A SANSKRIT-ENGLISH DICTIONARY

A SANSKRIT-ENGLISH DICTIONARY

ETYMOLOGICALLY AND PHILOLOGICALLY ARRANGED

WITH SPECIAL REFRENCE TO

GREEK, LATIN, GOTHIC, GERMAN, ANGLO-SAXON

AND OTHER COGNATE INDO-EUROPEAN LANGUAGES

BY

MONIER WILLIAMS, M.A.

BODEN PROFESSOR OF SANSKRIT IN THE UNIVERSITY OF OXFORD

PART I

GYAN

Published by

Gyan Publishing House
5, Ansari Road
Daryaganj, New Delhi-110002
Phone: 011-47034999, 9811692060
E-mail: books@gyanbooks.com

Distribution Network
gyanbooks.com
India, USA, Canada, UK, Australia, France

ISBN : 978-81-212-3037-7 (PB)
First Published, 1872

2nd Impression 2020

Printed at: Gyan Press, Delhi.

A Sanskrit-English Dictionary
Author: Monier Williams

A SANSKRIT-ENGLISH DICTIONARY

ETYMOLOGICALLY AND PHILOLOGICALLY ARRANGED

WITH SPECIAL REFERENCE TO

GREEK, LATIN, GOTHIC, GERMAN, ANGLO-SAXON,

AND OTHER COGNATE INDO-EUROPEAN LANGUAGES

BY

MONIER WILLIAMS, M.A.

BODEN PROFESSOR OF SANSKRIT IN THE UNIVERSITY OF OXFORD.

Oxford:

AT THE CLARENDON PRESS.

SOLD BY MACMILLAN AND CO., PUBLISHERS TO THE UNIVERSITY,

29 AND 30, BEDFORD STREET, COVENT GARDEN, LONDON;

AND BY W. H. ALLEN AND CO.

13, WATERLOO PLACE, LONDON.

M DCCC LXXII.

PREFACE.

A WORK of the kind here submitted to the students of Sanskṛit must be left to prove its usefulness by actual experiment. Nevertheless the plan of the present Dictionary is so novel that I must crave permission to introduce it with a longer explanation than might otherwise be needed. To conduce to greater clearness I propose distributing my prefatory statements under the following separate heads:

1. Reasons for undertaking a New Sanskṛit Dictionary.
2. Plan and Arrangement of the Present Work.
3. Extent of Sanskṛit Literature comprehended.
4. Alphabet and System of Transliteration employed.
5. Principal Sources drawn upon in the Process of Compilation.
6. Aids and Encouragements received.
7. Defects and Inconsistencies acknowledged.

SECTION 1.

Reasons for undertaking a New Sanskṛit Dictionary.

In the forefront must be placed the growing importance assigned by philologists to the oldest branch of the great Indo-European speech-stem, of which English is a modern offshoot. An intricate language destined to occupy the foremost rank throughout Europe as an instrument of linguistic training needs greater facilities for its acquisition. Some may smile at the idea of any Oriental language acquiring greater weight as an instrument of training among Occidental peoples whose vigorous mental faculties require a more suitable discipline for their development. Be it remembered, however, that Sanskṛit is, in one sense, the property of Europe as well as of India. Its relationship to some of our own languages is as close as to some of the Hindū dialects. It is a better guide than either Greek or Latin to the structure, historical connection, and correlation of the whole Indo-European family. It is a more trustworthy authority in the solution of recondite philological problems. Its study involves a mental discipline not to be surpassed.

Not even the most superficial observer can possibly be blind to the educational movement now spreading everywhere. Perhaps, however, some of us, trained under the old system, are scarcely yet alive to the forces which are at work for infusing new blood (if I may be allowed the phrase) into the whole body of our teaching. Not only must Greek and Latin be taught more thoroughly and scientifically, if they are to hold their own as the best trainers of thought and enforcers of accuracy *, but modern languages and modern literature can no longer be thrust aside or only employed to fill up the gaps in our system of instruction. All the nations of the

* Thoroughness in our teaching of Greek and Latin will never be effected until we lead our pupils to look more into the intimate internal constitution of these languages in their correlation to each other and to the other members of the Āryan family. To this end Sanskṛit is indispensable. French again will never be taught as it ought to be till our boys are made to understand its connection with Latin in every part of its grammatical structure. I hail such an excellent work as the 'Historical Grammar of the French Tongue by Auguste Brachet,' translated by the Rev. G. W. Kitchin, as an evidence that we are beginning to realize the defects in our present system of linguistic training.

civilized world are being drawn into closer intercommunion. The rapid advance of science in England, Germany, France, and Italy has forced natural science upon us as a necessary element of all mental culture, making also an interchange of thought between these countries indispensable. Eastern languages too, both Semitic and Āryan, are pressing peremptorily on the attention of our Universities *. Hebrew and Aramaic must now be studied by all our younger clergy, if they are to hold their own in the conflict of theological parties or present a bold front towards sceptical assailants. A knowledge of Arabic is essential to a right understanding of the literature, religion, and social institutions of the millions of our Muslim fellow-subjects. Some of the dialects of India must be mastered by all who have communication with the tens of millions of our Hindū brethren. Lastly, all the branches of the two great stems of speech are now proved to be so closely interdependent, and the permutations of sounds in passing through the varying organs of varying types of the human family are shewn to obey such curiously definite laws, that a new science has been established †. This science has for its field of investigation not any one particular language, but the whole area of human speech, and as it inquires into the laws governing the living organs of utterance as well as the living organic growth of the actual sounds themselves, may be said to trench not only on Ethnology, but even on Biology. This 'science of language' might with more propriety be called 'Glossology' than Philology. In its method of investigation it has much in common with the natural sciences, and though its analogy to these ought not to be strained beyond a mere analogy, yet as a veritable science dealing with one of the grandest distinctive attributes of human nature, it can no more be left out of any modern educational programme than any of the natural sciences properly so called. With the 'Glossologist' every spoken word is like a plant or animal in the hands of a Biologist; its birth, growth, transformations, and decay must all be accounted for; its whole structure dissected limb by limb; every appendage traced to its appropriate use and function; its deepest internal constitution analyzed.

Will it be denied, then, that Sanskṛit is destined to increasing cultivation, as the one typical scientific language whose structure is a master-key to the structure of all languages, whose very name implies 'Synthesis,' and whose literature, commencing with the Ṛig-veda about 1500 B.C., extends in a continuous line for nearly 3000 years, throwing a flood of light on the operation of linguistic laws?

In point of fact the Hindūs may be said to be the original inventors of the 'science of language.' Like the Greeks, they are the only nation who have worked out for themselves the laws of thought and of grammar independently. If their system of logic is inferior to that of Aristotle, they are unequalled in their examination into the constitution of speech. The name Vyākaraṇa, which they give to their grammar, implies 'decomposition' or 'resolution of a compound into its parts,' just as Saṇskaraṇa implies the re-composition or re-construction of the same decomposed elements. Every single word in their classical language is referred to a Dhātu or Root, which is also a name for any constituent elementary substance, whether of rocks or living organisms. In short, when we follow out their grammatical system in all the detail of its curious subtleties and technicalities, we seem to be engaged, like a Geologist, in splitting solid substances, or, like a Chemist, in some elaborate process of analysis.

* See the notes on the Semitic and Āryan languages at pp. viii, ix of this Preface. Cambridge is at this moment engaged in establishing both a Semitic and Indian languages Tripos. Although our system of 'Schools' at Oxford is somewhat different, yet, I hope, we shall not be behind the Sister University in our encouragement of these languages.

† The debt which we English scholars owe to Professor Max Müller for having first introduced us to this science by his well-known lectures, is too universally acknowledged to require notice here. I am not sure whether twelve lectures on the principles of linguistic science by William Dwight Whitney, Professor of Sanskṛit in Yale College, are quite so well known in this country. If they are not, I here commend them to all interested in the study of language, merely remarking that their excellence is too obvious to require any praise from me.

Having said so much in support of an effort to facilitate and generalize the study of Sanskṛit, I have now to state my reasons for having addressed myself to a task like the present.

It may not be generally known that the late Professor H. H. Wilson once intended the compilation of a Dictionary not wholly dissimilar in character and plan to that here offered to the students of Sanskṛit and its cognate languages. This I have heard from himself was what he intended by the last words of the Preface to his second edition, in which he stated that it would be his wish as Boden Professor to offer to the cultivators of Sanskṛit 'other and better assistance.'

It is perhaps also not known that he actually made some progress in carrying out this intention, though eventually debarred from its prosecution by his other numerous literary labours. He therefore, about the year 1852, when I had completed the printing of the English-Sanskṛit Dictionary compiled by me for the East-India Company, made over a large manuscript volume, containing the commencement of his new work, to me, with a request that I would continue it on the plan sketched out by himself. At the same time he generously presented me with a copious selection of examples and quotations made by Pandits at Calcutta, under his direction, from a considerable range of Sanskṛit literature. It has become necessary for me to state these circumstances at the risk of being charged with egotism, because the publication of the first part of Professor Goldstücker's Dictionary has made Orientalists aware that Professor Wilson entrusted the printing of a third edition of his Dictionary to that learned scholar, whose recent death is felt by all Sanskṛitists to be an irreparable loss *. From what I have now notified, however, it will, I trust, be quite understood that the work committed to me by one who was first my master, and afterwards my wisest guide and truest friend, was not a new edition of his Dictionary, but an entire remodelling of his scheme of lexicography, consisting of a re-arrangement of all the words under Roots, according to native principles of etymology, with addition of the examples collected as above described. Having already completed the English-Sanskṛit part of a Dictionary of my own, I naturally undertook as a sequel the work thus assigned me, especially as the plan commended itself to my own judgment and predilections. Moreover, I actually carried on the task for a considerable period between the intervals of other undertakings. Soon, however, it began to be manifest that the third edition of Professor Wilson's Dictionary was assuming, under Professor Goldstücker's editorship, almost interminable proportions, so as to become no longer a new edition of a previous Lexicon, but rather a many-volumed Encyclopædia of Sanskṛit learning, which no one scholar, however persistent, could hope to carry beyond the letter A. At the same time the Sanskṛit-German Wörterbuch of Professors Böhtlingk and Roth, though conducted by two of the most energetic scholars of the day, and put forth with singular perseverance, appeared to be expanding into vast dimensions, so as to be quite beyond the compass of ordinary English students. These circumstances having forced themselves upon my observation, I suddenly determined to abandon the design of a wholly Root-arranged Dictionary—which could only be useful, like the works above-named, to the highest class of scholars—and to commence a work on a more

* It is stated in a notice of the late Professor Goldstücker's life, which appeared in a recent number of a well-known scientific periodical, that many thousands of notes and references for the new edition of Wilson's Sanskṛit Dictionary and other works, the result of an unremitting study of the MSS. treasures at the India House &c., are left behind by Professor Goldstücker. With reference to this matter, I ought in justice to the present learned and courteous librarian of the India Office, as well as in justice to my own Dictionary, to put on record, that soon after his appointment, Dr. Rost offered to allow me also the use of any of these MSS. treasures if I would name any likely to be useful to myself. Knowing, however, that about eighty MSS., including those I needed most, were doing good service at the house of Professor Goldstücker, aiding him day by day in the elaboration of his Dictionary, I did not feel justified in interrupting the prosecution of so large a work for the sake of any advantage that might have accrued to my own less weighty performance. Moreover, I felt that I could not in justice interrupt the continuity of Professor Goldstücker's labours, when I had the use of the Wilsonian Collection belonging to the Bodleian, which, however inferior to those at the India Office in the departments required by a lexicographer, were still freely placed at my command by our own learned and obliging librarian, the Rev. H. O. Coxe.

practical plan, which, although raised as far as my powers went, to the level of modern scholarship, so as to be a sufficiently trustworthy aid in studying the chief departments of literature, including the Veda, should yet be procurable at a moderate cost, and not extend beyond the limits of one compact volume. This leads me therefore to

SECTION 2.

Plan and Arrangement of the Present Work.

Those who appreciate the value of Sanskṛit in its bearing on the philosophy of language will understand my motive in endeavouring so to arrange this lexicon as to exhibit most effectively that peculiarity of construction which distinguishes the highest type of the great Indo-European line of speech. Such persons will comprehend without much explanation the plan pursued by me throughout these pages in the collocation of words connected by mutual affinities. For the benefit, however, of younger students, I now proceed briefly to point out the one grand distinctive peculiarity of the Āryan dialects which the arrangement of the present Dictionary is intended to demonstrate—a peculiarity separating them by a sharp line of demarcation from the other great family of human speech usually called Semitic*.

Happily it is now a familiar fact to most educated persons that the Indo-European or Āryan languages (of which Sanskṛit is the eldest sister †, and English one of the youngest) proceeded from a common but nameless and unknown parent, whose very home in Asia cannot be absolutely fixed, though the locality may conjecturally be placed somewhere in the region of Bokhāra, near the river Oxus. From this centre radiated, as it were, eight principal lines of speech; first, the two Asiatic lines, 1. Indian, 2. Īrānian, (the former eventually comprising Sanskṛit, Pāli, Prākṛit, and the modern Prākṛits or spoken languages of the Hindūs, such as Hindī, Marāṭhī, Gujarātī, Bengālī, &c.; the latter comprising (*a*) Zand, old Persian, Pahlavī, modern Persian, and Pushtū; (*b*) Armenian); and then the six European lines, viz. 1. Keltic, 2. Hellenic, 3. Italic, 4. Teutonic, 5. Slavonic, 6. Lithuanian, each branching into various sub-lines or ramifications as exhibited in the present languages of Europe ‡. Now, if the question be asked, What most striking feature distinguishes all

* I use the term 'Semitic' out of deference to established usage, though it leads to some confusion of ideas, because if 'Semitic,' or more properly 'Shemitic,' be used for the languages of the descendants of Shem, then 'Japhetic' (instead of 'Āryan') should be used for the descendants of Japhet. We cannot, however, give up the epithet Āryan (from the Sanskṛit *ārya*, 'noble') for our own Indo-European languages, suited as it certainly is to that noblest of all families of speech. The Rev. F. W. Farrar suggests adopting the term 'Syro-Arabian' as well as Semitic for the other family. Still the name Semitic may well be applied to Hebrew, Aramaic [including perhaps one set of cuneiform inscriptions, Chaldee and Syriac], and Arabic, because in the tenth chapter of Genesis, Shem is represented as father of Elam (who peopled Elymais), Assur (Assyria), Lud (Lydia), Aram (Syria), and of Arphaxad, grandfather of Eber, from whom came the Hebrews—or Trans-Euphratian race, the name Hebrew really meaning 'one who lives beyond a river'—and Joktan, father of Sheba, father of Himyar, whence came the Arabians. Mr. Farrar states in his useful lectures that the Semitic nations may number about 40 millions, compared with about 400 millions of the Indo-Europeans. Among Semitic races come the people of Abyssinia. These have special languages of their own, viz. the Ethiopic or Geez, which is their sacred and literary language only, and the spoken dialects called Tigré, Tigriña, for the north and north-east, and Amharic, for the centre and south; the former being nearer to Ethiopic than the latter, and all being connected with the Semitic, as derived through the ancient Himyaritic Arabic of South Arabia (Yaman).

† Though the younger sisters sometimes preserve older forms.

‡ As this is the first Oriental Dictionary put forth by any English scholar which attempts to introduce abundant comparisons between the various members of the Indo-European family, I here append a brief account of the Āryan cognate languages beginning with the Indian. 1. By Pāli or Pālī is meant one of the oldest forms of the ancient provincial Hindū-ī language of which Sanskṛit is the learned form, (see p. xiii of Preface.) It must have been spoken either in Magadha or in some district not far from Oude, where Buddha flourished, and being carried by the Buddhists into Ceylon became their sacred language, and is preserved in their canonical scriptures called Tri-piṭaka. Prākṛit is the name given to other and later provincial forms of Sanskṛit, which were the precursors and parents of the present Hindū dialects, Hindī, Marāṭhī, &c., see note, p. xvii. These latter may be called modern Prākṛits. 2. Now as to the Īrānian: (*a*) Zand or Zend (old Bactrian) is to old Persian and Pahlavī what Sanskṛit is to Pāli and Prākṛit. It is that ancient language of Persia in which the sacred books are written, called Zand Avastā, belonging to the Pārsīs (or fugitives from Persia scattered on the coast of India, and still believers in the religion founded by Zardusht or Zoroaster). Old Persian is a name given to the dialect preserved in one set of cuneiform inscriptions, about contemporaneous with Zand. Pahlavī (sometimes written

these languages from the Semitic? My answer is, that the main distinction lies in the character of their roots or radical sounds; for although both Āryan and Semitic forms of speech are called 'inflective *,' it should be well understood that the inflectiveness of the root in the two cases implies two wholly different processes.

Let me first briefly advert to the Semitic form. A Semitic root then may be described as a kind of hard frame-work consisting generally of three consonants which resemble three sliding but inflexible upright limbs, moveable hither and thither to admit on either side the intervenient vowels and certain merely ancillary consonants, usually called 'servile.' These subservient letters are, it is true, of the utmost importance to the diverse colouring of the radical idea, and the perfect precision of their operation is noteworthy, but their presence within and without the rigid frame of the root is, so to speak, almost overpowered by the ever prominent consonantal skeleton. In illustration of this we may take the Arabic triliteral root KTB, using capitals for these radical consonants to indicate their prominence; the third pers. sing. past tense is KaTaBa, 'he wrote,' and from the same three consonants, by means of various vowels and servile letters, are developed a number of other forms, of which the following are specimens: KaTB, writing; KāTiB, a writer; maKTūB, written; taKTīB, causing to write; muKāTaBat, corresponding by letter; iKTāB, dictating; taKāTuB, writing to one another; mutaKāTiB, one who keeps up a correspondence; maKTaB, the place of writing, a writing-school; KiTāB, a book; KiTBat or KiTāBat, inscription †.

Pehlevi) is a later Īrānian dialect, which once possessed an extensive literature. A more recent Īrānian dialect is Pārsī or Pāzand, leading to the modern Persian which sprang up in Persia not long after the Muhammadan conquest (about A. D. 1000), the earliest form of which, as represented in the Shāh-nāmah of Firdausī, has little admixture of Arabic, while the later is flooded with it. Pushtū is the present language of Afghānistān. (*b*) Armenian is of course the language of Armenia; it has two forms, the old Armenian or literary language, which is dead, and the modern Armenian, said to be split into four dialects containing many Turkish words. Connected with these is the Ossetic of the Ossetes, a Caucasian tribe. We now come to the six European lines: 1. The Keltic or Celtic (of the Κελτοί, Herod. II. 33) is the oldest of the Āryan family in Europe, and as it has had the longest life, so it presents the greatest divergence from Sanskṛit: it has been driven into a corner of the continent, viz. Brittany, by Romanic French, and into the extremities of Cornwall, Wales, Ireland, and the Highlands of Scotland by Germanic English: it has two lines, (*a*) the principal Keltic or Gaelic (of the Galli), comprising the Irish, Highland-Scotch, and Manx, of which the Irish is most interesting in relation to Sanskṛit; (*b*) the Kymric form of Keltic, including Welsh, Cornish (now extinct), and Armorican, which last is the name given to the language of Brittany. 2. The Hellenic comprises ancient Greek with its dialects (most interesting in its close affinity to Sanskṛit, and most important in its bearing on the original of the New Testament, though far less remarkable in its bearing on other European languages than Latin), and modern Greek, usually called Romaic (infinitely nearer to the ancient Greek than the Romanic languages are to Latin). 3. The Italic comprises, of course, Latin with its Romanic (or Romance) offspring, viz. Italian, French, Spanish, Portuguese, Wallachian, and Provençal; and includes some old Italian dialects, such as the Oscan of the Samnites in southern Italy, Umbrian spoken in north-eastern Italy and Sabine. 4. The Teutonic comprises (*a*) Gothic, which is the Sanskṛit of the Teutonic languages, especially of Low German; it was spoken by the ancient Gothic peoples who belonged to the Germanic race, and were divided into eastern and western Goths; a part of the latter being allowed by the Romans to settle in the province of Mœsia, near the mouth of the Danube, became converts to Christianity, and happily their bishop Ulfilas fixed their language by translating nearly all the Bible; a remnant of his translation has been preserved, otherwise this dialect, sometimes called Mœso-Gothic, would have been lost, and with it a most important key to Teutonic philology: (*b*) German, divided into two branches, viz. 1st, Low German, which is subdivided into four, viz. Saxon (sometimes called Old Saxon), leading to Anglo-Saxon and English; Frisian, once largely spoken by the Frisian tribes (Lat. *Frisii*) who dwelt on the north-west coast of Germany, and closely connected with English; Dutch, current of course in Holland; Flemish, spoken in that part of Belgium called Flanders; 2ndly, High German, subdivided into old, middle, and new, the last bringing us to modern German: (*c*) Scandinavian, divided into four, viz. Norse, i. e. old and new Icelandic (nearly alike and most valuable as preserving the original structure of the whole Scandinavian group), Swedish, Norwegian, and Danish, the two latter only differing in pronunciation. 5. The Slavonic comprises (*a*) old Slavonic or old Bulgarian, being to the Slavonic what Gothic is to the Teutonic, and similarly preserved in a translation of the Bible made by Cyril: (*b*) Russian, divided into Russian proper, Little Russian: (*c*) Polish, with other less noticeable Slavonic dialects, viz. Polabian, Bohemian, Sorbian, Servian, Kroatian, and Slovenian. 6. The Lithuanian is sometimes regarded as a branch of the Slavonic line, to which it is more nearly related than to the Teutonic; it is interesting as coming nearer to Sanskṛit in some of its forms than any other member of the Āryan family, and as having a dual, like the Gothic, and seven cases; it is still spoken by a limited number in Russian and Prussian provinces on the coast of the Baltic, but is disappearing before Russian and German; a more modern form of it is Lettish, spoken in Livonia: another kindred dialect is Old Prussian, once spoken in north-eastern Prussia, but now extinct.

* As distinguished from 'monosyllabic,' like the Chinese; and 'agglutinative,' like the Drāviḍian, Turkish, and other members of an immense class of languages in which the termination is easily separable from the body of the word. These are still called by some Tūrānian (from Tūr, eldest son of Farīdūn, to whom he assigned Turkistān, thence called Tūrān).

† For a further insight into these Arabic formations, the student is referred to a chapter on the use of Arabic words in my 'Practical Hindūstānī Grammar,' published by Longman & Co.

An Āryan root on the other hand, as best typified by a Sanskṛit radical, is generally a single monosyllable, which may be compared to a malleable substance capable of being drawn out to express every modification of an original conception. And this malleability, as it were, arises chiefly from the circumstance that the vowel is recognized as a constituent part of the radical; blending with its very substance, and even sometimes standing alone as itself the only root. Sanskṛit exhibits better than any other member of the Āryan line of speech this characteristic root-expansibility. More than this, it exemplifies better than any other that excessive *root-accretiveness* (if I may use the term) by which not only terminations and prefixes are grafted upon or welded into the original monosyllabic stock, but affix is affixed to affix, prefix is prefixed to prefix, derivative is derived from derivative, compound is compounded with compound in an almost interminable chain. In illustration of this the student is referred to such roots as 1. *kṛi*, p. 245; 1. *bhū*, p. 714; 1. *śru*, p. 1026; 1. *sthā*, p. 1145 of this volume.

Hence it becomes evident that the original plan of Professor Wilson, by which every single word would have been represented in regular sequence, growing, as it were, from its own parent stem, would have realized the true conception of a perfect Sanskṛit Dictionary. Verily if Greek lexicography has been occasionally so treated, much more has Sanskṛit, the great type of linguistic constructiveness, a right so to be.

I have now to show how far the present work satisfies this ideal. It is sometimes calculated, that there are about two thousand distinct roots in this language. If it be supposed that there are about eighty thousand distinct words growing out of these two thousand roots, a Dictionary on the usual alphabetical plan must have consisted of a series of eighty thousand monographs, each independent of the other; and, indeed, such a Dictionary might have been thought most agreeable to the common notion of a really practical work. It seemed to me, however, that a Dictionary so planned would have afforded little effective aid to the study of Sanskṛit, in its connection with comparative philology. On the other hand, it must be confessed that the idea of taking root by root, and writing, as it were, two thousand biographies, each giving a connected history of a distinct family allied together by a common pedigree was a philological dream too unpractical to be wholly realized. Some middle course, therefore, satisfying the requirements both of philology and of ordinary practice seemed most to be desired, and the following publication, though not answering the perfect philological ideal, is intended as an attempt at combining a partial root-arrangement with a convenient alphabetical order suited to ready reference.

In unison with this design, the roots of the language—always brought prominently before the eye by large Nāgarī type—will be found treated more exhaustively in the present work, both as regards the meanings given and the forms exhibited, than in any other Sanskṛit-English Dictionary yet published *. It is evident that a great many of these roots, or Dhātus, as they are called by native lexicographers, are not really elementary radicals, but compounds or developments of simpler elements. I have not always ventured to pronounce categorically as to which of two or more roots is the simplest form, but when roots are evidently allied, their connection is conspicuously indicated in the following pages. Thus I hope to have drawn attention to a point which English scholars have hitherto greatly overlooked †.

* I cannot sufficiently acknowledge my debt to Westergaard's Radices. The copy I have had for about thirty years tells a tale of constant reference. Indeed we have to thank Danish, quite as much as German scholars, for what they have done towards promoting linguistic culture.

† The number of distinct radical forms in Wilkins' collection is 1750, but as many forms having the same sound have different meanings, and are conjugated differently, they are held to be distinct roots, and the number is thereby swelled to 2490. Probably, the real number of elementary radicals in Sanskṛit might be reduced to a comparatively small catalogue. Some roots containing dentals have been cerebralized or vice versâ, and both forms are allowed to co-exist, as *bhan* and *bhaṇ*, *dhan* and *dhaṇ*; others whose initials are aspirated consonants have passed into other aspirated consonants or retained only the aspirate; and all forms co-exist in *bhṛi*, *dhṛi*, *dhvṛi*, *hvṛi*, &c. Again, such a

Furthermore, the plan now first carried out of arranging all verbs formed from roots by prefixing prepositions in their proper alphabetical order and at the head of their own derivatives, will be noted as a marked feature of originality and individuality. The labour entailed by the simple process of thus re-arranging the verbs in a language so rich in prepositions, can only be understood by other lexicographers *. But even this re-arrangement has not caused so much difficulty as the attempt to exhibit what may be termed *the kinship of words*, by distributing the greater part of the vocabulary of the language in families, or rather, if I may so express myself, in family-groups †. These groups are, as far as possible, collected under roots or leading words, which stand, as it were, at the head of the family, and are always distinguished from the rest by Nāgarī type in the manner more fully explained in the table of directions at the end of the Preface. Such a re-distribution of the vocabulary has often necessitated the separation of roots and homonyms under two, three, or more heads, each with its train of derivatives, subderivatives, and associated words, which in other Dictionaries would be brought together under one article ‡. An abundant return, however, has been reaped, if philological precision has been thus promoted, and facility afforded for viewing synoptically and comparing together the etymological history of the words so collocated.

Besides the obvious advantage of this arrangement to the philologically-minded student, great saving of space has been thus effected; all necessity for repeating derivations under each head being thus avoided, and the power gained of leaving many meanings to be inferred from one or other member of a group, instead of constantly reiterating them. For it must be borne in mind that all the series included under the same heading in Nāgarī type are to be regarded as cohering; so that all derivatives, whether primary or secondary, and all compound words following in regular sequence, may be studied in their mutual bearing and correlation both as illustrating each other and as contributing to throw light on the modifications of meaning evolved from the radical idea. These meanings, too, have not been thrown together in a heap, as they have been hitherto in some Oriental Dictionaries, but an attempt has been made to set them forth according to their logical development. The further advantage gained in space by the free use of Roman type will be explained under Section 4.

Conspicuously, again, in an enumeration of the more noteworthy features of the present publication, should certainly be placed the introduction of abundant comparisons from cognate languages, which no other Lexicon published by English scholars has, I believe, hitherto attempted to the same extent. I must at once distinctly notify that for these comparisons I have not trusted to my own judgment, but have followed the authority of the eminent German scholars whose names will be mentioned subsequently.

Another distinctive characteristic of this Dictionary consists in the articles on mythology, literature, religion, and philosophy, which will be found scattered everywhere throughout its pages. By consulting Professor Aufrecht's catalogues, Dr. Ballantyne's works, Dr. Fitz-Edward Hall's writings, Dr. Muir's Sanskṛit Texts, Professor M. Müller's Ancient Sanskṛit Literature, Dr. Weber's Indische Studien, Wilson's Vishṇu-Purāṇa, some Oriental Articles in Chambers' Encyclopædia—written, I believe, by the late Professor Goldstücker,—and my own collection of notes, I have been able to furnish the student with much valuable information on many subjects not hitherto treated of in any

root as *svad* is probably nothing but a compound of *su* and root *ad*, and such roots as *stubh*, *stumbh*, *stambh* are plainly mere modifications of each other.

* Why should not Sanskṛit lexicons have been brought into harmony with Greek in this respect long ere this? Greek is almost as free in its use of prepositions, e. g. *συμπαραβάλλω*, *συμπαρακαθέζομαι*.

† Even in English this might advantageously be done, as, for example, it would be very instructive to see such words as *share*, *shire*, *shore*, *shears*, &c. arranged under '*shear*,' to cut off, separate. Richardson in his great Dictionary has to a certain extent carried out this idea. See on this subject 'Archbishop Trench on the Study of Words.'

‡ See, for example, the roots 1. *su*, 2. *su*, 3. *su*, 4. *su*, at p. 1117, and 1. *kāla*, 2. *kāla*, at pp. 224, 225.

Dictionary. Let him observe, for instance, what is written under the words Vishṇu, Śiva, Veda, Manas, Sāman, Soma, Sāṅkhya, Sauptika-parvan. It will be doubtless said that too many names of persons, places, and books are introduced. In excuse I have to plead that greater liberty ought to be allowed to a Sanskṛit Dictionary in this respect than to Greek and Latin Lexicons, because Oriental alphabets have no capital letters. As to the names of books, it may often be useful to have attention drawn to works, still unprinted, ascertained to exist either in Europe or India.

It may perhaps be objected that there are too many compound words; but again it may be urged that a Sanskṛit Dictionary must not be tried by ordinary laws in this respect, for here again Sanskṛit stands eminently forth as the grand typical representative of the whole Āryan line of speech, which is throughout distinguished by its love of composition. To exclude compounds from a Sanskṛit Lexicon, would be, so to speak, to 'Unsanskṛitize' it. Not only are there certain compounds quite peculiar to Sanskṛit, but in the grammar composition almost takes the place of syntax, and the various kinds of compound words are classified and defined with greater subtlety and minuteness than would be possible in any other known language of the world. When a student is in doubt whether to translate compounds like *Indra-śatru* as Bahuvrīhis or Tatpurushas, the Dictionary is surely bound to aid in clearing up his perplexities. Moreover, as few examples are given or passages quoted in the present work, a limited admission of compounds, under certain restrictions, serves to illustrate the use of a leading word; for to such words, let it be observed, they have always been subordinated. After I had formulated my plan, and a large portion of the work was in type, the Sanskṛit Dictionary of Professor Benfey appeared *, and I was glad to find that, working independently, I had devised a system supported in some of these particulars by that philologist. All must agree that as Sanskṛit exceeds every other language in its infinite capacity for composition, no Sanskṛit Lexicon, if it admits compounds at all, ought to treat them as if they were independent entities entitled to a separate existence of their own.

Nevertheless I could never have followed Professor Benfey in placing compound words under their last member. This method, however philosophical, seems to sacrifice at the shrine of logical propriety what I have set before myself as a paramount consideration in arranging my own Dictionary—*facility of reference.* For a further explanation of points of detail the student is referred to the table of directions at the end of the Preface. I now therefore pass on to my third point.

SECTION 3.

Extent of Sanskṛit Literature comprehended.

I have sometimes been gravely asked by men learned in all the classical lore of Europe, Has Sanskṛit any literature? Such a question proves the urgent need for a work like the present, which aims at facilitating and making more general the study of a language closely allied to our own, and still more closely connected with the spoken dialects of our great Indian Empire—a language, therefore, about whose history every well-educated Englishman ought surely to know something.

Conscious, then, as my present office has made me of the general ignorance prevalent on Indian subjects, I may be excused if I preface this part of my Introduction by stating precisely what I conceive to me implied by the words Sanskṛit and Sanskṛit literature. By Sanskṛit, then, is not meant any really spoken language of India or even, I hold, any once generally spoken language. What the word Sanskṛit properly represents is, I conceive, *a certain form* of the

* The Sanskṛit-French Dictionary of M. Emile Burnouf, which also appeared after much of my work was in type, is an independent working out of some ideas similar to my own.

language brought by the Indian branch of the great Āryan race into India, the ancient spoken language of the Hindūs being more suitably styled Hindū-ī, just as its principal later development is called Hindī *. For in fact that happened in India which has come to pass in all civilized countries. The spoken vernacular of the people has separated into two lines, the one elaborated by the learned, the other popularized and variously provincialized by the unlearned †. In India, however, from the greater exclusiveness of the educated few, the greater ignorance of the masses and the desire of a bigoted priesthood to keep the key of knowledge in their own possession, this separation became more marked, more diversified, and progressively intensified. Hence, the very grammar which with other nations was regarded only as a means to an end, came to be treated by Indian Paṇḍits as the end itself, and was subtilized into an intricate science, fenced round by a bristling barrier of technicalities. The language, too, elaborated *pari passu* with the grammar, rejected the natural name of Hindū-ī, or 'the speech of the Hindūs,' and adopted an artificial designation, viz. Sanskṛita, or 'the perfectly constructed speech,' to denote its complete severance from the common tongue (called by contrast Prākṛita), and its exclusive dedication to literary and religious purposes. This of itself is a remarkable circumstance; for although something similar has happened in Europe, yet we do not find that Latin and Greek ceased to be called Latin and Greek when they became the language of the learned, any more than we have at present two names for the common and literary languages of modern nations. These remarks will perhaps conduce to a right appreciation of the nature of a literature which, although elaborated by a learned caste, is still the only real literature of the Hindū race, the vernaculars having hitherto produced little worthy of consideration.

Sanskṛit literature, it should be remembered, embraces two distinct periods, Vedic and post-Vedic. The former, beginning with the Ṛig-veda, and extending through the other three Vedas (viz. the Yajur-veda, Sāma-veda, and Atharva-veda), with their Brāhmaṇas, Upanishads, and Sūtras, is most valuable to philologists as presenting them with the nearest approach to the original Āryan language, its earlier works being composed in an ancient form of Sanskṛit, which is to the later what Chaucer's writings are to modern English. The latter commencing with the Code of Manu, with its train of subsequent important law-books, and extending through the six systems of philosophy ‡, the vast grammatical literature, the immense epics ||, the lyric, erotic, and didactic poems, the Nīti-śāstras, moral tales and apothegms, the dramas, the various treatises on mathematics, rhetoric, prosody, music, medicine, &c., brings us at last to the eighteen Purāṇas with their succeeding Upa-Purāṇas, and the more recent Tantras, all of which are worthy of study as the great repositories of the modern mythologies and popular creeds of India. No one person, indeed, with limited powers of mind and body, can hope to master more than one or two departments of so vast a range, in which scarcely a subject can be named, with the single exception of Historiography, not furnishing a greater number of treatises than any other language of the ancient world. In some

* I use the word Hindū-ī as a convenient term for the ancient Bhāshā of the Āryan settlers in the neighbourhood of the Sindhu or rather of the Hapta Hendu = *sapta sindhavas*. It may be thought that this Bhāshā was identical with the language of the Vedic hymns. But even Vedic Sanskṛit represents a considerable amount of elaboration scarcely compatible with the notion of a vernacular dialect (as, for example, in the use of complicated grammatical forms like Intensives). Pāṇini, in distinguishing between the common language and the Vedic, uses the terms Bhāshā and Loka.

† Of course the provincialized Prākṛits, though not, as I conceive, derived directly from the learned language, borrowed largely from the Sanskṛit after it was thus elaborated.

‡ The systems of philosophy are properly only three: 1. the Nyāya by Gautama, which is the most practical, and contains the Hindū system of logic; 2. the Sāṅkhya by Kapila, which is dualistic, asserting the separate existence of soul and matter; 3. the Vedānta by Vyāsa or Bādarāyaṇa, which asserts the unity of all being: but of each of these respectively there are branches, viz. (*a*) the Vaiśeshika by Kaṇāda; (*b*) the Yoga by Patañjali; (*c*) the Pūrva-mīmāṃsā by Jaimini.

|| Some idea of the extent of Sanskṛit literature may be gained by comparing the two great epic or heroic poems called the Mahā-bhārata and Rāmāyaṇa with the Iliad and Odyssey, as I have attempted to do in the small volume called 'Indian Epic Poetry,' published by Messrs. Williams and Norgate. The Mahā-bhārata, printed at Calcutta, contains 107,389 verses, each verse being supposed to consist of two lines. See also my edition of the 'Story of Nala,' published at the Clarendon Press.

subjects too, especially in poetical descriptions of nature and domestic affection, Indian works do not suffer by a comparison with the best specimens of Greece and Rome, while in the wisdom, depth, and shrewdness of their moral apothegms they are unrivalled. More than this, the learned Hindūs had probably made great advances in astronomy, algebra, arithmetic, botany, and medicine, not to mention their admitted superiority in grammar, long before any of these sciences were cultivated by the most ancient nations of Europe. Hence it has happened that I have been painfully reminded during the progress of this Dictionary that a Sanskṛit lexicographer ought to aim at a kind of quasi omniscience. Nor will any previous classical education, such at least as has been hitherto usual, enable him to explain correctly the scientific expressions which—not borrowed from the Greeks—are liable to be brought before him. To pretend therefore that the present work, although probably containing nearly three times as much matter as any other Sanskṛit Dictionary yet published (excepting of course the great Thesaurus of Professors Böhtlingk and Roth, and that of Rādhākānta-deva), is competent to satisfy the student in every branch of Sanskṛit literature, would manifestly display either ignorance or conceit. Perhaps the departments in which it must be admitted to be weakest are those of the Veda and philosophy with their respective native commentaries. Still an attempt has been made to supply what has hitherto been almost entirely neglected by English lexicographers.

In truth, I have felt that no modern Lexicon ought to exclude Vedic words, important as these are in their philological bearings. I must nevertheless plainly confess that the interpretation of these words is often so doubtful—often so purely tentative—that I have been sorely perplexed in my efforts to furnish the student with trustworthy renderings. Of course with the Veda, as with every other profoundly obscure subject, there is a natural craving for an infallible guide. At the same time no priestly infallibility is here thought to be attainable; for although the great Brāhman and Ācārya, Sāyaṇa, lived about five hundred years ago at Vijaya-nagara, an ancient Indian capital and seat of learning, yet this eminent authority has been altogether put out of court by modern philological critics. When, however, it is found that modern scholars themselves frequently differ as much from each other as they do from that once trusted and certainly most learned Brāhman, it seems hopeless to expect security from error in any particular sect or section of modern critics and philologists. Notwithstanding these perplexities, I cannot express too strongly my appreciation of what German scholars have effected in this difficult field of research, and my gratitude for the aid received from the interpretations of Professors Böhtlingk and Roth. The authority of these scholars has been generally followed by me, though I have been careful to give, in addition, the renderings of Sāyaṇa (according to Professor Max Müller's edition *), feeling, as I do, rather enthusiastically that this great native commentator, even if he occasionally misleads, ought never to be ignored.

The foregoing sketch of the nature of Sanskṛit literature will, I trust, explain the impossibility of covering its vast area by any Dictionary in one volume. It will also explain my non-admission into my pages of the ample store of examples made over to me by my predecessor, the late Professor H. H. Wilson. These would, at least, have swelled out my one compact volume to an inconvenient size, if they had not expanded it into two. For the same reason I have been obliged, as a rule, to forego authenticating my meanings by more than a few scattered references either to passages in

* It should be mentioned however, that for the latter part of the Ṛig-veda I have not had the advantage of Professor Max Müller's editorial skill. The first volume of his edition of this work, with Sāyaṇa's commentary, was brought out under the patronage of the East India Company in 1849. Three other volumes have since appeared, completing as far as the end of the eighth Maṇḍala. For the remainder I have been obliged to trust to an imperfect MS. of Sāyaṇa's commentary in the Wilsonian Collection belonging to the Bodleian Library. This is the only Ṛig-veda MS. of any value that I have had it in my power to employ, as I have not been able to consult the excellent MSS. belonging to the India Office Library, which others had a greater right to use than myself. I am informed that a fifth volume of the Ṛig-veda is about to appear.

the literature or to the modern authorities on which I have depended for guidance. In this I had better ground for abstention than my predecessor, seeing that the great work of Professors Böhtlingk and Roth, the completion of which may be looked for in a few years, will provide advanced scholars with abundant examples and references to every department of the literature. I should add that as my main object has been to facilitate and generalize the study of a difficult language, I have of course abstained from complicating the typography of this volume by placing accents on Vedic words *. For a knowledge of these the scholar must again apply to the great German Wörterbuch.

I come in the next place to a feature in the present publication which, as the four Governments of India have liberally patronized this work, demands an ample explanation.

SECTION 4.

Alphabet and System of Transliteration employed.

I fear the great Indian Paṇḍits, if they deem this Dictionary worthy of their notice, will be somewhat surprised that a work intended as an aid to the study of their literature should exhibit their venerable Sanskṛit clothed in a modern European dress †. Let me then crave leave to remind them that the Romanized character employed in these pages will be found, if its history be investigated, to be neither modern nor European, and may possibly turn out to be even more ancient than their sacred Nāgarī, and even more suited to the expression of their sacred Sanskṛit.

After all, we English are not only Eastern in our origin, but in many of our most important surroundings. First, we have received our religion and our Bible through an Eastern people; next, our language is certainly Asiatic in its affinities; thirdly, we are known to have derived our invaluable decimal notation, commonly called the ten Arabic numerals, from India through the Arabs; lastly, the written symbols which I am now employing, and by which this useful vernacular of ours is, as it were, materialized and sent to the ends of the earth, are certainly Asiatic too.

The East is, we must candidly own, the first source of all our light. We cannot, indeed, localize in Asia the precise spot whence issued the springs of that grand flow of speech which spread in successive waves—commencing with the Keltic—over the whole area of Europe; but the local source of the first alphabet, without which each of these waves of speech must have been in the end swallowed up and lost in its successor, is well known to have been Phœnicia. The great centre of the commerce of antiquity naturally gave birth to what was felt to be indispensable to the intercommunion of national as well as individual life. By the very necessities of trade Phœnicia invented the first, so to speak, locomotive power which enabled language, embodied in a kind of material form, to be in a manner exported to distant countries and bartered, like any other commodity, for language imported in return.

Probably the first Phœnician graphic signs were, like the Chinese, of an ideographic character, but of this there is said to be no certain evidence. However that may be, it is tolerably clear that the first Phœnician graphic system, about which we know anything, had not advanced beyond

* See the note on Vedic accents, p. xix of this Preface.

† Though some Sanskṛit books—such as Professor Aufrecht's Ṛig-veda—printed in the Roman character are much used by European scholars, it is doubtful whether these have obtained even a limited circulation in India. I trust, therefore, that when this volume falls into the hands of any great Paṇḍit, to whom one of our Indian Governments may present it, he will not consider that I am degrading Sanskṛit like the man who pollutes cow's milk by putting it into a dog's skin. *Nahi pūtaṃ syād go-kshīraṃ śva-dṛitau dhṛitam*; cf. Muir's Sanskṛit Texts, vol. ii. p. 53, note 97. Of course I know that many native books are printed in which Sanskṛit words are transliterated by Roman letters, but my desire is to see some standard texts accurately printed in this character and circulated throughout India. At present the loose and careless way in which the Roman alphabet is applied tends to bring the whole system into disrepute. This is exemplified in writing the names of places and persons as well as in books. A little work called the Durga-puja [sic] by Pratápachandra Ghosha has just been received by me from Calcutta. It contains much useful information, but here we have Sanskṛit words transliterated without any attempt at exactness, e.g. *Devi, Durga, puja, Purana, ashtami, Krshna, Savitri*, and numberless others.

the second stage of alphabetic progress. It was, in fact, essentially syllabic, and even to this day the Semitic alphabets coming immediately from it—viz. the Hebrew, Syriac, and Arabic—are very little better than syllabic systems. Such an alphabet then, though well suited to Eastern calligraphic tastes, was manifestly imperfect. It provided chiefly for consonants, as if they were the lords of sound, instead of its dependents, and often its impediments. The real want for civilized nations, eager for intercommunication, was a phonetic alphabet, by which neither ideas nor consonants, but rather *sounds* should be symbolized. As therefore vowels are the only real representatives of sound, and indeed the very life of the word which without them would be a mere hard and helpless skeleton, it was essential to an effective phonetic system of graphic symbols that vowels should have at least as prominent a position in a written word as their attendant consonants. This was very soon felt by the Greeks, who no sooner received a consonantal alphabet from Phœnicia than they began to remedy its defects, and forthwith invented a system by which the vowel sounds were properly symbolized and distributed side by side with their consonantal fellows—not as mere appendages, but as close companions. The Greek expansion of the Phœnician alphabet was still further developed by the more practical Romans, and by them spread everywhere throughout Europe *.

Now, although the Semitic origin of Indian alphabets has not yet been satisfactorily proved, it is still probable that the Eastern branch of the Āryan stock which settled down in India, derived their first idea of symbolizing language by written marks indirectly from Phœnicia through some neighbouring country whose system was borrowed from Semitic models †. They appear also, like the Greeks, to have felt the defects of a syllabic or merely consonantal method, and just as they worked out for themselves their own theory of grammar, so they elaborated for themselves their own 'vowelized' system of writing. Note, however, how the subtle-minded Hindūs, working out their own ideas in their own philosophical way, have produced an alphabet, not only free from the defects of the Semitic, but so overdone in its abundance of vowel symbols and its theory of the mutual relationship of vowels and consonants, that this very elaboration becomes practically a serious hindrance.

Let me for the benefit of those who may use this Dictionary for philological purposes, without having acquired a complete familiarity with the Nāgarī letters, briefly point out the most conspicuous merits and demerits of the European and Indian systems.

From what I have before advanced, it will, I think, be clear that it ought to be a fixed rule in all good alphabets, 1st, That every vowel, short and long, should be properly symbolized and admitted to close companionship with its consonant, no vowel symbol being ever allowed to stand for any other vowel sound but its own. For example, the 'a' sound of 'ka' should be properly symbolized; it should not be supposed to inhere in 'k;' nor should it be represented by a mere dot or stroke, above or below the 'k,' as if it were a simple appendage to the consonant, as in Semitic alphabets. Nor should the symbol 'a' be allowed to stand for different vowel sounds short and long, as in 'tape,' 'tap,' 'tall,' 'tar,' 'mortar,' in every one of which the vowel ought to be variously symbolized. 2ndly, That every simple consonant should have one single fixed symbol, and never more than one. For example, the symbol 'k' should not be interchangeable with 'c' to express the same consonantal power as in 'cap' and 'keep.' 3rdly, That modifications of any particular simple

* The Romans, however, having no proper aspirated consonantal sounds, rejected the Greek θ, φ, χ, and to represent these unhappily originated the clumsy *th*, *ph*, *ch*, writing also *ps* for ψ.

† According to Mr. Edward Thomas (Prinsep's Indian Antiquities, vol. ii. p. 42), the theory by which Professor Weber has sought to establish a Phœnician origin for the Indian alphabets is untenable. There are, however, two sets of Buddhist inscriptions, and that of Kapurdigiri is decidedly traceable to a Phœnician source. Those on the rock of Girnar (Giri-nagara) in Kattywar, Gujarāt, which are said to be most important in their relation to the present Indian alphabets, are not so clearly traceable. Mr. Thomas appears to have good ground for thinking that many of the Nāgarī letters were derived from the Drāviḍians of the South.

vowel or consonantal power should not be represented by two letters, but by some modification of a single symbol. For example, the long form of the vowels *a, i, u* should not be denoted by two letters, as in our word 'hoop,' but by some mark or stroke placed over these vowels (so that 'hoop' should be written 'hūp'). Similarly, the aspiration of *k, t, p,* ought not to be represented by two letters as in *kh, th, ph,* but by some mark attached to *k, t, p;* thus such a word as *phala* should be written *ṗala*, and *dhana, ḋana;* or perhaps according to the Anglo-Saxon method with a horizontal stroke above, as in đ for the *dh* sound of *the*.

Tried by these rules, the Nāgarī alphabet shows itself in many respects superior to the old Roman alphabet, and certainly to our use or *abuse* of the Roman symbols commonly called the English alphabet. But tried by the same rules, it will be found, I believe, inferior to the Indo-Romanic system, by which name I call the modification of Sir William Jones' method of applying the Roman alphabet to the languages of India, adopted in the present Dictionary.

The fact of the matter is, that Hindū grammarians have so overdone the true theory of the necessary vocalization of consonants, that they declare it impossible for any consonant to stand alone without its associated vowel, not only in a single word, but in a whole sentence, unless, indeed, the consonant come at the end of all, when the mark ◌्, called a Virāma or stop, must be employed. Moreover, the dependent position of a consonant is so insisted on that every simple consonant must perforce possess an inherent vowel by a necessary condition of its own existence, so that when it is written without vowel or stop the vowel 'a' must always be pronounced after it. Hence, such a word as 'bind,' would have to be pronounced 'binada,' unless a conjunct symbol be employed, compounding *n* and *d* into one letter, the use of the Virāma or stop, except at the end of a sentence, being an infraction of orthographic laws. Thus it arises that an immense assortment of conjunct consonants is needed. More than this, the excessive elaboration of their vowel-system by the Hindūs necessitates the introduction of two new vowels, *ṛi* and *lṛi*. Again, each of the fourteen vowels (except *ă*) has two symbols, according as it is initial or non-initial, and the form of some of these obliges them to be printed before the letter after which they are pronounced and in various awkward places, thereby exposing them to fracture, and increasing the general complication. So that with unusually numerous vowel-symbols, with thirty-five consonants and an almost indefinite number of intricate conjunct consonants, the number of distinct types necessary to equip a perfect Sanskṛit fount amounts to about 500 (see the table opposite to page 1).

Now will any one maintain, that in these days of railroads, electric telegraphs, cheap printing, and the Suez canal, such an overstraining of alphabetical precision can be maintained much longer for the expression of any language belonging to the same family as our own, and in any country forming an integral part of the British Empire? Indeed Sanskṛit ought to be made a potent instrument for uniting England more closely with India, and a powerful means for exciting more real sympathy and fellow-feeling between Englishmen and their Indian fellow-subjects; but on this very account it requires every facility to be conceded to its acquisition, and every contrivance to be adopted for harmonizing it with those kindred European tongues whose structure it is above all capable of illustrating.

Be it remembered that we are not expecting either absurdities or impossibilities. We are not so foolish as to suppose that the Hindūs will ever abandon their own national forms of speech. On the contrary, we expect that they will tenaciously adhere to them, even as their brethren of Wales hold to their own separate and distinct branch of the same speech-stem. But because we cannot change the organs of speech or fuse the twenty-two languages* of India into one common

* Viz. Sanskṛit, with its kindred Hindī, Marāṭhī, Gujarātī, Bengālī, Uriya, Asamese, Panjābī, Gurumukhī, Sindhī, Nepalese, Kaśmīrī, the Singhalese of Ceylon; the Pushtū of Afghānistān; the five Drāviḍian languages, Tamil, Malayālam, Telugu, Kanarese, Tulu; the half Ḍrāviḍian Brahū-ī; the composite Urdū or Hindūstānī current throughout India; and lastly Burmese.

tongue, are we therefore not to do what we really can to promote intercourse and communion between kindred races united under one government and descended from the same ancestors? If our great Indian Paṇḍits are made familiar with our graphic systems, will they not be more likely to study our language and literature, to benefit by our knowledge, and to use our numerous appliances for economizing time, labour, and money? In short, is it fatuous to expect our fellow-subjects to imitate us in adopting a common system of symbols for a common line of cognate languages?—a system, be it thoroughly understood, not to be confounded with our English 'free and easy' abandonment of all system in our treatment of the Roman alphabet—but a system capable of complete adjustment to the expression of Āryan sounds, whether Roman, Greek, Welsh, English, or Indian, and probably little more different in form from the present Nāgarī than that Nāgarī is from the characters prevalent in India when Sanskṛit was first committed to writing *. For since the fact is patent, that the further we go back, the more plainly do the Indian alphabets point to a foreign origin, the power of ancient and sacred association cannot certainly be pleaded for the maintenance of the present Nāgarī.

Nor can our Indian brethren shelter themselves under any plea of impossibility, when all the logic of historical facts is against them. Is any nation more tenacious of everything national than the Jews? and yet have they not abandoned their ancient character for a more modern form? Have not also the Arabs and Persians, not to mention the Keltic and Teutonic races, done the same? Have not the Hindūs themselves renounced many of their most ancient usages, and allowed the rigidity of caste to relax under the pressure of steam and other European forces. Even in the very matter of alphabets the facts of their own history are also against them, for if they deny the foreign origin of their venerated Nāgarī, they have confessedly adopted the modern Persianized Arabic alphabet—a consonantal, if not a purely syllabic system—to express Hindūstānī. Now, Hindūstānī, notwithstanding its flood of Arabic and Persian words, is as much a form of Hindī—the language of 'pakka' Hindūstān—as English with its flood of Norman French is of Anglo-Saxon. Surely then all must admit that Hindūstānī, at least, has a far better right to the Indo-Romanic alphabet derived from kindred British rulers, than it has to be saddled with the consonantal system of foreign Muslim invaders. For that system, be it noted, is wholly Semitic in its essential features, and therefore quite unsuited to the fundamental Āryan structure of a Persianized Āryan dialect.

If after what I have thus advanced, our great Indian Paṇḍits remain, as I fear some of them will, unconvinced, let any ordinary scholar who consults the pages of this work say whether they do not derive much of their typographical clearness from certain apparently trifling, but really important contrivances, possible in our Indo-Romanic, impossible in the usual Nāgarī type. One of these, of course, is the power of leaving spaces between the words of the Sanskṛit examples given. Will any student say that such an example as *sādhu-mitrāṇy akuśalād vārayanti* does not gain in clearness by being properly spaced †? Again, the power of using capitals and what are called italics (to say nothing of 'Egyptian' and other forms of European type) is manifestly an advantage to be placed to the credit of Indo-Romanic typography. Who will deny the gain in clearness by the ability to make a distinction between smith and Smith—brown and Brown—bath and Bath? And will any one examine the pages of this Dictionary, and then compare those of the Śabda-kalpadruma, without admitting the advantage gained in the power of employing italic type? Lastly, the

* It is certainly remarkable that the whole Vyākaraṇa of Pāṇini, unlike the Greek grammar or γράμμα, appears to ignore written symbols, as if Sanskṛit was never intended to have any peculiar graphic system of its own. In South India Sanskṛit is written in different characters; and the first inscriptions found on rocks are in Pāli and Prākṛit, not in Sanskṛit. They are referred to the Buddhist sovereigns who possessed political power in India about three centuries B.C. The present form of Nāgarī is thought to be little older than the tenth or eleventh century of our era.

† What should we think of an English Dictionary which, disdaining to aid our overtried vision by any typographical contrivances at the supposed sacrifice of euphonic propriety, should insist on presenting the corresponding example in proper phonetic conjunction thus—'goodfriendsguardfromevil?'

power of applying the hyphen to separate long compounds in a language where compounds prevail more than simple words *, will surely be appreciated by all. I can only say, that without that most useful little mark, the present volume must have lost much of its clearness, and probably half its compactness, for besides the obvious advantage of being able to indicate the difference between such compounds as *su-tapa* and *suta-pa*, which could not be done in Nāgarī type, it is manifest that even the simplest compounds, like *sad-asad-viveka*, *sv-alpa-keśin*, would have required without its use an extra line to explain their analysis †.

Notwithstanding all my advocacy of the Indo-Romanic graphic system, it is still my duty to point out that so long as the natives of India continue to use their own alphabets, so long is it incumbent upon us Englishmen who study Sanskṛit in its bearing upon the Indian vernaculars, to master the Nāgarī character. Under any circumstances there must be a long transition period during which the Indian and Romanic systems will co-exist, and however the struggle between them may terminate, the end is not likely to be witnessed by the existing generation. For this reason the Nāgarī alphabet is by no means ignored in these pages. On the contrary, it is pressed into the service of the Romanic, and made to minister to a most useful purpose, being employed to distinguish the leading word of a group in a manner best calculated to strike the eye and arrest the attention.

Fairness, moreover, demands that a few of the obvious defects of the system of transliteration adopted in this volume should be specified. In certain cases it confessedly offends against philosophical exactness; nor does it always consistently observe the rules stated in a preceding paragraph. The vowels *ṛi* and *ṛī* ought to be represented by some one symbol—such as that used by many German scholars—though *ṛ*, *ṝ* seem to me somewhat unsuitable for vowel sounds. So again the aspirated consonants ought not to be represented by a second letter attached to them. In the case of *ch* employed by Sir W. Jones for च and *chh* for छ, the inconvenience appeared to me so great that in the third edition of my Sanskṛit Grammar, I ventured to adopt *ć* for च, the pronunciation, however, being the same as *ch* in *church*, which might therefore be written *ćurć*. Had I dared to innovate further, I should have written *k'* for *kh*, *t'* for *th*, *p'* for *ph;* and so with the other aspirated consonants, *c* being then employed for च. The fact, of course, is that an aspirated consonant is merely a consonant pronounced with an emphatic emission of the breath, much as an Irishman would pronounce *p* in *penny*, and to indicate this, a stroke placed on one side or over the letter seems more appropriate than the mark of the Greek hard breathing adopted by Bopp, which may well be used alone to utter a vowel, but is scarcely suitable to emphasize a consonant ‡.

I also prefer the symbol *ṣ* for the cerebral sibilant. Should a second edition of this Dictionary be ever called for, some of these improvements may possibly be adopted. With regard to the letter *w*, I have discarded it, and retained only *v*, because the Nāgarī only possesses one character for the labial semivowel, viz. व, and to transliterate this or any other single Oriental character by two Roman representatives must certainly lead to confusion. As to the German method of using

* Forster gives an example of one compound word consisting of 152 syllables. I rather think this might be matched by even longer specimens from Ćampū composition.

† At any rate, it is to be hoped that the hyphen will not be denied to Sanskṛit for the better understanding of the more complex words, such, for example, as *vaidika-manv-ādi-praṇīta-smṛititvāt*, *karma-phala-rūpa-śarīra-dhāri-jīva-nirmitatvābhāva-mātreṇa*, taken at hap-hazard from Dr. Muir's Texts. We may even express a hope that German scholars and other Europeans, who speak forms of Āryan speech, all of them equally delighting in composition, may condescend more frequently to the employment of the hyphen for some of their own Sesquipedalia Verba, thereby imitating the practical Englishman in his Parliamentary compounds, such, for example, as habeas-corpus-suspension-act-continuance-Ireland-bill.

‡ A hint might be taken from Anglo-Saxon đ, as before observed, especially if ^ be used for long vowels. The mark ′ is perhaps too much like that required for accentuation. I hope, however, that the system of accentuating classical Sanskṛit will never be allowed. Why complicate a subject already sufficiently intricate by introducing another element of perplexity which native scholars themselves do not sanction? Let accentuation be kept for the Veda; and in Vedic words a more upright and conspicuous stroke might, in my opinion, be used with advantage.

k, *kh* for *ć*, *ćh*, and *ǵ*, *ǵh* for *j*, *jh*, the philological advantage gained by thus exhibiting the phonetic truth of the interchange of gutturals and palatals, appears to me outweighed by the disadvantage of representing sounds differing so greatly in actual pronunciation by similar symbols.

Notwithstanding the shortcomings and inconsistencies thus fairly acknowledged, I have no hesitation in asserting that the Romanic system expanded by the marks and signs now generally agreed upon and still further to be improved hereafter, may be adapted to the Āryan languages of India quite as completely and appropriately as to the Āryan languages of Europe.

Having felt obliged by the form in which this Dictionary is printed to dwell thus at length on a point of vast importance both to the general cultivation of Sanskṛit and the diffusion of knowledge in our Eastern Empire, I must now beg permission to record my sense of the great assistance this cause has received from the energetic efforts of one who has ever been a true friend to the natives of India, Sir Charles E. Trevelyan. He was the first Indian officer of eminence who appreciated the real bearing of this matter upon native education, and the first writer who in his able minute, dated Calcutta, January 1834*, cleared away the confusion of ideas with which the subject was then perplexed by many prejudiced persons and even by some scholars. He also was the first to awaken an interest in the question throughout England about thirteen years ago, aided as he was by the able advocacy of 'the Times' newspaper. To him and to 'the Times' I owe the first impressions which corrected my own prejudices. Since then, many Oriental books printed on a plan substantially agreeing with Sir W. Jones' Indo-Romanic system have been published, both by eminent scholars in Europe and by missionaries in India †, and the form in which the present Sanskṛit Dictionary is now put forth affords, I trust, another evidence of the reality of the movement and of its gradual advance.

Section 5.

Principal Sources drawn upon in the Process of Compilation.

I have now to enumerate the various works consulted by me in compiling this Dictionary. My only reason for not indicating these authorities in the body of the various articles as they have been written, has been that the volume—which even now has outgrown the dimensions originally fixed—would have thereby lost much of its convenient compactness, and could not have been produced at a moderate cost. The eye, too, would have been confused in passing from one meaning to another. Justice, however, requires that before commencing my enumeration, I should specially record my debt to particular authorities most frequently consulted and relied upon. I do so with a deep consciousness that nothing I am about to state can add to the celebrity of any one of the eminent scholars to whom I owe most. Indeed, it is impossible for me to express adequately my sense of obligation to the great work of Professors Böhtlingk and Roth. Although I have referred to every other dictionary, glossary, and vocabulary, including those of Professor Benfey and Westergaard and the eight-volumed Encyclopædia of Rādhākānta-

* This will be found at p. 3 of the 'Original Papers illustrating the History of the Application of the Roman Alphabet to the Languages of India,' edited by me at the request of Sir Charles Trevelyan in 1859, and published by Messrs. Longman. I commend this volume to every one interested in the diffusion of education among the natives of our Indian Empire.

† Amongst other publications the Ṛig-veda itself, edited by Professor Aufrecht, has been printed and published in the Roman character; also part of the Kathā-sarit-sāgara by Dr. Hermann Brockhaus. Dr. Muir in his Sanskṛit Texts has also extensively used the Indo-Romanic system, as well as Dr. Weber in the Indische Studien, where some of the Upanishads are so transliterated. Let any one compare Professor Aufrecht's one compact and cheap octavo volume with the six massive quartos to which the Ṛig-veda will extend, now being edited in the native character. Even if the Romanized edition had the commentary, it would probably not extend beyond two moderate octavo volumes. With regard to the series of valuable Hindūstānī works printed in the Anglo-Hindūstānī character by missionaries in India, a full account of them will be found in Sir Charles Trevelyan's 'Original Papers' referred to in a previous note. The whole Bible has been beautifully printed in this form, and carried through the press by the Rev. R. Cotton Mather; also a glossary to part of the Bible by his son Mr. Cotton Mather.

deva, commonly called the Śabda-kalpa-druma *, and although I have striven to weigh and verify for myself all the words and meanings given by my fellow lexicographers, yet I have always considered an appeal to the St. Petersburg Wörterbuch as the most satisfactory available means for deciding doubtful questions.

Naturally, I have kept Professor H. H. Wilson's Dictionary on my working-table, and have constantly had recourse to its pages. Indeed, I must own that I commenced by looking to my predecessor's labours as my chief authority. And let me here assert most emphatically, not only that, considering the condition of Sanskṛit scholarship when it was compiled, Professor Wilson's was a wonderful production, but that, like many other scholars, I could never have learnt Sanskṛit at all without its aid. Nevertheless, sincerity obliges me to confess, what other lexicographers may perhaps admit to be not without a parallel in their own mental history, that my mind has had to pass through a kind of painful discipline involving a gradual weakening of faith in the performances of my fellow men, not excepting those of my own venerated teacher. I began, indeed, with much confidence in the thought that one man existed on whom I could lean as an almost infallible guide; but as the work grew under my hands and my sensitiveness to error sharpened, I discovered to my surprise that I was compelled to reject much of his teaching as doubtful. Moreover, the truth must be told, that as I advanced further my trustfulness in others, besides my old master, began to experience occasional disagreeable and unexpected shocks; till now that I am arrived at the end of my work, I find myself left with my confidence in the accuracy of human beings generally—certainly not excepting myself—rather painfully disturbed. Nevertheless, I am bound thankfully to acknowledge that my faith in the general scholarlike exactness of the great German authorities already named has never been materially shaken. I ought also to make particular mention of Dr. John Muir's 'Sanskṛit Texts,' which have been constantly referred to by me, and have been found by experience to be invaluable, both for their general accuracy and for the judgment the author has displayed in his interpretation of Vedic words.

To these acknowledgments of special obligations I now subjoin an alphabetical list of all the principal works (not including of course all the mere texts and manuscripts) consulted by me, or in any way drawn upon for information, during the progress of my labours.

Andrew's (E. A.) Latin-English Dictionary.
Asiatic Researches.
Asiatic Society's (Royal) Journal.
Aufrecht's (Th.) Catalogue of Sanskṛit MSS. in the Bodleian Library, Oxford.
— Catalogue of Sanskṛit MSS. in the Library of Trinity College, Cambridge.
— Halāyudha's Vocabulary.
— Ṛig-veda-saṃhitā.
— Uṇādi-sūtras.

Ballantyne's (James) various lectures on Hindū Philosophy, and translations of some of the Aphorisms.
— translation of the Sāhitya-darpaṇa.
— Laghu-kaumudī.
Banerjea's (K. M.) Hindū Philosophy.
Banerjea's Kumāra-sambhava (with notes).
Benfey's Chrestomathie (with vocabulary).
— Sāma-veda (with vocabulary).
— Sanskṛit-English Dictionary.
— Sanskṛit Grammar.
Böhtlingk's (and Roth's) Sanskṛit-Wörterbuch.
Böhtlingk's Indische Sprüche.
— edition of Pāṇini's Grammar.
— edition of Vopa-deva's Grammar.
— (and Rieu's) Hemaćandra's Glossary.
Bombay edition of the Mahā-bhārata.
— of the Rāmāyaṇa.
Bopp's Glossary (first and second editions).
— Comparative Grammar (Eastwick).
Bosworth's (Dr. J.) Anglo-Saxon Dictionary and Grammar.
Brockhaus' (Hermann) Kathā-sarit-sāgara.
Burgess' translation of the Sūrya-siddhānta.
Burnouf's (Eugène) Bhāgavata-Purāṇa (books I–III, translated by Burnouf).
Burnouf's (Émile) Sanskṛit-French Dictionary.

Chambers' Encyclopædia.
Colebrooke's Amara-kosha.
— Indian Algebra.
— Essays on the Religion and Philosophy of the Hindūs.
— Dāya-bhāga.
— Mitāksharā.
Cowell's (E. B.) Kusumāñjali (with translation).

* A fine copy of this valuable work, now very difficult to procure in its perfect state, was searched for, some years ago, at Calcutta and most kindly presented to me by my friend Mr. Walter Scott Seton-Karr, Foreign Secretary to the Governments of Lord Lawrence and Lord Mayo, and Vice-Chancellor of the Calcutta University.

Cowell's (E. B.) translation of the Vikramorvaśī.
— edition of Elphinstone's History of India.
Curtius' (Georg) Grundzüge der Griechischen Etymologie.

Farrar's (F. W.) Families of Speech.
Foucaux's (Ph. Ed.) Episodes of the Mahā-bhārata.

Goldstücker's (Theodor) Sanskṛit-English Dictionary (parts I–VI).
Griffith's (Ralph T. H.) Specimens of Old Indian Poetry.

Hall's (Fitz-Edward) edition of the Sūrya-siddhānta.
— Contribution towards an Index to the Bibliography of the Indian Philosophical Systems.
— translation of Nīlakaṇṭha's Rational Refutation of the Hindū Philosophical Systems.
— Sāṅkhya-pravaćana-bhāshya.
— edition of Wilson's Vishṇu-Purāṇa.
Haughton's (Graves C.) Bengālī Dictionary.
Haug's (Martin) Aitareya-Brāhmaṇa (with translation.)
Hilpert's (J. D.) German Dictionary.

Johnson's (Francis) Hitopadeśa (first and second editions, with translation and vocabulary).
— Selections from the Mahā-bhārata (with vocabulary).
— Megha-dūta (1st and 2nd editions, with vocabulary).
Jones' (Sir William) translation of Manu.
Journal of the Royal Asiatic Society.

Lassen's Sanskṛit Anthology (with glossary).
Liddell's and Scott's Greek-English Lexicon.
Ludvig's Infinitiv im Veda.

Molesworth's (James T.) Murathee Dictionary.
Moor's Hindū Pantheon.
Müller's (Max) Ancient Sanskṛit Literature.
— Chips from a German Workshop.
— Hymns to the Maruts.
— Lectures on the Science of Language.
— Ṛig-veda-saṃhitā.
— Ṛig-veda-prātiśākhya.
— Sanskṛit Grammar.
Muir's (John) Original Sanskṛit Texts (five volumes).

Prinsep's (James) Indian Antiquities (edited with notes and addenda by Edward Thomas).

Rādhākānta-deva's Śabda-kalpa-druma.
Rājendralāla-Mitra's notices of Sanskṛit MSS.
Regnier's Étude sur l'idiome des Védas.
— Ṛigveda-prātiśākhya.
Rieu's (and Böhtlingk's) Hemaćandra.
Röer's (E.) Upanishads (with translations).
— (and Montriou's) Hindū Law.
Roth's (and Böhtlingk's) Sanskṛit-Wörterbuch).
Roth's Nirukta.
— (and Whitney's) Atharva-veda-saṃhitā.

Schlegel's (A. G.) Rāmāyaṇa.
Scott's and Liddell's Greek-English Lexicon.

Stenzler's edition of the Raghu-vaṇśa.
— Yājñavalkya.

Tāranātha Tarkavāćaspati's Dhātu-rūpādarśa.
Thompson's (J. C.) Bhagavad-gītā (with translation).
Thornton's Gazetteer.
Troyer's Rāja-taraṅgiṇī.

Vigfusson's (G.) Cleasby's Icelandic Dictionary.

Weber's (Albrecht) Vājasaneyi-saṃhitā.
— Śatapatha-Brāhmaṇa.
— Kātyāyana-śrauta-sūtra.
— Indische Studien.
— Indische Streifen.
Westergaard's Radices Linguæ Sanscritæ.
Whitney's (W. D.) Atharva-veda-prātiśākhya.
— (and Roth's) Atharva-veda-saṃhitā.
— Language and the Study of Language (twelve lectures).
Wilson's (H. H.) Glossary of Indian Terms.
— Sanskṛit-English Dictionary.
— Sanskṛit Grammar.
— Sāṅkhya-kārikā.
— Theatre of the Hindūs.
— translation of the Ṛig-veda (vols. I–IV).
— translation of the Vishṇu-Purāṇa.

Yates' (W.) octavo edition of Wilson's Sanskṛit Dictionary with addenda (partly edited by J. Wenger).

Zeitschrift der Deutschen morgenländischen Gesellschaft.

SECTION 6.

Aids and Encouragements received.

My first acknowledgments are due to the Delegates of the Clarendon Press, without whose kind patronage this work could never have been published. It does not become me to commend the efforts these gentlemen are making for the furtherance of education, except so far as to say that they fitly represent the mind and wishes of the University of Oxford. Nor does the Clarendon Press itself need any monument of my rearing. Let those who desire proofs of its efficiency look around and note the series of valuable educational books constantly issuing from its founts, models of clear and accurate typography, in almost every department of science.

Perhaps, however, I may be permitted to mention specially the name of one who has recently left us, but who was a member of the Press-Delegacy when the publication of this

Dictionary was undertaken, the late Master of Balliol and now Dean of Rochester, Dr. Robert Scott. He has been one of my kindest friends and wisest counsellors ever since the day I went to him for advice during my first undergraduate days at Balliol, on receiving an appointment in the Indian Civil Service. It is not too much, I think, to aver that without his support, encouragement, and sympathy,—all the more prized as coming from an experienced fellow-labourer, able to estimate the difficulties of a less experienced disciple,—I could not have persevered in this work to its termination.

My next acknowledgments must be tendered to the Representatives of the Governments of Bengal, Madras, Bombay, and the North-West Provinces of India, as well as of the India Office, for the substantial aid received from them in the patronage they have accorded to this undertaking.

I have in the third place to express in the most cordial manner my thanks to each and all of the gentlemen who have aided me in the compilation of this Dictionary.

No one but those who have taken part in similar labours can at all realize the amount of tedious toil—I might almost say drudgery—involved in the daily routine of small details, such as verifying references and meanings, making indices and lists of words, sorting and sifting an ever-increasing store of materials, revising old work, arranging and re-arranging new, correcting and re-correcting proofs, writing and re-writing and interlineating 'copy,' till reams upon reams of paper have been filled, putting the eye-sight, patience, and temper of compilers, readers, and compositors to a severe trial. I mention these matters, not to magnify the labours undergone, but to show that I could not have prosecuted them persistently single-handed. This statement may also give an idea of what I owe to the persevering co-operation of my kind assistants, whose names in the chronological order of their services are as follow: the Rev. J. Wenger, who is now I believe engaged in valuable literary work connected with the Baptist Mission in Calcutta; Dr. Franz Kielhorn, who is now Superintendant of Sanskṛit Studies in Deccan College, Poona; Dr. Hermann Brunnhofer (whose assistance was not of very long duration); Mr. A. E. Gough, M.A., of Lincoln College, Oxford, now Professor of Sanskṛit at the Government College, Benares; lastly, Mr. E. L. Hogarth, M.A., of Brasenose College, and formerly Head Master of the Government Provincial School at Calicut, who has been my constant and painstaking assistant for about three years and a half, continuing with me to the termination of the work. I must also thank my old friend Professor Francis Johnson, who was one of my first instructors in Sanskṛit when a student at Haileybury, and afterwards my colleague as Professor, for the kind interest he has shown in my labours, and the aid I have received from him at various times, including recently a list of words collected by himself in preparing a new volume of Selections from the Mahā-bhārata, shortly to be published.

Finally, I must express my gratitude for the extreme care with which the reading of my often intricate manuscript has been conducted by the Oriental Reader, and the printing of the whole book executed by the Managers of the Clarendon Press.

SECTION 7.

Defects and Inconsistencies acknowledged.

When some one pointed out to Dr. Johnson the imperfections of his great Dictionary, he is said to have retorted on his critics that mere fault-finding was often an indication of ignorance. His work was too large, he affirmed, not to take in errors, and the quicksightedness to these was a symptom of the dulness which could not comprehend the merit of the performance as a whole. Without imitating this convenient way of disposing of criticism in my own case,

I may yet request leave to inform any mere *Ĉhidrānveshin*, of whom it may be said *ĉhidraṃ nirūpya sahasā praviśati*, that no one can be more keenly alive to the flaws and defects of this volume than I am myself. No one, indeed, can be more desirous to criticize it, with a view to its improvement in a future edition.

If any real scholars—always considerate and temperate even if severe—having had practical experience of lexicography, will aid me in my efforts to attain greater accuracy, I shall be thankful. From them I do not fear but rather court criticism. Such critics will quite understand how a compiler's sense of responsibility may grow with the growth of a work like this, putting him out of conceit with his own performance, and filling him with earnest cravings after an accuracy more than human. Such critics will appreciate the difficulties besetting the production of so many closely printed pages abounding with countless dots and diacritical marks. Nor will they be surprised at inequalities of execution and occasional inconsistencies in a work representing efforts spread over numerous years. Nor will they need to be reminded that occasional distractions, trials of health and weariness of spirit, are incident not only to a human compiler but to his human assistants. Indeed it is no disparagement to those who have contributed to the detail of this work to assume that a compilation which has passed through many different hands must reflect the infirmities of all. No other apology will here be attempted for its errors and inadvertencies; nor do I ask that the blame be laid at the door of any one but myself, who alone am responsible. Some explanation, however, of a few intentional inconsistencies and almost unavoidable defects is here appended.

In the first place, there has not been absolute consistency in the collocation of words connected by a common etymology. I have not bound myself in this respect by any fixed rules. Hence some words are given in the usual alphabetical order of the Nāgarī type which might be expected to fall under a previous classification in the Indo-Romanic order. Facility of reference has been my only guide in this matter.

Again, in the arranging of a whole chain of words etymologically allied, some formations have been placed under compounds which ought properly to have a separate line assigned to them. Others again have separate lines which ought more consistently to come under compounds. For example, abstract nouns formed with the affixes *tā* and *tva*, and possessive adjectives formed with *vat*, *mat*, &c. are placed in the order of the compounds, when they are really not compounds at all. Still it is plain that such a word as *svāmi-tā*, 'ownership,' is really equivalent to *svāmi-bhāva*, and such a word as *śrī-mat*, 'possessed of fortune,' to *śrī-yukta*. In these cases my motive for sacrificing absolute consistency has rather been to gain space. Other liberties indulged in with regard to the use of the hyphen are noticed in the table of directions following the Preface.

With regard to the nominative cases of adjectives and of a few participles—such as those of Parasmai-pada Intensives—and even of a few substantives, I fear this Dictionary cannot always be quite trusted; though it may perhaps be conceded that I have improved upon my predecessor in this respect. In point of fact it has not been possible to settle with certainty the nominative cases, especially in the feminine forms, of all adjectives. The German Wörterbuch avoids exhibiting the nominative cases of adjectives and participles, and rarely gives their feminines, leaving also the nominative cases of substantives to be inferred from their gender. Although I studied Pāṇini's chapter on feminine formations with great care, I was unable to discover either in his Grammar or in any other Grammar or Dictionary a solution of all my difficulties. My rule has been to give the nominative cases both of substantives and adjectives in all their genders wherever there was ground for certainty or for a reasonable inference, and in other rare cases to exhibit only the crude base. Sometimes I have merely given the nominative case masculine of adjectives, omitting the feminine when that alone appeared doubtful, and leaving the neuter to be inferred; but throughout the Dictionary the omission of a nominative case has been quite an exception. Thus I have endeavoured to increase the usefulness of this publication even at the risk of occasionally misleading.

Another point requires a few words of explanation. I shall probably be told that meanings and synonyms are needlessly multiplied; but before the book is hastily censured on this score, let it be fairly tested by a repeated and extended application to various branches of the literature. I can with truth affirm that having myself constantly put these pages to a trial during their progress through the press, so far from having to regret any superfluity or surplusage, I have too often had to lament sins of omission, and have frequently discovered, when too late, that some one meaning has been rejected, because thought to be a mere synonym, when this very apparent synonym was really the precise word required to suit a particular passage.

With reference to the philological comparisons given throughout this work, I fear that occasional inconsistencies and violations of orthography will be found. For indeed I do not pretend to even a limited knowledge of some of the numerous languages compared, and my private library has not furnished the means of verifying all the words. It should be noted that I have not generally indicated the cognate English words with the Anglo-Saxon, because these are self-evident, and will generally be found among the meanings. As to other comparisons, I can only say that when I commenced my compilation, Bopp was considered the chief authority in comparative philology. I have not generally adopted what more modern scholars substitute for his teaching, because some of these later writers have themselves yet to undergo the full test of an extended criticism, which may not always support their opinions. Besides trusting to Bopp, I have generally followed Professors Benfey and Curtius, and I request that the comparisons given be accepted on the authority of these three scholars, subject to the understanding that more recent views have been propounded on many points.

Most of the errors and omissions hitherto discovered, whether typographical or caused by my own want of knowledge, have, I trust, been corrected and supplied in the supplementary matter at the end of the volume.

With these explanations I close my present labours, profoundly conscious of their imperfection, but full of thankfulness that my life has been spared to bring them, such as they are, to a completion.

MONIER WILLIAMS.

OXFORD, *May* 1872.

DIRECTIONS TO BE STUDIED BEFORE USING THIS DICTIONARY.

THERE are two alphabetical orders: 1. that in the Nāgarī; 2. that in the Indo-Romanic type.

Roots are always in large Sanskṛit type.

Verbs formed by prefixing prepositions to roots are arranged in the alphabetical order of the prepositions so affixed, e.g. *anu-kṛi* must *not* be looked for under the root *kṛi*, as in other Sanskṛit Dictionaries, but in its own alphabetical order, as in Greek lexicons, and at the head of its own group of derivatives. See p. 32, col. 1.

All the Sanskṛit words in Indo-Romanic type arranged in alphabetical order under a leading word—which leading word is always either a root in large Nāgarī type or some other word in small Nāgarī type—must be regarded as mutually connected. They must be supposed to form a family of words bound together by a common origin or dependent on each other by some tie of relationship. The derivation or etymology is generally given in a parenthesis after the leading word in Sanskṛit type, and this etymology is supposed to apply to all the group which follows, until a new classification of words is introduced by a *new word in Nāgarī type*. Other derivations are sometimes noticed when authorities differ in explaining the etymology of particular words.

The Nāgarī type is thus employed to strike the eye and direct it to the leading word in each group. By this means also a repetition of the etymology is avoided.

All the meanings of a word belonging to a group are not always given in full, if they may be manifestly gathered from its other members; this applies especially to participles and participial formations, e. g. the meaning 'charged with,' which belongs to *ā-ropita*, p. 128, col. 3, may readily be inferred from *ā-ropa*, which stands above it in the same classification.

Again, all the derivatives from a Radical or Verb at the head of a family are not always given when they may be readily supplied; this applies especially to participles, and occasionally to verbal nouns, e. g. under *vi-hiṉs* at the head of a group, p. 952, it is easy to supply *vi-hiṉsana, am*, n. the act of injuring.

Observe, that meanings which appear to be mere amplifications of preceding meanings are separated by a comma, whereas those which do not clearly run into each other are divided by a semicolon. All remarks upon meanings and all descriptive and explanatory statements are given between ( ); comparisons, between [ ].

Compound words are always arranged in alphabetical order *under the first word* in the compounds, a hyphen marking the division of each member of the compound, and when the final and initial vowel of two members of a compound blend, the separation of these vowels is denoted by a hyphen in brackets, (see, for example, *kṛitodaka* for *kṛita-udaka*, p. 248, col. 1, line 4.) For greater clearness, some words are thus treated, which are formed by Taddhita affixes, *supposed to be added to the whole word*, and which therefore ought not strictly to have a hyphen at all.

Compound words divided by a hyphen or hyphens have no etymology given because the employment of the hyphen makes their several elements manifest at once, so that it is always easy to refer to the separate members of the compound for the several etymologies, e. g. *an-oka-śāyin* is manifestly separable into *an* + *oka* + *śāyin*, to each of which it is easy to refer for an explanation of the several etymologies.

When no etymology of a simple word is exhibited its derivation is either unknown or too doubtful to deserve recording.

The nominative cases of all nouns, substantive and adjective, and of all participles, are given immediately after the crude base, except in the cases explained at the end of the preceding Preface. Thus *guru, us, vī, u*, means that the adjective *guru* makes in its nominative case masc. fem. and neut., *gurus, gurvī, guru*; similarly *vividvas, ān, ushī, at* (p. 919, col. 2), stands for nom. masc. fem. and neut., *vividvān, vividushī, vividvat*.

Under roots and verbs the 3rd pers. singular of the various tenses is given, other forms being noticed in parentheses. The names of the tenses are generally left to be inferred, except when an unusual tense, like the Precative, is given, and the form of the 1st Future can always be inferred from the Infinitive: thus the Infinitive being *veditum*, the 1st Future 3rd pers. sing. will be *veditā*; similarly from *dagdhum* will be inferred 1st Future 3rd pers. sing. *dagdhā*.

When words really dissimilar appear similar either in Roman or Nāgarī type, the figures 1, 2, 3, &c. are placed before them; see, for example, 1. *sa*, 2. *sa*, 3. *sa*, 4. *sa*, 5. *sa*; 1. *suta-pa*, 2. *su-tapa*; 1. *sam-āna*, 2. *samāna*; 1. *saha*, 2. *saha*; 1. *sv-ap*, 2. *svap*.

It is believed that few common words or meanings likely to be met with in the classical literature have been omitted in this work; nevertheless the Supplement at the end of the volume should occasionally be consulted: thus in the two pages, 623, 624, one or two words and the common meaning 'affix,' belonging to *praty-aya*, have accidently dropped out, but are supplied in the supplementary pages.

ABBREVIATIONS AND SYMBOLS USED IN THIS DICTIONARY.

[*In the progress of a work extending over several years it has been found almost impossible to preserve uniformity in the use of symbols, but it is hoped that most of the inconsistencies are noticed in the following table.*]

A. = Ātmane-pada; the long mark over the A. has been omitted for convenience in printing.
abl. *or* abl. c. = ablative case.
acc. *or* acc. c. = accusative case.
accord. = according.
Ādi-p. = Ādi-parvan of the Mahā-bhārata.
adj. = adjective.
Æol. = Æolic.
alg. = algebra.
Angl. Sax. = Anglo-Saxon.
anom. = anomalous, irregular.
Aor. = Aorist.
Arab. = Arabic.
arithm. = arithmetic.
Arm. *or* Armor. = Armorican or the language of Brittany.
Armen. = Armenian.
astrol. = astrology.
astron. = astronomy.
Atharva-v. = Atharva-veda, edited by Roth and Whitney.
Bhāgavata-P. = Bhāgavata-Purāṇa, Burnouf's edition, or Bombay edition for the later books.
Bhaṭṭi-k. = Bhaṭṭi-kāvya, Calcutta edition.
Boh. *or* Bohem. = Bohemian.
B. R. = Böhtlingk and Roth.
Br. = Brāhmaṇa.
Bret. = Breton.
Buddh. = Buddhist.
c. = case.
Cambro-Brit. = the language of Wales.
Caus. = Causal.
cf. = confer, compare.
chap. = chapter.
cl. = class.
Class. = Classical.
col., cols. = column, columns.
comm. = commentator or commentary.
comp., comps. = compound, compounds.
compar. = comparative degree.
Cond. *or* Condit. = Conditional.
cons. = consonant.
dat. *or* dat. c. = dative case.
defect. = defective.
Desid. = Desiderative.
dimin. = diminutive.
Dor. = Doric.
du. = dual number.
ed. *or* edit. = edition.
e. g. = exempli gratiâ.
Eng. = English.
Ep. *or* ep. = Epic, i. e. such works as the Mahā-bhārata, Rāmāyaṇa, &c.
epith. = epithet.
esp. = especially.
etym. = etymology.
explet. = expletive.
f. *or* fem. = feminine.
fr. = from.
Fut. = Future.
Gaël. = Gaëlic.
gen. *or* gen. c. = genitive case.
gend. = gender.
geom. = geometry.
Germ. = German or High-German.
Goth. = Gothic.
Gr. = Greek.
Gram. = A Practical Sanskrit Grammar by Monier Williams, third edition, published at the Clarendon Press.
gram. = grammar.
Hib. = Hibernian or Irish.
Hind. = Hindī.
Icel. = Icelandic.
i. e. = id est.
impers. = impersonal, i. e. used impersonally.
Impf. = Imperfect tense.
Impv. = Imperative.
ind. = indeclinable, either an indeclinable participle or an adverb or a case used adverbially.
Inf. *or* infin. = Infinitive mood.
inst. *or* inst. c. = instrumental case.
Intens. = Intensive.
Ion. = Ionic.
Island. = the German form of Icelandic.
Kirāt. *or* Kirātārj. = Kirātārjunīya.
Kumāra-s. = Kumāra-sambhava.
Lat. = Latin.
lat. = latitude.
Lett. = Lettish.
lit. = literally.
Lith. = Lithuanian.
loc. *or* loc. c. = locative case.
long. = longitude.
m. *or* masc. = masculine gender.
Mahā-bh. &c. = Mahā-bhārata, Calcutta edition.
mathem. = mathematics.
medic. = medicine.
Megh. = Megha-dūta, Johnson's second edition.
Mod. = Modern.
MS., MSS. = manuscript, manuscripts.
N. = Name.
n. *or* neut. = neuter gender.
Naigh. = Naighaṇṭuka.
neg. = negative.
Nir. = Nirukta.
Nom. *or* nom. = Nominal verb.
nom. *or* nom. c. = nominative case.
num. *or* numb. = number.
obs. = obsolete.
occ. = occasionally.
Osc. *or* Osk. = Oscan or Oskan.
Osset. = Ossetic (see p. ix).
P. = Parasmai-pada.
p. = page.
-p. = parvan or section of the Mahā-bhārata.
Pāṇ. = Pāṇini.
Part. *or* part. = Participle.
Pass. = Passive voice.
patron. = patronymic.
Perf. = Perfect tense.
Pers. = Persian.
pers. = person.
phil. = philosophy.
pl. *or* plur. = plural number.
poet. = poetry, poetic license.
Pol. = Polish.
Pot. = Potential.
Pr. = proper.
Prāk. = Prākṛit.
Prep. = Preposition.
Pres. = Present tense.
priv. = privative.
pronom. = pronominal.
Pruss. = Prussian.
q. v. = quod vide.
Raghu-v. = Raghu-vaṇśa.
Reflex. = Reflexive or used reflexively.
Ṛig-v. = Ṛig-veda.
rt., rts. = root, roots.
Russ. = Russian.
Śabda-k. = Śabda-kalpa-druma.
Sabin. = Sabine or Sabellian (old Italic dialect).
Sāma-v. = Sāma-veda.
Sans. = Sanskṛit.
Sax. = Saxon.
Sāy. = Sāyaṇa or according to Sāyaṇa.
Schol. = Scholiast or Commentator.
scil. = scilicet.
Scot. = Scotch or Highland-Scotch.
sing. = singular number.
Slav. = Slavonic or Slavonian.
subst. = substantive.
superl. = superlative degree.
s. v. = sub voce.
Them. = Thema or base.
Umbr. = Umbrian.
Uṇādi-s. = Uṇādi-sutras (Aufrecht's edition).
usu. = usually.
Vājasaneyi-s. = Vājasaneyi-saṃhitā.
Vārt. *or* Vārtt. = Vārttika.
Ved. = Vedic or Veda.
Vish.-Pur. = Vishṇu-Purāṇa.
voc. *or* voc. c. = vocative case.
=, equal, equivalent to, the same as, explained by.
\+ plus.
&c. = et cetera.
◡ denotes that a vowel or syllable is to be noted as short.
\- that a vowel or syllable is long.
° that the rest of a word is to be supplied, e. g. °*ri-in*° after *karīndra* is for *kari-indra*.

THE DICTIONARY ORDER OF THE NĀGARĪ LETTERS

WITH THEIR INDO-ROMANIC EQUIVALENTS AND THEIR PRONUNCIATION EXEMPLIFIED BY ENGLISH WORDS.

Vowels.

Initial.	Medial.	Equivalents and Pronunciation.	
अ	—	a	*in* mica, rural.
आ	ा	ā	,, tar, father (tār, fāther).
इ	ि	i	,, fill, lily.
ई	ी	ī	,, police (polīce).
उ	ु	u	,, full, bush.
ऊ	ू	ū	,, rude (rūde).
ऋ	ृ	ṛi	,, merrily (merṛily).
ॠ	ॄ	ṛī	,, marine (maṛīne).
ऌ	ॢ	lṛi	,, revelry (revelṛi).
ॡ	ॣ	lṛī	,, the above prolonged.
ए	े	e	,, prey, there.
ऐ	ै	ai	,, aisle.
ओ	ो	o	,, go, stone.
औ	ौ	au	,, Haus (German).

SIGNS OR SYMBOLS.

ं	n̲ or ṃ	either the true Anusvāra, sounded like *n* in French *mon*, or the symbol of any nasal.
ः	ḥ	symbol for the sibilant called Visarga.

Consonants.

	Equivalents and Pronunciation.			Equivalents and Pronunciation.	
क्	k	*in* kill, seek.	द्	d	*in* dice (more like *th* in *this*).
ख्	kh	,, ink-horn (inkhorn).	ध्	dh	,, adhere (but more dental).
ग्	g	,, gun, get, dog.	न्	n	,, not, nut, in.
घ्	gh	,, log-hut (loghut).	प्	p	,, put, sip.
ङ्	n·	,, sing, king, sink (sin·k).	फ्	ph	,, uphill.
च्	ć	,, dolće (in music).	ब्	b	,, bear, rub.
छ्	ćh	,, church-hill (ćurćhill).	भ्	bh	,, abhor.
ज्	j	,, jet, jump.	म्	m	,, map, jam.
झ्*	jh	,, hedge-hog (hejhog).	य्	y	,, yet, loyal.
ञ्	ṅ	,, singe (siṅj).	र्	r	,, red, year.
ट्	ṭ	,, true (ṭrue).	ल्	l	,, lull, lead.
ठ्	ṭh	,, ant-hill (anṭhill).	ळ्	ḷ	,, (sometimes for ड् *ḍ* in Veda).
ड्	ḍ	,, drum (ḍrum).	ळ्ह्	ḷh	,, (sometimes for ढ् *ḍh* in Veda).
ढ्	ḍh	,, red-haired (reḍhaired).	व्	v	,, ivy (but like *w* after cons.).
ण्	ṇ	,, none (ṇoṇe).	श्	ś	,, sure, session (śure, seśśion).
त्	t	,, water (in Ireland).	ष्	sh	,, shun, bush.
थ्	th	,, nuthook (more dental).	स्	s	,, saint, sin, hiss.
			ह्	h	,, hear, hit.

* Sometimes printed in the form झ्, see pp. 147, 354.

Note—The conjunct consonants are too numerous to be exhibited above, but the most common will be found at the end of 'A Practical Sanskṛit Grammar by Monier Williams,' published by the Delegates of the Clarendon Press, third edition.

For the correct pronunciation of the aspirated consonants, *kh, ćh, ṭh, th, ph,* &c., see p. xix of the preceding Preface.

THE DICTIONARY ORDER OF THE INDO-ROMANIC LETTERS

WITHOUT THEIR NĀGARĪ EQUIVALENTS.

a, ā; i, ī; u, ū; ṛi, ṛī; lṛi, lṛī; e, ai; o, au;—n̲ or ṃ, ḥ;—k, kh; g, gh; n·;—ć, ćh; j, jh; ṅ;—ṭ, ṭh; ḍ, ḍh; ṇ;—t, th; d, dh; n;—p, ph; b, bh; m;—y, r, l, ḷ, ḷh, v;—ś, sh, s;—h.

Observe—*n̲* represents the true Anusvāra in the body of a word before the sibilants and *h*, as in *an̲śa, an̲sa, an̲hati:* *ṃ* as the symbol of any nasal will often be found at the end of a word, as in *dānaṃ ća;* but may also represent Anusvāra, when final *m* is followed by initial sibilants and *h*, and in words formed with preposition *sam*, like *saṃ-śaya, saṃ-hata:* in the word Sanskṛit the second *s* is not initial, but introduced into the body of the word, so that we might properly write San̲skṛit. Visarga as a substitute for final *s* is a distinctly audible aspirate, so that the *ḥ* at the end of *devaḥ* must be clearly heard.

अ 1. *a*, the first letter of the alphabet; the first short vowel inherent in consonants. – *A-kāra*, *as*, m. the letter or sound *a*.

अ 2. *a*, ind. an interjection of pity (Ah !).

अ 3. *a* (before a vowel *an*), a prefix corresponding to Gr. ἀ, ἀν, Lat. *in*, Goth. and Germ. *un*, Eng. *in* or *un*, and having a negative or privative or depreciative sense; e. g. *eka* one, *an-eka* not one; *anta* end, *an-anta* endless; *paśyat* seeing, *a-paśyat* not seeing. Sometimes this prefix denotes comparison. It is occasionally an expletive.

अ 4. *a*, the base of some pronouns and pronom. forms; (substituted for *idam*, in *asya*, *atra*, &c.)

अ 5. *a*, the augment prefixed to the root in the formation of the imperfect, aorist, and conditional tenses, by some considered as connected with 3. *a*, and by others as connected with 4. *a*.

अ 6. *a*, *as*, m., N. of Vishṇu (especially as the first of the three sounds in the sacred syllable *om*), also of Brahmā, Śiva, and Vaiśvānara; (*am*), n. Brahma.

अऋणिन् *a-ṛiṇin*, *ī*, *inī*, *i*, free from debt.

अंश् *anś*, cl. 10. P. *anśayati*, *-yitum*, to divide, distribute; also occasionally A. *anśayate*; also *anśāpayati*.

Anśa, *as*, m. a share, portion, part, party; partition, inheritance; a share of booty; earnest money; a fraction; the denominator of one; a degree of lat. or long.; N. of an Āditya; the shoulder or shoulder-blade, more usually spelt *anṣa*, q. v. [cf. Old Germ. *ahsala*; Mod. Germ. *achsel*; Lat. *axilla*]. – *Anśa-karaṇa*, *am*, n. act of dividing. – *Anśa-bhāj*, *k*, *k*, *k*, one who has a share, an heir, a co-heir. – *Anśa-vat*, *ān*, m. a species of the Soma plant. – *Anśa-savarṇana*, *am*, n. reduction of fractions. – *Anśa-svara*, *as*, m. the key-note. – *Anśa-hara*, *as*, *ā* or *ī*, *am*, or *anśa-hārin*, *ī*, *iṇī*, *i*, one who takes a share, a sharer. – *Anśānśa* (°*śa-an*°), *as*, m. part of a portion (of a deity), a secondary incarnation. – *Anśānśi*, ind. share by share. – *Anśāvataraṇa* (°*śa-av*°), *am*, n. descent of parts of the deities; partial incarnation; title of sections 64–67 of the first book of the Mahā-bhārata.

Anśaka, *as*, *ā* or *ikā*, *am*, having a share; m. f. a co-heir, a relative; m. a share; n. a day.

Anśana, *am*, n. the act of sharing or dividing.

Anśanīya or *anśayitavya*, *as*, *ā*, *am*, divisible.

Anśayitṛi, *tā*, *trī*, *tṛi*, a divider, sharer.

Anśala. See *anṣala* next col.

Anśita, *as*, *ā*, *am*, divided, shared.

Anśin, *ī*, *inī*, *i*, a sharer, co-heir.

Anśu, *us*, m. a filament, especially of the Soma plant; end of a thread; a minute particle; a point or end; a garment, decoration; a ray, light, the sun; N. of a Ṛishi or of a prince. – *Anśu-jāla*, *am*, n. a collection of rays, a blaze of light. – *Anśu-dhara*, *as*, m. the bearer of rays, the sun. – *Anśu-paṭṭa*, *am*, n. a kind of cloth. – *Anśu-pati*, *is*, or *-bhartṛi*, *tā*, m. the lord of rays, the sun. – *Anśu-mat*, *ān*, *atī*, *at*, fibrous, rich in filaments; radiant, luminous; pointed; (*ān*), m. the sun, the moon; N. of various persons, especially of a prince of the solar race, son of A-samañjas, grandson of Sagara; (*tī*), f. the celestial river Yamunā; a plant, Hedysarum Gangeticum. – *Anśumat-phalā*, f. a plant, Musa Paradisiaca. – *Anśu-mālā*, f. a garland of light, halo. – *Anśu-mālin*, *ī*, m. the sun. – *Anśu-vāṇa*, *as*, m. having rays for arrows, the sun. – *Anśu-hasta*, *as*, m. having rays in his hand, the sun.

Anśuka, *am*, n. a leaf; cloth; fine or white cloth; muslin, an upper garment; a mantle.

Anśula, *as*, *ā*, *am*, radiant; (*as*), m., N. of the sage Cāṇakya.

Anśya, *as*, *ā*, *am*, divisible.

अंस् *ans*, cl. 10. P. *ansayati*, &c., = *anś*.

अंस *ansa*, *as*, m. (fr. rt. *am*), the shoulder, shoulder-blade; N. of a king; a share, see *anśa*; (*au*), m. du. the two shoulders or angles of an altar [cf. Goth. *amsa*; Gr. ὤμος; Lat. *humerus*, *ansa*]. – *Ansa-kūṭa*, *as*, m. a bull's hump, the protuberance between the shoulders of the Indian ox. – *Ansa-tra*, *am*, n. armour to protect the shoulder; a bow. – *Ansa-dhrī*, f. a cooking vessel (?). – *Ansa-phalaka*, *as*, m. upper part of the spine. – *Ansa-bhāra* or *anse-bhāra*, *as*, m. a yoke or burden put upon the shoulder. – *Ansa-bhārika* or *anse-bhārika*, *as*, *ī*, *am*, or *ansa-bhārin* or *anse-bhārin*, *ī*, *iṇī*, *i*, bearing a yoke.

Ansala, *as*, *ā*, *am*, lusty, strong.

Ansya, *as*, *ā*, *am*, belonging to the shoulder.

अंह् *anh* (allied to *angh*), cl. 1. A. *anhate*, *-hitum*, to go, set out, commence; to approach: cl. 10. P. *anhayati*, to send; to speak; to shine. [The rt. *anh* seems to have had originally another meaning, viz. to press together, strangle; = Gr. ἄγχω.]

Anhati, *is*, f. (probably fr. the preceding rt., said to be here a substitute for *han*), anxiety, distress, trouble, illness [cf. Lat. *ango*]; a gift, (in this sense also *anhatī*, f.)

Anhas, n. (said to be connected with rt. *am*), anxiety, trouble; sin [cf. *agha*, *āgas*; Gr. ἄχνυμαι, ἄχος, ἄγος]. – *Anhasas-pati*, *is*, m., Ved. lord of the perplexity, i. e. an intercalary month. – *Anhas-vat*, *ān*, *atī*, *at*, sinful. – *Anho-muć*, *k*, *k*, *k*, Ved. delivering from distress.

Anhiti, *is*, f. a gift, donation. See *anhati*.

Anhu, *us*, *us*, *u*, Ved. strait, narrow; (*us*), m., N. of an Asura; (*u*), n. anxiety, distress; Pudendum Muliebre [cf. Gr. ἐγγύς; Goth. *aggvus*; Lat. *angustus*, *anxius*, &c.]. – *Anhu-bhedī*, f. having a narrow slit, having the pudendum divided.

Anhura, *as*, *ā*, *am*, straitened, distressed; sinful.

Anhūraṇa, *as*, *ā*, *am*, distressing, sinful; (*am*), n. sin, distress.

Anhoyu, *us*, *us*, *u*, Ved. troublesome; freed from sin.

Anhri, *is*, m. a foot, the root of a tree [cf. *anghri*]. – *Anhri-pa*, *as*, m. a tree (foot-drinker). – *Anhri-skandha*, *as*, m. a part of the foot between the ancle and the heel.

अक् *ak*, cl. 1. P. *akati*, *akitum*, to move tortuously, like a snake [cf. Gr. ἀγκή, ἀγκαί, ἀγκών; Lat. *angulus*]. Compare rt. *ag*.

Aka, *as*, *ā*, *am*, moving tortuously; (*am*), n. pain, trouble, sin (also derived from *a*, not + *ka*, happiness).

अकच *a-kaća*, *as*, *ā*, *am*, destitute of hair, bald; (*as*), m., N. of Ketu, the dragon's tail or descending node, the symbol of which is a headless trunk.

अकण्टक *a-kaṇṭaka*, *as*, *ā*, *am*, free from thorns, troubles, difficulties, or enemies.

अकत्थन *a-katthana*, *as*, *ā*, *am*, not boastful.

अकथ्य *a-kathya*, *as*, *ā*, *am*, unspeakable; not to be uttered or mentioned.

अकनिष्ठ *a-kanishṭha*, *as*, *ā*, *am*, not the youngest; elder, superior; (*as*), m. a deified Buddhist saint, Buddha. – *Akanishṭha-ga*, *as*, m. Buddha.

अकन्या *a-kanyā*, f. no virgin.

अकपीवत् *akapīvat*, *ān*, m., N. of a Ṛishi.

अकम्पित *a-kampita*, *as*, *ā*, *am*, unshaken, firm; (*as*), m., N. of a Jaina saint, a pupil of the last Tīrtha-kara.

A-kampya, *as*, *ā*, *am*, not to be shaken.

अकर *a-kara*, *as*, *ā* or *ī*, *am*, handless, maimed; exempt from tax or duty, privileged; not acting; (*ā*), f. Emblic Myrobalan, Phyllanthus Emblica.

अकरण *a-karaṇa*, *am*, n. absence of action.

A-karaṇi, *is*, f. non-accomplishment, failure, disappointment (used in imprecations, e. g. *tasyākaraṇir evāstu*, may he experience a failure !).

A-karaṇīya, *as*, *ā*, *am*, not to be done.

अकरुण *a-karuṇa*, *as*, *ā*, *am*, merciless, relentless. – *Akaruṇa-tva*, *am*, n. harshness, cruelty.

अकर्कश *a-karkaśa*, *as*, *ā*, *am*, not hard, not rugged, soft, tender.

अकर्ण *a-karṇa* or *a-karṇaka*, *as*, *ā*, *am*, without ears, deaf.

A-karṇya, *as*, *ā*, *am*, not fit for the ears; not in the ears.

अकर्णधार *a-karṇadhāra*, *as*, *ā*, *am*, without a helmsman, destitute of a pilot.

अकर्तन *a-kartana*, *as*, m, a dwarf (?).

अकर्तृ *a-kartṛi*, *tā*, m. not an agent; an inferior agent. – *Akartṛi-tva*, *am*, n. condition of an inferior agent, a subordinate station.

अकर्मन् *a-karman*, *ā*, *ā*, *a*, without work, idle; inefficient; disqualified for performing essential rites, destitute of good works; (in grammar) intransitive; (*a*), n. absence of work; absence of essential observances; improper work, crime. – *Akarma-bhoga*, *as*, m. renunciation of self-righteousness; enjoyment of freedom from the fruits of action. – *A-karmānvita* (°*ma-an*°), *as*, *ā*, *am*, unoccupied, disqualified; criminal.

A-karmaka, *as*, *ā*, *am*, (in grammar) intransitive.

A-karmaṇya, *as*, *ā*, *am*, improper to be done; unfit for work; inefficient.

अकल *a-kala*, *as*, *ā*, *am*, not in parts, entire.

अकल्क *a-kalka*, *as*, *ā*, *am*, free from sediment; pure; sinless; (*ā*), f. moonlight. – *Akalka-tā*, f. honesty.

अकल्कन *a-kalkana* or *a-kalkala*, *as*, *ā*, *am*, free from pride, modest, honest.

अकल्प *a-kalpa*, *as*, *ā*, *am*, not subject to rules, uncontrolled; incomparable; unable, weak.

A-kalpita, *as*, *ā*, *am*, not manufactured, not artificial, not pretended; natural, genuine.

अकल्मष *a-kalmasha*, *as*, *ā*, *am*, sinless, faultless.

अकल्माष *a-kalmāsha*, *as*, m., N. of a son of the fourth Manu.

अकल्य *a-kalya*, *as*, *ā*, *am*, unwell, ill, sick.

A-kalyāṇa, *as*, *ā*, *am*, not prosperous, inauspicious; (*am*), n. adversity.

अकव *a-kava*, *as*, *ā*, *am* (fr. 1. *ku*, q. v.), Ved. not contemptible, not bad. – *A-kavāri* (°*va-ari*), *is*, *is*, *i*, Ved. not contemptible as an enemy, or to his enemies, or in his enemies; not having weak enemies.

अकवच *a-kavaća*, *as*, *ā*, *am*, Ved. without a coat of mail.

अकवि *a-kavi, is, is, i,* Ved. unwise.

अकस्मात् *a-kasmāt,* ind. without a why or a wherefore, accidentally, suddenly.

अकाण्ड *a-kāṇḍa, as, ā, am,* 'without a trunk,' causeless, unexpected. — *Akāṇḍa-pāta-jāta, as, ā, am,* dying as soon as born. — *Akāṇḍa-śūla, am,* n. sudden attack of colic.
A-kāṇḍe, ind. causelessly, unexpectedly.

अकातर *a-kātara, as, ā, am,* not down-hearted, cheerful, hearty.

अकाम *a-kāma, as, ā, am,* without desire or affection, without intention; unintentional, reluctant; (in grammar) the Sandhi which causes the dropping of a final *r* before a succeeding *r;* (*as*), m. absence of desire or affection. — *A-kāma-karśana, as,* m., Ved. not disappointing desires. — *Akāma-tas,* ind. unintentionally, unwillingly. — *Akāma-tā,* f. freedom from desire or affection or intention. — *A-kāma-hata, as, ā, am,* not smitten with desire or affection; free from desire, calm.
A-kāmin, ī, inī, i, the same as *a-kāma.*

अकाय *a-kāya, as, ā, am,* incorporeal.

अकारण *a-kāraṇa, as, ā, am,* causeless; (*am*), n. absence of a cause; ind. causelessly. — *A-kā-raṇotpanna* (°*ṇa-ut*°), *as, ā, am,* produced spontaneously.
A-kārin, ī, iṇī, i, inactive, not performing.

अकार्णवेष्टकिक *a-kārṇaveshṭakika, as, ī, am,* not adapted for ear-rings. See *karṇa-veshṭaka.*

अकार्य *a-kārya, as, ā, am,* not to be done, impracticable, improper; (*am*), n. a criminal action. — *Akārya-kārin, ī, iṇī, i,* an evil-doer; one who neglects his duty.

अकार्ष्ण्य *a-kārshṇya, am,* n. absence of blackness.

अकाल *a-kāla, as,* m. a wrong or bad or inauspicious time; (*as, ā, am*), unseasonable. — *A-kāla-kushmāṇḍa, as,* m. a pumpkin produced out of season; a useless birth. — *Akāla-kusuma, am,* n. a flower blossoming out of season. — *Akāla-ja* or *akāla-jāta* or *a-kālotpanna* (°*la-ut*°), *as, ā, am,* born or produced at a wrong time, unseasonable. — *Akāla-jaludodaya* (°*da-ud*°) or *akāla-megho-daya* (°*gha-ud*°), *as,* m. unseasonable rise of clouds; a mist. — *Akāla-velā,* f. unseasonable or unusual time. — *Akāla-saha, as, ā, am,* unable to bide one's time.
A-kālya, as, ā, am, unseasonable.

अकिञ्चन *a-kiñćana, as, ā, am,* without anything, utterly destitute, poor; disinterested; (*am*), n. that which is nothing, or worth nothing. — *A-kiñćana-tā,* f. voluntary poverty (as the duty of a Jaina ascetic).
A-kiñćaniman, ā, m. destitution, poverty.

अकितव *a-kitava, as,* m. no gambler.

अकिल्विष *a-kilvisha, as, ā, am,* sinless, faultless.

अकीर्त्ति *a-kīrtti, is,* f. bad repute. — *Akīrtti-kara, as, ā, am,* disreputable.

अकुण्ठ *a-kuṇṭha, as, ā, am,* not blunted or worn out; fresh, vigorous, fixed. — *A-kuṇṭha-dhishṇya, am,* n. heaven.
A-kuṇṭhita, as, ā, am, = *akuṇṭha* above.

अकुतस् *a-kutas,* ind. (usually found in composition), not from anywhere or any cause. — *A-kutaś-ćala, as,* m. not moveable from any cause; a title of Śiva. — *A-kuto-bhaya, as, ā, am,* not afraid or threatened from any quarter, secure.
A-kutra or *a-kutrā,* ind., Ved. nowhere, i. e. astray.

अकुत्सित *a-kutsita, as, ā, am,* unreproached.

अकुध्र्यञ्च् *a-kudhryańć, an, dhrīćī, ak* (*ku-dhri* for *kadha* for *kuha* = *kutra*), Ved. going nowhere, coming to nothing; (Sāy.) fruitless, worthless.

अकुप्य *a-kupya, am,* n. 'not base metal,' gold or silver; any base metal, (see 3. *a* at end.)

अकुमार *a-kumāra, as,* m. not a boy; an epithet of Vishṇu.

अकुल *a-kula, as, ā, am,* not of a good family, low; (*as*), m., N. of Śiva; (*ā*), f., N. of Pārvatī. — *Akula-tā,* f. lowness of family.
A-kulīna, as, ā, am, not of a good family.

अकुशल *a-kuśala, as, ā, am,* inauspicious, evil; not clever; (*am*), n. evil, an inauspicious or evil word.

अकुसीद *a-kusīda, as, ā, am,* not wishing for interest or gain; (also *a-kuśīda.*)

अकुसुम *a-kusuma, as, ā, am,* destitute of flowers or blossoms.

अकुह *a-kuha, as,* m. no deceiver.

अकूपार *a-kū-pāra, as, ā, am* (probably fr. *akū* for *a-ku,* not bad, not contemptible, and *pāra,* opposite shore or limit), having a good issue or effect; unbounded; (*as*), m. the sea; the sun; the king of tortoises, who upholds the world; any tortoise or turtle.
A-kūvāra = *a-kū-pāra* above.

अकूर्च *a-kūrća, as, ā, am,* guileless; (*as*), m. Buddha.

अकृच्छ्र *a-kṛićchra, as, am,* m. n. absence of difficulty; facility.
A-kṛićchrin, ī, iṇī, i, free from trouble.

अकृत *a-kṛita, as, ā, am,* undone, unperformed; not made, uncreated; not prepared, not ready, incomplete; one who has done no works; (*am*), n. an unperformed act; an unheard-of action or crime; (*ā*), f. a daughter not placed on a level with sons. — *Akṛita-kāram,* ind. as has not been done before. — *Akṛita-jña, as, ā, am,* ungrateful. — *Akṛita-jña-tā,* f. ingratitude. — *Akṛita-buddhi, is, is, i,* having an unformed mind. — *A kṛitabuddhi-tva, am,* n. ignorance. — *Akṛita-vraṇa, as,* m., N. of an expounder of the Purāṇas. — *Akṛitātman* (°*ta-āt*°), *ā, ā, a,* having an unformed mind; not yet identified with the supreme spirit. — *Akṛitārtha* (°*ta-ar*°), *as, ā, am,* having one's object unaccomplished, unsuccessful. — *A-kṛitāstra* (°*ta-as*°), *as, ā, am,* unpractised in arms. — *A-kṛitainas* (°*ta-en*°), *ās, ās, as,* innocent. — *Akṛitodvāha* (°*ta-ud*°), *as, ā, am,* unmarried.
A-kṛitin, ī, inī, i, unfit for work, clumsy. — *Akṛiti-tva, am,* n. unfitness for work.
A-kṛitya, as, ā, am, not to be done, criminal; (*am*), n. crime. — *Akṛitya-kārin, ī, iṇī, i,* evil-doer.

अकृत्त *a-kṛitta, as, ā, am,* uncut, unimpaired. — *Akṛitta-ruć, k, k, k,* possessing unimpaired splendor.

अकृत्रिम *a-kṛitrima, as, ā, am,* inartificial, unfeigned, natural.

अकृत्स्न *a-kṛitsna, as, ā, am,* incomplete.

अकृप *a-kṛipa, as, ā, am,* merciless, unkind.

अकृपण *a-kṛipaṇa, as, ā, am,* not miserly.

अकृश *a-kṛiśa, as, ā, am,* not slender or emaciated; strong, full. — *A-kṛiśa-lakshmī, is, is, i,* enjoying full prosperity. — *A-kṛiśāśva* (°*śa-aś*°), *as,* m., N. of a king of Ayodhyā.

अकृषीवल *a-kṛishīvala, as, ā, am,* not agricultural.

अकृष्ट *a-kṛishṭa, as, ā, am,* unploughed, untilled; not drawn. — *Akṛishṭa-paćya, as, ā, am,* ripening in unploughed land, growing wild.

अकृष्णकर्मन् *a-kṛishṇa-karman, ā, ā, a,* free from black deeds, guiltless, virtuous.

अकेतन *a-ketana, as, ā, am,* houseless.

अकेतु *a-ketu, us, us, u,* Ved. shapeless, unrecognisable; (Sāy.) unconscious.

अकेश *a-keśa, as, ā, am,* destitute of hair.

अकोट *a-koṭa, as,* m. the Areca or Betel-nut palm, ('without a bend.')

अकोपन *a-kopana, as, ā, am,* not irascible.

अकोविद *a-kovida, as, ā, am,* unwise, stupid, ignorant.

अकौशल *a-kauśala, am,* n. want of dexterity or skill; evil [cf. *a-kuśala*].

अक्का *akkā,* f. a mother. [Supposed to be a term of foreign origin; cf. Lat. *Acca.*]

अक्त 1. *akta, as, ā, am* (part. of rt. *ańć* or *añj* in the sense 'to go'), gone.

अक्त 2. *akta, as, ā, am* (part. of rt. *añj*), smeared over; diffused; bedaubed, tinged, characterized. It is often the last part of a compound word; as, *raktākta,* tinged with red or blood; (*am*), n. oil, ointment.
Aktā, f., Ved. night.
Aktu, us, f. (m.?), Ved. ointment; tinge, ray, light, star (?); dark tinge, darkness, night.
Aktos, aktubhis, ind., Ved. at night.
Aktvā (ind. part. of rt. *añj*), having besmeared.

अक्न *akna, as, ā, am* (fr. rt. *ańć*), bent.
1. *akra, as, ā, am,* Ved. violent [Lat. *acer?*].

अक्र 2. *a-kra, as, ā, am* (fr. 3. *a* and rt. 1. *kṛi?*), Ved. inactive, bootless.

अक्रतु *a-kratu, us, us, u,* Ved. destitute of will or energy; powerless, foolish; (Sāy.) without sacrifices.

अक्रम *a-krama, as,* m. want of order, confusion.

अक्रविहस्त *a-kravi-hasta, as, ā, am,* Ved. not having bloody hands; (Sāy.) not having niggardly hands, not close-fisted.

अक्रव्याद *a-kravyāda, as, ā, am,* or *a-kra-vyād, t, t, t,* not carnivorous, not eating flesh.

अक्रान्त *a-krānta, as, ā, am,* unpassed, unsurpassed, unconquered; (*ā*), f. the Egg plant.

अक्रिय *a-kriya, as, ā, am,* without works; inactive, torpid; abstaining from religious rites; good for nothing; (*ā*), f. inactivity; neglect of duty.

अक्रीडत् *a-krīḍat, an, antī, at,* not playing.

अक्रूर *a-krūra, as, ā, am,* not cruel, gentle; (*as*), m., N. of Kṛishṇa's paternal uncle and friend.

अक्रोध *a-krodha, as,* m. suppression of anger, one of the chief virtues among Hindūs; (*as, ā, am*), free from anger.
A-krodhana, as, ā, am, free from anger; (*as*), m., N. of a prince, son of Ayutāyu.

अक्लम *a-klama, as,* m. freedom from fatigue.

अक्लिका *aklikā,* f. the Indigo plant.

अक्लिष्ट *a-klishṭa, as, ā, am,* untroubled; undisturbed; unwearied. — *Aklishṭa-karman, ā, ā, a,* or *aklishṭa-kārin, ī, iṇī, i,* unwearied in action. — *Aklishṭa-vrata, as, ā, am,* unwearied in keeping religious vows.
A-kleśa, as, m. freedom from trouble.

अक्लेद्य *a-kledya, as, ā, am,* incapable of moisture, not to be wetted.

अक्ष् *aksh* (probably not a simple rt., perhaps a kind of old Desid. form of rt. 1. *aś*), cl. 1. P. *akshati,* cl. 5. *akshṇoti, ānaksha, akshishyati, akshyati, ākshīt, akshitum* or *ashṭum,* to reach; to pass through, penetrate, pervade, embrace; to accumulate (to form the cube?): Caus. *akshayati,*

-yitum, ăćikshat, to cause to pervade: Desid. *aćikshishati* or *aćikshati.*

अक्ष 1. *aksha, as,* m. (fr. rt. 1. *aś* or *aj?*), an axle, axis, pivot, (in this sense also *am,* n.); a wheel, car, cart; pole of a car; the beam of a balance or string which holds the pivot of the beam; a snake; terrestrial latitude; the lower part of the temples [cf. Lat. *axis;* Gr. ἄξων; Old Germ. *ahsa;* Mod. Germ. *Achse;* Lith. *assis*]. — *Aksha-karṇa, as,* m. the hypotenuse, especially of the triangle formed with the gnomon of a dial and its shadow; (in astronomy) argument of the latitude. — *Aksha-ja, as,* m. a diamond; a thunderbolt; a N. of Vishṇu. — *Aksha-dhur, ūr,* f. the yoke attached to the fore part of the pole of a car. — *Aksha-dhūrtila, as,* m. a bull, an ox, i. e. yoked to the pole of a cart. — *Aksha-pīḍā,* f., N. of a plant. — *Aksha-bhāga, as,* m. a degree of latitude. — *Aksha-bhāra, as,* m. cart-load, carriage-load. — *Akshāṅsa* (°*sha-aṅ*°), *as,* m. a degree of latitude. — *Akshāgra* (°*sha-ag*°), *am,* n. the end of an axle; the anterior end of the pole of a car; an axle. — *Akshāgra-kīla* or *-kīlaka, as,* m. a linchpin; the pin which fastens the yoke to the pole. — *Akshā-nah, t, t, t,* Ved. tied to a cart or its pole.

अक्ष 2. *aksha, as,* m. (said to be from rt. 1. *aś*), a die for playing with; a cube; a seed of which rosaries are made (in compound words, like *Indrāksha, Rudrāksha*); a shrub producing that seed (Eleocarpus Ganitrus); a weight called *karsha,* equal to 16 māshas; Beleric Myrobalan (Terminalia Belerica), the seed of which is used as a die; (*am*), n. sochal salt; blue vitriol (from its crystallized shape). — *Aksha-kuśala, as, ā, am,* skilled in dice. — *Aksha-glaha, as,* m. gambling, playing at dice. — *Aksha-jña, as, ā, am,* skilled in gambling. — *Aksha-tattva, am,* n. science of dice. — *Akshatattva-vid, t, t, t,* skilled in the principles of gambling. — *Aksha-devana, am,* n. gambling, dice-playing. — *Aksha-devin, ī,* m. a gamester. — *Aksha-dyū, ūs,* m. a gambler, a dice-player. — *Aksha-dyūta, as,* m. a gambler, a dice-player; (*am*), n. gambling. — *Aksha-dyūtika, am,* n. dispute at play. — *Aksha-drugdha, as, ā, am,* hated by, i. e. unlucky at dice. — *Aksha-dhara, as, ā* or *ī, am,* one who has dice; (*as*), m. a plant, Trophis Aspera; see *śākhoṭa.* — *Aksha-dhūrta, as,* m. a gamester, a gambler, i. e. a dice-rogue. — *Aksha-naipuṇa* or *-naipuṇya, am,* n. skill in gambling. — *Aksha-parājaya, as,* m. loss in gambling. — *Aksha-pāta, as,* m. cast of dice. — *Aksha-pātana, am,* n. act of casting dice. — *Aksha-priya, as, ā, am,* fond of dice, or (perhaps) favoured by the dice, lucky. — *Aksha-mada, as,* m. intoxicating passion for dice. — *Aksha-mātra, am,* n. dice, anything as big as dice; the twinkling of an eye, a moment of time. — *Aksha-mālā,* f. a rosary, a string or necklace of beads, especially of the seeds of the Eleocarpus; a N. of Arundhatī, wife of Vasishṭha, from her wearing a rosary; (*as, ā, am*), or *aksha-mālin, ī, inī, i,* wearing a rosary of seeds. — *Aksha-rāja, as,* m. the king of dice, the die called Kali. — *Aksha-vat, ān, atī, at,* having dice, relating to dice, gambling; (*tī*), f. a game of dice. — *Aksha-vāma, as,* m. an unfair gambler. — 1. *aksha-vid, t, t, t,* skilful in gambling. — *Aksha-vṛitta, as, ā, am,* what has occurred in gambling. — *Aksha-śauṇḍa, as, ā, am,* fond of gambling. — *Aksha-sūtra, am,* n. a string or rosary of Eleocarpus seeds. — *Aksha-stusha, as,* m. Beleric Myrobalan. — *Aksha-hṛidaya, am,* n. innermost nature of dice, perfect skill in gambling. — *Akshahṛidaya-jña, as, ā, am,* perfectly skilled in gambling. — *Akshāvapana* (°*sha-āv*°), *am,* n. a dice-board. — *Akshāvāpa* or *akshātivāpa* (°*sha-at*°), *as,* m. the keeper of the dice, or of a gambling table.

Akshaka or *akshika, as,* m. the tree Dalbergia Oujeinensis.

अक्ष 3. *aksha, am,* n. (fr. rt. 1. *aś?*), an organ of sense, an object of sense; (*ās*), m. the soul; knowledge, religious knowledge; the law; a lawsuit; a person born blind; N. of Garuḍa, of a son of Rāvaṇa, of a son of Narā, &c. — *Aksha-darśaka, as,* m. a judge, i. e. one who sees lawsuits; also *aksha-dṛiś, k.* — *Aksha-paṭala, am,* n. court of law; depository of legal document. — *Aksha-pāṭa, as,* m. an arena, a wrestling ground, place of contest. — *Aksha-pāṭaka* or *aksha-pāṭika, as,* m. a judge, i. e. arranger of a lawsuit. — *Aksha-pāda, as,* m. a follower of the Nyāya or logical system of philosophy; N. of the Ṛishi Gotama. — *Aksha-vāṭa,* see *aksha-pāṭa.* — 2. *aksha-vid, t, t, t,* versed in law.

अक्ष 4. *aksha, am,* n. the eye, especially substituted for *akshi* at the end of adjective compounds, the fem. being *akshī* [cf. Gr. ὄσσο, ὄκκο, for ὄξο; Lat. *oculus;* Germ. *Auge;* Russ. око].

अक्षण *a-kshaṇa, as, ā, am,* inopportune.

अक्षत *a-kshata, as, ā, am,* not crushed; uninjured, unbroken, whole; (*as*), m. Śiva; thrashed and winnowed rice which has been dried in the sun; barley; (*as, am*), m. n. an eunuch; (*ā*), f. a virgin; N. of a plant, Karkaṭaśriṅgī or Kankaḍaśriṅgī; (*am*), n. and (*ās*), m. pl. whole grain, fried grain. — *Akshata-yoni, is,* f. a virgin, an unblemished maiden.

अक्षत्र *a-kshatra, as, ā, am,* destitute of the Kshatriya caste, apart from the Kshatriya caste.

अक्षन् *akshan,* substituted for *akshi,* the eye, in the weakest cases, see Gram. 122 [cf. Goth. *augan*].

Akshaṇ-vat, ān, atī, at, having eyes.

अक्षम *a-kshama, as, ā, am,* unable to endure, impatient; incompetent. — *A-kshamā* or *akshama-tā,* f. impatience, envy; incompetence.

अक्षय *a-kshaya, as, ā, am,* exempt from decay, undecaying; (*as*), m., N. of the twentieth year in the cycle of Jupiter; (*ā*), f. the seventh day of a lunar month, if it fall on Sunday or Monday; the fourth, if it fall on Wednesday. — *Akshaya-guṇa, as, ā, am,* possessing imperishable qualities; (*as*), m. Śiva. — *Akshaya-tā,* f. or *akshaya-tva, am,* n. imperishableness. — *Akshaya-tṛitīyā,* f. a festival, the third day of the bright half of Vaiśākha, which is the first day of the Satya-yuga, and secures permanency to actions then performed. — *Akshaya-puruhūta, as,* m. Śiva. — *Akshaya-mati, is,* m., N. of a Bodhi-sattva. — *Akshaya-loka, as,* m. the undecaying world, heaven. — *Akshayā-lalitā,* f. festival observed by women on the seventh day of the second half of Bhādra.

A-kshayin, ī, iṇī, i, undecaying; (*iṇī*), f., N. of Śiva's wife.

A-kshayya, as, ā, am, undecaying.

अक्षर *a-kshara, as, ā, am,* imperishable; unalterable; (*as*), m. a sword; Śiva; Vishṇu; (*am*), n. a syllable; the syllable *om;* a letter; a vowel, a sound; a word; speech; Brahma; final beatitude; abiding merit, religious austerity; sacrifice; right, justice; the sky; water; a plant (Achyranthes Aspera). — *Akshara-ćañću* or *akshara-ćuñću, us,* or *akshara-ćaṇa* or *akshara-ćana, as,* m. a writer, scribe. — *Akshara-ććhandas, as,* n. metre regulated by the number and quantity of syllables. — *Akshara-jananī,* f. a reed or pen. — *Akshara-jīvaka* or *akshara-jīvika, as,* or *akshara-jīvin, ī,* m. a scribe. — *Akshara-jur, ūr,* m. a sage, one who knows and enjoys Brahma. — *Akshara-tūlikā,* f. a reed or pen. — *Akshara-nyāsa* or *akshara-vinyāsa, as,* m. array of syllables or letters, writing; scripture; the alphabet. — *Akshara-pankti, is, is, i,* containing five syllables; (*is*), f., N. of a metre of four lines, each containing one dactyl and one spondee; also called *pankti* or *haṅsa.* — *Akshara-bhāj, k, k, k,* Ved. entitled to a share in the syllables (of a prayer). — *Akshara-mukha, as,* m. having the mouth full of syllables, a student, scholar. — *Akshara-vinyāsa,* see *akshara-nyāsa.* — *Akshara-śas,* ind. syllable by syllable. — *Akshara-śūnya, as, ā, am,* inarticulate. — *Akshara-saṃsthāna, am,* n. scripture, writing. — *Aksharāṅga* (°*ra-aṅga*), *am,* n. part of a syllable.

Aksharaka, am, n. a vowel.

Aksharya, as, ā, am, relating to syllables or letters.

अक्षान्ति *a-kshānti, is,* f. impatience, jealousy, intolerance.

अक्षार *a-kshāra, as, ā, am,* free from factitious salt; (*as*), m. natural salt. — *Akshāra-lavaṇa* or *akshāralavaṇa, am,* n. natural salt; food that may be eaten at a season unfit for performing religious duties.

अक्षि *akshi,* n. (fr. rt. 1. *aś* or *añj?* Instr. *akshṇā,* Dat. *akshṇe* &c., fr. *akshan,* substituted for *akshi* in the weakest cases. At the end of comp. *aksha* is substituted, see 4. *aksha*), the eye; the number two; (*ī*), du., Ved. the sun and moon [cf. Lith. *aki-s*]. — *Akshi-kūṭa* or *akshi-kūṭaka, am,* n. the eyeball, the pupil of the eye. — *Akshi-gata, as, ā, am,* visibly present, seen; hated. — *Akshi-gola, as,* m. the eyeball. — *Akshi-jāha, am,* n. the root of the eye. — *Akshi-tārā,* f. the pupil of the eye. — *Akshi-pakshman, a,* n. the eyelash. — *Akshi-paṭala, am,* n. a coat of the eye. — *Akshi-pat, t, t, t,* Ved. (falling into the eyes), hurtful; (*t*), ind. as much as could fall into the eyes, a little. — *Akshi-bhū, ūs, ūs, u,* visible, perceptible, manifest, present. — *Akshi-bheshaja, am,* n. a medicament for the eyes, collyrium, &c.; (*as*), m. a tree, Red Lodh. — *Akshi-bhruva, am,* n. the eyes and eyebrows together. — *Akshi-mat, ān, atī, at,* provided with eyes. — *Akshi-loman, a,* n. the eyelash. — *Akshi-vikūṇita, am,* n. a glance, a look with the eyelids partially closed.

Akshika or *akshīka, as,* m. the tree Dalbergia Oujeinensis. See *akshaka.*

अक्षिणी *akshiṇī,* f. (fr. 3. *aksha?*), one of the eight conditions or privileges attached to landed property.

अक्षित *a-kshita, as, ā, am,* undecayed, uninjured; undecaying; (*am*), n. water. — *Akshitā-vasu, us,* m., Ved. epithet of Indra (possessed of undecaying wealth). — *Akshitoti* (°*ta-ūti*), *is,* m., Ved. epithet of Indra (granting permanent help).

A-kshiti, is, f. imperishableness; (*is, is, i*), imperishable.

अक्षियत् *a-kshiyat, an, atī, at,* Ved. not inhabiting, destitute of a dwelling, unsettled; (Sāy.) not decreasing (in riches).

अक्षिव *akshiva* or *akshīva, as,* m. a plant, Guilandina or Hyperanthera Moringa; (*am*), n. sea salt.

अक्षीक *akshīka, as,* m. See *akshika.*

अक्षीव *a-kshīva, as, ā, am,* not intoxicated, sober. See also *akshiva.*

अक्षु *akshu, us,* m., Ved. a kind of net.

अक्षुण्ण *a-kshuṇṇa, as, ā, am,* unbroken, uncurtailed, unconquered; inexperienced, inexpert. — *A-kshuṇṇa-tā,* f. uncurtailed condition; inexperience.

अक्षुद्र *a-kshudra, as, ā, am,* not small.

अक्षुध् *a-kshudh, t,* f., Ved. satiety.

A-kshudhya, as, ā, am, not liable to hunger.

अक्षेत्र *a-kshetra, as, ā, am,* destitute of fields, uncultivated; (*am*), n. not a proper field, a bad field; not a proper geometrical figure. — *Akshetra-jña, as, ā, am,* or *akshetra-vid, t, t, t,* destitute of spiritual knowledge.

A-kshetrin, ī, iṇī, i, having no fields.

Akshaitrajñya, am, n. spiritual ignorance.

अक्षोट *akshoṭa, as,* m. a walnut (Pistacio nut?); N. of a tree, Pīlu; of another tree, Aleurites Triloba. Also spelt *akshoḍa, akshoḍaka, ākshoṭa, ākshoḍaka, ākhoṭa.*

अक्षोभ *a-kshobha, as, ā, am,* unagitated, unmoved; (*as*), m. the post to which an elephant is tied; freedom from agitation, imperturbability.

A-kshobhya, as, ā, am, immoveable, imperturbable; (*as*), m., N. of a Buddha; an immense number, said by Buddhists to be 100 vivaras.

अक्षौहिणी *akshauhiṇī,* f. an army consisting

of ten anîkinîs, or 21,870 elephants, 21,870 chariots, 65,610 horse, and 109,350 foot. (The anîkinî consists of 27 vâhinîs; and 27 being the cube, *aksha*, of 3, it is probable that *akshauhiṇī* is a compound from *aksha* and *vāhinī*.)

अक्ष्ण *akshṇa, am,* n. (fr. rt. 1. *aś*), Ved. time (= *a-khaṇḍa* Schol. to Uṇ-sūtras).

अक्ष्णया *akshṇayā* (probably the Instr. of an obs. word *akshṇā*, fr. *anć*), ind., Ved. circuitously (like a wheel), in a tortuous way; wrongly. — *Akshṇayā-druh, -dhruk, k, k,* Ved. seeking to injure in a tortuous manner. — *Akshṇa-yāvan, ā, arī, a,* Ved. going across; (Sāy.) going through, penetrating.

अखट्ट *akhaṭṭa, as,* m., N. of a tree, Buchanania Latifolia.

अखट्टि *akhaṭṭi, is,* m. childish whim.

अखण्ड *a-khaṇḍa, as, ā, am,* not fragmentary, entire, whole; (*am*), n. time (?). *A-khaṇḍā dvādaśī* is the twelfth day of the first half of the lunar month Mārgaśīrsha.
A-khaṇḍana, am, n. not breaking; leaving entire; non-refutation, admission; (*as*), m. time.
A-khaṇḍita, as, ā, am, not reduced to pieces, unbroken, undivided, unimpaired; unrefuted. — *Akhaṇḍitartu* (°*ta-ṛitu*), *us, us, u,* bearing fruit every season. — *Akhaṇḍitotsava* (°*ta-ut*°), *as, ā, am,* ever festive.

अखर *a-khara, as, ā, am,* not hard, soft.

अखर्व *a-kharva, as, ā, am,* not short, not stunted, not small, not dwarfish.

अखात *a-khāta, as, ā, am,* not dug (by man); unburied; (*as, am*), m. n. a natural pond or lake, a pool before a temple.

अखाद्य *a-khādya, as, ā, am,* uneatable.

अखिद्र *a-khidra, as, ā, am,* unwearied. — *A-khidra-yāman, ā, ā, a,* Ved. unwearied in course.

अखिल *a-khila, as, ā, am,* without a gap, complete, whole. — *Akhilātman* (°*la-āt*°), *ā,* m. the universal spirit, Brahma.
Akhilena, ind. completely.

अखेटिक *akheṭika* or *ākheṭika, as,* m. a dog trained to the chase.

अखेदिन् *a-khedin, ī, inī, i,* not wearisome; unwearied. — *Akhedi-tra, am,* n. continuous flow (of speech); one of the vāgguṇas of the Jainas.

अख्खल *akhkhala,* ind., Ved. an exclamation of joy. — *Akhkhalī-kṛi,* cl. 8. P. *-karoti, -kartum,* Ved. to utter the exclamation *akhkhala.*

अख्यात *a-khyāta, as, ā, am,* not famous, unknown, obscure; infamous.
A-khyāti, is, f. want of fame; infamy, bad repute. — *Akhyāti-kara, as, ā, am,* disreputable.

अग् *ag,* cl. 1. P. *agati, āga, agitum,* to move tortuously, wind: Caus. *agayati, -yitum,* to cause to move tortuously [cf. rt. *ang*].
1. *aga, as,* m. a snake; the sun; a water-jar.

अग 2. *a-ga, as, ā, am* (fr. rt. *gam*), unable to walk; unapproachable; (*as*), m. a mountain, a tree; (in arithm.) seven. — *Aga-ja, as, ā, am,* produced on a mountain, or from a tree; (*am*), n. bitumen. — *Agātmajā* (*aga-āt*°), f., N. of Pārvatī, the daughter of Himālaya. — *Agāvaha* (*aga-āv*°), *as,* m., N. of a son of Kṛishṇa and of others. — *Agaukas* (*aga-ok*°), *ās,* m. a lion; a bird; the *śarabha,* a fabulous animal with eight legs.
A-gaććha, as, ā, am, not going; (*as*), m. a tree.

अगणित *a-gaṇita, as, ā, am,* uncounted. — *Agaṇita-lajja, as, ā, am,* disregarding shame.

अगत *a-gata, as, ā, am,* not gone; unfrequented; (*am*), n., Ved. not coming, non-return (?).
A-gati, is, f. want of resort or resource, necessity.

A-gatika or *a-gatīka, as, ā, am,* destitute of resort or of resources. — *Agatika-gati, is,* f. the resort of one who has no resort, a last resource.

अगद *a-gada, as, ā, am,* free from disease, healthy, salubrious; free from judicial affliction; (*as*), m. freedom from disease, health; a medicine, medicament, drug; the science of antidotes. — *Agadaṅkāra, as, ī,* m. f. a physician, ('who makes well.')
Agadya, nom. P. *agadyati,* to have good health.

अगदित *a-gadita, as, ā, am,* untold.

अगम *a-gama, as, ā, am,* not going, unable to go; (*as*), m. a mountain, a tree [cf. 2. *a-ga*].
A-gamya or *a-gantavya, as, ā, am,* unfit to be walked in, or to be approached; inaccessible (physically or metaphorically), inapproachable; unattainable, incomprehensible, unsurpassable. — *Agamya-rūpa, as, ā, am,* of unsurpassed form, nature, or beauty. — *Agamyā-gamana, am,* n. illicit sexual intercourse. — *Agamyāgamanīya, as, ā, am,* relating to illicit intercourse. — *Agamyā-gāmin, ī, inī, i,* practising illicit intercourse.

अगरी *a-garī,* f. a kind of grass, commonly called Deotar, Andropogon Serratus [cf. *garī*].

अगरु *agaru, us, u,* m. n. Agallochum, Amyris Agallocha.

अगर्व *a-garva, as, ā, am,* free from pride.

अगर्हित *a-garhita, as, ā, am,* undespised, unreproached, blameless.

अगव्यूति *a-gavyūti, is, is, i,* Ved. without good pasturage for cattle, barren.

अगस्ति *agasti, is,* m. (said to be fr. 2. *a-ga,* a mountain, and *asti,* fr. rt. 2. *as,* thrower), N. of a Ṛishi, author of several Vedic hymns, (he is said to have been the son of both Mitra and Varuṇa by Urvasī; to have been born in a water-jar; to have been of short stature; to have swallowed the ocean, and compelled the Vindhya mountains to prostrate themselves before him; to have conquered and civilized the South; to have written on medicine, &c.); the star Canopus, of which Agastya is the regent; a plant, Sesbana (or Æschynomene) Grandiflora. — *Agasti-dru, us,* f. a plant, Sesbana Grandiflora.
Agastayas, m. pl. the descendants of Agastya.
Agastī, f. a female descendant of Agastya.
Agastīya, as, ā, am, relating to Agasti.
Agastya, a, m. = *agasti,* N. of Śiva. — *Agastya-gītā, ās,* f. pl. Agastya's hymns, forming part of the Ādi-varāha-Purāṇa. — *Agastya-ćāra, as,* m. the course of Canopus. — *Agastya-saṃhitā,* f. Agastya's collection (of law). — *Agastyodaya* (°*ya-ud*°), *as,* m. the rise of Canopus; the seventh day of the second half of Bhādra.

अगा *a-gā, ās,* m. f., Ved. not going.

अगाध *a-gādha, as, ā, am* (see *gādha*), very deep, unfathomable, bottomless; (*as, am*), m. n. a hole, chasm; (*as*), m., N. of one of the five fires at the Svāhākāra [cf. Gr. ἀγαθός and Goth. *gôths,* fr. the crude form *gôda*]. — *Agādha-jala, as, ā, am,* having deep water; (*as*), m. a deep lake.

अगार *a-gāra, as, am,* m. n. house, apartment [cf. *ā-gāra*].

अगिन *agina, as,* m. the sun (?). See *agira.*

अगिर *agira, as,* m. (fr. rt. *ag*), the sun; fire; a Rākshasa.

अगिरौकस् *a-giraukas, ās, ās, as* (fr. *a* + *girā,* Instr. of *gir* and *okas*), Ved. not to be stopped by threatening shouts (lit. 'having no station by speech'), epithet of the Maruts.

अगु *a-gu, us, us, u* (fr. *go* with *a*), Ved. destitute of cows, or of rays; poor; destitute of hymns, wicked; (*us*), m., N. of Rāhu or the ascending node.
A-go, aus, aus, u, Ved. destitute of cows. — *Ago-tā,* f. want of cows.

अगुण *a-guṇa, as, ā, am,* destitute of qualities or attributes (sometimes said of the supreme being); destitute of good qualities; (*as*), m. a fault. — *Aguṇa-tā,* f. absence of good qualities. — *Aguṇa-vat, ān, atī, at,* destitute of qualities, especially of good qualities. — *Aguṇa-vādin, ī, inī, i,* fault-finding, censorious. — *Aguṇa-śīla, as, ā, am,* of a worthless character.

अगुप्त *a-gupta, as, ā, am,* unhidden, unconcealed; unprotected; not keeping a secret.

अगुरु *a-guru, us, ū* or *vī, u,* not heavy, light; (in prosody) short as a short vowel alone or before a single consonant; (*us, u*), m. n. the fragrant Aloe wood and tree, Aquilaria Agallocha; the Śiśu tree; the tree which yields Bdellium, Amyris Agallocha. — *Aguru-śiṃśapā,* f. the Śiśu tree, (probably distinct words, *śiṃśapā* being added to explain *aguru*.)

अगूढ *a-gūḍha, as, ā, am,* unconcealed, manifest. — *Agūḍha-gandha, as, ā, am,* having an unconcealed smell; (*am*), n. Asa Fœtida. — *Agūḍha-bhāva, as, ā, am,* having a transparent disposition.

अगृभीत *a-gṛibhīta, as, ā, am,* Ved. not seized or taken, unsubdued. — *Agṛibhīta-śoćis, is, is, is,* Ved. having inconceivable splendor; (Sāy.) of unsubdued splendor.

अगृह *a-gṛiha* or *a-graha, as,* m. a houseless man, a Vānaprastha or Brāhman of the third order.

अगोचर *a-goćara, as, ā, am,* not obvious, imperceptible by the senses; (*am*), n. anything that is beyond the cognizance of the senses; Brahma; the not being seen, absence.

अगोपा *a-gopā, ās, ās, am,* Ved. without a cowherd, not tended by one.

अगोरुध *a-go-rudha, as, ā, am,* Ved. not repulsing the cow; (Sāy.) not repelling or disdaining praise.

अगोह्य *a-gohya, as, ā, am,* Ved. unconcealable, not to be covered, bright.

अगौकस् *agaukas.* See 2. *a-ga,* col. 1.

अग्नायी *agnāyī.* See p. 6, col. 1.

अग्नि *agni, is,* m. (fr. rt. *ang* or *ag* or *añj*?), fire; sacrificial fire of three kinds, Gārhapatya, Āhavanīya, and Dakshiṇa; the number three; the god of fire; the fire of the stomach, the digestive faculty; the gastric fluid; bile; gold; N. of various plants, Semicarpus Anacardium, Plumbago Zeylanica and Rosea, Citrus Acida; mystical substitute for the letter *r* [cf. Lat. *igni-s;* Lith. *ugni-s;* Slav. *ognj;* Goth. *auhn'-s;* αἴγλη and ἀγλαός may be related to *agni*]. — *Agnā-marutau,* m. du. Agni and Marut. — *Agnā-vishṇū,* m. du. Agni and Vishṇu. — *Agni-kaṇa, as,* m. a spark. — *Agni-karman, a,* n. action of fire or of Agni; cauterization. — *Agni-kārikā,* f. and *agni-kārya, am,* n. kindling or feeding the sacrificial fire with clarified butter, &c. — *Agni-kāshṭha, am,* n. Agallochum. — *Agni-kukkuṭa, as,* m. a lighted wisp of straw, firebrand. — *Agni-kuṇḍa, am,* n. a hole or enclosed space for the consecrated fire. — *Agni-kumāra, as,* m. a particular preparation of various drugs. — *Agni-kṛita, as, ā, am,* made by fire, offered by fire. — *Agni-ketu, us,* m., N. of a Rakshas. — *Agni-koṇa, as,* m. the south-east quarter, ruled over by Agni. — *Agni-kriyā,* f. obsequies or any other religious act performed by means of fire. — *Agni-krīḍā,* f. firework, illumination, &c. — *Agni-garbha, as, ā, am,* pregnant with fire; (*as*), m. a gem supposed to contain and give out solar heat, sūryakānta; N. of a plant, Agnijāra; (*ā*), f., N. of a plant, Mahājyotishmatī. — *Agni-gṛiha, am,* n. house or place for keeping the sacred fire. — *Agni-grantha, as,* m., N. of a work. — *Agni-ćaya, as,* m. a heap of fire. — *Agni-ćayana, am,* n. or *agni-ćiti, is,* f. or *agni-ćityā,* f. arranging or preparing the sacred or sacrificial fire-place. — *Agni-ćit,* ind., Ved. like Agni;

(*t*), m. one who has arranged a sacred fire-place. — *Agnićit-vat, ān, atī, at*, having householders or inhabitants that have prepared a sacred fire-place. — *Agni-ja* or *agni-jāta, as, ā, am*, produced by fire, born of or in fire; digestive; (*as*), m., N. of Vishṇu; a medicinal plant, Agnijāra. — *Agni-janman, ā*, m. Skanda, the god of war. — *Agni-jāra* or *agni-jāla, as*, m. a medicinal plant. — *Agni-jihva, as, ā, am*, having a fiery tongue; (*ā*), f. a tongue or flame of fire; a tongue of Agni (who is said to have seven tongues); a medicinal plant, Lāngalī. — *Agnijvalita-tejana, as, ā, am*, having a point hardened in fire. — *Agni-jvālā*, f. glow or flame of fire; a plant with red blossoms, used by dyers, Grislea Tomentosa; another plant with red blossoms, Jalapippalī. — *Agni-tap, p*, Ved. enjoying the warmth of a fire. — *Agni-tapas, ās, ās, as*, hot as fire, glowing. — *Agni-tapta, as, ā, am*, heated by fire, glowing. — *Agni-tā*, f. the state of fire. — *Agni-tejas, ās, ās, as*, having the power of fire or of Agni; (*ās*), m., N. of one of the seven Ṛishis of the eleventh Manvantara. — *Agni-traya, am*, n. or *agni-tretā*, f. the three sacred fires, called respectively Gārhapatya, Āhavanīya, and Dakshiṇa. — *Agni-trā, ās, ās, am*, Ved. protected by Agni. — *Agni-da* or *agni-dāyaka, as, ā, am*, supplying with fire, stomachic, tonic, incendiary. — *Agni-dagdha, as, ā, am*, burnt with fire; burnt on the funeral pile; burnt at once, without having fire put into the mouth, because destitute of issue; (*ās*), m. pl. a class of Pitṛis or those who on earth maintained the sacred fire. — *Agni-datta, as*, m., N. of a prince. — *Agni-damanī*, f. a narcotic plant, Solanum Jacquini. — *Agni-dāyaka*, see *agnida*. — *Agni-dāha, as*, m., N. of a disease. — *Agni-diś, k*, f. Agni's quarter, i. e. the south-east. — *Agni-dīpana, as, ī, am*, stimulating digestion. — *Agni-dīpta, as, ā, am*, blazing, glowing; (*ā*), f., N. of a plant, Mahājyotishmatī. — *Agni-dīpti, is*, f. active state of digestion. — *Agni-dūta, as, ā, am*, Ved. having Agni for a messenger. — *Agni-dūshita, as, ā, am*, branded. — *Agni-deva, as*, m. Agni; a worshipper of Agni; (*ā*), f. the third lunar mansion, i. e. the Pleiades. — *Agni-devatā*, f. the deity Agni. — *Agni-devatya* or *agni-daivata* or *agni-daivatya, as, ā, am*, referring to Agni or to his divinity. — *Agnidh* or *agnīdh, t*, m. (fr. *agni-idh*), Ved. the priest who kindles the sacred fire. — *Agni-dhāna, am*, n. the receptacle for keeping the sacred fire. — *Agni-nakshatra, am*, n. the third lunar mansion, the Pleiades. — *Agni-nayana* or *agni-praṇayana, am*, n. bringing out the sacrificial fire. — *Agni-niryūsa, as*, m. a medicinal plant, Agnijāra. — *Agni-nunna, as, ā, am*, Ved. struck by Agni or lightning. — *Agni-netra, as, ā, am*, Ved. having Agni for a guide. — *Agni-pakva, as, ā, am*, cooked with fire. — *Agni-pada, am*, n., N. of a plant or a man. — *Agni-parikriyā*, f. care of the sacred fire. — *Agni-paricchada, as*, m. the whole apparatus used in a sacrifice with fire. — *Agni-paridhāna, am*, n. enclosing the sacrificial fire with a kind of screen. — *Agni-parīkshā*, f. ordeal by fire. — *Agni-parvata, as*, m. a volcano. — *Agni-pućcha, as, am*, m. n. end or extinction of the fire, lit. tail of the fire. — *Agni-purāṇa, am*, n., N. of a Purāṇa. — *Agni-purogama, as, ā, am*, having Agni for a leader. — *Agni-praṇayana, am*, n. bringing out the sacrificial fire. — *Agni-praṇayanīya, as, ā, am*, referring to the bringing out that fire. — *Agni-pratishṭhā*, f. consecration of fire, especially the nuptial fire. — *Agni-praveśa, as*, m. or *agni-praveśana, am*, n. entering the fire; self-immolation of a widow on the funeral pile of her husband. — *Agni-prastara, as*, m. stone producing fire; flint. — *Agni-bāhu* or *agni-vāhu, us*, m. smoke; N. of a son of the first Manu; N. of a son of Priyavrata and Kāmyā. — *Agni-bha, am*, n. (shining like fire), gold. — *Agni-bhu, u*, n. water. — *Agni-bhū, ūs*, m. Skanda; N. of a teacher, Kāśyapa, who was taught by Agni; (in arithm.) six. — *Agni-bhūti, is*, m., N. of a pupil of the last Tīrthakara, being one of the eleven chiefs of the Jaina Ṛishis. — *Agni-bhrājas, ās, ās, as*, Ved. possessing fiery splendour. — *Agni-maṇi, is*, m. the sun-stone or sūryakānta. — *Agni-mat, ān, atī, at*, having a fire, enjoying it; maintaining a sacrificial fire, having a good digestion. — *Agni-mantha, as, ā, am*, producing fire by friction; (*as*), m., N. of a plant, Premna Spinosa. — *Agni-manthana, am*, n. production of fire by friction. — *Agnimanthanīya, as, ā, am*, referring to such friction. — *Agni-maya, as, ī, am*, fiery. — *Agni-māṭhara, as*, m., N. of an expounder of the Ṛig-veda. — *Agni-māndya, am*, n. dyspepsia. — *Agni-māruti, is*, m., N. of Agastya. — *Agni-mitra, as*, m., N. of a prince of the Śunga dynasty. — *Agnim-indha, as*, m. the priest who kindles the sacrificial fire. — *Agni-mukha, as*, m. a deity; a Brāhmaṇa; a tonic medicine; N. of two plants, Semicarpus Anacardium and Plumbago Zeylanica. — *Agni-mukhī*, f. Semicarpus Anacardium; Gloriosa Superba. — *Agni-mūḍha, as, ā, am*, Ved. made insane by Agni or lightning. — *Agni-yuta, as*, m., N. of the author of a hymn in the Ṛig-veda. — *Agni-yojana, am*, n. causing the sacrificial fire to blaze up. — *Agni-rakshaṇa, am*, n. preservation of the sacred (especially the domestic) fire. — *Agni-raja, as*, or *agni-rajas, ās*, m. a scarlet insect. — *Agni-rahasya, am*, n. mystery of Agni, the title of the tenth book of the Śatapatha Brāhmaṇa. — *Agni-rāśi, is*, m. a heap of fire, a burning pile. — *Agni-ruhā*, f. a plant, Māṉsarohiṇī. — *Agni-rūpa, as, ī, am*, fire-shaped. — *Agni-retasa, as, ā, am*, sprung from the seed of Agni. — *Agni-rohiṇī*, f. a hard inflammatory swelling in the arm-pit. — *Agni-loka, as*, m. the world of Agni. — *Agni-vat, ān, atī, at*, having or enjoying a fire, maintaining a sacrificial fire, having a good digestion; (*vat*), ind. like Agni, fire. — *Agni-varćas, ās*, m., N. of a teacher of the Purāṇas. — *Agni-varṇa, as, ā, am*, having the colour of fire; closely related to fire, hot, fiery; (*as*), m., N. of a prince, the son of Sudarśana; (*ā*), f. a kind of strong liquor. — *Agni-vardhaka, as, ā* or *ī, am*, feeding or exciting fire; tonic; (*as*), m. a tonic, stomachic. — *Agni-vallabha, as*, m. a tree, Shorea Robusta; the resinous juice of it. — *Agni-vāṇa, as*, m. a fiery arrow, a rocket. — *Agni-vāsas, ās, ās, as*, wearing a fiery or red garment. — *Agni-vāha, as*, m. the vehicle of fire, i. e. smoke. — *Agni-vāhu, us*, m. = preceding; N. of two men, see *agni-bāhu*. — *Agni-vimoćana, am*, m. the ceremony of lowering the sacrificial fire. — *Agni-visarpa, as*, m. spread of inflammation, pain arising from an inflamed tumour. — *Agni-viharaṇa, am*, n. removing the sacrificial fire from the Agnīdhra to the Sadas Maṇḍapa. — *Agni-vīja* or *agni-vīrya, am*, n. gold. — *Agni-vṛiddhi, is*, f. improved digestion. — *Agni-veśa, as*, m., N. of an early medical authority. — *Agnivaiśya, as, ā, am*, descended from Agniveśa. — *Agni-śaraṇa* or *agni-śāla, am*, n. or *agni-śālā*, f. house or place for keeping the sacrificial fire. — *Agni-śikha, as, ā, am*, having a crest of fire, fiery; (*as*), m. a lamp; a fiery arrow, rocket; an arrow; the Safflower plant; saffron; N. of Vararući's father; (*am*), n. saffron, gold. — *Agni-śikhā*, f. a flame; N. of two plants, Gloriosa Superba and Menispermum Cordifolium. — *Agni-śuśrūshā*, f. careful attention to the sacrificial fire. — *Agni-śekhara, am*, n. saffron. — *Agni-śesha, as*, m. appendix to the chapter on Agni in the Taittirīya Saṃhitā. — *Agni-śri, īs, īs, i*, Ved. visiting Agni or fire. — *Agni-shṭut, t*, m. (laudatory of Agni), the first day of the Agnishṭoma sacrifice; one day of the Sattra Pańćadaśarātra. — *Agni-shṭubh, p*, m. son of the sixth Manu, Ćākshusha, by Naḍvalā; see the next. — *Agni-shṭoma, as*, m. (praise of Agni), N. of a protracted ceremony or sacrifice, extending over several days in spring, and forming an essential part of the Jyotishṭoma; a passage of the Sāma-veda chanted at the Agnishṭoma; the first day of the Sattra Pańćadaśarātra; a species of the Soma plant; N. of the son of the sixth Manu; see *agnishṭubh*. — *Agnishṭoma-yājin, ī, inī, i*, one who has performed the Agnishṭoma. — *Agni-shṭha, as, ā, am*, placed in, or over, or near the fire; (*as*), m. an iron frying-pan; in the Aśvamedha sacrifice, the eleventh Yūpa or sacrificial post which, of all the twenty-one, is nearest the fire; (*ā*), f. the corner of the sacrificial post which, of all the eight, is nearest the fire. — *Agni-shvātta* or *agni-svātta, as, ā, am*, tasted by the funeral fire; (*ās*). m. pl. Manes, especially of those who on earth neglected the sacrificial fire. — *Agni-saṉskāra, as*, m. the consecration of fire; performance of any rite in which the application of fire is essential, as the burning of the dead body. — *Agni-sankāśa, as, ā, am*, resplendent like fire. — *Agni-sańćaya, as*, m. preparing the sacrificial fire-place, see *agnićayana*. — *Agni-sakha, as*, m. the wind. — *Agni-sambhava, as, ā, am*, sprung from fire; (*as*), m. wild safflower; the result of digestion, lymph. — *Agni-sahāya, as*, m. the wind; a wild pigeon. — *Agni-sākshika, as, ā, am*, taking Agni, or the domestic or nuptial fire, for a witness. — *Agnisākshika-maryāda, as, ā, am*, one who, taking Agni for a witness, gives a solemn promise of conjugal fidelity. — *Agni-sāra, am*, n. a medicine for the eyes, a collyrium. — *Agni-sāvarṇi, is*, m., N. of a Manu. — *Agni-siṉha, as*, m., N. of the father of the seventh black Vāsudeva. — *Agnisiṉha-nandana, as*, m. the son of Agnisiṉha. — *Agni-sūtra, am*, n. thread of fire; a girdle of sacrificial grass put upon a young Brāhman at his investiture. — *Agni-stambha, as*, m. the (magical) quenching of fire. — *Agni-stoka, as*, m. a spark. — *Agni-svātta*, see *agni-shvātta*. — *Agni-hut, t, t, t*, or *agni-huta, as, ā, am*, sacrificed by fire. — *Agni-hotṛi, tā*, m., Ved. sacrificing to Agni, or having Agni for a priest; see *agni-hotrin*. — *Agni-hotra, as*, m., Ved. oblation to Agni; the sacred fire; (*am*), n. an oblation to Agni, chiefly of milk, oil, and sour gruel;—there are two kinds of Agnihotra, one is *nitya*, i. e. of constant obligation; the other *kāmya*, i. e. optional;—the sacred fire; the maintenance of it; the placing the sacrificial fire on the ground prepared for it, see *agny-ādhāna*; (*as, ī, am*), Ved. sacrificing to Agni; destined for the Agnihotra, or connected with it. — *Agnihotra-havaṇī*, f. a ladle used for sacrificial libations. — *Agnihotra-hut, t*, Ved. offering the Agnihotra. — *Agnihotrāhuti* (°*tra-āh*°), *is*, f. invocation connected with the Agnihotra. — *Agni-hotrin, ī, iṇī, i*, practising the Agnihotra; maintaining the sacrificial fire; one who has prepared the sacred fire-place, or conveyed the sacrificial fire to it. — *Agnihotroććhishṭa* (°*tra-uć*°), *am*, n. that which is left of the Agnihotra. — *Agnīdh* (°*ni-idh*), *t*, m. the priest who kindles the fire. — *Agnīdhra, as*, m. = the preceding; N. of two men, see *agni-bāhu*. — *Agnīdhrī*, f. feeding the sacrificial fire. — *Agnīndra* (°*ni-in*°), *au*, m. du., Ved. Agni and Indra. — *Agnīndhana* (°*ni-indh*°), *am*, n. kindling or feeding the fire. — *Agnī-parjanya, au*, m. du., Ved. Agni and Parjanya. — *Agnī-varuṇa, au*, m. du., Ved. Agni and Varuṇa. — *Agnī-shoma, au*, m. du. Agni and Soma. — *Agnīshoma-praṇayana, am*, n. bringing out the fire and the Soma, a ceremony in the Jyotishṭoma sacrifice. — *Agnī-shomīya* or *agnī-shomya, as, ā, am*, relating or sacred to Agni and Soma. — *Agnīshomīya-nirvāpa, as*, m. making libations with the cake sacred to Agni and Soma, a ceremony in the Darśapūrṇamāsa sacrifice. — *Agnīshomīya-paśu, us*, m. a victim, generally a sheep or goat, sacred to Agni and Soma. — *Agnīshomīyapaśv-anushṭhāna, am*, n. the proceedings with that victim, at the Jyotishṭoma sacrifice. — *Agnīshomīya-puroḍāśa, as*, m. cake sacred to Agni and Soma, which must be baked in eleven bowls. — *Agnīshomīya-yāga, as*, m. one of the three sacrifices of the Pūrṇamāsa. — *Agnīshomīyaikādaśa-kapāla* (°*ya-ek*°), *as*, m. cake sacred to Agni and Soma, see above. — *Agnī-shomya*, see *agnī-shomīya*. — *Agny-agāra* or *agny-āgāra, as*, m. house or place for keeping the sacred fire. — *Agny-abhāva, as*, m. lack or loss of the sacred fire; loss of appetite. — *Agny-astra, am*, n. fire serving as a weapon, a rocket, fire-arms (?). — *Agny-āgāra*, see *agny-agāra*. — *Agny-ātmaka, as, ā, am*; Ved. having Agni's nature. — *Agny-ādhāna* or *agny-ādheya, am*, n. or *agny-āhiti, is*, f. placing the fire on the sacrificial fire-place or ground previously prepared. — *Agny-ālaya, as*, m. a house or place for keeping the sacred fire; a cavity with several compartments, for the several sacred fires. — *Agny-āhita, as*, m. one who has performed the Agnyādhāna. — *Agny-utpāta, as*, m. a fiery portent, meteor, a comet. — *Agny-uddharaṇa, am*, n. taking the sacred fire from its usual place, previous to a sacrifice. — *Agny-upasthāna, am*, n. worship of Agni, at the conclusion of the Agnihotra, &c. — *Agny-edha, as*, m. an incendiary.

Agnāyī, f. the wife of Agni, and goddess of fire; the Tretā-yuga.

Agnika, as, m. an insect of scarlet colour, Coccinella.

Agnisāt, ind. to the state of fire, used in composition with *kṛi* and *bhu*, as *agnisāt kṛi*, to reduce to fire, to subject to fire.

Agnīya, as, ā, am, referring to fire or to Agni, fiery.

अग्मन् *agman, a*, n. conflict, battle; see *ajman*, with which it is connected.

अग्र *agra, as, ā, am* (said to be fr. rt. *ang*, the nasal being dropped), foremost; anterior, first; chief; prominent, best; projecting, supernumerary, excessive; much; (*am*), n. foremost point or part; tip; front; uppermost part, top, summit, surface; point, and hence, figuratively, sharpness; the nearest end, the beginning; the climax or best part; goal, aim, resting-place; multitude, assemblage; a weight, equal to a pala; a measure of food given as alms; (in astronomy) the sun's amplitude; (*am*), ind. in front, before, ahead of, chiefly in answer to the question whither? [cf. Gr. ἄκρον]. — *Agra-kara, as*, m. the fore part of the hand or arm; the right hand; the fore part of rays, the focal point. — *Agra-kāya, as*, m. the fore part of the body. — *Agra-ga, as*, m. a leader. — *Agra-gaṇya, as, ā, am*, that should be counted or regarded as the foremost, best, principal. — *Agra-gāmin, ī, inī, i*, preceding, taking the lead. — *Agra-ja, as, ā, am*, or *agra-jā, ās, ās, am*, Ved. born first or earlier; (*as*), m. the first-born; an elder brother; a Brāhman; Vishṇu; (*ā*), f. an elder sister. — *Agra-janghā*, f. the fore part of the thigh. — *Agra-janman, ā*, m. the first-born; an elder brother; a Brāhman; a member of one of the three highest castes; Brahmā. — *Agra-jātaka, as*, or *agra-jāti, is*, m. a Brāhman. — *Agra-jihva, am*, n. the tip of the tongue. — *Agra-jyā*, f. (in astron.) the sine of the amplitude. — *Agra-ṇī, īs, īs, i*, taking the lead, foremost, first. — *Agra-ṇīti, is*, f., Ved. the first offering. — *Agra-dānin, ī*, m. a degraded Brāhman who receives presents from Śūdras, or takes things previously offered to the dead. — *Agra-nakha, as*, m. the tip of the nail. — *Agra-nāsikā*, f. the tip of the nose. — *Agra-nirūpaṇa, am*, n. determining beforehand, predestination, prophecy. — *Agra-parṇī*, f. cowage, Carpopogon Pruriens. — *Agra-pāṇi, is*, or *agra-hasta, as*, m. the fore part of the hand or arm; the right hand. — *Agra-pūjā*, f. the first or highest mark or act of reverence. — *Agra-peya, am*, n. precedence in drinking. — *Agra-bhāga* or *agrānśa* (°*ra-an*°), *as*, m. part of the top, &c., fore part; (in astron.) degree of amplitude. — *Agra-bhuj, k, k, k*, having the precedence in eating. — *Agra-bhūmi, is*, f. the place aimed at, goal, object. — *Agra-mahishī*, f. the principal queen. — *Agra-mānsa, am*, n. the heart; morbid protuberance of the liver. — *Agra-yāna, am*, n. stepping in front to defy the enemy. — *Agra-yāyin, ī, inī, i*, going before, taking the lead; (ī), m. a leader. — *Agra-yāvan, ā, ā, a*, Ved. going before. — *Agra-yodhin, ī*, m. the foremost man or leader in a fight; a champion. — *Agra-lohitā*, f. a kind of pot-herb, red pepper (?). — *Agra-vīja, as, ā, am*, (said of a plant) propagating itself by means of the top; (*as*), m. a viviparous plant, according to Hindū notions. — *Agra-vīra, as*, m. the principal hero. — *Agra-sandhānī*, f. the register of human actions, kept by Yama. — *Agra-sandhyā*, f. early dawn. — *Agra-sara, as, ī, am*, going in front, taking the lead; (in Bengālī), going ahead, advancing. — *Agra-sānu, us*, m. the front part of a table land. — *Agra-sārā*, f. a compendious method of counting immense numbers. — *Agra-sena, as*, m., N. of Janamejaya's son. — *Agra-hasta, as*, m. = *agra-pāṇi*, the tip of an elephant's trunk. — *Agra-hāyaṇa, as*, m. commencement of the year; N. of a Hindū month, commencing about the 12th of November. — *Agra-hāra, as*, m. royal donation of land to Brāhmans; land thus given. — *Agrānśa*, see *agra-bhāga*. — *Agrānśu* (°*ra-an*°), *us*, m. the end of a ray of light, the focal point. — *Agrākshan, a*, or *agrākshi* (°*ra-ak*°), *i*, n. the fore part of the eye, sharpness of vision. — *Agrānguli* (°*ra-ang*°), *is*, m. the tip of the finger. — *Agrādvan* (°*ra-ad*°), *ā, ā, a*, having precedence in eating. — *Agrānīka* (°*ra-an*°), *as, am*, m. n. the front of an army, vanguard. — *Agrāyaṇīya*, (°*ra-ay*°), *am*, n. title of the second of the fourteen oldest Jaina books. — *Agropaharaṇa* (°*ra-up*°), *am*, n. first or principal supply. — *Agropaharaṇīya, as, ā, am*, that which has to be first or principally supplied.

Agratas, ind. in front of, before, in the presence of; at the head, first. — *Agrataḥ-kṛi*, cl. 8. P. A. *-karoti, -kurute, -kartum*, to place in front or at the head, to consider most important. — *Agrataḥ-sara, as, ī, am*, going in front, taking the lead; (*as*), m. a leader.

Agrima, as, ā, am, foremost; prior, preceding; elder, eldest; principal, best; furthest advanced, first ripe; further; (*ā*), f. a fruit, Annona Reticulata.

Agriya, as, ā, am, foremost, oldest, best; (*as*), m. elder brother; (*am*), n. the first fruits, the best part.

Agrīya, as, ā, am, Ved. same as the preceding.

Agre, ind. (loc. of *agra*), in front; before; in the presence of; at the head; first; ahead, beyond, further on, i. e. subsequently to. — *Agre-ga, as, ā, am*, going in front or before; (*as*), m. a leader. — *Agre-gā, ās*, or *agre-gū, ūs*, or *agre-nī, īs*, m. a leader. — *Agretvan* (°*gra-it*°), *ā, arī, a*, Ved. going in front or before. — *Agre-didhishu, us*, m. a man belonging to one of the first three classes, who at his first marriage takes a wife that was married before; (*us* or *ū, ūs*), f. a married woman whose elder sister is still unmarried. — *Agre-pā, ās, ās*, or *agre-pū, ūs, ūs*, m. f. having the precedence in drinking. — *Agre-bhrū, ūs*, m. roaming in front. — *Agre-vaṇa, am*, n. the border of a forest. — *Agre-vadha, as*, m. hitting or killing whatever is in front. — *Agre-sara, as, ā* or *ī, am*, going in front, preceding, taking the lead. — *Agre-sara* or *agre-sarika, as*, m. a leader.

Agrya, as, ā, am, foremost, topmost, principal, best, proficient; pointed, i. e. intent, closely attentive; (*as*), m. an elder or eldest brother; (*am*), n. a roof.

अग्रभण *a-grabhaṇa, as, ā, am* (fr. *grabh*, old form of rt. *grah*), Ved. having nothing which can be grasped.

A-graha, as, m. non-acceptance. — *A-graha* or *a-gṛiha, as*, m. a houseless man, i. e. a Vānaprastha, a Brāhman of the third class.

A-grāhin, ī, iṇī, i, not taking, (said of a leech) not holding.

A-grāhya, as, ā, am, unfit or improper to be received, accepted, perceived, obtained, admitted, trusted; deserving to be rejected or refused.

अग्राम्य *a-grāmya, as, ā, am*, not rustic, town-made; not tame, wild.

अग्रु *agru, us*, m. unmarried; (*ū*), f. a finger; a river [cf. Zend *aghru*].

अघ *agh*, cl. 10. P. *aghayati, -yitum*, to go wrong, sin.

Agha, am, n. a going wrong; mishap, evil; misdeed, a fault; sin; passion; impurity; pain, suffering; (*as, ā, am*), evil, bad, sinful, subject to passion, miserable, unclean; (*as*), m., N. of an Asura, the general of Kansa; (*ā*), f. the goddess of sin; (*ās*), f. pl. the constellation usually called Maghā. — *Agha-kṛit, t, t, t*, doing evil or harm, an evil-doer. — *Agha-dvishṭa, as, ā, am*, Ved. hated by the wicked. — *Agha-nāśaka, as, ā, am*, or *agha-ghna, as, ī, am*, or *agha-nāśana, as, ī, am*, sin-destroying, expiatory; (*as*), m. an expiator; an epith. of Vishṇu. — *Agha-nishkṛita, as, ā, am*, freed from guilt. — *Agha-maya, as, ī, am*, sinful. — *Agha-marshaṇa, as, ā, am*, expiatory, usually applied to a particular prayer daily offered by Brāhmans; (*as*), m., N. of the author of that prayer, son of Madhućchandas. — *Agha-malāpaha* (°*la-ap*°), *as, ā, am*, removing the filth of sin. — *Agha-māra, as, ā, am*, Ved. fearfully fatal. — *Agha-rud, t, t, t*, fearfully howling. — *Agha-vat, ān, atī, at*, sinful; [voc. *aghavan* or *aghos*, see s. v.] — *Agha-visha, as, ā, am*, Ved. fearfully venomous. — *Agha-śansa, as, ā, am*, wicked; sin-destroying; (*as*), m. a wicked man. — *Aghaśansa-han, ā*, m. slaying the wicked. — *Agha-śansin, ī, inī, i*, Ved. reporting sin. — *Agha-haraṇa, am*, n. removal of guilt. — *Agha-hāra, as*, m., Ved. remover of guilt, pious (?); or, a wicked (notorious) robber (?). — *Aghāśva* (°*gha-aś*°), *as*, m. a bad or vicious horse; N. of a snake. — *Aghāsura* (°*gha-as*°), *as*, m. Agha, Kansa's general. — *Aghāha* (°*gha-ah*°), *as*, m. an inauspicious day, time of impurity from the death of a relative, &c. — *Aghaugha-marshaṇa* (°*gha-ogha-*), *as, ā, am*, destroying the mass or whole of sin.

Aghala, as, ā, am, Ved. evil, sinful.

Aghāya, nom. P., Ved. *aghāyati, -yitum*, to be malicious, to sin, to threaten. — *Aghāyu, us, us, u*, malicious, wicked.

अघटमान *a-ghaṭamāna, as, ā, am*, incongruous, incoherent.

अघन *a-ghana, as, ā, am*, not dense or solid, liquid.

अघर्म *a-gharma, as, ā, am*, not hot, cool. — *Agharma-dhāman, ā*, m. the moon, whose light is supposed to be cool.

अघातिन् *a-ghātin, ī, inī, i*, not fatal, not injurious, harmless.

अघारिन् *a-ghārin, ī, iṇī, i*, not anointing.

अघृण *a-ghṛiṇa, as, ā, am*, destitute of compassion. — *A-ghṛiṇin, ī, inī, i*, not contemptuous, not disdainful.

अघोर *a-ghora, as, ā, am*, not terrific; (*as*), m. a euphemistic title of Śiva; a worshipper of Śiva and Durgā; (*ā*), f. the fourteenth day of the dark half of Bhādra, which is sacred to Śiva. — *Aghora-ghora-rūpa, as*, m. a name of Śiva ('having a form or nature both not terrific and terrific'). — *Aghora-pathin, -nthās*, or *aghora-mārga, as*, m. a follower of Śiva. — *Aghora-pramāṇa, am*, n. a terrific oath.

अघोष *a-ghosha, as*, m. (in grammar) the hard sound of a consonant; (*as, ā, am*), hard-sounding; destitute of cowherds.

अघोस् *aghos*, ind. a vocative particle; properly another form for *aghavan*, voc. of *aghavat*, q. v.

अघ्नत् *a-ghnat, an, antī, at* (fr. rt. *han*), not killing, not injurious.

A-ghnya, as, ā, am, improper to be killed; (*as*), m. Brahmā; a bull; (*ā*), f. a cow; a cloud (?).

अघ्रेय *a-ghreya, as, ā, am* (fr. rt. *ghrā*), improper to be smelled at.

अङ्क् *ank*, cl. 1. A. *ankate, ānanke, ankishyate, ankitum*, to move in a curve; to mark; cl. 10. P. *ankayati, -yitum*, to move in a curve; to mark, stamp, brand; (this rt. is related to *anć*.)

अङ्क *anka, as*, m. (fr. rt. *anć*, but connected with preceding rt. *ank*), a hook; a curve or bend; the curve in the human, especially the female, figure above the hip, where infants (sitting astride) are carried by Hindū mothers or nurses (hence often equivalent to the English breast or lap); the side or flank; the body; proximity, place; the bend in the arm; any hook or crooked instrument; a curved line; a numerical figure, cipher; a figure or mark branded on an animal, &c.; any mark, line, stroke, ornament, stigma; a number; the number nine; a coefficient; an act of a drama; a drama; a military show or sham-fight; a misdeed, a sin; moving in a curve [cf. Gr. ὄγκος and Lat. *uncus*]. — *Anka-karaṇa, am,* n. the act of marking or stamping. — *Anka-tantra, am,* n. title of a book treating of magical marks or figures. — *Anka-dhāraṇā,* f. manner of holding the body, figure. — *Anka-parivartana, am,* n. turning the body, turning on the other side. — *Anka-pāda-vrata, am,* n. title of a chapter in the Bhavishyottara Purāṇa. — *Anka-pāli, is,* f. or *ānka-pālikā,* f. embracing, an embrace. — *Anka-pālī,* f. an embrace; a nurse; a plant, Piring or Medicago Esculenta. — *Anka-pāśa, as,* m. a peculiar concatenation of numerals or numbers. — *Ankapāśa-vyavahāra, as,* m. the use of that concatenation. — *Ankapāśādhyāya* (°*śa-adh*°), *as,* m. the study or use of that concatenation. — *Anka-bandha, as,* m. branding with a mark that resembles a headless body. — *Anka-bhāj, k, k, k,* an infant carried on the hip; forced fruit, nearly ripe, early ripe. — *Anka-mukha, am,* n. the act of a drama which gives a clue to the whole plot. — *Anka-loḍya, as,* m., N. of a plant or its root, ginger, Ciñcoḍa or Ciñcoṭaka. — *Anka-vidyā,* f. arithmetic. — *Ankānka* (°*ka-an*°), *am,* n., Ved. water. — *Ankāvatāra* (°*ka-av*°), *as,* m. the closing part of a dramatic scene.

Ankati, is, m. wind; fire; Brahmā; a Brāhman who maintains the sacred fire.

Ankana, am, n. the act of marking, stamping, branding, ciphering, writing; (*as, ā, am*), marking.

Ankas, as, n. tortuous motion, a mark; the body.

Ankasa, am, n. the flanks (?) or the trappings of a horse.

Ankita, as, ā, am, marked, branded; numbered, counted, calculated.

Ankin, ī, inī, i, having an *anka,* q. v.; (*ī*), m. a small drum; (*inī*), f. a number of marks, &c.

Ankī, f. a small drum.

Ankuṭa, as, m. a key.

Ankupa, am, n., Ved. water.

Ankura or *ankūra, as,* m. a sprout, shoot, blade; a hair; blood; water; a swelling, a tumour.

Ankuraka, as, m. a nest.

Ankurita, as, ā, am, sprouted.

Ankuśa, as, am, m. n. a hook, especially an elephant-driver's hook; (*ā*) or (*ī*), f. one of the twenty-four Jaina goddesses [cf. Gr. ἄγκιστρον; Germ. *Angel*]. — *Ankuśa-graha, as,* m. an elephant-driver. — *Ankuśa-durdhara, as,* m. a restive elephant.

Ankuśita, as, ā, am, urged on by the hook.

Ankuśin, ī, inī, i, having a hook, laying hold of with a hook.

Ankūyat, an, antī, at, Ved. (fr. a nom. *ankūya,* related to *anka*), moving tortuously (to escape).

Ankūra, as, m. a sprout. See *ankura.*

Ankūsha, as, am, m. n. a hook; an ichneumon.

Ankya, as, ā, am, fit or proper to be marked or counted; (*as*), m. a small drum [cf. *ankī*].

अङ्कार *ankāra, as,* m. diminution in music.

अङ्कोट *ankoṭa* or *ankoṭha* or *ankola* or *ankolaka, as,* m. a plant, Alangium Hexapetalum. — *Ankolla-sāra, as,* m. a poison, probably prepared from the plant called Ankola, &c.

अङ्कोलिका *ankolikā,* f. (a corruption of *anka-pālikā,* q. v.), an embrace.

अङ्क्त्वा *anktvā,* ind. (part. fr. rt. *añj*), having besmeared.

अङ्ख् *ankh,* cl. 10. P. *ankhayati, -yitum,* to move slowly, to crawl; to cling to, to hold back.

अङ्ग् *ang,* cl. 1. P. *angati, ānanga, angitum,* to walk, go round (connected with rt. *ag*); cl. 10. P. *angayati, -yitum,* to walk, go round; to mark (in the last sense connected with rt. *ank*); [cf. Gr. ἐγγύς, ἐγγίζω ?].

Angana, am, n. walking; place to walk in, yard; see s. v.

अङ्ग 1. *anga,* ind. a particle implying attention, assent or desire, and sometimes impatience; it may be rendered by well; indeed, true; please; rather; quick. It is often used (changed to *angī,* q. v.) to form compound words, as *angī-kartum,* to assent, promise; see under *angī* [cf. ἄγχι].

अङ्ग 2. *anga, am,* n. (said to be fr. rt. *am,* but rather fr. rt. *ang*), a round limb; a member; the body; a division or department, especially of a science, as the six Vedāngas; science; a subdivision, a supplement; (in grammar) the base of a word; (in rhetoric) an illustration; (in the drama) the whole of the subordinate characters; an expedient; a mental organ, the mind; the number six; (*as*), m. sing. or (*ās*), m. pl., N. of Bengal proper, near Bhagalpur, or its inhabitants; in the sing. it may denote the name of a king of Anga; (*as, ā, am*), having members or divisions, contiguous. — *Anga-kartana, am,* n. cutting off a limb. — *Anga-karman, a,* n. or *anga-kriyā,* f. a supplementary sacrificial act. — *Anga-graha, as,* m. seizure of a limb, i. e. spasm. — *Anga-ja, as, ā, am,* produced from or on the body; ornamental; produced by a supplementary ceremony; (*as*), m. a son; hair of the head; love personified; intoxicating passion; drunkenness; a disease; (*ā*), f. a daughter; (*am*), n. blood. — *Anga-janus, us,* m. a son. — *Anga-jāta, as, ā, am,* produced from or on the body, ornamental, produced by a supplementary ceremony. — *Anga-jvara, as, ā, am,* Ved. causing fever. — *Anga-dvīpa, as,* m. one of the six minor Dvīpas. — *Anga-nyāsa, as,* m. ceremony of touching certain parts of the body. — *Anga-pāli, is,* f. an embrace. — *Anga-prāyaścitta, am,* n. expiation of bodily impurity, especially that arising from death in a family. — *Anga-bheda, as, ā, am,* Ved. causing rheumatism. — *Anga-marda* or *anga-mardaka, as,* m. or *anga-mardin, ī,* m. a servant who has to shampoo his master's body. — *Anga-marsha, as,* m. pain in the limbs, rheumatism. — *Angamarsha-praśamana, am,* n. alleviation of, or medicine for, rheumatism. — *Anga-yāga, as,* m. a subordinate sacrificial act. — *Anga-rakta, as,* m. a plant, Guṇḍārocanī. — *Anga-rakshaṇī* or *anga-rakshiṇī,* f. a body-protector, i. e. a coat of mail, cloak, garment. — *Anga-rāga, as,* m. application of scented unguents or cosmetics to the body, especially after bathing; scented cosmetic. — *Anga-rāj, ṭ,* or *anga-rāja, as,* m., N. of Karṇa, the king of Anga. — *Anga-rājya, am,* n. the kingdom of Anga. — *Anga-ruha, as, ā, am,* what grows on the body, as hair, wool, down, &c. — *Anga-lipi, is,* f. written character of Anga. — *Anga-loka, as,* m. the country called Anga. — *Anga-loḍya, as,* m. a sort of grass, ginger, or its root, commonly ćenćrā. — *Anga-vāk-pāṇi-mat, ān, atī, at,* possessing mind (?), speech, and hands. — *Anga-vikṛiti, is,* f. change of bodily appearance, collapse; fainting, apoplexy. — *Anga-vikshepa, as,* m. gesticulation; a kind of dance with movement of the arms. — *Anga-vidyā,* f. knowledge of lucky or unlucky marks on the body. — *Anga-vaikṛita, am,* n. a wink, nod, sign. — *Anga-sanskāra, as,* m. or *anga-sanskriyā,* f. embellishment of person, doing what is needed to secure a fine personal appearance, as bathing, perfuming, and adorning the body. — *Anga-saṃhati, is,* f. compactness, symmetry or strength of the body. — *Anga-sanga, as,* m. bodily contact, coition. — *Anga-skandha, as,* m. a subdivision of a science. — *Anga-sparśa, as,* m. bodily contact. — *Anga-hāra, as,* or *anga-hāri, is,* m. gesticulation. — *Anga-hīna, as, ā, am,* mutilated; incorporeal; (*as*), m. Kāmadeva. — *Angāngi* (°*ga-an*°), ind. (lit. limb and limb), jointly or reciprocally, in consequence of being related, as one limb to another or to the body. — *Angāngi-tā,* f. intimate relation, as between the limbs, or a limb and the body, or the subordinate and the principal. — *Angāngi-bhāva, as,* m. existence or working of such intimate relation. — *Angādhipa* (°*ga-adh*°), *as,* m. Karṇa, the king of Anga. — *Angānulepana* (°*ga-an*°), *am,* n. anointing the body. — *Angāpūrva* (°*ga-ap*°), *am,* n. effect of a secondary sacrificial act. — *Angeśvara* (°*ga-īś*°), *as,* m. the king of Anga. — *Ange-shṭhā, ās, ās, am,* Ved. situated in a member or in the body.

Angaka, am, n. a limb, member, body; (*ikā*), f. a bodice, a jacket.

Angin, ī, inī, i, having limbs, corporeal, having subordinate parts, principal; having expedients.

Angīya, as, ā, am, referring to the Anga country. — *Angya,* see s. v.

अङ्गण *angaṇa, am,* n. (a place to walk in), a yard, court, area; see *angana* below.

अङ्गति *angati, is,* m. (fr. rt. *ag*), fire; a Brāhman who maintains a sacred fire; Brahmā; Vishṇu.

अङ्गद *anga-da, as,* m. (fr. *anga* + *da*), N. of a brother of Rāma; of a son of Gada; of an ape son of Bāli; (*ā*), f. the female elephant of the south (or the north?); (*am*), n. a bracelet worn on the upper arm.

अङ्गन *angana, am,* n. (fr. rt. *ang,* q. v.), the act of walking; place to walk in, yard, court, area; (*ā*), f. a woman with well-rounded limbs; any woman or female; (in astronomy) Virgo; the female elephant of the north. — *Anganā-gaṇa, as,* m. a number of women. — *Anganā-jana, as,* m. a female person. — *Anganā-priya, as,* m. (lit. dear to women), N. of the tree Jonesia Asoca.

अङ्गव *angava, as,* m. (fr. *angu?,* a corruption of *agni*), dried or withered fruit.

अङ्गस् *angas, as,* n. (fr. rt. *añj?*), a bird.

अङ्गार *angāra, as,* m.; (rarely *am*), n. (said to be fr. rt. *ag* or *ang,* cf. *agni*), charcoal, either heated or not heated; (*as*), m. the planet Mars; N. of a prince of the Maruts; a plant, Hitāvalī; (*ās*), m. pl., N. of a people and country [cf. Lith. *angli-s*; Russ. *ūgolj*; also Germ. *Kohle*; Old Germ. *col* and *colo*; Engl. *coal*]. — *Angāra-kushṭhaka, as,* m. a plant, Hitāvalī. — *Angāra-dhānī* or *angāra-dhānikā,* f. a portable fire-place. — *Angāra-paripāćita, am,* n. roasted food. — *Angāra-parṇa, as,* m. an epith. of Ćitraratha, the chief of the Gandharvas. — *Angāra-pātrī,* f. a portable fire-place. — *Angāra-pushpa, as,* m. a plant, Ingudī; Vulg. Ingua. — *Angāra-mañjarī* or *angāra-mañjī,* f. a shrub, Cesalpinia Banducella. — *Angāra-vallarī* or *angāra-vallī,* f., N. of various plants; Galedupa Arborea; Ovieda Verticallata; Bhārgī; Guñjā. — *Angāra-śakaṭī,* f. a portable fire-place or wheels. — *Angāra-setu, us,* m., N. of a prince, father of Gāndhāra. — *Angārā-vakshayaṇa* (°*ra-av*°), *am,* n. vessel or receptacle for extinguishing coals.

Angāraka, as, m. charcoal; heated charcoal; the planet Mars; Tuesday; N. of a prince of Sauvīra; also of a Rudra; N. of two plants, Eclipta (or Verbesina) Prostrata, and white or yellow Amaranth; (*am*), n. a medicated oil in which turmeric and other vegetable substances have been boiled. — *Angāraka-dina, as, am,* m. n. a festival of Mars on the fourteenth of the latter half of Ćaitra. — *Angāraka-maṇi, is,* m. coral (amber). — *Angāraka-vāra, as,* m. Tuesday.

Angārakita, as, ā, am, charred, roasted, burnt.

Angāri, is, f. a portable fire-place.

Angārikā, f. the stalk of the sugar-cane; the bud of the Kiṇśuka or Butea Frondosa.

Angāriṇī, f. a small fire-place; the region heated by the sun, though no longer exposed to its rays; N. of a creeper.

Angārita, as, ā, am, charred, roasted, burnt; (*ā*), f. a portable fire-place; a bud; N. of a creeper; of a river; (*am*), n. the early blossom of the Kiṇśuka.

Angārīya, as, ā, am, fit for making charcoal of.

Angāryā, f. a heap of charcoal.

अङ्गिका aṅgikā, f. a bodice, a jacket. See aṅgaka.

अङ्गिर् aṅgir, ir, m. (fr. rt. aṅg?), N. of a Ṛishi, who received the Brahmavidyā from Atharvan, and imparted it to Satyavāha, the teacher of Aṅgiras.

Aṅgira, as, or usually *aṅgiras, ās,* m. (related to ἄγγελος or ἄγγαρος!), a celebrated mythological name, usually ascribed to a Ṛishi, the author of a number of hymns in the Ṛig-veda, of a code of laws, and of a treatise on astronomy; he is said by some to have been born from Brahmā's mouth, and to have been the husband of Smṛiti, of S'raddhā, of two daughters of Maitreya, of several daughters of Daksha, &c.; he is considered as one of the seven Ṛishis of the first Manvantara, as a Prajāpati, as a teacher of the Brahmavidyā, which he had learnt from Satyavāha, a descendant of Bharadvāja, &c. Among his sons, the chief is Agni, others are Saṃvarta, Utathya, and Bṛihaspati; among his daughters are mentioned Sinīvālī, Kuhū, Rākā, and Anumati; but the Ṛićas (or Vedic hymns), the manes of Havishmat, and mankind itself are styled his offspring. In astronomy he is the planet Jupiter, and a star in Ursa Major. (*asas*), m. pl. descendants of Aṅgiras or of Agni, mostly personifications of luminous objects; the hymns of the Atharva-veda; priests who, by using the magical formulas of those hymns, protect the sacrifice against the effects of inauspicious accidents. — *Aṅgiras-tama, as, ā, am,* very rapid, especially (like Agni) in devouring food. — *Aṅgiras-vat,* ind. like Aṅgiras; (*ān, atī, at*), connected with or accompanied by the Aṅgirasas.

Aṅgirasa, as, m. an enemy of Vishṇu in his incarnation of Paraśurāma.

Aṅgirasām-ayana, am, n. a Sattra sacrifice.

अङ्गी aṅgī (substituted for aṅga in compound words) implies assent.

Aṅgī-kṛi, cl. 8. P. A. *-karoti, -kurute, -kartum,* to agree to, promise, confess.

Aṅgī-karaṇa, am, n. act of assenting, agreeing, promising.

Aṅgī-kāra, as, m. agreement, promise.

Aṅgī-kṛita, as, ā, am, agreed to, promised.

Aṅgī-kṛiti, is, f. agreement, promise.

अङ्गुरि aṅguri, is, or aṅgurī, f. (for aṅguli, q. v.), a finger; a toe. — *Aṅgurīya* or *aṅgurīyaka, as, am,* m. n. a finger-ring; the ring-finger (?).

अङ्गुल aṅgula, as, m. (for rt. ag or aṅg), a finger; the thumb; a finger's breadth, a measure equal to eight barley-corns, twelve aṅgulas making a vitasti or span, and twenty-four a hasta or cubit; (in astron.) a digit, or twelfth part; N. of the sage Ćāṇakya. — *Aṅgula-pramāṇa* or *aṅgula-māna, am,* n. the measure or length of an aṅgula; (*as, ā, am*), having the length of an aṅgula.

Aṅgulaka at the end of compounds = *aṅgula,* i. e. so many aṅgulas or fingers long.

Aṅguli, is, or *aṅgulī,* f. a finger; a toe; the thumb; the great toe; the finger-like tip of an elephant's trunk; the measure aṅgula. — *Aṅguli-toraṇa, am,* n. a sectarial mark on the forehead consisting of three fingers or lines shaped like an arch or doorway (*toraṇa*), drawn with sandal or the ashes of cow-dung. — *Aṅguli-tra, am,* n. or *aṅguli-trāṇa, as, am,* m. (?), n. a finger-protector, a contrivance like a thimble, used by archers to protect the thumb or finger from being injured by the bow-string. — *Aṅgulitra-vat, ān, atī, at,* provided with such a finger-protector. — *Aṅguli-mukha* or *aṅguli-mukha, am,* n. the tip of the finger. — *Aṅguli-mudrā* or *aṅguli-mudrikā,* f. a seal-ring. — *Aṅguli-moṭana, am,* n. snapping or cracking the fingers. — *Aṅguli-shaṅga, as,* m. contact of the fingers; act of fingering; (*as, ā, am*), sticking to the fingers. — *Aṅguli-sandeśa, as,* m. snapping or cracking the fingers as a sign. — *Aṅguli-sphoṭana, am,* n. snapping or cracking the fingers. — *Aṅguli-pañćaka, am,* n. the five fingers. — *Aṅgulī-parvan, a,* n. a finger-joint. — *Aṅgulī-sambhūta, as,* m. produced from or on the finger, i. e. a finger nail.

Aṅgulika or *aṅgulīya* or *aṅgulīyaka, as, am,* m. n. a finger-ring.

अङ्गुष्ठ aṅgushṭha, as, m. (the smallest aṅga or limb?), the thumb; the great toe; a thumb's breadth, usually regarded as equal to an aṅgula. — *Aṅgushṭha-mātra, as, ī, am,* or *aṅgushṭha-mātraka, as, ikā, am,* having the length or size of a thumb.

Aṅgushṭhya, as, m. the thumb nail.

अङ्गूष aṅgūsha, as, m. (rapid in motion, fr. rt. aṅg or ag), an ichneumon; an arrow.

अङ्गोषिन् aṅgoshin, ī, iṇī, i, Ved. resonant (?), praiseworthy (?).

अङ्ग्य aṅgya, as, ā, am (fr. aṅga), belonging to or connected with the limbs of the body, corporeal, &c.

अंघ् aṅgh, cl. 1. A. *aṅghate, ānaṅghe, aṅghitum,* to go, set out, set about, commence; to hasten; to speak hastily, scold, blame.

Aṅgha (not in use, but equivalent to *agha*), evil, sin. — *Aṅghas, as,* n. sin. — *Aṅghāri* (°*gha-ari*), *is,* m. (an enemy to sin or evil), epith. of Soma, and of a particular altar.

Aṅghi, or better *aṅghri, is,* m. a foot; the root of a tree [cf. *aṃhri*]. — *Aṅghri-nāmaka, as,* m. or *aṅghri-nāman, a,* n. a synonym of *aṅghri,* a root. — *Aṅghri-pa, as,* m. (drinking with the foot or root), a tree. — *Aṅghri-parṇī* or *aṅghri-valli, is,* or *aṅghri-vallikā,* f. a plant, Hedysarum Lagopodioides. — *Aṅghri-pāna, as, ā, am,* sucking his foot or toes (as an infant). — *Aṅghri-skandha, as,* m. the ancle.

अच् ać (connected with *añć,* q. v.), cl. 1. P. A. *aćati, añćati, -te, ānañća, -e, añćitum,* to go, move, tend; to honour; to make round or carved; to request, ask; to speak indistinctly. See 2. *aćita, aćishṇu.*

अचक्र a-ćakra, as, ā, am, having no wheels; immoveable; not vacillating; automatous (?).

अचक्षुस् a-ćakshus, us, n. a bad or miserable eye, no eye; (*us, us, us*), blind. — *A-ćakshur-vishaya, as, ā, am,* not or no longer within reach of the eyes, invisible. — *Aćakshush-ṭva, am,* n. blindness.

A-ćakshushka, as, ā, am, destitute of eyes, blind.

अचण्ड a-ćaṇḍa, as, ā or ī, am, not of a hot temper, gentle, tractable; (*ī*), f. a tractable cow.

अचतुर a-ćatura, as, ā, am, destitute of four, having less than four; not cunning, not dexterous.

अचन्द्र a-ćandra, as, ā, am, moonless.

अचपल a-ćapala, as, ā, am, not oscillating or vibrating; unmoveable, steady.

A-ćāpalya, am, n. freedom from unsteadiness, firmness.

अचर a-ćara, as, ā, am, or a-ćarat, an, antī, at, immoveable.

अचरम a-ćarama, as, ā, am, not last, not least.

अचल a-ćala, as, ā, am, not staggering or moving, immoveable; (*as*), m. a mountain or rock; a bolt or pin; the number seven; N. of S'iva and of the first of the nine deified persons, called 'white Balas' among the Jainas; (*ā*), f. the earth; one of the ten earths of the Buddhists. — *Aćala-kīlā,* f. the earth. — *Aćala-tvish, ṭ,* m. the Kokila or Indian cuckoo. — *Aćala-dhṛiti, is,* f. a metre of four lines, of sixteen short syllables each, also called Gītyāryā. — *Aćala-bhrātṛi, tā,* m., N. of a Brāhman from Oude, who became one of the eleven heads of Gaṇas among the Jainas. — *Aćala-mati, is,* m., N. of a Rākshasa. — *Aćala-śreshṭha, as,* m. chief of mountains. — *Aćalādhipa* (°*la-adh*°), *as,* m. (king of mountains), the Himālaya. — *Aćalā-saptamī,* f. title of a book in the Bhavishyottara Purāṇa.

अचारु a-ćāru, us, vī, u, not pretty, inelegant.

अचिक्कण a-ćikkaṇa, as, ā, am, not smooth, rough.

अचित् 1. a-ćit, t, t, t (fr. rt. ćit), without understanding.

A-ćikitvas, ān, ushī, as, Ved. not knowing, ignorant of.

A-ćitta, as, ā, am, unnoticed, unexpected; not an object of thought; inconceivable; destitute of intellect or sense.

A-ćitti, is, f., Ved. want of sense, infatuation; an infatuated man (?).

अचित् 2. a-ćit, t, t, t (fr. ćit or ćiti, a pile; rt. ći), neglecting the Agnićayana, irreligious.

1. *a-ćita, as, ā, am,* not collected.

अचित 2. aćita, as, ā, am (fr. rt. ać), gone.

Aćishṇu, us, us, u, Ved. going everywhere.

अचित्र a-ćitra, as, ā, am (not variegated), undistinguishable, indistinct.

अचिन्ता a-ćintā, f. thoughtlessness, disregard.

A-ćintita, as, ā, am, not thought of, unexpected, disregarded.

A-ćintya, as, ā, am, surpassing all thought or conception; (*as*), m., N. of S'iva. — *Aćintya-karman, ā, ā, a,* having or performing inconceivable actions. — *Aćintya-rūpa, as, ā* or *ī, am,* possessing inconceivable beauty.

अचिर a-ćira, as, ā, am, not of long duration, brief; not of long date, recent. — *Aćira-dyuti, is,* f. or *aćira-prabhā,* f. lightning. — *Aćira-prasūtā,* f. (having recently brought forth), a cow that has recently calved. — *Aćira-bhās, ās,* f. lightning. — *Aćira-mṛita, as, ā, am,* recently deceased. — *Aćira-roćis, is,* f. or *aćirāṃśu* (°*ra-aṃ*°), *us,* f. or *aćirābhā* (°*ra-ābhā*), f. lightning.

Aćiram or *aćirāt* or *aćireṇa,* ind. not long, not for long; not long ago; soon, speedily.

Aćirā, f. the mother of the Jaina-saint S'ānti.

अचिष्णु aćishṇu, Ved. See under 2. *aćita.*

अचेतन a-ćetana, as, ā, am, or a-ćetas, ās, ās, as, destitute of consciousness, inanimate; (of men) inconscious, insensible, senseless, fainting, &c.

A-ćetāna, as, ā, am, Ved. thoughtless, infatuated.

A-ćaitanya, am, n. unconsciousness; insensibility; senselessness, ignorance in spiritual things; that which is destitute of consciousness, i. e. the material world; matter.

अचेष्ट a-ćeshṭa, as, ā, am, effortless, motionless. — *Aćeshṭa-tā,* f. loss of motion from fainting, &c.

अचोदस् a-ćodas, ās, ās, as, Ved. free from compulsion or external stimulus, spontaneous.

अच्छ 1. a-ććha, as, ā, am (not shaded or covered, fr. a + ćha for ćhad or ćhāyā, rt. ćhad), pellucid, transparent, clear; (*as*), m. a crystal. — *Aććhoda* (*aććha-uda*), *as, ā, am,* having clear water; (*ā*), f., N. of a river; a covering or garment of Vishṇu (?); (*am*), n., N. of a lake in the Himālaya formed by the river Aććhodā.

A-ććhāya, as, ā, am, without shadow, casting no shadow.

अच्छ 2. aććha, as, m. (corruption of ṛiksha), a bear. — *Aććha-bhalla, as,* m. a bear; (*bhalla* itself means 'a bear.')

अच्छ 3. aććha or usually aććhā, rarely aććham, ind., Ved. to, towards (governing the accusative and rarely the locative). It is a kind of separable preposition or prefix to verbs and verbal derivatives, as in the following.

Aććha-i, cl. 2. P. *-eti, -tum*, or *aććhā-gam*, cl. 1. P. *-gaććhati, -gantum*, to attain, go towards.

Aććha-naksh, cl. 1. P. A., Ved. *-nakshati, -te, -kshitum*, to go towards, approach.

Aććha-naś, cl. 1. P., Ved. *-naśati, -śitum*, to come near.

Aććha-nī, cl. 1. P., Ved. *-nayati, -netum*, to lead towards or to.

Aććha-nu, cl. 2. P., Ved. *-nauti, -navitum* or *-nuvitum*, to call out to, to cheer.

Aććha-pat, cl. 1. P., Ved. *-patati, -titum*, and Caus. P. *-patayati, -yitum*, to fly towards.

Aććha-vad, cl. 1. P., Ved. *-vadati, -ditum*, to salute.

Aććhā-vać, cl. 2. P., Ved. *-vakti, -ktum*, to invite. — *Aććhā-vāka, as*, m. 'the inviter,' title of a particular priest or Ṛitvij, one of the sixteen required to perform the great sacrifices with the Soma juice. — *Aććhāvākīya, as, ā, am*, referring to the Aććhāvāka; containing the word *aććhāvāka*.

Aććheta (°*ćha-ita*), *as, ā, am*, Ved. approached, attained.

Aććhokti (°*ćha-uk*°), *is*, f., Ved. invitation.

अच्छिद्र *a-ććhidra, as, ā, am* (free from clefts or flaws), unbroken, uninterrupted, uninjured; (*am*), n. unbroken or uninjured condition, an action free from defect or flaw; (*ena*), ind. uninterruptedly, from first to last. — *Aććhidra-kāṇḍa, am*, n. title of a chapter of the Taittirīya-Brāhmaṇa. — *Aććhidroti* (°*dra-ūti*), *is, is, i*, affording perfect protection. — *Aććhidrodhnī* (°*ra-ūdh*°), f., Ved. (a cow) having a faultless udder.

A-ććhidyamāna, as, ā, am, uncut, uncurtailed; not fragile.

A-ććhinna, as, ā, am, uncut, uncurtailed, uninjured; undivided, inseparable. — *Aććhinna-pattra, as, ā, am* (of a bird, or, in the Vedas, of an altar shaped like a bird), having the wings uncurtailed, uninjured; having uninjured leaves. — *Aććhinna-parṇa, as, ī, am*, having uninjured leaves.

A-ććhedika or *a-ććhaidika, as, ā* or *ī, am*, not fit or needing to be cut.

A-ććhedya, as, ā, am, improper or impossible to be cut, indivisible.

अच्छुप्ता *a-ććhuptā*, f. (not touched by sin), N. of one of the sixteen Vidyādevīs of the Jainas.

अच्छोटन *aććhoṭana, am*, n. hunting.

अच्युत *a-ćyuta, as, ā, am*, what has not given way or fallen; firm, solid; imperishable, permanent; not leaking or dripping; (*as*), m., N. of Vishṇu or Kṛishṇa; also of a physician; N. of a plant, Morinda Tinctoria; N. of a gift to Agni. — *Aćyuta-kshit, t*, m., Ved. having solid ground, an epithet of Soma. — *Aćyuta-ćyut, t, t, t*, Ved. throwing down that which is fixed. — *Aćyuta-ja, ās*, m. pl. a class of Jaina deities produced by Vishṇu. — *Aćyuta-jallakin, ī*, m., N. of a commentator of the Amara-Kosha. — *Aćyuta-danta* or *aćyutanta, as*, m., N. of the ancestor of a warrior tribe called Āćyutadanti or Āćyutanti, though possibly the names refer to two distinct persons and tribes. — *Aćyuta-mūrti, is*, m., N. of Vishṇu. — *Aćyuta-rush, ṭ*, f. inveterate hatred. — *Aćyuta-vāsa, as*, m. the sacred fig-tree, Ficus Religiosa. — *Aćyuta-sthala, am*, n., N. of a place in the Pañjāb. — *Aćyutāgraja* (°*ta-ag*°), *as*, m. (Vishṇu's elder brother), Balarāma; Indra. — *Aćyutopādhyāya* (°*ta-up*°), *as*, m. = *aćyuta-jallakin*, q. v.

अज् *aj*, cl. 1. P. (defect. verb, supplemented fr. rt. *vī*), *ajati, ājīt, ajitum*, to go, to drive, propel, throw, cast: Desid. *ajijishati*, to be desirous of driving [cf. Gr. ἄγω; Lat. *ago*].

1. *aja, as*, m. a drove; a driver, mover, instigator, leader; epithet given in the Vedas to Indra, Rudra, one of the Maruts, Agni, and the sun; in later works to Brahmā, Vishṇu, Śiva, and Kāma (see also 2 *a-ja*); the leader of a flock; a he-goat or ram [cf. Gr. αἴξ, αἰγός; Lith. ożys]; the sign Aries; the vehicle of the sun; N. of a descendant of Viśvāmitra, and of Daśaratha's or Dīrghabāhu's father; N. of a mineral substance; of a kind of rice; of the moon; (*as*), m. pl., N. of a class of Ṛishis; of a people mentioned in the Vedas; (*ā*), f., N. of Prakṛiti or Nature, of Māyā or Illusion; a she-goat; N. of a plant whose bulbs resemble the udder of a goat. — *Aja-karṇa, as*, m. a goat's ear; a plant or tree, Terminalia Alata Tomentosa. — *Aja-karṇaka, as*, m. the Sāl-tree, Shorea Robusta. — *Aja-kūlā*, f., N. of a town of the Bodhis. — *Aja-kshīra, am*, n., Ved. goat's milk. — *Aja-gandha, as*, m. smell of a he-goat; (*as, ā, am*), smelling like a goat. — *Aja-gandhā* or *aja-gandhikā*, f. shrubby basil, Ocymum Gratissimum. — *Aja-gandhinī*, f. a plant, also called *ajaśṛiṅgī*, q. v. — *Aja-gara, as*, m. (that swallows a goat), a huge serpent, probably boa constrictor; (*ī*), f., N. of a plant. — *Aja-gallikā*, f. 'goat's cheek,' an infantile disease. — *Aja-jīva* or *aja-jīvika, as*, m. 'who lives by goats,' a goat-herd. — *Aja-tā*, f. a multitude of goats; the being a goat. — *Aja-tva* or *ajā-tva, am*, n. the being a goat. — *Aja-daṇḍī*, f. a plant, also called *brahmadaṇḍī*. — *Aja-devatā, ās*, f. pl. the 25th lunar mansion. — *Aja-nāmaka, as*, m. (named Aja or Vishṇu), a mineral substance. — *Aja-pa, as*, m. a goat-herd. — *Aja-patha, as*, m. 'goat's road,' probably synonymous with *aja-vīthī*, q. v. — *Aja-pada* or *aja-pāda, as, ā, am*, goat-footed. — *Aja-pād, t*, m., Ved. epithet of the divinity called *Aja*. — *Aja-pārśva, as*, m. (having black sides like a goat), epithet of Śvetakarṇa's son Rājīvaloćana. — *Aja-pāla, as*, m. a goat-herd; N. of Daśaratha's father. — *Aja-bhaksha, as*, m. 'goat's food,' N. of a plant, Varvūra. — *Aja-māyu, us*, m., Ved. bleating like a goat. — *Aja-māra, as*, m., N. of a tribe or a prince. — *Aja-mīḍha* or *aja-mīlha, as*, m., N. of a son of Suhotra, the author of some Vedic hymns; of a grandson of Suhotra; surname of Yudhishṭhira. — *Aja-mukha, as, ī, am*, goat-faced; (*ī*), f., N. of a Rākshasī. — *Aja-meru*, N. of a place, Ajmir (?). — *Aja-moda, as*, m. or *aja-modā* or *aja-modikā*, f. 'goat's delight,' N. of various plants, common Carroway, the species called Ajwaen (Ligusticum Ajwaen), and especially a species of Parsley, Apium Involucratum. — *Ajarshabha* (°*ja-ṛish*°), *as*, m. the best goat. — *Aja-lambana, am*, n. antimony. — *Aja-loman, ā*, m. or *aja-lomī*, f., N. of a plant, Cowage, Carpopogon Pruriens; (*a*), n. goat's hair. — *Aja-vasti, is*, m., N. of a tribe; (*ayas*), m. pl. the members of that tribe. — *Aja-vāha, as*, m., N. of a district. — *Aja-vīthī*, f. 'goat's road,' N. of one of the three divisions of the southern path, or one of the three paths in which the sun, moon, and planets move, comprehending the asterisms *mūlā, pūrvāshāḍha*, and *uttarāshāḍha*. — *Aja-śṛiṅgī*, f. 'goat's horn,' N. of a shrub, Odina Wodier, used as a charm and as a remedy for sore eyes,—the fruit resembles a goat's horn. — *Aja-stunda, am*, n., N. of a town. — *Aja-hā*, f. Cowage, Carpopogon Pruriens. — *Ajā-kṛipāṇīya, as, ā, am*, like the goat and shears in the fable. — *Ajā-kshīra, am*, n. goat's milk. — *Ajā-gala, as*, m goat's neck. — *Ajāgala-stana, as*, m. nipple or fleshy protuberance on the neck of some Indian goats, and an emblem of any useless or worthless object or person. — *Ajā-jīva, as*, m. (who lives by goats), a goat-herd. — *Ajā-taulvali, is*, m., N. of a Muni who lived on the milk of goats; (given by grammarians as an example of compounds in which the middle term is left out). — *Ajāda* (*aja-ada*), *as*, m. 'goat-eater,' the ancestor of a warrior tribe. — *Ajādanī* (°*ja-ad*°), f. a species of prickly night-shade. — *Ajāntrī* (°*ja-an*°), f. a pot-herb, Convolvulus Argenteus. — *Ajā-payas, as*, n. goat's milk. — *Ajā-pālaka, as, ā, am*, tending goats; (*as*), m. a goat-herd. — *Ajāvika* (*aja-av*°), *am*, n. goats and sheep, small cattle. — *Ajāśva* (*aja-aś*°), *am*, n. goats and horses; (*as*), m. Pūshan or the Sun who has goats for horses. — *Ajaikapād* (*aja-ek*°), *t*, m. epithet of Vishṇu; of one of the eleven Rudras. — *Ajaiḍaka* (*aja-eḍ*°), *am*, n. goats and rams.

Ajaka, as, m., N. of a descendant of Purūravas; also of a king of Magadha; *ajakā* or *ajikā*, f. a young she-goat; a disease of the pupil of the eye, small reddish tumours (compared to kids), protruding through the transparent cornea and discharging pus. — *Ajakā-jāta, am*, n. the same disease of the eyes.

Ajana, ajani, aji, ajma, &c., see s. v.

अज 2. *a-ja, as, ā, am*, not born, existing from all eternity; (*as*), m. Brahmā, Vishṇu, Śiva, Kāma; (*ā*), f. Prakṛiti or Nature, Māyā or Illusion (see also 1. *aja*, s. v. *aj* and 1. *ajana*).

अजकव *ajakava, as*, m. (etymology unknown), Śiva's bow. — *Ajakāva, as, am*, m. n. Śiva's bow; (*as*), m. a venomous kind of vermin, centipede or scorpion; (*am*), n. sacrificial vessel dedicated to Mitra and Varuṇa. — *Ajagava* or *ajagāva, am*, n. Śiva's bow; the southern portion of the path of the sun, moon, and planets; N. of a snake priest.

अजघन्य *a-jaghanya, as, ā, am*, not last; not least.

अजघ्निवस् *a-jaghnivas, ān, ushī, at* (perf. part. fr. rt. *han*), not having killed.

अजटा *a-jaṭā*, f. a plant, Flacourtia Cataphracta; also *ajaḍā* and *ajjhaṭā*.

अजड *a-jaḍa, as, ā, am*, not torpid or stupid; (*ā*), f., N. of two plants; see *Ajaṭā* and *Kapikaććhu*, Carpopogon Pruriens. — *Ajaḍa-dhī, is, is, i*, of a vigorous mind, energetic, bold.

अजथ्या *ajathyā*, f. yellow jasmin (fit for goats?).

अजन 1. *ajana, as*, m. (fr. rt. *aj*.), Brahmā 'the agitator;' (*am*), n. act of instigating or moving. — *Ajana-yoni-ja, as*, m. (born fr. *Ajana*, i. e. Brahmā); N. of Daksha.

Ajani, is, f. a path, road; see also *aji*.

अजन 2. *a-jana, as, ā, am* (rt. *jan*), destitute of living beings, especially of men; desert; (*as*), m. an insignificant person.

A-janani, is, f. privation of birth, cessation of existence; *ajananir astu tasya*, 'may he cease to exist!'

A-janya, as, ā, am, improper to be produced or born; unfit or unfavourable for mankind; (*am*), n. any portent or natural phenomenon unfavourable to mankind, as an earthquake.

अजप 1. *a-japa, as*, m. (rt. *jap*), one who does not repeat prayers; a reader of heterodox works; (*ā*), f. the mantra or formula called haṅsa, which consists only of a number of inhalations and exhalations.

अजप 2. *aja-pa, as*, m. a goat-herd. See s. v. 1. *aja*.

अजमीढ *aja-mīḍha, as*, m. See s. v. 1. *aja*.

अजम्भ *a-jambha, as*, m. (toothless), a frog.

अजय *a-jaya, as*, m. non-victory, defeat; (*as, ā, am*), unconquered, unsurpassed, invincible; (*as*), m., N. of Vishṇu; of a lexicographer; of a river; (*ā*), f. hemp; N. of a friend of Durgā; Māyā or Illusion.

A-jayya, as, ā, am, invincible, improper to be won at play.

अजर *a-jara, as, ā, am* (rt. *jṛī*), not subject to old age, undecaying, ever young; (*ā*), f., N. of two plants, Aloe Perfoliata and Jīrṇapañjhī. — *Ajarāmaravat* (°*ra-am*°), ind. as if undecaying and immortal.

A-jarat, an, antī, at, not suffering from old age, not decaying.

A-jarayu, us, us, u, not subject to old age or decay.

A-jaras, another form for *ajara*, used only in some cases.

A-jarya, as, ā, am, not friable, not digestible; not subject to old age or decay; (*am*), n. friendship.

अजवस् *a-javas, ās, ās, as*, Ved. not quick, inactive.

अजस्र *a-jasra, as, ā, am* (rt. *jas*, 'to injure' not to be killed or interrupted), perpetual. — *Ajasram* or *ajasreṇa*, ind. perpetually, for ever, ever.

अजहत् *a-jahat* (pres. part. fr. rt. *hā* with *a*), not dropping or losing (used in compounds). — *Ajahat-svārthā*, f., N. of a rhetorical figure, an elliptical use of words in which their original meaning is not dropped, as "white ones" for "white horses," "lances" for "men with lances." — *Ajahal-liṅga, as*, m. (in grammar) said of a noun not dropping its original gender, when used like an adjective.

अजा *ajā*, f. a goat; Prakṛiti; Māyā. See s.v. 1. *aja*, where the compounds of *ajā* will also be found.

अजागर *a-jāgara, as, ā, am*, not awake, not wakeful; (*as*), a plant, Eclipta or Verbesina Prostrata.

अजाजि *ajā-ji, is*, or *ajā-jī*, f. (*ajā* with rt. *ji ?*, that overcomes goats); Cumin seed, Cuminum Cyminum; Ficus Oppositifolia; Nigella Indica.

अजात *a-jāta, as, ā, am*, unborn, not yet born, not yet developed. — *Ajāta-kakud, t*, m. a young bull whose hump (*kakud*) is yet undeveloped. — *Ajāta-paksha, as, ā* or *ī, am*, having undeveloped wings. — *Ajāta-vyañjana, as, ā, am*, having an undeveloped beard. — *Ajāta-vyavahāra, as*, m. having his majority unattained, a minor, a youth under fifteen. — *Ajāta-śatru, us, us, u*, having no enemy; having no adversary of equal standing; (*us*), m., N. of S'iva, of Yudhishṭhira, of a king of Kāśī, of a son of S'amīka, of a son of Vidmisāra or Bimbisāra, and contemporary of S'ākyamuni. — *Ajātānuśaya* (°*ta-anu*°), *as, ā, am*, having no regret. — *Ajātāri* (°*ta-ari*), *is*, m. (having no enemy), Yudhishṭhira.

अजानत् *a-jānat, an, atī, at* (pres. part. of rt. *jñā* with *a*), not knowing, unaware.

अजानि *a-jāni, is*, or *a-jānika, as*, m. having no wife.

अजानेय *ajāneya*, better *ājāneya, as, ā, am* (from *ājāna*, *ājāni*, birth, descent), of high breed; undaunted, fearless; (*as*), m. a horse of high breed.

अजामि *a-jāmi, is, is, i*, Ved. not of kin, not related; unfriendly; (in grammar) not corresponding. — *Ajāmi-tā*, f., Ved. absence of connection, friendliness, or similarity.

अजायमान *a-jāyamāna, as, ā, am* (rt. *jan*), not being born, not subject to birth.

अजि *aji*, f. (fr. *aj*, q. v.), a road.

अजिका *ajikā*, f. (fr. *ajā*), a young goat [cf. 1. *aja*].

अजित *a-jita, as, ā, am*, not conquered, unsubdued, unsurpassed, invincible, irresistible; (*as*), m., N. of an antidote, a poisonous sort of rat; N. of various persons, viz. Vishṇu; S'iva; one of the Saptarshis of the fourteenth Manvantara; Maitreya or a future Buddha; the second of the Arhats or saints of the present (Jaina) Avasarpiṇī, a descendant of Ikshvāku; the attendant of Suvidhi, who is the ninth of those Arhats; (*ās*), m. pl. a class of deified beings in the first Manvantara. — *Ajita-keśa-kambala, as*, m., N. of a Brāhman. — *Ajita-balā*, f., N. of a Jaina deity, who acts under the direction of the Arhat Ajita. — *Ajita-vikrama, as*, m. (having invincible power), epithet of king C'andragupta the second. — *Ajitātman* (°*ta-āt*°), *ā, ā, a*, having an unsubdued self or spirit. — *Ajitāpīḍa* (°*ta-āp*°), *as*, m. having an unsurpassed crown; N. of a king. — *Ajitendriya* (°*ta-ind*°), *as, ā, am*, having an unsubdued sensuous nature, whose passions are not controlled.

अजिन *ajina, am*, n. (probably at first the skin of a goat, *aja*, with the hair on, then any skin which would answer the same purpose); the hairy skin of an antelope, especially a black antelope, which serves the religious student for a couch, seat, covering, &c.; the hairy skin of a tiger, &c.; (*as*), m., N. of a descendant of Pṛithu. — *Ajina-pattrā* or *ajina-pattrī* or *ajina-pattrikā*, f. a bat. — *Ajina-phalā*, f., N. of a plant (?). — *Ajina-yoni, is*, m. (origin of the skin), an antelope, deer. — *Ajina-vāsin, ī, inī, i*, clad in a skin. — *Ajina-sandha, as*, m. (who joins or prepares skins), a furrier.

अजिर *ajira, as, ā, am* (fr. rt. *aj*), agile, quick, rapid; (*as*), m., N. of a snake priest; (*ā*), f., N. of Durgā, and of a river; (*am*), n. place to run or fight in, area, court [Lat. *ager ?*]; the body; any object of sense, air, wind; a frog; (*am*), ind. quickly. — *Ajira-vatī*, f., N. of the river on which the town S'rāvastī was situated. — *Ajira-śoćis, is*, m., Ved. having a quick light, glittering, epithet of Agni and Soma. — *Ajirādhirāja* (°*ra-adh*°), *as*, m., Ved. an agile emperor, epithet of death.

Ajirāya, nom. A. *ajirāyate, -yitum*, Ved. to be agile or quick.

Ajirīya, as, ā, am, connected (by proximity or ownership &c.) with an ajira or court &c.

अजिह्म *a-jihma, as, ā, am*, not crooked, straight, straightforward, upright; (*as*), m. a frog, a fish; see *a-jihva*, of which this may be a corruption. — *Ajihma-ga, as, ā, am*, going straight on; (*as*), m. an arrow. — *Ajihmāgra* (°*hma-ag*°), *as, ā, am*, having a straight point.

अजिह्व *a-jihva, as, ā, am*, tongueless; (*as*), m. a frog.

अजीकव *ajīkava, am*, n. S'iva's bow. See *ajakava*.

अजीगर्त *a-jīgarta, as*, m. (that has nothing to swallow), N. of a Ṛishi, S'unaḥśepha's father.

अजीत *a-jīta, as, ā, am* (rt. *jyā* usually makes *jīna*), not faded, not faint. — *Ajīta-punarvaṇya, am*, n., Ved. (unfaded and recoverable), N. of a twofold rite to be performed by Kshatriyas.

A-jīti, is, f., Ved. unfadingness; freedom from decay, prosperity.

अजीर्ण *a-jīrṇa, as, ā, am* (rt. *jṝ*), not decomposed; unimpaired; undigested; (*am*), n. freedom from decay, indigestion.

A-jīrṇi, is, f. indigestion.

A-jīrṇin, ī, inī, i, suffering from indigestion.

अजीव *a-jīva, as*, m. (non-life), non-existence, death; (*as, ā, am*), lifeless.

A-jīvat, an, antī, at, not living, destitute of a livelihood.

A-jīvana, am, n. non-existence, death; (*as, ā, am*), destitute of a livelihood.

A-jīvani, is, f. non-existence, death; *ajīvanis tasya bhūyāt*, 'may death befal him!'

A-jīvita, am, n. non-existence, death.

अजुगुप्सित *a-jugupsita, as, ā, am*, not blamed.

अजुर *a-jura* or *a-jurya, as, ā, am* (rt. *jūr*), Ved. not subject to old age or decay.

अजुष्ट *a-jushṭa, as, ā, am*, Ved. not enjoyed, unsatisfactory.

A-jushṭi, is, f., Ved. non-enjoyment, feeling of disappointment.

अजेतव्य *a-jetavya, as, ā, am*, invincible, insuperable, irresistible.

A-jeya, as, ā, am, invincible; (*am*), n., N. of an antidote.

अजैकपाद् *ajaikapād* (*aja-eka*°), *t*, or *ajaikapāda, as*, m. an epithet of Vishṇu; N. of one of the eleven Rudras.

अजैडक *ajaiḍaka* (*aja-eḍaka*), *am*, n. goats and sheep.

अजोष *a-josha, as, ā, am*, Ved. not gratified, not yet satisfied. — *A-joshya, as, ā, am*, Ved. not easily gratified, never satisfied.

अज्जुका *ajjukā*, f. (in the drama) a courtezan; (corruption of *arjukā*.)

अज्झटा *ajjhaṭā*, f. a plant, Flacourtia Cataphracta. (Also *ajaṭā* and *ajaḍā*.)

अज्झल *ajjhala, as*, m. (corruption of *ujjvala ?*), a burning coal; (*am*), n. a shield (?).

अज्ञ *a-jña, as, ā, am* (fr. *a* and rt. *jñā*), not knowing; ignorant, inexperienced; unconscious; unwise, stupid. — *Ajña-tva, am*, n. or *ajña-tā*, f. ignorance.

Ajñakā or *ajñikā*, f. diminutive form for *ajñā*, an ignorant woman.

A-jñāta, as, ā, am, unknown; unexpected; unaware. — *Ajñāta-kula-śīla, as, ā, am*, whose lineage and character are unknown. — *Ajñāta-keta, as, ā, am*, Ved. having unknown or secret designs. — *Ajñāta-bhukta, as, ā, am*, eaten unawares. — *Ajñāta-yakshma, as*, m., Ved. (insidious consumption ?), N. of a disease. — *Ajñāta-vāsa, as, ā, am*, whose dwelling is unknown. — *Ajñāta-śīla, as, ā, am*, whose character is unknown.

Ajñātaka, as, ā, am, unknown, unaware.

A-jñāti, is, m. not a kinsman, not related.

A-jñātvā, ind. not having known or ascertained.

अज्ञान *a-jñāna, am*, n. non-cognisance; ignorance, especially (in philosophy) spiritual ignorance; not merely a negative, but an active principle, which consisting of the three Guṇas (fetters or qualities) *sattva, rajas*, and *tamas*, and preventing the soul from realizing its identity with Brahma, causes self to appear a distinct personality, and matter to appear a reality; hence equivalent to Prakṛiti or Nature, and termed a divine S'akti (power), synonymous with Māyā, Illusion; (*as, ā, am*), ignorant, unwise. — *Ajñāna-tas* or *ajñānāt*, ind. unawares, ignorantly, inadvertently. — *Ajñāna-kṛita, as, ā, am*, done inadvertently. — *Ajñāna-tva, am*, n. or *ajñāna-tā*, f. ignorance. — *Ajñāna-bandhana, am*, n. the bond of ignorance.

A-jñānin, ī, inī, i, ignorant, unwise.

A-jñās, ās, m., Ved. not a kinsman.

A-jñeya, as, ā, am, baffling or passing knowledge, unfit to be known.

अज्म *ajma, as*, m. (fr. rt. *aj*), Ved. career, march, battle [cf. ὄγμος].

Ajman, a, n., Ved. career, passage, battle; a house, a habitation [Lat. *agmen*].

अज्यानि *a-jyāni, is*, f., Ved. undecaying nature.

अज्येष्ठ *a-jyeshṭha, as, ā, am*, not the oldest or best; having no elder brother. — *A-jyeshṭha-vṛitti, is, is, i*, not behaving as the eldest brother ought to behave, or (*ajyeshṭha-vṛitti*) behaving like one who has no elder brother.

अज्र *ajra, as*, m., Ved. a field, a plain; (*as, ā, am*), Ved. agile, quick [Lat. *ager*; Gr. ἀγρός: cf. *ajira*].

Ajrya, as, ā, am, Ved. being in or connected with a field or plain.

अज्विन *ajvin, ī, inī, i* (fr. rt. *aj*), Ved. active, agile.

अञ्च 1. *añć* (connected with *ać*, q. v.), cl. 1. P. A. *añćati, -te, ānañća, -e, añćishyati, -te, añćitum*, to bend, curve, incline, curl; to reverence (with inclined body), to honour; to tend, move, go, wander about; to request: cl. 10. or Caus. *añćayati, -yitum*, to unfold, make clear, produce: Desid. P. A. *añćićishati, -te*, to be desirous of bending: Pass. *añćyate* or *aćyate*, to be bent.

2. *añć* (at the end of compounds), turned to, going or directed towards; see *akudhryañć, avāñć, udañć, devadryañć*, &c. It may also mean honouring, see *prāñć*.

Añća, as, m. (only used as the last part of compound words), curling, as in *romāñća*, sensation of the hairs of the body curling, thrill of rapture.

Añćati, is, m. or *añćatī,* f. wind; fire.

Añćana, am, n. act of bending or curving.

Añćala, as, m. (perhaps also *am*), n. the border or corner of a garment, especially of a woman's garment, of a veil, shawl. (In Bengālī, a strip of country, district.)

Añćita, as, ā, am, bent, curved, curled, arched, handsome; gone, walked in; reverenced, honoured, distinguished. — *Añćita-pattra, as,* m. lotus with curved leaves. — *Añćitapattrāksha* (°*ra-aksha*), *as, ī, am,* having lotus eyes. — *Añćita-bhrū, ūs,* f. woman with arched or handsome eyebrows. — *Añćita-lāṅgūla, as, ā, am,* having a curved tail (as a monkey).

अञ्ज् *añj,* cl. 7. P. A. *anakti, aṅkte, ānañja, añjishyati* or *aṅkshyati, āñjīt, añjitum* or *aṅktum,* to apply an ointment or pigment, smear with, anoint; to decorate, prepare; to honour, celebrate; to cause to appear, to make clear, distinguish, represent; to be beautiful; to go: Caus. *añjayati, -yitum, āñjijat,* to smear with; to speak, shine, to cause to go [cf. Lat. *ungo*].

Añjaka, as, m., N. of a son of Vipraćitti; of a son of Yadu.

Añjana, as, m. a kind of domestic lizard; N. of a fabulous serpent; of a tree; of a mountain; of a king of Mithilā; of the elephant of the west or south-west quarter; (*am*), n. act of applying an ointment or pigment, embellishing, &c.; black pigment or collyrium applied to the eye-lashes or the inner coat of the eye-lids; special kind or material of this pigment, as lamp-black, Antimony, an extract of Ammonium, Xanthorrhiza, &c.; paint, especially as a cosmetic; magic ointment; ink; night; fire. (In rhetoric) suggesting the special meaning alluded to in an expression, as in a pun, &c. — *Añjana-keśī,* f., N. of a vegetable perfume. — *Añjana-nāmikā,* f. a swelling of the eyelid, stye. — *Añjana-vat,* ind. like collyrium. — *Añjanādhikā* (°*na-adh*°), f. a species of lizard. — *Añjanāmbhas* (°*na-am*°), *as,* n. eye-water.

Añjanaka, as, m. portion of the Vedas containing the word *añjana.* — *Añjanakī,* f., N. of a medicinal plant.

Añjanā, f., N. of Hanumat's mother; of Pravarasena's mother. — *Añjanā-giri, is,* m., N. of a mountain. — *Añjanā-vatī,* f. the female elephant of the north-east (or the west?) quarter.

Añjanika, as, ā, am, connected with collyrium; (*ā*), f. a species of lizard; a small mouse.

Añjanī, f. a woman fit for the application of ointments, pigments, sandal, &c.; N. of two medicinal plants.

Añjala, añjali, see s. v. below.

Añjas, as, n., Ved. ointment, preparation (?); smoothness, sliding, speed (?); a good fit, adaptation (?); (according to others, *ās, ās, as*), level, straight, right. — *Añjas-pā, ās, ās, am,* Ved. drinking the Soma preparation. — *Añjah-sava, as,* m. rapid preparation of Soma.

Añjasa, as, ā, am, straight, straightforward, honest; (*ī*), f., Ved., N. of a heavenly river.

Añjasā or *añjas,* ind. straight on, right, truly, justly; quickly, soon, instantly.

Añjasāyana (°*sā-ay*°), *as, ī, am,* having a straight course, going straight on.

Añjasīna, as, ā, am, Ved. going straight on, straightforward.

Añji, is, is, i, applying an ointment or pigment; ointment, brilliancy, unctuous, slimy; shining, brilliant; (*is, i*), m. n. the sexual organ, i. e. distinguishing the sex; (*is*), m. a sender, commander. — *Añji-mat, ān, atī, at,* Ved. coloured, bright, adorned. — *Añji-saktha, as,* m. (a victim) that has coloured thighs.

Añjin, ī, inī, i, Ved. making clear or manifest.

Añjiva, as, ā, am, Ved. slippery, smooth.

Añjishṭha, as, m., Ved. (highly brilliant), the sun; also *añjishṇu, us,* m.

अञ्जल *añjala* (only at the end of compounds), another form for *añjali,* q. v.

अञ्जलि *añjali, is,* m. (fr. rt. *añj*), the open hands placed side by side and slightly hollowed, as if by a beggar to receive food; hence when raised to the forehead, a mark of supplication, reverence, salutation or benediction; a libation; a measure of corn, sufficient to fill both hands when placed side by side, equal to a kuḍava. — *Añjali-karman, a,* n. making the *añjali* or respectful salutation. — *Añjali-kārikā,* f. an earthen doll, making the *añjali;* N. of a plant, probably Mimosa Natans. — *Añjali-puṭa, as, am,* m. n. cavity produced in making the *añjali.* — *Añjali-bandhana, am,* n. salutation with the *añjali* raised to the forehead. — *Añjali-krita, as, ā, am,* (hands) placed together to form the *añjali.*

Añjalika, as, am, m. n., N. of one of Arjuna's arrows; see *Karṇa-parva,* 4788; (*ā*), a young mouse.

अञ्जिक *añjika, as,* m., N. of a son of Yadu. See *añjaka.*

अञ्जिहिषा *añjihishā,* f. (fr. Desid. of rt. *aṅh*), desire of going.

अञ्जी *añjī,* f. a blessing (?).

अञ्जीर *añjīra, am,* n. a species of fig-tree (Ficus Oppositifolia); a fig. (In Bengālī) a guava. (*Añjīra* is a Persian word.)

अट् *aṭ,* cl. 1. P. A. *aṭati, -te, āṭa, aṭishyati, āṭīt, aṭitum,* to roam, wander about (sometimes with acc.), frequently used of religious mendicants: Intens. *aṭāṭyate,* to roam or wander about zealously or habitually, especially as a religious mendicant: Desid. *aṭiṭishati,* to be desirous of roaming.

Aṭa, as, ā, am, roaming, wandering; (*ā*), f. the act or habit of roaming or wandering about, especially as a religious mendicant.

Aṭaka, as, ī, am, roaming.

Aṭana, am, n. act or habit of wandering about.

Aṭani, is, f. or *aṭanī,* f. the notched extremity of a bow.

Aṭamāna, as, ā, am, roaming about, vagabond.

Aṭavi, is, or *aṭavī,* f. (place to roam in), a forest. — *Aṭavi-śikhara, ās,* m. pl., N. of a people or country.

Aṭavika, better *āṭavika, as,* m. a woodman, forester.

Aṭāṭā, f. (habit of) roaming or wandering about.

Aṭāṭyamāna, as, ā, am, roaming excessively.

Aṭāṭyā, f. (habit of) roaming.

Aṭāya, nom. A. *aṭāyate,* to enter upon a roaming life, to become a religious mendicant.

Aṭyā, f. act or habit of roaming about as a religious mendicant.

अटनि, अटवि, अटाट्या, &c., see under *aṭ* above.

अटरूष *aṭarusha* or *aṭarūsha* or *aṭarūshaka, as,* m., N. of the shrub Justicia Adhatoda.

अटल *a-ṭala, as, ā, am,* not shaky, firm, solid.

अट्ट् *aṭṭ,* cl. 1. A. *aṭṭate, ānaṭṭe, aṭṭitum,* to exceed, kill; cl. 10. P. *aṭṭayati, -yitum,* to contemn, lessen, diminish.

Aṭṭa, ind. high, lofty, loud; (*as*), m. top-heavy (?), exceeding; shaking; injuring; N. of a Yaksha; (*as, am*), m. n. addition to a building, apartment on the roof, upper story; tower, buttress, back of a building; (corruption of *haṭṭa*), a market, a market-place; (*ā*), f. overbearing conduct?; (*am*), n. (corruption of *anna?*), boiled rice, food; (*as, ā, am*), dried, dry. — *Aṭṭa-pati-bhāgākhya-griha-kritya* (°*ga-ākh*°), *am,* n. business of the house called the market-master's department (an office in Kashmir). — *Aṭṭa-sthalī,* f. (site of an *aṭṭa*), a name. — *Aṭṭa-hasita, am,* n. loud laughter, a horse-laugh. — *Aṭṭa-hāsa, as,* m. idem; a name of Śiva. — *Aṭṭa-hāsaka, as,* m., N. of a shrub, Jasminum Multiflorum or Hirsutum. — *Aṭṭa-hāsin, ī,* m. epithet of Śiva. — *Aṭṭa-hāsya, am,* n. loud laughter; a horse-laugh. — *Aṭṭāṭṭa-hāsa* (°*ṭṭa-aṭṭ*°), *as,* m. very loud laughter.

Aṭṭaka, as, m. an apartment on the roof.

Aṭṭaṭṭa, ind. very high, very loud.

Aṭṭana, am, n. a weapon shaped like a discus.

Aṭṭā, f. overbearing conduct (?), excess (?).

Aṭṭāya (nom. fr. *aṭṭā*), A. *aṭṭāyate* (meaning doubtful), to be overbearing (?).

अट्टाल *aṭṭāla, as,* or *aṭṭālaka, as,* m. an apartment on the roof, an upper story; (*ikā*), f. a house of two or more stories, a lofty house, palace; N. of a country. — *Aṭṭālikā-kāra, as,* m. a bricklayer, mason. — *Aṭṭālikā-bandha, as,* m. (in architecture) a kind of base.

अट्टिलिका *aṭṭilikā,* f., N. of a town.

अट्णार *aṭṇāra, as,* m. a king of Kośala.

अट्या *aṭyā,* f.; see under rt. *aṭ.*

अठ् *aṭh,* cl. 1. P. A. *aṭhati, -te,* to go.

अठिल्ला *aṭhillā,* f., N. of a Prākṛit metre.

अड् 1. *aḍ,* cl. 1. P. *aḍati,* to endeavour.

अड् 2. *aḍ,* cl. 5. P., Ved. *aḍnoti,* to pervade, attain; various reading for *ah* (?).

अडकवती *aḍakavatī,* N. of a fabulous palace on Meru; also of a city.

अड्ड् *aḍḍ,* cl. 1. P. *aḍḍati, ānaḍḍa, aḍḍitum,* to join; to infer, argue, meditate, discern; to attack.

Aḍḍana, am, n. a shield.

अण् 1. *aṇ,* cl. 1. P. *aṇati, āṇa, aṇitum,* to sound.

अण् 2. *aṇ,* cl. 4. A. *aṇyate,* to breathe; another form of rt. *an,* q. v.

Aṇaka, as, ā, am, insignificant, small, contemptible.

Aṇakiya, as, ā, am, connected with what is insignificant, &c.

Aṇavya, am, n. a field of (*aṇu*) Panicum Miliaceum; see *aṇu.*

Aṇi, is, m. or *aṇī,* f. the point of a needle; the linch-pin; the pin or bolt at the end of the pole of a carriage; the corner or part of a house which serves for slaughtering; a bound, boundary, limit. — *Aṇi-māṇḍavya, as,* m., N. of a Ṛishi said to have been impaled on an *aṇi* or linch-pin.

Aṇiman, ā, m. (fr. *aṇu,* q. v.), minuteness, fineness, thinness; atomic nature; the superhuman power of becoming as small as an atom; (*a*), n., Ved. the smallest particle.

Aṇishṭha, as, ā, am (fr. *aṇu,* q. v.), most minute.

Aṇīyas, ān, asī, as (fr. *aṇu,* q. v.), or *aṇīyaska, as, ā, am,* more minute than usual.

Aṇu, us, us or *vī, u,* fine, minute, atomic; (*us*), m. an atom of matter; an atom of time; the 54,675,000th part of a muhūrta (of 48 minutes); N. of a grain, Panicum Miliaceum; N. of Śiva; (*u*), n. (in prosody) the fourth part of a mātrā. — *Aṇu-tara, as, ā, am,* very fine or minute, gentle. — *Aṇu-taila, am,* n., N. of a medical oil. — *Aṇu-tva, am,* n. or *aṇu-tā,* f. minuteness, atomic nature. — *Aṇu-bhā,* f. lightning. — *Aṇu-madhya-vīja, am,* n. title of a hymn. — *Aṇu-mātra, as, ī, am,* having the size of an atom. — *Aṇu-mātrika, as, ā, am,* having the size of an atom; containing the atomic elements (*mātrā*) of the body. — *Aṇu-reṇu, us,* m. f. atomic dust (as seen in sun-beams). — *Aṇu-reṇu-jāla, am,* n. an aggregate of such atomic dust. — *Aṇu-revatī,* f., N. of a plant, Croton Polyandrum. — *Aṇu-vedānta, am,* n. title of a book. — *Aṇu-vrīhi, is,* m., N. of a fine sort of rice. — *Aṇu-śas,* ind. into or in minute particles. — *Aṇū-bhū,* cl. 1. P. *-bhavati, -vitum,* to become minute or atomic. — *Aṇū-bhāva, as,* m. the becoming an atom. — *Aṇv-anta, as,* m. a hair-splitting question.

Aṇuka, as, ā, am, fine, minute, atomic; acute, clever, subtle.

Aṇva, am, n., Ved. fine interstice or hole in the strainer used for the Soma juice.

Aṇvī, f., Ved. a finger.

अणुह *aṇuha, as,* m., N. of a son of Vibhrāja.

अण्ठ् *aṇṭh* or *aṭh,* cl. 1. A. *aṇṭhate, ānaṇṭhe, aṇṭhitum,* to go, move, tend.

Aṇṭhita, as, ā, am, gone; pained.

अण्ड *aṇḍa, as, am,* m. n. (fr. rt. *am*), an egg, a testide; the scrotum; the musk bag; Semen Virile; epithet of Śiva, from his being identified with the Brahmāṇḍa or mundane egg. — *Aṇḍa-kaṭāha, as,* m. the shell of the mundane egg. — *Aṇḍa-koṭara-pushpī,* f., N. of a plant, Convolvulus Argenteus (?). — *Aṇḍa-kośa* or *aṇḍa-kosha* or *aṇḍa-koshaka, as,* m. the scrotum. — *Aṇḍa-ja, as, ā, am,* born from an egg; (*as*), m. a bird; a fish; a snake; a lizard; (*ā*), f. musk. — *Aṇḍajeśvara* (°*ja-īś*°), *as,* m. Garuḍa, the king of birds. — *Aṇḍa-dhara, as,* m. epithet of Śiva. — *Aṇḍa-vardhana, am,* n. or *aṇḍa-vriddhi, is,* f. swelling of the scrotum, hydrocele. — *Aṇḍa-sū, ūs,* f. oviparous. — *Aṇḍākarshaṇa* (°*ḍa-āk*°), *am,* n. castration. — *Aṇḍākāra* (°*ḍa-āk*°), *as, ā, am,* egg-shaped, oval, elliptical; (*as*), m. an ellipsis. — *Aṇḍākriti* (°*ḍa-āk*°), *is, is, i,* egg-shaped, oval, elliptical; (*is*), f. an ellipsis.

Aṇḍaka, as, m. the scrotum; (*am*), n. a small egg, an egg.

Aṇḍara, as, ī, am, N. or epithet of a tribe. — *Aṇḍarāya,* nom. A. *aṇḍarāyate, -yitum,* to behave like an Aṇḍara.

Aṇḍālu, us, m. a fish (full of eggs).

Aṇḍīra, as, m. a full male, a man; strong.

अत् 1. *at,* ind. a prefix said to imply 'surprise,' probably a contraction of *ati,* meaning 'extraordinary.' — *Ad-bhuta, as, ā, am,* extraordinary, mysterious, wonderful; see s. v.

अत् 2. *at,* cl. 1. P. *atati, āta, atishyati, ātīt, atitum,* sometimes A. *atate,* &c., to go constantly, walk, run; to obtain.

Atana, as, m. a passer on; (*am*), n. act of passing on. — *Atana-vat, ān,* m. one who wanders.

Atasi, atka, see s. v.

अतज्ज्ञ *a-taj-jña* (for *a-tad-jña*), *as, ā, am,* ignorant of (*tat*) that, i. e. Brahma and the soul's identity with it.

अतट *a-taṭa, as, ā, am,* having no beach or shore, precipitous; (*as*), m. a precipice; the third hell.

अतत्त्वविद् *a-tattva-vid, t, t, t,* ignorant of (*tattva*) the soul's identity with Brahma.

A-tattvārtha-vat (°*tva-ar*°), *ān, atī, at,* not conformable with the nature of truth.

अतथा *a-tathā, ās,* m., Ved. not such, different; saying *a-tathā,* 'not so,' 'no,' refusing; careless. — *A-tathoćita* (°*thā-uć*°), *as, ā, am,* not deserving of such (a fate), not thus deserving, not used to this (with gen.).

A-tathya, as, ā, am, untrue, unreal, not really so.

अतदर्ह *a-tad-arha, as, ā, am,* not deserving that; (*am*), ind. undeservedly, unjustly.

A-tad-guṇa, as, m. (in rhetoric) the use of predicates not descriptive of the essential nature of the object.

अतन्त्र *a-tantra, as, ī, am,* having no ropes or no (musical) strings; unrestrained; (*am*), n. not the object of a rule or of the rule under consideration.

अतन्द्र *a-tandra, as, ā, am,* or *a-tandrita, as, ā, am,* or *a-tandrin, ī, iṇī, i,* free from lassitude, alert, unwearied.

अतप *a-tapa, as, ā, am* (rt. *tap*), not hot, not excited, not eager; cool; impassible, unostentatious; unemployed; (*ās*), m. pl. a class of deities among the Buddhists.

A-tapas, ās, ās, as, or *a-tapaska, as, ā, am,* or *a-tapasya, as,* m. one who neglects *tapas* or the practice of ascetic austerities; an irreligious character.

A-tapta, as, ā, am, not heated, cool. — *Atapta-tanū, ūs,* m., Ved. whose body or mass is cool. — *Atapta-tapas, ās,* m. whose ascetic austerity has not been (fully or properly) endured.

A-tapyamāna, as, ā, am, not suffering.

अतमिस्र *a-tamisra, as, ā, am,* not dark, not benighted.

अतमेरु *a-tameru, us, us, u,* Ved. not languid.

अतर्क *a-tarka, as,* m. an illogical reasoner; bad logic.

A-tarkita, as, ā, am, unconsidered, unthought of; unexpected; (*am*), ind. unexpectedly.

A-tarkya, as, ā, am, baffling or surpassing thought or reasoning. — *Atarkya-sahasra-śakti, is,* m. incomprehensibly endowed with a thousand powers.

अतल *a-tala, am,* n. bottomless; N. of a hell beneath the earth; (*as*), m. Śiva. — *Atala-sparśa, as, ā, am,* or *atala-spriś, k, k, k,* touching the *atala;* bottomless; (or it may be *a-tala-sparśa,* whose bottom cannot be touched or reached.)

अतव्यस् *a-tavyas, ān, asī, as,* Ved. not stronger, not very strong.

अतस् *atas,* ind. (ablative of the pronom. base *a,* synonymous with *asmāt*), from this, than this; hence; henceforth, from that time; from this (or from that) cause or reason. — *Ata-ūrdhvam,* ind. henceforth, afterwards. — *Ata-eva,* ind. for this very reason; therefore. — *Ataḥ-param,* ind. henceforth, further on. — *Ato-nimittam,* ind. on this ground, for this reason. — *Ato-nya* (*tas-an*°), *as, ā, at,* differing from this. — *Ato-rtham* (*tas-ar*°), ind. for this object.

अतस *atasa, as,* m. (fr. rt. अत्), wind, air; the soul; a (missile) weapon; a garment made of the fibre of (*atasī*) flax; (*am*), n., Ved. shrubs.

Atasī, f. common flax, Linum Usitatissimum; Śaṇa, Bengal sun used as hemp, Crotolaria Juncea.

अतसि *atasi, is,* m. (fr. rt. अत्), Ved. a wandering mendicant.

Atasāyya, as, ā, am, Ved. to be got by begging.

अति *ati,* ind. [probably neut. of an obsolete adj. *atin,* passing, going, beyond; see rt. *at* and cf. Old Germ. *anti, unti, inti, unde, indi,* &c.; Eng. *and;* Germ. *und;* Gr. ἔτι, ἀντί; Lat. *ante;* Lith. *ant;* Arm. *ti;* Zend *aiti*]. As a prefix to verbs and nouns, expresses beyond, over; too far past; as *atikramitum,* to overstep. — *Ati-krama,* transgression.

When prefixed to nouns, not derived from verbs, it expresses beyond, surpassing; as *ati-kaśa,* past the whip; *ati-mānusha,* superhuman, &c.; see s. v.

As a separable adverb or preposition (with acc.), Ved. beyond.

Ati is often prefixed to nouns and adjectives, and rarely to verbs, in the sense excessive, extraordinary, intense; excessively, too; exceedingly, very. — *Ati-kaṭhora, as, ā, am,* very hard, too hard. — *Ati-kathā,* f. an exaggerated tale; (*as, ā, am*), exaggerated; see also s. v. — *Ati-karshaṇa, am,* n. excessive exertion. — *Ati-kalyam,* ind. very early, too early. — *Ati-kānta, as, ā, am,* excessively beloved. — *Ati-kāya, as, ā, am,* of extraordinary body or size, gigantic; (*as*), m., N. of a Rākshasa. — *Ati-kutsita, as, ā, am,* greatly despised. — *Ati-kulva, as, ā, am,* Ved. too bald. — *Ati-kriććhra, as,* m. extraordinary pain or hardship; extraordinary penance. — *Ati-krita, as, ā, am,* overdone, exaggerated. — *Ati-kriśa, as, ā, am,* very thin, emaciated. — *Ati-krishṇa, as, ā, am,* very or too dark, very or too deep blue. — *Ati-kruddha, as, ā, am,* excessively angry. — *Ati-krushṭa, am,* n. extraordinary cry or wailing. — *Ati-khara, as, ā, am,* very pungent or piercing. — *Ati-gaṇḍa, as, ā, am,* having large cheeks or temples; (*as*), m., N. of the *yoga* (or index), star of the 6th lunar mansion. — *Ati-gandha, as, ā, am,* having an overpowering smell; (*as*), m. sulphur; lemon-grass (Andropogon Schænanthes); the Champac flower (Michelia Champaca); a kind of jasmin. — *Ati-gandhālu, us,* m., N. of a creeper, Putradātrī. — *Ati-garīyas, as,* n. (compar. of *ati-guru*), a higher price. — *Ati-garvita, as, ā, am,* very conceited. — *Ati-gahana, as, ā, am,* very impenetrable. — *Ati-guṇa, as, ā, am,* having extraordinary qualities. — *Ati-gupta, as, ā, am,* closely concealed, very mysterious. — *Ati-guru, us, us* or *vī, u,* very heavy. — *Ati-go, aus,* f. an excellent cow. — *Ati-grāhya, as, ā, am,* very acceptable; (*as*), N. of three successive libations made (or cups filled) at the Jyotishṭoma sacrifice. — *Ati-ćaṇḍa, as, ā, am,* very violent. — *Ati-ćaraṇa, am,* n. excessive practice. — *Ati-ćāpalya, am,* n. extraordinary mobility or unsteadiness. — *Ati-ćhattra* or *ati-ćhattraka, as,* m. (extraordinary parasol), a mushroom; (*ā*), f. Anise, principally Anisum or Anethum Sowa; another plant, Barleria Longifolia. — *Ati-jara, as, ā, am,* or (as a supplementary form) *ati-jaras, ās, ās, as,* very aged. — *Ati-jala, as, ā, am,* well watered. — *Ati-java, as,* m. extraordinary speed; (*as, ā, am*), very fleet. — *Ati-jāgara, as, ā, am,* very wakeful; (*as*), m. the black curlew. — *Ati-jīrṇa, as, ā, am,* very aged. — *Atijīrṇa-tā,* f. extreme old age. — *Ati-jīva, as, ā, am,* quite alive, very lively. — *Ati-ḍīna, am,* n. extraordinary flight (of birds). — *Ati-tapasvin, ī, inī, i,* very ascetic. — *Ati-tīkshṇa, as, ā, am,* very sharp. — *Ati-tīvra, as, ā, am,* very sharp, pungent or acid; (*ā*), f. dūb grass. — *Ati-triṇṇa, as, ā, am,* seriously hurt. — *Ati-tripti, is,* f. too great satiety. — *Ati-trishṇā,* f. excessive thirst, rapacity; (*as, ā, am*), excessively thirsty, rapacious. — *Ati-trasnu, us, us, u,* very timid, over timid. — *Ati-dagdha, as, ā, am,* badly burnt; (*am*), n. (in medicine) N. of a bad kind of burn. — *Ati-darpa, as,* m. excessive conceit; N. of a snake; (*as, ā, am*), excessively conceited. — *Ati-darśin, ī, inī, i,* very far-sighted. — *Ati-dātṛi, tā,* m. a very liberal man. — *Ati-dāna, am,* n. munificence. — *Ati-dāruṇa, as, ā, am,* very terrible. — *Ati-dāha, as,* m. great heat; violent inflammation. — *Ati-dīrgha, as, ā, am,* very long, too long. — *Ati-duḥkhita* or *ati-dushkhita, as, ā, am,* greatly afflicted, very sad. — *Ati-duḥsaha, as, ā, am,* very hard to bear, quite unbearable. — *Ati-durgata, as, ā, am,* very badly off. — *Ati-durdharsha, as, ā, am,* very hard to approach, very haughty. — *Ati-durlambha, as, ā, am,* very hard to attain or obtain. — *Ati-dushkara, as, ā, am,* very difficult. — *Ati-dūra, as, ā, am,* very distant; (*am*), n. a great distance. — *Ati-dosha, as,* m. a great fault. — *Ati-dhavala, as, ā, am,* very white. — *Ati-dhenu, us, us, u,* distinguished for his cows. — *Ati-nidrā,* f. excessive sleep; (*as, ā, am*), given to (or overpowered by) excessive sleep; (*am*), ind. past (or after) sleeping time. — *Ati-nipuṇa, as, ā, am,* very able or skilful. — *Ati-nīća, as, ā, am,* excessively low. — *Ati-pathin, anthās,* m. a better road than common. — *Ati-pada, as, ā, am,* (in prosody) too long by one *pada* or foot. — *Ati-paroksha, as, ā, am,* far out of sight, i. e. no longer discernible. — *Atiparoksha-vritti, is, is, i,* (in grammar) having a nature that is no longer discernible, i. e. obsolete. — *Ati-pātaka, am,* n. a very heinous sin, incest. — *Ati-purusha* or *ati-pūrusha, as,* m. a first-rate man or hero. — *Ati-pūta, as, ā, am,* quite purified; refined to excess. — *Ati-peśala, as, ā, am,* very dexterous or clever. — *Ati-prakāśa, as, ā, am,* Ved. very manifest, notorious. — *Ati-prage,* ind. very early. — *Ati-praṇaya, as,* m. excessive kindness, partiality. — *Ati-praṇudya,* ind. having pushed far forward. — *Ati-prabandha, as,* m. complete continuity. — *Ati-pravaraṇa, am,* n. excess in choosing. — *Ati-pravritti, is,* f. issuing abundantly or too freely. — *Ati-pravriddha, as, ā, am,* enlarged to excess, overbearing. — *Ati-praśna, as,* m. an extravagant question, a question regarding transcendental objects. — *Ati-praśnya, as, ā, am,* fit to be asked such an extravagant question. — *Ati-prasakti, is,* f. or *ati-prasaṅga, as,* m. excessive attachment; unwarrantable stretch of a rule or principle. — *Ati-prasiddha, as, ā, am,* very famous, notorious.

— *Ati-praudha, as, ā, am,* full-grown. — *Ati-praudha-yauvana, as, ā, am,* being in the full enjoyment of youth. — *Ati-bala, as, ā, am,* very strong or powerful; (*as*), m. an active soldier; N. of a king; (*ā*), f., N. of a medicinal plant (Sidonia Cordifolia and Rhombifolia, or Annona Squamosa); N. of a powerful charm; N. of one of Daksha's daughters. — *Ati-bālaka, as,* m. an infant; (*as, ā, am*), childish. — *Ati-bāhu, us,* m. 'having extraordinary arms;' N. of a Ṛishi of the fourteenth Manvantara. — *Ati-bībhatsa, as,* m. excessive aversion. — *Ati-brahmaćarya, am,* n. excessive abstinence or continence. — *Ati-bhara,* usually *ati-bhāra, as,* m. an excessive burden; excessive obscurity (of a sentence); N. of a king. — *Atibhāra-ga, as,* m. a mule. — *Ati-bhī, īs,* m. (very terrific), lightning. — *Ati-bhīshaṇa, as, ā, am,* very terrific or formidable. — *Ati-bhṛita, as, ā, am,* well filled. — *Ati-bhojana, am,* n. eating too much; morbid voracity. — *Ati-bhrū, ūs, ūs, u,* having extraordinary eyebrows. — *Ati-maṅgalya, as, ā, am,* very auspicious; (*as*), m. a fruit, Ægle or Cratæva Marmelos. — *Ati-mati, is,* f. haughtiness. — *Ati-madhyandina, am,* n. the height of noon. — *Ati-marśa, as,* m. close contact. — *Ati-māna, as,* m. great haughtiness. — *Ati-mānin, ī, inī, i,* very haughty. — *Atimāni-tā,* f. great haughtiness. — *Ati-māruta, as, ā, am,* very windy; (*as*), m. a hurricane. — *Ati-mukta, as, ā, am,* entirely liberated; quite free from sensual or worldly desire; seedless, barren; (*as*), m., N. of a tree, Dalbergia Oujeinensis; of a creeper, Gærtnera Racemosa. — *Ati-muktaka, as,* m. = the preceding; mountain ebony; a tree called Harimantha. — *Ati-mukti, is,* f. final liberation (from death). — *Ati-mūrti, is,* f. 'highest shape,' N. of a ceremony. — *Ati-maithuna, am,* n. excess of sexual intercourse. — *Ati-moksha, as,* m. final liberation (from death). — *Ati-modā,* f. extraordinary fragrance; N. of a tree, Jasminum Arboreum. — *Ati-yava, as,* m. a sort of barley. — *Ati-yaśa, as, ā, am,* or *ati-yaśas, ās, ās, as,* very celebrated or illustrious. — *Ati-yāja, as,* m. 'great sacrificer,' N. of a Ṛishi. — *Ati-yuvan, vā, vatī,* or *ūnī, va,* very youthful. — *Ati-yoga, as,* m. (in medicine) excessive union, excess. — *Ati-raṇhas, ās, ās, as,* extremely rapid. — *Ati-rakta, as, ā, am,* very red; (*ā*), f. one of Agni's seven tongues. — *Ati-ratha, as,* m. a very great warrior fighting from a car. — *Ati-rabhasa, as,* m. excessive or extraordinary speed. — *Ati-rasā,* f. (very succulent); N. of various plants, as Mūrvā, Rāsnā, Klītanaka. — *Ati-rājan, ā,* m. an extraordinary or excellent king; one who surpasses a king [cf. also s. v.]. — *Ati-rućira, as, ā, am,* very lovely; (*ā*), f., N. of two metres, one a variety of the *Ati-jagatī,* the other also called *Cuḍikā* or *Culikā.* — *Ati-rush, ṭ, ṭ, ṭ,* very angry. — *Ati-rūpa, as, ā* or *ī, am,* very beautiful; (*am*), n. extraordinary beauty. — *Ati-roga, as,* m. consumption. — *Ati-romaśa, as, ā, am,* very hairy, too hairy; (*as*), m. a wild goat, or a kind of monkey. — *Ati-lakshmī, is, īs, i,* very prosperous; (*īs*), f. extraordinary prosperity. — *Ati-laṅghana, am,* n. excessive fasting. — *Ati-lamba, as, ā, am,* very extensive. — *Ati-lubdha* or *ati-lobha, as, ā, am,* very greedy or covetous. — *Ati-lulita, as, ā, am,* closely attached or adhering. — *Ati-lobha, as,* m. or *atilobha-tā,* f. excessive greediness or covetousness. — *Ati-loma* or *ati-lomaśa, as, ā, am,* very hairy, too hairy. — *Ati-lomaśā,* f. a pot-herb, Convolvulus Argenteus. — *Ati-lohita, as, ā, am,* very red. — *Ati-laulya, am,* n. excessive eagerness or desire. — *Ati-vaktṛi, ā, rī, ṛi,* very loquacious. — *Ati-vakra, as, ā, am,* very crooked or curved; (*ā*), f. one of the eight descriptions of planetary motion. — *Ati-vartula, as, ā, am,* very or quite round; (*as*), m., N. of a grain or pot-herb. — *Ati-vāta, as,* m. high wind, a storm. — *Ati-vāda, as,* m. extraordinary, i. e. abusive language; (reproof); N. of a Vedic verse recited on certain occasions. — *Ati-vādin, ī, inī, i,* talkative. — *Ati-vālaka, as, ā, am,* childish; (*as*), m. an infant. — *Ati-vāhana, am,* n. excessive toiling. — *Ati-vikaṭa, as, ā, am,* very fierce; (*as*), m. a vicious elephant. — *Ati-vipina, as, ā, am,* having many forests. — *Ati-vilambin, ī, inī, i,* very dilatory. — *Ati-viśrabdha-navoḍhā* (°*va-ūḍhā*), f. a fond but pert young wife. — *Ati-visha, as, ā, am,* exceedingly poisonous; counteracting poison; (*ā*), f. a very poisonous yet medicinal plant, Aconitum Ferox. — *Ati-vṛiddhi, is,* f. extraordinary growth or increase. — *Ati-vṛishṭi, is,* f. excessive rain. — *Ativṛishṭi-hata, as, ā, am,* injured by heavy rain. — *Ati-vepathu, us,* m. excessive tremor; (*us, us, u*), or *ativepathu-mat, ān, atī, at,* trembling excessively. — *Ati-vaićakshaṇya, am,* n. great proficiency. — *Ati-vaiśasa, as, ā, am,* very adverse or destructive. — *Ati-vyathana, am,* n. infliction of (or giving) excessive pain. — *Ati-vyathā,* f. excessive pain. — *Ati-vyaya, as,* m. lavish expenditure. — *Ati-vyāpta, as, ā, am,* stretched too far (as a rule or principle). — *Ati-vyāpti, is,* f. unwarrantable stretch (of a rule or principle). — *Ati-śakta, as, ā, am,* or *ati-śakti, is, is, i,* very powerful; (*is*), f. or *atiśakti-tā,* f. great power or valour. — *Atiśakti-bhāj, k, k, k,* possessing great power. — *Ati-śaṅkā,* f. excessive timidity. — *Ati-śarvara, am,* n., Ved. the dead of night. — *Ati-śasta, as, ā, am,* very excellent. — *Ati-śukra, as, ā, am,* too bright. — *Ati-śukla, as, ā, am,* very white, too white. — *Ati-śobhana, as, ā, am,* very handsome, distinguished. — *Ati-śrī, īs, īs, i,* very prosperous. — *Ati-sanskṛita, as, ā, am,* highly finished or adorned or educated. — *Ati-sakti, is,* f. excessive attachment. — *Atisakti-mat, ān, atī, at,* excessively attached. — *Ati-sańćaya, as,* m. excessive accumulation, a hoard. — *Ati-santapta, as, ā, am,* greatly afflicted. — *Ati-sandheya, as, ā, am,* easy to be settled or conciliated. — *Ati-samartha, as, ā, am,* very competent. — *Ati-samīpa, as, ā, am,* very near. — *Ati-samparka, as,* m. excessive sexual intercourse. — *Ati-sādhvasa, am,* n. excessive fear or alarm. — *Ati-sāntapana, am,* n. a species of severe penance, inflicted especially for eating unclean animal food. — *Ati-sāyam,* ind. very late or in the dusk. — *Ati-siddhi, is,* f. great perfection or proficiency. — *Ati-sujana, as, ā, am,* very moral, very friendly, very respectable. — *Ati-sundara, as, ā* or *ī, am,* very handsome, very beautiful; (*as, ā*), m. f. a metre belonging to the class *Ashṭi,* also called *Citra* or *Cańćalā.* — *Ati-sulabha, as, ā, am,* very easily obtainable. — *Ati-suhita, as, ā, am,* excessively kind, over-kind. — *Ati-sṛishṭi, is,* f. an extraordinary or excellent creation. — *Ati-sevā,* f. excessive indulgence (of a habit). — *Ati-saurabha, as, ā, am,* very fragrant; (*am*), n. extraordinary fragrance. — *Ati-sauhitya, am,* n. excessive fondness, or the effect of it, e. g. being spoiled, stuffed with food, &c. — *Ati-stuti, is,* f. extraordinary praise. — *Ati-sthira, as, ā, am,* very stable or durable. — *Ati-sthūla, as, ā, am,* excessively thick, or stout, or big, or clumsy; excessively stupid. — *Ati-snigdha, as, ā, am,* very smooth, very nice, very affectionate. — *Ati-sparśa, as,* m. too marked contact (of the tongue and palate) in pronunciation. — *Ati-sphira, as, ā, am,* very tremulous. — *Ati-svapna, as,* m. excessive sleep; (*am*), n. excessive tendency to dreaming. — *Ati-svastha, as, ā, am,* enjoying excellent health. — *Ati-hasita, am,* n. or *ati-hāsa, as,* m. excessive laughter. — *Ati-hrasva, as, ā, am,* excessively short. — *Aty-agni, is,* m. morbidly rapid digestion. — *Aty-adbhuta, as, ā, am,* very wonderful. — *Aty-adhvan, ā,* m. a long way or journey, excessive travelling. — *Aty-amarshin, ī, iṇī, i,* quite out of temper. — *Aty-amla, as, ā, am,* very acid; (*as*), m. a tree, Spondias Mangifera; (*ā*), f. a tree, a species of citron. — *Atyamla-parṇī,* f. having very acid leaves, N. of a medicinal plant or creeper. — *Aty-alpa, as, ā, am,* very little. — *Aty-aśana, am,* n. immoderate eating. — *Aty-aśnat, an, atī, at,* eating too much. — *Aty-asama, as, ā, am,* very uneven, very rough. — *Aty-ādara, as,* m. excessive deference. — *Aty-ādāna, am,* n. taking away too much. — *Aty-āpti, is,* f. complete attainment. — *Aty-ārūḍhi, is,* f. mounting too high. — *Aty-āśā,* f. extravagant hope. — *Aty-āhāra, as,* m. excess in eating. — *Aty-āhārin, ī, iṇī, i,* eating immoderately, gluttonous. — *Aty-āhita, am,* n. great calamity; great danger; facing great danger; a daring action. — *Aty-ukti, is,* f. excessive talking; exaggeration; hyperbole. — *Aty-ugra, as, ā, am,* very fierce; very pungent; (*am*), n. Asa Fœtida. — *Aty-uććais,* ind. very loudly. — *Atyuććair-dhvani, is,* m. a very loud sound; a very high note. — *Aty-utkaṭa, as, ā, am,* very imposing, immense, extraordinary. — *Aty-utsāha, as,* m. (in medicine) excessive vigour or activity. — *Aty-udāra, as, ā, am,* very liberal. — *Aty-ulbaṇa* or *aty-ulvaṇa, as, ā, am,* very conspicuous, immense, excessive. — *Aty-ushṇa, as, ā, am,* very hot.

अतिकथ **ati-katha** or **iti-katha**, *as, ā, am,* past tradition or law, deviating from the rules of his caste, lawless; (see also under *ati.*)

अतिकन्दक **ati-kandaka**, *as,* m., N. of a plant or tree, Hastikanda.

अतिकश **ati-kaśa**, *as, ā, am,* past the whip, i. e. unmanageable.

अतिकुप् **ati-kup**, cl. 4. P. *-kupyati, -kopitum,* to become very angry.

अतिकूर्द् **ati-kūrd**, cl. 1. P. *-kūrdati, -ditum,* to jump about.

अतिकृति **ati-kṛiti** or **abhikṛiti**, *is,* f., N. of a metre of four lines, each containing twenty-five syllables.

अतिकृष् **ati-kṛish**, cl. 1. P. *-karshati, -karshṭum* or *-krashṭum,* to drag over or beyond.

अतिकेशर **ati-keśara**, *as,* m. an aquatic plant, Trapa Bipinosa.

अतिक्रम् **ati-kram**, cl. 1. P. A., 4. P. *-krāmati, -te, -krāmyati, -kramitum,* to step or go or get beyond or over or across; to pass, cross; to surpass, excel, overcome; to pass by, neglect; to overstep, transgress, violate; to pass on or away; to step out; to part from, lose: Caus. *-krāmayati* or *-kramayati, -yitum,* to allow to pass, to leave unnoticed.

Ati-krama, as, m. act of passing or overstepping; lapse (of time); overcoming, surpassing, conquering; excess, imposition, transgression, violation; neglect; determined onset.

Ati-kramaṇa, am, n. passing, surpassing, overstepping; excess; spending (time).

Ati-kramaṇīya, as, ā, am, proper or practicable to be passed by or neglected or overcome.

Ati-kramin, ī, iṇī, i, exceeding, violating, &c.

Ati-kramya, ind. having passed beyond, behind, &c.

Ati-krānta, as, ā, am, having passed or transgressed; exceeded, surpassed, overcome. — *Atikrānta-nishedha, as, ā, am,* guilty of neglecting a prohibition.

Ati-krāmaka, as, ā, am, exceeding, transgressing, &c.

अतिक्षर् **ati-kshar**, cl. 1. P., Ved. *-ksharati, -ritum,* to overflow.

अतिक्षिप् **ati-kship**, cl. 6. P. *-kshipati, -ksheptum,* to throw beyond.

Ati-kshipta, as, ā, am, thrown beyond; (*am*), n. (in medicine) sprain or dislocation of a particular kind.

अतिखट्व **ati-khaṭva**, *as, ā, am,* past the bedstead, able to do without a bedstead.

अतिख्या **ati-khyā**, cl. 2. P., Ved. *-khyāti, -khyātum,* to survey, overlook, neglect, abandon, repudiate.

अतिगम् **ati-gam**, cl. 1. P. *-gaććhati, -gantum,* or *ati-gā,* cl. 3. P. *-jigāti, -gātum,* to pass, overcome, succeed; to escape; to pass by, pass over, neglect; to pass away, die.

Ati-ga, as, ā, am (used at the close of compounds), exceeding, overcoming, surpassing; as *śokātiga* (°*ka-at*°), overcoming grief.

Ati-gata, as, ā, am, having passed; being past.

अतिगव **ati-gava**, *as, ā, am,* having passed or surpassed a cow.

अतिगाह् *ati-gāh*, cl. 1. A. *-gāhate, -hitum*, or *-gāḍhum*, to emerge over; to rise upon.

अतिगुर् *ati-gur*, cl. 6. P., Ved. *-gurati, -ritum*, to shout, exclaim (?).

अतिगुहा *ati-guhā*, f. a plant, Hemionites Cordifolia.

अतिग्रह् *ati-grah*, cl. 9. P., Ved. *-gribhṇāti* or *-grihṇāti, -grahītum*, to take beyond or over the usual measure; to overtake, surpass.

Ati-graha, as, m. act of overtaking or surpassing; one who takes or seizes to an extraordinary extent; (in philosophy) the same as *atigrāha*.

Ati-grāha, as, m. object of a *graha*, i.e. of an apprehensive organ; there are eight such grahas, viz. *prāṇa*, 'inhaling or nose;' *vāć*, 'speech;' *jihvā*, 'tongue;' *ćakshus*, 'eye;' *śrotra*, 'ear;' *manas*, 'mind;' *hasta*, 'hand;' *tvać*, 'skin:' these have eight corresponding *ati-grāhas* or objects, viz. *apāna*, 'exhaling substance;' *nāman*, 'name;' *rasa*, 'sap or taste;' *rūpa*, 'form;' *śabda*, 'sound;' *kāma*, 'desire;' *karman*, 'action;' and *sparśa*, 'touch.'

Ati-grāhya, as, m., Ved., N. of three successive libations made (or cups filled) at the Jyotishṭoma sacrifice; (very acceptable; see under *ati*.)

अतिघ *ati-gha, as*, m. (fr. *ati* and rt. *han*, 'very destructive'), a weapon, a bludgeon; wrath.

Ati-ghna, as, ī, am, Ved. very or utterly destructive; (ī), f., Ved. a happy state of utter oblivion or profound sleep obliterating all that is disagreeable in the past.

Ati-ghnya, as, ā, am, Ved. overpowering, overcoming (?).

अतिचमू *ati-ćamū, ūs, ūs, u*, victorious over armies.

अतिचर् *ati-ćar*, cl. 1. P. *-ćarati, -ritum*, to pass or pass by; to overtake, surpass; to transgress, offend, be unfaithful to.

Ati-ćara, as, ā, am, transient, changeable; (ā), f., N. of the shrub Hibiscus Mutabilis.

Ati-ćaraṇa. See s. v. *ati*.

Ati-ćāra, as, m. act of passing, overtaking, surpassing; accelerated motion, especially of planets.

Ati-ćārin, ī, iṇī, i, surpassing, transgressing.

अतिचृत् *ati-ćrit*, cl. 1. P. *-ćartati, -titum*, to stick on, fasten together.

अतिचेष्ट् *ati-ćesht*, cl. 1. A. *-ćeshṭate, -ṭitum*, to make extraordinary or excessive efforts.

अतिच्छन्द *ati-ććhanda, as, ā, am*, past worldly desires, free from them.

Ati-ććhandas, ās, ās, as, Ved. past worldly desires, free from them; (*ās, as*), f. n., N. of two extensive classes of metres; (*as*), n., N. of a particular brick in the sacrificial fire-place.

अतिजगती *ati-jagatī*, f., N. of a genus of metres (belonging to the class *Atiććhandas*), of four lines, each containing thirteen syllables.

अतिजन *ati-jana, as, ā, am* ('past men'), uninhabited.

अतिजात *ati-jāta, as, ā, am*, superior to his parentage.

अतिजि *ati-ji*, cl. 1. P. *-jayati, -jetum*, to conquer.

अतिजीव् *ati-jīv*, cl. 1. P. *-jīvati, -vitum*, to survive; to surpass in the mode of living.

अतितत *ati-tata, as, ā, am* (fr. *ati-tan*), far-stretched, making one's self very big, conceited.

अतितप् *ati-tap*, cl. 1. P. *-tapati, -taptum*, to be very hot; to heat; to affect greatly: Caus. *-tāpayati, -yitum*, to heat much.

अतितराम् *ati-tarām*, ind. (compar. of *ati*), above in rank (with acc.); better, higher, more (with abl.); very much, exceedingly, excessively.

अतितृद् *ati-trid*, cl. 7. P. *-triṇatti, -tarditum*, to pierce, penetrate.

अतितृप् *ati-trip*, cl. 4. P. *-tripyati, -tarptum* or *-traptum*, to be or become satisfied, satiated or glutted.

अतितॄ *ati-trī*, cl. 1. P. *-tarati, -taritum* or *-tarītum*, to pass, cross, get over, overcome, escape; to attain: Desid. *-titīrshati*, to be desirous of crossing or overcoming.

Ati-tārin, ī, iṇī, i, crossing.

Ati-tārya, as, ā, am, proper or practicable to be got over or overcome.

अतित्यद् *ati-tyad*, surpassing that; (a fictitious compound coined by grammarians.)

अतित्वम् *ati-tvam*, surpassing thee; (a grammatical compound, see the last); *atitvām, ati-tvān* (acc. sing. and pl.), him that surpasses thee, them that surpass thee.

अतित्वर् *ati-tvar*, cl. 1. A., occasionally P., *-tvarate, -ti, -ritum*, to hasten greatly.

अतिथि *atithi, is, ī, i*, m. f. n. (etymology uncertain; if, according to native authorities, fr. rt. *at*, it would then first mean 'a traveller;' if fr. *a* and *tithi*, the first idea would be 'one who has no fixed time for coming or staying;' if from *ati* and *sthā*, 'one who has the pre-eminence over the members of the household'), a guest, entitled to hospitality; (*is*), m. wrath; N. of Agni or an attendant of Soma; N. of Suhotra, king of Ayodhyā, and grandson of Rāma. — *Atithi-kriyā*, f. hospitality, as (religiously) due to a guest. — *Atithi-gva, as*, m. ('to whom guests should go'), an epithet of Divodāsa. — *Atithi-tva, am*, n. condition of a guest, hospitality. — *Atithi-deva, as, ā* or *ī, am*, treating the guest as a divinity. — *Atithi-dvesha, as*, m. inhospitality. — *Atithi-dharma, as*, m. title to hospitality. — *Atithi-dharmin, ī, iṇī, i*, entitled to hospitality. — *Atithi-pati, is*, m. the host or entertainer of a guest. — *Atithi-pūjana, am*, n. or *atithi-pūjā*, f. honourable and religious reception of a guest. — *Atithi-vat*, ind. like a guest. — *Atithi-satkāra, as*, m. honourable treatment of a guest. — *Atithi-sevā*, f. attention paid to a guest.

Atithin, ī, inī, i (fr. rt. *at*), Ved. travelling; (ī), m., N. of a king, also called Suhotra and Atithi, q. v.

अतिदत्त *ati-datta, as*, m., N. of a brother of Datta and son of Rājādhideya.

अतिदह् *ati-dah*, cl. 1. P., poet. also A., *-dahati, -te, -dagdhum*, to burn or blaze across; to burn or distress greatly.

अतिदा *ati-dā*, cl. 3. P. *-dadāti, -dātum*, to surpass in giving; to pass over or neglect in giving.

अतिदान्त *ati-dānta, as*, m., N. of a prince.

अतिदिव् *ati-div*, cl. 4. P. *-dīvyati, -devitum*, to play high, lose at play.

अतिदिश् *ati-diś*, cl. 6. P. *-diśati, -deshṭum*, to assign, make over, transfer: Pass. *-diśyate*, (in grammar) to be overruled or attracted or assimilated.

Ati-dishṭa, as, ā, am, overruled, attracted, influenced, inferred, substituted.

Ati-deśa, as, m. transfer, extended application, inference, analogy, overruling influence, assimilation; a rule providing for more than the usual rule; putting one thing instead of another, substitution; *rūpāti-deśa*, such a rule as affecting the form of a word; (*as, ā, am*), overruling, previously stated.

अतिदीप्य *ati-dīpya, as*, m. (very brilliant), a plant, Plumbago Rosea.

अतिदृप् *ati-drip*, cl. 4. P. *-dripyati, -darptum* or *-draptum*, to be excessively conceited.

अतिदृश् *ati-driś*, cl. 1. P., Ved. *-paśyati, -drashṭum*, to look beyond, look through.

अतिदेव *ati-deva, as*, m. a superior god; surpassing the gods.

अतिधन्वन् *ati-dhanvan, ā*, m., N. of a descendant of Śunaka.

अतिधाव् *ati-dhāv*, cl. 1. P. *-dhāvati, -vitum*, to run or rush over.

अतिधृति *ati-dhriti, is*, f., N. of a genus of metres belonging to the class *Atiććhandas*, and consisting of four lines, each containing nineteen syllables; (in arithm.) nineteen.

अतिनम् *ati-nam*, cl. 1. P. *-namati, -nantum*, to bend aside, keep on one side.

अतिनामन् *ati-nāman, ā*, m., N. of a Saptarshi of the sixth Manvantara.

अतिनाष्ट्र *ati-nāshṭra, as, ā, am*, past danger, out of danger.

अतिनिचृत् *ati-nićrit* or *ati-nivrit, t*, f., N. of a Vedic metre of three pādas, containing respectively seven, six and seven syllables.

अतिनिद्रम् *ati-nidram*, ind. past sleeping time. See s. v. *ati*.

अतिनिष्टन् *ati-nish-ṭan (-nis-tan)*, cl. 8. P., Ved. *-tanoti, -nitum*, to penetrate.

अतिनी *ati-nī*, cl. 1. P. *-nayati, -netum*, to lead over or beyond, to help a person over anything; to allow to pass away: Intens. A. *-nenīyate*, to bring forward.

अतिनु *ati-nu*, Caus. *-nāvayati, -yitum*, to turn away.

अतिनुद् *ati-nud*, cl. 6. P. A., Ved. *-nudati, -te, -nottum*, to drive by.

अतिनेद् *ati-ned*, cl. 1. P., Ved. *-nedati, -ditum*, to stream or flow over, to foam over.

अतिनौ *ati-nau, aus, aus, u*, disembarked.

अतिपञ्चा *ati-pańćā*, f. a girl who is past five.

अतिपटीक्षेप *ati-paṭīkshepa* or *a-paṭīkshepa, as*, m. omission of removing the theatrical curtain.

अतिपठ् *ati-paṭh*, Pass. *-paṭhyate*, to be proclaimed, named or celebrated.

अतिपत् *ati-pat*, cl. 1. P. *-patati, -titum*, to fall or fly by, past, beyond, over; to neglect: Caus. *-pātayati, -yitum*, to cause to fly by; to drag away; to make effectless.

Ati-patana, am, n. act of falling or flying beyond, passing, missing, transgressing.

Ati-patita, as, ā, am, missed, transgressed, past.

Ati-pāta, as, m. passing away, lapse; neglect, transgression; ill-usage, opposition, contrariety.

Ati-pātita, as, ā, am, quite displaced or broken; (*am*), n. (in medicine) complete fracture of a bone.

Ati-pātin, ī, inī, i, overtaking, excelling in speed; (in medicine) running a rapid course, acute.

Ati-pātya, as, ā, am, fit or proper to be neglected.

अतिपत्त्र *ati-pattra, as*, m. the Teak tree; another tree, Hastikanda.

अतिपद् *ati-pad*, cl. 4. A. *-padyate, -pattum*, to go beyond (with acc.), jump over, neglect, transgress: Caus. *-pādayati, -yitum*, to allow to pass by.

Ati-patti, is, f. going beyond, passing, lapse; *kriyātipatti*, the passing by of an action unaccomplished.

Ati-panna, as, ā, am, gone beyond, transgressed, missed; past.

अतिपर *ati-para, as, ā, am*, having overcome his enemy or enemies; (*as*), m. a great enemy.

अतिपा *ati-pā,* Caus. P. *-pāyayati, -yitum,* to give to drink in great quantity.

अतिपादनिचृत् *ati-pādanićṛit* or *ati-pāda-nivṛit, t,* f., N. of a Vedic metre of three pādas, containing respectively six, eight and seven syllables.

अतिपितृ *ati-pitṛi, -tā,* m. surpassing his own father. — *Ati-pitāmaha, as,* m. surpassing his own paternal grandfather.

अतिपू *ati-pū,* cl. 9. P., Ved. *-punāti, -pavitum,* to purify by overflowing.

अतिपॄ *ati-pṝī,* P., Ved. *-priṇāti* (?), Caus. *-pārayati, -yitum,* to convey across.

अतिप्रकित् *ati-pra-kit* or *-ćit,* cl. 3. A., Ved. *-ćekite,* to be distinct or distinguishable.

अतिप्रच्यु *ati-pra-ćyu,* cl. 1. A. *-ćyavate, -ćyotum,* to pass by: Caus. *-ćyāvayati, -yitum,* to cause or allow to pass by.

अतिप्रणश् *ati-pra-ṇaś* (rt. *naś*), cl. 4. P. *-naśyati, -naśitum* or *-nanshṭum,* to be deprived of (with acc.).

अतिप्रणी *ati-pra-ṇī* (rt. *nī*), cl. 1. P. *-ṇayati, -ṇetum,* to lead past.

अतिप्रणुद् *ati-pra-ṇud* (rt. *nud*), cl. 6. P. A. *-ṇudati, -te, -ṇottum,* to press a person very strongly.

अतिप्रमाण *ati-pramāṇa, as, ā, am,* past measure, immense.

अतिप्राणम् *ati-prāṇam,* ind. above life. — *Atiprāṇa-priya, as, ā, am,* dearer than life.

अतिप्रेषित *ati-preshita, am,* n. the time after the ceremony in which the Praisha Mantras are used.

अतिब्रह्मन् *ati-brahman, ā,* m., N. of a king.

अतिब्रू *ati-brū,* cl. 2. P. *-bravīti, -vaktum,* to insult, abuse.

अतिभू *ati-bhū,* cl. 1. P. *-bhavati, -vitum,* to excel, overcome.

Ati-bhāva, as, m, superiority; overcoming.

अतिभूमि *ati-bhūmi, is,* f. extensive land; culmination, eminence, superiority; excess.

अतिभूष् *ati-bhūsh,* cl. 10. A. *-bhūshayate, -yitum,* to precede in adorning oneself.

अतिमनुष्यबुद्धि *ati-manushya-buddhi, is, is, i,* having a superhuman intellect.

अतिमर्त्य *ati-martya, as, ā, am,* superhuman.

अतिमर्याद *ati-maryāda, as, ā, am,* exceeding the proper limit; (*am*), ind. beyond bounds.

अतिमात्र *ati-mātra, as, ā, am,* exceeding the proper measure; (*am*), ind. or *atimātra-śas,* ind. beyond measure.

अतिमानुष *ati-mānusha, as, ī, am,* superhuman, divine.

अतिमाम् *ati-mām* (acc. of *aty-aham,* q. v.), him or her that surpasses me.

अतिमाय *ati-māya, as, ā, am,* emancipated from Māyā or Illusion; finally liberated.

अतिमार *ati-māra* or *ati-bhāra, as,* m., N. of a prince.

अतिमित 1. *ati-mita, as, ā, am,* over measured, beyond measure, exceeding.

अतिमित 2. *a-timita, as, ā, am,* not moistened, not wet.

अतिमुक्त *ati-mukta* and *ati-muktaka, as,* m. (rt. *muć*), N. of certain shrubs or trees; see under *ati* (surpassing pearls in whiteness).

Ati-mukti, is, f. final liberation. See under *ati.*

Ati-mućya, ind. part. having dismissed or given up.

अतिमृत्यु *ati-mṛityu, us, us, u,* overcoming death.

अतिया *ati-yā,* cl. 2. P. *-yāti, -tum,* to pass by.

अतियूयम् *ati-yūyam* (nom. pl. of *ati-tvam,* q. v.), persons surpassing thee.

अतिराजन् *ati-rājan, ā,* m. an extraordinary king; superior to a king. — *Ati-rājakumārī, is, is* or *ī, i,* superior to a princess.

Atirājaya, nom. P. *atirājayati, -yitum,* to surpass a king.

Ati-rājñī, f. (a woman) superior to a king.

अतिरात्र *ati-rātra, as, ā, am,* Ved. prepared or performed over-night; (*as*), m. an optional part of the Jyotishṭoma sacrifice; commencement and conclusion of certain sacrificial acts; concluding Vedic verse chanted on such occasions; N. of a son of Cākshusha the sixth Manu. — *Atirātra-savanīya-paśu, us,* m. the victim sacrificed at the Atirātra.

अतिरि *ati-ri,* neut. of *ati-rai,* q. v.

अतिरिच् *ati-rić,* Pass. *-rićyate,* to be left with a surplus, to surpass (in a good or bad sense with abl. or acc.).

Ati-rikta, as, ā, am, left with or as a surplus, left apart; redundant, unequalled. — *Atirikta-tā,* f. redundancy, &c. — *Atiriktāṅga* (°*ta-an*°), *as, ā, am,* having a redundant limb or finger or toe; (*am*), n. a redundant limb or finger or toe.

Ati-reka or *atī-reka, as,* m. surplus, excess; redundancy; difference; (*as, ā, am*), redundant.

Ati-rekin, ī, iṇī, i, surpassing.

अतिरुच् *ati-ruć,* cl. 1. P. *-roćati, -ćitum,* to outshine.

Ati-ruć, k, m. a horse's fetlock or knee.

अतिरै *ati-rai, ās, ās, i* ('exceeding one's income'), extravagant.

अतिलिहा *atilihā* or *aṭhillū,* f. (etymology uncertain), N. of a Prākṛit metre of four lines, each containing sixteen Mātras.

अतिवयम् *ati-vayam* (nom. pl. of *aty-aham,* q. v.), persons surpassing me.

अतिवर्तन *ati-vartana.* See under *ati-vṛit.*

अतिवलित *ati-valita, as, ā, am,* well surrounded or covered (?), full of folds (?), well supplied (?).

अतिवह् *ati-vah,* cl. 1. P. *-vahati, -voḍhum,* to carry over or across: Caus. *-vāhayati, -yitum,* to let time pass, spend.

Ati-vāhana, am, n. excessive toiling or enduring.

Ati-vāhita, as, ā, am, swifter than the wind; (according to Colebrooke) an epithet of the Sūkshma-śarīra, also (according to Carey) of the Preta-śarīra, or misery-enduring body, which is of the size of a thumb; (*as*), m. an inhabitant of the lower world.

Ati-vāhya, as, ā, am, practicable or proper to be passed (as time, &c.); (*am*), n. the passing of time.

Ati-voḍhṛi, ḍhā, m. one who carries over or across.

अतिवास *ati-vāsa, as,* m. fast on the day before performing the Srāddha.

अतिविद्ध *ati-viddha, as, ā, am* (rt. *vyadh*), transfixed, badly wounded. — *Atividdha-bheshaja, as, ī, am,* curing deep wounds.

अतिविश्व *ati-viśva, as,* m. ('superior to all or to the universe'), N. of a Muni.

अतिवृत् *ati-vṛit,* cl. 1. A. *-vartate, -titum,* to pass, surpass, cross; to get over, overcome; to transgress, violate, offend, especially by unfaithfulness; to pass away; to delay.

Ati-vartana, am, n. a pardonable offence or misdemeanour.

Ati-vartin, ī, inī, i, crossing, passing; guilty of a pardonable offence or of pardonable irregularity.

Ati-vṛitti, is, f. surpassing; hyperbolical meaning; (in medicine) excessive action.

अतिवेल *ati-vela, as, ā, am,* passing its proper boundary, excessive; (*am*), ind. excessively.

अतिव्याधिन् *ati-vyādhin, ī, inī, i* (rt. *vyadh*), piercing, wounding.

Ati-vyādhya, as, ā, am, vulnerable.

अतिशक्करी *ati-śakkarī* or *ati-śakvarī,* f. a class of metres of four lines, each containing fifteen syllables. It has eighteen varieties.

अतिशक्र *ati-śakra, as, ā, am,* superior to Indra.

अतिशङ्क् *ati-śaṅk,* cl. 1. A. *-śaṅkate, -kitum,* to suspect; to be concerned about.

अतिशय *atiśaya,* &c. See under *ati-śī* below.

अतिशस्त्र *ati-śastra, as, ā, am,* superior to weapons or missiles.

अतिशाक्वर *atiśākvara, as, ā, am,* written in or connected with the Ati-śakvarī metre.

अतिशी *ati-śī,* cl. 2. A. *-śete, -śayitum,* to precede in lying down; to surpass, excel, exceed; to act as an incubus, annoy.

Ati-śaya, as, m. pre-eminence, eminence; superiority in quality or quantity or numbers; advantageous result; one of the superhuman qualities attributed to Jaina Arhats; (*as, ā, am*), pre-eminent, superior, abundant. — *Atiśayam* or *atiśayena,* ind. eminently, very. — *Atiśayokti* (°*ya-uk*°), *is,* f. hyperbolical language; extreme assertion; verbosity.

Ati-śayana, as, ā, am, eminent, abundant; (*am*), ind. excessively. — *Ati-śayanī,* f., N. of a metre of four lines, also called *Citralekhā.*

Ati-śayita, as, ā, am, superior.

Ati-śayin, ī, inī, i, excelling, abounding.

Ati-śāyana, am, n. act of excelling; excessiveness.

Ati-śāyin, ī, inī, i, excelling, abounding; excessive.

Ati-śeta, as, ā, am, excelling, exceeding; superior.

अतिशीतम् *ati-śītam,* ind. past the cold, after the winter.

अतिशेष *ati-śesha, as,* m. remainder, remnant, especially of time.

अतिश्रेष्ठ *ati-śreshṭha, as, ā, am,* superior to the best, best of all. — *Atiśreshṭha-tva, am,* n. pre-eminence.

Ati-śreyasi, is, m. a man superior to the most excellent woman.

अतिश्लिष् *ati-ślish,* cl. 4. P. *-ślishyati, -śleshṭum,* to fasten or tie over.

अतिश्व *ati-śva, as, ī, am,* superior to, or worse than, a dog; (*ā*), m., N. of a tribe.

अतिषेल् *ati-shel* (rt. *sel* or *śel*), Caus. P. *-shelayati, -yitum,* to make one go to a great distance.

अतिष्कद्वरी *ati-shkadvarī,* f. (rt. *skand*), (transgressor), a dissolute woman.

अतिष्ठत् *a-tishṭhat, an, antī, at,* not standing, unstable.

अतिष्ठा *ati-shṭhā* (rt. *sthā*), cl. 1. P. *-tishṭhati, -shṭhātum,* to excel.

Ati-shṭhā, f. precedence, superiority; (*ās*), m. f., Ved. or *ati-shṭhāvan, ā,* m. or *atishṭhā-vat, ān, atī, at,* superior in standing, surpassing.

अतिसन्धा *ati-san-dhā* (*-sam-dhā*), cl. 3. P. A. *-dadhāti, -dhatte, -dhātum,* to overreach, deceive.

Ati-sandham, ind. in violation of an agreement or of the settled order.

Ati-san-dhāna, am, n. overreaching, cheating.
Ati-san-dhita, as, ā, m, overreached, cheated.
Ati-san-dheya, as, ā, am, easy to be conciliated or settled.

अतिसर्व *ati-sarva, as, ā, am*, superior to all; (*as*), m. the supreme.

अतिसांवत्सर *ati-sāṃvatsara, as, ī, am*, extending over more than a year.

अतिसाम्या *ati-sāmyā*, f. the sweet juice of the Bengal Madder, Rubia Manjith.

अतिसृ *ati-sṛi*, Caus. P. *-sārayati, -yitum*, to extend; to exert (?).
Ati-sara, as, m., Ved. effort, exertion.
Ati-sāra or *atī-sāra, as*, m. violent straining at stool, dysentery.
Ati-sārakin or *atī-sārakin* or *ati-sārin* or *atī-sārin, ī, iṇī, i*, afflicted with dysentery.

अतिसृज् *ati-sṛij*, cl. 6. P. *-sṛijati, -srashṭum*, to dismiss, abandon; to leave as a remnant; to remit, forgive; to give away.
Ati-sarga, as, m. act of parting with, dismissal, giving away, granting permission.
Ati-sarjana, am, n. liberality, granting, engaging, a gift; sending out of the world, killing.
Ati-sṛijya, ind. part. having dismissed, &c.; excessively.

अतिसृप् *ati-sṛip*, cl. 1. P. *-sarpati, -sarptum* or *-sraptum*, to glide over, get over.

अतिसेन *ati-sena, as*, m., N. of a prince, a son of Śambara.

अतिसौपर्ण *ati-sauparṇa, as, ī, am*, superior to Suparṇa's or Garuḍa's (vision, &c.).

अतिस्त्रि *ati-stri, is, is* or *ī, i*, surpassing a woman; Gram. 123. *b*. The feminine may end in *ī*.

अतिहस्तय *ati-hastaya*, Nom. (fr. *ati-hasta*), P. *atihastayati, -yitum*, to stretch out the hands; (fr. *atihastin*), to overtake on an elephant.

अतिहिमम् *ati-himam*, ind. after the cold or the frost.

अती *atī* (*ati-i*), cl. 2. P. *aty-eti, -tum*, to pass, elapse, pass over, overflow; to pass on; to get over; to defer; to enter; to overcome, overtake, outdo; to pass by, neglect; to overstep, violate; to be redundant; to die: Intens. *atīyate*, to overcome.
Atīta, as, ā, am, gone by, past, passed away, dead; having gone through, having got over or beyond, having passed by, having neglected; negligent; passed, left behind; excessive; (*as*), m. modern N. of a particular Śaiva sect; (*am*), n. the past. — *Atīta-kāla, as*, m. the past time or tense. — *Atīta-nauka, as, ā, am*, landed.
Atītvarī (°*ti-it*°), f., Ved. (transgressor), a bad woman. — *Aty-aya, aty-āya*, see s. v.

अतीक्ष्ण *a-tīkshṇa, as, ā, am*, not sharp, blunt, dull.

अतीन्द्रिय *atīndriya* (*ati-in*°), *as, ā, am*, beyond the cognisance of (*indriya*) the senses; (*as*), m. in the Sāṅkhya phil. the soul or *purusha*; (*am*), n. in the Sāṅkhya phil. nature or *pradhāna*; in the Vedānta phil. the mind or *manas*.

अतीरेक, अतीसार. See under *ati-riċ, ati-sṛi*.

अतीव *atīva* (*ati-iva*), ind. exceedingly, very; excessively, too; quite; surpassing (with the acc.).

अतीव्र *a-tīvra, as, ā, am*, not sharp, blunt; not pungent.

अतुङ्ग *a-tuṅga, as, ā, am*, not tall, short, dwarfish.

अतुन्द *a-tunda, as, ā, am*, not stout, thin, lank.

अतुर *a-tura, as, ā, am*, Ved. not liberal, not rich.

अतुल *a-tula, as, ā, am*, unequalled; (*as*), m. (destitute of weight), the Sesamum seed and plant. — *A-tulya, as, ā, am*, unequalled.

अतुष *a-tusha, as, ā, am*, without husks.

अतुषारकर *a-tushāra-kara, as*, m. (having not cold rays), the sun.

अतुष्टि *a-tushṭi, is*, f. displeasure, discontent.

अतुहिन *a-tuhina*, Ved. not cold; used in compounds, thus *atuhina-dhāman, ā*, or *atuhina-raśmi, is*, or *atuhina-ruċi, is*, m. the sun.

अतूतुजि *a-tūtuji, is, is, ī*, Ved. not quick, slow.

अतूर्त *a-tūrta, as, ā, am*, Ved. not in a hurry; not outrun or outdone or obstructed; unhurt; (*am*), n. illimited space. — *Atūrta-daksha, as*, m., Ved. having designs that cannot be obstructed (epithet of the Aśvins). — *Atūrta-pathin, anthās*, m., Ved. having a path that cannot be obstructed.

अतृणाद *a-tṛiṇāda* (°*ṇa-ada*), *as*, m. (not an eater of grass), a newly-born calf.

अतृण्या *a-tṛiṇyā*, f. a small quantity or short supply of grass.

अतृदिल *a-tṛidila, as, ā, am*, Ved. not fragile, solid, or 'having no holes.'

अतृप *a-tṛipa, as, ā, am*, Ved. not satisfied.
Atṛipṇuvat, ān, atī, at, Ved. insatiable.
A-tṛipta, as, ā, am, unsatisfied, insatiable, eager. — *Atṛipta-dṛiś, k, k, k*, looking with eagerness.
A-tṛipti, is, f. unsatisfied condition, insatiability.

अतृषित *a-tṛishita, as, ā, am*, Ved. not thirsty, not greedy.
A-tṛishṇaj, k, k, k, Ved. not thirsty.
A-tṛishya, as, ā, am, Ved. beyond the reach of thirst.
A-tṛishyat, an, antī, at, Ved. not thirsting after, not greedy, not eager.

अतेजस् *a-tejas*, n. absence of brightness or vigour; dimness, shade, shadow; feebleness, dulness, insignificance; (*ās, ās, as*), or *a-tejaska, as, ā, am*, or *a-tejasvin, ī, inī, i*, not bright, dim, not vigorous.

अतोषणीय *a-toshaṇīya, as, ā, am*, impossible or improper to be pleased or appeased.

अत्क *atka, as, ā, am* (fr. rt. *at*), travelling; (*as*), m. a traveller; a limb or member; (Ved.) water, liquid; lightning; armour, mail; garment; N. of an Asura.

अत्कील *atkīla* or *utkīla, as*, m., N. of the author of some Vedic hymns, a descendant of Viśvāmitra.

अत्तलि *attali, is*, m., N. of a man.

अत्तव्य *attavya, as, ā, am* (fr. rt. *ad*), fit or proper to be eaten.
Atti, is, m., Ved. an eater; f., see also s. v. *attā*.
Attṛi, tā, m. an eater.

अत्ता *attā*, f. (etym. uncertain, probably a word borrowed from the Deccan, occurring chiefly in dramas); a mother; mother's sister; elder sister; (in Prākṛit) a mother-in-law. See *akkā*.
Atti, is, or *attikā*, f. elder sister.

अत्त्र, अत्त्रि, अत्त्रिन्, *attra*, &c. See अत्र, अत्रि, अत्रिन्.

अत्न *atna, as*, or *atnu, us*, m. (fr. *at*), the sun.
Atya, as, m., Ved. a courser, steed.

अत्यंहस् *aty-aṃhas, ās, ās, as*, Ved. beyond the reach of (or emancipated from) sin or evil.

अत्यग्नि *aty-agni, is*, m. morbidly rapid digestion, see s. v. *ati*; (*is, is, i*), surpassing fire. — *Aty-agni-somārka* (°*ma-ar*°), *as, ā, am*, brighter than fire or the moon or the sun.

अत्यग्निष्टोम *aty-agnishṭoma, as*, m., N. of the optional second part of the Jyotishṭoma sacrifice; the Vedic verse chanted at the close of that ceremony.

अत्यङ्कुश *aty-aṅkuśa, as, ā, am*, past the (elephant-driver's) hook, unmanageable.

अत्यङ्गुल *aty-aṅgula, as, ā, am*, exceeding an aṅgula (finger's breadth).

अत्यतिक्रम् *aty-ati-kram*, cl. 1. P. *-krāmati, -kramitum*, to approach for sexual intercourse.

अत्यनिल *aty-anila, as, ā, am*, surpassing the wind.

अत्यन्त *aty-anta, as, ā, am*, past its proper end or limit; excessive, very great or strong, &c.; endless, unbroken, perpetual; absolute, perfect; (*am*), ind. excessively, exceedingly; in perpetuity; absolutely, completely; to the end. — *Atyanta-kopana, as, ā, ām*, very passionate, outrageous. — *Atyanta-ga, as, ā, am*, going or walking very much or very fast. — *Atyanta-gata, as, ā, am*, completely pertinent; always applicable. — *Atyanta-gati, is*, f. complete accomplishment; (in grammar) the sense of 'completely.' — *Atyanta-gāmin, ī, inī, i*, going or walking very much or very fast. — *Atyanta-guṇin, ī, inī, i*, having extraordinary qualities. — *Atyanta-tiraskṛita-vāċya-dhvani, is*, f. (in rhetoric) a metaphoric or hyperbolical use of depreciating language. — *Atyanta-pīḍana, am*, n. act of giving excessive pain. — *Atyanta-vāsin, ī*, m. a Brāhman who perpetually lodges as a student with his teacher. — *Atyanta-saṃyoga, as*, m. (in grammar) immediate proximity. — *Atyanta-samparka, as*, m. excessive sexual intercourse. — *Atyanta-sukumāra, as, ī, am*, very tender; (*as*), m. a kind of grain, Panicum Italicum. — *Atyantābhāra* (°*ta-abh*°), *as*, m. absolute non-existence.
1. *atyantika* or *atyantīna, as, ā, am*, going much or fast or far.

अत्यन्तिक 2. *aty-antika, as, ā, am*, too close, too near, very close; (*am*), n. too great nearness.

अत्यय *aty-aya, as*, m. (fr. rt. *i* with *ati*, see *atī*), passing, lapse, passage; passing away, perishing, death; danger, risk, evil, suffering; transgression, guilt, vice; getting at, attacking; overcoming, mastering (mentally); a class.
Atyayika, better *ātyayika, as, ā, am*, temporary, occasional.
Atyayin, ī, inī, i, passing, surpassing.

अत्यराति *aty-arāti, is*, m., N. of a son of Janantapa.

अत्यर्थ *aty-artha, as, ā, am* (beyond its proper worth), exorbitant, excessive. — *Atyartham*, ind. excessively, exceedingly.

अत्यर्द् *aty-ard*, cl. 1. P. *-ardati, -ditum*, to press hard, to distress greatly.

अत्यर्ह् *aty-arh*, cl. 1. P. *-arhati, -hitum*, to excel in worth.

अत्यवि *aty-avi, is*, m., Ved. passing over or through the strainer, which consisted of sheep's wool or a sheep's tail (an epithet of Soma).

अत्यश् *aty-aś*, cl. 9. P. *-aśnāti, -aśitum*, to precede in eating.

अत्यष्टि *aty-ashṭi, is*, f. a metre of four lines, each containing seventeen syllables; the number seventeen. — *Atyashṭi-sāmagrī*, f. title of a particular book.

अत्यस् 1. *aty-as* (*ati-as*), cl. 2. P. *-asti*, to excel, surpass.

अत्यस् 2. *aty-as* (*ati-as*), cl. 4. P. *-asyati*, *-situm*, to shoot beyond or at, overpower (with arrows).

Aty-asta, *as*, *ā*, *am*, having shot beyond, having surpassed.

अत्यहम् *aty-aham*, surpassing me, (a fictitious word coined by grammarians.)

अत्यह्न *aty-ahna*, *as*, *ā*, *am*, exceeding a day in duration.

अत्याकार *aty-ā-kāra*, *as*, m. (rt. *kṛi*), contempt, blame.

अत्याक्रम् *aty-ā-kram* (*ati-ā°*), cl. 1. P. *-krāmati*, *-kramitum*, to walk past.

अत्याचार *aty-āćāra*, *as*, m. performance of works of supererogation; (*as*, *ā*, *am*), negligent of or departing from the established customs.

अत्यादित्य *aty-āditya*, *as*, *ā*, *am*, surpassing the sun.

अत्याधान *aty-ā-dhāna*, *am*, n. act of imposing or placing upon; imposition, deception.

अत्यानन्दा *aty-ānandā*, f. morbid indifference (of a wife) to the pleasure of sexual intercourse.

अत्याय *aty-āya*, *as*, m. (fr. rt. *i* with *ati*), transgression, excess; (*as*, *ā*, *am*), going beyond, transgressing.

अत्यायत् *aty-ā-yat* (*ati-ā°*), cl. 1. A. *-yatate*, *-titum*, to make extraordinary efforts.

अत्याल *aty-āla*, *as*, m., N. of a plant, Plumbago Rosea.

अत्याश्रमिन् *aty-āśramin*, *ī*, m. (superior to the four Āśramas), an ascetic of the highest degree.

अत्यास *aty-āsa*, *as*, m. act of allowing to elapse; only used in the acc. as the concluding part of compound words, thus *dvyahātyāsam*, after an interval of two days.

अत्युक्ता *aty-uktā* or *aty-ukthā*, f., N. of a class of metres of four lines, each containing two syllables.

अत्युक्ष् *aty-uksh* (*ati-uksh*), cl. 1. P. *-ukshati*, *-kshitum*, to surpass.

अत्युत्क्रम् *aty-ut-kram* (*ati-ut°*), cl. 1. P. *-krāmati*, *-kramitum*, to surpass, excel.

अत्युपध *aty-upadha*, *as*, *ā*, *am*, superior to any test, tried, trustworthy.

अत्युह् *aty-uh*. See *aty-ūh*.

अत्यूमशा *aty-ūmaśā*, ind. (etym. unknown), particle of abuse, used in comp. with *as*, *bhū*, *kṛi*.

अत्यूर्मि *aty-ūrmi*, *is*, *is*, *i*, Ved. overflowing, bubbling over.

अत्यूह् *aty-ūh* (*ati-ūh*), cl. 1. P. *ūhati*, *-hitum*, to convey across. Spelt *aty-uh* in some forms.

अत्यूह *aty-ūha*, *as*, m. close meditation; a gallinule, a peacock; (*ā*), f. a plant, Jasminum Villosum or Nyctanthes Tristis.

अत्यृज् *aty-ṛij* (*ati-ṛij*), cl. 1. P. A. *-arjati*, *-te*, *-jitum*, to convey across, admit; to remove.

अत्येष् *aty-esh*, cl. 1. P. *-eshati*, *-shitum*, to glide over.

अत्र 1. *a-tra* or Ved. *a-trā*, ind. (fr. pronominal base *a* substituted for *etad*; the word *atra* being often used for the loc. case *etasmin*), in this matter, in this respect; in this place, here; at this time; there; then. — *Atra-daghna*, *as*, *ī*, *am*, reaching so far up, having this (or that) stature. — *Atra-bhavat*, *ān*, *atī*, *at*, honourable (used chiefly in dramatic language, to indicate a person who is present).

Atratya, *as*, *ā*, *am*, connected with this place, produced or found here.

अत्र 2. *a-tra*, *as*, *ā*, *am* (rt. *trai*), Ved. not enjoying (or not affording) protection.

अत्र 3. *atra*, *as*, m. (for *at-tra*, fr. rt. *ad*), Ved. a devourer, demon; a Rākshasa; (*am*), n., Ved. food.

Atri, *is*, m. (etymologically *at-tri*, fr. rt. *ad*), a devourer; N. of a great Ṛishi, author of a number of Vedic hymns; (in astronomy) one of the seven stars of the Great Bear. — *Atrayas*, pl. m. the descendants of Atri. — *Atri-ćaturaha*, *as*, m. (the four days of Atri), N. of a sacrifice. — *Atri-jāta*, *as*, m. the moon, said to have been produced by Atri's look; for *a-tri-jāta*, see below. — *Atri-dṛig-ja*, *atri-netra-ja* or *atri-netra-prasūta* or *atri-netra-prabhava* or *atri-netra-sūta*, *as*, or *atri-netra-bhū*, *ūs*, m. the moon; (in arithm.) the number one. — *Atri-bhāradvājikā*, f. marriage of Atri and Bhāradvājī. — *Atri-vat*, ind. like Atri. — *Atri-saṃhitā*, *ā*, or *atri-smṛiti*, *is*, f. the code ascribed to Atri.

Atrin, *ī*, m. a devourer, demon; a Rākshasa.

अत्रप *a-trapa*, *as*, *ā*, *am*, destitute of shame.

अत्रवस् *atravas*, ind. (a doubtful word), the year before last.

अत्रस्नु *a-trasnu*, *us*, *us*, *u*, or *a-trāsa*, *as*, *ā*, *am*, fearless.

अत्रिजात *a-tri-jāta*, *as*, *ā*, *am* (not born thrice, but twice); a man belonging to one of the first three classes [for *atri-jāta*, see s. v. *atri*].

अत्रैव *atraiva* (*atra-eva*), ind. on this very spot.

अत्वच् *a-tvać*, *k*, *k*, *k*, skinless.

अत्वरा *a-tvarā*, f. freedom from or absence of haste.

अथ *atha* or Ved. *athā*, ind. (probably fr. pronom. base *a*), an auspicious and inceptive particle, often not easily expressed in English; now; then; moreover; rather; certainly; but; else; what? how else? &c. — *Atha-kim*, ind. how else? what else? certainly, assuredly, sure enough. — *Atha-kimu*, ind. how much more; so much the more. — *Atha-ća*, ind. moreover, and likewise. — *Atha-tu*, ind. but, on the contrary. — *Atha-vā*, ind. or; (when repeated) either or; or rather; or perhaps; what? is it not so? &c. — *Athavāpi* (°*vā-api*), ind. or, rather. — *Athātas* (°*tha-at°*), ind. now. — *Athānantaram* (°*tha-an°*), ind. now. — *Athāpi* (°*tha-api*), ind. so much the more; moreover; therefore; thus.

Atho, ind. (has much the same meaning as *atha*, and probably the same etymology), now; likewise; next; therefore. — *Atho-vā*, ind. the same as *atha-vā*.

अथरि *athari*, *is*, or *atharī*, f. (generally in the plural; etymology doubtful; said to be fr. rt. *at*, to go, or fr. an obsolete rt. *ath*), meaning doubtful, probably spark or flame having a pointed shape; (according to others) the point of a lance; (according to others) a finger.

Atharya, *as*, m., Ved. lambent; moving constantly; or (according to some) pointed like a lance; or (according to some) shooting forth points like those of a lance.

Atharya, nom. P. *atharyati*, Ved. to move constantly.

Atharyu, *us*, m., Ved. = *atharya*, *as*.

अथर्वन् *atharvan*, *ā*, m. (said to be fr. an obsolete word *athar*, fire), a priest who has to do with fire and Soma; a Brāhman; N. of the priest who is said to have been the first to obtain fire and offer Soma and prayers: he is represented as a Prajāpati, as Brahmā's eldest son, as the first learner and earliest teacher of the Brahma-vidyā, as the author of the Atharva-veda, as identical with Aṅgiras, as the father of Agni, &c.: epithet of Śiva, Vaśishṭha, Soma, Prāṇa; (*ā*, *a*), m. n. the fourth or Atharva-veda, consisting chiefly of formulas intended to obviate the effects of any mistake or untoward incident attending the performance of a sacrifice. — *Atharvāṇas*, pl. m. descendants of Atharvan, often coupled with those of Aṅgiras and Bhṛigu; the hymns of the Atharva-veda. — *Atharva-bhūta*, *ās*, m. pl. (who have become Atharvans), epithet of the twelve Maharshis. — *Atharva-vat*, ind. like Atharvan or his descendants. — *Atharva-vid*, *t*, m. one versed in the Atharva-veda (a qualification essential to the special class of priests called Brāhmaṇas). — *Atharva-veda*, *as*, m., N. of the fourth Veda, which strictly speaking is not a Veda at all, like the Ṛig, Yajur, and Sāma-vedas, but a collection of formulas to avert the consequences of mistakes or mishaps in sacrifices. — *Atharva-śikhā*, f. title of an Upanishad. — *Atharva-śiras*, n. = preceding; (*ās*), m. an epithet of Mahāpurusha. — *Atharva-hṛidaya*, *am*, n. title of a Pariśishṭa.

Atharva, *as*, m., N. of Brahmā's eldest son, to whom he revealed the Brahma-vidyā. See *atharvan*.

Atharvaṇa, *as*, m., N. of Śiva.

Atharvaṇi, *is*, better *ātharvaṇi*, m. a Brāhman versed in the Atharva-veda; a family priest.

Atharvāṅgiras (°*va-aṅ°*), *ās*, m. a member of the sacerdotal race or class called *Atharvāṅgirasas*, m. pl., i. e. the descendants of Atharvan and of Aṅgiras; this latter word is also a name of the hymns of the Atharva-veda.

Atharvāṅgirasa, *as*, *ī*, *am* (fr. the preceding), connected with the sacerdotal class called Atharvāṅgiras; (*am*), n. the work or office of the Atharvāṅgiras; (*ās*), m. pl. the hymns of the Atharva-veda.

Atharvāṇa, *am*, n. the work, i. e. ritual of the Atharva-veda. — *Atharvāṇa-vid*, *t*, m. one versed in that ritual.

Atharvī, f., Ved. (doubtful) not moving (?); pierced by a lance (?); surrounded by fire (?).

अद् *ad*, cl. 2. P. *atti*, *āda*, *atsyati*, *attum*, to eat, devour; to destroy [cf. Lith. *edmi*; Slav. *jamj* for *jadmj*; Gr. ἔδω; Lat. *edo*; Goth. rt. *AT*, pres. *ita*; Germ. *essen*; Eng. *to eat*; Arm. *utem*].

Ad, *t*, *t*, *t*, at the end of compounds, eating; as *matsyād*, *t*, *t*, *t*, eating fish.

Ada or *adaka*, *as*, *ā*, *am*, eating.

1. *adat*, *an*, *atī*, *at*, eating. (For *a-dat*, see below.)

Adana, *am*, n. act of eating; food.

Adanīya, *as*, *ā*, *am*, to be eaten, what may be eaten.

Attavya, *atti*, *attri*, *adman*, *adya*, *advan*, &c., see s. v.

अदक्ष *a-daksha*, *as*, *ā*, *am*, not handy, unskilful, awkward.

अदक्षिण *a-dakshiṇa*, *as*, *ā*, *am*, not handy; not right, left; not giving or bringing in a dakshiṇā or present to the priest. — *Adakshiṇa-tva*, *am*, n. awkwardness; peculiarity of not bringing in a dakshiṇā. — *Adakshiṇīya* or *adakshiṇya*, *as*, *ā*, *am*, not entitled to a dakshiṇā.

अदग्ध *a-dagdha*, *as*, *ā*, *am*, not burnt, not scorched.

अदण्ड *a-daṇḍa*, *as*, *ā*, *am*, free from punishment; (*am*), n. impunity.

A-daṇḍya or *a-daṇḍanīya*, *as*, *ā*, *am*, not deserving punishment; exempt from it.

अदत् 2. *a-dat*, *an*, *atī*, *at*, or *adatka*, *as*, *ā*, *am*, toothless. (For *adat*, see above.)

अदत्त *a-datta*, *as*, *ā*, *am*, not given; given unjustly; not given in marriage; having given nothing;

(ā), f. an unmarried girl; (am), n. a donation which is null and void.

A-dattrā, ind. not having given, without having given.

A-datrayā, ind., Ved. not through a present.

अदद्र्यञ्च् adadry-anć, an, īćī, ak (a word coined by grammarians, fr. adas + anć), inclining or going to that.

अदन adana, adanīya. See under ad.

अदन्त 1. a-danta or a-dantaka, as, ā, am, toothless; (as), m. a leech.

A-dantya, as, ā, am, not suitable for the teeth; not dental; injurious to the teeth; (am), n. toothlessness.

अदन्त 2. ad-anta, as, ā, am, (in gram.) ending in at, i.e. in the short inherent vowel a.

अदब्ध a-dabdha, as, ā, am (rt. dambh or dabh), Ved. not deceived or tampered with, unimpaired, unbroken, pure. — Adabdha-dhīti, is, is, i, Ved. whose works are unimpaired. — Adabdha-vrata, as, m., Ved. whose devotions or religious observances are unbroken. — Adabdha-vrata-pramati, is, m., Ved. of unbroken observances and superior mind; of superior mind from having unbroken observances. — Adabdhāyu (°dha-āyu), us, m., Ved. having unimpaired vigour or pure food; leaving uninjured the man who sacrifices. — Adabdhāsu (°dha-asu), us, us, u, Ved. having a pure life.

A-dabha, as, ā, am, Ved. free from deceit, unimpaired.

A-dabhra, as, ā, am, not scanty, plentiful.

A-dambha, as, ā, am, free from deceit, straightforward; (as), m. an epithet of Śiva; freedom from or absence of deceit; straightforwardness.

A-dambhi-tva, am, n. sincerity.

अदमुद्र्यञ्च् adamudry-anć, an, īćī, ak, inclining or going to that. (Like adadryanć, coined by grammarians from adas + anć.)

Adamuy-anć or adamūy-anć = the preceding.

अदम्य a-damya, as, ā, am, untameable.

अदय a-daya, as, ā, am (rt. day), merciless, unkind; (am), ind. ardently.

A-dayālu, us, us, u, unkind.

अदर a-dara, as, ā, am, not little, much. — Adaraka, as, m., N. of a man.

अदर्श 1. a-darśa (for ā-darśa), as, m. a mirror.

अदर्श 2. a-darśa, as, m. day of new moon.

A-darśana, am, n. non-vision, not seeing; disregard, neglect; non-appearance, latent condition, disappearance; (as, ā, am), invisible, latent. — Adarśana-patha, am, n. a path beyond the reach of vision.

A-darśanīya, as, ā, am, invisible; (am), n. invisible condition.

अदल a-dala, as, ā, am, leafless; (as), m. a plant, Eugenia (or Barringtonia) Acutangula; (ā), f. Socotorine Aloe, a Perfoliata or Indica.

अदशन् a-daśan, a, not ten. — A-daśa-māsya, as, ā, am, not ten months old.

अदस् 1. adas, m. asau, f. asau, n. adas, pron. that; a certain. — Adas, ind. thus, so; ever. — Adaḥ-kṛitya, having done that. — Ado-bhavati, he becomes that. — Ado-maya, as, ī, am, made of that, containing that. — Ado-mūla, as, ā, am, rooted in that.

Adasya, nom. P. adasyati, to become that.

अदस् 2. adas, eating, (only at the close of compound words.)

अदाक्षिण्य a-dākshiṇya, am, n. unkindness, rudeness.

अदातृ a-dātṛi, tā, trī, tṛi, not giving; not liberal, miserly; not giving (a daughter) in marriage; not paying, not liable to payment.

अदादि ad-ādi, is, is, i, having ad at the head, i.e. belonging to the second class of roots headed by ad.

अदान a-dāna, am, n. (rt. dā), not giving, act of withholding; (as, ā, am), not giving.

A-dānya, as, ā, am, not giving, miserly.

A-dāman, ā, ā, a, Ved. not liberal, miserly.

A-dāyin, ī, inī, i, not giving.

A-dāśu, us, us, u, Ved. or a-dāśuri, is, m. or a-dāśvas, ān, m. not giving, not sacrificing, impious.

1. a-diti, is, f., Ved. having nothing to give, destitution; for 2. aditi, 3. a-diti, see below.

अदान्त a-dānta, as, ā, am, unsubdued.

अदाभ्य a-dābhya, as, ā, am, Ved. free from deceit, trusty; not to be trifled with; (as), m., N. of a libation (graha) in the Jyotishṭoma sacrifice.

अदायाद a-dāyāda, as, ā, am, not entitled to be an heir; destitute of heirs.

A-dāyika, as, ī, am, unclaimed from want of persons entitled to inherit; not relating to inheritance.

अदार 1. a-dāra, as, m. having no wife.

अदार 2. a-dāra, as, m. (rt. dṛī), non-injuring. — Adāra-sṛit, t, t, t, Ved. escaping unhurt.

अदास a-dāsa, as, m. (not a slave), a free man.

अदाह्य a-dāhya, as, ā, am, incombustible.

अदिक्क a-dikka, as, ā, am, Ved. having no share in the horizon, banished from beneath the sky.

अदिति 2. aditi, is, m. (fr. rt. ad), Ved. devourer, i.e. death; for 1. a-diti, see above.

अदिति 3. a-diti, is, is, i (rt. 4. dā or do, dyati; for 1. a-diti, see above), not tied, free; boundless; unbroken, entire, unimpaired; happy; pious; (is), f. freedom, security, safety; boundlessness, immensity; inexhaustible abundance; unimpaired condition, perfection; creative power; Aditi, the mother of the Ādityas, or of the gods; a cow; a wife; milk; the earth; speech (as symbols of the above ideas). — Aditī, du., Ved. heaven and earth. — Aditi-ja or aditi-nandana, as, m. a son of Aditi, an Āditya, a divine being. — Aditi-tva, am, n. the condition of Aditi, or of freedom, unbrokenness, &c.

अदित्सत् a-ditsat, an, antī, at, or a-ditsu, us, us, u (Desid. fr. rt. dā), not inclined to give.

अदिप्रभृति adi-prabhṛiti, is, m., ad &c., i.e. belonging to the second class of roots [cf. ad-ādi].

अदीक्षित a-dīkshita, as, ā, am, one who has not performed the consecrating ceremony (dīkshā) connected with the Soma sacrifice; one who is not concerned in that ceremony; one who has not received Brāhmanical consecration.

अदीन a-dīna, as, ā, am, not depressed; not low; noble-minded; rich, happy; (as), m., N. of a prince, also called Ahīna. — Adīna-sattra, as, ā, am, possessing undepressed (or unimpaired) goodness or mettle. — Adīnātman (°na-āt°), ā, ā, a, undepressed in spirit; high-spirited.

अदीपित a-dīpita, as, ā, am, not illuminated.

अदीर्घ a-dīrgha, as, ā, am, not long. — Adīrgha-sūtra, as, ā, am, not dilatory, not tedious, prompt.

अदुःख a-duḥkha, as, ā, am (free from evil or trouble), propitious. — Aduḥkha-navamī, f. the propitious ninth day in the first fortnight of Bhādrapada, when the women worship Devī to avert evil for the ensuing year.

अदुग्ध a-dugdha, as, ā, am, not milked out, not sucked out.

अदुच्छुन a-dućchuna, as, ā, am, Ved. free from evil, propitious.

अदुर्ग a-durga, as, ā, am, not difficult of access; destitute of a strong hold or fort. — Adurga-vishaya, as, m. an unfortified country.

अदुर्मख a-durmakha, as, ā, am, Ved. not reluctant, unremitting, cheerful.

अदुर्मङ्गल a-durmangala, as, ā, am, Ved. not inauspicious.

अदुर्वृत्त a-durvṛitta, as, ā, am, not of a bad character or disposition.

अदुष्ट a-dushṭa, as, ā, am, not vitiated, not bad, not guilty; innocent. — Adushṭa-tva, am, n. the being not vitiated; innocence.

अदू a-dū, ūs, ūs, u, Ved. dilatory, without zeal, not worshipping.

अदून a-dūna, as, ā, am (rt. du), uninjured, unimpaired.

अदूर a-dūra, as, ā, am, not distant, near; (am), n. vicinity. — Adūre or adūrāt or adūratas, ind. (with abl. or gen.) not far, near; soon. — Adūra-bhava, as, ā, am, situated at no great distance.

अदूषित a-dūshita, as, ā, am, unvitiated; unspotted, irreproachable. — Adūshita-dhī, īs, m. possessing an uncorrupted mind.

अदृढ a-dṛiḍha, as, ā, am, not firm; not decided, irresolute.

अदृपित a-dṛipita, as, ā, am (rt. dṛip), Ved. not treated haughtily (?), not thoughtless.

Adṛipta, as, ā, am, Ved. not conceited, not vain. — Adṛipta-kratu, us, us, u, having not vain designs; sober-minded.

Adṛipyat, an, antī, at, Ved. not conceited.

अदृश् a-dṛiś, k, k, k (rt. dṛiś), sightless, blind.

A-dṛiśya, as, ā, am, invisible, latent; not fit to be seen. — Adṛiśya-karaṇa, am, n. act of rendering invisible; title of a part of a treatise on magic.

A-dṛiśyat, an, antī, at, invisible; (ī), f., N. of Vasishṭha's daughter-in-law.

A-dṛishṭa, as, ā, am, unseen, unforeseen; invisible; not experienced; unobserved, unknown; unsanctioned; (as), m., Ved., N. of some venomous substance or vermin; (am), n. unforeseen danger or calamity; that which is beyond the reach of observation or consciousness; especially the merit or demerit attaching to a man's conduct in one state of existence (such as a former birth), and the corresponding (apparently arbitrary) reward or punishment with which he is visited in another (which may be either the present life or a future birth); destiny, fate; luck, bad luck. — Adṛishṭa-karman, ā, ā, a, one who has not seen practice. — Adṛishṭa-kāma, as, m. passionate attachment to an object that has never been seen. — Adṛishṭa-ja, as, ā, am, produced or resulting from fate. — Adṛishṭa-nara or adṛishṭa-purusha, as, m. (no third person or mediator being seen), a treaty concluded by the parties personally. — Adṛishṭa-para-sāmarthya, as, m. one who has not experienced the power of an enemy. — Adṛishṭa-pūrva, as, ā, am, never seen before. — Adṛishṭa-phala, as, ā, am, having consequences that are not yet visible; (am), n. result or consequence which is not yet visible, i.e. hidden in the future. — Adṛishṭa-rūpa, as, ā, am, having an invisible shape. — Adṛishṭa-vat, ān, atī, at, connected with or coming from destiny; lucky or unlucky; fortunate. — Adṛishṭa-han, ā, m., Ved. destroyer of venomous vermin. — Adṛishṭārtha (°ṭa-ar°), as, ā, am, having a transcendental object, metaphysical, having an object not evident to the senses (as a science). — Adṛishṭāśruta-pūrvatva (°ṭa-aś°), am, n. quality of never having been seen or heard before.

A-drishṭi, is, or *a-drishṭikā,* f. a displeased or malicious look, an evil eye.

अदेय *a-deya, as, ā, am,* improper or unfit to be given; (*am*), n. an object which, in law, it is either not right or not necessary to give or surrender. — *Adeya-dāna, am,* n. an illegal gift.

अदेव *a-deva, as, ā, am* (rt. *div*), not divine, not of divine origin, not referring to any deity; godless, impious; (*as*), m. one who is not a god. — *Adeva-mātṛika, as, ā, am,* not having the gods as mothers, not suckled by any deity, i. e. not rained upon.

A-devaka, as, ā, am, not referring to or intended for any deity.

A-devatā, f. one who is not a deity.

A-devatra or *a-devatrā,* ind., Ved. not towards the gods.

A-devayat, an, antī, at, or *adevayu, us, us, u,* Ved. indifferent to the gods, irreligious.

A-daiva, as, ī, am, not referring to or connected with the gods or with their action; not predetermined by them or by fate.

अदेवृघ्नी *a-devṛi-ghnī,* f., Ved. not destructive to her brother-in-law.

अदेश *a-deśa, as,* m. (rt. *diś*), a wrong place, an improper place. — *A-deśa-kāla, am,* n. wrong place and time. — *Adeśa-ja, as, ā, am,* grown in a wrong place. — *Adeśa-stha, as, ā, am,* out of place, in the wrong place, one absent from his country, an absentee.

A-deśya, as, ā, am, improper or unfit to be ordered or advised or indicated; not on the spot, not present on the occasion referred to.

अदोमद *a-doma-da* or *a-doma-dha, as, ā, am,* Ved. not occasioning inconvenience.

अदोमय *ado-maya,* &c. See *adas.*

अदोह *a-doha, as,* m. (rt. *duh*), season when milking is impracticable.

A-dogdhṛi, dhā, dhṛī, dhṛi (not milking), not exacting; considerate.

अद्ग *adga, as,* m. (fr. rt. *ad*), a sacrificial cake, also called *puroḍāśa;* (according to others) an oblation of clarified butter.

अट्ट् *aḍḍ* or **अद्ड्** *adḍ.* See s. v. *aṭṭ.*

अद्धा *ad-dhā,* ind. (fr. *ad* or *a,* this), Ved. in this way; manifestly; certainly, truly. — *Addhā-tamām,* ind., Ved. most certainly. — *Addhā-purusha, as,* m., Ved. a veritable or true man. — *Addhā-bodheya, ās,* m. pl. adherents of a particular S'ākhā or recension of the white Yajur-veda.

Addhāti, is, m., Ved. a wise man, a seer.

अद्ध्यालोहकर्णा *addhyā-loha-karṇa, as, ā* or *ī, am,* Ved. having ears quite red (?).

अद्भुत *adbhuta, as, ā, am* (perhaps corrupted from *ati-bhūta,* 'exceeding that which is;' see 1. *at*), transcendental, supernatural, prodigious, wonderful, marvellous; (*as*), m. the marvellous (in style); surprise; N. of the Indra of the ninth Manvantara; (*am*), n. a marvel, a wonder, a prodigy. — *Adbhuta-karman, ā, ā, a,* performing wonderful works; exhibiting wonderful workmanship. — *Adbhuta-kratu, us, us, u,* Ved. possessing wonderful intelligence. — *Adbhuta-gandha, as, ā, am,* having a wonderful smell. — *Adbhuta-tama, am,* n. an extraordinary wonder. — *Adbhuta-tva, am,* n. wonderfulness. — *Adbhuta-darśana, as, ā, am,* having a wonderful aspect. — *Adbhuta-dharma, as,* m. a system or series of marvels or prodigies. — *Adbhuta-brāhmaṇa, am,* title of a portion of a Brāhmaṇa belonging to the Sāma-veda. — *Adbhuta-bhīma-karman, ā, ā, a,* performing wonderful and fearful works. — *Adbhuta-rasa, as,* m. the marvellous style (of poetry). — *Adbhuta-rāmāyaṇa, am,* n. title of a work ascribed to Vālmīki. — *Adbhuta-rūpa, as, ā* or *ī, am,* having a wonderful shape. — *Adbhuta-śānti, is,* m. or f. (?), N. of the sixty-seventh Pariśishṭa of the Atharva-veda. — *Adbhuta-saṅkāśa, as, ā, am,* resembling a wonder. — *Adbhuta-sāra, as,* m. the wonderful resin (of the Khadira tree, Mimosa Catechu); title of a book on the "Essence of Prodigies." — *Adbhuta-svana, as,* m. (having a wonderful sound or voice), a N. of S'iva. — *Adbhutainas* (°*ta-en*°), *ās, ās, as,* Ved. one in whom no fault is visible. — *Adbhutottarakāṇḍa* (°*ta-utt*°), *am,* n., N. of a work, an appendix to or rather an imitation of the Rāmāyaṇa. — *Adbhutopama* (°*ta-up*°), *as, ā, am,* resembling a wonder.

अद्मन् *adman, a,* n. (fr. rt. *ad*), Ved. eating; a meal; a house. — *Adma-sad, t,* m., Ved. seated (with others) at a meal (?); seated at or busy in the preparation of a meal (?); a cook (?); a mother (?). — *Admasadya, am,* n., Ved. the condition of an *admasad.* — *Admasadvan, ā, ā, a,* Ved. fit to be a companion at a meal.

Admani, is, m. fire.

Admara, as, ā, am, gluttonous.

1. *adya, as, ā, am,* fit or proper to be eaten; (*am*), n. food, anything eatable.

अद्य 2. *a-dya* or Ved. *adyā,* ind. (fr. pronom. base *a,* this, with *dya* for *dyu,* Lat. *ho-die*), to-day; now-a-days; now. — *Adya-dina* or *adya-divasa, as, am,* m. n. the present day. — *Adya-pūrvam,* ind. before now. — *Adya-prabhṛiti,* ind. from and after to-day. — *Adya-śvīna, as, ā, am,* likely to happen to-day or (*śvas*) to-morrow; (*ā*), f. a female near delivery. — *Adya-sutyā,* f. preparation and consecration of the Soma on the same day. — *Adyāpi* (°*ya-api*), ind. even now, just now; to this day; down to the present time; henceforth. — *Adyāvadhi* (°*ya-av*°), *is, is, i,* beginning or ending to-day; from or till to-day. — *Adyaiva* (*adya-eva*), ind. this very day.

Adyatana, as, ī, am, extending over or referring to to-day; occurring or current to-day or now-a-days, modern; (*as*), m. the period of a current day, either from midnight to midnight, or from dawn to dark; (*ī*), f. (in gram.) the aorist tense from its relating what has occurred on the same day. — *Adyatana-bhūta, as,* m. the aorist.

Adyatanīya, as, ā, am, extending over or referring to to-day; current now-a-days.

अद्यु *a-dyu, us, us, u,* Ved. blunt.

अद्युत् *a-dyut, t, t, t,* Ved. destitute of brightness.

अद्यूत्य *a-dyūtya, am,* n., Ved. unlucky gambling; (according to others) the watch just before the dawn; (*as, ā, am*), not derived from gambling, honestly obtained.

अद्रव *a-drava, as, ā, am,* not liquid.

अद्रव्य *a-dravya, am,* n. a nothing, a worthless thing.

अद्रि *adri, is,* m. (said to be fr. rt. *ad,* but perhaps from *a,* not, and *dṛī,* to split, not liable to be split), a stone, a rock, a mountain; a stone for pounding Soma with or grinding it on; a stone for a sling, a thunderbolt; a mountain-shaped mass of clouds; a cloud (the mountains are the clouds personified, and regarded as the enemies of Indra); a tree; the sun; N. of a measure; the number seven; N. of a grandson of Pṛithu. — *Adri-karṇī,* f. a plant, Clitoria Ternatea Lin. — *Adri-kīlā,* f. the earth. — *Adri-kṛita-sthalī,* f., N. of an Apsaras. — *Adri-ja, as, ā, am,* produced from or found among rocks or mountains; (*ā*), f., N. of a plant, Saiṃhalī; N. of Pārvatī or Durgā; (*am*), n. red chalk. — *Adri-jā, ās,* m., Ved. produced from (the friction of) stones. — *Adri-jūta, as, ā, am,* Ved. excited by (the friction of) stones. — *Adri-tanayā,* f. the mountain-daughter, i. e. Pārvatī; N. of a metre of four lines, each containing twenty-three syllables. — *Adri-dugdha, as, ā, am,* Ved. milked, i. e. expressed with stones. — *Adri-drish, t,* m. the enemy of mountains or clouds, i. e. Indra. — *Adri-nandinī,* f., N. of Pārvatī. — *Adri-pati, is,* m. the Himālaya as the lord of mountains. — *Adri-barhas, ās, ās, as,* Ved. mountain-high. — *Adri-budhna, as, ā, am,* Ved. rooted in or produced on a rock or mountain. — *Adri-bhid, t, t, t,* Ved. splitting mountains or clouds; (*t*), m., N. of Indra. — *Adri-bhū, ūs, ūs, u,* mountain-born, found or living among mountains; (*ūs*), f. a plant, probably Salvinia Cucullata. — *Adri-mātṛi, tā, tṛī, tṛi,* Ved. having a rock or mountain for a mother. — *Adri-mūrdhan, ā,* m. the head or summit of a mountain. — *Adri-rāj, ṭ,* or *adri-rāja, as,* m. Himālaya as the king of mountains. — *Adri-vat, ān,* voc. *as,* m., Ved. armed with stones or thunderbolts. — *Adri-vahni, is,* m. fire on or in a mountain or rock. — *Adri-śayya, as,* m. having the mountain for his couch, i. e. S'iva. — *Adri-śṛiṅga, am,* n. a mountain-peak. — *Adri-shuta, as, ā, am,* Ved. prepared with stones. — *Adri-saṃhata, as, ā, am,* Ved. expressed with stones. — *Adri-sānu, us, us, u,* Ved. lingering on the mountains. — *Adri-sāra, as,* m. essence of stones, i. e. iron. — *Adri-sāra-maya, as, ī, am,* made of iron. — *Adrīndra* (°*dri-in*°) or *adrīśa* (°*dri-īś*°), *as,* m. the lord of mountains, i. e. Himālaya.

Adrikā, f., N. of an Apsaras.

अद्रुह् *a-druh, dhruk, k, k,* or *adruhvan, ā, ā, a* (rt. *druh*), Ved. free from malice or treachery.

A-drogha, as, ā, am, Ved. free from falsehood, true; (*am*), ind. without falsehood. — *Adrogha-vāć, k, k, k,* Ved. free from malice or treachery in speech. — *Adroghāvita* (°*gha-av*°), *as, ā, am,* Ved. loving freedom from malice or treachery.

A-droha, as, m. freedom from malice or treachery. — *Adroha-vṛitti, is,* f. conduct free from malice or treachery.

A-drohin, ī, iṇī, i, free from malice or treachery.

अद्वन् *advan, ā, ā, a* (fr. rt. *ad*), eating; (used at the end of compound words.)

अद्वय *a-dvaya, as, ā, am,* not two, without a second, only, unique; (*as*), m., N. of Buddha; (*am*), n. non-duality, unity; identity, especially the identity of Brahma with the universe or with the soul, or of spirit and matter; the ultimate truth. — *Advaya-vādin* or *advaita-vādin, ī,* m. Buddha; a Jaina; one who teaches *advaya* or identity. — *Advayānanda* (°*ya-ān*°), *as,* m., N. of an author, and of a founder of the Vaishṇava sect in Bengal, who lived at the close of the fifteenth century.

A-dvayat, an, or *a-dvayas, ās,* m., Ved. free from duplicity.

A-dvayāvin, ī, or *a-dvayu, us,* m., Ved. free from double dealing or duplicity.

अद्वार *a-dvāra, am,* n. a place without a door; an entrance which is not the proper door.

अद्विज *a-dvija, as, ā, am,* destitute of Brāhmans.

अद्वितीय *a-dvitīya, as, ā, am,* without a second, sole, unique; matchless.

अद्विषेण्य *a-dvisheṇya, as, ā, am* (rt. *dvish*), Ved. not to be disliked; not malevolent.

A-dvesha, as, ā, am, Ved. not malevolent. — *A-dvesha-rāgin, ī, iṇī, i,* free from malevolence and passionate desire.

Adveshas, ind., Ved. without malevolence, without opposition.

Adveshin, ī, iṇī, i, free from malevolence.

Adveshṭṛi, ā, m. not an enemy; a friend.

अद्वैत *a-dvaita, as, ā, am,* destitute of duality, having no duplicate; peerless; sole, unique; epithet of Vishṇu; (*am*), n. non-duality; identity, especially the identity of Brahma with the universe or with the soul, or of spirit and matter; the ultimate truth; title of an Upanishad. — *Advaitena,* ind. solely. — *Advaitānanda* (°*ta-ān*°), *as,* m. =

advayānanda, q. v. — *Advaitopanishad* (°*ta-up*°), *t*, f., N. of an Upanishad.

अध *adha* or *adhā*, ind., Ved. (much the same as *atha*, used chiefly as an inceptive particle), now; then, therefore; moreover, so much the more; and, partly. — *Adha-adha*, as well as, partly-partly. — *Adha-priya, as, ā, am*, or *adha-prī, is, is, i*, Ved. pleased or glad then.

अधः *adhaḥ*, &c. See **अधस्**.

अधन *a-dhana, as, ā, am*, destitute of wealth or property.

A-dhanya, as, ā, am, not richly supplied with corn or other produce; not prosperous; unhappy, wretched.

अधम *adhama, as, ā, am* (see etymology of *adhara*), lowest, vilest, worst; very low or vile or bad; often used at the close of comp., as in *narādhama*, the vilest or worst of men; (*as*), an unblushing paramour; (*ā*), a low or bad mistress [cf. Lat. *infimus*]. — *Adhama-bhṛita* or *adhama-bhṛitaka, as*, m. a servant of the lowest class, a porter. — *Adhamarṇa* (°*ma-ṛi*°), *as*, or *adhamarṇika, as*, m. one reduced to inferiority by debt, a debtor. — *Adhama-śākha, as* or *am* (?), m. or n. (?), N. of a region. — *Adhamāṅga* (°*ma-an*°), *am*, n. (the lowest member), the foot. — *Adhamāćāra* (°*ma-āć*°), *as, ā, am*, guilty of vile conduct. — *Adhamārdha* (°*ma-ar*°), *am*, n. the lower half, the lower part. — *Adhamārdhya, as, ā, am*, connected with or referring to the lower part.

अधमर्ण, अधमर्णिक, &c. See above, under *adhama*.

अधर *adhara, as, ā, am* (said to come from *adhas* or from a base *adh*, whence *adhas* may be derived), lower, inferior; tending downwards; low, vile; worsted, silenced; prior; (*as*), m. the lower lip, the lip; (*ā*), f. the lower region, nadir; (*am*), n. the lower part; a reply; Pudendum Muliebre [Ossetic, *dalag;* Goth. *dalathrô;* Lat. *inferus*]. — *Adhara-tas* or *adharastāt* or *adharasmāt* or *adharāt* or *adhareṇa*, ind. below, beneath; in the lower region. — *Adhara-kaṇṭha, as, am*, m. n. the lower neck. — *Adhara-kāya, as*, m. the lower part of the body. — *Adhara-pāna, am*, n. drinking the lower lip, kissing. — *Adhara-madhu, u*, n. the moisture of the lips. — *Adhara-svastika, am*, n. the nadir. — *Adharāmṛita* (°*ra-am*°), *am*, n. the nectar of the lips. — *Adharāraṇi* (°*ra-ar*°), *is*, f., Ved. the lower of the two pieces of wood used in producing fire by friction. — *Adharāvalopa* (°*ra-av*°), *as*, m. biting the lip. — *Adharottara* (°*ra-ut*°), *as, ā, am*, lower and higher; worse and better; question and answer; nearer and further; sooner and later; upside down, topsy-turvy. — *Adharoshṭha* or *adharaushṭha* (°*ra-osh*°), *as*, m. the lower lip; (*am*), n. the lower and upper lip.

Adharāk, ind. beneath, in the lower region.

Adharāćīna or *adharāćya, as, ā, am*, or *adharāñć, āṅ, āćī, āk*, Ved. tending downwards, to the nadir or the lower region, tending towards the south (or west?).

Adharāttāt, ind., Ved. below, beneath.

Adharī-kṛita, as, ā, am, worsted; invalidated.

Adharīṇa, as, ā, am, vilified.

Adharī-bhūta, as, ā, am, worsted; invalidated.

Adhare-dyus, ind. the day before yesterday; on a previous day.

Adhareya, as, ā, am, inferior in quality or worth.

अधर्म *a-dharma, as*, m. unrighteousness, injustice, irreligion, wickedness; demerit, guilt; N. of a Prajāpati, son of Brahmā, husband of Hiṃsā or Mṛishā; N. of an attendant of the sun; (*ā*), f. unrighteousness personified and represented as the bride of death. — *Adharma-ćārin, ī, iṇī, i*, practising wickedness. — *Adharma-tas*, ind. unrighteously, unjustly. — *Adharma-daṇḍana, am*, n. unjust punishment. — *Adharma-maya, as, ī, am*, made up of wickedness; downright wicked. — *Adharmātman* (°*ma-āt*°), *ā, ā, a*, having a wicked spirit or disposition. — *Adharmāstikāya* (°*ma-as*°), *as*, m. the category (*astikāya*) of *adharma*.

Adharmin, ī, iṇī, i, unrighteous, wicked, impious.

Adharmishṭha, as, ā, am, most wicked, impious.

Adharmya, as, ā, am, unlawful, contrary to law or religion, wicked.

अधवा *a-dhavā*, f. a widow (usually *vidhavā*, without a husband).

अधस् *adhas*, ind. (said to come from *adh*, see *adhara*), below, down; in the lower region; beneath, under; from under (with acc., gen., and abl.); also applied to the lower region and to the Pudendum Muliebre [cf. Lat. *infra*]. — *Adhas-taram*, ind. very far down. — *Adha-upāsana, am*, n. sexual intercourse. — *Adhaḥ-kara, as*, m. the lower part of the hand. — *Adhaḥ-kāya, as*, m. the lower part of the body. — *Adhaḥ-kṛita, as, ā, am*, put down, cast down. — *Adhaḥ-kṛishṇājinam* (°*ṇa-aj*°), ind. under the black skin. — *Adhaḥ-khanana, am*, n. undermining. — *Adhaḥ-padma, am*, n. (in architecture) a certain part of the cupola. — *Adhaḥ-pāta, as*, m. a downfall. — *Adhaḥ-pushpī*, f. (having flowers looking downwards), N. of two plants, Pimpinella Anisum and Elephantopus Scaber (or Hieracium?). — *Adhaḥ-pravāha, as*, m. a downward current. — *Adhaḥ-prastara, as*, m. seat or bed of turf or grass for persons in a state of impurity. — *Adhaḥ-prāṅ-śāyin, ī, inī, i*, sleeping on the ground, towards the east. — *Adhaś-ćara, as*, m. a thief ('creeping on the ground'). — *Adhaḥ-śaya, as, ā, am*, sleeping on the ground. — *Adhaḥ-śayya, as, ā, am*, having a peculiar couch on the ground; (*ā*), f. act of sleeping on the ground and on a peculiar couch. — *Adhaḥ-śiras, ās, ās, as*, holding the head downward; head foremost; (*as*), n., N. of a hell. — *Adhas-tala, am*, n. the room below anything. — *Adhas-pada, am*, n. the place under the feet. — *Adhaspadam*, ind. under foot. — *Adhaḥ-stha, as, ā, am*, placed low or below; inferior. — *Adhaḥ-sthita, as, ā, am*, standing below; situated below. — *Adhaḥ-svastika, am*, n. the nadir. — *Adho-'ṅśuka, am*, n. a lower garment. — *Adho-'ksha* or *adho-aksha, as, ā, am*, Ved. (situated) below the axle or under a car; (*am*), ind. under the axle. — *Adho-'ksha-ja, as*, m. an epithet of Vishṇu or Kṛishṇa; the sign Śravaṇā. — *Adho-ghaṇṭā*, f. a plant, Achyranthes Aspera. — *Adho-gata, as, ā, am*, gone down, descended. — *Adho-gati, is*, f. or *adho-gama, as*, m. or *adho-gamana, am*, n. descent, downward movement, degradation. — *Adho-gati, is, is, i*, going downwards, descending. — *Adho-gāmin, ī, inī, i* = preceding. — *Adho-ghaṇṭā*, f. a plant, Achyranthes Aspera. — *Adho-'ṅga, am*, n. the anus, Pudendum Muliebre. — *Adho-jānu*, ind. below the knee. — *Adho-jihvikā*, f. the uvula. — *Adho-dāru, u*, n. the under timber. — *Adho-diś, k*, f. the lower region, the nadir. — *Adho-dṛishṭi, is*, f. a downcast look; (*is, is, i*), having a downcast look. — *Adho-deśa, as*, m. the lower or lowest part, especially of the body. — *Adho-dvāra, am*, n. the anus, Pudendum Muliebre. — *Adho-nābham*, ind. below the navel. — *Adho-'para, am*, n. the anus. — *Adhopahāsa* (°*dhas-up*°), *as*, m., Ved. sexual intercourse. — *Adho-bandhana, am*, n. an under girth. — *Adho-bhakta, am*, n. a dose of medicine to be taken after eating. — *Adho-bhara, as, ā, am*, lower. — *Adho-bhāga, as*, m. the lower or lowest part, especially of the body. — *Adho-bhāga-dosha-hara, as, ā, am*, curing or strengthening the lower part of the body. — *Adho-bhuvana, am*, n. the lower world. — *Adho-bhūmi, is*, f. lower ground; land at the foot of a hill. — *Adho-marman, a*, n. the anus. — *Adho-mukha, as, ā* or *ī, am*, having the face downwards; headlong; upside down; (*as*), m. Vishṇu; (*ā*), f. a plant, Premna Esculenta; (*am*), n. a division of hell. — *Adho-yantra, am*, n. the lower part of an apparatus; a still. — *Adho-rakta-pitta, am*, n. discharge of blood from the anus and the urethra. — *Adho-rāma, as*, m., Ved. (a goat) having peculiar white or black marks on the lower part of the body. — *Adho-lāmba, as*, m. a plummet; the perpendicular; (*as*), m. the lower world. — *Adho-vadana, as, ā, am*, the same as *adho-mukha*. — *Adho-varćas, ās, ās, as*, powerful in the lower regions. — *Adho-vaśa, as*, m. the bottom, Pudendum Muliebre. — *Adho-vāyu, us*, m. vital air passing downwards; flatulency. — *Adho-'vekshi* (*adhas + ava + ikshin*), looking down. — *Adho-'sra-pitta*, see *adho-raktapitta*. — *Adho-'śvam*, ind. under the horse.

Adhastana, as, ī, am, lower, being underneath.

Adhastāt, ind. the same as *adhas*, q. v.

Adhastād-diś, k, f. the lower region, the nadir.

अधा *adhā*, Ved. See *adha*.

अधामार्गव *adhāmārgava, as*, m. a plant, Achyranthes Aspera.

अधारणक *a-dhāraṇaka, as, ā, am*, unable to support, unremunerative.

अधार्मिक *a-dhārmika, as, ī, am*, unjust, unrighteous, wicked.

अधार्य *a-dhārya, as, ā, am*, unfit or improper to be held or carried or kept up.

अधि 1. *adhi, is*, m. (better **आधि**, q. v.), anxiety, perplexity; f. a woman in her courses.

अधि 2. *adhi*, ind., as a prefix to verbs and nouns, expresses above, over and above, besides.

As a separable adverb or preposition; (with abl.) Ved. over; from above; from; from the presence of; for; (with gen.) Ved. among; (with loc.) Ved. over; on; at; subject to; (with acc.) over, upon, concerning. — *Adhy-adhi*, ind. on high, just above.

Adhika, as, ā, am, additional; subsequent, later; surpassing (in number or quantity or quality), superior, more numerous; abundant; excellent; supernumerary, redundant; secondary, inferior; intercalated; (*am*), n. surplus; abundance; redundancy; hyperbole: ind. exceedingly; too much; more. — *Adhikam-tu*, moreover. — *Adhika-kshaya-kārin, ī, iṇī, i*, causing excessive waste. — *Adhika-tā*, f. or *adhika-tva, am*, n. addition, excess, redundancy, preponderance. — *Adhika-tithi, is*, m. f. an intercalary lunar day. — *Adhika-danta* or *adhi-danta, as*, m. a redundant tooth which grows over another. — *Adhika-dina* or *adhi-dina, am*, n. an intercalated day. — *Adhika-māṅsārman* (°*sa-ar*°), *a*, n. proud flesh in the eye; see *adhimāṅsa*. — *Adhika-māsa, as*, m. an intercalated month. — *Adhikarddhi* (°*ka-ṛid*°), *is, is, i*, abundantly prosperous. — *Adhika-vākyokti* (°*kya-uk*°), *is*, f. exaggeration, hyperbole. — *Adhika-shāshṭika, as, ī, am*, (containing or costing) more than sixty. — *Adhika-saṃvatsara, as*, m. an intercalated month. — *Adhika-sāptatika, as, ī, am* (containing or costing) more than seventy. — *Adhikāṅga* (°*ka-an*°), *as, ā* or *ī, am*, having some redundant member or members; (*am*), n. belt worn over the coat of mail. — *Adhikādhika* (°*kha-adh*°), *as, ā, am*, outdoing one another. — *Adhikārtha* (°*ka-ar*°), *as, ā, am*, exaggerated. — *Adhikārtha-vaćana, am*, n. exaggeration, hyperbole,

अधिकर्मकर *adhi-karmakara, as*, m. or *adhi-karmakṛit, t*, m. an overseer of workmen.

अधिकल्पिन् *adhi-kalpin, ī*, m., Ved. a sharp gambler.

अधिकार्म *adhi-kārma, am*, n., N. of some place unknown.

अधिकृ *adhi-kṛi*, cl. 8. P. *-karoti, -kartum*, to place at the head, appoint; to aim at, regard; to refer or allude to; to superintend, be at the head of: A. *-kurute*, to be or become entitled to; to be or become superior to.

Adhi-karaṇa, am, n. the act of placing at the head or of subordinating government, supremacy, magistracy, court of justice; a receptacle, support; a claim; a topic, subject; (in philosophy) a substratum; a subject (e.g. *ātmā* is the *adhi-karaṇa* of knowledge); a category; a relation; (in grammar) regimen, government, comprehension, location, the sense of the locative case; relationship of words in a sentence, which agree together, either as adjective and substantive, or as subject and predicate, or as two substantives in apposition; (in rhetoric) a topic; a paragraph or minor section; (*as, ī*), m. f. one who has to superintend. — *Adhikaraṇa-bhojaka, as,* m. a judge. — *Adhikaraṇa-maṇḍapa, as, am,* m. n. the hall of justice. — *Adhikaraṇa-siddhānta, as,* m. a syllogism or conclusion which involves others. — *Adhikaraṇaitāvattva* (°*ṇa-et*°), *am,* n. fixed quantity of a substratum.

Adhi-karaṇika or better *ādhikaraṇika, as,* m. a government official; a judge or magistrate.

Adhi-karaṇya, am, n. authority, power.

Adhi-karman, a, n. superintendence. — *Adhi-karmakṛit* or *adhi-karmakara,* see s. v. — *Adhi-karma-kṛita, as,* m. person appointed to superintend an establishment.

Adhikarmika, as, m. the overseer of a market.

Adhi-kāra, as, m. authority; office; government, rule, administration, jurisdiction; royalty, prerogative; title; rank; claim, right, especially to perform sacrifices with benefit; privilege; ownership; possession; property; reference, relation; exertion, effort; a topic, subject; a paragraph or minor section; (in grammar) government; a heading-rule; (*as, ī*), m. f. having much to superintend. — *Adhikāra-stha, as, ā, am,* established in an office. — *Adhikārāḍhya* (°*ra-āḍh*°), *as, ā, am,* invested with authority.

Adhi-kārin, ī, iṇī, i, possessing authority; entitled to; fit for; (*ī*), m. a superintendent, governor; an official; a rightful claimant; a proprietor, master; one possessing the right of sacrificing; a man proficient in the Vedānta; man as the lord of creation. — *Adhikāri-tva, am,* n. or *adhikāri-tā,* f. authority; rightful claim; ownership, &c.

Adhi-kṛita, as, ā, am, placed at the head of; appointed; ruled, administered; claimed; (*as*), m. a superintendent, especially a comptroller of public accounts. — *Adhikṛita-tva, am,* n. the being engaged in or occupied with.

Adhi-kṛiti, is, f. a right, privilege; possession.

Adhi-kṛitya, ind. having placed at the head, having made the chief subject; regarding; concerning; with reference to.

अधिक्रम् *adhi-kram,* cl. 1. P. *-krāmati, -kramitum,* to ascend, mount up to; to attack, scale.

Adhi-krama, as, m. an invasion, attack.

Adhi-kramaṇa, am, n. act of invading or scaling.

अधिक्षि *adhi-kshi,* cl. 6. or cl. 2. P., Ved. *-kshiyati* or *-ksheti, -kshetum,* to be settled in or over, rest upon; to inhabit, to obtain; (occasionally *adhi-kship* occurs for this rt. by mistake.)

अधिक्षित् *adhi-kshit, t,* m., Ved. a lord, ruler (fr. rt. 2. *kshi* and not fr. *adhi-kshi* above).

अधिक्षिप् *adhi-kship,* cl. 6. P. *-kshipati, -ksheptum,* to lay upon; to bespatter; to insult, abuse, scold; to superinduce (disease); (occasionally this rt. appears to be used by mistake for *adhi-kshi,* q.v.)

Adhikshipad-abja-netra, as, ā or *ī, am,* having eyes which eclipse the lotus.

Adhi-kshipta, as, ā, am, insulted; scolded; thrown down; placed, fixed; despatched.

Adhi-kshepa, as, m. abuse, contempt; dismissal.

अधिगण् *adhi-gaṇ,* cl. 10. P. *-gaṇayati, -yitum,* to enumerate, to value highly.

अधिगम् *adhi-gam,* cl. 1. P. *-gaććhati, -gantum,* to go up to, approach, overtake; to have sexual intercourse with; to fall in with; to meet, find, discover, obtain; to accomplish; to study, read: Desid. P. *adhi-jigamishati,* to seek; A. *adhi-jigāṅsate,* to be desirous of studying or reading.

Adhi-gata, as, ā, am, found, obtained, acquired; gone over, studied, learnt.

Adhi-gantavya, as, ā, am, attainable.

Adhi-gantṛi, tā, m. one who attains or acquires.

Adhi-gama, as, m. the act of attaining, acquisition; acquirement, mastery, study, knowledge; mercantile return, profit, &c.

Adhi-gamana, am, n. acquisition; finding; acquirement, reading, study; marriage, copulation.

Adhi-gamanīya or *adhi-gamya, as, ā, am,* attainable, practicable to be learnt.

अधिगर्त्य *adhi-gartya, as, ā, am,* Ved. (found) on the driver's seat.

अधिगव *adhi-gava, as, ī, am,* Ved. (found) on or in a cow, derived from a cow.

अधिगा *adhi-gā,* cl. 2. P. A. or cl. 3. P. *-gāti, -te, -jigāti, -gātum,* to fall in with, obtain; to notice, to go over, learn, read, study, remember; to attempt, resolve: Caus. P. *adhi-gāpayati, -yitum,* to cause to go over or teach: Desid. of the Caus. *adhi-jigāpayishati,* to be desirous of teaching.

अधिगुण *adhi-guṇa, as, ā, am,* possessing superior qualities.

अधिगुप्त *adhi-gupta, as, ā, am,* protected, guarded.

अधिचङ्क्रम *adhi-ćankrama, as, ā, am,* Ved. walking or creeping over something.

अधिचर् *adhi-ćar,* cl. 1. P. *-ćarati, -ritum,* to walk or move on or over something.

Adhi-ćaraṇa, am, n. the act of walking or moving or being on or over something.

अधिचि *adhi-ći,* cl. 5. P. *-ćinoti, -ćetum,* to pile or build upon.

अधिजन् *adhi-jan,* cl. 4. A. *-jāyate, -janitum,* to be born.

Adhi-ja, as, ā, am, born, superior by birth.

Adhi-janana, am, n. birth.

अधिजानु *adhi-jānu,* ind. on the knees.

अधिजि *adhi-ji,* cl. 1. P. *-jayati, -jetum,* to win in addition, conquer.

अधिजिह्व *adhi-jihva, as,* m. or *adhi-jihvikā,* f. a peculiar swelling of the tongue or epiglottis.

अधिज्य *adhi-jya, as, ā, am,* having the bowstring (*jyā*) up or stretched, i.e. strung.

अधिज्योतिषम् *adhi-jyotisham,* ind. on the subject of light or the mundane luminaries (a chapter in the Upanishads).

अधितिष्ठति *adhi-tishṭhati.* See अधिष्ठा.

अधित्य *adhitya, as, ā, am* (fr. *adhi*), being above.

Adhityakā, f. land on the upper part of a mountain, table land.

अधिदण्डनेतृ *adhi-daṇḍa-netṛi, tā,* m. (ruler appointed to punish), epithet of Yama.

अधिदन्त *adhi-danta, as,* m. a redundant tooth which grows over another.

अधिदार्व *adhi-dārva, as, ī, am* (fr. *dāru*), wooden.

अधिदिन *adhi-dina, am,* n. an intercalated day.

अधिदेव *adhi-deva, as,* m. or *adhi-devatā,* f. a presiding or tutelary deity. — *Adhi-devam* or *adhi-devatam,* ind. concerning the gods or the deity.

अधिदेवन *adhi-devana, am,* n., Ved. part of the house allotted to gambling; the table or board for gambling.

अधिदैव *adhi-daiva* or *adhi-daivata, am,* n. a presiding or tutelary deity; the supreme deity; the divine agent operating in material objects. — *Adhi-daivam* or *adhidaivatam,* ind. on the subject of the deity or the divine agent.

Adhi-daivika, as, ī, am, spiritual.

अधिधा *adhi-dhā,* cl. 3. P. *-dadhāti, -dhātum,* to give, present; A. *-dhatte,* to acquire additionally.

अधिधृ *adhi-dhṛi,* Caus. P. *-dhārayati, -yitum,* to carry over or across.

अधिनाथ *adhi-nātha, as,* m., N. of the author of the Kālayoga-śāstra.

अधिनिधा *adhi-ni-dhā,* cl. 3. P. *-dadhāti, -dhātum,* to deposit, impart.

अधिनिर्णिज् *adhi-nirṇij, k, k, k,* Ved. veiled.

अधिनिवस् *adhi-ni-vas,* cl. 1. P. *-vasati, -vastum,* to dwell.

अधिनी *adhi-nī,* cl. 1. P. *-nayati, -netum,* to lead away from (with abl.); to raise above the ordinary measure, enhance.

अधिनृत् *adhi-nṛit,* cl. 4. P. *-nṛityati, -nartitum,* to dance upon (with acc.).

अधिप *adhi-pa, as,* m. a ruler, commander, regent, king.

Adhi-pati, is, m. same as *adhi-pa,* (in medic.) a particular part of the head, where a wound proves instantly fatal. — *Adhipati-vatī,* f., Ved., N. given to certain female divinities.

Adhi-patnī, f. a female sovereign or ruler.

Adhi-pā, ās, m., Ved. a ruler, king, sovereign.

अधिपथम् *adhi-patham,* ind. over or across a road.

अधिपांशुल *adhi-pāṅśula, as, ā, am,* become dusty from above; dusty. Also *adhi-pāṅsula.*

अधिपुरुष *adhi-purusha, as,* m. the supreme spirit.

अधिपू *adhi-pū,* cl. 9. P., Ved. *-punāti, -pavitum,* to besprinkle, to sprinkle.

अधिपूतभृतम् *adhi-pūta-bhṛitam,* ind., Ved. over the (vessel) full of purified Soma.

अधिपेषण *adhi-peshaṇa, as, ā, am,* serving to pound or grind upon.

अधिप्रजम् *adhi-prajam,* ind. on the subject of procreation as a means of preserving the world (a chapter in the Upanishads).

अधिप्रष्टियुग *adhi-prashṭi-yuga, am,* n. yoke laid upon the *prashṭi* or foremost of three horses, used on certain sacrificial occasions, to which a fourth horse could be attached; (*as*), m. the fourth horse thus attached (?).

अधिबाध् *adhi-bādh,* cl. 1. A. *-bādhate, -dhitum,* to vex, annoy.

अधिब्रू *adhi-brū,* cl. 2. P. *-bravīti, -vaktum,* to give orders to.

अधिभुज् *adhi-bhuj,* cl. 7. A. *-bhunkte, -bhoktum,* to enjoy.

अधिभू *adhi-bhū, ūs,* m. (rt. *bhū* with *adhi*), a master, a superior.

Adhi-bhūta, am, n. the spiritual or fine substratum of material or gross objects; the all-penetrating influence of the supreme spirit; the supreme spirit himself; nature. — *Adhi-bhūtam,* ind. on the subject of material objects (a chapter in the Upanishads).

Adhi-bhautika (better *ādhibhautika,* q. v.), *as, ī, am,* natural (?).

अधिभोजन *adhi-bhojana, am,* n. an additional gift.

अधिमन्थ *adhi-mantha* or *adhī-mantha, as,* m. (churning of the eyes), severe ophthalmia.

Adhi-manthana, am, n., Ved. friction for producing fire; *(as, ā, am),* suitable for such friction (as wood).

Adhi-manthita, as, ā, am, suffering from ophthalmia.

अधिमांस *adhi-māṇsa* or *adhi-māṇsaka, as,* m. proud flesh or cancer, especially in the eyes or the back part of the gums. — *Adhimāṇsārman* (°*sa-ar*°), *a,* n. ophthalmic disease produced by proud flesh or cancer.

अधिमात्र *adhi-mātra, as, ā, am,* past or above measure, excessive; *(am),* ind. on the subject of prosody. — *Adhimātra-kāruṇika, as,* m. (exceedingly merciful), N. of a Mahā-brāhmaṇa among the Buddhists.

अधिमास *adhi-māsa, as,* m. an intercalary month.

अधिमुक्ति *adhi-mukti, is,* f. (with Buddhists) intuition (?); implicit faith (?). — *Adhimukti-sāra, as, ā, am,* wholly given to intuition or to implicit faith (?).

Adhi-muktika, as, m. (with Buddhists) an epithet of Mahā-kāla.

अधिमुह्य *adhi-muhya, as,* m., N. of Śākya-muni in one of his thirty-four former births.

अधियज्ञ *adhi-yajña, as,* m. the chief or principal sacrifice; influence or agency affecting a sacrifice; *(as, ā, am),* relating to a sacrifice; *(am),* ind. on the subject of sacrifices.

अधियत् *adhi-yat,* cl. 1. A., Ved. *-yatate, -titum,* to fasten, fix, stick.

अधियम् *adhi-yam,* cl. 1. P. *-yacchati, -yantum,* to give, present.

अधिया *adhi-yā,* cl. 2. P. *-yāti, -tum,* to escape.

अधियाङ्ग *adhiyāṅga, am,* n. a redundant limb; (better *adhikāṅga.*)

अधियोध *adhi-yodha, as,* m. a warrior who fights in the first lines (?).

अधिरज्जु *adhi-rajju, us, us, u,* Ved. carrying a rope, fastening, fettering.

अधिरथ *adhi-ratha, as, ā, am,* being upon or over a car; *(as),* m. a charioteer; N. of a charioteer who was a prince of Aṅga and Karṇa's foster-father; *(am),* n. a cart-load.

Adhi-rathi, is, m. (various reading for *uḍa-rathi*), the sun (?); the sea (?).

Adhi-rathyam, ind. on the high road.

अधिराज् *adhi-rāj, ṭ,* m. a supreme king, emperor.

Adhi-rāja, as, or *adhi-rājan, ā,* m. an emperor.

Adhi-rājya or *adhi-rāshṭra, am,* n. supremacy, imperial dignity; an empire; N. of a country. — *Adhirājya-bhāj, k,* m. possessor of imperial dignity.

अधिरुक्म *adhi-rukma, as, ā, am,* wearing gold.

अधिरुह् *adhi-ruh,* cl. 1. P. or poet. A. *adhi-rohati, -te, -roḍhum,* to rise above, to ascend, mount: Caus. *-ropayati, -yitum,* to raise, place above.

Adhi-rūḍha, as, ā, am, ascended, mounted. — *Adhirūḍha-samādhi-yoga, as, ā, am,* engaged in profound meditation.

Adhi-ropaṇa, am, n. the act of raising or causing to mount.

Adhi-ropita, as, ā, am, raised, placed above.

Adhi-roha, as, m. ascent, mounting, overtopping.

Adhi-rohaṇa, am, n. act of ascending or mounting or rising above; *(ī),* f. a ladder, flight of steps.

Adhi-rohin, ī, iṇī, i, rising above, ascending, &c.; *(iṇī),* f. a ladder, flight of steps.

अधिलोकम् *adhi-lokam,* ind. on the subject of the universe (a chapter in the Upanishads). — *Adhi-loka-nātha, as,* m. lord of the universe.

अधिवच् *adhi-vac,* cl. 2. P., Ved. *-vakti, -vaktum,* to speak in favour of; to advocate; to side with.

Adhi-vaktṛi, tā, m., Ved. an advocate; a comforter; an orator.

Adhi-vacana, am, n. advocacy; speaking in favour of; an appellation, epithet.

Adhi-vāka, as, m., Ved. advocacy, protection.

अधिवप् *adhi-vap,* cl. 1. A., Ved. *-vapate, -vaptum,* to put on; to shatter.

अधिवस् 1. *adhi-vas,* cl. 1. P. *-vasati, -vastum,* to inhabit; to settle or perch upon.

1. *adhi-vāsa, as,* m. an inhabitant, a neighbour; one who dwells above; a habitation, abode, settlement, site; sitting before a person's house without taking food till he ceases to oppose or refuse a demand, commonly called 'sitting in dharṇā;' pertinacity; (for 2. 3. *adhi-vāsa,* see below.) — *Adhivāsa-bhūmi, is,* f. a dwelling-place, settlement.

1. *adhi-vāsana, am,* n. act of causing the divinity to take up its abode in an image; sitting in dharṇā [cf. s. v. *adhi-vāsa* above]. (For 2. *adhi-vāsana,* see below.)

Adhi-vāsin, ī, inī, i, inhabiting, settled in. — *Adhivāsi-tā,* f. settled residence.

Adhy-ushita, see s. v.

अधिवस् 2. *adhi-vas,* cl. 2. A. *-vaste, -vasitum,* to put on or over (as clothes &c.).

Adhi-vastra, as, ā, am, clothed.

2. *adhi-vāsa* or *adhī-vāsa, as,* m. an upper garment, mantle.

1. *adhi-vāsita, as, ā, am,* invested with, clothed with; see also s. v. *adhi-vās* below.

अधिवाज्य *adhi-vājya, am,* n., N. of a country; correctly *adhi-rājya.*

अधिवास् *adhi-vās,* cl. 10. P. *-vāsayati, -yitum,* to scent, perfume.

3. *adhi-vāsa, as,* m. application of perfumes or fragrant cosmetics. (For 1. 2. *adhi-vāsa,* see above.)

2. *adhi-vāsana, am,* n. application of perfumes, &c.; touching a vessel containing fragrant objects, that have been presented to an idol, as a ceremony; preliminary purification of the image.

2. *adhi-vāsita, as, ā, am,* scented.

अधिवाहन *adhi-vāhana, as,* m., N. of a man, said to be a son of Aṅga.

अधिविकर्तन *adhi-vi-kartana, am,* n. the act of cutting off.

अधिविक्रम् *adhi-vi-kram,* cl. 1. A. *-kramate, -mitum,* to step forth towards or for some one.

अधिविद् *adhi-vid,* cl. 6. P. *-vindati, -veditum,* to obtain; to marry in addition to.

Adhi-vinnā, f. a wife whose husband has married again; a neglected or superseded wife.

Adhi-vettavyā or *adhi-vedanīyā* or *adhi-vedyā,* f. a wife in addition to whom it is proper to marry another.

Adhi-vettṛi, tā, m. a husband who marries an additional wife.

Adhi-vedana, am, n. marrying an additional wife.

अधिविद्यम् *adhi-vidyam,* ind. on the subject of science (a chapter in the Upanishads).

अधिवेदम् *adhi-vedam,* ind. concerning the Veda.

अधिशी *adhi-śī,* cl. 2. A. *-śete, -śayitum,* to lie down upon, to lie upon, to sleep upon.

Adhi-śayana, as, ā, am, lying on, sleeping on.

Adhi-śayita, as, ā, am, recumbent upon; used for lying or sleeping upon.

अधिश्रि *adhi-śri,* cl. 1. P. *-śrayati, -yitum,* Ved. *-śrayitavai,* to ascend; to put on fire, make hot.

Adhi-śraya, as, m. a receptacle.

Adhi-śrayaṇa, am, n. act or ceremony of putting (a kettle) on the fire; *(ī),* f. a fire-place, oven. — *Adhi-śrayaṇīya, as, ā, am,* relating to or connected with the Adhi-śrayaṇa.

Adhi-śrita, as, ā, am, put on the fire (as a pot).

अधिषवण *adhi-shavaṇa, am,* n. (fr. rt. *su* with *adhi*), Ved. hand-press for extracting and straining the Soma juice; *(as, ā, am),* used for extracting and straining the Soma juice.

अधिष्ठा *adhi-shṭhā* (*adhi-sthā*), cl. 1. P. or poet. A. *-tishṭhati, -te, -shṭhātum,* to stand upon, depend; to inhabit, abide; to be, stand; to superintend, govern; to step over or across; to overcome; to ascend, mount.

Adhi-shṭhātṛi, tā, trī, tṛi, superintending, presiding, governing, tutelary; *(ā),* m. a ruler; especially the supreme ruler, or Providence personified and identified with one or another of the Hindū gods; a chief; a protector.

Adhi-shṭhāna, am, n. standing by, being at hand, approach; standing or resting upon; a basis, base; a wheel (as the basis of a car); a position, site, residence, abode, seat; a settlement, town; government, authority, power, dominion; a precedent, rule; a benediction. — *Adhishṭhāna-śarīra, am,* n. (in Sāṅkhya phil.) a body which forms the medium between the subtle and the gross body.

Adhi-shṭhāyaka, as, ā, am, governing, superintending, guarding.

Adhi-shṭhita, as, ā, am, settled; inhabited; superintended; regulated; appointed; superintending.

अधिस्त्रि *adhi-stri,* ind. concerning a woman or a wife. — *Adhi-strī,* f. a superior or distinguished woman.

अधिहरि *adhi-hari,* ind. concerning Hari.

अधी *adhī* (*adhi-i*), cl. 2. P. *adhy-eti, -tum,* to meet with, attain, notice, observe, understand; to mind, remember, care for, long for; to know, know by heart; to go over; study, learn, read, recite, declare; A. *adhīte,* to study, learn by heart, read, recite, declare: Caus. P. *adhy-āpayati, -yitum,* to make one read or study, teach, instruct; Desid. of the Caus. *adhy-āpipayishati,* to be desirous of teaching: Desid. *adhīshishati,* to be desirous of teaching.

Adhīta, as, ā, am, attained; studied, read; well read, learned. — *Adhīta-veda, as,* m. one who has studied the Vedas or whose studies are finished.

Adhīti, is, f. perusal, study; Ved. desire, recollection.

Adhītin, ī, inī, i, well read, proficient.

Adhītya, ind. having gone over, having studied.

Adhīyat, an, atī, at, remembering, proficient in study.

Adhīyāna, as, m. a student; one who goes over the Veda either as a student or a teacher.

Adhy-ayana, adhy-āpaka, adhy-āpana, adhy-etavya, adhy-etṛi, &c., see s. v.

अधीकार *adhī-kāra* = *adhi-kāra,* q. v.

अधीक्ष *adhīksh* (*adhi-īksh*), cl. 1. A. *adhīkshate, -kshitum,* to discover.

अधीन *adhīna, as, ā, am* (fr. *adhi*), subject, subservient (generally forming the last member of a compound). — *Adhīna-tā,* f. or *adhīna-tva, am,* n. subjection, dependence.

अधीमन्थ *adhī-mantha* = *adhi-mantha,* q. v.

अधीर *a-dhīra, as, ā, am,* not fixed, moveable; confused; deficient in calm self-command; excited, excitable; fitful, capricious; querulous; weak-minded, foolish; *(ā),* f. lightning; a capricious or bellicose mistress. — *Adhīra-tā,* f. want of confidence.

अधीवास *adhī-vāsa* = *adhi-vāsa,* q. v.

Adhī-vāsas, ind. over the garment.

अधीश *adhīśa* (*adhi-īśa*), *as,* m. a lord, a master over (others).

Adhīśvara (*adhi-īś*°), *as,* m. a supreme lord or king, an emperor; (among the Jainas) an Arhat.

अधीष्ट *adhīshṭa* (*adhi-ishṭa*), *as, ā, am*, solicited, honorary; (*am*), n. solicitation; honorary office.

अधुना *a-dhunā*, ind. (fr. the pronom. base *a*, substituted for *idam*), at this time, now.
Adhunātana, as, ī, am, belonging to or extending over the present time.

अधुर *a-dhura, as, ā, am*, not laden.

अधूमक *a-dhūmaka, as, ā, am*, smokeless.

अधृत *a-dhṛita, as, ā, am*, not held, unrestrained, uncontrolled; (*as*), m. an epithet of Vishṇu.
A-dhṛiti, is, f. want of firmness or fortitude; laxity, absence of control or restraint; incontinence; (*is, is, i*), unsteady.

अधृष्ट *a-dhṛishṭa, as, ā, am* (rt. *dhṛish*), not bold, modest; not put down, invincible, irresistible.
A-dhṛishya, as, ā, am, unassailable, invincible; unapproachable; proud; (*ā*), f., N. of a river.

अधेनु *a-dhenu, us, us, u*, Ved. yielding no milk or advantage; not nourishing.

अधैर्य *a-dhairya, am*, n. want or loss of calm self-command; paroxysm of excitement; excitability; (*as, ā, am*), deficient in self-command; swayed by excitement or violent feeling.

अधो *adho*. See under *adhas*.

अध्यंस *adhy-aṇsa, as, ā, am*, (placed) on the shoulder.

अध्यक्त *adhy-akta, as, ā, am* (rt. *añj*), equipped, prepared.

अध्यक्ष *adhy-aksha, as, ā, am*, observable; exercising supervision; (*as*), m. an eye-witness; an inspector, superintendent; N. of a plant, Mimusops Kauki (*Kshīrikā*).

अध्यक्षरम् *adhy-aksharam*, ind. on the subject of syllables; above all syllables (as the mystic *om*).

अध्यग्नि *adhy-agni*, ind. over or by the nuptial fire, property given to the bride. — *Adhyagni-kṛita, am*, n. property given to the wife at the wedding. — *Adhyagny-upāgata, am*, n. property received by a wife at the wedding.

अध्यञ्च् *adhy-añć, an, īćī, ak*, tending upwards, eminent, superior.

अध्यण्डा *adhyaṇḍā*, f., N. of two plants, Cowage (Carpopogon Pruriens) and Flacourtia Cataphracta.

अध्यधिक्षेप *adhy-adhikshepa, as*, m. excessive censure; gross abuse.

अध्यधीन *adhy-adhīna, as, ā, am*, completely subject or dependent, as a slave.

अध्यय *adhy-aya* or better *adhy-āya, as*, m. (fr. *adhi-i*, see *adhī*), a lesson, lecture, chapter.
Adhy-ayana, am, n. reading, studying, especially the Vedas (one of the six duties of a Brāhman). — *Adhyayana-tapasī*, n. nom. du. study and penance. — *Adhyayana-puṇya, am*, n. religious merit acquired by studying.
Adhy-ayanīya, as, ā, am, fit or proper to be read or studied.

अध्यर्ध *adhy-ardha, as, ā, am*, having an additional half, i. e. one and a half; (in compounds synonymous with) *adhy-ardhaka, as, ikā, am*, amounting to or worth one and a half. — *Adhyardha-kaṇsa, as, am*, m. n. one and a half kaṇsa; (*as, ī, am*), amounting to or worth one and a half kaṇsa. — *Adhyardha-kākiṇika, as, ā, am*, amounting to or worth one and a half kākiṇī. — *Adhyardha-kārshāpaṇa* or *adhyardha-kārshāpaṇika, as, ī, am*, amounting to or worth one and a half kārshāpaṇa. — *Adhyardha-khārīka, as, ā, am*, amounting to or worth one and a half khārī. — *Adhyardha-paṇya, as, ā, am*, amounting to or worth one and a half paṇa. — *Adhyardha-pādya, as, ā, am*, amounting to one foot and a half. — *Adhyardha-pratika, as, ī, am*, amounting to one and a half kārshāpaṇa. — *Adhyardha-māshya, as, ā, am*, amounting to or worth one and a half māsha. — *Adhyardha-viṇśatikīna, as, ā, am*, amounting to or worth one and a half score or thirty. — *Adhyardha-śata* or *adhyardha-śatya, as, ā, am*, amounting to or bought with one hundred and fifty. — *Adhyardha-śatamāna* or *adhyardha-śātamāna, as, ī, am*, amounting to or worth one and a half śatamāna. — *Adhyardha-śāṇa* or *adhyardha-śāṇya, as, ā, am*, amounting to or worth one and a half śāṇa. — *Adhyardha-śūrpa, as, ī, am*, amounting to or worth one and a half śūrpa. — *Adhyardha-sahasra* or *adhyardha-sāhasra, as, ī, am*, amounting to or worth one thousand five hundred. — *Adhyardha-suvarṇa* or *adhyardha-sauvarṇika, as, ī, am*, amounting to or worth one and a half suvarṇa.

अध्यर्बुद *adhy-arbuda* or *adhy-arvuda, am*, n. a tumour, goitre (dating from the time of birth).

अध्यवसो *adhy-ava-so*, cl. 4. P. *-syati, -sātum*, to undertake, grapple with, attempt; to determine, consider.
Adhy-ava-sāna, am, n. determining; attempt, effort, exertion; energy, perseverance; (in rhetoric) concise and forcible language.
Adhy-ava-sāya, as, m. = the preceding; (in philosophy) mental effort, apprehension. — *Adhyavasāya-yukta, as, ā, am*, or *adhyavasāyin, ī, inī, i*, resolute.
Adhy-ava-sāyita, as, ā, am, attempted.
Adhy-ava-sita, as, ā, am, mentally apprehended, ascertained, determined.

अध्यवहनन *adhy-avahanana, as, ā, am*, Ved. serving as an implement on which anything is peeled.

अध्यशन *adhy-aśana, am*, n. eating too soon after a meal, before the last meal is digested.

अध्यस् *adhy-as*, cl. 4. P. *-asyati, -situm*, to throw or place over or upon.
Adhy-asta, as, ā, am, placed over; disguised; supposed.

अध्यस्थि *adhy-asthi, i*, n. a bone growing over another.

अध्यह् *adhy-ah*, Defect. Perf. *-āha*, to address; to bless.

अध्याक्रम् *adhy-ā-kram*, cl. 1. P. *-krāmati, -kramitum*, to attack; to fix upon, occupy.

अध्यागम् *adhy-ā-gam*, cl. 1. P. *-gaććhati, -gantum*, to fall in with, meet with.

अध्याचर् *adhy-ā-ćar*, cl. 1. P. *-ćarati, -ritum*, to bestride, occupy as a seat.

अध्याण्डा *adhy-āṇḍā*, f., N. of a plant. See *adhyaṇḍā*.

अध्यात्म *adhy-ātma, am*, n. the supreme spirit; (*as, ā, am*), own, belonging to self; (*am*), ind. concerning self or individual personality. — *Adhyātma-ćetas, ās*, m. one who meditates on the supreme spirit. — *Adhy-ātma-jñāna, am*, n. or *adhyātma-vidyā*, f. knowledge of the supreme spirit or of *ātman*. — *Adhy-ātma-dṛiś, k*, or *adhyātma-vid, t*, m. a sage proficient in that knowledge. — *Adhyātma-rati, is*, m. a man delighting in the contemplation of the supreme spirits or of *ātman*. — *Adhyātma-rāmāyaṇa, am*, n. a Rāmāyaṇa, in which everything is referred to the universal spirit; it forms part of the Brahmāṇḍa-Purāṇa. — *Adhyātma-śāstra, am*, n., N. of a work. — *Adhyātmottara-kāṇḍa* (°*ma-ut*°), *am*, n., N. of the last book of the Adhyātmarāmāyaṇa.
Adhy-ātmika or better *ādhyātmika, as, ī, am*, connected with or relating to the soul or the supreme spirit.

अध्यापक *adhy-āpaka, as*, m. (fr. *adhi-i*, see *adhī*), a teacher or professor, especially of sacred knowledge; N. of a priest (?). — *Adhyāpakodita* (°*ka-ud*°), *as*, m. entitled an *adhyāpaka*, styled a professor.
Adhy-āpana, am, n. instruction or lecturing, especially on sacred knowledge.
Adhy-āpayitṛi, tā, m. a teacher.
Adhy-āpita, as, ā, am, instructed.
Adhy-āpya, as, ā, am, fit or proper to be instructed.
Adhy-āya, as, m. a lesson, lecture, chapter; reading; proper time for reading or for a lesson; (at the close of comp. words) a reader, student, as *Vedādhyāya*, a reader or student of the Vedas. — *Adhyāya-śata-pāṭha, as*, m. an index of the One Hundred Chapters, N. of a work.
Adhyāyin, ī, inī, i, studious, engaged in reading or study.

अध्यारुह् *adhy-ā-ruh*, cl. 1. P., poet. A. *-rohati, -te, -roḍhum*, to ascend, mount: Caus. *-ropayati, -yitum*, to cause or order to mount.
Adhy-ārūḍha, as, ā, am, mounted, ascended; (with the instr.) above, superior; (with the abl.) below, inferior.
Adhy-āropa, as, m. or *adhy-āropaṇa, am*, n. act of making one mount or of raising; act of attributing, especially through mistake.
Adhy-āropita, as, ā, am, falsely attributed; hyperbolical.

अध्यावस् *adhy-ā-vas*, cl. 1. P. *-vasati, -vastum*, to inhabit, dwell in (with acc. or loc.).

अध्यावाप *adhy-ā-vāpa, as*, m. (rt. *vap*), the act of sowing or scattering upon.

अध्यावाहनिक *adhy-ā-vāhanika, am*, n. that part of a wife's property which she receives when on a visit to her parents.

अध्यास् *adhy-ās*, cl. 2. A. *-āste, -situm*, to sit down or (of beasts) lie down upon, to settle upon; to occupy as one's seat or habitation; to get into, enter upon; to be directed to or upon; to affect, concern; to influence, rule; to cohabit with: Caus. P. *adhy-āsayati, -yitum*, to make (one) sit down: Des. *adhy-āsisishate*, to be about to get upon (a seat &c.).
Adhy-āsana, am, n. act of sitting down upon; presiding over; a seat, settlement.
Adhyāsa-yoga, as, m. (with Buddhists) a kind of meditation (?).
Adhy-āsita, as, ā, am, seated on; seated in the presidential chair; settled, inhabited.
Adhy-āsin, ī, inī, i, sitting down or seated upon.
Adhy-āsīna, as, ā, am, seated upon.

अध्यास *adhy-āsa, as*, m. (rt. 2. *as*), imposing; erroneously attributing; an appendage.

अध्याहरण *adhy-ā-haraṇa, am*, n. or *adhy-ā-hāra, as*, m. (rt. *hṛi*), act of supplying (elliptical language); supplement; act of inferring or arguing.
Adhy-āharaṇīya or *adhy-āhartavya* or *adhy-āhārya, as, ā, am*, proper to be supplied; proper to be argued.
Adhy-āhṛita, as, ā, am, supplied, argued.

अध्युषित *adhy-ushita, as, ā, am* (rt. *vas*, see 1. *adhi-vas*), inhabited; obtained (?). — *Adhy-ushitāśva* or *adhyushitāśva* (°*ta-aś*°), *as*, m., N. of a prince descended from Daśaratha.

अध्युष्ट *adhy-ushṭa, as, ā, am* (rt. *ush* = *ućć h?*), coiled up three and a half times. — *Adhy-ushṭa-valaya, as*, m. (snake) forming a ring coiled up three and a half times.

अध्युष्ट्र *adhy-ushṭra, as*, m. conveyance borne or drawn by camels.

अध्यूढ *adhy-ūḍha, as, ā, am* (past pass. part. fr. rt. *vah* with *adhi*), raised, exalted; affluent; abundant; (*as*), m. Śiva; (*ā*), f. a wife whose husband has married an additional wife.

अध्यूध्नी *adhy-ūdhnī*, f. (fr. *ūdhan* or *ūdhas*,

udder, with *adhi*), a tubular vessel above the udder, or above the scrotum, i. e. urethra (?).

अध्यूषिवस् *adhy-ūshivas, ān, ushī, as* (perf. part. of rt. *vas* with *adhi*), having inhabited.

अध्यूह् *adhy-ūh*, cl. 1. P. *-ūhati, -hitum*, to lay on, overlay; to place upon, to raise above.

Adhy-ūhana, am, n. putting on a layer (of ashes or cinders).

अध्यृध् *adhy-ṛidh*, cl. 5. P. *-ṛidhnati, -ardhitum*, to expand.

अध्येतव्य *adhy-etavya* or *adhy-eya, as, ā, am* (fr. rt. *i* with *adhi*, see *adhī*), fit or proper to be studied or read.

Adhy-etṛi, t, ā, m. a student, reader.

Adhy-eshyamāṇa, as, ā, am (fut. part.), intending to study.

अध्येध् *adhy-edh*, cl. 1. A. *-edhate, -dhitum*, to increase, prosper.

अध्येषण *adhy-eshaṇa, am, ā*, n. f. (fr. rt. 3. *ish* with *adhi*), solicitation, entreaty.

अध्रि *a-dhri, is, is, i* (rt. *dhṛi*), unrestrained, irresistible. — *Adhri-gu, us*, plur. *āvas*, m., Ved. irresistible; N. of a heavenly killer of victims; N. of a formula concluding with an invocation of Agni. — *Adhri-ja, as, ā, am*, Ved. irresistible. — *Adhri-pushpalikā*, f. a species of the Pān plant, Piper Betel.

A-dhriyamāṇa, as, ā, am (pres. pass. part. of rt. *dhṛi* with *a*), not held; not to be got hold of, not forthcoming, not surviving or existing, dead.

अध्रुव *a-dhruva, as, ā, am*, not fixed, not permanent; uncertain, doubtful; separable, admitting of severance without disastrous effects.

अध्रुष *adhrusha, as*, m. quinsy, a kind of sore throat (etymology doubtful).

अध्वन् *adhvan, ā*, m. (said to be from *ad*, 'to eat,' *d* being changed to *dh*, or fr. rt. *at*), a road, way, orbit; a journey, course; distance; time; means, method, resource; the zodiac (?), sky, air; a place; a recension of the Vedas and the school upholding it; assault (?). *Adhvan* becomes *adhva, as*, at the end of some compounds. — *Adhva-ga, as, ā, am*, travelling; (*as*), m. a traveller; a camel, a mule; the sun; (*ā*), f. Gangā (the river). — *Adhva-gat, t*, m. a traveller. — *Adhva-gatyanta* or *adhva-gantavya, as*, m. measure of length applicable to roads. — *Adhvaga-bhogya, as*, m. (traveller's delight), N. of a tree (Spondias Mangifera). — *Adhva-gamana, am*, n. act of travelling. — *Adhva-gāmin, ī, inī, i*, wayfaring. — *Adhva-jā*, f. a plant, also called Svarṇulī. — *Adhva-pati, is*, m. (lord of the orbits or of the zodiac), the sun. — *Adhva-ratha, as*, m. a travelling car. — *Adhva-śalya, as*, m. a plant, Achyranthes Aspera. — *Adhvādhipa* (°*va-adh*°) or *adhveśa* (°*va-īś*°), *as*, m. officer in charge of the police on the public roads.

Adhvanīna or *adhvanya, as, ā, am*, speeding on a journey; (*as*), a traveller.

Adhvayat, an, antī, at, Ved. running, quick.

अध्वर *a-dhvara, as, ā, am* (fr. *a*, not, and *dhvara*, crookedness, injury), Ved. not crooked, unbroken, uninterrupted; durable; sound; intent; (*as*), m. a religious or liturgical service, a sacrifice, especially the Soma sacrifice; N. of a Vasu; of the chief of a family; (*am*), n. sky or air. — *Adhvara-karman, a*, n. performance of the Adhvara or connected with it. — *Adhvara-kalpā*, f., N. of an optional sacrifice (Kāmyeshṭi). — *Adhvara-kāṇḍa, am*, n. title of the book in the Śatapatha-Brāhmaṇa which refers to Adhvaras. — *Adhvara-kṛit, t*, m. performing an Adhvara. — *Adhvara-ga, as, ā, am*, intended for an Adhvara. — *Adhvara-dīkshaṇīyā*, f. consecration connected with the Adhvara. — *Adhvara-prāyaścitti, is*, f. expiation connected with the Adhvara. — *Adhvara-vat, ān, atī, at*, containing the word Adhvara. — *Adhvara-śrī, īs*, m., Ved. glory (i. e. patron) of the Adhvara. — *Adhvara-samishṭa-yajus, us*, n., N. of an aggregate of nine libations connected with the Adhvara. — *Adhvara-stha, as, ā, am*, or *adhvare-shṭhā, ās, ās, am*, Ved. standing at (or engaged in) an Adhvara.

Adhvarayu, etymological substitute for *adhvaru*.

Adhvarīya or *adhvarya*, nom. (fr. *adhvara*), P. *adhvarīyati* or *adhvaryati*, P. to be desirous of having an Adhvara performed; to institute one (?).

Adhvaryu, us, m. one who institutes an Adhvara; any officiating priest; technical name of a priest of a particular class (as distinguished from the *Hotṛi*, the *Udgātṛi*, and the *Brahman* classes). The Adhvaryavas "had to measure the ground, to build the altar, to prepare the sacrificial vessels, to fetch wood and water, to light the fire, to bring the animal and immolate it." Whilst engaged in these duties, they had to repeat, without interruption or mistake, the hymns of the Yajur-veda; hence that Veda itself is also called Adhvaryu or Adhvaryavas, and the latter word also means adherents of the Yajur-veda. — *Adhvaryu-kāṇḍa, am*, n. title of a book of mantras or prayers intended for Adhvaryavas. — *Adhvaryu-kratu, us*, m. sacrificial act performed by the Adhvaryu. — *Adhvaryu-veda, as*, m. the Yajur-veda.

अध्वस्मन् *a-dhvasman, ā, ā, a*, Ved. imperishable (?); not causing to fall (?); unveiled, open to the light (?).

अध्वान्त *a-dhvānta, am*, n. (not positive darkness), twilight, gloom, shade. — *Adhvānta-śātrava, as*, m. a plant, Cassia Fistula or Bignonia Indica (not an enemy to darkness, i. e. blossoming in the shade).

अन् 1. *an-*, occasionally अन *ana-*, (before a vowel) the substitute for 3. *a*, or *a* privative.

(Before terminations commencing with vowels) the substitute for the pronominal base *a*, as in *anena* (*ana-ina*).

अन् 2. *an*, cl. 2. P. *aniti* or Ved. *anati*, *āna, anishyati, ānīt, anitum*, to breathe, gasp, move, go, live [cf. Gr. ἄνεμος; Lat. *animus*]: Caus. *ānayati, -yitum*: Desid. *aninishati*.

Ana, as, m. breath, spiration.

Anana, am, n. breathing, living.

अनंश *an-anśa, as, ā, am*, or *an-anśin, ī, inī, i*, portionless; not entitled to a share in an inheritance.

अनंशुमत्फला *an-anśumat-phalā*, f. a plantain (the same as *anśumat-phalā*).

अनक *anaka, as, ā, am*, inferior = *aṇaka*, q. v.

अनकदुन्दुभ *anaka-dundubha, as*, m. a name of Kṛishṇa's grandfather. — *Anaka-dundubhi* or better *ānakadundubhi, is*, m. a name given to Kṛishṇa's father, Vasudeva; (a name said to be derived from the beating of drums at his birth.)

अनकस्मात् *an-akasmāt*, ind. not without a cause or an object; not accidentally, not suddenly.

अनक्ष् *an-aksh, k, k, k*, Ved. or *an-aksha, as, ī, am*, sightless, blind.

An-aksht, n. a bad eye.

अनक्षर *an-akshara, as, ā, am*, unfit to be uttered; unable to articulate.

अनक्षस्तम्भम् *an-aksha-stambham*, ind. so as not to interfere with the axle-tree.

अनगार *an-agāra, as*, m. (houseless), an ascetic who has adopted a houseless or vagrant condition.

An-agārikā, f. the houseless life of such an ascetic.

अनग्न *a-nagna, as, ā, am*, not naked. — *Anagna-tā*, f. the not being naked.

अनग्नि *an-agni, is*, m. non-fire; substance differing from fire; absence of fire; (*is, is, i*), requiring no fire or fire-place; not maintaining the sacred fire, irreligious; unmarried; dispensing with the use of fire; dyspeptic. — *An-agni-tra, as, ā, am*, or *an-agni-trā, ās, ās, am*, not maintaining the sacred fire, irreligious (?); not enjoying Agni's protection (?). — *An-agni-dagdha, as, ā, am*, not burnt with fire; not burnt on the funeral pile (but buried); (*ās*), m. pl., N. of a class of manes. — *Anagni-shvātta, ās*, m. pl. = preceding; see *agni-dagdha* and *agni-shvātta* under *agni*.

अनघ *an-agha, as, ā, am*, sinless, innocent; faultless; handsome; (*as*), m. white mustard; N. or epithet of various persons, especially Śiva. — *Anaghāshṭamī* (°*gha-ash*°), f., N. of the fifty-fifth Adhyāya of the Bhavishyottara-Purāṇa.

अनङ्कुश *an-ankuśa, as, ā, am*, unrestrained, ungovernable.

अनङ्ग *an-anga, as, ā, am*, incorporeal; (*as*), m. Love, N. of Kāma, the god of love, so called because he was reduced to ashes by a flash from the eye of Śiva, for having attempted to disturb his penance by filling him with love for Pārvatī; (*am*), n. the ether, air, sky; the mind, *manas*; that which is not the *anga*, q. v. — *Ananga-krīḍā*, f., N. of a metre of two verses, the first containing sixteen long syllables, the second thirty-two short ones. — *Ananga-devī*, f., N. of a queen-consort of Kashmīr. — *Ananga-pāla, as*, m., N. of a king's chamberlain at Kashmīr. — *An-angam-ejaya, as, ā, am*, not shaking the body (?). — *Ananga-ranga*, N. of an erotic work. — *Ananga-lekhā*, f. a love letter; N. of a queen of Kashmīr. — *Ananga-śekhara, as*, m., N. of a metre of four verses, each containing fifteen iambi. — *Ananga-senā*, f., N. of a dramatic personage. — *Anangāpīḍa* (°*ga-āp*°), *as*, m., N. of a king of Kashmīr. — *Anangāsuhṛid* (°*ga-as*°), *t*, m. Kāma's enemy, i. e. Śiva.

An-angaka, am, n. the mind.

अनङ्गुरि *an-anguri, is, is, i*, destitute of fingers.

अनच्छ *an-aććha, as, ā, am*, not pellucid, turbid.

अनजका *an-ajakā* or *an-ajikā*, f. a miserable little goat.

अनञ्जन *an-añjana, as, ā, am*, free from collyrium or pigment or paint; (*am*), n. the sky, atmosphere; Vishṇu.

अनडुह् *anaḍ-uh, ḍvān*, m. (fr. *anas*, a cart, q. v., and *vah*, to drag), an ox; bull; the sign Taurus. — *Anaḍuj-jihvā*, f. a plant, also called Gojihvā, Elephantopus Scaber. — *Anaḍud-da, as*, m. donor of a bull or ox. — *Anaḍuhī* or *anaḍvāhī*, f. a cow.

Anaḍutka, as, ā, am, having oxen (?).

Anaḍuha, as, m., N. of the chief of a certain Gotra.

अनणु *an-aṇu, us, us* or *vī, u*, not minute or fine, coarse; (*us*), m. coarse grain, peas, &c.

अनत *a-nata, as, ā, am*, not bent, not bowed down; erect; stiff; haughty.

अनति- *an-ati-*, not very-, not too-, not past-. (Words commencing with *an-ati* are so easily analysed by referring to *ati*, &c., that few need be enumerated). — *An-ati-krama, as*, m. moderation, propriety. — *An-atikramaṇīya, as, ā, am*, not to be avoided, not to be transgressed, inviolable. — *An-atidṛiśya, as, ā, am*, Ved. not transparent, opaque; (or equivalent to *aty-adṛiśya*), quite indiscernible. — *An-atidbhuta, as*, m., Ved. unsurpassed. — *An-ativṛitti, is*, f. congruity. — *An-ativyādhya, as, ā, am*, Ved. invulnerable. — *An-atyanta-gati, is*, f. the sense of "not exceedingly," sense of diminutive words. — *An-atyaya, as, ā, am*, unperishable, unbroken. — *An-atyudya, as, ā, am*, Ved. (equivalent to *aty-an-udya*), quite unfit to be mentioned.

अनदत् *an-adat, an, atī, at,* not eating, not consuming.

अनद्धा *an-addhā* or (with part. *u*) *an-addho,* ind., Ved. not truly, not really; not clearly. — *An-addhā-purusha, as,* m., Ved. one who is not a true man, one who is of no use either to gods or men or the manes.

अनद्य *an-adya, as, ā, am,* not fit to be eaten; (*as*), m. white mustard.

अनद्यतन *an-adyatana, as,* m. tense which is not applicable to the current day.

अनधिक *an-adhika, as, ā, am,* incapable of being enlarged or excelled; boundless; perfect.

अनधिकार *an-adhikāra, as,* m. absence of authority or right or claim. — *Anadhikāra-ćarćā,* f. intermeddling, officiousness.

An-adhikārin, ī, iṇī, i, not entitled to.

An-adhikṛita, as, ā, am, not placed at the head of, not appointed.

अनधिगत *an-adhigata, as, ā, am,* not obtained, not acquired; not studied. — *Anadhigata-manoratha, as, ā, am,* disappointed. — *Anadhigata-śāstra, as, ā, am,* unacquainted with the Śāstras.

An-adhigamya, as, ā, am, unattainable.

अनधिष्ठान *an-adhishṭhāna, am,* n. want of superintendence.

An-adhishṭhita, as, ā, am, not appointed; not present.

अनधीन *an-adhīna* or *an-adhīnaka, as, ā, am,* independent; (*as*), m. an independent carpenter who works on his own account, see *kauṭa-taksha.*

अनध्यक्ष *an-adhyaksha, as, ā, am,* not observable; destitute of a superintendent.

अनध्ययन *an-adhyayana, am,* n. not studying; intermission of study.

An-adhyāya, as, m. = the preceding; time when there is or ought to be an intermission of study. — *Anadhyāya-divasa, as,* m. a vacation day.

अनन *anana, am,* n. (fr. rt. *an*), breathing, living.

अननङ्गमेजय *an-anaṅgamejaya, as, ā, am,* not leaving the body unshaken; see under *an-aṅga.*

अननुज्ञात *an-anujñāta, as, ā, am,* not agreed to, not permitted, denied.

अननुभावक *an-anubhāvaka, as, ī, am,* unable to comprehend. — *Ananubhāvaka-tā,* f. non-comprehension; unintelligibility.

अननुभाषण *an-anubhāshaṇa, am,* n. not repeating (for the sake of challenging) a proposition; tacit assent.

अननुभूत *an-anubhūta, as, ā, am,* not perceived, not experienced, unknown.

अननुमत *an-anumata, as, ā, am,* not honoured, not liked, disagreeable, unfit.

अननुषङ्गिन् *an-anushaṅgin, ī, iṇī, i,* not attached to, indifferent to.

अननुष्ठान *an-anushṭhāna, am,* n. non-observance, neglect; impropriety.

अननूक्त *an-anūkta, as, ā, am,* not recited or studied; not responded to.

अनन्त *an-anta, as, ā, am,* endless, boundless, eternal, infinite; (*as*), m., N. of many persons, particularly of Vishṇu; of Vishṇu's couch, the snake king Śesha; of Śesha's brother Vāsuki; of Kṛishṇa; of his brother Baladeva; of Śiva, Rudra, one of the Viśva-devas, the 14th Arhat, &c.; a plant, Sinduvāra, Vitex Trifolia; Talc; the 23rd lunar asterism, Śravaṇa; a silken cord tied round the right arm at a particular festival; the letter *ā*; a periodic decimal fraction?; (*ā*), f. the earth; the number one; N. of various females, especially of Pārvatī; N. of various (perennial?) plants, particularly one also called Śārivā, Periploca Indica or Asclepias Pseudosarsa (or Asthmatica), the root of which supplies a valuable medicine; (*am*), n. the sky, atmosphere; Talc. — *Ananta-kara, as, ī, am,* rendering endless, magnifying indefinitely. — *Ananta-ga, as, ā, am,* going or moving for ever or indefinitely. — *Ananta-guṇa, as, ā, am,* having boundless excellencies. — *Ananta-ćaturdaśī,* f. the fourteenth lunar day (or full moon) of Bhādra, when Ananta is worshipped. — *Ananta-ćāritra, as,* m., N. of a Bodhisattva. — *Ananta-jit, t,* m., N. of the fourteenth Jaina Arhat of the present Avasarpiṇī. — *Ananta-tā,* f. or *ananta-tva, am,* n. eternity, infinity. — *Ananta-tāna, as, ā, am,* extensive. — *Ananta-tīrtha, as,* m., N. of an author. — *Ananta-tīrtha-kṛit, t,* m. the same as Anantajit. — *Ananta-tṛitīyā,* f. the third day of Bhādra, said to be sacred to Vishṇu. — *Anantatṛitīya-vrata,* the twenty-fourth Adhyāya of the Bhavishyottara-Purāṇa. — *Ananta-dṛishṭi, is,* m. epithet of Śiva. — *Ananta-deva, as,* m., N. of various persons, especially of a king of Kashmīr. — *Ananta-nemi, is,* m., N. of a king of Mālava, a contemporary of Śākyamuni. — *Ananta-pāra, as, ā, am,* of boundless width. — *Ananta-pāla, as,* m., N. of a warrior chief in Kashmīr. — *Ananta-bhaṭṭa, as,* m., N. of a man. — *Ananta-mati, is,* m., N. of a Bodhisattva. — *Ananta-māyin, ī, inī, i,* endlessly illusory or delusive or deceitful. — *Ananta-mūla, as,* m. a medicinal plant, also called Śārivā. — *Ananta-rāma, as,* m., N. of a man. — *Ananta-rāśi, is,* m. (in arithm.) an infinite quantity; a periodic decimal fraction (?). — *Ananta-rūpa, as, ā* or *ī, am,* having innumerable forms or shapes. — *Ananta-vat, ān, atī, at,* eternal, infinite; (*ān*), m. (in the Upanishads) one of Brahmā's four feet, earth, intermediate space, heaven, and ocean. — *Ananta-varman, ā,* m., N. of a king. — *Ananta-vāta, as,* m. a disease of the head, somewhat like tetanus. — *Ananta-vikramin, ī,* m., N. of a Bodhisattva. — *Ananta-vijaya, as,* m., N. of Yudhishṭhira's conch-shell. — *Ananta-vīrya, as,* m., N. of the twenty-third Jaina Arhat of a future age. — *Ananta-vrata, am,* n. ceremony or festival in honour of Ananta or Vishṇu on the day of the full moon in Bhādra; title of the 102nd Adhyāya of the Bhavishyottara-Purāṇa. — *Ananta-śakti, is, is, i,* omnipotent; (*is*), m., N. of a king. — *Ananta-śayana, am,* n. Travancore. — *Ananta-śīrshā,* f., N. of the snake king Vāsuki's wife. — *Ananta-śushma, as, ā, am,* Ved. possessing boundless strength (?); endlessly blowing (?). — *Anantātman* (°*ta-āt*°), *ā,* m. the infinite spirit. — *Anantāśrama, ananteśvara,* &c., names of persons unknown.

Anantaka, as, ā, am, endless, boundless, eternal, infinite; (*am*), n. (among the Jainas) the eternal (i. e. the aggregate of spirit and matter); the infinite (i. e. infinite space).

Anantya, as, ā, am, infinite, eternal; (*am*), n. infinity, eternity.

अनन्तर *an-antara, as, ā, am,* having no interior; having (or leaving) no interstice or interval or pause; uninterrupted, unbroken; continuous; immediately adjoining, contiguous; next of kin, &c.; compact, close; (*am*), n. contiguousness; Brahma, the supreme soul, as being of one entire essence; (*am*), ind. immediately after; after; afterwards.

Anantara-ja, as, m. (next-born), the son of a Kshatriyā or Vaiśyā mother by a father belonging to the caste immediately above the mother's. — *An-antara-jāta, as,* m. = preceding; also the son of a Śūdrā mother by a Vaiśya father.

An-antarāyam, ind. without a break.

An-antarita, as, ā, am, not separated by any interstice; unbroken.

Anantarīya, as, ā, am, concerning (or belonging to) the next of kin, &c.

अनन्तर्हित *an-antar-hita, as, ā, am* (past part. Pass. of *antar-dhā,* q. v., with *an*), not concealed, manifest; not separated by a break.

अनन्द *a-nanda, as, ā, am,* joyless, cheerless; (*ās*), m. pl., Ved., N. of a purgatory.

अनन्न *an-anna, am,* n. rice or food undeserving of its name.

अनन्य *an-anya, as, ā, am,* no other, not another, not different, identical; self; not having a second, unique; not more than one, sole; having no other (object), undistracted. — *Ananya-gati, is,* f. sole resort or resource. — *Ananya-gati, is, is, i,* or *ananya-gatika, as, ā, am,* having only one (or no other) resort or resource left. — *Ananya-gāmin, ī, inī, i,* going to no other. — *Ananya-ćinta, as, ā, am,* or *ananya-ćetas, ās, ās, as,* giving one's undivided thought to, (with loc.). — *Ananya-ćodita, as, ā, am,* self-impelled. — *Ananya-ja, as,* m. epithet of Kāma or Love. — *Ananya-tā,* f. or *ananya-tva, am,* n. identity. — *Ananya-dṛishṭi, is, is, i,* gazing intently. — *An-anya-deva, as, ā, am,* having no other god. — *Ananya-nishpādya, as, ā, am,* (requiring) to be accomplished by no other. — *An-anya-pūrvā,* f. a female who never belonged to another, a virgin. — *Ananya-pratīkriya, as, ā, am,* having no other means of resistance or redress. — *Ananya-bhava, as, ā, am,* originating in or with no other. — *Ananya-bhāva, as, ā, am,* thinking of the only one, i. e. of the supreme spirit. — *Ananya-manas, ās, ās, as,* or *ananya-manaska, as, ā, am,* or *ananya-mānasa, as, ī, am,* exercising undivided attention. — *Ananya-yoga, as,* m. not suitable to any others. — *Ananya-vishaya, as, ā, am,* exclusively applicable. — *Ananya-vishayātman* (°*ya-āt*°), *ā, ā, a,* having the mind fixed upon one (or the sole) object. — *Ananya-vṛitti, is, is, i,* closely attentive. — *An-anya-hṛita, as, ā, am,* not carried off by another, safe. — *Ananyānubhava* (°*ya-an*°), *as,* m., N. of the teacher of Prakāśātman. — *Ananyārtha* (°*ya-ar*°), *as, ā, am,* not subservient to another object; principal. — *Ananyāśrita* (°*ya-āś*°), *as, ā, am,* not having resorted to another; independent; (*am*), n. (in law) unencumbered property.

An-anyādṛiśa, as, ī, am, not like others, singular.

अनन्वय *an-anvaya, as,* m. want of connexion; (in rhetoric) comparison of an object with its own ideal, (as, a lady-like lady.)

An-anvita, as, ā, am, unconnected, inconsecutive, desultory, incoherent, irrelevant, irregular; not attended with, destitute of.

अनप *an-apa, as, ā, am,* destitute of water.

अनपकरण *an-apakaraṇa, am,* n. (rt. *kṛi*), not injuring; (in law) non-payment, non-delivery.

An-apakarman, a, n. or *anapakriyā,* f. = preceding.

An-apakāra, as, m. harmlessness.

An-apakārin, ī, iṇī, i, innocuous.

An-apakṛita, as, ā, am, unharmed.

अनपकर्ष *an-apakarsha, as,* m. (rt. *kṛish*), m. non-degradation, superiority.

अनपग *an-apaga, as, ā, am,* not departing from.

अनपच्युत *an-apaćyuta, as, ā, am,* Ved. not fallen off, not declined; not displaced.

अनपजय्य *an-apajayya, as, ā, am* (rt. *ji*), Ved. impossible to have its victorious character reversed or neutralized.

अनपत्य *an-apatya, as, ā, am,* childless; Ved. causing childlessness, unpropitious; (*am*), n. childlessness. — *Anapatya-tā,* f. childlessness. — *An-apatya-vat, ān, atī, at,* Ved. childless.

Anapatyaka, as, ā or *ī, am,* childless.

अनपत्रप *an-apatrapa, as, ā, am,* shameless,

अनपनिहित *an-apanihita, as, ā, am*, Ved. not curtailed or mutilated.

अनपयति *an-apayati*, ind., Ved. (before the sun makes a start); very early. (*Apayatī* is said to be fr. rt. *i* with *apa*, perhaps the loc. of the pres. part.)

अनपर *an-apara, as, ā, am*, without another; having no follower; sole (as an epithet of Brahma).

अनपराद्ध *an-aparāddha, as, ā, am*, having sustained no injury; (*am*), ind. without injury.
An-aparādha, as, m. innocence, innocuousness; (*as, ā, am*), innocent, faultless; free from defects. — *Anaparādha-tva, am*, n. freedom from fault.
Anaparādhin, ī, inī, i, innocent.

अनपलाशुक *an-apalāshuka, as, ā, am*, not thirsty.

अनपवाचन *an-apavāćana, as, ā, am*, Ved. impossible to be talked away or wished away.

अनपवृज्य *an-apavṛijya, as, ā, am*, Ved. clear of objects that should be shunned as impure.

अनपव्ययत् *an-apavyayat* (*apa-vy-ayat*), *an, antī, at*, Ved. unremitting, not letting go, able.

अनपसर *an-apasara, as, ā, am* (having no hole to creep out of), inexcusable, unjustifiable; (*as*), m. an usurper.
An-apasaraṇa, am, n. absence of an outlet.

अनपस्पृश् *an-apaspriś, k, k, k*, Ved. not refusing, not obstinate.

अनपस्फुर् *an-apasphur, ūs*, or *an-apasphura, as, ā, am*, or *an-apasphurat, an, antī, at*, Ved. (a cow) not withdrawing, i. e. not refusing to be milked.

अनपहतपाप्मन् *an-apahata-pāpman, ā, ā, a*, Ved. not freed from evil (epithet of the Pitṛis).

अनपहृत *an-apahṛita, as, ā, am*, not carried off, not stolen.

अनपाकरण *an-apākaraṇa, am*, n. or *an-apākarman, a*, n. (in law) non-payment, non-delivery.

अनपाय *an-apāya, as, ā, am*, free from loss, undiminished; not passing away, imperishable; (*as*), m. freedom from loss or from wear and tear; permanence, imperishable nature; epithet of Śiva.
Anapāyin, ī, inī, i, not transient, imperishable; unfailing.

अनपावृत् *an-apāvṛit*, ind., Ved. not turned away, unremittingly.

अनपाश्रय *an-apāśraya, as, ā, am*, not dependent.

अनपुंसक *a-napuṉsaka, am*, n. (in gram.) not a neuter.

अनपूपीय *an-apūpīya* or *an-apūpya, as, ā, am*, unfit for (*apūpa*) cakes. See *apūpa*.

अनपेक्ष *an-apeksha, as, ā, am*, regardless, careless; indifferent; impartial; irrespective; irrelevant; (*ā*), f. disregard, carelessness, indifference; (*am*), ind. without regard to; regardlessly, carelessly, accidentally. — *Anapeksha-tva, am*, n. disregard; irrelevance; irrespectiveness; (*-trāt*), from having no reference to, since (it) has no reference to.
An-apekshita, as, ā, am, disregarded; unheeded; unexpected.
An-apekshin, ī, iṇī, i, regardless, careless; indifferent, &c.
An-apekshya, ind. disregarding, irrespective of.

अनपेत *an-apeta, as, ā, am*, not gone off, not past; not separated, faithful to, possessed of.

अनप्त *an-apta, as, ā, am*, Ved. not watery.

अनप्नस् *an-apnas, ās, ās, as*, Ved. destitute of means (?), merit (?), shape (?), [cf. Lat. *inops*.]

अनप्सरस् *an-apsaras, ās*, f. unlike an Apsaras, unworthy of an Apsaras.

अनफा *anaphā*, f. a particular configuration of the planets. [Gr. ἀναφή.]

अनभिज्ञ *an-abhijña, as, ā, am*, unacquainted with, ignorant.

अनभिद्रुह् *an-abhidruh, dhruk, k, k*, Ved. not malicious.

अनभिप्रेत *an-abhipreta, am*, n. something different from (or the reverse of) what was intended.

अनभिभूत *an-abhibhūta, as, ā, am*, not overcome, unsurpassed; not beset, unobstructed.

अनभिमत *an-abhimata, as, ā, am*, not to one's mind, disliked.

अनभिम्लात *an-abhi-mlāta, as, ā, am*, unfaded. — *Anabhimlāta-varṇa, as, ā, am*, Ved. of unfaded colour or brightness.
An-abhimlāna, as, m. (non-fading), N. of the chief of a Gotra.

अनभिरूप *an-abhirūpa, as, ā* or *ī, am*, not handsome, not pleasing.

अनभिलक्षित *an-abhilakshita, as*, m. destitute of (masonic?) marks or symbols, an impostor.

अनभिलाष *an-abhilāsha, as*, m. non-relish; want of appetite; want of desire.
An-abhilāshin, ī, iṇī, i, not desirous.

अनभिव्यक्त *an-abhivyakta, as, ā, am*, indistinct.

अनभिशस्त *an-abhiśasta, as, ā, am*, or *an-abhiśasti, is, is, i*, or *an-abhiśastya, as, ā, am*, Ved. blameless, faultless. — *Anabhiśaste-nī, īs, īs, i*, Ved. leading to perfection or to heaven.

अनभिषङ्ग *an-abhishanga* or *an-abhishvanga, as*, m. absence of connection or attachment.

अनभिसन्धान *an-abhisandhāna, am*, n. or *an-abhisandhi, is*, m. absence of a (latent) design; disinterestedness. — *Anabhisandhi-kṛita, as, ā, am*, done undesignedly.

अनभिसम्बन्ध *an-abhisambandha, as, ā, am*, unconnected.

अनभिस्नेह *an-abhisneha, as, ā, am*, not affectionate, impassible.

अनभिहित *an-abhihita, as, ā, am*, not named; (Ved.) not fastened; (*as*), m., N. of the chief of a Gotra.

अनभीशु *an-abhīśu, us, us, u*, Ved. unbridled; epithet of the sun.

अनभ्यनुज्ञा *an-abhyanujñā* (*abhy-anu-jñā*), f. non-permission.

अनभ्यारूढ *an-abhyārūḍha, as, ā, am*, not ascended, not mounted.

अनभ्याश *an-abhyāśa* or *an-abhyāsa, as, ā, am*, not near, distant. — *Anabhyāśam-itya, as, ā, am*, improper to be approached.

अनभ्यास *an-abhyāsa, as*, m. want of practice or skill.

अनभ्रक *an-abhraka, as*, m. 'cloudless;' N. of a class of Bauddha divinities (generally in m. pl.).

अनभ्रि *an-abhri, is, is, i*, Ved. (requiring) no shovel or scraper; epithet of rain-water.

अनम *a-nama, as*, m. one who needs not make a salutation to others; a Brāhman.
A-namasya, as, ā, am, unworthy of a salutation.

अनमितम्पच *an-amitam-paća, as, ā, am*, (the same as *mitam-paća*), not cooking what has not first been weighed, niggardly, miserly.

अनमित्र *an-amitra, as, ā, am*, having no enemies; (*am*), n. condition of having no enemies; (*as*), m., N. of various persons, particularly a king of Ayodhyā.

अनमीव *an-amīva, as, ā, am*, Ved. free from disease, well, comfortable; salubrious, salutary; sinless; (*am*), n. good health, happy state, comfort, prosperity.

अनम्बर *an-ambara, as, ā, am*, wearing no clothing, naked; (*as*), m. a Buddhist mendicant.

अनय 1. *a-naya, as*, m. bad management; bad conduct (gambling, &c.).

अनय 2. *an-aya, as*, m. evil course, ill luck; misfortune, adversity. — *Anayan-gata, as, ā, am*, unfortunate.

अनरण्य *an-araṇya, as*, m., N. of a king of Ayodhyā, said by some to have been Pṛithu's father.

अनरुस् *an-arus, us, us, us*, Ved. not sore or wounded, healed, well, sound.

अनर्गल *an-argala, as, ā, am*, free from bars, free, licentious.

अनर्घ *an-argha, as, ā, am*, priceless, invaluable; (*as*), m. wrong value. — *Anargha-rāghava, am*, n. title of a drama by Murāri, treating of Rāma.
An-arghya, as, ā, am, priceless, not to be had at any price; anything but valuable. — *Anarghya-tva, am*, n. pricelessness.

अनर्थ *an-artha, as*, m. non-value; a worthless or useless object; disappointing occurrence, reverse, evil; nonsense; (*as, ā, am*), worthless, useless; unfortunate; having no meaning; having not that (but another) meaning; nonsensical. — *Anartha-kara, as, ī, am*, doing what is useless or worthless; unprofitable; producing evil or misfortune. — *Anartha-tva, am*, n. uselessness, &c. — *Anartha-darśin, ī, inī, i*, minding useless or worthless things. — *Anartha-nāśin, ī*, m. (destroyer of evil), Śiva. — *Anartha-buddhi, is, is, i*, having a nonsensical intellect. — *Anartha-bhāva, as, ā, am*, malicious. — *Anartha-lupta, as, ā, am*, freed from all that is worthless. — *An-artha-saṃśaya, as*, m. not a risk of one's money; safety of one's money or wealth.
An-arthaka, as, ā, am, useless, vain, worthless; meaningless, nonsensical.
An-arthya, as, ā, am, worthless, useless.

अनर्पण *an-arpaṇa, am*, n., Ved. non-surrendering, not giving up.

अनर्व *an-arva, as, ā, am*, or *an-arvan, ā, ā, a*, Ved. not liable to be stayed or limited; unobstructed; irresistible; permanent.

अनर्विश् 1. *anar-viś, ṭ*, m., Ved. seated on the car (*anas*) or cart; a driver.

अनर्विश् 2. *an-ar-viś, ṭ*, m. (*ar* for *aram*, rt. *ṛi*), one who fails to reach his destination.

अनर्शनि *an-arśani, is*, m., Ved., N. of a demon slain by Indra; (etym. doubtful.)

अनर्शराति *an-arśa-rāti, is, is, i*, Ved. giving of uninjurious things, one whose gifts do not hurt.

अनर्ह *an-arha, as, ā, am*, or *an-arhat, an, antī, at*, undeserving of punishment or of reward; unworthy; inadequate, unsuitable.
Anarhya-tā, f. condition of not being properly estimated; inadequacy, unsuitableness.

अनल *anala, as*, m. (fr. rt. *an*, q. v.), fire;

Agni, the god of fire; digestive power, gastric juice, bile; wind; N. or epithet of Vasudeva; of a certain Muni; of one of the eight Vasus; of a certain monkey; N. of various plants, as Plumbago Zeylanica and Rosea, and Semicarpus Anacardium; the letter *r;* the number three; (in astron.) the fiftieth year of Bṛihaspati's cycle; the third lunar mansion or Kṛittikā(?). — *Anala-dīpana, as, ī, am,* stomachic. — *Anala-prabhā,* f. a plant, Halicacabum Cardiospermum. — *Anala-priyā,* f. Agni's wife. — *Anala-vāṭa, as,* m., N. of ancient Pattana. — *Anala-sāda, as,* m. dyspepsia. — *Analānanda* (°*la-ān*°), *as,* m., N. of a Vedantic writer, author of the Vedāntakalpataru.

अनलङ्करिष्णु *an-alankarishṇu, us, us, u,* not given to the use of ornaments; not ornamented.

अनलम् *an-alam,* ind. not enough; insufficiently.

अनलस *an-alasa, as, ā, am,* not lazy, active.

अनलि *anali, is,* m. a tree, Sesbana Grandiflora.

अनल्प *an-alpa, as, ā, am,* not a little, much, numerous. — *Analpa-ghosha, as, ā, am,* very clamorous, very noisy. — *Analpa-manyu, us, us, u,* greatly enraged.

अनव *anava, as,* m., N. of a man or a tribe, = *anu.*

अनवकाश *an-avakāśa, as, ā, am,* having no opportunity; uncalled for (there being no "occasion" for it), inapplicable.

अनवगाहिन् *an-avagāhin, ī, inī, i* (rt. *gāh*), not dipping into, not studying.

An-avagāhya, as, ā, am, unfathomable.

अनवगीत *an-avagīta, as, ā, am,* not made an object of a contemptuous song, not blamed.

अनवग्रह *an-avagraha, as, ā, am,* resistless; not to be intercepted.

अनवग्लायत् *an-avaglāyat, an, antī, at,* Ved. not growing remiss.

अनवच्छिन्न *an-avaććhinna, as, ā, am,* not intersected, uninterrupted; not marked off, unbounded, unlimited, immoderate; undefined, undiscriminated. — *Anavaććhinna-hāsa, as,* m. continuous or immoderate laughter.

अनवत् *ana-vat, ān, atī, at* (fr. *ana,* see under rt. *an*), endowed with breath or life. — *Anavat-tva, am,* n. condition of being endowed with life.

अनवतप्त *an-avatapta, as,* m., (among Buddhists) N. of a serpent king; N. of a lake, = Rāvaṇa-hrada.

अनवद्य *an-avadya, as, ā, am,* irreproachable, faultless; unobjectionable; (*ā*), f., N. of an Apsaras. — *Anavadya-tā,* f. or *anavadya-tva, am,* n. faultlessness. — *Anavadya-rūpa, as, ā* or *ī, am,* of faultless form or beauty. — *Anavadyāṅga* (°*ya-aṅ*°), *as, ā* or *ī, am,* having faultless body or limbs.

अनवद्राण *an-avadrāṇa, as, ā, am* (rt. *drā*), Ved. not going to sleep, not sleepy.

अनवधर्ष्य *an-avadharshya, as, ā, am,* Ved. not to be defied.

अनवधान *an-avadhāna, am,* n. inattention, inadvertence; (*as, ā, am*), inattentive, careless. — *Anavadhāna-tā,* f. inadvertency.

अनवधि *an-avadhi, is, is, i,* unlimited.

अनवधृष्य *an-avadhṛishya, as, ā, am,* impossible to be put down or injured.

अनवन *an-avana, as, ā, am,* affording no help or protection.

अनवनामितवैजयन्त *an-avanāmita-vaijayanta, as,* m. (having victorious banners unlowered, ever prosperous; Buddhist term for) a future universe.

अनवपृग्ण *an-avapṛigṇa, as, ā, am* (rt. *pṛić*), Ved. not closely united, but spreading all around.

अनवबुध्यमान *an-avabudhyamāna, as, ā, am,* deranged.

अनवब्रव *an-avabrava, as, ā, am,* Ved. not speaking without effect; speaking authoritatively; or irreproachable (?).

अनवभ्र *an-avabhra, as, ā, am,* Ved. not carried off (?); undiminished (?); enduring (?). — *An-avabhra-rādhas, ās, ās, as,* Ved. having undiminished (or durable) wealth; able to give a lasting reward.

अनवम *an-avama, as, ā, am,* not low; exalted.

अनवमर्शम् *an-avamarśam,* ind. without touching.

अनवर *an-avara, as, ā, am,* not inferior; excellent.

अनवरत *an-avarata, as, ā, am,* incessant; (*am*), ind. incessantly.

अनवरथ *an-avaratha, as,* m., N. of a son of Madhu and father of Kuruvatsa.

अनवरार्ध्य *an-avarārdhya, as, ā, am,* chief, principal.

अनवलम्ब *an-avalamba, as, ā, am,* having no prop or support.

An-avalambana, am, n. independence.

An-avalambita, as, ā, am, not propped up, not supported, not dependent.

अनवलेप *an-avalepa, as, ā, am,* free from (moral) veneer, unvarnished, unassuming.

अनवलोभन *an-avalobhana, am,* n. ('non-longing'), N. of a ceremony to be observed by a pregnant woman; title of a particular treatise in an Upanishad.

अनवस *an-avasa, as, ā, am,* Ved. not stopping to eat by the way.

अनवसर *an-avasara, as, ā, am,* having no interval of leisure, busy; coming when there is no such interval, inopportune; (*as*), m. absence of leisure; unseasonableness.

अनवसाद्य *an-avasādya,* ind. (part. of Caus. of *ava-sad* with 3. *a*), without annoying.

अनवसान *an-avasāna, as, ā, am* (rt. *so*), having no setting, free from death; endless.

An-avasita, as, ā, am, not set, not terminated; (*ā*), f., N. of a species of the Trishṭubh metre, consisting of four lines with eleven feet in each.

An-avasyat, an, antī, at, unceasing.

अनवस्कर *an-avaskara, as, ā, am,* free from dirt, clean, cleansed.

अनवस्थ *an-avastha, as, ā, am,* unsettled, unstable; (*ā*), f. unsettled condition or character; instability, unsteady or loose conduct; (in phil.) non-finality (of a proposition), endless series of statements.

An-avasthāna as, ā, am, unstable, fickle; (*as*), m. wind; (*am*), n. instability; unsteadiness or looseness of conduct.

An-avasthāyin, ī, inī, i, transient.

An-avasthita, as, ā, am, unsettled, unsteady, loose in conduct. — *Anavasthita-ćitta, as, ā, am,* or *an-avasthitātman* (°*ta-āt*°), *ā, ā, a,* unsteady-minded. — *Anavasthitaćitta-tva, am,* n. unsteadiness of mind. — *Anavasthita-tva, am,* n. unsteadiness, instability.

An-avasthiti, is, f. instability; unsteadiness; looseness of character.

अनवस्यत् *an-ava-syat.* See *an-avasāna.*

अनवहित *an-avahita, as, ā, am,* heedless, inattentive.

अनवह्वर *an-avahvara, as, ā, am,* Ved. not crooked, straightforward.

अनवाच् *an-avāć, k, k, k,* not speechless, the reverse of speechless.

अनवाञ्च् *an-avāñć, āṅ, āćī, āk,* not inclining downwards, looking up or straightforward.

अनवानम् *an-avānam,* ind. without breathing (between), in one breath, without interruption, *uno tenore.* — *Anavāna-tā,* f. uninterruptedness, contiguity.

अनवाप्त *an-avāpta, as, ā, am,* not obtained.

An-avāpti, is, f. non-attainment.

अनवायम् *an-avāyam,* ind., Ved. uninterruptedly, unyieldingly.

अनविथ्य *an-avithya, as, ā, am* (fr. *avi,* q. v.), not suited to sheep.

अनवेक्ष *an-aveksha, as, ā, am,* regardless; (*am*), ind. irrespectively; without regard to; (*ā*), f. or *an-avekshaṇa, am,* n. regardlessness.

अनव्रत *an-avrata, as, ā, am,* not (wholly) destitute of ascetic performances; (*as*), m. a Jaina devotee of that description.

अनशन *an-aśana, am,* n. abstinence from food, fasting, especially as a form of suicide adopted from vindictive motives; (*as, ā, am*), fasting. — *Anaśana-tā,* f. not eating.

An-aśanāya, as, ā, am, Ved. not hungry.

An-aśita, am, n. condition of not having eaten, fasting.

An-aśnat, an, atī, at, not eating, not enjoying. — *Anaśnant-sāngamana, as,* m., Ved. the sacrificial fire in the Sabhā (which is approached before breakfast).

An-aśnāna, as, ā, am, not eating.

अनश्रु *an-aśru, us, us, u,* tearless.

अनश्व *an-aśva, as, ā, am,* having no horse or horses; (*as*), m. something that is not a horse. — *An-aśva-dā, ās, ās, am,* Ved. one who does not give horses.

अनश्वन् *an-aśvan, ā,* m., N. of Parīkshit's father.

अनश्वर *a-naśvara, as, ī, am,* imperishable.

A-nashṭa, as, ā, am, undestroyed, unimpaired. — *Anashṭa-paśu, us, us, u,* Ved. having his cattle unimpaired. — *Anashṭa-vedas, ās, ās, as,* Ved. having his property unimpaired.

अनस् *anas, as,* n. (said to be fr. rt. *an*), a cart; a mother; birth; offspring, living creature; boiled rice. — *Anas-vat, ān, atī, at,* Ved. yoked to a cart.

Anaḍ-uh, anar-viś, see s. v. (*s* changed to *ḍ* and *r*).

अनसूय *an-asūya, as, ā, am,* not spiteful, not envious; (*ā*), f. freedom from spite; absence of ill-will or envy; N. of a daughter of Daksha, and of one of S'akuntalā's friends.

An-asūyaka, as, ā, am, or *an-asūyu, us, us, u,* not spiteful or envious.

अनसूरि *an-a-sūri, is, is, i,* Ved. not unwise, wise.

अनस्तमित *an-astam-ita, as, ā, am,* not gone down; not subject to setting or declining.

अनस्थ *an-astha, as, ā, am,* or *an-asthi, is, is, i,* or *anasthika, as, ā, am,* or *anasthi-mat, ān, atī, at,* boneless.

अनहङ्कार *an-ahankāra, as,* m. (non-ego-tism), absence of or freedom from self-conceit, or the tendency to regard self as something distinct from the supreme spirit; freedom from pride; (as, ā, am), free from self-conceit or pride.

An-ahankṛita, as, ā, am, or an-aham-vādin, ī, inī, i, free from self-conceit or pride.

An-ahankṛiti, is, f. = an-ahankāra; (is, is, i), free from self-conceit or pride.

अनहन् an-ahan, as, n. a day which is no day, an evil or unlucky day.

अना anā, ind., Ved. (inst. of pronom. base a), hereby, thus, indeed; also said to be a substitute for an or ana, 'not,' in one or two words.

अनाकार an-ākāra, as, ā, am, shapeless.

अनाकारित an-ākārita, as, ā, am, not claimed, not exacted.

अनाकाल an-ākāla, as, m. unseasonable time; famine.—Anākāla-bhṛita, as, m. a slave who became one voluntarily to avoid starvation in a time of scarcity; also spelt annākāla-bhṛita.

अनाकाश an-ākāśa, as, ā, am, having no transparent atmosphere, differing from it; opaque, dark; (as, am), m. n. air or atmosphere undeserving of its name.

अनाकुल an-ākula, as, ā, am, not beset; not confused; unperplexed, calm, consistent, regular.

अनाकृत an-ākṛita, as, ā, am, Ved. unreclaimed, unreclaimable.

अनाक्रान्त an-ākrānta, as, ā, am, unassailed, unassailable; (ā), f. a plant, Prickly Nightshade, Solanum Jacquini.

अनाक्षारित an-ākshārita, as, ā, am, unreproached.

अनाक्षित् an-ākshit, t, t, t, Ved. not residing or resting.

अनाग an-āga, as, ā, am, Ved. sinless; see an-āgas; (ā), f., N. of a river.

अनागत an-āgata, as, ā, am (rt. gam), not come, not arrived; future; not attained, not learnt; unknown; (am), n. the future.—Anāgata-vat, ān, atī, at, connected with or relating to the future.—Anāgata-vidhātṛi, ā, m. (disposer of the future), provident; N. of a fish.—Anāgatābādha (°ta-āb°), as, m. future trouble.—Anāgatārtavā (°ta-ār°), f. a girl who has not yet attained to puberty.—Anāgatāvekshaṇa (°ta-av°), am, n. act of looking at that which is to come next.

An-āgati, is, f. non-arrival; non-attainment, non-accession.

An-āgama, as, m. non-arrival, non-attainment; (as, ā, am), not come, not present; (in law) not constituting an accession to previous property, but possessed from time immemorial, and therefore without documentary proof.—Anāgamopabhoga (°ma-up°), as, m. enjoyment of such property.

An-āgamishyat, an, antī, at, one who will not approach.

An-āgamya, as, ā, am, unapproachable, unattainable.

An-āgāmin, ī, inī, i, not coming, not arriving; not future, not subject to returning; (ī), m. epithet of the third among the four Buddhist orders.

An-āgāmuka, as, ā am, not in the habit of coming, not likely to come.

अनागस् an-āgas, ās, ās, as, sinless, blameless; conferring sinlessness or bliss.—Anāgās-tva, am, n., Ved. sinlessness.—Anāgo-hatyā, f. murder of an innocent person.

अनाचरण an-āćaraṇa, am, n. or better an-āćāra, as, m. Improper behaviour; departure from that which is customary or right.

An-āćāra, as, ā, am, or anāćārin, ī, iṇī, i, improper in behaviour; regardless of custom or propriety or law; unprincipled.

अनाचार्यभोगीन an-āćārya-bhogīna, as, ā, am, unfit or improper for a spiritual teacher to eat or enjoy.

अनाज्ञप्त an-ājñapta, as, ā, am (rt. jñā), not commanded.—Anājñapta-kārin, ī, iṇī, i, doing what has not been commanded.

अनाज्ञात an-ājñāta, as, ā, am, unknown, surpassing all that has ever been known.

अनाढ्य an-āḍhya, as, ā, am, not wealthy, poor.—An-āḍhyam-bhavishṇu, us, us, u, not becoming wealthy; becoming poor (?).

अनातत an-ātata, as, ā, am, not stretched or strung (as a bow).

अनातप an-ātapa, as, m. freedom from the blaze of the sun; shade; coolness.

अनातुर an-ātura, as, ā, am, Ved. free from suffering or weariness; well.

अनात्मन् an-ātman, ā, m. not self, another; something different from spirit or soul; (ā, ā, a), not spiritual, corporeal; destitute of spirit or mind.—An-ātma-jña, as, ā, am, destitute of spiritual knowledge or true wisdom.—Anātma-pratyavekshā, f. (with Buddhists) reflection that there is no spirit or self.—An-ātma-vat, ān, atī, at, not self-possessed; (vat), ind. unlike one's self.

An-ātmaka, as, ā, am, (with Buddhists) unreal.

An-ātmanīna, as, ā, am, not adapted to self; disinterested.

An-ātmya, as, ā, am, impersonal; (am), n. want of affection for one's own family.

अनात्यन्तिक an-ātyantika, as, ī, am, not perpetual, not final; intermittent, recurrent.

अनाथ a-nātha, as, ā, am, having no master or natural protector; widowed; fatherless; helpless, poor; (am), n., Ved. want of a protector, helplessness.—Anātha-piṇḍa-da or a-nātha-piṇḍika, as, m. ('giver of cakes or food to the poor'), N. of a merchant, in whose garden Sākyamuni used to instruct his disciples.—Anātha-sabhā, f. a poor-house.

अनाद a-nāda, as, m. absence of sound (in pronouncing aspirated letters).

A-nādin, ī, inī, i, not sounding.

अनाददान an-ādadāna, as, ā, am, not accepting.

अनादर an-ādara, as, m. disrespect, contemptuous neglect; (as, ā, am), Ved. not awe-struck, calm; indifferent.

An-ādaraṇa, am, n. disrespectful behaviour, neglect.

An-ādarin, ī, iṇī, i, disrespectful, irreverent.

अनादि an-ādi, is, is, i, having no beginning, existing from eternity.—Anādi-tva, am, n. state of having no beginning.—An-ādi-nidhana, as, ā, am, having neither beginning nor end, eternal.—Anādi-mat, ān, atī, at, having no beginning.—An-ādi-madhyānta (°dhya-an°), as, ā, am, having no beginning, middle or end.—Anādy-ananta, as, ā, am, without beginning and without end.—An-ādyanta, as, ā, am, without beginning and end; (as), m., N. of Śiva.

अनादिष्ट an-ādishṭa, as, ā, am, not indicated; not commanded or instructed; not allowed.

अनादीनव an-ādīnava, as, ā, am, faultless.

अनादृत an-ādṛita, as, ā, am, not respected, disrespected, despised.

An-ādṛitya, ind. without respecting, regardless of.

अनादेय an-ādeya, as, ā, am, unfit or improper to be received, unacceptable, inadmissible.

अनादेशकर anādeśa-kara, as, ā, am, doing what is not commanded or not allowed.

अनाद्य 1. an-ādya, as, ā, am, = an-ādi, having no beginning.

अनाद्य 2. an-ādya, as, ā, am, = an-adya, not eatable.

अनाधृष् an-ādhṛish, k, k, k (rt. dhṛish), Ved. not checking.

An-ādhṛishṭa, as, ā, am, Ved. unchecked, unimpaired, invincible, perfect.

An-ādhṛishṭi, is, m. ('superior to any check'), N. of a son of Śūra; also of a son of Ugrasena and general of the Yādava.

An-ādhṛishya, as, ā, am, Ved. invincible, not to be meddled with.

अनानत an-ānata, as, ā, am, Ved. unbent, not humbled; (as), m., N. of a Ṛishi.

अनानुकृत्य an-ānukṛitya, as, ā, am (rt. kṛi with ānu for anu), Ved. inimitable, unparalleled.

अनानुद an-ānuda, as, ā, am (rt. dā with ānu for anu), Ved. not giving way, unyielding, obstinate; unaided (?), unsurpassed in giving (?).

अनानुदिष्ट an-ānudishṭa, as, ā, am (rt. diś with ānu for anu), Ved. unsolicited.

अनानुपूर्व्य an-ānupūrvya, am, n. separation of the different parts of a compound word by the intervention of others; the not coming in regular order, tmesis.—An-ānupūrvya-saṃhitā, f. the manner of constructing a sentence with the above tmesis.

अनानुभूति an-ānubhūti, is, f., Ved. inattention, neglect; (tayas), pl. neglectful or irreligious people.

अनापद् an-āpad, t, f. absence of misfortune or calamity.

अनापन्न an-āpanna, as, ā, am, not realized, unattained.

अनापान an-āpāna, as, m., N. of a prince, son of Aṅga.

अनापि an-āpi, is, is, i, Ved. having no kindred or friends (epithet of Indra).

अनापूयित an-āpūyita, as, ā, am, Ved. not stinking.

अनाप्त an-āpta, as, ā, am, unattained, unobtained; unsuccessful in the effort to attain or obtain; not apt, unfit; (as), m. a stranger.

An-āpti, is, f. non-attainment.

An-āpya, as, ā, am, unattainable, unobtainable.

अनाप्लुत an-āpluta, as, ā, am, unbathed, unwashed.—An-āplutāṅga (°ta-aṅ°), as, ā or ī, am, having an unwashen body.

अनाबाध an-ābādha, as, ā, am, free from obstacles or troubles.

अनाभयिन् an-ābhayin, ī, inī, i, Ved. fearless (epithet of Indra).

अनाभू an-ābhū, ūs, ūs, u, Ved. neglectful, disobliging, irreligious.

अनाभ्युदयिक an-ābhyudayika, as, ī, am, inauspicious, ill-omened, unlucky.

अनामन् a-nāman, ā, ā, a, nameless; infamous; (ā), m. the ring-finger.—Anāma-tva, am, n. namelessness.

A-nāmaka, as, ā, am, nameless, infamous; (as), m. the intercalary month; (am), n. piles, hæmorrhoids.

A-nāmikā, f. the ring-finger.

अनामय an-āmaya, as, ā, am, free from disease, healthy, salubrious; (as), m. Śiva; (am), n. health.

An-āmayat, an, antī, at, Ved. not causing pain, not hurting; (t), n., Ved. health.

An-āmayitnu, us, us, u, Ved. salubrious, curative.

अनामिन् *a-nāmin, ī, inī, i,* Ved. unbending.
A-nāmya, as, ā, am, impossible to be bent.

अनामिष *an-āmisha, as, ā, am,* without flesh; bootless, profitless.

अनामृण *an-āmṛiṇa, as, ā, am,* Ved. having no enemy that can injure.

अनामृत *an-āmṛita, as, ā, am,* immortal.

अनायक *a-nāyaka, as, ā, am,* having no leader or ruler, disorderly.

अनायत *an-āyata, as, ā, am,* unchecked, unrestrained; not propped or supported; close, continuous, unseparated; unextended, having no length.

अनायतन *an-āyatana, am,* n. that which is not really a resting-place or an altar; *(as, ā, am),* having no resting-place or altar. — *Anāyatana-vat, ān, atī, at,* = the last.

अनायत्त *an-āyatta, as, ā, am,* independent, uncontrolled. — *Anāyatta-vṛitti, is, is, i,* having an independent livelihood. — *Anāyattavṛitti-tā,* f. independence.

अनायसाग्र *an-āyasāgra* (°*sa-ag*°), *as, ā, am,* having no iron point.

अनायास *an-āyāsa, as,* m. absence of exertion, facility, ease, idleness, neglect; *(as, ā, am),* easy, ready; *(ena),* ind. easily. — *Anāyāsa-kṛita, as, ā, am,* done readily or easily; *(am),* n. an infusion prepared extemporaneously (in medicine).

अनायुध *an-āyudha, as, ā, am,* Ved. weaponless; having no implements (for sacrifice).

अनायुषा *an-āyushā,* f. or *an-āyus,* f., N. of the mother of Bala and Vṛitra.
An-āyushya, as, ā, am, not imparting long life, fatal to long life.

अनारत *an-ārata, as, ā, am,* eternal; *(am),* ind. eternally.

अनारभ्य 1. *an-ārabhya, as, ā, am,* improper or impracticable to be commenced or undertaken. — *Anārabhya-tva, am,* n. impossibility of being commenced.
2. *an-ārabhya,* ind. without commencing: this is used in compounds in the sense 'detached;' thus, *anārabhya-vāda, as,* m. a detached remark (upon sacrifices, &c.); *anārabhyādhīta* (°*ya-adh*°), *as, ā, am,* taught or studied or read as a detached subject (not as part of a regular or authoritative treatise).
An-ārambha, as, m. absence of beginning, non-commencement, not attempting or undertaking; *(as, ā, am),* having no commencement.

अनारम्बण *an-ārambaṇa, as, ā, am,* Ved. (for *anālambana*) having no support.

अनारम्भण *an-ārambhaṇa, as, ā, am,* Ved. without support (?), or intangible (?).

अनारुह्य *an-āruhya,* ind. not having surmounted.

अनारोग्य *an-ārogya, am,* n. sickness; *(as, ā, am),* unhealthy. — *Anārogya-kara, as, ā* or *ī, am,* unwholesome, unhealthy, causing sickness.

अनार्जव *an-ārjava, am,* n. crookedness, moral or physical; disease.

अनार्तव *an-ārtava, as, ī, am,* unseasonable.

अनार्त्विजीन *an-ārtvijīna, as, ā, am,* unfit or unsuitable for a priest.

अनार्य *an-ārya, as, ā, am,* not respectable, vulgar, unworthy, inferior, bad, vile; destitute of Āryas; *(as),* m. not an Ārya. — *Anārya-karmin, ī,* m. doing work unbecoming an Ārya or becoming only a non-Ārya. — *Anārya-ja, as, ā, am,* of vile or unworthy origin; *(am),* n. Agallochum, being a produce of the country of Mleććhas or barbarians. — *Anārya-jushṭa, as, ā, am,* practised, observed, or possessed by men who are not Āryas. — *Anārya-tā,* f. or *anārya-tva, am,* n. vileness, unworthiness, baseness. — *Anārya-tikta, as,* m. a medicinal plant, a kind of Gentian (Gentiana Cherayta Rox).
An-āryaka, am, n. Agallochum or Aloe wood (Aquila Agallocha Rox).

अनार्ष *an-ārsha, as, ī, am,* not referring or belonging to a Ṛishi or to the genuine text of a Vedic hymn; e. g. the word *iti,* added for grammatical purposes in the Pada-pāṭha to certain words, which in the Saṃhitā-pāṭha are not followed by *iti;* not applied to a Ṛishi, not added to his name, as an affix.
An-ārsheya, as, ī, am, the same as the last.

अनालम्ब *an-ālamba, as, ā, am,* unsupported, without stay or support; *(as),* m. want of support; despondency.
An-ālambana, as, ā, am, unsupported; desponding.
An-ālambī, f. Śiva's lute.
An-ālambukā or *an-ālambhukā,* f. a woman during menstruation.

अनालाप *an-ālāpa, as, ā, am,* reserved, taciturn; *(as),* m. reserve, taciturnity.

अनालोचित *an-āloćita, as, ā, am,* unseen, unbeheld; unweighed, unconsidered, rash, imprudent.
An-āloćya, ind. not having considered.

अनावया *an-āvayā, ās, ās, am,* Ved. unyielding, not desisting.

अनावर्ति *an-āvarti, is,* f. non-return, i. e. final emancipation. See *an-āvṛit* below.

अनाविद्ध *an-āviddha, as, ā, am,* not wounded, unhurt, unmoved by.

अनाविल *an-āvila, as, ā, am,* not turbid, clear, pure, not marshy.

अनावृत् *an-āvṛit, t, t, t,* Ved. not returning.
An-āvṛitta, as, ā, am, not turned about or round; not retreating; not freqented or approached; not chosen.
An-āvṛitti, is, f. non-return; final emancipation.

अनावृत *an-āvṛita, as, ā, am,* uncovered, undressed, uninclosed, open.

अनावृष्टि *an-āvṛishṭi, is,* f. want of rain, drought.

अनावेदित *an-āvedita, as, ā, am,* not notified, not made known.

अनाव्याध *an-āvyādha, as, ā, am,* Ved. impossible to be broken or forced open.

अनाव्रस्क *an-āvraska, as,* m. (rt. *vraść*), uninjured condition; *(as, ā, am),* not injurious.

अनाश 1. *an-āśa, as, ā, am* (fr. *āśā*), hopeless, despairing.

अनाश 2. *a-nāśa, as, ā, am* (rt. *naś*), undestroyed, living.
A-nāśin, ī, inī, i, imperishable.
A-nāśya, as, ā, am, indestructible.

अनाशक *an-āśaka, am,* n. fasting, abstaining from food even to death. — *Anāśaka-nivṛitta, as,* m. one who has abandoned the practice of fasting. — *Anāśakāyana* (°*ka-ay*°), *am,* n. a course of fasting (as a penance).

अनाशस्त *an-āśasta, as, ā, am,* not praised; not commendable (?), inglorious (?), hopeless (?).

अनाशीर्दा *an-āśīr-dā, ās,* m. not giving a blessing; ungrateful.

अनाशु 1. *an-āśu, us, us, u,* not quick, slow.

अनाशु 2. *an-āśu, us, us, u* (rt. *aś*), not diffusive, not pervading.

अनाशु 3. *a-nāśu, us, us, u,* Ved. indestructible.

अनाश्चर्य *an-āśćarya, as, ā, am,* not wonderful.

अनाश्रमिन् *an-āśramin, ī,* m. one who does not belong to or follow any of the four Āśramas or religious orders to which Brāhmans at different periods of life are bound to attach themselves.
An-āśrama-vāsa or *an-āśrame-vāsa, as,* m. one who does not belong to the Āśramas; non-residence in a religious retreat.

अनाश्रय *an-āśraya, as,* m. absence or want of any person or thing to depend upon; defencelessness, self-dependence, isolation; *(as, ā, am),* defenceless; unprotected; isolated.
An-āśrita, as, ā, am, detached; disengaged; unconnected with, independent; non-inherent.

अनाश्वस् *an-āśvas, vān, ushī, vat,* not having eaten, fasting.

अनाष्ट्र *a-nāshṭra, as, ā, am,* free from dangers or dangerous opponents.

अनास् *an-ās, ās,* m. f. having no mouth or face.

अनास *a-nāsa, as, ā, am,* Ved. without a nose (epithet of demons).
A-nāsika, as, ā, am, noseless.

अनासादित *an-āsādita, as, ā, am,* not met with, not found or obtained, not encountered or attacked; not occurred; not having happened; non-existent. — *Anāsādita-vigraha, as, ā, am,* unused to war.

अनास्था *an-āsthā,* f. unfixedness, want of confidence; disrespect; want of consideration; want of faith or devotedness; unconcern, indifference.
An-āsthāna, as, ā, am, having or yielding no basis or fulcrum; without a fixed seat or site.

अनास्वाद *an-āsvāda, as,* m. want of taste, insipidity; *(as, ā, am),* without taste, insipid.
An-āsvādita, as, ā, am, untasted.

अनाहत *an-āhata, as, ā, am,* unbeaten, unwounded, intact; new and unbleached (as cloth); produced otherwise than by beating; not multiplied; *(as),* m. the fourth of the mystical *ćakras* or circles of the body. — *Anāhata-nāda, as,* m. a sound produced otherwise than by beating; the sound *om.*

अनाहार *an-āhāra, as,* m. abstinence, not taking food; non-seizure; non-production; *(as, ā, am),* one who abstains from food.
An-āhārin, ī, iṇī, i, not taking (food); fasting.
An-āhārya, as, ā, am, not to be seized or taken, not producible; not to be eaten.

अनाहिताग्नि *an-āhitāgni* (°*ta-ag*°), *is,* m. a householder who has neglected to perform the Agnyādhāna.

अनाहुति *an-āhuti, is,* f. non-sacrificing; a sacrifice unworthy of its name.

अनाहूत *an-āhūta, as, ā, am,* uncalled, uninvited. — *Anāhūtopajalpin* (°*ta-up*°), *ī,* m. an uncalled-for boaster. — *Anāhūtopavishṭa* (°*ta-up*°), *as, ā, am,* seated as an uninvited guest.

अनाह्लाद *an-āhlāda, as,* m. absence of joy; *(as, ā, am),* gloomy, not cheerful.
An-āhlādita, as, ā, am, not exhilarated.

अनिःशस्त *a-niḥśasta, as, ā, am,* unpraised.

अनिकामतस् *a-nikāmatas,* ind. involuntarily, unintentionally.

अनिकेत *a-niketa* or *a-niketana, as, ā, am,* houseless.

अनिक्षिप्तधूर *a-nikshipta-dhūra, as,* m., N. of a Bodhisattva or deified Buddhist saint.

अनिक्षु *an-ikshu, us,* m. not (true) sugarcane; a sort of long grass or reed, Saccharum Spontaneum. (*An* may here denote 'comparison,' see 3. *a.*)

अनिगीर्ण *a-nigīrṇa, as, ā, am,* not swallowed, not supplied (as an ellipsis).

अनिग्रह *a-nigraha, as, ā, am,* unrestrained; (*as*), m. non-restraint; non-refutation; not owning one's self refuted. — *Anigraha-sthāna, am,* n. (in philosophy) occasion of non-refutation.

अनिघातेषु *a-nighāteshu* (°*ta-ishu*), *us,* m., N. of a man (having arrows that strike no one).

अनिङ्ग्य *an-iṅgya, as, ā, am,* not divisible; a word not divisible.

अनिच्छ *an-iććha* or *an-iććhaka, as, ā, am,* or *an-iććhat, an, antī* or *atī, at,* or *an-iććhu, us, us, u,* or *an-iććhuka, as, ā, am,* undesirous, averse, unwilling; not intending.

An-iććhā, f. absence of wish or design, indifference.

अनिजक *a-nijaka, as, ā, am,* not one's own, belonging to another.

अनित *anita, as, ā, am* (etym. doubtful), destitute of. — *Anita-bhā*, f., Ved. not endowed with splendor, N. of a river (?).

अनित्य *a-nitya, as, ā, am,* not everlasting, transient; occasional, incidental; irregular, unusual; unstable; uncertain; (*am*), ind. occasionally. — *Anitya-karman, a,* n. or *anitya-kriyā,* f. an occasional act of worship, sacrifice for a special purpose. — *Anitya-tā,* f. or *anitya-tva, am,* n. transient or limited existence. — *Anitya-datta* or *anitya-dattaka* or *anitya-datrima, as,* m. a son surrendered by his parents to another for temporary or preliminary adoption. — *Anitya-pratyavekshā,* f. (Buddhist) consciousness that all is passing away. — *Anitya-bhāva, as,* m. transitoriness. — *Anitya-sama, as, ā,* m. f. sophism, consisting in generalizing what is exceptional (as perishableness). — *Anitya-sama-prakaraṇa, am,* n. a section in the Nyāya discussing that sophism. — *Anitya-samāsa, as,* m. a compound, the sense of which may be equally expressed by resolving it into its constituent parts.

अनिदान *a-nidāna, as, ā, am,* causeless, groundless.

अनिद्र *a-nidra, as, ā, am,* sleepless, awake; (*ā*), f. sleeplessness.

A-nidrita, as, ā, am, not asleep, awake.

अनिधृष्ट *a-nidhṛishṭa, as, ā, am,* unchecked, unsubdued.

अनिध्म *an-idhma, as, ā, am,* having or requiring no fuel.

अनिन *an-ina, as, ā, am,* Ved. having no master.

अनिन्दित *a-nindita, as, ā, am,* irreproachable, not despised, pious, virtuous, free.

A-nindya or *a-nindanīya, as, ā, am,* unblamable, faultless.

अनिन्द्र *an-indra, as, ā, am,* deprived of Indra; dispensing with or disregarding Indra.

अनिन्द्रिय *an-indriya, am,* n. that which is not the senses, the soul, the reason.

अनिपद्यमान *a-nipadyamāna, as, ā, am,* not falling down (to sleep), untiring.

अनिपात *a-nipāta, as,* m. (not a fall), continuance of life.

अनिपुण *a-nipuṇa, as, ā, am,* unskilled, not clever or conversant.

अनिबद्ध *a-nibaddha, as, ā, am,* not tied down, not bound, unattached, incoherent, unconnected. — *Anibaddha-pralāpin, ī, inī, i,* chattering incoherently, talking at random.

अनिबाध *a-nibādha, as, ā, am,* unobstructed, unlimited; (*as*), m. liberty.

अनिभृत *a-nibhṛita, as, ā, am,* not private, not reserved, immodest, bold, public.

अनिभृष्ट *a-nibhṛishṭa, as, ā, am,* Ved. unabated; unimpaired; undefeated. — *Anibhṛishṭa-tavi-hi, is,* m., Ved. having unabated power.

अनिभ्य *an-ibhya, as, ā, am,* not wealthy.

अनिमन् *animan, ā,* m. a mote. See *aṇiman.*

अनिमन्त्रित *a-nimantrita, as, ā, am,* uninvited. — *A-nimantrita-bhojin, ī, inī, i,* eating without being invited.

अनिमान *a-nimāna, as ā, am,* Ved. unbounded, immense.

अनिमित्त *a-nimitta, as, ā, am,* having no adequate occasion, causeless, groundless; (*am*), n. absence of an adequate cause or occasion, groundlessness. — *Animitta-tas,* ind. groundlessly. — *A-nimitta-nirākṛita, as, ā, am,* groundlessly rejected. — *Animitta-liṅga-nāśa, as,* m. (unaccountable loss of distinct vision); N. of an ophthalmic disease, ending in total blindness, perhaps amaurosis.

अनिमिष् *a-nimish,* f., Ved. absence of winking (only used in acc. and inst. cases). — *Animisham* or *animishā* or *animesham,* ind., Ved. without winking, i. e. vigilantly or incessantly.

A-nimisha or *a-nimesha, as, ā, am,* not winking, looking steadily, vigilant; open as eyes or flowers; (*as*), m. not winking; a god; a fish. — *Animishāksha* (°*sha-ak*°), *as, ī,* m. f. one whose eyes are fixed. — *Animishāćārya* (°*sha-āć*°), *as,* m., N. of Vṛihaspati.

Animishīya, as, ā, am, relating to those who do not wink (i. e. to the gods).

अनियत *a-niyata, as, ā, am,* not regulated, uncontrolled, not fixed, uncertain, unrestricted, irregular, casual. — *A-niyata-puṇskā,* f. a woman irregular or unchaste in conduct. — *Aniyata-vṛitti, is, is, i,* having no fixed or regular employment or income. — *Aniyatāṅka* (°*ta-aṅ*°), *as,* m. (in arithm.) an indeterminate digit. — *A-niyatātman* (°*ta-āt*°), *ā,* m. one whose self or spirit is not regulated or under proper control.

A-niyama, as, m. absence of control or rule or fixed order or obligation, unsettledness; indecorous or improper conduct; uncertainty, doubt; (*as, ā, am*), having no rule, irregular.

A-niyamita, as, ā, am, having no rule or law; irregular.

अनियुक्त *a-niyukta, as, ā, am,* not appointed, not authoritative; (*as*), m. an assessor at a court who has not been formally appointed and is not entitled to vote.

A-niyogin, ī, inī, i, not attached or clinging to.

अनिर *an-ira, as, ā, am,* Ved. destitute of food (or vigour?), or of a sacrificial offering; (*ā*), f. want of food (languor?).

अनिराकरिष्णु *a-nirākarishṇu, us, us, u,* not obstructive, not censorious.

A-nirākṛita, as, ā, am, unobstructed.

अनिरुक्त *a-nirukta, as, ā, am,* unuttered, not articulated, not clearly explained, unspeakable, not plain, vague. — *Anirukta-gāna, am,* n. indistinct singing; humming (of hymns), a particular mode of chanting the Sāma-veda.

अनिरुद्ध *a-niruddha, as, ā, am,* unobstructed, ungovernable, self-willed; (*as*), m. a spy, a secret emissary (?); the son of Pradyumna, a form of Kāma, and husband of Ushā; Śiva; N. of an Arhat contemporary of Śākyamuni; N. of a descendant of Vṛishṇi; (*am*), n. the rope for fastening cattle. — *A-niruddha-patha, am,* n. an unobstructed path; the atmosphere, ether. — *A-niruddha-bhāvinī,* f. Aniruddha's wife.

अनिरूपित *a-nirūpita, as, ā, am,* not determined, undefined.

अनिर्जित *a-nirjita, as, ā, am,* unconquered, unvanquished.

अनिर्णय *a-nirṇaya, as,* m. uncertainty, want of decision.

A-nirṇīta, as, ā, am, unascertained, undetermined.

A-nirṇeya, as, ā, am, not to be decided.

अनिर्दश *a-nirdaśa* or *a-nir-daśāha* (°*śa-ah*°), *as, ā, am,* within the ten days of impurity after childbirth or a death; (*am*), ind. = preceding, used adverbially.

अनिर्दिष्ट *a-nirdishṭa, as, ā, am* (rt. *diś*), unexplained, undefined.

A-nirdeśa, as, m. absence or unsatisfactoriness of rule or direction.

A-nir-deśya or *a-nirdiśya, as, ā, am,* undefinable, inexplicable, incomparable.

अनिर्धारित *a-nirdhārita, as, ā, am,* undetermined, unascertained, undefined.

A-nirdhārya, as, ā, am, undeterminable, not to be agreed upon.

अनिर्भर *a-nirbhara, as, ā, am,* little, slight, light.

अनिर्भेद *a-nirbheda, as,* m. (the act of not blurting out), not revealing.

अनिर्मल *a-nirmala, as, ā, am,* dirty, foul, turbid.

A-nirmālyā, f. a plant (Mendicago Esculenta, Rox).

अनिर्लोचित *a-nirloćita, as, ā, am,* not carefully looked at, not considered.

अनिर्वचनीय *a-nirvaćanīya* or *a-nirvāćya, as, ā, am,* unutterable, indescribable; improper to be mentioned.

अनिर्वर्त्यमान *a-nirvartyamāna, as, ā, am,* not being brought to a close.

अनिर्वाण *a-nirvāṇa, as, ā, am,* unextinguished.

अनिर्वाह *a-nirvāha, as,* m. non-accomplishment, non-completion; inconclusiveness; insufficiency of income, the state of being straitened in means.

A-nirvāhya, as, ā, am, difficult to be managed.

अनिर्विण्ण *a-nirviṇṇa, as, ā, am,* not downcast.

A-nirvid, t, t, t, free from causes of depression.

A-nirveda, as, m. non-depression, self-reliance.

अनिर्वृत *a-nirvṛita* or *a-nirvṛitta, as, ā, am,* unaccomplished, unfulfilled; discontented; unhappy, ill at ease, unquiet, discomposed.

A-nirvṛiti or *a-nirvṛitti, is,* f. incompleteness, discontent, misery.

अनिर्वेश *a-nirveśa, as, ā, am,* destitute of employment, wretched.

अनिल *anila, as,* m. (fr. rt. *an,* cf. Irish *anal*), air or wind, considered also as a deity; one of the subordinate deities, forty-nine of whom form the class of Anilas or winds; one of the eight demi-gods, called Vasus; wind, as one of the humors or *rasas* of the body; rheumatism, paralysis, or any affection referred to disorder of the wind; N. of a Ṛishi and other persons; the letter *y;* the number forty-nine; (*ī*), f. the fifteenth Nakshatra (?). — *Anila-kumāra, ās,* m. pl. among the Jainas, a class of deities. — *Anila-ghna, as, ī, am,* or *anila-han, hā, -ghnī, ha,* or *anila-hṛit, t, t, t,* or *anilāpaha* (°*la-ap*°), *as, ā, am,* curing disorders arising from wind. — *Anila-ghnaka, as,* m. a large tree (Terminalia Belerica). — *Anila-paryaya* or *anila-paryāya, as,* m. pain and swelling of the eyelids and outer parts of the eye. — *Anila-prakṛiti, is, is, i,* having an airy or windy nature. — *Anila-vyādhi,* *is*, m. derangement of the (internal) wind. — *Anila-sakha, as*, m., N. of fire (the friend of wind). — *Anilātmaja* (°*la-āt*°), *as*, m. the son of the wind, Hanumat or Bhīma. — *Anilāntaka* (°*la-an*°), *as*, m., N. of a plant, Iṅgudī or Aṅgāra-pushpa (wind-destroying). — *Anilāmaya* (°*la-ām*°), *as*, m. morbid affection of the wind, flatulence, rheumatism. — *Anilāyana* (°*la-ay*°), *am*, n. way or course of the wind. — *Anilāśin* (°*la-āś*°), *ī, inī, i*, fasting, lit. feeding on the wind.

अनिलम्भसमाधि *a-nilambha-samādhi, is*, m. (i. e. unpropped meditation), N. of a peculiar kind of meditation among Buddhists.

अनिलयन *a-nilayana, as, ā, am*, having no (fixed) home.

अनिलोचित *a-nilocita*. See *anirlocita*.

अनिलोडित *a-nilodita, as, ā, am*, inexperienced.

अनिवर्तन *a-nivartana, as, ā, am*, not turning away, firm, steadfast; improper to be abandoned, right.

A-nivartin, ī, inī, i, not turning back, brave, not returning. — *Anivarti-tva, am*, n. not turning back, brave resistance.

अनिवारित *a-nivārita, as, ā, am*, unchecked, unimpeded, unopposed, unforbidden.

A-nivārya, as, ā, am, not to be warded off, inavertible, unavoidable, irresistible.

अनिविशमान *a-niviśamāna, as, ā, am*, Ved. not retiring to rest, restless.

अनिवृत *a-nivṛita, as, ā, am*, unchecked, not impeded.

अनिवेदित *a-nivedita, as, ā, am*, untold, unmentioned. — *Anivedita-vijñāta, as, ā, am*, known without being told.

A-nivedya, ind. not having announced.

अनिवेशन *a-niveśana, as, ā, am*, Ved. having no place of rest.

अनिश *a-niśa, as, ā, am*, Ved. nightless, i. e. sleepless, uninterrupted, incessant. — *Aniśam*, ind. incessantly.

A-niśita, as, ā, am, Ved. incessant. — *Aniśita-sarga, as, ā, am*, Ved. having an incessant flow.

अनिश्चित *a-niśćita, as, ā, am*, unascertained, not certain.

A-niśćitya, ind. not having ascertained.

अनिश्चिन्त्य *a-niśćintya, as, ā, am*, not to be comprehended (by thought), inconceivable.

अनिषङ्ग *a-nishanga, as, ā, am*, Ved. having no quiver, unarmed.

अनिषव्य *a-nishavya, as, ā, am*, Ved. not to be killed.

अनिषिद्ध *a-nishiddha, as, ā, am*, unprohibited, unforbidden.

A-nisheddhra, as, ā, am, Ved. unimpeded, unchecked.

अनिषु *an-ishu, us, us, u*, having no arrows, having bad arrows.

अनिष्कृत *a-nishkṛita, as, ā, am*, not done with, unfinished, not settled. — *Anishkṛitainas* (°*ta-en*°), *ās, ās, as*, having one's guilt not settled, i. e. unexpiated.

अनिष्ट 1. *an-ishṭa, as, ā, am* (rt. *ish*), unwished, undesirable, disadvantageous, disagreeable, unfavourable; bad, wrong, evil, unlucky, ominous; (*ā*), f. a plant, Sida Alba; (*am*), n. evil, detriment, disadvantage, calamity, crime. — *Anishṭa-graha, as*, m. an evil planet. — *Anishṭa-dushṭa-dhī, is, is, i*, having an evil and corrupt mind. — *Anishṭa-prasanga, as*, m. connection with a wrong object or a wrong argument or a wrong rule. — *Anishṭa-phala, am*, n. evil result. — *Anishṭa-śankā*, f. foreboding or fear of evil or misfortune. — *Anishṭa-sūćaka, as, ikā, am*, foreboding evil, ominous. — *Anishṭa-hetu, us*, m. an evil omen. — *An-ishṭāpādana* (°*ṭa-āp*°), *am*, n. not obtaining what is desired or (fr. *anishṭa* and *āpādana*) obtaining what is not desired. — *An-ishṭāpti* (°*ṭa-āp*°), *is*, f. = preceding. — *Anishṭāśansin* (°*ṭa-āś*°), *ī, inī, i*, indicating or boding evil. — *Anishṭotprekshaṇa* (°*ṭa-ut*°), *am*, n. expectation of evil.

अनिष्ट 2. *an-ishṭa, as, ā, am* (rt. *yaj*), not offered in sacrifice, not honoured with a sacrifice.

An-ishṭin, ī, m. one who does not sacrifice or has not sacrificed.

अनिष्टृत *a-nishṭṛita, as, ā, am*, Ved. unhurt, unchecked.

अनिष्ठा *a-nishṭhā*, f. unsteadfastness, unsteadiness.

अनिष्ठुर *a-nishṭhura, as, ā, am*, not harsh, not scurrilous.

अनिष्णात *a-nishṇāta, as, ā, am*, unskilled.

अनिष्पत्ति *a-nishpatti, is*, f. non-accomplishment, incompletion.

A-nishpanna, as, ā, am, imperfect, incomplete.

अनिष्पत्त्रम् *a-nish-pattram*, ind. so that the arrow does not come out (on the other side), i. e. not with excessive force.

अनिसर्ग *a-nisarga, as, ā, am*, unnatural, unnaturally affected.

अनिस्तब्ध *a-nistabdha, as, ā, am*, not rendered immoveable or stiff; not paralysed; not fixed.

अनिस्तीर्ण *a-nistīrṇa, as, ā, am*, not crossed over; not set aside; not rid of; unanswered, unrefuted. — *Anistīrṇābhiyoga* (°*ṇa-abh*°), *as*, m. (a defendant) who has not yet (by refutation) got rid of a charge.

अनीक *anīka, as, am*, m. n. (fr. rt. *an*), face; appearance, splendor; edge, point; front, row, array, march; army, forces; war, combat. — *Anīka-vat, ān*, m., Ved. having a face, or constituting the face, or occupying the front or foremost rank (epithet of Agni). — *Anīka-vidāraṇa, as*, m. (shatterer of armies), N. of a man. — *Anīka-śas*, ind. in rows or marching columns. — *Anīka-stha, as*, m. a warrior or combatant; an armed or royal guard, a sentinel; the trainer of an elephant, an elephant-driver; a mark, a sign, signal; a military drum.

Anīkinī, f. an army, a host, forces; a certain force; three Camūs or one-tenth of an Akshauhiṇī, i.e. a complete army; 2187 elephants and as many cars, 6561 horses, and 10935 foot; a lotus.

अनीक्षण *an-īkshaṇa, am*, n. not seeing or looking at.

अनीच *a-nīća, as, ā, am*, not low, decent, respectable; not pronounced with the Anudātta accent. — *A-nīćānuvartin* (°*ća-an*°), *ī, inī, i*, not keeping low company; (*ī*), m. a faithful lover or husband.

A-nīći-darśin, ī, m., N. of a Bauddha saint (?).

Anīćais, ind. not in a low voice, loudly.

अनीड *a-nīḍa, as, ā, am*, having no nest or settled abode, i. e. incorporeal; (*as*), m. an epithet of Agni or fire.

अनीति 1. *a-nīti, is*, f. impropriety, immorality, injustice; impolicy, foolish conduct, indiscretion. — *Anīti-jña, as, ā, am*, or *anīti-vid, t, t, t*, clever in immoral conduct or (fr. *a* and *nītijña*) ignorant of morality or policy, not politic or discreet.

अनीति 2. *an-īti, is*, f. freedom from a calamitous season.

अनीदृश *an-īdṛiśa, as, ī, am*, unlike, dissimilar.

अनीप्सित *an-īpsita, as, ā, am*, undesired.

अनीरसन *a-nīrasana* (*a-nir-rasana*), *as, ā, am*, not destitute of a waistband.

अनीश *an-īśa, as, ā, am*, one who has not a lord or superior, paramount; powerless, unable; (*as*), m. Vishṇu; (*ā*), f. powerlessness, helplessness. — *Anīśa-tva, am*, n. powerlessness.

An-īśvara, as, ā, am, without a superior; unchecked, uncontrolled, paramount; without power, powerless, unable; not belonging to the deity; atheistical. — *Anīśvara-tā*, f. or *anīśvara-tva, am*, n. absence of a supreme ruler. — *An-īśvara-vādin, ī*, m. an atheist, one who denies a supreme ruler of the universe.

अनीह *an-īha, as, ā, am*, listless, indifferent; (*as*), m., N. of a king of Ayodhyā.

An-īhā, f. indifference, apathy, disinclination.

An-īhita, as, ā, am, disagreeable, displeasing, unwished; (*am*), n. displeasure.

अनीळ *a-nīḷa*, Ved. See *a-nīḍa*.

अनु 1. *anu, us, vī, u*. See *aṇu*.

अनु 2. *anu, us*, m., Ved. man; N. of a king, one of Yayāti's sons; (possibly) N. of a non-Āryan tribe.

अनु 3. *anu*, ind. as a prefix to verbs and nouns, expresses after, along, alongside, lengthwise, near to, under, subordinate to, with.

(When prefixed to nouns, especially in adverbial compounds) it implies repetition, according to, severally, each by each, orderly, methodically.

(As a separable preposition, with accusative) after, along, over, near to, through, to, towards, at, according to, in order, agreeably to, in regard to.

(As a separable adverb) after, afterwards, thereupon, again, further, then, next.

अनुक *anu-ka, as, ā, am*, lustful (fr. *anu-kam*, q. v.; or, according to others, fr. 3. *anu* with affix *ka*).

अनुकथ् *anu-kath*, cl. 10. P. *-kathayati, -yitum*, to relate after (some one else); to repeat (what has been heard).

Anu-kathana, am, n. orderly narration, discourse, conversation.

Anu-kathita, as, ā, am, related, repeated.

अनुकनीयस् *anu-kanīyas, ān, asī, as*, the next youngest.

अनुकम् *anu-kam*, Caus. P. *-kāmayati, -yitum*, to desire.

Anu-ka, as, ā, am, libidinous; see s. v. above.

Anu-kāma, as, m., Ved. desire; (*as, ā, am*), according to one's desire, agreeable; (*am*), ind. as desired, at pleasure; wish after wish (?), after one's wish (?). — *Anukāma-kṛit, t, t, t*, Ved. fulfilling one's desire.

Anukāmīna, as, m. one who acts as he pleases.

अनुकम्प् *anu-kamp*, cl. 1. A. *-kampate, -pitum*, to sympathize with, compassionate: Caus. *-kampayati, -yitum*, = the same.

Anu-kampaka, as, m. (sympathizer), N. of a king; (*as, ā, am*), (at the close of compounds) sympathizing with, compassionating.

Anu-kampana, am, n. or *anu-kampā*, f. sympathy, compassion.

Anu-kampāyin, ī, inī, i, condoling.

Anu-kampita, as, ā, am, compassionated. — *Anu-kampitātman* (°*ta-āt*°), *ā, ā, a*, having a compassionate spirit.

Anu-kampin, ī, inī, i, sympathizing with, compassionating.

Anu-kampya or *anu-kampanīya, as, ā, am*, pitiable, worthy of sympathy; (*as*), m. an ascetic; a courier.

अनुकर्ष *anu-karsha*. See under *anu-kṛish*.

अनुकल्प *anu-kalpa*. See under अनुक्लृप्.

अनुकाङ्क्ष् *anu-kānksh*, cl. 1. P. A. *-kānkshati, -te, -kānkshitum*, to long for, desire, seek.

Anu-kānkshā, f. desire after.

Anu-kānkshin, ī, iṇī, i, longing for.

अनुकाल *anu-kāla, as, ā, am*, opportune, occasional; (*am*), ind. opportunely, occasionally, on a proper occasion.

अनुकीर्तन *anu-kīrtana*. See *anu-kṛīt*.

अनुकुञ्चित *anu-kuńćita, as, ā, am*, bent, made crooked.

अनुकुष् *anu-kush*, cl. 9. P. *-kushṇāti, -koshitum*, to pull or drag along (to lift?).

अनुकूज् *anu-kūj*, cl. 1. P. *-kūjati, -jitum*, to follow in cooing or singing or groaning.

अनुकूल *anu-kūla, as, ā, am*, following the bank (*kūla*), slope or declivity, according to the current, favourable, agreeable; conformable to; friendly, kind, well-disposed; (*as*), m. a faithful or kind and obliging husband; (*ā*), f. Croton Polyandrum; N. of a metre; (*am*), n. favour, kindness (often in an ironical sense). — *Anukūla-tā*, f. concord, good-will, favour, conformity, consent; prosperity. — *Anukūla-nāyaka, as*, m. a kind husband or lover. — *Anukūla-vāyu, us*, m. a favourable wind.

Anukūlaya, nom. P. *anukūlayati, -yitum*, to act in a friendly way.

अनुकृ *anu-kṛi*, cl. 8. P. or poet. A. *-karoti, -kurute, -kartum*, to do afterwards, to follow in doing, imitate, equal, requite, adopt: Caus. *-kārayati, -yitum*, to cause one to imitate.

Anu-kara, as, ā, am, imitating; (*as*), m. an assistant.

Anu-karaṇa, am, n. imitation, following an example; resemblance, similarity.

Anu-kartṛi, tā, trī, tṛi, an imitator, imitating; (*tā*), m. a mimic, actor, performer.

Anu-karman, a, n. imitation; a subsequent rite or ceremony.

Anu-kāra, as, m. imitation, resemblance.

Anu-kārin, ī, iṇī, i, imitating, an imitator, acting, mimicing.

Anu-kārya, as, ā, am, fit to be imitated or (dramatically) acted; (*am*), n. subsequent business; subsequent day (?).

Anu-kṛita, as, ā, am, copied, imitated, made or done like.

Anu-kṛiti, is, f. imitation, a copy, compliance.

Anu-kṛitya, as, ā, am, fit to be imitated or represented.

Anu-kriyā, f. imitation, doing anything subsequently or in like manner; a subsequent rite.

Anu-krī, f. a subsequent rite or ceremony.

अनुकृत् *anu-kṛit*, cl. 6. P. *-kṛintati, -kartitum*, to go on shattering or destroying.

अनुकृप् *anu-kṛip*, cl. 6. A., Ved. *-kṛipate*, to mourn; nom. A. *-kṛipāyate, -yitum*, to compassionate, condole with.

अनुकृष् *anu-kṛish*, cl. 1. P. *-karshati, -karshṭum* or *-krashṭum*, to drag after one's self, attract: Caus. *-karshayati, -yitum*, = the same; to subject.

Anu-karsha, as, m. or *anu-karshaṇa, am*, n. attraction, drawing; invoking, summoning by incantation; the bottom or the axle-tree of a carriage; grammatical attraction; including a subsequent in a preceding rule; lagging behind in a ceremony; delayed performance of a duty.

Anu-karshan, ā, m. the bottom of a carriage.

Anu-kṛishṭa, as, ā, am, attracted; included or implied in a subsequent rule.

अनुकॄ *anu-kṝi*, cl. 6. P. *-kirati, -karitum, -rītum*, to scatter along, to crowd: Pass. *-kīryate*, to become crowded or filled.

Anu-kīrṇa, as, ā, am, crowded.

अनुकृत् *anu-kṛīt*, cl. 10. P. *-kīrtayati, -yitum*, to relate after (or in order), to narrate.

Anu-kīrtana, am, n. act of proclaiming or publishing.

अनुक्लृप् *anu-klṛip*, cl. 1. A. *-kalpate, -kalpitum, -kalptum*, to follow duly: Caus. *-kalpayati, -yitum*, to get (others) to follow or imitate duly.

Anu-kalpa, as, m. permission to adopt an alternative or substitute, as "instead of Kuśa grass you may use Dūrbā."

Anu-kalpita, as, ā, am, followed, attended.

अनुक्त *an-ukta, as, ā, am* (rt. *vać*), unuttered, unsaid, unheard of, extraordinary. — *Anukta-nimitta, am*, n. a reason which is unuttered or unheard of or extraordinary; (*as, ā, am*), having such a reason.

An-ukti, is, f. the not speaking, improper speech.

अनुक्थ *an-uktha, as, ā, am*, Ved. hymnless, not singing hymns.

अनुक्रकच *anu-krakaća, as, ā, am*, serrated, dentated like a saw.

अनुक्रन्द् *anu-krand*, cl. 1. A. *-krandate, -ditum*, to shout or cry after one.

अनुक्रम् *anu-kram*, cl. 1. P. *-krāmati, -kramitum*, to go on, go after, follow; to go through in order, enumerate, supply with an abstract or index.

Anu-krama, as, m. succession, arrangement, order, method; an index showing the successive contents of a book; (*am*), ind. in due order.

Anu-kramaṇa, am, n. proceeding methodically or in order; following.

Anu-kramaṇikā or *anu-kramaṇī*, f. a table or chapter of contents, especially of the collection of hymns &c. in Vedic books.

Anu-krānta, as, ā, am, gone over, read, or done in due order.

अनुक्रीड् *anu-krīḍ*, cl. 1. A. *-krīḍate, -ḍitum*, to play.

अनुक्रुश् *anu-kruś*, cl. 1. P. *-krośati, -kroshṭum*, to shout at: Caus. *-krośayati, -yitum*, to join in lamenting, show sympathy.

Anu-krośa, as, m. tenderness, compassion.

अनुक्षणम् *anu-kshaṇam*, ind. momentarily, perpetually, every instant.

अनुक्षत्तृ *anu-kshattṛi, tā*, m. the door-keeper's or charioteer's mate or attendant.

अनुक्षपम् *anu-kshapam*, ind. night after night.

अनुक्षर् *anu-kshar*, cl. 1. P. *-ksharati, -ritum*, to flow into or upon.

अनुक्षि *anu-kshi*, cl. 6. P., Ved. *-kshiyati, -kshetum*, to overspread, reach: Pass. *-kshīyate*, to decay or vanish gradually.

अनुक्षेत्र *anu-kshetra, am*, n. stipend (in commutation probably of the proceeds of an endowment) given to temple-servants in Orissa.

अनुखञ्ज *anu-khańja, as*, m., N. of a country.

अनुख्या *anu-khyā*, cl. 2. P., Ved. *-khyāti, -tum*, to descry.

Anu-khyāti, is, f. act of descrying or revealing or reporting.

Anu-khyātṛi, tā, m. a discoverer, revealer, reporter.

अनुगङ्गम् *anu-gangam*, ind. along the Ganges.

अनुगण् *anu-gaṇ*, cl. 10. P. *-gaṇayati, -yitum*, to count over.

Anu-gaṇita, as, ā, am, counted over.

Anu-gaṇitin, ī, inī, i, one who has counted over.

अनुगम् *anu-gam*, cl. 1. P. *-gaććhati, -gantum*, to go after, follow, seek, approach, visit, arrive; to practise, observe, obey, imitate; to enter into; to die out, be extinguished: Caus. *-gamayati, -yitum*, to imitate, cause to die out.

Anu-ga, as, ā, am, going after, following, corresponding with, adapted to; a companion; a follower, a servant; (at the close of compounds) having followers, as *balānuga*, having a force following him, i. e. leader of a force or army; (*ā*), f., N. of an Apsaras.

Anu-gata, as, ā, am, followed (lit. or fig.), as by a dependant; covered (as by a dress hanging behind); following; a follower; acquired; extinguished; tallying with; (*am*), n. moderate time in music. — *Anugatārtha* (°*ta-ar*°), *as, ā, am*, having a corresponding (easily discoverable) meaning.

Anu-gatika, as, m. a follower, an imitator.

Anu-gantavya or *anu-gamya, as, ā, am*, proper to be followed (especially in death); worthy of being imitated.

Anu-gama, as, m. or *anu-gamana, am*, n. following, going after in life or death; postcremation of a widow; imitating, approaching.

Anu-gamya, as, ā, am, to be followed or imitated.

Anu-gāmin, ī, inī, i, following, a follower, a companion.

Anu-gāmuka, as, ā, am, habitually or constantly following or attending.

अनुगर्ज् *anu-garj*, cl. 1. P. *anu-garjati, -jitum*, to shout or roar after.

Anu-garjita, am, n. roaring echo.

अनुगवम् *anu-gavam*, ind. so as to suit the oxen.

अनुगवीन *anu-gavīna, as*, m. a cowherd.

अनुगा *anu-gā*, cl. 3. P. *-jigāti, -gātum*, to go after, follow, seek, be guided by.

अनुगादिन् *anu-gādin, ī, inī, i*, following in speaking, echoing.

अनुगाह् *anu-gāh*, cl. 1. A. *-gāhate, -gāhitum, -gāḍhum*, to plunge after, be immersed in.

Anu-gāḍha, as, ā, am, plunged, immersed.

अनुगिरम् *anu-giram*, ind. on the mountain.

अनुगु *anu-gu*, ind. behind the oxen or cows.

अनुगुण *anu-guṇa, as, ā, am*, having similar qualities, congenial with; according or suitable to; (*am*), ind. naturally; (*as*), m. natural peculiarity.

अनुगुप् *anu-gup*, cl. 1. P. *-gopāyati, -goptum*, to protect.

Anu-gupta, as, ā, am, protected, sheltered, concealed.

अनुगृध् *anu-gṛidh*, cl. 4. P. *-gṛidhyati, -gardhitum*, to be greedy after.

अनुगॄ *anu-gṝi*, cl. 9. P. *-gṛiṇāti, -garitum, -rītum*, Ved. to join in praising; to rejoin, answer, repeat.

अनुगै *anu-gai*, cl. 1. P. *-gāyati, -gātum*, to sing after or to (a person or a tune); to celebrate in song: Caus. *-gāpayati, -yitum*, to make one sing after or to.

Anu-gīti, is, f., N. of a metre of two verses, the first containing twenty-seven, the second thirty-two mātrās.

अनुग्र an-ugra, as, ā, am, not harsh or violent, mild, gentle.

अनुग्रह् anu-grah, cl. 9. P. -gṛihṇāti or Ved. -gribhṇāti, or cl. 9. A. -gṛihṇīte, -grahītum, to follow in taking or plundering; to support; uphold; to receive, welcome; treat with kindness, favour, oblige; foster.

Anu-gṛihīta, as, ā, am, favoured, obliged.

Anu-graha, as, m. or anu-grahaṇa, am, n. favour, kindness, showing favour, conferring benefits, promoting or furthering a good object; assistance; facilitating by incantations; rear-guard; (in the Purāṇas) N. of the eighth or fifth creation. — Anugraha-kātara, as, ā, am, anxious to please or for favour. — Anugraha-sarga, as, m. (in Sāṅkhya phil.) creation of the feelings or mental conditions.

Anu-grahin, ī, m., Ved. proficient in magic skill.

Anu-grāhaka, as, ikā, am, favouring, furthering, facilitating; favourable, kind, gracious.

Anu-grāhita or anu-grahita (?), as, ā, am, favoured.

Anu-grāhin, ī, iṇī, i, gracious, favourable.

Anu-grāhya, as, ā, am, fit or deserving to be favoured or furthered.

Anu-jighṛikshā, f. desire to show favour or kindness.

अनुग्रामम् anu-grāmam, ind. village after village.

अनुग्रासक anu-grāsaka, as, m. a mouthful (of boiled rice), the equivalent of a mouthful.

अनुघट्ट् anu-ghaṭṭ, cl. 10. P. -ghaṭṭayati, -yitum, to stroke, rub lengthwise.

अनुघुष् anu-ghush, cl. 1. P., Ved. -ghoshati, -shitum, to name aloud.

अनुचक्ष् anu-ćaksh, cl. 2. A., Ved. -ćashṭe, -ćashṭum, to look at or up to.

अनुचर् anu-ćar, cl. 1. P. -ćarati, -ritum, to walk or move after or along, to follow, pursue, traverse, seek after; to follow out, adhere to, attend, to behave: Caus. -ćārayati, -yitum, to let or cause to traverse.

Anu-ćara, as, ī, am, following, attending; (as), m. companion, follower, servant; (ā or ī), f. a female attendant.

Anu-ćāraka, as, m. a follower, attendant; (ā), f. a female follower or attendant.

Anu-ćārin, ī, iṇī, i, following, attending.

अनुचर्चि anu-ćarći, is, is, i, Ved. reciting or repeating (in a chorus).

अनुचि 1. anu-ći, cl. 5. P. -ćinoti, -ćetum, to set or place along or in regular order.

1. anu-ćita, as, ā, am, set or placed along or lengthwise or in rows.

अनुचि 2. anu-ći, cl. 3. P., Ved. -ćiketi, to remember.

अनुचित 2. an-ućita, as, ā, am, improper, wrong, unusual, strange. — Anućitārtha (°ta-ar°), as, m. an unusual meaning.

अनुचिन्त् anu-ćint, cl. 10. P. -ćintayati, -yitum, to meditate, consider, recal to mind: Caus. to make to consider.

Anu-ćintā, f. or anu-ćintana, am, n. thinking of, meditating upon, recalling, recollecting; anxiety.

Anu-ćintita, as, ā, am, recollected, recalled, thought of.

अनुच्च an-ućća, as, ā, am, not high, low, humble.

An-uććais, ind. not aloud, in a low voice.

अनुच्चार an-uććāra, non-pronunciation, skipping words. See uć-ćar.

अनुच्छाद anu-ććhāda, as, m. (fr. rt. ćhad with anu), a garment which hangs down, or probably that part of the lower garment which hangs down in front from the waist to the feet.

अनुच्छित्ति an-uć-ćhitti, is, f. or an-uć-ćheda, as, m. (rt. ćhid with ud), not cutting off, non-extirpation, non-destruction, indestructibility. — Anuććhitti-dharman, ā, ā, a, possessing the virtue (or law) of being indestructible.

1. an-uć-ćhindat, an, atī, at, not destroying.

An-uć-ćhinna, as, ā, am, not cut off, unextirpated, undestroyed.

An-uć-ćhedya, as, ā, am, indestructible, not severable.

अनुच्छिद् anu-ććhid (anu-ćhid), cl. 7. P. -ććhinatti, -ććhettum, to cut along or lengthwise.

2. anu-ććhindat, an, atī, at, cutting lengthwise.

अनुच्छिष्ट an-uććhishṭa, as, ā, am (rt. śish with ud), not rejected, pure (by austerity and devotion).

अनुच्छो anu-ććho (anu-ćho), cl. 4. P. -ćhyati, -ćhātum, to cut open or cut up.

अनुजन् anu-jan, cl. 4. A. -jāyate, -janitum, to follow in being born or produced or arising; to take after (one's parents).

Anu-ja, as, ā, am, born after, later, younger; (as), m. a younger brother, a cadet; N. of a plant, also called Trāyamāṇa; (am), n., N. of a plant, also called Prapauṇḍarīka; (ā), f. a younger sister.

Anu-janman, ā, m. a younger brother, younger.

Anu-jāta, as, ā, am, after-born, later, younger; taking after (the parents); after teething (?); born again, i. e. invested with the sacred cord; (as), m. a younger brother; (ā), f. a younger sister.

अनुजनम् anu-janam, ind. according to people, popularly.

अनुजप् anu-jap, cl. 1. P. -japati, -pitum, to follow or imitate in muttering.

अनुजल्प् anu-jalp, cl. 1. P. -jalpati, -pitum, to follow in talking; A. -jalpate, to entertain by conversation.

अनुजागृ anu-jāgṛi, cl. 2. P. -jāgarti, -jāgaritum, to watch as an attendant.

अनुजि anu-ji, cl. 1. P. -jayati, -jetum, to subdue: Desid. -jigīshate, to be desirous of subduing.

अनुजिघृक्षा anu-jighṛikshā. See under anu-grah.

अनुजीव् anu-jīv, cl. 1. P. -jīvati, -vitum, to follow or imitate in living; to live for any one; to live by or upon something; to live submissively under: Caus. -jīvayati, -yitum, to restore to life.

Anu-jīvin, ī, inī, i, living by or upon; dependent; (ī), m. a dependent, follower. — Anujīvi-sāt-kṛita, as, ā, am, made wholly subservient.

Anu-jīvya, as, ā, am, to be followed in living.

अनुजुष् anu-jush, cl. 6. A., Ved. -jushate, -joshitum, to seek.

अनुजॄ anu-jṝi, cl. 4. P. -jīryati, or cl. 1. P., Ved. -jarati, -jaritum, -rītum, to follow in getting old or decaying.

Anu-jīrṇa, as, ā, am, grown old or decayed after or in consequence of.

अनुज्झत् an-ujjhat, an, antī or atī, at, not quitting, not leaving.

An-ujjhita, as, ā, am, undiminished, unimpaired, not left or lost.

अनुज्ञा 1. anu-jñā, cl. 9. P. rarely A. -jānāti, -jānīte, -jñātum, to permit, grant, allow, consent; to excuse, forgive; to authorize; to allow one to take leave, dismiss, bid farewell; to entreat; to behave kindly: Caus. -jñāpayati, -yitum, to request, ask permission, ask for leave, to take leave: Desid. -jijñāsati or -te, to be willing to grant.

2. anu-jñā, f. or anu-jñāna, am, n. assent, assenting, permission; leave to depart; allowance made for faults; an order or command. — Anujñā-prārthanā or anujñaishaṇā (°jñā-esh°), f. asking permission, taking leave.

Anu-jñāta, as, ā, am, assented to, permitted, allowed; ordered, directed, instructed; accepted; authorized, honoured; allowed to depart, dismissed.

Anu-jñāpaka, as, m. one who commands or enjoins.

Anu-jñāpana, am, n. or anu-jñapti, is, f. authorization; issuing an order or permission.

अनुज्येष्ठ anu-jyeshṭha, as, ā, am, next eldest; (am), ind. after the eldest, according to seniority.

अनुतक्ष् anu-taksh, cl. 1. P., Ved. -takshati, -kshitum, -tashṭum, to sharpen or stimulate by offerings.

अनुतन् anu-tan, cl. 8. P. -tanoti, -tanitum, to extend along, to carry on, continue, develop.

अनुतप् anu-tap, cl. 1. P. -tapati, -taptum, to heat, to vex, annoy: Pass. -tapyate or poet. -tapyati, to suffer afterwards, repent; to desiderate, miss: Caus. -tāpayati, -yitum, to distress.

Anu-tapta, as, ā, am, heated; filled with regret.

Anu-tāpa, as, m. repentance, heat.

Anu-tāpana, as, ī, am, occasioning remorse, repentance or sorrow.

Anu-tāpin, ī, inī, i, penitent, regretting.

अनुतर anu-tara. See anu-tṝi below.

अनुतर्क् anu-tark, cl. 10. P. or poet. A. -tarkayati, -te, -yitum, to follow in thought, to regard as or take for.

अनुतर्ष anu-tarsha, as, m. thirst, wish, desire; a drinking vessel, one used for drinking spirituous liquors.

Anu-tarshaṇa, am, n. a vessel from which spirituous liquor is drunk; distributing liquor.

अनुतिलम् anu-tilam, ind. grain after grain (of Sesamum), i. e. very minutely or by grains.

अनुतिष्ठमान anu-tishṭhamāna. See anu-shṭhā.

अनुतुन्न anu-tunna, as, ā, am (rt. tud), Ved. depressed or repressed (in sound), muffled.

अनुतूलय anu-tūlaya, nom. P. -tūlayati, -yitum, to rub lengthwise (with a brush or cotton?).

अनुतृद् anu-tṛid, cl. 7. P. -tṛinatti, -tarditum, to let go, let out; split, sever, open.

अनुतृप् anu-tṛip, cl. 4. A. -tṛipyate, -tarpitum, -tarptum, -traptum, to take one's fill (or refreshment) after or later than another.

अनुतॄ anu-tṝi, cl. 1. P. -tarati, -ritum or -rītum, to follow across or to the end; to stretch lengthwise or prostrate: Pass. -tīryate, to be laid or lay one's self lengthwise.

Anu-tara, am, n. fare, freight.

अनुत्क an-utka, as, ā, am, free from regret, not regretting, self-complacent, not repenting of.

अनुत्कर्ष an-utkarsha, as, m. inferiority, non-elevation.

अनुत्त a-nutta, as, ā, am, Ved. not cast down, invincible; (or, not moistened, = an-utta?). — Anutta-manyu, us, m. of invincible wrath, i. e. Indra.

अनुत्तम an-uttama, as, ā, am, unsurpassed, incomparably the best or chief, excellent; not the best; (in gram.) not used in the uttama or first person. — An-uttamāmbhas (°ma-am°), as, n. (in Sāṅkhya phil.) indifference to and consequent abstinence from sensual enjoyment, as fatiguing.—*An-uttamāmbhasika, am*, n. indifference to and abstinence from sensual enjoyment as involving injury to external objects.

अनुत्तर *an-uttara, as, ā, am*, chief, principal; best, excellent; without a reply, unable to answer, silent; fixed, firm; low, inferior, base; south, southern; (*am*), n. a reply which is coherent or evasive and therefore held to be no answer; (*as*), m. a class of gods among the Jainas.—*Anuttara-yoga-tantra, am*, n. title of the last of the four Bauddha-tantras.—*An-uttaropapātika* (°*ra-up*°), *ās*, m. pl. the same class of gods.—*Anuttaropapātika-daśā, ās*, f. pl. title of a book treating of those gods.

अनुत्तान *an-uttāna, as, ā, am*, lying with the face towards the ground; not supine.

अनुत्थान *an-utthāna, am*, n. (rt. *sthā*), the not rising, want of exertion.

An-utthita, as, ā, am, not risen, not grown up (as grain).

अनुत्पत्ति *an-utpatti, is*, f. failure, non-production; (*is, is, i*), or *an-utpattika, as, ī, am*, not (yet) produced.—*Anutpattika-dharma-kshānti, is*, f. (with Buddhists) acquiescence in the state (and moral condition) which is still future, preparation for a future state.—*Anutpatti-sama, as, ā*, m. f. (in Nyāya phil.) arguing against a thing by trying to show that nothing exists from which it could spring.

An-utpanna, as, ā, am, unborn, unproduced; uneffected, unaccomplished.

An-utpāda, as, m. the not coming into existence; the not taking effect.—*Anutpāda-kshānti, is*, f. acquiescence in not having to undergo another birth.

An-utpādana, am, n. not producing, non-production.

An-utpādya, as, ā, am, not to be produced or created, i. e. eternal.

अनुत्साह *an-utsāha, as*, m. want of adequate effort; want of energy or determination; listlessness; (*as, ā, am*), deficient in determination.—*Anutsāha-tā*, f. want of determination.

अनुत्सुक *an-utsuka, as, ā, am*, not eager, calm, retiring; moderate.—*Anutsuka-tā*, f. moderateness.

अनुत्सूत्र *an-utsūtra, as, ā, am*, not anomalous.

अनुत्सेक *an-utseka, as*, m. absence of arrogance or highmindedness.

An-utsekin, ī, inī, i, not arrogant or puffed up.

अनुदक *an-udaka, as, ā, am*, waterless.

अनुदग्र *an-udagra, as, ā, am*, not lofty, low; not projecting.

अनुदय *an-udaya, as*, m. non-rising, the not rising (of a luminary).

1. *an-udita, as, ā, am*, not risen, not appeared. (For 2. *an-udita*, see next column.)

अनुदर *an-udara, as, ā, am*, thin, lank.

अनुदह् *anu-dah*, cl. 1. P. *-dahati, -dagdhum*, to burn over again, to burn up.

अनुदा *anu-dā*, cl. 3. P. *-dadāti, -dātum*, to give back, restore, give way, yield, grant, remit; to pay one out (?).

Anu-da, as, ā, am, Ved. yielding, emulating others in giving, a follower.

Anu-datta, as, ā, am, granted, remitted, given back.

Anu-deya, as, ā, am, to be given back or restored.

Anu-deyī, f., Ved. restitution; a female follower or companion.

अनुदात्त *an-udātta, as, ā, am*, not raised, not elevated, not pronounced with the Udātta accent, grave; accentless, having the neutral general tone neither high nor low: the term *Anudātta* is used by Pāṇini both for the grave or non-elevated accent (explained by him as *sannatara*, q. v.) which immediately precedes the Udātta, and also for the general accentless, neutral tone, neither high nor low, explained as *eka-śruti*, i. e. the one monotonous ordinary intonation which belongs to the generality of syllables in a sentence; (*as*), m. one of the three accents to be observed in reading the Vedas, the grave accent.—*Anudātta-tara, as*, m. more than Anudātta, still lower in sound than Anudātta, i. e. the *very* Anudātta accent (or a syllable having this accent) which immediately precedes a syllable having the Udātta or Svarita accent, and is therefore more depressed than the ordinary Anudātta.—*Anudāttādi* (°*tta-ād*°), n. (in gram.) a nominal base of which the first syllable is Anudātta.—*Anudāttet* (°*tta-it*°), *t*, m. a verbal root having for its Anubandha the Anudātta accent to indicate that it takes the Ātmane-pada terminations only; also *anudāttopadeśa*.—*Anudāttodaya* (°*tta-ud*°), *am*, n. a syllable immediately preceding the Anudātta accent.

अनुदार 1. *an-udāra, as, ā, am*, niggardly, mean; liberal, munificent.

अनुदार 2. *anu-dāra, as, ā, am*, adhered to or followed by a wife.

अनुदित 2. *an-udita, as, ā, am*, unsaid, unuttered, interdicted (see 1. *an-udita* under *an-udaya*).

अनुदिनम् *anu-dinam* or *anu-divasam*, ind. daily, every day.

अनुदिश् *anu-diś*, cl. 6. P. *-diśati, -deshṭum*, to point out, to assign.

Anu-diśam, ind. in every quarter.

Anu-deśa, as, m. a rule or injunction, especially one that points back to a previous rule; reference to something prior.

Anu-deśin, ī, inī, i, pointing back, referring back; being the object of an Anudeśa.

अनुदृभ् *anu-dṛibh*, cl. 6. P., Ved. *-dṛibhati, -darbhitum*, to make into bundles or chains.

अनुदृश् *anu-dṛiś*, cl. 1. P. *-paśyati, -drashṭum*, to survey, behold; to keep in view or in mind, to foresee: Caus. P. *-darśayati, -yitum*, to show, tell, teach: Pass. *-dṛiśyate*, to become or be visible.

Anu-darśana, am, n. consideration, regard, reference.

Anu-darśin, ī, inī, i, considering, foreseeing.

Anu-dṛishṭi, is, f., N. of the ancestress of Ānu-dṛishṭineya.

An-udrashṭavya, as, ā, am, capable of being observed, visible.

अनुदॄ *anu-dṛī*, Pass. *-dīryate*, to break through after (another); to be scattered or confused (in consequence of the confusion of others).

अनुदेहम् *anu-deham*, ind. behind the body.

अनुदैर्घ्य *anu-dairghya, as, ā, am*, longitudinal.

अनुद्गीर्ण *an-udgīrṇa, as, ā, am*, not vomited forth, not disdained; not spurned.

अनुद्धत *an-uddhata, as, ā, am* (rt. *han*), not lifted up, humble, unsurpassed, unequalled, unopposed.

अनुद्धरण *an-uddharaṇa, am*, n. (rt. *hṛi*), non-removal; not offering, not establishing or proving.

An-uddhāra, as, m. non-partition, not taking a share; non-removal.

An-uddhṛita, as, ā, am, non-removed, not taken away; uninjured, undestroyed; unoffered; undivided, unpartitioned; unestablished, unproved.—*An-uddhṛitābhyastamaya* (°*ta-abh*°), *as*, m. sunset (*abhy-astamaya*), taking place whilst the Āhavanīya fire continues (*an-uddhṛita*) unremoved from the Gārhapatya.

अनुद्भट *an-udbhaṭa, as, ā, am*, not exalted, unassuming.

अनुद्य *an-udya, as, ā, am*, unutterable.

अनुद्यत *an-udyata, as, ā, am* (rt. *yam*), inactive, idle, destitute of perseverance.

अनुद्योग *an-udyoga, as*, m. absence of exertion or effort, inactivity, laziness.

An-udyogin, ī, inī, i, inactive, lazy, indifferent.

अनुद्र *an-udra, as, ā, am*, waterless.

अनुद्रु *anu-dru*, cl. 1. P. *-dravati, -drotum*, to run after, follow; accompany; to pursue.

Anu-druta, as, ā, am, followed, pursued; (*am*), n. a measure of time in music, half a Druta, or one-fourth of a Mātrā or of the time taken to articulate a short vowel.

अनुद्वाह *an-udvāha, as*, m. non-marriage, celibacy.

अनुद्विग्न *an-udvigna, as, ā, am*, free from apprehension or perplexity, easy in mind.

An-udvega, as, ā, am, free from anxiety; (*as*), m. freedom from uneasiness.—*An-udvega-kara, as, ī, am*, not causing apprehension, not overawing.

अनुधा *anu-dhā*, cl. 3. P. *-dadhāti, -dhātum*, to welcome, receive kindly.

अनुधाव् 1. *anu-dhāv*, cl. 1. P. *-dhāvati, -vitum*, to run after, to run up to.

Anu-dhāvat, an, antī, at, running after.

1. *anu-dhāvana, am*, n. chasing, pursuing, running after; close pursuit of any object, going after a mistress.

Anu-dhāvita, as, ā, am, pursued, run after, literally or figuratively.

अनुधाव् 2. *anu-dhāv*, cl. 1. P. A. *-dhavati, -te, -vitum*, to cleanse.

2. *anu-dhāvana, am*, n. cleansing, purification.

अनुध्यै *anu-dhyai*, cl. 1. P. *-dhyāyati, -dhyātum*, to consider attentively, to think of, to muse, to be anxious.

Anu-dhyāna, am, n. meditation, religious contemplation, solicitude.

Anu-dhyāyin, ī, inī, i, contemplating, meditating.

अनुनद् *anu-nad*, cl. 1. P. *-nadati, -ditum*, to sound towards, (with acc.): Caus. P. *-nādayati, -yitum*, to make resonant or musical.

Anu-nāda, as, m. sound, vibration, reverberation, echo.

Anu-nādita, as, ā, am, made to resound.

Anu-nādin, ī, inī, i, resounding, echoing, resonant.

अनुनम् *anu-nam*, cl. 1. P. *-namati, -nantum*, to incline to.

अनुनय *anu-naya, anu-nayin*, &c. See *anu-nī*.

अनुनासिक *anu-nāsika, as, ā, am*, nasal, uttered through the nose (as one of the five nasal consonants, or a vowel, or the three semivowels *y, v, l*, under certain circumstances; in the case of vowels and semivowels, the mark ँ is used to denote this nasalization); the nasal mark ँ; (*am*), n. a nasal twang.—*Anunāsika-tva, am*, n. nasality.—*Anunāsika-lopa, as*, m. dropping of a nasal sound or letter.—*Anunāsikātva* (°*ka-āt*°), *am*, n. nasal pronunciation of *ā*.—*Anunāsikādi* (°*ka-ādi*), *is*, m. a compound letter commencing with a nasal.—*Anunāsikānta* (°*ka-an*°), *as*, m. a radical ending in a nasal.—*Anunāsikopadha* (°*ka-up*°), *as, ā, am*, having a nasal penultimate; succeeding a syllable with a nasal sound.

अनुनिक्रम् *anu-ni-kram*, cl. 1. P. *-krāmati, -kramitum*, to follow in the steps.

अनुनिक्ष् *anu-niksh*, cl. 1. P., Ved. *-nikshati, -kshitum*, to pierce along.

अनुनितुद् *anu-ni-tud*, cl. 6. P. *-tudati, -tottum*, to wound with a stab, to goad.

अनुनिपद् *anu-ni-pad*, cl. 4. A. *-padyate, -pattum*, to lie down by the side of.

अनुनिर्जिहान *anu-nir-jahāna, as, ā, am* (rt. *hā*), proceeding out of (?).

अनुनिर्दह् *anu-nir-dah*, cl. 1. P. *-dahati, -dagdhum*, to burn down in succession.

अनुनिर्देश *anu-nirdeśa, as*, m. description or relation following a previous model.

अनुनिर्वाप *anu-nirvāpa, as*, m. subsequent libation (with clarified butter).

Anu-nirvāpyā, f. ceremony connected with this subsequent libation.

अनुनी *anu-nī*, cl. 1. P. *-nayati, -netum*, to bring near, to lead after; to persuade, induce, win over, conciliate, to coax, pacify, supplicate.

Anu-naya, as, m. conciliation, salutation, courtesy, civility, showing respect or adoration to a guest or a deity; humble entreaty or supplication, reverential deportment; regulation of conduct, discipline, tuition; (*as, ā, am*), conciliatory, kind; (*am*), ind. fitly, becomingly. — *Anunaya-pratigha-prahāṇa, am*, n. (with Buddhists) abandoning the obstacles to conciliatory behaviour. — *Anunayāmantraṇa* (°*ya-ām*°), *am*, n. conciliatory address.

Anu-nayamāna, as, ā, am, conciliating, honouring, showing respect.

Anu-nayin, ī, inī, i, courteous, humble, supplicating.

Anu-nāyaka, as, ikā, am, submissive, humble.

Anu-nāyikā, f. a female character, subordinate to a *nāyikā* or leading female character in a drama.

Anu-ninīshu, us, us, u, desirous of conciliating or gratifying.

Anu-nīta, as, ā, am, trained, disciplined, obtained, acquired, taught, respected; pleased, pacified, appeased, humbly entreated.

Anu-nīti, is, f. conciliation, courtesy, supplication.

Anu-neya, as, ā, am, easily conciliated.

अनुनु *anu-nu* or *-nū*, cl. 6. and cl. 2. P., Ved. *-nuvati* or *-nauti, -navitum* or *-nuvitum*, to praise again and again: Intens. *-nonavīti*, to cheer after.

अनुनृत् *anu-nṛit*, cl. 4. P. *-nṛityati, -nartitum*, to dance after (with acc.); to dance before (with acc.).

अनुन्नत *an-unnata, as, ā, am*, not elevated, not lifted up. — *Anunnata-gātra, as, ā, am*, (with Buddhists) having limbs that are not too stout, prominent or protuberant. — *Anunnatānata* (°*ta-ān*°), *as, ā, am*, not raised nor lowered, level.

अनुन्मत्त *an-unmatta* or *an-unmadita* or *an-unmāda, as, ā, am*, sane, sober, not wild, not mad.

अनुप *anupa, as, ā, am*, watery, marshy; see *anūpa*. — *Anupa-ja* or better *anūpa-ja, am*, n. ginger (in its undried state).

अनुपकारिन् *an-upakārin, ī, iṇī, i*, not assisting, disobliging, ungrateful, not making a return for benefits received; unserviceable, useless.

An-upakṛita, as, ā, am, unassisted.

अनुपक्षित *an-upakshita, as, ā, am*, uninjured, undestroyed.

अनुपगीत *an-upagīta, as, ā, am*, not praised or celebrated (?); not accompanied in singing (?); (*am*), ind. so that no other person accompanies in singing.

अनुपघातार्जित *an-upaghātārjita* (°*ta-arj*°), *as, ā, am*, acquired without detriment (to the paternal estate).

An-upaghnat, an, atī, at, not detrimental (to the paternal estate).

अनुपच् *anu-paċ*, cl. 1. P. *-paċati, -paktum*, to make ripe by degrees: Pass. *-paċyate*, to become ripe by degrees.

अनुपजीवनीय *an-upajīvanīya, as, ā, am*, yielding (or granting) no livelihood; having no livelihood.

अनुपठ् *anu-paṭh*, cl. 1. P. *-paṭhati, -ṭhitum*, to say after, repeat.

Anu-paṭhita, as, ā, am, read through (aloud), recited.

Anu-paṭhitin, ī, m. (one who has read through or recited), proficient.

अनुपत् *anu-pat*, cl. 1. P. *-patati, -titum*, to fly to (with acc.); fly after, run after, go after, follow: Caus. *-pātayati, -yitum*, to fly to; to throw a person down together with oneself.

Anu-patana, am, n. falling on or upon; following; (in mathem.) proportion.

Anu-patita, as, ā, am, fallen, descended; followed.

Anu-pāta, see s. v.

अनुपति *anu-pati*, ind. after the husband.

अनुपथ *anu-patha, as, ā, am*, following the road; having favourable roads?; (*as*), m. a road; (*am*), ind. along the road.

अनुपद् 1. *anu-pad*, cl. 4. A. *-padyate, -pattum*, to follow, attend, be fond of; to enter; to enter upon; to notice, understand; to handle.

2. *anu-pad, t, t, t*, Ved. coming to pass; or (*t*), f. food (?).

Anu-pada, as, ā, am, following closely; (*as*), m., N. of a man or tribe; (*am*), n. a chorus, burden of a song or words sung again after regular intervals; (*am*), ind. step by step, word for word; on the heels of, close behind or after. — *Anupada-sūtra, am*, n. title of a commentary explaining the text (of a Brāhmaṇa) word for word.

Anu-padavī, f. a way.

Anu-padin, ī, m. a searcher, an inquirer, one who follows or seeks for.

Anupadīnā, f. a boot, a buskin.

अनुपदस्वत् *an-upadasvat, ān, atī, at*, Ved. not drying up, not decaying (?).

अनुपदिष्ट *an-upadishṭa, as, ā, am*, untaught, uninstructed.

An-upadeshṭṛi, ṭā, m. one who does not point out or teach.

अनुपध *an-upadha, as*, m. (having no penultimate), a letter or syllable (as a sibilant or *h*) when not preceded by another.

अनुपधिशेष *an-upadhi-śesha, as*, m. that in which there is no longer a condition of individuality (?).

अनुपनाह *an-upanāha, as*, m. (with Buddhists) want of close attachment or adherence (?).

अनुपन्यस्त *an-upanyasta, as, ā, am*, not laid down clearly, not established.

An-upanyāsa, as, m. failure of proof or determination, uncertainty, doubt.

अनुपपत्ति *an-upapatti, is*, f. non-accomplishment, failure, inconclusive argumentation; irrelevancy, inapplicability, impossibility, insufficiency of means, penury, adversity.

An-upapanna, as, ā, am, not done, unaccomplished, uneffected; unproved, undemonstrated; irrelevant, inconclusive, inapplicable, impossible, inadequately supported.

An-upapādaka, ās, m. pl. (having no material parent), N. of a class of Buddhas, called Dhyāni-buddhas.

अनुपप्लव *an-upaplava, as, ā, am*, free from any overwhelming calamity.

An-upapluta, as, ā, am, not overwhelmed (with calamity).

अनुपबाध *an-upabādha, as, ā, am*, Ved. unobstructed, unimpaired.

अनुपभुक्त *an-upabhukta, as, ā, am*, unenjoyed, unpossessed.

An-upabhujyamāna, as, ā, am, not being enjoyed.

अनुपम *an-upama, as, ā, am*, incomparable, matchless; excellent, best; (*ā*), f. the female elephant of the south-east or of the north-east. — *Anupama-mati, is*, m., N. of a contemporary of Śākya-muni.

An-upamita, as, ā, am, uncompared, matchless.

An-upameya, as, ā, am, incomparable.

अनुपमर्दन *an-upamardana, am*, n. non-demolition or refutation of a charge.

अनुपयुक्त *an-upayukta, as, ā, am*, unsuited, unsuitable, improper; useless, unserviceable.

An-upayoga, as, m. unserviceableness, uselessness.

An-upayogin, ī, inī, i, unsuitable, useless.

अनुपरत *an-uparata, as, ā, am*, uninterrupted, not stopped.

अनुपरापत् *anu-parā-pat*, cl. 1. P. *-patati, -titum*, to fly or hasten by the side of another.

अनुपरिकॄ *anu-pari-kṝ*, cl. 6. P. *-kirati, -karitum, -rītum*, to scatter alongside, to bestrew.

अनुपरिक्रम् *anu-pari-kram*, cl. 1. P. *-krāmati, -kramitum*, to walk round in order, to make the circuit of, visit in a regular round.

अनुपरिगा *anu-pari-gā*, cl. 3. P. *-jigāti, -gātum*, to make the round of, traverse.

अनुपरिणी *anu-pari-ṇī* (*-nī*), cl. 1. P. *-ṇayati, -ṇetum*, to lead or carry about.

अनुपरिधि *anu-paridhi*, ind. along or at the three Paridhis of the sacrificial fire.

अनुपरिश्रित् *anu-pariśrit*, ind. along or at the surrounding fence.

अनुपरी *anu-parī* (*-pari-i*), cl. 2. P. *-paryeti, -tum*, to follow in going round, to make the round of.

अनुपरे *anu-pare* (*-parā-i*), cl. 2. P. *-paraiti, -tum*, to follow in walking off.

अनुपर्यागा *anu-pary-ā-gā*, cl. 3. P. *-jigāti, -gātum*, to revolve, accomplish a revolution.

अनुपर्ये *anu-parye* (*-pari-ā-i*), cl. 2. P. *-paryaiti, -tum*, to make the whole round of.

अनुपलक्षित *an-upalakshita, as, ā, am*, untraced, unperceived, unmarked, undiscriminated.

An-upalakshya, as, ā, am, not to be traced. — *Anupalakshya-vartman, ā, ā, a*, having ways (or a way) that cannot be traced.

अनुपलब्ध *an-upalabdha, as, ā, am*, unobtained, unperceived, unascertained.

An-upalabdhi, is, f. non-perception, non-recognition. — *Anupalabdhi-sama, as, ā*, m. f. sophism, trying to establish a fact (e. g. the reality and eternity of sound) from the impossibility of perceiving the non-perception of it.

An-upalabhyamāna, as, ā, am, not being perceived.

An-upalambha, as, m. non-perception.

An-upalambhana, am, n. want of apprehension or knowledge.

अनुपवीतिन् an-upavītin, ī, m. one who does not wear the sacred cord, uninvested with the sacrificial thread.

अनुपशय an-upaśaya, as, m. any aggravating thing or circumstance that increases a disease.

अनुपशान्त an-upaśānta, as, ā, am, not calm; (as), m., N. of a Buddhist mendicant.

अनुपश्य anu-paśya, as, ā, am, following with his looks, keeping in view or in mind.

अनुपसर्ग an-upasarga, as, m. a word that is not an Upasarga, that has not the force of one, that is destitute of one; that which needs no additions or supplements (as a divine being).

अनुपसेचन an-upasećana, as, ā, am, having nothing (e. g. no sauce) for moistening.

अनुपस्कृत an-upaskṛita, as, ā, am, unfinished, unpolished; not cooked, i. e. genuine, blameless; unrequited.

अनुपस्थान an-upasthāna, am, n. absence, the not being at hand.

An-upasthāpana, am, n. not producing, not offering, not placing; not having ready or at hand.

An-upasthāpayat, an, antī, at, not presenting, not having at hand.

An-upasthāpita, as, ā, am, not ready, not at hand, not offered or produced.

An-upasthāyin, ī, inī, i, absent, distant.

An-upasthita, as, ā, am, not come near, not present, not at hand, not current; (am), n. a word not upasthita (q. v.) in the grammatical sense of that term.

An-upasthiti, is, f. absence, not being at hand.

अनुपहत an-upahata, as, ā, am, unimpaired, unvitiated; not rendered impure. — An-upahata-krushṭa, as, ā, am, (with Buddhists) neither affected by injury nor by anger.

अनुपहूत an-upahūta, as, ā, am, not called upon or invited; not called upon aloud; not accompanied with invitations.

अनुपा 1. anu-pā, cl. 1. P. -pibati, -pātum, to drink after or thereupon, follow in drinking, drink at: Caus. -pāyayati, -yitum, to cause to drink afterwards.

Anu-pāna, am, n. a fluid vehicle in medicine; drink taken with or after medicine; drink close at hand.

Anu-pānīya, am, n. drink close at hand; (as, ā, am), fit to be drunk after; serving as a liquid vehicle of medicine.

अनुपा 2. anu-pā, Caus. P. A. -pālayati, -te, -yitum, to preserve, keep.

Anu-pālana, am, n. preserving, keeping up.

Anu-pālayat, an, antī, at, keeping, maintaining.

Anu-pālin, ī, inī, i, preserving, keeping up.

Anu-pālu, n., N. of a plant, wild Calladium (?).

अनुपाकृत an-upākṛita, as, ā, am, not rendered fit for sacrificial purposes. — Anupākṛita-mānsa, am, n. flesh of an animal not prepared for sacrifice.

अनुपाख्य an-upākhya, as, ā, am, not clearly discernible.

अनुपात anu-pāta, as, m. falling subsequently upon, alighting or descending upon in succession; following; going, proceeding in order, or as a consequence; a degree of latitude opposite to one given, the Antæci (?); proportion (in arithm.); arithmetical progression, rule of three.

Anu-pātaka, am, n. a heinous crime, as falsehood, fraud, theft, adultery.

Anu-pātam, ind. in succession.

Anu-pātin, ī, inī, i, following as a consequence or result.

अनुपान anu-pāna. See s. v. 1. anu-pā.

अनुपानत्क an-upānatka, as, ā, am, shoeless.

अनुपायिन् an-upāyin, ī, inī, i, not using means or expedients.

अनुपार्श्व anu-pārśva, as, ā, am, lateral; along or by the side.

अनुपावृत्त an-upāvṛitta, ās, m. pl., N. of a people.

अनुपासन an-upāsana, am, n. want of attention to.

An-upāsita, as, ā, am, not attended to, neglected.

अनुपुरुष anu-purusha, as, m. the before-mentioned man, a follower.

अनुपुष्प anu-pushpa, as, m. a kind of reed (Saccharum Sara Roxb.).

अनुपूर्व anu-pūrva, as, ā, am, regular, orderly, successive, from the preceding. Anupūrveṇa or anupūrva-śas, ind. in regular order or succession, from the first, from the beginning, from above downwards. — Anupūrva-keśa, as, m. one who has regular hair. — Anupūrva-gātra, as, m. one who has regularly shaped limbs. — Anupūrva-ja, as, ā, am, descended in a regular line. — Anupūrva-danshṭra, as, ā, am, having regular teeth. — Anupūrva-nābhi, is, m. having a regularly shaped navel. — Anupūrva-pāṇi-lekha, as, ā, am, having regular lines in the hands. — Anupūrva-vatsā, f. a cow which calves regularly.

Anupūrvya, as, ā, am, regular, orderly, successive.

अनुपृक्त anu-pṛikta, as, ā, am, mixed with.

अनुपृष्ठ्य anu-pṛishṭhya, as, ā, am (held or extended), lengthwise.

अनुपॄ anu-pṝī, Caus. P. -pūrayati, -yitum, to fill, to fulfil.

अनुपेत an-upeta, as, ā, am, not endowed with, not invested with (the sacred cord).

अनुपोषण an-uposhaṇa, am, n. not fasting.

अनुप्त an-upta, as, ā, am (rt. vap), unsown (as seed). — Anupta-śasya, as, ā, am, fallow, meadow (ground, &c.).

An-uptrima, as, ā, am, grown without being sown.

अनुप्रकम्प् anu-pra-kamp, Caus. A. -kampayate, -yitum, to follow in swinging or agitating.

अनुप्रछ् anu-prać, cl. 6. P. -pṛiććhati, -prashṭum (with two acc. cases of the person and thing), to ask, to inquire after.

Anupraśna, see s. v.

अनुप्रजन् anu-pra-jan, cl. 4. A. -jāyate, -janitum, to be born after; to procreate again and again: Caus. -janayati, -yitum, to cause to be born subsequently.

अनुप्रज्ञा anu-pra-jñā, cl. 9. P. -jānāti, -jñātum, to track, trace, discover.

Anu-prajñāna, am, n. tracking, tracing.

अनुप्रणुद् anu-pra-ṇud (-nud), cl. 6. P. A. -nudati, -te, -nottum, to push away from one's self; to frighten away, put to flight.

अनुप्रतिक्रम् anu-prati-kram, cl. 1. P. -krāmati, -kramitum, to return.

अनुप्रथ् anu-prath, cl. 1. A. -prathate, -thitum, to praise, celebrate.

अनुप्रदा anu-pra-dā, cl. 3. P. -dadāti, -dātum, to surrender, make over.

Anu-pradāna, am, n. a gift, donation.

अनुप्रधाव् anu-pra-dhāv, cl. 1. P. -dhāvati, -vitum, to rush after.

Anu-pradhāvita, as, ā, am, hurried, eager.

अनुप्रपत् anu-pra-pat, cl. 1. P. -patati, -titum, to fly towards.

Anu-prapātam, ind. going in succession.

अनुप्रपद् anu-pra-pad, cl. 4. A. -padyate, -pattum, to follow.

Anu-prapanna, as, ā, am, following after, conformed to.

Anu-prapādam, ind. going in succession.

अनुप्रपा anu-pra-pā, cl. 1. P. A. -pibati, -te, -pātum; P. to drink one after the other; A. to drink after another (with acc.).

अनुप्रमाण anu-pramāṇa, as, ā, am, having a suitable size or length.

अनुप्रयुज् anu-pra-yuj, cl. 7. A. -yunkte, -yoktum, to employ, apply.

Anu-prayujyamāna, as, ā, am, employed in addition.

Anu-prayoktavya, as, ā, am, proper to be joined or employed in addition.

Anu-prayoga, as, m. additional use.

अनुप्ररोह anu-praroha, as, ā, am, coming up or growing in accordance with.

अनुप्रवह् anu-pra-vah, cl. 1. P. -vahati, -voḍhum, to drag (or carry) about.

अनुप्रविश् anu-pra-viś, cl. 6. P. -viśati, -veshṭum, to follow in entering, to attack, enter; to sleep with.

Anu-praviśya, ind. having entered.

Anu-praveśa, as, m. or anu-praveśana, am, n. return, entrance; imitation.

Anu-praveśanīya, as, ā, am, connected with returning or with entering.

अनुप्रशुच् anu-pra-śuć, cl. 1. P. -śoćati, -ćitum, to regret or mourn deeply.

अनुप्रश्न anu-praśna, as, m. (fr. anu-prać), a subsequent question having reference to what has been previously said by the teacher.

अनुप्रसक्त anu-prasakta, as, ā, am, strongly attached, closely connected.

Anu-prasakti, is, f. close connection with.

अनुप्रस्थ anu-prastha, as, ā, am, latitudinal; according to width, following the breadth or latitude.

अनुप्रहरण anu-praharaṇa, am, n. knocking into or throwing into.

अनुप्राण् anu-prāṇ (-pra-an), cl. 2. P. -prāṇiti, -ṇitum, to breathe after.

अनुप्राप् anu-prāp (-pra-āp), cl. 5. P. -āpnoti, -āptum, to come or go up to, reach, attain, overtake (?); to arrive, to get, obtain; to get back; to imitate.

Anu-prāpta, as, ā, am, arrived, returned; obtained; having reached, having got.

अनुप्रास् anu-prās (-pra-as), cl. 4. P. -asyati, -asitum, to throw or shoot after.

Anu-prāsa, as, m. alliteration, repetition of similar letters, syllables, and words.

अनुप्रे anu-pre (-pra-i), cl. 2. P. -praiti, -tum, to follow; to follow in death; to seek after.

अनुप्रेक्ष् anu-preksh (-pra-īksh), cl. 1. A. -prekshate, -kshitum, to follow with the eyes.

अनुप्रेष् anu-presh (-pra-ish), Caus. P. -preshayati, -yitum, to send forth after.

अनुप्लव anu-plava, as, m. (rt. plu), a companion or follower.

अनुबन्ध् *anu-bandh,* cl. 9. P. *-badhnāti, -banddhum,* to attach, tie; to bind (by an obligation); to stick, adhere, follow, endure.

Anu-baddha, as, ā, am, bound to, obliged to, connected with, related to, belonging to.

Anu-bandha, as, m. binding, connection, attachment, the encumbrance or clog of a family; uninterrupted succession; sequence, consequence, result; intention, design, motive or cause of an action; obstacle; the inseparable adjunct or sign of anything, secondary or symptomatic affection, supervening on the principal disease; an indicatory letter or syllable, marking some peculiarity in the inflection of the word to which it is attached (for instance, an *i* attached to roots, denotes the insertion of a nasal before their final consonant); a child or pupil, who imitates an example set by the parent or preceptor; commencement, beginning; anything small or little, a part, a small part; (in arithm.) the junction of fractions; (in phil.) an indispensable element of the Vedānta; (ī), f. hickup; thirst.

Anu-bandhaka, as, ikā, am, connected, allied; related.

Anu-bandhana, am, n. binding, connection, succession, unbroken series.

Anu-bandhin, ī, inī, i, connected with, attached; having in its train or as a consequence, resulting. — *Anubandhi-tva, am,* n. the state of being accompanied.

Anu-bandhya, as, ā, am, principal, primary, what may receive an adjunct, as a root, a disease; (*as*), m. one of the three principal sacrificial animals at the Jyotishṭoma sacrifice.

अनुबल *anu-bala, am,* n. rear-guard, or an auxiliary army following another.

अनुबाध् *anu-bādh,* cl. 1. A. *-bādhate, -dhitum,* to press closely, pursue.

अनुबुध् *anu-budh,* cl. 4. A. *-budhyate, -bodhitum,* to awake, to recollect, to learn (by information).

Anu-bodha, as, m. reviving the scent of a faded perfume, replacing perfumes removed by bathing; an after-thought.

Anu-bodhana, am, n. recollecting.

Anu-bodhita, as, ā, am, informed or convinced by recollection.

अनुब्राह्मण *anu-brāhmaṇa, am,* n. a work resembling a Brāhmaṇa.

Anu-brāhmaṇika (or perhaps more correctly *ānu-brāhmaṇika*), *as,* or *anu-brāhmaṇin, ī,* m. a knower of an *anu-brāhmaṇa.*

अनुब्रू *anu-brū,* cl. 2. P. *-bravīti, -vaktum,* to pronounce, utter, vow.

अनुभाष् *anu-bhāsh,* cl. 1. A. *-bhāshate, -shitum,* to pronounce clearly, to confess.

Anu-bhāshaṇa, am, n. repeating what has been said; repeating a proposition in order to refute it.

अनुभास *anu-bhāsa, as,* m. a species of crow.

अनुभिद् *anu-bhid,* cl. 7. P. *-bhinatti, -bhettum,* to split, break.

Anu-bhitti, ind. along a cleft.

अनुभुज् *anu-bhuj,* cl. 7. A. *-bhuṅkte, -bhoktum,* to suffer the due consequence of one's actions.

Anu-bhoga, as, m. (in law) enjoyment, a grant of hereditary land in return for service.

अनुभू *anu-bhū,* cl. 1. P. *-bhavati, -vitum,* to be after, to notice, perceive, understand; to experience, to attempt.

Anu-bhava, as, m. perception, apprehension, fruition; understanding; impression on the mind not derived from memory; experience, knowledge derived from personal observation or experiment; result, consequence. — *Anubhava-siddha, as, ā, am,* established by experience or perception. — *Anubhavārūḍha* (°*va-ār*°), *as, ā, am,* subjected to trial or experiment.

Anu-bhāva, as, m. a sign or indication of a feeling (*bhāva*) by look or gesture; dignity, authority, consequence; firm opinion, ascertainment, good resolution, belief.

Anu-bhāvaka, as, ikā, am, causing to apprehend, making to understand. — *Anubhāvaka-tā,* f. understanding.

Anu-bhāvana, am, n. the act of indicating feelings by sign or gesture.

Anu-bhāvin, ī, inī, i, perceiving, knowing, an eye-witness; showing signs of feeling.

Anu-bhū, ūs, ūs, u, perceiving, understanding.

Anu-bhūta, as, ā, am, perceived, understood, judged, experienced, apprehended; resulted, followed as a consequence; that has experienced, tasted, tried or enjoyed.

Anu-bhūti, is, f. perception, apprehension; knowledge from any source but memory; (in phil.) knowledge from four sources, viz. perception by the senses, inference, comparison, and verbal knowledge; dignity, consequence. — *Anubhūti-prakāśa, as,* m. title of a metric paraphrase of the twelve principal Upanishads, by Vidyāraṇya-muni. — *Anubhūti-svarūpāćārya* (°*pa-āć*°), *as,* m., N. of the author of the grammar Sārasvatī-prakriyā.

Anu-bhūya, ind. having perceived, having experienced.

Anu-bhūyamāna, as, ā, am, under trial, under enjoyment.

अनुभृ *anu-bhṛi,* cl. 1. P., Ved. *-bharati, -bhartum,* to praise conformably (?), to commit to, throw into.

Anu-bhartṛi, tā, trī, tṛi, Ved. praising conformably, imitating.

अनुभ्राज् *anu-bhrāj,* cl. 1. P. *-bhrājati, -jitum,* to illuminate.

अनुभ्रातृ *anu-bhrātṛi, tā,* m. a younger brother.

अनुमद् *anu-mad,* cl. 1. P., Ved. *-madati, -ditum,* to rejoice over, to gladden, to praise.

Anu-matta, as, ā, am, intoxicated (with joy, &c.); recovered from intoxication (?).

Anu-mādya, as, ā, am, to be praised in succession, to be granted with acclamation or praise.

अनुमध्यमम् *anu-madhyamam,* ind. next oldest to the middle.

अनुमन् *anu-man,* cl. 4. A. *-manyate, -mantum,* to approve, assent to, permit, grant: Caus. P. *-mānayati, -yitum,* to ask for permission, to honour.

Anu-mata, as, ā, am, approved, assented to, permitted, allowed; agreeable, pleasant; loved, beloved; concurred with, being of one opinion; (*am*), n. consent, permission, approbation. *Anumate,* loc. c. with consent of. — *Anumata-karma-kārin, ī, iṇī, i,* doing what is allowed, acting according to an agreement.

Anu-mati, is, f. assent, permission, approbation; the fifteenth day of the moon's age, on which it rises one digit less than full, when the gods or manes receive oblations with favour; the former personified as a goddess and worshipped especially in the Rājasūya sacrifice; oblation made to this goddess. — *Anumati-pattra, am,* n. (in law) a deed expressing assent.

Anu-manana, am, n. assenting; independance.

Anu-mantṛi, tā, trī, tṛi, consenting to, permitting.

Anu-manyamāna, as, ā, am, minding, assenting.

अनुमन्त्र् *anu-mantr,* cl. 10. A. (P.?) *-mantrayate, -ti, -yitum,* to accompany with or consecrate by magic formulas; to dismiss with a blessing.

Anu-mantraṇa, am, n. consecration by hymns and prayers. — *Anumantraṇa-mantra, as,* m. a hymn used in consecrating.

Anu-mantrita, as, ā, am, so consecrated.

अनुमरण *anu-maraṇa.* See *anu-mṛi.*

अनुमरु *anu-maru, us,* m. a country next to a desert.

अनुमा 1. *anu-mā,* cl. 3. A. *-mimīte, -mātum,* to infer, conclude, guess, conjecture; to reconcile, to equal: Pass. *-mīyate,* to be inferred or supposed.

2. *anu-mā,* f. inference, a conclusion from given premises.

Anu-māna, am, n. the act of inferring or drawing a conclusion from given premises; inference, consideration, reflection; guess, conjecture; one of the means of obtaining knowledge (*pramāṇa*) according to the Sāṅkhya or Nyāya systems, but not according to the Vedānta. — *Anumāna-khaṇḍa, am,* n., N. of a work on inference, by Cintāmaṇi. — *Anumāna-prakāśa, as,* m. a similar work by Rućidatta. — *Anumāna-maṇi-dīdhiti, is,* f. a similar work by Raghunātha. — *Anumānokti* (°*na-uk*°), *is,* f. reasoning, logic.

Anu-māpaka, as, ikā, am, causing an inference, as an effect.

Anu-mita, as, ā, am, inferred, conjectured.

Anu-miti, is, f. inference, conclusion from given premises.

Anu-mimāna, as, ā, am, concluding, inferring.

Anu-mīyamāna, as, ā, am, being inferred.

Anu-meya, as, ā, am, inferable, to be inferred, proved or conjectured.

अनुमाद्य *anu-mādya.* See under *anu-mad.*

अनुमाषम् *anu-māsham,* ind. like a kidney bean.

अनुमास *anu-māsa, as,* m. the following month.

अनुमुद् *anu-mud,* cl. 1. A. *-modate, -ditum,* to join in rejoicing, to sympathize with, to rejoice; to allow with pleasure, to express approval, applaud, permit.

Anu-moda, as, m. a subsequent pleasure, the feeling of pleasure from sympathy.

Anu-modaka, as, ikā, am, assenting, showing sympathetic joy.

Anu-modana, am, n. pleasing, causing pleasure, applauding; assent, acceptance; sympathetic joy.

Anu-modita, as, ā, am, pleased, delighted, applauded; agreeable, acceptable.

अनुमुह् *anu-muh,* cl. 4. P. *-muhyati, -mogdhum* or *-moḍhum,* to feel distressed at, to be troubled about.

अनुमृ *anu-mṛi,* cl. 6. A. *-mriyate, -martum,* to follow in death.

Anu-maraṇa, am, n. following in death; post-cremation of a widow whose husband's corpse is not on the spot, and with part of whose dress she therefore ascends the pile; this is prohibited to Brāhman women: it is often synonymous with the opposite term *saha-maraṇa,* con-cremation or burning with the body.

Anu-marishyat, an, atī or *antī, at,* about to follow in death.

Anu-mṛitā, f. the woman who burns with a part of her husband's dress.

अनुमृग्यदाशु *anumṛigya-dāśu, us,* m. (rt. *mṛig* and *dā*), granting all that is sought.

अनुमृज् *anu-mṛij,* cl. 2. P. *-mārshṭi, -mārjitum* or *-mārshṭum,* to purify.

अनुमृश् *anu-mṛiś,* cl. 6. P. *-mṛiśati, -marshṭum* or *-mrashṭum,* to consider, think of, reflect.

Anu-marśam, ind. having repeatedly considered.

अनुम्लोचा *anu-mloćā* or *anu-mloćantī,* f., N. of an Apsaras.

अनुयजुस् *anu-yajus,* ind. (rt. *yaj*), according to the Yajur-veda.

Anu-yāga, as, m. a subsequent or after-sacrifice.

Anu-yāja, as, m. a secondary or final sacrifice or offering. — *Anuyāja-prasava, as,* m. permission to perform an Anuyāja. — *Anuyāja-praisha, ās,* m. pl. the formulas belonging to the Anuyāja. — *Anuyāja-vat, ān, atī, at,* having secondary sacrifices. — *Anuyājānumantraṇa* (°*ja-an*°), *am,* n. reciting those formulas. — *Anuyājārtha* (°*ja-ar*°), *as, ā, am,* belonging to or used at an Anuyāja.

अनुयम् *anu-yam,* cl. 1. P., Ved. *-yaććhati, -yantum,* to covet.

अनुयवम् *anu-yavam,* ind. like barley.

अनुया 1. *anu-yā,* cl. 2. P. *-yāti, -tum,* to follow, attend; to take (off) seriatim.

2. *anu-yā, ās, ās, am,* following; (*ās*), f., Ved. food.

Anu-yata, as, ā, am, followed, pursued, practised.

Anu-yātavya, as, ā, am, to be followed.

Anu-yātṛi, tā, m. a follower, companion.

Anu-yātra, am, ā, n. f. retinue, attendance, that which is required for a journey.

Anu-yātrika, as, ā, am, following as attendant.

Anu-yāna, am, n. going after, following.

Anu-yāyin, ī, inī, i, going after; a follower, a dependant or attendant; following, consequent upon. — *Anuyāyi-tā,* f. or *anuyāyi-tva, am,* n. the state of being a follower, succession.

अनुयुज् *anu-yuj,* cl. 7. A. *-yuṅkte, -yoktum,* to examine, question, put upon trial; to order; enjoin; to select (a husband).

Anu-yukta, as, ā, am, ordered, enjoined; asked, inquired; examined, questioned, reprehended, censured.

Anu-yuktin, ī, m. one who has enjoined, examined.

Anu-yugam, ind. according to the Yugas or four ages.

Anu-yoktṛi, tā, m. an examiner, inquirer, teacher.

Anu-yoga, as, m. a question, examination, asking, solicitation; censure, reproof; religious meditation, spiritual union. — *Anuyoga-kṛit, t,* m. an Āćārya or spiritual teacher.

Anu-yogin, ī, inī, i, what combines or unites; connected or combined with, situated in or on, questioning, examining.

Anu-yojana, am, n. question, questioning, examining.

Anu-yojya, as, ā, am, to be examined or questioned; to be enjoined or, ordered; censurable; a servant, agent, delegate.

अनुयूपम् *anu-yūpam,* ind. along the Yūpa or sacrificial post.

अनुरक्ष् *anu-raksh,* cl. 1. P. *-rakshati, -shitum,* to preserve.

Anu-rakshaṇa, am, n. the act of preserving.

अनुरज्जु *anu-rajju,* ind. along the rope.

अनुरञ्ज् *anu-rañj,* cl. 4. A. *-rajyate, -raṅktum,* to be attached or devoted; P. *-rajyati,* to blush, be deeply affected: Caus. P. *-rañjayati, -yitum,* to win, conciliate, gratify.

Anu-rakta, as, ā, am, fond of, attached or devoted to, pleased; beloved. — *Anurakta-praja, as, ā, am,* beloved by his subjects. — *Anurakta-loka, as,* m. a person to whom every one is attached.

Anu-rakti, is, f. affection, attachment, love, devotion.

Anu-rañjaka, as, ikā, am, attaching, conciliating, causing affection, gratifying, pleasing.

Anu-rañjana, am, n. attachment, the act of attaching or conciliating affection, love; pleasing, giving delight to.

Anu-rañjita, as, ā, am, conciliated, inspired with affection, pleased, delighted.

Anu-rāga, as, m. attachment, affection, love, passion, goodwill. — *Anurāga-vat, ān, atī, at,* affectionate, attached, in love with. — *Anurāgengita* (°*ga-iṅg*°), *am,* n. gesture expressive of passion.

Anu-rāgin, ī, iṇī, i, impassioned, attached, enamoured, causing love; (*iṇī*), f. personification of a musical note. — *Anurāgi-tā,* f. the state of being in love with.

अनुरणन *anu-raṇana, am,* n. sounding conformably to.

अनुरत *anu-rata, as, ā, am,* fond of, attached, devoted to.

Anu-rati, is, f. love, affection; attachment, goodwill.

अनुरथ *anu-ratha, as,* m., N. of a son of Kuruvatsa and father of Puruhotra.

Anu-rathyā, f. a path along the margin of a road; a side road, the margin of a street.

अनुरस *anu-rasa, as,* m. (in poetry) a subordinate feeling or passion; (in medic.) a secondary flavour, as a little sweetness in a sour fruit, &c.

अनुरहस *anu-rahasa, as, ā, am,* solitary, private; (*am*), ind. in secret, apart.

अनुरात्रम् *anu-rātram,* ind. every night.

अनुराद्ध *anu-rāddha, as, ā, am* (rt. *rādh*), effected, accomplished.

Anu-rādha, as, ā, am, causing welfare; see *anūrādha;* born under the asterism Anurādhā; (*ā*), f. the seventeenth of the twenty-eight Nakshatras or lunar mansions, a constellation described as a row of oblations. — *Anurādha-grāma, as,* m. or *anurādha-pura, am,* n. the ancient capital of Ceylon founded by a man named Anurādha.

अनुरी *anu-rī,* cl. 4. A. *-rīyate, -retum,* to flow after.

अनुरु *an-uru, us, us* or *vī, u,* not great, not large.

अनुरुच् *anu-ruć,* Caus. P. *-roćayati, -yitum,* to choose, prefer.

अनुरुद् *anu-rud,* cl. 2. P. *-roditi, -tum,* to lament.

अनुरुध् 1. *anu-rudh,* cl. 7. P. *-ruṇaddhi, -roddhum,* to retain, keep back; cl. 4. A. *-rudhyate* or poet. P. *-rudhyati,* to love, to be fond of or to spare; to coax, soothe, entreat (especially in Bengālī).

Anu-ruddha, as, ā, am, checked, restrained, opposed; soothed, coaxed, pacified; (*as*), m., N. of a cousin of S'ākya-muni.

2. *anu-rudh, t, t, t,* Ved. loving, adhering to, favouring.

Anu-rodha, as, m. or *anu-rodhana, am,* n. obliging another or fulfilling his wishes; obligingness, compliance, gratification, satisfaction, conformity, consideration, respect; reference or bearing of a rule.

Anu-rodhaka, as, ikā, am, or *anu-rodhin, ī, inī, i,* complying with, compliant, obliging, conforming to, having respect or regard to. — *Anurodhi-tā,* f. the state of being so.

अनुरुहा *anu-ruhā,* f., N. of a grass (Cyperus Pertenius).

अनुरूप *anu-rūpa, as, ā, am,* following the form, conformable, corresponding, like, resembling; fit, suitable; adapted to, agreeable to, according to; (*as*), m. the Antistrophe which has the same metre as the Stotriya or Strophe (understand *pragātha* or *tṛića*); the second of three verses recited together; (*am*), n. conformity, suitability. *Anurūpam* or *anurūpeṇa* or *anurūpatas,* ind. conformably, agreeably to, according. — *Anurūpa-ćeshṭa, as, ā, am,* endeavouring to act becomingly.

अनुरेवती *anu-revatī,* f., N. of a plant.

अनुलग्न *anu-lagna, as, ā, am,* attached to; followed; intent on, pursuing after.

अनुला *anulā,* f., N. of a female Arhat or Buddhist saint; also of a queen of Ceylon.

अनुलाप *anu-lāpa, as,* m. (rt. *lap*), repetition of what has been said, tautology.

अनुलास *anu-lāsa, as,* m. or *anu-lāsya, as,* m. a peacock.

अनुलिप् *anu-lip,* cl. 6. P. *-limpati, -leptum,* to anoint, besmear; cl. 6. A. *-limpate,* to anoint one's self (previous to or after bathing); to bathe: Caus. *-lepayati, -yitum,* to get one anointed.

Anu-lipta, as, ā, am, smeared, anointed. — *Anuliptāṅga* (°*ta-aṅ*°), *as, ā, am,* having the limbs anointed.

Anu-lepa, as, m. unction, anointing, smearing, bedaubing.

Anu-lepaka, as, ikā, am, or *anu-lepin, ī, inī, i,* anointing the body with unguents, who or what anoints.

Anu-lepana, am, n. anointing the body; unguent so used; oily or emollient application.

अनुलुभ् *anu-lubh,* Caus. *-lobhayati, -yitum,* to entice; to go astray (?).

अनुलोम *anu-loma, as, ā, am,* in a natural direction, in regular order, regular, successive, with the hair (*loman*) or grain (opposed to *prati-loma*); (*ā*), f. a woman of a lower caste than that of the man's with whom she is connected; (*ās*), pl. mixed castes. — *Anuloma-kalpa, as,* m. the thirty-fourth of the Pariśishṭas belonging to the Atharva-veda. — *Anuloma-kṛishṭa, as, ā, am,* ploughed in the regular direction (with the grain). — *Anuloma-ja, as, ā, am,* produced or born in due gradation; applied especially to the mixed tribes; or offspring of a mother inferior in caste to the father, as the Mūrdhāvasikta of a Brāhman father and Kshatriyā mother, and so on with the Ambashṭha, Nishāda or Pāraśava, Māhishya, Ugra, Karaṇa. — *Anuloma-pariṇītā,* f. married in regular gradation. — *Anulomāya* (°*ma-aya*), *as, ā, am,* having fortune favourable.

Anu-lomana, am, n. due regulation, sending or putting in the right direction; (in medicine) carrying off by the right channels, purging.

Anu-lomaya, nom. P. *anu-lomayati, -yitum,* to stroke or rub with the hair or the grain, to go with the grain, to send in the right direction or carrying off by the right channels.

अनुल्बण *an-ulbaṇa* or *an-ulvaṇa, as, ā, am,* not excessive, not prominent, smooth (?), free from disturbing circumstances.

अनुवंश *anu-vanśa, as,* m. a genealogical list or table; (*am*), ind. according to race or family, a new family.

Anuvanśya, as, ā, am, relating to a genealogical list or table.

अनुवक्र *anu-vakra, as, ā, am,* somewhat crooked or oblique. — *Anuvakra-ga, as, ā, am,* having a somewhat oblique course (as a planet, &c.).

अनुवच् *anu-vać,* cl. 2. P. *-vakti, -tum,* to repeat, reiterate, recite, speak after, reply.

Anu-vaktavya, as, ā, am, to be repeated.

Anu-vaktṛi, tā, trī, tṛi, speaking after, repeating, replying.

Anu-vaćana, am, n. or *anu-vāć, k,* f. speaking after, repetition, reciting, reading; lecture; a chapter, a section; recitation of certain texts (*mantra*) in consequence of and in connection or conformity with injunctions (*praisha*) spoken by other priests.

Anu-vaćanīya, as, ā, am, referring to the *anuvaćana.*

Anu-vāka, as, m. saying after, reciting, repeating, reading; a chapter of the Vedas, a subdivision or section; a compilation from the Ṛig or Yajur-vedas. — *Anuvāka-sankhyā,* the fourth of the eighteen Pariśishṭas of the Yajur-veda. — *Anuvākānukramaṇī* (°*ka-an*°), f. a work referring to the Ṛig-veda, attributed to S'aunaka.

Anu-vākyā, f. the verse to be recited by the Hotṛi priest, in which the god is invoked to partake of the offering intended for him. — *Anuvākya-vat* or *anuvākyā-vat, ān, atī, at,* furnished or accompanied with an Anuvākyā.

Anu-vāćana, am, n. the act of causing to recite; the recitation of mantras or passages of the Ṛig-veda by the Hotṛi in obedience to the injunction (*praisha*) of the Adhvaryu priest. — *Anuvāćana-praisha, as,* m. an injunction to recite as above.

Anu-vāćita, as, ā, am, before-mentioned, before-named.

Anūkta, &c. See s. v., p. 42.

अनुवत्सर *anu-vatsara, as,* m. a year; (in astronomy) the fifth of five cycles of twelve years in the Vṛihaspati cycle. — *Anu-vatsaram,* ind. every year, yearly.

अनुवद् *anu-vad,* cl. 1. P. *-vadati* (with acc.), or Ā. *-vadate, -ditum* (with gen.), to imitate in speaking, to mock, to repeat.

Anu-vāda, as, m. saying after or again, repeating by way of explanation, explanatory repetition or reiteration with corroboration or illustration, explanatory reference to anything already said, translation; any portion of the Brāhmaṇas which comments on, explains or illustrates an injunction (*vidhi*) previously propounded, and which does not itself propound rules (such a passage is sometimes called *anuvāda-vaćana*); confirmation; report, rumour, *on dit;* slander, reviling.

Anu-vādaka, as, ikā, am, or *anu-vādin, ī, inī, i,* repeating with comment and explanation, corroborative, concurrent, conformable, in harmony with. The masculine of the last is also the name of any one of the three notes of the gamut.

Anu-vādya, as, ā, am, to be explained by an Anuvāda, to be made the subject of one; (*am*), n. the subject of a predicate. — *Anuvādya-tva, am,* n. the state of requiring to be explained by an Anuvāda.

Anūdita. See s. v., p. 42.

अनुवनम् *anu-vanam,* ind. along side of the wood.

अनुवर्ण् *anu-varṇ,* cl. 10. P. *-varṇayati, -yitum,* to mention, describe, recount.

अनुवर्तन, अनुवर्तिन्, &c. See *anu-vṛit.*

अनुवश *anu-vaśa, as,* m. obedience to the will of another; (*as, ā, am*), obedient to the will of another.

अनुवषट्कार *anu-vashaṭkāra, as,* m. or *anu-vashaṭkṛita, am,* n. a secondary exclamation of *vashaṭ,* on making an oblation to a deity.

अनुवस् *anu-vas,* cl. 1. P. *-vasati, -vastum,* to dwell near to; to inhabit along with.

Anu-vāsin, ī, inī, i, residing, resident.

अनुवसित 1. *anu-vasita, as, ā, am* (fr. rt. *vas,* to put on), dressed up, wrapped.

अनुवसित 2. *anu-va-sita, as, ā, am* (for *anv-ava-sita,* rt. *si*), fastened to, bound to, attached.

अनुवह *anu-vaha, as,* m. (rt. *vah*), one of the seven tongues of fire; ('bearing after.')

अनुवा *anu-vā,* cl. 2. P. *-vāti, -tum,* to blow upon, fan.

Anu-vāte, ind. with the wind blowing in the same direction, with the wind from behind, to windward.

अनुवाक *anu-vāka.* See under *anu-vać.*

अनुवारम् *anu-vāram,* ind. time after time, repeatedly.

अनुवास *anu-vāsa, as,* m. or *anu-vāsana, am,* n. (rt. *vās*), perfuming the clothes, especially dipping the ends of the clothes in perfumes; perfuming, scenting in general; an oily enema; administering oily enemata.

Anu-vāsita, as, ā, am, scented, perfumed, fumigated; prepared or administered as an enema.

Anu-vāsya, as, ā, am, or *anu-vāsanīya, as, ā, am,* to be scented or fumigated, requiring an enema.

अनुविकस् *anu-vi-kas,* cl. 1. P. *-kasati, -situm,* to blow, expand, as a flower.

अनुविकृ *anu-vi-kṛi,* cl. 8. P. *-karoti, -kartum,* to follow in shaping.

अनुविकॄ *anu-vi-kṝi,* cl. 6. P. *-kirati, -karitum, -rītum,* to bestrew.

अनुविक्रम् *anu-vi-kram,* cl. 1. A., Ved. *-kramate, -mitum,* to walk after, follow.

अनुविचर् *anu-vi-ćar,* cl. 1. P. *-ćarati, -ritum,* to walk or pass through, to walk up to.

अनुविचल् *anu-vi-ćal,* cl. 1. P. *-ćalati, -litum,* to follow in changing place.

अनुविचाकश् *anu-vi-ćākaś,* Intens., Ved. *-ćākaśīti,* to penetrate with one's vision.

अनुविचिन्त् *anu-vi-ćint,* cl. 10. P. *-ćintayati, -yitum,* to recal to mind.

अनुवितन् *anu-vi-tan,* cl. 8. A. *-tanute, -nitum,* to extend all along or all over.

अनुविद् 1. *anu-vid,* cl. 2. P., Ved. *-vetti, -veditum,* to know thoroughly.

अनुविद् 2. *anu-vid,* cl. 6. P. A. *-vindati, -te, -veditum,* to find, discover; to deem; to marry.

Anu-vitta, as, ā, am, found.

Anu-vitti, is, f. finding, obtaining.

अनुविदृश् *anu-vi-dṛiś,* cl. 1. P. *-paśyati, -drashṭum,* to perceive, view.

अनुविधा *anu-vi-dhā,* cl. 3. P. *-dadhāti, -dhātum,* to regulate, lay down a rule: Pass. *-dhīyate,* to be trained to follow rules; to obey.

Anu-vidhātavya, as, ā, am, to be performed according to an order.

Anu-vidhāna, am, n. obedience, acting conformably to order.

Anu-vidhāyin, ī, inī, i, conforming to, compliant, obedient.

अनुविनद् *anu-vi-nad,* Caus. P. *-nādayati, -yitum,* to make resonant or musical.

अनुविनर्द् *anu-vi-nard,* cl. 1. P. *-nardati, -ditum,* to answer with roars.

अनुविनश् *anu-vi-naś,* cl. 4. P. *-naśyati, -naśitum* or *-nanshṭum,* to disappear, perish, vanish after or with another.

Anu-vi-nāśa, as, m. perishing after.

अनुविन्द *anu-vinda, as,* m., N. of a king of Oujein.

अनुविपत् *anu-vi-pat,* cl. 1. P. *-patati, -titum,* to fly away towards (with acc.).

अनुविमृश् *anu-vi-mṛiś,* cl. 6. P. *-mṛiśati, -marshṭum, -mrashṭum,* to consider, think over.

अनुविश् *anu-viś,* cl. 6. P. *-viśati, -veshṭum,* to follow.

Anu-veśa, as, m. or *anu-veśana, am,* n. entering after, following.

अनुविश्व *anu-viśva, ās,* m. pl., N. of a people in the north-east.

अनुविष्टम्भ *anu-vishṭambha, as,* m. the being impeded in consequence of.

अनुविष्णु *anu-vishṇu,* ind. after Vishṇu.

अनुवी *anu-vī* (*-vi-i*), cl. 2. P. *-vyeti, -tum,* to follow or join in going off or separating.

अनुवीक्ष् *anu-vīksh* (*-vi-īksh*), cl. 1. A. *-vīkshate, -kshitum,* to survey, examine.

अनुवीज् *anu-vīj,* cl. 10. P. *-vījayati, -yitum,* to fan.

अनुवृत् *anu-vṛit,* cl. 1. A. *-vartate,* poet. P. *-vartati, -titum,* to go after; to follow, pursue; to attend; obey, respect, imitate; to resemble; to assent, to expect: Caus. P. *-vartayati, -yitum,* to roll after or forward; to follow up, carry out.

Anu-vartana, am, n. obliging, serving or gratifying another; compliance, obedience; following, attending; concurring; consequence, result; continuance; supplying from a previous rule.

Anu-vartanīya, as, ā, am, to be supplied from a previous rule.

Anu-vartin, ī, inī, i, following, compliant, obedient, resembling. — *Anuvarti-tva, am,* n. the state of being so.

Anu-vartman, ā, ā, a, following, attending.

Anu-vṛitta, as, ā, am, following, obeying, complying; rounded off; (*am*), n. obedience, conformity, compliance.

Anu-vṛitti, is, f. following, acting suitably to, having regard or respect to, complying with, the act of continuance, continued course or influence of a preceding rule or assertion on what follows; reverting to; imitating, doing or acting in like manner.

अनुवृध् *anu-vṛidh,* cl. 1. A. *-vardhate, -dhitum,* to grow, increase.

Anu-vṛiddhi, is, is, i, Ved. increasing (as in clearness or emphasis) in regular ratio.

अनुवेदि *anu-vedi,* ind. along the ground prepared for sacrifice. — *Anu-vedy-antam,* ind. along the edge of this sacrificial ground.

अनुवेलम् *anu-velam,* ind. constantly.

अनुवेल्लित *anu-vellita, am,* n. (rt. *vel* or *vell* or *vehl*), bandaging, securing with bandages (in surgery); a kind of bandage applied to the extremities; (*as, ā, am*), bent in conformity with, bent under.

अनुवैनेय *anuvaineya,* N. of a country.

अनुव्यञ्जन *anu-vyañjana, am,* n. a secondary mark or token.

अनुव्यध् *anu-vyadh,* cl. 4. P. *-vidhyati, -vyaddhum,* to follow in striking; to hit again and again; to wound.

Anu-viddha, as, ā, am, pierced; obstructed, checked, variegated; full of, abounding in; set (as a jewel).

Anu-vedha or *anu-vyādha, as,* m. piercing; obstructing; blending.

अनुव्यम् *anu-vyam,* ind. (rt. *vī* with *anu*), Ved. behind, after, following.

अनुव्यवगा *anu-vy-ava-gā* (*-vi-ava-gā*), cl. 3. P. *-jigāti, -gātum,* to come between successively or in succession to another.

अनुव्यवे *anu-vy-ave* (*-vi-ava-i*), cl. 2. P. *-avaiti, -tum,* to follow in intervening or coming between.

अनुव्यश् *anu-vy-aś* (*-vi-aś*), cl. 3. A. *-vyaśnute, -śitum,* to overtake, reach.

अनुव्याख्या *anu-vy-ā-khyā* (*-vi-ā-khyā*), cl. 2. P. *-khyāti, -tum,* to explain further.

Anu-vyākhyāna, am, n. that portion of a Brāhmaṇa which explains or illustrates difficult Sūtras, texts, or obscure statements occurring in another position.

अनुव्याहरण *anu-vyāharaṇa* (*-vi-ā-haraṇa*), *am,* n. or *anu-vyāhāra, as,* m. cursing, execration; repeating, repeated utterance.

Anu-vyāhārin, ī, iṇī, i, execrating, cursing.

अनुव्युच्चर् *anu-vy-uć-ćar (-vi-ud-ćar)*, cl. 1. P. *-ćarati, -ritum*, to follow in going forth or stepping forward.

अनुव्यूह् *anu-vy-ūh (-vi-ūh)*, cl. 1. P. *-vy-ūhati, -hitum*, to distribute.

अनुव्रज् *anu-vraj*, cl. 1. P. *-vrajati* or poet. A. *-vrajate, -jitum*, to follow, especially a departing guest, as a mark of respect; to visit seriatim; to obey, do homage.

Anu-vrajana, am, n. or *anu-vrajyā*, f. following as above.

Anu-vrājya, as, ā, am, to be followed, as by the relatives of a dead person to the cemetery.

अनुव्रत *anu-vrata, as, ā, am*, devoted to, faithful to, ardently attached to; *(as)*, m. a particular kind of Jaina devotee.

अनुशक् *anu-śak*, Desid. Caus. P. *-śikshayati, -yitum*, to teach, instruct.

Anu-śikshin, ī, iṇī, i, exercising one's self in, practising.

अनुशतिक *anu-śatika, as, ā, am*, accompanied with or bought for a hundred (the derivative *ānuśātika* has Vṛiddhi in both members).

अनुशय *anu-śaya*, &c. See under *anu-śī*.

अनुशर *anu-śara, as*, m. (rt. *śṛī* with *anu*), a Rākshasa, a sort of demon.

अनुशस्त्र *anu-śastra, am*, n. anything used in place of a regular surgical instrument, as a finger-nail or bambu; any subsidiary weapon or instrument.

अनुशास् *anu-śās*, cl. 2. P. or poet. A. *-śāsti, -te, -situm*, to rule, govern; to order; to teach, direct, advise, address; to punish, chastise, correct.

Anu-śāsaka, as, ikā, am, or *anu-śāsin, ī, inī, i*, or *anu-śāstṛi, tā, trī, tṛi*, one who governs, instructs, directs or punishes.

Anu-śāsat, t, tī, t, instructing, ruling.

Anu-śāsana, am, n. instruction, direction, command, giving rules, order, precept, law. — *Anuśāsana-para, as, ā, am*, obedient.

Anu-śāsanīya or *anu-śāsya, as, ā, am*, to be instructed.

Anu-śāsita, as, ā, am, directed, governed, defined by rule.

Anu-śāsitṛi, tā, trī, tṛi, ruling, governing, commanding, directing, a ruler.

Anu-śishṭa, as, ā, am, taught, revealed; adjudged, done conformably to law.

Anu-śishṭi, is, f. instruction, teaching, ordering.

Anu-śishya, ind. part. having ruled or ordered.

अनुशिक्षिन् *anu-śikshin*. See *anu-śak*.

अनुशिख *anu-śikha, as*, m., N. of a serpent which at a certain sacrifice officiated as Potṛi priest.

अनुशिवम् *anu-śivam*, ind. after Śiva.

अनुशिशु *anu-śiśu, us*, f. (an animal) followed by its young (as by a foal, &c.).

अनुशी *anu-śī*, cl. 2. A. *-śete, -śayitum*, to sleep or spend the night with, to lie along or close, to adhere closely to.

Anu-śaya, as, m. close connection as with a consequence, close attachment to any object; (in phil.) the consequence itself, the evil result of an act which clings to it and causes the soul after enjoying the temporary freedom from transmigration, which is the reward of its good deeds, to enter other bodies; repentance, regret; hatred; ancient or intense enmity; *(ī)*, f. a disease of the feet, a boil or abscess on the upper part; also one on the head. — *Anuśaya-vat, ān, atī, at*; see *anu-śayin*.

Anu-śayāna, as, ā, am, repenting, regretting; *(ā)*, f. a particular kind of heroine or female character.

Anu-śayitavya, as, ā, am, to be regretted.

Anu-śayin, ī, inī, i, having the consequence of an act, connected as with a consequence; devotedly attached to, faithful; repentant, penitent, regretful, sorry for; hating deeply.

Anu-śāyin, ī, inī, i, adhering to, lying along or upon.

अनुशीलन *anu-śīlana, am*, n. constant study or pursuit (of a science, &c.), repeated and devoted service.

Anu-śīlita, as, ā, am, studied carefully, attended to.

अनुशुच् *anu-śuć*, cl. 1. P. *-śoćati, -ćitum*, to mourn over, regret, bewail: Caus. P. *-śoćayati, -yitum*, to mourn over.

Anu-śućikā, f. any ceremony enjoined by the Vedas?. (This word, given by Wilson, is very doubtful.)

Anu-śoka, as, m. sorrow, repentance, regret.

Anu-śoćaka, as, ikā, am, grieving, one who repents; occasioning repentance.

Anu-śoćana, am, n. sorrow, repentance.

Anu-śoćita, as, ā, am, regretted, repented of.

Anu-śoćin, ī, inī, i, penitent, regretful, sorrowful.

अनुशोभिन् *anu-śobhin, ī, inī, i*, shining.

अनुश्रु *anu-śru*, cl. 5. P. *-śṛiṇoti, -śrotum*, to hear repeatedly, especially from a sacred authority: Desid. A. *-śuśrūshate*, to obey.

Anu-śrava, as, m., Vedic tradition (acquired by repeated hearing).

Anu-śruta, as, ā, am, handed down by Vedic tradition.

अनुषञ्ज् *anu-shañj (-sañj)*, cl. 1. A. or Pass. *-shajjate, -shajyate, -shanktum*, to cling to, adhere, be attached to.

Anu-shak or *anu-shaṭ*, ind. in continuous or close order; one after the other [cf. *ānu-shak*].

Anu-shakta, as, ā, am, closely connected with, supplied from something preceding.

Anu-shanga, as, m. close adherence, connection, association, conjunction, coalition, commixture; connection of word with word, or effect with causes; necessary consequence, the connection of a subsequent with a previous act; the nasals connected with certain roots ending in consonants (such as *trimph*); tenderness, compassion.

Anu-shangika, as, ī, am, consequent, following as a necessary result; connected with, adhering to, inherent, concomitant.

Anu-shangin, ī, iṇī, i, addicted or attached to; connected with; common, prevailing.

Anu-shañjana, am, n. connection with what follows, concord; grammatical relation.

Anu-shañjanīya, as, ā, am, to be connected, supplied.

अनुषण्ड *anushaṇḍa, as* or *am* (?), m. or n. (?), N. of a place or country (?).

अनुषिच् *anu-shić*. See *anu-sić*.

Anu-shikta, as, ā, am, re-watered or sprinkled.

Anu-sheka, as, m. or *anu-shećana, am*, n. re-watering or sprinkling over again.

अनुषिध् *anu-shidh (-sidh)*, Ved., Intens. *-seshidhīti*, to bring back.

अनुष्टुति *anu-shṭuti, is*, f. (rt. *stu*), praise.

अनुष्टुभ् 1. *anu-shṭubh (-stubh)*, cl. 1. P., Ved. *-shṭobhati, -bhitum*, to praise after, to follow in praising.

2. *anu-shṭubh*, p. f. following in praise or invocation; speech; Sarasvatī; a kind of metre consisting of four Pādas or quarter-verses of eight syllables each (so called because it *anushṭobhati* follows with its praise the Gāyatrī, which consists of three Pādas); in later metrical systems, the Anushṭubh constitutes a whole class of metres, consisting of four times eight syllables. — *Anushṭub-garbhā*, f. a metre in the Vedas of the class Ushṇih.

Anu-shṭobhana, am, n. praising after.

अनुष्ट्र *an-ushṭra, as*, m. no camel, i. e. a bad camel.

अनुष्ठा *anu-shṭhā (-sthā)*, cl. 1. P. *-tishṭhati, -shṭhātum*, to stand near or by, to follow out, to carry out, attend to, perform, do, practise; to govern, rule, superintend; to appoint: Pass. *-shṭhīyate*, to be done, to be followed: Desid. *-tishṭhāsati*, to be desirous of doing, &c.

Anu-tishṭhamāna, as, ā, am, following, performing, attending to.

Anu-shṭha, as, ā, am, standing after, i. e. in succession.

Anu-shṭhātavya, as, ā, am, to be done or accomplished.

Anu-shṭhātṛi, tā, m. the undertaker of any work.

Anu-shṭhāna, am, n. commencing, undertaking; doing or engaging in any work, performance, religious practice; acting in conformity to; *(ī)*, f. performance, action. — *Anushṭhāna-krama, as*, m. the order of performing religious ceremonies. — *Anushṭhāna-śarīra, am*, n. (in Sāṅkhya phil.) a body presumed to be intermediate between the *linga-śarīra* or *sūkshma-śarīra* and the *sthūla-śarīra*. — *Anushṭhāna-smāraka, as, ikā, am*, reminding of religious ceremonies.

Anu-shṭhāpaka, as, ikā, am, causing to perform.

Anu-shṭhāpana, am, n. the causing to perform an act.

Anu-shṭhāyin, ī, inī, i, doing, performing an act.

Anu-shṭhi, is, f., Ved. proper order, succession; only used in inst. *anu-shṭhyā*.

Anu-shṭhita, as, ā, am, done, practised; effected, executed, accomplished; followed, observed; done conformably.

Anu-shṭhu, us, f., Ved. proper order, succession; only used in inst. *anu-shṭhuyā*; *(u)*, ind. in proper order, in regular succession, properly.

Anu-shṭheya, as, ā, am, to be effected, done or accomplished; to be observed; to be proved or established.

अनुष्ण *an-ushṇa, as, ā, am*, not hot, cold, chilly, apathetic; lazy, sluggish; *(am)*, n. a blue lotus, Nymphæa Cærulea; *(ā)*, f., N. of a river. — *Anushṇa-gu, us*, m. (having cold rays), the moon. — *Anushṇa-vallikā*, f., N. of a plant, Nīla-dūrbā. — *Anushṇāśīta* (°*ṇa-aś*°), *as, ā, am*, neither hot nor cold.

An-ushṇaka, as, ā, am, not hot, cold, chilly, &c.

अनुष्यन्द *anu-shyanda, as*, m. (rt. *syand*), a hind-wheel.

अनुष्वध *anu-shvadha, as, ā, am*, accompanied by food: *(am)*, ind. according to food, through food; after food; after every sacrifice; according to one's will, voluntary.

अनुसंया *anu-saṃ-yā*, cl. 2. P. *-yāti, -tum*, to advance against seriatim, attack one after the other.

अनुसंरक्त *anu-saṃrakta, as, ā, am*, attached or devoted to.

अनुसंवत्सरम् *anu-saṃvatsaram*, ind. year after year.

अनुसंविचर् *anu-saṃ-vi-ćar*, cl. 1. P. *-ćarati, -ritum*, or Ved. *-radhyai, -ritave, -rase*, to visit successively, make the round of.

अनुसंविश् *anu-saṃ-viś*, cl. 6. P. *-viśati, -veshṭum*, to follow in retiring for sleep.

अनुसंसर्पम् *anu-saṃsarpam*, ind. at each occasion of approaching.

अनुसंसृ *anu-saṃ-sṛi*, Caus. P. *-sārayati, -yitum*, to dismiss.

अनुसंस्मृ *anu-saṃ-smṛi*, cl. 1. P. *-smarati*, *-smartum*, to remember, to long for (the dead or absent).

अनुसंहितम् *anu-saṃhitam*, ind. according to the Saṃhitā text.

अनुसङ्कल् *anu-saṅ-kal* (*-sam-kal*), cl. 10. P. *-kālayati*, *-yitum*, to follow in driving.

अनुसङ्क्रम् *anu-saṅ-kram* (*-sam-kram*), cl. 1. P. *-krāmati*, *-kramitum*, to walk or go up to, to reach.

अनुसङ्ख्या *anu-saṅ-khyā* (*-saṃ-khyā*), Caus. P., Ved. *-khyāpayati*, *-yitum*, to show, to cause one to observe.

अनुसङ्ग्रह् *anu-saṅ-grah* (*-sam-grah*), cl. 9. P. *-gṛihṇāti*, *-grahītum*, to oblige, favour; to salute one by laying hold of the feet.

अनुसञ्चर् *anu-sañ-ćar* (*-sam-ćar*), cl. 1. P. *-ćarati*, *-ritum*, Ved. *-radhyai*, *-ritave*, *-rase*, to walk along side, to follow, join; to visit; to pursue, seek after; to penetrate, traverse, cross; to become assimilated: Caus. P. *-ćārayati*, *-yitum*, to join, become identified or assimilated with.

Anu-sañćaraṇam, ind. at each occasion of coming.

अनुसञ्चिन्त् *anu-sañ-ćint* (*-sam-ćint*), cl. 10. P. *-ćintayati*, *-yitum*, to meditate.

अनुसञ्ज्वर् *anu-sañ-jvar* (*-sam-jvar*), cl. 1. P. *-jvarati*, *-ritum*, to take after (another) in feeling distressed, to be troubled, become envious.

अनुसन्तन् *anu-san-tan* (*-sam-tan*), cl. 8. P. *-tanoti*, *-nitum*, to overspread, diffuse, extend everywhere, to join on, continue.

अनुसन्तॄ *anu-san-tṝi* (*-sam-tṝi*), cl. 1. P. *-tarati*, *-rītum*, Ved. *-taradhyai*, to follow to the end.

अनुसन्दह् *anu-san-dah* (*-sam-dah*), cl. 1. P. *-dahati*, *-dagdhum*, to burn up along the whole length.

अनुसन्दिश् *anu-san-diś* (*-sam-diś*), cl. 6. P. *-diśati*, *-deshṭum*, to assign, to make over.

अनुसन्दृश् *anu-san-dṛiś* (*-sam-dṛiś*), cl. 1. P. *-paśyati*, *-drashṭum*, to consider successively.

अनुसन्धा *anu-san-dhā* (*-sam-dhā*), cl. 3. P. A. *-dadhāti*, *-dhatte*, *-dhātum*, to explore, ascertain, inspect, plan, arrange, calm, compose, set in order, aim at.

Anu-sandhātavya, *as*, *ā*, *am*, to be explored, to be investigated, to be looked after, &c.

Anu-sandhāna, *am*, n. investigation, inquiry, searching into, close inspection, setting in order, arranging, planning, aiming at, plan, scheme, congruous or suitable connection; (in the Vaiśeshika phil.) the fourth step in a syllogism, i. e. the application.

Anu-sandhānin or *anu-sandhāyin*, *ī*, *inī*, *i*, investigating, searching, skilful at concerting plans or continuing schemes.

Anu-sandheya, *as*, *ā*, *am*, to be investigated, worthy of inquiry or scrutiny, &c.

अनुसन्ध्यम् *anu-sandhyam*, ind. evening after evening, every twilight.

अनुसमय *anu-samaya*. See under *anu-sam-i* next col.

अनुसमश् *anu-sam-aś*, cl. 5. A. *-aśnute*, *-aśitum* or *-ashṭum*, to overtake, reach.

अनुसमस् *anu-sam-as*, cl. 4. P. *-asyati*, *-situm*, to add further.

अनुसमाचर् *anu-sam-ā-ćar*, cl. 1. P. *-ćarati*, *-ritum*, Ved. *-radhyai*, *-ritave*, *-rase*, to carry out, accomplish.

अनुसमाधा *anu-sam-ā-dhā*, cl. 3. P. A. *-dadhāti*, *-dhatte*, *-dhātum*, to calm, compose.

अनुसमाप् *anu-sam-āp*, Caus. P. *-āpayati*, *-yitum*, to complete or accomplish further or subsequently.

Anu-samāpana, *am*, n. regular completion.

अनुसमि *anu-sam-i*, cl. 2. P. *-eti*, *-tum*, to visit conjointly or successively; to join in following or being guided by; to join, become assimilated with.

Anu-samaya, *as*, m. regular connection (as of words).

अनुसमीक्ष् *anu-sam-īksh*, cl. 1. A. *-īkshate*, *-kshitum*, to keep in view, have in view.

अनुसमुद्रम् *anu-samudram*, ind. along the sea.

अनुसम्प्राप् *anu-sam-prāp* (*-pra-āp*), cl. 5. P. *-prāpnoti*, *-prāptum*, to arrive, reach, get.

Anu-samprāpta, *as*, *ā*, *am*, arrived, come.

अनुसम्बद्ध *anu-sambaddha*, *as*, *ā*, *am* (rt. *bandh*), connected with, accompanied by.

अनुसवनम् *anu-savanam*, ind., Ved. at every sacrifice.

अनुसातम् *anu-sātam*, ind. according to delight.

अनुसाम *anu-sāma*, *as*, *ā*, *am*, conciliated, appeased, friendly.

अनुसायम् *anu-sāyam*, ind. evening after evening, every evening.

अनुसार *anu-sāra*, *anu-sārin*, &c. See under *anu-sṛi* below.

अनुसिच् *anu-sić*, cl. 6. P. *-siñćati*, *-sektum*, to water or sprinkle consecutively; (better spelt *anu-shić*, q. v.)

अनुसीतम् *anu-sītam*, ind. along the furrow.

अनुसीरम् *anu-sīram*, ind. along the plough.

अनुसू *anu-sū*, *ūs*, m., N. of a work.

अनुसूचक *anu-sūćaka*, *as*, *ikā*, *am* (rt. *sūć*), indicative of, pointing out.

Anu-sūćana, *am*, n. pointing out, indication.

अनुसूपम् *anu-sūpam*, ind. in every condiment.

अनुसृ *anu-sṛi*, cl. 1. P. *-sarati*, *-sartum*, to follow: Caus. P. *-sārayati*, *-yitum*, to pursue.

Anu-sara, *as*, m. a companion.

Anu-saraṇa, *am*, n. following, going after; conformity to, consequence of; custom, habit, usage.

Anu-sāra, *as*, m. going after, following; custom, usage; nature, natural state or condition of anything; prevalence, currency; received or established authority, especially of codes of law; conformity to usage; consequence, result. — *Anusāra-tas* or *anusāreṇa*, ind. conformably to.

Anu-sāraka, *as*, *ā*, *am*, or *anu-sārin*, *ī*, *iṇī*, *i*, following, attendant on, according or conformable to; penetrating, scrutinizing, investigating.

Anu-sāryaka, *am*, n. a fragrant substance.

Anu-sṛita, *as*, *ā*, *am*, followed, conformed to.

Anu-sṛiti, *is*, f. going after, following, conforming to; N. of a woman (?).

अनुसृप् *anu-sṛip*, cl. 1. P. *-sarpati*, *-sarptum* or *-sraptum*, to glide after or towards, to approach.

Anu-sarpa, *as*, m. a serpent-like being.

अनुसृष्ट *anu-sṛishṭa*, *as*, *ā*, *am* (rt. *sṛij*), Ved. created in succession.

अनुसेव् *anu-sev*, cl. 1. A. *-sevate*, *-vitum*, to practise, observe.

Anu-sevin, *ī*, *inī*, *i*, practising, observing, habitually addicted.

अनुसैन्य *anu-sainya*, *am*, n. the rear of an army.

अनुसोमम् *anu-somam*, ind. near the Soma, as with the Soma.

अनुस्कन्दम् *anu-skandam*, ind. having gone into in succession.

अनुस्तरण *anu-staraṇa*, *as*, *ī*, *am* (rt. *stṛi*), strewing round; (*ī*), f. the cow sacrificed at the funeral ceremony.

अनुस्तोत्र *anu-stotra*, *am*, n. praising after; N. of a treatise relating to the Sāma-veda.

अनुस्नेहम् *anu-sneham*, ind. after (adding) oil.

अनुस्पष्ट *anu-spashṭa*, *as*, *ā*, *am*, plain, manifest.

अनुस्फुर *anu-sphura*, *as*, *ā*, *am*, Ved. whizzing (as an arrow).

अनुस्मृ *anu-smṛi*, cl. 1. P. *-smarati*, *-smartum*, to remember, recollect: Caus. P. *-smārayati* or *-smarayati*, *-yitum*, to remind (painfully).

Anu-smaraṇa, *am*, n. remembering, repeated recollection.

Anu-smṛita, *as*, *ā*, *am*, remembered.

Anu-smṛiti, *is*, f. cherished recollection, recalling some idea to the exclusion of all others.

अनुस्यूत *anu-syūta* or *anu-shyūta*, *as*, *ā*, *am* (rt. *siv*), sewed consecutively, strung together or connected regularly and uninterruptedly.

अनुस्रयामन् *an-usra-yāman*, *ā*, m., Ved. not going (in a waggon drawn) by oxen.

अनुस्वान *anu-svāna*, *as*, m. sounding conformably.

अनुस्वार *anu-svāra*, *as*, m. (rt. *svṛi*), after-sound, the nasal sound which is marked by a dot above the line, and which always belongs to a preceding vowel. — *Anusvāra-vat*, *ān*, *atī*, *at*, having the Anusvāra. — *Anusvāra-vyavāya*, *as*, m. separation between two sounds caused by an Anusvāra. — *Anusvārāgama* (°*ra-āg*°), *as*, m. an augment consisting in the addition of an Anusvāra.

अनुह *anuha*, *as*, m., N. of a son of Vibhrātra and father of Brahma-datta.

अनुहव *anu-hava*, *as*, m. (rt. *hvā* for *hve*), Ved. inviting, stirring up.

अनुहा *anu-hā*, cl. 3. A., Ved. *-jihīte*, *-hātum*, to grant.

अनुहुङ्कृ *anu-huṅ-kṛi*, cl. 8. A. *-kurute*, *-kartum*, to roar in imitation of.

अनुहृ *anu-hṛi*, cl. 1. P. *-harati*, *-hartum*, to imitate, to exhibit; A. *-harate*, to take after (one's parents).

Anu-haraṇa, *am*, n. or *anu-hāra*, *as*, m. imitation; resemblance.

Anu-harat, *an*, *antī*, *at*, imitating; (*an*), m., N. of a man (?); (the deriv. *ānuhārati* takes Vṛiddhi in both members.)

Anu-haramāṇa, *as*, *ā*, *am*, imitating.

Anu-hāraka, *as*, *ikā*, *am*, imitating.

Anu-hārya, *as*, *ā*, *am*, to be imitated; (*as*), m. monthly obsequies on the day of the new moon.

अनुहोड *anu-hoḍa*, *as*, m. a cart (?); (the deriv. *ānuhauḍika* takes Vṛiddhi in both members.)

अनुह्राद *anu-hrāda* or *anu-hlāda*, *as*, m., N. of a son of Hiraṇya-kaśipu.

अनूक *anūka, as, am,* m. n. (fr. *añć* with *anu*), the backbone, spine; the back part of the altar; a former state of existence; (*am*), n. race, family; peculiarity of race, disposition, character; (*ā*), f., N. of an Apsaras.

Anūkya, am, n. backbone; flesh on the skull.

अनूकाश *anū-kāśa, as,* m. (rt. *kāś*), reflection (of light), clearness; regard, reference.

अनूक्ष् *anūksh* (*anu-uksh*), cl. 1. A. *anūkshate, -kshitum,* to sprinkle, bedew.

अनूचीन *anūćīna, as, ā, am* (fr. *anv-añć*), coming after, successive; *anūćīnāham,* on the following day.—*Anūćīna-garbha, as, ā, am,* born in successive order.

1. *anūćya, am,* n., Ved. the board on the side of a couch. (For 2. *anūćya,* see below.)

अनूच्यते *anūćyate* (°*nu-uć*°), Pass. of *anuvać,* q. v., p. 38.

Anūkta, as, ā, am, spoken after, recited after; occurring in the (sacred) text; studied; (*am*), n. = the next.

Anūkti, is, f. mentioning after, repeated mention, repetition by way of explanation; study of the Veda. —*Anūkti-tva, am,* n. state of requiring repetition or explanation.

Anūćāna, as, ā, am, devoted to study; one so well versed in the Vedas and Vedāngas as to be able to repeat them; one who repeats his lesson after his master; well-behaved.

2. *anūćya, as, ā, am,* to be studied.

अनूज्जि *anūj-ji* (*anu-ud-ji*), cl. 1. P. *-jayati, -jetum,* to follow in being victorious.

अनूढ *an-ūḍha, as, ā, am* (rt. *vah*), not borne, not carried; unmarried; (*ā*), f. an unmarried woman.—*Anūḍha-māna, as, ā, am,* bashful. —*Anūḍhā-gamana, am,* n. fornication.—*Anūḍhā-bhrātri, tā,* m. the brother of an unmarried woman; the brother of the concubine of a king.

अनूति *an-ūti, is,* f., Ved. not helping, not coming to aid.

अनूत्क्रम् *anūt-kram* (*anu-ud-kram*), cl. 1. P. *-krāmati, -kramitum,* to follow in going up or out.

अनूत्त *anūtta, as, ā, am* (for *anu-datta,* rt. *dā*), given back.

अनूत्था *anūtthā* (*anu-ud-sthā*), cl. 1. P. *anūttishṭhati, anūtthātum,* to follow in rising; Ved. to approach.

अनूत्पत् *anūt-pat* (*anu-ud-pat*), cl. 1. P. *-patati, -titum,* to fly up after another (with acc.), raise one's self into the air, jump up afterwards.

अनूत्पा *anūt-pā* (*anu-ud-pā*), cl. 1. P., Ved. *-pibati, -pātum,* to empty by drinking after another.

अनूदक *an-ūdaka, am,* n. (for *an-udaka*), want of water, aridity.

अनूदस् *anūd-as* (*anu-ud-as*), cl. 4. P. *-asyati, -situm,* to toss up behind or after.

अनूदि *anūd-i* (*anu-ud-i*), cl. 2. P. *-eti, -tum,* to follow in going up or out.

अनूदित *anūdita* (°*nu-ud*°), *as, ā, am* (rt. *vad*), spoken after, spoken according to.

1. *anūdya, as, ā, am,* to be spoken to afterwards or in reply to.

2. *anūdya,* ind. having said in reply.

Anūdyamāna, as, ā, am, spoken in reply to, according to.

अनूदे *anūd-e* (*anu-ud-ā-i*), cl. 2. P. *anūdaiti, -tum,* to follow in coming up or rising.

अनूद्देश *anūddeśa* (*anu-ud*°), *as,* m. (rt. *diś*), describing, mentioning according to or conformably with.

अनूधस् *an-ūdhas, ās,* f., Ved. udderless.

अनून *an-ūna* or *an-ūnaka, as, ā, am,* whole, entire; having full power; not less, not inferior; (*ā*), f., N. of an Apsaras.—*Anūna-guru, us, us* or *vī, u,* of undiminished weight, very heavy. —*Anūna-varćas, ās,* m., Ved. having full splendor.

अनून्नी *anūn-nī* (*anu-ud-nī*), cl. 1. P. *-nayati, -netum,* to take out and fill after another.

अनूप 1. *anūpa, as, ā, am* (fr. *ap,* q. v., with *anu*), situated near the water, watery, wet, a watery country; (*as*), m. pond, bank of a river; a buffalo; N. of a king.—*Anūpa-ja, am,* n. moist ginger. —*Anūpa-deśa, as,* m. a marshy country.—*Anūpa-prāya, as, ā, am,* marshy.—*Anūpa-vilāsa, as,* m. title of a work.

Anūpya, as, ā, am, being in ponds or bogs (as water).

अनूप 2. *anūpa, as, ā, am* (fr. *anu-vap*), Ved. bestowing in order. (For 1. *anūpa,* see above.)

अनूपदस् *anūpa-das* (*anu-upa-das*), cl. 4. P. *-dasyati, -situm,* to fail (or become extinct) in consequence.

अनूपसदम् *anūpasadam* (*anu-up*°), ind. at every Upasad (a kind of religious ceremony).

अनूबन्ध्य *anū-bandhya, as, ā, am* (rt. *bandh*), Ved. to be fastened (as a sacrificial animal); see also *anu-bandhya,* p. 37.

अनूयाज *anū-yāja.* See *anu-yāja,* p. 37.

अनूराध *anū-rādha, as, ā, am,* Ved. causing welfare, happiness; (*ā*), f. = *anu-rādhā,* q. v., p. 38.

अनूरु *an-ūru, us, us, u,* thighless; (*us*), m. the charioteer of the sun, the dawn.—*Anūru-sārathi, is,* m. whose charioteer is Anūru, i. e. the sun.

अनूर्जित *an-ūrjita, as, ā, am,* not strong, weak; not proud.

अनूर्ध्व *an-ūrdhva, as, ā, am,* not high, low. —*Anūrdhva-bhās, ās,* m., Ved. one whose splendor does not rise, who lights no sacred fires.

अनूर्मि *an-ūrmi, is, is, i,* Ved. not waving, not fluctuating; inviolable.

अनूला *anūlā,* f., N. of a river in Kāśmīra.

अनूवृज् *anū-vrij, k,* m. f. (?), Ved. a part of the body near the ribs.

अनूषर 1. *an-ūshara, as, ā, am* (fr. *ūshara* with 3. *a* as an expletive or denoting comparison), saline.

अनूषर 2. *an-ūshara, as, ā, am,* not saline.

अनूषित *anūshita, as, ā, am* (rt. *vas* with *anu*), living near another.

अनूष्मपर *an-ūshma-para, as, ā, am,* (in gram.) not followed by a sibilant.

अनूह *an-ūha, as, ā, am,* thoughtless, careless.

अनृक्क *an-rikka.* See *an-rić* below.

अनृक्षर *an-rikshara, as, ā, am,* Ved. thornless (as a path or a couch).

अनृच् *an-rić, k, k, k,* or *an-rića, as, ā, am,* not containing a verse from the Rig-veda, hymnless, not conversant with the Rig-veda.

An-rikka or *an-rićka, as, ā, am,* containing no Rić.

अनृजु *an-riju, us, us, u,* not straight, crooked, perverse, wicked.

अनृण *an-riṇa, as, ā, am,* free from debt. —*Anriṇa-tā,* f. or *anriṇa-tva, am,* n. freedom from debt.

An-riṇin, ī, inī, i, unindebted, free from debt.

अनृत *an-rita, as, ā, am,* not true, false; (*am*), n. falsehood, lying, cheating; agriculture. —*Anrita-deva, as,* m., Ved. one whose gods are not true; playing unfairly (?).—*Anrita-dvish, ṭ, ṭ, ṭ,* Ved. persecuting untruth.—*Anrita-maya, as, ī, am,* full of untruth, false.—*Anrita-vadana, am,* n. or *anrita-bhāshaṇa, am,* n. or *anritākhyāna* (°*ta-ākh*°), *am,* n. speaking falsehood, lying.—*Anrita-vādin, ī, inī, i,* or *anrita-vāć, k, k, k,* speaking untruth.—*Anrita-vrata, as, ā, am,* false to vows or engagements.

Anritin, ī, inī, i, one who tells untruths, lying, a liar.

अनृतु *an-ritu, us,* m. unfit season.—*Anritu-kanyā,* f. a girl before menstruation.

अनृशंस *a-nriśaṇsa, as, ā, am,* not cruel, mild.—*Anriśaṇsa-tā,* f. mildness, kindness.

अनेक *an-eka, as, ā, am,* not one, many, much; separated.—*Aneka-kālam,* ind. a long time, for a long time.—*Anekakālāvadhi* (°*la-av*°), ind. long since.—*Aneka-krit, t,* m. doing much, epithet of Śiva.—*Aneka-gotra, as,* m. having more families than one, i. e. two, belonging to two families (or to one as an adopted son).—*Aneka-ćara, as, ā, am,* gregarious.—*Aneka-ćitta-mantra, as,* m. one whose counsels are many-minded.—*Aneka-ja, as, ā, am,* born more than once; (*as*), m. a bird.—*Aneka-tā,* f. or *aneka-tva, am,* n. muchness, manifold condition.—*Aneka-tra,* ind. in many places.—*Aneka-dharma-kathā,* f. different exposition of the law. —*Aneka-dhā,* ind. in various ways, often.—*Anekadhā-prayoga, as,* m. using several times.—*Aneka-pa, as, ā, am,* drinking oftener than once; (*as, ā*), m. f. an elephant, because he drinks with his trunk and with his mouth.—*Aneka-bhārya, as, ā, am,* having more wives than one.—*Aneka-mukha, as, ā, am,* having several faces, having different ways. —*Aneka-yuddha-vijayin, ī,* m. victorious in many battles.—*Aneka-randhra, as, ā, am,* having many holes, weaknesses or troubles.—*Aneka-rūpa, as, ā, am,* multiform; of various kinds or sorts; fickle, of variable mind.—*Aneka-loćana, as,* m. having several (three) eyes, N. of Śiva.—*Aneka-vaćana, am,* n. the plural number.—*Aneka-varṇa,* (in arithmetic compounded with various words to denote) many unknown quantities (colours representing *x, y, z,* &c.), e. g. *aneka-varṇa-guṇana,* multiplication of many unknown quantities. (Similarly, if for *guṇana* be substituted *bhajana* 'division,' *madhyamāharaṇa* 'taking away the middle term,' *vyavakalana* 'subtraction,' *saṅkalana* 'addition,' other algebraical processes may be expressed).—*Aneka-vāram,* ind. many times, repeatedly.—*Aneka-vidha, as, ā, am,* of many kinds, in different ways, various.—*Aneka-śapha, as, ā, am,* cloven-hoofed.—*Aneka-śabda, as, ā, am,* expressed by several words, synonymous. —*Aneka-śas,* ind. in great numbers, several times, repeatedly, by large numbers or quantities.—*Anekākāra* (°*ka-āk*°), *as, ā, am,* multiform.—*Anekākshara* (°*ka-ak*°), *as, ā, am,* polysyllabic, having more than one syllable.—*Anekāgra* (°*ka-ag*°), *as, ā, am,* engaged in various pursuits.—*Anekāć* (°*ka-ać*), having more than one vowel or syllable (*ać* in gram. being the technical term for vowel).—*Anekārtha* (°*ka-ar*°), *as, ā, am,* having more than one meaning (as a word).—*Anekārtha-dhvani-mañjarī,* f. and *anekārtha-saṅgraha, as,* m. titles of two works on such words.—*Anekāl* (°*ka-al*), consisting of more than one *al* or letter (in the technical phras. of gram.).—*Anekāśraya* (°*ka-āś*°), *as,* m. or *anekāśrita* (°*ka-āś*°), *as, ā, am,* (in Vaiśeshika phil.) dwelling, abiding in more than one.

An-ekākin, ī, inī, i, not alone, accompanied by.

An-ekānta, as, ā, am, not alone and excluding every other, uncertain. — *Anekānta-tva, am,* n. uncertainty. — *Anekānta-vāda, as,* m. scepticism. — *Anekānta-vādin, ī,* m. a sceptic; a Jaina, an Arhat of the Jainas.

Anekī-karaṇa, am, n. making manifold.

Anekī-bhavat, an, antī, at, being manifold, i. e. divided in two.

Anekīya, as, ā, am, having several.

अनेजत् *an-ejat, an, antī, at* (rt. *ej* with *an*), not moving, immoveable.

अनेड *an-eḍa, as,* m. (*an* being an expletive or denoting comparison), stupid, foolish.

An-eḍa-mūka, as, ā, am, deaf and dumb; blind; wicked, fraudulent.

अनेद्य 1. *a-nedya, as, ā, am* (rt. *nid*), Ved. not to be blamed.

अनेद्य 2. *a-nedya, as, ā, am* (fr. *a* and *nedyas*, a contraction of *nedīyas*?), Ved. not near, infinite.

अनेन 1. *an-ena, as, ā, am,* Ved. (according to native authorities) sinless, faultless; (according to German scholars) without a variegated set (of horses). See *eta.*

An-enas, ās, ās, as, blameless, sinless, not liable to error; N. of various personages.

An-enasya, am, n. freedom from fault, sin.

अनेन 2. *anena, as,* m. (fr. *ina* and *ana* for *an*); this doubtful word may signify one who has no superior, 'a sovereign or paramount lord;' see *ina* and *ana* for *an.*

अनेमन् *a-neman, ā, ā, a,* Ved. to be praised.

अनेव *an-eva,* ind. otherwise(?), or (?).

अनेहस् *an-ehas, ā, ā, as* (fr. rt. *īh* with *an*), Ved. without a rival, incomparable, unattainable; unmenaced, unobstructed; (*ā*), m. time.

अनैकान्त *an-aikānta, as, ā, am* (fr. *ekānta*), variable, unsteady; (in logic) occasional, as a cause not invariably attended by the same effects.

An-aikāntika, as, ī, am, unsteady, variable, having many objects or purposes. — *Anaikāntika-tva, am,* n. unsteadiness, uncertainty.

अनैक्य *an-aikya, am,* n. (*eka*), want of oneness, plurality, the existence of many; want of union, anarchy.

अनैपुण *a-naipuṇa* or *a-naipuṇya, am,* n. unskilfulness. See *ānaipuṇa.*

अनैश्वर्य *an-aiśvarya, am,* n. weakness. See *ānaiśvarya.*

अनो *ano,* ind. no, not. (An unusual form of *no.*)

अनोकशायिन् *an-oka-śāyin, ī,* m. not sleeping in a house (as a beggar).

An-oka-ha, as, m. not quitting the house, a tree; (*oka* is for *okas,* q. v.)

अनोङ्कृत *an-oṅ-kṛita, as, ā, am,* not accompanied by the holy syllable *om.*

अनोदित *anodita* (*ana-ud*°), *as, ā, am,* unaddressed (?).

अनोवाह्य *ano-vāhya, as, ā, am,* to be carried on a carriage.

अनौचित्य *an-aucitya, am,* n. unfitness.

अनौजस्य *an-aujasya, am,* n. want of vigour.

अनौद्धत्य *an-auddhatya, am,* n. freedom from haughtiness.

अनौपम्य *an-aupamya, as, ā, am,* unparalleled.

अनौरस *an-aurasa, as,* m. not one's own son, adopted.

अन्त् *ant,* cl. 1. P. *antati, -titum,* to bind [cf. *and, int*].

अन्त *anta, as,* m. (fr. rt. *am*?), end, limit, boundary, term; end of a texture; end, conclusion; end of life, death, destruction (in these latter senses sometimes neut.); a final syllable, termination; last word of a compound; pause, settlement, definite ascertainment, certainty; whole amount; border; nearness, proximity, presence (e. g. *grāmānte,* in the neighbourhood of the village); inner part, inside; condition, nature; *ante,* loc. c. in the end, at last; in the inside; *antam* at the end of a compound means 'as far as,' thus *udakāntam,* as far as the water; (*as, ā, am*), near, handsome, agreeable [cf. Goth. *andeis,* Theme *andja;* Germ. *Ende;* Eng. *end:* with *anta* are also compared the Greek ἄντα, ἀντί; Lat. *ante;* the Goth. *anda* in *anda-vaurd,* &c.; and the Germ. *ent,* e. g. in *entsagen*]. — *Anta-kara, as, ī, am,* or *anta-karaṇa, as, ī, am,* or *anta-kārin, ī, iṇī, i,* causing death, mortal, destructive. — *Anta-kāla, as,* m. time of death, death. — *Anta-kṛit, t, t, t,* making an end; (*t*), m. death. — *Antakṛid-daśā, ās,* f. pl. a sacred book of the Jainas, containing ten chapters. — *Anta-ga, as, ā, am,* going to the end, thoroughly conversant with. — *Anta-gati, is, is, i,* or *anta-gāmin, ī, inī, i,* going to the end, perishing. — *Anta-gamana, am,* n. the going to the end of something, finishing; the going to the end, dying. — *Anta-ćara, as, ī, am,* going to the frontiers, walking about the frontiers. — *Anta-ja, as, ā, am,* last born. — *Anta-jāti,* see *antya-jāti.* — *Anta-tas,* ind. from the end, from the term; lastly, finally; in the lowest way; in part; within. — *Anta-dīpaka, am,* n. a figure in rhetoric. — *Anta-pāla, as,* m. a frontier-guard. — *Anta-bhara, as, ā, am,* being at the end, last. — *Anta-bhāj, k, k, k,* standing at the end (of a word). — *Anta-rata, as, ā, am,* delighting in destruction. — *Anta-līna, as, ā, am,* hidden, concealed. — *Anta-lopa, as,* m. the dropping of the final of a word (in grammar). — *Anta-vat, ān, atī, at,* having an end or term, limited, perishable; (*-vat*), ind. like the end. — *Antavat-tva, am,* n. limited existence, perishableness. — *Anta-vahni, is,* m. the fire of the end, by which the world is to be burnt. — *Anta-vāsin* or *ante-vāsin, ī, inī, i,* dwelling near the boundaries, dwelling close by; (*ī*), m. a pupil who dwells near or in the house of his teacher; a Caṇḍāla (who lives at the end of the town). — *Anta-velā,* f. hour of death. — *Anta-śayyā,* f. a bed or mat on the ground; death; the place for burial or burning; bier. — *Anta-satkriyā,* f. the funeral ceremonies. — *Anta-sad, t,* m. a pupil (who dwells near his teacher). — *Anta-stha, as, ā, am,* standing at the end; see also *antaḥ-stha.* — *Anta-svarita, as,* m. the Svarita accent on the last syllable of a word; (*am*), n. a word thus accentuated. — *Antādi* (°*ta-ādi*), *ī,* du. m. end and beginning. — *Antārasāyin* or *antāraśāyin* (°*ta-av*°), *ī,* m. a barber; a Caṇḍāla; N. of a Muni or saint; see *antyārasāyin.* — *Ante-vāsa, as,* m. a neighbour, a companion, a pupil. — *Ante-vāsi,* ind. in statu pupillari; see *anta-vāsin* above. — *Antodātta* (°*ta-ud*°), *as,* m. the acute accent on the last syllable; (*as, ā, am*), having the acute accent on the last syllable.

Antaka, as, m. border, boundary; (*as, ā, am*), making an end, causing death; (*as*), m. death; Yama, king or lord of death. — *Antaka-druh, -dhruk, k, k,* Ved. offending or provoking destructive demons, or death, or Yama.

Antaki, is, m. wind (?).

Antama, as, ā, am, next, nearest, intimate (as a friend); Ved. last.

Antaya, nom. P. *antayati, -yitum,* to make an end of.

Antika, antima, antya, &c. See *antika,* p. 45.

अन्तः *antaḥ.* See *r*

अन्तःख्या *antaḥ-kh* *as,* m. worms in the intes-

Ved. *-khyāti, -tum,* ' 1. P. *andati, -ditum,* to

अन्तम *antama.*

अन्तर् *antar,* ir ıding.

andū, ūs, f. or *anduka* or *an-*

in the middle or ichain for an elephant's feet; a ring

(As a prep. with the ancle.

to; (with acc.) be

(When used at the (for *antikā,* q. v.), fire-

in the middle of, between, ou.

Zend *antarĕ;* Lat. *inter;* Goth. u. *andolayati,*

Sometimes *antar* is compounded with a word like an adjective, meaning interior, intermediate. — *Antaḥ-karaṇa, am,* n. the in... and spiritual part of man, the seat of thought and feeling, the mind, the thinking faculty, the heart, the conscience, the soul. — *Antaḥ-kalpa, as,* m. a certain number of years (in Buddhism). — *Antaḥ-kuṭila, as, ā, am,* internally crooked; fraudulent; (*as*), m. a couch. — *Antaḥ-krimi, is,* m. a disease caused by worms in the body. — *Antaḥ-koṭara-pushpī,* a various reading for *aṇḍa-koṭara-pushpī,* q. v. — *Antaḥ-koṇa, as,* m. the inner corner. — *Antaḥ-kopa, as,* m. inward wrath. — *Antaḥ-kośa, am,* n., Ved. the interior of a store-room. — *Antaḥ-paṭa, as, am,* m. n. a cloth held between two persons who are to be united (as bride and bridegroom, or pupil and teacher) until the right moment of union is arrived. — *Antaḥ-padam,* ind. in the middle of an inflected word. — *Antaḥ-paridhāna, am,* n. the innermost garment. — *Antaḥ-paridhi,* ind. in the inside of an enclosure. — *Antaḥ-parśavya* or *antaḥ-pārśvya, as, ā, am,* being between the ribs (as flesh). — *Antaḥ-pavitra,* the Soma when in the straining-vessel (?). — *Antaḥ-paśu,* ind. from evening till morning (while the cattle is in the stables). — *Antaḥ-pāta* or *antaḥ-pātya, as,* m. (in gram.) insertion of a letter; a post fixed in the middle of the place of sacrifice. — *Antaḥ-pātita, as, ā, am,* or *antaḥ-pātin, ī, inī, i,* inserted, included in. — *Antaḥ-pātra, am,* n., Ved. the interior of a vessel. — *Antaḥ-pādam,* ind. within the Pāda of a verse. — *Antaḥ-pāla, as,* m. one who watches the inner apartments of a palace. — *Antaḥ-pura, am,* n. the king's palace, the female apartments, gynæceum; those who live in the female apartments; a queen. — *Antaḥpura-ćara, as,* m. guardian of the women's apartments. — *Antaḥpura-jana, as,* m. the women of the palace. — *Antaḥpura-praćāra, as,* m. the gossip of the women's apartments. — *Antaḥpura-rakshaka, as,* m. or *antaḥpura-vartin, ī,* m. or *antaḥpurādhyaksha* (°*ra-adh*°), *as,* m. superintendent of the gynæceum, chamberlain. — *Antaḥ-pura-sahāya, as,* m. belonging to the gynæceum (as an eunuch, &c.). — *Antaḥ-purika, as,* m. superintendent of the gynæceum; (*ā*), f. a woman in the gynæceum. — *Antaḥ-pūya, as, ā, am,* ulcerous. — *Antaḥ-peya, am,* n., Ved. supping up, drinking. — *Antaḥ-prakṛiti, is,* f. the heart, the soul, the internal nature or constitution of a man. — *Antaḥ-prajña, as, ā, am,* internally wise, knowing one's self. — *Antaḥ-pratishṭhāna, am,* n. residence in the interior. — *Antaḥ-pratishṭhita, as, ā, am,* residing inside. — *Antaḥ-śara, as,* m. an internal arrow or disease. — *Antaḥ-śarīra, am,* n. the internal and spiritual part of man. — *Antaḥ-śalya, as, ā, am,* having a pin or extraneous body sticking inside. — *Antaḥ-śilā,* f., N. of a river. — *Antaḥ-ślesha, as,* m. or *antaḥ-śleshaṇa, am,* n., Ved. internal support. — *Antaḥ-sañjña, as, ā, am,* internally conscious. — *Antaḥ-sattvā,* f. a pregnant woman; the marking nut (Semecarpus Anacardium L.). — *Antaḥ-sadasam,* ind. in the middle of the assembly. — *Antaḥ-sāra, as, ā, am,* having internal essence; (*as*), m. internal treasure, inner store or contents. — *Antaḥ-sukha, as, ā, am,* internally happy. — *Antaḥ-senam,* ind. into the midst of the armies. — *Antaḥ-stha, as, ā, am,* being in the midst or between; a term applied to the semivowels, as standing between the consonants and vowels; (*ā*), f. the god of the vital

अनूक anūka, as, am, of the Rig-veda mantras. anu), the backbone, spine; m. (in anatomy) the altar; a former state of exist rala, as, m. an ele- family; peculiarity of race, dispo āṇsa (°rā-aṇ°), as, f., N. of an Apsaras. between the shoul-

Anūkya, am, n. backbone; fles m. the interior fire, , ā, am, interior,

अनूकाश anū-kāśa, as, m., or having refer- flection (of light), clearness; regar orga or base of a

अनूक्ष् anūksh (anu-uksh am, not essential beyond or external to it. kshate, -kshitum, am, n. the state or condition of

अनूचीन – Antar-arayava, as, m. an inner coming art. – Antar-ākāśa, as, m. the sacred ether lowin mma in the interior part or soul of man. – Antar-ākūta, am, n. hidden intention. – Antar-āgama, as, m. an additional augment between two letters (in gram.). – Antar-āgāra, as, m. the interior of a house – Antar-ātman, ā, m. the soul, the inherent supreme spirit; the internal feelings, the heart or mind. – Antar-ātmeshṭakam (°man-ish°), ind. in the space between one's self and the (sacrificial) bricks. – Antar-āpaṇa, as, m. a market inside (a town). – Antarāya, see antar-i. – Antar-ārāma, as, ā, am, rejoicing in one's self (not in the exterior world). – Antar-āla or antar-ālaka, am, n. intermediate space; antarāle, in the midst, in midway; (āla is probably for ālaya). – Antar-indriya, am, n. an internal organ, of which there are four, viz. manas, buddhi, ahankāra, and ćitta. – Antar-īpa, as, am, m. n. (fr. ap), an island, a promontory. – Antar-ushya, am, n. (rt. vas), Ved. a secret abode. – Antar-gangā, f. the Ganges, as supposed to communicate under-ground with a sacred spring in Mysore. – Antar-gaḍu, us, us, u, unprofitable, useless (filled with worms). – Antar-gata, &c.; see under antar-gam. – Antar-garbha, as, ā, am, inclosing young; pregnant. – Antar-giram or antar-giri, ind. among the mountains. – Antar-guda-valaya, as, m. (in medicine) the sphincter muscle. – Antar-gūḍha-visha, as, ā, am, having hidden poison within. – Antar-gṛiha, am, n. an inner apartment of the house; antar-gṛiham or antar-geham, ind. in the interior of a house. – Antar-ghaṇa, as, or antar-ghana, as, m. a place between the entrance-door and the house; N. of a village. – Antar-ghāta, as, m. striking in the middle. – Antar-ja, as, ā, am, bred in the interior (of the body, as a worm). – Antar-jaṭhara, am, n. the stomach. – Antar-janman, a, n. inward birth. – Antar-jambha, as, m. the inner part of the jaws. – Antar-jala-ćara, as, ī, am, going in the water. – Antar-jāta, as, ā, am, inborn, inbred, innate. – Antar-jānu, ind. between the knees; (us, us, u), being between the knees. – Antar-jñāna, am, n. inward knowledge. – Antar-jyotis, is, is, is, having the soul enlightened, illuminated. – Antar-jvalana, am, n. internal heat, inflammation. – Antar-dagdha, as, ā, am, burnt inwardly. – Antar-dadhana, am, n. the distillation of spirituous liquor, or a substance used to cause fermentation. – Antar-dadhāna, as, ā, am, vanishing, disappearing, hiding one's self [cf. antar-dhā]. – Antar-daśā, f. a technical term in astrology. – Antar-daśāha, am, n. an interval of ten days; so antar-daśāhāt, before the end of ten days. – Antar-dāva, as, ā, am, Ved. containing fire. – Antar-dāha, as, m. internal heat, or fever. – Antar-duḥkha, as, ā, am, afflicted in mind, sad. – Antar-dushṭa, as, ā, am, internally bad, wicked, vile. – Antar-drishṭi, is, is, i, looking into one's own soul. – Antar-deśa, as, m., Ved. an intermediate region of the compass. – Antar-dvāra, am, n. a private or secret door within the house. – Antar-dhā, &c.; see s.v. antar-dhā, p. 45. – Antar-dhyāna, am, n. profound inward meditation. – Antar-nagara, am, n. the palace of a king. – Antar-nirishṭa, as, ā, am, gone within, being within. – Antar-nishṭha, as, ā, am, engaged in internal reflection. – Antar-bharana, am, n. the interior of a house. – Antar-bhāva, &c.; see antar-bhū, p. 45. – Antar-bhāvanā, f. inward meditation or anxiety; a technical term in arithmetic; rectification of numbers by the differences of the products. – Antar-bhūmi, is, f. the inner part of the earth. – Antar-bhauma, as, ā, am, being in the interior of the earth; subterranean. – Antar-manas, ās, ās, as, sad, perplexed. – Antar-mukha, as, ā, am, going into the mouth; (am), n. a kind of scissors used in surgery. – Antar-mudra (?), sealed inside; N. of a certain form of devotion. – Antar-mṛita, as, ā, am, still-born. – Antar-yāma, as, m. the suppression of the breath and voice; a Soma libation during this act. – Antar-yāma-graha, as, m. the Soma libation Antar-yāma; the performing of such a libation. – Antar-yāmin, ī, m. checking or regulating the internal feelings; the soul; providence; the supreme spirit as regulating and guiding mankind; Brahmā. – Antar-yoga, as, m. deep thought, abstraction. – Antar-lamba, as, ā, am, acute-angular; (as), m. a triangle in which the perpendicular falls within, an acute-angled triangle. – Antar-līna, as, ā, am, inherent. – Antar-loma, as, ā, am, covered with hair on the inner side. – Antar-vanśa, as, m. the gynæceum; see antaḥ-pura. – Antar-vanśika, as, m. superintendent of the women's apartments. – Antar-vaṇa, as, ā, am, situated in a forest; (am), ind. within a forest. – Antar-vat, ān, atī, at, being in the interior. – Antar-vatī, Ved. or antar-vatnī, f. a pregnant woman. – Antar-vami, is, m. flatulence, indigestion. – Antar-vartin, ī, inī, i, or antar-vasat, an, antī, at, internal, included, dwelling in. – Antar-vasu, us, m., N. of a Soma sacrifice. – Antar-vastra, am, n. an under garment. – Antar-vāṇi, is, is, i, skilled in sacred sciences. – Antar-vāvat, ān, antī or atī, at, Ved. abounding internally with precious things, hidden; (vat), ind. inwardly. – Antar-vāshpa, as, m. suppressed tears; (as, ā, am), containing tears. – Antar-vāsas, as, n. an inner or under garment. – Antar-vigāhana, am, n. entering within. – Antar-vidvas, vān, ushī, vas, Ved. knowing (the paths) between (earth and heaven); knowing exactly. – Antar-vega, as, m. internal uneasiness or anxiety; inward fever. – Antar-vedi, is, is, i, belonging to the inside of the sacrificial ground; (i), ind. within this ground; (is or ī), f. the Doab or district between the Gangā and Yamunā rivers. – Antar-veśman, a, n. the inner apartments, the interior of a building. – Antar-veśmika, as, m. superintendent of the women's apartments. – Antar-haṇana, am, n. striking in the middle. – Antar-hanana, as, m., N. of a village. – Antar-hastam, ind. in the hand, within reach of the hand. – Antar-hastīna, as, ā, am, being in the hand or within reach. – Antar-hāsa, as, m. laughing inwardly; suppressed laughter; (am), ind. with suppressed laugh. – Antar-hita, see antar-dhā, p. 45. – Antar-hṛidaya, am, n. the interior of the heart. – Antas-tapta, as, ā, am, internally heated or harassed. – Antas-tāpa, as, m. inward heat; (as, ā, am), burning inwardly, burning with passion. – Antas-tushāra, as, ā, am, having dew in the interior. – Antas-toya, as, ā, am, containing water. – Antas-patha, as, ā, am, Ved. going within the clefts or hollows (of mountains), being on the way.

Antastya, am, n. intestines, bowels, entrails.

अन्तर antara, as, ā, am, being in the interior, interior; near, proximate, related, intimate; lying adjacent to; distant; different from; exterior; (am), n. the interior; a hole, opening; the interior part of a thing, the contents; soul, heart, supreme soul; interval, intermediate space or time; period; term; opportunity, occasion; distance, absence; difference, remainder; property, peculiarity; weakness, weak side; representation; surety, guaranty; respect, regard; (at the end of compounds) different, other, another, e. g. deśāntaram, another country [cf. Goth. anthar, Theme anthara; Lith. antra-s, 'the second;' Lat. alter]. Antaram or antara-tas, ind. in the interior, within. – Antara-ćakra, am, n. a technical term in augury. – Antara-jña, as, ā, am, knowing the interior, prudent, provident, foreseeing. – Antara-tat, t, t, t (rt. tan), spreading death or destruction. – Antara-tama, as, ā, am, nearest; immediate, intimate, internal; like, analogous; (as), m. a congenial letter, one of the same class. – Antara-tara, as, ā, am, nearer, more intimate. – Antara-da, as, ā, am (rt. dā for do), cutting or hurting the interior or heart. – Antara-diśā, f. or antarā-diś, k, f. or antar-deśa, as, m. an intermediate region or quarter of the compass. – Antara-pūrusha, as, m. the internal man, the soul. – Antara-prabhava, as, ā, am, of mixed origin or caste. – Antara-praśna, as, m. an inner question; a question which is contained in and arises from what has been previously stated. – Antara-stha, as, ā, am, or antara-sthāyin, ī, inī, i, or antara-sthita, as, ā, am, interposed, internal, situated inside, inward; separate, apart. – Antarāpatyā (°ra-ap°), f. a pregnant woman. – Antarābhara, as, m., Ved. (if fr. antara and ābhara) taking away intervals; (if fr. antarā and bhara) bringing into the midst or near; procuring.

Antarā, ind. in the middle, in the interior, inside, within, among, between; on the way, by the way; in the neighbourhood, near, nearly, almost; in the meantime, now and then; for some time; (with acc. and loc.) between, during, without. – Antarānsa, see under antar. – Antarā-bhava-deha, as, m. or antarā-bhava-sattra, am, n. the soul in its middle existence between death and regeneration. – Antarā-vedi, is or ī, f. a veranda resting on columns. – Antarā-śṛingam, ind. between the horns.

Antarīya, am, n. an under or lower garment.

Antare, ind. amidst, among, between.

Antareṇa, ind. amidst, between; (with acc.) within, between, amidst, during; except, without, with regard to, with reference to, on account of.

Antarya, as, ā, am, interior.

अन्तरञ्ज् antar-añj, cl. 7. P., Ved. -anakti, -anktum, -añjitum, to assume, take upon one's self.

अन्तरय, अन्तराय, &c. See antar-i.

अन्तराल antar-āla. See under antar.

अन्तरि antar-i, cl. 1. P. -ayati, -etum, to come between; cl. 2. P. -eti, -tum, to stand in any one's way, to separate; to exclude from (with abl.); to pass over, omit; to disappear: Ved., Intens. or Pass. -īyate, to walk to and fro between (as a mediator).

Antar-aya, as, m. impediment, hindrance.

Antar-ayaṇa, am, n. going under, disappearing.

Antar-āya, as, ā, am, going between; (as), m. intervention, obstacle, impediment.

Antar-ita, as, ā, am, gone within, interior, hidden, concealed, screened, shielded; departed, retired, withdrawn, disappeared, vanished, perished, dead; separated, detached; impeded, hindered; (am), n. (?) remainder (in arithmetic); a technical term in architecture.

अन्तरिक्ष antariksha or antarīksha, am, n. (either fr. antar, 'within,' and īksh, 'to see,' or fr. antari, loc., and ksha, 'dwelling within bodies;' ksha being fr. rt. kshi), the intermediate space between heaven and earth; (in the Veda) the middle of the three spheres or regions of life; the atmosphere or sky; the air; talc. – Antariksha-kshit, t, t, t, dwelling in the atmosphere. – Antariksha-ga or antariksha-ćara, as, m. a bird. – Antariksha-prā, ās, ās, m. f., Ved. filling the sky, irradiating the firmament; travelling through the atmosphere (?). – Antariksha-prut, t, t, t (rt. pru for plu), Ved. floating over the atmosphere. – Antariksha-loka, as, m. the intermediate region or sky as a peculiar world. – Antariksha-saṃśita, as, ā, am, sharpened in the atmosphere. – Antariksha-sad, t, t, t, Ved. dwelling in the atmosphere. – Antariksha-sadya, am, n., Ved. residence in the atmosphere. – Antar-ikshodara (°ksha-ud°), as, ā, am, having an interior as comprehensive as the atmosphere. – Antar-īksha-ga, as, ā, am, going in the atmosphere; (as), m. a bird. – Antarīksha-ćara, as, ī, am, moving through the atmosphere. – Antarīksha-jala or antariksha-jala, am, n. the water of the atmosphere.

Antarikshya, as, ā, am, atmospheric, aërial.

अन्तरुपाती *antar-upātī* (*-upa-ati-i*), cl. 2. P. *-upātyeti*, *-tum*, to enter over a threshold or boundary.

अन्तर्गम् *antar-gam*, cl. 1. P. *-gaććhati*, *-gantum*, to go between (so as to exclude from, with abl.); to disappear.

Antar-gata, as, ā, am, or *antar-gāmin, ī, inī, i*, gone between or into, being in, included in; being in the interior, internal, hidden, secret; disappeared, perished; slipped out of the memory, forgotten. — *Antargata-manas, ās, ās, as*, whose mind is turned inwards, engaged in deep thought, sad, perplexed. — *Antargatopamā* (°*ta-up*°), f. a concealed simile (the particle of comparison being omitted).

अन्तर्गा *antar-gā*, cl. 3. P. *-jigāti*, *-gātum*, to go between, separate (so as to exclude from; with abl.).

अन्तर्दृश् *antar-dṛiś*, cl. 1. P., Ved. *-paśyati*, *-drashṭum*, to look between or into.

अन्तर्धा 1. *antar-dhā*, cl. 3. A. *-dhatte*, *-dhātum*, to place within, deposit; to receive within; to hide, conceal, obscure; to hide one's self: Pass. *-dhīyate*, to be received within, to be absorbed; to be rendered invisible; to disappear, vanish; to cease: Caus. *-dhāpayati*, *-yitum*, to render invisible, to cause to disappear.

2. *antar-dhā*, f. concealment, covering, disappearing.

Antar-dhāna, am, n. disappearance, invisibility; *antardhānam i* or *gam*, to disappear; (*as*), m., N. of a son of Pṛithu. — *Antardhāna-gata, as, ā, am*, disappeared. — *Antardhāna-ćara, as, ī, am*, going invisibly.

Antar-dhāpita, as, ā, am, rendered invisible.

Antar-dhāyaka, as, ikā, am, rendering invisible, concealing.

Antar-dhi, is, m. concealment, covering, disappearance.

Antar-hita, as, ā, am, placed between, separated; covered, concealed, hidden, made invisible, vanished, invisible; hidden from (with abl.). — *Antar-hitātman* (°*ta-āt*°), *ā*, m. epithet of Śiva ('of concealed mind').

अन्तर्भू *antar-bhū*, cl. 1. P. *-bhavati*, *-vitum*, to be (contained or inherent or implied) in.

Antar-bhava, as, ā, am, being within, inward, internal, generated internally.

Antar-bhavana, antar-bhāvanā. See s. v. *antar.*

Antar-bhāva, as, m. the being included by, internal or inherent nature or disposition.

Antar-bhāvita, as, ā, am, included, involved, implied.

Antar-bhūta, as, ā, am, being within, internal, inner. — *Antarbhūta-tva, am*, n.; see *antar-bhāva.*

Antar-bhūmi. See under *antar.*

अन्तश्चर् *antaś-ćar* (*antar-ćar*), cl. 1. P. A. *-ćarati, -te, -ritum*, Ved. *-radhyai*, to move between, to move within.

अन्तश्छिद् *antaś-ćhid* (*antar-ćhid*), cl. 7. P. *-ćhinatti, -ćhettum*, to cut off, to intercept.

अन्तस् *antas.* See *antar.*

अन्ति 1. *anti*, ind. before, in the presence of, near; (with gen.) within the proximity of, to [cf. Lat. *ante*, Gr. ἀντί]. — *Anti-gṛiha, am*, n., Ved. a house near one's own dwelling; a place before the house, the neighbourhood of the house. — *Anti-tama, as, ā, am*, very near. — *Anti-tas*, ind., Ved. from near. — *Anti-deva, as, ā, am*, Ved. being in the presence of the gods, near the gods; playing against another, an adversary (at dice). — *Anti-mitra, as, ā, am*, Ved. near or at hand with friendship. — *Anti-rāma, as, ā, am*, Ved. near with wealth or loveliness. — *Anti-shad, t, t, t*, Ved. sitting near. — *Anti-shumna, as, ā, am*, Ved. near with happiness or kindness. — *Anty-ūti, is, is, i*, Ved. near with help.

1. *antika, as, ā, am*, (with gen. or abl.) near, proximate; compar. *nedīyas*, superl. *nedishṭha*; (*am*), n. vicinity, proximity, near, e. g. *antika-stha*, remaining near; (*am*), ind. (with abl., gen., or as last member of a compound) until, near to, into the presence of; (*āt*), ind. from the proximity; near, close by; within the presence of; (*e*), ind. (with gen. or as last member of a compound) near, close by, in the proximity or presence of; (*ena*), ind. (with gen.) near. — *Antika-gati, is*, f. going near. — *Antika-tā*, f. nearness, vicinity, contiguity. — *Antikāśraya* (°*ka-āś*°), *as*, m. contiguous support (as that given by a tree to a creeper).

1. *antima, as, ā, am*, immediately following (in this sense as the last member of a compound, e. g. *daśāntima*, 'the eleventh'); very near.

Antiya, as, ā, am, Ved. near; (*am*), n. a proximate place.

अन्ति 2. *anti, is*, f. an elder sister (in theatrical language). For 1. *anti*, see last col.

Antikā, f. an elder sister (in theatrical language; perhaps a corruption of *attikā*); a fire-place; a plant, Echites Scholaris.

Antī, f. an oven.

अन्तिक 2. *antika, as, ā, am* (fr. *anta*), reaching to the end of, reaching to (e. g. *nāsāntika*, reaching to the nose), lasting till, until.

2. *antima, as, ā, am*, final, ultimate, last. — *Anti-māṅka* (°*ma-aṅ*°), *as*, m. the last unit, nine.

Antya, as, ā, am, last in place, in time, or in order; immediately following (used as the last member of a compound, e. g. *ashṭamāntya*, 'the ninth'); lowest in place or condition, undermost, inferior, belonging to the lowest caste; (*as*), m., N. of the plant Cyperus Hexastachyus Communis; (*am*), n. the number 1000 billions; the twelfth sign of the zodiac; the last member of a mathematical series. — *Antya-karman, a*, n. or *antya-kriyā*, f. funeral rites. — *Antya-ja, as, ā, am*, younger, latest born; of the lowest caste; (*as*), m. a Śūdra; a man of one of seven inferior tribes; a washerman, currier, mimic, Varuḍa, fisherman, Meda or attendant on women, and mountaineer or forester. — *Antyaja-gamana, am*, n. intercourse (between a woman of the higher caste) with a man of the lowest caste. — *Antya-janman, ā, ā, a*, or *antya-jāti, is, is, i*, or *antya-jātīya, as, ā, am*, of the lowest caste. — *Antyajā-gamana, am*, n. intercourse (between a man of the higher caste) with a woman of the lowest caste. — *Antya-dhana, am*, n. last member of an arithmetical series. — *Antya-pada* or *antya-mūla, am*, n. (in arithm.) the last or greatest root (in the square). — *Antya-bha, am*, n. the last Nakshatra (Revatī); the last sign of the zodiac, the sign Pisces. — *Antya-yuga, as*, m. the last or Kali age. — *Antya-yoni, is*, f. the lowest source; (*is, is, i*), of the lowest origin. — *Antya-varṇa, as, ā*, m. f. a man or woman of the last tribe, a Śūdra. — *Antya-vipulā*, f., N. of a metre. — *Antyāvasāyin* (°*ya-av*°), *ī, inī*, m. f. a man or woman of low caste, the son of a Ćāṇḍāla by a Nishādī, especially one of the following classes: Ćāṇḍāla, Śvapaća or executioner, Kshattṛi, Sūta, Vaidehaka, Māgadha or bard, and Āyogava. — *Antyāhuti* (°*ya-āh*°), *is*, f. funeral oblation or sacrifice. — *Antyeshṭi* (°*ya-ish*°), *is*, f. funeral sacrifice. — *Antyeshṭi-kriyā*, f. funeral ceremonies.

Antyaka, as, m. a man of the lowest tribe.

अन्त्र *antra, am*, n. (contraction of *antara*; or fr. rt. *am*?; Gr. ἔντερον), entrail, intestine; (*ī*), f., N. of a plant, either Convolvulus Argenteus or Ipomœa Pes Capræ Roth (?). — *Antra-kūja, as*, m. or *antra-kūjana, am*, n. or *antra-vikūjana, am*, n. rumbling of the bowels. — *Antran-dhami, is*, f. indigestion, inflation of the bowels from wind. — *Antra-pāćaka, as*, m., N. of a plant, Æschynomene Grandiflora. — *Antra-maya, as, ī, am*, consisting of entrails. — *Antra-vṛiddhi, is*, f. inguinal hernia, rupture. — *Antra-śilā*, f., N. of a river. — *Antra-sraj, k*, f. a kind of garland worn by Nara-siṅha. — *Antrāda* (°*ra-ād*°), *as*, m. worms in the intestines.

अन्द् *and*, cl. 1. P. *andati*, *-ditum*, to bind.

Anda, as, m. binding.

Andu, us, f. or *andū, ūs*, f. or *anduka* or *andūka, as*, m. the chain for an elephant's feet; a ring or chain worn on the ancle.

अन्दिका *andikā*, f. (for *antikā*, q. v.), fire-place.

अन्दोलय *andolaya*, nom. P. *andolayati*, *-yitum*, to agitate, to swing.

Andolana, am, n. swinging, oscillating.

Andolita, as, ā, am, agitated, swung.

अन्द्रक *andraka, as*, m., N. of a king.

अन्ध् *andh*, cl. 10. P. *andhayati*, *-yitum*, to be or become blind.

Andha, as, ā, am, blind; making blind, preventing the sight, dark; (*am*), n. darkness; turbid water, water; (*ās*), m. pl., N. of a people. — *Andhakāra, as, am*, m. n. darkness. — *Andhakāra-maya, as, ī, am*, dark. — *Andhakāra-sañćaya, as*, m. intensity of darkness. — *Andha-kārita, as, ā, am*, made dark, dark. — *Andha-kūpa, as*, m. a well of which the mouth is hidden; a well over-grown with plants, &c.; a particular hell. — *Andhaṅ-karaṇa, as, ī, am*, making blind. — *Andha-tamasa* or *andha-tāmasa* or *andhā-tamasa, am*, n. great darkness. — *Andha-tā*, f. or *andha-tva, am*, n. blindness. — *Andha-tāmisra, as*, m. complete darkness of the soul; (*am*), n. a division of Tartarus, the second or eighteenth of the twenty-one hells; doctrine of annihilation after death. — *Andha-dhī, is, is, i*, mentally blind. — *Andha-pūtanā*, f. a female demon causing diseases in children. — *Andha-mūshā*, f. a small covered crucible with a hole in the side. — *Andha-mūshikā*, f., N. of a grass, Lepeocercis Serrata. — *Andham-bhāvuka, as, ā, am*, or *andha-bhavishṇu, us, us, u*, becoming blind. — *Andha-rātrī*, f., Ved. dark night. — *Andhālajī* (°*dha-al*°), f. a blind boil, one that does not suppurate. — *Andhāhi* (°*dha-ahi*), *is*, or *andhāhika, as*, m. a blind snake, not poisonous; (*is, is*), m. f., N. of a fish, commonly called kućikā.

Andhaka, as, ā, am, blind; (*as*), m., N. of an Asura, a son of Kaśyapa and Diti; N. of a descendant of Yadu and ancestor of Kṛishṇa and his descendants; N. of a Muni. — *Andhaka-ghātin, ī*, m. or *andhaka-ripu, us*, m. or *andhakāri* (°*ka-ari*), *is*, m. or *andhakāsuhrid* (°*ka-as*°), m. epithet of Śiva, the slayer or enemy of the Asura Andhaka. — *Andhaka-varta, as*, m., N. of a mountain. — *Andhaka-vṛishṇi, ayas*, pl. m. descendants of Andhaka and Vṛishṇi.

1. *andhas, as*, n., Ved. darkness, obscurity.

Andhikā, f. night; a kind of game, blindman's buff; a woman of a particular character; one of the classes of women; a disease of the eye; another disease; see *sarshapī.*

Andhī-kṛi, cl. 8. P. *-karoti*, *-kartum*, to make blind, to blind. — *Andhī-kṛita, as, ā, am*, made or become blind. — *Andhīkṛitātman* (°*ta-āt*°), *ā, ā, a*, blinded in mind.

Andhī-gu, us, m., N. of a Ṛishi.

Andhī-bhū, cl. 1. P. *-bhavati*, *-vitum*, to become blind. — *Andhī-bhūta, as, ā, am*, become blind.

अन्धस् 2. *andhas, as*, n. (fr. rt. *ad*, to eat?; Gr. ἄνθος), food, Soma, ghee, boiled rice; herb in general, herb of the Soma plant, Soma juice, juice; grassy ground. (For 1. *andhas*, see above.)

अन्धु *andhu, us*, m. (fr. rt. *am* or *andh*?), a well.

अन्धुल *andhula, as*, m., N. of a tree, Acacia Sirissa.

अन्ध्र *andhra, as*, m., N. of a people, probably modern Telingana; N. of a dynasty; a man of a low caste, the offspring of a Vaideha father and Kārāvara mother, who lives by killing game. — *Andhra-jāti, is,* f. the Andhra tribe. — *Andhra-jātīya, as, ā, am,* belonging to this tribe. — *Andhra-bhṛitya, ās,* m. pl. a dynasty of the Andhras.

अन्न 1. *anna, as,* m. (fr. rt. *at* or *am?*), the sun.

अन्न 2. *anna, as, ā, am* (fr. rt. *ad*), eaten; (*am*), n. food or victuals in general; food in a mystical sense, or the lowest form in which the supreme soul is manifested, the coarsest envelope of the supreme spirit; boiled rice; bread corn; Ved. water; Vishṇu; earth. — *Anna-kāma, as, ā, am,* desirous of food. — *Anna-kāla, as,* m. meal-time, proper hour for eating. — *Anna-koshṭhaka, as,* m. cupboard, granary; Vishṇu; the sun. — *Anna-gati, is,* f. the oesophagus, gullet. — *Anna-gandhi, is,* m. dysentery, diarrhœa. — *Anna-ja* or *anna-jāta, as, ā, am,* springing from or occasioned by food as the primitive substance. — *Anna-jala, am,* n. food and water, bare subsistence. — *Anna-jit, t, t, t,* Ved. obtaining food by conquest. — *Anna-jīvana, as, ī* (?), *am,* living by food. — *Anna-tejas, ās, ās, as,* Ved. having the vigour of food. — *Anna-da, as, ā, am,* or *anna-dātṛi, tā, trī, tṛi,* or *anna-dāyin, ī, inī, i,* or *anna-prada, as, ā, am,* giving food; epithet of Śiva and Durgā. — *Anna-dāna, am,* n. the giving of food. — *Anna-devatā,* f. the divinity supposed to preside over articles of food. — *Anna-dosha, as,* m. a fault committed by eating prohibited food. — *Anna-dvesha, as,* m. want of appetite, dislike of food. — *Anna-pati, is,* m. possessor of food, an epithet of Savitṛi, Agni, Śiva. — *Anna-pū, ūs,* m., Ved. purifying food, epithet of the sun. — *Anna-pūrṇa, as, ā, am,* filled with or possessed of food; (*ā*), f. a goddess, a form of Durgā. — *Anna-pūrvā* (?), f., N. of Durgā. — *Anna-peya, am,* n., Ved. another name for the Vāja-peya sacrifice. — *Anna-pralaya, as, ā, am,* being resolved into food or the primitive substance after death. — *Anna-prāśa, as,* m. or *anna-prāśana, am,* n. putting rice into a child's mouth for the first time, after oblations to fire, a ceremony performed between the fifth and eighth month: it is one of the sixteen Saṇskāras mentioned in the second book of Manu. — *Anna-bubhukshu, us, us, u,* desirous of eating food. — *Anna-brahman, a,* n. or *annātman* (°*na-āt*°), *ā,* m. Brahma as represented by food. — *Anna-bhaksha, as,* m. or *anna-bhakshaṇa, am,* n. or *anna-bhukti, is,* f. eating of food. — *Anna-bhāga, as,* m., Ved. a share of food. — *Anna-bhuj, k, k, k,* eating food; (*k*), m. an epithet of Śiva. — *Anna-maya, as, ī, am,* made from food, composed of food or of boiled rice; (*am*), n. plenty of food. — *Annamaya-kośa* or *annamaya-kosha, as,* m. the gross material body, that which is sustained by food (the sthūla-śarīra). — *Anna-mala, am,* n. excrement; spirituous liquor. — *Anna-rakshā,* f. caution in eating food. — *Anna-rasa, as,* m. essence of food, chyle; meat and drink, nutriment, taste in distinguishing food. — *Anna-lipsā,* f. desire for food, appetite. — *Anna-vat, ān, atī, at,* possessed of food. — *Anna-vastra, am,* n. food and clothing, the necessaries of life. — *Anna-vāhi-srotas, as,* n. the oesophagus, gullet. — *Anna-vikāra, as,* m. transformation of food; disorder of the stomach from indigestion; the seminal secretion. — *Anna-vid, t, t, t,* Ved. knowing food; possessed of food. — *Anna-śesha, as,* m. leavings, offal. — *Anna-saṇskāra, as,* m. consecrating of food. — *Anna-hartṛi, tā, trī, tṛi,* taking away food. — *Anna-homa, as,* m. a sacrifice connected with the Aśva-medha. — *Annākāla,* see *anākāla.* — *Annāććhādana* (°*na-āćh*°), *am,* n. food and clothing. — *Annāttṛi* (°*na-at*°), *tā,* m. or *annādin* (°*na-ād*°), *ī, inī, i,* eating food. — *Annāda* (°*na-ad*°), *as, ā, am,* eating food; (*as*), m., N. of Vishṇu. — *Annādana* (°*na-ad*°), *am,* n. eating of food. — *Annādya* (°*na-ad*°), *am,* n. food in general, proper food. — *Annādya-kāma, as,* m. desirous of food. — *Annāyu* or *annāyus* (°*na-āy*°), *us,* m. living by food, desirous of food. — *Annārthin* (°*na-ar*°), *ī, inī, i,* asking for food. — *Annāvṛidh* (final *a* lengthened), *t, t, t,* Ved. increasing food. — *Annāhārin* (°*na-āh*°), *ī, iṇī, i,* eating food.

अन्नम्भट्ट *annambhaṭṭa, as,* m., N. of the author of the Tarka-saṇgraha, or compendium of the Nyāya philosophy, especially the Vaiśeshika branch.

अन्य *anya, as, ā, at* (according to native authorities fr. rt. *an,* but more probably from a pronom. base *a* or *an*), other, different; (with abl. or as the last member of a compound) other than, different from, opposed to; another; another person; one of a number; *anya anya* or *eka anya,* the one, the other [cf. Zend *anya*; Armen. *ail*; Lat. *alius*; Goth. *aljis,* Them. *alja*; Gr. ἄλλος for ἄλjo-ς; cf. also ἔνιοι]. — *Anya-kāma, as, ā, am,* loving another. — *Anya-kārukā,* f. a worm bred in excrement. — *Anya-kṛita, as, ā, am,* or *anya-kārita, as, ā, am,* done by another. — *Anya-kshetra, am,* n. another territory or sphere. — *Anya-ga, as, ā, am,* or *anya-gāmin, ī, inī, i,* going to another, adulterous. — *Anya-gotra, as, ā, am,* of a different family. — *Anya-ćitta, as, ā, am,* whose mind is fixed on some one or something else. — *Anya-ćodita, as, ā, am,* moved by another. — *Anyać-ća* (°*yad-ća*), ind. and another, besides, moreover, on the contrary. — *Anya-ja* or *anya-jāta, as, ā, am,* born of another (family, &c.), of a different origin. — *Anya-janman, a,* n. another birth, being born again, metempsychosis. — *Anya-tā,* f. difference. — *Anyat-kāma, as, ā, am,* desirous of something else. — *Anyat-kṛi,* to make a mistake in reading, &c. — *Anyad-artha* or *anyārtha* (°*ya-ar*°), *as, ā, am,* having another meaning, purpose, sense. — *Anya-durvaha, as, ā, am,* difficult to be borne by another. — *Anya-devata* or *anya-devatya* or *anya-daivata, as, ā, am,* having another divinity, i. e. addressed to another divinity. — *Anya-dharma, as,* m. different characteristic; characteristic of another; (*as, ā, am*), having different characteristics. — *Anya-dhī, īs, īs, i,* one whose mind is alienated (from God). — *Anya-nābhi, is, is, i,* of another family. — *Anya-para, as, ā, am,* devoted to something else, zealous in something else. — *Anya-pushṭa* or *anya-bhṛita, as, ā,* m. f. the kokila or Indian cuckoo, supposed to be reared by the crow. — *Anya-pūrvā,* f. a woman previously promised or betrothed to one and married to another. — *Anya-bhṛit, t,* m. a crow ('nourishing another;' the crow being supposed to sit upon the eggs of the kokila). — *Anya-manas, ās, ās, as,* or *anya-manaska* or *anya-mānasa, as, ā, am,* one whose mind is fixed on something else, absent, fickle, versatile; having another mind in one's self, possessed by a demon. — *Anya-mātṛi-ja, as,* m. a half-brother, who has the same father but another mother. — *Anya-rājan, ā, ā, a,* having another for king, subject to another. — *Anya-rāshṭrīya, as, ā, am,* from another kingdom, belonging to another kingdom. — *Anya-rūpa, am,* n. another form; (*eṇa*), in another form, disguised; (*as, ā, am*), changed, altered. — *Anya-rūpin, ī, iṇī, i,* having another shape. — *Anya-liṅga* or *anya-liṅgaka, as, ā, am,* having the gender of another (word, viz. of the substantive), an adjective. — *Anya-varṇa, as, ā, am,* having another colour. — *Anya-vāpa, as,* m. the kokila or Indian cuckoo ('sowing for others,' i. e. leaving his eggs in the nests of other birds). — *Anya-vīja-ja* or *anya-vīja-samudbhava* or *anya-vījotpanna* (°*ja-ut*°), *as,* m. ('born from the seed of another'), an adopted son. — *Anya-vrata, as,* m., Ved. following other (than Vedic) observances; devoted to other (gods), infidel, unbelieving. — *Anya-śākhaka, as,* m. a Brāhman who has left his school; an apostate. — *Anya-saṅgama, as,* m. intercourse with another, adulterous intercourse. — *Anya-sādhāraṇa, as, ā, am,* common to others. — *Anya-strī-ga, as,* m. going to another's wife, an adulterer. — *Anyādṛiksha, as, ā, am,* or *anya-dṛiś, k, k, k,* or *anya-dṛiśa, as, ī, am,* of another kind, like another. — *Anyādhīna* (°*ya-adh*°), *as, ā, am,* subject to others, dependent. — *Anyāśrayaṇa* (°*ya-āś*°), *am,* n. going to another (as an inheritance). — *Anyāśrita* (°*ya-āś*°), *as, ā, am,* gone to another. — *Anyāsakta* (°*ya-ās*°), *as, ā, am,* intent on something else. — *Anyāsādhāraṇa* (°*ya-as*°), *as, ī, am,* not common to another, peculiar. — *Anyoḍhā* (°*ya-ūḍh*°), f. married to another, another's wife. — *Anyotpanna* (°*ya-ut*°), *as, ā, am,* begotten by another. — *Anyodarya* (°*ya-ud*°), *as, ā, am,* born from another womb; (*as*), m. a step-mother's son.

Anyaka, as, m. another, other.

Anya-tama, as, ā, am, any one of many, either, any.

Anya-tara, as, ā, at, either of two, other, different; *anyatara anyatara,* the one, the other; *anyatarasyām,* loc. f. either way. — *Anyatara-tas,* ind. on one of two sides. — *Anyatarato-danta, as, ā, am,* having teeth on one side (only). — *Anyatare-dyus,* ind. on either of two days.

Anya-tas, ind. from another; from another motive; on one side (*anyataḥ anyataḥ,* on the one, on the other side); elsewhere; on the other side, on the contrary, in one direction; towards some other place. — *Anyata-eta, etas, enī,* m. f., Ved. variegated on one side. — *Anyataḥ-kshṇut, t, t, t,* Ved. sharp on one side. — *Anyataḥ-plakshā,* f., N. of a Lotus pond in Kurukshetra. — *Anyato-ghātin, ī,* m., Ved. striking in one direction. — *Anyato-'raṇya* (°*tas-ar*°), *am,* n., Ved. a land which is woody here and there, or only on one side (?). — *Anyato-vāta, as,* m. a certain disease of the eye.

Anyatastya, as, m. opponent, adversary.

Anya-tra, ind. (equivalent to *anyasmin,* loc. of *anya*), elsewhere, in another place (with abl.); on another occasion; (as last member of a comp.) at another time than; otherwise, in another manner; to another place; except, without [cf. Goth. *aljathrō*]. — *Anyatra-manas, ās, ās, as,* whose mind is directed to something else, inattentive.

Anya-thā, ind. otherwise, in a different manner (with *atas, itas* or *tatas* = in a manner different from this; *anyathā anyathā,* in one way, in another way); inaccurately, untruly, falsely, erroneously; from another motive; in the contrary case, otherwise [cf. Lat. *aliuta*]. — *Anyathā-kāra, as,* m. doing otherwise, changing; (*am*), ind. otherwise, in a different manner. — *Anyathā-kṛi,* to act otherwise, alter, violate (a law), destroy (a hope), &c. — *Anyathā-kṛita, as, ā, am,* changed. — *Anyathā-khyāti, is,* f. erroneous conception of spirit; title of a philosophical work. — *Anyathā-tva, am,* n. an opposite state of the case, difference. — *Anyathā-bhāva, as,* m. alteration, difference. — *Anyathā-bhūta, as, ā, am,* changed. — *Anyathā-vādin* or *anya-vādin, ī, inī, i,* speaking differently; (*ī*), m. speaking inconsistently; (in law) prevaricating or a prevaricator. — *Anyathā-vṛitti, is, is, i,* altered, disturbed by strong emotion. — *Anyathā-siddha, as, ā, am,* wrongly defined, wrongly proved or established; effected otherwise, unessential. — *Anyathāsiddha-tva, am,* n. or *anyathā-siddhi, is,* f. wrong arguing, wrong demonstration; that demonstration in which arguments are referred to which are not the true causes. — *Anyathā-stotra, am,* n. irony. — (From *anyathā* comes the nom. verb *anyathaya,* P. *anyathayati, -yitum,* to alter.)

Anya-dā, ind. at another time; sometimes; one day, once; in another case [cf. Old Slav. *inogda, inūda*].

Anyadīya, as, ā, am, belonging to another.

Anyarhi, ind. at another time.

Anye-dyus, ind. on the other day, on the following day; the other day, once. — *Anyedyushka, as, ā, am,* occurring every other day, daily, diurnal; (*as*), m. a quotidian fever.

Anyonya or *anyo-'nya, as, ā, am,* one another, mutual [this word is said to be fr. *anyas,* nom. sing. m., and *anya*; cf. *paraspara.* In most cases, accordingly, it will be found that the first *anya* may be regarded as the subject of the sentence, while the latter assumes the acc., inst., gen., or loc. cases as required by the verb; there are many instances, however, in which the first *anya,* originally a nominative, must be regarded as equivalent to an oblique case]; *anyonyam* or *anyonya-tas*, ind. mutually. — *Anyonya-kalaha, as*, m. mutual quarrel. — *Anyonya-ghāta, as*, m. mutual conflict, killing one another. — *Anyonya-paksha-nayana, am*, n. transposing (of numbers) from one side to another. — *Anyonya-bheda, as*, m. mutual division or enmity. — *Anyonya-mithuna, am*, n. mutual union; (*as*), m. united mutually. — *Anyonya-vibhāga, as*, m. mutual partition (of an inheritance). — *Anyonya-vṛitti, is*, m. mutual effect of one upon another. — *Anyonya-vyatikara, as*, m. reciprocal action, relation or influence. — *Anyonya-saṃśraya, as*, m. reciprocal relation (of cause and effect). — *Anyonya-sāpeksha, as, ā, am*, mutually relating. — *Anyonya-hārābhihata* (°*ra-abh*°), *as, ā, am*, (two quantities) mutually multiplied by their denominators. — *Anyonyāpahṛita* (°*ya-ap*°), *as, ā, am*, taken or secreted from one another, taken secretly. — *Anyonyābhāva* (°*ya-abh*°), *as*, m. mutual non-existence, mutual negation, relative difference. — *Anyonyāśraya* (°*ya-āś*°), *as*, m. mutual or reciprocal support, connection or dependance; mutually depending. — *Anyonyāśrita* (°*ya-āś*°), *as, ā, am*, mutually supported or depending. — *Anyonyokti* (°*ya-uk*°), *is*, f. conversation.

अन्यङ्ग *a-nyaṅga, as, ā, am*, Ved. spotless. — *A-nyaṅga-śveta, as, ā, am*, Ved. white and without spot (as a sacrificial animal).

अन्यच, अन्यतस्, अन्यथा, अन्यदा, अन्योन्य. See under *anya*.

अन्या *a-nyā*, f., Ved. (*nyā* contracted fr. *niyā*?), not drying up (as the milk of a cow?); or *anyā*, f. of *anya*, other (the accent being altered?).

अन्याय *a-nyāya, as*, m. unjust or unlawful action; impropriety, indecorum; irregularity, disorder. — *Anyāya-vartin, ī, inī, i*, or *anyāya-vṛitta, as, ā, am*, acting unjustly; following evil courses.

A-nyāyin, ī, inī, i, or *a-nyāyya, as, ā, am*, unjust, improper, indecorous, unbecoming.

अन्यून *a-nyūna, as, ā, am*, not defective, entire, complete. — *A-nyūnādhika* (°*na-adh*°), *as, ā, am*, not too little and not too much; neither deficient nor excessive.

अन्योकस् *a-ny-okas, ās, ās, as*, not remaining in one's own (*okas*) habitation.

अन्वक्ष *anv-aksha, as, ā, am* (fr. *aksha*, the eye, with *anu*), following; (*am*), ind. afterwards; immediately after; directly.

अन्वक्षरसन्धि *anv-akshara-sandhi, is*, m. a kind of Sandhi in the Vedas, euphonic conjunction of a vowel and consonant.

अन्वङ्गम् *anv-aṅgam*, ind. after every member or part.

अन्वच् *anvañć, an, ūći, ak* (fr. rt. *añć* with *anu*), following the direction of another, going after, following; lying lengthwise; *anūći*, loc. c. in the rear, behind; (*ak*), ind. afterwards. — *Anvag-bhāvam*, ind. afterwards; friendly disposed. — *Anvag-bhūya*, ind. becoming friendly disposed.

अन्वती *anv-atī* (*anu-ati-i*), cl. 2. P. *-atyeti*, *-tum*, to follow in crossing or passing.

अन्वध्यायम् *anv-adhyāyam*, ind. according to the chapters (especially of the Veda), according to the sacred texts.

अन्वय *anv-aya, as, am*, m. n. (fr. rt. *i* with *anu*, see *anv-i*), following, succession; (*as*), m. connection, association, being linked to or concerned with; the natural order or connection of words in a sentence, syntax, construing; logical connection of words; logical connection of cause and effect, or proposition and conclusion; drift, tenor, purport; descendants, race, lineage, family. — *Anvaya-jña, as*, m. a genealogist. — *Anvaya-vat, ān, atī, at*, having a connection (as a consequence), following, agreeing with; belonging to race or family. — *Anvaya-vat*, ind. in connection with, in the sight of. — *Anvaya-vyatireka, am*, n. a positive and negative proposition; agreement and contrariety; species and difference; rule and exception; logical connection and disconnection. — *Anvaya-vyatirekin, ī, iṇī, i*, (in phil.) affirmative and negative. — *Anvaya-vyāpti, is*, f. an affirmative argument.

Anvayin, ī, inī, i, connected (as a consequence). — *Anvayi-tva, am*, n. the state of being a necessary consequence.

अन्वर्च् *anv-arć* (*anu-arć*), cl. 1. P. *-arćati*, *-ćitum*, to honour with shouts or songs of jubilee.

अन्वर्ज् *anv-arj* (*anu-arj*), cl. 1. P. *-arjati*, *-jitum*, to let go.

अन्वर्तितृ *anv-artitṛi, tā*, m. (fr. *anu-art* for *anu-ṛith*), Ved. an inviter, one who allows to take.

अन्वर्थ *anv-artha, as, ā, am*, having the meaning obvious, intelligible, clear. — *Anvartha-grahaṇa, am*, n. the literal acceptation of the meaning of a word (as opposed to the conventional). — *Anvartha-sañjñā*, f. a term whose meaning is intelligible in itself (opposed to such technical terms as *bha, ghu*, &c.).

अन्वव् *anv-av* (*anu-av*), cl. 1. P. *-avati*, *-vitum*, to encourage.

अन्ववकॄ *anv-ava-kṝi* (*anu-ava*°), cl. 6. P. *-kirati*, *-karitum* or *-rītum*, to scatter or strew about: Caus. P. *-kīrayati*, *-yitum*, to make one scatter about.

Anv-avakiraṇa, am, n. scattering about successively.

अन्ववक्रम् *anv-ava-kram* (*anu-ava*°), cl. 1. P. *-krāmati*, *-kramitum*, to descend or enter in succession.

अन्ववगा *anv-ava-gā* (*anu-ava*°), cl. 3. P. *-jigāti*, *-gātum*, to go and join another.

अन्ववचर् *anv-ava-ćar* (*anu-ava*°), cl. 1. P. *-ćarati*, *-ritum*, to insinuate one's self into, enter stealthily.

Anv-avaćāra, as, m., Ved. descending and going after.

अन्ववपा *anv-ava-pā*, cl. 1. P. *-pibati*, *-pātum*, to drink after others.

अन्ववसर्ग *anv-avasarga, as*, m. (fr. rt. *sṛij* with *anu* and *ava*), letting down, slackening; friendly invitation; permission to do as one likes.

अन्ववसित *anv-avasita, as, ā, am* (fr. rt. *si* with *anu* and *ava*), fastened to, bound to, attached; see *anuvasita*.

अन्ववार्ज् *anv-avārj* (*anu-ava-arj*), cl. 1. P. *-avārjati*, *-jitum*, to cause to go after or in a particular direction; to visit with anything.

अन्ववे *anv-ave* (*anu-ava-i*), cl. 2. P. *-avaiti*, *-tum*, to follow, walk up to or get into.

Anv-avāya, as, m. race, lineage.

Anv-avāyana, am, n., Ved. descending and going after.

अन्ववेक्ष् *anv-aveksh* (*anu-ava-īksh*), cl. 1. A. *-avekshate*, *-kshitum*, to look at, inspect.

Anv-avekshā, f. regard, consideration.

अन्वश् *anv-aś* (*anu-aś*), cl. 5. P. A. *-aśnoti*, *-nute*, *-aśitum* or *-ashṭum*, to reach, come up to, equal.

अन्वष्टका *anv-ashṭakā*, f. the ninth day in the latter half of the three months following the full moon in Āgrahāyaṇa, Pausha, Māgha, Phālguna.

Anvashṭakya, am, n. a Śrāddha or funeral ceremony performed on the Anvashṭakās.

अन्वस् *anv-as* (*anu-as*), cl. 2. P., Ved. *-asti*, to be at hand, to reach.

अन्वस्त *anv-asta, as, ā, am* (fr. rt. 2. *as*, *asyati*), shot along, shot; interwoven (as in silk), chequered.

अन्वह् *anv-ah* (*anu-ah*), perf. *-āha*, to pronounce, especially a ceremonial formula (Gram. 384. *b*).

अन्वहम् *anv-aham* (*anu-aham*), ind. day after day, every day.

अन्वाक्रम् *anv-ā-kram* (*anu-ā*°), cl. 1. A. *-kramate*, *-mitum*, to ascend towards or to; P. *-krāmati*, to visit in succession.

अन्वाख्या *anv-ā-khyā* (*anu-ā*°), cl. 2. P. *-khyāti*, *-tum*, to enumerate.

Anv-ākhyāna, am, n. enumeration; section; chapter.

अन्वागम् *anv-ā-gam* (*anu-ā*°), cl. 1. P. *-gaććhati*, *-gantum*, to follow, come after: Desid. *-jigāṅsati*, to wish or intend to follow.

अन्वागा *anv-ā-gā* (*anu-ā*°), cl. 3. P., Ved. *-jigāti*, *-gātum*, to follow.

अन्वाचक्ष् *anv-ā-ćaksh* (*anu-ā*°), cl. 2. A. *-ćashṭe*, Ved. Inf. *-ćakshase*, to name after.

अन्वाचम् *anv-ā-ćam* (*anu-ā*°), cl. 1. P. *-ćāmati*, *-ćamitum*, to follow in rinsing the mouth.

अन्वाचय *anv-āćaya, as*, m. (rt. *ći*), laying down a rule of secondary importance after that which is *pradhāna* or primary; connecting of a secondary action with the main action (e. g. the conjunction *ća* is sometimes used *anvāćaye*). — *Anvāćaya-śishṭa, as, ā, am*, propounded as a rule or matter of secondary importance.

Anv-āćita, as, ā, am, secondary, inferior.

अन्वाचर् *anv-ā-ćar* (*anu-ā*°), cl. 1. P. *-ćarati*, *-ritum*, to follow or imitate in doing.

अन्वाजे *anvāje* (fr. *anu* and *aj*?), only used in connection with rt. *kṛi*, e. g. *anvāje kṛi*, to support, aid, assist.

अन्वातन् *anv-ā-tan* (*anu-ā*°), cl. 8. P. *-tanoti*, *-nitum*, to extend, spread; to overspread, extend over.

अन्वादा *anv-ā-dā* (*anu-ā*°), cl. 3. A. *-datte*, *-dātum*, to resume.

अन्वादिश् *anv-ā-diś* (*anu-ā*°), cl. 6. P. *-diśati*, *-deshṭum*, to name or mention afresh; to employ again.

Anv-ādishṭa, as, ā, am, mentioned after or according to, employed again; inferior.

Anv-ādeśa, as, m. mentioning after, a repeated mention, referring to what has been stated previously, re-employment of the same word in a subsequent part of a sentence, the employment again of the same thing to perform a subsequent operation.

अन्वाधान *anv-ādhāna, am*, n. (fr. rt. *dhā* with *anu* and *ā*), putting fuel (on the three sacred fires), depositing.

1. *anv-ādhi, is*, m. a bail or deposit delivered to a third person, see *anv-āhita* below; a second deposit.

Anv-ādheya or *anv-ādheyaka, am*, n. property presented after marriage to the wife by her husband's family.

Anv-āhita, as, ā, am, deposited with a person to be delivered ultimately to the right owner.

अन्वाधि 2. *anv-ādhi, is*, m. (rt. *dhyai*), repentance, remorse, melancholy reflection after (the commission of a bad act).

Anv-ādhya, as, m. a kind of divinity.

अन्वानी *anv-ā-nī*, cl. 1. P. *-nayati*, *-netum*, to lead to, to lead along.

अन्वानु *anv-ā-nu*, Intens., Ved. *-nonavīti*, to sound through.

अन्वान्त्र्य *anv-āntrya, as, ā, am*, Ved. being in the entrails.

अन्वायतन *anv-āyatana, as, ā, am*, latitudinal.

अन्वायत्त *anv-āyatta, as, ā, am* (fr. rt. *yat* with *ā* and *anu*), Ved. following after, in accordance with.

अन्वायात्या *anv-āyātyā*, f. a deity invoked by the verb *anv-ā-yā*.

अन्वारभ् *anv-ā-rabh* (*anu-ā°*), cl. 1. Ā. *-rabhate, -rabdhum*, to commence; to receive; to touch.

Anv-ārabdha, as, ā, am, in contact with.

Anv-ārabhya, as, ā, am, to be touched, tangible.

Anv-ārambha, as, m. or *anv-ārambhaṇa, am*, n. touching, contact.

Anv-ārambhaṇīyā, f. an initiatory ceremony.

अन्वारुह् *anv-ā-ruh* (*anu-ā°*), cl. 1. P. *-rohati, -roḍhum*, to follow or join by ascending.

Anv-ārohaṇa, am, n. (a widow's) ascending the funeral pile after or with the body of a husband.

Anv-ārohaṇīya, as, ā, am, belonging to the Anvārohaṇa, or rite of cremation.

अन्वाविश् *anv-ā-viś* (*anu-ā°*), cl. 6. P. *-viśati, -veshṭum*, to enter, occupy, possess, engross.

अन्वाश्रि *anv-ā-śri* (*anu-ā°*), cl. 1. P. *-śrayati, -yitum*, to resort to, repair, to go (or come) up to.

अन्वास् *anv-ās* (*anu-ās*), cl. 2. Ā. *-āste, -situm*, to follow in taking a seat; to be seated at or near or round; to be engaged in (especially in a religious act).

Anv-āsana, am, n. sitting down after (another), service; regret, affliction; a place where work is done, a manufactory, a house of industry; an unctuous or cooling enema.

Anv-āsita, as, ā, am, made to sit down after or alongside.

Anv-āsīna, as, ā, am, sitting down after, seated alongside of.

Anv-āsyamāna, as, ā, am, being accompanied by, attended by.

अन्वास्था *anv-ā-sthā* (*anu-ā°*), cl. 1. P. *-tishṭhati, -sthātum*, to go towards, to meet.

अन्वाहार्य *anv-āhārya, as, am*, m. n. or *anv-āhāryaka, am*, n. (rt. *hṛi*), a certain gift presented to the priests; (*am* or *akam*), n. the monthly Śrāddha or funeral repast in honour of the manes, held on the day of new moon; according to Manu, it should be of meat eaten after the presentation of a Piṇḍa or ball of rice. — *Anvāhārya-paćana, as*, m. the southern sacrificial fire, used in the Anvāhārya sacrifice.

अन्वाहिक *anv-āhika, as, ī, am*, daily, diurnal.

अन्वाहित *anv-āhita*. See *anv-ādhāna*, p. 47.

अन्वि *anv-i* (*anu-i*), cl. 2. P., Ved. *-eti, -tum, -tave, -tavai*, to go after or alongside, to follow; to seek; to be guided by; to fall to one's share.

Anv-aya. See s. v., p. 47, col. 1.

Anv-ita or *anv-īta, as, ā, am*, joined, attended, connected with, linked to; having as an essential or inherent part, endowed with, possessed of, possessing; acquired, reached by the mind, understood; following; connected as in grammar or construction. — *Anvitārtha* (°*ta-ar*°), *as, ā, am*, having a clear meaning understood from the context, perspicuous.

Anv-iti, is, f. following after; food (as the companion of the body?).

Anv-īyamāna, as, ā, am, being followed.

अन्विध् *anv-idh* or *anv-indh* (*anu-indh*), cl. 7. or cl. 1. Ā. *-inddhe* or *-indhate, -dhitum*, to kindle.

अन्विष् 1. *anv-ish* (*anu-ish*), cl. 1. P. *-iććhati, -eshitum, -eshṭum*, to desire, seek, seek after, search, aim at.

अन्विष् 2. *anv-ish* (*anu-ish*), cl. 4. P. *-ishyati, -eshitum*, to go after, seek, search: Caus. *-eshayati, -yitum*, to seek.

Anv-ishṭa or *anv-ishyamāṇa, as, ā, am*, sought, required.

Anv-esha, as, m. or *anv-eshaṇa, am, ā*, n. f. seeking for, searching, investigating.

Anv-eshaka, as, ikā, am, or *anv-eshin, ī, iṇī, i*, or *anv-eshṭṛi, tā, tṛī, tṛi*, searching, enquiring.

Anv-eshṭavya or *anv-eshya, as, ā, am*, to be searched, to be investigated.

अन्वीक्ष् *anv-īksh* (*anu-īksh*), cl. 1. Ā. *-īkshate, -shitum*, to follow with one's looks, to keep looking or gazing, to keep in view.

Anv-īkshaṇa, am, n. or *anv-īkshā*, f. reflection, meditation, searching.

अन्वीप *anvīpa, as, ā, am* (fr. *ap*, q.v., with *anu*), near the water; or (fr. rt. *āp* with *anu*), attainable; friendly (?).

अन्वृ *anv-ṛi* (*anu-ṛi*), cl. 3. P. *-iyarti, -artum* or *-aritum* or *-arītum* (?), to follow; to follow in rising.

अन्वृचम् *anv-ṛićam*, ind. verse after verse.

अन्वृध् *anv-ṛidh* (*anu-ṛidh*), cl. 6. P., Ved. *-ṛidhati, -ardhitum*, to carry out, accomplish.

अन्वे *anv-e* (*anu-ā-i*), cl. 2. P. *-aiti, -tum*, to come after, to follow as an adherent or attendant.

अप् *ap* (in the Vedas used in sing. and plur., but in the classical language only in plur.), *āpas*, f. water; air, the intermediate region; the star δ Virginis. Sometimes, particularly in the Vedas, the *Āpaḥ* are considered as divinities. As the last member of a compound, *ap* may become *apa, īpa, ūpa*. [Cf. Lat. *aqua*; Goth. *ahva*, 'a river;' Old Germ. *aha*, and *affa* at the end of compounds; Lith. *uppê*, 'a river;' perhaps Lat. *amnis*, 'a river,' for *apnis*; cf. also ἀφρός]. — *Apa-vat, ān, atī, at*, Ved. watery. — *Apaḥ-saṃvarta, as*, m. (Buddh.) destruction (of the world) by water. — *Apāṃ-vatsa, as*, m., N. of a star ('calf of the waters'). — *Apāṃ-napāt, t*, or *apāṃ-naptṛi, tā*, or *apāṃ-garbha, as*, or *apān-napāt*, or *apo-napāt, t*, &c., m., Ved., N. of Agni or fire as sprung from water. — *Apāṃ-naptriya* or *apāṃ-naptrīya* or *apa-naptriya* or *apo-naptriya, as, ā, am*, Ved. relating to Agni. — *Apāṃ-nātha, as*, m. the ocean. — *Apāṃ-nidhi, is*, m. the ocean. — *Apām-pati* or *ap-pati, is*, m. the ocean; N. of Varuṇa. — *Apāṃ-pitta* or *ap-pitta, am*, n. fire; a plant. — *Ap-kṛitsna, am*, n. deep meditation performed by means of water. — *Ap-ćara, as*, m. an aquatic animal. — *Ap-saras*, see s. v.

Aptya, apya. See s. v.

Apsava, apsavya, apsā. See s. v.

Apsu, for words beginning thus. See *apsu-*.

Ab-, for words beginning thus. See *ab-indhana*, &c.

अप *apa*, ind. (as a prefix to nouns and verbs, expresses) away, off, back (opposed to *upa, anu, sam, pra*), down (opposed to *ud*).

When prefixed to nouns, it may sometimes = the neg. particle *a*, e. g. *apa-bhī*, fearless; or may express deterioration, inferiority, &c., e. g. *apa-pāṭha*, q. v.

(As a separable preposition or adverb, with abl.) away from, on the outside of, without, with the exception of. It is separated only in the Vedas [cf. Gr. ἀπό; Lat. *ab*; Goth. *af*; Eng. *of*].

अपकरुण *apa-karuṇa, as, ā, am*, cruel.

अपकलङ्क *apa-kalaṅka, as*, m. an indelible disgrace, a deep stain.

अपकल्मष *apa-kalmasha, as, ā, am*, stainless.

अपकष् *apa-kash*, cl. 1. P. *-kashati, -shitum*, to scrape off.

अपकाम *apa-kāma, as*, m., Ved. aversion, abhorrence; abominableness; deprivation of what is dear; (*am*), ind. against one's liking, unwillingly.

अपकीर्ति *apa-kīrti, is*, f. infamy, disgrace.

अपकुक्षि *apa-kukshi, is*, m. a bad or ill-shaped belly (?). This word may also be used as a *Bahu-vrīhi* and as an *Avyayī-bhāva*.

अपकुञ्ज *apa-kuñja, as*, m., N. of a younger brother of the serpent king Śesha.

अपकृ *apa-kṛi*, cl. 8. P. Ā. *-karoti, -kurute, -kartum*, to carry away, remove, drag away; (with gen. or acc.) to hurt, wrong, injure (any one): Caus. *-kārayati, -yitum*, to hurt, wrong.

Apa-karaṇa, am, n. acting improperly; doing wrong; ill-treating, offending, injuring.

Apa-kartṛi, tā, trī, tṛi, injurious, offensive, hostile, inimical, an enemy.

Apa-karman, a, n. discharge (of a debt); evil doing, improper conduct, wickedness; oppression, violence; laziness, incompetence; any impure or degrading act or rite.

Apa-kāra, as, ā, am, acting wrong, offending; (*as*), m. wrong, offence, injury, hurt; wickedness; oppression, enmity. — *Apakāra-gir, īs*, f. or *apakāra-śabda, as*, m. an offending or menacing speech. — *Apakāra-tā*, f. wrong, offence. — *Apakārārthin* (°*ra-ar*°), *ī, inī, i*, malicious, malevolent.

Apa-kāraka, as, ikā, am, or *apa-kārin, ī, iṇī, i*, (with gen.) acting wrong, doing ill (to any one), offending, injuring.

Apa-kṛita, as, ā, am, done wrong, maliciously, offensively or wickedly committed; observed or practised as a degrading or impure act, as servile duties, funeral rites, &c.; (*am*), n. injury, offence.

Apa-kṛiti, is, f. oppression, wrong, injury; enmity, opposition; any degrading or impure act or rite.

Apa-kṛitya, am, n. damage, injury, hurt.

Apa-kriyā, f. delivery, clearing off (debts); offence; any impure act or rite.

अपकृत् *apa-kṛit*, cl. 6. P. *-kṛintati, -karttum*, to cut off.

अपकृष् *apa-kṛish*, cl. 1. and 6. P. Ā. *-karshati, -te, -kṛishati, -te, -karshṭum* or *-krashṭum*, to draw off or aside, drag down, carry away, take away, remove; to omit, diminish; to put away; to anticipate something which occurs later (as a word of a sentence); to bend (a bow); to detract, debase, dishonour: Caus. *-karshayati, -yitum*, to remove, diminish, detract.

Apa-karsha, as, m. drawing or dragging off or down, detraction, deficiency, diminution, decay; lowering, deterioration, depression; decline, degradation, inferiority, infamy; anticipated performance of a duty; (in poetry) anticipation of a word occurring later. — *Apakarsha-sama, as, ā*, m. f. a sophism in the Nyāya, e. g. 'sound has not the quality of shape as a jar has, therefore sound and a jar have no qualities in common.'

Apa-karshaka, as, ikā, am, drawing down, detracting (with gen.).

Apa-karshaṇa, as, ī, am, taking away, forcing away, removing, diminishing; (*am*), n. taking away, depriving of; drawing down; abolishing, denying.

Apa-kṛishṭa, as, ā, am, drawn away, taken away, removed, lost; dragged down, brought down, depressed; low, vile, inferior; (*as*), m. a crow. — *Apakṛishṭa-ćetana, as, ā, am*, mentally debased. — *Apakṛishṭa-jāti, is, is, i*, of a low tribe. — *Apakṛishṭa-tā*, f. or *apakṛishṭa-tva, am*, n. inferiority, vileness.

अपकृ *apa-kṛī*, cl. 6. P. *-kirati*, *-karitum*, *-rītum*, to spout out, spurt, scatter; to throw down; to scrape with the feet.

अपकौशली *apa-kauśalī*, f. news, information.

अपक्ति *a-pakti*, *is*, f. (rt. *pać*), immaturity; indigestion.

A-pakva, *as*, *ā*, *am*, unripe, immature; undigested. — *Apakva-tā*, f. immaturity; incompleteness. — *Apakva-buddhi*, *is*, *is*, *i*, of immature understanding. — *Apakvāśin* (°*va-āś*°), *ī*, *inī*, *i*, eating raw, uncooked food.

अपक्रम् *apa-kram*, cl. 1. P. *-krāmati*, poet. A. *-kramate*, *-mitum*, to go away, fly, retreat, retire from; to glide away; to measure off by steps.

Apa-krama, *as*, m. going away; passing off or away; flight, retreat.

Apa-kramaṇa, *am*, n. or *apa-krāma*, *as*, m. passing off or away, retiring.

Apa-kramin, *ī*, *iṇī*, *i*, going away, retiring.

अपक्री *apa-krī*, cl. 9. P. A. *-krīṇāti*, *-ṇīte*, *-kretum*, to buy, purchase.

अपक्रुश् *apa-kruś*, cl. 1. P. *-krośati*, *-kroshṭum*, to revile.

Apa-krośa, *as*, m. reviling, abusing.

अपक्ष *a-paksha*, *as*, *ā*, *am*, without wings; not on the same side or party; adverse, opposed to. — *Apaksha-tā*, f. opposition, hostility. — *A-paksha-pāta*, *as*, m. impartiality.

अपक्षि *apa-kshi*, cl. 5. 9. or 1. P. *-kshiṇoti*, *-kshiṇāti*, *-kshayati*, *-kshetum*, to destroy, annihilate; bring to an end: Pass. *-kshīyate*, to decline, wane (as the moon).

Apa-kshaya, *as*, m. decline, decay, wane.

Apa-kshita, *as*, *ā*, *am*, waned.

Apa-kshīṇa, *as*, *ā*, *am*, declined, decayed, diminished.

अपक्षिप् *apa-kship*, cl. 6. P. A. *-kshipati*, *-te*, *-ksheptum*, to throw away or down, take away, remove.

Apa-kshipta, *as*, *ā*, *am*, thrown or cast down or away.

Apa-kshepaṇa, *am*, n. casting away, throwing down.

अपगम् *apa-gam*, cl. 1. P. *-gaććhati*, *-gantum*, to go away, depart; to give way, vanish.

Apa-ya, *as*, *ā*, *am*, going away, turning away; (*ā*), f. a river.

Apa-gata, *as*, *ā*, *am*, gone, departed, remote, gone off; dead, diseased. — *Apagata-vyādhi*, *is*, *is*, *i*, one who has recovered from a disease.

Apa-gama, *as*, m. or *apa-gamana*, *am*, n. going away; giving way; separation, departure, death.

अपगर *apa-gara*, *as*, m. (rt. *gṛī*), reviler.

अपगर्जित *apa-garjita*, *as*, *ā*, *am*, thunderless (as a cloud).

अपगल्भ *apa-galbha*, *as*, m., Ved. failing in boldness; abortive; being on the side (not in the middle?); separated from the oldest by one.

अपगा *apa-gā*, cl. 3. P. *-jigāti*, *-gātum*, to go away, vanish, retire.

अपगुर् *apa-gur*, cl. 6. A. *-gurate*, sometimes P. *-gurati*, *-ritum*, to reject, disapprove, threaten; to inveigh against any one; to deprive of (?): part. of the Intens. *apa-jargurāṇa*, *as*, *ā*, *am*, Ved. rejecting, &c.

Apa-gāram or *apa-goram*, ind. having raised.

अपगुह् *apa-guh*, cl. 1. P. A. *-gūhati*, *-te*, *-gūhitum*, *-goḍhum*, to conceal, hide.

Apa-goha, *as*, m., Ved. hiding place; secret.

अपगोपुर *apa-gopura*, *as*, *ā*, *am*, without gates (as a town).

अपग्रह् *apa-grah*, cl. 9. P. A. *-gṛihṇāti*, *-ṇīte*, *-grahītum*, to take away, disjoin, tear off.

अपघन *apa-ghana*, *as*, m. (fr. rt. *han* with *apa*), a limb or member, as a hand or foot.

Apa-ghāta, *as*, m. striking or cutting off; warding off; killing; a violent death.

Apa-ghātaka, *as*, *ikā*, *am*, warding off.

Apa-ghātin, *ī*, *inī*, *i*, murderous, killing. See *apa-han*.

अपङ्क्त्य *apaṅktya*. See *apāṅktya*.

अपच *a-paća* or *a-paćamāna*, *as*, m. not cooking; not being able to cook; a bad cook.

अपचर् *apa-ćar*, cl. 1. P. *-ćarati*, *-ritum*, to depart; to act wrongly.

Apa-ćarita, *as*, *ā*, *am*, gone away, departed, dead; (*am*), n. fault, offence.

Apa-ćāra, *as*, m. want, absence; defect; fault, improper conduct, offence; unwholesome or improper regimen.

Apa-ćārin, *ī*, *iṇī*, *i*, doing wrong, wicked, bad.

अपचाय् *apa-ćāy*, cl. 1. P. A. *-ćāyati*, *-te*, *-yitum*, to fear; to respect, honour.

Apa-ćāyita, *as*, *ā*, *am*, honoured, respected.

अपचि 1. *apa-ći*, cl. 3. P., Ved. *-ćiketi*, *-ćetum*, to pay attention to, to respect; to invite respectfully.

1. *apa-ćita*, *as*, *ā*, *am*, honoured, respected, saluted; (*am*), n. honouring, esteeming.

1. *apa-ćiti*, *is*, f. honouring, worship, reverence. — *Apaćiti-mat*, *ān*, *atī*, *at*, honoured.

अपचि 2. *apa-ći*, cl. 5. P. A. *-ćinoti*, *-nute*, *-ćetum*, to gather, collect: Pass. *-ćīyate*, to be injured in health or prosperity; to grow less; to wane; (with abl.) to lose anything.

Apa-ćaya, *as*, m. diminution, decay, decrease, loss, privation, decline; N. of several planetary mansions.

2. *apa-ćita*, *as*, *ā*, *am*, diminished, expended, wasted; emaciated, thin.

2. *apa-ćiti*, *is*, f. loss; expense; exclusion; compensation; punishing; N. of a daughter of Marīći.

Apa-ćī, f. a disease consisting in an enlargement of the glands of the neck.

Apa-ćetṛi, *tā*, m. a spendthrift.

अपचिकीर्षा *apa-ćikīrshā*, f. (rt. *kṛi* in Desid.), desire of hurting any one.

अपचित् 1. *apa-ćit*, Caus. P. A. *-ćetayati*, *-te*, or Ved. *-ćitayati*, *-te*, *-yitum*, to become faithless: Desid. *-ćikitsati*, *-te*, to wish to leave or to abandon any one.

2. *apa-ćit*, *t*, f., Ved. a noxious flying insect.

अपच्छत्त्र *apa-ććhattra*, *as*, *ā*, *am*, not having a parasol.

अपच्छाय *apa-ććhāya*, *as*, *ā*, *am*, shadowless, having no shadow, as a deity or celestial being; having a bad or unlucky shadow; (*ā*), f. an unlucky shadow, a phantom, apparition.

अपच्छेद *apa-ććheda*, *as*, m. or *apa-ććhedana*, *am*, n. (rt. *ćhid*), cutting off or away; loss; interruption.

अपच्यु *apa-ćyu*, cl. 1. A. *-ćyavate*, poet. P. *-ćyavati*, *-ćyotum*, to fall off, to perish, to go off, desert, withdraw: Caus. *-ćyāvayati*, to expel.

Apa-ćyava, *as*, m., Ved. going or coming out; moving down (as a pestle?).

Apa-ćyuta, *as*, *ā*, *am*, fallen off, departed, gone away, perished.

अपजात *apa-jāta*, *as*, m. a bad son who has turned out ill.

अपजि *apa-ji*, cl. 1. P. *-jayati*, *-jetum*, to defeat, conquer, to ward off, keep off or out.

Apa-jaya, *as*, m. defeat, discomfiture, overthrow.

Apa-jayya, *as*, *ā*, *am*, conquerable, to be defeated.

अपजिघांसु *apa-jighāṅsu*, *us*, *us*, *u* (fr. *apa-han* in Desid.), desirous of keeping off, wishing to avert.

अपजिहीर्षु *apa-jihīrshu*, *us*, *us*, *u* (fr. *apa-hṛi*, q. v., in Desid.), wishing to carry off or take away.

अपज्ञा *apa-jñā*, cl. 9. A. *-jānīte*, *-jñātum*, to deny, repudiate; to dissemble, conceal; to cause not to be recognized.

Apa-jānāna, *as*, *ā*, *am*, denying, concealing.

अपञ्चीकृत *a-pańćī-kṛita*, *am*, n. simple elementary substance, not compounded of the five (*pańćan*) gross elements; the five subtle elements.

अपटान्तर *a-paṭāntara* (°*ṭa-ant*°), *as*, *ā*, *am*, not separated by a curtain; adjoining, contiguous.

अपटी *apaṭī*, f. a screen or wall of cloth, especially the *kanāt* or screen surrounding a tent. — *Apaṭī-kshepa* or *apaṭā-kshepa*, *as*, m. tossing aside the curtain; *apaṭī-kshepeṇa*, with a toss of the curtain, precipitate entrance on the stage, indicating hurry and agitation.

अपटु *a-paṭu*, *us*, *us* or *vī*, *u*, not clever, awkward, uncouth; ineloquent; sick, diseased. — *A-paṭu-tā*, f. or *apaṭu-tva*, *am*, n. awkwardness; sickness.

अपठ *a-paṭha*, *as*, m. unable to read, not reading.

अपण्डित *a-paṇḍita*, *as*, *ā*, *am*, unlearned, illiterate.

अपण्य *a-paṇya*, *as*, *ā*, *am*, unsaleable, unfit for sale.

अपतक्ष् *apa-taksh*, cl. 1. P., Ved. *-takshati*, *-shitum* or *-tashṭum*, to chip off.

अपतन्त्रक *apa-tantraka*, *as*, m. spasmodic contraction of the body or stomach, emprosthotonos.

अपतानक *apa-tānaka*, *as*, m. spasmodic contraction.

Apa-tānakin, *ī*, *inī*, *i*, affected with spasmodic contraction.

अपति *a-pati*, *is*, m., Ved. not a husband or master; (*is*, *is*, *i*), without a husband or master, unmarried. — *A-pati-ghnī*, f. not killing the husband. — *Apati-tā*, f. state of being without a husband. — *Apati-putra*, *as*, *ā*, *am*, without a husband and children. — *A-pati-vratā*, f. an unfaithful or unchaste wife.

A-patika, *as*, *ā*, *am*, without a husband.

अपतीर्थ *apa-tīrtha*, *as*, *am*, m. n. a bad or improper Tīrtha, q. v.

अपतृप् *apa-tṛip*, Caus. P. *-tarpayati*, *-yitum*, to starve, cause to fast.

Apa-tarpaṇa, *am*, n. fasting (in sickness).

अपत्त्र *a-pattra*, *as*, *ā*, *am*, leafless; (*ā*), f., N. of a plant.

अपत्नीक *a-patnīka*, *as*, *ā*, *am*, without a wife.

अपत्य *apatya*, *am*, n. (fr. *apa* or according to native etym. fr. rt. *pat* with *a*, because a family is by offspring prevented from falling into decay); offspring, child, descendant; a patronymical affix. — *Apatya-kāma*, *as*, *ā*, *am*, desirous of offspring. — *Apatya-jīva*, *as*, m., N. of a plant. — *Apatya-tā*, f. state of childhood. — *Apatya-da*, *as*, *ā*, *am*, giving offspring; (*ā*), f., N. of various plants. — *Apatya-patha*, *as*, m. the vulva. — *Apatya-pratyaya*, *as*, m. a patronymical affix. — *Apatya-vat*, *ān*, *atī*, *at*, possessed of offspring. — *Apatya-vikrayin*, *ī*, m. a seller of his offspring; a father who receives a gratuity from his son-in-law. — *Apatya-śatru*, *us*, m. 'having his descendants for enemies,' a crab (said to perish in producing young). — *Apatya-sāć, k, k, k*, Ved. accompanied with offspring. — *Apatyārtha-śabda* (°*ya-ar*°), *as*, m. a patronymic.

अपत्रप् *apa-trap*, cl. 1. A. or poet. P. *-trapate, -ti, -trapitum, -traptum*, to be ashamed or bashful, turn away the face.

Apa-trapaṇa, am, n. or *apa-trapā*, f. bashfulness; embarrassment.

Apa-trapishṇu, us, us, u, bashful.

अपत्रस् *apa-tras*, cl. 1. 4. P. *-trasati, -syati, -situm*, to be deterred, to be afraid of, to flee from in terror.

Apa-trasta, as, ā, am, (with abl.) afraid of, fleeing or retiring from in terror.

अपथ *a-patha, am*, n. not a way, absence of a road, pathless state, irregularity, deviation; heresy, heterodoxy; the vulva; (*as, ā, am*), pathless, roadless; (*ā*), f., N. of various plants. — *Apatha-gāmin, ī, inī, i*, going by a wrong road, pursuing bad practices, heretical. — *Apatha-prapanna, as, ā, am*, out of place, in the wrong place, misapplied.

A-pathin, -nthās, m. absence of road, pathless state.

A-pathya, as, ā, am, unfit; unsuitable; inconsistent; (in medic.) unwholesome as food or drink in particular complaints. — *Apathya-nimitta, as, ā, am*, caused by unfit food or drink. — *Apathya-bhuj, k, k, k*, eating what is forbidden.

अपद् *a-pad, t, t, t*, or *āt, āt* or *adī, āt*, Ved. footless, having no feet; going on a road which does not exist or is unknown (?).

A-pada, as, ā, am, footless; having no office; (*as*), m. a reptile; (*am*), n. no place, no abode; the wrong place or time; ether. — *A-pada-ruhā* or *a-pada-rohiṇī*, f., N. of a parasitical plant, Epidendron Tesselloides. — *A-pada-stha, as, ā, am*, out of office. — *A-padāntara* (°*da-an*°), *as, ā, am*, not separated by a foot, adjoining, contiguous; (*am*), n. proximity.

अपदक्षिणम् *apa-dakshiṇam*, ind. away from the right, to the left side.

अपदम *apa-dama, as, ā, am*, without self-restraint; of wavering fortune.

अपदव *apa-dava, as, ā, am*, free from forest-fire. — *Apadavāpad* (°*va-āp*°), *t, t, t*, free from the calamity of fire.

अपदश *apa-daśa, as, ā, am*, (any number) off ten.

अपदस् *apa-das*, cl. 4. P., Ved. *-dasyati, -situm*, to fail, i. e. become dry.

अपदह् *apa-dah*, cl. 1. P. *-dahati, -dagdhum*, to burn up, to burn out so as to drive out.

अपदान *apa-dāna* or *apa-dānaka, am*, n. (rt. *dai*), correct or pure conduct, approved occupation; a great or noble work; work well or completely done (for *avadāna*, q. v.).

अपदार्थ *a-padārtha* (°*da-ar*°), *as*, m. non-entity, nothing.

अपदिश् *apa-diś*, cl. 6. P. *-diśati, -deshṭum*, to assign, to point out, indicate, betray, to pretend, hold out as a pretext or disguise.

Apa-diśam, ind. in an intermediate region (of the compass), half a point.

Apa-dishṭa, as, ā, am, assigned as a reason or pretext.

Apa-deśa, as, m. turning away, refusal; pretence, feint, pretext, disguise, contrivance; the second step in a syllogism, according to the Vaiśeshikas, i. e. the statement of the reason, adducing a reason or cause; a butt or mark; place, quarter; fame, reputation.

Apa-deśin, ī, inī, i, assuming the appearance or semblance of.

Apa-deśya, as, ā, am, to be shown, to be stated.

अपदृ *apa-dṛi*, used in part. of Intens., Ved. *apa-dardrat, at, atī, at*, tearing open.

अपदेवता *apa-devatā*, f. an evil spirit, a goblin.

अपदोष *apa-dosha, as, ā, am*, free from blame.

अपद्रव्य *apa-dravya, am*, n. any bad thing.

अपद्वार *apa-dvāra, am*, n. a side-entrance (not the regular door).

अपधा *apa-dhā*, f., Ved. hiding, shutting up.

अपधाव् *apa-dhāv*, cl. 1. P. *-dhāvati, -vitum*, to depart (from a previous statement), prevaricate.

अपधूम *apa-dhūma, as, ā, am*, free from smoke.

अपधृ *apa-dhṛi*, Caus. P. *-dhārayati, -yitum*, to carry off.

अपध्मा *apa-dhmā*, cl. 1. P. *-dhamati, -dhmātum*, to blow away or off.

अपध्यै *apa-dhyai*, cl. 1. P. *-dhyāyati, -dhyātum*, to have a bad opinion of, to curse mentally.

Apa-dhyāna, am, n. evil thoughts, wickedness.

अपध्वंस् *apa-dhvaṇs*, cl. 1. P., better A., *-dhvaṇsati, -te, -situm*, to scold, revile, repel; to fall away, be degraded.

Apa-dhvaṇsa, as, m. falling away, degradation, disgrace; concealment. — *Apadhvaṇsa-ja, as*, m. a man of a mixed or impure caste (whose father belongs to a lower caste than his mother's).

Apa-dhvaṇsin, ī, inī, i, causing to fall, destroying, abolishing.

Apa-dhvasta, as, ā, am, reviled, cursed; abandoned, pounded or pounded badly; (*as*), m. a vile wretch lost to all sense of right.

अपध्वान्त *apa-dhvānta, as, ā, am* (rt. *dhvan*), sounding wrong.

अपनत *apa-nata, as, ā, am*, bulging out.

अपनश् *apa-naś*, cl. 4. P. *-naśyati, -naśitum* and *-nanshṭum*, to disappear, go away.

अपनस *apa-nasa, as, ā, am*, without a nose.

अपनह् *apa-nah*, cl. 4. P. A. *-nahyati, -te, -naddhum*, to unbind; to loosen.

अपनामन् *apa-nāman, a*, n. a bad name; (*ā, ā, a*), having a bad name.

अपनिद्र *apa-nidra, as, ā, am*, sleepless.

अपनिर्वाण *apa-nirvāṇa, as, ā, am*, not yet extinct.

अपनी *apa-nī*, cl. 1. P. *-nayati, -netum*, to lead away or off; to rob, steal, take or drag away; to remove, frighten away; to put off or away (as garments, ornaments, or fetters); to extract, take from; to deny; to except, exclude from a rule: Desid. *-ninīshati*, to wish to remove.

Apa-naya, as, m. leading away, taking away; bad policy.

Apa-nayana, am, n. taking away, withdrawing, removing; destroying, healing; acquittance of a debt or obligation.

Apa-nīta, as, ā, am, taken away, removed; paid, discharged; led away from, contradictory; badly executed, spoiled; (*am*), n. imprudent or bad behaviour.

Apa-netṛi, tā, m. a remover, taking away.

अपनुद् *apa-nud*, cl. 6. P. A. *-nudati, -te, -nottum*, to remove.

Apa-nutti, is, f. or *apa-noda* or *apa-nodaka, as*, m. removing, taking or sending away; expiation.

Apa-nuda, as, ā, am, removing, driving away.

Apa-nunutsu, us, us, u, desirous of removing, expiating.

Apa-nodana, as, ī, am, removing, driving away; (*am*), n. removing, destroying.

Apa-nodya, as, ā, am, to be removed.

अपन्नगृह *a-panna-gṛiha, as, ā, am*, Ved. having an indestructible house.

अपपद् *apa-pad*, cl. 4. A. *-padyate, -pattum*, to escape, run away.

अपपाठ *apa-pāṭha, as*, m. a mistake in reading; a wrong reading in a text.

अपपात्र *apa-pātra, as, ā, am*, using separate vessels (from which no one else will eat); of low caste.

Apa-pātrita, as, m. a person not allowed by his kindred to eat or drink from a common vessel; a person who has lost his caste.

अपपादत्र *apa-pādatra, as, ā, am*, having no protection for the feet, shoeless.

अपपान *apa-pāna, am*, n. a bad or improper drink.

अपपित्व *apa-pitva, am*, n. (for *apa-apitva*, fr. rt. *āp* or *ap* with *apa*), Ved. severance; turning away, separation.

अपपूत *apa-pūta, au*, m. du. badly formed buttocks; (*as, ā, am*), having badly formed buttocks.

अपपृ *apa-pṛi*, cl. 3. P., Ved. *-piparti*, to take away, remove.

अपप्रजाता *apa-prajātā*, f. a female that has had a miscarriage.

अपप्रदान *apa-pradāna, am*, n. a bribe.

अपप्रे *apa-pre* (*-pra-i*), cl. 2. P. *-praiti, -tum*, to go away, to withdraw.

अपप्रोषित *apa-proshita* (*-pra-ush*°, rt. *vas*), *am*, n., Ved. the having departed, a wrong departure or evil caused thereby.

अपबध् *apa-badh* or *apa-vadh* (defect. verb), to repel, avert.

अपबर्हिस् *apa-barhis, is, is, is*, not having the portion constituting the Barhis.

अपबाध् *apa-bādh*, cl. 1. A. *-bādhate, -dhitum*, to drive away, repel, remove.

अपबाहुक *apa-bāhuka, as*, m. a bad arm, stiffness in the arm.

अपभय *apa-bhaya, as, ā, am*, or *apa-bhī, is, is, i*, fearless, undaunted.

अपभरणी *apa-bharaṇī*, f. (fr. rt. *bhṛi* with *apa*), the last lunar mansion.

Apa-bhartṛi, tā, trī, tṛi, Ved. taking away, destroying.

अपभाष् *apa-bhāsh*, cl. 1. A. *-bhāshate, -shitum*, to revile.

Apa-bhāshaṇa, am, n. abuse, bad words, vituperation.

अपभू *apa-bhū*, cl. 1. P. *-bhavati, -vitum*, to be absent.

Apa-bhūti, is, f., Ved. defect, damage.

अपभ्रंश *apa-bhraṇśa* or *apa-bhraṇsa, as*, m. falling down or away; a bad fall; a corrupted word, a corruption; ungrammatical language, the most corrupt of the Prākrit dialects. (The spelling *apa-bhraṇsa* is incorrect according to some grammarians.)

Apa-bhrashṭa, as, ā, am, fallen away, corrupted (as a Prākrit dialect).

अपम *apama, as, ā, am* (fr. *apa*), Ved. the

most distant, the last; (*as*), m. the declination in astronomy; the ecliptic. — *Apama-kshetra*, see *krānti-kshetra*. — *Apama-jyā*, f. the sine of the ecliptic. — *Apama-maṇḍala* or *apa-maṇḍala* or *apama-vṛitta*, *am*, n. the ecliptic.

अपमन्यु *apa-manyu*, *us*, *us*, *u*, free from grief.

अपमर्द *apa-marda*, *as*, m. (rt. *mṛid*), what is swept away, dirt.

अपमर्श *apa-marśa*, *as*, m. (rt. *mṛiś*), touching, grazing.

अपमान *apa-māna*, *as*, *am*, m. n. (rt. *man*), disrespect, contempt, disgrace.

Apa-mānita, *as*, *ā*, *am*, dishonoured, disgraced.

Apa-mānin, *ī*, *inī*, *i*, dishonouring, despising.

Apa-mānya, *as*, *ā*, *am*, disreputable, dishonourable.

अपमार्ग *apa-mārga*, *as*, m. a by-way.

अपमित्य 1. *apa-mitya*, *as*, *ā*, *am* (rt. *mi?*), Ved. to be thrown away; see under *apa-me* below.

अपमुख *apa-mukha*, *as*, *ā*, *am*, having the face averted; having an ill-formed face or mouth; (*am*), ind. except or without the face, &c.

अपमूर्धन् *apa-mūrdhan*, *ā*, *ā*, *a*, headless.

अपमृज् *apa-mṛij*, cl. 2. P. *-mārshṭi*, *-mārjitum*, *-mārshṭum*, to wipe off, remove.

Apa-mārjana, *am*, n. cleansing; shaving, paring, chips.

Apa-mṛishṭa, *as*, *ā*, *am*, cleansed.

अपमृत्यु *apa-mṛityu*, *us*, m. sudden death, dying by some accident, not of sickness or decay; a great danger or illness, from which a person, contrary to expectation, recovers.

अपमृषित *apa-mṛishita*, *as*, *ā*, *am*, unintelligible (as a speech).

अपमे *apa-me*, cl. 1. A. *-mayate*, *-mātum*, to change.

2. *apa-mitya* or *apa-mityaka*, *am*, n. debt.

अपयशस् *apa-yaśas*, *as*, n. disgrace, infamy. — *Apayaśas-kara*, *as*, *ī*, *am*, occasioning infamy, disgraceful.

अपया *apa-yā*, cl. 2. P. *-yāti*, *-tum*, to go away, to depart, fall off, go over to.

Apa-yāta, *as*, *ā*, *am*, gone away, having retired.

Apa-yātavya, *am*, n. to be gone away (used impersonally).

Apa-yāna, *am*, n. retreat, flight.

अपयु *apa-yu*, cl. 3. P., Ved. *-yuyoti*, to repel, disjoin.

अपर 1. *a-para*, *as*, *ā*, *am*, having nothing beyond or after, having no rival or superior. — *A-para-vat*, *ān*, *atī*, *at*, having nothing following.

अपर 2. *apara*, *as*, *ā*, *am* (fr. *apa*), posterior, hinder, later, latter (opposed to *pūrva* and often occurring as the first member of a comp.); following; western; inferior, lower (opposed to *para*); other, another (opposed to *sva*); different (with abl.); distant, opposite. Sometimes *apara* is used as a conjunction to connect words or sentences, e. g. *aparañća*, moreover. (*as*), m. the hind foot of an elephant; (*ā*), f. the west; the hind quarter of an elephant; the womb; (*ī*), f., Ved. the future times, future; (*am*), n. the future; the hind quarter of an elephant; (*am*), ind. in future, for the future; again, moreover; (*eṇa*), ind. (with acc.) behind, west, to the west of [cf. Goth. and Old Germ. *afar*; and the Mod. Germ. *aber*, in such words as *Aber-mal*, *Aberwitz*]. — *Apara-kānyakubja*, *as*, *ī*, *am*, situated in the western part of Kānyakubjā. — *Apara-kāya*, *as*, m. the hind part of the body. — *Apara-kāla*, *as*, m. another or later period. — *Apara-godāna*, *am*, n. (in Buddhist cosmogony) a country west of the Mahā-meru. — *Apara-ja*, *as*, m., Ved. born later, or at the end of the world (the destroying fire). — *Apara-jana*, *as*, m. an inhabitant of the west. — *Apara-tā*, f. or *apara-tva*, *am*, n. distance; posteriority (in place or time); opposition, contrariety, relativeness; nearness. — *Apara-tra*, ind. in another place; *ekatra*, *aparatra*, in one place, in the other place. — *Apara-dakshiṇam*, ind. south-west. — *Apara-nidāgha*, *as*, m. the latter part of the summer. — *Apara-paksha*, *as*, m. the latter half of the month, the other or opposing side, the defendant. — *Apara-pakshīya*, *as*, *ā*, *am*, belonging to the latter half of the month. — *Apara-pañćāla*, *ās*, m. pl. the western Pañćālas. — *Apara-para*, *ās* or *e*, *ās*, *āṇi*, pl. one and the other, various. — *Apara-praṇeya*, *as*, *ā*, *am*, easily led by others, tractable. — *Apara-bhāva*, *as*, m. existing after, succession, continuation. — *Apara-rātra*, *as*, m. the latter half of the night, the end of the night, the last watch. — *Apara-loka*, *am*, n. another world, paradise. — *Apara-vaktrā*, f. a kind of metre of four lines, having every two lines the same. — *Apara-vat*, ind. like what comes after. — *Apara-varshā*, *ās*, f. pl. the latter part of the rains. — *Apara-śarad*, *t*, f. the latter part of the autumn. — *Apara-saktha*, *am*, n. the hind thigh. — 1. *aparas-para*, *as*, *ā*, *am*, one after another; continued, uninterrupted. — *Apara-svastika*, *am*, n. the western point in the horizon. — *Apara-hemanta*, *as*, *am*, m. n. the latter part of winter. — *Apara-haimana*, *as*, *ī*, *am*, belonging to the latter half of the winter season. — *Aparāgni* (°*ra-ag*°), *ī*, m. du. the *dakshiṇa*, i. e. southern, and *gārhapatya*, i. e. western fire (of a sacrifice). — *Aparānta* (°*ra-an*°), *as*, *ā*, *am*, living at the western border; (*as*), m. the western extremity, the country or the inhabitants of the western border; the extreme end or term; death. — *Aparāntaka*, *as*, m. the same as *aparānta*; N. of a song; (*ikā*), f. a metre consisting of four times sixteen mātrās. — *Aparānta-jñāna*, *am*, n. prescience of one's latter end. — *Aparāpara* (°*ra-ap*°), *ās* or *e*, *ās*, *āṇi*, pl. another and another, various. — *Aparārka* (°*ra-ar*°), *as*, m. the oldest known commentator of Yājñavalkya's law-book. — *Aparārka-ćandrikā*, f. the name of his comment. — *Aparārdha* (°*ra-ar*°), *as*, m. the latter, the second half.

Aparāhṇa (°*ra-ah*°), *as*, m. afternoon, the last watch of the day. — *Aparāhṇatana* or *aparāhṇetana*, *as*, *ī*, *am*, belonging to or produced in the close of the day.

Aparetarā (°*ra-it*°), f. opposite to or other than the west, the east.

Apare-dyus, ind. on the following day.

अपरक्त *apa-rakta*, *as*, *ā*, *am*, colourless, bloodless, pale.

अपरति *apa-rati*, *is*, f. (rt. *ram*), stopping, ceasing.

अपरव *apa-rava*, *as*, m. contest, dispute; discord. — *Aparavojjhita* (°*va-uj*°), *as*, *ā*, *am*, free from dispute, undisturbed, undisputed.

अपरस्पर 2. *a-paraspara*, *as*, *ā*, *am*, not reciprocal, not one (by) the other. — *A-paraspara-sambhūta*, *as*, *ā*, *am*, not produced one by the other; or (fr. 1. *aparas-para* above), produced by an uninterrupted series (?).

अपराग *apa-rāga*, *as*, m. (rt. *rañj*), aversion, antipathy, enmity.

अपराच् *a-parāć*, *ān*, *āćī*, *āk*, not averted, i. e. fronting, in front. — *A-parāṅ-mukha*, *as*, *ā* or *ī*, *am*, with unaverted face, not turned away; presenting a firm front.

अपराजित *a-parājita*, *as*, *ā*, *am* (rt. *ji*), unconquered, unsurpassed; (*as*), m. a poisonous insect; Vishṇu; Śiva; one of the eleven Rudras; a class of divinities, constituting one portion of the so-called Anuttara divinities of the Jainas; N. of a sage; (*ā*), f. Durgā; a name applied to several plants, Clitoria Ternatea, Marsilea Quadrifolia, Sesbania Ægyptiaca; a species of the Śaṅkarī metre of four lines, each containing fourteen syllables. — *Aparājitā-diś*, *k*, f. the north-east quarter.

A-parājishṇu, *us*, *us*, *u*, or *a-parājeya*, *as*, *ā*, *am*, unconquerable, invincible.

अपराध् *apa-rādh*, cl. 4. or 5. P. *-rādhyati*, *-rādhnoti*, *-rāddhum*, to wrong (with gen.), to offend, sin; to annoy, prohibit.

Apa-rāddha, *as*, *ā*, *am*, sinned; criminal, guilty; erring. — *Aparāddha-pṛishatka*, *as*, or *aparāddheshu* (°*dha-ish*°), *us*, m. an archer whose arrows always miss the mark.

Apa-rāddhi, *is*, f. wrong, mistake.

Apa-rāddhṛi, *dhā*, *dhrī*, *dhṛi*, offending, an offender.

Apa-rādha, *as*, m. offence, transgression, fault; mistake; e. g. *aparādhaṃ kṛi*, (with gen.) to offend any one. — *Aparādha-bhañjana*, *as*, m. the destroyer of sin, epithet of Śiva. — *Aparādhabhañjana-stotra*, *am*, n. a poem of Śaṅkarāćārya, in praise of Śiva.

Apa-rādhin, *ī*, *inī*, *i*, offending; criminal; guilty. — *Aparādhi-tā*, f. or *aparādhi-tva*, *am*, n. criminality, guilt.

अपरापरण *a-parāparaṇa*, *as*, m. not having descendants or offspring.

अपरामृष्ट *a-parāmṛishṭa*, *as*, *ā*, *am*, not touched.

अपरिकलित *a-parikalita*, *as*, *ā*, *am*, unknown, unseen.

अपरिक्रम *a-parikrama*, *as*, *ā*, *am*, unable to walk round.

A-parikrāmam, ind. without going about, standing still.

अपरिक्लिन्न *a-pariklinna*, *as*, *ā*, *am*, not moist, not liquid, dry.

अपरिगण्य *a-parigaṇya*, *as*, *ā*, *am*, incalculable.

अपरिगत *a-parigata*, *as*, *ā*, *am*, unobtained, unknown.

अपरिग्रह *a-parigraha*, *as*, m. non-acceptance, renouncing; deprivation, destitution, poverty; (*as*, *ā*, *am*), destitute of or without attendants.

A-parigrāhya, *as*, *ā*, *am*, unfit or improper to be accepted, not to be taken.

अपरिचयिन् *a-parićayin*, *ī*, *inī*, *i* (rt. *ći*), having no acquaintances, misanthropic.

A-parićita, *as*, *ā*, *am*, unacquainted with, unknown to.

A-parićeya, *as*, *ā*, *am*, unsociable.

अपरिच्छद *a-pariććhada*, *as*, *ā*, *am* (rt. *ćhad*), without retinue, not wealthy, poor.

A-pariććhanna or *a-pariććhādita*, *as*, *ā*, *am*, uncovered, unclothed.

अपरिच्छिन्न *a-pariććhinna*, *as*, *ā*, *am*, without interval or division, continuous, connected, undistinguished.

A-pariććheda, *as*, m. want of distinction or division; want of arrangement or order; want of discrimination or discernment; want of judgment; continuance.

अपरिज्यानि *a-parijyāni*, *is*, f. not growing old; not losing; *ishṭāpūrtasyāparijyāni* (°*ya-ap*°), *is*, f., N. of a sacrificial ceremony.

अपरिणयन *a-pariṇayana*, *am*, n. (rt. *nī*), celibacy.

A-pariṇītā, f. an unmarried woman.

अपरिणाम *a-pariṇāma*, *as*, m. (rt. *nam*), unchangeableness. — *A-pariṇāma-darśin*, *ī*, *inī*, *i*, not providing for a change, improvident.

A-pariṇāmin, *ī*, *inī*, *i*, unchanging.

अपरितोष *a-paritosha*, *as*, *ā*, *am*, unsatisfied, discontented.

अपरिपक्व *a-paripakva, as, ā, am,* not quite mature.

अपरिपर *a-paripara, as, ā, am,* Ved. not going by a tortuous course.

अपरिमाण *a-parimāṇa, as, ā, am,* without measure, immeasurable, immense.

A-parimita, as, ā, am, unmeasured, unlimited, unbounded. — *Aparimita-guṇa-gaṇa, as, ā, am,* of unbounded excellences.

A-parimeya, as, ā, am, immeasurable, illimitable.

अपरिम्लान *a-parimlāna, as, ā, am,* not withering, not decaying; (*as*), m., N. of a plant, Gomphrena Globosa.

अपरियाणि *a-pariyāṇi, is,* f. not walking about (used in execrations only); a various reading has *a-paripāṇi.*

अपरिलोप *a-parilopa, as,* m. non-violation.

अपरिवर्तनीय *a-parivartanīya, as, ā, am,* not to be exchanged.

अपरिवाद्य *a-parivādya, as, ā, am* (rt. *vad*), not to be reprimanded.

अपरिविष्ट *a-parivishṭa, as, ā, am,* Ved. not enclosed, unbounded.

अपरिवृत *a-parivṛita, as, ā, am,* uninclosed, unsurrounded.

अपरिशेष *a-pariśesha, as, ā, am,* not leaving a remainder, all-surrounding, all-enclosing.

अपरिष्कार *a-parishkāra, as,* m. want of polish or finish, moral or physical; coarseness, rudeness.

A-parishkṛita, as, ā, am, unpolished, unadorned, coarse, rude, morally or physically.

अपरिसमाप्तिक *a-parisamāptika, as, ā, am* (rt. *āp* with *pari* and *sam*), not ending, endless.

अपरिसर *a-parisara, as, ā, am,* non-contiguous, distant.

अपरिस्कन्द *a-pariskanda, as, ā, am,* not moving, motionless.

अपरिहरणीय *a-pariharaṇīya* or *a-parihārya, as, ā, am,* not to be avoided, inevitable; not to be abandoned or lost; not to be degraded.

अपरिह्वृत *a-parihvṛita, as, ā, am,* Ved. unafflicted, not endangered; going straightforward.

अपरीक्षित *a-parīkshita, as, ā, am* (rt. *īksh*), inconsiderate; untried, unproved.

अपरीत *a-parīta, as, ā, am* (rt. *i*), Ved. unobstructed, irresistible; (*as*), m., N. of a nation.

अपरुष *a-parusha, as, ā, am,* not rough, not harsh.

अपरूप *apa-rūpa, as, ā* or *ī, am,* deformed, ugly, ill-looking, ill-made, strange, odd-shaped; (*am*), n. monstrosity, deformity.

अपरेद्युस् *aparedyus.* See under *apara.*

अपरोक्ष *a-paroksha, as, ā, am,* not invisible; perceptible; (*am*), ind. (with gen.) in the sight of; (*āt*), ind. perceptibly, manifestly.

Aparokshaya, nom. P. *aparokshayati, -yitum,* to make perceptible.

अपरोध *apa-rodha, as,* m. (rt. *rudh*), exclusion, prohibition.

अपर्ण *a-parṇa, as, ā, am,* leafless; (*ā*), f. N. of Durgā or Pārvatī; (the goddess not having even leaves for food during her performance of religious austerities.)

अपर्तु *apartu* (*apa-ṛitu*), *us, us, u,* Ved. untimely, unseasonable.

अपर्यन्त *a-paryanta, as, ā, am,* unbounded, unlimited.

अपर्याप्त *a-paryāpta, as, ā, am* (rt. *āp*), incomplete, unable, insufficient; not enough; unlimited, unbounded.

अपर्याय *a-paryāya, as,* m. want of order or method.

अपर्वन् *a-parvan, a,* n. no joint or point of junction; a day which is not a *parvan,* i. e. a certain day in the lunar month, as the full and change of the moon, and the eighth and fourteenth of each half month; (*ā, ā, a*), without a joint. — *Aparva-daṇḍa, as,* m. a kind of sugar-cane.

A-parvaka, as, ikā, am, jointless.

अपल 1. *apala, am,* n. a pin or bolt.

अपल 2. *a-pala, as, ā, am,* fleshless.

अपलप् *apa-lap,* cl. 1. P. or poet. A. *-lapati, -te, -pitum,* to explain away, to deny, refuse, conceal; to detract from slander: Caus. A. *-lāpayate, -yitum,* to outwit.

Apa-lapana, am, n. or *apa-lāpa, as,* m. denial or concealment of knowledge, evasion, turning off the truth, detraction; concealing, hiding; affection, regard; (in medic.) the part between the shoulder and the ribs. — *Apalāpa-daṇḍa, as,* m. (in law) a fine laid on one who denies his conviction.

Apa-lapita, as, ā, am, denied, concealed.

Apa-lāpin, ī, inī, i, one who denies, evades; concealing (with the object in the gen. case).

अपलाल *a-palāla, as,* m., N. of a Rakshas or of a Nāga ('not fond of flesh?').

अपलाश *a-palāśa, as, ā, am,* Ved. leafless.

अपलाषिका *apa-lāshikā* or *apa-lāsikā,* f. thirst.

Apa-lāshin, ī, inī, i, or *apa-lāshuka, as, ā, am,* thirsty; free from desire.

अपलित *a-palita, as, ā, am,* not grey.

अपलुप् *apa-lup,* used in the acc. case *apa-lupam* as Ved. inf. of the verb *apa-lup,* to cut off.

अपल्यूलनकृत *a-palyūlana-kṛita, as, ā, am,* not cleaned by cleansing substances. Some read *palpūlana.*

अपवक्तृ *apa-vaktṛi, tā,* m., Ved. speaking away, i. e. warning off, averting.

Apa-vaćana, am, n. the act of speaking away or warning off, removing.

अपवद् *apa-vad,* cl. 1. P. A. *-vadati, -te, -ditum,* to revile, abuse; (A. only) to disown, deny, contradict: Caus. *-vādayati, -yitum,* to oppose as unadvisable.

Apa-vadamāna, as, ā, am, (with dat.) reviling.

Apa-vaditṛi. See *apa-vaktṛi.*

Apa-vāda, as, m. evil speaking, reviling, blaming (with the gen.); denial, refutation, contradiction; a special rule setting aside a general one; exception (opposed to *utsarga*); order, command. — *Apavāda-pratyaya, as,* m. an exceptional affix. — *Apavāda-sthala, am,* n. case for a special rule or exception.

Apa-vādaka, as, ikā, am, or *apa-vādin, ī, inī, i,* reviling, blaming, defaming; opposing, objecting to; excepting, excluding.

Apa-vādita, as, ā, am, blamed, censured; opposed, objected to.

Apa-vādya, as, ā, am, to be censured, to be excepted.

अपवध् *apa-vadh* (defective in most of its tenses, see *vadh*), to repel, avert.

अपवन 1. *a-pavana, as, ā, am,* without air, sheltered from wind.

अपवन 2. *apa-vana, am,* n. a grove.

अपवरक *apa-varaka, apa-varaṇa, apa-vāraṇa.* See *apa-vṛi* below.

अपवर्ग *apa-varga, apa-varjita.* See *apa-vṛij* below.

अपवर्त *apa-varta,* &c. See under *apa-vṛit.*

अपवह् *apa-vah,* cl. 1. P. *-vahati, -vaḍhum,* to carry off; to deduct: Caus. P. *-vāhayati, -yitum,* to have (something) carried off or taken away.

Apa-vāha, as, m. or *apa-vāhana, am,* n. deduction, subtraction (of fractions); N. of a metre; N. of a people.

Apa-vāhya, as, ā, am, to be carried away.

Apoḍha. See s. v., p. 56.

अपवाद *apa-vāda,* &c. See *apa-vad* above.

अपवास *apa-vāsa, as,* m. (rt. *vas*), Ved. disappearance, going away, vanishing; N. of a plant.

अपविक्षत *apa-vikshata, as, ā, am,* unwounded; unviolated.

अपविघ्न *apa-vighna, as, ā, am,* unobstructed, unimpeded; (*am*), ind. free from obstruction.

अपवित्र *a-pavitra, as, ā, am,* impure, unclean.

अपविद्ध *apa-viddha* and *apa-vedha.* See *apa-vyadh,* p. 53.

अपविष *apa-visha, as, ā, am,* free from poison; (*ā*), f. a species of grass, Kyllingia Monocephala.

अपविष्णु *apa-vishṇu,* ind. except or without Vishṇu.

अपवीण *apa-vīṇa, as, ā, am,* having a bad or no lute; (*ā*), f. a bad lute; (*am*), ind. without a lute.

अपवीरवत् *a-pavīra-vat, ān, atī, at,* Ved. not armed with a lance.

अपवृ *apa-vṛi,* cl. 5. P. *-vṛiṇoti, -varitum, -rītum,* to open, uncover, exhibit.

Apa-varaka, as, m. an inner apartment, the lying-in chamber.

Apa-varaṇa, am, n. covering, screening; garment.

Apa-vāraṇa, am, n. covering, concealment, disappearance.

Apa-vārita, as, ā, am, covered, concealed, disappeared.

Apa-vāritaka, am, n. concealed, secret manner; *apavāritakena,* (in theatrical language) apart, aside (speaking so that only the addressed person may hear; opposed to *prakāśam*).

Apa-vārya, ind. apart, aside; having concealed.

Apa-vṛita, as, ā, am, uncovered, opened.

Apa-vṛiti, is, f. uncovering; concealing (?).

अपवृज् *apa-vṛij,* Caus. P. *-varjayati, -yitum,* to quit, get rid of, to pay, to fulfil.

Apa-varga, as, m. completion, end (e. g. *pañća-pavarga,* coming to an end in five days); exception (to a rule); gift, donation; the emancipation of the soul from the body and exemption from further transmigration; final beatitude. — *Apavarga-da, as, ā, am,* conferring final beatitude.

Apa-varjana, am, n. abandoning, abandonment; gift or donation, making good a promise, discharging a debt or obligation; final emancipation or beatitude.

Apa-varjanīya or *apa-vṛijya, as, ā, am,* to be abandoned, to be avoided.

Apa-varjita, as, ā, am, abandoned, quitted, got rid of, given or cast away; made good as a promise, discharged as a debt.

Apa-varjya, ind. excepting, except.
Apa-vṛikta, as, ā, am, finished, completed.
Apa-vṛikti, is, f. fulfilment, completion.

अपवृत् *apa-vṛit,* cl. 1. A. *-vartate, -titum,* to turn away, depart; to turn back, to come to an end.

Apa-varta, as, m. taking away; (in arithmetic or algebra) reduction to a common measure; the divisor, which is applied to both or either of the quantities of an equation.

Apa-vartaka, as, m. a common measure.

Apa-vartana, am, n. taking away; removal; transferring from one place to another; abbreviation, abridging; reduction of a fraction to its lowest terms; division without remainder; divisor.

Apa-vartita, as, ā, am, taken away; removed; divided by a common measure without remainder.

Apa-vṛitta, as, ā, am, reversed, inverted, overturned; ended; *(am),* n. ecliptic (in astronomy).

Apa-vṛitti, is, f. end.

अपव्यध् *apa-vyadh,* cl. 4. P. *-vidhyati, -vyaddhum,* to pierce badly, to throw away, to neglect.

Apa-viddha, as, ā, am, pierced; thrown away, rejected, dismissed, removed.—*Apaviddha-putra, as,* m. a son rejected by his natural parents and adopted by a stranger; one of the twelve objects of filiation in law.—*Apaviddha-loka, as, ā, am,* dead.

Apa-vedha, as, m. piercing anything in the wrong direction or manner (spoiling a jewel by so piercing it).

अपव्यय *apa-vyaya, as,* m. (rt. *i* with *apa* and *vi*), prodigality.

Apa-vyayat, an, antī, at, going away.

Apa-vyayamāna, as, ā, am, squandering; denying a debt.

Apa-vyayin, ī, inī, i, squandering, wasting, prodigal.

अपव्यादा *apa-vy-ā-dā (-vi-ā-dā),* cl. 3. P. *-dadāti, -dātum,* to open.

अपव्रत *apa-vrata, as, ā, am,* Ved. disobedient, unfaithful; not performing holy acts, irreligious; perverse.

अपशकुन *apa-śakuna, am,* n. a bad omen.

अपशङ्क *apa-śanka, as, ā, am,* fearless, having no fear or hesitation; *(am),* ind. fearlessly.

अपशद *apa-śada* or *apa-sada, as,* m. a low man.

अपशब्द *apa-śabda, as,* m. common or vulgar speech; a bad word; any form of language not Sanskṛit; ungrammatical language. See *apabhraṇśa.*

अपशम *apa-śama, as,* m. cessation.

अपशिरस् *apa-śiras, ās, ās, as,* or *apa-śirsha, as, ā, am,* or *apa-śirshan, ā, ā, a,* headless.

अपशु *a-paśu, us,* m. not cattle; *(us, us, u),* deprived of cattle, poor.—*A-paśu-han, hā, ghnī, ha,* not killing cattle.

अपशुच् 1. *apa-śuć,* Intens. P., Ved. *-śośokti,* to disappear, vanish.

2. *apa-śuć, k,* m. (without sorrow), the soul.

Apa-śoka, as, ā, am, sorrowless; *(as),* m. a tree, Jonesia Aśoka.

अपश्चादघ्वन् *a-paśćā-daghvan* or *a-paśćād-daghvan, ā,* m., Ved. not staying behind; not coming short of, not being a loser.

अपश्चिम *a-paśćima, as, ā, am,* not having another in the rear, last; having no end.

अपश्य *a-paśya, as, ā, am* Ved., or *a-paśyat, an, antī, at,* not seeing.

A-paśyanā, f. not seeing (?).

अपश्रय *apa-śraya, as,* m., Ved. a bolster; see *upa-śraya.*

अपश्री *apa-śrī, īs, īs, i,* deprived of beauty.

अपश्वास *apa-śvāsa, as,* m. one of the five vital airs; see *apāna.*

अपष्ठ *apa-shṭha, am,* n. (rt. *sthā*), the end or point of the hook for driving an elephant.

Apa-shṭhu, us, us, u, contrary, opposite; perverse; left; *(u),* ind. contrary, perversely, badly; well, properly; handsomely; *(us),* m. time.

Apa-shṭhura or *apa-shṭhula, as, ā, am,* opposite, contrary.

अपस् *apas, as,* n. (fr. obs. rt. *ap*), Ved. work, action; sacred act, sacrificial act; water; *(ās),* m. f. *(asas),* m. f. pl., Ved. active, skilful in any art: *apasas,* f. pl., is a name of the hands and fingers which are busy in kindling the sacred fire and in performing the sacrifices; also a name of the three goddesses of sacred speech, or of the three divinities, fire, wind, and sun; also of the active or running waters [cf. Lat. *opus*].

Apas-tama, as, ā, am (superl.), Ved. most active or rapid.

1. *apasya, as, ā, am,* active, fit for an act, running away; watery; *(ā),* f. a kind of brick (twenty are used in building the sacrificial altar); activity; water.

2. *apasya,* nom. P. *apasyati,* to be active.

Apasyu, us, us, u, Ved. active.

अपसद *apa-sada, as,* m. the children of six degrading connections, viz. of a Brāhman with the women of the three lower classes, of a Kshatriya with women of the two lower, and of a Vaiśya with one of the Śūdra; a low man; an outcast (in this sense generally as last member of a comp., e. g. *brāhmaṇāpasada*).

अपसमम् *apa-samam,* ind. last year (?).

अपसर्जन *apa-sarjana, am,* n. (rt. *sṛij*), abandonment; gift or donation; final emancipation of the soul [cf. *apa-vṛij*].

अपसलवि *apa-salavi,* ind., Ved. to the left (opposed to *pra-salavi*); the space between the thumb and the forefinger (sacred to the Manes).

अपसव्य *apa-savya, as, ā, am,* or *apa-savyaka, as, ikā, am,* not on the left side, right; opposite, contrary; *(am),* ind. to the right; the same as *apa-salavi.*—*Apasavyam kṛi = pradakshiṇam kṛi,* to circumambulate a person keeping the right side towards him; to put the sacred cord on the right shoulder.—*Apasavya-vat, ān, atī, at,* having the sacred thread worn on the right shoulder, (as during a Śrāddha, &c.)

अपसिद्धान्त *apa-siddhānta, as,* m. (rt. 1. *sidh*), an erroneous conclusion.

अपसिध् *apa-sidh,* cl. 1. P. *-sedhati, -seddhum, -sedhitum,* to ward off, remove, drive away.

अपसृ *apa-sṛi,* cl. 1. P. *-sarati, -sartum,* to walk off, go away: Caus. *-sārayati, -yitum,* to make or let one go away, to remove.

Apa-sara, as, m. excuse, apology.

Apa-saraṇa, am, n. going away, retreating; egress.

Apa-sāra, as, m. going out; egress, passage for going forth; escape.

Apa-sāraṇa, am, n. removing to a distance.

Apa-sārita, as, ā, am, removed, put away, thrown aside.

अपसृप् *apa-sṛip,* cl. 1. P. *-sarpati, -sarptum, -sraptum,* to glide or move off.

Apa-sarpa or *apa-sarpaka, as,* m. a secret emissary or agent, spy.

Apa-sarpaṇa, am, n. going back, retreating.

Apa-sṛipti, is, f. going away.

अपस्कम्भ *apa-skambha, as,* m., Ved. fastening, making firm.

अपस्कर *apa-skara, as,* m. any part of a carriage, a wheel, &c.; fæces; anus; vulva.

Apa-skāra, as, m. the root or under part of the knee.

अपस्खल *apa-skhala, as,* m. leaping off, jumping off; outside of a threshing floor (?).

अपस्तम *apas-tama.* See under *apas.*

अपस्तम्भ *apa-stambha, as,* m. a vessel in the side of the breast containing vital air.

Apa-stambhinī, f., N. of a plant.

अपस्नात *apa-snāta, as, ā, am,* bathed or bathing after death or mourning, or upon the death of a connection, preparatory to other ceremonies.

Apa-snāna, am, n. funeral bathing, upon the death of a connection, after mourning, &c.; impure bathing, or bathing in water in which a person has previously washed.

अपस्पति *apas-pati, is,* m., N. of a son of Uttānapāda.

अपस्पृश् 1. *apa-spṛiś,* cl. 6. P. *-spṛiśati, -sparshṭum, -sprashṭum,* to touch.

Apa-sparśa, as, ā, am, having no touch, insensible.

2. *apa-spriś, k, k, k,* Ved. not letting one's self be touched.

अपस्पृश् 3. *a-paspṛiś, k, k, k,* Ved. not touching, not hurting.

अपस्फिग *apa-sphiga, as, ā, am,* one who has badly formed buttocks; *(am),* ind. except the buttocks.

अपस्फुर् *apa-sphur, ūs, ūs, ūs,* or *apa-sphura, as, ā, am,* or *apa-sphurat, an, antī, at,* Ved. bounding or bursting forth, swelling, increasing. According to native authorities, both *apa-sphura* and *apa-sphurat* may mean 'injured.'

अपस्मार *apa-smāra, as,* m. or *apa-smṛiti, is,* f. forgetfulness; epilepsy, falling sickness.

Apa-smārin, ī, iṇī, i, epileptic, convulsed.

Apa-smṛiti, is, is, i, forgetful.

अपस्य *apasya, apasyu.* See under *apas.*

अपस्वर *apa-svara, as,* m. an unmusical note or sound.

अपहन् *apa-han,* cl. 2. P. *-hanti, -tum,* to beat off, ward off, repel, destroy.

Apa-ha, as, ā, am, keeping back, repelling, removing, destroying (e. g. *śokāpaha, as, ā, am,* removing sorrow).

Apa-hata, as, ā, am, destroyed, warded off, killed.

Apa-hati, is, f. removing, destroying.

Apa-hanana, am, n. or *apa-ghāta* (q. v.), warding off.

Apa-hantṛi, tā, m. beating off, destroying.

Apa-ghātin, apa-jighāṇsu. See s. v.

अपहल *apa-hala, as, ā, am,* having a bad plough.

अपहस् *apa-has,* cl. 1. P. *-hasati, -situm,* to deride: Caus. P. *-hāsayati, -yitum,* to deride, ridicule.

Apa-hasita, am, n. or *apa-hāsa, as,* m. silly or causeless laughter.

Apa-hāsya, as, ā, am, to be laughed at.

अपहस्त *apa-hasta, am,* n. taking or throwing away or off; stealing, plundering.

Apa-hastaya, nom. P. *apa-hastayati, -yitum,* to throw away, lose.

Apa-hastita, as, ā, am, thrown away, lost, parted with.

अपहा 1. *apa-hā,* cl. 3. A. *-jihīte, -hātum,* to go off, come to an end.

अपहा 2. *apa-hā*, cl. 3. P. *-jahāti, -hātum*, to leave, abandon.

Apa-hāna, as, ā, am (or fr. 1. *apa-hā?*), leaving, abandoning; also written *apa-hāyana*.

Apa-hāni, is, f. leaving; leaving off, abandonment, stopping, vanishing; exception, exclusion.

Apa-hāya, ind. leaving out of view, excepting, except, besides.

अपहिङ्कार *apa-hin-kāra, as, ā, am*, without the syllable *him*, which is pronounced in singing the Sāma verses.

अपहृ *apa-hṛi*, cl. 1. P. A. (?) *-harati, -te, -hartum*, to snatch away, carry off, plunder; to remove, to throw away: Caus. *-hārayati, -yitum*, to have (anything) carried off.

Apa-haraṇa, am, n. taking away, carrying off; stealing.

Apa-haraṇīya or *apa-hartavya* or *apa-hārya, as, ā, am*, to be taken away, carried off, stolen, &c.; to be taken back or resumed.

Apa-hartṛi, tā, m. (with gen. or acc.) taking away; expiating.

Apa-hāra, as, m. taking away, stealing; spending another person's property; secreting, concealment; e.g. *ātmāpahāram kṛi*, to conceal one's real character.

Apa-hāraka, as, ikā, am, or *apa-hārin, ī, iṇī, i*, one who takes away, seizes, steals, &c.; a plunderer, a thief.

Apa-hāraṇa, am, n. causing to take away, spoiling.

Apa-hṛita, as, ā, am, taken away, carried off, stolen, &c.; taken back, resumed. — *Apahṛita-vijñāna, as, ā, am*, bereft of sense.

अपहेला *apa-helā*, f. disrespect, contempt.

अपह्नु *apa-hnu*, cl. 2. A. *-hnute, -hnotum*, to conceal, disguise; to refuse, deny, disown.

Apa-hnava, as, m. concealment of knowledge; denial of or turning off of the truth; dissimulation; appeasing, satisfying; affection, love.

Apa-hnuta, as, ā, am, concealed, denied.

Apa-hnuti, is, f. denial, concealment of knowledge; a figure of rhetoric, applying a description or simile to other than its obvious application.

Apa-hnuvāna, as, ā, am, concealing, denying.

Apa-hnotṛi, tā, trī, tṛi, one who conceals or denies or disowns.

अपह्रास *apa-hrāsa, as*, m. diminishing, reducing.

अपाक् *apāk*, ind. westward, southward; see *apāć* next col.

अपाक 1. *apāka, as, ā, am* (fr. *apa*), situated aside or behind; distant; coming from a distant place; incomparable. — *Apāka-ćakshas, ās*, m., Ved. looking or shining far; of incomparable brightness.

Apākā or *apākāt*, ind., Ved. aside, distant. — *Apāke-stha, as, ā, am*, Ved. standing behind.

Apāktāt, ind., Ved. from behind, from the west.

अपाक 2. *a-pāka, as, ā, am* (rt. *pać*), immature, raw, unripe, undigested; (*as*), m. immaturity, indigestion. — *A-pāka-ja, as, ā, am*, not produced by cooking or ripening; original; natural. — *Apāka-śāka, am*, n. ginger.

A-pākin, ī, inī, i, unripe, undigested.

अपाकृ *apā-kṛi* (*apa-ā°*), cl. 8. P. A. *-karoti, -kurute, -kartum*, or Ved. *-kartos*, to remove, drive away, keep away; to take away; to reject (an opinion); to cast off, reject; to desist from, to drop; to free one's self from; to pay.

Apā-karaṇa, am, n. driving away, removal; payment, liquidation.

Apā-karishṇu, us, us, u, driving away; excelling.

Apā-karman, a, n. payment, liquidation.

Apā-kṛita, as, ā, am, taken away, removed, destroyed, void of; paid.

Apā-kṛiti, is, f. taking away, removal.

अपाकृष् *apā-kṛish* (*apa-ā°*), cl. 1. 6. P. A. *-karshati, -te, -kṛishati, -te, -karshṭum, -krashṭum*, to turn off or away, to avert.

अपाकॄ *apā-kṝi* (*apa-ā°*), cl. 6. P. *-kirati, -karitum, -rītum*, to throw any one off; to abandon, to contemn.

अपाक्रम् *apā-kram* (*apa-ā°*), cl. 1. P. poet. A. *-krāmati, -kramate, -kramitum*, to retire from.

अपाक्ष *apāksha* (*apa-ak°*), *as, ā, am*, present, perceptible; (*as, ī, am*), eyeless, having bad eyes.

अपाङ्क्त *a-pāṅkta* or *a-pāṅkteya* or *a-pāṅktya, as, ā, am*, not in a line or row; not in the same degree or class, unworthy, inadmissible into society, ejected from caste, excluded, outcast. — *A-pāṅktyopahata* (*°ya-up°*), *as, ā, am*, defiled or contaminated by the presence of impure or improper persons.

अपाङ्ग *apāṅga* (*apa-aṅ°*) or *apāṅgaka, as, ā, am*, maimed, crippled; wanting or deformed in some limb; (*as*), m. the outer corner of the eye (sometimes as last member of a feminine comp. ending in *ā* or *ī*); a sectarial mark or circlet on the forehead; N. of Kāma, the god of love; a plant, Achyranthes Aspera. — *Apāṅga-darśana, am*, n. a side glance, a leer, a wink. — *Apāṅga-deśa, as*, m. the place round the outer corner of the eye. — *Apāṅga-netra, as, ā, am*, having eyes with beautiful outer angles.

अपाच् *apāć* or *apāñć, n, ćī, k* (fr. *añć* with *apa*), going or situated backwards, behind; western (opposed to *prāñć*); southern (opposed to *udañć*); (*k*), ind. behind, westward, southward.

Apāćī, f. the south. — *Apāćītarā* (*°ćī-it°*), f. the north, i.e. other than the south.

Apāćīna, as, ā, am, situated backwards, behind; western; turned back; southern.

Apāćya, as, ā, am, western, southern.

अपाज् *apāj* (*apa-aj*), cl. 1. P. *apājati, -jitum*, to drive away.

अपाञ्च् *apāñć* (*apa-añć*), cl. 1. P. A. *apāñćati, -te, -ćitum*, to push away, to drive away.

अपाटव *a-pāṭava, am*, n. awkwardness, inelegance; sickness, disease.

अपाठ्य *a-pāṭhya, as, ā, am*, illegible.

अपाणिग्रहण *a-pāṇigrahaṇa, am*, n. celibacy.

A-pāṇi-pāda, as, ā, am, without hands and feet.

अपात्र *a-pātra, am*, n. a worthless or common utensil; an inferior, undeserving or worthless person, unfit as a recipient, unworthy to receive gifts. — *A-pātra-kṛityā*, f. or *a-pātrī-karaṇa, am*, n. acting unbecomingly, doing degrading offices (as for a Brāhman to receive wealth improperly acquired, to trade, to serve a Śūdra, and to utter an untruth); excommunication, disqualification. — *Apātra-dāyin, ī, inī, i*, giving to the undeserving. — *Apātra-bhṛit, t, t, t*, supporting the unworthy, cherishing the undeserving.

अपाद् *a-pād*, footless. See *apad*, p. 50.

A-pādya, as, ā, am, anything (as water) unfit for the feet.

अपादा *apā-dā* (*apa-ā°*), cl. 3. A. *-datte, -dātum*, to take off or away, to remove.

Apā-dāna, am, n. taking away, removal, ablation; a thing from which another thing is removed; the sense of the fifth or ablative case.

अपादादिभाज् *a-pādādi-bhāj* (*°da-ād°*), *k, k, k*, not standing at the beginning of a Pāda.

A-pādāntīya, as, ā, am, not standing at the end of a Pāda.

अपाध्वन् *apādhvan* (*apa-adh°*), *ā*, m. a bad road.

अपान् *apān* (*apa-an*), cl. 2. A. *apāniti, -nitum*, to breathe out or away, to expire, respire.

Apāna, as, m. expiration, breathing out (opposed to *prāṇa*); that of the five vital airs which goes downwards and out at the anus; (*am*), n. the anus; ventris crepitus. — *Apāna-dā, ās*, m., Ved. giving the vital air Apāna. — *Apāna-dvāra, am*, n. the anus. — *Apāna-pavana, as*, m. the vital air Apāna. — *Apāna-pā, ās*, m., Ved. protecting the Apāna. — *Apāna-bhṛit, t*, f. cherishing the vital air, a sacrificial brick. — *Apāna-vāyu, us*, m. the air Apāna; ventris crepitus.

अपानुद् *apā-nud* (*apa-ā°*), cl. 6. P. A. *-nudati, -te, -nottum*, to remove, repel, repudiate.

अपानृत *apānṛita* (*°pa-an°*), *as, ā, am*, free from falsehood, true.

अपान्नपात् *apān-napāt* or *apam-napāt*, &c. See under *ap*, p. 48.

अपाप *a-pāpa, as, ā, am*, or *a-pāpin, ī, inī, i*, sinless, virtuous, pure. — *A-pāpa-kāśin, ī, inī, i*, not ill-looking; not revealing evil. — *A-pāpa-kṛit, t, t, t*, not committing sin. — *A-pāpa-vasyasa, am*, n., Ved. non-increase of evil; health, prosperity. — *A-pāpa-viddha, as, ā, am*, not afflicted with evil.

अपाम् *apām*. See under *ap*, p. 48.

अपामार्ग *apā-mārga, as*, m. (rt. *mṛij*), N. of a plant (Achyranthes Aspera), employed very often in incantations, in medicine, in washing linen, and in sacrifices.

Apā-mārjana, am, n. cleansing, keeping back, removing (of diseases and other evils).

अपामृत्यु *apā-mṛityu, us*, m. sudden death; see *apa-mṛityu*.

अपाय *apāya*. See under *ape*.

अपार् *apār* (*apa-ṛi*), cl. 5. P. *apārṇoti, apārtum, -ritum* or *-rītum* (?), to remove; to open.

अपार 1. *apāra, am*, n. the opposite bank of a river; the same as *pāra*, q.v.

अपार 2. *a-pāra, am*, n. (in the Sāṅkhya) a bad shore, i.e. a kind of mental indifference or acquiescence (*tushṭi*); it may also mean the reverse of *pāra* or of *pārapāra*, i.e. the reverse of mental acquiescence; (*as, ā, am*), shoreless, unbounded, boundless, interminable; an epithet of heaven and earth; out of reach; inexhaustible. — *A-pārapāra, am*, n. non-acquiescence.

A-pāraka, as, ikā, am, or *a-pārayat, an, antī, at*, incompetent, impotent.

A-pāraṇīya, as, ā, am, out of reach.

अपारमार्थिक *a-pāramārthika, as, ī, am*, not concerned about the highest truth.

अपार्छ् *apārćh* (*apa-ṛićh*), cl. 6. P. *apārććhati, -ćhitum*, to go away, retire.

अपार्जित *apārjita, as, ā, am* (rt. *ṛij* with *apa*), flung away.

अपार्ण *apārṇa, as, ā, am* (rt. *ard*), distant, far.

अपार्थ *apārtha* (*apa-ar°*), *as, ā, am*, or *apārthaka, as, ikā, am*, without any object, useless, unprofitable; unmeaning; (*am*), n. incoherent argument. — *Apārtha-karaṇa, am*, n. a false plea in a lawsuit.

अपाल *a-pāla* or *a-pālana* or *a-pālita, as, ā, am*, unguarded, unprotected, undefended.

अपालङ्क *apālanka, as*, m., N. of a plant, Cassia Fistula.

अपालम्ब *apā-lamba, as*, m., Ved. the

hinder part of a carriage; mechanism to stop a carriage (?).

अपालि apāli (apa-ali), is, is, i, free from ali or bees, &c.

अपावृ apā-vṛi (apa-ā°), cl. 5. P., Ved. -vṛiṇoti, -varitum, -rītum, to open; to cover; (in the first sense apāvṛi is said to be for apa-vṛi, the final of apa being lengthened.)

Apā-vṛita, as, ā, am, open, laid open; covered, concealed, enclosed; unrestrained, self-willed.

Apā-vṛiti, is, f. or apā-varaṇa, am, n. laying open, enclosing, surrounding; covering, concealing, screening.

अपावृत् apā-vṛit (apa-ā°), cl. 1. A. -vartate, -titum, to turn away, to return, to abstain from, to come to nought.

Apā-vartana, am, n. turning away or from; retreat, returning; repulse.

Apā-vṛit, t, t, t, Ved. returning.

Apā-vṛitta, as, ā, am, (with abl.) turned away from; averted; abstaining from, rejecting, despising; reversed, repelled; (am), n. the rolling on the ground (of a horse).

Apā-vṛitti, is, f. retreat, returning; repulse.

अपाश्या a-pāśyā, f. no great number of nooses or fetters (i. e. a few).

अपाश्रय 1. apāśraya (apa-āś°), as, ā, am, helpless, destitute.

अपाश्रि 1. apā-śri (apa-ā°), cl. 1. P. -śrayati, -yitum, to resort to; to use, practice.

2. apā-śraya, as, m. refuge, recourse, the person or thing to which recourse is had for refuge; an awning spread over a court or yard.

Apā-śrita, as, ā, am, resting on; resorting to.

अपाष्टि apāshṭi, is, f., Ved. the heel.

अपाष्ठ apā-shṭha, as, m., Ved. barb of an arrow; (am), n. what remains of the Soma plant after it has been pressed out. — Apāshṭha-vat, ān, atī, at, Ved. having barbs; (vat), ind. like the remainder of the Soma plant (?).

अपास् apās (apa-as), cl. 4. P. apāsyati, -situm, to fling away, throw away or off, to discard; to scare, drive away; leave behind, leave in a deserted condition; to desert, to take no notice of, disregard; reject.

Apāsana, am, n. throwing away; quitting, foregoing, discarding; killing, slaughter.

Apāsita, as, ā, am, thrown or cut down, injured, destroyed.

Apāsta, as, ā, am, thrown off, set aside; driven away, expelled; abandoned, discarded; disregarded, contemned.

Apāsya, ind. having thrown away or discarded, having left, having disregarded, having excepted.

Apāsyat, an, antī, at, discarding, throwing off, &c.

अपासङ्ग apā-saṅga, as, m. (rt. sañj), a quiver; also upāsaṅga.

अपासरण apā-saraṇa, am, n. (rt. sṛi), departing, departure, removal.

Apā-sṛita, as, ā, am, gone, departed, gone away.

अपासि apāsi (apa-asi), is, is, i, having a bad or no sword.

अपासु apāsu (apa-asu), us, us, u, lifeless.

अपाहा apā-hā (apa-ā°), cl. 3. P. -jahāti, -hātum, to leave, omit, reject.

Apā-hāya, ind. excepting; except.

अपि api, or sometimes pi (as a particle or preposition prefixed to verbs and nouns), expresses placing near or over, uniting to, annexing, reaching to, proximity, &c. [cf. Gr. ἐπί; Zend api; Germ. and Eng. prefix be]; in later Sanskṛit its place seems frequently supplied by abhi.

(As a separable adv.) and, also, moreover, besides, assuredly, surely; api api or api-ća, as well as; na vāpi or na apivā or na naćāpi, neither, nor; ćāpi, (and at the beginning of a sentence) api-ća, moreover.

Api is often used to express emphasis, in the sense of even, also, very; e. g. anyad api, also another, something more; adyāpi, this very day, even now; tathāpi, even thus, notwithstanding; yady api, even if, although; yadyapi tathāpi, although, nevertheless; na kadāćid api, never at any time: sometimes in the sense of but, only, at least, e. g. muhūrtam api, only a moment.

Api may be affixed to an interrogative to make it indefinite, e. g. ko'pi, any one; kutrāpi, anywhere.

Api imparts to numerals the notion of totality, e. g. ćaturṇām api varṇānām, of all the four castes.

Api may be interrogative at the beginning of a sentence.

Api may strengthen the original force of the potential, or may soften the imperative, like the English 'be pleased to;' sometimes it is a mere expletive.

Api tu, but, but yet.

Api-tva, am, n., Ved. having part, share. — Api-tvin, ī, inī, i, Ved. having part, sharing.

Api-nāma, perhaps, in all probability.

अपिकक्ष api-kaksha, as, m., Ved. the region of the arm-pits and shoulder-blades, especially in animals; N. of a man; (ās), m. pl. the descendants of this man.

Api-kakshya, as, ā, am, Ved. connected with the region of the arm-pits, or that which binds to the kaksha.

अपिकर्ण api-karṇa, am, n., Ved. the region of the ears.

अपिकृत् api-kṛit, cl. 6. P. -kṛintati, -kartitum, to cut off.

अपिक्षि api-kshi, Caus. -kshāpayati, -yitum, to annihilate, to make away with.

अपिगम् api-gam, cl. 1. P. -gaććhati, -gantum, to go into, enter, approach, join; to approach a woman.

Api-gata, as, ā, am, gone into, entered, come near, approached, joined.

अपिगा api-gā, cl. 3. P. -jigāti, -gātum, to enter, get into, mingle with.

अपिगीर्ण api-gīrṇa, as, ā, am, praised, celebrated.

अपिग्रह् api-grah, cl. 9. P. A. -gṛihṇāti, -ṇīte, -grahītum, to receive; to stop; to close (the mouth, nose, &c.).

Api-gṛihya Ved., or api-grāhya, as, ā, am, to be received.

अपिघस् api-ghas, cl. 1. P. -ghasati, -ghastum, to eat off or away.

अपिच्छिल a-piććhila, as, ā, am, clear, free from sediment or soil.

अपिज api-ja, as, m. born after, born again; epithet of several divinities.

अपिण्ड a-piṇḍa, as, ā, am, without funeral cakes.

अपित् 1. a-pit, t, t, t (rt. pi), Ved. not swelling, dry; waterless.

अपित् 2. a-pit, t, t, t, (in gram.) not having the it or Anu-bandha p.

अपितृ a-pitṛi, tā, m. not a father.

A-pitṛika, as, ā, am, not ancestral or paternal, uninherited; fatherless.

A-pitrya, as, ā, am, uninherited, not ancestral or paternal.

अपिदह् api-dah, cl. 1. P., Ved. -dahati, -dagdhum, to singe.

अपिदृभ् api-dṛibh, cl. 6. P., Ved. -dṛibhati or -dṛimbhati, -darbhitum, to rely upon.

अपिदो api-do, cl. 4. P., Ved. -dyati, -dātum, to cut off.

अपिधा api-dhā, cl. 3. P. A. -dadhāti, -dhatte, -dhātum, to put to, shut, close, cover, conceal.

Api-dhāna or pi-dhāna, am, n. covering, concealment; a cover, a lid, a cloth for covering. — Api-dhāna-vat, ān, atī, at, Ved. having a cover; concealed.

Api-dhi, is, m. concealment.

Api-hita or pi-hita, as, ā, am, shut, covered, concealed.

अपिनह् api-nah or pi-nah, cl. 4. P. -nahyati, -naddhum, to tie on, fasten.

Api-naddha or pi-naddha, as ā, am, tied on; clothed, accoutred.

अपिनी api-nī, cl. 1. P. -nayati, -netum, to lead towards or to, bring to a state or condition.

अपिपद् api-pad, cl. 4. A. -padyate, -pattum, to go in, enter.

अपिपास a-pipāsa, as, ā, am, free from thirst; satisfied.

अपिपृच् api-pṛić, cl. 7. P. A., Ved. -pṛiṇakti, -pṛinkte, -parćitum, to mix with.

अपिप्राण api-prāṇa, as, ī, am, Ved. breathing upon, vivifying, animating (?).

अपिबद्ध api-baddha, as, ā, am, fastened; connected with.

अपिभाग api-bhāga, as, ā, am, Ved. having part in, sharing in.

अपिमृष् api-mṛish, cl. 4. P. A. -mṛishyati, -te, -marshitum, to forget, neglect.

अपिवृ api-vṛi, cl. 5. P. -vṛiṇoti, -varitum, -rītum, to conceal.

Api-vṛita, as, ā, am, concealed, covered.

अपिव्रत api-vrata, as, m. sharing in the same religious acts, related by blood.

अपिशर्वर api-śarvara, as, ā, am, Ved. contiguous to the night; being at the beginning or end of the night; (am), n. evening-time or morning-time.

अपिशल apiśala, as, m., N. of a man; (ās), m. pl. the descendants of Apiśala.

अपिशस् api-śas, f. (only used in abl.), Ved. slitting, ripping up.

अपिशुन a-piśuna, as, ā, am, unmalicious, upright, honest.

अपिष्टुत api-shṭuta, as, ā, am (rt. stu), praised.

अपिसिच् api-sić, cl. 6. P. -sinćati, -sektum, to sprinkle with.

अपिहित api-hita. See api-dhā.

अपी apī (api-i), cl. 2. P. apy-eti, -tum, to go in or near, to enter into or upon; to come near, approach; to partake, have a share in; to suffer; to join; to pour out (as a river); to dissolve; to enter the other world, to die.

Api-yat, an, atī, at, coming near.

1. apīta, as, ā, am, gone into, entered, approached.

Apīti, is, f., Ved. entering into, encountering, joining battle, junction; dissolving.

Apy-aya, coming near, union. See s. v.

अपीच्य apīćya, as, ā, am (fr. api-añć), Ved. secret, hidden (incorrectly for apīvya, q. v.).

अपीजू api-jū, ūs, ūs, u, Ved. stirring up, impelling.

अपीडन a-pīḍana, am, n. or a-pīḍā, f. not giving pain, gentleness, kindness.

A-pīḍayat, an, antī, at, without distressing, not paining.

अपीत 2. a-pīta, as, ā, am, not drunk.

A-pītvā, ind. not having drank, without drinking.

अपीनस apī-nasa or pī-nasa, as, m. (apī for api and nasa for nāsikā), dryness of the nose, want of the pituitary secretion and loss of smell, cold.

अपीवृत apī-vṛita = api-vṛita, as, ā, am, covered.

अपीव्य apīvya, as, ā, am, very handsome, most excellent (?).

अपुंस् a-puṅs, -pumān, m. not a man, a eunuch. — Apuṅs-tva, am, n. the state of a eunuch.

A-puṅskā, f. without a husband.

अपुच्छ a-puććha, as, ā, am, tailless; (ā), f. the tree Dalbergia Sisu.

अपुण्य a-puṇya, as, ā, am, unclean, impure, wicked, bad. — Apuṇya-kṛit, t, t, t, acting wickedly, wicked, bad.

अपुत्र a-putra, as, m. not a son; (as, ā, am), or a-putraka, as, ikā, am, having no son, sonless. — Aputra-tā, f. sonlessness.

A-putrikā, f. the daughter of a sonless father, who herself has no male offspring; (as), m. the father of such a daughter.

अपुनर् a-punar, ind. not again, once for ever. — A-punaḥ-prāpya, as, ā, am, irrecoverable. — A-punar-anvaya, as, ā, am, not returning, dead. — A-punar-āvṛitti, is, f. final exemption from life or transmigration. — A-punar-dīyamāna, as, ā, am, not being given back. — A-punar-bhava, as, m. not being again; exemption of the soul from further transmigration, final beatitude. — A-punar-bhāva, as, m. not being born again.

अपुराण a-purāṇa, as, ā, am, or a-purātana, as, ī, am, not old, modern, new.

अपुरूष a-purusha, as, ā, am, unmanly. — A-purushārtha (°sha-ar°), as, m. a rite which is not for the benefit of the sacrificer; not the chief object of the soul.

अपुरोऽनुवाक्यक a-puro-'nuvākyaka, as, akā or ikā, am, without a Puronuvākyā.

A-purorukka, as, ā, am, without a Puroruć.

अपुष्कल a-pushkala, as, ā, am, not eminent; mean, low.

अपुष्ट a-pushṭa, as, ā, am, unnourished, lean; soft.

अपुष्प a-pushpa, as, ā, am, not flowering; (as), m. the glomerous fig tree. — A-pushpa-phala or a-pushpa-phala-da, as, ā, am, bearing fruits without flowering; having neither flowers nor fruits; (as), m. the jack tree, Artocarpus Integrifolia, the glomerous fig tree.

अपुस् apus, us, n., Ved. shape; the same as rapus, q. v.

अपूजक a-pūjaka, as, ikā, am, irreverent, irreligious.

A-pūjā, f. irreverence, disrespect.

A-pūjita, as, ā, am, not reverenced or worshipped, contemned, disregarded.

A-pūjya, as, ā, am, not to be worshipped or revered.

अपूत a-pūta, as, ā, am, impure; not having received the invocatory rite.

अपूप apūpa, as, m. cake of flour, meal, &c.; a sort of bread; wheat; honey-comb (?). — Apūpa-nābhi, is, m., Ved. having a navel which consists of or is decorated with cake. — Apūpa-maya, as, ī, am, consisting of cake. — Apūpa-vat, ān, atī, at, accompanied with cake. — Apūpāpihita (°pa-ap°), as, ā, am, covered with cake.

Apūpīya, as, ā, am, belonging to cake.

Apūpya, am, n. flour, meal.

अपूरणी apūraṇī, f. the silk cotton tree, Bombax Heptaphyllum.

अपूरुष a-pūrusha, as, ā, am, lifeless, inanimate; soulless; unpeopled. — A-pūrusha-ghna, as, m., Ved. not killing men.

अपूर्ण a-pūrṇa, as, ā, am, not full or entire, imperfect, incomplete, deficient; (am), n. an incomplete number, a fraction. — Apūrṇa-kāla, as, ā, am, premature; (as), m. incomplete time. — Apūrṇa-kāla-ja, as, ā, am, born before the proper time, abortive. — Apūrṇa-tā, f. incompleteness.

A-pūryamāṇa, as, ā, am, not being full, incomplete.

अपूर्व a-pūrva, as, ā, am, unpreceded, unprecedented; not having existed before, quite new; unparalleled, incomparable, wonderful, extraordinary; not first; (in Pāṇini) preceded by a or ā; (am), n. the remote or unforeseen consequence of an act, as heaven of religious rites; a consequence not immediately preceded by its cause. — Apūrva-karman, a, n. a religious rite or sacrifice, the power of which on the future is not before seen. — Apūrva-tā, f. or apūrva-tva, am, n. the being unpreceded, not having existed before, incomparableness, &c. — A-pūrva-pati, is, f. one who has had no husband before. — Apūrva-vat, ind. singularly, unlike anything else. — A-pūrveṇa, ind. never before.

A-pūrvīya, as, ā, am, referring to the remote or unforeseen consequence of an act.

A-pūrvya, as, ā, am, Ved. unpreceded, first; having nothing similar before one's self, incomparable, unheard of.

अपृक्त a-pṛikta, as, ā, am, unmixed, uncombined; (as), m. (in Pāṇini) a word or an affix consisting of a single letter, i. e. of one not combined with another; (in the Prātiśākhyas) the preposition ā and the particle u.

अपृणत् a-pṛiṇat, an, atī, at, Ved. not filling, not propitiating by gifts; stingy.

अपृथक् a-pṛithak, ind. not separately, with, together with, collectively. — Apṛithag-dharma-śīla, as, ā, am, of the same religion. — Apṛithag-dhī, is, is, i, regarding God in all things.

अपृष्ट a-pṛishṭa, as, ā, am, unasked, unaddressed, not spoken to.

अपे ape (apa-i), cl. 2. P., cl. 1. A. apaiti, apāyate, apaitum, to go away, withdraw, retire, run away, escape, vanish; to be wanting, to be omitted; to start.

Apāya, as, m. going away, departure; destruction, death, annihilation; injury, detriment, loss; misfortune, evil, ill, calamity, danger; end (of a word).

Apāyin, ī, inī, i, going away, departing, vanishing, perishable.

Apeta, as, ā, am, escaped, departed, gone; having retired from, free from (with abl. or as last member of a comp.). — Apeta-bhī, īs, īs, i, one whose fear is gone. — Apeta-rākshasī, f., N. of a plant, Ocimum Sanctum.

Apeya, as, ā, am, removed (?).

Apehi. See s. v. next col.

अपेक्ष् apeksh (apa-īksh), cl. 1. A. apekshate, -shitum, to look away, to look round, to look about for something; to have some design; to have regard to, to respect; to look for, wait for, expect, hope; to require, to have an eye to; with na, not to like.

Apekshaṇa, am, n. or apekshā, f. looking round or about; (with the object either in loc. or as the preceding member of a compound) consideration, reference, regard; connection of cause with effect or of individual with species; expectation, hope, desire, need, requirement. — Apekshayā, with reference to. — Apekshā-buddhi, is, f. a mental process in the Vaiśeshika philosophy, the faculty of arranging and methodising; clearness of understanding.

Apekshaṇīya or apekshitavya or apekshya, as, ā, am, to be considered or regarded, to be looked for or expected, to be wished, desired, or required; desirable.

Apekshita, as, ā, am, considered, regarded, referred to, looked for, expected; wished, hoped, required; (am), n. consideration, reference, regard.

Apekshin, ī, iṇī, i, (with the object in gen. or as the preceding member of a compound) considering, respecting, regarding, looking to; looking for, expecting, hoping, requiring.

Apekshya, ind. having considered, having regard to, with regard or reference to.

अपेज् apej (apa-ej), cl. 1. A. apejate, -jitum, to remove, drive away. (See Gram. 784. a.)

अपेन्द्र apendra (°pa-in°), as, ā, am, without Indra.

अपेय a-peya, as, ā, am, unfit for drinking, undrinkable.

अपेशल a-peśala, as, ā, am, not clever, inexpert.

अपेशस् a-peśas, ās, ās, as, Ved. formless, shapeless.

अपेष् 1. apesh (apa-ish), cl. 4. A. apeshyate, -shitum, to strive after, aspire to.

अपेष् 2. apesh (apa-īsh), cl. 1. A. apeshate, -shitum, to withdraw from, to retire.

अपेहि apehi (imperative of rt. i with apa), at the beginning of several compounds, means excluding, expelling, denying admission; e. g. apehi-prakasā, f. a ceremony where people are not admitted. — Apehi-bāṇijā, f. a ceremony from which merchants are excluded. — Apehi-vātā, f., N. of a plant useful in expelling wind (Pœderia).

अपैशुन a-paiśuna, am, n. integrity, honesty, uprightness.

अपोगण्ड a-pogaṇḍa, as, ā, am, not under sixteen years of age; a child or infant; timid, fearful; flaccid; having a limb too many or too few.

अपोच्छद् apoććhad (apa-ud-ćhad), cl. 10. P. A. -ćhādayati, -te, -yitum, to uncover.

अपोढ apoḍha, as, ā, am (fr. rt. vah with apa), carried off, removed, taken away.

अपोत्कृष् apot-kṛish (apa-ud-kṛish), cl. 1. 6. P. A. -karshati, -te, -kṛishati, -te, -karshṭum, -krashṭum, to separate, disjoin.

अपोदक apodaka (°pa-ud°), as, ā, am, waterless, water-tight; not watery, not fluid; (ikā), f. a pot-herb, Basella Rubra or Lucida.

अपोदि apod-i (apa-ud-i), cl. 2. P. -eti, -tum, to go away altogether, to give way, to withdraw.

Apod-itya, as, ā, am, to be completely gone away from or left.

अपोद्धार्य apod-dhārya, as, ā, am (fr. rt. hṛi with apa and ud), liable to have something taken away.

अपोनपात् apo-napāt, &c. See under ap.

अपोभ् apobh (apa-ubh), cl. 6. P., Ved. apobhati, -ombhati, -bhitum, to bind, fetter.

अपोर्णु *aporṇu* (*apa-ūrṇu*), cl. 2. P. A. *aporṇauti, -ṇoti, -ṇute, -ṇavitum, -ṇuvitum,* to uncover, to unveil, to open; A. to uncover one's self.

अपोष् *aposh* (*apa-ush*), cl. 1. P., Ved. *aposhati, apoććhati,* to dispel darkness (said of the dawn).

अपोह् *apoh* (*apa-ūh*), cl. 1. P. A. *apohati, -te, -hitum,* to strip off, to push away, to frighten away; to remove, to heal (sickness); A. to keep away from one's self, to avoid, to give up; (in disputation) to object, to deny, to reason, argue.

Apoha, as, m. or *apohana, am,* n. pushing away, removing; removal of doubt by the exercise of the reasoning faculty; reasoning, arguing.

Apohanīya or *apohya, as, ā, am,* to be taken away, or removed, or expiated.

Apohita, as, ā, am, taken away, removed; established by reason.

अपौरुष *a-paurusha, am,* n. unmanliness, cowardice; superhuman power; (*as, ā, am*), unmanly, cowardly; superhuman.

अपौष्कल्य *a-paushkalya, am,* n. immaturity.

अप्त *apta, as, ā, am* (fr. obs. rt. *ap* for later *āp*), Ved. obtained; watery (?).

Aptas, as, n. a sacrificial act.

Aptu, us, m., Ved. busy, active, diligent; the body; Soma; a sacrificial animal.

Aptur, ūs, m., Ved. active, busy; giving water; running as water.

Aptūrya, am, n., Ved. zeal, activity; the giving of water.

Aptor-yāma, as, or *aptor-yāman, ā,* m., Ved., N. of a sacrificial ceremony, and of a verse in the Sāma-veda closing that ceremony [cf. *vairāja*].

Aptya, as, ā, am, active, spacious; watery (?).

Apna, as, m. or *apnas, as,* n., Ved. possession, property; work, sacrificial act; progeny; shape [cf. Lat. *ops*]. — *Apnaḥ-stha, as,* m., Ved. superintending work. — *Apna-rāj, ṭ,* m., Ved. possessing property; illustrious through work. — *Apnas-vat, ān, atī, at,* Ved. productive, having sacrificial acts or work.

Apnavāna, as, m., Ved. having progeny; the arm; N. of a Ṛishi; poor (?).

Apya, as, ā, am, obtainable, to be reached; active, belonging to or connected with work or sacrificial acts, watery.

अप्प *appa, as,* m., N. of an author of a book on prosody.

अप्पति *appati, is,* m. See under *ap.*

अप्पदीक्षित *appadīkshita* or *apyadīkshita* or *apyayadīkshita, as,* m., N. of an author of the sixteenth century.

अप्पित्त *ap-pitta, am,* n. fire; see under *ap.*

अप्यच् *apy-ać, yan, īćī, yak* (rt. *ańć*), reaching, gone into, hidden.

अप्यत्यर्ज् *apy-aty-arj* (*api-ati°*), cl. 1. P., Ved. *-arjati, -jitum,* to add over and above.

अप्यय *apy-aya, as,* m. (fr. rt. *i* with *api,* see *apī*), approach, meeting, joining; pouring out; entering, vanishing; junction; (e.g. *svāpyaya,* entering into one's self, absorption.) — *Apyaya-dīkshita, as,* m., N. of a Drāviḍa saint and writer, the author of various works, celebrated as a Śaiva, and thought to be an incarnation of Śiva; (also *apyāya°* or *apyai°,* &c.)

Apy-ayana, am, n. union, joining; copulating.

अप्यर्धम् *apy-ardham,* ind., Ved. within proximity, near.

अप्यस् *apy-as* (*api-as*), cl. 2. P. *-asti,* (with loc. or with an adv. of place) to be in anything; to be closely connected with, to belong to.

अप्युत *apy-uta* = *api* and *uta,* q. v.

अप्रकट *a-prakaṭa, as, ā, am,* unmanifested, unapparent, obscure.

अप्रकम्प *a-prakampa, as, ā, am,* unshaken, literally and metaphorically; firm, steady; unanswered, unrefuted. — *Aprakampa-tā,* f. firmness, stability, unanswerableness.

अप्रकर *a-prakara, as, ā, am,* not acting excellently.

A-prakaraṇa, am, n. not the principal topic, not relevant to the main subject.

A-prakṛita, as, ā, am, not principal, not relevant to the main topic under discussion, not chief; occasional or incidental, not natural.

A-prakṛiti, is, f. not the inherent or inseparable property, accidental property or nature; spiritual being.

अप्रकर्षित *a-prakarshita, as, ā, am,* not exceeded, not more than; unsurpassed.

A-prakṛishṭa, as, ā, am, low, vile; (*as*), m. a crow.

अप्रकल्पक *a-prakalpaka, as, ikā, am,* not prescribing as obligatory.

A-prakḷipta, as, ā, am, not explicitly enjoined.

अप्रकाण्ड *a-prakāṇḍa, as, ā, am,* stemless; (*as*), m. a bush, a shrub.

अप्रकाश *a-prakāśa, as, ā, am,* not shining, dark; self-illuminated; not visible, hidden, secret; not manifest or evident; (*am*), ind. in secret; (*as*), m. indistinctness, secresy, a secret.

A-prakāśaka, as, ikā, am, not rendering bright; making dark.

A-prakāśamāna or *a-prakāśita, as, ā, am,* not manifested, undivulged, unrevealed, not evident or public.

A-prakāśya, as, ā, am, not to be manifested or divulged.

अप्रकेत *a-praketa, as, ā, am,* Ved. indiscriminate, unrecognizable.

अप्रक्षित *a-prakshita, as, ā, am,* Ved. undiminished, undecayed.

अप्रखर *a-prakhara, as, ā, am,* dull, obtuse; bland, mild.

अप्रगम *a-pragama, as, ā, am,* going too fast for others to follow, not to be surpassed.

अप्रगल्भ *a-pragalbha, as, ā, am,* not arrogant, modest.

अप्रगीत *a-pragīta, as, ā, am,* not chaunted aloud.

अप्रगुण *a-praguṇa, as, ā, am,* confounded, perplexed.

अप्रग्राह *a-pragrāha, as, ā, am,* unrestrained, unbridled.

अप्रचङ्कश *a-praćankaśa, as, ā, am,* Ved. without power of seeing; not beautiful (?).

अप्रचुर *a-praćura, as, ā, am,* little, few.

अप्रचेतस् *a-praćetas, ās, ās, as,* Ved. deficient in understanding, foolish.

A-praććtita, as, ā, am, unknown.

अप्रचोदित *a-praćodita, as, ā, am,* undesired, not bidden or commanded; undeclared, not said; unasked.

अप्रच्छेद्य *a-praććhedya, as, ā, am,* inscrutable.

अप्रच्युत *a-praćyuta, as, ā, am,* unmoved; (with abl.) not fallen or deviating from, observing, following.

अप्रज *a-praja, as, ā, am* (rt. *jan*), without progeny, childless; unborn; unpeopled; (*ā*), f. not bearing, unprolific, having no child.

1. *a-prajajñi, is, is, i* (rt *jan*), without progeny.

A-prajas, ās, ās, as, without progeny, childless. — *Aprajas-tā,* f. or *aprajas-tva* or *aprajās-tva, am,* n. childlessness.

A-prajāta, as, ā, am, childless, having no progeny.

अप्रजज्ञि 2. *a-prajajñi, is, is, i* (rt. *jñā*), Ved. inexperienced, inexpert.

अप्रणीत *a-praṇīta, as, ā, am* (rt. *nī*), unconsecrated, profane, common; (*am*), n. the act of frying clarified butter without consecrated water.

अप्रणोद्य *a-praṇodya, as, ā, am* (rt. *nud*), not to be turned away.

अप्रत् *a-prat, n, tī, t* (rt. *prā*), Ved. not affluent; *apratā,* inst. c. without wealth.

अप्रतर्क्य *a-pratarkya, as, ā, am,* not to be discussed; incomprehensible by reason, undefinable.

अप्रताप *a-pratāpa, as,* m. want of brilliancy, dulness; meanness, want of dignity.

अप्रति *a-prati, is, is, i,* Ved. without opponents, irresistible; unequalled; (*i*), ind. irresistibly. — 1. *aprati-rūpa, as, ā, am,* of unequalled form, incomparable [cf. 2. *a-pratirūpa,* p. 58]. — *Aprati-rūpa-kathā,* f. incomparable or unanswerable discourse. — *Aprati-vīrya, as, ā, am,* of irresistible power.

अप्रतिकर *a-pratikara, as, ā, am,* trusted, trusting, confidential.

A-pratikarman, ā, ā, a, of unparalleled deeds.

A-pratikāra or *a-pratīkāra, as,* m. not remedying, non-requital, non-retaliation; (*as, ā, am*), irremediable, helpless, defenceless.

A-pratikārin, ī, iṇī, i, not remedying, not counteracting.

अप्रतिगृह्य *a-pratigṛihya, as, ā, am,* one from whom one must not accept anything.

A-pratigrāhaka, as, ikā, am, not accepting.

A-pratigrāhya, as, ā, am, not to be taken, unacceptable.

अप्रतिघ *a-pratigha, as, ā, am* (rt. *han*), not to be kept off, not to be vanquished.

अप्रतिद्वन्द्व *a-pratidvandva, as, ā, am,* not having an adversary in battle; not to be vanquished; irresistible. — *Apratidvandva-tā,* f. unrivalledness.

अप्रतिधुर *a-pratidhura, as, ā, am,* Ved. without a match in carrying burdens or the yoke (said of a horse).

अप्रतिधृष्ट *a-pratidhṛishṭa, as, ā, am,* not to be opposed, irresistible. — *Apratidhṛishṭa-śavas, ās, ās, as,* Ved. of irresistible power.

A-pratidhṛishya, as, ā, am, Ved. irresistible.

अप्रतिपक्ष *a-pratipaksha, as, ā, am,* without a rival or opponent.

अप्रतिपण्य *a-pratipaṇya, as, ā, am,* not to be bartered or exchanged.

अप्रतिपत्ति *a-pratipatti, is,* f. non-ascertainment; non-performance, failure; neglect, disregard.

A-pratipad, t, t, t, not stopping; not to be depended on.

A-pratipanna, as, ā, am, unascertained, unaccomplished, neglected.

अप्रतिबन्ध *a-pratibandha, as,* m. absence of obstruction; (*as, ā, am*), unimpeded, undisputed, direct (inheritance), not collateral or presumptive.

अप्रतिबल *a-pratibala, as, ā, am,* of unequalled power.

अप्रतिबोधवत् *a-pratibodhavat, ān, atī, at,* without the sense of personal consciousness.

अप्रतिब्रुवत् *a-pratibruvat, an, atī, at,* Ved. not speaking against, not contradicting.

अप्रतिभ *a-pratibha, as, ā, am,* modest, bashful; (*ā*), f. shyness, timidity.

Q

अप्रतिम *a-pratima, as, ā, am,* unequalled, incomparable, without a match.

अप्रतिमन्यूयमान *a-pratimanyūyamāna, as, ā, am,* Ved. being unable to show one's resentment to another, or to retaliate anger for anger.

अप्रतियत्न *a-pratiyatna, as,* m. natural or spontaneous state or condition.

अप्रतियोगिन् *a-pratiyogin, ī, inī, i,* without adversary; not opposed (to one another), having no opposite.

अप्रतिरथ *a-pratiratha, as,* m. having no antagonist, an invincible warrior; N. of a Rishi; *(am),* n., N. of a hymn composed by Apratiratha.

अप्रतिरव *a-pratirava, as, ā, am,* uncontested, undisputed.

अप्रतिरूप 2. *a-pratirūpa, as, ā, am,* not corresponding with, unfit. (For 1. see under *a-prati.*)

अप्रतिलब्धकाम *a-pratilabdha-kāma, as, ā, am,* unsatiated in one's desires.

अप्रतिषिद्ध *a-pratishiddha, as, ā, am* (rt. 2. *sidh*), unprohibited, unforbidden.

A-pratishedha, as, m. non-prohibition, non-negation.

अप्रतिष्कुत *a-pratishkuta, as, ā, am,* Ved. not to be kept off, not to be resisted, not contradicted, not refused.

अप्रतिष्ठ *a-pratishṭha, as, ā, am,* having no solid ground, fluctuating; thrown away, unprofitable; infamous, disreputable; *(as),* m., N. of a hell; *(ā),* f. instability, absence of reputation, ill-fame, dishonour.

A-pratishṭhāna, as, ā, am, Ved. without solid or firm ground; *(am),* n. instability.

A-pratishṭhita, as, ā, am, unsettled, unfixed; unconsecrated; uncelebrated, obscure.

अप्रतिसङ्क्रम *a-pratisankrama, as, ā, am,* having no intermixture.

अप्रतिसङ्ख्य *a-pratisankhya, as, ā, am,* unobserved. — *Apratisankhya-nirodha, as,* m. the unobserved nullity or annihilation of an object.

अप्रतिहत *a-pratihata, as, ā, am,* uninterrupted, unobstructed, irresistible; unaffected, unimpaired, indestructible, uninjured; not disappointed. — *Apratihata-netra, as,* m., N. of a Buddhist deity (whose eyes are unimpeded).

अप्रतीकार *a-pratīkāra.* See under *a-pratikāra,* p. 57.

अप्रतीक्षम् *a-pratīksham,* ind. without looking backward.

अप्रतीत *a-pratīta, as, ā, am* (rt. *i* with *prati*), unapproached, unattackable; unopposed; unintelligible, not understood. — *Apratīta-tā,* f. unintelligibleness.

A-pratīti, is, f. the state of not being understood; mistrust, want of confidence.

अप्रतीत्त *a-pratītta, as, ā, am* (for *a-pratidatta,* fr. rt. *dā* with *prati*), Ved. not given back.

अप्रतीप *a-pratīpa, as,* m., N. of a king of Magadha.

अप्रतुल *a-pratula, as,* m. want of weight, want, necessity.

अप्रत्त *a-pratta, as, ā, am* (for *a-pradatta,* fr. rt. *dā* with *pra*), not given away; *(ā),* f. not given away in marriage, a girl.

अप्रत्यक्ष *a-pratyaksha, as, ā, am,* not present to the sight, invisible, imperceptible; unknown. — *Apratyaksha-tā,* f. imperceptibility. — *A-pratyaksha-śishṭa, as, ā, am,* not distinctly taught.

अप्रत्यय *a-pratyaya, as,* m. distrust, disbelief, doubt; not an affix; *(as, ā, am),* distrustful (with loc.); having no affix. — *A-pratyaya-stha, as, ā, am,* (in gram.) not pertaining to an affix.

अप्रत्याख्यात *a-pratyākhyāta, as, ā, am,* uncontradicted, unrefuted, assented to.

A-pratyākhyāna, am, n. non-refutation.

A-pratyākhyeya, as, ā, am, not to be contradicted, undeniable.

अप्रत्यृत *a-pratyṛita, as, ā, am,* not attacked.

अप्रथित *a-prathita, as, ā, am,* unpublished; unnoted, unknown, not celebrated.

अप्रदीप्ताग्नि *a-pradīptāgni* (°*ta-ag*°), *is, is, i,* dyspeptic.

अप्रदुग्ध *a-pradugdha, as, ā, am,* Ved. not milked to the end.

अप्रदृपित *a-pradṛipita, as, ā, am,* Ved. not proud, not arrogant; not humbled, not careless (?).

अप्रधान *a-pradhāna, as, ā, am,* not principal, subordinate, secondary. — *Apradhāna-tā,* f. or *apradhāna-tva, am,* n. subordination, inferiority.

अप्रधृष्य *a-pradhṛishya, as, ā, am,* not to be vanquished, invincible.

अप्रपदन *a-prapadana, am,* n., Ved. a bad place of refuge.

अप्रबल *a-prabala, as, ā, am,* inefficacious, weak.

अप्रभ *a-prabha, as, ā, am,* without radiance, obscure; dull; mean.

अप्रभु *a-prabhu, us, us, u,* wanting power, unable, incompetent (with loc.). — *Aprabhu-tva, am,* n. want of power, insufficiency.

A-prabhūta, as, ā, am, insufficient, inadequate.

A-prabhūti, is, f. little effort.

अप्रमत्त *a-pramatta, as, ā, am,* not careless, careful, attentive, vigilant, sober.

A-pramāda, as, m. care, vigilance; *(as, ā, am),* careful, cautious, steady; *(am),* ind. attentively, carefully; without interruption.

A-pramādin, ī, inī, i, careful, attentive.

अप्रमद *a-pramada, as, ā, am,* without pleasure, joyless.

अप्रमय *a-pramaya, as, ā, am,* Ved. unlimited, imperishable.

अप्रमा *a-pramā,* f. a rule which is no authority (see *a-pramāṇa*); incorrect knowledge.

अप्रमाण *a-pramāṇa, as, ā, am,* immeasurable, unlimited; without weight or proof, without authority; *(am),* n. a rule which is no standard of action. — *A-pramāṇa-vid, t, t, t,* incapable of weighing evidence. — *Apramāṇa-śubha, ās,* m. pl. of immeasurable virtue; N. of a class of Buddhist divinities. — *Apramāṇābha* (°*ṇa-ābha*), *ās,* m. pl. of unlimited splendor; N. of a class of divinities in Buddhism.

A-pramāṇika, as, ā, am, unauthorized; properly *a-prāmāṇika,* q. v.

A-pramita, as, ā, am, unbounded, unmeasured; not proved, not established by authority.

A-prameya, as, ā, am, immeasurable; unfathomable, inscrutable; not to be proved. — *Aprameyātman* (°*ya-āt*°), *ā,* m. of inscrutable spirit, an epithet of Śiva. — *Aprameyānubhāva* (°*ya-an*°), *as, ā, am,* of unlimited energy.

अप्रमायुक *a-pramāyuka, as, ā, am,* Ved. not dying suddenly (?), immeasurably long (?).

अप्रमीय *a-pramīya, as, ā, am,* Ved. not to be killed.

अप्रमूर *a-pramūra,* Ved. or *a-pramūrććhita, as, ā, am,* not foolish, prudent.

अप्रमृष्य *a-pramṛishya, as, ā, am,* not to be destroyed, indestructible.

अप्रमोद *a-pramoda, am,* n. inability to remove pain.

अप्रयत्न *a-prayatna, as,* m. absence of effort, indifference, laziness; *(as, ā, am),* not energetic, indifferent, apathetic, not devoted to (with loc.).

अप्रयाणि *a-prayāṇi, is,* f. not going, not moving.

A-prayāpaṇi or *a-prayāpani, is,* f. not causing to go on; not allowing to progress.

अप्रयावम् *a-prayāvam,* ind. (rt. *yu*), Ved. without interruption, attentively.

A-prayućchat, an, antī, at, Ved. unceasing, careful, attentive.

A-prayuta, as, ā, am, Ved. unaltered, continual.

A-prayutvan, ā, ā, a, Ved. not separate, combined, careful.

अप्रयास *a-prayāsa, as,* m. ease, absence of trouble.

अप्रयोग *a-prayoga, as,* m. non-applicability, bad application.

A-prayojaka, as, ikā or *akā, am,* inapplicable, causeless, irrelevant.

अप्रलम्ब *a-pralamba, as, ā, am,* not slow, quick, expeditious.

अप्रवर्तक *a-pravartaka, as, ikā, am,* abstaining from action, inert; not exciting to action.

A-pravartana, am, n. the act of refraining from, not engaging in; not exciting to any action.

A-pravṛitta, as, ā, am, not acting, not engaged in, not commenced, not instigated.

A-pravṛitti, is, f. not proceeding; abstaining from action, inertion; non-excitement; (in medic.) suppression of the natural evacuations, constipation, ischury, &c.

अप्रवीण *a-pravīṇa, as, ā, am,* unskilful.

अप्रवीत *a-pravīta, as, ā, am,* Ved. unapproached; not approaching (to impregnate); not impregnated.

अप्रवृद्ध *a-pravṛiddha, as, ā, am,* not excessively grown.

अप्रवेद *a-praveda, as, ā, am,* Ved. difficult to be found or obtained; silent (?).

अप्रशक्त *a-praśakta, a-praśakti,* probably for *a-prasakta, a-prasakti,* q. v. below.

अप्रशस्त 1. *a-praśasta, as, ā, am* (rt. *śaṇs*), not praised, worthless, contemptible; not approved, forbidden.

A-praśasya, as, ā, am, not praiseworthy, not good.

अप्रशस्त 2. *a-praśasta, as, ā, am* (rt. *śās*), Ved. indocile, disobedient.

अप्रसक्त *a-prasakta, as, ā, am* (rt. *sañj*), not addicted, not attached to; moderate, temperate.

A-prasakti, is, f. or *a-prasanga, as,* m. non-addiction, non-attachment, moderation.

अप्रसन्न *a-prasanna, as, ā, am* (rt. *sad*), not quiet, not clear, turbid, muddy; displeased, dissatisfied, unfavourable.

A-prasāda, as, m. disfavour, disapprobation.

A-prasādya, as, ā, am, not to be propitiated; unappeasable, implacable.

अप्रसव *a-prasava, as, ā, am* (rt. *su* or *sū*), not being prolific; *(as),* m. the not being born.

A-prasūta, as, ā, am, not having offspring, barren, childless.

अप्रसह्य *a-prasahya, as, ā, am,* intolerable, insufferable.

अप्रसिद्ध *a-prasiddha, as, ā, am,* not settled or established; unknown, uncelebrated; unusual, uncommon, of no real existence, not current or generally known.—*Aprasiddha-pada, am,* n. an obsolete word.

अप्रस्तुत *a-prastuta, as, ā, am,* unconnected with, irrelevant, unsuitable to the time or subject; not principal, not being the chief subject-matter; accidental or extraneous; not ready.

A-prastāvika, as, ī, am, irrelevant to the subject-matter.

अप्रहत *a-prahata, as, ā, am,* unhurt, intact; untilled, waste; uncultivated.

A-prahan, ā, ā, a, or *a-prahantṛi, tā, trī, tṛi,* not hurting.

अप्रहित *a-prahita, as, ā, am,* Ved. not stirred up, not sent out, unassailed (by foes).

अप्राकृत *a-prākṛita, as, ā, am,* not principal; not original; special, particular; not vulgar.

अप्राग्र्य *a-prāgrya, as, ā, am,* secondary, subordinate.

अप्राचीन *a-prāćīna, as, ā, am,* modern, recent; not eastern, western.

अप्राज्ञ *a-prājña, as, ā, am,* unlearned, ignorant; unconscious.—*Aprājña-tā,* f. ignorance, unconsciousness.

अप्राण *a-prāṇa, as, ā, am,* or *a-prāṇin, ī, inī, i,* inanimate, lifeless.

अप्राधान्य *a-prādhānya, am,* n. inferiority, subordination.

अप्राप्त *a-prāpta, as, ā, am* (rt. *āp* with *pra*), unobtained; unarrived; unproved.—*Aprāpta-kāla, as, ā, am,* out of season, inopportune, ill-timed; under age; (*am*), n. an irregular debate.—*Aprāpta-yauvana, as, ā, am,* not arrived at puberty.—*A-prāpta-vyavahāra* or *aprāpta-vayas, ās, ās, as,* a minor in law; under age, not of years to engage in law or public business.—*Aprāptāvasara* (°*ta-av*°), *as, ā, am,* unseasonable, inopportune.

A-prāpti, is, f. non-attainment, non-acquisition, scarcity.

A-prāpya, ind. not having found; (*as, ā, am*), unobtainable, unattainable, scarce.

अप्रामाणिक *a-prāmāṇika, as, ī, am,* unauthentic, unwarranted, unauthoritative, unworthy of being trusted or believed.

A-prāmāṇya, am, n. absence or insufficiency of proof or authority.

अप्रामिसत्य *a-prāmi-satya, as, ā, am* (rt. *mī* with *pra*), Ved. of unimpaired truthfulness; unalterably true.

अप्रायत्य *a-prāyatya, am,* n. impurity, ungovernableness.'

अप्रायु *a-prāyu, us, us, u,* Ved. assiduous, unceasing, not going forth (?).

A-prāyus, us, m., Ved. not ceasing; with undeparted life, with unimpaired or ever brilliant vigour.

अप्रिय *a-priya, as, ā, am,* disagreeable, disliked; unkind, unfriendly; (*as*), m. a foe, an enemy; N. of a Yaksha; (*ā*), f. a sort of skeat fish, Silurus Pungentissimus.—*Apriya-kara, as, ā* or *ī, am,* or *apriya-kārin, ī, iṇī, i,* doing an unkindness; unfriendly, ill-disposed.—*Apriya-bhāgin, ī, inī, i,* unfortunate.—*Apriya-vādin, ī, inī, i,* or *apriyaṃ-vada, as, ā, am,* speaking unkindly or harshly.

A-prīti, is, f. dislike, aversion, unfriendliness, enmity; pain.—*Aprīti-kara, as, ī, am,* unkind, adverse; disagreeable, offensive.—*Aprīty-ātmaka, as, ikā, am,* consisting of pain.

अप्रेतराक्षसी *apreta-rākshasī,* f., N. of a plant, Ocimum Sanctum; see *apeta-rākshasī,* p. 56.

अप्रेमन् *a-preman, a,* n. dislike, aversion; (*ā, ā, a*), unfriendly.

अप्रैष *a-praisha, as, ā, am,* not invoked with a *praisha* (q. v.) mantra.

अप्रोषिवस् *a-proshivas, -vān, -shushī, -vat* (rt. *vas,* perf. part.), Ved. not gone away, staying.

अप्रौढ *a-prauḍha, as, ā, am,* not arrogant, timid, gentle; (*ā*), f. an unmarried girl, or one very recently married and not come to womanhood.

अप्लव *a-plava, as, ā, am,* without a ship; not swimming.—*A-plaveśa* (°*va-īśa*), *as, ā, am,* unable to swim.

अप्वा *apvā,* f. (fr. *apa* or fr. obs. rt. *ap*?), disease; danger; the region of the throat or neck.

अप्स 1. *ap-sa, as,* m., Ved. giving or yielding (*ap*) water [cf. *ap-sā* below].

अप्स 2. *a-psa, as,* m., Ved. not destroying.

अप्सर *ap-sara, as,* m. water-goer, any aquatic animal (see etym. of next).

अप्सरस् *apsaras, ās,* or *apsarā,* f. (fr. *ap,* q. v., and rt. *sṛi,* 'going in the waters or between the waters of the clouds'); certain female divinities, who reside in the sky and are the wives of the Gandharvas; they have the faculty of changing their shapes, are very fond of bathing, and are said to have been produced at the churning of the ocean.—*Apsarah-pati, is,* m. Indra, lord of the Apsarasas.—*Apsaras-tīrtha, am,* n. a pool in which the Apsarasas bathe.—*Apsarā-pati, is,* m. lord of the Apsarasas; N. of the Gandharva S'ikhaṇḍin.

Apsarāya, nom. A. *apsarāyate, -yitum,* to behave like an Apsaras.

अप्सव *apsava, as, ā, am,* Ved. (if from *apsas*) possessed of form or shape; (if from *ap*) giving water.

Apsavya, as, ā, am, fit for water, being in the water.

अप्सस् *apsas, as,* n. (fr. obs. rt. *ap*), Ved. cheek; shape, beauty (?).

अप्सा *ap-sā, ās,* m. (fr. *ap* and rt. *san*), Ved. giving water.

अप्सु 1. *a-psu, us, us, u,* Ved. without food; not beautiful (?).

अप्सु 2. *apsu* (loc. pl. of *ap,* q. v.), in the water or waters. This word forms the first member of various compounds, thus:—*apsu-kshit, t,* m., Ved. dwelling within the clouds, in the region between heaven and earth.—*Apsu-ćara, as, ī, am,* Ved. going in the waters.—*Apsu-ja, as, ā, am,* or *apsu-jā, ās, ās,* m. f., Ved. born in the waters.—*Apsu-jit, t, t, t,* Ved. vanquishing between the waters or in the region of the clouds.—*Apsu-mat, ān, atī, at,* possessed of what is in the waters; not losing one's nature in the water (e. g. the lightning does not lose his fiery nature in the clouds); containing the word *apsu.*—*Apsu-yoga, as,* m. the connecting power in water.—*Apsu-yoni, is,* m., Ved. born from the waters.—*Apsu-vāh, ṭ,* m., Ved. driving in water.—*Apsu-shad, t, t, t,* Ved. dwelling in the waters.—*Apsu-shoma, as,* m. Soma in water; a cup filled with water.—*Apsu-saṃśita, as, ā, am,* Ved. raised or excited in the waters.

अफल *a-phala, as, ā, am,* unfruitful, barren; vain, unproductive; deprived of virility; (*as*), m., N. of a plant, Tamarix Indica; (*ā*), f. the Aloe plant, Aloes Perfoliata; another plant, Flacourtia Cataphracta.—*A-phala-kāṅkshin, ī, iṇī, i,* disinterested, not looking to beneficial consequences.—*Aphala-tā,* f. or *aphala-tva, am,* n. barrenness, unprofitableness.—*A-phala-prepsu, us, us, u,* one who desires no recompense.

अफल्गु *a-phalgu, us, us, u,* not vain, productive, profitable.

अफुल्ल *a-phulla, as, ā, am,* unblown.

अफेन 1. *a-phena, as, ā, am,* frothless, without scum or foam.

अफेन 2. *a-phena, am,* n. (corruption of *ahi-phena,* foam of a snake?), opium.

अबद्ध *a-baddha, as, ā, am,* or *a-baddhaka, as, ikā, am* (rt. *bandh*), unbound, at liberty; unmeaning, nonsensical.—*Abaddha-mukha, as, ā, am,* foul-mouthed, scurrilous; mendacious.

1. *a-badhya, as, ā, am,* unmeaning, nonsensical.

A-bandhaka, as, ikā, am, not binding; (*as*), m., N. of a man; (*ās*), m. pl. the descendants of this man.

A-bandhana, as, ā, am, without fetters, free.

A-bandhya. See s. v. below.

A-bandhra, as, ā, am, Ved. without bonds or ligatures, falling asunder.

अबध *a-badha, as,* m. (rt. *badh*), not killing; (*ā*), f. a segment of the base of a triangle, see *a-vadha.*—*Abadhārha* (°*dha-ar*°), *as, ā, am,* not worthy of death.

2. *a-badhya, as, ā, am,* not to be killed, inviolable; see also *a-vadhya.*—*Abadhya-bhāva, as,* m. immunity, sacredness of character, as that of an ambassador.

अबन्धु *a-bandhu, us, us, u,* without kindred, without companions, friendless.—*Abandhu-kṛit, t, t, t,* Ved. causing want of companions.

A-bāndhava, as, ā, am, having no relation or kindred, lone, unacknowledged, unowned.

अबन्ध्य *a-bandhya, as, ā, am,* not barren, not unfruitful, fruitful, productive.

अबल *a-bala, as, ā, am,* weak, feeble, infirm; (*as*), m., N. of a plant, Tapia Cratæva; N. of a king of Magadha; (*ā*), f. a woman; one of the ten Buddhist earths; (*am*), n. want of strength, weakness [with *abala* have been compared, Goth. *ubils,* Them. *ubila;* Mod. Germ. *uebel;* Eng. 'evil'].—*Abala-dhanvan, ā, ā, a,* possessing a weak bow.—*Abalābala* (°*la-ab*°), *as,* m. 'neither powerful nor powerless;' an epithet of Siva.

A-balāsa, as, ā, am, not consumptive.

Abalīyas, ān, asī, as, weaker.

A-balya, am, n. weakness, sickness.

अबहु *a-bahu, us, us,* or *vī, u,* not many, few.—*Abahv-akshara, as, ā, am,* or *abahv-ać, ć, ć, ć,* having not more than two syllables.

अबाध *a-bādha, as, ā, am,* unobstructed, unrestrained; free from pain; (*ā*), f. segment of the base of a triangle [cf. *a-badhā* under *a-badha* above].

A-bādhaka, as, ikā, am, or *a-bādhita, as, ā, am,* unimpeded, unobstructed; unrefuted.

A-bādhya, as, ā, am, improper to be opposed or pained.

अबान्धव *a-bāndhava.* See *a-bandhu.*

अबालिश *a-bāliśa, as, ā, am,* not childish.

अबालेन्दु *a-bālendu* (°*la-in*°), *us,* m. full-moon.

अबाह्य *a-bāhya, as, ā, am,* not exterior, internal; without an exterior.

अबिन्धन *ab-indhana, as,* m. 'having (*ap*) water for fuel,' submarine fire.

अबिभीवस् *a-bibhīvas, ān, bhyushī, at,* or *a-bibhyat, at, atī, at,* Ved. fearless, confident.

अबुद्ध *a-buddha, as, ā, am,* unwise, foolish.—*A-buddha-tva, am,* n. foolishness.

A-buddhi, is, f. want of understanding; ignorance; stupidity; (*is, is, i*), ignorant, stupid.—*A-buddhi-pūrva* or *a-buddhi-pūrvaka, as, ā, am,* not preceded by intelligence; beginning with non-intelligence; (*am*), ind. ignorantly. — *Abuddhi-mat, ān, atī, at*, unwise, ignorant, foolish.

A-budh, bhut, t, t, or *a-budha, as, ā, am*, stupid, foolish; (*as*), m. a fool.

A-budhya, as, ā, am, Ved. not to be perceived; not to be awakened.

A-budhyamāna, as, ā, am, not being awake.

A-bodha, as, m. ignorance, stupidity; (*as, ā, am*), ignorant, stupid; puzzled, perplexed. — *A-bodha-gamya, as, ā, am*, incomprehensible.

A-bodhanīya, as, ā, am, unintelligible; not to be awakened or aroused.

अबुध्न *a-budhna, am*, n., Ved. 'having no bottom or root,' the air or intermediate region.

अब्ज *ab-ja, as, ā, am* (fr. *ap* and rt. *jan*), born in water; (*as*), m. the conch; the moon; the tree Barringtonia Acutangula; Dhanvantari, physician of the gods, produced at the churning of the ocean; N. of a son of Viśala; (*am*), n. a lotus; a large number of millions. — *Abja-ja, as*, m. an epithet of Brahmā (sprung at the creation from the lotus, which arose from the navel of Vishṇu). — *Abja-dṛiś, k, k, k*, or *abja-nayana, as, ā, am*, or *abja-netra, as, ā, am*, lotus-eyed, having large fine eyes. — *Abja-bāndhava, as*, m. the sun (friend of the lotus). — *Abja-bhava, as*, m. Brahmā, a Brāhman. — *Abja-bhoga, as*, m. the root of a lotus. — *Abja-yoni, is*, m. epithet of Brahmā [cf. *abja-ja*]. — *Abja-vāhana, as*, m. epithet of Śiva, 'carrying the moon' on his forehead. — *Abja-hasta, as*, m. the sun (represented as holding a lotus in one hand).

Ab-jā, ās, m., Ved. born in water.

Abjinī, f. a multitude of lotus flowers. — *Abjinī-pati, is*, m. the sun.

अब्जस् *abjas, as*, n. shape, beauty [cf. *apsas*].

अब्जित् *ab-jit, t, t; t* (fr. *ap* and rt. *ji*), Ved. conquering waters.

अब्द *ab-da, as, ā, am* (fr. *ap* and rt. *dā*), giving water; (*as*), m. a cloud; a year; the grass Cyperus Rotundus; N. of a mountain. — *Abda-tantra, am*, n., N. of an astronomical work. — *Abda-vāhana, as*, m., N. of Śiva (? borne on a cloud or bearing the clouds). — *Abda-śata, am*, n. a century. — *Abda-sahasra, am*, n. a thousand years. — *Abda-sāra, as*, m. a kind of camphor. — *Abdārdha* (°*da-ar*°), *am*, n. a half year.

Abdayā, ind., Ved. out of desire of giving water.

Ab-di, is, m., Ved. a cloud. — *Abdi-mat, ān, atī, at*, Ved. possessed of clouds, giving water, impregnating (?).

अब्दुर्ग *ab-durga, am*, n. (see *ap*), a fortress surrounded by a moat or lake.

अब्देवताक *ab-devatāka* or *ab-daivata, as, ā, am* (see *ap*), having the waters as divinities, praising the waters.

अब्धि *ab-dhi, is*, m. (fr. *ap* and rt. *dhā*), a pond, lake; the ocean; sometimes used to denote the numerals 4 or (?) 7. — *Abdhi-kapha, as*, m. cuttle fish bone, being considered as the froth of the sea. — *Abdhi-ja, as, ā, am*, born in the ocean; (*au*), m. the Aśvins; (*ā*), f. spirituous liquor. — *Abdhi-jhasha, as*, m. a sea-fish. — *Abdhi-dvīpā*, f, earth; an island surrounded by the ocean. — *Abdhi-nagarī*, f., N. of Dvārakā, the capital of Kṛishṇa. — *Abdhi-navanītaka, as*, m. the moon. — *Abdhi-phena, as*, m. cuttle fish bone. — *Abdhi-maṇḍūki*, f. the pearl oyster. — *Abdhi-śayana, as*, m., N. of Vishṇu, sleeping on the ocean at the periods of the destruction and renovation of the world. — *Abdhi-sāra, as*, m. a gem. — *Abdhy-agni, is*, m. submarine fire.

अब्भक्ष *ab-bhaksha, as, ā, am* (fr. *ap* and rt. *bhaksh*), living upon water; (*as*), m. a snake.

Ab-bhakshaṇa, am, n. living upon water, a kind of fasting.

अब्भ्र *ab-bhra.* See *abhra*, &c.

अब्रह्मचर्य *a-brahmaćarya, as, ā, am*, unchaste.

A-brahma-ćaryaka, am, n. incontinence, coition.

अब्रह्मण्य *a-brahmaṇya, am*, n. act not proper for a Brāhman; an unbrahmanical or sacrilegious act; in theatrical language an exclamation, meaning 'help!' 'to the rescue!' 'a disgraceful deed is perpetrated!'

A-brahman, ā, ā, a, Ved. unaccompanied by devotion or devotional hymns, wanting in knowledge or divine wisdom; separated from the Brāhmans. — *Abrahma-tā*, f., Ved. want of devotion or true divine knowledge. — *A-brahma-vid, t, t, t*, not knowing Brahma or the supreme spirit.

A-brāhmaṇa, as, m. not a Brāhman; (*as, ā, am*), without Brāhmans.

A-brāhmaṇya, am, n. violation of sanctity, or of the duty of a Brāhman.

अब्रुवत् *a-bruvat, an, atī, at*, not speaking, silent.

अब्रूकृत *abrū-kṛita, am*, n. making (*abrū*) a growling; indistinctness of speech caused by shutting the lips.

अब्लिङ्ग *ab-linga, am*, n. (see *ap*), a *Sūkta* or verse addressed to the waters.

अब्विन्दु *ab-vindu, us*, m. (see *ap*), a tear.

अभ् *abh.* See *ambh.*

अभक्त 1. *a-bhakta, as, ā, am*, unbelieving, not devoted, not worshipping; not attached to, detached, unconnected with; not accepted.

A-bhakti, is, f. want of devotion to, want of faith, unbelief, incredulity. — *Abhakti-mat, ān, atī, at*, undevoted to, unbelieving.

अभक्त 2. *a-bhakta, as, ā, am*, not eaten. — *A-bhakta-ććhandas, as*, n. or *a-bhakta-ruć, k*, f. want of appetite.

अभक्ष *a-bhaksha, as*, m. or *a-bhakshaṇa, am*, n. not eating anything, fasting.

A-bhakshya, as, ā, am, not to be eaten. — *A-bhakshya-bhakshaṇa, am*, n. eating of prohibited food. — *Abhakshya-bhakshin, ī, iṇī, i*, eating forbidden food.

अभग *a-bhaga, as, ā, am*, without enjoyment, unfortunate.

अभग्न *a-bhagna, as, ā, am*, unbroken, entire; uninterrupted.

A-bhaṅgura, as, ā, am, unbroken; firm; undisturbed.

A-bhajyamāna, as, ā, am, not being detached, associated, attended with.

अभद्र *a-bhadra, as, ā, am*, not good, bad, wicked; (*am*), n. badness, sin, wickedness.

अभय *a-bhaya, as, ā, am*, unfearful, not dangerous, secure; fearless, undaunted; (*as*), m., N. of Śiva; a son of Dharma; (*ā*), f. a plant, Terminalia Citrina; (*am*), n. absence or removal of fear, peace, safety, security; N. of a sacrificial hymn; the root of a fragrant grass, Andropogon Muricatum. — *Abhaya-giri-vāsin, ī*, m. dwelling on the mountain of safety; N. of a division of Kātyāyana's pupils. — *Abhaya-giri-vihāra, as*, m. Buddhist monastery on the Abhayagiri. — *Abhayaṅ-kara, as, ā, am*, or *abhayaṅ-kṛit, t, t, t*, causing peace or safety. — *Abhaya-jāta, as*, m., N. of a man. — *Abhaya-ḍiṇḍima, as*, m. a war-drum. — *A-bhaya-da* or *abhayan-dada* or *abhayam-prada, as, ā, am*, giving fearlessness or safety; (*as*), m. an Arhat of the Jainas; N. of a king, the son of Manasyu and father of Su-dhanvan. — *Abhaya-dakshiṇā*, f. promise or present of protection from danger; a gift to a Brāhman, which he may receive even from a Śūdra. — *Abhaya-dāna* or *abhaya-pradāna, am*, n. giving assurance of safety or protection. — *Abhaya-pattra, am*, n. (a modern term), a written document or paper granting assurance of safety, a safe conduct. — *Abhaya-vaćana, am*, n. or *abhaya-vāć, k*, f. assurance of safety, encouragement. — *Abhaya-sani, is, is, i*, Ved. giving safety. — *Abhayānanda* (°*ya-ān*°), *as*, m., N. of a man.

अभर्तृका *a-bhartṛikā*, f. an unmarried woman; a widow.

अभव *a-bhava, as*, m. non-existence; destruction, end of the world.

A-bhavanīya or *a-bharitavya, as, ā, am*, what is not to be, what will not be.

A-bhavan-mata-yoga or *a-bhavan-mata-sambandha, as*, m. (in rhetoric) a defect in composition; want of harmony between the ideas, which are to be expressed, and the words by which they are expressed.

A-bhavya, as, ā, am, not to be, not predestined; what ought not to be, improper, inauspicious.

अभस्त्र *a-bhastra, as, ā, am*, without bellows.

A-bhastrakā or *a-bhastrikā* or *a-bhastrākā*, f. a badly made or inferior pair of bellows. The former two are said to mean also, 'a small woman who has no bellows.'

अभाग *a-bhāga, as, ā, am*, or *a-bhāgin, ī, inī, i*, not sharing or dividing.

A-bhāgya, as, ā, am, unfortunate, wretched.

अभाव *a-bhāva, as*, m. non-existence, absence; non-entity, negation, nullity, the seventh category in Kaṇāda's system; annihilation, death.

A-bhāvanā, am, f. n. absence of judgment or right perception; absence of religious meditation or contemplation.

A-bhāvanīya, as, ā, am, not to be inferred or contemplated, inconceivable.

A-bhāvayitṛi, tā, trī, tṛi, not perceiving, not inferring, not comprehending.

A-bhāvin, ī, inī, i, or *a-bhāvya, as, ā, am*, what is not to be or will not be, not destined to be.

अभाषण *a-bhāshaṇa, am*, n. not speaking, silence.

अभि *abhi*, ind. (a prefix to verbs and nouns, expressing) to, towards, into, over, upon.

(As a prefix to verbs of motion) it expresses the notion of moving or going towards, approaching, &c.

(As a prefix to nouns not derived from verbs) it expresses superiority, intensity, &c.; e. g. *abhi-tāmra, abhi-nava*, q. v.

(As a separable adverb or preposition) it expresses (with acc.) to, towards, in the direction of, against; in, into, to; for, for the sake of; on account of; on, upon, with regard to; by, before, in front of; over. It may even express one after the other, severally; e. g. *vṛiksham vṛiksham abhi*, tree after tree [cf. Gr. ἀμφί; Lat. *ob*; Zend *aibi*; Goth. *bi*; Old High Germ. *bī*].

Abhika, as, ā, am, lustful, libidinous; (*as*), m. a lover, a husband. Some regard this as derived from *abhi-kam* [cf. *anuka*].

Abhi-tarām, abhi-tas. See s. v.

अभिकम् *abhi-kam*, perf. *-ćakame, -kamitum*, to desire, love.

Abhi-kāma, as, m. affection, desire; (*as, ā, am*), affectionate, loving, desirous, with obj. in acc. or gen.; (*am*), ind. with desire.

Abhi-kāmika, as, ā, am, voluntary.

अभिकम्प् *abhi-kamp*, cl. 1. A. *-kampate, -pitum*, to tremble vehemently, to shake: Caus. *-kampayati, -yitum*, to stir, allure.

अभिकाङ्क्ष् *abhi-kāṅksh*, cl. 1. P. *-kāṅkshati, -shitum*, to ask, request, long for, desire; to strive.

Abhi-kāṅkshā, f. longing, wish, desire.

Abhi-kāṅkshita, as, ā, am, longed for, wished, desired.

Abhi-kāṅkshin, ī, iṇī, i, longing for, wishing, desiring.

अभिकाल *abhi-kāla, as,* m., N. of a town; see Rāmāyaṇa II. 68.

अभिकाश् *abhi-kāś,* Intens., Ved. *-ćākaśīti, -ćākaśyate,* to illuminate, irradiate; to look on, to perceive.

अभिकुत्स् *abhi-kuts,* cl. 10. P. A. *-kutsayati, -te, -yitum,* to revile, to inveigh against.

अभिकुष् *abhi-kush,* cl. 9. P. *-kushṇāti, -koshitum,* to pull, to tear.

अभिकूज् *abhi-kūj,* cl. 1. P. *-kūjati, -jitum,* to twitter, warble, coo.

अभिकृ *abhi-kṛi,* cl. 8. P. *-karoti, -kartum,* to do with reference to or in behalf of; to procure, effect; to render, make: Desid. *-ćikīrshati,* to wish to do; to long for.

Abhi-karaṇa, am, n. effecting; incantation.

Abhi-kṛiti, is, f., N. of a metre, containing one hundred syllables.

Abhi-kṛitvan, vā, varī, m. f., Ved. magical; a magician, a spirit (producing diseases?).

अभिकृष् *abhi-kṛish,* cl. 1. 6. P. A. *-karshati, -te, -kṛishati, -te, -karshṭum* or *-krashṭum,* to overpower, to pull down.

अभिकॄ *abhi-kṝ,* cl. 6. P. *-kirati, -karitum* or *-rītum,* to pour over, throw over, cover; to fill.

अभिकॢप् *abhi-klṛip,* cl. 1. A. *-kalpate, -pitum* or *-ptum,* to be adequate to, to answer; to have the same meaning: Caus. *-kalpayati, -yitum,* to put in order.

Abhi-klṛipta, as, ā, am, prepared, produced.

अभिक्नूय् *abhi-knūy,* cl. 1. A. *-knūyate, -yitum,* to bemoisten, bedew.

अभिक्रतु *abhi-kratu, us,* m., Ved. insolent, haughty (as an enemy).

अभिक्रन्द् *abhi-krand,* cl. 1. P. *-krandati, -ditum,* to shout at, roar at, to neigh or whinny at.

Abhi-kranda, as, m. a shout.

अभिक्रम् *abhi-kram,* cl. 1. P. A., cl. 4. P. *-krāmati, -kramate, -krāmyati, -kramitum,* to step or go near to, approach; to fly at, attack; to step upon; to undertake, begin: Caus. *-kramayati, -yitum,* to bring near.

Abhi-krama, as, m. assault, attack; ascending, mounting; undertaking, attempt, beginning. — *Abhi-krama-nāśa, as,* m. unsuccessful effort.

Abhi-kramaṇa, am, n. or *abhi-krānti, is,* f. stepping near, approaching.

Abhi-krānta, as, ā, am, approached; attacked, begun.

Abhi-krāntin, ī, inī, i, one who has undertaken; conversant with (with loc.).

Abhi-krāmam, ind. having stepped near.

अभिक्री *abhi-krī,* cl. 9. P. A. *-krīṇāti, -ṇīte, -kretum,* to buy for a certain purpose.

अभिक्रुध् *abhi-krudh,* cl. 4. P. *-krudhyati, -kroddhum,* to be angry with (with acc.).

अभिक्रुश् *abhi-kruś,* cl. 1. P. *-krośati, -kroshṭum,* to cry out at, call out to; to call to any one in a scolding manner; to lament with tears, to bemoan.

Abhi-krośaka, as, m. a reviler, one who calls out; a herald (?).

अभिक्षत्तृ *abhi-kshattṛi, tā,* m., Ved. murderer, destroyer.

अभिक्षदा *abhi-kshadā,* f., Ved. (according to native interpretation) destroying, a destroyer. It is better, perhaps, to divide thus, *a-bhiksha-dā, ās,* m. giving without having been asked.

अभिक्षम् *abhi-ksham,* cl. 1. A. *-kshamate, -kshantum,* to be gracious, propitious, to allow, to pardon.

अभिक्षर् *abhi-kshar,* cl. 1. P. A. *-ksharati, -te, -ritum,* Ved. *-radhyai,* to flow near or round, to pour on.

अभिक्षिप् *abhi-kship,* cl. 6. P. *-kshipati, -ksheptum,* to fling at (as the lash of a whip at a horse), to insult; to excel.

Abhi-kshipat, an, atī or *antī, at,* surpassing.

अभिखन् *abhi-khan,* cl. 1. P. A. *-khanati, -te, -nitum,* to dig up, to turn up (the soil).

अभिख्या 1. *abhi-khyā,* cl. 2. P., Ved. *-khyāti, -tum,* to see, view, perceive; to cast a kind or gracious look upon any one, to be gracious: in later Sanskrit the rt. *khyā* conveys the idea of telling, making known: Caus. *-khyāpayati, -yitum,* to make known.

2. *abhi-khyā,* f. look, view; splendor; beauty; fame, glory; notoriety; telling; calling, addressing; a name, appellation.

Abhi-khyāta, as, ā, am, become known, manifested.

Abhi-khyātṛi, tā, trī, tṛi, Ved. looking, supervising, superintending.

Abhi-khyāna, am, n. fame, glory.

अभिगम् *abhi-gam,* cl. 1. P. *-gaććhati, -gantum,* to go near to, approach (with acc.); to follow; to meet with, to find; to cohabit, have intercourse with a woman; to undertake; to get, gain, obtain: Caus. *-gamayati, -yitum,* to cause to obtain, to cause to apprehend, to explain.

Abhi-gaććhat, an, antī, at, approaching, &c.

Abhi-gata, as, ā, am, approached, &c.

Abhi-gantṛi, tā, m. one who approaches, one who has intercourse with a woman; one who understands.

Abhi-gama, as, m. or *abhi-gamana, am,* n. approaching, visiting; sexual intercourse.

1. *abhi-gamya, as, ā, am,* to be visited; accessible; inviting.

2. *abhi-gamya,* ind. having approached.

Abhi-gāmin, ī, inī, i, having intercourse with.

अभिगर *abhi-gara.* See *abhi-gṝ* below.

अभिगर्ज् *abhi-garj,* cl. 1. P. *-garjati, -jitum,* to roar at, to bawl at; to raise savage or ferocious cries.

Abhi-garjana, am, n. ferocious roaring, uproar.

Abhi-garjita, am, n. a savage cry, uproar.

अभिगा *abhi-gā,* cl. 3. P. *-jigāti, -gātum,* to go near to, to approach, arrive at; to get, gain.

अभिगाह् *abhi-gāh,* cl. 1. A. *-gāhate, -hitum, -gāḍhum,* to penetrate into.

अभिगुप् *abhi-gup,* cl. 1. P. *-gopāyati, -goptum,* or Caus. *-gopayati, -yitum,* to guard, protect.

Abhi-gupta, as, ā, am, guarded, protected, hidden, concealed.

Abhi-gupti, is, f. guarding, protecting.

Abhi-goptṛi, tā, trī, tṛi, guarding, protecting.

अभिगुर् *abhi-gur,* cl. 6. P. A. *-gurati, -te, -ritum,* to assent, agree, approve of.

Abhi-gūrta, as, ā, am, approved of, destined for (an offering, &c.), accompanied with applause (?).

Abhi-gūrti, is, f., Ved. making resolution or effort, song of praise, hymn (?).

अभिगॄ *abhi-gṝ,* cl. 9. P. A., Ved. *-gṛiṇāti, -ṇīte, -garitum* or *-rītum,* to call to or address with approbation; to join in; to welcome, praise; to approve of, to accept propitiously, to allow.

Abhi-gara, as, m., Ved. song of praise; praising.

अभिगै *abhi-gai,* cl. 1. P. *-gāyati, -gātum,* to call to, to sing to; to fill with song; to enchant; to sing, celebrate in song.

अभिग्रस् *abhi-gras,* cl. 1. A. *-grasate, -situm,* to overcome.

Abhi-grasta, as, ā, am, subdued, overcome.

अभिग्रह् *abhi-grah,* Ved. *-grabh,* cl. 9. P. A. *-gṛihṇāti, -ṇīte,* Ved. *-gṛibhṇāti, -ṇīte, -grahītum,* to seize, catch, take hold of; accept; to set (as a blossom); to lay together, to fold; to receive (as a guest): Caus. *-grāhayati, -yitum,* to catch, surprise in the act; to let one's self be caught; e. g. *rūpābhigrāhita, as, ā, am,* taken in the very act.

Abhi-gṛihīta, as, ā, am, seized, taken hold of. — *Abhigṛihīta-pāṇi, is, is, i,* having the hands joined.

Abhi-graha, as, m. attack, onset; defiance, challenge; seizing, robbing, plundering; authority, weight.

Abhi-grahaṇa, am, n. robbing, seizing anything in presence of the owner.

अभिघर्षण *abhi-gharshaṇa, am,* n. (rt. *ghṛish*), rubbing, friction; possession by an evil spirit.

अभिघात *abhi-ghāta, as,* m. (rt. *han*), striking, attack, infliction of injury, damage; striking back, driving away, warding off; abrupt or vehement articulation of Vedic texts; *(am),* n. the combination of the fourth letter of any class with the first or third letter; of the second with the first letter; and of the third with the second letter of any class.

Abhi-ghātaka, as, ikā, am, keeping back, removing.

Abhi-ghātin, ī, inī, i, striking, attacking, hurting; inflicting injury; (ī), m. an assailant, enemy.

अभिघृ *abhi-ghṛi,* Caus. P. *-ghārayati, -yitum,* to cause to trickle down; to sprinkle with.

Abhi-ghāra, as, m. ghee or clarified butter, dropping it on the oblation.

Abhi-ghāraṇa, am, n. the act of sprinkling ghee, besprinkling.

Abhi-ghārita, as, ā, am, sprinkled (as ghee), dropped upon.

Abhi-ghārya, as, ā, am, to be sprinkled.

अभिघ्रा *abhi-ghrā,* cl. 1. P. *-jighrati, -ghrātum,* to snuffle, smell at; to bring the nose close to another's forehead in caressing, or as a token of affection.

अभिचक्ष् *abhi-ćaksh,* cl. 2. A. *-ćashṭe, -shṭum,* to look at, view, perceive; to oversee; to cast a kind or gracious look upon any one; to address, to assail with harsh language; to call.

Abhi-ćakshaṇa, am, n., Ved. caution, means of defence; magic remedy; (ā), f., Ved. viewing, indicating (?).

Abhi-ćakshya, as, ā, am, to be spoken of everywhere.

अभिचर् *abhi-ćar,* cl. 1. P. *-ćarati, -ritum,* Ved. *-ritave, -vai, -rase, -radhyai,* to act wrongly towards any one; to be faithless (as a wife); to charm, enchant, exorcise; to possess.

Abhi-ćara, as, m. a servant.

Abhi-ćaraṇa, am, n. enchanting, exorcising.

Abhi-ćaraṇīya, as, ā, am, fit for enchanting or exorcising.

Abhi-ćarat, an, antī, at, employing spells or enchantments.

Abhi-ćaritu, us, f., Ved. enchanting. — *Abhi-ćaritos,* to enchant.

Abhi-ćāra, as, m. exorcising, incantation, employment of spells for a malevolent purpose; magic, one of the Upapātakas or minor crimes. — *Abhićāra-kalpa, as,* m. title of a work on incantations, belonging to the Atharva-veda. — *Abhićāra-jvara, as,* m. a fever caused by magical spells. — *Abhićāra-mantra, as,* m. a formula or prayer for working a charm, an incantation. — *Abhićāra-yajña* or *abhićāra-homa, as,* m. a sacrifice for the same purpose.

Abhi-ćāraka, as, ikā, am, or *abhi-ćārin, ī, iṇī, i,* enchanting, exorcising, conjuring; a conjurer, a magician.

Abhi-ćāraṇīya or *abhi-ćārya, as, ā, am,* to be enchanted.

Abhi-ćārita, as, ā, am, enchanted, charmed.

अभिचाकशीति **abhi-ćākaśīti.** See *abhi-kāś*, p. 61, col. 1.

अभिचिन्त् **abhi-ćint**, cl. 10. P. *-ćintayati, -yitum*, to reflect on.

अभिचिह्नय **abhi-ćihnaya**, nom. P. *-ćihnayati, -yitum*, to mark, characterize.

अभिचुद् **abhi-ćud**, Caus. P. *-ćodayati, -yitum*, to impel, drive; to inflame, animate, embolden; to invite; to fix, settle; to announce, inquire for.

अभिचैद्य **abhi-ćaidya**, *as*, m., N. of Śiśupāla.

अभिच्छद् **abhi-ććhad** (*-ćhad*), cl. 10. P. *-ććhādayati* or *-ććhadayati, -yitum*, to cover over.

अभिच्छायम् **abhi-ććhāyam**, ind., Ved. in darkness.

अभिजग्मिवस् **abhi-jagmivas**, *vān, mushī, vat*, perf. part. of *abhi-gam*, q. v., p. 61, col. 2.

अभिजन् **abhi-jan**, cl. 4. A. *-jāyate, -janitum*, to be born for or to; to claim as one's birth-right; to be born or produced; to be reproduced or born again; to become.

Abhi-ja, as, ā, am, produced all around.

Abhi-jana, as, m. family, race; descendants; ancestors; noble descent; the head or ornament of a family; native country; fame, notoriety. — *Abhijana-vat, ān, atī, at*, of noble descent.

Abhi-janitu, us, f., Ved. the being born or produced. — *Abhi-janitos*, to produce.

Abhi-jāta, as, ā, am, produced all around; born in consequence of; born, produced; noble, well-born; obtained by birth, inbred; fit, proper; wise, learned; handsome; (*am*), n. nativity. — *Abhijāta-tā*, f. high birth, nobility.

Abhi-jāti, is, f. descent, birth.

अभिजप् **abhi-jap**, cl. 1. P. *-japati, -pitum*, to mutter over or whisper to.

अभिजभ् **abhi-jabh**, Intens., Ved. *-jañjabhyate*, to try to swallow, open the mouth to do so.

अभिजल्प् **abhi-jalp**, cl. 1. P. *-jalpati, -pitum*, to address, to accompany with remarks; to advocate, to settle by conversation.

अभिजि **abhi-ji**, cl. 1. P. *-jayati, -jetum*, to conquer completely, to acquire by conquest: Desid. *-jigīshati*, to try to win, to attack.

Abhi-jaya, as, m. conquest, complete victory.

Abhi-jit, t, t, t, victorious; born under the constellation Abhijit; (*t*), m., N. of Vishṇu; of a Soma sacrifice, part of the great sacrifice Gavām-ayana; N. of a son of Punarvasu, or of his father; (*t*), f., N. of a star (α Lyræ); one of the Nakshatras or lunar mansions; (*t*), n. the eighth Muhūrta of the day; midday. — *Abhijin-muhūrta, as*, m. the eighth Muhūrta, or period comprising twenty-four minutes before and twenty-four after midday.

Abhi-jita, as, m., N. of an asterism.

Abhi-jiti, is, f., Ved. victory, conquest.

अभिजिघ्रण **abhi-jighraṇa**, *am*, n. the act of smelling at or touching the forehead of another with the nose. See *abhi-ghrā*, p. 61, col. 3.

अभिजुष् **abhi-jush**, cl. 6. A., or Ved. P. *-jushate, -ti, -joshitum*, to visit, to frequent, to be pleased with, to be contented with, to like.

Abhi-jushṭa, as, ā, am, visited, frequented, surrounded by, possessed of.

अभिजृम्भ् **abhi-jṛimbh**, cl. 1. A. *-jṛimbhate, -bhitum*, to open the mouth wide (for swallowing).

अभिज्ञा **abhi-jñā**, cl. 9. P. A. *-jānāti, -nīte, -jñātum*, to recognize, perceive, know, be or become aware of; to acknowledge, agree to, own.

Abhi-jña, as, ā, am, knowing, skilful, clever; (with gen.) one who understands or is conversant with; (*ā*), f. remembrance, recollection, recognition; supernatural science or faculty, of which five are enumerated, viz. 1. taking any form at will; 2. hearing to any distance; 3. seeing to any distance; 4. penetrating men's thoughts; 5. knowing their state and antecedents.

Abhi-jñāna, am, n. remembrance, recollection; knowledge; ascertainment; a sign or token of remembrance. — *Abhijñāna-pattra, am*, n. certificate. — *Abhijñāna-śakuntala, am*, n. title of a play of Kālidāsa, i. e. (the *nāṭaka* or play) on the subject of 'token-(recognized)-Śakuntalā.'

Abhi-jñāpaka, as, ikā, am, making known, informing.

Abhi-jñāya, ind. having recognized.

अभिज्ञु **abhi-jñu**, ind., Ved. on the knees, up to the knees.

अभिज्वल् **abhi-jval**, cl. 1. P. *-jvalati, -litum*, to blaze forth, burst into flame.

अभिडीन **abhi-ḍīna**, *am*, n. (rt. *ḍī*), act of flying towards.

अभितंस् **abhi-taṇs**, cl. 1. 10. P., Ved. *-taṇsati, -situm, -sayati, -yitum*, to shake out of, to rob.

अभितड् **abhi-taḍ**, cl. 10. P. *-tāḍayati, -yitum*, to thump, hit, knock, beat, wound, bruise; (in astron.) to eclipse the greater part of a disk.

Abhi-tāḍita, as, ā, am, knocked, struck.

अभितन् **abhi-tan**, cl. 8. P. *-tanoti, -nitum*, to stretch or spread in front of or across or over; to place in front of.

अभितप् **abhi-tap**, cl. 1. P. *-tapati, -ptum*, to irradiate with heat, to heat; to pain, distress: Pass. *-tapyate*, to suffer intensely: Caus. *-tāpayati, -yitum*, to distress.

Abhi-tapta, as, ā, am, scorched, burnt, afflicted.

Abhi-tāpa, as, m. extreme heat; agitation, affliction, emotion; great pain.

अभितराम् **abhi-tarām**, ind. (compar. fr. *abhi*), nearer to.

अभितर्ज् **abhi-tarj**, cl. 1. P. or poet. A. *-tarjati, -te, -jitum*; cl. 10. P. or poet. A. *-tarjayati, -te, -yitum*, to scold, abuse.

अभितस् **abhi-tas**, ind. (Lat. *apud*, Eng. *about*), near to, towards; near, in the proximity or presence; (with acc.) on both sides; before and after; on all sides, everywhere, about, round; quickly; entirely. — *Abhito-bhāva, as*, m. the state of being on both sides. — *Abhito-rātram*, ind., Ved. near the night, i. e. either just at the beginning or end. — *Abhito-'sthi* (°*tas-as*°), *is, is, i*, surrounded by bones.

अभिताम्र **abhi-tāmra**, *as, ā, am*, dark-red, very red, murry-coloured.

अभितिग्मरश्मि **abhi-tigmaraśmi**, ind. towards the sun.

अभितृद् **abhi-tṛid**, cl. 7. P., Ved. *-tṛiṇatti, -tarditum*, to burst open; to let out; get at, procure.

अभितृप् **abhi-tṛip**, Caus. P. *-tarpayati, -yitum*, to satiate, refresh.

Abhi-tṛipta, as, ā, am, satiated, refreshed.

अभितॄ **abhi-tṛī**, cl. 1. P. *-tarati, -ritum* or *-rītum*, to overtake, get up to.

अभित्ति **a-bhitti**, *is*, f. not splintering or breaking.

अभित्वर् **abhi-tvar**, cl. 1. A. *-tvarate, -ritum*, to be in haste.

अभित्सर् **abhi-tsar**, cl. 1. P., Ved. *-tsarati, -ritum*, to catch, entrap.

अभिदक्षिणम् **abhi-dakshiṇam**, ind. to or towards the right.

अभिदधत् **abhi-dadhat**, *at, atī, at*, addressing. See 1. *abhi-dhā* below.

अभिदर्शन **abhi-darśana.** See *abhi-dṛiś* below.

अभिदष्ट **abhi-dashṭa**, *as, ā, am* (rt. *daṇś*), bitten.

अभिदह् **abhi-dah**, cl. 1. P. *-dahati, -dagdhum*, to singe, burn.

अभिदा **abhi-dā**, cl. 3. P. *-dadāti, -dātum*, to give, bestow (for a purpose).

Abhi-dāpana, am, n. the being trampled on by elephants as a punishment (?).

अभिदास् **abhi-dās**, cl. 1. P., Ved. *-dāsati, -situm*, to consider and treat as an enemy.

अभिदिग्ध **abhi-digdha**, *as, ā, am* (rt. *dih*), besmeared, especially with poison.

अभिदिप्सु **abhi-dipsu**, *us, us, u* (*dips*, Desid. of rt. *dambh*), Ved. wishing to deceive, inimical, cunning.

अभिदिश् **abhi-diś**, cl. 6. P. *-diśati, -deshṭum*, to point out.

Abhi-dishṭa, as, ā, am, pointed out.

अभिदुष् **abhi-dush**, cl. 10. or Caus. P. *-dūshayati, -yitum*, to contaminate, to wound.

Abhi-dushṭa, as, ā, am, contaminated, polluted.

Abhi-dūshita, as, ā, am, wounded, injured.

अभिदूति **abhi-dūti**, ind. to or towards a female messenger.

अभिदृश् **abhi-dṛiś**, cl. 1. P. *-paśyati, -drashṭum*, to look at: Caus. P. *-darśayati, -yitum*, to show, point out; to show one's self, i. e. appear: Pass. *-dṛiśyate*, to be visible, be in view, appear; to be considered or thought.

Abhi-darśana, am, n. seeing; becoming visible, appearance.

अभिद्यु **abhi-dyu**, *us, us, u*, Ved. directed to heaven, tending or going to heaven; heavenly, bright; (*us*), m. a half month.

अभिद्युत् **abhi-dyut**, cl. 1. A. *-dyotate, -titum*, to burn.

अभिद्रु **abhi-dru**, cl. 1. P. and poet. A. *-dravati, -te, -drotum*, to run up to or near; to attack, overrun, infest.

Abhi-druta, as, ā, am, run towards, attacked.

Abhi-drutya, ind. having attacked.

अभिद्रुह् 1. **abhi-druh**, cl. 4. P. *-druhyati, -drogdhum, -droḍhum*, to hate, seek to injure or maliciously assail.

Abhi-drugdha, as, ā, am, injured, oppressed.

2. *abhi-druh, -dhruk, k, k*, Ved. seeking to injure, inimical, cunning.

Abhi-druhyamāṇa, as, ā, am, being injured or oppressed.

Abhi-droha, as, m. injuring, hurting, oppression, cruelty.

अभिधन्व् **abhi-dhanv**, cl. 1. P. A., Ved. *-dhanvati, -te, -vitum*, to come up in haste.

अभिधर्म **abhi-dharma**, *as*, m. the supreme truth according to the Buddhists, the dogmas of Buddhist philosophy or metaphysics. — *Abhidharma-kośa, as*, m. title of a work on the preceding. — *Abhidharma-piṭaka, as*, m. 'basket of metaphysics,' title of that section of Buddhist writings which contains the *abhi-dharma*.

अभिधर्षण **abhi-dharshaṇa**, *am*, n. (rt. *dhṛish*), possession by demoniac spirits.

Abhi-dhṛishṇu, us, us, u, Ved. overpowering, subduing (with acc.).

अभिधा 1. **abhi-dhā**, cl. 3. P. A. *-dadhāti*,

-dhatte, -dhātum, to set forth, explain, tell, speak to, address, say, name; A., Ved. to receive; P. (corruption of *abhi-dhāvati?*), to assail: Pass. *-dhīyate,* to be named or called.

2. *abhi-dhā,* f. name, appellation; the literal power or sense of a word; a word, sound; (*ās, ās*), m. f., Ved. naming; praised; invoked (?). — *Abhidhā-dhvaṅsin, ī, inī, i,* losing one's name. — *Abhidhā-mūla, as, ā, am,* founded on the literal meaning of a word.

Abhi-dhātavya, as, ā, am, to be told or named, to be manifested.

Abhi-dhāna, am, n. telling, naming, speaking, speech, manifesting; (*as, am*), m. n. a name, title, appellation, expression, word; a vocabulary, a dictionary. — *Abhidhāna-ćintāmaṇi, is,* m. title of Hemaćandra's vocabulary of synonyms (the jewel that gives every word that can be imagined). — *Abhidhāna-tva, am,* n. the state of being used as a name or expression. — *Abhidhāna-mālā,* f. a dictionary. — *Abhidhāna-ratnamālā,* f. title of Halāyudha's vocabulary.

Abhi-dhānaka, am, n. a sound, a noise.

Abhi-dhānī, f., Ved. a halter, a rope.

Abhi-dhānīya, as, ā, am, to be named.

Abhi-dhāya, ind. having said, having called.

Abhi-dhāyaka, as, ikā, am, or *abhi-dhāyin, ī, inī, i,* naming, expressing, expressive of, denominating; telling, speaking. — *Abhidhāyaka-tva, am,* n. the state of being expressive.

Abhi-dhāyam, ind. expressing.

Abhi-dhitsā, f. desire of expressing or naming.

Abhi-dheya, as, ā, am, to be named or mentioned; to be expressed, to be spoken of; (*am*), n. signification, meaning. — *Abhidheya-rahita, as, ā, am,* having no sense or meaning, unmeaning, nonsensical.

Abhi-hita, abhi-hiti. See s. v. below.

अभिधाव् *abhi-dhāv,* cl. 1. P. A. *-dhāvati, -te, -vitum,* to run up towards, to rush upon, attack.

Abhi-dhāvaka, as, ikā, am, running up, hastening towards, assailing; an assailant.

Abhi-dhāvana, am, n. running up, pursuit, chase, attack.

अभिधृ *abhi-dhṛi,* Caus. P. *-dhārayati, -yitum,* to uphold, maintain.

अभिध्यै *abhi-dhyai,* cl. 1. P. *-dhyāyati, -dhyātum,* to consider, reflect, meditate upon.

Abhi-dhyā, f. coveting another's property; desire, wish, longing for in general.

Abhi-dhyāna, am, n. desiring, longing for; wish; meditation, profound thought.

Abhi-dhyāyat, an, antī, at, coveting, desiring.

Abhi-dhyāyamāna, as, ā, am, being meditated on.

अभिध्वन् *abhi-dhvan,* cl. 1. P. *-dhvanati, -nitum,* to resound, shout.

अभिनक्ष् *abhi-naksh,* cl. 1. P. *-nakshati, -kshitum,* to encompass; Ved. to bring, to approach, come to, arrive at.

अभिनद् *abhi-nad,* cl. 1. P. *-nadati, -ditum,* to sound towards a person (with acc.); to sound, raise a noise: Caus. *-nādayati, -yitum,* to cause to sound, fill with noise: Pass. to resound.

अभिनद्ध *abhi-naddha, as, ā, am* (rt. *nah*), bound, tied round, fastened on or upon. — *Abhinaddhāksha* (°*dha-ak*°), *as, ī, am,* blindfold.

अभिनन्द् *abhi-nand,* cl. 1. P. A. *-nandati, -te, -ditum,* to rejoice at, salute, welcome, address, congratulate; to praise, applaud, approve, respect, care for; to acknowledge: Caus. *-nandayati, -yitum,* to gladden.

Abhi-nanda, as, m. rejoicing, delighting; applauding; wish, desire; N. of a commentator or commentary on the Amara-kosha; N. of another author; (*ā*), f. delight, wish.

Abhi-nandana, am, n. delighting, rejoicing; praising, applauding, approving; wish, desire; (*as*), m. the fourth Jaina Arhat of the present Avasarpiṇī.

Abhi-nandanīya or 1. *abhi-nandya, as, ā, am,* to be acknowledged or applauded.

Abhi-nandita, as, ā, am, delighted, made happy, saluted, applauded, &c.

Abhi-nandin, ī, inī, i, rejoicing at, wishing, desiring, &c.

2. *abhi-nandya,* ind. having rejoiced at, having gladdened.

अभिनभ्यम् *abhi-nabhyam,* ind., Ved. towards the clouds or heaven.

अभिनम् *abhi-nam,* cl. 1. P. *-namati, -nantum,* to bow, bend, curve; to turn towards a person.

Abhi-nata, as, ā, am, bent, inclined.

Abhi-namra, as, ā, am, bent, deeply bowed or curved.

अभिनय *abhi-naya.* See 1. *abhi-nī,* p. 64.

अभिनर्द् *abhi-nard,* cl. 1. P., ep. also A. *-nardati, -te, -ditum,* to roar towards.

अभिनव *abhi-nava, as, ā, am,* quite new or young, very young, fresh; not having experience. — *Abhinava-ćandrārgha-vidhi* (°*ra-ar*°), *is,* m. a ceremony performed at the time of the new moon. — *Abhinava-yauvana, as, ā, am,* youthful. — *Abhinava-vaiyākaraṇa, as,* m. one who has just begun grammar. — *Abhinavodbhid* (°*va-ud*°), *t,* m. a new bud.

Abhinavī-bhū, cl. 1. P. *-bhavati, -vitum,* to become new. — *Abhinavī-bhūta, as, ā, am,* renewed.

अभिनश् *abhi-naś,* cl. 1. P. A., Ved. *-naśati, -te, -śitum,* to attain, seize; to assail.

अभिनह् *abhi-nah,* cl. 4. P. A. *-nahyati, -te, -naddhum,* to bind up (as the eyes).

Abhi-nahana, am, n. a bandage (especially over the eyes.)

अभिनासिकाविवरम् *abhi-nāsikāvivaram,* ind. to the opening of the nose.

अभिनिःस्तन् *abhi-niḥ-stan* (*-nir-stan*), cl. 1. P. *-stanati, -nitum,* to sound.

Abhi-nishṭāna, as, m. a sound which dies away; the Visarga; a letter of the alphabet.

अभिनिक्रम् *abhi-ni-kram,* cl. 1. P. A., cl. 4. P. *-krāmati, -kramate, -krāmyati, -kramitum,* to tread down.

अभिनिगद् *abhi-ni-gad,* cl. 1. P. *-gadati, -ditum,* to speak to.

अभिनिधन *abhi-nidhana, am,* n., N. of certain verses of the Sāma-veda.

अभिनिधान *abhi-nidhāna, am,* n. putting on; an euphonic suppression or weakening (in the pronunciation of words), especially the suppression of an initial *a* after *e, o.*

Abhi-nidhīyamāna, as, ā, am, being suppressed.

अभिनिध्यै *abhi-ni-dhyai,* cl. 1. P. *-dhyāyati, -dhyātum,* to investigate.

अभिनिनी *abhi-ni-nī,* cl. 1. P. A. *-nayati, -te, -netum,* to pour out (water &c.) upon.

अभिनिनृत् *abhi-ni-nṛit,* cl. 4. P., Ved. *-nṛityati, -nartitum,* to accomplish step by step, repeat separately.

अभिनिपत् *abhi-ni-pat,* Caus. P. *-pātayati, -yitum,* to throw down.

अभिनिपीड् *abhi-ni-pīḍ,* cl. 10. P. *-pīḍayati, -yitum,* to press, squeeze, trouble.

Abhi-nipīḍita, as, ā, am, exceedingly pained, tormented.

अभिनिम्रुच् *abhi-ni-mluć,* cl. 1. P. *-mloćati, -ćitum,* to set (as the sun) upon a person (while some act is being done by him).

अभिनियुक्त *abhi-niyukta, as, ā, am* (rt. *yuj*), occupied in.

अभिनिर्गम् *abhi-nir-gam,* cl. 1. P. *-gaććhati, -gantum,* to go out, go away from.

अभिनिर्जित *abhi-nirjita, as, ā, am* (rt. *ji*), conquered.

अभिनिर्णुद् *abhi-nir-ṇud* (*-nir-nud*), cl. 6. P. A. *-ṇudati, -te, -ṇottum,* to drive out, frighten away, remove.

अभिनिर्दिश् *abhi-nir-diś,* cl. 6. P. *-diśati, -deshṭum,* to point out, indicate, appoint, characterize.

अभिनिर्भर्त्स् *abhi-nir-bharts,* cl. 10. A. or P. *-bhartsayate, -ti, -yitum,* to scold, threaten.

अभिनिर्मित *abhi-nirmita, as, ā, am* (rt. *mā*), made, created.

अभिनिर्मुक्त *abhi-nirmukta, as, ā, am* (rt. *muć*), left, quitted (by the sun when it sets), i. e. one asleep at sunset.

अभिनिर्या *abhi-nir-yā,* cl. 2. P. *-yāti, -tum,* to march out.

Abhi-niryāṇa, am, n. march of an assailant, invasion.

अभिनिर्वृत्त *abhi-nirvṛitta, as, ā, am,* accomplished.

Abhi-nirvṛitti, is, f. accomplishment.

अभिनिवर्त *abhi-nivarta, as,* m. turning towards; (*am*), ind. having turned towards.

अभिनिविश् *abhi-ni-viś,* cl. 1. A. *-viśate, -veshṭum,* to enter into possession of; to sit down in or be settled in, to occupy: Caus. *-veśayati, -yitum,* to make one enter into or sit down, apply, &c.

Abhi-nivishṭa, as, ā, am, well versed or proficient in, conversant or familiar with; intent on; attentive, engrossed; endowed with; determined; (*am*), n. persevering. — *Abhinivishṭa-tā,* f. state of being so.

Abhi-niveśa, as, m. application, perseverance, intentness, study, affection, devotion; determination to effect a purpose or attain an object; tenacity, adherance; ignorant fear causing death (?).

Abhi-niveśita, as, ā, am, made to enter into, plunged into.

Abhi-niveśin, ī, inī, i, intent upon, devoted to, determined.

अभिनिशम् *abhi-ni-śam,* cl. 4. P. *-śāmyati, -śamitum,* or Caus. P. *-śāmayati, -yitum,* to observe, perceive.

अभिनिश्चित *abhi-niśćita, as, ā, am* (rt. *ći*), quite convinced of.

अभिनिष्कारिन् *abhi-nish-kārin, ī, iṇī, i* (rt. *kṛi*), Ved. intending anything evil against, injuring.

Abhi-nishkṛita, as, ā, am, directed against (as an evil action).

अभिनिष्क्रम् *abhi-nish-kram* (*-nis-kram*), cl. 1. P. A., cl. 4. P. *-krāmati, -kramate, -krāmyati, -kramitum,* to go out or forth, to lead towards.

Abhi-nishkramaṇa, am, n. going forth; (with Buddhists) leaving the house in order to become an anchorite.

Abhi-nishkrānta, as, ā, am, gone out or forth.

अभिनिष्टान *abhi-nishṭāna.* See *abhi-niḥ-stan* last col.

अभिनिष्पत् *abhi-nish-pat* (*-nis-pat*), cl. 1. P. *-patati, -titum,* to fly away, rush out; to spring forth, shoot forth.

Abhi-nishpatana, am, n. issuing, sallying.

अभिनिष्पद् *abhi-nish-pad* (*-nis-pad*), cl. 4. A. *-padyate, -pattum,* to come to; to enter into, become (with acc.); to appear: Caus. *-pādayati, -yitum,* to bring to, help to.

Abhi-nishpatti, is, f. completion, end, termination; appearance (?).

Abhi-nishpanna, as, ā, am, finished, completed.

अभिनिह्नव *abhi-nihnava, as,* m. (rt. *hnu*), denial.

अभिनी 1. *abhi-nī,* cl. 1. P. *-nayati, -netum,* to bring near, conduct towards, adduce, introduce, quote; represent dramatically, act.

Abhi-naya, as, m. indication of a passion or purpose by look, gesture, &c.; acting, dramatic action expressive of sentiment, dramatic personification.

Abhi-nīta, as, ā, am, brought near, adduced; performed; highly finished or ornamented; fit, proper; friendly, kind, patient; impatient, passionate (?).

Abhi-nīti, is, f. gesture, expressive gesticulation; friendship, civility, kindness.

Abhi-niyamāna, as, ā, am, being brought near, &c.

Abhi-netavya or *abhi-neya, as, ā, am,* to be represented dramatically.

Abhi-netṛi, tā, trī, m. f. an actor, an actress.

अभिनी 2. *abhi-nī (abhi-ni-i),* cl. 2. P. *-nyeti, -tum,* to go in to, to approach a woman.

अभिनील *abhi-nīla, as, ā, am,* very black, very dark.

अभिनु 1. *abhi-nu,* cl. 2. 6. P. *-nauti, -nuvati, -navitum* or *-nuvitum,* to extol, praise.

अभिनु 2. *abhi-nu,* cl. 1. A., Ved. *-navate,* to turn one's self towards.

अभिनुद् *abhi-nud,* cl. 6. P. A. *-nudati, -te, -nottum,* to push, press: Caus. *-nodayati, -yitum,* to excite, to spur or urge on.

अभिन्न *a-bhinna, as, ā, am* (rt. *bhid*), uncut, unbroken; unchanged, unaltered, not different; undivided, one; same, identical; *(as),* m. an integer, a whole number (in arithmetic). — *Abhinna-tā,* f. wholeness, identity. — *Abhinna-parikarmāshṭaka* (°*ma-ash*°), *am,* n. eight processes in working integers or whole numbers. — *Abhinnātman* (°*na-āt*°), *ā, ā, a,* of undaunted spirit, firm.

अभिन्यस् *abhi-ny-as (-ni-as),* cl. 4. P. *-asyati, -situm,* to depress.

Abhi-nyāsa, as, m. a kind of fever.

अभिन्युब्ज् *abhi-ny-ubj (-ni-ubj),* cl. 6. P. *-ubjati, -jitum,* to press down, to hold down.

अभिपच् *abhi-pać,* cl. 1. P. A. *-paćati, -te, -paktum,* to boil up (as milk).

अभिपठित *abhi-paṭhita, as, ā, am,* denominated, named.

अभिपत् 1. *abhi-pat,* cl. 1. P. *-patati, -titum,* to fly near, hasten near; to assail; to fall down, fall; to fall into, come into; to overtake in flying: Caus. *-pātayati, -yitum,* to throw on or down.

Abhi-patana, am, n. approaching, assailing, seizing; falling into.

अभिपत् 2. *abhi-pat,* cl. 4. A., Ved. *-patyate,* to be master or lord over, to possess.

अभिपद् *abhi-pad,* cl. 4. A. *-padyate, -pattum,* to draw near, approach; to come up (as an auxiliary), assist; to honour; to seize, catch, overpower, master; to take possession of; to accept; to undertake, devote one's self to anything.

Abhi-patti, is, f. drawing near, approaching.

Abhi-panna, as, ā, am, gone near; approached, obtained; flown, fugitive; seeking refuge; subdued; unfortunate, calamitous; guilty; removed to a distance, dead.

अभिपद्म *abhi-padma, as, ā, am,* exceedingly handsome (lit. superior to the lotus).

अभिपरिग्लान *abhi-pariglāna, as, ā, am* (rt. *glai*), tired, exhausted.

अभिपरिप्लु *abhi-pari-plu,* cl. 1. A. *-plavate, -plotum,* to stream or flow so as to inundate, to overflow.

Abhi-pariplutā, as, ā, am, overwhelmed, overflowed, filled with; shaken; attacked, affected by.

अभिपरिष्वञ्ज् *abhi-pari-shvañj (-svañj),* cl. 1. A. *-shvajate, -shvanktum,* to embrace.

अभिपरीत *abhi-parīta, as, ā, am* (rt. *i* with *abhi-pari*), surrounded, overpowered by, overwhelmed with.

अभिपरे *abhi-pare (-parā-i),* cl. 2. P. *-paraiti, -tum,* to go away towards.

अभिपर्ये *abhi-pary-e (-pari-ā-i),* cl. 2. P. *-paryaiti, -tum,* to go about; glide away, pass away.

अभिपा 1. *abhi-pā,* cl. 1. P. *-pibati, -pātum,* to drink of.

Abhi-pīta, as, ā, am, watered (as cattle), filled with drink.

अभिपा 2. *abhi-pā,* cl. 2. P. *-pāti, -tum,* to protect: Caus. P. *-pālayati, -yitum,* to protect, to assist.

अभिपित्व *abhi-pitva, am,* n. (for *abhi-apitva,* fr. obs. rt. *ap;* see *apa-pitva*), Ved. approaching, visiting, putting up (for the night at an inn), close or departure of day, evening; dawn; sacrifice.

अभिपीड् *abhi-pīḍ,* cl. 10. P. *-pīḍayati, -yitum,* to oppress, torment, afflict.

Abhi-pīḍita, as, ā, am, harassed.

अभिपुथ् *abhi-puth,* Caus. P. *-pothayati, -yitum,* to throw with violence; dash against.

अभिपुष्प *abhi-pushpa, as, ā, am,* covered with flowers; *(am),* n. an excellent flower.

अभिपू *abhi-pū,* cl. 1. A., Ved. *-pavate, -vitum,* to be cleared, to flow purified towards or for; to blow against; to make bright, glorify.

अभिपूज् *abhi-pūj,* cl. 10. P. *-pūjayati, -yitum,* to honour, approve, assent to.

Abhi-pūjita, as, ā, am, honoured; approved.

Abhi-pūjyamāna, as, ā, am, being greatly reverenced.

अभिपूर्वम् *abhi-pūrvam,* ind. one after the other.

अभिपृण् *abhi-priṇ,* cl. 6. P. *-priṇati, -partum,* to be filled; to be glad.

अभिपॄ *abhi-prī,* cl. 3. 9. P. *-piparti, -priṇāti, -paritum* or *-rītum,* to fill: Pass. *-pūryate,* to fill one's self, become full: Caus. *-pūrayati, -yitum,* to fill, make full; to load with, cover with; to present with; to master completely.

Abhi-pūraṇa, am, n. filling.

Abhi-pūrṇa, as, ā, am, full of (with inst. or gen.); filled; fraught; laden.

अभिप्यै *abhi-pyai,* cl. 1. A., Ved. *-pyāyate, -pyātum* or *-pyāyitum,* to swell, to abound with.

अभिप्रकम्प् *abhi-pra-kamp,* Caus. P. *-kampayati, -yitum,* to stir, allure.

अभिप्रकाश् *abhi-pra-kāś,* cl. 1. 4. A. *-kāśate, -kāśyate, -śitum,* to become visible, to show one's self.

अभिप्रक्रम् *abhi-pra-kram,* cl. 1. P. A., cl. 4. A. *-krāmati, -kramate, -krāmyati, -kramitum,* to go up to, approach.

अभिप्रक्षर् *abhi-pra-kshar,* cl. 1. P. A. *-ksharati, -te, -ritum,* Ved. *-radhyai,* to stream towards a place.

अभिप्रक्षल् *abhi-pra-kshal,* cl. 10. P. *-kshālayati, -yitum,* to clean thoroughly, polish up.

अभिप्रगाह् *abhi-pra-gāh,* cl. 1. A. *-gāhate, -hitum, -gāḍhum,* to penetrate, dip or plunge into, join: Caus. *-gāhayati, -yitum,* to immerse, dip.

अभिप्रगै *abhi-pra-gai,* cl. 1. P. *-gāyati, -gātum,* to begin to praise.

अभिप्रचक्ष् *abhi-pra-ćaksh,* cl. 2. A., Ved. *-ćashṭe, -shṭum,* to throw light upon; to see (?).

अभिप्रचुद् *abhi-pra-ćud,* Caus. P. *-ćodayati, -yitum,* to impel, induce, persuade.

अभिप्रच्यु *abhi-pra-ćyu,* cl. 1. A. *-ćyavate, -ćyotum,* to move towards, arrive at.

अभिप्रछ् *abhi-prać h,* cl. 6. P. *-pṛiććhati, -prashṭum,* to ask or inquire after.

अभिप्रजन् *abhi-pra-jan,* Caus. P. *-janayati, -yitum,* to beget for (a purpose).

अभिप्रज्वल् *abhi-pra-jval,* cl. 1. P. *-jvalati, -litum,* to flare up.

अभिप्रणक्ष् *abhi-pra-ṇaksh (-naksh),* cl. 1. P., Ved. *-ṇakshati, -shitum,* to overpower.

अभिप्रणद् *abhi-pra-ṇad (-nad),* cl. 1. P. A. *-ṇadati, -te, -ditum,* to shout at, to scream; to begin to roar or sound.

अभिप्रणम् *abhi-pra-ṇam (-nam),* cl. 1. P. A. *-ṇamati, -te, -ṇantum,* to bow before (with dat. or acc.).

Abhi-praṇata, as, ā, am, bent, bowing before.

अभिप्रणी *abhi-pra-ṇī (-nī),* cl. 1. P. *-ṇayati, -ṇetum,* to lead forth; bring towards.

Abhi-praṇaya, as, m. propitiation; affection, favour.

Abhi-praṇīta, as, ā, am, brought, attracted; consecrated; invoked, propitiated.

अभिप्रणु *abhi-pra-ṇu (-nu),* cl. 2. 6. P., Ved. *-ṇauti, -ṇuvati, -ṇavitum* or *-ṇuvitum,* to praise highly, extol.

अभिप्रतप्त *abhi-pratapta, as, ā, am* (rt. *tap*), intensely heated; dried up; exhausted with pain or fever.

अभिप्रतारिन् *abhi-pratārin, ī,* m., N. of a descendant of Kaksha-sena.

अभिप्रतिगॄ *abhi-prati-grī,* cl. 9. P. A. *-griṇāti, -ṇīte, -garitum* or *-rītum,* to call out to; to welcome; to answer in singing; to assent.

अभिप्रतिपद् *abhi-prati-pad,* cl. 4. A. *-padyate, -pattum,* to begin with or at.

अभिप्रतिपिष् *abhi-prati-pish,* cl. 7. P., Ved. *-pinashṭi, -peshṭum,* to dash or crush out.

अभिप्रत्यवे *abhi-praty-ave (-prati-ava-i),* cl. 2. P. *-pratyavaiti, -tum,* to step down towards.

अभिप्रत्ये *abhi-praty-e (-prati-ā-i),* cl. 2. P. *-pratyaiti, -tum,* to come back towards, return.

अभिप्रथन *abhi-prathana, am,* n. (rt. *prath*), spreading or extending over.

अभिप्रदक्षिणम् *abhi-pra-dakshiṇam,* ind. to the right; (e. g. with *kṛi,* to circumambulate keeping the object on the right.)

अभिप्रदिश् *abhi-pra-diś,* Caus. P. *-deśayati, -yitum,* to urge on.

अभिप्रदृश् *abhi-pra-dṛiś,* cl. 1. P., Ved. *-paśyati, -drashṭum,* to look at, look out for.

अभिप्रदॄ *abhi-pra-drī,* Pass. *-dīryate,* to be scattered or divided asunder.

अभिप्रपच् *abhi-pra-pać,* cl. 1. P. A. *-paćati, -te, -paktum,* to cause to cook, ripen; to develope.

अभिप्रपद् *abhi-pra-pad,* cl. 4. A. *-padyate,*

-pattum, to come towards, enter, hasten towards, resort to (with acc.); to undertake.

Abhi-prapanna, as, ā, am, approached, attained.

अभिप्रपीड् *abhi-pra-pīḍ,* Caus. P. *-pīḍayati, -yitum,* to cause pain, torture.

अभिप्रपॄ *abhi-pra-pṝ,* Pass. *-pūryate,* to be filled, fill one's self completely.

अभिप्रभङ्गिन् *abhi-pra-bhangin, ī, iṇī, i* (rt. *bhañj*), Ved. breaking completely.

अभिप्रमन्द् *abhi-pra-mand,* cl. 1. P., Ved. *-mandati, -ditum,* to gladden.

अभिप्रमुर् *abhi-pra-mur, ūr, ūr, ūr,* Ved. (if fr. rt. *murćh* or *mur*) completely raised, surrounded; (if fr. rt. *mṛi*) destroying (?).

अभिप्रमृश् *abhi-pra-mṛiś,* cl. 6. P., Ved. *-mṛiśati, -marshṭum, -mrashṭum,* to offer, grant.

अभिप्रया *abhi-pra-yā,* cl. 2. P. *-yāti, -tum,* to march against.

Abhi-prayāyam, ind. by approaching, having approached.

अभिप्रवृत् *abhi-pra-vṛit,* cl. 1. A. *-vartate, -titum,* to advance up to; to flow or fall into; to become conversant with.

Abhi-pravartana, am, n. coming forth, flowing; advancing up to.

Abhi-pravṛitta, as, ā, am, advancing; occurring; occupied or engaged in.

अभिप्रवृध् *abhi-pra-vṛidh,* Caus. P. *-vardhayati, -yitum,* to enlarge, render prosperous.

अभिप्रवृष् *abhi-pra-vṛish,* cl. 1. P. *-varshati, -shitum,* to pour down rain.

अभिप्रशंस् *abhi-pra-śans,* cl. 1. P. *-śansati, -situm,* to praise highly.

अभिप्रश्निन् *abhi-praśnin, ī, inī, i* (rt. *praćh*), desirous of asking many questions.

अभिप्रसद् *abhi-pra-sad,* cl. 1. P., Ved. *-sīdati, -sattum,* to come near, approach: Caus. P. *-sādayati, -yitum,* to propitiate, make happy, console.

अभिप्रस्था *abhi-pra-sthā,* cl. 1. P. *-tishṭhati, -sthātum,* to step up towards.

अभिप्रहत *abhi-prahata, as, ā, am* (rt. *han*), struck at, hurt.

अभिप्राण् *abhi-prāṇ (-pra-an),* cl. 2. P. *-prāṇiti, -ṇitum,* to exhale, breathe forth.

Abhi-prāṇana, am, n. exhaling (opposed to *apānana,* q. v.).

अभिप्रातर् *abhi-prātar,* ind., Ved. towards morning, early.

अभिप्राप् *abhi-prāp (-pra-āp),* cl. 5. P. *-prāpnoti, -ptum,* to reach, obtain, arrive at.

Abhi-prāpta, as, ā, am, reached, obtained, arrived.

Abhi-prāpti, is, f. reaching, obtaining, arrival.

Abhi-prepsu, us, us, u, desirous of gaining, &c.

अभिप्राय *abhi-prāya.* See *abhi-pre.*

अभिप्रार्च् *abhi-prārć (-pra-arć),* cl. 1. P. *-prārćati, -ćitum,* to celebrate in song.

अभिप्रार्थ् *abhi-prārth (-pra-arth),* cl. 10. A. *-prārthayate, -yitum,* to long for, desire.

अभिप्रास् *abhi-prās (-pra-as),* cl. 4. P. *-prāsyati, -prāsitum,* to throw on or upon.

अभिप्री *abhi-prī, īs, īs, i,* Ved. gladdening, pleasing, gaining.

Abhi-prīti, is, f. rejoicing in; wish, desire.

अभिप्रुष् *abhi-prush,* cl. 5. A., 1. P., Ved. *-prushṇute, -prushāyati, -proshitum,* to sprinkle with.

अभिप्रे *abhi-pre (-pra-i),* cl. 2. P. *-praiti, -tum,* to go near to, approach; to approach with one's mind, to think of, aim at, intend.

Abhi-prāya, as, ā, am, going near, approaching; aiming at; (*as*), m. aim, purpose, intention, wish, desire; goal; meaning, sense, reference.

Abhi-preta, as, ā, am, meant, intended; wished; accepted, approved; wishing, desirous.

Abhi-pretya, ind. aiming at, intending, meaning by.

अभिप्रेक्ष् *abhi-preksh (-pra-īksh),* cl. 1. A. *-prekshate, -shitum,* to look at, to see, view.

Abhi-prekshya, ind. having looked at or towards.

अभिप्रेप्सु *abhi-prepsu.* See *abhi-prāp* above.

अभिप्रेर् *abhi-prer (-pra-īr),* Caus. *-prerayati, -yitum,* to drive forward, impel towards: Pass. *-preryate,* to be impelled towards.

Abhi-preryamāṇa, as, ā, am, being driven towards.

अभिप्रेष् *abhi-presh (-pra-ish),* cl. 4. P. *-preshyati, -shitum,* to summon, command.

अभिप्रोक्षण *abhi-prokshaṇa, am,* n. (rt. *uksh*), sprinkling upon, affusion.

अभिप्लु *abhi-plu,* cl. 1. A. *-plavate, -plotum,* to overflow, to overwhelm.

Abhi-plava, as, m., N. of a religious ceremony, performed as part of the sacrifice Gavām-ayana.

Abhi-pluta, as, ā, am, overflowed, overrun; filled with; overwhelmed, affected by, labouring under.

अभिबल *abhi-bala, am,* n. an agreement to meet at some place of rendezvous in disguise (the technical name of a dramatic scene in rhetoric).

अभिबुद्धि *abhi-buddhi, is,* f. a Buddhīndriya or organ of apprehension.

अभिभङ्ग *abhi-bhanga, as,* m. (rt. *bhañj*), Ved. breaking down, one who destroys.

Abhi-bhañjat, an, atī, at, breaking down, &c.

अभिभर्तृ *abhi-bhartṛi,* ind. to a lover, before a husband.

अभिभर्त्स् *abhi-bharts,* cl. 10. A. P. *-bhartsayate, -ti, -yitum,* to scold at, threaten so as to terrify.

अभिभव *abhi-bhava.* See *abhi-bhū* below.

अभिभा 1. *abhi-bhā,* cl. 2. P. *-bhāti, -tum,* to glitter (around).

2. *abhi-bhā,* f., Ved. apparition, phenomenon, inauspicious omen; state of being overpowered, calamity; act of overpowering, superiority. — *Abhibhāyatana* (°*bhā-āy*°), *am,* n. abode of superiority; N. of the eight sources of superiority with Buddhists.

अभिभार *abhi-bhāra, as, ā, am,* very heavy.

अभिभाष् *abhi-bhāsh,* cl. 1. A. *-bhāshate, -shitum,* to address, converse with, speak to, confess.

Abhi-bhāshaṇa, am, n. the act of addressing or speaking to.

Abhi-bhāshamāṇa, as, ā, am, speaking to.

Abhi-bhāshita, as, ā, am, addressed, spoken to.

Abhi-bhāshin, ī, iṇī, i, addressing, speaking to.

Abhi-bhāshya, as, ā, am, to be addressed.

Abhi-bhāshyamāṇa, as, ā, am, being addressed.

अभिभू 1. *abhi-bhū,* cl. 1. P. *-bhavati, -vitum,* to overcome, overpower, predominate, conquer, surpass, overspread; to attack, defeat, humiliate.

Abhi-bhava, as, ā, am, overpowering; (*as*), m. addition; prevailing, overpowering, excessive power, predominance; defeat, subjugation; disregard, disrespect; humiliation, mortification, disgrace.

Abhi-bhavana, am, n. overpowering, overcoming.

Abhi-bhavanīya, as, ā, am, to be overcome or surpassed.

Abhi-bhāvaka, as, ikā, am, or *abhi-bhāvin, ī, inī, i,* or *abhi-bhāvuka, as, ā, am,* overpowering, surpassing, overspreading.

Abhi-bhāvana, am, n. causing to overcome, making victorious.

Abhi-bhu, us, or 2. *abhi-bhū, ūs,* m., Ved. one who surpasses, a superior.

Abhi-bhūta, as, ā, am, surpassed, defeated, subdued, humbled; overcome, aggrieved, injured.

Abhi-bhūti, is, f. superior power, overpowering, defeating; disrespect, disgrace, humiliation; (*is, is, i*), Ved. overpowering, superior. — *Abhibhūty-ojas, as,* n., Ved. superior power; (*ās, ās, as*), having superior power.

Abhi-bhūya, am, n., Ved. superiority.

Abhi-bhūvan, vā, vari, m. f., Ved. superior, victorious over.

अभिमद् *abhi-mad,* cl. 1. P., Ved. *-madati, -ditum,* to gladden, inebriate.

Abhi-māda, as, m. intoxication, inebriety.

Abhi-mādyat, an, antī, at, being inebriated.

Abhi-mādyatka, as, ā, am, partially intoxicated, half-drunk, stammering.

अभिमन् *abhi-man,* cl. 8. A. *-manute, -ntum,* to think one's self equal to, to think of self; cl. 4. A. and poet. P. *-manyate, -ti,* to assent to, approve of; to covet, desire; to consider, imagine, fancy, think.

Abhi-mata, as, ā, am, admitted, assented to; agreed, accepted; wished, desired; honoured, respected; (*am*), n. desire, wish. — *Abhimata-tā,* f. agreeableness, desirableness; desire, love.

Abhi-manas, ās, ās, as, having the mind directed towards; desirous of, longing for.

Abhi-manāya, nom. A. *-nāyate, -yitum,* to be desirous of, to long for.

Abhi-mantavya, as, ā, am, to be considered; to be desired.

Abhi-mantu, us, f. injuring, destroying. — *Abhimantos,* ind., Ved. to injure.

Abhi-mantṛi, tā, trī, tṛi, admonishing, longing for, referring all objects to self, self-conceited.

Abhi-manyamāna, as, ā, am, conceiving, imagining, regarding.

Abhi-māna, as, m. high opinion of one's self, self-conceit, pride, haughtiness, honourable feeling; consciousness; referring all objects to self (as the act of Ahankāra or personality); conception, conceit; affection, love, desire; laying claim to; injury, hurting. — *Abhimāna-tā,* f. pride, arrogance. — *Abhimāna-vat, ān, atī, at,* conceiving or having ideas about self; proud, arrogant. — *Abhimāna-śūnya, as, ā, am,* void of conceit, humble.

Abhi-mānita, am, n. the condition of an egotist; copulation, sexual intercourse.

Abhi-mānin, ī, inī, i, thinking of one's self, proud, self-conceited, arrogant; imagining; (*ī*), m., N. of a deity. — *Abhimāni-tā,* f. or *abhimāni-tva, am,* n. the state of self-conceitedness.

Abhi-mānuka, as, ā, am, Ved. striving to hurt.

अभिमन्त्र् *abhi-mantr,* cl. 10. A. *-mantrayate, -yitum,* to consecrate or accompany with Mantras or magic formulas; to address, invite.

Abhi-mantraṇa, am, n. calling out to, addressing, inviting; counselling; charming, consecrating; making anything sacred by a special formula, called *abhimantraṇa-mantra.*

Abhi-mantrita, as, ā, am, consecrated, charmed; made sacred by a certain formula.

अभिमन्थ *abhi-mantha, as,* m. ophthalmia, disease of the eyes.

अभिमन्यु *abhi-manyu, us,* m., N. of a son of Manu Cākshusha; of a son of Arjuna by Subhadrā; of two kings. — *Abhimanyu-pura, am,* n., N. of a town. — *Abhimanyu-svāmin, ī,* m., N. of a temple.

अभिमर *abhi-mara, as,* m. (rt. *mṛi*), killing, slaughter; war, combat; treachery, danger from one's own party or friends; binding, confinement.

अभिमर्द *abhi-marda.* See *abhi-mṛid,* p. 66.

अभिमर्शन. See *abhi-mṛiś* next col.

अभिमाति *abhi-māti, is, is, i* (rt. *mā=man*),

Ved. striving to injure, hurting, inimical; (*is, is*), m. f. striving to injure, hurting, plotting against; an enemy, foe. — *Abhimāti-jit, t, t, t,* Ved. subduing enemies. — *Abhimāti-shāh, ṭ, ṭ, ṭ,* Ved. conquering enemies. — *Abhimāti-han, ā,* m., Ved. striking, destroying one's enemies.

Abhi-mātin, ī, m., Ved. injuring; an enemy.

अभिमाद *abhi-māda.* See *abhi-mad* above.

अभिमान *abhi-māna.* See *abhi-man* above.

अभिमाय *abhi-māya, as, ā, am,* perplexed, bewildered, stupid, ignorant.

अभिमिह्य *abhi-mihya, as, ā, am* (rt. *mih*), Ved. to be wetted (by urining upon).

अभिमीलित *abhi-mīlita, as, ā, am,* closed (as the eyes).

अभिमुख *abhi-mukha, as, ā* or *ī, am,* with the face directed towards; turned towards, facing; going near, approaching; disposed to, intending to, ready for; taking one's part; nearly related to; friendly disposed; (*ī*), f. one of the ten earths of Buddhists; (*am*), ind. towards, in the direction of, in front or presence of, near to. — *Abhimukha-tā,* f. presence, proximity.

Abhimukhī-karaṇa, am, n. causing to turn the face towards, addressing.

Abhimukhī-bhūta, as, ā, am, being in presence of or facing.

अभिमूर्च्छित *abhi-mūrććhita, as, ā, am,* distracted, utterly confused.

अभिमृद् *abhi-mṛid,* cl. 1. P. *-mardati, -di-tum,* to oppress, to devastate.

Abhi-marda, as, m. rubbing, friction; oppression, devastation of a country &c. by an enemy; war, battle; spirituous liquor.

Abhi-mardana, as, ā, am, oppressing; (*am*), n. oppression.

Abhi-mardin, ī, inī, i, oppressing, one who devastates.

अभिमृश् *abhi-mṛiś,* cl. 6. P. *-mṛiśati, -marshṭum* or *-mrashṭum,* to touch, stroke, come in contact with.

Abhi-marśa, as, m. or *abhi-marśana, am,* n. (less correctly) *abhi-marsha, as,* m. or *abhi-marshaṇa, am,* n. touching, contact; (*as, ā, am*), rubbing, destroying.

Abhi-marśaka or (less correctly) *abhi-marshaka, as, ikā, am,* touching, coming in contact with.

Abhi-mṛishṭa, as, ā, am, touched, rubbed, brought close to, grazing.

अभिमेथिका *abhi-methikā,* f. (rt. *meth*), Ved. insulting or injurious speech; obscene expression; imprecation.

अभिम्लात *abhi-mlāta* or *abhi-mlāna, as, ā, am* (rt. *mlai*), Ved. altogether withered, faded; decayed.

अभियज्ञगाथा *abhi-yajña-gāthā,* f. a sacrificial verse.

अभिया 1. *abhi-yā,* cl. 2. P. *-yāti, -tum,* to go up to, approach, encounter, attack, assail.

2. *abhi-yā, ās, ās,* m. f. going up to, approaching, assailing.

Abhi-yāt, ān, ātī or *āntī, āt,* assailing, an assailant.

Abhi-yāta, as, ā, am, approached, attacked.

Abhi-yāti, is, m. or *abhi-yātin, ī,* m. or *abhi-yātṛi, tā,* m. an assailant, foe, enemy.

Abhi-yāna, am, n. coming near, approaching, attacking.

Abhi-yāyin, ī, inī, i, coming near, approaching, attacking.

अभियाच् *abhi-yāć,* cl. 1. A. or ep. P. *-yāćate, -ti, -ćitum,* to ask for, solicit, request.

Abhi-yāćana, am, n. or *abhi-yāćñā,* f. asking for, entreaty, request.

Abhi-yāćita, as, ā, am, asked for, requested.

अभियुज् 1. *abhi-yuj,* cl. 7. A. *-yuṅkte, -yoktum,* to apply to, exert effort, make one's self ready; to encounter, attack, assail; to accuse; to hurt: Pass. *-yujyate,* to be accused, &c.

Abhi-yukta, as, ā, am, applied, intent on, diligent, absorbed in meditation, versed in; appointed; said, spoken; attacked by an enemy, assaulted, assailed; blamed, rebuked; (in law) charged, prosecuted, a defendant.

Abhi-yugvan, ā, m., Ved. hurting, attacking; an enemy.

2. *abhi-yuj, k,* f. attacking; an enemy.

Abhi-yujyamāna, as, ā, am, being prosecuted (as a defendant).

Abhi-yoktavya or *abhi-yojya, as, ā, am,* to be reproved or rebuked; to be prosecuted, indictable; assailable.

Abhi-yoktṛi, tā, trī, tṛi, assailing, attacking; (*tā*), m. an enemy; a plaintiff, a claimant, a pretender, an accuser; a stronger party.

Abhi-yoga, as, m. application; energetic effort, exertion, perseverance, learning; attack, assault, challenging to fight, war, battle; (in law) a plaint, a charge, an accusation. — *Abhiyoga-pattra, am,* n. a petition or writing of complaint.

Abhi-yogin, ī, inī, i, intent upon, absorbed (in meditation); attacking; (*ī*), m. a plaintiff, a prosecutor.

Abhi-yogya, as, ā, am, assailable.

Abhi-yojana, am, n., Ved. harnessing (one horse) on to another.

अभियुध् *abhi-yudh,* cl. 4. A. P. *-yudhyate, -ti, -yoddhum,* to fight against, to acquire by fighting, to conquer for (another).

अभिरक्ष् *abhi-raksh,* cl. 1. P. or ep. A. *-rakshati, -te, -shitum,* to succour, to protect, to preserve; to govern or command.

Abhi-rakshā, f. universal protection, wide benevolence.

Abhi-rakshita, as, ā, am, protected, preserved, guarded; governed.

Abhi-rakshitṛi, tā, trī, tṛi, preserving, protecting, guarding.

Abhi-rakshya, as, ā, am, to be protected or governed.

अभिरञ्ज् *abhi-rañj,* cl. 4. A. or Pass. *-rajyate, -raṅktum,* to be coloured, to be flushed with pleasure: Caus. P. *-rañjayati, -yitum,* to colour.

Abhi-rañjita, as, ā, am, tinted, flushed, kindly affected.

अभिरम् *abhi-ram,* cl. 1. A. *-ramate, -rantum,* to delight in, to be delighted.

Abhi-rata, as, ā, am, pleased or contented with, satisfied; engaged in; attentive to; performing, practising.

Abhi-rati, is, f. pleasure, delighting in; occupation, practice.

Abhi-ramaṇa, am, n. delighting in, delighting.

Abhi-ramaṇīya, as, ā, am, to be delighted in, delightful.

Abhi-rāma, as, ā, am, pleasing, delightful, agreeable, beautiful; an epithet of Śiva; (*am*), ind., see s. v. next col. — *Abhirāma-tā,* f. or *abhirāma-tva, am,* n. loveliness, beauty, splendor.

अभिरम्भित *abhi-rambhita, as, ā, am,* obtained (?).

अभिराज् 1. *abhi-rāj,* cl. 1. A. *-rājate, -jitum,* to shine, be brilliant.

2. *abhi-rāj, ṭ, ṭ, ṭ,* reigning everywhere.

Abhi-rāja, as, m., N. of a Burmese king.

Abhi-rāshṭra, as, ā, am, Ved. one who has gained dominion.

अभिराध् *abhi-rādh,* Pass. *-rādhyate,* to be rendered propitious.

अभिरामम् *abhi-rāmam,* ind. referring to Rāma (see also under *abhi-ram* last col.).

अभिरुच् *abhi-ruć,* Caus. P. *-roćayati, -yitum,* to long for, desire, be inclined to, have a taste for, to like.

Abhi-rući, is, f. desire, delight, taste, relish, pleasure; desire of fame, ambition; splendor.

Abhi-rućita, as, ā, am, pleased, delighted, delighting in.

Abhi-rućira, as, ā, am, very pleasant, desirable or pretty.

अभिरुत *abhi-ruta, as, ā, am* (rt. *ru*), sounded; cooed, vocal (as the voices of birds, &c.).

अभिरुह् *abhi-ruh,* cl. 1. P. *-rohati, -roḍhum,* to ascend, mount.

Abhi-ruhya, ind. having ascended.

अभिरूप *abhi-rūpa, as, ā, am,* corresponding with; conformable to, congruous; in accordance with; pleasing, handsome, desirable, well formed, beautiful; wise, learned; (*as*), m. the moon; Śiva; Vishṇu; Kāmadeva. — *Abhirūpa-pati, is,* m. having an agreeable master (a rite) to secure such a master in the next world.

Abhi-rūpaka, as, ā, am, corresponding; pleasing, handsome; learned.

अभिरोरुद *abhi-roruda, as, ā, am* (Intens. of rt. *rud*), Ved. causing tears (of earnest desire).

अभिलक्षित *abhi-lakshita, as, ā, am,* marked with signs, bearing marks.

Abhi-lakshya, as, ā, am, to be marked or noted; (*am*), ind. towards a mark or aim.

अभिलङ्घ् *abhi-laṅgh,* cl. 10. P. *-laṅghayati, -yitum,* to jump across or over.

Abhi-laṅghana, am, n. jumping across or over.

अभिलभ् *abhi-labh,* Desid. A. or poet. P. *-lipsate, -ti,* to desire to obtain, covet.

Abhi-lambhana, am, n. obtaining transition (?).

Abhi-lipsā, f. desire of obtaining.

अभिलष् *abhi-lash,* cl. 1. 4. P. *-lashati, -lashyati, -shitum,* to desire or wish for, covet, crave.

Abhi-lashaṇa, am, n. craving after, desiring.

Abhi-lashaṇīya, as, ā, am, desirable, to be coveted.

Abhi-lashita, as, ā, am, desired, wished; (*am*), n. desire, wish, will, pleasure.

Abhi-lāsha or (less correctly) *abhi-lāsa, as,* m. desire, wish, covetousness, affection, love.

Abhi-lāshaka, as, ikā, am, or *abhi-lāshin, ī, iṇī, i,* or *abhi-lāshuka, as, ā, am,* or (less correctly) *abhi-lāsin, ī, inī, i,* wishing, desiring, desirous, covetous, greedy.

अभिलाप *abhi-lāpa, as,* m. (rt. *lap*), expression, word, speech; declaration of the object of a vow or religious obligation.

अभिलाव *abhi-lāva, as,* m. (rt. *lū*), cutting, reaping, mowing.

अभिलिखित *abhi-likhita, as, ā, am,* inscribed, inserted in writing.

Abhi-lekhana, am, n. writing upon, inscribing.

अभिलीन *abhi-līna, as, ā, am* (rt. *lī*), adhering to, shrouding; embraced; embracing.

अभिलुप्त *abhi-lupta, as, ā, am,* disturbed, injured.

अभिलुलित *abhi-lulita, as, ā, am,* playful, unsteady; agitated, disturbed, injured.

अभिलूता *abhi-lūtā,* f. an insect, a kind of spider.

अभिवच् *abhi-vać,* cl. 2. P. *-vakti, -ktum,* to speak to, address; to tell.

अभिवञ्चित *abhi-vañćita, as, ā, am* (rt. *vañć*), cheated, deceived.

अभिवत् *abhi-vat, ān, atī, at,* containing the word *abhi.*

अभिवद् *abhi-vad,* cl. 1. P. A. *-vadati, -te, -ditum,* to address or salute with reverence: Caus. *-vādayati, -te, -yitum,* to address or salute reverently; to salute through another person; to play on an instrument.

Abhi-vadana, am, n. addressing, salutation.

Abhi-vāda, as, m. reverential salutation; (for *ati-vāda*), opprobrious or unfriendly speech, abuse.

Abhi-vādaka, as, ikā, am, a saluter, saluting, offering salutation; civil, polite.

Abhi-vādana, am, n. respectful salutation, including sometimes the name or title of the person so addressed and followed by the mention of the person's own name; salutation of a superior or elder by a junior or inferior, and especially of a teacher by his disciple; (in general it is merely lifting the joined hands to the forehead and saying *aham abhivādaye,* I salute). — *Abhivādana-śīla, as, ā, am,* one who habitually salutes, respectful.

Abhi-vādayitṛi, tā, trī, m. f. a respectful saluter.

Abhi-vādita, as, ā, am, saluted respectfully.

Abhi-vādin, ī, inī, i, telling, enunciating, describing.

Abhi-vādya or *abhi-vādanīya, as, ā, am,* to be respectfully saluted.

अभिवन्द् *abhi-vand,* cl. 1. A. *-vandate, -ditum,* to salute respectfully.

Abhi-vandana, am, n. saluting respectfully.

अभिवप् *abhi-vap,* cl. 1. P., Ved. *-vapati, -ptum,* to join, come together.

अभिवयस् *abhi-vayas, ās, ās, as,* Ved. very youthful, fresh; possessed of food.

अभिवर्त *abhi-varta,* &c. See *abhi-vṛit.*

अभिवर्षण *abhi-varshaṇa,* &c. See *abhi-vṛish.*

अभिवस् *abhi-vas,* Caus. P. *-vāsayati, -yitum,* to clothe, cover.

Abhi-vāsa, as, m. or *abhi-vāsana, am,* n. covering.

Abhi-vāsas, ind. over the cloth or covering.

अभिवह *abhi-vaha, as, ā, am,* conveying near or towards, driving near.

Abhi-vahana, am, n. conveying towards or near.

Abhi-vāhya, as, ā, am, to be carried near; (*am*), n. conveyance, transmission; presentation, offering.

अभिवा *abhi-vā,* cl. 2. P. *-vāti, -tum,* to blow upon or towards.

Abhi-vātam, ind. towards the wind, windwards.

अभिवाञ्छ् *abhi-vāñćh,* cl. 1. P. *-vāñćhati, -ćhitum,* to long for, desire.

अभिवान्या *abhi-vānyā* or *abhivānya-vatsā,* f. (fr. *abhivā,* obtained?, and *anya*), Ved. a cow who suckles an adopted calf.

अभिविख्या *abhi-vi-khyā,* cl. 2. P. *-khyāti, -tum,* Ved. to look at, view. In later Sanskrit, to tell, to call.

Abhi-vikhyāta, as, ā, am, universally known, renowned, known as, called.

अभिविचक्ष् *abhi-vi-ćaksh,* cl. 2. A. *-ćashṭe,* Ved. to look towards. In later Sanskrit the idea of speaking is usually inherent in *ćaksh.*

अभिविचर् *abhi-vi-ćar,* cl. 1. A. *-ćarate, -ritum,* Ved. *-tave, -tavai, -rase, -radhyai,* to approach; cl. 10. P. *-ćārayati, -yitum,* to discuss.

अभिविजंह् *abhi-vi-jaṅh* Ved., Intens. 3rd sing. *-jaṅgahe,* to twitch convulsively.

अभिविज्ञा *abhi-vi-jñā,* cl. 9. P. *-jānāti, -jñātum,* to be aware, to know, perceive.

Abhi-vijñapta, as, ā, am, notified, made known.

अभिविज्वल् *abhi-vi-jval,* cl. 1. P. *-jvalati, -litum,* to flame or blaze against or opposite to.

अभिवितन् *abhi-vi-tan,* cl. 8. P. A., Ved. *-tanoti, -nute, -nitum,* to stretch (the string) over or across (the bow); to stretch over, cover.

अभिविद् *abhi-vid,* cl. 6. P. A. *-vindati, -te, -veditum,* to find, obtain; to seek.

अभिविदृश् *abhi-vi-dṛiś,* cl. 1. P., Ved. *-paśyati, -drashṭum,* to look at, behold.

अभिविधि *abhi-vidhi, is,* m. complete coincidence, complete comprehension or inclusion.

अभिविनद् *abhi-vi-nad,* cl. 1. P. *-nadati, -ditum,* to raise a loud noise.

अभिविनी *abhi-vi-nī,* cl. 1. P. A. *-nayati, -te, -netum,* to inform, instruct.

Abhi-vinīta, as, ā, am, well-behaved; well-disciplined; pious, pure, devout.

अभिविनुद् *abhi-vi-nud,* Caus. P. *-nodayati, -yitum,* to gladden, cause to rejoice.

अभिविभा *abhi-vi-bhā,* cl. 2. P., Ved. *-bhāti, -tum,* to illuminate.

अभिविमान *abhi-vimāna, as, ā, am,* of unlimited dimensions.

अभिविया *abhi-vi-yā,* cl. 2. P., Ved. *-yāti, -tum,* to approach, visit.

अभिविराज् *abhi-vi-rāj,* cl. 1. A. *-rājate, -jitum,* to shine, be radiant.

अभिविशङ्किन् *abhi-viśaṅkin, ī, inī, i,* afraid.

अभिविश्रुत *abhi-viśruta, as, ā, am,* widely celebrated.

अभिविश्वस् *abhi-vi-śvas,* Caus. P. *-śvāsayati, -yitum,* to render confident or secure.

अभिवी *abhi-vī (-vi-i),* cl. 2. P. *-veti, -tum,* to come together towards, meet together in.

अभिवीक्ष् *abhi-vīksh (-vi-īksh),* cl. 1. A. *-vīkshate, -kshitum,* to look at, view, perceive; to aim at, to examine; to be affected towards.

Abhi-vīkshita, as, ā, am, seen, perceived.

Abhi-vīkshya, ind. having seen or observed.

अभिवीर *abhi-vīra, as,* m., Ved. surrounded by men or heroes.

अभिवृत् *abhi-vṛit,* cl. 1. A. *-vartate, -titum,* to go towards, to face, to approach, come up, attack, to turn up, arise.

Abhi-vartin, ī, inī, i, going towards, approaching, attacking.

Abhi-vṛitta, as, ā, am, gone towards; turning towards.

अभिवृत *abhi-vṛita, as, ā, am* (rt. *vṛi*), chosen, selected.

अभिवृध् *abhi-vṛidh,* cl. 1. A. *-vardhate, -dhitum,* to increase, prosper.

Abhi-vṛiddha, as, ā, am, increased, augmented.

Abhi-vṛiddhi, is, f. increase, addition, success.

अभिवृष् *abhi-vṛish,* cl. 1. P. *-varshati, -shitum,* to rain upon, water, bedew, cover with a shower (e. g. of blossoms); to shower down; to cause to rain.

Abhi-varshaṇa, am, n. watering, bedewing; raining upon.

Abhi-varshin, ī, iṇī, i, bedewing; raining upon.

Abhi-vṛishṭa, as, ā, am, bedewed; rained upon.

अभिवेग *abhi-vega, as,* m. (rt. *vij*), consideration, determination.

अभिव्यञ्ज् *abhi-vy-añj (-vi-añj),* cl. 7. P. *-anakti, -añjitum* or *-aṅktum,* to manifest, reveal.

Abhi-vyakta, as, ā, am, manifest, evident, distinct, plain; declared, revealed; (*am*), ind. manifestly, plainly.

Abhi-vyakti, is, f. manifestation, distinction; declaration, revelation.

Abhi-vyaṅgya, as, ā, am, to be manifested or made clear.

Abhi-vyajyamāna, as, ā, am, being manifested.

Abhi-vyañjaka, as, ikā, am, revealing, manifesting; indicative, showing.

Abhi-vyañjana, am, n. making manifest, act of revealing.

अभिव्यन् *abhi-vy-an (-vi-an),* cl. 2. P. *-aniti, -nitum,* to breathe through, to fill with breath.

अभिव्यादा *abhi-vy-ā-dā (-vi-ā-dā),* cl. 3. P. A. *-dadāti, -datte, -dātum,* to open one's mouth (for swallowing).

Abhi-vyādāna, am, n. suppressed sound; repetition of the same sound.

अभिव्याधिन् *abhi-vyādhin, ī, inī, i* (rt. *vyadh*), striking at, hurting much, injuring greatly.

अभिव्याप् *abhi-vy-āp (-vi-āp),* cl. 5. P. *-āpnoti, -āptum,* to extend to, to comprehend, include, pervade, surround.

Abhi-vyāpaka, as, ikā, am, or *abhi-vyāpin, ī, inī, i,* including, comprehending.

Abhi-vyāpta, as, ā, am, included, comprehended, co-extended, &c.

Abhi-vyāpti, is, f. co-extending, universal pervasion, inclusion, comprehension.

1. *abhi-vyāpya,* ind. up to a certain point inclusive.

2. *abhi-vyāpya, as, ā, am,* to be included; (*am*), n. validity of a rule (?).

अभिव्याहृ *abhi-vy-ā-hṛi (-vi-ā-hṛi),* Caus. P. *-hārayati, -yitum,* to utter, pronounce, tell, explain.

Abhi-vyāharaṇa, am, n. or *abhi-vyāhāra, as,* m. pronunciation, utterance; an articulate significant word or phrase.

Abhi-vyāhārin, ī, iṇī, i, pronouncing, telling.

Abhi-vyāhṛita, as, ā, am, pronounced, spoken, told.

अभिव्युक्ष् *abhi-vy-uksh (-vi-uksh),* cl. 1. P. *-ukshati, -shitum,* to sprinkle towards.

अभिव्लङ्ग *abhi-vlaṅga, as,* m. (rt. *vlaṅg*), Ved. assault, shaking off.

अभिशंस् *abhi-śaṅs,* cl. 1. P. *-śaṅsati, -situm,* to accuse, blame, calumniate, abuse.

Abhi-śaṅsaka, as, ikā, am, or *abhi-śaṅsin, ī, inī, i,* accusing; insulting; abusive.

Abhi-śaṅsana, am, n. accusation; insult.

1. *abhi-śas, as,* f., Ved. accusation, imprecation, solicitation (?). For 2. see next col.

1. *abhi-śasta, as, ā, am,* falsely accused, calumniated; defamed, infamous; sinful, wicked. See next col.

Abhi-śastaka, as, ikā, am, falsely accused, cursed; caused by imprecation.

Abhi-śasti, is, f. imprecation; curse, damnation; effect of imprecation, misfortune, evil; one who curses or injures; calumny, defamation, scandal; asking, begging. — *Abhiśasti-ćātana, as,* m., Ved. keeping off imprecation. — *Abhiśasti-pā, ās,* or *abhiśasti-pāvan, ā,* m., Ved. defending from insults or imprecations.

अभिशक् *abhi-śak,* Desid. Caus. *-śikshayati, -yitum,* to teach.

अभिशङ्क् *abhi-śaṅk,* cl. 1. A. *-śaṅkate, -kitum,* to doubt, suspect, be suspicious.

Abhi-śaṅkā, f. doubt, alarm, suspicion.

Abhi-śaṅkita, as, ā, am, doubtful, frightened, alarmed.

अभिशप् *abhi-śap,* cl. 1. P. A. *-śapati, -te, -śaptum,* to execrate, curse.

Abhi-śapana, am, n. or *abhi-śāpa, as,* m. curse,

imprecation; charge, accusation; false accusation, calumny.—*Abhiśāpa-jvara, as,* m. fever caused by a curse.

Abhi-śapta, as, ā, am, cursed, accursed; falsely accused, calumniated; reviled.

Abhi-śāpana, am, n. pronouncing a curse or malediction.

अभिशब्दित *abhi-śabdita, as, ā, am,* declared, announced.

अभिशस् 2. *abhi-śas,* cl. 1. P. *-śasati, -situm,* to hurt, injure, attack. (See under *abhi-śaṅs.*)

3. *abhi-śas,* f., Ved. injuring (?). For 1. *abhi-śas,* see under *abhi-śaṅs,* p. 67, col. 3.

2. *abhi-śasta, as, ā, am,* injured, hurt, attacked.

Abhi-śastṛi, tā, trī, tṛi, an injurer, an enemy.

अभिशस्त, अभिशस्ति. See *abhi-śaṅs* and *abhi-śas.*

अभिशान्त्व् *abhi-śāntv,* cl. 10. P. *-śāntvayati, -yitum,* to pacify, appease, reconcile, comfort. See *abhi-sāntv.*

Abhi-śāntva, am, n. graciousness, complaisance.

अभिशीत *abhi-śīta* or *abhi-śyāta, as, ā, am* (rt. *śyai*), cold, chilly.

Abhi-śīna or *abhi-śyāna, as, ā, am,* coagulated, congealed.

अभिशोक 1. *abhi-śoka, as,* m. (rt. 1. *śuć*), Ved. intense grief.

1. *abhi-śoća, as, ā, am,* Ved. causing great grief.

Abhi-śoćana, am, n. great grief, pain; a tormenting spirit or demon.

1. *abhi-śoćayishṇu, us, us, u,* tormenting.

अभिशोक 2. *abhi-śoka, as,* m. (rt. 2. *śuć*), Ved. ardour.

2. *abhi-śoća, as, ā, am,* shining, glowing with heat.

2. *abhi-śoćayishṇu, us, us, u,* glowing with heat.

अभिशौरि *abhi-śauri,* ind. towards Sauri or Kṛishṇa.

अभिश्रवण *abhi-śravaṇa, am,* n. (rt. *śru*), repeating Vedic texts, sitting down to a Sráddha.

Abhi-śrāva, as, m. hearing, becoming renowned.

अभिश्रि *abhi-śri,* cl. 1. P. *-śrayati, -yitum,* to resort to.

Abhi-śrī, īs, īs, m. f. (from *śri* connected with *śrī*), Ved. joining, connecting one's self with, mixing; combining, holding together, arranging, putting in order, united, approaching; having recourse to, worthy to be had recourse to; respected; shining; powerful.

अभिश्रिष् *abhi-śrish* or *abhi-ślish, ṭ* (rt. *ślish*), Ved. a ligature.

Abhi-śleshaṇa, am, n. a bandage, ligature.

अभिश्वस् *abhi-śvas, as,* m., Ved. one who breathes upon or towards.

Abhi-śvasa, as, m., Ved. breathing forth or on, eructation.

Abhi-śvāsa, as, m. breathing upon or towards, blowing into a flame.

अभिषञ्ज् *abhi-shañj* (*-sañj*), cl. 1. P. *-shajati, -shanktum,* to be in contact with; to revile, curse.

Abhi-shakta, as, ā, am, possessed by evil spirits, humiliated, defeated, reviled, cursed.

Abhi-shaṅga, as, m. or *abhi-shañjana, am,* n. complete contact, union; connection, copulation, association, company; embracing; possession by evil spirits; oath; curse or imprecation; false accusation, calumny; defeat, blow, shock, sudden affliction. —*Abhishaṅga-jvara, as,* m. a fever supposed to be caused by evil spirits.

अभिषव *abhi-shava.* See *abhi-shu.*

अभिषह् *abhi-shah* (*-sah*), cl. 1. A. *-shahate, -hitum* or *-shoḍhum,* to attack.

Abhi-shahya, ind. violently, by force, insolently.

अभिषाच् *abhi-shāć, k, k, k* (rt. *sać*), Ved. following; honouring, paying attention to, devoted; defeating.

अभिषिच् *abhi-shić* (*-sić*), cl. 6. P. A. *-shiñćati, -te, -shektum,* to sprinkle; to water, wet; to consecrate, anoint, appoint by consecration; A. to be consecrated or inaugurated: Desid. *-shishikshati,* to be desirous of watering, &c.: Caus. *-shećayati, -yitum,* to have (another) consecrated.

Abhi-shikta, as, ā, am, sprinkled; anointed, installed, inaugurated, enthroned.

Abhi-shishikshat, an, antī, at, desiring to inaugurate.

Abhi-sheka, as, m. sprinkling, anointing; inaugurating or consecrating by sprinkling water; inauguration of a king, royal unction; the water or liquid used at an inauguration; religious bathing; ablution; bathing of the divinity to whom worship is offered. —*Abhisheka-śālā,* f. the hall of coronation. —*Abhishekārdra-śiras* (°*ka-ār*°), *ās, ās, as,* wet on the head with the royal unction. —*Abhi-shekāha* (°*ka-ah*°), *as,* m. day of inauguration.

Abhi-shektṛi, tā, m. an anointer, one who inaugurates.

Abhi-shećana, am, n. sprinkling; initiation, inauguration.

Abhi-shećanīya or *abhi-shećya* or *abhi-shekya, as, ā, am,* worthy of inauguration; belonging to inauguration; (*-nīyas*), m., N. of a sacrificial ceremony performed at the inauguration of a king.

Abhi-shećita, as, ā, am, caused to be sprinkled, inaugurated.

अभिषु *abhi-shu* (*-su*), cl. 5. P. *-shuṇoti, -shotum,* to express the Soma juice or any other juice; to moisten.

Abhi-shava, as, m. or *abhi-shavaṇa, am,* n. pressing out the juice of the Soma plant; distillation; religious bathing, ablution preparatory to religious rites; drinking Soma juice, sacrifice; ferment, yeast, any substance producing vinous fermentation; (*am*), n. sour gruel.

Abhi-shavaṇī, f. an apparatus for pressing the Soma.

Abhi-shavaṇīya, as, ā, am, to be expressed as Soma juice.

Abhi-shāvaka, as, or *abhi-shotṛi, tā,* m. the priest or any one who expresses the Soma juice.

Abhi-shāvakīya, nom. P. *-yati, -yitum,* to long for such a priest.

Abhi-shuta, as, ā, am, expressed as Soma juice; (*am*), n. sour gruel.

अभिषुक *abhi-shuka, as,* m., N. of a plant.

अभिषेण *abhi-sheṇa, as,* m., Ved. approaching as an enemy with an army; directing arrows against.

Abhi-sheṇana, am, n. march to attack or repel an enemy.

Abhi-sheṇaya, nom. P. *-sheṇayati, -yitum,* to approach with an army, to march with an army against the enemy. —*Abhi-shisheṇayishu, us, us, u,* desirous of approaching with an army.

अभिषो *abhi-sho* (*-so*), cl. 4. P. *-shyati, -shātum,* to put an end to, to destroy.

Abhi-shyat, an, antī, at, destroying, killing.

अभिष्टन *abhi-shṭana, as,* m. (rt. *stan*), Ved. roaring, bawling, a shout.

अभिष्टि *abhi-shṭi, is,* m. (fr. 1. *abhy-as;* according to other authorities fr. *abhīsh* or fr. *abhi-shṭhā,* q. v.), Ved. an assistant, a protector; one who is to be praised or worshipped (as a protector); one who approaches in order to assist, one who approaches to attack; one who assails an enemy, one who overpowers an enemy, one who approaches in order to obtain; desiring, desire; (*is*), f. assistance, protection; favour, help, worshipping, praising; a sacrifice, a hymn; approaching in order to assist, approaching in general, access. —*Abhishṭi-kṛit, t, t, t,* Ved. assisting; granting desires. —*Abhishṭi-dyumna, as, ā, am,* Ved. giving happiness. —*Abhishṭi-pā, ās,* m., Ved. guarding from enemies, keeping off enemies. —*Abhishṭi-mat, ān, atī, at,* Ved. desirable, favourable. —*Abhishṭi-śavas, ās,* m., Ved. rendering assistance, able to overcome enemies.

अभिष्टु *abhi-shṭu* (*-stu*), cl. 2. P. *-shṭauti, -shṭotum,* to praise, extol.

Abhi-shṭava, as, m. praise, eulogy.

Abhi-shṭuta, as, ā, am, praised.

Abhi-shṭuvat, an, atī, at, praising.

अभिष्ठा *abhi-shṭhā* (*-sthā*), cl. 1. P. *-tishṭhati, -shṭhātum,* to trample upon, destroy.

अभिष्यत् *abhi-shyat.* See under *abi-sho.*

अभिष्यन्द *abhi-shyanda* or *abhi-syanda, as,* m. (rt. *syand*), oozing or flowing; weakness of or running at the eyes; great increase or enlargement.

Abhi-shyandin or *abhi-syandin, ī, inī, i,* oozing, trickling; laxative; causing defluxions or serous effusion. —*Abhishyandi-ramaṇa* or *abhisyandi-ramaṇa, am,* n. a suburb, a smaller city appended to a larger one.

अभिष्वङ्ग *abhi-shvaṅga, as,* m. (rt. *svañj*), intense attachment or affection.

अभिसंयोग *abhi-saṃyoga, as,* m. intimate union, close contact.

अभिसंरभ् *abhi-saṃ-rabh,* cl. 1. A., Ved. *-rabhate, -rabdhum,* to support one's self on.

अभिसंरुध् *abhi-saṃ-rudh,* cl. 7. P. *-ruṇaddhi, -roddhum,* to ward off.

अभिसंवृत *abhi-saṃvṛita, as, ā, am* (rt. *vṛi*), covered, clad, clothed.

अभिसंशीन *abhi-saṃśīna* or *abhi-saṃśyāna, as, ā, am* (rt. *śyai*), coagulated, congealed.

अभिसंश्रय *abhi-saṃśraya, as,* m. (rt. *śri*), refuge.

अभिसंसार *abhi-saṃsāra, as,* m. (rt. *sṛi*), approaching together or in multitudes; (*am*), ind. having approached together.

अभिसंस्कृ *abhi-saṅs-kṛi* (*-sam-kṛi*), cl. 8. P. *-karoti, -kartum,* to shape, form; to make, render; to consecrate.

Abhi-saṅskāra, as, m. imagination; vain or profitless performance.

अभिसंस्तम्भ् *abhi-sam-stambh,* cl. 5. P. *-stabhnoti, -stambhitum,* to support, render firm.

अभिसंस्तव *abhi-saṃstava, as,* m. (rt. *stu*), praise, praising highly.

Abhi-saṃstuta, as, ā, am, highly praised.

अभिसंस्पृश् *abhi-saṃ-spṛiś,* cl. 6. P. *-spṛiśati, -sprashṭum, -sparshṭum,* to wash one's self.

अभिसंस्मृ *abhi-saṃ-smṛi,* cl. 1. P. *-smarati, -smartum,* to recollect.

अभिसंहन् *abhi-saṃ-han,* cl. 2. P. *-hanti, -tum,* to surround, enclose.

Abhi-saṃhata, as, ā, am, joined, united.

अभिसंहित. See under *abhi-sandhā.*

अभिसंक्रुध् *abhi-saṅ-krudh* (*-sam-krudh*), cl. 4. P. *-krudhyati, -kroddhum,* to be angry with.

Abhi-saṅkruddha, as, ā, am, angry with (with gen.).

Abhi-saṅkrudhyat, an, antī, at, being angry with (with acc.).

अभिसंक्रुश् *abhi-saṅ-kruś* (*-sam-kruś*), cl. 1. P. *-krośati, -kroshṭum,* to call out to.

अभिसङ्क्षिप् *abhi-saṅ-kship* (*-sam-kship*), cl. 6. P. *-kshipati, -ksheptum*, to compress, to crowd together in a small space.
Abhi-saṅkshipta, as, ā, am, thrown together or at; casting, throwing, shooting, aiming or aimed at.
Abhi-saṅkshepa, as, m. compressing, comprehending.

अभिसङ्ख्या *abhi-saṅ-khyā* (*-sam-khyā*), cl. 2. P. *-khyāti, -tum*, to enumerate; infer.
Abhi-saṅkhya, as, ā, am, inferable, clearly ascertainable.
Abhi-saṅkhyeya, as, ā, am, to be enumerated.

अभिसङ्गम् *abhi-saṅ-gam* (*-sam-gam*), cl. 1. P. *-gaććhati, -gantum*, to approach together; to join in welcoming; to meet with.

अभिसङ्गुप्त *abhi-saṅgupta, as, ā, am*, guarded, protected.

अभिसङ्गॄ *abhi-saṅ-gṝ* (*-sam-gṝ*), cl. 9. P. A. *-gṛiṇāti, -ṇīte, -garitum, -rītum*, to promise.

अभिसङ्ग्रह् *abhi-saṅ-grah* (*-sam-grah*), cl. 9. P. A. *-gṛihṇāti, -ṇīte, -grahītum*, to grasp at once with all the fingers.

अभिसच् *abhi-sać*, cl. 1. A., Ved. *-saćate, -ćitum*, to follow; to revere, favour.

अभिसञ्चर् *abhi-saṅ-ćar* (*-sam-ćar*), cl. 1. P. *-ćarati, -ritum*, Ved. *-ritave, -rase, -radhyai*, to go up to, to seek for, to move or wander about.
Abhi-saṅćārin, ī, iṇi, i, moving in every direction, inconstant, changeable.

अभिसञ्चि *abhi-saṅ-ći* (*-sam-ći*), cl. 5. P. A. *-ćinoti, -nute, -ćetum*, to arrange with reference to (anything).

अभिसञ्चिन्त् *abhi-saṅ-ćint* (*-sam-ćint*), cl. 10. P. *-ćintayati, -yitum*, to remember.

अभिसञ्जात *abhi-saṅjāta, as, ā, am* (rt. *jan*), produced, coming into existence.

अभिसञ्ज्ञा *abhi-saṅ-jñā* (*-sam-jñā*), cl. 9. A. *-jānīte, -jñātum*, to allow, acquiesce in.

अभिसञ्ज्वर् *abhi-saṅ-jvar* (*-sam-jvar*), cl. 1. P. *-jvarati, -ritum*, to envy, regard with spite.

अभिसत्वन् *abhi-satvan, ā*, m., Ved. surrounded by brave beings or heroes.

अभिसन्तन् *abhi-san-tan* (*-sam-tan*), cl. 8. P., Ved. *-tanoti, -nitum*, to spread or stretch across, to use for bridging over or stretching across.
Abhi-santata, as, ā, am, stretched across, spread over, covering.

अभिसन्तप् *abhi-san-tap* (*-sam-tap*), cl. 1. P. *-tapati, -ptum*, to press hard on all sides.
Abhi-santapta, as, ā, am, tormented.
Abhi-santāpa, as, m. war, battle.

अभिसन्तॄ *abhi-san-tṝ* (*-sam-tṝ*), cl. 1. P. *-tarati, -ritum, -rītum*, to cross over towards.

अभिसन्त्यज् *abhi-san-tyaj* (*-sam-tyaj*), cl. 1. P. *-tyajati, -tyaktum*, to abandon, give up, desist from.

अभिसन्त्रस्त *abhi-santrasta, as, ā, am* (rt. *tras*), terrified, much alarmed.

अभिसन्दष्ट *abhi-sandashṭa, as, ā, am* (rt. *daṅś*), compressed, tightened.

अभिसन्देह *abhi-sandeha, as*, m. (rt. *dih*), exchange; organ of generation. In the last sense also written *abhi-sandoha.*

अभिसन्धा 1. *abhi-san-dhā* (*-sam-dhā*), cl. 3. P. *-dadhāti, -dhātum*, to aim at; overcome; deceive; calumniate; declare; add; prefer.
Abhi-saṃhita, as, ā, am, agreed, contracted; attached to, interested, following any object eagerly.
Abhi-sandha or *abhi-sandhaka, as*, m. a deceiver, a calumniator.
2. *abhi-sandhā*, f. speech, declaration, promise.
Abhi-sandhāna, am, n. speech, deliberate declaration; attachment or interest in any object; special agreement; cheating, deceiving; making peace or alliance.
Abhi-sandhāya, ind. having aimed at, shooting at.
Abhi-sandhi, is, m. speaking or declaring deliberately, purpose, intention, object, meaning; special agreement; cheating, deceiving; making peace or alliance; joint, junction. — *Abhisandhi-kṛita, as, ā, am*, done intentionally or on purpose.

अभिसन्नम् *abhi-san-nam* (*-sam-nam*), cl. 1. P. *-namati, -nantum*, to inflect.

अभिसन्नह् *abhi-san-nah* (*-sam-nah*), cl. 4. P. A. *-nahyati, -te, -naddhum*, to bind or string together; to arm one's self against (?).
Abhi-sannaddha, as, ā, am, accoutred, armed.

अभिसन्नी *abhi-san-nī* (*-sam-nī*), cl. 1. P. A. *-nayati, -te, -netum*, to lead to or upon.

अभिसन्नु *abhi-san-nu* (*-sam-nu*), cl. 2. P., Ved. *-nauti, -navitum, -nuvitum*, to rejoice or cheer together at or towards.

अभिसमवाय *abhi-samavāya, as*, m. (rt. *i*), union, association.

अभिसमागम् *abhi-sam-ā-gam*, cl. 1. P. *-gaććhati, -gantum*, to approach together, come to.

अभिसमापद् *abhi-sam-ā-pad*, cl. 4. A. *-padyate, -pattum*, to approach, enter upon.

अभिसमि *abhi-sam-i*, cl. 2. P. *-eti, -tum*, to come together or meet at (a particular place); to invade.

अभिसमीक्ष् *abhi-sam-īksh*, cl. 1. A. *-īkshate, -shitum*, to see, look at, have in view; to comprehend, examine.

अभिसमीर् *abhi-sam-īr*, Caus. P. *-īrayati, -yitum*, to put in motion.

अभिसमूह् *abhi-sam-ūh*, cl. 1. P. A. *-ūhati, -te, -hitum*, to cover by bringing together.

अभिसमृ *abhi-sam-ṛi*, cl. 5. A., Ved. *-ṛiṇute, -artum, -ritum, -rītum*, to reach, seize.

अभिसमे *abhi-sam-e* (*-ā-i*), cl. 2. P. *-aiti, -tum*, to join in coming near or approaching, to go in quest of.

अभिसम्पच् *abhi-sam-pać*, Pass. *-paćyate*, to become ripe at a certain time (with acc.).

अभिसम्पत् *abhi-sam-pat*, cl. 1. P. *-patati, -titum*, to fly to, hasten to, jump upon; to fly along.
Abhi-sampāta, as, m. concourse, war, battle.

अभिसम्पद् 1. *abhi-sam-pad*, cl. 4. A. *-padyate, -pattum*, to become anything, become similar to, be changed to; to come to, arrive at; to obtain: Caus. *-pādayati, -yitum*, to make equal, change into.
Abhi-sampatti, is, f. becoming or being effected completely; transition.
2. *abhi-sampad, t*, f. becoming complete, complete number.
Abhi-sampanna, as, ā, am, complete, completely effected.

अभिसम्पराय *abhi-samparāya, as*, m. (rt. *i* with *parā* and *sam*), futurity.

अभिसम्पूज् *abhi-sam-pūj*, cl. 10. P. *-pūjayati, -yitum*, to honour, revere greatly.

अभिसम्प्रपद् *abhi-sam-pra-pad*, cl. 4. A. *-padyate, -pattum*, to come towards, share in.

अभिसम्प्राप् *abhi-sam-prāp* (*-pra-āp*), cl. 5. P. *-āpnoti, -āptum*, to reach, come to, arrive at, get, obtain.

अभिसम्प्रेक्ष् *abhi-sam-preksh* (*-pra-īksh*), cl. 1. A. *-prekshate, -shitum*, to look at, perceive.

अभिसम्बन्ध् *abhi-sam-bandh*, Pass. *-badhyate*, to be connected with, to relate or refer to.
Abhi-sambaddha, as, ā, am, connected with, referring to.
Abhi-sambandha, as, m. connection; contact, conjunction, relation; sexual connection.

अभिसम्बाध *abhi-sambādha, as, ā, am*, very confined or contracted.

अभिसम्भू *abhi-sam-bhū*, cl. 1. P., Ved. *-bhavati, -vitum*, to be near to, to enjoy.

अभिसम्मुख *abhi-sammukha, as, ā* or *ī, am*, fronting, facing; looking respectfully towards.

अभिसर *abhi-sara, abhi-sarga*, &c. See *abhi-sṛi, abhi-sṛij.*

अभिसर्पण *abhi-sarpaṇa, am*, n. (rt. *sṛip*), coming near.

अभिसान्त्व् *abhi-sāntv* or better *abhi-śāntv*, cl. 10. P. *-sāntvayati, -yitum*, to conciliate, pacify, comfort.
Abhi-sāntva or *abhi-śāntva, as*, m. consolation, conciliation.

अभिसायम् *abhi-sāyam*, ind. about evening, at sunset.

अभिसावक *abhi-sāvaka*, &c. See *abhi-shu.*

अभिसुसूष् *abhi-susūsh, ūs, ūs, ūs*, or *abhi-soshyat, an, atī* or *antī, at*, desirous of expressing Soma juice. See *abhi-shu.*

अभिसूच् *abhi-sūć*, cl. 10. P. *-sūćayati, -yitum*, to point out, show.
Abhi-sūćita, as, ā, am, pointed out.

अभिसूद् *abhi-sūd*, cl. 10. P. *-sūdayati, -yitum*, to kill outright, destroy utterly.

अभिसृ *abhi-sṛi*, cl. 1. P. *-sarati, -sartum*, to approach, go towards, advance in order to meet, to attack: Caus. P. *-sārayati, -yitum*, to visit, approach.
Abhi-sara, as, m. a companion, a follower; N. of a people.
Abhi-saraṇa, am, n. approaching, meeting, rendezvous, going to meet.
Abhi-sarat, an, antī, at, going to meet, attacking.
Abhi-sartṛi, tā, trī, tṛi, attacking, assailant.
Abhi-sāra, as, m. attack, assault; meeting, rendezvous; companion, follower; war, battle; a purificatory rite; going to meet a lover, an assignation, appointment; (*ās*), m. pl., N. of a people; (*ī*), f., N. of a town.
Abhi-sārikā, f. a woman who goes to meet her lover or keeps an assignation.
Abhi-sārin, ī, iṇī, i, going to meet, visiting, attacking; (*iṇī*), f. a woman who keeps an assignation or goes to meet her lover; N. of a species of the Trishṭubh metre, in which two Pādas contain twelve instead of eleven syllables, and which therefore is said to *approach* another metre called Jagatī.
Abhi-sāryamāṇa, as, ā, am, being approached.
Abhi-sṛitya, ind. having gone near.

अभिसृज् *abhi-sṛij*, cl. 6. P. *-sṛijati, -srashṭum*, to pour forth, to give.
Abhi-sarga, as, m. creation.
Abhi-sarjana, am, n. gift, donation; killing (?).
Abhi-sṛishṭa, as, ā, am, given.

अभिसेवन *abhi-sevana, am*, n. practising, cultivating.

अभिस्कन्द *abhi-skanda, as*, m., Ved. assault; an assailant; (*am*), ind. by assailing.

अभिस्थिरम् *abhi-sthiram*, ind. very firmly.

अभिस्नेह *abhi-sneha, as*, m. attachment, affection, desire.

अभिस्फुरित abhi-sphurita, as, ā, am, expanded to the full (as a blossom).

अभिस्मि abhi-smi, cl. 1. A., poet. P. -smayate, -ti, -smetum, to smile upon.

अभिस्यन्द abhi-syanda, &c. See abhi-shyanda, &c.

अभिस्वयमातृण्णम् abhi-svayamātṛiṇṇam, ind., Ved. on the brick (used in sacrifices and called) svayam-ātṛiṇṇa (perforated in itself, i. e. full of holes).

अभिस्वृ abhi-svṛi, cl. 1. P., Ved. -svarati, -svartum, -ritum, to approve, praise, invoke.
Abhi-svar, ar, f., Ved. invocation; calling into (one's) presence; a hymn or song of praise.
Abhi-svartṛi, tā, m., Ved. invoking, praising, an invoker.

अभिहन् abhi-han, cl. 2. P. -hanti, -tum, to thump at, strike, kill; to beat off, drive off.
Abhi-hata, as, ā, am, struck; beaten; smitten; killed; humbled, subdued, broken down; obstructed; multiplied.
Abhi-hati, is, f. striking; (in arithm.) multiplication.
Abhi-hanyamāna, as, ā, am, being smitten, killed, &c.
Abhi-ghāta. See s. v.

अभिहव 1. abhi-hava, as, m. (rt. hve), invocation; (for 2. see under abhi-hu below.)
Abhi-hūti, is, f. invocation, worshipping.

अभिहस्य abhi-hasya, as, ā, am (rt. has), Ved. ridiculous, laughable.
Abhi-hāsa, as, m. jest, joke, mirth.

अभिहित abhi-hita, as, ā, am (fr. abhi-dhā, q. v.), held forth, said, declared, spoken; determined; spoken to, addressed, accosted; whispered, prompted to say; placed upon; (as), m., N. of a chief; (am), n. a name, expression, word. — Abhihita-tva, am, n. the state of being said or spoken; a holding forth, declaration; authority, test.
Abhi-hiti, is, f. telling, manifesting, title. See abhi-dhāna.

अभिहु abhi-hu, cl. 3. P. -juhoti, -hotum, Ved. -hotavai, to make an oblation, sacrifice.
2. abhi-hava, as, m. oblation, sacrifice. See above.
Abhi-homa, as, m. making the oblation of clarified butter.

अभिहृ abhi-hṛi, cl. 1. P. -harati, -hartum, to snatch away, carry off; to bring: Caus. P. -hārayati, -yitum, to make a sudden attack.
Abhi-hara, as, ā, am, carrying off, removing.
Abhi-haraṇa, am, n. bringing near, conveying, robbing.
Abhi-haraṇīya or abhi-hartavya or abhi-hārya, as, ā, am, to be brought near.
Abhi-hartṛi, tā, trī, tṛi, one who snatches away, seizes, takes by violence; a ravisher.
Abhi-hāra, as, m. robbing, seizing anything in the owner's presence; a brisk attack; effort; arming, taking up arms; mingling together.

अभिह्रुत् abhi-hrut, t, t, t (rt. hvṛi), Ved. bending, causing crookedness, acting injuriously; (t), f. fall, defeat, damage.
Abhi-hruti, is, f. causing to fall; defeat, damage, offence; offensive, injurious.
Abhi-hvara or abhi-hvāra, as, ā, am, falling off; crookedness, sin.

अभी 1. a-bhī, is, is, i, without fear, fearless.

अभी 2. abhī (abhi-i), cl. 2. P. abhy-eti, -tum, to come near, approach; to go up to or towards (with acc.); to go along, go after; to go into, enter; to join; to go over to; to reach; to come to, to fall to one's share (with acc.); to get; to fall into: Ved. Intens. or Pass. -īyate, to ask, request; sakāśam or samīpam abhī, to go near.
1. abhīti, is, f., Ved. approach, assault. See next col.
Abhītvan, vā, varī, m. f., Ved. approaching, attacking: also written abhītvara, as, ī, am.
Abhy-aya. See s. v., p. 71, col. 2.

अभीक 1. abhīka, as, ā, am (= abhika, q. v., fr. abhi), longing after; lustful, libidinous; anxious, desirous; (as), m. a lover, a husband, a master.

अभीक 2. abhīka, am, n. (fr. abhi-ać; cf. anūka, apāka, pratīka), Ved. meeting together, closeness, nearness; collision, combat, opposition; abhīke, ind. in the neighbourhood, at the same place or time, at the right time, just in time; in a moment, instantaneously; (with abl.) from, out of; on account of, with regard to; from (in connection with verbs expressing defending from, &c.).

अभीक 3. a-bhīka, as, ā, am (fr. bhī), fearless; (as), m. a poet; a master.

अभीक्ष् abhīksh (abhi-īksh), cl. 1. A. -īkshate, -shitum, to look towards.

अभीक्ष्ण abhīkshṇa, as, ā, am (contraction of abhi-kshaṇa), repeated, frequent; constant, perpetual; (am), ind. repeatedly, again and again; perpetually, constantly; very, exceedingly; quickly. — Abhīkshṇa-śas, ind. repeatedly.

अभीघात abhī-ghāta. See abhi-ghāta.

अभीज्य abhījya, as, ā, am (rt. yaj), to be sacrificed to, one to whom sacrifice is offered; (as), m. a god.

अभीत a-bhīta, as, ā, am, not terrified, fearless. — Abhīta-vat, ind. as one not afraid, fearlessly.
2. a-bhīti, is, f. fearlessness. See last line first col.

अभीन्ध् abhīndh (abhi-indh), cl. 7. A. -inddhe, -indhitum, to surround with flames, to inflame.
Abhīddha, as, ā, am, inflamed, shining.

अभीपत् abhīpat, m. (fr. abhi and ap; cf. anūpa), Ved. a pond or any spot in which water collects; favour (?).

अभीपतस् abhīpatas, ind. (fr. rt. āp with abhi), Ved. according to the event, at the right time (?).

अभीप्सित abhīpsita, as, ā, am (īps, Desid. of rt. āp; see abhy-āp), desired, wished.
Abhīpsin, ī, inī, i, or abhīpsu, us, us, u, desirous of obtaining, wishing.

अभीम a-bhīma, as, ā, am, unterrific, causing no fear; (as), m., N. of Vishṇu.

अभीमान abhī-māna, as, m. (rt. man), pride, &c. See abhi-māna under abhi-man.

अभीमोद abhī-moda, as, m. (rt. mud), joy. — Abhīmoda-mud (only used in pl.), Ved. intense joy and pleasure; or abhī-modamud, excessively joyful (fr. irreg. intens. of rt. mud).

अभीर abhīra, as, m. a cowherd; N. of a people; (ī), f. the language of this people; (am), n., N. of a metre, containing four Pādas with eleven Mātrās in each Pāda.

अभीरणी abhīraṇī, f. (rt. īr?), a kind of serpent.

अभीराजी abhīrājī, f. a kind of poisonous insect.

अभीरु a-bhīru, us, us or ūs, u, unterrific; fearless, undaunted; (us), m., N. of Bhairava or Śiva; (us or ūs), f., N. of a plant, Asparagus Racemosus. — Abhīru-pattrī, f. a plant, the leaves of which are like those of the plant Abhīru (see above); the plant Abhīru.
A-bhīruṇa, as, ā, am, unterrific, fearless, innocent.
A-bhīlu, us, us, u (for a-bhīru), or abhīluka, as, ā, am, fearless.

अभीरुच् abhī-ruć. See abhi-ruć.

अभीलापलप् abhīlāpa-lap (only used in pl.), Ved. discourse and talk; or abhī-lāpalap, talking excessively, whimpering (fr. irreg. intens. of rt. lap, cf. abhī-modamud last col.).

अभीवर्ग abhī-varga, as, m. (rt. vṛij), circuit, compass.

अभीवर्त abhī-varta, as, m. (fr. abhi-vṛit, q. v.), Ved. existing everywhere, going towards, approaching, attacking successfully; successful assault, victory; a hymn recited in attacking the enemy.
Abhī-vṛit, t, t, t, Ved. abiding everywhere.

अभीवृत abhī-vṛita, as, ā, am (rt. vṛi), covered, surrounded.

अभीशाप abhī-śāpa, as, m. (rt. śap), curse, imprecation. See abhi-śapana.

अभीशु abhīśu or less correctly abhīshu, us, m. (rt. īś or 1. aś with abhi?), Ved. rein, bridle; arm, finger; ray of light. — 1. abhīshu-mat, ān, atī, at, splendid, brilliant.

अभीष् abhīsh (abhi-ish), cl. 6. P. abhīććhati, abhy-eshitum, -shṭum, to seek for, long for, endeavour to gain.
Abhīććhat, an, atī or antī, at, wishing, desiring.
Abhīshu, us, m. attachment, love, lust, passion [cf. abhīśu above]. — 2. abhīshu-mat, ān, atī, at, attached, enamoured.
Abhīshṭa, as, ā, am, wished, desired; acceptable, dear, favourite, darling; optional; (ā), f. a mistress; betel. — Abhīshṭa-tā, f. state of being desired. — Abhīshṭa-devatā, f. beloved goddess, favourite deity. — Abhīshṭa-lābha, as, m. or abhīshṭa-siddhi, is, f. the gaining a desired object.

अभीषङ्ग abhī-shanga, as, m. curse, imprecation. See abhi-shañj.

अभीषया a-bhīshayā, ind. (inst. case of abhīshā), fearlessly.

अभीषाह् abhī-shāh, ṭ, ṭ, ṭ, Ved. overpowering; (ṭ), f. immense power.

अभुक्त a-bhukta, as, ā, am (rt. bhuj), uneaten; unenjoyed, unused, unexpended; one who has not eaten, enjoyed or expended. — Abhukta-vat, ān, atī, at, one who has not eaten.
A-bhuj, k, k, k, Ved. one who has not experienced or enjoyed, one who does not keep (a promise).
A-bhuñjat, an, atī, at, not eating; Ved. not allowing to enjoy; not protecting.

अभुग्न a-bhugna, as, ā, am, not bent, straight; well, free from disease.

अभुज a-bhuja, as, ā, am, armless, maimed.

अभुजिष्य a-bhujishya, as, ā, m. f. not a slave, not a servant.

अभू a-bhū, ūs, m. unborn; an epithet of Vishṇu.
A-bhūta, as, ā, am, non-existent, whatever is not or has not been. — Abhūta-tadbhāva, as, m. the coming into being of that which has not existed before. — A-bhūta-pūrva, as, ā, am, unprecedented. — A-bhūta-prādurbhāva, as, m. the becoming manifest of what has not been before. — Abhūta-rajas, asas, m. pl., N. of some deities supposed to have existed in the fifth Manvantara. — A-bhūta-śatru, us, us, u, having no enemy.
A-bhūti, is, f. non-existence; want of power; poverty.

अभूमि a-bhūmi, is, f. non-earth, anything but earth; no proper object, unfit place or object. — Abhūmi-ja, as, ā, am, produced in unfit or unsuitable ground.

अभूयिष्ठ a-bhūyishṭha, as, ā, am, few, scanty.

अभूरि a-bhūri, is, is, i, few, some, several.

अभूष a-bhūsha or a-bhūshita, as, ā, am, unadorned.

अभृत a-bhṛita or a-bhṛitrima, as, ā, am, not receiving hire, not hired, not paid.

अभृश a-bhṛiśa, as, ā, am, not much, little, few.

अभेद a-bheda, as, m. absence of difference or distinction; identity; not breaking, compactness, closeness of array; (as, ā, am), undivided, identical, alike.

A-bhedaka, as, ikā, am, not dividing, not distinguishing.

A-bhedya, as, ā, am, or a-bhaidika, as, ī, am, not to be divided or broken or pierced; indivisible; (-yam), n. a diamond. — *Abhedya-tā*, f. indivisibility, impenetrability.

अभोक्तृ a-bhoktṛi, tā, trī, tṛi, or a-bhogin, ī, inī, i, not enjoying, not using, abstemious.

A-bhoktavya, as, ā, am, not to be enjoyed or used.

A-bhoga, as, m. non-enjoyment, not making use of.

A-bhogya, as, ā, am, not to be enjoyed.

A-bhoj, k, m., Ved. not affording enjoyment (to the gods, i. e. refusing to sacrifice). — *Abhog-ghan*, ā, m., Ved. killing the stingy (who will not sacrifice).

A-bhojana, am, n. not eating, fasting, abstinence.

A-bhojita, as, ā, am, not fed, not feasted.

A-bhojin, ī, inī, i, not eating, fasting.

A-bhojya, as, ā, am, not to be eaten, prohibited as food, impure. — *A-bhojyānna* (°ya-an°), as, ā, am, one whose food is not allowed to be eaten.

अभौतिक a-bhautika, as, ī, am, not elemental, not relating to or produced by the gross elements, mental.

अभ्यग्नि abhy-agni, is, m., N. of a son of Etaśa or Aitaśa; (i), ind. towards the fire.

अभ्यग्र abhy-agra, as, ā, am, near; fresh, new; (am), n. proximity.

अभ्यङ्क abhy-anka, as, ā, am, recently marked.

अभ्यज् abhy-aj (abhi-aj), cl. 1. P. -ajati, -jitum, to unite, join.

अभ्यञ्ज् abhy-añj (abhi-añj), cl. 7. P. -anakti, -añjitum, -anktum, to smear, anoint; to decorate.

Abhy-akta, as, ā, am, oiled, anointed.

Abhy-anga, as, m. rubbing with unctuous substances, smearing the body with oil, inunction; unguent, liniment.

Abhy-añjana, am, n. smearing the body with oil, inunction; oil; applying collyrium to the eyelashes; ornament; embellishment.

अभ्यत् abhy-at (abhi-at), cl. 1. P. -atati, -titum, to visit.

अभ्यतिक्रम् abhy-ati-kram (abhi-ati°), cl. 1. P. A., cl. 4. P. -krāmati, -kramate, -krāmyati, -kramitum, to step over, to walk through; to overpower; to transgress; to violate.

अभ्यतिक्षर् abhy-ati-kshar (abhi-ati°), cl. 1. P. A. -ksharati, -te, -ritum, Ved. -radhyai, to flow over to.

अभ्यतिनी abhy-ati-nī (abhi-ati°), cl. 1. P. A. -nayati, -te, -netum, to mix with (?).

अभ्यती abhy-atī (abhi-ati-i), cl. 2. P. abhy-aty-eti, -tum, to go past, glide away; to pass over; to get through.

Abhy-atīta, as, ā, am, dead, passed away.

अभ्यधिक abhy-adhika, as, ā, am, surpassing (in number, power, kind); exceeding the common measure, excellent; pre-eminent, extraordinary; superior, more excellent, having more authority or power; (am), ind. exceedingly.

अभ्यध्वम् abhy-adhvam, ind. towards the way, on the way; (e), ind. on the way, near.

अभ्यनुज्ञा 1. abhy-anu-jñā (abhi-anu°), cl. 9. P. -jānāti, -jñātum, to allow, permit; to authorize, direct; to allow one to depart, dismiss; to take leave: Caus. -jñāpayati, -yitum, to ask for leave to depart, to take leave.

2. *abhy-anujñā*, f. or *abhy-anujñāna*, am, n. assent, permission; granting leave of absence, dismissing; order, command.

Abhy-anujñāta, as, ā, am, allowed, permitted, assented to, dismissed; ordered, commanded.

अभ्यनुप्रछ् abhy-anu-prach (abhi-anu°), cl. 6. P. -pṛicchati, -prashṭum, to inquire after, ask for.

अभ्यनुमुद् abhy-anu-mud (abhi-anu°), Caus. P. -modayati, -yitum, to permit one to leave, to dismiss.

अभ्यनूक्त abhy-anūkta (-anu-uk°), as, ā, am (rt. vać), said conformably to what was declared before.

अभ्यन्तर abhy-antara, as, ā, am, interior, being inside; initiated in, conversant with; next, nearly related, intimate: (am), n. inner part, interior, inside, middle; included space; (am or atas), ind. in the interior, inwards. — *Abhyantara-karaṇa*, see antaḥkaraṇa. — *Abhyantara-kalā*, f. the secret art or the art of coquetry. — *Abhyantarāyāma* (°ra-āy°), as, m. curvature of the spine by spasm; emprosthonos.

Abhy-antaraka, as, m. an intimate friend.

Abhyantarī-kṛi, cl. 8. P. -karoti, -kartum, to initiate, inaugurate; to make a near friend (of a person); to familiarize. — *Abhyantarī-karaṇa*, am, n. initiating in, inaugurating; making a near friend (of a person). — *Abhyantarī-kṛita*, as, ā, am, put between, made interior; initiated; made intimate or familiar with.

अभ्यपक्रम् abhy-apa-kram (abhi-apa°), cl. 1. P. A., cl. 4. P. -krāmati, -kramate, -krāmyati, -kramitum, to go away to, to go up to.

अभ्यपान् abhy-apān (abhi-apa-an), cl. 2. P., Ved. -apāniti, -nitum, to breathe on.

अभ्यम् abhy-am (abhi-am), cl. 1. P., Ved. -amati, -mitum, to advance violently against, to attack, to pain, hurt; to be angry with; to overcome.

Abhy-amana, am, n. attacking, assault, disease. — *Abhyamana-vat*, ān, atī, at, with assaults or attacks, with diseases.

Abhy-amita, as, ā, am, diseased, sick.

Abhy-amin, ī, inī, i, attacking, inclined to attack.

Abhy-ānta. See s. v.

अभ्यमित्र abhy-amitra, am, n. assault on an enemy; (am), ind. towards or against the enemy.

Abhy-amitrīṇa or *abhy-amitrīya* or *abhy-amitrya*, as, m. a soldier who faces the enemy valiantly.

अभ्यय abhy-aya, as, m. (fr. abhi-i, see abhī), going near, approaching, arriving; entering; setting (of the sun).

अभ्यरि abhy-ari, ind. towards or against the enemy.

अभ्यर्कबिम्बम् abhy-arkabimbam, ind. towards the disk of the sun.

अभ्यर्च् abhy-arć (abhi-arć), cl. 1. P. -arćati, -ćitum, to praise, celebrate in song; to worship, reverence: Pass. -arćyate, to be honoured.

Abhy-arćat, an, antī, at, worshipping, reverencing.

Abhy-arćana, am, n. or *abhy-arćā*, f. worship, reverence.

Abhy-arćanīya or *abhy-arćya*, as, ā, am, to be worshipped, to be reverenced.

Abhy-arćita, as, ā, am, praised, worshipped.

अभ्यर्ण abhy-arṇa, as, ā, am (fr. rt. ṛi or ard with abhi?), near, proximate; (am), n. nearness, proximity.

अभ्यर्थ् abhy-arth (abhi-arth), cl. 10. A. -arthayate, -yitum, to ask, request.

Abhy-arthana, am, ā, n. f. petition, request.

Abhy-arthanīya or *abhy-arthya*, as, ā, am, to be requested or asked. — *Abhy-arthayamāna*, as, ā, am, asking, one who asks.

Abhy-arthita, as, ā, am, asked, invited.

Abhy-arthin, ī, inī, i, asking.

अभ्यर्द् abhy-ard (abhi-ard), cl. 1. P. -ardati, -ditum, to oppress, afflict, pain.

Abhy-ardita, as, ā, am, distressed, oppressed.

अभ्यर्ध abhy-ardha, as, ā, am (fr. ardh for ard with abhi, cf. abhy-arṇa), Ved. being on this side; proximate, near; increasing; (am), n. the being situated on this side, near. — *Abhyardha-yajvan*, ā, m., Ved. granting gifts; increasing the worshipper's prosperity.

अभ्यर्ष् abhy-arsh (abhi-arsh), cl. 1. P. -arshati, -shitum, to flow near, to run near (with acc.); to cause to flow near.

अभ्यर्हणीय abhy-arhaṇīya, as, ā, am (rt. arh), to be greatly honoured, venerable. — *Abhy-arhaṇīya-tā*, f. honourableness, honour.

Abhy-arhita, as, ā, am, greatly honoured, venerable; fit, proper, becoming.

अभ्यलङ्कृ abhy-alankṛi (abhi-alam-kṛi), cl. 8. P. -karoti, -kartum, to decorate.

Abhy-alankṛita, as, ā, am, decorated.

अभ्यवकर्षण abhy-avakarshaṇa, am, n. (rt. kṛish), extraction, drawing out.

अभ्यवकाश abhy-avakāśa, as, m. (rt. kāś), an open space.

अभ्यवकॄ abhy-ava-kṝ (abhi-ava°), cl. 6. P. -kirati, -karitum, -rītum, to throw or cast on, to pour on, to cover.

अभ्यवचर् abhy-ava-ćar (abhi-ava°), cl. 1. P. -ćarati, -ritum, Ved. -tave, -tavai, -rase, -radhyai, to press on, penetrate: Caus. -ćārayati, -yitum, to send away.

अभ्यवतन् abhy-ava-tan (abhi-ava°), cl. 8. P., Ved. -tanoti, -nitum, to extend along or to.

अभ्यवदान्य abhy-avadānya, as, ā, am, Ved. withholding gifts, not liberal.

अभ्यवदो abhy-ava-do (abhi-ava°), cl. 4. P. -dyati, -dātum, to divide into pieces for any purpose.

अभ्यवधा abhy-ava-dhā (abhi-ava°), cl. 3. P. A. -dadhāti, -dhatte, -dhātum, to lay down on all sides, overlay.

Abhy-avahita, as, ā, am, allayed, laid, e. g. dust.

अभ्यवनम् abhy-ava-nam (abhi-ava°), Caus. P. -nāmayati, -yitum, to bow, incline.

अभ्यवनिज् abhy-ava-nij (abhi-ava°), cl. 3. P. A. -nenekti, -nenikte, -nektum, to wipe or wash off, clean: Caus. -nejayati, -yitum, to cause to wash off.

अभ्यवनी abhy-ava-nī (abhi-ava°), cl. 1. P. A. -nayati, -te, -netum, to lead down, pour into.

अभ्यवपत् abhy-ava-pat (abhi-ava°), cl. 1. P. -patati, -titum, to fly or fall down.

अभ्यवमन् abhy-ava-man (abhi-ava°), cl. 4. A. -manyate, -mantum, to despise, scorn, reject.

अभ्यवस्कन्द् abhy-ava-skand (abhi-ava°), cl. 1. P. -skandati, -skantum, to jump up (or out?).

Abhy-avaskanda, as, m. or *abhy-avaskandana*, am, n. impetuous assault, facing an enemy; striking so as to disable an enemy.

अभ्यवहृ abhy-ava-hṛi (abhi-ava°), Caus.

-hārayati, -yitum, to get one to oppose another; to cause one to take or eat.
Abhy-avaharaṇa, am, n. throwing away or down; taking food, eating.
Abhy-avahāra, as, m. taking food, eating, enjoying; food.
Abhy-avahārya, as, ā, am, eatable, fit for eating; (am), n. food, eating.
Abhy-avahṛita, as, ā, am, taken (as food), devoured.

अभ्यवास् abhy-avās (abhi-ava-as), cl. 4. P. -asyati, -situm, to throw upon.

अभ्यवे abhy-ave (abhi-ava-i), cl. 2. P. -avaiti, -tum, to go down; to descend; to get an insight, to condescend; to perceive.
Abhy-avāyana, am, n. going down, descending.
Abhy-aveta, as, ā, am, descended, immersed.

अभ्यवेक्ष् abhy-aveksh (abhi-ava-īksh), cl. 1. A. -avekshate, -shitum, to look at or upon.

अभ्यश् abhy-aś (abhi-aś), cl. 5. P. A. -aśnoti, -nute, -aśitum, -ashṭum, to pervade, reach to, gain; to make one's self master of.
Abhy-aśana, am, n. reaching to, pervading, gaining.
Abhy-āśa, as, m. reaching to, pervading; proximity, neighbourhood, result, consequence, prospect, hope of gaining; (as, ā, am), near, proximate (also written abhy-āsa). Abhy-āśam or abhy-āśe, ind. near (also written abhy-āse). Abhyāśād-āgata, as, ā, am, arrived from near at hand.

अभ्यस् 1. abhy-as (abhi-as), cl. 2. P. -asti, to fall to one's share; to be over; to excel; to reign over, tyrannize over.

अभ्यस् 2. abhy-as (abhi-as), cl. 4. P. -asyati, -asitum, to throw down, throw to, heap one on the other, accumulate, to shoot off at, to concentrate one's attention in one direction; to repeat, practice, exercise; to study, read, recite; to learn by heart.
Abhy-asana, am, n. concentrating of the faculties of the mind in one direction; practice, exercise; repetition, study.
Abhy-asanīya or abhy-asitavya or abhy-asya, as, ā, am, to be studied, to be repeated or reduplicated.
Abhy-asta, as, ā, am, accumulated, practised, exercised; learnt by heart, repeated, studied; multiplied; reduplicated in grammar; (am), n. the reduplicated base of a root.
Abhy-asyat, an, antī, at, studying, practising.
Abhy-āsa, as, m. repetition; practice, military practice, permanent or repeated exercise, discipline, use, habit, custom; repeated reading, reciting, study; learning by heart; education; practising archery; (in grammar) repeating twice, reduplication; the first syllable of a reduplicated radical; (in poetry) repetition of the last verses of a stanza; (in arithmetic) multiplication: see also under abhy-aś. — Abhyāsa-gata, as, ā, am, approached, gone near (see abhy-āśa above). — Abhyāsa-tā, f. constant practice, use, habit. — Abhyāsa-nimitta, am, n. the cause of the reduplication in grammar. — Abhyāsa-parivartin, ī, inī, i, wandering about or near, for abhyāśa°. — Abhyāsa-yoga, as, m. the practice of frequent and repeated meditation on any deity or on abstract spirit, repeated recollection. — Abhyāsa-vyavāya, as, m. interval caused by the reduplication-syllable.
Abhyāsin, ī, inī, i, practising, repeating.
Abhyāse, ind. near; more correctly written abhyāśe.

अभ्यसूय abhy-asūya, nom. P. A. -asūyati, -te, -yitum, to show indignation, to detract.
Abhy-asūya, as, ā, am, angry, vexed, impatient.
Abhy-asūyaka, as, ikā, am, detracting, a detractor, calumniator; envious.
Abhy-asūyā, f. detraction, envy, calumny.

अभ्यस्तमि abhy-astam-i, cl. 2. P. -eti, -tum, or abhy-astan-gā, cl. 3. P. -jigāti, -gātam, to go down or set (as the sun) during or with reference to (some act).
Abhy-astamaya, as, m. setting of the sun during or with reference to.
Abhy-astamita, as, ā, am, one on whom the sun has gone down while asleep.

अभ्याकर्ष abhy-ākarsha, as, m. (rt. kṛish), a striking of the flat of the hand upon the breast in defiance (a practice common to wrestlers and pugilists).

अभ्याकाङ्क्षित abhy-ākāṅkshita, am, n. a groundless complaint, a false accusation.

अभ्याकृ abhy-ā-kṛi (abhi-ā°), cl. 8. P. -karoti, -kartum, to draw near to one's self, attract.
Abhy-ākāram, ind. by or in drawing near to one's self.

अभ्याक्रम् abhy-ā-kram (abhi-ā°), cl. 1. P. A., cl. 4. P. -krāmati, -kramate, -krāmyati, -kramitum, to step near.
Abhy-ākrāmam, ind. by or in stepping near or mutually, in stepping rapidly.

अभ्याक्रुश् abhy-ā-kruś (abhi-ā°), cl. 1. P. -krośati, -kroshṭum, to assail with harsh language, to revile.

अभ्याख्यात abhy-ākhyāta, as, ā, am, accused falsely, calumniated.
Abhy-ākhyāna, am, n. a false or groundless accusation, calumny.

अभ्यागम् abhy-ā-gam (abhi-ā°), cl. 1. P. -gaććhati, -gantum, to come near to, approach, visit; to come to, fall into.
Abhy-āgata, as, ā, am, come, arrived; (as), m. a guest, a visitor.
Abhy-āgama, as, m. or abhy-āgamana, am, n. approaching, arrival, visit, visitation; neighbourhood; arriving at or enjoying a result; rising, getting up; war, battle; encountering, striking, killing; enmity.

अभ्यागा abhy-ā-gā (abhi-ā°), cl. 3. P. -jigāti, -gātum, to come to, approach, arrive.

अभ्यागारिक abhy-āgārika, as, ā, am (fr. āgāra, q. v., with abhi), diligent in supporting a family.

अभ्याघात abhy-āghāta, as, m. (rt. han), assault, attack.
Abhy-āghātin, ī, inī, i, attacking, assailing.

अभ्याचक्ष् abhy-ā-ćaksh (abhi-ā°), cl. 2. A. -ćashṭe, -shṭum, to look at; to speak.

अभ्याचर् abhy-ā-ćar (abhi-ā°), cl. 1. P. A. -ćarati, -te, -ritum, Ved. -itave, -itavai, -rase, -radhyai, to approach, practice.
Abhy-āćāra, as, m., Ved. approaching (as an enemy), disturbing.

अभ्याज् abhy-āj (abhi-ā-aj), cl. 1. P. -ājati, -jitum, to drive near.

अभ्याज्ञाय abhy-ājñāya, as, m. (rt. jñā), Ved. order, command.

अभ्यातन् abhy-ā-tan (abhi-ā°), cl. 8. A., Ved. -tanute, -nitum, to take aim at, shoot.
Abhy-ātāna, as, m. spreading over; expansion.

अभ्यातप् abhy-ā-tap (abhi-ā°), cl. 1. P. -tapati, -ptum, to distress, torment.

अभ्यातॄ abhy-ā-tṝi (abhi-ā°), cl. 1. P. -tarati, -rītum, -ritum, to come up.

अभ्यात्म abhy-ātma, as, ā, am, Ved. directed towards one's self; (am), ind. towards one's self. — Abhyātma-taram, ind. more towards one's self.

अभ्यादा abhy-ā-dā (abhi-ā°), cl. 3. A. -datte, -dātum, to seize, snatch away; to put on; to take up the conversation, or commence speaking after another.
Abhy-ātta, as, ā, am (for abhy-ādatta), obtained; having gained, encompassing.
Abhy-ādāna, am, n. beginning, commencement; first beginning.

अभ्यादिश् abhy-ā-diś (abhi-ā°), cl. 6. P. -diśati, -deshṭum, to aim at (in talk), to have in view.

अभ्याधा abhy-ā-dhā (abhi-ā°), cl. 3. P. -dadhāti, -dhātum, to lay on (fuel, &c.), to add, apply.
Abhy-ādhāna, am, n. laying or placing on, adding.
Abhy-āhita, as, ā, am, laid on, put on. — Abhyāhita-paśu, us, m. a present usual in some districts of India.

अभ्यानी abhy-ā-nī (abhi-ā°), cl. 1. P. A. -nayati, -te, -netum, to pour into, mix with.

अभ्यानृत् abhy-ā-nṛit (abhi-ā°), cl. 4. P., Ved. -nṛityati, -nartitum, to dance towards, to hasten near.

अभ्यान्त abhy-ānta, as, ā, am (fr. rt. am with abhi, see abhy-am), sick, diseased.

अभ्याप् abhy-āp (abhi-āp), cl. 5. P. -āpnoti, -ptum, to reach to, to get, to obtain: Caus. -āpayati, -yitum, to bring to an end: Desid. -īpsati, to strive to reach, to ask for, to desire.
Abhīpsita, as, ā, am, desired, acceptable, dear.

अभ्यापत् abhy-ā-pat (abhi-ā°), cl. 1. P. -patati, -titum, to jump on, to hasten near to, rush towards.
Abhy-āpāta, as, m. calamity, misfortune.

अभ्यापद् abhy-ā-pad, cl. 4. A. -padyate, -pattum, to come to, to approach.

अभ्यामर्द abhy-āmarda, as, m. or abhy-āmardana, am, n. (rt. mṛid), war, battle, fighting.

अभ्यायम् abhy-ā-yam (abhi-ā°), cl. 1. P. -yaććhati, -yantum, to restrain.
Abhy-āyaṃsenya, as, m., Ved. to be restrained; to be made subject.

अभ्याया abhy-ā-yā (abhi-ā°), cl. 2. P. -yāti, -tum, to come up to, attain.

अभ्यारभ् abhy-ā-rabh (abhi-ā°), cl. 1. A. or P. -rabhate, -ti, -rabdhum, to commence.
Abhy-ārambha, as, m. beginning, commencement.

अभ्यारम् abhy-āram, ind. (rt. ṛi), near, at hand, by coming near.

अभ्यारूढ abhy-ārūḍha, as, ā, am (rt. ruh), ascended; gone up to; surpassed.
Abhy-āroha, as, m. or abhy-ārohaṇa, am, n. going up to, ascending; transition from one place to another; progress; ascending in devotion, praying.
Abhy-ārohaṇīya, as, m., N. of a sacrificial ceremony.
Abhy-ā-rohya, as, ā, am, to be ascended, to be gained.

अभ्यावृत् abhy-ā-vṛit (abhi-ā°), cl. 1. A., Ved. P. -vartate, -ti, -titum, to come up to, come towards, approach.
Abhy-āvarta, as, m. repetition; a hymn, the verses of which are repeated in singing; (am), ind. repeatedly, by repeating.
Abhy-āvartin, ī, inī, i, repeatedly coming; (ī), m., N. of a king.
Abhy-āvṛitta, as, ā, am, come near to, approached, repeated.
Abhy-āvṛitti, is, f. repetition.

अभ्याश abhy-āśa, as, m. See abhy-aś.

अभ्यास abhy-āsa. See 2. abhy-as.

अभ्यासद् abhy-ā-sad (abhi-ā°), cl. 1. P. -sīdati, -sattum, to attain, obtain.
Abhy-āsādana, am, n. striking so as to disable an enemy, facing an enemy.

अभ्याहन् *abhy-ā-han* (*abhi-ā°*), cl. 2. P. *-hanti, -tum,* to strike, wound, smite, impede.

Abhy-āhata, as, ā, am, struck, wounded, impeded.

Abhy-āhanana, am, n. striking, hurting, killing, impeding.

अभ्याहित *abhy-āhita.* See under *abhy-ā-dhā,* p. 72, col. 3.

अभ्याहृ *abhy-ā-hṛi* (*abhi-ā°*), cl. 1. P. *-harati, -hartum,* to bring towards, bring near; to give, hand over.

Abhy-āhāra, as, m. bringing near; robbery.

Abhy-āhārya, as, ā, am, to be eaten.

अभ्युक्त *abhy-ukta, as, ā, am* (rt. *vać*), declared with reference to (some particular point).

अभ्युक्ष् *abhy-uksh* (*abhi-uksh*), cl. 6. 1. P. A. *-ukshati, -te, -shitum,* to sprinkle over, besprinkle.

Abhy-ukshaṇa, am, n. sprinkling over, wetting.

Abhy-ukshita, as, ā, am, besprinkled.

Abhy-ukshya, ind. having sprinkled over.

अभ्युच् *abhy-uć* (*abhi-uć*), cl. 4. P. *-ućyati, -ćitum,* to like, to take pleasure in visiting.

अभ्युचित *abhy-ućita, as, ā, am,* usual, customary.

अभ्युच्चगामिन् *abhy-ućća-gāmin, ī, inī, i,* going exceedingly high; (*ī*), m., N. of a Buddha.

अभ्युच्चय *abhy-uććaya, as,* m. (rt. *ći*), increase, augmentation.

Abhy-uććita, as, ā, am, increased, augmented.

अभ्युच्चर् *abhy-uć-ćar* (*abhi-ud-ćar*), cl. 1. P. *-ćarati, -ritum,* Ved. *-tave, -tavai, -rase, -radhyai,* to rise over.

अभ्युच्छ्रित *abhy-uććhrita, as, ā, am* (fr. rt. *śri* with *abhi* and *ud*), raised aloft, elevated. — *Abhy-uććhrita-kara, as, ā, am,* with uplifted proboscis.

अभ्युज्जीव् *abhy-uj-jīv* (*abhi-ud°*), cl. 1. P. *-jīvati, -vitum,* to live for others.

अभ्युत्क्रम् *abhy-ut-kram* (*abhi-ud°*), cl. 1. P. A., cl. 4. P. *-krāmati, -kramate, -krāmyati, -kramitum,* to go up to: Caus. P. *-kramayati, -yitum,* to cause to go up to, to cause to ascend.

अभ्युत्क्रुश् *abhy-ut-kruś* (*abhi-ud°*), cl. 1. P. *-krośati, -kroshṭum,* to raise loud acclamations.

Abhy-utkrushṭa, as, ā, am, applauded with loud acclamations.

Abhy-utkrośana, am, n. loud acclamation. — *Abhy-utkrośana-mantra, as,* m. a hymn of applause.

अभ्युत्तॄ *abhy-ut-trī* (*abhi-ud°*), cl. 1. P., Ved. *-tarati, -ritum, -rītum,* to cross over towards, penetrate to.

अभ्युत्था *abhy-ut-thā* (*abhi-ud-sthā*), cl. 1. P. *-tishṭhati, -thātum,* to rise, rise from a seat to do any one honour.

Abhy-utthāna, am, n. rising from a seat through politeness; rising, elevation, obtaining a high position, gaining authority, dignity, respectability; sunrise.

Abhy-utthāyin, ī, inī, i, rising from a seat to do any one honour.

Abhy-utthita, as, ā, am, risen, arisen, elevated, exalted. — *Abhyutthitāśva* (*°ta-aś°*), *as,* m., N. of a prince descended from Daśaratha.

Abhy-uttheya, as, ā, am, to be greeted reverentially, i. e. by rising from one's seat.

अभ्युत्पत् *abhy-ut-pat* (*abhi-ud°*), cl. 1. P. *-patati, -titum,* to fly up to, jump up to: Caus. *-pātayati, -yitum,* to cause to fly up to (with acc.).

Abhy-utpatana, am, n. springing or leaping against any one.

अभ्युत्सद् *abhy-ut-sad* (*abhi-ud°*), Caus. P., Ved. *-sādayati, -yitum,* to destroy (?).

अभ्युत्सह् *abhy-ut-sah* (*abhi-ud°*), cl. 1. A. *-sahate, -sahitum, -soḍhum,* to feel competent, to venture, to dare.

अभ्युत्स्मि *abhy-ut-smi* (*abhi-ud°*), cl. 1. A. or poet. P. *-smayate, -ti, -smetum,* to smile.

अभ्युदन् *abhy-ud-an* (*abhi-ud°*), cl. 2. P. *-aniti, -anati, -anitum,* to breathe on or upon.

अभ्युदाहरण *abhy-udāharaṇa, am,* n. (rt. *hṛi*), an example or illustration of a thing by its reverse.

अभ्युदि *abhy-ud-i* (*abhi-ud°*), cl. 2. P. *-eti, -tum,* to go up; to rise over; to happen; to engage in combat with.

Abhy-udaya, as, ā, am, rising; (*as*), m. the rise of luminaries (especially with reference to some other occurrence), sunrise; beginning, commencing; elevation, increase, prosperity; happiness; good result; a festival, any religious celebration; accident, occurrence. — *Abhyudayeshṭi* (*°ya-ish°*), *is,* f., N. of a particular expiatory sacrifice.

Abhy-udayin, ī, inī, i, rising, arising.

1. *abhy-udita, as, ā, am,* risen (as the sun); arisen, happened; elevated, exalted; asleep at sunrise; celebrated as a festival; (*ā*), f., N. of a religious ceremony; (*am*), n. rising, sunrise.

अभ्युदित 2. *abhy-udita, as, ā, am* (rt. *vad*), mentioned, referred to.

अभ्युदीक्ष् *abhy-ud-īksh* (*abhi-ud°*), cl. 1. A. *-īkshate, -shitum,* to look towards.

अभ्युदीर् *abhy-ud-īr* (*abhi-ud°*), Caus. P. *-īrayati, -yitum,* to raise (one's voice); to speak aloud; to incite, stir up.

Abhy-udīrita, as, ā, am, thrown over or upon.

अभ्युदूह् *abhy-ud-ūh* (*abhi-ud°*), cl. 1. P. A. *-ūhati, -te, -hitum,* to move or push farther out.

अभ्युदे *abhy-ude* (*abhi-ud-ā-i*), cl. 2. P. *-aiti, -tum,* to go up to, approach.

अभ्युद्गम् *abhy-ud-gam* (*abhi-ud°*), cl. 1. P. *-gaććhati, -gantum,* to extend; to go out to meet.

Abhy-udga, as, ā, am, rising, uprisen.

Abhy-udgata, as, ā, am, extended; gone out in order to meet (another); risen, elevated. — *Abhy-udgata-rāja, as,* m., N. of a Buddhist Kalpa.

Abhy-udgama, as, m. or *abhy-udgamana, am,* n. rising from a seat to honour any one; setting out to pay a visit.

अभ्युद्गा *abhy-ud-gā* (*abhi-ud°*), cl. 3. P. *-jigāti, -gātum,* to rise over or before.

अभ्युद्दृष्ट *abhy-uddrishṭa, am,* n. (rt. *dṛiś*), the becoming visible (of a star); (*ā*), f., N. of a ceremony.

अभ्युद्धृ *abhy-ud-dhṛi* (*abhi-ud-hṛi*), cl. 1. P. *-uddharati, -rtum,* to take up, take out; to destine, set apart: Caus. *-uddhārayati, -yitum,* to snatch away.

Abhy-uddhṛita, as, ā, am, taken out, taken up, delivered.

अभ्युद्यम् *abhy-ud-yam* (*abhi-ud°*), cl. 1. P. *-yaććhati, -yantum,* to bring, offer; to lift up.

Abhy-udyata, as, ā, am, brought or given unsolicited; prepared, exerting one's self, lifted up.

अभ्युन्द् *abhy-und* (*abhi-und*), cl. 7. P. *-unatti, -unditum,* to wet, bedew; flow over.

Abhy-undat, an, atī, at, bedewing, wetting; flowing over.

अभ्युन्नत *abhy-unnata, as, ā, am* (rt. *nam*), raised, elevated; projecting upwards, very high or full.

Abhy-unnati, is, f. great elevation or prosperity.

अभ्युन्नी *abhy-un-nī* (*abhi-ud-nī*), cl. 1. P. A. *-nayati, -te, -netum,* to pour upon, scoop towards.

अभ्युपगम् *abhy-upa-gam* (*abhi-upa°*), cl. 1. P. *-gaććhati, -gantum,* to go near to, approach, arrive at; to obtain; to assent, agree to, promise, believe: Caus. *-gamayati, -yitum,* to prevail on any one to assent.

Abhy-upagata, as, ā, am, gone near to, approached, arrived at; promised, agreed, assented to; admitted, implied; inferred, probable; similar, analogous.

Abhy-upagantavya, as, ā, am, to be approached or assented to, to be admitted.

Abhy-upagantṛi, tā, trī, tṛi, one who approaches or assents, &c.

Abhy-upagama, as, m. going near to, approaching, arriving at; a promise, an agreement, contract; granting, allowing, admitting, believing; probable ascertainment; supposition, inference, analogy, affinity. — *Abhyupagama-siddhānta, as,* m. an admitted axiom.

Abhy-upagamita, as, ā, am, made to consent, obtained by assent or free consent; (*as*), m. a slave for a fixed term.

अभ्युपपद् *abhy-upa-pad* (*abhi-upa°*), cl. 4. A. *-padyate, -pattum,* to approach in order to help; to deliver; to honour, to comfort; to ask for help; to furnish with.

Abhy-upapatti, is, f. approaching in order to assist, protection, defence; favour, the conferring of a benefit or kindness, affection; agreement, assent; impregnation of a woman (especially of a brother's widow, as an act of duty).

Abhy-upapanna, as, ā, am, protected, rescued, delivered, agreed to, agreeing to, proved, admitted.

अभ्युपयुक्त *abhy-upayukta, as, ā, am* (rt. *yuj*), employed, used.

अभ्युपशान्त *abhy-upaśānta, as, ā, am* (rt. *śam*), allayed, calmed.

अभ्युपसेव् *abhy-upa-sev* (*abhi-upa°*), cl. 1. A. *-sevate, -vitum,* to observe religiously.

अभ्युपस्था *abhy-upa-sthā* (*abhi-upa°*), cl. 1. P. *-tishṭhati, -sthātum,* to accompany, attend, assist.

Abhy-upasthita, as, ā, am, accompanied, attended, assisted by.

अभ्युपाकृत *abhy-upākṛita, as, ā, am,* summoned to take part (in a ceremony?).

अभ्युपागम् *abhy-upāgam* (*abhi-upa-ā-gam*), cl. 1. P. *-gaććhati, -gantum,* to come to.

अभ्युपादा *abhy-upādā* (*abhi-upa-ā-dā*), cl. 3. A. *-datte, -dātum,* to pick up.

अभ्युपावृत्त *abhy-upāvṛitta, as, ā, am* (rt. *vṛit*), approached, come to.

अभ्युपे 1. *abhy-upe* (*abhi-upa-i*), cl. 2. P. *-upaiti, -tum,* to go near, approach, arrive at, enter; to enter a state or condition; to agree with, approve of; to be faithful, obey, submit.

Abhy-upāya, as, m. an agreement, a promise, an engagement; a means, an expedient.

Abhy-upāyana, am, n. a bribe, douceur, complimentary gift, an inducement.

Abhy-upeta, as, ā, am, approached; promised, assented or agreed to (as by contract, &c.), admitted. — *Abhyupetārthakṛitya* (*°ta-ar°*), *as, ā, am,* pledged to the peformance of a required act.

Abhy-upetavya or *abhy-upeya, as, ā, am,* to be admitted or assented to.

Abhy-upetya, ind. having arrived at, having assented or agreed to. — *Abhyupetyāśuśrūshā* (*°tya-aś°*), f. a head or title of law, breach of engagement or contract between master and servant.

Abhy-upeyivas, vān, yushī, vat, (having) arrived at.

अभ्युपे 2. abhy-upe (abhi-upa-ā-i), cl. 2. P. -upaiti, -tum, to go towards, approach.

अभ्युपेक्ष् abhy-upeksh (abhi-upa-iksh), cl. 1. A. -upekshate, -shitum, to leave, abandon.

अभ्युष abhy-usha or abhy-ūsha or abhy-osha, as, m. (rt. ush), a kind of cake of grain &c. half dressed, slightly scorched, or parched so as to be eaten from the hand; bread.

Abhyushīya or abhyūshīya or abhyushya or abhyūshya or abhy-oshīya or abhy-oshya, as, ā, am, consisting of, or belonging to, or fit for the above cake or preparation of parched grain.

अभ्युषित abhy-ushita, as, ā, am (rt. 1. vas), dwelling near to, dwelling with.

अभ्यूढ 1. abhy-ūḍha, as, ā, am (fr. rt. vah with abhi), brought near.

अभ्यूर्णु abhy-ūrṇu (abhi-ūrṇu), cl. 2. P. A. -ūrṇoti, -ṇute, -ūrṇavitum or -ṇuvitum, to cover, hide, conceal; to cover one's self (?).

अभ्यूह् abhy-ūh (abhi-ūh), cl. 1. P. A. -ūhati, -te, -ūhitum, to cover over, to clothe; A. -ūhate, Ved. -ohate, to watch for, to form a plot against; to infer, to guess.

2. abhy-ūḍha, as, ā, am, reasoned upon, concluded, inferred.

Abhy-ūha, as, m. discussion, reasoning, deduction, inference; supplying an ellipsis; understanding.

Abhy-ūhitavya or abhy-ūhya, as, ā, am, to be inferred or guessed.

Abhy-uhya (the u being shortened after abhi before the ya of the ind. part., but sometimes wrongly written with long ū), ind. having concluded or inferred, having reasoned; having supplied an ellipsis.

अभ्यृ abhy-ṛi (abhi-ṛi), cl. 3. 5. P. abhīyarti, -ṛṇoti, -artum, -ritum, -rītum, to go to, to pervade.

Abhy-arṇa. See s. v., p. 71, col. 2.

अभ्यृच्छ् abhy-ṛich (abhi-ṛich), cl. 6. P. -ṛicchati, -chitum, to come to, to visit or afflict with; to strive against, to strive to overpower.

अभ्यृञ्ज् abhy-ṛiñj (abhi-ṛiñj), cl. 6. P. A. -ṛiñjati, -te, -jitum, to stretch out the hand for, to hasten to or towards.

अभ्यृष् abhy-ṛish (abhi-ṛish), cl. 1. P. -arshati, -shitum, to flow or run towards a place; to let flow or run towards a place.

अभ्ये abhye (abhi-ā-i), cl. 2. P. -aiti, -tum, to go near, to come to.

Abhy-etya, ind. having approached, having come to.

अभ्येषण 1. abhy-eshaṇa, am, n. (rt. 3. ish), desiring, wishing for.

Abhy-eshaṇīya, as, ā, am, to be desired.

अभ्येषण 2. abhy-eshaṇa, am, n. (rt. 1. ish), going towards, attacking.

अभ्र् abhr, cl. 1. P. abhrati, abhritum, to go; to err or wander about.

अभ्र abhra (sometimes spelt abbhra, according to the derivation ab-bhra, 'water-bearer'), am, n. cloud; sky, atmosphere, ether, heaven; dust (?); talc, mica; gold; camphor; the ratan (Calamus Rotang); Cyperus Rotundus; (in arithmetic) a cypher; [cf. Gr. ὄμβρος and Lat. imber.] — Abhram-liha, as, ā, am, cloud-licking; what touches or sweeps the clouds; sky-scraper; (as), m. wind. — Abhra-ghana, as, ā, am, thickly covered with clouds. — Abhran-kasha, as, ā, am, grazing (hurting) the clouds, very high; (as), m. air, wind, a mountain. — Abhra-jā, ās, ās, am, Ved. born from clouds, caused by vapours. — Abhra-nāga, as, m. one of the elephants supporting the globe. — Abhra-piśāća or abhra-piśāćaka, as, m. sky-demon, N. of Rāhu, the descending node personified. — Abhra-pushpa, as, m., N. of a cane, Calamus Rotang; (am), n. water; a flower in the clouds, castle in the air, anything impossible. — Abhra-prush, ṭ, f., Ved. the sprinkling of the clouds, rain. — Abhra-māṅsī, f., N. of a plant, Valeriana Jaṭāmāṅsī. — Abhra-mātanga, as, m. Airāvata, Indra's elephant. — Abhra-mālā, f. a line or succession of clouds. — Abhra-roha, am, n. Lapis Lazuli. — Abhra-lipta, as, ā, am, overspread with clouds. — Abhra-varsha, as, ā, am, Ved. pouring water from the clouds. — Abhra-vāṭika, as, m., N. of a plant, Spondias Magnifera. — Abhra-śiras, as, n. a head formed of the sky. — Abhrāvakāśa (°ra-av°), as, m. fall of rain, clouds as the only shelter. — Abhrāvakāśika, as, ā, am, or abhrāvakāśin, ī, inī, i, exposed to the rain (and so doing penance), not seeking shelter from the rain, having the clouds for shelter, open to the sky. — Abhrottha (°ra-ut°), as, m. sky-born, i. e. Indra's thunderbolt.

Abhraka, am, n. talc, mica; the same as abhra, q. v. — Abhraka-bhasman, a, n. calx of talc. — Abhraka-sattva, am, n. steel.

Abhrāya, nom. A. abhrāyate, -yitum, to create clouds, make cloudy.

Abhrita, as, ā, am, clouded, covered with clouds.

Abhriya, as, ā, am, belonging to or produced from clouds; (as), m. lightning; (am), n. a collection of thunder-clouds.

Abhrya, as, m. a naked ascetic, who is clothed only by the air.

अभ्रम a-bhrama, as, ā, am, not blundering; steady, clear; (as), m. steadiness, composure.

A-bhramu, us, f. the female elephant of the east, the mate of Airāvata. — Abhramu-priya or abhramu-vallabha, as, m. the male elephant of the east or Airāvata.

अभ्रातृ a-bhrātṛi, tā, tṛi, Ved. or a-bhrātṛika, as, ā, or a-bhrātṛi-mat, ān, atī, m. f. brotherless. — A-bhrātṛi-han, hā, ghnī, m. f., Ved. not killing a brother.

अभ्रातृव्य a-bhrātṛivya, as, ā, am, having no rival, without an enemy.

अभ्रान्त a-bhrānta, as, ā, am, unperplexed, not mistaken or in error, clear, composed.

A-bhrānti, is, f. absence of perplexity or error.

अभ्रि abhri or abbhri, is, or abhrī, f. (fr. rt. abhr), a wooden scraper or shovel for cleaning a boat, a spatula, a spade, a pointed stick. — Abhri-khāta, am, n., Ved. dug up with the above instrument, as a ploughed field.

अभ्रेष a-bhresha, as, m. non-deviation, fitness, propriety.

अभ्व a-bhva, as, ā, am (etymology doubtful, bhva = bhava or bhuva?), Ved. huge, immense, mighty; monstrous, terrible; (as), m. a powerful man, applied to an enemy; (am), n. immense power, monstrosity, the great pervading principle of the universe; embarrassed state, great calamity; sultriness (?); a monster; offspring; water, a cloud.

अम् 1. am, ind. quickly, a little.

अम् 2. am, cl. 1. P. amati, -mitum, Ved. amiti or amīti, to go; to go to or towards; to serve or honour; to sound: Caus. āmayati, -yitum, to afflict with sickness or pain from disease; to be afflicted or sick.

1. ama, as, m., Ved. going, pressure, heavy weight, violence, strength, power, depriving of sensation, fright, terror; disease, sickness; a servant; companion; (as, ā, am), unripe; unfortunate (?). — Ama-vat, ān, atī, at, Ved. impetuous, violent, strong; powerful, bold, persevering, constant; attended by ministers, attended by diseases, possessed of self; (vat), ind. impetuously. — Ama-hata, as, ā, am, injured by disease, &c. — Ama-han, hā, ghnī, ha, destroying diseases, &c.

1. amata, as, m. sickness; disease; death; time.

1. amati, is, m. moon, time; (is), f., Ved. form, shape, a splendid shape; splendor, glitter; (is, is, i), Ved. poor, indigent; (is), f. want, indigence.

1. amatī-van, ā, m., Ved. poor, indigent.

Amatra, amani, amavishṇu. See s. v.

अम 2. ama, as, m. (connected with amu), this; self; (ā), f. soul.

Amā, ind., Ved. at home, in the house; with; together with; near: see also p. 75, col. 3. — Amā kṛi, to take or carry with one's self.

1. amāt, ind., Ved. from near at hand, from the neighbourhood. (For 2. see p. 75, col. 3.)

अम 3. a-ma, as, m. or a-mā, f. (rt. mā), unmeasured state.

2. a-mati, is, is, i, Ved. of unmeasured lustre (the sun).

अमङ्गल a-mangala or a-mangalya, as, ā, am, inauspicious, unlucky, evil; (las), m. the castor oil tree, Ricinus Communis; (am), n. inauspiciousness, ill-luck.

अमण्ड amaṇḍa, as, m. the castor oil tree, Ricinus Communis.

अमण्डित a-maṇḍita, as, ā, am, unadorned.

अमत 2. a-mata, as, ā, am (rt. man), not felt, not perceptible by the mind; (for 1. amata, see under 2. am.) — Amata-parārtha, as, ā, am, incompatible with the principal subject or subject-matter.

अमति 3. a-mati, is, f. unconsciousness, ignorance, feebleness of intellect, absence of forethought, knowledge or intention; (is, is, i), evil-minded, unworthy of credit, depraved. — Amati-pūrva, as, ā, am, unconscious, unintentional, without forethought.

2. amatī-van, ā, m., Ved. evil-minded, weak-minded.

अमत्र amatra, as, ā, am (rt. am), Ved. overpowering, overcoming, strong, violent, impetuous; (am), n., Ved. strength, power; a vessel, a utensil.

Amatrin, ī, iṇī, i, Ved. strong, powerful; having a drinking-vessel.

अमत्सर a-matsara, as, ā, am, unenvious, charitable.

अमद a-mada, as, ā, am (rt. mad), cheerless, grave, sorrowful.

A-matta, as, ā, am, not inebriated, sober, sane, not mad.

अमधव्य a-madhavya, as, ā, am, not worthy of the sweetness (of the Soma).

अमधुपर्क्य a-madhuparkya, as, ā, am, not worthy of the madhu-parka, q. v.

अमध्यम a-madhyama, as, ā, am, non-central, not being in the middle.

अमध्यस्थ a-madhyastha, as, ā, am, not indifferent.

अमनस् a-manas, as, n. not the organ of desire, non-perception, want of perception; (ās, ās, as), = the next.

A-manaska, as, ā, am, without the organ of desire, without perception; without intellect, unconscious.

A-manasvin, ī, inī, i, unintelligent, inhuman (as a Rākshasa).

अमनाक् a-manāk, ind. not little, much, greatly.

अमनि amani, is, f. (fr. rt. am), a road, a way.

अमनुष्य a-manushya, as, ā, am, not human, unfrequented by men; (as), m. not a man, a demon. — Amanushya-tā, f. unmanliness. — A-manushya-nishevita, as, ā, am, not inhabited by men.

अमनोगत a-manogata, as, ā, am, unthought of, unknown.

अमनोज्ञ a-manojña, as, ā, am, unwelcome to the mind, disagreeable, disliked.

अमनोनीत *a-manonīta, as, ā, am,* disapproved; reprobate.

अमनोयोग *a-manoyoga, as,* m. inattention. *A-manoyogin, ī, inī, i,* inattentive.

अमनोहर *a-manohara* or *a-manoramya, as, ā, am,* or *a-manohārin, ī, iṇī, i,* disagreeable, displeasing, unattractive.

अमन्तव्य *a-mantavya* or *a-mananīya, as, ā, am* (rt. *man*), not to be regarded, inadmissible. *A-mantu, us, us, u,* Ved. unwise, foolish, indocile; (for *ava-mantu*), despising.

अमन्त्र *a-mantra, as,* m. not a Vedic verse or text; *(as, ā, am),* or *a-mantraka, as, ikā, am,* unaccompanied by Vedic verses or texts; unentitled to or not knowing Vedic texts, as a Śūdra, a female, &c. — *A-mantra-vid, t, t, t,* not knowing the formulas or texts of the Veda; *(t),* m., N. of a man.

अमन्द *a-manda, as, ā, am,* not slow, active, violent; not stupid; not little, important; *(as),* m., N. of a tree.

अमन्यमान *a-manyamāna, as, ā, am,* Ved. not understanding, offering no homage; not expecting, not being aware of.

अमन्युत *a-manyuta, as, ā, am,* Ved. not affected with secret anger, not bearing ill-will against a person.

अमम *a-mama, as, ā, am,* without egotism, devoid of all selfish or wordly attachment or desire; *(as),* m. the twelfth Jaina saint of a future Utsarpiṇī. — *Amama-tā,* f. or *amama-tva, am,* n. disinterestedness, indifference.

अमम्रि *a-mamri, is, is, i* (rt. *mṛi*), Ved. immortal, undying.

अमर *a-mara, as, ā, am* (rt. *mṛi*), undying, immortal, imperishable; *(as),* m. a god, a deity; N. of a Marut; a plant, Euphorbia Tirucalli; another plant, Tiaridium Indicum; a species of pine; quicksilver, gold; N. of Amara-siṇha; of a mountain; mystical signification of the letter *u;* the number 33, such being the number of gods according to the later mythology; *(ā),* f. the residence of Indra; the umbilical cord; the womb; a house-post; N. of several plants, Panicum Dactylon, Cocculus Cordifolius, &c.; *(ī),* f. the same as *amarā* in many of its senses. — *Amara-kanṭaka, am,* n. 'peak of the immortals,' N. of part of the Vindhya range near the source of the Soṇa and Narmadā. — *Amara-koṭa, as,* m. the fortress of immortals; N. of the capital of a Rājput state. — *Amara-kosha, as,* m., N. of the Sanskrit dictionary of Amara or Amara-siṇha. — *Amara-kosha-kaumudī,* f. title of a commentary on Amara-siṇha's dictionary. — *Amara-gaṇa, as,* m. the assemblage of immortals. — *Amara-ćandra, as,* m., N. of the author of the Bāla-bhārata. — *Amara-ja, as,* m., N. of a plant. — *Amara-taṭinī,* f. river of the gods; an epithet of the Ganges. — *Amara-tā,* f. or *amara-tva, am,* n. immortality; the condition of the gods. — *Amara-datta, as,* m., N. of a lexicographer. — *Amara-dāru, us,* m., N. of a tree (Pinus Deodaru Roxb.). — *Amara-deva, as,* m. a N. of Amara-siṇha. — *Amara-dvija, as,* m. a Brāhman who lives by attending a temple or idol; superintending a temple. — *Amara-pati, is,* m. the lord of the gods; an epithet of Indra. — *Amara-pura, am,* n. the residence of the immortals, paradise; N. of various towns. — *Amara-pushpa* or *amara-pushpaka, as,* m., N. of several plants; a kind of grass, Saccharum Spontaneum, Pandanus Odoratissimus, Magnifera Indica. — *Amara-pushpikā,* f. a kind of anise, Anethum Sowa Roxb. — *Amara-prakhya* or *amara-prabha, as, ā, am,* like an immortal. — *Amara-prabhu, us,* m. 'lord of the immortals,' one of the thousand names of Vishṇu. — *Amara-bhartṛi, tā,* m. lord of the gods; an epithet of Indra. — *Amara-mālā,* f. title of a dictionary, said to be by the same author as the Amara-kosha. — *Amara-ratna, am,* n. crystal. — *Amara-rāja, as,* m. king of the gods; an epithet of Indra. — *Amararāja-śatru, us,* m. an enemy of the king of the gods; an epithet of Rāvaṇa. — *Amara-loka, as,* m. the abode of the gods, heaven. — *Amaraloka-tā,* f. the bliss of heaven. — *Amara-vat,* ind. like an immortal. — *Amara-vallarī,* f., N. of a plant, Cassyta Filiformis Lin. — *Amara-śakti, is,* m., N. of a king. — *Amara-sarit, t,* f. the river of the gods; epithet of the Ganges. — *Amara-siṇha, as,* m. 'god-lion,' N. of a renowned lexicographer; he was a Buddhist, and is supposed to have adorned the court of Vikramāditya, being included among the nine gems. — *Amara-strī,* f. an Apsaras or nymph of heaven. — *Amarāćārya* (°*ra-āć*°), *as,* m. Vṛihaspati, teacher of the gods. — *Amarāṅganā* (°*ra-aṅg*°), f. a nymph of Indra's heaven. — *Amarādri* (°*ra-ad*°), *is,* m. the mountain of the gods; an epithet of the mount Sumeru or Meru. — *Amarādhipa* (°*ra-adh*°), *as,* m. lord of the gods; an epithet of Indra. — *Amarāpagā* (°*ra-ap*°), f. the river of the gods; an epithet of the Ganges. — *Amarejya* (°*ra-ij*°), *as,* m., N. of Vṛihaspati. — *Amareśa* (°*ra-iś*°), *as,* m. lord of the gods; an epithet of Śiva or Indra. — *Amareśvara* (°*ra-iś*°), *as,* m. an epithet of Vishṇu, Śiva, or Indra. — *Amarottama* (°*ra-ut*°), *as, ā, am,* best of the immortals. — *A-maropama* (°*ra-up*°), *as, ā, am,* like an immortal.
A-maraṇa, am, n. the not dying, immortality.
A-maraṇīya, as, ā, am, immortal. — *Amaraṇīya-tā,* f. immortality.
Amarā-vatī, f. the abode of the immortals, residence of Indra; N. of a town in Berar.
A-marishṇu, us, us, u, Ved. immortal.
A-marta, as, ā, am, Ved. immortal.
A-martya, as, ā, am, immortal, imperishable, divine; *(as),* m. god. — *Amartya-tā* or *amartya-tva, am,* n. immortality. — *Amartya-bhuvana, am,* n. the world of the immortals, heaven.

अमरु *amaru, us,* m., N. of a king, the author of the *Amaru-śataka, am,* n. or the hundred verses of Amaru.

अमरुत *a-maruta, as, ā, am,* without wind, calm.

अमर्दित *a-mardita, as, ā, am* (rt. *mṛid*), unthreshed, unsubdued, not trodden down.

अमर्धत् *a-mardhat, an, antī, at,* Ved. not injuring; indefatigable (?).

अमर्मन् *a-marman, ā,* m., Ved. not a vital part of the body, without a joint, having no joint, having no vital part. — *A-marma-jāta, as, ā, am,* not produced in a vital organ. — *A-marma-vedhin, ī, inī, i,* not injuring vital organs, mild.

अमर्याद *a-maryāda, as, ā, am,* having no limits, transgressing every bound; *(ā),* f. the transgressing or overstepping due bounds; disrespect, impropriety of conduct; violation of decorum or due reverence; forwardness or pertness.

अमर्ष *a-marsha, as,* m. (rt. *mṛish*), nonendurance; impatience; impetuosity, determination of purpose; anger, passion; *(as, ā, am),* unenduring, not bearing; *(as),* m., N. of a prince. — *Amarsha-ja, as, ā, am,* springing from impatience or indignation. — *Amarsha-hāsa, as,* m. an angry laugh, a sarcastic sneer.
A-marshaṇa, as, ā, am, or *amarsha-vat, ān, atī, at,* or *a-marshita, as, ā, am,* or *a-marshin, ī, iṇī, i,* not suffering, not bearing; impatient, intolerant; passionate, wrathful, angry, impetuous, determined.

अमल *a-mala, as, ā, am,* spotless, stainless, clean, pure, shining, white; *(ā),* f., N. of the goddess Lakshmī; the umbilical cord; N. of a tree, Emblica Officinalis Gærtn.; N. of a plant; *(am),* n. purity; the supreme spirit; talc. — *A-mala-garbha, as,* m., N. of a Bodhi-sattva. — *Amala-patatrin, ī, iṇī,* m. f. the wild goose. — *Amala-ratna, am,* n. or *amala-maṇi, is,* m. f. crystal. — *Amalātman* (°*la-āt*°), *ā, ā, a,* of undefiled mind.
Amalaya, nom. P. *amalayati, -yitum,* to make spotless.
A-malina, as, ā, am, stainless, free from dirt, clean.

अमलानक *amalānaka, am,* n. globe-amaranth (Gomphræna Globosa). See *amilātaka.*

अमवत् *ama-vat, ān, atī, at.* See under 1. *ama.*

अमविष्णु *amavishṇu, us, us, u* (fr. rt. *am*), going in different directions, up and down.
Amasa, as, m. disease; stupidity, a fool, time.

अमसृण *a-masṛiṇa, as, ā, am,* not soft, harsh, hard; violent, intense.

अमस्तक *a-mastaka, as, ā, am,* headless.

अमस्तु *a-mastu,* n. curds. See *mastu.*

अमा 1. *amā,* f. day of conjunction of sun and moon or new moon; see *amā-vasī,* p. 76, col. 1. — *Amānta* (*amā-anta*), *as,* m. the end of the day of new moon.

अमा 2. *amā,* ind. at home, in the house; see also under 2. *ama,* p. 74. — *Amākta* (*amā-akta*), *as, ā, am,* Ved. met, come together. — *Amā-jur, ūr,* f., Ved. living at home during life, growing old at home; being without husband in the same dwelling with her parents (as a maiden).

अमांस *a-māṇsa, am,* n. not flesh, anything but flesh; *(as, ā, am),* without flesh, feeble, thin. — *A-māṇsaudanika* (°*sa-od*°), *as, ī, am,* not relating to a preparation of rice with meat.

अमात् 2. *a-māt, ān, āti* or *ānti, āt,* not measuring. (For 1. see p. 74, col. 3.)

अमातृक *a-mātṛika, as, ā, am,* without a mother, motherless.
A-mātā-putra, as, m. having neither mother nor son.
A-mātṛibhogiṇa, as, ā, am, not fit for the use of a mother.

अमात्य *amātya, as,* m. (fr. 2. *amā* above), inmate of the same house, belonging to the same house or family; a companion, follower, counsellor, minister.

अमात्र *a-mātra, am,* n. non-measure, not a measure or quantity (said of the universal spirit); *(as, ā, am),* boundless; not whole or entire; not elementary; having the measure or quantity of the letter *a.* — *Amātravat-tva, am,* n. deficiency, defect; spirit, spiritual essence.

अमानन *a-mānana, am,* n. disrespect, contempt, disobedience.

अमानव *a-mānava, as, ā, am,* not human, animal; superhuman.

अमानस्य *a-mānasya, am,* n. pain.

अमानिता *a-mānitā,* f. or *a-mānitva, am,* n. (rt. *man*), modesty, humility.
A-mānin, ī, inī, i, humble, modest.
A-mānya or *a-mānitavya* or *a-mānanīya, as, ā, am,* to be disrespected.

अमानुष *a-mānusha, as, ī, am,* not human, anything but man; supernatural, inhuman, a monster; not well disposed towards man.
A-mānushya, as, ā, am, not human, superhuman, &c.

अमामसी *amā-masī* or *amā-māsī* for *amā-vasī,* p. 76, col. 1.

अमाय *a-māya, as, ā, am,* not cunning, not sagacious; free from error or deceit, guileless, sincere; (*ā*), f. absence of delusion, deceit, or guile; knowledge of the truth; sincerity, honesty.

A-māyika, as, ā, am, or *a-māyin, ī, inī, i,* without illusion or deceit, void of trick or guile; true, honest; real.

अमार *a-māra, as,* m. not dying.

अमार्ग *a-mārga, as,* m. want of a road; (*as, ā, am*), pathless, without a road.

अमार्गित *a-mārgita, as, ā, am,* unsought, not hunted after.

अमार्जित *a-mārjita, as, ā, am,* uncleansed, unwashed, unadorned.

अमावसु *amā-vasu, us,* m., N. of a son of Purūravas, of a son of Kuśa and others.

अमावास्या *amā-vāsyā,* f. (fr. rt. *vas,* 'to dwell,' with *amā,* 'together,' i. e. *rātri,* night of new moon), the first day of the first quarter on which the moon is invisible; a sacrifice offered at that time; the sacrificial cake?; (*as, ā, am*), or *amā-vāsyaka, as, ā, am,* produced in a night of new moon.

Amā-vasī or *amā-vasyā* or *amā-vāsī,* f. the night of new moon; that night during which the moon dwells together with or in the same quarter as the sun.

अमाष *a-māsha, as, ā, am,* or *a-māshaka, as, ikā, am,* having no kidney-beans.

अमित 1. *amita, as, ā, am* (fr. rt. *am*), gone, served, honoured, sounded.

अमित 2. *a-mita, as, ā, am* (rt. *mā*), unmeasured, boundless, infinite; without a certain measure; neglected; unpolished, unclean. — *Amita-kratu, us,* m., Ved. of unbounded wisdom; of unbounded energy. — *Amita-gati, is,* m., N. of a Jaina author. — *Amita-tejas, ās, ās, as,* of boundless glory. — *Amita-dyuti, is, is, i,* of infinite splendor. — *Amita-dhvaja, as,* m., N. of a son of Dharma-dhvaja. — *Amita-vikrama, as,* m. of unbounded valour, a N. of Vishṇu. — *Amita-vīrya, as,* m. of immense strength. — *Amitākshara* (°*ta-ak*°), *as, ā, am,* not containing a fixed number of syllables, unbound, prosaic. — *Amitābha* (°*ta-ābh*°), *as, ā, am,* of unmeasured splendor; (*as*), m. a kind of deity; N. of a Dhyāni-buddha. — *Amitāyus* (°*ta-āy*°), *us,* m., N. of a Dhyāni-buddha. — *Amitaujas* (°*ta-oj*°), *ās, ās, as,* of unbounded energy, all-powerful, almighty.

अमित्र *a-mitra, as, ā,* m. f. not a friend, an enemy, adversary, foe. (According to some authorities this is not derived from *a* and *mitra,* a friend, but fr. rt. *am,* 'to attack.') — *Amitra-khāda, as,* m., Ved. swallowing or devouring his enemies; an epithet of Indra. — *Amitra-gaṇa-sūdana, as, ā, am,* destroying the hosts of one's enemies. — *A-mitra-ghāta, as, ā, am,* Ved. killing enemies; (*as*), m. a N. of Vindusāra, the son of Ćandragupta. — *Amitra-ghātin, ī, inī, i,* or *amitra-ghna, as, ā* or *ī, am,* the same as the preceding. — *Amitra-jit, t,* m. conquering one's enemies; a son of Suvarṇa. — *Amitra-tā,* f. enmity. — *Amitra-dambhana, as, ā, am,* Ved. hurting enemies. — *Amitra-sāha, as,* m., Ved. enduring or overcoming enemies; epithet of Indra. — *Amitra-senā,* f. hostile arrow. — *Amitra-han, ā,* m., Ved. killing enemies. — *Amitrā-yudh, t, t, t,* Ved. subduing one's enemies.

Amitraya or *amitrāya,* nom. *amitrayati, -trāyate, -yitum,* to act like an enemy, have hostile intentions, to hate.

A-mitrin, ī, iṇī, i, hostile, an adversary, enemy.

A-mitriya, as, ā, am, or *a-mitrya, as, ā, am,* hostile; inimical.

अमिथित *a-mithita, as, ā, am,* Ved. not reviled; unprovoked.

अमिथ्या *a-mithyā,* ind. not falsely, truthfully.

अमिन् *amin, ī, inī, i* (fr. *ama,* see *am*), sick, diseased.

1. *amina, as, ā, am* (fr. rt. *am*), Ved. going everywhere, violent, tempestuous (?); loved by all (?).

अमिन 2. *a-mina, as, ā, am,* Ved. unmeasured, unparalleled, inviolable.

अमिनत् *a-minat, an, atī, at* (rt. *mī*), Ved. not hurting; unhurt.

अमिलातक *amilātaka, am,* n. globe-amaranth.

अमिश्र *a-miśra, as, ā, am,* unmixed, unmixing; without participation of others.

A-miśraṇīya, as, ā, am, immiscible.

A-miśrita, as, ā, am, unmixed, unblended.

अमिष 1. *amisha, am,* n. luxury, object of enjoyment, flesh. See *āmisha.*

अमिष 2. *a-misha, am,* n. honesty, simplicity, absence of fraud; dishonesty (?).

अमीतवर्ण *a-mīta-varṇa, as, ā, am* (*mīta* fr. rt. *mī*), Ved. of infinite hue; of unhurt or unextinguishable colour.

अमीमांसा *a-mīmāṇsā,* f. (rt. *man*), absence of reasoning or investigation.

A-mīmāṇsya, as, ā, am, not to be reasoned about or discussed, not to be demonstrated by reason.

अमीवा *amīvā,* f. (fr. rt. *am*), pain, distress, terror, fright; tormenting spirit, demon; affliction, disease; (*as*), m. an enemy, one who afflicts; (*am*), n. affliction, pain, grief. — *Amīva-ćātana, as, ī, am,* Ved. driving away pains, diseases, enemies, or tormenting spirits. — *Amīva-han, ā,* m., Ved. killing evil spirits, destroying pains.

अमु *amu,* a pronominal base, used in the declension of the pronom. *adas.*

Amuka, as, ā, am, a certain person or thing, anything or person referred to without a name.

Amutas, ind. from there, there; from that place, from above, i. e. from the other world, from heaven; hereupon, upon this; henceforth.

Amutra, ind. there; there, i. e. in what precedes or has been said; there above, i. e. in the other world, in the life to come; here. — *Amutra-bhūya, am,* n., Ved. being there above or in the other world; dying.

Amutratya, as, ā, am, belonging to a future state, being of the next world.

Amuthā, ind. thus, in that manner, like that; *amuthā as,* to be thus, a euphemistic expression used in the sense of, to fare very ill.

Amuyā, ind., Ved. in that manner, thus or thus; (with rt. *as* or *bhū*) to be thus; to be gone, to be lost.

Amurhi, ind. at that time, then.

Amu-vat, ind. like a person or thing referred to without name.

Amushmin (loc. sing. of *adas*), in the other world.

Amushya (gen. sing. of *adas*), of such a one. — *Amushya-kula, as, ā, am,* belonging to the family of such a one. — *Amushya-putra, as, ī,* m. f. the son or daughter of such a one; of a good family, of known origin. — *Amushyāyaṇa* (°*ya-ay*°), *as, ā,* m. f. offspring of such a one; of respectable birth, of known origin.

Amū-dṛiś, k, k, k, or *amū-dṛiśa,* or *amū-dṛiksha, as, ā, am,* like that, such like, such a one, of such form or kind.

अमुक्त *a-mukta, as, ā, am,* not loosed, not let go; not liberated from birth and death; (*am*), n. a weapon that is always grasped and not thrown, as a knife, a sword, &c. — *Amukta-hasta, as, ā, am,* one whose hand is not open (to give); sparing; stingy; frugal, prudent.

A-mukti, is, f. non-liberation; want of freedom or liberty.

A-muć, k, f., Ved. non-liberation.

A-mući, f., Ved. not unbinding, not setting at liberty (epithet of an evil spirit).

अमुख *a-mukha, as, ā, am,* having no mouth.

A-mukhya, as, ā, am, not chief, inferior, ordinary.

अमुग्ध *a-mugdha, as, ā, am,* not confounded, not perplexed, not foolish.

अमूढ *a-mūḍha, as, ā, am* (rt. *muh*), not infatuated, wise; not perplexed.

अमूर *a-mūra, as, ā, am* (for *a-mūḍha,* q. v.), Ved. without error or mistake, infallible, not ignorant, not bewildered.

अमूर्त *a-mūrta, as, ā, am,* formless, shapeless, incorporeal, unembodied; (*as*), m., N. of Śiva. — *Amūrta-rajas, ās,* or *amūrta-rajasa, as,* m. a son of Kuśa by Vaidarbhī.

A-mūrti, is, f. shapelessness, absence of shape or form; (*is, is, i*), formless; (*is*), m., N. of Vishṇu; (*-ayas*), m. pl. a class of Manes, who have no definite form. — *Amūrti-mat, ān, atī, at,* formless.

अमूल *a-mūla* or *a-mūlaka, as, ā, am,* rootless, baseless; without support; without authority; without material cause or origin; not fixed in the earth; having locomotive powers; (*ā*), f., N. of a plant, Methonica Superba Lam.

अमूल्य *a-mūlya, as, ā, am,* invaluable, not to be purchased, priceless.

अमृक्त *a-mṛikta, as, ā, am,* Ved. unhurt, unharmed, safe.

अमृणाल *a-mṛiṇāla, am,* n. the root of a fragrant grass, used for taties or screens, &c., commonly called Kaskas, Andropogon Muricatus.

अमृत *a-mṛita, as, ā, am,* not dead; immortal, imperishable, causing immortality; beautiful, beloved, desired; (*as*), m. a god, an immortal; N. of Indra, of the sun, of Prajāpati, of the soul, of Vishṇu, of Śiva, of Dhanvantari as physician of the gods, &c.; N. of a plant, Phaseolus Trilobus Ait.; N. of the root of a plant; (*ā*), f. spirituous liquor; N. of several plants, Emblica Officinalis, Terminalia Citrina Roxb., Cocculus Cordifolius, Piper Longum, Ocymum Sanctum, &c.; N. of the mother of Parikshit; (*am*), n. immortality; the collective body of immortals; the world of immortality, heaven, paradise, eternity; the immortal light; the nectar conferring immortality, ambrosia; the Soma juice; antidote against poison; a drug; the residue of a sacrifice; unsolicited alms; water; clarified butter; milk; food; boiled rice; anything sweet, a sweetmeat; property; gold, quicksilver; poison; splendor; final emancipation; N. of a sacred place; N. of various conjunctions of planets supposed to confer long life; the number 'four.' — *Amṛita-kuṇḍa, am,* n. the vessel containing the Amṛita or nectar. — *Amṛita-keśava, as,* m., N. of a temple, built by Amṛita-prabhā. — *Amṛita-kshāra, am,* n. sal ammoniac. — *Amṛita-gati, is,* f., N. of a metre consisting of four times ten syllables. — *A-mṛita-garbha, as,* m., Ved. the immortal fetus, i. e. sleep; (*as, ā, am*), filled with nectar. — *Amṛita-ćiti, is,* f. the accumulation or arrangement of sacrificial bricks conferring immortality. — *Amṛita-ja, as, ā, am,* produced by the Amṛita; (*ā*), f., N. of a plant, Yellow Myrobalan. — *Amṛita-jaṭā,* f., N. of a plant, Valeriana Jaṭāmāṇsī. — *Amṛita-taraṅgiṇī,* f. moonlight. — *Amṛita-tā,* f. or *amṛita-tva, am,* n. immortality. — *Amṛita-dīdhiti* or *amṛita-dyuti, is,* m. the moon. — *Amṛita-drava, as, ā, am,* shedding ambrosia. — *Amṛita-dhāra, as, ā, am,* shedding or distilling ambrosia; (*ā*), f., N. of a metre. — *Amṛita-nādopanishad* (°*da-up*°), *t,* f., N. of an Upanishad, lit. 'the sound of immortality.' — *Amṛita-pa, as, ā, am,* drinking nectar; (*as*), m. a deity.

— *Amṛita-paksha, as,* m. the immortal or golden wing (of sacrificial fire); having immortal or golden wings. — *Amṛita-prabhā,* f., N. of several women. — *Amṛita-phala, as, am,* m. n., N. of a plant, Trichosanthes Dioeca, Roxb.; (*ā*), f. a bunch of grapes; the plant Emblica Officinalis Gærtn. — *Amṛita-bandhu, us,* m., Ved. friend of immortality, keeper of immortality; a horse (so called because a horse was produced in the ocean along with the Amṛita). — *Amṛita-bhavana, am,* n., N. of a monastery. — *Amṛita-bhuj, k,* m. an immortal, a deity. — *Amṛita-bhū, ūs, ūs, u,* free from birth and death. — *Amṛita-mati, is,* f., N. of the metre Amṛitagati. — *Amṛita-manthana, am,* n. the churning for the Amṛita. — *Amṛita-maya, as, ī, am,* immortal; consisting of or full of Amṛita. — *Amṛitamālinī,* f., N. of Durgā. — *Amṛita-rasa, as,* m. nectar, ambrosia; (*ā*), f. dark-coloured grapes. — *Amṛita-latā* or *amṛita-latikā,* f. a nectar-giving creeping plant. — *Amṛita-vapus, us,* m. of immortal form, Śiva. — *Amṛita-varsha, as,* m. a shower of nectar. — *Amṛita-vallarī* or *amṛita-vallī,* f. a creeping plant, Cocculus Cordifolius. — *Amṛita-vākā,* f. a kind of bird. — *Amṛita-vindūpanishad* (*°du-up°*), *t,* f., N. of an Upanishad of the Atharva-veda, lit. 'drop of nectar.' — *Amṛita-sambhavā,* f. a creeping plant, Cocculus Cordifolius. — *Amṛita-sāra, as,* m. essence of ambrosia. — *Amṛitasāra-ja, as,* m. raw sugar, molasses. — *Amṛita-sū, ūs,* m. the moon (as distilling nectar). — *Amṛita-sodara, as,* m. a horse, lit. 'brother of nectar,' born together with the Amṛita at the churning of the ocean. — *Amṛita-sravā,* f., N. of a plant and tree. — *Amṛita-srut, t, t, t,* shedding nectar. — *Amṛitākara* (*°ta-āk°*), *as,* m. 'a mine of nectar;' N. of a man. — *Amṛitākshara* (*°ta-ak°*), *as, ā, am,* immortal and imperishable. — *Amṛitānanda* (*°ta-ān°*), *as,* m., N. of a man. — *Amṛitāndhas* (*°ta-an°*), *ās,* m. a deity, whose food is ambrosia. — *Amṛitā-phala, am,* n. the fruit of the Trichosanthes. — *Amṛitāśa* (*°ta-āśa*), *as,* m., N. of Vishṇu. — *Amṛitāśana* (*°ta-aś°*), *as,* or *amṛitāśin* (*°ta-āś°*), *ī,* m. eating ambrosia; a deity. — *Amṛitāsaṅga* (*°ta-ās°*), *am,* n. a collyrium, extracted from the Amomum Anthoriza. — *Amṛitāsu* (*°ta-asu*), *us, us, u,* whose soul is immortal. — *Amṛitāharaṇa* (*°ta-āh°*), *as,* m., N. of Garuḍa, the bird of Vishṇu, who upon one occasion stole the Amṛita. — *Amṛitāhva* (*°ta-āh°*), *am,* n. a kind of fruit. — *Amṛiteśa* or *amṛiteśvara* (*°ta-īś°*), *as,* m. epithet of Śiva. — *Amṛiteśaya, as,* m. sleeping on the Amṛita, epithet of Vishṇu. — *Amṛiteshṭakā* (*°ta-ish°*), f. a kind of sacrificial brick, shaped like golden heads (of men, animals, &c.). — *Amṛitotpatti* (*°ta-ut°*), *is,* f. the production of the Amṛita. — *Amṛitotpannā* (*°ta-ut°*), f. a fly; (*am*), n. a kind of collyrium. — *Amṛitodana* (*°ta-od°*), *as,* m., N. of a son of Siṇhahanu. — *Amṛitodbhava* (*°ta-ud°*), *am,* n. a kind of collyrium.

Amṛitaka, am, n. the nectar of immortality.

Amṛitāya, nom. A. *amṛitāyate, -yitum,* to be like nectar.

अमृत्यु *a-mṛityu, us,* m. not death, immortality; (*us, us, u*), immortal, causing immortality.

अमृध्र *a-mṛidhra, as, ā, am,* Ved. uninjured, not to be impaired, invulnerable; unremitting, unceasing, indefatigable (?).

अमृषा *a-mṛishā,* ind. not falsely, certainly, surely; rightly. — *Amṛishā-bāshin, ī, iṇī, i,* speaking truly.

अमृष्ट *a-mṛishṭa, as, ā, am* (rt. *mṛij*), not rubbed. — *Amṛishṭa-mṛija, as, ā, am,* of unimpaired purity.

अमृष्य *a-mṛishya, as, ā, am,* unbearable, insufferable.

A-mṛishyamāṇa, as, ā, am, not enduring, not bearing or tolerating.

अमेक्षण *a-mekshaṇa, as, ā, am,* having no *mekshaṇa* or mixing-instrument.

अमेघ *a-megha, as, ā, am,* cloudless.

अमेदस्क *a-medaska, as, ā, am,* without fat, lean.

अमेधस् *a-medhas, ās, ās, as,* foolish; an idiot.

अमेध्य *a-medhya, as, ā, am,* not able or not allowed to sacrifice, not fit for sacrifice, impure, unholy, nefarious, foul; (*am*), n. fæces, excrement; an unlucky omen. — *Amedhya-kuṇapāśin* (*°pa-āś°*), *ī, inī, i,* feeding on carrion. — *Amedhya-tā,* f. or *amedhya-tva, am,* n. impurity, foulness, filthiness. — *A-medhya-yukta, as, ā, am,* filthy, foul. — *A-medhya-lipta, as, ā, am,* smeared with ordure, foul, defiled. — *Amedhya-lepa, as,* m. smearing with ordure. — *Amedhyākta* (*°ya-ak°*), *as, ā, am,* soiled by ordure.

अमेन *a-mena, as,* m., Ved. having no wife, a widower.

अमेनि *a-meni, is, is, i,* Ved. not shooting, not able to shoot, not injuring.

अमेय *a-meya, as, ā, am,* immeasurable. — *Ameyātman* (*°ya-āt°*), *ā, ā, a,* possessing extraordinary powers of mind, magnanimous; (*ā*), m. a N. of Vishṇu.

अमेष्ट *ameshṭa* (*°mā-ish°*), *as, ā, am,* Ved. sacrificed at home. See 2. *amā,* p. 75.

अमोक्य *a-mokya, as, ā, am* (rt. *muć*), Ved. that cannot be unloosed.

A-moćana, am, n. not loosening or letting go; non-liberation.

A-moćanīya, as, ā, am, not to be liberated, not to be let go.

A-moćita, as, ā, am, not liberated, confined.

अमोक्ष *a-moksha, as, ā, am* (rt. *moksh*), unliberated, unloosed; (*as*), m. want of freedom, bondage, confinement; non-liberation from mundane existence.

अमोघ *a-mogha, as, ā, am,* unerring, unfailing, not vain, efficacious, succeeding, reaching the mark; productive, fruitful; (*as*), m. the not erring, the not failing; unerringness; N. of Śiva and Vishṇu; N. of a river; (*ā*), f. trumpet flower, Bignonia Suaveolens, Roxb.; a plant of which the seed is used as a vermifuge, Erycibe Paniculata, Roxb.; Terminalia Citrina, Roxb.; N. of a spear; N. of Śiva's wife; mystical name of the double consonant *ksh.* — *Amogha-daṇḍa, as,* m. (unerring in punishment), N. of Śiva. — *Amogha-darśin, ī,* m., N. of a Bodhi-sattva. — *Amogha-dṛishṭi, is, is, i,* of unerring view or mind. — *Amogha-bala, as, ā, am,* of never-failing strength. — *Amogha-bhūti, is,* m., N. of a king of the Pañjāb. — *Amogha-rāja, as,* m., N. of a Bhikshu. — *Amogha-vāć, k,* f. words that are not vain or idle. — *Amogha-vāñćhita, as, ā, am,* never disappointed. — *Amogha-vikrama, as,* m. of unerring valour; N. of Śiva. — *Amogha-siddha, as,* m., N. of the fifth Dhyāni-buddha. — *Amoghāćārya* (*°gha-āć°*), *as,* m., N. of an author.

अमोत *amota* (*amā-uta*), *as, ā, am,* Ved. woven at home, taken care of at home; see 2. *amā.* — *Amota-putrakā,* f., Ved. a maiden protected at home.

Amotaka, as, m., Ved. protected at home (a child); a weaver (?).

अमौत्रधौत *a-mautra-dhauta, as, ā, am,* not washed by a washerman.

अमौन *a-mauna, am,* n. non-silence; knowledge of soul.

अम्नस् *amnas* (liable to become *amnar*), Ved. unawares, quickly; at present; a little. (The etymology is doubtful, but cf. 1. *am.*)

अम्ब् *amb,* cl. 1. P. *ambati, -bitum,* to go; cl. 1. A. *ambate,* to sound.

Amba, as, m. a father; sound, the Veda, one who sounds; (*ā*), f. a mother, see *ambā;* (*am*), n. the eye; water?; (*a*), ind. a particle of affirmation, well! well now! — *Amba-sthala, am,* n., N. of a mountain peak.

Ambaka, am, n. a father (?), an eye [cf. *try-ambaka*]; copper?; (*ikā,* f.), see under *ambā.*

Ambayā, f., Ved. mother, good woman (as a respectful title?), conveying water (?).

अम्बर *ambara, am,* n. (fr. rt. *amb?* or rt. *vṛi,* to surround, with *am* prefixed), circumference, compass; surrounding country, neighbourhood; clothes, apparel; cotton; sky, atmosphere, ether; saffron; talc; a perfume (Ambergris); N. of a people. — *Ambara-ga, as, ā, am,* sky-going. — *Ambara-da, am,* n. cotton. — *Ambara-yuga, am,* n. the two principal female garments, or upper and lower cloths or mantles. — *Ambara-śaila, as,* m. a high mountain touching the sky. — *Ambara-sthalī,* f. the earth. — *Ambarānta* (*°ra-an°*), *as,* m. the end of a garment; the horizon. — *Ambaraukas* (*°ra-ok°*), *ās,* m. dwelling in heaven; a god.

Ambarya, nom. P. *ambaryati, -yitum,* to bring together.

अम्बरीष *ambarīsha, as, am,* m. n. (fr. rt. *amb?*), a frying-pan (in this sense also written with short *i, ambarisha*); one of the hells; remorse, war, battle; (*as*), m. a young animal, a colt; the sun; the hog-plum plant, Spondias Magnifera; N. of Vishṇu; of Śiva; of a king of the solar race, celebrated as a worshipper of Vishṇu. — *Ambarīsha-putra, as,* m. son of Ambarīsha, whence the N. of a country.

अम्बष्ठ *amba-shṭha, as,* m. (fr. *amba* and *sthā?*), N. of a country and of its inhabitants; the offspring of a man of the Brāhman and a woman of the Vaiśya tribe, a man of the medical caste; (*ā*), f., N. of several plants, Jasminum Auriculatum, Clypea Hernandifolia, Oxalis Corniculata; (*ā*) or (*ī*), f. an Ambashṭha woman.

Ambashṭhakī, f. the plant Clypea Hernandifolia.

Ambashṭhikā, f. the plant Clerodendrum Siphonanthus.

अम्बा *ambā,* f. (fr. rt. *amb?* the voc. case in the Veda is *ambe* or *amba;* in later Sanskrit *amba* only), a mother, good woman (as a title of respect); N. of a plant; N. of Durgā, the wife of Śiva; N. of an Apsaras; N. of a daughter of a king of Kāśi; a sister of Pāṇḍu's mother; a term in astrology to denote the fourth condition (?). In the South-Indian languages, *ambā* is corrupted into *ammā,* and is often affixed to the names of goddesses, and females in general [with *ambā* has been compared the Germ. *Amme,* 'a nurse;' Old Germ. *amma,* Them. *ammôn, ammûn*]. — *Ambā-gaṅgā,* f. a river in Ceylon. — *Ambā-janman, a,* n., N. of a Tīrtha.

Ambāḍā or *ambālā* or *ambāyu, us,* f. mother.

Ambālikā, f. mother, good woman (as a term of respect); N. of a plant; N. of a daughter of a king of Kāśi, wife of Vićitra-vīrya, and mother of Pāṇḍu.

Ambi, is, f., Ved. water; woman, mother, nurse. — *Ambi-tamā,* f., Ved. the best of waters or mothers.

Ambikā, f. mother, good woman (as a term of respect); N. of the plant Wrightia Antidysenterica; a sister of Rudra; N. of Pārvatī, the wife of Śiva; the wife of Rudra Ugraretas; one of the female domestic deities of the Jainas; daughter of a king of Kāśi, wife of Vićitra-vīrya, and mother of Dhṛita-rāshṭra; N. of a place in Bengal. — *Ambikā-pati, is,* m., N. of Śiva. — *Ambikā-putra, as,* m., N. of Dhṛita-rāshṭra.

Ambikeya or *ambikeyaka, as,* m., N. of Gaṇeśa, Kārttikeya, and Dhṛita-rāshṭra. See *āmbikeya.*

अम्बु *ambu,* n. (fr. rt. *amb?*), water; the watery element of the blood [cf. ὄμβρος, *imber*]; the plant Andropogon Schœnanthus; N. of a metre; a term in astrology = *ambā.* — *Ambu-kaṇa, as,* m. a drop of water. — *Ambu-kaṇṭaka, as,* m. the short-nosed alligator. — *Ambu-kirāta, as,* m. an alligator. — *Ambu-kīśa* or *ambu-kūrma, as,* m. a porpoise, especially the Gangetic, Delphinus Gangeticus. — *Ambu-keśara, as,* m. lemon tree. — *Ambu-kriyā,* f. a funeral rite = *jala-kriyā.* — *Ambu-ga, as, ā, am,* water-goer, living in water. — *Ambu-ghana, as,* m. hail, frozen rain. — *Ambu-ćara, as, ī, am,* moving in the water, aquatic. — *Ambu-ćāmara, am,* n. water-chowrī, an aquatic plant, Valisneria. — *Ambu-ćārin, ī, iṇī, i,* moving in water, as a fish, &c. — *Ambu-ja, as, ā, am,* produced in water, water-born, aquatic; (*as*), m., N. of a plant, Barringtonia Acutangula Gærtn.; a lotus, Nymphæa Nelumbo; the thunderbolt of Indra. — *Ambu-janman, a,* n. a lotus, Nymphæa Nelumbo. — *Ambuja-bhū, ūs,* m. the god Brahmā. — *Ambuja-stha, as, ā, am,* sitting on a lotus. — *Ambu-taskara, as,* m. water-thief, the sun. — *Ambu-tāla, as,* m. the plant Valisneria. — *Ambu-da, as, ā, am,* shedding or giving water; (*as*), m. a cloud; the plant Cyperus Hexastychius Communis. — *Ambu-dhara, as,* m. a cloud. — *Ambu-dhi, is,* m. (receptacle of waters), the ocean; the number 'four.' — *Ambudhi-sravā,* f., N. of a plant, Aloes Perfoliata. — *Ambu-nidhi, is,* m. (treasury of waters), the ocean. — *Ambu-pa, as, ā, am,* drinking or imbibing water; (*as*), m. a plant, Cassia Tora or Alata. — *Ambu-pattrā,* f., N. of a plant, Cyperus Hexastychius Communis Nees. — *Ambu-paddhati, is,* f. or *ambu-pāta, as,* m. current, stream, flow of water. — *Ambu-prasāda, as,* m. or *ambu-prasādana, am,* n. the clearing nut tree, Strychnos Potatorum: the nuts of this plant are generally used in India for purifying water; they are rubbed upon the inner surface of a vessel, and so precipitate the impurities of the fluid it contains. — *Ambu-bhṛit, t,* m. a cloud; the ocean (?); a grass, Cyperus Pertenuis; talc. — *Ambu-mat, ān, atī, at,* watery, having or containing water; (*tī*), f., N. of a river. — *Ambu-mātra-ja, as, ā, am,* produced only in water; (*as*), m. a bivalve shell. — *Ambu-muć, k,* m. a cloud. — *Ambu-rāja, as,* m. the ocean; N. of Varuṇa. — *Ambu-rāśi, is,* m. (heap of waters), the ocean. — *Ambu-ruha, am,* n. the lotus; (*ā*), f. Hibiscus Mutabilis. — *Ambu-rohiṇī,* f. the lotus. — *Ambu-vāći,* f. four days in Āshāḍha, the tenth to the thirteenth of the dark half of the month, when the earth is supposed to be unclean, and agriculture is prohibited. — *Ambu-vāći-tyāga,* the thirteenth of the same. — *Ambu-vāći-prada, am,* n. the tenth in the second half of the month Āshāḍha. — *Ambu-vāsinī* or *ambu-vāsī,* f. the trumpet flower, Bignonia Suaveolens. — *Ambu-vāha, as,* m. a cloud; the grass Cyperus Pertenuis; a water-carrier; talc; the number 'seventeen.' — *Ambu-vāhin, ī, inī, i,* carrying or conveying water; (*inī*), f. a wooden baling vessel; N. of a river. — *Ambu-vetasa, as,* m. a kind of cane or reed growing in water. — *Ambu-śirishikā,* f., N. of a plant. — *Ambu-śitā,* f., N. of a river. — *Ambu-sarpiṇī,* f. a leech. — *Ambu-secanī,* f. a wooden baling vessel.

Ambū-kṛita, as, ā, am, pronounced indistinctly, so that the words remain too much in the mouth; sputtered (as speech, accompanied with emission of saliva).

अम्ब्य *ambya, as,* m., Ved. a chanter.

अम्भ् *ambh,* cl. 1. A. *ambhate, -bhitum,* to sound.

अम्भस् 1. *ambhas,* n. also ind., power, splendor, fruitfulness; a philos. term = *tushṭi:* (the etymology is doubtful; perhaps connected with obs. rt. *ap,* or fr. *bhā,* 'to shine,' with prefix *am.*)

अम्भस् 2. *ambhas,* n. (said to be fr. rt. *āp;* perhaps connected with 1. *ambhas* or with *ap, abbhra, ambu*), water; the sky; the fourth sign of the zodiac; collective N. for gods, men, manes, and Asuras; mystical name of the letter *v* [cf. ὄμβρος, *imber*]. — *Ambhaḥ-sāra, am,* n. a pearl. — *Ambhaḥ-sū, ūs,* m. smoke; cloudiness. — *Ambhaḥ-stha, as, ā, am,* what holds or contains water; abiding in water. — *Ambhasā-kṛita, as, ā, am,* done by water. — *Ambho-ja, as, ā, am,* produced in water, water-born, aquatic; (*as*), m. the moon; the sārasa or Indian crane; (*am*), n. the lotus. — *Ambhoja-khaṇḍa, am,* n. a group of lotus flowers. — *Ambhoja-janman, ā,* m. or *ambhoja-jani, is,* m. or *ambhoja-yoni, is,* m. an epithet of Brahmā, being born secondarily from a lotus. — *Ambhojinī,* f. an assemblage of lotus flowers or a place where they abound. — *Ambho-da, as,* m. a cloud; the plant Cyperus Hexastychius Communis Nees. — *Ambho-dhara, as,* m. a cloud. — *Ambho-dhi, is,* m. (receptacle of waters), the ocean. — *Ambhodhi-vallabha, as,* m. coral. — *Ambho-nidhi* or *ambho-rāśi, is,* m. a pool, the ocean. — *Ambho-ruh, t,* n. or *ambho-ruha, am,* n. the lotus; (*as*), m. the Indian crane.

अम्भिणी *ambhiṇī,* f., Ved., N. of an instructress, who transmitted the white Yajur-veda to Vāć (speech).

अम्भृण 1. *ambhṛiṇa, as, ā, am* (connected with 1. *ambhas*), Ved. powerful, great, violent [cf. ὄβριμος, ὄμβριμος].

अम्भृण 2. *ambhṛiṇa, as, ā, am* (fr. rt. *bhraṇ?*), crying violently, roaring terribly.

अम्भृण 3. *ambhṛiṇa, as,* m. (rt. *bhṛi* with *am?*), Ved. a vessel used in preparing the Soma juice; N. of a Ṛishi, the father of Vāć. See *ām-bhṛiṇī.*

अम्मय *am-maya, as, ī, am* (for *ap-maya*), formed from or consisting of water, watery.

अम्यक् *amyak,* ind., Ved. (rt. *ać* with *am,* *i* being inserted), towards, here (?).

अम्र *amra, as,* m. (fr. rt. *am?*), the mango tree. See *āmra.*

Amrāta or *amrātaka, as,* m. a species of Spondias or hog-plum, Spondias Magnifera. See *āmrāta.*

अम्ल *amla, as, ā, am* (fr. rt. *am,* to make sick), sour, acid; (*as*), m. sourness; acidity; vinegar; wood sorrel, Oxalis Corniculata; (*ī*), f. Oxalis Corniculata; (*am*), n. sour curds. — *Amla-kāṇḍa, am,* n., N. of a plant. — *Amla-keśara, as,* m. citron tree. — *Amla-ćukrikā,* f. or *amla-ćūḍa, as,* m. a kind of sorrel. — *Amla-jambīra, as,* m. lime tree. — *Amla-tā,* f. sourness. — *Amla-nāyaka, as,* m. sorrel. — *Amla-nimbūka, as,* m. the lime. — *Amla-niśā,* f., N. of a plant, Curcuma Zerumbet, Roxb. — *Amla-pañćaka* or *amla-pañća-phala, am,* n. a collection of five kinds of sour vegetables and fruits. — *Amla-pattra, as,* m., N. of the plant Oxalis, and other plants. — *Amla-panasa, as,* m. a tree, Artocarpus Lacucha, Roxb. — *Amla-pitta, am,* n. acidity of stomach. — *Amla-phala, as,* m. the tamarind tree, Magnifera Indica; (*am*), n. the fruit of this tree. — *Amla-bhedana, as,* m. sorrel. — *Amla-meha, as,* m. a urinary disease. — *Amla-rasa, as, ā, am,* sour, having a sour taste; (*as*), m. sourness, acidity. — *Amla-ruhā,* f. a kind of betel. — *Amla-loṇikā* or *amla-loṇī* or *amla-lolikā,* f. wood sorrel, Oxalis Corniculata. — *Amla-varga, as,* m. a class of plants with acid leaves or fruits, as the lime, orange, pomegranate, tamarind, sorrel, and others. — *Amla-vallī,* f., N. of a plant, Pythonium Bulbiferum Schott. — *Amla-vāṭaka, as,* m. hog-plum, Spondias Magnifera. — *Amla-vāṭikā,* f. a sort of betel. — *Amla-vāstūka, am,* n. sorrel. — *Amla-vṛiksha, as,* m. the tamarind tree. — *Amla-vetasa, as,* m. a kind of dock or sorrel, Rumex Vesicarius. — *Amla-śāka, as,* m. a sort of sorrel, commonly used as a pot-herb. — *Amla-sāra, as,* m. the lime; a sort of sorrel; (*am*), n. rice water after fermentation. — *Amla-haridrā,* f. the plant Curcuma Zerumbet, Roxb. — *Amlākta* (°*la-ak*°), *as, ā, am,* acidulated. — *Amlāṅkuśa* (°*la-an*°), *as,* m. a kind of sorrel. — *Amlādhyushita* (°*la-adh*°), *am,* n. a disease of the eyes. — *Amlodgāra* (°*la-ud*°), *as,* m. sour eructation.

Amlaka, as, m. the plant Artocarpus Lacucha.

Amlikā or *amlīkā,* f. a sour taste in the mouth, acidity of stomach; the tamarind tree; wood sorrel, Oxalis Corniculata. — *Amlikā-vaṭaka, as,* m. a sort of cake.

Amliman, ā, m. sourness.

Amlī-bhūta, as, ā, am, become sour.

Amvla, as, m. sourness.

अम्लान *a-mlāna, as, ā, am* (rt. *mlai*), not withered, clean, clear; bright, unclouded; (*as*), m. globe-amaranth, Gomphræna Globosa L.

A-mlāni, is, f. vigour, freshness, verdure; (*is, is, i*), vigorous, unfading.

A-mlānin, ī, inī, i, clean, clear; (*inī*), f. an assemblage of globe-amaranths.

अय् *ay* (connected with rt. *i,* q. v.), cl. 1. A. *ayate, -yitum,* to go.

Aya, as, m. (fr. rt. *i*), going; a move towards the right at chess; good luck, favourable fortune; a die; N. of a Prajāpati; (*as, ā, am*), going, moving. — *Aya-tā,* f. good luck. — *Aya-vat, ān, atī, at,* happy. — *Aya-śobhin, ī, inī, i,* bright with good fortune. — *Ayānvita* (*aya-an*°), *as, ā, am,* fortunate, lucky.

Ayatha, am, n., Ved. a leg, foot (?).

Ayana, as, ā, am (fr. rt. *i*), going; especially at the end of a compound, e. g. *samudrāyaṇa,* going to the ocean; (*am*), n. going, walking, walk; a road, a path; a place, a site (?); course, circulation, period; final emancipation; a commentary, treatise; N. of certain sacrificial performances; the sun's road north and south of the equator, the half year; the equinoctial and solstitial points; way, progress, manner; a Śāstra or inspired writing. — *Ayana-kāla, as,* m. the interval between the equinoxes. — *Ayana-devatā,* f. a deity or an idol placed near a road (?). — *Ayana-bhāga, as,* m. or *ayanāṅśa* (°*na-aṅ*°), *as,* m. the arc between the vernal equinoctial point and the beginning of the fixed zodiac or first point in Aries. — *Ayana-valana, am,* n. deviation of the ecliptic. — *Ayana-vṛitta, am,* n. the ecliptic.

अयक्ष्म *a-yakshma, as, ā, am,* Ved. not consumptive; not sick, healthy; causing health; (*am*), n. health. — *Ayakshma-karaṇa, as, ī, am,* Ved. producing health. — *Ayakshma-tāti, is,* f. or *ayakshma-tva, am,* n., Ved. freedom from consumption; health.

अयक्ष्यमाण *a-yakshyamāṇa, as,* m. not wishing or not about to sacrifice.

अयजुष्क *a-yajushka, as, ā, am,* Ved. without a sacrificial formula or verse.

अयज्ञ *a-yajña, as,* m. no sacrifice; a bad sacrifice; (*as, ā, am*), not offering sacrifice. — *A-yajña-sāć, k, k, k,* Ved. not performing a sacrifice, performing worthless sacrifices.

A-yajñaka, as, ā, am, unfit for sacrifice.

A-yajñiya, as, ā, am, not fit for sacrifice; not worthy of sacrifice, profane, common.

A-yajyu, us, us, u, Ved. not sacrificing, impious, profane, wicked.

A-yajvan, ā, ā, a, Ved. not offering sacrifice, profane.

अयज्ञदत्त *a-yajñadatta, as,* m. not Yajñadatta, i. e. the vile Yajñadatta.

अयत् *a-yat, t, t, t* (rt. *yam*), not making efforts.

A-yata, as, ā, am, unrestrained, uncontrolled, unchecked.

A-yatin, ī, inī, i, of unsubdued appetite; incontinent.

Ayatna, as, m. absence of effort or exertion; *ayatnena* or *ayatnāt* or *ayatnatas,* without effort or exertion. — *A-yatna-kārin, ī, iṇī, i,* making no exertion, indifferent, idle. — *A-yatna-kṛita* or *a-yatna-ja, as, ā, am,* easily or readily produced, spontaneous. — *Ayatna-vat, ān, atī, at,* inactive, indifferent, idle.

अयथा *a-yathā,* ind. not as it should be, unfitly, unsuitably. — *A-yatham,* Ved. without effort. — *A-yathā-tatha, as, ā, am,* not so as it should be, unfit, unsuitable; useless, unprofitable, vain; (*am*), ind. unfitly, unsuitably. — *A-yathā-tathya, am*, n. unsuitableness, unprofitableness, incompatibility. — *A-yathā-dyotana, am*, n. intimation of something unexpected. — *A-yathā-pūrva* or *a-yathā-pura, as, ā, am*, unprecedented. — *A-yathā-balam*, ind. not according to one's power. — *A-yathā-mātra, as, ā, am*, not according to measure. — *A-yathāmukhīna, as, ā, am*, having the face turned away. — *A-yathārtha* (°*thā-ar*°), *as, ā, am*, not according to the sense or object, incongruous, unmeaning, nonsensical; improper, unfitting. — *A-yathā-vat*, ind. inaccurately, erroneously. — *A-yathāśāstra-kārin, ī, iṇī, i*, not acting in accordance with the scripture. — *A-yatheshṭa* (°*thā-ish*°), *as, ā, am*, not as wished; disliked, disapproved of; insufficient, not enough. — *A-yathoćita* (°*thā-uć*°), *as, ā, am*, unworthily, unsuitably.

अयदीक्षित *aya-dīkshita, as*, m., N. of an author.

अयन *ayana*, &c. See under *ay*, p. 78.

अयन्त्र *a-yantra, am*, n., Ved. non-restraint, not a means of restraining; having no restraint; a powerful weapon for restraining enemies.

A-yantrita, as, ā, am, unhindered, unrestrained, self-willed.

अयमित *a-yamita, as, ā, am*, unchecked, untrimmed, unpaired, unclipped.

अयव 1. *ayava, as, ā, am*, deficient; (*as*), m., N. of a worm bred in the intestines.

अयव 2. *a-yava, as*, m. or *a-yavan, ā*, m. or *a-yavas, as*, n. the dark half of the month.

अयव 3. *a-yava, as, ā, am*, or *a-yavaka, as, ikā, am*, having worthless or no barley.

A-yavya, as, ā, am, unfit for barley.

अयशस् *a-yaśas, as*, n. infamy; (*ās, ās, as*), infamous, disagreeable. — *Ayaśas-kara, as, ā* or *ī, am*, disgraceful, degrading.

A-yaśasya, as, ā, am, infamous.

अयस् *ayas, ās, ās, as* (fr. rt. *i*), going, nimble; (*as*), n. iron, steel, gold, metal [cf. Lat. *æs, ær-is* for *æs-is*; Goth. *ais*, Them. *aisa*; Old Germ. *ēr*, 'iron;' Goth. *eisarn*; Mod. Germ. *Eisen*]; (*ās*), m. fire. — *Ayaḥ-pāna, am*, n. a particular hell. — *Ayaḥ-pratimā*, f. iron image. — *Ayaḥ-śanku, us*, m., N. of an Asura. — *Ayaḥ-śaya, as, ā, am*, Ved. lying in iron, made of iron (said of fire). — *Ayaḥ-śipra, as, ā, am*, Ved. having jaws or a nose of iron. — *Ayaḥ-śiras, ās*, m., N. of an Asura. — *Ayaḥ-śīrshan, ā, ā, a*, Ved. having a head of iron. — *Ayaḥ-śūla, am*, n. an iron lance; fraudulent or cunning artifice. — *Ayaḥ-sthūṇa* or *ayas-sthūṇa* or *aya-sthūṇa, as, ī, am*, Ved. having iron pillars or spikes; (*as*), m., N. of a Ṛishi. — *Ayaś-ćūrṇa, am*, n. iron filings. — *Ayas-kaṃsa, as, am*, m. n. an iron goblet. — *Ayas-kāṇḍa, as, am*, m. n. an iron arrow. — *Ayas-kānta, as*, m. a precious stone, the loadstone. — *Ayas-kāra, as*, m. a blacksmith; the upper part of the thigh (?). — *Ayas-kīṭa, am*, n. rust of iron. — *Ayas-kumbha, as, ī*, m. f. an iron pot or boiler. — *Ayas-kuśā*, f. a rope partly consisting of iron. — *Ayas-kṛiti, is*, f. preparation of iron. — *Ayas-tāpa, as, ā, am*, making iron red-hot. — *Ayas-pātra, am*, n. an iron vessel. — *Ayas-maya, as, ī, am*, Ved. made of iron or of metal; (*as*), m., N. of a son of Manu Svārośisha; (*ī*), f., N. of one of the three residences of the Asuras.

For compounds beginning *ayo*, see s. v. *ayo-guḍa*. *Ayasa* may be used for *ayas* at the end of compounds, as *kṛishṇāyasa*, q. v.

अया *ayā*, ind. (fr. pronominal base *a* = *anayā*), Ved. in this manner, thus.

अयाचक *a-yāćaka, as, ikā, am* (rt. *yāć*), one who does not ask or solicit.

A-yāćita, as, ā, am, unasked, unsolicited; *ayāćitam*, ind. without being asked; (*as*), m., N. of the Ṛishi Upavarsha. — *Ayāćita-vṛitti, is*, f. or *ayāćita-vrata, am*, n. subsisting on alms without begging.

A-yāćin, ī, inī, i, not soliciting.

अयाज्य *a-yājya, as, ā, am* (rt. *yaj*), a person or thing for whom or for which one must not offer sacrifices; outcast, degraded; not competent to offer sacrifice; incapable of or inadmissible to religious ceremonies. — *Ayājya-tva, am*, n. the state of an outcast. — *Ayājya-yājana* or *ayājya-saṃyājya, am*, n. sacrificing for an outcast.

अयातपूर्व *a-yāta-pūrva, as, ā, am*, following, subsequent to, succeeding.

अयातयाम *a-yātayāma, as, ā, am*, Ved. not weak; not worn out by use; fresh; (*am*), n., N. of certain texts of the Yajur-veda, revealed to Yājñavalkya. — *Ayātayāma-tā*, f., Ved. unweakened strength, freshness.

A-yātayāman, ā, mnī, a, Ved. not weak, fresh.

अयातु *a-yātu, us, us, u*, Ved. not demoniacal; free from evil spirits; (*us*), m. not a demon, the opposite of an evil spirit.

अयाथार्थिक *a-yāthārthika, as, ī, am*, improper, unjust; not genuine, not real, incongruous, absurd.

A-yāthārthya, am, n. impropriety, unfitness, absurdity, nonsense.

अयान *a-yāna, am*, n. not moving, halting, stopping; natural disposition or temperament: (in the last sense the etymology is doubtful.)

अयानय *ayānaya* (°*ya-an*°), *am*, n. good and bad luck; (*as*), m. a particular position of the pieces on a chess or backgammon board.

Ayānayīna, as, m. a piece at chess or backgammon so moved.

अयावक *a-yāvaka, as, ā, am*, unstained with lac-dye, naturally red.

अयावन *a-yāvana, am*, n. not causing to unite.

अयाशु *a-yāśu, us, us, u*, Ved. unfit for copulation.

अयास् *a-yās* (?), *ās*, m. (rt. *yas*), Ved. agile (without effort), dexterous, nimble; (*ās*), ind. fire (?).

A-yāsya, as, ā, am, Ved. not to be obtained by effort, indefatigable; valiant; enterprising; (*as*), m., N. of an Aṅgiras; mystical name of the chief vital air.

अयासोमीय *ayāsomīya, am*, n., N. of some verses of the Sāma-veda.

अयि *ayi*, ind. a vocative particle; a particle of encouragement or introducing a kind enquiry.

अयिन् *ayin, ī, inī, i* (rt. *i*), at the end of compounds, going, e. g. *atyayin*, q. v.

अयुक्त *a-yukta, as, ā, am* (rt. *yuj*), not yoked, not joined, not united, not married; not harnessed; not connected; not suited, unfit, unsuitable; not attentive, not devout; negligent, not dexterous, unpractised, untrue, wrong; indecent. — *A-yukta-kṛit, t, t, t*, committing wrong acts. — *Ayukta-ćāra, as*, m. (a king &c.) who does not appoint spies. — *Ayukta-tā*, f. or *ayukta-tva, am*, n. the not being used. — *Ayukta-padārtha, as*, m. the sense of a word to be supplied. — *Ayukta-rūpa, as, ā, am*, unfit, unsuitable.

A-yukti, is, f. disunion, separation; unreasonableness, want of conformity to correct principles or to analogy; impropriety, unfitness.

A-yuga or *a-yugala, as, ā, am*, separate, single, odd. — *Ayugārćis* (°*ga-ar*°), *is*, m. fire.

A-yugapad, ind. not at once, gradually, seriatim. — *Ayugapad-grahaṇa, am*, n. apprehending gradually and not simultaneously. — *Ayugapad-bhāva, as*, m. successiveness.

A-yugma, as, ā, am, not in couples, separate, single; odd, uneven. — *Ayugma-ććhada, as*, m., N. of the plant Alstonia Scholaris. — *Ayugma-netra, as*, m., N. of Śiva. — *Ayugma-śara, as*, m., N. of the god of love ('having an odd number of arrows').

A-yuj, k, k, k, not existing in couples; odd, uneven. — *Ayuk-ćhada, as*, m., N. of a plant, Alstonia Scholaris. — *Ayuk-palāśa, as*, m., N. of a tree. — *Ayuk-pāda-yamaka, am*, n. a kind of alliteration, viz. the same syllables in the first and third Pāda of a word in a different sense. — *Ayuk-śakti, is*, m., N. of Śiva. — *Ayug-ishu, us*, m., N. of Kāma, from his having five arrows; see *pañćeshu*. — *Ayug-dhātu, us, us, u*, having an odd number of elements. — *Ayug-vāṇa, as*, m., N. of Kāma. — *Ayun-netra* or *ayug-aksha, as*, m., N. of Śiva, from his having three eyes; see *tri-netra*.

A-yuja, as, ā, am, Ved. without a companion, not having an equal; not existing by pairs, separate, odd.

A-yoga, as, m. separation, disjunction; interval; unfitness, unsuitableness, unconformity; inefficacy of a remedy; medical treatment counter to the symptoms; non-application or mis-application of remedies; vigorous effort, exertion; a widower, an absent lover or husband; inauspicious conjunction of the planets; a conjunction of two planets; (*as, ā, am*), unconnected with; indistinctly connected with; making vigorous efforts. — *Ayoga-vāha, as*, m. a term for Anusvāra, Visarjanīya, Upadhmānīya, and Jihvāmūlīya, as standing between vowels and consonants. (For *ayo-ga*, hammer, see *ayo-'gra* below.)

A-yogya, as, ā, am, unfit, unsuitable, useless; immaterial; (in phil.) not ascertainable &c. by the senses. — *Ayogya-tā*, f. or *ayogya-tva, am*, n. unfitness, unsuitableness.

A-yojana, am, n. disunion, separation.

A-yauktika, as, ī, am, not conformable to, inconsistent with.

A-yaugapadya, am, n. uncontemporaneous existence, unsimultaneousness.

A-yaugika, as, ī, am, having no regular derivation.

अयुङ्ग *a-yunga, as, ā, am*, Ved. not existing in couples; odd, uneven.

अयुत 1. *a-yuta, as, ā, am* (rt. 2. *yu*), Ved. not disturbed or interrupted; (*as*), m., N. of a son of Rādhika. — *Ayuta-siddha, as, ā, am*, proved to be not separated or interrupted, proved to be inherent. — *Ayuta-siddhi, is*, f. proof that certain things or notions are not separable.

A-yuva, as, ā, am, Ved. undisturbed, unshaken.

अयुत 2. *a-yuta, as, ā, am* (rt. 1. *yu*, to mix), disjoined, detached, not counted; (*am*), n. ten thousand, a myriad. — *Ayuta-jit, t*, m., N. of a son of Bhajamāna. — *Ayuta-nāyin, ī*, m., N. of a king. — *Ayuta-śas*, ind. by myriads. — *Ayuta-homa, as*, m. a kind of sacrifice. — *Ayutādhyāpaka* (°*ta-adh*°), *as*, m. a good teacher. — *Ayutāyus* (°*ta-āy*°), *us*, m., N. of a son of Jayasena Ārāvin; of a son of Śrutavat. — *Ayutāśva* (°*ta-aś*°), *as*, m., N. of a son of Sindhu-dvīpa.

अयुद्ध *a-yuddha, as, ā, am* (rt. *yudh*), Ved. unconquered; not fighting; (*am*), n. not war, absence of war, peace. — *A-yuddha-sena, as*, m., Ved. whose arrows or armies are unconquered, irresistible.

A-yuddhvī, ind., Ved. without fighting.

A-yudha, as, m. a non-fighter.

A-yudhya, as, ā, am, unconquerable.

A-yudhvin, ī, m., Ved. not conquering, not a valiant warrior.

A-yoddhṛi, dhā, m. no warrior, a bad fighter; unmatched by other warriors.

A-yodhya, as, ā, am, Ved. not to be warred against, irresistible; (*ā*), f. the capital of Rāma, the modern Oude, on the river Sarayu. — *Ayodhyādhipati* (°*yā-adh*°), *is*, m. the sovereign of Ayodhyā. — *Ayodhyā-vāsin, ī, inī, i*, inhabiting Ayodhyā.

A-yaudhika, as, m. not a warrior.

अयूप *a-yūpa, as,* m. no sacrificial post.

अये *aye,* ind. a vocative particle, an interjection of surprize, recollection, fatigue, fear, passion; used also in the same meanings as *ayi.*

अयोगव *ayogava, as, ā* or *ī,* m. f. or *ayogū?* (etymology uncertain; perhaps connected with *ayas,* iron, or fr. *a-yoga*), the offspring of a Śūdra man and Vaiśya woman, whose business is carpentry. See *āyogava.*

अयोगुड *ayo-guḍa, as,* m. (*ayo* for *ayas,* iron), a chalybeate pill, one made of some preparation of iron; an iron ball.

Ayo-'gra or *ayo-'graka* (*ayas-ag°*), *am,* n. a hammer, a forge hammer; a mace or club tipped with iron; a pestle for cleaning grain. (A form *ayo-ga, as,* m., is also given in the sense 'iron hammer.')

Ayo-ghana, as, m. a hammer, a forge hammer.

Ayoćchishṭa (*ayas-uć°?*), *am,* n. rust of iron.

Ayo-jāla, as, ā, am, furnished with iron nets; (*am*), n. iron net-work.

Ayo-danshṭra, as, ā, am, Ved., or *ayo-dat, at, atī, at,* iron-toothed, having iron weapons.

Ayo-dāha, as, m. the burning quality of iron.

Ayo-'pāshṭi (*ayas-ap°*), *is, is, i,* Ved. furnished with iron claws or heels.

Ayo-maya, as, ī, am, made of iron. See also s. v. *ayas.*

Ayo-mala, am, n. rust of iron.

Ayo-mukha, as, ā, am, having an iron mouth, face, or beak; tipped or pointed with iron; (*as*), m. an arrow; N. of a Dānava; N. of a mountain.

Ayo-raja, am, n. or *ayo-rajas, as,* n. rust of iron.

Ayo-rasa, as, m. iron rust or filings.

Ayo-vatsa, as, m., N. of a man.

Ayo-vikāra, as, m. iron-work, any iron fabric.

Ayo-hata, as, ā, am, Ved. embossed in iron-work; made or performed by a priest &c. who wears a golden ring on his finger.

Ayo-hanu, us, us, u, Ved. iron-jawed.

Ayo-hṛidaya, as, ā, am, iron-hearted, stern, unrelenting.

अयोद्ध, अयोध्य. See *a-yuddha,* p. 79, last col.

अयोनि *a-yoni, is,* f. not the womb; anything but the womb; not a particular verse of the Sāma-veda; (*is, is, i*), without origin; not born from the womb, born in a manner not approved by law or religion; (*is*), m., N. of Brahmā and Śiva; a pestle (for *ayo-'gra* above?). — *A-yoni-ja, as, ā, am,* not born from the womb, not produced in the ordinary course of generation, generated equivocally; (*am*), n., N. of a Tīrtha. — *Ayonija-tva, am,* n. the state of not being born from a womb. — *Ayonijeśa* (°*ja-īśa*), *as,* m., N. of Śiva. — *Ayonijeśvara* (°*ja-īś°*) or *ayonijeśvara-tīrtha, am,* n., N. of a Tīrtha. — *A-yoni-sambhava, as, ā, am* = *ayonija,* q. v.

A-yonika, as, ā, am, without the verse containing the word *yoni.*

अर *ara, as, ā, am* (fr. rt. *ṛi*), swift, speedy; little; (at end of comp.) going; (*as, am*), m. n. the spoke or radius of a wheel, see also *aram,* col. 3; (*as*), m. a spoke of the time-wheel, viz. a Jaina division of time, the sixth of an Avasarpiṇī or Utsarpiṇī; the eighteenth Jaina saint of the present Avasarpiṇī; N. of an ocean in Brahmā's world. — *Ara-ghaṭṭa* or *ara-ghaṭṭaka, as,* m. a wheel or machine for raising water from a well (Hind. ارهت); a deep well. — *Ara-nemi, is,* m., N. of Brahma-datta, king of Kośala. — *Arāntareshu* (°*ra-an°*), loc. pl. in the intervals of the spokes.

Araka, as, m. the spoke of a wheel; a Jaina division of time [cf. *ara*]; the plant Blyxa Octandra; another plant, Gardenia Enneandra.

अरक्षस् *a-rakshas, ās, ās, as,* Ved. harmless, honest; not disturbed &c. by evil spirits.

अरक्षित *a-rakshita, as, ā, am,* unprotected, undefended; not preserved, not kept.

अरगराट *aragarāṭa, as,* m., Ved. a valley (?).

अरङ्कृ *aran-kṛi,* cl. 8. P., Ved. *-karoti, -kartum,* to prepare, make ready; serve. See *aram,* col. 3.

Aran-kṛit, t, t, t, Ved. acting satisfactorily; preparing, serving as a worshipper.

Aran-kṛita, as, ā, am, Ved. prepared, ready; gratified.

Aran-kṛiti, is, f., Ved. service, gratification.

अरङ्गम् *aran-gam,* cl. 1. P., Ved. *-gaććhati, -gantum,* to be present, come near (in order to help), become visible, appear. See *aram,* col. 3.

Aran-gama, as, ā, am, Ved. coming near or into the presence, appearing (in order to help), becoming visible.

अरङ्गर *aran-gara, as,* m., Ved. praising readily (?); factitious or made up poison. See *aram.*

अरङ्गिन् *a-rangin, ī, iṇī, i,* passionless. — *Arangi-sattva, as,* m. a passionless being, a class of gods with Buddhists.

अरङ्घुष *aran-ghusha, as, ā, am,* Ved. praising readily, sounding aloud. See *aram,* col. 3.

अरजस् *a-rajas, ās, ās, as,* or *a-raja* or *a-rajaska, as, ā, am,* dustless; free from passion or desire; clean, pure; not having the monthly courses; (*ās*), f. a young girl.

Arajāya, nom. A. *arajāyate, -yitum,* to become dustless; to lose the monthly courses.

अरज्जु *a-rajju, us, us, u,* Ved. not consisting of cords; not furnished with cords.

अरटु *araṭu* or *araḍu, us,* m., N. of the tree Calosanthes Indica Bl.

Araṭva, as, ā, am, made of the wood of the above tree; (*as*), m., N. of a man.

अरण 1. *araṇa, as, ī, am* (rt. *ṛi*), Ved. departed, gone away; strange, foreign; distant; (*am*), n. moving, entering; being inserted; a refuge.

1. *araṇi, is, ī,* m. f. the wood of the Ficus Religiosa used for kindling fire by attrition; the lower one (*adharāraṇi*) of the two Araṇis; (*ī*), du. the two pieces of wood used in kindling the sacred fire; (*is*), m., N. of several plants, especially Premna Integrifolia; the sun; fire; 'a flint?; (*is*), f. a way, a path. — *Araṇi-mat, ān, atī, at,* related to the two Araṇis; to be produced by the Araṇis. — *Araṇi-ketu, us,* m. the Premna Integrifolia.

अरण 2. *a-raṇa, as, ā, am,* not fighting, without fighting.

अरणि 2. *a-raṇi, is,* f., Ved. stinginess.

अरण्य *araṇya, as, am,* m. n. (fr. rt. *ṛi*), land neither cultivated nor grazed; a wilderness, desert, forest; N. of a plant; N. of a Sādhya. — *Araṇya-kaṇā,* f. wild cumin seed. — *Araṇya-kadalī,* f. the wood or wild plantain. — *Araṇya-kāṇḍa* (?), *am,* n. title of the third book of the Rāmāyaṇa. — *Araṇya-kārpāsī,* f. the wild cotton. — *Araṇya-kulatthikā,* f., N. of the plant Glycine Labialis Lin. — *Araṇya-kusumbha, as,* m., N. of the plant Carthamus Tinctorius. — *Araṇya-gaja, as,* m. a wild elephant. — *Araṇya-gata, as, ā, am,* gone into a forest. — *Araṇya-gāna* (?), *am,* n. one of the four Gānas or hymn-books of the Sāma-veda. — *Araṇya-gholī,* f., N. of a plant. — *Araṇya-ćaṭaka, as,* m. a wild pigeon. — *Araṇya-ćara, as, ī, am,* living in forests, wild. — *Araṇya-ja, as, ā, am,* produced or born in a forest. — *Araṇya-jārdrakā* (°*ja-ārd°*), f. wild ginger. — *Araṇya-jīra, as,* m. wild cumin. — *Araṇya-jīva, as, ā, am,* living in a forest. — *Araṇya-damana, as,* m. a wild plant, called *Dona.* — *Araṇya-dvādaśī,* f. or *araṇyadvādaśī-vrata, am,* n., N. of a ceremony performed on the twelfth day of the month Mārgaśīrsha. — *Araṇya-dharma, as,* m. forest usage, wild or savage state. — *Araṇya-dhānya, am,* n. wild rice. — *Araṇya-nṛipati, is,* m. king of the forest. — *Araṇya-bhava, as, ā, am,* growing in a forest, wild. — *Araṇya-makshikā,* f. the gad-fly. — *Araṇya-mārjāra, as,* m. wild cat. — *Araṇya-mudga, as,* m. a kind of bean. — *Araṇya-yāna, am,* n. going into a forest. — *Araṇya-rakshaka, as,* m. forest-keeper, superintendent of a forest district. — *Araṇya-rāj, ṭ,* m. king of the forest; epithet of a lion or tiger. — *Araṇya-rājya, am,* n. the sovereignty of the forest. — *Araṇya-rudita, am,* n. weeping in a forest, i. e. weeping in vain, with no one to hear. — *Araṇya-vat,* ind. like a wilderness. — *Araṇya-vāyasa, as,* m. a raven. — *Araṇya-vāsa, as,* m. a hermitage. — *Araṇya-vāsin, ī, inī, i,* living in a forest, wild; (*ī*), m. forest-dweller, a hermit, anchorite; (*nī*), f., N. of a plant. — *Araṇya-vāstuka* or *araṇya-vāstūka, as,* m., N. of a plant. — *Araṇya-śāli, is,* m. wild rice. — *Araṇya-śūkara, as,* m. a wild hog. — *Araṇya-śūraṇa, as,* m., N. of a plant. — *Araṇya-śvan, ā,* m. a wolf. — *Araṇya-shashṭhī,* f., N. of a festival celebrated by females in the month Jyaishṭha. — *Araṇya-sabhā,* f. a forest court. — *Araṇyādhyaksha* (°*ya-adh°*), *as,* m. forest-keeper or ranger, a head-man or superintendent of a forest district. — *Araṇyāyana* (°*ya-ay°*), *am,* n. going into the forest, becoming a hermit. — *Araṇye-tilaka, as,* m. wild sesamum growing in a forest and containing no oil; hence, anything which disappoints expectation. — *Araṇye-'nūćya* (°*ye-an°*), *as,* m., Ved. a kind of oblation. — *Araṇyaukas* (°*ya-ok°*), *ās,* m. living in a forest, a Brāhman who has left his family and become an anchorite.

Araṇyaka, am, n. a forest, a desert; N. of a plant.

Araṇyānī, is, or *araṇyānī,* f. a wilderness, desert, large forest; the goddess of the wilderness and desert, and mother of wild animals.

Araṇyīya, as, ā, am, containing a forest, near to one.

अरत *a-rata, as, ā, am* (rt. *ram*), dull, languid, apathetic; disgusted, discontented; (*am*), n. non-copulation. — *A-rata-trapa, as, ā, am,* not ashamed of copulation; (*as*), m. a dog.

1. *a-rati, is,* f. dissatisfaction, discontent; absence of pleasure, pain; dulness, languor; anxiety, distress, regret; a bilious disease; (*is, is, i*), discontented, unhappy; dull, languid, restless. — *Arati-jña, as, ā, am,* dull, spiritless.

अरति 2. *arati, is,* m. (fr. rt. *ṛi,* cf. *ara, aram*), Ved. going, approaching; moving quickly; moving flame; occupying; attacking; a servant, assistant, manager, administrator; a master; an intelligent being of all-piercing intellect; anger, passion; anxiety.

अरत्नि *aratni, is,* m. (said to be fr. rt. *ṛi*), the elbow, a corner; a cubit of the middle length, from the elbow to the tip of the little finger, a fist. — *Aratni-mātra, as, ī, am,* one ell in length.

Aratnika, as, m. the elbow.

अरथ *a-ratha, as, ā, am,* having no carriage.

A-rathin, ī, m. a warrior who does not fight in a car, or owns no car.

A-rathī, īs, m., Ved. not a charioteer.

अरध्र *a-radhra, as, ā, am,* Ved. not lazy; not to be subdued; unprosperous.

अरन्तुक *arantuka, as,* m., N. of a Tīrtha.

अरप *a-rapa, as, ā, am,* Ved. unhurt; sinless, pure.

A-rapas, ās, ās, as, Ved. unhurt, safe; not hurting, beneficial, charitable; sinless, pure.

अरपचन *arapaćana, as,* m. a mystical collective N. of the five Buddhas, each being represented by a letter.

अरम् *aram,* ind. (fr. rt. *ṛi,* see *ara*), Ved. swiftly, at hand, near, present; readily, fitly, suitably, so as to answer a purpose; enough, sufficient [cf. *alam* and Gr. ἄρα]. — *Aran-kṛi* and *aran-gam*, see p. 80, col. 2. — *Aramaṇas, ās, ās, as* (for *aram-m°*), Ved. ready to serve, obedient, devoted to the worship of God; (according to native interpretation) having hostile intentions. — *Aramati, is*, f. (for *aram-m°*), Ved. readiness to serve, obedience, devotion; a goddess, described in the Vedas as protecting the worshippers of the gods and pious works in general; (according to others) not resting, active, going everywhere; splendor. — *Aram-ish, ṭ, ṭ, ṭ*, Ved. hastening near (?).

अरमण *a-ramaṇa, as, ī, am* (rt. *ram*), not gratifying, not pleasing.

A-ramaṇīya, as, ā, am, unpleasant, disagreeable. — *Aramaṇīya-tā*, f. disagreeableness.

A-ramamāṇa, as, ā, am, not gratifying; Ved. unremitting, unceasing.

A-ramayitṛi, tā, trī, tṛi, not causing gratification.

अरमुडि *aramuḍi, is*, m. a king of Nepāl.

अरर *arara, am*, n. a covering, a sheath; (*as, ī, am*), m. f. n. the leaf of a door, a door; the sheath of the shoot of a bamboo; (*as*), m. an awl; a part of a sacrifice; fighting, war.

Arari, is, i, m. n. a door; a door-leaf.

अररका *ararakā*, f., N. of the ancestress of a celebrated Hindū family.

Ararakya, as, m. a descendant of Ararakā.

अररिन्द *ararinda, am*, n., Ved. water; a vessel used in preparing the Soma juice (?).

अररिवस् *a-rarivas, vān, ushī*, m. f. (rt. *rā*), Ved. not offering; envious, hard, cruel, unfriendly; an epithet of evil spirits, who strive to disturb the happiness of man; an enemy.

1. *a-raru, us*, m. = the preceding; N. of an Asura; (*us*), m. f. (?) a weapon.

अररु 2. *araru, us, us, u* (rt. *ṛi*), Ved. moving.

अररे *arare*, ind. a vocative particle, expressing haste.

अरर्य *ararya*, nom. P. *araryati, -yitum*, to work with an awl; to try, put to the proof (?).

अरलु *aralu, us*, or *araluka, as*, m. a plant, Bignonia Indica.

अरव *a-rava, as, ā, am* (rt. *ru*), noiseless.

अरविन्द *aravinda, am*, n. (fr. *a*, 'like,' and *ravinda*, q. v., for *ravi-da?*), a lotus, Nelumbium Speciosum or Nymphæa Nelumbo; (*as*), m. the Indian crane; copper. — *Aravinda-dala-prabha, am*, n. copper. — *Aravinda-nābhi, is*, m. Vishṇu, from whose navel sprung the lotus that bore Brahmā at the creation. — *Aravinda-sad, t*, m., N. of Brahmā, 'sitting on a lotus.'

Aravindinī, f. an assemblage of lotus flowers.

अरश्मन् *a-raśman, ā, ā, a*, Ved. having no ropes or reins.

अरस *a-rasa, as, ā, am*, sapless, tasteless; weak, effectless, having no strength; dull, flat; insipid; (*as*), m. no juice, absence of juice. — *Arasāśa* (°*sa-āśa*), *as*, m. the eating of sapless food; maceration of the body. — *Arasāśin* (°*sa-āś°*), *ī, inī, i*, eating sapless food; macerating the body.

A-rasika, as, ā, am, devoid of taste, unfeeling, dull; insipid, flavourless.

अरहस् *a-rahas, as*, n. absence of secrecy.

Arahāya, nom. A. *-yate, -yitum*, to become public.

अरहित *a-rahita, as, ā, am*, not deprived of, possessed of, having.

अराग *a-rāga, as, ā, am*, or *a-rāgin, ī, iṇī, i*, unimpassioned, cool.

अराजक *a-rājaka, as, ā, am*, having no king or governor, anarchical.

A-rājan, ā, m., Ved. not a king.

A-rājabhogīna, as, ā, am, not fit for the enjoyment or use of a king.

A-rājasthāpita, as, ā, am, not allowed or licensed by government.

A-rājin, ī, inī, i, Ved. having no splendor; unchecked, uncontrolled.

अराटकी *arāṭakī*, f., Ved., N. or epithet of the plant Ajaśṛiṅgī.

अराति *a-rāti, is*, f. (rt. *rā*), Ved. the non-offering (of sacrifices); stinginess, hardness, disfavour, severity; malignity, malevolence; failure; adversity; malignity personified; particular evil spirits, who frustrate the good intentions and disturb the happiness of man; (*is*), m. an enemy; the number 'six.' — *Arāti-dūshaṇa, as, ī, am*, or *arāti-dūshi, is, is, i*, or *arāti-ha, as, ā, am*, Ved. destroying enemies or adversity. — *Arāti-bhaṅga, as*, m. defeat of a foe.

Arātiya or *arātīya*, nom. P., Ved. *-yati, -yitum*, to desire not to offer; to act like an enemy. — *Arātīyat, an, antī, at*, Ved. envious, unfriendly, not offering; behaving like an enemy, striving to cause adversity.

Arātiyu, us, us, u, Ved. not in the habit of offering.

Arāti-van, ā, m., Ved. not offering, not giving; unfriendly, malicious.

अराद्धि *a-rāddhi, is*, f., Ved. transgression, sin, envy.

अराधस् *a-rādhas, ās, ās, as*, Ved. too poor to perform sacrifices, not making oblations, unkind, hard, stingy, selfish.

अराय *a-rāya, as*, m., Ved. too poor to make oblations, obstructing a sacrifice; niggard, stingy; (*as, ī*), m. f. any evil spirit. — *Arāya-kshayaṇa, as, ī, am*, Ved. overpowering malignant spirits; (*am*), n. destruction of malignant spirits. — *Arāya-ćātana, as, ī, am*, Ved. destroying evil spirits; (*am*), n. destruction of evil spirits.

अराल *arāla, as, ā, am* (connected with *ara*, fr. rt. *ṛi*; Intens. for *arāra*?), crooked, curved; spreading like the spokes of a wheel; (*as*), m. a bent or crooked arm; the resin of the plant Shorea Robusta; an elephant in rut; (*ā*), f. a disloyal or unchaste woman; a modest woman. — *Arāla-pakshma-nayana, as, ā, am*, whose eyelashes are curved.

अरावन् *a-rāvan, ā, vṇī, a*, Ved. not offering, envious, inimical, odious; an epithet of evil spirits.

अराष्ट्र *a-rāshṭra, am*, n., Ved. loss of royal power or of a kingdom.

अरि 1. *ari, is, is, i* (fr. rt. *ṛi*), Ved. going, moving; reaching, obtaining, making an effort to get; aspiring after; desiring, sacrificing, devoted to; (*is*), m. the wind; a lord, a master; a pious man. — *Ari-gūrta, as*, m., Ved. praised by devoted men or by worshippers; (according to others) ready for the destruction of enemies. — *Ari-dhāyas, ās, ās, as*, Ved. willingly yielding milk (as a cow); (according to others) to be held by lords only, very precious. — *Ari-shṭuta, as, ā, am*, Ved. praised with zeal.

अरि 2. *a-ri, is*, m. (rt. *rā*; but by some written *ari*, and identified with 1. *ari*), Ved. ungenerous, malicious; not worshipping; inimical, hostile; an enemy; a species of Khadira or Mimosa; N. of the numeral 'six;' N. of a condition in astronomy. — *Ari-karshaṇa, as*, m. tamer of enemies. — *Ari-kula, am*, n. family of an enemy. — *Ari-kshipa, as*, m., N. of a son of Svaphalka. — *Ari-ghna, as*, m. a destroyer of enemies. — *Ari-ćintana, am*, n. or *ari-ćintā*, f. a plot directed against an enemy, administration of foreign affairs. — *Ari-tā*, f. or *ari-tva, am*, n. enmity. — 1. *ari-tra, as, ā, am*, protecting from enemies (for 2. see next col.). — *Ari-dānta, as*, m. enemy-subdued; N. of a man. — *Ari-nandana, as, ā, am*, gratifying an enemy, affording triumph to an enemy; an enemy's joy. — *Ari-nipāta, as*, m. an invasion made by enemies. — *Ari-nuta, as, ā, am*, praised even by enemies. — *Arin-dama, as, ā, am*, conquering, victorious; (*as*), m. a conqueror of enemies; N. of a man; N. of a Muni. — *Ari-pura, am*, n. an enemy's town or country. — *Ari-marda, as*, m., N. of a plant. — *Ari-mardana, as, ā, am*, foe-trampling, enemy-destroying; (*as*), m., N. of a son of Svaphalka. — *Ari-mitra, as*, m. an ally or friend of an enemy. — *Arim-ejaya, as*, m., N. of a son of Kuru, or of S'vaphalka. — *Ari-meda, as*, m. a fetid Mimosa, Vachellia Farnesiana; N. of a country. — *Ari-medaka, as*, m., N. of an insect. — *Ari-rāshṭra, am*, n. an enemy's country. — *Ari-loka, as*, m. a hostile tribe or an enemy's country. — *Ari-shṭhānaka, am*, n. consternation, defeat. — *A-ri-sūdana* or *ari-hiṅsaka, as*, m. destroyer of foes. — *Ari-ha, as*, m. a son of Avaćīna, a son of Devātithi.

अरिक्त *a-rikta, as, ā, am*, not empty.

अरिक्थभाज् *a-riktha-bhāj, k, k, k*, not entitled to a share of property, not an heir.

A-rikthīya, as, ā, am = the preceding.

अरिणिन् *ariṇin, ī*, m. a cock.

अरितृ *aritṛi, tā*, m. (fr. rt. *ṛi*), Ved. a rower; a helmsman [cf. Gr. ἐρέτης, ἐρετμόν, &c.; Lat. *ratis, remex*, &c.].

2. *aritra, as, ā, am*, Ved. propelling, driving; (*am*), n. an oar; a rudder, helm; a ship, a boat; a part of a carriage; a Soma vessel; (*as*), m. a Soma vessel; N. of a person. [For 1. see under 2. *a-ri*; also cf. Lat. *aratrum*.] — *Aritra-gādha, as, ā, am*, oar-deep, shallow. — *Aritra-paraṇa, as, ī, am*, Ved. passing over by means of oars.

अरिन् *arin, i*, n. a wheel, a discus.

अरिपु *a-ripu, us*, m. the father of Nala.

अरिप्र *a-ripra, as, ā, am*, Ved. spotless, clean, clear; faultless, blameless.

अरिफित *a-riphita, as, ā, am*, not changed to *r*, said of Visarga.

A-repha, as, ā, am, without the letter *r*.

अरिषण्य *a-rishaṇya, as, ā, am* (rt. *rish*), Ved. not hurting, defending from injury.

A-rishaṇyat, an, antī, at, Ved. not being hurt.

A-rishṭa, as, ā, am, unhurt; unharmed; perfect; secure, safe; (*as*), m. a heron; a crow; N. of several plants, the soap-berry tree, Sapindus Detergens Roxb.; Azadirachta Indica; garlic; a distilled mixture; N. of an Asura, son of Bali, slain by Kṛishṇa (Vishṇu); N. of a son of Manu Vaivasvata; (*ā*), f. a bandage; a medical plant; N. of a daughter of Daksha and one of the wives of Kaśyapa; (*am*), n. bad or ill-luck, misfortune; a natural phenomenon boding misfortune; sign or symptom of approaching death; good fortune, happiness; buttermilk; vinous spirit; a woman's apartment, the lying-in chamber. — *Arishṭa-karman, ā*, m., N. of a king of the Andhra dynasty. — *A-rishṭa-gātu, us, us, u*, Ved. having a secure residence. — *Arishṭa-gu, us, us, u*, Ved. whose cattle are unhurt. — *Arishṭa-gṛiha, am*, n. a lying-in chamber. — *Arishṭa-grāma, as*, m., Ved. whose troop is complete in number (said of the Maruts). — *Arishṭa-tāti, is*, f., Ved. safeness, security; (*is, is, i*), auspicious, making fortunate or happy. — *Arishṭa-dushṭa-dhī, īs, īs, i*, apprehensive of death, alarmed at its approach. — *Arishṭa-nemi, is, is, i*, Ved. the felly of whose wheel is unhurt; an epithet of Tārkshya; the twenty-second of the twenty-four Jaina Tīrthakāras of the present Avasarpiṇī. — *Arishṭa-pura, am*, n., N. of a town. — *Arishṭa-bharman, ā*, m., Ved. yielding security. — *Arishṭa-mathana, as*, m. Vishṇu (Siva?) as killer of the Asura. — *Arishṭa-ratha, as*, m., Ved. whose carriage is unhurt. — *Arishṭa-vīra, as*, m., Ved. whose heroes are unhurt. — *Arishṭa-śayyā*, f. a lying-in couch. — *Arishṭa-sūdana, as*, m. or *arishṭa-han, ā*, m. Vishṇu as killer of the Asura. — *Arishṭā-śrita-pura* (°*ṭa-āś°*), *am*, n., N. of a town. — *Arishṭāsu* (°*ṭa-asu*), *us, us, u*, Ved. whose vital power is unhurt.

A-rishṭaka, as, m. the same as *arishṭa,* m. above.
A-rishṭi, is, f., Ved. safeness, security.
A-rishyat, an, antī, at, Ved. not being hurt.

अरीळ्ह *a-rīḷha, as, ā, am* (for *a-rīḍha,* rt. *rih=lih*), Ved. not licked.

अरु *aru, us,* m. the sun; N. of a plant.

अरुंषिका *arunshikā,* f. scab on the head.

अरुच् *a-ruć, k, k, k,* Ved. having no light, lightless.

अरुचि *a-rući, is,* f. aversion, dislike; want of appetite, disrelish, disgust.
A-rućira, as, ā, am, disagreeable, disgusting.
A-rućya, as, ā, am, disagreeable.

अरुज् *a-ruj, k, k, k,* not breaking, not suppurating, not festering; free from disease, sound, healthy.
A-rugṇa, as, ā, am, not broken, not diseased.
A-ruja, as, ā, am, not breaking; not suppurating; sound; (*as*), m., N. of a plant, Cassia Fistula; N. of a Dānava.

अरुण *aruṇa, as, ā* or *ī, am* (said to be fr. rt. *ṛi*), reddish-brown, tawny, red; ruddy; the colour of the morning opposed to the darkness of night; perplexed; dumb; (*as*), m. red colour, the colour of the dawn; dawn; the dawn personified as the charioteer of the sun; the sun; a kind of leprosy, with red spots and insensibility of the skin; a little poisonous animal; N. of a plant, Rottleria Tinctoria; molasses; N. of several persons; (*ā*), f., N. of several plants; a plant Betula; madder, Rubia Manjith; another plant, commonly Téori; a black kind of the same; Colocynth or bitter apple; the plant that yields the red and black berry used for the jewellers' weight, called Retti; N. of a river; (*ī*), f. a red cow; the dawn; (*am*), n. red colour; gold. — *Aruṇa-kamala, am,* n. the red lotus. — *Aruṇa-jyotis, is,* m. an epithet of Śiva. — *Aruṇa-tā,* f. red colour. — *Aruṇa-datta, as,* m., N. of an author. — *Aruṇa-dūrvā,* f. reddish fennel. — *Aruṇa-priyā,* f., N. of an Apsaras. — *Aruṇa-psu, us, us, u,* Ved. having a red shape. — *Aruṇa-babhru, us, us, u,* Ved. reddish-yellow. — *Aruṇa-yuj, k, k, k,* Ved. furnished with red (rays of light), an epithet of the dawn. — *Aruṇa-loćana, as, ā, am,* red-eyed; (*as*), m. a pigeon. — *Aruṇa-sārathi, is,* m. whose charioteer is Aruṇa; epithet of the sun. — *Aruṇāgra-ja* (°*ṇa-ag*°), *as,* m. Garuḍa, the bird of Vishṇu. — *Aruṇātmaja* (°*ṇa-āt*°), *as,* m., N. of Jaṭāyu, a fabulous bird, said by some to be the son of Aruṇa, but more generally of Garuḍa. — *Aruṇārćis* (°*ṇa-ar*°), *is,* m. the sun. — *Aruṇāvara-ja* (°*ṇa-av*°), *as,* m. the younger brother of Aruṇa, a N. of Garuḍa. — *Aruṇāśva* (°*ṇa-aś*°), *as,* m., Ved. driving with red horses, an epithet of the Maruts. — *Aruṇekshaṇa* (°*ṇa-īk*°), *as, ā, am,* red-eyed. — *Aruṇoda* (°*ṇa-ud*°), *as, am,* m. n., N. of a lake. — *Aruṇodaya* (°*ṇa-ud*°), *as,* m. break of day, dawn, the period preceding sunset. — *Aruṇopala* (°*ṇa-up*°), *as,* m. a ruby.
Aruṇita, as, ā, am, reddened, dyed red, impurpled.
Aruṇiman, ā, m. redness, ruddiness.
Aruṇī-kṛita, as, ā, am, reddened, turned or become red.
Aruṇīya or *aruṇīya-yoga, as,* m. the twenty-fifth Upanishad of the Atharva-veda.

अरुतहनु *a-ruta-hanu, us, us, u,* Ved. whose cheeks or jaws cannot be broken.

अरुद्ध *a-ruddha, as, ā, am* (rt. *rudh*), not obstructed, not hindered.

अरुन्तुद *arun-tuda, as, ā, am,* inflicting wounds, causing torments; sharp, corrosive; acrimonious, sour (as disposition). — *Aruntuda-tva, am,* n. infliction of pain; acrimoniousness, causticity.

अरुन्धती *a-rundhatī,* f. (rt. *rudh*), a medicinal climbing plant; the wife of Vasishṭha; the wife of Dharma; the morning star, personified as the wife of Vasishṭha or of the seven Ṛishis; also one of the Pleiades. At marriage ceremonies Arundhatī is invoked as a pattern of conjugal excellence by the bridegroom. — *Arundhatī-jāni, is,* or *arundhatī-nātha, as,* m. Vasishṭha, one of the seven Ṛishis or saints, and stars in the great bear.

अरुर्मघ *arur-magha, as,* m., Ved., N. of certain miserly evil spirits (as the Paṇis, &c.).

अरुशहन् *aruśa-han, ā,* m. (*aruśa = arusha?*), Ved. striking the red (clouds), an epithet of Indra.

अरुष् *a-rush, ṭ, ṭ, ṭ,* not angry, good-tempered.
A-rushṭa, as, ā, am, not angry, calm.

अरुष *arusha, as, ī, am* (said to be fr. rt. *ṛi* and connected with *aruṇa*), Ved. red, reddish; the colour of Agni and his horses; (*as*), m. the red horse of Agni, flame; the sun; the day; a red storm-cloud; (*ī*), f. the dawn; a red horse; flame; N. of the wife of Bhṛigu and the mother of Aurva. — *Arusha-stūpa, as, ā, am,* Ved. having brilliant masses of flame.
Arusha or *arushya,* nom. P. *arushati* or *arushyati, -shitum, -yitum,* to go.

अरुस् *arus, us, us, us* (fr. rt. *ṛi*), wounded, sore; (*us*), n. a sore or wound; ind. a joint. — *Arushkara, as, ā, am,* causing wounds, wounding; (*as*), m. the plant Semecarpus Anacardium; the nut of this tree. — *Arush-kṛita, as, ā, am,* wounded. — *A-ruḥ-srāṇa, am,* n., Ved. a kind of medical preparation for wounds.
Arushka, as, m., N. of a tree, Semecarpus Anacardium.
Arusikā, f. eruptions on the scalp with acute pain (?).
Arū-kṛi, cl. 8. P. *-karoti, -kartum,* to wound.

अरुहा *a-ruhā,* f., N. of a plant.

अरूक्ष *a-rūksha, as, ā, am,* Ved. soft. — *Arūksha-tā,* f., Ved. softness.
A-rūkshita, as, ā, am, Ved. soft, supple.
A-rūkshṇa, as, ā, am, Ved. soft, tender.

अरूप *a-rūpa, as, ā, am,* formless, shapeless; ugly, ill-formed; dissimilar, unlike. — *Arūpatā,* f. shapelessness, ugliness; dissimilarity. — *Arūpavat, ān, atī, at,* shapeless, ugly.
A-rūpaka, as, ā, am, without figure or metaphor, not figurative, literal.
A-rūpin, ī, iṇī, i, shapeless.

अरूष *arūsha, as,* m. (fr. rt. *ṛi*), the sun, a kind of snake.

अरे *are,* ind. interjection of calling.

अरेणु *a-reṇu, us, us, u,* Ved. not dusty, not touching the dust (of the earth); (*u*), n. what is not dusty, the ether.

अरेतस् *a-retas, ās, ās, as,* or *a-retaska, as, ā, am,* seedless, not receiving seed.

अरेपस् *a-repas, ās, ās, as,* Ved. spotless, clear, clean, shining.

अरेरे *arere,* ind. interjection of calling to inferiors or of calling angrily.

अरोक *a-roka, as, ā, am* (rt. *ruć*), darkened, obscured, dimmed. — *Aroka-dat, at, atī, at,* or *aroka-danta, as, ā, am,* having black or discoloured teeth, having bad teeth.

अरोग *a-roga, as, ā, am,* free from disease, healthy, well; (*as*), m. health.
A-rogaṇa, as, ā, am, Ved. not rendering sick, freeing from disease.
A-rogin, ī, iṇī, i, or *a-rogya, as, ā, am,* healthy. — *Arogi-tā* or *arogya-tā,* f. healthiness, health.

अरोचक *a-roćaka, as, ikā, am* (rt. *ruć*), not shining; causing want of appetite or disgust; (*as*), m. want or loss of appetite, disgust, indigestion.
A-roćakin, ī, inī, i, suffering from want of appetite or indigestion.
A-roćamāna, as, ā, am, not shining.
A-roćishṇu, us, us, u, dark, disagreeable, ugly.

अरोदन *a-rodana, am,* n. (rt. *rud*), not weeping.

अरोध्य *a-rodhya, as, ā, am* (rt. *rudh*), not to be hindered or obstructed, unobstructed.

अरोपण *a-ropaṇa, am,* n. (rt. *ruh*), not planting or fixing.

अरोष *a-rosha, as,* m. calmness, gentleness.

अरौद्र *a-raudra, as, ī, am,* not formidable or fierce.

अर्क् *ark,* cl. 10. P. *arkayati, -yitum,* to heat or warm; to praise.

अर्क *arka, as,* m. (fr. rt. *arć*), a ray, flash of lightning; the sun; fire; crystal; copper; a N. of Indra; Sunday; membrum virile; N. of the plant Calotropis Gigantea; a religious ceremony; praise, hymn; praising; a singer; a learned man; an elder brother; food. — *Arka-kāntā,* f., N. of the plant Polanisia Icosandra W. — *Arka-kshetra, am,* n. 'the field of the sun,' N. of a sacred place in Orissa. — *Arka-ćikitsā,* f. 'the medical art of the sun,' title of a work on medicine. — *Arka-ja, au,* m. du. the two sons of Sūrya or the sun and Aśvinī, and physicians of Svarga or heaven. — *Arka-tanaya, as,* m. offspring of the sun, an epithet of Karṇa, Manu Vaivasvata, Manu Sāvarṇi, and Śani; (*ā*), f. an epithet of the rivers Yamunā and Tapatī. — *Arka-tva, am,* n. brightness, &c. — *Arka-tvish, ṭ,* f. a ray of light, the light of the sun. — *Arka-dina, am,* n. a solar day. — *Arka-nandana, as,* m. a son of the sun; a N. of the planet Saturn; an epithet of Karṇa. — *Arka-nayana, as,* m., N. of an Asura. — *Arka-pattra, as,* m., N. of the plant Calotropis Gigantea; (*ā*), f. a kind of birth-wort, Aristolochia Indica; (*am*), n. the leaf of the plant Calotropis Gigantea. — *Arka-parṇa, as,* m. the plant Calotropis Gigantea; (*am*), n. the leaf of this plant. — *Arka-pādapa, as,* m., N. of the tree Melia Azadirachta Lin. — *Arka-putra, as,* m. the child of the sun, i. e. Karṇa. — *Arka-pushpikā,* f., N. of the plant Gynandropsis Pentaphylla. — *Arka-pushpī,* f., N. of the plant Kuṭumbinī. — *Arka-prakāśa, as,* m. 'the revelation of the sun,' title of a work on medicine and jurisprudence. — *Arka-priyā,* f., N. of the plant Hibiscus Rosa Sinensis L. — *Arka-bandhu, us,* or *arka-bāndhava, as,* m. a N. of Buddha Śākya-muni. — *Arka-bhaktā,* f., N. of the plant Polanisia Icosandra W. and A. — *Arka-maṇḍala, am,* n. the disc of the sun. — *Arka-mūlā,* f. a kind of birth-wort, Aristolochia Indica. — *Arka-reto-ja, as,* m. Revanta, the son of Sūrya. — *Arka-lūsha, as,* m., N. of a man. — *Arkavat, ān, atī, at,* containing flashes of lightning. — *Arka-varsha, as,* m. a solar year. — *Arka-vallabha, as,* m., N. of the plant Pentapetes Phœnicea Lin. — *Arka-vedha, as,* m., N. of a plant. — *Arka-vrata, as,* m. the rule or law of the sun; i. e. levying taxes, subjecting the people to imposts, or drawing their wealth as imperceptibly as the sun evaporates water. — *Arka-śoka, as,* m., Ved. brilliancy of rays. — *Arka-sāti, is,* f., Ved. invention of hymns, poetical inspiration. — *Arka-sūnu, us,* m. son of the sun, an epithet of Yama. — *Arka-sodara, as,* m. Airāvata, the elephant of Indra. — *Arka-hitā,* f., N. of the plant Polanisia Icosandra W. — *Arkāṅśa* (°*ka-aṅ*°), *as,* m. a digit or the twelfth part of the sun's disc. — *Arkāśman* (°*ka-aś*°), *ā,* m. heliotrope, girasol, crystal. — *Arkāhva* (°*ka-āh*°), *as,* m. swallow wort. — *Arkendu-sangama* (°*ka-in*°), *as,* m. the instant of conjunction of the sun and moon. — *Arkopala* (°*ka-up*°), *as,* m. the sun-stone, a ruby.
Arkin, ī, iṇī, i, Ved. shining; praising.

Arkīya or *arkya, as, ā, am*, belonging to *arka*.

अर्गड *argaḍa, as, ā*, m. f. (for *argala*), an impediment.

अर्गल *argala, as, ā* or *ī, am*, m. f. n. (said to be fr. rt. *arj*), a wooden bolt or pin for fastening a door or the cover of a vessel; a bar; a wave or billow.

Argalikā, f. a small door pin, a bolt.

Argalita, as, ā, am, fastened by a bolt or pin.

Argalīya or *argalya, as, ā, am*, belonging to a bolt or pin.

अर्घ् *argh*, cl. 1. P. *arghati, -ghitum*, to be worth, to cost; to hurt? [cf. Germ. *arg, ärgern*; Old Germ. *arg, ark*, and with *a* inserted, *arag, arak*, miserly, wicked, impious; *arg*, evil].

अर्घ *argha, as*, m. (fr. rt. *arh*), worth, value, price; a respectful offering of various ingredients to a god or Brāhman. — *Argha-dāna, am*, n. presentation of a respectful offering. — *Argha-balābala* (°*la-ab*°), *am*, n. rate of price, proper price, the cheapness or dearness of commodities. — *Argha-saṅkhyāpana, am*, n. fixing the price of commodities, appraising, assize: it is the act of the king or ruler, in concert with the traders, and should be done once a week or once a fortnight. — *Arghārha* (°*gha-ar*°), *as, ā, am*, worthy of or requiring a respectful offering, a superior. — *Arghāshṭa-puraka* (°*gha-ash*°), *am*, n., N. of a town. — *Arghīśa* (°*gha-īśa*?), *as*, m. a N. of Śiva.

Arghya, as, ā, am, valuable; venerable; deserving a respectful oblation; (*am*), n. a respectful oblation to gods or venerable men, of rice, dūrva-grass, flowers, &c., with water; or of water only in a small boat-shaped vessel; a kind of honey. — *Arghya-tas*, ind. of true value.

अर्घट *arghaṭa, am*, n. ashes. See *pārghaṭa*.

अर्च् *arć*, cl. 1. P. *arćati, ānarća, arćishyati, ārćīt, arćitum*, to shine; to praise; to honour or treat with respect, to worship; to salute: Caus. *arćayati, -te, -yitum*, to cause to shine; to praise; to honour; worship, salute: Desid. *arćićishati*, to wish to honour: Ved. Pass. *ṛićyate*.

Arća, as, ā, am, Ved. shining. See also *arćā* below.

Arćaka, as, ā, am, worshipping; (*as*), m. a worshipper.

Arćatri, is, is, i, Ved. sounding, neighing, roaring.

Arćatrya, as, ā, am, Ved. to be praised.

Arćad-dhūma, as, ā, am, Ved. whose smoke is shining.

Arćana, as, ī, am, praising, celebrating with praise; (*ā* or *am*), f. n. worship, the homage paid to deities and to superiors. — *Arćanānas* (°*na-an*°), *ās*, m., Ved., N. of a Ṛishi ('he who has a sounding carriage').

Arćanīya, as, ā, am, to be worshipped, respectable, venerable, adorable.

Arćā, f. worship, adoration; an image or idol destined to be worshipped. — *Arćā-vat, ān, atī, at*, worshipped. — *Arćā-viḍambana, am*, n. false or feigned worship.

Arći, is, m. ray, flame (of fire or of the dawn, &c.). — *Arći-ketu, us*, m., N. of a man. — *Arći-netrādhipati* (°*ra-adh*°), *is*, m., N. of a Yaksha. — *Arći-mat, ān, atī, at*, shining, blazing; (*ān*), m., N. of a man. — *Arći-vat, ān, atī, at*, Ved. blazing.

Arćita, as, ā, am, honoured, worshipped, respected, saluted; offered with reverence.

Arćitin, ī, inī, i, honouring.

Arćitri, tā, m. a worshipper.

Arćin, ī, inī, i, Ved. praising, honouring; shining (as a ray of light), radiating; (*ī*), m., N. of a man; a ray of light.

Arćis, is, f. n. ray of light, flame; light, lustre; (*is*), f., N. of the wife of Kṛiśāśva and mother of Dhūmaketu. — *Arćish-mat, ān, atī, at*, brilliant, resplendent; (*ān*), m. fire, the god of fire; (*atī*), f. one of the ten earths with Buddhists.

1. *arćya, as, ā, am*, to be honoured or worshipped.

2. *arćya*, ind. having honoured or worshipped.

अर्ज् 1. *arj*, cl. 1. P. *arjati, ānarja, arjishyati, -jitum*, to procure; to acquire, reach, gain, earn: Caus. *arjayati, -yitum*, to procure, acquire; to work or manufacture; to make or prepare.

Arjaka, as, ikā, am, procuring, acquiring; (*as*), m., N. of several plants, Ocymum Gratissimum L., &c.

Arjana, am, n. procuring; acquiring, gaining, earning; gathering.

Arjita, as, ā, am, acquired, gained, earned.

अर्ज् 2. *arj* (a doubtful root, probably distinct from the last, and connected with *raj, rāj*, and *arć*), to shine, to be white (?).

Arjuna, as, ā or *ī, am*, white, clear, the colour of day; of silver; (*as*), m. the white colour; a peacock; cutaneous disease; the tree Terminalia Arjuna W. and A.; a N. of Indra; N. of the third of the Pāṇḍava princes, who was a son of Indra and Kuntī; N. of a son of Kṛitavīrya, who was slain by Paraśurāma; N. of a Śākya; N. of a country; the only son of his mother; (*ī*), f. a procuress, a bawd; cow; a kind of serpent; Ushā, wife of Aniruddha; N. of a river, more commonly called Bāhudā or Karatoyā; (*nyau* or *nyas*), du. or pl., N. of the constellation Phalgunī; (*am*), n. silver; gold; slight inflammation of the conjunctiva or white of the eye; grass; (*ās*), m. pl. the descendants of Arjuna. — *Arjuna-kāṇḍa, as, ā, am*, Ved. having a white appendage. — *Arjuna-ćchavi, is, is, i*, of a white colour, white. — *Arjuna-tas*, ind. on the side or party of Arjuna. — *Arjuna-dhvaja, as*, m. having a white banner, an epithet of Hanumat. — *Arjuna-pākī*, f., N. of a plant and its fruits. — *Arjunārishṭa-sañćhanna* (°*na-ar*°), *as, ā, am*, covered with Arjuna and Nimb trees. — *Arjunopama* (°*na-up*°), *as*, m. the teak tree, Tectona Grandis L.

Arjunaka, as, ā, am, belonging to Arjuna; (*as*), m. a worshipper of Arjuna.

Arjunasa, as, ā, am, overgrown with Arjuna plants.

अर्ण *arṇa, as, ā, am* (fr. rt. *ṛi*), being in motion, agitated; foaming, effervescing; restless; (*as*), m. a wave, flood, stream; the teak tree, Tectona Grandis L.; a letter; N. of a metre, comprising ten feet, and belonging to the class called Daṇḍaka; N. of a man; (*am*), n. tumult or din of battle. — *Arṇa-sāti, is*, f., Ved. tumult of battle.

Arṇava, as, ā, am, being agitated; foaming; restless; (*as*), m. a wave, flood, stream; the foaming sea, high water; the ocean of air; N. of a metre; title of a work on jurisprudence. — *Arṇava-ja, as, ā, am*, sea-born, marine; (*as, am*), m. n. cuttle fish. — *Arṇava-pota, as*, m. a boat or ship. — *Arṇava-mandira, as*, m. an epithet of Varuṇa, regent of the waters. — *Arṇava-yāna, am*, n. a boat or ship. — *Arṇavānta* (°*va-an*°), *as*, m. the extremity of the ocean. — *Arṇavodbhava* (°*va-ud*°), *as*, m., N. of a plant.

Arṇas, as, n. a wave, flood, stream; the sea, ocean; the ocean of air; river, water. — *Arṇas-vat, ān, atī, at*, Ved. containing many waves. — *Arṇo-da, as*, m. a cloud; N. of the plant Cyperus Rotundus. — *Arṇo-bhava, as*, m. a shell. — *Arṇo-vṛit, t, t, t*, Ved. including the waters.

अर्तगल *arta-gala, as*, m., N. of a plant, Barleria Cærulea Roxb.

अर्तन *artana, as, ā, am* (rt. *ṛit*), blaming, reviling; (*am*), n. censure, approach, abuse.

Artuka, as, ā, am, Ved. provoking, contentious, quarrelsome.

अर्ति *arti, is*, f. (a weakened form of *ārti*, fr. rt. *ṛi* with *ā*), pain; the end of a bow.

अर्तिका *artikā*, f. an elder sister (in theatrical language), [cf. *attikā* and *antikā*].

अर्थ् *arth*, cl. 10. A. *arthayate, -yitum*, Aor. *ārtithata*, ep. cl. 1. A. *arthate, -thitum*, to strive to obtain, to desire, wish, request; to supplicate or entreat any one, to sue.

Artha, as, am, m. n., in Ṛig-veda generally n., but in later Sanskṛit only m. (said to be fr. rt. *ṛi*, but connected with rt. *arth*), object; purpose; cause, motive, reason; advantage, use, utility; thing; substance, wealth, property, opulence; affair, concern; request, suit, petition; asking, begging, want, need; sense, meaning, notion; manner, sort, kind; prohibition, prevention, abolition; price; N. of a son of Dharma. (*Artha* in some of its first senses may govern an inst. case; e. g. *ko me jīvitena arthaḥ*, 'what concern have I with life?'). — *Artha-kara, as, ā* or *ī, am*, producing or yielding advantage or wealth; useful; enriching. — *Artha-karman, a*, n. a principal or main action. — *Artha-kāma, au*, m. du. utility and desire, wealth and pleasure; (*as, ā, am*), desirous of wealth. — *Artha-kṛićchra, am*, n. a difficult matter. — *Artha-kṛit, t, t, t*, causing profit, useful. — *Artha-kṛityā, am*, f. n. an action aiming at profit. — *Artha-gata, as, ā, am* (= *gatārtha*), without an object, useless. — *Artha-garīyas, ān, asī, as*, highly significant. — *Artha-ghna, as, ī, am*, wasteful, extravagant. — *Artha-jāta, as, ā, am*, significant, full of meaning; worth the money. — *Artha-jña, as, ā, am*, understanding the meaning of anything. — *Artha-tattva, am*, n. truth, the real object, nature or cause of anything; the true state of the case, the fact of the matter. — *Artha-tas*, ind. towards a particular object; with reference to the meaning; in fact, really, truly; namely, that is to say; on account of, (at the end of a compound). — *Artha-da, as, ā, am*, conferring advantage; profitable, useful, compliant, favourable; liberal, munificent. — *Artha-dūshaṇa, am*, n. spoiling of another's property; unjust seizure of property, or a withholding of what is due; waste, prodigality, extravagance; finding fault with the meaning of a passage. — *Artha-nibandhana, as, ā, am*, having its cause in wealth, contingent on affluence and respectability. — *Artha-niśćaya, as*, m. determination, decision. — *Artha-pati, is*, m. the lord of riches; a king; an epithet of Kuvera; N. of a man. — *Artha-para, as, ā, am*, intent on gaining wealth; parsimonious, niggardly. — *Artha-prayoga, as*, m. application of wealth, as to trade, usury, &c.; the profession of usury. — *Artha-prāpti, is*, f. acquisition of wealth; attainment of an object. — *Artha-bandha, as*, m. that which binds together the sense; the text. — *Artha-buddhi, is, is, i*, selfish. — *Artha-bodha, as*, m. indication of the real import. — *Artha-bhāj, k, k, k*, entitled to a share in the division of property. — *Artha-bhṛita, as, ā, am*, having high wages (as a servant). — *Artha-bheda, as*, m. distinction, difference of meaning. — *Artha-mātra, ā, am*, f. n. property, money. — *Artha-lābha, as*, m. acquisition of wealth. — *Artha-lubdha, as, ā, am*, greedy of wealth, covetous, niggardly. — *Artha-leśa, as*, m. a little wealth. — *Artha-lobha, as*, m. desire of wealth, avarice. — *Artha-vat, ān, atī, at*, wealthy, rich; significant, full of sense or meaning; (*ān*), m. a man; (*-vat*), ind. according to a purpose. — *Arthavat-tva, am*, n. significance, importance. — *Arthavargīya, as, ā, am*, concerning the category of objects. — *Artha-vāda, as*, m. explanation of an affair, explanatory remark, exegesis; affirmation or narrative; declaration of purpose or object; speech or expression having a certain object; sentence; praise, eulogium. — *Artha-vijñāna, am*, n. comprehension of meaning, one of the six exercises of the understanding. — *Artha-vid, t, t, t*, sagacious, sensible, wise. — *Artha-viniśćaya, as*, m. title of a Buddhist Sūtra work. — *Artha-vṛiddhi, is*, f. accumulation of wealth. — *Artha-vaikalpa, am*, n. deviation from truth, perversion or disguise of fact; prevarication. — *Artha-vyaya, as*, m. expenditure. — *Artha-vyaya-jña, as, ā, am*, liberal in giving and using. — *Artha-vyaya-saha, as, ā, am*, prodigal. — *Artha-śāstra, am*, n. institutes of the science of what is useful in life; science of polity or moral and political government. — *Artha-śauća, am*, n. purity, honesty in money matters. — *Artha-sam-*

sthāna, am, n. accumulation of wealth; treasury. — Artha-saṅgraha, as, m. accumulation of wealth; treasure. — Artha-sañćaya, as, m. acquisition of wealth; wealth, property. — Artha-sambandha, as, m. connection of the sense with the word or sentence. — Artha-sādhaka, as, m. bringing any matter to a conclusion; N. of a minister of king Daśaratha. — Artha-sāra, as, m. a considerable property. — Artha-siddhaka, as, m., N. of the plant Vitex Negundo L. — Artha-siddhi, is, f. success. — Artha-hara, as, ā, am, inheriting or taking wealth. — Artha-hīna, as, ā, am, unmeaning, nonsensical; poor, deprived of wealth; failing. — Arthāgama (°tha-āg°), as, m. receipt or collection of property; income, acquisition of wealth. — Arthādhikāra (°tha-adh°), as, m. office of treasurer, charge of money or property. — Arthādhikārin (°tha-adh°), ī, m. a treasurer, a paymaster. — Arthāntara (°tha-an°), am, n. another matter, a different or new circumstance, a new affair; a different meaning; opposite or antithetical meaning, difference of meaning or purport. — Arthāntara-nyāsa, as, m. antithesis. — Arthānvita (°tha-an°), as, ā, am, possessed of wealth, rich; significant. — Arthāpatti (°tha-āp°), is, f. an inference from circumstances; one of the five arguments of the Mīmāṇsakas; presumption, supposition. — Arthārthin (°tha-ar°), ī, inī, i, one who solicits wealth, or endeavours to gain any object. — Arthet (°tha-it), t, t, t, Ved. active, industrious; hasty. — Arthepsu (°tha-īp°), us, us, u, desirous of wealth. — Arthepsutā, f. desire of wealth. — Arthehā (°tha-īhā), f. desire of wealth. — Arthopama (°tha-up°), am, n. a simile in which the object of comparison is stated without any particle of comparison, e. g. 'he is a dog.' — Arthopārjana (°tha-up°), am, n. acquisition of wealth or property. — Arthoshman (°tha-ush°), a, n. wealth, the glow or pride of wealth, the condition of being wealthy; (so, Anglice, 'a warm man'). — Arthaugha (°tha-ogh°), as, m. a treasure.

Arthanā, f. request, begging, asking, entreaty.

Arthanīya, as, ā, am, to be requested, asked, &c.

Artham or arthe, ind. (generally at the end of compounds) on account of, in behalf of, for the sake of.

Arthāt, ind. according to the state of the case, according to the circumstances, as a matter of fact; in fact; that is to say.

Arthāpaya, nom. P. arthāpayati, -yitum. See rt. arth.

Arthāya, ind. on account of, for the sake of.

Arthika, as, m. a crier, a watchman, a minstrel, a servant, whose duty it is to announce, by song or music, fixed periods of the day, such as the hours of rising and going to rest.

Arthita, as, ā, am, asked, desired, requested; (am), n. wish, desire, supplication, petition.

Arthitavya, as, ā, am, to be asked, requested.

Arthin, ī, inī, i, one who seeks to effect or gain a purpose or object; one who asks or begs for anything (with inst.); desirous of (with inst.); supplicating or entreating any one (with gen.); a beggar, a petitioner, suitor; a plaintiff, a prosecutor; a servant; a follower, a companion or partizan. — Arthi-tā, f. the condition of a beggar, asking, wishing; begging. — Arthi-tva, am, n. the condition of a suppliant. — Arthi-sāt, ind. with kṛi, to dispose of anything in favour of one who asks or begs for it.

Arthīya, as, ā, am, (as last member of a compound) destined for; relating to.

Arthe, ind. on account of; see artham. — Arthe-kṛi, to act on behalf of (?).

Arthya, as, ā, am, proper, fit; rich; to be asked or sought for; intelligent, wise; (am), n. red chalk.

अर्द् ard cl. 1. P. ardati, ānarda, ardishyati, ārdīt, arditum, Ved. 3 pl. impv. ṛidantu and cl. 7. P. ṛiṇatti, to move; to be moved; to be scattered as dust; to dissolve; to go; to ask, beg; to torment, hurt, kill: Caus. ardayati, -yitum, to make agitated or restless; to stir up, shake vehemently; to distort; to torment, distress; to strike, hurt, kill: Desid. ardidishati [cf. Lat. ardeo].

Ardana, as, ā, am, moving restlessly; disturbing, distressing; (ā), f. going; asking, begging, giving pain, killing; (am), n. pain, trouble, excitement, disturbance.

Ardani, is, m. sickness, disease; asking, begging; fire.

Ardita, as, ā, am, gone; asked, requested, begged; killed, injured, pained, afflicted; (am), n. a disease, spasm of the jaw-bones; trismus, tetanus; or hemiplegia, i. e. paralysis of the muscles on one side of the face and neck.

Arditin, ī, inī, i, having spasms of the jaw-bones.

Ardyamāna, as, ā, am, being distressed.

अर्ध 1. ardha, as, m. (said to be fr. rt. ṛidh), Ved. side, part; place, region, country [cf. Lat. ordo, Germ. ort]. The accent is on the first syllable.

2. ardha, as, ā, am, half, halved, forming a half [cf. Osset. ardag]; ardha ardha, one part, the other part; (as, am), m. n. the half; one part of two, a part, a party; half a short syllable. The accent is on the last syllable. (Ardha may be compounded in a peculiar way with an ordinal, e. g. ardha-tṛitīya, containing (two and) the third (only) half, i. e. two and a half; ardha-ćaturtha, three and a half, &c.) — Ardha-kāla or ardha-kūṭa, as, m. an epithet of Śiva. — Ardha-kṛita, as, ā, am, half-done, half-performed. — Ardha-ketu, us, m., N. of a Rudra. — Ardha-koṭi, f. half a crore, five millions. — Ardha-kosha, as, m. a moiety of one's treasure. — Ardha-krośa, as, m. half a league. — Ardha-khāra, am, ī, n. f. a measure, half a khārī. — Ardha-gaṅgā, f., N. of the river Kāverī. — Ardha-garbha, as, ā, am, Ved. in the middle of the womb. — Ardha-guććha, as, m. a necklace of twenty-four strings. — Ardha-gola, as, m. a hemisphere. — Ardha-ćakravartin or ardha-ćakrin, ī, m. half a ćakravartin; N. of the nine black Vāsudevas and the nine enemies of Vishṇu. — Ardha-ćandra, as, m. half-moon; the semicircular marks on a peacock's tail; the semicircular scratch of the finger nail; an arrow, the head of which is like a half-moon; the hand bent into a semicircle or the shape of a claw, as for the purpose of seizing or clutching anything; (ā), f., N. of the plant Convolvulus Torpethum; (as, ā, am), crescent-shaped, of a semilunar form. — Ardha-ćandrākāra (°ra-āk°), as, ā, am, or ardha-ćandrākṛiti, is, is, i, half-moon-shaped, crescent-shaped; (as), m. or (is), f. a meniscus. — Ardha-ćandrikā, f., N. of a climbing plant. — Ardha-ćolaka, as, m. a short bodice. — Ardha-jāhnavī, f., N. of the river Kāverī. — Ardha-tanu, us, f. half a body. — Ardha-tikta, as, m., N. of a plant. — Ardha-tūra, as, m. a particular kind of musical instrument. — Ardha-dagdha, as, ā, am, half-burnt. — Ardha-divasa, as, m. half a day, midday; a day containing one half of a whole day, a day of twelve hours. — Ardha-deva, as, m., Ved. demi-god. — Ardha-dhāra, am, n. a knife or lancet with a single edge, the blade two inches long, the handle six. — Ardha-nārāyaṇa, as, m. a form of Vishṇu. — Ardha-nārīśa (°ri-īśa), as, m. one of the forms of Śiva (half male and half female). — Ardha-nāra, am, n. half a boat. — Ardha-niśā, f. midnight. — Ardha-pañćāśat, f. twenty-five. — Ardha-paṇa, am, n. a measure containing half a paṇa. — Ardha-patha, am, n. half-way; (e), ind. midway. — Ardha-pādika, as, ā, am, having only half a foot. — Ardha-pārāvata, as, m a kind of pigeon. — Ardha-pulāyita, am, n. a half-gallop, canter. — Ardha-pūrṇa, as, ā, am, half-full. — Ardha-prahara, as, m. half a watch, one hour and a half. — Ardha-bṛihatī, f., Ved. half the usual breadth. — Ardha-bhāga, as, m. a half; a part. — Ardha-bhāgika, as, ī, am, or ardha-bhāgin, ī, inī, i, taking or sharing half. — Ardha-bhāj, k, k, k, taking or sharing half; (k), m. a sharer, companion. — Ardha-bhāskara, as, m. midday. — Ardha-bhoṭikā, f. a kind of cake. — Ardha-māgadhī, f. a variety of the Māgadhī dialect. — Ardha-māṇava or ardha-māṇavaka, as, m. a necklace of twelve strings. — Ardha-mātrā, f. half a short syllable. — Ardha-mārge, ind. half-way, midway. — Ardha-māsa, as, m. half a month; ardhamāsa-śas, ind. every half month, or fortnight. — Ardhamāsatama, as, ā, am, or ardhamāsika, as, ā, am, done or happening every half month; lasting half a month, or a fortnight. — Ardha-mushṭi, is, m. f. a half-clenched hand. — Ardha-yāma, as, m. half a watch, an hour and a half. — Ardha-ratha, as, m. a warrior who fights on a car along with another. — Ardha-rātra, as, m. midnight; a night containing half a whole day of twenty-four hours. — Ardha-rātra-samaya, as, m. the time of midnight. — Ardharātrārdhadivasa (°rātra-ardha°), am, n. the equinox. — Ardharća (°dha-ṛića), as, am, m. n. half a verse or hemistich. — Ardharća-śas, ind. in every hemistich. — Ardha-vastra-saṃvīta, as, ā, am, clothed or enveloped in half-garments. — Ardha-visarga, as, m. the sound Visarga before k, kh, p, ph, so called because its sign (✕) is the half of that of Visarga (ঃ). — Ardha-vīkshaṇa, am, n. a side-look, a glance, a leer. — Ardha-vṛiddha, as, ā, am, middle-aged. — Ardha-vaināśika, as, m., N. of the followers of Kaṇāda ('arguing half-perishableness'). — Ardha-vyāsa, as, m. the radius of a circle. — Ardha-śata, am, n. fifty; one hundred and fifty. — Ardhaśana, am, for ardhāśana (°dha-aś°), am, n. half a meal. — Ardha-śaphara, as, m. a kind of fish. — Ardha-śabda, as, ā, am, having a low voice. — Ardha-śesha or ardhāvaśesha (°dha-av°), as, ā, am, having only half left. — Ardha-śyāma, as, ā, am, half-clouded. — Ardha-śloka, as, m. half a Śloka. — Ardha-sañjāta-sasya, as, ā, am, having its crops half-grown. — Ardha-sīrin, ī, m. a cultivator, a ploughman, who takes half the crop for his labour. — Ardha-hāra, as, m. a necklace of sixty-four or of forty strings. — Ardha-hrasva, am, n. half a short syllable. — Ardhāṇśa (°dha-aṇ°), as, m. a half, the half. — Ardhāṇśin (°dha-aṇ°), ī, inī, i, sharing a half. — Ardhākāra (°dha-a°), as, m. half the letter a; another name for avagraha, q. v. — Ardhāṅga (°dha-aṅ°), am, n. half the body. — Ardhārdha (°dha-ar°), as, m. half of a half, a quarter; half and half. — Ardhāvabhedaka (°dha-av°), as, m. pain in half the head, hemicrania; (am), n. dividing in equal parts. — Ardhāvaśesha (°dha-av°), as, ā, am, having only one half left. — Ardhāśana (°dha-aś°), am, n. half a meal. — Ardhāsana (°dha-ās°), am, n. half a seat (it is considered a mark of high respect to make room for a guest on the same seat with one's self); greeting kindly or with respect; exemption from censure. — Ardhendu (°dha-in°), us, m. a half-moon or crescent; the semicircular impression of a finger nail; an arrow with a crescent-shaped head; the hand expanded in a semicircular form like a claw. — Ardhendu-mauli (°dha-in°), is, m. Śiva, whose diadem is a half-moon. — Ardhendra (°dha-in°), as, ā, am, that of which a half belongs to Indra. — Ardhokta (°dha-uk°), as, ā, am, half-uttered, said imperfectly or indistinctly. — Ardhokti (°dha-uk°), is, f. speaking indistinctly or incompletely, broken or interrupted speech. — Ardhodaya (°dha-ud°), as, m. the rising of the half-moon. — Ardhodita (°dha-ud°), as, ā, am (rt. i with ud), half-risen; (rt. vad), half-uttered. — Ardhoruka (°dha-ūru), as, ā, am, reaching to the middle of the thighs; (am), n. a short petticoat.

Ardhaka, as, am, m. n. the same as ardha. — Ardhaka-ghātin, ī, m., N. of Rudra.

Ardhan-kṛi, cl. 8. P., Ved. -karoti, -kartum, to prefer, to favour.

Ardhika, as, ī, am, measuring a half, relating to a half.

Ardhin, ī, inī, i, entitled to half or sharing a half.

अर्धुक ardhuka, as, ā, am (fr. rt. ṛidh), Ved. succeeding, prospering.

Ardhya, as, ā, am, to be accomplished; to be obtained.

अर्पय arpaya, Caus. of rt. ṛi; arpayati,

-yitum, to throw, cast; insert, fix; pierce, place in or upon; offer, deliver, consign, entrust, give back.

Arpaṇa, *am*, n. throwing, casting; inserting, fixing; piercing; placing in or upon; offering, delivering, consigning, entrusting; giving back.

Arpaṇīya, *as*, *ā*, *am*, to be delivered, to be placed.

Arpita, *as*, *ā*, *am*, delivered, consigned; placed in or upon. — *Arpita-kara*, *as*, *ī*, *am*, extending or giving the hand; married.

Arpisa, *as*, m. the heart.

Arpya, *as*, *ā*, *am*, to be delivered, consignable.

अर्ब् *arb*, cl. 1. P. *arbati*, *ānarba*, *arbitum*, to go, to go to or towards; to hurt or kill.

अर्बुद *arbuda*, *as*, *am*, m. n. (said to be fr. the preceding rt.), a serpent; a serpent-like demon conquered by Indra; a long round mass; a swelling, a tumour, a polypus; a hundred millions; N. of a mountain in the west of India, commonly called Abū, a place of pilgrimage, especially of the Jainas; N. of a people; N. of a hell.

Arbudi, *is*, m., Ved. a serpent-like demon conquered by Indra.

Arbudin, *ī*, *inī*, *i*, afflicted with swelling or tumour.

अर्भ *arbha*, *as*, *ā*, *am* (said to be fr. rt. *ṛi*), little, small, unimportant; (*as*), m. child, pupil [cf. Lat. *orbus*; Gr. ὀρφανός].

Arbhaka, *as*, *ā*, *am*, small, minute; weak, little; emaciated; young, childish; like, similar; (*as*), m. a boy, a child, the young of any animal; a fool, an idiot.

Arbhaga, *as*, *ā*, *am*, Ved. youthful.

अर्म *arma*, *as*, *am*, m. n. (said to be fr. rt. *ṛi*), a disease of the eyes.

Armaka, *as*, *ā*, *am*, narrow, thin; (*am*), n. narrowness.

Armaṇa, *as*, m. a measure of one droṇa.

Arman, *a*, n. a disease of the eyes.

अर्य *arya*, *as*, *ā*, *am* (fr. rt. *ṛi*), attached to, true, devoted, dear; kind; excellent; (*as*), m. a master, lord; an Āryan; a man of the third tribe, a Vaiśya; (*ā*), f. a woman of the third tribe, the wife of a Vaiśya. — *Arya-jārā*, f., Ved. the mistress of an Āryan. — *Arya-patnī*, f., Ved. wife of a true, legitimate husband. — *Arya-varya*, *as*, m. a Vaiśya of rank. — *Arya-śveta*, *as*, m., N. of a man.

Aryaman, *ā*, m., Ved. a bosom friend, play-fellow, companion, especially a friend who asks a woman in marriage for another; N. of an Āditya, who is commonly invoked together with Varuṇa and Mitra; N. of the chief of the manes; the sun; the Asclepias plant. — *Aryama-datta*, *as*, m., N. of a man. — *Aryama-devā*, f., N. of the twelfth lunar mansion.

Aryamya, *as*, *ā*, *am*, Ved. intimate, very friendly; (*as*), m. bosom friend, companion.

Aryayāṇī, f. a multitude of women of the Vaiśya tribe (?).

Aryāṇī, f. a mistress; a woman of the third or Vaiśya tribe.

अर्व् *arv*, cl. 1. P. *arvati*, *ānarva*, *arvitum*, to hurt, kill.

अर्व *arva*, (in comp.) hither, towards, near to. — *Arva-vasu*, *us*, m. one of the seven principal rays of the sun.

अर्वट *arvaṭa*, *am*, n. (said to be fr. rt. *arv*), ashes.

अर्वन् *arvan*, *ā*, m. (fr. rt. *ṛi*), going, running; epithet of a horse or its driver; a horse; one of the ten horses of the moon; epithet of Indra; a short span; (*tī*), f. a mare; a bawd, a procuress; (*ā*, *atī*, *at*), low, contemptible, inferior, vile. — *Arvanās*, *ās*, *ās*, *as*, whose nose is like that of a horse.

Arvaśa, *as*, *ā*, *am*, Ved. possessed of coursers, quick.

अर्वाच् *arvāć*, *vān*, *vāćī*, *vāk* (fr. rt. *añć* with *arva*; cf. *arvan*), coming hitherward; turned towards, coming to meet any one; being on this side (as the bank of a river); being below or behind, turned down or downwards; following, subsequent.

Arvāk, ind. (with abl.) hitherward; on this side; from a certain point; before, after; on the lower side of, behind, downwards; (with loc.) within; near. — *Arvākkālika*, *as*, *ā*, *am*, belonging to proximate time, modern. — *Arvākkālika-tā*, f. modernness, posteriority of time. — *Arvāk-kūla*, *am*, n. the near bank of a river. — *Arvāk-sāman*, *ā*, *ā*, *a*, Ved. epithet of three days, during which a Soma sacrifice is performed. — *Arvāk-srotas*, *ās*, *ās*, *as*, N. of a creation of beings in which the current of nutriment tends downwards. — *Arvāg-bila*, *as*, *ā*, *am*, Ved. having the mouth hitherward. — *Arvāg-vasu*, *us*, *us*, *u*, Ved. offering riches.

Arvāke, ind., Ved. in the proximity of, near to.

Arvāćīna, *as*, *ā*, *am*, turned towards; favouring; being on this side or below (with abl.); born afterwards, posterior, recent, modern; reverse, contrary. — *Arvāćīna-tā*, f. or *arvāćīna-tva*, *am*, n. state of being posterior, recent or contrary.

Arvāćīnam, ind. (with abl.) on this side of; thenceforward, thence onward; less than.

अर्वावत् *arvā-vat*, *t*, f., Ved. proximity [cf. *parā-vat*]; being near.

अर्वावसु *arvā-vasu*, *us*, m., Ved., N. of the Hotṛi; N. of the Brahman of the gods.

अर्वुक *arvuka*, *as*, m., N. of a tribe or people in the Mahā-bhārata.

अर्श *arśa*, *as*, m. (fr. rt. *ṛiś*), damage, hurt; hemorrhoids, piles.

Arśas, *as*, n. piles, hemorrhoids. — *Arśo-ghna*, *as*, *ī*, *am*, destroying the hemorrhoids; (*as*), m., N. of the plant Amorphophallus Campanulatus Blume; one part of buttermilk with three parts of water; (*ī*), f., N. of the plant Curculigo Archioides Lin. — *Arśo-yuj*, *k*, *k*, *k*, afflicted with hemorrhoids. — *Arśo-roga*, *as*, m. the hemorrhoids. — *Arśoroga-yuta*, *as*, *ā*, *am*, or *arśorogin*, *ī*, *iṇī*, *i*, afflicted with hemorrhoids, having hemorrhoids. — *Arśo-hita*, *as*, m. the marking nut plant, Semecarpus Anacardium.

Arśasa, *as*, *ā*, *am*, afflicted with hemorrhoids.

Arśasāna, *as*, *ā*, *am*, Ved. striving to hurt, malicious; (*as*), m. fire.

Arśin, *ī*, *inī*, *i*, afflicted with hemorrhoids.

अर्षण *arshaṇa*, *as*, *ā*, *am* (fr. rt. *ṛish*), flowing, movable.

Arshaṇī, f., Ved. a pricking or piercing pain.

अर्सस् *arsas*, *as*, n. hemorrhoids. See *arśas* above.

अर्ह् *arh*, cl. 1. P., ep. A. *arhati*, *-te*, *ānarha*, *arhishyati*, *ārhīt*, *arhitum*, Ved. *arhase*, to deserve, merit, be worthy; to have a claim to anything, to be entitled to (with acc.); to be allowed to do anything (with inf.); to be obliged or required to do anything (with acc.); to be worthy; to be worth; to counterbalance; to be able; (the 2nd pers. pres. of *arh* with an infinitive is often used as a softened form of imperative; e. g. *dātum arhasi*, 'be pleased to give;' *śrotum arhasi*, 'deign to listen,' for *śriṇu*): Caus. *arhayati* (aor. *ārjihat*), *-yitum*, to honour: Desid. *arjihishati* [cf. Gr. ἄρχω].

Arha, *as*, *ā*, *am*, meriting, deserving, worthy of, having a claim or being entitled to (with acc. or inf.); being required, obliged, or allowed (with inf.); becoming, proper, fit; worth (in money), costing; (*as*), m. a N. of Indra; (*ā*), f. worship; (*āṇi*), Ved. n. pl. worship.

Arhaṇa, *am*, *ā*, n. f. worship, adoration, honour, treating with veneration or respect; (*ā*), ind., Ved. according to what is due; according to one's means.

Arhat, *an*, *antī*, *at*, deserving, entitled to; able, allowed to; worthy; venerable, respectable; praised, celebrated; (*an*), m. a Buddha; the highest rank in the Buddhist hierarchy; an Arhat or superior divinity with the Jainas. — *Arhat-tama*, *as*, *ā*, *am*, most worthy, best, most venerable.

Arhanta, *as*, *ā*, *am*, worthy; (*as*), m. a Buddha; a Buddhist mendicant; N. of Śiva.

Arhita, *as*, *ā*, *am*, honoured, worshipped, saluted.

Arhya, *as*, *ā*, *am*, worthy; respectable; right, fit.

अर्हरिष्वणि *arhari-shvaṇi*, *is*, *is*, *i*, Ved. making enemies (*arhari*) cry aloud; (if formed by redupl. of *hṛish* with affix *vani*) exultant.

अल् *al*, cl. 1. P. *alati*, *alitum*, to adorn; to be competent or able; to prevent. See *alam*.

अल *ala*, *am*, n. (said to be fr. rt. *al*), the sting in the tail of a scorpion; yellow orpiment. See *āla*.

अलक *alaka*, *as*, *am*, m. n. (said to be fr. rt. *al*), a curl, lock; (*as*), m. a mad dog [cf. *alarka*]; (*ā*), f. a girl from eight to ten years of age; N. of the capital of Kuvera, situated on a peak of the Himālaya inhabited also by Śiva. — *Alaka-tva*, *am*, n. the state of a curl or tress. — *Alaka-nandā*, f. a young girl from eight to ten years old; N. of the Gaṅgā river; N. of a river that runs from the Himālaya mountains and falls into the Gaṅgā. — *Alaka-prabhā*, f. the capital of Kuvera. — *Alaka-priya*, *as*, m., N. of the plant Terminalia Tomentosa W. and A. — *Alaka-saṃhati*, *is*, f. rows of curls. — *Alakādhipa* (°*kā-adh*°), *as*, m. or *alakādhipati* (°*kā-adh*°), *is*, m. a N. of Kuvera. — *Alakānta* (°*ka-an*°), *as*, m. the end of a curl, a ringlet. — *Alakeśvara* (°*kā-īś*°), *as*, m. a N. of Kuvera.

अलकम् *alakam*, ind., Ved. in vain, for nothing.

अलक्त *alakta* or *alaktaka*, *as*, m. (said to be for *a-rakta*), the red resin of certain trees; or perhaps the cochineal or its red sap. — *Alakta-rasa*, *as*, m. the Alakta juice [cf. the preceding].

अलक्षण *a-lakshaṇa*, *am*, n. (rt. *laksh*), a bad, inauspicious sign; (*as*, *ā*, *am*), having no signs or marks; without characteristic, having no good marks, inauspicious, unfortunate.

A-lakshita, *as*, *ā*, *am*, unseen, unperceived, unobserved, unlooked for; uncharacterized, having no particular mark. — *Alakshitāntaka* (°*ta-an*°), *as*, *ā*, *am*, suddenly dead. — *Alakshitopasthita* (°*ta-up*°), *as*, *ā*, *am*, one who has approached unobserved.

A-lakshya or *a-lakshaṇīya*, *as*, *ā*, *am*, invisible; unmarked, not indicated; having no particular marks, insignificant in appearance; (*as*), m., N. of a certain weapon. — *Alakshya-gati*, *is*, *is*, *i*, moving invisibly. — *Alakshya-liṅga*, *as*, *ā*, *am*, disguised, incognito.

अलक्ष्मी *a-lakshmī*, *īs*, f. evil fortune, bad luck, distress, poverty.

अलखान *alakhāna*, *as*, m., N. of a king of Gurjara.

अलगर्द *alagarda* or *alagardha*, *as*, m. a water-serpent, the black variety of the Cobra de Capello (Coluber Nāga); (*ā*), f. a large poisonous leech: (etymology doubtful.)

अलग्न *a-lagna*, *as*, *ā*, *am* (rt. *lag*), not joined or connected.

अलग्ल *a-lagla*, *as*, *ā*, *am*, speaking unconnectedly; stammering.

अलघु *a-laghu*, *us*, *vī*, *u*, not light, heavy; not short, long; weighty; serious, solemn; intense, violent. — *Alaghu-pratijña*, *as*, *ā*, *am*, solemnly pledged or promised. — *Alaghūpala* (°*ghu-up*°), *as*, m. a rock. — *Alaghūshman* (°*ghu-ush*°), *ā*, m. intense heat.

अलङ्करण *alaṅkaraṇa*, *alaṅkāra*. See under *alam*, p. 86, col. 1.

अलङ्घन *a-laṅghana*, *am*, n. (rt. *laṅgh*), not surmounting, not transgressing, not passing over or beyond.

A-laṅghanīya or *a-laṅghya*, *as*, *ā*, *am*, insurmountable, impassable, not to be crossed; not to be transgressed, inviolable, venerable. — *Alanghanīya-tā* or *alanghya-tā*, f. impassableness, insurmountableness, inaccessibility; inviolability; respectability; authoritative or absolute rule; superiority.

अलज *alaja, as,* m. a kind of bird.

अलजी *alajī,* f. inflammation of the eye, at the edge of the cornea.

अलज्ज *a-lajja, as, ā, am,* shameless.

अलञ्जर *alañjara, as,* m. an earthen water-jar. See *aliñjara.*

अलति *alati, is,* m. a kind of song.

अलपत् *a-lapat, an, antī, at,* not speaking.

अलब्ध *a-labdha, as, ā, am* (rt. *labh*), unobtained. — *Alabdha-nātha, as, ā, am,* friendless, without a patron. — *Alabdhābhīpsita* (°*dha-abh*°), *as, ā, am,* disappointed in one's desire.

A-labhamāna, as, ā, am, not gaining, &c.

A-labhya, as, ā, am, unobtainable, unattainable.

अलम् *alam,* ind. (said to be fr. rt. *al*), enough, sufficient, adequate, equal to, competent, able. (*Alam* may govern a dat., e. g. *alaṃ jīvanāya,* sufficient for living; also a loc. or inf., e. g. *alaṃ vijñāne* or *vijñātum,* able to conceive; also inst., e. g. *alaṃ śaṅkayā,* enough, i. e. away with fear! It may be used with the future tense, e. g. *alam hanishyati,* he will be able to kill; or with an indecl. part., e. g. *alam bhuktvā,* enough of eating, i. e. do not eat more; *alaṃ vićārya,* enough of consideration.)

Alan-kṛi, cl. 8. P. *-karoti, -kartum,* to prepare, make ready; to ornament, decorate; to prevent from, impede (with gen.).

Alan-karaṇa, am, n. preparation, the act of decorating, decoration; ornament.

Alan-karishṇu, us, us, u, fond of ornament; decorating, skilled in decorating; ornamented; (*us*), m. an epithet of Śiva.

Alan-kartṛi, tā, trī, tṛi, decorating, skilled in decoration, a decorator.

Alankarmīṇa, as, ā, am, competent to any act, skilful, clever.

Alan-kāra, as, m. the act of decorating; ornament, decoration; a figure or rhetorical expression. — *Alankāra-ćandrikā,* f. title of a commentary on Kuvalayānanda. — *Alankāra-vat, ān, atī, at,* decorated, ornamented; (*tī*), f. title of the ninth Lambaka in the Kathāsaritsāgara; (*vat*), ind. like an ornament. — *Alankāra-śāstra, am,* n. a manual or text-book of rhetoric. — *Alankāra-suvarṇa, am,* n. gold used for ornaments. — *Alankāra-sūra, as,* m., N. of a kind of meditation in Buddhism. — *Alankāra-hīna, as, ā, am,* unadorned.

Alankāraka, as, m. ornament, decoration.

Alan-kṛita, as, ā, am, prepared, made ready; ornamented, adorned.

Alan-kṛiti, is, f. ornament; rhetorical ornament, figure or rhetorical expression.

Alan-kriyā, f. adorning, ornamenting.

Alan-gāmin, ī, inī, i, going after or following in due or proper manner.

Alañ-jīvika, as, ā, am, sufficient for livelihood.

Alañ-jusha, as, ā, am, sufficient, adequate to.

Alan-tama, as, ā, am, able, sufficient, having power.

Alan-dhana, as, ā, am, possessing sufficient wealth.

Alan-dhūma, as, m. thick smoke, smoke enough.

1. *alam-paṭa, as,* m. the interior of a house; woman's apartment.

Alam-paśu, us, us, u, able to keep cattle.

Alampurushīṇa, as, ā, am, fit for a man, becoming a man; sufficient for a man.

Alam-bala, as, m. strong enough, having sufficient power; an epithet of Śiva.

Alam-bhūshṇu, us, us, u, able, competent.

अलम्पट 2. *a-lampaṭa, as, ā, am,* not libidinous, chaste.

अलम्बुष *alambusha, as,* m. (etymology doubtful, though connected with *alam* above), the palm of the hand with the fingers extended; vomiting; N. of a Rākshasa or evil spirit; (*ā*), f. a barrier, a line or anything not to be crossed; a sort of sensitive plant; N. of an Apsaras.

अलय *a-laya, as,* m. (rt. *lī,* to be dissolved, or to rest, cling to), non-dissolution, permanence; (*as, ā, am*), houseless, homeless; vagrant.

अलर्क *alarka, as,* m. (etymology doubtful), a mad dog or one rendered furious; a fabulous animal, like a hog with eight legs; N. of the plant Calatropis Gigantea Alba; N. of a prince.

अलर्षि *alarshi.* See s. v. *ṛi.*

Alarshi-rāti, is, is, i, Ved. eager to bestow, ready to grant gifts, one whose gifts are granted quickly.

अललाभवत् *alalā-bhavat, an, antī, at,* Ved. becoming active or lively.

अलले *alale,* ind. a word of no import occurring in the dialect or gibberish of the Piśāćas, a class of imps or goblins, introduced in plays, &c.

अलवाल *alavāla* or *alavālaka, am,* n. a basin for water at the root of a tree.

अलस् *a-las, as, as, as* (rt. *las,* to shine), not shining.

अलस *a-lasa, as, ā, am* (rt. *las,* to labour), inactive, without energy, lazy, idle, indolent, tired, faint; (*as*), m. sore or ulcer between the toes; N. of a small poisonous animal; N. of a plant; (*ā*), f., N. of the climbing plant Vitis Pedata Wall. — *Alasa-tā,* f. or *alasa-tva, am,* n. idleness. — *Alasekshaṇā* (°*sa-īk*°), f. a woman with languishing looks.

A-lasaka, as, ā, am, indolent; (*as*), m. tympanitis, flatulence, intumescence of the abdomen, with constipation and wind.

A-lāsya, as, ā, am, idle, lazy.

अलाण्डु *alāṇḍu, us,* m., N. of a small noxious insect or other animal.

अलात *alāta, am,* n. a fire-brand, coal.

अलातृण *a-lātṛiṇa, as,* m. (rt. *lā = rā?*), Ved. not granting anything; a cloud.

अलाबु *a-lābu, us* or *ū, ūs,* f. (fr. *a,* 'not,' and *lab,* 'to sink?'), the bottle-gourd, Lagenaria Vulgaris Ser; (*us, u*), m. n. a vessel made of the preceding. — *Alābu-pātra, am,* n. a jar made of the bottle-gourd. — *Alābu-maya, as, ī, am,* made of a bottle-gourd. — *Alābū-kaṭa, am,* n. the down of the bottle-gourd.

अलाभ *a-lābha, as,* m. (rt. *labh*), non-acquirement; loss.

अलाय्य *alāyya, as,* m. (fr. rt. *ṛi?*), Ved. epithet of Indra or N. of a man; an assailant.

अलार *alāra, am,* n. (said to be fr. rt. *ṛi*), a door.

अलास *a-lāsa, as,* m. (said to be fr. *a* + *lāsa,* saliva), inflammation and abscess at the root of the tongue.

अलास्य *a-lāsya.* See *a-lasa* above.

अलि *ali, is,* m. (fr. rt. *al?*), a crow; the Indian cuckoo; a scorpion; a large black bee; spirituous liquor. — *Ali-kula, am,* n. a flight or number of bees. — *Alikula-saṅkula, as,* m. the water plant Trapa Bispinosa. — *Ali-jihvā* or *ali-jihvikā,* f. the uvula or soft palate. — *Ali-dūrvā,* f., N. of a plant. — *Ali-pattrikā,* f., N. of a shrub. — *Ali-parṇī,* f., N. of the plant Tragia Involucrata Lin. — *Ali-priya, am,* n. the red lotus, Nymphæa Rubra; (*ā*), f. the trumpet flower, Bignonia Suaveolens. — *Ali-mālā,* f. a flight of bees. — *Ali-modā,* f., N. of a plant, Premna Spinosa. — *Ali-virāva, as,* m. or *ali-viruta, am,* n. song or hum of the bee.

Alin, ī, m. a scorpion; a large black bee.

Alinī, f. a swarm of bees.

अलिंश *aliṃśa, as,* m., Ved. a kind of demon.

अलिक *alika, am,* n. (fr. rt. *al?*), the forehead.

अलिक्लव *aliklava, as,* m., Ved. a kind of carrion bird.

अलिगर्द *aligarda, as,* m. a snake. See *alagarda.*

अलिङ्ग *a-linga, am,* n. absence of marks; (*as, ā, am*), having no marks; (in gram.) having no gender.

A-lingin, ī, inī, i, an impostor, a pretended ascetic or student, one wearing the usual frontal marks, skin, staff, &c., without belonging to a religious order.

अलिञ्जर *aliñjara, as,* m. a small earthen water-jar.

अलिन *alina, as,* m., Ved., N. of a tribe (?).

अलिन्द *alinda* or *alindaka, as,* m. (fr. rt. *al!*), a terrace before a house-door; (*ās*), pl., N. of a people.

अलिपक *alipaka, as,* m. a dog; the Indian cuckoo; a bee.

अलिप्सा *a-lipsā,* f. (Desid. of rt. *labh*), freedom from desire or cupidity.

अलिमक *alimaka* or *alimpaka* or *alimbaka, as,* m. the Indian cuckoo; a frog; a bee; N. of the plant Bassia Latifolia; the filaments of the lotus.

अलीक *alīka, as, ā, am* (said to be fr. rt. *al,* 'to adorn,' i. e. dress out in false colour; perhaps fr. *a,* 'not,' and *līka,* but the latter does not occur), unpleasing, disagreeable; untrue, false; small, little; (*am*), n. anything displeasing; falsehood, untruth; the forehead; heaven. — *Alīka-tā,* f. falsehood, vanity. — *Alīka-matsya, as,* m. a kind of dish resembling the taste of fish ('mock-fish'), made of the flour of a sort of bean fried with Sesamum oil.

Alīkayu, us, m., N. of a Brāhman.

Alīkāya, nom. A. *alīkāyate, -yitum,* to be deceived.

Alīkin, ī, inī, i, disagreeable; false, deceiving.

Alīkya, as, ā, am, belonging to falsehood, false.

अलीगर्द *alīgarda, as,* m. a snake. See *aligarda.*

अलु *alu, us,* f. a small water-pot. See *ālu.*

अलुप्त *a-lupta, as, ā, am* (rt. *lup*), not cut off, undiminished. — *Alupta-mahiman, ā, ā, a,* of undiminished glory.

अलुब्ध *a-lubdha, as, ā, am,* or *a-lubhyat, an, antī, at* (rt. *lubh*), Ved. moderate, content, not covetous. — *Alubdha-tva, am,* n. freedom from covetousness, moderation, contentment.

A-lobha, as, m. non-confusion; right process (?); absence of cupidity, moderation.

A-lobhin, ī, inī, i, not wanting or desiring anything.

अलूक्ष *a-lūksha, as, ā, am,* soft. See *a-rūksha.*

अलून *a-lūna, as, ā, am* (rt. *lū*), uncut, unshorn.

अले *ale* or *alele,* ind. unmeaning words in the dialect of the demons or Piśāćas, introduced in plays, &c.

अलेपक *a-lepaka, as, ikā, am,* stainless.

अलेश *a-leśa, as, ā, am,* not little, much, large; (*am*), ind. not at all. — *A-leśaija* (°*śa-ej*°), *as, ā, am,* firm, steady.

अलोक *a-loka*, *as*, m. (rt. *lok*), not the world; the end of the world; the immaterial or spiritual world; not the people; (*as*, *ā*, *am*), not having space, finding no place.

A-lokana, *am*, n. invisibility, disappearance.

A-lokanīya, *as*, *ā*, *am*, invisible, imperceptible.

A-lokita, *as*, *ā*, *am*, unseen.

A-lokya, *as*, *ā*, *am*, unusual, unallowed. — *Alokya-tā*, f. unfitness for heaven.

A-laukika, *as*, *ī*, *am*, not current in the world, not relating to this world, uncommon, supernatural; (in gram.) not current in the usual language; unusual, rare; theoretical; Vedic (as opposed to the later usage of a word). — *Alaukika-tva*, *am*, n. rare occurrence of a word.

अलोपाङ्ग *a-lopāṅga* (°*pa-an*°), *as*, *ā*, *am*, Ved. not defective in a single limb.

अलोमहर्षण *a-lomaharshaṇa*, *as*, *ā*, *am*, not causing erection of the hair of the body (from joy).

अलोल *a-lola*, *as*, *ā*, *am*, unagitated, firm, steady, tranquil; (*ā*), f., N. of a metre containing four lines, each of fourteen syllables. See *lolā*.

A-lolu, *us*, *us*, *u*, indifferent to sensual objects. — *Alolu-tva*, *am*, n. indifference to sensual objects.

अलोलुप *a-lolupa*, *as*, *ā*, *am*, free from desire; not greedy or covetous, apathetic.

अलोह *aloha*, *as*, m., N. of a person? (Gaṇa to Pāṇini IV. 2, 97).

अलोहित *a-lohita*, *as*, *ā*, *am*, bloodless; (*am*), n. Nymphæa Rubra.

अलौकिक *a-laukika*. See above.

अल्क *alka*, *as*, m. (a doubtful word), a tree; a member of the body.

अल्प *alpa*, *as*, *ā*, *am* (fr. rt. *al?* perhaps connected with *arbha*), small, minute, trifling; little; seldom, rare; of short existence. *Alpam*, ind. little; *alpāt*, ind. without much trouble, easily; *alpena*, ind. easily [cf. Lith. *alpstu*, *ap-alpstu*, 'to faint']. — *Alpa-kārya*, *am*, n. small matter. — *Alpa-keśī*, f., N. of a plant; or perhaps the root of sweet flag. — *Alpa-krīta*, *as*, *ā*, *am*, bought for little money, cheap. — *Alpa-gandha*, *am*, n. the red lotus. — *Alpa-ćeshṭita*, *as*, *ā*, *am*, inert. — *Alpa-ććhada*, *as*, *ā*, *am*, scantily clad. — *Alpa-jña*, *as*, *ā*, *am*, knowing little, ignorant, shallow, superficial. — *Alpa-tanu*, *us*, *us*, *u*, small-bodied; short, thin. — *Alpa-tā*, f. or *alpa-tva*, *am*, n. smallness, minuteness; inferiority, insignificance. — *Alpa-dakshiṇa*, *as*, *ā*, *am*, defective in presents (as a ceremony). — *Alpa-dṛishṭi*, *is*, *is*, *i*, of confined views, narrow-minded. — *Alpa-dhana*, *as*, *ā*, *am*, of little wealth, not affluent. — *Alpa-dhī*, *īs*, *īs*, *i*, weak-minded, having little sense, foolish. — *Alpa-pattra*, *as*, m., N. of a plant, a species of the Tulasi. — *Alpa-padma*, *am*, n. the red lotus. — *Alpa-parīvāra*, *as*, *ā*, *am*, having a small train or retinue. — *Alpa-paśu*, *us*, *us*, *u*, Ved. having a small number of cattle. — *Alpa-puṇya*, *as*, *ā*, *am*, whose religious merits are small. — *Alpa-prajas*, *ās*, *ās*, *as*, having few descendants or few subjects. — *Alpa-prabhāva*, *as*, *ā*, *am*, of little weight or consequence, insignificant. — *Alpa-prabhāva-tva*, *am*, n. insignificance. — *Alpa-pramāṇa* or *alpapramāṇaka*, *as*, *ā*, *am*, of little weight or measure; of little authority, resting on little evidence; (*as*), m. common cucumber, Cucumis Sativus. — *Alpa-prayoga*, *as*, *ā*, *am*, of rare application or use. — *Alpa-prāṇa*, *as*, m. (in gram.) slight breathing or weak aspiration; the effort in uttering the vowels, the semivowels *y*, *r*, *l*, *v*, the consonants *k*, *ć*, *ṭ*, *t*, *p*, *g*, *j*, *ḍ*, *d*, *b*, and the nasals, is said to be accompanied with slight aspiration, but practically *alpa-prāṇa* is here equivalent to unaspirated, as opposed to *mahā-prāṇa*, q. v.; (*as*, *ā*, *am*), having little or short breath, asthmatic. — *Alpa-bala*, *as*, *ā*, *am*, of little strength, feeble. — *Alpa-bādha*, *as*, *ā*, *am*, causing little annoyance or inconvenience. — *Alpa-buddhi*, *is*, *is*, *i*, weak-minded, unwise, ignorant, silly. — *Alpa-bhāgya*, *as*, *ā*, *am*, having little fortune. — *Alpa-bhāshin*, *ī*, *iṇī*, *i*, speaking little, taciturn. — *Alpa-madhyama*, *as*, *ā*, *am*, thin-waisted. — *Alpa-mātra*, *am*, n. a little, a little merely; a short time, a few moments. — *Alpa-mārisha*, *as*, m. a kind of amaranth, Amaranthus Polygamus. — *Alpa-mūrti*, *is*, *is*, *i*, small-bodied, diminutive; (*is*), f. a small figure or object. — *Alpa-mūlya*, *as*, *ā*, *am*, of small value — *Alpa-medhas*, *ās*, *ās*, *as*, of little understanding, ignorant, silly. — *Alpam-paća*, *as*, *ā*, *am*, cooking little, stingy. — *Alpa-vayas*, *ās*, *ās*, *as*, young in age. — *Alpa-vādin*, *ī*, *inī*, *i*, speaking little, taciturn. — *Alpa-vidya*, *as*, *ā*, *am*, ignorant, ill-taught, uneducated. — *Alpa-vishaya*, *as*, *ā*, *am*, of limited range or capacity, engaged in trifling matters. — *Alpaśaḥ-pankti*, *is*, f., N. of a metre. — *Alpa-śakti*, *is*, *is*, *i*, of little strength, weak, feeble. — *Alpa-śas*, ind. in a low degree, a little; separately; seldom, now and then. — *Alpa-saras*, *as*, n. a basin, a small pond, one which is shallow or dry in the hot season. — *Alpa-snāyu*, *us*, *us*, *u*, having few sinews. — *Alpākāṅkshin* (°*pa-āk*°), *ī*, *iṇī*, *i*, desiring little, contented or satisfied with little. — *Alpāñji* (°*pa-añ*°), *is*, *is*, *i*, Ved. covered with minute spots. — *Alpāyus* (°*pa-āy*°), *us*, *us*, *us*, short-lived; young, of few years; (*us*), m. a goat. — *Alpārambha* (°*pa-ār*°), *as*, m. a gradual beginning. — *Alpālpa* (°*pa-al*°), *as*, *ā*, *am*, very little, minute; little by little. — *Alpāhāra* (°*pa-āh*°), *as*, m. the taking little food; moderation, abstinence; (*as*, *ā*, *am*), abstinent. — *Alpāhārin* (°*pa-āh*°), *ī*, *iṇī*, *i*, eating little, moderate, abstemious. — *Alpećchu* (°*pa-ić*°), *us*, *us*, *u*, moderate in wishes, seeking little. — *Alpetara* (°*pa-it*°), *as*, *ā*, *am*, large, lit. other than small. — *Alpeśākhya* (*alpa-īśa-ākhya*), *as*, *ā*, *am*, named after an insignificant chief or master, of low origin. — *Alpona* (°*pa-ūn*°), *as*, *ā*, *am*, slightly defective, not quite complete or not finished. — *Alpopāya* (°*pa-up*°), *as*, m. small means.

Alpaka, *as*, *ikā*, *am*, small, minute, trifling; (*am*), ind. little; (*as*), m., N. of a plant, Hedysarum Alhagi.

Alpita, *as*, *ā*, *am*, diminished.

Alpishṭha, *as*, *ā*, *am*, least, smallest, very small. — *Alpishṭha-kīrti*, *is*, *is*, *i*, of little note.

Alpī-kṛi, cl. 8. P. *-karoti*, *-kartum*, to make small.

Alpī-kṛita, *as*, *ā*, *am*, made small; comminuted; reduced in number.

Alpī-bhūta, *as*, *ā*, *am*, become small; diminished, reduced in number.

Alpīyas, *ān*, *asī*, *as*, smaller, less, very small.

अल्ला *allā*, f. a mother; voc. *alla*.

अव् *av*, cl. 1. P. *avati*, *āva*, *āvīt*, *avishyati*, *avitum*, to be glad, to enjoy one's self, to satisfy one's self with (with loc.); to do good to any one; to satisfy, to fill; to like, wish, desire, love; to be pleased with, to bestow great care upon; to favour, promote, animate; to help, guard, defend, protect. (The following meanings are doubtful): to move; to know or apprehend; to enter; to be near; to have a right; to obey; to shine; to embrace; to kill or hurt; to take; to be; to grow, to burn, to divide: Caus. P. *āvayati*, *-yitum*, to consume, devour [cf. Lat. *aveo*; Gr. ἄω].

1. *ava*, *as*, *ā*, *am*, Ved. desiring, loving.

Avana, *avani*, &c. See s. v.

अव 2. *ava* or sometimes *va*, ind. (as a prefix to verbs and nouns expresses) off, away, down; implying sometimes depreciation, disrespect, diminution, &c.

(As a separable adverb or preposition with abl.) away, off, away from or down [cf. the Zend pron. *ava*, to which corresponds the Slav. *ovo*, *ova*, 'this, that:' cf. also the syllable αὐ in αὐ-τός, αὖ, αὖθι, αὖθις, αὖτις, αὖτε, αὐτάρ; Lat. *au-t*, *au-tem*, &c.].

Avakaṭa, *as*, *ā*, *am*, opposite, contrary; backwards, downwards; (*am*), n. opposition, contrariety, reverse.

Avakaṭikā, f. dissimulation.

Avakuṭāra, *as*, *ā*, *am*, opposite, contrary; backwards, downwards; (*am*), n. reverse, contrariety.

Avakuṭārikā, f. dissimulation.

अवंश *a-vanśa*, *as*, m. a low or despised family; (*am*), n., Ved. that which has no beams or support, the ether.

अवकट, अवकुटार. See above.

अवकलित *ava-kalita*, *as*, *ā*, *am*, seen, observed; wicked, perverse (?).

अवका *avakā*, f. a grassy plant growing in marshy land, Blyxa Octandra Rich; otherwise called Saivāla. — *Avakāda* (°*kā-ada*), *as*, *ā*, *am*, Ved. eating the plant Blyxa Oct. R. — *Avakolba* (°*kā-ul*°), *as*, *ā*, *am*, covered or surrounded with Avakā plants.

अवकाश् *ava-kāś*, cl. 1. 4. A. *-kāśate*, *-kāśyate*, *-śitum*, to be visible, to be manifest: Caus. P. *-kāśayati*, *-yitum*, to cause to look at: Intens. part. *-ćākaśat*, *at*, *atī*, *at*, shining; seeing.

Ava-kāśa, *as*, m. a glance cast on anything; N. of certain verses, during the recitation of which the eyes must be fixed on certain objects; place, space, open or wide space, room, occasion, opportunity; interval, aperture; intermediate time; *avakāśam kṛi* or *dā*, to make room, to give way, to admit; *avakāśam labh*, to get a footing; to obtain a favourable opportunity; to find scope, happen, take place; *avakāśam rudh*, not to give way; to hinder, impede. — *Avakāśa-vat*, *ān*, *atī*, *at*, spacious.

Avakāśya, *as*, *ā*, *am*, admitted in the recitation of the Avakāśa verses.

अवकुञ्चन *ava-kunćana*, *am*, n. bending, curving, flexure, contraction.

अवकुट्टित *ava-kuṭṭita*, *as*, *ā*, *am*, vexed, inflamed; cut off.

अवकुण्ठन *ava-kunṭhana*, *am*, n. investing, surrounding; attracting.

Ava-kunṭhita, *as*, *ā*, *am*, invested, surrounded, attracted.

अवकुत्स् *ava-kuts*, cl. 10. P. A. *-kutsayati*, *-te*, *-yitum*, to blame, revile, contemn.

Ava-kutsita, *as*, *ā*, *am*, reviled, despised; (*am*), n. blame, censure.

अवकुष् *ava-kush*, cl. 9. P. *-kushṇāti*, *-koshitum*, to draw or rub downwards; to prove (?); to display (?).

अवकूल् *ava-kūl*, cl. 10. P. *-kūlayati*, *-yitum*, to singe, burn.

अवकृत् *ava-kṛit*, cl. 6. P. *-kṛintati*, *-kartitum*, to cut off or away: Caus. P. *-kartayati*, *-yitum*, to cause to cut off.

Ava-karta, *as*, m. a part cut off, a strip.

Ava-kartana, *am*, n. cutting off, excision.

Ava-kartin, *ī*, *inī*, *i*, cutting off, cutting out.

अवकृश् *ava-kṛiś*, Caus. *-karśayati*, *-yitum*, to emaciate, make lean or meagre or mean-looking; to deform.

अवकृष् *ava-kṛish*, cl. 1. P. *-karshati*, *-karshṭum*, *-krashṭum*, to draw off or away, to pull off or out, to extract, to take off; to drag down.

Ava-karshaṇa, *am*, n. taking or pulling out, off or down, extraction; expulsion.

Ava-kṛishṭa, *as*, *ā*, *am*, drawn away or down, sent away, removed, dropped; expelled, turned out; dragged down; being below; inferior, low; degraded, outcast; (*as*), m. a servant who performs the lowest office, a sweeper, a waterman, &c.

Ava-kṛishya, ind. having drawn away or down.

अवकॄ *ava-kṝī*, cl. 6. P. *-kirati*, *-karitum*,

-rītum, to pour out or down, to spread, to scatter; to shake off, throw off, leave; to bestrew, pour upon, cover with, fill: A. -kirate, to extend; to fall asunder; to pass away, fall off, become faithless.

Ava-kara, as, m. dust or sweepings.

Ava-kīrṇa, as, ā, am, thrown off, left; scattered, disregarded, violated, coarsely pounded.

Ava-kīrṇin, ī, inī, i, violating a vow or engagement of chastity, continence, temperance, &c.; (ī), m. a religious student who has committed an act of incontinency. — *Avakīrṇi-vrata, am,* n. penance for an act of incontinency.

Ava-kīryamāṇa, as, ā, am, being scattered or strewed.

अवक्लृप् *ava-klṛip,* cl. 1. A. *-kalpate, -pitum, -ptum,* to correspond with, to answer; to be right; to be fit; to help to, to serve: Caus. *-kalpayati, -yitum,* to put in order; to prepare, make ready; to employ becomingly; to consider as possible: Desid. of Caus. *-ćikalpayishati,* to wish to prepare or to make ready.

Ava-kalpita, as, ā, am, corresponding with, right, fit.

Ava-klṛipti, is, f. considering as possible; possibility, suitableness.

अवकेश *ava-keśa, as, ā, am,* Ved. having the hair hanging down.

Ava-keśin, ī, inī, i, unfruitful, barren; (ī), m. a tree without fruit.

अवकोकिल *ava-kokila, as, ā, am,* called down to by the koil (singing in a tree above?).

अवकोल्ब *avakolba.* See s. v. *avakā.*

अवक्तव्य *a-vaktavya, as, ā, am* (rt. *vać*), not to be said, improper; indescribable.

अवक्त्र *a-vaktra, as, ā, am,* having no mouth (as a vessel).

अवक्र *a-vakra, as, ā, am,* not crooked, straight, upright, honest.

अवक्रक्षिन् *ava-krakshin, ī, iṇī, i* (rt. *kraksh* connected with *kṛish?*), Ved. dashing down, overcoming.

अवक्रन्द् *ava-krand,* cl. 1. P. A. *-krandati, -te, -ditum,* or Caus. P. *-krandayati, -yitum,* to cry out, roar.

Ava-kranda, as, m., Ved. roaring, neighing.

Ava-krandana, am, n. crying out, weeping aloud.

अवक्रम् *ava-kram,* cl. 1. 4. P. *-krāmati, -krāmyati, -kramitum,* to step down or away, run away, escape; to tread down, overcome; to descend: Caus. P. *-kramayati, -yitum,* to cause to go down.

Ava-krānti, is, f. descending, descent; approach.

Ava-krāmin, ī, iṇī, i, Ved. running away, escaping.

अवक्रिया *ava-kriyā,* f. neglect, omission, non-performance of prescribed acts.

अवक्री *ava-krī,* cl. 9. P. A. *-krīṇāti, -ṇīte, -kretum,* to purchase; to let out to hire; to bribe.

Ava-kraya, as, m. letting out to hire; rent; revenue; price.

अवक्रीड् *ava-krīḍ,* cl. 1. P. A. *-krīḍati, -te, -ḍitum,* to play (?).

अवक्रुश् *ava-kruś,* cl. 1. P. *-krośati, -kroshṭum,* to call down to; to revile.

Ava-krushṭa, as, ā, am, sounded ill or badly; reviled, abused.

Ava-krośa, as, m. a discordant noise; a curse, an imprecation; abuse.

अवक्लम् *ava-klam,* ? Caus. P. *-klamayati, -yitum,* to bring water for washing; (this word, given by Westergaard, is doubtful.)

अवक्लेद *ava-kleda, as,* m. (rt. *klid*), trickling, descent of moisture; ichor, malignant or fetid discharge.

Ava-kledana, am, n. trickling, falling as dew or moisture.

अवक्वण *ava-kvaṇa, as,* m. a discordant or false note.

अवक्वाथ *ava-kvātha, as,* m. imperfect digestion or decoction.

अवक्षर् *ava-kshar,* Caus. P. *-ksharayati, -yitum,* to cause to flow down upon.

अवक्षल् *ava-kshal,* cl. 10. P. *-kshālayati, -yitum,* to wash by dipping in.

अवक्षाम *ava-kshāma, as,* m., Ved. propitiatory offering, satisfaction of claims, compensation.

अवक्षि *ava-kshi,* cl. 9. 5. 1. P. *-kshiṇāti, -ṇoti, -kshayati, -kshetum,* to remove: Pass. *-kshīyate,* to waste away.

Ava-kshaya, as, m. destruction, waste, loss.

Ava-kshayaṇa, am, n. a means for extinguishing (a fire, &c.).

Ava-kshiṇa, as, ā, am, wasted, emaciated.

अवक्षिप् *ava-kship,* cl. 6. P. A. *-kshipati, -te, -ksheptum,* to throw down; to cause to fly down or away; to hurl; to reprimand, revile any one; to grant, yield: Caus. P. *-kshepayati, -yitum,* to cause to fall down.

Ava-kshipta, as, ā, am, thrown down, badly thrown; said sarcastically, imputed, insinuated; blamed, reviled.

Ava-kshepa, as, m. blaming, reviling, scolding.

Ava-kshepaṇa, am, n. throwing down, overcoming; censure, blame; despising; (ṇī), f. rein, bridle.

अवक्षु *ava-kshu,* cl. 2. P. *-kshauti, -kshavitum,* to sneeze upon.

Ava-kshuta, as, ā, am, sneezed upon.

अवक्षुद् *ava-kshud,* cl. 1. P. *-kshodati, -ditum,* to stamp or pound; to rub to pieces.

अवक्षै *ava-kshai,* cl. 1. P. *-kshāyati, -kshātum,* to burn down or to the end.

Ava-kshāṇa, as, ā, am, burnt down.

अवक्ष्णु *ava-kshṇu,* cl. 2. P. *-kshṇauti, -kshṇavitum,* to rub to pieces.

अवखण्ड् *ava-khaṇḍ,* cl. 10. P. *-khaṇḍayati, -yitum,* to divide, annihilate, destroy.

Ava-khaṇḍana, am, n. dividing, destroying.

अवखाद *ava-khāda, as,* m., Ved. a bad or contemptible meal, eating to no purpose, an unworthy oblation.

अवख्या *ava-khyā,* cl. 2. P., Ved. *-khyāti, -khyātum,* to look down, perceive: Caus. P. *-khyāpayati, -yitum,* to cause to look at.

अवगण् *ava-gaṇ,* cl. 10. P. *-gaṇayati, -yitum,* to disregard, disrespect, pay no attention; to despise.

Ava-gaṇana, am, n. contempt, disregard.

Ava-gaṇita, as, ā, am, disregarded, despised.

अवगण *ava-gaṇa, as, ā, am,* separated from one's companions, isolated, alone.

अवगण्ड *ava-gaṇḍa, as,* m. a boil or pimple upon the face.

अवगथ *ava-gatha, as, ā, am* (rt. *gā,* to go), bathing or bathed early in the morning.

अवगदित *ava-gadita, as, ā, am* (rt. *gad*), unsaid, unuttered.

अवगम् *ava-gam,* cl. 1. P. *-gaćchati, -gantum,* to go down, descend; to come to, visit; to go near, undertake; to reach, obtain; to hit upon, think of, conceive; to learn, understand, assure one's self, be convinced; to recognize, consider: Caus. P. *-gamayati, -yitum,* to bring near, procure; to cause to know, teach.

Ava-gata, as, ā, am, gone, gone away; obtained, conceived, known, learnt, understood, comprehended; assented, promised.

Ava-gati, is, f. perception, knowledge, comprehension.

Ava-gantavya or *ava-gamya, as, ā, am,* to be known or understood, to be judged, intended to be understood, meant.

Ava-gama, as, m. or *ava-gamana, am,* n. going near, descending, understanding, comprehension, intelligence; knowledge, getting acquainted with.

अवगर्हित *ava-garhita, as, ā, am,* despised.

अवगल् *ava-gal,* cl. 1. P. *-galati, -litum,* to fall down, slip down.

अवगल्भ् *ava-galbh,* cl. 1. A. *-galbhate, -bhitum,* to be brave, valiant.

अवगाद *avagāda, as,* m. a small wooden bason for baling water out of a boat; (etym. doubtful.)

अवगाह् *ava-gāh,* cl. 1. A. *-gāhate, -gāhitum, -gāḍhum,* to plunge into; to go deep into, to be absorbed in (with loc. or acc.).

Ava-gāḍha, as, ā, am, immersed, bathed, plunged into; that in which one bathes; deepened, low; concealed, curdling (as blood). — *Avagāḍha-vat, ān, atī, at,* bathing, plunging, diving.

Ava-gāha, as, m. plunging, bathing; a bucket (?).

Ava-gāhana, am, n. immersion, plunging, diving, bathing.

Ava-gāhita, as, ā, am, bathed, immersed.

अवगुण्ठ् *ava-guṇṭh,* cl. 10. P. *-guṇṭhayati, -yitum,* to cover with; to draw over, conceal.

Ava-guṇṭhana, am, n. hiding, veiling, a veil; a peculiar joining of the fingers in certain religious ceremonies; sweeping. — *Avaguṇṭhana-vat, ān, atī, at,* covered with a veil.

Ava-guṇṭhikā, f. a veil.

Ava-guṇṭhita, as, ā, am, covered, concealed, veiled, screened. — *Avaguṇṭhita-mukha, as, ī, am,* having the face veiled.

अवगुण्डित *ava-guṇḍita, as, ā, am,* pounded, ground, pulverulent.

अवगुर् *ava-gur,* cl. 6. A. *-gurate, -ritum,* to assail with threats, to attack, to raise a weapon for the purpose of striking a blow.

Ava-goraṇa, am, n. menacing, assaulting with intent to kill, assailing with weapons.

अवगुह् *ava-guh,* cl. 1. P. A. *-gūhati, -te, -gūhitum, -goḍhum,* to cover; to hide, conceal; to put into or inside; to embrace.

Ava-gūhana, am, n. hiding, concealing, embracing.

अवगॄ *ava-gṝ,* cl. 6. A. *-girate* or *-gilate, -garitum* or *-galitum, -garītum* or *-galītum,* to swallow up.

Ava-girṇa, as, ā, am, swallowed up.

अवगै *ava-gai,* cl. 1. P. *-gāyati, -gātum,* to sing in a discordant tone, sing depreciatingly, satirize in song, reproach, revile.

Ava-gīta, as, ā, am, sung in a discordant tone, sung badly; sung depreciatingly, satirized in song, destroyed by incantation; reproached, abused, censured; wicked, vile; seen frequently (= *muhur-dṛishṭa*), sung of frequently, well known, 'decantatus;' (*am*), n. satire in song; reproach, blame, bad or discordant singing.

अवग्रह् *ava-grah,* cl. 9. P. A. *-gṛihṇāti, -ṇīte,* or Ved. *-gṛibhṇāti, -ṇīte, -grahītum,* to let loose, to let go; to divide; (in gram.) to break off, separate, discontinue; to distinguish: Caus. P. *-grāhayati, -yitum,* to knead, make dough.

Ava-gṛihīta, as, ā, am, obstructed, impeded, restrained.

1. *ava-gṛihya, as, ā, am,* (in gram.) separable.

2. *ava-gṛihya,* ind. having separated, laying hold with the feet, leaning against with force or violence.

Ava-graha, as, m. separation of the component parts of a compound, or of other grammatical forms, occurring in some Pāṭhas, e. g. in the Pada-text of the Vedas; the mark or the interval of such a separation; the syllable or letter after which the separation occurs; the chief member of a word so separated; obstacle, impediment, restraint; drought; nature, original temperament; a sort of knowledge, a false idea (?); an imprecation or term of abuse; an elephant's forehead; a herd of elephants; an iron hook with which elephants are driven.

Ava-grahaṇa, am, n. obstacle, impediment, restraint, disrespect.

Ava-grāha, as, m. breaking off, discontinuing; obstacle, impediment, imprecation; drought; the forehead of an elephant.

Ava-grāham, ind. in breaking off or discontinuing.

अवघट्ट *ava-ghaṭṭ,* cl. 1. A. *-ghaṭṭate, -ṭṭitum,* cl. 10. P. *-ghaṭṭayati, -yitum,* to push or brush away or off; to touch, feel, rub; to stir up.

Ava-ghaṭṭa, as, m. a hole in the ground, a cave, a cavern.

Ava-ghaṭṭana, am, n. rubbing away or off.

Ava-ghaṭṭita, am, n. pushing or rubbing together; rubbing off.

अवघात *ava-ghāta, as,* m. (rt. *han*), striking, hurting, killing; a violent or fatal blow; threshing corn by bruising it with a wooden pestle in a mortar of the same material.

Ava-ghātin, ī, inī, i, striking, killing.

अवघुष् *ava-ghush,* cl. 1. P. *-ghoshati, -shitum,* to proclaim aloud; to convoke, send for, summon; to fill with cries or clamour.

Ava-ghushṭa, as, ā, am, proclaimed, summoned.

Ava-ghoshaṇa, am, n. crying, proclaiming, denouncing.

अवघूर्ण् *ava-ghūrṇ,* cl. 1. P. A. *-ghūrṇati, -te, -ṇitum,* to whirl round, brandish, move to and fro.

Ava-ghūrṇa, as, m. a whirling round; a whirlpool.

Ava-ghūrṇana, am, n. rolling or whirling round.

Ava-ghūrṇita, as, ā, am, whirled round.

अवघृष् *ava-ghrish,* cl. 1. P. A. *-gharshati, -te, -shitum,* to rub off, rub to pieces: Caus. *-gharshayati, -yitum,* to rub off, scratch off.

Ava-gharshaṇa, am, n. rubbing off, scrubbing.

Ava-gharshita, as, ā, am, rubbed off, scrubbed.

अवघोटित *ava-ghoṭita, as, ā, am* (rt. *ghuṭ,* cf. rt. *guṇṭh* with *ava*), covered, concealed.

अवघ्रा *ava-ghrā,* cl. 1. P. *-jighrati, -ghrātum,* to smell at, to touch with the mouth; to kiss: Caus. *-ghrāpayati, -yitum,* to cause to smell at.

Ava-ghrāṇa, am, n. the act of smelling at.

Ava-ghrāta, as, ā, am, smelled, smelled at; kissed.

अवच *avaća,* lower. This word is connected with *ava* as *uća* is with *ud,* but only found in *uććāvaća,* q. v.

अवचक्ष् *ava-ćaksh,* cl. 2. A. *-ćashṭe, -ćashṭum,* to look down upon, to perceive.

Ava-ćakshaṇa, am, n. looking down upon? (Gaṇa to Pāṇini VIII. 1. 27, 57).

अवचन *a-vaćana, am,* n. absence of assertion, silence, taciturnity; (*as, ā, am*), not speaking, silent. — *A-vaćana-kara, as, ā, am,* not doing what one is bid, disobedient.

A-vaćanīya, as, ā, am, not to be spoken, improper. — *Avaćanīya-tā,* f. or *avaćanīya-tva, am,* n. impropriety of speech.

A-vaćas-kara, as, ā or *ī, am,* silent, not speaking, taciturn.

अवचन्द्रमस *ava-ćandramasa, am,* n., Ved. the looking down of the moon.

अवचर् *ava-ćar,* cl. 1. P. A. *-ćarati, -te, -ritum,* Ved. *-ritave* or *-vai, -rase, -radhyai,* to move or come down; to go down towards: Caus. *-ćārayati, -yitum,* to cause to move or descend upon; to employ.

Ava-ćara, as, ā, am, going or moving down or in or upon; (*as*), m. place of descent, road, field of action.

Ava-ćāraṇa, am, n. employing, application, mode of proceeding.

Ava-ćārya, as, ā, am, to be cast down, to be given, to be put on or applied.

अवचि 1. *ava-ći,* cl. 3. P., Ved. *-ćiketi, -ćetum,* to worship, honour, respect.

अवचि 2. *ava-ći,* cl. 5. P. A. *-ćinoti, -nute, -ćetum,* to gather, pick off; to take off; to let down (one's cloak) behind, to open (one's cloak).

Ava-ćaya, as, m. gathering, especially flowers, fruits, &c.

Ava-ćāyin, ī, inī, i, gathering, picking off.

Ava-ćita, as, ā, am, gathered; filled, inhabited.

अवचूड *ava-ćūḍa, as,* m. the pendent crest or streamer of a standard. See *ava-ćūla.*

अवचूर्ण् *ava-ćūrṇ,* cl. 10. P. *-ćūrṇayati, -yitum,* to sprinkle with meal, dust, &c.; to cover.

Ava-ćūrṇana, am, n. sprinkling with powder; pounding, reducing to powder.

Ava-ćūrṇita, as, ā, am, sprinkled with powder; coarsely pounded, ground, crushed.

अवचूल *ava-ćūla, as,* m. (fr. *ćūla* for *ćūḍa*), an ornament hanging downwards from the top of a banner, the top ornaments (such as streamers, peacocks' tails, &c.) of a standard hanging downward; a chowrī.

Ava-ćūlaka, as, m. a chowrī or brush, formed of a cow's tail, peacock's feathers, &c., for fanning off flies.

अवचृत् *ava-ćrit,* cl. 6. P. *-ćritati, -ćartitum,* to let loose.

अवच्छद् *ava-ćchad* (*-ćhad*), cl. 10. P. *-ćchādayati, -yitum,* to cover over, overspread; to conceal, to obscure, leave in darkness.

Ava-ćchada, as, m. a cover, covering.

Ava-ćchanna, as, ā, am, covered over, overspread, filled.

Ava-ćchādya, ind. having covered over; having obscured.

अवच्छिद् *ava-ćchid* (*-ćhid*), cl. 7. P. A. *-ćchinatti, -ćchinte, -ćchettum,* to cut off, detach, separate, to tear in pieces, break asunder; to excerpt, distinguish, discriminate; to interrupt.

Ava-ćchinna, as, ā, am, cut off, separated, divided, detached, excerpted; broken; (in logic) predicated, i. e. separated from everything else by the properties predicated; bounded.

Ava-ćcheda, as, m. anything cut off; part, portion; separation, distinction; discrimination; distinguishing; boundary, limit; a predicate, the property of a thing by which it is distinguished from everything else. — *Avaćchedāvaćcheda* (°*da-av*°), *as,* m. generalising, removing distinctions.

Ava-ćchedaka, as, ikā, am, separating, distinguishing, particularising, determining; bounding, separating one thing from another; peculiar; (*as*), m. that which distinguishes, &c.; a predicate, characteristic, property; boundary, limit.

Ava-ćchedana, am, n. cutting off; separating, dividing; discriminating, distinguishing.

Ava-ćchedya, as, ā, am, to be cut off, separated, &c.

अवच्छुरित *ava-ćchurita* or *ava-ćchuritaka, am,* n. (fr. rt. *ćhur,* 'to split,' with *ava,* 'that which splits one's sides?'), a horse-laugh.

अवच्छो *ava-ćcho* (*-ćho*), cl. 4. P. *-ćchyati, -ćchātum,* to cut off or away, to flay, to skin, to reap.

Ava-ćchāta, as, ā, am, cut off, flayed, emaciated by abstinence; reaped.

अवजनित *ava-janita, as, ā, am* (rt. *jan*), born, brought forth.

अवजि *ava-ji,* cl. 1. P. *-jayati, -jetum,* to spoil (i. e. deprive by conquest), to win; recover; to ward off; conquer: Desid. *-jigīshati,* to wish to win or recover.

Ava-jaya, as, m. the act of overcoming, victory.

Ava-jita, as, ā, am, conquered; contemned, disregarded.

अवजुष्ट *ava-jushṭa, as, ā, am* (rt. *jush*), visited.

अवज्ञा 1. *ava-jñā,* cl. 9. P. *-jānāti, -jñātum,* to disesteem, have a low opinion of, despise, treat with contempt.

2. *ava-jñā,* f. or *ava-jñāna, am,* n. contempt, disesteem, disrespect (with obj. in loc. or gen.). — *Avajñopahata* (°*jñā-up*°), *as, ā, am,* treated with contempt, humiliated, degraded.

Ava-jñāta, as, ā, am, despised, disrespected.

Ava-jñeya, as, ā, am, contemptible, to be treated with disrespect, disreputable.

अवज्युत् *ava-jyut* (rt. *jyut* for *dyut*), Caus. *-jyotayati, -yitum,* to light up or bring a light to bear upon, to illumine.

Ava-jyotya, ind. having lighted (a lamp).

अवज्वल् *ava-jval,* Caus. *-jvālayati, -yitum,* to set on fire.

अवट *avaṭa, as,* m. (fr. 2. *ava,* q. v.), a hole, a vacuity; a hole in the ground, a chasm, a pit; any depressed part of the body, a cavity, a fosse, a sinus; a well; a juggler; N. of a man. — *Avaṭa-kaććhapa, as,* m. a tortoise in a hole (said of an inexperienced man, who has seen nothing of the world). — *Avaṭa-virodhana, am,* n. a particular hell.

Avaṭi, is, m. a hole in the ground; a sinus; a hollow, a cavity.

Avaṭīṭa, as, ā, am, flat-nosed.

Avaṭu, us, m. f. the back or nape of the neck; a hole in the ground; a well; N. of a tree; (*u*), n. a hole, a rent. — *Avaṭu-ja, as,* m. a hind curl, the hair on the back of the head.

Avaṭya, as, ā, am, Ved. being in a hole.

Avata, as, m., Ved. a well, a cistern.

अवडङ्ग *avaḍanga* or *avaḍranga* or *avaṭanka* (?) or *avaṭanga* (?), *as,* m. a market, a mart.

अवडीन *ava-ḍīna, am,* n. (rt. *ḍī*), the flight of a bird, flying downwards.

अवण्ड *a-vaṇḍa, as, ā, am,* Ved. not without a tail.

अवतंस *ava-tansa* or *ava-tansaka, as, am,* m. n. (rt. *tans*), a garland; a ring-shaped ornament, ear-ring, crest.

Ava-tansita, as, ā, am, having a garland or earring, crested.

अवतक्षण *ava-takshaṇa, am,* n. (rt. *taksh*), anything cut in pieces; chopped straw.

अवतड् *ava-taḍ,* Caus. P. *-tāḍayati, -yitum,* to strike downwards.

अवतन् *ava-tan,* cl. 8. P. *-tanoti, -nitum,* to stretch or extend downwards: to overspread, cover; to loosen, undo, especially a bowstring.

Ava-tata, as, ā, am, overspread, canopied, covered; loosened — *Avatata-dhanvan, ā,* m., Ved. whose bow is unbent.

Ava-tati, is, f. stretching, extending.

Ava-tāna, as, m. stretching, extending; unbending of a bow; cover; awning.

अवतप् *ava-tap,* cl. 1. P. *-tapati, -taptum,* to radiate heat (or light) downwards: Caus. *-tāpayati, -yitum,* to irradiate; to heat; to illuminate.

Ava-tapta, as, ā, am, heated. — *Avatapte-nakula-sthita, am,* n. an ichneumon's standing on hot ground (metaphorically said of the inconstancy of man).

Ava-tāpin, ī, inī, i, a place where the sun strikes vertically down.

अवतमस *ava-tamasa, am,* n. slight darkness, obscurity.

अवतरम् *ava-taram,* ind. (fr. *ava* with compar. affix), Ved. farther away, more distantly.

Ava-tas, ind. below, in the lower world.

अवतर्पण *ava-tarpaṇa, am,* n. (rt. *tṛip*), soothing remedy.

अवतृद् *ava-tṛid,* cl. 7. P., Ved. *-tṛiṇatti, -tarditum,* to chip off, sever; to silence.

अवतॄ *ava-tṛī,* cl. 1. P. *-tarati, -taritum* or *-rītum,* to descend (especially as a deity in becoming incarnate); to alight; to betake one's self to; to make one's appearance; to undertake, overcome: Caus. *-tārayati, -yitum,* to make or let one descend, to bring or fetch down; to pour down, take down, take off, remove; to bring down towards; to introduce, set a-going, render current; to descend (?).

Ava-taraṇa, am, n. descending, alighting; rushing along, sudden disappearance; crossing; translating.

Ava-taraṇikā, f. the short prayer (e. g. *gaṇeśāya namaḥ*) at the beginning of a work, which causes the divinity so addressed to descend from heaven.

Ava-taritavya, as, ā, am, to be descended.

Ava-tāra, as, m. descent (especially of a deity from heaven), the appearance of any deity upon earth, but more particularly the incarnations of Vishṇu in ten principal forms, viz. the fish, tortoise, boar, man-lion, dwarf, the two Rāmas, Kṛishṇa, Buddha, and Kalki; any new and unexpected appearance; (any distinguished person in the language of respect is called an Avatār or incarnation of a deity); aiming at an object (with gen.); a landing-place, a Tīrtha or sacred place; a pond; translation, translating, crossing; *avatāraṃ labh,* to gain one's aim or object with regard to anything (with gen.). — *Avatāra-kathā,* f. account of an Avatāra; N. of a chapter in the work entitled 'Saṅkara-vijaya,' supposed to have been composed by Anantānanda-giri. — *Avatāra-dvādaśa-kīrtana, am,* n. title of a chapter of the work 'Ūrdhvāmnāya-saṃhitā.' — *Avatāra-mantra, as,* m. a prayer causing the descent of a deity. — *Avatāra-vādāvalī,* f., N. of a controversial work by Purushottama.

Ava-tāraka, as, ikā, am, making one's appearance; making a descent.

Ava-tāraṇa, am, n. causing to descend; translation; worship, adoration; possession by an evil spirit; the ends or border of a garment.

Ava-tārita, as, ā, am, taken off or out, laid down or aside; descended; translated.

Ava-tārin, ī, iṇī, i, making one's appearance; making a descent.

Ava-tārya, ind. having caused to alight.

Ava-tīrṇa, as, ā, am, descended, alighted; crossed, passed over; translated. — *Avatīrṇarṇa* (°*ṇa-ṛiṇa*), *as, ā, am,* freed from debt.

Ava-tīrya, ind. having alighted or descended.

अवतोका *ava-tokā,* f. a woman or a cow miscarrying from accident.

अवत्क *avatka, am,* n. (fr. *avata,* q. v.), Ved. a small well.

अवत्त, अवत्तिन्. See under *ava-do.*

अवत्रस्त *ava-trasta, as, ā, am* (rt. *tras*), terrified.

अवत्विष् *ava-trish,* cl. 1. P. *-treshati, -treshṭum,* to glitter, shine; to move (?); to take (?).

अवत्सर् *ava-tsar,* cl. 1. P. *-tsarati, -ritum,* to fly away.

Ava-tsāra, as, m., N. of a descendant of Kaśyapa.

अवत्सीय *a-vatsīya, as, ā, am,* not suitable for a calf.

अवदंश *ava-daṇśa, as,* m. any pungent food which excites thirst; a stimulant.

अवदत्त *ava-datta, as, ā, am* (fr. rt. *dā* with *ava*), given away; finished, accomplished.

अवदय् *ava-day,* cl. 1. A. *-dayate, -yitum,* to give or pay an instalment (for the purpose of silencing or keeping one off).

अवदल् *ava-dal,* cl. 1. P. *-dalati, -litum,* to burst, to crack asunder.

Ava-dalita, as, ā, am, burst, cracked, destroyed.

अवदह् *ava-dah,* cl. 1. P. *-dahati, -dagdhum,* to burn down, destroy.

Ava-dāgha, as, m. (Gaṇa to Pāṇini VII. 1. 3, 53.)

Ava-dāha, as, m. burning down, the root of the fragrant grass Andropogon Muricatus. — *Avadāheshṭa* (°*ha-ish*°), *am,* n. = the last.

अवदात *ava-dāta, as, ā, am,* or *ava-dātaka, as, ā, am* (fr. rt. *dai* with *ava*), clean, clear; white; yellow; beautiful; (*as*), m. white colour.

1. *ava-dāna, am,* n. a pure or approved occupation; an act accomplished; a great or glorious act, achievement; object of a legend.

अवदान 2. *ava-dāna, am,* n. See under *ava-do.*

अवदान्य *a-vadānya, as, ā, am,* niggardly, stingy [cf. *abhy-avadānya*].

अवदावद *a-vadāvada, as, ā, am,* Ved. having no bad reputation.

अवदिश् *ava-diś,* cl. 6. P. *-diśati, -deshṭum,* to show or practice (kindness &c.): Caus. *-deśayati, -yitum,* to inform.

अवदिह् *ava-dih,* cl. 2. P. *-degdhi, -dhum,* to besmear.

अवदृश् *ava-dṛiś,* cl. 1. P. A. *-paśyati, -te, -drashṭum,* P. to look at, observe; A. to see, live to see: Pass. *-dṛiśyate,* to be inferred or inferrible.

अवदॄ *ava-dṛī,* cl. 9. P. *-dṛiṇāti, -daritum* or *-rītum,* to split or force open, to rend or tear asunder: Caus. *-dārayati, -yitum,* to cause to burst, to rend or split: Pass. *-dīryate,* to be split, to burst.

Ava-daraṇa, am, n. breaking (as a boil &c.), bursting, separating.

Ava-dāraṇa, am, n. tearing, dividing; a spade or hoe.

Ava-dārita, as, ā, am, torn off or away, rent.

Ava-dīrṇa, as, ā, am, torn, rent; melted, fused, liquefied; bewildered.

अवदो *ava-do,* cl. 4. P. *-dyati, -dātum,* to cut off, divide; Ved. A. to take away (anger), pacify.

Ava-tta, as, ā, am, cut off, divided.

Avattin, ī, inī, i, (after a cardinal num.) dividing into so many parts; e. g. *pañcāvattin,* dividing into five parts.

2. *ava-dāna, am,* n. cutting or dividing into pieces, a part, portion; the root of a fragrant grass, see *ava-dāha.* (For 1. *ava-dāna,* see under *ava-dāta.*)

अवदोह *ava-doha, as,* m. (fr. rt. *duh* with *ava*), milk.

अवद्य *a-vadya, as, ā, am* (rt. *vad*), not to be praised; low, inferior; disagreeable, blamable, disliked; (*am*), n. anything blamable, or not to be spoken of with praise; want, imperfection, vice, sin; blame, censure; shame, reproach. — *Avadya-gohana, as, ā, am,* Ved. concealing or keeping off want. — *Avadya-bhī, is,* f., Ved. fear of vices or sin. — *Avadya-vat, ān, atī, at,* Ved. disgraceful, lamentable.

अवद्योतिन् *ava-dyotin, ī, inī, i* (rt. *dyut*), shining down upon, illuminating [cf. *ava-jyut*].

अवद्रङ्ग *avadranga, as,* m. a market. See *avaḍanga.*

अवध *a-vadha, as,* m. (rt. *vadh* or *badh*), no murder; (*as, ā, am*), Ved. inviolable, invulnerable; see *a-badha.* — *A-vadhārha* (°*dha-ar*°), *as, ā, am,* not worthy of death.

A-vadhya, as, ā, am, not to be killed, inviolable. — *Avadhya-tā,* f. or *avadhya-tva, am,* n. inviolability.

अवधर्ष्य *ava-dharshya, as, ā, am* (rt. *dhṛish*), to be defied.

अवधा *ava-dhā,* cl. 3. A. *-dhatte, -dhātum,* to place down, deposit, apply (as the mind &c.); to be attentive: Pass. *-dhīyate,* to be placed, applied or directed (as the mind).

Ava-dhātavya or *ava-dhānīya* or *ava-dheya, as, ā, am,* to be attended to, deserving attention and care.

Ava-dhāna, am, n. attention, attentiveness, intentness; care, carefulness, devotion. — *Avadhāna-tā,* f. or *avadhāna-tva, am,* n. attentiveness.

Ava-dhānin, ī, inī, i, attentive.

Ava-dhi, is, m. application, attention, care; a term, a limit, conclusion, termination; a district, division, department; period, time; agreement, engagement; a hole, a pit. — *Avadhi-tā,* f. or *avadhi-tva, am,* n. limit, limitation. — *Avadhi-mat, ān, atī, at,* limited, bounded.

Ava-dhīyamāna, as, ā, am, being placed down or in, deposited.

Ava-hita, as, ā, am, deposited, applied; attentive, careful, done with care; celebrated, known. — *Avahita-karaṇa-kalāpa, as, ā, am,* having all the senses at rest, imperturbable. — *Avahita-tā,* f. application, attention. — *Avahitāñjali* (°*ta-añj*°), *is, is, i,* with joined hands.

अवधाव् *ava-dhāv,* cl. 1. P. A. *-dhāvati, -te, -vitum,* to run down, drop down; to run after.

1. *ava-dhāvana, am,* n. running after, pursuing; seizure.

Ava-dhāvanīya, as, ā, am, to be run after.

1. *ava-dhāvita, as, ā, am,* chased, pursued.

अवधावन 2. *ava-dhāvana, am,* n. (rt. 2. *dhāv*), cleaning, washing.

2. *ava-dhāvita, as, ā, am,* cleaned, cleansed.

अवधीर् *avadhīr,* cl. 10. P. *-dhīrayati, -yitum,* to disregard, disrespect; to despise, repudiate.

Avadhīraṇa, am, n. treating with disrespect, despising, repudiating.

Avadhīrita, as, ā, am, disrespected, disregarded, despised.

Avadhīrin, ī, iṇī, i, despising, scorning, excelling.

अवधू *ava-dhū,* cl. 5. P. A. *-dhūnoti, -dhūnute, -dhavitum* or *-dhotum,* to shake off or out, shake, toss; to discard; to lie down (?): Caus. *-dhūnayati, -yitum,* to shake.

Ava-dhūta, as, ā, am, shaken off, removed, shaken, tossed, compelled; discarded, rejected, spurned; trodden upon; separated from worldly feeling and obligation. — *Avadhūta-praṇipāta, as, ā, am,* rejecting an act of homage. — *Avadhūta-veśa, as, ā, am,* undressed, naked.

Ava-dhūnana, am, n. shaking, causing to shake; expelling; agitation, trembling; trampling on, treading on.

अवधूक *a-vadhūka, as,* m. having no wife.

अवधूपित *ava-dhūpita, as, ā, am,* perfumed with incense.

अवधृ *ava-dhṛi,* Caus. P. *-dhārayati, -yitum,* to consider, ascertain, determine accurately, make out, limit, restrict.

Ava-dhāra, as, m. accurate determination, limitation.

Ava-dhāraka, as, ikā, am, determining accurately, restricting one's self to anything.

Ava-dhāraṇa, am, n. ascertainment, affirmation, emphasis; stating or holding with positiveness or assurance, accurate determination, limitation (of the sense of words); restriction to a certain instance or instances with exclusion of any other; *(as, ā, am),* restrictive.
Ava-dhāraṇīya or *ava-dhārya, as, ā, am,* to be ascertained, determined or known.
Ava-dhārita, as, ā, am, ascertained, known, certain.

अवध्य *a-vadhya.* See *a-vadha.*

अवध्यै *ava-dhyai,* cl. 1. P. (A.?) *-dhyāyati, -te, -dhyātum,* to think ill of, despise.
Ava-dhyāta, as, ā, am, spurned, disdained.

अवध्र *a-vadhra, as, ā, am,* Ved. innoxious, beneficent.

अवध्वंस् *ava-dhvaṇs,* Caus. P. *-dhvaṇsayati, -yitum,* to cast down.
Ava-dhvaṇsa, as, m. falling off or from; sprinkling; meal, dust; abandoning, quitting; disrespect, censure, blame.
Ava-dhvasta, as, ā, am, sprinkled; pounded coarsely; abandoned, quitted; censured; scattered.

अवन *avana, am,* n. (rt. *av*), satisfaction; joy, happiness; desire; favour, preserving, protection, defence; speed; going, obtaining, asking; seizing, killing; power; increase; existence; adorning; embracing; bearing; entrance.
Avani, is, f. (said to be fr. rt. *av,* but rather connected with ? *ava,* down), course, bed of a river; stream, river; the earth; a finger. — *Avanin-gata, as, ā, am,* prostrate on the ground. — *Avani-ćara, as, ā, am,* roving over the earth, vagabond. — *Avani-pati, is,* m. lord of the earth, a king; Vishṇu; Yudhishṭhira. — *Avani-pāla, as,* m. protector of the earth, a king. — *Avani-maṇḍala, am,* n. the globe. — *Avani-ruh, ṭ,* m. a tree.
1. *avanī,* f. the earth; N. of a plant. — *Avanī-pati, is,* m. or *avanīśa* or *avanīśvara* (°*nī-īś*°), *as,* m. lord of the earth, a king. (For 2. see next col.)

अवनक्ष् *ava-naksh,* cl. 1. P., Ved. *-nakshati, -shitum,* (with gen.) to overtake (a person).
Ava-nakshatra, am, n. the disappearance of the stars.

अवनम् *ava-nam,* cl. 1. P. *-namati, -nantum,* to bow down, to bend down, bend: Caus. *-nāmayati, -yitum,* to bend down, bend.
Ava-nata, as, ā, am, bowed; bent down, downcast; bending, stooping, deepened, not projecting. — *Avanata-kāya, as, ā, am,* bending the body, crouching down. — *Avanata-mukha, as, ī, am,* with downcast countenance. — *Avanata-śirshan, ā, ā, a,* bowing the head.
Ava-nati, is, f. bowing down, stooping; setting.
Ava-namra, as, ā, am, bowed, bent.
Ava-nāma, as, m. causing to bend down, bending, bowing.
Ava-nāmaka, as, ikā, am, what depresses or causes to bow or bend.
Ava-nāmin, ī, inī, i, bending or bowing down.

अवनर्द् *ava-nard,* cl. 1. P. *-nardati, -ditum* (a technical term applicable to chanting in the Hindū ritual), to slur or trill, &c.

अवनश् *ava-naś,* cl. 4. P. *-naśyati, -naśitum* and *-nanshṭum,* to disappear, perish.

अवनह् *ava-nah,* cl. 4. P. A. *-nahyati, -te, -naddhum,* to bind on, tie on, put over, cover with.
Ava-naddha, as, ā, am, bound on, tied, covered; *(am),* n. a drum.
Ava-nāha, as, m. binding, girding, putting on.

अवनाट *ava-nāṭa, as, ā, am,* flat-nosed; *(am),* n. the condition of having a flat nose.

अवनि *avani.* See *avana.*

अवनिज् *ava-nij,* cl. 3. P. A. *-nenekti, -nenikte, -nektum,* to wipe or wash off, purify, clean; A. to wash one's self: Caus. *-nejayati, -yitum,* to cause to wash off.
Ava-negya, as, ā, am, used for washing off.
Ava-nejana, am, n. washing, washing off, ablution; water for washing, foot-bath.

अवनिनी *ava-ni-nī,* cl. 1. P. A. *-nayati, -te, -netum,* to put or bring into (water); to pour down.

अवनिश्चय *ava-niśćaya, as,* m. deduction, ascertainment.

अवनिष्ठिव् *ava-ni-shṭhiv* (or *-shṭhīv*), cl. 1. P. *-shṭhīvati, -shṭhevitum,* to spit upon.
Ava-nishṭhīvana, am, n. spitting upon.

अवनी 2. *ava-nī,* cl. 1. P. *-nayati, -netum,* to lead or bring down, to push into, to cause to descend or to flow; to lead away; to pour down or over.
Ava-naya or *ava-nāya, as,* m. causing to descend; throwing down, precipitating.
Ava-nayana, am, n. leading down, pouring down.
Ava-nāyaka, as, ikā, am, causing to descend.

अवनु *ava-nu,* cl. 1. A., Ved. *-navate,* to move or go towards.

अवनुद् *ava-nud,* Caus. *-nodayati, -yitum,* (with two acc.) to cause a person to drive away another.

अवन्ति *avanti, is,* m., N. of a country and its inhabitants; N. of a city, the modern Oujein (one of the seven sacred cities of the Hindūs, to die at which secures eternal happiness); N. of a river. — *Avanti-khaṇḍa, am,* n. a portion of the Skanda-purāṇa. — *Avanti-deva, as,* m. = *avanti-varman,* q. v. — *Avanti-pura, am,* n. the city of the Avantis, Oujein; N. of a town in Kāśmīra, built by Avanti-varman; (ī), f. Oujein. — *Avanti-brahma, as,* m., N. of a district inhabited by Brāhmans. — *Avanti-bhūpāla, as,* m. the king of Avanti, i. e. Bhoja. — *Avanti-varman, ā,* m., N. of a king; also of a poet. — *Avanti-soma, as,* m. sour gruel, prepared from the fermentation of rice-water.
Avantikā, f. the modern Oujein.
Avantī, f. Oujein; the queen of Oujein; N. of a river. — *Avantī-deśa, as,* m. the region of Avantī. — *Avantīśvara* (°*tī-īś*°), *as,* m., N. of a sanctuary built by Avanti-varman.

अवन्ध्य *avandhya, as*(?) or *(ā),* m. f., N. of a place.

अवपट् *ava-paṭ,* cl. 10. P. *-pāṭayati, -yitum,* to split: Pass. *-pāṭyate,* to split one's self; to be split.
Ava-pāṭikā, f. laceration of the prepuce.

अवपत् *ava-pat,* cl. 1. P. *-patati, -titum,* to fly down, jump down, fall down, alight: Caus. *-pātayati, -yitum,* to throw down.
Ava-patana, am, n. alighting, descending.
Ava-pāta, as, m. falling down; descent, descending; flying down; a hole or pit for catching game in.
Ava-pātana, am, n. felling, knocking or throwing down.

अवपद् *ava-pad,* cl. 4. A. *-padyate, -pattum,* to go down, glide down, descend; to be deprived of (with abl.); to fall, meet with an accident: Caus. *-pādayati, -yitum,* to cause to glide or go down.
Ava-panna, as, ā, am, fallen on or into; descended, alighted; thrown down.

अवपाक *a-vapāka, as, ā, am,* without a net.

अवपात्रित *ava-pātrita, as, ā, am,* a person not allowed by his kindred to eat or drink from a common vessel; one who has lost his caste [cf. *apa-pātrita*].

अवपान *ava-pāna, am,* n., Ved. drinking, giving to drink; a pond or pool for watering.

अवपालित *ava-pālita, as, ā, am* (fr. *pāl,* Caus. of rt. 3. *pā* with *ava*), unprotected, neglected.

अवपाशित *ava-pāśita, as, ā, am,* snared, having a snare laid over.

अवपीड् *ava-pīḍ,* cl. 10. P. *-pīḍayati, -yitum,* to press down, compress.
Ava-pīḍa, as, m. pressing down; a sternutatory; any drug producing sneezing.
Ava-pīḍana, am, n. the act of pressing down; a sternutatory; *(ā),* f. damage, violation.

अवपूर्ण *ava-pūrṇa, as, ā, am* (rt. *pṛī*), full of, filled.

अवप्रज्जन *ava-prajjana, as,* m. (rt. *pṛij*), the end of the warp of a web.

अवप्लु *ava-plu,* cl. 1. A. *-plavate, -plotum,* to jump down or off.
Ava-plutya, ind. having jumped down.

अवफ *ava-pha, as,* m. flatulence, wind from the bowels.

अवबधा *ava-badhā,* f. segment of the base of a triangle [cf. *a-badhā* and *ā-bādhā*].

अवबन्ध *ava-bandha, as,* m. falling or palsy of the eyelids, Blepharoptosis.

अवबाहुक *ava-bāhuka, as,* m. spasm in the arm.

अवबुध् *ava-budh,* cl. 4. A. *-budhyate, -boddhum,* to awake, become sensible or aware of, perceive, know: Caus. *-bodhayati, -yitum,* to make one aware of, inform, explain.
Ava-bodha, as, m. waking, being awake; perception, knowledge; discrimination, judgment; teaching.
Ava-bodhaka, as, m. an awakener, a teacher. — *Avabodhaka-tva, am,* n. instruction, guidance, explanation.
Ava-bodhana, am, n. perception, knowledge, &c.

अवब्रव *ava-brava, as,* m. (rt. *brū* with *ava*), ill report, defamation.

अवभञ्ज् *ava-bhañj,* cl. 7. P. *-bhanakti, -bhanktum,* to break off, smash.
Ava-bhajya, ind. having broken off.
Ava-bhañjana, am, n. breaking off, tearing.

अवभर्त्स् *ava-bharts,* cl. 10. P. (or A.?) *-bhartsayati, -yitum,* to deter by scolding or threatening, to menace.

अवभा *ava-bhā,* cl. 2. P. *-bhāti, -tum,* to shine downwards.

अवभाषण *ava-bhāshaṇa, am,* n. speaking.

अवभास् *ava-bhās,* cl. 1. A. *-bhāsate, -situm,* to shine forth, become manifest: Caus. *-bhāsayati, -yitum,* to illuminate.
Ava-bhāsa, as, m. splendor, lustre, light; appearance, manifestation; space, reach, compass. — *Avabhāsa-kara, as,* m., N. of a divinity. — *Avabhāsa-prabha, ās,* m. pl., N. of a whole class of deities. — *Avabhāsa-prāpta,* N. of a world.
Ava-bhāsaka, as, ikā, am, irradiating, luminous. — *Avabhāsaka-tva, am,* n. luminousness.
Ava-bhāsita, as, ā, am, illumined, lighted, radiant; evident, manifest.
Ava-bhāsin, ī, inī, i, shining, bright; *(nī),* f. the outer skin or cuticle.

अवभिद् *ava-bhid,* cl. 7. P. *-bhinatti, -bhettum,* to break off, shatter.
Ava-bhinna, as, ā, am, broken off, pierced, divided.
Ava-bhedin, ī, inī, i, breaking off, shattering, dividing.

अवभुज् *ava-bhuj,* cl. 6. P. *-bhujati, -bhoktum,* to bend down, curve.
Ava-bhugna, as, ā, am, contracted, bent.

अवभृथ *ava-bhṛitha, as,* m. (fr. rt. *bhṛi* with

ava), carrying off, removing; purification by bathing of the sacrificer and the sacrificial vessels after a sacrifice; the water of purification; a supplementary sacrifice to atone for defects in a principal and preceding one. — Avabhṛitha-snāna, am, n. bathing or ablution after a sacrificial ceremony.

Ava-bhra, as, m. abduction, carrying off.

अवभ्रट ava-bhraṭa, as, ā, am, flat-nosed; (am), n. state of having a flat nose.

अवम avama, as, ā, am (fr. 2. ava), undermost, inferior, lowest, base; next, intimate; last, youngest; growing less, decreasing; (am), n. a lunar day exactly coinciding with a solar one.

अवमन् ava-man, cl. 4. A. or poet. P. -manyate, -ti, -mantum, to despise, treat contemptuously: Caus. -mānayati, -yitum, to despise, &c.

Ava-mata, as, ā, am, despised, disregarded, contemned. — Avamatāṅkuśa (°ta-aṅ°), as, m. a restive elephant that disdains the hook, one in rut.

Ava-mati, is, m. a master, an owner; (is), f. aversion, dislike; disregard, contempt.

Ava-matya, ind. having scorned, despising.

Ava-mantavya or ava-manya, as, ā, am, contemptible, to be treated with disrespect.

Ava-mantṛi, tā, trī, tṛi, despising; contemptuous, disrespectful; arrogant.

Ava-māna, as, m. disrespect, contempt. — Avamāna-tā, f. or avamāna-tva, am, n. dishonourableness, contempt.

Ava-mānana, am, ā, n. f. disrespect.

Ava-mānanīya or ava-mānya, as, ā, am, to be disrespected, contemptible, despicable.

Ava-mānita, as, ā, am, disrespected, despised.

Ava-mānin, ī, inī, i, contemning, despising, behaving disrespectfully. — Avamāni-tā, f. or avamāni-tva, am, n. disrespectfulness.

अवमन्थ ava-mantha or ava-manthaka, as, m. (rt. manth), swellings caused by boils or contusions.

अवमर्श ava-marśa, as, m. See ava-mṛiś.

अवमर्षण ava-marshaṇa, am, n. (rt. mṛish), intolerance, impatience; effacing, obliterating, banishing from recollection.

अवमुच् ava-muć, cl. 6. P. -muñćati, -moktum, to loosen; to let go; to take off (a garment, &c.); to unharness.

Ava-mućya, ind. having unloosed or unharnessed.

Ava-moćana, am, n. letting go, loosening; setting at liberty.

अवमूत्र् ava-mūtr, cl. 10. P. -mūtrayati, -yitum, to urine upon.

Ava-mūtrayat, an, antī, at, urining upon.

अवमूर्धशय ava-mūrdha-śaya, as, ā, am, lying with the head hanging down.

अवमृज् ava-mṛij, cl. 2. P. -mārshṭi, -mārjitum or -mārshṭum, to wipe or rub off, to strip off, remove; to efface.

Ava-mārjana, am, n., Ved. what is stripped or rubbed off.

Ava-mṛijya, ind. having stripped, having pulled off; having wiped away.

अवमृद् ava-mṛid, cl. 9. P. -mṛidnāti, -marditum, to grind down, to reduce by friction (or otherwise); to crush, to tread down; to rub.

Ava-marda, as, m. trampling, oppression, driving one into straits; giving pain; devastation, inflicting pain or punishment on an enemy by laying his country waste, &c.

Ava-mardana, as, ā, am, treading down, grinding, crushing, oppressing; (am), n. rubbing, washing; oppression.

Ava-mardita, as, ā, am, ground, rubbed, crushed, oppressed.

अवमृश् ava-mṛiś, cl. 6. P. -mṛiśati, -marshṭum, -mrashṭum, to touch.

Ava-marśa, as, m. touch, contact.

Ava-mṛiśya, as, ā, am, to be touched.

अवय avaya. See śatāvaya.

अवयज् ava-yaj, cl. 1. A. -yajate, -yashṭum, to expiate; not to worship, to abandon.

Ava-yajana, am, n., Ved. expiating; purification.

Ava-yāj, ās, f., Ved. a particular portion of a sacrifice; m. a kind of priest. Gram. 176. f.

अवयव ava-yava, as, m. (fr. rt. 1. yu with ava), a limb, a member; a part, a portion; a member or component part of a logical argument or syllogism. — Avayava-śas, ind. part by part, severally. — Avayavārtha (°va-ar°), as, m. the meaning of the component parts of a word.

Avayavin, ī, inī, i, limbed, having limbs; having portions or subdivisions; a whole; (ī), m. a syllogism, a logical argument.

अवया 1. ava-yā, cl. 2. P. A. -yāti, -te, -yātum, to go down, to give way, desist; to remove.

2. ava-yā, ās, ās, am, Ved. giving way, desisting, ceasing.

Avayāta-heḍas, ās, m., Ved. one whose anger is appeased.

Ava-yātṛi, tā, m., Ved. turning away; appeasing, one who appeases.

Ava-yāna, am, n. going down, retreat; appeasing, expiation.

अवयुन a-vayuna, as, ā, am, Ved. not to be recognized; indistinct, confused.

अवर avara, as, ā, am (fr. 2. ava), below, inferior; low, mean, unimportant, of small value; posterior, hinder, later, last, younger; western; nearer; (at the end of a compound signifying quantity) the least, the lowest degree, lowest value; (ā), f. the hind thigh of an elephant; a N. of Durgā; (am), n. the hind thigh of an elephant; [with avara have been compared Gr. οὐρά, οὗρος, οὖρον, ὅρος, ὄρρος; Lat. eurus; also the Lat. aver-nus]. — Avara-ja, as, ā, am, of low birth, inferior; younger, junior; (as), m. a Śūdra; a younger brother; (ā), f. a younger sister. — Avara-tas, ind. behind, afterwards, hinder, posterior, downwards. — Avara-param, ind., Ved. one after another. — Avara-purusha, ās, m. pl. the descendants. — Avara-varṇa, as, m. a low or despised tribe; (as, ā, am), belonging to a low caste or tribe; a Śūdra, a man or woman of the fourth tribe. — Avara-varṇaka or avara-varṇa-ja, as, ā, am, belonging to or born in a low tribe. — Avara-vrata, as, m. the sun [cf. arka-vrata]. — Avara-śilā, f., N. of a Buddhist monastery. — Avara-śaila, ās, m. pl., N. of a Buddhist school. — Avaras-para, as, ā, am, Ved. having the last first, or the hindermost foremost; inverted, confused. — Avarārdha (°ra-ar°), as, m. the least part, the minimum; the last half; (am), ind. in a certain succession of parts; successively. — Avarārdha-tas, ind. from below. — Avarārdhya, as, ā, am, being on the lower or nearer side; beginning from below; belonging to the last half; (am), n. the least or smallest part, the minimum. — Avarāvara (°ra-av°), as, ā, am, lowest, most inferior of all. — Avarokta (°ra-uk°), as, ā, am, named last.

Avarastāt, ind. behind, hinder, posterior; below, downwards.

Avarīṇa, as, ā, am, degraded, debased; censured, blamed.

Avareṇa, ind. (with acc.) below.

Avarya, nom. P. avaryati, -yitum, to become lower.

अवरङ्गसाह avaraṅga-sāha, the Sanskrit form of the Muhammedan name Aurungzeb. (Sāha = the Persian شاه).

अवरम् ava-ram, cl. 1. A. -ramate, -rantum, to leave off, cease.

Ava-rata, as, ā, am, stopped, ceased, desisted from.

Ava-rati, is, f. stopping, ceasing, cessation, relaxation, repose, end.

अवरीयस् a-varīyas, ān, m., N. of a son of Manu Sāvarṇa.

अवरुज् ava-ruj, cl. 6. P. -rujati, -roktum, to break off, to break.

Ava-rugṇa, as, ā, am, broken off, torn; diseased.

Ava-rujya, ind. having broken off.

अवरुध् ava-rudh, cl. 7. P. A. -ruṇaddhi, -rundhe, -roddhum, to obstruct, restrain, hinder, shut up, besiege; to keep back: Pass. -rudhyate: Intens. P. -roroddhi, to injure, hurt.

Ava-ruddha, as, ā, am, checked, stopped, hindered; shut up or in, enclosed; imprisoned, secluded, as in the inner apartments. — Avaruddha-deha, as, ā, am, incarcerated.

Ava-ruddhi, is, f. restraint, besieging; gaining.

Ava-rudhyamāna, as, ā, am, being enclosed or surrounded.

1. ava-rodha, as, m. hindrance, obstruction; restraint; an enclosure, confinement, besieging, a siege; a covering, lid; a fence, a pen; a watchman; the inner apartments of a palace, the queen's or women's apartments; a palace; pl. the wives of a king. (For 2. ava-rodha, see below under ava-ruh.) — Avarodhāyana (°dha-ay°), am, n. a seraglio.

Ava-rodhaka, as, ikā, am, obstructive, hindering, impeding; (as), m. a guard; (ikā), f. a female of the inner apartments; (am), n. a barrier, a fence.

1. ava-rodhana, am, n. siege, blockade; hindering, obstructing; obstacle, impediment; a closed or private place, the innermost part of anything; the inner or women's apartments in a royal palace. (For 2. ava-rodhana, see below under ava-ruh.)

Ava-rodhika, as, ī, am, obstructive, impeding; (as), m. a guard of the queen's apartments.

Ava-rodhin, ī, inī, i, obstructing, hindering.

अवरुह् ava-ruh, cl. 1. P. -rohati, -roḍhum, to descend, alight, dismount: Caus. -ropayati or -rohayati, -yitum, to cause to descend; to bring down; to lower, lessen.

Ava-rūḍha, as, ā, am, descended, dismounted, alighted.

2. ava-rodha, as, m. (rt. rudh for ruh), Ved. moving down, descending; a shoot sent out by the root of a plant, a slip (for planting), the pendent shoots of the Indian fig tree.

2. ava-rodhana, am, n. (rt. rudh for ruh), Ved. descending motion, descending.

Ava-ropaṇa, am, n. causing to descend; uprooting; taking away, depriving, diminishing; descending; setting (as of the sun).

Ava-ropita, as, ā, am, caused to descend; uprooted, deprived of, curtailed, diminished, lost.

Ava-ropya, ind. having made to descend; rooting up.

Ava-roha, as, m. descent, passing from or over; mounting, ascending (?); a shoot sent out by a plant; a pendent branch, one that strikes fresh root into the earth, as those of the Indian fig tree; the growth of a creeping plant or vine; a creeping plant climbing up to the top of a tree; heaven or Svarga. — Avaroha-vat, ān, or avaroha-śāyin, ī, m. the Indian fig tree.

Ava-rohaṇa, am, n. alighting, descending, dismounting; ascending.

Ava-rohikā, f., N. of the plant Physalis Flexuosa L.

Ava-rohin, ī, iṇī, i, descending, what descends, what ascends; (ī), m. the Indian fig tree.

अवरूप ava-rūpa, as, ā, am, mis-shapen, deformed; degenerated.

अवरोकिन् ava-rokin, ī, iṇī, i (fr. rt. ruć with ava), Ved. shining, brilliant.

Ava-roćuka, as, m. want of appetite.

अवर्चस् a-varćas, ās, ās, as, Ved. without splendor, insignificant in form, mean-looking.

अवर्जिवस् *a-varjivas, ān, jushī, at,* Ved. not hindering, not being able to prevent.

अवर्ण *a-varṇa, as, ā* or *ī, am,* colourless; having no marks; bad, low, destitute of good qualities; (*as*), m. blame, censure. — *Avarṇa-vāda, as,* m. censure, blame, reproach.

अवर्तन *avartana,* N. of an *upa-dvīpa* or island, mentioned in the Purāṇic descriptions of the earth.

अवर्तमान *a-vartamāna, as, ā, am,* non-existent, not present, absent.

अवर्ति *avarti, is,* f. (*ava-ṛiti,* fr. rt. *ṛi* with *ava*), Ved. bad fortune, poverty, distress, want.

अवर्त्र *a-vartra, as, ā, am,* Ved. (rt. *vṛit*), not turning back; (if fr. rt. *vṛi*) not to be kept back.

अवर्धमान *a-vardhamāna, as, ā, am,* not increasing, not growing, not thriving.

अवर्मन् *a-varman, ā, ā, a,* Ved. having no armour.

अवर्ष *a-varsha, as,* m. or *a-varshaṇa, am,* n. want of rain, drought.

A-varshuka, as, ā, am, Ved. not raining.

Avarshya, as, ā, am, Ved. being active in rainless bright weather.

अवलक्ष *avalaksha* or *valaksha, as, ā, am,* white; (*as*), m. the white colour.

अवलग्न *ava-lagna, as, ā, am* (rt. *lag*), hanging down; placed contiguously, impressed, attached, &c.; (*as, am*), m. n. the waist.

अवलङ्घ् *ava-langh,* cl. 10. P. A. *-langhayati, -te, -yitum,* to pass (time), spend.

अवलम्ब् *ava-lamb,* cl. 1. A. or poet. P. *-lambate, -ti, -bitum,* to hang, glide or slip down, descend; to catch hold of, cling to, hang to, hold on or support one's self by; rest upon as a support, to depend upon: Caus. *-lambayati, -yitum,* to make one rest upon or catch hold of.

Ava-lamba, as, m. hanging down; hanging on or from; depending; resting upon; asylum, dependance, support; a prop, a stay; suspender; an appendage; a perpendicular.

Ava-lambaka, as, m., N. of a metre.

Ava-lambana, am, n. depending upon, dependance; hanging on or from; a prop.

Ava-lambita, as, ā, am, hanging on or upon, suspended from, clinging to; depending upon, trusting to, supported by, protected, cherished; alighting, descending; expeditious (?).

Ava-lambitavya, as, ā, am, to be caught hold of or grasped, to be clung to; expeditious, quick.

Ava-lambin, ī, inī, i, hanging down so as to rest upon, hanging on or from, depending on; clinging to, reclining, resting upon.

Ava-lambya, ind. leaning on, having depended or relied on, supporting one's self; trusting to; waiting.

अवलिप्त *ava-lipta, as, ā, am* (rt. *lip*), anointed, plastered, smeared; proud, arrogant, vain. — *Avalipta-tā,* f. or *avalipta-tva, am,* n. unction; pride, arrogance, vanity.

Ava-lepa, as, m. smearing, anointing; ornament; union, association; pride, haughtiness.

Ava-lepana, am, n. anointing; proud behaviour; daring, proud or arrogant purpose.

अवलिह् *ava-lih,* cl. 2. P. A. *-leḍhi, -līḍhe, -leḍhum,* to lick off, to lick, to lap: Intens. *-leleḍhi,* to lick again and again.

Ava-līḍha, as, ā, am, licked, lapped; devoured, destroyed: (*ā*), f. disregard, contempt.

Ava-leha, as, m. or *ava-lehikā,* f. licking, lapping; an extract, an electuary, confection.

Ava-lehana, am, n. licking with the tongue, lapping.

Ava-lehya, as, ā, am, to be licked; thick, viscid.

अवली *ava-lī,* cl. 4. A. *-līyate, -letum* or *-lātum,* to stick to, hang to.

Ava-līna, as, ā, am, sticking to, cleaving to.

अवलीला *ava-līlā,* f. sport, play, mirth.

अवलुञ्च् *ava-luñć,* cl. 1. P. *-luñćati, -ćitum,* to pull down or out.

Ava-luñćana, am, n. tearing or cutting off, pulling out.

अवलुण्ठन *ava-luṇṭhana, am,* n. (rt. *luṇṭh*), robbing; rolling or wallowing on the ground.

Ava-luṇṭhita, as, ā, am, robbed; rolled on the ground.

अवलुप् *ava-lup,* cl. 6. A. or P. *-lumpate, -ti, -loptum,* to rush or dash upon as a wild beast on its prey, to burst or break in upon.

Ava-lumpana, am, n. leaping on suddenly.

Ava-lopya, as, ā, am, that can be broken in upon or assailed with a sudden rush.

अवलून *ava-lūna, as, ā, am,* cut off.

अवलेख *ava-lekha, as,* m. (rt. *likh*), anything scraped off.

Ava-lekhana, am, ī, n. f. scraping off.

Ava-lekhā, f. rubbing; adorning the person.

अवलेप *ava-lepa.* See under *ava-lipta* last col.

अवलोक् *ava-lok,* cl. 1. A. *-lokate, -kitum,* or cl. 10. P. *-lokayati, -yitum,* to look down upon, look at, view, behold, see, consider.

Ava-loka, as, m. sight, seeing; looking down upon with compassion.

Ava-lokaka, as, ikā, am, looking at, wishing to see.

Ava-lokana, am, n. act of looking at; beholding; sight; seeing; review.

Ava-lokayitṛi, tā, trī, tṛi, looking upon, considering.

Ava-lokita, as, ā, am, seen; (*as*), m., N. of a Bodhi-sattva; (*am*), n. a look, a glance. — *Avalokiteśvara* (°*ta-īś*°), *as,* m., N. of a Bodhi-sattva, worshipped by the northern Buddhists.

Ava-lokin, ī, inī, i, looking at, beholding; considering.

अवलोभन *ava-lobhana, am,* n. (rt. *lubh*), sensual desire.

अवल्गुज *a-valgu-ja, as,* m., N. of the plant Vernonia Anthelmintica.

अवल्गुली *avalgulī,* f., N. of a poisonous insect.

अववद् *ava-vada, as,* m. or *ava-vadana, am,* n. (rt. *vad*), evil report or reputation.

Ava-vaditṛi, tā, m., Ved. one who speaks finally or decisively (?), an adjudicator.

Ava-vāda, as, m. evil report or reputation; censure, reproach; a command, an order; trust, confidence; information.

अववर्षण *ava-varshaṇa, am,* n. raining upon.

अववा *ava-vā,* cl. 2. P., Ved. *-vāti, -tum,* to radiate (?), to prevail (?), to rage (as fire ?).

अवविद्ध *ava-viddha, as, ā, am* (rt. *vyadh*), cast down.

अवव्रश्च् *ava-vraść,* cl. 6. P. *-vṛiśćati, -vraśćitum, -vrashṭum,* to splinter, cut off.

Ava-vraśća, as, m. splinter, chip.

अवश *a-vaśa, as, ā, am* (rt. *vaś*), unsubmissive to another's will; independent, unrestrained, free; not having one's own free will; doing something against one's liking or unwillingly; necessary, certain. — *Avaśaṅ-gama, as, ā, am,* not submitting to another's will. — *Avaśendriya-ćitta* (°*śa-in*°), *as, ā, am,* whose mind and senses are not held in subjection.

A-vaśī-bhūta, as, ā, am, unrestrained, independent; uninfluenced by magic.

A-vaśya, as, ā, am, untameable, ungovernable, inevitable; (*am*), ind. necessarily, inevitably, certainly, at all events, by all means; *avaśyam eva,* most surely. If compounded with a fut. pass. part. the final nasal is dropped; e. g. *avaśya-pāćya,* to be necessarily cooked; *avaśya-kārya,* to be necessarily done: but retained in *avaśyan-kārin,* doing what is necessary; *avaśyam-bhāvin,* necessarily being.

A-vaśyaka, as, ā, am, necessary, inevitable, indispensable. — *Avaśyaka-tā,* f. or *avaśyaka-tva, am,* n. necessity, obligation, certainty.

अवशक्थिका *ava-śakthikā,* f. a cloth tied round the legs and knees of a person sitting on his hams [cf. *ava-sakthikā*].

अवशस् *ava-śas, as,* f. (rt. *śaṃs*), Ved. wrong desire.

अवशा *a-vaśā,* f., Ved. not a cow, a bad cow.

अवशातन *ava-śātana, am,* n. (Caus. of rt. *śad*), withering, drying up.

अवशिरस् *ava-śiras, ās, ās, as,* or *ava-śirshaka, as, ā, am,* having the head turned down.

अवशिष् *ava-śish,* Pass. *-śishyate,* to be left last or as a remnant, to remain over.

Ava-śishṭa, as, ā, am, left, remaining; (*am*), n. or *ava-śishṭaka, am,* n. rest, remainder.

Ava-śesha, as (*am?*), m. (n.?) leavings, remainder; end, close, termination. Frequently as the last member of a compound; thus, *ardhāvaśesha,* having only one half left; *kathāvaśesha-tā,* the condition of one who survives only in narrations.

Ava-śeshita, as, ā, am, left remaining.

अवशॄ *ava-śṝ,* Pass. *-śīryate,* to be shattered.

अवश्या *ava-śyā,* f. (rt. *śyai* with *ava*), hoar-frost; a fog or mist.

Ava-śīna, as, m. a scorpion.

Ava-śyāya, as, m. hoar-frost; white dew; pride.

अवश्रयण *ava-śrayaṇa, am,* n. (rt. *śri*), taking (anything) from off the fire (opposed to *adhi-śrayaṇa,* q. v.).

अवश्वसम् *ava-śvasam,* ind. (rt. *śvas*), Ved. as if blown away.

अवष्कयणी *avashkayaṇī,* f. (= *vashkayaṇī*), a cow that bears a calf after a long interval.

अवष्टम्भ् *ava-shṭambh* (*-stambh*), cl. 5. 9. P. *-shṭabhnoti* or *-nāti, -shṭambhitum,* to lean or rest upon; to be contiguous or near; to be astounded or bewildered.

Ava-shṭabdha, as, ā, am, supported, rested on, protected; hanging from or upon; stopped, obstructed, stayed; paralysed; bound, tied, attached; wrapped up, enfolded; opposed; surpassed, overcome; near.

Ava-shṭabhya, ind. leaning upon, resting on, holding; stopping, arresting.

Ava-shṭambha, as, m. leaning or resting upon, having recourse to any one; stopping, standing still, staying; self-confidence, resoluteness; commencement, beginning; excellence; obstruction, impediment; support, stay; paralysis; a post or pillar; gold. — *Ava-shṭambha-maya, as, ī, am,* golden, made of gold.

Ava-shṭambhana, am, n. resting upon, having recourse to; supporting, protecting; stopping, staying; paralysing; a pillar or post.

अवष्वन् *ava-shvan* (*-svan*), cl. 1. P. *-shvaṇati, -ṇitum,* to smack (one's lips) or otherwise make a noise in eating.

Ava-shvāṇa, as, m. noisy eating, smacking.

अवस् 1. *avas,* n. (fr. rt. *av*), Ved. satisfaction, pleasure, enjoyment; wish, desire, aspiring; favour, furtherance, protection, assistance. — *Avas-vat, ān, atī, at*, Ved. striving, desirous.

Avasa, am, n., Ved. refreshment, food, provisions, viaticum; preserving, protecting; (*as*), m. a king; the sun.

अवस् 2. *avas*, ind. (fr. 2. *ava*), Ved. adv. below, downwards, hitherward.

(As a prep. with inst. or abl. it expresses) below, at the lowest place of; without, on the outside.

Avastāt. See s. v.

अवसक्थिका *ava-sakthikā* or *ava-saktikā*, f. a cloth tied round the legs and knees of a person sitting on his hams; a wrapper; a girth or band [cf. *ava-śakthikā*].

अवसञ्ज् *ava-sañj*, cl. 1. P. *-sajati, -sanktum*, to suspend, attach, cling to.

Ava-sakta, as, ā, am, suspended from, attached to or by, in contact with, bound round, begirt; engaged in, intent on, eager, placed upon.

Ava-sañjana or *ava-sajjana, am*, n. embracing, clinging.

अवसण्डीन *ava-saṇḍīna, am*, n. (rt. *ḍī*), the united downward flight of birds.

अवसथ *a-vasatha, as*, m. (for *ā-vasatha*, q. v.), habitation; a village; a college, a school; (*am*), n. a house. See *ā-vasatha*.

Avasathya, as, m. a college, a school.

अवसद् *ava-sad*, cl. 1. P. *-sīdati, -sattum*, to sink down, to faint; become disheartened, be exhausted, perish, come to an end: Caus. *-sādayati, -yitum*, to cause to sink, dispirit, render downhearted, to ruin.

Ava-sanna, as, ā, am, sunk down, bowed, bent; languid, enervated; melancholy, dispirited, unhappy; ended, terminated, separated; non-suited. — *Avasanna-tā*, f. or *avasanna-tva, am*, n. affliction, low spirits; dejection; termination, completion.

Ava-sāda, as, m. sitting down; sinking, fainting; exhaustion, fatigue, lassitude, want of energy or spirit, especially as proceeding from doubtful or unsuccessful love; (in law) badness of a cause; end, termination.

Ava-sādaka, as, ikā, am, causing to sink, frustrating; exhausting, tiresome, wearisome; ending, finishing.

Ava-sādana, am, n. oppressing, disheartening; finishing; an escharotic; removing proud flesh by escharotic applications.

Ava-sādita, as, ā, am, made to sink, exhausted, faint, languid.

अवसभ *ava-sabha, as, ā, am*, Ved. excluded from society.

अवसर *ava-sara, as*, m. (fr. rt. *sṛi* with *ava*), descent, place of descent; descent of water; rain, raining; occasion, moment, favourable opportunity; leisure, advantageous situation; consultation in private; a year. — *Avasara-kāle*, at a favourable opportunity, at a time of leisure.

Ava-sāraṇa, am, n. removing, causing to move.

अवसर्ग *ava-sarga*. See *ava-sṛij*.

अवसर्प *ava-sarpa, as*, m. (rt. *sṛip*), a spy, a secret emissary.

Ava-sarpaṇa, am, n. stepping down.

Ava-sarpin, ī, iṇī, i, stepping down; (*iṇī*), f. a long period of time with the Jainas.

अवसव्य *ava-savya, as, ā, am*, not left, right.

अवसान 1. *a-vasāna, as, ā, am* (rt. 2. *vas*), Ved. not dressing. (For 2. *ava-sāna*, see under *ava-so* next col.)

अवसिच् *ava-sić*, cl. 6. P. *-sinćati, -sektum*, to sprinkle, bedew, bespatter.

Ava-sikta, as, ā, am, sprinkled. — *Avasiktāṅga* (*°ta-aṅ°*), *as, ī, am*, having the limbs sprinkled.

Ava-seka, as, m. sprinkling, irrigating, bedewing.

Avasekima, as, m. a kind of cake, pulse ground and fried with oil or butter.

Ava-sećana, am, n. sprinkling, water used for sprinkling; bleeding.

अवसुप्त *ava-supta, as, ā, am* (rt. *svap*), asleep.

अवसृज् *ava-sṛij*, cl. 6. P. *-sṛijati, -srashṭum*, to let off, to let loose, let go, fling down, pour out, dismiss, remit, liberate.

Ava-sarga, as, m. letting off, letting go, emission, remission, laxity, relaxation, following one's own inclinations, independence.

Ava-sarjana, am, n., Ved. liberation.

Ava-sṛishṭa, as, ā, am, dismissed, let go.

अवसो *ava-so*, cl. 4. P. *-syati, -sātum*, to finish, accomplish; to destroy: Caus. *-sāyayati, -yitum*, to destroy; to cause to be completed.

Ava-sā, f., Ved. liberation, setting free, deliverance.

Ava-sātṛi, tā, m., Ved. a deliverer, liberator.

2. *ava-sāna, am*, n. place of dismounting from a horse or alighting from a carriage, stopping, resting-place, residence; conclusion, termination, cessation; death; boundary, limit; (in gram.) the last part of a word or period, disjunction of letters; a pause; the end of a verse or the verse itself: (for 1. *a-vasāna*, see last col.) — *Avasāna-darśa, as, ā, am*, Ved. looking at one's place of destination or residence.

Ava-sānaka, as, ikā, am, coming to an end, perishing.

Avasānya, as, ā, am, Ved. belonging to the end of a verse.

1. *ava-sāya, as*, m. conclusion, end; termination, completion; remainder; determination, ascertainment, certainty.

2. *ava-sāya*, ind. having finished; having loosened, having set free.

Ava-sāyin, ī, inī, i, residing, dwelling in.

Ava-sāyya, ind. having caused to be completed.

Ava-sita, as, ā, am, having settled in a place, residing; ended, terminated; finished, completed; standing in a pause; known, understood; stored (as grain, &c.); gone; (*am*), n. a dwelling-place. — *Avasita-mati, is, is, i*, frustrated, disappointed.

Ava-seya, as, ā, am, to be destroyed, destructible, perishable.

अवस्कन्द् *ava-skand*, cl. 1. P. *-skandati, -skantum*, to storm, to assault.

Ava-skanda, as, m. assault, attack, storm; a camp; descending, bathing.

Ava-skandana, am, n. attacking, assaulting, storm; refutation; descending; bathing.

Ava-skandita, as, ā, am, attacked; gone down; refuted; bathed, bathing.

Ava-skandin, ī, inī, i, leaping upon, covering; attacking, assaulting.

अवस्कर *avas-kara, as*, m. (fr. rt. *kṛī* with *avas*), something to be concealed or swept away; a privity; ordure, fæces; dirt; sweepings; the privities; a place for fæces, &c. — *Avaskara-mandira, am*, n. a privy, water-closet.

Avas-karaka, as, m. existing in the fæces, an insect; a sweeper; a brush, broom, &c.

अवस्कव *ava-skava, as*, m. a kind of worm.

अवस्तात् *avastāt*, ind. (fr. 2. *avas*, q. v.), below, from below, downwards, hitherwards; (with gen.) below. — *Avastāt-prapadana, as, ā, am*, (anything) attained from below (as heaven, &c.).

अवस्तु *a-vastu, u*, n. a worthless thing; nothing; insubstantiality, the unreality of matter. — *Avastu-tā*, f. or *avastu-tva, am*, n. insubstantiality, unreality.

अवस्तृ *ava-stṛi*, cl. 9. P., Ved. *-stṛiṇāti, -startum, -starītum* or *-rītum*, to cover; to spread or lay down a covering.

Ava-staraṇa, am, n. spreading out or laying down a covering.

Ava-stāra, as, m. a screen or wall of cloth surrounding a tent.

अवस्त्र *a-vastra, as, ā, am*, without clothes, garmentless, naked. — *Avastra-tā*, f. nakedness.

अवस्था *ava-sthā*, cl. 1. A. *-tishṭhate, -sthātum*, to take one's stand, remain standing; to stay, abide, stop, stand apart, stand by or near; Ved. to place: Caus. *-sthāpayati* or *-te, -yitum*, to cause to stand or stop, to place, fix, settle, set, array.

Ava-stha, as, m. membrum virile, see *upa-stha*; (*ā*), f. appearance (in a court of justice); stability, consistence; state, condition, situation, circumstance of age or position; degree, proportion; the female organ of generation. — *Avasthā-ćatushṭaya, am*, n. the four periods or states of human life, viz. childhood, youth, manhood, and old age. — *Avasthā-traya, am*, n. the three states, or waking, dreaming, and sound sleep. — *Avasthā-dvaya, am*, n. the two states of life, viz. happiness and misery.

Ava-sthāna, am, n. standing on or placing one's self on (anything), residing, abiding, dwelling; residence, abode; place or period of abiding or staying; situation, station.

Ava-sthāpana, am, n. fixing, settling.

Ava-sthāpita, as, ā, am, fixed.

Ava-sthāpya, ind. having fixed, placed, set or put.

Ava-sthāya, ind. having stayed or remained.

Ava-sthāyin, ī, inī, i, staying, residing in; placed.

Ava-sthita, as, ā, am, standing on or in, remaining, staying, abiding, residing, lasting, remaining firm or fixed, &c.; firm of purpose, steady; engaged in, prosecuting, following. — *Avasthita-mati, is, is, i*, of fixed mind.

Ava-sthiti, is, f. abiding; residence; following, practising.

अवस्पृ *ava-spṛi*, cl. 5. P., Ved. *-spṛiṇoti, -spartum*, to defend, preserve from.

Ava-spartṛi, tā, m., Ved. a preserver, saviour.

अवस्य *avasya* (fr. 1. *avas*), nom. P. *avasyati*, Ved. to seek favour or assistance.

Avasyu, us, us, u, Ved. desiring favour or assistance.

अवस्रंसन *ava-sraṅsana, am*, n. falling off or down.

अवस्वन् *ava-svan*, cl. 1. P. *-svanati, -nitum*, to sound, to smack (the lips) or otherwise make a noise in eating. See *ava-shvan*.

Ava-svanya, as, ā, am, Ved. roaring, boisterous.

अवहन् *ava-han*, cl. 2. P. *-hanti, -tum*, to strike, hit, beat off.

Ava-hata, as, ā, am, beaten, bruised; threshed, winnowed.

Ava-hanana, am, n. threshing, pounding of rice, winnowing; the lungs.

अवहस् *ava-has*, cl. 1. P. *-hasati, -situm*, to smile at, laugh at, deride.

Ava-hāsa, as, m. jest, joke.

Ava-hāsya, as, ā, am, to be derided, exposed to jest, ridiculous.

अवहस्त *ava-hasta, as*, m. the back of the hand.

अवहा *ava-hā*, Pass. *-hīyate*, to be left remaining.

अवहालिका *avahālikā*, f. (rt. *hal*), a wall, a bound hedge.

अवहित *ava-hita*. See under *ava-dhā*.

अवहित्था *a-vahi-tthā*, f., *am*, n. (corrupted fr. *a-vahiḥ-sthā*), dissimulation.

अवहृ *ava-hṛi*, cl. 1. P. *-harati, -hartum*, to lay aside, throw away, take away; Ved. to throw or knock down (?).

Ava-haraṇa, am, n. throwing away; taking away; stealing, plundering; taking back, redeeming; fining, mulcting.

Ava-hāra, as, m. truce, suspension of arms, cessation of gambling, fighting, &c.; a thief; a shark; a water elephant; summoning, inviting; any object fit or able to be brought near; apostacy, abandoning a sect or cast; re-delivery.

Ava-hāraka, as, ikā, am, one who stops fighting, &c.; (*as*), m. a shark, a marine monster.

Ava-hārya, as, ā, am, to be made to restore or compensate; finable, punishable; recoverable, redeemable; (anything) which one is compelled to restore.

Ava-hṛita, as, ā, am, taken off, back, or away; seized; stolen; fined.

अवहेल *ava-hela, am, ā,* n. f. or *ava-helana, am,* n. (fr. rt. *hel* for *heḍ* with *ava*), disrespect.

Ava-helita, as, ā, am, disrespected; (*am*), n. disrespect.

अवह्वर *ava-hvara, as,* m. (rt. *hvṛi*), a crooked way; trick; deceit.

अवाकिन् *a-vākin, ī, inī, i* (rt. *vać*), not speaking.

1. *a-vākka, as, ā, am,* Ved. speechless.

1. *a-vāć, k, k, k,* speechless, dumb. — *Avāk-śruti, is, is, i,* deaf and dumb.

1. *a-vāćya, as, ā, am,* not to be addressed; improper to be uttered; vile, bad; not distinctly expressed. — *Avāćya-tā,* f. or *avāćya-tva, am,* n. impropriety; reproach, calumny. — *Avāćya-deśa, as,* m. unmentionable region, the vulva.

अवाकृ *avā-kṛi* (*ava-ā-kṛi*), cl. 8. 5. P. *-karoti, -kriṇoti, -kartum,* to remove.

अवाकॄ *avā-kṝi* (*ava-ā-kṝi*), cl. 6. P. *-kirati, -karitum, -rītum,* to strew, pour upon.

Avā-kara, as, m. a mint (?).

अवाक्ष *avāksha, as, ī, am* (fr. 2. *aksha* for *akshi* with *ava*), who or what looks down upon or defends, a guardian, a keeper.

अवाग्र *avāgra* (*ava-ag°*), *as, ā, am,* having a bent top; stooping, bending, bowed.

अवाच् 2. *avāć, ān, āćī, āk* (fr. 2. *ava* and *ańć*), turned downwards, being or situated below, lower than (with abl.); looking downwards, headlong; south; (*ī*), f. the south quarter, the lower regions [with *avāć* has been compared the Lat. *au-ster* for *ava-ster*].

Avāk, ind. downwards; south, southward, southern. — *Avāk-pushpī,* f., N. of the plant Anethum Sowa Roxb. — *Avāk-śākha, as, ā, am,* having the branches turned downwards; epithet of the Ficus Religiosa. — *Avāk-śiras, ās, ās, as,* having the head downwards, headlong. — *Avāg-bhāga, as,* m. the part below. — *Avāṅ-mukha, as, ī, am,* looking down or away, having the face turned downwards, headlong; (*as*), m., N. of a weapon. — *Avāṅ-jñāna, am,* n. disrespect.

2. *avākka, as, ā, am,* Ved. a word formed for the etymology of *avakā.*

Avāćīna, as, ā, am, down-looked, headlong; south, southern; descended, gone down; (*as*), m., N. of a king.

2. *avāćya, as, ā, am,* southern, southerly.

अवाचि *avā-ći* (*ava-ā-ći*), cl. 5. P. A. *-ćinoti, -nute, -ćetum,* to heap up, accumulate, gather.

अवाच्छिद् *avā-ććhid* (*ava-ā-ćhid*), cl. 7. P. A. *-ććhinatti, -ććhinte, -ććhettum,* to tear or snatch away.

Avā-ććhidya, ind. having snatched away.

अवाज् *avāj* (*ava-aj*), cl. 1. P. *avājati, -jitum,* to drive down, to throw down.

अवाजिन् *a-vājin, ī,* m., Ved. a bad horse.

अवात् *avāt* (*ava-at*), cl. 1. P., Ved. *avātati, -titum,* to go down; (formed for the etym. of *avata,* q. v.)

Avātita (*ava-at°*), *as, ā, am,* gone down.

अवात 1. *a-vāta, as, ā, am,* Ved. windless, not moved by wind, calm.

अवात 2. *a-vāta, as, ā, am* (rt. *van,* whence the part. pass. *vāta*), Ved. unattacked, untroubled, untouched; unconquered.

अवातुल *a-vātula, as, ā, am,* not flatulent.

अवाद् *avād* (*ava-ad*), cl. 2. P., Ved. *avātti, -ttum,* to cause to eat food.

अवादिन् *a-vādin, ī, inī, i,* no speaker, no disputer, one who does not prosecute or bring an action, peaceable.

अवान् *avān* (*ava-an*), cl. 2. P. *avāniti, -nitum,* to breathe or inhale.

1. *avāna, as,* m. breathing, inhaling.

अवान 2. *a-vāna, as, ā, am* (for *an-avāna*?), dried, dry. See *vāna.*

अवान्तर *avāntara* (*ava-an°*), *as, ā, am,* situated between; included, involved. — *Avāntara-diś, k,* or *avāntara-diśā,* f. an intermediate region of the compass. — *Avāntara-deśa, as,* m. a place situated in an intermediate region.

Avāntarām, ind., Ved. between.

अवाप् *avāp* (*ava-āp*), cl. 5. P. A. *-āpnoti, -nute, -āptum,* to reach, enter; to receive; to attain, obtain, gain; to get, suffer.

Avāpta, as, ā, am, reached, received, obtained, got. — *Avāpta-vat, ān, atī, at,* reaching, obtaining, receiving, taking; entertaining (as a belief).

Avāptavya, as, ā, am, to be obtained or gained.

Avāpti, is, f. obtaining, getting, receiving.

1. *avāpya,* ind. having obtained.

2. *avāpya, as, ā, am,* to be obtained or gained; unattainable, unobtainable (?).

अवापित *a-vāpita, as, ā, am* (rt. *vap*), not sown (as grain) but planted.

अवापोह् *avāpoh* (*ava-apa-ūh*), cl. 1. P. A. *avāpohati, -te, -hitum,* to remove.

अवाय *avāya, as, ā, am* (fr. rt. *i* with *ava*), giving way, yielding, complying.

अवार *avāra, as, am,* m. n. (fr. 2. *ava* or 2. *avas,* as *pāra* fr. *para* or *paras,* q. v.), this side, the near bank of a river. — *Avāra-tas,* ind., Ved. to this side. — *Avāra-pāra, as,* m. the ocean. — *Avāra-pārīṇa, as, ā, am,* belonging to the ocean; crossing a river.

Avārīṇa, as, ā, am, crossing a river.

1. *avārya, as, ā, am,* being on the near side of a river.

अवारण *a-vāraṇa, as, ā, am* (rt. *vṛi*), incurable, not to be remedied.

1. *avāraṇīya, as, ā, am,* treating of incurable sicknesses.

2. *a-vāraṇīya, as, ā, am,* not to be warded off.

Avārikā, f., N. of the plant Coriandrum Sativum.

A-vārita, as, ā, am, unimpeded, unobstructed; innumerable. — *Avārita-dvāra, as, ā, am,* having open doors.

A-vāritavya, as, ā, am, not to be impeded or hindered, not to be kept off.

2. *a-vārya, as, ā, am,* unrestrainable, irresistible; not to be warded off; incurable. — *A-vārya-kratu, us, us, u,* Ved. of irresistible courage. — *Avārya-tā,* f. incurableness.

अवार्छ् *avārćh* (*ava-ṛićh*), cl. 6. P., Ved. *avārććhati, -ććhitum,* to unharness, to fall down.

अवार्ज् *avārj* (*ava-arj*), cl. 1. P., Ved. *avārjati, -jitum,* to dismiss.

अवालोच् *avā-loć* (*ava-ā-loć*), cl. 1. A. *-loćate, -ćitum,* to consider.

अवावट *avāvaṭa, as,* m. the son of a woman by any other man than her first husband.

अवावन् *avāvan, ā,* m. (fr. rt. *ṛn*), a thief.

अवाश्य *a-vāśya, as, ā, am* (rt. *vaś*), undesirable.

अवास् *avās* (*ava-as*), cl. 4. P. *avāsyati, -situm,* to throw down.

अवासस् *a-vāsas, ās, ās, as,* unclothed, naked.

अवास्तव *a-vāstava* or *a-vāstavika, as, ī, am,* unsubstantial, unreal; fictitious; unfounded, irrational (as an argument).

अवास्तु *a-vāstu, us, us, u,* Ved. having no dwelling, homeless.

अवाहन *a-vāhana, as, ā, am,* Ved. having no team or carriage, not driving in a carriage.

अवि *avi, is, is, i* (fr. rt. *av*), Ved. favourable, attached to, kindly disposed; (*is*), m. f. a sheep; the woollen Soma strainer; (*is*), m. a master; the sun; air, wind; a mountain; a wall or enclosure; a cover made of the skin of mice; a rat; a blanket; the shawl goat; (*is*), f. an ewe; a woman in her courses [cf. Lith. *awi-s;* Slav. *ovjza;* Lat. *ovi-s;* Gr. ὄϊς; Goth. *avistr*]. — *Avi-kaṭorana, as,* m. a kind of tribute (perhaps consisting of sheep). — *Avi-gandhikā,* f., N. of a plant = *Aja-gandhā.* — *Avi-dugdha* or *avi-dūsa* or *avi-marīsa* or *avi-sodha, am,* n. the milk of an ewe. — *Avi-paṭa, as,* m. sheep's skin, woollen cloth. — *Avi-pāla, as,* m. a shepherd. — *Avi-priya, as,* m. 'liked by sheep,' N. of the grass Oplismenus Frumentaceus; (*ā*), f., N. of another plant. — *Avi-mat, ān, atī, at,* Ved. possessing sheep. — *Avi-sthala, am,* n. 'sheep-place,' N. of a town.

Avika, as, m. a sheep; (*ā*), f. an ewe; (*am*), n. a diamond.

Avikaṭa, as, m. a flock of sheep.

Avitā, f. an ewe, a sheep.

Avithya. See below, s. v.

अविकच *a-vikaća, as, ā, am,* closed, shut (as a flower).

A-vikaćita, as, ā, am, unblown.

अविकथ *a-vikatha, as, ā, am,* not boasting, not talking vainly or idly.

A-vikathana, as, ā, am, one who does not boast; (*am*), n. not boasting.

अविकर्ष *a-vikarsha, as,* m. absence of separation.

A-vikrishṭa, as, ā, am, not drawn apart, not separated.

अविकल *a-vikala, as, ā, am,* unimpaired, perfect, entire; regular, orderly, consistent.

अविकल्प *a-vikalpa, as,* m. absence of doubt or alternative, positive act or precept; (*as, ā, am*), unchangeable; (*am*), ind. without any doubt.

अविकार *a-vikāra, as, ā, am,* or *a-vikārya, as, ā, am,* immutable, unchangeable; permanent; (*am*), n. unchangeableness.

A-vikṛita, as, ā, am, unchanged, permanent.

A-vikriya, as, ā, am, showing no alteration or difference, unchangeable, always alike.

अविक्रम *a-vikrama, as, ā, am,* powerless, feeble, without courage; (*as*), m. cowardice.

A-vikrānta, as, ā, am, unsurpassed; feeble, powerless.

अविक्रय *a-vikraya, as,* m. (rt. *krī*), non-sale.

A-vikrīta, as, ā, am, unsold; one who has not sold.

A-vikreya, as, ā, am, unsaleable, not to be sold.

अविक्लम *a-viklama, as,* m. vigour, freshness, absence of fatigue.

A-viklānta, as, ā, am, unwearied, vigorous.

अविक्लव *a-viklava, as, ā, am,* calm, composed, firm.

अविक्षत *a-vikshata, as, ā, am,* undiminished, entire; unhurt.

अविक्षित् *a-vikshit, t,* m., N. of a king.

A-vikshita, as, ā, am, Ved. undiminished, unhurt.

अविक्षिप *a-vikshipa, as,* m. unable to distribute, dispense, &c.; distributing badly; different from one who distributes; one who is no distributer.

A-vikshipta, as, ā, am, not thrown away, retained; attentive, composed.

अविक्षोभ *a-vikshobha, as,* m. (rt. *kshubh*), quiet, quiescence.

A-vikshobhita, as, ā, am, undisturbed, tranquil.

अविखण्डित *a-vikhaṇḍita, as, ā, am,* undisturbed. — *Avikhaṇḍita-manas, ās, ās, as,* imperturbable.

अविगत *a-vigata, as, ā, am,* unseparated, retained, present.

A-vigama, as, ā, am, unseparated, unremoved; (*as*), m. non-separation, association, inherence, presence.

अविगर्हित *a-vigarhita, as, ā, am,* unreproached.

अविगीत *a-vigīta, as, ā, am,* uncensured, unreproached.

अविगुण *a-viguṇa, as, ā, am,* compatible, consistent with, not contrary to.

अविग्न *a-vigna, as,* m., N. of the fruit tree Carissa Carandas L.

अविग्रह *a-vigraha, as, ā, am,* bodiless, incorporeal.

अविघात *a-vighāta, as, ā, am* (rt. *han*), unimpeded, having no obstacle. — *Avighāta-gati, is, is, i,* unimpeded or unobstructed in (its) course.

A-vighna, as, ā, am, uninterrupted, unimpeded; (*am*), n. undisturbedness, want of obstacle; *avighnena,* ind. without obstacle, uninterruptedly.

अविचक्षण *a-vićakshaṇa, as, ā, am,* unlearned, ignorant.

अविचल *a-vićala, as, ā, am,* immoveable.

अविचाचल *a-vićāćala, as, ā, am,* or *a-vićāćalat, at, atī, at,* or *a-vićāćali, is, is, i,* Ved. not staggering or fluctuating, standing firmly.

अविचार *a-vićāra, as, ā, am,* undiscriminating, ill-judging, unwise; unhesitating, prompt; (*as*), m. want of judgment or discrimination, error, folly; promptitude.

A-vićārita, as, ā, am, ill-judged, badly investigated, unconsidered; determined, certain, clear, not requiring deliberation. — *Avićārita-nirṇaya, as,* m. prejudice.

A-vićārin, ī, iṇī, i, nothinking, inconsiderate.

A-vićārya, ind. without considering, inconsiderately, unreflectingly.

अविचालित *a-vićālita, as, ā, am,* unmoved; unshaken; victorious.

अविचृत्य *a-vićṛitya, as, ā, am,* Ved. not to be loosened.

अविचेतन *a-vićetana, as, ā, am,* Ved. unintelligible.

अविच्छिन्न *a-viććhinna, as, ā, am,* unseparated, undivided, uninterrupted. — *A-viććhinna-pātam,* ind. fallen on one's knees.

A-viććheda, as, ā, am, uninterrupted; undivided, entire, whole; (*as*), m. the not being separated, entireness; connection, continuity. — *Aviććhedena,* ind. uninterruptedly.

अविच्युत *a-vićyuta, as, ā, am,* not deviated from, observed, followed; eternal, permanent.

अविजात *a-vijāta, as, ā, am* (rt. *jan*), Ved. not having brought forth, not having offspring.

A-vijātīya, as, ā, am, of the same species.

अविजानत् *a-vijānat, an, atī, at* (rt. *jñā*), Ved. not understanding.

A-vijña, as, ā, am, ignorant, untaught; clumsy, stupid. — *Avijña-tā,* f. or *avijña-tva, am,* n. ignorance, folly.

A-vijñāta, as, ā, am, unknown; undistinguished, unintelligible, indistinct, doubtful. — *Avijñāta-gati, is,* m., N. of a son of Anila and Śivā. — *Avijñāta-gada, as, ā, am,* Ved. speaking in an unintelligible manner.

A-vijñāya, ind. not having understood, without distinguishing.

A-vijñeya, as, ā, am, undistinguishable, undiscernible, unintelligible, not to be recognized or known.

अविजित्य *a-vijitya,* ind. not having conquered.

अविडीन *a-viḍīna, am,* n. a direct flight.

अवित *avita, as, ā, am* (rt. *av*), preserved, protected.

Avitṛi, tā, trī, m. f., Ved. a favourer, patron, protector.

अवितथ *a-vitatha, as, ā, am,* not untrue, true; not vain, not false or futile; effective; (*am*), n. truth; a species of the Atyashṭi metre; (*am*), ind. not falsely, according to truth.

अवितारिन् *a-vitārin, ī, iṇī, i* (rt. *tṝ*), Ved. not passing away, not departing, remaining.

अवितृप्त *a-vitṛipta, as, ā, am,* unsatisfied. — *Avitṛipta-kāma, as, ā, am,* having the desires unsatisfied.

अवित्त *a-vitta, as, ā, am* (rt. *vid,* to find), not found; unknown, poor.

A-vitti, is, f., Ved. the not finding, the not possessing, poverty.

अवित्यज *a-vityaja, as, am,* m. n. quicksilver.

अविथुर *a-vithura, as, ā, am,* Ved. not staggering; not fragile.

अविथ्य *avithya, as, ā, am* (fr. *avi*), fit or suited to a sheep.

अविदग्ध *a-vidagdha, as, ā, am* (rt. *dah*), unlearned, inexperienced, stupid; undigested.

A-vidāhin, ī, inī, i, imperfectly digested, producing heartburn.

अविदस्य *a-vidasya, as, ā, am* (rt. *das*), Ved. not ceasing, inexhaustible.

A-vidāsin, ī, inī, i, perennial, perpetual.

अविदित *a-vidita, as, ā, am,* unknown.

A-viditvā, ind. not knowing, without having ascertained.

अविदीधयु *a-vidīdhayu, us, us, u* (rt. *dhī*), Ved. not deliberating, not delaying; shining, resplendent.

अविदूर *a-vidūra, as, ā, am,* not very distant, near, contiguous; (*am*), n. proximity; (*am*), ind. near to. — *Avidūrāt* or *avidūra-tas* or *avidūre,* ind. near, not far off (with abl.).

अविद्ध *a-viddha, as, ā, am,* unpierced. — *Aviddha-karṇā* or *aviddha-karṇī* (also *viddha-karṇī*), f., N. of the plant Cissampelos Hexandra. — *Aviddha-dṛiś, k, k, k,* all-seeing. — *Aviddha-varćas, ās, ās, as,* of unimpaired glory.

अविद्य *a-vidya, as, ā, am* (rt. 1. *vid,* to know), unlearned, unwise, foolish; not relating to knowledge; (*ā*), f. ignorance, spiritual ignorance, illusion, personified illusion or Māyā; (with Buddhists) ignorance together with non-existence. — *Avidyā-maya, as, ī, am,* caused by ignorance or illusion.

A-vidvas, ān, ushī, as, unwise, unlearned.

अविद्यमान *a-vidyamāna, as, ā, am* (rt. 2. *vid,* to find), not present, absent; non-existent.

अविद्रिय *a-vidriya, as, ā, am* (rt. *dṛī*), Ved. without a rent; impenetrable, solid, dense.

अविद्विष् *a-vidvish, ṭ, ṭ, ṭ* (rt. *dvish*), not hating, not an enemy.

A-vidvesha, as, m., Ved. absence of hatred or hostility.

अविधवा *a-vidhavā,* f. not a widow.

अविधा *avidhā,* ind. an interjection corresponding to the Prākṛit *avihā* or *aviha,* used in calling for help in danger.

अविधान *a-vidhāna, am,* n. (rt. *dhā*), deviation from or absence of fixed rule, irregularity. — *Avidhāna-tas,* ind. irregularly.

A-vidhi, is, is, i, void of or contrary to rule; (*is*), f. irregularity. — *A-vidhi-pūrvaka, as, ā, am,* not according to rule.

अविन *avina, as,* m. (rt. *av*), a sacrificer, one who performs a sacrifice or causes it to be performed; an officiating priest at a sacrifice.

अविनय *a-vinaya, as, ā, am* (rt. *nī*), without proper training, ill-behaved, indecorous; (*as*), m. want of good manners or modesty; bad training; rude behaviour; indecorum, impropriety, fault; incivility, disrespect; offence, crime.

A-vinīta, as, ā, am, badly trained, badly brought up, ill-mannered, misbehaving, acting ill or improperly, wicked, vile; (*ā*), f. an immodest, unchaste, or disloyal woman.

अविनश्वर *a-vinaśvara, as, ī, am,* or *a-vināśya, as, ā, am,* indestructible.

A-vinaśyat, an, antī, at, not perishing.

A-vināśa, as, m. non-destruction, preservation.

A-vināśin, ī, inī, i, indestructible.

अविनाभाव *a-vinābhāva, as,* m. inherent and essential character.

अविनिगम *a-vinigama, as,* m. an illogical conclusion.

अविनिर्मोक *a-vinirmoka, as, ā, am,* without an exception.

अविनिवर्तिन् *a-vinivartin, ī, inī, i,* not turning back, holding on, advancing.

अविन्ध्य *avindhya, as,* m., N. of a minister of Rāvaṇa; (*ā*), f., N. of a river.

अविपक्व *a-vipakva, as, ā, am* (rt. *pać*), not ripe, immature, undigested. — *Avipakva-buddhi, is, is, i,* inexperienced.

A-vipāka, as, m. indigestion; immaturity; not suffering the consequence of actions in a former life; (*as, ā, am*), suffering from indigestion.

अविपक्ष *a-vipaksha, as, ā, am,* having no adversary, unopposed.

अविपद् *a-vipad, t,* f. (rt. *pad*), prosperity, ease.

A-vipanna, as, ā, am, uninjured, unhurt; not soiled or contaminated, pure, clean.

अविपश्चित् *a-vipaśćit, t, t, t,* unwise, ignorant.

अविपुल *a-vipula, as, ā, am,* small, insignificant, slender.

अविप्र *a-vipra, as, ā, am,* Ved. not spiritually excited, not inspired; not a worshipper, not a praiser.

अविप्रकृष्ट *a-viprakṛishṭa, as, ā, am,* not remote, near.

अविप्रिय *avi-priya.* See under *avi.*

अविप्लुत *a-vipluta, as, ā, am,* undeviating, steadily observing; unviolated, observed without deviation.

अविफल *a-viphala, as, ā, am,* fruitful, productive.

अविफुल्ल *a-viphulla, as, ā, am,* unblown.

अविभक्त *a-vibhakta, as, ā, am* (rt. *bhaj*), undivided, unpartitioned; unseparated, joint, not sharing (applied to co-heirs who have not divided their inheritance).

A-vibhāga, as, ā, am, unpartitioned, unportioned; (*as*), m. undivided inheritance.

A-vibhāgin, ī, inī, i, one who does not share; not sharing, not dividing.

A-vibhājya, as, ā, am, not to be divided, not to be partitioned. — *Avibhājya-tā,* f. or *avibhājya-tva, am,* n. indivisibility, unfitness for partition.

अविभावना *a-vibhāvanā,* f. or *a-vibhāvana, am,* n. (rt. *bhū*), non-perception, non-discrimination, imperceptibility, disappearance.

A-vibhāvanīya, as, ā, am, imperceptible, undistinguishable.

A-vibhāvita, as, ā, am, unperceived, unobserved.

A-vibhārya, as, ā, am, undistinguishable, imperceptible.

अविभ्रान्त *a-vibhrānta, as, ā, am,* uninterrupted.

अविमत्त *a-vimatta, as,* m., N. of a man (?).

अविमल *a-vimala, as, ā, am,* not clear, foul, turbid.

अविमुक्त *a-vimukta, as, ā, am* (rt. *muć*), unloosed, not quitted; (*as*), m., N. of a Tīrtha near Benares. — *Avimuktāpīḍa* (°*ta-āp*°), *as,* m., N. of a king. — *Avimukteśvara* (°*ta-īś*°), *as,* m. a celebrated Śiva-linga at Benares.

A-vimokya, as, ā, am, Ved. not to be loosened.

अवियुक्त *a-viyukta, as, ā, am* (rt. *yuj*), undivided, conjoined; not separated or absent.

A-viyoga, as, m. conjunction, association; the not being parted or absent, presence. — *Aviyoga-tṛitīyā,* f., N. of a certain festival or holiday. — *Aviyogatṛitīyā-vrata,* N. of the sixteenth Adhyāya of the Bhavishyottara-Purāṇa.

अविरक्त *a-virakta, as, ā, am,* not indifferent or estranged; attached to, interested in.

अविरण *a-viraṇa, as,* m., Ved. continuation.

अविरत *a-virata, as, ā, am* (rt. *ram*), not desisting from (with abl.); uninterrupted, continual, eternal; abandoned; (*am*), ind. eternally, continually.

A-virati, is, f. incontinence, intemperance.

A-virāma, as, ā, am, uninterrupted, continuous; (*as*), m. uninterrupted succession, continuance; (*am*), ind. uninterruptedly.

अविरल *a-virala, as, ā, am,* contiguous, close; coarse, gross, substantial; uninterrupted; (*am*), ind. contiguously, closely. — *Avirala-dhārāsāra, as,* m. incessant down-pour of heavy rain.

अविरहित *a-virahita, as, ā, am,* not separated from, abounding in.

अविराधयत् *a-virādhayat, an, antī, at,* Ved. not withdrawing one's self, not avoiding; not desisting.

अविरुद्ध *a-viruddha, as, ā, am* (rt. *rudh*), unobstructed, unimpeded; allowed, permitted, proper; compatible, consistent with.

A-virodha, as, m. absence of impediment; assent, concurrence, non-opposition; consistency, compatibility.

A-virodhita, as, ā, am, unimpeded, unobstructed.

अविरेचन *a-virećana, am,* n. anything which constipates or stops the passage of the food.

A-virećya, as, ā, am, not to be purged.

अविलक्षित *a-vilakshita, as, ā, am,* concealed, veiled.

अविलङ्घन *a-vilanghana, am,* n. non-transgression, not exceeding, not trespassing.

A-vilanghanīya, as, ā, am, not to be exceeded or transgressed; prescribed, fixed.

अविलम्ब *a-vilamba* or *a-vilambana, as, ā, am,* not delaying, prompt, quick, expeditious; (*bas*), m. non-delay. — *A-vilambam* or *a-vilambena,* ind. without delay, quickly.

A-vilambita, as, ā, am, not delaying, not slow, quick, expeditious; (*am*), ind. going quickly, a swift pace.

अविला *avilā,* f. an ewe. See under *avi.*

अविलास *a-vilāsa, as, ā, am,* free from caprice, faithful, constant.

अविलिख *a-vilikha, as,* m. unable to write or paint, writing or painting badly; different from one who writes or paints; one who is not a writer or painter.

अविलुप्त *a-vilupta, as, ā, am,* uninterrupted.

अविवक्षित *a-vivakshita, as, ā, am* (rt. *vać*), not intended to be said, unasserted, undeclared.

A-vivākya, as, ā, am, not admitting censure or correction; N. of the tenth day of a certain Soma sacrifice.

अविवाद *a-vivāda, as,* m. non-disagreement, concurrence, consent.

A-vivādin, ī, inī, i, uncontentious, quiet, peaceable.

अविवाहित *a-vivāhita, as, ā, am* (rt. *vah*), unmarried.

A-vivāhin, ī, inī, i, not marrying, single; not relating to marriage; interdicted as to marriage.

अविविक्त *a-vivikta, as, ā, am* (rt. *vić*), undiscriminated, uninvestigated; indiscriminate, confounded; common, public. — *A-vivikta-dṛiś, k, k, k,* viewing all as one with God.

A-viveka, as, ā, am, without judgment or discrimination; (*as*), m. absence of discrimination or judgment, ignorance. — *Aviveka-kṛita, as, ā, am,* done thoughtlessly. — *Aviveka-tā,* f. or *aviveka-tva, am,* n. want of judgment, inconsiderateness, imprudence.

A-vivekin, ī, inī, i, or *a-vivećaka, as, ikā, am,* undiscriminating, ignorant, having no judgment, superficial, short-sighted.

A-vivećanā, f. want of judgment or discrimination.

अविवेन *a-vivena, as, ā, am,* Ved. not disaffected; (*am*), ind., Ved. not disaffectedly, favourably.

अविशङ्क *a-viśanka, as, ā, am* (rt. *śank*), having no fears or doubts, fearless; (*ā*), f. unapprehensiveness, confidence, certainty. — *A-viśankena,* ind. undoubtingly, without hesitation.

A-viśankita, as, ā, am, unapprehensive, confiding, trusting.

अविशस्तृ *a-viśastṛi, tā,* m., Ved. an unskilful cutter up or killer (of animals at a sacrifice).

अविशुद्ध *a-viśuddha, as, ā, am,* pure, clear, free from fault or defect; valid, perfect, unimpeached.

अविशेष *a-viśesha, as, ā, am,* uniform, alike, without any difference; (*am*), n. equability, uniformity. — *A-viśesha-jña, as, ā, am,* not perceiving the difference in things, undiscriminating.

अविश्रान्त *a-viśrānta, as, ā, am,* unwearied.

अविश्वमिन्व *a-viśvam-inva, as, ā, am,* Ved. not all-embracing, not pervading everything.

अविश्वविन्न *a-viśva-vinna, as, ā, am,* Ved. not perceived everywhere.

अविश्वास *a-viśvāsa, as, ā, am* (rt. *śvas*), not causing confidence, mistrusted; (*as*), m. mistrust, suspicion; (*ā*), f. a cow calving after long intervals.

A-viśvasta, as, ā, am, not trusted, suspected, doubted.

A-viśvāsin, ī, inī, i, mistrustful, unbelieving.

अविष *a-visha, as, ā, am,* not poisonous, anti-venomous, antidote; (*as*), m. the ocean; sky; (*ā*), f., N. of the plant Curcuma Zedoaria; (*ī*), f. a river; the earth; heaven.

अविषक्त *a-vishakta, as, ā, am,* unimpeded, unrestrained, unchecked.

अविषय *a-vishaya, as, ā, am,* unperceived, invisible; insensible; disregarding objects of sense; (*as*), m. disappearance; absence; disregard of objects of sense. — *A-vishayī-karaṇa, am,* n. the not making anything an object.

अविषाद *a-vishāda, as, ā, am,* not dejected, unwearied, persevering; (*as*), m. cheerfulness.

अविष्ठ *avishṭha, as, ā, am* (superl. of rt. *av*), Ved. gladly accepting; very attentive.

अविष्या *avishyā,* f. (fr. *avi*), Ved. wish, desire, ardour; wish to go.

Avishyu, us, us, u, Ved. assailing; desirous, vehement, violent; wishing to eat; wishing to protect.

अविस् *avis, is,* m. an extender, enlarger (?).

अविसंवादिन् *a-visaṃvādin, ī, inī, i,* not contradictory.

अविसर्गिन् *a-visargin, ī, iṇī, i,* not quitting, retaining, adhering to; (*ī*), m. an unintermittent fever.

अविसोढ *avi-soḍha.* See under *avi.*

अविस्तर *a-vistara, as, ā, am* (rt. *stṛī*), of small extent or circuit.

A-vistāra, as, m. absence of amplification.

A-vistīrṇa, as, ā, am, not extended, not amplified, contracted.

A-vistṛita, as, ā, am, compact, compressed, close.

अविस्पष्ट *a-vispashṭa, as, ā, am,* not clear or plain, indistinct, obscure; (*am*), n. indistinct speech.

अविस्मरण *a-vismaraṇa, am,* n. or *a-vismṛiti, is,* f. not forgetting, remembering, recollection.

अविहत *a-vihata, as, ā, am,* unobstructed, unimpeded. — *Avihata-gati, is, is, i,* one whose course is unobstructed.

अविहर्यतक्रतु *a-viharyata-kratu, us, us, u,* Ved. whose will cannot be averted; (Sāy.) doer of acts undesired (by his foes).

अविहित *a-vihita, as, ā, am,* undone, uneffected; unprescribed, not directed or ruled.

अविहृत *a-vihruta, as, ā, am* (rt. *hvṛi*), Ved. unbent, unbroken; not curved.

A-vihvarat, an, antī, at, Ved. not slipping, not falling; undeviating.

अविह्वल *a-vihvala, as, ā, am,* unagitated, composed, calm.

अवी 1. *avī,* wrong reading for *ambya,* q. v.

अवी 2. *a-vī, īs,* f. (fr. rt. *vī* with *a*), a woman in her courses.

अवीक्षण *a-vīkshaṇa, am,* n. (rt. *īksh*), not looking at, not regarding.

A-vikshita, as, ā, am, unseen, unbeheld.

अवीचि *a-vīći, is, is, i*, waveless; (*is*), m. a particular hell.—*Avīći-maya, as*, m. a hell, the place of punishment for liars.

अवीज *a-vīja, as, ā, am*, seedless, impotent; (*am*), n. bad seed, bad grain; absence of seed.

A-vījaka, as, ā, am, seedless; unsown.

अवीर *a-vīra, as, ā, am*, unmanly, effeminate, weak; helpless; having no sons; destitute of men; (*ā*), f. a woman who has neither husband nor son.—*Avīra-tā*, f., Ved. want of sons.—*A-vīra-han, ā, ghnī, a*, Ved. not killing men, not pernicious to men.

A-vīrya, as, ā, am, Ved. weak, ineffective.

अवृक *a-vṛika, as, ā, am*, Ved. not hurting, inoffensive, true; unendangered, safe; free from one who obscures; (*am*), n. safety, peace; quiet.

अवृक्ष *a-vṛiksha* or *a-vṛikshaka, as, ā, am*, treeless; destitute of trees.

अवृजिन *a-vṛijina, as, ā, am*, Ved. not intriguing, straightforward, sincere, not deserting (friends), an epithet of the Ādityas.

अवृत *a-vṛita, as, ā, am*, Ved. unchecked, unimpeded; unsubdued; unselected; uncovered, unprotected.

अवृत्ति *a-vṛitti, is*, f. inadequate support, absence of subsistence or allowance; want; (*is, is, i*), not existing, not present.—*Avṛitti-tva, am*, n. non-existence.

अवृथा *a-vṛithā*, ind. not in vain, successfully, profitably.—*Avṛithārtha* (°*thā-ar*°), *as, ā, am*, successful, gaining one's object.

अवृद्धिक *a-vṛiddhika, as, ī, am* (rt. *vṛidh*), not augmentative; not bearing interest.

A-vṛidha, as, ā, am, Ved. not promoting, not honouring.

अवृष्टि *a-vṛishṭi, is*, f. want of rain, drought; famine.

अवृह *a-vṛiha* or *a-bṛiha, ās*, m. pl. (rt. *vṛih*), a class of Buddhist divinities.

A-vṛihita, as, ā, am, few, not much or large.

अवे *ave* (*ava-i*), cl. 2. P. *avaiti, -tum*, to go away, to move away; to go to (with acc.); to come down upon, rush upon; to look upon, consider; perceive, conceive, understand, learn, know: Intens. or Pass. *aveyate*, to beg pardon for, conciliate.

Aveta, as, ā, am, elapsed, past; one who has gained, obtained, attained; joined with.

अवेक्ष् *aveksh* (*ava-īksh*), cl. 1. A. *avekshate, -shitum*, to look towards, look at, consider; to perceive, observe, experience; to have in view, aim at; to have regard to, respect; to expect, hope for: Caus. *avekshayati, -yitum*, to cause to look at.

Avekshaṇa, am, n. looking towards or at; the act of considering, attention, observation.

Avekshaṇīya, as, ā, am, to be looked at, to be respected.

Avekshamāṇa, as, ā, am, looking at, inspecting, examining.

Avekshā, f. seeing, looking at; observation, care, regard, attention to (with loc.); agreement, engagement.

Avekshita, as, ā, am, looked at, perceived, regarded.

Avekshin, ī, iṇī, i, observing, seeing, looking at.

1. *avekshya, as, ā, am*, to be regarded, to be respected.

2. *avekshya*, ind. having beheld, having regarded.

अवेणि *a-veṇi, is, is, i*, not braided, having no braid of hair; not commingled (as the waters of rivers).

अवेदयान *a-vedayāna, as, ā, am* (rt. 1. *vid*), not knowing, not ascertaining.

A-veda-vid, t, m. a Brāhman who has not studied the Vedas.

A-veda-vihita, as, ā, am, not enjoined in the Vedas, unscriptural.

1. *a-vedya, as, ā, am*, not to be known; unascertainable, secret.

अवेद्य 2. *a-vedya, as, ā, am* (rt. 2. *vid*), not to be married; (*as*), m. a calf.

अवेनत् *a-venat, an, antī, at*, Ved. unconscious, not perceiving.

अवेन्व् *avenv* (*ava-inv*), cl. 1. P., Ved. *avenvati, -vitum*, to send away.

अवेल *avela* (*ava-ilā?*), *as*, m. denial or concealment of knowledge; (*ā*), f. chewed betel.

अवेष्टि *aveshṭi, is*, f. (fr. rt. *yaj* with *ava*), Ved. appeasing or expiation by sacrifices.

अवैदिक *a-vaidika, as, ī, am*, not Vedic, not belonging to the Veda.

अवैध *a-vaidha, as, ī, am*, irregular, heterodox, contrary or not conformable to rule.

अवैधव्य *a-vaidhavya, as, ā, am*, free from widowhood.

अवैरहत्य *a-vairahatya, am*, n., Ved. the non-destruction of men, security from slaughter.

अवोक्षण *avokshaṇa, am*, n. (fr. rt. *uksh* with *ava*), Ved. besprinkling, bedewing.

अवोद *avoda, as*, m. (fr. rt. *ud* with *ava*), dripping down, sprinkling, moistening; (*as, ā, am*), wet, moist.

अवोदेव *avo-deva, as, ā, am* (fr. 2. *avas*, q. v.), Ved. bringing down the gods.

अवोह् *avoh* (*ava-ūh*), cl. 1. P. A. *avohati, -te, -hitum*, to push down.

अव्द *avda, as*, m. (= *abda*), a cloud; a year.

अव्य *avya, as, ā, am* (fr. *avi*), Ved. coming from or belonging to sheep.

अव्यक्त *a-vyakta, as, ā, am* (rt. *añj*), unapparent, indistinct, not manifest, not to be discerned, invisible, imperceptible, unperceived, undetermined; (in algebra) unknown as quantity or number; (*as*), m. a fool; primary matter which has not yet entered into real existence; N. of Vishṇu; of Śiva; of Kāma or Kandarpa; (*am*), n. the supreme being or universal spirit; (in Sāṅkhya phil.) 'the undiscrete,' the primary germ of nature, the primordial element or productive principle whence all the phenomena of the material world are developed; the soul; nature, temperament; (*am*), ind. imperceptibly, indistinctly, secretly.—*Avyakta-kriyā*, f. algebraic calculation; any act of an indistinct character or aim.—*Avyakta-gati, is, is, i*, going imperceptibly.—*Avyakta-pada, as, ā, am*, inarticulate.—*Avyakta-mūrti, is, is, i*, whose form is incomprehensible.—*Avyakta-rāga, as*, m. dark-red, the colour of the dawn.—*Avyakta-rāśi, is*, f. an unknown number or indistinct quantity (in algebra).—*Avyakta-lakshaṇa* or *avyakta-vyakta, as*, m. epithet of Śiva, whose qualities are not perceptible.—*Avyakta-vartman, ā, ā, a*, or *avyakta-mārga, as, ā, am*, mysterious in his ways.—*Avyakta-vāć, k, k, k*, speaking indistinctly.—*Avyakta-sāmya, am*, n. equation of unknown quantities.—*Avyaktādi* (°*ta-ādi*), *is, is, i*, whose beginning is inscrutable.—*A-vyaktānukaraṇa* (°*ta-an*°), *am*, n. the imitating of unarticulated or unmeaning sound.

A-vyañjana, as, ā, am, indistinct; plain, not figurative; (*as*), m. an animal without horns, though of an age to have them.

अव्यग्र *a-vyagra, as, ā, am*, steady, cool, deliberate; indifferent, undisturbed; attentive.

अव्यङ्ग *a-vyanga, as, ā, am*, not mutilated, sound, perfect; not figurative, plain; (*ā*), f., N. of the plant Carpopogon Pruriens Roxb. [cf. Zend *aiwyâṅhanem*].—*Avyangānga* (°*ga-anga*), *as, ī, am*, well made, symmetrical, perfect, entire.

अव्यचस् *a-vyaćas, ās, ās, as*, Ved. not spacious.

अव्यण्डा *avyaṇḍā*, f. (for *adhy-aṇḍā?*), N. of the plant Carpopogon Pruriens Roxb.

अव्यति *avyati, is*, f. (fr. rt. *av*), Ved. the act of satiating, satisfaction; desire.

अव्यतिकीर्ण *a-vyatikīrṇa, as, ā, am*, unmixed, unblended, distinct, specific, separate.

अव्यथ *a-vyatha, as, ā, am* (rt. *vyath*), free from pain; not inflicting pain, merciful; (*as*), m. a snake; (*ā*), f., N. of the plant Terminalia Citrina Roxb., and of the plant Hibiscus Mutabilis L.; Ved. firmness, steadiness, absence of tremor.

A-vyathamāna, as, ā, am, Ved. not moving unsteadily, not trembling.

A-vyathi, is, is, i, Ved. not tremulous, not tottering; not unsteady, stepping firmly and safely, sure-footed, undaunted; epithet of the horses of the Aśvins; (*is*), f. a firm step, sure-footedness; undauntedness.—*A-vyathi-dhī, īs*, f. the earth; night.

A-vyathin, ī, inī, i, free from pain, not inflicting pain.

A-vyathisha, as, m. the ocean; the sun; (*ī*), f. the earth; midnight.

A-vyathya, as, ā, am, free from pain, not giving pain, not paining.

अव्यनत् *a-vyanat, an, atī, at* (rt. *an*), Ved. not breathing, lifeless.

अव्यपदेश्य *a-vyapadeśya, as, ā, am*, not to be defined.

अव्यभिचार *a-vyabhićāra, as*, m. steadiness, consistency, constancy.

A-vyabhićārin, ī, iṇī, i, not going astray, constant; virtuous, moral; steady, steadfast, permanent, faithful.

अव्यय 1. *avyaya, as, ī, am* (fr. *avi*, q. v.), Ved. coming from sheep, made of sheep's skin.

अव्यय 2. *a-vyaya, as, ā, am* (rt. *i* with *a* and *vi*), not liable to change, imperishable, undecaying, immutable, eternal; unexpended, unwasted; economical, parsimonious; (*as*), m. a N. of Vishṇu or of Śiva; N. of a son of Manu Raivata; (*as, am*), m. n. an indeclinable word, a particle; (*am*), n. (in the Vedānta) a member or corporeal part of an organized body.—*Avyaya-tva, am*, n. imperishableness.—*Avyaya-varga, as*, m. the class of indeclinables.—*Avyayātman* (°*ya-āt*°), *ā, ā, a*, imperishable, eternal; (*ā*), m. soul, spirit.

Avyayī-bhāva, as, m. unchangeable state, imperishableness; an indeclinable compound.

अव्यर्थ *a-vyartha, as, ā, am*, not useless, profitable, fruitful; effectual, efficacious.

अव्यलीक *a-vyalīka, as, ā, am*, not false, true, veracious, not disagreeable.

अव्यवधान *a-vyavadhāna, as, ā, am* (rt. *dhā*), close, contiguous, immediate: not screened, not concealed, open, careless.—*Avyavadhāna-tā*, f. or *avyavadhāna-tva, am*, n. contiguity, carelessness.

A-vyavahita, as, ā, am, adjoining, contiguous.

अव्यवसाय *a-vyavasāya, as*, m. (rt. *so*), negligence, inactivity.—*Avyavasāya-vat, ān, atī, at*, negligent, inactive, remiss.

A-vyavasāyin, ī, inī, i, negligent, inactive, remiss.

अव्यवस्था *a-vyavasthā*, f. (rt. *sthā*), irregularity, deviation from established rule; incorrect legal opinion.

A-vyavasthita, as, ā, am, not conformable to law or practice; unacquainted with the law or custom; ill-regulated; displaced, disordered, not in due order, unmethodical.

अव्यवहार्य *a-vyavahārya, as, ā, am* (rt. *hṛi*), unactionable, not to be discussed in law.

A-vyavahṛita, as, ā, am, not determined or investigated by law; not spoken.

अव्यवाय *a-vyavāya, as*, m. absence of interval, non-separation.

अव्यसन *a-vyasana, as, ā, am*, or *a-vyasanin, ī, inī, i*, free from evil practices, not vicious, moral, correct, steady.

अव्यस्त *a-vyasta, as, ā, am*, undecomposed, simple; not separated, undispersed, collected.

अव्याकुल *a-vyākula, as, ā, am*, not disturbed, composed, calm, firm.

अव्याकृत *a-vyākṛita, as, ā, am*, undecomposed, simple; (*am*), n. elementary substance from which all things were created, considered as one with the substance of Brahma.

अव्याख्या *a-vyākhyā*, f. (rt. *khyā*), want of clearness of explanation, obscurity.

A-vyākhyāta, as, ā, am, unexplained, obscure.

A-vyākhyāna, am, n. non-explanation, absence of explicitness.

A-vyākhyeya, as, ā, am, inexplicable, unintelligible; not requiring to be explained, easy.

अव्याज *a-vyāja, as*, m. absence of fraud, simplicity, honesty.

अव्यापक *a-vyāpaka, as, ā, am* (rt. *āp*), not spread over or pervading the whole, not an invariable concomitant, special, individual, peculiar. — *Avyāpaka-tā*, f. or *avyāpaka-tva, am*, n. non-comprehensiveness or generalization, speciality, individuality.

A-vyāpin, ī, inī, i, not pervading, not comprehensive, not invariably concomitant, special, individual; partial, limited. — *Avyāpi-tā*, f. or *avyāpi-tva, am*, n. non-generalization, speciality.

A-vyāpta, as, ā, am, not pervaded with, peculiar, individual, limited.

A-vyāpti, is, f. inadequate pervasion or extent (of a definition); e. g. 'man is a cooking animal,' which does not extend to savages who eat raw food.

A-vyāpya, as, ā, am, not to be pervaded generally, not extending to the whole circumstances, peculiar; (*a*), ind. not pervading. — *A-vyāpya-vṛitti, is, is, i*, (in logic) a category of limited application, partial inherence, with reference to place and time, as pain, pleasure, love, hatred, virtue, vice, &c.

अव्यापन्न *a-vyāpanna, as, ā, am*, not dead, not quite extinct, just alive.

अव्यापार *a-vyāpāra, as*, m. vacation from work, state of being unemployed; a business not practised or understood, not one's own business.

अव्यायाम *a-vyāyāma, as*, m. (rt. *yam*), non-exertion, absence of lassitude or of fatigue from exertion.

A-vyāyata, as, ā, am, not occupied, not detached, holding firm (?).

अव्यावर्तन *a-vyāvartana, am*, n. not returning, not coming back, not circulating.

अव्याहत *a-vyāhata, as, ā, am*, unresisted, unimpeded; not disappointed.

अव्याहारिन् *a-vyāhārin, ī, iṇī, i*, not uttering (?).

अव्याहित *a-vyāhita, as, ā, am*, undisputed.

अव्युच्छिन्न *a-vy-ućchinna, as, ā, am*, not interrupted.

अव्युत्पन्न *a-vyutpanna, as, ā, am*, not accomplished, not proficient, inexperienced.

अव्युष्ट *a-vyushṭa, as, ā, am*, Ved. not yet shining (as the dawn).

अव्यृद्धि *a-vyṛiddhi, is*, f., Ved. not failing.

अव्येष्यत् *a-vyeshyat, an, atī* or *antī, at* (rt. *i*), Ved. not disappearing, not vanishing.

अव्रण *a-vraṇa, as, ā, am*, without rents or scars, without splinters; unhurt, unscarred, sound; *avraṇam śukram*, a peculiar disease of the eyes.

अव्रत *a-vrata* or *a-vratika, as, ā, am*, lawless, disobedient, wicked; not observing religious rites or obligations, uninitiated.

Avratya, am, n., Ved. offence against the rule of an ascetic, violation of a religious obligation.

A-vrātya, as, m., Ved. one who is not a Vrātya.

अव्राजिन् *a-vrājin, ī, inī, i*, not wandering or travelling as a mendicant (?).

अश् 1. *aś*, cl. 5. P. A. (in classical Sanskrit A. only), *aśnoti, -nute, āśa, ānanśa, ānaśe, aśishyate* or *akshyate, āśishṭa* and *ashṭa, aśitum*, to reach, come to, arrive at; to get, gain, obtain; to become master of, to master, to be able; to pervade, penetrate, pierce through, fill; to heap, accumulate: Caus. *āśayati, āśiśat*: Desid. *aśiśishate*: Intens. *aśāśyate*.

Aśan, ā, m., Ved. a missile-stone, or stone for slinging, stone, rock; a cloud.

1. *aśana, as, ā, am*, reaching, reaching across.

Aśani, is, m. f. a missile, especially the thunderbolt and flash of lightning; the tip of a missile; N. of a warrior-tribe. — *Aśani-prabha, as*, m., N. of a Rākshasa. — *Aśani-mat, ān, atī, at*, Ved. throwing the thunderbolt, endowed with it.

1. *aśitra, as*, m. a thief.

Aśin, ī, inī, i, reaching far, enduring; Vedic superlative *aśitama* and *aśishṭha*.

अश् 2. *aś*, cl. 9. P. *aśnāti, āśa, aśishyati, āśīt, aśitum*, to eat, consume; to taste, enjoy: Caus. *āśayati, -yitum*, to cause to eat, to give to eat, to feed: Desid. *aśiśishati*, to wish to eat: Intens. *aśāśyate*.

2. *aśana, am*, n. eating, feeding; food (often at the end of compounds, e. g. *mūla-phalāśana, as, ā, am*, having roots and fruit for food). — *Aśana-kṛit, t, t, t*, Ved. preparing food. — *Aśana-pati, is*, m., Ved. lord of food. — *Aśana-vat, ān, atī, at*, Ved. possessed of food.

Aśanāya, nom. P. *-yati, -yitum*, to desire food, to be hungry.

Aśanāyā, f. hunger.

Aśanāyita or *aśanāyuka, as, ā, am*, Ved. hungry.

Aśita, as, ā, am, eaten, satisfied. — *Aśitan-gavīna* or *āśitan-gavīna, as, ā, am*, formerly grazed by cattle.

Aśitavya, as, ā, am, to be eaten.

Aśitṛi, tā, m. eating, an eater.

2. *aśitra, am*, n. an oblation of rice, &c.

Āśita, as, ā, am, fed, satiated, satiate; given to eat; (*am*), n. food.

अशकुन *a-śakuna, am*, n. an inauspicious omen.

अशकुम्भी *aśa-kumbhī*, f., N. of the aquatic plant Pistia Stratiotes Lin.

अशक्त *a-śakta, as, ā, am* (rt. *śak*), unable, incompetent. — *Aśakta-tā*, f. or *aśakta-tva, am*, n. weakness, inability.

A-śakti, is, f. inability, incapability, weakness, impotence.

A-śakya, as, ā, am, impossible, impracticable; not to be done. — *Aśakyārtha* (°*ya-ar*°), *as, ā, am*, unavailing.

अशग *aśaga, as*, m., N. of the author of the Śāntipurāṇa.

अशङ्क *a-śanka, as, ā, am* (rt. *śank*), fearless, undaunted; secure, certain.

A-śankita, as, ā, am, certain, undoubted; fearless.

अशठ *a-śaṭha, as, ā, am*, virtuous, sincere.

अशत्रु *a-śatru, us, us, u*, Ved. one who has no adversary; one whom no enemy defies; without opposition from enemies; (*us*), m. the moon; (*u*), n. condition of having no enemy.

अशन 3. *aśana, as*, m. = *asana*, N. of the tree Terminalia Tomentosa W. and A. — *Aśana-parṇī* or *asana-parṇī*, f., N. of a plant.

अशन, अशनि. See under 1. *aś*, 2. *aś*.

अशपत् *a-śapat, an, antī, at*, Ved. not cursing, not imprecating.

अशम् *a-śam*, ind. (rt. *śam*), Ved. non-welfare, harm, mischief.

A-śama, as, m. disquietude, uneasiness.

A-śānta, as, ā, am, unappeased, indomitable, violent, wild; restless, anxious, unresigned; unconsecrated, not sacred, irreligious, profane. — *Aśānta-tā*, f. want of tranquillity, passionateness.

A-śānti, is, f. restlessness, anxiety. — *Aśānti-kara, as, ī, am*, causing anxiety.

A-śāmya, as, ā, am, unappeasable.

अशरण *a-śaraṇa, as, ā, am*, destitute of refuge, defenceless.

अशरीर *a-śarīra, as, ā, am*, bodiless, incorporeal; (*as*), m. a N. of Kāma, the god of love.

A-śarīrin, ī, iṇī, i, incorporeal.

अशर्मन् *a-śarman, a*, n. unhappiness, pain, affliction; (*ā, ā, a*), unhappy, afflicted.

अशस् *a-śas, as, as, as* (rt. *śas* for *saṇs*), Ved. not blessing, not wishing well, not praising, cursing, hating.

A-śasta, as, ā, am, Ved. inexpressible, ineffable, not esteemed, hated, ill-starred. — *Aśasta-vāra, as, ā, am*, Ved. having indescribable treasures; (Sāy.) who is not asked for wealth, i. e. who grants it of his own accord.

A-śasti, is, f., Ved. not wishing well, imprecation, evil design, curse; a curser, hater. — *Aśasti-han, ā, ghnī, a*, Ved. averting imprecations or curses.

अशस्त्र *a-śastra, as, ā, am* (rt. *śas*, to hurt), weaponless, unarmed.

अशाखा *a-śākhā*, f., N. of a grass.

अशारीरिक *a-śārīrika, as, ī, am*, not relating to or endowed with body, incorporeal.

अशाश्वत *a-śāśvata, as, ī, am*, perishable, transient, temporary.

अशासन *a-śāsana, am*, n. (rt. *śās*), want of government, anarchy, disorder.

A-śāsanīya or *a-śāsya, as, ā, am*, ungovernable.

A-śāsita, as, ā, am, ungoverned, undisciplined.

A-śāstra, as, ā, am, unscriptural, not conformable to sacred authority, heterodox. — *A-śāstra-vihita* or *a-śāstra-siddha, as, ā, am*, not enjoined by the Śāstras.

A-śāstrīya, as, ā, am, unscriptural, heterodox, illegal, immoral, irreligious.

अशिक्षित *a-śikshita, as, ā, am*, untaught.

अशित *aśita, aśitavya*, &c. See under 2. *aś*.

अशित्र *aśitra*. See under 1. *aś*, 2. *aś*.

अशिथिल *a-śithila, as, ā, am*, not loose, firm, tight, hard.

अशिन् *aśin*. See under 1. *aś*.

अशिपद *a-śipada, as, ā, am*, Ved. not causing the sickness called Śipada.

अशिमिद *a-śimida, as, ā, am*, Ved. not destructive like a Śimidā.

अशिमिविद्विष् *aśimi-vidvish, ṭ, ṭ, ṭ,* Ved. epithet of the seven Parjanyas or rain-clouds (perhaps the true reading may be *Śimi-vidvish,* 'hater of the Śimis').

अशिर *aśira, as,* m. (fr. rt. 2. *aś*), fire; a N. of the sun, 'consumer or devourer;' N. of a Rākshasa or goblin; (*ā*), f., N. of the wife of this Rākshasa; (*am*), n. a diamond.

अशिरस् *a-śiras, ās, ās, as,* or *a-śiraska, as, ā, am,* headless [cf. ἀκάρηνος]. — *A-śiraḥ-snāna, am,* n. bathing the whole body except the head.

अशिव *a-śiva, as, ā, am,* unfriendly, unkind, envious; pernicious, dangerous; causing or threatening mischief; unlucky, unfortunate; (*as*), m., N. of a certain divine being; (*ī*), f. a female demon or goblin; (*am*), n. ill-luck, evil fortune, mischief.

अशिशिर *a-śiśira, as, ā, am,* not cold, warm. — *Aśiśira-tā,* f. heat, warmth.

अशिशिषु *aśiśishu, us, us, u* (fr. rt. 2. *aś,* in Desid.), hungry.

अशिशु *a-śiśu, us, vī, u,* childless, without young ones. — *Aśiśvī* or *aśiśvikā,* f. a childless woman.

अशिष्ट *a-śishṭa, as, ā, am* (rt. *śās*), untrained, badly trained, ill-regulated, ill-behaved, rude, barbarous, profligate. — *Aśishṭa-tā,* f. or *aśishṭa-tva, am,* n. rudeness. — *Aśishṭâcāra* (°*ṭa-āc*°), *as,* m. bad behaviour, rudeness, profligacy.

A-śishya, as, ā, am, not to be taught, not to be informed.

अशिष्ठ *aśishṭha, as, ā, am* (superl. of *aśin,* see 1. *aś*), Ved. reaching very far.

अशीत 1. *aśīta, as, ī, am,* the eightieth.

Aśīti, is, f. eighty. — *Aśīti-bhāga, as,* m. the eightieth part, one part out of eighty.

Aśītika, as, ā, am, an octogenarian, one eighty years of age.

अशीत 2. *a-śīta, as, ā, am,* not cold, warm, hot. — *Aśīta-kara, as,* or *aśīta-ruć, k,* m. the sun, 'having hot rays.'

A-śītala, as, ā, am, hot.

अशीर्ण *a-śīrṇa, as, ā, am,* undecayed, unimpaired.

अशीर्षन् *a-śīrshan, ā, ā, a,* Ved. or *a-śīrshika, as, ā, am,* headless.

अशील *a-śīla, as, ā, am,* ill-behaved, vulgar, offensive; indifferent; (*am*), n. bad manners, bad conduct, depravity.

अशुचि *a-śući, is, is, i* (rt. 2. *śuć*), foul, impure; (*is*), f. impurity, disgrace, degradation. — *Aśući-tā,* f. or *aśući-tva, am,* n. impurity.

A-śauća, am, n. impurity, foulness; legal impurity, contamination, defilement contracted by the death of a relation, or by the commission of prohibited acts, &c. — *Aśauća-tva, am,* n. impure or abandoned nature or disposition; defilement, contamination.

अशुद्ध *a-śuddha, as, ā, am* (rt. *śudh*), impure; inaccurate; unknown, unascertained. — *Aśuddha-vāsaka, as,* m. a vagrant, a suspicious character.

A-śuddhi, is, is, i, impure; (*is*), f. impurity.

A-śodhana, am, n. uncleanness; inaccuracy.

A-śodhita, as, ā, am, uncleansed, unclean; inaccurate, uncorrected, unrevised.

अशुभ *a-śubha, as, ā, am,* unlucky, inauspicious; (*am*), n. sin, a shameful deed, misfortune. — *Aśubhodaya* (°*bha-ud*°), *as,* m. inauspicious omen.

अशुश्रूषा *a-śuśrūshā,* f. inattention, neglect of service or respect.

अशुष *aśusha, as, ā, am* (fr. rt. 2. *aś*), Ved. eating, consuming, voracious; (Sāy.) not causing to dry up, not extinguished (as if fr. rt. *śush*).

अशुष्क *a-śushka, as, ā, am* (rt. *śush*), not dry, moist, fresh, green.

A-śoshaṇīya or *a-śoshya, as, ā, am,* not to be dried up.

अशूद्र *a-śūdra, as,* m. one who is not a Śūdra.

अशून्य *a-śūnya, as, ā, am,* not empty. — *Aśūnya-śayana, am,* n., *aśūnyaśayana-dvitīyā,* f., *aśūnyaśayana-vrata, am,* n., N. of certain ceremonies.

अशूला *a-śūlā,* f. the tree Vitex Alata.

अशृङ्ग *a-śṛinga, as, ā, am,* having no horn or top.

अशृण्य *a-śṛiṇya, as, ā, am,* untameable, unbridled.

अशृत *a-śṛita, as, ā, am,* not cooked, unripe.

अशृथित *a-śṛithita, as, ā, am* (rt. *śrath*), Ved. not loosened.

अशेव *a-śeva, as, ā, am,* Ved. pernicious, dangerous, not causing pleasure.

अशेष *a-śesha, as, ā, am,* without remainder, entire, perfect, all, whole, every; infinite, endless; (*as*), m. non-remainder; *aśesham* or *aśeshena* or *aśeshatas,* ind. entirely, wholly. — *Aśesha-tā,* f. totality. — *Aśesha-sāmrājya, as,* m. an epithet of Śiva.

Aśeshaya, nom. P. *aśeshayati, -yitum,* to finish entirely.

A-śeshas, ās, ās, as, Ved. without offspring or descendants.

अशैक्ष *a-śaiksha, as,* m. an Arhat (lit. 'no longer a pupil').

अशोक 1. *a-śoka, as, ā, am* (rt. 2. *śuć*), Ved. without heat.

अशोक 2. *a-śoka, as, ā, am* (rt. 1. *śuć*), without sorrow, not feeling or not causing sorrow; (*as*), m., N. of the tree Jonesia Aśoka Roxb. (it is a tree of moderate size, belonging to the leguminous class, with magnificent red flowers); N. of a minister of king Daśaratha; N. of a king in Pāṭaliputra; (*ā*), f., N. of a medicinal plant; one of the female domestic deities of the Jainas; (*am*), n. the blossom of the Aśoka plant; quicksilver. — *Aśoka-taru, us,* m. or *aśoka-naga, as,* m. or *aśoka-vṛiksha, as,* m. an Aśoka tree. — *Aśoka-trirātra, as,* m., N. of a feast which lasts during three nights. — *Aśoka-datta* or *aśoka-vega, as,* m., N. of a man. — *Aśoka-pūrṇimā,* f., N. of a certain holiday. — *Aśoka-mañjarī,* f., N. of a metre. — *Aśoka-rohiṇī,* f., N. of a medicinal plant. — *Aśoka-vardhana, as,* m., N. of a king. — *Aśoka-shashṭhī,* f., N. of a certain holiday. — *Aśokāri* (°*ka-ari*), *is,* m., N. of the plant Nauclea Kadamba Roxb. — *Aśokāshṭamī* (°*ka-ash*°), f. the eighth day in the first half of the month Caitra.

A-śoća, as, m. absence of care or vanity; content, tranquillity, modesty.

A-śoćya, as, ā, am, not to be sorrowed for.

अशोधन *a-śodhana.* See under *a-śuddha.*

अशोषणीय, अशोष्य. See under *a-śushka.*

अशौच *a-śauća.* See under *a-śući.*

अशौर्य *a-śaurya, am,* n. want of heroism, cowardice.

अश्न 1. *aśna, as, ā, am* (fr. rt. 2. *aś*), Ved. voracious; (*as*), m., N. of a demon.

Aśnayā, f., Ved. hunger.

Aśnita-pibatā, f. invitation to eat and to drink. — *Aśnitapibatīyati,* nom. he invites to eat and drink.

1. *aśman, ā,* m., Ved. eating.

अश्न 2. *aśna, as,* m. (fr. rt. 1. *aś?*), Ved. a stone; a cloud.

Aśma, as, m. a mountain, a rock; Ved. a cloud.

Aśmaka, as, ī, m. f., N. of several persons.

2. *aśman, ā,* m. a stone, especially one fit for slinging; flint; hard stone, rock; a cloud; thunderbolt; sky (?); N. of a Brāhman [cf. Zend *aśman;* Pers. *asmān;* Lith. *akmů,* Them. *akmen;* Slav. *kamy,* Them. *kamen*]. — *Aśma-kadalī,* f., N. of a plant. — *Aśma-kuṭṭa* or *aśma-kuṭṭaka, as, ā, am,* breaking or bruising anything with a stone, bruised or broken by stones. — *Aśma-keta, us,* m., N. of a plant. — *Aśma-gandhā,* f., N. of a plant. — *Aśma-garbha, am,* n. or *aśmagarbha-ja, am,* n. an emerald. — *Aśma-ghna, as,* m., N. of a plant. — *Aśma-ćakra, as, ā, am,* Ved. furnished with a disk of stone. — *Aśma-ja, am,* n. red chalk; iron. — *Aśma-jatuka, am,* n. bitumen. — *Aśma-dāraṇa, as,* m. an axe or crow for breaking stones; (*am*), n. splitting stones or rocks. — *Aśma-didyu, us, us, u,* Ved. throwing rocks or thunderbolts; (Sāy.) one who has obtained a weapon, having adamantine weapons. — *Aśman-maya, as, ī, am,* Ved. made of stone. — *Aśman-vat, ān, atī, at,* Ved. of stone, stony. — *Aśma-pushpa, am,* n. benzoin (styrax). — *Aśma-bhāla, am,* n. a mortar of stone or iron. — *Aśma-bhid, t,* m. the plant Coleus Scutellarioides, supposed to dissolve stone in the bladder. — *Aśma-bheda* or *aśma-bhedaka, as,* m. the same. — *Aśma-maya, as, ī, am,* made or consisting of stone, stony. — *Aśma-yoni, is,* m. an emerald. — *Aśma-vat, ān, atī, at,* stony, of stone. — *Aśma-varman, a,* n., Ved. a wall or shield of stone. — *Aśma-vraja, as, ā, am,* Ved. included in rocks. — *Aśma-sāra, as, am,* m. n. iron; sapphire. — *Aśmasāra-maya, as, ī, am,* made or consisting of iron. — *Aśma-hanman, a,* n., Ved. a stroke of the thunderbolt. — *Aśmāsya* (°*man-ās*°), *as, ā, am,* Ved. having a stone-mouth or stone-source, i. e. flowing from a rock. — *Aśmottha* (°*man-ut*°), *am,* n. asphalt, bitumen.

Aśmara, as, ā, am, stony, rocky, appertaining to stone or rock; (*ī*), f. strangury, stone or gravel (the disease). — *Aśmarī-ghna, as,* m., N. of the tree Cratæva Roxburghii R. Br., used as a lithontriptic. — *Aśmarī-bhedana, am,* n. a lithontriptic. — *Aśmarī-hara, as,* m., N. of the tree Pentaptera Arjuna, used as a lithontriptic.

Aśmīra, as, am, m. n. stone or gravel (the disease).

अश्मन्त *aśmanta, am,* n. (fr. 2. *aśman?*), a fire-place; a field, a plain; death; (*as, ā, am*), unauspicious, unlucky; unbounded, unlimited; (*as*), m., N. of a Marut; [with this word compare Gr. κάμινος and Lat. *caminus.*]

Aśmantaka, am, n. a fire-place; a shade for a lamp; (*as*), m., N. of a plant, from the fibres of which a Brāhman's girdle may be made.

अश्र 1. *aśra, as,* m. (fr. rt. 1. *aś,* wrongly spelt *asra*), a corner [cf. *aśri*].

अश्र 2. *aśra, am,* n. = *aśru,* a tear, q. v.

Aśrāya, nom. A. *aśrāyate, -yitum,* to shed tears.

Aśrin, ī, iṇī, i, having tears, in tears.

अश्र 3. *aśra, am,* n. = *asra,* blood, q. v. — *Aśra-pa, as,* m. fiend, a cannibal, 'a blood-drinker.'

अश्रद्ध *a-śraddha, as, ā, am* (rt. *dhā* with *śrad*), not trusting in (with loc. c.); unbelieving; (*ā*), f. want of trust, unbelief.

A-śraddadhāna, as, ā, am, unbelieving, incredulous, having no faith.

A-śraddheya, as, ā, am, not to be believed, incredible.

A-śrāddha, as, ā, am, not performing funeral rites, not entitled to them, not belonging or relating to them; (*as*), m. non-performance of funeral rites. — *A-śrāddha-bhojin, ī, inī, i,* one who has taken the vow not to eat during the performance of the Śrāddha ceremonies.

अश्रम a-śrama, *as*, m. (rt. *śram*), freedom from fatigue, freshness; absence of toil, laziness; (*as, ā, am*), Ved. indefatigable.

A-śramaṇa, as, ā, am, Ved. indefatigable; (*as*), m. one who is not an ascetic or Buddhist mendicant.

A-śrānta, as, ā, am, untired, unwearied, eternal, continual; (*am*), ind. unweariedly, continually, uninterruptedly.

अश्रवण a-śravaṇa, *am*, n. (rt. *śru*), loss of hearing, deafness.

A-śrāvya, as, ā, am, not to be heard, unfit to be heard, not to be spoken of.

अश्रातस् a-śrātas, ind. (rt. *śrā*), Ved. in an uncooked manner, raw.

अश्रि aśri, *is*, or *aśrī*, f. (fr. rt. 1. *aś?*), the sharp side of anything, a corner, angle of a room or house; the edge of a sword [cf. Lat. *acies, acer;* Lith. *assmů*]. — *Aśri-mat, ān, atī, at*, cornered.

अश्रित a-śrita, *as, ā, am*, Ved. unapproached, difficult of access; not stopping (?).

अश्रिन् aśrin. See under 2. *aśra*.

अश्रीक a-śrīka, *as, ā, am* (fr. *śrī*, q. v.), unlucky, unpropitious.

A-śrīmat, ān, atī, at, unfortunate, inglorious.

A-śrīra, as, ā, am, Ved. unpleasant, ugly.

A-śrīla, as, ā, am, unprosperous, unlucky.

A-ślīka, as, ā, am (*ślī* substituted for *śrī*), unlucky, unpropitious.

A-ślīla, as, ā, am, unpleasant, ugly; coarse, vulgar; abusive, blackguard; (*am*), n. rustic language, untruth, low abuse.

अश्रु aśru, *u*, n. a tear [supposed to stand for *daśru* fr. rt. *daṅś:* cf. Gr. δάκρυ; Lat. *lacryma* for *dacryma;* Goth. *tagrs*, Them. *tagra;* Eng. *tear;* Mod. Germ. *Zähre;* Lith. *aszara*]. — *Aśru-kalā*, f. a tear-drop. — *Aśru-nālī*, f. Fistula Lachrymalis. — *Aśru-paripūrṇāksha* (°*ṇa-ak*°), *as, ī, am*, whose eyes are filled with tears. — *Aśru-paripluta, as, ā, am*, bathed in tears. — *Aśru-pāta, as*, m. flow of tears. — *Aśru-pūrṇa, as, ā, am*, filled with tears. — *Aśru-pūrṇākula* (°*ṇa-āk*°), *as, ā, am*, troubled and filled with tears. — *Aśru-pūrṇāksha* (°*ṇa-ak*°), *as, ī, am*, whose eyes are filled with tears. — *Aśru-mukha, as, ī, am*, having tears on the face. — *Aśru-loćana, as, ā, am*, having tears in the eyes. — *Aśrūpahata* (°*ru-up*°), *as, ā, am*, affected by tears.

अश्रुत a-śruta, *as, ā, am* (rt. *śru*), unheard, inaudible; contrary to the Vedas; (*as*), m., N. of a son of Kṛishṇa, also of Dyutimat. — *Aśruta-vat*, ind. as if it were not heard. — *Aśruta-vraṇa, as*, m., N. of a man.

A-śruti, is, f. not hearing, forgetfulness; not being directed by the Vedas. — *A-śruti-dhara, as, ā, am*, not striking the hearing; not knowing the Veda.

अश्रेयस् a-śreyas, *ān, asī, as*, not the better, inferior, worse; worthless, useless, unprofitable, bad; (*as*), n. mischief, unhappiness.

A-śreshṭha, as, ā, am, not the best, inferior, worse; bad, vile.

अश्रेष्मन् a-śreshman, *ā, ā, a*, Ved. without bands (?).

अश्रोत्रिय a-śrotriya, *as*, m. a Brāhman who has not read the Vedas; not a theologian.

अश्लाघा a-ślāghā, f. (rt. *ślāgh*), absence of self-applause, modesty, reserve.

A-ślāghya or *a-ślāghanīya, as, ā, am*, undeserving of honour or praise, worthless; base, mean.

अश्लेषा a-śleshā, f. (rt. *ślish*), the ninth Nakshatra or lunar mansion, containing five stars; disunion, disjunction. — *Aśleshā-bhava, as*, or *aśleshā-bhū, ūs*, m. a N. of Ketu, i. e. the descending node or dragon's tail; (as formed of the lower extremities of the Daitya Saiṅhika, who was cut in two by Vishṇu at the churning of the ocean.)

अश्लोन a-ślona, *as, ā, am*, Ved. not lame, not crippled.

अश्व 1. aśva, *as*, m. (rt. 1. *aś?*), a horse, especially a stallion; the number 'seven' (that being the number of the horses of the sun); a race of men horse-like in strength; N. of a son of Ćitraka, also of a Dānava; (*ā*), f. a mare; (*au*), du. a horse and a mare [cf. Zend *aśpa;* Lat. *equus;* Gr. ἵππος; Lith. *aszwa;* Old Sax. *ehuscalc*]. — *Aśva-kandikā*, f., N. of the plant Physalis Flexuosa. — *Aśva-karṇa, as*, m. the ear of a horse; N. of the tree Vatica Robusta W. and A., so called from the shape of its leaves; a term in surgery for a particular fracture of the bones; N. of a mountain. — *Aśva-karṇaka, as*, m. = the preceding in all but its last sense. — *Aśva-kuṭī*, f. a stable for horses. — *Aśva-kuśala* or *aśva-kovida, as, ā, am*, skilled in horses. — *Aśva-kranda, as*, m., N. of a bird. — *Aśva-khura, as*, m. a horse's hoof; a perfume, apparently a dried shell-fish; (*ā* or *ī*), f. the plant Clitoria Ternatea Lin. — *Aśva-gati, is*, f. the pace of a horse; N. of a metre containing four verses of sixteen syllables each. — *Aśva-gandhā*, f. the plant Physalis Flexuosa Lin. — *Aśva-goyuga, am*, n. a pair of horses. — *Aśva-goshṭha, am*, n. a stable. — *Aśva-grīva, as*, m. 'horse-neck,' N. of a demon, a foe of Vishṇu, more commonly called Haya-grīva. — *Aśva-ghāma, as*, m., N. of a place. — *Aśva-ghāsa, as*, m. pasture for horses. — *Aśva-ghosha, as*, m., N. of a Buddhist. — *Aśva-ghna, as*, m. 'horse-bane,' N. of a kind of Oleander, Nerium Odorum Ait. — *Aśva-ćalana-śālā*, f. a riding-house. — *Aśva-ćikitsaka, as*, m. a farrier, a veterinary surgeon. — *Aśva-ćikitsā*, f. farriery. — *Aśva-jaghana, as*, m. a kind of centaur, a being with lower limbs like those of a horse. — *Aśva-jit, t, t, t*, Ved. gaining horses by conquest; (*t*), m., N. of a Buddhist Bhikshu. — *Aśva-tīrtha, am*, n., N. of a place of pilgrimage near Kānyakubja on the Gaṅgā. — *Aśva-da, as, ā, am*, giving horses. — *Aśva-daṅshṭrā*, f. the plant Tribulus Lanuginosus Lin. — *Aśva-dā, ās*, m., Ved. or *aśva-dāvan, ā*, m., Ved. giving horses. — *Aśva-dūta, as*, m. a riding messenger. — *Aśva-nadī*, f., N. of a river. — *Aśva-nāya, as*, m. a horse-herd, i. e. one who has the charge of a drove of grazing horses. — *Aśva-nibandhika, as*, m. lit. 'a horse-fastener,' a groom. — *Aśva-nirṇij, k, k, k*, Ved. decorated or embellished with horses. — *Aśva-pa, as*, m., Ved. a groom. — *Aśva-pati, is*, m., Ved. lord of horses; N. of several persons, of a king of Madra and father of Sāvitrī; and of an Asura. — *Aśva-parṇa, as, ā, am*, Ved. having horses for wings. — *Aśva-pastya, as, ā, am*, Ved. having horses for (its) home or seat or source, consisting in horses (?), depending on horses (?). — *Aśva-pāda, as, ā, am*, horse-footed. — *Aśva-pāla, as*, m. a groom. — *Aśva-pućchī*, f. the plant Glycine Debilis Ait. — *Aśva-prishṭha, am*, n. horseback. — *Aśva-peśas, ās, ās, as*, Ved. decorated or embellished with horses. — *Aśva-baḍava* or *aśva-vaḍava, am*, n. horses and mares; (*au*), m. du. a horse and a mare. — *Aśva-bandha, as*, m. lit. 'a horse-fastener,' a groom, an ostler. — *Aśva-bandhana, am*, n. fastening of horses; (*as, ī, am*), used for fastening horses. — *Aśva-balā*, f., N. of a vegetable. — *Aśva-bāla* or *aśva-vāla, as*, m. tail or hair of a horse; a kind of reed, Saccharum Spontaneum Lin. — *Aśva-bāhu, us*, m., N. of a son of Ćitraka. — *Aśva-budhna, as, ā, am*, Ved. based on horses, having its origin in horses, standing on horses, i. e. on a carriage drawn by horses. — *Aśva-budhya, as, ā, am*, Ved. based on horses, having its origin in horses (as wealth), distinguished by horses. — *Aśva-bhā*, f. lightning. — *Aśva-mahishikā*, f. the natural enmity of a horse and a buffalo. — *Aśva-māra* or *aśva-māraka, as*, or *aśva-hantri, tā*, m. 'horse-destroying,' a kind of Oleander, Nerium Odorum. — *Aśva-māla, as*, m. a kind of serpent. — *Aśvam-ishṭi, is, is, i*, Ved. seeking or wishing for horses; procuring horses, an epithet of Agni; (Sāy.) whose rites are pervasive, or who desires quick worship. — *Aśva-mukha, as, ī, am*, having the head or countenance of a horse; (*as*), m. a Kinnara or celestial chorister (so represented); according to others, a kind of demi-god distinct from the preceding; N. of a peculiar race of people. — *Aśva-muć, k*, m. a horse-stealer. — *Aśva-medha, as*, m. the horse-sacrifice; (a celebrated ceremony, the antiquity of which reaches back to the Vedic period. For example, hymns 162 and 163 in the first Maṇḍala of the Rig-veda were used at this sacrifice. In later times its efficacy was so exaggerated, that a hundred such sacrifices entitled the sacrificer to displace Indra from the dominion of Svarga; kings who engaged in it spent enormous sums in gifts to the Brāhmans. It is said that the horse was sometimes not immolated, but kept bound during the ceremony); N. of a son of Bharata. — *Aśvamedha-kāṇḍa, am*, n., N. of the thirteenth book of the Śatapatha-Brāhmaṇa. — *Aśvamedha-datta, as*, m., N. of a king. — *Aśvamedhika* or *aśvamedhīya, as, ā, am*, relating to the horse-sacrifice; (*as*), m. a horse fit for the sacrifice, called Aśva-medha. — *Aśva-yuj, k, k, k*, Ved. harnessing horses; having horses put to (as a carriage); (*k*), f., N. of a constellation, the head of Aries; the first lunar mansion; m. the month Āśvina (Sept.–Oct.); (*k, k, k*), born under the constellation Aśvayuj. — *Aśva-yuja, as*, m. the month Āśvina. — *Aśva-yūpa, as*, m., Ved. the post to which the sacrificial horse was bound. — *Aśva-yoga, as, ā, am*, Ved. causing the yoking of horses, joining or reaching as quickly as horses. — *Aśva-raksha, as*, m. the keeper or rider of a horse, a groom. — *Aśva-ratha, as*, m. a carriage drawn by horses; (*ā*), f., N. of a river. — *Aśva-rādhas, ās, ās, as*, Ved. furnishing horses. — *Aśva-rodhaka, as*, m., N. of the plant Nerium Odorum Ait. — *Aśva-lalita*, N. of a species of the Vikṛiti metre. — *Aśva-lālā*, f. a kind of snake. — *Aśva-loman, ā*, m. horse-hair; a kind of snake. — *Aśva-vaktra, as*, m. a Kinnara or Gandharba. — *Aśva-vaḍava, am*, n. a stud of horses and mares; (*au*), m. du. a horse and a mare; (*ās*), m. horses and mares, see *aśva-baḍava*. — 1. *aśva-vat*, ind. like a horse. — 2. *aśva-vat*, or Ved. *aśvā-vat, ān, atī, at*, possessed of horses, consisting of horses. — *Aśva-vadana, as*, m., N. of a people. — *Aśva-vaha, as*, m. a horseman. — *Aśva-vāra* or *aśva-vāla, as*, m. a horseman, a groom. — *Aśva-vāraka, as*, m. a horseman, a groom. — *Aśva-vāraṇa, as*, m., N. of the Bos Gavæus. — *Aśva-vāha* or *aśva-vāhaka, as*, m. a horseman. — *Aśva-vikrayin, ī*, m. a horse-dealer. — *Aśva-vid, t, t, t*, skilled in taming horses, an epithet of Nala; a jockey; Ved. procuring horses. — *Aśva-vṛisha, as*, m., Ved. a stallion. — *Aśva-vaidya, as*, m. a farrier, a veterinary surgeon. — *Aśva-śaka, am*, n., Ved. excrements of a horse. — *Aśva-śakṛit, t*, n. excrements of a horse, horse-dung; N. of a river. — *Aśva-śaṅku, us*, m., N. of a Dānava. — *Aśva-śālā*, f. a stable. — *Aśva-śāva, as*, m. a foal, a colt. — *Aśva-śāstra, am*, n. a manual or text-book of veterinary science. — *Aśva-śiras, as*, n. a horse's head; (*ās, ās, as*), having the head of a horse, an epithet of Nārāyaṇa; (*ās*), m., N. of a Dānava. — *Aśva-śṛigālikā*, f. the natural enmity between the horse and the jackal. — *Aśva-śćandra, as, ā, am*, Ved. causing joy (by means of) horses; brilliant with horses. — *Aśva-shaṅgava, am*, n. a set or team of six horses. — *Aśva-sani, is, is, i*, Ved. or *aśva-sā* or *aśva-shā, ās, ās, am*, Ved. gaining or procuring horses. — *Aśva-sāda, as*, or *aśva-sādin, ī*, m. a horseman, a rider, a horse-soldier. — *Aśva-sārathya, am*, n. management of horses and cars, horsemanship and driving, coachmanship, charioteership. — *Aśva-sūkti, is*, m., N. of an author of Vedic hymns. — *Aśva-sūnṛita, as, ā, am*, Ved. praised sincerely for (the gift of) horses; whose praise for (giving) horses is agreeable and true. — *Aśva-sena, as*, m., N. of a Nāga. — *Aśvasena-nṛipa-nandana, as*, m., N. of a king and saint, also Sanatkumāra.

— *Aśvastomīya, as, ā, am,* Ved. relating to the praise of the sacrificial horse. — *Aśva-sthāna, am,* n. a stable or stall for horses; (*as, ā, am*), born in a stable. — *Aśva-haya, as, ā, am,* Ved. driving or spurring a horse. — *Aśva-hāraka, as,* m. a horse-stealer. — *Aśva-hṛidaya, am,* n. horsemanship. — *Aśvāksha* (°*va-ak*°), *as,* m., N. of a plant. — *Aśvājanī* (°*va-aj*°), f. a whip. — *Aśvādhika* (°*va-adh*°), *as, ā, am,* strong in cavalry, superior in horses. — *Aśvādhyaksha* (°*va-adh*°), *as,* m. a guardian of horses. — *Aśvā-magha, as, ī, am,* Ved. rich in horses. — *Aśvāyur-veda* (°*va-āy*°), *as,* m. veterinary science. — *Aśvāri* (°*va-ari*), *is,* m. a buffalo. — *Aśvārūḍha* (°*va-ār*°), *as, ā, am,* mounted, sitting on horseback. — *Aśvāroha* (°*va-ā*°), *as, ā, am,* riding or mounted on a horse; (*as*), m. a horseman; (*ā*), f., N. of the plant Aśvagandhā. — *Aśvārohaka* (°*va-ār*°), *as,* m., N. of the plant Aśvagandhā. — *Aśvārohin* (°*va-ār*°), *ī, iṇī, i,* mounted or riding on horseback. — *Aśvā-vat, ān, atī, at,* furnished with horses. — *Aśvāvarohaka* (°*va-av*°), *as,* m., N. of the plant Aśvagandhā. — *Aśveshita* (°*va-ish*°), *as, ā, am,* hurried along by horses. — *Aśvorasa* (°*va-ur*°), *as, ī, am,* broad-chested like a horse.

2. *aśva,* nom. P. *aśvati,* to behave like a horse.

Aśvaka, as, ā, am, horse-like, acting like a horse, &c.; (*as*), m. a small horse; a bad horse, a hack; a stray horse, one whose owner is not known; any horse.

Aśvakinī, f. the first Nakshatra or lunar mansion.

Aśvatara, as, ā, am, swift, speedy; (*as, ī*), m. f. a mule; (*as*), m. a male calf; N. of a Gandharva; one of the chiefs of the Nāgas or serpent-race, inhabiting the regions under the earth.

Aśvattha, as, m. the holy fig tree, Ficus Religiosa L. (under which horses stand; *ttha = stha*); Ved. a vessel made of its wood; N. of another tree (= *gardabhāṇḍa*); the fruit of the Ficus Religiosa; the time at which it bears; an epithet of the sun; N. of a man; N. of a people; (*ā*), f. day of full moon in the month Āśvina, in which month the fruits of the Ficus Religiosa generally become ripe; day of full moon; (*ī*), f., N. of a plant. — *Aśvattha-kuṇa, as,* m. the fruit season of the holy fig tree. — *Aśvattha-bheda, as,* m., N. of a tree, Bignonia Suaveolens.

Aśvatthaka, as, ā, am, to be given or to be done &c. when the Aśvattha tree bears; (*am*), n. the petals of the Arabian jasmine.

Aśvatthāman, ā, m. (*tthāman* for *sthāman* ?), N. of a saint and warrior, the son of Droṇa and one of the chiefs of the Kurus.

Aśvatthikā, f., N. of a plant.

Aśvaya, nom. P. *aśvayati, -yitum,* to wish for horses.

Aśvayā, f., Ved. desire to get horses.

Aśvayu, us, us, u, Ved. desiring horses.

Aśvala, as, m., N. of the Hotṛi-priest of Janaka, king of Videha.

Aśvasya, nom. P. *aśvasyati, -yitum,* to wish for the stallion.

Aśvāya, nom. P. *aśvāyati, -yitum,* Ved. to wish for horses.

Aśvika, as, ī, am, drawn by horses, carried by horses.

Aśvin, ī, inī, i, Ved. possessed of horses, consisting of horses; (*ī*), m. a cavalier, a horse-tamer; (*nau*), m. du. the two charioteers; N. of two divinities, who appear in the sky before the dawn in a golden carriage drawn by horses or birds; they bring treasures to men and avert misfortune and sickness; in later times they are considered as the physicians of Svarga or heaven; (in astronomy) they are the twins of the zodiac; (*inī*), f. a nymph, considered in later times as the mother of the Aśvins; she was the wife of Sūrya or the sun, who concealed herself in the form of a mare; (in astronomy) the head of Aries or the first of the twenty-eight Nakshatras or lunar mansions; (*i*), n., Ved. richness in horses. — *Aśvi-devatāka, as, ā, am,* whose divinities are the Aśvins. — *Aśvinī-kumāra* or *aśvinī-putra* or *aśvinī-suta, au,* m. du. the twin sons of Sañjñā, the sun's wife, in the form of Aśvinī, commonly called the Aśvins. — *Aśvi-mat, ān, atī, at,* (any Mantra &c.) containing the word Aśvin. — *Aśvi-sālokya, am,* n. the heaven or station of the Aśvins, to which the giver of a horse is raised.

Aśviya, as, ā, am, Ved. referring to horses; (*ā*), Ved. neut. pl. a troop of horses.

Aśvīna, as, ā, am, distant a day's journey for a horse; more usually *Āśvīna.*

Aśvīya, as, ā, am, belonging or relating to a horse, conducive to horses; (*am*), n. a number of horses.

Aśvya, as, ā, am, Ved. belonging to or coming from horses; consisting of horses; (*am*), n., Ved. a number of horses, possession of horses; (*as*), m., N. of Vaśa, the son of Aśva.

अश्वन्त *aśvanta, am,* n. (connected with *aśmanta,* q. v.), death; a field; a fire-place; termination, limit; (*as, ā, am*), unlucky, inauspicious, unbounded, unlimited. [In the first sense *aśvanta* may be for *asu-anta,* 'end of life.']

अश्वस्तन *a-śvastana, as, ī, am,* or *a-śvastanika, as, ā, am,* of to-day, not of or not for to-morrow; one who makes no provision for to-morrow. — *A-śvastana-vid, t, t, t,* ignorant of the future.

अष *ash,* cl. 1. P. A. *ashati, -te, -shitum,* to go or move; to take or receive; to shine.

अषडक्षीण *ashaḍakshīṇa, am,* n. (fr. *a, shash, akshi*), anything not seen by six eyes, i. e. known or determined by two persons to the exclusion of a third; a secret.

अषतर *ashatara, as, ā, am,* Ved. (fr. a positive, which is not preserved, but may be referred to rt. 1. *aś*), more accessible or acceptable.

अषाढ *a-shāḍha,* or Ved. *a-shālha, as, ā, am,* not to be overcome, invincible; born under the constellation Ashāḍhā; (*as*), m. the month Ashāḍha (or Āshāḍha), commencing with the sun's entrance into Gemini (June–July); a staff made of the wood of Palāśa, carried by a student during the performance of certain vows; N. of a teacher; N. of the Malaya mountain; (*ā*), f., N. of a sacred brick; N. of a constellation; pl. the eighteenth and nineteenth or twentieth and twenty-first lunar mansions.

Ashāḍhaka, as, m. the month Ashāḍha (or Āshāḍha).

अष्टन् *ashṭan, a* or *au* (but *ashṭau* is more common for nom., acc., and voc. cases), pl. eight [cf. Lat. *octo;* Gr. ὀκτώ; Goth. *ahtau;* Mod. Germ. *acht;* Eng. *eight;* Lith. *asztûni;* Slav. *osmj*]; in comp. with other numerals often *ashṭā,* e. g. *ashṭādaśan,* eighteen; *ashṭādaśa, as, ī, am,* the eighteenth, divided into eighteen parts; *ashṭādaśa-dhā,* eighteen-fold; *ashṭā-viṅśati,* twenty-eight; *ashṭāviṅśa, as, ī, am,* the twenty-eighth, divided into twenty-eight parts; *ashṭātriṅśa, as, ī, am,* the thirty-eighth, containing thirty-eight; *ashṭāćatvāriṅśa, as, ī, am,* the forty-eighth. — *Ashṭa-karṇa, as, ā, am,* one who has the number eight as a mark burnt in his ear; (*as*), m. eight-eared, an epithet of Brahmā, who is supposed to have four heads; (*ī*), m., N. of a man. — *Ashṭa-kṛitvas,* ind. eight times. — *Ashṭa-koṇa, as,* m. an octagon. — *Ashṭa-khaṇḍa, as,* m. title of a collection of several sections of the Ṛig-veda. — *Ashṭa-gava, am,* n. a flock of eight cows. — *Ashṭa-gādh* (?), *t,* m. a fabulous animal (called Sarabha), supposed to have eight legs; a spider (?). — *Ashṭa-guṇa, as, ā, am,* eight-fold; (*am*), n. the eight qualities. — *Ashṭaguṇāśraya* (°*ṇa-āś*°), *as, ā, am,* endowed with the eight qualities, epithet of a king. — *Ashṭa-tva, am,* n. condition of eight. — *Ashṭa-daṅshṭra, as,* m., N. of a son of Virūpa, author of a hymn of the Ṛig-veda; N. of a Dānava. — *Ashṭa-dala,* an octagon. — *Ashṭa-dik-pāla, ās,* m. pl. the regents of the cardinal points, as Indra of the East, Agni or Vahni of the S. E., Yama of the South, Nairṛita of the S. W., Varuṇa of the West, Marut of the N. W., Kuvera of the North, and Īśa or Śiva of the N. E. — *Ashṭa-diś, k,* f. the eight cardinal points of the compass collectively. — *Ashṭa-dhā,* ind. eight-fold, eight times, in eight parts or sections. — *Ashṭa-dhātu, u,* n. the eight metals collectively, as gold, silver, copper, tin, lead, brass, iron, and steel. — *Ashṭa-pada, as,* m. a Vedic metre of eight Padas. — *Ashṭa-pād, t, t, t,* having eight legs; (*t*), m. a spider; a fabulous animal with eight legs. — *Ashṭa-pāda, as, ā, am,* having eight legs; (*as*), m. a kind of spider with a small body and long legs. — *Ashṭa-pādikā,* f., N. of the plant Vallaris Dichotomus Wall. — *Ashṭa-maṅgala, as,* m. a horse with a white face, tail, mane, breast, and hoofs; (*am*), n. a collection of eight lucky things to be assembled on certain occasions (such as a coronation &c.), e. g. a lion, a bull, an elephant, a water-jar, a fan, a flag, a trumpet, and a lamp; or, according to others, a Brāhman, a cow, fire, gold, ghee, the sun, water, and a king. — *Ashṭa-māna, am,* n. a measure, one kuḍava. — *Ashṭa-māsika, as, ā, am,* occurring once in eight months. — *Ashṭa-mūrti, is,* m. eight-formed, an epithet of Śiva (as identified with the five elements, mind, egotism, and matter; or, according to the opening of the Sakuntalā, with the five elements, the sun and moon and the sacrificing priest). — *Ashṭamūrti-dhara, as,* m. possessing eight forms, an epithet of Śiva. — *Ashṭa-ratna, am,* n. the eight jewels, title of a collection of eight Ślokas on ethics. — *Ashṭa-rasāśraya* (°*sa-āś*°), *as, ā, am,* endowed or furnished with the eight rasas or sentiments of poetry. — *Ashṭarća* (°*ṭan-ṛić*), *as,* m. a psalm or hymn consisting of eight verses. — *Ashṭa-lohaka, am,* n. a class of eight metals, gold, silver, copper, tin, lead, the magnet, muṇḍaloha (?), and tīkshṇaloha or steel (?). — *Ashṭa-varga, as,* m. a class of three principal medicaments (mostly the roots of plants from the hills), named Ṛishabha, Jīvaka, Medā, Mahāmedā, Ṛiddhi, Vṛiddhi, Kākolī, and Kshīrakākolī. — *Ashṭa-vidha, as, ā, am,* eight-fold, of eight kinds. — *Ashṭa-śata, am,* n. eight hundred. — *Ashṭa-śravaṇa, as,* or *ashṭa-śravas, ās,* m., N. of Brahmā (eight-eared, see *ashṭa-karṇa*). — *Ashṭasāhasrika, as, ā, am,* consisting of eight thousand. — *Ashṭā-kapāla, as, ī, am,* (an oblation) prepared or offered in eight pans; (*as*), m. a sacrifice in which ghee or clarified butter is offered in eight pans. — *Ashṭākshara* (°*ṭan-ak*°), *as, ā, am,* containing eight syllables; (*as*), m., N. of an author. — *Ashṭā-gava, am,* n. a car or wain, one drawn by eight oxen. — *Ashṭāṅga* (°*ṭan-aṅ*°), *am,* n. eight parts of the body with which very profound obeisance is performed (viz. the hands, breast, forehead, eyes, throat, and middle of the back; or the first four, with the knees and feet; or these six, with the speech and mind); the eight parts of a court, or the law, the judge, assessors, scribe, and astrologer, gold, fire, and water; any whole consisting of eight parts or members; a die, dice; (*as, ā, am*), consisting of eight parts or members. — *Ashṭāṅga-naya, as,* m. = *ashṭāṅga.* — *Ashṭāṅga-pāta* or *ashṭāṅga-praṇāma, as,* m. prostration of the eight parts of the body as in reverence. — *Ashṭāṅga-hṛidaya, am,* n. title of a medicinal work. — *Ashṭāṅgārghya* (°*ga-ar*°), *as,* m. an offering of eight articles, water, milk, kuśa grass, curds, ghee, rice, barley, and mustard; or honey, red oleander flowers, and sandal are substituted for the last three. — *Ashṭā-daṅshṭra* = *ashṭa-daṅshṭra,* q. v. — *Ashṭādaśa-bhujā,* f., N. of the wife of Śiva. — *Ashṭādaśāṅga* (°*śan-aṅ*°), *as,* m. a decoction of eighteen ingredients. — *Ashṭādhyāyī* (°*ṭan-adh*°), f. title of the eleventh Kāṇḍa of the Śatapatha-Brāhmaṇa, consisting of eight lectures. — *Ashṭānavata, as, ī, am,* the ninety-eighth. — *Ashṭā-pada, as,* m. a spider; a worm; a fabulous animal with eight legs, the Sarabha; a wild sort of jasmin; a pin or bolt; the mountain Kailāsa or abode of Kuvera; (*as, am*), m. n. a kind of chequered cloth or board for drafts, dice, &c.; gold. — *Ashṭā-pada-pattra, am,* n. gold-leaf; a sheet of gold. — *Ashṭā-pād, t, -padī,* m. f., Ved. having eight legs, consisting of eight members; (in ritual language) a term for a pregnant animal; (*padī*), f. a wild sort of jasmin. — *Ashṭā-pāda, as, ā, am,* quartered by eight, having eight for the root. — *Ashṭā-pādya, as, ā, am,* eight-fold. — *Ashṭāra-ćakra-vat* (°*ṭan-ar*°), *ān,* m. having a wheel with eight spokes, an epithet of Mañju-śrī, a Jaina saint and ruler. — *Ashṭā-ratha, as,* m., N. of a son of Bhīmaratha. — *Ashṭā-vakra, as,* m., N. of a Brāhman, a son of Kahoḍa. — *Ashṭāsra* (°*ṭan-as*°), *am,* n. an octagon. — *Ashṭāsraya* (°*ṭan-as*°), *as, ā, am,* octangular. — *Ashṭāha* (°*ṭan-ah*°), *as, ā, am,* lasting eight days.

Ashṭaka, as, ā, am, consisting of eight parts, eight-fold; one who studies or is acquainted with the eight books of Pāṇini's grammar or the formulas of the Veda; (*as*), m. the eighth part, e. g. of the Rig-veda; N. of a son of Viśvāmitra; (*ā*), f. the eighth day after full moon; especially the eighth day of three months, on which the progenitors or manes are worshipped; worship of the progenitors or manes on certain days, vegetables, flesh, and cake being severally offered upon these occasions, and the Brāhmans feasted; (*am*), n. a whole consisting of eight parts, e. g. the eight sections of Pāṇini's grammar. — *Ashṭakāṅga* (°*ka-an*°), *am,* n. a kind of board or cloth for playing with dice on, having eight divisions.

Ashṭakin, ī, m. one who performs an Ashṭakā.

Ashṭataya, am, n. a conjunction or aggregate of eight.

Ashṭama, as, ī, am, the eighth; (*as*), m. the eighth part; (*ī*), f. (scil. *rātri*), the eighth day (night) in a half-month; N. of the medicinal plant Kshīrakākolī, the last of a class of eight medicinal plants. — *Ashṭama-kālika, as, ā, am,* one who omitting seven meals partakes only of the eighth. — *Ashṭamāṅśa* (°*ma-aṅ*°), an eighth part.

Ashṭamaka, as, ā, am, the eighth.

Ashṭamikā, f. a śukti or weight of four tolas.

Ashṭātaya, as, ī, am, consisting of eight parts; (*am*), n. collection of eight things.

1. *ashṭi, is,* f., N. of a metre consisting of sixty-four syllables.

Ashṭin, ī, inī, i, consisting of eight members or syllables.

अष्टि *2. ashṭi, is,* f. (fr. rt. 1. *as*), Ved. reaching.

अष्ट्रा *ashṭrā,* f. (fr. rt. 1. *aś?*), Ved. a prick or goad for driving cattle; (sometimes regarded as the badge of the agriculturist, as the staff is of the Brāhman); [cf. Zend *astrâ*; Lith. *akstinas.*] — *Ashṭrā-vin, ī, inī, i,* Ved. obeying the goad.

अष्ठि *ashṭhi, is,* f. (fr. rt. 1. *aś?* connected with *aśan* and *aśman*), seed; a kernel, a stone.

Ashṭhīlā, f. a globular body; a round pebble or stone; kernel; seed-corn; a globular swelling below the navel, produced by wind; contusion.

Ashṭhīlikā, f. a kind of abscess; a pebble.

Ashṭhī-vat, vān, vat, m. n. the knee, knee-bone; (by native grammarians derived fr. *asthi.*)

अस 1. *as,* cl. 2. P. *asti,* (2nd sing. *asi,* Impf. *āsīt,* Pot. *syāt,* Impv. *astu,* 2nd sing. *edhi,* Perf. *āsa*), to be, live, exist, be present; to take place, happen; to belong to, be in the possession of (e. g. *tasya na kiṅćit svam asti,* there is no property belonging to him); to fall to the share of, to happen to any one (with gen.); to abide, dwell, stay; to turn out, tend towards any result, prove (with dat.); to be sufficient for (with dat.); to become: *na as,* to be lost, to perish; [cf. Gr. ἐσ-τί; Lat. *es-t*; Goth. *is-t*; Lith. *es-ti*; Slav. *jes-tj.*]

अस् 2. *as,* cl. 4. P. *asyati, āsa, asishyati, āsthat, asitum,* to throw, cast, shoot at (with dat., loc., or gen. of the mark); to drive or frighten away; to throw away, take away, let go, leave.

Asana, am, n. the act of throwing, &c. See s.v.

अस् 3. *as,* cl. 1. P. A. *asati, -te, -situm,* to go; to shine; to take.

असंयत् *a-saṃyat, an, atī, at* (rt. *i*), Ved. not entering, not pleasing.

असंयत्त *a-saṃyatta, as, ā, am* (rt. *yat*), Ved. undisturbed, (various reading for *a-saṃyata.*)

असंयम *a-saṃyama, as,* m. (rt. *yam*), absence of check or restraint, especially of the senses.

A-saṃyata, as, ā, am, unrestrained, unassailed. — *Asaṃyatātman* (°*ta-āt*°), *ā, ā, a,* having the soul uncontrolled.

असंयुक्त *a-saṃyukta, am,* n. (rt. *yuj*), non-combination, hiatus (in Vedic grammar).

A-saṃyoga, as, m. absence of union or connection.

असंयुत *a-saṃyuta, as,* m. unmixed, unblended; an epithet of Vishṇu.

असंरुद्ध *a-saṃruddha, as, ā, am,* unobstructed.

असंलग्न *a-saṃlagna, as, ā, am,* disjoined, detached, separate.

असंवत्सरभृत *a-saṃvatsara-bhṛita, as, ā, am,* Ved. not supported a whole year (as a sacred fire).

A-saṃvatsarabhṛitin, ī, inī, i, Ved. one who does not support (a fire) a whole year.

असंविदान *a-saṃvidāna, as, ā, am,* ignorant, unwise; not promising or covenanting.

असंवृत *a-saṃvṛita, as, ā, am,* uncovered, exposed; imperfectly or scarcely covered.

असंव्यवहितम् *a-saṃvyavahitam,* ind. immediately, without interval.

असंशय *a-saṃśaya, as,* m. absence of doubt; (*as, ā, am*), free from doubt, certain. — *A-saṃśayam,* ind. without doubt, certainly, verily.

असंश्रव *a-saṃśrava, as,* m. (rt. *śru*), the being out of hearing; (*e*), ind. out of the hearing of; (*as, ā, am*), out of hearing, inaudible.

A-saṃśrāvam, ind. inaudibly, out of the hearing of (with gen. of the person).

असंश्लिष्ट *a-saṃślishṭa, as,* m. not joined, not in contact, an epithet of Śiva.

असंसक्त *a-saṃsakta, as, ā, am,* not attached to, not joined together, disunited, indifferent to.

असंसिद्ध *a-saṃsiddha, as, ā, am,* unaccomplished, incomplete.

असंसूक्तगिल *a-saṃsūkta-gila, as, ā, am,* Ved. swallowing whole or without chewing (said of Rudra's dogs).

असंसृति *a-saṃsṛiti, is,* f. not returning to a new course of existence, absorption into the supreme spirit.

असंसृष्ट *a-saṃsṛishṭa, as, ā, am,* unmixed with, separate, not living in common.

असंस्कृत *a-sanskṛita, as, ā, am,* not perfect, unpolished, rude, common; uninitiated, not having gone through the proper rites of caste, state, sex, or age.

असंस्तुत *a-saṃstuta, as, ā, am,* unknown, unacquainted, not known as acquaintances; not on terms of friendship.

असंस्थान *a-saṃsthāna, am,* n. (rt. *sthā*), absence of cohesion or configuration; disorder, confusion; want, destitution.

A-saṃsthita, as, ā, am, not arranged or arrayed, disordered, irregular; not collected; not finished, not accomplished; not ceasing, not stopping; destitute.

A-saṃsthiti, is, f. disorder, confusion; want, destitution.

असंहत *a-saṃhata, as, ā, am,* not joined; scattered, loose, straggling, uncompressed; (*am*), n. a form of array, loose or open order of troops.

असंहार्य *a-saṃhārya, as, ā, am,* irresistible, insuperable.

असंहित *a-saṃhita, as, ā, am,* not included in the *Saṃhitā* of the Veda.

असकल *a-sakala, as, ā, am,* not all, not entire, a part.

असकृत् *a-sakṛit,* ind. not once, oftener than once, again and again, repeatedly. — *Asakṛit-samādhi, is,* m. repeated meditation. — *Asakṛid-garbha-vāsa, as,* m. repeated birth.

असक्त *a-sakta, as, ā, am,* detached, disunited; detached from worldly feelings or passions; not interested in, unattached to, indifferent to.

असक्थ *a-saktha, as, ā, am,* without thighs, thighless.

असक्र *a-sakra, as, ā, am* (rt. *saść*), Ved. not ceasing to flow, not drying up; not going elsewhere.

असखि *a-sakhi, ā,* m. an untrustworthy friend.

A-sakhin, ā, m. an enemy, an adversary.

असगोत्र *a-sagotra, as, ā, am,* of a different family.

असङ्कल्प *a-sankalpa, as, am,* m. n. absence of predetermination, absence of interested purpose, sincerity.

A-sankalpita, as, ā, am, not purposed, not resolved or determined on.

असङ्कसुक *a-sankasuka, as, ā, am,* not fickle, unfluctuating, firm, steady.

असङ्कीर्ण *a-sankīrṇa, as, ā, am,* unmixed, uncompounded, uncollected.

असङ्कुल *a-sankula, as, ā, am,* not crowded, open, clear, broad; (*as*), m. a broad road.

असङ्केत *a-sanketa, as, ā, am,* not appointed, not agreed upon.

A-sanketita, as, ā, am, uninvited.

असङ्ख्य *a-sankhya, as, ā, am* (rt. *khyā*), without number, innumerable, exceedingly numerous. — *Asankhya-tā,* f. or *asankhya-tva, am,* n. innumerableness, immensity, infinity.

A-sankhyāta, as, ā, am, uncounted, innumerable.

A-sankhyeya, as, ā, am, innumerable; (*as*), m. an epithet of Śiva; (*am*), n., Ved. an innumerable multitude; an exceedingly large number. — *Asankhyeya-guṇa, as, ā, am,* innumerable, unnumbered. — *Asankhyeya-tā,* f. innumerableness.

असङ्ग 1. *a-sanga, as,* m. (rt. *sañj*), non-attachment; (*as, ā, am*), not attached, having no attachment or inclination for or interest in, independent, free from ties, not hindered, moving without hindrance. — *Asanga-vat, ān, atī, at,* not attached to.

A-sangin, ī, inī, i, not attached to the world.

Asajjitātman (°*ta-āt*°), *ā, ā, a,* having a soul free from attachments.

असङ्ग 2. *a-sanga, as, ā, am* (rt. *gam* with *sam* and *a* prefixed), not united, unassociated, solitary; (*as*), m., N. of a son of Yuyudhāna.

A-sangata, as, ā, am, ununited, unaccompanied, unassociated with; uneven, unequal; improbable, inconsistent; unpreferred, disesteemed; unbecoming, unseemly; rude, ill-mannered, unpolished, clownish. — *Asangatāćaraṇa* (°*ta-āć*°), *am,* n. inconsistent conduct.

A-sangati, is, f. not associating; incongruity, improbability.

A-sangama, as, m. not associating with; separation, disunion; incongruity; inequality.

असचद्विष् *a-saća-dvish, ṭ, ṭ, ṭ,* Ved. persecuting those who are not (his) worshippers; having no enemies.

असच्छाखा *asać-ćhākhā, asaj-jana,* &c. See under *asat.*

असजात *a-sajāta, as, ā, am,* Ved. not related by blood.

A-sajātya, as, ā, am, Ved. without consanguinity.

असंज्ञ *a-sañjña, as, ā, am,* insensible; (*ā*), f., Ved. disunion, disagreement, discord.

A-sañjñi-sattva, ās, m. pl. a class of Buddhist divinities (otherwise *a-rangi-sattva*).

असत् *a-sat, an, atī, at,* not being, not existing, unreal; not as it should be, not answering its purpose, untrue, wrong, wicked, bad, vile; (*ī*), f. an unfaithful or unchaste wife; (*n*), m. Indra; (*t*), n. non-existence, non-entity; untruth, falsehood, a lie; evil. — *Asać-ćhākhā* (*asat-śākhā*), f., Ved. an unreal branch, a seeming member (?). — *Asać-ćhāstra* (*asat-śāstra*), *am,* n. heretical or heterodox doctrine. — *Asaj-jana, as,* m. a bad, wicked, or contemptible man. — *Asaj-jāti-miśra, as,* m., N. of a person. — *Asat-kalpanā,* f. an untrue action, or one which never took place; fabrication of falsehood. — *Asat-tā,* f. non-existence; untruth; wickedness. — 1. *asat-tva, am,* n. non-existence; untruth; wickedness. — *Asat-patha, as,* m. a bad road; evil practice or doctrine. — *Asat-parigraha, as,* m. receiving unfit presents, or from improper persons. — *Asat-putra, as,* m. a childless man; a wicked or disreputable son. — *Asat-saṃsarga, as,* m. evil company. — *Asat-sanga, as, ā, am,* attached to evil; (*as*), m., N. of a doorkeeper or porter in the Prabodha-ćandrodaya. — *Asad-adhyetṛi, tā,* m. a Brāhman who reads heterodox works; a heterodox student. — *Asad-āćāra, as, ā, am,* following evil practices, wicked; (*as*), m. evil practice. — *Asad-āćārin, ī, iṇī, i,* one who follows bad or heterodox practices, wicked, vile. — *Asad-graha* or *asad-grāha, as,* m. mischievous or wicked trick; caprice, idle or childish desire. — *Asadgrahin, ī, iṇī, i,* performing mischievous or malicious tricks. — *Asad-dṛiś, k, k, k,* evil-eyed. — *Asad-bhāva, as,* m. non-existence, absence; an evil temperament or disposition. — *Asad-vṛitti, is,* f. low or degrading occupation or profession; wickedness. — *Asad-vyavahāra, as, ā, am,* following evil practices; (*as*), m. evil practices. — *Asadvyavahārin, ī, iṇī, i,* following evil courses. — *Asan-mantra, as,* m., Ved. untrue or false counsel or speech.

A-satāyī, f. wickedness.

A-satī, f. an unfaithful or unchaste wife. See above. — *Asatī-suta, as,* m. the son of an unchaste wife, a bastard.

Asat-kṛi, cl. 8. P. *-karoti, -kartum,* to do no good, to harm, injure, dishonour.

Asat-karman, ā, ā, a, wicked; (*a*), n. wickedness.

Asat-kāra, as, m. offence, doing injury; (*a-sat-kāra*), not honouring.

Asat-kṛita, as, ā, am, ill-done, done from improper motives or in an unbecoming manner; (*a-satkṛita*), not honoured; (*am*), n. wicked deed.

Asat-kṛitya, as, ā, am, one who has done evil or wicked actions.

2. *a-sattva, as, ā, am,* strengthless, without energy; (for 1. *asat-tva,* see under *a-sat* above.)

A-satya, as, ā, am, false, untrue; lying, a liar; (*am*), n. untruth, falsehood. — *Asatya-vādin, ī, inī, i,* speaking falsely, giving false evidence, a liar. — *Asatya-sandha, as, ā, am,* treacherous, base, wicked. — *A-satya-sannibha, as, ā, am,* improbable, unlikely.

असदृश *a-sadṛiśa, as, ī, am,* unlike, dissimilar. — *Asadṛiśa-vyavahārin, ī, iṇī, i,* behaving improperly.

असद्यस् *a-sadyas,* ind. not on the same day, not immediately.

असन् *asan,* the base of some of the cases of *asṛij,* blood, q.v.; thus, inst. *asnā,* gen. *asnas,* &c.

असन *asana, am,* n. (fr. rt. 2. *as*), throwing, sending; a shot; (*as*), m., N. of the tree Terminalia Tomentosa, see *aśana.* — *Asana-parṇī,* f., N. of the plant Marsilea Quadrifolia, see *aśana-parṇī.*

Asanā, f., Ved. a missile, an arrow.

असन्तति *a-santati, is, is, i* (rt. *tan*), childless, having no posterity; (*is*), f. want of posterity.

A-santāna, as, ā, am, childless; (*as*), m. want of posterity.

असन्ताप *a-santāpa, as, ā, am* (rt. *tap*), Ved. not suffering pain or sorrow; not causing pain or sorrow.

असन्तुष्ट *a-santushṭa, as, ā, am* (rt. *tush*), discontented, displeased.

A-santosha, as, m. displeasure.

असन्दिग्ध *a-sandigdha, as, ā, am* (rt. *dih*), not indistinct; not vanished; certain, confident; undoubted, unsuspected; (*am*), ind. without any doubt, certainly.

असन्दित *a-sandita* or *a-sandina, as, ā, am* (rt. 4. *dā,* to bind), Ved. unbound, unrestrained.

असन्दिष्ट *a-sandishṭa, as, ā, am* (rt. *diś*), unapprised, uncommunicated.

असन्धान *a-sandhāna, am,* n. (rt. *dhā*), want of aim or object, disjunction.

A-sandhi, is, m. want of union or connection.

A-sandhita, as, ā, am, untied, unbound, at liberty, loose.

A-sandheya, as, ā, am, not to be made peace with.

असन्न *a-sanna, as, ā, am,* Ved. restless, without rest or repose.

असन्नद्ध *a-sannaddha, as, ā, am* (rt. *nah*), unarmed; born, produced; pretending to knowledge, conceited as a Paṇḍit or teacher; proud.

असन्निकर्ष *a-sannikarsha, as,* m. (rt. *kṛish*), non-perception of objects, not bringing them to the mind, remoteness.

A-sannikṛishṭa, as, ā, am, unperceived, undistinguished; not near, remote.

असन्निधि *a-sannidhi, is,* m. or *a-sannidhāna, am,* n. (rt. *dhā*), absence, distance; confidence, absence of doubt.

A-sannihita, as, ā, am, not near, far.

असन्न्यस्त *a-sannyasta, as, ā, am,* one who has not renounced the world.

असन्मान *a-sanmāna, am,* n. disrespect, impropriety.

असपत्न *a-sapatna, as, ī, am,* Ved. without another wife, without a rival; not attacked; without an adversary; not rivalling; (*am*), n. undisturbed condition, peace.

असपिण्ड *a-sapiṇḍa, as, ā, am,* unconnected by funeral offerings.

असबन्धु *a-sabandhu, us, us, u,* Ved. not related.

असभ्य *a-sabhya, as, ā, am,* unfit for an assembly, vulgar, low.

असम *a-sama, as, ā, am,* uneven, unequal either in surface or number; odd; unequalled, individual, without a fellow or equal; (*as*), m. a N. of Buddha or a Buddha. — *Asama-ratha, as, ā, am,* Ved. possessed of an unequalled chariot. — *Asama-bāṇa* or *asama-sāyaka, as,* m. or *asameshu* (°*ma-ish*°), *us,* m. having an odd number of arrows, i.e. the five-arrowed, an epithet of Kāma. — *Asamaujas* (°*ma-oj*°), *ās,* m., N. of a person.

A-samana, as, ā, am, going asunder or in different directions; uneven, unequal; (if, according to Sāy., derived fr. *manas*), of different minds, of different colours.

A-samāna, as, ā, am, not the same, not homogeneous, not of equal birth; unlike, unequal, different. — *Asamāna-kāraṇa, as, ā, am,* not having the same cause.

असमक्ष *a-samaksha, as, ā, am,* not visible, not present, absent.

असमग्र *a-samagra, as, ā, am,* incomplete, unentire, partial, part.

असमञ्ज *a-samañja, as,* or *a-samañjas, ās,* m., N. of a descendant of Ikshvāku, a son of Sagara by Keśinī and father of Aṇśumat.

A-samañjasa, as, ā, am, unequal, unlike; (*am*), n. unconformity, disparity, difference; (*am*), ind. unfitly, unbecomingly; in a fluctuating or confused manner.

असमद् *a-samad, t,* f., Ved. non-conflict, harmony, concord.

असमय *a-samaya, as,* m. unseasonableness; unfit or unfavourable time.

असमर्थ *a-samartha, as, ā, am,* unable, incompetent; feeble, weak.

असमर्पण *a-samarpaṇa, am,* n. non-delivery, not committing or intrusting anything to another.

A-samarpita, as, ā, am, unconsigned, unintrusted, undelivered.

असमवायिन् *a-samavāyin, ī, inī, i* (rt. *i* with *sam* and *ava*), accidental, not inherent, not intimate and inseparable. — *Asamavāyi-kāraṇa, am,* n. (in logic) accidental cause, not intimate or inherent relation (e.g. the separable conjunction of two different objects). — *Asamavāyi-tva, am,* n. the condition of something that is not inherent and inseparable.

A-samaveta, as, ā, am, not classed together, not connected, incoherent. — *Asamaveta-rūpam,* ind. incoherently.

असमष्टकाव्य *a-samashṭa-kāvya, as, ā, am,* Ved. of unattainable wisdom.

असमस्त *a-samasta, as, ā, am,* uncompounded, separate, several; uncollected; incomplete, imperfect.

असमाति *a-samāti, is, is, i,* Ved. having nothing equal, unparalleled; (*is*), m., N. of a king. — *Asamāty-ojas, ās, ās, as,* Ved. of unequalled strength.

असमान *a-samāna.* See *a-sama* above.

असमापित *a-samāpita* or *a-samāpta, as, ā, am,* unfinished, unaccomplished, incomplete.

A-samāpti, is, f. incompleteness.

असमावर्तक *a-samāvartaka, as,* or *a-samāvṛittika, as,* m. a religious student who has not completed the period of his residence with his teacher.

असमाहार *a-samāhāra, as,* m. non-recovery of anything; disjunction, disconnection.

A-samāhārya, as, ā, am, irrecoverable, not to be combined or united.

असमीक्ष्य *a-samīkshya,* ind. not having considered. — *Asamīkshya-kārin, ī, iṇī, i,* acting inconsiderately.

असमीचीन *a-samīćīna, as, ā, am,* improper, incorrect.

असमृद्ध *a-samṛiddha, as, ā, am,* Ved. not increased, not prosperous; one whose wishes are frustrated.

A-samṛiddhi, is, f. non-increase; failing, perishing; *(is, is, i),* unfortunate.

असम्पत्ति *a-sampatti, is,* f. (rt. *pad*), ill-luck, want of success; non-accomplishment, failure.

A-sampanna, as, ā, am, uneffected, unaccomplished.

असम्पर्क *a-samparka, as, ā, am* (rt. *pṛić*), destitute of contact, without connection or relation.

A-samparkīya, as, ā, am, unconnected with, not belonging to.

असम्पूर्ण *a-sampūrṇa, as, ā, am,* incomplete, not entire.

असम्प्रति *a-samprati,* ind., Ved. not according to the moment or to present circumstances.

असम्प्राप्य *a-samprāpya,* ind. without reaching.

असम्बद्ध *a-sambaddha, as, ā, am* (rt. *bandh*), not closely associated, distant, not related; unconnected, incoherent, unmeaning; improper, wrong; speaking unconnectedly or unmeaningly.

A-sambandha, as, ā, am, unconnected, not relating or belonging to; *(as),* m. non-connection.

असम्बाध *a-sambādha, as, ā, am* (rt. *bādh*), unconfined, spacious, wide, large; open, accessible; *(ā),* f. a species of the S'arkarī metre, consisting of fifty-six syllables; *(am),* n., Ved. non-confinement, open space.

असम्भव *a-sambhava, as, ā, am* (rt. *bhū*), inconsistent, improbable, unlikely; non-existent; *(am, ā),* n. f. any extraordinary event; non-existence.

A-sambhavyam, ind., Ved. in an incomprehensible or extraordinary manner.

A-sambhāvanā, f. difficulty or impossibility of conceiving or comprehending.

A-sambhāvanīya or *a-sambhāvya, as, ā, am,* inconceivable, incomprehensible, impossible. — *Asambhāvyam,* ind. in an incomprehensible or impossible manner.

A-sambhūta, as, ā, am, unproduced.

A-sambhūti, is, f., Ved. non-existence, the not being born again.

असम्भोग *a-sambhoga, as,* m. non-enjoyment, not using or enjoying.

असम्भ्रम *a-sambhrama, as, ā, am,* free from flurry, composed, cool; *(as),* m. calmness, steadiness.

असम्मत *a-sammata, as, ā, am* (rt. *man*), disapproved, despised; dissentient, differing from; averse, contrary. — *Asammatādāyin* (°*ta-ād*°), *ī, inī, i,* taking without the consent of the possessor; a thief.

A-sammati, is, f. dissent, difference of opinion; dislike, aversion.

A-sammāna, am, n. disrespect, disgrace.

असम्मित *a-sammita, as, ā, am,* Ved. not measured, immeasurable.

असम्मूढ *a-sammūḍha, as, ā, am* (rt. *muh*), calm, deliberate, cool, clear seeing, judging well.

A-sammoha, as, m. steadiness, calmness, composure.

असम्मृष्ट *a-sammṛishṭa, as, ā, am,* Ved. unpurified, uncleansed.

असम्मोष *a-sammosha, as,* m. the allowing nothing to escape (one's cognizance?).

असम्यञ्च् *a-samyańć, myan, mīćī, myak,* improper, incorrect; imperfect, incomplete. — *Asamyak-kārin, ī, iṇī, i,* acting unskilfully, inexpert, incompetent; acting improperly, ill-conducted, profligate.

असरु *asaru, us,* m. (rt. 2. *as*), the medicinal plant Blumea Lacera.

असर्वज्ञ *a-sarva-jña, as, ā, am,* not knowing everything.

असर्ववीर *a-sarva-vīra, as, ā, am,* Ved. not having all one's men collected round.

असल *asala, am,* n. iron; arms; a mantra.

असवर्ण *a-savarṇa, as, ā, am,* of a different caste, of a different colour.

असवस् *asavas,* m. pl. (of *asu,* q. v.), the vital airs or breath.

असश्चत् *a-saśćat, an, antī, at* (rt. *saść*), Ved. not ceasing, not sticking, not closed up, not drying up, untouched (as by any one attempting to enter a door). — *Asaśćatas,* f. pl. (i. e. *dhārās*), inexhaustible streams. — *Asaśćatā,* ind. in an inexhaustible manner.

A-saśćivas, ān, ćushī, as, Ved. not ceasing, not drying up.

अससत् *a-sasat, an, atī, at,* Ved. not sleeping.

असह *a-saha, as, ā, am* (rt. *sah*), not bearing, not enduring, intolerant, impatient; *(am),* n. the middle of the breast.

A-sahana, as, ā, am, unenduring, envious, jealous; *(as),* m. an enemy; *(am),* n. intolerance, impatience.

A-sahanīya or *a-sahitavya* or *a-sahya, as, ā, am,* unbearable, insufferable, insuperable. — *Asahya-pīḍa, as, ā, am,* causing intolerable pain.

A-sahamāna, as, ā, am, impatient, not bearing, not enduring.

A-sahishṇu, us, us, u, impatient, unenduring, envious; quarrelsome. — *Asahishṇu-tā,* f. impatience, envy.

असहाय *a-sahāya, as, ā, am,* without companions, friendless, lonely, solitary. — *Asahāya-tā,* f. or *asahāya-tva, am,* n. loneliness, solitude, the life of a hermit; friendlessness, being without a friend or patron. — *A-sahāya-vat, ān, atī, at,* without companions, friendless.

A-sahita, as, ā, am, unassociated, unaccompanied.

असाक्षात् *a-sākshāt,* ind. [cf. 2. *aksha* and *akshi,* the eye], not before the eyes, invisible, imperceptible; not present.

A-sākshika, as, ī, am, unattested, unwitnessed.

A-sākshin, ī, iṇī, i, incompetent as a witness, not an eye-witness.

A-sākshya, am, n. want of evidence.

असात्म्य *a-sātmya, as, ā, am,* unwholesome, disagreeing (as food?).

असाद *a-sāda, as, ā, am,* Ved. seatless, not sitting.

असाधन *a-sādhana, as, ā, am* (rt. *sādh*), without means, destitute of means, resources, materials, instruments or implements; *(am),* n. non-accomplishment, not proving or establishing.

A-sādhanīya or *a-sādhya, as, ā, am,* not to be effected or completed, not proper or able to be accomplished; incurable, irremediable, not susceptible of proof.

A-sādhita, as, ā, am, unaccomplished.

असाधारण *a-sādhāraṇa, as, ā, am,* not common, special, specific; *(am),* n. speciality, species, special property.

असाधु *a-sādhu, us, us* or *vī, u,* not good, wicked, bad; *(vī),* f. an unchaste wife. — *Asādhu-tā,* f. or *asādhu-tva, am,* n. wickedness. — *Asādhu-vṛittā,* f. an unchaste woman.

असान्द्र *a-sāndra, as, ā, am,* not close, fine, delicate but with interstices, transparent.

असान्निध्य *a-sānnidhya, am,* n. non-proximity, distance.

असामयिक *a-sāmayika, as, ī, am,* unseasonable.

असामर्थ्य *a-sāmarthya, am,* n. weakness.

असामान्य *a-sāmānya, as, ā, am,* peculiar, not common; *(am),* n. peculiar or special property.

असामि *a-sāmi, is, is, i,* Ved. not half, entire, whole, complete; *(i),* ind. completely. — *Asāmi-śavas, ās, ās, as,* Ved. having complete strength.

असाम्प्रत *a-sāmprata, as, ī, am,* not fit, not becoming, improper. — *A-sāmpratam,* ind. unfitly, improperly, inopportunely.

असाम्य *a-sāmya, am,* n. (fr. *a-sama*), difference, dissimilarity; unsuitableness (in medicine or diet), unwholesomeness; disagreeableness.

असार *a-sāra, as, ā, am,* sapless; without genuine strength and value; without vigour, spoiled, unfit, vain, unprofitable; weak, feeble, infirm, fragile; *(as),* m., N. of the plant Ricinus Communis or castor-oil tree; *(am),* n. Agallochum. — *Asāra-tā,* f. saplessness; unfitness, fragility.

असावधान *a-sāvadhāna, as, ā, am,* careless, inadvertent. — *Asāvadhāna-tā,* f. or *asāvadhāna-tva, am,* n. carelessness.

असाहस *a-sāhasa, am,* n. absence of violence, gentleness.

A-sāhasika, as, ī, am, not violent, peaceable, gentle.

असाहाय्य *a-sāhāyya, am,* n. want of assistance or co-operation.

असि *asi, is,* m. (fr. rt. 2. *as*), a sword, a cimeter, a knife used for killing animals. — *Asi-gaṇḍa, as,* m. a small pillow for the cheek. — *Asi-danshṭra* or *asi-danshṭraka, as,* m. the marine monster Makara, painted on the banner of Kāmadeva. — *Asi-danta, as,* m. a crocodile. — *Asi-dhārā,* f. the edge of a sword. — *Asidhārā-vrata, am,* n. a vow of standing on the edge of a sword, used figuratively for any hopelessly difficult task. — *Asi-dhāva* or *asi-dhāvaka, as,* m. an armourer, a furbisher, a sword or tool cleaner. — *Asi-dhenu, us,* or *asi-dhenukā,* f. a knife. — *Asi-pattra, as, am,* m. n. the blade of a sword; a sheath, a scabbard; *(as, ā, am),* whose leaves are swords, having sword-shaped leaves; *(as),* m. the sugar-cane, Scirpus Kysoor Roxb.; a kind of tree which grows in the lower world; a hell paved with swords. — *Asi-pattraka, as,* m. sugar-cane. — *Asipattra-vana, am,* n. a hell where the trees have leaves as sharp as swords. — *Asi-patha, am,* n., Ved. the course of a sacrificial knife (?). — *Asi-puććhaka, as,* m. the Gangetic porpoise, Delphinus Gangeticus. — *Asi-putrikā* or *asi-putrī,* f. a knife, lit. daughter of a sword. — *Asi-mat, ān, atī, at,* Ved. furnished with knives or daggers. — *Asi-meda, as,* m. the fetid Mimosa Vachellia Farnesiana W. and A. — *Asi-loman, ā,* m., N. of a Dānava. — *Asi-hatya, am,* n. fighting with knives or swords. — *Asi-heti, is,* m. a swordsman or soldier armed with a sword. — *Asy-asi,* ind. sword to sword, sword against sword.

Asika, am, n. (fr. *asi* ?), the part of the face between the underlip and the chin.

असिक्नी *asiknī.* See 2. *asita.*

असित 1. *a-sita, as, ā, am* (rt. *si*), Ved. unbound.

असित 2. *asita, as,* f. *asitā* or Ved. f. *asiknī, am,* (*sita,* 'white,' appears to have been formed from this word, which is probably original, and not a compound of *a* and *sita;* cf. the formation of *sura* fr. *asura*), dark-coloured, black, dark-blue; *(as),* m. the black colour; N. of the planet Saturn; the dark fortnight of a lunar month; N. of a being presiding over darkness and magic; N. of a descendant of Kaśyapa and several other persons; N. of a mountain; a black snake; *(tā),* f. the indigo plant; N. of an Apsaras; *(asiknī),* f., Ved. 'the dark one,' the night; a girl attending upon the inner or women's apartments (whose hair is not whitened by age); N. of a daughter of Vīraṇa and wife of Daksha; N. of the river Akesines (afterwards Ćandra-bhāga) in the Pañjāb. — *Asita-keśānta, as, ā, am,* having black locks. — *Asita-grīva, as, ā, am,* Ved. having a black neck. — *Asita-jñu, us, ūs, u,* Ved. having black knees. — *Asita-nayana, as, ā, am,* black-eyed. — *Asita-bhrū, ūs, ūs, u,* having black eyelids. — *Asita-mṛiga, as,* m., N. of a family. — *Asitābhra-śekhara* (°*ta-abh*°), *as,* m., N. of a Buddha. — *Asitāmburuha* (°*ta-am*°), *as,* m. the blue lotus. — *Asitārćis* (°*ta-ar*°), *is,* m. fire. — *Asitālu* (°*ta-āl*°), *us,* m., N. of a plant. — *Asitāśman* (°*ta-aś*°), *ā,* m. the lapis lazuli; any black or dark-blue stone. — *Asitotpala* (°*ta-ut*°), *am,* n. the blue lotus, Nymphæa Cærulea. — *Asitopala* (°*ta-up*°), *am,* n. lapis lazuli.

Asiknikā, f. a woman-servant [cf. *asiknī*].

Asitakī, f., N. of a plant.

असिद्ध *a-siddha, as, ā, am,* imperfect, incomplete; unaccomplished, uneffected; unproved; unripe.

A-siddhi, is, f. imperfect or incomplete accomplishment, failure; (in logic) want of proof, conclusion not warranted by the premises.

असिन्व *a-sinva, as, ā, am,* or *a-sinvat, an, atī, at,* Ved. insatiable.

असिर *asira, as,* m. (fr. rt. 2. *as,* to throw), Ved. a beam, a ray; an arrow, a bolt.

Asishṭha, as, ā, am, (superl.) Ved. most skilful in shooting (arrows &c.).

असी *asī,* f., N. of a river, = *asi.*

असीमकृष्ण *asīma-kṛishṇa, as,* m., N. of a prince.

असु *asu, us,* m. (fr. rt. 1. *as,* to be), breath, life, spiritual life; life of the spiritual world or departed spirits; water?; [cf. ἀάζω, ἄσθμα]; (*asavas*), nom. pl. the five vital breaths or airs of the body; animal life; (*u*), n. reflection, thought or the heart as the seat of it; grief. — *Asu-dhāraṇa, am,* n. life, existence. — *Asu-nīta, am,* n., Ved. the world of spirits, or (*as*), m. the lord of the spirits. — *Asu-nīti, is,* f., Ved. the life or the world of spirits; that life personified as a female deity invoked for the preservation of life, or as Yama, lord of the dead. — *Asu-bhaṅga, as,* m. breaking of life; fear about life; danger of life. — *Asu-bhṛit, t,* m. breathing, living, a creature. — *Asu-mat, ān, atī, at,* living, breathing; (*mān*), m. life, the principle of vitality, the portion of spirit connected with the attributes of existence. — *Asu-sama, as, ā, am,* dearly loved, as dear as life; (*as*), m. a husband, a lover.

Asura, as, ā, am, Ved. living, alive, spiritual; an epithet of the supreme spirit; Varuṇa; incorporeal, superhuman, divine; (*as*), m. spirit; an incorporeal being of an evil kind; an evil spirit, a demon; a ghost or spectre; a general name for the chief of the Asuras [these Asuras are often regarded as the children of Diti by Kaśyapa, see *daitya;* as such they are demons of the first order in perpetual hostility with the gods, and must not be confounded with the Rākshasas or imps who animate dead bodies and disturb sacrifices]; the sun; Rāhu; an elephant; N. of a warrior-tribe; (according to Sāy.) a cloud?; (*ā*), f. night; a zodiacal sign; a prostitute; (*ī*), f. a female demon, the wife of an Asura; N. of the plant Sinapis Racemosa Roxb. [Observe, in later Sanskṛit, *sura* has been formed from *asura,* as *sita* from *asita,* q. v.] — *Asura-kumāra, ās,* m. pl. a class of deities belonging to the Bhavanādhīśas. — *Asura-kshayaṇa, as, ā, am,* or *asura-kshiti, is, is, i,* Ved. destroying the Asuras. — *Asura-tva, am,* n., Ved. spirituality, supernatural or divine dignity. — *Asura-māyā,* f., Ved. demoniacal magic. — *Asura-rakshasa, āni,* n. pl., Ved. the Asuras and Rākshasas; (*am*), n. sing. a demoniacal being, partaking of the qualities of both the classes of evil spirits. — *Asura-rāj, ṭ,* m. king of the Asuras, epithet of the Asura Baka. — *Asura-ripu, us,* m. enemy of the Asuras, epithet of Vishṇu. — *Asura-sūdana, as,* m. destroyer of the Asuras, epithet of Vishṇu. — *Asura-han, ā, ghnī, a,* Ved. destroying the Asuras, epithet of Agni, Indra, &c. — *Asurāćārya* (°*ra-āć*°), *as,* m. teacher of the Asuras; epithet of the regent of the planet Venus. — *Asurādhipa* (°*ra-adh*°), *as,* m. lord of the Asuras; N. of Bali Vairoćani and of Māyādhara. — *Asurāhva* (°*ra-āh*°), *am,* n. bell-metal, named after an Asura.

Asurya, as, ā, am, Ved. incorporeal, spiritual, divine; demoniacal, belonging to the Asuras; (*am*), n. spirituality, divine nature; the incorporeal, the collective body of spiritual beings; (according to Sāy.) the water of the clouds.

असुकर *a-sukara, as, ā, am,* not easy to be done, difficult, arduous.

असुक्षण *asukshaṇa,* a various reading for *asūkshaṇa,* q. v.

असुख *a-sukha, as, ā, am,* unhappy, sorrowful, melancholic; (*am*), n. sorrow, pain, affliction. — *Asukha-jīvikā,* f. a joyless life. — *Asukha-pīḍita, as, ā, am,* pained with grief. — *Asukhāvaha* (°*kha-āv*°), *as, ā, am,* producing unhappiness. — *Asukhāvishṭa* (°*kha-āv*°), *as, ā, am,* afflicted with grief, pain, or unhappiness. — *Asukhodaya* (°*kha-ud*°), *as, ā, am,* causing or ending in unhappiness. — *Asukhodarka* (°*kha-ud*°), *as, ā, am,* productive of or ending in unhappiness.

A-sukhin, ī, inī, i, unhappy, sorrowful, afflicted.

असुगम *a-sugama, as, ā, am,* difficult of attainment or accomplishment, hard, unattainable; difficult to be understood.

असुत 1. *a-suta, as, ā, am* (rt. 2. *su*), Ved. not pressed out, not cleared or purified, not ready (as the Soma juice).

A-sunva, as, ā, am, or *a-sunvat, an, atī, at,* or *a-sushvi, is, is, i,* Ved. not pressing out the Soma juice, not worshipping the gods, wicked.

असुत 2. *a-suta, as, ā, am* (rt. 1. *su*), childless. See *a-sū.*

असुतर *a-sutara, as, ā, am* (rt. *tṛi*), not to be easily passed.

असुतृप् *a-sutṛip, p, p, p,* Ved. insatiable, not easily satiated.

असुनिरस *a-sunirasa, as, ā, am,* disagreeable, unpleasant, offensive.

असुन्दर *a-sundara, as, ā* or *ī, am,* plain, ugly; improper, unbecoming.

असुप्त *a-supta, as, ā, am,* not asleep. — *A-supta-dṛiś, k, k, k,* never closing the eyes in sleep, ever-seeing.

असुम्न *a-sumna, as, ā, am,* Ved. contrary, adverse.

असुर *asura.* See under *asu.*

असुरक्ष *a-suraksha, as, ā, am,* perishable, volatile, transitory.

A-surakshya, as, ā, am, difficult of retention or preservation.

असुरसा *a-surasā,* f. the plant Basilicum Pilosum Benth.

असुलभ *a-sulabha, as, ā, am,* difficult of attainment.

असुष्वि *a-sushvi.* See under 1. *a-suta.*

असुस्थ *a-sustha, as, ā, am,* unwell, indisposed, not well placed, uncomfortable. — *Asustha-tā,* f. indisposition, sickness.

असुहृद् *a-suhṛid, t,* m. not a friend, an enemy.

असू *a-sū, ūs, ūs,* m. f. (rt. 1. *su,* to bring forth), Ved. not bringing forth, barren.

A-sūta or *a-sūtika, as, ā, am,* Ved. one who has not brought forth, barren.

A-sūti, is, f. non-production; obstruction, removal; barrenness.

A-sūsu, us, us, u, Ved. not bringing forth, barren.

असूक्षण *asūkshaṇa* or *asukshaṇa* or *asurkshaṇa* or *asūrkshaṇa* or *astarkshaṇa, am,* n. (etymology doubtful), disrespect.

असूक्ष्म *a-sūkshma, as, ā, am,* not fine, not minute, large, thick, gross.

असूय *asūya* (fr. *asu*), nom. P. A. *asūyati, -te, -yitum,* to murmur at, to detract from, depreciate; to envy, scorn, be displeased or discontented with, or grumble at (with dat. or acc.): Caus. *asūyayati, -yitum,* to cause to murmur or be displeased or discontented.

Asūyaka, as, ikā, am, detracting, envious, calumnious, discontented, displeased; (by some written *asūka?*).

Asūyana, am, n. calumny, detraction.

Asūyayitvā, ind. having scorned, having cursed.

Asūyā, f. displeasure, indignation, especially at the merits or the happiness of another, envy, jealousy; calumny, detraction; aversion; N. of the wife of Atri.

Asūyitṛi, tā, trī, tṛi, murmuring, detracting, displeased.

Asūyu, us, us, u, envious, displeased; (*us*), m. calumny.

असूर *a-sūra, am,* n., Ved. absence of a person to press out the Soma juice; (Sāy.) a place or country devoid of praise or worship.

असूर्क्षण *asūrkshaṇa, am,* n. disrespect. See *asūkshaṇa.*

असूर्त *a-sūrta, as, ā, am,* Ved. not moving, remote (?).

असूर्य *a-sūrya, as, ā, am,* Ved. sunless.

A-sūryam-paśyā, f. the wife of a king who being shut up in the inner apartments never sees the sun; a chaste and loyal wife.

असृज् *asṛij, k,* n. (said to be fr. rt. *sṛij* with *a,* which may stand for *ava* or *ā*), blood; saffron; (*k*), m. a kind of religious abstraction; [cf. Lat. *sanguis.*] — *Asṛik-kara, as,* m. the essence of the body, lymph, serum, &c. — *Asṛik-pa, as,* m. a Rākshasa or imp of malicious propensities, who drinks blood. — *Asṛik-pāta, as,* m. the falling of blood; (*ās*), m. pl. drops of blood, as from a wound. — *Asṛik-pāvan, ā, ā, a,* Ved. drinking blood. — *Asṛik-śrāva, as,* m. bleeding, letting blood. — *Asṛik-śrāvin, ī, iṇī, i,* bleeding, who or what takes away blood. — *Asṛig-dara, as,* m. irregular or excessive menstruation, mœnorrhagia. — *Asṛig-doha, as, ā, am,* shedding blood, bleeding. — *Asṛig-dharā,* f. the skin. — *Asṛig-dhārā,* f. a stream of blood; the skin. — *Asṛig-vahā,* f. a blood-vessel. — *Asṛig-vimokshaṇa, am,* n. blood-letting, bleeding. — *Asṛiṅ-miśra, as, ā, am,* mixed or covered with blood. — *Asṛiṅ-mukha, as, ī, am,* Ved. whose face is bloody. — *Asṛi-pāṭa, as, ī,* m. f. (for *asṛik-pāta*), a stream of blood.

असृणि *a-sṛiṇi, is, is, i,* unrestrained.

असृष्ट *a-sṛishṭa, as, ā, am* (rt. *sṛij*), uncreated; undistributed, not presented; continued. — *Asṛishṭānna* (°*ṭa-an*°), *as, ā, am,* one who does not distribute food.

असेचन *a-sećana* or *a-sećanaka, as, ā, am,* that on which one cannot look enough; charming, lovely [cf. *ā-sećanaka*].

असेन्य *a-senya, as, ā, am,* Ved. not worthy of an army; not striking, not wounding (?).

असेवन *a-sevana, am,* n. or *a-sevā,* f. (rt.

sev), disregarding, neglecting; not following or practising, shunning; disregard, inattention, disobedience.

A-sevita, as, ā, am, neglected, unattended to, disobeyed; abstained from, disused. — *A-seviteśvara-dvāra* (°*ta-iś*°), *as, ā, am,* not waiting at the doors of the great.

A-sevya, as, ā, am, not to be served or attended to; not to be used or practised, not to be eaten, drank, &c.

असौकृ *asau-kṛi*, cl. 8. P. *-karoti, -kartum,* to do such and such a thing.

Asau-nāman, ā, ā, a, Ved. having such and such a name.

असौन्दर्य *a-saundarya, am,* n. ugliness.

असौम्य *a-saumya, as, ā, am,* ugly, unlovely; disagreeable, displeasing. — *Asaumya-svara, as, ā, am,* having a bad or croaking voice.

असौष्ठव *a-saushṭhava, am,* n. ugliness, deformity; demerit, worthlessness.

अस्कन्न *a-skanna, as, ā, am* (rt. *skand*), Ved. not spilt, not effused, not fallen; not sprinkled, not covered; permanent, durable.

A-skandita, as, ā, am, not spilt, not fallen, not gone, not attacked. — *Askandita-vrata, as, ā, am,* true to vows.

अस्कम्भन *a-skambhana, am,* n., Ved. want of a pillar or support.

अस्कृधोयु *a-skṛidhoyu, us, us, u,* Ved. not narrow or deficient, abundant.

अस्खलित *a-skhalita, as, ā, am,* unshaken, unyielding, firm, permanent; not stumbling or slipping, undeviating. — *A-skhalita-prayāṇa, as, ā, am,* not stumbling in progress, with unfaltering step.

अस्त 1. *asta, as, ā, am* (fr. rt. 2. *as*), thrown, cast; expelled, sent away; sent, despatched; removed, laid or set aside; finished; (*ā*), f., Ved. a missile, an arrow. — *Asta-kopa, as, ā, am,* whose anger is laid aside. — *Asta-dhī, īs, īs, i,* foolish. — *Asta-vat, ān, atī, at,* obstructed (?). — *Asta-vyasta, as, ā, am,* scattered hither and thither, confused, disordered, irrelevant. — *Asta-saṅkhya, as, ā, am,* innumerable.

Astṛi, tā, m., Ved. throwing, a shooter.

अस्त 2. *asta, am,* n. (fr. rt. 1. *as*?), Ved. home; death, end; (*as*), m. the western mountain, behind which the sun is supposed to set; sunset; (in astronomy) the seventh lunar mansion. — *Astam,* ind. at home, home. — *Astam i* or *gam* or *yā,* to go home; to go down, to set; *astaṃ nī* or *vah,* to conduct or lead home; to lead to setting, to cause to set; *astaṃ gam* or *i* or *prāp,* to go to one's eternal home, to cease, to vanish, to die. — *Asta-gata, as, ā, am,* set (as the sun). — *Asta-gamana, am,* n. setting. — *Asta-giri, is,* m. the western mountain. — *Astam-aya, as,* m. or *astam-ayana, am,* n. disappearance, setting. — *Astam-ita, as, ā, am,* set (as the sun). — *Astāćala* (°*ta-ać*°), *as,* m. the western mountain. — *Astāćalāvalambin* (°*la-av*°), *ī, inī, i,* reclining on the western mountain, about to set. — *Astādri* (°*ta-ad*°), *is,* m. the western mountain. — *Astāvalambana* (°*ta-av*°), *am,* n. the resting of a heavenly body on the western part of the horizon. — *Astāvalambin, ī, inī, i,* setting as the sun, on the point of setting.

Astaka, am, n., Ved. home; (*as*), m. going to one's eternal home, beatitude, eternal felicity.

Astatāti, is, f., Ved. home.

Astamati, f. (perhaps a corruption of *aṅśu-mati*), the plant Desmodium Gangeticum.

Astamana, am, n. corruption of (*astam-ayana*), setting.

Astamīke, ind., Ved. at home, near.

Astā, ind., Ved. at home.

अस्तब्ध *a-stabdha, as, ā, am,* not firm or self-possessed, confounded. — *Astabdha-tva, am,* n. being confused or confounded, want of self-possession.

अस्तर्क्षण *astarkshaṇa, am,* n. disrespect. See *asūkshaṇa.*

अस्ताग *astāga, as,* m., N. of the fifteenth Arhat of the past Utsarpiṇī.

अस्ताघ *astāgha, as, ā, am,* very deep. See *asthāgha.*

अस्ति *asti,* ind. (3rd sing. pres. of rt. 1. *as*), being, existent, present; (*is*), f., N. of a sister of Prāpti, daughter of Jarāsandhas and wife of Kaṅsa. — *Asti-kāya, as,* m. a category or predicament. — *Asti-kshīra, as, ā, am,* having milk. — *Asti-tva, am,* n. existence. — *Asti-nāsti* (°*na-as*°), ind. doubtful, partly true and partly not. — *Astināsti-tva, am,* n. or *astināsti-tā,* f. uncertain or doubtful existence; partial existence. — *Asti-pravāda, am,* n. title of the fourth of the fourteen Pūrvas or older writings of the Jainas. — *Asti-mat, ān, atī, at,* possessed of property, wealthy, opulent.

Astu (3rd sing. impv. of rt. 1. *as*), let it be, be it so, implying assent, also reluctance and pain. — *Astun-kāra, as, ā, am,* efficacious, as a medicament; (*astum* is here the acc. of *astu,* 'producing that which the physician promises shall be.') — *Astv-evam,* ind. be it so.

अस्तुत *a-stuta, as, ā, am* (rt. *stu*), Ved. not praised, not deserving praise; not recited in prayer.

A-stuti, is, m. the absence of praise.

अस्तृत *a-stṛita, as, ā, am,* Ved. not overcome, invincible, indestructible. — *Astṛita-yajvan, ā, ā, a,* Ved. sacrificing indefatigably or invincibly.

अस्तेन *a-stena, am,* or *a-steya, am,* n. absence of theft, honesty.

अस्त्य *astya, am,* n., Ved. a house. See 2. *asta.*

अस्त्यान *a-styāna, am,* n. reproach, blame.

अस्त्र *astra, am,* n. (fr. rt. 2. *as*), a missile weapon, bolt, arrow; bow; a weapon in general, a sword; [with *astra* cf. Gr. ἄστρον and ἀστήρ, perhaps that which throws out or emits rays of light.] — *Astra-kaṇṭaka, as,* m. an arrow. — *Astra-kāraka* or *astra-kāra, as,* or *astra-kārin, ī,* m. an armourer, maker of weapons. — *Astra-kshepaka, as, ā, am,* shooting arrows. — *Astra-ćikitsaka, as,* m. a surgeon. — *Astra-ćikitsā,* f. surgery. — *Astra-jit, t,* n., N. of a plant. — *Astra-jīva, as,* m. a soldier, a warrior. — *Astra-dhāraṇa, am,* n. the bearing of arms. — *Astra-dhārin, ī,* m. one who bears arms, a soldier. — *Astra-nivāraṇa, am,* n. warding off a blow. — *Astra-mārja* or *astramārjaka, as,* m. an armourer, a sword-polisher or tool-cleaner, furbisher. — *Astra-yuddha, as,* m. fighting with weapons. — *Astra-lāghava, am,* n. dexterity in arms. — *Astra-vid, t, t, t,* skilled in the science of arms or war. — *Astra-vidyā,* f. the military science. — *Astra-vidvas, ān, ushī, as,* skilled in the use of arms. — *Astra-vṛishṭi, is,* f. shower of arrows. — *Astra-veda, as,* m. the science of arms and war. — *Astra-śastra, am,* n. all sorts of arms (as arrows and swords). — *Astra-śikshā,* f. military exercise, passage of arms. — *Astra-sāyaka, as,* m. an iron arrow. — *Astra-hīna, as, ā, am,* unarmed, defenceless. — *Astrāgāra* (°*tra-āg*°), *as,* m. an arsenal, an armoury. — *Astrāghāta* (°*tra-āgh*°), *as,* m. a wound, a cut. — *Astrāhata* (°*tra-āh*°), *as, ā, am,* struck, wounded, killed.

Astrin, ī, iṇī, i, fighting with a missile weapon, an archer.

अस्त्री *a-strī,* f. not a woman; (in gram.) the masculine and neuter genders.

A-strīka, as, ā, am, having no wife, without a woman.

A-straiṇa, as, ī, am, Ved. without a wife.

अस्थन् *asthan,* the base of some of the cases of *asthi,* 'a bone,' q.v.; thus, inst. *asthnā,* &c.

Astha = *asthi* at the end of some compounds.

अस्थला *a-sthalā,* f., N. of an Apsaras.

अस्था *asthā,* f. (?), Ved. a thunderbolt.

अस्थाग *asthāga, as, ā, am* (rt. *sthā* with *a*?), very deep; also written *astāga, asthāgha, asthāna, asthāra.*

अस्थान *a-sthāna, as, ā, am* (rt. *sthā*), very deep; (*am*), n. no place, a place where there is no firm footing, a bad or wrong place; (*am*), ind. unsuitably, unseasonably; *a-sthāne,* ind. unseasonably, inopportunely.

A-sthāyin, ī, inī, i, not permanant, perishable, transient.

A-sthāvara, as, ā, am, moveable, moving, not fixed; (in law) personal, as property, money, cattle, &c., opposed to land.

A-sthita, as, ā, am, not standing still, not fixed.

A-sthiti, is, f. want of place or condition, want of firm continuance.

अस्थि *asthi, i,* Ved. *asthan, a,* n. (said to be fr. rt. 2. *as*; perhaps fr. *a-sthā* for *ā-sthā*), a bone; the kernel or stone of a fruit. At end of compounds *astha* is found, e. g. *an-astha,* q. v. The weakest cases of *asthi* are derived from *asthan,* q. v.; the Veda has also *asthāni, asthabhis,* &c. [cf. Lat. *os, ossis,* assimilated fr. *ostis*; Gr. ὀστέον; Slav. *kosti,* with *k* prefixed]. — *Asthan-vat, ān, atī, at,* Ved. having bones, bony. — *Asthi-kṛit, t, t, t,* m. f. n. marrow. — *Asthi-ććhallita, am,* n. a particular fracture of the bones. — *Asthi-ja, as, ā, am,* Ved. produced in the bones; (*as*), m. marrow; the thunderbolt; in the last sense a various reading for *aksha-ja.* — *Asthi-jña, as,* m. marrow. — *Asthi-tuṇḍa, as, ā,* m. f. a bird (whose mouth or beak consists of bone). — *Asthi-tejas, as,* n. marrow. — *Asthi-toda, as,* m. pain in the bones. — *Asthi-tvać, k,* f. the periosteum. — *Asthi-dhanvan, ā,* m. a N. of Śiva. — *Asthi-pañjara, as,* m. a skeleton; lit. a cage of bones. — *Asthi-bhaksha, as,* m. a dog (eating bones). — *Asthi-bhaṅga, as,* m. fracture of the bones; N. of the plant Vitis Quadrangularis. — *Asthi-bhuj, k,* m. a bone-eater, a dog. — *Asthi-bhūyas, ān, asī, as,* Ved. consisting chiefly of bones, dried up. — *Asthi-bheda, as,* m. fracturing, breaking or wounding a bone; a sort of bone, a bone. — *Asthi-bhedaka, as, ā, am,* a bone-breaker, who or what breaks bones. — *Asthi-mat, ān, atī, at,* having bones, vertebrated. — *Asthi-maya, as, ī, am,* bony, consisting of bones. — *Asthi-mālā,* f. a necklace of bones. — *Asthi-mālin, ī,* m. an epithet of Śiva (this deity being commonly represented with a necklace of skulls). — *Asthi-yoga, as,* m. the joining of a broken bone. — *Asthi-vat, ān, atī, at,* bony, osseous. — *Asthi-vigraha, as,* m. a N. of Bhṛiṅgin, one of Śiva's attendants. — *Asthi-śṛiṅkhalā,* f. or *asthi-saṃhāra, as, ī,* m. f., N. of the plant Heliotropium Indicum. — *Asthi-śosha, as,* m. dryness and decay of the bones. — *Asthi-saṃhāraka, as,* m. 'bone-seizer,' the adjutant bird. — *Asthi-sańćaya, as,* m. collecting the bones or their ashes after burning a corpse. — *Asthi-sandhi, is,* m. a joint, an articulation; uniting of a broken bone. — *Asthi-samarpaṇa, am,* n. throwing the bones of a dead body into the Ganges. — *Asthi-sāra, as,* m. marrow. — *Asthi-sthūṇa, as,* m. the body, 'having the bones for its pillars.' — *Asthi-sneha, as,* m. marrow. — *Asthi-sraṅsa, as, ī, am,* Ved. causing the bones to fall asunder.

Asthika, am, n. a bone; used at the end of compounds, e. g. *an-asthika, as, ā, am,* boneless.

अस्थिर *a-sthira, as, ā, am,* unsteady; trembling, shaking; uncertain, unascertained; unworthy of confidence. — *Asthira-tā,* f. or *asthira-tva, am,* n. unsteadiness, fickleness, mutability.

A-stheyas, ān, asī, as, unsteady, not firm.

A-sthairya, am, n. instability, unsteadiness.

अस्थूरि *a-sthūri, is, is, i,* Ved. furnished with more than one horse; not one-sided.

अस्थूल *a-sthūla, as, ā, am,* not bulky, delicate.

अस्नातृ *a-snātṛi, tā, trī, tṛi,* Ved. not fond of bathing, not a bather.

अस्नाविर *a-snāvira, as, ā, am,* Ved. without sinews, without bands.

अस्निग्ध *a-snigdha, as, ā, am* (rt. *snih*), not smooth, harsh, hard, dry; unkind.—*Asnigdha-dāru, u,* n. a kind of pine tree.

A-sneha, as, ā, am, unkind; harsh, hard, dry; (*as*), m. unkindness, want of affection; absence of oiliness.

अस्पन्द *a-spanda, as, ā, am,* not trembling, not moving, fixed, unchangeable.

अस्पर्श *a-sparśa, as, ā, am* (rt. *spṛiś*), not touching, not in contact; (*as*), m. not touching, non-contact.

A-sparśana, am, n. non-contact, avoiding the contact of anything, especially of one who is impure.

A-sparśanīya, as, ā, am, not to be touched, impure.

A-sparśita, as, ā, am, untouched.

A-spṛiśya, as, ā, am, not to be touched, intangible.

A-spṛishṭa, as, ā, am, untouched.—*Aspṛishṭa-rajas-tamaska, as, ā, am,* perfectly pure.—*Aspṛishṭa-vahni, is, is, i,* unscathed by fire.

A-spṛishṭi, is, f. not touching, avoiding contact.

अस्पष्ट *a-spashṭa, as, ā, am,* indistinct.

अस्पृत *a-spṛita, as, ā, am,* Ved. unconquered, irresistible.

अस्पृह *a-spṛiha, as, ā, am,* undesirous, content; indifferent.

A-spṛihaṇīya, as, ā, am, undesirable.

अस्फुट *a-sphuṭa, am,* n. indistinct speech; (*as, ā, am*), indistinct, obscure, invisible, unblown.—*Asphuṭa-phala, am,* n. indistinct result; (in geom.) gross area of a triangle, &c.—*A-sphuṭa-vāć, k, k, k,* lisping, speaking indistinctly.

अस्म *a-sma,* a pronominal base (supposed to be compounded fr. *a* and *sma*) from which several cases of the pronoun of the 1st person plur. and of the 3rd sing. are derived. See also the next.

अस्मद् *asmad,* the plural base of the 1st personal pronoun (said to be fr. 2. *as,* 'to throw', Uṇ-sūt. I. 138; or fr. 1. *as,* 'to be'), nom. sing. *aham,* 'I,' du. *āvām,* 'we two,' pl. *vayam,* 'we;' acc. pl. *asmān,* inst. *asmābhis,* dat. *asmabhyam,* abl. *asmat* or *asmattas,* gen. *asmākam,* loc. *asmāsu.* Native grammarians derive the sing. as well as plur. from the base, *asmad.* The form *asme,* common to all oblique cases of the plur., is confined to the Vedas; and sometimes a form *asmāka* is used for the gen. *asmākam.* The form *nas* for acc., dat., and gen. is enclitic. The form *asma* is met with in the Vedas as well as the *asmad* of the classical language, especially at the beginning of compounds [cf. Gr. ἄμμες fr. ἄσμες; Goth. *unsa* for *usna;* Mod. Germ. *unser*].—*Asma-trā,* ind., Ved. to us, with us, among us.—*Asmatrāńć, āṅ, āćī, āk,* Ved. turned towards us.—*Asmad-rāta, as, ā, am,* Ved. given by us.—*Asma-druh, -dhruk, k, k,* Ved. forming a plot against us or me, inimical.—*Asmad-vidha, as, ā, am,* or *asmādṛiśa, as, ī, am,* or *asmādṛiś, k, k, k,* similar, or like us or me; one of us.—*Asme-hiti, is,* f., Ved. errand or message for us.

Asmadīya, as, ā, am, our, ours.

Asmadryańć, āṅ, drīćī, ak, Ved. turned towards us; (*k*), ind. towards us.

Asmayu, us, us, u, Ved. endeavouring to attain us, desiring us, favourable to us.

Asmāka, as, ā, am, Ved. our, ours.

अस्मन्त *asmanta, am,* n. a furnace or fire-place. See *aśmanta.*

अस्मरण *a-smaraṇa, am,* n. (rt. *smṛi*), forgetfulness, forgetting.

A-smaraṇīya, as, ā, am, not to be recollected.

A-smārta, as, ī, am, immemorial, not within memory; illegal, not according to law; not belonging to the Hindū institutes.

A-smṛita, as, ā, am, not remembered, forgotten.

A-smṛiti, is, f. want of memory, forgetfulness; the not being part of the institutes of law; (*i*), ind., Ved. inattentively.

अस्मिता *asmi-tā,* f. (abstract noun formed fr. *asmi,* 1st pers. sing. pres. of 1. *as,* 'I am'), egotism.

अस्मेर *a-smera, as, ā, am* (rt. *smi*), Ved. not sullen, confiding.

अस्यन्दमान *a-syandamāna, as, ā, am,* Ved. not gliding away.

अस्यवामीय *asyavāmīya, am,* n. the hymn beginning with the words *asya vām* (Ṛig-veda I. 164).

अस्यहत्य *asya-hatya,* अस्यहेति *asya-heti.* See Gaṇa Anuśatikādi to Pāṇini VII. 3, 20.

अस्युद्यत *asy-udyata, as, ā, am* (for *udyatāsi*), having the sword raised.

अस्र *asra, as,* m. (said to be fr. 2. *as*), hair of the head; a corner, an angle, see *aśra;* (*am*), n. blood; a tear, see *asṛij* and *asan.*—*Asra-kaṇṭha, as,* m. an arrow; (perhaps a variation from *astra-kaṇṭha?*).—*Asra-khadira, as,* m. a red Mimosa.—*Asra-ja, am,* n. flesh.—*Asra-jit, t,* m. a plant; see *astra-jit.*—*Asra-pa, as,* m. a Rākshasa or goblin; (*ā*), f. a leech; a Ḍākinī or female imp.—*Asra-pattraka, as,* m., N. of a plant, Rubia Cordifolia L. (?).—*Asra-pitta, am,* n. plethora, hemorrhage, epistaxis, involuntary discharge of blood from the mouth, nostrils, anus, &c.—*Asra-phalā,* f. the plant Boswellia Thurifera Roxb.—*Asra-mātṛikā,* f. chyle, chyme.—*Asra-rodhinī,* f. the plant Mimosa Pudica.—*Asra-vindu-ćchadā,* f., N. of a tuberous plant.—*Asrārjaka* (°*ra-ar*°), *as,* m. the white Tulasī plant.

Asrāya, nom. A. *asrāyate, -yitum,* to shed tears.

अस्रवत् *a-sravat, an, antī, at* (rt. *sru*), not flowing; Ved. not leaky (as a ship).

A-sruva, am, n. granulation (of a running sore).

अस्राम *a-srāma, as, ā, am,* Ved. not stiff, not lame.

अस्रि *asri, is,* f. an angle; ten millions. See *aśri.*

अस्रिध् *a-sridh, t, t, t,* or *a-sridhāna, as, ā, am,* or *a-sredhat, an, antī, at,* Ved. not doing harm; uninjured, unfatigued; pious, peaceable.

अस्रीवयस् *asrī-vayas,* Ved. having food which falls or drops down (?).

अस्रु *asru,* n. a tear, &c. See *aśru.*

अस्रेमन् *asreman, ā,* m., Ved. praiseworthy, to be praised; (if fr. rt. *sriv*) undecaying, immortal.

अस्व *a-sva, as, ā, am,* or *a-svaka, as, akā* or *ikā, am,* or *a-svakīya, as, ā, am,* not one's own, belonging to another.—*A-sva-ga, as, ā, am,* Ved. not going to one's own home, homeless.—*A-svaga-tā,* f., Ved. homelessness.—*A-sva-jāti, is, is, i,* of a different caste, of a different species.—*Asva-tva, am,* n. or *asva-tā,* f. want of claim or right to anything, having no indefeasible property in it, absence of ownership

A-svaćchanda, as, ā, am, docile; not self-willed, dependant.

A-svatantra, as, ā, am, not self-willed, dependant, subject; docile, humble.

A-svabhāva, as, m. unnatural or unusual character or temperament; (*as, ā, am*), of a different nature.

A-svarūpa, as, ā, am, essentially different or unlike.

A-svaveśa, as, ā, am, Ved. having no home of one's own, expelled from home.

A-svādhyāya (°*sva-adh*°), *as,* m. a Brāhman who has not performed his studies, who has not read the Vedas previously to his investiture; interruption or interval of study, prohibited on certain days of the moon, at eclipses, &c.

A-svārtha (°*sva-ar*°), *as, ā, am,* not for one's self; not for a proper object; having a different meaning.

A-svīkāra, as, m. non-acquiescence, dissent.

A-svīkṛita, as, ā, am, dissented from, refused, not promised.

अस्वच्छ *a-svaććha, as, ā, am,* not clear, opaque.

अस्वन्त *a-svanta* (*a-su-anta*), *as, ā, am,* ending ill, leading to or having an unfavourable issue; (fr. *asu-anta?*) approaching the end of life; a fire-place, see *aśvanta.*

अस्वप्न *a-svapna, as, ā, am,* Ved. sleepless, awake; (*as*), m. sleeplessness, the being awake; a god, a deity [cf. ἄυπνος].

A-svapnaj, k, k, k, Ved. not sleepy, sleepless.

अस्वर *a-svara, as, ā, am,* not aloud, speaking in an under tone, indistinct; having a bad or croaking voice; (*am*), ind. not aloud, in a low tone, indistinctly.

अस्वर्ग्य *a-svargya, as, ā, am,* not leading to heaven, unheavenly.

अस्वस्थ *a-sva-stha, as, ā, am,* not in good health, not one's self, sick.—*Asvastha-tā,* f. want of firmness; weakness, illness.

A-svāsthya, am, n. indisposition, sickness, discomfort, indigence.

अस्वादु *a-svādu, us, us, u,* tasteless, insipid.

अस्वामिक *a-svāmika, as, ā* or *ī, am,* unowned, unclaimed.

A-svāmin, ī, inī, i, having no right or title to anything, not being master of it; that which has no master or owner.—*A-svāmi-vikraya, as,* m. sale without ownership.

A-svāmya, am, n. absence of right or title to property.

अस्वार्थ *a-svārtha, as, ā, am,* unselfish, disinterested.

अस्वेद *a-sveda, as,* m. suppressed perspiration; (*as, ā, am*), not perspiring.

अह् 1. *ah* (connected with rt. *nah*), cl. 1. P., Ved. *ahati,* 2nd pl. perf. *anāha,* to string together (?), to compose, to celebrate, to prepare, to increase.

अह् 2. *ah,* cl. 5. P., Ved. *ahnoti* or *aḍnoti,* to pervade or occupy; to go or move; cl. 10 (?) to cause to shine (?).

Ahana, as, ā, am, illuminating, spreading light (epithet of the dawn).

अह् 3. *ah* (defect. verb, preserved only in five persons of the perfect, viz. *āttha, āha, āhathus, āhatus, āhus,* which may have a present signification), to say, speak; to acknowledge, accept, state; to declare, express, signify; to call; to attribute; to call (with two acc.); to hold, consider, regard; to adjudge anything (acc.) to any one (gen.). [To this rt. are referred, Hib. *ag-all,* 'speech;' *ag-aill,* 'to speak;' *eigh-im,* 'I call:' Goth. *af-aika,* 'I deny:' Lat. *nego* for *n'—ego,* 'to say no:' also *ajo.*]

अह aha, ind. (as a particle implying ascertainment, affirmation, certainty, &c.) surely, certainly, yes, well; (as explaining, defining, admitting, limiting, &c.) namely; I grant you, granted, indeed, of course; at least. This particle is also said to imply rejecting, sending; deviation from custom, impropriety.

अहंयाति, अहंयु, &c. See under *aham.*

अहत *a-hata, as, ā, am* (rt. *han*), unhurt, uninjured, not struck, not killed; unbeaten (as clothes in washing); unwashed, new; unblemished, unsoiled; not disappointed; (*am*), n. unwashed or new clothes.

A-hati or *a-hanti, is,* f., Ved. safeness.

A-hatvā, ind. not having killed.

A-hananīya or *a-hantavya, as, ā, am,* not to be killed.

A-hantya or *a-hantra* or *a-hanya, as, ā, am,* Ved. indestructible, invincible.

अहन् *ahan* and *ahas*, n. (said to be fr. 2. *hā* with *a*, 'not;' according to others, who compare the Goth. *daga*, Germ. *tag*, Eng. *day*, a corruption of *dahan* fr. rt. *dah*; the nom. acc. voc. sing. and the middle cases come fr. *ahas*, the others fr. *ahan*; in the Vedas the middle cases also are sometimes formed fr. *ahan*, e. g. *ahabhyas, ahabhis*); a day; a sacrificial or festival day; a day's work; a portion of a book appointed for one day's reading; day personified as one of the eight Vasus; N. of a Tīrtha; *ahany-ahani* or *ahar-ahaḥ*, day by day, daily; *ahanī*, du. day and night; *tad ahas*, on that very day; *yad ahas*, on which day. (As the last member of a compound *ahan* generally appears in the form *aha*, m., rarely n., but sometimes also in the form *ahan*, e. g. *puṇyāha, ekāhan*, q. v. As the first member of a compound *ahas* and *ahar* are the usual forms; as in the following examples.) — *Ahaḥ-pati, is,* m. lord of the day, the sun; see *ahar-pati*. — *Ahaḥ-śesha, am,* n. evening. — *Ahar-āgama, as,* m. the approach of day. — *Ahar-gaṇa, as,* m. a series of sacrificial days; a month; any calculated term. — *Ahar-jara, as,* m., Ved. the year (as making days become old). — *Ahar-jāta, as, ā, am,* Ved. born in the day or from day, not belonging to night or to the spirits of darkness. — *Ahar-diva, as, ā, am,* Ved. existing every day; (*am*), ind. daily, day by day. — *Ahar-divi*, ind., Ved. day by day, every day, constantly. — *Ahar-dṛiś, k, k, k,* Ved. beholding the day, living. — *Ahar-niśa, am,* n. day and night, a whole day; (*am*), ind. day and night, during the whole day, continually. — *Ahar-pati, is,* m., Ved. lord of the day; the sun; epithet of Śiva; also written *ahaḥ-pati*. — *Ahar-bāndhava, as,* m. the sun. — *Ahar-bhāj, k, k, k,* Ved. partaking of the day. — *Ahar-maṇi, is,* m. the sun. — *Ahar-mukha, am,* n. commencement of the day, morning, dawn. — *Ahar-loka, as, ā, am,* Ved. taking the place of day. — *Ahar-vid, t, t, t,* Ved. existing (many) days; known long ago; knowing the (fit) time or season. — *Ahaś-śas*, ind., Ved. every day. — *Ahas-kara, as,* m. the sun. — *Ahas-pati, is,* m. the sun; swallow wort.

Aho-rātra, &c. See s. v.

अहन *ahana*. See 2. *ah*.

अहम् *aham*, nom. sing. 'I.' The supposed base of this 1st personal pronoun is *asmad*, q. v. [cf. Zend *azem*; Gr. ἐγών, ἐγώ, ἰών; Lat. *ego*; Goth. *ik*; Mod. Germ. *ich*; Lith. *asz*; Slav. *az*; Cambro-brit. *ym*; Bret. *am, em*].

Ahaṃ-yāti, is, m., N. of a son of Saṃyāti.

Ahaṃyu, us, us, u, selfish, proud, haughty; (*us*), m. a warrior.

Ahaṃ-vādin, ī, inī, i, speaking only of one's self, presumptuous, haughty.

Ahaṃ-śreyas, as, or *ahaṃ-śreyasa, am,* n. claiming superiority for one's self.

Ahaṃ-sana, as, ā, am, Ved. gaining for one's self, obtaining for one's self.

Ahan-kartavya, as, ā, am, to be referred to self; (*am*), n. the object of Ahan-kāra.

Ahan-kāra, as, m. the making of self, sense of self, thinking of self, egotism, individuality; self-consciousness, pride, haughtiness; (in the Sān-khya phil.) the third of the eight producers or elements of creation, viz. the conceit or conception of individuality, individualization. — *Ahankāra-vat, ān, atī, at,* conscious, selfish, proud.

Ahan-kārin, ī, iṇī, i, self-important, proud.

Ahan-kārya, am, n. that which is to be done by one's self, any personal object, business or matter.

Ahan-kṛita, as, ā, am, egotistic; proud, haughty; conscious.

Ahan-kṛiti, is, f. egotism, high opinion of one's self, pride.

Aham-agrikā, f. or *aham-uttara, am,* n. a contest for superiority, rivalry.

Aham-ahamikā, f. assertion or conceit of superiority, boasting, egotism; military vaunting.

Aham-pūrva, as, ā, am, Ved. desirous of being first.

Aham-pūrvikā, f. or *aham-prathamikā*, f. emulative onset, the running forward of soldiers with emulation; conceit, vaunting.

Aham-bhadra, am, n. self-conceit, a high notion of one's own superiority.

Aham-mati, is, f. or *aham-māna, am,* n. self-illusion, spiritual ignorance, conceit, self-love.

अहर *a-hara, as,* m. (rt. *hṛi*), N. of the twelfth Manu; a Dānava.

A-haraṇīya, as, ā, am, not to be taken away.

A-hārin, ī, iṇī, i, not taking (?).

A-hārya, as, ā, am, not to be stolen, not to be removed; (*as*), m. a mountain. — *Ahārya-tā*, f. or *ahārya-tva, am,* n. the state of not being liable to be taken away, security.

अहरित *a-harita, as, ā, am,* Ved. not yellow.

अहर्ष *a-harsha, as, ā, am* (rt. *hṛish*), unhappy, gloomy, sorrowful.

A-harshita, as, ā, am, unhappy, sorrowful.

अहल *a-hala, as, ā, am,* or *a-hali, is, is, i,* unploughed, unfurrowed.

A-halya, as, ā, am, not arable, unploughed; (*ā*), f., N. of an Apsaras; N. of the wife of Gautama or Śaradvat; N. of a sea.

अहल्लिक *ahallika, as,* m., Ved. a talker, tattler (?).

अहवनीय *a-havanīya, as, ā, am* (rt. *hu*), not to be offered as an oblation, not fit or proper to be sacrificed.

A-havis, is, is, is, Ved. without oblations, sacrificeless.

अहस्त *a-hasta, as, ā, am,* handless.

अहह *ahaha* or *ahahā*, ind. a particle or interjection, as Ah! Aha! &c., implying surprise, fatigue, pain, sorrow, pleasure, calling.

अहार्य *a-hārya*, &c. See under *a-hara*.

अहावस् *ahāvas*, Ved., said to be a sound like a flourish at the end of a hymn.

अहि *ahi, is,* m. (fr. rt. *aṇh*; according to Sāy. fr. rt. *han* with *ā* prefixed and shortened, 'one that destroys on all sides'), a snake; the serpent of the sky, the demon Vṛitra; a cloud; water; lead; a traveller; the sun; a N. of Rāhu, the ascending node; the navel; [cf. *agha* and *aṇhu*, pp. 1, 6; Lat. *anguis*; Gr. ἔχι-ς, ἔχιδνα, ἔγχε-λυς, and ὄφις; Lith. *angury-s*; Russ. *ûgorj*; Armen. *ôz*; Germ. *unc*; Mod. Gr. ἀχέλι.] — *Ahi-kānta, as,* m. air, wind; (snakes being supposed to feed upon air.) — *Ahi-kosha, as,* m. the slough or cast skin of a snake. — *Ahi-kshatra* and *ahi-kshetra, as,* m., N. of a country. — *Ahi-gopa, as, ā, am,* Ved. guarded by a serpent. — *Ahi-ghna, am,* n., Ved. the slaying of the serpent or demon (Vṛitra) who obstructs the heavenly waters. — *Ahi-ghni, is,* m., Ved. killing snakes. — *Ahi-ććhatra, as,* m. a kind of vegetable poison; the plant Gymnema Sylvestre (?); N. of a country; (*ā*), f. sugar; the city of Ahiććhatra. — *Ahi-ććhatraka, am,* n. a mushroom. — *Ahi-jit, t,* m., N. of Kṛishṇa, also of Indra. — *Ahi-tuṇḍika, as,* m. a snake-catcher or exhibiter; see *āhituṇḍika*. — *Ahi-dat, an, atī, at,* or *ahi-danta, as, ī, am,* having the teeth of a serpent. — *Ahi-dvish, ṭ, ṭ, ṭ,* enemy of the serpents or of Vṛitra; (*ṭ*), m. an ichneumon; a peacock; Garuḍa, the bird of Vishṇu; Indra. — *Ahi-nakulikā*, f. the natural enmity between a snake and an ichneumon. — *Ahi-nāma-bhṛit, t,* m., N. of Baladeva (as identified with Śesha). — *Ahi-nirmoka, as,* m. or *ahi-nirvlayanī*, f. the cast off skin of a snake. — *Ahi-patāka, as,* m. a kind of snake, not venomous. — *Ahi-pati, is,* m., N. of Śesha, sovereign of the snakes, also of Vāsuki and others; any large serpent. — *Ahi-putraka, as,* m. a kind of boat. — *Ahi-pūtana, as, ā,* m. f. sores on the hinder part of the body (of children). — *Ahi-phena, am,* n. opium, the saliva or venom of a snake [cf. 2. *a-phena*]. — *Ahi-bradhna, as,* m., N. of Śiva; one of the Rudras; corrupted fr. *ahir-budhnyas*. — *Ahi-bradhna-devatā*, f. the twenty-sixth lunar mansion. — *Ahi-bhaya, as,* m. fear of a lurking snake; apprehension of treachery. — *Ahibhaya-dā*, f., N. of the plant Flacourtia Cataphracta Roxb. — *Ahi-bhānu, us, us, u,* Ved. shining like serpents; epithet of the Maruts. — *Ahi-bhuj, k,* m. Garuḍa, the bird of Vishṇu; a peacock; N. of a plant. — *Ahi-bhṛit, t,* m. 'carrying serpents,' N. of Śiva. — *Ahi-manyu, us, us, u,* Ved. enraged like serpents, epithet of the Maruts; (Sāy.) 'endowed with destructive anger,' or 'with unimpaired knowledge.' — *Ahi-mardanī*, f., N. of a plant. — *Ahi-māya, as, ā, am,* Ved. multiform or versatile like a snake, showing the same variety of colour and shape. — *Ahi-māra* or *ahi-medaka, as,* m., N. of a plant. — *Ahi-ripu, us,* m. a peacock. — *Ahir-budhna, as,* m., N. of Śiva; corrupted fr. *ahir-budhnyas*. — *Ahirbudhna-devatā, ās,* f. pl. the twenty-sixth lunar mansion. — *Ahir-bradhna, as,* m., N. of a Rudra. — *Ahi-latā*, f., the plant Betel; another plant. — *Ahi-locana, as,* m., N. of a servant of Śiva. — *Ahi-vidashṭa, as, ā, am,* snake-bitten. — *Ahi-vidvish, ṭ,* m. Garuḍa; Indra. — *Ahi-śushmasattvan, ā,* m., Ved. one whose men (the Maruts) hiss like serpents; epithet of Indra; (according to Sāy. *ahi-śushma* means 'of all-pervading strength,' and is to be separated from *sattvan*.) — *Ahi-hatya, am,* n. the slaying of the serpent or demon (Vṛitra) who obstructs the heavenly waters. — *Ahi-han, ā,* m., Ved. killing serpents or Vṛitra. — *Ahy-arshu, us, us, u,* Ved. gliding like a snake.

1. *ahika, as,* m. a blind snake, not venomous, see *andhāhika*; (*ā*), f., N. of the silk-cotton tree, Bombax Heptaphyllum Salmalia Malabarica. (For 2. *ahika*, see below.)

अहिंसक *a-hiṇsaka, as, ā, am,* or *a-hiṇsat, an, antī, at,* or *a-hiṇsāna, as, ā, am* (rt. *hiṇs*), Ved. not hurting, harmless, innocuous.

A-hiṇsā, f. harmlessness, not injuring anything, one of the cardinal virtues of most Hindū sects, but particularly of the Buddhists and Jainas; security, safeness. — *Ahiṇsā-nirata, as, ā, am,* devoted to harmlessness or gentleness.

A-hiṇsita or *a-hiṇsyamāna, as, ā, am,* Ved. uninjured, being unharmed.

A-hiṇsra, as, ā, am, innocuous, innocent, harmless; (*am*), n. harmless behaviour; (*ā*), f., N. of the plant Momordica Cochinchinensis, Spreng, (commonly called Kūrkavāli.)

अहिक 2. *ahika, as, ā, am* (fr. *ahan*, q. v.), is found at the end of a few compounds in the sense of lasting a certain number of days, e. g. *daśāhika*, lasting for ten days. See 1. *ahika* above.

अहिण्डुका *ahiṇḍukā*, f. a kind of small poisonous animal.

अहित a-hita, as, ā, am (rt. dhā), not placed, not put, not fixed; unfit, improper; unadvantageous, noxious; hurtful, prejudicial; hostile, inimical; (as), m. an enemy; (am), n. damage; food &c. contra-indicated in a disease. — Ahita-kārin, ī, iṇī, i, adverse, inimical, acting unkindly. — A-hita-nāman, ā, ā, a, Ved. having as yet no name. — A-hita-manas, ās, ās, as, not friendly-minded, hating, adverse, inimical. — Ahita-hita-vićāra-śūnya-buddhi, is, is, i, whose intellect is incapable of discriminating between good and evil. — Ahiteććhu (°ta-ić°), us, us, u, not wishing well, malevolent.

अहिमकर a-hima-kara, as, or a-hima-tejas, ās, or a-hima-rući, is, or a-himāṅśu (°ma-aṅ°), us, m. the sun.

अही ahī, īs, m., Ved., N. of a demon conquered by Indra and his companions; a serpent (see ahi); a cow; (ī), du. heaven and earth.

अहीन 1. ahīna, as, ā, am (fr. ahan), lasting several days; (as), m. a sacrifice lasting several days; one lasting twelve days (i. e. stoma or yajña).

अहीन 2. ahīna, as, m. (fr. ahi, q. v.), a large snake (?).

अहीन 3. a-hīna, as, ā, am (rt. 2. hā), unimpaired, whole, entire; full, luxurious; not deprived of, not withdrawing; possessed of; not outcast or vile. — A-hīna-gu, us, m., N. of a prince, son of Devānīka. — A-hīna-vādin, ī, m. a witness capable of giving evidence.

अहीर ahīra, as, m. a cowherd. See abhīra.

अहीरणि ahīraṇi, is, or ahīraṇin, ī, m. a kind of snake, said to be two-headed.

अहीशुव ahīśuva, as, m., Ved., N. of a demon conquered by Indra.

अहु ahu, us, vī, u, (in compounds) narrow. See aṅhu.

अहुत a-huta, as, ā, am (rt. hu), unsacrificed, unoffered, not yet sacrificed; one who has not received any sacrifice; not gained or obtained by sacrifice; (as), m. religious meditation, prayer, and study of the Veda, considered as one of the five great sacraments, otherwise called Brahma-yajña. — A-hutâd (°ta-ad), t, t, t, Ved. not eating of a sacrifice; not allowed to partake of a sacrifice.

अहूत a-hūta, as, ā, am (rt. hve), uncalled, unsummoned, unchallenged. (The form a-huta with the sense 'uncalled,' given by Wilson, is very questionable.)

अहृणान a-hṛiṇāna, as, ā, am, Ved. not being angry, friendly.

A-hṛiṇīyamāna, as, ā, am, Ved. not being angry, jealous, or envious; not discontented, willing; that which is bestowed willingly.

अहृद्य a-hṛidya, as, ā, am, not desired, not agreeable. — Ahṛidya-kṛit, t, t, t, disagreeable, causing disgust.

अहे ahe, ind. a particle implying reproach, rejection, separation.

अहेतु a-hetu, us, m. absence of cause or reason. — Ahetu-tā, f. or ahetu-tva, am, n. absence of cause, reason, or necessity.

A-hetuka, as, ā, am, causeless, groundless.

A-haituka, as, ī, am, having no reason or foundation; causeless, having no motive, disinterested.

अहेरु aheru, us, f. the plant Asparagus Racemosus.

अहेळत् a-heḷat, an, antī, at, or a-heḷamāna, as, ā, am, or a-heḷayat, an, antī, at (rt. heḍ, Ved. heḷ with a), Ved. not angry, not displeased, favourable.

अहो aho, ind. (as a particle and interjection of joyful or painful surprise) Ah! (of enjoyment or satisfaction) Oh! (of fatigue, discontent, compassion, sorrow, regret) Alas! Ah! (of praise) Bravo! (of reproach) Fie! (of calling) Ho! Halo! (of doubt, deliberation) either, or; (of contempt) Pshaw! It is also sometimes an expletive.

Aho-purushikā, f. self-confidence; boasting.

अहोतृ a-hotṛi, tā, m., Ved. not sacrificing; not competent to sacrifice.

अहोरात्र aho-rātra, as, am, m. n. (fr. ahan, q. v. + rātri, q. v.), a day and night, νυχθήμερον; a day of twenty-four hours or thirty Muhūrtas, from sunrise to sunrise; a day and night of the Pitṛis = a month of the gods = a year of Brahmā = 2000 Yugas of the gods; (am), ind. day and night, continually, always.

Aho-rūpa, am, n. the appearance of day.

अहोवत ahovata, ind. a particle of calling, of compassion, of fatigue.

अहोहि ahohi, ind. in a variegated or wonderful manner (?).

अह्न ahna, as, m. as last member of a compound = ahan, a day, q. v.; e. g. madhyāhna, midday; aparāhṇa, afternoon.

Ahnāya, ind. formerly; instantly; soon, speedily.

Āhnika, as, ā, am, as last member of a compound = ahan; e. g. dvy-ahnika, as, ā, am, lasting two days.

Ahnī, f. and ahnīya, as, ā, am, or ahnya, as, ā, am (all fr. ahan), used at the end of compounds; e. g. rathāhnya, am, n. the daily journey of a chariot.

अह्नवाय्य a-hnavāyya, as, ā, am (rt. hnu), Ved. not to be denied or set aside; (as), m. according to Sāy. the N. of a king.

अह्यर्षु ahy-arshu. See under ahi.

अह्रय a-hraya or a-hrayāṇa, as, ā, am (fr. hrī, shame, q. v.), Ved. luxurious, proud, bold, conscious of one's own power.

A-hri, is, is, i, Ved. luxurious, fat.

A-hrī, īs, īs, i, Ved. shameless, importunate.

A-hrīka, as, ā, am, shameless; (as), m. a Buddhist mendicant.

अह्रुत a-hruta, as, ā, am (rt. hvṛi), Ved. not fluctuating, not stumbling; going in a straight line; not crooked, straight. — Ahruta-psu, us, us, u, Ved. of straight or upright appearance.

अह्वला a-hvalā, f., Ved. not fluctuating, not stumbling, firmness; the plant Semecarpus Anacardium.

आ

आ 1. ā, the second letter of the alphabet, corresponding to a long, as in far.

आ 2. ā, (as a particle or interjection of assent) yes, verily; (of compassion or pain) Ah! Alas! in the latter sense it is more correctly written ās; (of reminiscence) Ah! Oh! (a conjunction disjunctive) but; (a conjunction copulative) and. This particle remains unaltered in orthography even before vowels.

आ 3. ā, a prefix to verbs and nouns, (expressing) near, near to, towards, from all sides, all around; and sometimes redundant. As a prefix to verbs of motion it expresses the notion of moving or going towards; e. g. ā-krāmati, he goes towards. When prefixed to roots like gam, yā, and i, to go, and dā, to give, it reverses the action; e. g. ā-gaććhati, he comes; ā-datte, he takes.

As unconnected with verbs and prefixed to nouns it forms with them either compound adverbs or adjectives, implying the limit conclusive (until, unto, as far as), or the limit inceptive (from, from thence or that time); e. g. ā-maraṇam, till death; ā-kumāram, from childhood [cf. a puero]; ā-gopālā dvijātayaḥ, the twice-born including the cowherds.

(Prefixed to adjectives &c. it implies) diminution; e. g. ā-pāṇḍu, a little pale; ā-pakva, half-cooked.

(As a separable adverb ā implies) near, near to, towards; thereto, further, also, and; especially, even. In many places in the Vedas ā gives force to the word which precedes it (e. g. mahimā vām Indrāgnī panishṭha ā, 'your greatness, O Indra and Agni, is praiseworthy indeed'); and in a similar manner we find it in the Veda placed after prepositions, the sense of which is strengthened by it.

(As a separable preposition with acc. or abl.) near to, up to, to, as far as; e. g. śatam ā jātis, as far as a hundred births; ā samudrāt, as far as the ocean: (with abl.) away from, from; out of, of, from among; e. g. ā mūlāt, from the beginning; bahubhya ā, from among many: (with loc.) in, at; e. g. dama ā, in a house.

आ 4. ā, ās, m., N. of Śiva; (ā), f., N. of Lakshmī.

आ-इ ā-i. See e.

आ-इन्ध् ā-indh. See endh.

आ-इन्व् ā-inv. See env.

आ-इष् ā-ish. See esh.

आ-ईक्ष् ā-īksh. See eksh.

आ-ईर् ā-īr. See er.

आ-ईष् ā-īsh. See esh.

आ-उ ā-u. See o.

आ-उक्ष् ā-uksh. See oksh.

आ-ऊर्णु ā-ūrṇu. See orṇu.

आ-ऊह् ā-ūh. See oh.

आ-ऋ ā-ṛi. See ār.

आ-ऋच् ā-ṛić. See ārć.

आ-ऋञ्ज् ā-ṛiñj. See ārñj.

आ-ऋध् ā-ṛidh. See ārdh.

आकच् ā-kać, cl. 1. A. -kaćate, -ćitum, to tie on, to fasten on.

आकत्थन ā-katthana, as, ā, am, boasting, swaggering.

आकन् ā-kan, cl. 1. P. -kanati, -nitum, or Intens. -ćākanti, to be pleased with (with loc.); to endeavour to obtain; to love, to desire, solicit, praise.

आकम्प् ā-kamp, cl. 1. A. -kampate, -pitum, to tremble: Caus. -kampayati, -yitum, to cause to tremble.

Ā-kampa, as, m. or ā-kampana, am, n. trembling motion, shaking, trembling.

Ā-kampita or ā-kampra, as, ā, am, shaken, trembling; moved, agitated.

आकर ā-kara, ākarin, &c. See under ā-kṛī.

आकरण ā-karaṇa. See under ā-kṛi.

आकर्ण् ā-karṇ, cl. 10. P. -karṇayati, -yitum, to give ear to, listen to, hear.

Ā-karṇa, up to the ear, (occurs at the commencement of several compounds to denote the end of an arrow reaching to the ear in drawing a bow.)

Ā-karṇana, am, n. hearing, listening.

Ā-karṇita, as, ā, am, heard, listened to; overheard.

Ā-karṇya, ind. having heard or listened to.

आकर्ष ā-karsha, ā-karshin, &c. See under ā-kṛish.

आकल् *ā-kal*, cl. 10. P. *-kalayati*, *-yitum*, to shake, agitate, throw, cast; to lay hold of, seize; to tie, fasten; to surrender, transfer; to observe, take into consideration; to consider [cf. Gr. ὀκέλλω].

Ā-kalana, *am*, n. binding, confinement; counting, reckoning; laying hold of; wish, desire.

Ā-kalita, *as*, *ā*, *am*, bound; counted, reckoned; seized, held.

आकल्प *ā-kalpa*, *as*, m. (rt. *klṛip* with *ā*), adding to, improving, increasing; ornament, decoration; sickness, disease.

Ā-kalpaka, *as*, m. remembering with regret, missing; joy; fainting, loss of sense or perception; darkness; a knot or joint.

Ā-kalpam, ind. till the end of a kalpa.

आकल्य *ākalya*, *am*, n. (fr. *a-kalya*), sickness, disease.

आकष *ā-kasha*, *as*, m. (fr. rt. *kash*, 'to rub,' with *ā*), a touchstone.

Ā-kashaka, *as*, *ikā*, *am*, cutting, rubbing, or testing with a touchstone, touching, assaying.

Ā-kashika, *as*, *ī*, *am*, touching, testing.

आकस्मिक *ākasmika*, *as*, *ī*, *am* (fr. *a-kasmāt*), causeless, unforeseen, unexpected, sudden. — *Ākasmika-tva*, *am*, n. suddenness, &c.

आकाङ्क्ष् *ā-kāṅksh*, cl. 1. P. A. *-kāṅkshati*, *-te*, *-shitum*, to desire, long for, hope for, endeavour to gain, expect (with acc.); to endeavour to reach a place, turn to; (in gram.) to require some word or words to be supplied for the completion of the sense.

Ā-kāṅksha, *as*, *ā*, *am*, desiring, wishing; (in gram.) requiring a word or words to complete the sense; (*ā*), f. desire, wish; (in gram.) the requiring of a word or period for the completion of the sense; looking at or towards; purpose, intention; enquiry, asking; the significancy of a word.

Ā-kāṅkshaṇīya or *ā-kāṅkshitavya*, *as*, *ā*, *am*, to be desired or expected, desirable.

Ā-kāṅkshat, *an*, *antī*, *at*, wishing, expecting; looking at, looking to or towards.

Ā-kāṅkshita, *as*, *ā*, *am*, wished, desired; asked, enquired; regarded, looked at; wanted, necessary.

Ā-kāṅkshin, *ī*, *iṇī*, *i*, wishing, desirous, wishful, hopeful; asking, enquiring, expectant.

Ā-kāṅkshya, *as*, *ā*, *am*, desirable; (*am*), n. need of supplying a word or words for the completion of the sense.

आकाय *ā-kāya*, *as*, m. (fr. rt. *ći* with *ā*), a funeral pile; abode, residence.

आकाय्य *ā-kāyya*, *as*, *ā*, *am* (fr. rt. *ki* with *ā*), Ved. desirable; in every way praiseworthy or commendable.

आकार *ā-kāra*. See under *ā-kṛi*.

आकाल *ā-kāla*, *as*, m. the right time; (for *a-kāla*) wrong or inauspicious time.

Ākālika, *as*, *ā* or *ī*, *am*, not filling a space of time, momentary, instantaneous; unseasonable; (*ī*), f. lightning. — *Ākālika-tva*, *am*, n. unseasonableness, suddenness.

आकाश् *ā-kāś*, cl. 1. A. *-kāśate*, *-śitum*, to shine, be bright; to view, recognize.

Ā-kāśa, *as*, *am*, m. n. (in Ved. m.) light, clearness; a free space, vacuity; the ether, the sky or atmosphere considered as the fifth element; Brahma as identical with ether. *Ākāśa* is the subtle and ethereal fluid, supposed to fill and pervade the universe and to be the peculiar vehicle of life and of sound. *Ākāśe*, ind. in the air; a stage direction implying something said by or to a person out of sight. — *Ākāśa-kakshā*, f. the horizon, 'girdle of the sky.' — *Ākāśa-ga*, *as*, *ā*, *am*, going through the atmosphere. — *Ākāśa-garbha*, *as*, m., N. of a Bodhisattva. — *Ākāśa-ćamasa*, *as*, m. the moon, ('a cup or vessel with ether.') — *Ākāśa-ja*, *as*, *ā*, *am*, produced in the sky. — *Ākāśa-jananin*, *ī*, m. a loop-hole, a casement, an embrasure. — *Ākāśa-dīpa* or *ākāśa-pradīpa*, *as*, m. a lamp or torch lighted in honour of Lakshmī or Vishṇu and elevated on a pole in the air at the Dīvāli (Dīpāli) festival, in the month Kārttika; a beacon, a lantern on a pole. — *Ākāśa-pratishṭhita*, *as*, m., N. of a Buddha. — *Ākāśa-buddha-laksha*, *as*, m. (in theatrical language) fixing the gaze on some object out of sight of the audience. — *Ākāśa-bhāshita*, *am*, n. (in dramatic language) speaking outside or off the stage; a supposed speech, which is replied to as if it had been spoken; a voice or sound in the air. — *Ākāśa-maṇḍala*, *am*, n. the celestial sphere; the atmosphere. — *Ākāśa-maya*, *as*, *ī*, *am*, consisting of ether. — *Ākāśa-māṃsī*, f. the plant Nardostachys Jaṭāmāṃsī. — *Ākāśa-mūlī*, f. the aquatic plant Pistia Stratiotes. — *Ākāśa-yāna*, *am*, n. a heavenly car, one moving through the air. — *Ākāśa-rakshin*, *ī*, m. a warder, a watchman on the outer battlements. — *Ākāśa-vat*, *ān*, *atī*, *at*, filling a certain place, spacious, extensive. — *Ākāśa-vartman*, *a*, n. the atmosphere, the firmament, the air. — *Ākāśa-vallī*, f. a sort of creeper, a parasite, Cassyta Filiformis. — *Ākāśa-vāṇī*, f. a voice from heaven; m., N. of the author of a Hanumat-stotra. — *Ākāśa-salila*, *am*, n. rain. — *Ākāśa-stha*, *as*, *ā*, *am*, abiding in the sky, aerial. — *Ākāśa-sphaṭika*, *as*, m. a kind of crystal supposed to be formed in the atmosphere. It is of two kinds, Sūrya-kānta and Candra-kānta, q. v. — *Ākāśānantyāyatana* (°*śa-anantya-āy*°), *am*, n. abode of infinity or of infinite space; N. of a world with Buddhists. — *Ākāśeśa* (°*śa-īś*°), *as*, m. epithet of Indra, as ruler of the firmament; (in law) any helpless person, as a child, a woman, a pauper or invalid (who has no other possession than the air).

Ākāśīya, *as*, *ā*, *am*, or *ākāśin*, *ī*, *inī*, *i*, atmospherical.

Ākāśya, *as*, *ā*, *am*, being in the atmosphere.

आकिञ्चन *ākiñćana* or *ākiñćanya*, *am*, n. (fr. *a-kiñćana*), want of any possession, poverty.

आकिदन्ति *ākidanti*, *is*, and *ākidantīya*, *as*, m., N. of a warrior-tribe and its chief.

आकीम् *ā-kīm*, ind., Ved. (with abl.) from.

आकुञ्च् *ā-kuñć*, cl. 6. P., 1. A. *-kućati*, *-kuñćate*, *-ćitum*, to bend: Caus. *-kuñćayati*, *-yitum*, to draw together, contort, contract; to bend inwards, shorten.

Ā-kuñćana, *am*, n. compression, contraction, shrinking; collecting, heaping; curving, flexure; contortion.

Ā-kuñćita, *as*, *ā*, *am*, bent, contorted, contracted; twisted, crooked.

आकुण्ठित *ā-kuṇṭhita*, *as*, *ā*, *am*, confounded, abashed.

आकुर्वती *ā-kurvatī*. See under *ā-kṛi*.

आकुल *ā-kula*, *as*, *ā*, *am* (rt. *kul*, to compact or compress together), filled, full, overburdened with (with inst.); confounded, confused, agitated, flurried; confused (in order), disordered; taken out of one's natural condition; incoherent, contradictory; (*am*), n. an inhabited place. — *Ākula-tā*, f. or *ākula-tva*, *am*, n. accumulation, multitude; perplexity, confusion, bewilderment. — *Ākulendriya* (°*la-in*°), *as*, *ā*, *am*, confused in mind.

Ākulaya, nom. P. *ākulayati*, *-yitum*, to confound, make disordered.

Ākuli, *is*, m., N. of an Asura priest.

Ākulita, *as*, *ā*, *am*, confounded; bewildered, flurried, agitated; distressed.

Ākulī-kṛi, cl. 8. P. *-karoti*, *-kartum*, to fill with; to confound. — *Ākulī-karaṇa*, *am*, n. confounding. — *Ākulī-kṛita*, *as*, *ā*, *am*, confounded; perplexed, bewildered.

Ākulī-bhū, cl. 1. P. *-bhavati*, *-ritum*, to become perplexed. — *Ākulī-bhūta*, *as*, *ā*, *am*, perplexed, confounded.

आकुष्ट *ā-kushṭa*, *as*, *ā*, *am*, expelled, extracted.

आकूज् *ā-kūj*, cl. 1. P. *-kūjati*, *-jitum*, to twitter, warble, coo.

आकूत *ā-kūta*, *am*, n. (rt. *kū* or *ku*, to sound), meaning, intention, purpose; wish, desire.

Ā-kūti, *is*, f. intention, wish, desire; N. of a daughter of Manu Svāyambhuva and of Śatarūpā. — *Ākūtī-pra*, *as*, *ā*, *am*, Ved. accomplishing one's intentions.

आकूवार *ākūvāra*, *as*, m. = *a-kū-pāra*, q. v.

आकृ *ā-kṛi*, cl. 8. 5. P. *-karoti*, *-kṛiṇoti*, *-kartum*, to bring near or towards, to bring down, to make or form wholly; to drive near to or together: Caus. P. *-kārayati*, *-yitum*, to ask any one (acc.) for anything (acc.); to invite to a place, to call into existence, to cause to appear: Desid. *-ćikīrshati*, to intend to accomplish: Intens. *-karikrati*, 3rd pl., Ved. to attract repeatedly towards one's self.

Ā-kāra, *as*, m. form, figure, shape, stature, appearance, aspect, behaviour, external gesture or aspect of the body, the expression of the face, as furnishing a clue to the disposition of mind; hint, sign, token; the letter *ā*. — *Ākāra-gupti*, *is*, f. or *ākāra-gopana*, *am*, n. dissimulation, suppressing all sign or inclination of the feelings. — *Ākāra-vat*, *ān*, *atī*, *at*, having a shape, embodied, symmetrical, handsome, well-formed. — *Ākāra-varṇa-suślakshṇa*, *as*, *ā*, *am*, delicate in shape and colour.

Ā-kāraṇa or *ā-karaṇa*, *am*, *ā*, n. f. calling, inviting, a call or summons; challenging, a challenge.

Ā-kāraṇīya, *as*, *ā*, *am*, to be called.

Ā-kārita, *as*, *ā*, *am*, called, summoned; stipulated, agreed; demanded, exacted.

Ā-kurvatī, f., N. of a certain rocky hill. (Rām. II. 71. 3.)

Ā-kṛita, *as*, *ā*, *am*, Ved. brought near to; being near.

Ā-kṛiti, *is*, f., Ved. a constituent part; form, figure, shape, appearance, aspect; character, specimen; the body; tribe, species; a metre consisting of four lines with twenty-two syllables to each line. — *Ākṛiti-gaṇa*, *as*, m. a list of specimens, a collection of words belonging to a certain grammatical rule, which does not exhibit every word belonging to that rule, but only specimens; whereas a simple Gaṇa exhibits every word; (explained by native authorities to mean a list of words, the fact of a word belonging to which can only be determined by observing the forms used by classical authors.) — *Ākṛiti-ććhatrā*, f. the plant Achyranthes Aspera. — *Ākṛiti-mat*, *ān*, *atī*, *at*, having shape, embodied.

आकृष् *ā-krish*, cl. 1. P., 6. P. A. *-karshati*, *-kṛishati*, *-te*, *-karshṭum* or *-krashṭum*, to draw towards, attract, put on, draw away; to bend (e. g. *ćāpam*, a bow); to draw or tear off, draw out of; to withdraw, deprive of, take away; to borrow: Caus. *-karshayati*, *-yitum*, to draw near to one's self.

Ā-karsha, *as*, m. drawing or attracting towards one's self, pulling to or towards, dragging, attracting, hawling; drawing the bow; attraction, fascination; spasm; playing with dice; a die or dice; a board for such a game; an organ of sense; magnetic attraction; a magnet, a loadstone; N. of a prince.

Ā-karshaka, *as*, *ikā*, *am*, attractive, what draws or attracts; (*as*), m. a magnet or loadstone; (*ikā*), f., N. of a town.

Ā-karshaṇa, *am*, n. pulling, drawing, attracting; (*ī*), f. a crooked stick for pulling down fruit, &c.; any instrument for pulling.

Ā-karshika, *as*, *ī*, *am*, magnetic, attractive.

Ā-karshita, *as*, *ā*, *am*, drawn, attracted.

Ā-karshin, *ī*, *iṇī*, *i*, attractive; (*ṇī*), f. a rod with a hook at the end for pulling down boughs in order to gather fruit.

Ā-kṛishṭa, as, ā, am, drawn, pulled, attracted. — *Ākṛishṭa-mānasa, as, ā, am,* distracted in mind. — *Ākṛishṭa-vat, ān, atī, at,* pulling, dragging, pulling up or out; pulling to, attracting; charming, fascinating.

Ā-kṛishṭi, is, f. attracting, drawing near, bending of a bow. — *Ākṛishṭi-mantra, as,* m. an incantation by which another person is attracted.

Ā-kṛishya, ind. having drawn, extracted, pulled or dragged.

Ā-kṛishyamāṇa, as, ā, am, being drawn or attracted.

आकॄ *ā-kṝ*, cl. 6. P. *-kirati, -karitum* or *-rītum,* to scatter or sprinkle over, fill, fill up, give abundantly, cover, replenish, heap up, accumulate.

Ā-kara, as, m. one who scatters over or fills; accumulation, collection, plenty, multitude; a mine, a rich source of anything; best, excellent; N. of a country; N. of the Mahā-bhāshya.

Ākarin, ī, iṇī, i, produced in a mine, mineral.

Ā-kīrṇa, as, ā, am, scattered, spread; overspread, filled; crowded, impervious; covered, surrounded. — *Ākīrṇa-tā,* f. or *ākīrṇa-tva, am,* n. fulness, crowd, multitude.

आके *āke,* ind. (fr. rt. *añć* with *ā*), Ved. hitherward, near, in the neighbourhood. — *Āke-nipa, as, ā, am,* Ved. considering or regarding from a near place; wise; (Sāy.) falling down near at hand, advancing near (as rays of light).

आकै *ā-kai,* cl. 1. P. A., Ved. *-kāyati, -te, -kātum,* to implore, appeal to, solicit; praise.

आकोकेर *ākokera, as,* m. the constellation Capricornus (Αἰγόκερως).

आकौशल *ākauśala, am,* n. (fr. *a-kuśala*), inexpertness, want of skill or practice.

आक्न *ākna, as, ā, am* (rt. *ać* or *añć*), bent, curved.

आक्रन्द् *ā-krand,* cl. 1. P. A. *-krandati, -te, -ditum,* to shout at, roar at; to invoke; to cry with sorrow, lament, weep: Caus. P. *-krandayati, -yitum,* to cause to weep or cry; inspire courage by its sound (as a drum?); to shout at, roar at; to cry without interruption.

Ā-kranda, as, m. calling, crying, crying out; shouting; weeping, sobbing; sound; war-cry; furious or violent combat; war, battle; violence; a friend; a brother; a king, a lord; usurper; a king who prevents an ally from aiding another; *(as, ā, am),* one who checks or restrains.

Ā-krandana, am, n. lamentation, weeping.

Ākrandika, as, ī, am, going to where cries of distress are heard.

Ā-krandita, as, ā, am, roaring, crying wofully; invoked; *(am),* n. a cry, a roar; lamentation.

Ā-krandin, ī, inī, i, shouting at; invoking in a weeping tone, weeping.

आक्रम् *ā-kram,* cl. 1. P. A., cl. 4. P. *-krāmati, -kramate, -krāmyati, -kramitum,* to step near to; to come towards, approach; to enter; to visit; arrive at; to step or tread upon, to lie heavily on, to press; to hold fast with the hands, seize; to attack, invade, take possession of, become master of, conquer, overcome; to undertake, begin; to rise, mount, ascend; to cover: Caus. P. *-kramayati, -yitum,* to cause to come or step near: Desid. *-ćikraṇsate,* to wish to ascend.

Ā-krama, as, m. coming near, approaching, arriving, attaining; overcoming, obtaining; invading, attacking, falling upon, an attack; spreading or going over or upon, surpassing, overloading; might, valour.

Ā-kramaṇa, as, ā, am, Ved. coming near, approaching, stepping upon; *(am),* n. attacking, marching against, invading; overpowering, subduing; spreading or extending over or upon; going over or beyond; attacking.

1. *ā-kramya* or *ā-kramaṇīya, as, ā, am,* to be approached; to be attacked; to be ascended or surpassed or overcome, to be seized.

2. *ā-kramya,* ind. having attacked, invaded, seized upon, overrun or encroached.

Ā-krānta, as, ā, am, come near; obtained; possessed; overspread; overcome, overrun; attacked; surpassed, surmounted; accompanied, attended; agitated or overcome by (any feeling); pained, distressed. — *Ākrānta-mati, is, is, i,* mentally overcome or overpowered; having the mind engrossed or deeply impressed.

Ā-krānti, is, f. ascending, rising; stepping upon; going over or beyond; overpowering; might, valour.

Ā-krāmaka, as, ikā, am, an invader, attacker.

आक्री *ā-krī,* cl. 9. P. A. *-krīṇāti, -ṇīte, -kretum,* to purchase.

Ā-kraya, as, m., Ved. a dealer, small trader, pedlar.

आक्रीड् *ā-krīḍ,* cl. 1. P. A. *-krīḍati, -te, -ḍitum,* to play, sport, take one's pleasure.

Ā-krīḍa, as, m. a play, sport, pleasure; *(as, am),* m. n. a playing-place, pleasure-grove, garden, royal garden; *(as),* m., N. of a son of Karutthāma.

Ā-krīḍana, am, n. sporting, taking pleasure.

Ā-krīḍin, ī, inī, i, sporting, playing.

आक्रुश् *ā-kruś,* cl. 1. P. *-krośati, -krashṭum,* to cry out at, call out aloud to; to call to any one in an abusive manner, to assail with angry and menacing words; to scold at any one; to curse, revile, express displeasure.

Ā-krushṭa, as, ā, am, scolded, reviled; vociferated; abused, calumniated, accused; cursed; *(am),* n. calling out.

Ā-krośa, as, m. calling or crying out, vociferation; scolding, reviling, blaming, censuring, abuse; a curse or oath.

Ā-krośaka, as, ī, am, vociferous, abusing, abusive.

Ā-krośana, am, n. assailing with harsh language, scolding, censuring; imprecation, curse.

Ā-krośanīya or *ā-krośitavya* or *ā-krośya, as, ā, am,* censurable, to be reviled or cursed.

Ā-krośita, as, ā, am, cursed, abused.

Ā-kroshṭṛi, ṭā, m. a reviler; one who vociferates.

आक्ली *ā-klī,* an undeclinable word joined to the roots *as, kṛi,* and *bhū.* See Gaṇa to Pāṇini I. 4, 61.

आक्लेद *ā-kleda, as,* m. moistening, sprinkling.

आक्षद्यूतिक *ākshadyūtika, as, ī, am,* effected or completed by gambling. See *aksha-dyūta* under 3. *aksha.*

आक्षपण *ā-kshapaṇa, am,* n. (rt. 1. *kshap*), fasting, purification by fasting, abstinence.

आक्षपाटिक *ākshapāṭika, as,* m. a judge. See *aksha-pāṭaka* under 2. *aksha.*

आक्षपाद *ākshapāda, as,* m. a follower of the Nyāya doctrine; a logician. See under 2. *aksha.*

आक्षभारिक *ākshabhārika.* See Gaṇa to Pāṇini V. 1, 50.

आक्षर् *ā-kshar,* cl. 10. P. *-kshārayati, -yitum,* to abuse, revile, accuse, punish. (Sometimes regarded as a nom. fr. the next.)

Ā-kshāra, as, m. calumny, accusation.

Ā-kshāraṇa, am, ā, n. f. abuse; calumnious accusation (especially of adultery).

Ā-kshārita, as, ā, am, calumniated, falsely accused; accused of adultery or fornication; guilty, criminal; reviled, abused.

आक्षि *ā-kshi,* cl. 2. 6. P. *-ksheti, -kshiyati, -kshetum,* to abide, dwell in, stay at (with acc.); to inhabit; to exist; to possess, take possession of (with acc.).

Ā-kshit, t, t, t, Ved. abiding, dwelling in, staying at.

आक्षिक *ākshika, as, ī, am* (fr. 3. *aksha*), relating or belonging to a die or to gambling, &c.; won at dice; *(am),* n. a gambling debt, money lost at play; *(as),* m., N. of the tree Morinda Tinctoria. — *Ākshika-paṇa, as,* m. a stake, a wager, a bet.

आक्षिप् *ā-kship,* cl. 6. P. A. *-kshipati, -te, -ksheptum,* to cast or throw at or down; to strike with a bolt; to draw near or together, to contract, convulse, cause to tremble; to draw or take off or away, withdraw; to chase or drive out of a place; to hang out or expose to view; put into; point to, apply to, refer to, hint, indicate; to refuse, not to have regard to, refuse as wrong; to insult, deride; to say or state ironically: Caus. P. *-kshepayati, -yitum,* to cause to throw down.

Ā-kshipat, an, atī or *antī, at,* casting, striking, tossing, sending; reviling, abusing; excelling so as to reproach or put to shame.

Ā-kshipta, as, ā, am, cast, thrown, tossed; thrown down or away; taken away; borne, carried; insulted, reviled, abused, blamed, ridiculed; equal or equivalent to.

Ā-kshiptikā, f. a particular air or song which is sung by a person approaching the stage.

Ā-kshipya, ind. having spurned, having insulted.

Ā-kshepa, as, m. throw, toss, drawing together or near to one's self, attraction, convulsion, palpitation; hinting; applying, laying on (as a colour); throwing away, giving up; sustaining (as a sound); reviling, abuse, censure, blame, reproach; objection; doubt, irony (as a figure in rhetoric).

Ā-kshepaka, as, ikā, am, blaming, censuring, reviling; *(as),* m. a thrower, a detractor, a calumniator or accuser; sickness, disease; convulsion, spasm.

Ā-kshepaṇa, am, n. throwing, tossing.

Ā-kshepin, ī, iṇī, i, applying to, concerning; (also = *ā-kshepaka.*)

आक्षीव *ākshīva, as,* m., N. of the plant Morunga Guilandina and Hyperanthera. See *akshīva.*

आक्षैत्रज्ञ्य *ākshaitrajñya, am,* n. (fr. *a-kshetrajña,* q. v.), spiritual ignorance.

आक्षोट *ākshoṭa* or *ākshoḍa, as* or *am* (?), m. or n. (?) a walnut (Pistacio nut?); N. of a tree, Pīlu; also of another tree, Aleurites Triloba. See *akshoṭa.*

आक्षोदन *ākshodana, am,* n. hunting (also *āćhodana*).

आक्ष्णु *ā-kshṇu,* cl. 2. P. *-kshṇauti, -kshṇavitum,* to rub, polish up; sharpen.

आक्ष्यत् *ākshyat, an, antī, at* (fut. part. fr. *aksh* or *aś* with *ā* !); *ākshyanti ahāni,* days leading to completion, complemental days; the N. of certain days on which the ceremony Ayana, performed for the Ādityas and Aṅgirasas, is finished.

आखण *ākhaṇa, as, ā, am,* hard.

आखण्डयितृ *ā-khaṇḍayitṛi, tā,* m. (rt. *khaṇḍ*), a breaker, a destroyer.

Ā-khaṇḍala, as, ā, am, breaking, destroying; destroying enemies; *(as),* m. a N. of Indra.

आखन् *ā-khan,* cl. 1. P. *-khanati, -nitum,* to dig. (It is doubtful whether *ā-khan* is used as a verb, but the nouns which follow are all derived from it.)

Ā-kha, as, m. a spade, a hoe.

Ā-khana, as, m. a digger, a spade.

Ā-khanika, as, m. a digger, a ditcher, a miner; a thief; a hog; a rat; a mouse; a spade. — *Ākhanika-baka* or *ākhanika-vaka, as,* m. a stork in relation to a mouse; (metaphorically) a man who behaves as an hero towards a weak person; a digger, a spade.

Ā-khara, as, m., Ved. the hole or cover of any animal; a stable; a spade, a digger. — *Ākhare-shṭha, as, ā, am,* Ved. abiding or dwelling in a hole.

Ā-khāta, as, am, m. n. a natural pond. See *a-khāta.*

Ā-khāna, as, m. a spade, a digger.

Ā-khu, us, m. a mouse, a rat, a mole; the grass Lipeocercis Serrata; a thief; a hog; a digger, a spade. — *Ākhu-karīsha, am,* n., Ved. a mole-hill. — *Ākhu-karṇī,* f., N. of the plant Salvinia Cucullata. — *Ākhu-ga, as,* m. (riding on a rat), an epithet of Gaṇeśa and of Kārttikeya. — *Ākhu-ghāta, as,* m. a Śūdra or man of low caste and profession, lit. 'a rat-catcher.' — *Ākhu-parṇikā* or *ākhu-parṇī,* f., N. of the plant Salvinia Cucullata Roxb. (?). — *Ākhu-pāshāṇa, as,* m. a kind of mineral, a loadstone. — *Ākhu-bhuj, k,* m. 'a mouse-eater,' a cat. — *Ākhu-ratha, as,* m. a N. of Gaṇeśa, 'having a rat for his vehicle.' — *Ākhu-visha-hā,* f. a kind of grass, Andropogon Serratum, considered as a remedy for a rat's bite. — *Ākhūtkara* (°*khu-ut*°), *as,* m. a mole-hill. — *Ākhūttha* (°*khu-ut*°), *as,* m. the rising up or appearance of rats or moles, a swarm of rats or moles.

आखाद् *ā-khād,* cl. 1. P. *-khādati, -ditum,* to chew, to bite into pieces; to eat, consume.

आखिद् *ā-khid,* cl. 6. P., Ved. *-khidati,* Class. *-khindati, -khettum,* to take away and appropriate to one's self, to draw to one's self.

आखिल्य *ākhilya, am,* n. (fr. *a-khila*), the whole.

आखेट *ā-kheṭa, as,* m. (rt. *khiṭ?*), chase, hunting; terror, fright. — *Ākheṭa-śīrshaka, am,* n. a cavern, a mine.

Ā-kheṭaka, as, ā, am, hunting, a hunter; frightening, frightful; (*am*), n. hunting, chase.

Ākheṭika, as, ī, am, who or what hunts; terrible, frightful; (*as*), m. a hound; a hunter.

आखोट *ākhoṭa, as,* m. the walnut tree. See *akshoṭa.*

आख्या 1. *ā-khyā,* cl. 2. P. *-khyāti, -tum,* Ved. to look at; to count, number; to recite; to tell, notify; inform, communicate, declare, make known; to announce; to call, signify (with two acc.); Caus. P. *-khyāpayati, -yitum,* to make known, declare; A. to cause to tell.

Ā-khyas, ās, m., N. of Prajāpati, the lord of creation.

2. *ā-khyā,* f. appellation, name; (*as, ā, am*), often at the end of a compound in the sense of 'named,' 'called.'

Ā-khyāta, as, ā, am, counted, recited; said, spoken; called; declared, made known; inflected, declined, conjugated; (*am*), n. a verb.

Ā-khyātavya, as, ā, am, to be told; to be declared, to be made known.

Ā-khyāti, is, f. telling, communication, publication of a report; fame; name, appellation.

Ākhyātika, adj. fr. *ā-khyāta.* Pāṇini IV. 3, 72.

Ā-khyātṛi, tā, m. one who tells or speaks.

Ā-khyāna, am, n. saying, declaring; speech; a tale, story, legend.

Ākhyānaka, am, n. a tale, a short narrative; (*ī*), f., N. of a metre, being a combination of the Indravajrā and Upendravajrā.

Ā-khyāpana, am, n. causing one to tell, making known.

Ā-khyāyaka, as, m. a messenger, a teller, an announcer or relater; (*ikā*), f. a tale or short narrative; a true or probable story.

Ā-khyāyin, ī, inī, i, telling, declaring, informing.

Ā-khyeya, as, ā, am, to be told or related; fit or proper to be said.

आग 1. *āga* = *āgas* in *an-āga,* q. v.

आगम् *ā-gam,* cl. 1. P. *-gaćchati, -gantum,* to come; to make one's appearance; to come near, go towards or to or into; to arrive at, attain, reach, strike; to return; to fall into (any state of mind); have recourse to: Caus. P. *-gamayati, -yitum,* to cause to come near; to lead towards; to convey; to announce the arrival (of any one); to obtain information about anything, ascertain (with acc.); A. to wait for, to have patience: Intens. Ved. *-ganīganti,* to approach repeatedly: Desid. *-jigamishati,* to be about to come.

2. *ā-ga, as, ā, am,* accidental; happening accidentally. — *Āga-tva, am,* n. accident, chance.

Ā-gata, as, ā, am, come, arrived; occurred, happened; living or residing in; returned; fallen to one's share; fallen into; received, obtained; passed; (*am*), n. occurrence, event [cf. *an-āgata, sv-āgata*]. — *Āgata-kshobha, as, ā, am,* confounded, perplexed. — *Āgata-sādhvasa, as, ā, am,* terrified, afraid.

Ā-gati, is, f. arrival, coming; return; origin; accident, chance.

Ā-gatya, ind. having come, having arrived.

Ā-gantavya, as, ā, am, to be arrived, what is likely to arrive; to be come to (with acc. or loc. of the place); obliged to come.

Ā-gantu, us, us, u, coming, arriving; what is added, adhering; coming from the outside, external; adventitious, incidental; (*us*), m. a new comer, a stranger, a guest; an accident, any accidental hurt or wound. — *Āgantu-ja, as, ā, am,* arising accidentally.

Āgantuka, as, ā or *ī, am,* coming, arriving; arriving of one's own accord; stray; incidental, accidental, adventitious (as pleasure, pain, ornament, &c.); (*as*), m. a new comer, a stranger, a guest; an interpolated *pāṭha* or various reading (which has crept in without authority).

Ā-gama, as, ā, am, coming near, approaching, supplying; (*as*), m. arrival, appearance; coming, approach; addition; course; the mouth of a river; supply of money, income, revenue; increase of property (especially in the compound *arthāgama*), lawful acquisition of anything; increase of knowledge (especially in the compound *vidyāgama*); knowledge, science, intelligence; a traditional doctrine or precept, a collection of such doctrines or precepts, a sacred work, scripture; a manual; an affix; the interpolation of a letter in grammar, a grammatical augment, a meaningless syllable or letter inserted in any part of the radical word; record, title-deed, legal title, a voucher or written testimony; (*am*), n. a Tantra or any work inculcating the mystical worship of Śiva and Śakti. — *Āgama-nirapeksha, as, ā, am,* independent of a written voucher or title. — *Āgama-nīta, as, ā, am,* studied, read, examined. — *Āgama-rahita, as, ā, am,* devoid of a written title or a voucher; without a Śāstra. — *Āgama-vat, ān, atī, at,* having an augment or addition of any kind; having approached for sexual intercourse. — *Āgama-sāpeksha, as, ā, am,* with or supported by legal vouchers. — *Āgamāpāyin* (°*ma-ap*°), *ī, inī, i,* transient, of short duration. — *Āgamāvartā* (°*ma-āv*°), f., N. of the plant Tragia Involucrata Lin.

Ā-gamana, am, n. coming, approaching, arriving; returning; arising; approaching a woman for sexual intercourse. — *Āgamana-kāraṇa, am,* n. reason of one's coming. — *Āgamana-tas,* ind. on account of an arrival.

Ā-gamayya, ind. having explored or discovered.

Ā-gamita, as, ā, am, read over, perused, studied; understood, ascertained.

Āgamin, ī, inī, i, (in gram.) receiving an augment.

Ā-gamishṭha, as, ā, am (superl.), Ved. coming with pleasure or very quickly.

1. *ā-gamya, as, ā, am,* to be approached, accessible; to be acquired.

2. *ā-gamya,* ind. having arrived or come.

Ā-gāntu, us, m. a guest. See *ā-gantu.*

Āgāmika, as, ā, am, relating or belonging to the future.

Ā-gāmin, ī, inī, i, coming, about to come, arriving, impending; future. — *Āgāmi-kāla, as,* m. future time.

Ā-gāmuka, as, ā, am, coming, arriving; future.

आगर *āgara,* Ved. = *ā-gāra* (?).

आगलित *ā-galita, as, ā, am,* drooping, languishing, dejected.

आगविष्ठ *ā-gavishṭha, as, ā, am* (either a false reading for *ā-gamishṭha* or fr. an adj. *ā-gu*), Ved. coming near (?).

आगवीन *ā-gavīna, as, ā, am,* occupied with any business till the return of the cows.

आगस् *āgas, as,* n. (said to be fr. rt. *i* with *āga* substituted), transgression, offence, sin, fault [cf. Gr. ἄγος]. — *Āgas-kṛita, as, ā, am,* offending; offended.

आगस्त्य *āgastya, as, ā, am,* referring to the sage Agasti, q. v.; originating from the plant Agasti Grandiflorum.

Āgastīya, as, ā, am, relating to or tending to the advantage of Agasti.

आगा 1. *ā-gā,* cl. 2. P. *-gāti, -tum,* to come towards or into; to approach, make one's appearance; to meet with; to visit.

2. *ā-gā, ās, ās, am,* coming towards, &c.

आगाध *āgādha* = *a-gādha,* q. v.

आगार *ā-gāra, am,* n. (probably fr. *ā-gṛī,* 'to swallow down,' and denoting first any inner receptacle), room, covered place, dwelling, house, receptacle [cf. *a-gāra*]. — *Āgāra-godhikā,* f. a lizard (?). — *Āgāra-dāha, as,* m. arson, setting a house on fire. — *Āgāra-dāhin, ī,* m. an incendiary. — *Āgāra-dhūma, as,* m., N. of a plant.

आगुर् 1. *ā-gur,* cl. 6. A. *-gurate, -ritum* (*gur* = rt. *gṛī,* see *ā-gṛī*), to approve, to agree or assent to, to promise, to pronounce the Āgur.

2. *ā-gur, ūr,* f., Ved., N. of a class of plauditory or approving exclamations or formularies used by the priests in sacrificial rites; assent, an agreement.

Ā-guraṇa or *ā-gūraṇa* or *ā-gūrṇa, am,* n. recitation of the Āgur.

Ā-gū, ūs, f. an agreement (?).

Ā-gūrtin, ī, inī, i, Ved. performing or pronouncing the Āgur.

आगुरव *āgurava, as, ī, am* (fr. *a-guru*), originating from or formed of Agallochum. See *a-guru.*

आगॄ *ā-gṛī,* cl. 9. P. A., Ved. *-gṛiṇāti, -ṇīte, -garitum* or *-rītum,* to approve, to praise.

आगै *ā-gai,* cl. 1. P., Ved. *-gāyati, -gātum,* to sing to, to obtain by singing.

Ā-gātṛi, tā, trī, tṛi, obtaining by singing.

Ā-gāna, am, n. the act of obtaining by song.

आग्नापौष्ण *āgnāpaushṇa, as, ī, am,* Ved. belonging or referring to Agni and Pūshan.

Āgnāvaishṇava, as, ī, am, Ved. belonging or referring to Agni and Vishṇu.

आग्निक *āgnika, as, ī, am* (fr. *agni*), fiery, belonging to fire or to a sacrifice performed with fire.

Āgnimāruta, as, ī, am, belonging or referring to Agni and the Maruts; (*as*), m. an epithet of Agastya; (*am*), n. a hymn praising Agni and the Maruts [cf. Pāṇini VII. 3, 21; VI. 3, 28].

Āgnivāruṇa, as, ī, am, belonging or referring to Agni and Varuṇa.

Āgniveśya and *āgniveśyāyana, as,* m., N. of two teachers.

Āgnishṭomika, as, ī, am, belonging to the Agnishṭoma; one who recites or is conversant with the Agnishṭoma.

Āgnihotra, as, ī, am, fit for the Agnihotra.

Āgnīdhra, as, ā, am, Ved. originating from or belonging to the Agnīdh, i. e. to the priest who kindles the fire; (*as*), m. the priest who kindles the fire; (*ā*), f. care of the sacred fire; (*am*), n. the place where a sacrificial fire is kindled; the function of the priest who kindles the sacred fire.

Āgnīdhrīya, as, ā, am, being within the Āgnīdhra or the place where a sacrificial fire is kindled; (*as*), m. the fire (*agni*) within the Āgnīdhra; the fire-place (*dhishṇya*) within the Āgnīdhra.

Āgnīdhrya, as, ā, am, belonging to the Āgnīdhra or the priest who kindles the sacred fire.

Āgnendra, as, ī, am, Ved. consecrated to Agni and Indra.

Āgneya, as, ī, am, fiery, belonging or relating or consecrated to fire or its deity Agni; similar to fire or Agni; belonging to Agnāyī, wife of Agni; (*as*), m. epithet of Skanda; of Agastya; (*ās*), m. pl., N. of a people; (*ī*), f., N. of Agnāyī, wife of Agni; the wife of Ūru and daughter of Agni (?); the south-east quarter, of which Agni is the regent; (*am*), n. blood; ghee or boiled butter; gold; N. of a region. — *Āgneya-kīṭa, as,* m. an insect (*kīṭa*) which flies into the fire (applied to a thief who breaks into a room and extinguishes the lamp). — *Āgneya-purāṇa, am,* n. the same as the *agni-purāṇa*, q. v.

Āgnyādheyika, as, ā, am, belonging to the Agnyādheya. See under *agni*.

आग्रन्थ् *ā-granth*, cl. 9. 1. P. *-grathnāti, -granthati, -thitum,* to wind round, to intwine.

आग्रभोजनिक *āgrabhojanika, as, ī, am* (fr. *agra-bhojana*), one to whom food is first offered.

आग्रयण *āgrayaṇa, as,* m. (fr. *agra*), the first Soma libation at the Agnishṭoma sacrifice (see *graha*); a form of Agni; (*ī*), f. an oblation consisting of first-fruits or firstlings; (*am*), n. oblation consisting of first-fruits at the end of the rainy season.

आग्रस्त *ā-grasta, as, ā, am,* bored, perforated.

आग्रह् *ā-grah*, Ved. *-grabh*, cl. 9. P. A. *-gṛihṇāti, -ṇīte,* Ved. *-gṛibhṇāti, -ṇīte, -grahītum,* to seize, take hold of; to draw tight (as reins).

Ā-graha, as, m. seizing, taking; attack; surpassing, surmounting; favour; patronage; power, ability; moral power, courage.

Āgrahikā, f. favour, patronage, help.

आग्रहयण *āgrahayaṇa, as, ī, am,* belonging to the month Agra-hayaṇa (= *agra-hāyaṇa*, q. v.).

Āgrahāyaṇa, as, m. 'commencement of the year,' N. of a Hindū month commencing about the 12th of November, see *agra-hāyaṇa*; (*ī*), f. the day of full moon (*paurṇamāsī*) in the month Agra-hāyaṇa; a particular kind of Pāka-yajña, q. v.; N. of a constellation consisting of three stars, one of which is λ Orionis, figured by an antelope's head, hence also called Mṛiga-śiras.

Āgrahāyaṇaka, as, ī, am, to be paid (as a debt &c.) on the day of full moon in the month Agrahāyaṇa.

Āgrahāyaṇika, as, m. the month Agra-hāyaṇa; (*as, ī, am*), to be paid on the day of full moon in the month Agra-hāyaṇa.

आग्रहारिक *āgrahārika, as, ī, am,* one who appropriates to himself an Agra-hāra, viz. an endowment of lands or villages conferred upon Brāhmans.

आग्रायण *āgrāyaṇa, as,* m., N. of a grammarian; a sacrifice offered when the new rice or wheat ripens; (see *āgrayaṇa*, which is the correct reading.) — *Āgrāyaṇeshṭi* (°*ṇa-ish*°), *is,* f. the ceremony Āgrāyaṇa.

आघट्टक *ā-ghaṭṭaka, as,* m. (rt. *ghaṭṭ* or *ghaṭ*), a rubber; anything which causes friction; the plant Desmochæta Atropurpurea.

Ā-ghaṭṭana, am, n. friction, rubbing, contact, shaking.

Ā-ghaṭṭita, as, ā, am, rubbed, touched, shaken.

Ā-ghāṭa, as, m., Ved. a musical instrument used for accompanying a dance; a cymbal or rattle; boundary, limit; the plant Achyranthes Aspera; (at the end of some compounds) = *ā-ghāta*, see next col.

Ā-ghāṭi, is, is, m. f., Ved. a musical instrument which sounds on being shaken, a cymbal or rattle.

आघर्ष *ā-gharsha, as,* m. (rt. *ghṛish*), rubbing, friction.

Ā-gharshaṇa, as, ī, am, scratching, rubbing; (*am*), n. rubbing, friction; (*ī*), f. a brush, a rubber.

Ā-gharshita, as, ā, am, rubbed, brushed.

आघात *ā-ghāta, as,* m. (fr. rt. *han* with *ā*), striking, a blow, a wound; killing; a beater, striker; retention of urine; misfortune, pain; a slaughter-house, a place for killing animals or victims.

Ā-ghātana, am, n. striking, killing; a slaughter-house.

Ā-ghnat, an, atī, at, striking, beating.

आघार *ā-ghāra*. See under *ā-ghṛi*.

आघुष् *ā-ghush*, cl. 1. P. *-ghoshati, -ghoshitum,* to make one's self audible; to cry aloud, to proclaim; to praise; to listen to: Caus. *-ghoshayati, -yitum,* to make a noise, to cause to sound; to proclaim or cause to proclaim aloud; to complain continually.

Ā-ghosha, as, m. calling out to, invocation.

Ā-ghoshaṇa, am, ā, n. f. a crying or proclaiming, public announcement.

आघूर्ण् *ā-ghūrṇ*, cl. 6. P., 1. A. *-ghūrṇati, -ghūrṇate, -ṇitum,* to fluctuate, stagger; to roll, whirl.

Ā-ghūrṇana, am, n. rolling, tossing; fluctuating, whirling round.

Ā-ghūrṇita, as, ā, am, rolled, rolling; whirled round, fluctuating.

आघृ *ā-ghṛi*, cl. 1., and Ved. cl. 3. P. *-gharati, -jigharti, -ghartum,* to sprinkle towards or upon: Caus. *-ghārayati, -yitum,* to sprinkle.

Ā-ghāra, as, m. sprinkling, sprinkling clarified butter upon the fire at certain sacrifices; ghee or clarified butter.

आघृणि *ā-ghṛiṇi, is, is, i,* Ved. glowing with heat; endowed with spendor; epithet of the god Pūshan. — *Āghṛiṇi-vasu, us, us, u,* Ved. rich with heat, epithet of Agni; (Sāy.) having splendid wealth.

आघ्रा *ā-ghrā*, cl. 1. P. *-jighrati, -ghrātum,* to smell, smell at; to kiss: Caus. *-ghrāpayati, -yitum,* to cause to smell at.

Ā-ghrāṇa, am, n. smelling; satisfaction, satiety; (*as, ā, am*), satisfied, satiated.

Ā-ghrāta, as, ā, am, smelled, scented; satisfied, satiated; surmounted, surpassed.

Ā-ghreya, as, ā, am, to be smelled at.

आङ्कुशायन *āṅkuśāyana,* adj. formed fr. *aṅkuśa*. See Gaṇa to Pāṇini IV. 2, 80.

आङ्कृति *āṅkṛiti, is,* m., N. of a prince.

आङ्क्ष्ी *āṅkshī,* f. a musical instrument, a tabor.

आङ्ग *āṅga, as, ī, am* (fr. 2. *aṅga*), relating to the base (*aṅga*) of a word in grammar; bodily, corporeal; having limbs or parts or relating to them; relating to the inferior persons of a drama, to a portion of the Vedas, &c.; (*am*), n. a soft delicate form or body; (*as, ī, am,* pl. *āṅgās*), produced or born in the country Aṅga; a prince of that country.

Āṅgaka, as, m. the ruler of the country Aṅga; an inhabitant of the same.

Āṅgavidya, as, ī, am, occurring in or being familiar with chiromancy or the knowledge of lucky and unlucky marks on the body. See *aṅga-vidyā*.

Āṅgika, as, ī, am, bodily, corporeal; gesticulated, expressed by bodily action (dramatic sentiment, passion &c., exhibited by attitude, gesture &c.); (*as*), m. a player on a tabor or drum.

आङ्गदी *āṅgadī,* f., N. of the capital of Aṅgada's kingdom.

आङ्गार *āṅgāra, am,* n. (fr. *aṅgāra*), a multitude of firebrands.

आङ्गिरस *āṅgirasa, as, ī, am* (fr. *aṅgiras*), descended from or belonging to or referring to the Aṅgirasas or to Aṅgiras; (*as*), m. a descendant of Aṅgiras; especially a N. of Vṛihaspati, the preceptor of the gods; a Kshatriya by will of Brahmā and by profession.

आङ्गुलिक *āṅgulika, as, ī, am* (fr. *aṅguli*, q. v.), like a finger.

आङ्गूष *āṅgūsha, as,* m., Ved. praising aloud, a hymn [cf. *aṅgūsha, aṅgoshin*].

Āṅgūshya, as, ā, am, Ved. praising aloud, sounding; fit for praise.

आङ्गेयी *āṅgeyī* probably = *āṅgī*. See *āṅga*.

Āṅgya, adj. fr. *aṅga*, q. v.

आच 1. *āća, as,* m., N. of a man.

आच 2. *āća,* in the words *āća-parāća* and *āćopaća*, 'turned towards and away from' (?).

आचक्ष् *ā-ćaksh*, cl. 2. A. *-ćashṭe, -shṭum,* to look at, inspect; to tell, relate, make a communication about anything (with acc.); to announce, declare; to make known, confess; to acquaint, introduce to; to address any one (with acc.); to call, name.

Ā-ćakshamāṇa, as, ā, am, saying, declaring.

Ā-ćakshus, us, m. a learned man, a Paṇḍit.

आचतुरम् *ā-ćaturam,* ind. till the fourth generation.

आचतुर्य *āćaturya, am,* n. (fr. *a-ćatura*), clumsiness, stupidity.

आचम् *ā-ćam*, cl. 1. P. *-ćāmati, -ćamitum,* to sip; to rinse the mouth (with inst. of the thing); to lap up, lick up, to cause to disappear (as the wind licks up moisture): Caus. *-ćāmayati, -yitum,* to cause to sip water.

Ā-ćama, as, m. rinsing the mouth.

Ā-ćamana, am, n. rinsing the mouth, sipping water (before religious ceremonies, before meals &c., from the palm of the hand. It is usual to spit the water out again; the ceremony also includes touching the body in various parts); gargling the throat; the water used for rinsing the mouth.

Ā-ćamanaka, as, m. a spitting pot.

Āćamanīya, as, ā, am, used for rinsing the mouth; (*am*), n. water for rinsing the mouth, a gargle.

Ā-ćamya, ind. having rinsed the mouth, having sipped and ejected a little water.

Ā-ćānta, as, ā, am, sipped and ejected (as water); one who has rinsed his mouth.

Ā-ćāma, as, m. sipping water, rinsing the mouth; the water or foam of boiled rice.

Ā-ćāmaka, as, ā, am, rinsing the mouth.

Ā-ćāmanaka, as, m. a spitting pot.

Ā-ćāmya, am, n. rinsing the mouth, water so used, a gargle; (*as, ā, am*), to be rinsed.

आचय *ā-ćaya, as,* m. (fr. rt. *ći* with *ā*), collection, plenty.

Āćayaka, as, ā, am, collecting, skilful in collecting.

आचर् *ā-ćar*, cl. 1. P. ep. A. *-ćarati, -te, -ritum,* Ved. *-radhyai, -ritave, -rase,* to come near to, approach; to step upon, pass through; to proceed, manage, behave one's self towards (with loc.); to treat; to have intercourse with, frequent; to act, undertake, do, exercise, practice, perform; to devour, eat into; to help forward, put into.

Ā-ćaraṇa, am, n. approaching, arrival; following, observing, conduct, usage, practice; an institute, rite or rule of conduct; a cart, carriage.

Ā-ćaraṇīya, as, ā, am, to be done or performed; to be followed or observed, right, proper.

Ā-ćarat, an, antī, at, following, practising, observing.

Ā-ćarita, as, ā, am, observed, practised, as a rite or usage; usual, customary; enjoined, fixed by rule.

Ā-ćaritavya, as, ā, am, to be performed in a customary manner; to be done or performed.

Ā-ćarya, as, ā, am, to be gone to or approached; to be done or performed.

Ā-ćāra, as, m. conduct, manner of action; behaviour; good conduct, good behaviour; custom, practice, usage; an established rule of conduct, an ordinance, an institute, a precept; manner of conducting one's self, diet; rule; [cf. Hib. *acara,* 'convenience, conveniency, use.'] — *Āćāra-ćandrikā,* f. title of a work on the religious customs of the Śūdras. — *Āćāra-tantra, am,* n. one of the four classes of Tantras with Buddhists. — *Āćāra-dīpa, as,* m. 'lamp of religious customs,' title of a work. — *Āćāra-bhrashṭa, as, ā, am,* fallen from established usage, apostate. — *Āćāra-mayūkha, as,* m. 'ray of religious customs,' title of a work. — *Āćāra-vat, ān, atī, at,* well-conducted, virtuous. — *Āćāra-varjita, as, ā, am,* irregular, out of rule; outcast. — *Āćāra-viruddha, as, ā, am,* contrary to custom. — *Āćāra-vedī,* f. 'altar of religious customs,' a N. of Āryāvarta. — *Āćāra-hīna, as, ā, am,* deprived of established ordinances, outcast. — *Āćārāṅga* (°*ra-an*°), *am,* n. title of the first of the twelve sacred books of the Jainas. — *Āćārādarśa* (°*ra-ād*°), *as,* m. 'looking-glass of religious customs,' title of a work. — *Āćārārka* (°*ra-ar*°), *as,* m. 'sun of religious customs,' title of a work. — *Āćārollāsa* (°*ra-ull*°), *as,* m. 'light of religious customs,' title of a work.

Āćārika, as, ī, am, conformable to rule or practice, prescriptive, authorized; (*am*), n. rules for the preservation of health, habit of life, regimen, diet.

Āćārin, ī, iṇī, i, following established rites or practice.

Ā-ćārī, f. the plant Hingtsha Repens, also called Hilamoćikā.

Ā-ćārya, as, m. lit. 'one to whom one must have recourse' or 'one who is to be attended to or waited on' or 'one whose precepts are to be followed' or 'one who knows the *āćāra* or rules;' a spiritual guide or teacher, especially one who invests the student with the sacrificial thread, and instructs him in the Vedas, in the law of sacrifice and religious mysteries (Manu 2. 140, 171); an epithet of Droṇa the teacher of the Pāṇḍus; (*ā*), f. a spiritual preceptress. The title *āćārya* affixed to names of learned men is rather like our Dr.; e. g. *Rāghavāćārya,* &c. — *Āćārya-karaṇa, am,* n. acting as teacher. — *Āćārya-tā,* f. or *āćārya-tva, am,* n. the office or proficiency of a holy teacher. — *Āćārya-deva, as,* m. one whose preceptor is his god. — *Āćārya-bhogīna, as, ā, am,* delighting the holy teacher. — *Āćārya-miśra, as, ā, am,* venerable, honourable. — *Āćārya-vat, ān, atī, at,* one who has a teacher. — *Āćāryopāsana* (°*ya-up*°), *am,* n. waiting upon or serving the spiritual preceptor.

Āćāryaka, as, ā, am, originating from a spiritual teacher; (*am*), n. the proficiency of a holy teacher.

Āćāryānī, f. (with dental *n,* Pāṇini IV. 1, 49. Vārt. 6), the wife of an Āćārya or holy teacher.

Ā-ćīrṇa, as, ā, am (anom. past pass. part.), devoured, eaten into.

आचरण्य *ā-ćaraṇya* (nom. fr. *ćaraṇa*), P. *-ćaraṇyati, -yitam,* to move one's self, to move or extend towards.

आचल् *ā-ćal,* Caus. P. *-ćālayati, -yitum,* to move, draw away from one's place, stir up.

आचान्त, आचाम. See under *ā-ćam.*

आचि *ā-ći,* cl. 5. P. A. *-ćinoti, -nute, -ćetum,* to accumulate; to collect; to heap up, load with; to cover.

Ā-ćita, as, ā, am, collected, accumulated, heaped; filled, loaded with, covered; spread, diffused; inlaid, set (e. g. *ardhāćitā rasanā,* a girdle half set with gems); larded; (*as, am*), m. n. a cart-load; a measure of ten bhāras or cart-loads.

Āćitika, as, ī, am, or *āćitīna, as, ā, am,* holding or being equal to or cooking a quantity equal to the preceding measure; (a numeral may be placed before these forms, e. g. *dvyāćitika,* &c.).

आचिख्यासा *ā-ćikhyāsā,* f. (fr. Desid. of rt. *khyā* with *ā*), desire or intention of expressing or denoting something.

आचित् 1. *ā-ćit,* cl. 1. 3. P. *-ćetati, -ćiketti,* A. *-ćikite, -ćettum,* to attend to, to keep in mind; to comprehend, understand, know; to invent; to appear, become visible, distinguish one's self: Desid. *-ćikitsati, -te,* to wait for, watch clandestinely, lurk.

2. *ā-ćit, t,* f., Ved. taking notice or cognizance, attention to; (according to Sāy. the form *ā-ćitā* may stand for *ā-ćite* fr. *ā-ćita* above.)

आचीर्ण *ā-ćīrṇa, as, ā, am.* See under *ā-ćar* last col.

आचूषण *ā-ćūshaṇa, am,* n. suction; sucking out; application of cupping-glasses to the skin.

आचृत् *ā-ćṛit,* cl. 6. P. *-ćṛitati, -ćartitum,* to fasten, tie, affix.

आचेश्वर *āćeśvara* (°*ća-īś*°), *as,* m., N. of a sanctuary built by Āća.

आचेष्ट् *ā-ćeshṭ,* cl. 1. P. A. *-ćeshṭati, -te, -ṭitum,* to undertake; to do.

आचोपच *āćopaća.* See 2. *āća.*

आच्छद् 1. *ā-ććhad* (*-ćhad*), cl. 10. P. *-ććhadayati* or *-ććhādayati, -yitum,* to cover, hide; to clothe, to dress, put on clothes; to conceal.

2. *ā-ććhad, t,* f., Ved. a cover, covering; a sheath. — *Āććhad-vidhāna, am,* n., Ved. an arrangement made for defence, a means of covering; or (*as, ā, am*), one who has such means.

Ā-ććhanna, as, ā, am, covered, concealed, clothed.

Ā-ććhāda, as, m. cloth, clothes.

Ā-ććhādaka, as, ā, am, concealing, hiding.

Ā-ććhādana, am, n. covering, concealing, hiding; disappearance; a covering, a sheath; cloth, clothes; mantle, cloak, &c.; the wooden frame of a roof.

Ā-ććhādita, as, ā, am, covered, clothed.

Ā-ććhādin, ī, inī, i, covering, concealing.

1. *ā-ććhādya,* ind. having clothed or put on.

2. *ā-ććhādya, as, ā, am,* to be covered or clothed.

आच्छाक *āććhāka, as,* m., N. of the tree Morinda Tinctoria; (better *āććhuka,* q. v.)

आच्छिद् *ā-ććhid* (*-ćhid*), cl. 7. P. A. *-ććhinatti, -ććhinte, -ććhettum,* to tear or cut off; to cut or break in pieces; to take out of; to draw off; remove; to cut off, exclude; to snatch away, to tear from, to rob; to disregard, not to take notice of.

Ā-ććhidya, ind. cutting off; cutting, excluding, disregarding; setting aside, in spite of, notwithstanding.

Ā-ććhinna, as, ā, am, cut, cut off.

Ā-ććheda, as, m. cutting, cutting off, excision.

Ā-ććhedana, am, n. excision, cutting off, exclusion.

आच्छुक *āććhuka, as,* m., N. of the plant Morinda Tinctoria. See *ākshika* and *āććhāka.*

आच्छुरित *ā-ććhurita, as, ā, am* (fr. rt. *ćhur* with *ā*), scratched; irritated; (*am*), n. making a noise with the finger-nails by rubbing them on one another; a horse-laugh.

Āććhuritaka, am, n. a scratch with a finger-nail; a horse-laugh.

आच्छृद् *ā-ććhṛid* (*-ćhṛid*), cl. 7. P. A. *-ććhṛinatti, -ććhṛinte, -ććharditum,* to pour upon, to fill.

आच्छो *ā-ććho* (*-ćho*), cl. 4. P. *-ććhyati, -ććhātum,* to skin, to flay.

आच्छोदन *ā-ććhodana, am,* n. (rt. *ćhud* for *ćud?*), hunting, the chase. See *aććhoṭana, ākshodana.*

आच्यु *ā-ćyu,* Caus. P. A. *-ćyāvayati, -te, -yitum,* to cause to flow over, pour out; to draw or bring near; to induce (any one) to come near.

आच्युतदन्ति *āćyutadanti* (fr. *aćyutadanta*) or *āćyutanti* (fr. *aćyutanta*), *ayas,* m. pl., N. of a warrior-tribe.

आज् *āj* (*ā-aj*), cl. 1. P. A. *ājati, -te, -jitum,* to drive or bring towards; to procure; to drive near, i. e. to come near in a carriage.

Ājani, is, f., Ved. a stick for driving.

1. *āji, is,* m. f. (Ved. m.), a running-match; (*ājim aj* or *i* or *dhāv* or *sṛi,* to run with or against any one for the prize); a fighting-match, fighting, combat, battle, war; place for running, course, level ground; abuse, invective; an instant; [cf. Scot. *àgh,* 'fight;' Hib. *agh.*] — *Āji-kṛit, t, t, t,* Ved. running or fighting for a prize; making war. — *Āji-kriyā,* f. fighting, making war. — *Āji-tur, ūr, ūr, ūr,* Ved. victorious in battles. — *Āji-pati, is,* m., Ved. lord of the battle. — *Ājy-anta, as,* m. the goal in a race-course.

आज *āja, as, ī, am* (fr. 1. *aja*), coming from goats, belonging to goats, produced by goats; (*as*), m. a vulture; (*am*), n. boiled or clarified butter; ghee.

Ājaka, am, n. a flock of goats.

आजकार *ājakāra, as,* m. Śiva's bull.

आजगर *ājagara, as, ī, am* (fr. *aja-gara*), treating of the boa or large serpent; (a chapter in the Mahā-bhārata.)

आजगव *ājagava, as,* m. the bow of Śiva [cf. *ajakāva*].

आजन् *ā-jan,* cl. 4. A., Ved. *-jāyate, -janitum,* to be born or come into existence, to be produced or born from; to beget, cause to be born, render prolific.

Ā-janana, am, n. birth, origin.

Ā-janma, ind. from birth, since birth. — *Ājanma-surabhi-pattra, as,* m., N. of a plant (the leaves of which are fragrant from their first appearance).

Ā-jāti, is, f. birth, origin.

Ā-jāna, am, n. birth, descent, species; birth-place.

Ā-jāni, is, f., Ved. birth, descent; noble birth; (Sāy.) a mother.

Ājāneya, as, ī, am, of noble origin, of good breed (as a horse), fearless, undaunted; (*as*), m. a well-bred horse.

Ājāneyya, as, ā, am, Ved. of good breed, well-bred.

आजप् *ā-jap,* cl. 1. P. *-japati, -pitum,* to mutter or whisper to.

आजमीढ *ājamīḍha, as,* m., N. of a king in the Mahā-bhārata.

आजरसम् *ā-jarasam* or *ā-jarasāya,* ind., Ved. till old age.

आजवन *ā-javana, am,* n. (fr. rt. *ju* with *ā*), rushing at, attacking, fighting.

आजवस्तेय *ājavasteya* (patronymic fr. *ajavasti* Pāṇini IV. 1, 136).

आजवाह *ājavāha* or *ājavāhaka* fr. *aja-vāha* Pāṇini IV. 2, 133.

आजातशत्रव *ājātaśatrava, as,* m. (fr. *ajāta-śatru*), epithet of Bhadrasena in the Śatapatha-Brāhmaṇa V. 5. 5, 14.

आजाद्य *ājādya, as, ā, am,* originating from the warrior-tribe called Ajādas or a chief of that tribe.

आजान *ā-jāna, ājāneya.* See under *ājan.*

आजि 1. *āji.* See under *āj* above.

आजि 2. *ā-ji*, cl. 1. P. *-jayati, -jetum*, to conquer, win, acquire: Desid. *-jigīshati*, to try or desire to conquer or win.

Ā-jayana, am, n. conquering.

Ā-jigīshu, us, us, u, ambitious, wishing to excel or overcome.

आजिग्रह *ā-jigraha, as, ā, am* (rt. *grah*), who or what takes or seizes.

आजिज्ञासेन्य *ā-jijñāsenya, as, ā, am* (fr. Desid. of rt. *jñā* with *ā*), Ved. liable to investigation; (*ās*), f. pl., N. of a short section of the Kuntāpa hymns in the Aitareya-Brāhmaṇa; (the word *ṛićas* must be supplied.)

आजिहीर्षु *ā-jihīrshu, us, us, u* (fr. Desid. of rt. *hṛi* with *ā*), about to bring towards (with acc.); wishing to take.

आजीकूल *ājīkūla*, N. of a region.

आजीगर्ति *ājīgarti*, a patronymic fr. *ajīgarta*.

आजीव् *ā-jīv*, cl. 1. P. *-jīvati, -vitum*, to live by; to have the use or enjoyment of; to subsist.

Ā-jīva, as, m. livelihood, subsistence; a Jaina beggar.

Ā-jīvaka, as, m. a beggar, one who obtains his livelihood everywhere.

Ā-jīvana, am, n. livelihood, subsistence. — *Ājīvanārtha* (°*na-ar*°), *as*, m. (*am*, n.?) means of livelihood or subsistence, business, profession.

Ā-jīvin, ī, m. having a livelihood; a peculiar kind of beggar.

Ā-jīvya, as, ā, am, to be practised as a means of living; fit for or affording a livelihood; habitable, fertile; fruitful; (*am*), n. means of living.

आजुर् *ā-jur, ūr*, f. or *ā-jū, ūs*, f. (fr. rt. *jṛī* with *ā*!), unpaid labour, working without wages; consigning to hell; infirm age (?).

आज्ञा 1. *ā-jñā*, cl. 9. P. *-jānāti, -jñātum*, to know, understand, learn, obtain information, ascertain, notice, perceive: Caus. *-jñāpayati, -yitum*, to publish, order, command, direct; to assure.

Ā-jñapta, as, ā, am, ordered, commanded.

Ā-jñapti, is, f. order, injunction, command.

2. *ā-jñā*, f. an order, a command; allowance, permission; [cf. Hib. *agna*, 'wisdom.'] — *Ājñā-kara, as, ī, am*, executing an order, obeying, obedient; (*as*), m. a servant. — *Ājñā-karaṇa, am*, n. execution of orders, obedience. — *Ājñākara-tva, am*, n. the office of a servant. — *Ājñā-kārin, ī, iṇī, i*, one who obeys or executes orders, obedient, ministrant. — *Ājñā-ćakra, am*, n. a mystical circle or diagram, one of six described by the Tantras. — *Ājñānuyāyin* or *ājñānuvartin* (°*jñā-an*°), *ī, inī, i*, obeying or executing orders, obedient. — *Ājñānusārin* (°*jñā-an*°), *ī, iṇī, i*, executing orders, obedient. — *Ājñā-pattra, am*, n. an edict, written order. — *Ājñā-pratighāta as*, m. disobedience, rebellion. — *Ājñā-bhanga, as*, m. disobedience, insubordination, disloyalty. — *Ājñā-vaha, as, ā, am*, obedient, subject, ministrant. — *Ājñā-sampādin, ī, inī, i*, executing an order, obedient, submissive.

Ā-jñāta, as, ā, am, ordered, commanded; (*as*), m., N. of one of the first five pupils of Sākya-muni.

Ā-jñātṛi, tā, m., Ved. one who orders or directs.

Ā-jñāna, am, n. the act of noticing, perceiving.

Ā-jñāpaka, as, ā, am, giving orders, commanding, a commander.

Ā-jñāpana, am, n. ordering, commanding, making known.

Ā-jñāpita, as, ā, am, ordered, commanded.

Ā-jñāpya, as, ā, am, to be directed or commanded.

Ā-jñāyin, ī, inī, i, perceiving, understanding.

आज्य *ājya, am*, n. (fr. rt. *añj* with *ā*), melted or clarified butter used for oblations, or for pouring into the holy fire at the sacrifice, or for anointing anything sacrificed or offered; (in a wider sense) oil and milk used instead of clatified butter at a sacrifice; N. of a sort of chant or religious service; turpentine. — *Ājya-pa, as, ā, am*, Ved. drinking the clarified butter; (*ās*), m. pl. a class of Manes who are the sons of Pulastya and the ancestors of the Vaiśya order. — *Ājya-pātra, am*, n. a vessel or dish to hold clarified butter. — *Ājya-bhāga, as*, m. a portion of clarified butter; (*au*), m. du. the two portions of clarified butter belonging to Agni and Soma; (*as, ā, am*), partaking of the clarified butter; offering clarified butter at certain ceremonies. — *Ājya-bhuj, k*, m. 'consumer of clarified butter,' epithet of Agni. — *Ājya-vāri, is*, m. 'sea of clarified butter,' one of the seven seas. — *Ājya-sthālī*, f., see *ājya-pātra*.

आञ्च् *āñć* (*ā-añć*), cl. 1. P. A. *āñćati, -te, -ćitum*, to bend, crook, curve.

Āñćana, am, n. partial extraction of thorns or arrows and the like from the body.

आञ्छ् *āñćh*, cl. 1. P. *āñćhati, āñćha* or *ānāñćha, āñćhitum*, to make straight; to lengthen or stretch; to regulate, draw into the right position; to set (a bone or leg).

Āñćhana, am, n. setting (a bone or leg), bringing back into the right place by stretching, bending, or drawing.

आञ्ज् *āñj* (*ā-añj*), cl. 7. P. *ānakti, āñjitum* or *āṅktum*, to anoint; to smooth, polish, prepare; to honour, receive respectfully.

Āñjana, am, ī, n. f. ointment, especially for the eyes; fat. — *Āñjanābhyañjanīya* (°*na-abhy*°), *am, ā*, n. f., N. of a certain ceremony. — *Āñjani-kārī*, f. a woman who anoints or makes ointments.

आञ्जनेय *āñjaneya, as*, m. (fr. *añjanā*, his mother), N. of the monkey Hanumat.

आञ्जलिक्य *āñjalikya* (fr. *añjalika*). See Gaṇa to Pāṇini V. 1, 128.

आञ्जिक *āñjika, as*, m., N. of a Dānava.

आञ्जिनेय *āñjineya, as*, m. an insect, a kind of lizard, Lacerta Unjinensis. See *añjana* and *añjanikā*.

आट *āṭa, as*, m., N. of a serpent.

आटरूष *āṭarūsha, as*, m., N. of the tree Justicia Adhenatoda. See *aṭarūsha* or *aṭarūshaka*.

आटविक *āṭavika, as*, m. (fr. *aṭavī*), the inhabitant of a forest; a woodman, a pioneer.

Āṭavī, f., N. of a town in the Mahā-bhārata (2. 1175).

आटव्य *āṭavya, as*, m., N. of a teacher in the Vāyu-Purāṇa.

आटि *āṭi, is*, f. (rt. *aṭ*, to wander), N. of the bird Turdus Ginginianus [cf. *āḍi* and *āṭī*]. — *Āṭi-mukha, as* or *am*?, m. or n.? a surgical instrument employed in blood-letting, the top of which is like the beak of the bird *āṭi*.

Āṭika, as, ī, am, able to wander; (*ī*), f., N. of the wife of Ushasti.

Āṭikya, as, ā, am, being on a voyage.

आटीकन *ā-ṭīkana* or *ā-ṭīlaka, am*, n. (fr. rt. *ṭīk* with *ā*), the leaping motion of a calf [cf. *āḍhīlaka* and *ālīḍhaka*].

Ā-ṭīkara, as, m. a bull (etym. probably the same as the last).

आटोप *āṭopa, as*, m. (said to be fr. a Sautra rt. *ṭup* with *ā*), puffing, swelling; flatulence, borborygmi; pride, self-conceit.

आट्टस्थलक *āṭṭasthalaka* (fr. *aṭṭa-sthalī*) Gaṇa to Pāṇini IV. 2, 127.

आट्णार *āṭṇāra, as*, m. (fr. *aṭṇāra*), Ved., N. of Para in the Śatapatha-Brāhmaṇa; (*as, ā, am*), fond of wandering (?).

आडम्बर *āḍambara, as*, m. (etym. doubtful, probably rt. *ḍamb* with *ā*), a drum used in battle; charge sounded by musical instruments; the sounding of a trumpet as a sign of attack; the roaring of elephants; pride, arrogance (in this sense perhaps connected with *saṃrambha*?); commencement (in this sense perhaps connected with *ārambha*?); anger, passion; happiness, pleasure; the eyelid; (*am*), n. rubbing and kneading the body; (sometimes this word is written *āḍampara*.) — *Āḍambarāghāta* (°*ra-āgh*°), *as*, m., Ved. one who beats a drum.

Āḍambarin, ī, iṇī, i, arrogant, proud.

आडि *āḍi, is*, f. a bird, the Śarāli (Turdus Ginginianus); a kind of fish. See *āṭi*.

आडु *āḍu, us, us, u* (fr. rt. *aḍ*), striving to obtain anything.

आडू *āḍū, ūs*, m. (or f.?) a raft, a float. See *āṭu*.

आढक *āḍhaka, as, am*, m. n. (etym. doubtful), a measure of grain, the 4th of a droṇa and equal to 4 prasthas = 16 kuḍavas = 64 palas = 256 karshas = 4096 māshas; or containing nearly 7 lbs. 11 ozs. avoirdupois. In Bengal an *āḍhaka* is equal to two mans or 164 lbs. avds.; (*ī*), f. a kind of pulse, Cajanus Indicus Spreng.; a kind of fragrant earth. — *Āḍhaka-jambu*, N. of a country. — *Āḍhakajambuka, as, ī, am*, relating to that country.

Āḍhakika, as, ī, am, or *āḍhakīna, as, ā, am*, holding or containing an āḍhaka; sown with an āḍhaka of seed, as a field &c.

आढीलक *āḍhīlaka*, a various reading for *ā-ṭīlaka*. See *ā-ṭīkana*.

आढ्य *āḍhya, as, ā, am* (etym. doubtful, perhaps for *ārdhya* fr. *ṛidh*), opulent, wealthy, rich; (with an inst. or as last member of a comp.) rich in, abounding in, productive; possessing abundantly; mixed with, watered with; abundant, existing in abundance. — *Āḍhyakulīna, as, ā, am*, descended from a rich family. — *Āḍhyaṅ-karaṇa, as, ī, am*, enriching; (*am*), n. the means of enriching, wealth, prosperity. — *Āḍhya-ćara, as, ī, am*, once opulent (?). — *Āḍhyatā*, f. opulence, wealth. — *Āḍhyam-bhavishṇu, us, us, u*, or *āḍhyam-bhāvuka, as, ī, am*, becoming rich or eminent. — *Āḍhya-vāta, as*, m. (abundant wind), a convulsive or rheumatic palsy of the loins. — *Āḍhyāḍu* (°*ḍhya-āḍu*), *us, us, u*, striving to get wealth.

Āḍhyaka, am, n. wealth, opulence, abundance.

आणक *āṇaka, as, ā, am* (fr. *aṇu*, q. v.), low, inferior. See *aṇaka*.

Āṇava, am, n. exceeding smallness; (*as, ī, am*), very small, fine (?).

Āṇavīna, as, ā, am, bearing or fit to bear Panicum Miliaceum.

आणि *āṇi, is*, m. f. [cf. *aṇi*], the pin of the axle of a cart, the linch-pin; the part of the leg just above the knee; the corner of a house; a limit, a boundary; the edge of a sword.

आण्ड *āṇḍa, am*, n. (fr. *aṇḍa*, q. v.), an egg; a multitude of eggs, a brood; (*au*), m. du., Ved. the testicles [cf. *aṇḍa*]. — *Āṇḍa-ja, as, ā, am*, born from an egg. — *Āṇḍa-vat, ān, atī, at*, possessed of eggs or testicles. — *Āṇḍād* (°*ḍa-ad*), *t*, m., Ved. one who eats eggs, N. of a demon.

Āṇḍī, f., Ved. a testicle.

Āṇḍīka, as, ā, am, Ved. bearing eggs, as a plant with egg-shaped fruits or bulbs.

Āṇḍīra, as, ā, am, having many eggs.

आत् *āt*, ind. (fr. 4. *a*), Ved. afterwards, then; (in which senses it is often used in a concluding paragraph antithetically to *yad, yadā, yadi*, being then sometimes strengthened by the particles *aha, id, īm, u*; e.g. *yaded ayukta haritaḥ sadhasthād ād rātrī vāsas tanute simasmai*, 'at the very time when he has unyoked his coursers from his car, then night extends the veiling darkness over all;' *Vṛitram yad Indra śavasāvadhīr ahim ād it sūryam divy ārohayo dṛiśe*, 'when, O Indra, thou didst slay with thy power the dragon Vṛitra, then indeed thou didst raise the sun in the sky, that it might be seen.' In other passages *āt* is simply used like a conjunction, equivalent to 'then, further, also, and.' Sometimes it only serves to strengthen the meaning of another word, or to give emphasis to an interrogative pronoun, in the same way as *u, nu, anga*, &c.; e. g. *ya eka id apratir manyamāna ād asmād anyo ajanishṭa tavyān*, 'he who considered himself alone irresistible, another was born mightier even than he;' *Kim āt pra bravāma*, 'How can we at all proclaim?'

आत *āta, as, ā*, m. f. (fr. *ā-tan* below?), Ved. a scaffold; the frame of a door; (Sāy.) a quarter of the sky.

आतंस् *ā-tans*, Caus. A., Ved. *-tansayate, -yitum*, to shake out; (Sāy) to decorate from all sides.

आतक *ātaka, as*, m., N. of a Nāga.

आतक्ष् *ā-taksh*, cl. 1. P. A., Ved. *-takshati, -te, -kshitum, -tashṭum*, to bring from all sides, to procure.

आतञ्च् *ā-tanć*, cl. 7. P. *-tanakti, -tanktum* or *-tanćitum*, to cause to shrink or contract, to coagulate.

Ā-tanka, as, m. (this word may also be connected with rt. *tank*, q. v.), disease or sickness of the body; pain or affliction of mind, disquietude, apprehension, fear; fever; the sound of a drum or tabor.

Ā-tanćana, am, n. casting one thing into another to effect some change, as butter-milk into fresh milk to turn it; the act of causing to contract; that which causes coagulation; runnet; curdled milk; a sort of whey; calcining, adding a powder or flux to metals in fusion; the flux so used; casting away, destroying; danger, calamity (as a pestilence or epidemic); speed, velocity; gratifying, satisfying; making fat.

आतड् *ā-taḍ*, cl. 10. P. *-tāḍayati, -yitum*, to thump, strike.

आतन् *ā-tan*, cl. 8. P. *-tanoti, -nitum*, to extend over, stretch over, penetrate, to spread, overspread; to illuminate; to take hold of, seek to attain, assume a (hostile) attitude; to stretch (as a bow for shooting); to diffuse; to bring to pass, effect: Caus. *-tānayati, -yitum*, to stretch (a bow); [cf. rt. *tāy*, with which some of the following forms are connected.]

Ā-tata, as, ā, am, spread, extended, stretched (as a bow), &c.

Ātatāyin, ī, inī, i, one whose bow is stretched to take another's life; endeavouring to kill some one; a felon, a thief, a murderer, incendiary, ravisher. — *Ātatāyi-tā*, f. or *ātatāyi-tva, am*, n. persecuting, murdering, destroying, stealing.

Ātatā-vin, ī, inī, i, Ved. one whose bow is stretched. See *ātatāyin*.

Ā-tana, am, n. spreading, expanding; sight, view.

Ā-tani, is, is, i, Ved. spreading, penetrating.

Ā-tāna, as, m., Ved. an extended cord, string, &c.

Ā-tāyin, ī, m. a falcon, a kite. See *ātāpin*.

आतप् 1. *ā-tap*, cl. 1. P. *-tapati, -taptum*, to radiate heat; to blaze, to heat; to cause to glow: Pass. *-tapyate*, to suffer pain, be afflicted; to inflict (austerities) upon one's self.

2. *ā-tap, p*, f., Ved. heat.

Ā-tapa, as, ā, am, Ved. causing pain or affliction; (*as*), m. heat of the sun, sunshine. — *Ātapa-tra, am*, n. a large umbrella of silk or leaves used in the East as a parasol. — *Ātapatraka, am*, n. a small umbrella, a mat or basket carried on the head as one. — *Ātapa-vat, ān, atī, at*, irradiated by the sun. — *Ātapa-varshya, as, ā, am*, Ved. (water &c.) produced by rain during sunshine. — *Ātapa-vāraṇa, am*, n. a parasol. — *Ātapa-śushka, as, ā, am*, dried in the sun, evaporated by the solar heat. — *Ātapābhāva* (°*pa-abh*°), *as*, m. non-existence of sunshine, shadow.

Ā-tapana, as, m. causing heat, an epithet of Śiva.

Ātapīya, as, ā, am (adj. fr. *ā-tapa*), sunshiny (?).

Ātapya, as, ā, am, Ved. being in the sunshine.

आतम् *ā-tam*, cl. 4. P. *-tāmyati, -tamitum*, to faint, to swoon, to become senseless; to despond, to languish, fade away.

आतमाम् *ā-tamām?* (a superlative form fr. 3. *ā?*).

आतर *ā-tara*. See under *ā-tṛī*.

आतर्ज् *ā-tarj*, cl. 10. P. *-tarjayati, -yitum*, to scold, abuse.

आतर्दन *ā-tardana*. See under *ā-tṛid*.

आतर्पण *ā-tarpaṇa*. See under *ā-tṛip*.

आतव *ātava*, a proper N. (whence the patron. *ātavāyana* Pāṇini IV. 1, 110. Gaṇa.)

आतान *ā-tāna*. See under *ā-tan*.

आतापिन् *ātāpin* or *ātāyin, ī*, m., N. of the bird Falco Cheela. See under *ā-tan*.

आतार *ā-tāra, ā-tārya*. See under *ā-tṛī*.

आताली *ātālī*, an indeclinable word compounded with *as, bhū*, and *kṛi* (see Pāṇini I. 4, 61).

आति *āti, is*, m. f. (fr. rt. *at*), Ved. a kind of water-bird; the bird Turdus Ginginianus (see *āṭi*); going.

आतिथेय *ātitheya, as, ī, am* (fr. *atithi*, q. v.), proper for a guest, hospitable, attentive to a guest; (*ī* or *am*), f. n. hospitality.

Ātithya, as, ā, am, proper for a guest, hospitable, attentive to a guest; (*as*), m. a guest; (*am*), n. hospitable reception; hospitality; a particular rite, the reception of the Soma when it is brought to the place of sacrifice, also called *ātithyeshṭi*. — *Ātithya-rūpa, as, ā, am*, Ved. being in the place of the Ātithya rite. — *Ātithya-satkāra, as*, m. the rites of hospitality.

आतिदेशिक *ātideśika, as, ī, am*, (in gram.) connected with an *ati-deśa*, q. v.; having reference to substitution or putting one thing for another.

आतिरश्चीन *ā-tiraśćīna, as, ā, am*, a little transverse or across.

आतिरैक्य *ātiraikya, am*, n. (fr. *ati-reka*), superfluity, excess.

आतिविज्ञान्य *ātivijñānya, as, ī, am* (fr. *ati-vijñāna*), surpassing the perception or understanding.

आतिशय्य *ātiśayya, am*, n. (fr. *ati-śaya*), excess, quantity.

आतिष्ठ *ātishṭha, am*, n. (fr. *ati-shṭha*), Ved. the being placed at the head of something, being a universal ruler.

आतु *ātu, us*, m. (said to come fr. *ā-tṛī* next col.; but probably fr. rt. *at*), a raft, a float. See *āḍū*.

आतुच् *ā-tuć, k*, f., Ved. growing dusk, evening.

आतुज् 1. *ā-tuj*, cl. 1. 6. P., Ved. *-tojati, -tujati, -tojitum*, to bring near, to procure.

2. *ā-tuj*, m. (Sāy.) destroyer of enemies, or giver of wealth.

Ā-taji, is, is, i, Ved. rushing on, hastening towards; carrying off (as booty), injuring.

आतुद् *ā-tud*, cl. 6. P. A. *-tudati, -te, -tottum*, to strike, to push, spur on, stir up.

Ā-todin, ī, inī, i, Ved. striking, pushing, pricking.

Ā-todya, am, n. 'to be struck,' a musical instrument.

आतुर *ā-tura, as, ā, am* (fr. rt. *turv* with *ā*), hurt, injured; suffering; sick in body or mind, disabled, diseased; feeble, weak, incapable of doing anything (with inf.).

आतुल् *ā-tul*, cl. 10. P. *-tolayati, -yitum*, to lift up, raise, elevate.

आतृद् *ā-tṛid*, cl. 7. P. *-tṛiṇatti, -tarditum*, to split, sever, pierce; to push open, open; A. *-tṛinte*, to become split or severed, to sever one's self.

Ā-tardana, am, n. pushing open, opening.

Ā-tṛiṇṇa, am, n. an opening, hole; an open wound.

आतृप् *ā-tṛip*, cl. 4. 5. 6. P. *-tṛipyati, -tṛipnoti, -tṛimpati, -tarptum* or *-traptum*, to be satisfied: Caus. *-tarpayati, -yitum*, to satisfy.

Ā-tarpaṇa, am, n. satisfying, gratification, satisfaction; whitening the wall, floor or seat on festive occasions; the pigment used for that purpose.

Ā-tṛipya, as, ā, am, satisfiable, to be satisfied; (*as*), m. the custard apple tree Annona Reticulata; (*am*), n. the fruit of this tree.

आतॄ *ā-tṛī*, cl. 1. P., Ved. *-tarati, -taritum* or *-rītum*, to pass through or over; to cross over; to overcome; to enlarge, increase.

Ā-tara, as, m. fare for being ferried over a river, passage money, freight.

Ā-tāra, as, m. landing, coming to shore, fare, freight.

Ā-tārya, as, ā, am, to be crossed; (Ved.) landing, coming to shore, relating to landing.

आत्त *ā-tta, as, ā, am* (contracted fr. *ā-datta*, part. pass. of *ā-dā*, q. v.), taken, accepted; assumed; attracted. — *Ātta-gandha, as, ā, am*, one whose smell is taken away, one who is throttled; hence one whose pride is humbled, insulted. — *Ātta-garva, as, ā, am*, whose pride has been taken down, humiliated, degraded. — *Ātta-manaska, as, ā, am*, whose mind is transported or carried away (with joy). — *Ātta-lakshmī, īs, īs, i*, stripped of wealth. — *Ātta-vaćas, ās, ās, as*, Ved. destitute of speech.

आत्थ *āttha*, thou saidst. See under rt. 3. *ah*.

आत्मन् *ātman, ā*, m. (fr. rt. *an*, to breathe, or *at*, to go; or, according to some, fr. rt. *ah* and connected with *aham*, I; or, according to others, a contraction of *avatman* fr. rt. *av* = *vā*; but the existence of the old Vedic form *tman* makes all these etymologies doubtful); the breath, soul, the principle of life and sensation, the individual soul, the self, the abstract individual (e. g. *ātman* Ved. loc. *dhatte*, 'he places in himself, he makes his own;' *ātmanā vi-yuj*, 'to lose one's life;' *ātmanā saptamas*, 'made the seventh by one's self,' i. e. 'being one's self the seventh with six others'); self, one's self, used as a reflexive pronoun for all three persons (e. g. *ātmānam sā hanti*, 'she strikes herself'); and used in the singular even when it refers to a dual or plural (e. g. *putram ātmanaḥ sprishṭvā nipetatuḥ*, 'they two having touched their son fell down'); the natural temperament or disposition; essence, nature, character, peculiarity; the person or whole body considered as one and opposed to the separate members of the body; the body; the understanding, intellect, the mind, the faculty of thought or reason, the thinking faculty; the highest personal principle of life, Brahma, the supreme deity and soul of the universe (but *paramātman* is more usual in this latter sense); care, effort, pains; firmness; the sun; fire; wind; air; a son; [cf. Goth. *ahma*; Old Germ. *ātum*, Them. *ātuma*; Angl. Sax. *ædhm*; Mod. Germ. *Athem, Odem*; Hib. *adhm*, 'knowledge,' and *adhma*, 'knowing;' Gr. ἀϋτμήν, ἀϋτμή (?); ἀτμός, ἀτμή (?): cf. also rt. ἄω &c. = rt. *vā*.] — *Ātma* is used at the end of some compounds for *ātman ;* e. g. *pratyayātma, as, ā, am,* whose natural disposition is confidence. — *Ātma-karman, a,* n. one's own act. — *Ātma-kāma, as, ā, am,* loving one's self, possessed of self-conceit; loving Brahma, the supreme spirit. — *Ātma-kāmeya, ās,* m. pl., N. of a people. — *Ātma-kāmeyaka, as, ā, am,* inhabited by the Ātmakāmeyas. — *Ātma-kārya, am,* n. one's own business, private affairs. — *Ātma-kṛita, as, ā, am,* self-executed, done of one's self; done against one's self. — *Ātma-gatam,* ind. lit. 'gone to one's self,' aside (used in theatrical language, like the English 'aside,' to denote that the words which follow are supposed to be spoken privately, as if to the speaker's self and not in the hearing of any one but the audience). — *Ātma-gati, is,* f. course of the soul's existence, life of the spirit; one's own course. — *Ātma-gatyā,* ind. by one's own act (without the intervention of another). — *Ātma-guptā,* f., N. of the plant Mucuna Pruritus Hook.; (according to others) Cowach or Cowhage. — *Ātma-gupti, is,* f. a cave, the hiding-place of an animal. — *Ātma-grāhin, ī, iṇī, i,* selfish, greedy, taking care of one's self, appropriating, taking for one's self. — *Ātma-ghāta, as,* m. suicide; heresy, schism. — *Ātma-ghātin, ī, inī, i,* a suicide, a heretic, a schismatic, one who disregards moral or religious institutions. — *Ātma-ghosha, as,* m. a crow; a cock ('one who calls out to himself'). — *Ātma-ja, as,* m. a son; (*ā*), f. a daughter; a descendant; the reasoning faculty, understanding. — *Ātma-janman, a,* n. the birth of one's self, i. e. the birth of a son; (*ā*), m. a son. — *Ātma-jaya, as,* m. one's own victory; victory over one's self. — *Ātma-jña, as,* m. a sage, one who knows his own nature and that of spirit, self-knowing. — *Ātma-jñāna, am,* n. knowledge of the soul or supreme spirit, spiritual knowledge, philosophical knowledge of the spiritual principle in creation; self-knowledge, true wisdom. — *Ātma-tattva, am,* n. the true nature of the soul or of the supreme spirit. — *Ātmatattva-jña, as,* m. a sage versed in the Vedānta doctrines. — *Ātma-tā,* f. or *ātma-tva, am,* n. identity with self, spirituality. — *Ātma-tyāga, as,* m. self-sacrifice, giving up one's own life, suicide. — *Ātma-tyāgin, ī,* m. one who gives up his own life, a suicide: a heretic, an unbeliever. — *Ātma-trāṇa, am,* n. self-preservation, a body-guard. — *Ātma-darśa, as,* m. 'self-shower,' a mirror. — *Ātma-darśana, am,* n. seeing one's self; knowledge of man's real nature, spiritual knowledge. — *Ātma-dā, ās, ās, am,* Ved. granting personal existence or life. — *Ātma-dāna, am,* n. gift of self, self-sacrifice, resignation. — *Ātma-dūshi, is, is, i,* Ved. corrupting the soul, soul-destroying. — *Ātma-devatā,* f. a tutelary deity. — *Ātma-drohin, ī, iṇī, i,* self-tormenting, fretful, miserable. — *Ātma-nitya, as, ā, am,* constantly in the heart, greatly endeared to one's self. — *Ātma-nindā,* f. self-reproach. — *Ātma-nivedana, am,* n. offering one's self as a living sacrifice to the deity. — *Ātman-vat, ān, atī, at,* Ved having a soul, animated, alive, personal. — *Ātman-vin, ī, inī, i,* Ved. animated, having a soul. — *Ātma-parājita, as, ā, am,* Ved. one who has lost himself. — *Ātma-parityāga, as,* m. self-sacrifice. — *Ātma-prabodha, as,* m. cognition of soul or supreme spirit; title of an Upanishad. — *Ātma-prabha, as, ā, am,* shining by one's own light, self-illuminated. — *Ātma-pravāda, as,* m. conversation about the soul or supreme spirit; N. of the seventh of the fourteen Pūrvas or most ancient sacred writings of the Jainas. — *Ātma-praśaṇsā,* f. self-applause. — *Ātma-prīti, is,* f. self-enjoyment, self-indulgence. — *Ātma-badha,* see *ātma-vadha.* — *Ātma-bandhu, us,* m. one's own kinsman, a first cousin or father's sister's son, mother's brother's son, mother's sister's son. — *Ātma-buddhi, is,* f. self-knowledge. — *Ātma-bodha, as,* m. knowledge of soul or supreme spirit; self-knowledge; N. of a work of Śaṅkarāćārya; N. of one of the Upanishads of the Atharva-veda; (*as, ā, am*), possessed of a knowledge of soul or the supreme spirit. — *Ātma-bhava, as,* m. becoming or existing of one's self; (*as, ā, am*), produced in one's self, caused by one's self. — *Ātma-bhāva, as,* m. existence of the soul; the self, proper or peculiar nature; the body. — *Ātma-bhū, ūs,* m. self-born, self-existent; an epithet of Brahmā, Vishṇu, Śiva, and Kāmadeva, the god of love. — *Ātma-bhūta, as, ā, am,* self-produced, become one's self, own, peculiar, belonging to; attached to, faithful. — *Ātma-bhūya, am,* n. peculiarity, own nature. — *Ātma-maya, as, ī, am,* spiritual. — *Ātma-mātrā,* f. a particle of the supreme spirit. — *Ātma-mānin, ī, inī, i,* self-honouring, self-respecting, decorous, respectable. — *Ātma-mūla, as, ā, am,* self-existent; (*ī*), f., the plant Alhagi Maurorum ('striking root in self'). — *Ātmam-bhari, is, is, i,* self-nourishing, one who takes care only of his own person, selfish, greedy. — *Ātma-yājin, ī, inī, i,* sacrificing for one's self; one who sacrifices himself; (*ī*), m. a wise or learned man, one who studies his own nature and that of the soul. — *Ātma-yoni, is,* m. one whose birth-place is self; an epithet of Brahmā, Vishṇu, Śiva, and Kāmadeva, the god of love. — *Ātma-rakshā,* f. the plant Cucumis Colocynthis or Trichosanthes Bracteata (a creeper with a poisonous fruit). — *Ātma-rāma-yogendra* (°*ga-in*°), *as,* m., N. of a man. — *Ātma-loman, a,* n. the hair of the body; the beard. — *Ātma-vañćaka, as, ā, am,* self-deceiver. — *Ātma-vañćanā,* f. self-delusion. — *Ātma-vat, ān, atī, at,* self-possessed, composed, prudent; knowing spirit; (*t*), ind. like one's self. — *Ātma-vat-tā,* f. self-possession, self-regard, prudence; self-resemblance, proportion, analogy. — *Ātma-vadha, as,* m. or *ātma-vadhyā,* f. suicide. — *Ātma-vaśa, as,* m. subjection of the mind, self-control, self-government; (*as, ā, am*), depending on one's own will. — *Ātma-vikraya, as,* m. sale of one's self, sale of one's liberty. — *Ātma-vid, t,* m. a wise man, a sage, one who knows the nature of the soul or spirit; a sensible man, one who knows himself; a N. of Śiva. — *Ātma-vidyā,* f. knowledge of soul or the supreme spirit; spiritual knowledge. — *Ātma-vivṛiddhi* or *ātma-vṛiddhi, is,* f. self-advantage. — *Ātma-vīra, as, ā, am,* existent, sentient; appropriate, good for one's self, suitable as diet &c.; (*as*), m. a mighty man; a son; a wife's brother; the jester or Vidūshaka in a play. — *Ātma-vṛittānta, as,* m. one's own story, account of one's self, autobiography. — *Ātma-vṛitti, is,* f. one's own circumstances; practising one's own duties or occupation. — *Ātma-śakti, is,* f. inherent or own power or effort. — *Ātma-śalyā,* f. the plant Asparagus Racemosus Willd. — *Ātma-śuddhi, is,* f. self-purification. — *Ātma-ślāghā,* f. self-praise, boasting. — *Ātma-saṃyama, as,* m. self-restraint, stoicism. — *Ātma-sad, t, t, t,* Ved. dwelling in self. — *Ātma-sani, is, is, i,* Ved. granting the breath of life. — *Ātma-sandeha, as,* m. internal doubt, personal risk. — *Ātma-sambhava, as,* m. a son; (*ā*), f. a daughter. — *Ātma-sāt,* ind. one's own; (used in connection with rt. *kṛi,* see *ātmasāt-kṛi* next col.) — *Ātma-siddhi, is,* f. personal aggrandizement, self-advantage. — *Ātma-sukha, as,* m., N. of a man. — *Ātma-stuti, is,* f. self-praise. — *Ātma-hatyā,* f. self-destruction, suicide. — *Ātma-han, ā,* m. one who kills his soul, or does not concern himself about the welfare of his soul; a heretic, an unbeliever; a self-murderer, a suicide; a priest in a temple, a servant or attendant upon an idol; (the priest subsisting by appropriating to himself offerings to deities, for which future punishment is assigned) — *Ātma-hanana, am,* n. suicide. — *Ātma-hita, as, ā, am,* beneficial to one's self; (*am*), n. one's own profit or advantage. — *Ātmādishṭa* (°*ma-ād*°), *as, ā, am,* self-counselled; (*as*), m. a treaty dictated by the party wishing it himself. — *Ātmādhīna* (°*ma-adh*°), *as, ā, am,* depending on self, independent; sentient, existent; (*as*), m. a son; a wife's brother; the jester or Vidūshaka in a play, see *ātmanīna* and *ātma-vīra.* — *Ātmāparādha* (°*ma-ap*°), *as,* m. own offence, personal transgression. — *Ātmāpahāraka* (°*ma-ap*°), *as,* m. an impostor, one who pretends to belong to a higher class than his own. — *Ātmābhilāsha* (°*ma-abh*°), *as,* m the soul's desire. — *Ātmārtha* (°*ma-ar*°), *as, ā, am,* for one's own sake, for the sake of one's self. — *Ātmāśin* (°*ma-āś*°), *ī,* m. a fish, supposed to eat its young. — *Ātmāśraya* (°*ma-āś*°), *as,* m. self-dependance; innate idea, abstract knowledge which is independant of the thing to be known. — *Ātmeśvara* (°*ma-īś*°), *as,* m. master of one's self, self-possessed; God. — *Ātmodaya* (°*ma-ud*°), *as,* m. self-advantage or elevation. — *Ātmodbhava* (°*ma-ud*°), *as, ā, am,* born or produced from one's self; (*as*), m. a son; (*ā*), f. a daughter; N. of the plant Glycine Debilis Roxb. — *Ātmopajīvin* (°*ma-up*°), *ī, inī, i,* one who lives by his own labour; one who lives by his wife; a public performer, actor, singer, dancer, &c.; a day-labourer. — *Ātmopanishad* (°*ma-up*°), *t,* f. title of an Upanishad which treats of the supreme spirit. — *Ātmopama* (°*ma-up*°), *as, ā, am,* like one's self. — *Ātmaupamya* (°*ma-aup*°), *am,* n. likeness to self, analogy to one's own self.

Ātmaka, as, ikā, m. f. = *ātman,* essence, nature, character, property, peculiarity; (*as, ā, am*), belonging to the nature or essence of a thing, of the same nature as. *Ātmaka* often occurs as the last member of a compound; e. g. *saṅkalpātmaka,* whose characteristic is *saṅkalpa; pañćātmaka,* five-fold, composed of five; *vishātmaka,* poisonous; *Ṛig-ātmaka,* belonging to the Rig-veda.

Ātmakīya or *ātmīya, as, ā, am,* belonging to one's self, one's own, own; cognate, related of kin. Used reflexively for all three persons.

Ātmanīna, as, ā, am, belonging to self, own; appropriate, good for, fit for, suitable (as diet &c.), existent, sentient; (*as*), m. a son; any living being; a wife's brother; the jester or Vidūshaka (q. v.) in a drama.

Ātmane-pada, am, n. 'word to one's self,' form for one's self; that form of the verb which implies an action belonging or reverting to self; that voice which corresponds to the Greek middle; the terminations of that voice.

Ātmanepadin, ī, inī, i, taking the terminations of the middle voice, inflected in this voice.

Ātmane-bhāshā, f. the Sanskrit middle voice.

Ātmasāt-kṛi, to make one's own, to acquire or gain for one's self, to place upon one's self.

Ātmasāt-kṛita, as, ā, am, made one's own, appropriated.

Ātmī-bhāva, as, m. becoming part of the supreme spirit.

Ātmya, as, ā, am, belonging to self, personal; (at the end of a comp.) having the nature of.

आत्यन्तिक *ātyantika, as, ī, am* (fr. *aty-anta*), continual, uninterrupted, infinite, endless; excessive, superlative, abundant; supreme. — *Ātyantika-pralaya, as,* m. the grand or universal destruction of the world.

आत्ययिक *ātyayika, as, ī, am* (fr. *aty-aya*), having a rapid course, rushing quickly to a termination, not suffering delay, pressing, urgent; destructive, disastrous, distressing, painful, ill-omened, unpropitious.

आत्यूह *ātyūha, as,* m. a gallinule. See *dātyūha.*

आत्रेय *ātreya, as, ī, am* (fr. *atri*), originating from Atri; (*as*), m. a descendant of Atri; a priest who is closely related to the Sadasya (perhaps because this office was generally held by a descendant of Atri); an epithet of Śiva; an essential humor or juice of the body; (*ī*), f. a female descendant of Atri; a woman in her courses; any woman of the Brāhmanical order; N. of a river in the north of Bengal, otherwise called Tistā. — *Ātreyī-putra, as,* m., N. of a teacher.

Ātreyikā, f. a woman in her courses.

आथर्वण *ātharvaṇa, as, ī, am* (fr. *atharvan*), originating from, or belonging or relating to Atharvan or the Atharvans; (*as*), m. a descendant of Atharvan; a priest whose ritual is comprised in the Atharva-veda; a Brāhman versed in the Atharva-veda; a house-priest; the Atharva-veda; (*am*), n. a private apartment in which, after a sacrifice, the sacrificer is informed of the happy event of the sacrifice by the officiating Brāhman.

Ātharvaṇika, as, m. a Brāhman who has studied the Atharva-veda.

Ātharvaṇīya-rudropanishad (°*ra-up*°), *t*, f., N. of an Upanishad.

आद् ād (*ā-ad*), cl. 2. P., Ved. *ātti*, *āttam*, to eat.

आदंश् ā-danś, cl. 1. P. *-danśati*, *-danshṭum*, to nibble, bite or peck at.

Ā-danśa, as, m. a bite, a wound caused by biting.

Ā-dashṭa, as, ā, am, nibbled, pecked at.

आदघ्न ā-daghna, *as, ī, am* (fr. *ās-d*°), Ved. reaching up to the mouth (as water).

आदम्भ् ā-dambh, cl. 5. P., Ved. *-dabhnoti*, *-dambhitum*, to harm, hurt, injure, treat injuriously.

आदर ā-dara. See under *ā-dṛi*.

आदर्श ā-darśa. See under *ā-dṛiś*.

आदह् ā-dah, cl. 1. P. *-dahati*, *-dagdhum*, to burn, burn up: Caus. *-dāhayati*, *-yitum*, to cause to burn: Caus. Pass. *-dāhyate*, to be burnt.

Ā-dahana, am, n., Ved. a place where anything is burnt.

आदा 1. ā-dā, cl. 3. A. (Ved. sometimes P.) *-datte*, *-dadāti*, *-dātum*, to give to one's self, appropriate to one's self, take, receive, accept, seize, take away, separate; to carry off, to put on (as clothes), to perceive, comprehend; to agree to; to undertake, begin; to begin to speak; to repeat (with *punar*): Caus. *-dāpayati*, *-yitum*, to cause one to take: Desid. A. *-ditsate*, to desire to take, to be on the point of taking or seizing.

Ā-da, as, ā, am, (at the end of some compounds) taking, receiving.

Ā-datta, as, ā, am (sometimes contracted to *ātta*, q. v.), taken, seized, put on; agreed to, undertaken, begun.

Ā-dadāna, as, ā, am, taking, accepting, undertaking, beginning.

Ā-dadi, is, is, i, Ved. procuring, gaining; taking or carrying away or off.

Ā-dātavya, as, ā, am, to be taken or received.

Ā-dātṛi, tā, m. a receiver.

1. *ā-dāna, am*, n. taking, seizing; receipt, acceptance; taking for one's self, drawing near to one's self; receiving; taking away or off; a symptom: (for 2. *ā-dāna* see below under 2. *ā-dā*.) — *Ādāna-vat, ān, atī, at*, one who receives something.

Ā-dānī, f., N. of a plant, commonly called *hastighoshā*.

Ā-dāpana, am, n. inviting or causing another to accept something.

1. *ā-dāya, as, ā, am*, receiving, taking.

2. *ā-dāya*, ind. having taken. — *Ādāya-ćara, as, ā, am*, one who goes away after having taken anything.

Ā-dāyamāna, as, ā, am (epic form for *ā-dadāna*), taking, seizing.

Ā-dāyin, ī, inī, i, receiving, inclined to receive (gifts), taking gifts for one's self.

Ā-deya, as, ā, am, to be taken or received, receivable, leviable.

आदा 2. ā-dā, cl. 2. 4. P. *-dāti*, *-dyati*, *-dātum*, to bind, fasten.

2. *ā-dāna, am*, n., Ved. binding, fettering; a horse's trappings. (For 1. *ā-dāna* see under 1. *ā-dā*.)

आदादिक ādādika, *as, ī, am* (fr. *ad-ādi*), belonging to that class of roots of which the first is *ad*, i. e. to the second class.

आदि ādi, *is*, m. (fr. 1. *ā-dā ?*), beginning, commencement; a firstling, first-fruits; first, prior, prime, pre-eminent; (very often at the end or in the middle of a compound in the sense) beginning with, et cætera, and so on (e. g. *Indrādayaḥ surāḥ*, the gods beginning with Indra, i. e. Indra &c.; *gṛihādi-yukta*, possessed of houses, &c.; *evam-ādīni vastūni*, such and similar things; *śayyā khaṭvādiḥ*, the word *śayyā* means a bed &c.); *ādau*, ind. in the commencement or beginning, at first; [with this word has been compared the Slav. *jedin*, 'one.'] — *Ādi-kara, as*, m. the creator; an epithet of Brahmā. — *Ādi-kartṛi, tā*, m. the creator; an epithet of Brahmā, Kṛishṇa or Vishṇu. — *Ādi-karman, a*, n. (in gram.) the beginning or commencement of an action (as in the example *sūryaḥ pradyotitaḥ*, 'the sun has begun to shine;' see Gram. 895. *a*). — *Ādi-kavi, is*, m. the first poet; an epithet of Brahmā, or of Vālmīki. — *Ādi-kāṇḍa, am*, n. first part or chapter; title of the first book of the Rāmāyaṇa. — *Ādi-kāraṇa, am*, n. a primary cause; analysis, algebra. — *Ādi-kāla, as*, m. primitive time, remote antiquity. — *Ādi-kāvya, am*, n. the first poem, an epithet of the Rāmāyaṇa. — *Ādi-krit, t*, m. the creator; see *ādi-kartṛi* above. — *Ādi-keśava, as*, m. the first keśava, an epithet of Vishṇu. — *Ādi-tas*, ind. from the beginning, from the first, in the beginning, at first, at the head of (with gen.). — *Ādi-tā*, f. or *ādi-tva, am*, n. priority, precedence. — *Ādi-deva, as*, m. the first god, the creator; N. of Brahmā, Vishṇu or Kṛishṇa, or Nārāyaṇa; the sun. — *Ādi-daitya, as*, m. epithet of Hiraṇyakaśipu. — *Ādi-nātha, as*, m., N. of Ādi-buddha; N. of an author. — *Ādi-parvan, a*, n. first section or chapter, title of the first book of the Mahā-bhārata. — *Ādi-purāṇa, am*, n. the primitive Purāṇa, N. of the Brahma-Purāṇa. — *Ādi-purusha* or *ādi-pūrusha, as*, m. the first male or progenitor, usually applied to Vishṇu; the primeval spirit. — *Ādi-bala, am*, n. generative power (first vigour). — *Ādi-buddha, as, ā, am*, perceived in the beginning; (*as*), m. the primitive Buddha, the chief deity of the northern Buddhists. — *Ādi-bhava, as, ā, am*, produced at first; (*as*), m. epithet of Brahmā. — *Ādi-bhūta, as, ā, am*, first-born or existent; (*as*), m., a N. of Brahmā. — *Ādi-mat, ān, atī, at*, having a beginning. — *Ādi-mūla, am*, n. primitive foundation, primeval cause. — *Ādi-yogāćārya* (°*ga-āć*°), *as*, m. primitive teacher of devotion; an epithet of Śiva. — *Ādi-rasa, as*, m. the first or chief of the eight rasas, the principal sentiment or emotion, i. e. śriṅgāra or love. — *Ādirasa-śloka, as*, m., N. of a poem supposed to be written by Kālidāsa. — *Ādi-rāja, as*, m. the first king; an epithet of Manu; of a son of Kuru; of Pṛithu. — *Ādi-vanśa, as*, m. primeval race, primitive family. — *Ādi-varāha, as*, m. the first boar; N. of Vishṇu, alluding to his incarnation in that form. — *Ādivārāha, as, ī, am*, relating to the first boar. — *Ādi-vipulā*, f., N. of a metre. — *Ādi-śarīra, am*, n. the primitive body. — *Ādi-sarga, as*, m. primitive creation. — *Ādi-śūra, as*, m., N. of a prince. — *Ādīśvara* (°*di-īś*°), *as*, m., N. of a prince. — *Ādy-anta, as, ā, am*, having beginning and end; from the beginning to the end; (*am*), n. beginning and end, first and last. — *Ādyanta-vat, ān, atī, at*, having beginning and end, finite. — *Ādy-antāntara-vartin, ī, inī, i*, containing beginning, end, and middle; being all in all. — *Ādy-udātta, as, ā, am*, having the acute accent on the first syllable. — *Ādyudātta-tva, am*, n. the condition of having the acute accent on the first syllable. — *Ādyopāntam* (°*dya-up*°), ind. from first to last.

Ādika, as, ā, am, (used like *ādi*, q. v., at the end of compounds) beginning with, et cætera, and so on.

Ādima, as, ā, am, first, prior, primitive, original.

1. *ādya, as, ā, am*, being at the beginning, first, primitive; beginning with (used in this sense like *ādi*; e. g. *Indrādyāḥ surāḥ*, the gods beginning with Indra, i. e. Indra &c.); immediately preceding (e. g. *ekādaśādya*, immediately before the eleventh, i. e. the tenth; *saṃyuktādya*, immediately preceding a double consonant); being at the head, unparalleled, unprecedented, excellent; (*am*), n. the beginning; *ādye*, in the beginning; (*ās*), m. pl., N. of a class of deities; (*ā*), f. an epithet of Durgā. — *Ādya-kavi, is*, m. the first poet, a N. of Vālmīki, the author of the Rāmāyaṇa. — *Ādya-māshaka, as*, m. a māsha, a weight equal to five guñja or retti seeds, about 17½ grains troy. — *Ādya-vīja, am*, n. a primary cause.

आदिग्ध ā-digdha, *as, ā, am* (rt. *dih*), besmeared.

आदितेय āditeya, *as*, m. (fr. *aditi*), a son of Aditi; a god, a deity, a divinity.

Āditya, as, ā, am, belonging or devoted to, or originating from Aditi; belonging or relating to, or originating from the Ādityas; (*as*), m. a son of Aditi. In the earliest times this is the N. of seven deities of the heavenly sphere, of whom Varuṇa is the chief and to whom therefore especially belongs the title Āditya. The names of six of the seven are Varuṇa, Mitra, Aryaman, Bhaga, Daksha, and Anśa; that of the seventh is not clearly ascertained. Sometimes their number is supposed to be eight; and in the period of the Brāhmaṇas twelve, as representing the sun in the twelve months of the year. The name Āditya was afterwards applied to any god, though especially applicable to Sūrya, the sun; N. of Vishṇu in his Vāmana or dwarf avatār, as son of Kaśyapa and Aditi and younger brother of Indra; the plant Calotropis Gigantea; N. of a man; (*au*), m. du., N. of a constellation, the seventh lunar mansion. — *Āditya-ketu, us*, m., N. of a son of Dhṛita-rāshṭra. — *Āditya-garbha, as*, m., N. of a Bodhi-sattva. — *Āditya-ćandrau*, m. du. sun and moon. — *Āditya-dāsa, as*, m., N. of a man. — *Āditya-pattra, as*, m. a plant = *arka-pattra*. — *Āditya-parṇinī*, f. a creeping plant with gold-coloured flowers, growing near the banks of water. — *Āditya-purāṇa, am*, n., N. of an Upa-purāṇa. — *Āditya-pushpikā*, f. red swallow wort. — *Āditya-prabha, as*, m., N. of a king. — *Āditya-bhaktā*, f. = *arka-bhaktā*, q. v. — *Āditya-maṇḍala, am*, n. the disc or orb of the sun. — *Āditya-vat, ān, atī, at*, surrounded by the Ādityas. — *Āditya-vani, is, is, i*, Ved. winning the (favour of the) Ādityas. — *Āditya-varṇa, as, ā, am*, having the colour of the sun; (*as*), m., N. of a man. — *Āditya-varman, ā*, m., N. of a king. — *Āditya-vrata, am*, n. = *arka-vrata*, q. v. — *Āditya-sadṛiśa, as, ī, am*, like the sun. — *Āditya-sūnu, us*, m., son of the sun; N. of Sugrīva, the monkey-king; of Yama, Saturn, Sāvarṇi Manu, and Vaivasvata Manu. — *Āditya-sena, as*, m., N. of a king of Ujjayinī. — *Ādityāćārya* (°*tya-āć*°), *as*, m., N. of an author.

आदित्सा ā-ditsā, f. (fr. Desid. of 1. *ā-dā*), desire to seize or take.

Ā-ditsu, us, us, u, wishing to take or have (with acc.).

आदिन् ādin, *ī, inī, i* (rt. *ad*), eating (used at the end of compounds; cf. *annādin* &c.).

आदिनव ādinava, *am*, n. (?), Ved. misfortune, hinderance, want of luck (in dice); see *ādīnava*. — *Ādinava-darśa, as, ā, am*, Ved. having evil designs towards a fellow-player at dice.

आदिश् 1. ā-diś, cl. 6. P. A. *-diśati*, *-te*, *-deshṭum*, to aim at, to assign; to point out, indicate, report, announce, teach, determine, specify, foretel; to order, direct, command; to provoke, challenge; to undertake, try; to profess as one's purpose or duty: Caus. *-deśayati*, *-yitum*, to indicate, announce.

2. *ā-diś, k*, f., Ved. aiming at, design, intention; project, proposition; proposal, declaration; region, quarter; (Sāy.) a sacrifice offered or assigned (to a particular deity).

Ā-diśya, ind. announcing, apprising, aiming at.

Ā-dishṭa, as, ā, am, advised, enjoined; directed, commanded; said; (*am*), n. command, order; fragments or leavings of a meal.

Ādishṭin, ī, inī, i, or (*ī*), m. one who receives instruction, a pupil, a student, a Brāhman in the first order or quarter of his life; a penitent, one engaged in any expiatory rite.

Ā-deśa, as, m. account, information; advice, instruction, precept, rule; an order, command; foretelling; (in gram.) a substitute, substituted form or

letter, &c.; (in astrology) event, result, consequence of stellar conjunctions.—Ādeśa-kārin, ī, iṇī, i, obedient.
Ā-deśana, am, n. the act of instructing, commanding or prescribing.
Ā-deśin, ī, inī, i, ordering, commanding, instigating, exciting (e.g. kapola-pāṭalādeśin, exciting a glow on the cheek); (ī), m. a commander, a director; an astrologer, a fortune-teller.
Ā-deśya, as, ā, am, to be ordered or commanded.
Ā-deshṭṛi, ṭā, m. an adviser, a director, a commander; an employer of priests.

आदीनव ādīnava, as, m. distress, pain, uneasiness; fault, transgression; an afflicter of distress.

आदीप् ā-dīp, Caus. P. -dīpayati, -yitum, to cause to blaze, kindle, set on fire, illuminate.
Ā-dīpana, am, n. setting on fire, inflaming, exciting, embellishing; whitening the wall, floor or seat &c. upon festival occasions.
Ā-dīpita, as, ā, am, illuminated, inflamed.
Ā-dīpta, as, ā, am, set on fire, blazing up.

आदु ā-du, cl. 5. P. A. -dunoti, -te, -dotum, to feel pain.

आदृ ā-dṛi, cl. 6. A. or poet. P. -driyate, -ti, -dartum, to feel timid from veneration; to respect, mind; to honour, reverence; to enjoy honour, be honoured.
Ā-dara, as, m. respect shown to a person or thing, notice, care; reverence; commencement, beginning; [cf. Hib. adharadh, 'adoration;' adharach, 'one who adores.']
Ā-daraṇa, am, n. notice, respect.
Ā-daraṇīya, as, ā, am, venerable, respectable; to be attended to.
Ā-dartavya, as, ā, am, to be respected or regarded.
Ā-darya, as, ā, am, venerable, respectable.
Ā-dāra, as, m., Ved. allurement, attraction; (Sāy.) an instigator; N. of a plant used instead of the Soma plant, if this cannot be had.—Ādāra-bimbī, f., N. of a plant.
1. ā-dārin, ī, iṇī, i, Ved. attracting, alluring; (Sāy.) destroying (as if fr. ā-dṛī).
1. ā-duri, is, is, i, Ved. careful, attentive. (For 2. ā-duri see under ā-dṛī below.)
Ā-dṛita, as, ā, am, respected, honoured, worshipped; zealous, diligent; respectful.
1. ā-dṛitya, as, ā, am, venerable, respectable.
2. ā-dṛitya, ind. having respected, having honoured.

आदृश् ā-dṛiś, cl. 1. P., Ved. -paśyati, -drashṭum, to look at: Caus. P. -darśayati, -yitum, to show, exhibit.
Ā-darśa, as, m. a looking-glass, a mirror; copy of a work; the original manuscript from which a copy is taken; a commentary; N. of a son of the eleventh Manu; N. of a country.—Ādarśa-maṇḍala, having mirror-like spots; N. of a snake.
Ā-darśaka, as, m. a mirror.
Ā-darśana, am, n. showing, making apparent or seen; a mirror.
Ā-darśita, as, ā, am, shown, made apparent.
Ā-dṛishṭi, is, f. looking at, power of looking.

आदॄ ā-dṛī, cl. 9. P. A. -dṛiṇāti, -ṇīte, -daritum or -rītum, to crush, to force or split open, make accessible, bring to light: Intens. -dardarīti, to crush.
Ā-dardari, is, is, i, Ved. crushing, splitting.
2. ā-dārin, ī, iṇī, i, crushing, destroying.
Ā-dīrya, ind. having split, showing fissures.
2. ā-duri, is, is, i, Ved. crushing, bruising.

आदेय ā-deya. See under 1. ā-dā last page.

आदेवक ā-devaka, as, ī, am (fr. rt. div with ā), one who sports or plays.
Ā-devana, am, n. a place for playing.
1. ā-dyūna, as, ā, am, shamelessly voracious (said to come fr. ā-div, but the connection of this meaning with rt. div is not very apparent). For 2. ādy-ūna see next col.

आदो ā-do, cl. 4. P. -dyati, -dātum, to reduce to pieces or fragments; to tie, fetter. (In this last sense, the rt. is better written dā; see 2. ā-dā.)

आद्य 2. ādya, as, ā, am (fr. rt. ad), to be eaten, edible; (am), n. grain, food. (For 1. ādya see s. v. ādi last page, col. 2.)

आद्यून 2. ādy-ūna, as, ā, am, without beginning. (For 1. ā-dyūna see last col.)

आद्योत ā-dyota, as, m. (rt. dyut), light, brilliance.

आद्रिसार ādrisāra, as, ī, am (fr. adri-sāra), made of iron, iron.

आद्रु ā-dru, cl. 1. P., Ved. A. -dravati, -te, -drotum, to run towards, to hasten towards, to approach running; to bring running.

आद्वादशम् ā-dvādaśam, ind., Ved. up to twelve.

आधमन ā-dhamana, am, n. (fr. ā-dhā below or fr. ā-dham for ā-dhmā?), a deposit, pledge; fraudulent puffing of goods at a sale (?).

आधमर्ण्य ādhamarṇya, am, n. (fr. adhamarṇa), the state of being indebted.

आधर्मिक ādharmika, as, ī, am (fr. a-dharma), unjust, unrighteous.

आधर्षण ā-dharshaṇa. See ā-dhṛish.

आधा ā-dhā, cl. 3. P. A. -dadhāti, -dhatte, -dhātum, to place, deposit, apply, appoint, direct, propose, supply, give, make, constitute; (only A.) to appropriate to one's self, hold, possess, take.
Ā-dadhāna, as, ā, am, having, possessing.
Ā-dhāna, am, n. putting near or upon, placing; taking, having; receiving, recovering; the containing anything, the being in possession of a thing; a ceremony performed with consecrated fire (see agnyādhāna); a ceremony performed previous to conception (see garbhādhāna); a pledge, a deposit; a surety; assigning, attributing, employing; the place in which anything is deposited or rests; a receptacle; enclosure, circuit.
Ādhānika, am, n. a ceremony performed after cohabitation to procure or favour conception.
Ā-dhāya, ind. having deposited or placed.
Ā-dhāyaka, as, ikā, am, placing, assigning, attributing, applying.
1. ā-dhi, is, m. (for 2. ā-dhi see under ā-dhyai), place, situation; a pledge, deposit; a pawn, a mortgage; location fixing, site; definition, epithet.—Ādhi-tva, am, n. the nature or circumstance of a pledge.—Ādhitvopādhi (°tva-up°), is, m. the object or purpose with which a pledge is given, the conditions or terms of a mortgage.—Ādhi-bhoga, as, m. enjoyment or use of a deposit, use of a horse, cow, &c., when pledged.
Ādhī-kṛi, cl. 8. P. -karoti, -kartum, to pledge, mortgage, pawn, make a deposit.
Ādhī-karaṇa, am, n. pledging, mortgaging, a pledge.
Ādhī-krita, as, ā, am, pledged, pawned, mortgaged.
Ādhī-kṛitya, ind. having pledged, mortgaged, &c.
Ā-dhīyamāna, as, ā, am, being placed, being deposited.—Ādhīyamāna-citta, as, ā, am, having the heart applied or intent on.
Ā-dheya, as, ā, am, to be deposited or placed; to be pledged or mortgaged; what is put down or has a place assigned to it; to be assigned, attributed or given; to be received, held or supported; (am), n. = ā-dhāna, q. v.

आधार ā-dhāra. See under ā-dhṛi.

आधाव् ā-dhāv, cl. 1. P. -dhāvati, -vitum, to come running, to run towards.
Ā-dhāvamāna, as, ā, am, running, rushing onwards or at.

आधि ā-dhi. See under ā-dhā above for 1. ā-dhi, and under ā-dhyai for 2. ā-dhi.

आधिकारण्य ādhikāraṇya, am, n. (fr. adhikaraṇya), possession, location.
Ādhikārika, as, ī, am (fr. adhi-kāra), supreme, superior, relating or belonging to anything or person in authority; official, relating to any office or duty.

आधिक्य ādhikya, am, n. (fr. adhika), excess, abundance, superabundance, high degree, overweight, preponderance; superiority.

आधिदैविक ādhidaivika, as, ī, am (fr. adhideva), relating to a tutelary or presiding deity.

आधिपत्य ādhipatya, am, n. (fr. adhi-pati), supremacy, sovereignty, power.

आधिभौतिक ādhibhautika, as, ī, am (fr. adhi-bhūta), relating to beings; elementary, derived or produced from the primitive elements, material.

आधिराज्य ādhirājya, am, n. (fr. adhi-rājan), royalty, royal government, supreme sway.

आधिवेदनिक ādhivedanika, am, n. (fr. adhivedana), property, gifts &c. given to a first wife upon marrying a second.

आधु ā-dhu or -dhū, cl. 5. 9. P. -dhunoti, -dhunāti or -dhūnoti, -nāti, -dhavitum or -dhotum, to stir, agitate.
Ā-dhava, as, m., Ved. one who stirs up or agitates; that which is agitated, mixture; throwing; also = ā-dhavanīya (?).
Ā-dhavana, am, n. agitating, moving.
Ā-dhavanīya, as, m. a vessel in which the Soma plant is shaken and cleansed.
Ā-dhāva, as, m., Ved. that which is shaken or cleansed by shaking.
Ā-dhuta or ā-dhūta, as, ā, am, shaken, agitated, trembling.

आधुनिक ādhunika, as, ī, am (fr. adhunā), new, recent, of the present moment.

आधूर्य ādhūrya, am, n. weakness (?).

आधृ ā-dhṛi, cl. 1. P. -dharati, -dhartum, to hold, keep, support: Caus. P. -dhārayati, -yitum, to bring, supply: Pass. -dhriyate, to be brought.
Ā-dhāra, as, m. support, prop, stay; the power of sustaining, or the support given, aid, patronage, assistance; that which contains; a vessel or receptacle; a dike, dam; a canal; a basin round the foot of a tree; comprehension, location, the sense of the locative case; relation.—Ādhārādheya-bhāva (°ra-ādh°), as, m. the influence or action of the support or recipient upon the thing received or supported.
Ā-dhāraka, as, m. foundation.
Ā-dhāraṇa, am, n. bearing, holding, supporting.
Ā-dhārya, as, ā, am, to be located, that to which a location is to be assigned.—Ādhāryādhāra-sambandha, as, m. the relation of the recipient or receptacle and the thing to be received or located.
Ā-dhṛita, as, ā, am, Ved. contained, supported.

आधृष् ā-dhṛish, cl. 5. P., Ved. -dhṛishṇoti, -dharshitum, to assail, defy, injure, overcome; cl. 10. P. -dharshayati, -yitum, to injure, hurt, overcome, defy; refute, convict: Intens. Ved. -dadharshati or Leṭ of Caus. to overcome.
Ā-dharshaṇa, am, n. conviction of crime or error; sentence, refutation; injuring, annoying.
Ā-dharshita, as, ā, am, convicted, sentenced; refuted in argument, disproved, injured, aggrieved.
Ā-dhṛishṭa, as, ā, am, checked, overcome.
Ā-dhṛishṭi, is, f. assailing, attacking.

आधेनव ādhenava, am, n. (fr. a-dhenu), want of cows.

आधोरण ādhoraṇa, as, m. the rider or driver of an elephant.

आध्मा ā-dhmā, cl. 1. P. -dhamati, -dhmātum, to inflate, puff up; to sound.

Ā-dhmāta, as, ā, am, sounded, sounding; inflated, burnt; *(as),* m. flatulence, borborygmi, swelling of the abdomen with noise, war, battle.

Ā-dhmāna, am, n. blowing, inflation; boasting; a bellows; intumescence, swelling of the body, dropsy.

Ā-dhmāpana, am, n. a means of inflating.

आध्यक्ष्य *ādhyakshya, am,* n. (fr. *adhy-aksha*), Ved. superintendence.

आध्यश्वि *ādhyaśvi,* N. of a place.

आध्यात्मिक *ādhyātmika, as, ī, am* (fr. *adhy-ātman*), relating to self (as *ādhyātmikī rić,* a hymn sung by any deity or other personage in praise of himself); relating to the supreme spirit; spiritual, holy.

आध्यान *ā-dhyāna.* See under *ā-dhyai.*

आध्यापक *ādhyāpaka, as,* m. a teacher, a scriptural preceptor; = *adhy-āpaka,* q. v.

आध्यायिक *ādhyāyika, as, ī, am* (fr. *adhy-āya,* q. v.), occupied or employed with reading or studying.

आध्यै *ā-dhyai,* cl. 1. P. *-dhyāyati, -dhyātum,* to think on, meditate on, remember.

2. *ā-dhi, is,* m. (for 1. see under *ā-dhā*), thought, care, anxious reflection, mental agony, anxiety, pain; misfortune; reflection on religion or duty; hope, expectation; a man solicitous for his family's livelihood. — *Ādhi-ja, as, ā, am,* produced by pain, &c. — *Ādhi-jña, as, ā, am,* suffering pain, distressed; crooked. — *Ādhi-manyu, avas,* m. pl. feverish heat or burning. — *Ādhi-mlāna, as, ā, am,* withered with anxiety.

Ā-dhī, f., Ved. thinking, longing, care. — *Ādhī-parṇa, as, ā, am,* Ved. winged with longing or hope.

Ā-dhīta, as, ā, am, Ved. reflected or meditated upon; *(am),* n. the object or subject of one's thoughts, anything intended or hoped for.

Ā-dhyā, f. recollection, remembering especially with regret.

Ā-dhyāna, am, n. remembering with regret, pensive or sorrowful recollection, dwelling or meditating upon, &c.

आध्र *ādhra, as, ā, am* (rt. *dhrai?*), Ved. poor, destitute, indigent, weak.

आध्वनिक *ādhvanika, as, ī, am* (fr. *adhvan*), being on a journey.

आध्वरिक *ādhvarika, as, ī, am* (fr. *a-dhvara*), belonging to a Soma sacrifice.

आध्वर्यव *ādhvaryava, as, ī, am* (fr. *adh-varyu*), belonging to the Adhvaryu or to the Yajur-veda; *(am),* n. service at a sacrifice, especially the office of an Adhvaryu priest.

आन *āna, as,* m. (fr. rt. *an*), inhalation, breath inspired; Ved. mouth, nose; breathing, blowing.

Ānana, am, n. the mouth, the face. — *Ānanābja* (°*na-ab*°), *am,* n. face-lotus (i. e. lotus-like face).

आनक *ānaka, as,* m. (fr. rt. *an?*), a large military drum beaten at one end, a double drum, a small drum or tabor; the thunder-cloud or a cloud to which the noise of the thunder is ascribed. — *Ānaka-dundubhi, is,* m. (a patronymic fr. *anaka-dundubha,* q. v.), an epithet of Vasudeva the father of Krishṇa; *(is, ī),* m. f. a large drum beaten at one end, a large *d'hol,* a kettle-drum. — *Ānaka-sthalī,* f., N. of a country.

आनक्य *ānakya, as,* m. (?), N. of a sage (for Cāṇakya?).

आनक्ष *ā-naksh,* cl. 1. P. *-nakshati, -shitum,* to approach, obtain, reach, present.

आनडुह *ānaḍuha, as, ī, am* (fr. *anaḍ-uh*), originating from a bull; *(am),* n., N. of a Tīrtha.

आनद् *ā-nad,* Caus. P. *-nādayati, -yitum,* to make resonant, cause to sound.

Ā-nādayat, an, antī, at, causing to sound, making to ring.

आनद्ध *ā-naddha.* See under *ā-nah.*

आनन *ānana.* See s. v. *āna* above.

आनन्तर्य *ānantarya, am,* n. (fr. *an-antara*), immediate consequence or succession; proximity, absence of interval.

आनन्त्य *ānantya, am,* n. (fr. *an-anta*), infinity; immortality, future happiness.

आनन्द् *ā-nand,* cl. 1. P. *-nandati, -ditum,* to rejoice: Caus. P. *-nandayati, -yitum,* to gladden; A. to amuse one's self.

Ā-nanda, as, m. happiness, joy, enjoyment, sensual pleasure; N. of the forty-eighth year of the cycle of Jupiter; an epithet of Śiva; N. of a Bala-rāma according to the Jaina doctrine of many Krishṇas and many Bala-rāmas; N. of a cousin and a zealous follower and favourite disciple of Buddha Śākya-muni, compiler of the Sūtras: (*ā* and *ī*), f., N. of two plants; *(am),* n. God, the supreme spirit according to the Vedānta. — *Ānanda-giri, is,* or *ānanda-jñāna, as,* or *ānanda-jñāna-giri, is,* m., N. of an annotator on Śaṅkarāćārya. — *Ānanda-tā,* f. joyfulness, joy. — *Ānanda-tīrtha, as,* m., N. of a scholiast. — *Ānanda-da* or *ānanda-kara, as, ā, am,* exhilarating, delighting. — *Ānanda-datta, as,* m. membrum virile. — *Ānanda-paṭa, am,* n. a bridal garment. — *Ānanda-pūrṇa, as,* m., N. of a man. — *Ānanda-prabhava, am,* n. the seminal fluid. — *Ānanda-bodhendra* (°*dha-in*°), *as,* m., N. of a scholiast. — *Ānanda-bhairava, as, ā, am,* causing both enjoyment and fear. — *Ānanda-maya, as, ī, am,* blissful, made up or consisting of happiness; *(am),* n. the supreme spirit. — *Ānandamaya-kosha, as,* m. the innermost case of the body, or causal frame enshrining the soul. — *Ānanda-rāma, as,* m., N. of a man. — *Ānanda-laharī, is* or *ī,* f. 'wave of enjoyment,' title of a hymn by Śaṅkarāćārya, addressed to Pārvatī. — *Ānanda-vana, as,* m., N. of a scholiast. — *Ānanda-vardhana, as, ā, am,* enhancing enjoyment; *(as),* m., N. of a poet. — *Ānanda-vallī,* f. title of the second part of the Taittirīya-Upanishad. — *Ānanda-veda, as,* m., N. of a man. — *Ānandānandana* (°*da-ān*°), *as,* m. a king. — *Ānandāśrama* (*da-āś*°), *as,* m., N. of a scholiast.

Ā-nandaka, as, ā, am, gladdening, rejoicing.

Ā-nandathu, us, us, u, happy, joyful; *(us),* m. happiness, joy.

Ā-nandana, am, n. delighting, making happy; civility, courtesy, courteous treatment of a friend or guest at meeting and parting; what gives or occasions delight.

Ā-nandayitavya, am, n. the object of enjoyment or sensual pleasure.

Ā-nandayitṛi, tā, m. one who gladdens or makes joyful.

Ā-nandi, is, ī, m. f. happiness, enjoyment, pleasure.

Ā-nandita, as, ā, am, rejoiced, delighted, happy; *(as),* m., N. of a man.

Ā-nandin, ī, inī, i, happy, joyful.

आनपत्य *ānapatya, am,* n. (fr. *an-apatya*), childlessness.

आनभिम्लात *ānabhimlāta, as,* m. a descendant of An-abhimlāta.

आनम् *ā-nam,* cl. 1. P. *-namati, -nantum,* to bend, bend down, bow, incline; to humble; to salute reverently: Caus. P. *-nāmayati, -yitum,* to cause to bend.

Ā-nata, as, ā, am, bending, stooping, bowed; pacified, conciliated; humbled; submissive, obedient; saluted reverently. — *Ānata-ja, ās,* m. pl. a class of divine beings.

Ā-nati, is, f. bending, bowing, stooping; saluting.

Ā-nama, as, m. bending, stretching (a bow).

Ā-namita, as, ā, am, bent, bowed down.

1. *ā-namya* or *ā-nāmya, as, ā, am,* to be bent.

2. *ā-namya* or *ā-natya,* ind. having bent.

Ā-namra, as, ā, am (3. *ā* prefixed in the sense of diminution), a little bent, bowing, stooping, bowed down.

आनय *ā-naya,* &c. See under *ā-nī.*

आनर्त *ā-narta, as,* m. (fr. *ā-nṛit,* q. v.), a stage, a theatre; war; N. of a country and its inhabitants in the peninsula Gujarat with its capital Dvārakā or Kuśasthalī. — *Ānarta-nagarī,* f. the capital of Ānarta.

Ānartīya, as, ā, am, belonging to or coming from Ānarta; *(as),* m., N. of a man.

आनर्थक्य *ānarthakya, am,* n. (fr. *an-arthaka*), unfitness, impropriety; uselessness, unprofitableness.

आनलवि *ānalavi, is,* m., N. of a man.

आनव *ānava, as, ī, am* (fr. *anu*), Ved. kind to men, benevolent (?); human; *(as),* m. men, people; foreign men or people.

आनस *ānasa, as, ī, am* (fr. *anas*), Ved. belonging to a waggon.

आनह् *ā-nah,* cl. 4. P. A. *-nahyati, -te, -naddhum,* to bind to; A. to be stopped up.

Ā-naddha, as, ā, am, bound, tied, costive; *(am),* n. a drum in general, dressing, putting on clothes or ornaments. — *Ānaddha-vasti-tā,* f. retention of urine.

Ā-nāha, as, m. epistasis, suppression of urine, or constipation; length, especially of cloth.

Ānāhika, as, ī, am, to be used in cases of epistasis.

आनाथ्य *ānāthya, am,* n. (fr. *a-nātha*), state of being unprotected or without a guardian, orphanism.

आनिर्हत *ānirhata, as, ī, am* (fr. *a-nirhata*), Ved. indestructible nature; (according to Mahī-dhara) wholly gone out of the world.

आनिल *ānila, as, ī, am* (fr. *anila*), proceeding from or produced by wind, windy; *(as),* m., N. of Hanumat and Bhīma; *(ī),* f., N. of the fifteenth lunar mansion.

Ānili, is, m., N. of Hanumat and Bhīma.

आनी *ā-nī,* cl. 1. P. *-nayati, -netum,* to lead towards or near; to bring, fetch, bring back or take back: Caus. P. *-nāyayati, -yitum,* to have anything brought, to cause to be fetched: Pass. *-nīyate,* to be brought or fetched.

Ā-naya, as, m. bringing, investiture with the sacred thread.

Ā-nayana, am, n. bringing or leading near to; investiture with the sacred thread.

Ā-nayitavya, as, ā, am, to be brought or led near.

1. *ā-nāya, as,* m. a net.

2. *ānāya,* nom. A. *ānāyate, -yitum,* to form or represent a net.

Ānāyin, ī, m. a fisherman, a fisher.

1. *ā-nāyya, as, ā, am,* to be brought near; *(as),* m. consecrated fire, taken from the Gārhapatya or household fire, and placed on the south side, whence it is called Dakshiṇāgni.

2. *ā-nāyya,* ind. having caused to be brought, having caused to be introduced, having brought together, having convened.

Ā-nīta, as, ā, am, taken, brought, obtained.

Ā-nīti, is, f. leading near.

Ā-nīya, ind. having taken, having brought.

Ā-netavya or *ā-neya, as, ā, am,* to be brought, to be fetched.

Ā-netṛi, tā, m. a bringer, bringing.

आनील *ā-nīla, as, ā, am,* darkish; slightly black or blue; *(as),* m. a black horse.

आनु *ā-nu,* cl. 2. P. *-nauti, -navitum* or *-nuvitum,* Ved. 1. A. *-navate,* to sound, scream, warble: Intens. Ved. *-navīnoti,* to sound through.

आनुकल्पिक *ānukalpika, as,* m. one who knows the *anu-kalpa,* q. v.

आनुकूलिक ānukūlika, as, ī, am (fr. anu-kūla), favourable, conformable.

Ānukūlya, am, n. conformity, suitableness; favour, kindness.

आनुकृष्ट ānukṛishṭa = anu-kṛishṭa, q. v.

आनुगत्य ānugatya, am, n. (fr. anu-gata), acquaintance, familiarity.

Ānugatika, as, ī, am, relating to a follower.

आनुगादिक ānugādika = anu-gādin, q. v.

आनुग्रामिक ānugrāmika, as, ī, am (fr. anu-grāma), about or belonging to a village, rustic, rural.

आनुजावर ānujāvara, as, ī, am (fr. anu-jāvara, rt. jan), Ved. posthumous.

आनुदृष्टिनेय ānudṛishṭineya, as, m. a patronymic from anu-dṛishṭi, q. v.

आनुनासिक्य ānunāsikya, am, n. (fr. anu-nāsika), nasality (of a sound).

आनुपदिक ānupadika, as, ī, am (fr. anu-pada), following, pursuing, tracking.

आनुपूर्व ānupūrva, am, ī, n. f. (fr. anu-pūrva), order, series, succession: (in law) direct order of the castes; (in logic) a conclusion, regularly or syllogistically deduced. — Ānupūrveṇa or ānupūrvyā, ind. one after the other, in due order.

Ānupūrvya, am, n. order, series, succession.

आनुमत ānumata, as, ī, am (fr. anu-mata, rt. man), relating to the consent or favour (of another).

आनुमानिक ānumānika, as, ī, am (fr. anu-māna, rt. mā), relating to a conclusion; derived from inference, subject to inference, inferable, inferred. — Ānumānika-tva, am, n. the state of being inferable.

आनुरक्ति ānurakti, is, f. passion, affection; the same as anu-rakti, q. v.

आनुलोम्य ānulomya, as, ī, am (fr. anu-loma), in the direction of the hair, produced in natural or direct order; (am), n. a direction similar to that of the hairs, natural or direct order; favourable direction, fit disposition, favourableness; regular series or succession; bringing to one's right place.

Ānulomika, as, ī, am, regular, orderly, in due course or series; favourable.

आनुविधित्सा ānuvidhitsā, f. (corrupted fr. an-anuvidhitsā fr. rt. dhā?), ingratitude.

आनुवेश्य ānuveśya, as, m. (fr. anu-veśa), a neighbour who lives in the same house.

आनुशासनिक ānuśāsanika, as, ī, am (fr. anu-śāsana), relating to or treating of instruction.

आनुशूक ānuśūka, as, ī, am (fr. anu-śūka), being with or within the awns (as rice).

आनुश्रविक ānuśravika or ānuśrāvika, as, ī, am (fr. anu-śrava), according to hearing, resting on tradition.

आनुषक् ānushak, ind. (fr. anu-sañj, q. v.), Ved. in continuous order, uninterruptedly, one after the other.

Ānushangika, as, ī, am, connected with, concomitant, necessarily following, adherent, inherent, implied; proportionate, like, analogous, relative; necessary as a result or consequence, inevitable; (in gram.) elliptical, including or agreeing with words not comprised in the sentence.

आनुषण्ड ānushaṇḍa or ānushaṇḍaka, as, ī, am. See Gaṇa to Pāṇini IV. 2, 133. 134.

आनुषूक ānushūka, as, ī, am (either = ānuśūka or fr. rt. sū?), promoting, driving forward.

आनुष्टुभ ānushṭubha, as, ī, am (fr. anu-shṭubh), consisting of Anushṭubhs, formed like the Anushṭubh metre (e.g. composed of four divisions).

आनुसूय ānusūya, as, ī, am, coming from Anusūyā.

आनूकम् ānūkam, ind. (fr. ā-anūkam?), Ved. in abundance.

आनूप ānūpa, as, ī, am (fr. anūpa), wet, watery, marshy; (as), m. any animal frequenting watery or marshy places, as a buffalo, &c. — Ānūpa-mānsa, as, m. the flesh or meat of animals frequenting marshes.

Ānūpaka, as, ī, am, living or happening in marshy places.

आनृण्य ānṛiṇya, am, n. (fr. an-ṛiṇa), acquittance of debt or obligation, the not being indebted to (with gen.).

आनृत् ā-nṛit, cl. 4. P. -nṛityati, -nartitum, to dance towards, hasten near, dance: Caus. P. -nartayati, -yitum, to agitate gently.

Ā-narta, as, m. a stage, theatre; war. See s. v.

आनृत ānṛita, as, ī, am (fr. an-ṛita), untruthful; (as), m., N. of a people (?).

Ānṛitaka, as, ī, am, inhabited by the Ānṛitas.

आनृशंस ānṛiśansa or ānṛiśansya, am, n. (fr. a-nṛiśansa), mildness, kindness, mercy, compassion; cruelty (?).

आनेतव्य ā-netavya, ā-neya. See under ā-nī.

आनैपुण ānaipuṇa, am, n. (fr. a-nipuṇa), clumsiness, stupidity; = a-naipuṇa, q. v.

आनैश्वर्य ānaiśvarya, am, n. (fr. an-īśvara), absence of power or supremacy. See an-aiśvarya.

आन्त 1. ānta, as, ā, am (fr. rt. am), gone.

आन्त 2. ānta, as, ī, am (fr. anta), final, terminal, relating to the end.

Āntya, as, m., Ved. one who finishes; personified as Bhauvana.

आन्तम् āntam, ind. (fr. ā + antam), to the end, completely, from head to foot.

आन्तरतम्य āntaratamya, am, n. (fr. antaratama), nearest or closest relationship (as of two letters).

Āntarya, am, n. (fr. antara), near relationship (of two letters).

आन्तरिक्ष āntariksha or āntarīksha, as, ī, am (fr. antariksha), belonging to the intermediate space between earth and heaven, atmospherical, heavenly, celestial, produced in the atmosphere; (am), n. the firmament, the intermediate region between earth and sky.

आन्तर्गणिक āntargaṇika, as, ī, am (fr. antar-gaṇa), included, comprehended (as in a class or troop).

आन्तर्गेहिक āntargehika, as, ī, am (fr. antar-geha), being inside a house.

आन्तर्वेश्मिक āntarveśmika, as, ī, am (fr. antar-veśman), produced or occurring within a house.

आन्तिका āntikā, f. an elder sister. See antikā.

आन्त्र āntra, am, n., Ved. the bowels, entrails.

Āntrika, as, ī, am, visceral, within, or relating to the bowels.

आन्द ānda, as, m., N. of a despised class of men.

आन्दोलय् āndolay, cl. 10. P. āndolayati, -yitum, to swing. See andolay.

Āndola, as, m. swinging.

Āndolana, am, n. swinging, a swing; trembling, oscillation.

Āndolita, as, ā, am, swung, shaken.

आन्धस āndhasa, as, m. (fr. andhas, q. v.), the scum of boiled rice.

Āndhasika, as, m. a cook.

आन्ध्य āndhya, am, n. (fr. andha), blindness.

आन्ध्र āndhra, ās, m. pl. the Telugu country, Telingana, see andhra; (as, ā, am), anything relating to this country (as the Telugu language).

आन्न ānna, as, ī, am (fr. anna), fed, having food; relating to food, derived from it, &c.

आन्यतरेय ānyatareya, as, m., N. of a grammarian.

आन्वयिक ānvayika, as, ī, am (fr. anv-aya), of a good family, well born; orderly, according to order or arrangement.

आन्वाहिक ānvāhika, as, ī, am (fr. anv-aham), daily.

आन्वीक्षिकी ānvīkshikī, f. (fr. anv-īkshā), logic, logical philosophy, metaphysics.

आप् āp, cl. 5. 1. P. āpnoti or āpati, āpa, āpsyati, āpat, āptum, to reach, overtake, meet with, fall upon; to obtain, gain, take possession of, undergo, suffer; to enter, pervade, occupy, to equal: Pass. āpyate, to be reached, found, met with, obtained; to arrive at one's aim or end, become filled: Caus. P. āpayati, -yitum, aor. āpipat, to cause to reach or obtain or gain; to cause any one to feel; to hit: Desid. P. īpsati, to strive to reach or obtain: Desid. of the Caus. āpipayishati, to strive to reach; [cf. Lat. apio, aptus; adipiscor: Old Germ. uoban: Mod. Germ. üben.]

1. āpa, as, ā, am, at the end of compounds; e. g. dur-āpa, difficult to be obtained.

Āpana, am, n. reaching, obtaining; pepper.

Āpaneya, as, ā, am, to be reached or obtained.

Āpayitṛi, tā, trī, tṛi, one who procures, procuring.

Āpi, is, m., Ved. an ally, a friend, an acquaintance. — Āpi-tva, am, n., Ved. confederation, friendship.

Āpta, as, ā, am, reached, overtaken, equalled; got, gained, obtained; reaching to, extending; abundant, full; apt, fit, true, exact, clever, trusted, trustworthy, confidential; intimate, related, acquainted; appointed; generally received; commonly used; authentic; accused, prosecuted; (as), m. a fit person, a credible person, a warranter, guarantee; a friend; an Arhat; N. of a Nāga; (ā), f. a twisted band or lock of hair; (am), n. a quotient; equation of a degree. — Āpta-kāma, as, ā, am, one who has gained his wish, satisfied. — Āpta-kārin, ī, iṇī, i, managing things in a fit or confidential manner; (ī), m. a trusty agent, a confidential servant. — Āpta-garbhā, f. a pregnant woman. — Āpta-garva, as, ā, am, proud, arrogant. — Āpta-dakshiṇa, as, ā, am, having proper gifts, or furnished with gifts. — Āpta-vaćana, am, n. received text, revelation, authority. — Āpta-vajra-sūći, is, f., N. of an Upanishad. — Āpta-vākya, am, n. a correct sentence. — Āpta-vāć, k, f. the evidence of a credible person; (k), m. one whose evidence is credible. — Āptokti (°ta-uk°), is, f. augment or affix; a word of received acceptation and established by usage only.

Āptavya, as, ā, am, to be reached, obtainable.

Āpti, is, f. reaching, meeting with; obtaining, gain, acquisition; binding, connection, relation, fitness, aptitude; (ayas), f. pl., N. of twelve sacrificial verses beginning with āpaye (dat. case of āpi).

1. āpya, as, ā, am, obtainable. See āptavya.

2. āpya, am, n., Ved. confederation, alliance, relationship, friendship.

आप 2. āpa, as, m. (probably connected with ap, āpas, q. v.), N. of one of the eight demigods called Vasus. (For 1. āpa see above.)

आपकर *āpakara, as, ī, am* (fr. *apa-kara*), offensive, mischievous, unfriendly.

आपक्व *ā-pakva, as, ā, am* (rt. *pać* with 3. *ā*, implying diminution), half-baked, crude, raw; nearly ripe, not quite ripe; undressed, what is eaten without further preparation (as bread &c.).

आपगा *āpagā*, f. (fr. rt. *gā* with *apa?*), a river, a stream; N. of a stream.

Āpageya, as, m. the son of a river; an epithet of Kṛishṇa or Bhīma.

आपट् *ā-paṭ*, cl. 10. P. *-pāṭayati, -yitum*, to split; to sever.

आपण *ā-paṇa, as*, m. (rt. *paṇ* with *ā*), a market, a shop.

Āpaṇika, as, ī, am, mercantile, relating to traffic, to a market &c.; *(as)*, m. a merchant, a dealer, a shop-keeper; tax on markets or shops; assize, market-rate.

आपत् *ā-pat*, cl. 1. P. *-patati, -titum*, to fly towards, to come flying, to come in haste, to rush in or on; to assail; to approach; to fall to one's share, to befal, happen: Caus. P. *-pātayati, -yitum*, to throw down, let fall, shed; *-patayati, -yitum*, to go towards, approach.

Ā-patat, an, antī, at, approaching, preparing to assail.

Ā-patana, am, n. coming, approaching; descending, alighting, happening.

Ā-pati, is, is, i, Ved. coming in haste, rushing on.

Ā-patika, as, ī, am, accidental, unforeseen, sent from heaven; *(as)*, m. a hawk, a falcon.

Ā-patita, as, ā, am, happened, befallen; alighted, descended.

Ā-pāta, as, ā, am, rushing upon, attacking, approaching; *(as)*, m. rushing upon, pressing against, falling, descending; throwing down; causing to descend; happening, becoming apparent, appearance; the instant, the current moment; *(atas)*, ind. at the first attack, instantly, immediately.

Ā-pātin, ī, inī, i, falling on, descending, happening.

आपतालिका *āpatālikā*, f. (fr. *apa-tāla?*), N. of a metre.

आपत्य *āpatya, as, ī, am* (fr. *apatya*), relating to offspring; (in gram.) relating to the formation of patronymic nouns.

आपथि *ā-pathi, is, is, i* (fr. *pathin* with *ā*), Ved. being on the way or on a voyage.

Ā-pathī, is, or *ā-pathya, as*, m., Ved. a traveller, wanderer.

आपद् 1. *ā-pad*, cl. 4. A. *-padyate, -pattum*, to come, walk towards; to enter into, attain; to get into trouble, fall into misfortune; to happen: Caus. P. *-pādayati, -yitum*, to bring on, bring to pass.

Ā-patti, is, f. entering into a state or condition, entering into relationship with anything, changing into; obtaining, procuring; misfortune, calamity, fault, transgression; remonstrance, expostulation.

2. *ā-pad, t*, f. misfortune, calamity; [cf. Hib. *âpadh*, 'death;' *âpthach*, 'mortal.'] — *Āpat-kāla, as*, m. season of distress. — *Āpatkālika, as, ā* or *ī, am*, occurring in a time of calamity, belonging to such a time. — *Āpat-prāpta, as, ā, am*, unfortunate, unhappy, afflicted. — *Āpad-gata, as, ā, am*, fallen into misfortune. — *Āpad-grasta, as, ā, am*, seized by misfortune, unfortunate, unhappy, in misfortune. — *Āpad-dharma, as*, m. practice or profession other than that proper to caste, but allowable in time of distress.

Ā-padā, f. misfortune, calamity.

Ā-panna, as, ā, am, gained, obtained, acquired; afflicted, unfortunate. — *Āpanna-sattva, as, ā, am*, impregnated, pregnant; *(ā)*, f. a pregnant woman. — *Āpannārti-praśamana-phala* (°*na-ār*°), *as, ā, am*, fruitful in the relieving of the pains of the afflicted.

Ā-pāda, as, m. reward, remuneration.

Ā-pādana, am, n. causing to arrive at, leading to.

आपन *āpana, āpaneya*. See under rt. *āp*.

आपनिक *āpanika, as*, m. an emerald; a kirāta or barbarian.

आपमित्यक *āpamityaka, as, ī, am* (fr. *apa-mitya*, rt. *mā* with *apa*; cf. *apa-mityaka*), received by barter; *(am)*, n. property &c. obtained by barter.

आपया *āpayā*, f., Ved., N. of a river near the Sarasvatī.

आपयितृ *āpayitṛi*. See under rt. *āp*.

आपराह्णिक *āparāhṇika, as, ī, am* (fr. *aparāhṇa*), occurring in the afternoon.

आपर्तुक *āpartuka, as, ī, am* (fr. *apa-ṛitu*), not bound to fixed times, not restricted to particular seasons.

आपव *āpava, as*, m. an epithet of Vaśishṭha.

आपवर्ग्य *āpavargya, as, ī, am* (fr. *apa-varga*), conferring final beatitude.

आपस् *āpas*, n. a religious ceremony; water (see *ap*); sin [cf. *apas*].

आपस्कार *āpaskāra, am*, n. (fr. *apa-skara*), the root or extremity of the trunk or body.

आपस्तम्ब *āpastamba, as*, m., N. of a renowned sage and writer on ritual.

Āpastambi, is, m. a patronymic from the preceding.

आपस्तम्भिनी *āpastambhinī*, f., N. of a plant, perhaps Eriocaulon Quinquangulare Lin.

आपा *ā-pā*, cl. 1. P. *-pibati* or *-pivati, -pātum*, to drink up, to drink out of or at; to drink with the ears or eyes, hear, see: Caus. *-pāyayati, -yitum*, to cause to drink.

Ā-pāna, am, n. a drinking-party, a banquet; a tavern, a liquor shop, a place for drinking in company.

Āpānta-manyu, us, us, u, Ved. giving zeal or courage when drunk (said of the Soma juice).

Ā-pāyin, ī, inī, i, fond of drinking.

1. *ā-pīta, as, ā, am*, drunk up, exhausted.

आपाक *ā-pāka, as*, m. (fr. rt. *pać* with *ā*), a baking oven, a potter's kiln. — *Āpāke-stha, as, ā, am*, Ved. standing in an oven.

आपाङ्ग्य *āpāngya, am*, n. (fr. *apānga*), anointing the corners of the eyes.

आपाण्डुर *ā-pāṇḍura, as, ā, am*, slightly pale, palish.

आपात *ā-pāta*. See under *ā-pat*.

आपाद *ā-pāda, ā-pādana*. See under *ā-pad*.

आपालि *ā-pāli, is*, m. a louse.

आपि *āpi*. See under rt. *āp*.

आपिञ्जर *ā-piñjara, as, ā, am*, somewhat red, reddish.

आपिश् *ā-piś*, cl. 6. P., Ved. *-piṅśati, -peśitum*, to shape, configurate; to decorate, ornament.

आपिशलि *āpiśali, is*, m., N. of an old grammarian.

Āpiśala, as, ī, am, originating from Āpiśali; *(as)*, m. a pupil of Āpiśali.

आपिष् *ā-pish*, cl. 7. P., Ved. *-pinashṭi, -peshṭum*, to press, touch.

आपी *āpī*, **आपीन** *ā-pīna*. See *ā-pyai*.

आपीड् *ā-pīḍ*, cl. 10. P. *-pīḍayati, -yitum*, to press, weigh down; to press hard, give pain, perplex.

Ā-pīḍa, as, m. compressing, squeezing; giving pain, hurting; a chaplet tied on the crown of the head; *(ā)*, f., N. of a metre.

Ā-pīḍana, am, n. compressing, squeezing, tying or drawing tightly; embracing, clasping; giving pain, hurting.

Ā-pīḍita, as, ā, am, compressed, squeezed; bound tightly, embraced; hurt; decorated with chaplets.

आपीत 2. *ā-pīta, as, ā, am*, yellowish; *(am)*, n. a pyritic mineral. (For 1. *ā-pīta* see under *ā-pā*.)

आपू *ā-pū*, cl. 1. A. *-pavate, -vitum*, to be pure; to flow towards after purification; to carry towards in its course (said of a stream).

आपूपिक *āpūpika, as, ī, am* (fr. *apūpa*), selling cakes; accustomed to eat cakes; fond of cakes, eating cakes (with benefit); a good maker of cake; *(as)*, m. a baker; a confectioner; *(am)*, n. a multitude of cakes.

Āpūpya, am, n. flour, meal.

आपूय् *ā-pūy*, cl. 1. P. *-pūyati, -yitum*, to be putrescent, putrify.

आपूष *āpūsha, am*, n. tin.

आपृच् *ā-pṛić*, cl. 7. P. A. *-pṛiṇakti, -pṛiṅkte, -parćitum*, to fill, pervade; A. to satiate one's self; to mix with.

Ā-pṛik, ind., Ved. in a mixed manner, confusedly.

आपृच्छा *ā-pṛiććhā*, &c. See under *ā-prach*.

आपृ *ā-pṛī*, Caus. P. *-pūrayati, -yitum*, to fill, fulfil: Pass. *-pūryate*, to be filled, become full.

Ā-pūra, as, ā, am, becoming full.

Ā-pūraṇa, as, ā, am, becoming full; *(as)*, m., N. of a Nāga; *(am)*, n. filling, making full.

Ā-pūrti, is, f. filling; fulness, satisfaction.

Ā-pūrya, ind. filling, having filled.

Ā-pūryamāṇa, as, ā, am, becoming full, being filled. — *Āpūryamāṇa-paksha, as*, m. the crescent or waxing moon.

आपेक्षिक *āpekshika, as, ī, am* (fr. *apekshā*), raising expectations.

आपोक्लिम *āpoklima, as*, m., in astronomy = Gr. ἀπόκλιμα.

आपोमय *āpo-maya, as, ī, am* (fr. *āpas*, nom. pl. of *ap*, q. v.), consisting of water. — *Āpo-mātrā*, f. the subtle elementary principle of water. — *Āpo-mūrti, is*, m., N. of a deity under Manu Svārocisha, one of the seven Ṛishis of the tenth Manvantara.

आपोशान *āpośāna, as*, m., N. of a kind of prayer spoken before and after eating; perhaps contracted from *āpo 'śāna*, 'drink the water,' with which words the prayer began.

आप्त, आप्ति, आप्तोक्ति, &c. See under rt. *āp*.

आप्तोर्यामन् *āptor-yāman*. See *aptor-yāma*.

आप्त्य *āptya, as*, m., Ved., N. of a class of deities, and especially of the deity Trita, as one of that class.

आप्य 3. *āpya, as, ā, am* (fr. *ap*), belonging or relating to water; watery; consisting of water; living in water. (For 1. 2. *āpya* see under rt. *āp*.)

आप्य 4. *āpya, as*, m. (for *āptya*), N. of a class of deities in the sixth Manvantara.

आप्य 5. *āpya, am*, n., N. of a plant, a kind of Costus. See *vāpya*.

आप्यै *ā-pyai*, cl. 1. A. *-pyāyate, -pyātum*, to grow fat or comfortable, to increase, become full, enlarge: Caus. P. *-pyāyayati, -yitum*, to make fat or comfortable; to enlarge.

Āpī, is, f. the twentieth Nakshatra or lunar mansion.

Ā-pīna, as, ā, am, stout, fat; *(as)*, m. a well;

(*am*), n. an udder.—*Āpīna-vat*, *ān*, *atī*, *at*, Ved. containing the rt. *pyai* with *ā* (said of a *ṛić* or verse).

Ā-pyāna, *as*, *ā*, *am*, stout, robust.

Ā-pyāya, *as*, m. becoming full or fat.

Āpyāyana, *as*, *ā*, *am*, causing fulness or stoutness, increasing welfare; (*am*), n. the act of making full or fat; satisfying, refreshing, pleasing; satiety, satisfaction; advancing; anything which causes corpulency or good condition; strengthening medicine; corpulency, growing or being fat or stout; (in certain ceremonies) the act of pouring water &c. on the Soma and so causing it to swell.—*Āpyāyana-śīla*, *as*, *ā*, *am*, satisfying.

Ā-pyāyita, *as*, *ā*, *am*, satisfied, increased, improved, pleased, gratified; stout, fat.

आप्र *āpra*, *as*, *ā*, *am* (fr. rt. *prī* with *ā*?), Ved. busy, zealous; (Sāy.) able to reach.

आप्रछ् *ā-prach*, cl. 6. A. or poet. P. *-pṛiććhate*, *-ti*, *-prashṭum*, to bid farewell; to salute on receiving or parting with a visitor; to extol.

Ā-pṛićchā, f. conversation, speaking to or with; bidding farewell.

1. *ā-pṛićchya*, *as*, *ā*, *am*, Ved. to be saluted, to be welcomed, to be honoured; laudable, commendable, beautiful.

2. *ā-pṛićchya*, ind. having saluted, having bid adieu. (In Rāmāyaṇa I. 72, 20, a form *ā-pṛishṭvā* occurs.)

Ā-praććhana, *am*, n. expressions of civility on receiving or parting with a visitor, welcome, bidding adieu, &c.

आप्रतिनिवृत्त *ā-pratinivṛitta*, *as*, *ā*, *am*, prevented, turned back (?).

आप्रदिवम् *ā-pradivam*, ind., Ved. for ever.

आप्रपद *ā-prapada*, *am*, n. a dress reaching to the feet; (*am*), ind. to the end of the foot, reaching to the feet.

Āprapadīna, *as*, *ā*, *am*, reaching from the shoulders to the feet (as a dress).

Āprapadīnaka, *am*, n. a dress reaching to the feet.

आप्रावृषम् *ā-prāvṛisham*, ind. until the rainy season.

आप्री *ā-prī*, f. (fr. rt. *prī* with *ā*), Ved. gaining one's favour, conciliation, propitiation; (*ā-priyas*), propitiatory verses; N. of certain invocations addressed to a series of deified objects in order, and said to be introductory to the animal sacrifice. According to others, the objects propitiated by these hymns are the real āpris or *āpriyas*; whence the hymns themselves are called *āprī* hymns. The objects invoked are in a series of twelve verses, as follows: 1. Su-samiddha (or the fuel); 2. and 3. Tanūnapāt and Narāśaṇsa (these are sometimes invoked in one verse as mystic names of fire); 4. The divine being who bears the invocations to the gods (see under *iḍ*); 5. Barhis (or the sacred grass); 6. The doors of the chambers in which the sacrifice is offered; 7. Night and dawn; 8. The two divine beings, sometimes called Praćetasas, who preside over and protect the sacrificial rite; 9. The three goddesses, Ilā (see under *iḍā*), Sarasvatī (goddess of eloquence), and Mahī (a form of Bhāratī or speech); 10. Tvashṭṛi (the maker or creator); 11. Vanas-pati (the tree or wooden column to which the victim is tied); 12. Svāhā (the exclamation used in inviting the gods to the sacrifice when finally offered in the fire). All these are by Sāy. regarded as forms of Agni. See Ṛig-veda I. 13.

Ā-prīta-pā, *ās*, m., Ved. epithet of Vishṇu, 'guarding those who have appeased his anger.'

आप्लु *ā-plu*, cl. 1. A. *-plavate*, *-plotum*, to bathe, wash, immerse one's self; to jump up, dance: Caus. P. *-plāvayati*, *-yitum*, to cause to be bathed or washed; to wash or wet; to overflow, overwhelm; to set in commotion; A. *-plāvayate*, to bathe.

Ā-plava, *as*, m. bathing, sprinkling with water. —*Āplava-vratin*, *ī*, m. an initiated householder, who has passed through the first order (Brahma-ćārin), and is admitted into the second. See *snātaka*.

Ā-plavana, *am*, n. immersing, bathing, sprinkling with water.

Ā-plāva, *as*, m. bathing, sprinkling, wetting; a submerging; a flood, an inundation.

Ā-plāvita, *as*, *ā*, *am*, inundated, overflowed.

Ā-plāvya, ind. having wetted or sprinkled.

Ā-pluta, *as*, *ā*, *am*, bathed; wetted, sprinkled. In comp. sometimes used figuratively (e.g. *snehāpluta*, overflowing with affection); (*as*), m. an initiated householder, see *āplava-vratin*; (*am*), n. bathing.—*Āpluta-vratin*, *ī*, m. an initiated householder; see *āplava-vratin*.—*Āplutāṅga* (°*ta-an*°), *as*, *ī*, *am*, bathed all over.

Ā-plutya, ind. having bathed, having washed; having jumped up.

आप्वन् *āpvan*, *ā*, m. (fr. rt. *āp*), air, wind.

Āpvā, f. the neck.

आप्सव *āpsava*, *as*, m. (fr. *apsu*, loc. pl. of *ap*), epithet of a Manu.

आफूक *āphūka*, *am*, n. opium. See 2. *a-phena*.

आबन्ध *ā-bandh*, cl. 9. P. *-badhnāti*, *-banddhum*, to bind or tie on.

Ā-baddha, *as*, *ā*, *am*, tied, bound, joined; (*as*), m. a binding, a yoke; ornament; affection.—*Ābaddha-māla*, *as*, *ā*, *am*, forming a wreath.

Ā-badha, *as*, m., Ved. binding.

Ā-bandha, *as*, m. a tie or bond; the tie of a yoke, that which fastens the ox to the yoke, or the latter to the plough; ornament, decoration; affection.

Ā-bandhana, *am*, n. tying, binding on or round.

आबयु *ābayu*, *us*, Ved., perhaps the N. of a plant.

आबर्ह *ā-barha*, *as*, *ā*, *am* (rt. *vṛih* or *bṛih* with *ā*), having the property or power of tearing or pulling out; (*as*), m. tearing out.

Ā-barhaṇa, *am*, n. the act of tearing out.

Ā-barhin, *ī*, *iṇī*, *i*, fit for tearing out.

आबल्य *ābalya*, *am*, n. (fr. *a-bala*), weakness.

आबाध् *ā-bādh*, cl. 1. A. *-bādhate*, *-dhitum*, to check, rein in, restrain; to interrupt, molest, attack.

Ā-bādha, *as*, m., Ved. attack; molestation, trouble, interruption, damage; (*ā*), f. pain, distress, segment of the base of a triangle.

आबाल्य *ā-bālya*, *am*, n. age ending with infancy.

आबिलम् *ā-bilam*, ind., Ved. to the hole or aperture [cf. *vila*].

आबुत्त *ābutta*, *as*, m. (perhaps corrupted fr. *ārya-putra*), a sister's husband (in theatrical language).

आबुध् *ā-budh*, cl. 1. P., Ved. *-bodhati*, *-boddhum*, to perceive, notice, understand.

Ā-bodhana, *am*, n. knowledge, understanding; instructing, informing.

आब्दिक *ābdika*, *as*, *ī*, *am* (fr. *abda*), annual, yearly.

आभज् *ā-bhaj*, cl. 1. P., Ved. *-bhajati*, *-bhaktum*, to make one share, cause one to partake.

Ā-bhaga, *as*, m., Ved. a partaker of (with loc.); (Sāy.) to be shared in.

आभरण *ā-bharaṇa*, *am*, n. See under *ā-bhṛi*.

आभा 1. *ā-bhā*, cl. 2. P. *-bhāti*, *-tum*, to shine, blaze; to irradiate; to outshine; to appear, to look like.

2. *ā-bhā*, f. splendor, light; a flash; colour, appearance, beauty; a reflected image, shade; likeness, resemblance: (*as*, *ā*, *am*, at the end of compounds) like, resembling, appearing; e.g. *hemābha*, *as*, *ā*, *am*, shining like gold; [cf. Hib. *aoibh*, 'likeness, similitude;' *aoibe*, 'neatness, elegance;' *aoibheal*, 'a spark of fire.']

Ā-bhāti, *is*, f. splendor, light; shade.

आभाष् *ā-bhāsh*, cl. 1. A. *-bhāshate*, *-shitum*, to address, speak to; to talk, shout.

Ā-bhāsha, *as*, m. addressing; introduction, preface.

Ā-bhāshaṇa, *am*, n. addressing, speaking to.

1. *ā-bhāshya*, *as*, *ā*, *am*, to be addressed, worthy of being spoken to.

2. *ā-bhāshya*, ind. having addressed, having spoken to.

आभास् 1. *ā-bhās*, cl. 1. A. *-bhāsate*, *-situm*, to shine, blaze; to be bright: Caus. *-bhāsayati*, *-yitum*, to illuminate.

2. *ā-bhās*, f. splendor, lustre, light.

Ā-bhāsa, *as*, m. splendor, light, colour, appearance; semblance, phantom; mere appearance; fallacious appearance; reflection; intention, purpose; (in logic) fallacy, semblance of a reason, sophism, an erroneous though plausible argument (regarded by logicians as of various kinds).

Ā-bhāsana, *am*, n. illuminating, making apparent or clear.

Ā-bhāsura, *as*, m., N. of a class of deities or demigods, sixty in number.

Ā-bhāsvara, *as*, m. a demi-god, of a class consisting of sixty-four.

आभिचरणिक *ābhićaraṇika*, *as*, *ī*, *am* (fr. *abhi-ćaraṇa*), maledictory, imprecatory, serving for malediction or cursing.

Ābhićārika, *as*, *ī*, *am* (fr. *abhi-ćāra*), magical, relating to magic; (*am*), n. incantation, magic.

आभिजन *ābhijana*, *as*, *ī*, *am* (fr. *abhi-jana*, rt. *jan*), relating to descent; (*am*), n. loftiness of birth.

Ābhijātya, *am*, n. (fr. *abhi-jāta*, rt. *jan*), the nature or state of a man of noble birth, nobility; birth, family, rank, learning.

आभिजित *ābhijita*, *as*, *ī*, *am* (fr. *abhi-jit*), born under the constellation Abhijit.

आभिधा *ābhidhā*, f. or *ābhidhātaka*, *am*, n. a sound, a word, a name. See *abhi-dhā*.

Ābhidhānika, *as*, *ī*, *am*, contained in a dictionary, lexicographical; (*as*), m. a lexicographer.

Ābhidhānīyaka, *as*, *ī*, *am* (fr. *abhi-dhāna*), relating or belonging to a name or word; (*am*), n. the property of a name.

आभिप्रविक *ābhiplavika*, *as*, *ī*, *am* (fr. *abhi-plava*), relating to the religious ceremony called Abhi-plava.

आभिमुख्य *ābhimukhya*, *am*, n. (fr. *abhi-mukha*), direction towards anything; wish or desire directed towards anything; presence, being in front of or face to face.

आभिषेचनिक *ābhishećanika*, *as*, *ī*, *am* (fr. *abhi-shećana*), relating to the inauguration of a king; serving for it.

आभिहारिक *ābhihārika*, *as*, *ī*, *am* (fr. *abhi-hāra*), taken by force or fraud; (*am*), n. a room.

आभीक *ābhīka*, *am*, n., N. of a Sāma melody.

आभीक्ष्ण *ābhīkshṇa*, *as*, *ī*, *am* (fr. *abhīkshṇa*), much, exceeding, eternal; (*am*), ind. exceedingly, eternally.

Ābhīkshṇya, *am*, n. continued repetition.

आभीय *ābhīya*, *as*, *ā*, *am* (fr. *ā-bhāt*, 'up to *bha*'), contained in a chapter of Pāṇini which ends with *bha*.

आभीर *ābhīra*, *as*, m., N. of a people; a cowherd sprung from a Brāhman and female of the

Ambashṭha or medical tribe; N. of a metre; (ī), f. a cowherd's wife or woman of the Ābhīra tribe; the language of the Ābhīra. — *Ābhīra-palli, is* or *ī* or *ikā*, f. a station of herdsmen, a village inhabited by cowherds only, an abode of cowherds &c.

आभील *ā-bhīla, as, ā, am* (fr. rt. *bhī* with *ā*), formidable, fearful; suffering pain; (*am*), n. bodily pain; [cf. Hib. *abhéil*, 'terrible, dreadful.']

आभु *ābhu, us, us, -u*, Ved. empty; one whose hands are empty; stingy; (Sāy.) pervading, reaching.

Ābhūka, as, ā, am, Ved. empty, having no contents, powerless.

आभुग्न *ā-bhugna, as, ā, am* (rt. 1. *bhuj* with 3. *ā* implying diminution), a little curved or bent.

आभू 1. *ā-bhū*, cl. 1. P. *-bhavati, -vitum*, to be present, continue one's existence.

2. *ā-bhū, ūs, ūs, u*, Ved. strong, sufficient, efficacious; (Sāy.) approaching (as a praiser); a prison, a place of confinement; applied according to rule (as a hymn); very prosperous.

Ā-bhūti, is, f., Ved. capability, efficiency; (Sāy.) overpowering strength; (*is*), m., N. of a man.

Ā-bhūshenya, as, ā, am, Ved. to be obeyed; (Sāy.) praiseworthy.

आभूष् *ā-bhūsh*, cl. 1. P., Ved. *-bhūshati, -shitum*, to adorn, to adorn with one's presence, i. e. to come.

आभृ *ā-bhṛi*, cl. 1. P., Ved. *-bharati, -bhartum*, to bring; to carry; to bear; to support.

Ā-bharaṇa, am, n. ornament, decoration (as jewels &c.); act of nourishing; title of several works.

Ā-bharat, an, antī, at, bringing. — *Ābharad-vasu, us, us, u*, Ved. bringing property, goods, &c.; (*us*), m., N. of a man.

आभेरी *ābherī*, f. one of the Rāgiṇīs or modes of music, personified as a female.

आभोग 1. *ā-bhoga, as*, m. (fr. rt. 1. *bhuj*, to curve, bend, with prep. *ā*), winding, curving, curve, crease; crumpling; circuit, circumference, environs, extension, fulness, expanse; a serpent; the expanded hood of the Cobra Capella (used by Varuṇa as his umbrella); effort, pains.

आभोग 2. *ā-bhoga, as*, m. (fr. rt. 2. *bhuj*, to eat, enjoy), enjoyment, satiety, fulness, completion.

Ā-bhogaya, am, n., Ved. means of supporting life, livelihood; (Sāy.) to be enjoyed (as Soma juice).

Ā-bhogi, is, f., Ved. living, supporting life; (Sāy.) enjoyment.

आभ्यन्तर *ābhyantara, as, ī, am* (fr. *abhyantara*), being inside, interior, inner.

आभ्यवकाशिक *ābhyavakāśika, as, ī, am* (fr. *abhy-avakāśa*), living in the open air.

आभ्याशिक *ābhyāśika, as, ī, am* (fr. *abhyāśa*), being near to each other, neighbouring; (less correctly in this sense written *ābhyāsika*.)

आभ्यासिक *ābhyāsika, as, ī, am* (fr. *abhyāsa*), resulting from practice, practising, repeating.

आभ्युदयिक *ābhyudayika, as, ī, am* (fr. *abhy-udaya*), connected with the rising or beginning of anything; relating to or granting prosperity; high, exalted, important; (*am*), n. a Srāddha or offering to ancestors on occasions of rejoicing.

आभ्रिक *ābhrika, as, ī, am* (fr. *abhri*), one who digs with a spade or a hoe.

आम् *ām*, ind. an interjection of assent or recollection, (a vocative following this particle is *anudātta*.)

आम 1. *āma, as, ā, am* (fr. rt. 2. *am ?*), raw, uncooked (the opposite to *pakva*, q. v.; in the Veda often an epithet of the cow considered as the raw material which produces the milk); unbaked, unannealed; undressed; unripe, immature; undigested; (*am*), n. condition of being raw; constipation, passing hard and unhealthy excretions; grain freed from chaff; [cf. Gr. ὠμό-ς; Hib. *amh*, 'raw, unsodden, crude, unripe.'] — *Āma-kumbha, as*, m. a water-jar of unbaked clay. — *Āma-gandhi*, n. smell of raw meat or of a burning corpse. — *Āma-gandhika, am*, n. the smell of raw meat. — *Āma-tā*, f. rawness, unreadiness. — *Āma-tvaċ, k, k, k*, tender-skinned. — *Āma-pātra, am*, n. an unannealed vessel. — *Āma-pīnasa, am*, n. running at the nose, defluxion. — *Āma-māṅsa, as*, m. raw flesh. — *Āmamāṅsāśin* (°*sa-āś*°), *ī*, m. a cannibal, eater of raw flesh. — *Āma-rakta, as*, m. dysentery. — *Āma-rasa, as*, m. imperfect chyme. — *Āma-vāta, as*, m. constipation or torpor of the bowels with flatulence and intumescence. — *Āma-śūla, as*, m. the cholic, pain arising from indigestion. — *Āmātisāra* (°*ma-at*°), *as*, m. dysentery or diarrhœa produced by vitiated mucus in the abdomen; the excretion being mixed with hard and fetid matter. — *Āmād* (°*ma-ad*), *t, t, t*, eating raw flesh or food. — *Āmānna* (°*ma-an*°), *am*, n. undressed rice. — *Āmāśaya* (°*ma-āś*°), *as*, m. the receptacle of the undigested food, the upper part of the belly to the navel, the stomach.

Āmaka, as, ā, am, raw, uncooked, &c. See 1. *āma*.

Āmisha, am, n. flesh. See s. v. next col.

आम 2. *āma, as*, m. or *āmana, am*, n. (fr. rt. 2. *am*), sickness, disease.

Āmaya, as, m. damage, hurt; disease, sickness; indigestion; (*am*), n., N. of the medical plant Costus Speciosus.

Āmayāvin, ī, inī, i, sick, diseased, affected with indigestion, dyspeptic. — *Āmayāvi-tva, am*, n. indigestion, dyspepsia.

आमण्ड *āmaṇḍa, as*, m. the castor-oil plant [cf. *amaṇḍa* and *maṇḍa*].

आमन *ā-mana, am*, n. (rt. *man*), Ved. friendly disposition, inclination, affection.

Ā-manas, ās, ās, as, friendly disposed, kind, favourable.

आमनस्य *āmanasya* or *āmānasya, am*, n. (fr. *a-manas*), pain.

आमन्त्र् *ā-mantr*, cl. 10. A. *-mantrayate, -yitum*, to address, especially in saluting and in bidding farewell; to ask, invite.

Ā-mantraṇa, am, ā, n. f. addressing, speaking to, calling or calling to; greeting, courtesy, welcome, bidding adieu, taking leave; inviting, invitation; deliberation, interrogation; the vocative case.

Ā-mantraṇīya, as, ā, am, Ved. to be addressed or asked, to be asked for advice or consulted.

Ā-mantrayitṛi, tā, trī, tṛi, asking, inviting, calling; (*tā*), m. an inviter, entertainer, especially of Brāhmans.

Ā-mantrita, as, ā, am, invited, summoned, called; (*am*), n. addressing; the vocative case.

1. *ā-mantrya, as, ā, am*, to be addressed or called to; to be invited; (*am*), n. a word standing in the vocative case.

2. *ā-mantrya*, ind. having taken leave, bidding farewell.

आमन्थ् *ā-manth* or *ā-math*, cl. 1. P. *-manthati, -thitum*, to agitate.

आमन्द्र *ā-mandra, as, ā, am*, having a slightly deep tone, making a low muttering sound (like thunder).

आमरणान्त *ā-maraṇānta, as, ā, am*, or *ā-maraṇāntika* (°*ṇa-ant*°), *as, ī, am*, having death as the limit, continuing till death, lasting for life.

आमरितृ *ā-maritṛi, tā*, m. (rt. *mṛi* or *mṛiṇ* with *ā*), Ved. one who hurts or destroys; a destroyer.

आमर्द, आमर्दिन्. See under *ā-mṛid*.

आमर्ष *ā-marsha, as*, m. (for *a-marsha*, q. v.), impatience, anger, wrath. (For *ā-marśa* see under *ā-mṛiś*.)

Ā-marshaṇa, am, n. anger.

आमलक *āmalaka, as, ī, am*, m. f. n. the plant Emblic Myrobalan, Emblica Officinalis Gærtn.; (*as*), m. another plant, Gendarussa Adhatoda; (*am*), n. the fruit of the Emblic Myrobalan.

आमहीया *āmahīyā*, f. designation of a particular (*ṛiċ*) verse of the Ṛig-veda (viz. Ṛig-veda VIII. 48, 3).

Āmahīyava, as, m., N. of a Ṛishi.

आमा *ā-mā*, cl. 3. A. *-mimīte, -mātum*, to effect, accomplish.

आमात्य *āmātya, as*, m. a minister, a counsellor, an adviser; a general. See *amātya*.

आमालक *āmālaka, as, am*, m. n. land near a mountain (?).

आमावास्य *āmāvāsya, as, ī, am* (fr. *amāvāsyā*), belonging to the new moon or its festival; born at the time of new moon; occurring on the day of conjunction; (*am*), n. the new moon oblation.

आमिक्षा *āmikshā*, f. curd of two-milk whey, a mixture of boiled and coagulated milk.

Āmikshya or *āmikshīya, as, ā, am*, suitable for the preparation of Āmikshā; made of curds.

आमित्र *āmitra, as, ī, am* (fr. *a-mitra*), produced by an enemy, inimical, odious.

आमिश्ल *ā-miśla, as, ā, am*, Ved. having a tendency to mix, readily mixing.

आमिष *āmisha, am*, n. (connected with 1. *āma*), flesh, enjoyment; an object of enjoyment, a pleasing or beautiful object &c.; a bribe; coveting, longing for; lust, desire; food; form. — *Āmisha-priya, as, ā, am*, fond of flesh-meat, carnivorous; (*as*), m. a heron. — *Āmisha-bhuj, k, k, k*, carnivorous. — *Āmishāśin* (°*sha-āś*°), *ī, inī, i*, carnivorous, eating flesh and fish.

Āmis, m. (occurring in loc. c. *āmishi*), Ved. raw flesh, meat; a dead body.

आमी *ā-mī*, cl. 9. P., Ved. *-mīnāti, -mātum*, to destroy, neutralize, curtail; A. *-minīte*, to destroy or neutralize mutually.

आमीक्षा *āmīkshā*, f. = *āmikshā*, q. v.

आमील् *ā-mīl*, cl. 1. P. *-mīlati, -litum*, to close the eyes.

Ā-mīlana, am, n. closing of the eyes.

आमीवत् *ā-mīvat, an, antī, at*, or *āmīvatka, as, ā, am*, Ved. attacking, pressing.

आमुख *ā-mukha, am*, n. commencement; prelude, prologue; (*am*), ind. to the face.

आमुच् *ā-muċ*, cl. 6. P. *-muñċati, -moktum*, to loosen, let go; to put on a garment.

Ā-mukta, as, ā, am, loosed, let go; liberated; discharged, cast, shot off; put on as clothes or armour; dressed, accoutred.

Ā-mukti, is, f. liberation, the being let loose; final liberation; (*ī*), ind. to the end of existence.

Ā-moċana, am, n. the act of loosing, liberating; emitting, shedding, letting forth, putting or tying on.

आमुप *āmupa, as*, m. the cane Bambusa Spinosa Hamilt. Roxb.

आमुर् *ā-mur, ūr*, or *ā-muri, is*, m. (fr. rt. *mṛi* with *ā*), Ved. destroying, hurting.

आमुष्मिक *āmushmika, as, ī, am* (fr. *amushmin*, loc. of 1. *adas*), of that state, being there, belonging to the other world.

Āmushyakulaka, am, n., *āmushyaputraka, am,* n., Gaṇa to Pāṇini V. 1, 133.

Āmushyāyaṇa, as, m. (fr. *amushya,* gen. of 1. *adas*), son or descendant of such a one, son or descendant of an illustrious person; (*as, ī, am*), well-born, well descended.

आमूलम् *ā-mūlam,* ind. to the root, by the root, entirely, radically.

आमृज् *ā-mṛij,* cl. 1. 2. P. *-mārjati, -mārshṭi, -mārjitum, -mārshṭum,* to wipe, rub.

Ā-mṛijya, ind. having wiped or rubbed.

Ā-mṛishṭa, as, ā, am, wiped, rubbed.

आमृण *ā-mṛiṇa, as, ā, am,* vulnerable. See *an-āmṛiṇa.*

आमृत *ā-mṛita, as, ā, am* (fr. rt. *mṛi* with *ā*), mortal.

आमृत्योस् *ā-mṛityos,* ind. until death.

आमृद् *ā-mṛid,* cl. 9. P. *-mṛidnāti, -marditum,* to crush by rubbing; to crumple; to press, to squeeze.

Ā-marda, as, m. crushing, handling roughly; pressing, squeezing; N. of a town.

Ā-mardin, ī, inī, i, crushing; pressing.

आमृश् *ā-mṛiś,* cl. 6. P. *-mṛiśati, -marshṭum* or *-mrashṭum,* to touch, handle roughly, rub, injure.

Ā-marśa, as, m. advice, counsel.

Ā-marśana, or less correctly *ā-marshaṇa, am,* n. rubbing, wiping.

आमेन्य *ā-menya, as, ā, am* (fr. *meni* with *ā*), Ved. to be reached with an arrow or bolt; (Sāy.) to be measured from all sides.

आमोक्षण *ā-mokshaṇa, am,* n. the act of fixing or tying on or to.

आमोचन *ā-moćana.* See under *ā-muć.*

आमोद *ā-moda, as, ā, am* (fr. rt. *mud* with *ā*), gladdening, cheering up; (*as*), m. joy, serenity, pleasure; fragrancy, a diffusive perfume; strong smell.

Ā-modana, am, n. rejoicing, delighting.

Ā-modita, as, ā, am, pleased, delighted, fragrant.

Ā-modin, ī, inī, i, fragrant; happy, delighted; (at the end of compounds) fragrant or perfumed with, e. g. *kadambāmodin,* perfumed with kadambas; (*ī*), m. a perfume for the mouth made up in the form of a pill or bolus of camphor &c.

आमोष *ā-mosha, as,* m. (fr. rt. *mush* with *ā*), robbing, stealing.

Ā-moshin, ī, iṇī, i, who or what steals, a thief.

आमोहनिका *ā-mohanikā,* f. (fr. rt. *muh* with *ā*), a particular fragrant odour.

आम्ना *ā-mnā,* cl. 1. P., Ved. *-manati, -mnātum,* to keep in mind, to repeat, commit to memory, hand down in sacred texts; to celebrate, to hail.

Ā-mnāta, as, ā, am, kept in mind, remembered, committed to memory, learnt by heart, repeated, handed down in sacred texts, celebrated.

Ā-mnāna, am, n. mention, repetition, handing down by sacred texts.

Ā-mnāya, as, m. sacred tradition, sacred texts handed down by repetition; that which is to be remembered, studied or learnt by heart; a Veda or the Vedas in the aggregate; received doctrine; traditional usage, family or national customs; advice, instruction in past and present usage; a Tantra; an element of being, a property of substance (?); a family, series of families. — *Āmnāya-sārin, ī, iṇī, i,* observing the Vedas and traditional customs, pious; containing the essence of the Veda.

आम्प्रत्यय *ām-pratyaya, as, ā, am,* having *ām* for its affix (e. g. a root like *iś*).

आम्बरीषपुत्रक *āmbarīshaputraka, as,* m. a country inhabited by the Ambarīsha-putras.

आम्बष्ठ *āmbashṭha, as,* m. an inhabitant of Ambashṭha.

आम्बिकेय *āmbikeya, as,* m. (fr. *ambikā*), an epithet of Dhṛita-rāshṭra; also of Kārttikeya.

आम्भस *āmbhasa, as, ī, am* (fr. 2. *ambhas*), watery, fluid.

Āmbhasika, as, ī, am, living in water, aquatic; (*as*), m. a fish.

आम्भृणी *āmbhṛiṇī,* f. a N. of Vāć, the daughter of the Ṛishi Ambhṛiṇa. See 3. *ambhṛiṇa.*

आम्र *āmra, as,* m. (said to be fr. rt. 2. *am*), the mango tree, Mangifera Indica; (*am*), n. the fruit of the mango tree. — *Āmra-kūṭa, as,* m., N. of a mountain. — *Āmra-gandhaka, as,* m., N. of a plant. — *Āmra-gupta, as,* m., N. of a man. — *Āmra-pālī,* f., N. of a woman. — *Āmra-peśī,* f. a portion of dried mango fruit. — *Āmra-maya, as, ī, am,* made of mangoes (as sauce). — *Āmra-vaṇa, am,* n. a mango forest. — *Āmrāvarta* (°*ra-āv*°), *as,* m. inspissated mango juice.

Āmrāta, as, m. the hog-plum, Spondias Mangifera.

Āmrātaka, as, m. the hog-plum, Spondias Mangifera; inspissated mango juice; N. of a mountain.

Āmrāvatī, f., N. of a town.

Āmriman, ā, m., Gaṇa to Pāṇini V. 1, 123.

आम्रेडन *ā-mreḍana, am,* n. tautology, reiteration of words or sounds.

Ā-mreḍita, as, ā, am, reiterated, repeated; (*am*), n. repetition of a sound or word; (in gram.) reduplication, the second word in reduplications.

आम्ल *āmla, as, ā,* m. f. (fr. *amla*), the tamarind tree, Tamarindus Indica; (*am*), n. sourness, acidity. — *Āmla-vetasa, as,* m. the plant Rumex Vesicatorius.

Āmlikā, f. the tamarind tree; sourness in the mouth, acidity of stomach.

Āmlīkā, f. the tamarind tree.

आय *āya, as,* m. (fr. rt. *i* with *ā*), arrival, approach; income, revenue; gain, profit; the guard of the women's apartments; the eleventh lunar mansion. — *Āya-vyaya, am* or *au,* n. or m. du. receipt and disbursement, income and expenditure. — *Āya-sthāna, am,* n. a place where revenues are collected.

1. *ā-yat, an, atī, at,* coming, approaching. — *Āyatīgavam,* ind. at the time when the cows come home. — *Āyad-vasu, us, us, u,* Ved. one to whom goods come.

Āyana, am, n., Ved. coming.

Āyin, ī, inī, i, Ved. driving near.

आयःशूलिक *āyaḥśūlika, as, ī, am* (fr. *ayaḥśūla*), active, diligent, indefatigable; (*as*), m. a man who, in order to obtain an object, uses forcible instead of gentle means; as, for instance, a beggar who holds a lance to your breast in asking for alms.

आयज् *ā-yaj,* cl. 1. A. *-yajate, -yashṭum,* to honour (the gods); to give, present.

Ā-yaji, is, is, i, Ved. procuring, granting; (Sāy.) accomplishing sacrifices from all sides.

Ā-yajishṭha, as, ā, am, Ved. procuring most or best; (Sāy.) sacrificing best.

Ā-yajyu, us, us, u, Ved. endeavouring to gain; inclined to sacrifice.

Ā-yāga, as, m. a gift given at a sacrifice. — *Āyāga-bhūta, as, ā, am,* obtained by sacrifice.

आयत् 2. *ā-yat,* cl. 1. A. *-yatate, -titum,* to make effort; to rest on, to depend on, to have the upper hand (?).

Ā-yatana, am, n. resting-place, support, seat, place, home, house, abode; the place of the sacred fire, an altar, a shed for sacrifices; a sanctuary; a ground-plot, the site of a house; a barn; (with Buddhists) an inner seat (the five senses and Manas are considered as the six inner seats or āyatanas); the cause of disease. — *Āyatana-tva, am,* n. state of being an altar or seat. — *Āyatana-vat, ān, atī, at,* Ved. having a certain seat or home; (*ān*), m., N. of the fourth foot of Brahmā.

Ā-yatta, as, ā, am, dependant, tractable, docile. — *Āyatta-tā,* f. or *āyatta-tva, am,* n. dependence, humility, tractableness, docility.

Ā-yatti, is, f. dependence, subjection, subjecting; affection; power, strength; day; boundary, limit; sleeping; length (? for *ā-yati* below); majesty, dignity; future time (? for *ā-yati*); continuance in the right way, steadiness of conduct.

आयथातथ्य *āyathātathya, am,* n. (fr. *a-yathātatha*), unsuitableness, unfitness, incompatibility.

आयम् *ā-yam,* cl. 1. P. *-yaććhati, -yantum,* to stretch, lengthen out, extend, restrain; A. *-yaććhate,* to stretch one's self or be stretched, to grow long; to grasp, possess: Caus. *-yāmayati, -te, -yitum,* to lengthen, &c.

Ā-yata, as, ā, am, long; diffuse, prolix; (*as*), m. an oblong figure (in geometry). — *Āyata-ććhadā,* f. the plantain tree Musa Paradisiaca Lin. — *Āyata-stū, ūs,* m. a panegyrist. — *Āyatāksha* (°*ta-ak*°), *as, ī, am,* having large eyes or long eyelids. — *Āyatāpāṅga* (°*ta-ap*°), *as, ī, am,* having a long-cornered eye. — *Āyatāyati* (°*ta-āy*°), *is,* f. long continuance, remote futurity. — *Āyatārdha* (°*ta-ardh*°), *as,* m., (in geometry) half an oblong. — *Āyatekshaṇa* (°*ta-īk*°), *as, ā, am,* long-eyed, having long or large eyes.

Ā-yati, is, f. extension, length; stretching the hand, accepting, obtaining; connection, junction; meeting; following or future time; the future, 'the long run;' majesty, dignity; restraint of mind; N. of a daughter of Meru. — *Āyati-mat, ān, atī, at,* long, extended; stately, dignified; self-restrained.

Ā-yantṛi, tā, m., Ved. one who fastens or raises; (Sāy.) one who approaches.

Ā-yamana, am, n. stretching (as a bow).

1. *ā-yamya, as, ā, am,* to be stretched; to be restrained.

2. *ā-yamya* or *ā-yatya,* ind. having restrained, suppressed or stretched.

Ā-yāma, as, m. stretching, extending; restraining, restraint, stopping; expansion, length (either in space or time), breadth (in mensuration). — *Āyāma-vat, ān, atī, at,* extended, long.

Ā-yāmita, as, ā, am, lengthened out, extended.

Ā-yāmin, ī, inī, i, one who restrains, long in space or time.

आयल्लक *āyallaka, am,* n. impatience, longing for, missing, regretting (etym. doubtful).

आयवन *ā-yavana, am,* n. (fr. rt. *yu* with *ā*), Ved. a spoon for stirring, any similar implement.

आयवस *ā-yavasa, as* or *am* (?), m. n., Ved. pasture-ground, place for feeding; (*as*), m., N. of a man (?).

आयस् *ā-yas,* cl. 4. P. *-yasyati, -situm,* to exert one's self, to weary one's self, become exhausted: Caus. *-yāsayati, -te, -yitum,* to weary, worry.

Ā-yasta, as, ā, am, pained, distressed; vexed, angry; hurt, killed; managed or effected with difficulty; labouring, toiling, making effort or exertion; sharpened, whetted; thrown, cast, sent.

Ā-yāsa, as, m. effort, exertion (of bodily or mental power), trouble, labour; fatigue, weariness.

Ā-yāsaka, as, ī, am, causing effort, fatigue or weariness.

Ā-yāsin, ī, inī, i, making exertion, active, laborious; exhausted by labour, wearied.

आयस *āyasa, as, ī, am* (fr. *ayas*), of iron, made of iron or metal, metallic; armed with an iron weapon; zealous?; (*ī*), f. armour for the body, a breastplate, a coat of mail; (*am*), n. iron; anything made of iron; a weapon; a wind-instrument.

आयस्कार *āyaskāra, as,* m. the upper part of the thigh of an elephant. See *ayas-kāra.*

आया *ā-yā,* cl. 2. P. *-yāti, -tum,* to come, arrive, approach, reach, attain; Ved. to bring.

Ā-yāta, as, ā, am, come; *(am),* n. excess, superabundance.

Ā-yāti, is, f. coming near, arrival; *(is),* m., N. of a son of Nahusha.

Ā-yāna, am, n. coming, arrival; the natural temperament or disposition.

Ā-yāpana, am, n. causing to come, inviting.

आयाचित *ā-yāćita, as, ā, am* (rt. *yāć*), urgently requested or desired.

आयु *āyu, us, us, u* (perhaps fr. rt. *an,* but said to be fr. rt. *ay,* to go), Ved. living, movable; *(us),* m. a living being, man; living beings collectively; mankind; the human race; the first man; life, duration of life; wind; a son, descendant, offspring; the son of Purūravas and Urvaśī; N. of a man persecuted by Indra, also of one protected by him; N. of a Ṛishi; of a son of Hrada; of a king of frogs. — *Āyu-shak,* ind. (*shak* fr. rt. *sać*), Ved. joined with men, with the co-operation of men; (Sāy.) attached to.

Āyus, n. life, vital power, health, duration of life, long life, vital power; N. of a ceremony, commonly called Āyushṭoma, performed to obtain longevity and forming part together with the Go and Jyotis of the Abhi-plava ceremony; food; [cf. Dor. αἰές; perhaps also αἰών]; *(us),* m. the son of Purūravas and Urvaśī. — *Āyuḥ-śesha, as,* m. end of life, death. — *Āyuḥ-śesha-tā,* f. the state of having nothing left but life. — *Āyur-dad, t, t, t,* or *āyur-dā, ās, ās, am,* or *āyur-dāvan, ā, ā, a,* Ved. giving life. — *Āyur-dravya, am,* n. a medicament. — *Āyur-veda, as,* m. the science of health or medicine; it is classed among sacred sciences, and considered as a supplement of the Atharva-veda; it contains eight departments: 1. Śalya, surgery; 2. Śālākya, inquiry into diseases of the head and its organs; 3. Kāya-ćikitsā, treatment of diseases affecting the whole body; 4. Bhūta-vidyā, treatment of diseases of the mind supposed to be produced by demoniacal influence; 5. Kaumāra-bhṛitya, treatment of children; 6. Agada-tantra, doctrine of antidotes; 7. Rāsāyana-tantra, doctrine of elixirs; 8. Vājīkaraṇa-tantra, rules for increasing generative power. — *Āyurveda-dṛiś, k,* m. a physician. — *Āyurveda-maya, as, ī, am,* acquainted with medical science. — *Āyurvedika, as,* m. acquainted or familiar with medical science, a physician. — *Āyurvedin, ī, inī, i,* belonging to medicine, of the medical profession, medical, medicinal, &c.; (ī), m. a practiser of physic, a physician or surgeon. — *Āyush-kāma, as, ā, am,* wishing for life or health. — *Āyush-kṛit, t, t, t,* Ved. producing or creating life. — *Āyushṭoma, as,* m. (fr. *āyus-stoma*), a sacrifice to obtain longevity. — *Āyush-pā, ās, ās, am,* Ved. preserving life. — *Āyush-pratarana, as, ī, am,* Ved. prolonging life. — *Āyush-mat, ān, atī, at,* possessed of vital power, healthy, long-lived; alive, living; lasting; old; *(ān),* m. the third of the twenty-seven Yogas or divisions of the ecliptic; the Yoga star in the third lunar mansion; N. of a son of Uttānapāda, also of Saṃhrāda. — *Āyus-kara, as, ā* or *ī, am,* promoting longevity, supporting life. — *Āyus-tejas, ās,* m., N. of a Buddha.

Āyusha, am, n. (at the end of some compounds) = *āyus,* life.

Āyushka, (with Jainas) union or connection with the body or person; that which proclaims (*kāyate*) age (*āyus*) or duration of life.

Āyushya, as, ā, am, giving long life, vital, preservative of life, for the sake of life, relating or belonging to it; *(am),* n. vital power, abundance of life; 'vivifying,' N. of a ceremony performed after a child's birth.

आयुज् 1. *ā-yuj,* cl. 7. P. A. *-yunakti, -yunkte, -yoktum,* to yoke to (anything); to join; to appoint.

Ā-yukta, as, ā, am, appointed, charged with; united, joined, obtained; *(as),* m. a minister, an agent or deputy.

2. *ā-yuj, k, k, k,* Ved. uniting, joining.

Ā-yoga, as, m. appointment; action, the performance of an act; presenting or offering flowers, perfumes, &c.; a shore or bank, a quay to which boats are attached.

Ā-yojana, am, n. effort, exertion; taking, seizing; collecting.

Ā-yojita, as, ā, am, collected together.

आयुत *ā-yuta, as, ā, am* (rt. *yu*), melted, mixed, mingled; *(am),* n. (with *ā* implying diminution), half-melted butter.

Ā-yuvamāna, as, ā, am, Ved. mixing, mingling.

आयुध् *ā-yudh,* cl. 4. P. A. *-yudhyati, -te, -yoddhum,* to war against, attack, oppose: Caus. *-yodhayati, -te, -yitum,* to attack, oppose.

Ā-yudha, as, am, m. n. a weapon; Ved. a vessel; *(ānī),* n. pl., Ved. water; *(am),* n. gold used for ornaments. — *Āyudha-jīvin, ī, inī, i,* living by one's weapon; (ī), m. a warrior. — *Āyudha-dharmiṇī,* f. the plant Sesbania Ægyptiaca, commonly called Jayantī. — *Āyudhāgāra* (°*dha-ag*°), *am,* n. an armoury, arsenal.

Āyudhika, as, ī, am, relating to arms; *(as),* m. a soldier, warrior.

Āyudhin, ī, inī, i, bearing weapons; (ī), m. a warrior.

Āyudhīya, as, ā, am, relating to or connected with arms; *(as),* m. a warrior.

Ā-yodhana, am, n. war, battle; slaughter, killing; battle-field.

आये *āye,* ind. an interjection of calling, expressive of affection.

आयोगव *āyogava, as,* m. a man belonging to the tribe of Ayogu; a man of a mixed tribe sprung from a Śūdra man and Vaiśya woman; his business is carpentry &c.; (ī), f. a woman of this tribe.

आयोद *āyoda, as,* m., N. of a Ṛishi.

आर् 1. *ār, āryati* Ved. to praise; (Sāy.) to approach or to make master of.

आर् 2. *ār* (*ā-ṛi*), cl. 3. P. *eyarti,* or cl. 5. P. *ārṇoti, ārtum, āritum* or *arītum,* to come; to reach, obtain, fall into; to inflict; to insert, place in: Caus. *ārpayati, -yitum,* to cause to partake of; to fix, settle, annex; to ordain.

1. *āra, as, am,* m. n. (? fr. rt. *ṛi*), an angle, a corner; N. of a tree; N. of a lake; brass; oxide of iron; *(as),* m. the planet Mars, Ἄρης; the planet Saturn; *(ā),* f. a shoemaker's awl or knife, a bore, a probe, a spoke. — *Āra-kūṭa, as, am,* m. n. brass. — *Ārāgra* (°*rā-ag*°), *am,* n. the point of an awl; the iron thong at the end (of a whip); the edge of a semicircular arrow-head; *(as, ā, am),* sharpened, sharp at the top and broad at the bottom like an awl. — *Ārāvalī* (°*rā-āv*°), f., N. of a chain of mountains, a spur of the Vindhya.

Ārta, as, ā, am, afflicted, pained. See s. v.

Ārpita, as, ā, am, fastened to, annexed; depending on.

आर 2. *āra* (contained in *ārāt, āre,* q. v.), distance; proximity (?).

Ārakāt, ind., Ved. (with abl.) far from.

आर 3. *āra,* probably a wrong reading for *ara,* a spoke, q. v.

आरक्त *ā-rakta, as, ā, am* (see 3. *ā*), reddish.

आरक्ष *ā-raksha, as, ā, am* (rt. *raksh*), preserved, defended, proper or worthy to be preserved; *(as),* m. protection, guard, preservation; the junction of the frontal sinuses of an elephant; the part of the forehead below this junction.

Ā-rakshaka, as, ā, am, who or what guards or protects; *(as),* m. a watchman; see the next.

Ā-rakshika, as, m. a watchman, a patrol; a village or police magistrate.

Ā-rakshya, as, ā, am, to be preserved or guarded.

आरग्वध *ārag-badha, as,* m. the tree Cathartocarpus (Cassia) Fistula; *(am),* n. its fruit.

आरङ्गर *ārangara, as,* m., Ved. epithet of a bee.

आरचित *ā-raćita, as, ā, am* (rt. *rać*), arranged, prepared.

आरट *āraṭa, am,* n. flesh. (This word is also one of the Gaṇa *gaurādi* Pāṇini IV. 1, 41.)

आरट्ट *āraṭṭa, ās,* m. pl., N. of a people and country in Pańća-nada or the Pańjāb. — *Āraṭṭa-ja, as, ā, am,* born in Āraṭṭa; *(as),* m. an inhabitant of this country; a horse from it.

आरडव *āraḍava, as, ī, am* (fr. *araḍu*), Pāṇini IV. 2, 71.

आरण *āraṇa, am,* n. (probably related to 1. *araṇa*), Ved. depth, abyss, precipice.

आरणज *āraṇaja, ās,* m. pl., N. of a class of deities forming part of the Kalpa-bhavās.

आरणि *āraṇi, is,* m. an eddy.

आरणेय *āraṇeya, as, ī, am* (fr. *araṇi,* q. v.), relating to the Araṇis or two pieces of wood by the attrition of which sacred fire is kindled; *(am),* n. or *āraṇeya-parvan, a,* n. title of the last section of the third book of the Mahā-bhārata.

आरण्य *āraṇya, as, ā, am* (fr. *araṇya*), forest, relating to a forest, forest-born, wild; *(ās),* m. pl. wild animals. — *Āraṇya-gāna, am,* n. one of the four Gānas or psalm-books of the Sāma-veda. — *Āraṇya-parvan, a,* n., N. of the third book of the Mahā-bhārata, more usually called *vana-parvan.* — *Āraṇya-paśu, us,* m. a wild or forest animal (as a buffalo, monkey, &c.). — *Āraṇya-mudgā,* f. a kind of bean, Phaseolus Trilobus Ait. — *Āraṇya-rāśi, is,* m. (in the zodiac) the sign Leo; Aries and Taurus; the former half of Capricorn.

Āraṇyaka, as, ā, am, forest, wild, forest-born, produced in a forest, relating to a forest; the *āraṇyakam parva* of the Mahā-bhārata is either the whole third book or only the first section of it; *(as),* m. a forester, an inhabitant of the woods; *(am),* n. an *āraṇyaka,* i. e. one of a class of religious and philosophical writings (closely connected with the Brāhmaṇas) which are either composed in forests or must be studied there; the Upanishads are considered to be attached to them. — *Āraṇyaka-kāṇḍa, am,* n. title of the third book of the Rāmāyaṇa and of the fourteenth book of the Śatapatha-Brāhmaṇa.

आरद्ध *āraddha, as,* or *āradvat, ān,* m., N. of a son of Setu.

आरनाल *āranāla* or *āranālaka, am,* n. sour gruel made from the fermentation of boiled rice.

आरभ् *ā-rabh,* cl. 1. A. *-rabhate, -rabdhum,* to commence, begin, undertake; to be active or energetic; to rely, obtain.

Ā-rabdha, as, ā, am, begun, commenced.

Ā-rabdhi, is, f. beginning, commencement.

Ā-rabhaṭa, as, m. an enterprising, courageous man; *(as, ī),* m. f. boldness, confidence; (ī), f. a branch of the dramatic art, the machinery of the drama, the representation of supernatural and horrible events on the stage.

Ā-rabhamāṇa, as, ā, am, beginning, commencing resolutely with a determination to finish.

Ā-rabhya, ind. having begun, beginning from.

Ā-rabhyamāṇa, as, ā, am, being commenced.

Ā-rambha, as, m. undertaking, beginning; a thing begun; commencement; haste, speed; effort, exertion; pride; killing, slaughter; an introduction, a prologue, &c. — *Ārambha-tā,* f. beginning.

Ā-rambhaka, as, ī, am, undertaking, beginning.

Ā-rambhaṇa, *am*, n. taking hold of, seizing, using; the place of seizing, a handle.—*Ārambhaṇa-vat*, *ān*, *atī*, *at*, seizable.

Ā-rambhaṇīya, *as*, *ā*, *am*, that with which one must begin, forming the commencement.

Ā-rambhin, *ī*, *iṇī*, *i*, enterprising, one who makes many new projects.

आरम् *ā-ram*, cl. 1. P. *-ramati*, *-rantum*, to delight in; to rest; to leave off.

Ā-rata, *as*, *ā*, *am*, quiet, gentle.

Ā-rati, *is*, f. stopping, ceasing; waving lights before an image.

Ā-ramaṇa, *am*, n. taking delight; cessation, pause; resting-place.

Ā-rāma, *as*, m. delight, pleasure; place of pleasure, a garden, a grove; [with this word cf. ἠρέμα and ἔρημος.]—*Ārāma-śītalā*, f., N. of a fragrant plant.

Ārāmika, *as*, m. a gardener.

आरम्बण *ā-rambaṇa*, *am*, n. (= *ā-lambana*), support.

आरव, आराव. See under 1. *ā-ru*.

आरस् *ā-ras*, cl. 1. P. *-rasati*, *-situm*, to bewail, to lament.

आरस्य *ārasya*, *am*, n. (fr. *a-rasa*), insipidity, want of flavour or spirit.

आरा *ārā*, f. a probe, an awl. See under 2. *ār*.

आराग *ā-rāga*, *as*, m. (fr. rt. *rañj* with *ā*), one of the seven suns at the end of a period of the world.

आराज्ञी *ā-rājñī*, f. (fr. *rājan* with 3. *a*), N. of a region.

आराड *ārāḍa*, *as*, m. with the epithet *kālāpa*, N. of a teacher of Śākya-muni.

आराढि *ārāḍhi*, *is*, m. a patronymic of a teacher named Saugata in the Aitareya-Brāhmaṇa.

आरात् *ārāt*, ind. (see 2. *āra*), from a distant place; distant; to a distant place; far from (with abl.); near; directly, immediately.

Ārātīya, *as*, *ā*, *am*, remote; near, proximate.

Ārāttāt, ind., Ved. from a distant place.

आराति *ārāti*, *is*, m. an enemy. See *a-rāti*.

आरात्रिक *ā-rātrika*, *am*, n. the light or the vessel containing it which is waved at night before an idol; N. of this ceremony; N. of another ceremony.

आराध् *ā-rādh*, cl. 5. P. *-rādhnoti*, *-rāddhum*, or Caus. P. *-rādhayati*, *-yitum*, to conciliate, propitiate; strive to obtain the favour of; to honour, worship; to deserve, merit: Pass. *-rādhyate*, to be effected or accomplished.

Ā-rādhaka, *as*, *ā*, *am*, who or what worships, a worshipper.

Ā-rādhana, *am*, n. propitiating, rendering favourable to one's self; (*am*), n. accomplishment, undertaking; cooking; acquirement, attainment; gratifying, propitiating, worshipping; (*ā*), f. service; (*ī*), f. worship, adoration, propitiation of the deities.

Ā-rādhanīya or *ā-rādhitavya*, *as*, *ā*, *am*, to be worshipped or adored, to be conciliated or propitiated.

Ā-rādhayitṛi, *tā*, *trī*, *tṛi*, endeavouring to conciliate or propitiate.

Ā-rādhayishṇu, *us*, *us*, *u*, propitiatory; = the preceding.

Ā-rādhita, *as*, *ā*, *am*, accomplished, effected; propitiated, pleased; worshipped, honoured, reverenced.

Ā-rādhya, *as*, *ā*, *am*, to be made favourable, to be worshipped.

Ā-rādhyamāna, *as*, *ā*, *am*, being in course of fulfilment, being accomplished; being worshipped, receiving worship.

Ā-rirādhayishu, *us*, *us*, *u*, endeavouring to gain one's favour, desirous of worshipping.

आरालिक *ārālika*, *as*, *ī*, m. f. a cook, (etymology doubtful, said to be fr. *arāla*, i. e. bending over dishes.)

आरावली *ārāvalī*, f. See under 2. *ār*.

आरिच् *ā-rić*, cl. 7. P. A. *-riṇakti*, *-riṅkte*, *-rektum*, to empty.

Ā-reka, *as*, m. emptying, doubt.

Ā-rećita, *as*, *ā*, *am*, emptied, contracted, mixed.

आरित्रिक *āritrika*, adj. fr. *aritra*. Pāṇini IV. 2, 116.

आरिन्दम *ārindama*, *as*, m. patronymic of the prince Sana-śruta.

आरी *ā-rī*, cl. 4. A. *-rīyate*, *-retum*, to trickle or flow upon, to flow over, water.

आरु 1. *ā-ru*, cl. 2. P. *-rauti* or *-ravīti*, *-ravitum*, to shout, to cry out; to praise.

Ā-rava, *as*, m. cry, crying, howling, crash, sound; N. of a people.

Ā-rāva, *as*, m. cry, crying; humming (of bees &c.); sound.

Ā-rāvin, *ī*, m. epithet of Jayasena.

आरु 2. *āru*, *us*, m. a hog; a crab; the tree Lagerstrœmia Regina; (*us*), f. a pitcher.

आरुक *āruka*, *am*, n. a medicinal plant of cooling properties growing on the Himālaya mountains.

आरुच् *ā-ruć*, Caus. *-roćayati*, *-yitum*, to regard as pleasant, to choose.

Ā-roka, *as*, m. shining through; small points of light between the threads of a web.

Ā-roćana, *as*, *ā*, *am*, shining.

आरुज् *ā-ruj*, *k*, *k*, *k* (rt. *ruj*), breaking.

Ā-ruja, *as*, *ā*, *am*, Ved. breaking, destroying; (*as*), m., N. of a Rakshas attendant on Rāvaṇa.

Ā-rujatnu, *us*, *us*, *u*, Ved. breaking.

Ā-roga, *as*, m., N. of a sun [cf. *ā-rāga*].

आरुणपराजिन् *āruṇaparājin*, *ī*, m., N. of an ancient Kalpa work on the ritual of the Brāhmaṇas.

आरुणि *āruṇi*, *is*, m. (fr. *aruṇa*), N. of Uddālaka, a renowned Brāhmaṇa teacher, son of Aruṇa Aupaveśi and father of Śvetaketu; N. of Auddālaki, i. e. of Śvetaketu; of Suparṇeya, son of Prajāpati; of Vainateya, son of Vinatā.

Āruṇeya, *as*, m. epithet of Śvetaketu.

आरुणिन् *āruṇin*, *inas*, m. pl., N. of a school derived from Vaiśampāyana Āruṇi.

आरुणी *āruṇī*, f., Ved. 'the red one,' a N. given to the horses of the Maruts, which are females. See *aruṇa*.

आरुध् *ā-rudh*, cl. 7. P. *-ruṇaddhi*, *-roddhum*, to keep off: Caus. *-rodhayati*, *-yitum*, to obstruct, impede.

Ā-rodhana, *am*, n., Ved. secret place, innermost part.

आरुषी *ārushī*, f. (fr. *arusha*), N. of a daughter of Manu and mother of Aurva.

आरुष्कर *ārush-kara*, *am*, n. the fruit of the Semecarpus Anacardium.

आरुह् 1. *ā-ruh*, cl. 1. P. *-rohati*, *-roḍhum*, to ascend, mount, bestride; to venture upon, undertake; to attain, gain: Caus. *-rohayati* or *-ropayati*, *-yitum*, to cause to mount or ascend, raise; to cause to grow; to plant; to place, fasten; to attribute.

Ā-rurukshamāṇa, *as*, *ā*, *am* (Desid.), wishing to ascend.

Ā-rurukshu, *us*, *us*, *u*, desirous to rise or ascend or advance, &c.

2. *ā-ruh*, *k*, *k*, *k*, Ved. ascending; (*k*), f. excrescence, shoot (of a plant).

Ā-ruha, *as*, *ā*, *am*, leaping up, mounting, ascending; (*as*), m. ascent.

Ā-ruhya, ind. having mounted, having ascended.

Ā-rūḍha, *as*, *ā*, *am*, mounted, ascended, risen; raised up, elevated on high: often used in compounds, e. g. *indriyārūḍha*, brought under the cognizance of the senses, perceived.—*Ārūḍha-vat*, *ān*, *atī*, *at*, mounting, rising.

Ā-rūḍhi, *is*, f. ascent, mounting, ascending.

Ā-roḍhavya, *as*, *ā*, *am*, to be ascended or mounted.

Ā-roḍhṛi, *ḍhā*, *ḍhrī*, *ḍhṛi*, who or what mounts or rides, &c.

Ā-ropa, *as*, m. imposing (as a burden), burdening with, charging with; placing in or on; assigning or attributing to; relating to; superior position.

Ā-ropaka, *as*, *ā*, *am*, planting, fixing, causing to ascend.

Ā-ropaṇa, *am*, n. the act of placing or fixing in or on; causing to mount or ascend, raising to heaven; planting; trusting, delivering; the stringing of a bow.

Ā-ropaṇīya, *as*, *ā*, *am*, to be made to ascend; to be raised, placed, &c.

Ā-ropita, *as*, *ā*, *am*, raised, elevated; fixed, placed, made; strung (as a bow); deposited, intrusted; consecrated; accidental, adventitious.

1. *ā-ropya*, *as*, *ā*, *am*, to be placed or fixed on or in.

2. *ā-ropya*, ind. having made to ascend, having caused to mount, having placed upon.

Ā-ropyamāṇa, *as*, *ā*, *am*, being strung, being tried to be strung.

Ā-roha, *as*, m. one who mounts or ascends, a rider (on a horse &c.), one who is seated in a carriage; ascent, rising, creeping up, mounting, riding; haughtiness, pride; elevation, elevated place, altitude; a heap, mountain; a woman's waist, the buttocks; length; measure; descending (= *ava-roha*?); a mine.

Ā-rohaka, *as*, *ā*, *am*, ascending; rising; raising up; (*as*), m. a rider; a tree.

Ā-rohaṇa, *am*, n. the act of rising, ascending; the rising or growing of new shoots, growing (of plants); Ved. a carriage; an elevated stage for dancing; a ladder, a staircase; riding on (a horse &c.).

Ārohaṇika, *as*, *ī*, *am*, relating to ascent or mounting.

Ā-rohin, *ī*, *iṇī*, *i*, ascending, mounting; one who mounts or rides.

आरू *ārū*, *ūs*, *ūs*, *u*, of a tawny colour; (*ūs*), m. tawny (the colour).

आरे *āre*, ind. (see 2. *āra*), Ved. far, far from (with abl.); near.—*Āre-agha*, *as*, *ā*, *am*, Ved. having evil far removed.—*Āre-avadya*, *as*, *ā*, *am*, Ved. one from whom blame or insult is far removed.—*Āre-śatru*, *us*, *us*, *u*, Ved. one whose enemies are driven far away.

आरेवत *ārevata*, *as*, m. a tree, = *ārag-badha*, q. v.; (*am*), n. the fruit of this tree.

आरेहण *ā-rehaṇa*, *am*, n. (fr. rt. *rih* for *lih* with *ā*), Ved. licking, kissing.

आरोग्य *ārogya*, *am*, n. (fr. *a-roga*), freedom from disease, health.

आर्कि *ārki*, *is*, m. a son of Arka or the sun; epithet of the planet Saturn.

आर्क्ष *ārksha*, *as*, *ī*, *am* (fr. *ṛiksha*), stellar, regulated by the stars or constellations; (*as*), m. a son or descendant of Ṛiksha; epithet of Āśvamedha, of Śrutarvan, of Saṃvaraṇa.—*Ārksha-varsha*, *as*, m. a stellar year or revolution of a constellation.

Ārkshya, patronymic of *ṛiksha* Pāṇini IV. 1, 105.

आर्क्षोद *ārkshoda*, *as*, *ī*, *am*, inhabiting the mountain Ṛikshoda.

आर्गल *ārgala*, *as*, *ī*, m. f. a bolt or bar. See *argala*.

आर्ग्बध *ārgbadha*, *as*, m. = *ārag-badha*, q. v.

आर्घा *ārghā*, f. a sort of yellow bee.

Ārghya, as, ā, am, relating to this bee; (am), n. its honey.

आर्च ārća, as, ī, am (fr. arćā or fr. ṛić), devout, worshipping; relating to the Ṛić or Ṛig-veda.

Ārćika, as, ī, am, relating to the Ṛig-veda; (am), n. an epithet of the Sāma-veda.

आर्चत्क ārćatka, as, m. a patronymic of Śara.

आर्चाभिन् ārćābhin, inas, m. pl., N. of a school, founded by a pupil of Vaiśampāyana.

आर्छ् ārćh (ā-ṛićh), cl. 6. P. ārćhati, -ćhitum, to fall into (mischief); to obtain; to partake of.

आर्जव ārjava, am, n. (fr. ṛiju), straightness, straight direction; rectitude, propriety of act or observance; honesty, open behaviour; sincerity.

आर्जीक ārjīka, as, m. (cf. ṛijīka), Ved. originally perhaps a milk-vessel. This word probably denotes a celestial vessel, in which the heavenly Soma is purified, or one of the rivers which it forms in the sky; (Sāy.) a lake in the country Ṛijīkā.

Ārjīkīya, as, m. = the preceding; (ā), f. a terrestrial river; N. of the river Vipāśā.

आर्जुनायन ārjunāyana, ās, m. pl. (fr. arjuna), N. of a people.

Ārjunāyanaka, as, ī, am, inhabited by the Ārjunāyanas.

आर्जुनि ārjuni, is, m. a patronymic from Arjuna.

Ārjuneya, as, m. a patronymic of Kutsa.

आर्ञ्ज् ārñj (ā-ṛiñj), cl. 1. A. ārñjate, -jitum, to strive after, to endeavour to obtain, to wish to possess.

आर्त ārta, as, ā, am (probably past pass. part. of rt. ṛi with prep. ā, but according to some fr. rt. ṛit, and according to others an irreg. formation fr. rt. ard, which ought to form arṇa with prep. sam, ni and vi, and ardita in other cases), struck by calamity, afflicted, pained, disturbed; injured; oppressed, suffering, sick, unhappy. — Ārta-gala, as, m., N. of the plant Barleria Cærulea. — Ārta-tara, as, ā, am, extremely pained, disturbed, confounded. — Ārta-tā, f. state of affliction, pain. — Ārta-nāda or ārta-svara, as, m. a cry of pain. — Ārta-bandhu, us, m. friend of the distressed.

Ārti, is, f. painful occurrence, pain, injury, mischief, evil; sickness; the end of a bow [cf. arti and ārtnī]. — Ārti-mat, ān, atī, at, having or suffering pain; (ān), m., N. of a serpent. — Ārti-han, ā, ā, a, or ārti-hara, as, ā, am, destroying pain. — Ārty-apaharaṇa, am, n. the relieving of distress, pain, &c.

आर्तना ārtanā, f. (according to Sāy. derived fr. ārta above), Ved. a destructive combat; (as an adj.?) uncultivated, wild ground (? connected with āra, araṇa, araṇya, &c.).

आर्तपर्णि ārtaparṇi, is, m. the son of Ṛitaparṇa, a patronymic of Sudāsa.

आर्तभाग ārtabhāga, as, m. son of Ṛitabhāga, a patronymic of Jarat-kārava.

आर्तव ārtava, as, ā or ī, am (fr. ṛitu), belonging or conforming to the seasons or periods of time, seasonable; menstrual, relating to or produced by this discharge; (as), m. a section of the year, a combination of several seasons; (ī), f. a mare; (am), n. the menstrual discharge, certain days after the menstrual discharge fit for generation; fluid discharged by the female of an animal at the time of rut; a flower.

Ārtveyī, f. a woman during her courses.

आर्त्नी ārtnī, f., Ved. the end of a bow, the place where the string or sinew is fastened; (κορώνη.)

आर्त्विजीन ārtvijīna, as, ī, am (fr. ṛitvij), fit for the office of a priest.

Ārtvijya, am, n. the office or business of a sacrificing priest, his rank or order.

आर्त्व्य ārtvya, as, m. a patronymic of Dvi-mūrdhan, a kind of Asura.

आर्थ ārtha, as, ī, am (fr. artha), relating to a thing or object; material, significant (opposed to śābda, q. v.).

Ārthapatya, am, n. (fr. artha-pati), power over or possession of a thing.

Ārthika, as, ī, am, significant, wise, rich; substantial, real, pertaining to the true substance of a thing.

आर्द्र ārdra, as, ā, am (said to be fr. rt. ard), wet, moist, damp; fresh, not dry, succulent, green (as a plant), living; fresh, new; soft, tender, full of feeling, warm; loose, flaccid; (as), m., N. of a grandson of Pṛithu; (ā), f. the fourth or sixth Nakshatra or lunar mansion. — Ārdra-kāshṭha, am, n. green wood, timber not dry. — Ārdra-tā, f. or ārdra-tva, am, n. wetness, moisture; freshness, greenness; softness, tenderness. — Ārdra-dānu, us, us, u, Ved. granting moisture. — Ārdra-nayana, as, ā, am, moist-eyed, weeping, suffused with tears. — Ārdra-pavi, is, is, i, Ved. having moist or dripping fellies (said of a carriage). — Ārdra-pavitra, as, ā, am, Ved. having a wet strainer; epithet of the Soma. — Ārdra-māshā, f. a leguminous shrub, Glycine Debilis. — Ārdra-śāka, am, n. fresh ginger. — Ārdra-hasta, as, ā, am, Ved. moist-handed. — Ārdrā-lubdhaka, as, m. the dragon's tail or descending node.

Ārdraka, am, n. ginger in its undried state; (as, ī, am), born under the constellation Ārdrā; (as), m., N. of a son of Vasumitra.

Ārdraya, nom. P. ārdrayati, -yitum, to make wet, moisten.

आर्ध् ārdh (ā-ṛidh), Desid. A. ertsate, to wish to obtain or to collect.

आर्ध ārdha (fr. ardha), used at the beginning of compounds to express 'half.'

Ārdhadrauṇika, as, ī, am, bought with half a droṇa, containing it, &c.

Ārdhadhātuka, as, ī, am, applicable to half the root or to the shorter form of the verbal base; this is the name of those terminations and affixes which belong to the six non-conjugational or general tenses. These terminations are supposed to be affixed immediately to the root or with the interposition only of an augment, such as the inserted i.

Ārdhaprasthika, as, ī, am, bought &c. with half a prastha.

Ārdhamāsika, as, ī, am, lasting &c. for half a month; observing or practising (continence &c.) for a fortnight.

Ārdharātrika, ās, m. pl. (fr. ardha-rātra), N. of an astronomical school who reckoned the beginning of the motions of the planets from midnight.

Ārdhika, as, ī, am, sharing half, an equal partner; relating to half; (as), m. one who ploughs the ground for half the crop.

आर्धुक ārdhuka, as, ī, am (fr. rt. ṛidh), Ved. conducive to success, useful, beneficial.

आर्पय् ārpay, Caus. fr. rt. ṛi with ā: See 2. ār.

Ārpayitṛi, tā, m., Ved. one who injures or hurts.

आर्भव ārbhava, as, ī, am (fr. ṛibhu), belonging or sacred to the Ṛibhus.

आर्य ārya, as, ā, m. f. (fr. arya, rt. ṛi), a loyal or faithful man, a man of one's own race; one who is faithful to the deities of his country; N. of the Hindū and Iranian people (opposed to an-ārya, dasyu, dāsa); in later times N. of the first three castes (opposed to śūdra); a man highly esteemed, a respectable, honourable man; a master, an owner; a friend; a Vaiśya; Buddha; (with Buddhists) a man who has thought on the four chief principles of Buddhism and lives according to them; a son of Manu Sāvarṇa; (as, ā or ī, am), Aryan, favourable to the Āryan people; behaving like an Āryan, worthy of one, honourable, respectable, noble; of a good family; excellent; wise; suitable; (ā), f. a name of Pārvatī; a kind of metre of two lines, each line consisting of seven and a half feet; each foot containing four instants, except the sixth of the second line, which contains only one, and is therefore a single short syllable; hence there are thirty instants in the first line and twenty-seven in the second; [with ārya cf. the Old Germ. êra and Mod. Germ. Ehre.] — Ārya-gṛihya, as, ā, am, easily to be got by honourable men, to be received with honour by noble men; decorous, respectable, right. — Ārya-tā, f. or ārya-tva, am, n. honourable behaviour. — Ārya-deva, as, m., N. of a pupil of Nāgārjuna. — Ārya-deśa, as, m. a region inhabited by Āryans or followers of the Āryan laws. — Āryadeśya, as, ā, am, originating from such a region. — Ārya-putra, as, m. son of an Āryan or honourable man; the son of a spiritual preceptor; honorific designation of the son of an elder brother; of a husband by his wife; of a prince by a general; a husband (in theatrical language). — Ārya-prāya, as, ā, am, inhabited by Āryan people; abounding with respectable persons. — Ārya-bhaṭṭa, as, m., N. of a renowned astronomer, the inventor of algebra, among the Hindūs. — Ārya-bhāva, as, m. honourable character or behaviour. — Ārya-mārga, as, m. the way of the honourable, the respectable way. — Ārya-miśra, ās, m. pl. an assembly of respectable or honourable men; (as, ā, am), distinguished, respectable; (as), m. a gentleman, a man of consequence. — Ārya-yuvan, ā, m. an Āryan youth. — Ārya-rāja, as, m., N. of a king. — Ārya-rūpa, as, ā, am, one who has only the form of an Āryan; a hypocrite, an impostor. — Āryalingin, ī, inī, i, one who bears the external semblance of an Āryan or honourable man, an impostor. — Ārya-varman, ā, m., N. of a king. — Ārya-vṛitta, am, n. the behaviour of an Āryan or noble man; (as, ā, am), behaving like an Āryan; virtuous, good, pious. — Ārya-veśa, as, ā, am, dressed like an Āryan, well clothed, fine. — Ārya-vrata, as, ā, am, one who observes the laws and ordinances of the Āryans or honourable men. — Ārya-sangha, as, m. the whole body of the Āryans, the collective body of noblemen; N. of a renowned philosopher, founder of the school of the Yogākāras. — Ārya-satya, am, n. a noble or sublime truth; four such truths form the four chief principles of Buddhism. — Ārya-siṅha, as, m., N. of a Buddhist patriarch. — Ārya-hṛidya, as, ā, am, beloved by the noble. — Āryā-gīti, is, f. a variety of the Āryā metre, containing eight equal feet or thirty-two syllabic instants in each verse of the couplet. — Āryāvarta (°ya-āv°), as, m. abode of the noble or excellent; the sacred land or place of residence of the Āryans; N. of the land extending from the eastern to the western sea, and bounded on the north and south by the Himālaya and Vindhya mountains. — Āryā-vilāsa, as, m. title of a work. — Āryāshṭaśata (°ya-ashṭa-śa°), am, n. title of a work of Ārya-bhaṭṭa's, consisting of eight hundred distichs.

Āryaka, as, m. an honourable, respectable man; a grandfather; N. of a cowherd who became king; of a Nāga. — Āryakā or āryikā, f. a respectable woman; (ikā), f., N. of a Nakshatra; (akam), n. a ceremony performed to the manes, the vessel &c. used in sacrifices made to the manes.

Āryāṇaka, N. of a country.

आर्वाक् ārvāk, ind. after, afterwards, behind. See arvāk.

आर्श ārśa, as, ī, am (fr. ṛiśya), Ved. belonging to the antelope.

आर्ष ārsha, as, ī, am (fr. ṛishi), relating or belonging to or derived from Ṛishis, i. e. the poets of the Vedic and other old hymns, archaistic; (as), m. a form of marriage derived from the Ṛishis, the father of the bride receiving one or two pairs of kine from the bridegroom; (am), n. the speech of a

Rishi, the holy text, the Vedas; sacred descent; the derivation (of a poem) from a Rishi author; (*ā*), f. a class of Vedic metres. — *Ārshoḍhā* (°*sha-ūḍh*°), f. a wife married according to the Ārsha form.

Ārsheya, as, ī, am, relating or belonging to or derived from a Rishi, of sacred descent; venerable, respectable; (*am*), n. sacred descent. — *Ārsheya-vat, ān, atī, at,* Ved. connected with sacred descent.

आर्षभ *ārshabha, as, ī, am* (fr. *ṛishabha*), derived from a bull, produced by one.

Ārshabhi, is, m., N. of the first Ćakravartin in Bhārata; a son of the first Tīrthakṛit Ṛishabha.

Ārshabhya, as, ā, am, a steer sufficiently full-grown to be used or one fit to be castrated.

आर्ष्टिषेण *ārshṭisheṇa, as,* m. a patronymic of Devāpi.

आर्हत *ārhata, as, ī, am* (fr. *arhat*), belonging to the doctrine of Jina or the Jains; (*as*), m. a Jaina, a follower of the doctrines of Jina.

Ārhatya, am, n. the quality or practice of an Arhat or Jain saint.

आल *āla, am,* n. spawn, any discharge of venomous matter from poisonous animals; yellow arsenic, orpiment; (*as, ā, am*), not small, large, extensive. — *Ālākta* (°*la-ak*°), *as, ā, am,* Ved. anointed with poison (as an arrow).

आलक्ष् *ā-laksh,* cl. 10. P. A. *-lakshayati, -te, -yitum,* to descry, behold.

1. *ā-lakshya, as, ā, am,* to be observed, visible, apparent.

आलक्षण्य *ālakshaṇya, am,* n. (fr. *a-lakshaṇa*), misfortune, crime.

आलक्ष्य 2. *ā-lakshya, as, ā, am* (3. *ā* preprefixed in the sense of diminution), scarcely visible.

आलगर्द *ālagarda, as,* m. a species of Cobra. See *alagarda.*

आलप् *ā-lap,* cl. 1. P. *-lapati, -pitum,* to address, speak to, converse: Caus. *-lāpayati, -yitum,* to engage (another) in conversation, to question.

Ā-lāpa, as, m. speaking to, addressing, speech, conversation, communication; statement of the question in an arithmetical or algebraic sum; a question. — *Ālāpa-vat, ān, atī, at,* speaking, addressing.

Ā-lāpana, as, ā, am, causing to speak or converse about; (*am*), n. speaking to, conversing with.

Ā-lāpanīya or *ā-lāpya, as, ā, am,* to be said or spoken, to be spoken to or addressed.

Ā-lāpin, ī, inī, i, speaking or conversing with; (*inī*), f. a lute made of a gourd.

आलभ् *ā-labh,* cl. 1. A. *-labhate, -labdhum,* to take hold of, touch, handle.

Ā-labhana, am, n. taking hold of, bringing (?).

1. *ā-labhya, as, ā, am,* Ved. fit to be killed or sacrificed.

2. *ā-labhya,* ind. having received or obtained.

Ā-lambha, as, m. taking hold of, seizing, touching; tearing off, rooting out (of plants); the killing of the animal at a sacrifice.

Ā-lambhana, am, n. taking hold of, touching; killing.

Ā-lambhanīya, as, ā, am, to be taken hold of or handled, to be touched.

Ā-lambhin, ī, inī, i, touching, taking hold of.

Ā-lambhya, as, ā, am, obtainable, to be obtained; fit or proper to be killed.

आलम्ब् *ā-lamb,* cl. 1. A. *-lambate, -bitum,* to rest or lean upon; to hang from; to depend; to lay hold of, support, seize; to strike up (a tune or note).

Ā-lamba, as, ā, am, hanging down; (*as*), m. that on which one rests or leans; support; receptacle; a prop; an asylum; depending on or from; a perpendicular; (*ā*), f., N. of a plant with poisonous leaves.

Ā-lambana, am, n. depending on or resting upon, hanging from; supporting, sustaining; fundament, base; reason, cause; (in rhetoric) the natural and necessary connection of feeling with the cause which excites it; the mental exercise practised by the Yogin in endeavouring to realize the gross form of the eternal; silent repetition of a prayer; (with Buddhists) the five attributes of things corresponding to the five senses, viz. form, sound, smell, taste, and touch; also *dharma* or law corresponding to *manas.*

Ālambāyana or *ālambāyanī-putra, as,* m., N. of a teacher.

Ā-lambi, is, m., N. of a pupil of Vaiśampāyana.

Ā-lambita, as, ā, am, pendent, suspended, hanging from or on; supported, upheld; protected.

Ā-lambin, ī, inī, i, hanging from, resting or leaning upon; depending on or from; laying hold of, supporting, maintaining; wearing; (*inas*), m. pl. N. of a school.

Ā-lambya, ind. having supported; supporting, sustaining; taking by the hand.

आलय *ā-laya.* See under 2. *ā-lī.*

आलर्क *ālarka, as, ī, am* (fr. *alarka*), caused by or relating to a mad dog.

आलवण्य *ālavaṇya, am,* n. (fr. *a-lavaṇa*), ugliness, insipidity.

आलवाल *ālavāla, am,* n. a basin for water round the root of a tree. See *alavāla, āvāla.*

आलस *ālasa, as, ī, am* (fr. *a-lasa*), idle, slothful, lazy.

Ālasya, as, ī, am, idle, slothful, apathetic; (*am*), n. idleness, sloth, want of energy. — *Ālasya-nibandhana, as, ā, am,* originating in indolence.

आलाक्त *ālākta.* See under *āla.*

आलाट्य *ālāṭya, as, ā, am* (rt. *laṭ* for *raṭ*), Ved. being amongst the breakers of the sea (?).

आलात *ālāta, am,* n. a firebrand; a coal burning or extinguished. See *alāta.*

आलान *ālāna, am,* n. (etym. doubtful), the post to which an elephant is tied; the rope that ties him; a fetter, a tie; a rope or string; tying, binding; (*as*), m., N. of a minister of Śiva.

Ālānika, as, ā, am, serving as a post to which an elephant is tied.

आलाप *ā-lāpa,* &c. See under *ā-lap.*

आलाबु *ālābu, us,* or *ālābū, ūs,* f. a pumpkin gourd. See *a-lābu.*

आलावर्त *ālāvarta* (°*la-āv*° ?), *am,* n. a fan made of cloth.

आलास्य *ālāsya* (°*la-ās*°), *as,* m. a crocodile (' poison-mouthed;' see *āla*).

आलि *āli, is,* m. (see *ali*), a scorpion; a bee; (*is*), f. a woman's female friend; a row, range, continuous line [cf. *āvali*]; a ridge or mound of earth crossing ditches, dividing fields, &c.; a dike; a line, a race, family; (*is, is, i*), useless, idle, unmeaning; pure, honest, sincere.

Ālin, ī, m. a scorpion [cf. *alin*].

Ālī, f. a female friend, row, range, line, &c.

आलिख् *ā-likh,* cl. 6. P. *-likhati, -lekhitum,* to write, delineate.

Ā-likhat, an, m. scratching; N. of an evil spirit.

Ā-likhya, ind. pourtraying, delineating, sketching.

Ā-lekhana, as, ā, am, scratching, painting; (*as*), m., N. of a teacher; (*ī*), f. a brush, a pencil; (*am*), n. scratching, writing, painting.

Ā-lekhya, as, ā, am, to be written, to be delineated or painted; (*am*), n. a painting, writing. — *Ālekhya-lekhā,* f. painting. — *Ālekhya-śesha, as, ā, am,* having nothing left but a painting, deceased.

आलिगी *āligī,* f., Ved., N. of a serpent.

आलिङ्ग् *ā-liṅg,* cl. 1. P. A. *-liṅgati, -te, -gitum,* or cl. 10. P. *-liṅgayati, -yitum,* to clasp, join the limbs closely; to encircle, embrace.

Ā-liṅga, as, m. embracing; a kind of drum.

Ā-liṅgana, am, n. clasping, embracing, an embrace.

Ā-liṅgita, as, ā, am, embraced; (*am*), n. an embrace. — *Āliṅgita-vat, ān, atī, at,* one who has embraced.

Ā-liṅgin, ī, inī, i, embracing; (*ī*), m. a small drum, shaped like a barley corn and carried upon the breast.

1. *ā-liṅgya, as, ā, am,* to be embraced; (*as*), m. a small drum.

2. *ā-liṅgya,* ind. having embraced.

आलिञ्जर *āliñjara, as,* m. a large clay water-jar.

आलिन्द *ālinda* or *ālindaka, as,* m. a terrace before a house, a raised place or terrace for sleeping upon. See *alinda.*

आलिप् *ā-lip,* cl. 6. P. *-limpati, -leptum,* to anoint, besmear.

Ā-lipta, as, ā, am, anointed, smeared, plastered.

Ā-limpana, am, n. whitening or painting the floor, wall, &c., on festival occasions.

Ā-lepa, as, m. smearing, plastering, anointing; liniment.

Ā-lepana, am, n. smearing, plastering; liniment.

आली 1. *ālī,* f. See under *āli* last col.

आली 2. *ā-lī,* cl. 4. A. *-līyate, -letum* or *-lātum,* to settle down upon; to melt; faint.

Ā-laya, as, am, m. n. a house, a dwelling, a receptacle, an asylum; (frequently at the end of a compound, e. g. *himālaya,* the abode of snow.)

Ā-līna, as, ā, am, melted, fused.

Ālīnaka, am, n. tin; lead (from its melting easily).

आलीढ *ā-līḍha, as, ā, am* (rt. *lih*), eaten, licked, lapped by the tongue, scraped; (*as*), m., N. of a man; (*am*), n. an attitude in shooting, the right knee advanced, the left leg retracted.

आलीढक *ālīḍhaka, am,* n. the frolicing of a calf; (etym. doubtful, perhaps for *āḍhīlaka.*)

आलु *ālu, us,* m. (said to be for *āru* fr. rt. *ṛi*), an owl; an esculent root, Arum Campanulatum; in the modern dialects this name is applied to the yam, potatoe, &c.; ebony, black ebony; (*us* or *ūs*), f. a pitcher, a small water-jar; (*u*), n. a raft, a float.

Āluka, as, m. a kind of ebony; an epithet of Śesha, the chief of the Nāgas or serpent race; (*am*), n. the esculent root of Amorphophallus Campanulatus.

आलुञ्चन *ā-luñćana, am,* n. (rt. *luñć*), tearing in pieces, rending.

आलुड् *ā-luḍ,* cl. 1. P. *-loḍati, -loḍitum,* to stir up, mix, agitate.

Ā-loḍana, am, n. mixing, blending; stirring, shaking, agitating.

Ā-loḍita, as, ā, am, mixed, blended, shaken, agitated.

आलून *ā-lūna, as, ā, am* (rt. *lū*), cut, cut off.

आलेखन *ā-lekhana,* &c. See under *ā-likh.*

आलोक् *ā-lok,* cl. 1. A., 10. P. *-lokate, -kitum, -lokayati, -yitum,* to look forth; to behold; to consider, contemplate, regard.

Ā-loka, as, m. looking, seeing, beholding, sight, aspect; light, lustre, splendor; flattery, praise, complimentary language, panegyric; section, chapter.

Ā-lokana, am, n. seeing, looking, sight, beholding.

Ā-lokanīya, as, ā, am, visible; to be considered, regarded. — *Ālokanīya-tā,* f. the being visible.

Ā-lokita, as, ā, am, seen, beheld.

Ā-lokin, ī, inī, i, seeing, beholding.

Ā-lokya, ind. having seen or looked at, beholding.

आलोच् *ā-loć,* cl. 1. A. *-loćate, -ćitum,* to behold, view, perceive, consider, reflect.

Ā-loćaka, as, ā, am, beholding; causing to see; (*am*), n. the faculty of vision or the cause of sight.
Ā-loćana, am, ā, n. f. seeing, perceiving; considering, reflecting.
Ā-loćita, as, ā, am, seen, beheld, considered.
1. *ā-loćya* or *ā-loćanīya, as, ā, am*, to be seen, thought of or considered.
2. *ā-loćya*, ind. having considered, having reflected.

आलोल **ā-lola, as, ā, am**, trembling slightly, rolling (as an eye); shaken, agitated; (*as*), m. trembling, agitation.
Ā-lolita, as, ā, am, shaken, agitated.

आव **āva**, the base of the dual cases of the pronoun of the 1st person; Nom. Acc. *āvām* (Ved. *āvam*); Inst. Dat. Abl. *āvābhyām*; Gen. Loc. *āvayos*.

आवच् **ā-vać**, cl. 3. P., Ved. *-vivakti, -vaktum*, to invoke.

आवत् **ā-vat, t**, f. (fr. 3. *ā*), Ved. proximity, (opposed to *parā-vat*.)

आवद् **ā-vad**, cl. 1. P., Ved. *-vadati, -ditum*, to shout at, invoke, celebrate.

आवनेय **āvaneya, as**, m. (fr. *avani*), son of the earth; epithet of the planet Mars.

आवन्तिक **āvantika, as, ī, am** (fr. *avanti*), coming from or belonging to Avanti or the district of Oujein; (*ās*), m. pl., N. of a Buddhist school; (*ā*), f., N. of the daughter of a Brāhman.
Āvantya, as, ā, am, coming from or being in the country Avanti; (*as*), m. a prince or an inhabitant of Avanti or of Oujein; the offspring of a degraded Brāhman.

आवप् **ā-vap**, cl. 1. P. A. *-vapati, -te, -vaptum*, to sow, scatter; to pour out; to offer: Caus. P. *-vāpayati, -yitum*, to shave, cut off, trim.
Ā-vapana, am, n. the act of sowing, throwing, scattering, placing upon; instilling, inserting; capacity, a vessel, a jar, a ewer; sowing seed, weaving; (*ī*), f., Ved. a vessel, a jar.
Ā-vapantika, as, ā, am, Ved. scattering.
Ā-vāpa, as, ā, am, scattering, throwing; (*as*), m. scattering, throwing; sowing seed; casting, directing; (in pharmacy) throwing additional ingredients into any compound in course of preparation; mixing, inserting; setting out or arranging vessels, jars, &c.; a kind of drink; a bracelet; a basin for water round the root of a tree; uneven ground; hostile purpose, intention of going to war; a vessel; principal oblation to fire.
Āvāpaka, as, m. a bracelet of gold, &c.
Ā-vāpana, am, n. a loom, an implement for weaving; a reel or frame for winding thread.
Āvāpika, as, ā, am, additional, inserted, supplementary.

आवय **1. āvaya, am**, n. (fr. 2. *a-vī*), Ved. non-conception, barrenness.

आवय **2. āvaya, as, ā**, m. f. water.

आवयाज् **āvayāj, s**, m. (fr. *ava-yāj*), Ved. one who expiates or averts by means of sacrifice; (Sāy. as if from rt. *vī* with *ā*) one who causes the sacrifice to go to the gods.

आवरसमक **āvarasamaka, as, ī, am** (fr. *avarasama*), to be paid in the following year.

आवर्जित **ā-varjita**. See under *ā-vṛij*.

आवर्त **ā-varta**, &c. See under *ā-vṛit*.

आवर्हित **ā-varhita, as, ā, am**, eradicated, plucked up by the roots.

आवलि **āvali, is** or **ī**, f. (fr. rt. *val* with *ā*?), a row, a range, a continuous line; a series, dynasty, a lineage.

आवल्ग् **ā-valg**, cl. 1. P. A. *-valgati, -te, -gitum*, to spring, to jump, to leap up.

आवल्गुज **āvalguja, as, ī, am** (fr. *a-valgu-ja*), produced from the plant Vernonia Anthelminthica.

आवशीर **āvaśīra, ās**, m. pl., N. of a people.

आवश्य **āvaśya, am**, n. (fr. *avaśya*), necessity, inevitable act or conclusion.
Āvaśyaka, as, ī, am, necessary, inevitable; (*am*), n. necessity, inevitable act or conclusion; (*āvaśyakaṃ kṛi*, to do what nature makes necessary.) — *Āvaśyaka-tva, am*, n. or *āvaśyaka-tā*, f. necessity, inevitability.

आवस् **ā-vas**, cl. 1. P. *-vasati, -vastum*, to inhabit, be occupied or engaged in (with acc.): Caus. P. *-vāsayati, -yitum*, to cause or allow one to dwell, receive hospitably; to inhabit, settle in a place.
Ā-vasati, is, f. the night, i. e. the time during which one rests.
Ā-vasatha, as, m. a dwelling-place, habitation; a house; a fire-temple or place where sacrificial fire is preserved; a dwelling for pupils and ascetics; a particular religious observance; a treatise on the Āryā metre.
Āvasathika, as, ī, am, inhabiting a house, household, domestic; keeping a sacred fire in one's house.
Āvasathya, as, ā, am, being in a house; (*as*), m. the sacred fire kept in a house; (*as, am*), m. n. a dwelling for pupils and ascetics; (*am*), n. placing a sacred fire within a house.
Ā-vāsa, as, m. abode, residence, dwelling, house.

आवसायिन् **āvasāyin, ī, inī, i** (fr. *avasaāyin*), Ved. going after a livelihood or provisions.

आवसित **āvasita, as, ā, am**, stored (as grain), winnowed; ripe, full-grown. See *ava-sita*.

आवस्थिक **āvasthika, as, ī, am** (fr. 2. *avasthā*), founded on circumstances, suitable, adapted to.

आवह् **ā-vah**, cl. 1. P. *-vahati, -voḍhum*, to bring, to bring to pass: Caus. P. *-vāhayati, -yitum*, to have brought, cause to be brought, send for; to make one bring.
Ā-vaha, as, ā, am, bringing, bringing to pass, producing; what bears or conveys; (*as*), m., N. of one of the seven winds or bands of air, that which is usually assigned to the *bhuvar-loka* or atmospheric region between the *bhūr-loka* and *svar-loka*; one of the seven tongues of fire.
Ā-vahat, an, antī, at, bringing, receiving.
Ā-vahana, am, n. bringing near.
Ā-vahamāna, as, ā, am, bearing along, bringing near, followed by, succeeded, bringing in succession.
Ā-vāha, as, m. marrying; N. of a son of S'vaphalka.
Ā-vāhana, am, n. sending for, inviting, calling; offering oblations with fire; (*ī*), f. a particular position of the hands, the palms being placed together, and the thumbs turned towards the root of the ring-finger.
Ā-vāhita, as, ā, am, invoked, invited.

आवा **ā-vā**, cl. 2. P. *-vāti, -tum*, to blow from all quarters, to blow upon: Desid. P. A. *-vivāsati, -te*, to care for, be attentive to, favour.
Ā-vāt, ān, ātī or *āntī, āt*, blowing.

आवाधा **ā-vādhā**, f. (see *ā-bādhā*), pain, distress; segment of the base of a triangle.

आवाप **āvāpa**, &c. See under *ā-vap*.

आवाल **āvāla, am**, n. a basin of water round the foot of a tree. See *ālavāla*.

आवास **ā-vāsa**. See under *ā-vas*.

आविक **āvika, as, ī, am** (fr. *avi*), relating to or derived from sheep; woollen; (*am*), n. a woollen cloth, blanket. — *Āvika-sautrika, as, ī, am*, made of woollen thread.

आविक्षित **āvikshita, as**, m. (fr. *a-vikshit*), a patronymic of Marutta.

आविग्न **āvigna, as**, m. the fruit tree Carissa Carandas L. See *a-vigna*.

आविज्ञान्य **āvijñānya, as, ī, am** (fr. *a-vijñāna*), Ved. undistinguishable.

आवितन् **ā-vi-tan**, cl. 8. A. *-tanute, -nitum*, to diffuse light over, illuminate.

आविद् **1. ā-vid**, Caus. P. *-vedayati, -yitum*, to make known, report, declare, announce.
2. *ā-vid, t*, f., Ved. knowledge, the being or becoming known; technical designation of the Vedic formulas beginning with *āvis* and *āvitta*.
Ā-vidvas, ān, ushī, as, Ved. acquainted with, knowing thoroughly, skilled in.
Ā-vedaka, as, ā, am, making known, reporting, announcing; (*as*), m. an appellant, a suitor; one who makes known, an informer.
Ā-vedana, am, n. representation, stating a complaint, addressing or apprising respectfully.
Ā-vedanīya, as, ā, am, to be declared or reported or announced.
Ā-vedita, as, ā, am, made known, communicated, represented.
Ā-vedin, ī, inī, i, announcing, declaring.
1. *ā-vedya*, ind. having made known.
2. *ā-vedya, as, ā, am*, to be represented or made known.
Ā-vedyamāna, as, ā, am, being made known, stated or represented.

आविदूर्य **āvidūrya, am**, n. (fr. *a-vidūra*), proximity.

आविभा **ā-vi-bhā**, cl. 2. P., Ved. *-bhāti, -tum*, to kindle on all sides (with dat. of the thing kindled, Ṛig-veda I. 71, 6).

आविर्भाव **āvir-bhāva**. See under *āvis*.

आविल **āvila, as, ā, am** (said to be fr. rt. *vil* with *ā*), turbid (as a fluid), foul, not clear. — *Āvila-kanda, as*, m., N. of a root.
Āvilaya, nom. P. *āvilayati, -yitum*, to make turbid, to blot.

आविश् **ā-viś**, cl. 6. P. *-viśati, -veshṭum*, to go towards, approach; to enter; to take possession of; to arise: Caus. *-veśayati, -yitum*, to cause to enter.
Ā-viśat, an, atī or *antī, at*, approaching, entering.
Ā-vishṭa, as, ā, am, entered; possessed (by a demon &c.); possessed, engrossed, filled (by any sentiment or feeling), intent. — *Āvishṭa-linga, as, ā, am*, (a noun) which possesses or has the force of all three genders (or which in every relationship preserves its own gender, e. g. *pradhānam, upasarjanam*, &c.).
Ā-veśa, as, m. joining one's self; entering, entrance, taking possession of; absorption of the faculties in one wish or idea, intentness, devotedness to an object; demoniacal frenzy, possession, &c.; pride, arrogance; indistinctness of idea, apoplectic or epileptic giddiness.
Ā-veśana, am, n. entering, entrance; possession by devils, &c.; passion, anger, fury; a house in which work is carried on, a workshop, a manufactory, &c.; the disk of the sun or moon.
Āveśika, as, ī, am, own, peculiar; inherent; (*as, ī, am*), m. f. n. a guest, a visitor; (*am*), n. entering into; hospitable reception, hospitality.

आविष् **ā-vish**, cl. 3. P. A., Ved. *-veveshṭi, -veveshṭe, -veshṭum*, to pervade, penetrate, visit, go through.

आविस् **āvis**, ind. (said to be connected with *vahis* and *ava*; or, according to others, fr. *ā-vid*: cf. Gr. ἐξ; Lat. *ex*?), before the eyes, openly, manifestly, evidently; (very often joined to the roots *as, bhū*, and *kṛi*.)
Āvir-bhū, cl. 1. P. *-bhavati, -vitum*, to be or become apparent or visible, to appear, become manifest, be present before the eyes. — *Āvir-bhāva, as*, m. manifestation, becoming visible, presence. — *Āvir-bhūta, as, ā, am*, manifest, become visible, appeared.
Āvish-kṛi, cl. 8. P. *-karoti, -kartum*, to make

apparent, reveal, uncover, show. — *Āvish-karaṇa, am*, n. or *āvish-kāra, as*, m. making visible, manifestation. — *Āvish-kṛita, as, ā, am*, made visible, revealed, uncovered, evident, manifest, known.

Āvishṭya, as, ā, am, Ved. apparent, manifest.

Āvis-tarām, ind., Ved. in a more manifest way.

आवी 1. *ā-vī*, cl. 2. P., Ved. *-veti, -tum*, to go towards, approach, enter.

2. *ā-vī*, f. the pangs of child-birth. (For *āvī*, f. of *ārya*, see *ārya* next col.)

Ā-vīta, as, ā, am, entered, passed, gone; placed, hung; (*as*), m. the sacrificial cord worn in a particular manner.

Āvītin, ī, m. a Brāhman who wears the sacrificial cord in a particular manner, especially on the right shoulder.

आवुक *āvuka, as*, m. a father (in theatrical language).

आवृ *ā-vṛi*, cl. 5. 9. P. A. *-vṛiṇoti, -vṛiṇute, -vṛiṇāti, -ṇīte, -varitum* or *-rītum*, to choose, desire; to cover, hide, conceal; fill, surround; to enclose, comprehend, shut, hem in; to keep off: Caus. P. *-vārayati, -yitum*, to cover, enclose, ward off, keep off.

Ā-varaka, as, ā, am, what covers or conceals, a cover, a veil.

Ā-varaṇa, as, ā, am, covering, hiding, concealing; (*am*), n. covering, concealing, hiding; shutting, enclosing; an obstruction, interruption; a covering, a garment, cloth; anything that protects, an outer bar or a fence, a wall; a shield; a bolt, lock; mental blindness. — *Āvaraṇa-śakti, is*, f. the power of illusion, that which veils the real nature of things.

Ā-vāra, enclosing, keeping off, in the words *dur-āvāra, skandhāvāra*, q. q. v. v.

Ā-vāri, is, m. a shop, a stall.

Ā-vārya, ind. having enclosed, having covered; concealing; warding off.

Ā-vṛita, as, ā, am, enclosed, encompassed, surrounded (by a ditch, wall, &c.); covered, screened, concealed; invested, involved; spread, overspread, overcast; filled with, abounding with; (*as*), m. a man of mixed origin, the son of a Brāhman by a woman of the Ugra caste.

Ā-vṛiti, is, f. covering, enclosing, hiding.

आवृज् *ā-vṛij*, cl. 1. A. *-varjate, -jitum*, to bestow, give: Caus. P. *-varjayati, -yitum*, to turn over, incline, bend, pour out, to cause to yield, overcome.

Ā-varjita, as, ā, am, inclined, poured down, made to flow downwards.

Ā-varjya, ind. turning down slantwise, inclining, pouring out.

आवृत् 1. *ā-vṛit*, cl. 1. A. *-vartate, -titum*, to turn or go towards, to turn round, turn back, revolve, return: Caus. P. *-vartayati, -yitum*, to cause to turn; to roll; to cause to roll down, shed; to attract; A. *-vartayate*, to turn round or back.

Ā-varta, as, m. turning, winding, turning round, revolving; whirl, gulf, whirlpool; deliberation, revolving (in the mind); a lock of hair that curls backwards, especially on a horse; the two depressions of the forehead above the eyebrows; a crowded place where many men live close together; a kind of jewel; N. of a form of cloud personified; (*ā*), f., N. of a river; (*am*), n. a mineral substance, pyrites, marcasite.

Ā-vartaka, as, m. a kind of poisonous insect; N. of a form of cloud personified; depression above the frontal ridge or over the eyebrows; whirlpool; revolution; revolution of the mind from the influence of the senses; a curl of hair; (*ī*), f., N. of a creeping plant.

Ā-vartana, as, ā, am, Ved. turning round or towards; revolving; (*am*), n. turning, turning round, returning; circular motion, gyration, churning, stirring anything in fusion; melting metals together, alligation; the time when the sun begins to cast shadows towards the east or when shadows are cast in an opposite direction; repeating, doing over again; study, practising; (*ī*), f. a crucible. — *Āvartana-maṇi, is*, m. a gem of secondary order, generally known as Rājāvarta.

Ā-vartanīya, as, ā, am, to be turned round or whirled; to be reversed; to be repeated.

Ā-vartamāna, as, ā, am, going round, revolving; advancing, proceeding.

Ā-vartita, as, ā, am, turned round, stirred round.

Ā-vartin, ī, inī, i, what whirls or turns upon itself; returning; (*ī*), m. a horse having curls of hair on various parts of his body, considered as a lucky mark; (*inī*), f. a whirlpool; N. of the plant Odina Pinnata.

2. *ā-vṛit, t*, f. turning towards or round, entering; (Sāy.) causing to turn towards; turn of a path or way, course, process, direction; progress of an action, occurrence, a series of actions, order, method. — *Āvṛit-vat, ān, atī, at*, Ved. turned or turning towards.

Ā-vṛitta, as, ā, am, turned round, stirred, whirled; reverted, averted; retreated, fled.

Ā-vṛitti, is, f. turning towards, entering, turning back or from, reversion, retreat, flight; recurrence to the same point; repetition; turn of a way, course, direction; occurrence; revolving, going round; worldly existence, the revolution of births; use, employment, application. — *Āvṛitti-dīpaka, am*, n. (in rhetoric) laying stress upon a word by repeating it.

Ā-vṛitya, ind. having turned, turning towards.

आवृध् *ā-vṛidh*, cl. 1. A. *-vardhate, -dhitum*, to increase.

आवृष् *ā-vṛish*, cl. 1. P. A., Ved. *-varshati, -te, -shitum*, to rain, to pour out (a libation).

Ā-vṛishṭi, is, f. raining, pouring.

आवेग *ā-vega, as*, m. (rt. *vij*), hurry, haste produced by excitement; flurry, agitation; (*ī*), f. the plant Convolvulus Argenteus.

आवेणिक *āveṇika, as, ī, am* (fr. *a-veṇi*), not connected with anything else; independant.

आवेदक, आवेदन, &c. See under 1. *ā-vid*.

आवेश *ā-veśa*, &c. See under *ā-viś*.

आवेष्ट *ā-veshṭa, as*, m. (rt. *veshṭ*), surrounding, covering with.

Ā-veshṭaka, as, m. a wall, a fence, an enclosure.

Ā-veshṭana, am, n. wrapping round, binding, tying; a wrapper, an envelope, a bandage; an enclosure.

Ā-veshṭita, as, ā, am, surrounded, enveloped, inclosed, bound or tied.

आव्य *āvya, as*, f. *āvī, am*, Ved. belonging to sheep; woollen.

आव्यध् *ā-vyadh*, cl. 4. P. *-vidhyati, -vyaddhum*, poet. *-veddhum*, to shoot at, to throw; to hit, pierce, wound; to pin on.

Ā-viddha, as, ā, am, cast, thrown, sent; pierced, wounded; disappointed; crooked; false, fallacious; stupid, foolish. — *Āviddha-karṇī* or *āviddha-karṇikā*, f., N. of a plant.

Ā-vidha, as, m. an awl, a drill, a kind of gimlet worked by a string.

Ā-vedhya, as, ā, am, to be pierced, pinned on, put on.

Ā-vyādhin, ī, inī, i, Ved. wounding, attacking; (*inī*), f. a band of robbers.

आव्युषम् *ā-vyusham* Ved., ind. till the dawn.

आव्रज् *ā-vraj*, cl. 1. P. A. *-vrajati, -te, -jitum*, to walk towards or up to; to return.

आव्रश्च् *ā-vraść*, cl. 6. P., Ved. *-vṛiśćati, -vraśćitum* or *-vrashṭum*, to tear off, cut off, tear in pieces, interrupt.

Ā-vraśćana, am, n., Ved. the stump of a tree.

Ā-vraska, as, m., Ved. the being torn off or tearing itself off.

आश् 1. *āś* (*ā-aś*), cl. 5. P. A. (Class. only A.) *āśnoti, -nute, āśitum*, to reach to; to obtain, gain; to addict one's self to.

आश् 2. *āś* (*ā-aś*), cl. 9. P. *āśnāti, āśitum*, to eat: Caus. *āśayati, -yitum*, to give to eat.

आश *āśa, as, ā, am* (fr. rt. 2. *aś*), an eater, eating; often in this sense at the end of compounds; (*as*), m. eating.

Āśaka, am, n. eating.

Āśayitṛi, tā, trī, tṛi, feeding, a feeder, one who gives food; protecting, a protector.

1. *āśi, is*, f. the act of eating food.

Āśita, as, ā, am, eaten; given to eat; voracious. — *Āśitan-gavīna, as, ā, am*, formerly grazed by cattle. — *Āśitam-bhava, as, ā, am*, satiating; (*am*), n. food, victuals; (*as* or *am*), m. n. satisfaction, satiety.

Āśitṛi, tā, trī, tṛi, voracious, gluttonous, eating excessively.

Āśin, ī, inī, i, eating.

1. *āśira, as, ā, am*, voracious; (*as*), m. fire; a Rakshas. (For 2. *āśira* see under *āśir*.)

आशंस् *ā-śaṇs*, cl. 1. P. *-śaṇsati, -situm*, to tell; A. or ep. P. *-śaṇsate*, to hope for, desire, believe: Caus. P. Ved. *-śaṇsayati, -yitum*, to render famous or celebrated.

Ā-śaṇsana, am, n. expecting, wishing; declaring, asserting.

Ā-śaṇsā, f. wish, desire, hope; speech, declaration.

Ā-śaṇsita, as, ā, am, wished, hoped, expected; declared, said.

Ā-śaṇsitṛi, tā, trī, tṛi, wishing, desiring; asserting.

Ā-śaṇsin, ī, inī, i, declaring, announcing.

Ā-śaṇsu, us, us, u, wishing, hoping, desiring.

Ā-śas, as, f., Ved. wish, desire, hope; (Say.) praise.

1. *ā-śā*, f. wish, desire, hope, expectation, prospect; hope personified as the wife of a Vasu: (for 2. *āśā* see next page.) — *Āśā-kṛita, as, ā, am*, lit. 'made expectation,' attended with the expectation (of being gratified) or hope of success. — *Āśānvita* (°*śā-an*°), *as, ā, am*, having hope. — *Āśā-piśāćikā*, f. fallacious hopes. — *Āśā-prāpta, as, ā, am*, successful, possessing the object hoped for. — *Āśā-bandha, as*, m. band of hope, confidence, trust, expectation; a spider's web. — *Āśā-bhanga, as*, m. disappointment. — *Āśā-vat, ān, atī, at*, hoping, having hope, trusting. — *Āśā-vaha, as*, m. bringing hope; N. of a son of heaven; of a Vṛishṇi. — *Āśā-vibhinna, as, ā, am*, disappointed in expectation. — *Āśā-hīna, as, ā, am*, one who has lost all hope, desponding, despairing.

आशक् *ā-śak*, cl. 5. P., Ved. *-śaknoti, -śaktum*, to render one capable, to make one master or possessor of: Desid. Ved. *-śikshati*, to render one master of, impart.

Ā-śakta, as, ā, am, able, powerful, capable.

Ā-śakti, is, f. power, ability, might.

Ā-śikshā, f., Ved. desire of learning.

आशङ्क् *ā-śaṅk*, cl. 1. A. *-śaṅkate, -kitum*, to fear, suspect, doubt, hesitate.

Ā-śaṅkanīya, as, ā, am, to be doubted; to be apprehended; questionable.

Ā-śaṅkamāna, as, ā, am, fearing, apprehending.

Ā-śaṅkā, f. fear, apprehension; doubt, uncertainty; distrust, suspicion. — *Āśaṅkānvita* (°*kā-an*°), *as, ā, am*, apprehensive, doubting, uncertain; afraid.

Ā-śaṅkita, as, ā, am, feared, dreaded; doubted.

Ā-śaṅkin, ī, inī, i, fearing, doubting, hesitating.

Ā-śaṅkya, ind. having suspected, fearing, apprehending, doubting.

आशद् *ā-śad*, cl. 6. A. *-śīyate, -śattum*, to go.

आशन *āśana, as*, m., N. of the tree Pentaptera Tomentosa. See 3. *aśana*.

आशय *āśaya*. See under 3. *ā-śī*.

आशयाश *āśayāśa*. See under *ā-śaya* below.

आशर *ā-śara, as*, m. (rt. *śrī*), fire; a Rakshas, a goblin; the wind? [cf. 1. *āśira*].

Ā-śarika, as, m., Ved., N. of a disease, violent and acute pain in the limbs.

आशल *āśala, as*, m. a tree. See *jīvaka*.

आशव *āśava, am*, n. (fr. *āśu*), speed, quickness; (for *ā-sava*, q.v.) a spirit distilled from molasses.

आशसन *ā-śasana, am*, n. (rt. *śas*), Ved. cutting up an animal when killed.

आशा 2. *āśā*, f. (fr. rt. 1. *aś*; for 1. *ā-śā* see last page under *ā-śaṅs*), space, region, quarter of the compass, an intermediate region.—*Āśā-gaja, as*, m. an elephant of a quarter or point of the compass, supporting one division of the globe.—*Āśā-dāman, ā*, m., N. of a king.—*Āśāditya* (°*śā-ād*°) or *āśārka* (°*śā-ar*°), *as*, m., N. of a commentator.—*Āśā-pāla, as*, m., Ved. a defender or guardian of the regions or quarters.—*Āśā-pura, am*, n., N. of a town.—*Āśā-pura-guggulu, us*, or *āśāpura-sambhava, as*, m. a kind of Bdellium.

आशाढ *āśāḍha* for *āshāḍha*, q.v.

आशार *ā-śāra, as*, m. (fr. rt. *śri* with *ā*), shelter.—*Āśāraishin* (°*ra-esh*°), *ī, iṇī, i*, Ved. seeking shelter.

आशास् *ā-śās*, cl. 2. P. *-śāsti, -śāsitum*, to order, command, relate; A. *-śāste*, to wish well towards, pray for; to praise; to desire.

Ā-śāsya, as, ā, am, to be wished, desirable; (*am*), n. wish, benediction.

1. *ā-śis, is*, f. asking for, prayer, wish; blessing, benediction; bestowing or praying for a blessing upon others; one of the eight chief medicaments.—*Āśir-vāda* or *āśīr-vāda, as*, m. expression of a prayer or wish, benediction.—*Āśīr-geya, am*, n. a song accompanied with benedictions.—*Āśīr-dā*, f., Ved. the offering of a prayer.—*Āśīr-vaćana, am*, n. a blessing, a benediction.

1. *ā-śī*, f. wishing or bestowing a blessing.

आशि 2. *ā-śi*, cl. 3. P., Ved. *-śiśeti, -śetum*, to incite. (For 1. *āśī* see under *āśa* last page.)

आशिक्षा *ā-śikshā*. See under *ā-śak*.

आशिञ्जित *ā-śiñjita, as, ā, am*, tinkling (as of the ornaments worn on the hands and feet).

आशित, आशिन्, आशिर. See under *āśa* last page.

आशिन *āśina, as, ā, am* (fr. 1. *aś*), Ved. aged; (reaching to many years.)

आशिमन् *āśiman*. See under *āśu* next col.

आशिर् *āśir, is*, f. (fr. rt. *śrī* for *śri* with *ā*), Ved. the milk which is mixed with the Soma juice to purify it (e.g. *dadhyāśiraḥ Somāsaḥ* = Soma offerings purified by mixture with thickened milk).—*Āśir-vat, ān, atī, at*, Ved. mixed with milk (as Soma).

2. *āśira*, a form sometimes used for *āśir*. See also under *āśa*.

आशिरःपादम् *ā-śiraḥ-pādam*, ind. from head to foot.

आशिस् 2. *āśis, is*, f. (fr. rt. 1. *aś*), a serpent's fang: (for 1. *ā-śis* see above.)—*Āśir-visha, as*, m. a snake (having venom in its fang).

2. *āśī*, f. a serpent's fang; a kind of venom, the venom of a snake.—*Āśī-visha*, see *āśīr-visha*.

आशी 3. *ā-śī*, cl. 2. A. *-śete, -śayitum*, to lie or sleep on, pass (the night) in sleep; to inhabit, have for one's home.

Ā-śaya, as, m. bed-chamber, resting-place, seat, place, an asylum, an abode or retreat; a receptacle; any recipient, any vessel or viscus of the body (e.g. *raktāśaya*, the heart; *āmāśaya*, the stomach, &c.); the stomach in particular; the seat of feelings and thoughts, the mind, heart; the thought lying in the mind, meaning, intention; disposition of mind, mode of thinking; will or pleasure; virtue, vice; fate, fortune; property, possessions; a miser, a niggard; N. of the plant Artocarpus Integrifolia.—*Āśayāśa* (°*ya-āśa*), *as*, m. fire; [cf. *āśrayāśa* under 1. *ā-śri*.]

आशु *āśu, us, us, u* (said to be fr. 1. *aś*), fast, quick, going quickly; (*u*), ind. quickly, quick, immediately, directly; (*us*), m., Ved. the quick one, a horse; (*us* or *u*), m. n. rice ripening quickly in the rainy season; [cf. Gr. ὠκύς, ὤκιστος; Lat. *acu* in *acupedeus, ōcissimus*: of the same origin may be the Lat. *aquila* and *accipiter*.]—*Āśu-kārin, ī, iṇī, i*, doing anything quickly, smart, active; (in medic.) operating speedily.—*Āśu-kopin, ī, inī, i*, easily provoked, irritable.—*Āśu-kriyā*, f. quick procedure.—*Āśu-ga, as, ā, am*, going or moving quickly, swift, fleet; (*as*), m. the wind; the sun; an arrow; N. of one of the first five followers of Śākya-muni.—*Āśu-gāmin, ī, inī, i*, going or moving quickly; (*ī*), m. an epithet of the sun.—*Āśuṅ-ga, as*, m., Ved. N. of an animal, perhaps a bird; going to the horse (?).—*Āśu-tosha, as, ā, am*, easily pleased or appeased; (*as*), m., N. of Śiva.—*Āśu-tva, am*, n. quickness.—*Āśu-pattrī*, f. a tree which yields frankincense, Boswellia Serrata.—*Āśu-patvan, ā*, m., Ved. flying quickly.—*Āśu-phala, as*, m. a kind of weapon.—*Āśu-bodha*, 'easily understood,' 'teaching quickly,' title of a grammar.—*Āśu-mat, ān, atī, at*, Ved. quick; (*at*), ind. quickly.—1. *āśu-yā, ās, ās, am*, Ved. (Sāy.) going quickly.—*Āśu-ratha, as, ā, am*, Ved. possessing a fast chariot.—*Āśu-vrīhi, is*, m. rice ripening quickly in the rainy season.—*Āśu-sheṇa, as, ā, am*, Ved. having swift arrows.—*Āśu-heman, ā*, m., Ved. urged to fast course, running on quickly; inciting his horses (as an epithet of Agni, especially when regarded as Apām-napāt).—*Āśu-heshas, ās, ās, as*, Ved. having neighing horses; (Sāy.) having quick horses or quickly praised; epithet of the Aśvins.—*Āśv-apas, ās, ās, as*, Ved. acting quickly.—*Āśv-aśva, as, ā, am*, Ved. possessed of quick horses; an epithet of the Maruts.—*Āśvaśvya, am*, n., Ved. possession of quick horses.

Āśiman, ā, m. quickness, rapidity; = *āśava*, q.v.

2. *āśuyā*, ind., Ved. quickly, rapidly.

आशुशुक्षणि *ā-śuśukshaṇi, is, is, i* (fr. rt. *śuć* with *ā*), Ved. shining forth; (Sāy.) 'being worshipped on account of shining very quickly' or 'causing sorrow (to one's enemies)'; (*is*), m. fire, wind; air.

आशेकुटिन् *āśekuṭin, ī*, m. a mountain (etymology doubtful).

आशोषण *ā-śoshaṇa, am*, n. the act of drying.

आशौच *āśauća, am*, n. (fr. *a-śući*), impurity.

आश्चर्य 1. *āśćarya, as, ā, am* (fr. rt. *ćar* with *ā*, with a sibilant inserted), appearing rarely, curious, marvellous, astonishing, wonderful, extraordinary; (*am*), ind. rarely, wonderfully; (*am*), n. strange appearance; a wonder, miracle, marvel, prodigy; wonder, surprise, astonishment.—*Āśćarya-tā*, f. or *āśćarya-tva, am*, n. wonderfulness, wonder, astonishment.—*Āśćarya-bhūta, as, ā, am*, having a marvellous appearance, wonderful.—*Āśćarya-maya, as, ī, am*, wonderful, marvellous, miraculous.

2. *āśćarya*, nom. P. (?) *-yati, -yitum*, to be wonderful.

आश्चोतन *ā-śćotana* or *ā-śćyotana, am*, n. (fr. rt. *śćut* or *śćyut* with *ā*), aspersion, sprinkling; applying ghee &c. to the eyelids.

आश्म *āśma, as, ī, am* (fr. *aśman*), stony, made of stone.—*Āśmabhārika, as, ī, am* (fr. *aśma-bhāra*), having a mass of stones.—*Āśmarathya, as*, m., N. of a teacher of ritual.

Āśmana, as, ī, am, stony, made of stone; (*as*), m., N. of Aruṇa, the charioteer of the sun.

Āśmarika, as, ī, am, suffering from stone in the bladder.

Āśmika, as, ī, am, made of stone, consisting of stone, &c.

आश्यै *ā-śyai*, cl. 1. A. *-śyāyate, -śyātum*, to become coagulated or congealed, to congeal, to become dry.

1. *ā-śyāna, as, ā, am*, consolidated, coagulated, congealed.

2. *ā-śyāna, as, ā, am* (*ā* implying diminution), partially dried.

आश्रपण *ā-śrapaṇa, am*, n. (rt. *śrī* with *ā*), the act of cooking slightly.

आश्रम *ā-śrama, as, am*, m. n. (fr. rt. *śram* with *ā*), a hermitage, the abode of ascetics, the cell of a hermit or of retired saints or sages; a period in the religious life of a Brāhman, of which there are four referable to the different periods of life (viz. 1st, that of the Brahma-ćārin or student; 2nd, that of the Gṛiha-stha or householder; 3rd, that of the Vāna-prastha or anchorite; and 4th, that of the Bhikshu or beggar: in some places the law-givers mention only three such periods of religious life, the first period being then omitted); a college, a school; a wood or thicket.—*Āśrama-guru, us*, m. the head of a religious order, a preceptor, a principal.—*Āśrama-dharma, as*, m. the special duty or duties of each order or period of life.—*Āśrama-pada, am*, n. a hermitage; a period in the religious life of a Brāhman.—*Āśrama-parvan, a*, n. the first section of the fifteenth book of the Mahā-bhārata.—*Āśrama-bhrashṭa, as, ā, am*, fallen or apostatising from an *āśrama* or religious order.—*Āśrama-maṇḍala, am*, n. the circle of a hermitage, a hermitage.—*Āśramavāsika, as, ī, am*, relating to residence in a hermitage; *āśramavāsikam parva*, title of the fifteenth book of the Mahā-bhārata.—*Āśrama-vāsin, ī*, or *āśrama-sad, t*, m. an inhabitant of a hermitage, an ascetic.—*Āśrama-sthāna, am*, n. the abode of hermits, a hermitage.—*Āśramālaya* (°*ma-āl*°), *as*, m. an inhabitant of a hermitage, an ascetic.—*Āśramopanishad* (°*ma-up*°), *t*, f. title of an Upanishad.

Āśramika, as, ī, am, or *āśramin, ī, iṇī, i*, belonging to one of the four orders or periods of religious life; belonging to a hermitage, a hermit, an anchorite, &c.

आश्रव 1. *ā-śrava, as*, m. (more correctly written *ā-srava*, q.v.), stream, flow, river; distress, fatigue; fault, transgression. (For 2. *ā-śrava* see under *ā-śru* next page.)

आश्रि 1. *ā-śri*, cl. 1. P. A. *-śrayati, -te, -yitum*, to resort to, betake one's self to; seek refuge in, enter, inhabit; depend on, choose, prefer; to assist, adhere to, be subject to, keep in mind.

Ā-śraya, as, m. that to which anything is annexed, or with which anything is closely connected, or on which anything depends or rests; a recipient, the person or thing in which any quality or article is inherent or retained or received; seat, resting-place; dwelling, asylum, place of refuge, shelter; depending on, having recourse to; help, assistance, protection; authority, sanction, warrant; a plea, an excuse; being inclined or addicted to, following, practising; attaching to, choosing, taking; joining, union, attachment; dependance, contiguity, vicinity; relation; connection; appropriate act or one consistent with the character of the agent; (in gram.) the subject, that to which the predicate is annexed; (with Buddhists) the five organs of sense with *manas* or mind (the six together being the recipients of the *āśrita* or objects which enter them by way of their *ālambana* or qualities); source, origin. *Āśraya* may occur at the end of compounds in the sense of 'depending on, resting on, endowed or furnished with' (e.g. *ashṭa-guṇāśraya*, see under *ashṭa*).—*Āśraya-tas*, ind. in consequence of the proximity.—*Āśraya-tva, am*, n. the state of *ā-śraya* above.—*Āśraya-bhuj, k*, m. fire; see *āśrayāśa*.—*Āśraya-bhūta, as, ā, am*, one who is the refuge.

or support of another person, protecting, supporting. — *Āśraya-liṅga, as, ā, am,* a word the gender of which must agree with the gender of the word to which it is referred, an adjective. — *Āśraya-vat, ān, atī, at,* having help or support. — *Āśrayāśa* (°*ya-āśa*), *as, ā, am,* consuming everything with which (it) comes in contact; (*as*), m. fire; a forfeiter of an asylum, one who by misconduct &c. loses patronage or protection.

Ā-śrayaṇa, as, ī, am, resorting to, seeking refuge in; relating to; (*am*), n. betaking one's self to; joining, accepting, choosing; refuge, asylum, means of protection or security.

Ā-śrayaṇīya, as, ā, am, to be had recourse to, to be practised or followed.

Ā-śrita, as, ā, am, inhabiting, dwelling in, resorting to as a retreat or asylum; having recourse to; following, practising, observing; using, employing; receiving anything as an inherent or integral part; taking one's station at a window or seat &c.; dependant on, a dependant; (*āni*), n. pl. the objects perceived by the senses and *manas* or mind. — *Āśrita-tva, am,* n. dependance.

Ā-śritya, ind. having sought or obtained an asylum; having recourse to, employing, practising.

आश्रि 2. *āśri, is,* f. the edge of a sword. See *aśri.*

आश्रु *ā-śru,* cl. 5. P. *-śriṇoti, -śrotum,* to listen to, to hear; to accept, promise: Caus. *-śrāvayati, -yitum,* to cause to hear, to call, to tell: Desid. *-śuśrūshati,* to wish to hear; to listen.

2. *ā-śrava, as, ā, am,* obedient, compliant; (*as*), m. a promise, an engagement. (For 1. *ā-śrava* see last page.)

Ā-śrāvaṇa, am, n. calling out so as to make one listen; designation of certain short words uttered at ceremonies.

Ā-śrāvya, as, m., N. of a man.

Ā-śruta, as, ā, am, heard, promised, agreed; (*am*), n. calling so as to make one listen.

Ā-śruti, is, f., Ved. hearing; range of hearing.

Āśrut-karṇa, as, ī, am, Ved. one whose ears listen all around.

आश्लिष् *ā-ślish,* cl. 4. P. A. *-ślishyati, -te, -śleshṭum,* to embrace.

Ā-śresha, as, m. (for *ā-ślesha*), Ved. one who embraces; N. of an evil spirit or goblin; (*ās*), f. pl., N. of the seventh Nakshatra or lunar mansion.

Ā-ślishṭa, as, ā, am, embraced; embracing, who or what embraces; connected, interwoven, blended; attaching to, joining, who or what adheres to; invested, spread; connected as a consequence, deduced, concluded.

Ā-ślesha, as, m. embracing, embrace, intwining; intimate connection, contact; site of any act; (*ās*), f. pl., N. of the seventh Nakshatra.

आश्व *āśva, as, ī, am* (fr. *aśva*), relating or belonging to a horse, equestrian, coming from a horse (e. g. *āśvam mūtram,* 'the urine of a horse'); drawn by horses (e. g. *āśvo rathaḥ,* 'a chariot drawn by horses'); (*am*), n. a number of horses, a chariot drawn by horses; the state or action of a horse. — *Āśva-ghna, as,* m., Ved., N. of a man.

Āśvatara, as, m. (fr. *aśva-tara*), patronymic of Buḍila (Bulila); a descendant of Aśvatara, son of Aśva.

Āśvattha, as, ī, am (fr. *aśvattha*), taken from or made of the tree Ficus Religiosa; relating to the fruit-bearing season of this tree; (*am*), n. the fruit of the holy fig tree.

Āśvatthika, as, ī, am, relating to or produced by the Aśvattha tree; relating to its fruit-bearing season.

Āśvapejin, inas, m. pl. (fr. *aśva-peja*), the pupils or followers of Aśva-peja.

Āśvabala, as, ī, am (fr. *aśva-balā*), produced by the plant Aśva-balā.

Āśvabāla or *āśvavāla, as, ī, am* (fr. *aśva-bāla*), made of the cane Aśva-bāla.

Āśvamedhika, as, ī, am (fr. *aśva-medha*), belonging to the horse-sacrifice; (*āśvamedhikam parva* is the N. of the fourteenth book of the Mahābhārata.)

Āśvayuja, as, ī, am (fr. *aśva-yuj*), born under the constellation Aśvayuj, belonging to or occurring in the month Āśvina; (*as*), m. the month Āśvina; (*ī*), f. the day of full moon in Āśvina.

Āśvayujaka, as, ī, am, sown at the day of full moon in the month Āśvina.

Āśvaratha, as, ī, am (fr. *aśva-ratha*), belonging to a chariot drawn by horses.

Āśvalakshaṇika, as, ī, am (fr. *aśva-lakshaṇa*), knowing the marks of horses; (*as*), m. a farrier, a groom.

Āśvāyana, as, m. (fr. *aśva* + *ayana*), a descendant of Aśva.

Āśvika, as, ī, am, equestrian, cavalier, relating to a horse, drawn by horses.

Āśvina, as, ī, am, (if fr. 1. *aśvin*) Ved. like riders; belonging to or devoted to the Aśvins; (if fr. rt. 1. *aś,* to pervade), pervading, penetrating; (*as*), m., N. of a month of the rainy season, during which the moon is near to the constellation Aśvinī; (*ī*), f., N. of certain (*ishṭakā*) bricks; (*am*), n. a day's journey for a horse or rider.

Āśvineya, as, m. (a patronymic fr. *aśvinau,* the fathers of the twins Nakula and Sahadeva), N. of Sahadeva, the youngest of the Pāṇḍava princes; (fr. their mother *Aśvinī*), an epithet of either of the two Aśvins.

Āśvīna, as, ī, am, passed over by a horse in one day; (*am*), n. a day's journey for a horse.

Āśvīya, am, n. a number of horses.

Āśreya, as, m. a patronymic from Aśva.

आश्वपस् *āśv-apas,* &c. See under *āśu.*

आश्वलायन *āśvalāyana, as,* m. (patronymic fr. *aśvala*), N. of the author of a ritual work, called the Āśvalāyana Sūtras; he was a disciple of Śaunaka; (*as, ī, am*), belonging to Āśvalāyana.

आश्वस् *ā-śvas,* cl. 2. P. *-śvasiti, -situm,* to breathe, breathe again, breathe freely, take breath, recover breath, take heart or courage; to revive: Caus. P. *-śvāsayati, -yitum,* to cause one to take breath; to encourage, comfort, cheer up; to conciliate.

Ā-śvasat, an, atī, at, taking breath, breathing anew; reviving; recovering.

Ā-śvasita, as, ā, am, encouraged, cheered, consoled.

Ā-śvāsa, as, m. breathing again, taking breath, breathing freely, recovery; cheering up, consolation; a chapter or section, the division of a book; a probable story; cessation, completion.

Ā-śvāsaka, as, ikā, am, consolatory, consoling, comforting; (*as*), m. clothing.

Ā-śvāsana, am, n. making or letting one take breath, consoling, encouraging, reviving; cheering up.

Ā-śvāsayat, an, antī, at, encouraging, animating.

Ā-śvāsita, as, ā, am, encouraged, animated, comforted, consoled.

Ā-śvāsin, ī, inī, i, breathing freely, reviving, becoming cheerful; consoling.

Ā-śvāsya, ind. having consoled, having cherished; having recovered or revived.

आषाढ *āshāḍha, as,* m. (fr. *a-shāḍhā*), N. of a month, corresponding to part of June and July, in which the full moon is near the constellation Ashāḍhā; a staff of the wood of the Palāśa, carried by an ascetic during certain vows in the month Āshāḍha; N. of a prince; the Malaya mountain; (*ā*), f. the twenty-first and twenty-second lunar mansions, commonly compounded with *pūrva* and *uttara*; (*ī*), f. the day of full moon in the month Āshāḍha. — *Āshāḍha-bhava, as, ā, am,* produced in the month Āshāḍha; (*as*), m. the planet Mars. — *Āshāḍha-bhūti, is,* m., N. of a man. — *Āshāḍhā-bhū, ūs,* m. produced in the month Āshāḍha; the planet Mars.

Āshāḍhaka, as, m. the month Āshāḍha; N. of a man.

Āshāḍhikā, f., N. of a Rākshasī.

Āshāḍhīya, as, ā, am, born under the constellation Ashāḍhā.

आष्टक *āshṭaka,* N. of a region.

आष्टम *āshṭama, as,* m. (fr. *ashṭama*), the eighth part.

आष्ट्र *āshṭra, am,* n. (fr. rt. 1. *aś*), ether, sky, atmosphere.

आष्ट्री *āshṭrī,* f., Ved. kitchen, fire-place; (if fr. rt. 1. *aś,* according to Sāy.) an extensive forest.

आष्ठा *āshṭhā,* f. [cf. 2. *āśā*], region, quarter.

आस् 1. *ās,* ind. (an interjection implying joy, anger, menace, pain, affliction, recollection) Ah! Oh! &c.

आस् 2. *ās* (*ā-as*), cl. 4. P., Ved. *āsyati, -situm,* to enclose, border; to admit (as water) into.

3. *ās* (fr. 2. *ās* above? or fr. rt. 2. *as*; cf. Lat. *os*), mouth, face; only used in two forms, as follows: *āsas,* abl., Ved. from mouth to mouth, in close proximity; *āsā,* inst., Ved. before one's eyes; by word of mouth, personally; present; in one's own person; immediately. — *Ās-pātra, am,* n., Ved. a vessel which is as it were the mouth of the gods.

आस् 4. *ās,* cl. 2. A. *āste* (Ved. and poet. also cl. 1. A. *āsate*), *āsāñ-cakre, āsishyate, āsishṭa, -situm,* to sit, sit down, rest, lie; to be present, to exist, to inhabit, dwell in; to make one's abode in; to sit quietly, abide, remain, continue; to cease, have an end; to solemnize, celebrate; to do anything without interruption, to continue doing anything, to continue in any situation, to last. It is used in the sense of 'continuing,' with a participle, adj., or subst. (e. g. *etat sāma gāyann āste,* 'he continues singing this verse'); with an indeclinable participle in *tvā, ya,* or *am* (e. g. *uparudhya arim āsīta,* 'he should continue blockading the foe'); with an adverb (e. g. *tūshṇīm āste,* 'he continues quiet;' *sukham āsva,* 'continue well'); with an inst. case (e. g. *sukhena āste,* 'he continues well'); with a dat. case (e. g. *āstāṃ tushṭaye,* 'may it be to your satisfaction'): Caus. *āsayati, -yitum,* to cause any one to sit down: Desid. *āsisishate*; [cf. Gr. ἧ(σ)-μαι, ἧσ-ται: Lat. *āsa* changed to *āra*; *ā-nus* for *ās-nus.*]

1. *āsa,* seat (e. g. in the compound *svāsa-stha,* 'staying in one's own seat'); (*am*), n. the seat or lower part of the body; proximity.

1. *āsana, am,* n. sitting, sitting down; sitting in peculiar postures, according to the custom of devotees, (five or, in other places, even eighty-four postures are enumerated; see *padmāsana, bhadrāsana, vajrāsana, vīrāsana, svastikāsana*: the manner of sitting forming part of the eight-fold observances of ascetics); halting, stopping, encamping; abiding, dwelling; seat, place, stool; the withers of an elephant, the part where the driver sits; maintaining a post against an enemy; (*ā*), f. stay, abiding; (*ī*), f. stay, abiding, sitting; a shop, a stall; a small seat, a stool.

Āsita, as, ā, am, seated, at rest, one who has sat down, one who is seated or dwells; (*am*), n. sitting, sitting down; a seat; place where one has lived, place of abode, a city; *dur-āsitam,* an improper way of sitting.

Āsīna, as, ā, am, sitting, seated. — *Āsīna-pracalāyita, am,* n. nodding, nodding when seated, falling asleep.

Āsyā, f. sitting, abiding, abode, state of rest.

आस् 5. *ās* (*ā-ās*), cl. 2. P., Ved. *āste, -situm,* to sit down upon.

आस 2. *āsa, as,* m. (fr. rt. 2. *as,* to throw),

Ved. ashes, dust which easily flies away; (*as, am*), m. n. a bow. (For 1. *āsa* see under 4. *ās.*)

2. *āsana, am,* n. throwing; (*as*), m., N. of a tree. See *asana.*

आसंसार *ā-saṃsāra, as, ā, am* (rt. *sṛi*), liable to continuous flow, progress or alteration; (*am*), ind. as long as the world goes on, till the end of the world.

आसङ्गत्य *āsaṅgatya, am,* n. (fr. *a-saṅgata*), detachment, disunion.

आसञ्ज् *ā-sañj,* cl. 1. P. *-sajati, -sanktum,* to fasten on, attach, fix; to fasten on one's self, put on (as dress, armour, &c.); to take up: Caus. *-sañjayati, -yitum,* to cause to attach, have (anything) fastened or put on: Pass. *-sajyate,* to adhere, cohere, to be attached.

Ā-sakta, as, ā, am, attached strongly to or intent on; zealously following or pursuing; trusting to, confiding in, eternal; (*am*), ind. eternally.— *Āsakta-ćitta, as, ā, am,* having the mind deeply engaged in, intent on, devoted to, absorbed in.— *Āsakta-ćetas, ās, ās, as,* having the mind fixed or intent on any object.— *Āsakta-manas, ās, ās, as,* having the mind fixed upon any object.

Ā-sakti, is, f. devotedness or attachment (as to one object or pursuit), diligence, application; Ved. lying wait for, way-laying; (*i*), ind., Ved. purposely, intentionally.

Ā-saṅga, as, m. fastening to, fixing; association, connection; attachment to any object; proximity, contact; Ved. way-laying; N. of a man; (*am*), n. a kind of fragrant earth; (*as, ā, am*), uninterrupted, eternal; (*am*), ind. without interruption; eternally.

Ā-saṅginī, f. a whirlwind.

Āsaṅgima, as, m. (in surgery) a kind of bandage.

Ā-sañjana, am, n., Ved. putting on (dress, armour, ornaments, &c.); fastening to, fixing; a handle, a hook.— *Āsañjana-vat, ān, atī, at,* having a handle, hook, loop, &c.

आसद् *ā-sad,* cl. 1. P. *-sīdati, -sattum,* to sit down, sit near; to place; to approach, meet with, find; encounter, attack, commence, undertake; cl. 10. P. *-sādayati, -yitum,* to approach, meet with, find; encounter, attack; commence, undertake; Ved. to make one sit down.

Ā-satti, is, f. intimate union, meeting, junction; gain, profit, acquirement; (in logic) connection or relation between two or more proximate terms and the sense they convey.

Ā-sadana, am, n. the act of sitting down; a seat.

Ā-sanna, as, ā, am, near, proximate; (*as*), m. the setting sun.— *Āsanna-kāla, as,* m. the hour of death; one whose last hour is at hand.— *Āsanna-tara, as, ā, am,* nearer.— *Āsannatara-tā,* f. greater nearness.— *Āsanna-prasava, as, ā, am,* near parturition, about to bring forth or to lay eggs.

Ā-sāda, as, m., Ved. a cushion.

Ā-sādana, am, n. putting or laying down; attacking, making war upon; going to or towards; meeting with; obtaining, attaining; accomplishing.

Ā-sādayitavya, as, ā, am, to be attacked, to be encountered; attainable.

Ā-sādita, as, ā, am, obtained, acquired, gained, reached, gone to; spread, extended, overspread; effected, completed; met with, attacked.

1. *ā-sādya, as, ā, am,* attainable, obtainable.

2. *ā-sādya,* ind. having attained or reached; having obtained, according to.

Ā-sisādayishu, us, us, u, about to attack; wishing to attack.

आसन् *āsan,* n. [cf. 2. *ās* and *āsya*], Ved. the mouth, the jaws; (this word occurs in inst., dat., abl., loc. sing., and inst. plur.)— *Āsann-ishu, us, us, u,* Ved. one who has arrows in his mouth.

Āsanya, as, ā, am, Ved. being in the mouth.

आसन *āsana.* See under 4. *ās* and 2. *āsa.*

आसन्द *āsanda, as,* m. (fr. rt. *sad* with *ā?*), an epithet of Vishṇu; (*ī*), f. a small couch or oblong chair, the seat of which is made of basket work; a chair, arm-chair.— *Āsandī-vat, ān,* m., N. of a country.

आसन्वत् *āsanvat, ān, atī, at* (fr. rt. 1. *as?*), Ved. what exists or is present (?).

आसमुद्रात् *ā-samudrāt,* ind. as far as the ocean.

आसम्बाध *ā-sambādha, as, ā, am,* blocked up, obstructed, confined.

आसया *āsayā,* ind. (irreg. inst. case fr. 3. *ās,* q. v.), Ved. together with, from mouth to mouth, near to, in the presence of.

आसव *ā-sava.* See under *ā-su.*

आसात् *āsāt,* ind. (fr. 1. *āsa*), Ved. from or in the proximity, near.

आसाधन *ā-sādhana, am,* n. (rt. 1. *sidh*), accomplishment, attainment.

1. *ā-siddha, as, ā, am,* accomplished, effected. (For 2. *ā-siddha* see below.)

आसार *ā-sāra, as,* m. (rt. *sṛi*), surrounding an enemy; incursion; attack; a hard shower; the army of an ally or of a king, whose dominions are separated by other intervening states; provision, food.

आसाव्य *ā-sāvya.* See under 2. *ā-su.*

आसिक *āsika, as,* m. (fr. *asi*), a swordsman.

आसिका *āsikā,* f. (fr. rt. 4. *ās*), turn or order of sitting; sitting; (*as, ā, am*), one who sits.

आसिच् 1. *ā-sić,* cl. 6. P. *-sinćati, -sektum,* to pour in or on, besprinkle, wet, water: Caus. *-sećayati, -yitum,* to have (anything) poured in.

Ā-sikta, as, ā, am, poured in or on; sprinkled.

2. *ā-sić, k,* f., Ved. a dish, vessel; (Say.) an oblation which is poured out.

Ā-seka, as, m. wetting, sprinkling, pouring in.

Ā-sećana, am, n. the act of pouring into, wetting, sprinkling; Ved. a reservoir or vessel for fluids; (*as, ī, am*), charming, lovely, beloved [cf. *a-sećana,* for which it may be a substitute].— *Āsećana-vat, ān, atī, at,* containing a reservoir or cavity, hollow, concave.

Āsećanaka, as, ā, am (?), beloved, desired, charming [cf. *a-sećana*].

आसिद्ध 2. *ā-siddha, as, ā, am* (rt. 2. *sidh*), put under restraint, imprisoned. (For 1. see above.)

Ā-seddhṛi, dhā, m. one who confines or arrests another.

Ā-sedha, as, m. arrest, custody, legal restraint of four kinds, viz. *kālāsedha,* limitation of time; *sthānāsedha,* confinement to a place; *pravāsāsedha,* prohibition against removal or departure; *karmāsedha,* restriction from employment.

Ā-sedhaka, as, ā, am, restraining, confining.

Ā-sedhanīya or *ā-sedhya, as, ā, am,* to be placed in custody, restrained; confined, prohibited, interrupted.

आसु 1. *ā-su,* cl. 5. P., Ved. *-sunoti, -sotum,* to press out Soma juice, to distil.

1. *ā-sava, as,* m. distilling, distillation; decoction; rum, spirit distilled from sugar or molasses, spirituous liquor in general: (for 2. *ā-sava* see next col.)— *Āsava-dru, us,* m., N. of the Palmyra tree, Borassus Flabelliformis; (its juice on fermenting affording a spirituous liquor.)

Ā-sāva, as, m., Ved. one who presses out the Soma juice; (Say.) a praiser (?).

1. *ā-suti, is,* f. distilling; decoction; a draught so prepared; distillation: (for 2. *ā-suti* see next col.)— *Āsutī-vala, as,* m. a sacrificing priest; a sacrificer at the full and change of the moon; one who prepares or sells spirituous liquors, a distiller; one who sells female slaves (?).

आसु 2. *ā-su,* cl. 2. P., Ved. *-sauti, -sotum,* to bring forth, excite.

2. *ā-suva, as,* m., Ved. exciting, enlivening.

Ā-savitṛi, tā, trī, tṛi, Ved. exciting, an exciter.

Ā-sāvya, as, ā, am, to be born.

2. *ā-suti, is,* f., Ved. exciting, enlivening.

आसुर *āsura, as, ī, am* (fr. *asura*), spiritual, divine; belonging to or devoted to evil spirits; belonging or relating to the Asuras; infernal, demoniacal; (*as*), m. an Asura or demon; a form of marriage in which the bridegroom purchases the bride from her father and paternal kinsmen; (*ās*), m. pl. the stars of the southern hemisphere; a prince of the warrior-tribe Asura; (*ī*), f. a division of medicine, surgery, curing by cutting with instruments, applying the actual cautery; N. of the plant Sinapis Ramosa; (*am*), n. blood; black salt.

Āsurāyaṇa, as, m., N. of a teacher.

Āsuri, is, m. (patron. fr. *asura*), N. of a teacher.— *Āsuri-vāsin, ī,* m. an epithet of Prāśnīputra.

Āsurīya, as, ā, am, belonging to or coming from Āsuri.

आसू *ā-sū,* cl. 6. P., Ved. *-suvati, -savitum,* to bring or send quickly, yield, grant.

आसूत्रित *ā-sūtrita, as, ā, am,* tied on or round, forming or wearing a garland.

आसृज् *ā-sṛij,* cl. 6. P., Ved. *-sṛijati, -srashṭum,* to pour out upon, pour in.

आसेध *ā-sedha.* See 2. *ā-siddha* last col.

आसेव् *ā-sev,* cl. 1. A. or poet. P. *-sevate, -ti, -vitum,* to attend to, accomplish; carry out, practice, perform assiduously; to indulge in, enjoy.

Ā-sevana, am, n. assiduous practice or performance of any action.

Ā-sevā, f. zealous cultivation of any pursuit; commerce, intercourse.

Ā-sevin, ī, inī, i, performing assiduously, acting.

आस्कन्द् *ā-skand,* cl. 1. P. *-skandati, -skantum,* to invade, attack.

Ā-skanda, as, m. ascending, mounting; assault, attack; an assailant.

Ā-skandana, am, n. going towards, assailing, attack; battle, war; reproach, abuse; effacing, destroying; drying (?).

Ā-skandita or *ā-skanditaka, am,* n. the walk of an horse.

Ā-skandin, ī, inī, i, jumping upon, assailing; causing to flow; granting.

आस्कु *ā-sku,* cl. 5. P., Ved. *-skunoti, -skotum,* to snatch up.

आस्क्र *ā-skra, as, ā, am* (fr. *skṛi* = rt. *kṛi?*), Ved. joined, united; (Say.) attacking, assailing enemies, approaching.

आस्तर, आस्तरण, &c. See under *ā-stṛi.*

आस्ताव *ā-stāva, as,* m. (rt. *stu*), Ved. the place of reciting a particular hymn.

आस्तिक *āstika, as, ī, am* (fr. *asti,* 3rd pers. sing. of rt. 1. *as*), a believer in sacred tradition; one who believes in God and another world; believing, pious, faithful; (*as*), m., N. of a Muni or saint, more correctly written *āstīka,* q. v.— *Āstika-tā,* f. or *āstika-tva, am,* n. belief in God.

Āstikārthada or *āstīkārthada* (°*ka-artha-da*), *as,* m. an epithet of king Janam-ejaya (who granted the request of the sage Āstīka, and spared the Nāga Takshaka from the destruction to which he had doomed the serpent-race).

Āstikya, am, n. belief in God, piety, faithfulness, a believing nature or disposition.

Āstīka, as, m., N. of an old saint, the son of Jarat-kāru; (*as, ī, am*), relating to or treating of that saint; *āstīkam parva,* a section of the first book of the Mahā-bhārata. — *Āstīka-jananī*, f. the wife of Jarat-kāru and mother of Āstīka.

Āstīkya, *am*, n. (? error for *āstikya*), belief.

आस्तृ *ā-stṛi* or *ā-stṛī*, cl. 5. 9. P. A. *-stṛiṇoti*, *-ṇute*, *-ṇāti*, *-ṇīte*, *-startum*, *-ritum*, *-rītum*, to spread (as a carpet &c.), deck, bestrew, scatter over, cover.

Ā-stara, *as*, m. a covering, coverlet, blanket thrown over the back of a horse or elephant; a carpet, bed; spreading (clothes &c.); N. of a man.

Ā-staraṇa, *am*, *ī*, n. f. the act of spreading; a carpet, a rug, a cushion, a quilt, bed-clothes; a bed; a layer of sacred grass spread out at a sacrifice; an elephant's housings, a painted cloth or blanket worn on his back. — *Āstaraṇa-vat*, *ān*, *atī*, *at*, covered with a cloth or carpet.

Āstaraṇika, *as*, *ā*, *am*, resting on a cloth or carpet.

Ā-stāra, *as*, m. spreading, strewing, scattering. — *Āstāra-paṅkti*, *is*, f., N. of a metre, the first verse of which consists of two Pādas of eight syllables each, the second of two Pādas of twelve syllables each.

Ā-stīrṇa, *as*, *ā*, *am*, spread, strewed, scattered.

Ā-stṛita, *as*, *ā*, *am*, spread, covered, strewed.

आस्त्रबुध्न *āstrabudhna*, *as*, m., Ved., N. of a man.

आस्था 1. *ā-sthā*, cl. 1. P. or poet. A. *-tishṭhati*, *-te*, *-sthātum*, to stand or remain on or by; to stay near, go towards, resort to; to ascend, mount; to undertake, perform, do, carry out, practise, use; to behave; to exhibit, aim at; to undertake, i. e. promise.

2. *ā-sthā*, f. consideration, regard, care, care for (with loc., e. g. *mayi āsthā*, care for me); assent, promise; confidence, hope; prop, stay, support; place or means of abiding; an assembly; state, condition.

Ā-sthātṛi, *tā*, *trī*, *tṛi*, Ved. standing on, mounting on.

Ā-sthāna, *am*, n. place, site, ground, base; an assembly; a hall of audience; (*ī*), f. an assembly. — *Āsthāna-gṛiha*, *am*, n. an assembly-room.

Ā-sthāpana, *am*, n. placing, fixing, causing to stay or remain; a strengthening remedy; an enema of oil, ghee, &c.

Ā-sthāpita, *as*, *ā*, *am*, placed, fixed, &c.

Ā-sthāya, ind. having recourse to, using, employing; having ascended; standing, standing by.

Ā-sthāyikā, f. audience; (e. g. *āsthāyikām dā*, to give an audience.)

Ā-sthita, *as*, *ā*, *am*, stayed, dwelt, abiding, abode; having recourse to; applied to; occupied, engrossed by, engaged in; spread, overspread; obtained; observing, adhering to, following, practising.

Ā-stheya, *as*, *ā*, *am*, to be approached, to be seized, to be applied or practised.

आस्नान *ā-snāna*, *am*, n. (rt. *snā*), Ved. water for washing, a bath.

आस्नेय *āsneya*, *as*, *ā*, *am* (fr. *asan*), Ved. bloody, being in blood.

आस्पद *āspada*, *am*, n. (fr. *pada* with *ā* prefixed, *s* being inserted), place, site, seat, office; rank, station; dignity, authority; business, affair. Often used in comp.; e. g. *ahankārāspadam*, the seat of consciousness.

आस्पन्दन *ā-spandana*, *am*, n. trembling, throbbing.

आस्पर्धा *ā-spardhā*, f. emulation, rivalry, endeavour after.

Ā-spardhin, *ī*, *inī*, *i*, emulous, striving after.

आस्पर्श *ā-sparśa*, *as*, m. (rt. *spṛiś*), contact; *āsparśa-tas*, by the contact.

आस्पात्र *ās-pātra*. See 3. *ās*.

आस्फल् *ā-sphal* or *ā-sphul*, Caus. *-sphālayati*, *-yitum*, to cause to flap, rock or shake.

Ā-sphāla, *as*, m. striking, rubbing, causing to move gently; flapping, clapping; the flapping motion of an elephant's ear.

Ā-sphālana, *am*, n. rubbing, stirring, flapping, moving gently; striking; pride, arrogance.

Ā-sphālita, *as*, *ā*, *am*, struck gently, rubbed, touched, stirred; flapped, clapped, struck together.

आस्फाय् *ā-sphāy*, cl. 1. A. *-sphāyate*, *-yitum*, to grow, increase.

आस्फुजित् *āsphujit* = Ἀφροδίτη, N. of the planet Venus.

आस्फुल् *ā-sphul*. See *ā-sphal* above.

आस्फोट *ā-sphoṭa*, *as*, m. (rt. *sphuṭ*), moving or flapping to and fro, quivering, trembling, shaking, the sound of clapping or striking on the arms as made by combatants, wrestlers, &c.; a plant, see *ā-sphota*; (*ā*), f. a wild variety of Jasmin.

Ā-sphoṭaka, *as*, m., the plant Careya Arborea.

Ā-sphoṭana, *am*, n. moving to and fro, flapping, trembling; shaking; blowing, expanding; contracting, closing, sealing; slapping or clapping the arms, or the noise made by it; (*ī*), f. a gimlet or auger.

Ā-sphota or *ā-sphotaka*, *as*, m. (probably an incorrect form of *ā-sphoṭa*), N. of several plants, Calotropis Gigantea, Bahinia Variegata L., Echites Dichotoma Roxb.; (*ā*), f., N. of several plants, Jasminum Sambac, Clitoria Terneata, Echites Frutescens or Echites Dichotoma.

आस्माक *āsmāka*, *as*, *ī*, *am*, or *āsmākīna*, *as*, *ā*, *am* (fr. *asmākam*), our, ours.

आस्य *āsya*, *am*, n. (see 3. *ās*), mouth, jaws; face; a part of the mouth as the organ of pronouncing letters; mouth, opening; (*as*, *ā*, *am*), belonging or relating to the mouth or face. — *Āsyandhaya*, *as*, *ī*, *am*, drinking the mouth, kissing. — *Āsya-pattra*, *am*, n. a lotus. — *Āsya-lāṅgala*, *as*, m. 'whose face is a plough;' a hog, a boar. — *Āsya-loman*, *a*, n. the hair of the face, the beard. — *Āsyāsara* (°*ya-ās*°), *as*, m. spittle, saliva.

आस्यन्दन *ā-syandana*, *am*, n. flowing near. — *Āsyandana-vat*, *ān*, *atī*, *at*, flowing near.

आस्यहात्य *āsyahātya*, *as*, *ā*, *am*, containing the word *asyahatya* (a chapter).

आस्या *āsyā*, f. See under 4. *ās*.

आस्रप *āsrapa*, *as*, m. (fr. *asra-pa*), the nineteenth lunar mansion.

आस्रव *ā-srava*, *as*, m. (fr. rt. *sru* with prep. *ā*), the foam on boiling rice; flowing, running, discharge; distress, pain, affliction; (with Jainas) that which directs the embodied spirit towards eternal objects, (viz. the occupation or employment of the senses or organs on sensible objects; or the association or connection of body with right and wrong deeds.)

Ā-srāva, *as*, m. flow, issue, running, discharge; pain, affliction; a disease of the body. — *Āsrāva-bheshaja*, *am*, n., Ved. a medicament, medicine.

Āsrāvin, *ī*, *iṇī*, *i*, flowing, emitting fluid, discharging humor; an epithet of the elephant (a fluid issuing from its temples during the rutting-time).

आस्रस्त *ā-srasta*, *as*, *ā*, *am*, fallen off, loose.

आस्वद् *ā-svad* or *-svād*, cl. 1. A. *-svadate* or *-svādate*, *-ditum*, to taste, eat.

Ā-svāda, *as*, *ā*, *am*, tasting, eating; (*as*), m. tasting, enjoying, eating; flavour. — *Āsvāda-vat*, *ān*, *atī*, *at*, having a good taste, palatable; delicious in flavour.

Ā-svādaka, *as*, *ikā*, *am*, tasting, enjoying.

Ā-svādana, *am*, n. tasting, enjoying, eating.

Ā-svādita, *as*, *ā*, *am*, tasted, enjoyed, possessed; eaten.

Ā-svādya, *as*, *ā*, *am*, to be tasted or enjoyed, to be eaten; having a good taste, palatable, delicious. — *Āsvādya-toya*, *as*, *ā*, *am*, having sweet or palatable water.

आस्वन् *ā-svan*, cl. 1. P. *-svanati*, *-nitum*, to sound.

Ā-svanita or *ā-svānta*, *as*, *ā*, *am*, sounded.

आह 1. *āha*, ind. (an interjection implying reproof, severity, command, casting, sending) Ah! Aha! &c.

आह 2. *āha*. See rt. 3. *ah*.

आहक *āhaka*, *as*, m. a peculiar disease of the nose, inflammation of the Schneiderian membrane.

आहङ्कार्य *āhankārya*, *am*, n. (fr. *ahan-kāra*), conceitedness.

आहन् *ā-han*, cl. 2. P. A. *-hanti*, *-hate*, *-hantum*, to strike at, hit, beat, kill; commit slaughter.

Ā-hata, *as*, *ā*, *am*, struck, beaten; injured, killed; multiplied; known, understood; uttered falsely; (*as*), m. a drum; (*am*), n. old cloth or raiment; new cloth or clothes; assertion of an impossibility. — *Āhata-lakshaṇa*, *as*, *ā*, *am*, noted for good qualities.

Ā-hati, *is*, f. hitting, striking, a blow, a hit; killing.

Ā-hanana, *am*, n. the act of striking at, beating; killing of an animal.

Āhananya, *as*, *ā*, *am*, Ved. making one's self known by beating (a drum &c.).

आहनस् *āhanas*, *ās*, *ās*, *as* (fr. rt. *han*?), Ved. swelling, tumid, crammed full; fat, luxuriant, lascivious; (Sāy.) to be beaten or pressed out (as Soma).

Āhanasya, *am*, n., Ved. luxuriancy, lasciviousness; (*ās*), f. pl. verses (*ṛićas*) of a lascivious character. — *Āhanasya-vādin*, *ī*, *inī*, *i*, Ved. uttering lascivious words.

आहलक् *āhalak*, ind., Ved. a smacking sound.

आहव, आहवन, आह्व, &c. See under *ā-hu* and *ā-hve*.

आहिक *āhika*, *as*, m. (fr. *ahi*), the descending node; an epithet of the grammarian Pāṇini.

आहिकम् *āhikam*, a particle = *ā hi kam* (?).

आहिण्ड् *ā-hiṇḍ*, cl. 1. A. *-hiṇḍate*, *-ḍitum*, to roam about.

आहिण्डिक *āhiṇḍika*, *as*, m. a man of mixed origin, the son of a Nishāda father and a Vaidehī mother, employed as a watchman on the outside of gaols &c.

आहित *ā-hita*, *as*, *ā*, *am* (fr. rt. *dhā* with prep. *ā*), placed, deposited; entertained, felt; comprising, containing; performed, done. — *Āhita-klama*, *as*, *ā*, *am*, exhausted. — *Āhita-lakshaṇa*, *as*, *ā*, *am*, noted or known for good qualities; [cf. *āhata-lakshaṇa*.] — *Āhita-vyatha*, *as*, *ā*, *am*, pained, grieved. — *Āhita-svana*, *as*, *ā*, *am*, uttering or making a sound, noisy. — *Āhitāgni* (°*ta-ag*°), *is*, *is*, *i*, one who has placed the sacred fire upon the altar, a sacrificer; a Brāhman who has kept alive a sacred fire perpetually in a family &c. — *Āhitāṅka* (°*ta-aṅ*°), *as*, *ā*, *am*, marked, spotted, stained.

Ā-hiti, *is*, f., Ved. placing on; anything placed on.

आहितुण्डिक *āhituṇḍika* or *ahituṇḍika*, *as*, m. (fr. *ahi-tuṇḍa*), a snake-catcher, a juggler.

आहीरणिन् *āhīraṇin*, *ī*, m. a two-headed snake.

आहु *ā-hu*, cl. 3. P. A. *-juhoti*, *-juhute*, *-hotum*, to sacrifice, to offer an oblation, to worship.

1. *ā-hava*, *as*, m. sacrificing, sacrifice. (For 2. *ā-hava* see under *ā-hve*.)

Ā-havana, am, n., Ved. offering an oblation, offering sacrifice, sacrifice.

Ā-havanīya, as, ā, am, to be offered as an oblation; (*as*), m. a consecrated fire taken from the householder's perpetual fire and prepared for receiving oblations; the eastern of the three fires burning at a sacrifice.

Āhavanīyaka, as, ā, am, fit for a burnt offering; (*as*), m. a consecrated fire.

1. *ā-hāva, as*, m., Ved. a trough, a pail, a vessel; a trough near a well for watering cattle.

Ā-huta, am, n. an offering made to men, hospitality; the nourishment of all created beings considered as one of the five sacraments or principal sacrifices of the Hindūs.

1. *ā-huti, is*, f. offering oblations with fire to the deities; any solemn rite accompanied with oblations: (for 2. *ā-huti* see under *ā-hve*.) — *Āhuti-vṛidh, t, t, t*, Ved. delighting in sacrifices.

आहुक **āhuka, as**, m., N. of a prince, great-grandfather of Kṛishṇa, a son or grandson of Abhijit; (*ī*), f. a sister of this prince; (*ās*), m. pl., N. of a people.

आहुल्य **āhulya, am**, n., N. of the leguminous shrub Tabernæmontana Coronaria.

आहृ **ā-hṛi**, cl. 1. P. A. *-harati, -te, -hartum*, to fetch, bring, bring near, give; to recover, bring back; to get, take; to offer in sacrifice: Caus. P. *-hārayati, -yitum*, to make one pay or give or fetch or bring; to exact; to exert, exhibit: Desid. A. *-jihīrshate*, to seek to recover or get back.

Ā-hara, as, ā, am, (at the end of compounds) bringing, fetching; (*as*), m. taking, seizing; accomplishing, offering of a sacrifice; drawing in breath, inhaling, inhaled air; breath inspired, inspiration.

Ā-haraṇa, as, ā, am, taking away, robbing; (*am*), n. taking, seizing, bringing near; extracting, removing; accomplishing, offering at a sacrifice; causing, inducing.

Āharaṇī-kṛi, cl. 8. P. *-karoti, -kartum*, to give as a present.

Ā-hartṛi, tā, trī, tṛi, one who takes, seizes, brings or procures; inducing, causing; offering; (*tā*), m. a copy holder (in law).

Ā-hāra, as, ā or *ī, am*, bringing near, procuring; going to fetch; (*as*), m. taking, fetching, bringing near; employing; taking food, food (e. g. *āhāram kṛi*, to take food, eat). — *Āhāra-viraha, as*, m. want of food. — *Āhāra-sambhava, as*, m. the juice of the body, chyle, lymph, serum. — *Āhārārthin* (°*ra-ar*°), *ī, inī, i*, begging or seeking for food.

Ā-hāraka, as, ā, am, going to fetch.

Ā-hārika, (with Jainas) one of the five bodies belonging to the soul; described by Colebrooke as a minute form, issuing from the head of a meditative sage to consult an omniscient saint and returning with the desired information.

Ā-hārya, as, ā, am, to be taken or seized; to be fetched or brought near; to be extracted or removed; what may be removed, adventitious, accessary, incidental; to be eaten; (*as*), m. a kind of bandage; (*am*), n. any disease to be treated by the operation of extracting; extraction; a vessel; the ornamentative part of the drama, the dress, decorations, &c. — *Āhārya-śobhā*, f. adventitious beauty, beauty not natural but the effect of paints, ornaments, &c.

Ā-hṛita, as, ā, am, brought, taken, collected. — *Āhṛita-yajña-kratu, us, us, u*, Ved. intending (to offer) a prepared sacrifice; preparing a sacrificial act (?).

Ā-hṛitya, ind. having taken or received, having brought.

आहेय **āheya, as, ī, am** (fr. *ahi*), belonging or relating to a snake.

आहो **āho**, ind. (an interjection of doubt and of asking) or, or perhaps. — *Āho-purushikā*, f. great self-conceit, boasting, military vaunting; a vain determination to accomplish an object, vaunting of one's power. — *Āho-svit*, ind. a particle implying doubt.

आह्न **āhna, as, am**, m. n. (fr. *ahan*), a series of days, many days.

Āhnika, as, ī, am, daily, diurnal, performed on a day, performed every day; (*am*), n. a religious ceremony to be performed every day at a fixed hour; a day's work, what may be read on one day, the division or section of a book; constant occupation, daily work; daily food, &c. — *Āhnikāćāra* (°*ka-āć*°), *as*, m. daily observance, the prayers and practices necessary for bodily and mental purification.

Āhneya, as, m. a patronymic of Sauća.

आह्लाद् **ā-hlād**, Caus. P. *-hlādayati, -yitum*, to gladden.

Ā-hlāda, as, m. joy, delight. — *Āhlāda-dugha, as, ā, am*, conferring delight.

Ā-hlādana, am, n. gladdening.

Ā-hlādi, is, m., N. of a son of Babhru.

Ā-hlādita, as, ā, am, delighted, rejoiced.

आह्वृ **ā-hvṛi**, cl. 1. P., Ved. *-hvarati, -hvartum*, to make crooked, to injure.

Ā-hūrya, as, ā, am, Ved. to be bent down or brought near; to be made favourable, one towards whom one must bow; (Sāy.) to be invoked (fr. rt. *hve*).

Ā-hruta, as, ā, am, injured. — *Āhruta-bheshaja, as, ā, am*, Ved. curing what is bent or injured.

Ā-hvara, as, m., N. of a fortress of the Uśīnaras.

Ā-hvaraka, as, m. a low or expelled man who, after having offered a sacrifice to the manes, takes the sacrificial food for himself.

Āhvāraka, ās, m. pl. the Āhvārakas, a recension of the black Yajur-veda (distinct from the Taittirīya) named from Ahvāra or Āhvāra.

Ā-hvriti, is, m., N. of a prince.

आह्वे **ā-hve**, cl. 1. P. or poet. A. *-hvayati, -te, -hvātum*, to call near; to summon; to invite, ask; A. to provoke, challenge, emulate: Caus. *-hvāyayati, -yitum*, to send for; to cause to invite or summon or challenge; provoked: Desid. *-juhūshati*, to wish to call near or invite: Intens. *-johavīti*, to call.

2. *ā-hava, as*, m. challenge, provoking, calling; war, battle. — *Āhava-kāmyā*, f. desire of war: (for 1. *ā-hava* see under *ā-hu*, page 136, col. 3.)

2. *ā-hāva, as*, m. calling, invoking; battle, war.

2. *ā-huti*, calling, invoking. (This word may sometimes have this sense in the oldest Vedic texts, but see the more correct form *ā-hūti*. For 1. *ā-huti* see under *ā-hu* last col.)

Ā-huva, as, ā, am, Ved. (Sāy.) to be invoked.

Ā-hū, f., Ved. calling, invoking.

2. *ā-hūta, as, ā, am*, called, summoned, invoked, invited. — *Āhūta-prapalāyin, ī*, m. a defendant or witness absconding or not appearing when summoned.

Ā-hūti, is, f. calling, invoking.

Ā-hūya, ind. having invited.

Ā-hva, as, ā, am, who or what calls, a crier; named, called; (*ā*), f. a name, appellation.

Ā-hvaya, as, m. a lawsuit arising from a dispute about games with animals, as cock-fighting &c.; appellation, name (generally as last member of a compound, the first member of which, though commonly an appellative noun, is used as a proper name).

Ā-hvayat, an, antī, at, calling, challenging.

Ā-hvayana, am, n. appellation, name.

Ā-hvayitavya, as, ā, am, to be summoned or invited.

Ā-hvāna, am, n. calling, invitation, a call or summons; invocation of a deity; challenge; legal summons; an appellation, a name; designation of a liturgical formula. — *Āhvāna-darśana, am*, n. day of trial.

Āhvānaya, nom. P. *āhvānayati, -yitum*, (in law) to summon.

Ā-hvāya, as, m. a summons, a name.

Ā-hvāyaka, as, m. a messenger, a courier.

Ā-hvāyayitavya, as, ā, am, to be called before a tribunal.

इ

इ 1. **i**, the third vowel of the alphabet, corresponding to *i* short, and pronounced as that letter in *kill* &c. — *I-kāra, as*, m. the letter or sound *i*.

इ 2. **i**, ind. an interjection of anger, calling, sorrow, distress, compassion, &c.

इ 3. **i**, pronominal base of the 3rd person; [cf. *itara, itas, iti, id, idam, idā, iyat, iva, iha*: cf. also Lat. *id*; Goth. *ita*; Eng. *it*; Old Germ. *iz*; Mod. Germ. *es*.]

इ 4. **i, is**, m. a N. of Kāmadeva.

इ 5. **i**, cl. 2. P., 1. P. A. *eti, ayati, -te, iyāya, eshyati, etum*, Ved. *etave, etavai, etos*, to go; to go to or towards (with acc.); to come; to go away, escape, pass, retire; to return; to arrive at, reach, obtain; to fall into; to arise from, come from; to approach with prayers, ask; to undertake anything (with acc.); to appear, to be; to go on well, to prosper (e. g. *tasmin yuktasya eti pretakṛityā*, 'the funeral ceremony of one engaged in that goes on well or prospers'); to be employed in, go on with, be in any condition or relation (with a part. or inst., e. g. *Asura-rakshasāni mṛidyamānāni yanti*, 'the Asuras and Rakshas are being trampled upon;' *Gavāmayanena īyuḥ*, 'they were engaged in the Gavāmayana'): Intens. or cl. 4. A. *īyate*, inf., Ved. *īyadhyai*, to go quickly or repeatedly; to come, wander, run; to appear, make one's appearance; to approach any one with requests (with two acc.), ask, request; to be asked or requested: Caus. *āyayati, -yitum*, to cause to come; [cf. Gr. εἶ-μι, ἴ-μεν; Lat. *eo, īmus*; Lith. *ei-mi*, 'I go;' Slav. *i-dû*, 'I go,' *i-ti*, 'to go;' Goth. *i-ddja*.]

It, (at the end of a few compounds) going; cf. *arthet*.

Ita, as, ā, am, gone; returned; obtained; remembered; (*am*), n. way. — *Itāsu* (°*ta-as*°), *us, us, u*, Ved. whose vital spirits have departed.

1. *iti, is*, f., Ved. going, moving.

Itya, as, ā, am, to be gone to or towards.

Ityā, f., Ved. going, a way; a litter, a palanquin.

Itvan, ā, ā, a, going.

Itvara, as, ī, am, going, travelling, a traveller; cruel, harsh; poor, indigent; low, vile; contemned; (*ī*), f. a disloyal or unchaste woman.

इक्कट **ikkaṭa, as**, m. a kind of reed. See *itkaṭa*.

इक्कवाल **ikkavāla** in astrology = اقبال *iqbāl*, good fortune, prosperity.

इक्षु **ikshu, us**, m. (fr. rt. 3. *ish*?), the sugar-cane (twelve species of it are enumerated); N. of a river. — *Ikshu-kāṇḍa, as, am*, m. n. the stem or cane of the Saccharum Officinale, the sugar-cane; (*as*), m., N. of two different species of sugar-cane, viz. Saccharum Munja Roxb. and Saccharum Spontaneum L. — *Ikshu-kuṭṭaka, as*, m. a gatherer or reaper of sugar-cane. — *Ikshu-gandha, as*, m. Saccharum Spontaneum; a kind of Asteracantha Longifolia; (*ā*), f. Saccharum Spontaneum, Asteracantha Longifolia, Capparis Spinosa, Batatas Paniculata. — *Ikshu-gandhikā*, f. Batatas Paniculata. — *Ikshu-ja, as, ā, am*, coming from sugar-cane. — *Ikshu-tulyā*, f. Saccharum Spontaneum. — *Ikshu-daṇḍa, am*, n. the stem or cane of the Saccharum Officinale. — *Ikshu-darbhā*, f. a kind of grass or sugar-cane. — *Ikshu-dā*, f., N. of a river; see *ikshulā, ikshu-mālinī, ikshu-mālavī*. — *Ikshu-netra, am*, n. a kind of sugar-cane. — *Ikshu-pattra, as*, m. the grain Penicillaria Spicata. — *Ikshu-pāka, as*, m. molasses. — *Ikshu-pra, as*, m. the plant Saccharum Sara. — *Ikshu-bālikā*, f. Saccharum Spontaneum, = *ikshu-tulyā*. — *Ikshu-bhakshikā*, f. a meal of sugar or molasses. — *Ikshu-matī*, f., N. of a river in Kurukshetra. — *Ikshu-mālavī* or *ikshu-mālinī*, f., N. of a river; see *ikshu-dā*. — *Ikshu-mūla, am*, n. a kind of sugar-cane; the root of sugar-cane. — *Ikshu-meha, as*, m. diabetes or diabetes mellitus; see *madhu-meha*. — *Ikshumehin, ī, inī, i*, diabetic. — *Ikshu-yantra, am*, n. a sugar-mill. — *Ikshu-yoni, is*, m. Saccharum Officinarum. — *Ikshu-rasa, as*, m. the juice of the sugar-cane; molasses, unrefined sugar; the cane Saccharum Spontaneum. — *Ikshurasa-krātha, as*, m. raw or unrefined sugar, molasses. — *Ikshurasoda* (°*sa-ud*°), *as*, m. the sea of syrup. — *Ikshu-vaṇa, am*, n. a sugar-cane wood. — *Ikshu-vallarī* and *ikshu-vallī*, f. Batatas Paniculata. — *Ikshu-vāṭikā* or *ikshu-vāṭī*, f. Saccharum Officinarum, the common yellow cane. — *Ikshu-vāri*, n. the sea of syrup, one of the seven seas. — *Ikshu-vikāra, as*, m. sugar, molasses; any sweetmeat. — *Ikshu-veshṭana, as*, m. a kind of sugar-cane. — *Ikshu-śākaṭa* or *ikshu-śākina, am*, n. a kind of sugar-cane. — *Ikshu-samudra, as*, m. the sea of syrup, one of the seven seas. — *Ikshu-sāra, as*, m. molasses, raw or unrefined sugar. — *Ikshvāri, is*, m. (for *ikshu-vāri?*), Saccharum Spontaneum. — *Ikshvālika, as*, m. (for *ikshu-bālika*), Saccharum Spontaneum; (*ā*), f. another sort, Saccharum Fuscum, (native reed-pens are made from its stem.)

Ikshuka, as, m. sugar-cane.

Ikshukīyā, f. a region abounding in sugar-cane.

Ikshura, as, m. Capparis Spinosa; Asteracantha Longifolia; Saccharum Spontaneum.

Ikshuraka, as, m. Capparis Spinosa; Saccharum Spontaneum.

Ikshulā, f., N. of a river. See *ikshu-dā*.

इक्ष्वाकु *ikshvāku, us*, m., N. of a son of Manu Vaivasvata, father of Kukshi and first king of the solar dynasty in Ayodhyā; a descendant of Ikshvāku; the Jainas derive their Cakravartins and many of their Arhats from Ikshvāku; (*ās*), m., N. of a warrior-tribe derived from Ikshvāku; (*us*), f. a bitter gourd; according to some, the Coloquintida (Citrillus Colocynthis), the fruit of a wild species of Lagenaria Vulgaris. — *Ikshvāku-kula-ja, as, ā, am*, born in the family of Ikshvāku.

इख् *ikh*, cl. 1. P. *ekhati, iyekha, ekhishyati, ekhitum*, to go, move; [cf. Gr. εἴκω, οἴχομαι?].

इङ्कार *in-kāra* and *in-kṛita* = *hin-kāra, hin-kṛita*, q. v.

इङ्ख् *inkh*, cl. 1. P. *inkhati, inkhāñ-cakāra, inkhishyati, inkhitum*, to go, move; [cf. Hib. *imchim*, 'I go on, proceed, march.']

इङ्ग् *ing*, cl. 1. P., ep. A. *ingati, -te, ingāñ-cakāra, ingishyati, ingitum*, to go, go to or towards; to move or agitate: Caus. P. *ingayati, -yitum*, to move, agitate, shake; (in gram.) to divide or separate the members of a compound word, to use a word or bring it into such a grammatical relation that it is considered *ingya*; see below; [cf. Hib. *ing*, 'a stir, a move.']

Inga, as, ā, am, movable, locomotive; surprising, wonderful; (*as*), m. a hint or sign, an indication of sentiment by gesture, knowledge; (*ā*), f. a kind of counting.

Ingana, am, n. shaking; (in gram.) the operation by which one member of a compound is separated from another, as by the *ava-graha* or mark of tmesis.

Ingita, am, n. palpitation, change of the voice, internal motion, motion of various parts of the body as indicating the intentions; hint, sign, gesture; aim, intention, real but covert purpose. — *Ingita-kovida* or *ingita-jña, as, ā, am*, understanding signs, acquainted with the gesture of another, skilled in the expression or interpretation of the internal sentiments by the external gesture.

Ingya, as, ā, am, movable from its place; in the Prātiśākhyas a term for those words or rather parts of a compound word which in certain grammatical operations may be separated from the preceding parts, a word which in the Pada-pāṭha is divided by the *ava-graha* or mark of tmesis.

इङ्गिड *ingiḍa*, N. of a plant, = *inguda* (?).

इङ्गुद *inguda, as, ī*, m. f., N. of a medicinal tree, Terminalia Catappa; in Bengal confounded with Putrañjīva Roxburghii Wall.; (*am*), n. the nut of the tree Terminalia Catappa.

Ingula, as, ī, m. f., N. of the tree Terminalia Catappa.

इचिकिल *icikila, as*, m. a pond, mud, mire.

इच्छक 1. *icchaka, as*, m. the citron, Citrus Medica L.

इच्छक 2. *icchaka*, इच्छा *icchā*, &c. See under 3. *ish* at page 142.

इज्जल *ijjala, as*, m. a small tree growing in wet and saline soil, or on low grounds near the sea, Barringtonia Acutangula Gærtn.

इज्य *ijya, as*, m. (fr. rt. *yaj*), a teacher; an epithet of Bṛihaspati the teacher or Guru of the gods; (*ā*), f. a sacrifice, making offerings to the gods or manes; a gift, a donation; worship, reverence; meeting, union; a cow; a bawd or procuress. — *Ijyā-śīla, as*, m. a frequent sacrificer.

इञ्चाक *iñcāka, as*, m. a shrimp or prawn.

इट् *iṭ*, cl. 1. P. *eṭati, eṭitum*, to go, to go to or towards; Ved. to make haste, to err.

इट *iṭa, as*, m., Ved. cane or grass; a web made of it, a mat. — *Iṭa-sūna, am*, n., Ved. a texture of reed, a mat.

इटत *iṭata, as*, m., N. of a Bhārgava, author of a hymn of the Ṛig-veda.

इट्चर *iṭ-cara, as*, m. (fr. 4. *ish* and *cara*), a bull or steer allowed to go at liberty.

इठिमिका *iṭhimikā*, f. title of a section of the Kāṭhaka recension of the Yajur-veda.

इड् *iḍ*, Ved. (only in inst., gen., abl. sing., and acc. pl. *iḍā* and *iḍas*; or, according to the spelling of the Ṛig-veda, *iḷā* and *iḷas*), a refreshing draught, refreshment, libation offered to the gods; the flow of speech, the stream of sacred words and worship, prayer; (Sāy.) the earth, food; (*iḍas* or *iḷas*), pl. the object of devotion, addressed in the third or fourth verses of the Āprī hymns, (so used only in Ṛig-veda 3, 4. 3; but also erroneously referred to in the Brāhmaṇas &c. as if etymologically connected with the words *īḍya, īḍita, īḷita*, 'the praiseworthy,' 'the praised,' which are used in the third or fourth verses of the other Āprīs as the designation of the same object of worship.) — *Iḍas-pati, is*, m., N. of Vishṇu. — *Iḍ-devatā*, f. deity of the libation. — *Iḷas-pati, is*, m., Ved. a N. of Pūshan. — *Iḷas-pade*, in the place of sacred libation, i. e. at the altar or place of offering.

Iḍa, as, m., Ved. This word occurs only in one sacred formula as an epithet of Agni, who is to be addressed with prayers, or invoked with the stream or flow of praise.

Iḍā, f. or (in Ṛig-veda) *iḷā*, (not to be confounded with the inst. case of *iḍ* above), refreshing draught, refreshment, animation, recreation, comfort, vital spirit; food; offering, libation, especially a holy libation, coming between the Prayāga and Anuyāga, and consisting of four preparations of milk, poured into a vessel containing water, and then partially drank by the priest and sacrificers; (metaphorically cf. *iḍ*) stream or flow of praise and worship, personified as the goddess of sacred speech and action, invoked together with Aditi and other deities, but especially in the Āprī hymns together with Sarasvatī and Mahī or Bhāratī; (Sāy.) the earth, food; (*iḍā*, as the libation and offering of milk is personified in the cow, the symbol of feeding and giving, whence the word *iḍā* is given as a synonym of 'cow.' The goddess *Iḍā* or *Ilā* is the daughter of Manu or of man thinking on and worshipping the gods; she is the wife of Budha and mother of Purū-ravas; in another aspect she is called Maitrāvaruṇī as daughter of Mitra-Varuṇa, two gods who were objects of the highest and most spiritual devotion. *Ilā* is also a N. of Durgā, of a daughter of Daksha and wife of Kaśyapa, of a wife of Vasudeva and of the Rudra, Ṛita-dhvaja); heaven; a tubular vessel, one of the principal channels of the vital spirit, that which is on the right side of the body. *Iḷāyās-pade*, at the place of Iḍā, i. e. of worship and libation, earth. — *Iḍā-vat, ān, atī, at*, Ved. refreshing, granting fresh vital spirits; possessed of refreshment, refreshed; (Sāy.) possessed of sacrificial food.

Iḍācikā, f. (fr. *iḍā?*), a wasp.

Iḍikā, f. the earth.

इडिक्क *iḍikka, as*, m. a wild goat.

इड्वर *iḍvara, as*, m. a bull fit to be set at liberty. See *iṭ-cara*.

इण्डीन्थ *iṇḍīntha, as*, m. a knife (?).

इण्ड्व *iṇḍva, am*, n., Ved. (used in du.) two round small plates made of Muñja reed, used as coverings for the hands in taking the fire-pans from the fire.

इण्वीन्दु *iṇvīndu, us*, m. the tree Trochis Aspera (?).

इण्वेरिका *iṇverikā*, f. a kind of cake.

इतर *i-tara, as, ā, at*, Ved. *am* (comparative form of pronom. base 3. *i*; cf. Lat. *iterum*; Hib. *iter*), the other (of two), another; (pl.) the rest; (with abl.) different from; low, vile; expelled, rejected; *itara itara*, the one—the other, this—that. (*Itara* connected antithetically with a preceding word often signifies the contrary idea, e. g. *vijayāya itarāya vā*, to victory or defeat; so in Dvandva compounds, *sukhetareshu*, in happiness and distress. It sometimes, however, forms a Tat-purusha compound with another word to express the one idea implied in the contrary of that word, e. g. *dakshiṇetara*, the left hand.) — *Itara-jana, ās*, m. pl. other men; a euphemistic title of certain beings who appear to be considered as spirits of darkness; Kuvera belongs to them. — *Itara-tas*, ind. otherwise than, different from; *itaścetarataśca*, hither and thither. — *Itara-thā*, ind. in another manner, in a contrary manner; perversely; on the other hand, else.

Itarā, f., N. of the mother of Aitareya.

Itaretara, as, ā, am (occurring chiefly in oblique cases of sing. and in comp.; fr. *itara-itara*, which may be for *itaras-itara*, cf. *anyo'nya, paras-para*), one another, one with another, mutual, respective, several; (*am*), n. or adv. mutually, &c. — *Itaretara-kāmyā*, f. respective or several fancies or inclinations. — *Itaretarāśraya* (°*ra-āś*°), *as, ā, am*, affecting or concerning mutually.

Itare-dyus, ind. at another or different day.

I-tama, as, ā, at (superlative form of 3. *i*), another (of many?).

इतस् *i-tas*, ind. (fr. 3. *i* with affix *tas*, used like the abl. case of the pronoun *idam*), from hence, hence, here (opposed to *amu-tas* and *amu-tra*); from this point; from this world, in this world; *itas itas*, here—there; *itaścetaśca*, hence and thence, hither and thither, here and there, to and fro; from this time, now; therefore. — *Ita-ūti, is, is, i*, Ved. extending or reaching from hence; existing or lasting longer than the present time, future; (Sāy.) one who has obtained help. — *Itas-tatas*, ind. here and there, hither and thither.

इति 2. *iti*, ind. (fr. pronominal base 3. *i*), in this manner, thus. In its original signification *iti* refers to something that has been said or thought, or lays stress on what precedes. In the Brāhmaṇas it is often equivalent to 'as you know,' reminding the hearer or reader of certain customs, conditions, &c., supposed to be known to him.

In quotations of every kind *iti* means that the preceding words are the very words which some person has or might have spoken, and placed thus at the end of a speech it serves the purpose of inverted commas (e.g. *ity uktvā*, having so said; *iti kṛitvā*, having so considered, having so decided). It may often have reference merely to what is passing in the mind, e.g. *bālo 'pi nāvamantavyo manushya iti bhūmipaḥ*, a king, though a child, is not to be despised, saying to one's self, 'he is a mortal,' (Gram. 928.) In theatrical language *iti tathā karoti* = after these words he acts so.

Sometimes *iti* is used to include under one head a number of separate objects aggregated together (e.g. *ijyādhyayanadānāni tapaḥ satyam kshamā damaḥ alobha iti mārgo 'yam*, 'sacrificing, studying, liberality, penance, truth, patience, self-restraint, absence of desire,' this course of conduct, &c.).

Iti is sometimes followed by *evam*, *iva*, or a demonstrative pronoun pleonastically (e.g. *tām brūyād bhavatīty evam*, her he may call 'lady,' thus).

Iti may form an adverbial compound with the name of an author (e.g. *itipāṇini*, thus according to Pāṇini). It may also express manifestation (lo! behold!), something additional (as in *ity-ādi*, et cetera), order, arrangement specific or distinctive, and identity. It is used by native commentators after quoting a rule to express 'according to such a rule' (e.g. *anudāttanita ity Ātmanepadam bhavati*, according to the rule of Pāṇini I. 3, 12, the Ātmane-pada takes place). *Kim iti* = *kim*, wherefore, why? (In the Śatapatha-Brāhmaṇa *ti* occurs for *iti*; cf. Prākṛit *ti* and *tti*.) — *Iti-katha*, *as*, *ā*, *am*, unworthy of trust, not fit to be credited; wicked, lost; (*ā*), f. unmeaning or nonsensical discourse; (? for *ati-katha*, q. v.) — *Iti-karaṇa*, *am*, n. or *iti-kāra*, *as*, m. the word *iti*. — *Iti-kartavya*, *as*, *ā*, *am*, proper or necessary to be done according to certain conditions; (*am*), n. duty, obligation. — *Itikartavya-tā*, f. or *itikārya-tā* or *itikṛitya-tā*, f. any proper or necessary measure, obligation. — *Itikartavyatā-mūḍha*, *as*, *ā*, *am*, embarrassed, dumbfounded, wholly at a loss what to do. — *Iti-tha*, *as*, *ī*, *am*, Ved. such a one, such, e.g. *puretithyai* (? *rātryai* dat. sing.) *marishyasi*, before such and such a day thou wilt die. — *Iti-mātra*, *as*, *ā*, *am*, of such extent or quality. — *Iti-vat*, ind. in the same manner. — *Iti-vṛitta*, *am*, n. occurrence, event. — *Ity-artham*, ind. for this purpose. — *Ity-ādi*, *is*, *is*, *i*, having such (thing or things) at the beginning, thus beginning, and so forth, et cetera. — *Ity-ukta*, *am*, n. information, report, narrative.

Iti-ha, ind. thus indeed, (according to tradition.)

Iti-hāsa, *as*, m. (*iti-ha-āsa*, 'so indeed it was'), talk, legend, tradition, history, traditional accounts of former events, heroic history, as the Mahā-bhārata.

इतिहास *iti-hāsa*. See under 2. *iti* above.

इतीक *itīka*, *as*, m., N. of a people.

इत्कट *itkaṭa*, *as*, m. a kind of reed or grass. See *ikkaṭa*.

इत्किला *itkilā*, f., N. of a perfume. See *rocanā*.

इत्थ *ittha*, *am*, n. in astronomy = ἰχθύς.

इत्थम् *ittham*, ind. (fr. *id*, q. v.), thus, in this manner; [cf. Lat. *item*.] — *Itthaṃ-vidha*, *as*, *ā*, *am*, of such a kind, endowed with such qualities. — *Itthaṅ-kāram*, ind. in this manner. — *Ittham-bhāva*, *as*, m. the being thus endowed. — *Ittham-bhūta*, *as*, *ā*, *am*, become thus, being thus or in such manner; so circumstanced.

इत्थशाल *itthaśāla*, (in astrology) N. of the third Yoga, = Arabic إتّصال.

इत्था *itthā*, ind., Ved. thus; (often used in the Ṛig-veda, and sometimes only to lay stress on a following word; therefore by native etymologists considered as a particle of affirmation.) *Itthā* is often connected with words expressing devotion to the gods &c. in the sense of thus, truly, really; especially with *dhī* as an adjective. Hence *itthā-dhī* = such, i. e. true (*satyā*) or real worship. Similarly, *itthā-dhī*, *is*, *is*, *i*, so devout, so pious, i. e. very devout; (Sāy.) performing such or true works.

इत्थात् *itthāt*, ind. (= *ittham*), Ved. thus, in this way.

इद् *id*, ind., Ved. (probably the neut. form of the pronom. base *i*, see 3. *i*; a particle of affirmation), even, just, only; (especially in strengthening an antithesis, e.g. *yathā vaśanti devās tathā id asat*, as the gods wish it, thus indeed it will be; *dipsanta id ripavo nāha debhuḥ*, the enemies wishing indeed to hurt were in nowise able to hurt.)

Id is often added to words expressing excess or exclusion (e.g. *viśva it*, everyone indeed; *śaśvad it*, constantly indeed; *eka it*, one only). At the beginning of sentences it often adds emphasis to pronouns, prepositions, particles (e.g. *tvam it*, thou indeed; *yadi it*, if indeed, &c.).

Id occurs often in the Ṛig-veda, seldom in the Brāhmaṇas, and its place is taken in classical Sanskṛit by *eva* and other particles.

इदम् *idam*, *ayam*, *iyam*, *idam* (fr. *id*, a kind of neut. of the pronom. base 3. *i* with *am*; cf. Lat. *is*, *ea*, *id*, and *idem*: the regular forms are partly derived from the pronom. base *a*; see Gram. 224. The Veda exhibits various irregular formations, e.g. fr. pronom. base *a*, an inst. *enā*, *ayā*, and gen. loc. du. *ayos*; fr. the base *ima*, a gen. sing. *imasya*, &c.: the forms derived fr. *a* are used enclitically if they take the place of the third personal pronoun, do not stand at the beginning of a verse or period, and have no peculiar stress laid upon them), this, this here, referring to something near the speaker; known, present; (opposed to *adas*, e.g. *ayaṃ lokaḥ* or *idaṃ viśvam* or *idaṃ sarvam*, this earthly world, this universe; *ayam agniḥ*, this fire which burns on the earth; but *asāv agniḥ*, that fire in the sky, i. e. the lightning: so also *idam* or *iyam* alone signifies 'this earth;' *ime smaḥ*, here we are.)

Idam often refers to something immediately following, whereas *etad* points to what precedes (e.g. *śrutvā etad idam ūcuḥ*, having heard that they said this).

Idam occurs connected with *yad*, *tad*, *etad*, *kim*, and a personal pronoun, partly to point out anything more distinctly and emphatically, partly pleonastically (e.g. *tad idam vākyam*, this speech here following; *so 'yaṃ Vidūshakaḥ*, this Vidūshaka here).

Idam, ind., Ved. here, to this place; now, even, just; there; with these words. — *Idaṃ-rūpa*, *as*, *ā*, *am*, Ved. having this shape. — *Idaṃ-vid*, *t*, *t*, *t*, knowing this or conversant with this. — *Idan-kāryā*, f. the plant Hedysarum Alhagi. — *Idad-vasu*, *us*, *us*, *u*, Ved. rich in this and that. — *Idan-tā*, f. identity. — *Idam-prakāram*, ind. in this manner. — *Idam-prathama*, *as*, *ā*, *am*, doing anything for the first time. — *Idam-maya*, *as*, *ī*, *am*, Ved. made or consisting of this.

Idamyu, *us*, *us*, *u*, wishing this.

इदा *i-dā*, ind. (fr. pronom. base 3. *i*), Ved. now, at this moment; (often connected with a gen. of *ahan*, e.g. *idā ahnaḥ* or *ahna idā*, this present day, 'now-a-days;' and with *hyas*, e.g. *idā hyaḥ*, only yesterday.) — *Idā-vatsara*, *as*, m. originally perhaps 'the present or current year;' then one of the names given to the single years of a period of five years; one of the five years in which gifts of clothes and food are productive of great rewards. — *Idāvatsarīya*, *as*, *ī*, *am*, belonging to such a year. — *Idu-vatsara* and *id-vatsara* = *idā-vatsara* above. — *Id-vatsarīya* = *idāvatsarīya* above.

I-dānīm, ind. now, at this moment, in this case, just, even; (with gen. of *ahan*, e.g. *idānīm ahnaḥ*, this present day, 'now-a-days;' *idānīm eva*, just now; immediately; *idānīm api*, in this case too; *tata idānīm*, thereupon, then.) In rare cases it is an expletive, affecting but slightly the sense. *Idānīm* as a measure of time is the fifteenth part of an *etarhi*, and is then declinable (e.g. *yāvanty Etarhīṇi tāvanti pañcadaśakṛitva Idānīni*, as many Etarhis, so many Idānīms fifteen times repeated). — *Idānīn-tana*, *as*, *ī*, *am*, present, momentary, of the present moment.

इद्ध, इध्म, &c. See under *indh*.

इन् *in*, cl. 8. P., Ved. *inoti*, *ainot*, 2nd sing. impv. *inuhi* or *inu*, cl. 9. P., 1st pl. *inīmasi*, cl. 6. P. (fr. *inv*) *invati*, perf. 3rd pl. *invire*, to advance upon, press upon, drive; to infuse strength, invigorate; to use force, to force; drive away, keep back, remove; to have in one's power, to take possession of, pervade; dispose; to be lord or master of a thing or an art. See *inv*.

Ina, *as*, *ā*, *am*, Ved. able, strong, energetic, determined, bold; powerful, mighty, wild; glorious; (*as*), m. a lord, a master; a king; the sun; the lunar mansion Hasta. — *Ina-sabha*, *am*, n. a royal court or assembly.

इनक्ष् *inaksh*, *inakshati* (a Ved. Desid. of *naksh*), to endeavour to reach, strive to obtain.

इनानी *inānī*, f., N. of a plant (= Vaṭapattrī).

इनु *inu*, *us*, m., N. of a Gandharva.

इन्थिहा *inthihā*, f., an astrological term taken from the Arabic.

इन्द् *ind*, cl. 1. P. *indati*, *aindat*, *indām-babhūva*, *inditum*, to be powerful; (this root seems to be formed merely for the etymology of the word *indra*, q. v.)

इन्दम्बर *indambara*, *am*, n. the blue lotus, Nymphæa Cærulea. See *indī-vara*.

इन्दिन्दिर *indindira*, *as*, m. a large bee.

इन्दिरा *indirā*, f. epithet of Lakshmī, wife of Vishṇu. — *Indirā-mandira*, *as*, m. epithet of Vishṇu. — *Indirālaya* (°*rā-āl*°), *am*, n. (lit. 'the abode of *Indirā* or Lakshmī'), the blue lotus, Nymphæa Stellata and Cyanea. (The goddess *Indirā* issued at the creation from the petals of the flower.) — *Indirā-vara*, *am*, n. = preceding.

इन्दीवर *indī-vara* or *indī-vāra* or *indi-vara*, *am*, m. (contracted fr. *indirā-vara*), the blue lotus, Nymphæa Stellata and Cyanea, see *indirā*; (*ī*), f. the plant Asparagus Racemosus; (*ā*), f., N. of another plant.

Indīvariṇī, f. a group of blue lotuses.

इन्दु *indu*, *us*, m. (said to be fr. rt. *und*; perhaps connected with *vindu*, which last is unknown in the Ṛig-veda), Ved. a drop, especially of Soma, Soma; a bright drop, a spark; the moon; (*avas*), m. pl. the moons, i. e. the periodic changes of the moon; time of moonlight, night; (*us*), m. camphor. (In the Brāhmaṇas *indu* is used only for the moon; but the connection between the senses 'Soma juice' and 'moon' in the word *indu* has led to the same two ideas being transferred in classical Sanskṛit to the word *Soma*, although the latter has properly only the sense 'Soma juice.') — *Indu-kamala*, *am*, n. the white lotus. — *Indu-kalā*, f. a digit of the moon; N. of several plants, Cocculus Cordifolius, Sarcostema Viminale, Ligusticum Ajowan. — *Indu-kalikā*, f. the plant Pandanus Odoratissimus. — *Indu-kānta*, *as*, m. the lunar gem, the moon-stone; (*ā*), f. night. — *Indu-ja*, *as*, m. epithet of the planet mercury, 'son of the moon;' (*ā*), f., N. of the river Revā or Narmadā in the Dekhan. — *Indu-janaka*, *as*, m. the ocean, lit. 'father of the moon,' (the moon being produced amongst other things at the churning of the ocean.) — *Indu-dala*, *as*, m. a portion of the moon, a digit, crescent. — *Indu-putra*, *as*, m. epithet of the planet Mercury. — *Indu-pushpikā*, f. the plant Methonica Superba. — *Indu-bhṛit, t*, m. epithet of S'iva, 'bearing the crescent on his forehead.' — *Indu-maṇi, is*, m. the moon-stone. — *Indu-maṇḍala, am*, n. the orb or disc of the moon. — *Indu-mat, ān*, m., Ved. (in liturgical language) an epithet of Agni, because in the verses in which he is addressed the word *indu* occurs; (*tī*), f. day of full moon; N. of the sister of Bhoja and wife of Aja; N. of a river. — *Indu-mauli, is*, m. epithet of S'iva; see *indu-bhṛit*. — *Indu-ratna, am*, n. a pearl. — *Indu-rāj, ṭ*, m. the moon, king of the stars. — *Indu-rekhā*, f. a digit of the moon. — *Indu-lekhā*, f. a digit of the moon; the plant Menispermum Glabrum; the moon-plant Asclepias Acida; a kind of lovage, Ligusticum Ajwæn. — *Indu-lohaka, am*, n. silver. — *Indu-vadanā*, f. a metre of four verses of which each contains fourteen syllables. — *Indu-vallī*, f. the plant Sarcostemma Viminale. — *Induvāra* in astrology = the Arabic إنبار. — *Indu-vrata, am*, n. a religious observance depending on the age of the moon; diminishing the quantity of food by a certain portion daily, for a fortnight or a month, &c. — *Indu-s'ekhara, as*, m. 'moon-crested,' an epithet of S'iva.

Induka, as, m., N. of a plant, = *aśmantaka*.

इन्दूर *indūra, as*, m. a rat, a mouse [cf. *undura, unduru*].

इन्द्र *indra, as*, m. (fr. rt. *in* or *ind* or obsolete rt. *id?*), the god who in Vedic mythology reigns over the deities of the intermediate region or atmosphere; he fights against and conquers with his thunderbolt (*vajra*) the demons of darkness, and is in general a symbol of generous heroism; (*Indra* was not originally lord of the gods of the sky, but his deeds were most useful to mankind, and he was therefore addressed in prayers and hymns more than any other deity, and ultimately superseded the more lofty and spiritual Varuṇa. In the later mythology *Indra* is subordinated to the triad Brahmā, Vishṇu, and S'iva, but remained the chief of all other deities in the popular mind; he is also regent of the east quarter, and considered one of the twelve Ādityas: in the Vedānta he is identified with the supreme being); the first, the chief (of any class of objects); a prince; the pupil of the right eye (that of the left being called Indrāṇī or Indra's wife); N. of the plant Wrightia Antidysenterica, &c. (see *kuṭaja*); a vegetable poison; N. of the twenty-sixth Yoga or division of a circle on the plane of the ecliptic; the Yoga star in the twenty-sixth Nakshatra, γ Pegasi; the human or animal soul, the portion of spirit residing in the body; night; one of the nine divisions of Jambu-dvīpa or the known continent; best, excellent (in compounds); (*ā*), f. the wife of Indra, see *indrāṇī*; N. of a plant, Marjoram (?), see *phaṇijjhava*. — *Indra-ṛishabha, as, ā, am*, Ved. having Indra as a bull, or impregnated by Indra, epithet of the earth. — *Indra-karman, ā*, m. epithet of Vishṇu, 'performing Indra's deeds.' — *Indra-kīla, as*, m., N. of a mountain; a rock. — *Indra-kuñjara, as*, m. Indra's elephant; see *airāvata*. — *Indra-kūṭa, as*, m., N. of a mountain. — *Indra-kṛishṭa, as, ā, am*, ploughed by Indra, growing in a wild state. — *Indra-ketu, us*, m. Indra's banner; N. of a man. — *Indra-kośa* or *indra-kosha* or *indrakoshaka, as*, m. a platform, a scaffold; a projection of the roof of a house, forming a kind of balcony or terrace; a pin or bracket projecting from the wall. — *Indra-giri, is*, m., N. of a mountain. — *Indra-gupta, as, ā, am*, Ved. guarded or protected by Indra; (*as*), m., N. of a Brāhman. — *Indra-guru, us*, m. teacher of Indra; an epithet of Kaśyapa. — *Indra-gopa, as*, or *ā, ās*, m., Ved. having Indra as one's protector; (*as*), m. the insect cochineal of various kinds; in this sense also *indragopaka*. — *Indra-ghosha, as*, m., Ved. noise of Indra personified; having the name Indra. — *Indra-ćandana, am*, n. = *hari-ćandana*. — *Indra-ćāpa, as*, m. Indra's bow, a rainbow. — *Indra-ćirbhiṭī*, f., N. of a plant. — *Indra-ćhandas*, n. a necklace consisting of 1008 strings. — *Indra-janana, am*, n. Indra's birth. — *Indrajananīya, as, ā, am*, treating of Indra's birth. — *Indra-jā, ās, ās, am*, Ved. originating from Indra. — *Indra-jānu, us*, m., N. of a monkey. — *Indra-jāla, am*, n., Ved. the net of Indra; a weapon employed by Arjuna, stratagem or trick in war; deception, cheating; conjuring, juggling. — *Indrajālika, as, ī, am*, a juggler, a conjurer; deceptive, unreal. — *Indrajālin, ī*, m., N. of a Bodhi-sattva. — *Indra-jit, t*, m. 'conqueror of Indra,' N. of the son of Rāvaṇa; of a Dānava; of the father of Rāvaṇa and king of Kāśmīra; an author of the seventeenth century. — *Indrajid-vijayin, ī*, m. 'conqueror of Indrajit,' an epithet of Lakshmaṇa. — *Indra-jūta, as, ā, am*, Ved. promoted, excited, or procured by Indra. — *Indra-jyeshṭha, as, ā, am*, Ved. whose chief is Indra, led by Indra. — *Indra-tama, as, ā, am*, Ved. most Indra-like, mighty, powerful. — *Indra-tā*, f. power and dignity of Indra. — *Indra-tāpana, as*, m., N. of a Dānava. — *Indra-tūla* or *indratūlaka, am*, n. a flock of cotton, a flocculent seed &c. blown about in the air. — *Indra-toyā*, f., N. of a river. — *Indra-tva, am*, n. Indra's power and dignity; kingship. — *Indra-tvota, as, ā, am* (fr. *indra-tvā-ūta*), Ved. favoured or protected by thee, O Indra. — *Indra-datta, as*, m., N. of a Brāhman. — *Indra-dāru, us*, m., the tree Pinus Devadāru. — *Indra-devī*, f., N. of the wife of king Meghavāhana, who built a monastery called *indradevī-bhavana*. — *Indra-dyumna, as*, m., N. of a man with the patronymic Bhāllaveya; (*am*), n., N. of a lake. — *Indra-dru, us*, m. the plants Terminalia Arjuna and Wrightia Antidysenterica. — *Indra-druma, as*, m. the plant Terminalia Arjuna. — *Indra-dvīpa, as, am*, m. n. one of the nine dvīpas or divisions of the known continent. — *Indra-dhanus, us*, n. Indra's bow, the rainbow. — *Indra-dhvaja, as*, m., N. of a Tathāgata or of a Nāga. — *Indra-nakshatra, am*, n., Ved., Indra's lunar mansion; an epithet of Phalgunī. — *Indra-nīla, as*, m. a sapphire. — *Indranīlaka, as*, m. an emerald. — *Indra-patnī*, f., Ved. the wife of Indra. — *Indra-parṇī*, f., N. of a plant, perhaps Methonica Superba. — *Indra-parvata, as*, m., N. of a mountain. — *Indra-pātama, as, ā, am*, Ved. drunk by Indra with more pleasure than by any one else. — *Indra-pāna, as, ā, am*, Ved. drunk by Indra (anything which serves as his drink). — *Indra-pālita, as*, m. 'protected by Indra,' N. of a king; also of a Vaiśya. — *Indra-pita, as, ā, am*, Ved. drunk by Indra. — *Indra-putrā*, f., Ved. daughter of Indra. — *Indra-purogama, as, ā, am*, preceded or led on by Indra, having Indra as leader. — *Indra-purohitā*, f. the asterism Pushya. — *Indra-pushpā* or *indra-pushpikā* or *indra-pushpī*, f. the medicinal plant Methonica Superba. — *Indra-pramati, is*, m. a descendant of Vasishṭha, author of some verses of the Ṛig-veda. — *Indra-pramada, as*, m., N. of a man. — *Indra-prasūta, as, ā, am*, Ved. caused or impelled by Indra. — *Indra-prastha, as, am*, m. n., N. of a city on the Yamunā (now Delhi), the residence of the Pāṇḍavas. — *Indra-praharaṇa, am*, n. Indra's weapon, the thunderbolt. — *Indra-brāhmaṇa, as*, m., N. of a man. — *Indra-bhaginī*, f. 'Indra's sister,' epithet of the wife of S'iva. — *Indra-bhūti, is*, m., N. of one of the eleven Gaṇādhipas of the Jainas. — *Indra-bheshaja, am*, n. dried ginger. — *Indramaha, am*, n., N. of a ceremony beginning with the words *indram aham*. — *Indramaha-kāmuka, as*, m. a dog. — *Indra-mādana, as, ā, am*, Ved. animating or delighting Indra. — *Indra-mārga, as*, m., N. of a Tīrtha. — *Indra-medin, ī, inī, i*, Ved. whose friend or ally is Indra. — *Indra-yava, am*, n. Indra-grain; the seed of the Wrightia Antidysenterica. — *Indra-yoga, as*, m., Ved., Indra's union or uniting power. — *Indra-lupta, as, am*, m. n. or *indra-luptaka, am*, n. morbid baldness of the head; loss of beard. — *Indra-loka, as*, m. Indra's world; Svarga or paradise. — *Indralokāgamana* (°*ka-āg*°), *am*, n. (Arjuna's) approach to Indra's world. — *Indra-lokeśa* (°*ka-īś*°), *as*, m. the lord of Indra's world, i. e. Indra; a guest (as conferring paradise on his host). — *Indra-vaṇśā*, f. a metre of four lines, each of which contains twelve syllables. — *Indra-vajrā*, f. a metre of four lines occurring frequently in epic poetry; each line contains eleven syllables. — *Indra-vat*, or in some cases *indrā-vat, ān, atī, at*, Ved. associated with or accompanied by Indra. — *Indra-varman, ā*, m., N. of a warrior. — *Indra-vallarī* or *indra-vallī*, f. the plant Cucumis Colocynthis (?). — *Indra-vasti, is*, m. f. (?) the calf (of the leg). — *Indra-vātatama, as, ā, am*, Ved. much desired by Indra. — *Indra-vāyu, ū*, m. du. Indra and Vāyu. — *Indra-vāruṇikā* or *indra-vāruṇī*, f. Colocynth, a wild bitter gourd, Cucumis Colocynthis; the favourite plant of Indra and Varuṇa. — *Indra-vāh, ṭ*, m., Ved. carrying Indra. — *Indra-vīja, am*, n. the seed of the Wrightia Antidysenterica. — *Indra-vṛiksha, as*, m. = *indra-dāru*. — *Indra-vṛiddhā*, f. a kind of abscess. — *Indra-vṛiddhika, as*, m. a kind of horse. — *Indra-vaidūrya, am*, n. a kind of precious stone. — *Indra-vrata, am*, n. 'Indra's rule of conduct,' one of the duties of a king, viz. to distribute benefits, as Indra pours down rain. — *Indra-śakti, is*, f. Indrāṇī the wife or personified energy of Indra. — *Indra-śatru, us, us, u*, Ved. whose enemy or conquerer is Indra, conquered by Indra (with the Udātta on the first syllable; differently accented the word might mean 'an enemy of Indra'); (*us*), m. 'Indra's enemy,' epithet of Prahlāda. — *Indra-śalabha, as*, m., N. of a man. — *Indra-śaila, as*, m., N. of a mountain. — *Indra-śreshṭha, as, ā, am*, Ved. having Indra as chief, led by Indra; see *indra-jyeshṭha*. — *Indra-sakhi, ā*, m., Ved. one whose ally or companion is Indra. — *Indra-sandhā*, f. connection or alliance with Indra. — *Indra-sārathi, is, is, i*, Ved. driving in the same carriage with Indra, an epithet of Vāyu. — *Indra-sāvarṇi, is*, m., N. of the fourteenth Manu. — *Indra-suta, as*, m. 'son of Indra,' N. of the monkey-king Bali; also an epithet of Arjuna and Jayanta. — *Indra-surasa, as*, m. a shrub, the leaves of which are used in discutient applications, Vitex Negundo. — *Indra-surā*, f. or *indra-surisa, as*, m., N. of the same plant (?). — *Indra-sūnu, us*, m. 'the son of Indra,' epithet of the monkey-king Bali. — *Indra-sena, as*, m., N. of several men; N. of a Nāga; (*ā*), f., N. of several women. — *Indrasena-dvitīya, as, ā, am*, attended by Indrasena. — *Indra-senā*, f., Ved., Indra's missile. — *Indra-stut, t*, m. or *indra-stoma, as*, m. 'praise of Indra;' N. of particular hymns to Indra in certain ceremonies. — *Indras-vat, ān, atī, at*, Ved. similar to Indra; (Sāy.) accompanied by Indra, possessed of power (?). — *Indra-hava, as*, m., Ved. invocation of Indra. — *Indra-hasta, as*, m. a kind of medicament. — *Indrāgni-devatā* (°*ra-ag*°), f. the sixteenth lunar mansion. — *Indrāgni-dhūma, as*, m. frost, snow. — *Indrānuja* (°*ra-an*°), *as*, m. 'the younger brother of Indra,' an epithet of Vishṇu or Kṛishṇa. — *Indrābha* (°*ra-ābh*°), *as*, m., N. of a grandson (?) of Dhṛita-rāshṭra. — *Indrāyudha* (°*ra-āy*°), *am*, n. Indra's weapon, the rainbow; (*as*), m., N. of a horse; a horse marked with black about the eyes; (*ā*), f. a kind of leech having rainbow tints on the back. — *Indrāyudha-śikhin, ī*, m., N. of a Nāga. — *Indrāri* (°*ra-ar*°), *is*, m. Indra's enemy, an Asura or demon. — *Indrāvaraja* (°*ra-av*°), *as*, m. 'the younger brother of Indra,' an epithet of Vishṇu or Kṛishṇa. — *Indrāśana* (°*ra-aś*°), *as*, m. hemp, dried and chewed; the shrub which bears the seed used as a jeweller's weight, Albus Precatorius. — *Indrāsana* (°*ra-ās*°), *am*, n. the throne of Indra, any throne; a foot of five short syllables. — *Indrejya* (°*ra-ij*°), *as*, m., N. of Vṛihaspati, the preceptor of the gods. — *Indreshita* (°*ra-ish*°), *as, ā, am*, Ved. sent or driven or instigated by Indra. — *Indrota* (°*ra-ūta*), *as*, m., N. of a son of Ṛiksha and of Devāpi. — *Indrotsava* (°*ra-ut*°), *as*, m. a festival honouring Indra.

Indraka, am, n. an assembly-room, a hall.

Indraya, nom. A., Ved. *indrayate, -yitum*, to behave like Indra.

Indrayu, us, us, u, Ved. longing for or wishing to approach Indra.

Indrāṇikā, f. the plant Vitex Negundo.

Indrāṇī, f. the wife of Indra; N. of Durgā, reckoned as one of the eight mothers (*mātṛikā*) or divine energies; a kind of coitus; the plant Vitex Negundo.

Indriya, as, ā, am, fit for or belonging to or agreeable to Indra; (*as*), m. a companion of Indra; (*am*), n. power, force, the quality which belongs especially to the mighty Indra; exhibition of power, powerful act; bodily power, power of the senses; virile power; semen virile; faculty of sense, sense, organ of sense; the number five as symbolical of the five senses. (In addition to the five organs of perception, *buddhīndriyāṇi* or *jñānendriyāṇi*, i. e. eye, ear, nose, tongue, and skin, the Hindūs enumerate five organs of action, *karmendriyāṇi*, i. e. larynx, hand, foot, anus, and parts of generation; between these ten organs and the soul or *ātman* stands *manas* or mind, considered as an eleventh organ. In the Vedānta, *manas, buddhi, ahankāra*, and *ćitta* form the four inner or internal organs, *antar-indriyāṇi*, so that according to this reckoning the organs are fourteen in number, each being presided over by its own ruler or *niyantṛi*; thus, the eye by the Sun, the ear by the Quarters of the world, the nose by the two Aśvins, the tongue by Praćetas, the skin by the Wind, the voice by Fire, the hand by Indra, the foot by Vishṇu, the anus by Mitra, the parts of generation by Prajāpati, manas by the Moon, buddhi by Brahman, ahankāra by Śiva, ćitta by Vishṇu as Aćyuta. In the Nyāya philosophy each organ is connected with its own peculiar element, the nose with the Earth, the tongue with Water, the eye with Light or Fire, the skin with Air, the ear with Ether. The Jainas divide the whole creation into five sections, according to the number of organs attributed to each being.) — *Indriya-kāma, as, ā, am*, Ved. desiring or endeavouring to obtain power. — *Indri-yagoćara, as, ā, am*, perceptible, capable of being ascertained by the senses. — *Indriya-grāma, as*, m. the assemblage of the organs, the senses or organs of sense collectively. — *Indriya-jñāna, am*, n. the faculty of perception, sense, consciousness. — *Indriya-nigraha, as*, m. restraint of the organs of sense. — *Indriya-buddhi, is*, f. perception by the senses, the exercise of any sense, the faculty of any organ. — *Indriya-bodhana, as, ā, am*, exciting power, arousing or sharpening the senses; (*am*), n. any excitement of sense, an object of perception, a stimulus, &c. — *Indriya-varga, as*, m. the assemblage of organs, the organs of sense collectively. — *Indriya-vipratipatti, is*, f. perversion of the organs, erroneous or perverted perception. — *Indriya-svāpa, as*, m. sleep of the senses, unconsciousness, insensibility; the end of the world. — *Indriyāgoćara* (°*ya-a-goć*°), *as, ā, am*, imperceptible. — *Indriyātman* (°*ya-āt*°), *ā*, m. an epithet of Vishṇu. — *Indriyāyatana* (°*ya-āy*°), *am*, n. the residence of the senses; the body. — *Indriyārtha* (°*ya-ar*°), *as*, m. an object of sense (as sound, smell, &c.), anything exciting the senses. — *Indriyā-vat, ān, atī, at*, or *indriyā-vin, ī, inī, i*, Ved. powerful, mighty; sometimes also *indriya-vat*. — *Indriyā-saṅga* (°*ya-a-s*°), *as*, m. non-attachment to sensual objects, stoicism, philosophy.

इन्द्रिय ***indriya.*** **See above.**

इन्ध् ***indh***, **cl. 7. A.** ***inddhe, indhāñ-ćakre*** or ***īdhe, indhishyate, aindhishṭa, indhitum***, to kindle, light, set on fire: Pass. *idhyate*, to be lighted; to blaze, flame; [with *indh* cf. Gr. αἴθω, ἰθαρός; αἰθήρ, Αἴτνη; Ἥφ-αισ-τος: Lat. *æs-tus, æs-tas*: Old Germ. *eit*, 'fire.']

Iddha, as, ā, am, kindled, lighted, alight; shining, glowing, blazing; clean, clear, bright; wonderful; obeyed, unresisted?; (*am*), n. sunshine, light, heat; a wonder. — *Iddha-manyu, us, us, u*, having the anger excited or kindled. — *Iddhāgni* (°*dha-ag*°), *is, is, i*, Ved. one whose fire burns.

Idh, (at the end of compounds) lighting; [cf. *agnīdh*.]

Idhma, as, am, m. n. fuel, especially that which is used for the sacred fire; [cf. Hib. *adhmad*; Zend *aiśma*.] — *Idhma-jihva, as*, m., N. of a son of Priya-vrata. — *Idhma-pravraśćana, as*, m. a hatchet, an axe. — *Idhma-bhṛiti, is, is, i*, Ved. bringing fuel. — *Idhma-vāha, as*, m. epithet of Dṛiḍhasyu or Dṛiḍhadasyu.

Idhyā, f. kindling, lighting. See *vājedhyā*.

Indha, as, ā, am, lighting, kindling.

Indhana, am, n. kindling, lighting; [cf. *agnindhana*]; fuel; wood, grass &c. used for this purpose. — *Indhana-vat, ān, atī, at*, possessed of fuel. — *Indhan-van, ā, ā, a*, Ved. possessed of fuel; flaming.

इन्व् ***inv***, **cl. 6. P.** ***invati, invāñ-ćakāra, invishyati, ainvīt, invitum***, to pervade, surround, embrace, seize, take possession of; to invigorate, gladden. See *in*.

Inva, as, ā, am, pervading (in *viśvam-inva*).

इन्वका ***invakā, ās***, **f. pl. stars in the head** of Orion.

इभ ***ibha, as*** **or** ***am?***, **m. or n.? (said to be** fr. rt. *i*, to go), Ved. servants, dependants, domestics, household, family; (Sāy.) fearless power; (*as, ā, am*), followed by attendants; (*as*), m. an elephant; (*ī*), f. a female elephant; [with this word cf. the Gr. ἐλ-έφας and the Lat. *ebur*.] — *Ibha-kaṇā*, f. a plant with an aromatic seed, Scindapsus Officinalis. — *Ibha-keśara, as*, m. the tree Mesua Roxburghii. — *Ibha-gandhā*, f., N. of a poisonous fruit. — *Ibha-dantā*, f. the plant Tiaridium Indicum. — *Ibha-nimīlikā*, f. smartness, shrewdness, sagacity (like that of an elephant). — *Ibha-pālaka, as*, m. the driver or keeper of an elephant. — *Ibha-poṭā*, f. a young elephant, a cub. — *Ibham-aćala, as*, m. a lion. — *Ibha-yuvati, is*, f. an elephant's cub. — *Ibhākhya* (°*bha-ākh*°), *as*, m. the plant Mesua Roxburghii. — *Ibhāri* (°*bha-ar*°), *is*, m. a lion ('enemy of the elephant'). — *Ibhoshaṇā* (°*bha-ush*°), f. a kind of aromatic plant.

Ibhya, as, ā, am, Ved. belonging to one's servants or attendants; wealthy, opulent, having many attendants; (Sāy.) (*as*), m. an enemy; (*ā*), f. a female elephant; N. of the Olibanum tree, Boswellia Serrata. — *Ibhya-tilvala, as, ā, am*, Ved. abundantly possessed of household requisites.

इम ***ima***, **a pronominal base. See** ***idam.***

Imaka, as, ā, am, diminutive of *ima*.

Imathā, ind., Ved. as in this place, as here, as now.

इयक्ष् ***iyaksh*** **(Anomalous Desid. of rt.** ***yaj***), Ved. occurring only in the part. pres. *iyakshat* and *iyakshamāṇa*, and in impf. subj. *iyakshān*, to go towards, approach; to request, endeavour to gain; to long for, seek.

Iyakshu, us, us, u, Ved. longing for, seeking to gain.

इयत् ***iyat, ān, atī, at*** **(fr. pronominal base** 3. *i*), so large, only so large; so much, only so much; [with *iyat* cf. the syllable *iens* or *ies* in such Lat. words as *totiens, toties, quotiens, quoties*, and in numeral adverbs as *quinquies*.] — *Iyat-tā*, f. or *iyat-tva, am*, n. quantity, fixed measure or quantity, so much.

Iyattaka, as, ikā, am, Ved. so small, very small, wee.

इयस्य ***iyasya*** **(Anomalous Intens. of rt.** ***yas***), A., Ved. *iyasyate*, to relax, weaken; to vanish.

Iyasā, f., Ved. lassitude, dejection, low spirits.

इर् ***ir***, **cl. 6. P.** ***irati***, **to go; [cf.** ***il.***]

इरज्य ***irajya*** **(Anomalous Intens. of** ***raj, rāj***), P. rarely A., Ved. *irajyati, -te*, to order, prepare, arrange; to lead; to dispose, be master of; (Sāy.) to grow.

Irajyu, us, us, u, Ved. busy with preparations for the sacrificial rite.

इरण ***iraṇa***, **desert; salt or barren (soil);** = *iriṇa*, q. v.

इरध् ***iradh*** **(Anomalous Intens. of** ***rādh***), *iradhate* and *iradhyati*, Ved. to endeavour to gain; (Sāy.) to worship. The inf. *iradhyai* is by some referred to this form, and regarded as a shortened form of *iradhadhyai*; but Sāy. refers it to rt. *īr*.

इरंमद ***iram-mada, as***, **m., Ved. delighting** in drink; an epithet of Agni, in the form of lightning and Apām-napāt; a flash of lightning or the fire attending the fall of a thunderbolt; submarine fire.

इरस्य ***irasya***, **P., Ved.** ***irasyati***, **to behave** insolently, be angry; (with dat.) to be ill-affected towards; [cf. Lat. *ira, irasci*.]

Irasyā, f., Ved. ill-will, malevolence; (Sāy.) wish for food.

इरा ***irā***, **f. (closely allied to** ***iḍā*** **and** ***ilā***), Ved. any drinkable fluid; a draught (especially of milk); refreshment, comfort, enjoyment; N. of an Apsaras, a daughter of Daksha and wife of Kaśyapa; water; ardent spirits; the earth; speech; the goddess of speech, Sarasvatī; [cf. *iḍā*.] — *Irā-kshira, as, ā, am*, Ved. whose milk is a refreshment or enjoyment. — *Irā-ćara, am*, n. hail; (*as, ā* or *ī, am*), earth-born, terrestrial, aquatic. — *Irā-ja, as*, m. a N. of Kāma, god of love, 'born from water.' — *Irā-mukha, am*, n., N. of an Asura-town near Meru. — *Irā-vat, ān, atī, at*, Ved. granting drink or refreshment, satiating, giving enjoyment; endowed with provisions; comfortable; (*ān*), m., N. of a son of Arjuna; the ocean, a cloud; a king; (*ī*), f., N. of a plant; N. of Durgā, the wife of Rudra, daughter of the Nāga Suśravas; N. of a river in the Pañjāb, now called Rāvī. — *Irā-vellikā*, f. pimples or pustules on the head. — *Ireśa* (°*rā-īś*°), *as*, m. a N. of Vishṇu; a king, a sovereign; Varuṇa.

इरिका ***irikā***, **f., N. of a plant or tree.** — *Irikā-vana, am*, n. a grove of such trees.

इरिण ***iriṇa, am***, **n. (said to be fr. rt.** ***ṛi***, to go; connected with *irā*), Ved. a water-course, a rivulet, a well; any incision in the ground, a hollow, hole; a desert, an inhospitable region; a bare plain, barren soil; salt soil.

Iriṇya, as, ā, am, Ved. belonging or relating to a desert &c.

इरिन् ***irin, ī, iṇī, i*** **(connected with** ***ina?***), Ved. powerful, violent; an overbearing fellow; (Sāy.) an instigator; [cf. *irasya* &c.]

इरिमेद ***irimeda, as***, **m., N. of a plant,** = *ari-meda*.

इरिम्बिठि ***irimbiṭhi, is***, **m., N. of a man of** the family of Kāṇva, author of several hymns of the Ṛig-veda.

इरिविल्ला ***irivillā*** **or** ***irivellikā***, **f. pimples** or pustules on the head.

इर्य ***irya, as, ā, am***, **Ved. active, powerful,** energetical; epithet of Pūshan and of the Aśvins; (Sāy.) instigating; destroying enemies; a lord.

इर्वारु ***irvāru, us***, **m. f., N. of an eatable** cucumber, Cucumis Utilissimus; of another kind, Cucumis Colocynthis; see *irvālu, īrvāru, urvāru, ervāru*. — *Irvāru-śuktikā*, f. a kind of melon, commonly Sphuti or Sphut, Cucumis Momordica.

Irvāruka, as, m. an animal living in caves.

Irvālu, us, m. f. Cucumis Utilissimus Roxb. or Cucumis Colocynthis.

इल् ***il***, **cl. 6. P.** ***ilati, iyela, elishyati, ailīt, elitum***, or cl. 10. P. *ilayati* or *elayati, -yitum*, aor. *aililat* or *ailayīt*, to keep still, not to move; to become quiet; to send, to cast; to sleep; to move, to go; [a various reading has the form *il*: cf. Old Germ. *illu, illo*, for *ilju*; Mod. Germ. *Eile*; Cambro-Brit. *il*, 'progress, motion;' Gr. ἐλάω.]

Ilaya, as, ā, am, Ved. resting, motionless.

इलव *ilava, as, ā, am,* Ved. sounding, noisy, loud; [cf. *ailaba.*]

इलविल *ilavila, as,* m., N. of a son of Daśaratha; (*ā*), f., N. of a daughter of Tṛiṇavindu, wife of Viśravas and mother of Kuvera.

इला *ilā,* f. flow, speech, the earth, &c.; see *iḍā.* — *Ilā-gola, am,* n. the earth, the globe. — *Ilā-tala, am,* n. the fourth place in the circle of the zodiac; the surface of the earth. — *Ilā-dadha, as,* m., N. of a certain sacrifice. — *Ilān-da, am,* n. 'granting refreshment or food,' N. of a ceremony or of a verse; N. of a Sāman. — *Ilā-vṛita, as,* m., N. of a son of Agnīdhra, who received the Varsha *ilā-vṛita* as his kingdom; (*am*), n. one of the nine Varshas or divisions of the known world, comprehending the highest and most central part of the old continent.

Ilikā, f. the earth.

इलिनी *ilinī,* f., N. of a daughter of Medhātithi.

इली *ilī,* f. a cudgel, a stick shaped like a sword or a short sword. See *īlī.*

इलीबिश *ilībiśa, as,* m., Ved., N. of a demon conquered by Indra.

इलीश *ilīśa, as,* m. (said to be fr. *il,* to go), a fish, commonly the hilsa or sable, Clupea Alosa; the fish being one of high flavour, and very abundant at certain seasons, is generally eaten both by the natives of Bengal and by Europeans residing there; [cf. *illiśa.*]

इलूष *ilūsha, as,* m., N. of the father of Kavasha. See *ailūsha.*

इल्प *ilpa, as,* m., N. of a wonderful tree in the other world.

इल्लक *illaka, as,* m., N. of a merchant's son.

इल्लल *illala, as,* m., N. of a bird.

इल्लिश *illiśa, as,* m. the fish Clupea Alosa; [cf. *ilīśa.*]

इल्वका *ilvakā, ās,* f. pl. the five stars in Orion's head. See *ilvala.*

इल्वल *ilvala, as,* m. a kind of fish; N. of a Daitya, the brother of Vātāpi; (*ās*), f. pl., N. of the five stars in Orion's head.

इव *iva,* ind. (fr. pronominal base 3. *i*), like, in the same manner as (in this sense = *yathā,* and used correlatively to *tathā*); as it were (after a metaphorical expression, e. g. *pathā iva yantau,* on a path going as it were); in a certain manner, in some measure, a little, perhaps (in qualification or mitigation of a strong assertion); nearly, almost, about (e. g. *muhūrtam iva,* almost an hour); so, just so, just, exactly, indeed, very (especially after words which involve some restriction, e. g. *īshad iva,* just a little; *kiñćid iva,* just a little bit: and after a negation, e. g. *naćirād iva,* very soon). *Iva* is connected vaguely, and somewhat pleonastically, with an interrogative pronoun or adverb (e. g. *kim iva,* what? *katham iva,* how could that possibly be? *kveva,* where, I should like to know?). In the Pada texts of the Ṛig, Yajur, and Atharva-veda, and by native grammarians, *iva* is considered to be compounded with the word after which it stands, and is therefore enclitic.

इवीलक *ivīlaka, as,* m., N. of a son of Lambodara.

इशीका *iśīkā,* f. an elephant's eyeball. See *ishīkā.*

इष 1. *ish,* cl. 4. P. *ishyati, iyesha, eshishyati, aishīt, eshitum,* to move, to cause to move; to let fly, to throw, cast; to raise (as one's voice); to sprinkle; cl. 9. P. *ishṇāti,* to cause to move quickly, to cast, let fly, swing; to strike; to fly off, escape; to impel, incite, animate, promote: Caus. P. *eshayati, -yitum,* to bring, offer: Desid. *eshishishati.*

2. *ish,* (at the end of some compounds) moving quickly, speedy. See *aram-ish.*

Ishaṇaya, nom. (from the next) A., Ved. *ishaṇayate, -yitum,* to move, excite.

1. *ishaṇi, is,* f., Ved. impulse, desire. (For 2. see under 3. *ish.*)

Ishaṇya, nom. P., Ved. *ishaṇyati, -yitum,* to cause to make haste, to excite, drive.

Ishaṇyā, f., Ved. impulse, desire.

Isharya, as, ā, am (fr. *ishu* below), Ved. skilled in archery.

Ishikā = ishīkā and *īshīkā,* q. v.

Ishita, as, ā, am, moved, driven, tossed, sent; caused, excited, animated; quick. — *Ishita-tvatā,* ind., Ved. by impulse or excitement.

Ishīka, as, m., N. of a people, = *aishīka;* (*ā*), f. reed, rush, stem or stalk of grasses; an arrow; a sort of sugar-cane, Saccharum Spontaneum; a brush; a small stick of wood or iron used for trying whether or not the gold in a crucible is melted; the eyeball of an elephant; see *ishikā, īshikā, īshīkā, iśīkā.* — *Ishīka-tūla, am,* n. the point or upper part of a reed.

Ishu, us, m. f. an arrow; (in mathematics) a versed sine; N. of a Soma ceremony. — *Ishu-kāra, as,* or *ishu-kṛit, t,* m., Ved. an arrow-maker. — *Ishu-dhara, as,* m. an archer. — *Ishu-dhi,* see s. v. below. — *Ishu-pa, as,* m., N. of an Asura, who appeared on earth as king Magna-jit. — *Ishu-patha, as,* m. the range of an arrow. — *Ishu-pushpā,* f., N. of a plant. — *Ishu-bala, as, ā, am,* Ved. powerful by arrows. — *Ishu-bhṛit, t, t, t,* carrying arrows, an archer. — *Ishu-mat, ān, atī, at,* Ved. possessed of arrows. — *Ishu-mātra, as, ī, am,* having the length of an arrow, i. e. about five short spans or three feet; (*am*), ind. as far as the range of an arrow. — *Ishus-trikāṇḍā,* f. the threefold arrow, N. of a constellation, perhaps the girdle of Orion. — *Ishu-hasta, as, ā, am,* 'arrow-handed,' carrying arrows in the hand. — *Ishv-agra, am,* n. the point of an arrow. — *Ishv-anīka, am,* n. the point of an arrow. — *Ishvarga, as,* m. (for *ishu-varga*), Ved. one who averts arrows, a shield-bearer. — *Ishv-asana* or *ishv-astra, am,* n. a bow ('arrow-thrower'). — *Ishv-āyudha, am,* n., Ved. arrow and weapons. — *Ishv-āsa, as, ā, am,* throwing arrows; (*as*), m. a bow; an archer, a warrior.

Ishuka, as, ī, am, arrow-like; (*ā*), f., Ved. an arrow.

Ishu-dhi, is, m. f. (rt. *dhā*), a quiver. — *Ishudhi-mat, ān, atī, at,* Ved. possessed of a quiver.

Ishudhya, nom. P., Ved. *-dhyati, -yitum,* to be a quiver, to contain arrows; to implore, request; (Sāy.) to desire oblations.

Ishudhyā, f., Ved. imploring, request.

Ishudhyu, us, us, u, Ved. imploring, requesting; (Sāy.) going.

1. *ishṭi, is,* f. impulse, acceleration, hurry; invitation, order, despatch.

Ishmin, ī, iṇī, i, Ved. going quickly, speedy, impetuous; an epithet of the winds.

इष 3. *ish,* cl. 6. P., ep. also A. *iććhati, -te, iyesha, eshishyati, aishīt, eshitum* or *eshṭum,* to endeavour to obtain, strive, seek for; to endeavour to make favourable; desire, wish, long for; to request; to be willing, to be about to do anything, to intend; to strive to obtain anything (acc.) from any one (abl. or loc.); to expect anything from any one; to assent; to be favourable; to ask anything (acc.) from any one (loc.); to acknowledge, to regard: Pass. *ishyate,* to be wished or liked; to be asked, requested, prescribed; to be approved, acknowledged, accepted, regarded as; to be worth; to be wanted as a desideratum, see 2. *ishṭi:* Caus. P. *eshayati, -yitum, aishishat:* Desid. *eshishishati;* [with *ish* cf. Old Germ. *eiscôm,* 'I ask;' Mod. Germ. *heische:* cf. also Gr. προΐσσομαι, προ-ΐκτης, προ-ΐξ; and perhaps Gr. ἰό-της and ἵ-μερος.]

Iććhaka, as, ikā, am, wishing, desirous of; (*as*), m. demand, the sum sought (in arithmetic).

Iććhat, an, atī or *antī, at,* wishing, wishful, desirous.

Iććha-tā, f. or *iććha-tva, am,* n. desire, wishfulness.

Iććhā, f. wish, desire, inclination; (in mathematics) a question or problem; (in gram.) the desiderative form; *iććhayā,* according to one's wish or desire; *iććhām ni-grah,* to suppress one's desire. — *Iććhā-dāna, am,* n. the granting or gratification of a wish. — *Iććhā-nivṛitti, is,* f. suppression of desire. — *Iććhānvita* (°*ćhā-an*°), *as, ā, am,* having a desire, wishing, wishful. — *Iććhā-phala, as,* m. (in mathematics) the solution of a question or problem. — *Iććhā-vat, ān, atī, at,* wishing, wishful, desirous; (*tī*), f. a woman desirous of anything. — *Iććhā-vasu, us,* m. an epithet of Kuvera ('possessing wealth according to wish'). — *Iććhā-sampad, t,* f. fulfilment or attainment of wishes.

Iććhu, us, us, u, wishing, desiring (with acc. or inf.).

Iććhuka, as, ā or *ī, am,* wishing, desirous.

4. *ish, ṭ,* f. wish; [cf. *iṭ-ćara.*]

2. *ishaṇi, is,* f., Ved. wish, desire. (For 1. see under 1. *ish.*)

Ishūya, P., Ved. *ishūyati, -yitum,* to request, ask; (Sāy.) to wish for food, wish to approach.

1. *ishṭa, as, ā, am* (for 2. see next page), sought; wished, desired; liked, beloved; agreeable; cherished; worshipped, reverenced, respected; regarded as good, approved; valid; (*as*), m. a lover, a husband; the plant Ricinus Communis; (*ā*), f., N. of a plant; (*am*), n. wish, desire; (*am*), ind. voluntarily. — *Ishṭa-karman, a,* n. (in arithmetic) rule of supposition, operation with an assumed number. — *Ishṭa-kāpatha, as,* m. the root of the fragrant grass Andropogon Muricatus. — *Ishṭa-kāma-duh, dhuk,* f. 'granting the wished-for desires,' epithet of the cow of plenty. — *Ishṭa-gandha, as, ā, am,* fragrant; (*as*), m. any fragrant substance; (*am*), n. sand. — *Ishṭa-jana, as,* m. a beloved person, man or woman; a loved one. — *Ishṭa-tama, as, ā, am,* most desired, best beloved, beloved, dearest. — *Ishṭa-tara, as, ā, am,* more desired, more dear, dearer. — *Ishṭa-tas,* ind. according to one's wish or desire. — *Ishṭa-tā,* f. or *ishṭa-tva, am,* n. desirableness, the state of being beloved or reverenced. — *Ishṭa-deva, as,* m. or *ishṭa-devatā,* f. a chosen or tutelary deity, a favourite god, one particularly worshipped. — *Ishṭa-yāman, ā, ā, a,* Ved. going according to one's desire. — *Ishṭa-raśmi, is, is, i,* Ved. having desired or best reins or bridles. — *Ishṭa-vrata, as, ā, am,* Ved. obeying one's wish; (Say.) that by which good works succeed. — *Ishṭā-kṛita, am,* n., Ved. wish and deed, i. e. accomplishment of a wish (?); N. of a certain sacrificial ceremony. — *Ishṭā-pūrta, am,* n., Ved. wish and fulfilment, i. e. fulfilment of one's wishes; any religious duty or pious act, as oblation, sacrifice, penance, holy study, digging a well, planting a tree, &c. — *Ishṭārtha* (°*ṭa-ar*°), *as,* m. anything desired or agreeable. — *Ishṭārthodyukta* (°*tha-ud*°), *as, ā, am,* zealously active, diligent for a desired object. — *Ishṭāśva* (°*ṭa-aś*°), *as, ā, am,* Ved. having desired or best horses.

2. *ishṭi, is,* f. seeking, endeavouring to obtain; wish, request, desire; any desired object, a desired rule, a desideratum (a term applied to Patañjali's additions to Pāṇini's rules); (*is*), m., Ved. seeking, going after, guarding.

Ishṭu, us, f. wish, desire.

Ishma, as, m. the spring; love or the deity Kāma.

Ishya, as, am, m. n. the spring season.

Ishva, as, m. a spiritual teacher. See *īshva.*

इष 5. *ish, ṭ,* f., Ved. that which is drunk, a draught, refreshment, enjoyment; libation; the refreshing waters of the sky; sap, strength, freshness, comfort, increase; good condition, affluence.

Isha, as, m. one who possesses sap and strength;

the month Āśvina (September–October); strength, vigour (?). — *Isha-vat, ān, atī, at,* Ved. vigorous. — *Isha-stut, t,* m., Ved. a praiser of the desired (Sun); (*t*), f. praise of comfort.

Ishaya, nom. P. A., Ved. *ishayati, -te, -yitum,* to be succulent, swell; to be fresh, active, powerful; to refresh, strengthen, animate.

Ishira, as, ā, am, Ved. succulent, refreshing, fresh, flourishing; vigorous, active, quick; [cf. Gr. ἱερός]; (*as*), m. fire ?; (*am*), ind. quick.

Ishetvāka, as, ā, am (an Adhyāya or Anuvāka), containing the words *ishe tvā,* 'for rain thee.'

इषु *ishu, ishu-dhi,* &c. See 1. *ish* last page.

इष्कृ *ish-kṛi,* cl. 8. P., Ved. *-karoti, -kartum,* to arrange, set in order, prepare.

Ish-kartṛi, tā, trī, tṛi, Ved. arranging, preparing, setting in order.

Ish-kṛita, as, ā, am, Ved. arranged. — *Ishkṛitā-hāva* (°*ta-āh*°), *as, ā, am,* Ved. whose Soma vessel is prepared or ready.

इष्ट 2. *ishṭa, as, ā, am* (fr. rt. *yaj;* for 1. *ishṭa* see last page), sacrificed, worshipped with sacrifices; (*as*), m. sacrifice; (*am*), n. sacrificing; sacred rite, sacrament. — *Ishṭa-yajus, us, us, us,* Ved. one to whom sacrificial verses have been offered or addressed. — *Ishṭā-vat, ān, atī, at,* possessed of sacrifices.

Ishṭakā, f. a brick, especially one used in building the altar of a sacrifice. — *Ishṭakā-gṛiha, am,* n. a brick house. — *Ishṭakā-ćita, as, ā, am,* built of bricks. — *Ishṭakā-nyāsa, as,* m. laying the foundation of a house. — *Ishṭakā-rāśi, is,* m. a pile of bricks.

3. *ishṭi, is,* f. sacrificing, sacrifice; oblation consisting of butter, fruits, &c., opposed to the sacrifice of an animal or of Soma. — *Ishṭi-paća, as,* or *ishṭi-mush, ṭ,* m. an Asura, a demon. — *Ishṭy-ayana, am,* n. a series of oblations, a sacrifice lasting a long time.

Ishṭikā, f. a brick, especially one used in building the sacrificial altar. See *ishṭakā* above.

Ishṭin, ī, inī, i, one who has sacrificed.

Ishṭvā, ind. having sacrificed or worshipped.

इष्टनि *ishṭani, is, is, i,* Ved. (if fr. rt. *yaj*), to be worshipped; (if instead of *ni-shṭani,* fr. rt. *stan*), rustling, rushing.

इस् *is,* ind. an interjection of anger, pain, or sorrow.

इह *iha,* ind. (fr. pronom. base 3. *i*), in this place, here; to this place; in this world; in this book or system; in this case (e. g. *tena iha na,* 'therefore not in this case,' i. e. the rule does not apply here); now, at this time; [cf. Zend *idha,* 'here;' Gr. ἰθα or ἰθαι in ἰθα-γενής and ἰθαι-γενής; Goth. *ith;* perhaps Lat. *igi-tur.*] — *Iha-kāla, as,* m. this life. — *Iha-kratu, us, us, u,* or *iha-ćitta, as, ā, am,* Ved. whose intentions or thoughts are in this world or place. — *Iha-tra,* ind. here, in this world. — *Iha-bhojana, as, ā, am,* Ved. whose goods and gifts come hither. — *Iha-loka, as,* m. this world, this life; (*e*), ind. in this world. — *Iha-samaye,* ind. here, now, on the present occasion, at such a time as this. — *Iha-stha, as, ā, am,* standing here. — *Iha-sthāna, as, ā, am,* whose place or residence is on the earth; (*e*), ind. in this place. — *Ihāgata* (°*ha-āg*°), *as, ā, am,* come or arrived hither. — *Ihāmutra* (°*ha-am*°), ind. here and there, in this world and in the next. — *Iheha* (*iha-iha*), ind. here and there, now and then, repeatedly. — *Iheha-mātṛi, tā,* m., Ved. of whose mothers one is here and one there; (Say.) whose mother is here and there, i. e. everywhere.

Ihatya, as, ā, am, or *ihatyaka, as, ikā, am,* being here.

ई

ई 1. *ī,* the fourth letter of the alphabet, corresponding to *i* long, and having the sound of *ee* in *feel.*

ई 2. *ī, īs,* m., N. of Kandarpa, the god of love; *ī* or *īs,* f., N. of Lakshmī.

ई 3. *ī,* ind. an interjection of pain, anger, consciousness or perception, consideration, compassion.

ई 4. *ī* for rt. *i.* See under 5. *i.*

ईक्ष् *īksh,* cl. 1. A. *īkshate, īkshāñ-ćakre, īkshishyate, aikshishṭa, īkshitum,* to see, look, view, behold, look at, gaze at (with acc. or rarely loc.); to see in one's mind, think, have a thought, regard, consider; to look to the welfare of any one (with dat.): Caus. *īkshayati, -yitum,* to make one look at (with acc.). (This root is perhaps connected with *akshi,* q. v.)

Īkshaka, as, m. a spectator, a beholder.

Īkshaṇa, am, n. a look, view, aspect, sight; regarding, looking after, caring for; an eye.

Īkshaṇika, as, ā, m. f. a looker into the future, a fortune-teller.

Īkshamāṇa, as, ā, am, looking at, surveying.

Īkshā, f. sight, viewing, considering.

Īkshita, as, ā, am, seen, beheld, regarded.

Īkshitṛi, tā, trī, tṛi, seeing, beholding, a beholder.

Īksheṇya, as, ā, am, Ved. deserving to be seen, curious.

Īkshyamāṇa, as, ā, am, being beheld, being viewed.

ईख् *īkh* or *ikh,* cl. 1. P. *ekhati, iyekha,* or *īkhati, īkhāñ-ćakāra, ekhitum* or *īkhitum,* to go, move.

ईङ्ख् *īṅkh* or *iṅkh,* cl. 1. P. *iṅkhati, iṅkhāñ-ćakāra,* or *īṅkhati, īṅkhāñ-ćakāra, iṅkhitum* or *īṅkhitum,* to go, move: Caus. *īṅkhayati, -yitum,* to move backwards and forwards, to move up and down, to swing.

ईज् *īj* or *īñj,* cl. 1. P. *ījati, ījāñ-ćakāra, ījitum* or *īñjati,* &c., to go; to blame or censure.

ईजिक *ījika, ās,* m. pl., N. of a people.

ईड् 1. *īḍ,* cl. 2. A. *īṭṭe* (2nd sing. pres. *īḍishe,* Ved. *īḷishe*), *īḍāñ-ćakre, īḍishyate, aiḍishṭa, īḍitum,* Ved. *īḷe,* &c., to implore, request, ask for (with two acc.); to praise: Caus. P. *īḍayati, -yitum,* to ask; to praise.

Īḍana, am, n. the act of praising.

Īḍā, f. praise, commendation.

Īḍita or *īḷita, as, ā, am,* praised, commended.

Īḍenya or *īḷenya* or *īḍya, as, ā, am,* Ved. to be invoked or implored, to be praised or glorified, praiseworthy, laudable.

Īḍyamāna, as, ā, am, being praised.

ईड् 2. *īḍ, īṭ,* f., Ved. = *iḍ,* refreshment, libation.

ईढ *īḍha, as, ā, am* (? fr. *īh*), sought (?).

ईति *īti, is,* f. (fr. 4. *ī?*), plague, distress, any calamity of the season (as drought, excessive rain, swarm of rats, foreign invasion, &c.); infectious disease; an affray; travelling in foreign countries, sojourning.

ईदृक्ष *īdṛiksha, as, ī, am* (fr. *id,* neut. of pronom. base 3. *i,* and *dṛiksha,* rt. *dṛiś,* dropping one *d* and lengthening the preceding *i,* as in *tādṛiksha* from *tad,* &c.), of this aspect, of such a kind, endowed with such qualities, such like.

Ī-dṛiś, k, Ved. *n,* endowed with such qualities, such; (*k*), n., Ved. such a condition, such occasion. — *Īdṛik-tā,* f. quality.

Īdṛiśa, as, ī, am, or *īdṛiśaka, as, ikā, am,* endowed with such qualities, such; [with the final syllables *dṛiś* and *dṛiśa* of these words cf. the Gr. λικ in ἡλίκ, λικο in τηλίκο-ς, &c.; Goth. *leika* in *hvēleiks,* 'welcher,' *svaleik-s,* 'such;' Mod. Germ. *solcher;* Slav. *liko,* nom. *lik,* e. g. *tolik,* 'such;' Lat. *li* in *tālis, quālis.*]

ईन्त् *īnt,* cl. 1. P. *īntati, -titum,* to bind; [cf. *ant* and *and.*]

ईप्स् *īps* (Desid. of rt. *āp,* q. v.), to wish to obtain.

Īpsana, am, n. desiring, wishing to obtain.

Īpsā, f. asking, desire, wish to obtain.

Īpsita, as, ā, am, wished, desired.

Īpsu, us, us, u, striving to obtain; wishing to get or obtain, desirous of (with acc.). — *Īpsu-yajña, as,* m. a particular Soma sacrifice.

ईम् *īm,* ind. (fr. pronominal base 3. *i*), Ved. a particle of affirmation and restriction, generally after short words at the beginning of a period, or after the relative pronouns, the conjunction *yad,* prepositions and particles such as *āt, uta, atha,* &c. *Īm* has also the sense 'now' (= *idānīm*), and is by Sāy. sometimes considered as an acc. case for *enam.*

ईयचक्षस् *īya-ćakshas, ās, ās, as* (*īya* fr. rt. *i*), Ved. one whose eyes go or look about everywhere; (Sāy.) of pervading sight.

Īyivas, ān, -yushī, as, gone, having gone, having obtained.

ईर् *īr,* cl. 2. A. *īrte, īrāñ-ćakre, īrishyati, airishṭa, īritum,* Ved. inf. *iradhyai,* to go, move, rise, arise from; to go away, retire; to agitate, elevate, raise (one's voice): Caus. P. *īrayati, -yitum,* to agitate, throw, cast; to excite; to cause to rise; to bring to life; to raise one's voice, utter, pronounce, proclaim, cite; to elevate; A. to raise one's self.

Īraṇa, as, ā, am, agitating, driving; (*as*), m. the wind.

Īrita, as, ā, am, sent, despatched; said, uttered. — *Īritākūta* (°*ta-āk*°), *am,* n. declared purpose or intention.

Īrya, as, ā, am, to be excited. — *Īrya-tā,* f., Ved. the condition of one who is to be excited.

Īryā, f. wandering about as a religious mendicant. — *Īryā-patha, as,* m. the observances of a religious mendicant; the four positions of the body, viz. going, standing upright, sitting and lying down.

ईरामा *īrāmā,* f., N. of a river.

ईरिण *īriṇa, as, ā, am* (fr. rt. *īr?*), desert; (*am*), n. salt and barren soil. See *iriṇa.*

ईरिन् *īrin, ī,* m., N. of a man; (*iṇas*), m. pl. the descendants of this man.

ईर्क्ष्य् *īrkshy.* See *īrshy.*

ईर्म 1. *īrma,* ind., Ved. in this place, here, to this place; (Sāy.) going constantly, or instigating everything.

ईर्म 2. *īrma, as,* m., Ved. the arm, the fore-quarter of an animal; (*am*), n. a sore or wound.

ईर्मान्त *īrmānta, as, ā, am,* Ved. epithet of a team of horses or of the horses of the sun's car; full-haunched (lit. full-ended); thin-haunched; (perhaps) having the biggest horses on both sides of the team.

ईर्वारु *īrvāru, us,* m. a cucumber, Cucumis Utilissimus. See *irvāru.*

ईर्ष्य् *īrshy* or *īrkshy,* cl. 1. P. *īrshyati, īrshyāñ-ćakāra, īrshyitum* or *īrkshyati,* &c., to envy, to feel impatient at another's prosperity (with dat.): Desid. *īrshyishishati* or *īrshyiyishati.*

Īrshā, f. impatience, envy of another's success; more properly read *īrshyā.*

Īrshālu, us, us, u, impatient of another's success, envious.

Īrshita, as, ā, am, envied; (*am*), n. envy.

Īrshitavya, as, ā, am, to be envied.

Īrshu, us, us, u, envious, jealous.

Īrshya, as, ā, am, envious, envying; (*ā*), f. envy or impatience of another's success; spite, malice. — *Īrshyā-vat, ān, atī, at,* or *īrshyā-maya, as, ī, am,* envious, spiteful. — *Īrshyā-vaśa, as, ā, am,* overcome with envy.

Irshyaka, *as*, *ā*, *am*, envious, envying.
Irshyamāṇa, *as*, *ā*, *am*, envying, envious.
Irshyālu, *us*, *us*, *u*, envious, jealous.
Irshyin, *ī*, *iṇī*, *i*, envious, spiteful.
Irshyu, *us*, *us*, *u*, Ved. zealous.

ईलिन **īlina**, *as*, m., N. of a son of Taṇsu and father of Dushyanta.

ईली **īlī** or *īli*, *is*, f. a weapon, sometimes considered as a cudgel and sometimes as a short sword or stick shaped like a sword.

ईळ् **īḷ**, *īḷā*, &c. See under *īḍ*.

ईवत् **ī-vat**, *ān*, *atī*, *at* (fr. pronominal base 3. *i*), Ved. so large, so stately, so magnificent, so much.

ईश् 1. **īś**, cl. 2. A. *īshṭe*, or Ved. *īśe*, *īśāñ-ćakre*, *īśishyati*, *īśitum*, to own, possess; to belong to; to dispose of, be valid or powerful, to be master of (with gen., or Ved. with gen. of an inf., or with a common inf., or the loc. of an abstract noun); to command; to rule, reign; to behave like a master, allow; [with this word are perhaps connected Goth. *aigan*, 'to have;' Old Germ. *eigan*, adj. *eigan*, 'own;' Mod. Germ. *eigen*.]

2. *īś*, *ṭ*, m., Ved. master, lord, the supreme spirit. — *Iśā-vāsya*, *am*, n. 'to be clothed or pervaded by the supreme,' a title of the Īśa-upanishad, which commences with that expression.

Iśa, *as*, *ā*, *am*, owning, possessing, sharing; one who is completely master of anything; capable of (with gen.); powerful, supreme; a ruler, a master, a lord; (*as*), m. a husband; a Rudra; the number 'eleven' (as there are eleven Rudras); N. of Śiva as regent of the north-east quarter; (*ā*), f. faculty, power, dominion. — *Iśa-tva*, *am*, n. supremacy, superiority. — *Iśa-sakhi*, *ā*, m. Śiva's friend, an epithet of Kuvera. — *Iśādhyāya* (°*śa-adh*°), *as*, m., N. of the Īśa-upanishad. — *Iśopanishad* (°*śa-up*°), *t*, f., N. of an Upanishad.

Iśana, *am*, n. commanding, reigning.

Iśāna, *as*, *ā*, *am*, owning, possessing, wealthy; reigning; (*as*), m. a ruler, master, one of the older names of Śiva-Rudra; one of the Rudras; the sun as a form of Śiva; a Sādhya; epithet of Vishṇu; N. of a man; (*ī*), f. an epithet of Durgā; (*as* or *ī*), m. or f. the silk-cotton tree, Bombax Heptaphyllum; (*am*), n. light, splendor. — *Iśāna-kṛit*, *t*, *t*, *t*, Ved. acting like a competent person, making use of one's possessions or faculties; (Sāy.) rendering one a master or able. — *Iśāna-ćandra*, *as*, m., N. of a physician. — *Iśāna-ja*, *ās*, m. pl. a class of deities forming a section of the Kalpa-bhavas. — *Iśāna-devī*, f., N. of a woman.

Iśitṛi, *tā*, m. a master, an owner or proprietor; a king.

Iśin, *ī*, *inī*, *i*, commanding, reigning; (*inī*), f. supremacy. — *Iśi-tā*, f. or *iśi-tva*, *am*, n. superiority, supremacy, one of the eight attributes of Śiva.

Iśvara, *as*, *ā*, *am*, able to do, capable of (with gen. of Vedic inf., or with common inf.), liable, exposed to; (*as*, *ī*), m. f. master, lord, prince, king, mistress, queen; (*as*), m. a husband; god, the supreme, especially Śiva, one of the Rudras, the god of love, the soul or supreme soul (*ātman*); N. of a prince; (*ā* or *ī*), f., N. of Durgā; of Lakshmī or of any other of the Śaktis or female energies of the deities. — *Iśvara-krishṇa*, *as*, m., N. of the author of the Sāṅkhya-kārikā. — *Iśvara-gītā*, f. pl. a section of the Kūrma-Purāṇa. — *Iśvara-tā*, f. or *īśvara-tva*, *am*, n. superiority, supremacy. — *Iśvara-datta*, *as*, m., N. of a prince. — *Iśvara-nishedha*, *as*, m. atheism. — *Iśvara-nishṭha*, *as*, *ā*, *am*, trusting in God. — *Iśvara-pūjaka*, *as*, *ā*, *am*, pious. — *Iśvara-pūjā*, f. worship of God. — *Iśvara-prasāda*, *as*, m. divine grace. — *Iśvara-bhāva*, *as*, m. royal or imperial state. — *Iśvara-sadman*, *a*, n. a temple. — *Iśvara-sabha*, *am*, n. a royal court or assembly. — *Iśvara-sevā*, f. the worship of God. — *Iśvarādhīna* (°*ra-adh*°), *as*, *ā*, *am*, subject to a king, dependant on a master or on God. — *Iśvarādhīna-tā*, f. or *īśvarādhīna-tva*, *am*, n. dependance upon God, subjection to a ruler. — *Iśvarānanda* (°*ra-ān*°), *as*, m., N. of a scholiast.

ईष् **īsh**, cl. 1. A. (with prep. also P.) *īshate*, *-ti*, *īshāñ-ćakre* or *-ćakāra*, and Ved. *īshe*, *ishitum*, to go, to fly away, escape; to attack, to hurt; to glean, to collect a few grains; to look.

Ishaṇa, *as*, *ā*, *am*, hastening; (*ā*), f. haste.
Ishaṇin, *ī*, *inī*, *i*, hastening.

ईष **īsha**, *as*, m. the month Āśvina; see *isha*; a son of the third Manu; a servant of Śiva.

ईषत् **īshat**, ind. (said to be a pres. part. fr. rt. *īsh*), little, a little, slightly. — *Ishać-ćhvāsa*, *as*, *ā*, *am*, slightly resounding. — *Ishaj-jala*, *am*, n. shallow water, a little water. — *Ishat-kara*, *as*, *ī*, *am*, doing little; easy to be accomplished. — *Ishat-kārya*, *as*, *ā*, *am*, connected with slight effort. — *Ishat-pāṇḍu*, *us*, m. a pale or light brown colour. — *Ishat-pāna*, *as*, *ā*, *am*, that of which a little is drunk; (*am*), n. a little draught. — *Ishat-purusha*, *as*, m. a mean man. — *Ishat-pralambha*, *as*, *ā*, *am*, to be gained for little. — *Ishat-sprishṭa*, *as*, *ā*, *am*, slightly touched (applied to the semivowels). — *Ishad-ushṇa*, *as*, *ā*, *am*, tepid, slightly warm. — *Ishad-ūna*, *as*, *ā*, *am*, not quite complete or entire. — *Ishad-guṇa*, *as*, *ā*, *am*, of little merit. — *Ishad-darśana*, *am*, n. a glance, a slight inspection. — *Ishad-dhāsa* (*īshat-hāsa*), *as*, m. slight laughter, a smile. — *Ishad-rakta*, *as*, *ā*, *am*, pale red. — *Ishad-vivṛita*, *as*, *ā*, *am*, slightly open. — *Ishan-nāda*, *as*, *ā*, *am*, slightly sounding (applied to unaspirated soft consonants). — *Ishan-nimaya*, *as*, *ā*, *am*, exchanged for a little. — *Ishal-labha*, *as*, *ā*, *am*, to be obtained for a little.

ईषा **īshā**, f. (said to be fr. *īsh*), the pole or the shafts of a carriage or plough; (e), du. the double or fork-shaped pole. — *Ishā-daṇḍa*, *as*, m. the handle of a plough. — *Ishā-danta*, *as*, m. an elephant with a large tusk or tooth, the tusk of an elephant. — *Ishādhāra* (°*shā-ādh*°), *as*, m., N. of a Nāga.

ईषिका **īshikā**, f. an elephant's eyeball; a painter's brush, &c.; a weapon, a dart or arrow. See *ishīkā* and *īshīkā*.

ईषिर **īshira**, *as*, m. fire. See *ishira*.

ईषीका **īshīkā**, f. a painter's brush, a fibrous stick used as one; an ingot-mould; a dipping rod or something cast into a crucible to examine if the metal it contains is in fusion. See *īkshikā*.

ईष्म **īshma** and *īshva*, *as*, m. Kāmadeva; spring. See *ishma* and *ishva*.

ईष्व **īshva**, *as*, m. a spiritual teacher.

ईह् **īh**, cl. 1. A. *īhate*, *īhāñ-ćakre*, *īhishyate*, *īhitum*, rarely P. *īhati*, &c., to endeavour to obtain; to aim at or attempt; to long for, desire; to take care of; to have in mind, think of (with acc.): Caus. *īhayati*, *-yitum*, to impel.

Iha, *as*, m. attempt (e.g. *ūrdhveha*, attempt to rise).

Ihamāna, *as*, *ā*, *am*, attempting, undertaking, performing.

Ihā, f. effort, exertion, activity; request, desire, wish. — *Ihā-tas*, ind. diligently, energetically, by or with labour or exertion. — *Ihā-mṛiga*, *as*, m. a wolf; a division of the drama. — *Ihārthin* (*īhā-ar*°), *ī*, *inī*, *i*, aiming at any object, seeking wealth. — *Ihā-vṛika*, *as*, m. a wolf.

Ihita, *as*, *ā*, *am*, sought, attempted, striven for; wished, desired; (*am*), n. desire, request, wish, effort.

उ

उ 1. **u**, the fifth letter and third short vowel of the alphabet, pronounced as the *u* in *full*. — *U-kāra*, *as*, m. the letter or sound *u*.

उ 2. **u**, ind. an interjection of assent, calling, compassion, anger, and command.

उ 3. **u**, ind. an enclitic copula, used frequently in the Vedas; (as a particle implying restriction and antithesis, generally after pronominals, prepositions, particles, and before *nu* and *su*, equivalent to) and, also, further; on the other hand (especially in connection with a relative, e. g. *ya u*, he on the contrary who &c.).

This particle may serve to give emphasis, like *id* and *eva*, especially after prepositions or demonstrative pronouns, in conjunction with *nu*, *vai*, *hi*, *ćid*, &c. (e. g. *ayam u vām purutamo johavīmi*, I this very person invoke you constantly). It is especially used in the figure of speech called Anaphora, and particularly when the pronouns are repeated (e. g. *tam u stusha Indram tam griṇīshe*, him I praise, Indra, him I sing). It may be used in drawing a conclusion, like the English 'now' (e. g. *tad u tathā na kuryāt*, that now he should not do in such a manner), and is frequently found in interrogative sentences (e. g. *ka u tać ćiketa*, who, I ask, should know that?).

Pāṇini calls this particle *uñ* to distinguish it from the interrogative *u*. In the Pada-pāṭha it is written *ūṃ*.

In the classical language *u* occurs only after *atha*, *na*, and *kim*, with a slight modification of the sense, and often only as an expletive (see *kim*); *u-u* or *u-uta*, on the one hand—on the other hand; partly—partly; as well—as.

उ 4. **u**, cl. 1. A. *avate*, *ūve*, *oshyate*, *aushṭa*, *otum*, to sound, to make a noise; to roar, bellow: Caus. P. *āvayati*, *-yitum*, to cause to sound.

उ 5. **u**, cl. 5. P., Ved. *unoti*, *otum*, to animate, ask, demand.

उ 6. **u**, *us*, m., N. of Śiva; also of Brahmā.

उकनाह **ukanāha**, *as*, m. a horse of a red and yellow or red and black colour, a bay or chesnut horse.

उकुण **ukuṇa**, *as*, m. a bug; also *utkuṇa*.

उक्त **ukta**, *as*, *ā*, *am* (past pass. part. of rt. *vać*), uttered, said, spoken; (*am*), n. word, sentence; (*am*, *ā*), n. f. a stanza of four lines with one syllabic instant, one long or two short syllables in each; [cf. Zend *ukhta*.] — *Ukta-tva*, *am*, n. the being spoken or uttered. — *Ukta-nirvāha*, *as*, m. maintaining an assertion. — *Ukta-puṇska*, a (feminine or neuter) word, of which also a masculine is mentioned or exists, and whose meaning only differs from that of the masculine by the notion of gender (e. g. the word *Gaṅgā* is not *ukta-puṇska*, whereas the word *śobhanā* is so; cf. *bhāshita-puṇska*). — *Ukta-pratyukta*, *am*, n. speech and reply, discourse, conversation. — *Ukta-vat*, *ān*, *atī*, *at*, one who has spoken. — *Ukta-varjam*, ind. except the cases mentioned. — *Ukta-vākya*, *as*, *ā*, *am*, one who has given an opinion; (*am*), n. a dictum, a decree. — *Uktānukta* (°*ta-an*°), *as*, *ā*, *am*, spoken and not spoken. — *Uktopasaṃhāra* (°*ta-up*°), *as*, m. any brief or compendious phrase or description.

Ukti, *is*, f. sentence, proclamation, speech, expression, word.

Uktvā, ind. having spoken or said.

Uktha, *am*, n. a saying, sentence, verse, eulogy, praise; (in the ritual) a kind of recitation or certain recited verses forming a subdivision of the Śastras. They generally form a series, and are spoken or recited in opposition to those verses which are sung (*Sāman*) and to the muttered sacrificial formulas (*Yajus*). The great *Uktha* (*Mahad-uktham* or *Bṛihad-uktham*) forms a series of verses, in three sections, each containing eighty threefold verses (*Trića*), recited at the end of the Agnićayana; a N. of the Sāma-veda; (*ā*), f. a kind of metre, a stanza of four lines having one long or two short syllables in each; (*as*), m. a form of Agni; N. of a prince. — *Uktha-pattra*, *as*, *ā*, *am*, Ved. having verses as wings. — *Uktha-pātra*, *am*, n. vessels or libations offered during the recitation of an uktha. — *Uktha-bhṛit*, *t*, *t*, *t*, Ved. offering ukthas. — *Uktha-vat, ān, atī, at,* Ved. connected with an uktha. — *Uktha-vardhana, as, ā, am,* Ved. strengthening one's self by or delighting in praise; (Sāy.) to be celebrated in praise. — *Uktha-vāhas, ās, ās, as,* Ved. offering verses; one to whom verses are offered. — *Uktha-śansin, ī, inī, i,* Ved. praising; uttering the ukthas. — *Uktha-śas, as, as,* or *uktha-śās, ās, ās,* m. f. or *uktha-śasa, as, ā, am,* Ved. uttering a verse, praising. — *Uktha-śushma, as, ā, am,* Ved. loudly resonant with verses, moving on with the sound of verses (as with the roaring of waters), accompanied by sounding verses; (Sāy.) whose strength is praise. — *Ukthā-mada, am,* n., Ved. praise and rejoicing. — *Ukthārka* (°*tha-ar*°), *am,* n., Ved. recitation and hymn. — *Ukthā-vi, īs, īs, i,* Ved. fond of verses. — *Ukthā-śastra, am,* n., Ved. recitation and praise.

Ukthin, ī, inī, i, Ved. uttering verses, praising, lauding; accompanied by praise, or (in ritual) by ukthas.

Ukthya, as, ā, am, Ved. accompanied by verse or praise, consisting of praise, deserving praise, skilled in praising; accompanied by ukthas; (*as*), m. a libation (*graha*) at the morning and midday sacrifice; (scil. *kratu*) N. of a liturgical ceremony, forming part e. g. of the Jyotishṭoma; a Soma-yajña.

उक्ष् 1. *uksh,* cl. 1. 6. P. A. *ukshati, -te, ukshāñ-ćakāra* (Ved. *vavaksha, -she*), *ukshitum,* to sprinkle, moisten, wet; to sprinkle or scatter in small drops, to emit; to throw out, scatter (as sparks); to clean; [cf. Lith. *ûkana:* Hib. *uisg, uisge,* 'water, a river;' *uisgeach,* 'aquatic, watery, fluid, moist, pluvial.']

1. *uksha, as,* m. (at the end of some compounds) = *ukshan* below; (*as, ā, am*), clean (?).

Ukshaṇa, am, n. sprinkling, consecrating.

Ukshaṇya, nom. P., Ved. *ukshaṇyati,* to do or behave like Ukshan; (Sāy.) to desire one who pours down riches &c.

Ukshaṇyāyana, as, m., Ved. a patronymic from Ukshaṇya.

Ukshaṇyu, us, us, u, Ved. behaving or doing like Ukshan; (Sāy.) desirous of one who pours down riches &c.

Ukshan, ā, m. an ox or bull (especially as drawing the chariot of Ushas or dawn); epithet of the Soma (as sprinkling or scattering small drops); of the Maruts; of the sun and Agni; one of the eight chief medicaments (*ṛishabha*); N. of a man; (*ā, ā, a*), large (?); [cf. Zend *ukhshan;* Goth. *auhsa* and *auhsu;* Armen. *eṣn.*] — *Uksha-tara, as,* m. a small bull or ox; a large bull. — *Uksha-vaśa, as,* m., Ved. a bull-calf, male calf. — *Uksha-vehat, at,* m., Ved. an impotent bull (?). — *Ukshānna* (°*ksha-an*°), *as, ā, am,* Ved. one whose food is oxen.

1. *ukshita, as, ā, am,* sprinkled, moistened, cleansed, perfumed.

उक्ष् 2. *uksh,* cl. 1. P., Ved. *ukshati, vavaksha,* and A. *vavakshe, ukshitum,* to grow up, to grow strong; A. to strengthen one's self; become strong: Caus. *ukshayate, -yitum,* to strengthen.

2. *uksha, as, ā, am,* large.

Ukshāla, as, ā, am (?), swift, excellent, terrible, high, much; (*as*), m. a monkey (?).

2. *ukshita, as, ā, am,* adult, of full growth, strong; old.

उख् *ukh,* cl. 1. P. *okhati, uvokha, okhitum,* to go, move.

उख *ukha, as,* m. (fr. rt. *khan* with *ud?*), Ved. a boiler, a pot, a vessel; N. of a pupil of Tittiri; (*ā*), f. a boiler, any saucepan, a pot or vessel which can be put on the fire; a part of the body. — *Ukhaććhid, t, t, t,* Ved. breaking the pot.

Ukhya, as, ā, am, Ved. being in a dish; boiled, dressed in a pot (flesh, &c.).

उखर्वल *ukharvala* or *ukhala, as,* m. a kind of grass, a sort of Andropogon.

उखुली *ukhulī,* f., N. of a deity.

उगण *ugaṇa, as, ā, am* (corrupted fr. *ud-gaṇa* or *uru-gaṇa?*), Ved. consisting of extended troops (used as an epithet of *senā,* an army).

उग्र *ugra, as, ā, am* (said to be fr. rt. *uć,* but probably fr. a rt. *uj* or *vaj,* fr. which also *ojas, vāja, vajra,* may be derived; comparative *ugratara* and *ojīyas;* superl. *ugratama* and *ojishṭha*), powerful, violent, mighty, strong beyond measure, huge, formidable, terrible; high, noble; cruel, fierce, ferocious, savage; angry, passionate, wrathful; hot, sharp, pungent, acrid; (*as*), m., N. of Rudra or Śiva; N. of a mixed tribe, from a Kshatriya father and Śūdra mother, (the employment of this caste, according to Manu, is the killing or catching of animals that live in holes, as of snakes &c.; but according to the Tantras the Ugra is an encomiast or bard); the tree Hyperanthera Moringa; N. of a Dānava; a son of Dhṛita-rāshṭra; the Guru of Narendrāditya, who built a temple called Ugreśa; a group of asterisms (viz. *pūrvaphālgunī, pūrvāshāḍhā, pūrvabhādrapada, maghā, bharaṇī*); N. of the Malabar country; (*ā*), N. of different plants, Artemisia Sternutatoria, Coriandrum Sativum, &c.; (*ī*), f. a being belonging to the class of demons; (*am*), n. a certain poison, the root of Aconitum Ferox; wrath, anger; [cf. Zend *ughra.*] — *Ugra-karman, ā, ā, a,* fierce in action, violent, cruel. — *Ugra-kāṇḍa, as,* m. a sort of gourd, Momordica Charantia. — *Ugra-gandha, as, ā, am,* strong-smelling; (*as*), m. the plant Michelia Champaca; garlic; (*ā*), f. orris root; a medicinal plant; Artemisia Sternutatoria; Pimpinella Involucrata; the common carraway (Carum Carui, &c.); Ligusticum Ajowan; (*am*), n. Asa Fœtida. — *Ugragandhin, ī, inī, i,* strong-smelling. — *Ugraćaya, as,* m. strong desire. — *Ugra-ćāriṇī,* f., N. of Durgā. — *Ugra-jāti, is, is, i,* base-born. — *Ugra-jit, t,* f., Ved., N. of an Apsaras. — *Ugra-tā,* f. or *ugratva, am,* n. violence, passion, anger; pungency, acrimony. — *Ugra-tejas, ās, ās, as,* endowed with great or terrible energy; (*ās*), m., N. of a Nāga; of a Buddha; of another divine being. — *Ugra-danshṭra, as, ā, am,* having terrific teeth. — *Ugra-daṇḍa, as, ā, am,* lit. 'stern-sceptred' or holding a terrible rod; relentless, remorseless. — *Ugra-darśana, as, ā, am,* of a frightful appearance, frightful, terrible. — *Ugra-duhitṛi, tā,* f. daughter of a powerful man. — *Ugra-dhanvan, ā, ā, a,* Ved. having a powerful bow, epithet of Indra. — *Ugra-nāsika, as, ā, am,* large-nosed. — *Ugra-putra, as,* m. son of a powerful man; (*as, ā, am*), having mighty sons. — *Ugra-bāhu, us, us, u,* Ved. whose arms are large or powerful. — *Ugram-paśya, as, ā, am,* frightful, hideous, fierce looking; malignant, wicked; (*ā*), f., N. of an Apsaras. — *Ugra-retas, ās,* m. a form of Rudra. — *Ugra-vīra, as, ā, am,* Ved. having powerful men. — *Ugra-vīrya, as, ā, am,* terrible in might. — *Ugra-vega, as, ā, am,* of terrible velocity. — *Ugra-vyagra, as,* m., N. of a Dānava. — *Ugra-śakti, is,* m., N. of a son of king Amara-śakti. — *Ugra-śāsana, as, ā, am,* severe in command, strict in orders. — *Ugra-śekharā,* f. 'crest of Śiva,' N. of the Gangā. — *Ugra-śoka, as, ā, am,* sorely grieving. — *Ugra-śravaṇa-darśana, as, ā, am,* terrible to hear and see. — *Ugra-śravas, ās,* m., N. of a man. — *Ugra-sena, as,* m., N. of several princes, e. g. of a brother of Janam-ejaya; (*ā*), f., N. of the wife of Akrūra. — *Ugrasena-ja, as,* m. a N. of Kansa, the uncle and enemy of Kṛishṇa. — *Ugrāćārya* (°*gra-āć*°), *as,* m., N. of an author. — *Ugrā-deva, as,* m., Ved. having mighty deities, N. of a Ṛishi. — *Ugrāyudha* (°*gra-āy*°), *as, ā, am,* Ved. having powerful weapons; (*as*), m., N. of a prince. — *Ugreśa* (°*gra-īś*°), *as,* m. the mighty or terrible lord, an epithet of Śiva; N. of a sanctuary built by Ugra.

Ugraka, as, m., N. of a Nāga.

उङ्कार *un-kāra, as,* m., N. of a companion of Vishṇu.

उङ्कुण *unkuṇa, as,* m. a bug. See *ut-kuṇa.*

उच् *uć,* cl. 4. P. *ućyati, uvoća, ućishyati, ućitum,* to take pleasure in; to delight in, to be fond of; to be accustomed, to be suitable, to suit, to fit.

Ućita, as, ā, am, delightful, pleasurable, agreeable; customary, usual; proper, suitable, convenient; acceptable, fit or right to be taken; known, understood; intrusted, deposited; measured, adjusted, accurate; delighting in, used to.

उचथ *ućatha, am,* n. (fr. rt. *vać*), Ved. verse, praise.

Ućathya, as, ā, am, Ved. deserving praise; (*as*), m., N. of an Āngirasa, author of some hymns of the Ṛig-veda.

उच्च *ućća, as, ā, am* (said to be fr. 1. *ud* with *ća* fr. rt. *aṅć*), high, lofty, elevated; tall; deep; high-sounding, loud, pronounced with the Udātta accent; intense, violent; (*as*), m. the apex of the orbit of a planet; [cf. Hib. *uchdan,* 'a hillock;' Cambro-Brit. *uched,* 'cleve.'] — *Ućća-tama, as, ā, am,* highest. — *Ućća-tara, as, ā, am,* higher, more lofty. — *Ućća-taru, us,* m. the cocoa-nut tree; any lofty tree. — *Ućća-tā,* f. or *ućća-tva, am,* n. height, superiority. — *Ućća-tāla, am,* n. music and dancing at feasts, drinking parties, &c. — *Ućća-deva, as,* m. an epithet of Vishṇu or Kṛishṇa. — *Ućća-devatā,* f. time personified, chronos. — *Ućća-dhvaja, as,* m., N. of Śākya-muni as teacher of the gods among the Tushitas, q. v. — *Ućća-nīća, as, ā, am,* high and low, variegated, heterogeneous; (*am*), n. the upper and lower station of the planets; change of accent. — *Ućća-pada, am,* n. a high situation, a high office. — *Ućća-bhāshaṇa, am,* n. speaking aloud. — *Ućća-bhāshin, ī, iṇī, i,* speaking with a loud voice, shouting, brawling. — *Ućća-lalāṭā* or *-ikā,* f. a woman with a high or projecting forehead. — *Uććāvaća, as, ā, am* (fr. *ućća* = *ud* + *ća* and *ava* + *ća?*), high and low, great and small, variegated, heterogeneous; various, multiform; uneven, irregular, undulating.

Uććakais, ind. excessively lofty; tall; loud.

Uććā, ind., Ved. above (in heaven), from above, upwards; *uććā kṛi,* to carry upwards. — *Uććā-ćakra, as, ā, am,* Ved. having a wheel above (epithet of a well). — *Uććā-budhna, as, ā, am,* Ved. having the bottom upwards.

Uććais, ind. (used adjectively in comp.) aloft, high, above, upwards, from above; loud, accentuated; intensely, much, powerfully. — *Uććaiḥ-kara, as, ā, am,* making acutely accented. — *Uććaiḥ-kula, am,* n. a high family; (*as, ā, am*), of high family. — *Uććairghushṭa, am,* n. making a loud noise, clamour. — *Uććair-ghosha, as, ā, am,* Ved. sounding aloud, crying, neighing, roaring, rattling. — *Uććair-bhujataru, us, us, u,* having trees like outstretched arms. — *Uććaiḥ-śiras, ās, ās, as,* carrying one's head high, a man of high rank. — *Uććaiḥ-śravas, ās,* m. long-eared or neighing aloud; epithet of the horse of Indra, produced at the churning of the ocean, (regarded as the prototype and king of horses.) — *Uććaiḥśravasa, as,* m. = the same. — *Uććaiḥ-svara, as,* m. a loud sound or voice; (*as, ā, am*), making a loud sound. — *Uććais-tama, as, ā, am,* very high, tall or lofty; very loud. — *Uććais-tamām,* ind. exceedingly high; on high; loudly, aloud. — *Uććais-tara, as, ā, am,* higher, very high, loftier, louder; pronounced with a higher accent. — *Uććaistara-tva, am,* n. state of being too high. — *Uććais-tva, am,* n. height. — *Uććaiḥ-sthāna, am,* n. a high place; (*as, ā, am*), of high rank or family. — *Uććaiḥ-stheya, am,* n. lofty, firmness (of character).

उच्चक् *uć-ćak* (*ud-ćak*), cl. 1. P. A. *ćakati, -te, -kitum,* to look up at, behold.

उच्चक्षुस् *uć-ćakshus* (*ud-ća*°), *us, us, us,* whose eyes are directed upwards.

उच्चघन *uććaghana, am,* n. laughter in the mind not expressed in the countenance.

उच्चट् uć-ćaṭ (*ud-ćaṭ*), cl. 1. P. *-ćaṭati, -ṭitum*, to go away, disappear: Caus. P. *-ćāṭayati, -yitum*, to drive away, expel, scare.

Uć-ćāṭana, am, n. eradicating (as a plant), expulsion; ruining (an adversary), causing a person to quit his occupation by means of magical incantations, exciting disgust for one's profession.

Uć-ćāṭanīya, as, ā, am, to be driven away.

Uć-ćāṭita, as, ā, am, driven away.

उच्चटा uććaṭā, f. (perhaps connected with *ućća* or in some senses fr. *uć-ćaṭ* above), pride, arrogance; habit, usage; N. of different plants, a species of cyperus, a kind of garlic, Abrus Precatorius, Flacourtia Cataphracta.

उच्चण्ड uć-ćaṇḍa (*ud-ća°*), *as, ā, am*, quick, expeditious; passionate, violent; hanging down.

उच्चन्द्र uć-ćandra (*ud-ća°*), *as*, m. the moonless period of the night, the last watch of the night.

उच्चर् uć-ćar (*ud-ćar*), cl. 1. P. *-ćarati, -ritum* (ep. sometimes *-ćartum*), Ved. *-ritave* or *-vai, -rase, -radhyai*, to go upwards, ascend, rise (as the sun), issue forth, go forth; to rise (as the voice); to let the contents (of anything) issue out, to empty the body by evacuations; to emit (sounds), utter, pronounce; to quit, leave; to sin against, to be unfaithful to a husband; to transgress against: Caus. *-ćārayati, -yitum*, to cause to go forth, to evacuate the body by excretion, to discharge feces, to emit, to cause to sound, utter, pronounce, declare.

Uć-ćaraṇa, am, n. going up or out, uttering, articulating.

Uć-ćaraṇya, nom. P. *-ćaraṇyati, -yitum*, to move out, stretch out to.

Uć-ćarita, as, ā, am, gone up or out, risen; uttered, articulated; (*am*), n. excrement, dung.

Uć-ćāra, as, m. feces, excrement; discharge; pronunciation, utterance.

Uć-ćāraka, as, ā, am, pronouncing, making audible.

Uć-ćāraṇa, am, n. pronunciation, articulation, enunciation; making audible. — *Uććāraṇa-jña, as*, m. a linguist, one skilled in utterances or sounds. — *Uććāraṇa-sthāna, am*, n. the part of the throat whence certain sounds such as nasals, gutturals &c. proceed. — *Uććāraṇārtha* (°*ṇa-ar*°), *as, ā, am*, useful for pronunciation; necessary for pronunciation, a redundant letter &c. only used to make pronunciation easy.

Uć-ćāraṇīya, as, ā, am, to be pronounced.

Uć-ćārita, as, ā, am, pronounced, uttered, articulated; having excrements.

1. *uć-ćārya*, ind. having spoken, uttered.

2. *uć-ćārya, as, ā, am*, to be spoken, to be pronounced.

Uć-ćāryamāṇa, as, ā, am, being uttered or pronounced.

उच्चल् uć-ćal (*ud-ćal*), cl. 1. P. *-ćalati, -litum*, to go or move away from; to free one's self from, loosen one's self from.

Uć-ćala, am, n. the mind, the understanding.

Uć-ćalana, am, n. going off or out, moving away.

Uć-ćalita, as, ā, am, gone up or out, winnowed.

उच्चि uć-ći (*ud-ći*), cl. 5. P. A. *-ćinoti, -nute, -ćetum*, to gather, collect.

Uć-ćaya, as, m. gathering, picking up from the ground; adding to, annumeration; collection, heap, plenty, multitude; the knot of the string or cloth which fastens the lower garments round the loins tied in front; the opposite side of a triangle. — *Uććayāpaćaya* (°*ya-ap*°), *au*, m. du. prosperity and decline, rise and fall.

उच्चिङ्गट uććiṅgaṭa, *as*, m. a passionate or angry man; a kind of crab; a sort of cricket. See *uććiṭiṅga, ćiṅgaṭa, ćiććiṭiṅga*.

उच्चिटिङ्ग uććiṭiṅga, *as*, m. a small poisonous animal living in water, a crab; [cf. the last.]

उच्चूड uć-ćūḍa or *uć-ćūla, as*, m. (fr. *ud* + *ćūḍā*), the flag or pennon of a banner; an ornament tied on the top of a banner.

उच्च्यु uć-ćyu (*ud-ćyu*), Caus. P. *-ćyāvayati, -yitum*, to loosen, make free from, emancipate.

उच्छद् uć-ćhad (*ud-ćhad*), cl. 10. P. *-ćhādayati, -yitum*, to uncover (one's body), undress.

Uć-ćhādya, ind. having undressed.

उच्छन्न uććhanna, *as, ā, am* (for *ut-sanna* by a Prākrit corruption?), destroyed.

Uć-ćhādana, am, n. (for *ut-sādana*), cleaning or rubbing the body with perfumes.

उच्छल् uć-ćhal (*ud-śal*), cl. 1. P. A. *-ćhalati, -te, -litum*, to fly upwards or away, to move onwards.

Uć-ćhalat, an, antī, at, flying up or away; going or moving on or against.

Uć-ćhalana, am, n. moving upwards, going on or against.

Uć-ćhālita, as, ā, am, moved, waved, waved above; gone; shaken.

उच्छास् uć-ćhās (*ud-śās*), cl. 2. P., Ved. *-ćhāsti, -situm*, to clean or purify thoroughly.

उच्छास्त्रवर्तिन् uć-ćhāstra-vartin (*ud-śāstra-va*°), *ī, inī, i*, deviating from the law-books, transgressing the ritual-books.

उच्छिख uć-ćhikha, *as, ā, am* (fr. *ud* + *śikhā*), having the flame pointed upwards; flaming, blazing up; radiant; high-crested; (*as*), m., N. of a Nāga ('with erected crest').

उच्छिङ्घन uć-ćhiṅghana, *am*, n. (fr. *ud-śiṅgh*), breathing through the nostrils, snuffing, snoring; (the word is also written *uććhiṅhana*.)

उच्छिद् uć-ćhid (*ud-ćhid*), cl. 7. P. A. *-ćhinatti, -ćhinte, -ćhettum*, to cut out or off, extirpate, destroy; to interfere, interrupt, stop: Caus. P. *-ćhedayati, -yitum*, to cause to extirpate or destroy: Pass. *-ćhidyate*, to be cut off, stopped, or interrupted; to cease, be deficient, fail.

Uć-ćhitti, is, f. extirpation, destroying, destruction.

Uć-ćhidya, ind. having cut off, destroyed, killed, &c.

Uć-ćhinna, as, ā, am, cut out or off; destroyed, killed; abject, vile; (*as*), m. peace obtained by ceding valuable lands.

Uć-ćhettṛi, tā, m. an extirpator, a destroyer.

Uć-ćheda, as, m. cutting off or out; extirpation; destruction; cutting short, putting an end to; excision.

Uć-ćhedana, am, n. cutting off, extirpating, destroying, destruction.

Uć-ćhedanīya, as, ā, am, to be cut off.

Uć-ćhedin, ī, inī, i, destroying.

Uć-ćhedya, as, ā, am, to be cut off, to be destroyed.

उच्छिरस् uć-ćhiras (*ud-śi*°), *ās, ās, as*, having the head elevated, with upraised head, N. of a mountain also called Urumuṇḍa.

उच्छिलीन्ध्र uć-ćhilīndhra (*ud-śi*°), *am*, n. a mushroom.

उच्छिष् uć-ćhish (*ud-śish*), cl. 7. P. *-ćhinashṭi, -ćheshṭum*, to leave (as a remainder), to reject: Pass. *-ćhishyate*, to be left remaining.

Uć-ćhishṭa, as, ā, am, left, rejected, stale; having the remains of food on the mouth or hands, one who has not washed his hands and mouth and therefore is considered impure; (*am*), n. leavings, fragments, remainder (especially of a sacrifice or of food). — *Uććhishṭa-kalpanā*, f. a stale invention. — *Uććhishṭa-gaṇapati, is*, m. (opposed to *śuddha-gaṇapati*), Gaṇeśa as worshipped by the Uććhishṭas or men who leave the remains of food in their mouth during prayer. — *Uććhishṭa-tā*, f. the being left, state of being a remnant or remainder. — *Uććhishṭa-bhojana, am*, n. eating the leavings of another man; (*as*), m. one who eats another's leavings; the attendant upon an idol, whose food is the leavings of offerings. — *Uććhishṭa-bhojin, ī, inī, i*, or *uććhishṭa-bhoktṛi, tā, trī, tṛi*, an eater of leavings, a mean person. — *Uććhishṭa-modana, am*, n. wax. — *Uććhishṭānna* (°*ṭa-an*°), *as, ā, am*, leavings, offal.

Uć-ćhesha, as, m. or *uć-ćheshaṇa, am*, n. rest, remainder; leavings.

उच्छीर्षक uć-ćhīrshaka (*ud-śī*°), *as, ā, am*, having the head raised; (*am*), n. a pillow ('that which raises the head').

उच्छुष् uć-ćhush (*ud-śush*), Caus. *-ćhoshayati, -yitum*, to dry up, make dry.

Uć-ćhushka, as, ā, am, dry, dried up, withered.

Uć-ćhoshaṇa, as, ā, am, drying up, making dry; (*am*), n. drying up, parching.

Uć-ćhoshuka, as, ā, am, drying up, making dry.

उच्छुष्म uć-ćhushma, *am*, n. or *uć-ćhushman, a*, n. (fr. rt. *śvas* with *ud*?), confusion.

उच्छूडा uć-ćhūḍā, f. (see the more correct *uć-ćūḍa*), the head of a banner or part above the flag.

उच्छून uć-ćhūna, *as, ā, am* (fr. rt. *śvi* with *ud*), swollen, turgid; lofty, high; fat, bulky.

उच्छृङ्खल uć-ćhṛiṅkhala (*ud-śṛi*°), *as, ā, am*, unbridled, uncurbed, unrestrained, perverse, self-willed; irregular, desultory, unmethodical.

उच्छोचन uć-ćhoćana, *as, ā, am* (fr. *ud-śuć*), Ved. burning.

उच्छोषण uć-ćhoshaṇa. See *uć-ćhush* above.

उच्छ्रि uć-ćhri (*ud-śri*), cl. 1. P. A. *-ćhrayati, -te, -ćhrayitum*, P. to raise, erect, extol; A. to rise, be erected.

Uć-ćhraya, as, m. rising, raising, erecting; elevation of a tree, mountain, &c.; rising of a planet, &c.; height; growth, increase, intensity; the upright side of a triangle. — *Uććhrayopeta* (°*ya-up*°), *as, ā, am*, possessing height, high, lofty, elevated.

Uć-ćhrayaṇa, am, n. raising, erecting.

Uć-ćhrāya, as, m. rising upwards, elevation, height; growth, increase, intensity; (*ī*), f. an upraised piece of wood, plank.

Uć-ćhrāyin, ī, iṇī, i, high, raised, lofty.

Uć-ćhrita, as, ā, am, raised, lifted up; high, tall; advancing, increasing, prosperous; born, produced; increased in size or bulk, grown. — *Uććhrita-pāṇi, is, is, i*, with outstretched hand.

Uć-ćhriti, is, f. rising upwards, elevation, increase; the upright side of a triangle; the upright elevation or height of a figure.

Uć-ćhreya, as, ā, am, high, lofty.

उच्छ्लक uććhlaka, *as*, m., Ved. a part of the human body, (used only in du.)

उच्छ्वङ्क uććhvaṅka, *as*, m. (fr. rt. *śvaṅć* with *ud*), Ved. gaping, cleaving open, forming a fissure.

उच्छ्वस् uć-ćhvas (*ud-śvas*), cl. 2. P. *-ćhvasiti, -situm*, to breathe, take a deep breath, sigh, pant, respire.

Uć-ćhvasat, an, atī, at, breathing hard, panting.

Uć-ćhvasana, am, n. breathing, sighing; taking a deep breath.

Uć-ćhvasita, as, ā, am, heaving, beating, breathed, inspired, blown, expanded; blooming, enlivened, gladdened; (*am*), n. sighing.

Uć-ćhvāsa, as, m. breath, breathing, deep inspiration; sigh; breathing out, expiring, dying; consolation, encouragement; division of a book, pause in a narration; an air-hole.

Uć-ćhvāsita, as, ā, am, breathless, out of breath, much, excessive, loosened, released, desisted from, disjointed, divided.

Uć-ćhvāsin, ī, inī, i, breathing, inhaling air; sighing, breathing out, expiring; pausing; rising, coming forward.

उछ् ućh, cl. 1. 6. P. *uććhati, uććhāñćakāra, uććhitum*, to finish; to bind; to abandon, transgress.

उज्जन् *uj-jan* (*ud-jan*), cl. 3. P. *-jajanti*, *-janitum*, to beget, produce; cl. 4. A. *-jāyate*, to be born, originate.

उज्जयन *uj-jayana*, &c. See s.v. *uj-ji* below.

उज्जस् *uj-jas* (*ud-jas*), Caus. *-jāsayati*, *-yitum*, to destroy, extirpate (with gen.).

Uj-jāsana, *am*, n. killing, slaughter.

उज्जानक *ujjānaka*, *as*, m., N. of a Tīrtha; also spelt *ujjālaka*.

उज्जि *uj-ji* (*ud-ji*), cl. 1. P. *-jayati*, *-jetum*, to win, conquer, acquire by conquest; to be victorious: Caus. *-jāpayati*, *-yitum*, to assist any one to win; to cause to conquer (with two acc.): Desid. *-jigīshati*, to wish to conquer.

Uj-jayana, *as*, m., N. of a man; (*ī*), f. Ujjayinī or Oujein, the Gr. Οζήνη, a city so called in Avanti (Mālava), formerly the capital of Vikramāditya; it is one of the seven sacred cities of the Hindūs, and the first meridian of their geographers, from which they calculate longitude; the modern Oujein is about a mile south of the ancient city.

Uj-jayanta, *as*, m., N. of a mountain in Surāshṭra in the west of India, part of the Vindhya range. See *raivata*.

Uj-jayinī, f. the city Oujein. See *uj-jayanī*.

Uj-jiti, *is*, f., Ved. victory; N. of certain verses in the Vājasaneyi-Saṃhitā, so called because the words *udajayat tam ujjesham* occurs in them.

Uj-jesha, *as*, *ā*, *am*, Ved. victorious. — *Ujjesha-vat*, *ān*, *atī*, *at*, Ved. containing the word *ujjesha*.

उज्जिहान *ujjihāna*, N. of a region.

उज्जिहीर्षा *uj-jihīrshā*, f. (fr. Desid. of rt. *hṛi* with *ud*), wishing to take or seize.

उज्जीव् *uj-jīv* (*ud-jīv*), cl. 1. P. *-jīvati*, *-vitum*, to revive, return to life: Caus. P. *-jīvayati*, *-yitum*, to restore to life, animate.

Uj-jīvin, *ī*, m., N. of a counsellor of Meghavarṇa, the king of the crows.

उज्जृम्भ् *uj-jṛimbh* (*ud-jṛimbh*), cl. 1. A., poet. P. *-jṛimbhate*, *-ti*, *-bhitum*, to gape, to open; to part asunder; to show one's self, become visible, come forth, break forth, expand, arise.

Uj-jṛimbha, *as*, *ā*, *am*, gaping, parting asunder, open, apart; blown, expanded.

Uj-jṛimbhaṇa, *am*, n. the act of gaping, opening the mouth.

Uj-jṛimbhita, *as*, *ā*, *am*, opened, stretched; expanded, blown; (*am*), n. effort, exertion.

उज्ज्य *uj-jya*, *as*, *ā*, *am* (fr. *ud* + *jyā*), having the bow-sinew loosened.

उज्ज्वल् *uj-jval* (*ud-jval*), cl. 1. P., ep. A. *-jvalati*, *-te*, *-litum*, to blaze up, flame, shine: Caus. P. *-jvalayati*, *-yitum*, to light up, cause to shine, illuminate.

Uj-jvala, *as*, *ā*, *am*, blazing up, luminous, splendid, light; burning; clean, clear; lovely, beautiful; blown, expanded; (*as*), m. love, passion; (*am*), n. gold; (*ā*), f. splendor, clearness, brightness; a form of the Jagatī metre. — *Ujjvala-tā*, f. or *ujjvala-tva*, *am*, n. splendor, radiance; beauty. — *Ujjvala-datta*, *as*, m., N. of the author of a commentary on the Uṇādi-sūtras.

Uj-jvalana, *am*, n. burning, shining; fire, gold (?).

Uj-jvalita, *as*, *ā*, *am*, lighted, shining, flaming, &c.

उज्झ् *ujjh*, cl. 6. P. *ujjhati*, *ujjhāṅ-ćakāra*, *ujjhitum*, &c., to leave, abandon, quit; to avoid, escape.

Ujjha, *as*, *ā*, *am*, quitting, forgetting.

Ujjhaka, *as*, m. a cloud, a devotee.

Ujjhana, *am*, n. abandoning, removing.

Ujjhita, *as*, *ā*, *am*, left, abandoned; left off, discontinued.

Ujjhitṛi, *tā*, *trī*, *tṛi*, who or what leaves.

उज्झटित *uj-jhaṭita*, *as*, *ā*, *am* (rt. *jhaṭ*), perplexed, bewildered.

उञ्छ् *uñćh*, cl. 1. 6. P. *uñćhati* (cl. 1. and 6. differing only in the accent), *uñćhitum*, to gather, glean.

Uñćha, *am*, n. gleaning, gathering grains. — *Uñćha-vritti*, *is*, *is*, *i*, one who lives by gleaning, a gleaner. — *Uñćha-śila*, *am*, n. gleaning corn or grains. — *Uñćha-śila*, *as*, *ā*, *am*, one who lives by gleaning &c.

Uñćhana, *am*, n. gleaning, gathering grains of corn in market-places &c.

उट *uṭa*, *as*, m. leaves, grass, &c., used in making huts, thatches, &c. — *Uṭa-ja*, *as*, *am*, m. n. a hut made of leaves, the residence of hermits or saints; a house in general.

उठ् *uṭh* or *ūṭh*, cl. 1. P. *oṭhati* or *ūṭhati*, *-ṭhitum*, to strike or knock down.

उडु *uḍu*, *us*, *u*, f. n. a lunar mansion or constellation in the moon's path; (*u*), n. water. — *Uḍu-pa*, *as*, *am*, m. n. a raft or float; (*as*), m. the moon, (the half-moon being formed like a boat.) — *Uḍu-pati*, *is*, m. or *uḍu-rāj*, *ṭ*, m. the moon; the Soma. — *Uḍu-patha*, *as*, m. the ether, firmament (the path of the stars). — *Uḍu-rāj*, *ṭ*, m. the moon. — *Uḍu-loman*, *ā*, m., N. of a man. — *Uḍū-pa*, *as*, *am*, m. n. a raft, a float; (*as*), m. the moon.

उडुम्बर *uḍumbara*, *as*, m. (in Ved. written with *ḍ*, in Class. generally with *d*), the tree Ficus Glomerata; a species of leprosy with coppery spots; the threshold of a house; a eunuch; a kind of worm supposed to be generated in the blood and to produce leprosy; (*am*), n. the fruit of the tree Ficus Glomerata; copper; a karsha, a measure of two tolas. — *Uḍumbara-dalā* or *uḍumbara-parṇī*, f. the plant Croton Polyandra. — *Uḍumbarā-vatī*, f., N. of a river; see also *udumbara*.

उड्डामर *uḍḍāmara*, *as*, *ā*, *am* (fr. *ud-ḍā*° ?), excellent, respectable, of high rank or consequence.

उड्डी *uḍ-ḍī* (*ud-ḍī*), cl. 1. 4. A. *-ḍayate* or *-ḍīyate*, *-ḍayitum*, to fly up: Caus. *-ḍapayati* (*-ḍāpayati* ?), to scare.

Uḍ-ḍayana, *am*, n. flying up, flying, soaring.

Uḍ-ḍīna, *as*, *ā*, *am*, flown up, flying up; (*am*), n. flying as a bird; flying up, soaring.

Uḍ-ḍīyana, *am*, n. flying up, soaring.

Uḍ-ḍīyamāna, *as*, *ā*, *am*, flying up, soaring, one who flies or soars.

उड्डीश *uḍḍīśa*, *as*, m. a work so called, containing charms and incantations; a N. of Śiva.

उड्र *uḍra*, *ās*, m. pl., N. of a people.

उण्डुक *uṇḍuka*, *as*, m. a texture, a net; a part of the body, the peritoneum ?; (this word is perhaps connected with *uḍupa*.)

उण्डेरक *uṇḍeraka*, *as*, m. a ball of flour, a roll, a loaf. — *Uṇḍeraka-sraj*, *k*, f. a string of rolls, balls of meal or flour upon a string.

उत् *ut*, ind. a particle of doubt or deliberation = how, what (?), either, or; see 2. *uta*. (For the prep. *ud* see 1. *ud*, page 153.)

उत 1. *uta*, *as*, *ā*, *am* (fr. rt. *ve*), sewn, woven.

उत 2. *uta*, ind. (as a particle of doubt or deliberation) and, also, even, or. Often used for the sake of emphasis, especially at the end of a line after *iti* or a verb (e. g. *sarva-bhūtāni tam pārtha sadā paribhavanty uta*, all creatures, O king, certainly always despise him).

(As an interrogative particle, generally at the beginning of the second or following part of a double interrogation) or, utrum-an (e. g. *katham nirṇīyate kiṃ syān nishkāraṇo bandhur uta viśvāsa-ghātakah*, how can it be decided whether he be a friend without a motive or a violator of confidence ?). In this sense it may be strengthened by *āho* (e. g. *kaććit tvam asi mānushī utāho surāṅganā*, art thou a mortal woman or divine ?), or by *āho-svit* (e. g. *Śālihotraḥ kiṃ nu syād utāhosvid rājā Nalaḥ*, can it be Śālihotra or king Nala ?). Rarely *kim* is repeated before *uta* used in this sense (e. g. *kiṃ nu svargāt prāptā tasyā rūpeṇa kimuta anyā āgatā*, has she arrived from heaven or has another come in her form ?).

(As a particle of wishing, especially at the beginning of a sentence followed by a potential) would that! utinam! (e. g. *uta adhīyīta*, would that he would read !).

(*Uta* preceded by *kim*) on the contrary, how much more, how much less (e. g. *samartho 'si sahasram api jetum kimuta ekam*, thou art able to conquer even a thousand, how much more one ?).

(*Uta* preceded by *prati*) on the contrary, rather (e. g. *esha prishṭo 'smābhir na jalpati hanti pratyuta pāshāṇaiḥ*, this one questioned by us does not speak, but rather throws stones at us). *Uta vā*, or else, and (e. g. *samudrād uta vā purīshāt*, from the sea or from the moisture in the air); *vā-uta vā* or *utāho vāpi-vā*, either—or; *uta-uta*, both—and (e. g. *uta balavān uta abalaḥ*, both the strong and the weak); *kim-uta vā*, whether—or else.

उतङ्क *utanka*, *as*, m., N. of a Ṛishi. — *Utanka-megha*, *as*, m. a kind of cloud named after that Ṛishi.

उतथ्य *utathya*, *as*, m., N. of a son of Aṅgiras and elder brother of Bṛihaspati. — *Utathya-tanaya*, *as*, m. an epithet of Gautama. — *Utathyā-nuja*, *as*, m. or *utathyānujanman* (°*ya-anu-ja*°), *ā*, m. a N. of Bṛihaspati, regent of the planet Jupiter (younger brother of Utathya).

उताहो *utāho*, ind. (fr. 2. *uta* + *āho*), a particle of doubt or deliberation = either, or; see under 2. *uta* above. — *Utāho-svit*, see under 2. *uta*.

उतूल *utūla*, *ās*, m. pl., N. of a people; also *kulūṭa* or *ulūṭa*.

उत्क *utka*, *as*, *ā*, *am* (fr. 1. *ud*), excited by the desire of obtaining anything; wishing for (with inf.), desirous of, longing for; regretting, sad, sorrowful; absent, thinking of something else; (*as*), m. desire; opportunity, occasion. — *Utka-tā*, f. a state of longing or regret; the plant Pothos Officinalis having aromatic seeds.

Utkāya, nom. A. *-yate*, *-yitum*, to long for.

उत्कच *ut-kaća*, *as*, *ā*, *am*, having the hairs erect.

उत्कच्छा *ut-kaććhā*, f. a metre of six verses, each verse containing eleven syllabic instants.

उत्कञ्चुक *ut-kañćuka*, *as*, *ā*, *am*, having no coat of mail, without bodice or jacket.

उत्कट *ut-kaṭa*, *as*, *ā*, *am* (fr. 1. *ud*), exceeding the usual measure, important; richly endowed with, abounding in; drunk, mad, furious; excessive, much; superior, high, proud, haughty; uneven; difficult; (*as*), m. fluid dropping from the temples of an elephant in rut; the plant Saccharum Sara, or a similar kind of grass; intoxication, pride; (*ā*), f. the plant Laurus Cassia; N. of a town; (*am*), n. the fragrant bark of Laurus Cassia.

उत्कटुकासन *utkaṭukāsana*, *am*, n. sitting on the hams, squatting.

उत्कणिका *ut-kaṇikā*, f. a raised particle.

उत्कण्ठ 1. *ut-kaṇṭha*, *as*, *ā*, *am*, having the neck uplifted, on the point of doing anything; (*as* or *ā*), m. f. longing for a beloved person or thing; regretting, missing anything or person.

2. *utkaṇṭha*, nom. A. *utkaṇṭhate*, *-ṭhitum*, to long

for, regret, sorrow for: Caus. *utkaṇṭhayati, -yitum,* to excite longing, inspire with tender emotions.

Utkaṇṭhita, as, ā, am, regretting, wishing or sorrowing for, distressed, sorrowful; (*ā*), f. a woman longing after her absent lover or husband.

उत्कन्द् *ut-kand* (*ud-skand*), cl. 1. P. *-kandati, -kantum,* to leap, jump over.

Ut-kandaka, as, m. a kind of disease.

उत्कन्धर *ut-kandhara, as, ā, am,* having the neck erect or uplifted; (*am*), n. bending back the neck.

उत्कम्प् *ut-kamp* (*ud-k°*), cl. 1. A. *-kampate, -pitum,* to tremble: Caus. P. *-kampayati, -yitum,* to cause to tremble; to cause to swing upwards, agitate, shake.

Ut-kampa, as, ā, am, trembling, tremor, agitation; (*as*), m. trembling.

Ut-kampana, am, n. the act of trembling, agitation.

Ut-kampin, ī, inī, i, trembling, agitating, causing to tremble.

उत्कर *ut-kara.* See under *ut-kṛī.*

उत्कर्कर *ut-karkara, as,* m. a kind of musical instrument.

उत्कर्ण *ut-karṇa, as, ā, am,* having the ears erect; (*as*), m. an erect ear.

उत्कर्ष *ut-karsha,* &c. See under *ut-kṛish.*

उत्कल् 1. *ut-kal* (*ud-k°*), cl. 10. P. *-kalayati, -yitum,* to unbind, loosen.

Ut-kalita, as, ā, am, unbound, loosened; opened, blossoming; prosperous, rising, increasing; regretting, grieving for.

उत्कल् 2. *ut-kal* (*ud-k°*), cl. 10. P. *-kālayati, -yitum,* to drive out, expel.

उत्कल *utkala, ās,* m. pl., N. of the inhabitants of Orissa, in the south of India; a subdivision of Brāhmans, derived from *Utkala,* a son of Sudyumna; (*as, ā, am*), m. f. n. a porter, one who travels with a burden or load; (*as*), m. a fowler, a bird-catcher.

उत्कलाप *ut-kalāpa, as, ā, am,* having the tail erect and expanded.

Utkalāpaya, nom. P. *-payati, -yitum,* to cause the peacock to spread its tail, to cause any one to be proud; to inspire conceit by an acknowledgment of merit; to return thanks (?).

उत्कलि *utkali, is,* m., N. of a deity; (a various reading has *utkharin.*)

उत्कलिका *utkalikā,* f. (fr. 1. *ut-kal?*), longing for, regretting, missing anything or person; wanton sportfulness, dalliance; a bud, an unblown flower; a wave. — *Utkalikā-prāya,* (prose) abounding in compound words.

उत्कषण *ut-kashaṇa, am,* n. (rt. *kash*), tearing or pulling up, drawing through (as a plough).

उत्कस् *ut-kas* (*ud-k°*), cl. 1. P., Ved. *-kasati, -situm,* to gape, to open.

उत्काका *ut-kākā,* f. a cow calving every year.

उत्काश् *ut-kāś* (*ud-k°*), cl. 1. A. *-kāśate, -śitum,* to flash upwards, shine.

Utkāśana, am, n. giving orders, commanding.

उत्कास *utkāsa, as,* m., N. of a man.

उत्कासन *ut-kāsana, am,* n. (rt. *kās*), hemming, clearing the throat of mucus.

उत्कीर्ण *ut-kīrṇa.* See under *ut-kṛī* 3rd col.

उत्कीर्त् *ut-kīrt.* See *ut-kṛīt* 3rd col.

उत्कीर्तन *ut-kīrtana,* &c. See *ut-kṛīt.*

उत्कील *utkīla, as,* m., N. of a man.

उत्कुच् *ut-kuć* or *ut-kuñć* (*ud-k°*), cl. 6. P., 1. A. *-kućati, -kuñćate, -kuñćitum,* to bend upwards; to bend aside, to bend from the right course, to go or lead any one astray, to corrupt.

Ut-kuñćikā or *ut-kuñćitā,* f. the plant Nigella Indica.

Ut-koća, as, m. a bribe.

Utkoćaka, as, ikā, am, corrupted with bribes; (*as*), m. the receiver of a bribe, a bribe; N. of a Tīrtha.

उत्कुट् *ut-kuṭ* (*ud-k°*), Caus. *-koṭayati, -yitum,* to bend upwards.

Ut-kuṭa, am, n. lying stretched out on the back, lying with the face upwards, sleeping with the head erect.

Ut-kuṭaka, as, ā, am, stretched out on the back with the face upwards, erect. — *Utkuṭaka-prahāna, am,* n. avoiding the above position. — *Utkuṭakāsana* (*°ka-ās°*), *am,* n. a position like that just described.

उत्कुण *ut-kuṇa, as,* m. a bug; a louse.

उत्कुल *ut-kula, as, ā, am,* degenerating, dishonouring one's family.

उत्कूज् *ut-kūj* (*ud-k°*), cl. 1. P. *-kūjati, -jitum,* to utter monotonous sounds.

Ut-kūja, as, m. the singing of the kokila.

उत्कूट *ut-kūṭa, as,* m. an umbrella or parasol.

उत्कूर्द् *ut-kūrd* (*ud-k°*), cl. 1. P. A. *-kūrdati, -te, -ditum,* to jump up, spring upwards.

Ut-kūrdana, am, n. jumping up, springing upwards.

उत्कूल *ut-kūla, as, ā, am,* Ved. being on an elevation, going up-hill; (*am*), ind. up-hill.

Ut-kūlita, as, ā, am, brought to the bank or shore.

उत्कृ *ut-kṛi* (*ud-k°*), cl. 8. A. *-kurute, -kartum,* to inform against.

Ut-kṛiti, is, f. a metre of four times twenty-six syllables.

उत्कृत् *ut-kṛit* (*ud-k°*), cl. 6. P. *-kṛintati, -kartitum,* to cut out or off, to tear out or off; to cut up, cut in pieces, carve, butcher.

Ut-kartana, am, n. cutting up, cutting to pieces, cutting off.

Ut-kṛitya, ind. having cut off or up, having cut out.

Ut-kṛityamāna, as, ā, am, being cut to pieces, being cut up.

उत्कृष् *ut-kṛish* (*ud-k°*), cl. 1. P. sometimes A. *-karshati, -te, -karshṭum* or *-krashṭum,* to draw or drag or pull up; to raise; to draw or take out, to extract; to pull or put off; to bend (as a bow); to tear asunder: Caus. *-karshayati, -yitum,* to elevate, raise, increase: Pass. *-kṛishyate,* to be lifted or drawn up, to be raised, to rise, become powerful, become eminent.

Ut-karsha, as, ā, am, superior, eminent; much, excessive; exaggerated, boastful; attractive; (*as*), m. pulling upwards, drawing, pulling; elevation, increase, rising to something better, prosperity; excellence, eminence; excess, abundance; self-conceit; boasting; joy, pleasure (?).

Ut-karshaka, as, ikā, am, drawing upwards, raising.

Ut-karshaṇa, am, n. drawing upwards, taking off.

Ut-karshita, as, ā, am, drawn upwards, elevated.

Ut-kṛishṭa, as, ā, am (opposed to *apa-kṛishṭa* and *ava-kṛishṭa*), drawn up or out; attracted; extracted; taking a high position; excellent, eminent; superior, best; much, most, excessive; *jñānotkṛishṭa* (*°na-ut°*), *as, ā, am,* eminent through knowledge. — *Utkṛishṭa-tā,* f. or *utkṛishṭa-tva, am,* n. excellence, superiority, eminence. — *Utkṛishṭa-bhūma, as,* m. a good soil. — *Utkṛishṭa-vedana, am,* n. marrying a man of a higher caste; the best or most respectable form of marriage (?). — *Utkṛishṭopādhitā* (*°ṭa-up°*), f. state of high illusion.

उत्कॄ *ut-kṛī* (*ud-k°*), cl. 6. P. A. *-kirati, -te, -karitum* or *-rītum,* to scatter upwards, pile up, heap up; to dig up or out, excavate; to engrave.

Ut-kara, as, ā or *ī, am,* what piles or heaps, what makes up or raises; (*as*), m. what is dug out, rubbish; heap, multitude; a pile, a stack.

Ut-karikā, f. a sort of sweetmeat made with milk, treacle, and ghee.

Utkarīya, as, ā, am, relating or belonging to a heap &c.

Ut-kāra, as, m. winnowing corn; piling it up.

Ut-kārikā, f. a poultice.

Ut-kīrṇa, as, ā, am, heaped up, scattered, dug out, perforated.

उत्कृत् *ut-kṛīt* (*ud-k°*), cl. 10. P. *-kīrtayati, -yitum,* to proclaim, celebrate, praise, promulgate.

Ut-kīrtana, am, n. crying out, proclaiming; praising, celebrating.

Ut-kīrtita, as, ā, am, proclaimed, promulgated; praised, celebrated, renowned.

उत्कॢप् *ut-klṛip* (*ud-k°*), Caus. P. *-kalpayati, -yitum,* to form, fashion, create.

उत्कोच *ut-koća.* See under *ut-kuć.*

उत्क्रम् *ut-kram* (*ud-k°*), cl. 1. P. A., 4. P. *-krāmati, -kramate, -krāmyati, -kramitum,* to step up, go up, ascend; to step out, go out or away; to pass away, die; to go over; pass over; omit; not to notice; to neglect, transgress: Caus. P. *-kramayati, -yitum,* to cause to go up or ascend: Desid. Ved. *-ćikrāmishati* or *-ćikramishyati,* to wish to go up or out.

Ut-krama, as, m. going up or out; progressive increase; going astray, acting improperly, deviation, transgression.

Ut-kramaṇa, am, n. going up or out, soaring aloft, stepping out; surpassing, exceeding; (*prāṇotkramaṇa, am,* n. the flight of the soul.)

Ut-kramaṇīya, as, ā, am, to be abandoned, to be given up.

Ut-krānta, as, ā, am, gone forth or out, gone over or beyond, passed, surpassed; trespassing, exceeding.

Ut-krānti, is, f. stepping up to, going out.

Utkrāntin, ī, inī, i, passing, passing away, gone, departed.

Ut-krāma, as, m. going from or out, going above, surpassing, deviating from propriety, transgression; opposition, contrariety.

Ut-krāmat, an, antī, at, going out, going over or above, surpassing.

उत्क्रुश् *ut-kruś* (*ud-k°*), cl. 1. P. *-krośati, -kroshṭum,* to cry out, to call to (with acc.), exclaim; proclaim.

Ut-krushṭa, as, ā, am, crying, speaking out or aloud; (*am*), n. crying out, calling, exclaiming, conversation.

Ut-krośa, as, m. clamour, outcry, proclamation; an osprey.

उत्क्रोद *ut-kroda, as,* m. (fr. *krud = kurd* with *ud?*), Ved. exultation (?); cf. *ut-kūrd.*

उत्क्लिश् *ut-kliś* (*ud-k°*), cl. 9. P. *-kliśnāti, -kleśitum* or *-kleshṭum,* to feel uneasy, to be uncomfortable or distressed: Caus. P. *-kleśayati, -yitum,* to excite, stir up, expel.

Ut-kleśa, as, m. excitement, disquietude; disorder or corruption of the humors (of the body); sickness, nausea.

Ut-kleśaka, as, m. a kind of poisonous insect.

Ut-kleśana, as, ā, am, or *ut-kleśin, ī, inī, i,* exciting, stirring up, causing disorder (e. g. *kaphotkleśin,* exciting phlegm).

उत्क्लेद *ut-kleda, as,* m. (fr. rt. *klid* with *ud*), the becoming wet or moist.

Ut-kledin, ī, inī, i, wet, becoming moist.

उत्क्वथ् *ut-kvath* (*ud-k°*), cl. 1. P. *-kvathati, -thitum,* to boil out, extract by boiling &c.

उत्क्षिप् *ut-kship* (*ud-k°*), cl. 6. P. A. *-kshipati, -te, -ksheptum*, to throw up, raise, set up, erect; to throw away, reject, get rid of, vomit up.

Ut-kshipta, as, ā, am, thrown upwards, tossed, raised; thrown out, ejected; vomited; rejected, dismissed; (*as*), m. the thorn apple (Datura Metel and Fastuosa).

Utkshiptikā, f. an ornament in the shape of a crescent worn in the upper part of the ear.

Ut-kshepa, as, m. throwing or tossing up; throwing away; sending, despatching; bringing up, vomiting; the region above the temples; N. of a country; also of a man.

Ut-kshepaka, as, ā, am, throwing, a thrower, who or what elevates or raises; one who sends or orders; (*as*), m. a stealer of clothes &c.

Ut-kshepaṇa, am, n. throwing upwards, tossing; sending, sending away; vomiting, taking up; a kind of basket or bowl used for cleaning corn; a fan; a measure of sixteen paṇas.

उत्खचित *ut-khaćita, as, ā, am*, intermixed with.

उत्खन् *ut-khan* (*ud-kh°*), cl. 1. P. A. *-khanati, -te, -nitum*, to dig up or out, to excavate; to tear out by the roots, root up; to draw or tear out; to destroy entirely.

Ut-khāta, as, ā, am, dug up; excavated, eradicated, pulled up by the roots; destroyed, annihilated; (*am*), n. a hole, a cavity, a deepening, uneven ground.

Utkhātin, ī, inī, i, having cavities or holes, uneven; destructive.

उत्खरिन् *ut-kharin, ī*, m., N. of a deity; (a various reading has *utkali*.)

उत्खला *utkhalā*, f. (fr. *ud* and *khala?*), a kind of perfume.

उत्खिद् *ut-khid* (*ud-kh°*), cl. 6. P. *-khindati* (Ved. *-khidati*), *-khettum*, to draw out, extract.

उत्त *utta, as, ā, am*, wet, moistened. See 2. *ud*, page 153.

उत्तंस *ut-taṇsa, as, am*, m. n. (rt. *taṇs*), an earring; a crest, a chaplet, a wreath worn on the crown of the head.

Uttaṇsika, as, m., N. of a Nāga.

Uttaṇsita, as, ā, am, having earrings, crested.

उत्तक्ष् *ut-taksh* (*ud-t°*), cl. 1. 5. P., Ved. *-takshati, -kshṇoti, -kshitum* or *-tashṭum*, to form (anything) out of any other thing; (Sāy.) to take (anything) out of any other thing.

उत्तङ्ग *uttanga, as*, m., N. of a servant of S'iva.

उत्तट *ut-taṭa, as, ā, am*, overflowing its banks (as a river).

उत्तन् *ut-tan* (*ud-t°*), cl. 8. P. A. *-tanoti, -nute, -nitum*, to stretch upwards, stretch out; endeavour to rise.

Ut-tāna, as, ā, am, stretched out, spread out, lying on the back, sleeping supinely or with the face upwards; upright; turned so that the mouth or opening is uppermost (as a vessel), concave; spreading out over the surface; shallow; open. — *Uttāna-kūrmaka, am*, n. a particular posture in sitting. — *Uttāna-pattraka, as*, m. a species of Ricinus. — *Uttāna-pad*, f., Ved. one whose legs are extended (in parturition or creation); epithet of a peculiar creative agency described in Ṛig-veda X. 72; (Sāy.) vegetation, the whole creation of upward-germinating plants. — *Uttāna-parṇa, as, ā, am*, Ved. having extended leaves. — *Uttāna-pāda, as*, m. the star β in the little bear, personified as son of Vīra or Manu Svāyambhuva and father of Dhruva, the polar-star. — *Uttānapāda-ja, as*, m. a N. of Dhruva or the polar-star. — *Uttāna-barhis, is*, m., N. of a prince. — *Uttāna-śaya, as, ā, am*, lying on the back, sleeping with the face upwards; (*as, ā*), m. f. a little child. — *Uttāna-śīvan, ā, arī, a*, Ved. lying extended, stagnant. — *Uttāna-hasta, as, ā, am*, Ved. having the hands extended, extending them in prayer; (*au*), m. du. the two hands with the fingers stretched out, but with the backs towards the ground.

Uttānaka, as, m. a species of Cyperus grass.

Uttānikā, f., N. of a river.

उत्तप् *ut-tap* (*ud-t°*), cl. 1. P. rarely A. *-tapati, -te, -ptum*, to make warm or hot, to heat thoroughly; to pain, torment; to excite, urge on, press hard: Caus. P. *-tāpayati, -yitum*, to warm up, heat.

Ut-tapta, as, ā, am, burnt, seared; bathed, washed; anxious, excited; (*am*), n. dried flesh.

Ut-tāpa, as, m. great heat, affliction, distress, anxiety, excitement, ardour, effort, energy.

Ut-tāpita, as, ā, am, heated, made hot, pained, distressed, roused, excited.

उत्तम् *ut-tam* (*ud-t°*), cl. 4. P. *-tāmyati, -tamitum*, to be distressed, to lose heart, to faint.

उत्तम *ut-tama, as, ā, am* (superlative fr. 1. *ud*; opposed to *avama, adhama*, &c.; cf. *an-uttama*), uppermost, highest, chief; most elevated, principal; best, excellent (often at the end of compounds, e.g. *dvijottamas*, best of the twice-born); first, greatest; the highest (tone); the most removed or last in place, order, or time; (*am*), ind. most, in the highest degree; (*as*), m. the last person (= in European grammars the first person); N. of a brother of Dhruva, son of Uttāna-pāda and nephew of Priya-vrata; a son of Priya-vrata and third Manu; the twenty-first Vyāsa; (*ās*), m. pl., N. of a people; (*ā*), f. a kind of piḍakā or pustule; the plant Oxystelma Esculentum (Asclepias Rosea Roxb.); an excellent woman, one who is handsome, healthy, and affectionate. — *Uttama-gandhāḍhya* (*°dha-āḍh°*), *as, ā, am*, possessing abundantly the most delicate scent or delicious fragrance. — *Uttama-tā*, f. or *uttama-tva, am*, n. excellence, superiority; goodness, good quality. — *Uttama-pada, am*, n. a high office. — *Uttama-purusha* or *uttama-pūrusha, as*, m. the last person in verbal conjugation, i. e. I, we two, we (= in European grammars the first person, our third person being regarded in Hindū grammars as the *prathama-purusha*, q. v.; cf. also *madhyama-purusha*); the supreme spirit; an excellent man. — *Uttama-phalinī*, f. the plant Oxystelma Esculentum (Asclepias Rosea Roxb.). — *Uttamarṇa* (*°ma-ṛiṇa*), *as*, m. a creditor; (*ās*), m. pl., N. of a people. — *Uttamarṇika, as*, m. a creditor. — *Uttamarṇin, ī*, m. a creditor. — *Uttama-lābha, as*, m. great profit, a double return. — *Uttama-veśa, as*, m. 'having the most excellent dress,' N. of S'iva. — *Uttama-śākha, as*, m., N. of a region. — *Uttama-sangraha, as*, m. intriguing with another man's wife, addressing her privately, casting amorous looks &c. — *Uttama-sāhasa, am*, n. the highest of the three fixed mulcts or fines; a fine of 1000 or of 80,000 paṇas; capital punishment, branding, banishment, confiscation, mutilation, and death. — *Uttama-sukha, as*, m., N. of a man. — *Uttamānga* (*°ma-an°*), *am*, n. the highest or chief part of the body, the head. — *Uttamādhama* (*°ma-adh°*), *as, ā, am*, high and low. — *Uttamādhama-madhyama, as, ā, am*, good, bad, and indifferent; high, low, and middling. — *Uttamāraṇī* (*°ma-ar°*), f. the plant Asparagus Racemosus. — *Uttamārdha* (*°ma-ar°*), *as*, m. the last half or part; the best half. — *Uttamārdhya, as, ā, am*, relating to or connected with the last part or the best half. — *Uttamāha* (*°ma-ah°*), *as*, m. the last or latest day, a fine day (?), a lucky day (?). — *Uttamopapada* (*°ma-up°*), *as, ā, am*, one to whom the best term is applicable, best, good. — *Uttamaujas* (*°ma-oj°*), *ās*, m. 'of excellent valour,' N. of one of the warriors of the Mahā-bhārata.

Uttamāyya, as, ā, am (fut. pass. part. fr. a nom. *uttamāya?*), Ved. to be raised or celebrated.

Uttamīya, as, ā, am, uppermost, highest, chief, best.

1. *ut-tara, as, ā, am* (comparative fr. 1. *ud*; opposed to *adhara*; declined Gram. 238. *a*), upper, higher, superior (e.g. *uttare dantās*, the upper teeth); northern (because the northern part of India is high); left (opposed to *dakshiṇa* or right, because in praying the face being turned to the east the north would be on the left-hand); later, following, subsequent, latter, concluding, posterior, future (opposed to *pūrva*, &c., e.g. *uttaraḥ kālaḥ*, future time; *uttaraṃ vākyam*, a following speech, answer, reply; *phalam uttaram*, subsequent result, future consequence; *varshottareshu*, in future years); superior, chief, excellent, dominant, predominant, more powerful; better, more excellent; (*as*), m., N. of a son of Virāṭa; a king of the Nāgas; N. of a mountain; (*ā*), f. the north (i. e. the northern *diś* or quarter); N. of a daughter of Virāṭa and daughter-in-law of Arjuna; (*am*), n. upper surface or cover; the north; the following member, the last part of a compound; answer, reply; (in law) a defence, a rejoinder; (in the Mīmāṇsā philosophy) the answer, the fourth member of an adhikaraṇa or case; superiority, excellence, competency; result, the chief or prevalent result or characteristic, what remains or is left, conclusion, remainder, excess, over and above, (often at the end of a compound, e.g. *shashṭyuttaram sahasram*, one thousand with an excess of sixty, i. e. 1060; *saptottaraṃ śatam*, 107; *bhayottara*, attended with danger, having danger as the result; *dharmottara*, chiefly characterized by virtue); remainder, difference (in arithmetic); N. of a song; (*am*), ind. at the conclusion, at the end, e.g. *bhavad-uttaram*, with the word 'bhavad' at the end; *asrottaram ikshitā*, looked at with tears at the end, i. e. with a glance ending in tears; [cf. Gr. ὕστερος.] — *Uttara-kāṇḍa, am*, n. following or concluding book; the seventh book of the Rāmāyaṇa. — *Uttara-kāya, as*, m. the upper part of the body. — *Uttara-kāla, as*, m. future time; time reckoned from full moon to full moon. — *Uttara-kuru, us* or *u*, m. n. one of the nine divisions of the world, the country of the northern Kurus, situated in the north of India, and described as the country of eternal beatitude. — *Uttara-kośalā*, f. the city Ayodhyā, the modern Oude. — *Uttara-kriyā*, f. the last sacred action, funeral rites, obsequies. — *Uttara-khaṇḍa, am*, n. last section; the concluding book of the Padma-purāṇa, also of the S'iva-purāṇa. — *Uttara-khaṇḍana, am*, n. cutting off a reply, refutation. — *Uttara-grantha, as*, m. title of a supplement of the Yoni-grantha. — 1. *uttaran-ga, am*, n. a wooden arch surmounting the door frame. — *Uttara-ććhada, as*, m. a cover, what is thrown over anything. — *Uttara-ja, as, ā, am*, born in the latter (or last-mentioned kind of wedlock); born subsequently or afterwards, posterity. — *Uttara-jyā*, f. the versed sine of an arc, or rather the second half of the chord halved by the versed sine. — *Uttara-jyotisha, am*, n., N. of a country. — *Uttara-tantra, am*, n. 'concluding doctrine,' N. of a supplementary section in the medical manual of Suśruta. — *Uttara-tara, as, ā, am* (compar. fr. *uttara*), still further removed, still more distant, still higher. — *Uttara-tas*, ind. at the top, above, from the north, northward, to the left (opposed to *dakshiṇa-tas*); afterwards; behind. — *Uttarataḥ-paśćāt*, ind. north-westward (with gen.). — *Uttara-tāpanīya*, title of the second part of the Nṛisiṇha-tāpanīyopanishad. — *Uttara-tra*, ind. in what follows, after, subsequently, later, further on, beyond, below (in a work), northward; (*pūrvatra uttaratra*, in the first case or place—in the second.) — *Uttara-dāyaka, as, ā, am*, replying, giving an answer, impertinent. — *Uttaradik-stha, as, ā, am*, situated in the north, northern. — *Uttara-diś, k*, f. the north quarter. — *Uttara-deśa, as*, m. the country towards the north, the up-country. — *Uttara-dheya, as, ā, am*, to be done subsequently. — *Uttara-paksha, as*, m. the northern or left wing (side); second or following part of an argument, the reason *pro*, the reply, refutation;

the answer to the first or objectionable argument, the right argument, demonstrated truth, or conclusion; the minor proposition in a syllogism. — *Uttarapaksha-tā*, f. or *uttarapaksha-tva, am*, n. conclusion, demonstration, reply. — *Uttara-paṭa, as*, m. an upper garment. — *Uttara-patha, as*, m. the northern way, the way leading to the north. — *Uttarapathika, as, ī, am*, inhabiting the northern country. — *Uttara-pada, am*, n. the last member of a compound word. — *Uttarapadika, as, ī, am*, or *uttarapadakīya, as, ā, am*, relating to or studying the last word or term. — *Uttara-parvata, as*, m. the northern mountain. — *Uttara-paśćārdha* (°*ća-ar*°), *as*, m. the north-western half. — *Uttara-paśćima, as, ā, am*, north-western; (*ā*), f. the north-west (scil. *diś*). — *Uttara-pāda, as*, m. a division of legal practice, that part which relates to the reply or defence, four divisions being admitted in every suit. — *Uttara-purastāt*, ind. north-eastward (with gen.). — *Uttara-purusha, as*, m. = *uttama-purusha* (?). — *Uttara-pūrva, as, ā, am*, north-eastward; one who takes the north for the east. — *Uttara-praććhada, as*, m. a coverlid, a quilt. — *Uttara-pratyuttara, am*, n. a dispute, an altercation, a discussion; the pleadings in a law-suit. — *Uttara-phalgunī* or *uttara-phālgunī*, f. the twelfth lunar mansion, containing two stars, figured by a bed. — *Uttara-bhādrapad, t*, f. or *uttara-bhādrapadā*, f. the twenty-sixth lunar mansion, figured by a couch, and comprehending two stars, of which one is α Andromedæ. — *Uttara-mati, is*, m., N. of a man. — *Uttara-mandrā*, f. a loud but slow manner of singing. — *Uttara-mātra, am*, n. a mere reply, even a reply. — *Uttara-mānasa, am*, n., N. of a Tīrtha. — *Uttara-mīmāṅsā*, f. the Vedānta philosophy, an inquiry into the Jñāna-kāṇḍa or second portion of the Veda (opposed to *pūrva-mīmāṅsā*; see *mīmāṅsā*). — *Uttara-rahita, as, ā, am*, devoid of reply, having no answer. — *Uttara-rāma-ćarita* or *-ćaritra, am*, n. 'the further or later deeds of Rāma,' title of a drama of Bhavabhūti. — *Uttara-lakshaṇa, am*, n. the indication of an actual reply; (*as, ā, am*), marked on the left side. — *Uttara-loman, ā, ā, a*, having the hairs turned upwards or outwards. — *Uttara-vayasa, am*, n. the latter or declining years of life. — *Uttara-vallī*, f. title of the second section of the Kaṭhakopanishad when divided into two Adhyāyas. — *Uttara-vasti, is*, f. a small syringe, a urethra injection pipe. — *Uttara-vastra, am*, n. an upper garment. — *Uttara-vādin, ī*, m. a replicant; a defendant; one whose claims are of later date than another's. — *Uttara-vāsas, as*, n. an upper garment. — *Uttara-vedi, is* or *ī*, f., Ved. the northern altar made for the sacred fire. — *Uttara-saktha, am*, n. the left thigh. — *Uttara-sañjñita, as, ā, am*, designated in the reply (a witness &c.); hear-say evidence, see the next. — *Uttara-sākshin, ī*, m. witness for the defence; a witness testifying from the report of others. — *Uttara-sādhaka, as, ā, am*, finishing what remains or follows, assisting at a ceremony, befriending; an assistant, a helper, a friend; who or what establishes a reply. — *Uttara-hanu, us*, m., Ved. the upper jawbone. — *Uttarādhara* (°*ra-adh*°), *as, ā, am*, superior and inferior, higher and lower; (*am*), n. the upper and under lip; the lips; see *adharottara*. — *Uttarādhikāra* (°*ra-adh*°), *as*, m. right to property &c. in succession to another person, heirship, inheritance. — *Uttarādhikāri-tā*, f. or *uttarādhikāri-tva, am*, n. right of succession. — *Uttarādhikārin, ī, iṇī, i*, an heir or claimant subsequent to the death of the original owner, an heir who claims as the second in succession. — *Uttarānvita* (°*rā-an*°), *as, ā, am*, accompanied by Uttarā. — *Uttarā-patha, am*, n. the northern road or direction, the northern country, north. — *Uttarābhāsa* (°*ra-ābh*°), *as*, m. a false, indirect or prevaricating reply. — *Uttarābhāsa-tā*, f. or *uttarābhāsa-tva, am*, n. inadequacy of a reply, the semblance without the reality. — *Uttarāyaṇa* (°*ra-ay*°), *am*, n. the progress (of the sun) to the north; the period of the sun's progress to the north of the equator, the summer solstice. — *Uttarāraṇi* (°*ra-ar*°), *is* or *ī*, m. f. the upper *araṇi* (q. v.) which by cutting becomes the *pramantha* or churner. — *Uttarārtha* (°*ra-ar*°), *as, ā, am*, for the sake of what follows. — *Uttarārdha* (°*ra-ar*°), *am*, n. the upper part (of the body); the northern part; the latter half; the further end. — *Uttarārdhya, as, ā, am*, Ved. being on the northern side. — *Uttarā-vat, ān, atī, at*, Ved. victorious, overpowering. — *Uttarāśā* (°*ra-āśā*), f. the northern quarter, the north. — *Uttarāśādhipati* (°*śā-adh*°) or *uttarāśā-pati, is*, m. the regent of the northern quarter, an epithet of Kuvera. — *Uttarāśman* (°*ra-aś*°), *ā*, m., N. of a rocky river in the north. — *Uttarāshāḍhā* (°*ra-ash*°), f. the twenty-first of the lunar mansions, figured by an elephant's tooth or a bed, and containing two stars, one of which is β in Sagittarius. — *Uttarāsanga* (°*ra-ās*°), *as*, m. an upper or outer garment. — *Uttarāha* (°*ra-ah*°), *as*, m. the following day. — *Uttaretarā* (°*ra-it*°), f. the southern quarter. — *Uttarottara* (°*ra-ut*°), *as, ā, am*, more and more, higher and higher, further and further; always increasing, always following; (*am*), ind. higher and higher, more and more, in constant continuation, one on the other; (*am*), n. reply to an answer, reply on reply; conversation; a rejoinder; excess, exceeding quantity or degree; succession, gradation; descending. — *Uttarottarin, ī, iṇī, i*, constantly increasing; one following the other. — *Uttaroshṭha* or *uttaraushṭha* (°*ra-osh*°), *as*, m. the upper lip.

Uttaram, ind. further on, forward; hereafter, in the following part (of a book).

Uttarā, ind. north, northerly, northward (with gen. or abl.). — *Uttarā-sad, t, t, t*, Ved. seated northward or on the left.

Uttarāt, ind. from the left, from the north, northward.

Uttarāttāt, ind., Ved. from the north.

Uttarāhi, ind. northerly, from the north (with abl.).

Uttarin, ī, iṇī, i, superior.

Uttarīya or *uttarīyaka, am*, n. an upper or outer garment.

Uttareṇa, ind. (with gen., abl., acc., or at the end of a compound) northward, on the left side of; posterior, subsequent.

Uttare-dyus, ind. a subsequent day, a day following, to-morrow.

उत्तमर्ण *uttamarṇa*. See under *ut-tama*.

उत्तम्भ् *ut-tambh* (*ud-stambh*), cl. 5. 9. P. *-tabhnoti, -nāti, -tambhitum*, to stay, prop, support.

Ut-tambhana, am, n. upholding, staying, supporting; stopping, arresting; a prop, a stay.

Ut-tambhita, as, ā, am, upheld, supported; stopped, arrested; erect (as the hair of the head), standing on end.

Ut-tambhitavya, as, ā, am, to be upheld.

उत्तर *ut-tara*. See above and under *ut-tṝ*.

उत्तरङ्ग 2. *ut-taranga, as, ā, am* (for 1. see under 1. *ut-tara*, p. 149), flooded, inundated, washed over by waves.

उत्तर्जन *ut-tarjana, am*, n. violent threatening.

उत्तान *ut-tāna*. See under *ut-tan*, p. 149.

उत्ताप *ut-tāpa*. See under *ut-tap*, p. 149.

उत्तार *ut-tāra*. See under *ut-tṝ* next col.

उत्ताल *ut-tāla, as, ā, am* (fr. *ud* and *tāla*?), great, strong; formidable; arduous, difficult; speedy, swift, best, excellent; elevated, lofty, tall, loud; (*as*), m. an ape; (*am*), n. a particular number.

उत्तिज् *ut-tij* (*ud-t*°), Caus. P. *-tejayati, -yitum*, to excite, stimulate, incite, instigate, urge on, stir up, animate.

Ut-tejaka, as, ā, am, instigating, stimulating.

Ut-tejana, am, ā, n. f. incitement, instigation, exciting, animating; sending, despatching; urging, driving; whetting, sharpening, furbishing, polishing; an inspiring or exciting speech; an incentive, inducement, stimulant.

Ut-tejita, as, ā, am, incited, animated, excited, urged; sent, despatched; whetted, sharpened, furbished, polished; (*am*), n. an incentive, inducement; sidling, one of a horse's five paces; moderate velocity in a horse's pace.

उत्तु *ut-tu* (*ud-tu*), cl. 2. P., Ved. *-tavīti* or *-tauti, -totum* or *-tavitum*, to effect, bring about; (Sāy.) to increase, prosper.

उत्तुङ्ग *ut-tunga, as, ā, am*, lofty, high, tall, swollen (as a stream). — *Uttunga-tā*, f. or *uttunga-tva, am*, n. height, loftiness, elevation.

उत्तुण्डित *ut-tuṇḍita, am*, n. the head of a thorn &c. which has entered the skin.

उत्तुद् *ut-tud* (*ud-t*°), cl. 6. P. A., Ved. *-tudati, -te, -tottum*, to push up, tear up, stir up, push open.

Ut-tuda, as, m., Ved. one who stirs up.

उत्तुल् *ut-tul* (*ud-t*°), cl. 10. P. *-tolayati* or *-tulayati, -yitum*, to raise up (by means of a counterpoise), to erect, set up; to weigh.

Ut-tolana, am, n. lifting up, raising, elevating (by means of a counterpoise or balance).

Ut-tolita, as, ā, am, raised, lifted up.

उत्तुष *ut-tusha, as*, m. fried grain; (freed from the husks.)

उत्तृद् *ut-tṛid* (*ud-t*°), cl. 7. P. A. *-tṛiṇatti, -tṛinte, -tarditum*, to split, cut through.

उत्तॄ *ut-tṝ* (*ud-t*°), cl. 1. 6. P. *-tarati, -tirati, -taritum* or *-rītum*, to pass out of (especially *jalāt*, the water &c., with abl. c.), to disembark, to come out of; to escape from (a misfortune, affliction, &c.); to come down, descend, alight, put up at; to pass over; to cross (as a river, with acc.), to vanquish; to give up, leave; to elevate, strengthen, increase: Caus. *-tārayati, -yitum*, to cause to come out, to deliver, assist, rescue; to make any one alight, take down, take off; to cause to pass over, to convey or transport across, land, disembark; to vomit up: Desid. *-titīrshati*, to wish to cross.

2. *ut-tara, as, ā, am* (for 1. see p. 149, col. 3), crossing over; to be crossed (in the word *dur-uttara*, difficult to be come out of or escaped from).

Ut-taraṇa, as, ā, am, coming out of, crossing over; (*am*), n. coming forth or out of (especially out of water), landing, disembarking; crossing rivers &c.

Ut-tarat, an, antī, at, coming out of (water &c.), crossing, going over.

Ut-tarikā, f., N. of a river.

Ut-tāra, as, m. transporting over; landing; delivering, rescuing; ejecting, getting rid of; vomiting; passing away, instability; (*as, ā, am*), surpassing others, excellent, pre-eminent. — *Uttāra-loćana, as, ā, am*, having the eyes turned up.

Ut-tāraka, as, m. a deliverer, epithet of Śiva.

Ut-tāraṇa, as, ā, am, transporting over, bringing over, rescuing; (*am*), n. the act of landing, delivering, rescuing; helping to cross over or escape, transportation.

Ut-tārin, ī, iṇī, i, transporting across; unsteady; inconstant, changeable, tremulous, sick.

Ut-tārya, as, ā, am, to be made to land, to be ejected, to be thrown up by vomiting.

Ut-titīrshu, us, us, u, about to pass out of (water), wishing to land.

Ut-tīram, ind. on the bank, on land, ashore.

Ut-tīrṇa, as, ā, am, landed, crossed, traversed; rescued, liberated, escaped; released from obligation; thrown off; one who has completed his studies, experienced, clever.

Ut-tīrya, ind. having crossed, having landed.

उत्तेरित *utterita, am*, n. (said to be fr. *ut-tṝ*, but perhaps connected with rt. *īr*), one of the five paces of a horse in Hindū jockeyship.

उत्तोरण *ut-toraṇa, as, ā, am*, decorated with raised or upright arches.

उत्तोलन *ut-tolana*. See under *ut-tul*.

उत्त्यक्त *ut-tyakta, as, ā, am* (fr. rt. *tyaj* with *ud*), abandoned, left; thrown, tossed; free from passion or affection.

Ut-tyāga, as, m. abandonment, quitting; throwing, throwing up; secession from worldly attachments.

उत्त्रस् *ut-tras* (*ud-t°*), Caus. P. *-trāsayati, -yitum*, to frighten, alarm.

Ut-trasta, as, ā, am, frightened.

Ut-trāsa, as, m. fear, terror.

उत्त्रिपद *ut-tripada, am*, n. an upright tripod.

उत्था *ut-thā* (*ud-sthā*), cl. 1. P. A. *-tishṭhati, -te, -thātum*, to stand up, rise, raise one's self; come forth, arise, originate from; to rise (from the dead); to become animated; to be active or brave; to make efforts, take pains with, to excel: Caus. *-thāpayati, -yitum*, to cause to stand up, raise, set up, erect; to lift up; to arouse, awaken, raise to life, make alive.

Ut-tishṭhamāna, as, ā, am, standing up, rising; increasing, augmenting.

Ut-tha, as, ā, am, (generally at the end of a compound) rising, arising; coming forth, originating, derived from; standing up; (*as*), m. arising, coming forth; [cf. Zend *usta*.]

Ut-thātṛi, tā, m., Ved. one who rises; resolving.

Ut-thāna, am, n. the act of standing up or rising; rising (of the moon &c.); resurrection; rising up to depart; leaving off; starting on a warlike expedition; rise, origin; effort, exertion; manly exertion, manhood; evacuating (by stool &c.); an army; joy, pleasure; a book; a court-yard; a shed where sacrifices are offered; a term, a limit; business of a family or realm, the care of subjects or dependants; reflection; proximate cause of disease; (*as, ā, am*), causing to arise or originate. — *Utthāna-vat, ān, atī, at*, ready for action. — *Utthānaikādaśī* (°*na-ek°*), f. the eleventh day in the light or former half of the month Kārttika, when Vishṇu rises from his sleep.

Ut-thāpaka, as, ā, am, lifting up, causing to get up, who or what raises &c.; exciting, animating.

Ut-thāpana, am, n. causing to rise or get up; raising, elevating; causing to leave (a house &c., with acc. of the person made to leave); causing to come forth, bringing forth; exciting, instigating; bringing about; causing to cease, finishing; (in mathem.) the finding of the quantity sought, answer to the question, substitution of a value; (*ī*), f. a concluding verse (*ṛić*).

Ut-thāpita, as, ā, am, raised, lifted up, elevated; made to get up (from a seat, bed, &c.); aroused, instigated.

1. *ut-thāpya*, ind. having raised or caused to rise, having roused or instigated.

2. *ut-thāpya, as, ā, am*, to be raised; Ved. to be sent away.

Ut-thāya, ind. having risen (from a seat &c.); having risen (in rank &c.). — *Utthāyotthāya* (°*ya-ut°*), every time one rises (from one's bed).

Ut-thāyin, ī, inī, i, rising, coming forth, becoming visible.

Ut-thita, as, ā, am, risen or rising (as from a seat &c.); arisen, born, produced; happened, occurring; endeavouring, striving; advancing, increasing; high, lofty, eminent; extended; N. of a Pragātha consisting of ten Pādas. — *Utthita-tā*, f. state of activity or of readiness to serve others. — *Utthitāṅguli* (°*ta-aṅ°*), *is*, m. the palm of the hand with the fingers extended.

Ut-thiti, is, f. elevation, rising up.

उत्पक्ष्मन् *ut-pakshman, ā, ā, a*, or *ut-pakshmala, as, ā, am*, with upraised eyelids.

उत्पचिष्णु *ut-paćishṇu, us, us, u*, apt to ripen or cook.

उत्पट् *ut-paṭ* (*ud-p°*), Caus. *-pāṭayati, -yitum*, to tear up or out, root up, eradicate, extirpate.

Ut-paṭa, as, m. sap issuing from the cleft of a tree.

Ut-pāṭa, as, m. pulling up by the roots, destroying; a disease of the external ear.

Ut-pāṭaka, as, m. the above disease; (*ikā*), f. the external bark of a tree.

Ut-pāṭana, am, n. pulling up by the roots, eradicating; destroying, destruction.

Ut-pāṭita, as, ā, am, pulled up by the roots, eradicated, torn out.

Ut-pāṭin, ī, inī, i, (often at the end of compounds) eradicating, extirpating.

Ut-pāṭya, ind. having plucked up.

उत्पत् *ut-pat* (*ud-p°*), cl. 1. P. *-patati, -titum*, to fly or jump up, to rise, to be produced, originate: Caus. *-pātayati, -yitum*, to cause to fly up.

Ut-pata, as, m. a bird; going upwards or up. — *Utpata-nipatā*, f. flying up and down.

Ut-patat, an, antī, at, flying upwards or onwards.

Ut-patana, am, n. rising, ascending, going up; birth, production.

Ut-patita, as, ā, am, springing up, risen, ascended.

Ut-patitavya as, ā, am, to be flown upwards.

Ut-patitṛi, tā, trī, tṛi, rising, jumping up, going upwards.

Ut-patishṇu, us, us, u, rising, jumping up.

Ut-pāta, as, m. flying up, a spring, jump; an unusual or startling event boding calamity, a portent, prodigy, phenomenon; any public calamity, as an eclipse, meteor, earthquake. — *Utpāta-vāta, as*, m. a whirlwind, a hurricane.

Ut-pātaka, as, m. a fabulous animal with eight legs, (written also *ut-pādaka*, q. v.); N. of a Tīrtha.

उत्पताक *ut-patāka, as, ā, am*, with raised flags; with uplifted banners; (*ā*), f. a raised banner or flag. — *Ut-patāka-dhvaja, as, ā, am*, with raised banners and flags.

उत्पथ *ut-patha, as*, m. wrong road, bad way, error, evil; (*am*), ind. astray, on the wrong road.

उत्पद् *ut-pad* (*ud-p°*), cl. 4. A. *-padyate, -pattum*, to arise, rise, originate, be produced: Caus. *-pādayati, -yitum*, to produce, beget, generate, cause, effect; to cause to issue or come forth, bring forward.

Ut-patti, is, f. arising, birth, production, origin; becoming visible, coming into existence; production in general, profit, productiveness; producing as an effect or result, giving rise to or generating as a consequence; resurrection. — *Utpatti-kālīna, as, ā, am*, taking place at the time of birth. — *Utpatti-prayoga, as*, m. production by the joint operation of cause and effect; purport, meaning. — *Utpatti-mat, ān, atī, at*, produced, born. — *Utpatti-vyañjaka, as*, m. a type of birth (as investiture); a mark of the twice-born.

Ut-panna, as, ā, am, risen, gone up; arisen, born, produced; produced unexpectedly; acquired, gained; occurred, happened; effected, accomplished; known, ascertained. — *Utpanna-tantu, us, us, u*, having a line of descendants. — *Utpanna-tva, am*, n. origin, production. — *Utpanna-bhakshin, ī, inī, i*, living from hand to mouth. — *Utpanna-vināśin, ī, inī, i*, perishing as soon as produced.

Ut-pāda, as, m. coming forth, birth, production. — *Utpāda-pūrva, am*, n. title of the first of the fourteen Pūrvas or older sacred writings of the Jainas. — *Ut-pāda-śayana*, see s. v. next col.

Ut-pādaka, as, ā, am, bringing forth, producing, productive, effective; (*as*), m. a producer, a generator; a fabulous animal, called Sarabha, with eight legs; written also *utpātaka*; (*ikā*), f. a certain insect, perhaps the white ant (termes); N. of the pot-herb Enhydra Hingtsha, also of Basilla Rubra or Lucida; (*am*), n. origin, cause.

Ut-pādana, as, ā, am, bringing forth, producing, productive; (*am*), n. producing, generating, begetting, causing.

Ut-pādita, as, ā, am, produced, effected; generated, begotten.

Ut-pādin, ī, inī, i, produced, born; (at the end of compounds) bringing forth, producing.

Ut-pādya, ind. having produced; having begotten; having inspired.

Ut-pādyamāna, as, ā, am, being produced or generated.

उत्पल 1. *utpala, am*, n. (fr. rt. *pal* for *paṭ* with *ud*, to burst upwards as a blossom?), the blue lotus, Nymphæa Cærulea, a seed of the Nymphæa; the plant Costus Speciosus; any water-lily; a plant in general; (*as*), m., N. of a man who built a sanctuary, of an astronomer; N. of a lexicographer; (*ā*), f., N. of a river; (*ī*), f. a kind of cake made with unwinnowed corn. — *Utpala-gandhika, am*, n. a species of sandal of the colour of brass and very fragrant. — *Utpala-ćakshus, us, us, us*, lotus-eyed, fine-eyed. — *Utpala-pattra, am*, n. the leaf of a Nymphæa; a wound caused by the finger-nail of a woman; a Tilaka or mark on the forehead, made with sandal &c. by the Hindūs; a broad-bladed knife or lancet. — *Utpala-pattraka, am*, n. a broad-bladed knife or lancet used by surgeons. — *Utpala-pura, am*, n., N. of a town built by Utpala. — *Utpala-bhedyaka, as*, m. a kind of bandage. — *Utpala-mālā*, f., N. of a lexicon. — *Utpala-rāja, as*, m., N. of a poet. — *Utpala-vatī*, f., N. of a river. — *Utpala-varṇā*, f., N. of a woman. — *Utpala-śāka, as*, m., N. of a plant. — *Utpala-śārivā*, f. the plant Ichnocarpus Frutescens. — *Utpalāksha* (°*la-ak°*), *as*, m., and *utpalāpīḍa* (°*la-āp°*), *as*, m., N. of two princes. — *Utpalābha* (°*la-ābh°*), *as, ā, am*, lotus-like, resembling a lotus. — *Utpalā-vana, am*, n., N. of a region in Pañćāla.

Utpalaka, as, m., N. of a man; of a king of the Nāgas.

Utpalin, ī, inī, i, abounding in lotus flowers; (*inī*), f. an assemblage of lotus flowers; a species of the Atijagatī metre, the same as Ćandrikā; N. of a river; title of a dictionary.

उत्पल 2. *ut-pala, as, ā, am* (fr. *ud* and *pala*, flesh), fleshless, emaciated; (*am*), n., N. of a hell.

उत्पवन *ut-pavana*. See under *ut-pū*.

उत्पश्य *ut-paśya, as, ā, am*, looking up or upwards.

उत्पादशयन *ut-pāda-śayana, as*, m. a kind of partridge, Parra Jacana or Gœnsis, (sleeping with legs erect.)

उत्पारण *ut-pāraṇa, am*, n., Ved. transporting over, transportation.

उत्पाली *utpālī*, f. health (etym. doubtful).

उत्पिञ्जर *ut-piñjara, as, ā, am*, uncaged, unconfined.

Ut-piñjala, as, ā, am (*l* substituted for *r*), out of order, disordered, excessively confused; uncaged.

उत्पित्सु *ut-pitsu, us, us, u* (Desid. of *ut-pat*, q. v.), desirous of rising or flying away or proceeding.

उत्पिष् *ut-pish* (*ud-p°*), cl. 7. P. *-pinashṭi, -peshṭum*, to rub together; to crush, grind.

Ut-pishṭa, as, ā, am, rubbed, ground; (*am*), n. a disease, a grating of the bones or of the joints upon each other.

उत्पीड् *ut-pīḍ* (*ud-p°*), cl. 10. P. *-pīḍayati, -yitum*, to press upwards, to press out of.

Ut-pīḍa, as, m. pressing out, pressure; foam, froth, a gush.

Ut-pīḍana, am, n. the act of pressing out.

उत्पुच्छय *ut-pućchaya*, nom. (fr. *ud-pućcha*) A. *utpućchayate*, to raise or cock the tail; P. *-yati*, to make one raise the tail.

उत्पुटक *ut-puṭaka, as*, m. a disease of the external ear; [cf. *ut-pāṭa*.]

उत्पुलक *ut-pulaka, as, ā, am,* joyful, delighted.

उत्पू *ut-pū (ud-pū),* cl. 9. P. A. *-punāti, -punīte, -paritum,* to cleanse, purify; to extract anything that has been purified.

Ut-pavana, am, n. cleaning, cleansing; straining liquids for domestic or religious uses; any implement for cleaning; the act of sprinkling clarified butter or other fluids on the sacrificial fire with two blades of Kuśa grass, the ends of which are held in either hand and the centre dipped into the liquid.

Ut-pavitṛi, tā, trī, tṛi, purifying; a purifier.

Ut-pāva, as, m. purifying ghee &c.

उत्पोषध *ut-poshadha, as,* m., N. of an old king.

उत्प्रभ *ut-prabha, as, ā, am,* flashing forth or diffusing light, shining.

उत्प्रसव *ut-prasava, as,* m. abortion.

उत्प्रास *ut-prāsa, as,* m. (fr. rt. 2. *as* with *pra* and *ud*), hurling, throwing afar; violent burst of laughter; ridicule, derision; excess.

Ut-prāsana, am, n. = the preceding.

उत्प्रुष् *ut-prush, ṭ,* f., Ved. that which bubbles up, a bubble.

उत्प्रेक्ष् *ut-preksh (ud-pra-īksh),* cl. 1. A. *-prekshate, -shitum,* to look up to with attention (as a pupil to his teacher); to perceive; to transfer (with loc.); to compare one thing with another, illustrate by a simile.

Ut-prekshaṇa, am, n. looking into, perceiving, foreseeing, comparing.

Ut-prekshā, f. overlooking, disregarding, carelessness, indifference; (in rhetoric) comparison in general, simile, illustration, metaphor; a parable; an ironical comparison. — *Utprekshā-vallabha, as,* m., N. of a poet.

Ut-prekshita, as, ā, am, compared (as in a simile).

Ut-prekshya, as, ā, am, that with which anything is compared.

उत्प्लु *ut-plu (ud-p°),* cl. 1. A. *-plavate, -plotum,* to jump up, leap up; to bound; to spring or jump upon; to float upon.

Ut-plava, as, m. a jump, leap, bound; *(ā),* f. a boat.

Ut-plavana, am, n. jumping or leaping up, springing upon; skimming off impure oil or ghee, or any dirt floating on a fluid, by passing a blade of Kuśa grass over it.

Ut-pluta, as, ā, am, jumped up or upon, sprung upon suddenly.

Ut-plutya, ind. having sprung up or jumped upon.

उत्फल् *ut-phal (ud-ph°),* cl. 1. P. *-phalati, -litum,* to spring; to part asunder, to expand (as a flower): Caus. P. *-phālayati, -yitum,* to open, open wide, cause to expand.

Ut-phāla, as, m. a jump, a spring, leaping up or out of, moving or shuffling of feet.

Ut-phulla, as, ā, am (*phulla* pass. part. of rt. *phal*), widely opened (as the eyes); blown as a flower; swollen, increased in bulk; sleeping supinely; *(am),* n. a kind of coitus.

उत्फल *ut-phala, am,* n. excellent fruit.

उत्स *utsa, as,* m. (fr. 2. *ud*), Ved. a spring, a fountain (metaphorically applied to the clouds). — *Utsa-dhi, is,* m., Ved. the receptacle of a spring, a well.

उत्सक्थ *ut-saktha, as, ī, am,* Ved. opening the thighs.

उत्सङ्ग *ut-sanga, as,* m. (fr. rt. *sañj* with *ud*), embrace, association, union; slope, side; the haunch or part above the hip; the lap; the acclivity or edge of a hill; the roof of a house; the bottom or deep part of an ulcer; a high number = 100 Vivāhas.

Ut-sangita, as, ā, am, associated, combined, joined.

Ut-sangin, ī, inī, i, associating or combining with, an associate, a partner; deep-seated, as an ulcer; *(ī),* m. an ulcer, a deep sore; *(inī),* f. pimples on the inner edge of the eyelids.

Ut-sañjana, am, n. leading upwards.

उत्सद् *ut-sad (ud-s°),* cl. 1. P. *-sīdati, -sattum,* to sink, settle down, fall into ruin or decay; to leave off; to rise up: Caus. P. *-sādayati, -yitum,* to destroy, overturn.

Ut-sanna, as, ā, am, decayed, in ruins; destroyed, overturned; disused, fallen into disuse; risen, increased. — *Utsanna-dharma, as,* or *utsanna-yajña, as,* m. an interrupted or suspended sacrifice.

Ut-sāda, as, m., Ved. a particular part of the sacrificial animal.

Ut-sādaka, as, ā, am, destroying, overturning.

Ut-sādana, am, n. destroying, overturning; suspending, interrupting, omitting; cleaning the person with perfumes, rubbing or chafing the limbs; healing a sore, causing it to fill up; going up, ascending, rising; raising, elevating; ploughing a field twice or thoroughly.

Ut-sādanīya, as, ā, am, to be destroyed; to be effected; to be gone up or ascended; *(am),* n. any application to a sore producing granulations.

Ut-sādita, as, ā, am, destroyed, overturned; cleansed, purified with oil, perfumes, &c.; risen, ascended; raised, elevated.

Ut-sāditavya or *ut-sādya, as, ā, am,* to be destroyed.

उत्सर, उत्सारक, &c. See under *ut-sṛi.*

उत्सर्ग *ut-sarga.* See under *ut-sṛij.*

उत्सव *utsava, as,* m. (fr. rt. 2. *su* with *ud?*), enterprise, beginning; a festival, a jubilee; joy, gladness; merry-making; height, elevation, insolence; passion, wrath; wish; rising of a wish; a section of a book. — *Utsava-sanketa, ās,* m. pl., N. of a people.

उत्सह् *ut-sah (ud-s°),* cl. 1. A. *-sahate, -sahitum* or *-sodhum,* to be able, to be adequate, to have power (with inf., or with dat. of an abstract noun); to act with courage or energy: Caus. *-sāhayati, -yitum,* to animate, encourage, excite; Desid. of the Caus. *-sisāhayishati,* to wish to excite.

Ut-sāha, as, m. power, strength, strength of will, resolution; effort, perseverance, strenuous and continued exertion, energy; firmness, fortitude; happiness; a thread. — *Utsāha-vat, ān, atī, at,* active, energetic, persevering. — *Utsāha-vardhana, as,* m. the heroic *rasa* or feeling; *(am),* n. increase of energy, heroism. — *Utsāha-sampanna, as, ā, am,* active, persevering.

Ut-sāhana, am, n. effort, perseverance.

Utsāhin, ī, inī, i, active, persevering.

उत्सिच् *ut-sić (ud-s°),* cl. 6. P. A. *-sinćati, -te, -sektum,* to sprinkle, pour, to spread; to make proud: Pass. *-sićyate,* to spout or foam up or over; to be puffed up; to overflow, increase.

Ut-sikta, as, ā, am, sprinkled; flooded, abundantly furnished; elevated, raised, haughty, proud, rude; enlarged, increased; disordered, disturbed in mind &c.

Ut-sićyamāna, as, ā, am, foaming or spouting up, showering; increasing, overflowing, growing.

Ut-seka, as, m. sprinkling, pouring; foaming upwards, spouting out or over, showering; overflow, increase, enlargement; haughtiness, pride.

Utsekin, ī, inī, i, overflowing; proud, haughty, puffed up.

Ut-sećana, am, n. the act of showering or spouting upwards, boiling or foaming over.

उत्सुक *utsuka, as, ā, am* (fr. 1. *ud* and *suka;* the latter does not exist separately, but may be derived from the particle *su,* as *anuka* fr. *anu, abhika* fr. *abhi;* cf. also *utka*), restless, uneasy, unquiet, anxious; anxiously desirous, zealously active, striving or making exertions for any object (e. g. *jayotsuka,* anxiously striving for victory); eager for, fond of, attached to; regretting, repining, missing, sorrowing for; *(as),* m. (?) longing for. — *Utsuka-tā,* f. or *utsuka-tva, am,* n. restlessness, uneasiness, unquietness, zeal; attachment, affection; sorrow, regret.

Utsukāya, nom. A. *utsukāyate,* to become unquiet &c.

उत्सूत्र *ut-sūtra, as, ā, am,* unstrung; irregular, out of rule, loose, detached.

उत्सूर *ut-sūra, as,* m. evening, twilight (when the sun sets).

Utsūrya. See under *otsūryam.*

उत्सृ *ut-sṛi (ud-sṛi),* Caus. P. *-sārayati, -yitum,* to expel, turn out, drive away.

Ut-sara, as, m. a species of the Ati-śakvarī metre, consisting of four verses of fifteen syllables each.

Ut-saryā, f. a cow when grown up and fit to take the bull.

Ut-sāraka, as, m. one who drives away the mob from a person of rank, a policeman; a guard, a guardian.

Ut-sāraṇa, am, n. moving, causing to move, removing, keeping at a distance, driving out of the way; assisting any one to step out (of a palanquin &c.); reception of a guest.

उत्सृज् *ut-sṛij (ud-s°),* cl. 6. P. *-sṛijati, -srashṭum,* to pour out, emit, send forth; to let loose; to cast forth or away; to lay aside, quit, leave, abandon, avoid, eschew; to abolish (a rule &c.).

Ut-sarga, as, m. pouring out, pouring forth, emission, dejection, excretion, voiding by stool &c.; laying aside, abandoning, resigning, quitting, retiring from, suspending; loosening, delivering; oblation, libation; presentation of anything promised to a god or Brāhman with suitable ceremonies; giving, donation; a particular ceremony on suspending a Vedic lecture; (in gram.) any general precept or rule (opposed to *apavāda,* special rule or exception, and so called because only abolished in express cases by a substitute). — *Utsarga-tas,* ind. generally, i. e. without any special limitation.

Utsargin, ī, iṇī, i, leaving out or off; omitting, abandoning, quitting.

Ut-sarjana, am, n. letting loose, abandoning, leaving, &c.; gift, donation, oblation; suspending (a lecture in the Veda), a ceremony connected with it.

Ut-sisṛikshu, us, us, u, wishing to create.

Ut-sṛijya, ind. having abandoned, having quitted.

Ut-sṛishṭa, as, ā, am, left, abandoned; given up, given, presented; poured forth, cast into or upon. — *Utsṛishṭa-paśu, us,* m. a bull set at liberty upon particular occasions, as on a marriage &c., and allowed to go about at will. — *Utsṛishṭa-vat, ān, atī, at,* one who has let fall, who has shed (a tear &c.).

Ut-sṛishṭi, is, f. abandonment, letting go, emission.

Utsrashṭu-kāma, as, ā, am, wishing to let go or put down.

उत्सृप् *ut-sṛip (ud-s°),* cl. 1. P. *-sarpati, -sarptum* or *-sraptum,* to go, glide or soar upwards, to spread out.

Ut-sarpa, as, m. going or gliding upwards; swelling, heaving.

Ut-sarpaṇa, am, n. gliding upwards; swelling, heaving.

Ut-sarpita, as, ā, am, gliding or going upwards; heaving, heaved, undulating.

Ut-sarpin, ī, iṇī, i, moving or gliding upwards; rising; soaring; *(iṇī),* f. a Jaina division of time, a long period described as ten crores of crores of oceans of years; this period alternates with one of similar duration. See *ava-sarpiṇī.*

उत्सेध *ut-sedha, as,* m. (fr. rt. 1. *sidh* with *ud*), height, elevation; thickness, fatness, obesity; intumescence; excelling, sublimity; the body; *(am),* n. killing, slaughter.

उत्स्थल *ut-sthala, am,* n., N. of an island.

उत्स्मि *ut-smi (ud-s°),* cl. 1. A. *-smayate, -smetum,* to smile at, deride: Caus. P. *-smāyayati, -yitum,* to make a fool of one.

Ut-smaya, as, m. a smile.

Ut-smayat, an, antī, at, smiling.

उत्स्य *utsya, as, ā, am* (fr. *utsa*), Ved. coming from a well or fountain (as water).

उत्स्वप्नाय *utsvapnāya,* nom. (fr. *ud-svapna*) A. *utsvapnāyate,* to talk in one's sleep; to dream uneasily.

उद् 1. *ud,* a particle and prefix to verbs and nouns. (As implying superiority in place, rank, station, or power) up, upwards; upon, on; over, above. (As implying separation and disjunction) out, out of, from, off, away from, apart. (According to native authorities *ud* may also imply publicity, pride, indisposition, weakness, helplessness, binding, loosing, existence, acquisition.)

Ud is not used as a separable adverb or preposition; in those rare cases, in which it appears in the Veda uncompounded with a verb, the latter has to be supplied from the context (e.g. *ud utsam śatadhāram,* out (pour) a fountain of a hundred streams).

Ud is sometimes repeated in the Veda to fill out the verse (e.g. *kim na ud ud u harshase*).

[Cf. Zend *uś;* Hib. *uas* and in composition *os, ois,* e.g. *os-car,* 'a leap, bound,' &c. See also *ut-tama,* 1. *ut-tara,* &c.]

उद् 2. *ud* or *und,* cl. 7. P. *unatti, undāñćakāra, undishyati, aundīt, unditum,* to flow or issue out, to spring (said of water); to wet, bathe: Caus. *undayati,* aor. *aundidat:* Desid. *undidishati;* [cf. Gr. ὕδωρ; Lat. *unda;* Goth. *vato;* Lit. *wandū'.*]

Uda, am, n. (only at the beginning or end of a compound) water. — *Uda-kīrṇa* or *uda-kīrya, as,* m. the tree Galedupa Piscidia, the bark of which is rubbed and scattered into water to stun the fishes. — *Uda-kumbha, as,* m. a water-jar, a jar with water. — *Uda-grābha, as,* m., Ved. holding water. — *Uda-ćamasa, as,* m. a cup containing water. — 1. *uda-ja, as, ā, am* (for 2. see *ud-aj* 3rd col.), aquatic, watery, produced in or by water. — *Uda-jña, as,* m., N. of a man. — *Uda-dhāna, as, ā, am,* containing water. — *Udha-dhi, is, is, i,* Ved. containing water; (*is*), m. a water-jar, a reservoir for water; a cloud; a lake; the ocean. — *Udadhi-kumāra, ās,* m. pl. a class of divinities, belonging to the Bhavanādhīśās. — *Udadhi-krama, as,* m. or *udadhi-krā, ās,* m., Ved. a voyager, a mariner. — *Udadhi-mala, as,* m. cuttle-fish bone. — *Udadhi-mekhalā,* f. the earth (girdled by the ocean). — *Udadhi-rāja, as,* m. the king of the waters, the ocean. — *Udadhi-sutā,* f. the daughter of the ocean; an epithet of Lakshmī; and of Dvārakā, the capital of Krishṇa. — *Uda-pa, as, ā, am,* crossing the water, as a boat. — *Uda-pātra, am, ī,* n. f. a water-jug, a ewer. — *Uda-pāna, as, am,* m. n. a well. — *Udapāna-maṇḍūka, as,* m. a frog in a well; (metaphorically) an inexperienced man of limited ideas who knows only his own neighbourhood. — *Uda-pū, ūs, ūs, u,* Ved. cleansing one's self with water, purified with water. — *Uda-pesha, am,* n. a paste, anything ground with water; (*am*), ind. by grinding in water. — *Uda-prut, t, t, t,* Ved. swimming or splashing in water; (Say.) causing water to flow. — *Uda-pluta, as, ā, am,* Ved. swimming in water. — *Uda-bhāra, as,* m. a water-carrier, a cloud. — *Uda-bhrijja* and *uda-majja, as,* m., N. of two men. — *Uda-mantha, as,* m. barley-water. — *Uda-megha, as,* m. a watery cloud; a shower of rain. — *Uda-lāvaṇika, as, ī, am,* salted, prepared with brine. — *Uda-vajra, as,* m. a thunder-shower, a water-spout. — *Uda-vāpa, as,* m., N. of a man. — *Uda-vāsa, as,* m. residence in water; (*am*), n. a house on the margin of a stream or pond, a marine grotto &c. — *Uda-vāha, as, ā, am,* Ved. bringing water; epithet of the Maruts. — *Uda-vāhana, am,* n. any water-vessel; a cloud. — *Uda-vindu, us,* m. a drop of water. — *Uda-vīvadha, as,* m. a yoke for carrying water. — *Uda-vraja, as,* m., N. of a man. — *Uda-śarāva, as,* m. a jar filled with water. — *Uda-śuddha, as,* m. a water-jar. — *Uda-śrit, t,* n. two portions of buttermilk and one portion of water. — *Uda-sthālī,* f. a caldron, a kettle. — *Uda-haraṇa, as,* m. a vessel for drawing water. — *Uda-hāra, as, ī, am,* Ved. fetching or carrying water; (*as*), m. a water-carrier, a cloud. — *Udaudana,* see *udakaudana.*

Udaka, am, n. water; *udakam dā* or *pradā* or *kṛi,* to offer a libation of water to a dead person (with gen. or dat. of the person); *udakam upa-spriś,* to touch certain parts of the body with water, as prescribed by law; (the word *udaka* may be used alone to express this ceremony, e.g. *udakārtham,* for the sake of the *udaka* ceremony.) — *Udaka-karman, a,* n. or *udaka-kriyā,* f. presentation of water to dead ancestors as far as the fourteenth degree. — *Udaka-kārya, am,* n. a religious ceremony performed with water; ablution of the body; oblations to the dead. — *Udaka-kumbha, as,* m. a water-jar. — *Udaka-krīḍana, am,* n. sporting about in water. — *Udaka-gāha* or *uda-gāha, as,* m. entering the water. — *Udaka-giri, is,* m. a mountain abounding in streams of water. — *Udaka-ćandra,* a kind of magic. — *Udaka-da, as, ā, am,* a giver of water, yielding water, offering water to the manes; (*as*), m. an heir, a near kinsman. — *Udaka-dātṛī, tā,* or *udaka-dāyin, ī,* m. one who presents libations of water to the manes, an heir or kinsman. — *Udaka-dāna, am,* n. gift of water, especially to the manes, as a religious or obsequial rite. — *Udaka-dānika, as, ā, am,* referring to the above obsequial rite. — *Udaka-dhara, as,* m. 'water-holder,' a cloud. — *Udaka-parvata, as,* m.; see *udaka-giri.* — *Udaka-pūrvakam,* ind. preceded by the water-rite, i.e. by pouring water on the hand as preparatory to or confirmatory of a gift or promise. — *Udaka-pratīkāśa, as, ā, am,* like water, watery, fluid. — *Udaka-bhāra, as,* m. a yoke for carrying water. — *Udaka-bhūma, as,* m. humid soil. — *Udaka-mañjarī,* f. title of a work on medicine. — *Udaka-maṇḍalu, us,* m., Ved. a water-pitcher. — *Udaka-mantha* or *uda-mantha, as,* m. a kind of peeled grain. — *Udaka-meha, as,* m. a sort of diabetes, passing watery urine. — *Udakamehin, ī, inī, i,* suffering from this disease. — *Udaka-vajra, as,* m. a thunder-shower, a thunderstorm with rain; [cf. *uda-vajra.*] — *Udaka-vat, ān, atī, at,* furnished with water. — *Udaka-vindu, us,* m. a drop of water. — *Udaka-vīvadha, as,* m. a yoke for carrying water; [cf. *uda-vīvadha.*] — *Udaka-śāka, am,* n. any aquatic herb. — *Udaka-śānti, is,* f. sprinkling consecrated water over a sick person to allay fever. — *Udaka-saktu, us,* m. ground rice moistened with water. — *Udaka-sparśa, as, ā, am,* touching different parts of the body with water; touching water in confirmation of a promise. — *Udaka-hāra, as,* m. a water-carrier. — *Udakātman* (°*ka-āt*°), *ā, ā, a,* chiefly consisting of water, whose chief substance is water. — *Udakādhāra* (°*ka-ādh*°), *as,* m. a reservoir, a cistern, a well. — *Udakānta* (°*ka-an*°), *as,* m. margin of water, bank, shore. — *Udakārthin* (°*ka-ar*°), *ī, inī, i,* desirous of water, thirsty. — *Udakāhāra* (°*ka-āh*°), *as,* m. the drawing up of water. — *Udake-ćara, as, ā, am,* moving or living in or inhabiting water. — *Udake-viśīrṇa, as, ā, am,* dried in water, (a metaphorical expression for anything unheard of or impossible.) — *Udakodañjana* (°*ka-ud*°), *as,* m. a water-jar. — *Udakodara* (°*ka-ud*°), *am,* n. dropsy. — *Udakodarin, ī, iṇī, i,* dropsical. — *Udakaudana* (°*ka-od*°), *as,* m. rice boiled with water.

Udakala, as, ā, am, watery, containing water.

Udakila, as, ā, am, watery, containing water.

Udakya, as, ā, am, being in water; (*ā*), f. a woman in her courses (requiring water for purification).

1. *udan,* n. (not used in the nom. sing. du. plur. and the acc. sing. and du.), Ved. a wave, water. — *Udan-vat, ān, atī, at,* Ved. wavy, watery, abounding in water; (*ān*), m. the ocean; N. of a Rishi.

Udani-mat, ān, atī, at, Ved. abounding in waves or water.

1. *udanya,* nom. P., Ved. *udanyati,* to irrigate; to thirst, be thirsty.

2. *udanya, as, ā, am,* Ved. watery; (*ā*), f. thirst. — *Udanya-ja, as, ā, am,* Ved. born in or living in water.

Udanyu, us, us, u, Ved. liking or seeking water, walking in water.

Undana, unna, &c. See under *und,* p. 159.

उदक् *udak.* See under 2. *ud-añć.*

उदग्र *ud-agra, as, ā, am,* with elevated top, having the top upwards, over-topping, towering or pointing upwards; projecting; high, tall, long; advanced (in age); increased, large, vast, fierce, intense; excited, enraptured. — *Udagra-dat, an, atī, at,* having projecting teeth, large-toothed; (*an*), m. an elephant with a large tusk.

उदज् *ud-aj,* cl. 1. P. A. *-ajati, -te, -ajitum,* to drive out, expel, pull off.

2. *ud-aja, as,* m. (for 1. see under *uda* 1st col.), the driving out or forth (of cattle &c.).

Ud-āja, as, m. leading up or out.

उदजलक *udajalaka, as,* m., N. of a wheelwright in the Pañća-tantra.

उदञ्च् 1. *ud-añć* or *ud-ać,* cl. 1. P. A. *-añćati, -te, -ćitum,* to elevate, raise up, lift up, throw up; to send forth, utter, cause to resound.

Ud-akta, as, ā, am, gone up, raised up, risen, ascended; sent forth; uttered.

Ud-aṅka, as, m. a vessel or bucket (for oil &c., but not for water); Pāṇini III. 3, 123, N. of a man.

2. *ud-añć* or *ud-ać, an, īćī, ak,* turned or going upwards; upper, upwards; turned to the north, northern (opposed to *adharāñć* and *dakshiṇa*); subsequent, posterior; (*k*), ind. above; northward; subsequently; *udīćī,* the northern *diś* or quarter, the north. — *Udaktāt,* ind., Ved. towards the north, northward. — *Udak-patha, as,* m. the northern country. — *Udak-pravaṇa, as, ā, am,* sloping towards the north; proceeding well (as a sacrifice?). — *Udak-sena, as,* m., N. of a prince. — *Udag-adri, is,* m. the northern mountain; the Himālaya mountain to the north of Hindūstan. — *Udag-ayana, am,* n. the sun's progress north of the equator, the half-year from the winter to the summer solstice. — *Udag-daśa, as, ā, am,* having the border turned upwards or to the north. — *Udag-bhūma, as,* m. fertile soil (turned upwards or towards the north). — *Udag-bhūmi, is,* m. good or fertile soil. — *Udan-mukha, as, ī, am,* facing the north.

Ud-añćana, am, n. a bucket, a pail for drawing water out of a well; (*am*), n. directing or throwing upwards; rising, ascending; a cover or lid.

Ud-añćita, as, ā, am, raised up, thrown up, tossed; worshipped.

Ud-añću, us, m., N. of a man.

उदञ्जलि *ud-añjali, is, is, i,* hollowing the palms and then raising them.

उदण्डपाल *ud-aṇḍa-pāla, as,* m. a kind of fish; a sort of snake.

उदधि *uda-dhi.* See under *uda.*

उदन् 2. *ud-an,* cl. 2. P. *-aniti, -nitum,* to breathe upwards, emit the breath in an upward direction; to breathe.

Ud-āna, as, m. breathing upwards, breathing, breath; one of the three or five vital airs, that which rises up the throat and passes into the head; (with Buddhists) an expression of joy or praise; the navel; an eyelash; a kind of snake.

उदन्त *ud-anta, as, ā, am,* reaching to the end or border of anything; (*as*), m. 'telling to the end,' full tidings, intelligence; news; a pure and virtuous man; supporting one's self by sacrificing for others; one who gets a livelihood by a trade &c.

Udantaka, as, m. news, tidings, intelligence.
Ud-antikā, f. satisfaction, satiety.
Udantya, as, ā, am, living beyond a limit or boundary.

उदन्य *udanya.* See under 2. *ud.*

उदय *ud-aya,* &c. See under *ud-i* 3rd col.

उदर *udara, am,* n. (fr. rt. *ṛi* with *ud?*), the belly; a cavity, the interior or inside of anything (e. g. *udare,* inside, in the interior); enlargement of the abdomen from dropsy or flatulence, any morbid abdominal affection, as liver, spleen, &c., a class of eight different diseases; the thick, inner side of the *angushṭha* or thumb; slaughter; [cf. Lat. *uterus.*] — *Udara-granthi, is,* m. disease of the spleen, lit. 'knot of the belly' (a chronic affection of this organ not uncommon in India). — *Udara-trāṇa, am,* n. a cuirass, armour covering the front of the body; a girth, a belly-band. — *Udara-dāra, as,* m., Ved. a particular disease of the belly. — *Udara-piśāća, as,* m. a glutton, voracious, one who devours everything, flesh, fish, &c. — *Udara-pūram,* ind. till the belly is full. — *Udara-poshaṇa, am,* n. feeding the belly, supporting life. — *Udara-bharaṇa-mātra-kevalećchu* (°*la-ić*°), *us, us, u,* desirous only of the mere filling of the belly. — *Udaram-bhari, is, is, i,* nourishing only one's own belly, selfishly voracious, gluttonous. — *Udara-vat, ān, atī, at,* having a large belly, corpulent. — *Udara-śaya, as, ā, am,* sleeping on the face or belly. — *Udara-śāṇḍilya, as,* m., N. of a sage. — *Udara-sarvasva, as,* m. an epicure, a glutton. — *Udarādhmāna* (°*ra-ādh*°), *am,* n. flatulence of the body. — *Udarāmaya* (°*ra-ām*°), *as,* m. disease of the belly, dysentery, diarrhœa. — *Udarāmayin, ī, iṇī, i,* suffering from dysentery or diarrhœa. — *Udarāvarta* (°*ra-āv*°), *as,* m. the navel. — *Udarāveshṭa* (*ra-āv*°), *as,* m. tape worm.
Udaraka, as, ī, am, abdominal.
Udarika, as, ā, am, having a large belly.
Udarin, ī, iṇī, i, having a large belly, fat, corpulent; abdominal; (*iṇī*), f. a pregnant woman.
Udarila, as, ā, am, fat, corpulent.
Udarya, as, ā, am, belonging to the belly; (*am*), n., Ved. contents of the belly or what forms the belly.

उदरथि *ud-arathi, is,* m. (fr. rt. *ṛi* with *ud?*), the sun; the ocean.

उदर्क *ud-arka.* See under *ud-ṛić* at p. 155.

उदर्चिस् *ud-arćis, is, is, is,* shining or blazing upwards, luminous; (*is*), m. a N. of fire; of Śiva, of Kandarpa.

उदर्ज् *ud-arj,* cl. 1. P., Ved. *-arjati, -jitum,* to drive out, remove.

उदर्द् *ud-ard,* cl. 1. P. *-ardati, -ditum,* to strike or beat upon.
Ud-arda, as, m. (in medic.) erysipelas.

उदर्द्ध *ud-arddha, as,* m. (fr. rt. *ṛidh* with *ud*), scarlet fever.

उदल *udala, as,* m., N. of a man.

उदव् *ud-av,* cl. 1. P. *-avati, -vitum,* to regard, attend to; to wait for; to promote, impel.

उदवग्रह *ud-avagraha, as,* m. a Svarita accent depending on an Udātta which stands in the *ava-graha* (q. v.). See *tairovirāma.*

उदवसानीय *ud-avasānīya, as, ā, am* (fr. rt. *so* with *ava* and *ud*), Ved. concluding, final.
Ud-avasita, am, n. a house, dwelling.

उदश् *ud-aś,* cl. 5. P. A. *-aśnoti, -nute, -aśitum* or *-ashṭum,* to reach to the top of, reach, attain; to be able, be master of.

उदश्रु *ud-aśru, us, us, u,* one whose tears gush forth, weeping.

उदस् *ud-as,* cl. 4. P. *-asyati, -situm,* to cast or throw up; to raise, erect, elevate; to throw out, expel.
Ud-asana, am, n. throwing up, raising, erecting.
Ud-asta, as, ā, am, thrown or cast up, raised, thrown; cast out, expelled; removed, scattered, humbled, shamed.
Ud-asya, ind. having cast up, having tossed upwards, having thrown; having expelled, having scattered; having made efforts, having taken pains.
1. *ud-āsa, as,* m. throwing or directing upwards, elevation.

उदाकृ *ud-ā-kṛi,* cl. 8. 5. P. A. *-kṛiṇoti, -ṇute, -karoti, -kurute, -kartum,* to expel; to fetch out of; to select; A. to overpower.

उदाख्या *ud-ā-khyā,* cl. 2. P. *-khyāti, -tum,* to relate aloud; enunciate.

उदागा *ud-ā-gā,* cl. 3. P. *-jigāti, -gātum,* to come up or out towards.

उदाचक्ष् *ud-ā-ćaksh,* cl. 2. A. *-ćashṭe,* to declare aloud.

उदाचर् *ud-ā-ćar,* cl. 1. P., Ved. *-ćarati, -ritum, -rtum,* Ved. *-ritave, -tavai, -rase, -radhyai,* to rise from or out of.

उदाजन् *ud-ā-jan,* cl. 4. A., Ved. *-jāyate, -janitum,* to arise from; to become visible above.

उदातन् *ud-ā-tan,* cl. 8. P. A. *-tanoti, -nute, -nitum,* to erect one's self, to rise.

उदादा *ud-ā-dā,* cl. 3. P., Ved. *-dadāti, -dātum,* to lift up, elevate.
Ud-ātta, as, ā, am (for *ud-ā-datta*), elevated, high, upraised, lofty; highly or acutely accented; great, illustrious; generous, gentle, and bountiful; giving, a donor; dear, beloved; (*as*), m. the acute accent, a high or sharp tone; a gift, donation; a kind of musical instrument, a large drum; an ornament or figure of speech in rhetoric; work, business; (*am*), n. an ornament or figure in rhetoric. — *Udāttatara, as, ā, am,* more elevated, more acute. — *Udātta-tva, am,* n. the state of having the acute accent. — *Udātta-maya, as, ī, am,* similar to the high tone or accent. — *Udātta-rāghava, am,* n. title of a drama. — *Udātta-vat, ān, atī, at,* pronounced with the acute accent. — *Udātta-śruti, is, is, i,* pronounced with the Udātta accent. — *Udāttaśruti-tā,* f. the state of being pronounced with the acute accent.

उदाद्यन्त *ud-ādy-anta, as, ā, am,* preceded and followed by an Udātta.

उदान *ud-āna.* See under 2. *ud-an,* p. 153.

उदानी *ud-ā-nī,* cl. 1. P. A. *-nayati, -te, -netum,* to lead up (out of water); to elevate.

उदाप् *ud-āp,* cl. 5. P., Ved. *-āpnoti, -āptum,* to reach up to, reach, attain.

उदापि *ud-āpi, is,* m., N. of a son of Sahadeva.

उदाप्यम् *ud-āpyam,* ind., Ved. up the stream, against stream.

उदायम् *ud-ā-yam,* cl. 1. P. *-yaććhati, -yantum,* to show, to make known.

उदायस *ud-āyasa, as,* m., N. of a prince.

उदायुध *ud-āyudha, as, ā, am,* with uplifted weapon, upraising weapons.

उदार *ud-āra, as, ā* or *ī, am* (fr. rt. *ṛi* with *ud*), high, lofty, exalted, noble, illustrious, generous, liberal, gentle, munificent, great, best; upright, honest, sincere; proper, right; eloquent; unperplexed; Ved. causing to rise, exciting, driving forth; (*am*), ind. aloud; (*as*), m., Ved. a rising fog or vapour; a sort of grain with long stalks; a figure in rhetoric, attributing nobleness to an inanimate object; (*ās*), pl. nebulous forms, spirits (?). — *Udāra-ćarita, as, ā, am,* of a generous disposition, noble-minded. — *Udāra-ćetas, ās, ās, as,* high-minded, magnanimous. — *Udāra-tā,* f. liberality, generosity. — *Udāra-dhī, īs, īs, i,* highly intelligent, wise, sagacious, noble-minded. — *Udāra-vīrya, as, ā, am,* of great power. — *Udāra-sattva, as, ā, am,* generous-minded.
Udāraka, as, m., N. of a man.

उदारथि *ud-ārathi, is, is, i* (fr. rt. *ṛi* with *ud ?*), Ved. steaming (as a hot dish); (Sāy.) rising, or enlightening the organs of sense; (*is*), m. an epithet of Vishṇu.

उदावत्सर *udāvatsara, as,* m. a year, one of the five years forming a period. See *idāvatsara.*

उदावर्त *ud-āvarta, as,* m. a class of diseases, marked by the retention of the excrements; disease of the bowels, iliac passion; (*ā*), f. painful menstruation with foamy blood.
Udāvartin, ī, inī, i, suffering from such diseases.

उदावसु *udāvasu, us,* m., N. of a king of Videha, a son of Janaka; [cf. *upāvasu.*]

उदावह् *ud-ā-vah,* cl. 1. P. A. *-vahati, -te, -voḍhum,* to extol, to praise; to draw, lead along; to marry.

उदास् *ud-ās,* cl. 2. A. *-āste, -āsitum,* to sit separate or away from, to sit on one side or apart, not to share in, not to show interest in; to be unconcerned about, to be indifferent or passive.
2. *ud-āsa, as, ā, am* (for 1. see under *ud-as*), indifferent, unconcerned, apathetic; (*as*), m. a stoic, a philosopher; indifference, apathy, stoicism.
Ud-āsitṛi, tā, trī, tṛi, indifferent, disregarding, stoical, one void of concern or affection.
Ud-āsin, ī, inī, i, indifferent, disregarding; (*ī*), m. a stoic, a philosopher; one who has no passion nor affection for anything; in popular acceptation, a religious mendicant in general, or one of a particular order.
Ud-āsīna, as, ā, am, sitting apart, indifferent, free from affection; (in law) not involved in the dispute; (*as*), m. a stranger, a neutral, a common acquaintance, a person neither a friend nor a foe. — *Udāsīna-tā,* f. indifference, apathy.

उदास्थित *ud-āsthita, as,* m. (fr. rt. *sthā* with *ā* and *ud*), a superintendent, a doorkeeper; a spy, an emissary; an ascetic who has given up his vow; (*as, ā, am*), set over.

उदाहित *ud-āhita, as, ā, am* (fr. rt. *dhā* with *ā* and *ud*), elevated, raised.

उदाहृ *ud-ā-hṛi,* cl. 1. P. A. *-harati, -te, -hartum,* to relate, declare, announce; illustrate.
Ud-āharaṇa, am, n. relating, saying, declaring, declaration; referring a general rule to a special case, an example or illustration; an apposite argument, the third of the five premises of rhetorical reasoning; the example or third member in a fivefold syllogism.
Ud-āhāra, as, m. an example or illustration; the beginning of a speech.
Ud-āhārya, as, ā, am, to be referred as a general rule to a special case.
Ud-āhṛita, as, ā, am, said, illustrated, called, named, entitled.
Ud-ā-hṛiti, is, f. an example, an illustration.

उदि *ud-i,* cl. 2. P. *-eti, -etum,* to go up or proceed; to rise (e. g. as a star), to come up (as a cloud); to go out of; to come out or arise from; to escape; to start up; to rise up against.
Ud-aya, as, ā, am, (in gram.) following, coming after or upon (as one letter, accent &c. upon another); (*as*), m. going upwards; rising (of the sun or planets or of a cloud); the eastern mountain behind which the sun is supposed to rise; coming forth, creation, production, becoming visible, appearance, development; light, splendor; conclusion, result, consequence; rising, reaching one's aim, elevation; profit, advantage, income, revenue, interest; outlet, exit; N. of the seventh Arhat of the future Utsarpiṇī, = Udayā-

śva; a son of Yājñika; a follower of Sākya-muni. — *Udaya-gupta, as,* m., N. of a man. — *Udaya-jit, t,* m., N. of a son of Guṇala. — *Udaya-dhavala, as,* m., N. of a prince. — *Udaya-parvata, as,* m. or *udaya-giri, is,* m. or *udaya-śaila, as,* m. or *udayāćala* (°*ya-ać*°), *as,* m. or *udayādri* (°*ya-ad*°), *is,* m. the eastern mountain behind which the sun rises. — *Udaya-pura, am,* n., N. of the capital of Marvar. — *Udaya-prastha, as,* m. the plateau of the mountain behind which the sun rises. — *Udaya-rāja, as,* m., N. of a man. — *Udaya-vat, ān, atī, at,* risen. — *Udaya-siṇha, as,* m., N. of a king. — *Udayāditya* (°*ya-ād*°), *as,* m., N. of a man. — *Udayāśva* (°*ya-aś*°), *as,* m., N. of a grandson of Ajāta-śatru.

Ud-ayat, an, antī, at, going upwards, rising.

Ud-ayana, am, n. rising, ascending (of the sun); exit, result; conclusion, end; (*as*), m. an epithet of Agastya; N. of a king of Vatsa; N. of a Purohita of king Suddhodana. — *Udayana* or *Udayanāćārya, as,* m. a philosopher and violent persecutor of the Buddhists. — *Udayana-ćarita, am,* n. title of a play.

Udayanīya, as, ā, am, belonging to an end or conclusion, finishing (as a ceremony).

Ud-ayin, ī, inī, i, rising, ascending, prosperous, flourishing; (*ī*), m., N. of a man. — *Udayi-bhadra, as,* m., N. of a son of Ajāta-śatru.

Ud-āya. See s. v. *try-udāya.*

1. *ud-ita, as, ā, am,* risen, ascended, being above; high, tall, lofty; grown, augmented, born, produced; incurred, experienced. — *Udita-homin, ī, inī, i,* Ved. sacrificing after sunrise.

1. *ud-iti, is,* f., Ved. ascending, rising (of the sun); going away or down, setting (of the sun).

Ud-iyamāna, as, ā, am, rising.

उदिङ्ग् *ud-iṅg,* Caus. P. *-iṅgayati, -yitum,* to impart a tremulous motion, to vibrate; to utter with a whirring or vibratory sound; to cause to whir (said of the pronunciation of certain letters).

उदित 2. *udita, as, ā, am* (fr. rt. *vad*), said, spoken. — *Uditodita, as, ā, am* (fr. 2. *udita* with 1. *ud-ita*), well-grounded in the Sāstras.

2. *uditi, is,* f., Ved. speech.

उदित 3. *udita, as, ā, am* (incorrectly spelt for *ud-dita,* see 4. *dā*), bound, tied.

उदिनक्ष *ud-inaksh* (irreg. Desid. of rt. *naksh*), Ved. *-inakshati,* to attain, obtain, reach; to wish to gain, to pretend to.

उदीक्ष् *ud-īksh,* cl. 1. A. *-īkshate, -shitum,* to look up to; to look at, regard, view, behold; to wait, to delay, to expect: Caus. *-īkshayati, -yitum,* to cause to look up.

Ud-īkshaṇa, am, n. looking up, seeing, beholding.

Ud-īkshya, ind. having looked up at, having seen.

उदीचीन *udīćīna, as, ā, am* (fr. 2. *ud-aṅć*), turned towards the north, northern.

Udīćya, as, ā, am, being or living in the north; (*as*), m. the country to the north and west of the river Sarasvatī, the northern region; (*ās*), m. the inhabitants of this country; (*am*), n. a kind of perfume. — *Udīćya-vritta, am,* n. the metre of the inhabitants of the northern country, a species of the Vaitālīya metre.

उदीप *ud-īpa, as,* m. (fr. 1. *ud* and *ap,* water), high water, an inundation; (*as, ā, am*), flooded.

उदीर् *ud-īr,* cl. 2. A. *-īrte, -īritum,* to rise; to start (in order to go or to come); to move upwards, ascend; to arise, originate: Caus. *-īrayati, -yitum,* to cause to rise or move; to throw or cast upwards, to cast, throw, discharge, to drive forward; to rouse up, excite; to raise one's voice; to utter, speak; to effect; to make visible: Pass. *-īryate,* to be cast or thrown upwards; to be excited; to be uttered, announced, enunciated; to sound; to issue forth.

Ud-īraṇa, am, n. throwing, casting, discharging (a missile); speaking, saying.

Ud-īrita, as, ā, am, said, uttered; excited, animated. — *Udīrita-dhī, īs, īs, i,* whose mind is active, acute-minded.

Ud-īrṇa, as, ā, am, issued out, excited, increased, intense; generous, great, excellent. — *Udīrṇa-tā,* f. excitement, activity, agility. — *Udīrṇa-dīdhiti, is, is, i,* intensely bright. — *Udīrṇa-vega, as, ā, am,* impetuous in its course (as a torrent), violent.

1. *ud-īrya, as, ā, am,* to be raised, uttered, spoken.

2. *ud-īrya,* ind. having uttered, having spoken.

Ud-īryamāṇa, as, ā, am, being cast or discharged; being spoken or uttered.

उदीष् *ud-īsh,* cl. 1. A. *-īshate, -īshitum,* to rise.

Ud-īshita, as, ā, am, risen, elevated.

उदुक्ष् *ud-uksh,* cl. 1. P., Ved. *-ukshati, -shitum,* to sprinkle upwards or outwards.

उदुब्ज् *ud-ubj,* cl. 6. P. *-ubjati, -jitum,* to cleave asunder (?); to set up, erect.

उदुम्बर *udumbara, as,* m. (Ved. written with *d,* in later books generally with *ḍ*), the glomerous fig tree, Ficus Glomerata; a kind of leprosy; a threshold; a eunuch; (*am*), n. the fruit of the glomerous fig tree; copper; the weight karsha. — *Udumbara-parṇī* or *udumbara-dalā,* f., N. of the plant Croton Polyandra. — *Udumbarā-vatī,* f., N. of a river.

Udumbala, as, ā, am, Ved. copper-coloured?; (Say.) of extended power (for *uru-bala;* said of the two dogs, the messengers of Yama).

Udumbhara, a word coined for the etymological explanation of *udumbara.*

उदुष् *ud-ush,* cl. 1. P. *-oshati, -shitum,* to expel by heat.

Udushṭa-mukha, as, ā, am, Ved. having a red mouth (as a horse).

उदूखल *udūkhala, as, am,* m. n. a wooden mortar used for pounding rice and separating the husk; any mortar; bdellium; a mortar-shaped joint.

उदूढ *ud-ūḍha, as, ā, am* (fr. rt. *vah* with *ud*), married; coarse, gross, heavy, fat; material, substantial; much, exceeding.

उदूह् *ud-ūh,* cl. 1. P. A. *-ūhati, -te, -hitum,* to push or press upwards, move or bear upwards.

उदृ *ud-ṛi,* cl. 3. P. *-iyarti* (Ved. aor. A. *-ārta*), *-artum, -aritum* or *-rītum,* to start up, rise; to move up, raise, excite: Caus. *-arpayati, -yitum,* to cause to rise.

उदृच् *ud-ṛić, k,* f. (fr. rt. *rić* with *ud*), Ved. that which reaches beyond (the present time) or what follows, future time; remainder, conclusion, end, aim; concluding part or hymn (?).

Ud-arka, as, m. reaching or extending beyond, surpassing; the future result of actions; consequence, futurity, future time; a remote consequence, reward; conclusion, end; elevation of a building, a tower, look-out place; the plant Vanguiera Spinosa.

उदृष् *ud-ṛish,* cl. 6. P., Ved. *-ṛishati, -arshitum,* to split, pierce through.

उदे *ud-e* (*ud-ā-i*), *-aiti, -tum,* to come up, come out of, arise from; to step up (to an altar), to go out.

उदेज् *ud-ej,* cl. 1. P. *-ejati, -ejitum,* to move, rise, shake, tremble.

Ud-ejaya, as, ā, am, shaking, making tremble.

उदोजस् *ud-ojas, ās, ās, as,* Ved. exceedingly powerful or violent.

उद्गन्धि *ud-gandhi, is, is, i,* fragrant.

उद्गम् *ud-gam,* cl. 1. P. *-gaććhati, -gantum,* to go up, rise, ascend; to shoot up; to go out, come from, break out, depart; to spread.

Ud-gata, as, ā, am, gone up, risen, ascended; gone, departed; proceeded forth or from; vomited, cast up; (*ā*), f. a stanza of four lines, with ten syllables in the first three and thirteen in the last. — *Udgata-śriṅga, as, ā, am,* (a calf) whose horns are just appearing. — *Udgatāsu* (°*ta-asu*), *us, us, u,* deceased, dead.

Ud-gati, is, f. going up, rising, ascent; coming forth; bringing up, vomiting.

Ud-gama, as, m. going up, rising, ascending, elevation (as of a mountain); rising (of the stars); going out or away; coming forth, becoming visible, production, creation; shoot (of a plant); bringing up, vomiting.

Ud-gamana, am, n. rising, ascending; coming forth, becoming visible.

Ud-gamanīya, as, ā, am, to be gone up or ascended; (*am*), n. a pair of bleached cloths or sheets.

उद्गल् *ud-gal,* cl. 1. P. *-galati, -litum,* to trickle out, ooze out; issue in drops.

उद्गा *ud-gā,* cl. 3. P. *-jigāti, -gātum,* to rise (as the sun &c.); to come forward, to begin.

उद्गातृ *ud-gātṛi,* &c. See *ud-gai* below.

उद्गार *ud-gāra,* &c. See *ud-gṛī* below.

उद्गाह् *ud-gāh,* cl. 1. A. *-gāhate, -gāhitum* or *-gāḍhum,* to emerge.

Ud-gāḍha, as, ā, am, excessive, violent, much; (*am*), ind. excessively, much.

उद्गुर् *ud-gur,* cl. 6. A. *-gurate, -ritum,* to raise the voice in a threatening manner.

Ud-gūrṇa, as, ā, am, raised, lifted, held up; erected, excited.

उद्गुह् *ud-guh,* cl. 1. P. A. *-gūhati, -te, -gūhitum* or *-goḍhum,* to pierce through and through, to twist through.

उद्गॄ *ud-gṛī,* cl. 6. P. *-girati* or *-gilati, -garitum* or *-lītum,* or *-garītum* or *-lītum,* to eject (from the mouth), spit out, vomit out or up, belch out, pour out, discharge; breathe out; to rise from: Caus. P. *-girayati, -yitum,* to cause to pour forth, to raise (a sound), to cause to utter sounds.

Ud-gāra, as, m. spitting out, ejecting anything from the mouth, vomiting; belching, eructation; relating repeatedly; spittle, saliva; speaking in the throat, sound, roaring, hissing.

Ud-gārin, ī, iṇī, i, ejecting, spitting, vomiting.

Ud-giraṇa, am, n. vomiting; ejecting anything (as saliva &c.) from the mouth, slavering.

Ud-gīrṇa, as, ā, am, vomited forth, ejected, cast forth, breathed out, exhaled, disdained.

उद्गै *ud-gai,* cl. 1. P. *-gāyati, -gātum,* to begin to sing; to sing or chant (applied especially to the singing or chanting of the Sāma-veda, from which one order of priests take the name of Udgātṛi); to announce, to celebrate in song; to sing before any one (with acc.); to fill with song.

Udgātu-kāma, as, ā, am, wishing to sing.

Ud-gātṛi, tā, m. one of the four chief-priests, viz. the one who chants the hymns of the Sāma-veda; a chanter.

Ud-gāthā, f. a variety of the Āryā measure, the same as the Gīti, a stanza of four half-lines, containing alternately twelve and eighteen instants.

Ud-gīti, is, f. singing; chanting of the Sāma-veda; a variety of the Āryā metre, a verse of four half-lines, containing twelve, fifteen, twelve, eighteen instants.

Ud-gītha, as, m. chanting of the Sāma-veda, the office of the Udgātṛi; the second part of the Sāma-veda; N. of a son of Bhava; N. of a commentator of Vedic texts; designation of *Om* or the triliteral name of God.

उद्ग्रन्थ् *ud-granth,* cl. 9. 1. P. A. *-grathnāti, -nīte,* or *-granthati, -te, -granthitum,* to bind up, tie into bundles; to tie up, truss; to fasten, wind; to unbind, loosen.

Ud-grathita, as, ā, am, interlaced; unbound, loosened.

Ud-grantha, as, m. a section, chapter.

Ud-granthi, is, is, i, untied, free from worldly ties.

उद्ग्रह् *ud-grah*, cl. 9. P. A. *-gṛihṇāti* or Ved. *-gṛibhṇāti, -ṇīte, -grahītum*, to take or lift up; to set up, erect, elevate; to take out, draw out, take away; to take away from, to preserve; to cease, especially to cease to rain; to break off, discontinue (speaking); A. to raise one's self: Caus. *-grāhayati, -yitum*, to cause to take up or out, to cause to pay; to extol, extol with praise.

Ud-gṛihīta, as, ā, am, taken up, turned up, upraised.

Ud-grabhaṇa, am, n., Ved. taking up, raising.

Ud-graha, as, m. taking up; any object that may be accomplished by religious or other acts.

Ud-grahaṇa, am, n. taking up, lifting up, taking away or out.

Ud-grābha, as, m., Ved. raising, elevating.

Ud-grāha, as, m. taking up or away; (in the Prātiśākhyas) the rule of Sandhi which causes the change of the terminations *aḥ, e*, and *o*, to *a* before a following vowel; replying in argument; objection. — *Udgrāha-padavṛitti, is*, f. the Sandhi called Udgrāha before a long vowel. — *Udgrāha-vat*, ind. (in the Prātiśākhyas) 'like the Udgrāha,' a term applied to that kind of Sandhi by which final *a* and *ā* appear as *ă* before *ṛi*.

Udgrāhaṇikā, f. replying in argument.

Ud-grāhita, as, ā, am, taken away, lifted up; deposited, delivered; seized; bound, tied; excellent, exalted; recalled, remembered.

उद्ग्रीव *ud-grīva, as, ā, am*, or *ud-grīvin, ī, iṇī, i*, one who lifts up or raises the neck (in trying to see anything).

उद्घ *ud-gha, as*, m. (fr. rt. *han* with *ud*), excellence, happiness; the hollow hand; fire; a model, a pattern; organic air in the body.

Ud-ghana, as, m. a carpenter's bench, a plank on which he works.

Ud-ghāta, as, m. striking, wounding, inflicting a hurt; a wound, a blow; slipping, tripping; raising, elevation; a beginning, a thing begun; breathing through the nostrils as a religious exercise; a club, a mallet, a weapon; the division of a book, a chapter, a section.

Udghātin, ī, inī, i, uneven, having elevations, rough.

उद्घट् *ud-ghaṭ*, Caus. *-ghāṭayati, -yitum*, to open, unlock, unfasten; to peel, shell; to reveal, expose; to undertake, commence; to rub over, stroke, tickle.

Ud-ghāṭa, as, m. a watch or guard-house.

Ud-ghāṭaka, as, m. an opener, the instrument or implement for opening anything, a key; (*am*), n. the rope and bucket of a well, a leather bucket used for drawing water.

Ud-ghāṭana, am, n. opening, unlocking; an opener, the instrument or means of opening, a key, &c.; the rope and bucket of a well, a leather bucket used for drawing water; hoisting, raising, lifting up.

Ud-ghāṭanīya, as, ā, am, to be opened.

Ud-ghāṭita, as, ā, am, opened, manifested; undertaken, commenced; raised, hoisted or lifted up; done with effort, exerted. — *Udghāṭita-jña, as, ā, am*, wise, intelligent. — *Udghāṭitāṅga* (°*ta-an*°), *as, ā, am*, naked; intelligent, wise.

Ud-ghāṭin, ī, inī, i, opening, commencing.

उद्घट्टक *ud-ghaṭṭaka, as*, m. (fr. rt. *ghaṭṭ* with *ud*), a kind of time (in music).

Ud-ghaṭṭana, am, n. kicking of a horse (?); friction; opening, opening upwards as a lid.

Ud-ghaṭṭita, as, ā, am, opened, unlocked.

उद्घस *ud-ghasa, as*, m. (fr. rt. *ghas*), flesh.

उद्घुष् *ud-ghush*, cl. 1. P. *-ghoshati, -shitum*, to sound, cry out, fill with cries: Caus. *-ghoshayati, -yitum*, to cause to sound aloud, to declare aloud; proclaim, noise abroad.

Ud-ghushṭa, as, ā, am, sounded out; proclaimed; (*am*), n. sound, noise.

Ud-ghosha, as, m. announcing or proclaiming aloud; popular talk, general report.

उद्घृष् *ud-ghṛish*, cl. 1. P. *-gharshati, -shitum*, to rub, comminute by rubbing; to rub over, strike against.

Ud-gharshaṇa, am, n. rubbing, rubbing up; rubbing the skin with hard substances, as vitrified brick &c.; a cudgel.

Ud-ghṛishṭa, am, n. a peculiar fault in pronunciation.

उद्दंश *ud-daṇśa, as*, m. (rt. *daṇś*), a bug; a mosquito, a gadfly.

उद्दण्ड *ud-daṇḍa, as, ā, am*, whose staff is raised, whose stalk is erect; raised on a staff or pole. — *Uddaṇḍa-pāla, as*, m. a punisher, whether king or magistrate; a sort of snake, a kind of fish; [cf. *ud-aṇḍa-pāla.*]

उद्दन्तुर *ud-dantura, as, ā, am*, large-toothed, having projecting teeth; high, tall; terrific, formidable.

उद्दम् *ud-dam*, cl. 4. P. *-dāmyati, -damitum*, cl. 10. P. *-damayati, -yitum*, to subdue, to overpower, become master of.

Ud-dama, as, m. subduing, overpowering.

Ud-dānta, as, ā, am, energetic, humble, elevated; (? for *ud-vānta*), vomited by an elephant.

उद्दा *ud-dā*, cl. 3. P. *-dadāti, -dātum*, to take away, snatch away.

उद्दान *ud-dāna, am*, n. (fr. rt. 4. *dā*, to bind, with *ud*), binding, confinement; taming, subduing; the middle, the waist; a fire-place; submarine fire; entrance of the sun into a sign of the zodiac.

Ud-dāma, as, ā, am (fr. *ud* and *dāman*, a bond), unrestrained, unbound, set free; self-willed; unlimited, extraordinary; proud, haughty; large, great; (*as*); m. an epithet of Yama ('whose noose is raised'); an epithet of Varuṇa; (*am*), ind. in an unrestrained manner, without any limits.

Ud-dita, as, ā, am, bound, tied.

उद्दाल *ud-dāla, as*, m. (fr. *dṛi* with *ud*?), the plant Cordia Myxa or Latifolia; also Paspalum Frumentaceum. — *Uddāla-vat, ān*, m., N. of a Gandharba.

Uddālaka, as, m., N. of the above plants; N. of a teacher; (*am*), n. a kind of honey. — *Uddālaka-pushpa-bhañjikā*, f. 'breaking of Uddālaka flowers,' a sort of game played by people in the eastern districts.

Uddālin, ī, m., N. of a teacher.

उद्दिधीर्षा *ud-didhīrshā*. See under 1. *ud-dhṛi*.

उद्दिन *ud-dina, am*, n. midday.

उद्दिश् 1. *ud-diś*, cl. 6. P. A., 3. P. *-diśati, -te, -dideshṭi, -deshṭum*, to show or direct towards; to point out, signify, declare, determine; to enunciate, prophesy; to mean; to aim at, intend, destine; to explain, instruct, teach.

2. *ud-diś, k*, f., Ved. a particular direction or quarter of the sky.

Ud-diśya, ind. having shown or explained; stipulating for, demanding; aiming at, in the direction of, with reference to; towards; with regard to, for, for the sake of, in the name of.

Ud-dishṭa, as, ā, am, mentioned, particularized, described, promised.

Ud-deśa, as, m. pointing to or at, direction; ascertainment; brief statement; exemplification, illustration, explanation; mentioning a thing by name; assignment, prescription; stipulation, bargain; quarter, spot, region, place; an object, a motive; upper region, high situation; (in Nyāya phil.) the enunciation of a thing that is to be further discussed and elucidated; (at the end of compounds) relative to. — *Uddeśa-tas*, ind. pointedly, distinctly; by way of explanation.

Ud-deśaka, as, ā, am, illustrative, explanatory; (*as*), m. an illustration, an example; an illustrator, a guide; (in mathematics) a question, problem.

Ud-deśya, as, ā, am, to be illustrated or explained; anything to which one refers or which one has in view; (*am*), n. the end in view, an incentive.

Ud-deshṭṛi, ṭā, ṭrī, ṭṛi, pointing out &c.; one who acts with a certain scope or design.

उद्दिह् *ud-dih*, cl. 2. P. A., Ved. *-degdhi, -digdhe, -degdhum*, to throw or heap up.

Ud-dehika, as, m., N. of a people; (*ā*), f. the white ant.

उद्दीप् *ud-dīp*, cl. 4. A. *-dīpyate, -dīpitum*, to flame, blaze up, be kindled: Caus. *-dīpayati, -yitum*, to light up, inflame, illuminate, excite, animate.

Ud-dīpa, as, m. inflaming, lighting; an inflamer; animating, who or what animates; (*am*), n. a gummy and resinous substance, bdellium.

Ud-dīpaka, as, ā, am, inflaming, exciting, rendering more intense; lighting, setting alight.

Ud-dīpana, am, n. inflaming (as passion), exciting, animating; illuminating; burning of a body &c.; any aggravating thing or circumstance, giving poignancy to feeling or passion.

Ud-dīpamāna, as, ā, am, lighting up, brightening, becoming light.

Ud-dīpta, as, ā, am, lighted, set on fire or alight; shining; inflamed, aggravated (as passion).

Ud-dīpra, am, n. bdellium.

उद्दृश् *ud-dṛiś*, cl. 1. P. *-paśyati, -drashṭum*, to see above (in the sky), to look upwards; to look into the future, expect; to become aware of; to doubt: Caus. *-darśayati, -yitum*, to make visible, cause to appear.

Ud-darśana, as, m., N. of a king of the Nāgas.

उद्दॄ *ud-dṝi*, cl. 9. P. *-dṛiṇāti, -daritum* or *-rītum*, to tear out.

उद्द्युत् *ud-dyut*, cl. 1. A. *-dyotate, -titum*, to blaze up, shine: Caus. *-dyotayati, -yitum*, to cause to shine: Intens. Ved. *-davidyutiti*, to shine intensely.

Ud-dyota, as, ā, am, flashing up, shining; (*as*), m. light, lustre; revelation.

Ud-dyotita, as, ā, am, lighted up, emblazoned.

उद्द्राव *ud-drāva, as*, m. (rt. *dru*), flight, retreat, going upwards; (*as, ā, am*), running away.

Ud-druta, as, ā, am, fled, retreated, run away; ascended; gone up or upwards.

उद्धन् *ud-dhan* (*ud-han*), cl. 2. P. *-dhanti* (Ved. cl. 1. P. *-dhanati*), *-dhantum*, to raise up, elevate.

Ud-dhata, as, ā, am, raised, elevated; exceeding, excessive; haughty, vain, puffed up; excited, intense; rude, ill-behaved; (*as*), m. a king's wrestler. — *Uddhata-manas, ās, ās, as*, or *uddhata-manaska, as, ā, am*, high-minded, haughty, proud. — *Uddhata-manaska-tva, am*, n. pride, arrogance. — *Uddhatārṇava-nisvana* (°*ta-ar*°), *as, ā, am*, raising a noise like the ocean.

Ud-dhati, is, f. elevation; pride, haughtiness; a stroke, shaking.

उद्धम *ud-dhama*. See under *ud-dhmā*.

उद्धय *ud-dhaya, as, ā, am* (fr. rt. *dhe* with *ud*), who or what drinks.

उद्धर *ud-dhara*, &c. See 2. *ud-dhṛi*.

उद्धर्ष 1. *ud-dharsha, as*, m. (fr. rt. *dhṛish* with *ud*), courage to undertake a thing.

1. *ud-dharshaṇa, as, ā, am* (or fr. next?), animating, encouraging; (*am*), n. animating, encouraging.

उद्धर्ष 2. *ud-dharsha, as*, m. (fr. rt. *hṛish* with *ud*), great joy; a festival (especially a religious one).

2. ud-dharshaṇa, am, n. erection of the hair of the body, occasioned by great pleasure.

Ud-dharshin, ī, iṇī, i, Ved. whose hair is erected; (iṇī), f., N. of a metre of four verses, of fourteen syllables each.

उद्धव ud-dhava, as, m. (fr. rt. hu with ud), a sacrificial fire; a festival, a holiday; N. of a Yādava, the friend and counsellor of Kṛishṇa. — Uddhava-dūta and uddhava-sandeśa, as, m. title of two poems. — Uddhava-brāhmaṇa, as, m., N. of a copyist.

उद्धस्त ud-dhasta, as, ā, am (fr. hasta and ud), extending the hands, raising the hands.

उद्धा 1. ud-dhā, cl. 3. P., Ved. -dadhāti, -dhātum, to abandon or expose (an infant); to set up, erect, build up.

Ud-dhi, is, m., Ved. a particular part of a carriage, perhaps the part which rests on the axles; an earthen stand on which the Ukhā rests.

Ud-dhita, as, ā, am, set up, erected.

उद्धा 2. ud-dhā (ud-hā), cl. 3. A. uj-jihīte, ud-dhātum, to go upwards, move upwards; to raise; to go away from.

1. ud-dhāna, as, ā, am, gone up, ascended.

उद्धान 2. uddhāna, as, ā, am (for ud-vānta, ud-dhmāta, and ud-dhmāna?), ejected, vomited; inflated, corpulent; (am), n. ejecting, vomiting; a fire-place.

उद्धान्त uddhānta, as, ā, am (for ud-vānta?), ejected, vomited; (as), m. an elephant out of rut (from whose temples the juice ceases to flow).

उद्धुर ud-dhura, as, ā, am (fr. ud and dhur), freed from a yoke or burden; ceasing from, leaving off; unrestrained, lively, cheerful; heavy, thick, gross, firm; high.

उद्धुषण uddhushaṇa, a corruption of 2. ud-dharshaṇa, q. v.

उद्धू ud-dhū, cl. 5. P. A. -dhūnoti or -dhunoti, -nute, -dhavitum or -dhotum, to rouse up, shake up, move; to disturb, excite; to shake off, throw off; to expel.

Ud-dhūta, as, ā, am, shaken off, fallen from or off; tossed up, scattered above; exalted; high, loud. — Uddhūta-pāpa, as, ā, am, one who has shaken off (his) sins.

उद्धूपन ud-dhūpana, am, n. fumigating.

उद्धूलय uddhūlaya, nom. P. -dhūlayati, -yitum, to powder, sprinkle with dust or powder.

उद्धूषण uddhūshaṇa, am, n. horripilation; also uddhushaṇa. See 2. ud-dharshaṇa.

Uddhūshita, as, ā, am, having the hairs erected.

उद्धृ 1. ud-dhṛi, cl. 1. P. A. -dharati, -te, -dhartum, to draw out, raise up, make honoured.

Ud-didhīrshā, f. wish to remove.

उद्धृ 2. ud-dhṛi (ud-hṛi), cl. 1. P. A. -dharati, -te, -dhartum, to draw out, take out, to extricate, deliver; to tear out, pull out, eradicate; to extend, elevate, raise: Caus. -dhārayati, -yitum, to cause to draw out; to raise: Desid. uj-jihīrshati, to wish to elevate or draw out, to elevate.

Ud-dhara, as, m., N. of a Rakshas; (as, ā, am) = ud-dhura (?).

Ud-dharaṇa, am, n. the act of drawing out, taking out, tearing out; taking off (clothes); extricating, delivering, rescuing; raising, lifting; eradication; extermination; act of destroying; taking a part or share; taking from the Gārhapatya fire to supply the other sacred fires; vomiting, bringing up; vomited food; final emancipation; (as), m., N. of the father of king Śantanu, the author of a commentary on a portion of the Mārkaṇḍeya-Purāṇa.

Ud-dharaṇīya, as, ā, am, to be raised or taken up, to be extracted.

Ud-dhartavya, as, ā, am, to be drawn out.

Ud-dhartṛi, tā, trī, tṛi, one who raises or lifts up; a sharer, a coheir; one who recovers property; (tā), m. a destroyer, exterminator; redeemer, deliverer.

Ud-dhāra, as, m. raising, elevating, lifting up; drawing out, extraction, deliverance, redemption, extrication; taking away; deduction, a part to be set aside, selected part; a portion, share, a surplus given by the Hindū law to the eldest son beyond the shares of the younger ones; the first division of a patrimony; the sixth part of booty taken in war which belongs to the prince; debt, especially a debt not bearing interest, obligation; recovering property; selecting (a passage), quoting; (ā), f. the plant Cocculus Cordifolius; (am), n. a fire-place. — Uddhāra-vibhāga, as, m. division of shares, partition.

Ud-dhāraka, as, ā, am, who or what raises or lifts, drawing out.

Ud-dhāraṇa, am, n. raising, elevating; drawing out of (a danger), delivering; sharing, dividing.

Ud-dhārita, as, ā, am, taken out, drawn forth, extricated, released.

Ud-dhṛita, as, ā, am, drawn up or out as water from a well &c., raised, elevated; lifted up, thrown up or upwards; extracted, pulled up or out, eradicated or broken off; separated, set apart; divided, partitioned; selected, taken from or out of, recovered; uncovered; dispersed, scattered; holding, containing; vomited. — Uddhṛita-sneha, as, ā, am, skimmed (as milk). — Uddhṛitāri (°ta-ari), is, is, i, destroying an enemy. — Uddhṛitoddhāra (°ta-ud°), as, ā, am, one who has received his share; that from which a share has been deducted.

Ud-dhṛiti, is, f. drawing out; extraction, an extract; delivering, rescue.

Ud-dhṛitya, ind. having raised up or drawn out.

उद्ध्मा ud-dhmā, cl. 1. P. -dhamati, -dhmātum, to breathe out, to puff, to pant, to blow; to inflate, to make known by blowing (a trumpet &c.).

Ud-dhama, as, ā, am, who or what blows; (as), m. breathing hard, panting; blowing, sounding.

Ud-dhmāna, am, n. a stove.

Ud-dhmāya, ind. breathing out &c.

उद्ध्य uddhya, as, m. (fr. rt. ujjh?), a river; N. of a river.

उद्ध्वंस ud-dhvaṇsa, as, m. (rt. dhvaṇs), hoarseness.

उद्बन्ध् ud-bandh, cl. 9. P. -badhnāti, -bandhum, to tie up, hang.

Ud-baddha, as, ā, am, tied up, hung.

Ud-bandha, as, m. or ud-bandhana, am, n. tying up, hanging; hanging one's self.

Ud-bandhuka, as, ā, am, Ved. one who hangs up.

उद्बल ud-bala, as, ā, am, strong, powerful.

उद्बाहु ud-bāhu, us, us, u, having the arms raised; extending the arms; having the trunk upraised (as an elephant).

उद्बिल ud-bila, as, ā, am, out of the hole, (an animal) that has quitted its hole.

उद्बुध् ud-budh, cl. 1. P. A., Ved. -bodhati, -te, -bodhitum, to awaken, arouse, excite, remind.

Ud-buddha, as, ā, am, awakened, excited, reminded, made to think of, recalled; blown, budded. — Udbuddha-saṇskāra, as, m. association of ideas, recalling anything to remembrance.

Ud-bodha, as, m. awaking, reminding, incipient knowledge.

Ud-bodhaka, as, ā, am, exciting; reminding, what reminds or calls to remembrance; discovering, exhibiting.

Ud-bodhana, am, n. awaking, arousing; recalling, reminding.

उद्भट udbhaṭa, as, ā, am, excellent; exalted, magnanimous; (as), m. a tortoise; a fan for winnowing corn; the sun (?).

उद्भव ud-bhava. See 1. ud-bhū below.

उद्भा ud-bhā, cl. 2. P. -bhāti, -tum, to become visible, appear.

उद्भास् ud-bhās, Caus. P. -bhāsayati, -yitum, to illuminate, render beautiful.

Ud-bhāsa, as, m. radiance, splendor. — Udbhāsavat, ān, atī, at, shining, radiant.

Ud-bhāsayat, an, antī, at, lighting up, irradiating.

Ud-bhāsita, as, ā, am, lighted up, illuminated, splendid; ornamented, graced, beautified.

Ud-bhāsin, ī, inī, i, or ud-bhāsura, as, ā, am, shining, radiant.

उद्भिद् 1. ud-bhid, cl. 7. P. A. -bhinatti, -bhinte, -bhettum, to break out, burst forth.

2. ud-bhid, t, t, t, breaking forth, sprouting, germinating; penetrating, coming to the top, destroying; (Sāy.) causing to come forth; (t), m. a sprout or shoot of a plant, a plant; a spring, a fountain; a kind of sacrifice. — Udbhij-ja (°bhid-ja), as, ā, am (less correctly udbhija), sprouting, germinating (as a plant or some lower animals). — Udbhid-vidyā, f. the science of plants, botany.

Ud-bhida, as, ā, am, sprouting, germinating; (am), n. culinary salt.

Ud-bhinna, as, ā, am, opened, burst, budded.

Ud-bheda, as, m. breaking through or out, becoming visible; a spring of water; treason.

Ud-bhedana, am, n. a spring of water, fountain.

उद्भू 1. ud-bhū, cl. 1. P. -bhavati, -vitum, to exist, spring from, arise: Caus. -bhāvayati, -yitum, to cause to exist; to produce; to use, employ.

Ud-bhava, as, m. existence, generation, production, birth, springing from, growing. (Often at the end of adj. compounds, e. g. medhya-vṛikshodbhavāni phalāni, fruits produced by pure trees.) — Udbhava-kara, as, ā or ī, am, productive.

Ud-bhāva, as, m. production, generation; magnanimity.

Ud-bhāvana, am, n. passing over, inattention, neglect, disregard; saying, speaking.

Ud-bhāvayitṛi, tā, trī, tṛi, raising upwards, exalting, lifting up.

Ud-bhāvita, as, ā, am, neglected, disregarded; said, declared.

2. ud-bhū, ūs, ūs, u, Ved. having persistency, lasting.

Ud-bhūta, as, ā, am, born, produced; lofty, literally or figuratively; visible, perceptible, present. — Udbhūta-rūpa, am, n. visible shape or form.

Ud-bhūti, is, f. elevation, increase.

उद्भृ ud-bhṛi, cl. 1. 3. P. A. -bharati, -te, -bibharti, -bibhṛite, -bhartum, to carry off, bear away.

उद्भ्यस ud-bhyasa, as, ā, am, Ved. raising, elevating.

उद्भ्रम् ud-bhram, cl. 1. 4. P. -bhramati, -bhrāmyati, -bhramitum, to move about in a wide space, wander, err.

Ud-bhrama, as, m. whirling, flourishing; regret; N. of a class of beings attending on Śiva.

Ud-bhramaṇa, am, n. moving or wandering about, ascending, rising.

Ud-bhrānta, as, ā, am, agitated, bewildered, distressed; whirled, flourished, waved (as a sword); (am), n. waving a sword.

Udbhrāntaka, am, n. rising into the air.

उद्मन् udman, a, n. (fr. rt. ud), Ved. surging, flooding.

उद्य udya, as, m. a river; [cf. uddhya.]

उद्यत् ud-yat, an, atī, at (fr. ud-i, q. v.), rising; (an), m. a star; N. of a mountain.

उद्यम् ud-yam, cl. 1. P. -yaććhati, -yantum, to raise, elevate, uplift, raise in a menacing manner;

to offer; to strive, be diligent: Intens. Ved. *-yamyamīti*, to raise.

Ud-yata, as, ā, am, raised, held up; active, persevering, labouring diligently and incessantly; trained, exercised, disciplined; eager, prepared, ready; *(as)*, m. time (in music); a section, a chapter, the division of a book. — *Udyata-kārmuka, as, ā, am*, with raised bow. — *Udyata-gada, as, ā, am*, with uplifted mace. — *Udyata-śūla, as, ā, am*, with raised spear. — *Udyata-sruć, k, k, k*, Ved. raising the ladle to offer a libation. — *Udyatāyudha* (°*ta-āy*°), *as, ā, am*, with uplifted weapon or weapons.

Ud-yati, is, f., Ved. raising, elevation.

Ud-yantṛi, tā, trī, tṛi, raising, elevating.

Ud-yama, as, m. raising or lifting up, elevation; raising the hands for work, undertaking anything; strenuous and continued effort, exertion, perseverance. — *Udyama-bhanga, as*, m. breaking the efforts, discouragement, dissuasion; desisting. — *Udyama-bhṛit, t, t, t*, bearing or undergoing exertions.

Ud-yamana, am, n. raising, elevation.

Ud-yamin, ī, inī, i, undertaking, persevering, making effort, active.

Ud-yamīyas, ān, asī, as, Ved. extending more widely; (Sāy.) excessively raising.

1. *ud-yamya, as, ā, am*, requiring exertion.

2. *ud-yamya*, ind. having lifted or taken up, having made exertion.

Ud-yāma, as, m. erecting, stretching out; a rope, cord.

उद्या ud-yā, cl. 2. P. *-yāti, -tum*, to go up or out, to rise, originate.

Ud-yāna, am, n. going out; walking out; a garden, a royal garden, a park; purpose, motive; N. of a country to the north of India. — *Udyāna-pāla, as*, m. a gardener; the master or owner or keeper of a garden. — *Udyāna-pālaka, as, ikā*, m. f. a gardener; superintendent or keeper of a garden. — *Udyāna-rakshaka, as*, m. a keeper of a garden; a gardener.

Udyānaka, am, n. a garden, a park.

Ud-yāpana, am, n. bringing to a conclusion, finishing, performing, accomplishing.

Ud-yāpita, as, ā, am, brought to a conclusion, finished, accomplished.

उद्याव ud-yāva, *as*, m. (rt. 1. *yu*), mixing, joining.

उद्यास ud-yāsa, *as*, m. (rt. *yas*), Ved. exertion, effort.

उद्युज् ud-yuj, cl. 7. P. A. *-yunakti, -yunkte, -yoktum*, to excite, incite, make active or quick, stimulate to exertion.

Ud-yukta, as, ā, am, zealously active, labouring for some desired end.

Ud-yoga, as, m. undertaking anything, exertion, perseverance, strenuous and continuous endeavour; active preparation. — *Udyoga-parvan, a*, n. title of the fifth book of the Mahā-bhārata. — *Udyoga-samartha, as, ā, am*, capable of exertion.

Ud-yogin, ī, inī, i, active, laborious, persevering, energetic, one who makes effort.

उद्र udra, *as*, m. (fr. 2. *ud*), a kind of aquatic animal, perhaps a crab, or an otter; (at the end of some compounds = *udaka*) water; see *an-udra*. — *Udra-pāraka, as*, m., N. of a Nāga.

Udraka, as, m., N. of a Ṛishi.

Udrin, ī, iṇī, i, Ved. springing (said of water), abounding in water.

उद्रङ्क udranka or *udranga, as*, m., N. of the town of Hariśćandra, floating in the air; a town in general, = *dranga*.

उद्रथ ud-ratha, *as*, m. the pin of the axle of a carriage; a cock.

उद्राव ud-rāva, *as*, m. (fr. rt. *ru*), a loud noise.

उद्रिच् ud-rić, Pass. *-rićyate*, to excel, increase, exceed, preponderate; to abound in: Caus. *-rećayati, -yitum*, to cause to excel, augment.

Ud-rikta, as, ā, am, increased, augmented; distinct; evident.

Ud-reka, as, m. excess, preponderance, increase, overplus, abundance, commencement; *(ā)*, f. the plant Melia Sempervirens. — *Udreka-bhanga, as*, m. the stifling or discouraging a thing at the outset.

Udrekin, ī, iṇī, i, (at the end of compounds) abounding in, giving preponderance.

उद्रुज ud-ruja, *as, ā, am* (rt. *ruj*), destroying, breaking down; undermining, rooting up.

उद्रोधन ud-rodhana, *am*, n. (rt. *rudh*=*ruh*), rising, growing.

उद्वत् ud-vat, *t*, f. (fr. 1. *ud*), Ved. elevation, a hill.

उद्वत्सर ud-vatsara, *as*, m. a year; (a wrong reading for *id-vatsara*, q. v.)

उद्वप् ud-vap, cl. 1. P. A. *-vapati, -te, -vaptum*, to pour out; to raise, elevate.

Ud-vapana, am, n. pouring out, shaking out.

Ud-vāpa, as, m. ejection; (in logic) non-existence of a subsequent resulting from the absence of an antecedent.

उद्वम् ud-vam, cl. 1. P. *-vamati, -mitum*, to throw up, eject, vomit.

Ud-vamat, an, antī, at, casting up, vomiting.

Ud-vamana, am, n. ejecting, emitting, vomiting.

Ud-vānta, as, ā, am, vomited; *(as)*, m. an elephant out of rut.

Ud-vānti, is, f. ejecting, vomiting.

उद्वयस् ud-vayas, *ās, ās, as*, Ved. (perhaps) exciting or increasing the strength.

उद्वर्त ud-varta, &c. See *ud-vṛit* next col.

उद्वर्धन ud-vardhana, *am*, n. sly or suppressed laughter.

उद्वर्हित ud-varhita. See under *ud-vṛih*.

उद्वस् ud-vas, Caus. P. *-vāsayati, -yitum*, to cause to live away, to banish, expel.

1. *ud-vāsa, as*, m. (for 2. see next col.), banishment, exile; abandonment, setting free; carrying out for slaughter, killing.

Ud-vāsana, am, n. taking out of or away (from the fire); expelling, banishing; quitting, abandoning; taking out in order to kill, killing, slaughter.

Udvāsya, as, ā, am, relating to the killing of a sacrificial animal.

उद्वह् ud-vah, cl. 1. P. A. *-vahati, -te, -voḍhum*, to carry out or away, elevate; to take or lead away; to bear up, raise up, elevate; to marry; to vomit (?): Caus. P. *-vāhayati, -yitum*, to cause to marry, to allow any one to expel his wife.

Ud-vaha, as, ā, am, carrying or leading up, carrying away, taking up or away; continuing, propagating; eminent, superior, best; *(as)*, m. son, offspring; the fourth of the seven winds or courses of air, viz. that of the Nakshatras supporting these lunar constellations and causing their revolution; the vital air that conveys nourishment upwards; one of the seven tongues of fire; N. of a prince; *(ā)*, f. a daughter.

Ud-vahat, an, antī, at, upholding, supporting, bearing, containing; having, possessing, assuming.

Ud-vahana, am, n. lifting or bringing up; carrying, drawing; being carried on, riding; possessing; leading home, marrying.

Ud-vāha, as, m. bearing up, supporting, marriage, wedding. — *Udvāha-karman, a*, n. the marriage ceremony. — *Udvāha-tattva, am*, n., N. of a work of Raghunandana on marriage ceremonies; [cf. *vivāha-tattva*.]

Ud-vāhana, as, ā, am, drawing up, that which raises or draws up; *(am)*, n. lifting up; ploughing a field twice; anxiety, anxious regret; marriage; *(ī)*, f. a cord, rope; the small shell used as a coin, a cowri.

Udvāhika, as, ā, am, relating to marriage, matrimonial.

Ud-vāhita, as, ā, am, raised, lifted or pulled up; eradicated.

Ud-vāhin, ī, inī, i, what raises or draws up; who or what marries, relating to marriage; *(inī)*, f. a rope.

Udvoḍhu-kāma, as, ā, am, desirous of marrying.

उद्वाचन ud-vāćana, *as, ā, am*, Ved. crying out (?).

उद्वादन ud-vādana, *am*, n. crying aloud.

उद्वान udvāna, *as, ā, am* (probably a corrupt form), ejected, vomited; *(am)*, n. ejecting, vomiting; a stove; [cf. *uddhāna, ud-dhmāna, ud-vānta*.]

उद्वाष्प ud-vāshpa, *as, ā, am*, shedding tears. — *Udvāshpa-tva, am*, n. the act of shedding tears.

उद्वास 2. *ud-vāsa, as, ā, am*, or *ud-vāsas, ās, ās, as*, one who has put off his clothes. (For 1. *ud-vāsa* see under *ud-vas*.)

उद्विघुष् ud-vi-ghush, Caus. P. *-ghoshayati, -yitum*, to declare or proclaim aloud, to cause to declare aloud.

उद्विज् ud-vij, cl. 6. A. (ep. also cl. 6. P. and cl. 1. P. A.) *-vijate, -ti, -vejati, -te, -vejitum*, to tremble, shake; to be agitated, grieved, or afflicted; to fear, be afraid of (with abl. or gen.); to grieve, afflict, frighten: Caus. P. *-vejayati, -yitum*, to terrify, frighten.

Ud-vigna, as, ā, am, sorrowful, anxious, grieving for an absent lover. — *Udvigna-ćitta, as, ā, am*, or *udvigna-manas, ās, ās, as*, depressed in mind, sorrowful, anxious, distressed.

Ud-vijamāna, as, ā, am, agitated, afraid.

Ud-vega, as, ā, am, going swiftly, an express messenger, a runner, a courier, &c.; steady, composed, tranquil; ascending, mounting, going up or upwards; an ascetic whose arms by long habit continue always raised above the head; *(as)*, m. trembling, waving, shaking; agitation, anxiety; regret, fear, distress occasioned by separation from a beloved object; admiration, astonishment; *udvegaṃ kṛi*, to disturb, to be disturbed in mind; *(am)*, n. the fruit of the Areca Faufel; the Areca nut, called betel nut because eaten with the betel leaf.

Udvegin, ī, inī, i, causing anxiety or agitation of mind; suffering distress, anxious, unhappy.

Ud-vejaka, as, ā, am, agitating, distressing, annoying, causing pain or sorrow.

Ud-vejana, as, ā, am, causing to shake with terror, hurting the feelings; *(am)*, n. shaking with terror, agitation, anxiety, affliction; infliction of pain, torture; regret, sorrowing for one absent. — *Udvejana-kara, as, ā* or *ī, am*, inflicting pain, punishing, torturing, painful.

Udvejanīya, as, ā, am, causing terror or shaking (with gen. of the person).

Ud-vejita, as, ā, am, grieved, pained, afflicted.

उद्वीक्ष् ud-vīksh (*ud-vi-īksh*), cl. 1. A. *-vīkshate, -shitum*, to look up or upwards, view, look at, perceive; to examine, consider.

Ud-vīkshaṇa, am, n. looking up or upwards; seeing, looking at.

Ud-vīkshya, ind. having looked upwards.

उद्वीज् ud-vīj, cl. 10. P. *-vījayati, -yitum*, to blow upon, blow towards; to fan upon.

उद्वृ ud-vṛi, cl. 5. 9. 1. P. A. *-vṛiṇoti, -ṇute, -vṛiṇāti, -ṇīte, -varati, -te, -varitum* or *-rītum*, to elect, select, choose.

उद्वृंहण ud-vṛinhaṇa, *am*, n. increase.

उद्वृत् ud-vṛit, cl. 1. A. *-vartate, -titum*, to go upwards, rise, ascend, swell; to be puffed up with pride, to be haughty: Caus. *-vartayati, -yitum*, to cause to come out, extirpate, eradicate, destroy.

Ud-varta, as, ā, am, superfluous, redundant, plentiful; left over as a remainder; *(as)*, m. a remainder, a surplus.

Ud-vartaka, as, ā, am, causing to rise, increasing; rubbing and cleaning the body, who or what does so; *(as)*, m. a mathematical term, the quantity assumed for the purpose of the operation.

Ud-vartana, am, n. going up, rising, ascending; prosperity, elevation; springing up of plants or grain &c.; drawing out metal, laminating, wire drawing; grinding, pounding; rubbing or kneading the body; rubbing and cleaning it with fragrant unguents; the unguents used for that purpose or to relieve pains in the limbs &c.; bad behaviour, bad conduct.

Ud-vartita, as, ā, am, risen, elevated; sprung up, drawn out; perfumed, scented, rubbed, kneaded, shampooed.

Ud-vṛitta, as, ā, am, raised, elevated; exalted, prosperous; vomited up; left as a remainder; ill-conducted, ill-mannered.

उद्वृह् *ud-vṛih,* cl. 6. P. *-vṛihati, -varhitum* or *-vardhum,* to raise up, elevate; to draw up, pull out by the roots, eradicate.

Ud-varhita, as, ā, am, raised, drawn or lifted up, eradicated.

उद्वेग *ud-vega.* See under *ud-vij,* p. 158.

उद्वेदि *ud-vedi, is, is, i,* furnished with an elevated altar.

उद्वेप् *ud-vep,* cl. 1. A. *-vepate, -pitum,* to tremble, to be agitated.

उद्वेल *ud-vela, as, ā, am,* overflowing its banks (as a river).

उद्वेल्लित *ud-vellita, as, ā, am,* tossed up.

उद्वेष्ट *ud-veshṭa, as, ā, am,* investing, enveloping, surrounding; *(as)*, m. surrounding, enclosing; investing a town, besieging or surrounding it.

Ud-veshṭana, am, n. the act of surrounding; oppressing; an enclosure; pain in the back of the body; *(hṛidayodreshṭana,* convulsive pain in the heart); *(as, ā, am)*, unbound, unfettered, freed from bonds or ties.

Ud-veshṭanīya, as, ā, am, to be unbound or unfastened.

Ud-veshṭita, as, ā, am, surrounded, invested, enclosed.

उधस् *udhas, as,* n. an udder. See *ūdhas.*

उध्य *udhya, as,* m., N. of a river.

उध्रस् *udhras* (another form of rt. *dhras,* q.v.), cl. 9. 10. P. *udhrasnāti, udhrāsayati,* to glean or gather by little at a time; to throw or cast upwards.

उन्द् *und.* See 2. *ud,* p. 153.

Undana, am, n. moistening.

Unna, as, ā, am, wetted, wet, moist; kind, humane.

उन्दुरु *unduru, us,* or *undura, as,* or *unduru, us,* m. a rat. — *Unduru-karṇikā* or *unduru-karṇī,* f. the plant Salvinia Cucullata.

उन्नट् *un-naṭ (ud-naṭ),* Caus. P. *-nāṭayati, -yitum,* to play a trick upon (with gen.).

उन्नत *un-nata.* See *un-nam* below.

उन्नद् *un-nad (ud-nad),* cl. 1. P. *-nadati, -ditum,* to cry out, sound, roar.

Un-nāda, as, m. crying out, humming, chirping.

उन्नम् *un-nam (ud-nam),* cl. 1. P. *-namati, -nantum,* to rise, ascend; to bend up, raise, elevate, erect: Caus. P. *-namayati, -yitum,* to bend upwards, raise, erect.

Un-nata, as, ā, am, raised, held or lifted up; high, tall; projecting, plump, full; great, eminent; *(as)*, m. a boa *(aja-gara)*; N. of a Buddha; *(am)*, n. elevation, ascension. — *Unnata-caraṇa, as, ā, am,* with uplifted paws, rampant. — *Unnata-tva, am,* n. height, sublimity, majesty. — *Unnata-nābhi, is, is, i,* having a projecting navel, i. e. corpulent. — *Unnata-śiras, ās, ās, as,* holding up the head, carrying the head high; with head upraised. — *Unnatānata* (°*ta-ān*°), *as, ā, am,* elevated and depressed, uneven, undulating, wavy.

Un-nati, is, f. elevation, height; rising, ascending; increase, advancement, prosperity; N. of a daughter of Daksha and wife of Dharma; the wife of Garuḍa. — *Unnati-mat, ān, atī, at,* elevated, projecting, plump; high, sublime. — *Unnatīśa* (°*ti-īśa*), *as,* m. a N. of Garuḍa.

Un-namana, am, n. bending upwards, raising, lifting up.

Un-namayya, ind. having raised.

Un-namita, as, ā, am, raised, elevated, lifted or pulled up; heightened, increased.

Un-namra, as, ā, am, erect, upright, elevated, lofty, high. — *Unnamra-tā,* f. erectness, uprightness (of the body).

Un-nāma, as, m. bending upwards, raising, lifting up.

उन्नय *un-naya.* See under 1. *un-nī* below.

उन्नयनपङ्क्ति *un-nayana-paṅkti, is, is, i,* having the line of the eyelids uplifted.

उन्नस *un-nasa (ud-nas), as, ā, am,* having a prominent nose.

उन्नह् *un-nah (ud-nah),* cl. 4. P. *-nahyati, -naddhum,* to tie up, bind up.

Un-naddha, as, ā, am, tied up; swelled, increased; unbound.

Un-nāha, as, m. sour gruel made from the fermentation of rice.

उन्नाभ *un-nābha, as,* m. (fr. *ud* + *nābhi*), N. of a prince.

उन्निद्र *un-nidra (ud-n°), as, ā, am,* sleepless, awake; expanded as a flower; budded, blown; shining (as the moon, supposed to be awake when others are asleep). — *Unnidra-tā,* f. sleeplessness.

उन्नी 1. *un-nī (ud-nī),* cl. 1. P. *-nayati, -netum,* to lead upwards or up to, bring up; to set up, erect; to bring out of, free from, help, rescue, redeem; to draw up (as water); to lead away; to stroke, smooth; to lead out; press out, extract; to find out, ascertain by inference, infer; lead off (in singing): Desid. A. *-ninīshate,* to intend or wish to lead out &c.

Un-naya, as, m. raising, elevating, hoisting, leading upwards; analogy, resemblance, consequence.

Un-nayana, am, n. raising, elevating, lifting up; taking out of, drawing water; the vessel out of which a fluid is taken; leading away; making straight, smoothing; deliberation, discussion, logic, reasoning, inference.

Un-nāya, as, m. raising, elevating.

Un-nāyaka, as, ā, am, what raises; what leads to an inference or conclusion.

2. *un-nī, īs, īs, i,* bringing or leading upwards.

Un-nīta, as, ā, am, led up, led away, inferred.

Un-netṛi, tā, m. one who pours a fluid out of one vessel into another, especially the priest who pours the Soma juice into the cups.

Unnetra, am, n. the office of the Unnetṛi.

Un-neya, as, ā, am, to be inferred, to be ascertained by analogy.

उन्मज्ज् *un-majj (ud-m°),* cl. 6. P. *-majjati, -manktum,* to emerge: Caus. *-majjayati, -yitum,* to cause to emerge.

Un-majjana, as, m., N. of an attendant of Siva.

उन्मत्त *un-matta.* See *un-mad* next col.

उन्मथ् *un-math* or *un-manth (ud-m°),* cl. 1. 9. P. *-mathati* or *-manthati, -mathnāti, -manthitum,* to shake up, disturb, excite; to shake, tear, or cut off; to strike, kill.

Un-mathana, am, n. shaking off, throwing off or down, slaughter.

Un-mathita, as, ā, am, shaken, agitated.

Un-mantha, as, m. agitation; killing, slaughter; a disease of the outer ear.

Un-manthaka, as, ā, am, shaking up or off, agitating, stirring; throbbing, beating; *(as)*, m. inflammation of the outer ear.

Un-manthana, am, n. the act of shaking or agitating; hurting, killing; probing, stirring a weapon &c. lodged in the body.

Un-manthita, as, ā, am, shaken up, moved, agitated, distressed.

Un-mātha, as, ā, am, destroying, killing; *(as)*, m. shaking; killing, slaughter; a snare or trap.

Un-māthin, ī, inī, i, shaking, agitating.

उन्मद् *un-mad (ud-m°),* cl. 4. P. *-mādyati, -maditum,* to be or become mad: Caus. P. *-madayati* or *-mādayati, -yitum,* to madden, inebriate, render drunk.

Un-matta, as, ā, am, insane, frantic, mad; drunk, intoxicated; *(as)*, m. the thorn-apple, Datura Metel and Fastuosa; another tree, Pterospermum Acerifolium; N. of a Rakshas. — *Unmatta-kīrti, is,* m. an epithet of Siva. — *Unmatta-gaṅga, am,* n., N. of a region ('where the Gaṅgā roars'). — *Unmatta-tā,* f. or *unmatta-tva, am,* n. insanity, intoxication. — *Unmatta-darśana* or *unmatta-rūpa, as, ā, am,* maniac-like, mad. — *Unmatta-pralapita, as, ā, am,* spoken in drunkenness or madness. — *Unmatta-bhairava-tantra, am,* n., N. of a Tantra. — *Unmatta-liṅgin, ī, inī, i,* feigning madness. — *Unmatta-vat,* ind. like one mad, as if mad, like a maniac. — *Unmatta-veśa, as,* m. an epithet of Siva. — *Unmattāvanti* (°*ta-av*°), *is,* m., N. of a prince.

Unmattaka, as, ā, am, insane, mad; drunk.

Un-mada, as, ā, am, mad, furious, extravagant; drunk, intoxicated; *(as)*, m. insanity, either morbid or as the effect of temporary excitement, intoxication, ecstacy.

Un-madana, as, ā, am, inflamed with love.

Un-madishṇu, us, us, u, mad, insane, crazed, intoxicated; in rut (as an elephant).

Un-māda, as, ā, am, mad, insane, extravagant; *(as)*, m. madness, extravagance; (in medicine) mania. — *Unmāda-vat, ān, atī, at,* mad, insane, wild, extravagant.

Un-mādana, as, ā, am, maddening, exciting, intoxicating; *(as)*, m. one of the five arrows of the god of love.

Unmādin, ī, inī, i, mad, intoxicated; *(nī)*, f., N. of a princess.

Un-māduka, as, ā, am, Ved. fond of drinking.

उन्मनस् *un-manas, ās, ās, as,* or *un-manaska (ud-ma°), as, ā, am,* excited or disturbed in mind, perplexed, disturbed; regretting, missing, repining for a lost or departed friend.

Unmanāya, nom. A. *unmanāyate, -yitum,* to become excited or disturbed in mind, to repine.

Unmanī-kṛi, cl. 8. P. *-karoti, -kartum,* to make excited, to excite, disturb.

Unmanī-bhū, cl. 1. P. *-bhavati, -vitum,* to become disturbed in mind, to repine.

उन्मयूख *un-mayūkha (ud-m°), as, ā, am,* shining, radiant.

उन्मर्दन *un-mardana, am,* n. (fr. rt. *mṛid* with *ud*), rubbing off, rubbing; a fragrant essence used for this purpose.

उन्मा *un-mā,* f. (fr. rt. *mā* with *ud*), Ved. a measure.

Un-māna, am, n. a measure of size or quantity; price.

Un-mita, as, ā, am, meted, measured.

Un-miti, is, f. measure, price.

Un-meya, as, ā, am, to be weighed, what is weighed; *(am)*, n. weight.

उन्मार्ग *un-mārga (ud-m°), as, ā, am,* m. f. n.

a wrong road, deviation from the right way, improper conduct, an evil course, error. — *Unmārga-gata, as, ā, am,* erred, erring, going wrong. — *Unmārga-gamana, am,* n. going on a wrong road, following evil courses. — *Unmārga-gāmin, ī, inī, i,* or *un-mārga-vartin, ī, inī, i,* going wrong, erring, following evil courses; taking a wrong road. — *Unmārga-jala-vāhin, ī, inī, i,* carrying its waters on a wrong way.

Unmārgin, ī, iṇī, i, going astray, finding an outlet.

उन्मार्जन *un-mārjana.* See *un-mṛij* below.

उन्मिश्र *un-miśra (ud-m°), as, ā, am,* mixed with, variegated.

उन्मिष् *un-mish (ud-mish),* cl. 6. P. *-mishati, -meshitum,* to open the eyes.

Un-misha, as, m. opening the eyes.

Un-mishat, an, atī or *antī, at,* opening the eyes, drawing up the eyelids, looking at, seeing.

Un-mishita, as, ā, am, opened (as the eye); blown as a flower.

Un-mesha, as, m. opening the eyes, looking at; winking, twinkling or upward motion of the eyelids; blowing or blossoming of a flower; awaking, becoming visible.

Un-meshaṇa, am, n. awaking, becoming visible.

उन्मील् *un-mīl (ud-mīl),* cl. 1. P. *-mīlati, -litum,* to open the eyes; to open; to expand, be diffused: Caus. P. *-mīlayati, -yitum,* to open.

Un-mīla, as, m. opening of the eyes, awaking, becoming visible.

Un-mīlana, am, n. winking, twinkling, opening of the eye; awaking, becoming visible; blowing, expanding.

Un-mīlita, as, ā, am, opened (as the eyes); blown as a flower; *(am),* n. unconcealed or open reference or allusion (to anything, in rhetoric).

उन्मुख *un-mukha (ud-m°), as, ī, am,* raising the face, looking at; waiting for, expecting; near to; *(as),* m., N. of an antelope (in the Hari-vaṇśa, in former births a hunter and a Brāhman). — *Unmukha-tā,* f. the state of one whose face is raised; state of watching or expectancy.

उन्मुखर *un-mukhara (ud-m°), as, ā, am,* loud-sounding, noisy.

उन्मुच् *un-muć,* cl. 6. P. A. *-muñćati, -te, -moktum,* to unfasten, pull off; take off (clothes &c.); to loosen, liberate; to elevate, raise: Caus. P. *-moćayati, -yitum,* to loosen, deliver.

Un-muća, as, m., N. of a man.

Un-moćana, am, n. unfastening, loosening.

उन्मुद्र *un-mudra (ud-m°), as, ā, am,* unsealed, opened; blown as a flower.

उन्मूल *un-mūla (ud-m°), as, ā, am,* eradicated, pulled up by the root.

Un-mūlana, am, n. eradicating, pulling up by the roots; destroying.

Unmūlaya, nom. P. *unmūlayati, -yitum,* to eradicate, pull up by the roots; to extirpate, destroy.

Un-mūlita, as, ā, am, eradicated, pulled up by the roots; destroyed.

उन्मृज् *un-mṛij (ud-m°),* cl. 2. P. *-mārshṭi, -mārjitum* or *-mārshṭum,* to rub off, wipe off; efface; blot out.

Un-mārjana, as, ā, am, rubbing or wiping off.

Unmṛijāvamṛijā (°ja-av°), f. repeatedly rubbing up and down.

Un-mṛishṭa, as, ā, am, worn off, blotted out, effaced.

उन्मृश्य *un-mṛiśya, as, ā, am* (rt. *mṛiś* with *ud*), Ved. to be reached, to be touched.

उन्मेदा *un-medā,* f. (fr. rt. *mid* with *ud*), corpulence, fatness.

उप *upa,* a prefix to verbs and nouns (expressing) towards, near to (opposed to *apa,* away), by the side of, with, together with, under, down (e. g. *upa-gam,* to go near, undergo; *upa-gamana,* approaching. In the Veda the verb has sometimes to be supplied from the context, and sometimes *upa* is placed after the verb with which it ought to have been compounded, e. g. *āyayur upa = upāyayuḥ,* they approached).

(As unconnected with verbs and prefixed to nouns *upa* expresses) direction towards, nearness, contiguity in space, time, number, degree, resemblance, and relationship, but with the idea of subordination and inferiority (e. g. *upa-kanishṭhikā,* the finger next to the little finger; *upa-purāṇam,* a secondary or subordinate Purāṇa; *upa-daśa,* nearly ten); sometimes forming with the nouns to which it is prefixed compound adverbs (e. g. *upa-mūlam,* at the root; *upa-pūrva-rātram,* towards the beginning of night; *upa-kūpe,* near a well), which adverbs lose their adverbial terminations if they are again compounded with nouns (e. g. *upakūpa-jalāśaya,* a reservoir in the neighbourhood of a well). Prefixed to proper names *upa* may express in classical literature 'a younger brother' (e. g. *Upendra,* 'the younger brother of Indra'), and in Buddhist literature 'a son.'

(As a separable adverb *upa* rarely expresses) thereto, further, moreover (e. g. *tatra upa brahma yo veda,* who further knows the Veda).

(As a separable preposition with locative) near to, towards, in the direction of, under, below (e. g. *upa āśāḥ,* towards the regions); near to, at, on, upon; at the time of, upon, up to, in, above (with loc., e. g. *upa sānushu,* on the tops of the mountains); with, together with, at the same time with, according to (with inst., e. g. *upa dharmabhiḥ,* according to the rules of duty).

Besides the meanings given above *upa* is said to imply disease, extinction; ornament; command; reproof; undertaking; giving; killing; diffusing; wish; power; effort; resemblance, &c.; [cf. Gr. ὑπό; Lat. *sub;* Goth. *up;* Old Germ. *oba;* Mod. Germ. *ob* in *obdach, obliegen,* &c.]

Upaka, as, m. a diminutive of all proper names beginning with *upa.*

उप-ॠ *upa-ṝi.* See *upār.*

उपकक्ष *upa-kaksha, as, ā, am,* Ved. reaching to the shoulder.

उपकण्ठम् *upa-kaṇṭham,* ind. upon the neck, near the throat; in the proximity of; *(am),* n. proximity, neighbourhood, contiguous space; space near a village or its boundary; one of a horse's paces; *(as, ā, am),* near, proximate.

उपकथा *upa-kathā,* f. a short story, tale.

उपकनिष्ठिका *upa-kanishṭhikā,* f. the last finger but one; the finger next to the little finger.

उपकन्यापुरम् *upa-kanyāpuram,* ind. near the women's apartments.

उपकरण, उपकार, &c. See *upa-kṛi* next col.

उपकर्णम् *upa-karṇam,* ind. close to the ear, into the ear, (whispered &c.)

Upakarṇikā, f. what goes from ear to ear, rumour, report.

उपकल्पन *upa-kalpana.* See *upa-klṛip,* p. 161.

उपकान्तम् *upa-kāntam,* ind. near a friend.

उपकाल *upa-kāla, as,* m., N. of a king of the Nāgas.

उपकिरण *upa-kiraṇa.* See *upa-kṝ* next col.

उपकीचक *upa-kīćaka, as,* m. a relation or follower of the Kīćakas.

उपकुञ्चि *upa-kuñći, is,* or *upa-kuñćikā,* f. the plant Nigella Indica; small cardamoms.

उपकुम्भ *upa-kumbha, as, ā, am,* near, proximate; solitary, lonely, retired; *(am),* ind. near the water-jar.

उपकुर्वाण *upa-kurvāṇa.* See *upa-kṛi* below.

उपकुल्या *upa-kulyā,* f. the plant Piper Longum; a canal, a trench, a ditch.

उपकुश *upa-kuśa, as,* m. gum-boil; N. of a Cakravartin, a son of Kuśa.

उपकूज् *upa-kūj,* cl. 1. P. *-kūjati, -jitum,* to fill with cooing, to make resonant.

Upa-kūjita, as, ā, am, made to resound (with cooing).

उपकूपे *upa-kūpe,* ind. near a well; *(am),* n. a well (?). — *Upakūpa-jalāśaya, as,* m. a trough near a well for watering cattle.

उपकूलम् *upa-kūlam,* ind. on the shore.

Upakūlaka, as, m., N. of a man.

उपकृ *upa-kṛi,* cl. 5. 8. P. A. *-kṛiṇoti, -ṇute, -karoti, -kurute, -kartum,* to place or bring near, to furnish with, provide; to assist, serve; favour, benefit; to foster, take care of; to serve, render homage to (with acc.); to undertake, begin, set about anything (with dat.); to place under, subdue; *upa-s-kṛi* (*s* inserted) A. to add, supply; to furnish with; to elaborate, prepare, furnish with anything beautiful, to adorn, ornament; to care for, take care of (with acc.); to furnish badly, deform; corrupt; to bring together.

Upa-karaṇa, am, n. doing anything for another, doing a service or favour, helping, assisting; instrument, implement, machine, engine, apparatus, paraphernalia, as the vessels and offerings at a sacrifice; anything added over and above, contribution, expedient, means of subsistence, anything supporting life; object of art or science, fabricating, composing, &c.; the insignia of royalty; the attendants of a king. — *Upakaraṇa-vat, ān, atī, at,* furnished with means, instruments or implements, competent to do anything.

Upa-kartṛi, tā, trī, tṛi, doing one a favour, assisting, befriending, one who helps or befriends.

Upa-kāra, as, m. help, assistance, benefit, service, favour, use, advantage, (*upakāre vṛit,* to be of service to another); preparation, ornament, garlands suspended at gateways as an embellishment on festivals, a flower &c.; (ī), f. a royal tent, a palace, a caravansera. — *Upakāra-para, as, ā, am,* beneficent, diligent in doing good. — *Upakārāpakārau (°ra-ap°),* m. du. kindness and injury.

Upa-kāraka, as, ikā, am, doing a service or favour, assisting, protecting, befriending; *(ikā),* f. a protectress, a female assistant; a palace, a caravansera; a kind of cake. — *Upakāraka-tva, am,* n. assistance, protection.

Upa-kārin, ī, iṇī, i, helping, assisting, doing one a favour, a benefactor; subsidiary, subservient; (often used in comp., e. g. *paropakārin,* helping others.) — *Upakāri-tā,* f. or *upakāri-tva, am,* n. aid, succour, protection.

Upa-kārya, as, ā, am, deserving assistance or favour; to be assisted; *(ā),* f. a king's house, a palace, a caravansera; a royal tent.

Upa-kurvāṇa, as, m. a Brāhman when passing from the state of a pupil (*Brahma-ćārin*) to that of a householder (*Gṛiha-stha*).

Upa-kṛita, as, ā, am, assisted, benefited; rendered as assistance, done kindly or beneficently; *(am),* n. a favour, a benefit.

Upa-kṛiti, is, f. aid, assistance, favour, kindness.

Upa-kṛitin, ī, inī, i, or *upakṛiti-mat, ān, atī, at,* one who has done a favour to any body.

Upa-kriyā, f. service, favour.

उपकृत् *upa-kṛit,* cl. 6. P. *-kṛintati, -kartitum,* to trim, clip off, carp at.

उपकृष् *upa-kṛish,* cl. 1. P. *-karshati, -karshṭum* or *-krashṭum,* to draw towards, take; to take away, remove, set aside.

उपकॄ *upa-kṝ,* cl. 6. P. *-kirati, -karitum* or *-rītum,* to scatter or throw down, to scatter upon, pour upon, besprinkle, bestrew. — *Upa-s-kṛī*, to cut up, split, hurt.

Upa-kiraṇa, am, n. scattering or throwing over, covering up (with earth &c.), burying.

Upa-kīrṇa, as, ā, am, besprinkled, strewed with, covered.

उपकॢप् *upa-klṛip*, cl. 1. A. *-kalpate*, *-kalpitum* or *-kalptum*, to be fit for; to be ready at hand; to serve as, lead to (with dat.); to take shape or form, become, be: Caus. *-kalpayati*, *-yitum*, to prepare, make ready, equip; to bring near, to fetch; to allot, assign; to set up, exhibit; to render (homage), to communicate; to assume.

Upa-kalpana, am, ā, n. f. preparation, preparing articles of food, medicine, &c.; fabricating, making, substituting.

Upa-kalpita, as, ā, am, prepared, made; secondary, substituted.

Upa-klṛipta, as, ā, am, brought near, at hand, ready, prepared, equipped, adapted, fitted for; formed, produced.

उपकोशा *upa-kośā*, f., N. of a daughter of Upa-varsha and wife of Vararući.

उपकोसल *upa-kosala, as*, m., N. of a man.

उपक्रम् *upa-kram*, cl. 1. P. A., 4. P. *-krāmati*, *-kramate* (ep. also *-krāmate*), *-krāmyati*, *-kramitum*, to go near, approach, come to; to go against, attack; to step over, stride; to approach with any object, have recourse to, to undertake, begin, set about (with acc. or dat. or inf.), to treat, act towards, attend on (as a physician).

Upa-krantṛi, tā, tṛī, tṛi, a beginner, one who undertakes.

Upa-krama, as, m. going near to, approach; undertaking; commencement, beginning; enterprise, planning, original conception, plan; what leads to any result, a means, an expedient, a stratagem, exploit; attendance (on a patient), treatment, practice of medicine, application of remedies, physicking; a particular ceremony preparatory to reading the Vedas; trying the fidelity &c. of a counsellor or friend; retiring from flight, retreat (?).

Upa-kramaṇa, am, n. approaching, undertaking, attendance (on a patient), treatment.

Upakramaṇīya, as, ā, am, to be gone to, to be approached, to be commenced or undertaken; relating to the attendance (on a patient).

Upa-kramitavya, as, ā, am, to be undertaken, to be commenced.

Upa-kramitṛi, tā, tṛī, tṛi, one who begins &c.

Upa-krāmya, as, ā, am, to be attended, to be treated.

उपक्री *upa-krī*, cl. 9. P. A. *-krīṇāti*, *-ṇīte*, *-kretum*, to purchase.

Upa-krīya, ind. having bought or purchased.

उपक्रीड् *upa-krīḍ*, cl. 1. P. (ep. also A.) *-krīḍati*, *-te*, *-ḍitum*, to approach playing, play around.

Upa-krīḍā, f. place for playing, play-ground.

उपक्रुश्य *upa-kruśya*, ind. (rt. *kruś*), chiding, blaming, affecting to be angry.

Upa-krośa, as, m. censure, reproach.

Upa-krośana, am, n. censuring, blaming.

Upa-kroshṭṛi, ṭā, m. a censurer, a reprover; an ass (which brays).

उपक्वण *upa-kvaṇa, as*, m. (rt. *kvaṇ*), the sound of a lute.

उपक्वस *upa-kvasa, as*, m., Ved. a kind of worm or insect.

उपक्षर् *upa-kshar*, cl. 1. P. (ep. also A.) *-ksharati*, *-te*, *-ritum*, Ved. *-radhyai*, to flow or stream towards.

उपक्षि 1. *upa-kshi*, Pass. *-kshīyate*, to waste away, decay, be consumed, be exhausted, disappear.

Upa-kshaya, as, m. waste, decay, loss, expenditure, outlay.

Upa-kshīṇa, as, ā, am, decayed, exhausted, consumed, disappeared.

उपक्षि 2. *upa-kshi*, cl. 2. 6. P. *-ksheti*, *-kshiyati*, *-kshetum*, to stay or dwell near or at (with acc.).

Upa-kshit, t, t, t, Ved. dwelling near; clinging to, attached to.

Upa-kshetṛi, tā, trī, tṛi, Ved. one who dwells near, attached to, a follower; (Sāy.) one who approaches.

उपक्षिप् *upa-kship*, cl. 6. P. A., 4. P. *-kshipati*, *-te*, *-kshipyati*, *-ksheptum*, to throw at, hurl against; to throw down; to strike with words, insult, accuse, insinuate, charge with (a crime).

Upa-kshepa, as, m. throwing at, mention, allusion, threatening; poetical or figurative style in composition.

Upa-kshepaṇa, am, n. throwing down, casting down, accusing.

उपख्या *upa-khyā*, cl. 2. P., Ved. *-khyāti*, *-tum*, to see.

उपगण *upa-gaṇa, as, ā, am*, constituting a small or subordinate class; (*as*), m. a small or inferior class; a small number less than a troop; N. of a man.

उपगन्ध *upa-gandha, as*, m. perfume, scent.

उपगम् *upa-gam*, cl. 1. P. *-gaććhati*, *-gantum*, to go near to, come towards, approach, arrive at, visit, reach, attain; to come upon, attack; to occur, happen, present itself; to undertake, begin; to approach a woman (for intercourse); to enter any state or relation, undergo; suffer, participate in, make choice of; to admit, agree to, allow, confess: Caus. *-gamayati*, *-yitum*, to cause to come near or approach: Desid. *-jigamishati*, to wish to approach, desire to go.

Upa-ga, as, ā, am, (at the end of a compound) approaching, following, joining; receiving.

Upa-gata, as, ā, am, gone to, met, approached, near at hand, approximate, arrived, occurred, happened, attained, obtained; undergone, experienced; become; furnished with; promised, agreed; feeling, suffering, entertaining; passed away, dead; (*am*), n. receipt, acquittance. — *Upagata-vat, ān, atī, at*, going to, having gone to or approached; possessing; feeling, suffering (as sorrow &c.); promising.

Upa-gati, is, f. going near, approach; undergoing.

Upa-gama, as, m. approach, approximation, coming to; obtaining; having; acquaintance, society, intercourse (as of the sexes); undergoing; suffering, feeling; agreement, promise; a particular high number.

Upa-gamana, am, n. coming to, obtaining; undertaking, addicting one's self to.

1. *upa-gamya, as, ā, am*, approachable, to be approached, attainable.

2. *upa-gamya* or *upa-gatya*, ind. having approached.

Upa-gāmin, ī, inī, i, coming near, approaching.

उपगहन *upa-gahana, as*, m., N. of a Ṛishi.

उपगा 1. *upa-gā*, cl. 3. P. *-jigāti*, *-gātum*, to go near to, arrive at, come into, undergo.

उपगाह् *upa-gāh*, cl. 1. A. *-gāhate*, *-gāhitum* or *-gāḍhum*, to penetrate, force one's way into.

उपगिरम् *upa-giram*, ind. at a mountain.

Upa-giri, is, m. a country near a mountain; (*i*), ind. near a mountain.

उपगु *upa-gu, us*, m. (fr. *upa* and *go*), N. of a prince; (*u*), ind. near a cow.

उपगुप्त *upa-gupta, as, ā, am*, hidden, concealed; (*as*), m., N. of a man, the son of Gupta. — *Upagupta-vitta, as, ā, am*, of concealed resources.

उपगुरु *upa-guru, us*, m. an assistant teacher; N. of a prince; (a various reading has *upa-gu*.)

उपगुह् *upa-guh*, cl. 1. P. A. *-gūhati*, *-te*, *-gūhitum* or *-goḍhum*, to hide, cover, conceal, clasp, embrace.

Upa-gūḍha, as, ā, am, hidden, concealed; lulled, suppressed; embraced; (*am*), n. an embrace. — *Upagūḍha-vat, ān, atī, at*, one who has embraced.

Upa-gūhana, am, n. hiding, concealing; embracing, an embrace; astonishment, surprise.

Upa-gohya, as, m. a kind of fire considered as impure (and therefore to be hidden).

उपगॄ 1. *upa-gṛī*, cl. 9. P. A., Ved. *-gṛiṇāti*, *-ṇīte*, *-garitum* or *-rītum*, to call out to, invoke with hymns of praise; to approach with praise (with acc. of the person).

उपगॄ 2. *upa-gṛī*, cl. 6. P. *-girati* or *-gilati*, *-garitum*, *-litum* or *-rītum*, *-lītum*, to swallow down.

उपगै *upa-gai*, cl. 1. P. *-gāyati*, *-gātum*, to sing to any one (with dat. or acc.), to join in singing; to sing before any one (with acc.); to fill with song, praise in song, sing, celebrate.

2. *upa-gā*, f. accompaniment of a song.

Upa-gātṛi, tā, m. one who accompanies the song or recitation of the Udgātṛi priest, a chorister.

Upa-gīta, as, ā, am, celebrated, proclaimed, sung by bards &c.

Upa-gīti, is, f. a variety of the Āryā metre, a stanza of four lines, containing twice 12 + 15 syllabic instants.

Upa-gīya, ind. having sung, having celebrated.

Upa-gīyamāna, as, ā, am, being celebrated.

Upa-geya, as, ā, am, to be sung or celebrated.

उपग्रन्थ् *upa-granth*, cl. 9. 1. 10. P. *-grathnāti*, *-granthati*, *-granthayati*, *-granthitum*, *-yitum*, to intwine or wind round.

Upa-grantha, as, m. title of a writing or of a class of writings.

उपग्रस् *upa-gras*, cl. 1. P. A. *-grasati*, *-te*, *-grasitum*, to swallow down, devour; to eclipse.

उपग्रह् *upa-grah*, cl. 9. P. A. *-gṛihṇāti*, *-ṇīte* (Ved. *-gṛibhṇāti*, *-ṇīte*), *-grahītum*, to collect (a fluid by holding one vessel under another), to hold under; to seize from below; to seize, take possession of, take, obtain; to subdue, become master of; to bring near to (one's self), take as one's ally, conciliate, make favourable; to conceive with one's mind (*dhiyā*); to decide, to determine; to accept, approve.

Upa-graha, as, m. seizure, confinement; a prisoner; subjoining, annexing; making favourable, appeasing, favour, encouragement, assistance; peace purchased by the cession of everything; the voice or pada of a verb; a heap of Kuśa grass; the presiding spirit or cause directing a planet's motion; (with *upa* implying inferiority) a minor planet or any heavenly body of a secondary kind, as a comet, a meteor, a falling star, &c.

Upa-grahaṇa, am, n. holding up, seizing from below; the taking any one prisoner, seizure, capture, taking, supporting, forwarding, promoting; holy study, reading the Vedas after initiation.

Upa-grāha, as, m. oblation, present, (what is accepted.)

Upa-grāhya, as, am, m. n. a present, an offering to a king or great man, a Nazr.

उपघात *upa-ghāta, as*, m. (fr. rt. *han* with *upa*), a stroke, injury, damage, offence; touch, contact, especially with intent to injure; personal violence, assault; disease, sickness; a kind of oblation offered in small portions at a time.

Upa-ghātaka, as, ikā, am, or *upa-ghātin, ī, inī, i*, injuring, hurting, offending.

Upa-ghna, as, m. contiguous support; a contiguous resting-place, shelter, support, stay, protection; what rests upon or is supported by.

उपघुष् *upa-ghush*, cl. 1. P. *-ghoshati*, *-shitum*, to fill with noise, make resonant.

Upa-ghushṭa, as, ā, am, resounding with; resonant; sounding.

Upa-ghoshaṇa, am, n. proclaiming, publication, making known.

उपघ्रा upa-ghrā, cl. 1. P. -jighrati, -ghrātum, to smell, smell at; to kiss: Caus. -ghrāpayati, -yitum, to cause to smell at or kiss.

उपचक्र upa-ćakra, as, m. a variety of the ruddy goose, Cakra or Cakravāka.

उपचतुर upa-ćatura, ās, ās, āṇi, pl. almost four, nearly four.

उपचय upa-ćaya. See 1. upa-ći.

उपचर् upa-ćar, cl. 1. P. A. -ćarati, -te, -ćaritum, Ved. -ritave, -vai, -rase, -radhyai, to come near, approach, go towards; to approach with the intention of serving, to assist, serve, attend, wait on (with acc.); to attend on a patient, to tend, nurse; to undertake; begin: Pass. -ćaryate, to be used figuratively or metaphorically, to be applied figuratively to any one (with loc.).

Upa-ćara, as, m. approach; attendance, cure.

Upa-ćaraṇa, am, n. going near to, approaching.

Upa-ćarita, as, ā, am, waited on, served, adored.

1. *upa-ćarya, as, ā, am,* to be served or waited on, to be worshipped; (ā), f. service, attendance; practice of medicine, physicking.

2. *upa-ćarya,* ind. having approached or attended to; having groomed or tended (horses).

Upa-ćāra, as, m. approach, service, attendance, act of civility, obliging or polite behaviour; proceeding, practice; profession, usage; physicking, the practice of medicine, tending the sick, nursing; behaviour, conduct; a ceremony, presenting offerings of water, betel, flowers, &c.; a present, a bribe; solicitation, request; incomplete act; a figure of speech, pretence, pretext, ellipsis, metaphor (e. g. *upaćārāt,* metaphorically); occurrence of *s* and *sh* in the place of Visarga in grammar; N. of a Pariśishṭa of the Sāma-veda. — *Upaćāra-karaṇa, am,* n. or *upaćāra-karman, a,* n. or *upaćāra-kriyā,* f. offering presents, especially of perfumes, flowers, &c.; attention, service. — *Upaćāra-para, as, ā, am,* diligent in service, serving diligently. — *Upaćāra-paribhrashṭa, as, ā, am,* void of civility, destitute of kindness, churlish, uncourteous.

Upa-ćārin, ī, iṇī, i, attending, serving.

Upa-ćārya, as, m. practice of medicine.

उपचर्म upa-ćarma or *am,* ind. on the skin, near the skin.

उपचारु upa-ćāru, us, m. and *upaćāru-mat, ān,* m., N. of two Cakravartins.

उपचि 1. upa-ći, cl. 5. P. A. -ćinoti, -nute, -ćetum, to gather together; to heap up, collect, hoard up, accumulate, increase, strengthen; to cover over with: Pass. -ćiyate, to be heaped together or accumulated, to increase, become strong; to better one's circumstances, be prosperous; to gain advantage, succeed, to be covered with.

Upa-ćaya, as, m. accumulation, increase, growth, prosperity; quantity, heap; elevation, excess; addition; the third, sixth, tenth, and eleventh degrees from the first of a zodiacal sign. — *Upaćaya-bhavana, am,* n. (?) according to some, a species of the Daṇḍaka metre. — *Upaćayāpaćayau* (°*ya-ap*°), m. du. prosperity and decay, rise and fall.

Upa-ćāyin, ī, inī, i, increasing, being in good circumstances.

Upa-ćāyya, as, m. a certain sacrificial fire; a place for holding sacrificial fire, a hearth, an altar.

Upa-ćit, t, f., Ved. a kind of disease, perhaps a swelling.

Upa-ćita, as, ā, am, collected, gathered together, heaped up, increased, assembled; thriving, increasing; abundantly furnished with, plastered, smeared; burnt (?). — *Upaćita-rasa, as, ā, am,* augmented in feeling.

Upa-ćiti, is, f. accumulation, collection, abundance.

Upa-ćīyamāna, as, ā, am, being collected or filled.

Upa-ćeya, as, ā, am, to be collected or heaped up.

उपचि 2. upa-ći, cl. 3. P., Ved. -ćiketi, -ćetum, to honour, worship.

उपचित्तचिन्त upaćitta-ćinta, as, m., N. of a son of Pāpīyas.

उपचित्र upa-ćitra, as, m., N. of a man; (ā), f. the plants Salvinia Cucullata and Croton Polyandra; N. of several metres, namely, 1. a variety of Mātrāsamaka, containing 4 × 16 syllabic instants; 2. a metre of four lines of eleven syllables each; 3. a metre of two lines of twenty-two syllables each.

उपचूलन upa-ćūlana, am, n. heating, burning (?).

उपचृत् upa-ćṛit, cl. 6. P. -ćṛitati, -ćartitum, to fasten, tie, bind on.

उपच्छद् 1. upa-ćhad (upa-ćhad), cl. 10. P. A. -ćhādayati, -te, -yitum, to cover, hide, conceal, keep secret.

Upa-ććhanna, as, ā, am, secret, concealed.

उपच्छद् 2. upa-ćhad or *-ććhand* (*upa-ćhad*), Caus. -ććhandayati, -yitum, to present any one (acc.) with anything (inst.); to persuade a person to do anything; to coax, to seek to seduce a person; to conciliate.

Upa-ććhandana, am, n. persuasion, persuading, coaxing.

उपच्यव upa-ćyava, as, m. (rt. *ćyu*), Ved. pressing close to (in sexual intercourse); (Sāy.) going into (the chamber).

उपजगती upa-jagatī, f. a variety of the Trishṭubh metre, in which three Pādas contain twelve syllables instead of eleven.

उपजन् upa-jan, cl. 4. A. -jāyate, -janitum, to be produced in addition, to be born, originate; to happen, become visible, appear; to be born again; to exist, be: Caus. -janayati, -yitum, to produce, cause.

Upa-ja, as, ā, am, being produced in addition, increasing; (*as*), m., N. of a divine being (?).

Upa-jana, as, m. additional production, addition, increase; appendage; addition of a letter in the formation of words; letters, syllables or affixes added.

Upa-jā, f., Ved. distant or not immediate posterity.

Upa-jāta, as, ā, am, produced, engendered, aroused. — *Upajāta-kopa* or *upajāta-krodha, as, ā, am,* provoked, excited, moved to anger. — *Upajāta-viśvāsa, as, ā, am,* believing, confiding, confident, trusting.

Upa-jāti, is, f. a mixed metre, especially a conjunction of Indravajrā and Upendravajrā, and a conjunction of Vaṇśastha and Indravaṇśa.

उपजप् upa-jap, cl. 1. P. -japati, -japitum, to whisper into the ears (of another), to bring over to one's own party by secretly suggesting anything in the ear, to instigate to rebellion or treachery; to make mischief.

Upa-japya, as, ā, am, to be brought over or instigated to rebellion by secret suggestions or whispering in the ear.

Upa-jāpa, as, m. the act of whispering into the ears, rousing to rebellion, bringing over to one's own party; treason, treachery; disunion, separation.

Upa-jāpaka, as, ā, am, whispering anything into the ears, rousing to rebellion; a traitor, treacherous; a mischief-maker, one who foments quarrels.

उपजरसम् upa-jarasam, ind. towards old age, in old age.

उपजला upa-jalā, f., N. of a river.

उपजल्प् upa-jalp, cl. 1. P. -jalpati, -pitum, to talk to, chatter, advise.

Upa-jalpita, am, n. talk.

Upa-jalpin, ī, inī, i, talking to a person, giving advice.

उपजायम् upa-jāyam, ind. near a wife.

उपजिगमिषु upa-jigamishu, us, us, u (fr. Desid. of rt. *gam*), desirous of going near.

उपजिहीर्षा upa-jihīrshā, f. (fr. Desid. of rt. *hṛi* with *upa*), desire, intention to rob.

उपजिह्वा upa-jihvā or *upajihvikā,* f. the uvula or soft palate, the epiglottis; enlargement of the under side of the tongue; a kind of ant.

उपजीक upajīka, as, m., Ved. a water deity.

उपजीव् upa-jīv, cl. 1. P. -jīvati, -vitum, to live or exist upon (food), subsist, support one's self on, be supported by, derive profit from, make use of (with acc.); to live under, be dependant on, to serve; to live for a profession, practice.

Upa-jīva, as, ā, am, Ved. living on &c. (?).

Upa-jīvaka, as, ā, am, living upon, subsisting by (with inst.); living under, depending upon, subject to, a dependant; (*am*), n. means of subsistence, act.

Upa-jīvana, am, n. means of living, subsistence.

Upa-jīvanīya, as, ā, am, granting means of subsistence, affording a livelihood.

Upa-jīvikā, f. subsistence, livelihood.

Upa-jīvin, ī, inī, i, living on, subsisting by (with acc. or gen.); living in dependance, dependant, subject.

Upa-jīvya, as, ā, am, that by which one lives, affording a livelihood; (*am*), n. means of subsistence, cause.

उपजोषम् upa-josham, ind. (rt. *jush*), according to one's desire or pleasure, quietly; an expression indicative of joy.

Upa-joshaṇa, am, n. enjoying, frequenting.

उपज्ञा 1. upa-jñā, cl. 9. A. -jānīte, -jñātum, to ascertain; excogitate, invent, find out, hit upon: Desid. A., ep. also P. -jijñāsate, -ti, to seek to ascertain or invent.

Upa-jijñāsya, as, ā, am, Ved. enigmatical, unintelligible, mysterious.

2. *upa-jñā,* f. a knowledge obtained by one's self and not handed down by tradition, primitive or untaught knowledge, invention; commencement of a thing not previously done; (at the end of a compound used in neut., e. g. *Pāṇiny-upajñam,* the grammar invented by Pāṇini.)

उपज्मन् upa-jman, ā, m., Ved. striding or stepping upon (?).

उपज्योतिष upa-jyotisha, N. of a region.

उपज्रि upa-jri, cl. 1. P., Ved. -jrayati, -jretum, to extend to; (Sāy.) to go near to, approach.

उपज्वलित upa-jvalita, as, ā, am, lighted up.

उपढौक् upa-ḍhauk, Caus. P. -ḍhaukayati, -yitum, to present an offering, make a respectful offering; carry out, accomplish.

Upa-ḍhaukana, am, n. a respectful offering or present, a Nazr.

उपतक्ष upa-taksha, as, m., N. of a certain semi-divine being, belonging to the class of Gandharvas or of Nāgas.

उपतटम् upa-taṭam, ind. near the skirt; (*as*), m. (?) the skirt.

उपतप् upa-tap, cl. 1. P. -tapati, -taptum, to make warm, to heat; to feel pain, become sick; to afflict, befal (as an illness; sometimes used impersonally with gen. or acc.): Pass. -tapyate, to feel pain, become ill, be afflicted with; to be emaciated with penance (*tapas*): Caus. -tāpayati, -yitum, to kindle, ignite, burn, consume; to cause pain, macerate the body by penance; torment, hurt, offend, oppress.

Upa-tapat, an, m., Ved. (scil. *agni*) interior heat, a disease.

Upa-tapta, as, ā, am, heated, parched; distressed, pained.

Upa-taptṛi, tā, m. morbid heat; any cause of heat, burning or inflammation.

Upa-tapyamāna, as, ā, am, being distressed.
Upa-tāpa, as, m. heat, warmth, heating, paining, pain, trouble, misfortune; sickness, disease, injury; haste, hurry.
Upa-tāpana, am, n. heating, distressing.
Upa-tāpin, ī, inī, i, heating, inflaming, exciting, causing pain; suffering heat or pain, sick.

उपतारक *upa-tāraka, as, ikā, am* (rt. *tṛī*), overflowing.

उपतिष्य *upa-tishya, as,* m., N. of a son of Tishya by S'ārikā.

उपतीरम् *upa-tīram,* ind. on the shore.

उपतुष् *upa-tush,* Caus. *-toshayati, -yitum,* to content, satisfy.

उपतूलम् *upa-tūlam,* ind. at the cotton.

उपतृण्य *upa-tṛiṇya, as,* m., Ved. epithet of a snake (lurking in grass).

उपत्य *upatya, as, ā, am* (fr. *upa*), situated under or below.
Upatyakā, f. low-land, land at the foot of a hill or mountain; a forest at the foot of a mountain; a vale, valley.

उपदंश् *upa-daṅś,* cl. 1. P. *-daśati, -daṅshṭum,* to bite or eat anything as a relish.
Upa-daṅśa, as, m. a relish, anything to excite drinking or appetite, anything eaten in addition; biting, stinging; the venereal disease, chancre; a tree, the scraped root of which is used for horse-radish, Morunga Hyperanthera.
Upadaṅśin, ī, inī, i, afflicted with the above disease.

उपदधि *upa-dadhi.* See under 1. *upa-dhā.*

उपदम्भ् *upa-dambh,* Caus. P., Ved. *-dambhayati, -yitum,* to lesson, diminish, destroy.

उपदश *upa-daśa, ās, ās, āni,* pl. almost ten, nearly ten.

उपदस् *upa-das,* cl. 4. P. *-dasyati, -situm,* to fail, be wanting, be extinguished, be exhausted, dry up; (in Ved. used impersonally with inst. or abl.): Caus. P. *-dāsayati, -yitum,* to cause to fail or cease, extinguish.
Upa-dāsuka, as, ā, am, Ved. failing, wanting.

उपदह् *upa-dah,* cl. 1. P. *-dahati, -dagdhum,* to burn, set fire to.

उपदा 1. *upa-dā,* cl. 3. P. A. *-dadāti, -datte, -dātum,* to give in addition, offer, grant, give; to add: Ved. cl. 1. A. *-dadate,* to take upon one's self; to erect, support.
2. *upa-dā, ās, ās, am,* Ved. giving a present; (*ā*), f. a present, an offering to a king or great man &c.; a Nazr.
Upa-dāna or *upadānaka, am,* n. an oblation, a present; a gift which is for the purpose of procuring favour or protection.

उपदानवी *upa-dānavī,* f., N. of the daughter of the Dānava Vṛisha-parvan and mother of Dushmanta.

उपदिग्ध *upa-digdha, as, ā, am* (fr. rt. *dih* with *upa*), smeared, covered; spotted over.
Upa-deha, as, m. a cover; liniment, ointment; (*upa* implying inferiority) a minor or secondary body growing on diseased parts of the body.
Upa-dehikā, f. a kind of ant; [cf. *upajihvikā.*]

उपदिश् 1. *upa-diś,* cl. 6. P. A. *-diśati, -te, -deshṭum,* to point out to; to indicate, specify, explain, instruct, teach; advise, admonish; to assign the right place to anything, arrange; to mention, exhibit; to inform; to settle, prescribe; to dictate, command, govern; to name: Pass. *-diśyate,* to be taught &c., to be called.
2. *upa-diś, k,* or *upa-diśā,* f. an intermediate region, as north-east &c.
Upa-diśa, as, m., N. of a son of Vasu-deva.
Upa-diśya, ind. having advised or instructed.
Upa-dishṭa, as, ā, am, specified, particularized; taught, instructed, advised; assigned as a plea or reason; initiated; (*am*), n. council, advice.
Upa-deśa, as, m. pointing out to, instruction, teaching, informing, advice, prescription; specification; plea, pretext; initiation, communication of the initiatory Mantra or formula; (in gram.) a form in a rule, an indicatory form, i. e. a root, base, affix, augment, or any other word or part of a word furnished with indicatory letters (anubandhas) which serve as a guide to the application of particular grammatical rules and are rejected when the word or part of a word is ready for use. — *Upadeśa-tā,* f. the state of being a precept or rule; injunction; manner of instructing; doctrine. — *Upadeśa-sahasrī,* f. title of a work of Saṅkara on philosophy. — *Upadeśārthavakya* (°*śa-ar*°), *am,* n. a parable.
Upa-deśaka, as, ā, am, giving instruction, instructing, instructive, didactic; (*as*), m. an instructor, a guide, especially a spiritual guide.
Upa-deśana, am, n. advising, instructing; (*ā*), f. information, doctrine.
Upa-deśin, ī, inī, i, advising, instructing, informing; (*ī*), m. a teacher, adviser; a word or affix &c. in the shape in which it appears in grammatical works.
Upa-deśya, as, ā, am, Ved. to be taught; that which is to be taught or learnt.
Upa-deshṭavya or *upa-deśanīya, as, ā, am,* to be taught or advised, fit or proper to be taught.
Upa-deshṭṛi, ṭā, ṭrī, ṭṛi, one who points out, an adviser, teacher; a Guru or spiritual guide.

उपदी *upadī,* f. the plant Vanda Roxburghii or Aërides Tesselata.

उपदीका *upadīkā,* f. a kind of ant; also *upa-dehikā.*

उपदीक्षिन् *upa-dīkshin, ī, iṇī, i,* sharing in an initiatory or other religious rite; a near relation.

उपदीप् *upa-dīp,* Caus. P. *-dīpayati, -yitum,* to kindle, set fire to.

उपदृश् 1. *upa-dṛiś,* cl. 1. P. *-paśyati, -drashṭum,* to look at; to perceive, observe: Pass. *-dṛiśyate,* to be or become visible, appear: Caus. *-darśayati, -yitum,* to cause to see, show, exhibit; to present a false show, impose upon another person by sham appearances; to illude; to explain, illustrate.
Upa-darśaka, as, m. a guide, one who shows the way, a door-keeper.
Upa-darśana, am, n. a commentary.
Upa-darśita, as, ā, am, perceived, distinguished.
2. *upa-dṛiś, k,* f., Ved. a view, aspect.
Upa-dṛishṭi, is, f. aspect, view, show.
Upa-drashṭṛi, ṭā, ṭrī, ṭṛi, Ved. a supervisor, inspector; overseeing, overlooking; (*ṭā*), m. a witness.

उपदृषद् *upa-dṛishad* or *upa-dṛishadam,* ind. near a boundary stone.

उपदेव *upa-deva, as,* m. an inferior deity; N. of a son of Akrūra; also of Devaka; (*ī*), f., N. of the wife of Vasu-deva; of a daughter of Devaka.
Upa-devatā, f. a minor deity, as a Yaksha, Gandarbha, Apsaras, &c.

उपदेश *upa-deśa,* &c. See under 1. *upa-diś.*

उपदोह *upa-doha, as,* m. (fr. rt. *duh* with *upa*), a nipple of the udder of a cow.

उपद्रु *upa-dru,* cl. 1. P. *-dravati, -drotum,* to run near to, run towards, run at, rush at, assault, attack.
Upa-drava, as, m. that which befalls suddenly, an unhappy accident, misfortune, calamity, mischief; national distress (whether the act of the seasons or the king, famine, exaction, &c.); national commotion, rebellion; violence, outrage; a symptom, a supervenient disease, one brought on whilst a person labours under another.
Upa-dravin, ī, iṇī, i, attacking, falling on; tyrannical, violent, factious; (*ī*), m. a tyrant, an oppressor, a rebel.
Upa-druta, as, ā, am, visited by calamities, oppressed, attacked, persecuted, tyrannized over; (in astron.) eclipsed; boding evil, inauspicious; (*am*), n. a term of the Bāshkalas for that kind of Sandhi, which is also called *udgrāhavat,* q. v.

उपद्वीप *upa-dvīpa, as,* m. an island.

उपधर्म *upa-dharma, as,* m. a minor or subordinate duty; a by-law; a heretic, a schismatic.

उपधा 1. *upa-dhā,* cl. 3. P. A. *-dadhāti, -dhatte, -dhātum,* to place or lay upon, place near to, put into; to place, lay; to put to (as horses to a carriage); to impose, lay upon, bestow upon, charge with (as a duty); to lay a command upon, enjoin, instruct in (with acc.); to place under one's self, to lie down upon; to place over, cover, conceal; to locate; to place in addition, to add; to communicate, cause to share in; (in gram.) to lie or be placed close to, to precede without the intervention of another syllable.
Upa-dadhi, is, is, i, Ved. placing upon.
2. *upa-dhā,* f. imposition, forgery, fraud, deceit, trick, a false pretence; trial or test of honesty &c., of four kinds, viz. of loyalty, disinterestedness, continence, and courage; (in gram.) a penultimate letter. — *Upadhā-bhṛita, as,* m. a servant who has been guilty of dishonesty. — *Upadhā-rañjana, am,* n. nasalization of the penultimate (?). — *Upadhā-śuci, is, is, i,* approved, tried, of approved loyalty &c.
Upa-dhāna, am, n. placing or resting upon; that on which one rests, a pillow, cushion; individuality, peculiarity; affection, kindness; religious observance or obligation; poison; excellence, excellent quality; (*as, ā, am*), employed in placing upon, i. e. used (as a Mantra) in the putting up (of the sacrificial bricks).
Upadhānīya, am, n. a pillow, cushion.
Upa-dhāya, ind. having placed or rested upon.
Upa-dhāyin, ī, inī, i, placing under.
Upa-dhi, is, m. the part of a wheel between the nave and the circumference; fraud, circumvention; fear, terror; foundation, (with Buddhists) substratum (?).
Upadhika, as, m. a cheat, a knave, especially one who imposes by threats, fraud.
Upa-dhīyamāna, as, ā, am, being preceded by.
Upa-dheya, as, ā, am, to be placed upon.
Upa-hita. See p. 170, col. 3.

उपधातु *upa-dhātu, us,* m. an inferior mineral, a semi-metal, (seven are specified; pyrites, sulphate of copper, talc, antimony, red orpiment, yellow orpiment, and calx of brass); secondary secretion of the body, as the milk, menses, adeps, sweat, teeth, hair, and lymph.

उपधारण *upa-dhāraṇa.* See under *upa-dhṛi* below.

उपधाव् *upa-dhāv,* cl. 1. P. A. *-dhāvati, -te, -vitum,* to run near to, approach hastily; have recourse to for assistance; A. to run, glide, soar.
Upa-dhāvana, as, m. a follower.

उपधि *upa-dhi.* See *upa-dhā* above.

उपधूपित *upa-dhūpita, as, ā, am,* fumigated; one to whom decline or death is near; being at the point of death; suffering extreme pain.

उपधृ *upa-dhṛi,* Caus. P. *-dhārayati, -yitum,* to hold up, support, bear, carry; to hold as, consider as, regard as; to hold in the mind, to comprehend, perceive, hear, experience, observe; to reflect or meditate on.
Upa-dhāraṇa, am, n. considering, consideration, reflection.
Upa-dhārya, ind. having taken or held up.
Upa-dhṛiti, is, f. a ray of light.

उपधे *upa-dhe*, Caus. A., Ved. *-dhāpayate, -yitum*, to rear by suckling.

उपध्मा 1. *upa-dhmā*, cl. 1. P. *-dhamati, -dhmātum*, to blow or breathe at or upon, fan.

2. *upa-dhmā*, f. blowing upon, breathing; the effort of the voice which produces the sound Upadhmānīya.

Upa-dhmāna, am, n. blowing upon, breathing.

Upadhmānin, ī, inī, i, blowing upon, fanning, breathing.

Upa-dhmānīya, as, m. the aspirate Visarga before the letters *p* and *ph*.

उपध्यै *upa-dhyai*, cl. 1. P., ep. also A. *-dhyāyati, -te, -dhyātum*, to think of, remember.

उपध्वस्त *upa-dhvasta, as, ā, am* (fr. rt. *dhvaṇs* with *upa*), Ved. spotted.

उपनक्षत्र *upa-nakshatra, am*, n., Ved. a secondary star.

उपनख *upa-nakha, am*, n. a disease of the finger-nails, whitlow, agnail.

उपनगर *upa-nagara, am*, n. a suburb.

उपनति *upa-nati*. See under *upa-nam*.

उपनदम् *upa-nadam* and *upa-nadi*, ind. near a river.

उपनन्द *upa-nanda, as*, m., N. of a son of Vasu-deva; a pupil of S'ākya-muni; a king of the Nāgas.

Upa-nandaka, as, m., N. of a son of Dhṛitarāshṭra.

उपनम् *upa-nam*, cl. 1. P. A. *-namati, -te, -nantum*, to bend towards, tend towards, approach; to come to, arrive at; to fall to the share of; share in (with acc., dat., or gen.): Caus. *-nāmayati, -yitum*, to lead towards or into the presence of (with gen.), introduce to; to offer.

Upa-nata, as, ā, am, bent towards, bent inwards; brought under, subjected, surrendered; dependent on (for protection &c.); brought near to; fallen to one's share; approached, approximate, near (either in time or space); brought about, produced, existing.

Upa-nati, is, f., Ved. inclination, affection.

Upa-nāmuka, as, ā, am, Ved. bending towards.

उपनय *upa-naya*. See under 1. *upa-nī*.

उपनर *upa-nara, as*, m., N. of a king of the Nāgas.

उपनह् *upa-nah*, cl. 4. P. A. *-nahyati, -te, -naddhum*, to tie up, tie together; to make up into a bundle, bind together; to inlay; to set with: Caus. *-nāhayati, -yitum*, to cause to bind together.

Upa-nahana, am, n., Ved. a cloth in which anything is bound up.

Upa-nāha, as, m. a bundle; a plaster, an unguent applied to a wound or sore; the tie of a lute, the lower part of the tail-piece where the wires are fixed; inflammation of the ciliary glands, stye.

Upa-nāhana, am, n. putting a plaster upon, applying an unguent, unction, anointing, plastering.

उपनामन् *upa-nāman, a*, n. a nickname, surname.

उपनासिक *upa-nāsika, am*, n. the part surrounding the nose, that which is near the nose.

उपनिक्षिप् *upa-ni-kship*, cl. 6. P. A., 4. P. *-kshipati, -te, -kshipyati, -ksheptum*, to throw down, place down, deposit.

Upa-nikshepa, as, m. a deposit sealed or covered up so that the contents are unknown; any article intrusted to one's keeping.

उपनिगम् *upa-ni-gam*, cl. 1. P. *-gaććhati, -gantum*, to meet with, fall into, fall upon, fall into any state.

उपनिग्रह् *upa-ni-grah*, cl. 9. P. A. *-grihṇāti, -ṇīte* (Ved. *-gribhṇāti, -ṇīte*), *-grahītum*, to press down upon, bring near to.

उपनिधा *upa-ni-dhā*, cl. 3. P. A. *-dadhāti, -dhatte, -dhātum*, to put or place near, to put down, place before any one (as a meal &c.), bring near, lead near to; to produce, cause; to deposit, to intrust.

Upa-nidhātṛi, tā, trī, tṛi, putting down, laying down.

Upa-nidhāna, am, n. a deposit.

Upa-nidhi, is, m. a deposit, pledge, property put under the care of a creditor, friend, &c.; in law this word ordinarily implies especially a sealed deposit, but according to some, any article intrusted to a friend which he may use whilst in his keeping; N. of a son of Vasu-deva.

Upa-nihita, as, ā, am, deposited with, intrusted to; placed near to; offered, presented.

उपनिपत् *upa-ni-pat*, cl. 1. P. *-patati, -titum*, to fly down to; to take place in addition; to be mentioned incidentally.

Upa-nipāta, as, m. sudden and unexpected attack.

Upa-nipātin, ī, inī, i, falling into; attacking suddenly.

उपनिपीड् *upa-ni-pīḍ*, cl. 10. P. *-pīḍayati, -yitum*, to oppress, disturb.

उपनिमन्त्र् *upa-ni-mantr*, cl. 10. A. *-mantrayate, -yitum*, to invite, consecrate, inaugurate.

Upa-nimantraṇa, am, n. invitation, inauguration.

उपनिवपन *upa-nivapana, am*, n. (rt. *vap*), scattering or pouring down upon.

उपनिवेशिन् *upa-niveśin, ī, inī, i* (rt. *viś*), attached to, inherent, annexed.

उपनिषद् *upa-nishad, t*, f. (rt. *sad* with *upa* and *ni*, implying originally sitting down at the feet of another in order to listen to his words, and hence confidential information given in this manner; but according to native authorities *upa-ni-shad* means 'to destroy ignorance by revealing the knowledge of the supreme spirit'); esoteric doctrine, secret doctrine, mysterious or mystical meaning, words of mystery &c.; certain mystical writings attached to the Brāhmaṇas, the aim of which is the ascertainment of the secret sense of the Veda, (they are more than a hundred in number, and are said to have been the source of the six darśanas or systems of philosophy; perhaps the most celebrated is the Bṛihad-āraṇyaka-upanishad attached to the S'ata-patha-Brāhmaṇa); true knowledge; a neighbouring mansion; a lonely place; (at the end of compounds *upanishad* sometimes becomes *upanishada*.) — *Upanishat-kṛi*, to regard as a mystical or secret doctrine.

Upa-nishādin, ī, inī, i, sitting at the feet of a person; subjected.

उपनिष्कर *upa-nishkara, am*, n. (rt. *kṛi*), a street, a principal or royal road.

उपनिष्क्रम् *upa-nish-kram* (*-nis-kram*), cl. 1. P. A., 4. P. *-krāmati, -kramate* (ep. also *-krāmate*), *-krāmyati, -kramitum*, to go out towards, step out, go out.

Upa-nishkramaṇa, am, n. going out towards; a particular religious rite, one of the Saṇskāras, taking a child in the fourth month of its age for the first time into the open air (see Manu II. 34); a main or royal road.

उपनी 1. *upa-nī*, cl. 1. P. A. *-nayati, -te, -netum*, to lead near to, bring near, bring, adduce, offer; bring information, communicate; to bring about, produce; to employ, to bring into any state, bring into one's possession, lead away, lead; to bring near to one's self (as a teacher receives a pupil for instruction), to invest with the sacred thread, initiate; A. to take into one's service: Caus. *-nāyayati, -yitum*, to cause (a master) to receive (a pupil), to cause to invest with the sacred thread.

Upa-naya, as, m. bringing near, procuring; attaining, gaining; employing; the fourth member in a fivefold syllogism, the application to the special case in question; leading a youth of the three first castes to a teacher; initiation; investiture with a peculiar thread or cord worn over the left shoulder and under the right, by which act spiritual birth is conferred and the youth is reckoned a member of the twice-born classes; (the cord of the Brāhman is of cotton, Munja or Kuśa grass; of the Kshatriya, of S'aṇa or hemp; and of the Vaiśya, of wool: the youths should be invested, respectively, from eight to sixteen, from eleven to twenty-two, and from twelve to twenty-four years of age.)

Upa-nayana, am, n. leading to, bringing; leading to a teacher, initiation. See *upa-naya*.

Upa-nāya, as, m. or *upa-nāyana, am*, n. leading to a teacher, initiation. See the preceding.

Upa-nāyika, as, ā, am, leading to; N. of a Sūtra work.

Upa-nīta, as, ā, am, brought near, approximated; presented; known; obtained, attained; cited, adduced; (*as*), m. the youth led to a teacher and invested with the characteristic cord.

Upa-nīya, ind. having led towards or brought, having invested (with the sacred thread).

Upa-nīyamāna, as, ā, am, being initiated.

Upa-netavya, as, ā, am, to be brought near; to be employed or observed.

Upa-netṛi, tā, m. one who leads or brings near.

उपनी 2. *upa-nī* (*upa-ni-i*), cl. 2. P. *-nyeti, -tum*, to enter into, penetrate.

उपनुद् *upa-nud*, cl. 6. P. A. *-nudati, -te, -nottum*, to drive or waft near, impel towards.

Upa-nunna, as, ā, am, sent, despatched; wafted, driven (by the wind).

उपनृत् *upa-nṛit*, cl. 4. P. A. *-nṛityati, -te, -nartitum*, to dance before any one (with acc.), to dance before any one with insulting gestures.

Upa-nṛitya, am, n. a place for dancing.

उपन्यस् *upa-ny-as* (*-ni-as*), cl. 4. P. *-asyati, -asitum*, to lay upon, place down, put down, deposit, intrust to any one (with dat.), commit to the care of; to explain minutely, describe in detail; suggest, plead, put forth or adduce arguments, state.

Upa-nyasta, as, ā, am, placed near to or upon; pledged, intrusted, deposited; given, communicated; brought forward as an example &c., adduced, hinted, suggested.

Upa-nyasya, ind. having delivered up, delivering up.

Upa-nyāsa, as, m. placing near to, juxta-position; intrusting, a deposit, pledge, a pawn, a hostage; statement, suggestion, hint, pretext, an exordium or introduction; a precept, a law.

Upa-nyāsya, as, ā, am, to be adduced or stated.

उपन्याचर् *upa-ny-ā-ćar* (*-ni-ā-*), cl. 1. P. A. *-ćarati, -te, -ritum* (Ved. *-ritave, -vai, -rase, -radhyai*), to enter into, penetrate.

उपपक्ष *upa-paksha, as*, m., Ved. the shoulder.

Upa-pakshya, as, ā, am, Ved. near the shoulder.

उपपत् *upa-pat*, cl. 1. P. *-patati, -titum*, to fly near, hasten towards.

Upa-pāta, as, m. accident, occurrence, misfortune, unlucky accident.

Upa-pātaka, am, n. (with *upa* implying inferiority) a crime or sin in the second degree (as killing a cow, selling a daughter, &c.).

Upapātakin, ī, inī, i, one who has committed a crime in the second degree; a sinner in any but the first degree.

Upa-pātin, ī, inī, i, falling into, hastening towards.

उपपति *upa-pati, is*, m. a paramour, a gallant.

उपपथम् *upa-patham*, ind. near the road.

उपपद् *upa-pad*, cl. 4. A. *-padyate, -pattum*, to go near, approach, come to, arrive at, to be obtained or gained, fall to one's share; to go against, attack; to take place, occur, to be produced, to be present, to be possible, to be adapted, to be fit for or adequate for (with loc.); put in a word or statement: Caus. *-pādayati, -yitum*, to bring into any state, cause to arrive or be obtained, offer, present any one (acc.) with (inst.); to cause to occur or happen; to accomplish, effect, cause; to make a statement, mention; to justify; to make fit or adequate for, to make conformable to; to furnish with; to pronounce, declare; to find out, ascertain; examine.

Upa-patti, is, f. happening, occurring, becoming visible, appearance, production, birth; gaining, effecting, accomplishing; cause, reason; termination, end; fitness, propriety; association, connection, possession; religious abstraction; proof, ascertained or demonstrated conclusion; (in arithm. or geom.) proof, demonstration; *upapattyā*, ind. suitably, in a fit manner.—*Upapatti-mat, ān, atī, at*, or *upapatti-yukta, as, ā, am*, right, fit, reasonable, proper; united, associated.

Upa-panna, as, ā, am, produced, effected, obtained, gained, demonstrated, proved, manifested, offered, presented, endowed with, possessed of, furnished with (e. g. *guṇopapanna*, endowed with good qualities); fit, suited to the occasion, adequate; physicked, cured.

Upa-pādaka, as, ā, am, producing, effecting, making visible.

Upa-pādana, am, n. effecting, doing, causing to appear; giving, delivering, presenting; proving or establishing by argument; explaining; examination; (*as, ā, am*), examining.

Upa-pādita, as, ā, am, effected, accomplished, performed, done; given, delivered, presented; proved, demonstrated.

1. *upa-pāduka, as, ā, am*, self-produced; (*as*), m. a superhuman being, a god, a demon, &c.; hell (?).

Upa-pādya, as, ā, am, to be effected, done, shown or proved; being produced, coming into existence.

उपपद *upa-pada, as*, m. a secondary word of a sentence (as for instance a subordinate word in a compound generally forming the first member; or a preposition, particle &c. prefixed to a verb or a noun derived from a verb qualifying or determining the idea contained in the verb; or a secondary word of any kind which is governed by or limits the general idea contained in the principal word); small, diminutive; a little.

उपपरीक्षण *upa-parīkshaṇa, am*, n. or *upa-parīkshā*, f. (fr. rt. *īksh* with *pari* and *upa*), inquiring into, investigation, examination.

उपपरे *upa-pare* (*-parā-i*), cl. 2. P. *-paraiti, -tum*, to go towards, approach.

उपपर्चन *upa-parćana, as, ā, am* (rt. *pṛić*), closely touching; in close contact; (*am*), n., Ved. admixture; (Sāy.) impregnation.

Upa-pṛić, k, k, k, Ved. closely attached, in close contact with.

उपपर्शुका *upa-parśukā*, f. the false ribs.

उपपली *upa-palī* (for *upa-pari-i*), cl. 2. P. *-palyeti, -tum*, to return, turn back.

उपपादुक 2. *upa-pāduka, as, ī, am*, having shoes, shod.

उपपाप *upa-pāpa, am*, n. a crime in the second degree; [cf. *upa-pātaka*.]

उपपार्श्व *upa-pārśva, as, am*, m. n. a shoulder; flank; the lesser ribs, the lesser flank; the opposite side.

उपपालित *upa-pālita, as, ā, am* (fr. rt. 2. *pā*), protected, nurtured.

उपपीड् *upa-pīḍ*, cl. 10. P. *-pīḍayati, -yitum*, to press down, disturb, distress; (in astron.) to eclipse.

Upa-pīḍana, am, n. pressing down, oppressing, devastating, laying waste; inflicting pain; pain, agony, torture.

Upa-pīḍita, as, ā, am, devastated; tortured, pained, distressed.

उपपुर *upa-puru, am*, n. a suburb, 'near the city.'

Upapaurika, as, ī, am, belonging to a suburb.

उपपुराण *upa-purāṇa, am*, n. a secondary or minor Purāṇa, a number of writings subordinate to the eighteen principal Purāṇas: viz. Ādi (by Sanatkumāra), Nṛisiṇha, Vāyu, Śivadharma, Durvāsas, Nārada, Nandikeśvara, Uśanas, Kapila, Varuṇa, Sāmba, Kālikā, Maheśvara, Padma, Deva, Parāśara, Marīća, Bhāskara.

उपपुष्पिका *upa-pushpikā*, f. yawning, gaping.

उपपौर्णमासम् *upa-paurṇamāsam* or *upa-paurnamāsi*, ind. at the time of full moon.

उपप्रगा *upa-pra-gā*, cl. 3. P. *-jigāti, -gātum*, to come near to, approach.

उपप्रछ् *upa-prać*, cl. 6. P. *-pṛiććhati, -prashṭum*, to ask a person (acc.) about anything.

उपप्रजन् *upa-pra-jan*, cl. 4. A. *-jāyate, -janitum*, to be born in addition.

उपप्रजिन्व् *upa-pra-jinv*, cl. 1. P. *-jinvati, -vitum*, to impel, stir up; (Sāy.) to gratify or please in approaching.

उपप्रतॄ *upa-pra-tṛī*, Caus. *-tārayati, -yitum*, to convey or transport across.

उपप्रदर्शन *upa-pradarśana, am*, n. pointing out, showing, indication.

उपप्रदा *upa-pra-dā*, cl. 3. P. A. *-dadāti, -datte, -dātum*, to deliver over, commit to (any one).

Upa-pradāna, am, n. delivering over, presenting; a present, a bribe.

उपप्रया *upa-pra-yā*, cl. 2. P. *-yāti, -tum*, to approach, attack.

उपप्रलोभन *upa-pralobhana, am*, n. (rt. *lubh*), seducing, alluring.

उपप्राण *upa-prāṇa, as*, m. a secondary or inferior vital air belonging to the body.

उपप्राप् *upa-prāp* (*-pra-āp*), cl. 5. P. *-prāpnoti, -ptum*, to come near, approach.

उपप्राया *upa-prā-yā* (*-pra-ā-yā*), cl. 2. P., Ved. *-yāti, -tum*, to go near, approach.

उपप्रुत् *upa-prut, t, t, t*, Ved. flowing or rushing near; (Sāy.) approaching.

उपप्रे *upa-pre* (*-pra-i*), cl. 2. P. *-praiti, -tum*, to go near, approach, invade; to undertake, begin; to set about anything (with acc. or dat.).

उपप्रेक्ष् *upa-preksh* (*-pra-īksh*), cl. 1. A. *-prekshate, -shitum*, to overlook, pass over unnoticed, disregard.

Upa-prekshaṇa, am, n. overlooking, looking at without interest, disregarding.

उपप्रेष् *upa-presh* (*-pra-ish*), cl. 4. P. *-preshyati, -preshitum*, to drive, impel; to invite or request (a priest to do anything at a sacrifice), to summon.

Upa-praisha, as, m. invitation, summons.

उपप्लु *upa-plu*, cl. 1. A. *-plavate, -plotum*, to assault violently, assail.

Upa-plava, as, m. (fr. rt. *plu* with *upa*), violent assault or attack; unlucky accident, misfortune, great calamity, disturbance; a portent or natural phenomenon, especially an eclipse; a N. of Rāhu, the ascending node, the author of eclipses; N. of Śiva.

Upaplavin, ī, inī, i, one who has met with a calamity.

Upa-plavya, am, n., N. of the capital of Virāṭa's country, Matsya.

Upa-pluta, as, ā, am, violently assaulted, assailed, beset; distressed, pained; harassed (by Rāhu &c.), eclipsed; marked by prodigies; wet, moistened; (*ā*), f. morbid sensibility of the uterus.—*Upaplutāksha* (°*ta-ak*°), *as, ī, am*, weeping.

उपबन्ध *upa-bandha, as*, m. (rt. *bandh*), connection; an affix; a mode of sitting.

Upa-baddha, as, ā, am, connected.

उपबर्ह *upa-barha, as*, m. (rt. *bṛih* or *bṛiṇh*; cf. *upa-vṛiṇh*, p. 168), a pillow.

Upa-barhaṇa, am, n., Ved. a cushion, coverlet, covering.

Upa-bṛiṇhin, ī, iṇī, i, supplementary, additional.

उपबहु *upa-bahu, us, us, u*, a few, a tolerable number.

उपबाहु *upa-bāhu, us*, m. the lower arm (from the elbow to the wrist); N. of a man.

उपब्द *upabda, as*, or *upabdi, is*, m., Ved. noise, sound, rattling, clanking.—*Upabdi-mat, ān, atī, at*, Ved. noisy, loud.

उपब्रू *upa-brū*, cl. 2. P. A. *-bravīti, -brūte*, to praise, celebrate.

उपभङ्ग *upa-bhanga, as*, m. (rt. *bhañj*), a division or member (of a verse).

उपभाषा *upa-bhāshā*, f. a secondary dialect.

उपभुज् *upa-bhuj*, cl. 7. P. A. *-bhunakti, -bhunkte, -bhoktum*, to enjoy, eat, possess, use; make use of, receive (as a reward).

Upa-bhukta, as, ā, am, enjoyed, used, possessed.—*Upabhukta-dhana, as, ā, am*, one who has enjoyed or makes use of his riches; (*as*), m., N. of a merchant's son.

Upa-bhuñjāna, as, ā, am, enjoying, using.

Upa-bhoktṛi, tā, trī, tṛi, an enjoyer, enjoying, possessing.

Upa-bhoga, as, m. enjoyment, use, eating; usufruct; pleasure, satisfaction, cohabitation.

Upa-bhogin, ī, inī, i, enjoying, using.

Upa-bhogya or *upa-bhoktavya* or *upa-bhojanīya, as, ā, am*, to be enjoyed, to be used; (*am*), n. object of enjoyment.

Upa-bhojin, ī, inī, i, eating, enjoying.

Upa-bhojya, as, ā, am, serving as food.

उपभू *upa-bhū*, cl. 1. P., Ved. *-bhavati, -vitum*, to be near to.

उपभृत् *upa-bhṛit, t*, f., Ved. a sacrificial vessel made of wood; a cup of round shape, made of the wood of the banian tree, and used in sacrifices.

उपम 1. *upama, as, ā, am* (fr. *upa*), Ved. uppermost, highest; nearest, next, first; most excellent, eminent, best.—*Upama-śravas, ās, ās, as*, Ved. of highest fame; (*ās*), m., N. of a son of Kuruśravaṇa and grandson of Mitrātithi.

1. *upamā*, ind., Ved. in the closest proximity or neighbourhood.

Upamām, ind., Ved. in the highest degree.

उपम 2. *upama*, at the end of compounds. See under 3. *upa-mā*.

उपमद्गु *upa-madgu, us*, m., N. of a son of Svaphalka and younger brother of Madgu.

उपमन्त्र् *upa-mantr*, cl. 10. A. *-mantrayate, -yitum*, to address, invoke, invite, persuade.

Upa-mantraṇa, am, n. the act of addressing, inviting, persuading.

Upa-mantrin, ī, iṇī, i, inviting, persuading.

उपमन्थनी *upa-manthanī,* f. (rt. *math*), a staff for stirring.

Upa-manthitṛi, tā, tṛi, tṛi, Ved. stirring up.

उपमन्यु *upa-manyu, us, us, u,* Ved. zealous, striving after; (Sāy.) knowing, understanding, intelligent; (*us*), m., N. of a pupil of Dhaumya Āyoda.

उपमा 2. *upa-mā,* cl. 2. P., 3 or 4. A. *-māti, -mimīte, -māyate, -mātum,* to measure one thing by another, compare; Ved. to give, grant.

3. *upa-mā,* f. resemblance, equality, similarity; a resemblance, as a picture, portrait, image, &c.; a simile; comparison, a particle of comparison; (*as, ā, am,* at the end of a Bahu-vrīhi compound) like, similar to, resembling (e. g. *amaropama,* resembling an immortal). — *Upamā-dravya, am,* n. any object used for a comparison. — *Upamā-rūpaka, am,* n. a figure in rhetoric combining comparison and metaphor. — *Upameta* (°*mā-ita?*), *as, ā, am,* compared with?; (*as*), m., N. of the tree Vatica Robusta.

1. *upa-mātṛi, tā,* m. an image-maker, a portrait-painter.

Upa-māna, am, n. comparison, resemblance, analogy; a simile; that with which anything is compared; a particle of comparison; (in the Nyāya phil.) recognition of likeness, comparison, the third of the four pramāṇas or means of correct knowledge. — *Upamāna-ćintāmaṇi, is,* m. title of a philosophical work. — *Upamānopameya-bhāva* (°*na-up*°), *as,* m. the connection between the subject of comparison and the comparison adduced.

Upa-mita, as, ā, am, compared, illustrated by comparison, similar.

Upa-miti, is, f. resemblance, comparison, a likeness, a picture, image, &c.; analogy; knowledge of things derived from analogy or resemblance; inference, induction.

Upa-meya, as, ā, am, (with inst. or as last member of a compound) to be compared, comparable with; (*am*), n. the subject of a comparison, that which is compared (opposed to *upa-māna,* that with which it is compared). — *Upameyopamā* (°*ya-up*°), f. the resemblance of any object to that compared with it; reciprocal comparison, as of the moon to a beautiful face.

उपमाति *upa-māti, is,* f. (fr. rt. *man* with *upa*), Ved. approaching with a prayer; addressing, address; (Sāy.) comparison; (*is*), m. approaching in a friendly way; obliging; one who may be addressed, affable, especially as an epithet of Agni; (Sāy.) granting wealth. — *Upamāti-vani, is, is, i,* Ved. one who receives addresses in a friendly way; (Sāy.) destroyer of an enemy.

Upa-mīmāṅsā, f., Ved. deliberation, investigation, consideration.

उपमातृ 2. *upa-mātṛi, tā,* f. (a second mother), a wet nurse; a near female relative.

उपमाद *upa-māda, as,* m., Ved. enjoyment, delight.

उपमारण *upa-māraṇa, am,* n. (fr. rt. *mṛi*), Ved. submerging (in water &c.).

उपमालिनी *upa-mālinī,* f. a species of the Ati-śakvarī metre.

उपमास्य *upa-māsya, as, ā, am,* Ved. occurring every month, monthly.

उपमित् *upa-mit, t,* f., Ved, a prop, a stay.

उपमूलम् *upa-mūlam,* ind. at the root.

उपमृद् *upa-mṛid,* cl. 9. P. *-mṛidnāti, -marditum,* to crush, bruise, dash to pieces, destroy; rub down.

Upa-marda, as, m. friction, rubbing down, bruising; destruction; reproach, abuse, refutation of a charge.

Upa-mardaka, as, ā, am, crushing, destroying, destructive; (*as*), m. refutation of a charge.

उपयज् *upa-yaj, ḍ,* f., Ved., N. of eleven additional formulas at a sacrifice.

Upa-yashṭṛi, ṭā, m., Ved. the priest who utters these verses.

Upa-yāja, as, m. additional formulas at a sacrifice; N. of a younger brother of Yāja.

उपयन्त्र् *upa-yantr,* cl. 10. P. *-yantrayati, -yitum,* to solicit or compel any one to do anything.

उपयम् *upa-yam,* cl. 1. P. A. *-yaććhati, -te, -yantum,* to take a wife, marry; to seize, take, receive, hold; to offer.

Upa-yantṛi, tā, m. a husband.

Upa-yantra, am, n. (with *upa* implying inferiority) a minor surgical instrument or implement; a secondary application of any kind, as actual cautery, escharotics, &c.

Upa-yama, as, m. marriage, marrying.

Upa-yamana, am, n. marrying; taking a wife; (*ī*), f. any support of stone, clay, gravel &c. for holding fire-wood; a sacrificial ladle; (*as, ā, am*), that upon which anything is placed, a support.

Upa-yāma, as, m., Ved. taking up with a ladle; a ladle (?); the verses or formulas uttered in ladling out the Soma juice; marriage.

उपया *upa-yā,* cl. 2. P. *-yāti, -tum,* to approach, undergo.

Upa-yāta, as, ā, am, arrived; (*am*), n. arrival, return.

Upa-yāna, am, n. coming near, approaching.

Upa-yāyin, ī, inī, i, coming towards, approaching.

उपयाचक *upa-yāćaka, as, ā, am* (rt. *yāć*), an asker, solicitor, begging.

Upa-yāćana, am, n. soliciting, approaching with a request or prayer.

Upa-yāćita, as, ā, am, requested, solicited; offered, especially to the deities to render them propitious; (*am*), n. prayer, request (to a deity).

उपयिचारिक *upayićārika, as,* m. any one employed to guard a Vihāra; a wrong reading for *upavihārika* (?).

उपयुज् *upa-yuj,* cl. 7. P. A. *-yunakti, yuṅkte, -yoktum,* to harness (as horses to a carriage); to occupy, take possession of; to use, employ, apply; to bestow upon; to attach one's self to, be devoted to; to appropriate, consume, eat.

Upa-yukta, as, ā, am, attached, adapted, suitable, appropriate, useful; worthy, serviceable; proper, right; taken, eaten, touched.

Upa-yuñjāna, as, ā, am, attaching, taking, appropriating.

Upa-yuyukshu, us, us, u, about to employ or apply.

Upa-yoktavya, as, ā, am, to be employed.

Upa-yoga, as, m. application, employment, use, service, utility; administration of medicines, preparation of them; fitness, suitableness; contact, proximity; any act tending to effect a desired object; good conduct, observing established practices. — *Upayogaṃ gam* or *vraj,* to be employed or used.

Upa-yogin, ī, inī, i, employing, using; what is employed, conducive or contributing to, serviceable, useful, convenient; appropriate; favourable, propitious; touching, in contact with. — *Upayogi-tā,* f. or *upayogi-tva, am,* n. usefulness; fitness, suitableness; occasion, need; favour, propitiousness.

Upa-yojana, am, n. harnessing a horse (by the side of another); a team.

Upa-yojya, as, ā, am, to be employed or used.

उपयोषम् *upa-yosham,* ind. a word expressing great pleasure; [cf. *upa-josham.*]

उपर *upara, as, ā, am* (fr. *upa*), Ved. situated below, under; posterior, later; nearer, approximate; *uparāsu* (loc. fem. pl.), in the proximity of, near to; (*as*), m. the lower stone on which the Soma is laid that it may be ground by means of other stones held in the hands; the lower part of the sacrificial post; a cloud; region (?). — *Upara-tāt,* ind., Ved. in the proximity or circumference.

उपरक्त *upa-rakta, as, ā, am* (fr. rt. *rañj* with *upa*), afflicted, overtaken by calamity; (*as*), m. eclipsed (as sun or moon), Rāhu the ascending node.

Upa-rāga, as, m. colour; darkening, an eclipse of the sun or moon; Rāhu or the ascending node; an inauspicious event, calamity, affliction; misbehaviour, ill conduct; reproach, abuse.

उपरक्षण *upa-rakshaṇa, am,* n. a guard, an outpost.

उपरचित *upa-raćita, as, ā, am,* made, prepared.

उपरत्न *upa-ratna, am,* n. a secondary or inferior gem, a diamond of low value.

उपरम् *upa-ram,* cl. 1. P. A. *-ramati, -te, -rantum,* to cease, end, terminate, be finished; to desist; to cause to cease or desist: Caus. *-ramayati, -yitum,* to cause to cease or desist, stop, render quiet.

Upa-rata, as, ā, am, ceased, stopped; dead; withdrawn or retired from. — *Uparata-karman, ā, ā, a,* ceasing from works or from relying on them. — *Uparata-rāsa, as, ā, am,* ceasing to dance or play. — *Uparata-vishayābhilāsha* (°*ya-abh*°), *as, ā, am,* ceasing from all desire after worldly things. — *Uparata-spṛiha, as, ā, am,* void of desire. — *Uparatāri* (°*ta-ari*), *is, is, i,* having no foe, being at peace with all.

Upa-rati, is, f. ceasing, stopping; death; refraining from sensual enjoyment, abstaining from prescribed acts; great or exquisite pleasure (?).

Upa-rama, as, m. stopping, ceasing; abstaining from, giving up; death.

Upa-ramaṇa, am, n. abstaining from the pleasures of sense or from ceremonial acts (with abl.); ceasing, discontinuance.

Upa-rāma, as, m. ceasing, stopping.

उपरव *upa-rava, as,* m. (fr. rt. *ru* with *upa*), a sound-hole, (designation of certain holes which increase the sound of the stones when the Soma is being ground.)

उपरस *upa-rasa, as,* m. a secondary mineral, as red chalk, bitumen, &c.; a secondary passion or feeling; a subordinate flavour.

उपराज *upa-rāja, as,* m. a viceroy.

Upa-rājam, ind. near a king.

उपरि *upari,* ind. (as a separable adverb) above, upon, on, upwards, towards the upper side of (opposed to *adhas* and *nića,* e. g. *upari yā,* to go upwards; sometimes written with a following word as if compounded with it, e. g. *upari-ćihnita,* marked above); besides, in addition to, further (*sahasraṃ śatāny upari ćāshṭau,* 1000 and 800 in addition); afterwards (e. g. *upari payaḥ pibet,* he should drink milk afterwards); *upari upari,* higher and higher; repeatedly, continuously.

(As a separable preposition, with acc., loc., or gen.) over, above, upon, on, at the head of, on the upper side of, beyond (e. g. *upari śailaṃ gam,* to go over the mountain; *upari Laṅkāyāṃ samprāptaḥ saḥ,* he arrived over Laṅkā; *upary upari sarveshām atishṭhat,* he stood at the very head of all; *ātmānaṃ tasya upari kshiptvā,* having thrown himself upon him); in connection with, with reference to, with regard to, towards (with gen., e. g. *mama upari vikāritaḥ,* changed in feeling with regard to me; *putrasya upari kruddhaḥ,* enraged towards his son); after (with abl., e. g. *muhūrtād upari,* after a minute); [cf. Zend *upara;* Goth. *ufar;* Old Germ. *obar;* Mod. Germ. *über;* Eng. *over;* Gr. ὑπέρ; Lat. *super.*]

Upari may also be used at the end of a compound; e. g. *tadupari gantum,* to fall upon him, to attack him.

Upari often stands at the beginning of a compound, as in the following examples. — *Upari-gata, as, ā, am,* gone up, ascended. — *Upari-ćara, as,* m. epithet of the king Vasu ('walking in the air'). — *Upari-ćita, as, ā, am,* piled over or above.

— Upari-ja, as, ā, am, growing up, produced above, elevated, high. — Upari-nihita, as, ā, am, laid over. — Upari-purusha, as, ā, am, having a man above. — Upari-prut, t, t, t, Ved. coming from above. — Upari-babhrava, as, m., N. of a teacher of the ritual. — Upari-budhna, as, ā, am, Ved. raised above the ground. — Upari-bhāga, as, m. the upper portion or side. — Upari-bhāva, as, m. the being above or higher. — Upari-bhūmi, is, f. the ground above. — Upari-bhram, cl. 1. 4. P. -bhramati, -bhrāmyati, -bhramitum, to wander over or above. — Upari-martya, as, ā, am, Ved. above men. — Upari-śayana, am, n., Ved. a place of rest. — Upari-śreṇika, as, ā, am, being in the upper series. — Upari-sad, t, t, t, Ved. sitting or dwelling above. — Upari-sadya, am, n., Ved. the act of sitting above. — Upari-stha, as, ā, am, staying or being above, upper. — Upari-sthāpana, am, n. placing upon or above. — Upari-sthita, as, ā, am, standing above, being above, upper. — Upari-spriś, k, k, k, Ved. raised, elevated. — Uparītaka (°ri-it°), as, m. a kind of coitus. — Upary-āsana, am, n. sitting on high.

Uparitana, as, ī, am, upper (opposed to adhastana).

Uparishṭāt, ind. (as an adverb) above, from above; behind (opposed to purastāt), further on (in a book), later; afterwards; (as a preposition) over, upon, down upon (with acc. and gen.); behind (with gen.). — Uparishṭāj-jyotishmatī, f., N. of a Vedic metre consisting of forty-three or forty-four syllables, the end of which is like the beginning of the metre Jyotishmatī. — Uparishṭāj-jyotis, is, f. a verse of the Trishṭubh metre, the last Pāda of which consists of eight syllables. — Uparishṭād-brihatī, f., N. of a Vedic metre consisting of four Pādas, the first of which contains twelve, each of the three others only eight syllables.

उपरुच् upa-ruć, cl. 1. A. -roćate, -roćitum, to shine, be brilliant.

उपरुध् upa-rudh, cl. 7. P. A. -ruṇaddhi, -rundhe, -roddhum, to obstruct, hinder, molest, trouble, disturb; to prevent; to conceal.

Upa-ruddha, as, ā, am, obstructed, impeded, molested, disturbed; covered, spread; protected, favoured.

Upa-rudhya, ind. having kept in check or obstructed, having blockaded or hemmed in.

Upa-rudhyamāna, as, ā, am, being besieged, besieged.

Upa-rodha, as, m. surrounding, blockading; obstruction, impediment, opposition, check, refusal; trouble, disturbance; binding, tying, taking hold of; protection, favour. — Uparodha-kārin, ī, iṇī, i, causing trouble, obstructing.

Upa-rodhaka, am, n. an inner room, a private apartment.

Upa-rodhana, am, n. obstruction, impediment.

Upa-rodhin, ī, inī, i, obstructing, impeding; obstructed, impeded.

उपरुह् upa-ruh, cl. 1. P. -rohati, -roḍhum, to ascend, rise.

Upa-ruhya, ind. having ascended.

उपरूपक upa-rūpaka, am, n. a drama of an inferior class, of which eighteen are enumerated.

उपल upala, as, m. (connected with upara, q. v.), a rock or stone; a precious stone or jewel; (ā), f. the upper and smaller mill-stone which rests on the drishad; refined or candied sugar; [cf. Gr. ὄπαλος; Lat. opalus.] — Upala-prakshin, ī, iṇī, i, Ved. arranging stones; (Sāy.) throwing grain on the mill-stone. — Upala-bhedin, ī, m., N. of a plant.

Upalaka, as, m. a stone.

उपलक्ष् upa-laksh, cl. 10. P. A. -lakshayati, -te, -yitum, to look at, observe, behold; to regard as, value as; to imply in addition: Pass. -lakshyate, to be observed &c.; to be likely.

Upa-lakshaka, as, ā, am, observing, designating.

Upa-lakshaṇa, am, n. looking at; observation; designation; implying something that has not been expressed, implying something in addition or any analogous object where only one is specified, using a term in a generic sense, metaphorical or elliptical expression, synecdoche of a part for the whole, of an individual for the species or of a quality for that in which it resides; mark. — Upalakshaṇa-tva, am, n. the being implied.

Upa-lakshayitavya, as, ā, am, to be observed.

Upa-lakshita, as, ā, am, comprehended, discovered, included, implied, metaphorically expressed, understood, characterized.

Upa-lakshya, as, ā, am, inferable; (as), m. a prop, stay, support, asylum; an inference.

उपलधिप्रिय upaladhipriya, as, m. the Bos grunniens; perhaps a wrong form for bāladhi-priya, 'valued for its tail.'

उपलभ् upa-labh, cl. 1. A. -labhate, -labdhum, to acquire, receive, accept, obtain, find; to conceive, become pregnant; to perceive, observe, hear, understand; [cf. Gr. ὑπολαμβάνω.]

Upa-labdha, as, ā, am, obtained, received; conceived; perceived, understood, known, guessed. — Upalabdha-sukha, as, ā, am, one who has experienced pleasure. — Upalabdhārtha (°dha-ar°), as, ā, am, having the meaning understood; (ā), f. a tale, a true or probable story.

Upa-labdhavya, as, ā, am, to be observed.

Upa-labdhi, is, f. obtaining, acquisition, gain; observation, perception, knowledge (especially religious), understanding, mind; a guess; appearance, perceptibility; [cf. Gr. ὑπόληψις.] — Upalabdhimat, ān, atī, at, perceptible, intelligible.

1. upa-labhya, as, ā, am, obtainable, perceivable, to be understood.

2. upa-labhya, ind. having perceived or observed.

Upa-labhyamāna, as, ā, am, being perceived. — Upalabhyamāna-tva, am, n. the being known.

Upa-lambha, as, m. acquisition; apprehension, conception, comprehension otherwise than from memory.

Upa-lambhaka, as, ā, am, causing to observe, reminding.

Upa-lambhana, am, n. apprehension.

Upa-lambhya, as, ā, am, obtainable, to be acquired; respectable, commendable, praiseworthy.

Upa-lābha, as, m., Ved. seizing or taking hastily.

Upa-lipsā, f. desire of obtaining.

Upa-lipsita, as, ā, am, wishing to take or seize.

Upa-lipsu, us, us, u, wishing to obtain or know.

उपलालिका upalālikā, f. thirst, oppression (?).

उपलिङ्ग upa-liṅga, as, m. a portent, a natural phenomenon considered as boding evil.

उपलिप् upa-lip, cl. 6. P. A. -limpati, -te, -leptum, to defile, anoint, smear, besmear: Caus. -lepayati, -yitum, to cause to anoint or besmear.

Upa-lipta, as, ā, am, anointed, smeared, plastered.

Upa-lepa, as, m. smearing, anointing, plastering; obstruction, the being concealed; becoming deadened or dull.

Upa-lepana, am, n. smearing, anointing, plastering; an ointment, an unguent.

Upa-lepin, ī, inī, i, serving as an ointment; anointing, smearing, obstructing.

उपलिप्सा upa-lipsā. See upa-labh above.

उपलेख upalekha, as, m. (fr. rt. likh with upa), title of a grammatical work connected with the Prātiśākhyas.

उपवक्तृ upa-vaktṛi, tā, m., Ved. one who directs and animates by his words; animating.

उपवङ्ग upa-vaṅga, ās, m. pl., N. of a country.

उपवञ्च् upa-vañć, Caus. -vañćayati, -yitum, to deceive; to repudiate.

उपवट upa-vaṭa, as, m. the tree Buchanania Latifolia.

उपवद् upa-vad, cl. 1. A. -vadate, -ditum, to talk over, conciliate; to flatter, cajole.

Upa-vāda, as, m., Ved. censure, blame.

Upa-vādin, ī, inī, i, Ved. censuring, blaming.

उपवन upa-vana, am, n. a small forest, a grove, a garden; a planted forest.

उपवर्ण् upa-varṇ, cl. 10. P. -varṇayati, -yitum, to tell or describe copiously.

Upa-varṇa, as, m. minute description, detail.

Upa-varṇana, am, n. description, minute description, delineation.

Upa-varṇita, as, ā, am, described.

उपवर्त upa-varta. See under upa-vrit.

उपवर्ष upa-varsha, as, m., N. of a son of Saṅkara-svāmin and younger brother of Varsha, author of writings on the Mīmāṅsā philosophy.

उपवल्गितनयन upavalgita-nayana, as, ā, am, swollen or dimmed with tears; (a various reading has apavalgita-°.)

उपवल्लिका upa-vallikā, f., N. of a plant.

उपवल्ह upa-valha, as, m., Ved. emulation, rivalry.

उपवस् upa-vas, cl. 1. P. -vasati, -vastum, to dwell in or at; to abide in a state of abstinence, abstain from food, to fast: Caus. -vāsayati, -yitum, to cause to fast.

Upa-vasatha, as, m., Ved. a fast-day, day of preparation for the Soma sacrifice, the day preceding a Soma sacrifice, day of a Soma sacrifice; a village (?).

Upavasathīya or upavasathya, as, ā, am, Ved. selected for an Upavasatha (as a day), belonging to or prepared for a Soma sacrifice.

Upa-vasta, am, n. a fast, fasting.

Upa-vastṛi, tā, trī, tṛi, one who fasts.

Upa-vāsa, as, am, m. n. a fast, fasting (as a religious act comprising abstinence from all sensual gratification, from perfumes, flowers, unguents, ornaments, betel, music, dancing, &c.); kindling a sacred fire, a fire altar.

Upa-vāsaka, am, n. a fast, fasting.

Upa-vāsin, ī, inī, i, fasting, one who observes a fast.

Uposhaṇa, uposhita, uposhya. See p. 173.

उपवह् upa-vah, cl. 1. P. A. -vahati, -te, -voḍhum, to bear or lead near, to lead towards, lead back; to bring about, commence.

Upa-vaha, am, n., Ved. anything placed on the neck of an ox under the yoke, to raise it to the right level for a yoke-fellow of greater height.

Upa-vāhana, am, n. carrying, bringing back.

Upa-vāhin, ī, inī, i, flowing or streaming towards.

Upa-vāhya, as, ā, am, to be drawn or led near to; (as), m. a king's elephant, any royal vehicle.

Upohyamāna, as, ā, am, being brought near, being commenced; [cf. upoh, fr. which this participle may also be derived.]

उपवा upa-vā, f., Ved. blowing at.

उपवाक 1. upa-vāka, as, m. (fr. rt. vać with upa), Ved. addressing, speaking to, praise.

Upavākya or upa-vāćya, as, ā, am, Ved. to be addressed or praised.

उपवाक 2. upavāka, as, ā, m. f., Ved., Indra-grain (see Indra-yava).

उपवाजन upa-vājana, am, n. (said to be derived fr. rt. vā), a fan.

उपवाद upa-vāda. See under upa-vad.

उपवासन upa-vāsana, am, n. (rt. 2. vas), Ved. a dress, a garment, a cover.

उपविद् *upa-vid, t,* f., Ved. investigating, inquiring into.

Upa-vidyā, f. profane science, inferior sort of knowledge.

Upa-veda, as, m. secondary knowledge, a class of writings subordinate or appended to the four Vedas. According to the Bhāgavata-Purāṇa their number is four, viz. *Āyur-veda, Dhanur-veda, Gāndharva-veda,* and *Sthāpatya-veda,* or medicine, military art, music, and mechanics.

उपविन्दु *upa-vindu, us,* m., N. of a man.

उपविपाशम् *upa-vipāśam,* ind. at or near the river Vipāśā.

उपविश् *upa-viś,* cl. 6. P. *-viśati, -veshṭum,* to sit down, take a seat; to pitch a camp; to enter; to seize, take possession of: Caus. *-veśayati, -yitum,* to cause to sit down.

Upa-viśya, ind. having sat down, sitting down.

Upa-vishṭa, as, ā, am, seated, sitting; arrived, entered.

Upa-veśa, as, m. sitting down, sitting, resting; fixing one's mind upon, being attached to; voiding by stool.

Upa-veśana, am, n. sitting down, resting; causing to sit down; devoting one's self to; voiding by stool.

Upa-veśita, as, ā, am, made to sit; seated.

Upa-veśin, ī, inī, i, sitting down; fixing one's mind upon, devoting one's self to.

Upa-veśya, ind. having seated or caused to sit.

Upa-veshṭṛi, ṭā, ṭrī, ṭṛi, he who sits, a sitter, sitting down.

उपविष *upa-visha, am,* n. factitious poison; a narcotic, any deterious drug, as opium, datura, &c.; (*ā*), f. a plant, Atis, Aconitum or Betula. See *ati-vishā.*

उपवीक्ष् *upa-vīksh (-vi-īksh),* cl. 1. A. *-vīkshate, -shitum,* to look at or towards.

उपवीज् *upa-vīj,* cl. 10. P. *-vījayati, -yitum,* to blow upon, fan.

उपवीणय *upavīṇaya,* nom. (fr. *upa-vīṇā*) P. *-vīṇayati, -yitum,* to play on the Vīṇā or Indian lute before or in the presence of any one.

उपवीत *upa-vīta, am,* n. (fr. rt. *vye* with *upa*), investiture with the sacred thread; the thread or cord worn by the first three classes of the Hindūs over the left shoulder and under the right arm.

Upavītin, ī, inī, i, wearing the string in the usual manner, or over the left shoulder and under the right arm.

उपवीर *upa-vīra, am,* n. a kind of demon.

उपवृ *upa-vṛi,* Intens. P., Ved. *-varvarti,* to put or place over or upon.

उपवृंह् *upa-vṛiṇh* or *-vṛih,* Caus. P. *-vṛiṇhayati, -yitum,* to increase.

Upa-varha, as, m. a pillow; [cf. *upa-barha,* p. 165.]

Upa-vṛiṇhaṇa, am, n. increasing, increase, collection.

Upa-vṛiṇhita, as, ā, am, increased, collected from, possessed of.

उपवृत् *upa-vṛit,* cl. 1. A. *-vartate, -titum,* to go towards, approach; to return.

Upa-varta, as, m. a particular high number.

Upa-vartana, am, n. a place for exercise, a country inhabited or not; a division, a district or Pergana; a kingdom.

Upa-vṛitti, is, f. motion towards.

उपवेणा *upa-veṇā,* f., N. of a river.

उपवेद *upa-veda.* See under *upa-vid.*

उपवेशि *upaveśi, is,* m., N. of a man.

उपवेष *upa-vesha, as,* m. (fr. rt. *vish* with *upa*), Ved. a stick (of green wood) used for stirring the sacrificial fire.

उपवेष्ट् *upa-vesht,* cl. 1. A. *-veshṭate, -ṭitum,* to surround, cover, dress.

उपवैणव *upavaiṇava, am,* n. (fr. *upa-veṇu?*), the three periods of the day, morning, midday, and evening.

उपव्याख्यान *upa-vyākhyāna, am,* n. subsidiary or supplementary explanation or interpretation.

उपव्याघ्र *upa-vyāghra, as,* m. the small hunting leopard.

उपशक् *upa-śak,* Desid. P. *-śikshati,* to learn.

Upa-śikshamāṇa, as, ā, am, training.

Upa-śikshā, f. learning, desire of learning, training.

Upa-śikshita, as, ā, am, learnt, studied, trained.

उपशम् *upa-śam,* cl. 4. P. *-śāmyati, -śamitum,* to become calm or quiet, to cease: Caus. *-śāmayati, -yitum,* to calm, tranquillize, appease, pacify, assuage, mitigate, make quiet, extinguish, kill.

Upa-śama, as, m. becoming quiet, assuagement, ceasing, stopping, cessation, relaxation, intermission; tranquillity, calmness, patience. — *Upaśama-śīla, as, ā, am,* placid, calm.

Upa-śamaka, as, ā, am, calming, affording repose, making patient.

Upa-śamana, am, n. quieting, calming, appeasing, mitigation, ceasing to burn, extinction; an anodyne.

Upa-śamanīya, as, ā, am, to be made quiet, to be appeased.

Upa-śānta, as, ā, am, calmed, appeased, pacified; calm, tranquil; intermitted, diminished. — *Upaśāntātman* (°*ta-āt*°), *ā, ā, a,* one whose mind is pacified, placid.

Upa-śānti, is, f. cessation, intermission, remission; appeasing, allaying, assuaging; abatement; tranquillity, calm.

Upaśāntin, ī, inī, i, appeased, tame, tranquil, calm; (*ī*), m. a tame elephant.

उपशय *upa-śaya,* &c. See *upa-śī* below.

उपशरदम् *upa-śaradam,* ind. at the time of autumn.

उपशल्य *upa-śalya, am,* n. an open place before a town or village (lit. 'a place where archers practice'?).

उपशाखा *upa-śākhā,* f. a secondary branch.

उपशान्त्व् *upa-śāntv,* cl. 10. P. *-śāntvayati, -yitum,* to appease, console, tranquillize.

Upa-śāntvana, am, n. appeasing, making quiet.

उपशाल *upa-śāla, am,* n. a place near a house, a court before a house; (*am*), ind. near a house.

उपशास्त्र *upa-śāstra, am,* n. a minor science or treatise.

उपशिक्षा *upa-śikshā.* See *upa-śak* above.

उपशिङ्घ् *upa-śiṅgh,* cl. 1. P. *-śiṅghati, -ghitum,* to kiss.

Upa-śiṅhana, am, n. (fr. rt. *śiṅgh* with *upa*), anything given to smell at (in medicine).

उपशिष्य *upa-śishya, as,* m. the pupil of a pupil.

उपशी *upa-śī,* cl. 2. A. *-śete, -śayitum,* to lie near.

Upa-śaya, as, ā, am, Ved. lying by the side of, lying down; productive of happiness or rest; (*ā*), f. a prepared piece of clay, i. e. *mṛid;* (*as*), m. lying by the side of; ascertainment of disease or diagnosis by the effect of certain articles of food or medicine; allaying disease by diet, regimen, &c.

Upa-śāya, as, m. turn or rotation for sleeping with (another).

Upa-śāyin, ī, inī, i, lying near to; lying, sleeping; going to bed; allaying, tranquillizing, what calms &c.; (in medicine) composing, narcotic. — *Upa-śāyi-tā,* f. or *upaśāyi-tva, am,* n. tranquillizing, calming; secondary means of cure, as diet &c.

उपशुनम् *upa-śunam,* ind. near a dog.

उपशुभ् *upa-śubh,* Caus. P. *-śobhayati, -yitum,* to adorn, ornament.

Upa-śobhana, am, n. adorning, ornamenting.

Upa-śobhita, as, ā, am, ornamented, adorned.

उपशुष् *upa-śush,* Caus. P. *-śoshayati, -yitum,* to make dry, dry up.

Upa-śoshaṇa, as, ā, am, drying up.

उपश्च्युत् *upa-śćyut* or *-śćut,* cl. 1. P. *-śćyotati, -titum,* to ooze or trickle down, fall in drops.

उपश्रि *upa-śri,* cl. 1. A. *-śrayate, -yitum,* to approach, go towards, go against; to attack; to surround.

Upa-śrī, f. a covering, anything thrown over.

उपश्रु *upa-śru,* cl. 5. P. *-śṛiṇoti, -śrotum,* to listen to, give ear to, to hear.

Upa-śruta, as, ā, am, listened to; promised, agreed.

Upa-śruti, is, f. giving ear to, listening to; range of hearing; a supernatural voice heard at night and personified as a nocturnal deity revealing the future; judicial astrology, aspect of the stars, fortune-telling; promise, assent.

Upa-śrutya, ind. listening to.

Upa-śrotṛi, tā, trī, tṛi, a listener, hearer, listening to.

उपश्लिष् *upa-ślish,* cl. 4. P. *-ślishyati, -śleshṭum,* to embrace: Caus. *-śleshayati, -yitum,* to cause to lay hold of, bring near, place at hand.

Upa-ślishṭa, as, ā, am, placed near, contiguous, adjoining.

Upa-ślesha, as, m. juxta-position, contiguity, an embrace.

उपश्लोकय *upaślokaya,* nom. (fr. *upa-śloka*) P. *-ślokayati, -yitum,* to praise in ślokas.

उपश्वस *upa-śvasa, as, ā, am,* Ved. sounding, roaring.

उपष्टुत् *upa-shṭut,* ind. (fr. rt. *stu* with *upa*), Ved. at command, (ready) at one's call.

उपसंयम *upa-saṃyama, as,* m. the end of the world.

उपसंयोग *upa-saṃyoga, as,* m. (rt. *yuj*), a secondary or subordinate connection, a modification.

उपसंरोह *upa-saṃroha, as,* m. (rt. *ruh*), growing over, growing together, cicatrizing.

उपसंवाद *upa-saṃvāda, as,* m. (rt. *vad*), agreeing together, agreement.

उपसंव्यान *upa-saṃvyāna, am,* n. an under garment.

उपसंव्रज् *upa-saṃ-vraj,* cl. 1. P. *-vrajati, -jitum,* to enter, go towards, approach.

उपसंस्कृ *upa-saṅs-kṛi (-sam-kṛi),* cl. 5. 8. P. A. *-kṛiṇoti, -ṇute, -karoti, -kurute, -kartum,* to prepare (as a meal); to ornament.

Upa-saṅskṛita, as, ā, am, cooked, dressed (as a meal).

उपसंहृ *upa-saṃ-hṛi,* cl. 1. P. A. *-harati, -te, -hartum,* to draw together, bring together, collect, to contract; to withdraw, take away, withhold.

Upa-saṃharaṇa, am, n. withdrawing, taking away; excluding; refusing, withholding; attacking, invading.

Upa-saṃharat, an, antī, at, withdrawing, taking away; refusing, excepting; going against, invading.

Upa-saṃhāra, as, m. drawing towards one's self,

drawing in or together, contracting; drawing away, taking away, withholding, excepting, excluding; collection, assemblage, winding or summing up, a compendium, brevity, conciseness, résumé; perfection; subduing, destruction, death, end; attacking, invading; (in logic) refutation; N. of the fourth section of the Vāyu-purāṇa.

Upa-saṃhārin, ī, iṇī, i, comprehending; exclusive; non-exclusive (?).

Upa-saṃhṛita, as, ā, am, withheld, refused, denied; excepted; excluded, compressed, comprehended, dead.

Upa-saṃhṛiti, is, f. comprehension, seizing, taking; a compound expressive of various meanings (?).

उपसङ्कॢप् *upa-san-klṛip* (*-sam-k°*), Caus. P. *-kalpayati, -yitum*, to fix, deposit, settle; to appoint, choose.

Upa-sanklṛipta, as, ā, am, placed over, built over.

उपसङ्क्रम् *upa-san-kram* (*-sam-k°*), cl. 1. P. A., 4. P. *-krāmati, -kramate* (ep. also *-krāmate*), *-krāmyati, -kramitum*, to go near to, approach: Caus. P. *-kramayati, -yitum*, to cause to approach.

उपसङ्क्षेप *upa-sankshepa, as*, m. (rt. *kship*), a concise abridgment, a summary; an abstract, compendium.

उपसङ्ख्यान *upa-sankhyāna, am*, n. (rt. *khyā*), annumeration, adding, addition; further enumeration; (in gram.) a substitute in form or sense, a consignificant term or affix.

उपसङ्गम् *upa-san-gam* (*-sam-g°*), cl. 1. P. *-gaććhati, -gantum*, to approach together, join in approaching, to enter into any condition or relation.

उपसङ्ग्रह् *upa-san-grah* (*-sam-g°*), cl. 9. P. A. *-gṛihṇāti, -ṇīte* (Ved. *-gṛibhṇāti, -ṇīte*), *-grahītum*, to clasp or embrace; to take upon one's self, to experience, suffer; to receive, accept; to seize, take into custody; to win over, conciliate, make favourable.

Upa-sangṛihya, ind. having clasped, having taken, holding.

Upa-sangraha, as, m. clasping (e. g. the feet of a person as a mark of great respect), respectful salutation; polite address; obeisance; bringing together, collecting, joining.

Upa-sangrahaṇa, am, n. respectful salutation (by clasping the feet of a person with the hands), polite address.

Upa-sangrāhya, as, ā, am, to be saluted reverentially, respectable, venerable.

उपसञ्चर् *upa-saṅ-ćar* (*-sam-ć°*), cl. 1. P. A. *-ćarati, -te, -ćaritum*, Ved. *-ritave*, &c., to enter, approach; to have sexual intercourse with.

Upa-saṅćara, as, m. manœuvre, flattery (?).

उपसद् 1. *upa-sad*, cl. 1. 6. P. *-sīdati, -sattum*, to sit near to, to go near to, approach; to worship; to obtain.

Upa-satti, is, f. connection with, union; service, worship; gift, donation.

Upa-sattṛi, tā, trī, tṛi, one who approaches, a worshipper; an inhabitant.

2. *upa-sad, t, t, t*, Ved. one who goes near to, serving, attending, waiting upon; (*t*), f. siege, assault; laying up, accumulating; service; N. of a ceremony lasting several days and forming part of the Jyotishṭoma ceremony. — *Upasad-van, ā, ā, a*, Ved. one who has attendants or worshippers, one who is worshipped. — *Upasad-vratin, ī, inī, i*, observing the rules of the Upasad, viz. drinking milk in certain quantities, sleeping on the bare earth, chastity, silence, &c.

Upa-sada, as, ā, am, going near to; (*as*), m. approach; gift, donation; N. of a ceremony. See 2. *upa-sad*.

Upa-sadana, am, n. approaching, going to (a teacher), sitting near (a master), becoming a pupil; going near to, being present at, partaking of; a neighbouring abode, a neighbourhood.

Upa-sadī, f., Ved. attendants collectively (?).

Upa-sadya, as, ā, am, to be attended on or worshipped.

Upa-sanna, as, ā, am, approached, approximate; worshipped. — *Upasanna-tā*, f. or *upasanna-tva, am*, n. proximity, approach.

Upa-sādita, as, ā, am, approached, come near to.

उपसन्तन् *upa-san-tan* (*-sam-t°*), cl. 8. P. A. *-tanoti, -nute, -nitum*, to bring into immediate connection with.

Upa-santāna, as, m. immediate connection, joining together; a descendant.

उपसन्धा *upa-san-dhā* (*-sam-dhā*), cl. 3. P. A. *-dadhāti, -dhatte, -dhātum*, to put together, add, increase; to join, connect, cause to partake of; to aim at.

Upa-saṃhita, as, ā, am, connected with, furnished with, accompanied or surrounded by; having regard or reference to, attached to one another.

उपसन्ध्यम् *upa-sandhyam*, ind. near or towards evening.

उपसन्न्यास *upa-sannyāsa, as*, m. (rt. 2. *as*), laying down, giving up.

उपसमश् *upa-sam-aś*, cl. 5. P. A. *-aśnoti, -nute, -śitum*, to reach, obtain.

उपसमस् *upa-sam-as*, cl. 4. P. *-asyati, -situm*, to put or place upon.

उपसमाकृ *upa-sam-ā-kṛi*, cl. 5. 8. P. A. *-kṛiṇoti, -ṇute, -karoti, -kurute, -kartum*, to connect, combine together.

उपसमाधा *upa-sam-ā-dhā*, cl. 3. P. A. *-dadhāti, -dhatte, -dhātum*, to put on (as wood on a fire), to place in order, arrange.

Upa-samādhāna, am, n. placing in or on, laying one upon the another.

उपसमाहार्य *upa-samāhārya, as, ā, am* (rt. *hṛi*), to be brought together, to be arranged.

उपसमि *upa-sam-i*, cl. 2. P. *-eti, -tum*, to approach together.

उपसमिद् *upa-samid* or *upa-samidham*, ind. near the fire-wood.

उपसमूह् *upa-sam-ūh*, cl. 1. P. *-ūhati, -hitum*, to draw together, contract, to collect together, to bring near.

उपसमे *upa-sam-e* (*-ā-i*), cl. 2. P. *-aiti, -tum*, to meet, meet with (with acc.).

उपसम्पद् *upa-sam-pad*, cl. 4. A. *-padyate, -pattum*, to come to, arrive at: Caus. P. *-pādayati, -yitum*, to bring near to, lead near, to give, grant; (with Buddhists) to receive into the order of priests, to ordain.

Upa-sampatti, is, f. approaching, arriving at, entering into any condition.

Upa-sampanna, as, ā, am, arrived at; gained, obtained; furnished with; familiar with; finished; enough, sufficient; dead, deceased; immolated, sacrificed as a victim &c.; dressed, cooked.

उपसम्प्रछ् *upa-sam-praćh*, cl. 6. P. *-pṛiććhati, -prashṭum*, to ask a person about anything.

उपसम्प्राप् *upa-sam-prāp* (*-pra-āp*), cl. 5. P. *-āpnoti, -ptum*, to reach, obtain, approach.

Upa-samprāpya, ind. having arrived at.

उपसम्भाषा *upa-sambhāshā*, f. talking over, friendly persuasion.

उपसर *upa-sara*. See *upa-sṛi* next col.

उपसर्ग *upa-sarga*. See *upa-sṛij* next col.

उपसर्पण *upa-sarpaṇa*. See *upa-sṛip* next col.

उपसान्त्व् *upa-sāntv*. See *upa-śāntv*.

उपसि *upasi*, ind., Ved. in the lap, on the hip.

उपसुन्द *upa-sunda, as*, m., N. of a Daitya, son of Nikumbha and younger brother of Sunda.

उपसूर्यक *upa-sūryaka, am*, n. the disk of the sun.

उपसृ *upa-sṛi*, cl. 1. and Ved. 3. P. *-sarati, -sisarti, -sartum*, to go towards, approach, go against, attack; to have intercourse (as a woman with a man).

Upa-sara, as, ā or *ī, am*, who or what approaches; (*as*), m. approaching (a cow); the first pregnancy or impregnation of a cow.

Upa-saraṇa, am, n. going or flowing towards, rapid flowing of the blood towards the heart in sickness; what is approached as a refuge.

Upa-sartavya, as, ā, am, to be approached for help, to be had recourse to.

Upa-saryā, f. 'to be approached,' a cow fit for a bull.

Upa-sārya, as, ā, am, to be approached or gone to.

Upa-sṛitya, ind. having gone towards, having approached.

उपसृज् *upa-sṛij*, cl. 6. P. *-sṛijati, -srashṭum*, to pour out or on, to offer, make an oblation; to join, attach, connect with; to beset with, oppress; to eclipse.

Upa-sarga, as, m. addition; trouble, misfortune; a portent, a natural phenomenon supposed to forbode future evil, an eclipse; a disease, possession by an evil spirit; change occasioned by any disease; indication or symptom of death; a disease superinduced on another; an inseparable particle or preposition prefixed to roots; see *karma-pravaćanīya*. — *Upasarga-vṛitti, is, is, i*, having the character of a preposition, to be treated like one.

Upa-sarjana, am, n. pouring on; misfortune, inauspicious phenomenon, portent, eclipse; passing by, leaving, eclipsing; any person or thing subordinate or subsidiary to another, a substitute, a representative; (in gram.) a word which by composition or derivation loses its original independance, while it also determines the sense of another word; for instance, in the derivative *Aupiśala*, a pupil of Apiśali, *Apiśali* has become the *upasarjana;* so also in the compound *rāja-purusha* (fr. *rājan* and *purusha*) the first loses its independant character when compounded and is therefore the *upasarjana;* (*ī*), f. an infusion.

Upa-sṛishṭa, as, ā, am, joined, attached, connected to or with, attended by or accompanied with; seized or possessed by (evil demons &c.); eclipsed, as the sun or moon; furnished with an *upasarga* or preposition (e. g. the root *dā* with *ā* prefixed is said to be *upasṛishṭa*); (*am*), n. coition, copulation.

उपसृप् *upa-sṛip*, cl. 1. P. A. *-sarpati, -te, -sarptum* or *-sraptum*, to creep near, approach; move onward, attack; [cf. ὑφέρπω.]

Upa-sarpa, as, m. approach, access, following a person.

Upa-sarpaṇa, am, n. approaching, advancing towards.

Upa-sarpin, ī, iṇī, i, creeping near, approaching.

Upa-sarpya, ind. having approached.

उपसेक्तृ *upa-sektṛi, tā*, m. (rt. *sić*), Ved. one who sprinkles or pours one thing on another.

Upa-sećana, as, ā, am, pouring or sprinkling one thing on another; (*am*), n. pouring or sprinkling upon, watering; infusion, juice; (*ī*), f. a ladle or cup for pouring.

उपसेन *upa-sena, as*, m., N. of a pupil of Śākya-muni.

उपसेव् *upa-sev*, cl. 1. A. *-sevate, -vitum*, to serve, worship, honour; to practise, pursue, cultivate, study, make use of, be addicted to, frequent, inhabit.

Upa-sevaka, as, ā, am, worshipping, following, practising.

Upa-sevana, am, n. worshipping, honouring; service, addiction to; using, enjoying.

Upa-sevā, f. service, worship, honour.

Upa-sevin, ī, inī, i, serving, worshipping, honouring; liking, pleased with.

उपस्कृ *upa-s-kṛi* (*s* inserted, see *upa-kṛi*), cl. 8. A. *-kurute, -kartum,* to prepare, elaborate, perfect, adorn, &c.

Upas-kara, as, m. any article which serves to make complete, an ingredient, condiment, spice or seasoning (mustard, pepper, &c.); an appurtenance, utensil, implement or instrument; an article of household use (as a broom, a basket, &c.), apparatus; blame, censure.

Upas-kāra, as, m. anything additional, a supplement.

Upas-kṛita, as, ā, am, prepared; blamed, censured.

Upas-kṛiti, is, f. a supplement, anything additional.

उपस्तम्भ् *upa-stambh,* cl. 5. 9. P. *-stabhnoti, -nāti, -stabdhum,* to stay, prop, support.

Upa-stambha, as, m. (also written *upa-shṭambha?*), stay, support, support of life (as food, sleep, and government of the passions); encouragement, incitement; base, basis, ground, occasion.

Upa-stambhaka, as, ā, am, supporting, promoting, encouraging.

Upa-stambhana, am, n., Ved. a support.

उपस्तरण *upa-staraṇa.* See *upa-stṛi* below.

उपस्ति *upa-sti, is,* m. (fr. rt. 1. *as* with *upa*), Ved. an attendant, a follower, a servant, a subject.

उपस्तु *upa-stu,* cl. 2. P. A. *-stauti* or *-staviti, -stute* or *-stuvīte, -stotum,* to praise, invoke.

Upa-stut, t, f., Ved. invocation, praise, invitation.

Upa-stuta, as, ā, am, invoked, praised; (*as*), m., N. of a Ṛishi.

Upa-stuti, is, f., Ved. invocation, praise.

Upa-stutya, as, ā, am, to be praised or invoked.

उपस्तृ *upa-stṛi* or *-stṝ,* cl. 5. 9. P. A. *-stṛiṇoti, -ṇute, -ṇāti, -ṇīte, -startum, -ritum* or *-rītum,* to spread, arrange, set in order; [cf. Lat. *substerno.*]

Upa-staraṇa, am, n., Ved. spreading out, scattering; what is spread out; a covering.

Upa-stir, f., Ved. scattering about, spreading; what is spread; a covering.

Upa-stīrṇa, as, ā, am, spread out, arranged.

उपस्त्री *upa-strī,* f. a concubine.

उपस्था 1. *upa-sthā,* cl. 1. P. A. *-tishṭhati, -te, -sthātum,* to stand near, stand by the side of in order to serve, wait on, attend on, serve (with acc.); to be or remain near; stay with; to come near, approach; to approach a god with prayer, worship; to stand under in order to support; to approach for intercourse, have intercourse with; to approach for assistance; to approach with hostile intentions, attack; to occur, come to pass, arise, be present; to meet with, obtain; to fall to one's share, come to the possession of; to conciliate: Caus. P. *-sthāpayati, -yitum,* to cause to stand near, to provide, present, furnish with, place upon or near; to produce.

Upa-stha, as, m. the lap, middle part in general, a secure place; (*as, am*), m. n. the organs of generation, especially of a woman; the anus; the haunch or hip; (*as, ā, am*), near, proximate; *upastham kṛi,* to sit down with the legs bent, make a lap; *upasthe kṛi,* to take on one's lap. — *Upastha-daghna, as, ī, am,* reaching to the lap. — *Upastha-nigraha, as,* m. restraint of sensual appetite; continence. — *Upastha-pattra, as,* m. the Indian fig tree. — *Upastha-sad, t, t, t,* Ved. sitting in the lap.

2. *upa-sthā, ās, ās, am,* Ved. standing on.

Upa-sthātṛi, tā, m. an attendant, servant.

Upa-sthāna, am, n. standing near, presence, proximity, nearness; approaching, appearing, coming into the presence of, introducing one's self; worshipping, waiting on; attendance; obeisance; abode; an assembly; any object approached with respect, a sanctuary; obtaining, getting; *upasthānam kṛi,* to give access or scope for action. — *Upasthāna-śālā,* f. the assembly-room of a Buddhist monastery.

Upa-sthānīya, as, ā, am, to be stayed with or near, to be kept near; to be attended on or served.

Upa-sthāpaka, as, ā, am, placing or bringing near, causing to obtain; explaining, teaching, a teacher.

Upa-sthāpana, am, n. placing near; attendance, service.

Upa-sthāpanīya or *upa-sthāpayitavya, as, ā, am,* to be placed near.

Upa-sthāpita, as, ā, am, placed near, attended.

Upa-sthāpya, as, ā, am, to be placed near, to be produced or made visible.

Upa-sthāya, ind. having approached, having brought near to or assembled.

Upa-sthāyaka, as, m. a servant; (with Buddhists) a follower of Buddha.

Upa-sthāyin, ī, inī, i, standing near, being present, appearing.

Upa-sthāvara, as, ā, am, Ved. stopping, not moving.

Upa-sthita, as, ā, am, approached, arrived, arisen, appeared, present; staying by or near at hand, impending, ready; received, obtained, gained; accomplished, taken place, happened; caused, occasioned; felt; known; clean, cleansed; (in Ved. gram.) in the Pada text followed by the particle *iti;* (*am*), n. the particle *iti* used in this manner; the position of words before and after *iti;* (*ā*), f., N. of a metre of four lines of ten syllables each; N. of another metre of four lines of eleven syllables each. — *Upasthita-pracupita,* N. of a metre consisting of four lines and fifty-one syllables. — *Upasthita-vaktṛi, tā,* m. a ready speaker, an eloquent man. — *Upasthita-samprahāra, as, ā, am,* about to engage in a battle, having battle at hand.

Upa-sthiti, is, f. standing near, approach, presence, proximity, arrival; obtaining, getting; effecting, accomplishing; remaining.

Upa-stheya, as, ā, am, to be attended to, to be worshipped.

उपस्नेह *upa-sneha, as,* m. (rt. *snih*), moistening, attracting moisture.

उपस्पिज् *upa-spij* (only used in acc. *-jam*), Ved. inconsiderate curiosity or jest (?).

उपस्पृश् 1. *upa-spṛiś,* cl. 6. P. *-spṛiśati, -sprashṭum* or *-sparshṭum,* to touch (water); to wash or rinse the mouth; to sip water, to sprinkle; to wash off; to gnash (the teeth).

Upa-sparśa, as, m. touching, contact; washing, bathing, ablution; rinsing the mouth, sipping water and ejecting it.

Upa-sparśana, am, n. touching; bathing; rinsing the mouth.

Upa-sparśin, ī, inī, i, touching, sipping water.

2. *upa-spṛiś, k, k, k,* Ved. touching.

Upa-spṛiśya, ind. having sipped water.

Upa-spṛishṭa, as, ā, am, touched, sipped.

उपस्मृति *upa-smṛiti, is,* f. a minor law-book; eighteen such books are mentioned.

उपस्रवण *upa-sravaṇa, am,* n. (rt. *sru*), flowing, the periodical flow of a woman.

उपस्वत्व *upasva-tva, am,* n. revenue, profit, what is derived from land or other capital.

Upasvā-vat, ān, m., N. of a son of Satrājit.

उपस्वेद *upa-sveda, as,* m. (rt. *svid*), moisture.

उपहन् *upa-han,* cl. 2. P. *-hanti, -tum,* to kill, injure, destroy, disturb, vex; to waste.

Upa-hata, as, ā, am, injured, impaired, evilly affected by; struck by lightning &c.; pained, hurt; destroyed; infected, polluted, vitiated; impure. — *Upahata-dṛiś, k, k, k,* dazzled, blinded. — *Upahata-dhī, īs, īs, i,* infatuated. — *Upahatātman* (°*ta-āt*°), *ā, ā, a,* agitated in mind, mentally affected as by passion.

Upahataka, as, ā, am, ill-fated, unfortunate, unlucky.

Upa-hatnu, us, us, u, Ved. assailing.

Upa-hatyā, f. dazzling of the eyes.

Upa-hantavya, as, ā, am, to be killed.

Upa-hantṛi, tā, trī, tṛi, having a contrary effect, disturbing.

उपहरण *upa-haraṇa.* See under *upa-hṛi.*

उपहस् *upa-has,* cl. 1. P. *-hasati, -situm,* to laugh at, deride.

Upa-hasita, am, n. satirical laughter, laughing; (*as, ā, am*), laughed at, derided.

Upa-hasvan, ā, ā, a, Ved. laughing at, a derider.

Upa-hāsa, as, m. fun, play, ridicule, derision, laughing at any one, satirical laughter. — *Upahāsāspada* (°*sa-ās*°), *am,* n. a laughing-stock.

Upa-hāsaka, as, ā, am, ridiculing others, jocose; (*as*), m. a jester.

Upa-hāsya, as, ā, am, to be laughed at, ridiculous, laughable. — *Upahāsya-tā,* f. ridiculousness. — *Upahāsya-tām gam,* to expose one's self to laughter.

उपहस्तिका *upahastikā,* f. (fr. *upa-hasta*), a small bag or box containing condiments or betel.

उपहा *upa-hā,* cl. 3. A. *-jihīte, -hātum,* to go down, descend.

उपहालक *upahālaka, ās,* m. pl., N. of a country, part of the peninsula of India.

उपहिंस् *upa-hiṇs,* cl. 7. 1. P. *-hinasti, -hiṇsati, -situm,* to injure, hurt, wound; to overpower.

उपहित *upa-hita, as, ā, am* (past pass. part. of 1. *upa-dhā,* p. 163), placed, deposited, placed in or upon; preceded by; laid aside, joined; mixed; ready, deputed to act as a spy, connected with. — *Upahita-bhara, as, ā, am,* having the weight carried; (a better reading has *apa-hṛita-.*)

उपहृ *upa-hṛi,* cl. 1. P. A. *-harati, -te, -hartum,* to bring near, offer; to take away, destroy: Caus. *-hārayati, -yitum,* to cause to offer: Desid. *-jihīrshati,* to wish to offer.

Upa-haraṇa, am, n. bringing near; offering gifts to superiors; presenting victims; distributing or serving out food; taking, seizing.

Upa-haraṇīya or *upa-hartavya, as, ā, am,* to be presented, to be offered as a victim.

Upa-hartṛi, tā, trī, tṛi, offering victims, serving out food &c.

Upa-hāra, as, m. oblation; a complimentary gift, a present to a superior &c.; an offering to a deity, a victim &c.; honour; tribute, indemnification, presents as the price of peace; food distributed to guests &c.; exultation, mirth (consisting in laughter, dance, song, bellowing as a bull, bowing, recital of prayer &c.).

Upa-hāraka, as, m. an oblation &c.

Upa-hārin, ī, iṇī, i, giving, presenting; sacrificing.

Upahārī-kṛi, cl. 8. P. A. *-karoti, -kurute, -kartum,* to make an oblation, to offer.

Upa-hṛita, as, ā, am, offered, presented; immolated, offered as a victim; served out as food; taken, collected, gathered.

उपहोम *upa-homa, as,* m. a supplementary sacrifice.

उपह्वर *upa-hvara, as,* m. (rt. *hvṛi*), Ved. bend, curve, arch, slope; declivity; the curved form of the Soma vessel; (*am*), n. proximity; a solitary or private place; (*as*), m. a car, a carriage; (*e*), ind. in the proximity of, near to, in a private place.

उपह्वे *upa-hve,* cl. 1. P. A. *-hvayati, -te, -hvātum,* to invoke, call near to.

Upa-hava, as, m. calling to, inviting, invitation; summoning, invoking; *upahavam ish,* to wish to receive an invitation from (with loc., e. g. *tasminn Indra upahavam aiććhata*, Indra wished to receive an invitation from him).

Upa-havya, as, m., N. of a ceremony.

Upa-hūta, as, ā, am, invoked, invited.

Upa-hūya, ind. having invoked or called or addressed.

Upa-hvāna, am, n. act of inviting.

उपांशु *upāṇśu*, ind. in a low voice, in a whisper; secretly, in secret (e. g. *upāṇśu-vrata*, a vow observed in secret); (*us*), m. a prayer uttered in a low voice; muttering prayers, reciting them in a low voice so as not to be overheard; N. of a Soma offering.—*Upāṇśu-krīḍita, as, ā, am*, played with in secret, made the companion of (a king's) private amusements.

उपाक *upāka, as, ā, am* (fr. rt. *anć* with *upa*), Ved. brought near to one another, joined, approximate; (*e*), Ved. du. an epithet of night and morning; (*e*), ind. in the next neighbourhood, in the presence of, before.—*Upāka-ćakshas, ās, ās, as*, Ved. standing present before the eyes.

उपाकृ *upā-kṛi* (*upa-ā-kṛi*), cl. 5. 8. P. A. *-kṛiṇoti, -ṇute, -karoti, -kurute, -kartum*, to bring near or towards, to fetch; to summon, invite; to deliver, commit to, offer, grant, bestow; to acquire, obtain; to bring about, make preparations for a sacred action; to undertake, begin; to enter.

Upā-karaṇa, am, n. bringing near, inviting, invitation to begin; a term applied to certain sentences, called Praishas &c., with which one priest invites another to perform a sacrifice; immolation, sacrifice of an animal duly consecrated; preparation, beginning; commencement of reading the Veda after the performance of a preparatory rite.

Upā-karman, a, n. preparation, beginning; a ceremony performed before reading the Vedas; beginning to read the Vedas.

Upā-kṛita, as, ā, am, brought near, invited, addressed with invitatory sentences; (*as*), m. a sacrificial animal killed during the recitation of prescribed prayers; attended with evil omens, disastrous, calamitous; (*as*), m. misfortune; a portent, a phenomenon announcing calamity.

उपाक्रम् *upā-kram* (*upa-ā-kram*), cl. 1. P. A., 4. P. *-krāmati, -kramate* (ep. also *-krāmate*), *-krāmyati, -kramitum*, to advance against in order to seize, to fall upon, take possession of.

उपाक्षम् *upāksham* (*upa-ak°*), ind. before the eyes.

उपाख्या *upā-khyā* (*upa-ā-*), cl. 2. P. *-khyāti, -tum*, to tell a story, narrate; to relate or give an account about anything (with acc.); to observe (?).

Upā-khya, as, ā, am, observable by the eyes; [cf. *nir-upākhya*]; (*as*), m., N. of a man.

Upākhyāna (*upa-ākh°*), *am*, n. a tale, a short narrative, an episode; telling or repetition of a story already heard from another.

Upākhyānaka, am, n. a short tale.

उपागम् *upā-gam* (*upa-ā-*), cl. 1. P. *-gaććhati, -gantum*, to go near or towards, to approach, visit; to return; to pass into any condition or relation; to undergo, suffer, endure; to occur, to come or fall to one's share.

Upā-gata, as, ā, am, approached, arrived; occurred, happened; promised; suffering, feeling.

Upā-gama, as, m. approach, arrival; occurrence; promise, agreement; the state of suffering, feeling.

Upā-gamya or *upā-gatya*, ind. having approached, having gone near or towards.

उपागा *upā-gā* (*upa-ā-gā*), cl. 3. P. *-jigāti, -gātum*, to come near, approach, come to.

उपाग्नि *upāgni* (*upa-agni*), ind. near a fire.

उपाग्र *upāgra* (*upa-ag°*), *am*, n. the part which is next to the end or top; a secondary member.

उपाग्रह् *upā-grah* (*upa-ā-grah*), cl. 9. P. A. *-gṛihṇāti, -ṇīte* (Ved. *-gṛibhṇāti, -ṇīte*), *-grahītum*, to comprehend, embrace.

Upā-grahaṇa, am, n. reading the Vedas after initiation.

उपाग्रहायणम् *upāgrahāyaṇam* or *upāgrahāyaṇi* (*upa-ag°*), ind. towards the day of full moon in the month Agrahāyaṇa.

उपाघ्रा *upā-ghrā* (*upa-ā-ghrā*), cl. 1. P. *-jighrati, -ghrātum*, to smell at; to kiss.

उपाङ्क्य *upāṅkya, as, ā, am* (fr. *upa-aṅka*), to be marked.

उपाङ्ग *upāṅga* (*upa-aṅ°*), *am*, n. a subdivision; any minor limb or member; a subsidiary or supplementary work of low value; a supplement of a supplement; secondary portion of science; (twelve Aṅgas and Upāṅgas constitute the sacred writings of the Buddhists); the sectarial mark made with Sandal &c. on the forehead.—*Upāṅga-gīta, am*, n. a kind of song.

उपाचर् *upā-ćar* (*upa-ā-*), cl. 1. P. A. *-ćarati, -te, -ritum*, Ved. *-tave*, &c., to come near to; to attend upon, be attached to, to wait on, serve; to be obedient; to treat.

Upā-ćarita, as, ā, am, attached to any one's service, obedient; (in gram.) that rule of Sandhi by which the sound Visarga becomes *s* before *k* and *p*.

Upā-ćāra, as, m. position (as of a word in a sentence); procedure; Sandhi by which the sound Visarga becomes *s* before *k* and *p*.

उपाच्छिद् *upā-ććhid* (*upa-ā-ćhid*), cl. 7. P. A. *-ććhinatti, -ććhinte, -ććhettum*, to tear away from, cut off from.

उपाज् *upāj* (*upa-aj*), cl. 1. P. A., Ved. *upājati, -te, -jitum*, to bring near to.

Upāje-kṛi, to support.—*Upāje-kṛitya* or *upāje-kṛitvā*, having supported.

उपाञ्च् *upāñć* (*upa-añć*) or *upāć* (*upa-ać*), cl. 1. P. A. *upāñćati, -te*, or *upāćati, -te, -ćitum*, to draw (water).

उपाञ्जन *upāñjana, am*, n. (fr. rt. *añj* with *upa*), anointing, plastering the ground with cow dung &c.

उपातिगम् *upāti-gam* (*upa-ati-gam*), cl. 1. P. *-gaććhati, -gantum*, to pass over, cross (a river).

उपाती *upātī* (*upa-ati-i*), cl. 2. P. *upātyeti, -tum*, to pass over; to be added as a surplus.

Upāty-aya, as, m. neglect or disobedience of customs; disorderly behaviour.

उपादा *upā-dā* (*upa-ā-dā*), cl. 3. A. *-datte, -dātum*, to receive, accept; to gain, acquire; to take, appropriate to one's self; to take away or off, carry off, steal; to seize, lay hold of, gather; to draw (water); to assume a form; to feel, perceive, consider, regard; to take in addition, include, comprise; to employ, apply, use; to undertake, begin; to mention, enumerate: Caus. *-dāpayati, -yitum*, to cause to employ or apply; to make use of: Desid. P. *-ditsati*, to strive to obtain.

Upā-tta, as, ā, am, received, accepted, acquired, gained, obtained; appropriated; taken away; seized, gathered; shaped; felt, perceived, regarded; comprised; employed, used; begun; enumerated; allowed in argument, granted, conceded; (*as*), m. an elephant out of rut.—*Upātta-raṇhas, ās, ās, as*, acquiring speed, quick, fleet.—*Upātta-śastra, as, ā, am*, taking up arms, armed.

Upā-dāna, am, n. taking, acquiring, taking away, abduction, appropriating to one's self, accepting, employment, using, becoming familiar with; mentioning, enumeration; saying, speaking; including, containing; abstraction, withdrawing the organs of sense and perception from the outer world; cause, motive; immediate or proximate cause; the formal or distinct form, the material cause; a double meaning, an expression conveying a sense besides that which appears intended; (with Buddhists) conception; effort or exertion of body or speech.—*Upādāna-kāraṇa, am*, n. a proximate cause.

Upā-dāya, ind. having seized, containing; including, inclusive of; together with; by means of.

Upā-deya, as, ā, am, to be taken or received, acceptable, admissible; to be chosen; to be selected, excellent, admirable.

उपादिक *upādika, as*, m. a sort of insect; [cf. *utpādaka*.]

उपादिश् *upā-diś* (*upa-ā-*), cl. 6. P. A. *-diśati, -te, -deshṭum*, to advise, show, point out, to indicate, inform, declare; to prescribe, give an order.

उपाद्रु *upā-dru* (*upa-ā-*), cl. 1. P. *-dravati, -drotum*, to run near to.

उपाधा *upā-dhā* (*upa-ā-*), cl. 3. P. A. *-dadhāti, -dhatte, -dhātum*, to place near, place upon; to offer; render, make, effect, fix; to keep, hold.

1. *upā-dhi, is*, m. (for 2. see below), deceit, deception, disguise (in the Vedānta this is especially applied to certain natural forms or properties, considered as disguises of the spirit); that which more closely defines, a discriminative or distinguishing property, an attribute, a peculiarity, an indispensable condition; limitation (e. g. *an-upādhi-ramaṇīyo deśaḥ*, a country beautiful without limitation, i. e. altogether beautiful); a title, a discriminative appellation, a nickname; a purpose, an occasion, an object; (in logic) a special cause for a general effect; (in rhetoric) the natural character of species, quality or action. *Upādhi-tas*, ind. in consequence of a peculiarity. (At the end of a compound the affix *ka* may be added to *upādhi*, e. g. *asty-upādhika*, having 'is' as an attribute.)

Upā-hita, as, ā, am, deposited, placed; put on, worn; joined, annexed; agreed upon, made or done mutually; (*as*), m. a fiery portent, a meteor, a comet.

उपाधि 2. *upā-dhi, is*, m. (fr. rt. *dhyai* with *upa-ā*), reflection on duty; virtuous reflection; a man who is careful to support his family. (For 1. see under *upā-dhā* above.)

उपाधिक *upādhika* (*upa-adh°*), *as, ā, am*, exceeding, supernumerary.

उपाध्याय *upādhy-āya, as*, m. (fr. rt. 5. *i* with *upa-adhi*), a sub-teacher who instructs in a part only of the Veda or in grammar and the other Vedāṅgas, and is therefore inferior to the Āćārya who instructs in the whole Veda with the Kalpa and Upanishads (see Manu II. 141); a spiritual teacher, a teacher in general; (*ā*), f. a female preceptor; (*ī*), f. a female teacher or the wife of a teacher.

Upādhyāyānī, f. the wife of a teacher.

उपानस *upānasa, as, ā, am* (fr. *upa* and *anas*), Ved. being on a carriage; (*am*), n. the space in a carriage; carriage-load; anything placed on a carriage.

उपानह् *upā-nah, t*, f. (rt. *nah*), a sandal, a shoe.—*Upānad-gūḍha, as, ā, am*, covered with a shoe.

उपानी *upā-nī* (*upa-ā-*), cl. 1. P. A. *-nayati, -te, -netum*, to lead or carry or bring near or towards; lead away, carry off; to initiate, consecrate; [cf. *upa-nī*.]

उपानुवाक्य *upānuvākya* (*upa-an°*), *as, ā, am*, Ved. an epithet of Agni; (*am*), n., N. of a section of the Taittirīya-Saṃhitā.

उपान्त *upānta* (*upa-an°*), *am*, n. proximity to the edge or margin, border, edge; the angle of the eye; immediate proximity; the last letter but one; (*as, ā, am*), near to the end, last but one; near.—*Upānta-sarpin, ī, iṇī, i*, coming near.

Upāntika, as, ī, am, near, proximate, neighbouring; *(am),* n. proximity.

Upāntya, as, ā, am, last but one; *(as),* m. the corner of the eye; *(am),* n. vicinity.

उपाप् *upāp (upa-āp),* cl. 5. P. *-āpnoti, -ptum,* to reach, to arrive at: Desid. *upepsati,* to wish to reach, to desire to win over or conciliate.

Upāpa in *dur-upāpa, as, ā, am,* difficult to be obtained.

Upāpti, is, f. reaching, obtaining.

Upepsā, f. desire to obtain.

उपाप्रछ् *upā-prach (upa-ā-),* cl. 6. P. *-pṛiććhati, -prashṭum,* to take leave of.

उपाभृति *upā-bhṛiti, is,* f. (fr. rt. *bhṛi* with *upa-ā*), Ved. act of bringing near.

उपामन्त्र्य *upā-mantrya (upa-ā-),* ind. having taken leave, having received permission to go.

उपाय *upāya.* See under 1. *upe* 3rd col.

उपाया *upā-yā (upa-ā-),* cl. 2. P. *-yāti, -tum,* to approach, arrive at.

Upā-yāta, as, ā, am, approached; *(am),* n. arrival; an event, an accident.

उपार् *upār (upa-ṛi),* cl. 3. P., Ved. *upeyarti, upārtum, -ritum* or *-rītum,* to offend against, make a mistake; to injure: Caus. P. *upārpayati, -yitum,* to bring near.

Upāra, as, m. or *upāraṇa, am,* n., Ved. a mistake, offence, sin.

उपारम् *upā-ram (upa-ā-),* cl. 1. A. *-ramate, -rantum,* to sport, take one's pleasure, delight in; to cease; to rest.

Upā-rata, as, ā, am, delighted; engaged in, occupied with; frequenting, resorting to.

Upā-rama, as, m. engaging in, going to or in.

उपाराध् *upā-rādh (upa-ā-),* cl. 5. P. *-rādhnoti, -rāddhum,* to serve, wait upon.

Upā-rādhya, ind. having served, having waited on.

उपारुद् *upā-rud (upa-ā-),* cl. 2. P. *-roditi, -roditum,* to weep, deplore.

उपारुह् *upā-ruh, k,* f. (rt. *ruh* with *upa* and *ā*), Ved. the shoot of a plant.

Upā-rūḍha, as, ā, am, grown, increased. — *Upārūḍha-sneha, as, ā, am,* whose affection has increased.

उपार्ज् *upārj (upa-arj),* cl. 1. P. *upārjati, -jitum,* to bring near to: Caus. *upārjayati, -yitum,* to cause to bring near, convey near, acquire, gain.

Upārjaka, as, ikā, am, acquiring, obtaining, earning, gaining.

Upārjana, am, n. bringing near to, acquiring.

Upārjanīya, as, ā, am, to be acquired, to be earned.

Upārjita, as, ā, am, gained, acquired, earned.

उपार्थ *upārtha (upa-ar°), as, ā, am,* of little worth.

उपार्ध् *upārdh (upa-ṛidh),* Desid. P. *upertsati,* to wish to accomplish, persevere, hold out.

उपार्ष् *upārsh (upa-ṛish),* cl. 6. P. *upārshati, -shitum,* to pierce, prick, goad.

उपालभ् *upā-labh (upa-ā-),* cl. 1. A. *-labhate, -labdhum,* to obtain; to censure, revile, abuse, scold.

Upā-labdha, as, ā, am, reproached, reviled.

Upā-labhya, as, ā, am, censurable, blamable.

Upā-lambha, as, m. or *upā-lambhana, am,* n. abuse, reviling, censure; deferring, delaying.

Upā-lambhya, as, ā, am, Ved. to be taken in addition.

उपालि *upāli, is,* m., N. of a man who arranged the Buddhist Vinaya.

उपाव् *upāv (upa-av),* cl. 1. P. *-vati, -vitum,* to cherish, behave friendly towards; to encourage (with dat. or acc.).

Upāvī, is, is, i, Ved. encouraging; attractive.

उपावरुह् *upāva-ruh (upa-ava-),* cl. 1. P. *-rohati, -roḍhum,* to descend towards.

उपावर्तन *upā-vartana.* See under 1. *upā-vṛit* below.

उपावसायिन् *upāva-sāyin, ī, inī, i* (fr. rt. *so* with *upa-ava*), Ved. submissive, compliant, obeying, accommodating.

उपावसु *upā-vasu, us, us, u,* Ved. bringing riches, granting wealth.

उपावहृ *upāva-hṛi (upa-ava-),* cl. 1. P. A. *-harati, -te, -hartum,* to bring or lead down towards.

Upāva-haraṇa, am, n. taking down, bringing down.

उपावृत् 1. *upā-vṛit (upa-ā-),* cl. 1. A. *-vartate, -titum,* to turn towards, go towards, approach; to turn away, return: Caus. P. *-vartayati, -yitum,* to cause to turn, lead back.

Upā-vartana, am, n. turning round, revolving; turning back, returning; approaching; ceasing.

2. *upā-vṛit, t,* f., Ved. return.

Upā-vṛitta, as, ā, am, turned round, rolling on the ground; ceased, ceasing, refraining; come, arrived; fit, proper; *(as),* m. a horse rolling on the ground; *(ās),* m. pl., N. of a people.

उपावे *upāve (upa-ava-i),* cl. 2. P., Ved. *-vaiti, -tum,* to go down, descend (into a bath &c.); to join in (singing &c.); to assent, show one's self willing.

उपावेक्ष् *upāveksh (upa-ava-iksh),* cl. 1. A. *-kshate, -kshitum,* to look at, look down at.

उपाव्याध *upā-vyādha, as,* m. (rt. *vyadh*), Ved. a vulnerable or unprotected spot.

उपाश् 1. *upāś (upa-aś),* cl. 5. P. A. *-śnoti, -śnute, -śitum,* to obtain, become master of.

उपाश् 2. *upāś (upa-aś),* cl. 9. P. *-śnāti, -śitum,* to eat, consume; to taste, enjoy.

उपाशंसनीय *upā-śansanīya, as, ā, am,* to be expected (as anything future).

उपाश्रि *upā-śri (upa-ā-),* cl. 1. P. A. *-śrayati, -te, -śrayitum,* to have recourse to.

Upā-śraya, as, m. recourse (for aid), asylum, support; reliance, dependance upon.

Upā-śrita, as, ā, am, relying or depending upon; supporting (literally or figuratively), bearing, holding, protecting.

उपास् 1. *upās (upa-as),* cl. 2. P., Ved. *upāsti,* to be near to or in.

उपास् 2. *upās (upa-as),* cl. 4. P. *upāsyati, -situm,* to throw near or upon or among, cast down upon.

1. *upāsana, am,* n. injuring, hurting; archery.

उपास् 3. *upās (upa-ās),* cl. 2. A. *upāste, -situm,* to sit near to (with acc.), sit at the side of (as a mark of submission and respect); to sit; to occupy, reside, abide in, be present at; to approach, go towards, invest (as an enemy's town); be intent upon, be engaged in; to undergo, suffer; to remain or continue in any action (with indecl. part., e. g. *kritvā upāsata,* they continued doing); to remain in expectation, expect, wait for; to approach respectfully, to serve, worship, honour; attach one's self to; to respect, recognize, acknowledge; to regard as; to employ, make subservient.

Upāsaka, as, ikā, am, serving, a servant; a Śūdra, a low fellow; worshipping, a worshipper, a follower; (with Buddhists) a worshipper of Buddha (as distinguished from the *Bhikshu* or Buddhist priest). — *Upāsaka-daśa, ās,* m. pl. title of the seventh of the twelve sacred books of the Jainas.

2. *upāsana, am,* n. sitting by the side of; being intent on, engaging in, serving, service, attendance, worship, respect, adoration; regarding as, reflecting on, religious meditation; the sacred fire; *(ā),* f. service, worship, adoration. — *Upāsanārtha* (°*na-ar*°), *as, ā, am,* worthy of attendance.

Upāsanīya, as, ā, am, to be attended on, worthy of attendance.

Upāsā, f. religious reflection or meditation; service, worship.

Upāsita, as, ā, am, served, honoured, worshipped; serving, paying worship or service.

Upāsitavya, as, ā, am, to be served or worshipped; to be attended to, to be accomplished; to be regarded or considered.

Upāsitṛi, tā, trī, tṛi, a worshipper.

Upāsīna, as, ā, am, sitting near to, occupying.

Upāsti, is, f. service, especially of a deity, worship, veneration.

1. *upāsya, as, ā, am,* to be served or worshipped; to be attended to or accomplished; to be respected; to be regarded or considered. — *Upāsya-tā,* f. or *upāsya-tva, am,* n. respectability, placability.

2. *upāsya,* ind. having served or worshipped; having associated (?).

Upāsyamāna, as, ā, am, being served, waited upon, attended, worshipped, receiving homage.

उपासङ्ग *upā-sanga, as,* m. (rt. *sañj*), proximity; a quiver.

उपास्तमन *upāstamana, am,* n. sunset.

Upāstamayam (upa-as°), ind. about the time of sunset.

उपास्त्र *upāstra (upa-as°), am,* n. a secondary or minor weapon.

उपास्था *upā-sthā (upa-ā-),* cl. 1. P. A. *-tishṭhati, -te, -sthātum,* to stand near, go near to, have intercourse with.

उपाहृ *upā-hṛi (upa-ā-),* cl. 1. P. A. *-harati, -te, -hartum,* to offer; to make, prepare.

Upāhāra (upa-āh°), as, m. slight refreshment (consisting of fruits, sweetmeats, &c.).

Upā-hṛita, as, ā, am, offered, prepared; seized.

उपाह्वे *upā-hve (upa-ā-),* cl. 1. P. A. *-hvayati, -te, -hvātum,* to challenge, invite.

उपे 1. *upe (upa-i),* cl. 2. P. *upaiti, -tum,* to go near, approach (as a friend or enemy); come near to, arrive at, reach; to go to (a master), become a pupil; to undergo, perform, undertake, devote one's self to; to pass into any state, to fall into (misfortune &c.), incur, be present at; to obtain; to fall to one's share; to befal; to regard as, admit, acknowledge.

Upāya, as, m. approaching, approach; that by which one reaches an aim, a means, an expedient, a way, stratagem; a means of success against an enemy (four of which are usually enumerated, sowing dissension, negotiation, bribery, and open attack); joining (in singing &c.). — *Upāya-ćatushṭaya, am,* n. the four expedients against an enemy; see above. — *Upāya-ćintā,* f. devising an expedient, thinking of a resource. — *Upāya-jña, as, ā, am,* fertile in expedients, contriving, provident. — *Upāya-tas,* ind. by some means or expedient. — *Upāya-turīya, as,* m. a fourth means, punishment. — *Upāya-tva, am,* n. state of being provided with means. — *Upāya-yoga, as,* m. application of means or combination of expedients. — *Upāyāntara* (°*ya-an*°), *am,* n. a remedy.

Upāyana, am, n. approaching, going near to, going to a teacher, becoming a pupil, engaging in any religious observance; undertaking, accepting; a present, a gift, a complementary or respectful gift.

Upāyika, as, ī, am, conducive to.

Upāyin, ī, inī, i, approaching; having sexual intercourse with; expert in the use of means.

Upāyu, us, us, u, Ved. going near to, approaching.

Upeta, as, ā, am, come near, approached, arrived at, come near to, present, existent; accompanied by, endowed with, possessed of, having, possessing; surrounded, invested; fallen into.

Upeti, is, f., Ved. approach, arrival.

Upetṛi, tā, trī, tṛi, approaching, going near to; contriving, a contriver, one who employs expedients, one who comes as an assailant.

Upetya, ind. having approached, having gone near.

Upeya, as, ā, am, to be gone to or approached, to be effected by any means; assailable; to be sought, to be had recourse to.

Upeyivas, ān, yushī, at, accompanied or followed by, associated with, united; obtained, got.

उपे 2. *upe (upa-ā-i),* cl. 2. P. *upaiti, -tum,* to come near to, go to, approach, visit; to have sexual intercourse with; to undergo, incur, fall into (misfortune &c.).

उपेक्ष् *upeksh (upa-īksh),* cl. 1. A. *upekshate, -shitum,* to look at, regard; to perceive; to notice, have regard to; to consider, expect; to overlook, disregard; to neglect, to quit, abandon; to despise.

Upeksha, as, m., N. of a son of Śvaphalka.

Upekshaka, as, ā, am, disregarding, neglecting, looking at inattentively, disdaining; patient, enduring.

Upekshaṇa, am, n. overlooking, looking at without interest or attention, disregarding, neglecting, disdaining; leaving, abandoning.

Upekshaṇīya, as, ā, am, to be neglected or disregarded.

Upekshā, f. overlooking, negligence, neglect; indifference, contempt, disdain; abandoning, leaving; endurance, patience; dissent; trick, deceit (as one of the minor expedients in war); regard.

Upekshita, as, ā, am, disregarded, disesteemed, neglected, disdained.

Upekshitavya, as, ā, am, to be looked at, to be regarded, to be examined; to be disregarded.

Upekshya, as, ā, am, to be regarded or examined; to be disregarded or neglected.

उपेन् *upen (upa-in),* cl. 8. P. *upenoti* (cl. 6. P. fr. *inv, upenvati*), to press in, force in.

Upenita, as, ā, am, driven or pressed in, turned in.

उपेन्द्र *upendra, as,* m. (fr. *upa-in°*), N. of Vishṇu or Kṛishṇa as the younger brother of Indra, (born subsequently to Indra, especially as son of Aditi, either as an Āditya or in the Vāmana Avatār); N. of a king of the Nāgas; (*ā*), f., N. of a river. — *Upendra-datta, as,* m., N. of a man. — *Upendra-bala, as,* m., N. of a man. — *Upendra-vajrā,* f. a metre of four lines of eleven syllables each.

उपेप्सा *upepsā.* See under *upāp.*

उपेष् 1. *upesh (upa-īsh),* cl. 1. A., Ved. *upeshate, -shitum,* to attack.

उपेष् 2. *upesh (upa-ā-īsh),* cl. 1. A., Ved. *upeshate, -shitum,* to approach with a request &c., to request.

उपेष् 3. *upesh (upa-esh),* cl. 1. P. *upeshati, -shitum,* to creep near, approach.

उपोक्ष् *upoksh (upa-uksh),* cl. 6. P. *upokshati, -shitum,* to sprinkle in addition.

उपोढ 1. *upoḍha, as, ā, am* (fr. *upa-vah*), brought near; brought about, advanced, begun; arranged, arrayed; near, proximate; married.

उपोढ 2. *upoḍha.* See *upoh* next col.

उपोती *upotī,* f. the pot-herb Basella Rubra or Lucida. See *upodikā.*

उपोत्क्रम् *upot-kram (upa-ud-kram),* cl. 1. and 4. P. *-krāmati, -krāmyati, -kramitum,* to go up towards, rise upwards, ascend.

उपोत्तम *upottama (upa-utt°), as, ā, am,* last but one; (*am*), n. (scil. *aksharam*) the last vowel but one.

उपोत्थित *upot-thita, as, ā, am* (rt. *sthā*), risen up.

उपोद् *upod (upa-ud),* cl. 7. P. *uponatti, upondītum,* to moisten.

उपोदक *upodaka (upa-ud°), as, ā, am,* near to water; (*akī* or *ikā*), f. the plant Basella Cordifolia.

उपोदयम् *upodayam (upa-ud°),* ind. about the time of sunrise.

उपोदि *upod-i (upa-ud-i),* cl. 2. P. *-eti, -tum,* to approach.

उपोदीका *upodīkā,* f. the plant Basella Cordifolia. See *upodikā.*

उपोदे *upode (upa-ud-ā-i),* cl. 2. P. *-aiti, -tum,* to go up towards, go up to.

उपोद्ग्रह् *upod-grah (upa-ud-grah),* cl. 9. P. A. *-gṛihṇāti, -ṇīte* (Ved. *-gṛibhṇāti, -ṇīte*), *-grahītum,* to erect, set up.

उपोद्घात *upod-ghāta, as,* m. (fr. rt. *han* with *upa-ud*), an example, an apposite argument or illustration; analysis, the ascertainment of the elements of anything; a beginning, a thing begun; an introduction, a preface. — *Upodghāta-pāda, as,* m., N. of the third part of the Vāyu-purāṇa.

उपोद्बलय *upodbalaya* (fr. *upa-udbala*), nom. P. *-balayati, -yitum,* to confirm.

Upodbalaka, as, ā, am, confirming.

उपोपविश् *upopa-viś (upa-upa-viś),* cl. 6. P. *-viśati, -veshṭum,* to sit down near, to take a seat near.

उपोष् *uposh (upa-ush),* cl. 1. P. *-oshati, -shitum,* to burn down, burn.

उपोषण *uposhaṇa, am,* n. (fr. rt. 1. *vas* with *upa*), a fast, fasting.

Uposhita, as, ā, am, fasted; (*am*), n. fasting.

Uposhya, ind. having fasted.

उपोषध *uposhadha, as,* m., N. of a Brāhman.

उपोह् *upoh (upa-ūh;* in some of its senses connected with *upa-vah*), cl. 1. P. *upohati, -hitum,* to push or impel towards; to push under, insert; to bring near, produce; to accumulate: Pass. *upohyate,* to be brought about, to advance, begin.

2. *upoḍha, as, ā, am,* brought near, brought about, advanced, commenced.

Upoha, as, m., Ved. adding, accumulating.

Upohyamāna, as, ā, am, being brought about or commenced.

उप्त *upta, as, ā, am* (past pass. part. of rt. *vap*), sown (as seed). — *Upta-kṛishṭa, as, ā, am,* ploughed after sowing.

Upti, is, f. sowing seeds. — *Upti-vid, t,* m. an agriculturist.

Uptrima, as, ā, am, sown, cultivated.

Upya, as, ā, am, to be scattered or sown.

Upyamāna, as, ā, am, being sown.

उब्ज् *ubj,* cl. 6. P. *ubjati, ubjāñ-ćakāra, ubjishyati, aubjīt, ubjitum,* to press down, subdue, keep under; to make straight: Desid. *ubjijishati.*

Ubja, as, m., N. of a man.

Ubjita, as, ā, am, pressed down, subdued.

उभ् *ubh* or *umbh,* cl. 6. 9. 7. P., Ved. *ubhati* or *umbhati, ubhnāti, unapti,* impf. *aunap, uvobha* or *umbhāñ-ćakāra, ubhitum* or *umbhitum,* to compact together; to confine; to cover over, fill with; (Sāy.) to break.

उभ *ubha,* pron. (nom. du. *ubhau,* pl. *ubhe;* said to be fr. rt. *ubh* above, and connected with Gr. ἄμφω; Lat. *ambo;* Slav. *oba;* Lith. *abbù;* Goth. *bai, ba*), both.

Ubhaya, as, i, am, (pl. m. f. n. *e, ās, āni,* only used in sing. and pl., but by some authorities also in dual), both. — *Ubhaya-guṇa, as, ā, am,* possessed of both qualities. — *Ubhayan-kara, as, ā, am,* Ved. effecting or accomplishing both. — *Ubhaya-ćara, as, ā, am,* 'moving in or on both,' living in water and on land or in the air, amphibious. — *Ubhaya-dyus,* ind., Ved. on both days, on two subsequent days; the day past and to come. — *Ubhaya-bhāga-hara, as, ā, am,* applicable to two purposes, taking two shares or parts; (*am*), n. a medicine that acts in two ways, as an emetic and a purge. — *Ubhaya-vat, ān, atī, at,* Ved. furnished with or containing both. — *Ubhaya-vidyā,* f. the twofold science, i.e. religious knowledge and acquaintance with worldly affairs. — *Ubhaya-vidha, as, ā, am,* appearing under two forms. — *Ubhaya-vipulā,* f., N. of a metre. — *Ubhaya-vetana, as, ā, am,* serving two masters, receiving wages from both. — *Ubhaya-vyañjana, as, ā, am,* having the marks of both sexes. — *Ubhaya-sambhava, as,* m. a dilemma. — *Ubhayātmaka* (°*ya-āt°*), *as, ā, am,* belonging to both. — *Ubhayānumata* (°*ya-an°*), *as, ā, am,* agreed to or accepted mutually or on both sides. — *Ubhayārtham* (°*ya-ar°*), ind. for a double object, as for prosperity on earth and happiness in heaven.

Ubhayatas, ind. from both sides, on both sides, to both sides; in both cases. — *Ubhayataḥ-kshṇut, t, t, t,* Ved. two-edged. — *Ubhayato-dat, an, atī, at,* having a double row of teeth (man, animal, &c.). — *Ubhayato-mukha, as, ī, am,* looking either way, two-faced. — *Ubhayato-hrasva, as, ā, am,* having a short vowel on both sides, (an accented vowel) produced by two short vowels.

Ubhayatra, ind. in both places, on both sides; in both cases, both times. — *Ubhayatrodātta* (°*ra-ud°*), *as, ā, am,* having an Udātta accent on both sides; resulting from the blending of two Udātta accents.

Ubhayathā, ind. in both ways; in both cases.

Ubhayā, ind., Ved. in both ways. — *Ubhayā-dat, an, atī, at,* Ved. having teeth on both sides. — *Ubhayā-vin, ī, inī, i,* Ved. being on both sides, partaking of both. — *Ubhayā-hasti,* ind., Ved. as much as may be grasped with both hands. — *Ubhayā-hastya, as, ā, am,* Ved. filling both hands.

Ubhayīya, as, ā, am, belonging to both.

Ubhaye-dyus, ind. on both days, on two subsequent days.

उम् *um,* ind. an interjection of anger, interrogation, promise or assent, of cordiality or pacification.

उम *uma, as,* m. a city, a town; a wharf, a landing-place.

उमा *umā,* f. (in the first sense perhaps fr. rt. *ve*), flax (Linum Usitatissimum); the plant Curcuma; N. of the daughter of Himavat and Menā, and wife of Rudra or Śiva (she is also called Pārvatī and Durgā); light, splendor; fame, reputation; quiet, tranquillity; night. According to the Kumāra-sambhava I. 26, the name *Umā* is derived from *u mā,* O do not (practice austerities)! the exclamation addressed to Pārvatī by her mother. — *Umā-kaṭa, as* or *am,* m. or n. the pollen of flax. — *Umā-guru, us,* m., N. of the mountain Himālaya as father of Umā. — *Umāguru-nadī,* f., N. of a river. — *Umā-pati, is,* m. epithet of Śiva as husband of Umā. — *Umā-pati-dhara, as,* m., N. of a poet. — *Umāpati-sevin, ī, inī, i,* worshipping Śiva. — *Umā-vana, am,* n., N. of the town Vana-pura or Devī-koṭa (Devi Cote). — *Umā-sahāya, as,* m., N. of Śiva as companion of Umā. — *Umā-suta, as,* m., N. of Kārttikeya as son of Umā. — *Umeśa* (*umā-īśa*), *as,* m., N. of Śiva as lord of Umā.

Umya, am, n. a field of linseed or of Curcuma.

उम्बर *umbara, as,* m. the upper timber of a door frame; N. of a Gandharva.

उम्बी *umbī,* f. the stalks of wheat or barley fried over a fire of wet grass, considered as a tonic.

उम्बुर *umbura, as,* m. the upper timber of a door frame; [cf. *umbara.*]

उम्लोचा *umloćā,* f., N. of an Apsaras.

उर् *ur,* to go; (a Sautra root, i. e. one occurring only in grammatical Sūtras and not in the Dhātu-pāṭha.)

उर *ura, as,* m., N. of a Ṛishi said to be of the family of Vāta.

उरक *uraka, as,* m., N. of one of Śiva's attendants.

उरग *ura-ga, as,* m. (fr. *ura* = *uras* and rt. *gam*), a snake ('going on the breast'); in mythology a Nāga or semi-divine serpent usually represented with a human face of great beauty; lead; (*ī*), f. a female snake; (*ā*), f., N. of a town. — *Uraga-pratisara, as, ā, am,* having a serpent for a wedding ring. — *Uraga-bhūshaṇa, as,* m. an epithet of Śiva, whose ornaments consist of snakes. — *Uraga-rāja, as,* m. the king of snakes, Śesha or Vāsuki. — *Uraga-sāra-ćandana, as, am,* m. n. a kind of sandal-wood. — *Uraga-sthāna, am,* n. the abode of the Nāgas, i. e. Pātāla, a region below the earth (not to be confounded with hell). — *Uragāri* (°*ga-ari*), *is,* m. Garuḍa, the bird of Vishṇu; a large crane; (lit. 'the enemy of the snakes.') — *Uragāśana* (°*ga-aś*°), *as,* m., N. of Garuḍa; a gigantic crane; ('whose food consists of serpents.') — *Uragāsya* (°*ga-ās*°), *am,* n. a kind of spade. — *Uragendra* (°*ga-in*°), *as,* m. the king of the snakes, Śesha or Vāsuki.

Uran-ga and *uran-gama, as,* m. a snake.

उरण *uraṇa, as,* m. (said to be fr. rt. 4. *ṛi*), a ram, a sheep, a young ram; a certain demon slain by Indra; a cloud?; (*ī*), f. a ewe. — *Uraṇāksha* (°*ṇa-ak*°) or *uraṇākshaka, as,* m. the plant Cassia Alata or Tora. — *Uraṇākhya* (°*ṇa-ākh*°) or *uraṇākhyaka, as,* m. the plant Tora.

Uraṇaka, as, m. a ram; a cloud.

उरभ्र *urabhra, as,* m. (fr. *ura* = *ūrṇā* and rt. *bhṛi?*), a ram; a kind of poisonous insect.

उररी *urarī,* ind. (perhaps connected with *uru*; cf. *urī, ūrī, ūrarī*), a particle implying assent, admission, extension, expansion, diffusion; often compounded with the roots *as, bhū,* and *kṛi.*

Urarī-kṛi, to allow, admit, assent. — *Urarī-kāra, as,* m. a promise, agreement; admission. — *Urarī-kṛita, as, ā, am,* promised, agreed; spread, extended, diffused.

उरश *uraśa, as,* m., N. of a country inhabited by a warrior-tribe; (*ā*), f., N. of a town; also *urasā.*

उरस् *uras,* n. (fr. rt. *vṛi,* to cover; cf. *uru*), the breast, the bosom; (*ās, ās, as*), best, excellent; *urasi kṛi,* to press any one to one's breast; to assent. — *Uraḥ-kshata, am,* n. injury to the chest, breaking a blood-vessel in the chest, consumption. — *Uraḥ-sūtrikā,* f. a pearl necklace hanging over the breast. — *Uraḥ-sthala, am,* n. the breast, the bosom. — *Uraś-ćhada, as,* m. a cuirass, breastplate, armour, mail. — *Urasi-ja* or *urasi-ruha, as,* m. the female breast (lit. 'produced on the chest'). — *Urasi-loman, ā, ā, a,* having hairs on the breast. — *Uras-kaṭa, as,* m. the sacrificial thread hung round the neck and upon the breast, as sometimes worn. — *Uras-tas,* ind. from the breast, in the direction of the breast. — *Uras-trāṇa, am,* n. a breastplate, cuirass, coat of mail. — *Uras-vat, ān, atī, at,* broad-chested, full-breasted, strong. — *Uro-gāmin, ī, inī, i,* going on the breast (as a reptile), creeping, crawling. — *Uro-graha, as,* m. disease of the chest, pleurisy. — *Uro-ghāta, as,* m. striking or beating the breast; pain in the chest. — *Uro-ja, as,* m. the female breast (lit. 'born on the chest'). — *Uro-bṛihatī,* f., N. of a metre. — *Uro-bhūshaṇa, am,* n. an ornament of the breast.

Urasa, as, ā, am, having a strong broad breast; (*am*), n. (at the end of compounds) best, most excellent.

Urasila, as, ā, am, broad-chested, having a full or broad breast.

1. *urasya,* nom. P. *urasyati, -yitum,* to be strong.

2. *urasya, as, ā, am,* situated in the breast; pectoral; (labour or exertion) requiring an effort of the chest; legitimate (as a son or daughter); one born from a married couple of the same tribe or caste; excellent (i. e. the very heart, the breast or best part).

उरा *urā,* f. (fr. rt. *vṛi?*), Ved. a ewe. — *Urā-mathi, is, is, i,* Ved. killing sheep.

उराह *urāha, as,* m. a horse of a pale colour with dark legs; (probably a foreign word.)

उरी *urī,* ind. (cf. *urarī, ūrarī, ūrī*), a particle implying (especially in composition with the roots *as, bhū,* and *kṛi*) promise, assent, admission, extension, diffusion, &c.

Urī-kṛi, to promise, allow, admit, assent. — *Urī-kāra, as,* m. promise, admission, extension. — *Urī-kṛita, as, ā, am,* promised, extended, spread.

उरु *uru, us, us* or *vī, u* (fr. rt. *vṛi,* to cover), wide, spacious; extended, great, large; much, excessive; excellent, precious, valuable; (*u*), n., Ved. wide space, space, room; *uru kṛi,* to grant space or scope, give opportunity; (*u*), ind. far, far off; (*vī*), f. the wide earth, see *urvī* next col.; comparative *varīyas,* superlative *varishṭha;* [cf. Gr. εὐρύς; Hib. *ur,* 'very;' *ur-ard,* 'very high;' *uras,* 'power, ability.'] — *Uru-kāla* or *urukālaka, as,* m. the creeper Cucumis Colocynthis. — *Uru-kṛit, t, t, t,* Ved. making room, granting space. — *Uru-krama, as, ā, am,* Ved. far-stepping, making wide strides; of high rank; (*as*), m. an epithet of Vishṇu. — *Uru-kshaya, as,* m., Ved. a spacious dwelling, a wide habitation; (*as, ā, am*), occupying spacious dwellings, an epithet of Mitra and Varuṇa and the Maruts; (*as*), m., N. of a prince. — *Uru-kshiti, is,* f., Ved. a spacious or comfortable dwelling. — *Uru-kshepa, as,* m., N. of a prince. — *Uru-gavyūti, is, is, i,* Ved. having a wide domain or territory. — *Uru-gāya, as, ā, am* (*gāya* fr. rt. *gā*), Ved. far-going, far-striding; an epithet of Vishṇu, the Aśvins, Soma, and Indra; offering wide space or scope for movement; (Sāy.) praised by the great; (*as*), m. an epithet of Vishṇu; (*am*), n. wide space, scope for movement or free and unconfined motion. — *Urugāya-vat, ān, atī, at,* offering ample space for motion, unconfined. — *Uru-gūlā* (?), f., Ved., N. of a snake. — *Uru-ćakra, as, ā, am,* Ved. having wide wheels. — *Uru-ćakri, is, is, i,* Ved. allowing unrestrained motion; (Sāy.) granting ample assistance. — *Uru-ćakshas, ās, ās, as,* Ved. far-seeing; epithet of Mitra-Varuṇa and of the Ādityas. — *Uru-jman, ā, ā, a,* Ved. having a wide path or range. — *Uru-jrayas, ās, ās, as,* or *uru-jri, is, is, i,* Ved. moving in a wide course, extending over a wide space; (Sāy.) of great impetuosity, of mighty impetus; epithet of Agni and of Indra. — *Uru-tama, as, ā, am,* widest, greatest. — *Uru-tara, as, ā, am,* wider, greater, larger. — *Uru-tā,* f., Ved. wideness; opening. — *Uru-tāpa, as,* m. great heat. — *Uru-tva, am,* n. magnitude, vastness. — *Uru-dhāra, as, ā, am,* Ved. giving a broad stream (of milk, as a cow). — *Uru-prathas, ās, ās, as,* Ved. wide-spreading, widely extended, far-spread. — *Uru-bila, as, ī, am,* Ved. having a wide opening. — *Urubja* (*uru-ubja?*), *as, ā, am,* Ved. widely opened; (Sāy.) excellent, pre-eminent. — *Uru-mārga, as,* m. a long road. — *Uru-muṇḍa, as,* m., N. of a mountain. — *Uru-yuga, as, ā, am,* Ved. furnished with a broad yoke. — *Uru-loka, as, ā, am,* Ved. containing wide space, widely extended; (Sāy.) widely illuminating. — *Uru-vikrama, as, ā, am,* valiant, mighty. — *Uru-vindu, us,* m., N. of a Flamingo (in the Hari-vaṇśa, whose condition was that of a hunter in a former birth). — *Uru-vilvā,* f., N. of a village. — *Uruvilvā-kalpa,* N. of a place. — *Uru-vyaćas, ās, ās, as,* Ved. occupying wide space, widely extending, widely capacious; (*ās*), m. a malignant spirit, an imp or goblin. — *Uru-vyańć, an, urūćī, ak,* Ved. extending far; far-reaching, capacious; perceived in a distant place (as a sound); containing wide spaces. — *Uru-vraja, as, ā, am,* Ved. having a wide domain or territory. — *Uru-śaṇsa, as, ā, am,* Ved. praising aloud; (Sāy.) to be praised by many; reigning over a wide territory; (Sāy.) praised by many; epithet of Varuṇa, Pūshan, the Ādityas, Indra, and Soma. — *Uru-śarman, ā, ā, a,* Ved. finding refuge everywhere throughout the universe, widely pervading. — *Uru-shā, ās, ās, am* (rt. *san*), Ved. granting wide space or free scope; (Sāy.) granting much. — *Uru-sattva, as, ā, am,* magnanimous, of a generous or noble nature. — *Uru-svana, as, ā, am,* stentorian. — *Uru-hāra, as,* m. a valuable necklace. — *Urū-ṇasa, as, ā, am,* Ved. broad-nosed, having a good scent (as a hound). — *Urv-anga, as,* m. a mountain; the ocean. — *Urv-ajra, as,* m., Ved. an extensive field.

Uruvu, us, m. or *uruvuka, as,* m. or *uruvūka, as, am,* m. n. the plant Ricinus Communis.

Urushya, nom. P., Ved. *urushyati,* to desire wide scope or freedom, to escape from (with acc.); to protect, preserve, secure, defend from (with abl.), to avert.

Urushyā, f., Ved. (only in inst.) with protecting hands; (Sāy.) with desire to protect.

Urushyu, us, us, u, Ved. going to a distant place; (Sāy.) desiring to protect.

Urūla, as, ā, am, liking space; fond of expatiating; free, unrestrained, disobedient.

Urviyā, ind., Ved. far, far off, far and near, widely.

Urvī, f. the wide earth, the earth, the soil; space, the open space or great expanse comprising the six spaces, viz. the four quarters of the sky with the upper and lower spaces; a river; (*vī*), du., Ved. the two worlds, or heaven and earth. — *Urvī-dhara, as,* m. a mountain; the serpent Śesha. — *Urvī-pati, is,* m. a king. — *Urvī-bhṛit, t,* m. a mountain. — *Urvī-ruha, as,* m. a tree, 'growing on the earth.' — *Urvīśa* (°*vī-īśa*), *as,* m. a king.

Urvyā, f. protection, security.

Urvy-ūti, is, is, i (fr. *urviyā-ūti?*), Ved. able to help or defend far and near; (Sāy.) granting extensive protection.

उरुण्ड *uruṇḍa, as,* m., N. of a demon; also of a man.

उरूरी *urūrī,* ind. a particle of assent and admission. See *urarī.*

उरूक *urūka, as,* m. an owl; [cf. *ulūka.*]

उरूची *urūćī.* See *uru-vyańć* under *uru.*

उर्जित *urjita, as, ā, am* (fr. rt. *vṛij*), abandoned, left.

उर्जिहाना *urjihānā,* f., N. of a town.

उर्णनाभ *urṇa-nābha, as,* m. a spider; [cf. *ūrṇa-nābha.*]

उर्णा *urṇā,* f. wool, felt, the hair of camels &c.; a circle of hair between the eyebrows. See *ūrṇā.*

उर्द् *urd,* cl. 1. A. *ūrdate, ūrdān-ćakre, ūrdishyate, aurdishṭa, ūrditum,* to measure; to play; to be easy or cheerful.

उर्द्र *urdra, as,* m. an otter. See *udra.*

उर्व् *urv,* cl. 1. P. *ūrvati, ūrvāń-ćakāra, ūrvitum,* to kill or hurt.

उर्व *urva, as,* m., N. of a man.

उर्वट *urvaṭa, as,* m. a year.

उर्वरा *urvarā,* f., Ved. fertile soil, yielding every kind of crop, field sown with corn; land in general; a mixed mass of fibres, wool, &c.; jocular term for curled hairs; N. of an Apsaras. — *Urvarā-jit, t, t, t,* Ved. acquiring fields. — *Urvarā-pati, is,* m., Ved. master of the fields sown with corn. — *Urvarā-sā, ās, ās, am,* Ved. granting fields.

Urvarī, f., Ved. tow, fibres drawn out of the distaff.

Urvarya, as, ā, am, Ved. belonging to a field which is sown with corn.

उर्वशी urvaśī, f. (fr. uru-vaśī), Ved. wish, ardour, hot desire; N. of an Apsaras or nymph of Indra's heaven, who became the wife of Purūravas; she is also identified with the Gangā. – Urvaśī-nāma-mālā, f., N. of a glossary of synonymous words by an anonymous author. – Urvaśī-ramaṇa, as, m. epithet of Aila or Purūravas, the second king of the lunar race and the husband of the Apsaras Urvaśī. – Urvaśī-vallabha or urvaśī-sahāya, as, m. epithet of Purūravas; see the preceding.

उर्वारु urvāru, us, m. a kind of cucumber, Cucumis Usitatissimus. See irvāru.

Urvāruka, am, n. the fruit of the above plant.

Urvārū, ūs, f., Ved. = the preceding.

उल् ul, ulati, to burn; (a Sautra root, i. e. one mentioned only in grammatical Sūtras but not occurring in the Dhātu-pāṭha.)

उल ula, as, m., Ved. a kind of wild animal; N. of a man.

उलप ulapa, as, m., Ved. a shrub, bush; a wick; the stalk of a shrub used as a wick (?); a creeping plant, a spreading creeper; the grass or reed Saccharum Cylindricum; N. of a pupil of Kalāpin.

Ulapya, as, ā, am, Ved. connected with or referring to a shrub &c.

उलिन्द ulinda, as, m., N. of a country; an epithet of Śiva.

उलुप ulupa, as, am, m. n. a spreading creeper; (as), m. the reed Saccharum Cylindricum. See ulapa.

उलुपिन् ulupin or ulapin or ulūpin, ī, m. a guinea-pig, a porpoise or fish resembling it.

उलुलि ululi, is, is, i or is, m., Ved. ululation, howling, a howl; [cf. Lat. ululabilis, ululatus.]

उलूक ulūka, as, m. (said to be fr. rt. val), an owl; N. of a country and people (pl.), and of their king, who appears in the Mahā-bhārata as a hero on the side of the Kurus; a son of Viśvā-mitra; of Śakuni; an epithet of Indra; N. of a king of the Nāgas; (am), n., N. of the reed Saccharum Cylindricum; [cf. Lat. ulula; Germ. Eule; Old Germ. uwila, ūla; Eng. owl; Fr. hulotte.] – Ulūka-yātu, us, m., Ved. a demon in the shape of an owl. – Ulūkāśrama (°ka-āś°), as, m. Indra's hermitage.

उलूखल ulūkhala, am, n. a wooden mortar used for cleansing rice from the husk &c.; bdellium, a gummy substance; (as), m. a staff of Udumbara wood, carried on certain occasions; N. of an evil spirit. – Ulūkhala-suta, as, ā, am, Ved. pressed out or pounded in a mortar.

Ulūkhalaka, am, n., Ved. a mortar; bdellium, a gummy substance, or the plant which produces it.

Ulūkhalika, as, ā, am, pounded in a mortar, cleansed from the husk; (at the end of a compound) using as a mortar (e. g. dantolūkhalika, using the teeth as a mortar).

उलूट ulūṭa or utūla or kulūṭa, ās, m. pl., N. of a people.

उलूत ulūta, as, m. a large snake, the Boa.

उलूप ulūpa, as, m. a spreading creeper; (am), n. a sort of grass; (ī), f., N. of a daughter of Nāga Kauravya, married to Arjuna.

उलूलु ulūlu, us, us, u or us, m. ululation, howling. See uluḷi.

उल्का ulkā, f. (said to be fr. rt. 1. ush), a fiery phenomenon in the sky, a meteor, fire falling from heaven; a firebrand; torch; fire, a flame, title of a grammar; [cf. Cambro-Brit. ulw, 'ashes.'] – Ulkā-jihva, as, m., N. of a Rakshas. – Ulkā-dhārin, ī, iṇī, i, a torch-bearer. – Ulkā-pāta, as, m. the fall of a meteor. – Ulkā-mālin, ī, m., N. of one of Śiva's attendants. – Ulkā-mukha, as, m. a demon or goblin (with a face or mouth of fire who eats what is vomited, having been a negligent Brāhman in his lifetime); N. of a descendant of Ikshvāku; (ī), f. a fox.

Ulkushī, f. a fiery phenomenon in the sky, a meteor; firebrand. – Ulkushī-mat, ān, atī, at, Ved. accompanied by fiery phenomena.

Ulmuka, am, n. a firebrand, wood burning or burnt as charcoal; N. of a son of Bala-rāma.

Ulmukya, as, ā, am, belonging to or connected with a firebrand.

उल्ब ulba or ulva, am, n. (fr. rt. vṛi), Ved. the bag which surrounds the embryo; the vulva; the womb; a cave; [cf. Lat. alvus, vulva; Lith. urwa, ūla; Hib. uile, 'a corner.']

Ulbaṇa or ulvaṇa, as, ā, am, thick, clotted, abundant; much, exceeding, superfluous, immense, strong, powerful; abundantly furnished with; manifest; (as), m., N. of a son of Vasishṭha.

Ulbya, as, ā, am, with āpaḥ, the fluid connected with the embryo; (am), n. excess and vitiation of any of the three humors of the body, bile, phlegm or wind; any calamity.

उल्लकसन ullakasana, am, n. horripilation, erection of the hairs of the body.

उल्लग्न ullagna, as, m. the lagna (q. v.) of any particular place.

उल्लङ्घ् ul-langh (ud-l°), cl. 1. P. A. -langhati, -te, -ghitum, to leap over, pass over or beyond, to cross over; transgress, exceed, violate, spurn.

Ul-langhana, am, n. leaping or passing over or beyond; transgression, exceeding.

Ul-langhanīya, as, ā, am, to be transgressed.

Ul-langhita, as, ā, am, jumped over or across, passed over or beyond; exceeded, transgressed, violated, apostatized. – Ullanghita-śāsana, as, ā, am, transgressing orders, rebellious, disobedient. – Ullanghitādhvan (°ta-adh°), ā, ā, a, having passed over the road.

Ul-langhya, as, ā, am, to be passed over or beyond, to be crossed; to be disregarded or neglected.

उल्लभ् ul-labh (ud-labh), cl. 1. A. -labhate, -labdhum, to obtain.

उल्लम्बित ul-lambita (ud-l°), as, ā, am, erected, elevated.

उल्लल ul-lala, as, ā, am (rt. lal), covered with thick hair; shaking, trembling.

Ul-lalat, an, antī, at, shaking, trembling; moving irregularly or convulsively.

Ul-lalita, as, ā, am, shaken, trembling, agitated.

Ul-lāla, N. of a metre of two verses, each containing 15 + 13 syllabic instants.

उल्लस् ul-las (ud-las), cl. 1. P. -lasati, -situm, to jump up, sport, play, dance, flash, shine: Caus. P. -lāsayati, -yitum, to cause to jump up or play; to cause to shine; to divert, delight.

Ul-lasa, as, ā, am, sporting, bright, shining; merry, happy; going out, issuing – Ullasa-tā, f. splendor, brilliancy; mirth, happiness, going forth, issuing.

Ul-lasat, an, antī, at, sporting, dancing, brilliant, shining; wantoning.

Ul-lasita, as, ā, am, shining, bright, splendid; happy; ejected, brought to the top or surface, drawn up, uplifted, brandishing. – Ullasita-hariṇa-ketana, as, ā, am, having its deer-marked banner gleaming or fluttering.

Ul-lāsa, as, m. jumping or leaping up, happiness, joy; light, splendor; (in rhetoric) giving prominence to any subject by comparison or opposition; division of a book, chapter, section (e. g. āćārollāsa, a chapter treating of customs and observances).

Ul-lāsana, as, ā, am, causing to leap or dance; (am), n. splendor.

Ul-lāsita, as, ā, am, delighted, overjoyed, rejoicing.

उल्लाघ ullāgha, as, ā, am (said to be fr. rt. lāgh; in some of its senses perhaps related to laghu), recovered from sickness, convalescent; dextrous, clever, intelligent; pure; happy, delighted; wicked; black.

उल्लाप ul-lāpa, as, m. (fr. rt. lap with ud), calling out in a loud voice; change of voice in grief, sickness, &c.

Ullāpika, as, ā, am, betraying, indicating.

Ul-lāpin, ī, inī, i, calling out.

Ul-lāpya, am, n. a kind of drama.

उल्लिख् ul-likh (ud-likh), cl. 6. P. -likhati, -lekhitum, to scratch, scrape, cut up, scarify.

Ul-likhat, an, atī or antī, at, scratching, scraping; scarifying, making lines or streaks above or on high; painting, writing; bearing, raising.

Ul-likhita, as, ā, am, scraped, scratched; scarified; thrown up, tossed; painted, delineated; written over or above; pared, made thin.

Ul-lekha, as, m. description; (in rhetoric) description of an object according to the different impressions caused by its apperance; speaking, utterance, pronunciation.

Ul-lekhana, am, n. scraping, scratching, scarifying, paring; digging; vomiting; raising up, elevating; uttering, utterance; writing, painting.

Ul-lekhya, as, ā, am, to be scraped or pared; to be written.

उल्लिङ्गित ul-lingita (ud-l°), as, ā, am, discriminated, distinguished, known.

उल्लुञ्चन ul-luñćana, am, n. plucking out the hair; cutting the hair; pulling.

उल्लुण्ठा ul-luṇṭhā, f. (fr. rt. luṇṭh with ud), irony.

उल्लू ul-lū, ūs, ūs, u (fr. rt. lū with ud), cutting up.

उल्लेख ul-lekha. See ul-likh above.

उल्लोच ul-loća, as, m. (rt. loć), an awning, a canopy.

उल्लोप्य ul-lopya, am, n. (rt. lup), N. of a song.

उल्लोल ul-lola (ud-l°), as, m. a large wave or billow; a surge.

उल्व ulva and ulvaṇa. See ulba and ulbaṇa.

उवट uvaṭa, as, m., N. of a scholiast on Vedic works.

उशङ्गव uśangava, as, m., N. of a king.

उशत् uśat, an, atī, at (fr. rt. vaś, to desire), loving, desirous, auspicious, pleasant.

Uśa-dhak, Ved. only in connection with vana, wood (fr. uśa, i. e. rt. vaś and dhaj, i. e. rt. dhe?; according to native etym. connected with rt. dah), (fire) consuming (wood &c.) with desire(?); (Sāy.) desiring and burning.

Uśanas, ā, m., N. of a sage mentioned in the Veda and having the epithet kāvya (uśanā kāvyaḥ); in the epic poems he is identified with Śukra, the regent of the planet Venus, and described as the preceptor of the Asuras or Daityas, and possessor of vast knowledge; N. of the author of a Dharma-śāstra.

Uśanā, ind., Ved. with desire, joyfully, with haste.

Uśānā, f., Ved. the desired one; N. of a plant, from which the Soma juice is produced.

Uśij, k, k, k, Ved. desiring, striving earnestly; devoted to, willing; (k), m. ghee or boiled butter; fire; (k), f., N. of a female slave, the mother of Kakshīvat.

Uśita, as, ā, am, wished, desired.

Uśi, is, f. wish, desire.

Uśenya, as, ā, am, Ved. to be wished, to be longed for.

उशती *uśatī,* f. (for *ruśatī,* scil. *vāć*), injurious discourse; cutting speech.

उशनस् *uśanas.* See under *uśat.*

उशीनर *uśīnara, ās,* m. pl., N. of a people or country, Kandahar; *(as),* m. the king of this country.

उशीर *uśīra, as, am,* m. n. (said to be fr. rt. *vaś*), the fragrant root of the plant Andropogon Muricatus; *(ī),* f. a sort of grass, a small sort of Saccharum. — *Uśīra-giri, is,* m., N. of a mountain. — *Uśīra-vīja, as,* m., N. of a mountain.

Uśīraka, am, n. the fragrant root of the plant Andropogon Muricatus.

Uśīrika, as, ī, am, trading in or selling Uśīra.

उष् 1. *ush,* cl. 1. P. *oshati, aushat, uvosha* or *oshāñ-ćakāra, oshishyati, aushīt, oshitum,* to burn; to punish; to consume; to kill, injure: Caus. *oshayati, -yitum:* Desid. *oshishishati;* [cf. Lat. *uro, ustus;* Gr. *αὔω, αὖος;* Hib. *usga,* 'incense.']

1. *usha, as,* m. bdellium; saline earth; *(am),* n. fossile salt. See *ūsha.*

Ushaṇa, am, n. black pepper; the root of Piper Longum; *(ā),* f. Piper Longum; Piper Chaba; dried ginger. See *ūshaṇa.*

Ushapa, as, m. fire; the sun.

1. *ushā,* f. burning, scorching. (For 2. see next col.)

1. *ushita* or *ushṭa, as, ā, am,* burnt; quick, expeditious. (For 2. see next col.)

Ushṇa, as, ā, am (opposed to *śīta*), hot, warm; pungent, acrid; sharp, active; impetuous, warm, passionate; *(as, am),* m. n. heat, warmth, the hot season (June and July); sunshine; a deep or feverish sigh; *(as),* m. an onion; N. of a prince; *(ā),* f. heat; consumption; bile. — *Ushṇa-kara, as,* m. the sun ('having hot rays'). — *Ushṇa-kāla, as,* m. the hot season. — *Ushṇa-ga, as,* m. the hot season. — *Ushṇa-gu, us,* m. the sun ('having hot rays'). — *Ushṇan-karaṇa, as, ī, am,* making hot or warm, heating. — *Ushṇa-tā,* f. or *ushṇa-tva, am,* n. heat, warmth. — *Ushṇa-dīdhiti, is,* m. the sun ('having hot rays'). — *Ushṇa-nadī,* f. the hot river; N. of the Vaitaraṇī or river of hell. — *Ushṇa-raśmi* or *ushṇa-rući, is,* m. the sun ('having hot rays'). — *Ushṇa-vāraṇa, as, am,* m. n. an umbrella or parasol, a chattar. — *Ushṇa-vāshpa, as,* m. hot vapour, steam; tears. — *Ushṇa-vīrya, as,* m. Delphinus Gangeticus. — *Ushṇa-vetālī,* f., N. of a female deity. — *Ushṇānśu* (°*ṇa-an*°), *us,* m. the sun ('having hot rays'). — *Ushṇāgama* (°*ṇa-āg*°), *as,* m. approach of the heat, the hot season, consisting of two months, about June and July. — *Ushṇābhigama* (°*ṇa-abh*°), *as,* m. the hot season. — *Ushṇāsaha* (°*ṇa-as*°), *as,* m. the cold season. — *Ushṇodaka* (°*ṇa-ud*°), *am,* n. warm or hot water, to be drunk on certain occasions; it belongs to the six prāṇa-karāṇi. — *Ushṇopagama* (°*ṇa-up*°), *as,* m. the hot season, summer.

Ushṇaka, as, ā, am, sharp, smart, active; suffering pain; sick of fever; warming, heating; bent, inclining, stooping; *(as),* m. the heat, the hot season (lasting for two months, about June and July); revolving, turning round.

Ushṇālu, us, us, u, suffering from heat.

Ushṇikā, f. rice-gruel.

Ushṇiman, ā, m. heat.

Ushṇī-kṛi, cl. 8. 5. P. A. *-karoti, -kurute, -kriṇoti, -ṇute, -kartum,* to make warm.

Ushṇī-ganga, the hot Gaṅgā, i. e. the Badarī, having hot sources; (perhaps merely a wrong reading for *tūshṇīnganga.*)

Ushma, as, m. heat; the hot season (June and July); spring (April and May); anger, warmth of temper; ardour, eagerness; [cf. *ushman* and *ūshman.*] — *Ushma-tā,* f. = *ushṇa-tā,* q. v. — *Ushma-pā, ās,* m. a spirit of an inferior order, a deceased ancestor; [cf. *ūshma-pa.*] — *Ushma-bhās, s,* m. the sun ('having hot beams'). — *Ushma-vat, ān, atī, at,* heated, burning, smoking. — *Ushma-sveda, as,* m. a vapour bath. — *Ushmāgama* (°*ma-āg*°), *as,* m. the hot season. — *Ushmānvita* (°*ma-an*°), *as, ā, am,* enraged. — *Ushmopagama* (°*ma-up*°), *as,* m. the hot season.

Ushmaka, as, m. the hot season.

Ushman, ā, m. heat, ardour, steam; the hot season.

Ushmāya, nom. A. *ushmāyate,* to emit heat or steam. See *ūshmāya.*

Ushmāyaṇa, as, m. the hot season.

उष् 2. *ush* (connected with rt. 3. *vas,* to shine; used as a noun but only in the form *ushas*), Ved. light, morning, dawn; *ushas tisraḥ,* morning, midday, and evening. (The words *ushas* and *ushā* below are connected by native authorities with 1. *ush.*)

2. *usha, as, ā, am,* Ved. shining, brilliant; *(as),* m. early morning, dawn, day-break.

Ushas, ās, f. morning light, dawn, morning; personified as the daughter of Heaven and sister of the Ādityas; evening light; *ushasau* or *ushāsau,* du. the two dawns, i. e. night and day; the outer passage of the ear; the Malaya range; *(sī),* f. the end of the day, twilight; [cf. Gr. *ἠώς;* Lat. *aurora;* Lith. *auszra;* Goth. *uh-tvô;* Old Germ. *uohta.*] — *Usharbudh, bhut, t, t,* Ved. awaking with the morning light, early awaked. — *Ushar-budha, as,* m. fire; a child. — *Ushāsā-naktā,* f. du., Ved. dawn and night. — *Usho-devatya, as, ā, am,* whose deity is the dawn.

1. *ushasya,* nom. P. *ushasyati, -yitum,* to become day.

2. *ushasya, as, ā, am,* sacred to the dawn.

2. *ushā,* f. morning light, dawn, morning; twilight, night; a cow; N. of a wife of Bhava (who was a manifestation of Rudra); of a daughter of Bāṇa and wife of Aniruddha; *(ā),* ind. at day-break; at night; at twilight (?). — *Ushā-kāla, as,* m. a cock. — *Ushā-pati, is,* m. an epithet of Aniruddha, the son of Kāmadeva and husband of Ushā. — *Ushā-ramaṇa, as,* m. an epithet of Aniruddha. — *Usheśa* (*ushā-īśa*), *as,* m. the same.

1. *usra, as, ā, am,* Ved. relating to or seen in the morning; bright; shining; clear; (Sāy. *utsaraṇa-śīla*) rising on high; *(as),* m. a ray of light; *(ā),* f. morning light, dawn, morning; light, bright sky. — *Usra-dhanvan, ā,* m. having a bright bow; an epithet of Indra. — *Usra-yāman, ā, ā, a,* Ved. going out in the early morning light (as the carriage of the Aśvins); going out at daylight.

Usriyā, f., Ved. brightness, light.

उष 3. *usha, as, ā, am* (connected with rt. *vaś*), wishing, desiring; *(as),* m. a lover.

Ushat, an, m., N. of a son of Suyajña.

उषङ्गु *ushaṅgu, us,* m. an epithet of Śiva; [cf. *uśaṅgava.*]

उषती *ushatī,* f. injurious discourse; cutting speech. See *uśatī.*

उषद्गु *ushadgu, us,* m., N. of a son of Svāhi.

उषद्रथ *ushadratha, as,* m. a son of Titikshu.

उषस्त *ushasta, as,* m., N. of a man, with the patronymic ćākrāyaṇa.

उषित 2. *ushita, as, ā, am* (rt. 1. *vas*), inhabited, dwelt; fixed, remaining in or on; stale. — *Ushitan-gavīna, as, ā, am,* formerly inhabited by cattle.

Ushitvā, ind. having resided in.

Ushya, ind. (irreg. form for *ushitvā*), having resided or dwelt.

उषीर *ushīra, as, am,* m. n. the root of Andropogon Muricatum. See *uśīra.*

उष्ट्र *ushṭra, as,* m. (said to be fr. 1. *ush*), a buffalo; a bull with a hump; a camel; a cart, a waggon; N. of an Asura; *(ī),* f. a she-camel; an earthen vessel in the shape of a camel. — *Ushṭra-karṇika, ās,* m. pl., N. of a people. — *Ushṭra-kāṇḍī,* f. a flower of a red colour. — *Ushṭra-krośin, ī, inī, i,* making a noise like a camel. — *Ushṭra-goyuga, am,* n. a couple of camels. — *Ushṭra-grīva, as,* m. hemorrhoids. — *Ushṭra-dhūsara-puććhikā,* f. the plant Tragia Involucrata. — *Ushṭra-pādikā,* f. the plant Jasminum Sambac. — *Ushṭra-yāna, am,* n. a camel-litter, a vehicle drawn by camels. — *Ushṭra-śiro-dhara, am,* n. hemorrhoids, piles, bleeding piles. — *Ushṭra-sthāna, am,* n. a stable for camels; *(as, ā, am),* born in a camel-stable.

Ushṭri, ṭā, m., Ved. a bull drawing a plough.

Ushṭrikā, f. a she-camel; an earthen vessel of the shape of a camel.

उष्णा *ushṇā.* See under 1. *ush* 1st col.

उष्णिह् *ushṇih, k,* f. (fr. *ud-snih?*), N. of a Vedic metre of three Pādas, the first two containing eight each, and the third twelve syllables; a classical metre of four Pādas of seven syllables; a brick sacred to the metre Ushṇih. — *Ushṇikćhandaska, as, ā, am,* having the metre Ushṇih. — *Ushṇig-garbhā,* f., N. of a Gāyatrī of three Pādas of six, seven, eleven syllables respectively.

Ushṇihā, f. the metre Ushṇih; *(ās),* pl., Ved. the nape of the neck.

उष्णीष *ushṇīsha, as, am,* m. n. (said to be connected with *ushṇa*), anything wound round the head; a turban, a diadem; a bandage of any kind; a distinguishing mark; the hair with which a Buddha is born and which indicates his future sanctity. — *Ushṇīsha-dhārin, ī, iṇī, i,* wearing a turban, turbaned.

Ushṇīshin, ī, iṇī, i, furnished with a turban; an epithet of Śiva.

उष्म *ushma.* See under 1. *ush.*

उष्य *ushya.* See under 2. *ushita.*

उष्यल *ushyala, am,* n., Ved. the frame (of a bed).

उस्र 2. *usra, as,* m. a bull; *(ā),* f. a cow; the plant Anthericum Tuberosum. (For 1. see last col.)

Usri, is, f., Ved. a cow (?).

Usrika, as, m., Ved. a small ox.

Usriya, as, ā, am, Ved. belonging to or coming from a cow or ox; *(as),* m. an ox; *(ā),* f. a cow; a calf; milk.

Usrīya, nom. P. *usrīyati, -yitum,* to desire or wish for a cow.

उह् *uh,* cl. 1. P. *ohati, uvoha, ohitum,* to hurt or give pain; to kill, to destroy. See *ūh.*

Uhan, Ved. a wrong reading for *udan.*

Uhāna, as, m., N. of a country.

उहू *uhū, ūs, ūs, u* (fr. rt. *vah*), Ved. bearing, carrying.

Uhyamāna, as, ā, am, being conveyed, borne along.

उह्यगान *uhyagāna,* a various reading for *ūhyagāna,* q. v.

ऊ

ऊ 1. *ū,* the sixth letter of the alphabet, corresponding to *u* long, and having the sound of that letter in the word *rule.* — *Ū-kāra, as,* m. the letter or sound *ū.*

ऊ 2. *ū,* ind. an interjection of compassion, of regard; an incipient particle used at the beginning of a sentence.

ऊ 3. *ū, ūs,* m. the moon; epithet of Śiva.

ऊ 4. *ū* (fr. rt. *av*), 'a preserver' (?).

1. *ūta, as, ā, am,* favoured, preserved, promoted, loved.

1. *ūti, is,* f. favouring, protecting, promoting, aid, assistance, help, favour, kindness, friendly feeling, affection, wish, desire, striving after, hastening towards, delight, enjoyment, sport, play, distillation; *(ayas),* pl. objects of enjoyment, as food &c.

Ūma, as, m., Ved. a good friend, an affectionate companion, an intimate associate; (am), n., N. of a town or country.

ऊवट ūaṭa, a various reading for uvaṭa, q.v.

ऊठ् ūṭh, a various reading for uṭh, q.v.

ऊढ 1. ūḍha, as, ā, am (fr. rt. vah or 1. ūh, for 2. ūḍha see 2. ūh), carried as a load or burden; married; (ā), f. a bride, a wife espoused according to the ritual. — Ūḍha-kaṅkaṭa, as, ā, am, armed, mailed. — Ūḍha-bhārya, as, ā, am, one who has married a wife. — Ūḍha-vayas, ās, m. a young man.

Ūḍhaya, nom. (fr. ūḍha or ūḍhi) P. ūḍhayati, aor. aujaḍhat or aujiḍhat, or auḍiḍhat, to carry (?).

Ūḍhi, is, f. carrying, bearing.

ऊणितेजस् ūṇī-tejas, ās, m., N. of a Buddha; (a various reading has ūrṇitejas.)

ऊत 2. ūta, as, ā, am (fr. rt. ve), woven.

2. ūti, is, f. weaving, sewing.

ऊधन् ūdhan and udhar, forms used in the Veda for some of the cases of ūdhas below.

ऊधस् ūdhas, n. (said to be fr. rt. vah. In the Veda the forms ūdhar and ūdhan are used for some of the cases, e.g. sing. nom. ūdhar, gen. abl. ūdhnas, loc. ūdhan or ūdhani; pl. inst. ūdhabhis, loc. ūdhassu), an udder; a covered secret place where only friends are admitted; the bosom; the breast of a mother; the udder of the sky, i.e. the clouds. In classical Sanskṛit the form ūdhan appears only in the fem. of adjective compounds, cf. adhy-ūdhnī, kuṇḍodhnī, ghaṭodhnī, pīnodhnī; [cf. Gr. οὖθαρ; Lat. uber; Germ. ūtar, euter; Angl. Sax. uder; Eng. udder; Hib. uit, uitche.] — Ūdhas-vatī, f. having a full udder.

Ūdhanya, as, ā, am, produced from the udder; (am), n. milk.

Ūdhasya, am, n. milk, 'produced from the udder.'

ऊन ūna, as, ā, am (said to be fr. rt. av and opposed to pūrṇa, ati-rikta, adhika), wanting, deficient, defective, short of any quantity, less than the right number, not sufficient; less (in number, size, or degree), minus, fewer, smaller, inferior, &c. (e.g. ūna-dvivarsha, not quite two years old; dvābhyām ūna, less by two; alpona, 'less by a little,' 'a little less.' Prefixed to any even decimal numeral from twenty up to a hundred, ūna serves to denote one less than the even ten, e.g. ūna-viṇśati, twenty minus one or nineteen; ūna-triṇśat, thirty minus one; ūnatriṇśa, the thirtieth minus one or twenty-ninth: so also with other numerals prefixed, e.g. pañćona-triṇśat, thirty minus five or twenty-five; ekonaćatvāriṇśa, the fortieth minus one or thirty-ninth.)

Ūnaka, as, ā, am, not sufficient, less, inferior.

Ūnaya, nom. P. ūnayati, -yitum, to leave deficient or unfinished; to deduct or lessen; to mete out in small quantities; to measure.

Ūnita, as, ā, am, lessened by subtraction or deduction, less, fewer, &c.

ऊम् ūm, ind. an interjection of interrogation; of anger; of reproach, abuse, envy, and arrogance.

ऊम ūma. See under 4. ū.

ऊय् ūy, cl. 1. A. ūyate = ve, vayati, to weave, sew.

ऊररी ūrarī, ind. a particle of assent and diffusion; ūrarī-kṛita, as, ā, am, allowed, promised. See urarī.

Ūrī, ind. = ūrarī; see urī. — Ūrī-kṛitya, ind. having promised, agreed, assented to.

ऊरु ūru, us, m. (said to be fr. ūrṇu), the thigh; N. of a son of Manu Ćākshusha; (vī), f. the middle of the thigh or a principal vein situated there. When ūru is used at the end of a compound the fem. form may end in either short or long u, but more properly in the latter (e.g. vāmorus or vāmorūs, a beautiful-thighed woman; rambhoru and raroru, O beautiful-thighed one; voc. cases of varorū and rambhorū). — Ūru-glāni, is, f. weakness of the thigh. — Ūru-ja, as, ā, am, born from the thigh; (as), m. a Vaiśya. — Ūru-daghna or ūru-dvayasa or ūru-mātra, as, ī, am, reaching to the thighs, as high as the thighs. — Ūru-parvan, ā or a, m. n. the knee. — Ūru-phalaka, am, n. the thigh-bone, the hip-bone. — Ūru-bhinna, as, ī, am, having a rent in the thigh (according to Pāṇini IV. 1, 52, used as a Bahu-vrīhi). — Ūru-sambhava, as, ā, am, sprung from the thigh. — Ūru-stambha, as, m. paralysis of the lower extremities, rheumatism of the thigh; (ā), f. the plantain tree. — Ūrūdbhava (ūru-ud°), as, ā, am, sprung from the thigh. — Ūrv-ashṭhīva, am, n. thigh and knee.

Ūravya, as, m. a man of the third or Vaiśya tribe as born from the thighs of Brahmā.

ऊरुरी ūrurī, ind. a particle implying assent, admission, promise, diffusion, &c.; [cf. ūrarī.]

ऊर्ज् ūrj, k, f. (fr. rt. vṛij; cf. Eng. work), food, strength, vigour, sap, juice; often occurring in conjunction with ish (e.g. isham ūrjam aśyuḥ, 'may they obtain food and strength'); [cf. Gr. ὀργάω and ὀργάς; Lat. urgeo; Hib. orc, 'a prince, a hero;' orcaim, 'I kill, I destroy.']

Ūrja, as, m., N. of the month Kārttika, i.e. November–December (as imparting food or strength); power, strength; effort, exertion; procreative power; life, breath; N. of a son of the second Manu; of Satyahita; of Vatsara; of the sons of Hiraṇya-garbha who are reckoned among the seven Ṛishis of the third Manvantara; (ā), f. food, strength, sap; N. of a daughter of Daksha and wife of Vasishṭha; (am), n. water. — Ūrja-yoni, is, m., N. of a son of Viśvāmitra. — Ūrja-vāha, as, m., N. of a son of Śući. — Ūrja-sani, is, is, i, Ved. granting strength. — Ūrja-stambha, as, m., N. of one of the seven Ṛishis of the second Manvantara. — Ūrjād (°jā-ad), t, t, t, Ved. an eater of strengthening food. — Ūrjā-vat, ān, atī, at, abounding in food. — Ūrjāhuti (°jā-āh°), is, is, i, Ved. offering nourishing or strength-giving sacrifices.

Ūrjaya, nom. P. ūrjayati, -yitum, to feed, strengthen; A. to become strong, to be powerful.

Ūrjayat, an, antī, at, Ved. strong, full of sap or juice, succulent; feeding, strengthening, nourishing.

Ūrjavya, as, ā, am, Ved. abounding in food or strength.

Ūrjas, a form for ūrj, used in compounds and with affixes, thus ūrjas-kara, as, ā, am, causing strength. — Ūrjas-vat, ān, atī, at, rich in food, abounding in sap or juice, juicy, succulent, powerful, vigorous, robust, strong; (tī), f., N. of a daughter of Daksha and wife of Dharma; of a daughter of Priya-vrata and wife of Uśanas; wife of Prāṇa. — Ūrjas-vala, as, ā, am, strong, powerful. — Ūrjas-vin, ī, inī, i, strong, powerful; (i), n. a figure of rhetoric, speaking of anything with disdain.

Ūrjānī, f., Ved. ūrjā personified.

Ūrjita, as, ā, am, powerful, strong, mighty, great, excellent, exceeding, much; (as), m., N. of a prince. — Ūrjitāśraya (°ta-āś°), as, ā, am, spirited, magnanimous.

Ūrjin, ī, inī, i, abounding in food.

ऊर्ण ūrṇa, am, ā, n. f. (fr. rt. vṛi, to cover, and connected with rt. ūrṇu next col.), wool; (ā), f. a circle of hair between the eyebrows; N. of the wife of Ćitra-ratha and mother of Samrāj; [cf. Lat. villus, vellus; Goth. vulla; Old Germ. wolla; Mod. Germ. Wolle; Eng. wool; Lith. wilna; Russ. volna; Gr. ἔρος, ἔριον, ἐρέα, εἶρος, εἴριον; Hib. olaun.] — Ūrṇa-nābha, as, m. a spider (as having wool on the navel or belly); N. of a son of Dhṛita-rāshṭra; of a Dānava. — Ūrṇa-paṭa, as, m. a spider. — Ūrṇa-mradas, ās, ās, as, or ūrṇa-mrada, as, ā, am, soft as wool. — Ūrṇa-vābhi, is, m. a spider ('wool-weaver?;' perhaps the original form of ūrṇa-nābhi, derived from an obsolete rt. vabh, to weave). — Ūrṇā-deśa, as, m., N. of a country. — Ūrṇā-piṇḍa, as, m. a ball of wool. — Ūrṇā-maya, as, ī, am, woollen, made of wool. — Ūrṇā-vat, ān, atī, at, woollen; (ān), m., N. of a man. — Ūrṇā-vala, as, ā, am, woollen. — Ūrṇā-sūtra, am, n., Ved. a thread of wool. — Ūrṇā-stukā, f., Ved. a tuft of wool.

Ūrṇāyu, us, us, u, woollen; (us), m. a ram; a woollen blanket; a spider; N. of a Gandharva.

ऊर्णु ūrṇu (connected with rt. vṛi), cl. 2. P. A. ūrṇoti and ūrṇauti, ūrṇute, ūrṇunāva, ūrṇunuve, ūrṇavishyati, -te, ūrṇuvishyati, -te, aurṇāvīt, aurṇavīt, aurṇuvīt, aurṇavishṭa, aurṇuvishṭa, ūrṇavitum, ūrṇuvitum, to cover, surround, hide; A. to cover one's self: Caus. ūrṇāvayati, aor. aurṇunuvat: Desid. ūrṇunūshati, -te, ūrṇunavishati, -te, ūrṇuvishati, -te: Intens. ūrṇonūyate, ūrṇonavīti, ūrṇonauti.

Ūrṇuta, as, ā, am, covered.

ऊर्द् ūrd, a various reading for rt. urd, q.v.

ऊर्दर ūrdara, as, m. (said to be in some of its meanings fr. ūrj and rt. dṛī), Ved. a vessel for measuring corn, a bushel; a hero, a champion; a Rakshas, a goblin or fiend.

ऊर्ध ūrdha and ūrdhaka, a wrong reading for ūrdhva and ūrdhvaka.

ऊर्ध्व ūrdhva, as, ā, am (fr. rt. vṛidh), rising, upwards, tending upwards, raised, elevated, erected, erect, upright; being above; above, high, superior, upper. In classical Sanskṛit an example of the uncompounded adjective as in ūrdhvaiḥ pādaiḥ, 'with raised feet,' is rare. (am), n. elevation, height, anything situated above; (am), ind. upwards, towards the upper part, aloft, above, in the upper regions, on the upper side of (with abl.); in the sequel (as of a book, the upper leaves of a MS. being read last); subsequent, after (with abl.); in a high tone, aloud; ūrdhvam dvitīyād aćaḥ, after the second vowel; ūrdhvam pituḥ, after the father's death; saṃvatsarād ūrdhvam, after a year; ata ūrdhvam, henceforward, from that time forward, hereafter; ūrdhvaṃ gam, to go upwards, to die; [cf. Gr. ὀρθός; Lat. arduus; Gaël. ard.] — Ūrdhva-kaća, as, m. an epithet of Ketu (whose hair streams upwards in the sky). — Ūrdhva-kaṇṭha, ās, m. pl., N. of a people; (ī), f., N. of a plant. — Ūrdhva-karṇa, as, ā, am, having the ears pricked up or erect. — Ūrdhva-karman, a, n. motion or action tending upwards; (ā), m., N. of Vishṇu (going upwards). — Ūrdhva-kāya, as, m. the upper part of the body. — Ūrdhva-kriśana, as, ā, am, Ved. effervescing, fermenting; epithet of the Soma; (Sāy.) having its sharp qualities stirred up. — Ūrdhva-ketu, us, m., N. of a son of Sanad-rāja. — Ūrdhva-keśa, as, ā, am, having the hair erect. — Ūrdhva-kriyā, f. motion or action tending upwards. — Ūrdhva-ga, as, ā, am, going upwards, ascending, hovering; being on high. — Ūrdhva-gata, as, ā, am, gone up, risen, ascended. — Ūrdhva-gati, is, is, i, going upwards; (is), f. ascent, elevation. — Ūrdhvaga-pura, am, n. the city of Hariśćandra, who with his subjects is supposed to be suspended in the atmosphere. — Ūrdhva-gama, as, m. upward motion of any kind. — Ūrdhva-gamana, am, n. going upwards, ascending; elevation in the scale of being. — Ūrdhva-gāmin, ī, inī, i, going up or above, ascending. — Ūrdhva-grāvan, ā, ā, a, Ved. raising the stones to press out the Soma plant. — Ūrdhva-ćaraṇa, as, ā, am, supine, having the feet upwards. — Ūrdhva-ćit, t, t, t, Ved. piling up, heaping up. — Ūrdhva-jānu, us, us, u, or ūrdhva-jña, as, ā, am, or ūrdhva-jñu, us, us, u, raising the knees, sitting on the hams; long-shanked. — Ūrdhva-tilakin, ī, inī, i, having a sectarian mark on the forehead. — Ūrdhva-tva, am, n. or ūrdhva-tā, f. height, elevation. — Ūrdhva-thā or ūrdhva-dhā, ind., Ved. upwards, erect. — Ūrdhva-danshṭrā-keśa, as, m. whose teeth and hair are erect; an epithet of Siva. — Ūrdhva-dṛishṭi, *is, is, i,* looking upwards, of high views, aspiring. — *Ūrdhva-deva, as,* m. a superior deity; an epithet of Vishṇu. — *Ūrdhva-deha, am,* n. ('the body gone above'), a funeral ceremony. — *Ūrdhva-nabhas, ās, ās, as,* Ved. being above in the clouds. — *Ūrdhvan-dama, as, ā, am,* going upwards, erected, exalted, elevated; (perhaps a wrong reading for *ūrdhvan-gama.*) — *Ūrdhva-patha, as,* m. the upper region, the ether. — *Ūrdhva-pātana, am,* n. causing to ascend, sublimation. — *Ūrdhva-pātra, am,* n. a sacrificial vessel. — *Ūrdhva-pāda, as, ā, am,* heels upwards; (*as*), m. a fabulous animal with eight legs; see *śarabha.* — *Ūrdhva-puṇḍra* or *ūrdhva-puṇḍraka, am,* n. a perpendicular line on the forehead of a Brāhman made with sandal &c., a Vaishṇava mark. — *Ūrdhva-pūram,* ind. full to the brim, full to overflowing. — *Ūrdhva-priśni, is, is, i,* Ved. spotted above. — *Ūrdhva-barhis, is, is, is,* Ved. being over the sacrificial grass. — *Ūrdhva-bāla, as, ā, am,* having the hair erect. — *Ūrdhva-bāhu, us, us, u,* having the arms raised; (*us*), m. a devotee who holds his arms above his head constantly till they are fixed in that position; N. of one of the seven Ṛishis of the fifth Manvantara; one of the seven Ṛishis of the south; one of the seven sons of Vasishṭha. — *Ūrdhva-budhna, as, ā, am,* Ved. bottom upwards, upside down. — *Ūrdhva-bṛihatī,* f., N. of a metre. — *Ūrdhva-bhāga, as,* m. the upper part; any part of a word coming after another part. — *Ūrdhva-bhāj, k, k, k,* partaking of the upper part; a N. of Baḍavāgni or submarine fire. — *Ūrdhva-manthin,* living in perpetual chastity; see *ūrdhva-retas.* — *Ūrdhva-māna, am,* n. an instrument for measuring altitudes. — *Ūrdhva-māyu, us, us, u,* giving forth a loud noise. — *Ūrdhva-māruta, am,* n. pressure of the wind (of the body) upwards. — *Ūrdhva-mukha, as, ī, am,* having the mouth or opening turned upwards. — *Ūrdhva-mauhūrtika, as, ī, am,* happening after a short time. — *Ūrdhva-rekhā-śavala, as, ā, am,* variegated with lines above. — *Ūrdhva-retas, ās, ās, as,* 'having the semen above,' abstaining from sexual intercourse, one who lives in perpetual chastity; a N. of Śiva, also of Bhīshma. — *Ūrdhva-roman, ā, ā, a,* having the hairs of the body erect; N. of a mountain. — *Ūrdhva-liṅga, as,* m., N. of Śiva. — *Ūrdhva-loka, as,* m. the upper world, the world above, heaven. — *Ūrdhva-vartman, ā,* m. the atmosphere, heaven. — *Ūrdhva-vāta, as,* m. or *ūrdhva-vāyu, us,* m. the wind in the upper part of the body. — *Ūrdhva-vṛita, as, ā, am,* put on above, put on over the head or shoulder (as the sacred thread of the Brāhman). — *Ūrdhva-śāyin, ī, inī, i,* sleeping upright; epithet of Śiva. — *Ūrdhva-śodhana, am,* n. 'purifying upwards,' i. e. vomiting. — *Ūrdhva-śosham,* ind. so as to dry (anything) above. — *Ūrdhva-śvāsa, as,* m. expiration. — *Ūrdhva-sānu, us, us, u,* Ved. carrying the neck high, with lofty or uplifted neck; (Sāy.) rising higher and higher. — *Ūrdhva-stha, as, ā, am,* being above, superior, situated on high. — *Ūrdhva-sthita, as, ā, am,* being or standing above. — *Ūrdhva-sthiti, is,* f. the rearing of a horse; a horse's back, the part where the rider sits; elevation, superiority. — *Ūrdhva-srotas, ās, ās, as,* N. of a creation of beings whose stream of life or current of nutriment tends upwards. — *Ūrdhvāṅguli* (°*va-aṅ*°), *is, is, i,* with raised finger. — *Ūrdhvāmnāya-saṃhitā* (°*va-ām*°), f. the doctrines of a particular Vaishṇava sect. — *Ūrdhvāyana* (°*va-ay*°), *ās,* m. pl., N. of a caste in Plaksha-dvīpa. — *Ūrdhvāvarta* (°*va-āv*°), *as,* m. rearing of a horse. — *Ūrdhvāsita* (°*va-as*°), *as,* m. the plant Momordica Charantia. — *Ūrdhveha* (°*va-īha*), *as,* m. motion or tendency upwards.

Ūrdhvaka as, m. a kind of drum.

Ūrdhvasāna, as, ā, am, Ved. rising, erecting one's self.

Ūrdhvī-kṛi, cl. 5. 8. P. A. *-kṛiṇoti, -ṇute, -karoti, -kurute, -kartum,* to raise aloft, to elevate.

ऊर्मि *ūrmi, is,* m. f. (fr. rt. *vṛi*), a wave; a current, the flowing of water; human infirmity (as grief, illusion, hunger, thirst, decay, death); speed, velocity; a fold or plait in a garment; a line, a row; manifestation, light; mental suffering, distress, uneasiness, pain; missing, regretting; association, number, quantity; [cf. Lith. *wilni-s;* Old Germ. *wella;* Mod. Germ. *Welle;* Eng. *well.*] — *Ūrmi-mat, ān, atī, at,* wavy, undulating, billowy; crooked; plaited, curled (as hair). — *Ūrmimat-tā,* f. undulation; crookedness. — *Ūrmimālin, ī, inī, i,* wreathed with waves, adorned with waves; (*ī*), m. the ocean.

Ūrmikā, f. a wave; a plait or fold in a garment; a finger ring; regret, sorrowing for anything lost; the buzzing of a bee.

Ūrmin, ī, iṇī, i, Ved. having waves, undulating.

Ūrmilā, f., N. of a daughter of Janaka and wife of Lakshmaṇa, mother of Gandharvī Somadā.

Ūrmya, as, ā, am, Ved. undulating, having waves, agitated; (*ā*), f. night.

ऊर्व 1. *ūrva, as,* m. (fr. rt. *vṛi*), Ved. a receptacle (for water), a reservoir; a cloud; an enclosed place, a stable for cattle; a prison, captivity (?); an epithet of the Pitṛis or manes of deceased ancestors.

Ūrvya, as, ā, am, Ved. being in reservoirs, lakes, &c.

ऊर्व 2. *ūrva, as,* m. (fr. *ūru ?*), N. of a saint from whose thighs sprang Aurva, a fiery being received by the ocean; the submarine fire; N. of a prince.

ऊर्वरा *ūrvarā,* f. fertile soil, land bearing any and every crop. See *urvarā.*

ऊर्वशी *ūrvaśī,* f., N. of an Apsaras. See *urvaśī.*

ऊर्वष्ठीव *ūrv-ashṭhīva.* See under *ūru.*

ऊर्वी *ūrvī.* See under *ūru.*

ऊर्व्यङ्ग *ūrvyaṅga, am,* n. (said to be fr. *ūrvī = urvī,* 'earth,' and *aṅga*), a mushroom.

ऊर्षा *ūrshā,* f. a kind of grass, Andropogon Serratum.

ऊलुपिन् *ūlupin, ī,* m. a porpoise. See *ulupin.*

ऊलूक *ūlūka, as,* m. an owl. See *ulūka.*

ऊवट *ūvaṭa,* a various reading for *uvaṭa* and *ūaṭa,* q. v.

ऊवध्य *ūvadhya* or *ūbadhya, am,* n., Ved. undigested grass &c. in the stomach (of an animal).

ऊष् *ūsh,* cl. 1. P. *ūshati, -shitum,* to be diseased or disordered, to be sick or ill.

ऊष *ūsha, as,* m. (fr. rt. 1. *ush* or fr. *ūsh* above ?), salt ground, soil impregnated with saline particles; a cleft, a hole; the cavity of the ear; dawn, daybreak (in the latter sense neut. according to some); the mountain Malaya; (*ī*), f. soil impregnated with saline particles or not fertile. — *Ūsha-puṭa, am,* n. particles of salt wrapped up in paper. — *Ūsha-vat, ān, atī, at,* consisting of saline soil.

Ūshaka, am, n. salt, pepper; dawn, day-break.

Ūshaṇa, am, n. black pepper; (*ā*), f. long pepper.

Ūshara, as, ā, am, impregnated with salt; (*am*), n. a barren spot with saline soil. — *Ūshara-ja, am,* n. salt produced from salt soil; a kind of magnet.

ऊषा *ūshā,* f., N. of the wife of Aniruddha. See *ushas,* &c.

ऊष्मन् *ūshman, ā,* m. (fr. rt. 1. *ush*), heat, steam, vapour, exhalation; ardour, passion, violence; the hot season; (in gram.) the sounds *ś, sh, s, h; shk, shp, aṃ, aḥ,* and more especially the first four of these sounds. — *Ūshma-pa, as, ā, am,* imbibing the steam of hot food; (*ās*), m. pl. a class of manes or deceased ancestors; (*as*), m. fire. — *Ūshma-para, as, ā, am,* followed by an Ūshman. — *Ūshma-prakṛiti, is, is, i,* produced from an Ūshman. — *Ūshma-vat, ān, atī, at,* hot, steaming. — *Ūshmānta* (°*ma-an*°), *as, ā, am,* ending in an Ūshman. — *Ūshmāntaḥstha* (°*ma-an*°), *ās,* m. pl. the sounds called Ūshman and the semivowels. — *Ūshmopagama* (°*ma-up*°), *as,* m. the approach of the heat.

Ūshmaṇa or *ūshmaṇya, as, ā, am,* Ved. steaming.

Ūshmāya, nom. A. *ūshmāyate, -yitum,* to emit heat or steam, to steam, perspire.

ऊह् 1. *ūh,* cl. 1. P. (with prep. also A.) *ūhati, -te, auhīt, ūhitum,* to change, modify; (with prep.) to push, thrust, move, remove, touch lightly. (This root is connected with rt. *vah;* and it is often difficult to decide to which of these two roots forms like 1. *ūḍha,* p. 177, are to be assigned.)

1. *ūha, as,* m. change, modification. — *Ūha-gāna, am,* n. or *ūha-gīti, is,* f., N. of the third Gāna or song book of the Sāma-veda.

Ūhanī, f. a broom.

Ūhya-gāna, am, n., N. of the fourth Gāna or song book of the Sāma-veda.

ऊह् 2. *ūh,* cl. 1. P. A. *ūhati, -te* (Ved. *ohate*), *ūhe* and *ūhāñ-ćakre, ūhishyate, auhishṭa, ūhitum,* to observe, mark, note, attend to (with acc.): to reckon on (with loc.); to wait for; to comprehend, conceive, conjecture, suppose, infer, reason, deliberate about; to be regarded as: Caus. *ūhayati, -yitum,* aor. *aujihat,* to cause to think, reason, infer, or conjecture; to attend to (?); to do, accomplish (?): Desid. *ūjihishate;* [cf. Hib. *uige;* Lat. *äugeo;* Goth. *auka;* Hib. *ugtar,* 'augmentation.']

2. *ūḍha, as, ā, am,* observed, inferred, &c.

2. *ūha, as,* m. deliberation, examination; reasoning; understanding; completing a defective sentence or verse, supplying an ellipsis; [cf. Hib. *uga,* 'choice, election.']

Ūhana, am, n. reasoning, inferring, concluding.

Ūhin, ī, inī, i, who or what reasons; who or what assembles, infers, or conjectures; (*inī*), f. an assemblage, a collection; arrangement, a multitude reduced to order; [cf. *akshauhiṇī.*]

Ūhya, as, ā, am, inferrible, to be investigated, requiring to be supplied, elliptical.

ऋ

ऋ 1. *ṛi,* the seventh vowel of the Sanskrit alphabet and peculiar to it, resembling the sound of *ri* in *merrily.* — *Ṛi-kāra, as,* m. the letter or sound *ṛi.*

ऋ 2. *ṛi,* ind. an interjection of abuse, laughter; a sound inarticulate or reiterated as in stammering.

ऋ 3. *ṛi, ā,* f. a N. of Aditi.

ऋ 4. *ṛi,* cl. 1. 9. (Ved. also 3. 4. 5. P.) *ṛićchati, ṛiṇāti* (Ved. *iyarti, āryate, ṛiṇoti* or *ṛiṇvati*), *āra* or *arāñ-ćakāra, arishyati* or *arīshyati* (?), *ārat, artum, aritum* or *arītum* (?), (Ved. 3rd pl. impf. *ranta*), to rise, tend upwards; to go, move; to meet with, fall upon or into, reach, obtain; to fall to one's share (with acc.); to move, excite, raise, raise (in singing, e. g. *vāćam iyarti,* he raises his voice; *stomān iyarti,* he sings hymns); to display; to injure, hurt: Caus. *arpayati, -yitum,* to throw, cast; to put, place, insert, fix, fasten; to direct towards, cast upon; to pierce; to place on, apply; to offer, give, give up, surrender; to give back, restore: Intens. Ved. 2nd pers. *alarshi,* 3rd pers. *alarti,* to move, come; strive, make effort, exert one's strength: Intens. Class. *arāryate,* to wander about; to run or fly towards: Desid. *aririshati;* [cf. Goth. *airus,* 'a messenger;' Hib. *ria* or rather *do ria,* 'he will come or arrive;' *ria,* 'running, speed;' *riach,* 'he came;' *riaehtaim,* 'I arrive;' *ar,* 'guiding, conducting.' With the Caus. have been compared Old Germ. *arbjan,* 'to inherit;' *kierpit,* 'possession;' Goth. *arbi,* Them. *arbja,* 'inheritance:' cf. also Lat. *aro;* Goth. *arja;* Old Germ. *erru;* Lith. *arù;* Lith. *orjù;* Gr. ἀίρω; Hib. *ar,* 'slaughter, destruction, plague, the slain in fight;' *aor,* 'a satire, a course.']

ऋक्छस् *ṛik-ćhas.* See under 2. *ṛić.*

ऋक्ण 1. ṛikṇa, as, ā, am (for vṛikṇa fr. rt. vraść), wounded. — Ṛikṇa-vaha, as, ā, am, whose shoulders are wounded or made sore by drawing.

ऋक्ण 2. ṛikṇa = ṛiktha below.

ऋक्थ ṛiktha, am, n. (fr. rt. ric), property, wealth, possessions, effects (especially left at death); gold; see riktha. — Ṛiktha-grahaṇa, am, n. receiving or inheriting property. — Ṛiktha-grāha, as, ā, am, an inheritor or receiver of property; (as), m. inheriting or receiving property. — Ṛiktha-jāta, as, ā, am, formed into property, accumulated (as property). — Ṛiktha-bhāga, as, m. division of property, inheritance, partition, a share. — Ṛiktha-bhāgin, ī, inī, i, an heir, a coheir; inheriting or sharing property. — Ṛiktha-hara, as, ī, am, an heir, a coheir. — Ṛiktha-hārin, ī, iṇī, i, inheriting or sharing property; an heir. — Ṛikthādāna (°tha-ād°), as, m. an inheritor.

ऋक्व ṛikva, as, ā, am, or ṛikvan, ā, ā, a (fr. rt. arć), Ved. praising, rejoicing.

ऋक्ष् ṛiksh, cl. 5. P. ṛikshṇoti, to kill; to hurt or seek to hurt; (a doubtful root.)

ऋक्ष 1. ṛiksha, as, ā, am, Ved. bald, bare.

ऋक्ष 2. ṛiksha, as, m. (fr. preceding rt. ṛiksh? or fr. rt. riś? or fr. rt. vraść?, cf. 1. ṛikṇa; or fr. rt. ṛić connected with rt. ark, to shine?; connected with rakshas?), Ved. one who hurts or destroys (?); a bear (as having a shining coat?); (ī), f. a female bear; (ās), m. pl. the seven stars, the Pleiades, Ἄρκτος, Ursa; in later times the seven Ṛishis; (as, am), m. n. a star, a constellation in general, a lunar mansion; the particular star in the twenty-seven mansions of the moon under which a person happens to be born; (as), m., N. of the plant Bignonia Indica, and of a similar species; N. of a man, a son of Ajamīḍha, or Ariha, or Vidūratha, or Revata; of Akrodhana; a descendant of Bhṛigu, identified with Valmīki; N. of a mountain; (ā), f., N. of the wife of Ajamīḍha; [cf. Gr. ἄρκτος; Lat. ursus; Hib. art; Lith. lokys for olkys; Armen. arj.] — Ṛiksha-gandhā, f. the plant Argyreia Argentea. — Ṛiksha-gandhikā, f. the plant Batatas Paniculata. — Ṛiksha-grīva, as, m., Ved. a kind of imp or demon. — Ṛiksha-nātha, as, m. lord of the stars, an epithet of the moon. — Ṛiksha-nemi, is, m. a N. of Vishṇu. — Ṛiksha-rāja, as, m. the king of the bears; king of the stars, an epithet of the moon. — Ṛiksha-vat, ān, m., N. of a mountain. — Ṛiksha-ranta, am, n., N. of a town. — Ṛiksha-vibhāvana, am, n. observing the stars. — Ṛiksha-harīśvara (°ri-īś°), as, m. the lord of bears and apes. — Ṛiksheśa (°sha-īśa), as, m. lord of the stars, an epithet of the moon. — Ṛiksheshṭi (°sha-ish°), is, f. offering worship to the planets and stars. — Ṛikshoda (°sha-uda), as, m., N. of a mountain.

Ṛikshīkā, f., Ved., N. of certain demons or evil spirits.

ऋक्ष 3. ṛiksha, as, ā, am (perhaps a wrong reading for ṛikṇa), pierced, cut, divided.

ऋक्षर ṛikshara, as, m. (fr. rt. 1. or 2. ṛish?), a thorn; a family priest; (am), n. a shower, a stream.

ऋक्षला ṛikshalā, f., Ved. a fetter; [cf. ṛiććharā.]

ऋघाय ṛighāya, nom. P. A. (fr. an obsolete noun ṛigha), Ved. ṛighāyati, -te, -yitum, to tremble; to tremble with passion, rage, rave; [cf. Zend ereghata; Germ. arg.]

Ṛighā-vat, ān, atī, at, Ved. raving, impetuous.

ऋच् 1. ṛić (connected with rt. arć and with rt. ark, q. q. v. v.), cl. 6. P. ṛićati, ānarća, arćishyati, arćitum, Ved. inf. ṛićase, to praise, extol, laud, celebrate; to cover, screen; to shine (?).

2. ṛić, k, f. (fr. preceding rt. or fr. rt. arć), lustre, splendor; a hymn; a single verse, stanza or text, especially verses recited or spoken at a sacrifice or religous ceremony (whereas the verses called sāman [pl. sāmāni] are sung, and the verses called yajus [pl. yajūṇshi] are some of them not metrical and are muttered in a peculiar manner; these three kinds of verse constitute the Mantra and are considered as sacred speech); a verse of the Ṛig-veda, the particular verse or text on the authority of which a ceremony is prescribed and to which the explanation in the Brāhmaṇa refers; the collective body of the Ṛić, i. e. the Ṛig-veda (but in this sense generally pl. ṛićas). — Ṛik-ćhas or ṛik-śas, ind. verse by verse, one verse after the other. — Ṛik-tantra-vyākaraṇa, am, n. one of the Pariśishṭas of the Sāma-veda. — Ṛik-tas, ind. from a Ṛić, with reference to a Ṛic. — Ṛik-prātiśākhya, am, n. the Prātiśākhya of the Ṛig-veda. — Ṛik-śata, am, n. a hundred texts. — Ṛik-shama (fr. ṛić and sama), as, ā, am, Ved. similar to a Ṛić; N. of a Sāman. — Ṛik-saṃśita, as, ā, am, Ved. instigated by the Ṛić. — Ṛik-saṃhitā, f. the arranged collection of the hymns of the Ṛig-veda. — Ṛik-sama, as, ā, am, Ved. similar to a Ṛić (as a Sāman). — Ṛik-sāma, e, n. du., Ved. the verses called Ṛić and Sāman. — Ṛik-sāman, a, n., N. of a Sāman. — Ṛiksāma-śṛinga, as, m. an epithet of Vishṇu. — Ṛig-āvānam, ind. (āvānam fr. rt. ve with ā), Ved. connecting one Ṛić with another, not interrupting their continuance. — Ṛig-gāthā, f., N. of a certain song. — Ṛig-bhāj, k, k, k, partaking of a Ṛić, as a deity who is addressed with it. — Ṛig-yajuḥ-sāma-vedin, ī, m. one who is familiar with the Ṛig, Yajur, and Sāma-veda. — Ṛig-vidhāna, am, n. title of a work of Śaunaka. — Ṛig-veda, as, m. the Ṛig-veda; the collective body of sacred verses which as being recited are called Ṛićas and differ from Sāmāni and Yajūṇshi in the manner described above; the arranged collection of these hymns as the most ancient sacred book of the Hindūs. (The Ṛig-veda consists of ten books or Maṇḍalas; the first eight books contain groups of hymns, each group ascribed to one author or to the members of one family; the ninth book contains the songs recited at the Soma ceremonies; the tenth contains hymns of a very different character, composed by a greater variety of individual authors. In its wider sense the term Ṛig-veda comprehends the Brāhmaṇas and the Sūtra works on the ritual connected with the hymns.) — Ṛigveda-prātiśākhya, am, n. the Prātiśākhya of the Ṛig-veda, attributed to Śaunaka. — Ṛigveda-vid, t, m. a Brāhman familiar with the Ṛig-veda. — Ṛigvedānukramaṇikā (°da-an°), f. the index of the Ṛig-veda, attributed to Kātyāyana. — Ṛig-vedin, ī, inī, i, conversant with the Ṛig-veda. — Ṛiṅ-maya, as, ī, am, consisting of Ṛićas.

Ṛigma, as, ā, am, Ved. having the character of a Ṛić.

Ṛigmin, ī, iṇī, i, Ved. praising, exulting with joy, jubilant with praise.

Ṛigmiya, as, ā, am, Ved. deserving praise, laudable.

Ṛića (at the end of some compounds) = Ṛić; (as), m., N. of a prince, a son of Sunīka.

ऋचीक ṛićīka, as, m., N. of the father of Jamadagni, a son of Heaven; N. of a country.

ऋचीष ṛićīsha, am, n. a frying-pan; (as), m. a hell.

ऋचीषम ṛićīshama, as, ā, am, Ved. (Sāy. fr. ṛić and sama) equal to the Ṛić; epithet of Indra; (perhaps this word is related to ṛijīsha, ṛijīshin, q. v.)

ऋचेयु ṛićeyu, us, m., N. of a man; a son of Raudrāśva.

ऋछ् ṛićh, cl. 6. P. ṛićchati, ānarćcha, arććhitum, to go, move; to fail in faculties; to become hard or stiff; [cf. Lat. rigere.]

ऋच्छका ṛićchakā, f. (fr. rt. 4. ṛi), wish, desire.

ऋच्छरा ṛićcharā, f., Ved. a fetter; a harlot, a courtezan.

ऋज् 1. ṛij, cl. 1. P. arjati, ānarja, arjitum, to bring near, obtain, get, acquire: Caus. arjayati, -yitum, to obtain, get, acquire.

ऋज् 2. ṛij, cl. 1. A. arjate, -jitum, to go; to stand or be firm; to acquire; to be healthy or strong; [cf. Lat. rego, rectus; Goth. raihts; Mod. Germ. recht; Gr. ὀρέγω; Hib. righim, 'I reach, arrive, stretch.']

ऋजिप्य ṛijipya, as, ā, am (fr. rt. 2. ṛiñj?), Ved. going quick, striving upwards; [cf. Zend ĕrĕzifja.]

ऋजिश्वन् ṛijiśvan, ā, m., Ved., N. of a man (protected by Indra) who has the epithet Vaidathina.

ऋजीक ṛijīka, as, ā, am (fr. 2. arj), Ved. coloured, variegated; mixed with; polluted; (as), m. smoke; an epithet of Indra; N. of a mountain.

Ṛijīti, is, is, i, Ved. burning, sparkling.

ऋजीष ṛijīsha, as, ā, am (fr. rt. 2. ṛiñj?), Ved. epithet of Indra, carrying or driving away, (or perhaps = ṛijīshin below); (am), n. the sediment or residue of Soma; a frying-pan; N. of a hell; (Sāy.) water.

Ṛijīshin, ī, iṇī, i, Ved. hastening towards, seizing; consisting of or receiving the sediment or residue of Soma.

ऋजु ṛiju, us, us, u (fr. rt. 2. ṛiñj), tending in a straight direction, straight; straight metaphorically as in morals, right, honest, upright; (in Ved. = sādhu and opposed to vṛijina; in classical Sanskṛit opposed to jihma and tiryać); comparative ṛijīyas, Ved. rajīyas; superlative ṛijishṭha, Ved. rajishṭha; (us), m., N. of a son of Vasu-deva; [cf. Hib. aroch; Zend ĕrĕśu.] — Ṛiju-kāya, as, ā, am, having a straight body; (as), m., N. of the saint Kaśyapa. — Ṛiju-kratu, us, us, u, Ved. intending what is honest; (Sāy.) acting honestly. — Ṛiju-ga, as, ā, am, Ved. going straight. — Ṛiju-gātha, as, ā, am, Ved. singing correctly. — Ṛiju-tā, f. or ṛiju-tva, am, n. straight direction, straightness; uprightness, sincerity, honesty. — Ṛiju-dāsa, as, m., N. of a son of Vasu-deva. — Ṛiju-dhā, ind. straight, right. — Ṛiju-nīti, is, f., Ved. right conduct. — Ṛiju-mitāksharā, f. title of a commentary on Yājñavalkya's law-book, generally called Mitāksharā. — Ṛiju-mushka, as, ā, am, Ved. having straight generative organs; (Sāy.) strong and muscular. — Ṛiju-raśmi, is, is, i, Ved. having straight rope-traces (said of a chariot). — Ṛiju-rohita, am, n. the straight red bow of Indra. — Ṛiju-vani, is, is, i, Ved. striving straightforward; (Sāy.) granting auspicious gifts. — Ṛiju-śansa, as, ā, am, Ved. desiring what is right. — Ṛiju-sarpa, as, m. a kind of snake. — Ṛiju-hasta, as, ā, am, Ved. extending the hand. — Ṛijū-nas, ās, m., N. of a man.

Ṛijūka, as, m., N. of a mountain.

Ṛijū-kṛi, cl. 8. P. -karoti, -kartum, to straighten, rectify. — Ṛijū-karaṇa, am, n. straightening. — Ṛijū-kṛita, as, ā, am, made straight.

Ṛijūya, nom. Ved. ṛijūyati, -te, -yitum, to walk straightforward, on the right or honest way; to direct one's way towards anything.

Ṛijūyā, ind., Ved. in a straight line.

Ṛijūyu, us, us, u, Ved. honest; upright.

Ṛijvać, ān, ūćī (?), ak, Ved. going straightforward.

ऋज्र 1. ṛijra, as, ā, am (rt. 2. arj), Ved. reddish, dark red, reddish brown.

Ṛijriya, as, ā, am, Ved. reddish, red.

ऋज्र 2. ṛijra, as, m. (fr. rt. 2. ṛiñj?), a leader. — Ṛijrāśva (°ra-aś°), as, m., N. of a man.

ऋञ्ज् 1. ṛiñj, cl. 1. A. ṛiñjate, ṛiñjāñćakre, -jitum, to fry.

ऋञ्ज् 2. ṛiñj, cl. 6. P. A. ṛiñjati, -te, -jitum, to spring forward, run; to strive after, long for; (Sāy.) to decorate.

Ṛiñjasāna, as, ā, am, running towards, striving after; (as), m. a cloud.

ऋण ṛiṇa, as, ā, am (said to be fr. rt. 4. ṛi;

cf. Lat. *reus*), Ved. guilty; (*am*), n. guilt; obligation, debt (opposed to *dhana* and *ṛiktha*, 'property'); a fort, a stronghold; water; a negative quantity, minus; (*as*), m. a N. of Vyāsa; *antyam ṛiṇam*, the last debt, a debt to the manes, i. e. the generation of a son; *ṛiṇam kṛi*, to get into debt; *ṛiṇam dhṛi*, to be indebted; *ṛiṇam dā* or *pra-yam* or *sam-nī*, to pay a debt; *ṛiṇam prāp*, to become indebted; *ṛiṇam parīps* (Desid. fr. rt. *āp* with *pari*), to require payment of a debt, call in a debt. — *Ṛiṇa-kartṛi, tā, trī, tṛi*, getting into debt, indebted. — *Ṛiṇa-kāti, is, is, i*, Ved. requiring payment of debts, 'taking revenge;' (Sāy.) one to whom praise is due as a debt, or one who receives praise as a debt to be repaid in benefits. — *Ṛiṇa-grasta, as, ā, am*, indebted, involved in debt. — *Ṛiṇa-graha, as*, m. borrowing; a borrower. — *Ṛiṇa-grāhin, ī, iṇī, i*, borrowing; a borrower. — *Ṛiṇa-ćit, t, t, t*, Ved. punishing offences or guilt; (Sāy.) acknowledging (praise) as an obligation to be paid for. — *Ṛiṇa-ćyut, t, t, t*, Ved. granting quittance of a debt or an offence. — *Ṛiṇañ-ćaya, as*, m., N. of a prince of the Ruśamas; N. of an author of a hymn in the Ṛig-veda (IX. 108). — *Ṛiṇa-da, as, ā, am*, or *ṛiṇa-dātṛi, tā, trī, tṛi*, or *ṛiṇa-dāyin, ī, inī, i*, one who pays a debt. — *Ṛiṇa-dāna, am*, n. payment of a debt. — *Ṛiṇa-dāsa, as*, m. lit. 'a debt-slave,' i. e. one who becomes a slave to his creditor till his debt is paid. — *Ṛiṇa-matkuṇa, as*, m. a security, a bail (which sticks to the debtor like an insect). — *Ṛiṇa-mārgaṇa, as*, m. a security. — *Ṛiṇa-mukta, as ā, am*, released from debt. — *Ṛiṇa-mukti, is*, f. discharge of a debt. — *Ṛiṇa-moksha, as*, m. paying a debt. — *Ṛiṇa-yā, ās, ās, am*, or *ṛiṇa-yāvan, ā, ā, a*, Ved. punishing or prosecuting guilt; keeping off debt or guilt. — *Ṛiṇa-vat, ān, atī, at*, one who is in debt, one who is under obligation (to another), indebted. — *Ṛiṇa-van, ā, ā, a*, Ved. guilty, indebted; obliged, under obligation (to another). — *Ṛiṇa-śodhana, am*, n. payment or discharge of a debt. — *Ṛiṇādāna* (°*ṇa-ād*°), *am*, n. recovery of a debt, receipt of money &c. lent (as one of the eighteen titles or subjects of judicial procedure). — *Ṛiṇāntaka* (°*ṇa-an*°), *as*, m. the planet Mars (as the patron of debtors). — *Ṛiṇāpanayana* (°*ṇa-ap*°), *am*, n. discharge of a debt. — *Ṛiṇāpanodana* (°*ṇa-ap*°), *am*, n. payment of a debt. — *Ṛiṇāpākāraṇa* (°*ṇa-ap*°), *am*, n. paying off a debt. — *Ṛiṇārṇa* (°*ṇa-ṛi*°), *am*, n. debt of a debt, compound interest; [cf. Gram. 38. *d.*] — *Ṛiṇodgrahaṇa* (°*ṇa-ud*°), *am*, n. recovering a debt in any way from the creditor by friendly or legal proceedings, by stratagem or by arrest.

Ṛiṇika, as, m. a debtor.

Ṛiṇin, ī, inī, i, a debtor, one under any obligation (to another), indebted, of or belonging to a debt; [cf. *an-ṛiṇin*.]

ऋत् *ṛit*, A. *ṛitīyate*, to reproach, contemn, pity; to rival, have power, domineer; hate; go; (a Sautra root, i. e. a root occurring only in grammatical Sūtras and not in the Dhātu-pāṭha.) [To this root have been referred Goth. rt. *lith* in *leithu, laith, lithum;* Hib. *rith*, 'course, flight, gallop, race;' *rithim*, 'I run, range, rush.']

ऋत *ṛita, as, ā, am* (fr. rt. 4. *ṛi*), proper, right; honest, brave, competent; true; worshipped, respected; enlightened, luminous; gone, risen, moved, affected by; (*am*), ind. right, duly, properly, energetically; *ṛitam i*, to go the right way, to live virtuously; (*as*), m., N. of a Rudra; of a prince; (*am*), n. fixed or settled order, law, rule (especially in religion); sacred or pious custom, pious action; divine law, faith, divine truth; (Sāy.) water, sacrifice, sacrificial rite; the sun (e. g. *ṛitam bṛihat*, the great divine law, supreme truth, or according to Sāy. a great sacrifice; *ṛitasya garbhaḥ* or *prajāḥ*, the offspring of divine truth, or according to Sāy. the offspring of the water or of sacrifice, as an epithet of Agni, of Soma, or of Vishṇu; *prathamajā ṛitasya*, the first-born of divine truth or Prajāpati; *ṛitasya sadanam* or *sadaḥ* or *sadma* or *padam* or *nābhiḥ*, the seat or centre of religious faith, as the altar &c., or according to Sāy. the seat of water or of the sun; *ṛitasya yoniḥ*, water; *ṛitasya gopāḥ* or *netā* or *rathīḥ* or *patiḥ*, the protector or leader or lord of divine truth, or according to Sāy. of the sacrifice, as an epithet of Agni, of Soma, of the Ādityas, and other gods, or sometimes applied to men who are guardians of the truth); truth in general, right (e. g. *pathyā* or *panthā ṛitasya*, the path of truth, the right way, a virtuous life, or according to Sāy. the way of the water); truth personified (as an object of worship, and hence enumerated among the sacred objects in the last chapter of the Nighaṇṭavas. In later Sanskrit he is regarded as a child of Dharma); gleaning, i. e. the lawful and right means of getting a livelihood for Brāhmans as opposed to the cultivation of the ground (this latter being metaphorically called *an-ṛita*, improper). — *Ṛita-ćit, t, t, t*, Ved. observing the sacred law, conversant or familiar with it; (Sāy.) knowing the sacrifice or water. — *Ṛita-jā, ās, ās, am*, or *ṛita-jāta, as, ā, am*, Ved. happening at the right time, of a true nature, sprung from sacred truth, according to sacred truth. — *Ṛita-jāta-satya, as, ā, am*, Ved. realizing what is according to the sacred law; (Sāy.) born for the sake of the sacrifice and having true result. — *Ṛita-jit, t, t, t*, Ved. gaining the right. — *Ṛita-jur, ūr, ūr, ur*, Ved. grown quite old; (Sāy.) growing old in religious worship. — *Ṛita-jña, ās, ās, am*, Ved. well informed; familiar with the sacred law; (Sāy.) knowing the sacrifice. — *Ṛita-jya, as, ā, am*, Ved. furnished with a good bow-string; (Sāy.) whose string is truth, truth-strung (said of a bow). — *Ṛita-dyumna, as, ā, am*, Ved. filled with sacred strength. — *Ṛita-dhāman, ā, ā, a*, Ved. of true or pure nature; (*ā*), m., N. of Vishṇu; of the thirteenth Manu; of the Indra in the twelfth Manvantara. — *Ṛita-dhīti, is, is, i*, Ved. of true or sacred disposition; epithet of the gods; (Sāy.) receiving true praise; whose actions are unobstructed. — *Ṛita-dhvaja, as*, m. epithet of Rudra; N. of a sage; a son of Kaṅka; epithet of Pratardana. — *Ṛita-nī, īs, īs, i*, Ved. leading in the right way; (Sāy.) leader of truth (as the Ādityas). — *Ṛita-parṇa, as*, m., N. of a prince (son of Ayutājit and friend of Nala). — *Ṛita-pā, ās, ās, am*, Ved. observing the truth; observing the law; (Sāy.) protecting truth or the sacrifice. — *Ṛita-peya, as*, m., N. of a certain ceremony. — *Ṛita-peśas, ās, ās, as*, Ved. having a perfect shape; epithet of Varuṇa; (Sāy.) one whose form consists of water. — *Ṛita-prajāta, as, ā, am*, Ved. happening at the right time, of true nature, born from sacred truth, according to sacred truth; (Sāy.) produced from water. — *Ṛita-pravīta, as, ā, am*, Ved. conceived in the right manner; (Sāy.) invested with truth, or with water, or with the sacrifice. — *Ṛita-psu, us, us, u*, Ved. having a perfect shape or aspect; (Sāy.) whose form is truth, or who consumes the sacrificial food. — *Ṛita-bhāga, as*, m., N. of a man, 'Αρταβάζης. — *Ṛitam-bhara, as, ā, am*, bearing the truth in one's self, an epithet of Brahmā, also of Vishṇu; (*ā*), f. intellect; N. of a river. — *Ṛita-yukti, is*, f., Ved. right union; (Sāy.) true application of a hymn. — *Ṛita-yuj, k, k, k*, Ved. well harnessed; well allied; (Sāy.) going to the sacrifice. — *Ṛita-vat, ān, atī, at*, being right, saying the truth. — *Ṛita-vāka, as*, m., Ved true or pious speech, speaking of truth. — *Ṛita-vādin, ī, inī, i*, Ved. saying right, speaking truth. — *Ṛita-vrata, ās*, m. pl., N. of the inhabitants of Śākadvīpa. — *Ṛita-sad, t, t, t*, Ved. dwelling or seated in truth; (Sāy.) dwelling in the sacrifice. — *Ṛita-sadana, am, ī*, n. f., Ved. the right or usual seat. — *Ṛita-sāp, p, p, p*, Ved. practising pious acts, of a pious disposition; steady in religious belief; (Sāy.) pervading truth. — *Ṛita-stubh, p*, m. 'praising in the right manner,' N. of a Ṛishi. — *Ṛita-sthā, ās, ās, am*, Ved. standing right. — *Ṛitas-pati, is*, m., Ved. lord of divine truth; an epithet of Vāyu; (Sāy.) lord of sacrifices. — *Ṛita-spṛiś, k, k, k*, Ved. loving sacred truth; an epithet of the Ādityas and of Mitra-Varuṇa; (Sāy.) touching water. — *Ṛitānṛita* (°*ta-an*°), *am*, n. truth and falsehood. — *Ṛitā-van, ā, arī, a*, Ved. of true nature or character, according to fixed order, epithet of any object in nature subject to fixed laws (e. g. of the moon, of plants, of waters, the dawn, &c.); true to sacred law; just, pious, faithful, believing; epithet of Agni, as always present at and presiding over sacrificial rites and the worship of the deities; epithet of Bṛihaspati, of Sarasvatī, of Soma, and especially of the Ādityas; (Sāy.) bestowing food; possessed of sacrifice. — *Ṛitā-vṛidh, t, t, t*, Ved. rejoicing in justice and piety, holy-minded, especially as an epithet of the Ādityas; (Sāy.) increasers of water, or of sacrifice, or of truth. — *Ṛitā-shah, -shāṭ, ṭ, ṭ*, Ved. maintaining the sacred law. — *Ṛitokti* (°*ta-uk*°), *is*, f. speaking truth. — *Ṛitodya* (°*ta-ud*°), *am*, n., Ved. true speech, truth; (Sāy.) born for sacrifice or religious rites.

Ṛitaya, nom. P. A. *ṛitayati, -te, -yitum* (generally used in pres. part. *ṛitayat* or *ṛitāyat*), to submit to divine ordinances, to act piously; to observe the sacred law, be obedient or pious; (Sāy.) to desire sacrifice.

Ṛitayā, inst., Ved. in right manner; (Sāy.) through desire of reward.

Ṛitayu or *ṛitāyu, us, us, u*, Ved. observing the sacred law, obedient, pious; (Sāy.) desirous of sacrifice.

Ṛitāyin, ī, inī, i, Ved. observing the sacred law. See *ṛitayu*.

Ṛite, ind. except, excepting, with the exception of, to the exclusion of, besides, without (with abl. or acc.); sometimes used at the beginning of a compound, e. g. *ṛite-rakshas, ās, ās, as*, (any rite &c.) from which the Rakshasas are excluded. — *Ṛite-karmam*, ind., Ved. acting according to fixed rule or settled law; (Sāy.) granting rain. — *Ṛite-jā, ās, ās, am*, Ved. living in truth, true to the law.

Ṛitena, ind. according to settled law, duly, properly, rightly, regularly, in the prescribed manner, justly, strictly, fairly, truly, honestly.

ऋति *ṛiti, is*, f. (fr. rt. 4. *ṛi*, and therefore connected with *ṛita* above), going, motion; assault, combat; abuse, censure, reproach; emulation, envy; manner of proceeding, manner; road, way; prosperity, felicity; fitness, trueness (?); remembrance; protection; misfortune; (some of the latter meanings are only found in lexicons); [cf. Hib. *raith*, 'prosperity, increase, profit, benefit, good;' *raite*, 'ways, passages, road.'] — *Ṛitiu-kara, as, ī, am*, unfortunate, propitious. — *Ṛitī-shah, -shāṭ, ṭ, ṭ*, Ved. enduring an assault, able to resist, enduring; (Sāy.) subduing an assailant.

Ṛitīya, nom. A. P. *ṛitīyate, -ti, -yitum*, to quarrel, litigate; to be in discord with one's self, be ashamed.

Ṛitīyā, f. censure, reproach; (according to others) shame.

ऋतु *ṛitu, us*, m. (fr. rt. 4. *ṛi ?*), any settled point of time, a fixed time, time appointed for sacrifices and other regular worship, right time, fit season (especially in the inst. pl. *ṛitubhis*, at the right time or at the appointed time for sacrifice or for a festival); an epoch, a period, a period of the year, a season; (the number of seasons is sometimes limited to three, or sometimes to five, viz. Vasanta, 'spring;' Grīshma, 'the hot season;' Varsha, pl. 'the rains;' Sarad, 'the autumn;' Hemanta-śiśira, du. 'the cold and dewy season:' but is more commonly reckoned as six, Hemanta and Śiśira being regarded as distinct: occasionally as seven, or even as twelve, in the latter case each season lasting one month. The Ṛitus or seasons are occasionally addressed in the Veda and libations offered to them); the menstrual evacuation, the time favourable for procreation, or sixteen days in each month; fixed order, order, rule; light, splendor; the number six (from the six seasons); a kind of collyrium; N. of the twelfth Manu; [cf. Hib. *raithe*, 'a quarter of a year;' *alt*, 'time, a joint, an article.'] — *Ṛitu-kāla, as*, m. the duration of a season; the period of menstruation, the period favourable for procreation, sixteen days of each month. — *Ṛitu-gaṇa, as*, m. the seasons collectively. — *Ṛitu-gāmin, ī,* m. having intercourse with a wife after the period of menstruation. — *Ṛitu-graha, as,* m., Ved. a libation offered to the seasons. — *Ṛitu-jit, t,* m., N. of a prince of Mithilā. — *Ṛitu-dhāman, ā,* m. epithet of Vishṇu; N. of the Indra of the twelfth Manvantara. — *Ṛitu-pati, is,* m., Ved. lord of the seasons; an epithet of Agni. — *Ṛitu-parṇa, as,* m., N. of a king of Ayodhyā. — *Ṛitu-paryāya, as,* m. the revolution of the seasons. — *Ṛitu-pā, ās, ās, am,* Ved. drinking or coming to the libation regularly or at the appointed seasons. — *Ṛitu-pātra, am,* n., Ved. the cup in which the libation to the seasons is offered. — *Ṛitu-prāpta, as, ā, am,* productive in due season, fruitful, fertile. — *Ṛitu-mat, ān, atī, at,* Ved. observing regular times, coming at regular times; enjoying the seasons; (*tī*), f. a woman during her courses, a woman during menstruation or in the period favourable for procreation; (*t*), n., N. of Varuṇa's grove or garden. — *Ṛitu-maya, as, ī, am,* consisting of the seasons. — *Ṛitu-mukha, am,* n. the beginning or first day of a season. — *Ṛitu-yāja, as,* m. sacrifice offered to the seasons; N. of a ceremony of the Prātaḥ-savana, just before the Ājya-śastra. — *Ṛitu-rāja, as,* m. the spring (king of the seasons). — *Ṛitu-linga, am,* n. characteristic or sign of the season; symptom of menstruation. — *Ṛitu-vṛitti, is,* m. revolution of the seasons, a year. — *Ṛitu-velā,* f. the period of menstruation; the period favourable for procreation, sixteen days of each month. — *Ṛitu-śas,* ind., Ved. in order, duly; at the right or fixed time. — *Ṛitu-shṭhā* and *ṛitu-sthā, ās, ā, am,* Ved. fixed at the proper seasons. — *Ṛitu-saṃhāra, as,* m. 'collection of the seasons,' title of a poem ascribed to Kālidāsa in praise of the six seasons. — *Ṛitu-sandhi, is,* m. the interval or junction between two seasons, the last seven days of one season and the first seven of the next. — *Ṛitu-samaya, as,* m. the period favourable for procreation. — *Ṛitu-sātmya, am,* n. diet &c. suited to the season. — *Ṛitu-sthalā,* f., N. of an Apsaras. — *Ṛitu-snātā,* f. a woman who has bathed after menstruation and so prepared herself for sexual intercourse. — *Ṛitu-snāna, am,* n. bathing after menstruation. — *Ṛitv-anta, as,* m. the close of a season, the termination of menstruation.

Ṛitavya, as, ā, am, devoted to the seasons, one who worships them as divinities, relating to the season, seasonable.

Ṛituthā, ind. in order, duly; distinctly, precisely, exactly; (Sāy.) at a right or fixed time.

Ṛitv-ij, k, k, k (*ij* fr. rt. *yaj*), Ved. sacrificing at the proper seasons, sacrificing regularly; (*k*), m. a priest; (the four chief Ṛitvijas or priests are the Hotṛi, Udgātṛi, Adhvaryu, and Brahman; sometimes eight are enumerated, and at very grand ceremonies sixteen, viz. Hotṛi, Ud-gātṛi, Adhvaryu, Brahman, Brāhmaṇāććhaṃsin, Pra-stotṛi, Maitrā-varuṇa, Prati-prasthātṛi, Potṛi, Prati-hartṛi, Aććhāvāka, Neshṭṛi, Agnīdh, Subrahmaṇya, Grāva-stut, and Un-netṛi.)

1. *ṛitviya, as, ā, am,* due, regular; happening at fixed or regular times; conforming to ceremonial rules, familiar with those rules. — *Ṛitviyā-vat, ān, atī, at,* Ved. conformable to law or rule, formal.

2. *ṛitviya* or *ṛitvya, as, ā, am,* menstruating; being in the period most favourable for procreation; (*am*), n. menstruation.

ऋते *ṛite.* See under *ṛita,* p. 180.

ऋत्विज् *ṛitv-ij.* See above.

ऋदूदर *ṛidūdara, as, ā, am* (perhaps related to *mṛidu*), Ved. mild, soft, kind, gracious.

Ṛidūpā, f. (for *mṛidu-pā?*), Ved. a bee or any other insect fond of sweets.

Ṛdū-vṛidh, t, t, t, Ved. rejoicing in sweets.

ऋध् *ṛidh,* cl. 4. 5. 7. P. *ṛidhyati, ṛidhnoti, ṛiṇaddhi* (and in some forms cl. 2, as pres. 2nd du. *ṛidhāthe,* pot. 1st pl. *ṛidhyāma,* impf. 1st pl. *ārdhma*), *ānardha, ardhishyati, ārdhīt, ardhitum,* to succeed, prosper; to grow, increase, flourish; to be prosperous and happy, to make prosperous, cause to succeed; to accomplish; to gratify, satisfy: Caus. *ardhayati, -yitum,* to cause to prosper, accomplish; to satisfy: Desid. *īrtsati;* [cf. Lat. *ol-esco, ad-ul-tus, radix;* Goth. *aurti,* 'plant,' in *aurti-gards;* Lat. *alo;* Gr. ἀλδαίνω; Goth. *alja;* Hib. *alt,* 'nursing.']

Ṛiddha, as, ā, am, prosperous; increased; thriving, rising; stored, as grain; (*am*), n. stored grain; a demonstrated conclusion, a distinct result.

Ṛiddhi, is, f. success, prosperity, good fortune, affluence, increase, growth, accomplishment; perfection, supernatural power or supremacy; N. of a medicinal plant; prosperity personified as the wife of Kuvera; N. of the goddess Pārvatī. — *Ṛiddhi-kāma, as, ā, am,* desiring increase or prosperity. — *Ṛiddhimat, ān, atī, at,* being in a prosperous state, prosperous, wealthy, respectable, rich; making a fine appearance, bringing happiness. — *Ṛiddhi-sākshāt-kriyā,* f. manifestation of supernatural power.

Ṛidhat, an, atī, at (pres. part. from a form in cl. 2), prospering, thriving, &c. — *Ṛidhad-ri, īs,* m. (*rī* = *rai*), N. of a man. — *Ṛidhad-vāra, as, ā, am,* Ved. increasing one's goods; (Sāy.) having desirable or prosperous wealth.

Ṛidhila, as, m., N. of a man.

ऋधक् *ṛidhak,* ind. (related to *ardha*), Ved. separately; aside, apart; singly, one by one; in a distinguished manner, particularly. — *Ṛidhan-mantra, as, ā, am,* Ved. one who is destitute of speech.

ऋधुक *ṛidhuka, as, ā, am,* short (?).

ऋफ् *ṛiph* or *ṛinph* or *ṛimph,* cl. 6. P. *ṛiphati, ānarpha* or *ṛimphāñ-ćakāra,* to injure, kill; [cf. rt. *riph.*]

ऋबीस *ṛibīsa, am,* n., Ved. a fissure, rent, gulf, abyss; warmth of the earth.

ऋभु *ṛibhu, us, us, u* (fr. rt. *rabh*), Ved. clever, skilful, inventive, prudent (often as an epithet of the gods Indra, Agni, and the Ādityas); handy (as a weapon), easy to be used; (Sāy.) shining far, diffusing light; (*us*), m. an artist, one who works in iron, a smith, a builder (especially of carriages); N. of three semi-divine beings (called Ṛibhu, Vibhvan, and Vāja, sons of Su-dhanvan, a descendant of Angiras, and called Ṛibhus from the name of the elder. Through their performance of good works [*sv-apas*] they obtained divinity, exercised superhuman powers, and became entitled to worship. They are supposed to dwell in the solar sphere, and are the artists who formed the horses of Indra, the carriage of the Aśvins, and the miraculous cow of Bṛihaspati; they made their aged parents young, and constructed four cups at a sacrifice from the one cup of Tvashṭṛi who, as the proper artificer of the gods, was in this respect their rival; they appear generally as accompanying Indra, especially at the evening sacrifice. In later mythology *Ṛibhu* is a son of Brahmā); a deity, a divinity in general; [cf. Ὀρφεύς.] — *Ṛibhu-mat, ān, atī, at,* Ved. clever, skilful, prudent; connected with or accompanied by the Ṛibhus; (Sāy.) wide-shining.

Ṛibhuksha, as, m. Indra; Indra's heaven or paradise; the thunderbolt of Indra. (This word does not seem to be used, but appears to owe its origin to the next.)

Ṛibhukshin, ās, m. (in the Ved. only the following forms occur, nom. sing. *-kshās,* acc. sing. *-kshaṇam,* nom. pl. *-kshās* and *-kshaṇas*), the first of the three Ṛibhus, who is the Ṛibhu par excellence; a Ṛibhu in general; a N. of Indra; N. of the Maruts; (the word means, according to the scholiasts, 'governing far or reigning over the Ṛibhus.')

Ṛibhva, as, ā, am, Ved. attacking, assailing, courageous, determined; extending far; clever; skilful.

Ṛibhvan, ā, ā, a, or *ṛibhvas, ās, ās, as,* Ved. attacking, assailing, courageous, determined; (Sāy.) shining widely or far extended.

ऋल्लक *ṛillaka, as,* m. a player on a kind of musical instrument; (perhaps a wrong reading for *jhallaka.*)

Ṛillarī, f. a kind of musical instrument.

ऋश्य *ṛiśya* or *ṛiśa, as,* m. the male of a species of antelope, the painted or white-footed antelope; [cf. *ṛishya* and *riśya.*] — *Ṛiśya-ketu, us,* m. an epithet of Aniruddha; (a various reading for *viśva-ketu.*) — *Ṛiśya-da, as,* m. (*da* fr. rt. 4. *dā,* 'to bind'), a pit for catching antelopes. — *Ṛiśya-pad, āt, adī, at,* Ved. having the feet of an antelope.

ऋष् 1. *ṛish* (connected with rt. *vṛish*), cl. 1. P. *arshati, ānarsha, arshitum,* to flow, flow quickly; to bring anything near by flowing; to glide, to move with a gliding or quick motion; [cf. Goth. *airz-ja;* Old Germ. *irru;* Lat. *erro.*]

Ṛishad-gu, us, m., N. of a son of Vṛijinīvat.

Ṛishabha, as, m. (fr. rt. *ṛish* as *vṛishabha* fr. *vṛish,* 'to sprinkle,' the idea of impregnating being involved), a bull, a young bull; (in comp. with other names of animals) the male animal; (in comp. with other nouns) the best or most excellent of any species or race (e. g. *purusharshabha,* an excellent man; *Bharatarshabha,* the most eminent of the Bharata race); the second of the seven notes of the Hindū gamut, in abbreviation Ṛi; the hollow of the ear; a boar's tail; a crocodile's tail; a dried plant, one of the eight principal medicaments; N. of an antidote; N. of a ceremony; N. of a king of the Śviknas; of a descendant of Viśvā-mitra and author of several hymns of the Ṛig-veda; of a Nāga; of a prince, a son of Nābhi and Meru; of a son of Kuśāgra; of one of the seven Ṛishis of the second Manvantara; of the first Arhat of the present Avasarpiṇī, a son of Nābhi and Marudevā; of a mountain; (*ī*), f. a woman with masculine peculiarities, as with a beard &c.; a widow; the plant Carpopogon Pruriens; N. of another plant; [cf. Zend *arshan;* Gr. ἄρσην.] — *Ṛishabha-kūṭa, as,* m., N. of a mountain. — *Ṛishabha-gaja-vilasita, am,* n., N. of a metre consisting of four lines of sixteen syllables each. — *Ṛishabha-tara, as,* m. a small bull. — *Ṛishabha-dāyin, ī, inī, i,* giving a bull. — *Ṛishabha-dvīpa, as,* m., N. of a country. — *Ṛishabha-dhvaja, as,* m. an epithet of Śiva; N. of an Arhat or Jaina saint.

Ṛishabhaka, as, m., N. of a medicinal plant.

ऋष् 2. *ṛish,* cl. 6. P. *ṛishati, ānarsha, arshishyati, ārshīt, arshitum,* to push; to pierce; to go, approach.

ऋषि *ṛishi, is,* m. (said to be either fr. rt. *driś,* 'to see,' or fr. 1. *ṛish;* perhaps related to *arć* or *ṛić,* 'to praise'), a singer of sacred hymns, an inspired poet or sage, any person who alone or with others invokes the deities in rhythmical speech or song, especially in song of a sacred character (e. g. the ancient hymn-singers Kutsa, Atri, Rebha, Agastya, Kuśika, Vasishṭha, Vy-aśva, who were regarded by later generations as patriarchal sages or saints, occupying the same position in Indian history as the heroes and patriarchs of other countries. These Ṛishis constitute a peculiar class of beings in the early mythical system, as distinct from gods, men, Asuras, &c.; they are the authors or rather seers of the Vedic hymns, i. e. according to orthodox Hindū ideas they are the inspired personages to whom these hymns were revealed, and such an expression as 'the Ṛishi says' is equivalent to 'so it stands in the sacred texts.' Seven Ṛishis, *sapta ṛishayaḥ* or *saptaṛishayaḥ* or *saptarshayaḥ,* are often mentioned in the Brāhmaṇas and later works as typical representatives of the character and spirit of the pre-historic or mythical period; in the Śatapatha-Brāhmaṇa their names are given as follows, Gotama, Bharadvāja, Viśvā-mitra, Jamadagni, Vasishṭha, Kaśyapa, and Atri; in the Mahā-bhārata thus, Marīći, Atri, Angiras, Pulaha, Kratu, Pulastya, Vasishṭha; in Manu they are called Prajāpatis or patriarchs, and are reckoned as ten, three other names being added, viz. Praćetas or Daksha, Bhṛigu, and Nārada, these ten being created by Manu Svāyambhuva for the production of all other beings including gods and men. The seven Ṛishis form in astronomy the constellation of 'the Great Bear.' Metaphorically, the seven Ṛishis may stand for the seven senses or the seven vital airs of the body); in later times a saint or sanctified sage in general, an ascetic, an anchorite, (sometimes three orders of these Ṛishis are enumerated, viz. Devarshis, Brahmarshis, and Rājarshis; sometimes seven, four others being added, viz. Maharshis, Paramarshis, S'rutarshis, and Kāṇḍarshis); a ray of light; an imaginary circle; the fish Cyprinus Ṛishi; [cf. Hib. *arsan*, 'a sage, a man old in wisdom;' *arrach*, 'old, ancient, aged.'] — *Ṛishi-kulyā*, f. 'the river of the Ṛishis,' a sacred river, as the Sarasvatī or Gaṅgā; a river in general; N. of the wife of Bhūman and mother of Udgītha. — *Ṛishi-kṛit*, *t*, *t*, *t*, Ved. rendering a poet inspired, inspiring; (Sāy.) making one's appearance, appearing. — *Ṛishi-gaṇa*, *as*, m. a company or number of sages, the host of patriarchal sages. — *Ṛishi-giri*, *is*, m., N. of a mountain in Magadha. — *Ṛishi-gupta*, *as*, m., N. of a Buddha. — *Ṛishi-ćodana*, *as*, *ā*, *am*, Ved. inspiring the singer. — *Ṛishi-ććhandas*, *as*, n. the metre of a Ṛishi. — *Ṛishi-jāṅgala*, *as*, m. or *ṛishi-jāṅgalikī*, f. the plant Convolvulus Argenteus. — *Ṛishi-tarpaṇa*, *am*, n. libation offered to the Ṛishis. — *Ṛishi-tva*, *am*, n. the order or state of a Ṛishi. — *Ṛishi-deva*, *as*, m., N. of a Buddha. — *Ṛishi-dvish*, *ṭ*, *ṭ*, *ṭ*, Ved. hating an inspired poet. — *Ṛishi-pańćamī*, f., N. of a festival on the fifth day in the second half of the month Bhādra. — *Ṛishi-patana*, N. of a country near Vārāṇasī. — *Ṛishi-putra*, *as*, m., N. of an author. — *Ṛishi-praśishṭa*, *as*, *ā*, *am*, Ved. instructed by the Ṛishi. — *Ṛishi-proktā*, f. the plant Glycine Debilis. — *Ṛishi-bandhu*, *us*, *us*, *u*, Ved. related to a Ṛishi, connected with a Ṛishi. — *Ṛishi-brāhmaṇa*, *am*, n. title of a work. — *Ṛishi-manas*, *ās*, *ās*, *as*, Ved. having the mind of a sacred poet, inspired. — *Ṛishi-mukha*, *am*, n. the beginning of a Maṇḍala composed by a Ṛishi. — *Ṛishi-yajña*, *as*, m. sacrifice offered to a Ṛishi, consisting of a prayer uttered in a low voice. — *Ṛishi-loka*, *as*, m. the world of the Ṛishis. — *Ṛishi-vat*, ind., Ved. like a Ṛishi. — *Ṛishi-vadana*, N. of a country; see *ṛishi-patana*. — *Ṛishi-vaha*, *as*, *ā*, *am*, bearing or conveying a Ṛishi. — *Ṛishi-shah*, *shāṭ*, *ṭ*, *ṭ*, Ved. intoxicating and inspiring the singer, as the Soma. — *Ṛishi-sheṇa*, *as*, m., N. of a man. — *Ṛishi-shṭuta*, *as*, *ā*, *am*, praised by the sacred poets. — *Ṛishi-sattama*, *as*, m. best or most excellent of the sages. — *Ṛishi-stoma*, *as*, m. praise of the Ṛishis. — *Ṛishi-svara*, *as*, *ā*, *am*, Ved. praised by a Ṛishi. — *Ṛishī-tata*, *as*, *ā*, *am*, celebrated by the sacred singers. — *Ṛishī-van*, *ā*, *ā*, *a*, Ved. equal to the Ṛishis; (Sāy.) accompanied by Ṛishis.

Ṛishika, *ās*, m. pl., N. of a people; (*as*), m. sing. a prince of this people; (*ā*), f., N. of a river.

Ṛishishāṇa, *as*, *ā*, *am*, Ved. attracted by the pious singer; (Sāy.) worshipped by the praiser.

ऋषु *ṛishu* (occurring only in gen. plur. *ṛishūṇām*), Ved. a firebrand; glowing fire; (Sāy.) one who approaches; a Ṛishi.

ऋष्टि *ṛishṭi*, *is*, m. f. (fr. rt. 2. *ṛish?*), a spear, a lance, a sword, the weapon of the Maruts; [cf. *rishṭi*.] — *Ṛishṭi-mat*, *ān*, *atī*, *at*, Ved. furnished with spears as the Maruts. — *Ṛishṭi-vidyut*, *t*, *t*, *t*, Ved. casting spears like lightning; (Sāy.) shining with weapons. — *Ṛishṭi-sheṇa*, *as*, m., N. of a man.

ऋष्य *ṛishya*, *as*, m. [cf. *riśya*], the painted or white-footed antelope; N. of a son of Devātithi; (*am*), n. a kind of leprosy. — *Ṛishya-ketana*, *as*, and *ṛishya-ketu*, *us*, m., N. of Aniruddha. — *Ṛishya-gatā*, f. the plant Asparagus Racemosus. — *Ṛishya-gandhā*, f. the plant Convolvulus Argenteus. — *Ṛishya-jihva*, *am*, n. a kind of leprosy. — *Ṛishya-proktā*, f., N. of several plants, Carpopogon Pruriens, Asparagus Racemosus, Sida Cordifolia or Rhombifolia. — *Ṛishya-mūka*, *as*, m. a mountain in the Dekhan, the temporary abode of Rāma with the monkey-chief Sugrīva. — *Ṛishya-śṛiṅga*, *as*, m., N. of a personage (son of the Ṛishi Vibhāṇḍaka) whose story is told in Rāmāyaṇa I. 9; N. of a legislator. — *Ṛishyāṅka* (°*ya-an*°), *as*, m. an epithet of Aniruddha.

Ṛishyaka, *as*, m. the painted or white-footed antelope.

ऋष्व *ṛishva*, *as*, *ā*, *am* (fr. rt. 1. *ṛish*), Ved. elevated, high, sublime, great; epithet of several deities, especially of Agni and Indra. — *Ṛishva-vīra*, *as*, *ā*, *am*, Ved. inhabited by sublime beings (as the sky). — *Ṛishvaujas* (°*va-oj*°), *ās*, *ās*, *as*, Ved. possessing high power.

ऋहत् *ṛihat*, *an*, *atī*, *at*, Ved. small, weak, powerless.

ॠ ऌ ॡ

No Sanskrit word begins with any of these vowels; *ṛī* appears only in the gen. plur. of nouns terminating in *ṛi*, in the acc. plur. of fem. nouns of relationship in *ṛi*, and in the nom. and acc. plur. of neuter nouns in *ṛi*. As to the vowel *ḷri* it occurs only in some forms of the root *klṛip*. The long *ḷrī* is a mere invention of grammarians.

ॠ 1. *ṛī*, ind. a particle uttered at the beginning of a speech; an interjection of warding off reproach and terror; (*rīs* or *rī*), f. the mother of the gods; also of the demons; recollection; (*ā*), m. a N. of Bhairava; a Dānava or demon; the breast; motion, going. — *Ṛī-kāra*, *as*, m. the letter or sound *ṛī*.

ॠ 2. *ṛī* for rt. 4. *ṛi*, q. v.

ऌ *ḷri*, ind. the earth; a mountain; the mother of the gods; the divine nature; a mystical letter. — *Ḷri-kāra*, *as*, m. the letter or sound *ḷri*. — *Ḷri-varṇa*, *am*, n. the vowel *ḷri*.

ॡ *ḷrī*, ind. a mother; a divine female; female nature; (*ḷrīs*), m. a N. of S'iva; (*ḷrīs*), f. the mother of the Dānavas; wife of a Daitya; the mother of the all-bestowing cow of plenty; ind. a mystical letter used once or repeatedly in Mantras or mystical formularies; (the letters *ṛī* and *ḷrī* are employed in the same manner; they have apparently no signification, but are personified and invested with mystical properties in the Tantras.)

ए

ए 1. *e*, the eleventh vowel of the alphabet, corresponding to the letter *e* as pronounced in most languages, and having the sound of *e* in *prey*, *grey*. In English, however, this sound is rarely given to *e*. — *E-kāra*, *as*, m. the letter or sound *e*.

ए 2. *e*, ind. an interjection of remembering, addressing, censure or contempt, and compassion.

ए 3. *e*, *es*, m. a N. of Vishṇu.

ए 4. *e* (*ā-i*), cl. 2. P. *aiti*, *-tum*, to come, come near, come to, to fall to one's share (with acc.); to arrive at, enter; to addict one's self to; to fall into; to gain: Intens. Ved. *eyate*, to hasten towards; to request, to obtain by entreaty.

एक *eka*, *as*, *ā*, *am* (said to be fr. rt. 5. *i*; perhaps fr. the pronom. base *e* contained in *etad*), one, alone, solitary, single, happening only once; the same, one and the same, identical; single of its kind, unique, singular, chief, pre-eminent, excellent; one of two or many [cf. *eka-tara*, *eka-tama*]; in later Sanskṛit used as an indefinite article; (*as*), m., N. of a man, the son of Raja.

Eka follows the declension of pronominals (see Gram. 200, 237), and may be declined in the plural (e. g. *eke*, some, several; *eke—eke* or *eke—apare* or *eke—anye* or *eke—eke—apare* or *eke—anye—eke—apare—apare*, some—others). Sometimes *eka* may be repeated in the sense of 'the one—the other, one—another' (e. g. *eka—eka* = *eka—anya* or *eka—dvitīya*, one—the other), or in the sense of 'one after another' (e. g. *eka ekaḥ purushaḥ*, one man after another). It is often used in the middle of compounds either substantively or adverbially (e. g. *puṇyaika-karmā*, practising only virtue; *svargaika-sammukhī*, f. looking only up to the sky; *kara-pādaika-hīnas*, deprived of one foot and one hand). In Vedic Sanskṛit it may sometimes be placed, together with *na*, before a decad to lessen it by one, being then used in the inst. or acc. fem., inst. or abl..neut. (e. g. *ekayā na triṁśat* or *ekām na triṁśat* = twenty-nine; *ekena na viṁśatiḥ* or *ekād na viṁśatiḥ* = nineteen). In compounds and derivatives *eka* never appears in its fem. form *ekā* (e. g. *ekasyāḥ kshīram*, the milk of one female, is compounded into *eka-kshīram* not *ekā-kshīram*); [cf. Lith. *ni-ékas*, 'no:' Hib. *each*, 'any;' *neach*, 'any one, one, some one, he;' *neach-tar*, 'neither;' *neachdarach*, 'neutral:' Gr. ἑκά-τερος; ἑκα-στος: Lat. *æquus*, *e-ocles* fr. *ĕc-ocles*: Goth. *ha* in compounds, as *haihs*, Them. *haiha*, *ha-iha*, 'one-eyed;' *ha-nfs*, Them. *ha-nfa*, 'one-handed;' *halts*, Them. *ha-lta*, 'lame;' *ha-lbs*, Them. *ha-lba*, 'half.'] — *Eka-ṛikthin*, &c.; see *eka-rikthin*, &c. — *Eka-kapāla*, *as*, *ā*, *am*, consisting of one cup, contained in one cup. — *Eka-kara*, *as*, *ī*, *am*, doing only one thing; (*as*, *ā*, *am*), one-handed, one-rayed. — *Eka-karma-kāraka*, *as*, *ā*, *am*, doing the same thing, of the same profession. — *Eka-kārya*, *am*, n. sole business, the same business or work; (*as*, *ā*, *am*), performing the same work, answering the same end. — *Eka-kāla*, *as*, m. one time, the same time; (*am*), ind. at one time, only once; (*e*), ind. at the same time, at once. — *Ekakāla-bhojana*, *am*, n. eating but one meal in any given time. — *Ekakālika*, *as*, *ā*, *am*, happening only once; happening once a day. — *Ekakālīna*, *as*, *ā*, *am*, contemporary, coeval, simultaneous. — *Eka-kuṇḍala*, *as*, m. an epithet of Kuvera; of Balabhadra; and of S'esha, the king of the Nāgas. — *Eka-kushṭha*, *am*, n. a kind of leprosy, ichthyosis. — *Eka-kshīra*, *am*, n. the milk of one (nurse &c.). — *Eka-guru*, *us*, or *eka-guruka*, *as*, m. a spiritual brother, pupil of the same preceptor; having the same preceptor. — *Eka-grāma*, *as*, m. the same village. — *Ekagrāmīṇa* or *eka-grāmīya*, *as*, *ā*, *am*, inhabiting the same village. — *Eka-ćakra*, *as*, *ā*, *am*, having only one wheel; passed over by the wheel (of the carriage) of only one (king), i. e. governed by only one king; (*as*), m., N. of a Dānava; (*ā*), f., N. of a town of the Kīćakas. — *Ekaćakravarti-tā*, f. state of being sole master of the whole earth. — *Ekaćakra-vartin*, *ī*, m. sole master of the whole earth. — *Ekaćatvāriṁśa*, *as*, *ī*, *am*, the forty-first. — *Eka-ćatvāriṁśat*, *t*, f. forty-one. — *Eka-ćara*, *as*, *ā* or *ī*, *am*, wandering or living alone, not living in company, segregarious, solitary, alone; having one follower; going together or at the same time; gregarious; (*as*), m. a rhinoceros. — *Eka-ćaraṇa*, *as*, *ā*, *am*, having only one foot; (*ās*), m. pl., N. of a fabulous race. — *Eka-ćārin*, *ī*, *iṇī*, *i*, living alone, not in society; going alone or with one follower only; (*ī*), m. a Pratyeka-buddha; a follower of Buddha; (*iṇī*), f. a loyal wife. — *Eka-ćitta*, *am*, n. fixedness of thought on one object; one and the same thought, unanimity; (*as*, *ā*, *am*), thinking of one thing only, intent upon, absorbed in (e. g. *tad-ekaćittā*, f. thinking only of him); having the same thought, of one mind, agreeing, concurring. — *Ekaćitta-tā*, f. fixedness of mind, agreement, unanimity. — *Ekaćittī-bhūya*, ind. having become unanimous. — *Eka-ćintana*, *am*, n. thinking of only one thing. — *Eka-ćūrṇi*, *is*, m., N. of an author. — *Eka-ćetas*, *ās*, *ās*, *as*, of one mind, unanimous. — *Eka-ćodana*, *am*, n. mentioning in the singular number; (*as*, *ā*, *am*), resting upon one rule. — *Eka-ććhāya*, *as*, *ā*, *am*, having only shadow, quite dark. — *Eka-ja*, *as*, *ā*, *am*, Ved. born alone or single, produced alone; growing alone (said of a tree); alone of its kind; of one kind, unchanging. — *Eka-janman*, *ā*, m. a king, a sovereign (whose birth is pre-eminent); once-born, a S'ūdra (opposed to *dvi-janman*, 'twice-born'). — *Eka-jāta, as, ā, am*, of one parentage, born of the same parents. — *Eka-jāti, is, is, i*, once-born; belonging to the same family or kind, of the same caste; (*is*), m. a Sūdra. — *Ekajāti-pratibaddha, as, ā, am*, bound only to one birth, not born again. — *Eka-jātīya, as, ā, am*, belonging to the same family or kind; of the same kind. — *Eka-jyā*, f. the cord of an arc; sine of 30° or of the radius. — *Eka-jyotis, is*, m. an epithet of Śiva. — *Eka-tama, as, ā, at*, one of many; one of two; one (used sometimes as an indefinite article). — *Eka-tara, as, ā, am* (neut. *am* not *at* by Pāṇini VII. 1, 26), one of two, either, other, different; one of many; [Gr. ἑκάτερος; Hib. *n'-eachtar*, 'neither of two.'] — *Eka-tā*, f. oneness, unity, union, coincidence, identity. — *Eka-tāna, as, ā, am*, directed to one object only, having the mind fixed on one object only, closely attentive; (*as*), m. attention fixed on only one object; musical harmony, (? a various reading for the next.) — *Eka-tāla, as*, m. harmony, unison, the accurate adjustment of song, dance, and instrumental music; (*ī*), f. an instrument for beating time, any instrument having but one note. — *Eka-tīrthin, ī, inī, i*, bathing in the same holy water, inhabiting the same hermitage; (*ī*), m. an associate in religious offices or objects, a spiritual brother. — *Eka-tejana, as, ā, am*, Ved. having one shaft (as an arrow). — *Ekatriṇśa, as, ī, am*, the thirty-first. — *Eka-triṇśat, t*, f. thirty-one. — *Eka-trika, as*, m., N. of a ceremony. — *Eka-tva, am*, n. oneness, unity, union, coincidence, identity; (in gram.) the singular number. — *Eka-danshṭra, as*, m. single-toothed or tusked; a N. of Gaṇeśa, as having one tusk, the fellow-tusk being broken off in a scuffle by Kārttikeya, or according to another legend by Paraśu-rāma. — *Eka-daṇḍin, ī, inī, i*, having only one stick; designation of a class of beggars; [cf. *tri-daṇḍin*.] — *Eka-danta, as*, m. a N. of Gaṇeśa; [cf. *eka-danshṭra*.] — *Eka-diś, k*, f. the same region. — *Eka-duḥkha-sukha, as, ā, am*, sympathizing, having the same joys and sorrows. — *Eka-dṛiś, k, k, k*, one-eyed; (*k*), m. a crow (as having excellent sight); an epithet of Śiva (as having one eye in his forehead). — *Eka-dṛiśya, as, ā, am*, alone worthy of being beheld, the sole object of vision. — *Eka-dṛishṭi, is*, f. gaze fixed upon one object. — *Eka-devata* or *eka-devatya, as, ā, am*, devoted or offered to one deity; directed to one deity. — *Eka-deśa, as*, m. one spot; a part, a portion or division of a whole; (*ena*), inst. partly; (*as, ā, am*), occupying the same place. — *Ekadeśa-stha, as, ā, am*, situated in the same region. — *Ekadeśin, ī, inī, i*, consisting of parts or portions, divided into parts (as a whole). — *Eka-deha, as, ā, am*, having only one body, single-bodied, consisting of only one individual; elegantly formed; (*as*), m. the planet Mercury. — *Eka-dyū, ūs*, m., N. of a son of Nodhas (mentioned Ṛig-veda VIII. 69, 6. Anukram.). — *Eka-dhana, am*, n. an excellent gift, an honorific offering; (*as*), m. a kind of jug with which water is taken up at certain religious ceremonies; (*ās*), f. pl. (scil. *āpaḥ*) the water taken up by means of these vessels. — *Ekadhana-vid, t, t, t*, Ved. taking or obtaining the vessels of water called Ekadhana; obtaining an honorific offering. — *Ekadhanin, ī, inī, i*, Ved. carrying the vessels called Ekadhana. — *Eka-dharmin, ī, iṇī, i*, having the same properties, of the same kind, professing the same religion. — *Eka-dhur, ūr*, f. a particular load or conveyance (?). — *Eka-dhura* or *ekadhurā-vaha* or *ekadhuriṇa, as, ā, am*, fit for but one kind of labour, or for only one yoke; cattle for special burden. — *Eka-nakshatra, am*, n. a lunar mansion consisting of only one star. — *Eka-naṭa, as*, m. the principal actor in a drama, the manager, who recites the prologue. — *Ekanavata, as, ī, am*, the ninety-first. — *Eka-navati, is*, f. ninety-one. — *Ekanavati-tama, as, ī, am*, the ninety-first. — *Eka-nātha, as, ā, am*, having one master; (*as*), m. sole master or lord; N. of a copyist. — *Eka-nāyaka, as*, m. an epithet of Śiva. — *Eka-niśćaya, as*, m. general agreement or conclusion; (*as, ā, am*), having come to the same conclusion or resolution, having the same aim. — *Eka-nishṭha, as, ā, am*, intently fixed on one object. — *Eka-nīḍa, as, ā, am*, having only one seat; having a common home. — *Eka-netra, as*, m. an epithet of Śiva ('one-eyed'). — *Eka-nemi, is, is, i*, Ved. having one circumference. — *Eka-paksha, as, ā, am*, of the same side or party, an associate, a firm partisan; partial, taking one view only; (*as*), m. one side; (*e*), ind. in one point of view. — *Eka-pańćāśa, as, ī, am*, the fifty-first. — *Eka-pańćāśat, t*, f. fifty-one. — *Ekapańćāśat-tama, as, ī, am*, the fifty-first. — *Eka-patika, as, ā, am*, having the same husband. — *Eka-pattrikā*, f. the plant Ocimum Gratissimum. — *Eka-patni, is, is, i*, having only one wife. — *Eka-patnī*, f. only one wife; the wife of one man, a faithful wife, one devoted to her husband; the wife of a man who has no other wives; the wife of the same man. — *Eka-pad* or *eka-pād, pāt, padī, pat*, having only one foot, limping, lame, incomplete; (*pāt*), m. an epithet of Śiva or of Vishṇu; N. of a Dānava; (*padī*), f. a foot-path; a path, a way, a road. (*Aja ekapād, t*, m., Ved. 'the one-footed driver,' probably a deity presiding over storms; according to the commentator a N. of the sun.) — *Eka-pada, am*, n. only one step; a simple word, a simple nominal formation; present time, same time; (*e*), ind. at the same moment, at once, suddenly; (*as, ā, am*), having only one foot; consisting of a single word, named with a single word; (*as*), m. a kind of coitus; (*ā*), f. (scil. *ṛić*) a verse consisting of only one Pāda or quarter-stanza; (*ās*), m. pl., N. of a fabulous race. — *Ekapada-vat*, ind. like one word. — *Ekapada-stha, as, ā, am*, standing in the same word. — *Eka-padi*, ind. upon one foot, with one foot. — *Eka-para, as, ā, am*, Ved. deciding by one (mark of the dice), an epithet of the dice in which one is decisive or of pre-eminent importance. — *Eka-pari*, ind. one over or under, a term at dice. — *Eka-parṇā*, f., N. of a younger sister of Durgā and wife of Asita-Devala; an epithet of Durgā. — *Eka-parvataka, as*, m. the same mountain, or N. of a certain mountain. — *Eka-palāśa, as*, m. a single Butea Frondosa. — *Eka-pāṭalā*, f., N. of a younger sister of Durgā and wife of Jaigīshavya; an epithet of Durgā. — *Eka-pāṇa, as*, m. a single wager or stake. — *Eka-pāta, as, ā, am*, happening at once, sudden, rapid, coming suddenly. — *Eka-pātin, ī, inī, i*, standing alone or solitary, independant; (*inī*), f. (scil. *ṛić*) a verse to be taken by itself or regarded independently of the hymn to which it belongs. — *Eka-pāda, as*, m. one foot; one and the same Pāda; (*as, ā, am*), having only one foot; standing on one foot, using only one foot; (*ās*), m. pl., N. of a fabulous race. — *Eka-pādikā*, f. title of the second book of the Śatapatha-Brāhmaṇa. — *Eka-pāduka, ās*, m. pl., N. of a fabulous race ('wearing only one shoe'). — *Eka-piṅga* or *eka-piṅgala, as*, m. an epithet of Kuvera ('having a yellow mark in the place of one of his eyes'). — *Eka-piṇḍa, as, ā, am*, related, near of kin, united by the offering of the funeral cake. — *Ekapiṇḍa-tā*, f. or *ekapiṇḍa-tva, am*, n. connection by the funeral cake, consanguinity. — *Eka-putra, as*, m. having only one son. — *Eka-purusha, as*, m. the one supreme spirit; (*as, ā, am*), consisting of only one man. — *Eka-pushpā*, f., N. of a plant. — *Eka-pṛithaktva, am*, n. unity and distinctness. — *Eka-prakāra, as, ā, am*, of the same kind. — *Eka-prakhya, as, ā, am*, singularly like, pre-eminently similar. — *Eka-prabhutva, am*, n. the sovereignty of one, monarchy. — *Eka-prayatna, as*, m. one effort (of the voice). — *Eka-prahārika, as, ā, am*, killed by one blow. — *Eka-prāṇa-yoga, as*, m. union in one breath. — *Eka-phala, as, ā, am*, having one or a principal result or object; (*ā*), f., N. of a plant. — *Eka-buddhi, is, is, i*, having only one thought; (*is*), m., N. of a frog in the Pańća-tantra. — 1. *eka-bhakta, as, ā, am*, serving one and the same master; worshipping one deity. — 2. *eka-bhakta, as, ā, am*, eating together; (*am*), n. eating but one meal (a day). — *Ekabhakta-vrata, am*, n. eating but once a day as a religious obligation. — 1. *eka-bhakti, is, is, i*, of one faith, believing in one deity. — 2. *eka-bhakti, is*, f. eating but one meal (a day). — *Eka-bhāva, as, ā, am*, of the same nature; of a simple or single nature or temperament; (*as*), m. becoming one, oneness, agreement. — *Eka-bhukta, as, ā, am*, eating but one meal (a day &c.); eating together. — *Eka-bhūta, as, ā, am*, being one, undivided; not distracted, closely attentive. — *Eka-bhojana, am*, n. eating one meal a day; eating in common, feeding together. — *Eka-mati, is*, f. the mind fixed upon one object; (*is, is, i*), unanimous. — *Eka-manas, ās, ās, as*, fixing the mind upon one object, having only one thought, attentive; unanimous. — *Eka-maya, as, ī, am*, consisting of one. — *Eka-mātra, as, ā, am*, of one syllabic instant. — *Eka-mukha, as, ā* or *ī, am*, having the face directed towards one spot, having the same aim; having one chief or head, having one overseer. — *Eka-mūrdhan, ā, ā, a*, Ved. having the face directed to one spot, directed towards the same aim. — *Eka-mūlā*, f. the plants Linum Usitatissimum and Desmodium (Hedysarum) Gangeticum. — *Eka-yakāra, as, ā, am*, containing only one *y*. — *Eka-yashṭi, is*, f. a single string of pearls. — *Eka-yashṭikā*, f. a single string of flowers, pearls, &c. — *Eka-yāvan, ā*, m., N. of a man. — *Eka-yoni, is, is, i*, of the same womb, uterine; of the same mother, family or caste. — *Eka-raja, as*, m. the plant Verbesina Scandens; see *bhṛiṅga-rāja*. — *Eka-rasa, as*, m. the only flavour, the only pleasure; (*as, ā, am*), of one flavour, relishing or finding pleasure in only one thing. — *Eka-rasika, as, ā, am*, influenced by one feeling, relishing one thing only. — *Eka-rāj, ṭ, ṭ, ṭ*, shining alone; (*ṭ*), m. single or absolute king, the king by himself as distinct from the people. — *Eka-rāja, as*, m. an absolute king. — *Eka-rātra, as*, m. a ceremony lasting one night; (*am*), n. duration of one night, one night, a night. — *Ekarātrika, as, ā, am*, sufficient for one night (or day). — *Eka-rāśi, is*, f. a heap, a crowd. — *Ekarāśi-bhūta, as, ā, am*, heaped or collected together. — *Eka-rikthin, ī*, m. a coheir. — *Eka-rūpa, am*, n. one form, one kind; (*as, ā, am*), uniform, of one kind, one-coloured. — *Ekarūpa-tas*, ind. in one form, unalterably. — *Ekarūpa-tā*, f. uniformity, unvariableness. — *Ekarūpya, as, ā, am*, formed or arising from one. — *Ekarća* (*eka-ṛića*), *as, ā, am*, consisting of one verse; (*am*), n., Ved. a hymn consisting of only one verse. — *Ekartu* (*eka-ṛitu*), *us*, m., Ved. one time or season. — *Ekarshi* (*eka-ṛishi*), *is*, m. the only or chief Ṛishi. — *Eka-lavya, as*, m., N. of a son of Hiraṇya-dhanus and king of the Nishādas. — *Eka-liṅga, am*, n. a place or district in which for five Krośas there is but one Phallus, an isolated Liṅga; (*as*), m. an epithet of Kuvera; [cf. *eka-piṅga*.] — *Eka-lū, ūs*, m., N. of a man. — *Eka-vaktra, as*, m., N. of a Dānava; perhaps a wrong form for *eka-ćakra*. — *Eka-vaćana, am*, n. the singular number. — *Eka-vat*, ind. like one, simple. — *Ekavad-bhāva, as*, m. an aggregate of many, as in grammar, the formation of a compound noun of several nouns. — *Eka-varṇa, as, ā, am*, of one colour, one-coloured; identical; of one tribe, of one caste; consisting of only one letter; of one quality; (*ī*), f. beating time, marking musical measure by clapping the hands, or the instrument which does so, a castanet; see *eka-tālī*. — *Ekavarṇa-vat*, ind. like one letter. — *Ekavarṇa-samīkaraṇa, am*, n. an equation involving only one unknown quantity; uniliteral equation. — *Ekavarṇika, as, ā, am*, of one colour, of one caste. — *Eka-varshikā*, f. a heifer one year old. — *Eka-vasana, as, ā, am*, having only one garment or robe. — *Eka-vastra, as, ā, am*, having only one garment, in one dress. — *Ekavastra-tā*, f. the state of having only one garment. — *Ekavastra-saṃvīta, as, ā, am*, clothed in one garment. — *Eka-vastrārdha-saṃvīta, as, ā, am*, clothed in half a single garment. — *Eka-vākya, am*, n. one opinion. — *Eka-vākya-tā*, f. unanimity. — *Ekavāṇa-vat*, ind. as one arrow. — *Eka-vāda, as*, m. a musical instrument, a kind of drum or tabor. — *Eka-vādyā*, f., Ved. a kind of imp or demon. — *Eka-vāram* or *eka-vāre,* ind. only once, at once, at one time, suddenly. — *Eka-vāsa, as, ā, am,* having one house or one residence. — *Eka-vāsas, ās, ās, as,* having only one garment, in one dress. — *Ekaviṇśa, as, ī, am,* the twenty-first; consisting of twenty-one; connected with the Ekaviṇśa-stoma; (*as*), m. the Ekaviṇśa-stoma; N. of one of the six Pṛishṭhya-stomas. — *Ekaviṇśaka, as, ī, am,* the twenty-first; containing twenty-one. — *Eka-viṇśat, t,* or *eka-viṇśati, is,* f. twenty-one, a combination or collection of twenty-one. — *Ekaviṇśati-tama, as, ī, am,* the twenty-first. — *Ekaviṇśati-dhā,* ind. twenty-one-fold, in twenty-one parts. — *Eka-viṇśa-vat, ān, atī, at,* Ved. connected with the Ekaviṇśa-stoma. — *Ekaviṇśa-stoma, as,* m., Ved. a Stoma consisting of twenty-one parts. — *Eka-vidha, as, ā, am,* of one kind, simple. — *Eka-vilocana, as, ā, am,* one-eyed; (*ās*), m. pl., N. of a fabulous race of people. — *Ekavishayin, ī,* m. having one common object or end, a rival. — *Eka-vīra, as,* m. a pre-eminent hero or warrior; N. of a plant. — *Eka-vṛiksha, as,* m. an isolated tree; a desert place in which but one tree is seen for four Krośas. — *Eka-vṛit, t, t, t,* Ved. simple. — *Eka-vṛinda, as,* m. a peculiar disease of the throat. — *Eka-vṛisha, as,* m., Ved. the chief bull, the master of the herd. — *Eka-veṇi, is* or *ī,* f. a single braid of hair (worn by a woman as a mark of mourning for an absent husband &c.); a woman whose hair is tied in a single braid. — *Eka-veśman, a,* n. a solitary house or room. — *Eka-vyavasāyin, ī,* m. following the same employment. — *Eka-vrātya, as,* m., Ved. the chief or principal Vrātya. — *Eka-śata, am,* n. 101; (*as, ī, am*), the 101st. — *Ekaśata-tama, as, ī, am,* the 101st. — *Ekaśata-dhā,* ind. 101-fold; in 101 parts. — *Ekaśata-vidha, as, ā, am,* 101-fold. — *Eka-śapha, as, ā, am,* Ved. whole-hoofed, not cloven-hoofed; (*as* or *am*), m. n. any animal whose hoof is not cloven; (*as*), m. a horse. — *Eka-śaraṇa, am,* n. one only hope or refuge, especially applied to a deity. — *Eka-śarīra, as, ā, am,* of one body or blood; consanguineous. — *Ekaśarīrānvaya* (°*ra-an*°), *as,* m. consanguineous descent. — *Ekaśarīrārambha* (°*ra-ār*°), *as,* m. commencement of consanguinity by the union of father and mother. — *Eka-śarīrāvayava* (°*ra-av*°), *as,* m. a descendant in a right line, a blood-kinsman. — *Ekaśarīrāvayava-tva* (°*ra-av*°), *am,* n. consanguineous descent or connection. — *Eka-śākha, as,* m. a Brāhman of the same branch or school. — *Eka-śāla, am,* n., N. of a town. — *Eka-śiti-pad, pāt, padī, pat,* Ved. having one white foot. — *Eka-śirshan, ā, ā, a,* Ved. having the face turned towards the same place. — *Ekaśīla-samācāra, as, ā, am,* one who leads one manner of life, whose manners are always the same. — *Eka-śuṅga, as, ā, am,* Ved. having one sheath. — *Eka-śṛiṅga, as, ā, am,* having only one horn; (*as*), m. a unicorn, a rhinoceros, an epithet of Vishṇu; (*ās*), m. a class of Pitṛis; (*ā*), f., N. of the mind-born daughter of the Pitṛis called Sukālas. — *Eka-śepa, as,* m., N. of a man. — *Eka-śesha, as,* m. 'the remainder of one only,' a term in grammar denoting that of two or more words only one remains or is retained (e.g. the dual *rāmau* is the one remainder of *rāmaḥ + rāmaḥ*). — *Eka-śruta, as, ā, am,* once heard. — *Ekaśruta-dhara, as, ā, am,* keeping in mind what one has heard once. — *Ekaśrutadhara-tva, am,* n. state of such a person. — *Eka-śruti, is,* f. the hearing of only one sound, monotony; the neutral accentless tone; (*ī*), ind. in a monotonous manner. — *Eka-śrushṭi, is, is, i,* Ved. obedient to one command. — *Ekashashṭa, as, ī, am,* the sixty-first; connected with sixty-one. — *Eka-shashṭi, is,* f. sixty-one. — *Ekashashṭi-tama, as, ī, am,* the sixty-first. — *Ekasaptata, as, ī, am,* the seventy-first. — *Eka-saptati, is,* f. seventy-one. — *Ekasaptati-tama, as, ī, am,* the seventy-first. — *Eka-sabha, am,* n. a common or general place of meeting. — *Eka-sarga, as, ā, am,* closely attentive, having the mind intent upon one object. — *Eka-sahasra, am,* n. 1001. — *Eka-sākshika, as, ā, am,* witnessed by one. — *Eka-sārtham,* ind. together, in one company. — *Eka-sūtra, am,* n. a small double drum played by a string and ball attached to the body of it. — *Eka-sūnu, us,* m. an only son. — *Eka-stoma, as,* m. 'consisting of one Stoma,' N. of a Soma ceremony. — *Eka-stha, as, ā, am,* standing together, remaining in one place, remaining in the same place, conjoined, collected, combined, assembled. — *Eka-sthāna, am,* n. one place, the same place. — *Eka-haṇsa, as,* m. the chief or highest Haṇsa (an allegorical designation of the soul); N. of a Tīrtha. — *Eka-hāyana, as, ī, am,* one year old; (*ī*), f. a heifer one year old; (*am*), n. the period of one year. — *Ekāṇśa* (*eka-aṇ*°), *as,* m. a distinct or separate part, a part in general. — *Ekāksha* (*eka-ak*°), *as, ī, am,* having only one axle; one-eyed; having an excellent eye; (*as*), m. a crow; an epithet of Śiva; N. of a Dānava. — *Ekākshara* (*eka-ak*°), *am,* n. a monosyllable; the sacred monosyllable *om.* — *Ekākshara-kosha, as,* m. a vocabulary of monosyllabic words by Purushottamadeva. — *Ekākshara-gaṇapati-stotra, am,* n. a hymn in honour of Gaṇeśa, a portion of the Rudrayāmala. — *Ekāksharī-bhāva, as,* m. the production of only one syllable, contraction. — *Ekāgra* (*eka-ag*°), *as, ā, am,* having one point, fixing one's attention on only one point or object, closely attentive, intent; undisturbed, unperplexed; known, celebrated; single-pointed; (*as*), m. (in mathematics) the whole of the long side of a figure which is subdivided. — *Ekāgra-citta, as, ā, am,* having the mind intent on one object. — *Ekāgra-tas,* ind. with undivided attention. — *Ekāgra-tā,* f. or *ekāgra-tva, am,* n. intentness in the pursuit of one object, close and undisturbed attention. — *Ekāgra-dṛishṭi, is, is, i,* fixing one's eyes on one spot. — *Ekāgra-manas, as,* n. intentness. — *Ekāgrya, as, ā, am,* closely attentive; (*am*), n. close attention. — *Ekāṅga* (*eka-aṅ*°), *am,* n. a single member, a single part; (*as*), m. a body-guard; the planet Mercury; the planet Mars; an epithet of Vishṇu; (*am*), n. sandal-wood. — *Ekāṅgikā,* f. a preparation made with sandal-wood. — *Ekātapatra* (*eka-āt*°), *as, ā, am,* characterized by one umbrella (said of universal sovereignty having an umbrella as one of its insignia). — *Ekātma-tā,* f. the unity of spiritual essence, the doctrine of one universal spirit. — *Ekātman* (*eka-āt*°), *ā,* m. the one spirit; (*ā, ā, a*), depending solely on self, solitary. — *Ekātmya, as, ā, am,* only, alone, homogeneous. — *Ekādaśa, as, ī, am,* the eleventh; consisting of eleven, lasting eleven months; (*ī*), f. the eleventh day of the half month, especially sacred to Vishṇu, when fasting is very efficacious; presentation of offerings to deceased ancestors or Pitṛis on the eleventh day after his decease, on which occasion Brāhmans are fed and the period of impurity for a Brāhman terminates; (*am*), n. the number eleven. — *Ekādaśaka, as, ā, am,* consisting of eleven, consisting of eleven parts; (*am*), n. the number eleven. — *Ekādaśa-kṛitvas,* ind. eleven times. — *Ekā-daśan, a,* pl. eleven. — *Ekādaśama, as, ī, am,* the eleventh. — *Ekādaśa-vidha, as, ā, am,* eleven-fold. — *Ekādaśāha* (°*śa-aha*), *as,* m. a sacrifice lasting eleven days. — *Ekādaśin, ī, inī, i,* consisting of eleven; (*inī*), f., Ved. the number eleven. — *Ekādaśīna, as, ā, am,* belonging to eleven (?). — *Ekādaśī-tattva, am,* n. part of the Smṛiti-tattva. — *Ekādaśī-vrata, am,* n. fasting on the eleventh day. — *Ekādaśottama* (°*śa-ut*°), *as,* m. chief of eleven; epithet of Śiva (chief among the eleven Rudras). — *Ekādeśa* (*eka-ād*°), *as,* m. one substitute for two or more letters (e.g. one vowel substituted for two other vowels either by the blending of the two vowels together or by the dropping of one). — *Ekādhipati* (*eka-adh*°), *is,* m. a sole monarch. — *Ekānaṇśā* (*eka-an-aṇśa*), f. 'the only (day) receiving no part (of the moon),' an epithet of Kuhū or the day of the new moon personified as a daughter of Aṅgiras and identified with Durgā, born together with Kṛishṇa, worshipped with Kṛishṇa and Baladeva. — *Ekānudishṭa* (*eka-an*°), *am,* n. (scil. *śrāddha*) a funeral ceremony performed for only one ancestor recently dead; (*as, ā, am*), left as a funeral feast; one who has recently partaken of it. — *Ekānta* (*eka-an*°), *as,* m. the only end or aim, exclusiveness; a lonely, retired or secret place; devotion to one, worship of one being, unitarian doctrine, monotheism; (*am* or *ena* or *e*), ind. solely, only exclusively, absolutely; necessarily; alone, apart, privately; much, exceedingly; (*as, ā, am*), directed towards one point or object; worshipping only one; excessive; solitary, lonely, retired; aside, apart. — *Ekānta-karuṇa, as, ā, am,* very compassionate, weakly charitable. — *Ekānta-tas,* ind. solely, only exclusively, apart; see *ekāntam.* — *Ekānta-tva, am,* n. exclusive worship. — *Ekānta-duḥshamā* (°*dus-samā*), f. 'containing only bad years,' with Jainas an epithet of two spokes in the wheel of time, the sixth of the Avasarpiṇī and the first of the Utsarpiṇī. — *Ekānta-bhūta, as, ā, am,* being alone or solitary. — *Ekānta-mati, is, is, i,* devoted to one object. — *Ekāntara* (*eka-an*°), *as, ā, am,* separated by one intermediate member, next but one. — *Ekānta-rāj, ṭ,* m., N. of a Bodhi-sattva. — *Ekānta-vihārin, ī, iṇī, i,* a solitary wanderer. — *Ekānta-sushamā* (°*su-samā*), f. 'containing exclusively good years,' with Jainas an epithet of two spokes in the wheel of time, the first of the Avasarpiṇī and the sixth of the Utsarpiṇī. — *Ekānta-sthita, as, ā, am,* staying or remaining alone or apart. — *Ekāntika, as, ā, am,* final, conclusive. — *Ekāntika-tva, am,* n. the being devoted to one object. — *Ekānti-tva, am,* n. devotion to one (with loc.). — *Ekāntin, ī, inī, i,* devoted to only one, having the mind fixed on only one object, worshipping only one (with gen.). — *Ekānna* (*eka-an*°), *am,* n. one and the same food; (*as*), m. a mess-mate. — *Ekānna-bhuj, k,* m. a mess-mate. — *Ekānnādin* (*eka-anna-ād*°), *ī, inī, i,* eating a supply of food from one person only. — *Ekābdā* (*eka-ab*°), f. a heifer one year old. — *Ekāyana* (*eka-ay*°), *am,* n. a lonely, retired place; a meeting-place; rendezvous of all thoughts, union of thoughts; devotion to one, doctrine of unity, monotheism; N. of a Śākhā or branch of the Veda; (*as, ā, am*), passable for only one, as a foot-path; fixing one's thoughts on one object, closely attentive, intent. — *Ekāyana-gata, as, ā, am,* one who has fixed all his thoughts on one object. — *Ekāyu* (*eka-āyu*), *us, us, u,* Ved. assembling or collecting all living beings; the first living being; (Sāy.) providing the most excellent food. — *Ekārṇava* (*eka-ar*°), *as, am,* m. n. a general inundation. — *Ekārtha* (*eka-ar*°), *as,* m. the same object; (*as, ā, am*), having one or the same aim or object; having one meaning; N. of a glossary; expressing one thing, forming only one notion. — *Ekārtha-tā,* f. or *ekārtha-tva, am,* n. state of having only one aim or object. — *Ekārtha-samupeta, as, ā, am,* arrived at one object. — *Ekārthī-bhāva, as,* m. the having one meaning. — *Ekāvama* (*eka-av*°), *as, ā, am,* inferior or less by one. — *Ekāvayava* (*eka-av*°), *as, ā, am,* made up of the same members or constituent parts. — *Ekāvalī* (*eka-āv*°), f. a single line, a single string of pearls, beads, flowers, &c.; (in rhetoric) a series of periods in which there is a regular transition from a predicate to a subject or from a subject to a predicate. — *Ekāśita, as, ī, am,* the eighty-first. — *Ekāśīti* (*eka-aś*°), *is,* f. eighty-one. — *Ekāśīti-tama, as, ī, am,* the eighty-first. — *Ekāśrama* (*eka-āś*°), *as,* m. a solitary hermitage. — *Ekāśrita* (*eka-āś*°), *as, ā, am,* resting upon or clinging to one object. — *Ekāśrita-guṇa, as,* m. a simple attribute or predicate, as form, taste, smell, &c. — *Ekāshṭakā* (*eka-ash*°), f. the first or chief Ashṭakā, either the first Ashṭakā after full moon (= *Ashṭakā*) or the first Ashṭakā of a year or a longer period of time. — *Ekāshṭī,* f. a pod or one seed of cotton. — *Ekāshṭhila* (*eka-ash*°), *as, ā, am,* having one kernel; (*as*), m., N. of the plant Agati Grandiflora Desv.; (*ā*), f. the plant Clypea Hernandifolia. — *Ekāsanika, as, ā, am* (fr. *eka* and *āsana*), having only one seat. — *Ekāha* (*eka-aha*), *as,* m. the period of one day; a ceremony or sacrifice lasting only one day, a Soma sacrifice in which Soma is only once prepared; (*am*), ind. during one day.

— *Ekāha-gama, as,* m. a day's journey. — *Ekāhāra* (*eka-āh°*), *as, ā, am,* taking food only once a day. — *Ekesha* (*eka-īshā*), *as, ā, am,* Ved. furnished with one pole. — *Ekaika* (*eka-eka*), *as, ā, am,* one by one, single, every single one; (*am*), ind. singly, one by one. — *Ekaika-tara, as, ā, am,* one by one (of many). — *Ekaika-vritti, is, is, i,* existing in every single one. — *Ekaika-śas,* ind. one by one, severally, seriatim. — *Ekaikaśya, am,* n. single state, severalty; (*ena*), ind. severally. — *Ekaishikā* (*eka-esh°*), f., N. of a medicinal plant. — *Ekokti* (*eka-uk°*), *is,* f. a single expression, a single word. — *Ekottara* (*eka-ut°*), *as, ā, am,* greater or more by one, increasing by one. — *Ekottarikā,* f. title of the fourth Āgama of the Buddhists. — *Ekodaka* (*eka-ud°*), *as, ā, am,* connected (as relatives) by the offering of funereal oblations of water to the same deceased ancestor. — *Ekodātta* (*eka-ud°*), *as, ā, am,* having one Udātta accent. — *Ekoddishṭa* (*eka-ud°*), *am,* n. (scil. *śrāddha*) the Srāddha or funeral rite performed for one definite individual deceased, not including other ancestors. — *Ekona* (*eka-ūna*), *as, ā, am,* less by one, minus one; (used in composition with *vinśati* and the following decads, e. g. *ekonavinśati* = nineteen.) — *Ekośikā,* f. the plant Cissampelos Hexandra (?). — *Ekaugha-bhūta* (*eka-ogha-bh°*), *as, ā, am,* collected into one mass, heaped or crowded together.

Ekaka, as, ā, am, single, alone, solitary.

Ekata, as, m., N. of a deity [cf. *dvita* and *trita*], one of the seven Dharmarājartvijas; N. of a Brāhman.

Ekatas, ind. from one side, on one side, on one part; singly, one by one; used sometimes as an abl. c. of *eka* (e. g. *ekato 'pi padāt,* 'after the same word'); *ekatas—ekatas,* on the one hand—on the other hand, on the one side—on the other side, here—there. — *Ekato-dat, an, atī, at,* having teeth on only one side.

Ekatra, ind. in one place, on one spot, in close connection; in a combined manner, together; used sometimes as a loc. c. of *eka* (e. g. *ekatra kare,* 'on one hand'); *ekatra—aparatra* or *ekatra—anyasmin,* on the one side—on the other side, here—there.

Ekadā, ind. at the same time, at once; once, sometimes; once on a time, one day; at one time.

Ekadhā, ind. simply, singly; in one way, together; at once, once.

Ekala, as, ā, am, alone, solitary.

Ekaśas, ind. one by one, singly.

Ekākin, ī, inī, i (fr. *eka* and rt. *anć?*), alone, solitary.

Ekī-kṛi, cl. 8. P. A. *-karoti, -kurute, -kartum,* to unite, associate, join together; combine.

Ekī-bhū, cl. 1. P. *-bhavati, -vitum,* to become one, to join together, blend, combine, mingle. — *Ekībhavat, an, antī, at,* blending together, contracted. — *Ekī-bhāva, as,* m. becoming one, combination, association; common nature or property. — *Ekībhāvin, ī, inī, i,* relating to the blending of vowels or accents.

Ekīya, as, ā, am, belonging to one, proceeding from one; belonging to the same party; a partisan or associate, a companion.

एकान्त, एकैक, &c. See under *eka* above.

एक्ष् *eksh* (*ā-īksh*), cl. 1. A. *ekshate, -shitum,* to look at.

एज् *ej,* cl. 1. P. A. *ejati, -te, ejāñ-ćakre, ejishyati, ejitum,* to stir, move, tremble, shake; A. to shine: Caus. *ejayati, -yitum,* to move: Desid. *ejijishati.*

Ejaka, as, ā, am, shaking.

Ejat, t, n., Ved. anything moving or living.

Ejatka, as, ā, am, trembling; (*as*), m., Ved. a kind of insect.

Ejathu, us, m., Ved. trembling, shaking (of the earth).

Ejana, am, n. trembling, shaking.

Ejaya, as, ā, am, or *ejayat, an, antī, at,* causing to shake or tremble, driving away.

Ejita, as, ā, am, shaken, agitated, trembling.

Ejitavya, as, ā, am, to be shaken.

Ejitri, tā, trī, tṛi, a shaker, shaking, trembling.

एजि *eji, is,* m., N. of a man.

एज्य *ejya, as, ā, am* (fr. rt. *yaj* with *ā*), Ved. to be offered (as an oblation or sacrifice).

एठ् *eṭh,* cl. 1. A. *eṭhate,* to annoy, resist or oppose.

एड *eḍa, as, ā, am,* deaf; (*as*), m. a kind of sheep. — *Eḍa-gaja, as,* m. the medicinal plant Cassia Tora or Alata, used for the cure of ring-worm. — *Eḍa-mūka, as, ā, am,* deaf and dumb; wicked, perverse.

Eḍaka, as, m. a kind of sheep, a ram, a wild goat; a certain medicinal plant; (*ā*), f. a ewe.

एडुक *eḍuka, am,* n. or *eḍūka* or *eḍoka, as, am,* m. n. a building constructed of rubbish, bones, &c., or of hard substances resembling bones; a wall enclosing bones, a tomb, &c.; (with Buddhists) a sanctuary filled with relics.

एण *eṇa, as, ī,* m. f. or *eṇaka, as,* m. a kind of deer or antelope, described as being of a black colour with beautiful eyes and short legs; (in astron.) Capricorn. — *Eṇa-tilaka, as,* m. the moon; (the marks of an antelope being fancifully visible on its disk.) — *Eṇa-driś, k,* m. Capricorn. — *Eṇa-bhṛit, t,* m. the moon. — *Eṇājina* (*eṇa-aj°*), *am,* n. deer-skin. — *Eṇī-paćana, ās,* m. pl., N. of a race (cooking antelopes for food). — *Eṇī-pada, as,* m. a kind of snake; (*ī*), f. a kind of poisonous insect.

एत 1. *eta, etas, etā* or *enī, etam* (said to be fr. rt. 5. *i*), of a variegated colour, shining, varying the colours; (Sāy.) going, flowing; (*as*), m. a deer or antelope; the hide of one; a variegated colour; (*nī*), f., Ved. a river.

Etagva, as, ā, am, Ved. of a variegated or dark colour; (Sāy. also) going on their way; epithet of the horses of the gods.

Etaśa, as, ā, am, Ved. of variegated colour, shining; epithet of Brahmaṇaspati; (*as*), m. a horse of variegated colour, a dappled horse, especially the horse or horses of the sun; N. of a favourite of Indra, who defends him from Sūrya; N. of one of the seven sons of Vātaraśana, author of two Ṛig-veda hymns; a Brāhman.

Etaśas, ās, m. a Brāhman.

एत 2. *eta, as, ā, am* (rt. 5. *i* with *ā*), arrived, come.

Eti, is, f., Ved. arrival, approach.

Etya, ind. having gone near to or approached.

एतद् *etad, eshas, eshā, etad* (fr. *e* with pronom. base *ta.* The vowel *e* appears also in *eka, eva,* &c.; and just as the simple base *ta* substitutes *sa* for the nom. sing. m. and f., so *eta* makes *eshas, eshā;* but *eta* appears in all the other cases, and the neut. *etad* is used as the base to form derivatives such as *etadīya* &c., and at the beginning of compounds), this, this here, here, especially as pointing to what is nearest to the speaker (e. g *esha vāṇaḥ,* this arrow here in my hand; *esha yāti panthāḥ,* here goes the way; *esha kālaḥ,* here, i. e. now, is the time; *etad,* this here, i. e. this world here below). *Etad* is sometimes used in this sense to give emphasis to the personal pronouns (e. g. *esho 'ham,* I this very person here) or with omission of those pronouns (e. g *esha tvāṃ svargam nayāni,* I standing here will convey you to heaven; *etau pravishṭau svaḥ,* we two here have entered). *Etad* as the subject of a sentence agrees in gender and number with the predicate without reference to the noun to be supplied (e. g. *etad me dhanam,* this [scil. cow] is my wealth); but may sometimes remain in the neut. sing. (e. g. *etad gurushu vrittiḥ,* this is the custom among Gurus)

Etad often refers to what precedes, especially when it is associated with *idam,* the latter then referring to what follows (e. g. *esha prathamaḥ kalpaḥ—anukalpas tv ayaṃ jñeyaḥ,* this before-mentioned is the first rule, but this following may be considered a secondary rule).

Etad may be used in connection with a relative clause, in which case the relative generally follows (e. g. *esha ćaiva gurur dharmo yam pravakshyāmy aham tava,* this is the important law, which I will proclaim to you).

Etad, ind. in this manner, thus, so, here, at this time, now (e. g. *etat suptaḥ,* asleep in this manner; *na vā u etad mriyase,* not at this time dost thou die).

Etad appears at the beginning of compounds, as in the following examples. — *Etaj-ja, as, ā, am,* arising from this. — *Etat-kāla, as,* m. the present time; (*e*), ind. now. — *Etatkālīna, as, ā, am,* belonging to the present time. — *Etat-kshaṇāt,* ind. from this moment, henceforth; (*e*), ind. now. — *Etat-tulya, as, ā, am,* similar to this. — *Etat-prathama, as, ā, am,* one who does anything for the first time. — *Etat-sama, as, ā, am,* equal to this. — *Etad-atirikta, as, ā, am,* besides this. — *Etad-anantaram,* ind. immediately after this. — *Etad-anta, as, ā, am,* terminating with this, ending thus. — *Etad-artha, as,* m. this matter; (*am* or *e*), ind. on this account, for this end, therefore; *etad-artham—yat,* for this end—that. — *Etad-avadhi,* ind. to this limit, so far. — *Etad-avastha, as, ā, am,* of such a state or condition. — *Etad-ātmya, as, ā, am,* being in this Ātman or supreme soul. — *Etad-ādi, is, is, i,* beginning thus, and so forth. — *Etad-eva,* ind. this very same. — *Etad-dvitīya, as, ā, am,* one who does anything for the second time. — *Etad-yonin, ī, inī, i,* residing or having one's origin in that. — *Etad-vat,* ind. like this, thus. — *Etan-na,* ind. not so. — *Etan-maya, as, ī, am,* consisting of this, of such a kind; [cf. Zend *aiśa, aita;* Old Pers. *aita;* Armen. *ais, aid;* Osk. *eiso;* Hib. *ise,* 'he, himself;' *isa* and *isi,* 'she, herself.']

Etadīya, as, ā, am, belonging to this.

Etarhi, ind., Ved. (very often in the Brāhmaṇas), now, at this time, at present, now-a-days; then (correlative to *yarhi*); a certain measure of time = fifteen *idānīms* or one fifteenth of a *kshipra.*

Etādṛiksha, as, ī, am, Ved., or *etādṛiś, k, k, k,* or *etādṛiśa, as, ī, am,* such, such like; so formed, of this kind, similar to this.

Etāvat, ān, atī, at, so great, so much, so many, of such a measure or compass, of such extent, so far, of such quality or kind; often found in connection with a relative clause, in which case the latter generally follows (e. g. *etāvān eva purusho yaj jāyātmā prajeti ha,* a man is of such a measure as [i. e. is made complete by] himself, his wife, and his progeny); (*vat*), ind. so far, thus far, so much, in such a degree, thus, &c. — *Etāvat-tva, am,* n. quantity, number; greatness; (with following *yad*) such a state or condition that; such extent.

एतन *etana, as,* m. expiration, breathing out, discharging air from the lungs; the fish Silurus Pelorius.

एतृ *etṛi, tā,* m. (rt. 5. *i*), Ved. going, approaching, asking, requesting.

Ema, as, m. or *eman, a,* n., Ved. a course, way.

एदिधिषुःपति *edidhishuḥpati, is,* m., Ved. the husband of a younger sister, whose elder sister has not yet been married. See *didhishu.*

एध् *edh* (connected with rt. *ṛidh*), cl. 1. A. (rarely P.) *edhate, edhāñ-ćakre, edhishyate, aidhishṭa, edhitum,* to prosper, increase, grow, become happy, grow strong, become great; to extend; to swell, rise (as waters): Caus. *edhayati, -yitum,* to cause to prosper, increase, celebrate, honour: Desid. *edidhishate;* [said to be related to Gr. οἶδος, οἰδάω; perhaps also to Lat. *æsculus.*]

1. *edhatu, us,* m. (for 2. see *endh* next page), Ved. prosperity, happiness; a man; (*us, us, u*), increased, grown.

Edhanīya or *edhitavya* or *edhya, as, ā, am*, to be increased or enlarged.

Edhamāna, as, ā, am, prospering, increasing. —*Edhamāna-dvish, ṭ, ṭ, ṭ*, Ved. hating the prosperous, especially those rendered insolent by prosperity; (Sāy.) hating the impious who prosper.

1. *edhas, as*, n. (in comp.) prosperity.

Edhā, f. happiness, prosperity.

Edhita, as, ā, am, grown, increased.

Edhitṛi, tā, trī, tṛi, increasing, growing, enlarging.

एन *ena*, a pronom. base (used for certain cases of the 3rd personal pronoun, and occurring only in the acc. sing. du. pl. (*enam, enām, enad*, &c.), inst. sing. (*enena, enayā*), gen. loc. du. (*enayos*, Ved. *enos*); the other cases are formed fr. the pronom. base *a*, see under *idam*), he, she, it; this, that. This pronoun is enclitic and cannot begin a sentence. It is generally used alone, so that *enam purusham*, 'that man,' would be very unusual if not incorrect. Grammarians assert that the substitution of *enam* for *imam* or *etam* takes place in case of the re-employment of these pronouns in the subsequent part of a sentence; see Gram. 836; [cf. Gr. ἕν, οἷος; Goth. *ains*; Old Pruss. *ains*; Lat. *oinos, unus*.]

Enā, ind., Ved. in this manner, thus; here, there; then, at that time; *para enā*, further on; *para enā prithivyā*, beyond the earth here.

एनस् *enas, as*, n. (fr. *in*, but said to be fr. rt. 5. *i*), mischief, crime; curse, unhappiness; sin, offence, fault; censure, blame. —*Enas-vat, ān, atī, at*, or *enas-vin, ī, inī, i*, wicked, sinful, a sinner.

Enasya, as, ā, am, Ved. caused by crime; sinful, wicked, wrong.

एनी *enī*. See under 1. *eta*.

एन्ध् *endh* (*ā-indh*), cl. 7. A. *endhe, endhitum*, to kindle, inflame; to be inflamed, to flame.

Edha, as, ā, am (fr. simple rt. *indh*), kindling, one who kindles, cf. *agny-edha*; (*as*), m. fuel, as wood, grass, &c.; [cf. Gr. αἶθος.] —*Edhāhāra* (*edha-āh°*), *as*, m. one who collects fuel.

2. *edhatu, us*, m. fire.

2. *edhas, as*, n. fuel.

एन्व् *env* (*ā-inv*), cl. 1. P. *envati, -vitum*, to bring near, to bestow.

एम *ema*. See under *etṛi* above.

एमूष *emūsha, as*, m., Ved. corrupted from *emusham*, the part. perf. of rt. *am*.

एर् *er* (*ā-īr*), cl. 2. A. *erte, eritum*, to go to or into: Caus. *erayati, -te, -yitum*, to bring near, procure; to obtain; to raise (the voice in singing &c.).

एरक *eraka, as*, m., N. of a Nāga; (*ā*), f. a sort of grass of emollient and diluent properties; (in the Mausala-parva of the Mahā-bh. this grass when plucked by Krishṇa and his family turned to clubs); (*am*), n. a woollen carpet; [cf. *airakya*.]

एरङ्ग *eranga, as*, m. a kind of fish; [cf. *elanga*.]

एरण्ड *eraṇḍa, as*, m. the castor-oil plant, Palma Christi or Ricinus Communis; (*ā*), f. long pepper. —*Eraṇḍa-pattrikā*, f. or *eraṇḍa-phalā*, f. the plant Croton Polyandrum.

Eraṇḍaka, as, m. the plant Ricinus Communis.

एरमत्तक *eramattaka, as*, m., N. of a man.

एरु *eru*, a word of doubtful meaning in Atharva-veda VI. 22, 3.

एर्त्स् *erts*, Desid. of *ārdh*, q. v.

एर्वारु *ervāru, us*, m. f. or *ervāruka, as*, m. a kind of cucumber, Cucumis Utilissimus.

एल *ela, am*, n. a particular number.

Elada, am, n. a particular number.

एलक *elaka, as*, m. a ram. See *eḍaka*.

एलङ्ग *elanga, as*, m. a kind of fish; [cf. *eranga*.]

एलपुर *elapura, am*, n., N. of a town.

एलवालु *elavālu*, n. or *elavāluka* or *elvavāluka, am*, n. the fragrant bark of Feronia Elephantum; a granular substance, apparently a vegetable of a reddish-brown colour (it is used as a drug and perfume).

एलविल *elavila, as*, m. an epithet of Kuvera. See *ailavila*.

एला *elā*, f. cardamoms, the seed of the Elettaria Cardamomum or Alpinia Cardamomum, it applies to both the large and small cardamom, but more commonly to the former; N. of a river; N. of a metre consisting of four lines of fifteen syllables each. —*Elā-pattra, as*, m., N. of a Nāga. —*Elā-parṇī*, f. the plant Mimosa Octandra. —*Elā-pura, am*, n., N. of a town.

Elāka, as, m., N. of a man.

Elikā, f. small cardamoms.

एलाय *elāya* (less correctly *ilāya*), nom. P. *elāyati, -yitum*, to be wantonly mischievous or wild in behaviour, to be merry.

एलु *elu*, n. a particular number.

एलुक *eluka*, N. of a medicinal substance or plant.

एलूक *elūka, am*, n. probably identical with *eḍūka*, a wall enclosing bones.

एव 1. *eva* (fr. pronom. base *e*, see *etad*, Zend *aiva*), so, just so, exactly so (e. g. *ya evedam iti bravat*, who may say 'it is so;' in this sense *eva* = the more modern word *evam*); like (e. g. *tvam eva yantā*, a driver like you; but examples of *eva* in the sense of *iva* are rare); indeed, truly, really (often in this sense found in the Veda at the beginning of a verse in conjunction with other particles of affirmation, especially with *id, id nu kam, hi*, &c., e.g. *evennu kaṃ tatāra*, be most certainly crossed; *evā hy asi vīrayuḥ*, thou art indeed hero-like.

(In its most frequent use of strengthening the idea expressed by any word, *eva*, if translateable, must be variously rendered by such adverbs as) just, exactly, very, merely, only, even, at the very moment, immediately on, scarcely, still, already, &c. (e. g. *tāvatīm eva rātrim*, just so long a night; *evam eva*, exactly so; *tān eva*, these very persons; *naćirād eva*, in no very long time; *apaḥ sprishṭvaiva*, by merely touching water; *japyenaiva*, by sole repetition; *abhuktvaira*, even without having eaten; *iti vadann eva*, at the very moment of saying so; *nāmni kīrtita eva*, scarcely had the name been mentioned; *sa jīvann eva*, he while still living.

Eva may often be connected with other adverbs in the sense of 'also,' 'likewise,' &c., as in the following examples: *tathaiva*, so also; *tathaiva ća*, and so likewise; *eva ća*, and also; *ćaiva*, and also; *eva vā*, or also; *na tv eva*, but not also. Grammarians assert that *eva* cuts off the final of *kva* when it follows that adverb, as *kv-eva*, where possibly? i. e. nowhere. Lexicographers affirm that *eva* may imply emphasis, affirmation, detraction, diminution, command, restraint; or be used as an expletive; [cf. Goth. *air*, Them. *aiva*; Old Germ. *eo, io*; Mod. Germ. *je*: perhaps also Lat. *ævum*; Goth. *ibus*; Old Germ. *ebanēr*; Mod. Germ. *ebener, eben*.]

Evathā, ind., Ved. indeed, certainly, even; (Sāy. either fr. rt. 5. *i*) assailing the strongholds of enemies, going to war; (or fr. rt. *ar*) protecting, protection, assistance.

एव 2. *eva, as, ā, am* (fr. rt. 5. *i*), Ved. going, moving, speedy, quick; (*as*), m. a course, way, (often in inst. pl., e. g. *sanād divam pari bhumā svebhir evair aktoshā ćarataḥ*, from all eternity day and night move round heaven and earth in their accustomed course); earth, world?; (Sāy.) a courser, a fleet horse; (*ās*), m. pl. way or manner of acting, mode of proceeding, custom, usage, habit; (Sāy.) desire, a hymn which goes or is directed to the object of praise (e. g. *abhi ćashṭe sūro arya evān*, the sun sees into the conduct of the worshipper; or according to Sāy. the sun being a lord makes manifest or grants desires). When the inst. c. is used, the meaning is hardly to be distinguished from that in the first example (e. g. *svair evaiḥ*, in his usual way of proceeding; *pūrvyebhir evaiḥ*, in the ancient mode; or according to Sāy. with ancient hymns). —*Eva-yā, ās, ās, am*, Ved. going in ways or courses, i. e. either going quickly or going the usual way; epithet of Vishṇu; (Sāy.) granting protection. —*Evayā-marut*, Ved., (Sāy.) N. of the author of a Ṛig-veda hymn, but perhaps rather an exclamation meaning either *eva-yā*, i. e. 'Vishṇu (cf. the preceding word) and the Maruts!' or 'moving Maruts.' —*Eva-yāvan, ā, ā, a*, Ved. going quickly, or going the usual way; epithet of Vishṇu and of the Maruts; (Sāy.) going with horses; granting desires.

एवम् *evam*, ind. (cf. 1. *eva* and *etad*), so, thus, in this way, in such a manner, such. *Evam* is not found in the oldest hymns of the Veda, where its place is taken by *eva*, but occurs in later hymns and in the Brāhmaṇas, especially in connection with the rt. *vid*, 'to know,' and its derivatives (e. g. *ya evaṃ veda*, he who knows so; cf. *evaṃ-vid* below). In classical Sanskṛit *evam* occurs very frequently, especially in connection with the roots *vać*, 'to speak,' and *śru*, 'to hear,' and refers to what precedes as well as to what follows (e. g. *evam uktvā*, having so said; *evamevaitat*, this is so; *evam astu* or *evam bhavatu*, be it so, I assent; *asty evam*, it is so; *yady evam*, if this be so; *kim evam*, how so? what is the meaning of it? what does this refer to? *maivam*, not so! *evam—yathā* or *yathā—evam*, so—as). *Evam* is often used like an adjective (e. g. *evaṃ te vaćane rataḥ*, rejoicing in such words of thine; where *evam* = *evaṃ-vidhe*). Sometimes *evam* is merely an expletive. According to lexicographers *evam* may imply likeness (so); sameness of manner (thus); assent (yes, verily); affirmation (certainly, indeed, assuredly); command (thus, &c.); and be used as an expletive. —*Evam-rūpa, as, ā, am*, of such a form or kind. —*Evaṃ-vāda, as*, m. such an expression. —*Evaṃ-vid, t, t, t*, or *evaṃ-vidvas, ān, ushī, as*, Ved. knowing so or such, well instructed, familiar with what is right. —*Evaṃ-vidha, as, ā, am*, of such a kind, in such form or manner, such. —*Evaṃ-vīrya, as, ā, am*, strong in such a manner, possessing such a power. —*Evaṃ-vritta, as, ā, am*, behaving or acting thus, of such a kind. —*Evaṃ-vṛitti, is, is, i*, behaving thus. —*Evan-kāram*, ind. in this manner. —*Evan-kāla, as, ā, am*, containing so many syllabic instants. —*Evan-kratu, us, us, u*, Ved. thus minded. —*Evan-gata, as, ā, am*, being in such a condition or state, so circumstanced, of such kind; (*e*), ind. under such circumstances. —*Evan-guṇa, as, ā, am*, possessing such qualities or such good qualities. —*Evan-duḥsaha, as, ā, am*, so hard to bear. —*Evan-nāman, ā, ā, a*, Ved. so called. —*Evam-avastha, as, ā, am*, so situated. —*Evam-ādi, is, is, i*, or *evam-ādya, as, ā, am*, having such a beginning, of such qualities or kind. —*Evam-prakāra* or *evam-prāya, as, ā, am*, of such a kind. —*Evam-prabhāva, as, ā, am*, possessed of such power. —*Evam-bhūta, as, ā, am*, of such quality, of such a description, in such a manner, so, such. —*Evambhūta-vat, ān, atī, at*, furnished with anything similar. —*Evam-bhūmi, is*, f. such a place, a place like the one just described.

एवार *evāra, as, ā, am* (fr. 1. *eva* and *aram*?), Ved. so prepared, ready; (Sāy.) N. of a man.

एवावद *evā-vada, as, ā, am*, Ved. so speaking, true; (*as*), m., (Sāy.) N. of a man.

एष् 1. *esh* (*ā-ish*), cl. 6. P. *eććhati, aishitum* or *-shṭum*, to wish, desire.

Eshṭa, as, ā, am, desired, wished.

एष् 2. esh (*ā-īsh*), cl. 1. P. A., Ved. *eshati, -te, eshitum*, to hasten near to or towards; to fly at; to attack any one; to endeavour to reach or gain; to desire; to request.

Eshṭi, is, f., Ved. seeking to go towards, desire, wish; (Sāy.) wishing; (or fr. rt. *yaj*) worshipping.

एष् 3. esh, cl. 1. P. A. *eshati, -te, eshāñ-ćakāra, eshāñ-ćakre, eshitum*, to creep, glide; to go or approach: Caus. *eshayati, -yitum*, to probe.

1. *esha, as, ā, am*, Ved. gliding, running; an epithet of Vishṇu; (Sāy.) to be desired, desirable; to be obtained.

एष 2. esha. See *etad.*

एष 3. esha, *as, ā, am* (fr. rt. 3. *ish*), seeking; (*as*), m. running or hastening towards; (according to Sāy. *eshe* is an inf. fr. rt. *i*, 'to go') seeking; wish, election; (*ā*), f. wish. — *Eshaishya* (*esha-esh°*), *as, ā, am*, Ved. to be sought, desirable.

Eshaṇa, as, ā, am, seeking; (*as*), m. an iron arrow; (*am*), n. driving, pressing; seeking; probing; wish, desire; (*ā*), f. seeking, wish, desire, begging, solicitation, request; (*ī*), f. an iron or steel probe; a goldsmith's balance, assay scales.

Eshaṇikā, f. a goldsmith's balance.

Eshaṇin, ī, inī, i, seeking, striving.

Eshaṇīya, as, ā, am, to be desired, desirable; to be aimed at; (at the end of a compound) relating to medical examination.

Eshitṛi, tā, trī, tṛi, wishing, desirous.

Eshin, ī, iṇī, i, driving, impelling; (at the end of compounds) seeking, desiring, desirous of, wishing (e. g. *hitaishin*, well-wishing).

Eshṭavya, as, ā, am, to be sought, desirable, wished.

Eshṭṛi, ṭā, ṭrī, ṭṛi, seeking, desiring.

Eshya, as, ā, am, to be sought for; to be investigated or probed.

एषवीर esha-vīra, *as*, m. designation of a despised Brāhmaṇic family.

एष्यत् eshyat, *an, atī* or *antī, at* (fut. part. fr. rt. 5. *i*), what is to come, future. — *Eshyatkālīya, as, ā, am*, future.

एह eha, *as, ā, am* (fr. rt. *īh*), Ved. desirous, wishing.

Ehas, as, n., Ved. anger.

एहि ehi (imperative of rt. 5. *i* with *ā*), come!

एहिमाय ehimāya, *as, ā, am*, Ved., = *ahi-māya*, q. v., an epithet of the Viśvedevās; (Sāy.) of all-pervading intelligence; or these deities may be so named because they uttered on one occasion the words 'Come near, do not go away' (*ehi mā yāsīḥ*. See Ṛig-veda I. 3, 9).

ऐ

ऐ 1. ai, the twelfth vowel of the alphabet, having the sound of *ei* in *heighth*. — *Ai-kāra, as*, m. the letter or sound *ai*.

ऐ 2. ai, ind. (an interjection of calling or summoning) Hola, Ho, Heigh; (and of remembering) Aye, Ha.

ऐ 3. ai, *ais*, m. an epithet of Śiva.

ऐकध्य aikadhya, *am*, n. (fr. *ekadhā*), singleness of time or occurrence; (*am* or *atas*), ind. at once, together.

Aikapatya, am, n. (fr. *eka-pati*), the sovereignty of one, absolute monarchy; supreme authority.

Aikapadika, as, ī, am (fr. *eka-pada*), belonging to a simple word; consisting of single words; the N. given to the Naigama section of Yāska's commentary on the Nighaṇṭavas, or collection of Vedic words.

Aikapadya, am, n. unity of words.

Aikabhāvya, am, n. (fr. *eka-bhāva*), singleness of nature.

Aikamatya, am, n. (fr. *eka-mati*), unanimity, sameness of doctrine or of opinion, agreement, consent, concurrence, confederation; (*as, ī, am*), connected with sameness of opinion.

Aikarājya, am, n. (fr. *eka-rāj*), monarchy.

Aikalavya, as, m. a patronymic fr. *eka-lū*.

Aikaśatika, as, ī, am (fr. *eka-śata*), provided with 101.

Aikaśapha, as, ī, am (fr. *eka-śapha*), produced by or belonging to animals with uncloven hoofs.

Aikaśrutya, am, n. (fr. *eka-śruti*, q. v.), the one accentless monotonous tone, monotony.

Aikasahasrika, as, ī, am (fr. *eka-sahasra*), provided with 1001.

Aikasvarya, am, n. (fr. *eka-svara*), oneness of accent (as in the case of a compound which has only one accent, though the separate members when uncompounded are each accented).

Aikāgārika, as, ī, m. f. (fr. *eka-āgāra*), a thief, a robber breaking into lonely houses; the possessor of one residence.

Aikāgrya, am, n. (fr. *ekāgra*), intentness on one object.

Aikāṅga, as, m. (fr. *ekāṅga*), a soldier of the body-guard.

Aikātmya, am, n. (fr. *eka-ātman*), unity of the soul, unity of being; oneness with the supreme spirit.

Aikādaśāksha, as, m. (fr. *ekādaśa + aksha*), N. of a man.

Aikādaśina, as, ī, am (fr. *ekādaśinī*), Ved. belonging to a collection or association of eleven.

Aikādhikaraṇya, am, n. (fr. *eka + adhikaraṇa*), oneness of relation.

Aikāntika, as, ī, am (fr. *ekānta*), absolute, complete, perfect.

Aikānyika, as, ī, am (fr. *eka + anya*), one who commits a single error in reading (who makes one thing another or otherwise than right).

Aikārthya, am, n. (fr. *ekārtha*), oneness of aim or intention.

Aikāhika, as, ī, am (fr. *ekāha*), ephemeral, quotidian, of one day, of the same day; belonging to a ceremony which lasts one day, belonging to a simple oblation.

Aikya, am, n. (fr. *eka*), oneness, unity, singleness, identity, harmony, sameness; the identity of the human soul or of the universe with the Deity; an aggregate, whole, total; (in alg.) the product of the length and depth of the portions, or of the little excavations differing in depth.

ऐक्षव aikshava, *as, ī, am* (fr. *ikshu*), produced from or relating to the sugar-cane, sugary; (*am*), n. sugar.

Aikshavya, as, ī, am, Ved. produced from or relating to the sugar-cane.

Aikshuka, as, ī, am, suitable for sugar-cane; bearing sugar-cane; (*as*), m. a carrier of sugar-canes; (*ās*), m. pl. the inhabitants of Ikshukīya.

Aikshubhārika, as, ī, am (fr. *ikshu-bhāra*), carrying a load of sugar-canes.

ऐक्ष्वाक aikshvāka, *as, ī, am* (fr. *ikshvāku*), belonging to Ikshvāku, of the family of Ikshvāku; (*as*), m. a descendant of Ikshvāku; epithet of Purukutsa, and of Daśaratha.

Aikshvāku, us, m. a descendant of Ikshvāku; epithet of Triśaṅku, and of Rāma.

ऐङ्गुद aiṅguda, *as, ī, am*, produced from the Iṅguda plant; (*am*), n. scil. *phalam*, the fruit of the Iṅguda plant.

ऐच्छिक aiććhika, *as, ī, am* (fr. *iććhā*), optional, voluntary, arbitrary, at will.

ऐड aiḍa, *as, ī, am* (fr. *iḍā*), Ved. containing anything refreshing or strengthening; containing the word *iḍā*; (*as*), m. the son of Iḍā, epithet of Purūravas; [cf. *aila*.]

ऐडक aiḍaka, *as, ī, am* (fr. *eḍaka*), produced from the animal Eḍaka; (*as*), m. a species of sheep.

ऐडविड aiḍaviḍa, *as*, m. an epithet of Kuvera; N. of a son of Daśaratha; also *aiḍavila*; [cf. *ailavila*.]

ऐडुक aiḍuka or *aiḍūka, am*, n. a wall &c. of bones and rubbish. See *eḍuka*.

ऐण aiṇa, *as, ī, am* (fr. *eṇa*), produced from or belonging to the male black antelope.

Aiṇika, as, ī, am, hunting black antelopes, a deer-killer.

Aiṇeya, as, ī, am (fr. *eṇī*), produced from the black doe or female antelope; produced from anything belonging to a black doe or female antelope; (*as*), m. the black antelope; (*am*), n. a kind of coitus.

ऐण्डिनेय aiṇḍineya, *ās*, m. pl., N. of a Śākhā or branch of the Veda.

ऐतदात्म्य aitadātmya, *am*, n. (abstr. noun of *etadātman*), the state of having this property or peculiarity.

ऐतरेय aitareya, *as*, m. a descendant of Itarā, to whom the Aitareya-Brāhmaṇa and Āraṇyaka were revealed; (*as, ī, am*), originating from Aitareya. — *Aitareya-brāhmaṇa* or *aitareyaka, am*, n. (scil. *brāhmaṇa*) title of a Brāhmaṇa attached to the Ṛig-veda and prescribing the duties of the Hotṛi priest. It consists of forty Adhyāyas, divided into eight Pañćikās. — *Aitareyopanishad* (°*ya-up*°), *t*, f., N. of an Upanishad forming part of the Aitareya-Āraṇyaka. — *Aitareyopanishad-bhāshya, am*, n. a commentary on the last by Saṅkarāćārya. — *Aitareyopanishadbhāshya-ṭippaṇī*, f., N. of a commentary on the last work by Anantānandagiri.

Aitareyin, ī, m. a follower of Aitareya, a reader of the Aitareya-Brāhmaṇa.

ऐतश aitaśa, *as*, m., N. of a Muni of the family of Aurva (Bhṛigu), author of the Aitaśa-pralāpa forming part of the Kuntāpa hymns of the Atharva-veda and used with these hymns in the ritual belonging to the Ṛig-veda.

Aitaśāyana, ās, m. pl. the descendants of Aitaśa.

Aitiśāyana, as, m., N. of a teacher.

ऐतिहासिक aitihāsika, *as, ī, am* (fr. *iti-hāsa*), derived from ancient legends, legendary, historical, traditional; (*as*), m. one who relates or knows ancient legends, an historian.

ऐतिह्य aitihya, *am*, n. (fr. *iti-ha*; see under *iti*, p. 139), traditional instruction.

ऐदंयुगीन aidaṃyugīna, *as, ā, am* (fr. *idaṃ-yuga*), fit for this yoke or team.

ऐध् aidh, f. or *aidha, as*, m. or *aidhā*, f. (fr. rt. *indh* with *ā*), Ved. flaming, a flame, splendor.

ऐन aina, *ās*, m. pl., N. of a people.

ऐनस ainasa, *am*, n. (fr. *enas*), sin.

ऐन्दव aindava, *as, ī, am* (fr. *indu*), lunar, belonging or relating or similar to the moon; (*ī*), f. the plant Serratula Anthelminthica; (*am*), n. the asterism Mṛigaśiras.

ऐन्द्र aindra, *as, ī, am* (fr. *indra*), belonging to or sacred to Indra, proceeding from Indra, similar to Indra; (*as*), m. the part of a sacrifice offered to Indra; (*ī*), f. (scil. *ṛić*) a verse addressed to Indra; (scil. *diś*) the east quarter, of which Indra is regent (e. g. *aindryāṃ diśi*, in the east); the eighteenth lunar mansion; the eighth day in the second half of the month Mārgaśīrsha, and of the month Pausha; Indra's energy, personified as his wife and by some identified with Durgā; epithet of Durgā; misfortune, misery (personified); N. of a plant, a kind of cucumber, Cucumis Madraspatanus; (am), n. the eighteenth lunar mansion (jyeshṭhā); wild ginger.

Aindrajālika, as, ī, am (fr. indra-jāla), familiar with or relating to magic, magical, deceptive, illusory; (as), m. a juggler.

Aindraturīya, as, ī, am, a libation (graha) &c., the fourth part of which is offered to Indra.

Aindradyumna, as, ī, am, relating to Indradyumna; N. of a country.

Aindraluptika, as, ī, am (fr. indra-lupta), afflicted with morbid baldness of the head.

Aindravāyava, as, ī, am, Ved. belonging to Indra and Vāyu.

Aindraśira, as, m. a species of elephant.

Aindrāgna, as, ī, am, Ved. sacred to or belonging to Indra and Agni, proceeding from Indra and Agni.

Aindrānairṛita, as, ī, am, belonging to Indra and Nirṛiti.

Aindrāpaushṇa, as, ī, am, belonging to Indra and Pūshan.

Aindrābārhaspatya, as, ī, am, belonging to Indra and Bṛihaspati.

Aindrāmāruta, as, ī, am, belonging to Indra and the Maruts.

Aindrāyudha, as, ī, am, relating to Indra's bow or the rainbow.

Aindrāvaruṇa, as, ī, am, sacred to Indra and Varuṇa.

Aindrāvaishṇava, as, ī, am, belonging to Indra and Vishṇu.

Aindrāsaumya, as, ī, am, belonging to Indra and Soma.

Aindri, is, m. a patronymic of Jayanta, the son of Indra; N. of Arjuna; N. of the monkey-king Bāli; a crow.

Aindrīya, as, ī, am (fr. indriya and connected with indra, q. v.), relating to or belonging to the senses, sensual; perceptible, perceived, present; (am), n. the world of the senses; a section of the Āyur-veda treating on the senses.

Aindriyaka, as, ī, am, relating to the senses; perceptible.

Aindriye-dhī, īs, īs, i, thinking only of sensual pleasure.

ऐन्धन *aindhana, as, ī, am* (fr. indhana), consisting of fuel; an epithet of the sun.

ऐभावत *aibhāvata, as*, m. (fr. ibhā-vat), a patronymic of Pratīdarśa.

ऐभी *aibhī*, f., N. of a plant; = ibhyā?

ऐयत्य *aiyatya, am*, n. (fr. iyat), quantity, number, value.

ऐरंमद *airammada, as*, m. (fr. irammada), a patronymic of Deva-muni, author of a Ṛig-veda hymn.

Airammadīya, am, n., N. of a sea in Brahmā's world.

ऐरावण *airāvaṇa, as*, m. (fr. irā-van = irā-vat, 'possessed of or proceeding from water'), N. of a king of the Nāgas; Indra's elephant, produced at the churning of the ocean.

Airāvata, as, m. a patronymic of a fabulous serpent-like being called Dhṛita-rāshṭra; a serpent, one of the chiefs of the Nāgas or serpent-race, inhabiting the lower world or Pātāla; N. of the elephant of Indra, produced at the churning of the ocean, and the prototype of the elephant race, considered also as the elephant of the east quarter; [cf. nāga, which means both serpent and elephant]; an excellent elephant; (as, am), m. n. a kind of rainbow, considered as the long and unbent bow of Indra; a kind of lightning; (as), m. the orange tree; another tree, Artocarpus Lacucha; (as, am), m. n. a vast and waterless region; (āni), n. pl., N. of a Varsha; N. of the northern path of the moon; the fruit of the tree Artocarpus Lacucha; (ī), f. the female of Indra's elephant; lightning; N. of a plant; N. of the Ravi river in the Pañjāb; N. of a particular portion of the moon's path.

ऐरिण *airiṇa, am*, n. (fr. iriṇa), fossil or rock salt.

ऐरेय *aireya, am*, n. (fr. irā), a spirituous liquor.

ऐर्म्य *airmya, as, ī, am* (fr. īrmā), good for healing wounds, (a plaster &c.)

ऐल *aila, as*, m. (= aiḍa), N. of Purūravas as son of Ilā; (am), n. a particular number. — *Aila-dhāna, am*, n., N. of a town.

ऐलब *ailaba, as*, m., Ved. noise, roaring, cry. — *Ailaba-kāra, as, ā, am*, Ved. making a noise, roaring (epithet of Rudra's dogs).

ऐलबृद *ailabṛida, as, ā, am*, Ved. bringing food; (perhaps related to ailaba.)

ऐलवालुक *ailavāluka, am*, n. a perfume. See elavālu.

ऐलविल *ailavila, as*, m., N. of Kuvera as son of Ilavilā; (also aiḍavida, aiḍavila, and elavila); N. of a king.

ऐलूष *ailūsha, as*, m. (fr. ilūsha), a patronymic of Kavasha, the author of two Ṛig-veda hymns.

ऐलेय *aileya, am*, n. a perfume; = elavālu.

ऐश *aiśa, as, ī, am* (fr. īśa), proceeding from or relating to Śiva; divine, supreme, regal.

Aiśāna, as, ī, am (fr. īśāna), belonging to Śiva; (ī), f. (scil. diś) the quarter of Śiva, the north-east quarter. — *Aiśāna-ja, ās*, m. pl. = īśāna-ja, q. v.

Aiśika, as, ī, am, belonging to Śiva; divine, heavenly; royal, regal.

Aiśvara, as, ī, am (fr. īśvara), fit for or belonging to or produced by a master, or by the supreme lord; mighty, majestic; divine, relating to God; supreme, royal; belonging to Śiva.

Aiśvarika, as, m. (with Buddhists) a theist.

Aiśvarya, am, n. power, might, sway; dominion; supremacy; superhuman power; the divine faculties of omnipresence, omnipotence, invisibility, &c. (sometimes their number is given as five, with reference to the five elements). — *Aiśvarya-vat, ān, atī, at*, endowed with superhuman faculties, possessed of supernatural powers, connected with them.

ऐषमस् *aishamas*, ind. (ai related to e or i in etad or idam, and samas from samā, 'year'), during this year, in the present year; [cf. Gr. σῆτες, σήμερον.]

Aishamastana, as, ī, am, or *aishamastya, as, ā, am*, of or belonging to the present year.

ऐषावीर *aishāvīra, as, ī, am* (fr. esha-vīra?), Ved. weak, powerless.

ऐषीक *aishīka, as, ī, am* (fr. ishīkā), consisting of stalks made of reeds or cane; (ās), m. pl., N. of a people; *aishīkam parva*, a section of the tenth book or Sauptika-parva of the Mahā-bhārata (Adhyāya 10–18).

ऐषुकारि *aishukāri, ayas*, m. pl. (fr. ishu-kāra), N. of a tribe or caste. — *Aishukāri-bhakta, am*, n. the country inhabited by this tribe.

ऐष्टक *aishṭaka, am*, n. (fr. ishṭakā), Ved. the sacrificial bricks collectively.

ऐष्टिक *aishṭika, as, ī, am* (fr. 3. ishṭi), sacrificial, ceremonial.

Aishṭikapaurtika, as, ī, am, belonging to the Ishṭāpūrta, ceremonial and meritorious.

ऐहलौकिक *aihalaukika, as, ī, am* (fr. iha-loka), of this world, happening in this world, terrestrial, sublunary; (opposed to pāralaukika.)

Aihika, as, ī, am (fr. iha), of this place, of this world, temporal, worldly, secular, local; (opposed to āmushmika.) — *Aihika-darśin, ī, inī, i*, worldly-minded, concerned about worldly affairs.

ओ

ओ 1. *o*, the vowel o, the thirteenth letter of the alphabet. — *O-kāra, as*, m. the letter or sound o.

ओ 2. *o*, ind. a vocative particle, Oh; an interjection of calling, Ho, Holla; of reminiscence, Ho, Ah; of compassion, Ah, Oh.

ओ 3. *o, aus*, m. a N. of Brahmā.

ओ 4. *o* (ā-u), only occurring in the past pass. part. — 1. *ota, as, ā, am*, Ved. invoked, summoned.

ओक *oka, as*, m. (fr. rt. uć), a house; an asylum, a refuge (see okas below); a bird?; [cf. Lith. ūkis, 'a dwelling;' ūkininkas: Gr. οἶκος belongs to rt. viś.]

Okas, as, n. gratification, pleasure; place of happiness or pleasure, a resting-place, a home, house; an asylum, a refuge.

Okivas, ān (irreg. perf. part. Par.?), Ved. delighting in anything; (Sāy.) meeting together, united.

Okya, as, ā, am, Ved. favourable to the (inmates of a) house; good for a house, kind to a household; (am), n. gratification, pleasure; a comfortable place; a resting-place, a house.

ओकण *okaṇa, as*, or *okaṇi, is*, m. a bug. See okodanī.

ओकुल *okula, as*, m. a cake of flour.

ओकोदनी *okodanī* or *okkaṇī*, f. a bug. See okaṇa.

ओक्ष् *oksh* (ā-uksh), cl. 1. P. *okshati, -shitum*, to sprinkle over or upon.

ओख् *okh*, cl. 1. P. *okhati, okhāñ-ćakāra, okhitum*, to be dry or arid; to be able or competent; to adorn, suffice; to refuse, prevent, ward off: Caus. *okhayati, -yitum*: Desid. *oćikhishati*.

ओगण *ogaṇa, as, ā, am* (fr. ava-gaṇa?), Ved. repudiated by one's companions, solitary, despised; (Sāy.) collected, united.

ओगीयस् *ogīyas* = ojīyas, comparative of ugra, q. v.

ओघ *ogha, as*, m. (fr. rt. vah), flood, stream; a torrent, a rapid flow of water, an inundation; a heap or quantity, flock, multitude, abundance; the whole; quick time in music; tradition, traditional advice or instruction; [cf. Gr. ὄχλος?]. — *Ogha-ratha, as*, m., N. of a son of Oghavat and brother of Oghavatī. — *Ogha-vat, ān, atī, at*, having a strong stream; (ān), m., N. of a prince, father-in-law or brother-in-law of Sudarśana; (tī), f., N. of a daughter of Oghavat; N. of the river Sarasvatī.

ओङ्कार *oṅkāra*. See under om.

ओज् *oj* (connected with ojas below), cl. 1. 10. P. *ojati, ojitum*, or *ojayati, -yitum*, to be strong or able; to increase, to have vital power.

ओज *oja, as, ā, am*, odd (as the first, third, fifth, &c., in a series).

ओजस् *ojas, as*, n. (fr. uj = vaj; see ugra), bodily strength, vigour, energy, ability; vitality, the principle of vital warmth and action diffused throughout the body; virility, the generative faculty; support, stay; (in rhetoric) a form of style, elaborate style, abounding with compounds; (in astrology) each alternate sign of the zodiac (as the first, third, fifth, &c.); water; light, splendor; metallic lustre;

manifestation, appearance; *ojasā*, with strength, resolutely, energetically (sometimes used at the beginning of a compound, e. g. *ojasā-kṛita*, done energetically); [cf. *amitaujas*, *uttamaujas*, &c.: cf. also Gr. ὑγιής; Zend *aušo*; Hib. *og*, 'young, juvenile, fresh;' *olg*, 'a champion;' *oighe*, 'entireness, virginity.'] — *Ojas-tara, as, ā, am* (comparative), more strong. — *Ojas-vat, ān, atī, at*, or *ojas-vin, ī, inī, i*, vigorous, powerful, strong, energetic; splendid, bright. — *Ojasvitā*, f. strength, power. — *Ojo-dā, ās, ās, am*, Ved. granting power, strengthening, possessed of strength. — *Ojo-balā*, f. (with Buddhists) N. of a goddess of Bodhidruma.

Ojasīna, as, ā, am, Ved. showing strength, powerful.

Ojasya, as, ā, am, showing strength, powerful.

Ojāya, nom. A. *ojāyate, -yitum*, to exhibit strength or energy, to make effort; to be strong.

Ojishṭha, as, ā, am (regarded as superlative of *ugra*, q. v.), strongest, most vigorous or vehement.

Ojīyas, ān, asī, as (regarded as comparative of *ugra*, q. v.), stronger, more vigorous or vehement.

Ojman, ā, m., Ved. strength; (Sāy.) speed; an instigator.

ओड *oḍa, as*, m., N. of a minister of Pratāpāditya.

ओडक *oḍaka* or *oḍava, as*, m. a musical mode which omits two of the notes of the scale, Ṛi and Pa.

ओडिका *oḍikā* or *oḍī*, f. wild rice.

ओड्र *oḍra, ās*, m. pl., N. of a people and country, the northern part of Orissa; (*as*), m. the China rose. — *Oḍra-pushpa, am*, n. Hibiscus Rosa Sinensis, and its flowers. — *Oḍrākhyā* (°*ra-ākh*°), f. the China rose.

ओढ *oḍha, as, ā, am* (past pass. part. of *ā-vah*, q. v.), brought or carried near.

ओण *oṇ*, cl. 1. P. *oṇati, oṇāñ-ćakāra, oṇitum*, to remove, take away, drag along: Caus. *oṇayati, -yitum, auṇiṇat*: Desid. *auṇiṇishati*.

ओणि *oṇi, is*, m. or f. (generally in du. *ī*; said to be fr. preceding rt.), Ved. a vessel used in the preparation of the Soma juice, and said to consist of two pieces (?), heaven and earth; preserving power; protection.

ओत 1. *ota*. See 4. *o*.

ओत 2. *ota, as, ā, am* (fr. rt. *ve* with *ā*), woven, sewn with the threads across; [cf. *prota*.] — *Ota-prota, as, ā, am*, sewn crosswise and lengthwise, extending to every quarter?; (*am*), ind. crosswise and lengthwise, vertically and horizontally.

Otu, us, m. the woof or cross-threads of a web; (*us*), m. f. a cat, (in this sense said to be fr. rt. *av*.) In a compound a final *a* preceding may optionally be dropped (e. g. *sthūlotu* or *sthūlautu*, a fat cat.)

ओत्स *otsa, as*, m., N. of an Agrahāra.

ओदती *odatī*, f. (part. of rt. 2. *ud*), Ved. flowing forth, issuing out, rising upwards; epithet of the dawn.

Odana, as, am, m. n. grain mashed and cooked with milk, boiled rice; a cloud; (*nī*), f. the plant Sida Cordifolia. When a name is given to a pupil to indicate his attachment to any particular master, *odana* may be prefixed to denote that the pupil's object is rather food than instruction (e. g. *odanapāṇinīyaḥ*, a pupil of Pāṇini whose object is only to be fed by Pāṇini). — *Odanāhvayā* (°*na-āh*°) or *odanāhvā* or *odanikā*, f., N. of a plant.

Odanīya, nom. P. *odanīyati, -yitum*, to wish to make mashed food of anything.

Odma, as, m. or *odman, a*, n. flowing, flooding; wetting, moistening.

ओधस् *odhas, as*, n. an udder; = *ūdhas*.

ओपश *opaśa, as*, m. (fr. rt. *paś?*), Ved. an ornament of the head, lock of hair, curl; tuft of hair?; (Sāy.) a horn (fr. *upa-śi* with *ā*).

Opaśin, ī, inī, i, Ved. adorned with curls.

ओम् *om*, ind. (said to be fr. rt. *av*; perhaps originally *oṃ*, which may be derived fr. *āṃ*, and this fr. *ā*), a word of solemn affirmation and respectful assent (sometimes translated by yes, verily, so be it, and in this sense compared with Amen). It is placed at the commencement of most Hindū works, and as a sacred exclamation may be uttered (but not so as to be heard by ears profane) at the beginning and end of a reading of the Vedas or previously to any prayer. It is also regarded as a particle of auspicious salutation (Hail!). *Om* appears first in the Upanishads as a mystic monosyllable, and is there set forth as the object of profound religious meditation, the highest spiritual efficacy being attributed not only to the whole word but also to the three sounds *a, u, m*, of which it consists. In later times *om* is the mystic name for the Hindū triad, and represents the union of the three gods, viz. *a* (Vishṇu), *u* (Śiva), *m* (Brahmā). It may also be typical of the three Vedas. *Om* is usually called *praṇava*, more rarely *aksharam* or *ekāksharam*, and only in later times *om-kāra*. The Buddhists use *om* at the commencement of their *vidyā shaḍ-aksharī* or mystical formulary in six syllables (viz. *om māni padme hūṃ*). Lexicographers affirm that besides the above uses, *om* may imply command or injunction, removal or warding off (Away! Hence!), and be used as an inceptive particle. Grammarians assert that before *om* a preceding *a* or *ā* at the end of a word should be cut off (e. g. *vijayonkāraḥ* for *vijayaunkāraḥ* (°*ya-on*°), thanksgiving for victory; see Gram. 38. *b*). — *Om-kāra, as*, m. the sacred and mystical syllable *om*; the exclamation *om*; pronouncing the syllable *om*; (*ā*), f. a Buddhist Śakti or female personification of divine energy. — *Oṃkāra-grantha, as*, m. title of a work of Nārāyaṇa. — *Oṃkāra-tīrtha*, N. of a Tīrtha. — *Oṃkāra-bhaṭṭa, as*, m., N. of a man.

ओम *oma, as*, m. (fr. rt. *av*, cf. 4. *ū*), Ved. a protector; any one favourably disposed (towards another); any one worthy of favour or protection.

Oman, ā, m., Ved. protection, assistance; favour, kindness; a kind person. — *Oman-vat, ān, atī, at*, Ved. friendly, agreeable; favourable, kind; satiating.

Omātrā, f., Ved. protection, assistance, kindness, readiness to help.

Omyā, f., Ved. favour, protection. — *Omyā-vat, ān, atī, at*, Ved. friendly, favourable.

ओमिल *omila, as*, m., N. of a man.

ओरिमिका *orimikā*, f. title of a section of the Kāṭhaka Recension of the Yajur-veda.

ओर्णु *orṇu* (*ā-ūrṇu*), cl. 2. P. A. *orṇati* or *-ṇauti, -ṇute, -ṇavitum* or *-ṇuvitum*, to cover.

ओल *ola* or *olla, as, ā, am*, wet, damp; (*as*), m. an esculent root, Arum Campanulatum.

ओलण्ड् *olaṇḍ*, cl. 10. P. *olaṇḍayati, -yitum*, to cast upwards, throw up; (various readings have *olaj* and *olj*.)

ओशिष्ठहन् *ośishṭha-han, ā, ghnī, a* (fr. *ośishṭha* = *oshishṭha* and *han*), Ved. striking very quickly; [cf. *oshishṭha-dāvan*.]

ओष *osha, as*, m. (fr. 1. *ush*), burning, combustion; [cf. Goth. *azgô*; Angl. Sax. *asca*; Old Germ. *asga*; Mod. Germ. *asche*; Eng. *ashes*.]

Oshaṇa, as, m. pungency, biting or pungent taste, sharp flavour; (*ī*), f. a pot-herb, commonly called Pūrya.

ओषधि *oshadhi, is*, or *ī*, f. (a contraction fr. *avasa* and *dhi*, 'containing refreshment or food?;' according to Pāṇini VI. 3, 132, the form in *ī* is only used for the oblique cases in the Veda; but this restriction does not seem to be universal), a herb, a plant, medicinal plant; an annual plant or herb, one that dies after becoming ripe. — *Oshadhi-garbha, as*, m. the moon (as containing the herbs in its interior). — *Oshadhi-ja, as, ā, am*, Ved. born or living among herbs; produced from plants. — *Oshadhi-pati, is*, m. a physician (master of the medicinal plants); the moon. — *Oshadhi-prastha, as*, m., N. of a mythic town, the town of Himavat. — *Oshadhī-pati, is*, m. the moon. — *Oshadhī-mat, ān, atī, at*, Ved. connected with herbs. — *Oshadhīśa* (°*dhi-īśa*), *as*, m. the moon (presiding over the plants). — *Oshadhī-saṃśita, as, ā, am*, Ved. impelled or influenced by herbs. — *Oshadhi-sūkta, am*, n., N. of a hymn.

ओषम् *osham*, ind. (fr. rt. 1. *ush?*), Ved. quickly, immediately.

Oshishṭha-dāvan, ā, ā, a, Ved. giving very quickly.

ओष्ठ *oshṭha, as*, m. (contracted fr. *avastha*), the down-hanging lip, i. e. the upper lip (opposed to *adhara*), a lip in general; *oshṭhau* or *drāv oshṭhau*, du. the lips, the two lips; (*ī*), f. a creeper bearing a red flower, to which the lip is commonly compared (Coccinia Grandis); [cf. *bimba*: cf. also Slav. *ûsta*, neut. pl.; *ûstna*, f.: Lat. *ostium*.] In compounds a final *a* or *ā* before *oshṭha* may be optionally dropped (e. g. *bimba* + *oshṭha* becomes either *bimboshṭha* or *bimbaushṭha*, 'red-lipped,' and the fem. of the comp. adj. may be formed in *ā* or *ī*). — *Oshṭha-karṇaka, ās*, m. pl., N. of a fabulous race who have their ears and lips very near each other. — *Oshṭha-kopa* or *oshṭha-prakopa, as*, m. a disease of the lips. — *Oshṭha-ja, as, ā, am*, produced by the lips, labial. — *Oshṭha-jāha, am*, n. the root of the ear. — *Oshṭha-pallava, am*, n. a lip or the lips. — *Oshṭha-puṭa, am*, n. the cavity made by opening the lips. — *Oshṭha-pushpa, am*, n. the plant Pentaptera Tomentosa. — *Oshṭha-roga, as*, m. any morbid affection of the lips. — *Oshṭhādhara* (°*ṭha-adh*°), *au*, du. or *am*, n. the upper and lower lip. — *Oshṭhopama-phalā* (°*ṭha-upamā-ph*°), f. the creeper Bryonia Grandis, whose flower resembles a lip.

Oshṭhaka (at the end of compounds) = *oshṭha*; (*as, ā, am*), taking care of the lips.

Oshṭhya, as, ā, am, being at the lips; belonging to or fit for the lips, labial (as the sounds *u, ū, o, au, p, ph, b, bh, m, v*, and the Upadhmānīya). — *Oshṭhya-yoni, is, is, i*, produced from labial sounds. — *Oshṭhya-sthāna, as, ā, am*, pronounced with the lips, as *o* and *au*.

ओष्ण *oshṇa, as, ā, am* (fr. *ā*, implying diminution, and *ushṇa*), a little warm, tepid.

ओह् *oh* (rt. 2. *ūh* with *ā*), cl. 1. A. *ohate, -hitum*, to understand, admit, receive.

Oha, as, m. (fr. 2. *ūh*), Ved. meditation; (Sāy.) bringing, performing; reaching. — *Oha-brahman, ā*, m., Ved. really a Brāhman, a Brāhman valued as one; (Sāy.) one who has sacred knowledge.

Ohala, as, m., N. of a man.

Ohas, as, n., Ved. idea, true notion; (Sāy.) praise.

Ohāna, as, ā, am, considering, reflecting on.

औ

औ 1. *au*, the fourteenth letter of the alphabet, having the same sound as *ou* in *our*. — *Au-kāra, as*, m. the letter or sound *au*.

औ 2. *au*, ind. an interjection of calling, Ho, Hola; of addressing, Oh; of prohibition and of asseveration.

औ 3. *au, aus*, m. sound; an epithet of Śesha or Ananta; (*aus*), f. the earth.

औक्थिक *aukthika, as*, m. (fr. *uktha*), a Brāhman acquainted with the Ukthas, reciting them.

Aukthikya, am, n. the text of the Ukthas.

Aukthya, am, n. a peculiar mode of recitation.

औक्ष *auksha, as, ī, am* (fr. *ukshan*), Ved.

relating to an ox, derived from one, &c. — *Auksha-gandhi, is,* f., N. of an Apsaras.

Aukshaka, am, n. a multitude of oxen.

Aukshṇa, as, ī, am, relating to an ox, derived from one; (*as*), m. a patronymic from Ukshan.

औखीय **aukhīya,** *ās,* m. pl. the followers of Ukha.

औख्य **aukhya,** *as, ā, am* (fr. *ukhā*), boiled or dressed in a pot.

औग्रसेनि **augraseni,** *is,* m. or *augrasenya, as,* m. a patronymic fr. *ugra-sena.*

Augrasainya, as, m. an epithet of Yudhāmśraushṭi.

Augrya, am, n. (fr. *ugra*), horribleness, dreadfulness, fierceness.

औघ **augha,** *as,* m. (fr. rt. *vah*), a flood; [cf. *ogha.*]

औचथ्य **aućathya,** *as,* m. (fr. *ućathya*), a patronymic of Dīrgha-tamas of the family of Aṅgiras; [cf. *autathya.*]

औचित्य **aućitya,** *am,* n. or *aućitī,* f. (fr. *ućita*), aptness, fitness, propriety, suitableness; taking pleasure in anything, habituation.

औच्चैःश्रवस **auććaiḥśravasa,** *as,* m. (fr. *uććaiḥ-śravas*), N. of Indra's horse.

औजस **aujasa,** *am,* n. (fr. *ojas*), gold.

Aujasika, as, ī, am, energetic, vigorous, acting with strength or energy; (*as*), m. a hero.

Aujasya, conducive to vitality or energy; (*am*), n. freshness or vigour of life, energy.

औज्जिहायनक **aujjihāyanaka,** *ās,* m. pl., N. of a grammatical school.

औज्ज्वल्य **aujjvalya,** *am,* n. (fr. *uj-jvala*), brightness, brilliancy.

औडवि **auḍavi,** *ayas,* m. pl., N. of a warrior-tribe.

Auḍavīya, as, m. a prince of this tribe.

औडुपिक **auḍupika,** *as, ī, am* (fr. *uḍupa*), crossing in a boat; (*as*), m. a passenger, one going in a raft or boat.

औडुम्बर **auḍumbara.** See *audumbara.*

औडुलोमि **auḍulomi,** *is,* m. (fr. *uḍuloman*), N. of a philosopher.

औड्र **auḍra,** *ās,* m. pl., N. of a people and the country inhabited by them. See *oḍra.*

औतङ्क **autaṅka,** *as, ī, am,* belonging to Utaṅka.

औतथ्य **autathya,** *as,* m. (fr. *utatha*), an epithet of Dīrgha-tamas.

औत्कण्ठ्य **autkaṇṭhya,** *am,* n. (fr. *utkaṇṭha*), desire, longing for. — *Autkaṇṭhya-vat, ān, atī, at,* desirous, longing for.

औत्कर्ष्य **autkarshya,** *am,* n. (fr. *ut-karsha*), excellence, superiority.

औत्तमि **auttami,** *is,* m. (fr. *uttama*), epithet of the third Manu.

Auttamika, as, ī, am, relating to the gods who are in the highest place (in the sky).

औत्तर **auttara,** *as, ī, am* (fr. 1. *uttara*), living in the north.

Auttarapathika, as, ī, am (fr. *uttara-patha*), going or coming in a northerly direction.

Auttarapadika, as, ī, am (fr. *uttara-pada*), comprehending the last word or term (?).

Auttaravedika, as, ī, am, belonging to the Uttara-vedi.

Auttarādharya, am, n. (fr. *uttarādhara*), state of being below and above.

Auttarāha, as, ī, am (fr. *uttarāha*), of or belonging to the following day.

Auttareya, as, m., N. of a son of Uttarā.

औत्तानपाद **auttānapāda,** *as,* and *auttānapādi, is,* m. (fr. *uttāna-pāda*), a N. of Dhruva; (in mythology) the son of Uttāna-pāda, and grandson of the first Manu; (in astronomy) the polar star or the north pole itself.

औत्पत्तिक **autpattika,** *as, ī, am* (fr. *ut-patti*), inborn, innate; natural; produced at the same time.

औत्पात **autpāta,** *as, ī, am* (fr. *ut-pāta*), treating of portents.

Autpātika, as, ī, am, portentous, prodigious, astounding, calamitous; (*am*), n. a portent.

औत्पाद **autpāda,** *as, ī, am* (fr. *ut-pāda*), relating to or treating of birth or production.

औत्पुटिक **autpuṭika,** *as, ī, am* (fr. *utpuṭa*), receiving anything with the mouth or beak turned upwards.

औत्र **autra,** *as, ī, am* (for *auttara?*), gross, rough, inexact.

औत्स **autsa,** *as, ī, am* (fr. *utsa*), born or produced in a well or fountain.

औत्सङ्गिक **autsaṅgika,** *as, ī, am* (fr. *ut-saṅga*), carried or placed upon the hip or flank.

औत्सर्गिक **autsargika,** *as, ī, am* (fr. *ut-sarga*), that which is abandoned (*utsṛijyate*) or liable to be abolished in exceptional cases, but valid generally (as a rule of grammar); general as opposed to special, not particular, not restricted, abandoning, omitting, leaving; terminating, completing, relating or belonging to a final ceremony by which a rite is dismissed; natural, inherent; produced directly and naturally; derivative. — *Autsargika-tva, am,* n. the generality of a rule.

औत्सुक्य **autsukya,** *am,* n. (fr. *utsuka*), anxiety, disquietude, uneasiness, regret; ardent desire, longing, eagerness, zeal.

औदक **audaka,** *as, ī, am* (fr. *udaka*), aquatic, watery, of or belonging to water. — *Audaka-ja, as, ā, am,* produced by aquatic plants.

Audaki, ayas, m. pl., N. of a warrior-tribe.

Audakīya, as, m. a prince of this warrior-tribe.

औदङ्कि **audaṅki,** *ayas,* m. pl., N. of a warrior-tribe.

Audaṅkīya, as, m. a prince of this tribe.

औदञ्चन **audañćana,** *as, ī, am* (fr. *ud-añćana*), contained in a pitcher.

औदनिक **audanika,** *as, ī, am* (fr. *odana*), one who knows how to cook mashed grain &c., a cook; one to whom mashed grain is given at regular times.

Audanya, as, m. a patronymic of Muṇḍibha.

औदपान **audapāna,** *as, ī, am* (fr. *uda-pāna*), raised from wells or drinking fountains (as a tax); coming from the village Udapāna.

औदमेघीय **audameghīya,** *as, ī, am,* belonging to Audameghi.

औदयक **audayaka,** *ās,* m. pl. (fr. *ud-aya*), a school of astronomers who reckoned the first motion of the planets from sunrise.

औदरिक **audarika,** *as, ī, am* (fr. *udara*), greedily voracious, gluttonous.

Audarya, being in the womb.

औदल **audala,** a patronymic from Udala; N. of a Sāman.

औदवापि **audavāpi,** a patronymic from Uda-vāpa.

Audavāpīya, as, ā, am, belonging to Audavāpi.

औदवाहि **audavāhi,** a patronymic from Uda-vāha; N. of a teacher.

औदश्वित **audaśvita** or *audaśvitka, as, ī, am* (fr. *uda-śvit*), made of buttermilk; (*am*), n. buttermilk with an equal proportion of water.

औदस्थान **audasthāna,** *as, ī, am* (fr. *uda-sthāna*), accustomed to stand in water.

औदात्त्य **audāttya,** *am,* n. (fr. *udātta*), the state of having the high tone.

औदारिक **audārika,** (with Jainas) the gross body which invests the soul.

औदार्य **audārya,** *am,* n. (fr. *udāra*), generosity, nobility, magnanimity, greatness.

औदासीन्य **audāsīnya,** *am,* n. (fr. *ud-āsīna*), indifference, apathy.

Audāsya, am, n. indifference, stoicism, philosophy, solitariness, loneliness.

औदुम्बर **audumbara,** *as, ī, am* (fr. *udumbara*), coming from the Udumbara tree, made of its wood; (*as*), m., N. of a region abounding in Udumbara trees; a form of Yama, the regent of death; (*ās*), m. pl., N. of a people; (*ī*), f. (scil. *śākhā*) a branch of the Udumbara tree; (*am*), n. the wood of the Udumbara tree or a piece of the wood; the Udumbara fruit; a kind of leprosy; copper.

Audumbaraka, as, m. the country inhabited by the Udumbaras.

Audumbarāyaṇa, as, m., N. of a grammarian.

Audumbari, is, m. a prince of the Udumbaras.

औद्गात्र **audgātra,** *as, ī, am* (fr. *ud-gātṛi*), relating to the Udgātṛi priest; (*am*), n. the office of the Udgātṛi priest. — *Audgātra-sāra-saṅgraha, as,* m., N. of a commentary of Rudraskanda on the Drāhyāyaṇa Sūtras.

औद्ग्रभण **audgrabhaṇa,** *am,* n. (fr. *ud-grabhaṇa;* scil. *yajus*), N. of certain sentences recited at the Dīkshā.

औद्दालक **auddālaka,** *am,* n. (fr. *uddāla* or *uddālaka;* scil. *madhu*), a bitter and acrid substance like honey, said to be found in the nest of the white ant; N. of a Tīrtha.

Auddālaki, is, m. an epithet of Svetaketu, of Kusuruvinda, and of Āruṇi.

औद्देशिक **auddeśika,** *as, ī, am* (fr. *ud-deśa*), pointing out, showing, indicative of; enumerating.

औद्धत्य **auddhatya,** *am,* n. (fr. *ud-dhata*), arrogance, insolence, overbearing manner, disdain.

औद्धारिक **auddhārika,** *as, ī, am* (fr. *ud-dhāra*), belonging to a portion or share, selected, portionable, heritable; (*am*), n. a portion or inheritance.

औद्बिल्य **audbilya,** *am,* n. (fr. *udbila*), joyful excitement.

औद्भारि **audbhāri,** *is,* m. (fr. *ud-bhāra*), a patronymic of Khaṇḍika.

औद्भिज्ज **audbhijja,** *as,* m. (fr. *udbhijja*), N. of a man; (*am*), n. fossil salt.

Audbhida, as, ī, am (fr. *ud-bhid*), springing forth, issuing (as from a well); forcing one's way towards an object, victorious; (*am*), n. spring water; fossil salt, rock or sambher salt.

Audbhidya, am, n., Ved. forcing one's way to victory, victoriousness.

औद्वाहिक **audvāhika,** *as, ī, am* (fr. *ud-vāha*), relating to marriage; (*am*), n. a gift made to a woman at her marriage.

औधस **audhasa,** *as, ī, am* (fr. *ūdhas*), being in the udder, contained in the udder (as milk).

औधेय *audheya, ās,* m. pl., N. of a family; N. of a school.

औन्नत्य *aunnatya, am,* n. (fr. *un-nata*), height.

औन्नेत्र *aunnetra, am,* n. (fr. *un-netṛi*), the office of the Un-netṛi.

औपकर्णिक *aupakarṇika, as, ī, am* (fr. *upa + karṇa*), being near the ears.

औपकलाप्य *aupakalāpya, as, ā, am* (fr. *upa + kalāpa*), being near the girdle.

औपकार्य *aupakārya, am,* n. (fr. *upa-kāryā*), a residence; a tent.

Aupakurvāṇaka, as, ī, am (fr. *upa-kurvāṇa,* q. v.), belonging to the Upa-kurvāṇa.

औपगव *aupagava, as, ī, am* (fr. *upa-gu*), belonging to Upagu; a patronymic from Upagu.

Aupagavaka, as, ī, am, belonging to the Aupagavas, coming from the Aupagavas; worshipping Aupagava; *(am),* n. an assemblage of Aupagavas.

औपग्रस्तिक *aupagrastika, as,* m. (fr. *upagrasta*) or *aupagrāhika, as,* m. (fr. *upa-graha*), an eclipse, the sun or moon in eclipse.

औपचारिक *aupaćārika, as, ī, am* (fr. *upaćāra*), metaphorical; figurative.

औपच्छन्दसिक *aupaććhandasika, am,* n. (fr. *upa + ćhandas*), N. of a metre of two lines, each containing 16 + 18 syllabic instants or 12 + 13 feet; see Gram. 970.

औपजन्धनि *aupajandhani, is,* m. a patronymic, N. of a teacher; also spelt *aupaćandhani.*

औपजानुक *aupajānuka, as, ī, am* (fr. *upa + jānu*), being upon or near the knees.

औपतस्विनि *aupatasvini, is,* m. patronymic of a Rāma mentioned in the Śatapatha-Brāhmaṇa.

औपदेशिक *aupadeśika, as, ī, am* (fr. *upadeśa*), living by teaching.

औपद्रविक *aupadravika, as, ī, am* (fr. *upadrava*), relating to symptoms, treating of them.

औपद्रष्ट्र्य *aupadrashṭrya, am,* n. (fr. *upadrashṭṛi*), Ved. the state of being an eye-witness; superintendence.

औपधर्म्य *aupadharmya, am,* n. (fr. *upadharma*), false doctrine, heresy; inferior virtue.

औपधिक *aupadhika, as, ī, am* (fr. *upa-dhi*), deceitful, deceptive.

औपधेनव *aupadhenava, as,* m. (fr. *upa + dhenu*), N. of a physician.

औपधेय *aupadheya, as, ī, am* (fr. *upa-dhi*), serving for the part of the wheel of a carriage, called Upadhi; *(am),* n. the wheel of a carriage.

औपनायनिक *aupanāyanika, as, ī, am* (fr. *upa-nāyana*), relating to or serving for the rite of investiture, belonging to it.

औपनासिक *aupanāsika, as, ī, am* (fr. *upa + nāsā*), being near the nose.

औपनिधिक *aupanidhika, as, ī, am* (fr. *upanidhi*), forming a deposit, relating to a deposit, deposited; *(am),* n. a deposit, the thing pledged or deposited.

औपनिषत्क *aupanishatka, as, ī, am* (fr. *upanishad*), living by an Upanishad.

Aupanishada, as, ī, am, contained in or taught in an Upanishad, scriptural, theological; *(as),* m. the follower of an Upanishad.

औपनीविक *aupanīvika, as, ī, am* (fr. *upa + nīvi*), being near the Nīvi, i. e. a cloth with which women cover their loins.

औपपक्ष्य *aupapakshya, as, ā, am* (fr. *upapaksha*), being in the arm-hole.

औपपत्तिक *aupapattika, as, ī, am* (fr. *upapatti*), present, ready, at hand, within reach, fit, proper, answering a purpose.

औपपातिक *aupapātika, as, ī, am,* one who has committed an Upa-pātaka, q. v.; *(am),* n. title of a Jaina Upāṅga.

औपपादुक *aupapāduka, as, ī, am* (fr. *upapāduka*), produced by one's self.

औपभृत *aupabhṛita, as, ī, am,* belonging to or being in the ladle called Upa-bhṛit.

औपमन्यव *aupamanyava, as,* m. a patronymic from Upa-manyu; N. of Mahāśāla Jābāla; of Prāćīnaśāla; of a grammarian.

औपमिक *aupamika, as, ī, am* (fr. 3. *upa-mā*), serving for or forming a comparison.

Aupamya, am, n. condition of resemblance or equality, similitude, comparison; often used in composition (e. g. *an-aupamya,* having no equal, unparalleled).

औपयज *aupayaja, as, ī, am,* belonging to the sentences called Upa-yaj.

औपयिक *aupayika, as, ī, am* (fr. *upāya*), leading to an object, answering a purpose, proper, fit, right; *(am),* n. a means, an expedient.

औपयौगिक *aupayaugika, as, ī, am* (fr. *upayoga*), relating to the employment or application of (a remedy &c.).

औपर *aupara, as,* m. (fr. *upara*), a patronymic of Daṇḍa.

औपराजिक *auparājika, as, ā* or *ī, am* (fr. *upa-rāja*), relating to a viceroy.

औपरिष्ट *auparishṭa, as, ī, am* (fr. *uparishṭāt*), being above, produced above.

Auparishṭaka, am, n. part of the Kāma-sūtra, an amatory work by Vātsyāyana.

औपरैधिक *auparaidhika, as,* m. (fr. *upara + edha?*; scil. *daṇḍa*), a staff made of the wood of the Pīlu tree.

औपरोधिक *auparaudhika, as, ī, am* (fr. *uparodha*), proceeding from or relating to kindness or favour; opposing, impeding, connected with or relating to a check or hindrance; *(as),* m. a staff of the wood of the Pīlu tree (used in guarding the women's apartments?).

औपल *aupala, as, ī, am* (fr. *upala*), stony, of stone; raised from stones (as a tax).

औपवसथिक *aupavasathika, as, ī, am,* or *aupavasathya, as, ā, am* (fr. *upa-vasatha*), designed for or belonging to the Upa-vasatha; *(am),* n., N. of a Pariśishṭa of the Sāma-veda.

Aupavasta, am, n. (fr. *upa-vasta*), fasting, a fast.

Aupavastra, am, n. fasting; food suitable for a fast.

Aupavastraka, am, n. food suitable for a fast.

Aupavāsa, as, ī, am, given during fasting, to be done during fasting.

Aupavāsika, as, ī, am, proper for fasting, able to fast.

Aupavāsya, am, n. fasting.

औपवाह्य *aupavāhya, as, ā, am* (fr. *upavāha*), designed for driving in a carriage or for riding; (a carriage) drawn for pleasure; *(as),* m. a king's elephant, any royal vehicle.

औपविन्दवि *aupavindavi, is,* m. a patronymic from Upavindu.

औपवेशि *aupaveśi, is,* m. (fr. *upa-veśa*), Ved. a patronymic of Aruṇa.

Aupaveśika, as, ī, am, living by entire devotion to any employment.

औपशिवि *aupaśivi, is,* m. a patronymic of Upaśiva; N. of a grammarian.

औपश्लेषिक *aupaśleshika, as, ī, am* (fr. *upaślesha*), relating to close or immediate contact.

औपसङ्क्रमण *aupasankramaṇa, as, ī, am,* anything presented or proper to be done at the Upa-saṅkramaṇa.

औपसङ्ख्यानिक *aupasankhyānika, as, ī, am* (fr. *upa-sankhyāna*), depending on the authority of any addition or supplement, mentioned in one; supplementary.

औपसद *aupasada, as, ī, am,* an Adhyāya or Anuvāka in which the word Upasad occurs; *(as),* m., N. of an Ekāha ceremony.

औपसर्गिक *aupasargika, as, ī, am* (fr. *upasarga*), superior to adversity, able to cope with calamity; portentous; relating to change &c.; superinduced, produced in addition to (or out of another disease); connected with a preposition, prepositive; *(as),* m. irregular action of the humors of the body, producing cold sweats &c.

औपसीर्य *aupasīrya, as, ā, am* (fr. *upa + sīra*), being near a plough.

औपस्थान *aupasthāna, as, ī, am* (fr. *upasthāna*), one whose business is to serve, wait on, or worship.

Aupasthānika, as, ī, am, living by waiting on or worshipping.

Aupasthika, as, ī, am (fr. *upa-stha*), living by fornication.

Aupasthya, am, n. cohabitation, sexual enjoyment.

औपस्थूण्य *aupasthūṇya, as, ā, am* (fr. *upa + sthūṇā*), being near a post.

औपस्वस्ती *aupasvastī,* f. a patronymic of a woman. — *Aupasvastī-putra, as,* m., N. of a teacher.

औपहस्तिक *aupahastika, as, ī, am,* living by Upa-hasta (?).

औपहारिक *aupahārika, am,* n. (fr. *upahāra*), an offering, oblation.

औपाधिक *aupādhika, as, ī, am* (fr. *upādhi*), conditional; pertaining to attributes or properties, an effect produced, a property or quality communicated (as colour, taste, &c.).

औपाध्यायक *aupādhyāyaka, as, ī, am* (fr. *upādhy-āya*), preceptral, of or relating to a spiritual teacher, coming from a teacher.

औपानह्य *aupānahya, as, ā, am* (fr. *upānah*), used for making shoes; to be tied or bound on (as grass, leather, &c.).

औपायिक *aupāyika* = *aupayika,* q. v.

औपावि *aupāvi, is,* m. (fr. *upāva*), a patronymic of Jānaśruteya.

औपासन *aupāsana, as,* m. (fr. *upāsana;* scil. *agni*), the fire used for domestic worship; (scil. *piṇḍa*), a small cake offered to the manes; *(as, ī, am),* performed with the fire called Aupāsana; connected with or belonging to worship or service, devotional, holy.

औपेय *aupeya,* a patronymic from Upeya (?).

औपोदिति *aupoditi, is,* m. (fr. *upodita*), Ved. a patronymic of Tumiñja.

Aupoditeya, as, m., N. of the son of Upoditā.

औम् *aum*, ind. the sacred syllable of the Sūdras; [cf. *om.*]

औम *auma* or *aumaka* or *aumika*, *as*, *ī*, *am* (fr. *umā*), flaxen, made of flax.

Aumīna, *am*, n. a field of flax.

औरग *auraga*, *as*, *ī*, *am* (fr. *ura-ga*), serpent, serpentine, relating or belonging to a snake; (*am*), n. the constellation Āśleshā.

औरभ्र *aurabhra*, *as*, *ī*, *am* (fr. *ura-bhra*), belonging to or produced from a ram or sheep; (*as*), m. a coarse woollen blanket; N. of a physician; (*am*), n. mutton, the flesh of sheep; woollen cloth.

Aurabhraka, *am*, n. a flock of sheep.

Aurabhrika, *as*, *ī*, *am*, relating to, produced by, &c., sheep; (*as*), m. a shepherd.

औरश *auraśa*, *as*, m. (fr. *uraśā*), an inhabitant of Uraśā.

औरस 1. *aurasa*, *as*, *ī*, *am* (fr. *uras*), belonging to or being in the breast; produced from the breast, i. e. the seat of manly strength, produced by one's self; legitimate; (*as*, *ī*), m. f. a legitimate child, i. e. one by a wife of the same caste.

Auraska, *as*, *ī*, *am*, excellent, distinguished; [cf. *urasya.*]

Aurasya (?), belonging to or being in the breast; legitimate.

औरस 2. *aurasa*, *as*, *ī*, *am* (fr. *uraśā* or *urasā*), coming from Uraśā.

औरुक्षयस *aurukshayasa*, a patronymic from Uru-kshayas = Uru-kshaya.

और्ण *aurṇa* or *aurṇaka*, *as*, *ī*, *am* (fr. *ūrṇā*), made of wool, woollen.

Aurṇanābha, a patronymic from Ūrṇa-nābha.

Aurṇanābhaka, *as*, *ī*, *am*, inhabited by the tribe of the Ūrṇa-nābhas.

Aurṇavābha, a patronymic of Ūrṇa-vābhi; N. of a grammarian.

Aurṇika, *as*, *ī*, *am*, woollen.

और्ध्वकालिक *aurdhvakālika*, *as*, *ā* or *ī*, *am* (fr. *ūrdhva-kāla*), relating to subsequent or later time.

Aurdhvadeha, *am*, n. (fr. *ūrdhva + deha*), a funeral ceremony.

Aurdhvadehika, *as*, *ā*, *am*, referring to the state after death, relating to a deceased person, any rite performed in honour of the dead; funereal, funeral; (*am*), n. the obsequies of a deceased person; funeral solemnities; whatever is given or performed on a person's decease, as burning of the body, offering cakes, distributing alms, &c.

Aurdhvadaihika, *as*, *ī*, *am*, funereal, funeral.

Aurdhvasadmana, *am*, n. (fr. *ūrdhva + sadman*), N. of a Sāman.

Aurdhvasrotasika or *aurdhvaśrotasika*, *as*, *ī*, *am* (fr. *ūrdhva-srotas*, a N. of Siva, 'above whom or in whose head is the river or the Ganges'), a Saiva or adherent of the sect which gives Siva the preeminence in the Hindū triad.

और्व *aurva*, *as*, m. (a patronymic fr. *urva*), N. of a Ṛishi, a son of Ūrva and descendant of Bhṛigu, mentioned in Ṛig-veda VIII. 102, 4. (This Aurva, who is called Bhārgava and described in Mahā-bh. I. 2610. as a son of Cyavana by his wife Ārushī and therefore grandson of Bhṛigu, is the subject of a legend told in Mahā-bh. I. 6802. There it is said that the sons of Kṛitavīrya, wishing to destroy the descendants of Bhṛigu in order to recover the wealth left them by their father, slew even the children in the womb. One of the women of the family of Bhṛigu, in order to preserve her embryo, secreted it in her thigh (*ūru*), whence the child at its birth was named Aurva; on beholding whom, the sons of Kṛitavīrya were struck with blindness, and from whose wrath proceeded a flame that threatened to destroy the world, had not Aurva at the persuasion of the Bhārgavas cast it into the ocean, where it remained concealed, and having the face of a horse. Aurva was afterwards preceptor to Sagara and gave him the Āgneyāstram, with which he conquered the barbarians who invaded his possessions; cf. *baḍavā-mukha*, *baḍavāgni*); a N. of a son of Vasishṭha; (*as*, *ī*, *am*), produced by Aurva, relating to Aurva; (*as*), m. submarine fire; (*am*), n. fossil salt. — *Aurvānala* (°*va-an*°), *as*, m. submarine fire.

और्वशे *aurvaśa*, *as*, *ī*, *am*, an Adhyāya or Anuvāka containing the word Urvaśī.

Aurvaśeya, *as*, m. an epithet of Agastya, the son of Urvaśī.

औलपि *aulapi*, *ayas*, m. pl. (a patronymic fr. *ulapa*), N. of a warrior-tribe.

Aulapin, *inas*, m. pl., N. of a school.

Aulapīya, *as*, m. a prince of the Aulapis.

औलान *aulāna*, Ved. a reservoir for water(?), a sacrificial oblation (?).

औलूक *aulūka*, *am*, n. (fr. *ulūka*), a number of owls.

Aulūkya, a patronymic from Ulūka; (*as*), m. a follower of the Vaiśeshika doctrine; ('like an owl;' this etymology, and perhaps the epithet itself, owes its origin to controversial animosity.) — *Aulūkya-darśana*, *am*, n., N. of the system of these philosophers treated of in the Sarvadarśana-saṅgraha.

औलूखल *aulūkhala*, *as*, *ī*, *am* (fr. *ulūkhala*), coming from a mortar; ground or pounded in a mortar.

औल्वण्य *aulvaṇya*, *am*, n. excess, superabundance.

औवेणक *auveṇaka*, *am*, n., N. of a song (Gītaka).

औशन *auśana* or *auśānasa*, *as*, *ī*, *am*, originating from Uśanas, peculiar to him; (*as*, *ī*), m. f. a patronymic from Uśanas; (*am*), n. (scil. *śāstra*) the law-book of Uśanas; N. of an Upa-purāṇa; N. of a Tīrtha.

औशिज *auśija*, *as*, *ī*, *am* (fr. *uśij*), Ved. desirous, zealous, wishing; a patronymic of Kakshīvat and others; (*as*), m., N. of a Muni.

औशीनर *auśīnara*, *as*, *ī*, m. f. a prince of the Uśīnaras; (*ī*), f. the wife of Purūravas.

Auśinari, *is*, m. a prince of the Uśīnaras.

औशीर *auśīra*, *as*, *am*, m. n. ('made of Uśīra'), the stick which serves as a handle to the cow's tail used as a fan or chowri; the cow's tail used as a fan, the chowri; (*am*), n. a bed, used also as a seat; a seat, a chair or stool; the root of a fragrant grass, Andropogon Muricatum; an unguent, made of Uśīra.

Auśīrikā, f. the shoot (of a plant); a basin, a bowl.

औषण *aushaṇa*, *am*, n. (fr. *ushaṇa*), pungency; black pepper.

औषदश्वि *aushadaśvi*, *is*, m. (fr. *oshadaśva*), a patronymic of Vasumat.

औषध *aushadha*, *as*, *ī*, *am* (fr. *oshadhi*), consisting of herbs; (*am*), n. a herb, herbs collectively; herbs used in medicine, a medicament, a drug, a medicine in general; a vessel for herbs; a mineral. — *Aushadhāvalī* (°*dha-āv*°), f. a medical work composed by Prāṇakṛishṇa.

Aushadhi, *is* or *ī*, f. a herb, a plant, a medicinal herb, an annual or deciduous plant, as grass &c.; a plant in general, = *oshadhi*, q. v.; (*ī*), f., N. of a goddess. — *Aushadhī-pati*, *is*, m. an epithet of the Soma, lord of the plants.

Aushadhī-kṛi, cl. 8. P. A. *-karoti*, *-kurute*, *-kartum*, to reduce to a medicament.

Aushadhīya, *as*, *ī*, *am*, medicinal, consisting of herbs, herby.

औषर *aushara* or *ausharaka*, *am*, n. (fr. *ūshara*), fossil salt; iron stone.

औषस *aushasa*, *as*, *ī*, *am* (fr. *ushas*), relating to dawn, early, matutinal; (*ī*), f. day-break; morning.

Aushasya, *as*, *ā*, *am*, sacred to Ushas or the dawn.

Aushika, *as*, *ī*, *am* (fr. 2. *ushā*), walking out at day-break; early, matutinal, &c., with the dawn.

औषिज *aushija* or *aushīja*, desirous &c.; = *auśija* above.

औष्ट्र *aushṭra*, *as*, *ī*, *am* (fr. *ushṭra*), derived from or relating to a camel; abounding in camels; (*am*), n. the camel genus or species, camel-nature.

Aushṭraka, *as*, *ī*, *am*, coming or derived from a camel; (*am*), n. a herd or multitude of camels.

Aushṭraratha, *as*, *ī*, *am* (fr. *ushṭra-ratha*), belonging to a carriage drawn by camels.

Aushṭrākshi, *is*, m. (fr. *ushṭra + aksha*), epithet of a teacher.

Aushṭrika, *as*, *ī*, *am*, coming from or relating to a camel.

औष्ठ *aushṭha*, *as*, *ī*, *am* (fr. *oshṭha*), lip-shaped.

औष्णिह *aushṇiha*, *as*, *ī*, *am*, Ved. in the Ushṇih metre.

औष्णीक *aushṇīka*, perhaps a wrong reading for *aushṇīsha*, = *ushṇīshin*.

औष्ण्य *aushṇya*, *am*, n. (fr. *ushṇa*) or *aushmya*, *am*, n. (fr. *ushman*), heat, warmth; burning.

क

क 1. *ka*, the first consonant of the alphabet, and the first of the guttural letters, corresponding in sound to *k* in *keep* or *king*. — *Ka-kāra*, *as*, m. the letter or sound *ka*. — *Kakāra-varga*, *as*, m. the guttural consonants collectively.

क 2. *ka*, *kas*, *kā*, *kim*, interrog. pron. (see *kim* and 2. *kad*, and cf. the following words in which the interrogative base *ka* appears, *katama*, *katara*, *kati*, *katham*, *kadā*, *karhi*, *kā*, &c.), who? which? what? In its declension *ka* follows the pronoun *tad* (Gram. 223) except in nom. acc. sing. neut., where *kim* has taken the place of *kad* or *kat* in classical Sanskṛit; but the old form *kad* is found in the Veda.

The interrogative sentence introduced by *ka* is often terminated by *iti* (e. g. *kasya sa putra iti kathyatām*, let it be said, 'whose son is he?'), but *iti* may be omitted and the sentence lose its direct interrogative character (e. g. *kasya sa putro na jñāyate*, it is not known whose son he is). *Ka* with or without *as*, 'to be,' may express 'how is it possible that?' 'what power have I, you, they, &c.?' (e. g. *ke mama dhanvino 'nye*, what can the other archers do against me? *ke āvām paritrātum*, what power have we to rescue you?). *Ka* is often connected with a demonstrative pron. (e. g. *ko 'yam āyāti*, who comes here?) or with the potential (e. g. *ko Hariṃ nindet*, who will blame Hari?). *Ka* is sometimes repeated (e. g. *kaḥ ko 'tra*, who is there? *kān kān*, whom? whom? i. e. which of them? cf. Gram. 53. *a*), and the repetition is often due to a kind of attraction (e. g. *keshāṃ kiṃ śāstram adhyayanīyam*, which book is to be read by whom? Gram. 836. *a*). When *kim* is connected with the inst. c. of a noun or with the indecl. participle it may express 'what is gained by doing so, &c.?' (e. g. *nīrujaḥ kim aushadhaiḥ*, what is the use of medicine to the healthy? *kiṃ vilambena*, what is gained by delay? *kim bahunā*, what is the use of more words? *kim paurushaṃ hatvā suptam*, what manliness is there in killing one asleep?).

Ka is often followed by the particles *iva, u, nāma, nu, vā, svid*, some of which serve merely to generalize the interrogation (e. g. *kim iva etad*, what can this be? *ka u śravat*, who can possibly hear? *ko nāma jānāti*, who indeed knows? *ko nv ayam*, who is this? *kiṃ nu kāryam*, what is to be done? *ko vā devād anyaḥ*, who possibly other than a god? *kasya svid hṛidayaṃ nāsti*, of what person is there no heart?).

Ka is occasionally used alone as an indefinite pronoun, especially in negative sentences (e. g. *na kasya ko vallabhaḥ*, no one is a favourite of any one; *nānyo jānāti kaḥ*, no one else knows; *kathaṃ sa ghātayati kam*, how does he kill any one? More usually, however, *ka* is only made indefinite when connected with the particles *ća, ćana, ćid, vā*, and *api*, in which case *ka* may sometimes be preceded by the relative *ya* (e. g. *ye ke ća*, any persons whatsoever; *yasyai kasyai ća devatāyai*, to any deity whatsoever; *yāni kāni ća mitrāṇi*, any friends whatsoever; *yat kiñća*, whatever). The particle *ćana*, being composed of *ća* and *na*, properly gives a negative force to the pronoun (e. g. *yasmād Indrād ṛite kiñćana*, without which Indra there is nothing), but the negative sense is generally dropped (e. g. *kaśćana*, any one; *na kaśćana*, no one), and a relative is sometimes connected with it (e. g. *yat kiñćana*, anything whatsoever). Examples of *ćid* with the interrogative are common; *vā* and *api* are not so common, but the latter is often found in classical Sanskrit (e. g. *kaśćid*, any one; *kećid*, some; *na kaśćid*, no one; *na kiñćid api*, nothing whatsoever; *yaḥ kaśćid*, any one whatsoever; *kećit—kećit*, some—others; *yasmin kasmin vā deśe*, in any country whatsoever; *na ko 'pi*, no one; *na kimapi*, nothing whatever).

Ka may sometimes be used, like 2. *kad*, at the beginning of a compound. See *ka-pūya*, &c.

क 3. *ka, as*, m. the Who? the Inexplicable, the Unknown. By a forced and erroneous interpretation of the interrogative pronoun occurring in a hymn of the Ṛig-veda (X. 121. *kasmai devāya havishā vidhema*, what god shall we worship with oblations?) the word *ka* is applied as a name to any chief god or object of worship, as Prajāpati, Brahmā, Vishṇu; air or wind; the sun; the mind; the soul; Yama; Kāma-deva, the god of love; fire; a peacock; a N. of Daksha (a clever or dexterous man?); a knot, joint; the king of the birds; a prince in general; the body; time; wealth, property; sound; light, splendor.

क 4. *ka, am*, n. (also regarded as ind.), happiness, joy, pleasure; water; the head, hair; a head of hair. (Perhaps this word has arisen from a far-fetched etymology of the word *nāka*, 'pleasure,' i. e. *na-a-ka*, 'not-not-pleasure.') — *Ka-ja, as, ā, am*, produced in or by water, watery, aquatic; (*am*), n. a lotus. — *Ka-da, as*, m. 'giving water,' a cloud.

Kam, ind. See 1. *kam*, s. v.

क 5. *ka*, a Taddhita affix much used in forming adjectives. It may also be added to nouns to express diminution, deterioration, or similarity (e. g. *putraka*, a little son; *aśvaka*, a bad horse or like a horse).

कंय्य *kaṃyya, as, ā, am*, or *kaṃyyu, us, us, u* (fr. 1. *kam*), happy, prosperous; according to other authorities also written *kaṃya* or *kaṃyu* or *kaṃva*.

कंवूल *kaṃvūla* or *kavūla, am*, n., N. of the eighth Yoga, = Arabic قبول.

कंश *kanśa, as, am*, m. n. = *kansa*, q. v.

कंस् *kans*, cl. 2. A. *kanste, -situm*, to go; to command; to destroy. See *kas*.

कंस *kansa, as, am*, m. n. (said to be fr. rt. 2. *kam*; according to others fr. the last), a vessel made of metal, a drinking vessel, a cup, a goblet (a noun ending in *as* followed by *kansa* in a compound does not change its final, e. g. *ayas-kansa, payas-kansa*, &c.); a particular measure; a metal, tutanag or white copper, brass, bell-metal; cf. *kansāsthi* and *kānsya*; (*as*), m., N. of a king of Mathurā, son of Ugra-sena and cousin of the Devakī who was mother of Kṛishṇa, (Ugra-sena being brother of Devaka, who was father of Devakī.) He is usually called the uncle, but was really a cousin of Kṛishṇa, and became his implacable enemy because it had been prophesied to him that he would be killed by a child of Devakī (Vish. Pur. p. 493); as the foe of the deity he is identified with the Asura Kālanemi; and, as he was ultimately slain by Kṛishṇa, the latter receives epithets like *Kansa-jit*, the conqueror of Kansa, &c.; (*ā*), f. N. of a daughter of Ugra-sena and sister of Kansa. — *Kansa-kāra, as, ī*, m. f. a worker in pewter or white brass, a bell-founder, considered as an intermediate caste. — *Kansa-jit, t*, m. an epithet of Kṛishṇa, the conqueror of Kansa. — *Kansa-vaṇij, k*, m. a brazier or seller of brass vessels. — *Kansa-badha, as*, m. the slaying of Kṛishṇa; title of a comedy of Śesha-Kṛishṇa. — *Kansa-mākshika, am*, n. a metallic substance in large grains, a sort of pyrites. — *Kansa-yajña, as*, m. a particular sacrifice. — *Kansa-vatī*, f., N. of a daughter of Ugra-sena and sister of Kansa and Kansā. — *Kansa-han, ā*, m. an epithet of Kṛishṇa, the destroyer of Kansa. — *Kansa-hanana, am*, n. the slaying of Kansa. — *Kansārāti* (°*sa-ar*°), *is*, or *kansāri* (°*sa-ari*), *is*, m. epithet of Kṛishṇa, the enemy of Kansa. — *Kansāsthi* (°*sa-as*°), *i*, n. tutanag, white copper, any alloy of tin and copper. — *Kansodbhavā* (°*sa-ud*°), f. a fragrant earth.

Kansaka, am, n. a mineral substance, a salt of iron used as an application to the eyes.

Kansika, as, ī, am, made of bell-metal &c.

Kansiya, as, ā, am, fit for or relating to a cup; (*am*), n. bell-metal.

कंसार *kaṃ-sāra, as, ā, am*, Ved. (rice) the grain of which hardens in the centre.

कक् *kak*, cl. 1. A. *kakate, ćakake, kakitum*, to be unsteady; to be proud; to be thirsty; [cf. Lat. *vacillo* for *qvacillo*.]

ककजाकृत *kakajā-kṛita, as, ā, am*, Ved. mutilated, torn to pieces.

ककन्द *kakanda, as*, m. gold; N. of a king.

ककर *kakara, as*, m., Ved. a kind of bird.

ककर्दु *kakardu, us*, m. (?), Ved. destruction of enemies.

ककाटिका *kakāṭikā*, f., Ved. a part of the back of the human head, (enumerated together with *mastishka, lalāṭa*, and *kapāla*.)

ककुञ्जल *kakuñjala, as*, m. the bird Ćātaka; [cf. *kapiñjala*.]

ककुत्सल *kakutsala, as*, m., Ved. an expression of endearment applied to a child (?).

ककुद् *kakud, t*, f. a peak or summit (culmen); chief, head; any projecting corner; the hump on the shoulders of the Indian bull; a horn; an ensign or symbol of royalty, as the white parasol &c.; N. of a daughter of Daksha and wife of Dharma. (According to native grammarians *kakud* is the form which must be substituted for *kakuda* at the end of compounds, e. g. *tri-kakud*, three-peaked.) — *Kakut-stha, as*, m., N. of a grandson of Ikshvāku and son of Śaśāda, said to be so called because in a battle he stood on the hump of Indra, who had been changed into a bull; according to the Rāmāyaṇa he is a son of Bhagīratha. — *Kakud-mat* or *kakun-mat, ān, atī, at*, running high (as a wave); furnished with a hump; (*ān*), m. a mountain; a buffalo with a hump on his shoulders; N. of a medicinal plant; (*tī*), f. the hip and loins; N. of a metre; [cf. Lat. *cacūmen* and *culmen* for *caculmen*.] — *Kakudmi-kanyā*, f. a river ('mountain-daughter'). — *Kakud-min, ī, inī, i*, peaked, humped; (*mī*), m. a mountain; a buffalo with a hump on his shoulders; an epithet of Vishṇu; N. of a prince of the Ānartas; (*inī*), f., N. of a river. — *Kakudruma, as*, m. (for *kakud-druma*?), N. of a jackal in the Pañćatantra. — *Kakud-vat, ān*, m. a buffalo with a hump on his shoulders; (*tī*), f., N. of the wife of Pradyumna.

Kakuda, as, am, m. n. the summit of a mountain; chief, pre-eminent; the hump on the shoulders of the Indian bull; a species of serpent; an ensign or symbol of royalty, as the white parasol, &c. — *Kakuda-kātyāyana, as*, m., N. of a Brāhman who was a violent adversary of Śākya-muni. — *Kakudāksha* (°*da-ak*°), *as*, m., N. of a man.

ककुन्दर *kakundara, am*, n. the cavities of the loins; (*kakudmatī-dara*?; cf. *kakudmatī* and *kukundara*.)

ककुभ् *kakubh, p*, f. (connected with *kakud*), a peak or summit (cacumen); space, region or quarter, as east, west, &c.; N. of a metre of three Pādas consisting of eight, twelve, and eight syllables respectively, so called because the second Pāda exceeds the others by four syllables; unornamented hair or the hair hanging down as a tail; a wreath of Ćampaka flowers; splendor, beauty; a Śāstra or sacred treatise: a Rāgiṇī or personified mode of music; the personified quarter of the sky; a daughter of Daksha and wife of Dharma.

Kakubha, as, ā, am, Ved. excelling, distinguished; (*as*), m. a kind of goblin or evil spirit; the tree Terminalia Arjuna; a part of a lute called the belly, a wooden vessel covered with leather placed under its neck to render the sound deeper, or a crooked piece of wood at the end of the lute; one of the Rāgas or personified musical modes; N. of a man; N. of a mountain; (*ā*), f. space, region, quarter; one of the Rāgiṇīs or female personifications of music. — *Kakubhādanī* (°*bhā-ad*°), f. 'food of the sky,' a kind of fragrance or perfume; [cf. *nalī*.]

Kakuha, as, ā, am, Ved. eminent, excelling others, excellent; (*as*), m., Ved. a part of a carriage, perhaps the seat.

ककेरुक *kakeruka, as*, m. a worm in the stomach.

कक्क् *kakk*, a various reading for *kakh*, q. v.

कक्कट *kakkaṭa, as*, m., Ved. a species of animal, perhaps a kind of bird.

कक्कुल *kakkula, as*, m., N. of a Bhikshu.

कक्कोल *kakkola, as*, m., N. of a plant bearing a berry, the inner part of which is a waxy and aromatic substance; (*am*), n. or *kakkolaka, am*, n. a perfume prepared from the berries of this plant.

कक्कल्ल *kakkvalla, as*, m. a patronymic of Guṇaćandra.

कक्ख् *kakkh*, a various reading for *kakh*, q. v.

कक्खट *kakkhaṭa, as, ā, am*, hard, solid; (*ī*), f. chalk. — *Kakkhaṭa-pattraka, as*, m. the plant Corchorus Olitorius; (rope is made from its fibre.)

कक्ष *kaksha, as*, m. (said to be fr. rt. *kash*), a lurking or hiding-place; an inner recess, the interior of a forest; a forest of dead trees, a dry wood (the lair of wild beasts), grass, dry grass; a spreading creeper, a climbing plant; the armpit (as the most concealed part of the human body); the side or flank; the orbit of a planet or the circle anciently termed a deferent; sin; a buffalo; a gate; the Beleric Myrobalan or Terminalia Belerica; (*ā*), f. painful boils in the armpit, side, shoulder, &c.; an elephant's rope, the string round his neck, also his girth; a woman's girdle or zone; a surrounding wall, a wall; a place surrounded by walls; a court or court-yard; an enclosure; a secluded portion of an edifice; a private or inner chamber, the private apartment for women &c., a room in general; a particular part of a carriage;

resemblance, similarity; objection or reply in argument; emulation, rivalry, object of emulation; the jeweller's weight, the Retti; (*as, ā*), m. f. the end of the lower garment which, after the cloth is carried round the body, is brought up behind and tucked into the waistband; a border, lace; the scale or basin of a balance; (*am*), n. a star, a constellation (perhaps a wrong reading for *ṛiksha*); (*ās*), m. pl., N. of a people. — *Kaksha-dhara, am*, n. the part of the body where the upper arm is connected with the shoulder, the shoulder-joint. — *Kaksha-pa, as*, m. one of the nine treasures of Kuvera; [cf. *kaććhapa.*] — *Kaksha-puṭa, as*, m. the armpit; title of a work on magic. — *Kaksha-ruhā*, f. a fragrant grass, Cyperus. — *Kaksha-śāya, as*, m. a dog; [cf. *kankaśāya.*] — *Kaksha-sena, as*, m., N. of a Rājarshi. — *Kaksha-stha, as, ā, am*, situated on the side, seated on the hip or flank. — *Kakshādhyāya* (°*sha-adh*°), *as*, m., N. of a part of a commentary by Bhūdhara on the Sūrya-siddhānta. — *Kakshāntara* (°*sha-an*°), *am*, n. the inner or private apartment. — *Kakshā-paṭa, as*, m. a cloth passed between the legs to cover the privities. — *Kakshā-puṭi, is*, m., N. of a physician; (wrong reading for *kākshapuṭi* ?). — *Kakshāvekshaka, as*, m. (*kakshā* + *avekshaka* fr. rt. *īksh* with *ava*), a guard of the inner or queen's apartments; keeper of a royal garden; a door-keeper; a poet; a debauchee; a player, a painter; warmth of feeling, strength of sentiment. — *Kakshī-kṛita, as, ā, am*, assented, promised, (touching the armpit with the hand was perhaps a manner of affirming anything; cf. *urasi kṛi* under *uras.*) — *Kakshotthā* (°*sha-ut*°), f. a fragrant grass, Cyperus.

Kakshaka, as, m., N. of a Nāga.

Kakshatu, us, m., N. of a plant.

Kakshāya, nom. A. *kakshāyate, -yitum*, to wait for any one in a hidden place, lie in ambush; to intend anything wicked.

Kakshīvat, ān, m. (fr. *kakshyā*), N. of a renowned Ṛishi, sometimes called Pajriya; he is the author of several hymns of the Ṛig-veda, and is described in legends as a son of Uśij and Dīrgha-tamas; (*antas*), m. pl. the family or the descendants of Kakshīvat.

Kaksheyu, us, m., N. of a son of Raudrāśva and Ghṛitāćī.

Kakshya, as, ā, am, Ved. consisting of shrubs or dry grass; secret; (Sāy.) filling the girth, as a well-fed horse; (*ā*), f. the girth of an elephant or horse, consisting of rope or leather; a woman's girdle or zone; metaphorically the fingers (encircling the Soma cup); an upper garment, the border or lace of one; the enclosure of an edifice, i. e. either the wall &c. so enclosing it, or the court or chamber constituting the enclosure, the inner apartment of a palace; similarity; effort, exertion; a shrub yielding the black and red berry that serves as a jeweller's weight, the Retti or Gunja, Abrus Precatorius; (*am*), n. the cup or receptacle of a balance; a part of a carriage. — *Kakshyapra, as, ā, am*, Ved. filling the girth (as a well-fed horse). — *Kakshyā-vat, ān, atī, at*, furnished with a girth. — *Kakshyāvekshaka, as*, m. = *kakshāvekshaka*, q. v. — *Kakshyā-stotra, am*, n., N. of a hymn by Divākara-vatsa.

काख् *kakh*, cl. 1. P. *kakhati, -khitum*, to laugh, laugh at or deride: Caus. P. *kakhayati, -yitum*, to cause to laugh; [cf. Lat. *cachinnare*; Gr. καχάζω, καγχάζω.]

कख्या *kakhyā*, f. an enclosure, a division of a large building; (a wrong reading for *kakshyā*.)

कग् *kag*, cl. 1. P. *kagati, -gitum*, to act, perform.

कङ्क् *kank*, cl. 1. A. *kankate, -kitum*, to go; [cf. Hib. *cichet*, 'walking;' *ciocair*, 'a way, a road:' Lith. *kankù*; *ifs-kankù*, 'to come to.']

कङ्क *kanka, as*, m. a heron (a bird of prey?); a kind of mango; an epithet of Yama; N. of a king; a Vṛishṇi; a son of Ugra-sena, a son of Śūra; pl., N. of a people; a title of Yudhishṭhira (from his assuming the disguise of a Brāhman before king Virāṭa); a false or pretended Brāhman; a man of the second or military tribe (perhaps a man of that caste pretending to be a Brāhman); one of the eighteen divisions of the continent; the brother of Kaṅsa; (*ā*), f. a sort of sandal; scent of the lotus; N. of a daughter of Ugra-sena and sister of Kanka. — *Kanka-ćit, t, t, t*, Ved. collected into a heap resembling a heron. — *Kanka-tuṇḍa, as*, m., N. of a Rakshas. — *Kanka-troṭa, as*, or *kanka-troṭi, is*, m. a kind of fish, commonly *kānkilā*; Esox Kankila. — *Kanka-pattra, am*, n. a heron's feather fixed on an arrow; (*as, ā, am*), furnished with the feathers of a heron; (*as*), m. an arrow furnished with heron's feathers. — *Kankapattrin, ī, iṇī, i*, furnished with heron's feathers. — *Kanka-parvan, ā*, m., N. of a serpent. — *Kanka-mālā*, f. a kind of musical instrument; beating time by clapping the hands. — *Kanka-mukha, as, ī, am*, shaped like a heron's mouth; (*as, am*), m. n. a pair of tongs, a sort of forceps. — *Kanka-śatru, us*, m. the plant Desmodium Gangeticum. — *Kanka-śāya, as*, m. a dog (sleeping like a heron).

कङ्कट *kankaṭa* or *kankaṭaka, as*, m. (said to be fr. rt. *kank*), mail, defensive armour; an iron hook to goad an elephant.

कङ्कटेरी *kankaṭerī*, f. turmeric.

कङ्कण *kankaṇa, as, am*, m. n. (said to be fr. rt. *kai*), a bracelet, an ornament of the wrist (used also as a weapon); a string or ribbon tied round the wrist; an ornament round the foot of an elephant; any ornament or trinket; a crest; (*ī*), f. a small bell or tinkling ornament; an ornament furnished with bells: see *kinkiṇī*; [cf. Lith. *kankala-s*.] — *Kankaṇa-pura, am*, n., N. of a town, called from *Kankaṇa-varsha*. — *Kankaṇa-priya, as*, m., N. of a servant of Śiva. — *Kankaṇa-bhūshaṇa, as, ā, am*, adorned with tinkling ornaments. — *Kankaṇa-maṇi*, f. the jewel in a bracelet. — *Kankaṇa-varsha, as*, m., N. of an alchimist; epithet of the king Kshemagupta.

Kankaṇin, ī, inī, i, ornamented with a bracelet.

Kankaṇikā, f. an ornament furnished with bells; a string tied round the wrist.

कङ्कत *kankata, as, ī, am*, m. f. n. or *kankatikā*, f. a comb, a hair-comb; (*as*), m. a tree; (according to Sāy.) a poisonous animal, a slightly venomous reptile (mentioned in a verse of Ṛig-veda I. 191, used as a mystical spell against poison).

Kankatīya, ās, m. pl., N. of a family.

कङ्कर *kankara, as, ī, am*, vile, bad; (*am*), n. buttermilk mixed with water; a high number, = 100 niyutas.

कङ्कोल *kankarola, as*, m. the plant Alangium Hexapetalum. See *nikoćaka*.

कङ्कलोड्य *kankalodya, am*, n. a kind of drug, = *alkalodya*.

कङ्काल *kankāla, as, am*, m. n. a skeleton; [cf. Mod. Gr. κόκαλον.] — *Kankāla-ketu, us*, m., N. of a Dānava. — *Kankāla-bhairava-tantra, am*, n., N. of a Tantra. — *Kankālamālin, ī*, m. an epithet of Śiva, whose necklace is formed of bones.

कङ्कालय *kankālaya* or *kalkālaya, as*, m., N. of an author.

कङ्कु *kanku, us*, m. = *kangu*, N. of a son of Ugra-sena and brother of Kaṅsa.

कङ्कुष्ठ *kankushṭha, as*, m. a medicinal earth, described as of two colours, one of a silvery and one of a gold colour, or one of a light and one of a dark yellow.

कङ्कूष *kankūsha*, (?) Atharva-veda IX. 8, 2.

कङ्केरु *kankeru, us*, m. a kind of crow.

कङ्केल्ल *kankella, as*, m. the tree Jonesia Aśoka; a kind of pot-herb, Chenopodium Esculentum.

Kankelli, is, m. Jonesia Aśoka.

कङ्कोल *kankola, as*, m. a king of the Nāgas; N. of the author of a hymn called Gaṇapatyārādhana.

कङ्ख *kankha, am*, n. enjoyment, fruition; (perhaps a combination of *ka* and *kha*.)

कङ्गु *kangu, us*, f. or *kangunī*, f. a kind of Panic seed, Panicum Italicum; several varieties of it are cultivated and form articles of food for the poor. — *Kangunī-pattrā*, f. a kind of grass, = *paṇyāndhā*.

कङ्गुल *kangula, as*, m. the hand; [cf. *angulī*.]

कच् *kać*, cl. 1. A. *kaćate, ćakaće, kaćitum*, to bind; to shine; P. *kaćati*, to sound, cry; [cf. *kanć*; cf. also Hib. *cacht*, 'a strait, a narrow place; bonds, fetters.']

Kaća, as, m. the hair (especially of the head); a cicatrix, a dry or healed sore, a scar; a binding, band; the hem of a garment; a cloud; N. of a son of Bṛihaspati; N. of a place; (*ā*), f. a female elephant; beauty, brilliancy; [cf. *a-kaća, ut-kaća*, &c.] — *Kaća-pa, as*, m. 'cloud-drinker,' grass; a leaf; (*am*), n. a vessel for vegetables; a leaf of a vegetable (?). — *Kaća-paksha* or *kaća-pāśa, as*, m. thick or ornamented hair. — *Kaća-māla, as*, m. smoke; (perhaps a wrong reading for *khatamāla* ?). — *Kaća-ripu-phalā*, f., N. of a tree; see *śamī*. — *Kaća-hasta, as*, m. thick or ornamented hair, a beautiful head of hair. — *Kaćā-kaći*, ind. hair against hair, pulling each other's hair. — *Kaćāćita* (°*ća-ać*°), *as, ā, am*, having long or dishevelled hair. — *Kaćāmoda* (°*ća-ām*°), *am*, n. a fragrant ointment for the hair.

कचङ्गन *kaćangana, am*, n. a free market, a place of sale paying no duty or custom; [cf. *karāngaṇa, angaṇa*, and *angana*.]

कचङ्गल *kaćangala, am*, n. the ocean; N. of a region.

कचाकु *kaćāku, us, us, u*, ill-disposed, wicked; intolerable, difficult to be borne; difficult to be attained; (*us*), m. a snake.

कचाटुर *kaćāṭura, as*, m. a gallinule. See *dātyūha*.

कचु *kaću, us*, f. an esculent root, Arum Colocasia and other kinds, many of which are cultivated for food. See *kaćvī*.

कचेल *kaćela, am*, n. a string or cover containing and keeping together the leaves of a manuscript; (perhaps a various reading for *kāćana*.)

कच्चट *kaććaṭa, am*, n. an aquatic plant, = *jalapippalī*.

कच्चर *kaććara* (*kad-ćara*,) *as, ā, am*, dirty, foul; spoiled, spoiled by dirt; vile, wicked, bad; (*am*), n. buttermilk diluted with water; [cf. *kankara, kaṭura*, &c.]

कच्चिद् *kać-ćid* (= *kad-ćid*). See under 2. *kad*.

कच्छ *kaććha, as, am*, m. n. (in the first sense a Prākrit form for *kaksha*; cf. *kaććhaṭikā*), the hem or end of a lower garment tucked into the girdle or waistband; (according to some m. f. n. in the next senses, according to others only m.) a bank or any ground bordering on water, as the margin of a river, lake, tank, &c.; a mound or causeway, watery soil, marshy ground, a marsh, a morass, low or flat land skirting mountains; N. of several places; (*ās*), m. pl. the people inhabiting them; (*as*), m. a part of a boat; a particular part of a tortoise; a tree, the timber of which is used for making furniture &c., Cedrela Toona or common Tūn; another tree, Hibiscus Populneoides; (*ā*), f. a cricket; the plant Lycopodium Imbricatum; see *vārāhī*. — *Kaććha-*

deśa, as, m., N. of a place.—*Kaććha-pa, as,* m. a turtle, a tortoise (as inhabiting marshy places); a tumour on the palate; an apparatus used in the distillation of spirituous liquor, a flat kind of still; an attitude in wrestling; the tree Cedrela Toona; one of the nine nidhis or treasures of Kuvera; N. of a Nāga; a son of Viśvā-mitra; N. of a country; (*ī*), f. a female tortoise or a small species of tortoise; a cutaneous disease, wart or blotch; a kind of lute, also the lute of Sarasvatī (so named from being similar in shape to the tortoise).—*Kaććha-pa-deśa, as,* m., N. of a place.—*Kaććha-bhū, ūs,* f. marshy ground, a swamp, a morass.—*Kaććha-ruhā,* f. a kind of grass, Dūrva, Agrostis Linearis, Panicus Dactilon.—*Kaććha-vihāra, as,* m., N. of a marshy region.—*Kaććhānta* (°*ćha-an*°), *as,* m. the border of a lake or stream.—*Kaććheśvara* (°*ćha-iś*°), *as,* m., N. of a town.

Kaććhaṭikā or *kaććhāṭikā* or *kaććhāṭī,* f. the end or hem of a lower garment or cloth gathered up behind and tucked into the waistband.

Kaććhapikā, f. a pimple, a blotch or wart; a wart accompanying gonorrhœa.

Kaććhara, ās, m. pl., N. of a people.

Kaććhoṭikā, f. = *kaććhaṭikā,* q. v.

कच्छिय **kaććhiya,** *ās,* m. pl., N. of a people; (various readings have *kaksha* and *kaććha.*)

कच्छु **kaććhu,** *us,* or **kaććhū,** *ūs,* f. (said to be fr. rt. *kash*), itch, formation of watery pustules on the hands &c., scab. (The form *kaććhū* is the older and more correct form.)—*Kaććhu-ghnī,* f. the plant Trichosanthes Diœca; another plant, = *hapuyābheda.*—*Kaććhū-matī,* f. the plant Carpopogon Pruriens, said to cause itching on being applied to the skin.

Kaććhura, as, ā, am, scabby, itchy; unchaste, libidinous; (*ā*), f. the plant Alhagi Maurorum; a species of Curcuma; the plant Carpopogon Pruriens.

Kaććhora, am, n. a kind of Curcuma.

कच्वी **kaćvī,** f. a plant with an esculent root (Arum Colocasia) cultivated for food.

कज् **kaj,** cl. 1. P. *kajati, -jitum,* to be happy; to be confused with joy, pride or sorrow; to grow, (in the last sense a Sautra root.)

कज **ka-ja.** See under 4. *ka.*

कजिङ्ग **kajinga,** *ās,* m. pl., N. of a people.

कज्जल **kajjala,** *as,* m. (in the first sense from *kad-jala*), a cloud; (*am*), n. lampblack, considered as a collyrium and applied to the eyelashes or eyelids medicinally or as an ornament, also sulphuret of lead or antimony so used; (*ā, ī*), f. the fish Cyprinus Atratus, or any kind peculiar to stagnant waters, whence the name; (*ī*), f. sulphuret of mercury, Æthiop's mineral; ink.—*Kajjala-dhraja, as,* m. a lamp.—*Kajjala-roćaka, as, am,* m. n. the wooden stand or tripod on which a lamp is placed, a candlestick.—*Kajjali-tīrtha, am,* n., N. of a Tīrtha.

Kajjalita, as, ā, am, covered with lampblack or with a collyrium prepared from it.

कज्ज्वल **kajjvala,** *am,* n. lampblack, especially considered as an application to the eyes; [cf. *kajjala.*]

कञ्च् **kañć,** cl. 1. A. *kañćate, ćakañće, kañćitum,* to bind; to shine; [cf. *kać* and *kāñć.*]

कञ्चट **kañćaṭa,** *as,* m. the aquatic plant Commelina Salicifolia and C. Bengalensis.

Kañćaḍa, as, m. the plant Commelina Bengalensis.

कञ्चार **kañćāra,** *as,* m. the sun.

कञ्चिका **kañćikā,** f. a small boil; the branch of a bamboo.

कञ्चुक **kañćuka,** *as,* m. (fr. rt. *kañć?*), a dress fitting close to the upper part of the body; armour, mail; a bodice, jacket; the skin of a snake; cloth, clothes; a kind of drawers or short breeches; a strap of leather; the cast-off skin of a snake; (*ī*), f., N. of a plant.

Kañćukālu, us, m. a snake.

Kañćukita, as, ā, am, furnished with armour or mail.

Kañćukin, ī, inī, i, furnished with armour or mail; (*ī*), m. an attendant on or overseer of the women's apartments, a chamberlain; a libidinous man, a debauchee, one addicted to women; a serpent; N. of several plants, Agallochum, barley, Cicer Arietinum.—*Kañćuki-rećaka, au,* m. du. the chamberlain and the forester.

Kañćulikā, f. a bodice or jacket.

Kañćūla, as, am, m. n. an article of female dress, perhaps a bodice.

कञ्ज **kañ-ja,** *as,* m. (fr. *kam* = head), the hair; (fr. *kam* = water), an epithet of Brahmā; (*am*), n. a lotus; the Amrita or food of the immortals; (*as, ā, am*), produced in or from water; (in composition *kañja* may follow or precede the term compounded with it, e. g. *kañja-vadana* or *vadana-kañja,* a lotus-face.)—*Kañja-ja, as,* m. an epithet of Brahmā (born from a lotus).—*Kañja-nābha, as,* m. an epithet of Vishṇu.

कञ्जक **kañjaka,** *as,* m. a kind of bird, Gracula Religiosa.

Kañjana, as, m. the bird Gracula Religiosa, the bird of Kandarpa; N. of Kandarpa, the deity of love.

Kañjala, as, m., N. of the bird Gracula Religiosa.

कञ्जर **kañjara,** *as,* m. the belly; an elephant; the sun; an epithet of Brahmā.

Kañjāra, as, m. (said to be fr. rt. *kaj*), a peacock; the belly; an elephant; a Muni or holy sage, an hermit; the sun; an epithet of Brahmā; also = *vyañjana* (?).

कञ्जाण **kañjāṇa,** *as* or *am,* m. or n. (?), N. of a place.

कञ्जिका **kañjikā,** f. the plant Siphonanthus Indica.

कट् 1. **kaṭ** or **kanṭ,** cl. 1. P. *kaṭati* or *kanṭati, -ṭitum,* to go.

कट् 2. **kaṭ,** cl. 1. P. *kaṭati, ćakāṭa, kaṭitum,* to rain; surround; to encompass, to cover or screen.

Kaṭa, as, m. a twist of straw or grass, a straw mat; a screen of straw; the hip; the hollow above the hip or the loins; the hip and loins; the temples of an elephant; a particular throw of the dice in hazard; (at the end of some compounds) much, excessive (but in the words *avakaṭa, utkaṭa, prakaṭa,* and *sankaṭa* considered as an affix); N. of a Rakshas; a corpse; a hearse, a bier, a bed &c. used for conveying a dead body; a place where dead bodies are burnt or buried, a place of sepulture; a time or season; excess, superabundance; the plant Saccharum Sara; an annual plant; grass; a thin piece of wood, a plank; (*am*), n. (considered as an affix at the end of compounds), dust of flowers; (*ī*), f. long pepper; (*as, ī, am*), an agent in any action.—*Kaṭa-khādaka, as, ā, am,* eating much, one who eats voraciously; (*as*), m. a jackal; a crow; a glass vessel, a tumbler or bowl.—*Kaṭa-ghosha, as,* m., N. of a region in the east of India.—*Kaṭa-nagara,* N. of a place in the East.—*Kaṭa-palli-kuñćikā,* f. a straw hut (?).—*Kaṭa-palvala,* N. of a place in the East.—*Kaṭa-pūtana, as,* m. a kind of demon (a Kshatriya not performing his duties is born after his death as such a goblin); a kind of Preta or inhabitant of the lower regions; see *pūtanā* and *andhapūtanā.*—*Kaṭa-prū, ūs,* m. a worm; one who gambles or plays with dice; an epithet of Śiva or Mahādeva; a Rakshas, an imp or goblin; a kind of demi-god, one of the class of Vidyādharas.—*Kaṭa-protha, as,* m. the buttocks.—*Kaṭa-bhanga, as,* m. gleaning, plucking or gathering corn with the hands; the destruction of a prince; royal misfortune, as deposure, defeat, &c.—*Kaṭa-bhī,* f., N. of several plants, Cardiospermum Halicacabum (an annual plant); Clitoria Ternatea = *aparājitā;* N. of a tree.—*Kaṭa-mālinī,* f. wine or any vinous liquor.—*Kaṭam-bhara, as,* m. the plant Bignonia Indica; another plant, = *kaṭubhī;* (*ā*), f. several plants, Pœderia Fetida; a medicinal plant, Kaṭukī; a sort of cucumber, Cucumis Madraspatanus; Bœrhavia Diffusa, Aletris Hyacinthoides; hog-weed; a female elephant; red arsenic.—*Kaṭa-vraṇa, as,* m. 'wounding in the hips,' a N. of Bhīma-sena.—*Kaṭa-śarkarā,* f. a fragment of a mat broken off, or of straw; the plant Guilandina Bonducella; [cf. *kaṭu-karañja.*]—*Kaṭa-sthala, am,* n. the hip and loins, an elephant's temples.—*Kaṭāksha* (°*ṭa-ak*°), *as,* m. a glance or side look, a leer.—*Kaṭāksha-kshetra,* N. of a place.—*Kaṭāksha-mushṭa, as, ā, am,* caught by a glance.—*Kaṭāksha-viśikha, as,* m. an arrow-like look of love.—*Kaṭākshāvekshaṇa* (°*sha-av*°), *am,* n. casting lewd or amorous glances, ogling.—*Kaṭāgni* (°*ṭa-ag*°), *is,* m. a fire kept up with dry grass or straw; the straw placed round a criminal who is to be burnt.

Kaṭaka, as, am, m. n. a string; a ring placed as an ornament upon an elephant's tusk; a bracelet of gold or of shell &c.; a zone; the link of a chain; a mat; the side or ridge of a hill or mountain; table land; a circle, a wheel, an army, a camp; a royal metropolis, a city or town, a village, a house or dwelling; N. of the capital of Orissa (Cuttack); sea-salt.

Kaṭakin, ī, m. a mountain.

Kaṭasī, f. a cemetery.

Kaṭāyana, am, n. the plant Andropogon Muricatus.

Kaṭi, is, f. the hip. See below.

Kaṭin, ī, inī, i, matted, screened; having handsome loins &c.; (*ī*), m. an elephant.

कटक **kaṭaka.** See above

कटकट **kaṭakaṭa,** *as,* m. an epithet of Śiva. See *kaṭankaṭa.*

कटकटा **kaṭakaṭā,** an onomatopoetic word supposed to represent the noise of rubbing together.

Kaṭakaṭāpaya, nom. P. *kaṭakaṭāpayati, -yitum,* to rub together, utter a creaking or grating noise.

कटकोल **kaṭakola,** *as,* m. a spitting-vessel.

कटङ्कट **kaṭankaṭa,** *as,* m. an epithet of Śiva or Gaṇeśa; [cf. *kaṭakaṭa, kaṭāṭanka.*]

कटङ्कटेरी **kaṭankaṭerī,** f. turmeric; yellow saunders; [cf. *dāru-haridrā.*]

कटन **kaṭana,** *am,* n. roof or thatch of a house.

कटम्ब **kaṭamba,** *as,* m. (said to be fr. rt. 2. *kaṭ*), a kind of musical instrument; an arrow.

कटम्बरा **kaṭambarā,** f. a medicinal plant, See *kaṭu-rohiṇī.*

कटाकु **kaṭāku,** *us,* m. a bird.

कटाक्ष **kaṭāksha.** See under *kaṭa* above.

कटाटङ्क **kaṭāṭanka,** *as,* m. an epithet of Śiva. See *kaṭankaṭa.*

कटार **kaṭāra,** *as,* m. a libidinous man, a lecher.

कटाह **kaṭāha,** *as,* m. (according to the Schol. m. f. n.), a frying-pan, a boiler or a frying-vessel of a semispheroidal shape and with handles; a shallow boiler for oil or butter; a turtle's shell; a well; a winnowing basket; a hill of earth; hell, the infernal regions; a young female buffalo whose horns are just appearing; a dvīpa or division of the known continent, so called, (perhaps the Katai of the Muhammedans or China.)

Kaṭāhaka, am, n. a pan, a pot.

कटि **kaṭi,** *is,* or **kaṭī,** f. (fr. rt. 2. *kaṭ?*), the hip; the buttocks; an elephant's cheek; (*ī*), f. long pepper.—*Kaṭi-kushṭha, am,* n. leprosy of the hip.—*Kaṭi-kūpa, as,* m. the hollow above the hip, the loins.—*Kaṭi-taṭa, am,* n. the loins, the hip.—*Kaṭi-tra, am,* n. anything to protect the hips; a cloth tied round the loins; a zone; an ornament of small bells worn round the loins; armour for the hip or loins. — *Kaṭi-deśa, as,* m. the loins. — *Kaṭi-protha* or *kaṭī-protha, as,* m. the buttocks; [cf. *kaṭa-protha.*] — *Kaṭī-mālikā,* f. a woman's zone. — *Kaṭi-rohaka, as,* m. the rider of an elephant who sits upon the hinder parts of the elephant, as distinct from the driver or the person sitting upon the loins. — *Kaṭi-śīrshaka, as,* m. the hip (as projecting like a head); the hip and loins or the hollow above the hip. — *Kaṭi-śṛinkhalā,* f. a girdle of small bells. — *Kaṭi-sūtra, am,* n. a female zone or waistband.

Kaṭikā, f. the hip.

Kaṭīra, as, am, m. n. the cavity of the loins or the iliac region; (*as*), m. Mons Veneris; a cave; (*am*), n. a hip.

Kaṭīraka, am, n. the posteriors.

कटिल्लक *kaṭillaka, as,* m. a species of the balsam apple, Momordica Charantia; [cf. *kaṭhillaka.*]

कटीतल *kaṭītala, as,* m. a crooked sword; a sabre or scymitar; [cf. *kaḍitula.*]

कटु *kaṭu, us, us* or *vī, u* (said to be fr. rt. *kaṭ*), pungent, acrid, sharp (one of the six kinds of flavour); pungent, stimulating (smell); strong-scented, ill-smelling; bitter, caustic (words); displeasing, disagreeable; fierce, impetuous, hot; envious; (*us*), m. pungency, acerbity (as a flavour); the plants Michelia Champaca, Trichosanthes Diœca, camphor, &c.; (*us*), f. various plants, = *kaṭu-rohiṇī,* a medicinal plant; Sinapis Ramosa; (*vī*), f., N. of a plant; (*u*), n. an improper action, an act which ought not to have been done; blaming, reviling, scandal. — *Kaṭu-kanda, as, am,* m. n. ginger, the fresh root or the plant; garlic; the plant Hyperanthera Moringa. — *Kaṭu-karañja, as,* m. the plant Guilandina Bonducella. — *Kaṭu-kīṭa* or *kaṭukīṭaka, as,* m. a gnat or musquito. — *Kaṭu-kvāṇa, as,* m. a species of chicken, Parra Jacana or Gœnsis (making a sharp or piercing noise). — *Kaṭu-granthi, i,* n. dried ginger; the root of long pepper. — *Kaṭu-ćāturjātaka, am,* n. an aggregate of four acid substances, as of cardamoms, the bark and leaves of Laurus Cassia and of black pepper. — *Kaṭu-ććhada, as,* m., N. of a tree with pungent leaves; [cf. *tagara.*] — *Kaṭu-ja, as, ā, am,* prepared from acid substances, as a kind of drink. — *Kaṭu-tiktika, as,* m. the plants Gentiana Cherayta and Cannabis Sativa; (*ā*), f., N. of a plant. — *Kaṭu-tuṇḍikā* and *kaṭu-tuṇḍī,* f., N. of a plant, = *tikta-tuṇḍī,* commonly *kaṭutarāī.* — *Kaṭu-tumbī,* f. a kind of bitter gourd. — *Kaṭu-traya, am,* n. the aggregate of three black substances or spices, ginger, black and long pepper. — *Kaṭu-dalā,* f., N. of a plant, = *karkaṭī.* — *Kaṭu-nishplāva, as,* m. grain not inundated. — *Kaṭu-pattra, as,* m. the medicinal plant Oldenlandia Biflora, and of another plant Sitārjaka. — *Kaṭu-pattrikā,* f., N. of a tree, = *kārī.* — *Kaṭu-padra,* N. of a place. — *Kaṭu-pāka, as, ā, am,* or *kaṭu-pākin, ī, inī, i,* producing acrid humors in digestion. — *Kaṭu-phala, as,* m. a sort of cucumber, Trichosanthes Diœca. — *Kaṭu-badarī,* f., N. of a plant and of a village called from this plant. — *Kaṭu-bhanga, as,* m. dried ginger. — *Kaṭu-bhadra, am,* n. dried ginger, or ginger in general. — *Kaṭu-mañjarikā,* f. the plant Achyranthes Aspera. — *Kaṭu-moda, am,* n. a certain perfume. — *Kaṭu-rava, as,* m. a frog. — *Kaṭu-rohiṇī,* f. the medicinal plant Helleborus Niger. — *Kaṭu-vārtākī,* f. a variety of Solanum. — *Kaṭu-vipāka, as, ā, am,* producing acrid humors in digestion. — *Kaṭu-vījā,* f. long pepper. — *Kaṭu-śṛingāla, am,* n., N. of a vegetable. — *Kaṭu-sneha, as,* m. the mustard-seed plant, Sinapis Dichotoma. — *Kaṭūtkaṭa* (°*ṭu-ut*°), *as,* m. ginger. — *Kaṭūtkaṭaka, am,* n. dry ginger. — *Kaṭphala, as,* m. (for *kaṭu-ph*°), a small tree found in the north-west of Hindūstan, the bark and seeds of which are used in medicine, and as aromatics; the fruit also is eaten; the common name is Kāyaphal; (*ā*), f., N. of several plants, as of Gmelina Arborea and different kinds of Solanum, = *devadālī* and *mṛigervāru.* — *Kaṭv-anga, as,* m. the tree Calosanthes Indica; an epithet of Dilīpa.

Kaṭuka, as, ā, am, sharp, pungent, bitter, fierce, impetuous, hot; (*as*), m. pungency, acerbity; N. of several plants, Trichosanthes Diœca, a fragrant kind of grass; gigantic swallow wort, Calotropis Gigantea; a plant the bark and seed of which have an acrid and bitter taste, and are used in medicine for worms, dysentery, &c., Wrigthia Antidysenterica; Sinapis Dichotoma or Ramosa; N. of a man; (*ā*), f., N. of several plants, = *kaṭvī* and *kaṭu-rohiṇī;* Areca Faufel or Catechu; Ruellia Longifolia; (*ī*), f. = *kaṭu-rohiṇī;* (*am*), n. pungency, acerbity (at the end of compounds in a bad sense, e. g. *dadhi-kaṭukam,* bad coagulated milk); a compound of pungent substances, as black pepper, long pepper, dry ginger. — *Kaṭuka-traya, am,* n. an aggregate of three pungent substances, as black pepper, long pepper, and ginger. — *Kaṭuka-tva, am,* n. pungency. — *Kaṭuka-phala, am,* n., N. of a perfume prepared from the berries of the plant Kakkola. — *Kaṭuka-bhakshin, ī,* m., N. of a man. — *Kaṭuka-rohiṇī,* f. = *kaṭu-rohiṇī.* — *Kaṭuka-vallī,* f. = *kaṭvī.* — *Kaṭukālābu* (°*ka-al*°), *us,* m. a kind of bitter gourd, Trichosanthes Diœca.

कटुङ्कटा *kaṭunkaṭā,* f. rough manners.

कटुर *kaṭura, am,* n. buttermilk mixed with water, = *takra;* [cf. *kankara, kaććara, kaṭvara, kadara, kadvara.*]

कटेरकग्राम *kaṭeraka-grāma, as,* m., N. of a village.

कटोदक *kaṭodaka, am,* n. (fr. *kaṭa* = *karta* = *garta?* and *udaka*), water for a funeral libation, a funeral rite.

कटोरा *kaṭorā,* f. a shallow cup.

कटोल *kaṭola, as,* m. (said to be fr. rt. *kaṭ*), a pungent flavour; a man of an inferior and degraded tribe, a Caṇḍāla, a Pariah, &c.; (*as, ā, am*), pungent. — *Kaṭola-vīṇā,* f. a kind of lute played by the common people or Caṇḍālas.

कट्टार *kaṭṭāra, as,* m. a weapon, a dagger.

कट्वर *kaṭvara, as, ā, am,* despised; (*am*), n. the skim or whey of curds; buttermilk with water; a sauce, condiment; [cf. *kankara, kaććara, kaṭura, kadara, kadvara.*]

कट्वाङ्ग *kaṭvānga,* a wrong reading for *khaṭvānga,* q. v.

कठ् *kaṭh,* cl. 1. P. *kaṭhati, -ṭhitum,* to live in distress.

कठ *kaṭha, as,* m., N. of a sage, a pupil of Vaiśampāyana and founder of a branch of the Yajur-veda, called after him; a Brāhman; a note or simple sound; (*ās*), m. pl. the followers or pupils of Kaṭha; (*ī*), f. a female follower of Kaṭha; the wife of a Brāhman. — *Kaṭha-kālāpāḥ,* the schools of Kaṭha and Kalāpin. — *Kaṭha-kauthumāḥ,* the schools of Kaṭha and Kuthumin. — *Kaṭha-dhūrta, as,* m. a Brāhman skilled in the Kaṭha branch of the Yajur-veda. — *Kaṭha-vallī* or *kaṭhavally-upanishad, t,* or *kaṭha-śruti, is,* or *kaṭhopanishad* (°*ṭha-up*°), *t,* f., N. of an Upanishad consisting of two Adhyāyas of three Vallī each. — *Kaṭha-śākhā,* f. a branch of the Yajur-veda; also of the Ṛig-veda (?). — *Kaṭha-śāṭha, as,* m., N. of a man; *Kāṭhaśāṭhin, inas,* m. pl., N. of a school. — *Kaṭha-śrotriya, as,* m. a Brāhman who has studied the Kaṭha branch of the Yajur-veda. — *Kaṭhādhyāpaka* (°*ṭha-adh*°), *as,* m. a teacher of the Kaṭha branch of the Yajur-veda. — *Kaṭhopanishad-bhāshya-ṭīkā,* f. a commentary by Anantānanda on a Kaṭhopanishadbhāshya. — *Kaṭhopanishadbhāshyaṭīkā-vivaraṇa, am,* n. a commentary by Vyāsatīrtha on the last.

कठमर्द *kaṭhamarda, as,* m. an epithet of Śiva; (fr. *kaṭha,* distress? *marda,* dissipating.)

कठर *kaṭhara, as, ā, am,* hard; [cf. *kaṭhina* and *kaṭhora.*]

कठल्य *kaṭhalya* or *kaṭhalla, as* or *am,* m. or n. (?), gravel.

कठाकु *kaṭhāku, us,* m. (said to be fr. rt. *kaṭh*), a bird (or more probably a particular bird).

कठाहक *kaṭhāhaka, as,* m. a gallinule. See *dātyūha.*

कठिका *kaṭhikā,* f. chalk; the plant commonly called Tulasī; [cf. *kaṭhinī* and *kaṭhiñjara.*]

कठिञ्जर *kaṭhiñjara, as,* m. the tree Ocymum Sanctum, commonly Tulasī.

कठिन *kaṭhina, as, ā, am* (said to be fr. rt. *kaṭh*), hard, stiff (opposed to *mṛidu*); inflexible; violent, as pain; (*as*), m. a thicket; (*ā*), f. crystallized sugar, a sweetmeat made with refined sugar; (*ī*), f. chalk; (*am*), n. an earthen vessel for cooking (according to some also f.); [cf. Lat. *catinum;* Gr. *κόφινος.*] — *Kaṭhina-tā,* f. or *kaṭhina-tva, am,* n. hardness, firmness; severity; difficulty, obscurity. — *Kaṭhina-pṛishṭha* or *kaṭhina-pṛishṭhaka, as,* m. a tortoise. — *Kaṭhina-hṛidaya* or *kaṭhina-ćitta, as, ā, am,* hard-hearted, cruel, unkind. — *Kaṭhināntaḥ-karaṇa* (°*na-an*°), *as, ā, am,* harsh, cruel, severe.

Kaṭhinikā, f. chalk.

Kaṭhinī-bhūta, as, ā, am, hardened, indurated.

कठिल्ल *kaṭhilla, as,* m. the plant Momordica Charantia.

Kaṭhillaka, as, m. the plant Momordica Charantia; Ocymum Sanctum [cf. *kaṭhiñjara*]; Bœrhavia Diffusa.

कठेर *kaṭhera, as,* m. (said to be fr. rt. *kaṭh*), a needy or distressed man, a pauper.

कठेरणि *kaṭheraṇi, is,* m., N. of a man; (*ayas*), m. pl. the descendants of this man.

कठेरु *kaṭheru, us,* m., N. of Kuvera (?).

कठोर *kaṭhora, as, ā, am* (said to be fr. rt. *kaṭh*), hard, solid, stiff; offering resistance; sharp, piercing; severe, cruel, hard-hearted; full, complete, full-grown; full (as the moon); [cf. *kaṭhina.*] — *Kaṭhora-giri-māhātmya, am,* n. a portion of the Brahmāṇḍa-Purāṇa. — *Kaṭhora-tā,* f. or *kaṭhora-tva, am,* n. hardness, firmness; severity, rigour.

Kaṭhola, as, ā, am, resisting, hard, &c., = *kaṭhora.*

कड् *kaḍ,* cl. 1. P. *kaḍati, -ḍitum,* to be confused or disturbed by pleasure or pain, to be elated or intoxicated; cl. 6. P. *kaḍati,* to consume; cl. 10. P. *kāḍayati, -yitum,* to break off a part, to tear, to separate or detach; to remove the chaff or husk of grain &c.; to preserve; [cf. *kaṇḍ.*]

Kaḍa, as, ā, am (said to be fr. preceding), dumb, hoarse; ignorant, stupid; [cf. *jaḍa.*] — *Kaḍan-kara* or *kaḍan-gara, as,* m. straw, the stalks of various sorts of pulse &c. (rendering hoarse). — *Kaḍankarīya* or *kaḍankarya* or *kaḍangarīya, as, ā, am,* to be fed with straw.

कडक *kaḍaka, am,* n. sea-salt obtained by evaporation.

कडङ्ग *kaḍanga, as,* m. (fr. rt. *kaḍ?*), a spirituous liquor, a kind of rum.

कडत्र *kaḍatra, am,* n. (said to be fr. rt. *gaḍ*), a kind of vessel or receptacle. See *kalatra.*

कडन्दिका *kaḍandikā,* f. science, = *kalandikā, kalindikā.*

कडम्ब *kaḍamba, as,* m. (said to be fr. rt. *kaḍ*), the end or point; the stalk of a pot-herb; (*ī*), f. the pot-herb Convolvulus Repens. See *kalamba.*

कडार *kaḍāra, as, ī, am* (said to be fr. rt. *gaḍ*), tawny; (*as*), m. tawny (the colour); a servant.

कडितुल *kaḍitula, as,* m. a sword, a scymitar, a sacrificial knife; [cf. *kaṭī-tala.*]

कड्ड *kaḍḍ,* cl. 1. P. *kaḍḍati, -ḍitum,* to be hard, rough; to be harsh or severe.

कण *kaṇ,* cl. 1. P. *kaṇati, ćakāṇa, kaṇishyati, akaṇīt* or *akāṇīt, kaṇitum,* to become small; to sound, cry as in distress; to go or approach: Caus. *kāṇayati, -yitum,* aor. *aćīkaṇat* and *aćakāṇat,* to sigh, sound; cl. 10. P. *kāṇayati, -yitum,* to wink; to close the eye with the lids or lashes.

Kaṇita, am, n. crying out with pain.

कण *kaṇa, as,* m. (said to be fr. rt. *kaṇ;* according to others related to *kanā, kanishṭha, kanīyas, kanyā,* in all of which the notion of smallness prevails), a grain, a single seed; a grain or particle of dust; flake (of snow); a drop of water; a spark of fire, the spark or facet of a gem; an ear of corn; an atom, a minute particle; small, minute; (*ā*), f. a kind of fly, commonly *kumīrāpokā;* long pepper; cummin seed; (*ī*), f. a drop, an atom; the plant Premna Spinosa or Longifolia; a kind of corn; see *kaṇikā.* — *Kaṇa-guggulu, us,* m., N. of a plant; [cf. *gandharāja, svarṇakarṇa,* and others.] — *Kaṇa-jīra, as,* m. a white kind of cummin seed. — *Kaṇa-jīraka, am,* n. small cummin seed. — *Kaṇa-bhaksha, as,* m. 'eating atoms or grains' (?), i.e. living on minute particles of food; a nickname of the philosopher Kaṇāda. — *Kaṇa-bhakshaka, as,* m. a kind of bird; [cf. *bhāriṭa, śyāmaćaṭaka, śaiśira.*] — *Kaṇa-bhakshaṇa, am,* n. the eating of grains. — *Kaṇa-bhuj, k,* m. nickname of Kaṇāda; see *kaṇa-bhaksha.* — *Kaṇa-lābha, as,* m. a whirlpool. — *Kaṇa-śas,* ind. in small parts, in minute particles. — *Kaṇānna* (°*ṇa-an*°), *as, ā, am,* one whose food consists of grains. — *Kaṇānna-tā,* f. the state of one who is made to feed on grains (of rice).

Kaṇika, as, m. a grain, an ear of corn; the meal of parched wheat, the heart of wheat (commonly suji or semoule); a small particle, as a crystal &c.; an enemy; N. of a purificatory ceremony, viz. whirling round lamps at sacrificial rites [cf. *nīrājana*]; N. of a minister of king Dhṛita-rāshṭra; (*ā*), f. a drop, an atom, a small particle; small, minute; the plant Premna Spinosa or Longifolia; a kind of corn or rice.

Kaṇiśa, as, am, m. n. an ear or spike of corn.

Kaṇishṭha, as, ā, am [cf. *kanishṭha*], the smallest, the most minute.

Kaṇīka, as, ā, am, small, diminutive.

Kaṇīyas, ān, asī, as, very small; young, younger; [cf. *kanīyas.*]

कणप *kaṇapa, as,* m. a kind of spear or lance; (various readings have *kaṇaya* and *kanaya.*)

कणभ *kaṇabha, as,* m. a kind of fly with a sting; [cf. *kaṇā.*]

कणाटीन *kaṇāṭīna* or *kaṇāṭīra* or *kaṇāṭīraka, as,* m. a wagtail.

कणाद *kaṇāda, as,* m., N. of a celebrated sage, considered as the author of the Vaiśeshika philosophy, a branch of the Nyāya. He is also called Kāśyapa, and considered as a Devarshi; the nicknames *kaṇa-bhaksha* and *kaṇa-bhuj* refer to the etymology of this name *kaṇa-ada,* 'eating atoms or grains;' a goldsmith; [cf. *kalāda.*]

कणित *kaṇita.* See under *kaṇ.*

कणीचि *kaṇīći, is,* and *kaṇīćī,* f. a sound; a tree (*pallavin*); a creeper in flower; the plant Abrus Precatorius; a cart; [cf. *kanīći.*]

कणूकय *kaṇūkaya,* nom. P. (connected with rt. *kaṇ*), Ved. to desire to utter words of blame or censure.

कणे *kaṇe,* ind. a particle expressing the satisfying of a desire. — *Kaṇe-hatya,* ind. (rt. *han*), satiating one's self (e.g. *kaṇe-hatya payaḥ pibati,* he drinks milk till he is satiated.)

कणेर *kaṇera, as,* m., N. of a tree, Cascaria Ovata [cf. *karṇikāra*]; (*ā*), f. a she-elephant; a courtezan.

Kaṇeru, us, m., N. of a tree; f. a she-elephant; a courtezan.

कण्ट *kaṇṭ,* cl. 1. P. *kaṇṭati, -ṭitum,* to go, to move.

कण्टक *kaṇṭaka, as, am,* m. n. (fr. rt. *kaṇṭ* ?), a thorn; anything pointed, the point of a pin or needle, a prickle, sting; a fish-bone; a finger-nail [cf. *kara-kaṇṭaka*]; the erection of the hair of the body in thrilling emotions, horripilation; any troublesome seditious person who is, as it were, a thorn to the state and an enemy of order and good government, a paltry foe (*kshudra-śatru*); a sharp stinging pain, symptom of a disease; a vexing or injurious speech; any annoyance or source of vexation; a term in the Nyāya philosophy implying refutation of argument, detection of error, &c.; impediment, obstacle; the first, fourth, seventh, and tenth lunar mansion; (*as*), m., N. of a barber; N. of the horse of Śākyamuni (a wrong form for *kanṭhaka*); N. of an Agrahāra; (according to lexicographers also) a bamboo; a workshop, a manufactory; fault, defect; N. of Makara or the marine monster, the symbol of Kāmadeva; (*ī*), f. a species of Solanum. (*Kaṇṭaka* takes the form *kaṇṭa* at the beginning of some compounds and in *kaṇṭala, kaṇṭālu, kaṇṭin;* cf. Gr. κεντέω, κεσ-τός, κέσ-τρον.) — *Kaṇṭaka-druma, as,* m. a tree with thorns, a thorn bush; the Sālmali or silk-cotton tree, Bombax Heptaphyllum. — *Kaṇṭaka-prāvṛitā,* f. the plant Aloe Perfoliata. — *Kaṇṭaka-phala, as,* m. the Jaka or bread-fruit tree, Artocarpus Integrifolia; another plant, Ruellia Longifolia (commonly called Go-kshura); the castor-oil tree; the Datura; the term is applicable to any plant the fruit of which is invested with a hairy or thorny coat; [cf. *kuṇṭaki-phala.*] — *Kaṇṭaka-bhuj, k,* m. a camel ('eating thorns'). — *Kaṇṭaka-mardana, as, ī, am,* treading down thorns; suppressing disturbances, annoyances, &c.; (*am*), n. the act of beating or treading down thorns; suppressing disturbances &c. — *Kaṇṭaka-yukta, as, ā, am,* having thorns, thorny. — *Kaṇṭaka-vṛintākī,* f. the plant Solanum Jacquini, a species of nightshade with thorny leaves. — *Kaṇṭaka-śreṇī,* f. the Solanum Jacquini; a porcupine. — *Kaṇṭaka-sthalī,* f., N. of a region. — *Kaṇṭakākhya* (°*ka-ākhyā*), *as,* m. the plant Trapa Bispinosa. — *Kaṇṭakāgāra* (°*ka-ag*°), *as,* m. a kind of lizard; a porcupine. — *Kaṇṭakāśana* (°*ka-aś*°), *as,* m. the camel (eating thorns, thistles, &c.; cf. *kaṇṭaka-bhuj*). — *Kaṇṭakāshṭhīla* (°*ka-ash*°), *as,* m. a kind of fish, having many bones. — *Kaṇṭakī-kāri,* f., Ved. working in thorns. — *Kaṇṭakī-druma, as,* m. Acacia Catechu. — *Kaṇṭakī-phala* = *kaṇṭaki-phala.* — *Kaṇṭa-kuraṇṭa, as,* m. = *jhiṇṭī,* Barleria Cristata. — *Kaṇṭakoddharaṇa* (°*ka-ud*°), *am,* n. weeding, extracting thorns &c.; removing annoyances; extirpating thieves, rogues, &c., or all national and public nuisances. — *Kaṇṭa-tanu, us,* f. a species of Solanum. — *Kaṇṭa-dalā,* f. the plant Pandanus Odoratissimus. — *Kaṇṭa-pattra, as,* m. the plant Flacourtia Sapida. — *Kaṇṭapattra-phalā,* f., N. of a plant, = *brahmadaṇḍī.* — *Kaṇṭa-pāda* = *kaṇṭa-pattra.* — *Kaṇṭa-phala, as,* m., N. of several plants, = *gokshura;* bread-fruit tree, Datura Fastuosa, = *latākarañja* = *tejaḥkhala* (?); Ricinus Communis; (*ā*), f. = *devadālīlatā.* — *Kaṇṭa-vallī,* f. = *śrīvallī-vṛiksha.* — *Kaṇṭa-vṛiksha, as,* m. = *tejaḥphala-vṛiksha.* — *Kaṇṭā-phala, as,* m. = *kaṇṭa-phala.* — *Kaṇṭārtagalā* (°*ṭa-ār*°), f. the plant Barleria Cærulea. — *Kaṇṭāhvaya* (°*ṭa-āh*°), *am,* n. the tuberous root of the lotus.

Kaṇṭakāra, as, m., N. of a plant; (*ī*), f., N. of several plants, Solanum Jacquini; Bombax Heptaphyllum, the silk-cotton tree; Flacourtia Sapida.

Kaṇṭakārikā, f. Solanum Jacquini; also the fruit of this plant.

Kaṇṭakāla, as, m. = *kaṇṭaka-phala,* q. v.

Kaṇṭakāluka, as, m. Hedysarum Alhagi.

Kaṇṭakita, as, ā, am, thorny; covered with erect hairs.

Kaṇṭakin, ī, inī, i, thorny, prickly; vexatious, annoying; (*ī*), m., N. of several thorny plants, Acacia Catechu; Vanguiera Spinosa; Ruellia Longifolia; Zizyphus Jujuba, bamboo; a fish; (*nī*), f., N. of several plants, Solanum Jacquini, red amaranth. — *Kaṇṭaki-ja, as, ā, am,* produced from a fish; produced by the Mimosa tree. — *Kaṇṭaki-phala, as,* m. the Indian bread-fruit tree or Jaka; see *kaṇṭaka-phala.* — *Kaṇṭaki-latā,* f. a gourd.

Kaṇṭakila, as, m. a thorny kind of bamboo, Bambusa Spinosa.

Kaṇṭala, as, m. the plant Mimosa Arabica; generally *Vāvala,* a tree yielding a species of Gum Arabic; the branches are prickly, whence the name.

Kaṇṭālu, us, m., N. of different plants; Solanum Jacquini; another species of Solanum; a bamboo.

Kaṇṭin, ī, m., N. of several plants, Achyranthes Aspera; Acacia Catechu; Ruellia Longifolia.

कण्ठ् *kaṇṭh,* cl. 1. P. A., 10. P. *kaṇṭhati, -te, -ṭhitum, kaṇṭhayati, -yitum,* to mourn; to long for; [cf. *utkaṇṭh;* cf. also Gr. πένθος, πόθος; Lat. *patior.*]

कण्ठ *kaṇṭha, as, am,* m. n. (said to be fr. rt. *kaṇ*), the throat, the neck (e.g. *ākaṇṭha-tṛipta,* filled up to the throat, quite satiated); the voice (e.g. *sanna-kaṇṭhena,* with broken voice); sound, especially guttural sound; the neck (of a pitcher or other vessel); the opening of the womb; metaphorically a bud on a stalk; immediate proximity; the space of an inch from the edge of the hole in which sacrificial fire is deposited; the tree Vanguiera Spinosa; N. of a Maharshi; (*ī*), f. neck, throat; a rope or leather round the neck of a horse; a necklace, a collar; [cf. *adhara-kaṇṭha, ut-kaṇṭhā;* cf. also Lat. *collum?*]. — *Kaṇṭha-kubja, as,* m. a kind of fever. — *Kaṇṭha-kubja-pratīkāra, as,* m. the cure of the preceding disease. — *Kaṇṭha-kūṇikā,* f. the Vīṇā or Indian lute. — *Kaṇṭha-ga, as, ā, am,* reaching or extending to the throat. — *Kaṇṭha-gata, as, ā, am,* being at or in the throat; approaching or reaching the throat. — *Kaṇṭha-taṭa, as, am,* m. n. the side of the neck. — *Kaṇṭha-talāsikā* (°*la-as*° ?), f. the leather or rope passing round the neck of a horse. — *Kaṇṭha-daghna, as, ī, am,* reaching to the neck. — *Kaṇṭha-dhāna, ās,* m. pl., N. of a people. — *Kaṇṭha-nīḍaka, as,* m. Falco Cheela; a kite. — *Kaṇṭha-nīlaka, as,* m. a torch, a whisp of lighted straw &c. (= *ulkā,* commonly *masālā*). — *Kaṇṭha-paṇḍita, as,* m., N. of a poet. — *Kaṇṭha-pāśaka, as,* m. a halter; a rope passing round an elephant's neck. — *Kaṇṭha-bandha, as,* m. a rope tied round an elephant's neck. — *Kaṇṭha-bhūshā,* f. a collar or short necklace. — *Kaṇṭha-maṇi, is,* m. a jewel worn on the throat, a dear or beloved object. — *Kaṇṭha-rava, as,* m., N. of an author; N. of a certain medical writer. — *Kaṇṭha-lagna, as, ā, am,* fastened or suspended round the throat; clinging to, embracing. — *Kaṇṭha-latā,* f. a collar; a horse's halter. — *Kaṇṭha-vartin, ī, inī, i,* being in the throat; [cf. *kaṇṭha-gata.*] — *Kaṇṭha-śālūka, am,* n. a hard tumour in the throat. — *Kaṇṭha-śuṇḍī,* f. swelling of the tonsils. — *Kaṇṭha-śosha, as,* m. drying the throat; fruitless expostulation. — *Kaṇṭha-śruty-upanishad, t,* f., N. of an Upanishad belonging to the Atharva-veda. — *Kaṇṭha-sajjana, am,* n. hanging on or round the throat. — *Kaṇṭha-sūtra, am,* n. a kind of embrace. — *Kaṇṭha-stha, as, ā, am,* sticking in the throat; being in or upon the throat; guttural; being in the mouth ready to be repeated by rote, learnt and ready to be recited. — *Kaṇṭhāgata* (°*ṭha-āg*°), *as, ā, am,* come to the throat (as the breath or soul of a dying person). — *Kaṇṭhāgni* (°*ṭha-ag*°), *is,* m. a bird (digesting in the throat or gizzard). — *Kaṇṭhā-*

bharaṇa (°*ṭha-ābh*°), *am*, n. a neck-ornament, a necklace; a shorter N. of the work called Sarasvatī-kaṇṭhābharaṇa. — *Kaṇṭhābharaṇa-darpaṇa, as,* m. a commentary of Rāmasiṃha-deva on the last. — *Kaṇṭhābharaṇa-mārjana,* a commentary by Hari-nātha on the same work. — *Kaṇṭhāvasakta* (°*ṭha-av*°), *as, ā, am,* clinging to the neck, embracing. — *Kaṇṭhī-rava, as,* m. a lion (roaring from the throat); an elephant in rut; a pigeon; (*ī*), f. the plant Gendarussa Vulgaris. — *Kaṇṭhe-kāla, as,* m. an epithet of Śiva ('blue on the neck'). — *Kaṇṭhe-viddha, as,* m., N. of a man. — *Kaṇṭheśvara-tīrtha* (°*ṭha-īś*°), N. of a Tīrtha. — *Kaṇṭhokta* (°*ṭha-uk*°), *am*, n. personal testimony.

Kaṇṭhaka, as, m., N. of a horse of Śākya-muni; [cf. *kaṇṭaka.*]

Kaṇṭhatas, ind. from the throat, with distinct words, explicitly.

Kaṇṭhikā, f. a necklace of one string or row.

Kaṇṭhin, ī, inī, i, belonging to the throat.

Kaṇṭhya, as, ā, am, being at or in the throat; suitable to the throat; belonging to the throat, pronounced from the throat, guttural; (according to a Prātiśākhya the guttural letters are *a, h,* and the *Jihvāmūlīya;* according to Pāṇini *a, k, kh, g, gh, n,* and *h;* according to Vopadeva also *e.*) — *Kaṇṭhya-varṇa, as,* m. a guttural letter. — *Kaṇṭhya-svara, as,* m. a guttural vowel, i. e. *a* and *ā.*

कण्ठाल *kaṇṭhāla, as,* m. a boat, a ship; a hoe, a spade; war; an esculent root, Arum Campanulatum; a camel [cf. *kaṇṭakāśana* and *kaṇḍola*]; a churning-vessel; (*ā*), f. a churning-vessel.

Kaṇṭhīla, as, m. a camel; (*as, ā*), m. f. a churning-vessel.

कण्ड् *kaṇḍ,* cl. 1. P. A. *kaṇḍati, -te, -ḍitum,* to be glad; cl. 10. P. *kaṇḍayati, -yitum,* to separate the chaff from the grain; to protect; [cf. *kaḍ:* cf. also Lith. *kándu,* 'to bite;' Cambro-Brit. *cat,* 'a fragment.']

Kaṇḍana, am, n. threshing, separating the chaff from the grain in a mortar; that which is separated from the grain, chaff; (*ī*), f. a wooden bowl or mortar in which the cleaning or threshing of grain is performed.

कण्डरा *kaṇḍarā,* f. a sinew (of which sixteen are considered to be in the human body); a principal vessel of the body, a large artery, vein, &c.

कण्डरीक *kaṇḍarīka, as,* m., N. of a son of Kauśika.

कण्डानक *kaṇḍānaka, as,* m., N. of a servant of Śiva.

कण्डिका *kaṇḍikā,* f. a short section, the shortest subdivision in the arrangement of certain Vedic compositions, as in the White Yajur-veda; [cf. *kāṇḍa* and *kāṇḍikā.*]

कण्डु *kaṇḍu, us,* m. f. or usually *kaṇḍū, ūs,* f. (fr. rt. *kaṇḍ*), scratching; itching, the itch; (*us*), m., N. of a Ṛishi. — *Kaṇḍū-kari,* f. the plant Mucuna Pruritus. — *Kaṇḍū-ghna, as,* m. the plant Cathartocarpus (Cassia) Fistula; white mustard. — *Kaṇḍūmakā,* f. (*makā* = *makshikā* or *maśaka?*), a kind of insect with a poisonous bite. — *Kaṇḍū-mat, ān, atī, at,* scratching, itching. — *Kaṇḍv-ādi, ayas,* m. pl. the nominal verbs, in the list of which *kaṇḍūyati* is the first.

Kaṇḍuka, as, m., N. of a barber.

Kaṇḍura, as, ā, am, scratching; (*as*), m. the plant Momordica Charantia, a species of reed; (*ā*), f. the plants Mucuna Pruritus and Aty-amlaparṇī.

Kaṇḍūti, is, f. scratching; itching, the itch.

Kaṇḍūya, nom. P. A. *kaṇḍūyati, -te, -yitum,* to scratch, scrape, rub: Desid. *kaṇḍūyiyishati.*

Kaṇḍūyat, an, antī, at, scratching, rubbing.

Kaṇḍūyana, am, n. scratching, scraping, rubbing, itching; (*ī*), f. a brush for rubbing.

Kaṇḍūyanaka, as, ī, am, scratching, scraping; (*as*), m. a tickler, one who tickles or scratches.

Kaṇḍūyamāna, as, ā, am, scratching.

Kaṇḍūyā, f. scratching, itching.

Kaṇḍūyita, am, n. scratching.

Kaṇḍūyitṛi, tā, trī, tṛi, scratching, a scratcher.

Kaṇḍūrā, f. the plant Mucuna Pruritus; 'what causes itching,' alluding to the irritating property of this plant.

Kaṇḍūla, as, ā, am, having or feeling the itch, itchy; (*as*), m. an esculent root (Arum Campanulatum).

कण्डोल *kaṇḍola, as,* m. a basket for holding grain, made of bamboo or canes; a safe, any place in which provisions are kept; a camel; [cf. *kaṇṭhāla;* (*ī*), f. the lute of the Caṇḍāla; [cf. *kaṭola, gaṇḍola.*] — *Kaṇḍola-vīṇā,* f. the lute of the Caṇḍāla, a vulgar lute.

Kaṇḍolaka, as, m. a basket, a safe, a store-room.

कण्डोष *kaṇḍosha, as,* m. a caterpillar.

कण्व *kaṇva, as, ā, am* (said to be fr. rt. *kaṇ*), deaf; (*as*), m., Ved. a peculiar class of evil spirits, against whom charms are used; a praiser; N. of a renowned Ṛishi, author of several hymns of the Ṛig-veda; he is called a son of Ghora and is said to belong to the family of Aṅgiras; (*ās*), m. pl. the family or descendants of Kaṇva; (besides the celebrated Ṛishi there occur a Kaṇva Nārshada, Kaṇva Śrāyasa, Kaṇva Kāśyapa; the founder of a Vedic school; a prince, son of Pratiratha and father of Medhātithi; a son of Apratiratha; a son of Ajamīḍha and father of Medhātithi; the author of a law-book; a grammarian.) The name *Kaṇva* was perhaps originally mythic, and afterwards transferred to a human family, as was the case with the name Aṅgiras; (*am*), n. sin, evil. — *Kaṇva-jambhana, as, ī, am,* Ved. consuming or destroying the evil spirits called Kaṇvas. — *Kaṇva-tama, as, ā, am,* Ved. very much like Kaṇva, very wise. — *Kaṇva-mat, ān, atī, at,* Ved. prepared after the manner of the Kaṇvas (as Soma); (Sāy.) united with praisers or with the Kaṇvas (as Indra). — *Kaṇva-vat,* ind. like Kaṇva. — *Kaṇva-sakhi, ā,* m., Ved. a friend of the Kaṇvas, friendly disposed towards them. — *Kaṇva-hotṛi, tā,* m., Ved. one whose Hotṛi priest is a Kaṇva.

Kaṇvāya, nom. A. *kaṇvā-yate, -yitum,* to do mischief; perhaps originally 'to act like a Kaṇva or evil spirit.'

कत *kata, as,* m. the clearing nut plant; see the following; N. of a Muni or saint. — *Kata-phala, as,* m. the clearing nut plant.

Kataka, as, m. the clearing nut plant, Strychnos Potatorum, (one of the seeds of this plant being rubbed upon the inside of the water-jars used in Bengal occasions a precipitation of the earthly particles diffused through the water and removes them.)

कतम *katama, as, ā, at* (superlative of 2. *ka;* declined as a pronom., Gram. 236), who or which of many? (e. g. *katamena pathā yātās te,* by which road have they gone?). *Katama* is often a mere strengthened substitute for *ka,* the superlative affix imparting emphasis. Hence it may occasionally be used for 'who or which of two?' (e. g. *tayoḥ katamasmai,* to which of these two?). It may optionally be compounded with the word to which it refers (e. g. *katamaḥ Kaṭhaḥ* or *katama-kaṭhaḥ,* which Kaṭha out of many?). When followed by *ća* and preceded by *yatama* an indefinite expression is formed equivalent to 'any whosoever,' 'any whatsoever,' &c. (e. g. *yatamad eva katamać ća vidyāt,* he may know anything whatsoever). In negative sentences *katama* with *ćana* or *katama* with *api* = not even one, none at all (e. g. *na katamaććanāhaḥ,* not even on a single day, on no day at all). In addition to the above uses *katama* is said to mean 'best,' 'excessively good-looking;' [cf. 3. *ka.*] — *Katamoraga* (°*ma-ur*°), *as,* m., N. of a man.

Katara, as, ā, at (comparative of 2. *ka;* declined as a pronom., Gram. 236), who or which of two? whether of two? Analogously to *katama* above *katara* may occasionally be used to express 'who or which of many' (e. g. *katarasyāṃ diśi,* in which quarter?), and may optionally be compounded with the word to which it refers (e. g. *kataraḥ Kaṭhaḥ* or *katara-kaṭhaḥ*). In negative sentences *katara* with *ćana* = neither of the two (e. g. *na kataraśćana jigye,* neither of the two was conquered; [cf. Gr. πότερος, κότερος; Goth. *hvathar;* Eng. *whether;* Lat. *uter;* Old Germ. *huedar;* Slav. *kotoryi.*]

Kataratas, ind. on which of the two sides?

1. *kati* (fr. 2. *ka,* declined in pl. only, Gram. 227. *a,* all the cases except the nom. voc. and acc. taking terminations, whereas the correlative *iti* has become fixed as an indeclinable adverb), how many? quot? several (e. g. *kati devāḥ,* how many gods? *kati vyāpādayati kati vā tāḍayati,* some he kills and some he strikes). In the sense of 'several,' 'some,' *kati* is generally followed by *ćid* or *api* (e. g. *katićid ahāni,* for several or some days). *Kati* may be used as an adverb with *ćid* in the sense of 'oftentimes,' 'much,' 'in many ways' (e. g. *katićit stutaḥ,* much or often praised). *Kati-kṛitvas,* ind. how many times? *kati-vidha, as, ā, am,* of how many kinds? *kati-śas,* how many at a time?

Katitha, as, ī, am, to what place or stage or degree advanced? (the how-maniest?) with *ćid* = advanced to such and such a point (e. g. *aham katithaśćid āsa,* I was so far advanced on to such and such a point).

Katidhā, ind. in how many places? in how many parts? how often? *katidhā ćit,* everywhere.

Katipaya, as, ā or *ī, am* (pl. m. *e* and *ās*), several, some; a certain number, so many; *katipayena ahargaṇena,* after some days; also *katipayaiṛ ahobhiḥ, katipayāhasya,* &c. — *Katipayena* or *katipayāt,* ind. with some exertion: [the affix *paya* has been compared with Gr. ποῖος.]

Katipayatha, as, ī, am, advanced to a certain place or degree.

कतमाल *katamāla, as,* m. fire; the right form is *khatamāla;* [cf. also *kaćamāla* and *karamāla.*]

कति 2. *kati, is,* m., N. of a sage, son of Viśvā-mitra and ancestor of Kātyāyana. (For 1. see above.)

Katika or *katikā,* f., N. of a town.

कतीमुष *katīmusha, am,* n., N. of an Agrahāra.

कत्ताशब्द *kattā-śabda, as,* m. the rattling sound of dice.

कत्तृण *kat-tṛiṇa, kat-toya, kat-tri.* See under 2. *kad.*

कत्थ् *katth,* cl. 1. A. *katthate, -thitum,* to boast; to mention with praise, to praise or celebrate; to flatter or coax; to abuse, revile.

Katthana, as, ā, am, boasting, praising; a boaster, praiser; (*am*), n. boasting.

कत्पय *kat-paya, as, ā, am* (fr. 2. *kad* and *paya* fr. *pī* = *pyai*), Ved. swelling, rising; (Sāy.) one whose waters cause happiness.

कत्र् *katr,* cl. 10. P. *katrayati, -yitum,* to loosen, slacken, remove.

कत्सवर *katsavara, am,* n. the shoulder, the shoulder-blade.

कथ् *kath* (this rt. is perhaps connected with *katham*), cl. 10. P., ep. also A. *kathayati, -te,* aor. *aćakathat* or *aćikathat, -yitum,* to converse with any one (with inst. c. alone or after *saha*); to tell, relate, narrate, report, inform, speak about, declare, explain (with acc. of the thing or person spoken about); to describe; to denounce, betray; to suppose, state: Pass. *kathyate,* to be called; be regarded or considered as: Desid. *ćikathayishati*, to desire to tell; [cf. Goth. *qvath;* Eng. *quoth* and *quote;* Gr. κωτίλος, κωτίλλω.]

Kathaka, as, ā, am, a narrator, a relater, one who recites a story or who publicly reads and expounds the Purāṇas &c., one who speaks or tells; (*as, ā*), m. f. the speaker of a prologue or monologue; a professional story-teller; chief actor; (*as*), m., N. of a man.

Kathana, as, ā, am, telling, talkative; (*am*), n. the act of telling, narration, relating, informing.

Kathanīya, as, ā, am, to be said, to be told or declared; worthy of relation, to be named.

Kathayāna, as, ā, am, telling, speaking.

Kathayitavya, as, ā, am, to be told, to be mentioned, to be communicated.

1. *kathā*, f. conversation, speech, tale; a fable, a feigned story; talk, mention; (in phil.) disputation; *kā kathā* (with gen. or more commonly with loc. and sometimes with *prati*), what should one say of? how should one speak of? (e. g. *eko 'pi kṛićchrād varteta, bhūyasām kathaiva kā*, even one person would live with difficulty, what should one say of many? i. e. how much more many?). — *Kathākrama* (°*thā-āk*°), *as*, m. the commencement of a conversation. — *Kathā-ćhala, am*, n. the device of a fable. — *Kathā-java, as*, m., N. of a man. — *Kathānurāga* (°*thā-an*°), *as*, m. attention, taking pleasure in a discourse. — *Kathānta* (°*thā-an*°), *as*, m. end of a conversation. — *Kathāntara* (°*thā-an*°), *am*, n. the course of a conversation. — *Kathā-pīṭha*, N. of the first Lambaka or book of the Kathā-sarit-sāgara. — *Kathā-prabandha, as*, m. a narrative, a tale, a composed story, a fiction. — *Kathā-prasanga, as*, m. connection of speeches or discourse, talking, conversation, speaking to or with, rumour, report; (*as, ā, am*), talkative, talking much and foolishly, half-witted, foolish; a conjuror, a dealer in antidotes &c. — *Kathā-prāṇa, as*, m. an actor, the speaker of a prologue or monologue, the introducer of a drama; a professed story-teller. — *Kathā-maya, as, ī, am*, consisting of tales. — *Kathā-mukha, am*, n. the introduction to a tale; N. of the second Lambaka or book of the Kathā-sarit-sāgara. — *Kathā-yoga, as*, m. conversation, talk, discourse. — *Kathārambha* (°*thā-ār*°), *as*, m. beginning of a story or narrative, story-telling. — *Kathārambha-kāla* (°*thā-ār*°), *as*, m. story-beginning-time. — *Kathārāma* (°*thā-ār*°), *as*, m. garden of fable. — *Kathārṇava* (°*thā-ar*°), *as*, m., N. of a collection of stories attributed to Śivadāsa. — *Kathālāpa* (°*thā-āl*°), *as*, m. speech, conversation. — *Kathāvaśesha* (°*thā-av*°), or *kathā-śesha, as, ā, am*, one of whom only the narrative remains, i. e. deceased, dead; *kathāvaśeshatām gataḥ*, deceased, dead. — *Kathā-virakta, as, ā, am*, reserved, taciturn, disliking conversation. — *Kathā-sangraha, as*, m. a collection of tales or fables. — *Kathā-sarit-sāgara, as*, m. the ocean of the rivers of stories; title of a work of Somadeva. — *Kathodaya* (°*thā-ud*°), *as*, m. the beginning of a tale, introduction to a tale. — *Kathodghāta* (°*thā-ud*°), *as*, m. the opening of a drama by the character that first enters overhearing and repeating the last words of the prelude. — *Kathopakathana* (°*thā-up*°), *am*, n. conversation, conference, narration. — *Kathopākhyāna* (°*thā-up*°), *am*, n. narration, narrative, relation, telling a story.

Kathānaka, am, n. a small tale; [cf. *krayāṇaka, bhayānaka*, &c.]

Kathāpaya, nom. P. *kathāpayati, -yitum*, to tell, relate, &c.

Kathika, as, ī, am, a narrator, a relater, a story-teller by profession.

Kathita, as, ā, am, told, said, related; (*am*), n. a conversation, discourse. — *Kathita-pada, am*, n. repetition, tautology.

Kathī-kṛi, cl. 8. P. A. *-karoti, -kurute, -kartum*, to transform into a tale. — *Kathī-kṛita, as, ā, am*, transformed into a tale, deceased, dead (e. g. *kathīkṛitam vapuḥ*, a body of which one can only give a history, a deceased body).

Kathya, as, ā, am, to be spoken about, to be told, fit to be mentioned.

Kathyamāna, as, ā, am, being told or mentioned, under narration.

कथम् *katham* (fr. 2. *ka*), ind. how? in what manner? whence? (e. g. *katham etat*, how is that? *katham idānīm*, how now? what is now to be done? *katham mārātmake tvayi viśvāsaḥ*, how can there be reliance on thee of murderous mind? *katham utsṛijya tvām gaććheyam*, how can I go away deserting you? *katham buddhvā bhavishyati sā*, how will she be when she awakes? *katham mṛityuḥ prabhavati vedavidām*, whence is it that death has power over those that know the Veda? *katham avagamyate*, whence is it inferred?). Sometimes *katham* merely introduces an interrogation (e. g. *katham ātmānam nivedayāmi katham vā ātmāpahāram karomi*, shall I declare myself or shall I withdraw?).

Katham is often found in connection with the particles *iva, nāma, nu, svid*, which appear to generalize the interrogation (how possibly? &c.); with *nu* it sometimes = *kimu* or *kutas* (e. g. *katham nu*, how much more! *na katham nu*, how much less!).

Katham is often connected, like *kim*, with the particles *ćana, ćid*, and *api*, which give an indefinite sense to the interrogative (e. g. *katham ćana*, in no way, not at all). When not itself negative *katham ćana* = in some way, some how; scarcely, with difficulty; *na katham ćana*, in no way; *kathańćit*, some how or other, by some means or other, in any way, with some difficulty, scarcely, in a moderate degree, a little; *na kathańćit*, not at all, in no way whatever; *na kathańćid na*, in no way not, i. e. most decidedly; *yathā kathańćit*, in any way whatsoever; *kathańćid yadi jīvati*, it is with difficulty that he lives; *katham api*, some how or other, with some difficulty, scarcely, a little; *katham api na*, by no means, not at all. In addition to the above senses lexicographers assert that *katham* may imply 'amazement, surprise, pleasure, abuse;' [with *katham* cf. Gr. κατά.]

At the beginning of an adjective compound *katham* may have the same sense as *kim*. — *Katham-rūpa, as, ā, am*, of what shape? — *Katham-vīrya, as, ā, am*, of what power? — *Kathan-kathika, as, ā, am* (fr. *katham katham*), one who is always asking questions, an inquisitive person. — *Kathan-kathika-tā*, f. questioning, inquiring, inquisitiveness. — *Kathan-kathita* (?), *as*, m. an interrogant, one who puts questions. — *Kathan-karman, ā, ā, a*, how acting? — *Kathan-kāram*, ind. in which manner? — *Kathan-tā*, f. enquiry, question, demand. — *Katham-pramāṇa, as, ā, am*, of what measure? — *Katham-bhāva, as*, m. what state? — *Katham-bhūta, as, ā, am*, how being? of what kind?

2. *kathā*, ind. (for *katham*), Ved. how? whence? why? Sometimes merely a particle of interrogation (e. g. *kathā śriṇoti Indraḥ*, does Indra hear? *yathā kathā ća*, in any way whatsoever).

कद् 1. *kad*, cl. 1. A. *kadate, -ditum*, perf. *ćakāda*, to be confused, suffer mentally; to grieve; to confound; to kill or hurt; to call; to cry or shed tears; *ćakāda kadanam*, he accomplished a destruction; [cf. Gr. κῆδος; Goth. *hatan:* cf. also *kand*.]

Kadana, am, n. destruction, killing, slaughter; war, sin. — *Kadana-pura, am*, n., N. of a town. — *Kadana-priya, as, ā, am*, loving slaughter.

कद् 2. *kad*, ind. (originally the neuter form of the interrogative pronoun *ka*), Ved. a particle of interrogation, where? *Kad* is used, like *kim*, with the particles *ćana* and *ćid* (e. g. *na kaććana upabdiḥ śriṇve rathasya*, not at any time or in any manner is heard the noise of thy chariot; *veti divaḥ kaććid ā*, he comes from heaven now and then). *Kaććid* is sometimes used, like the simple *kad*, as a particle of interrogation (e. g. *kaććid dṛishṭā tvayā Damayantī*, was Damayantī seen by thee?). *Kaććid* may sometimes be equivalent to 'I hope that' (e. g. *vyādhir na kaććit te śarīram pratibādhate*, I hope no illness afflicts thy body).

Kad at the beginning of a compound marks the uselessness, badness or defectiveness of anything; as in the following examples. — *Kat-tṛiṇa, am*, n. a fragrant grass; the plant Pistia Stratiotes. — *Kat-toya, am*, n. an intoxicating drink, wine or vinous spirit. — *Kat-tri, ayas*, m. pl. three inferior articles. — *Kad-akshara, am*, n. a bad letter, bad writing. — *Kad-agni, is*, m. some or a little fire. — *Kad-adhvan, ā*, m. a bad road. — *Kad-anna, am*, n. bad food. — *Kad-apatya, am*, n. bad posterity; bad children. — *Kad-abhyāsa, as*, m. a bad habit. — *Kad-artha, as*, m. a useless thing; (*as, ā, am*), useless, unmeaning; having what purpose or aim? — *Kadarthana, am, ā*, n. f. tormenting, torture. — *Kadarthaya*, nom. P. *kadarthayati, -yitum*, to despise, to estimate lightly; to torment, torture, trouble. — *Kadarthita, as, ā, am*, despised, disdained, rejected; rendered useless. — *Kadarthī-kṛi*, cl. 8. P. A. *-karoti, -kurute, -kartum*, to disdain, despise, to estimate at small value. — *Kadarthī-kṛita, as, ā, am*, despised, disdained, rendered useless and unavailing. — *Kad-arya, as, ā, am*, avaricious, miserly; little, insignificant, mean; bad, disagreeable; (*as*), m. a miser. — *Kadarya-tā*, f. or *kadarya-tva, am*, n. avarice; insignificance; badness. — *Kadarya-bhāva, as*, m. avarice, stinginess. — *Kad-aśva, as*, m. a bad horse. — *Kad-ākāra, as, ā, am*, ill-formed, ugly. — *Kad-ākhya, am*, n. the plant Costus Speciosus ('having a bad name,' i. e. *kushṭha* or *dushṭa*). — *Kad-āćāra, as, ā, am*, wicked, abandoned, following evil practices; (*as*), m. bad conduct. — *Kad-indriya, āṇi*, n. pl. bad organs of sense. — *Kad-ushṭra, as*, m. a bad camel. — *Kad-ushṇa, as, ā, am*, tepid, lukewarm; (*am*), n. warmth, lukewarmness, gentle warmth; [cf. *kavoshṇa, koshṇa*.] — *Kad-ratha, as*, m. a bad carriage. — *Kad-rat, ān, atī, at*, containing the word *ka*. — *Kad-vada, as, ā, am*, speaking ill or inaccurately or indistinctly; contemptible, vile, base. — *Kallola*, see s. v.

कद *ka-da, as*, m. a cloud. See 4. *ka*.

कदक *kadaka, as*, m. an awning; [cf. *kandaka*.]

कदन *kadana*. See under 1. *kad*.

कदम्ब *kadamba, as*, m. (said to be fr. 1. *kad*), the tree Nauclea Cadamba, a tree with orange-coloured fragrant blossoms; the mustard-seed plant, Sinapis Dichotoma; a kind of grass, Andropogon Serratus; a particular mineral substance; turmeric; (*ī*), f., N. of a plant; (*am*), n. a multitude, an assemblage or collection. — *Kadamba-pushpā* or *ī*, f. a plant, the flowers of which resemble those of the Kadamba, commonly called Mandiri. — *Kadamba-vāyu, us*, m. a fragrant breeze. — *Kadambānila* (°*ba-an*°), *as*, m. a fragrant breeze, spring.

Kadambaka, as, m. the plant Nauclea Cadamba, Sinapis Dichotoma, = *haridru;* (*am*), n. a multitude.

Kadambada, as, m. the mustard-seed plant, Sinapis Dichotoma.

कदर *kadara, as*, m. a saw; an iron goad for guiding an elephant; N. of a tree, which may be substituted for Khadira as a sacrificial post; a white sort of Mimosa; (*as, am*), m. n. a corn, a callosity of the feet caused by external friction; (*am*), n. coagulated milk; [cf. *kankara, kaććara, kaṭura*, &c.]

कदल *kadala, as, ī*, m. f. the plantain tree (Musa Sapientum), called also banana. It has a soft perishable stem, poetically a symbol of the frailty of human life; (*ā*), f., N. of several plants, Pistia Stratiotes; Bombax Heptaphyllum; (*ī*), f. a kind of deer, the hide of which is used as a seat &c.; a flag, a banner, a flag carried by an elephant. — *Kadalī-skandha, as*, m. a kind of illusion.

Kadalaka, as, m. the plantain or banana tree, Musa Sapientum.

Kadalin, ī, m. a kind of antelope.

कदलीक्षता *kadalīkshatā,* f. a sort of cucumber; a fine woman.

कदा *kadā,* ind. (fr. 2. *ka*), when? at what time? (with following fut. or pres. tense); how? *Kadā* is sometimes found with a following *ća* and preceding *yadā* (e.g. *yadā kadā ća sunavāma somam,* let us press out the Soma as often as may be or at all times); *kadā ćana,* (though originally negative, generally =) at some time, one day, once; *na kadā ćana,* never at any time; *kadā ćit,* at some time or other, sometimes, once; *na kadā ćit,* never; *kadāpi (kadā-api),* sometimes, now and then; *na kadāpi,* never; [cf. Gr. κότε and πότε; Lat. *quando;* Lith. *kadà;* Slav. *kogda.*] — *Kadā-matta, as,* m., N. of a man.

कदूहि *kadūhi, is,* m., N. of a man.

कद्रु *kadru, us, us* or *ūs, u* (said to be fr. rt. *kav*), tawny, reddish-brown; (*us*), m. tawny (the colour); N. of a Ṛishi; (*ūs*), f. a Soma vessel (?); a personification described in certain legends which relate to the bringing down of the Soma from heaven, according to the Brāhmaṇas 'the earth personified;' N. of a daughter of Daksha, wife of Kaśyapa and mother of the Nāgas or the serpent-race; N. of a plant. — *Kadru-putra, as,* m. or *kadru-suta, as,* m. a serpent.

कद्र्यच् *kadryać, ān, kadrīći, ak* (fr. 2. *ka* and rt. *añć*), Ved. turned towards what?

कद्वत् *kad-vat.* See under 2. *kad.*

कद्वर *kadvara, am,* n. whey; buttermilk mixed with water; [cf. *kankara, kaććara, kaṭura, kaṭvara,* and *kadara.*]

कधप्रिय *kadha-priya, as, ā, am,* or *kadha-prī, īs, īs, i,* Ved. friendly towards whom?; (Sāy.) fond of praise.

कन् *kan,* cl. 1. P., Ved. *kanati, ćakāna, akānīt, kantum* (of the simple root only the aor. is used), to be satisfied; to be contented with, to accept anything (acc.) with satisfaction; (Sāy.) to love, wish, desire; to shine; to go: Intens. *ćākanti,* impf. *ćākan,* perf. *ćākana* and *ćake,* to be satisfied, to like, enjoy anything (with loc., gen., or inst.); to be liked, wished, desired (with gen.); to strive after, seek, desire (with acc. or dat.); [cf. *kam* and *ćan:* cf. also Lat. *canus, caneo, candeo, candela;* Hib. *canu,* 'full moon.']

कन *kana,* a substitute for *alpa,* little, small, not occurring alone, but regarded as the source of the following derivatives; [cf. *kaṇa.*]

Kanaya, nom. P. *kanayati, -yitum,* to make less or smaller, diminish.

Kanā, f., Ved. a girl.

Kanishṭha, as, ā, am, the smallest, least (opposed to *bhūyishṭha*); the youngest, younger born (opposed to *jyeshṭha* and *vṛiddha*); (*ā*), f. (with or without *angulih*) the little finger; (*ās*), m. pl., N. of a class of deities of the fourteenth Manvantara; (*ā*), f. a kind of heroine. — *Kanishṭha-tā,* f. or *kanishṭha-tva, am,* n. the state of being younger or smaller. — *Kanishṭha-pada* or *kanishṭha-mūla, am,* n. the least or first root; that quantity of which the square multiplied by the given multiplicator and having the given addend added or subtrahend subtracted is capable of affording an exact square root.

Kanishṭhaka, as, ikā, am, Ved. the smallest; (*ā*), f. the little finger; (*am*), n. a kind of grass.

Kanī, f. a girl, a maiden.

Kanīna, as, ā, am, Ved. young; (*ī*), f. the pupil of the eye; the little finger.

Kanīnaka, as, m. a boy, a youth; the pupil of the eye; the caruncula lacrymalis; (*ā*), f. a maiden, a young girl, a virgin; the pupil of the eye; (*ikā*), f. the pupil of the eye; the little finger.

Kanīyas, ān, asī, as (opposed to *bhūyas, jyāyas, uttama*), smaller, less; younger, a younger brother or sister, a younger son or daughter.

Kanīyasa, as, ā, am, smaller, less; younger; (*am*), n. copper ('of less value'); [cf. *kanyasa.*]

Kanyakā, kanyā. See s. v.

कनक *kanaka, am,* n. (said to be fr. rt. *kan*), gold; N. of several plants, Datura Metel and Fastuosa, thorn apple; Mesua Ferrea; Michelia Champaka; Butea Frondosa; Bauhinia Variegata; a black sort of Agallochum or sandal-wood; (*as*), m., N. of a prince, a son of Durdama; N. of a son of a goddess; N. of a minister of Narendrāditya; (*ās*), m. pl., N. of a people; (*ā*), f. one of the seven tongues of fire. — *Kanaka-kuṇḍalā,* f. the mother of Harikeśa. — *Kanaka-kshāra, as,* m. borax. — *Kanaka-giri, is,* m., N. of the founder of a sect. — *Kanaka-ṭanka, as,* m. a golden hatchet. — *Kanaka-tālābha* (°*la-ābhā*), *as, ā, am,* bright as a golden palm tree. — *Kanaka-daṇḍaka, as,* m. the royal parasol (golden-sticked). — *Kanaka-datta, as,* m. the son of Nidhipati. — *Kanaka-dhvaja, as,* m., N. of a son of Dhṛita-rāshṭra. — *Kanaka-parāga, as,* m. gold-dust. — *Kanaka-pala, as,* m. a Pala, a weight of gold and silver equal to sixteen Māshakas, or about 280 grains troy. — *Kanaka-pingala,* N. of a Tīrtha. — *Kanaka-pura, am, ī,* n. f., N. of a town. — *Kanaka-prabhā,* f., N. of a plant; N. of a metre consisting of four lines of thirteen syllables each; N. of a princess; (*as, ā, am*), bright as gold. — *Kanaka-prasavā,* f., N. of a plant. — *Kanaka-bhanga, as,* m. a piece of gold. — *Kanaka-maya, as, ī, am,* golden, consisting or made of gold. — *Kanaka-muni, is,* m., N. of a Buddha. — *Kanaka-rambhā,* f., N. of a plant. — *Kanaka-rasa, as,* m. fluid gold; a yellow orpiment. — *Kanaka-rekhā,* f., N. of a daughter of Kanaka-prabhā. — *Kanakalodbhava, as,* m. (fr. *kanaka-kala-udbhava?*), resin of the plant Shorea Robusta. — *Kanaka-vatī,* f., N. of the residence of king Kanaka-varṇa; [cf. *kanakā-vatī.*] — *Kanaka-varṇa, as,* m., N. of a king supposed to be a former manifestation of Śākya-muni. — *Kanaka-vāhinī,* f., N. of a river ('gold stream'). — *Kanaka-vigraha, as,* m., N. of a king of Viśālapurī. — *Kanaka-śakti, is,* m. an epithet of Kārttikeya; [cf. *śakti-dhara.*] — *Kanaka-sūtra, am,* n. a gold cord. — *Kanaka-stambha-rućira, as, ā, am,* shining with columns of gold. — *Kanaka-sthalī,* f. a gold mine, golden soil. — *Kanakāngada* (°*ka-an*°), *as,* m., N. of a son of Dhṛita-rāshṭra. — *Kanakāćala* (°*ka-ać*°), *as,* m. the golden mountain; an epithet of the mountain Sumeru. — *Kanakādri-khaṇḍa* (°*ka-ad*°), *am,* n. a section of the Skanda-purāṇa. — *Kanakādhyaksha* (°*ka-adh*°), *as,* m. the treasurer or superintendent of the gold. — *Kanakāyu* (°*ka-āyu*), *us,* m., N. of a son of Dhṛita-rāshṭra; (a various reading has *karakāyu.*) — *Kanakālukā* (°*ka-āl*°), f. a golden jar or vase. — *Kanakā-vatī,* f. a proper name. — *Kanakārati-mādhava, as,* m. title of a work. — *Kanakāhva* (°*ka-āh*°), *am,* n. the blossom of the tree Mesua Ferrea. — *Kanakāhvaya, as,* m. the thorn apple; Mesua Ferrea; N. of a Buddha. — *Kanakeśvara-tīrtha* (°*ka-īś*°), *am,* n., N. of a Tīrtha.

Kanakāraka, as, m. the tree Bauhinia Variegata Lin.; [cf. *kāñćanāra* and *kāntāra.*]

कनक्नक *kanaknaka, as, ā, am,* Ved. epithet of a kind of poison.

कनखल *kanakhala, am,* n. and (*ās*), m. pl., N. of a Tīrtha and the mountains surrounding it.

कनटी *kanaṭī,* f. red arsenic, = *kunaṭī.*

कनदेव *kanadeva, as,* m., N. of a Buddhist patriarch.

कनन *kanana, as, ā, am,* one-eyed; [cf. *kāṇa.*]

कनप *kanapa,* a various reading for *kaṇapa,* q. v.

कनयक *kanavaka, as,* m., N. of a son of Śūra.

कनाठ *kanāṭha, as,* m., N. of a man.

कनिक्रद *kanikrada, as, ā, am* (an Intens. form of rt. *krand*), Ved. neighing.

कनिष्क *kanishka, as,* m., N. of an Indo-scythic king, celebrated in the history of Buddhism. — *Kanishka-pura, am,* n., N. of a town founded by Kanishka.

कनिष्ठ, कनी, कनीन, कनीयस्. See under *kana.*

कनीचि *kanīći, is,* f. a cart; a creeping plant with blossoms; the plant Abrus Precatorius.

कनूज *kanūja,* a corruption of *kanyā-kubja,* q. v. — *Kanūja-deśa, as,* m. the country round Kanyā-kubja.

कनेरा *kanerā,* f. a female elephant; a harlot. See *kaṇerā.*

कन्त *kanta, as, ā, am,* or *kanti, is, is, i* (fr. 1. *kam*), happy.

Kantu, us, us, u, happy; (*us*), m. the heart as the seat or faculty of perception and feeling; Kāma-deva, the deity of love; a granary.

कन्थक *kanthaka, as,* m., N. of a man.

कन्थरी *kantharī,* f., N. of a tree. See *kanthā, kanthārī, krūragandhā, tīkshṇakaṇṭakā,* &c.

कन्था *kanthā,* f. a rag, a patched garment, especially one worn by certain ascetics; a wall; a town (in composition the word is neuter if the compound imply a town of the Uśīnaras); a kind of tree; N. of a country. — *Kanthā-dhāraṇa, am,* n. wearing a patched garment as practised by certain Yogis. — *Kanthā-dhārin, ī, iṇī,* m. f. a Yogi, a religious mendicant. — *Kantheśvara-tīrtha* (°*thā-īś*°), *am,* n., N. of a Tīrtha.

कन्थारी *kanthārī,* f., N. of a tree.

कन्द् *kand,* cl. 1. P. *kandati, -ditum,* to cry, utter lamentations; A. *kandate,* to be confounded, confound; [cf. 1. *kad, krand, kland.*]

कन्द *kanda, as, am,* m. n. (said to be fr. rt. *kan*), a bulbous or tuberous root; a bulb; the bulbous root of Amorphophallus Campanulatus; garlic; a lump, swelling, knot; an affection of the feminine organ, considered as a fleshy excrescence, but apparently prolapsus uteri; N. of a metre of four lines of thirteen syllables each; a cloud (in this sense fr. *kam,* water, and *da*). — *Kanda-guḍūćī,* f., N. of a plant, = *kanda-rohiṇī,* &c. — *Kanda-ja, as, ā, am,* growing from bulbs. — *Kanda-da, as, ā, am,* giving or forming bulbs. — *Kanda-phalā,* f., N. of a plant. — *Kanda-bahulā,* f., N. of a plant. — *Kanda-mūla, am,* n. a radish. — *Kanda-latā,* f., N. of a plant with a bulbous root. — *Kanda-vat, ān,* m. a species of the Soma plant. — *Kanda-vardhana, as,* m. the esculent root of Amorphophallus Campanulatus. — *Kanda-vallī,* f., N. of a plant. — *Kanda-śūraṇa, as,* m. the plant Amorphophallus Campanulatus. — *Kanda-sañjña, am,* n. prolapsus uteri; [cf. *kanda.*] — *Kanda-sambhava, as, ā, am,* growing from bulbs. — *Kanda-sāra, am,* n. the garden or grove of Indra. — *Kandāḍhya,* (°*da-āḍh*°), *as,* m. a kind of tuberous plant. — *Kandāmṛitā* (°*da-am*°), f., N. of a plant, = *kanda-guḍūćī.* — *Kandārha* (°*da-ar*°), *as,* m. the plant Amorphophallus Campanulatus. — *Kandodbhavā* (°*da-ud*°), f., N. of a plant, = *kanda-guḍūćī.*

Kandālu, us, m., N. of several plants; an esculent root; a sort of Arum &c.

Kandin, ī, inī, i, having a bulbous root; (*ī*), m. the plant Amorphophallus Campanulatus.

कन्दक *kandaka, as,* m. a palanquin, = *kaḍaka.*

कन्दट *kandaṭa, am,* n. the white esculent water-lily; [cf. *kandoṭa* and *kandota.*]

कन्दर *kandara, as, ā* or *ī, am,* m. f. n. (perhaps fr. *kam-dara*), an artificial or natural cave; a glen, a defile, a valley; *(as),* m. a hook for driving an elephant; *(am),* n. dry ginger (in this sense fr. *kanda,* 'consisting of bulbs'?). — *Kandara-vat, ān, atī, at,* containing caves or valleys (as a mountain). — *Kandarākāra* (°*ra-āk*°), *as,* m. a mountain. — *Kandarāntara* (°*ra-an*°), *am,* n. the interior of a cave. — *Kandarāla* (°*ra-āla* = *ālaya*), *as,* m., N. of several plants, Hibiscus Populneoides; Ficus Infectoria. — *Kandarālaka, as,* m. the tree Ficus Infectoria. — *Kandarodbhavā* (°*ra-ud*°), f., N. of a plant.

कन्दर्प *kandarpa, as,* m. (fr. *kam-darpa,* 'how haughty;' or, according to others, 'the inflamer even of the chief of gods;' see 3. *ka*), N. of the deity Kāma, or the god of love, the Cupid of the Hindū mythology; love; *(ā),* f. one of the presiding female deities of the Jainas executing the orders of the fifteenth Arhat. — *Kandarpa-kūpa, as,* m. pudendum muliebre, ('a well of love.') — *Kandarpa-ketu, us,* m., N. of a prince. — *Kandarpa-keli, is,* m. title of a work. — *Kandarpa-jīva, as,* m., N. of a plant, = *kāma-vriddhi*. — *Kandarpa-jvara, as,* m. passion, desire. — *Kandarpa-dahana, am,* n. a section of the Śiva-purāṇa. — *Kandarpa-musala, as,* m. membrum virile. — *Kandarpa-śrinkhala, as,* m. a kind of coitus. — *Kandarpa-siddhānta, as,* m., N. of a scholiast on Supadma.

कन्दल *kandala, as, ā, am,* m. f. n. the skull (= *kapāla*); the cheek, or the cheek and temple; a new shoot or sprig; a low soft tone; a portent, a natural phenomenon supposed to forbode evil; reproach, censure; *(as),* m. gold; war, battle; *(ī),* f. a species of deer of which the hide is used; a plant, the plantain tree or banana tree (Musa Sapientum; see *kadalī*); lotus seed; a flag, a banner; *(am),* n. the flower of Musa Sapientum; perhaps a mushroom. — *Kandalī-kāra, as,* m., N. of an author. — *Kandalī-kusuma, am,* n. a mushroom.

Kandalita, as, ā, am, covered with mushrooms (?); budded, blown; put forth, emitted.

Kandalin, ī, inī, i, covered with mushrooms; *(ī),* m. a kind of antelope (?).

कन्दिरी *kandirī,* f. the plant Mimosa Pudica.

कन्दु *kandu, us,* m. f. (said to be fr. rt. *skand*), a boiler, a saucepan, or other cooking utensil of iron; an oven, or vessel serving for one; *(us),* m., N. of a Muni. — *Kandu-pakva, as, ā, am,* parched, roasted (as grain), fried &c. in a pan, dressed without water.

कन्दुक *kanduka, as, am,* m. n. (said to be fr. the preceding), a ball of wood or pith for playing with; *(am),* n. a pillow; a germ (?). — *Kanduka-prastha, as,* m., N. of a town. — *Kanduka-līlā,* f. any game with a ball, fives. — *Kandukeśa* (°*ka-īśa*), *as,* m., N. of a man. — *Kandukeśvara-linga* (°*ka-īś*°), *am,* n., N. of a Linga.

कन्दोट *kandoṭa, as,* m. the white lotus, Nymphæa Esculenta; *(am),* n. the blue lotus.

Kandota, as, m. the white lotus, Nymphæa Esculenta. See *kandaṭa.*

कन्ध *kan-dha, as,* m. (fr. *kam,* water, and *dha* fr. rt. *dhā*), a cloud.

Kan-dhara, as, ā, m. f. (fr. *kam,* head, and *dhara* fr. rt. *dhṛi*), the neck; *(as),* m. the plant Amaranthus Oleraceus; (*kam* = water), a cloud.

Kan-dhi, is, m. (fr. *kam,* water, and *dhi* fr. rt. *dhā*), the ocean; *(is),* f. (*kam* = head), the neck.

कन्न *kanna, as,* m., N. of a Rishi; *(am),* n. fainting, falling in a fit or state of insensibility; sin; (a various reading has *kalla.*)

कन्यका *kanyakā,* f. (see *kana*), a girl, a maiden; a young virgin; a daughter; the constellation Virgo in the zodiac; the plant Aloe Perfoliata. — *Kanyakā-guṇa, ās,* m. pl., N. of a people. — *Kanyakā-ćhala, am,* n. beguiling a maiden, seduction, betrayal. — *Kanyakā-jana, as,* m. a maiden. — *Kanyakā-jāta, as,* m. the son of an unmarried woman. — *Kanyakā-pati, is,* m. a daughter's husband.

Kanyanā or *kanyalā,* f., Ved. a girl.

Kanyā, f. (the gen. pl. in Ṛig-veda is *kanīnām*), a girl, a virgin, a daughter; (*kanyām dā* or *pra-dā* or *pra-yam* or *upa-pad* in Caus., to give one's daughter in marriage; *kanyām prati-grah* or *hṛi* or *vah,* to receive a girl in marriage, to marry); the sign of the zodiac Virgo; an epithet of Durgā; N. of a metre of four lines, each of them containing four long syllables; an annual plant; N. of several plants, the plant Aloe Perfoliata, a tuberous plant growing in Kāśmīra; large cardamoms; [cf. Zend *kainê;* Hib. *cain,* 'chaste, undefiled;' *caile,* 'a country-woman, a harlot;' *caileamhuil,* 'girlish, effeminate.'] — *Kanyā-kāla, as,* m. the time of virginity. — *Kanyā-kubja* or *kanya-kubja, am,* n., N. of an ancient city of great note, in the north of Hindūstan, situated on the *Kālī nadī,* a branch of the Ganges, in the modern district of Furruckabad. The popular spelling of the name presents, perhaps, greater variations than that of any place in India (e.g. *Kunnoj, Kunnouj, Kinoge, Kinnoge, Kinnauj, Kanoj, Kannauj, Kunowj, Canowj, Canoje, Canauj,* &c.). In antiquity this city ranks next to Ayodhyā in Oude. It is known to classical geography as Canogyza; but the name applies also to its dependencies and the surrounding district; the etymology (*kanyā,* a girl, and *kubja,* round-shouldered or crooked) refers to a legend relating to the hundred daughters of Kuśanābha, the king of this city, who were all rendered crooked by Vāyu for non-compliance with his licentious desires. The ruins of the ancient city are said to occupy a site larger than that of London. — *Kanyākubja-deśa, as,* m. the country round Kanyākubja. — *Kanyā-kumārī* or *kanya-kumāri, is,* f. the youthful goddess, an epithet of Durgā. — *Kanyā-kūpa, as,* m., N. of a Tīrtha. — *Kanyā-gata, as, ā, am,* inherent in or pertaining to a virgin; the position of a planet in the sign Virgo. — *Kanyā-garbha, as,* m. the offspring of an unmarried woman. — *Kanyā-grahaṇa, am,* n. taking a girl in marriage. — *Kanyāṭa* (°*yā-āṭa*), *as, ā, am,* following after young girls; *(as),* m. the middle of a house, the inner or private apartments for women. — *Kanyā-tīrtha, am,* n., N. of a Tīrtha. — *Kanyā-tva, am,* n. virginity. — *Kanyā-dātṛi, tā,* m. a father who gives a girl in marriage. — *Kanyādāna* (either °*yā-d*° or °*yā-ād*°), *am,* n. giving a girl in marriage; receiving a girl in marriage. — *Kanyā-dūshaka, as,* m. the violator or defiler of a virgin; the calumniator of a girl. — *Kanyā-dūshaṇa, am,* n. defiling a virgin, calumniating a girl. — *Kanyā-dosha, as,* m. a blemish in a virgin, disease, bad repute, &c. — *Kanyā-dhana, am,* n. a portion, dowry. — *Kanyā-pati, is,* m. a daughter's husband. — *Kanyā-pāla, as,* m. a dealer in slave girls; the father of a maiden; [cf. *kalyā-pāla.*] — *Kanyā-putra, as,* m. the offspring of an unmarried daughter. — *Kanyā-pura, am,* n. the women's apartments. — *Kanyā-pradāna, am,* n. giving a daughter in marriage. — *Kanyā-bhartṛi* or *kanyā-hartṛi* (?), *tā,* m. an epithet of Kārttikeya. — *Kanyā-bhāva, as,* m. virginity. — *Kanyā-maya, as, ī, am,* consisting in a girl (as property &c.), being a girl. — *Kanyā-ratna, am,* n. a jewel of a damsel, a lovely girl. — *Kanyā-rāma, as,* m., N. of a Buddha. — *Kanyā-rāśi, is,* m. the sign Virgo. — *Kanyā-vedin, ī,* m. a son-in-law. — *Kanyā-śulka, am,* n. the purchase-money of a maiden, money given to the bride's father. — *Kanyā-śrama* (°*yā-āś*°), *as,* m., N. of a hermitage. — *Kanyā-saṃvedya, am,* n., N. of a Tīrtha. — *Kanyā-samudbhava, as,* m. the son of an unmarried girl. — *Kanyā-sampradāna, am,* n. the giving away a maiden in marriage. — *Kanyā-svayaṃvara, as,* m. the choice of a husband by a maiden. — *Kanyā-haraṇa, am,* n. carrying off a girl, rape, ravishment. — *Kanyā-hrada, as,* m., N. of a Tīrtha.

Kanyākā or *kanyikā,* f. a young girl, a virgin.

कन्यस *kanyasa, as, ī, am* (fr. *kanīyas*), younger; *(ā),* f. the little finger.

कन्युष *kanyusha, am,* n. the hand below the wrist.

कप् *kap,* a various reading for *krap,* q. v.

कप *kapa, ās,* m. pl. a class of demons.

कपट *kapaṭa, as, am,* m. n. (said to be fr. rt. *kamp*), fraud, deceit, cheating, circumvention; *(as),* m., N. of a Dānava; *(ī),* f. a measure equal to the capacity of the hollows of the two hands joined. — *Kapaṭa-tā,* f. or *kapaṭa-tva, am,* n. deceitfulness. — *Kapaṭa-tāpasa, as,* m. one who deceitfully pretends to be an ascetic. — *Kapaṭa-daitya-badha, as,* m. title of a chapter of the Gaṇeśa-Purāṇa ('destruction of the Daitya Kapaṭa'). — *Kapaṭa-prabandha, as,* m. fraud, trick, fraudulent plot or contrivance. — *Kapaṭa-lekhya, am,* n. a forged document, a false or fraudulent statement. — *Kapaṭa-vaćana, am,* n. deceitful talk. — *Kapaṭa-veśa, as, ā, am,* assuming a false dress or appearance, masked, disguised; *(as),* m. disguise. — *Kapaṭaveśin, ī, inī, i,* disguised, in masquerade. — *Kapaṭeśvarī* (°*ṭa-īś*°), f., N. of a plant.

Kapaṭika, as, ī, am, acting deceitfully, fraudulent, dishonest, a rogue, a cheat.

Kapaṭin, ī, inī, i, fraudulent, dishonest, a cheat; *(inī),* f. a kind of perfume, = *ćiḍā.*

कपना *kapanā,* f. (said to be fr. rt. *kamp*), Ved. a worm, a caterpillar; [cf. κάμπη.]

कपर्द *kaparda, as,* m. a small shell or cowrie used as a coin and as a die in gambling, Cypræa Moneta; braided and knotted hair, especially that of Śiva (knotted so as to resemble the cowrie shell).

Kapardaka, as, m. = *kaparda* above; *(ikā),* f. Cypræa Moneta. See *kaparda.*

Kapardin, ī, inī, i, shaggy; wearing braided and knotted hair like the cowrie shell; epithet of Rudra, of Pūshan, of the descendants of Vasishṭha and of Durgā; *(ī),* m., N. of Śiva; N. of one of the eleven Rudras. — *Kapardi-kārikā, ās,* f. pl., N. of a work. — *Kapardi-svāmin, ī,* m., N. of a scholiast.

कपल *kapala, am,* n., Ved. a half, a part.

कपाट *kapāṭa, as, ī, am,* m. f. n. a door, the leaf or panel of a door. — *Kapāṭa-ghna, as,* m. one who breaks the door, a house-breaker, a thief. — *Kapāṭa-sandhi, is,* m. the junction of the leaves of a door; a mode of multiplying in which the multiplicand is placed in a certain manner under the multiplying quantity. — *Kapāṭasandhika, as, ā, am,* term used for a kind of bandage; similarly *ardha-kapāṭasandhika.* — *Kapāṭodghāṭana* (°*ṭa-ud*°), *am,* n. a door-key.

कपाल *kapāla, am,* n. (said to be fr. rt. *kamp*), a cup, a jar, a dish, used especially for the Puroḍāśa offering (often at the end of a compound, the first member of which is a numeral, e.g. *tri-kapāla,* 'consisting of three cups'); the shell of an egg, shell of a tortoise; the cotyla of the leg of a man or animal, any flat bone; a kind of leprosy; *(as, am),* m. n. the fragment of a vessel, a potsherd; a cover or lid; the skull, the cranium, the skull-bone; either half of a water-jar; multitude, assemblage, collection; a treaty of peace on equal terms, = *kapāṭa*?; *(as),* m., N. of an intermediate caste; N. of a man; *(am, ī),* n. f. a beggar's bowl; [cf. Gr. κεφαλή; Lat. *caput;* Germ. *haupt;* Goth. *haubith,* Them. *haubida.*] — *Kapāla-nālikā,* f. a sort of pin or spindle for winding cotton, thread, &c. — *Kapāla-pāṇi, is, is, i,* having a pot in hand to receive food (as a beggar). — *Kapāla-bhātī,* f. a particular sort of penance, consisting in alternate suppression and emission of the breath. — *Kapāla-bhrit, t,* m. an epithet of Śiva or Mahā-deva (who wears skulls). — *Kapālamālin, ī, inī, i,* bearing a garland of skulls; epithet of Śiva. — *Kapāla-moćana, am,* n., N. of a Tīrtha. — *Kapāla-śiras* (?), *ās,* m., N. of a Muni; (a various reading has *kalāpa-śiras.*) — *Kapāla-sandhi, is,* m. a treaty of peace on equal terms (= *kapāṭa-sandhi?*). — *Kapāla-sphoṭa, as,* m., N. of a Rakshas ('splitting the skull').

Kapālikā, f. a potsherd; the tartar of the teeth; [cf. *kāpālika.*]

Kapālin, ī, inī, i, furnished with or bearing skulls; (*ī, inī*), m. f. a man or woman of low caste, son or daughter of a Brāhman mother and a fisherman father; the follower of a certain Śaiva sect, [cf. *kāpālika*]; (*ī*), m. an epithet of Śiva (as wearing skulls); N. of one of the eleven Rudras; N. of a servant of Śiva; (*inī*), f. the goddess Durgā as the wife of Śiva-kapālin.

कपि *kapi, is, is, i* (said to be fr. rt. *kamp*), brown; (*is*), m. an ape or monkey; an elephant; the plant Emblica Officinalis or a species of Karañja; incense, storax or impure benzoin, [cf. *kapi-ja, kapi-taila,* &c.]; the sun; an epithet of Vishṇu or Kṛishṇa; N. of a Muni, the author of a Vedic verse, son of Uru-kshaya; (*is* or *ī*), f. a female ape or monkey; [cf. Gr. κῆπος, κεῖπος; Old Germ. *affo;* Angl.-Sax. *apa;* Eng. *ape.*] — *Kapi-kaććhu, us* or *ū, ūs,* f. the plant Mucuna Pruritus. — *Kapikaććhu-phalopamā* (°*la-up*°), f., N. of a plant. — *Kapi-kaććhurā,* f. the plant Mucuna Pruritus. — *Kapi-kanduka, am,* n. the skull, the cranium ('playing-ball of monkeys'). — *Kapi-ketana, as,* m. an epithet of Arjuna, the third son of Pāṇḍu. — *Kapi-keśa, as,* m. monkey's hair (?). — *Kapi-koli, is,* m., N. of a plant. — *Kapi-ćūḍā,* f. or *kapi-ćūta, as,* m. the tree Spondias Magnifera. — *Kapi-ja, as, ā, am,* born of a monkey; (*as*), m. incense, benzoin. — *Kapi-taila, am,* n. benzoin or storax. — *Kapi-tva, am,* n. the state of an ape, apishness. — *Kapi-dhvaja, as,* m. an epithet of Arjuna (having a monkey as his symbol, his ensign or arms). — *Kapi-nāman, ā,* m. incense. — *Kapi-pippali,* f., N. of two different kinds of plants. — *Kapi-prabhā,* f. the plant Mucuna Pruritus. — *Kapi-prabhu, us,* m. an epithet of Rāma, general of the monkey-force, with which he invaded Laṅkā. — *Kapi-priya, as,* m. the tree Spondias Magnifera and the tree Feronia Elephantum. — *Kapi-bhaksha, as,* m. the food of apes; N. of a certain eatable substance. — *Kapi-ratha, as,* m. an epithet of Rāma; [cf. *kapi-prabhu.*] — *Kapi-roma-phalā,* f. the plant Mucuna Pruritus. — *Kapi-loma-phalā,* f. the plant Mucuna Pruritus. — *Kapi-lomā,* f. a kind of perfume. — *Kapi-loha, am,* n. brass (monkey-coloured metal). — *Kapillikā,* f. (contracted from *kapi-vallikā?*), a plant which bears a seed resembling pepper, Scindapsus Officinalis, = *gaja-pippalī.* — *Kapi-vaktra, as,* m. a N. of Nārada, a saint and philosopher and friend of Kṛishṇa, having a face like a monkey. — *Kapi-vana, as,* m., N. of a man. — *Kapi-vallī,* f. the plant Scindapsus Officinalis. — *Kapi-śāka, as, am,* m. n. a cabbage. — *Kapi-śīrsha, am,* n. the upper part or coping of a wall. — *Kapi-śīrshaka, am,* n. vermilion, the red sulphuret of mercury. — *Kapi-śīrshṇī,* f. a kind of musical instrument. — *Kapi-shṭhala* (°*pi-stha*°), *as,* m., N. of a Ṛishi; (*ās*), m. pl. the descendants of this Ṛishi. — *Kapi-skandha, as,* m., N. of a Dānava. — *Kapi-sthala, am,* n. a place frequented by monkeys. — *Kapi-svara, as,* m., N. of a man. — *Kapī-kaććhu, us,* f. the plant Mucuna Pruritus; see *kapi-kaććhu.* — *Kapījya, as,* m. (*kapi-ijyā?*), the tree Mimusops Kauki. — *Kapīndra* (°*pi-in*°), *as,* m. the chief of the monkeys; an epithet of Vishṇu; of Jāmbavat, the father-in-law of Kṛishṇa; of Hanumat; of Sugrīva, &c. — *Kapīvat, ān,* m., N. of a sage; one of the seven sages of the fourth Manvantara; (*tī*), f., N. of a river. — *Kapishṭa* (°*pi-ish*°), *as,* m. the tree Feronia Elephantum. — *Kapy-ākhya, as,* m. incense.

Kapikā, f., N. of a plant.

Kapittha, as, m. (*ttha* = *stha* fr. rt. *sthā,* 'on which monkeys dwell;' cf. *aśvattha*), the elephant or wood apple tree, Feronia Elephantum; a particular position of the hands and fingers; (*am*), n. the fruit of Feronia Elephantum. — *Kapittha-tvać, k,* n. the bark of the tree Feronia Elephantum. — *Kapittha-parṇī* and *kapitthānī,* f., N. of a plant, = *ćitra-pattrikā,* &c. — *Kapitthāsya* (°*tha-āsya*), *as,* m. a kind of monkey (having a roundish face, in shape like the wood apple).

Kapitthaka, N. of a place in Avanti.

Kapitthinī, f. a region abounding in Kapitthas.

Kapiraka = *kapilaka,* q. v.

Kapila, as, ā, am, 'monkey-coloured,' brown, tawny, reddish; (*as*), m. the brown or tawny colour; a (brown) dog; incense; N. of an ancient sage, identified by some with Vishṇu and considered as the founder of the Sāṅkhya system of philosophy; a son of Vitatha; or a son of Vasu-deva by Naraći; or a son of Kardama by Devahūti; a form of fire; an epithet of the sun, considered as king of the Nāgas; N. of a Dānava; N. of a mountain; (*ās*), m. pl., N. of a people; (*ā*), f. a brown cow, a fabulous cow celebrated in the Purāṇas; N. of two plants, a kind of Śiṇśapā or Śiṇśapā itself; the plant Aloe Perfoliata; a sort of perfume; a kind of brass; the common leech; N. of a daughter of Daksha; N. of the female elephant of the south-east, the male being called Puṇḍarīka; N. of a river. — *Kapila-deva, as,* m., N. of the author of a Smṛiti. — *Kapila-dyuti, is,* m. a N. of Sūrya or the sun. — *Kapila-drākshā,* f. a vine with brown or tawny coloured grapes. — *Kapila-druma, as,* m., N. of a perfume or sweet scented wood (*kākshī*). — *Kapila-dhārā,* f. an epithet of the Gaṅgā; N. of a Tīrtha; a holy place, a place of pilgrimage. — *Kapila-phalā,* f. a vine with brown grapes. — *Kapila-bhadrā,* f., N. of a woman. — *Kapila-mata, am,* n., N. of a work. — *Kapila-rudra, as,* m., N. of a poet. — *Kapila-vastu, u,* n., N. of the town in which Śākya-muni or Buddha was born. — *Kapila-śiṇśapā,* f. a variety of Śiṇśapā with reddish flowers. — *Kapila-saṃhitā,* f. title of an Upa-purāṇa, a dialogue between Kapila and Satyajit. — *Kapilākshī* (°*la-ak*°), f. a kind of deer ('with brown eyes'); a variety of Śiṇśapā with reddish flowers. — *Kapilāñjana* (°*la-añ*°), *as,* m. an epithet of Śiva; [cf. *kapiśāñjana.*] — *Kapilā-tīrtha, am,* n., N. of a Tīrtha, (any one bathing there obtains 1000 brown cows.) — *Kapilāvaṭa* (°*la-av*°), *as,* m., N. of a Tīrtha. — *Kapilāśva* (°*la-aś*°), *as,* m. an epithet of the god of Indra; N. of a man, a son of Dhundhumāra. — *Kapilā-hrada, as,* m., N. of a Tīrtha.

Kapilaka, as, ikā, am, reddish; (*ikā*), f., N. of a woman.

Kapilī-kṛi, cl. 8. P. A. *-karoti, -kurute, -kartum,* to colour brown or reddish.

Kapiśa, as, ā, am, 'ape-coloured,' brown, reddish-brown; (*as*), m. brown or reddish colour, a compound of black and yellow; incense, storax or coarse benzoin; (*ā* or *ī*), f. a spirit, a sort of rum; (*ā*), f. the mother of the demons called Piśāćas; N. of a river. — *Kapiśāñjana* (°*śa-añ*°), *as,* m. an epithet of Śiva. — *Kapiśā-putra, as,* m. a Piśāća, an imp or goblin. — *Kapiśāyana* (°*śa-ay*°), *as,* m. a deity; a sort of spirit or rum. — *Kapiśāvadāna* (°*śa-av*°), N. of a Buddhist work.

Kapiśita, as, ā, am, embrowned, made brown or dusky red.

Kapiśikā, f. a kind of spirituous liquor.

Kapīta, as, m., N. of a tree.

Kapītana, as, m., N. of several plants; a tree bearing an acid fruit, Spondias Magnifera; the plant Thespesia Populnea; Acacia Sirisa; the holy fig tree, Ficus Religiosa; the betel nut tree, Areca Fausel; Ægle Marmelos.

कपिजङ्घिका *kapijanghikā,* f. a kind of ant; also spelt *kapijaṅghikā.*

कपिञ्जल *kapiñjala, as,* m. (fr. *ka* + *piñjala?,* sometimes *kapiṅgala*), a bird, the francoline partridge; the Caṭaka; N. of a man; also of a sparrow; (*ā*), f., N. of a river. — *Kapiñjalārma* (°*la-ar*°), *am,* n., N. of a region (?).

कपुच्छल *ka-pućchala, am,* n., Ved. the fore part of a sacrificial ladle, i. e. the part with which the fluid is skimmed off; hair hanging down to the ground, or a lock of hair tied on the right side of the crown of a young Brāhman, when he is invested with the sacerdotal thread.

कपुष्टिका *kapushṭikā,* f. a patch of hair on each side of the head; also written *kapushṇikā.*

कपूय *ka-pūya, as, ā, am* (see 2. *ka*), smelling badly, disgusting, disagreeable.

कपृथ् *ka-pṛith, t,* or *ka-pṛitha, as,* m. (see 4. *ka*), Ved. 'causing pleasure,' membrum virile.

कपोत *ka-pota, as,* m. (2. *ka* + *pota,* q. v.), a dove, pigeon, especially the spotty-necked pigeon; (in the Vedas often a bird of evil omen); a bird in general; a particular position of the hands; the gray colour of a pigeon; the brightness of antimony (of a gray colour). — *Kapota-ćaraṇā,* f. a kind of perfume. — *Kapota-pāka, ās,* m. pl., N. of a mountain-tribe; (*ā*), f. a princess of this tribe. — *Kapota-pāda, as, ī, am,* having feet like those of a pigeon. — *Kapota-pālikā* or *kapota-pālī,* f. a dove-cot, an aviary or pigeon-house. — *Kapota-rāja, as,* m. the king of the pigeons. — *Kapota-retasa, as,* m., N. of a man. — *Kapota-roman, ā,* m., N. of a prince. — *Kapota-vaṅkā,* f., N. of a medicinal plant (used as a remedy for the stone). — *Kapota-varṇa, as, ī, am,* of the colour of a pigeon, of a bright gray, lead-gray; (*ī*), f. small cardamoms. — *Kapota-vallī,* f., N. of a plant. — *Kapota-vāṇā,* f. a kind of perfume. — *Kapota-vegā,* f., N. of a plant. — *Kapota-sāra, am,* n. the brightness of antimony, antimony. — *Kapota-hasta* or *kapota-hastaka, as,* m. a mode of joining the hands in prayer, entreaty, or fear, &c. — *Kapotāṅghri* (°*ta-aṅ*°), *is,* f. a kind of perfume. — *Kapotāñjana* (°*ta-añj*°), *am,* n. = *kāpotāñjana,* the brightness of antimony, antimony. — *Kapotābha* (°*ta-ābhā*), *as, ā, am,* of the colour of a pigeon, of a bright gray; (*as*), m. a pale or dirty white colour. — *Kapotāri* (°*ta-ari*), *is,* m. a hawk, a falcon.

Kapotaka, as, m. a small pigeon or dove; a mode of joining the hands; (*am*), n. antimony.

Kapotakīyā, f. a region abounding in pigeons.

Kapotin, ī, inī, i, having pigeons, pigeon-shaped.

कपोल *kapola, as,* m. (said to be fr. rt. *kamp*), a cheek; (*ī*), f. the fore part of the knee, the knee-cap or pan; [cf. *kapāla.*] — *Kapola-kari, is,* m., N. of a poet. — *Kapola-kāsha, as,* m. any object against which the cheeks or temples are rubbed; the elephant's temples and cheeks. — *Kapola-phalaka, as,* m. the cheek; (perhaps) the cheek-bone. — *Kapola-bhitti, is,* m. the temples and cheek, the upper part of the face; (perhaps) the opening in the temples of an elephant during rut. — *Kapola-rāga, as,* m. colour or flush in the cheek.

कप्फिण *kapphiṇa, as,* m., N. of a man; (various readings have *kapphilla, kaphina, kaphin, kaphila, kamphilla.*)

कफ *kapha, as,* m. phlegm, one of the three humors of the body (the other two are *vāyu* and *pitta*), watery froth or foam in general. — *Kapha-kara, as, ā* or *ī, am,* or *kapha-da, as, ā, am,* producing phlegm; occasioning colds. — *Kapha-kūrćikā,* f. saliva, spittle. — *Kapha-kshaya, as,* m. pulmonary consumption. — *Kapha-ghna, as, ī, am,* removing phlegm, antiphlegmatic, curing colds (epithet of many plants); (*ī*), f., N. of a plant. — *Kapha-ja, as, ā, am,* arising from or produced by phlegm. — *Kapha-jvara, as,* m. fever arising from excess of phlegm. — *Kapha-nāśana, as, ī, am,* antiphlegmatic. — *Kapha-prāya, as, ā, am,* phlegmatic. — *Kapha-vardhaka, as, ī, am,* exciting or increasing phlegm. — *Kapha-vardhana, as, ī, am,* exciting or increasing phlegm; (*as*), m., N. of a plant, a species of Tabernæmontana. — *Kapha-virodhin, ī, inī, i,* obstructing the phlegm; (*i*), n. pepper. — *Kapha-sambhava, as, ā, am,* arising from phlegm. — *Kapha-hara, as, ā, am,* or *kapha-hṛit, t, t, t,* removing phlegm, antiphlegmatic. — *Kaphātmaka* (°*pha-āt*°), *as, ā, am,* phlegmatic. — *Kaphāntaka* (°*pha-an*°), *as,* m. a kind of plant, = *varvūra.* — *Kaphāri* (°*pha-ari*), *is,* m. dry ginger.

Kaphala, as, ā, am, phlegmatic, having phlegm.

Kaphin, ī, inī, i, phlegmatic; filled with mucus; (*ī*), m. an elephant; a various reading for *kapphiṇa;* (*inī*), f., N. of a river.

Kaphelū, ūs, ūs, u, phlegmatic, causing or exciting phlegm; (*ūs*), m. a plant, Cordia Latifolia.

कफणि *kaphaṇi, is,* m. f. the elbow.

Kaphoṇi, is, ī, m. f. the elbow. — *Kaphoṇi-ghāta, as,* m. a stroke with the elbow.

कफौड *kaphauḍa, as,* m., Ved. the elbow (?).

कब् *kab,* cl. 1. A. *kabate, -bitum,* to colour, to tinge with various hues; to praise; [cf. *kav.*]

कबन्ध *ka-bandha* or *ka-vandha, as* or *am,* m. or n. a big barrel or cask, a large-bellied vessel; (metaphorically) a cloud; the belly; the clouds which obscure the sun at sunset and sunrise (sometimes they are personified); water; a N. of Rāhu; a headless trunk (shaped like a barrel), especially one retaining vitality; (*as*), m., N. of an Ātharvaṇa and Gandharva; N. of a Muni; N. of the Dānava or Rākshasa called Danu, who was son of Śrī. (His story is told in Rāmāy. III. 75. It is there related that Indra punished him for his insolence in challenging the god to combat, by striking his head and thighs with his thunderbolt and so pressing them into his body. He had enormously long arms and a huge mouth in his belly. It was predicted that he would not recover his original shape until killed in a battle with Rāma and Lakshmaṇa. The whole story probably represents one of Indra's battles with the clouds.) — *Kabandha-tā,* f. or *kabandha-tva, am,* n. headlessness, decapitation. — *Kabandha-vadha, as,* m. 'the slaying of Kabandha,' title of a chapter of the Padma-purāṇa.

Kabandhin or *kavandhin, ī, inī, i,* Ved. 'bearing huge vessels of water or the clouds;' (Sāy.) 'endowed with water,' an epithet of the Maruts who open the clouds and send down rain; (*ī*), m., N. of a Kātyāyana.

कबित्थ *kabittha, as,* m. the elephant or wood apple tree, Feronia Elephantum. See *kapittha.*

कबिल *kabila, as, ā, am,* tawny-coloured; (*as*), m. tawny (the colour). See *kapila.*

कबुलि *kabuli, is,* f. the hinder part of an animal.

कब्रु *kabru,* Atharva-veda II. 3, 6.

कम् 1. *kam,* ind. (Gr. κεν), well, bene (opposed to *akam,* 'badly'), a particle placed after the word to which it belongs with an affirmative sense (Well, Yes), which sense, however, is generally so weak that the Indian grammarians are perhaps right in enumerating *kam* among the expletives; it is often found attached to a dat. case, giving to the latter a stronger meaning, and is generally placed at the end of the Pāda (e. g. *añjana oshadhīr bhojanāya kam,* thou didst create the plants for actual food); it is also used as an enclitic with the particles *nu, su,* and *hi,* but is nevertheless treated in the Padapāṭha as a separate word. Rarely *kam* seems to be used, like *kad* and *kim,* as an interrogative particle; sometimes it occurs, like *kim* and *kad,* at the beginning of compounds, marking the strange or unusual character of anything, [cf. *kandarpa*]: according to native lexicographers *kam* means also head; water; food. — *Kaṃ-vat, ān, atī, at,* Ved. lovely.

Kamba or *kambha, as, ā, am,* well (?).

कम् 2. *kam,* A. (not used in the conjugational tenses) *ćakame, kamishyate, aćakamata, kamitum,* to wish, desire, long for; to love, be in love with; to have sexual intercourse with: Caus. A. (ep. also P.) *kāmayate, -ti, kāmayāñ-ćakre, kāmayishyate, aćīkamata, kāmayitum,* to wish, desire, long for (with pot. or inf., e. g. *kāmaye bhuñjīta,* I wish he may eat; *kāmaye dātum,* I wish to give); to love, have sexual intercourse with; to be inflamed with love; (with *bahu* or *atyartham*) to rate or value highly; to cause any one to love, [cf. also *kan*]: Desid. *ćikamishate* and *ćikāmayishate:* Intens. *ćaṅkamyate;* [cf. Lat. *comis;* also *amo* with loss of the initial; *cā-rus* for *cam-rus;* Hib. *caemh,* 'love, desire; fine, handsome, pleasant;' *caomhach,* 'a friend, a companion;' *caomhaim,* 'I save, spare, protect:' perhaps Old Germ. *scim, scimo,* 'splendor;' Armen. *kamim.*]

Kamana, as, ā, am, wishing for, desirous; libidinous, beautiful, desirable, lovely; (*as*), m., N. of Kāma, the god of love; N. of Brahmā; the tree Jonesia Aśoka. — *Kamana-ćchada* (°*na-ćha*°), *as,* m. a heron (having beautiful plumage).

Kamanīya, as, ā, am, to be desired or wished for, desirable; lovely, pleasing, beautiful. — *Kamanīya-tā,* f. or *kamanīya-tva, am,* n. loveliness, beauty; desirableness.

Kamara, as, ā, am, desirous, lustful.

Kamala, as, ā, am, desirous, lustful; (*as*), m. a species of deer; the Indian crane, Ardea Sibirica; an epithet of Brahmā; N. of a man; (*am*), n. (according to some m. or n.) the lotus, Nelumbium; water; copper; the bladder; a medicament, a drug; N. of a town built by Kamalā; a particular high number; Ved., N. of a certain colour; (*am* or *ī*), n. f., N. of a metre of four lines of three short syllables each; (*ā*), f. an epithet of Lakshmī; an excellent woman; N. of a female dancer who afterwards became the wife of king Jayāpīḍa. — *Kamala-kīkara* and *kamala-kīṭa,* N. of two Grāmas or villages. — *Kamala-khaṇḍa, am,* n. an assemblage of lotuses. — *Kamala-garbhābha* (°*bha-ābhā*), *as, ā, am,* bright as the lotus-cup. — *Kamala-devī,* f., N. of the wife of king Lalitāditya and mother of king Kuvalayāpīḍa. — *Kamala-patrāksha* (°*ra-ak*°), *as, ā, am,* one whose eyes are like lotuses. — *Kamala-bhava, as,* m. or *kamala-yoni, is,* m. 'sprung from the lotus,' an epithet of Brahmā. — *Kamala-bhidā,* f., N. of a Grāma or village. — *Kamala-vatī,* f., N. of the wife of king Lalitāditya. — *Kamala-vadana, am,* n. a lotus face, i. e. a lovely face. — *Kamala-vardhana, as,* m., N. of a king of Kampana. — *Kamala-sambhava, as,* m. an epithet of Brahmā. — *Kamalākara* (°*la-āk*°), *as,* m. an assemblage of lotuses; a lake &c. where lotuses abound; N. of several authors. — *Kamalā-keśava, as,* m., N. of a sanctuary built by Kamalavatī. — *Kamalāksha* (°*la-ak*°), N. of a place. — *Kamalā-nandana, as,* m. son of Kamalā, an epithet of Miśra-dinakara. — *Kamalā-pati, is,* m., N. of a copyist. — *Kamalāyatāksha* (°*la-āyata-ak*°), *as, ā, am,* having large lotus eyes. — *Kamalāyudha* (°*la-āy*°), *as,* m., N. of a poet. — *Kamalālayā* (°*la-āl*°), f. an epithet of Lakshmī. — *Kamalāsana* or *kamalāsana-stha* (°*la-ās*°), *as,* m. an epithet of Brahmā. — *Kamalā-haṭṭa, as,* m., N. of a market-place founded by Kamalavatī. — 1. *kamalāhāsa* (°*la-āh*°), *as,* m. the shutting or opening of a lotus. — 2. *kamalāhāsa,* nom. (fr. the last) P. *-hāsati, -situm,* to smile like a lotus. — *Kamalekshaṇa* (°*la-ik*°), *as, ā, am,* lotus-eyed. — *Kamalottara* (°*la-ut*°), *am,* n. safflower, Carthamus Tinctorius.

Kamalaka, am, n., N. of a town.

Kamalinī, f. a number of lotus flowers or a lake or place abounding with them.

Kamā, f. loveliness, beauty, radiance.

Kamitṛi, tā, trī, tṛi, lustful, desirous, cupidinous.

Kamra, as, ā, am, desirous, cupidinous; beautiful, desirable.

कमक *kamaka, as,* m., N. of a man; (*ās*), m. pl. the descendants of this man.

कमठ *kamaṭha, as,* m. (said to be fr. 2. *kam*), a tortoise; a porcupine; a water-jar, especially one made of a hollow gourd or cocoa-nut, and used by ascetics; a bamboo; N. of a prince; of a Muni; and of a Daitya; (*ī*), f. a female tortoise, a small one. — *Kamaṭha-pati, is,* m. the king of tortoises. — *Kamaṭhāsura-vadha* (°*ṭha-as*°), *as,* m. 'the slaying of the Daitya Kamaṭha,' a section of the Gaṇeśa-Purāṇa.

कमण्डलु *kamaṇḍalu, us, u,* m. n. an earthen or wooden water-pot used by the ascetic and religious student; a vessel with a spout; the waved-leaf fig tree, Ficus Infectoria. — *Kamaṇḍalu-taru, us,* m. the tree Ficus Infectoria. — *Kamaṇḍalu-dhara, as,* m. an epithet of Śiva.

कमद्यू *kamadyū, ūs,* f. (fr. *kama* derived fr. 2. *kam* and *dyū?*), Ved., N. of a woman.

कमन्तक *kamantaka* and *kamandaka, as,* m., N. of two men; (*ās*), m. pl. the descendants of these men.

कमन्ध *kamandha, am,* n. water; (a various reading for *kabandha;* considered also as a compound of *kam* and *andha,* both being, according to native lexicographers, synonyms of water.)

कमल *kamala.* See under rt. 2. *kam* above.

कम्प् *kamp,* cl. 1. A. (ep. also P.) *kampate, kampati, ćakampe, kampishyate, akampishṭa, kampitum,* to tremble, shake: Caus. P. *kampayati, -yitum,* to cause to tremble, make tremble, shake; to pronounce in a tremulous manner, i. e. with a trill or shake: Desid. *ćikampishate:* Intens. *ćaṅkampyate, ćaṅkampti;* [cf. Gr. κάμπτω, πέμπω; Hib. *cabhóg,* 'hastening.']

Kampa, as, m. trembling, tremor, trembling motion, shaking; a tremulous or trilling pronunciation, a modification of the Svarita accent, which may take place if the Svarita syllable is followed by an Udātta syllable; N. of a man. — *Kampa-rāja, as,* m., N. of a man. — *Kampa-lakshman, ā,* m. air, wind. — *Kampānvita* (°*pa-an*°), *as, ā, am,* affected with trembling, agitated.

Kampana, as, ā, am, trembling, shaken, unsteady; causing to tremble, shaking; (*as*), m. a kind of weapon; the dewy season (November–December); N. of a prince; N. of a country near Kāśmīra; (*ā*), f., N. of a river; (*am*), n. trembling, quivering; quivering pronunciation, a modification of the Svarita accent (see *kampa*); shaking, swinging.

Kampanīya, as, ā, am, to be shaken, movable, vibratory.

Kampamāna, as, ā, am, trembling, shaking.

Kampayat, an, antī, at, shaking, causing to tremble.

Kampāka, as, m. (a wrong reading for *kampāṅka*), wind.

Kampita, as, ā, am, trembling, shaking; caused to tremble, shaken, swung; (*am*), n. trembling, a trembling, a tremor.

Kampin, ī, inī, i, trembling, quivering, shaking.

Kampila or *kampilya* or *kampilla* or *kampillaka* or *kampīla, as,* m., N. of a plant, Crinum Amaryllacee (?); commonly *kamalāguṇḍī;* [cf. *kāmpilla* and *śuṇḍā-roćanī.*]

Kampya, as, ā, am, to be shaken, to be made to tremble, to be moved away from one's place; to be pronounced in a quivering manner.

Kampra, as, ā, am, trembling, shaken, movable; agile, quick.

कम्ब् *kamb*, cl. 1. P. *kambati*, *-bitum*, to go, move; (a various reading for *karb.*)

कम्बर *kambara, as, ā, am*, variegated, spotted; (*as*), m. variegated colour; [cf. *karbura.*]

कम्बल *kambala, as, am*, m. n. (said to be fr. 2. *kam*), a woollen blanket or cloth; an upper cloth or garment of wool; (*as*), m. a dew-lap; a small worm or insect; a sort of deer; N. of a Nāga; N. of a man; (*am*), n. water; [cf. *kamala.*] — *Kambala-kāraka, as*, m. a woollen cloth manufacturer. — *Kambala-ćārāyaṇīya, ās*, m. pl. a nickname of a school of Cārāyaṇa. — *Kambala-dhāvaka, as*, m. one who cleans woollen clothes. — *Kambala-barhisha, as*, m., N. of a man. — *Kambala-vāhya, as*, m. or *kambala-vāhyaka, am*, n. a kind of carriage covered with a coarse blanket or woollen cloth and drawn by oxen. (The more correct spelling seems to be *kambali-vāhya* and *kambali-vāhyaka.*) — *Kambala-hāra, as*, m., N. of a man; (*ās*), m. pl. the descendants of this man.

Kambalaka, as, am, m. n. a woollen cloth, a garment of wool.

Kambalin, ī, inī, i, covered with a woollen cloth or blanket. — *Kambali-vāhyaka, am*, n. a carriage so covered and drawn by oxen.

Kambalīya, as, ā, am, fit for woollen blankets.

Kambalya, am, n. 100 Palas of wool (so much being necessary for making a woollen blanket).

कम्बालायिन् *kambālāyin, ī*, m. a sort of kite.

कम्बि *kambi, is*, f. a ladle or spoon; a shoot, a branch or joint of a bamboo.

कम्बु *kambu, us, u*, m. n. a conch, a shell; a bivalve shell; a bracelet, a ring made of shells; (*us*), m. an elephant; the neck; a tube-shaped bone; a vein or tubular vessel of the body; a sort of Curcuma. — *Kambu-kāshṭhā*, f. the tree Physalis Flexuosa. — *Kambu-grīva, as*, m., N. of a tortoise; (*ā*), f. a neck marked with three lines like a shell, and considered to be indicative of exalted fortune; a shell-shaped neck. — *Kambu-pushpī* and *kambu-mālinī*, f., N. of a plant. — *Kambv-ātāyin, ī*, m. the bird Falco Cheela.

Kambuka, as, m. a conch, a shell; a mean person; (*ā*), f. the tree Physalis Flexuosa; (*am*), n., N. of a town.

कम्बू *kambū, ūs, ūs, u* (said to be fr. 2. *kam*), stealing; (*ūs*), m. a thief, a plunderer; a bracelet.

कम्बूक *kambūka, as*, m., Ved. the husk of rice.

कम्बोज *kamboja, ās*, m. pl., N. of a country and its inhabitants; (*as*), m. the prince of this country; a shell; a kind of shell; a species of elephant; [cf. *kambu* and *kāmboja.*]

कम्भारी *kambhārī*, f. = *gambhārī*, the plant Gmelina Arborea.

कम्भु *kambhu, u*, n. the fragrant root of Andropogon Muricatus.

कय *kaya*, a Vedic form for 2. *ka*, occurring only in the genitive case with *ćid*; e. g. *kayasya ćid*, of every one; (*ni shū nama atimatim kayasya ćit*, bow well down the haughtiness of every one); [cf. Zend *kaya*; Armen. *ui.*]

कयस्था *kayasthā*, f. a medicinal plant, = *kākolī*; (probably a various reading for *vayasthā*: cf. *kāyasthā.*)

कया *kayā*, ind., Ved. (fr. 2. *ka* inst. fem.), in what manner?

कयाद् *kayād, t, t, t* (fr. *kaya* for *kāya?* and rt. *ad*), Ved. consuming the body; (a various reading for *kravyād.*)

कयाधू *kayādhū, ūs*, f., N. of the wife of Hiraṇyakaśipu.

कय्य *kayya, as*, m., N. of a prince, founder of a sanctuary (*śrīkayya-svāmin*) and of a Vihāra (*kayya-vihāra*) called after him.

कय्यक *kayyaka, as*, m., N. of a man.

कर 1. *kara, as, ā* or *ī, am* (fr. rt. *kṛi*, to do; for 2. *kara* see p. 205), who or what does or makes or causes; causing, doing, making (especially at the end of compounds, e. g. *bhayan-kara*, causing fear, frightful; *duḥkha-kara*, causing pain; *vriddhi-kara*, causing increase; *sampat-kara*, causing prosperity; *artha-karī vidyā*, a science productive of wealth &c.); (*as*), m. the hand ('the active one'); a measure, the breadth of twenty-four thumbs; an elephant's trunk; the act of doing, making, &c.; (at the end of several compounds with a passive sense, e. g. *īshat-kara* and *su-kara*, easy to be done; *dush-kara*, difficult to be done; *īshad-ādhyan-kara*, easy to be made rich); [cf. Lith. *kaire*, 'the left hand.'] — *Kara-kaṇṭaka, as*, m. a finger-nail ('thorn of the hand'). — *Kara-kamala, am*, n. the hand, especially of a lover or a mistress &c. (lit. 'hand-lotus;' similar compounds are *kara-padma, kara-pankaja, kara-pallava*, &c.). — *Kara-karṇa, as*, m., N. of a man. — *Kara-kalaśa, as*, m. the hand hollowed to receive water. — *Kara-kisalaya, as, am*, m. n. a hand which is like a branch; the finger ('shoot of the hand'). — *Kara-kudmala, am*, n. the finger ('bud of the hand'). — *Kara-kosha, as*, m. the hand hollowed to receive water; [cf. *kara-kalaśa.*] — 1. *kara-graha, as*, m. (for 2. see under 2. *kara*, p. 205), taking the hand (of the bride in the marriage ceremony; one part of the ceremony of marriage is the placing of the right hand of the bride, with the palm uppermost, in the right hand of the bridegroom), marriage. — 1. *kara-grahaṇa, am*, n. (for 2. see under 2. *kara*), taking the hand, marriage. — 1. *kara-grāhin, ī, iṇī, i*, taking the hand. — *Kara-gharshaṇa, as*, m. a churning-stick; (*am*), n. rubbing the hands together. — *Kara-gharshin, ī*, m. the churning-stick. — *Kara-ghāṭa, as*, m. a kind of poisonous tree. — *Kara-ććhada, as*, m. the teak tree, Trophis Aspera; (*ā*), f. a tree, commonly called *sindūra-pushpī-vriksha*. — *Kara-ja, as, ā, am*, produced in or from the hand; (*as*), m. a finger-nail; N. of a timber tree, = *karañja* or Pongamia Glabra; (*am*), n. a perfume, = *vyāghranakha*, resembling a nail in appearance. — *Karaja-vardhana, as*, m., N. of a prince. — *Karajākhya* (°*ja-ākh*°), *as*, m. a perfume, = *kara-ja*. — *Kara-jyoḍi, is*, m., N. of a tree, = *hasta-jyoḍi*. — *Kara-tala, as*, m. the palm of the hand; *karatalī-kṛi*, to take in the palm of the hands. — *Karatala-gata, as, ā, am*, being in the hand or in one's possession. — *Karatala-dhṛita, as, ā, am*, held in the hand. — *Karatala-stha, as, ā, am*, held in the hand, resting in the palm of the hand. — *Kara-tas*, ind. from the hand, out of the hand. — *Kara-tāla, am*, n. a musical instrument, a cymbal; (*ī*), f. beating time by clapping the hands. — *Karatālaka, am*, n. a musical instrument, a cymbal. — *Karatāla-dhvani, is*, m. the sound of cymbals. — *Kara-toyā*, f. the Karatoyā river in the north-east of Bengal, (at the wedding of Śiva and Pārvatī the water which had been poured into the hand of the former constituted, upon its being thrown on the ground, the source of this river.) — *Karatoyinī*, f., N. of a river, perhaps the same as the preceding (?). — 1. *kara-da, as, ā, am* (for 2. see under 2. *kara*), one who gives his hand &c. — *Kara-daksha, as, ā, am*, handy, dexterous, ready. — *Kara-druma, as*, m., N. of a tree, = *kāraskara*. — *Kara-dhṛita, as, ā, am*, held or supported by the hand. — *Kara-nihita, as, ā, am*, held in the hand. — *Karan-dhama, as*, m., N. of two princes. — *Kara-nyasta-kapolāntam*, ind. the end of the cheek held in the hand. — *Kara-pattra, am*, n. a saw; splashing water about while bathing, playing or gamboling in water; see *kara-pātra*. — *Karapattraka, am*, n. a saw. — *Karapattra-vat, ān*, m. the palmyra tree, Borassus Flabelliformis, (the leaves being compared to a saw.) — *Karapattrikā*, f. playing with water or in it, splashing it about &c.; [cf. *kara-pattra* and *kara-pātra.*] — *Kara-parṇa, as*, m., N. of two plants, commonly called *bhiṇḍā-vṛiksha* and *raktairaṇḍa*. — *Kara-pallava, as*, m. a finger, the hand; conversation with the fingers. — *Kara-pātra, am*, n. splashing water about while bathing, throwing water about in sport; the hand hollowed so as to hold anything; [cf. *kara-pattra* and *karapattrikā.*] — *Kara-pāla, as*, m. a sword, a scymitar ('protecting the hand'). — *Karapālikā*, f. a cudgel, a short club or wooden sword, a sword or one-edged knife. — *Kara-puṭa, as*, m. joining the palms of the hands in token of respect; the hands joined and hollowed to receive anything. — *Kara-pṛishṭha, am*, n. the back of the hand. — 1. *kara-praćeya, as, ā, am* (for 2. see under 2. *kara*), to be held, to be taken hold of by the hand. — 1. *kara-prada, as, ā, am*, giving the hand &c. — *Kara-prāpta, as, ā, am*, held in the hand; obtained, secured. — *Karabāla* and *karavāla, as*, m. (corruptions of *kara-pāla*), a sword, a scymitar; a finger-nail. — *Karabālikā*, f. a small sword; [cf. *karapālikā.*] — *Kara-bhañjaka, ās*, m. pl., N. of a people; (a various reading has *kara-bhañjika.*) — *Kara-bhājana, as*, m., N. of a Brāhman. — *Kara-bhū, ūs*, m. a finger-nail. — *Kara-bhūshaṇa, am*, n. a bracelet, an ornament worn round the wrist. — *Kara-marda, as, ī*, m. f. a small tree bearing an acid fruit, Carissa Carandas; (*am*), n. the fruit of this tree. — *Karamardaka, as*, m. the tree Carissa Carandas; see the preceding. — *Kara-mālā*, f. the hand used as a rosary, the joints of the fingers corresponding to the beads. — *Kara-mukta, am*, n. (scil. *astram*) a missile weapon thrown with the hand, a dart, a javelin, &c. — *Kara-ruddha, as, ā, am*, stopped by the hand, held tight or fast. — *Kara-ruha, as*, m. a finger-nail (growing from the hand). — *Kararddhi* (°*ra-riddhi*), *is*, f. a cymbal; a small musical instrument used for marking time, (a castanet?); clapping the hands together for that purpose; [cf. *kara-tāla.*] — *Kara-vāraka, as*, m. an epithet of Skanda. — *Karavālikā*, f. a small club; see *karabālikā*. — *Kara-vīra, as*, m. a fragrant Oleander, Nerium Odorum; a species of Soma; a sword or scymitar; a particular magical formulary or spell for recovering or attracting back a missile weapon of mystic properties after its discharge; a cemetery, a place for burning or interring the dead; N. of a Nāga; of a Daitya; of a mountain; of a town on the river Veṇvā, founded by Padma-varṇa; of a town on the river Dṛishadvatī, the residence of Candra-śekhara; (*ā*), f. red arsenic; (*ī*), f. a woman who has borne a son, a mother; a good cow; N. of Aditi, the mother of the gods; (*am*), n. the flower of Nerium Odorum. — *Karavīraka, as*, m. the poisonous root of the fragrant Oleander, a poison; the tree Terminalia Arjuna; a sword; N. of a Nāga. — *Karavīra-kanda-sañjña, as*, m. a species of onion or bulb, = *taila-kanda*. — *Karavīra-pura, am*, n., N. of a town founded by Padma-varṇa. — *Karavīra-bhujā*, f. Cajanus Indicus. — *Kara-vīrya, as*, m., N. of a physician. — *Kara-śākhā*, f. a finger. — *Kara-śīkara, as*, m. water expelled by an elephant's trunk. — *Kara-śūka, as*, m. a finger-nail. — *Kara-śotha, as*, m. œdematous swelling of the hands. — 1. *kara-sāda, as*, m. languor or weakness of the hands. — *Kara-sthālin, ī*, m. an epithet of Śiva, who uses his hands as a vessel for holding food. — *Kara-svana, as*, m. sound produced by beating the hands together. — *Karāgra* (°*ra-ag*°), *am*, n. the tip of an elephant's trunk. — *Karāgra-pallava, as*, m. finger. — *Karāghāta* (°*ra-āgh*°), *as*, m. a thumb, a blow with the hand. — *Karā-marda, as*, m. the tree Carissa Carandas; [cf. *kara-marda.*] — *Karāmbuka* or *karāmlaka, as*, m., N. of the same tree. — *Karāroṭa, as*, m. a finger-ring; (fr. *kara* and ?). — *Karārpita* (°*ra-ar*°), *as, ā, am*, taken in the hand. — *Karālamba* (°*ra-āl*°), *as*, m. the act of supporting with the hand, giving a helping hand;

(*as, ā, am*), stretching out one's hand to support or raise another. — *Karālambana, am,* n. extending the hand, taking by the hand, helping, sustaining. — *Karotpala* (°*ra-ut*°), *am,* n. a lotus-hand. — *Karodaka* (°*ra-ud*°), *am,* n. water held in or poured into the hand.

1. *karaka, as, am,* m. n. the water-pot of the student or ascetic; the shell of the cocoa-nut hollowed to form a vessel; shell of the cocoa-nut in general; (*as*), m. hand; a species of bird; N. of several plants, the pomegranate tree, = *dāḍima;* Pongamia Glabra; Butea Frondosa; Bauhinia Variegata; Mimusops Elengi; Capparis Aphylla; (*ās*), m. pl., N. of a people. — *Karaka-pātrikā,* f. a leather vessel for holding water. — *Karakāmbhas* (°*ka-am*°), *ās,* m. the cocoa-nut tree, Cocos Nucifera.

Karaṇa, as, ī, am, doing, making, effecting, causing (especially at the end of compounds; cf. *anta-karaṇa, andhan-karaṇa, ushṇan-karaṇa,* &c.); Ved. clever, skilled; (*as*), m., Ved. an assistant; a man of a mixed class, the son of a Śūdra woman by a Vaiśya, or (according to some) of an outcast Kshatriya (the occupation of this class is writing, accounts, &c.); a writer, a scribe; (*am*), n. making, doing, producing, effecting, accomplishing (very often as last member of a compound, e. g. *mushṭi-karaṇa,* committing theft; *virūpa-karaṇa,* producing deformity); an action, especially a religious action; business, occupation (as trade &c.); the special business of any tribe or caste; plastering, spreading anything with the hand; the usage or practice of the writer-caste; an act, a deed; an instrument or means of action, an expedient; an organ, an organ of sense or of speech; (in gram.) the immediate cause of an action, the idea expressed by the instrumental case, instrumentality; the body; (in law) an instrument, document, a bond; a cause, motive; the posture of an ascetic; posture in sexual intercourse, copulation; pronunciation, articulation; (in gram.) the term used in designating a sound or word when referring to it as an independent part of speech or as separated from its context, (*karaṇa* may be used in this way, like *kāra,* e. g. *iti-karaṇa,* the word *iti*); rhythm, time; dramatic action (?), singing (?); an astrological division of the day, (these Karaṇas are eleven, viz. *vava, vālava, kaulava, taitila, gara, vaṇija, vishṭi, śakuni, ćatushpada, kintughna,* and *nāga,* two being equal to a lunar day, or the time during which the moon's motion amounts to 6°; the first seven are called *a-dhruvāṇi* or movable, and fill, when eight times repeated, the space from the second half of the first day in the moon's increase to the first half of the fourteenth day in its wane; the four others are *dhruvāṇi* or fixed, and occupy the four half-days from the second half of the fourteenth day in the wane of the moon to the first half of the first day in its increase); title of a treatise of Varāha-mihira on the motions of the planets; a field; grain (?); the mind or heart (?); (*ī*), f. a woman of a mixed caste; a surd or irrational number, a surd root in arithmetic. — *Karaṇa-kutūhala, am,* n. title of a work on practical astronomy by Bhāskara. — *Karaṇa-grāma, as,* m. the senses collectively. — *Karaṇa-trāṇa, am,* n. the head ('protecting the organs of sense'). — *Karaṇa-tva, am,* n. instrumentality, mediate agency. — *Karaṇa-niyama, as,* m. suppression or restraint of the organs of sense. — *Karaṇa-vinyaya, as,* m. manner of pronunciation. — *Karaṇa-sāra, as,* m. title of a work on practical astronomy by Bhāskara. — *Karaṇa-sthāna-bheda, as,* m. difference of articulation or organ. — *Karaṇādhikāra* (°*ṇa-adh*°), *as,* m. a section on articulation.

Karaṇi, is, f. doing, making, effecting (only occurring with *a* privative, e. g. *a-karaṇi,* q. v.).

Karaṇīya, as, ā, am, to be done or made; feasible, to be accomplished; to be caused or effected.

Karabha, as, m. the metacarpus, the hand from the wrist to the root of the fingers; the trunk of an elephant; a young elephant; a camel; a young camel or any young animal; a camel three years old; a perfume (= *nakha,* commonly called *nakhi*); an epithet of Danta-vakra, prince of the Karūshas; (*ī*), f. a she-camel; the plant Tragia Involucrata; [cf. Gr. κάρπος.] — *Karabha-kāṇḍikā,* f., N. of a plant; [cf. *ushṭra-kāṇḍī.*] — *Karabha-priyā,* f. a plant, a sort of Hedysarum. — *Karabha-vallabha, as,* m. the tree Feronia Elephantum. — *Karabhādanī* (°*bha-adana*), f., N. of a plant; [cf. *karabha-priyā.*] — *Karabhorū* (°*bha-ūru*), *ūs,* f. a woman whose thighs resemble the trunk of an elephant; see *ūru.*

Karabhaka, as, m., N. of a messenger.

Karabhin, ī, m. an elephant ('having a trunk').

Karas, as, n., Ved. an action, a deed.

Karasna, as, m., Ved. the arm, the fore part of the arm; a finger-nail.

Kari, is, is, i, causing, accomplishing (at the end of a compound, e. g. *śakṛit-kari,* q. v.).

Karikā, f. a wound caused by a finger-nail.

Karin, ī, m. 'having a trunk,' an elephant; (*ṇī*), f. a female elephant. — *Kari-kaṇā-valli,* f. a species of pepper, Piper Chaba. — *Kari-kumbha, as,* m. the frontal globe of an elephant. — *Kari-kusumbha, as,* m. a fragrant powder prepared from the flowers of Nāga-kesara. — *Kari-kusumbhaka, as,* m. the same. — *Kari-garjita, am,* n. the roaring of elephants. — *Kari-ćarman, a,* n. an elephant's hide. — *Kari-ja, as,* m. a young elephant. — *Kariṇī-sahāya, as,* m. the mate of the female elephant. — *Kari-danta, as,* m. an elephant's tusk; ivory. — *Kari-dāraka, as,* m. a lion. — *Kari-nāsikā,* f. a musical instrument. — *Kari-pattra, am,* n., N. of a plant; see *tālīśa-pattra.* — *Kari-patha, as,* m. the way or habits of an elephant. — *Kari-pippalī,* f. a plant bearing a pungent fruit, Pothos Officinalis. — *Kari-pota, as,* m. a young elephant, one under ten years old. — *Kari-bandha, as,* m. the post to which an elephant is tied. — *Kari-makara, as,* m. a fabulous monster. — *Kari-māćala, as,* m. a lion, this animal being considered as the natural enemy and destroyer of the elephant; [cf. *gaja-māćala.*] — *Kari-mukha, as,* m. an epithet of Gaṇeśa, this deity having an elephant's trunk on his face. — *Kari-yādas,* n. a water-elephant, a hippopotamos. — *Kari-vara, as,* m. an excellent elephant. — *Kari-vaijayantī,* f. a flag carried by an elephant. — *Kari-śāvaka, as,* m. a young elephant under five years old, (according to some) also until ten years. — *Kari-skandha, as,* m. a troop of elephants. — *Karīndra* (°*ri-in*°), *as,* m. a large elephant, a war or state elephant; Indra's elephant (?).

कर 2. *kara, as,* m. (fr. rt. 1. *kṛī,* to scatter; for 1. *kara* see p. 204), a ray of light, a sun-beam, a moon-beam; hail; royal revenue, toll, tax, import, tribute. — 2. *kara-graha, as,* m. levying or gathering taxes, a tax-gatherer. — 2. *kara-grahaṇa, am,* n. levying or gathering taxes. — 2. *kara-grāhin, ī, iṇī, i,* levying a tax, a tax-collector. — *Kara-jāla, am,* n. a pencil of rays, a stream of light. — 2. *kara-da, as, ā, am,* paying taxes, subject to tax or duty, tributary. — *Karadī-kṛi,* cl. 8. P. A. *-karoti, -kurute, -kartum,* to render tributary. — *Karadī-kṛita, as, ā, am,* made tributary, subjugated. — *Kara-paṇya, am,* n. a commodity given as tribute. — 2. *kara-praćeya, as, ā, am,* to be collected by taxes. — 2. *kara-prada, as, ā, am,* paying taxes, subject to tax or duty, tributary. — *Kara-rudh, t, t, t,* ray-obstructing. — 2. *kara-sāda, as,* m. the fading away of rays. — *Karotkara* (°*ra-ut*°), *as,* m. a bundle of rays; a heavy tax.

2. *karaka, as, ā, am,* m. f. n. (according to some only m. and f.), hail; a thunderstone (?); (*as*), m. toll, tax, tribute (?). — 1. *karakāsāra* (°*ka-ās*°), *as,* m. a shower of hail. — 2. *karakāsāra,* nom. P. *karakāsārati,* to pour or shower down like hail.

Karī-kṛi, cl. 8. P. A. *-karoti, -kurute, -kartum,* to offer as a tribute.

कर 3. *kara, as, ā, am* (fr. rt. 2. *kṛī,* to praise), Ved. devoted, pious.

करकायु *karakāyu, us,* m., N. of a son of Dhṛita-rāshṭra. See *kanakāyu.*

करङ्क *karaṅka, as,* m. the skull, the head; a cocoa-nut hollowed to form a cup or vessel, a water-pot made from a cocoa-nut, [cf. 1. *karaka*]; a kind of sugar-cane; any bone of the body. — *Karaṅka-śāli, is,* m. a sort of sugar-cane.

करङ्गण *karaṅgaṇa, am,* n. a market or fair; (a various reading for *karāṅgaṇa.*)

करञ्ज *karañja, as,* m. the tree Pongamia Glabra, used medicinally; N. of an enemy of Indra, slain by this god. — *Karañja-phalaka, as,* m. Feronia Elephantum; see *kapittha.* — *Karañja-ha, as, ā, am,* Ved. pernicious to Karañja.

Karañjaka, as, m., N. of the tree Pongamia Glabra; also of Verbesina Scandens.

करट *karaṭa, as,* m. an elephant's cheek; a crow; a man of a low or degraded profession; a bad Brāhman; an atheist, an unbeliever, an impugner of the doctrines of the Vedas; a musical instrument (castanets?); the plant Carthamus Tinctorius; the first Srāddha or ceremony performed in honour of a deceased relative; (*ās*), m. pl., N. of a people; also of a family; (*ā*), f. an elephant's cheek; a cow difficult to be milked.

Karaṭaka, as, m. a crow; N. of a jackal in the Hitopadeśa.

Karaṭin, ī, m. an elephant; *karaṭi-kauluka,* a treatise on the elephant and his diseases.

करटु *karaṭu, us,* m. the numidian crane; [cf. *kareṭavyā, kareṭu, karkaṭa,* &c.]

करण *karaṇa.* See under 1. *kara.*

करणीसुता *karaṇīsutā,* f. an adopted daughter.

करण्ड *karaṇḍa, as,* m. (said to be fr. rt. 1. *kṛī*), a basket or covered box of bamboo wicker-work; a bee-hive, a honey-comb; a sword; a sort of duck; an aquatic weed called Vallisneria; (*ī*), f. a basket for flowers; [Lat. *corbis?*]. — *Karaṇḍa-vyūha, as,* m. title of a Buddhist work.

Karaṇḍaka, as, m. a basket. — *Karaṇḍaka-nivāpa, as,* m., N. of a region near Rājagṛiha.

Karaṇḍin, ī, m. a fish; (so called because caught in a basket?).

करथ *karatha, as,* m., N. of a physician.

करफु *karaphu,* a particular high number; [cf. *kalahu.*]

करभ *karabha.* See under 1. *kara.*

करभीर *karabhīra, as,* m. a lion.

करमट्ट *karamaṭṭa, as,* m. the betel-nut tree. See *guvākā.*

करमरिन् *karamarin, ī,* m. a prisoner, a captive; [cf. *kārā.*]

करमाल *karamāla, as,* m. smoke; (probably a corruption of *khatamāla.*)

करम्ब *karamba, as, ā, am* (said to be fr. 1. *kṛī*), mixed, intermingled; set, inlaid; (*as*), m. flour or meal mixed with curds. See *karambha.*

Karambita, as, ā, am, intermingled, mixed, blended, &c.; pounded, reduced to grains or dust; set, inlaid.

करम्भ *karambha, as,* m. groats or coarsely ground oats &c.; a dish of parched grain; a cake, flour or meal mixed with curds, a kind of gruel, generally offered to Pūshan (as having no teeth to masticate hard food); a mixture, a mixed odour; N. of a species of poisonous plant; N. of a son of Śakuni and father of Devarāta; N. of a brother of Rambha; (*ā*), f. the plant Asparagus Racemosus; another plant, = *priyangu-vṛiksha;* N. of a daughter of a king of Kaliṅga and wife of Akrodhana. — *Karambhād* (°*bha-ad*), *t, t, t,* Ved. eating groats or gruel, epithet of Pūshan.

Karambhaka, as, m., N. of a man; (*am*), n. groats, coarsely ground oats &c.; a cake, flour or meal mixed with curd.

Karambhi, is, m., N. of a son of Śakuni and father of Devarāta.

Karambhin, ī, iṇī, i, Ved. having groats.

करवी *karavī,* f. the leaf of the plant Asa Fœtida; [cf. *karvarī, kavarī, kāvarī.*]

करवीक *karavīka, as,* m., N. of a mountain; [cf. *kara-vīra.*]

करस् *karas.* See under 1. *kara.*

करस्न *karasna.* See under 1. *kara.*

करहञ्चा *karahañćā,* f., N. of a metre of four lines, each consisting of seven syllables.

करहाट *karahāṭa, as,* m. the tree Vangueria Spinosa; the fibrous root of a lotus; N. of a region.

Karahāṭaka, as, m. the tree Vangueria Spinosa; N. of an heretical prince.

कराङ्गण *karāṅgaṇa, as,* m. a market or fair visited by many men; [cf. *aṅgaṇa.*]

करायिका *karāyikā,* f. a bird, a small kind of crane.

कराल *karāla, as, ā, am,* opening wide, cleaving asunder, gaping (as a wound); having formidable projecting teeth, formidable, dreadful, terrible (especially as an epithet of the Rākshasas, of Śiva, of Kāla, of Vishṇu, and of a certain Devagandharva); great, large, high, lofty; spacious, wide; deformed; (*as*), m. a certain species of animal; resin, pitch, or a mixture of oil and the resin of the tree Shorea Robusta; N. of a region; (*ā*), f. the plant Hemidesmus Indicus; an epithet of Durgā; N. of a certain woman; (*ī*), f. one of the seven tongues and nine Samidhs of Agni; (*am*), n. a kind of Ocimum. — *Karāla-kara, as, ā, am,* having a powerful arm or hand; having a large trunk, as an elephant. — *Karāla-keśara, as,* m., N. of a lion in the Pañćatantra. — *Karāla-tripuṭā,* f. a species of corn. — *Karāla-daṇshṭra, as, ā, am,* having terrific teeth. — *Karāla-loćana, as, ā, am,* terrific. — *Karāla-vadanā,* f. an epithet of Durgā. — *Karālānana* (°*la-ān*°), *as, ā, am,* terrific.

Karālaka, am, n. a kind of Ocimum.

Karālika, as, m. a tree; a sword; (*ā*), f. an epithet of Durgā.

Karālita, as, ā, am, rendered formidable; afraid of, alarmed by or at; magnified.

करि *kari,* &c. See under 1. *kara.*

करिभ *karibha, as,* m. the tree Ficus Religiosa.

करिर *karira, as, am,* m. n. the shoot of a bamboo. See *karīra.*

करिष्ठ *karishṭha, as, ā, am* (superlative fr. 1. *kara*), doing most, doing very much.

Karishṇu, used in comp. See *alan-karishṇu* and *nir-ākarishṇu.*

Karīshya, as, ā, am (?), Ved. to be done (?).

Karishyat, an, atī or *antī, at,* willing to do, about to do.

Karishyamāṇa, as, ā, am, about to do, going to do.

Karīyas, ān, asī, as (comparative fr. 1. *kara*), doing more; one who does much.

करीकृ *karī-kṛi.* See under 2. *kara.*

करीति *karīti, ayas,* m. pl., N. of a people.

करीर *karīra, as, am,* m. n. (said to be fr. rt. 1. *kṛī*), the shoot of a bamboo; (*as*), m. a water-jar; a thorny plant, described as growing in deserts and fed upon by camels, Capparisaphylla; (*am*), n. the fruit of this plant; (*ā* or *ī*), f. the root of an elephant's tusk; a cricket, a small grasshopper. — *Karīra-kuṇa, as,* m. the fruit season of Capparisaphylla. — *Karīra-prastha, as,* m., N. of a town; (a various reading has *karīri-prastha.*)

Karīrikā, f. the root of an elephant's tusk.

करीरक *karīraka, am,* n. fight, battle.

करीलदेश *karīla-deśa, as,* m., N. of a region.

करीष *karīsha, as, am,* m. n. (fr. 1. *kṛī*), rubbish, refuse, dung; dry cow-dung; N. of a mountain; [cf. *ākhu-karīsha.*] — *Karīsha-gandhi, is,* m., N. of a man. — *Karīshan-kasha, as, ā, am,* sweeping away dung; (*ā*), f. a strong wind, a gale. — *Karīshāgni* (°*sha-ag*°), *is,* m. a fire of dry cow-dung; (this substance is very generally used as fuel in Hindūstan.)

Karīshaka, ās, m. pl., N. of a people.

Karīshin, ī, iṇī, i, abounding in dung; (*iṇī*), f. a region abounding in cow-dung; N. of a river.

करुण *karuṇa, as, ā, am* (said to be fr. rt. 1. *kṛī,* but in some of its meanings fr. 1. *kṛi*), mournful, miserable, lamenting; (*am*), ind. mournfully, wofully, pitifully, in distress; (*as*), m. that which causes pity, sorrow, affliction, tenderness, pity, compassion; one of the nine Rasas or sentiments of a poem, the pathetic sentiment; a fruit tree, the pamplemouse, Citrus Decumana; N. of a Buddha; a Jaina saint; N. of an Asura; (*ā*), f. pity, compassion; (*ī*), f., N. of a plant, also called *grīshma-pushpī, ćāriṇī,* &c.; (*am*), n., Ved. an action, a holy work. — *Karuṇa-dhvani, is,* m. a cry of distress. — *Karuṇa-puṇḍarīka, am,* n. title of a Buddhist work. — *Karuṇa-mallī,* f. the plant Jasminum Sambac; also read *karuṇā-mallī.* — *Karuṇa-vedi-tva, am,* n. compassion, sympathy. — *Karuṇa-vedin, ī, inī, i,* knowing affliction or distress, sympathising, pitiful. — *Karuṇākara* (°*ṇa-āk*°), *as,* m. the father of Padmanābha. — *Karuṇātmaka* (°*ṇa-āt*°), *as, ā, am,* compassionate, tender-hearted. — *Karuṇātman* (°*ṇa-āt*°), *ā, ā, a,* kind. — *Karuṇā-para, as, ā, am,* compassionate, tender. — *Karuṇā-maya, as, ī, am,* gentle, compassionate. — *Karuṇārambha* (°*ṇa-ār*°), *as, ā, am,* engaging in deplorable actions. — *Karuṇārdra* (°*ṇa-ār*°), *as, ā, am,* tender-hearted, soft, sensitive. — *Karuṇārdhita* (°*ṇa-ar*°), *as, ā, am,* kind. — *Karuṇā-vat, ān, atī, at,* being in a pitiful state, pitiable. — *Karuṇā-vipralambha, as,* m. grief of separation with the uncertainty of meeting again, fears occurring in absence. — *Karuṇā-vṛitti, is, is, i,* disposed to pity. — *Karuṇā-veditā,* f. charitableness, kindliness, sympathy.

Karuṇāya, nom. P. A. -*ṇāyati, -te, -yitum,* to be in a pitiful condition.

Karuṇin, ī, inī, i, being in a pitiful condition, pitiable.

करुत्थाम *karutthāma, as,* m., N. of a prince, a son of Dushyanta and father of Ākrīḍa; [cf. *aśvatthāman.*]

करुन्धक *karundhaka, as,* m., N. of a son of Sūra and brother of Vasu-deva.

करुम *karuma, as, ā, am,* Ved. an epithet of certain spectral or ghost-like appearances.

करूकर *karūkara, am,* n., Ved. the joint of the neck and the chine.

करूळतिन् *karūḷatin, ī, inī, i,* Ved. one whose teeth are decayed and broken; [cf. the next.]

करूष *karūsha, ās,* m. pl., N. of a people descended from a son of Manu Vaivasvata, (a prince of this people is named Danta-vakra.)

Karūshaka, as, m., N. of a son of Manu Vaivasvata; (*am*), n., N. of a species of fruit.

करेट *kareṭa, as,* m. a finger-nail.

करेटव्या *kareṭavyā,* f. or *kareṭu, us,* m. the numidian crane; [cf. *karaṭu, karkaṭa,* &c.]

करेणु *kareṇu, us,* m. f. (said to be fr. rt. 1. *kṛi;* cf. 1. *kara*), a male or female elephant, generally used for the latter; according to some also *kareṇū;* (*us*), m. the tree Pterospermum Acerifolium; (*us*), f., N. of a plant used as a drug and supposed to grow in Kāśmīra. — *Kareṇu-pāla, as,* m. the groom or keeper of a female elephant; N. of a man; [cf. *kāreṇupāli.*] — *Kareṇu-bhū, ūs,* m. an epithet of Pālakāpya. — *Kareṇu-matī,* f., N. of the wife of Nakula, daughter of a king of Ćedi. — *Kareṇu-varya, as,* m. a large or powerful elephant. — *Kareṇu-suta, as,* m. an epithet of Pālakāpya.

Kareṇuka, am, n. the poisonous fruit of the plant Kareṇu.

Kareṇū, ūs, m. f. a male or female elephant.

करेनर *karenara, as,* m. benzoin or storax. See *karevara.*

करेन्दुक *karenduka, as,* m. a species of grass, = *bhū-tṛiṇa.*

करेवर *karevara, as,* m. benzoin or storax.

करोट *karoṭa, as,* m. f. a basin, a cup; the bones of the head, the skull.

Karoṭaka, as, m., N. of a Nāga.

Karoṭi, is, or *karoṭī,* f. a basin, a cup; the skull.

करोत्कर *karotkara, karotpala,* &c. See under 1. and 2. *kara.*

कर्क् *kark,* to laugh; a Sautra root, or one occurring in grammatical Sūtras but not in the Dhātu-pāṭha.

कर्क *karka, as, ā, am* (said to be fr. 1. *kṛi*), white; good; excellent; (*as*), m. a white horse; a crab; the sign Cancer; a water-jar; fire; a mirror; N. of various plants, = *karkaṭa, karketana,* and *karketila;* beauty; N. of a commentator on Kātyāyana's Srauta-sūtras; (*ī*), f., Ved. a white cow (?). — *Karka-khaṇḍa, ās,* m. pl., N. of a people. — *Karka-ćirbhiṭī* (?), f. a small cucumber. — *Karka-phala, am,* n., N. of a plant. — *Karka-sāra, am,* n. flour or meal mixed with curds. — *Karkī-prastha, as,* m., N. of a town.

Karkaṭa, as, m. a crab; the sign Cancer; a kind of bird, the numidian crane, Lanius Excubitor; N. of a plant with poisonous tubers, the fibrous root of a lotus; the curved end of the beam of a balance (to which the strings supporting the scale are attached); a kind of coitus; the radius of a circle; compass, circuit; (*ā*), f. the plant Momordica Mixta; (*ī*), f. a female crab; a snake (?); a kind of cucumber, Cucumis Utilissimus; the fruit of the plant Bombax Heptaphyllum; the curved end of the beam of a balance &c.; a small water-jar; [cf. *karkara, karkaśa:* cf. also Gr. καρκῖνος; Lat. *cancer.*] — *Karkaṭa-pura, am,* n., N. of a town. — *Karkaṭa-śṛiṅga, am,* n. the claw of a crab. — *Karkaṭa-śṛiṅgikā* or *karkaṭa-śṛiṅgī,* f. a plant, the fruit of which is compared to the claw or feelers of a crab, the horn of a goat &c., see *aja-śṛiṅgī;* other names of this plant are *kāma-nāśinī, kaulīrā, kuliṅgī,* &c. — *Karkaṭākśha* (°*ṭa-ak*°), *as,* m. the plant Cucumis Utilissimus. — *Karkaṭākhyā* (°*ṭa-ākh*°), f. the plant Karkaṭa-śṛiṅgī. — *Karkaṭāṅgā* (°*ṭa-aṅ*°), f. the same plant. — *Karkaṭāsthi* (°*ṭa-as*°), n. the shell or crust of a crab. — *Karkaṭāhva* (°*ṭa-āh*°), *as,* m. the plant Ægle Marmelos; (*ā*), f. the plant Karkaṭa-śṛiṅgī. — *Karkaṭeśa* (°*ṭa-īśa*), *as,* m., N. of a sanctuary.

Karkaṭaka, as, m. a crab; the sign Cancer; the plant Momordica Mixta (?); a kind of sugar-cane; a hook shaped like the claw of a crab; N. of a Nāga; (*ī*), f. a female crab; (*am*), n. a poisonous root; a particular fracture of the bones. — *Karkaṭaka-rajju, us,* m. a rope with a hook attached to it, shaped like the claw of a crab. — *Karkaṭakāsthi* (°*ka-as*°), n. the shell or crust of a crab.

Karkaṭi, is, f. a sort of cucumber, Cucumis Utilissimus.

Karkaṭikā, f., N. of a plant, a kind of gourd; a kernel.

Karkaṭinī, f. the plant Curcuma Xanthorrhiza.

Karkaṭu, us, m. the numidian crane; [cf. *karaṭu,* &c.]

कर्कन्धु *karkandhu, us, ūs,* m. f. (considered

by some as an irregular compound of *karka* and *andhu*), the jujube tree, Zizyphus Jujuba; a species of this tree with a larger fruit; (*u*), n. the fruit of this tree, or the uneatable fruits of a wild species; (*ūs*), f. the berry of this tree; (*us*), m., N. of a man. — *Karkandhu-kuṇa, am*, n. the fruit season of the Karkandhu tree. — *Karkandhu-prastha, as*, m., N. of a town. — *Karkandhu-matī*, f., N. of a woman (?). — *Karkandhu-rohita, as, ā, am*, red like the berries of the jujube tree.

कर्कफल *karka-phala*. See under *karka*.

कर्कर *karkara, as, ā, am*, hard, firm; (*as*), m. a bone; a hammer; a mirror [cf. *karphara*]; a strap of leather (?); N. of a Nāga; (*am*), n. stone, limestone, especially the nodule found in Bengal under the name of Kan-kar; [cf. *karkaṭa, karkaśa*.] — *Karkarāksha* (°*ra-ak*°), *as*, m. a wagtail. — *Karkarāṅga* (°*ra-aṅ*°), *as*, m. a kind of bird, a gallinule (?). — *Karkarāndhuka* (°*ra-an*°), *as*, m. a blind well, one of which the mouth is overgrown with grass &c. so as to be hidden; also read *karkarāndhaka*; see *andha-kūpa*.

कर्कराटु *karkarāṭu, us*, m. a glance, a side-look.

कर्कराटुक *karkarāṭuka, as*, m. the numidian crane.

Karkareṭu, us, m. = the preceding; [cf. *karaṭu*, &c.]

कर्कराल *karkarāla, as, am*, m. n. a curl, a ringlet.

कर्करि *karkari, is* or *ī*, f., Ved. a kind of musical instrument, a lute; (*ī*), f. a water-jar.

Karkarikā, f. a small water-jar.

कर्करेट *karkareṭa, am*, n. the hand curved as a claw for the purpose of grasping anything.

कर्करेटु *karkareṭu*. See *karkarāṭuka*.

कर्कश *karkaśa, as, ā, am*, hard, harsh, rough (opposed to *komala, ślakshṇa*); intangible; violent, cruel; unfeeling, unmerciful; harsh, unkind, miserly; (*as*), m. a sword, a scymitar; N. of several plants, = *kāmpilla* = *gundārocanī* (commonly called Sunda Rochani); a kind of cassia, Cassia or Senna Esculenta; a species of sugar-cane; (*ā*), f. a thorny plant, Tragia Involucrata; (*ī*), f. the wild jujube; [cf. *karkaṭa, karkara*.] — *Karkaśa-ćchada, as*, m. the plants Trophis Aspera and Trichosanthes Dioeca; (*ā*), f. the plant Luffa Acutangula. — *Karkaśa-tva, am*, n. hardness, harshness, rough manners. — *Karkaśa-dala, as*, m. the plant Trichosanthes Dioeca; (*ā*), f. another plant. — *Karkaśa-vākya, am*, n. harsh or contumelious speech.

Karkaśikā, f. wild jujube.

कर्कसार *karka-sāra*. See under *karka*.

कर्कारु *karkāru, us, u*, m. n. a kind of gourd, Beninkasa Cerifera.

Karkāruka, as, m. the plant Convolvulus Paniculatus.

कर्कि *karki, is*, m. the sign of the zodiac, Cancer; also read *karkin, ī*, m.

कर्किप्रस्थ *karki-prastha*. See under *karka*.

कर्केतन *karketana* or *karketara, as*, m. (?) a kind of gem or precious stone.

कर्कोट *karkoṭa, as*, m. one of the principal serpents or Nāgas of Pātāla; (*ūs*), m. pl., N. of a people; (*am*), n. a poisonous fruit.

Karkoṭaka, as, m. several plants, Momordica Mixta; Ægle Marmelos; the sugar-cane; N. of a Nāga or serpent; (*ās*), m. pl., N. of a barbarous tribe of low origin; (*ī*), f., N. of a plant; (*kā*), f. the plant Momordica Mixta. — *Karkoṭaka-visha, am*, n. the poison of Karkoṭaka.

कर्चूर *karćūra, as*, m., N. of a plant, a kind of Curcuma; (*am*), n. gold; an orpiment; [cf. *karbura* and *karbūra*.]

Karćūraka, as, m. the plant Curcuma Zerumbet; also read *karbūraka*.

कर्ज् *karj*, cl. 1. P. *karjati, -jitum*, to pain or make uneasy.

कर्ण् *karṇ*, cl. 10. P. *karṇayati, -yitum*, to pierce, bore. See *ā-karṇ*.

कर्ण *karṇa, as*, m. (said to be fr. rt. 1. *kṛi*), the ear, the handle or ear of a vessel; the helm or rudder of a ship; the plants Cassia Fistula and Calotropis Gigantea; (in prosody) a spondee, a foot of two long syllables; (in geometry) the hypothenuse of a triangle or the diagonal of a tetragon; N. of a renowned hero in the Mahā-bhārata, king of Aṅga and elder brother by the mother's side of the Pāṇḍu princes, being the son of the god Sūrya by Pṛithā or Kuntī, before her marriage with Pāṇḍu. (Afraid of the censure of her relatives, Kuntī deserted the child and exposed it in the river, where it was found by a charioteer named Adhi-ratha and nurtured by his wife Rādhā; hence *Karṇa* is sometimes called Sūta-putra or Sūta-ja, sometimes Rādheya, though named by his foster-parents Vasu-sheṇa); N. of a son of Viśvajit; (with Buddhists) a son of Mahā-sammata and king in Potāla; N. of a king, father of Viśoka-deva; (*as, ā, am*), Ved. eared, furnished with long ears; furnished with chaff (as grain). *Karṇe*, (in theatrical language) into the ear, in a low voice, aside; *api karṇe*, Ved. behind the ear or back, from behind, after [cf. *api-karṇa*]; *karṇam dā*, to give ear to, listen to; *karṇam ā-gam*, to come to one's ears, become known to. — *Karṇa-kaṇḍu, us* or *ū, ūs*, m. f. painful itching of the ear. — *Karṇa-kīṭā*, f. an insect or worm with many feet and of a reddish colour, Julus Cornifex; a small centipede; according to some *karṇa-kīṭī*. — *Karṇa-kubja, am*, n., N. of an imaginary town. — *Karṇa-kshveḍa, as*, m. an affection of the ear, a roaring or constant noise in it. — *Karṇa-kharika, as*, m., N. of a Vaiśya. — *Karṇa-ga, as, ā, am*, touching the ear, hanging on it, next to the ear, extending to the ear. — *Karṇa-gūtha, am*, n. ear-wax; (*as*), m. or *karṇa-gūthaka, as*, m. hardening of the wax of the ear. — *Karṇa-grihīta, as, ā, am*, seized by the ear. — *Karṇa-grihya*, ind. seizing by the ear. — *Karṇa-gocara, as, ā, am*, perceptible to the ear, audible. — *Karṇa-grāha, as*, m. a helmsman. — *Karṇa-grāha-vat, ān, atī, at*, furnished with a helmsman (as a ship). — *Karṇa-ćchidra, am*, n. the outer auditory passage; [cf. *karṇa-puṭa, karṇa-randhra*, &c.] — *Karṇa-japa, as*, m. 'ear-whisperer,' an informer. — *Karṇa-jalūkā*, f. an insect, Julus; a small centipede; [cf. *karṇa-kīṭā*.] — *Karṇa-jalaukā*, f. or *karṇa-jalaukas, ās*, f. the same. — *Karṇa-jāpa* or *karṇa-japa, as*, m. whispering in the ear, tale-bearing, calumniating. — *Karṇa-jāha, am*, n. the root of the ear. — *Karṇa-jit, t*, m. 'the conqueror of Karṇa,' an epithet of Arjuna; (Karṇa having taken the part of the Kurus, was killed by Arjuna in one of the great battles between them and the Pāṇḍus.) — *Karṇa-tas*, ind. away from the ear. — *Karṇa-tāla, as*, m. the flapping of an elephant's ears. — *Karṇa-darpaṇa, as*, m. an ear-ring, an ornament for the ear. — *Karṇa-dundubhi, is*, f. a kind of worm (making a noise in the ear like a drum); see *karṇa-kīṭā*. — *Karṇa-deva, as*, m., N. of a king. — *Karṇa-dhāra, as*, m. a helmsman, a pilot. — *Karṇadhāra-tā*, f. the office of an helmsman. — *Karṇa-dhāriṇī*, f. a female elephant. — *Karṇa-nāda, as*, m. ringing in the ear. — *Karṇa-nāsā*, f. the ears and the nose. — *Karṇandu, us*, f. a woman's ear-ring; see *karṇāndu*. — *Karṇa-pa, as*, m., N. of a man. — *Karṇa-pattraka, as*, m. the tragus, a part of the external ear. — *Karṇa-patha, as*, m. the compass or range of hearing; *karṇapatham ā-yā* or *upe* (*upa-i*), to come within the range of the ear, to be heard. — *Karṇa-para, as*, m. an ornament for the ear. — *Karṇa-paramparā*, f. going from one ear to another. — *Karṇa-parākrama, as*, m. title of a work. — *Karṇa-parvan, a*, n. 'the Karṇa section,' title of the eighth book of the Mahā-bhārata. — *Karṇa-pāka, as*, m. inflammation of the outer ear. — *Karṇa-pāli, is*, f. the lobe of the ear; the outer and curving edge of the ear; (*ī*), f. an ornament of the ear, a garland or string of jewels pendent from it; N. of a river. — *Karṇa-pāśa, as*, m. a beautiful ear. — *Karṇa-puṭa, am*, n. the auditory passage of the ear. — *Karṇa-pur, ūr*, f. or *karṇa-purī*, f. the capital of Karṇa, i. e. Campā, the ancient N. of Bhagalpur. — *Karṇa-pushpa, as*, m., N. of a plant, = *moraṭa*. — *Karṇa-pūra, as*, m. an ornament of flowers worn round the ears; an ear-ring; N. of several plants, blue lotus; Acacia Sirissa; Jonesia Aśoka; N. of the father of Kavićandra, author of the Alaṅkāra Kaustubha. — *Karṇa-pūraka, as*, m. the Kadamba tree, Nauclea Cadamba; N. of a servant. — *Karṇa-pūraṇa, am*, n. the act of filling the ears (with cotton &c.); any substance used for that purpose; (*as*), m. = *karṇa-pūra*. — *Karṇa-pratināha* or *karṇa-pratīnāha, as*, m. a disease of the ear, suppression of its excretion or wax, which is supposed to have dissolved and pass by the nose and mouth. — *Karṇa-prayāga, as*, m., N. of the confluence of the river Gaṅgā and Pindar. — *Karṇa-prānta, as*, m. the lobe of the ear. — *Karṇa-prāvaraṇa, as, ā, am*, using the ears for a covering; (*ās*), m. pl., N. of a fabulous people. — *Karṇa-phala, as*, m. a sort of fish, Ophiocephalus Kurrawey. — *Karṇa-bhūshaṇa, am*, n. or *karṇa-bhūshā*, f. an ear ornament. — *Karṇa-madgura, as*, m. a sort of sheat fish, Silurus Unitus. — *Karṇa-mala, am*, n. the excretion or wax of the ear. — *Karṇa-mukura, as*, m. an ear ornament; an ear-ring. — *Karṇa-mukha, as, ī, am*, headed by Karṇa, having Karṇa as leader. — *Karṇa-mūla, am*, n. the root of the ear. — *Karṇamūlīya, as, ā, am*, near the root of the ear. — *Karṇa-moṭi, is*, f. an epithet of Devī or Durgā in one of her forms or incarnations (Cāmuṇḍā). — *Karṇa-yoni, is, is, i*, Ved. having the ear as a source or starting-point, going forth from the ear, an epithet of an arrow, because in shooting the bow-string is drawn back to the ear. — *Karṇa-randhra, as, am*, m. n. the orifice or auditory passage of the ear; [cf. *karṇa-ćchidra, karṇa-puṭa*, &c.] — *Karṇa-roga, as*, m. disease of the ear. — *Karṇaroga-pratishedha, as*, m. cure of a disease of the ear. — *Karṇaroga-vijñāna, am*, n. diagnosis of any disease of the ear. — *Karṇa-latā*, f. or *karṇa-latikā*, f. the lobe of the ear. — *Karṇa-vaṇśa, as*, m. an elevated platform of bamboo. — *Karṇa-vat, ān, atī, at*, having ears, long-eared; furnished with tendrils or hooks; having a helm. — *Karṇa-varjita, as, ā, am*, earless; (*as*), m. a snake. — *Karṇaviṭka, as, ā, am*, furnished with ear-wax. — *Karṇa-vidradhi, is*, f. ulceration of the ear. — *Karṇa-vivara, am*, n. the auditory passage of the ear. — *Karṇa-vish, ṭ*, f. ear-wax. — *Karṇa-vedha, as*, m. 'ear-piercing,' a religious ceremony performed to prevent a person from dying, if the birth of a third son be expected; piercing the ear to receive ear-rings. — *Karṇa-vedhanī* or *karṇa-vedhanikā*, f. an instrument for piercing the ear of an elephant. — *Karṇa-veshṭa, as*, m. an ear-ring; N. of a prince. — *Karṇa-veshṭaka, as*, m. the flaps of a cap protecting the ear; (*as* or *am*), m. n. (?) an ear-ring. — *Karṇa-veshṭana, am*, n. an ear-ring. — *Karṇa-śashkulī*, f. the outer part of the ear, the exterior cartilaginous portion leading to the auditory passage. — *Karṇa-śirīsha, as*, m. a Sirīsha flower fastened to the ear as an ornament. — *Karṇa-śūla, as, am*, m. n. ear-ache. — *Karṇaśūlin, ī, inī, i*, having ear-ache. — *Karṇa-śobhana, am*, n., Ved. an ear ornament. — *Karṇa-śrava, as, ā, am*, audible, loud. — *Karṇa-śravas, ās*, m., N. of a Brāhman. — *Karṇa-śrut, t*, m., N. of the author of several hymns of the Ṛig-veda. — *Karṇa-saṃsrāva* or *karṇa-srava* or *karṇa-srāva, as*, m. running of the ear, discharge of pus or ichorous matter from the ear.

— *Karṇa-sū, ūs,* m. the father of Karṇa, an epithet of Sūrya or the sun. — *Karṇa-sūċi, is,* m. a kind of insect. — *Karṇa-sphoṭā,* f. a sort of creeper (commonly *kāṇaphāṭā*). — *Karṇā-karṇi,* ind. from ear to ear, whispering into each other's ears. — *Karṇāñjali* (°*ṇa-añ*°), *is,* m. the auditory passage of the outer ear. — *Karṇāḍhaka* (°*ṇa-āḍh*°), *as,* m., N. of a man; (*ās*), m. pl. the descendants of this man. — *Karṇādeśa* (°*ṇa-ād*°), *as,* m. an ear-ring (?). — *Karṇānuja* (°*ṇa-an*°), *as,* m. an epithet of Yudhishṭhira, the younger brother of Karṇa, one of the five Pāṇḍu princes. — *Karṇāntika* (°*ṇa-an*°), *as, ā, am,* near or close to the ear. — *Karṇāndu* (°*ṇa-an*°), *us* or *ū, ūs,* f. an ornament for the ear; an ear-ring. — *Karṇābharaṇaka* (°*ṇa-ābh*°), *as,* m. the tree Cathartocarpus (Cassia) Fistula. — *Karṇārā* (°*ṇa* and rt. *ṛi?*), f. an instrument for perforating the ear of an elephant. — *Karṇāri* (°*ṇa-ari*), *is,* m. an epithet of Arjuna (as the enemy of Karṇa); the tree Terminalia Arjuna. — *Karṇārpaṇa* (°*ṇa-ar*°), *am,* n. applying the ear, giving ear, paying attention, listening to. — *Karṇālankāra* (°*ṇa-al*°), *as,* m. or *karṇālankriyā,* f. or *karṇālankṛiti, is,* f. an ear ornament, an ear-ring. — *Karṇāśva* (°*ṇa-aś*° ?), *as,* m., N. of a man. — *Karṇāsphāla* (°*ṇa-ās*°), *as,* m. the flapping to and fro of an elephant's ears. — *Karṇe-ċuruċurā,* f. tale-bearing. — *Karṇe-japa, as, ā, am,* a slanderous whisperer, a secret traducer, a tale-bearer, an informer. — *Karṇe-ṭiri-ṭirā,* f. tale-bearing. — *Karṇendu* (°*ṇa-in*°), *us,* f. a semicircular ornament of the ear, an ear-ring; [cf. *karṇāndu*.] — *Karṇotpala* (°*ṇa-ut*°), *as,* m., N. of a poet. — *Karṇodaya* (°*ṇa-ud*°), N. of a book. — *Karṇopakarṇikā* (°*ṇa-up*°), f. a female tale-bearer or informer. — *Karṇorṇa* (°*ṇa-ūr*°), *as, ā, am,* having wool on the ears (as any animal).

Karṇaka, as, m., Ved. a prominence, handle, or projection on the side or sides (of a vessel &c.); a tendril; applied also to the legs when spread out; N. of a man; (*ās*), m. pl. the descendants of this man. — *Karṇaka-vat, ān, atī, at,* Ved. furnished with tendrils or side branches.

Karṇakita, as, ā, am, furnished with tendrils.

Karṇala, as, ā, am, furnished with ears.

Karṇika, as, ā, am, having ears, having large or long ears; having a helm; (*as*), m. a steersman; pl., N. of a people; N. of a king in Potāla; (*ā*), f. an ear-ring or ornament for the ear; a knot, tubercle; round protuberance (e. g. the round protuberance at the end of a reed or cane); the pericarp of a lotus; a fruit-stalk; the tip of an elephant's trunk; the middle finger; chalk; a pen or small brush; a trowel; the plants Premna Spinosa or Longifolia, and Odina Pinnata; a bawd; N. of an Apsaras; N. of the wife of Kaṅka. — *Karṇikāċala, as,* m. an epithet of the fabulous mountain Meru; (fr. *karṇikā,* the seed vessel of a lotus, and *aċala,* a mountain, Meru being in the centre of the world, the divisions of which are compared to the leaves of a lotus); also *karṇikādri,* &c.

Karṇikāra, as, m. the tree Pterospermum Acerifolium; also Cassia Fistula; the pericarp of a lotus; (*am*), n. the flower of the tree Pterospermum Acerifolium and of Cassia Fistula. — *Karṇikāra-priya, as,* m. an epithet of Śiva.

Karṇikin, ī, m. an elephant.

Karṇin, ī, inī, i, having ears, relating to the ear; long-eared; (at the end of compounds) having (anything) attached to the ear; furnished with flaps or anything similar (said of shoes); barbed, furnished with knots &c. (as an arrow); having a helm; (*ī*), m. the side of the neck, the part near the ear; a steersman; N. of a mountain, one of the seven principal ranges of the mountains, dividing the universe; (*inī*), f. (scil. *yoni*) a disease of the uterus, prolapsus or polypus uteri. — *Karṇi-ratha, as,* m. (for *karṇi-ratha*), a covered car, or (according to some) a litter for the conveyance of women &c., borne on men's shoulders.

Karṇila, as, ā, am, long-eared.

Karṇī, a fem. form related to *karṇa* and appearing in compounds (e. g. *ayas-karṇī*). — *Karṇī-suta, as,* m. an epithet of Kaṃsa, the enemy of Kṛishṇa; according to the scholiast the author of a thieves' manual.

Karṇya, as, ā, am, being in or at the ear; suitable to the ear.

कर्णाट **karṇāṭa,** *ās,* m. pl., N. of a country and the people inhabiting it, whence the modern Karnatic; the name, however, was anciently applied to the central districts of the peninsula, including Mysore; (*ī*), f. a princess of Karṇāṭa; a plant, commonly Haṃsapadī; one of the Rāgiṇīs or female personifications of the musical modes, the bride of the Rāga Mālava. — *Karṇāṭa-deśa, as,* m. the Karṇāṭa country.

Karṇāṭaka, ās, m. pl., N. of a country and the people inhabiting it. — *Karṇāṭaka-deśa, as,* m. the Karṇāṭa country. — *Karṇāṭaka-bhāshā,* f. the dialect of Karṇāṭa.

कर्णार्पण **karṇārpaṇa.** See under *karṇa*.

कर्त् **kart** (a various reading for *katr, kartr*), cl. 10. P. *kartayati, -yitum,* to slacken or unloose, to remove.

कर्त **karta,** *as,* m. (fr. 1. *kṛit?*), Ved. a hole, a cavity; (a more recent form is *garta*.)

कर्तन 1. **kartana,** *am,* n. (fr. 1. *kṛit*), cutting, cutting off or in pieces, excision; (*ī*), f. scissors.

Kartari, is, f. scissors.

Kartarikā, f. a knife, a small sword or cutlass; a hunter's knife or sword, a couteau de chasse; scissors.

Kartarī, f. a scissors or shears; a knife; a small sword or cutlass; the part of an arrow to which the feathers are attached.

कर्तन 2. **kartana,** *am,* n. (fr. 2. *kṛit*), spinning cotton or thread.

कर्तरीय **kartarīya,** a kind of poisonous plant.

कर्तव्य **kartavya,** *as, ā, am* (fut. pass. part. fr. 1. *kṛi*), to be done, made or accomplished, what ought to be done; to be imposed (as a punishment); to be turned towards (as the mind); to be offered; to be acted; (*am*), n. what ought to be done, obligation, duty, task. — *Kartavya-tā,* f. or *kartavya-tva, am,* n. necessity, obligation; propriety, fitness; suitable measures.

Kartu, the base of several cases, used as infinitives of the verb *kṛi* in the Veda (e. g. *kartum, kartave, kartavai, kartos*). — *Kartu-kāma, as, ā, am,* desirous or intending to do.

Kartṛi, tā, trī, tṛi, a doer, a maker, one who makes or does, an agent, one who practises what he knows; one who acts in a religious ceremony, a priest; (very often at the end of compounds, e. g. *bhaya-kartṛi, rājya-kartṛi,* &c.); (*tā*), m. the creator of the world, an epithet of Brahmā, of Vishṇu, and of Śiva; (in gram.) an agent, one who acts of his own accord (*sva-tantraḥ*), the active noun, the nominative case. — *Kartṛi-tā,* f. the state of being the agent of an action. — *Kartṛi-tva, am,* n. agency, the act or property of an agent. — *Kartṛi-pura, am,* n., N. of a town. — *Kartṛi-vāċya, as,* m. the active voice. — *Kartṛi-stha, as, ā, am,* standing or being within the agent. — *Kartṛistha-kriyaka, as, ā, am,* any (root &c.) whose action stands within the agent. — *Kartṛistha-bhāvaka, as, ā, am,* any (root &c.) whose state or *bhāva* stands within the agent.

Kartṛika, as, ā, am, an agent, one who does anything. — *Kartṛika-tva, am,* n. agency, action.

Kartra, am, n., Ved. an incantation, charm.

Kartva, as, ā, am, Ved. to be done or accomplished; (*am*), n. obligation, duty; task.

कर्तित **kartita,** *as, ā, am* (fr. rt. 1. *kṛit*), cut, cut off.

Kartishyat, an, atī or *antī, at,* or *kartishyamāṇa, as, ā, am,* intending or wishing to cut.

Karttavya, as, ā, am, to be cut down, to be killed.

Karttṛikā, f. a small sword, a knife; [cf. the next.]

Karttrikā, f. a hunter's knife.

Karttrī, f. a pair of scissors.

Kartya, as, ā, am, to be cut down.

कर्त्र् **kartr,** cl. 10. P. *kartrayati, -yitum,* to unloose, remove; [cf. *kart* and *katr*.]

कर्द् **kard,** cl. 1. P. *kardati, -ditum,* to rumble, as the bowels; to caw, as a crow; or to make any similar noise; [cf. *pard;* Gr. χορδή.]

Kardana, am, n. rumbling of the bowels, borborygmi; (*ī*), f. the day of full moon in the month Caitra.

कर्द **karda,** *as,* m. (said to be fr. rt. *kard*), mud; clay.

Kardaṭa, as, m. mud, dirt; the fibrous root of the lotus (= *karahāṭa*); any aquatic weed, as Vallisneria &c.

Kardama, as, m. mud, slime; mire, clay; dirt, filth, sin; a kind of plant; a poisonous kind of bulb; N. of a Nāga; N. of a Prajāpati, born from the shadow of Brahmā, or son of that god by Ċhāyā, and the husband of Devahūti and father of Kapila; a son of Prajāpati Pulaha; (*ī*), f., N. of a plant; (*am*), n. flesh; (*as, ā, am*), furnished with mud, mire, dirt, filth. — *Kardama-rāja, as,* m. or *kardama-rājan, ā,* m., N. of a man, a son of Kshema-gupta. — *Kardamāṭaka* (°*ma-āṭ*°), *as,* m. a receptacle for filth, a sewer, &c.; [cf. *kanyāṭa, patnyāṭa*.]

Kardamaka, as, m. a kind of granulous fruit; a poisonous kind of bulb; a kind of serpent.

Kardamita, as, ā, am, furnished with mud, dirty.

Kardaminī, f. a marshy region.

Kardamila, am, n., N. of a region.

कर्पट **karpaṭa,** *as, am,* m. n. old or patched or ragged garments; [cf. *kārpaṭika* and *pañċa-karpaṭa*.] — *Karpaṭa-dhārin, ī,* m. a religious mendicant, a beggar in patched or ragged clothes, or sometimes with merely a cloth to cover the privities.

Karpaṭika, as, ā, am, or *karpaṭin, ī, inī, i,* covered with patched or ragged garments, clothed in beggar's raiment.

कर्पण **karpaṇa,** a kind of lance or spear; [cf. *kaṇapa* and *karpara*.]

कर्पर **karpara,** *as,* m. a cup, a pot, an iron saucepan or frying-pan (according to some also n. in this sense); the skull, the cranium; a kind of weapon; the plant Ficus Glomerata, [cf. *udumbara*]; (*ī*), f. a collyrium extracted from the Amomum Anthorhiza, [cf. *ghaṭa-karpara, kharpara*.]

Karparāla, as, m. a tree described as a Pīlu growing in the hills; (a various reading for *kandarāla*.)

Karparāśa, as, m. sand, gravel, a sandy soil; (a wrong reading for *karparāṃśa,* a potsherd.)

Karparikā, f. (diminutive fr. *karparī*) in *karparikātuttha, am,* n. a collyrium extracted from the Amomum Anthorhiza.

Karparīka (?), *as,* m. fire.

कर्पास **karpāsa,** *as, am,* m. n. (said to be fr. 1. *kṛi*), cotton, Gossypium Herbaceum; (*ī*), f. the cotton tree; [cf. *kārpāsa:* cf. also Gr. κάρπασος; Lat. *carbasus*.]

कर्पूर 1. **karpūra,** *as, am,* m. n. (said to be fr. rt. *kṛip*), camphor (the plant and resinous exudation and fruit); (*as*), m., N. of a poet; N. of the father of Gajamalla and uncle of Kalyāṇamalla.

Karpūra-kavi, is, m., N. of a poet. — *Karpūra-khaṇḍa, as,* m. a field of camphor. — *Karpūra-gaura, am,* n., N. of a lake or pond (yellowish-white like camphor). — *Karpūragaurākhya* (°*ra-ākh*°), *as, ā, am,* called Karpūragaura. — *Karpūra-tilaka, as,* m., N. of an elephant; (*ā*), f. an epithet of Jayā, one of Durgā's female attendants or confidantes. — *Karpūra-taila, am,* n. camphor liniment. — *Karpūra-nālikā,* f. a kind of food prepared with camphor, rice dressed with spices and camphor and ghee. — *Karpūra-prakaraṇa, am,* n. a Jaina work by Hari. — *Karpūra-mañjarī,* f. title of a dramatic work by Rāja-śekhara. — *Karpūra-maṇi, is,* m. a white mineral used medicinally. — *Karpūra-saras, as,* n., N. of a lake or pond.

2. *karpūra,* nom. P. *karpūrati, -ritum,* to spread like the smell of camphor.

Karpūraka, as, m. zedoary, Curcuma Zerumbet.

कर्फर *karphara, as,* m. a mirror; [cf. *karkara.*]

कर्ब् *karb,* cl. 1. P. *karbati, -bitum,* to go, move, approach.

कर्बर *karbara.* See *karvara.*

कर्बु *karbu, us, us, u* (said to be fr. rt. *kav,* to paint, colour), variegated, spotted. — *Karbu-dāra, as,* m. the tree Bauhinia Candida or Barleria Cærulea. — *Karbu-dāraka, as,* m. the tree Cordia Latifolia.

Karbuka, ās, m. pl., N. of a people.

Karbura and *karvura, as, ā, am,* variegated, of a spotted or variegated colour; white; (*as*), m. a variegated colour; sin; a Rakshas; the plant Curcuma Amhaldi or Zerumbet; rice growing amidst inundation; (*ā*), f. the plant Bignonia Suaveolens; another plant, commonly called Varvarā; (*ī*), f. an epithet of the goddess Durgā; (*am*), n. gold; the plant Datura, and the fruit of it; water. — *Karbura-phala, as,* m. a plant, commonly called Sākuruṇḍa.

Karbūra or *karvūra, as,* m. a Rakshas; the plant Curcuma Amhaldi or Zerumbet; (*ā*), f. a leech; (*am*), n. gold; a yellow orpiment.

Karbūraka, as, m. the plant Curcuma Amhaldi or Zerumbet.

Karbūrita, as, ā, am, variegated, many-coloured.

कर्बेल *karbela, as,* m. an epithet of the copyist Vishṇu-bhaṭṭa.

कर्मन् *karman, a,* n. (fr. rt. 1. *kṛi;* according to some also m.), action, work, deed; performance, business; office; specific action, moral duty, the obligation imposed by peculiarities of tribe, occupation, &c.; labour (as opposed to rest, *praśānti*); any religious action or rite (as sacrifice, ablution, &c., especially as originating in the hope of future recompense and as opposed to speculative religion or knowledge of spirit); action consisting in motion as the third among the seven categories of the Nyāya philosophy, (of these motions there are five, viz. *ut-kshepaṇa,* throwing upwards; *ava-kshepaṇa,* throwing downwards; *ā-kuñćana,* contraction; *prasāraṇa,* extension or dilatation; and *gamana,* going or motion in general); product, result, effect; organ of sense [cf. *karmendriya*]; natural or active property (as maturity, of heat; support, of earth; dispersion, of wind, &c.); the immediate object of an agent or act; (in grammar) the idea or notion expressed by the acc. case, (this object is of four kinds, viz. a. *nirvartya,* when anything new is produced, e. g. *kaṭam karoti,* 'he makes a mat;' *putram prasūte,* 'she bears a son:' b. *vikārya,* when change is implied either of the substance and form, e. g. *kāshṭham bhasma karoti,* 'he makes ashes out of fuel;' or of the form only, e. g. *suvarṇam kuṇḍalam karoti,* 'he fashions gold into an ear-ring:' c. *prāpya,* when any desired object is attained, e. g. *grāmam gaććhati,* 'he goes to the village;' *ćandram paśyati,* 'he sees the moon:' d. *anīpsita,* when an undesired object is abandoned, e. g. *pāpam tyajati,* 'he leaves the wicked'); fate, the certain consequence of previous acts [cf. *karma-pāka* and *karma-vipāka*]; (in astronomy) the tenth lunar mansion. — *Karma-kara, as, ī, am,* working for other people, a hired labourer, a servant of any kind (as a pupil &c.) who is not a slave, an agent, any one who does work or business; (*as*), m. an epithet of Yama, the regent of the dead; (*ī*), f. the plant Sanseviera Zeylonica; the plant Momordica Monadelpha. — *Karma-kartṛi, tā,* m. 'an object-agent' or 'object-containing agent,' i. e. an agent which is at the same time the object of an act on (this is the idea expressed by the reflexive passive, as in *odanaḥ paćyate,* 'the mashed grain cooks of itself,' see Gram. 461. *c*); *karma-kartārau,* m. du. the work and the person accomplishing it. — *Karma-kāṇḍa, as, am,* m. n. that department of the Veda which relates to ceremonial acts and sacrificial rites; N. of a Jaina work. — *Karma-kāra, as, ī, am,* a worker, one who does any business, an artisan, a mechanic; one who performs any act (without receiving wages for it, according to native lexicographers); (*as*), m. a bull; a blacksmith (forming a mixed caste regarded as the progeny of the divine artist Viśvakarman and a Śūdrā woman); (*ī*), f. the plants Sanseviera Zeylonica and Momordica Monadelpha. — *Karma-kāraka, as, ā, am,* one who does any act or work. — *Karmakārāpaya,* nom. (fr. *karmakāra*) A. *karmakārāpayate, -yitum,* to cause any one to work as a servant. — *Karma-kārin, ī, iṇī, i,* working, doing any work or act, (in compounds preceded by an adjective or pronoun, e. g. *śubha-karma-kārin,* doing good works; *tat-karma-kārin,* performing the same business.) — *Karma-kārmuka, as* or *am* (?), m. or n. 'the bow of action,' i. e. an efficacious or strong bow. — *Karma-kīlaka, as,* m. a washerman. — *Karma-kṛit, t, t, t,* performing any work, skilful in work (e. g. *tīkshṇa-karma-kṛit,* working with zeal); a workman, an artisan; a servant; one who has done any work. — *Karma-kṛitavat, ān,* m. the director of a religious rite, the reciter of Mantras or formularies. — *Karma-kṛitya, am,* n., Ved. activity, the state of active exertion. — *Karma-kshama, as, ā, am,* competent to perform an act, able to do it. — *Karma-kshetra, am,* n. the district or region of religious acts; [cf. *karma-bhūmi.*] — *Karma-granthi-prathama-vićāra,* title of a Jaina work. — *Karma-ghāta, as,* m. lit. 'the killing of work,' i. e. the act of leaving off work. — *Karma-ćandra, as,* m., N. of a prince of Mālava. — *Karma-ćit, t, t, t,* Ved. collected or accomplished by work. — *Karma-ćeshṭā,* f. active exertion, action. — *Karma-ćodanā,* f. the motive impelling to ritual acts. — *Karma-ja, as, ā, am,* resulting from or produced by any act whether religious or immoral; (*as*), m. the holy fig tree, Ficus Religiosa; the Kali-yuga or fourth and present age of the world, the age of iniquity. — *Karmaja-guṇa, as,* m. a property resulting from human acts (as separation, reunion, &c.). — *Karma-jit, t,* m., N. of a prince. — *Karma-jña, as, ā, am,* skilled in any work; acquainted with religious rites. — *Karmaṇi-vāćya, as,* m. the passive voice in grammar, (but according to Pāṇini the passive is an Ātmane-pada verb with the affix *yak* in four tenses, and *karman* expresses only one idea of the passive.) — *Karma-tyāga, as,* m. abandonment of worldly duties or ceremonial rites. — *Karma-tva, am,* n. or *karma-tā,* f. state of action, any act, the active discharge of the duties and functions of life. — *Karma-dushṭa, as, ā, am,* corrupt in action, wicked in practice, immoral, disreputable. — *Karma-deva, as,* m., Ved. a god by actions (opposed to *ājāna-deva,* a god by birth). — *Karma-dosha, as,* m. a sinful work, sin, vice; error, blunder; the evil consequence of human acts, discreditable conduct or business. — *Karma-dhāraya, as,* m., N. of a class of compounds (see Gram. 755); according to native grammarians a subdivision of the Tat-purusha class, the members of which are in the same relationship either as adjective and substantive or as two substantives in apposition (e. g. *śvetāśva,* 'a white horse;' Pāṇini I. 2, 42, calls a Karma-dhāraya comp. a Samānādhikaraṇa-tatpurusha; cf. *adhi-karaṇa*). — *Karma-dhvaṅsa, as,* m. loss of benefit arising from religious acts, destruction of any work, disappointment. — *Karma-nāman, a,* n. a participle. — *Karma-nāśā,* f., N. of a river between Kāśī and Vihāra, contact with which destroys the merit of works. — *Karma-nibandha, as,* m. necessary consequence of works. — *Karma-nirhāra, as,* m. removal of (bad) deeds or their effects. — *Karma-nishṭhā, ās, ās, am,* Ved. diligent in religious actions, engaged in active duties; (*as*), m. a Brāhman who performs sacrifices &c. — *Karma-patha, as,* m. the way or direction of an action. — *Karma-paddhati, is,* f. title of a work. — *Karma-pāka, as,* m. the ripening of actions, i. e. recompense for actions done in a former life; [cf. *karma-vipāka.*] — *Karma-pradīpa, as,* m. title of a work of Kātyāyana; N. of a work of Miśra. — *Karmapradīpa-vivṛiti,* N. of Śivarāma's commentary on the Karmapradīpa. — *Karma-pradīpikā,* f. title of a work of Kāma-deva. — *Karma-pravaćanīya,* employed for the definition of an action; (*as*), m. (scil. *śabdas*) a term for certain prepositions, particles, or adverbs, not connected with a verb, but with a case of a noun; (according to Pāṇini the first and general category to which prepositions belong is that of Nipātas or particles; they are Upasargas and Gatis when they are in connection with verbal action, i. e. with the tenses of a verb; but the term *gati* is more comprehensive than *upasarga,* and is applicable also when the verbal root becomes developed into a noun substantive, adjective, or participle. Moreover, the term *upasarga* is confined to the prepositions with *su* and *dus,* whereas the Gatis include many other adverbial prefixes such as *alam* and the nouns and adjectives which take the affix *ćvi* &c. Lastly, prepositions are Karmapravaćanīyas if they are unconnected with verbs and govern a noun either separated from it or forming a compound with it. A Karmapravaćanīya never loses its accent, and exercises no euphonic influence on the initial letters of a following verb.) — *Karma-pravāda, as,* m., N. of the eighth of the fourteen Pūrvas or oldest religious writings of the Jainas. — *Karma-phala, am,* n. the fruit or recompense of actions; pain, pleasure, &c., considered as the consequence of acts; the fruit of the tree Averrhoa Carambola; [cf. *karmaraṅga.*] — *Karmaphalodaya* (°*la-ud*°), *as,* m. the occurrence of consequences. — *Karma-bandha, as,* m. the tie of works (by which the soul is attached to pleasure &c.). — *Karma-bandhana, as, ā, am,* bound by acts; (*am*), n. confinement to repeated existence, as the consequence of acts. — *Karma-bhū, ūs,* f. tilled or cultivated ground. — *Karma-bhūmi, is,* f. the land or region of religious actions, i. e. where such actions are performed; (according to Hemaćandra the Karmabhūmis are Bharata, Airāvata, and Videha, but not the district of the Kurus; the other Varshas are *phala-bhūmayas,* i. e. lands of recompense; cf. *karma-kshetra.*) — *Karma-maya, as, ī, am,* consisting of works, resulting from works. — *Karma-mārga, as,* m. the way of work; a technical term used by thieves for the breaking of walls &c. — *Karma-mīmāṅsā,* see s. v. *mīmāṅsā.* — *Karma-mūla, am,* n. Kuśa or sacrificial grass, used as an essential part in many religious and sacred rites. — *Karma-yuga, am,* n. the fourth and present age of the world, the iron age, the Kali-yuga. — *Karma-yoga, as,* m. performance of a work or business or of worldly functions and religious duties; active exertion, industry; connection with a sacrifice. — *Karma-yoni, is,* m. f. source of action. — *Karmargha, as,* m. (fr. *karman* and *ṛigha* in *ṛighāya*), N. of a teacher. — *Karma-vaćana, am,* n. (with Buddhists) the ritual. — *Karma-vajra, as, ā, am,* 'whose thunderbolt is work;' an epithet of the Śūdra. — *Karma-vat, ān, atī, at,* busy with a work, employed in it. — *Karma-vaśa, as, ā, am,* being in the power of or subject to former actions; (*as*), m. the necessary influence of acts; fate, considered as the inevitable consequence of actions done in a former life. — *Karmavaśi-tā,* f. the condition of having power over works, a quality of a Bodhi-sattva. — *Karma-vaśin, ī, inī, i,* having power over works. — *Karma-vāṭī,* f. a lunar day or the thirtieth division of a lunar month (regulating all ceremonies, observances, religious actions, &c.). — *Karma-vighna, as,* m. an impediment to work, obstruction. — *Karma-vidhi, is,* m. rule of action, observance, practice, mode of conducting any ceremony. — *Karma-viparyaya, as,* m. succession of office or employment, revolving or alternating duty; contrariety or reverse of any act or business. — *Karma-vipāka, as,* m. 'the ripening of actions,' i.e. the good or evil consequences in this life of human acts performed in previous births; title of a work on this subject, explaining expiatory rites to be performed in cases of disease &c., supposed to be the punishment of offences committed in a previous existence (written in S'lokas in the form of a dialogue between S'akuntalā-Bharata and S'ātātapa-Bhṛigu), a work of Viśveśvara-bhaṭṭa. — *Karma-vipāka-saṅgraha,* title of a book. — *Karmavipāka-sāra,* title of a book composed by Dinakara, the brother of Kamalākara-bhaṭṭa. — *Karma-viśesha, as,* m. variety of act or actions. — *Karma-vīja, am,* n. the seed of works. — *Karma-śālā,* f. a workshop, a house of business. — *Karma-śālī,* f., N. of a river in Caturgrāma. — *Karma-śīla, as, ā, am,* assiduous, laborious, one who perseveres in his duties without looking to their reward. — *Karma-śuddha* (?), *am,* n. approved occupation. — *Karma-śūra, as, ā, am,* assiduous, laborious; *(as),* m. a skilful or clever workman. — *Karma-śauća, am,* n. humility. — *Karma-śreshṭha, as,* m., N. of a son of Pulaha by Gati. — *Karma-saṅgraha, as,* m. assemblage of acts, comprising the act, its performance and the performer. — *Karma-saćiva, as,* m. a minister, any officer employed upon active duties, as a judge, a deputy, &c. — *Karma-sannyāsika, as,* m. an ascetic, a religious person who has withdrawn from works. — *Karma-samādhi, is,* m. devotion, abstraction (?). — *Karma-sambhava, as, ā, am,* produced by or resulting from acts. — *Karma-sākshin, ī,* m. 'the witness of all acts,' epithet of the sun. — *Karma-sādhaka, as, ikā, am,* accomplishing a work. — *Karma-sādhana, am,* n. implement, means; articles essential to the performance of any religious act. — *Karma-siddhi, is,* f. accomplishment of an act, success. — *Karma-sena, as,* m., N. of the father of Rāma-ćandra. — *Karma-stha, as, ā, am,* standing or being within the object. — *Karmastha-kriyaka, as, ā, am,* any (root) whose action stands within the object. — *Karmastha-bhāvaka, as, ā, am,* any (root &c.) whose state (*bhāva*) stands within the object. — *Karma-sthāna, am,* n. a public office or place of business. — *Karma-hetu, us, us, u,* caused by acts, arising from acts. — *Karmākshama* (°*ma-ak*°), *as, ā, am,* incapable of business. — *Karmāṅga* (°*ma-aṅ*°), *as,* m. part of any act, part of a sacrificial rite. — *Karmātman* (°*ma-āt*°), *ā, ā, a,* one whose character is action, endowed with principles of action, active, acting. — *Karmāditya* (°*ma-ād*°), *as,* m., N. of a king. — *Karmādhikāra* (°*ma-adh*°), *as,* m. the right of action (in the Mīmāṃsa philosophy). — *Karmānubandha* (°*ma-an*°), *as,* m. connection with or dependance upon acts. — *Karmānubandhin, ī, inī, i,* connected with or involved in works. — *Karmānurūpa* (°*ma-an*°), *as, ā, am,* according to action, according to function or duty. — *Karmānurūpatas,* ind. conformably to act, function &c. — *Karmānushṭhāna* (°*ma-an*°), *am,* n. practising one's duties, discharging peculiar functions. — *Karmānushṭhāyin* (°*ma-an*°), *ī, inī, i,* practising duties, performing rites &c. — *Karmānusāra* (°*ma-an*°), *as,* m. consequence of or conformity to acts. — *Karmānusāratas,* ind. according to one's deeds. — *Karmānta* (°*ma-an*°), *as,* m. work, business, administration of an office; management of any business; the end of any task or act; the end or abandonment of ritual acts; tilled or cultivated ground. — *Karmāntara* (°*ma-an*°), *am,* n. interval between religious actions, suspense of such an action; difference or contrariety of action; penance, expiation. — *Karmāntika, as, ī, am,* final, completing; *(as),* m. a workman, a servant, one who finishes a work. — *Karmābhidhāyaka, as, ā, am,* or *karmābhidhāyin* (°*ma-abh*°), *ī, inī, i,* enjoining or prescribing duties or acts. — *Karmārambha* (°*ma-ār*°), *as,* m. commencement of any act. — *Karmārha* (°*ma-ar*°), *as, ā, am,* fit for work, able to do any work, suitable to any rite; *(as),* m. a man. — *Karmendriya* (°*ma-in*°), *am,* n. an organ of action (opposed to the *buddhīndriyāṇi* or perceptive organs of sense; five are reckoned, viz. the hand, the foot, the larynx or organ of the voice, the organ of generation and of excretion). — *Karmodāra* (°*ma-ud*°), *am,* n. any honourable or valiant act, magnanimity, prowess. — *Karmodyukta* (°*ma-ud*°), *as, ā, am,* actively labouring, busily engaged. — *Karmodyoga* (°*ma-ud*°), *as,* m. engaging actively in any work.

Karma, as, am, m. n. according to some lexicographers = *karman.*

Karmaka (at the end of some compounds) = *karman,* q. v.

Karmaṭha, as, ā, am, skilful or clever in work, clever; working diligently, accomplishing any rite, anxious to perform anything; *(as),* m. the director and performer of a sacrifice.

Karmaṇya, as, ā, am, Ved. skilful in work, clever, diligent; proper or fit for any act, suitable to it; (at the end of compounds) relating to any business or to the accomplishment of anything; *(ā),* f. wages, hire; *(am),* n. energy, activity. — *Karmaṇya-tā,* f. skilfulness, cleverness. — *Karmaṇya-bhuj, k, k, k,* receiving wages, working for hire; (a various reading for *bharaṇya-bhuj.*)

Karmatas, ind. according to actions.

Karmāra, as, m., Ved. an artificer, a mechanic, a blacksmith, a brazier, a carpenter, &c.; a bamboo; the plant Averrhoa Carambola, = *karmaraṅga* below. — *Karmāra-vana, am,* n., N. of a place.

Karmāraka, as, m. the plant Averrhoa Carambola.

Karmika, as, ā, am, acting, active.

Karmin, ī, iṇī, i, acting, active, busy; performing a religious action; engaged in any work or business; belonging or relating to any act.

Karmishṭha, as, ā, am (said to be a superlative of the last), very active, assiduous, diligent.

Karmīṇa = *karman* at the end of a compound; [cf. *alaṅkarmīṇa.*]

कर्मन्द *karmanda, as,* m., N. of a man, author of a Bhikshu-sūtra.

Karmandin, ī, m. a beggar, a religious mendicant, a member of the fourth order (lit. 'a follower of Karmanda').

कर्मर *karmara* and *karmaraka, as,* m. the plant Averrhoa Carambola.

Karmaraṅga, as, m., N. of the same plant; *(am),* n. the acid fruit of this plant.

कर्मरी *karmarī,* f. the manna of the bamboo; [cf. *vaṅśa-roćanā.*]

कर्मष *karmasha* = *kalmasha,* q. v.

कर्मस *karmasa, as,* m., N. of a son of Pulaha and Kshamā; [cf. *karma-śreshṭha.*]

कर्मीर *karmīra, as, ā, am,* variegated; (a various reading for *kirmīra.*)

Karmīraka, as, m. a small tree, Trophis Aspera.

कर्व् *karv,* cl. 1. P. *karvati, -vitum,* to be proud, to boast; [cf. *kharv* and *garv.*]

कर्व *karva, as,* m. (said to be fr. rt. 1. *kṛī*), love, desire; a rat.

कर्वट *karvaṭa, as, am,* m. n. declivity of a mountain; a village, market-town, the capital of a district (of two or four hundred villages) in a pleasant site and of handsome construction; *(as),* m., N. of a country or a people; *(ī),* f., N. of a river; *(am),* n. a city.

Karvaṭaka, as or *am,* m. or n. (?) declivity of a mountain.

कर्वर 1. *karvara, am,* n. (fr. rt. 1. *kṛī*), Ved. a deed, action.

कर्वर 2. *karvara* or *karbara, as, ā, am* (said to be fr. rt. 1. *kṛī*), variegated, spotted; *(as),* m. sin; a tiger; a Rakshas; a sort of medicament; *(ī),* f. an epithet of Durgā; night; a Rākshasī; a tigress; the leaf of the plant Asa Fœtida; [cf. *karavī, kavarī, kāravī.*] See *karbura.*

कर्शन *karśana, as, ā, am* (fr. rt. *kṛiś*), rendering lean, attenuating, causing emaciation; *(as),* m. fire; [cf. *kṛiśānu.*]

कर्शफ *karśapha, as,* m., Ved. an epithet of imps or goblins.

कर्श्य *karśya, as,* m., N. of a plant, = *karćūra;* [cf. *kārśya* and *kārshya.*]

कर्ष *karsha, as,* m. (fr. rt. *kṛish*), drawing, dragging, pulling; attracting; ploughing; a furrow, a trench; a scratch; *(as, am),* m. n. a weight of gold or silver, equal to 16 Māshas = $\frac{1}{4}$ Pala = $\frac{1}{400}$ of a Tulā = 11,375 French grains; according to the ancient division of 5 Rettis to the Māsha the Karsha would be equal to about 176 grains troy; in common use 8 Rettis are given to the Māsha, and the Karsha is then about 280 grains troy. — *Karsha-phala, as,* m. the tree Terminalia Bellerica; this tree is also called Aksha, because its fruits are used as dice; *(ā),* f. the plant Emblica Officinalis. — *Karshārdha* (°*sha-ar*°), *am,* n. a Tolaka, a weight of 16 Māshas (according to some calculations).

Karshaka, as, ā, am, a cultivator of the soil, one who ploughs or lives by tillage; a husbandman; who or what draws or drags, attractive, what attracts.

Karshaṇa, as, ā, am, pulling to and fro, dragging, attracting, overpowering, injuring; tormenting; harassed; extending (in time); *(am),* n. the act of dragging or pulling; drawing to and fro; removing, hurting, injuring; bending (a bow); ploughing, cultivating the ground; cultivated land.

Karshaṇi, is, f. an unchaste woman (attracting the men).

Karshaṇī, f., N. of a plant; [cf. *karshiṇī* and *kshīriṇī.*]

Karshaṇīya, as, ā, am, to be drawn or pulled; to be attracted; to be conciliated or won.

Karshayat, an, antī, at, dragging, pulling; attracting; harassing, annoying.

Karshita, as, ā, am, drawn, attracted; distracted, tormented, harassed; worn out; ploughed.

Karshin, ī, iṇī, i, who or what pulls or draws or attracts; attractive; inviting; who or what ploughs or furrows, a ploughman, peasant; *(iṇī),* f. the bit of a bridle; a medicinal moon-plant; [cf. *karshaṇī, kshīriṇī.*]

Karshū, ūs, f. a furrow, trench, incision; a river; a canal; a shallow trench for receiving the sacrificial fire; *(ūs),* m. a fire of dried cow-dung; agriculture, cultivation; livelihood.

कर्षापण *karshāpaṇa* = *kārshāpaṇa,* q. v.

कर्हि *karhi,* ind. (fr. 2. *ka*), Ved. when? at what time? (followed by the future or present tense) *karhi-ćid* or *karhy-api,* at any time; [cf. Goth. *hvar,* 'where?' Eng. *where?* Germ. *war* and *wor* in *warum, woraus,* &c.; Lith. *kur.*]

कल् 1. *kal,* cl. 1. A. *kalate, -litum,* to sound; to count; [Gr. καλέω? Lat. *calculo.*]

कल् 2. *kal,* cl. 10. P. *kālayati, -yitum,* to push on, drive forward, drive away; carry off; to drive together, collect; to throw; to announce the time.

कल् 3. *kal,* cl. 10. P. *kalayati, -yitum,* to impel, incite, urge on; to bear, carry; to do, make, accomplish; to tie on, attach, affix; to utter a sound, murmur; to furnish with; to observe, perceive, take notice of; to regard, consider, count, reckon, calculate; to go; to take hold of the die called Kali (in this last sense *kal* may be considered as a nom. fr. *kali*).

Kala, as, ā, am, dumb, hoarse, indistinct, inarticulate (especially in composition with *vāshpa* and *aśru,* e. g. *vāshpa-kala, aśru-kala,* having the speech impeded by tears, sobbing); emitting a low or soft tone, as humming, buzzing, &c.; weak; crude, undigested; (*as*), m. (scil. *svara*) a low or soft and inarticulate tone, as humming, buzzing, &c.; the tree Shorea Robusta; (in poetry) time equal to four Mātras or instants; (*ās*), m. pl. a class of manes or deceased ancestors; (*am*), n. semen virile; the jujube, Zizyphus Jujuba; (for *kalā* see below, s. v.) — *Kala-kaṇṭha, as*, m. a pleasing tone or note; a low murmuring tone; having a sweet voice, N. of several birds, as of the Indian cuckoo; a dove, a pigeon; a goose. — *Kala-kala, as*, m. a confused noise, the murmuring or buz of a crowd; resin, pitch, the resinous exudation of the tree Shorea Robusta; an epithet of Śiva; [cf. *kaṭakaṭa, kaṭankaṭa*.] — *Kalakala-vat, ān, atī, at*, causing humming or murmuring. — *Kala-kīṭa, as*, m., N. of a Grāma. — *Kala-kūjikā*, f. a wanton, a lascivious woman. — *Kala-kūṭa, as*, m., N. of a warrior-tribe and the country inhabited by it. — *Kala-kūṇikā*, f. a wanton, a lascivious woman. — *Kala-ghosha, as*, m. the Kokila or Indian cuckoo. — *Kalan-kasha, as*, m. a lion; a musical instrument; see *kara-tālī*. — *Kalan-kura, as*, m. an eddy, a whirlpool. — *Kalatā*, f. or *kala-tva, am*, n. melody, music. — *Kala-tūlikā*, f. a wanton or lascivious woman; [cf. *kala-kūṇikā*.] — *Kala-dhūta, am*, n. silver; (wrong reading for *kala-dhauta*?). — *Kala-dhauta, am*, n. gold and silver (sounding and shining); (*as, am*), m. n. a low or pleasing tone. — *Kaladhauta-lipi, is*, f. a streak of gold, illumination of a manuscript with gold. — *Kala-dhvani, is*, m. a low sweet tone; the Kokila or Indian cuckoo; the turtle-dove; a peacock. — *Kala-nāda, as*, m. a sort of goose; see *kala-haṅsa*. — *Kala-bhāshaṇa, am*, n. the prattle of childhood. — *Kala-bhairava, as* or *am*, m. or n. (?), N. of a deep ravine in the mountains between the rivers Tāpī and Narmadā. — *Kala-rava, as*, m. a low sweet tone; a dove; the Indian cuckoo; [cf. Lat. *columba*.] — *Kala-vaćas, ās, ās, as*, speaking sweetly, singing. — *Kala-svana, as, ā, am*, having a charming voice (a bird). — *Kala-svara, am*, n. a low musical sound. — *Kala-haṅsa, as*, m. a kind of duck or goose; a gander; another bird, Gallinula Porphyria; a drake or (according to some) a teal; an excellent king; Brahma or the supreme spirit; N. of a metre consisting of four lines of thirteen syllables each. — *Kalānunādin* (°*la-an*°), *ī*, m. a sparrow; a bee, but particularly one of a very large kind; the Ćātaka bird. — *Kalālāpa* (°*la-āl*°), *as*, m. a sweet humming sound, discourse; a bee. — *Kalottāla* (°*la-ut*°), *as, ā, am*, high, sharp.

Kalana, as, ā, am (at the end of compounds), causing, effecting; (*as*), m. a sort of cane; (*ā*), f. doing, making, effecting; subjection, submission; emitting (?); *kāla-kalanā*, fulfilling one's time, dying; (*am*), n. an embryo at the first stage after conception; a spot, a stain; an offence, fault, defect; murmuring, sounding.

Kalita, as, ā, am, impelled, driven, borne onwards; held, laid hold of; attached, affixed, furnished, endowed with; gained, acquired; considered, known, understood; numbered, counted, reckoned; separated, divided; sounded indistinctly, buzzed, murmured.

कलक *kalaka, as*, m. a kind of fish; a kind of prose.

कलङ्क *kalanka, as*, m. a spot, a mark; the rust of iron; a fault, defamation, abuse. — *Kalanka-kara, as, ī, am*, censorious, calumniating, defaming; spotting, staining. — *Kalanka-kalā*, f. a digit of the moon in shadow. — *Kalanka-maya, as, ī, am*, spotted, stained; calumniated, defamed. — *Kalanka-kṛit, t*, m. an epithet of Śiva.

Kalankaya, nom. P. *kalankayati, -yitum*, to spot, defame.

Kalankita, as, ā, am, spotted, soiled, stained; calumniated, defamed.

Kalankin, ī, inī, i, soiled, stained; disgraced, reviled, rusty.

कलञ्ज *kalañja, as*, m. an animal struck with a poisoned weapon; tobacco.

कलट *kalaṭa, am*, n. the thatch of a house; (other works read this *kuṭala*, q. v.)

कलत *kalata, as, ā, am*, = *khalati*, bald-headed.

कलत्र *kalatra, am*, n. (see *kaḍatra*), a wife; any female; the hip and loins; pudendum muliebre; a royal citadel, a strong hold or fastness; the seventh lunar mansion in astronomy. — *Kalatra-vat, ān, atī, at*, or *kalatrin, ī, iṇī, i*, having a wife, united to a wife.

कलन्तक *kalantaka* or *kalandaka, as*, m. a species of bird.

कलन्दन *kalandana, as*, m., N. of a man.

कलन्दर *kalandara, as*, m. a man of a mixed caste, the son of a Leṭa (?) man and a Tīvara woman.

कलन्दिका *kalandikā*, f. knowledge, intelligence, wisdom in general; (a various reading for *kalindikā*, q. v.)

कलन्धु *kalandhu, us*, m. a kind of vegetable; [cf. *gholī*.]

कलभ *kalabha, as*, m. (said to be fr. 3. *kal*), a young elephant; an elephant thirty years old; a young camel (perhaps also the young of other animals); the tree Datura Fastuosa [cf. *dhustūra*]; (*ī*), f. a sort of Ricinus (*ćaṅću*). — *Kalabha-vallabha, as*, m., N. of a tree; [cf. *pīlu*.]

कलम *kalama, as*, m. (said to be fr. 3. *kal*), rice, which is sown in May and June, and ripens in December or January; a white rice growing in deep water; a pen, a reed for writing with; a thief, a rogue; [cf. Gr. κάλαμος; Lat. *calamus, culmus*; and Arab. قلم.]

कलम्ब *kalamba, as*, m. the stalk of a pot-herb; an arrow; the tree Nauclea Cadamba; (*ī*), f. (according to a scholiast also m.), the pot-herb Convolvulus Repens; (*am*), n. Calumba root, Menispermum Calumba; [cf. *kaḍamba, kadamba*.]

Kalambaka, as, m., N. of a plant; [cf. *dhārā-kadamba*.]

Kalambikā, f. the nape of the neck (in this sense usually used in du.); the pot-herb Convolvulus Repens; [cf. *kalambī*.]

Kalambū, ūs, f. the same pot-herb.

कलम्बुट *kalambuṭa, am*, n. fresh butter.

कलल *kalala, as, am*, m. n. the womb, the uterus; a small round lump, a term for the embryo a short time after conception; [cf. *kalana*.]

कललज *kalalaja, as*, m. the resinous exudation of the Shorea Robusta; [cf. *kala-kala*.] — *Kalalajodbhava* (°*ja-ud*°), *as*, m. the tree Shorea Robusta.

कलविङ्क *kalaviṅka, as*, m. a sparrow; a spot, a stain [cf. *kalanka*]; a white Ćāmara; the plant Echites Antidysenterica [cf. *kalingaka*]; N. of a Tīrtha.

कलश *kalaśa, as, ī, am*, m. f. n. a water-pot, a pitcher, a jar, a dish; (*as*), m., N. of a poet; (*ī*), f. the plant Hemionitis Cordifolia; N. of a Tīrtha; a churn; [cf. *kalasa* and *droṇa-kalaśa*; Gr. κάλιξ; Lat. *calix*.] — *Kalaśa-dir, ir*, m., Ved. one whose pot or pitcher is broken. — *Kalaśa-potaka, as*, m., N. of a Nāga. — *Kalaśi-kaṇṭha, as*, m., N. of a man; (*ās*), m. pl. the descendants of this man. — *Kalaśi-padī*, f. having feet like a water-jar. — *Kalaśi-mukha, as*, m. a sort of musical instrument. — *Kalaśi-suta, as*, m. an epithet of Agastya. — *Kalaśodara* (°*śa-ud*°), *as*, m., N. of a Daitya.

Kalaśi, is, f. a water-pot, pitcher, dish, water-jar; the plant Hemionitis Cordifolia.

Kalasa, as, ī, am, m. f. n. a pot, a water-jar; (*as*), m. a Droṇa measure; a rounded pinnacle or ball on the top of a temple; (*ī*), f. the plant Hemionitis Cordifolia. — *Kalasodadhi* (°*sa-ud*°), *is*, m. the ocean.

कलह *kalaha, as, am*, m. n. strife, contention, quarrel, war, battle; the sheath of a sword, a scabbard; a road, a way; deceit, falsehood; violence without murderous weapons, abuse, beating, kicking, &c. — *Kalaha-kandala, as*, m., N. of an actor. — *Kalaha-kāra, as, ī, am*, quarrelsome, turbulent; contentious, pugnacious; (*ī*), f., N. of the wife of Vikramaćaṇḍa. — *Kalaha-kārin, ī, iṇī, i*, quarrelsome, contentious. — *Kalaha-nāśana, as*, m. the tree Cæsalpina Bonducella. — *Kalaha-priya, as, ā, am*, fond of contention, quarrelsome, turbulent; (*as*), m. an epithet of Nārada; (*ā*), f. the bird Gracula Religiosa. — *Kalahāntaritā* (°*ha-an*°), f. a heroine separated from her lover in consequence of a quarrel; an appeased wife, one who has been angry and is sorry for it. — *Kalahāpahṛita* (°*ha-ap*°), *as, ā, am*, taken away by force.

Kalahāya, nom. A. *kalahāyate, -yitum*, to quarrel, contend.

Kalahin, ī, inī, i, contentious, quarrelsome.

कलहु *kalahu*, a particular high number; [cf. *karaphu*.]

कला *kalā*, f. (said to be fr. 3. *kal*), a small part of anything, any single part or portion of a whole, but especially a sixteenth part; a digit or one sixteenth of the moon's diameter (personified as a daughter of Kardama and wife of Marīći); interest on capital, considered as a certain part of it; a division of time (according to some $\frac{1}{900}$ of a day, i. e. 1 minute and 36 seconds; according to others $\frac{1}{1800}$ of a day, i. e. 48 seconds; according to others $20\frac{1}{15}$ Kalās = 1 Muhūrta or $\frac{1}{30}$ of a day, therefore 1 Kalā = 2 minutes and $26\frac{54}{301}$ seconds; according to others $30\frac{1}{10}$ Kalās = 1 Muhūrta, therefore 1 Kalā = 1 minute and $35\frac{205}{301}$ seconds; according to others 1 Kalā = 8 seconds); the sixtieth part of one thirtieth of a zodiacal sign, a minute of a degree; (in prosody) a syllabic instant; a term for the seven substrata of the elements or Dhātus of the human body (which according to one reckoning are seven, as follows, flesh, blood, fat, phlegm, urine, bile, and semen; but according to Hemaćandra *rasa* 'chyle,' *asthi* 'bone,' and *majja* 'marrow,' take the place of phlegm, urine, and bile); an atom (there are 3015 Kalās or atoms in every one of the six Dhātus, not counting the *rasa*, therefore in all 18090); a small round lump, a term for the embryo shortly after conception [cf. *kalana*]; the menstrual discharge; any practical art, any mechanical or fine art (sixty-four such are enumerated, as carpentering, architecture, jewellery, farriery, acting, dancing, music, medicine, poetry, &c.); skill, ingenuity, contrivance, fraud, deceit; a boat; title of a grammatical commentary; N. of a deity; [cf. *a-kala, nishkala, sakala*.] — *Kalā-kuśala, as, ā, am*, skilled in the elegant arts, singing, dancing, &c. — *Kalā-keli, is, is, i*, gay, frolicsome, wanton; (*is*), m. an epithet of Kāma, the god of love. — *Kalā-dhara, as*, m. 'bearing a digit of the moon;' an epithet of Śiva; N. of a copyist. — *Kalā-nidhi, is*, m. 'a treasure or storehouse of digits,' the moon. — *Kalāntara* (°*lā-an*°), *am*, n. interest, profit. — *Kalāpa* (°*lā* + *āpa* fr. rt. *āp*), *as*, m. 'that which holds together the single parts,' a band, a bundle (e. g. *muktā-kalāpa*, an ornament consisting of several strings of pearls; *raśanā-kalāpa*, a zone consisting of several strings, worn by women round the waist; *jaṭā-kalāpa*, a tuft or knot of braided hair); totality, whole body or collection of a number of separate things, a zone, a string of bells worn by women round the waist; the rope round an elephant's neck; a bundle of arrows, a quiver with arrows, a quiver; a peacock's tail (as consisting of a multitude of single feathers); an ornament in general; N. of a grammar, supposed to be revealed by the god Kumāra or Kārttikeya to Sarva-varman; a village where the destroyer Kalki is to be born; the moon; a clever and intelligent man; a poem written in one metre;

(ī), f. a bundle of grass. — *Kalāpaka, as,* m. a band, a bundle; a string of pearls; the rope round an elephant's neck; a sectarian mark on the forehead; (*am*), n. a number of verses in one metre; a series of four stanzas on one subject; the eye in a peacock's feather?; (*as, ikā, am*), to be repaid when the peacocks spread their tails. — *Kalāpa-grāma, as,* m., N. of a Grāma or village. — *Kalāpa-ćhanda, as,* m. an ornament of pearls consisting of twenty-four strings. — *Kalāpa-tattvārṇava* (°*va-ar*°), title of a commentary on the Kalāpa grammar. — *Kalāpa-dvīpa,* N. of a place, perhaps the same as *kalāpa-grāma.* — *Kalāpa-śiras, ās,* m., N. of a Muni; (a various reading for *kapāla-śiras.*) — *Kalāpānusārin* (°*pa-an*°), *ī,* m. a follower of the Kalāpa grammar. — *Kalāpin, ī, inī, i,* furnished with a bundle of arrows, bearing a quiver with arrows; spreading its tail (said of a peacock &c.); (ī), m. a peacock; the Indian cuckoo; the waved-leaf fig tree, Ficus Infectoria; N. of an old teacher, a pupil of Vaiśampāyana; (according to some) the author of the Kalāpa grammar; the time (scil. *kālaḥ*) when peacocks spread their tails; (*inī*), f. night; the moon; a species of Cyperus. — *Kalā-pūrṇa, as, ā, am,* filled up by single or separate parts; (*as*), m. the moon. — *Kalā-bhṛit, t,* m. 'digit-bearer,' the moon; an artist, a mechanic, &c. — *Kalāyana* (°*lā-ay*°), *as,* m. a tumbler, a dancer, but especially one who dances or walks on a sharp edge, as the edge of a sword &c. — *Kalā-vat, ān,* m. 'having digits,' the moon; (*tī*), f. a mystical ceremony, the initiation of the Tantrika student, in which the goddess Durgā is supposed to be transferred from the water-jar to the body of the novice; N. of an Apsaras; N. of the mother of Rādhā; N. of the wife of Kṛita-varman, king of Ayodhyā; N. of the wife of Dāśārha; N. of the lute of the Gandharva Tumburu. — *Kalā-vāda-tantra, Kalā-vidhi-tantra, Kalā-sāra-tantra,* names of Tantras. — *Kalā-vilāsa, as,* m. a work on rhetoric. — *Kalā-śāstra, am,* n. a work by Viśākhila.

Kalikā, f. a digit of the moon. See below, s. v.

कलाकन्द *kalākanda* = *kanda,* a species of the Atijagatī metre.

कलाकुल *kalākula, am,* n. poison; [cf. *halāhala.*]

कलाङ्कुर *kalāṅkura, as,* m. the bird Ardea Sibirica, a crane; an epithet of the Asura Kaṇsa.

कलाङ्गल *kalāṅgala, as* or *am,* m. or n. (?) a kind of weapon (?).

कलाचिक *kalāćika, as* or *am,* m. or n. (?) a ladle; (*ā*), f. or *kalāćī,* f. the fore-arm, the arm below the elbow.

कलाटीन *kalāṭīna, as,* m. the white water wagtail.

कलाद *kalāda, as,* m. a goldsmith.

कलाधिक *kalādhika, as,* m. (fr. *kala* and *adhika*?), a cock; [cf. *kalāvika* and *ushākala.*]

कलानक *kalānaka, as,* m., N. of one of the attendants of Śiva.

कलाप *kalāpa,* &c. See under *kalā.*

कलापूर *kalāpūra, as* or *am* (?), m. or n. (?), and *ā,* f. a kind of musical instrument.

कलामक *kalāmaka, as,* m. a kind of rice ripening in the cold season; [cf. *kalama.*]

कलाम्बि *kalāmbi, is,* f. or *kalāmbikā,* f. lending, a loan; usury.

कलाय *kalāya, as,* m., N. of various leguminous seeds, chiefly of the order Phaseolus, particular kinds of pulse or vetches; (*ā*), f. a kind of Panicum, = *gaṇḍadūrvā.* — *Kalāya-khañja, as,* m. one who trembles and totters as he walks.

कलाविक *kalāvika, as,* m. a cock; [cf. *kalādhika.*]

कलाविकल *kalāvikala, as,* m. a sparrow; [cf. *kalaviṅka.*]

कलाहक *kalāhaka, as,* m. a kind of musical instrument; [cf. *kāhala.*]

कलि *kali, is,* m. (said to be fr. rt. 3. *kal*), N. of the die or side of a die, which is marked with one point (personified as a deity or evil genius in the poem of Nala); the plant Terminalia Bellerica, the nuts of which in olden times were used as dice; N. of the last and worst of the four Yugas, the present or iron age, the age of vice; (the four Yugas or ages have received their names from the marks on dice, the best mark being four points and the worst one; the Kali or fourth age contains, inclusive of the two dawns, 1200 years of the gods or 432,000 years of men, and begins the eighteenth of February 3102 B. C.; at the end of this Yuga the world is to be destroyed); strife (considered as the son of *Krodha* 'Anger' and *Hiṇsā* 'Injury,' and as generating with his sister *Durukti* 'Calumny,' two children, viz. *Bhaya* 'Fear' and *Mṛityu* 'Death'); dissension, war, battle; the worst in any class; a hero; an arrow; Ved., N. of a class of mythic beings related to the Gandharvas, and supposed by some to be fond of gambling; in epic poetry *Kali* is held to be the fifteenth of the Deva-gandharvas or children of the Munis; N. of a man; (*is* or *ī*), f. an unblown flower, a bud. — *Kali-kāra, as,* m., N. of several birds, the fork-tailed shrike; Loxia Philippensis, a small bird with a yellow head; a kind of chicken; a plant bearing a nut which is used as a febrifuge, Grey Bonduc, = *karañja* and *pūtikarañja*; an epithet of Nārada; (ī), f. the poisonous plant Methonica Superba. — *Kali-kāraka, as,* m. the plant Cæsalpinia Bonducella; (a various reading has *kali-māraka*); an epithet of Nārada ('the quarrelsome'). — *Kali-druma, as,* m. the plant Terminalia Bellerica or the tree of strife, being supposed to be the favourite haunt of imps or goblins. — *Kali-dharma-nirṇaya, as,* m., N. of a work. — *Kali-nātha, as,* m., N. of a writer on music. — *Kali-priya, as, ā, am,* quarrelsome, mischievous, mischief-making; (*as*), m. a monkey, an ape; an epithet of Nārada. — *Kali-māraka, as,* m. the plant Cæsalpinia Bonducella; (a various reading for *kali-kāraka,* q. v.) — *Kali-mālaka, as,* m. and *kali-mālya, as,* m. the plant Cæsalpinia Bonducella. — *Kali-yuga, am,* n., N. of the fourth age, the present or iron age. — *Kali-vṛiksha, as,* m. the tree Terminalia Bellerica. — *Kali-saṁśraya, as,* m. the act of betaking one's self to Kali.

कलिक *kalika, as,* m. a curlew.

कलिका *kalikā,* f. (fr. *kalā*), a digit or the sixteenth part of the moon; an unblown flower [cf. *kali*]; the bottom or peg of the Indian lute, made of cane; N. of several metres, a metre containing 4 x 8 + 16 syllabic instants; a metre of four lines, each containing fifteen syllables; a metre consisting of 12 + 8 + 16 + 20 syllables; title of a work on medicine.

कलिकाता *kalikātā,* f. the modern name Calcutta.

कलिकापूर्व *kalikāpūrva, am,* n. (fr. *kalikā* and *apūrva*?), acts leading to future consequences not connected with those of a previous birth.

कलिङ्ग *kaliṅga, as,* m., N. of a country; the name is applied in the Purāṇas to several places, but especially signifies a district on the Coromandel coast, extending from below Cuttack (Kaṭaka) to the vicinity of Madras; in this sense, like some other names of countries, it is usually confined to the plural number, confounding the place with the people inhabiting it, (these people are said to owe their origin to Kaliṅga, the son of Dīrgha-tamas and Sudeshṇā; Kaliṅga being sometimes identified with the epic Bali); N. of a scholiast on the Amara-kosha; N. of a poet; the fork-tailed shrike, Lanius Forficatus, (in this sense derived from *kalim* and *ga*?; cf. *kali-kāra*); the plants Cæsalpinia Bonducella, Wrightia Antidysenterica, Acacia Sirisa, Ficus Infectoria; (*ā*), f. a beautiful woman; the plant Ipomœa Turpethum; (*am*), n. Indra-grain [cf. *indra-yava*]; (*as, ā, am*), clever; cunning.

Kaliṅgaka, as, m. the seed of the Coraiya, Indra-grain.

Kaliṅgaḍī, f. (?) an epithet of Durgā.

कलिञ्ज *kaliñja, as,* m. a mat, a screen; (a various reading for *kiliñja.*)

कलित *kalita.* See 3. *kal.*

कलिन्द *kalinda, as,* m. the tree Terminalia Bellerica; the sun; (in these meanings perhaps a compound of *kalim* and *da*); N. of a mountain on which the river Yamunā rises; (*ās*), m. pl., N. of a people; (ī), f. a N. of the river Yamunā or Jumnā. — *Kalinda-kanyā* or *kalinda-nandinī* or *kalinda-śaila-jātā,* f. epithets of the river Yamunā or Jumnā.

कलिन्दिका *kalindikā,* f. science; (a various reading has *kalandikā.*)

कलिल *kalila, as, ā, am* (fr. rt. 1. *kṝ*?), covered with, full of; mixed, blended; impenetrable, impervious; (*am*), n. a large heap, thicket, confusion; [cf. *kalusha.*]

कलुक्क *kalukka, as,* m. a musical instrument, a cymbal; (*ā*), f. a tavern; a meteor.

कलुष *kalusha, as, ā, am* (fr. rt. 1. *kṝ*?, said to be fr. rt. 3. *kal*), turbid, foul, muddy, unclean; dark, opaque, without brilliancy; hoarse (as the voice); wicked, bad; lazy, idle; (*as*), m. a buffalo; (*am*), n. dirt, uncleanness; sin, wrath. — *Kalusha-tā,* f. or *kalusha-tva, am,* n. foulness, turbidness; darkness, opacity; agitation, trouble, anger. — *Kalusha-yoni, is, is, i,* of impure origin.

Kalushāya, nom. A. *kalushāyate, -yitum,* to become turbid.

Kalushita, as, ā, am, foul, impure; defiled, contaminated; wicked.

Kalushin, ī, iṇī, i, foul, impure; defiled, depraved; wicked.

Kalushī-kṛi, cl. 8. P. A. *-karoti, -kurute, -kartum,* to make turbid or unclean.

कलूतर *kalūtara, as* or *am* (?), m. or n. (?), N. of a place.

कलेवर *kalevara, as, am,* m. n. the body; [cf. Lat. *cadāver.*]

कल्क *kalka, as, am,* m. n. (said to be fr. 3. *kal*), a viscous sediment deposited by oily substances when ground; a kind of tenacious paste; dirt, filth; the wax of the ear; ordure, fæces; meanness, falsehood, deceit, sin, hypocrisy, pride; the tree Terminalia Bellerica; incense; levigated powder; (*as, ā, am*), sinful, wicked; [cf. *kalusha, kalmasha, kilvisha.*] — *Kalka-phala, as,* m. the pomegranate plant (*dāḍima*). — *Kalkālaya* (°*ka-āl*°), *as,* m., N. of a man.

Kalkana, am, n. falsehood, deceit, cheating, quarrelling.

Kalki, is, m. a N. of Vishṇu in his future capacity of destroyer of the wicked and liberator of the world from its enemies. This will constitute the tenth and last Avatāra or descent of the deity, and is to take place at the end of the four Yugas or ages. — *Kalki-prādurbhāva, as,* m. the apparition of Kalki.

Kalkin, ī, inī, i, foul, turbid, having sediment, dirty, wicked; (ī), m. = *kalki* above.

कल्कल *kalkala, ās,* m. pl., N. of a people.

कल्प *kalpa, as, ā, am* (fr. rt. *klṛip*), practicable, feasible, possible; proper, fit, able, competent (with gen., loc., inf., and at the end of a compound,

e. g. *dharmasya kalpaḥ*, competent for duty; *sva-karmaṇi na kalpaḥ*, not competent for his own work; *yadā na śāsitum kalpaḥ*, if he is not able to rule); strong, vigorous; *kalpe vayasi*, in the vigorous period of life; (*as*), m. a sacred precept, law, ordinance [cf. *vidhi, nyāya*]; manner of acting, proceeding, practice prescribed by the Vedas (e. g. *prathamaḥ kalpaḥ*, a rule to be observed before any other rule, first duty; *etena kalpena*, in this way; *paśu-kalpa*, the rites at the animal sacrifice; *na kalpa-mātre*, not according to the mere letter of the rule without regard to its spirit); the most complete of the six Vedāṅgas, that which prescribes the ritual and gives rules for ceremonial or sacrificial acts; (in medic.) treatment of the sick, manner of curing (e. g. *kalpetara*, one cured or treated differently); the doctrine of poisons and antidotes; (at the end of an adjective compound) having the manner or form of anything, similar to, resembling, like but with a degree of inferiority (e. g. *prabhāta-kalpā śarvarī*, the night which is something similar to dawn, i. e. the night at the approach of dawn; *mṛta-kalpa*, similar to a dead person, almost dead; *abhedya-kalpa*, almost impenetrable; according to native grammarians *kalpa* so used is an accentless affix, before which a final *s* is left unchanged, and final *ī* and *ū* shortened; native authorities also connect *kalpa* with a simple verb, thus *paćati-kalpam*, he cooks pretty well); a resolve, a determination; propriety, fitness (?); optionality, alternative [cf. *vi-kalpa*], doubt; a fabulous period of time, a day of Brahmā or 1000 Yugas, a period of four hundred and thirty-two million years of mortals, measuring the duration of the world; (a month of Brahmā is supposed to contain thirty such Kalpas; according to the Mahābhārata twelve months of Brahmā constitute his year, and one hundred such years his lifetime; fifty years of Brahmā are supposed to have elapsed, and we are now in the *śvetavārāha-kalpa* of the fifty-first. The Kalpa, in the same way as the Saṃvatsara or year, is personified as son of Dhruva and Bhrami; at the end of a Kalpa the world is annihilated; hence *kalpa* is sometimes used for *kalpānta* or the destruction of the world); N. of certain sentences or verses containing the verb *klṛp*; one of the trees of paradise, see *kalpa-taru* below; (with Jainas) a term for a particular abode of the deities [cf. *kalpa-bhava* and *kalpātīta*]; (*am* or *ā*), m. f. a kind of intoxicating liquor; [cf. *a-kalpa, anu-kalpa, upa-kalpa*, &c.] — *Kalpa-kāra, as*, m. an author of ritual or ceremonial rules. — *Kalpa-kedāra*, a medical work by Kāliśiva. — *Kalpa-kshaya, as*, m. the end of a Kalpa, end of the world, destruction of all things. — *Kalpa-gā*, f., N. of a river. — *Kalpa-taru, us*, m. one of the trees of Svarga or Indra's paradise, a fabulous tree, granting all desires, hence figuratively a generous person; title of a work on jurisprudence; also a work of Lakshmīdhara; also one of Vāćaspati. — *Kalpa-dru, us*, m. = *kalpa-taru*, also N. of a lexicon by Keśava. — *Kalpa-druma, as*, m. = *kalpa-taru*; a work on jurisprudence; also a Tantra work; the collection of roots by Vopadeva is called *Kavi-kalpadruma*, the tree from which poets obtain all desired roots; and the modern encyclopedia of Rādhākānta is entitled *Śabda-kalpadruma*, the tree which satisfies every desire for words. — *Kalpa-pādapa, as*, m. = *kalpa-taru* above. — *Kalpa-pāla, as*, m. a protector of order, a legitimate prince; a person who distils or sells spirituous liquors. — *Kalpa-bhava, ās*, m. pl., N. of a certain class of deities. — *Kalpa-mahīruh, t*, m. = *kalpa-vṛiksha*. — *Kalpa-yukti*, title of a work by Budha. — *Kalpa-latā*, f. a creeper yielding everything desired; *Kalpalatā-vatāra*, title of a commentary of Kṛishṇa on the Vīja-gaṇita; *Kalpalatā-prakāśa*, title of a commentary on the Vishṇu-bhaktilatā. — *Kalpa-latikā*, f. = *kalpa-latā* above; (*Śabda-k°*, title of a dictionary.) — *Kalpa-varsha, as*, m., N. of a son of Vasu-deva and Upa-devā. — *Kalpa-vallī*, f. = *kalpa-latā* above. — *Kalpa-vāyu, us*, m. the wind that is to blow at the end of the world. — *Kalpa-viṭapin, ī*, m. or *kalpa-vṛiksha, as*, m. the fabulous tree of Indra's heaven; see above. — *Kalpa-vidhi, is*, m. a rule resembling a ceremonial injunction. — *Kalpa-vṛiksha-latā*, f. a work by Lollaṭa. — *Kalpa-sūtra, am*, n. a Sūtra manual of ritual; also a medicinal work and a work of the Jaina sect so called. — *Kalpa-sūtra-vyākhyā*, f. a Jaina work on the Kalpasūtras. — *Kalpātīta* (°*pa-at*°), *ās*, m. pl., N. of a certain class of deities. — *Kalpādi* (°*pa-ādi*), *is*, m. the beginning of a Kalpa, the renovation of all things. — *Kalpānupada* (°*pa-an*°), *am*, n. title of a work belonging to the Sāma-veda. — *Kalpānta* (°*pa-an*°), *as*, m. the end of a Kalpa, the destruction of the world. — *Kalpāntara* (°*pa-an*°), *am*, n. another Kalpa. — *Kalpānta-sthāyin, ī, inī, i*, lasting to the end of a Kalpa.

Kalpaka, as, m. a rite, a ceremony; a barber [cf. *kalpanī*]; a kind of Curcuma, commonly *karćūra*. — *Kalpaka-taru, us*, m., N. of a tree of Indra's paradise; [cf. *kalpa-taru*.]

Kalpana, am, n. forming, fashioning; doing, performing; fixing, constituting; anything fixed or placed upon another thing for ornament; act of clipping, cutting; (*ā*), f. fixing, constituting, settling; making, performing; fabrication; composing, composition (of a poem &c.); inventing, invention; forgery; a fancy, an idea or image formed in the mind; an imagination, intention; contrivance, plan, inference; caparisoning or decorating an elephant; (*ī*), f. a scissors or shears. — *Kalpanā-śakti, is*, f. the power of forming ideas.

Kalpanīya, as, ā, am, to be made, fashioned or contrived, to be accomplished, possible, to be substituted or supplied.

Kalpika, as, ā, am, fit, proper.

Kalpita, as, ā, am, made, fabricated, artificial; composed, invented; arranged, put in order; prepared; brought; inferred; (*as*), m. an elephant armed or caparisoned for war. — *Kalpitārgha* (°*ta-ar*°), *as, ā, am*, one for whom a respectful offering is prepared.

Kalpin, ī, inī, i, Ved. a term used in gambling with dice.

Kalpya, as, ā, am, to be made or contrived or performed, to be prescribed; relating to ritual; to be substituted.

कल्मन् *kalman, a*, n. according to native grammarians = *karman*.

कल्मलि *kalmali*, Ved. splendor (of the stars?).

Kalmalīka, am, n. brightness, splendor.

Kalmalikin, ī, inī, i, Ved. burning, shining.

कल्मष *kalmasha, as, am*, m. n. stain, dirt, sin, dregs; *jala-kalmasha*, the dirt or sediment of water; (*am*), n. darkness, a division of the infernal regions; the hand below the wrist; (*as, ā, am*), dirty, foul. — *Kalmasha-dhvaṃsa-kārin, ī, iṇī, i*, destroying darkness or sin; preventing the commission of crime.

कल्माष *kalmāsha, as, ī, am*, variegated, spotted; black, black and white; (*as*), m. a variegated colour; a mixture of black and white, the black colour; a Rakshas, demon or goblin; a species of fragrant rice; N. of a Nāga; a form of fire; N. of a servant of the sun, identified with Yama; Śākya-muni in a former birth; (*ī*), f. the spotted cow of Jamadagni, the giver of all desires; N. of a river; (*am*), n. a stain. — *Kalmāsha-kaṇṭha, as*, m. an epithet of Śiva. — *Kalmāsha-grīva, as, ā, am*, Ved. having a variegated neck. — *Kalmāsha-tantura, as*, m., N. of a man. — *Kalmāsha-tā*, f. spottedness, the state of being variegated. — *Kalmāsha-pāda, as*, m., N. of a king; also Saudāsa, a descendant of Ikshvāku, transformed to a Rākshasa by Vasishṭha. — *Kalmāshāṅghri* (°*sha-an*°), *is*, m. another N. of the same king.

कल्य *kalya, as, ā, am* (rt. 3. *kal*?), well, sound, healthy, free from sickness; ready, prepared, armed; clever, dexterous; agreeable, auspicious (as a speech or discourse); instructive, admonitory; deaf and dumb [cf. *kala* and *kalla*]; (*am*), n. dawn, day-break; to-morrow; yesterday (?); *kalyam* or *kalye*, ind. at day-break; (*am* or *ā*), n. f. spirituous liquor; congratulation; good wishes; good tidings; (*ā*), f. Emblic Myrobalan, see *harītakī*; [cf. Gr. καλός, καλλίων, κάλλιστος, &c., for καλyος &c.] — *Kalya-jagdhi, is*, f. the morning-meal, breakfast. — *Kalya-tva, am*, n. or *kalya-tā*, f. health; recovery, convalescence. — *Kalya-pāla* or *kalyā-pāla* or *kalya-pālaka* or *kalyā-pālaka, as*, m. a distiller. — *Kalya-varta, as*, m. the morning-meal, breakfast; a light meal; (*am*), n. anything light, a trifle, a trivial or unimportant matter; [cf. *prātarāśa*.]

Kalyāṇa, as, ā or *ī, am*, beautiful, agreeable, friendly, illustrious, noble, excellent, happy, beneficial, salutary, prosperous; propitious, lucky, well, right, good; (*as*), m., N. of a prince, also called Bhaṭṭaśrīkalyāṇa; N. of the author of the poem Gītāgaṅgādhara; (*ī*), f. a cow; a leguminous shrub, Glycine Debilis; N. of two cities; N. of a river in Ceylon; N. of a deity; (*am*), n. good fortune, happiness, prosperity; virtue; a festival; gold; heaven; N. of the eleventh of the fourteen Pūrvas or most ancient writings of the Jainas. — *Kalyāṇa-kaṭaka, as*, m., N. of a place. — *Kalyāṇa-kara, as, ī, am*, propitious, auspicious, conferring good fortune &c. — *Kalyāṇa-kāra, as, ī, am*, or *kalyāṇa-kāraka, as, ā, am*, creating prosperity or profit. — *Kalyāṇa-kṛit, t, t, t*, virtuous, good; propitious, lucky. — *Kalyāṇa-ćandra, as*, m., N. of an astronomer in the twelfth century A. D. — *Kalyāṇa-ćāra, as, ī, am*, following virtuous courses; lucky, fortunate. — *Kalyāṇa-devī*, f., N. of the wife of Jayāpīḍa. — *Kalyāṇa-dharman, ā, ā, a*, virtuous, good. — *Kalyāṇa-pañćamīka, as*, m. a fortnight, the fifth lunar day of which is lucky. — *Kalyāṇa-pura, am*, n., N. of a town. — *Kalyāṇa-malla, as*, m., N. of a prince; N. of the author of a work called Anaṅgaraṅga; N. of a son of Gajamalla, author of the commentary called Mālatī. — *Kalyāṇa-mitra, am*, n. a friend of virtue, a religious counsellor. — *Kalyāṇa-rāja-ćaritra, am*, n. 'the life of king Kalyāṇa' by Madana. — *Kalyāṇa-vaćana, am*, n. friendly speech, good wishes. — *Kalyāṇa-vat, ān, atī, at*, happy. — *Kalyāṇa-vartman, ā*, f., N. of a princess, who erected a statue of Vishṇu, called Kalyāṇa-svāmi-keśava. — *Kalyāṇa-varman, ā*, m., N. of an astronomer. — *Kalyāṇa-vīja, as*, m. a sort of pulse, Ervum Hirsutum. — *Kalyāṇa-śarman, ā*, m., N. of a scholiast on Varāha-mihira. — *Kalyāṇa-sūtra, as*, m., N. of a Brāhman. — *Kalyāṇāćāra* (°*ṇa-āć*°), *as, ā, am*, following good practices, virtuous. — *Kalyāṇābhijana* (°*ṇa-abh*°), *as, ī, am*, of illustrious birth. — *Kalyāṇī-pañćamā, ās*, f. pl. (scil. *rātrayas*) nights of which the fifth is lucky.

Kalyāṇaka, as, ikā, am, auspicious, efficacious (as a drug), prosperous, happy; (*ikā*), f. red arsenic.

Kalyāṇin, ī, inī, i, happy, lucky, prosperous; illustrious; virtuous, good; (*inī*), f. the water-plant Sida Cordifolia.

कल्युष *kalyusha, am*, n. the wrist (?).

कल्ल् *kall*, cl. 1. A. *kallate, -litum*, to sound indistinctly; to sound; to be mute.

Kalla, as, ā, am, deaf; (also a various reading for *kanna*, q. v.) — *Kalla-tva, am*, n. or *kalla-tā*, f. deafness; indistinct articulation, hoarseness. — *Kalla-mūka, as, ā, am*, deaf and dumb. — *Kalla-vīra-tantra*, a Buddhist work, also called Ćaṇḍamahā-roshaṇa-tantra. — *Kallārya, as*, m., N. of an author.

कल्लट *kallaṭa, as*, m., N. of a prince; *śrī-kallaṭa*, N. of a sage.

कल्लि *kalli*, ind. to-morrow.

कल्लिनाथ *kallinātha, as*, m., N. of a writer on music.

कल्लोल *kallola, as, ā, am* (fr. 2. *kad* + *lola*),

inimical, hostile; (*as*), m. a wave; a surge, a billow; an enemy; joy, happiness, pleasure.

Kallolita, as, ā, am, surging, billowy.

Kallolinī, f. a surging stream, a river in general.

कल्हण *kalhaṇa, as,* m., N. of the author of the Rāja-taraṅgiṇī (often spelt *kahlaṇa*); N. of the father of the copyist Rāma.

कल्हार *kalhāra, am,* n. a water-lily.

कव् *kav,* cl. 1. A. *kavate, -vitum,* to describe (as a poet); to paint; to picture, colour; [cf. *kab.*]

कव 1. *kava,* a form substituted for *ka, kā,* and 1. *ku,* to express deterioration or deficiency.—*Kava-patha, as,* m., Ved. a bad way.—*Kavāgni* (°*va-ag*°), *is,* m. a little fire.—*Kavoshṇa* (°*va-ush*°), *as, ā, am,* slightly warm, tepid; (*am*), n. slight warmth.

2. *kava* in *a-kava* and *kavāsakha;* [cf. *kavatnu* and *kavāri.*]

कवक *kavaka, am,* n. a fungus, a mushroom; a mouthful.

कवच *kavaća, as, am,* m. n. (said to be fr. 3. *ku*), armour, mail, a coat of mail, a cuirass; the jacket of a boy; an amulet, a charm, the mystical syllable *hum* or *hūm,* forming part of a Mantra and considered as a preservative like armour; it is also inscribed on a birch leaf &c. and worn as an amulet, being carried about the person as a charm (this is the probable meaning in the titles *durgā-kavaća, sūryak°, śivak°, bhavānīk°,* &c.); a drum used in battle, a kettle-drum; the tree Hibiscus Populneoides.—*Kavaća-pattra, am,* n. the leaf of a birch tree; [cf. *bhūrja-pattra.*]—*Kavaća-pāśa, as,* m., Ved. the fastening of a cuirass or coat of mail.—*Kavaća-hara, as, ā* or *ī, am,* wearing armour or mail, or a jacket; wearing amulets; (*as*), m. a boy, a child.

Kavaćita, as, ā, am, dressed in armour.

Kavaćin, ī, inī, i, dressed in armour; (*ī*), m. an epithet of Śiva; N. of a son of Dhṛita-rāshṭra.

कवटी *kavaṭī,* f. the leaf or panel of a door; [cf. *kavāṭa.*]

कवड *kavaḍa, as,* m. water &c. for washing the mouth; [cf. *kavala.*]

कवत्नु *kavatnu, us, us, u* (fr. 1. *ku*), Ved. selfish, stingy; (Sāy.) a bad deed.

कवन *kavana, am,* n. water; (*as*), m., N. of a son of Śriṅgin.

कवन्तक *kavantaka, as,* m., N. of a man; (*ās*), m. pl. the descendants of this man.

कवन्ध *kavandha* and *kavandhin.* See *kabandha* and *kabandhin.*

कवपथ *kava-patha.* See under 1. *kava.*

कवयी *kavayī,* f. the fish Cojus Cobojus (commonly called Kavay or Kay), remarkable for going by land from one spot to another; [cf. *karikā.*]

कवर *kavara, as, ā* or *ī* (?), *am* (fr. rt. 3. *ku*), mixed, intermingled, blended; set, inlaid; (*as*), m. a lecturer; (*as, ī*), m. f. (according to some also n.) a braid or fillet of hair; (*as, am*), m. n. salt; sourness or acidity; (*ā*), f. the plant Ocimum Gratissimum; (*ī*), f. the leaf of the Asa Fœtida plant, Hiṅgupattrī.—*Kavara-pućchī,* f. having a twisted tail or one which resembles a braid.—*Kavarī-bhara* or *kavarī-bhāra, as,* m. a fine head of hair.—*Kavarī-bhṛit, t, t, t,* wearing a fillet of hair.

कवरकी *kavarakī,* f. a captive, a prisoner; [cf. *vandī.*]

कवल *kavala, as, am,* m. n. (fr. 3. *ku?*), a mouthful; an astringent wash for cleansing the mouth, a gargle; a kind of fish, commonly called Baliya; [cf. Hib. *caomhna, caomhnadh,* 'food, nourishment.']—*Kavala-prastha, as,* m., N. of a town.

Kavalikā, f. a piece of cloth over a sore or wound, a bandage.

Kavalita, as, ā, am, swallowed as a mouthful, eaten.

कवष *kavasha, as, ī, am,* Ved. according to Mahīdhara either 'sounding, creaking,' or 'pierced' (said of the leaves of a door); (*as*), m. a shield; N. of a man, son of Ilūsha or Ailūshī, author of several hymns of the Ṛig-veda; N. of a Muni; N. of the author of a Dharma-śāstra.

कवस *kavasa, as,* m. (said to be fr. rt. 3. *ku*), armour, a coat of mail; a prickly shrub.

कवाट *kavāṭa, as, ī, am,* m. f. n. (for *kapāṭa*), the leaf or panel of a door; a door; (at the end of a compound *kavāṭaka;* cf. *kavaṭī.*)—*Kavāṭa-ghna, as,* m. breaking the door, a thief; [cf. *kapāṭa-ghna.*]—*Kavāṭa-vakra, am,* n., N. of a plant; commonly called *kavāṭaveṭu;* or according to others *kavāḍaventuyā.*

कवार *kavāra, as,* m. the bird Tantalus Falcinellus; (*am*), n. a lotus; [cf. *kavela.*]

कवारि *kavāri, is, is, i,* Ved. selfish, stingy; [cf. *a-kavāri, a-kava, kavatnu.*]

Kavā-sakha, as, ā, am, Ved. a companion of the selfish man, selfish.

कवि *kavi, is, is* or *ī, i* (said to be fr. rt. 3. *ku;* but perhaps related to *ākūta, ākūti*), sensible, intelligent, prudent, clever, wise, learned; a thinker, a wise man, a sage, an intelligent man; (metaphorically) epithet of the gates of the sacrificial enclosure; epithet of the Ṛibhus (as skilful in contrivance); epithet of the old sages or patriarchs, now as spirits surrounding the sun; epithet of the gods, especially of Agni, Indra, Varuṇa, the Maruts, and Ādityas; epithet of the Soma priest &c.; (*is*), m. a poet, especially one who composes artificial poems; N. of a man, according to some genealogies a son of Bhṛigu and father of Śukra; epithet of Śukra, the regent of the planet Venus and preceptor of the demons; the sons of several Manus are also called Kavis; N. of a son of Kauśika and pupil of Garga; also a son of Ṛishabha; N. of Vālmīki, the inventor of poesy and author of the Rāmāyaṇa; the sun?; (*is* or *ī*), f. the bit of a bridle or the reins altogether; a ladle.—*Kavi-kaṇṭha-hāra, as,* m. 'the ornament of the neck of a poet,' title of a work on rhetoric.—*Kavi-kalpa-druma, as,* m. title of a collection of roots written in verse by Vopadeva.—*Kavi-kalpa-latā,* f. title of a work on rhetoric by Devendra.—*Kavi-kratu, us, us, u,* Ved. having wise designs, wise; (Sāy.) one who possesses wisdom or sacrifices.—*Kavi-ćandra, as,* m. the son of Karṇa-pūra and father of Kavi-vallabha, author of the Kāvya-ćandrikā; the author of the Dhātu-ćandrikā; the author of the Ratnāvalī; the author of the Rāmaćandra-ćampū; the author of the Śānti-ćandrikā; the author of a grammar called Sārala-harī; the author of a book named Stavāvalī.—*Kavi-ććhad, t, t, t,* Ved. delighting in wise men; (Sāy.) causing pleasure to the wise.—*Kavi-jyeshṭha, as,* m. an epithet of Vālmīki, the author of the Rāmāyaṇa, 'the oldest of poets.'—*Kavi-tama, as, ā, am,* wisest.—*Kavi-tara, as, ā, am,* wiser.—*Kavi-tā,* f. poesy, poetic style or composition.—*Kavitāmṛita-kūpa* (°*tā-am*°), *as,* m. title of a modern collection of verses, 'a well of nectar of poetry.'—*Kavitā-vedin, ī, inī, i,* understanding poesy, wise, learned, a poet, a genius.—*Kavi-tva, am,* n. wisdom; poesy.—*Kavi-tvana, am,* n., Ved. wisdom.—*Kavitva-ratnākara, as,* m. title of a modern work on rhetoric.—*Kavi-darpaṇa,* N. of a work by Raghu.—*Kavi-putra, as,* m., N. of a dramatic author.—*Kavi-praśasta, as, ā, am,* Ved. highly esteemed or praised by sages.—*Kavi-priyā,* f. a work on rhetoric by Keśava-dāsa.—*Kavi-bhaṭṭa, as,* m., N. of a poet.—*Kavi-bhūma, as,* m., N. of a man.—*Kavi-bhūshaṇa, as,* m. the son of Kavi-ćandra.—*Kavi-ratha, as,* m., N. of a prince, a son of Citra-ratha.—*Kavi-rahasya, am,* n. 'the secret of the learned,' title of a collection of roots by Halāyudha.—*Kavi-rāja, as,* m. king of the poets, N. of the author of the Rāghavapāṇḍavīya.—*Kavi-rāmāyaṇa, as,* m. an epithet of Vālmīki, the author of the Rāmāyaṇa, (an incorrect form for *rāmāyaṇa-kavi.*)—*Kavi-lāsikā* or *kavi-lāśikā,* f.(?) a kind of lute.—*Kavi-vallabha, as,* m., N. of the son of Kavi-ćandra.—*Kavi-vṛidha, as, ā, am,* Ved. prospering the wise.—*Kavi-śasta, as, ā, am,* Ved. praised by wise men.—*Kaviśvara* (°*vi-iś*°), *as,* m. a king of poets; N. of a poet.

Kavika, am, n. the bit of a bridle or the reins altogether; (*ā*), f. the bit of a bridle; N. of a flower, = *kevikāpushya;* a sort of fish, commonly called Kay.

Kavitri, tā, tri, tṛi (?), wise, learned.

Kaviya, as, am, m. n. the bit of a bridle or the reins.

1. *kavīya,* nom. P., Ved. *kavīyati, -yitum,* to act like a wise man; A. to claim wisdom for one's self, pretend to it.

2. *kavīya, as, am,* m. n. the bit of a bridle or the reins; [cf. *kaviya.*]

Kavīyas, ān, asī, as, Ved. (comparative for *kavitara*), wiser.

Kavya, as, ā, am, Ved. a wise, intelligent man; (*as*), m. a class of manes; N. of one of the seven sages of the fourth Manvantara; (*am*), n. the qualities or the actions of a sage; 'what must be offered to sages,' an oblation or offering of food to deceased ancestors; (generally connected with *havya.*)—*Kavya-tā,* f., Ved. the qualities or the actions or the state of a sage, wisdom.—*Kavya-vāḍa* or *kavya-vāla, as,* m. (formed fr. *kavya-vāh*), a class of manes or deified ancestors.—*Kavya-vāh, ṭ, ṭ, ṭ,* or *kavya-vāhana, as, ā, am,* Ved. an offering to sages, what must be offered or what belongs to them; (*as*), m. fire; an epithet of Śiva; (the word is formed like *havya-vāhana.*)

कविञ्जुक *kaviñjuka, as,* m. a kind of bird.

कवूल *kavūla* (in astrol.) = Arabic قبول.

कवेल *kavela, am,* n. a lotus; [cf. *kavāra.*]

कवोष्ण *kavoshṇa.* See under 1. *kava.*

कश् *kaś,* cl. 1. P. *kaśati, -śitum,* to sound; (*kaś* occurs also as a various reading for *kaṇs, kas, jhash,* and *śaś*); [cf. rt. *kāś;* cf. also Hib. *casgairim.*]

कश *kaśa, as,* m. (fr. rt. *kaś* above?; in the sense 'whip' connected with rt. *kash*), Ved. a species of small animal; a whip; (*ā*), f. a whip; whipping, flogging; a string, a rope; the mouth; a quality; (sometimes spelt *kashā.*)—*Kaśa-kṛitsna, as,* m., N. of a man.—*Kaśā-traya, am,* n. three modes of whipping (a horse), good, bad, and middling.—*Kaśārha* (°*śā-ar*°), *as, ā, am,* deserving a whipping.—*Kaśā-vat, ān, atī, at,* furnished with a whip.

Kaśya, as, ā, am, deserving the whip; (*am*), n. a horse's flank; spirituous liquor.

कशस् *kaśas, as,* n. water.—*Kaśo-jū, ūs, ūs, u,* Ved. running near the water; (perhaps a Pr. N.?)

कशिपु *kaśipu, us, u,* m. n. a mat; a pillow; (*us*), m. food; clothing; (*ū*), du. food and clothing; (sometimes spelt *kasipu;* cf. *hiraṇya-kaśipu.*)—*Kaśipūpabarhaṇa* (°*pu-up*°), *am,* n., Ved. a cover of a pillow, cloth.

कशीका *kaśīkā,* f., Ved. a weasel.

कशु *kaśu, us,* m., Ved., N. of a man.

कशेरक *kaśeraka, as,* m., N. of a Yaksha.

कशेरु *kaśeru* or *kaseru, us, u,* m. n. (fr. rt. *śrī* with *ka* prefixed?), the back-bone; a kind of grass, Scirpus Kysoor; (*us*), m. one of the nine divisions of Jambu-dvīpa; (*us*), f., N. of a daughter of Tvashṭṛi; (sometimes spelt *kaseru.*) — *Kaśeru-mat* or *kaseru-mat, ān*, m., N. of a Yavana; N. of a part of Bharata-varsha.

Kaśeruka or *kaseruka, as, ā, am*, m. f. n. a sort of grass, Scirpus Kysoor; (*ā*), f. the back-bone.

Kaśerus, us, n. or *kaśerū, ūs*, f. a sort of grass, Scirpus Kysoor.

कशोक *kaśoka, as*, m., Ved., N. of a class of demons.

कश्चन *kaśćana*, &c. See under 2. *ka*.

कश्मल *kaśmala, as, am*, m. n. (fr. rt. *kas?*), consternation, alarm; fainting, syncope; dejection of mind, depression of spirit, lowness, weakness; (*as, ā, am*), foul, dirty. — *Kaśmala-ćetas, ās, ās, as*, mentally debased.

कश्मश *kaśmaśa, as* or *am* (?), m. or n. (?), Ved. consternation (?).

कश्मीर *kaśmīra, as*, m. (said to be fr. rt. *kaś*), N. of a country; according to Burnouf a contraction of Kaśyapamīra; [cf. *kāśmīra*.] — *Kaśmīra-janman, ā* or *a*, m. n. saffron.

कश्य *kaśya*. See under *kaśa*.

कश्यत *kaśyata, as*, m., N. of a man.

कश्यप *kaśyapa, as, ā, am*, having black teeth; (*as*), m. a tortoise; a sort of fish; a kind of deer; a class of divine beings similar to or equal to Prajāpati, (also in pl. a peculiar class of semi-divine spirits or genii connected with or regulating the course of the sun); a mythical Ṛishi; N. of an old sage, conversant with the Mantras, author of several hymns of the Ṛig-veda, and according to the Anukramaṇī a descendant of Marīći. (In the later mythology he is the husband of Aditi and twelve other daughters of Daksha, and father by them of gods, demons, men, fish, reptiles, and all animals; he is also regarded as one of the seven sages, and in some legends as father of Vivasvat and of Vishṇu. He is supposed by some to be a personification of the race who resided in Caucasus, the Caspian, Kashmīr, &c.); the author of a Dharmaśāstra; (*ās*), m. pl. the descendants of Kaśyapa; *Kaśyapa* is also a constellation; (*ā*), f., N. of the authoress of a verse in the White Yajur-veda. — *Kaśyapa-nandana, as*, m. an epithet of Garuḍa, the bird of Vishṇu; ('son of Kaśyapa.') — *Kaśyapa-saṃhitā*, f. and *kaśyapa-smṛiti, is*, f., N. of two works.

कष् *kash*, cl. 1. P. A. *kashati, -te, ćakāsha, kashishyati, akashīt* and *akāshīt, kashitum*, to rub, scratch, scrape; to itch; to rub with a touchstone, test, try; to injure, hurt, destroy, kill; to leap: cl. 10. P. *kāshayati, -yitum*, to hurt.

Kasha, as, ā, am, rubbing, scraping, rubbing down; (*as*), m. rubbing; the touchstone; (*ā*), f. a whip; see *kaśa*. — *Kasha-pāshāṇa, as*, m. a touchstone. — *Kashāghāta* (°*shā-āgh*°), *as*, m. a cut, a stroke with a whip.

Kashaṇa, as, ā, am, unripe, immature; (*am*), n. rubbing, marking; touch or test of gold by the touchstone.

Kashan-mukha, as, m., N. of a man.

Kashāku, us, m. fire, the sun.

Kashi, is, is, i, injurious, mischievous.

Kashita, as, ā, am, hurt, injured.

Kashṭi, is, f. test, trial; pain, trouble.

कषापुत्र *kashāputra, as*, m. a Rakshas; [cf. *nikashātmaja*.]

कषाय *kashāya, as, ā, am* (fr. rt. *kash?*), astringent; fragrant; red, dark-red; brown, of a colour composed of red and yellow; (*as, am*), m. n. an astringent flavour or taste; the red colour; a decoction or infusion, that form of a decoction which has one part of a drug combined with four or (according to other authorities) with eight or sixteen parts of water, the whole being then boiled down until only one quarter is left; a kind of ointment, gum, resin, extract, exudation from a tree; plastering, anointing; colouring or perfuming the person; dirt, uncleanness, dulness, stupidity; decay, ruin; a mark of decay (of which, according to Buddhists, there are five, viz. *āyus-kashāya, dṛishṭi*°, *kleśa*°, *sattva*°, *kalpa*°); attachment to worldly objects; (*as*), m. passion, emotion; the Kali-yuga; the tree Bignonia Indica; N. of a teacher; (*as, ā, am*), m. f. n. the tree Grislea Tomentosa; (*ā*), f., N. of a plant, a small sort of Hedysarum; [cf. *kāshāya* and *pañća-kashāya*.] — *Kashāya-kṛit, t*, m. the tree Symplocos Racemosa, the bark of which is used in dyeing; also *rakta-lodhra*. — *Kashāya-ćitra, as, ā, am*, dyed or stained of a dull red colour. — *Kashāya-tā*, f. contraction. — *Kashāya-pāṇa, ās*, m. pl. a nickname of the Gāndhāras ('drinking decoctions'). — *Kashāya-yāvanāla, as*, m. a sort of grain. — *Kashāya-vāsika, as*, m. a kind of poisonous insect. — *Kashāyānvita* (°*ya-an*°), *as, ā, am*, astringent, harsh, styptic.

Kashāyita, as, ā, am, red, coloured; prepared for dyeing or colouring.

Kashāyin, ī, iṇī, i, yielding a resinous exudation, astringent, dyed of a red colour, worldly-minded; (*ī*), m., N. of several plants, Shorea Robusta; Artocarpus Lacucha; the wild Datura tree.

Kashāyī-kṛita, as, ā, am, made red. — *Kashāyī-kṛita-loćana, as, ā, am*, with reddened eyes.

Kashāyī-bhūta, as, ā, am, become red, reddened.

कषि *kashi*, &c. See under *kash*.

कषिका *kashikā*, f. (said to be fr. rt. *kash*), a bird in general.

Kashīkā, f. a species of bird.

कषेरुका *kasherukā*, f. the back-bone, the spine; [cf. *kaśerukā*.]

कष्कष *kashkasha, as*, m. (fr. *kash?*), Ved. a kind of poisonous insect.

कष्ट *kashṭa, as, ā, am*, bad; ill, evil, wrong; painful; grievous, severe; difficult; most grievous, most painful; mischievous, noxious, injurious; boding evil; (*am*), n. evil, difficulty, a bad state of things, misery, wretchedness, pain, suffering, hardship, uneasiness; *kashṭena*, with great difficulty or effort; (*am*), ind. an exclamation of grief or sorrow, Ah! Alas! [cf. Hib. *ceas*, 'sorrow, grief, sadness.'] — *Kashṭa-kara, as, ī, am*, giving pain or trouble. — *Kashṭa-kāraka, as, ā, am*, causing trouble or annoyance; (*as*), m. the world. — *Kashṭa-tapas, ās, ās, as*, one who performs many penitential exercises. — *Kashṭa-tara, as, ā, am*, more difficult, inconvenient or painful. — *Kashṭa-labhya, as, ā, am*, difficult to be obtained. — *Kashṭa-śrita, as, ā, am*, suffering pain or misfortune, undergoing hardships, performing penance. — *Kashṭa-sādhya, as, ā, am*, accomplishable with difficulty. — *Kashṭa-sthāna, am*, n. a bad situation, a disagreeable place or site. — *Kashṭāgata* (°*ṭa-āg*°), *as, ā, am*, with difficulty or hardly arrived.

Kashṭāya, nom. A. *kashṭāyate, -yitum*, to have wicked intentions.

कष्टि *kashṭi*. See under *kash*.

कष्फिल *kashphila, as*, m., N. of a Bhikshu.

कस् 1. *kas*, cl. 1. P. *kasati, ćakāsa, kasitum*, to go, move, approach: Intens. *ćanīkasīti, ćanīkasyate*; [cf. Hib. *cas, cos*, 'a foot;' *coisighim*, 'to go.']

Kasvara, as, ī, am, going, moving.

कस् 2. *kas, kaste*, a various reading for *kaṇs, kaṇste*.

कस *kasa, as*, m. = *kasha*, a touchstone; (*ā*), f. = *kaśā*, a whip.

कसना *kasanā*, f. a kind of poisonous spider.

कसनोत्पाटन *kasanotpāṭana, as*, m. the plant Gendarussa Vulgaris; (perhaps a wrong reading for *kāsanotp*°.)

कसर्णीर *kasarṇīra* or *kasarṇila, as*, m., Ved. a certain snake; also personified.

कसाम्बु *kasāmbu*, n., Ved. a heap of wood (?).

कसारस *kasāras*, a kind of bird.

कसिपु *kasipu, us*, m. food, boiled rice; [cf. *kaśipu*.]

कसेरु *kaseru, us*, m. a kind of grass. See *kaśeru*, &c.

Kaserukā, f. a sort of grass, back-bone, &c.

कस्तम्भी *ka-stambhī*, f., Ved. the prop of a carriage-pole.

कस्तीर *kastīra, am*, n. tin; [cf. κασσίτερος.]

कस्तुरिका *kasturikā* or *kastūrikā* or *kastūrī*, f. musk, the animal perfume so called, as brought from Kashmīr, Napal, and Western Asam or Butan, (the latter is said to be the best); the plant Hibiscus Abelmoschus, or the plant Amaryllis Zeylanica; (this word may be derived from the Gr. κάστωρ.) — *Kastūra-mallikā* or *kastūrī-mallikā*, f. the musk bag. — *Kāstūri-kāṇḍa-ja, as*, m. musk. — *Kastūrī-mṛiga, as*, m. the musk animal.

कस्फिल *kasphila, as*, m., N. of a Bhikshu; [cf. *kashphila*.]

कस्मल *kasmala, am*, n. consternation; fainting, syncope. See *kaśmala*.

कस्मात् *kasmāt*, ind. (abl. fr. 2. *ka*), where from? whence? why?

कस्वर *kasvara*. See under rt. 1. *kas*.

कहय *kahaya, as*, m., N. of a man.

कहाह *kahāha, as*, m. a buffalo.

कहूय *kahūya, as*, m., N. of a man.

कहोड *kahoḍa, as*, m., N. of a man, with the patronymic *kaushītaki* or *kaushītakeya*; (*am*), n. title of a work derived from him.

कह्लण *kahlaṇa*. See under *kalhaṇa*.

कह्लार *kahlāra, am*, n. the white esculent water-lily, Nymphæa Lotus; sometimes spelt *kalhāra*.

कह्व *kahva, as*, m. a kind of crane, Ardea Nivea.

का 1. *kā* = 2. *kad* and 1. *ku*, at the beginning of some compounds (e. g. *kāksha*), and perhaps a corruption of *kad*.

का 2. *kā*, a form for rt. *kan* in the Ved. participle *kāyamāna, as, ā, am*, wishing, desiring, loving, and in one or two other forms.

कांशि *kāṇśi, is*, m. a cup; [cf. *kāṇsya*.]

कांस् *kāṇs*, cl. 1. A. *kāṇsate, -situm*, to shine, glitter; [cf. *kāś*.]

कांस *kāṇsa, as, ī, am*, born in Kansa.

कांसीय *kāṇsīya, am*, n. white copper; [cf. the following.]

कांस्य *kāṇsya, as, ā, am* (fr. *kaṇsa*), consisting of white copper or brass; (*am*), n. white copper or brass, queen's metal, any amalgam of zinc and copper; a musical instrument, a sort of gong or plate of bell-metal struck with a stick or rod; a kind of measure; (*as, am*), m. n. a drinking vessel of brass, a goblet. — *Kāṇsya-kāra, as, ī*, m. f. a brazier, a pewterer, a worker in white or bell-metal. — *Kāṇsya-ja, as, ā, am*, made of brass. — *Kāṇsya-tāla, as*, m.

a cymbal. — *Kāṇsya-nīla, as,* m. blue vitriol considered as a collyrium; N. of a monkey; occasionally written *kāṇśya-nīla.* — *Kāṇsya-bhājana, am,* n. brass. — *Kāṇsya-maya, as, ī, am,* consisting or made of brass. — *Kāṇsya-mala, am,* n. verdigris. — *Kāṇsya-mākshika, am,* n. a metallic substance, probably a kind of pyrites. — *Kāṇsyābha* (°*ya-ābha*), *as, ā, am,* coloured like brass.

Kāṇsyaka, am, n. brass.

काक **kāka**, *as,* m. (said to be fr. rt. *kai*, to caw), a crow, (metaphorically an expression of contempt, e. g. *na tvāṃ kākam manye*, I value thee less than a crow); an impudent, insolent fellow; a lame man, a cripple; washing the head, bathing by dipping the head only into the water as crows do; a sectarial mark (*tilaka*); a particular measure; the plant Ardisia Humilis (see *kāka-jambu*); N. of a Dvīpa or division of the world; (*ās*), m. pl., N. of a people; (*ī*), f. a female crow, personified as a daughter of Kaśyapa by Tāmrā, and mother of the crows; a kind of medicinal plant (= *kākolī*); N. of one of the seven mothers of Śiśu; (*ā*), f., N. of several plants, Leea Hirta, also = *kāka-jaṅghā, kāka-nāsā;* Solanum Indicum, = *kāka-māći;* Ficus Oppositifolia, = *kākoḍumbara;* another medicinal plant, = *kākolī;* another plant, commonly *raktikā;* (*am*), n. a multitude or assemblage of crows; a modus coeundi. — *Kāka-kaṅgu, us,* f. a kind of panic-grass, Panicum Miliaceum. — *Kāka-kalā,* f. the plant Leea Hirta; [cf. *kāka-jaṅghā.*] — *Kāka-kūrma-mṛigākhu* (°*ga-ākhu*), *avas,* m. pl. the crow, tortoise, deer, and mouse. — *Kāka-kūrmādi* (°*ma-ādi*), *ayas,* m. pl. the crow, the tortoise, and the rest. — *Kāka-ghnī,* f. a tree, said to be a large kind of Karañja, Galedupa Arborea, = *mahā-karañja.* — *Kāka-ćaṇḍīśvara, as,* m., N. of a man. — *Kāka-ćiñćā,* f. the shrub which yields the red and black berry used in India as a jeweller's weight, Abrus Precatorius; also *kāka-ćiñći* and *kāka-ćiñćī.* — *Kāka-ćiñćika,* N. of a kind of soft substance; another reading of the word is *kāćilindi.* — *Kāka-ććhada, as,* m. a wagtail; side-locks of hair. — *Kāka-ććhadi, is,* m. or, according to another reading, *kāka-ććhardi, is,* m. a wagtail; a crow's vomit. — *Kāka-jaṅghā,* f. the plant Leea Hirta; also Abrus Precatorius. — *Kāka-jambu, us,* f. the plant Ardisia Humilis, commonly Bhumijamb; (*ūs*), f. another species of Jambu. — *Kāka-jāta, as,* m. the Indian cuckoo. — *Kāka-tā,* f. the state of a crow. — *Kāka-tālīya, as, ā, am,* unexpected, as in the fable of the fruit of the palm falling unexpectedly at the moment of the alighting of a crow and killing it; accidental; (*am*), ind. unexpectedly, suddenly; (*am*), n. the fable of the crow and the fruit of the palm. — *Kākatālīya-vat,* ind. suddenly, (said of any unexpected casualty.) — *Kāka-tālukin, ī, inī, i,* having the palate of a crow, contemptible, vile. — *Kāka-tiktā,* f. the plant Abrus Precatorius. — *Kāka-tinduka, as,* m. a kind of ebony, Diospyros Tomentosa. — *Kāka-tuṇḍa, as,* m. the dark species of Agallochum; (*ī*), f., N. of a tree, in Hindī called Kauāḍoḍi; a sort of brass. — *Kāka-tuṇḍikā,* f. the plant Abrus Precatorius. — *Kāka-tulya, as, ā, am,* like a crow, crow-like, crafty. — *Kāka-danta, as,* m. the tooth of a crow, i. e. anything impossible or not existing. — *Kāka-dantaki,* a patronymic from Kākadantaka; (*ayas*), m. pl., N. of a warrior-tribe; *kākadantakīya, as,* m. a prince of the Kākadantakis. — *Kāka-dhvaja, as,* m. submarine fire, a personage in Hindū mythology; [cf. *aurva.*] — *Kāka-nāman, ā,* m. the plant Agati Grandiflora. — *Kāka-nāśā,* f. the same plant. — *Kāka-nāsa, as,* m., N. of a plant, commonly called Vikaṇṭaka; (*ā*), f. the plant Leea Hirta. — *Kāka-nāsikā,* f. the plant Leea Hirta; N. of another plant, also called Rakta-trivṛit. — *Kāka-nidrā,* f. 'a crow's sleep,' a light slumber, one which is easily broken. — *Kāka-nīlā,* f. = *kāka-jambū.* — *Kāka-paksha, as,* m. side-locks of hair on the temples of boys and young men; three or five locks on each side left when the head is first shaved and allowed to remain there, especially in persons of the military caste; (also at the end of compounds *kāka-pakshaka.*) — *Kāka-pada, am,* n. the foot of a crow; an incision in the skin similar to a crow's foot; the sign V in MSS. marking that something has been left out; (*as*), m. a modus coeundi. — *Kāka-parṇī,* f. the plant Phaseolus Trilobus. — *Kāka-pīlu, us,* m., N. of several plants, = *kāka-tinduka, kāka-tuṇḍī,* and also a variety of Abrus Precatorius. — *Kāka-pīluka, as,* m. = *kāka-tinduka.* — *Kāka-puććha, as,* m. the Kokila or Indian cuckoo, (perhaps a Prākṛit form of the next.) — *Kāka-pushṭa, as,* m. the Indian cuckoo, (this bird, like the English cuckoo, being said to leave its eggs in the nests of other birds, as in that of the crow &c.) — *Kāka-pushpa, am,* n. = *gandha-parṇa* (?). — *Kāka-peya, as, ā, am,* what may be drunk by a crow, epithet of a shallow river. — *Kāka-phala, as,* m. the tree Azadirachta Indica; (*ā*), f. = *kāka-jambū.* — *Kāka-bandhyā,* f. a woman that bears only one child. — *Kāka-bhāṇḍī,* f. a species of Karañja. — *Kāka-bhīru, us,* m. an owl ('afraid of crows'). — *Kāka-madgu, us,* m. a water-hen, a gallinule; resembling a crow in colour. — *Kāka-marda, as,* m. a kind of gourd, Cucumis Colocynthis (*mahā-kāla*). — *Kāka-mardaka, as,* m. the same. — *Kāka-māćikā* or *kāka-māćī,* f. the plant Solanum Indicum, an esculent vegetable, commonly Gūrkamai. — *Kāka-mātā,* f. the same plant. — *Kāka-mukha, ās,* m. pl. 'crow-faced,' N. of a mythical people. — *Kāka-mudgā,* f. a plant, commonly Mugani; according to some a wild kind of bean, Phaseolus Trilobus. — *Kāka-mṛiga, au,* m. du. the crow and the deer. — *Kāka-yava, as,* m. barren corn, the ear of which has no grains. — *Kāka-rudra-saṃvāda, as,* m. title of a work on omens. — *Kāka-ruhā,* f. a parasite plant, Epidendrum Tesseloides &c. — *Kāka-vat,* ind. like a crow, in the manner of a crow. — *Kāka-varṇa, as,* m., N. of a prince. — *Kāka-varṇin, ī,* m., N. of a prince. — *Kāka-vartaka, au,* m. du. the crow and the quail. — *Kāka-vallabhā,* f. = *kāka-jambū.* — *Kāka-vallarī,* f., N. of a plant, = *svarṇa-vallī.* — *Kāka-vyāghra-gomāyu, avas,* m. pl. the crow, the tiger, and the jackal. — *Kāka-śabda, as,* m. the cawing of a crow. — *Kāka-śimbī,* f., N. of a plant, = *kāka-tuṇḍī.* — *Kāka-śīrsha, as,* m. the tree Agati Grandiflora, commonly called Vakapushpa. — *Kāka-śīrshi, is,* m., N. of a man. — *Kāka-strī,* f. the same plant. — *Kāka-sphūrja, as,* m. the plant Diospyros Tomentosa. — *Kāka-svara, as,* m. a shrill tone. — *Kākākshi* (°*ka-ak*°), n. the eye of a crow; *kākākshi-nyāyena,* ind. in the manner of a crow's eye, (crows are supposed to have but one eye or visual orb, which, as occasion requires, moves from the cavity on one side into that on the other); a term for a word which follows two rules. — *Kākāṅgā* or *ī* (°*ka-aṅ*°), f. the plant Leea Hirta, = *kāka-nāsā.* — *Kākāńći,* f. the plant Leea Hirta; an esculent vegetable, Solanum Indicum. — *Kākāṇḍa* (°*ka-aṇ*°), *as,* m., N. of two plants, Mahānimba and Kākatindu (?), a kind of bean; (*ā*), f. a kind of spider; N. of a plant; see *kolaśimbī.* — *Kākāṇḍaka, as,* m., N. of a crow or N. of a plant; a kind of spider. — *Kākāṇḍolā,* f., N. of a plant. — *Kākādanī* (°*ka-ad*°), f., N. of several plants, Abrus Precatorius; a white variety of this plant, commonly Śveta-guñjā. — *Kākāri* (°*ka-ari*), *is,* m. an owl. — *Kākekshu* (°*ka-ik*°), *us,* m. a kind of reed, Saccharum Spontaneum. — *Kākendu* (°*ka-in*°), *us,* m. a kind of ebony, Diospyros Melanoxylon, = *kāka-tinduka.* — *Kākeshṭa* (°*ka-ish*°), *as,* m. the tree Melia Azadirachta. — *Kākoḍumbara* (°*ka-uḍ*°), *as,* m. or *kākoḍumbarikā,* f. or *kākodumbarikā,* f. opposite-leaved fig tree, Ficus Oppositifolia. — *Kākodara* (°*ka-ud*°), *as,* m. a serpent. — *Kākolūka* (°*ka-ul*°), *am,* n. crow and owl. — *Kākolūkikā,* f. the natural enmity of the owl and crow. — *Kākolūkīya, am,* n. = the preceding; N. of the third book of the Pañćatantra. — *Kākoshṭhaka* and *kākaushṭhaka* (°*ka-oshṭha*), *as, ikā, am,* shaped like the beak of a crow; epithet of a bandage.

Kākaṇa, am, n. a leprosy with black and red spots, considered incurable; (called so from its similarity to the black and red seed of the plant Abrus Precatorius.)

Kākaṇantikā, f. the plant Abrus Precatorius.

Kākaṇi, a sort of small coin; [cf. *kākiṇī.*]

Kākananti, f. the plant Abrus Precatorius.

Kākāyu, us, m., N. of a plant, = *kākavallarī.*

Kākāla, as, m. a raven; [cf. *kāka* and *kākola.*]

Kākīya, as, ā, am, relating to a crow.

काकतीयरुद्र **kākatīya-rudra**, *as,* m., N. of a king of Nāgapura.

काकन्दि **kākandi**, *ayas,* m. pl., N. of a warrior-tribe.

Kākandī, f., N. of a country; Emblic Myrobalan.

Kākandīya, as, m. a prince of the above tribe.

काकम्बीर **kākambīra**, *as,* m., Ved., N. of a tree; (according to Sāy. literally 'a crow-bearer.')

काकरुक **kākaruka** or **kākarūka**, *as, ā, am,* timid, afraid, a coward; naked; poor, indigent; (*as*), m. a hen-pecked husband; an owl; fraud, deceit.

काकल **kākala**, *am,* n. a jewel worn upon the neck.

Kākalaka, as or *am,* m. or n. (?), the top of the windpipe; the thyroid cartilage; (*as*), m. an ornament of the neck; a species of rice.

काकलि **kākali**, *is,* f. a soft sweet sound [cf. *kala*]; N. of an Apsaras; (*ī*), f. a low and sweet tone; a musical instrument with a low tone played to ascertain whether a person is asleep or not. — *Kākalī-drākshā,* f. a kind of grape without a stone or with a very small one. — *Kākalī-rava, as,* m. the Kokila or Indian cuckoo.

Kākalika, as, am, m. n. (?) a low sweet tone.

काकार **kākāra**, *as, ī, am,* scattering water.

काकिणी **kākiṇī**, f. a small coin, a small sum of money equal to twenty Kapardas or cowries, or to a quarter of a Paṇa; the seed of Abrus Precatorius used as a weight; the shell Cypræa Moneta or cowrie used as a coin; a cubit, the fourth part of a Daṇḍa or short pole; a Daṇḍa; a part of a measure.

Kākiṇikā, f. = the preceding; an atom, a particle.

Kākiṇīka, as, ā, am, having the value of a Kākiṇī.

Kākinī, f. the fourth part of a Paṇa; a quarter of a Māna; the shell Cypræa Moneta.

काकिल **kākila**, *as,* m. a jewel worn upon the neck; [cf. *kākala.*]

काकु **kāku**, *us,* f. change of the voice in fear, anger, grief, &c. [cf. *sevā-kāku*]; muttering, murmuring; the tongue; stress, emphasis.

काकुत्स्थ **kākutstha**, *as,* m. a descendant of Kakutstha; an epithet of Anenas, Aja, Daśaratha, Rāma, Lakshmaṇa; N. of a sovereign, also Purañjaya; (*au*), du. Rāma and Lakshmaṇa.

काकुद् **kākud**, *t,* f., Ved. and **kākuda**, *am,* n. the hollow of the mouth, the palate.

Kākudra, as, ā, am, furnished with a palate (?), a palate (?).

Kākubh, a various reading for *kākud.*

काकुभ **kākubha**, *as, ā, am,* consisting of Kakubh verses; a patronymic from Kakubh. — *Kākubha-bārhata, as,* m. (scil. *pragātha*) a Pragātha beginning with a Kakubh and ending with a Bṛihatī.

काकोचिक **kākoćika**, *as,* m. or *kākoćī,* f. or *kākoćin, i,* m. the fish Cyprinus Cachius.

काकोल **kākola**, *as,* m. a raven [cf. *kāka* and *kākāla*]; a boar; a snake; a potter; (*as, am*), m. n. a poisonous substance of a black colour or the colour of a raven, whence its name; possibly the berry of the Cocculus Indicus; (*am*), n. a division of the infernal regions or hell; (*as, ī*), m. f. a vegetable substance used in medicine, described as sweet and cooling, allaying fever, removing phlegm, &c.; it is said to be a root brought from Nepal or Morung.

काक्ष kāksha (kā-ak°), as, ā, am, frowning, looking scornfully or in displeasure; (as), m. a glance, a wink or leer; (am), n. a frown, a look of displeasure; [cf. kaṭāksha.]

काक्षतव kākshatava, am, n. the fruit of Kakshatu.

काक्षसेनि kākshaseni, is, m. (a patronymic fr. kaksha-sena), an epithet of Abhipratārin.

काक्षि kākshi, is, m., N. of a man.

काक्षी kākshī, f. a perfume, a fragrant kind of earth; the plant Cytisus Cajan.

काक्षीव kākshīva, as, m. the plant Hyperanthera Moringa; N. of a son of Gautama and of Auśīnarī, (irregular patronymic fr. kakshīvat or kākshīvat.)

Kākshīvaka, as, m. the plant Hyperanthera Moringa.

काक्षीवत् kākshīvat, ān, m. = kakshīvat.

Kākshīvata, as, ī, am, composed by or relating to Kakshivat; (a patronymic fr. kakshīvat), epithet of Sambara.

काग kāga, as, m. a crow; (in the Prākṛit dialects, a raven; cf. kāka.)

काग्नि kāgni (kā-ag°), is, m. a little fire.

काङ्कायन kāṅkāyana, as, m. (a patronymic fr. kaṅka), N. of a Muni.

काङ्क्ष् kāṅksh, cl. 1. P. kāṅkshati, ća-kāṅksha, ep. also A. kāṅkshate, &c., kāṅkshitum, to wish, desire; to strive to obtain; to long for, hope for (with acc.), expect; to wait; to look for anything (with dat.): Caus. kāṅkshayati, aćakāṅkshat: Desid. ćikāṅkshishati: Intens. ćākāṅkshyate and ćākāṅshṭi; [cf. Hib. cachta, 'hunger;' Goth. huhru-s, 'hunger;' hungrja, 'to be hungry;' Germ. Hunger.]

Kāṅkshat, an, antī, at, or kāṅkshamāṇa, as, ā, am, wishing, desiring, hoping, expecting.

Kāṅkshā, f. wish, inclination, desire.

Kāṅkshita, as, ā, am, wished, desired; expected, longed for; (am), n. wish, desire.

Kāṅkshin, ī, iṇī, i, desiring, expecting, longing for (with acc. or at the end of a compound). — Kāṅkshitā, f. wish, desire.

काङ्क्षोरु kāṅkshoru, us, m. a heron; also written kāṅkshāru.

काङ्गा kāṅgā, f., N. of a plant, Orris root.

काङ्गुक kāṅguka, am, n. a kind of corn.

काच kāća, as, m. (fr. rt. kać), glass, crystal considered as a natural production and used as a jewel or ornament; alkaline ashes, any salt of potash or soda in a glassy or crystalline state; a class of diseases of the eye, especially an affection of the optic nerve or gutta serena; a loop, a swinging shelf, a string so fastened to the yoke as to hold or support burdens &c.; the string of the scale of a balance; (am), n. alkaline salt, black salt; wax. — Kāća-kūpī, f. a glass bottle. — Kāća-ghaṭī, f. a glass ewer. — Kāća-bhājana, am, n. a vessel of glass or crystal, a cup, a goblet. — Kāća-maṇi, is, m. 'a glass jewel,' crystal, quartz. — Kāća-mala, am, n. black salt or soda. — Kāća-lavaṇa, am, n. black salt, a medicinal salt, prepared by calcining fossil salt and the fruit of the Emblic Myrobalan together; it consists chiefly of muriate of soda, with a small quantity of iron, lime, and sulphur, and is a tonic aperient. — Kāća-vaka-yantra, am, n. a glass retort. — Kāća-sambhava, am, n. black salt. — Kāća-sauvarćala, am, n black salt. — Kāća-sthālī, f. the trumpet flower, Bignonia Suaveolens. — Kāćāksha (°ća-ak°), as, m. glass-eye, N. of an aquatic bird.

Kāćaka, as, m. glass, a stone; alkaline ashes &c.

Kāćana or kāćanaka, am, n. an enclosure, a string or tape which ties a parcel or bundle of papers or the leaves of a manuscript &c.; [cf. kaćela.]

Kāćanakin, ī, m. a writing, a manuscript.

Kāćita, as, ā, am, suspended by a swing or in a loop.

काचिघ kāćigha, as, m. a mouse, a rat; gold; a vegetable.

काचिञ्चिक kāćiñćika (a various reading for kākaćiñćika), a kind of soft substance.

काचित्कर kāćit-kara, as, ī, am, Ved. doing various things, serving various purposes; (kā-ćit, Ved. for kāni-ćit.)

काचिम kāćima, as, m. a tree considered as sacred, one growing near a temple, and being on that account an object of religious veneration or worship &c.

काचिलिन्दि kāćilindi and **kāćilindika** (various readings for kākaćiñćika), a kind of soft substance.

काच्छ kāććha, as, ī, am (fr. kaććha), being on the bank of a river (not applicable to a man).

Kāććhika, as, ī, am, being on the bank of a river (as a man).

काच्छप kāććhapa, as, ī, am (fr. kaććhapa), relating or belonging to a tortoise.

काच्छिम kāććhima, as, ā, am, clear (as water); [cf. aććha, svaććha.]

काच्छी kāććhī, f. a kind of fragrant earth; [cf. kākshī from which kāććhī is derived.]

काजल kā-jala, am, n. a little water.

काञ्च् kāñć, cl. 1. A. kāñćate, -ćitum, to shine; to bind; [cf. kać and kaṅć.]

Kāñćana, am, n. gold; property; wealth; the filament of the lotus; (as, ī, am), golden, made or consisting of gold; (as), m. several plants, Mesua Ferrea; Michelia Champaca; Ficus Glomerata; Bauhinia Variegata; Datura Fastuosa; another plant, = punnāga; N. of the fifth Buddha; N. of a son of Nārāyaṇa, author of the play Dhanañjaya-vijaya; N. of a prince [cf. kāñćana-prabha]; (ī), f. turmeric; a kind of Asclepias; a yellow pigment. — Kāñćana-kadalī, f. a variety of the plant Musa Sapientum. — Kāñćana-kandara, as, m. a gold mine. — Kāñćana-kāriṇī, f. the plant Asparagus Racemosus. — Kāñćana-kshīrī, f. a kind of Asclepias, = kshīriṇī-latā. — Kāñćana-giri, is, m. the golden mountain, an epithet of the mount Sumeru. — Kāñćana-gairika, am, n. a species of ochre. — Kāñćana-ćaya, as, m. a heap of gold. — Kāñćana-pura, am, n., N. of a town. — Kāñćana-pushpaka, am, n. the plant Tabernæmontana Coronaria. — Kāñćana-pushpī, f. the plant Premna Spinosa. — Kāñćana-prabha, as, m., N. of a prince, a son of Bhīma and father of Suhotra. — Kāñćana-bhū, ūs, f. gold-dust; a golden or yellow soil. — Kāñćana-maya, as, ī, am, golden. — Kāñćana-mālā, f., N. of the wife of Kunāla, the son of Aśoka; N. of another woman. — Kāñćana-vapra, as, m. a hill or mound of gold. — Kāñćana-varman, ā, m., N. of a prince. — Kāñćana-sandhi, is, m. a treaty of friendship between two parties on equal terms. — Kāñćana-sannibha, as, ā, am, like gold. — Kāñćanāksha (°na-ak°), as, m., N. of a Dānava; (ī), f., N. of the river Sarasvatī. — Kāñćanāṅga (°na-aṅ°), as, ī, am, golden-bodied. — Kāñćanābhidhāna-sandhi (°na-abh°), is, m. 'golden alliance,' (lit. golden-named.)

Kāñćanaka, as, m. the tree Bauhinia Variegata, mountain ebony; the fruit of rice or grain; (am), n. a yellow orpiment.

Kāñćanāra or kāñćanāla or kāñćanāraka, as, m. mountain ebony, Bauhinia Variegata.

Kāñćanīya, as, ā, am, golden; (ā), f. a yellow pigment, commonly Go-roćanā.

काञ्चि kāñći, ayas, m. pl., N. of a people; [cf. kāñći.]

काञ्चिक kāñćika, am, n. sour gruel; [cf. kāñjika.]

काञ्ची kāñćī or **kāñći**, is, f. (said to be fr. rt. kan), a girdle, especially a woman's zone or girdle furnished with small bells and other ornaments; the plant Abrus Precatorius; N. of an ancient city situated in the peninsula and one of the seven sacred cities of the Hindūs. — Kāñći-purī, f., N. of a town. — Kāñći-kshetra, N. of a region. — Kāñćī-nagara, am, n., N. of a town. — Kāñćī-pada, am, n. the hips and loins; mons veneris, the pubic region. — Kāñćī-pura, am, n., N. of a town. — Kāñći-prastha, as, m., N. of a town.

काञ्जिक kāñjika, am, n. sour gruel, the water of boiled rice in a state of spontaneous fermentation; (ā), f. the same; N. of two plants, = jīvantī-latā and palāśī-latā. — Kāñjika-vaṭaka, as, m. a dish consisting of sour gruel, meal, and several condiments.

Kāñji, f. sour gruel, = kāñjika; N. of a plant, = mahādroṇā.

Kāñjika, am, n. sour gruel.

काट kāṭa, as, am, m. n. (a Prākṛit form fr. karta), Ved. deepness, a hole; (Sāy.) a well.

Kāṭya, as, ā, am, Ved. being in a hole.

काटवेम kāṭavema, as, m., N. of a commentator on Kālidāsa's Sakuntalā.

काटुक kāṭuka, am, n. (fr. kaṭuka), acidity.

काठ kāṭha, as, ī, am, composed by Kaṭha; (as), m. a rock, a stone.

Kāṭhaka, as, m., N. of a work belonging to the Brāhmaṇa literature, and derived from the Kaṭha branch of the Vedas; (as, ī, am), according to the Kaṭha portion of the Vedas.

Kāṭhaśāṭhin, inas, m. pl. the pupils of Kaṭha-śāṭha.

काठिन kāṭhina, am, n. (fr. kaṭhina), hardness, sternness; (as), m. the date fruit.

Kāṭhinya, am, n. hardness, rigidity, stiffness, sternness, severity; firmness of character; difficulty, obscurity (of style). — Kāṭhinya-phala, as, m. the plant Feronia Elephantum, = kapittha.

काण kāṇa, as, ā, am, one-eyed, monoculous (akshṇā kāṇah, blind of one eye); perforated, as a cowrie broken or perforated by insects; (as), m. a crow; [cf. ekāksha and kāṇūka.] — Kāṇa-tva, am, n. one-eyedness. — Kāṇa-bhūti, is, m., N. of a Yaksha.

Kāṇeya, as, m. the son of a one-eyed woman; one-eyed. — Kāṇeya-vidha, am, n. a country inhabited by Kaṇeyas.

Kāṇera, as, m. son of a one-eyed woman; one-eyed.

काणाद kāṇāda, as, ī, am, composed by or relating to Kaṇāda.

काणूक kāṇūka or **kānūka**, as (?), m. (said to be fr. rt. kaṇ), a crow; the bird which makes a hanging nest on the tāl tree; a cock; a species of goose; [cf. kāṇa.]

काणेलीमातृ kāṇelīmātṛi, a name of reproach, occurring generally in the voc. case; (according to native commentators) one whose mother was an unmarried woman, a bastard; (connected with the word kāṇera ?).

काण्टकमर्दनिक kāṇṭakamardanika, as, ī, am (fr. kaṇṭaka-mardana), resulting from the treading down or crushing of thorns or enemies.

काण्टकार *kāṇṭakāra, as, ī, am,* made of the wood of Kaṇṭakāra.

काण्ठेविद्धि *kāṇṭheviddhi, is, ī* or *yā,* m. f. a patronymic fr. *kaṇṭhe-viddha.*

काण्ड *kāṇḍa, as, am,* m. n. (said to be fr. rt. 2. *kam*), a section, part; a single joint of the stalk or stem of a plant, i. e. the portion from one knot to another (e. g. *ishus tri-kāṇḍā,* an arrow made of a cane with three knots; but by Pāṇ. IV. 1, 21, the fem. should be *tri-kāṇḍī*); any part, portion or division of a work or action; any distinct portion or division of a sacrificial rite (as that belonging to the gods or to the manes); the section or chapter of a book, a separate department or subject (e. g. *karma-kāṇḍa,* the department of the Veda treating of sacrificial rites); a stalk or stem, a branch, a switch; the part of the trunk of a tree whence the branches proceed; a cluster, a bundle; a multitude, heap, quantity (at end of comp.); an arrow; a long bone, a bone of the arms or legs (e. g. *kāṇḍa-bhagna,* fracture of a bone); a cane, a reed (Saccharum Sara); a particular measure; water; opportunity, occasion; a private place, privacy, a secret place; praise, flattery; a horse. (At the end of a compound *kāṇḍa* may sometimes imply depreciation or deficiency, = vile, low, bad, sinful, wicked, &c.) — *Kāṇḍa-kaṭuka, as,* m. the plant Momordica Charantia, = *kāravella.* — *Kāṇḍa-kāṇḍaka, as,* m. a species of grass. — *Kāṇḍa-kāra, am,* n. the Areca or betel-nut tree, commonly Guvāka; the betel-nut. — *Kāṇḍa-kīlaka, as,* m. the tree Symplocos Racemosa. — *Kāṇḍa-kushku, us,* m. (?), N. of a man. — *Kāṇḍa-guṇḍa, as,* m. a species of grass. — *Kāṇḍa-goćara, as,* m. an iron arrow. — *Kāṇḍa-tikta* and *kāṇḍa-tiktaka, as,* m. a kind of gentian, Gentiana Cherayta. — *Kāṇḍa-dhāra, as,* m., N. of a country; (*as, am*), coming from or relating to this country. — *Kāṇḍa-nīla, as,* m. the plant Symplocos Racemosa. — *Kāṇḍa-paṭa, as, ī,* m. f. or *kāṇḍa-paṭaka, as,* m. (?) an outer tent, a screen surrounding a tent, a curtain. — *Kāṇḍa-patita, as,* m., N. of a serpent-king. — *Kāṇḍa-pāta, as,* m. an arrow's fall or flight. — *Kāṇḍa-puṅkhā,* f., N. of a plant, = *śara-puṅkhā.* — *Kāṇḍa-pushpa, am,* n. the flower Artemisia Indica, commonly Donā. — *Kāṇḍa-prishṭha, as, ā, am,* 'arrow-backed,' one who carries arrows on his back, one of the military profession, a soldier; (*as*), m. the husband of a Vaiśyā female; an adopted son, any other than one's own son; (*am*), n. the bow of Karṇa; the bow of Kāma; [cf. *kāṇḍa-sprishṭa.*] — *Kāṇḍa-bhagna, am,* n. a fracture or dislocation of the bones or limbs, complete fracture of a limb. — *Kāṇḍa-maya, as, ī, am,* consisting of pieces of cane; (*ī*), f. = *kāṇḍa-vīṇā,* q. v. — *Kāṇḍa-ruhā,* f. a medicinal plant, = *kaṭukī.* — *Kāṇḍarshi* (°*ḍa-rishi*), *is,* m. a Ṛishi or divine saint of a peculiar class, as Jaimini and others, who teach a peculiar Kāṇḍa or section of the Vedas. — *Kāṇḍa-lāva, as, ā, am,* cutting a cane or branch, intending to do so. — *Kāṇḍa-vat, ān, atī, at,* armed with an arrow, an archer. — *Kāṇḍa-vīṇā,* f. a musical instrument composed of joints of reed, a reed-pipe (?) played by the Ćaṇḍālas; [cf. *kaṇḍola-vīṇā.*] — *Kāṇḍa-sandhi, is,* m. a knot, a joint in the stem of a tree or of a reed. — *Kāṇḍa-sprishṭa, as, ā, am,* living by the military profession, living by arms, a soldier; (*as*), m. a Brāhman who lives by arms; [cf. *kāṇḍa-prishṭha.*] — *Kāṇḍa-hīna, am,* n. a fragrant grass, Cyperus Pertenuis. — *Kāṇḍānukrama* (°*ḍa-an*°), *as,* m. or *kāṇḍānukramaṇikā* or *kāṇḍānukramaṇī,* f. an index of the Kāṇḍas of the Taittirīya-Saṃhitā. — *Kāṇḍekshu* (°*ḍa-ik*°), *us,* m. the plant Asteracantha Longifolia and the plant Saccharum Spontaneum. — *Kāṇḍe-ruhā,* f., N. of a plant, = *kāṇḍa-ruhā.*

Kāṇḍanī, f., N. of a plant, = *sūkshma-parṇī* and *rāma-dūtī.*

Kāṇḍāla or *kāṇḍola, as,* m. a reed-basket.

Kāṇḍikā, f. a kind of corn (see *lankā*); a kind of gourd, Cucumis Utilissimus.

Kāṇḍin, ī, inī, i, Ved. reed-shaped, hollow.

Kāṇḍīra, as, ā, am, armed with arrows, an archer; (*as*), m. the plant Achyranthes Aspera and the plant Momordica Charantia; (*ā* and *ī*), f. the plant Rubia Munjista.

Kāṇḍeri, f. the plant Tiaridium Indicum.

काण्डणी *kāṇḍaṇī,* (?) f. a plant, commonly Rāmadūtī; [cf. *sūkshma-parṇī.*]

काण्डोल *kāṇḍola,* see above; [cf. *kaṇḍola.*]

काण्व *kāṇva, as, ī, am* (a patronymic fr. *kaṇva*), a descendant of Kaṇva; a follower of Kaṇva. — *Kāṇva-śākhin, ī,* m. a follower of the Kāṇva branch of the Veda. — *Kāṇvī-putra, as,* m., N. of a teacher.

Kāṇvaka, am, n., N. of a Sāman.

Kāṇvāyana, as, ā, am, a patronymic fr. *kāṇva.*

कातन्त्र *kā-tantra, am,* n. title of a grammar (= *kalāpa,* q. v.); there are several appendices to and commentaries on this grammar, called *Kātantra-gaṇadhātu,* °*ćatushṭayapradīpa,* °*ćandrikā,* °*dhātughoshā,* &c. — *Kātantra-pañjikā,* f. title of a commentary by Triloćana-dāsa.

कातर *kātara, as, ā, am* (fr. *katara ?*), cowardly, discouraged, timid, depressed, perplexed, shrinking, afraid; confused, agitated, disordered; (*as*), m. a large kind of fish, Cyprinus Catla, = *kātala.* — *Kātara-tā,* f. or *kātara-tva, am,* n. cowardice, timidity, agitation.

Kātarāyaṇa, as, m. a patronymic fr. *kātara.*

Kātarya, am, n. timidity, fear, dejection, depression of spirits.

कातल *kātala, as,* m. a large kind of fish, Cyprinus Catla; N. of a man; [cf. *kātara.*]

Kātalāyana, as, m. a patronymic fr. *kātala.*

काति *kāti, is, is, i* (fr. 2. *kā* = *kan*), wishing, desiring (in the compounds *ṛiṇa-kāti* and *kāma-kāti*).

कातीय *kātīya, as, ā, am* (fr. *kātya* below), composed by Kātya (e. g. in *kātīya-gṛihyasūtra, kātīya-kalpa-sūtra,* and *kātīya-sūtra*); a N. of Kātyāyana (?); a pupil of the same; also *kātyāyanīya* (?).

Kātya, as, m. a patronymic fr. *kata;* also = *kātyāyana* (?).

Kātyāyana, as, m. (a patronymic fr. *kati* or *kātya*), N. of the author of several treatises on ritual, grammar, &c.; he is generally identified with Vararući, the author of the Prākṛita-prakāśa. He is also the author of the Vārttikas or supplementary rules to Pāṇini, of the Yajur-veda Prātiśākhya, and the Srauta-sūtras; (*ī*), f., N. of one of the two wives of Yājñavalkya; an epithet of Durgā; a middle-aged widow dressed in red clothes. — *Kātyāyana-sūtra, am,* n. the Srauta-sūtras of Kātyāyana. — *Kātyāyana-sūtra-paddhati,* a commentary on the last by Yājñika-deva. — *Kātyāyanasūtra-bhāshya, am,* n. a commentary on the same by Karka. — *Kātyāyanī-putra, as,* m., N. of a teacher. — *Kātyāyanī-māhātmya, am,* n. a part of the Skanda-purāṇa.

Kātyāyanīya, as, ā, am, composed by Kātyāyana; e. g. *kātyāyanīya-śāstram,* 'the law-book composed by him;' (*as*), m. a pupil of Kātyāyana.

कातु *kātu, us,* m. a cave; a well (?); [cf. *kāṭa.*]

कातृण *kā-triṇa, am,* n. a species of grass, Rohisha-triṇa; [cf. *kat-triṇa.*]

कात्कृ *kāt-kṛi,* cl. 8. P. A. *-karoti, -kurute, -kartum* (fr. *kāt,* an exclamation of abuse, and 1. *kṛi*), to insult, dishonour.

Kāt-kṛita, as, ā, am, dishonoured, insulted.

कात्त्रेयक *kāttreyaka, as, ī, am* (fr. *kat-tri*), produced from or belonging to any combination of three inferior articles.

कात्थक्य *kātthakya, as,* m. (a patronymic fr. *katthaka*), N. of a commentator.

कात्यायन *kātyāyana.* See under *kātīya.*

काथक *kāthaka* and *kāthakya,* patronymics from Kathaka.

काथञ्चित्क *kāthañćitka, as, ī, am* (fr. *kathañćid*), accomplished with difficulty.

काथिक *kāthika, as, ī, am* (fr. 1. *kathā*), belonging to a tale, told in one; knowing stories; (*as*), m. a narrator of stories.

कादम्ब *kādamba, as,* m. (said to be fr. rt. 1. *kad*), a kind of goose with dark-grey wings (*kala-haṃsa*); a drake or (according to some) a teal; an arrow; the plant Nauclea Cadamba; (*ā*), f., N. of a plant, = *kadamba-pushpī;* (*am*), n. the flower of the plant Nauclea Cadamba.

Kādambaka, as, m. an arrow.

Kādambinī, f. a long line or bank of clouds.

कादम्बर *kādambara, as, am,* m. n. the surface or skim of coagulated milk; (*am, ī*), n. f. a spirituous liquor distilled from the flowers of the Cadamba; the rain-water which collects in clefts or hollow places of the tree Nauclea Cadamba when the flowers are in perfection, and which is supposed to be impregnated with the honey; wine, spirituous liquor in general; the fluid which issues from the temples of a rutting elephant; (*ī*), f. the female of the Kokila or Indian cuckoo; the female of another bird, = *śārikā,* i. e. Turdus Salica; an epithet of Sarasvatī; N. of a daughter of Ćitra-ratha and Madirā; a celebrated work of Vāṇa-bhaṭṭa, called 'Kādambarī,' derives its name from her. — *Kādambarī-vīja, am,* n. ferment, yeast, whatever occasions fermentation.

Kādambarya, as, m. = *kadamba,* Nauclea Cadamba.

कादाचित्क *kādāćitka, as, ī, am* (fr. *kadāćid*), appearing now and then, produced sometimes, occasional, incidental. — *Kādāćitka-tā,* f. the state of occurring occasionally.

कादिक्रमस्तुति *kādi-krama-stuti,* a work attributed to Saṅkarāćārya.

Kādi-mata, a Tantra work.

काद्रवेय *kādraveya, as,* m. (fr. *kadrū*), epithet of the Nāgas or serpents supposed to people the lower regions; an epithet of Arbuda; also of Kasarṇīra.

कानक *kānaka, as, ī, am* (fr. *kanaka*), golden; (*am*), n. the seed of Croton Jamalgota.

कानद *kānada, as,* m., N. of a son of Dhīmarana.

कानन 1. *kānana, am,* n. (said to be fr. rt. *kan*), a forest, grove; a house. — *Kānanāri* (°*na-ari*), *is,* m. a species of the Mimosa tree, Samī. — *Kānanaukas* (°*na-ok*°), *ās,* m. the inhabitant of a forest, a monkey; [cf. *vanaukas.*]

कानन 2. *kānana* (*ka-ān*°), *am,* n. the face of Brahmā.

कानीत *kānīta, as,* m. a patronymic of Pṛithu-śravas.

कानीन *kānīna, as, ī,* m. f. (fr. *kanīna*), the son or daughter of a young or unmarried woman; an epithet of Vyāsa, Karṇa, and Agniveśya; (*as, ā, am*), suitable to or designed for the eye-ball; [cf. *kanīnaka.*]

Kānīyasa (fr. *kanīyas*), less in number (used only in plur.).

कान्त *kānta, as, ā, am* (fr. 2. *kam*), desired, loved, dear; pleasing, agreeable; lovely, beautiful; (*as*), m. a lover, a husband; any one beloved; the moon; spring; the plant Barringtonia Acutangula [cf. *hijjala*]; iron; stone; a precious stone (in which sense it is compounded with *sūrya*, *ćandra*, and *ayas*); an epithet of Kṛishṇa, and of Skanda; (*ā*), f. a beloved or lovely woman, a wife, a mistress; the earth; N. of a plant (commonly called *priyaṅgu*); also of another plant (= *nāgara-mustā*); large cardamoms; a kind of perfume (see *reṇukā*); N. of a metre of four lines of seventeen syllables each; (*am*), n. saffron; a species of iron. — *Kānta-tā*, f. or *kānta-tva*, *am*, n. loveliness, beauty, agreeableness. — *Kānta-pakshin*, *ī*, m. a peacock ('the beautiful bird'). — *Kānta-pushpa*, *as*, m. the tree Bauhinia Variegata, mountain ebony. — *Kānta-miśra*, *as*, m., N. of a man. — *Kānta-loha*, *am*, n. the loadstone. — *Kānta-lauha*, *as* or *am* (?), m. or n. steel; [cf. *loha-kānta*.] — *Kāntāṅghri-dohada* (°*tā-aṅ*°), *as*, m. the tree Jonesia Aśoka (this tree being supposed to blossom upon coming in contact with the foot of a handsome female). — *Kāntā-ćaraṇa-dohada*, *as*, m. = the preceding. — *Kāntāyasa* (*ta-ayas*), *am*, n. the iron stone; [cf. *kānta-loha* and *ayas-kānta*.]

Kāntaka, *as*, m., N. of a man.

Kāntalaka, *as*, m. the tree Cedrela Toona, commonly Tunna, the wood of which sometimes resembles mahogany.

Kāntāya, nom. A. *-yate*, *-yitum*, to behave like a lover.

Kānti, *is*, f. desire, wish; loveliness, beauty; splendor; female beauty; personal decoration or embellishment; (in rhetoric) beauty enhanced by love; a lovely or desirable woman, personified as wife of the moon. — *Kānti-kara*, *as*, *ī*, *am*, causing beauty, beautifying, illuminating. — *Kānti-da*, *as*, *ā*, *am*, giving beauty; beautifying, adorning; (*ā*), f. the plant Serratula Anthelmintika; (*am*), n. bile, the bilious humor. — *Kānti-dāyaka*, *as*, *ikā*, *am*, granting beauty; beautifying, adorning; (*am*), n. a fragrant wood, a kind of Curcuma from the root of which a yellow die is prepared, C. Zanthorrhiza. — *Kānti-pura*, *am*, n., N. of a town in Nepal. — *Kānti-mat*, *ān*, *atī*, *at*, lovely, beautiful, splendid; (*tī*), f., N. of a metre; N. of a woman. — *Kānti-mat-tā*, f. loveliness, beauty. — *Kānti-hara*, *as*, *ī*, *am*, destroying beauty, making ugly, dulling, dimming. — *Kāntī-nagarī*, f. (for *kānti-n*°), N. of a city of the north; [cf. *kānti-pura*].

Kāntika, *ās*, m. pl., N. of a people.

कान्तार **kāntāra**, *as*, *am*, m. n. a wood or large forest; a bad or difficult road; a hole, a cavity; (*as*), m. a red variety of the sugar-cane; a bamboo; mountain ebony, Bauhinia Variegata; (*ī*), f. a kind of sugar-cane; (*am*), n. a symptom or symptomatic disease, a lotus. — *Kāntāra-ga*, *as*, *ā*, *am*, who or what goes into a wood. — *Kāntāra-patha*, *as*, m. a forest-way. — *Kāntāra-pathika*, *as*, *ī*, *am*, conveyed on difficult forest roads. — *Kāntāra-vāsinī*, f. an epithet of Durgā.

Kāntāraka, *as*, m. a kind of sugar-cane; (*ās*), m. pl., N. of a people; (*ikā*), f. a kind of bee.

कान्तोत्पाडा **kāntotpāḍā**, f. (for *kāntotpādā*?), N. of a metre consisting of four lines of twelve syllables each.

कान्थक **kānthaka** fr. *kanthā*, N. of a place on the river Varṇu.

कान्दव **kāndava**, *as*, *ī*, *am* (fr. *kandu*), roasted or baked, in an iron pan or oven, as bread, cakes, &c.

Kāndavika, *as*, *ī*, *am*, employed in baking; (*as*), m. a baker.

कान्दाविष **kāndā-visha**, *am*, n., Ved. a species of poison.

कान्दिश् **kāndiś**, *k*, *k*, *k*, or *kāndiśīka*, *as*, *ā*, *am*, put to flight, running away, flying; (fr. *kām diśam*, 'to which region' shall I fly?). — *Kāndig-bhūta*, *as*, *ā*, *am*, run away.

कान्यकुब्ज **kānyakubja**, *am*, n. = *kanya-kubja*, N. of a town; (*ī*), f. a princess or a female inhabitant of this town.

कान्यजा **kānyajā**, f. a kind of perfume, commonly Nālī.

कापटव **kāpaṭava**, a patronymic from Kāpaṭu.

Kāpaṭavaka, *as*, *ikā*, *am*, coming from the Kāpaṭavas.

कापटिक **kāpaṭika**, *as*, *ī*, *am* (fr. *kapaṭa*), fraudulent, dishonest; wicked, perverse, bad; (*as*), m. a flatterer, a parasite; a student, a scholar.

Kāpaṭya, *am*, n. wickedness, dishonesty, fraud.

कापथ **kā-patha**, *as*, m. a bad road; bad ways; (*am*), n. the fragrant root of Andropogon Muricatus; (*as*), m., N. of a Dānava.

कापा **kāpā**, f., Ved. a call (?).

कापाल **kāpāla**, *as*, *ī*, *am* (fr. *kapāla*), relating to the skull or cranium; made of skulls; (*as*), m. a follower of a certain Śaiva sect [cf. the following]; the plant Cucumis Utilissimus; (*ī*), f. a clever woman; (*am*), n. a kind of leprosy.

Kāpālika, *as*, *ī*, *am*, relating to or belonging to the skull; (*as*), m. a worshipper of Śiva of the left-hand order, characterized by carrying skulls of men as ornaments and by eating and drinking from them; N. of a mixed caste; (*as*, *ī*, *am*), peculiar to a Kāpālika.

Kāpālin, *ī*, m. a N. of Śiva; N. of a son of Kṛishṇa and Yaudhishṭhirī.

कापिक **kāpika**, *as*, *ī*, *am* (fr. *kapi*), shaped or behaving like a monkey.

Kāpittha, *as*, *ī*, *am* (fr. *kapittha*), belonging to the tree Feronia Elephantum.

Kāpitthaka, N. of a place.

Kāpila, *as*, *ī*, *am* (fr. *kapila*), peculiar or belonging to Kapila (or Vishṇu), derived from him; of a tawny colour; (*as*), m. a follower of the Sāṅkhya system of philosophy which was founded by Kapila; tawny (the colour); (*am*), n., N. of an Upa-purāṇa.

Kāpileya, a patronymic from Kapila or a metronymic from Kapilā.

Kāpivana, *as*, m. (fr. *kapi-vana*), N. of a festival lasting two days.

Kāpiśa, *am*, n. (fr. *kapiśa*), a spirituous liquor, wine; (*ī*), f., N. of a country.

Kāpiśāyana, *as*, *ī*, *am*, coming from Kapiśa (e. g. *madhu*, honey, or *drākshā*, grape); (*as*), m. a patronymic; (*am*), n. a spirituous liquor; a deity.

Kāpiśeya, *as*, m. (fr. *kapiśā*), a Piśāća, an imp or goblin

Kāpishṭhala, *as*, m. a patronymic fr. *kapishṭhala*; (*ās*), m. pl., N. of a people; [cf. καμβισθολοι.]

Kāpī, f., N. of a woman; N. of a river.

Kāpeya, *as*, *ī*, *am* (fr. *kapi*), belonging to or relating to or peculiar to a monkey; a patronymic fr. *kapi* (a descendant of Aṅgiras being meant); (*am*), n. the monkey species; monkey tricks.

Kāpya, *as*, *ā*, *am*, a patronymic fr. *kapi* (a descendant of Aṅgiras being meant).

कापुरुष **kā-purusha**, *as*, m. a mean contemptible man, a coward, a wretch; (*as*, *ā*, *am*), cowardly, miserable, mean. — *Kāpurusha-tā*, f. or *kāpurusha-tva*, *am*, n. meanness, cowardliness.

Kāpurushya, *am*, n. cowardice, meanness.

कापोत **kāpota**, *as*, *ī*, *am* (fr. *kapota*), peculiar to a pigeon; of the colour of a pigeon, grey, of a dirty white colour; (*as*), m. grey (the colour), a dirty white colour; natron, fossil alkali; antimony considered as a collyrium or application to the eyes; (*ī*), f., N. of a plant; (*am*), n. a flock of pigeons; antimony. — *Kāpotāñjana* (°*ta-añ*°), *am*, n. antimony especially considered as a collyrium or application to the eyes.

Kāpotaka, *ās*, m. pl. the inhabitants of Kapotakīyā.

Kāpotapākya, *as*, m. a prince of the Kapotapākas.

काप्यकर **kāpyakara**, *as*, m. (*kāpya ?-kara*), a penitent, one who acknowledges his faults.

Kāpya-kāra, *as*, m. avowal or confession of sin; a penitent, one who confesses a crime.

काफल **kāphala**, *as*, m. a bitter seed. See *kaṭphala*.

काबव **kābava**, *as*, m., Ved. an epithet of evil spirits.

काम् **kām**, ind. an interjection used in calling out to another.

काम **kāma**, *as*, m. (fr. 2. *kam*), wish, desire, longing (e. g. *prāpta-kāma*, one who has gained his wish), affection, love, the object of desire or love, the god of desire generally; Love, the god of love (son of Dharma and husband of Rati or, according to other authorities, son of Brahmā or Saṅkalpa); a N. of Agni in the Veda (either because he desires to consume all things or because he makes requests to the gods in behalf of man); a N. of Bala-deva [cf. *kāma-pāla*]; a species of the mango tree (= *mahā-rāja-ćūta*); N. of a metre consisting of four lines of two long syllables each; N. of a prince; (at the end of compounds) having a desire for, desiring (e. g. *go-kāma*, desiring cows; *dharma-kāma*, desiring justice; *tyaktu-kāma*, having a desire to leave; see Gram. 871). After the phrase *kāmo me*, 'my desire is,' the potential may be used; e. g. *kāmo me bhuñjīta bhavān*, my wish is that you should eat; (*ā*), f. wish, desire [cf. *kāmayā*]; N. of a daughter of Pṛithu-śravas and wife of Ayuta-nāyin; (*am*), n. object of desire; semen virile; N. of a Tīrtha; (*as*, *ā*, *am*), Ved. wishing, desiring. *Kāmena* or *kāmāt*, ind. out of affection or love for, of one's own accord, intentionally; *kāmāya* or *kāme*, ind. according to one's desire; out of love for (with gen. or dat. case). — *Kāma-karśana* in *a-kāma-karśana*, q. v. — *Kāma-kalā*, f. an epithet of Rati, the wife of Kāma. — *Kāma-kāti*, *is*, *is*, *i*, Ved. requesting the fulfilment of a wish; (Sāy.) uttering wishes. — *Kāma-kāma*, *as*, *ā*, *am*, or *kāma-kāmin*, *ī*, *inī*, *i*, wishing wishes; following the dictates of passion or desire. — *Kāma-kāra*, *as*, m. voluntary action, the act of following one's own inclinations, spontaneous deed; the operation or influence of desire, desire; (*as*, *ī*, *am*), following one's own inclinations, indulging one's desires. — *Kāmakāra-tas*, ind. according to one's desires or inclinations. — *Kāma-kūṭa*, *as*, m. the paramour of a harlot; wanton caresses, harlotry. — *Kāma-keli*, *is*, m. amorous sport, a euphemistic term for sexual intercourse; (*is*, *is*, *i*), having amorous sport, libidinous, wanton. — *Kāma-krīḍā*, f. amorous sport, N. of a metre consisting of four lines of fifteen long syllables each. — *Kāma-khaḍga-dalā*, f., N. of a plant; [cf. *svarṇa-ketakī*.] — *Kāma-ga*, *as*, *ā*, *am*, going or coming of one's own accord, able to move or act as one pleases; (*ā*), f. a libidinous woman. — *Kāma-gati*, *is*, *is*, *i*, or *kāma-gama*, *as*, *ā*, *am*, or *kāma-gāmin*, *ī*, *inī*, *i*, = *kāma-ga* above; (*kāma-gamās*), m. pl., N. of a class of deities of the eleventh Manvantara. — *Kāma-giri*, *is*, m., N. of a mountain. — *Kāma-guṇa*, *as*, m. the quality of desire, passion, affection; satiety, perfect enjoyment; an object of sense. — *Kāma-ćara*, *as*, *ā*, *am*, moving freely, unchecked, unrestrained. — *Kāma-ćaraṇa*, *am*, n. free or unchecked motion. — *Kāmaćara-tva*, *am*, n. unrestrainedness. — *Kāma-ćāra*, *as*, *ā*, *am*, moving freely, following one's own pleasure, unchecked, unrestrained; (*as*), m. free, unrestrained motion; independant, spontaneous action; following one's own wishes or pleasures, sensuality, selfishness. — *Kāmaćāra-tas*, ind. according to one's inclination. — *Kāma-ćārin*, *ī*, *iṇī*, *i*, moving according to one's inclination, acting unrestrainedly; behaving freely towards women, desirous, libidinous; self-willed; (*as*), m. a sparrow; an epithet of Garuḍa, the bird of Vishṇu. — *Kāma-ja*, *as*, *ā*, *am*, produced or caused by passion or desire; (a son) engendered in love; (*as*), m. the son of Kāma, i. e. Aniruddha. — *Kāma-jāna*, *as*, m. or (according to another reading) *kāma-jani*, *is*, m. the Indian cuckoo; [cf.

kāma-tāla.] — Kāma-jāla = kāma-tāla. — Kāma-jit, t, t, t, conquering desire; an epithet of Skanda. — Kāma-jyeshṭha, as, ā, am, Ved. having desire (personified) at the head; led by Kāma. — Kāma-tantra, N. of a work. — Kāma-taru, us, m. the god of love considered as a tree or parasitical plant; [cf. kāma-vṛiksha.] — Kāma-tas, ind. according to wish or affection, passionately, from passion or feeling (opposed to dharma-tas); of one's own accord, willingly, intentionally, by consent. — Kāma-tāla, as, m. the Indian cuckoo, (the song of this bird being poetically considered as an incentive to love.) — Kāma-da, as, ā, am, giving what is wished, granting desires; an epithet of the sun, and of Skanda; (ā), f. a fabulous cow, the cow of plenty; N. of a woman. — Kāma-dattā, f. title of a work. — Kāma-dattikā, f., N. of a woman. — Kāma-daminī, f. 'taming love,' N. of a libidinous woman in the Pañćatantra. — Kāma-dambhaka, as, m., N. of a man. — Kāma-darśana, as, ī, am, looking lovely. — Kāma-dugha, as, ā, am, milking all desires, i. e. yielding what one wishes; (ā), f. the cow of plenty, a fabulous cow yielding all desires. — Kāma-duh, -dhuk, f. and kāma-duhā, f. the cow of plenty. — Kāma-dūtikā, f. the plant Tiaridium Indicum. — Kāma-dūtī, f. the female of the Indian cuckoo; the plant Bignonia Suaveolens. — Kāma-deva, as, m. the god of love (according to some authorities a son of Sahishṇu and Yaśo-dharā); also a N. of Śiva; N. of a poet; N. of a king of Jayantīpurī; N. of the author of the Prāyaśćitta-paddhati. — Kāma-dohin, ī, inī, i, yielding desires; an epithet of the cow of plenty, which belonged to Vasishṭha. — Kāma-dharaṇa, am, n., Ved. procuring what is desired, fulfilment of desire. — Kāma-dhātu, us, m. the region of the wishes, the seat of the Kāmāvaćaras. — Kāma-dhenu, us, f. the cow of plenty, a cow belonging to the sage Vasishṭha, yielding all desires; title of a commentary of Vopadeva on his Kavi-kalpadruma, also called Kāvya-kāmadhenu. — Kāmadhenu-tantra, am, n. title of a work on the mystical signification of the letters of the alphabet. — Kāma-dhvaṇsin, ī, m. an epithet of Śiva as 'subduing the god of love.' — Kāma-nāśaka, as, ikā, am, destroying irregular desires, subduing any sensual appetite. — Kāmandhamin, ī, m. a brazier; [cf. kārandhamin.] — Kāma-pati, is, m. the lord of desires. — Kāma-patnī, f. the wife of Kāma, i. e. Rati. — Kāma-pāla, as, m. epithet of Bala-deva; also of Śiva; N. of a man. — Kāma-pīḍita, as, ā, am, tormented with lust or irregular desires. — Kāma-pūra, as, ā, am, fulfilling wishes, granting desires. — Kāma-pra, as, ā, am, Ved. granting desires; (am), n. the fulfilling of a desire. — Kāma-prada, as, ā, am, granting desires; (as), m. a kind of coitus. — Kāma-praśna, as, m. questioning as one pleases, asking unrestrainedly. — Kāma-prastha, as, m., N. of a town. — Kāmapri, is, m. (fr. kāma-pra), Ved. a patronymic of Marutta; (Sāy.) 'whose wishes are fulfilled.' — Kāma-phala, as, m. a species of the mango tree. — Kāma-baddha, as, ā, am, bound by love; (am), n. a wood. — Kāma-bhaksha or kāma-bhakshya, as, ā, am, eating anything or everything. — Kāma-bhāj, k, k, k, partaking of sensual enjoyment. — Kāma-bhoga, as, m. gratification of desires, sensual gratification (always used in plur.). — Kāma-mañjarī, f., N. of a woman. — Kāma-maya, as, ī, am, consisting of desire, answering all desires. — Kāma-mardana, as, m. epithet of Śiva, 'the destroyer of the god of love.' — Kāma-maha, as, m. the festival of the god of love (on the day of full moon in month Ćaitra or March-April). — Kāma-mālin, ī, m. epithet of Gaṇeśa. — Kāma-mūḍha, as, ā, am, infatuated by lust. — Kāma-mūta, as, ā, am, Ved. strongly affected by love. — Kāma-mohita, as, ā, am, overcome by or intoxicated with desire, love, or passion. — Kāma-rasa, as, m. seminal effusion. — Kāma-rasika, as, ī, am, libidinous. — Kāma-rāja, as, m., N. of a poet. — Kāma-rūpa, am, n. a shape changing at will; (as, ā, am), taking any shape at will; beautiful, pleasing; (as or ās), m. sing. or pl. a district lying east of Bengal, the western portion of Assam. — Kāmarūpa-dhara, as, ā, am, taking any shape at will. — Kāmarūpa-pati, is, m., N. of a commentary on the work Śāradātilaka. — Kāmarūpin, ī, iṇī, i, taking any shape at will; pleasing, beautiful; (ī), m. a pole-cat; a boar; a Vidyādhara, a kind of subordinate deity; (iṇī), f. the plant Physalis Flexuosa. — Kāma-rekhā, f. a harlot, a courtezan; [cf. kāma-lekhā.] — Kāma-latā, f. membrum virile; the plant Ipomœa. — Kāma-lekhā, f. a harlot, a courtezan; [cf. kāma-rekhā.] — Kāma-lola, as, ā, am, overcome with desire or passion. — Kāma-vat, ān, atī, at, being in love, enamoured, wanton; containing the word Kāma; (tī), f. a species of Curcuma [cf. dāru-haridrā]; N. of a town. — Kāma-vara, as, m. a gift chosen at will. — Kāma-vallabha, as, m. spring; the mango tree; (ā), f. moonlight. — Kāma-vaśa, as, m. subjection to love. — Kāma-vaśya, as, ā, am, being in subjection to the god of love, enamoured. — Kāma-vāṇa, as, m. an arrow of Kāma-deva, the deity of love. — Kāma-vāda, as, ā, am, saying anything at pleasure. — Kāma-vāsin, ī, inī, i, choosing one's residence at will. — Kāma-viddha, as, ā, am, wounded by the god of love; (as), m., N. of a man. — Kāma-vihantṛi, tā, trī, tṛi, disappointing desires. — Kāma-vīrya, as, ā, am, displaying heroism at will, an epithet of Garuḍa. — Kāma-vṛiksha, as, m. a parisitical plant (= vandāka). — Kāma-vṛitta, as, ā, am, indulging desires, licentious, dissipated, debauched. — Kāma-vṛiddhi, is, f. increase of desire or passion; (is, is, i), increasing love; (is), m. a shrub, called in Karṇāṭaka Kāma-ja, of supposed aphrodisiac properties. — Kāma-vṛintā, f. the trumpet flower, Bignonia Suaveolens. — Kāma-śara, as, m. love's shaft; the mango tree. — Kāma-śāstra, am, n. a manual of pleasure or of love, title of a work of Vātsyāyana. — Kāma-saṃyoga, as, m. attainment of desired objects. — Kāma-sakha, as, m. spring; the month Ćaitra; the mango tree. — Kāma-samūha, as, m., N. of a work of Ananta. — Kāma-suta, as, m. the son of Kāma-deva, god of love, i. e. Aniruddha. — Kāma-sū, ūs, ūs, u, granting wishes. — Kāma-sūtra, N. of a love-manual by Vātsyāyana. — Kāma-sena, as, m., N. of a king of Kāmavatī; (ā), f. the wife of Nidhipati. — Kāma-haituka, as, ī, am, caused or produced by mere desire, without any real cause; of one's own accord. — Kāmākshī (°ma-ak°), f. a form of Durgā. — Kāmākhyā (°ma-ākh°), f. a form of Durgā. — Kāmāgni (°ma-ag°), is, m. the fire of love, passion, lust, violent desire. — Kāmāgni-sandīpana, am, n. kindling the fire of lust, an aphrodisiac. — Kāmāṅkuśa (°ma-an°), as, m. a finger-nail; the membrum virile. — Kāmāṅga (°ma-an°), as, m. the mango tree, Mangifera Indica. — Kāmātura (°ma-āt°), as, ā, am, love-sick, in love, affected by love or desire. — Kāmātma-tā, f. passion, lust; wish, desire. — Kāmātman (°ma-āt°), ā, ā, a, whose very essence is desire, consisting of desire, libidinous, licentious; desiring, wishing for; enamoured. — Kāmādhikāra (°ma-adh°), as, m. the influence of passion or desire, aspiration; that part of a Śāstra which relates to human wishes or desires. — Kāmādhishṭhita (°ma-adh°), as, ā, am, influenced or overcome by love. — Kāmānala (°ma-an°), as, m. the fire of love, passion, lust, violent desire. — Kāmāndha (°ma-an°), as, m. the Indian cuckoo (blind from love); (ā), f. musk. — Kāmānnin (°ma-an°), ī, inī, i, having food at will. — Kāmābhikāma (°ma-abh°), as, ā, am, lustful. — Kāmāyudha (°ma-āy°), am, n. the weapon or arrow of the god of love; membrum virile; (as), m. a species of the mango tree. — Kāmāyus (°ma-āy°), us, m. a vulture; an epithet of Garuḍa, the bird of Vishṇu. — Kāmāraṇya (°ma-ar°), am, n. a pleasing grove or wood. — Kāmāri (°ma-ari), is, m. a mineral substance used in medicine, a sort of pyrites (see vīṭa-mākshika); an epithet of Śiva, the foe or conqueror of the god of love. — Kāmārta (°ma-ār°), as, ā, am, afflicted by love or passion, in love. — Kāmārthin (°ma-ar°), ī, inī, i, lascivious, wanton, amorous. — Kāmāvaćara (°ma-av°), ās, m. pl. a class of deities (with Buddhists). — Kāmāvatāra (°ma-av°), as, m., N. of a metre consisting of four lines of six syllables each; N. of a work. — Kāmāvasāya (°ma-av°), as, m. suppression or mortification of the passions, coldness, stoicism. — Kāmāvasāyi-tā, f. or kāmāvasāyi-tva, am, n. the power of suppressing desire, self-denial or mortification (one of the eight supernatural faculties of Śiva). — Kāmāvasāyitṛi, tā, trī, tṛi, who or what suppresses or destroys passion or desire. — Kāmāvasāyin, ī, inī, i, one who suppresses desire, destructive of love or desire. — Kāmāśana (°ma-aś°), am, n. eating at will, unrestrained enjoyment. — Kāmāśrama (°ma-āś°), as, m. or kāmāśrama-pada, am, n. the hermitage of the god of love. — Kāmāsakta (°ma-ās°), as, ā, am, overcome with desire or passion, impassioned, in love. — Kāmāsakti (°ma-ās°), is, f. passion, desire. — Kāmepsu (°ma-īp°), us, us, u, striving to obtain the fulfilment of a desire. — Kāmeśvara (°ma-īś°), as, m. an epithet of Kuvera. — Kāmodaka (°ma-ud°), am, n. a voluntary oblation of water; oblation of water to deceased friends &c. exclusive of those for whom it is directed by law. — Kāmodā, f. a Rāgiṇī, one of the female personifications of the musical notes. — Kāmopahata (°ma-up°), as, ā, am, overcome with passion or desire. — Kāmopahata-ćittāṅga (°ma-up°), as, ā, am, one whose mind and body are overcome with love.

Kāmana, as, ā, am, lustful, libidinous, desirous; (ā), f. desire, wish.

Kāmam, ind. (acc. c. of kāma), according to wish or desire, according to inclination; agreeably to desire; at will; willingly, joyfully; (as a particle of assent) well, very well; granted; admitted that; indeed, really, surely; (implying at the same time a contradiction to what precedes) but really, but. Kāmam — na or kāmam — na tu, rather — than (with pot. or impv. or fut. pass. part., e. g. kāmam ā maraṇāt tishṭhed gṛihe kanyā — na enām prayaććhet tu guṇa-hīnāya, 'rather should a girl stay at home till her death, than that he should give her to one void of excellent qualities'); in this sense the negative sentence with na or na tu may also precede or its place may occasionally be taken by an interrogative sentence (e. g. kāmaṃ nayatu māṃ devaḥ kim ardhena ātmano hi me, 'rather let the god take me, what is the use to me of half my existence?'). Kāmam — tu, or kāmam — kiṃ tu, or kāmam — athāpi, or kāmam — tathāpi, or kāmam — punar, well, indeed, surely, granted — however, notwithstanding, nevertheless (e. g. kāmaṃ tvayā parityaktā gamishyāmi — imaṃ tu bālaṃ santyaktuṃ nārhasi, 'granted that forsaken by thee I shall go — this child however thou must not forsake;' or the disjunctive particles are left out altogether). — Kāmaṅ-gāmin, ī, inī, i, going at will; going or coming according to one's inclination or of one's own accord.

Kāmayā, ind. (inst. c. of an obsolete base kāmā), only used with brūhi or prabrūhi (e. g. kāmayā me brūhi deva kas tvam, 'for love of me, say, O god, who thou art').

Kāmayāna, as, ā, am, desiring.

Kāmayitṛi, tā, trī, tṛi, libidinous, lustful, desirous.

Kāmala, as, ā, am, libidinous, lustful; (as), m. spring; dry and sterile soil, a desert; (as, ā), m. f. a form of jaundice, excessive secretion or obstruction of bile; (ā), f., N. of an Apsaras; (ī), f., N. of a daughter of Reṇu, also called Reṇukā.

Kāmalāyana or kāmalāyani (a patronymic fr. kamala), an epithet of the Upakosalas.

Kāmali, is, m., N. of a pupil of Vaiśampāyana.

Kāmalin, ī, inī, i, suffering from jaundice; (inas), m. pl., N. of a school derived from Kāmali (?).

Kāmi, is, m. a libidinous man, a lecher; (is), f. an epithet of Rati, the wife of the god of love.

Kāmika, as, ā, am, desired, wished for, one whose desires are fulfilled; (at the end of a compound) relating to or connected with a desire or wish; (as),

m. a kind of aquatic bird, a wild duck (*kāraṇḍava*); (*ā*), f. a mystical N. of the letter *t*.

Kāmita, as, ā, am, wished, desired; (*am*), n. a wish, desire.

Kāmin, ī, inī, i, desirous, cupidinous; loving, fond, impassioned, wanton; (*ī*), m. a lover, an uxorious husband; N. of several birds, the ruddy goose, Anas Casaca; a pigeon; Ardea Sibirica; a sparrow; an epithet of Śiva; the moon (?); (*inī*), f. a loving or affectionate woman, a timid woman; a woman in general; a climbing parasitical plant; a species of Curcuma; spirituous liquor. — *Kāmi-tā*, f. or *kāmi-tva, am*, n. the state of a lover, love, desire. — *Kāminī-kānta, as* or *am* (?), m. or n. (?), N. of a metre consisting of four lines of six syllables each. — *Kāminīśa* (°*nī-īśa*), *as*, m. the plant Hyperanthera Moringa (*śobhāñjana*).

Kāmīna or *kāmīla, as*, m. the plant Areca Triandra.

Kāmuka, as, ā or *ī, am*, wishing, desirous; loving; cupidinous, lustful, libidinous; (*as*), m. a lover; a sparrow; the plant Jonesia Aśoka; the creeping plant Gærtnera Racemosa; a bow (?); (*ā*), f. a woman desirous of wealth, food, &c.; (*ī*), f. a libidinous or lustful woman. — *Kāmuka-kāntā*, f. the plant Gærtnera Racemosa. — *Kāmuka-tva, am*, n. desire.

Kāmukāyana, as, m. (a patronymic fr. *kāmuka*), N. of a teacher.

1. *kāmya*, nom. P. *kāmyati* (in composition with an object), to have a desire for (e. g. *putra-kāmyati*, to have a desire for children).

2. *kāmya, as, ā, am*, desirable, beautiful; amiable, lovely, agreeable; optional, supererogatory, performed for some particular object and opposed to the *nitya-karma* or fixed and indispensable observance; relating to desire, will, &c., done through lust or passion; performed through the desire of some advantage (as a religious ceremony &c.); (*ā*), f., N. of an Apsaras, a daughter of Kardama. — *Kāmya-karman, a*, n. rites performed with a view to future fruition. — *Kāmya-gir, īr*, f. a pleasing sound, an agreeable speech or song. — *Kāmya-tā*, f. loveliness, beauty. — *Kāmya-tva, am*, n. love, desire; supererogation, will, pleasure. — *Kāmya-dāna, am*, n. an acceptable or desirable gift, a voluntary gift. — *Kāmya-maraṇa, am*, n. voluntary death, suicide. — *Kāmya-vrata, am*, n. a voluntary vow. — *Kāmyābhiprāya* (°*ya-abh*°), *as*, m. self-interested motive or purpose.

Kāmyaka, am, n., N. of a wood; also of a lake.

Kāmyā, f. wish, desire, longing for, striving after, will, intention; (generally compounded with an object, e. g. *putra-kāmyayā*, through desire for a son; *yat-kāmyā*, irreg. inst. c. with which intention.)

कामठ *kāmaṭha, as, ī, am* (fr. *kamaṭha*), peculiar to the tortoise.

Kāmaṭhaka, as, m., N. of a Nāga.

कामण्डलव *kāmaṇḍalava, am*, n. (fr. *kamaṇḍalu*), the business or trade of a potter.

Kāmaṇḍaleya, as, m. a patronymic fr. *kamaṇḍalu* or *kamaṇḍalū* (a species of quadruped).

कामन्दकि *kāmandaki, is*, m. a patronymic fr. *kamandaka*; (*ī*), f., N. of a Buddhist priestess.

कामालिका *kāmālikā*, f. a spirituous liquor.

कामालु *kāmālu, us*, m. the tree Bauhinia Variegata (= *rakta-kāñćana*).

काम्पिल *kāmpila, as*, m., N. of a country believed to be situated in the north of India; (*ī*), f. the capital of that region.

Kāmpilya, as, m., N. of a town of the Pañćālas or N. of a region; N. of one of the five sons of Hary-aśva or Bharmyāśva, called collectively Pañćālas; N. of a plant [cf. *kampila* and *kāmpīla*], a perfume, commonly called Sunda Roćanī.

Kāmpilla, as, m., N. of a plant, a perfume and drug so called; N. of a country said to be in the north-west of India.

Kāmpillaka, am, n. a kind of medicinal substance; (*ikā*), f. a drug and perfume, commonly Sunda Roćanī.

Kāmpīla, as, m., N. of a plant [cf. the preceding]; N. of a town (?); (*as, ī, am*), derived from this plant. — *Kāmpīla-vāsin, ī, inī, i*, living in the town Kāmpīla.

Kāmpīlaka, as, m., N. of a plant.

काम्बल *kāmbala, as, ī, am* (fr. *kambala*), covered with a woollen blanket; (*as*), m. a carriage covered with a woollen cloth or blanket.

काम्बलिक *kāmbalika, as*, m. a sour dish prepared with milk, whey, and vinegar; gruel, barley-water, &c.

काम्बविक *kāmbavika, as*, m. (fr. *kambu*), a dealer in shells, a vender of shell-ornaments.

काम्बुका *kāmbukā*, f. = *kambukā*, the plant Physalis Flexuosa (= *aśva-gandhā*).

काम्बुव *kāmbuva, as* or *am* (?), m. or n. (?), N. of a region.

काम्बोज *kāmboja, as, ī, am* (fr. *kamboja*), born in or coming from Kamboja; (*as*), m. a native of Kamboja, a foreign race who like the Yavanas shave the whole head, (one of the tribes was originally Kshatriya, but degraded by omission of the necessary rites); a prince of this tribe; a horse of the Kamboja breed; the plant Rottleria Tinctoria, commonly Punnag; a kind of Mimosa, the white sort of this plant; (*ī*), f., N. of several plants, Glycine Debilis; a kind of Mimosa, as above; the plant Abrus Precatorius; the plant Serratula Anthelmintica.

Kāmbojaka, as, ī, am, born in or coming from Kamboja.

Kāmboji, is, f. (?) the plant Glycine Debilis.

काम्ल *kāmla* (*kā-amla*), *as, ā, am*, slightly acid, acidulous.

काय 1. *kāya, as, ī, am* (fr. 3. *ka*), relating or devoted to the god Ka or Prajāpati; (with *havis*) clarified butter or any oblation to Brahmā; (*as*), m. scil. *vidhi* or *vivāha*, one of the eight modes of marriage, = Prājāpatya; (*am*), n. with or without *tīrtha*, part of the hand sacred to the creator Prajāpati, the root of the little finger or of the last two fingers.

काय 2. *kāya, as* or *am*, m. n. (fr. rt. *ći*), the body; the trunk of a tree; the body of a lute (i. e. the whole lute except the wires, including the gourd, neck, and belly); assemblage, collection, multitude; principal, capital; a house, a habitation; a butt or mark, an object to be hit or attained; natural temperament of anything or any being. — *Kāya-kāraṇa-kartṛi-tva, am*, n. activity exhibited in bodily acts. — *Kāya-kleśa, as*, m. bodily suffering, toil or pain. — *Kāya-ćikitsā*, f. a department of medical science, treatment of the diseases which affect the whole body. — *Kāya-bandhana, am*, n. a girdle. — *Kāya-valana, am*, n. armour, mail. — *Kāya-stha, as*, m. the supreme being or spirit; a caste or tribe or man of that tribe; the Kāyath or writer caste proceeding from a Kshatriya father and Śūdra mother; (*ī*), f. the wife of a Kāyath or scribe; (*ā*), f. a woman of this caste; N. of several plants, Myrobalanus Chebula; Emblica Officinalis; Ocimum Sanctum; a drug, commonly Kākolī; cardamoms. — *Kāya-sthita, as, ā, am*, situated in the body, corporeal. — *Kāyāgni* (°*ya-ag*°), *is*, m. the digestive faculty. — *Kāyārohaṇa* (°*ya-ār*°) and *kāyāvarohaṇa* (°*ya-av*°), N. of two places.

Kāyaka, as, ikā, am, belonging or relating to the body &c., bodily, corporeal; (*ikā*), f. with *vriddhis*, interest obtained from capital. — *Kāyikā-vṛiddhi, is*, f. interest consisting in the use of an animal or any capital stock pawned or pledged; service rendered by the body of an animal (as a cow &c.) pledged and used by the person to whom it is pledged; or (according to some) interest, of which the payment does not affect the principal.

Kāyika, as, ī, am, performed with the body; corporeal, relating to the body; belonging to an assemblage or multitude (especially at end of comp.).

कायमान *kāyamāna, am*, n. a hut made of grass or thatch.

कायव्य *kāyavya, as*, m., N. of a man.

कार 1. *kāra, as, ī, am* (fr. rt. 1. *kṛi*), at the end of a compound = making, doing, working; who or what does any act, an agent, a maker or doer, an author (e. g. *kumbha-kāra, as*, m. a potter, a maker of earthen vessels; *suvarṇa-kāra*, a goldsmith; *yajña-kāra*, one who performs a sacrifice; *vārttika-kāra*, the author of the Vārttikas); (*as*), m. act, action (e. g. *kāma-kāra, purusha-kāra*, &c.); the term used in designating a sound or a word which is not inflected (e. g. *a-kāra*, the sound *a*; *ka-kāra*, the sound *k*; *eva-kāra*, the word *eva*; *phūt-kāra*, the sound *phūt*; cf. *karaṇa*, p. 205); effort, exertion; determination; religious austerity; a husband, a master, a lord; (*ī*), f., N. of a plant, = *kārikā, kāryā*, &c. — *Kāra-kara, as, ī, am*, working, doing work, acting as agent. — *Kārāvara* (°*ra-av*°), *as*, m. a man of a mixed and low caste, one born from a Nishāda father and Vaidehī mother, employed in working in leather and hides.

1. *kāraka, as, ikā, am*, making, doing, who or what does, makes, creates, acts, &c.; an agent; one who effects or produces anything; (very often in composition with that which is produced or done, e. g. *siṅha-kāraka*, the creator of a lion; *kṛitsna-kāraka*, doing everything; *śilpa-kārikā*, a female mechanic or doer of a mechanical art); intending to act or do; (*ikā*), f. a female dancer; a business; trade; concise explanation and development of difficult rules by metrical lines, especially in philosophy and grammar, a memorial verse or collection of such verses; or sometimes two or three Vārttikas arranged in verse; torment, torture; interest; N. of a plant; (*ikās*), f. pl. Bhartṛihari's memorial verses on grammar; (*akam*), n. the relation of the noun to the verb in a sentence, the notion of a case but not co-extensive with the term case, (there are six such relations according to Pāṇini; a. *karman*, the object or nearest aim of an agent, the idea expressed by the acc. case; b. *karaṇa*, the instrument or idea expressed by the inst. case; c. *kartṛi*, the agent or doer of an action, also expressed by the inst. case, or if expressed by nom. case not considered a *kāraka*, i. e. the agent and instrument are both expressed by the inst. when they are not implied in the verbal termination; d. *sampradāna*, the recipient of the object of giving or of a gift, hence the idea expressed by the dat. case; e. *apādāna*, ablation, i. e. departure or removal from a fixed point, the idea expressed by the abl. case; f. *adhikaraṇa*, location, or the place of the action, i. e. the idea expressed by the loc. case. The idea of the genitive or possessive case is not considered a *kāraka*, because it expresses the relation of two nouns to each other, but not the relation of a noun and verb.) — *Kāraka-vat, ān, atī, at*, relating to one who is active in anything; instrumental, causal. — *Kāraka-vāda, as*, m. a treatise on logic by Rudra. — *Kāraka-hetu, us*, m. the efficient or active cause.

Kāraja, as, ī, am (fr. *kara-ja*), of or relating to the finger-nail; (*as*), m. a young elephant (?).

1. *kāraṇa, am*, n. cause, reason (with gen. and also often with loc.); instrument, means, motive, origin, principle, a cause (in phil.), i. e. that which is invariably antecedent to some product and is not otherwise constituted, (cause in the Nyāya philosophy is of three kinds, according to the distinction of a. *samavāyi*, intimate or inherent, as threads are the inherent cause of cloth; b. *a-samavāyi*, non-intimate or non-inherent, as the conjunction of the threads is the non-intimate cause of cloth; and c. *nimitta*, instrumental, as the weaver's loom is the instrumental cause of cloth); an element, elementary matter, the

origin or plot of a play or poem; that on which an opinion or judgment is founded; a sign, a mark, a document, a proof; a legal instrument; an organ of sense; an action; agency, instrumentality; a father (as the cause of being); a deity as the remote or proximate cause of creation; the body; a kind of musical instrument; a sort of song; a number of scribes or *kāyasthas*; (*ā*), f. pain, agony; casting into hell; an astronomical period; *kāraṇāt*, abl. c. from some cause or reason (e. g. *kasmāt kāraṇāt*, 'from what cause,' often with gen., e. g. *mama kāraṇāt*, 'for my sake,' and at the end of compounds; according to native grammarians every case of *kāraṇa* may be used in this manner, but only the inst., dat., abl., and loc. occur; *a-kāraṇena*, without a reason; *yena kāraṇena*, because; *yasmin kāraṇe*, from which motive, wherefore). — *Kāraṇa-kāraṇa*, *am*, n. a primary cause, an elementary cause, an atom. — *Kāraṇa-gata*, *as*, *ā*, *am*, referred to its cause, resolved into its principles. — *Kāraṇa-guṇa*, *as*, m. a quality of cause; an elementary or causal property. — *Kāraṇaguṇodbhava-guṇa* (°*ṇa-ud*°), *as*, m. a secondary or derivative property, as form, taste, smell, &c., produced by combinations of elementary or causal particles. — *Kāraṇa-tas*, ind. from a certain reason; [cf. *kārya-kāraṇatas*.] — *Kāraṇa-tā*, f. or *kāraṇa-tva*, *am*, n. causality, causation. — *Kāraṇa-dhvaṇsa*, *as*, m. the obviating or removing a cause or occasion. — *Kāraṇa-dhvaṇsaka*, *as*, *ikā*, *am*, or *kāraṇa-dhvaṇsin*, *ī*, *inī*, *i*, obviating or removing the cause or reason of a thing. — *Kāraṇa-bhūta*, *as*, *ā*, *am*, caused. — *Kāraṇa-mālā*, f. a series or chain of causes or events, a term for a figure in rhetoric. — *Kāraṇa-vādin*, *ī*, m. a complainant, a plaintiff. — *Kāraṇa-vāri*, *i*, n. the original water which was produced at the creation, from which, as from a reservoir, the Hindūs suppose all the water in the universe to be supplied. — *Kāraṇa-vihīna*, *as*, *ā*, *am*, without a cause or reason, unreasonable. — *Kāraṇa-śarīra*, *am*, n. the inner rudiment of the body or causal frame, the seat of the soul. — *Kāraṇānvita* (°*ṇa-an*°), *as*, *ā*, *am*, having a cause or reason, following as the effect from its cause. — *Kāraṇābhāva* (°*ṇa-abh*°), *as*, m. absence of cause. — *Kāraṇottara* (°*ṇa-utt*°), *am*, n. special plea, denial of the cause of complaint, admission of the charge generally, but denial of the issue; (thus with regard to the demand of a debt, acknowledgment that it was incurred, but assertion that the loan has been repaid &c.)

Kāraṇaka, at the end of compounds = *kāraṇa*, cause, reason.

Kāraṇika, *as*, *ā* and *ī*, *am*, causal, causative, investigating, ascertaining the cause.

Kāram, a kind of ind. part. fr. rt. *kṛi* at the end of compounds, e. g. *svāhā-kāram*, *namas-kāram*, making obeisance; also with an acc., e. g. *ćauraṅ-kāram ākrośati*, he abuses a person by calling him a thief; *svādunkāram*, making anything sweet &c.

Kārayat, *an*, *antī*, *at*, causing to do, giving power or authority to do &c.

Kārayamāṇa, *as*, *ā*, *am*, doing what is appointed, carrying into effect what has been ordered.

Kārayitavya, *as*, *ā*, *am*, to be caused to be done, to be effected, to be made to do anything. — *Kārayitavya-daksha*, *as*, *ā*, *am*, clever at performing what has to be done.

Kārayitṛi, *tā*, *trī*, *tṛi*, causing or instigating to act or do anything.

Kārayishṇu, *us*, *us*, *u*, causing to act or perform.

1. *kāri*, *is*, *is*, m. f. an artist, an artificer, a mechanic; (*is*), f. action, act, agency, work.

Kārita, *as*, *ā*, *am*, caused to be made or done, brought about, effected; (*ā*), f., scil. *vṛiddhiḥ*, interest, the amount of which is fixed by the debtor, he being forced to do so by the creditor; (*am*), n. the causal form of a verb. — *Kārita-vat*, *ān*, *atī*, *at*, having caused to be made or done. — *Kāritānta* (°*ta-an*°), *as*, *ā*, *am*, ending with a causal affix.

1. *kārin*, *ī*, *iṇī*, *i*, doing, making, effecting, producing, acting, an actor; (*ī*), m. a mechanic, a tradesman.

Kāru, &c. See s. v.

कार 2. *kāra*, *as*, m. (fr. 1. *kṝi*, to scatter), tax, toll, royal revenue, tribute; (*as*, *ī*, *am*, fr. 2. *kara*), produced by hail; (*as*), m. a heap of snow or a mountain covered with it. — *Kāra-kukshīya*, *as*, m., N. of the country of king Sālva on the skirts of the Himālaya ridge in the north-west of Hindūstān; (*ās*), m. pl. the people of this country.

2. *kāraka*, *am*, n. (fr. 2. *karaka*), scil. *salila*, water produced from hail.

कार 3. *kāra*, *as*, m. (fr. 2. *kṝi*, to praise), Ved. a song or hymn of praise, a battle-song.

2. *kāri*, *is*, *is*, *i*, Ved. raising hymns of praise.

2. *kārin*, *ī*, *iṇī*, *i*, Ved. rejoicing, praising.

कार 4. *kāra*, *as*, m. (fr. 2. *kṝi*, to kill), killing, slaughter.

2. *kāraṇa*, *am*, n. killing, injuring.

कारञ्ज *kārañja*, *as*, *ī*, *am*, produced by or coming from the tree Karañja.

कारण्डव *kāraṇḍava*, *as*, m. a sort of duck; [cf. *karaṇḍa*.] — *Kāraṇḍava-vatī*, f., N. of a river (?), abounding in Kāraṇḍavas.

कारण्डव्यूह *kāraṇḍavyūha*, *as*, m., N. of a Buddha; [cf. *karaṇḍa-vyūha*.]

कारन्धम *kārandhama*, *as*, m. (fr. *karandhama*), a patronymic of Avikshit; (*am*), n., N. of a Tīrtha.

Kārandhamin, *ī*, m. a brazier, a worker in mixed or white metal; a mineralogist, an assayer.

कारपचव *kārapaćava*, *as* or *am* (?), m. or n. (?), N. of a region near the Yamunā.

कारभ *kārabha*, *as*, *ī*, *am* (fr. *karabha*), produced by or coming from a camel.

कारमिहिका *kāramihikā*, f. camphor.

कारम्भा *kārambhā*, f., N. of a plant bearing a fragrant seed, commonly Priyangu; [cf. *karambhā*.]

कारव *kā-rava*, *as*, m. a crow; ['making a discordant sound;' cf. Lat. *corvus*, *cornix*; Gr. κόραξ, κορώνη; Germ. *Rabe*; Eng. *crow*.]

कारवल्ली *kāravallī*, f. the plant Momordica Charantia; [cf. *kāravella* and *kāṇḍīra*.]

कारवी *kāravī*, f. the Asa Fœtida plant or its leaf, = Hiṅgupatrī; the plant Celosia Cristata; a kind of anise, Anethum Sowa; another plant, Nigella Indica; a kind of fennel; a kind of Cucurbitaceous plant or small gourd.

कारवेल्ल *kāravella*, *as*, m. a kind of gourd, Momordica Charantia; (*am*), n. the fruit of this gourd.

Kāravellaka, *as*, m. and *kāravellikā*, f. the same.

कारव्य *kāravya*. See under 2. *kāru*.

कारस्कर *kāraskara*, *as*, m., N. of a poisonous medicinal plant; a tree in general; (*ās*), m. pl., N. of a people; (a various reading for *kāraskāra* and *kāraskṛita*.) — *Kāraskarāṭikā* (°*ra* + *āṭikā* fr. rt. *aṭ*), f. a centipede or worm resembling it.

कारा *kārā*, f. (fr. 1. *kṛi*?), a prison; binding, confinement, a fetter; the part of a lute below the neck, an instrument for deadening the sound of a lute; pain, affliction; a female messenger; a female worker in gold; [cf. Lith. *kaliu*, 'I am a captive;' *kalliny-s*, 'a captive;' *kaline*, 'a prison.'] — *Kārā-gāra* (°*rā-ag*°), *am*, n. a gaol or place of confinement. — *Kārā-gupta*, *as*, *ā*, *am*, captive, imprisoned, confined, a prisoner. — *Kārā-gṛiha*, *am*, n. a prison. — *Kārā-pāla*, *as*, m. the guard of a prison. — *Kārā-veśman*, *a*, n. a prison, a gaol.

काराधुनी *kārādhunī*, f., Ved., (Sāy.) a musical instrument, as the couch shell and the like, (or 'impelling the singer.')

कारापथ *kārāpatha*, *as* or *am* (?), m. or n. (?), N. of a country.

कारायिका *kārāyikā*, f. a female crane, = *karāyikā*.

कारिका *kārikā*. See under 1. *kāra*, p. 221.

कारीर *kārīra*, *as*, *ī*, *am* (fr. *karīra*), made of the shoots of reed; connected with the fruit of the plant Capparis Aphylla (as a sacrifice, in which this fruit is used).

Kārīrya, *as*, *ā*, *am*, connected with the fruit of the plant Capparis Aphylla.

कारीष *kārīsha*, *as*, *ī*, *am* (fr. *karīsha*), produced from or coming from dung; (*am*), n. a heap of dung, a great quantity of dried cow-dung.

Kārīshi, *is*, m., N. of a man; (*ayas*), m. pl., N. of a family.

कारु 1. *kāru*, *us*, *us* or *ūs*, *u* (fr. 1. *kṛi*), a maker, a doer, an agent, artificer, artisan, artist, a mechanic; terrible, horrible; (*as*), m. an epithet of Viśva-karman, the artist of the gods; an art, a science. — *Kāru-ćaura*, *as*, m. one who commits burglary. — *Kāru-ja*, *as*, m. the product of an artist or mechanic, a piece of mechanism, any product of manufacture; a young elephant; an ant hill, a hillock; froth, foam; sesamum growing spontaneously; the tree Mesua Ferrea; red orpiment. — *Kāru-hasta*, *as*, m. the hand of an artisan or artificer.

Kāruka, *as*, *ā*, m. f. an artisan, an artificer.

कारु 2. *kāru*, *us*, m. (fr. 2. *kṝi*), Ved. one who sings or praises, a poet. — *Kāru-dhāyas*, *ās*, *ās*, *as*, Ved. favouring or supporting the singer; (Sāy.) arranging works.

Kāravya, *as*, *ā*, *am*, Ved. belonging to the singer, epithet of certain verses (*ṛićas*) of the Atharva-veda.

कारुणिक *kāruṇika*, *as*, *ī*, *am* (fr. *karuṇa*), compassionate, tender, kind. — *Kāruṇika-tā*, f. compassion.

Kāruṇya, *am*, n. compassion, tenderness, kindness.

कारुण्डी *kāruṇḍī* or *kāruṇḍikā*, f. a leech.

कारूष *kārūsha*, *as*, m. a prince of the Karūshas; an epithet of Danta-vakra, the son of Kārūsha Vṛiddhaśarman; N. of a country; (*ās*), m. pl., N. of a people; (*as*), m. = *karūsha*, N. of a son of Manu; an intermediate caste, the son of the degraded or outcast Vaiśya tribe.

Kārūshaka, *as*, *ikā*, *am*, reigning over the Karūshas.

कारेणव *kāreṇava*, *as*, *ī*, *am* (fr. *kareṇu*), produced by or coming from the female elephant; a patronymic of Pālakāpya.

कारोतर *kārotara*, *as*, m., Ved. a filtering vessel, a cloth for purifying the liquor called surā.

Kārottama, *as*, m. yeast, barm, the froth of the surā liquor.

Kārottara, *as*, m. yeast, barm, the froth which rises on the surā; a well.

कार्कण *kārkaṇa*, *as*, *ī*, *am* (fr. *kṛikaṇa*), caused by or relating to a pheasant.

कार्कन्धव *kārkandhava*, *as*, *ī*, *am* (fr. *karkandhū*), produced by the plant Zizyphus Jujuba.

कार्कवाकव *kārkavākava*, *as*, *ī*, *am* (fr. *kṛikavāku*), relating to a cock, produced by a cock &c.

कार्कश्य *kārkaśya*, *am*, n. (fr. *karkaśa*), roughness, hardness; sternness, inflexibility; firmness, solidity; rough labour.

कार्कष *kārkasha*, *as*, m., N. of a man.

Kārkashāyaṇi, *is*, m. a patronymic from the last.

कार्कीक *kārkīka*, *as*, *ī*, *am* (fr. *karka*), like a white horse.

कार्कोटक *kārkoṭaka*, *am*, n., N. of a town.

कार्ण *kārṇa*, *as*, *ī*, *am* (fr. *karṇa*), being in

the ear, relating to the ear, auricular &c.; a patronymic from Karṇa; (*am*), n. the wax of the ear, an ear-ring.

Kārṇaććhidraka, as, m. (fr. *karṇa-ććhidra*), a sort of well, similar to the opening of the ear.

Kārṇaveshṭakika, as, ī, am (fr. *karṇa-veshṭaka*), ornamented with or fit for ear-rings; also read *kārṇaveshṭanika*.

Kārṇaśravasa, am, n. (fr. *karṇa-śravas*), N. of a Sāman or verse of the Sāma-veda.

Kārṇika, as, ī, am, relating to the ear.

कार्णाटभाषा *kārṇāṭa-bhāshā*, f. the dialect of Karṇāṭaka.

Kārṇāṭaka, as, m. a native of Karṇāṭa.

कार्त *kārta, as, ī, am* (fr. 1. *kṛit*), relating to or treating of the affixes called *kṛit*; (*as*), m. (fr. *kṛita*), N. of a son of Dharma-netra; a patronymic occurring in the compound Kārta-kaujapau.

Kārtayaśa, am, n. (fr. *kṛita* + *yaśa* for *yaśas*), N. of a Sāman or verse of the Sāma-veda.

Kārtayuga, as, ī, am (fr. *kṛita-yuga*), relating to the period of time called Kṛita.

Kārtavīrya, as, m. a patronymic from Kṛita-vīrya and epithet of Arjuna, a prince of the Haihayas, killed by Paraśu-rāma; N. of one of the Jaina Ćakravartins or emperors of the world in Bhārata.

Kārtasvara, am, n. (fr. *kṛita-svara*), gold; the thorn-apple.

Kārtāntika, as, m. (fr. *kṛitānta*), an astrologer who foretels destinies.

Kārti, is, m. a patronymic from Kṛita.

Kārtisiṇha-deva, as, m., N. of a man (*kārtisiṇha* being a patronymic fr. *kṛiti-siṇha*).

कार्त्तिक *kārttika, as*, m. (fr. *kṛittikā*, the Pleiades), scil. *māsa*, N. of the month Kārttika or October–November, when the moon is full and near the Pleiades, the twelfth month of the year; a metronymic of Skanda [cf. *kārttikeya*]; N. of a Varsha; N. of a medical author; (*ī*), f., scil. *rātri*, the night of full moon in the month Kārttika, the day on which the moon stands in the constellation Kṛittikā. — *Kārttika-mahiman, ā*, m. 'the greatness of the month Kārttika,' title of a treatise on the festivals of that month. — *Kārttika-māhātmya, am*, n. title of a section of the Padma-purāṇa. — *Kārttika-śāli, is*, m. the rice which ripens in the beginning of the cold season and forms the principal harvest in India. — *Kārttika-siddhānta, as*, m., N. of a scholiast on the Mugdhabodha. — *Kārttikotsava* (°*ka-ut*°), *as*, m. the day of full moon in the month Kārttika, a festival.

Kārttikika, as, m. the month Kārttika.

Kārttikeya, as, m., N. of Skanda, the god of war, so called because reared by the six Kṛittikās or Pleiades; (according to one legend he was son of Śiva without the intervention of his wife, his generative energy being cast into the fire and then received by the Ganges, whence he is sometimes described as son of Agni and Gaṅgā; when born he was fostered by the Pleiades, who offering their six breasts the child became six-headed. In other accounts he is described as a son of Śiva and Pārvatī or Durgā. Skanda may have been called Kārttikeya because the month Kārttikā is the best for warfare: he is sometimes described as presiding over thieves.) — *Kārttikeya-prasū, ūs*, f. an epithet of Durgā or Pārvatī, who, according to one legend, was the mother of Skanda.

कार्त्स्न *kārtsna, am*, n. (fr. *kṛitsna*), the whole, totality, all, entireness; (perhaps a wrong form for the following.)

Kārtsnya, am, n. the whole, totality, all, entireness. — *Kārtsnyena*, ind. in full, entirely.

कार्दम *kārdama, as, ī, am* (fr. *kardama*), made of mud, muddy, filled or covered with it; belonging to Prajāpati Kardama.

Kārdamika, as, ī, am, = the preceding.

कार्पट *kārpaṭa, as*, m. (fr. *karpaṭa*?), a petitioner, a suitor, one who begs for employment &c.; lac, the animal dye.

Kārpaṭika, as, m. a pilgrim, one who spends his life in pilgrimage, or who subsists by carrying water from holy rivers; a caravan of pilgrims; a parasite; an experienced man.

कार्पण्य *kārpaṇya, am*, n. (fr. *kṛipaṇa*), poverty, indigence; pitiful circumstances; poorness of spirit, weakness, parsimony, niggardliness, imbecility; compassion, pity.

कार्पाण *kārpāṇa, am*, n. (fr. *kṛipāṇa*), Ved. combat, fighting, battle.

कार्पास *kārpāsa, as, ī, am* (fr. *karpāsa*), made of cotton, cottony; (*as, am*), m. n. cotton, cotton cloth, &c.; paper; (*ī*), f. the cotton plant, Gossypium Hirsutum. — *Kārpāsa-nāsikā*, f. a spindle. — *Kārpāsāsthi* (°*sa-as*°), n. the seed of the cotton plant.

Kārpāsika, as, ī, am, made of or from cotton; (*ā*), f. the cotton plant.

कार्म *kārma, as, ī, am* (fr. *karman*), laborious, industrious, occupied.

Kārmaṇa, as, ī, am, finishing a work, doing it well or completely; (*am*), n. magic, sorcery, witchcraft; performing anything by means of magical incantations. — *Kārmaṇa-tva, am*, n. magic, fascination.

Kārmaṇeyaka, as or *am* (?), m. or n. (?), N. of a region.

Kārmāra, as, m., Ved. = *karmāra*, an artist, mechanic, a smith; a patronymic from Karmāra.

Kārmāraka, am, n. a smith's work.

Kārmika, as, ī, am, engaged or employed in any work, epithet of a Buddhist philosophical school; manufactured, made; worked, embroidered, intermixed with coloured thread (as cloth &c.); any variegated texture.

Kārmikya, am, n. activity, industry.

1. *kārmuka, as, ī, am*, finishing a work, doing it well or completely, fit for or able to do a work; (*as*), m. a bamboo.

कार्मुक 2. *kārmuka, as, ī, am* (fr. *kṛimuka*), consisting of the wood Kṛimuka; (*am*), n. a bow; an instrument shaped like a bow. — *Kārmuka-bhṛit, t*, m. the archer or Sagittarius in the zodiac; an archer in general, a soldier.

Kārmukāya, nom. A. *kārmukāyate, -yitum*, to form a bow.

Kārmukin, ī, iṇī, i, armed with a bow.

कार्य *kārya, as, ā, am* (fut. pass. part. fr. 1. *kṛi*), to be made, to be done, practised, performed, accomplished, &c., feasible; to be imposed (as a punishment), to be offered (as a libation) &c.; what ought to be done, fit, right; (*kārya-tama*, superl. what ought chiefly to be done, i. e. first duty); (*am*), n. work or business to be done, duty, affair; a religious action or performance; occupation, matter, thing, enterprise, emergency, occurrence, crisis; conduct, deportment; business, occasion, need (with inst. case, e. g. *triṇena kāryam*, there is need of a straw; *na bhūmyā kāryam asmākam*, we have no business whatever with the earth, the earth is not our concern); lawsuit, dispute; an operation in grammar (e. g. *sthāny-āśrayaṃ kāryam*, an operation which is borne by or rests on the primitive form as opposed to the *ādeśa* or substitute); an effect, the necessary result of a cause (in phil.); motive, object, aim, purpose (e. g. *kiṃ kāryam*, for what purpose? wherefore?); cause, origin; the denouement of a drama; (*ā*), f., N. of a plant, = *kārī, kārikā*. — *Kārya-kara, as, ī, am*, producing an effect, efficacious. — *Kārya-kartṛi, tā*, m. or *kārya-kāraka, as*, m. an agent, a workman. — *Kārya-kāraṇa, am*, n. object and motive, cause and effect, cause of a special or incidental kind, originating in some act or occasion. — *Kārya-kāraṇatas*, ind. from some special cause, with a particular design or motive. — *Kārya-kāraṇa-bhāva, as*, m. relation of cause and effect. — *Kārya-kārin, ī, iṇī, i*, performing a work. — *Kārya-kāla, as*, m. time for action, appointed time, season, opportunity. — *Kārya-kuśala, as, ā, am*, skilful or clever in work, doing it well or completely. — *Kārya-kshama, as, ā, am*, competent or fit for a work. — *Kārya-gurutā*, f. or *kārya-gurutva, am*, n. necessity or importance of any act. — *Kārya-gaurava, am*, n. importance of an affair or business. — *Kārya-ćintaka, as, ā, am*, one who takes care of a business, the manager of a business; prudent, considerate, cautious. — *Kārya-ćintā*, f. prudence, caution, consideration. — *Kārya-ćyuta, as, ā, am*, out of work, removed from an office. — *Kārya-tas*, ind. consequently, necessarily, actually. — *Kārya-tva, am*, n. the being an effect, the relation or condition of an effect or of what has been effected. — *Kārya-darśana, am*, n. inspection of work, revision. — *Kārya-darśin, ī*, m. an inspector or superintendent of affairs. — *Kārya-nirṇaya, as*, m. ascertainment of the fact; settlement or decision of an affair. — *Kārya-puṭa, as*, m. a man who does useless things; a madman, a crazy or hair-brained man; an impudent or shameless fellow; an idler, one who follows unprofitable pursuits. — *Kārya-pradvesha, as*, m. aversion from activity, idleness. — *Kārya-preshya, as*, m. one who is sent on any business, a messenger. — *Kārya-bhājana* or *kārya-pātra, am*, n. any one engaged in active life, one fit for business or the conduct of affairs. — *Kārya-bhrashṭa, as, ā, am*, = *kārya-ćyuta* above. — 1. *kārya-vat*, ind. actually, according to act or motive. — 2. *kārya-vat, ān, atī, at*, having business to transact, engaged in a business; having a cause or motive, doing one's duty. — *Kāryavat-tā*, f. or *kāryavat-tva, am*, n. the state of being engaged in a work, any business, act, action. — *Kārya-vaśa, as*, m. necessary consequence. — *Kārya-vastu, u*, n. anything that has to be done, an aim, object. — *Kārya-vipatti, is*, f. failure of an action, reverse, misfortune. — *Kārya-śesha, as*, m. the remainder of a business; completion of an affair. — *Kārya-sandeha, as*, m. uncertainty or doubt about a work, embarrassment, difficulty. — *Kārya-sāgara, as*, m. 'an ocean of business,' heavy or weighty affairs. — *Kārya-sādhaka, as, ā, am*, effective of any work, accomplishing any object, an agent. — *Kārya-sādhana, am*, n. means of effecting any object, instrument, implement, aid. — *Kārya-siddhi, is*, f. accomplishment of a work, success, fulfilment of any object. — *Kārya-sthāna, am*, n. a place of business, an office. — *Kārya-hantṛi, tā, trī, tṛi*, obstructing or counteracting the work of others, a mar-plot. — *Kāryākārya-vićāra, as*, m. deliberation on the arguments for and against any act. — *Kāryākshama* (°*ya-ak*°), *as, ā, am*, unfit for any work, incompetent, unable. — *Kāryādhipa* (°*ya-adh*°), *as*, m. the planet which determines or decides any inquiry or question in astrology. — *Kāryānta* (°*ya-an*°), *as*, m. the end of a business, termination of an affair. — *Kāryābdhi* (°*ya-ab*°), *is*, m. an ocean of business. — *Kāryārtha* (°*ya-ar*°), *as*, m. the object of a business or enterprise; any object or purpose; application for employment; (*am*), ind. for the sake of a business, for the sake of any particular object, to perform any work or duty. — *Kāryārtha-siddhi, is*, f. the accomplishment of any object or purpose. — *Kāryārthin* (°*ya-ar*°), *ī, inī, i*, making a request, seeking for business, applying for employment; pleading a cause in court, going to law. — *Kāryeśa* and *kāryeśvara* (°*ya-iś*°), *as*, m. = *kāryādhipa* above. — *Kāryoddhāra* (°*ya-ud*°), *as*, m. discharge of any duty, performance of any act. — *Kāryodyukta* (°*ya-ud*°), *as, ā, am*, engaged in any business, intent upon any object. — *Kāryodyoga* (°*ya-ud*°), *as*, m. active engagement in any business.

Kārytka, as, ī, am, having business, transacting business, seeking employment &c.; engaged in a suit at law, pleading a cause in court.

Kāryin, ī, iṇī, i, one who transacts business, active, assiduous; seeking for employment; having an object; a party to a suit, either as plaintiff or defendant; (in gram.) subject to the operation of a grammatical rule, requiring an affix &c. — *Kāryekshaṇa* (°*ya-ik*°), *am*, n. superintendence of public affairs.

काशकेय *kārśakeya*, a patronymic from Kṛiśaka. — *Kārśakeyī-putra, as*, m., N. of a teacher.

काशन *kārśana, as, ī, am* (fr. *kṛiśana*), Ved. consisting of pearl or mother-of-pearl.

काशानव *kārśānava, as, ī, am* (fr. *kṛiśānu*), fiery, hot, glaring, relating to fire.

काश्मरी *kārśmarī*, f., N. of a plant, = *kārshmarya, kāśmarī*.

कार्श्य 1. *kārśya, as*, m., N. of several plants, = *kārshya* and *kārshmarya*, = *karćūra;* another plant, Artocarpus Lacucha.

कार्श्य 2. *kārśya, am*, n. (fr. *kṛiśa*), emaciation, thinness, smallness.

कार्ष *kārsha, as, ī, am* (fr. rt. *kṛish*), one who ploughs a field, a peasant, a husbandman.

Kārshaka, as, m. a husbandman.

Kārshi, is, is, i, Ved. drawing, attracting; ploughing; (*is*), m. fire; (*is*), f. drawing, attracting; ploughing, cultivation.

Kārshika, as, ī, am (fr. *karsha*), deserving of pulling or dragging about; weighing a Karsha; (*as*), m. a coin of the weight of one Karsha; a husbandman.

Kārshīvaṇa, as, m. (fr. *kārshi* with *i* lengthened), Ved. one who ploughs a field, a husbandman.

Kārshman, a, n., Ved. the goal of a race-course (consisting of a line like a furrow).

कार्षापण *kārshāpaṇa, as, am*, m. n. (= *karshāpaṇa*), a coin or weight of different values, as synonymous with Karsha; if of gold, weighing 16 Māshas, which are variously calculated, see *karsha;* if of silver, it is in value = 16 Paṇas of Kowries, i. e. 1280 Kowries, commonly termed a Kāhan; if of copper, it weighs 80 Raktikās, or the same as of gold, about 176 grains; according to some it is the same as a Paṇa of Kowries, i. e. 80 Kowries; at the end of a compound it means 'worth so many Kārshāpaṇas;' (*am*), n. money, gold and silver; (*as*), m. a husbandman (?); N. of a warrior-tribe; the chief of this tribe. — *Kārshāpaṇārara* (°*ṇa-av*°), *as, ā, am*, having the value of at least one Kārshāpaṇa (as a fine).

Kārshāpaṇaka, as, am, m. n. a weight or measure of different values, as synonymous with Karsha.

Kārshāpaṇika, as, ī, am, worth one Kārshāpaṇa, bought &c. with one Kārshāpaṇa.

कार्ष्ण *kārshṇa, as, ī, am* (fr. *kṛishṇa*), coming from or belonging to the black antelope; made of the skin of the black antelope; belonging to the god Kṛishṇa or Kṛishṇa-dvaipāyana, composed by him &c. (e. g. *kārshṇam vedam*, the Mahā-bhārata); belonging to a descendant of Kṛishṇa; black; (*ī*), f. the plant Asparagus Racemosus; (*am*), n., Ved. the skin of the black antelope; (*as*), m. the black antelope (?).

Kārshṇājini, is, m. (fr. *kṛishṇājina*), a patronymic from Kṛishṇājina; N. of a teacher; N. of a philosopher; N. of the author of a law-book.

Kārshṇāyasa, as, ī, am (fr. *kṛishṇāyasa*), of iron, made of black iron; (*am*), n. iron.

Kārshṇi, is, m. a patronymic from Kṛishṇa; an epithet of Viśvaka; N. of a Devagandharva; an epithet of the god of love.

Kārshṇya, am, n. blackness, black colour, darkness.

कार्ष्मन् *kārshman*, See under *kārsha* above.

कार्ष्मर्य *kārshmarya, as*, m., Ved. the tree Gmelina Arborea. — *Kārshmarya-maya, as, ī, am*, made of this tree.

कार्ष्य *kārshya, as*, m. the tree Shorea Robusta. — *Kārshya-vaṇa, am*, n. a forest of these trees.

काल 1. *kāla, as, ī, am* (fr. rt. 3. *kal?;* for 2. *kāla*, 'time,' see next page), black, of a dark colour, especially dark-blue which is often confounded with black; (*as*), m. a black or dark-blue colour; the black part of the eye; the Indian cuckoo; the poisonous serpent, Coluber Naga (= *kāla-sarpa*); the plant Cassia Sophora; a plant, a red kind of plumbago; the resin of the plant Shorea Robusta; the planet Saturn; an epithet of Śiva; also of Rudra; N. of a son of Hrada; also of a prince; also of a brother of king Prasena-jit; also of a future Buddha; also of a Nāga-rāja; of a Rakshas; of an enemy of Śiva; N. of a mountain; (with the Jainas) N. of one of the nine treasures; a mystical name for the letter *m;* (*ā*), f., N. of several plants, Indigofera Tinctoria; Piper Longum; a plant nearly related to Ipomœa Turpethum, perhaps Ipomœa Atropurpurea; Nigella Indica; Rubia Munjista; Ruellia Longifolia; Physalis Flexuosa; Bignonia Suaveolens; the fruit of the Kālā (?); N. of a daughter of Daksha, the mother of the Kāleyas or Kālakeyas (a family of Asuras); an epithet of Durgā; (*ī*), f. black colour, ink or blacking; abuse, censure, defamation; a row or succession of black clouds; night; a worm or animalcule generated in the acetous fermentation of milk, = *kshīra-kīṭa* and *kshāra-kīṭa;* N. of several plants, = *kālāñjanī;* another plant, Cajanus Indicus; Ipomœa Turpethum; Bignonia Suaveolens; one of the seven tongues or flames of fire; a form of Durgā; one of the Mātṛis or divine mothers; N. of a female evil spirit, mother of the Kālakeyas; one of the sixteen Vidyādevīs; an epithet of Satyavatī, the wife of king Śāntanu and mother of Vyāsa or Kṛishṇa-dvaipāyana, but before her marriage. (After her marriage she had a son called Vićitra-vīrya, whose widows were married by Kṛishṇa-dvaipāyana and bore to him Dhṛita-rāshṭra and Pāṇḍu; according to other legends Kālī is the wife of Bhīma-sena and mother of Sarvagata); N. of a river, otherwise *kālā gangā;* (*am*), n. a black kind of Agallochum; a kind of perfume (= *kakkolaka*); iron; [cf. Gr. κηλίς, κελαινός; Lat. *caligo.*] — *Kāla-kaću, us*, f. the plant Arum Colocasia. — *Kāla-kaṇṭaka, as*, m. a gallinule; [cf. the next.] — *Kāla-kaṇṭha, as*, m., N. of several birds, a peacock; a water fowl, a gallinule; a wagtail; a sparrow; the plant Terminalia Tomentosa, = *pītaśāla* and *pītasāra;* an epithet of Śiva; [cf. *nīla-kaṇṭha.*] — *Kāla-kaṇṭhaka, as*, m. a gallinule. — *Kāla-kandaka, as*, m. a water-snake. — *Kāla-karṇikā* or *kāla-karṇī*, f. misfortune (predicted as the consequence of having black ears). — *Kāla-kalāya, as*, m. dark pulse, Phaseolus Max. — *Kāla-kastūrī*, f. the plant Hibiscus Abelmoschus, the seeds smelling of musk when rubbed. — *Kāla-kīrti, is*, m., N. of a king identified with the Asura Suparṇa. — *Kāla-kushṭha, as*, m. a kind of earth brought from mountains; [cf. *kankushṭha.*] — *Kāla-koṭi, is*, f., N. of a region. — *Kāla-klītaka, am*, n. the indigo plant. — *Kāla-khañja, ās*, m. pl. = *kālakañja*, perhaps only a wrong reading; (*am*), n. the liver. — *Kāla-khañjana, am*, n. the liver. — *Kāla-khaṇḍa, am*, n. the liver. — *Kāla-gangā*, f., N. of a river in Ceylon. — *Kāla-gaṇḍikā*, f., N. of a river. — *Kāla-gandha, as*, m. a kind of Cobra de Capella, = *kāla-kandaka.* — *Kāla-ghaṭa, as*, m., N. of a Brāhman. — *Kāla-joshaka, ās*, m. pl., N. of a people; (a various reading has *kālajoshika.*) — *Kāla-tāla, as*, m., N. of a plant, = *tamāla.* — *Kāla-tinduka, as*, m. a kind of ebony. — *Kāla-tīrtha, am*, n., N. of a Tīrtha. — *Kāla-toyaka, ās*, m. pl., N. of a people. — *Kāla-dantaka, as*, m., N. of a Nāga, a son of Vāsuki. — 1. *kāla-nara, as*, m., N. of a son of Sabhānara, a son of Anu; (for 2. *kāla-nara* see under 2. *kāla.*) — *Kāla-nābha, as*, m. (*nābha* = *nābhi*), N. of an Asura, a son of Hiraṇyāksha; also of a son of Hiraṇya-kaśipu; also of a son of Vipra-ćitti and Siṇhikā. — *Kāla-niryāsa, as*, m. a fragrant and resinous exudation from the plant Amyris Agallocha. — *Kāla-netra, as, ā, am*, black-eyed. — *Kāla-parṇa, as*, m., N. of a tree bearing dark-coloured leaves, Tabernæmontana Coronaria, commonly called Tagara. — *Kāla-parvata, as*, m., N. of a mountain. — *Kālapātrika, as*, m. (fr. *kāla-pātra*), a kind of mendicant whose alms-dish is painted black. — *Kāla-pālaka, am*, n. a kind of earth; [cf. *kankushṭha, kāla-kushṭha.*] — *Kāla-pīluka, as*, m., N. of a tree; see *kupīlu.* — *Kāla-puććha* or *kāla-puććhaka, as*, m. a species of animal living in marshes. — *Kāla-pushpa, am*, n., N. of a plant; see *kalāya.* — *Kāla-pūga, as*, m. the black multitude, i. e. the common people (?). — *Kāla-pṛishṭha, as*, m. a species of antelope (with a black back); a heron; (*am*), n., N. of the bow of Karṇa; a bow in general. — *Kāla-peśī*, f., N. of a plant; see *śyāmā.* — *Kāla-bhāṇḍikā*, f. the plant Rubia Munjista. — *Kāla-masī*, f., N. of a river; also called *kālamahī.* — *Kālamāna* and *kāla-māla, as*, m. the plant Ocimum Sanctum, a fragrant pot-herb. — *Kāla-mukha, as*, m. a kind of monkey; N. of a fabulous people; (*ā*), f., N. of a female. — *Kāla-mushkaka, as*, m. the plant Bignonia Indica; see *mushkaka.* — *Kāla-mūla, as*, m., N. of a plant, commonly Rakta-ćitraka. — *Kāla-meśikā* or *kāla-meshikā*, f. the plant Rubia Munjista; also the plant Ipomœa Atropurpurea (?). — *Kāla-meshī*, f., N. of several plants, Vernonia Anthelminthica; Rubia Munjista; and perhaps Ipomœa Atropurpurea. — *Kāla-yavana, as*, m., N. of a prince of the Yavanas; a tyrannical Asura, the foe of Kṛishṇa, destroyed by him by a stratagem. — 1. *kāla-rātri, is* or *ī*, f. a dark night; (for 2. see under 2. *kāla.*) — *Kāla-lavaṇa, am*, n. a kind of black factitious and purgative salt, commonly called *viḍ-lavaṇa.* — *Kāla-loćana, as*, m., N. of a Daitya. — *Kāla-lauha, am*, n. iron. — *Kāla-vadana, as*, m., N. of a Daitya; also called *śāla-vadana.* — *Kāla-vṛiksha* and *kāla-vṛinta, as*, m. a kind of vetch, Dolichos Biflorus [cf. *kulattha*]; (*ī*), f. the trumpet flower, Bignonia Suaveolens. — *Kāla-velā*, f. the time of Saturn, a particular time of the day at which any religious act is improper, half a watch in every day. — *Kāla-śambara, as*, m., N. of a Dānava. — *Kāla-śāka, am*, n. the pot-herb Ocimum Sanctum. — *Kāla-śāli, is*, m. a black sort of rice. — *Kāla-śivi, is*, m., N. of a man. — *Kāla-śaila, as*, m., N. of a mountain. — *Kāla-sankarshā*, f. a girl nine years old, who personates Durgā at a festival in honour of this goddess. — *Kāla-sarpa, as*, m. the black and most poisonous variety of the Cobra, Coluber Naga. — *Kāla-sāra, as*, m. the black antelope; (*am*), n. a yellow sort of sandal-wood. — *Kāla-skandha, as*, m., N. of several plants; a kind of ebony with a dark trunk, Diospyros Embryopteris; the Tamāla, a tree bearing dark blossoms, Xanthochymus Pictorius; another plant, = *jīraka;* another, = *dushkhadira;* the glomerous fig tree, Ficus Glomerata. — *Kālāguru* (°*la-ag*°), *u*, n. a black kind of aloe wood or Agallochum. — *Kālānga* (°*la-an*°), *as, ā, am*, having a dark-blue body, as a sword with a dark-blue edge. — *Kālājina* (°*la-aj*°), *as*, m., N. of a people. — *Kālāñjana* (°*la-añ*°), *am*, n. a black unguent; (*ī*), f. a small shrub used as a purgative. — *Kālāṇḍaja* (°*la-aṇ*°), *as*, m. the black bird, an epithet of the Indian cuckoo. — *Kālānuśārivā*, f., N. of two plants, = *tagara;* and *śilājatā*, commonly *śiulīćhop.* — *Kālānusāraka* (°*la-an*°), *am*, n., N. of a tree, = *tagara;* yellow sandal. — *Kālānusāri, is*, m. or *kālānusārin* (°*la-an*°), *ī*, m. or *kālānusārivā*, f. benzoin or benjamin. — *Kālānusārya, as, ā, am*, m. f. n. gum benjamin or benzoin; (*am*), n. a yellow fragrant wood from which a perfume is prepared, sandal-wood (?); N. of a tree, = *tagara;* (*as, am*), m. n. the tree Dalbergia Sissoo. — *Kālānusāryaka, am*, n. gum benzoin or benjamin. — *Kālāmra* (°*la-ām*°), *as*, m., N. of a Dvīpa. — *Kālāyasa* (°*la-ayas*), *am*, n. iron. — *Kālāyasamaya, as, ī, am*, of iron, consisting of iron. — *Kālāśoka* (°*la-aś*°), *as*, m., N. of a Buddhist king. — *Kālāsuhṛid* (°*la-as*°), *t*, m. an enemy of Kāla, epithet of Śiva. — *Kāleśvara* (°*la-īś*°), *as*, m., N.

of a mountain. — *Kālodaka* (°*la-ud*°), *am*, n., N. of a dark piece of water; N. of an ocean.

Kālaka, *as*, *ā*, *am*, dark-blue, coloured dark-blue; dark-coloured, black; (*as*), m. a mole, a freckle, a mark; the black part of the eye; a water-snake (*alagarda*); a kind of grain; N. of a Rakshas; also of an Asura; N. of a mountain; (*ās*), m. pl., N. of a Dānava family; (*ā*), f., Ved. a kind of bird; N. of a female evil spirit, mother of the Kālakeyas; a daughter of Daksha; also of Vaiśvānara; (*am*), n. the liver; N. of a plant. — *Kālaka-vṛikshīya*, *as*, m., N. of a sage. — *Kālakāksha* (°*ka-ak*°), *as*, m., N. of an Asura. — *Kālakāñja* (°*ka-añja?*), *as*, m. (?), Ved., N. of an animal ('black-spotted?'); N. of a constellation (?); N. of an Asura.

Kālakeya, *as*, m. (a metronymic fr. *kālakā*), N. of an Asura; (*ās*), m. pl., N. of a Dānava family; [cf. *kālakañja*, *kālakāñja*, 1. *kāleya*.]

1. *kālika*, *as*, m. a species of heron, Ardea Jaculator (also written *kālika*); N. of a king of the Nāgas; (*kā*), f. blackness or black colour; ink or blacking; cloudiness, a multitude or succession of clouds, a dark cloud threatening rain; a fault or flaw in gold; the liver; a particular blood-vessel in the ear; a line of hair extending from the pudenda to the navel; a kind of spirituous liquor; a female crow; a small singing bird with black wings (Turdus Macrourus, commonly Syāmā); a scorpion; a small worm or animalcule formed by the fermentation of milk; N. of several plants, a medicinal plant, commonly Vṛiśćikapattra; another plant, Valeriana Jaṭāmāṇsi; a kind of Terminalia; a branch of the plant Trichosanthes Dioeca; a kind of fragrant earth; a N. or form of Durgā; a girl of four years old, who personates the goddess Durgā at a festival held in honour of that deity; a kind of Yoginī; a species of Kinnarī; an epithet of Durgā; N. of a female evil spirit, daughter of Vaiśvānara; (with Jainas) N. of a kind of genius who executes the commands of the fourth Arhat; N. of a river; (*am*), n. black sandal-wood. — *Kālikā-krama*, *as*, m. title of a work. — *Kālikā-grantha*, *as*, m. a medical work. — *Kālikā-purāṇa*, *am*, n. the Purāṇa of Kālikā, i. e. of Durgā, title of an Upapurāṇa. — *Kālikā-mukha*, *as*, m., N. of a Rakshas. — *Kālikāśrama* (°*kā-āś*°), *as*, m., N. of a hermitage. — *Kālikopapurāṇa* (°*kā-up*°), *am*, n., N. of an Upa-purāṇa.

Kāliman, *ā*, m. blackness.

1. *kāliya*, *as*, m., N. of a Nāga or serpent inhabiting the Yamunā, slain by Kṛishṇa (also written *kālīya*, see below). — *Kāliya-damana*, *as*, or *kāliya-jit*, m., N. of Kṛishṇa or Vishṇu as destroyer of the serpent.

Kāliyaka = *kālīyaka* below.

Kālī, f., N. of Durgā, the wife of the god Śiva. — *Kālī-kula-sarvasva*, N. of a work. — *Kālī-tanaya*, *as*, m. a buffalo ('son or favourite of Durgā,' more correctly *haṇsakālī-tanaya*). — *Kālī-purāṇa*, *am*, n. the Purāṇa of Kālī, title of an Upapurāṇa. — *Kālī-māhātmya*, *am*, n. = *ćaṇḍikā-māhātmya*. — *Kālī-rahasya*, title of a work. — *Kālī-śiva*, *as*, m., N. of the author of the Kalpa-kedāra. — *Kālī-hṛidaya*, title of a work.

Kālīya, *as*, *ā*, *am*, relating to blackness; (*am*), n. a dark kind of sandal or perhaps of Agallochum; N. of a Nāga, see 1. *kāliya* above.

Kālīyaka, *as*, *am*, m. n. a species of aloe wood; a kind of turmeric (Curcuma Xanthorrhiza?), a kind of fragrant wood of a yellow colour; yellow sandal; a dark kind of sandal-wood; (*as*), m., N. of a Nāga, see 1. *kāliya* above.

1. *kāleya*, *am*, n. (for 2. see s. v.), the liver; saffron; a yellow fragrant wood; the black sandal-wood; (*as*, *ā*, *am*), dark-coloured; (*ās*), m. pl., N. of a family of Daityas (metronymic fr. *kālā*).

Kāleyaka, *as*, m. the plant Curcuma Xanthorrhiza, see *kālīyaka* above; (*am*), n. a fragrant wood, see above; a particular part of the intestines; a disease like jaundice; (*as*), m. a dog (for *kauleyaka*).

Kālyaka, *as*, m. zedoary (Curcuma Zerumbet). See *kālpaka*.

काल 2. *kāla*, *as*, m. (fr. rt. 3. *kal*), a fixed or right point of time, a space of time, time in general, (in the Ṛig-veda this word occurs only once, in the Brāhmaṇas oftener); the proper time or fit season for (with gen., dat., loc., pot., &c., e. g. *kālaḥ prasthānasya* or *prasthānāya* or *prasthāne*, time for departure; *kriyā-kālaḥ*, time for action; *na ayaṃ kālo vilambitum*, this is not the time to delay; *kālo yad bhuñjīta bhavān*, it is time for you to eat); the weather; time as leading to events, the causes of which are imperceptible to the mind of man; destiny, fate; time as destroying all things; death, time of death, often personified and represented with the attributes of Yama, regent of the dead, or even identified with him, (hence *kālam i* or *kālaṃ kṛi*, to die; *kāla-samāyukta*, dead; *kāla* in this sense is frequently connected with *antaka* and *mṛityu*, e. g. *abhyadhāvata prajāḥ kāla ivāntakaḥ*, he attacked the people like Time the destroyer, cf. *kālāntaka* below; *kāla* personified is also a Devarshi in Indra's court, and a son of Dhruva); a period of time, time of the world; measure of time, prosody; a section, a part; *deśa-kālau*, the right place and the right time, place and time; *kālaṃ kṛi*, to appoint or fix a time; *ubhau kālau*, both times, sunrise and sunset; *shashṭhe kāle 'hnaḥ*, at the sixth hour of the day, at midday; *shashṭhānna-kāla*, one who eats only at the sixth meal-time, i. e. who passes five meals without eating and has no meal till the evening of the third day; or without *anna*, e. g. *ćaturtha-kālam*, at the fourth meal-time, i. e. at the evening of the second day; *shashṭhe kāle*, at the evening of the third day; *ṛitu-kāla*, the time of a woman's courses; *gaććhatā kālena*, in the course of time, after some time; *nitya-kālam*, constantly, always; *dīrgha-kālam*, during a long time; *dīrgheṇa kāleṇa*, after a long time; *kālena*, in the course of time; *dīrghasya kālasya*, after a long time; *kasyaćit kālasya*, after some time; *kālāt* or *kālatas*, in the course of time &c.; [cf. Goth. *hveila*; Mod. Germ. *weile*; Gr. καιρός, ὥρα (?); Lat. *hora*, *calen-dæ*: cf. also Gr. κήρ; Hib. *ceal*, 'death and everything terrible.'] — *Kāla-karaṇa*, *am*, n. appointing or fixing a time. — *Kāla-karman*, *a*, n. death. — *Kāla-kalpa*, *as*, *ā*, *am*, like death, fatal, deadly. — *Kāla-kāra*, *as*, *ī*, *am*, making or producing time. — *Kāla-kārita*, *as*, *ā*, *am*, effected or brought about by or in time. — *Kāla-kuṇṭha*, *as*, m. an epithet of Yama. — *Kāla-kūṭa*, *as*, *am*, m. n. a deadly poison; see s. v. — *Kāla-kṛit*, *t*, m. the sun (producing the times, i. e. seasons). — *Kāla-kṛita*, *as*, *ā*, *am*, produced by time; fixed; appointed (as to time); lent or deposited by a giver for a certain time; (*as*), m. the sun; time (?). — *Kāla-kaumudī*, f., N. of a work. — *Kāla-krama*, *as*, m. lapse of time; *kāla-krameṇa*, in process of time. — *Kāla-kriyā*, f. fixing a time; title of the second chapter of the Sūrya-Siddhānta; death. — *Kāla-kshepa*, *as*, m. allowing time to pass away, delay, loss of time; spending or passing the time; *akāla-kshepam*, ind. without delay. — *Kāla-gati*, *is*, f. the lapse of time. — *Kāla-granthi*, *is*, m. 'a joint of time,' a year. — *Kāla-ghātin*, *ī*, *inī*, *i*, killing in the course of time, i. e. by degrees, slowly (as a poison). — *Kāla-ćakra*, *am*, n. the wheel of time, time represented as a wheel, which always turns round; a given revolution of time, a cycle; according to the Jainas, the wheel of time has twelve Aras or spokes and turns round once in 2000,000,000,000,000 Sāgaras of years [cf. *ava-sarpiṇī* and *ut-sarpiṇī*]; the wheel of fortune, the vicissitudes of life, the wheel of time or fate is sometimes regarded as a weapon; with Buddhists, a Tantra; (*as*), m. an epithet of the sun. — *Kāla-ćodita*, *as*, *ā*, *am*, summoned by the angel of death. — *Kālaćodita-karman*, *ā*, *ā*, *a*, acting under the influence of fate. — *Kāla-jña*, *as*, *ā*, *am*, one who knows the fixed times or seasons; (*as*), m. an astrologer; a cock. — *Kāla-jñāna*, *am*, n., N. of a medical work; N. of a work by Malladeva on the symptoms of diseases; a medical work by Śambhunātha. — *Kāla-jñānin*, *ī*, m. an epithet of Śiva. — *Kāla-tattvārṇava* (°*va-ar*°), 'the ocean of the truth of time,' title of a work. — *Kāla-taraṅga*, the first part of the Smṛity-artha-sāgara by Nṛisiṇha. — *Kāla-tā*, f. seasonableness, timeliness. — *Kāla-tulya*, *as*, *ā*, *am*, like death, deadly. — *Kāla-traya*, *am*, n. the three times, i. e. past, present, and future. — *Kāla-daṇḍa*, *as*, m. the staff of death, death. — *Kāla-damanī*, f. an epithet of Durgā. — *Kāla-dharma*, *as*, m. or *kāla-dharman*, *ā*, m. the line of conduct suitable to any time or season; the law, rule or operation of time, death, dying; influence of time, seasonableness; effects proper to the time or season. — *Kāla-dhāraṇā*, f. prolongation of time. — 2. *kāla-nara*, *as*, m. 'a time-man,' i. e. in astrology the figure of a man's body on the various limbs of which the twelve signs of the zodiac are distributed for the purpose of foretelling future destinies; [cf. *kāla-purusha*.] — *Kāla-nātha*, *as*, m. an epithet of Śiva. — *Kāla-nidhi*, *is*, m. an epithet of Śiva. — *Kāla-niyoga*, *as*, m. the command of time, fate, destiny. — *Kāla-nirūpaṇa*, *am*, n. chronology. — *Kāla-nirṇaya*, *as*, m. 'determination or fixing of times,' title of a work, also called *kāla-mādhavīya*, by Mādhavāćārya. — *Kāla-nirṇaya-dīpikā*, f. title of a metrical recension of the same work. — *Kāla-nirṇaya-prakāśa*, *as*, m. title of a work on jurisprudence (?). — *Kāla-nirvāha*, *as*, m. providing for daily wants. — *Kāla-nemi*, *is*, f. the felly or rim of the wheel of time, regarded as a terrible weapon; (*as*), m., N. of an Asura slain by Kṛishṇa, identified with Kaṇsa; N. of a Rakshas; N. of a son of the Brāhman Yajña-soma. — *Kāla-nemin*, *ī*, m., N. of an Asura; [cf. the preceding.] — *Kālanemi-ripu*, *us*, m. or *kālanemi-han*, *ā*, m. or *kālanemi-hara*, *as*, m. or *kālanemy-ari*, *is*, m. an epithet of Kṛishṇa or Vishṇu, the destroyer of the Asura Kālanemi. — *Kāla-pakva*, *as*, *ā*, *am*, ripened by time, i. e. spontaneously (opposed to *agni-pakva*). — *Kāla-patha*, *as*, m., N. of a son of Viśvā-mitra. — *Kāla-parivāsa*, *as*, m. standing for a time (so as to become stale or fermented). — *Kāla-pāśa*, *as*, m. the noose of Yama or death. — *Kāla-pāśika*, *as*, m. a hangman, an executioner, (one who has the noose of Yama.) — *Kāla-purusha*, *as*, m., cf. 2. *kāla-nara*. — *Kāla-prabhāta*, *am*, n. the dawning of the best season, the two months following the rainy season, autumn; the sultry season. — *Kāla-prarūḍha*, *as*, *ā*, *am*, over-blown, over-ripe. — *Kāla-bhaksha*, *as*, m. an epithet of Śiva. — *Kāla-bhṛit*, *t*, m. the sun; [cf. *kāla-kṛit*.] — *Kāla-mayūkha*, *as*, m. title of a part of Bhāskara. — *Kāla-mahiman*, *ā*, m. or *kāla-māhātmya*, *am*, n. the power or sway of time. — *Kāla-mādhava-kārikā*, f. title of a work. — *Kāla-mūrti*, *is*, f. time personified. — *Kāla-yāpa*, *as*, m. allowing time to pass away, putting off, delaying, procrastination. — *Kāla-yāpana*, *am*, n. passing away time, putting off, delaying. — *Kāla-yoga*, *as*, m. connection with time, with fate or destiny; fate, destiny. — *Kāla-yogin*, *ī*, *inī*, *i*, reigning over destiny, an epithet of Śiva. — *Kāla-yodhin*, *ī*, *inī*, *i*, fighting, or one who fights in season or at the proper time. — 2. *kāla-rātri*, *is* or *ī*, f. the night of all-destroying time, the night of destruction at the end of the world, often personified or identified with Durgā or with one of the Śaktis of Durgā; a particular night in the life of man, on the seventh day of the seventh month of the seventy-seventh year, after which period a man is exempt from attention to the usual ordinances; N. of a Brāhman woman, familiar with magic. — *Kāla-rūpa-dhṛish*, *k*, *k*, *k* (the last member of the compound being by some referred to rt. *dhṛi* or *dṛih*), wearing the form of Yama or death. — *Kāla-vat*, *ān*, *atī*, *at*, connected with time. — *Kāla-vikrama*, *as*, m. power of time, death. — *Kāla-vidhāna*, *am*, n. title of a work. — *Kāla-vidhvaṇsana*, *as*, m. (scil. *rasa*) a term for a particular drug or medicine. — *Kāla-viprakarsha*, *as*, m. prolongation of time. — *Kāla-viveka*, *as*, m., N. of a work by Jīmūta-vahana. — *Kāla-vṛiddhi*, *is*, f. periodical interest, payable monthly, &c. — *Kāla-vega*, *as*, m., N. of a Nāga, a son of Vāsuki. — *Kāla-vyāpin*, *ī*, *inī*, *i*, filling all time, everlasting.—*Kāla-saṃrodha, as,* m. keeping back or retaining for a long time; lapse of a long period of time.—*Kāla-saṃhitā,* f., N. of an astrological work.—*Kāla-sadṛiśa, as, ī, am,* opportune, seasonable; deathlike.—*Kāla-sampanna, as, ā, am,* effected by time, dated, bearing a date.—*Kāla-sāhvaya, as, ā, am,* named after Kāla.—*Kāla-sūtra* or *kāla-sūtraka, am,* n. the thread of time or death; N. of one of the twenty-one hells.—*Kāla-svarūpa, as, ā, am,* having the very form of death (applied to any terrific object).—*Kālākṛishṭa* (°*la-āk*°), *as, ā, am,* led to death or destruction, drawn to or by one's fate; produced or brought about by time.—*Kālāksharika, as,* m. (fr. *kāla + akshara*), a scholar, a pupil who has begun to read.—*Kālāgni* (°*la-ag*°), *is,* m. the fire that is to destroy the world; the conflagration at the end of time.—*Kālāgni-rudra, as,* m. Rudra regarded as the fire that is to destroy the world; (scil. *rasa*) N. of a particular drug or medicine.—*Kālāgnirudropanishad* (°*ra-up*°), *t,* f., N. of several Upanishads.—*Kālātīta* (°*la-at*°), *as, ā, am,* elapsed, passed by.—*Kālātmaka* (°*la-āt*°), *as, ikā, am,* depending on time or destiny.—*Kālātyaya* (°*la-at*°), *as,* m. lapse of time, loss or destruction by lapse of time.—*Kālātyayopadishṭa* (°*ya-up*°), *as, ā, am,* taught or rectified by the lapse of time; term for a vain argument (*hetv-ābhāsa*), also called *atīta-kāla* and *bādhita*.—*Kālādarśa* (°*la-ād*°), *as,* m. 'the mirror of time,' title of a work.—*Kālādhyaksha* (°*la-adh*°), *as,* m. the overseer or leader of time, an epithet of the sun.—*Kālānala* (°*la-an*°), *as,* m. the fire of all-destroying time, the universal conflagration at the end of all things; N. of a son of Sabhā-nara.—*Kālāntaka* (°*la-an*°), *as,* m. time regarded as the god of death.—*Kālāntaka-yama, as,* m. all-destroying time in the form of Yama.—*Kālāntara* (°*la-an*°), *am,* n. interval, intermediate time; period, process of time; a former or another time.—*Kālāntara-kshama, as, ā, am,* able to bear an interval of delay.—*Kālāntara-visha, as, ā, am,* poisonous at certain times; (*as*), m. a poisonous animal, venomous only when enraged or alarmed, as a rat &c.—*Kālāntarāvṛitta* (°*ra-āv*°), *as, ā, am,* hidden or concealed by time.—*Kālāntarāvṛitti-śubhāśubha* (°*bha-aś*°), *āni,* n. pl. good and evil things occurring within the revolutions of time.—*Kālāvadhi* (°*la-av*°), *is,* m. a fixed or appointed time.—*Kālāryavāya* (°*la-av*°), *as,* m. no interval of time.—*Kālāśuddhi, is,* m. or *kālāśauća* (°*la-aś*°), *am,* n. season of mourning or ceremonial impurity, as at the birth of a child, the death of a relation &c., when it is considered unlawful to perform any religious rites.—*Kāle-ja, as, ā, am,* born or produced at a fixed time or at due time.—*Kālottara* (°*la-ut*°), N. of a work.—*Kālotpādita* (°*la-ut*°), *as, ā, am,* produced in due season.—*Kālopta* (°*la-up*°), *as, ā, am,* sown in due season.

Kālaya, nom. P. *kālayati, -yitum,* to show or announce the time.

2\. *kālika, as, ī, am,* relating to time, connected with time, depending on time; fit for any particular season, seasonable; lasting a long time, of long standing (often at the end of a compound, e. g. *āsanna-kālika,* relating to a time near at hand, impending; *māsa-kālika,* monthly); *a-kālikam,* without delay; (*ā*), f. price of a commodity on credit, or a price to be paid at a fixed period or by instalments; periodical interest paid by the month &c.; change of complexion.—*Kālika-tā,* f. or *kālika-tva, am,* n. time, date, season.

Kālinī, f. 'bringing death,' N. of the sixth lunar mansion.

2\. *kāliya, as, ā, am,* relating to time. See col. 3.

Kālīna, as, ā, am (at the end of comp.), belonging or relating to any particular time, timely, seasonable.

2\. *kālīya, as, ā, am,* relating to time, timely.

Kālya, as, ā, am, timely, seasonable, fit for any particular season; being in a particular period; pleasant, agreeable, auspicious (as discourse; cf. *kalya*); (*as*), m., N. of a man; (*ā*), f. a cow fit for the bull; (*am*), n. day-break.

कालकञ्ज *kālakañja* or *kālakañjya, ās,* m. pl., N. of a Dānava family, the children of Kālakā.

कालकटङ्कट *kālakaṭaṅkaṭa, as,* m. an epithet of Śiva; (a various reading has *śālakaṭaṅkaṭa*); [cf. *kaṭaṅkaṭa.*]

कालकील *kālakīla* or *kālakīlaka, as,* m. a confused or mingled sound, a tumult; [cf. *kalakala.*]

कालकुञ्च *kālakuñća, as,* m. an epithet of Vishṇu.

कालकूट *kālakūṭa, as, am,* m. n. (fr. *kala-kūṭa*), a kind of poison contained in a bulbous root or tuber; a mortal or deadly poison; a poison produced at the churning of the ocean, swallowed by Śiva and causing the blueness of his neck; a poison in general; (*as*), m. myrrh; N. of a country near the Himālaya and the people inhabiting it; an epithet of Yama; [cf. *kāla-kuṇṭha.*]

Kālakūṭaka, as, am, m. n. a kind of poison contained in a bulbous root; a deadly poison produced at the churning of the ocean; a poison in general.

Kālakūṭi, is, m. a prince of the Kalakūṭas.

कालङ्कत *kālaṅkata, as,* m. the plant Cassia Sophora.

कालञ्जर *kālañjara, as,* m., N. of a mountain in Bundalkhand considered as sacred, the modern Kallinjer; N. of the adjacent country; an assembly or meeting-place of religious mendicants; Kallinjer is one of the places at which such assemblies meet, being enumerated amongst the Tapasyasthānas or spots adapted to practices of austere devotion; an epithet of Śiva; (*ā* or *ī*), f. an epithet of Durgā.

कालबलन *kālabalana, am,* n. armour, mail; (a wrong reading for *kāya-balana* or *kāya-valana.*)

कालबव *kālabava* or *kālavava, as,* m., N. of a man.

Kālabavin, inas, m. pl., N. of a school.

कालम्बी *kālambī,* f. or *kālambya, as* or *am* (?), m. or n. (?), N. of a caravansery.

कालव *kālava, ās,* m. pl., N. of a people.

कालवेय *kālaveya, ās,* m. pl., N. of a school.

कालशेय *kālaśeya, am,* n. (fr. *kalaśi* = *kalaśa*), buttermilk, produced in a jar or pitcher by churning; also *kālaseya.*

कालानर *kālānara, as,* m., N. of a son of Sabhā-nara; [cf. *kāla-nara* and *kālānala.*]

कालानुनादिन् *kālānunādin, ī,* m. = *kalānunādin,* a large black bee; a sparrow, the francoline partridge.

कालाप *kālāpa, as,* m. (fr. *kalāpa*), the hair of the head; a serpent's hood; a demon, an imp or goblin; a student of the Kalāpa grammar; one who knows or follows this grammar; (fr. *kalāpin*), a pupil of Kalāpin; epithet of Ārāḍa, a teacher of Śākya-muni.

Kālāpaka, as, ikā, am, belonging to the pupils of Kalāpin; (*am*), n. an assemblage of pupils of Kalāpin; N. of a grammar.

कालाम *kālāma, as,* m. an epithet of Ārāḍa, the teacher of Śākya-muni; [cf. *kālāpa.*]

कालामुख *kālāmukha, as,* m. (fr. *kāla-mukha?*), N. of a Śaiva sect.

कालायनि *kālāyani, is,* m., N. of a pupil of Bāshkali.

कालायनी *kālāyanī,* f. (fr. *kalā*), an epithet of Durgā.

कालिक *kālika.* See under 1. *kāla* and 2. *kāla* at page 224 and last col.

कालिङ्ग *kāliṅga, as,* m. (fr. *kaliṅga*), a prince of the Kaliṅgas; (pl.) the Kaliṅgas; an elephant; a snake; a species of cucumber, Cucumis Usitatissimus; a poisonous plant; a sort of iron; (*ī*), f. a princess of the Kaliṅgas; a kind of gourd or cucumber; N. of a river; (*am*), n. the water-melon; (*as, ī, am*), produced in or belonging to the Kaliṅga country.

Kāliṅgaka, as, m. a prince of the Kaliṅgas.

Kāliṅgikā, f. the plant Ipomœa Turpethum.

कालिञ्जर *kāliñjara, as,* m., N. of a mountain; [cf. *kālañjara.*]

कालिदास *kālidāsa, as,* m. (fr. *kālī,* the goddess Durgā, and *dāsa,* a slave, the final of *kālī* being shortened), N. of a celebrated poet, supposed to be the author of the Śakuntalā, Vikramorvaśī, Mālavikāgnimitra, the Megha-dūta, Raghu-vaṃśa, Nalodaya, and other poems; also of the Śruta-bodha: he was one of the nine poets or gems of Vikramāditya's court, and is supposed to have flourished in the century preceding the Christian era; the name is however applied to more persons than one, and seems, in some measure, to have been used as an honorary title; the works attributed to this author are amongst the most elegant compositions in the Sanskrit language.

Kālidāsaka, as, m. = the preceding.

कालिनी *kālinī.* See under 2. *kāla.*

कालिन्द *kālinda, am,* n. the water-melon; (*ī*), f. a sort of vessel; N. of a plant [cf. *kāliṅgikā*]; N. of a wife of Kṛishṇa; N. of the wife of Asita and mother of Sagara; an epithet of the river Yamunā; (*as, ī, am*), connected with the river Yamunā, coming from this river; [cf. *kalinda.*]—*Kālindī-karshaṇa, as,* m. an epithet of Bala-rāma, this hero having diverted the stream Yamunā into a new and devious channel, marked out by his ploughshare.—*Kālindī-bhedana, as,* m. an epithet of Bala-rāma; [cf. the preceding.]—*Kālindī-sū, ūs,* m. the father of the Yamunā, an epithet of Sūrya; (*ūs*), f. the mother of Yamunā, an epithet of one of the wives of Sūrya.—*Kālindī-sodara, as,* m. the brother of the Yamunā, an epithet of Yama.

Kālindaka, am, n. the water-melon.

कालिमन् *kāliman.* See under 1. *kāla.*

कालिम्मन्या *kālim-manyā,* f. (*kālim* instead of *kālīm*), thinking one's self to be Kālī, regarding one's self as Kālī.

कालिय 3. *kāliya, as,* m. (fr. *kali;* for 1. and 2. see under 1. and 2. *kāla*), the present age, commonly called the Kali-yuga.

कालीक *kālīka, as,* m. a heron; [cf. 1. *kālika.*]

कालीची *kālīćī,* f. (fr. 2. *kāla* and *añć?*), the judgment-hall of Yama, regent or judge of the dead.

कालीन *kālīna.* See under 2. *kāla,* col. 1.

कालीय 1. *kālīya.* See p. 225 and col. 1.

कालुष्य *kālushya, am,* n. (fr. *kalusha*), foulness, dirtiness, filth, turbidness, opacity; disturbance or interruption of harmony, disagreement.

कालेज *kāle-ja.* See under 2. *kāla.*

कालेय 2. *kāleya, am,* n. (fr. *kali;* for 1. see under 1. *kāla*), the Sāman of Kali; (*as, ā, am*), belonging to Kali, the Kali age &c.

कालेयक *kāleyaka.* See under 1. *kāla.*

कालेश्वर *kāleśvara, kālotpādita,* &c. See under 1. and 2. *kāla.*

कालोदायिन् *kālodāyin, ī,* m., N. of a pupil of Śākya-muni; (the right reading is perhaps *kālodayin.*)

काल्प kālpa, *as, ī, am* (fr. *kalpa*), preceptive, ritual; relating to a Kalpa or period so called; (*as*), m. the plant Curcuma Zerumbet.

Kālpaka, as, m. the same plant; [cf. also *kālyaka*.]

Kālpanika, as, ī, am (fr. *kalpanā*), existing only in fancy; fictitious, invented; counterfeit, hypocritical, artificial, fabricated. — *Kālpanika-tā*, f. contrivance, hypocrisy, forgery.

Kālpasūtra, as, m. (fr. *kalpa-sūtra*), one who is familiar with the Kalpasūtras.

काल्य kālya. See under 2. *kāla*.

काल्याणिनेय kālyāṇineya, *as, ī, am* (fr. *kalyāṇī*), sprung from a virtuous or fortunate woman; (*as*), m. the son of such a woman.

काल्वालीकृत kālvālī-kṛita, *as, ā, am*, Ved. made bald (?); [cf. Lat. *calvus*.]

काव kāva, *am*, n. (fr. *kavi*), N. of a Sāman.

कावचिक kāvaćika, *as, ī, am* (fr. *kavaća*), relating to armour, armorial; (*am*), n. a multitude of men in armour.

कावट kāvaṭa, *am*, n., N. of a district containing 100 Grāmas; [cf. *karvaṭa*.]

Kāvaṭikā, f. a district of 200 Grāmas.

कावरुक kāvaruka, *as, ī, am*, fearful; henpecked; (*as*), m. an owl; (a wrong form for *kākaruka* or *kākarūka*?).

कावष kāvasha, *am*, n. (fr. *kavasha*), N. of a Sāman.

Kāvasheya, as, m. a patronymic of Tura in the Brāhmaṇas.

कावार kāvāra (*kā-āv°*), *am*, n. the aquatic plant Vallisneria; (*ī*), f. an umbrella or chhattar, especially one without a stick and worn like a broad-brimmed hat.

काविराज् kā-virāj, *ṭ*, f. a metre consisting of 9 + 12 + 9 syllables.

कावृक kā-vṛika, *as*, m., N. of several birds; a gallinaceous fowl (= *kukkuṭa, kṛikavāku*); the ruddy goose, Anas Casaca (= *koka*); a small singing bird, Loxia Philippensis.

कावेर kāvera, *am*, n. saffron, Crocus Sativus; (*ī*), f. turmeric; a courtezan, a harlot; N. of a river in the Dekhan (according to a legend in the Hari-vaṇśa, a daughter of Yuvanāśva and wife of Jahnu, who by her father's curse was changed from one half of the Gaṅgā into the river Kāverī, therefore also called Ardha-gaṅgā or Ardha-jāhnavī).

Kāveraka, as, m. a patronymic of Rajata-nābhi.

Kāverikā, f., N. of a river, = *kāverī*.

काव्य kāvya, *as, ā, am* (fr. *kavi*), endowed with the qualities of a sage or poet, descended or coming from a sage; prophetic, inspired, poetical; a particular order of manes; a patronymic of Uśanas; (*ās*), m. pl. the descendants of Kavi; (*ā*), f. understanding, intelligence; a female fiend [cf. *pūtanā*]; (*am*), n. wisdom, intelligence; prophetic inspiration; high power and art; intellect, knowledge (often used in pl.); a poem, poetical composition, a work of poetic art; term for the first tetrastich in the metre Shaṭpada; happiness, welfare. — *Kāvya-kalpa-latā*, f. title of a work on artificial poems. — *Kāvyakalpalatā-vṛitti, is*, f. a commentary by Amara-ćandra on the last work. — *Kāvyakalpalatāvṛitti-parimala*, a commentary on the preceding work. — *Kāvya-kāma-dhenu, us*, f. title of a commentary by Vopadeva on his work called Kavi-kalpadruma. — *Kāvya-ćandrikā*, f. title of a work on artificial poems by Kavi-ćandra; another work on the same subject by Nyāyavāgīśa. — *Kāvya-ćaura, as*, m. a robber of other poems, a plagiarist. — *Kāvya-tā*, f. or *kāvya-tva, am*, n. the condition of a poetical composition. — *Kāvya-devī*, f., N. of a princess, who erected a statue of Śiva, called Kāvyadeveśvara. — *Kāvya-prakāśa* or *kāvya-pradīpa, as*, m. title of a work on artificial poems by Mammaṭa. — *Kāvya-mīmāṇsaka, as*, m. a poetaster, a rhetorician. — *Kāvya-rasika, as, ā, am*, one who has a taste for poetical compositions. — *Kāvya-rākshasa, am*, n. title of an artificial poem. — *Kāvya-śāstra, am*, n. title of a small work on poetics. — *Kāvya-sudhā*, f. title of a commentary on a work on artificial poems. — *Kāvya-hāsya, am*, n. a farce. — *Kāvyādarśa* (°*ya-ād*°), *as*, m. a work on poetics by Daṇḍin. — *Kāvyālankāra-vṛitti, is*, f. a work on poetics by Vāmana. — *Kāvyāshṭaka* (°*ya-ash*°), *am*, n. title of a work of Sūrya.

काश् kāś, cl. 1. and 4. A. *kāśate* and *kāśyate, ćakāśe* or *kāśāmāsa, kāśishyate, akāśishṭa, kāśitum*, to be visible, appear; to shine, be brilliant, have an agreeable appearance: Caus. *kāśayati, -yitum*: Desid. *ćikāśishate*: Intens. *ćākaśīti* and *ćākāśyate*, to shine brightly; to see clearly, survey; [cf. *kāś*.]

1. *kāśa, as*, m. the becoming visible, appearance; splendor; (*as, am*), m. n. a species of grass, Saccharum Spontaneum, used for mats, roofs, &c.; also personified, together with the Kuśa grass, as one of Yama's attendants; (*as*), m., N. of a man; a son of Sunahotra; also of another Sunahotra, the father of Kāśi-rāja. — *Kāśa-kṛitsna, as*, m., N. of a grammarian; also of a philosopher. — *Kāśakṛitsni, is*, m. (a patronymic from the preceding), N. of a teacher. — *Kāśa-pauṇḍra, ās*, m. pl., N. of a people. — *Kāśa-maya, as, ī, am*, consisting of the grass Saccharum Spontaneum.

Kāśaka, as, m. a species of grass, Saccharum Spontaneum; N. of a man, = *kāśa*.

1. *kāśin, ī, inī, i*, (at the end of compounds) shining, appearing, having the semblance of anything, e. g. *jita-kāśin*, one who appears as a conqueror or behaves like one; (*ī*), m., N. of a man, a son of Brahman Kavi (Mahā-bh. XIII. 4150).

Kāśila, as, ā, am, made of Kāśa grass, abounding in it.

Kāśishṇu, us, us, u, shining, brilliant.

काश 2. kāśa, *as*, m. (wrongly spelt for *kāsa*), cough, catarrh, irritation of the throat, sneezing. — *Kāśa-marda, as*, m. wrongly spelt for *kāsa-marda*, q. v.

2. *kāśin, ī, inī, i* (wrongly spelt for *kāsin*), having a cold or cough.

काशपरी kāśaparī, f., N. of a region (?).

Kāśapharī, f., N. of a region (?); (a various reading has *kāśaphārī*.)

काशब्द kā-śabda, *as*, m. the noise *kā*.

काशाल्मलि kā-śālmali, *is*, f. a kind of silk-cotton tree, Bombax Heptaphyllum.

काशि kāśi, *is*, m. the clenched hand, the fist; a handful; the sun (in this sense fr. rt. *kāś*); (*ayas*), m. pl., N. of the people of Kāśi; N. of the ancestors of the kings of Kāśi, of the family of Bharata; (*is*), m., N. of a son of Suhotra and grandfather of Dhanvantari; also N. of a son of Kāśya and grandson of Suhotra; (*ayas*), m. pl. the descendants of this man; (*is* or *ī*), f. a celebrated city and place of pilgrimage, the modern Benares; (*ī*), f., N. of the wife of Sudeva and mother of Supārśva. — *Kāśi-kanyā*, f. the virgin of Kāśi, daughter of the king of Kāśi. — *Kāśi-khaṇḍa*, a section of the Skanda-purāṇa. — *Kāśi-nagara, am*, n. the city of the Kāśis, i. e. Benares. — *Kāśi-nātha, as*, m., N. of several men. — *Kāśi-pa, as*, m. a sovereign of the Kāśis. — *Kāśi-pati, is*, m. the ruler of the Kāśis, epithet of Divodāsa Dhanvantari, a king of Benares, author of certain medical works and teacher of the Āyur-veda; he is often confounded with his celestial namesake, the physician of the gods. — *Kāśi-purī*, f. the city of the Kāśis, i. e. Benares. — *Kāśi-rāja, as*, m. a king of the Kāśis, identified with the Dānava Dīrghajihva; epithet of Divodāsa Dhanvantari; also of a grandfather of Dhanvantari. — *Kāśi-rājan, ā*, m. = the preceding. — *Kāśi-rāma, as*, m., N. of the author of a commentary on the Tithi-tattva and several other works. — *Kāśi-vilāsa* or *kāśi-vilāsa, as*, m. title of a work written in Sanskṛit and in one of the modern dialects. — *Kāśī-khaṇḍa, as, am*, m. n. title of a section of the Skanda-purāṇa, treating of Benares. — *Kāśī-nātha, as*, m. 'a lord or master of Benares;' an epithet of Śiva; N. of several men. — *Kāśī-māhātmya, am*, n. a section of the Brahma-vaivarta-purāṇa. — *Kāśī-rāja, as*, m. = *kāśi-rāja*, an epithet of Divodāsa. — *Kāśī-vilāsa, as*, m. = *kāśi-vilāsa*. — *Kāśīśa* (°*śī-īśa*), *as*, m. an epithet of Śiva; an epithet of Divodāsa or any king of Benares; (*am*), n. sulphate of iron. — *Kāśīśvara* (°*śi-īś*°), *as*, m. a prince of the Kāśis or a sovereign of Benares; N. of a grammarian; *Kāśīśvarī*, f. title of a grammar composed by Kaśīśvara (?); *Kāśīśvarī-gaṇa*, title of a treatise on grammar. — *Kāśī-setu, us*, m. title of a work.

Kāśika, as, m., N. of a man; (*ā*), f., scil. *purī*, the city of the Kāśis, i. e. Benares; *kāśikā vṛittiḥ* or only *kāśikā*, f. 'the commentary composed or used in Kāśi or Benares,' title of a commentary on Pāṇini's grammar by Vāmana Jayāditya. — *Kāśika-sūkshma, am*, n. fine cotton from Kāśi. — *Kāśikā-tilaka*, N. of a poem by Nīla-kaṇṭha. — *Kāśikā-priya, as*, m. an epithet of king Divodāsa, who was king of Benares.

Kāśeya, a patronymic from Kāśi; (*ī*), f. a daughter of the king of the Kāśis.

1. *kāśya, as, ā, am*, belonging to the race or tribe of the Kāśis, a prince of Kāśi; (*as*), m., N. of the father of Kāśyapa and ancestor of Kāśirāja Dhanvantari; also of a son of Suhotra, and of Senā-jit; (*ā*), f. the daughter of a king of Kāśi.

Kāśyaka, as, ā, am, belonging to the race or tribe of the Kāśis.

काशीत kāśīta, *am*, n., N. of a verse of the Sāma-veda.

काशूकार kāśūkāra, *as*, m. the Areca or betel-nut tree; (perhaps a wrong reading for *kāsūkāra*.)

काश्मरी kāśmarī, f. or *kāśmarya, as*, m. the plant Gmelina Arborea, commonly called Gambhārī; [cf. also *kārśmarī* and *kārshmarya*.]

काश्मीर kāśmīra, *as, ī, am* (fr. *kaśmīra*), born in or coming from Kaśmīra; (*as*), m. a king of Kaśmīra; (*ās*), m. pl. the inhabitants of Kaśmīra; the country Kaśmīra, also in sing.; (*ā*), f. a sort of grape; (*ī*), f. the tree Ficus Elastica; (*am*), n. the tuberous root of the plant Costus Speciosus; saffron; (= *ṭanka*.) — *Kāśmīra-ja, am*, n. saffron; a sort of drug; the tuberous root of the plant Costus Speciosus; (*ā*), f., N. of a plant, Atis or Betula, = *ati-vishā*. — *Kāśmīra-janman, a*, n. saffron.

Kāśmīraka, as, ī, am, born or produced in Kaśmīra, relating to Kaśmīra; (*ās*), m. pl. the inhabitants of Kaśmīra.

Kāśmīrika, as, ī, am, born or produced in Kāśmīra; *kāśmīrika-nivāsa, as*, m. the residence of the Kaśmīras.

काश्य 2. kāśya, *am*, n. = *kaśya*, a spirituous liquor.

काश्यप kāśyapa, *as, ī, am* (fr. *kaśyapa*), belonging to Kaśyapa, relating to or connected with him (e. g. *kāśyapī devī* or only *kāśyapī*, the earth); (*as*), m. a patronymic from Kaśyapa; N. of an old grammarian; an epithet of Aruṇa; a sort of deer; a fish; (*am*), n. flesh; (*ī*), f. the earth; (according to a legend of the Purāṇas, Paraśu-rāma, after the destruction of the Kshatriya race and the performance of an Aśva-medha sacrifice, presented the sovereignty of the world to Kāśyapa.) — *Kāśyapa-nandana, ās*, m. pl. the children of Kāśyapa, epithet of the gods. — *Kāśyapī-bālākyā-māṭharī-putra, as*, m., N. of a teacher.

Kāśyapi, is, m. (a patronymic fr. *kāśyapa*), an

epithet of Aruṇa, the charioteer of the sun; also of Garuḍa, the bird of Vishṇu.

Kāśyapin, inas, m. pl., N. of a school called after Kaśyapa.

Kāśyapiya, ās, m. pl., N. of a Buddhist school called after Kāśyapa.

Kāśyapeya, as, m. (a patronymic fr. *kaśyapa*), an epithet of the twelve Ādityas; also of the sun; and of Garuḍa, the bird of Vishṇu.

काश्मरी *kāśvarī*, f. the plant Gmelina Arborea, = *kāśmarī*.

काष *kāsha, as,* m. (fr. rt. *kash*), rubbing; that against which anything is rubbed.

काषाय *kāshāya, as, ī, am* (fr. *kashāya*), red, dyed of a reddish colour; a red cloth or garment; (*ī*), f. (with *makshikā*) a sort of fly or wasp. — *Kāshāya-grahaṇa, as,* m., N. of a Caitya, q. v. — *Kāshāya-vasana, as, ā, am,* having a dark or brown garment. — *Kāshāya-vāsika, as,* m. a kind of poisonous insect.

Kāshāyaṇa, as, m. (a patronymic fr. *kashāya* or *kāshāya*), N. of a teacher.

Kāshāyin, iṇas, m. pl., N. of a school called from Kashāya.

काष्ठ *kāshṭha, as,* m. (said to be fr. rt. *kāś*; cf. *kāshṭhā* next col.), N. of one of Kuvera's attendants; (*am*), n. a piece of wood or timber, a stick; wood or timber in general; an instrument for measuring lengths; a kind of measure; (metaphorically) a mere stick, a lanky thin man. At the beginning of a compound and before a simple verb *kāshṭha* may express excellence or superiority; [cf. Cambro-Brit. *coed;* Brit. *coat;* Gr. ξύ-λον.] — *Kāshṭha-kadalī,* f. the wild plantain, Musa Sapientum, (the fruit of this plant being hard and woody.) — *Kāshṭha-kīṭa, as,* m. a small insect or worm found in decayed wood. — *Kāshṭha-kuṭṭa* or *kāshṭha-kūṭa, as,* m. a bird, a sort of woodpecker, Picus Bengalensis. — *Kāshṭha-kuddāla, as,* m. a kind of wooden shovel or scraper used for baling water out of a boat, or for scraping and cleaning its bottom; also written °*kudāla* or °*kūddāla*. — *Kāshṭha-khaṇḍa, am,* n. a stick, a spar, a piece of wood. — *Kāshṭha-ghaṭita, as, ā, am,* formed of wood, wooden. — *Kāshṭha-jambū, ūs,* f., N. of a tree, = *bhūmi-jambū*. — *Kāshṭha-taksh, ṭ,* m. or *kāshṭha-takshaka, as,* m. a carpenter. — *Kāshṭha-tantu, us,* m. a caterpillar which secretes itself in wood and there passes into a chrysalis; a small worm found in timber. — *Kāshṭha-dāru, us,* m. the tree Pinus Deodora. — *Kāshṭha-dru, us,* m. the tree Butea Frondosa. — *Kāshṭha-dhātrī-phala, am,* n. the fruit of the plant Emblica Officinalis. — *Kāshṭha-pāṭalā,* f., N. of a plant (*sita-pāṭalikā*). — *Kāshṭha-pāshāṇa-vāsas, āṃsi,* n. pl. wood, stone, and clothes. — *Kāshṭha-puttalikā,* f. a wooden image. — *Kāshṭha-pradāna, am,* n. piling up wood, forming a funeral pile. — *Kāshṭha-bhāra, as,* m. a particular weight of wood. — *Kāshṭhabhārika, as,* m. a wood-carrier; a bearer of wood. — *Kāshṭha-bhūta, as, ā, am,* one who has become wood, or who is like a piece of wood; epithet of an ascetic, who stands without stirring; (*as*), m., N. of a divine being. — *Kāshṭha-bhṛit,* see under *kāshṭhā*. — *Kāshṭha-maṭhī,* f. a funeral pile. — *Kāshṭha-maya, as, ī, am,* made of wood, wooden, consisting of pieces of wood. — *Kāshṭha-malla, as,* m. a bier, a plank &c. on which dead bodies are carried. — *Kāshṭha-rajju, us,* m. or f. (?), a rope for binding together pieces of wood. — *Kāshṭha-lekhaka, as,* m. a small worm found in wood. — *Kāshṭha-lohin, ī,* m. a club, a short cudgel, especially if armed with iron. — *Kāshṭha-vat, ān, atī, at,* having wood for fuel &c.; (*vat*), ind. like a piece of wood, like a stick or stock, standing petrified with fear &c. — *Kāshṭha-vallikā,* f., N. of a plant, = *kaṭukā*. — *Kāshṭha-vāṭa, as* or *am,* m. or n. (?), a wall made of wood; N. of a place (?). — *Kāshṭha-vivara, am,* n. the hollow of a tree. — *Kāshṭha-śārivā,* f., N. of a plant, = *śārivā*. — *Kāshṭha-stambha, as,* m. a beam of wood. — *Kāshṭhāgāra* (°*ṭha-ag*°), *as* or *am,* m. or n. a house of wood, a wooden house or enclosure. — *Kāshṭhāmbuvāhinī* (°*ṭha-am*°), f. a wooden bucket or baling vessel; [cf. *ambu-vāhinī*.] — *Kāshṭhāluka* (°*ṭha-āl*°), *as* or *am,* m. or n. a species of Āluka. — *Kāshṭhekshu* (°*ṭha-ik*°), *us,* m. a kind of sugar-cane.

Kāshṭhaka, am, n. aloe wood or Agallochum.

Kāshṭhika, as, m. a bearer of wood; (*ā*), f. a small piece of wood.

Kāshṭhin, ī, inī, i, wooden; having wood.

काष्ठा *kāshṭhā*, f. [cf. *kāshṭha* last col.], a place for running, a race-ground, course; the course, path or track of the wind and clouds in the atmosphere; a quarter or region of the world, a cardinal point, space, tract; water; the mark, the goal; limit, boundary; the sun; a fixed place, place, site, especially the situation of the lunar mansions; a measure of time, = $\frac{1}{30}$ Kalā, = $\frac{1}{15}$ Laghu, = $\frac{1}{225}$ Nāḍikā, = $\frac{1}{450}$ Muhūrta; the plant Curcuma Xanthorrhiza; N. of a daughter of Daksha and wife of Kaśyapa, mother of the solidungulous quadrupeds; N. of a town. — *Kāshṭhā-bhṛit, t, t, t* (for *kāshṭhā-bhṛit*), Ved. leading to a mark or aim.

काष्ठील *kāshṭhīla* (*kā-ash*°), *as,* m. a large kind of Calotropis; (*ā*), f. a plantain, Musa Sapientum.

कास् 1. *kās*, cl. 1. A. *kāsate, ćakāse* or *kāsāmāsa, kāsishyate, akāsishṭa, kāsitum,* to cough; to make any disagreeable sound or one indicating disease; to shine (for rt. *kāś*, q. v.): Caus. *kāsayati, -yitum*: Desid. *ćikāsishate*: Intens. *ćākāsyate, ćākāsti*; [cf. Lith. *kostu, koseti*; Slav. *kašljati*; Old Germ. *huosto*; Scot. *casad*.]

2. *kās*, f., Ved. cough.

1. *kāsa, as, ā,* m. f. cough, catarrh. — *Kāsa-kanda, as,* m. a species of root, = *kāsālu*. — *Kāsa-kara, as, ī, am,* producing cough or catarrh. — *Kāsa-kuṇṭha, as, ā, am,* afflicted with cough; (*as*), m. an epithet of Yama; [cf. *kāśa*.] — *Kāsa-ghna, as, ī, am,* removing or alleviating cough, pectoral; (*ī*), f. a sort of prickly nightshade, Solanum Jacquini. — *Kāsa-jit, t,* f. the plant Clerodendrum Siphonanthus. — *Kāsa-nāśinī,* f., N. of a thorny plant, = *karkaṭa-śṛiṅgī*. — *Kāsa-marda, as,* m. the plant Cassia Sophora; a remedy against cough, an acid preparation, a mixture of tamarinds and mustard; also = *paṭala*. — *Kāsa-mardaka, as,* m. the plant Cassia Sophora. — *Kāsa-mardana, as,* m. the plant Trichosanthes Dioeca. — *Kāsa-vat, ān, atī, at,* having a cough. — *Kāsāri* (°*sa-ari*), *is,* m. the plant Cassia Sophora. — *Kāsālu* (°*sa-ālu*), *us,* m. an esculent root, a sort of yam.

Kāsikā, f. cough.

Kāsin, ī, inī, i, having a cough.

Kāsundīvaṭikā, f. a remedy against cough, an acid preparation, a mixture of tamarinds and mustard; (perhaps a wrong reading for *kāsandī*°.)

कास 2. *kāsa, as, am,* m. n. (for *kāśa*), a species of reed or long grass, Saccharum Spontaneum; another plant, Hyperanthera Moringa.

कासर *kāsara, as,* m. a buffalo; (fr. *ka,* water, and *sara,* going?; this animal being partial to marshy places.)

कासार *kāsāra, as, am,* m. n. (said to be fr. rt. *kās*), a pond, a pool.

कासीराम *kāsīrāma, as,* m., N. of a man; (more correctly *kāśī-rāma*?).

कासीस *kāsīsa, am,* n. green vitriol, green sulphate of iron; [cf. *kāśīśa*.]

कासू *kāsū, ūs,* f. (fr. rt. *kās*?), a sort of spear or lance; indistinct speech; speech in general; light, lustre; disease; devotion; understanding. — *Kāsū-tarī,* f. a short spear, a javelin.

कासृति *kā-sṛiti, is,* f. a by-way, a secret path.

कास्तीर *kāstīra, am,* n., N. of a town.

काहका *kāhakā*, f. a kind of musical instrument; [cf. *kāhalā*.]

काहल *kāhala, as, ā, am,* dry, withered; large, excessive; mischievous; (*as*), m. a cat; a cock; a sound in general; (*ā*), f. a kind of musical instrument; N. of an Apsaras; (*ī*), f. a young woman; (*am*), n. indistinct speech; a kind of musical instrument; (*as, ā, am*), m. f. n. a horn, either a cow-horn or an instrument of that shape; a large drum; (*am*), ind. much, excessively. — *Kāhalā-pushpa, as,* m. a thorn-apple, Datura Metel, = *dhūstūra*.

Kāhalin, ī, m., N. of a Ṛishi.

काहलि *kāhali, is,* m. an epithet of Śiva.

काहाबाह *kāhābāha, am,* n., Ved. a rumbling noise in the bowels.

काही *kāhī*, f. the plant Wrightia Antidysenterica; [cf. *kuṭaja*.]

काहूजी *kāhūji, īs,* m., N. of the father of the writer Mahādeva (author of an astronomical work).

कि 1. *ki*, a pronominal base, like *ka* and *ku*, in the words *kim, kiyat, kis, kīdṛiksha, kīdṛiś, kīdṛiśa, kīvat,* q. v.

कि 2. *ki*, a verbal root; [cf. *ći*; Lat. *scio*?; Hib. *ci*, 'see, behold;' *ci-thi*, 'you see;' *citear*, 'it seems, appears.']

किंस्त्य *kiṃstya, am,* n. a kind of fruit (?).

किकि *kiki, is,* m. a blue jay; the cocoa tree, Nārikela; [cf. the following.]

Kikidiva, as, m. or *kikidivi, is,* m. or *kikidīvi, is,* m. a blue jay; Ved. another kind of animal.

Kikin, ī, m. or *kikī,* f. a blue jay.

Kikīdiva, as, m. or *kikidivi* or *kikidīvi, is,* m. a blue jay.

किकिरा *kikirā*, ind., Ved. (with 1. *kṛi*) to tear in pieces, to rend into rags and tatters.

किक्किटा *kikkiṭā*, ind., Ved. an onomatopoetic word used like an interjection in invocations.

किक्किश *kikkiśa, as,* m. a kind of worm, pernicious to the hair, nails, and teeth.

किक्किसाद *kikkisāda, as,* m. a species of snake.

किक्नस *kiknasa, as,* m. particles of ground corn, bruised grain, groats.

किखि *kikhi, is,* m. a monkey, an ape; (*is*), f. a small jackal, a fox.

किङ्कणी *kinkaṇī*, f. a small bell; (a various reading for *kinkiṇī*, q. v.)

किङ्कर *kin-kara*, &c. See under *kim* below.

किङ्किण *kinkiṇa, as,* m. (an onomatopoetic word), a kind of musical instrument; N. of a son of Bhajamāna.

Kinkiṇi, is or *ī,* f. a small bell; a girdle of small bells, or any tinkling ornament; N. of an acid sort of grape (Vikankata).

Kinkiṇika, as or *am,* m. or n. (?), a small bell. — *Kinkiṇikāśrama* (°*ka-āś*°), *as,* m., N. of an hermitage.

Kinkiṇikin, ī, inī, i, ornamented or decorated with small bells.

किङ्किर *kinkira, as,* m. a horse; the Indian cuckoo, the Kokila or Koil; a large black bee; Kāmadeva, the god of love; (*ā*), f. blood; (*am*), n. the frontal sinus of an elephant.

Kinkirāta, as, m. a parrot; the Indian cuckoo or Kokila; Kāma-deva, the god of love; the tree Jonesia Aśoka; a species of amaranth; [cf. *kuraṇṭaka, raktāmlāna, pītāmlāna*.]

Kinkirāla, as, m., N. of a plant, = *varvūra*.

Kinkirin, ī, m., N. of a plant, commonly Buinchi, Flacourtia Sapida; [cf. *vikankata*.]

किङ्क्षण *kin-kshaṇa.* See under *kim* next col.

किञ्च *kiṅća*, ind. See under *kim* next col.

किञ्चन 1. *kiṅćana, as*, m. a species of the Palāśa or Butea Frondosa. (For 2. *kiṅ-ćana* see under 2. *ka* and *kim* below.)

किञ्चनक *kiṅćanaka, as*, m., N. of a king of the Nāgas.

किञ्चित् *kiṅćit, kiṅćit-kara*, &c. See under *kim* next col.

किञ्चिलिक *kiṅćilika* or *kiṅćulaka* or *kiṅćuluka, as*, m. an earth-worm.

किञ्ज *kiñja, am*, n. the blossom of the plant Mesua Ferrea [cf. *kiñjalka*]; the filament of a lotus.

Kiñjala, as, m. the filament of a plant, especially of a lotus.

Kiñjalka, as, m. the filament of a plant, especially the filament or blossom of a lotus; (*am*), n. the flower of the plant Mesua Ferrea.

Kiñjalkin, ī, inī, i, consisting of filaments.

किट् *kiṭ*, cl. 1. P. *keṭati, ćikeṭa, keṭitum*, to go or approach, to alarm or terrify; to dread, fear.

किटकिटाय *kiṭakiṭāya* (an onomatopoetic expression), A. *kiṭakiṭāyate*, to gnash the teeth.

किटि *kiṭi, is*, m. a hog; [cf. *kira, kiri*.]

किटिभ *kiṭibha, as*, m. a bug; a louse, = *keśa-kīṭa*; (*am*), n. a species of exanthema; [cf. the next.]

किटिम *kiṭima, as* or *am*, m. or n. (?), a species of leprosy.

किट्ट *kiṭṭa* or *kiṭṭaka, am*, n. secretion, excretion, excrement, dirt. — *Kiṭṭa-varjita, am*, n. semen virile.

Kiṭṭāla, as, m. scoria, rust of iron &c.; a copper vessel.

किट्टिम *kiṭṭima, am*, n. a kind of liquid.

किण *kiṇa, as*, m. a corn, a callosity; a scar; a wart, a mole; an insect found in wood. — *Kiṇa-vat, ān, atī, at*, callous. — *Kiṇāta* (°*ṇa-al*°), *as*, m. an epithet of Indra.

किणि *kiṇi, is*, f. or *kiṇihī*, f. the plant Achyranthes Aspera; [cf. *apāmārga*.]

किण्व *kiṇva, as, am*, m. n. ferment, a drug or seed used to produce fermentation in the manufacture of spirits from sugar, bassia, &c.; (*am*), n. sin.

किण्विन् *kiṇvin, ī*, m. a horse; [cf. *kindhin, kilkin*, and *kilvin*.]

कित् *kit*. See *ćit* and *ketaya*.

कित *kita, as*, m., N. of a man.

कितव *kitava, as, ī*, m. f. (perhaps fr. *kim tava*, 'what of you?' i. e. what is your stake?), a gamester, a gambler; a cheat, a fraudulent man or woman; a mad or crazy person; N. of a man; (*ās*), m. pl., N. of a people or race; (*as*), m. thorn-apple, Datura Metel [cf. *dhūrta* and *un-matta*]; a kind of perfume, commonly Roćana.

किनाट *kināṭa, am*, n. the inner bark of a tree.

किन्तनु *kin-tanu*, &c. See under *kim*.

किन्दुविल्व *kinduvilva, as* or *am*, m. or n. (?), or according to various readings *kinduvilla, kenduvilla*, or *tinduvilla*, N. of the place where Jaya-deva was born or where his family resided.

किन्धिन् *kindhin, ī*, m. a horse; (a various reading for *kilkin*.)

किन्नु *kin-nu*, ind. See under *kim* below.

किप्य *kipya, as*, m. a kind of worm.

किम् *kim*, ind. (originally nom. and acc. sing. n. of 2. *ka*, q. v.), how? whence? wherefore? why?

Kim is much used as a particle of interrogation like the Lat. *num, an*, sometimes translateable by 'whether?' but oftener serving only like a note of interrogation to mark a question (e. g. *kiṃ vyādhā vane 'smin sańćaranti*, do hunters roam about in this wood? In an interrogation the verb if uncompounded with a preposition generally retains its accent after *kim*). To this sense may be referred the *kim* expressing blame, deficiency, &c., at the beginning of compounds (e. g. *kiṃ-rājan*, what sort of a king? i. e. a bad king); also the *kim* prefixed to verbs with a similar meaning (e. g. *kim-adhīte*, he reads badly). *Kim—uta* or *kim—utavā* or *kim—uta—uta* or *kim—athavā—uta*, whether—or—or; [cf. *uta*.]

Kim is very frequently connected with other particles, as follows: *kim aṅga*, wherefore then? *atha kim*, how else? surely; *kim api*, somewhat, to a considerable extent, rather, much more, still further; *kim iti*, why? (see *iti*); *kimu* or *kimuta*, how much more? how much less? *kiṃ kila*, what a pity! (expressing dissatisfaction); *kiṅća*, moreover, further; *kiṅ-ćana* (originally negative = 'in no way'), to a certain degree, a little; *kiṅćit*, somewhat, a little; *kiṃ tarhi*, how then? but, however; *kintu*, but, however, nevertheless (bearing the same relation to *tu* that *kiṅća* bears to *ća*); *kin-nu*, whether indeed? (a stronger interrogative than *kim* alone); how much more? how much less? *kin nu khalu*, how possibly? (a still stronger interrogative); *kim punar*, how much more? how much less? *kiṃ vā*, whether? or whether? or, (often a mere particle of interrogation); *kiṃ svit*, whether? how? (a mere particle of interrogation like the last).

Kiṃ-yu, us, us, u, Ved. what wishing? — *Kiṃ-rājan, ā*, m. a bad king. — *Kiṃ-rūpa, as, ā, am*, of what shape? — *Kiṃ-vat, ān, atī, at*, poor, mean, insignificant. — *Kiṃ-vadanta, as*, m., N. of an imp or goblin who lies in wait for children. — *Kiṃ-vadanti, is* or *ī*, f. (lit. what do they say?), the common saying or rumour, report, tradition, tale. — *Kiṃ-varāṭaka, as, ā, am*, one who says 'what is a cowrie?' i. e. an extravagant careless man who does not value small coins. — *Kiṃ-vid, t, t, t*, what knowing? — *Kiṃ-vīrya, as, ā, am*, of what power? — *Kiṃ-vritta, as, ā, am*, one who says 'what is behaviour?' i. e. one who is not careful in his manners. — *Kiṃ-vyāpāra, as, ā, am*, following what occupation? — *Kiṃ-śāru, us, u*, m. n. the beard of corn; (*us*), m. an arrow; a heron. — *Kiṃ-śila, as, ā, am*, Ved. (land) having small stones or gravelly particles. — *Kiṃ-śīla, as, ā, am*, of what habits? in what manner generally existing or living? — *Kiṃ-śuka, as*, m. the tree Butea Frondosa, a tree bearing beautiful red blossoms, and hence often alluded to by poets; (*am*), n. the blossom of this tree; [cf. *palāśa* and *su-kiṃśuka*.] — *Kiṃśukodaka* (°*ka-ud*°), *am*, n. a decoction made from the blossoms of the tree Butea Frondosa and used for colouring. — *Kiṃ-śuluka, as*, m. a variety of the tree Butea Frondosa. — *Kiṃśulukā-giri, is*, m., N. of a mountain. — *Kiṃ-sakhi, ā*, m. a bad friend. — *Kiṅ-kara, as*, m. a servant, a slave; (Ved.) a particular part of a carriage; a kind of Rākshasa; N. of a people; (*ā*), f. a female servant; (*ī*), f. the wife of a servant. — *Kiṅkara-tva, am*, n. the condition of a servant or slave. — *Kiṅkartavya-tā* or *kiṅkārya-tā*, f. any situation or circumstances in which one asks one's self what ought to be done? [cf. *itikartavya-tā*.] — *Kiṅ-kala, as*, m., N. of a man. — *Kiṅ-kāmya*, nom. P. *-yati*, to wish what? — *Kiṅ-kāmyā*, ind. (old inst. for *-kāmyayā*), Ved. from a desire for what? — *Kiṅ-kāraṇa, as, ā, am*, having what reason or cause? — *Kiṅ-kshaṇa, as, ā, am*, one who says 'what is a moment?' i. e. a lazy fellow who does not value moments. — *Kiṅ-gotra, as, ā, am*, belonging to what family? — 2. *kiṅ-ćana*, see under 2. *ka* and *kim* above. — *Kiṅćana-tā*, f. something, somewhat. — *Kiṅćij-jña* (°*ćit-jña*), *as, ā, am*, knowing a little, a mere smatterer. — *Kiṅćit-kara, as, ī, am*, doing anything; (*a-kiṅćitkara*, one who has not done anything wrong.) — *Kiṅćit-kāla, as*, m. a little time, some time. — *Kiṅćit-pare*, ind. a little after. — *Kiṅćit-prāṇa, as, ā, am*, having a little life left. — *Kiṅćin-mātra, am*, n. only a little. — *Kiṅ-ćhandas, ās, ās, as*, conversant with which Veda? (which Veda does he know?) — *Kiṅ-japya, am*, n., N. of a Tīrtha. — *Kiṅ-jyotis, is, is, is*, having which light? — *Kin-tanu, us*, m. an insect described as having eight legs and a very slender body, a species of spider. — *Kin-tamām*, ind. whether? whether of many? — *Kin-tarām*, ind. whether? whether of two? — *Kintu-ghna, as*, m. one of the eleven periods called Karaṇa (destroying every 'but'). — *Kin-tva, as, ā, am*, Ved. an adj. formed from *kiṃ tvam*, 'what thou?' to denote the impudent manner in which a drunken man asks questions. — *Kin-data, as*, m., N. of a sacred well. — *Kin-dama, as*, m., N. of a Muni. — *Kin-darbha, as*, m., N. of a man. — *Kin-dāna, am*, n., N. of a Tīrtha. — *Kin-dāsa, as*, m., N. of a man. — *Kin-devata, as, ā, am*, having what deity? — *Kin-devatya, as, ā, am*, Ved. belonging to or devoted to what deity? — *Kin-nara, as*, m. (what sort of man?), a mythical being with a human figure and the head of a horse, originally perhaps a kind of monkey [cf. *vā-nara*], in later times (like the Naras) reckoned among the Gandharvas or celestial choristers and celebrated as musicians; also attached to the service of Kuvera; (with Jainas) one of the eight orders of the Vyantaras; (*as*), m., N. of a prince; an epithet of Nara, a son of Vibhīshaṇa; (with Jainas) the N. of the attendant of the fifteenth Arhat of the present Avasarpiṇī; N. of a place; a kind of musical instrument; (*ī*), f. a female Kinnara; the lute of the Caṇḍāla. — *Kinnara-varsha, as*, m. a division of the earth said to be north of the Himālaya mountains. — *Kinnareśa* or *kinnareśvara* (°*ra-iś*°), *as*, m. an epithet of Kuvera as lord of the Kinnaras. — *Kin-nāmadheya, as, ā, am*, or *kin-nāman, ā, ā, a*, having what name? — *Kin-nimitta, as, ā, am*, having what cause or reason? (*am*), ind. from what cause? for what reason? why? wherefore? — *Kim-artha, as, ā, am*, having what motives or aim? (*am*), ind. from what motive? what for? wherefore? why? — *Kim-ākhya, as, ā, am*, having what name? — *Kimiććhaka, as, ā, am* (fr. *kim* + *iććhā*), what one wishes or desires, anything desired. — *Kim-paća, as, ā, am*, cooking what? one who cooks nothing; miserly, avaricious. — *Kim-paćāna, as, ā, am*, miserly, niggardly, avaricious; [cf. *mitam-paća*.] — *Kim-parākrama, as, ā, am*, of what power? of what energy? — *Kim-paryantam*, ind. to what extent? how far? how long? — *Kim-pāka, as, ā, am*, unripe; ignorant; stupid; not arrived at mature age, childish; (*as*), m. a Cucurbitaceous plant, Trichosanthes Palmata; also Cucumis Colocynthus [cf. *mahā-kāla*]; (*am*), n. the fruit of this plant. — *Kim-punā*, f., N. of a river. — *Kim-purusha* or *kim-pūrusha, as*, m. a mongrel being (according to the Brāhmaṇas an evil being similar to man), perhaps originally a kind of monkey; in some instances the word seems to mean merely a low and despicable man; in later times the word is usually identified with *kin-nara*, though sometimes applied to other beings, in which the figure of a man and that of an animal are combined, (these beings are supposed to live on Hemakūṭa, and are regarded as the attendants of Kuvera; with Jainas the Kimpurushas, like the Kinnaras, belong to the Vyantaras); N. of one of the nine sons of Āgnīdhra, having the Varsha Kimpurusha as his hereditary portion; a division of the universe, one of the nine Khaṇḍas or portions into which the world is divided, and described as the country between the Himāćala and Hemakūṭa mountains, also called *kimpurusha-varsha*. — *Kimpurusheśvara* (°*sha-iś*°), *as*, m. an epithet of Kuvera. — *Kim-prakāram*, ind. in what manner? — *Kim-prabhāva, as, ā, am,* possessing what power? — *Kim-bala, as, ā, am,* possessing what strength or power? — *Kim-bharā* (?), f. a kind of perfume, commonly called Nalī. — *Kim-bhūta, as, ā, am,* being what? (*am*), ind. how? in what manner or degree? like what? — *Kim-maya, as, ī, am,* Ved. consisting of what?

Kimīya, as, ā, am, belonging or relating to whom or what?

किमीदिन् *kimīdin, ī, inī,* m. f., Ved., N. of a class of evil spirits.

कियत् *kiyat, ān, atī, at* (fr. 1. *ki*), how great? how large? how far? how much? of what extent? of what qualities? (Ved. loc. *kiyāti* with following *ā*, how long ago? since what time? e. g. *kiyāty ā prathamaḥ sarga āsām,* how long is it since their first creation? *kiyaty adhvani,* at what distance? how far off? *kiyad etad* with gen., of what importance is this to any one? *tena kiyān arthaḥ,* what profit arises from that? *kiyać ćirena,* in how long a time? *kiyad dūre,* how far?); little, small, unimportant, of small value (often in compounds, e. g. *kiyad-vakra,* a little bent; *kiyan-mātra,* of little importance; *kiyad api,* how large or how far soever, &c.; *yāvat kiyaćća,* how large or how much soever, of what qualities soever; (*kiyat*), ind. how far? how much? how? a little; *kiyat-kālam,* how long? some little time ago. — *Kiyad-etikā* or *kiyad-ehikā,* f. effort, vigorous and persevering exertions according to one's strength. — *Kiyad-dūra, as, ā, am,* for a short distance, a little way. — *Kiyan-mūlya, as, ā, am,* of what value? of what price?

कियाम्बु *kiyāmbu, u,* n., Ved. a kind of aquatic plant.

कियाह *kiyāha, as,* m. a fox, a horse of a red or bay colour.

कियेधा *kiye-dhā, ās, ās, am* (fr. *kiyad-dhā?*), Ved. containing or surrounding much, epithet of Indra.

किर *kira, as,* m. (fr. 1. *kṛī*), a hog.

Kiraka, as, m. a scribe.

Kiraṇa, as, m. dust, very small dust; a rein (?); a ray or beam of light, a sun or moon-beam; the sun; (*ā*), f., N. of a river. — *Kiraṇa-maya, as, ī, am,* radiant, bright, refulgent. — *Kiraṇa-mālin, ī,* m. the sun (having a garland of rays). — *Kiraṇāvali* (°*ṇa-av*°), f., N. of a work by Udayana; a commentary by Dādābhāī on the Sūrya-Siddhānta. — *Kiraṇāvalī-prakāśa, as,* m. title of a work.

Kirat, an, atī or *antī, at,* scattering, spreading; lighting, shedding light.

Kiri, is, m. a hog, = *kiṭi.*

Kirika, as, ā, am, Ved. sparkling, beaming.

Kiryāṇī, f. a wild hog.

किरात *kirāta, as,* m., N. of a degraded mountain-tribe, one of the barbarous tribes who inhabit woods and mountains and live by hunting (the Kirrhadæ of Arrian), having become Sūdras by their neglect of all prescribed religious rites (they are also regarded as Mleććhas); a savage; a pigmy, a dwarf; a groom, a horseman; N. of a plant, a kind of gentian [cf. *kirāta-tikta*]; N. of Siva, as a mountaineer opposed to Arjuna, the account of which is the subject of the celebrated poem by Bhāravi called Kirātārjunīya; (*ī*), f. a woman of the Kirāta tribe; a woman who carries a fly-flap or anything to keep off flies; an epithet of the goddess Durgā; a bawd, a procuress; an epithet of the river Gaṅgā; the celestial Gaṅgā or river of Svarga. — *Kirāta-tikta, as,* m. the plant Agathotes Chirayta, a kind of gentian; also *kirāta-tiktaka.* — *Kirātārjunīya, am,* n. (fr. °*ta + arjuna*), title of an artificial poem by Bhāravi, describing the combat of Arjuna with the god Siva in the form of a wild mountaineer or Kirāta, (this combat and its result is described in the Vana-parva or third book of the Mahā-bhārata 1538–1664.) — *Kirātāśin* (°*ta-aś*°), *ī,* m. an epithet of Garuḍa, the bird of Vishṇu ('swallowing the Kirātas').

Kirātaka, as, m. (at the end of compounds) the warrior or mountain-tribe of the Kirātas; N. of a plant, = *kirāta-tikta.*

Kirātī, is, f. an epithet of the river Gaṅgā; [cf. *kirātī.*]

Kirātinī, f., N. of a plant, the Indian spikenard; [cf. *jaṭāmāṅsī.*]

किरारि *kirāri, is,* m., N. of a people; (a various reading has *virāri.*)

किरिकिच्चिका *kirikiććikā,* f. a kind of musical instrument.

किरिटि *kiriṭi,* n. the fruit of the marshy date tree, Phœnix Paludosa.

किरिश *kiriśa, as,* m., N. of a man.

किरीट *kirīṭa, as* or *am,* m. or n. (said to be fr. rt. 1. *kṛī*), a diadem, a crest, a garland or any ornament used as a crown, a tiara; N. of a metre of four lines, each containing twenty-four syllables. — *Kirīṭa-dhāraṇa, am,* n. wearing a diadem, assuming the crown. — *Kirīṭa-dhārin, ī, iṇī, i,* crowned, having a tiara; (*ī*), m. a king. — *Kirīṭa-mālin, ī, inī, i,* ornamented with a diadem.

Kirīṭin, ī, inī, i, decorated with a diadem, crested, crowned; (*ī*), m. a king; an epithet of Indra; one of the attendants of Siva; a N. of Arjuna.

किरोडाट्य *kiroḍāṭya,* nom. P. *kiroḍāṭyati,* to cheat.

किर्मिर *kirmira, as, ā, am,* Ved. variegated; [cf. *kirmīra* below and *karbura.*]

किर्मी *kirmī,* f. a hall, a building, an apartment; an image of gold, a figure of iron; the Palāśa tree, Butea Frondosa.

किर्मीर *kirmīra, as, ā, am* (said to be fr. rt. 1. *kṛī*), variegated; (*as*), m. a variegated colour; the orange tree; N. of a Rākshasa or goblin conquered by Bhīma-sena; [cf. Gr. κιῤῥός.] — *Kirmīra-jit, t,* m. or *kirmīra-nisūdana, as,* m. or *kirmīra-bhid, t,* m. or *kirmīra-sūdana, as,* m. or *kirmīrāri* (°*ra-ari*), *is,* m. an epithet of Bhīma-sena, the enemy and conqueror of the Rākshasa Kirmīra. — *Kirmīra-tvać, k,* m. or f. (?), the orange tree.

Kirmīrita, as, ā, am, variegated, spotted.

किर्याणी *kiryāṇī.* See under *kira.*

किल् *kil,* cl. 6. P. *kilati, ćikela, kelitum,* to be or become white; to freeze; to play; cl. 10. P. *kelayati, -yitum,* to send, to throw or cast; [cf. Hib. *cal,* 'a joke.']

1. *kila, as,* m. play, trifling. — *Kila-kinćita, am,* n. amorous agitation, weeping, laughing, being angry, merry, &c., in the society of a lover.

किल 2. *kila,* ind. (a particle of asseveration or emphasis), indeed, verily, assuredly; (or of explanation) namely; *kila* is preceded by the word on which it lays stress, and occurs very rarely at the beginning of a sentence or verse; according to native lexicographers *kila* may be used in communicating intelligence, and may imply 'so said,' 'so reported,' 'probably,' 'possibly,' 'agreement,' 'dislike,' 'falsehood,' 'inaccuracy,' and 'reason.'

किल 3. *kila, as,* m., N. of a man.

किलकिल *kilakila, as,* m. an epithet of Siva; N. of a town; (*ā*), f. (an onomatopoetic word), sounds or cries expressing joy or the expression of pleasure by any sound or cry.

Kilakilāya, nom. P. *kilakilāyati,* to raise sounds expressing joy.

किलाट *kilāṭa, as, ī,* m. f. inspissated milk, coagulated milk; it may also be applied to cheese.

Kilāṭin, ī, m. a bamboo.

किलात *kilāta, as,* m., N. of an Asura; a dwarf.

किलास *kilāsa, as, ā, am,* Ved. leprous; (*ī*), f., Ved. a kind of spotted deer described as the vehicle of the Maruts; (*am*), n., Ved. a white leprous spot; a blotch, a scab; (in medic.) a species of leprosy resembling the so-called white leprosy, in which disease the skin becomes spotted without producing ulcers. — *Kilāsa-ghna, as,* m. a sort of gourd, Momordica Mixta ('what removes leprosy'). — *Kilāsa-nāśana, as, ī, am,* Ved. removing leprosy. — *Kilāsa-bheshaja, am,* n., Ved. a remedy against leprosy.

Kilāsin, ī, inī, i, leprous, having blotches.

किलिञ्च *kilinća, am,* n. a thin plank, a board; [cf. the following.]

किलिञ्ज *kilinja, as,* m. a mat; a thin plank of green wood.

Kilinjaka, as, m. a mat; a screen or twist of grass or straw.

किलिनकिल *kilinakila, as* or *am,* m. or n. (?), a various reading for *kilakila;* N. of a town (?).

किलिम *kilima, as,* m. a tree, a kind of fir or pine, Pinus Deodar [cf. *deva-dāru*]; (*am*), n. resin, the extract of the pine.

किल्किन् *kilkin, ī,* m. a horse; (also read *kindhin* and *kilvin.*)

किल्विष *kilbisha* or *kilvisha, am,* n. (fr. rt. *kil?*), fault, offence, sin, guilt; injustice, injury; disease, sickness. — *Kilvisha-spṛit, t, t, t,* Ved. removing or avoiding sins or offences.

Kilvishin, ī, iṇī, i, one who commits an offence, wicked, culpable, criminal, sinful, (often in compounds, e. g. *rāja-kilvishin,* one who as a king commits an offence.)

किल्विन् *kilvin, ī,* m. a horse; [cf. *kilkin.*]

किशल *kiśala, as, am,* m. n. a sprout, a shoot.

Kiśalaya, as, am, m. n. a young shoot. — *Kiśalaya-talpa, as,* m. or *kiśalaya-śayyā,* f. or *kiśalaya-śayana, am,* n. a bed of young leaves &c.; see *kisala, kisalaya,* &c.

किशोर *kiśora, as, ā, am* (said to be fr. *kim* and rt. *śṛī*), young, infantine; (*as*), m. a colt, the young of any animal; the sun; Benjamin or Styrax benzoin (= *tailaparṇy-oshadhi*); N. of a Dānava; a youth, a lad, one from his birth to the end of his fifteenth year, a minor in law (*ajāta-vyavahāra*) becoming after his fifteenth year subject to suits at law (or *jāta-vyavahāra*); (*ī*), f. a maiden, a young woman.

किष्क् *kishk,* cl. 10. A. *kishkayate, -yitum,* to injure, kill; (a various reading for *hishk* and *hikk*); [cf. Hib. *ceasaim,* 'I torment, crucify, vex.']

किष्किन्ध *kishkindha, as, ā* or *ī,* m. f., N. of a mountain in the south of India, in Odra, containing a cave, the residence of the monkey-prince Bālin. — *Kishkindha-parvata, as,* m., N. of a place. — *Kishkindhā-kāṇḍa, am,* n. title of the fourth book of the Rāmāyaṇa.

Kishkindhaka, ās, m. pl., N. of a people.

Kishkindhya, as, ā, am, m. f. (but generally f.), N. of a mountain and of a district = *kishkindha* above, said to be in the peninsula, in the northern part of Mysore, near the sources of the Pampā river, the territory of Bālin the monkey-king, from whom it was conquered by Rāma and transferred to Sugrīva, the brother of Bāli and rightful king. The story is told in the fourth book of the Rāmāyaṇa. The name *Kishkindhyā* is also applied to the capital city of the district, the mountain being called Ṛishya-mūka. — *Kishkindhyā-kāṇḍa, as,* m. title of the fourth book of the Rāmāyaṇa; also of the Adhyātma-rāmāyaṇa. — *Kishkindhyādhipa* (°*ya-adh*°), *as,* m. a N. of Bālin, a monkey-king slain by Rāma.

किष्कु *kishku, us, us, u,* vile, bad, contemptible; (*us*), m. f. the fore-arm, a cubit, a span; an instrument for measuring lengths = *hasta* or *kara* = twenty-four thumbs' breadths = $\frac{1}{400}$ of a Nalva. — *Kishku-parvan, ā,* m., N. of several kinds of reed, as bamboo, sugar-cane, Arundo Tibialis.

किस् *kis,* ind., Ved. a particle of interrogation, 'whether, if;' according to native commentators = *kartṛi,* 'a doer;' [cf. *nakis, mākis.*]

किस *kisa, as,* m., N. of an attendant of the sun.

किसर *kisara, am,* n. an article for sale(?).
Kisarika, as, ī, am, selling Kisara.

किसल *kisala* or *kisalaya, as, am,* m. n. a sprout or shoot, the extremity of a branch bearing new leaves.
Kisalayita, as, ā, am, furnished with leaf-buds or young shoots; [cf. *kiśala.*]

कीकट *kīkaṭa, as,* m., N. of a people not belonging to the Āryan race; N. of a son of Ṛishabha; also of Saṅkaṭa; N. of a country, Behar; a horse (originally perhaps a horse of the Kīkaṭas); (*as, ī, am*), poor, needy; miserly, avaricious.

कीकर *kīkara, as* or *am*(?), m. or n.(?), N. of a Grāma in the word *kamala-kīkara,* q. v.

कीकस *kīkasa, as, ā, am* (said to be fr. rt. *kak*), hard, firm; (*ās*), f. pl., Ved. the breast-bone and the cartilages of the ribs connected with it, cartilagines costarum; (*am*), n. a bone in general; (*as*), m. a bone, an insect. — *Kīkasa-mukha* or *kīkasāsya* (°*sa-ās*°), *as,* m. a bird in general.

कीकि *kīki, is,* m. a blue jay; [cf. *kiki.*]

कीचक *kīćaka, as,* m. (said to be fr. rt. *ćik*), a hollow bamboo; a bamboo whistling or rattling in the wind, Arundo Karka, a reed; a kind of tree; N. of a people, a tribe of the Kekayas, (a Kīćaka is chief of the army of king Virāṭa, and is conquered by Bhīma-sena); N. of a Daitya or demon; a certain Rākshasa or goblin. — *Kīćaka-jit, t,* or *kīćaka-nisūdana, as,* or *kīćaka-bhid, t,* m. an epithet of Bhīma-sena, conqueror of Kīćaka. — *Kīćaka-badha, as,* m. 'the killing of Kīćaka,' title of a poem.

कीज *kīja, as, ā, am,* Ved. wonderful.

कीट् *kīṭ,* cl. 10. P. *kīṭayati, -yitum,* to tinge or colour; to bind.

कीट *kīṭa, as, ā, am,* m. f. n. a worm, an insect; an expression of contempt, e. g. *pakshi-kīṭa,* a miserable bird; [cf. Gr. κίς.] — *Kīṭa-ghna, as,* m. sulphur ('destroying insects'). — *Kīṭa-ja, am,* n. silk; (*ā*), f. lac, an animal dye of a red colour. — *Kīṭa-pakshodbhava* (°*sha-ud*°), *as,* m. the change from the chrysalis or larva to the butterfly. — *Kīṭa-pādikā,* f. the plant Cissus Pedata. — *Kīṭa-maṇi, is,* m. a butterfly. — *Kīṭa-mātā,* f. the plant Cissus Pedata. — *Kīṭa-śatru, us,* m.(?) and *kīṭāri* (°*ṭa-ari*), *is,* m.(?) a species of plant.
Kīṭaka, as, m. a worm, an insect; a kind of bard (*māgadha-jāti*), a panegyrist, descended from a Kshatriya father and Vaiśya mother; N. of a prince; (*as, ā, am*), hard, harsh, unfeeling.

कीडेर *kīḍera, as,* m. the plant Amaranthus Polygamus.

कीदृक्ष *kīdṛiksha, as, ī, am* (fr. 1. *ki* or *kid* and *dṛiksha,* rt. *dṛiś,* see *īdṛiksha*), of what kind? of what sort? of what description? of what qualities? who or what like?
Kīdṛiś, k, k, k, Ved. *n,* of what kind? of what sort? &c., who or what like? *yādṛik-kīdṛik-ća,* of whatsoever kind or sort. — *Kīdṛig-vyāpāravat, ān, atī, at,* of what profession or vocation?
Kīdṛiśa, as, ī, am, of what kind? what like? [cf. Slav. *ko-lik,* Them. *ko-liko;* Gr. πη-λίκος; Goth. *hvê-leiks,* Them. *hvê-leika;* Mod. Germ. *we-lcher;* Lat. *quā-lis.*]

कीन *kīna, am,* n. flesh; [cf. *kīra.*]

कीनार *kīnāra, as,* m., Ved. = *kīnāśa* (?), a cultivator of the soil; (Sāy.) a vile man.

कीनाश *kīnāśa, as,* m. (said to be fr. rt. *kliś;* according to others fr. *kim* and *nāśa*), a labourer or cultivator of the soil; the poverty of this class of men in India was proverbial, so that *kīnāśa* meant sometimes 'a very poor man;' according to native lexicographers *kīnāśa* may be an adj. and has the following meanings, cultivating the soil; poor; covetous, niggardly; small, little, killing animals or killing secretly; (*as*), m. a kind of monkey [cf. *kīśa*]; an epithet of Yama; a kind of Rākshasa.

कीम् *kīm,* ind. a particle in *ākīm* and *mākīm,* q. v.

कीर *kīra, as,* m. a parrot; the country and (pl.) the people of Kaśmīra; (*am*), n. flesh; [cf. *kīna.*] — *Kīra-varṇaka, am,* n. a kind of perfume (*sthauṇeyaka*). — *Kīreshṭa* (°*ra-ish*°), *as,* m., N. of several plants; the tree Mangifera Indica; a species of mountain Pīlū Ākhoṭa; another plant, = *jala-madhūka.*

कीरक *kīraka, as,* m. gaining, obtaining; a Buddha; a kind of tree.

कीरि *kīri, is,* m. (fr. 2. *kṛi*), Ved. grateful or laudatory mention or remembrance; a poem, hymn, praise; one who praises, a poet. — *Kīri-ćodana, as, ā, am,* Ved. exciting praise, exciting the praiser.

कीर्ण *kīrṇa, as, ā, am* (fr. rt. 1. *kṛī*), scattered, thrown, cast; covered, secret, hidden; injured, hurt; full.
Kīrṇi, is, f. scattering, throwing; covering, concealing.
Kīrya, as, ā, am, what is scattered.
Kīryamāṇa, as, ā, am, being covered, bestrewed; being scattered; being thrown at.

कीर्तन, कीर्ति, &c. See under rt. *kṛīt.*

कीर्मी *kīrmī,* f. a house for straw (?).

कीर्शा *kīrśā,* f., Ved. a species of bird.

कील् *kīl,* cl. 1. or 10. P. *kīlati, kīlayati, -yitum,* to bind; to fasten; to stake; to pin.
Kīla, as, ā, m. f. a sharp piece of wood, a stake, a pin, a peg, a bolt, a wedge, &c.; a lance, a pike; a post, a post in a cow-house to which cows are fastened, a pillar; a weapon; the elbow; a blow or punch with the elbow; a blow, a thump; a blow in copulation; flame, lambent flame; a small or minute particle; a gnomon; a position of the foetus impeding delivery; an epithet of Śiva. — *Kīla-saṃsparśa, as,* m., N. of a plant, commonly Gāva, = Diospyros Glutinosa, a plant, the fruit of which yields a substance like turpentine used to cover the bottom of boats.
Kīlaka, as, m. a pin, a bolt, a wedge; a splint for confining a broken bone; a fence; also = *śivaka,* a pillar for cows &c. to rub themselves against, or one to which they are tied.
Kīlikā, f. the pin of an axle.
Kīlita, as, ā, am, staked, impaled; set up as a stake or pole; pierced, transfixed; pinned, fastened by a stake &c.; bound, tied, confined.

कीलाल *kīlāla, as,* m. a sweet beverage; also a heavenly drink similar to Amṛita, the food of the gods; honey; (*am*), n. blood; water. — *Kīlāla-ja, am,* n. flesh. — *Kīlāla-dhi, is,* m. the ocean. — *Kīlāla-pa, as, ā, am,* drinking blood; (*as*), m. a Rākshasa, a sort of goblin or imp. — *Kīlāla-pā, ās,* m., Ved. an epithet of Agni, 'drinking the beverage Kīlāla;' (*ās*), m. an attendant of Yama, or N. of one of the attendants of Yama. — *Kīlālodhan* (°*la-ūdhan*), *ā, dhnī, a,* Ved. carrying the beverage Kīlāla in one's udder.

कीवत् *kīvat, ān, atī, at* (fr. 1. *ki;* cf. *kiyat*), Ved. how much? how long?

कीश *kīśa, as, ā, am,* naked; (*as, ī*), m. f. an ape, a monkey; a bird; the sun. — *Kīśa-parṇa, as,* m. the tree Achyranthes Aspera (*apāmārga*); [cf. *keśa-parṇī.*]

कीस्त *kīsta, as,* m., Ved. one who praises, a singer, a poet; (related to *kīrti*?).

कु 1. *ku,* a pronominal base appearing in *kutas, kutra, kuvid, kuha, kva,* and as a prefix implying deterioration, depreciation, deficiency, want, diminution, littleness, prevention, hindrance, reproach, contempt, sin, guilt; originally perhaps *ku* signified how (strange!); (as a separate word *ku* occurs in the Vedas in the sense of 'where?' *ku ćid,* wherever, anywhere); [cf. *ku-kathā, ku-kara,* &c.]

कु 2. *ku, us,* f. the earth; the ground or base of a triangle or other plane figure. — *Ku-kīla, as,* m. a mountain ('a pin or bolt of the earth').

कु 3. *ku,* cl. 2. P. or cl. 1. A., Ved. *kauti* or *kavīti, kavate, ćukāva, ćukuve, kotum* or *kavitum* (?), to sound; to sound indistinctly; to cry, moan, groan; to cry as a bird, to coo, hum as a bee &c.: Caus. *kāvayati:* Desid. *ćukūshati, -te:* Intens. *ćokūyate* and *kokūyate,* to cry aloud.

कु 4. *ku* or *kū,* cl. 6. A. *kuvate, ćukuve, kutum* or *kuvitum:* Intens. *ćokūyate,* to cry, make a noise; to moan or groan; [cf. Hib. *caoi, caoidh,* 'lamentation, mourning;' *caoidhim,* 'I lament, mourn, grieve.']

कुंश् *kuṇś* or *kuṇs,* cl. 1. or 10. P. *kuṇśati, kuṇśayati,* or *kuṇsati, kuṇsayati, -yitum,* to speak; to shine.

कुक् *kuk,* cl. 1. A. *kokate, ćukuke, kokitum,* to take, accept, seize: Desid. *ćukokishate* or *ćukukishate.*
Kuka, as, ā, am, taking, accepting.

कुकथा *ku-kathā,* f. a bad, miserable tale.

कुकभ *kukabha, am,* n. a kind of spirituous liquor.

कुकर *ku-kara, as, ā, am* (see 1. *ku*), having a crooked or withered arm; acting wickedly, wicked.

कुकर्मन् *ku-karman, a,* n. (see 1. *ku*), a wicked deed; wickedness, depravity, villainy; (*ā, ā, a*), performing evil actions, wicked, depraved. — *Ku-karma-kārin, ī, iṇī, i,* wicked, depraved.
Ku-kārya, am, n. a bad action, sin, wickedness.

कुकीर्त्ति *ku-kīrtti, is,* f. (see 1. *ku*), ill-repute, notoriety.

कुकुट *kukuṭa, as,* m., N. of a pot-herb, = *sitāvara,* commonly *sushaṇiśāka,* Marsilea Quadrifolia.

कुकुटुम्बिनी *ku-kuṭumbinī,* f. a bad housewife.

कुकुद *kukuda, as,* m. one who gives away a girl in marriage after decoration with fit ornaments and the prescribed ceremonies; also *kūkuda,* q. v.

कुकुन्दर *kukundara* or *kukundura, am,* n., or *e,* du. n. the cavities of the loins just above the hips [cf. *kakundara*]; (*as*), m., N. of a plant, = *kukkura-dru,* q. v.

कुकुन्ध *kukundha, as,* m., Ved., N. of a kind of evil spirit.

कुकुभा *kukubhā,* f. one of the female personifications of music or Rāgiṇīs.

कुकुर *kukura, as,* m. (said to be fr. rt. *kuk*), a dog; N. of a plant and perfume, = *granthi-parṇī;* N. of a prince, a son of Andhaka; (*ās*), m. pl. the descendants of this prince; N. of a people, a branch of the Yadu race or Yādavas; the country of this people; [cf. *kukkura* and *kaukura*.] — *Kukura-jihvā*, f. a species of fish, Acheiris Kookor Zibha; the plant Leea Staphylea; another plant, Ixora Undulata. — *Kukurādhinātha* (°*ra-adh*°), *as*, m. lord of the Yādavas, an epithet of Kṛishṇa.

कुकूटी *kukūṭī*, f. the plant Salmalia Malabarica; [cf. *śālmali*.]

कुकूणक *kukūṇaka*, *as*, m. a kind of disease of the eyes in infants.

कुकूनन *kukūnana*, *as*, *ā*, *am*, Ved. (an onomatopoetic word), gargling.

कुकूरभ *kukūrabha*, *as*, m., Ved. a kind of evil spirit.

कुकूल *kukūla*, *as* or *am*, m. or n. chaff, conflagration of chaff, a fire made of chaff; (*am*), n. a hole filled with stakes; armour, mail.

कुकृत्य *ku-kṛitya*, *am*, n. (see 1. *ku*), an evil deed, evil, wickedness.

कुकोल *kukola*, *am*, n. the jujube, Zizyphus Jujuba; [cf. *koli*.]

कुक्कुट *kukkuṭa*, *as*, m. a cock, a wild cock; a whisp of lighted straw or grass, a firebrand, a spark of fire; the offspring of a Nishāda by a Śūdra woman or woman of the fourth caste; (*is* or *ī*), f. hypocrisy, interested observance of religious duties; (*ī*), f. a hen; a small house-lizard; the silk-cotton tree, Bombax Heptaphyllum, or the red cotton tree, Salmalia Malabarica. — *Kukkuṭa-kantha*, *am*, n., N. of a town. — *Kukkuṭa-dhvani*, *is*, m. the crowing of a cock, the cackling of fowls. — *Kukkuṭa-pakshaka*, *as* or *am* (?), m. or n. (?), a knife shaped like the wing of a cock. — *Kukkuṭa-pāda*, *as*, m., N. of a mountain (cock-foot). — *Kukkuṭa-maṇḍapa*, *as*, m., N. of a sanctuary in Benares standing on the right side of a statue of Śiva, a place where final emancipation may be attained; [cf. *mukti-maṇḍapa*.] — *Kukkuṭa-mastaka*, *as*, m. a sort of pepper, Piper Chaba. — *Kukkuṭa-vrata*, *am*, n. a religious observance (worship of Śiva) on the seventh of the light fortnight of the month Bhādra, by women, especially for the sake of obtaining offspring. — *Kukkuṭa-śikha*, *as*, m. safflower, Carthamus Tinctorius (cockscomb). — *Kukkuṭa-giri*, *is*, m., N. of a mountain. — *Kukkuṭāṇḍa* (°*ṭa-aṇ*°), *am*, n. a fowl's egg. — *Kukkuṭāṇḍaka*, *as* or *am* (?), m. or n. (?), a species of rice. — *Kukkuṭābha* (°*ṭa-ābhā*), *as*, m. a kind of snake compared to a fowl (perhaps from having a crest or comb). — *Kukkuṭārāma* (°*ṭa-ār*°), *as*, m., N. of a grove; N. of a celebrated hermitage near Gayā. — *Kukkuṭārma* (°*ṭa-ar*°), *am*, n., N. of a place. — *Kukkuṭāsana* (°*ṭa-ās*°), *am*, n. a particular posture of an ascetic in religious meditation. — *Kukkuṭāhi* (°*ṭa-ahi*), *is*, m. = *kukkuṭābha* above. — *Kukkuṭī-vrata*, *am*, n. a ceremony in honour of Śiva and Durgā; see *kukkuṭa-vrata*.

Kukkuṭaka, *as*, m. a cock, a wild cock; a man of a mixed caste, one sprung from a Śūdra and a Nishāda woman.

कुक्कुभ *kukkubha*, *as*, m. a wild cock, Phasianus Gallus; varnish, oily gloss.

कुक्कुर *kukkura*, *as*, m. (a more modern form for *kukura*), a dog; N. of a Muni; also of a prince, a son of Andhaka; (*ās*), m. pl., N. of a people; (*ī*), f. a bitch; (*am*), n. a vegetable perfume; [cf. *granthi-parṇa*.] — *Kukkura-dru*, *us*, m., N. of a plant, = *tāmra-ćūḍa*.

कुक्कुवाच् *kukku-vāć*, *k*, m. (fr. *kukku*, an onomatopoetic word, and *vāć*), a kind of deer, = *sāraṅga-mṛiga*.

कुक्रिया *ku-kriyā*, f. (see 1. *ku*), a bad action; (*as*, *ā*, *am*), wicked, sinful.

कुक्ष *kuksha*, *as*, m. (said to be fr. rt. *kush*), the belly.

Kukshi, *is*, m. the belly, the cavity of the abdomen (in the earlier language generally used in dual); the interior of anything; the womb, the part of the belly containing the fœtus; a cavity in general (e. g. *adri-kukshi*, cavity of a mountain); the cavity of the ocean, i. e. a bay, a gulf; a cavern; N. of a son (f. also of a daughter?) of Priya-vrata and Kāmyā; N. of Bali; of a king; of a son of Ikshvāku and father of Vikukshi; N. of a region; according to a native lexicographer *kukshi* means also the sheath of a sword, and steel; [cf. Lat. *coxa*, *coxendix*; Gr. *κοχώνη*? Old Germ. *bûh*; Mod. Germ. *Bauch*.] — *Kukshim-bhari*, *is*, *is*, *i*, one who nourishes only his belly, filling or pampering the belly, voracious, gluttonous. — *Kukshi-randhra*, *as*, m. a kind of reed. — *Kukshi-śūla*, *as*, m. pain in the belly, belly-ache, colic.

Kukshila, *as*, m., Ved. a species of evil spirit.

कुक्षितकि *kukshitaki*, *is*, m., N. of a man.

कुक्षेयु *kuksheyu*, *us*, m., N. of a son of Raudrāśva; (according to others *kaksheyu*.)

कुखाटि *kukhāṭi*, *is*, f. (said to be fr. rt. *khaṭ*), wantonness, dalliance, frolic.

कुख्याति *ku-khyāti*, *is*, f. (see 1. *ku*), evil report, infamy; a bad reputation, disrepute, disgrace.

कुगणिन् *kugaṇin*, *ī*, *inī*, *i* (fr. 1. *ku* + *gaṇa*), belonging to an evil set of people.

कुगो *ku-go*, *aus*, m. (see 1. *ku*), a miserable or weak bull.

कुग्रह *ku-graha*, *as*, m. (see 1. *ku*), an unpropitious planet; (five are reckoned by some, viz. Maṅgala, Ravi, Śani, Rāhu, and Ketu.)

कुग्राम *ku-grāma*, *as*, m. (see 1. *ku*), a petty village without a Rājā, an Agnihotrin, a physician, a rich man, or a river.

कुङ्कुण *kuṅkuṇa*, *as* or *am*, m. or n. (?), N. of a region.

कुङ्कुम *kuṅkuma*, *am*, n. saffron, Crocus Sativus, the plant and the pollen of the flowers; [cf. Gr. *κρόκος*; Lat. *crocus*?]. — *Kuṅkuma-tāmra*, *as*, *ā*, *am*, red, coppery red. — *Kuṅkuma-reṇu*, *us*, f. the dust or pollen of saffron. — *Kuṅkumākta* (°*ma-ak*°), *as*, *ā*, *am*, dyed or stained with saffron, orange, yellow. — *Kuṅkumāṅka* (°*ma-aṅ*°), *as*, *ā*, *am*, marked with saffron, dyed or stained of an orange colour. — *Kuṅkumāruṇa* (°*ma-ar*°), *as*, *ā*, *am*, red, ruddy.

कुङ्गनी *kuṅganī*, f., N. of a plant, = *mahā-jyotishmatī*.

कुच् *kuć*, cl. 6. 1. P. *kućati*, *koćati*, *ćukoća*, *kućitum* or *koćitum*, to sound high, to utter a shrill cry (as a bird); to polish; to go; to connect, mix; to bend, make curved or crooked, to be crooked; to oppose, impede; to mark with lines, to delineate, write; to contract or be contracted; to contend (?); [cf. *kuñć*.]

Kuća, *as*, m. (generally du. *kućau*), the female breast, a teat, a nipple, a pap. — *Kuća-kumbha*, *as*, m. the female breast. — *Kuća-taṭa*, *am*, n. the female breast. — *Kućataṭāgra* (°*ṭa-ag*°), *am*, n. a nipple. — *Kuća-phala*, *as*, m. the pomegranate (the fruit being shaped like the female breast). — *Kuća-mukha*, *am*, n. a nipple. — *Kućāgra* (°*ća-ag*°), *am*, n. a nipple.

Kućita, *as*, *ā*, *am*, closed, contracted; small, little.

कुचण्डिका *kućaṇḍikā*, f. a plant, Aletris Hyacinthoides, = *mūrvā*.

कुचन्दन *ku-ćandana*, *am*, n. (see 1. *ku*), red sanders, Pterocarpus Santalinus; sappan or log-wood, Cæsalpina Sappan [cf. *pattrāṅga*]; a leguminous plant, Adenanthera Pavonina; saffron.

कुचर *ku-ćara*, *as*, *ā* or *ī*, *am* (see 1. *ku*), going slowly, creeping; following evil practices, low, vile, wicked; speaking ill of any one, detracting, censorious; (*as*), m. a fixed star.

Ku-ćaryā, f. evil conduct, wickedness, impropriety.

कुचाङ्गेरी *ku-ćāṅgerī*, f. (see 1. *ku*), a kind of wood sorrel, Rumex Vesicarius, = *ćukrikā*.

कुचिक *kućika*, *as*, *ā*, m. f. a kind of fish, in shape like an eel, commonly Kuñćiya, Unibranchapertura Cuchiya, or Muræna Apterygia Synbrache; the Hindūs affirm that its bite is mortal to cows, though perfectly harmless to men; (also a various reading for *kuśika*, q. v.)

कुचीरा *kućīrā*, f., N. of a river.

कुचुमार *kućumāra*, *as*, m., N. of the author of the Aupanishadādhikaraṇa.

कुचेल *ku-ćela*, *am*, n. (see 1. *ku*), a bad garment; (*as*, *ā*, *am*), badly clothed, dressed in dirty or tattered garments; (*ā*), f., N. of a plant, = *avikarṇī* or *viddhaparṇī*; (*ī*), f., N. of a plant, = *ambashṭhā*, commonly Ākanādi, Cissampelos Hexandra.

कुचेष्टा *ku-ćeshṭā*, f. (see 1. *ku*), an evil design, a wicked contrivance.

कुच्छ *kuććha*, *am*, n. the white water-lily.

कुज् *kuj*, cl. 1. P. *kojati*, *kojitum*, to steal; cl. 6. P. *kujati*, to be crooked; [cf. *kuñj*.]

कुज *ku-ja*, *as*, m. (fr. 2. *ku* and rt. *jan*), a tree; the son of the earth, a N. of the planet Mars; N. of a Daitya, also called Naraka, conquered by Kṛishṇa; (*ā*), f. the daughter of the earth, an epithet of the goddess Durgā; also of Sītā. — *Kuja-pañćamī*, f. the fifth day of the moon occurring on a Tuesday or the day of Mars, by some thought unlucky.

कुजन *ku-jana*, *as*, m. (see 1. *ku*), a bad or wicked man, a low, mean or vulgar person.

कुजननी *ku-jananī*, f. (see 1. *ku*), a bad mother.

कुजन्मन् *kū-janman*, *ā*, *ā*, *a* (see 1. *ku*), low-born, of inferior origin.

कुजम्भ *ku-jambha*, *as*, m. (see 1. *ku*), N. of a Daitya, a younger brother of Jambha and son of Prahrāda or Prahlāda, a son of Hiraṇya-kaśipu.

कुजम्भल *kujambhala*, *as*, m. a thief who breaks into a house; also *kujambhira* and *kujambhila*; [cf. *kumbhila*.]

कुज्जिश *kujjiśa* or *kujjhiśa*, *as*, m. a sort of fish; [cf. *kuḍiśa*.]

कुज्झटि *kujjhaṭi*, *is* or *ī*, or *kujjhaṭikā*, f. a fog or mist.

कुञ्च् *kuñć*, cl. 1. P. *kuñćati*, *ćukuñća*, *kuñćitum*, to make crooked; to be crooked; to bend or curve, to move crookedly; to go; to go to or towards; to be or become small; to lessen, to make small; to shrink, to contract, to draw together: Caus. *kuñćayati*, *-yitum*: Desid. *ćukuñćishati*: Intens. *ćokućyate*; [cf. Hib. *cuachaim*, 'I fold, plait;' *cuach*, 'a curl;' *cuachach*, 'curled, frizzled.']

Kuñćana, *am*, n. curving, bending, contracting; contraction; a certain disease of the eyes, contracting the eyelids.

Kuñća-phalā, f. a kind of gourd, = *kushmāṇḍī*; (a wrong reading for *kuća-phala*?).

Kuñći, *is*, f. a measure of capacity equal to eight handfuls.

Kuñćikā, f. a key; a fish, commonly Kuñćiya, in shape like an eel and eaten as one, Unibranchapertura

Cuchiya, or the fish Muræna Apterygia, Synbrache [cf. *kućika*]; a plant bearing a red and black seed used as a weight, Abrus Precatorius; or another plant bearing a pungent seed, Nigella Indica; a sort of reed; the branch or shoot of a bamboo.

Kuñćita, as, ā, am, crooked, curved, bent, contracted, &c.; (*am*), n., N. of a plant. — *Kuñćitāṅguli* (°*ta-aṅ*°), *is, is, i*, with bent or curved fingers.

कुञ्ज् kuñj, cl. 1. P. *kuñjati, -jitum*, to murmur, = *kūj*.

कुञ्ज kuñja, *as, am*, m. n. a place overrun with plants or overgrown with creepers, a bower, an arbour; a cave; the lower jaw; an elephant's tusk or jaw; a tooth; (*as*), m., N. of a man. — *Kuñja-kuṭīra, as*, m. a bower, an arbour. — *Kuñja-vallarī*, f., N. of a plant, = *nikuñjikāmlā*.

Kuñjikā, f. another N. of the plant Kuñja-vallarī; fennel-flower seed, = *kuñćikā*, Nigella Indica.

कुञ्जर kuñjara, *as*, m. (fr. *kuñja?*), an elephant; anything pre-eminent in its kind (generally in compounds, e. g. *purusha-kuñjara*, an eminent man); the tree Ficus Religiosa; N. of a Nāga; N. of a prince of the Sauvīraka race; N. of a mountain; of a region; hair; (*ā* and *ī*), f. a female elephant; (*ā*), f. the plant Bignonia Suaveolens; another plant, Grislea Tomentosa. — *Kuñjara-kara, as*, m. an elephant's trunk. — *Kuñjara-kshāra-mūla, am*, n. a kind of radish (*mūlaka*). — *Kuñjara-graha, as*, m. an elephant-catcher. — *Kuñjara-darī*, f. 'elephant's cave,' N. of a place. — *Kuñjara-pippalī*, f., N. of a plant described as bearing a fruit resembling long pepper; [cf. *gaja-pippalī*.] — *Kuñjara-rūpin, ī, iṇī, i*, elephant-shaped. — *Kuñjarānīka* (°*ra-an*°), *am*, n. the division of an army consisting of elephants, an elephant-corps. — *Kuñjarārāti* (°*ra-ar*°), *is*, m. a lion; the Sarabha, a fabulous animal with eight legs, ('enemy of the elephant.') — *Kuñjarāluka* (°*ra-āl*°), *am*, n. a species of esculent root, a sort of yam. — *Kuñjarāśana* (°*ra-aś*°), *as*, m. the holy fig tree, Ficus Religiosa.

कुञ्जल kuñjala, *am*, n. sour gruel; [cf. *kāñjikā*.]

कुट् kuṭ, cl. 6. P. *kuṭati, ćukoṭa, kuṭishyati, akuṭīt, kuṭitum*, to be or become crooked or curved; to bend, curve, curl; to make crooked; to be dishonest, cheat or deceive; cl. 4. P. *kuṭyati*, or cl. 10. A. *koṭayate, -yitum*, to break to pieces, tear asunder, divide; to speak indistinctly; to be warm, burn: Caus. *koṭayati*: Desid. *ćukuṭishati*: Intens. *ćokuṭyate*; [cf. *kuṭṭ* and *kuṇṭ*.]

Kuṭa, as or *am*, m. n. a water-pot, a jar, pitcher; (*as*), m. a fort, a stronghold; a house [cf. *kuṭi, kuṭī*, and *kūṭa*]; a hammer, a mallet for breaking small stones; a tree; a mountain; N. of a man; (*am*), n., Ved. = *kṛita*, a work. — *Kuṭa-kārikā*, f. a female servant (bringing the water-jar). — *Kuṭa-ja, as*, m. the medicinal tree Wrightia Antidysenterica, commonly called Karaya; the seeds are used as a vermifuge [cf. *indra-yava*]; a N. of the sage Agastya ('born in a water-jar'); also of Droṇa, q. v. — *Kuṭaja-mallī*, f. a kind of plant.

Kuṭaka, as, m., N. of a people; N. of a mountain; the post round which the string of the churning-stick winds [cf. *kuṭara* and *kuṭhara*]; (*am*), n. a plough without a pole.

Kuṭi, is, ī, m. f. a curvature, a curve; a hut, cottage, house, hall, shop; (*ī*), f. a vessel with openings used for fumigations; a bawd, a procuress or go-between; a nosegay, a bundle or tuft of flowers or vegetables; a kind of perfume, commonly Murā; spirituous liquor; (*is*), m. the body; a tree; [cf. Eng. *hut*; Germ. *Hütte*.] — *Kuṭi-ćara, as*, m. a crocodile or porpoise. — *Kuṭi-pārthiva, as*, m., N. of a man. — *Kuṭī-kṛita, as, ā, am*, curved, curled, twisted, frizzled; (*am*), n. anything (as woollen cloth) curled or twisted. — *Kuṭī-gata, as, ā, am*, inside the house. — *Kuṭī-gu, us*, m., N. of a man. — *Kuṭī-ćaka, as*, m. a kind of religious mendicant, one who lives at his son's expense; (lit. 'delighting in staying in the house.') — *Kuṭī-ćara, as*, m. an ascetic of a particular order, one who consigns the care of his family to his son and remains at home engaged solely in devotion; or one who goes begging from one house to another. — *Kuṭī-maya, as, ī, am*, consisting of a house (?). — *Kuṭī-mukha, as*, m., N. of one of the attendants of Kuvera.

Kuṭika, as, ā, am, bent, crooked; (*ā*), f., N. of a river.

Kuṭita, as, ā, am, crooked, bent.

Kuṭitṛi, tā, trī, tṛi, making crooked; acting dishonestly; being bent.

Kuṭira, am, n. a hut, a cottage.

Kuṭila, as, ā, am, bent, crooked, curved, round, running in curved lines, crisped, curled; going crookedly, tortuous; insincere, dishonest, fraudulent; (*ā*), f., N. of a plant [cf. *tagarapādī*]; N. of a river; (according to some) N. of the Sarasvatī; N. of a metre containing four lines of fourteen syllables each; (*am*), n., N. of a plant [cf. *tagara, kuñćita, vakra*]; a kind of perfume; tin. — *Kuṭila-gati, is*, f. a species of the Atijagatī metre, = *ćandrikā*. — *Kuṭila-gāmin, ī, inī, i*, going crookedly, tortuous. — *Kuṭila-tā*, f. or *kuṭila-tva, am*, n. crookedness; guile, dishonesty. — *Kuṭila-pakshma, as, ā, am*, having curved eyelashes or brows. — *Kuṭila-svabhāva, as, ā, am*, crooked-minded, disingenuous. — *Kuṭilāśaya* (°*la-āś*°), *as, ā, am*, ill-intentioned, malevolent.

Kuṭilaka, as, ikā, am, bent, curved, crooked, winding; (*ikā*), f. crouching, coming stealthily as a hunter on his prey; a peculiar movement or gesture (in theatrical language); an instrument used by a blacksmith, a blacksmith's forge.

Kuṭikā, f. a small house.

Kuṭīya, nom. P. *kuṭīyati, -yitum*, to imagine one's self in a hut.

Kuṭīra, as or *am*, m. n. a small house, a hut, a hovel; a kind of plant; (*am*), n. sexual intercourse; exclusiveness.

Kuṭīraka, as, m. a hut.

कुटङ्क kuṭaṅka, *as*, m. (connected with *kuṭa* above), a roof, a thatch; [cf. *kuṭuṅgaka, kuḍaṅga, kuṇḍaṅga, kuṭala*.]

कुटङ्ग kuṭaṅga, N. of a place.

कुटङ्गक kuṭaṅgaka, *as*, m. an arbour formed by creeping plants overrunning a tree; a roof or thatch; a house, a small house, a hut or cottage; [cf. *kuṭuṅgaka*.]

कुटच kuṭaća, *as*, m. (for *kuṭa-ja*), the medicinal tree Wrightia Antidysenterica.

कुटज kuṭa-ja. See under *kuṭa* above.

कुटन्नक kuṭannaka, *am*, n. the fragrant grass Cyperus Rotundus; [cf. also the following.]

कुटन्नट kuṭannaṭa, *as*, m. the tree Calosanthes Indica; (*am*), n. the fragrant grass Cyperus Rotundus.

कुटप kuṭapa, *as*, m. (said to be fr. rt. *kuṭ*), a measure of grain &c. (= *kuḍava*); a saint, a divine sage or Muni; a garden or grove near a house (= *nishkuṭa*); (*am*), n. a lotus.

कुटर kuṭara, *as*, m. a post round which the string passes that works the churning-stick [cf. *kuṭaka* and *kuṭhara*]; N. of a Nāga.

कुटरु kuṭaru, *us*, m., Ved. a cock; a tent, a house of cloth or canvas.

कुटरुणा kuṭaruṇā, f. a plant, commonly Teōri, Ipomœa Turpethum.

कुटल kuṭala, *am*, n. a roof, a thatch; [cf. *kuṭaṅka*.]

कुटि kuṭi, kuṭira. See under rt. *kuṭ* above.

कुटिकोष्टिका kuṭikoshṭikā, f., N. of a river.

कुटिल kuṭila. See under rt. *kuṭ*, col. 2.

कुटीर kuṭīra. See under rt. *kuṭ*, col. 2.

कुटुङ्गक kuṭuṅgaka, *as*, m. an arbour or bower formed of creeping plants; a creeper winding round a tree; a thatch, a roof; a hut, a cottage; a granary, a store-room; [cf. *kuṭaṅka, kuṭaṅgaka, kuḍaṅga*.]

कुटुनी kuṭunī, f. a wrong reading for *kuṭṭanī*, q. v.

कुटुम्ब kuṭumba, *am*, n. a household, the collective members of a household, a family; the care of a family, house-keeping; the care taken by a householder for the members of his family, hence metaphorically care or anxiety about anything; (*as, am*), m. n. name; race; a kinsman, a relation by descent; a connection, a relation by marriage by the mother's side; offspring, progeny. — *Kuṭumba-kalaha, as, am*, m. n. domestic dissension, family feud. — *Kuṭumba-vyāpṛita, as*, m. a provident and attentive father of a family. — *Kuṭumbārtham* (°*ba-ar*°), ind. for the support or on account of a family. — *Kuṭumbaukas* (°*ba-ok*°), *as*, n. apartments &c. appropriated to the accommodation of relations &c.

Kuṭumbaka, as, ā, am, being of one family; (*am*), n. a household; the duties and cares of a householder; a family, kindred.

Kuṭumbaya, nom. A. *-yate*, to support a family.

Kuṭumbika, as, ā, am, taking care of a family or household; (*as*), m. the slave of a house.

Kuṭumbin, ī, m. a householder, a paterfamilias; one who supports or takes care of a family; metaphorically one who takes care of anything (especially at the end of a compound); a member of a family, any one belonging to a household; a peasant, a cultivator of the soil; (*inī*), f. the wife of a householder and mother of a family, a matron; a large household, a large family; a small shrub used in medicine, a kind of moon-plant, = *kshīriṇī*. — *Kuṭumbi-tā*, f. or *kuṭumbi-tva, am*, n. family connection or union, living as one family.

कुटेर kuṭera, *as*, m. a hut, a cottage; [cf. *kuṭīra*.]

कुट्ट् kuṭṭ, cl. 10. P. *kuṭṭayati, aćukuṭṭat, -yitum*, to cut, divide; to grind or pound; to multiply; to censure, abuse.

Kuṭṭa, as, ī, am, (at the end of compounds) cutting, dividing, making small; grinding, pounding; (*as*), m. a multiplier such that a given dividend being multiplied by it and a given quantity added to (or subtracted from) the product, the sum (or difference) may be measured by a given divisor. — *Kuṭṭaparānta* or *kuṭṭāparānta* (°*ṭa-ap*°), *ās*, m. pl., N. of a people. — *Kuṭṭa-praćaraṇa* and *kuṭṭa-prāvaraṇa, ās*, m. pl., N. of two nations.

Kuṭṭaka, as, ā, am, what cuts or divides, what pounds or grinds; (*as*), m. a grinder or pulverizer, a multiplier, &c. [cf. *kuṭṭa*]; a kingfisher. — *Kuṭṭaka-vyavahāra, as*, m. or *kuṭṭakādhyāya* (°*ka-adh*°), *as*, m. that branch or chapter of arithmetic which treats of the *kuṭṭa* or *kuṭṭaka*.

Kuṭṭana, am, n. cutting, dividing; pounding, grinding, beating, threshing; abusing; (*ī*), f. a bawd, a procuress, a go-between.

Kuṭṭantī, f. a kind of dagger.

Kuṭṭāka, as, ī, am, what cuts or divides.

Kuṭṭita, as, ā, am, cut, divided; pounded, flattened; (*ā*), f., scil. *sirā*, unskilful opening of a vein, the latter being cut to pieces by repeated application of the knife.

Kuṭṭin, ī, inī, i, what cuts or pounds; (*nī*), f. a bawd, a procuress.

Kuṭṭima, as, ā, am, plastered with small stones, decorated with mosaic; (*as, am*), m. n. an inlaid or paved floor, pavement, ground paved with mosaic or small stones, ground smoothed and plastered; ground prepared for the site of a mansion; a jewel mine; a hut, a cottage; the pomegranate.

कुट्टमित kuṭṭamita, am, n. one of the ten blandishments of women, affected repulse of a lover's caresses; [cf. kuṭṭumita.]

कुट्टार kuṭṭāra, as, m. a mountain; (am), n. sexual intercourse; pleasure; a woollen cloth or blanket; exclusion; oneness; [cf. kuṭīra and kuṭṭīra.]

कुट्टिहारिका kuṭṭihārikā, f. a female servant, a slave; [cf. kuṭa-hārikā.]

कुट्टीर kuṭṭīra, as, m. a mountain; [cf. kuṭīra and kuṭṭāra.]

कुट्टीरक kuṭṭīraka, am, n. (?) a small house, a hut; (a wrong reading for kuṭīraka ?).

कुट्टुमित kuṭṭumita, am, n. = kuṭṭamita above.

कुट्मल kuṭmala, as, ā, am (said to be fr. rt. kuṭ), opening or expanding as the blossom of a flower, blossoming; (as, am), m. n. an opening bud; (am), n. one of the twenty-one hells in which sinners are punished (where they are bound with ropes).

Kuṭmalita, as, ā, am, budded.

कुठ kuṭha, as, m. a tree; (generally written kuṭa.)

कुठर kuṭhara, as, m. the post round which the string of the churning-stick winds; [cf. kuṭara.]

कुठाकु kuṭhāku, us, m. a bird, the woodpecker, Picus Bengalensis, commonly Kāṭhṭhākro.

कुठाटङ्क kuṭhāṭaṅka, as, ā, m. f. an axe.

कुठार kuṭhāra, as, ī, m. f. an axe; a sort of hoe or spade; (as), m. a tree; N. of a man.

Kuṭhāraka, as, m. an axe; (ikā), f. a small axe or adze; also a similarly shaped instrument used in surgery for scarification; N. of a woman.

Kuṭhārika, as, m. a wood-cutter.

कुठारु kuṭhāru, us, m. an ape, a monkey; a tree; an armourer.

कुठि kuṭhi, is, m. a tree; a mountain; [cf. kuṭi.]

कुठिक kuṭhika, as, m., N. of a plant, = kushṭha, mṛitphalī, a kind of Costus, commonly called Kuṭh.

कुठुमि kuṭhumi, is, m., N. of a preceptor, author of a law-book; [cf. kuthumi.]

कुठेर kuṭhera, as, m. fire; a kind of Basilicum. — Kuṭhera-ja, as, m. a white kind of Basilicum, Ocimum Gratissimum.

Kuṭheraka, as, m. a kind of Basilicum, Ocimum Sanctum; a white sort of the same, Ocimum Gratissimum.

कुठेरु kuṭheru, us, m. the wind produced by a fan or chowrie.

कुड् kuḍ, cl. 6. P. kuḍati, ćukoḍa, kuḍitum, to play or act as a child, to trifle; to eat; to heap; to plunge under water, be immersed, dive (?).

कुडङ्ग kuḍaṅga, as, m. a bower, an arbour; [cf. kuṭaṅka, kuṭuṅgaka, kuṇḍaṅga.]

कुडप kuḍapa, as, am, m. n. = kuḍava below.

कुडव kuḍava, as, m. a measure of grain, wood, iron, &c., the fourth part of a Prastha, described by some as a vessel four fingers wide and as many deep and containing twelve Prakṛitis or handfuls; it is also said to contain 13½ cubic Angulas; or to be a finger and a half deep, and three fingers each in length and breadth; in medicine it is equal to two Prakṛitis or thirty-two Tolakas.

कुडि kuḍi, is, m. the body; [cf. kuṭi.]

कुडिका kuḍikā, f. an earthen or wooden water-pot used by ascetics; [cf. kuṭa.]

कुडिश kuḍiśa, as, m. a kind of fish, commonly Kūrchi, Cyprinus Curchius.

कुडी kuḍī, f. a small house, a hut; (a wrong reading for kuṭī ?).

कुडुप kuḍupa, as, m. the clasp or fastening of a necklace or bracelet.

कुड्मल kuḍmala, as, ā, am, opening or expanding as the blossom of a flower, blossoming; (as), m. an opening bud; (am), n. a particular hell; sometimes also spelt kudmala; [cf. kuṭmala.] — Kuḍmala-dantī, f., N. of a metre, = anukūlā; also spelt kudmala-dantī.

Kuḍmalita, as, ā, am, furnished with opening buds; budded, blossomed; cheerful, smiling (as the countenance).

कुड्य kuḍya, am, ā, n. f. a wall; plastering (a wall); eagerness, curiosity. — Kuḍya-ććhedin, ī, m. a housebreaker, a thief. — Kuḍya-ććhedya, am, n. an opening, a hole in a wall, a breach. — Kuḍya-matsī, f. or kuḍya-matsya, as, m. a house-lizard.

Kuḍyaka, am, n. a wall.

कुण् kuṇ, cl. 6. P. kuṇati, -ṇitum, to sound; to cherish, to support or aid with gifts &c.; to be in pain (?); cl. 10. P. kuṇayati, -yitum, to counsel or advise; to converse with, to speak to, address; to salute; to invite; [cf. Lat. cano, sono; Lith. zwanu.]

कुण kuṇa, as, m. in composition with aśvattha and other trees or flowers; the time when a plant bears fruit, e. g. pīlu-kuṇa, q. v.

कुणक kuṇaka, as, m. a young animal just born.

कुणञ्जर kuṇañjara, as, m. or kuṇañjā, f. or kṛiṇañja, as, m. a species of Chenopodium; (commonly Vanavetuā.)

कुणप kuṇapa, as, am, m. n. (said to be fr. rt. kvaṇ), a dead body, a corpse; a carcase; said contemptuously of living persons; (as), m. a spear; N. of a people; a stench, a foul smell; (ī), f. a small bird, a kind of Maina or Salik [cf. viṭ-sārikā]; (as, ī, am), mouldering, smelling like a dead body, foul smelling; stinking. — Kuṇapa-gandha, as, m. the smell of a dead body.

कुणरवाडव kuṇara-bāḍava, as, m., N. of a grammarian.

कुणारु kuṇāru, us, us, u, Ved. having a distorted arm (?); (Sāy. fr. rt. kuṇ) crying out.

कुणाल kuṇāla, as, m. (said to be fr. rt. kvaṇ), a kind of bird; N. of a son of Aśoka: N. of a country.

कुणि kuṇi, is, is, i, a cripple with a crooked or withered arm, or without a hand or finger; (is), m. a whitlow; the tree Cedrela Toona (tunna); N. of a prince, a son of Jaya and father of Yugan-dhara; N. of a Muni; N. of the author of a Dharma-śāstra. — Kuṇi-bāhu, us, m., N. of a Muni.

कुणिताहि kuṇitāhi, is, m., N. of the author of a Dharma-śāstra.

कुणिन् kuṇin, ī, inī, i, only in kuṇī kayābhaḥ, a kind of bug; [cf. utkuṇa, matkuṇa.]

कुणिन्द kuṇinda, as, m. (said to be fr. rt. kuṇ), sound, sounding.

कुण्ट् kuṇṭ = kuṇḍ, q. v.

कुण्टक kuṇṭaka, as, ī, am, fat, corpulent.

कुण्ठ् kuṇṭh, cl. 1. P. kuṇṭhati, -ṭhitum, to be lame or mutilated, to be blunted or dulled; to be lazy or stupid; cl. 10. P. kuṇṭhayati, -yitum, to cover, conceal.

Kuṇṭha, as, ā, am, blunt, dull; stupid; weak; indolent, lazy, slow; foolish; [cf. a-kuṇṭha.] — Kuṇṭha-tā, f. bluntness, dulness, indolence.

Kuṇṭhaka, as, ā, am, stupid, ignorant, a fool; (as), m., N. of a pupil of Luṇṭaka; (ās), m. pl., N. of a people.

Kuṇṭhita, as, ā, am, blunted, dulled; mutilated, stupid; grasped, held, encircled. — Kuṇṭhitāśri (°ta-aś°), is, is, i, having its edge or corners blunted.

कुण्ड् kuṇḍ, cl. 1. P. kuṇḍati, to mutilate; cl. 1. A. kuṇḍate, -ḍitum, to burn; cl. 10. P. kuṇḍayati, -yitum, to protect.

कुण्ड kuṇḍa, as, ī, am, m. f. n. (said to be fr. rt. kuṇ), a bowl-shaped vessel, a basin, bowl, pitcher, jar, pot, water-pot; (am), n. a particular measure; a clump, e. g. darbha-kuṇḍam, a clump of Darbha grass; (as, am), m. n. a round hole in the ground, a hole in the ground for receiving and preserving water; a hole in general (e. g. in comp. agni-kuṇḍa, a hole in the ground for receiving and preserving consecrated fire); a pit, a vat; a pool, a well, a spring or basin of water, especially consecrated to some holy purpose or person; (as), m. a son born in adultery, an adulterine, the son of a woman by another man than her husband, while the husband is alive; N. of a Nāga; a son of Dhṛita-rāshṭra; an epithet of Śiva; (ā), f. an epithet of Durgā. — Kuṇḍa-kīṭa, as, m. the son of a woman of the Brāhmanical tribe born in adultery with a man of an inferior caste; a keeper of concubines, a man who has female slaves; a follower of the Ćārvāka doctrine or the tenets of those who deny the authority of the Vedas. — Kuṇḍa-kīla, as, m. a low, a vile man; see nāgara. — Kuṇḍa-kaumudī or kuṇḍa-maṇḍapa-kaumudī, f. title of a work by Viśvanātha. — Kuṇḍa-gola, as, m. and kuṇḍa-golaka, am, n. sour rice, gruel; see kāñjika. — Kuṇḍa-ja, as, m., N. of a son of Dhṛita-rāshṭra. — Kuṇḍa-jaṭhara, as, m., N. of an old sage; [cf. kuṇḍodara.] — Kuṇḍa-dhāra, as, m., N. of a Nāga; also of a son of Dhṛita-rāshṭra. — Kuṇḍa-pāyin, ī, inī, i, drinking out of pitchers; kuṇḍa-pāyinām ayanam, a particular religious ceremony [cf. kauṇḍapāyina]. — Kuṇḍa-pāyya, as, ā, am, (scil. kratu, &c.), a particular ceremony or sacrifice at which ewers or pitchers are used for drinking; (as), m., N. of a man (?). — Kuṇḍa-prastha, as, m., N. of a town. — Kuṇḍa-bhedin, ī, m., N. of a son of Dhṛita-rāshṭra. — Kuṇḍa-maṇḍapa-siddhi, is, f., N. of a work by Viṭṭhaladīkshita. — Kuṇḍa-ratnākara, as, m., N. of a work by Viśvanātha. — Kuṇḍa-śāyin, ī, m., N. of a son of Dhṛita-rāshṭra. — Kuṇḍāgni (°ḍa-ag°), is or i (?), m. or n. (?), N. of a place; [cf. kauṇḍāgnaka.] — Kuṇḍāśin (°ḍa-āś°), ī, inī, i, one who is supported by a bastard; (ī), m. a pander, a pimp; N. of a son of Dhṛita-rāshṭra; also of a Nāga; also of one of the attendants of Śiva. — Kuṇḍoḍa (°ḍa-uḍa), as, m., N. of a mountain. — Kuṇḍodara (°ḍa-ud°), as, m., N. of a Nāga; a son of Janamejaya and brother of Dhṛita-rāshṭra; also a son of Dhṛita-rāshṭra. — Kuṇḍoddyota-darśana, N. of a work by Saṅkara-bhaṭṭa. — Kuṇḍodhnī (°ḍa-ūdh°), f. a cow with a full udder; a woman with a full bosom; [cf. ūdhas.] — Kuṇḍopadhānīyaka, as, ā, am (fr. °ḍa + upadhānīya), one who uses a pitcher as a pillow; an epithet of Pūrṇa; according to others kuṇḍopadhāna is the N. of a place. — Kuṇḍoparatha, cf. kauṇḍoparatha.

Kuṇḍaka, am, n. a pot; (as), m., N. of a son of Dhṛita-rāshṭra; also of Kshudraka.

Kuṇḍika, as, m., N. of a son of Dhṛita-rāshṭra; (ā), f. a pitcher; a student's water-pot, the Kamaṇḍalu.

Kuṇḍin, ī, inī, i, furnished with a pitcher or water-jar; (ī), m. a horse [cf. kiṅdhin &c.]; a bastard.

Kuṇḍina, as, m., N. of a son of Dhṛita-rāshṭra; N. of an author; (*am*), n. a city, the capital of the district Vidarbha, ruled over by Bhīma, the father-in-law of Nala, apparently the modern Kondavir in Berar; (according to some the city is also called Vidarbha, or m. pl. Vidarbhās, but this is rather the name of the territory.)

कुण्डङ्ग *kuṇḍaṅga, as*, m. a bower, an arbour; (a wrong reading for *kuḍaṅga*.)

कुण्डल *kuṇḍala, am*, n. a ring, an ear-ring; a bracelet; a fetter, a tie, a collar; the coil of a rope; (*as*), m., N. of a Nāga; (*ā*), f., N. of a woman; N. of a river; (*ī*), f., N. of several plants, mountain ebony, Bauhinia Variegata [cf. *kāñćana-dru*]; another plant, Cocculus Cordifolius [cf. *guḍūćī*]; another plant, Mucuna Pruritus [cf. *kapi-kaććhu*]; N. of two other plants, commonly called Sarpiṇī-vṛiksha and Kuṇḍalī-ćālana. — *Kuṇḍala-dhāraṇa, am*, n. the wearing of ear-rings. — *Kuṇḍala-dhārin, ī, iṇī, i*, wearing ear-rings. — *Kuṇḍalākāra* (°*la-āk*°), *as, ā, am*, shaped like an ear-ring or bracelet, circular, annular. — *Kuṇḍaloddyotitānana* (°*la-uddyotita-ān*°), *as, ā, am*, having his face radiant with glittering pendants.

Kuṇḍalanā, f. (fr. *kuṇḍalaya*, nom. fr. *kuṇḍala*), encircling a word or the circle round any word which is to be left out in a MS.

Kuṇḍalikā, f., N. of a metre in Prākrit poetry; [cf. *rāta-kuṇḍalikā*.]

Kuṇḍalin, ī, inī, i, having ear-rings or decorated with ear-rings; circular, annular, spiral, winding, coiling; (*ī*), m. a snake; the spotted or painted deer; a peacock; an epithet of Varuṇa, and of Siva; (*inī*), f. the plant Cocculus Cordifolius [cf. *guḍūćī*]; a particular dish, curds boiled with ghee and spices; a Sakti or form of Durgā worshipped by the Tantrikas.

Kuṇḍalī-kṛita, as, ā, am, forming a ring, formed into a circle, coiled, curled, moving in rings or circles.

Kuṇḍalī-bhūta, as, ā, am, formed into a ring, coiled, curled.

कुण्डीर *kuṇḍīra, as, ā, am*, strong, powerful, able; (*as*), m., N. of a man.

कुण्ड्रृणाची *kuṇḍriṇāćī*, f., Ved. a species of animal; (Sāy.) tortuous progress.

कुत् *kut* (a Sautra root, or one found in grammatical Sūtras only), to spread.

कुत *kuta, as*, m., N. of one of the eighteen attendants of the sun, identified with the god of the ocean.

कुतनय *ku-tanaya, as*, m. (see 1. *ku*), a degenerate son.

कुतनु *ku-tanu, us, vī, u* (see 1. *ku*), deformed; (*us*), m. an epithet of Kuvera or Kubera (this deity being of a monstrous appearance, having three legs and but eight teeth; see *kubera*).

कुतप *ku-tapa, as, ā, am* (see 1. *ku*), slightly hot, mild, tepid; (*as, am*), m. n. a sort of blanket made of the hair of the mountain-goat; the eighth Muhūrta or portion of the day from the last Daṇḍa of the second watch to the first of the third or about noon; an eligible time for the performance of sacrifices to the manes; a kind of sacrificial grass, Poa Cynosuroides; grain; a daughter's son; a sister's son; a twice-born man, one of the first three classes; a Brāhman; a guest; the sun; fire; an ox; a musical instrument. — *Kutapa-saptaka, am*, n. a Srāddha in which seven constituents occur, viz. noon, a horn platter, a Nepal blanket, silver, sacrificial grass, Sesamum, and Kine.

कुतपस्विन् *ku-tapasvin, ī*, m. (see 1. *ku*), a wicked or bad ascetic.

कुतर्क *ku-tarka, as*, m. (see 1. *ku*), fallacious argument, sophistry, fallacy, sophism. — *Ku-tarka-patha, as*, m. the way of sophists, i. e. a sophistical method of arguing.

कुतस् *kutas*, ind. (fr. 1. *ku*), from where? whence? from whence? whereto? where? in which direction? wherefore? why? from what cause or motive? because; how? in what manner? in which way? how much less? much less. *Kutas* is used sometimes for the abl. case of 2. *ka* = *kasmāt* (e. g. *kutaḥ kālāt*, since what time?). In *a-kutas*, which occurs at the beginning of some compounds, *kutas* has an indefinite sense (e. g. *akuto-mṛityu*, not fearing death from any quarter; cf. *akuto-bhaya*); *kutas* is also indefinite when connected with the particles *api, ćid*, and *ćana* (e. g. *kuto 'pi*, from any quarter, from any cause; *kutaśćid*, from any one, from anywhere; *akutaśćid-bhaya*, not fearing danger from any quarter, not presenting danger on any side; *kutaś ćana*, (in Ved.) from no side, to no side; *yataḥ kutaśćid*, from any person soever). — *Kutas-tarām*, ind. how? in what manner? — *Kuto-nimitta, as, ā, am*, having what cause or reason? — *Kuto-mūla, as, ā, am*, having what origin?

Kutastya, as, ā, am, whence come? how happened?

कुतापस *ku-tāpasa, as, ī*, m. f. (see 1. *ku*), a wicked ascetic.

कुतित्तिरि *ku-tittiri, is*, m. (see 1. *ku*), a species of bird resembling the partridge.

कुतीपाद *kutīpāda, as*, m., N. of one of the Ṛishis or poets of the Sāma-veda.

कुतीर्थ *ku-tīrtha, as*, m. (see 1. *ku*), a bad teacher.

कुतुक *kutuka, am*, n. eagerness, vehemence; desire, inclination; curiosity; [cf. *kautuka* and *kutūhala*.]

कुतुप *kutupa, as*, m. a small leathern oil-bottle [cf. *kutū*]; (*as, am*), m. n. the eighth Muhūrta or portion of the day from the last Daṇḍa of the second watch to the first of the third or about noon; an eligible time for the performance of sacrifices to the manes; [cf. *ku-tapa*.]

Kutū, ūs, f. a leathern oil-bottle.

कुतूणक *kutūṇaka, as*, m. weakness of the eyes, a disease of the eyes in infants; [cf. *kukūṇaka*.]

कुतूहल *kutūhala, am*, n. (fr. the interrogative adv. *kutas* and *hala*, calling out?), curiosity, interest in any extraordinary matter; desire, inclination; eagerness, vehemence, impetuosity; what excites curiosity or interest, anything interesting, fun; (*as, ā, am*), surprising, wonderful; excellent, best, praised, celebrated; [cf. *kautūhala*.] — *Kutūhala-vat, ān, atī, at*, curious, taking an interest in anything.

Kutūhalin, ī, inī, i, curious, highly interested in any extraordinary matter, inquisitive; eager, impatient.

कुतृण *ku-tṛiṇa, am*, n. (see 1. *ku*), an aquatic plant, water house-leek, Pistia Stratiotes.

कुत्थ *kuttha, as* or *am*, m. or n. (?), the fifteenth Yoga (in astronomy).

कुत्र *kutra*, ind. (fr. 1. *ku*), where? whereto? in which case? when? *kutra—kva*, where (this)—where (that), i. e. how distant or how different is this from that, how little is this consistent with that? *Kutra* becomes indefinite when connected with the particles *api, ćid, ćana*, e. g. *kutrāpi*, anywhere, somewhere, to any place wheresoever; *kutra ćid*, anywhere, somewhere, wheresoever, wherever, to any place; (sometimes *kutra ćid* = *kasminśćid*, e. g. *kutra ćid araṇye*, in a certain wood); *na kutra ćid*, nowhere, to no place whatsoever; *kutra ćid—kutra ćid*, in one case—in the other case; sometimes—sometimes; *yatra kutra ća* or *yatra kutra ćid*, wherever it be, here or there.

Kutratya, as, ā, am, where being? where living or residing?

कुत्स् *kuts* (perhaps related to *kutas*), cl. 10. P. A. *kutsayati, -te, -yitum;* rarely cl. 1. P. *kutsati*, to despise, abuse, revile, contemn; [cf. Lith. *kussinu*.]

Kutsana, as, ā, am, reviling, abusive, contemptuous; (*am*), n. abuse, reviling, contempt, reproach; reproachful or abusive language; (*ā*), f. contemning, expression of contempt.

Kutsā, f. reproach, contempt, censure. — *Kutsā-vādin, ī, inī, i*, censorious, abusive.

Kutsita, as, ā, am, despised, contemned, reviled; contemptible, low, mean, vile, hateful; (*am*), n., N. of a grass, Cyperus. — *Kutsita-tva, am*, n. meanness, vileness.

1. *kutsya, as, ā, am*, to be reproached, reviled, abused; blamable.

कुत्स *kutsa, as*, m., N. of a Ṛishi with the epithet Ārjuneya, author of several hymns of the Ṛig-veda (when attacked by the demon Sushṇa, Indra defended him and killed the demon; but in other hymns of the Ṛig-veda, Kutsa is represented as persecuted by Indra); N. of a descendant of Aṅgiras, author of several other hymns of the Ṛig-veda; (pl.) the descendants or the family of Kutsa; lightning, thunderbolt; [cf. *kautsa, puru-kutsa*, &c.] — *Kutsa-kuśikikā*, f. the intermarriage of the Kutsa and Kuśika families. — *Kutsa-putra* or *kutsa-vatsa, as*, m. a son of Kutsa.

2. *kutsya, as*, m. = *kutsa* (?).

कुत्सला *kutsalā*, f. the indigo plant; [cf. *nīlī*.]

कुथ् *kuth*, cl. 4. P. *kuthyati, ćukotha, akothīt, kothishyati, kothitum*, to stink, to become putrid: Caus. P. *kothayati, -yitum*, to cause to putrify.

कुथ *kutha, as, ā, am*, m. f. n. a painted or variegated cloth or blanket, serving as an elephant's housings; (*as*), m. sacrificial or Kuśa grass, Poa Cynosuroides; Sākya-muni in one of his former thirty-four births.

कुथुमि *kuthumi, is*, m., N. of a Muni.

कुथुमिन् *kuthumin, ī*, m., N. of a man.

कुद् *kud*, cl. 10. P. *kodayati, -yitum*, to tell a lie; (a various reading for *kundr*, q. v.)

कुदण्ड *ku-daṇḍa, as*, m. (see 1. *ku*), an unjust punishment.

कुदाल *kudāla, as*, m. mountain ebony; [cf. *kuddāla*.]

कुदिन *ku-dina, am*, n. (see 1. *ku*), an evil day; a rainy or cloudy day.

कुदिष्टि *ku-dishṭi, is*, f. (see 1. *ku*), a measure of length, longer than a Dishṭi, shorter than a Vitasti.

कुदृश्य *ku-dṛiśya, as, ā, am* (see 1. *ku*), ill-favoured, ugly, unseemly.

Ku-dṛishṭa, as, ā, am, seen wrongly or indistinctly.

Ku-dṛishṭi, is, is, i, having bad eyes; (*is*), f. weak sight, evil eye; a heterodox philosophical doctrine, as that of the Sāṅkhyas &c.

कुदेश *ku-deśa, as*, m. (see 1. *ku*), a bad country, where it is difficult to obtain the necessaries of life; a country subject to oppression.

कुदेह *ku-deha, as*, m. (see 1. *ku*), a bad, miserable body.

कुद्दल *kuddala, as,* m. mountain ebony; [cf. *kuddāla.*]

Kuddāra, as, m. or *kuddāla, as, am,* m. n. a kind of spade or hoe; (*as*), m. mountain ebony, Bauhinia Variegata.

Kuddālaka, as or *am,* m. or n. (?), a spade or hoe; (*am*), n. a copper pitcher. — *Kuddālaka-khāta, am,* n., N. of a region (?).

कुद्मल *kudmala, am,* n. an opening bud &c.; (a wrong spelling for *kuḍmala.*)

कुद्य *kudya, am,* n. a wall; (a wrong spelling for *kuḍya.*)

कुद्रङ्क *kudranka* or *kudranga, as,* m. a watch-house; a dwelling raised on a platform or scaffold; [cf. *dranka, dranga,* &c.]

कुद्रव *kudrava, as,* m. a kind of grass, the grain of which is eaten by the poor, Paspalum Scrobiculatum; [cf. *kodrava.*]

कुद्रि *kudri, is,* m., N. of a man; (*ayas*), m. pl. the descendants of this man.

कुधान्य *ku-dhānya, am,* n. (see 1. *ku*), a particular description of grain.

कुधी *ku-dhī, īs, īs, i* (see 1. *ku*), foolish, stupid; wicked; (*is*), m. a fool.

कुध्र *ku-dhra, as,* m. (fr. 2. *ku,* earth, and rt. *dhṛi?*), a mountain.

कुनक *kunaka, ās,* m. pl., N. of a people.

कुनख *ku-nakha, as, ī, am* (see 1. *ku*), having ugly nails; (*am*), n. a disease of the nails.

Kunakhin, ī, inī, i, having bad or diseased nails; (*ī*), m., N. of a man and N. of a book belonging to the Atharva-veda.

कुनट *kunaṭa, as,* m. a sort of trumpet flower, Bignonia (*śyonāka-prabheda*); (*ī*), f. a kind of coriander, Coriandrum Sativum; red arsenic.

कुनदिका *ku-nadikā,* f. (see 1. *ku*), a small river.

कुनन्नम *ku-nannama, as, ā, am* (see 1. *ku* and rt. *nam*), Ved. inflexible.

कुनलिन् *ku-nalin, ī,* m. (see 1. *ku*), the plant Agati Grandiflora.

कुनह *kunaha, ās,* m. pl., N. of a people; (a various reading for *kuṇapa.*)

कुनाथ *ku-nātha, as,* m. (see 1. *ku*), a bad protector; (*as, ā, am*), having a bad leader.

कुनादीका *ku-nādīkā,* f. (see 1. *ku*), a small river; also *ku-nadikā,* q. v.

कुनाभि *ku-nābhi, is,* m. (see 1. *ku*), a whirlwind; the collective treasures of Kuvera.

कुनामन् *ku-nāman, ā, ā, a* (see 1. *ku*), having a bad name; having a bad reputation; (*ā*), m., N. of a man; (*a*), n. a bad name, ill repute.

कुनायक *ku-nāyaka, as, ā, am* (see 1. *ku*), having a bad leader, unprotected.

कुनाल *kunāla, as,* m. a kind of bird living on the Himālaya; N. of a son of king Aśoka, named after the eyes of this bird.

कुनालिक *kunālika, as,* m. the Indian cuckoo or Kokila; [cf. the preceding.]

कुनाशक *ku-nāśaka, as,* m. (see 1. *ku*), the plant Alhagi Maurorum.

कुनि *kuni, is,* m., N. of a prince.

कुनिषञ्ज *ku-nishañja, as,* m. (see 1. *ku*), N. of a son of the tenth Manu.

कुनीति *ku-nīti, is,* f. (see 1. *ku*), ill conduct, misbehaviour; corrupt administration or policy, misgovernment; a low state of morals.

कुनेत्रक *ku-netraka, as,* m., N. of a Muni.

कुन्त *kunta, as,* m. a spear, a lance, a barbed dart [cf. Lat. *contus;* Gr. κοντός]; a small animal, an insect; a species of grain, Coix Barbata; passion; N. of a mountain.

Kuntala, as, m. (fr. *kunta?*), the hair of the head, a lock of hair; a drinking cup; a plough; barley; a kind of perfume, = *hrīvera;* (*ās*), m. pl., N. of a people and country in the north-west of the peninsula; (*as*), m. sing. the prince of this people. — *Kuntala-vardhana, as,* m., N. of a plant; [cf. *bhṛinga-rāja.*] — *Kuntalośīra* (°*la-uś*°), *am,* n. a perfume.

Kuntalikā, f. a butter knife or scoop; a species of plant.

कुन्ताप *kuntāpa, am,* n., Ved., N. of certain organs or glands (?), twenty in number, supposed to be in the belly; N. of a section of the Atharva-veda, according to Sāyaṇāćārya, thirty verses, constituting seven Sūktas of the twentieth book of this Veda.

कुन्ति *kunti, ayas,* m. pl., N. of a people; (*is*), m. sing. the prince of this people, also called Kunti-bhoja; *Kunti* is, according to different authorities, a son of either Dharmanetra, or of Netra and grandson of Dharma, or of Kratha, or of Vidarbha and father of Dhṛishṭa, or of Supārśva and grandson of Sampāti and great-grandson of Garuḍa; (*ī*), f. a N. of Pṛithā, the daughter of a Yādava prince named Sūra, who gave her to his childless cousin Kunti or Kunti-bhoja, by whom she was adopted. She afterwards became one of the two wives of Pāṇḍu. (On one occasion before her marriage she paid such respect to the powerful sage Durvāsas that he taught her an incantation or charm, by virtue of which she was to have a child by any god she liked to invoke. Out of curiosity she invoked the Sun, by whom she had a child, cf. *karṇa;* but the Sun afterwards restored to her her maidenhood. Soon after his marriage Pāṇḍu retired to the woods to indulge his passion for hunting. There he killed a male and female deer, who turned out to be a Ṛishi and his wife in the form of these animals. The sage cursed Pāṇḍu and predicted that he would die in the embrace of one of his wives. Hence Pāṇḍu lived apart from Kuntī, but with his approval she made use of her charm and had three sons, Yudhishṭhira, Bhīma, and Arjuna, by the three deities Dharma, Vāyu, and Indra respectively; cf. *mādrī*); N. of a Rākshasī; the wife of a Brāhman; the plant Boswellia Thurifera; a fragrant resin (= *guggulu*). — *Kunti-nandana, as,* m. a son of Kuntī (the final being sometimes shortened in a comp.), either of the three elder Pāṇḍava princes. — *Kunti-bhoja, as,* m., N. of a Yādava prince, king of the Kuntis, who adopted Kuntī. — *Kuntī-suta, as,* m. a son of Kuntī.

Kuntika, ās, m. pl., N. of a people.

कुन्थ् *kunth,* cl. 1. P. *kunthati, -thitum,* to hurt, injure; to suffer pain, want, &c.; to be distressed; cl. 9. P. *kuthnāti,* to injure; to cling to; to twine round or be connected with, embrace; [cf. Lat. *quatio, per-cutio.*]

कुन्थु *kunthu, us,* m., N. of the sixth Jaina Ćakravartin or emperor in Bhārata; also of the seventeenth Arhat of the present Avasarpiṇī.

कुन्द *kunda, as, am,* m. n. (said to be fr. rt. 3. *ku*), a kind of jasmine, Jasminum Multiflorum or Pubescens; (*as*), m. fragrant oleander, Nerium Odorum [cf. *karavīra*]; Olibanum, the resin of the plant Boswellia Thurifera; a turner's lathe; one of Kuvera's nine treasures; the number 'nine;' an epithet of Vishṇu; N. of a mountain. — *Kunda-kara, as,* m. a turner. — *Kunda-kundāćārya* (°*da-āć*°), *as,* m., N. of the author of the Pañćāstikāyasaṅgraha-sūtra. — *Kunda-mālā,* f. title of a work. — *Kunda-samāna-danta, as, ī, am,* one whose teeth are like the jasmine.

Kundaka, as, m. the plant Boswellia Thurifera; the resin of this plant.

Kundinī, f. an assemblage of lotus flowers or of jasmines.

कुन्दम *kundama, as,* m. a cat.

कुन्दर *kundara, as,* m. a sort of grass; an epithet of Vishṇu; [cf. *kaṇḍura* and *kunda.*]

कुन्दु *kundu, us,* m. a mouse, a rat; (*us*), f. the resin of the plant Boswellia Thurifera; gum olibanum or frankincense.

Kundura, as, m. or *kunduru, us,* m. f. the resin of the plant Boswellia Thurifera.

Kunduruka, as, ī, m. f. the resin of the plant Boswellia Thurifera; (*ī*), f. the plant Boswellia Thurifera.

कुन्द्र् *kundr,* cl. 10. P. *kundrayati, -yitum,* to tell a lie; [cf. *kud* and *gundr.*]

कुप् 1. *kup,* cl. 4. P. (ep. also A.) *kupyati, -te, ćukopa, kopishyati, akupat, kopitum,* to be moved, excited, agitated, to swell, heave or boil with rage or emotion, to be angry, to be angry with (with dat. or gen. or acc. or with *upari* and gen., e. g. *tasmai* or *tasya* or *tam* or *tasyopari ćukopa,* he was angry with him): Caus. *kopayati, -yitum,* to excite, agitate, affect strongly with anger &c.; to cause to swell or heave with passion; to stir up; to provoke, make angry; to be angry: Desid. *ćukupishati* and *ćukopishati:* Intens. *ćokupyate, ćokopti;* [cf. Lat. *cupio;* Eng. *hope;* Germ. *hoffe.*]

Kupa, as, m., Ved. the beam or lever of a pair of scales.

Kupana, as, m., N. of an Asura.

Kupaya, as, ī, am, Ved. heaving, swelling with emotion; disturbed; (Sāy.) to be guarded or protected (as if connected with rt. *gup*).

Kupita, as, ā, am, provoked, incensed, offended, angry, bristling. — *Kupita-vāyu, us,* m. aggravated flatulence, hypochondria. — *Kupitāntaka* (°*ta-an*°), *as,* m. imminent or threatening death.

Kupya, as, ā, am, to be excited; (*am*), n. a vile metal, any metal but silver and gold, base metal, copper, brass, &c.; zinc, lapis calaminaris, pewter, tutenag; (*as*), m., N. of a man; [cf. Lat. *cuprum.*] — *Kupya-śālā,* f. a braziery, a foundry, a place where metallic vessels &c. are made or sold.

Kupyaka at the end of compounds = *kupya.*

Kopa, as, m. passion, anger. See s. v.

कुप् 2. *kup,* cl. 10. P. *kopayati, -yitum,* to speak, to shine; [cf. Hib. *cubhas,* 'a word, a promise;' Lat. *cupo* in *nun-cupo;* Goth. *huf,* 'to lament.']

कुपङ्क *ku-panka, as,* m. (see 1. *ku*), a slough, a heap of filth and mud.

कुपट *ku-paṭa, as* or *am,* m. or n. (see 1. *ku*), miserable clothes, a miserable garment; (*as*), m., N. of a Dānava (covered with a miserable garment).

कुपत *kupata,* ind. excellent.

कुपथ *ku-patha, as,* m. (see 1. *ku*), a bad road, an evil way; bad conduct, evil way of living, immorality, profligacy; heterodox doctrine; (*as, ā, am*), walking in a bad or wrong road; (*as*), m., N. of an Asura or Dānava; (*ās*), m. pl., N. of a people. — *Kupatha-ga, as, ā, am,* or *kupatha-gāmin, ī, inī, i,* or *kupatha-ćara, as, ā, am,* going in a bad or wrong road, wicked.

Kupathya, as, ā, am, belonging to a bad way, literally or figuratively; unwholesome (as diet, regimen, &c.), improper, counter-indicated.

कुपरिज्ञात *ku-parijñāta, as, ā, am* (see 1. *ku*), badly understood, wrongly comprehended.

कुपरीक्षक *ku-parīkshaka, as, ikā, am* (see 1. *ku*), making a false estimate, not valuing rightly.

Ku-parīkshita, as, ā, am, badly examined or tested.

कुपाणि *ku-pāṇi, is, is, i* (see 1. *ku*), crooked-handed, having a deformed or maimed hand.

कुपात्र *ku-pātra, am,* n. an unfit recipient.

कुपिञ्जल *ku-piñjala, as,* m. (see 1. *ku*), N. of a man; [cf. *kaupiñjala.*]

कुपित *kupita.* See under rt. *kup* above.

कुपितृ *ku-pitṛi, tā,* m. (see 1. *ku*), a bad father.

कुपिनी *kupinī,* f. (fr. rt. 1. *kup?*), a kind of net for catching small fish, made of bamboos or rushes.

Kupinin, ī, m. a fisherman.

कुपिन्द *kupinda, as,* m. (said to be fr. 1. *kup*), a weaver; [cf. *kurinda.*]

कुपीलु *ku-pīlu, us,* m. (see 1. *ku*), a sort of ebony tree; [cf. *kāraskara.*]

कुपुत्र *ku-putra, as,* m. (see 1. *ku*), a bad son; a disobedient or wicked son; a son of an inferior degree, as an adopted son &c.

कुपुरुष *ku-purusha, as,* m. (see 1. *ku*), a low, vile, or miserable man; a poltroon. — *Kupurusha-janitā,* f., N. of a metre consisting of four lines of eleven syllables each.

कुपूय *ku-pūya, as, ā, am* (see 1. *ku*), inferior, low, vile, contemptible; [cf. *kapūya.*]

कुप्रावरण *ku-prāvaraṇa* or *ku-prāvṛita, as, ā, am* (see 1. *ku*), badly or miserably dressed.

कुप्रिय *ku-priya, as, ā, am* (see 1. *ku*), disagreeable, contemptible, low, vile, last, worst.

कुप्लव *ku-plava, as,* m. (see 1. *ku*), a weak or frail raft or float.

कुवधू *ku-badhū, ūs,* f. (see 1. *ku*), a wicked wife.

कुवन्ध *ku-bandha, as,* m. (see 1. *ku*), a disgraceful stigma; [cf. *anka-bandha.*]

कुवल *kubala, kubala-prastha, kubalāśva,* &c. See under *kuvala,* &c.

कुबुद्धि *ku-buddhi, is, is, i* (see 1. *ku*), a person of base or vile sentiments; stupid, foolish.

कुबेर *kubera,* or in later Sanskṛit *kuvera, as,* m. (said to be fr. rt. *kumb* or fr. 1. *ku* and *vera*), originally N. of the chief of the evil beings or spirits of darkness with the epithet Vaiśravaṇa; afterwards the god of riches and treasure, the regent of the northern quarter of the world, which is hence called Kubera-guptā dik; (*Kubera* is the son of Viśravas by Iḍaviḍā, the chief of the Yakshas, and a friend of Rudra; he is represented as having three legs and only eight teeth); with Jainas, the attendant of the nineteenth Arhat of the present Avasarpiṇī; N. of a prince of Deva-rāshṭra; or N. of the great-grandfather of Vāṇa-bhaṭṭa, the author of the Kādambarī; or of the author of the Dattaka-ćandrikā; the tree Cedrela Toona; (*as, ā, am*), deformed, monstrous; slow, lazy; [cf. *kuvera.*] — *Kubera-nalinī,* f., N. of a Tīrtha. — *Kubera-bāndhava, as,* m. an epithet of Śiva, 'the relation of Kubera.' — *Kubera-vana, am,* n. 'the forest of Kubera,' N. of a place. — *Kubera-vallabha, as,* m., N. of a Vaiśya. — *Kuberākshī* (°*ra-ak*°), f. the plant Bignonia Suaveolens. — *Kuberāćala* (°*ra-ać*°), *as,* m. 'the mountain of Kubera,' an epithet of the Kailāsa mountain. — *Kuberādri* (°*ra-ad*°), *is,* m. an epithet of the Kailāsa mountain.

Kuberaka, as, m. the tree Cedrela Toona (*tunna*); (*ikā*), f., N. of a woman.

कुबेरिण *kuberiṇa, as,* m. (?), N. of a mixed caste.

कुब्ज *kubja, as, ā, am* (fr. 1. *ku* and rt. *ubj?*), hump-backed, crooked; (*as*), m. a curved sword, scymitar; a sort of fish, Bola Cuja; the plant Achyranthes Aspera, = *apāmārga*; [cf. *nyubja* and *kanya-kubja*; cf. also Lith. *kupra, kupotas*; Gr. *κυφός, κύπτω*; Lat. *gibbus, gibba, gibber*; Germ. *Höcker?*]. — *Kubja-kaṇṭaka, as,* m. a white Mimosa. — *Kubja-kirāta* or *kubja-vāmana, am,* n. a hump-backed person and a dwarf. — *Kubjāmraka* (°*ja-ām*°), *as* or *am* (?), m. or n. (?), N. of a Tīrtha. — *Kubjālīḍha* (°*ja-āl*°), *as,* m., N. of the founder of a sect.

Kubjaka, as, ā, am, hump-backed, crooked; (*as*), m. the aquatic plant Trapa Bispinosa; (*ikā*), f. in the word *kubjikā-tantra,* N. of a Tantra; according to some authorities *kubjikā kumārī* is a girl eight years old personating the goddess Durgā at a festival of this deity.

Kubjita, as, ā, am, crooked, curved, bent.

कुब्र *kubra, am,* n. (said to be fr. rt. *kumb*), a forest; a hole for sacrificial fire; a ring, an ear-ring; a thread; a cart.

कुब्रह्म *ku-brahma, as,* m. or *ku-brahman, ā,* m. (see 1. *ku*), a degraded or contemptible Brāhman, one who officiates for Śūdras.

कुभन्यु *kubhanyu, us, us, u,* Ved. desirous of water.

कुभा *kubhā,* f., Ved., N. of a river falling into the Indus, the Kabul river (?); [cf. *κωφήν.*]

कुभार्य *ku-bhārya, as, ā, am* (see 1. *ku*), having a bad wife; (*ā*), f. a bad wife.

कुभुक्त *ku-bhukta, am,* n. (see 1. *ku*), bad food.

कुभृत्य *ku-bhṛitya, as,* m. (see 1. *ku*), a bad servant.

कुम् *kum,* ind. an interjection.

कुमति *ku-mati, is,* f. (see 1. *ku*), vile or base sentiment; slow or weak intellect; folly; (*is, is, i*), or *ku-manīsha, as, ā, am,* or *ku-manīshin, ī, iṇī, i,* of slow intellect, foolish.

कुमन्त्र *ku-mantra, as,* m. bad advice; evil counsel; a charm employed to secure success in a bad enterprise.

Ku-mantrin, ī, m. a bad counsellor.

कुमार *kumāra, as,* m. (fr. *ku* + *māra,* fr. rt. *mṛi?* 'easily dying;' by native authorities derived fr. rt. 2. *kam*), a child, a new-born child (especially in the earlier language); a boy, a youth, a son; a prince, the heir-apparent associated in the kingdom with the reigning monarch (especially in theatrical language); a groom; a N. of Skanda the god of war, who is also the reputed author of certain grammatical Sūtras (see *kalāpa*); N. of a son of Agni, who is the author of some Vedic hymns; an epithet of Agni; (with Jainas) N. of the attendant of the twelfth Arhat of the present Avasarpiṇī; N. of a Prajāpati; an epithet of Mañju-śrī; a parrot; the tree Capparis Trifoliata [cf. *kumāraka*]; an epithet of the river Sindhu; (*ās*), m. pl., N. of a people; (*ī*), f. a young girl, one from ten to twelve years old, a maiden; or (in the Tantras) any virgin up to the age of sixteen, or before menstruation has commenced; a daughter; N. of the wife of Bhīma-sena, the son of Parīkshit; or of a daughter of Vasu-deva by Rohiṇī; an epithet of Sītā, the wife of Rāma; an epithet of the goddess Durgā; the Syāmā, a bird so named; N. of several plants, Aloe Perfoliata, or the plant Clitoria Ternatea [cf. *aparājitā*]; also the plant Jasminum Sambac, and a plant commonly called Bandhyā-karkoṭakī; the blossom of the plants Taruṇī and Modinī; great cardamoms; the most southerly of the nine portions of the known continent, or of Jambu-dvīpa, the southern extremity of the peninsula, whence the modern name Cape Comorin (Kumārī); the central part of the universe, according to Hindū geography, Jambu-dvīpa or India; N. of a river flowing from the mountain Suktimat; N. of a metre consisting of four lines of sixteen syllables each; (when a name is given to a pupil to indicate his attachment to any particular master, *kumārī* may be prefixed to denote that the pupil's object is to gain the affections of the master's daughter, e. g. *kumārī-dāksha*); (*am*), n. pure gold; [Gr. *κόρος, κοῦρος; μεῖραξ, μειράκιον?*]. — *Kumāra-gupta, as,* m., N. of a prince ('protected by the god of war'). — *Kumāra-ghātin, ī,* m. the slayer of a child. — *Kumāra-jīva, as,* m., N. of a plant, = *putrañjīvaka.* — *Kumāra-tva, am,* n. boyhood, youth. — *Kumāra-datta, as,* m., N. of a son of Nidhipati. — *Kumāra-dāsa, as,* m., N. of a poet. — *Kumāra-devī,* f., N. of the mother of Samudra-gupta. — *Kumāra-deshṇa, as, ā, am,* Ved. granting perishable gifts; (Sāy.) granting children. — *Kumāra-dhārā,* f., N. of a river. — *Kumāra-pāla, as,* m., N. of a king, = *śālivāhana* (?), also N. of a king of Guzerat (?). — *Kumāra-bhaṭṭa, as,* m., N. of a poet. — *Kumāra-bhṛityā,* f. care of a young child, care of a pregnant or lying-in woman, midwifery. — *Kumāra-lalitā,* f. 'boy's play,' N. of a metre consisting of four lines of eight syllables each. — *Kumāra-vana, am,* n. Kumāra's (i.e. Kārttikeya's) grove. — *Kumāra-vāhin, ī,* m. a peacock, ('carrying the god of war;' this god being usually represented as borne by a peacock.) — *Kumāra-vrata, am,* n. a vow of eternal chastity. — *Kumāra-sambhava, as,* m. 'the birth of the god of war,' title of a poem by Kālidāsa. — *Kumāra-sū, ūs,* m. the father of the god of war, an epithet of Agni; (*ūs*), f. the mother of the god of war, an epithet of the river Gangā, also of the goddess Durgā. — *Kumāra-sena, as,* m., N. of a minister. — *Kumāra-svāmin, ī,* m., N. of the author of a commentary on the Mīmāṃsā-bhāshya. — *Kumāra-hārita, as,* m., N. of a teacher. — *Kumārābhisheka* (°*ra-abh*°), *as,* m. 'the inauguration of Kumāra,' title of the thirteenth book of the Kumāra-sambhava. — *Kumārī-tantra, am,* n., N. of a Tantra. — *Kumārī-pāla, as,* m. the guardian of a virgin or bride. — *Kumārī-putra, as,* m. the child of an unmarried woman. — *Kumārī-pura, am,* n. a gynæceum. — *Kumārī-pūjā,* f. the worship of Kumārī or Durgā, (a ceremony performed at the great Durgā festival, when a girl between ten and twelve years old is placed on a pedestal, as the representative of the goddess, and fed with offerings made to the idol.) — *Kumārī-śvaśura, as,* m. the father-in-law of a maiden.

Kumāraka, as, m. a child, a little boy, a boy, a lad, a youth; the pupil of the eye; N. of a Nāga; the plant Capparis Trifoliata; (*ikā*), f. a girl from ten to twelve years old, or generally a virgin; an insect, Sphex Asiatica; double jasmine, Jasminum Sambac; large cardamoms; N. of a part of Bhārata-varsha, a division of the known continent. — *Kumārikā-kshetra, am,* n., N. of a country. — *Kumārikā-khaṇḍa,* a section of the Skanda-purāṇa.

Kumāraya, nom. P. *kumārayati, -yitum,* to play, especially as a child.

Kumārayu, us, m. a prince, heir-apparent.

Kumārika, as, ī, am, furnished with girls, abounding in them.

Kumārin, ī, iṇī, i, abounding in girls.

Kumārila, as, m. or *kumārila-svāmin, ī,* m., N. of a renowned teacher of the Mīmāṃsā philosophy.

Kumārī, ī, ī, m. f. a man or woman desirous of a daughter.

कुमार्ग *ku-mārga, as,* m. (see 1. *ku*), a bad way, bad ways, (also used metaphorically.)

कुमालक *kumālaka, ās,* m. pl., N. of a people and country, = *kumāraka.*

Kumālaya, nom. P. *kumālayati, -yitum,* to play, especially as a child; [cf. *kumāraya.*]

कुमित्र *ku-mitra, am,* n. (see 1. *ku*), a bad friend.

कुमुख *ku-mukha, as,* m. (see 1. *ku*), a hog.

कुमुद् *ku-mud, t, t, t* (see 1. *ku*), unkind, unfriendly; avaricious, niggardly; (*t*), n. the plant Nymphæa Esculenta, the esculent white water-lily; the plant Nymphæa Rubra, the red lotus. — *Kumud-vat, ān, atī, at,* abounding in lotuses; (*atī*), f. an assemblage of lotuses; a place or pond filled with them; the flexible stalk of a water-lily; N. of a plant bearing a poisonous fruit, Villarsia (Menyanthes) Indica; N. of a sister of the serpent-king Kumuda and wife of Kuśa; N. of the wife of Vimarshaṇa; N. of a river. — *Kumudvatīśa* (°*tī-īśa*), *as,* m. an epithet of the moon; [cf. *kumuda-bandhu* and the following.]

Ku-muda, as, am, m. n. the esculent white water-lily, Nymphæa Esculenta ('exciting what joy!'); red lotus, Nymphæa Rubra; (*am*), n. silver; (*as*), m. camphor; N. of a Nāga; N. of the elephant of the south-west or southern quarter; N. of a Daitya; N. of an attendant of Vishṇu; N. of a son of Gada by Vṛihatī; N. of a confidant of king Unmattāvanti; one of the monkey-heroes of the Rāmāyaṇa; N. of a poet; N. of a mountain; N. of one of the smaller Dvīpas; (*ā*), f. several plants, Gmelina Arborea; Pistia Stratiotes; Desmodium Gangeticum; Grislea Tomentosa; N. of another plant, commonly called Kaṭphala; N. of a deity; (*ī*), f. a plant, commonly called Kaṭphala. — *Kumuda-khaṇḍa, am,* n. an assemblage of Kumudas. — *Kumuda-ghnī,* f., N. of a plant containing a poisonous milky juice. — *Kumuda-pattrābha* (°*tra-ābha*), *as, ā, am,* resembling the leaves of the white water-lily. — *Kumuda-bandhu, us,* m. or *kumuda-bāndhava, as,* m. the moon ('friend of the lotus;' the white esculent lotus expanding its petals during the night and closing them in the day time; hence other similar appellations of the moon, as *kumuda-priya,* &c.). — *Kumuda-vatī,* f. an assemblage of Kumudas, a place abounding in them, &c. — *Kumuda-suhṛid, t,* m. the moon; [cf. *kumuda-bandhu.*] — *Kumudākara* (°*da-āk*°), *as,* m. a number of water-lilies or place abounding in them. — *Kumudāksha* (°*da-ak*°), *as,* m., N. of a Nāga; also of an attendant of Vishṇu. — *Kumudādi* (°*da-ādi*), *is,* m., N. of a pupil of Pathya. — *Kumudāvāsa* (°*da-āv*°), *as, ā, am,* abounding or richly furnished with Kumudas; (*as*), m. a pool abounding in them. — *Kumudeśa* (°*da-īśa*), *as,* m. an epithet of the moon, 'lord of the lotus.'

Kumudika, as, ī, am, abounding with Kumudas; (*ikā*), f., N. of a plant, commonly called Kaṭphala; a small tree, the seeds of which are aromatic.

Kumudinī, f. an assemblage of Kumudas or a place abounding in them; the mother of Raghudeva. — *Kumudinī-nāyaka, as,* m. or *kumudinī-pati, is,* m. an epithet of the moon; [cf. *kumuda-bandhu.*] — *Kumudinī-vanitā,* f. any loved woman fancifully represented as an assemblage of lotus flowers.

कुमेधस् *ku-medhas, ās, ās, as* (see 1. *ku*), of little intellect, stupid; malicious.

कुमेरु *ku-meru, us,* m. (see 1. *ku*), the southern hemisphere or pole, the region of the demons and Titans.

कुमोदक *kumodaka, as,* m. an epithet of Vishṇu; [cf. *kaumodakī.*]

कुम्प् *kump,* cl. 10. P. *kumpayati, -yitum,* another form for *kumb, kumbayati.*

कुम्प *kumpa, as, ā, am,* crooked-armed.

कुम्ब् *kumb,* cl. 6. and 10. P. *kumbati* and *kumbayati, -yitum,* to cover; [cf. *kump* and *kumbh.*]

कुम्ब *kumba, as* or *am* (?), m. or n. (?), Ved. a kind of head-dress for women; the upper part or top of a club; (*ā*), f. a thick petticoat; an enclosure round a place of sacrifice to prevent profane intrusion.

कुम्बिक *kumbika, ās,* m. pl., N. of a people.

कुम्ब्या *kumbyā* or *kumvyā,* f., Ved. a kind of hymn or sacred formula.

कुम्भ् *kumbh,* cl. 10. P. *kumbhayati, -yitum,* another form for *kumb,* q. v.

कुम्भ *kumbha, as,* m. a jar, pitcher, water-pot, ewer, a small water-jar, (often in compounds, e. g. *ćhidra-kumbha,* a perforated pitcher; *āma-kumbha,* a jar of unbaked clay; *hema-kumbha,* a golden ewer; *jala-kumbha,* a water-pot); an urn in which the bones of a dead person are collected; the sign of the zodiac Aquarius; a measure of grain equal to twenty Droṇas, a little more than three bushels and three gallons (commonly called a comb, some make it two Droṇas or sixty-four Seers); the frontal globe on the upper part of the forehead of an elephant (there are two of these projections which swell in the rutting season); a religious exercise, viz. closing the nostrils and mouth so as to suspend breathing; the root of a plant used in medicine; the paramour of a harlot, a bully, a flash or fancy man; N. of a Muni; N. of a Dānava, son of Prahlāda and brother of Nikumbha; also of a Rākshasa, a son of Kumbha-karṇa; N. of the father of the nineteenth Arhat of the present Avasarpiṇī; N. of a monkey; one of the thirty-four jātakas or former births of Śākya-muni; title of a work; (*ī*), f. a small jar or pot, an earthen cooking vessel; a vessel for preserving grain, a measure of grain; N. of several plants, a small tree, the seeds of which are used in medicine, commonly called Kaṭphala; another plant, Bignonia Suaveolens; another plant, Pistia Stratiotes; another plant, commonly called Romaśa; another plant, Croton Polyandrum; (*ā*), f. a harlot, a whore; (*am*), n. the plant Ipomœa Turpethum; a fragrant resin (*guggulu*), or the plant which bears it; [cf. Gr. κύμβη; Lat. *cymba.*] — *Kumbha-karṇa, as,* m., N. of a Rākshasa, the gigantic brother of Rāvaṇa, who is described in the Yuddha-kāṇḍa of the Rāmāyaṇa as sleeping for six months at a time, and then waking to gorge himself; N. of a Muni; an epithet of Śiva; N. of a Dānava. — *Kumbhakarṇa-vadha, as,* m. 'the slaughter of Kumbhakarṇa,' a section of the Padma-purāṇa. — *Kumbha-kāmalā,* f. a bilious affection, a sort of jaundice together with swelling of the joints; [cf. *kumbha-pāda.*] — *Kumbha-kāra, as,* m. a potter, being according to some authorities the son of a Brāhman by a wife of the Kshatriya caste; a serpent; a kind of wild fowl; (*ī*), f. the wife of a potter; N. of a girl; a mineral substance used as an application to strengthen the eyes and beautify the eyelashes; red arsenic. — *Kumbha-kāraka, as,* m. a potter; (*ikā*), f. the wife of a potter, a woman of the potter caste; a sort of collyrium. — *Kumbha-kāra-kukkuṭa, as,* m. a kind of chicken, Phasianus Gallus. — *Kumbha-ketu, us,* m., N. of a son of Śambara. — *Kumbha-koṇa, as,* m. 'brim of a jar,' N. of a town. — *Kumbha-ghoṇa-tīrtha, am,* n., N. of a Tīrtha. — *Kumbha-janman, ā,* m. an epithet of Agastya. — *Kumbha-tumbī,* f. a kind of large round gourd. — *Kumbha-dāsī,* f. a bawd, a procuress. — *Kumbha-dhara, as,* m. the sign of the zodiac Aquarius. — *Kumbha-nābha, as,* m., N. of a son of Bali. — *Kumbha-pāda, as, -padī, am,* a person with swollen legs bulging like a pitcher; [cf. *kumbha-kāmalā.*] — *Kumbha-bāhu, us,* m., N. of a Daitya. — *Kumbha-maṇḍūka, as,* m. a frog in a pitcher; [cf. *kūpa-maṇḍūka.*] — *Kumbha-mushka, as, ā, am,* Ved. an epithet of certain demons, 'having a jar-shaped scrotum.' — *Kumbha-mūrdhan, ā,* m. a fabulous being mentioned in the Hari-vaṇśa. — *Kumbha-yoni, is,* m. 'born in a water-jar,' an epithet of the saint Agastya; of Vasishṭha; and of Droṇa, the military preceptor of the Kurus and Pāṇḍus; N. of a plant, commonly called Droṇa-pushpī; (*is*), f., N. of an Apsaras. — *Kumbha-rāśi, is,* m. the sign Aquarius. — *Kumbha-retas,* n. semen virile deposited in a Kumbha; (*ās*), m. a form of Agni. — *Kumbha-lagna, am,* n. that time of day in which Aquarius rises above the horizon. — *Kumbha-vījaka, as,* m., N. of a plant, commonly called Rīṭhā-karañja. — *Kumbha-śālā,* f. a pottery, a potter's kiln. — *Kumbha-sandhi, is,* m. the hollow on the top of an elephant's head, between the frontal globes. — *Kumbha-sambhava, as,* m. an epithet of the saint Agastya; also of Nārāyaṇa. — *Kumbha-sarpis, is,* n. butter placed in a jar. — *Kumbha-hanu, us,* m., N. of a Rākshasa. — *Kumbhāṇḍa* (°*bha-aṇ*°), *ās,* m. pl. (with Buddhists) a class of demons with testicles shaped like a Kumbha; N. of a minister of the Asura Bāṇa; (*ī*), f. a pumpkin gourd, (a various reading for *kushmāṇḍī.*) — *Kumbhī-dhānya, as,* m. grain stored in jars sufficient (according to some) for six days, or (to others) for one year's consumption. — *Kumbhī-dhānyaka, as,* m. a householder who preserves grain in store for six days &c. — *Kumbhī-nasa, as,* m. a kind of large venomous snake; a kind of poisonous insect; (*ī*), f., N. of the wife of the Gandharva Aṅgāraparṇa; also of a Rākshasī, the mother of Lavaṇa. — *Kumbhīnasi, is,* m., N. of a demon. — *Kumbhī-pāka, as,* m. the contents of a cooking vessel; (*as* or *ās*), m. sing. or pl. a hell, in which the wicked are baked like potters' vessels, or cooked like the contents of a cooking vessel. — *Kumbhī-vīja, am,* n. the nut of the croton; [cf. *kumbhinī-vīja.*] — *Kumbheśvara-tīrtha* (°*bha-īś*°), *am,* n., N. of a Tīrtha. — *Kumbhodara* (°*bha-ud*°), *as,* m., N. of an attendant of Śiva. — *Kumbholūka* (°*bha-ul*°), *as,* m. a kind of owl.

Kumbhaka, as, m. the base of a column; stopping the breath by shutting the mouth and closing both nostrils with the fingers of the right hand; a religious exercise.

Kumbhikā, f. a small pot or pitcher; N. of several plants, Pistia Stratiotes; another plant, Bignonia Suaveolens; another plant, commonly called Droṇa-pushpī; a disease of the eyes, hordeolum or stye.

Kumbhin, ī, inī, i, having a water-jar; shaped like a jar &c.; (*ī*), m., N. of a demon hostile to children; an elephant; a crocodile; a fish; a kind of poisonous insect; a sort of fragrant resin (*guggulu*), or the plant bearing this fragrant resin. — *Kumbhi-naraka, as* or *am* (?), m. or n. (?), N. of a hell, = *kumbhī-pāka* (?). — *Kumbhinī-vīja, am,* n. the croton-nut, Croton Jamalgota. — *Kumbhi-pākī,* f., N. of a plant, commonly called Kaṭphala. — *Kumbhi-mada, as,* m. the juice that exudes from an elephant's temples at certain seasons.

Kumbhila, as, m. a thief who breaks into a house, a plagiarist; a wife's brother; a child begotten at undue seasons or of an imperfect impregnation; a kind of fish, the gilt-head, Ophiocephalus Wrahl.

Kumbhīka, as, m. a pathic, a catamite; the plant Rottleria Tinctoria, or the plant Pistia Stratiotes, a plant the bark of which furnishes a yellow dye; (*ā*), f. a swelling, especially of the eyelids, similar to a seed or grain of the Kumbhīka; an affection of the eyes, hordeolum or stye, also *kumbhīka-piḍakā;* Ved., N. of a kind of demon.

Kumbhīkin, ī, inī, i, similar to a seed or grain of the Kumbhīka.

Kumbhīra, as, m. the crocodile of the Ganges, the long-nosed alligator; N. of a Yaksha. — *Kumbhīra-makshikā,* f. a sort of fly or aquatic insect.

Kumbhīraka, as, m. a thief.

Kumbhīla, as, m. a crocodile; [cf. *kumbhīra.*]

कुम्भरी *kumbharī,* f. an epithet of Durgā.

कुम्भला *kumbhalā,* f. a plant the flowers of which are compared to those of the plant Nauclea Cadamba; [cf. *muṇḍitikā.*]

कुम्भिल *kumbhila, kumbhīra,* &c. See under *kumbha* above.

कुयज्विन् ku-yajvin, ī, m. (see 1. ku), a bad sacrificer.

कुयव ku-yava, as, ā, am (see 1. ku), Ved. epithet of the demon S'ushṇa, who was slain by Indra, 'causing a bad harvest?;' (as), m., N. of another demon; (am), n. a bad harvest.

कुयवाच् kuya-vāć, k, m. (kuya = 1. ku), Ved. speaking ill, abusing; or N. of a demon who was slain by Indra (?).

कुयोग ku-yoga, as, m. (see 1. ku), an inauspicious conjunction of planets, signs, periods, &c.

Ku-yogin, ī, m. a false devotee, an impostor, a hypocrite.

कुयोनि ku-yoni, is, f. (see 1. ku), a base womb, the womb of a low woman.

कुर् kur, cl. 6. P. kurati, -ritum, to utter a sound, to sound in general.

कुरका kurakā, f. the olibanum tree, Boswellia Thurifera (= sallakī).

कुरङ्कर kurankara or **kurankura**, as, m. the Indian crane, Ardea Sibirica.

कुरङ्ग kuranga, as, m. (said to be fr. 1. kṛī), a species of antelope, an antelope or deer in general; N. of a mountain; (ī), f. a female antelope. — *Kuranga-nayanā*, f. a handsome woman ('fawn-eyed'). — *Kuranga-nābhi*, is, m. musk (formed in a bag attached to the belly of the deer above the navel).

Kurangaka, as, m. a species of antelope, an antelope, a deer; (ikā), f. a kind of bean (= mudga-parṇī).

Kurangama, as, m. a species of antelope or deer.

Kurangāya, nom. A. kurangāyate, -yitum, to become or take the shape of an antelope.

कुरचिल्ल kuraćilla, as, m. a crab; (a wrong reading for kuru-ćilla.)

कुरट kuraṭa, as, m. a shoemaker, a leather-seller, a currier; (ās), m. pl., N. of a people.

कुरण्ट kuraṇṭa, as, m. or kuraṇṭaka, as, ikā, m. f. yellow amaranth (pītāmlāna), and a yellow kind of barleria (pītajhiṇṭī); (am), n. the blossom of this plant. Also kuraṇḍaka and kuruṇṭaka.

कुरण्ड kuraṇḍa, as, m. enlargement of the testicles or rather of the scrotum, including inguinal hernia, hydrocele, &c.; N. of a plant, commonly called Sākuruṇḍa.

कुरण्डक kuraṇḍaka, as, m. yellow amaranth; a yellow kind of barleria; [cf. kuraṇṭa.]

कुरयाण kurayāṇa, as, m., N. of a man; [cf. kaurayāṇa.]

कुरर kurara, as, ā, m. f. (said to be fr. rt. 3. ku), an osprey; also another species of eagle; (ī), f. a female osprey; a sheep, an ewe; (as), m., N. of a mountain. — *Kurarānghri* (°ra-an°), is, m. a kind of mustard (deva-sarshapa). — *Kurarī-gaṇa*, as, m. a flight of ospreys.

Kurarāva, am, n. a place abounding with ospreys.

कुरल kurala, as, m. an osprey [cf. kurara]; a curl, a lock of hair upon the forehead.

कुरव ku-rava, as, ā, am (see 1. ku), having a bad voice; (as), m. a bad or harsh sound; N. of a plant, = sitamandāra; a red or a yellow kind of barleria.

Kuravaka, as, m. a crimson species of amaranth; a purple or a yellow sort of Jhiṇṭi or barleria; a species of rice or grain; (am), n. the blossom of the amaranth or of the barleria.

कुरस ku-rasa, as, ā, am (see 1. ku), having bad juice or flavour or essence; (as), m. spirituous or vinous liquor; (ā), f. a wild creeping plant, a species of hieracium; [cf. go-jihvā.]

कुराजन् ku-rājan, ā, m. (see 1. ku), a bad king.

Ku-rājya, am, n. bad dominion, bad administration.

कुराल kurāla, as, m. a light bay horse with black legs; (wrong reading for kurāha, which is a various reading for urāha.)

कुरी kurī, f. a kind of grass or corn.

कुरीर kurīra, am, n. (said to be fr. 1. kṛī), Ved. a kind of head-dress for women; copulation.

Kurīrin, ī, iṇī, i, Ved. decorated with the head-dress called kurīra.

कुरु kuru, avas, m. pl. (said to be fr. 1. kṛī), N. of a people of India and their country, situated near the country of the Pañćālas (hence often connected with Pañćāla or Pāñćāla; see kuru-pañćāla below); the Kurus derive their origin from Kuru (son of Saṃvaraṇa and Tapatī, daughter of the Sun), who is the ancestor of both Pāṇḍu and Dhṛita-rāshṭra, though the patronymic derived from his name is usually applied only to the sons of the latter, the sons and descendants of the former being called Pāṇḍavas; another Kuru is the son of Agnīdhra and grandson of Priya-vrata. The *uttara-kuravaḥ* or *uttarāḥ kuravaḥ* are the northern Kurus, the most northerly of the four Mahā-dvīpas or principal divisions of the known world (distinguished Mahā-bh. I. 4346. from the *dakshiṇāḥ kuravaḥ* or southern Kurus), by other systems regarded as one of nine divisions or Varshas of the same; it was probably a country beyond the most northern range of the Himālaya, often described as a country of everlasting happiness, and considered by some to be the ancient home of the Āryan race. *Kurū*, ūs, f. a princess of the Kuru race. According to native lexicographers the word kuru has also the following meanings: a priest; boiled rice; the plant Solanum Jacquini, = kaṇṭakārikā; [cf. kaurava, kauravaka, kauravya.] — *Kuru-kata*, ās, m. pl. the Kurus and Katas. — *Kuru-kandaka*, am, n. horse-radish, Raphanus Sativus (= mūlaka). — *Kuru-kurukshetra*, am, n. the country of the Kurus and Kurukshetra. — *Kuru-kshetra*, am, n. the field of the Kurus, N. of a region or extensive plain near Delhi, the scene of the great battles between the Kurus and Pāṇḍus; (ās), m. pl. the inhabitants of this country, renowned for their bravery. — *Kuru-kshetrin*, ī, iṇī, i, with yoga, a solar day, in the course of which three lunar days, three asterisms and three yogas occur. — *Kuru-ćilla*, as, m. a crab; [cf. kuraćilla.] — *Kuru-jāngala*, am, n., N. of a country; (ās), m. pl., N. of the people inhabiting it. — *Kuru-tīrtha*, am, n., N. of a Tīrtha. — *Kuru-nadikā*, f. according to native authorities, = ku-nadikā. — *Kuru-nandana*, as, m. a descendant of Kuru as Arjuna, Yudhishṭhira, &c. — *Kuru-pañćāla*, ās, m. pl. the Kurus and Pañćālas. — *Kurupañćālatrā*, ind., Ved. as among the Kurus and Pañćālas. — *Kuru-patha*, as, m., N. of a man (?); [cf. kaurupathi.] — *Kuru-pungava*, as, m. a Kuru chief. — *Kuru-rāj*, ṭ, m. an epithet of Duryodhana. — *Kuru-rāja*, as, m. an epithet of Yudhishṭhira. — *Kuru-rājya*, am, n. the Kuru realm. — *Kuru-vatsa*, as, m., N. of a prince. — *Kuru-varṇaka*, ās, m. pl., N. of a people; or perhaps (as, ā, am), belonging to the race of the Kurus. — *Kuru-vaśa*, as, m., N of a prince. — *Kuru-vājapeya*, as, m. a particular kind of Vājapeya. — *Kuru-vista*, as, m. a Pala of gold, a weight of gold equal to about 700 troy grains. — *Kuru-vriddha*, as, m. an epithet of Bhīshma. — *Kuru-śravaṇa*, as, m., N. of a prince. — *Kuru-śreshṭha* or *kuru-sattama*, as, m. an epithet of Arjuna. — *Kuru-hāra*, as or am (?), m. or n. (?), N of an Agra-hāra.

Kuruka, as, m., N. of a prince; (a various reading for ruruka.)

Kurukullā, f., N. of a Buddhist deity.

कुरुङ्ग kurunga, as, m., N. of a prince.

कुरुट kuruṭa, as, m. a kind of pot-herb; [cf. sitāvara.]

कुरुटिन् kuruṭin, ī, m. a horse.

कुरुण्ट kuruṇṭa, as, m. yellow amaranth; yellow barleria; (ī), f. a doll, a puppet made of wood; the wife of a Brāhman or teacher.

Kuruṇṭaka, as, m. yellow or white amaranth; a yellow species of barleria, B. Prionitis.

Kuruṇḍa, as, m. = kuruṇṭa.

कुरुतावि kurutāvi, a particular high number.

कुरुम्ब kurumba, am, n. a kind of orange, = kulapālaka; (ā), f., N. of a plant, commonly called Droṇa-pushpī; (ī), f. another plant, commonly called Saiṃhalī.

Kurumbikā, f., N. of a plant, commonly called Droṇa-pushpī.

कुरुरी kururī, f. a species of bird with a plaintive note; (a wrong reading for kurarī.)

कुरुल kurula, as, m. a curl or lock of hair, especially on the forehead.

कुरुवक kuruvaka, as, m. the crimson amaranth; a purple species of barleria; also a yellow kind; (am), n. the blossom of this flower; [cf. kuravaka.]

कुरुविन्द kuruvinda, as, m. (fr. kuru and vinda?), N. of several plants; a fragrant grass, Cyperus Rotundus; a kind of barley, see kalmāsha; the bud of a flower?; (as, am), m. n. a ruby; (am), n. black salt; cinnabar, or the plant Terminalia Catappa (?).

Kuruvindaka, as, m. a kind of Dolichos Biflorus, a wild variety.

कुरुविल्व kuruvilva or **kuruvilla** (?), as, m. a ruby; [cf. kuruvinda.]

Kuruvilvaka, as, m. a kind of barley. See kulmāsha and kuruvinda.

कुरुसुति kurusuti or **kurustuti**, is, m., N. of a Vedic poet.

कुरूटिन् kurūṭin, ī, inī, i, Ved. = kirīṭin (?).

कुरूप ku-rūpa, as, ā, am (see 1. ku), ill-made, of an ugly shape, deformed, ugly; (am), n. ugliness. — *Kurūpa-tā*, f. or *kurūpa-tva*, am, n. ugliness.

Ku-rūpin, ī, iṇī, i, ill-made, deformed, ugly, frightful.

Ku-rūpya, am, n. tin, (lit. bad silver.)

कुरूरु kurūru, us, m., Ved. a species of worm.

कुर्कुट kurkuṭa, as, m. [cf. kukkuṭa], a cock; rubbish, sweepings (?).

कुर्कुटाहि kurkuṭāhi, is, m. a kind of serpent; [cf. kukkuṭāhi and kukkuṭābha.]

कुर्कुर kurkura, as, m. (an onomatopoetic word), a dog or bitch; [cf. kukkura.]

कुर्चिका kurćikā, f. the milky juice of a bulbous root; a needle; (a wrong reading for kūrćikā.)

कुर्णज kurṇaja, as, m., N. of a plant, commonly called Kulañjana.

कुर्द् kurd and **kurdana**, incorrect forms for kūrd and kūrdana.

कुर्पर kurpara, as, m. the knee; the elbow; [cf. kūrpara.]

कुर्पास kurpāsa and **kurpāsaka**, as, m. a sort of bodice or jacket for women; [cf. kūrpāsa.]

कुर्वत् *kurvat, an, atī, at* (pres. part. fr. rt. 1. *kṛi*), doing, acting, &c.; acting as a servant, an agent, a servant. — *Kurvad-rūpa, am,* n. cause according to the Cārvākas.

Kurvāṇa, as, ā, am, doing, making, &c.

कुल् *kul,* cl. 1. P. *kolati, ćukola,* &c., *kolitum,* to accumulate, collect; to be of kin, to behave as a kinsman; to proceed continuously or without interruption; to count.

कुल *kula, am,* n. (fr. rt. *kul?*), a herd, a troop, a flock, an assemblage, a multitude, a number &c. (of quadrupeds, birds, insects, &c., or of inanimate objects, e. g. *go-kula,* a herd of cows; *mṛiga-kula,* a herd of deer; *mahishī-kula,* a herd of female buffaloes; *ali-kula,* a swarm of bees; *alaka-kula,* a multitude of curls); a race, family, community, tribe, caste, association, set, company (e. g. *brāhmaṇa-kula,* the caste of the Brāhmans); the residence of a family, seat of a community; (in a contemptuous sense) a lot, a gang (forming a comp. with a preceding gen. sing., e. g. *ćaurasya-kula,* a gang of thieves); an inhabited country; a house, an abode; a noble or eminent family or race; high station (often at the beginning of a compound = chief, principal; see *kula-giri* below); the body; the front, fore part; a blue stone; *(as),* m. the chief of a corporation or guild; [cf. Hib. *gaol,* 'a family or kindred.'] *Kuli* and *kulī,* see s. v. — *Kula-kajjala, as,* m. disgrace of the family. — *Kula-kaṇṭaka, as,* m. 'a family-thorn,' any one who is a trouble to his family. — *Kula-kanyā,* f. a girl of good family. — *Kula-kara, as, ī, am,* founding a family, the founder of a family or race, an ancestor. — *Kula-karkaṭī,* f. a kind of gourd; [cf. *ćīnākarkaṭī.*] — *Kula-kartṛi, tā,* m. the founder of a family or race, an ancestor. — *Kula-karman, a,* n. the peculiar or proper duty of a family or race, any observance or custom peculiar to a family. — *Kula-kalaṅka, as,* m. 'a family-stain,' any one who disgraces his family. — *Kula-kshaya, as,* m. decay or downfall of a race or family; *(ā),* f. a sort of cowach, Mucuna Pruritus (= *śūkaśimbī*). — *Kula-gariman, ā,* m. family pride. — *Kula-giri, is,* m. a chief mountain, any one of the seven principal mountains of Bhārata-varsha; see *kulāćala.* — *Kula-gṛiha, am,* n. a noble house. — *Kula-gopa, as,* m., Ved. the protector of a domicile. — *Kula-gaurava, am,* n. family importance. — *Kula-ghna, as, ā* or *ī, am,* destroying a family. — *Kula-ćandra, as,* m., N. of a scholiast on the Kātantra grammar; N. of the author of the Durgāvākya-prabodha. — *Kula-ćūḍāmaṇi,* title of a work. — *Kula-ćyuta, as, ā, am,* rejected by his family. — *Kula-ja* or *kula-jāta, as, ā, am,* born in a noble family, of a good or noble family, well-born, of good breed; ancestral, hereditary. — *Kula-jana, as,* m. a person belonging to a noble family, a high-born or distinguished person. — *Kula-tattva-vid, t, t, t,* knowing the true state of a family. — *Kula-tas,* ind. by birth. — *Kula-tithi, is,* m. f. an important lunar day, the fourth, eighth, twelfth, or fourteenth day of the half-month. — *Kula-tilaka, as,* m. the glory of a family, one who does honour to a family. — *Kula-damana, as, ā, am,* subduing a family, holding it in subjection. — *Kula-dīpa* or *kula-dīpaka, as,* m. the lamp or light or glory of a race or family; *(ikā),* f. title of a work treating on the noble families of Bengal. — *Kula-duhitṛi, tā,* f. the daughter of a noble family; a high-born maiden. — *Kula-devatā,* f. a principal deity; an epithet of the goddess Durgā. — *Kula-daiva, am,* n. family destiny; a principal deity. — *Kula-dharma, as,* m. practice or observance peculiar to a tribe or family, peculiar duty of caste or race. — *Kula-dhāraka, as,* m. 'upholder of the family,' a son. — *Kula-dhurya, as,* m. one who is able to support a family, a grown-up son. — *Kula-nakshatra, am,* n. any Nakshatra or lunar mansion distinguished above others; any auspicious asterism. — *Kula-nandana, as, ā, am,* causing joy to a family, doing honour to a family; a high-born virtuous child. — *Kula-nāyikā,* f. a girl worshipped at the celebration of the orgies of the left-hand Śāktas. — *Kula-nārī,* f. a woman of good family; a high-bred virtuous woman. — *Kula-nāśa, as,* m. a camel; a reprobate, an outcast. — *Kula-nindā,* f. family disgrace. — *Kulan-dhara, as, ā, am,* upholding a family. — *Kula-pa, as,* m., Ved. the chief of a family or race or tribe. — *Kula-pati, is,* m. the head or chief of a family. — *Kula-pattra, as,* m. a plant, commonly called Damanaka. — *Kula-paramparā,* f. the series of generations comprising a race. — *Kula-parvata* or *kula-śaila, as,* m. a principal mountain, any one of seven mountains in Bhārata; [cf. *kula-giri.*] — *Kula-pāṃsukā,* f. an unchaste woman. — *Kula-pālaka, as, ikā, am,* protecting a family, nourishing or providing for a family; *(am),* n. a kind of orange, = *kurumba,* commonly *kamalānevu.* — *Kula-pāli, is,* f. or *kula-pālikā,* f. or *kula-pālī,* f. a chaste, high-born, or noble woman. — *Kula-putra, as,* m. a son of a noble family, a noble or respectable youth; *(ī),* f. the daughter of a good family, a high-born or respectable girl; [cf. *kula-duhitṛi.*] — *Kula-putraka, as,* m., N. of a plant, = *kula-pattra* and *muni-putra.* — *Kulaputra-jana, as,* m. the son of a good family, a noble or respectable youth. — *Kula-purusha, as,* m. a man of good family, a noble or respectable man; an ancestor, any family progenitor. — *Kula-pūrvaga, as,* m. an ancestor. — *Kula-prakāśa, as,* m. title of a work. — *Kula-prasūta, as, ā, am,* born in a noble family. — *Kula-badhū, ūs,* f. a noble, virtuous, or respectable woman; [cf. *kula-yoshit.*] — *Kula-bālikā,* f. = *kula-pālikā* above. — *Kula-bhāryā,* f. a virtuous, noble, or high-bred wife. — *Kula-bhūbhṛit, t,* m. a principal mountain, one of the seven mountains in Bhārata. — *Kula-bhūshaṇa, as, ā, am,* 'family-adorning,' a family ornament. — *Kula-bhṛityā,* f. the nursing of a pregnant woman; a midwife, a nurse?; [cf. *kumāra-bhṛityā.*] — *Kula-bheda-kara, as,* m. one who causes discord in a family. — *Kula-bhrashṭa, as, ā, am,* expelled from a family. — *Kula-maryādā,* f. family honour or respectability. — *Kula-mārga, as,* m. the best or principal way, the way of honesty. — *Kula-mitra, am,* n. a friend of the family. — *Kulam-puna, as, ā, am,* purifying a family; *(am),* n., N. of a Tīrtha; *(ā),* f., N. of a river. — *Kulam-bhara, as, ā, am,* carrying or upholding a family; *(as),* m. a wrong form for *kujambhala,* a thief. — *Kula-yoshit, t,* f. a woman of noble family; a virtuous high-born woman. — *Kula-rakshaka, as, ā, am,* preserving a family. — *Kula-ratna-mālikā,* f. title of a work. — *Kula-vat, ān, atī, at,* belonging to a noble family. — *Kula-vadhū, ūs,* f. a virtuous wife, a respectable woman, one of good family. — *Kulavadhū-tā,* f. virtue in a wife. — *Kula-varṇā,* f. a species of the plant Convolvulus with red blossoms, = *rakta-trivṛit.* — *Kula-vardhana* or *kula-vardhaka, as, ā, am,* increasing or advancing or propagating a family. — *Kula-vāra, as,* m. a principal day, i. e. Tuesday and Friday. — *Kula-vidyā,* f. knowledge handed down in a family. — *Kula-vipra, as,* m. a family priest. — *Kula-vṛiddha, as,* m. the oldest member or head of a family. — *Kula-vṛiddhi, is,* f. family advancement. — *Kula-vyāpin, ī, inī, i,* attaching or applicable to tribe or caste. — *Kula-vrata, am,* n. a family vow. — *Kula-śīla, as, am,* m. n. character or conduct honourable to a family. — *Kula-śīla-samanvita, as, ā, am,* endowed with a noble character or disposition. — *Kula-śekhara, as,* m., N. of the author of Mukunda-mālā. — *Kula-śreshṭhin, ī, inī, i,* well-born; of good family, eminent in a family; *(ī),* m. the chief of a guild; an artificer or artisan of eminent birth. — *Kula-saṅkhyā,* f. ranking or being reckoned as a family, family respectability. — *Kula-sattra, am,* n. a family sacrifice. — *Kula-santati, is,* f. propagation of a family, posterity, descendants. — *Kula-sannidhi, is,* m. the presence of a number of persons or of witnesses, kindred, relations. — *Kula-samudbhava, as, ā, am,* born in a noble family. — *Kula-sambhava, as, ā, am,* sprung from a noble family; (in compounds) sprung from a family. — *Kula-sāra-tantra, am,* n., N. of a Tantra. — *Kula-sundarī,* f., N. of a deity. — *Kula-sevaka, as,* m. an excellent attendant or servant. — *Kula-saurabha, am,* n., N. of a plant, = *maruvaka.* — *Kula-strī,* f. a woman of good family, a respectable woman, a chaste or virtuous wife. — *Kula-sthiti, is,* f. antiquity or prosperity of a family. — *Kulākula* (°*la-ak*°), *as, ā, am,* excellent and not excellent, middling; of mixed character, of mixed origin; *(as),* m., N. of a Dānava. — *Kulākula-tithi, is,* m. f. the second, sixth, and tenth lunar days of a half-month. — *Kulākula-nakshatra, am,* n., N. of the lunar mansions Ārdrā, Mūlā, Abhijit, and Śatabhishā; an asterism of mixed character. — *Kulākula-vāra, as,* m. Wednesday. — *Kulāṅganā* (°*la-an*°), f. a woman of good family, a respectable or chaste woman. — *Kulāṅgāra* (°*la-an*°), *as,* m. 'a family firebrand,' metaphorically a man who foments domestic dissensions or ruins his family. — *Kulāćala* (°*la-ać*°), *as,* m. a principal mountain, one of a class of seven principal mountains which are supposed to exist in each Varsha or division of a continent; those of Bhārata-varsha or India are Mahendra, Malaya, Sahya, Śuktimat, Ṛiksha, Vindhya, and Pāripātra or Pāriyātra; N. of a Dānava. — *Kulāćāra* (°*la-āć*°), *as,* m. the peculiar or proper duty of a family or caste. — *Kulāćārya* (°*la-āć*°), *as,* m. a family teacher, a family priest; a person well versed in the pedigrees and customs of different families and employed to contract marriages between them; a genealogist. — *Kulādri* (°*la-ad*°), *is,* m. a principal mountain; one of seven principal mountains; see *kulāćala* above. — *Kulādhāraka* (°*la-ādh*°), *as,* m. a son; [cf. *kula-dhāraka.*] — *Kulānvita* (°*la-an*°), *as, ā, am,* sprung from a noble family. — *Kulābhimāna* (°*la-abh*°), *am,* n. pride of birth, family pride. — *Kulābhimānin, ī, inī, i,* proud of birth or of family descent. — *Kulāmṛita* (°*la-am*°), *am,* n. title of a work. — *Kulārṇava* (°*la-ar*°), *as,* m. title of a work. — *Kulārṇava-tantra, am,* n., N. of a Tantra. — *Kulālambin* (°*la-āl*°), *ī, inī, i,* supporting or maintaining a family. — *Kule-ćara, as* or *am* (?), m. or n. (?), a kind of plant. — *Kuleśvara* (°*la-īś*°), *as,* m. the chief of a family or race; the lord κατ' ἐξοχήν, an epithet of Śiva; *(ī),* f. an epithet of Durgā. — *Kulotkaṭa* (°*la-ut*°), *as, ā, am,* excellent by birth, high-born; *(as),* m. a horse of good breed. — *Kulotkarsha* (°*la-ut*°), *as,* m. family eminence. — *Kulotpanna* (°*la-ut*°), *as, ā, am,* sprung from a good family, well-born; belonging to a family (as property &c.). — *Kulodgata* (°*la-ud*°), *as, ā, am,* sprung from a noble family. — *Kulodbhava, as, ā, am,* or *kulodbhūta* (°*la-ud*°), *as, ā, am,* well-born, of good family; born or produced in a family. — *Kulodvaha* (°*la-ud*°), *as,* m. a chief, a leader, the head of a family. — *Kulopadeśa* (°*la-up*°), *as,* m. family name.

Kulaka, as, ā, am, relating to a tribe or family, of good family, of eminent birth; *(as),* m. the chief of a guild; any artisan of eminent birth; an ant-hill, a mole-hill; a green snake (*harita-sarpa*); N. of several plants, a kind of ebony, Diospyros Tomentosa; another species of ebony, commonly called Ku-pīlu; another plant, = *maruvaka, śuklapushpa, tilaka; (am),* n. a multitude; a sort of gourd, Trichosanthes Dioeca; a number of stanzas in grammatical connection, several verses in which the government of noun and verb is carried throughout, contrary to the practice of closing the sense with each verse; a kind of prose composition with few compound words.

Kulāyana, as, m., N. of a man.

Kulika, as, ā, am, of a good family, well-born; *(as),* m. a kinsman; the chief or head man of a tribe or caste; an artist or artificer of high birth; a thorny plant, Ruellia Longifolia or Asteracantha (Ruellia) Longifolia; one of the eight chiefs of the Nāgas or serpent-race, described as having a half-moon on the top of his head and being of a dusky-brown colour. — *Kulika-velā,* f. certain portions of each day on which it is improper to begin any good business.

Kulin, ī, inī, i, belonging to a noble family.

Kulīna, as, ā, am (at the end of compounds), belonging to a family; of high or eminent descent, of a good family, well-born; (*as*), m. a horse of good breed; a Brāhman of the highest class in Bengal, i. e. a member of one of the eight principal families of the Vārendra division or of one of the six chief families of the Rāḍha or Rāṛh division as classified by Balāl Sen, Rāja of Bengal, in the twelfth century, (common names of the latter families are Mukharji, Banarji, Chatoji, &c.); a worshipper of Śakti according to the left-hand ritual; (*ā*), f. a variety of the Āryā metre; (*am*), n. a disease of the nails. — *Kulīna-tā*, f. or *kulīna-tva, am*, n. birth, rank, family respectability.

Kulīnaka, as, ā, am, of good family; (*as*), m. a kind of wild kidney-bean.

Kuleya, as, ā, am (at the end of compounds) = *kulīna*.

1. *kulya, as, ā, am*, of or relating to a family or race; belonging to a congregation or corporation; of good family, well-born, well-descended; (*as*), m. a respectable man; (*ā*), f. a virtuous or decent woman; custom or habit of a family?; (*am*), n. friendly inquiry after family affairs or domestic accidents, condolence, congratulation, &c. (For 2. 3. see col. 3.)

कुलक्क **kulakka**, *as*, m. a cymbal; beating time in music.

कुलङ्गी **kulangī**, f. a thorny plant; (a wrong form for *kulingī*.)

कुलञ्ज **kulañja** or **kulañjana**, *as*, m. the plant Alpinia Galanga, = *gandha-mūla*.

कुलट **kulaṭa**, *as*, m. (fr. *kula* and rt. *aṭ*?), any son except one's own offspring, an adopted son, a bought son, &c.; (*ā*), f. an unchaste woman. — *Kulaṭā-pati, is*, m. the husband of an unchaste woman, a cuckold.

कुलटी **kulaṭī**, f. red arsenic, = *kunaṭī*.

कुलति **kulati**, *ayas*, m. pl., N. of a people.

कुलत्थ **kulattha**, *as*, m. (fr. *kula*? cf. *aśvattha* and *kapittha*), a kind of pulse, Dolichos Uniflorus; (*ās*), m. pl., N. of a people; (*ā*), f. a kind of Dolichos; a blue stone used in medicine and applied as a collyrium to the eyes, also as an astringent to sores &c.; a species of metre.

Kulatthikā, f. a blue stone used as a collyrium &c.; a sort of vetch, considered as a wild sort of the Dolichos Uniflorus.

कुलभ **kulabha**, *as*, m., N. of a Daitya; (another reading has *sulabha*.)

कुलहण्डक **kulahaṇḍaka**, *as*, m. an eddy, = *kūlahaṇḍaka*.

कुलाक्षुता **kulākshutā**, f. a bitch.

कुलाट **kulāṭa**, *as*, m. a kind of small fish.

कुलाद्य **kulādya**, *as*, m. (?), N. of a country or people.

कुलाभि **kulābhi**, *is*, m. a treasure.

कुलाय **kulāya**, *as, am*, m. n. (fr. *kula*?), a woven texture, a web; the nest of a bird; a case or investing integument, a receptacle; the body as the dwelling-place of the soul; the kennel or resting-place of a dog &c.; a place, a spot in general. — *Kulāya-nilāya, as*, m. the act of sitting in a nest, hatching, brooding. — *Kulāyanilāyi-tā*, f. the act or state of hatching, &c. — *Kulāya-nilāyin, ī, inī, i*, sitting in a nest, brooding, hatching. — *Kulāya-stha, as*, m. 'nest-dweller,' a bird.

Kulāyayat, an, antī, at (fr. nom. *kulāyaya*), Ved. building nests or a resting-place, hiding one's self in a nest.

Kulāyikā, f. a bird-cage, an aviary.

Kulāyin, ī, inī, i, Ved. forming a nest, shaped like a nest, homely; (*inī*), f., N. of a liturgical service.

कुलाल **kulāla**, *as*, m. (said to be fr. rt. *kul*), a potter; a wild cock, Phasianus Gallus; an owl; (*ī*), f. the wife of a potter; N. of a plant; a species of blue stone applied as a collyrium to the eyes (*kulatthikā*). — *Kulāla-vat*, ind. like a potter.

कुलालिका **kulālikā**, f. an aviary; (a wrong form for *kulāyikā*.)

कुलाह **kulāha**, *as*, m. a horse of a light-brown colour with black knees.

कुलाहक **kulāhaka**, *as*, m. a lizard, a chameleon; N. of a plant, commonly Rāṅgā Kulekhāḍā.

कुलाहल **kulāhala**, *as*, m., N. of a plant, = *alambusha, goććhāla, bhūkadamba*, commonly Kokaśimā, Coryza Terebinthina or Celsia Coromandelina, (a plant which dogs are fond of smelling before they eject urine.)

कुलि **kuli**, *is*, m. the hand; (*is*), f., N. of a plant, = *kaṇṭakārī*, a prickly nightshade.

कुलिङ्ग **ku-liṅga**, *as*, m. (see 1. *ku*), a kind of mouse; a species of bird, the fork-tailed shrike; N. of a man; (*ā*), f., N. of a town; (*ī*), f., N. of a plant [cf. *karkaṭa-śṛiṅgī*]; the female of the fork-tailed shrike. — *Kuliṅgākshī* (°*ga-ak*°), f., N. of a plant, = *peṭikā, kuverākshī*.

Kuliṅgaka, as, m. a sparrow.

कुलिज **kulija**, *as* or *am* (?), m. or n. (?), a sort of measure (occurring at the end of compounds in the forms *kulija, as, ī, am; kulijika, as, ī, am; kulijīna, as, ā, am*).

कुलिन्द **kulinda**, *ās*, m. pl., N. of a people; (*as*), m. sing. the prince of this people.

कुलिर **kulira**, *as*, m. a crab; also *kulīra*, q. v.

कुलिश **kuliśa**, *as, am*, m. n. (fr. 1. *ku* and *liśa*, = *riśa* fr. *riś*), Ved. an axe, a hatchet; the thunderbolt of Indra; a sort of fish; the plant Heliotropium Indicum; (*ī*), f., Ved., N. of a river supposed to be in the middle region of the sky. — *Kuliśa-nāyaka, as*, m. a kind of coitus. — *Kuliśa-bhṛit, t*, m. a N. of Indra, the bearer of the thunderbolt. — *Kuliśāṅkuśā* (°*śa-aṅ*°), f., N. of one of the sixteen Vidyā-devīs.

कुलिशासन **kuli-śāsana**, *as*, m. (fr. *kulin* and *śāsana*? or fr. *kuli* and *śāsana*, 'one who commands with his hand?'), an epithet of Śākya-muni.

कुली **kulī**, f. a wife's elder sister; the plant Solanum Jacquini or Solanum Longum (*vṛi-hatī*).

कुलीका **kulīkā**, f., Ved. a kind of bird.

कुलीनस **kulīnasa**, *am*, n. water.

कुलीपय **kulīpaya**, *as*, m., Ved. an aquatic animal.

कुलीर **kulīra**, *as, am*, m. n. (said to be fr. 1. *kṛī*), a crab; the sign of the zodiac Cancer; [cf. *kulira*.] — *Kulīra-śṛiṅgī*, f., N. of a plant; [cf. *karkaṭa-śṛiṅgī*.] — *Kulīrād* (°*ra-ad*), *t*, m. a young crab (destroying its parents; the old crab being supposed to perish on producing young).

Kulīraka, as, m. a small crab.

कुलीश **kulīśa**, *as, am*, m. n. Indra's thunderbolt; [cf. *kuliśa*.]

कुलुक **kuluka**, *am*, n. the fur or foulness of the tongue.

कुलुक्कगुञ्जा **kulukka-guñjā**, f. a firebrand; (for *ulkā-guñjā*?).

कुलुङ्ग **kuluṅga**, *as*, m., Ved. an antelope.

कुलुञ्च **ku-luñća**, *as*, m. (see 1. *ku*), Ved. one who plucks out hairs.

कुलूत **kulūta**, *ās*, m. pl., N. of a people.

कुल्फ **kulpha**, *as*, m. (said to be fr. 3. *kal*), Ved. the ancle; (*as, am*), m. n. a disease.

कुल्मल **kulmala**, *am*, n. (said to be fr. rt. *kush*), Ved. the part of an arrow or spear by which the head is attached to the shaft; sin. — *Kulmala-barhisha, as*, m., N. of a Vedic poet.

कुल्माष **kulmāsha**, *as* or *am*, m. or n. sour gruel prepared by the spontaneous fermentation of the juice of fruits or of boiled rice; (*am*), n. half-ripe barley; forced rice; a sort of Phaseolus, see *rāja-māsha*; a species of Dolichos, D. Biflorus, see *yāvaka*; (*as*), m. a kind of disease; (*ī*), f., N. of a river. — *Kulmāshābhishuta* (°*sha-abh*°), *am*, n. sour gruel.

Kulmāsa = *kulmāsha*.

कुल्य 2. **kulya**, *am*, n. (for 1. *kulya* see col. 1), a bone; flesh; a winnowing basket; a measure of eight Droṇas.

कुल्या 1. **kulyā**, f., Ved. a small river; a river in general; a canal, a channel for irrigation; a ditch, a dyke or trench; N. of a river.

3. *kulya, as, ā, am*, Ved. belonging to a river.

Kulyāya, nom. A. *kulyāyate, -yitum*, to become a river.

कुल्या 2. **kulyā**, f., N. of a drug or medicinal plant, Celtis Orientalis (*jīvantikaushadhi*); another plant, Solanum Longum (*sthūlāvārtāka*).

कुल्लूक **kullūka** or **kullūka-bhaṭṭa**, *as*, m., N. of a celebrated scholiast on Manu.

कुल्व **kulva**, *as, ā, am*, Ved. bald, bare [Lat. *calvus*] in *ati-kulva*, too bald.

कुल्वक **kulvaka**, *am*, n. fur upon the tongue; [cf. *kuvuka*.]

कुव **kuva**, *am*, n. a water-lily, a lotus; [cf. *kuvala, kuvalaya, kuvela*.]

कुवकालुका **kuvakālukā**, f., N. of a vegetable (*gholi-śāka*).

कुवङ्ग **ku-vaṅga**, *am*, n. (see 1. *ku*), lead.

कुवच **ku-vaća**, *as, ā, am* (see 1. *ku*), abusive, censorius, scurrilous, using bad language.

कुवज्रक **ku-vajraka**, *am*, n. (see 1. *ku*), crystal, a stone resembling a diamond.

कुवद **ku-vada**, *as, ā, am* (see 1. *ku*), censorious; [cf. *ku-vaća*.]

कुवम **kuvama**, *as*, m. a N. of Kaśyapa (?).

कुवर **kuvara**, *as, ā, am*, astringent in flavour; [cf. *tuvara*.]

कुवर्ष **ku-varsha**, *as*, m. (see 1. *ku*), a shower of rain, a sudden and violent shower.

कुवल **kuvala** or **kubala**, *as, ī*, m. f. the jujube tree, Zizyphus Jujuba; (*am*), n. the fruit of this tree; the water-lily; a pearl; (*ā*), f., N. of a pearl. — *Kuvala-kuṇa, as*, m. the time when the tree Zizyphus Jujuba bears fruits. — *Kuvala-prastha, as*, m., N. of a town. — *Kuvalāśva* or *kubalāśva* (°*la-aś*°), *as*, m., N. of a prince with the epithet Dhundhumāra. — *Kuvale-śaya, as*, m. an epithet of Vishṇu ('resting on a water-lily').

कुवलय **kuvalaya**, *am*, n. any water-lily; the blue water-lily; (*as, am*), m. n. the earth; (*as*), m., N. of the horse of Kuvalayāśva. — *Kuvalaya-pura, am*, n., N. of a town. — *Kuvalayāditya* (°*ya-ād*°), *as*, m., N. of a prince, = *kuvalayāpīḍa*. — *Kuvalayānanda* (°*ya-ān*°), *as*, m. title of a work on rhetoric by Apyadikshita. — *Kuvalayāpīḍa* (°*ya-āp*°), *as*, m., N. of a Daitya, who, changed to an elephant, became the vehicle of Kaṇsa; N. of a prince; [cf. *kuvalayāditya*.] — *Kuvalayāvalī* (°*ya-av*°), f., N. of a princess. — *Kuvalayāśva* (°*ya-aś*°), *as*, m., N. of a prince with the epitbet Dhundhumāra; an epithet of the prince Pratardana. — *Kuvalayāśvaka*, *as*, m., N. of a prince with the epithet Dhundhumāra. — *Kuvalayāśva-ćarita*, *am*, n. 'the adventures of Kuvalayāśva,' title of a Prākrit poem composed by Viśvanātha Kavirāja. — *Kuvalayāśvīya*, *am*, n. the story of Kuvalayāśva. — *Kuvalayeśa* (°*ya-īśa*), *as*, m. a ruler of the earth, a king. — *Kuvalayeśa-tā*, f. kingdom.

Kuvalayita, *as*, *ā*, *am*, decorated with water-lilies.

Kuvalayinī, f. an assemblage of water-lilies, a place abounding with them.

कुवाक्य *ku-vākya*, *am*, n. or *ku-vāć*, *k*, f. (see 1. *ku*), injurious or censorious language, speaking ill of any one.

कुवाट *kuvāṭa*, *as*, m. the fold of a door, = *karāṭa* and *kapāṭa*.

कुवाद *ku-vāda*, *as*, *ā*, *am* (see 1. *ku*), detracting, censorious, one who speaks ill of others.

कुवाहुल *kuvāhula*, *as*, m. a camel.

कुविक *kuvika*, *ās*, m. pl., N. of a people.

कुविद् *kuvid*, ind. (fr. 1. *ku* and *id*), Ved. a particle of interrogation, 'if, whether;' or used in direct questions; (a verb following this particle does not lose its accent.) — *Kuvit-sa*, *as*, m., Ved. any one, an unknown person; (Sāy.) N. of a man ('much destroying').

कुविन्द *kuvinda* or *kuvindaka*, *as*, m. a weaver, = *kupinda*.

कुविवाह *ku-vivāha*, *as*, m. (see 1. *ku*), a degrading or improper marriage.

कुवीणा *ku-vīṇā*, f. (see 1. *ku*), the lute of the Caṇḍālas.

कुवीर *kuvīra*, *as*, m. or *ā*, f. (?), N. of a river.

कुवृत्तिकृत् *kuvṛitti-kṛit*, m. the plant Cæsalpinia Bonducella (= *pūtika*).

कुवेणा *ku-veṇā*, f. (see 1. *ku*), N. of a river; a fish-basket; (various reading for the following.)

Ku-veṇī, f. a fish-basket; a badly braided tress of hair; a woman with her hair badly braided.

कुवेर *kuvera*, &c. See under *kubera*.

कुवेल *kuvela*, *am*, n. a water-lily, = *kuvalaya*, q. v.

कुवैद्य *ku-vaidya*, *as*, m. (see 1. *ku*), a bad physician.

कुव्र *kuvra*, *am*, n. a forest, a wood.

कुश् *kuś*, cl. 4. P. *kuśyati*, to embrace, enfold; (a various reading for *kus*, q. v.)

कुश *kuśa*, *as*, m. (used in Sūtra works, but the word *darbha* is more common in the Brāhmaṇas), grass, especially the sacred grass used at certain religious ceremonies (i. e. Poa Cynosuroides, a grass with long stalks and numerous pointed leaves); a rope made of Kuśa grass used for connecting the yoke of a plough with the pole; N. of a son of Vasu Uparićara; of a son of Balākāśva, grandson of Balāka, father of Kuśāmba and Kuśanābha; of a son of Suhotra [cf. *kāśa*]; of a son of Vidarbha; of a son of Rāma; of a son of Lava, king of Kaśmīra; one of the great Dvīpas or divisions of the universe, surrounded by the sea of liquified butter; (*ā*), f. a plank for covering anything; a piece of wood; a horse's bridle; N. of a plant, commonly called Madhukarkaṭikā; (*ī*), f. a sort of boat or ladle used in making libations; wrought iron; a ploughshare; a pod of cotton; (*am*), n. water; (*as*, *ā*, *am*), wicked, depraved; mad, inebriate. — *Kuśa-ćīra*, *am*, n. a garment made of Kuśa grass; (*as*, *ā*, *am*), covered with a garment made of Kuśa grass; (*ā*), f., N. of a river. — *Kuśa-dvīpa*, *as*, m., N. of one of the seven large Dvīpas or divisions of the universe. — *Kuśa-dhārā*, f., N. of a river. — *Kuśa-dhvaja*, *as*, m., N. of a prince, a son of Hrasva-roman; also a grandson of the latter; N. of a grandson of Vṛishadhvaja. — *Kuśa-nagara*, *am*, n., N. of the town in which Śākya-muni died. — *Kuśa-nābha*, *as*, m., N. of a son of Kuśa. — *Kuśa-netra*, *as*, m., N. of a Daitya. — *Kuśa-pushpa*, *am*, n., N. of a plant (= *granthi-parṇa*), a perfume so called. — *Kuśa-plavana*, *am*, n., N. of a Tīrtha. — *Kuśa-mushṭi*, *is*, *is*, *i*, having the hand full of sacrificial grass. — *Kuśa-lava*, *au*, m. du. the two sons of Rāma, called Kuśa and Lava. — *Kuśa-vat*, *ān*, *atī*, *at*, covered with Kuśa grass; (*tī*), f., N. of a town. — *Kuśa-vāri*, n. water in which Kuśa grass has been soaked. — *Kuśa-vindu*, *avas*, m. pl., N. of a people. — *Kuśa-vīrā*, f., N. of a river; (a various reading for *kuśa-ćīrā*.) — *Kuśa-stamba*, *as*, m. a heap of Kuśa grass; N. of a Tīrtha; N. of a prince. — *Kuśa-stava*, *as*, m. a bundle of Kuśa grass. — *Kuśa-sthala*, *am*, n. an epithet of the town Kānyakubja; (*ī*), f. an epithet of the town Dvārakā. — *Kuśa-hasta*, *as*, *ā*, *am*, having Kuśa grass in the hand or in the paw (as applied to the tiger in the Hitopadeśa). — *Kuśākara* (°*śa-āk*°), *as*, m. fire (the sacrificial fire being made upon a tuft of the Kuśa grass). — *Kuśāksha* (°*śa-ak*°), *as*, m. a monkey, an ape. — *Kuśāgra* (°*śa-ag*°), *am*, n. the sharp point of a blade of the Kuśa grass; (*as*), m., N. of a prince, the son of Bṛihadratha; (*as*, *ā*, *am*), sharp, shrewd, intelligent. — *Kuśāgra-buddhi*, *is*, *is*, *i*, sharp as the point of Kuśa grass, shrewd, intelligent; (*is*), f. shrewdness, subtlety; also similar compounds, as *kuśāgra-dhī*, &c. — *Kuśāgrīya*, *as*, *ā*, *am*, sharp as the point of Kuśa grass, subtile, penetrating. — *Kuśāgrīya-mati*, *is*, *is*, *i*, of subtile intellect, subtile, sharp-sighted, intelligent, possessing mental acumen; also other similar compounds, as *kuśāgrīya-dhī*, *kuśāgrīya-buddhi*, &c. — *Kuśāṅkura* (°*śa-aṅ*°), *as*, m. a blade of sacrificial grass. — *Kuśāṅgurīya* or *kuśāṅgurīyaka* (°*śa-aṅ*°), *am*, n. a ring of Kuśa grass worn at religious ceremonies. — *Kuśāraṇi* (°*śa-ar*°), *is*, m. 'one who may be irritated by a Kuśa blade,' epithet of the sage Durvāsas, famous for his irascibility. — *Kuśā-vatī*, f., N. of a town, the residence of Kuśa, son of Rāma. — *Kuśāvarta* (°*śa-āv*°), *as*, m., N. of a Tīrtha, or passage of the Ganges, personified as a son of Ṛishabha. — *Kuśāśva* (°*śa-aś*°), *as*, m., N. of a prince. — *Kuśāsana* (°*śa-ās*°), *am*, n. a small mat of sacrificial grass on which a Brāhman sits when performing his devotion. — *Kuśe-śaya*, *as*, *ā*, *am*, lying in grass or in water; (*as*), m. a kind of tree, = *karṇikāra*; the Indian crane; N. of a mountain in Kuśa-dvīpa; (*am*), n. 'lying in water,' a water-lily, a lotus. — *Kuśeśaya-kara*, *as*, m. the sun. — *Kuśottara* (°*śa-ut*°), *as*, *ā*, *am*, covered with sacrificial grass. — *Kuśodaka* (°*śa-ud*°), *am*, n. water in which Kuśa grass has been infused; (*ā*), f., N. of a deity.

Kuśaya or *kuśapa*, *as*, m. a drinking-vessel, a cup, a goblet, a cistern.

Kuśita, *as*, *ā*, *am*, mixed or combined with water; [cf. *kushita*.]

Kuśin, *ī*, *inī*, *i*, furnished with Kuśa grass; (*ī*), m. an epithet of Vālmīki (so called with reference to Kuśa, the son of Rāma). — *Kuśi-grāmaka*, *as*, m., N. of a village of the Mallas. — *Kuśi-nagara*, *am* or *ī*, n. or f., N. of the capital of the Mallas.

कुशज *kuśaja*, *ās*, m. pl., N. of a people; (a various reading for *kuśala*.)

कुशण्ड *kuśaṇḍa*, *ās*, m. pl., N. of a people.

कुशनामन् *kuśanāman*, *ā*, m. a camel; (probably a wrong form for *śiśu-nāman*.)

कुशनार *kuśanāra*, a various reading for *kuśa-dhārā*.

कुशय *kuśaya* or *kuśapa*. See last col.

कुशर *ku-śara*, *as*, m. (see 1. *ku*), Ved. a kind of reed.

कुशरीर *ku-śarīra*, *am*, n. (see 1. *ku*), a bad body; (*as*), m., N. of a Muni.

कुशल *kuśala*, *as*, *ā*, *am* (connected with *kuśa*?), right, proper, suitable, good (e. g. *kuśalam man*, to consider good, to approve), well, healthy, in good condition; happy, prosperous; fit for, competent, able, skilful, expert, clever, conversant with anything (with loc., gen., inf., and in compounds, e. g. *udgīthe* or *udgīthasya kuśalaḥ*, clever in song; *kuśalo vyākhyātum*, competent to explain; *aśva-kuśala*, skilled in horses); (*ās*), m. pl., N. of a people, the inhabitants of Kuśa-dvīpa; (*as*), m. an epithet of Śiva; N. of a prince; also of a grammarian, author of the Pañjikāpradīpa; (*ā*), f., N. of a woman; (*ī*), f. a plant, = *aśmantaka*; another plant, = *kshudrāmlikā*; (*am*), n. welfare, well-being; a good or happy or prosperous condition, happiness; virtue, virtuous action; cleverness, competence, ability; fitness; due order; *kuśalam praćh*, to ask after another's welfare, to say 'how do you do?' *kuśalaṃ te*, hail to thee! (used as a salutation, especially in greeting a Brāhman); *kuśalam* or *kuśalena*, ind. well, in a proper manner, properly, rightly; happily, cheerfully. — *Kuśala-kāma*, *as*, *ā*, *am*, desirous of happiness; (*as*), m. desire for happiness. — *Kuśala-tā*, f. or *kuśala-tva*, *am*, n. cleverness, ability, conversancy, experience; skilfulness, well-being. — *Kuśala-praśna*, *as*, m. friendly enquiry after a person's health or welfare; salutation, greeting, saying 'how do you do?' — *Kuśala-buddhi*, *is*, *is*, *i*, wise, able, intelligent. — *Kuśala-sāgara*, *as*, m., N. of a scribe, pupil of Lāvaṇyaratna.

Kuśalin, *ī*, *inī*, *i*, healthy, well, happy, prosperous; auspicious, favourable, good; virtuous; clever.

Kuśalī-kṛi, cl. 8. P. *-karoti*, *-kartum*, to make right or proper, to arrange in due order.

कुशाढ्य *kuśāḍhya* or *kuśāḍhya* (?), *ās*, m. pl., N. of a people; (a various reading for *kulāḍya*; cf. also *kuśāṇḍa*.)

कुशाम्ब *kuśāmba*, *as*, m., N. of a son of Vasu Uparićara; N. of a son of Kuśa, who was the founder of the town Kauśāmbī.

Kuśāmbu, *us*, m., N. of a son of Kuśa, the founder of Kauśāmbī.

कुशाल्मलि *ku-śālmali*, *is*, m. (see 1. *ku*), the plant Andersonia Rohitaka.

कुशिंशपा *ku-śiṅśapā*, f. a kind of Sisu tree, Dalbergia Sisu, = *kapila-śiṅśapā*.

कुशिक *kuśika*, *as*, *ā*, *am*, squint-eyed; (*as*), m., N. of the father of Viśvā-mitra; N. of the father of Gāthin or Gādhi or Gādhin, the latter being sometimes identified with Indra, who is called Kauśika or Kuśikottama; (according to the Mahā-bhārata and Rāmāyaṇa, Viśvā-mitra is son of Gādhi and grandson of Kuśika); (*ās*), m. pl. the descendants of Kuśika; N. of a people; (*as*), m. a ploughshare (in this sense more properly n.); the sediment of oil; the plant Shorea Robusta; also Terminalia Bellerica (*vibhītaka*); also Vatica Robusta (*aśva-karṇa*). — *Kuśikan-dhara*, *as*, m., N. of a Muni.

कुशित *kuśita*, &c. See under *kuśa*.

कुशिम्बि *ku-śimbi*, *is*, m. or f. (?), (see 1. *ku*), N. of a plant; [cf. *śimba*, *śimbi*, and *kusimbi*.]

कुशीद *kuśīda*, *am*, n. the profession of usury; red saunders; [cf. *kusīda*.]

कुशील *ku-śīla, as, ā, am* (see 1. *ku*), ill-behaved, rude, wicked; evil-disposed; ill-tempered. — *Kuśīla-tā*, f. or *kuśīla-tva, am*, n. misbehaviour, misconduct; bad disposition; ill-temper.

कुशीलव *kuśīlava, as*, m. (connected with *ku-śīla?*), a bard, herald; an actor, dancer, mime; a newsmonger; an epithet of Vālmīki; (*au*), m. du. the two sons of Rāma, Kuśa and Lava, who recited the Rāmāyaṇa, (probably these names were originally formed from the word Kuśīlava); [cf. *kuśa-lava*.]

कुशीवश *kuśīvaśa, as*, m. an epithet of Vālmīki; [cf. *kuśin* and *kuśīlava*.]

कुशुम्भ *kuśumbha, as*, m. a jar; the water-pot of an ascetic; [cf. *kusumbha*.]

कुशूल *kuśūla, as*, m. (fr. 1. *ku* and *śūla?*), a granary, a cupboard, a store-room, a place in which rice or other grain is kept; a conflagration of chaff. — *Kuśūla-dhānya, am*, n. grain stored for three years' consumption. — *Kuśūla-dhānyaka, as*, m. a householder &c. who has three years' grain in store. — *Kuśūla-pūraṇāḍhaka* (°*ṇa-āḍh*°), *as, ā, am*, being (like to mere empty) measures filling a granary.

कुशेशय *kuśe-śaya*, &c. See under *kuśa*.

कुश्रि *kuśri, is*, m., N. of a teacher.

कुश्रुत *ku-śruta, as, ā, am* (see 1. *ku*), indistinctly heard.

कुश्वभ्र *ku-śvabhra, am*, n. (see 1. *ku*), a small hole.

कुष् *kush*, cl. 9. P. *kushṇāti, ćukosha, koshishyati, akoshīt, koshitum*, to tear, tear asunder, to force or draw out, to extract, to expel; to test, assay, examine; to shine: Pass. *kushyati* and *kushyate*: Caus. *koshayati*: Desid. *ćukoshishati* and *ćukushishati*: Intens. *ćokushyate, ćokoshṭi*.

कुषण्ड *ku-shaṇḍa, as*, m. (see 1. *ku*), N. of a priest.

कुषल *kushala, as, ā, am*, clever, expert, &c.; (a wrong reading for *kuśala*.)

कुषवा *kushavā*, f., Ved., N. of a Rākshasī.

कुषाकु *kushāku, us, us, u* (fr. rt. *kush?*), burning, scorching, inflaming; wicked, detestable; (*us*), m. fire; the sun; a monkey; [cf. *kashāku*.]

कुषारु *kushāru, us*, m., N. of a man.

कुषित् *kushit*, ind. excellently; (for *kuvit?*).

कुषित *kushita, as, ā, am*, mixed with water [cf. *kuśita*]; (*am*), n. happy, well, right, fortunate, auspicious, &c. (?).

कुषीतक *kushītaka, as*, m., Ved. a kind of bird; N. of a man; (*ās*), m. pl. the descendants of this man.

कुषीद *ku-shīda, as, ā, am*, indifferent, apathetic, inert; (*am*), n. usury; (more correctly *ku-sīda*.)

कुषीदिन् *kushīdin, ī*, m., N. of a teacher.

कुषुभ्य *kushubhya*, nom. P. *kushubhyati*, to throw; to abuse; to despise.

कुषुम्भ *kushumbha, as*, m., Ved. the poison-bag of an insect.

कुष्ठ *kushṭha, as* or *am*, m. or n. (fr. 1. *ku* and *stha?*), a sort of medicinal plant (used as a remedy for the disease called *takman*, q. v.), Costus Speciosus or Arabicus; a sort of poison; leprosy, of which eighteen varieties are enumerated, seven severe and eleven of minor importance; (*ā*), f. the mouth or opening of a basket. — *Kushṭha-ketu, us*, m., N. of a plant, = *bhūmyāhulya*. — *Kushṭha-gandhi*, n. the fragrant bark of the plant Feronia Elephantum. — *Kushṭha-ghna, as, ī, am*, curing leprosy; (*as*), m., N. of a medicinal plant, commonly called Hiyāvalī [cf. *hitāvalī*]; (*ī*), f. an esculent root, Solanum Indicum, = *kākamāćī*; the opposite leaved fig tree. — *Kushṭha-ćikitsita, am*, n. the cure of leprosy. — *Kushṭha-nāśana, as*, m., N. of several plants which cure leprosy; the root of Dioscorea; white pepper or mustard; another plant, = *kshīrīśa-vṛiksha*. — *Kushṭha-nāśinī*, f. a plant, commonly Hākuca, Psoralia Corylifolia. — *Kushṭha-maya, as, ī, am*, full of leprosy, leprous. — *Kushṭha-roga, as*, m. leprosy, elephantiasis. — *Kushṭha-sūdana, as*, m. the Cassia tree, Cassia Fistula; [cf. *āragbadha*.] — *Kushṭha-hantṛi, tā*, m. a kind of bulbous plant, = *hasti-kanda*; (*trī*), f. another plant, generally called Vākućī. — *Kushṭha-hṛit, t*, m. the plant Acacia Catechu. — *Kushṭhāṅga* (°*ṭha-aṅ*°), *as, ā, am*, leprous. — *Kushṭhānvita* (°*ṭha-an*°), *as, ā, am*, afflicted with leprosy. — *Kushṭhāri* (°*ṭha-ari*), *is*, m. Acacia Catechu; another plant, Acacia Farnesiana (*viṭkhadira*); another plant, Trichosanthes Diœca, = *paṭola*; another plant, = *āditya-pattra* and *arka-pattra*; sulphur.

Kushṭhita, as, ā, am, or *kushṭhin, ī, inī, i*, leprous, a leper.

कुष्ठल *ku-shṭhala, am*, n. (fr. 1. or 2. *ku* and *sthala*), a bad place or spot; the surface of the earth.

कुष्ठिका *kushṭhikā, ās*, f. pl. (related to *kushṭhā?*), Ved. a part of the foot of a sacrificial animal considered worthless for sacrificial purposes; (Sāy.) the contents of the entrails.

कुष्मल *kushmala, am*, n. (said to be fr. rt. *kush*), cutting, dividing; a leaf.

कुष्माण्ड *kushmāṇḍa, as*, m. a kind of pumpkin-gourd, Benincasa Cerifera; false conception; a state of the womb in gestation (?); a particular religious formula; a class of demons; one of a class of demi-gods attached to Śiva; (*ī*), f. the gourd Benincasa Cerifera, a drug; a religious ceremony, a certain rite, performed as a penance or expiation; an epithet of the wife of Śiva.

Kushmāṇḍaka, as, m. the gourd Benincasa Cerifera; N. of a Nāga; N. of an attendant of Śiva.

कुस् *kus*, cl. 4. P. *kusyati*, to embrace, surround; [cf. *kuś*.]

कुसचिव *ku-saćiva, as*, m. (see 1. *ku*), a bad counsellor.

कुसरित् *ku-sarit, t*, f. (see 1. *ku*), a shallow stream.

कुसलम् *kusalam*, ind. well, happy, &c.; (more correctly *kuśala*, q. v.)

कुसहाय *ku-sahāya, as*, m. (see 1. *ku*), a bad companion.

कुसारथि *ku-sārathi, is*, m. (see 1. *ku*), a bad charioteer.

कुसित *kusita, as*, m. (said to be fr. *kus*), an inhabited country; N. of a country; a money-lender (?), see *kusīda*. — *Kusitāyī*, f. the wife of a money-lender (?); [cf. the following.]

कुसिदायी *kusidāyī*, f. the wife of a Kusida, of a money-lender (?), see *kusīdāyī*; a kind of demon (?).

कुसिन्ध *kusindha, am*, n., Ved. a trunk.

कुसिम्बी *kusimbī*, f. = *śimbī*.

कुसीद *ku-sīda, as, ā, am* (see 1. *ku*), Ved. sitting too long in one spot (?), lazy, slothful, inert; (*am*), n. any loan or thing lent to be repaid with interest; lending money; usury, the profession of usury; (*as, ā*), m. f. a money-lender, a usurer. — *Kusīda-patha, as*, m. usury, usurious interest, any exceeding five per cent. — *Kusīda-vṛiddhi, is*, f. interest on money.

Kusīdāyī, f. the wife of a usurer.

Kusīdika, as, ī, am, one who follows the profession of usury.

Kusīdin, ī, m. a usurer; N. of a descendant of Kaṇva, author of several hymns of the Ṛig-veda.

कुसुम *kusuma, as, am*, m. n. (said to be fr. rt. *kus*), a flower; (*am*), n. fruit; the menstrual discharge; a term for the shorter sections of Deveśvara's Kavi-kalpalatā (the longer chapters being called Stavaka); ophthalmia, disease of the eyes; (*as*), m. a form of fire; N. of the attendant of the sixth Arhat of the present Avasarpiṇī. — *Kusuma-kār-muka* or *kusuma-ćāpa, as*, m. or *kusuma-dhanvan, ā*, m. 'having flowers for his bow,' epithet of Kāma, the god of love. — *Kusuma-ketumaṇḍalin, ī*, m., N. of a Kinnara. — *Kusuma-komala, as, ā, am*, tender as a flower. — *Kusuma-ćita, as, ā, am*, heaped with flowers. — *Kusuma-deva, as*, m., N. of an author. — *Kusuma-naga, as*, m., N. of a mountain. — *Kusuma-pura, am*, n., N. of the town Pāṭaliputra. — *Kusuma-madhya, am*, n., N. of a tree bearing a large acid fruit, commonly Cālitā gāć, Cordia Myxa or Dillenia Indica. — *Kusuma-maya, as, ī, am*, consisting of flowers. — *Kusuma-latā*, f. a creeper in blossom. — *Kusuma-vat, ān, atī, at*, furnished with flowers, flowering, in flower; (*tī*), f. a female during menstruation; N. of the town Pāṭaliputra. — *Kusuma-vāṇa, as*, m. the flower-arrow of the god of love; 'flower-arrowed,' epithet of Kāma, the god of love, as having flowers for arrows. — *Kusuma-vićitrā*, f., N. of a metre consisting of four lines of twelve syllables each. — *Kusuma-śayana, am*, n. a couch of flowers. — *Kusuma-śara, as, ā, am*, 'flower-arrowed,' epithet of the god of love. — *Kusumaśara-tva, am*, n. the state of one who has flowers for arrows. — *Kusuma-śekhara-vijaya, as*, m. title of a play. — *Kusuma-sanātha, as, ā, am*, possessed of flowers, having flowers. — *Kusuma-stavaka, as*, m. a bunch of flowers, a nosegay, bouquet, a garland; N. of a metre. — *Kusumākara* (°*ma-āk*°), *as*, m. a quantity of flowers or place abounding with them, a parterre, a garden, a nosegay; spring, the vernal season. — *Kusumāñjana* (°*ma-añ*°), *am*, n. the calx of brass, used as a collyrium. — *Kusumāñjali* (°*ma-añ*°), *is*, f. 'handful of flowers,' the title of a philosophical work written to prove the existence of a Supreme being, by Udayana Āćārya, consisting of seventy-two Kārikās divided into five chapters. — *Kusumāñjali-makaranda, as*, m. title of a commentary by Rućidatta on the preceding work. — *Kusumātmaka* (°*ma-āt*°), *am*, n. saffron. — *Kusumādhipa* (°*ma-adh*°), *as*, m. 'the prince of flowers,' the champa, a tree which bears a yellow fragrant flower, Michelia Champaka. — *Kusumādhirāj* (°*ma-adh*°), *ṭ*, m. the same plant. — *Kusumāyudha* (°*ma-āy*°), *as*, m. 'flower-armed,' an epithet of Kāma, the god of love, his arrows being tipped with flowers. — *Kusumāvaćāya* (°*ma-av*°), *as*, m. gathering flowers. — *Kusumāvataṃsaka* (°*ma-av*°), *am*, n. a chaplet, a crown of flowers. — *Kusumāvalī* (°*ma-av*°), f. title of a medicinal work. — *Kusumāsava* (°*ma-ās*°), *am*, n. honey. — *Kusumāstra* (°*ma-as*°), *as*, m. 'flower-arrowed,' epithet of the god of love. — *Kusumeshu* (°*ma-ishu*), *us*, m. = *kusumāstra* above; (*u*), n. the bow of Kāma. — *Kusumojjvala* (°*ma-uj*°), *as, ā, am*, brilliant with blossoms.

Kusumaya, nom. P. *kusumayati, -yitum*, to produce flowers, cause to flower.

Kusumita, as, ā, am, furnished with flowers, flowered, budded, in flower. — *Kusumita-latā*, f. or *kusumitalatā-vellitā*, f., N. of a metre consisting of four lines of eighteen syllables each.

Kusumya, nom. P. *kusumyati*, to begin to flower.

कुसुमाल *kusumāla, as*, m. a thief (fr. *kusuma* + *āla*, 'living among flowers?').

कुसुम्भ *kusumbha, as, am*, m. n. (said to be

fr. rt. *kus*), safflower, Carthamus Tinctorius; saffron, Crocus Sativus; the water-pot of the student and Sannyāsin; (*am*), n. gold; (*as*), m. outward affection, compared with the colour of safflower; N. of a mountain.—*Kusumbha-vat, ān, atī, at,* furnished with a jar or water-pot.

कुसुरुविन्द **kusuruvinda** or **kusurubinda, as,** m., N. of a descendant of Uddālaka.

Kusurubindu or *kusuruvindu, us,* m., N. of an author of several verses of the Vājasaneyi-saṃhitā.

कुसू **kusū, ūs,** m. an earth-worm.

कुसूल **kusūla, as,** m., Ved. a kind of spiritual or supernatural being; a granary &c. See *kuśūla.*

कुसृति **ku-sṛiti, is,** f. (see 1. *ku*), evil conduct, wickedness, depravity; conjuring, sleight-of-hand, magic; (*is, is, i*), going evil ways, wicked.

कुस्तुभ **kustubha, as,** m. an epithet of Vishṇu (derived fr. *kaustubha?*).

कुस्तुम्बरी **kustumbarī,** f. a pungent seed used in condiments, coriander.

कुस्तुम्बरु **kustumbaru, us,** m., N. of one of Kubera's attendants.

कुस्तुम्बुरु **kustumburu, us,** m. (said to be fr. 1. *ku* and *tumburu*), the plant coriander; (*u*), n. the seed of this plant.

कुस्त्री **ku-strī,** f. (see 1. *ku*), a bad woman.

कुस्मय **kusmaya** (fr. *ku-smaya*), nom. A. *kusmayate,* to smile improperly; to see mentally, guess; to perceive, to imagine.

कुस्वप्न **ku-svapna, as,** m. (see 1. *ku*), a bad dream, a nightmare.

कुस्वामिन् **ku-svāmin, ī,** m. (see 1. *ku*), a bad master.

कुह् **kuh,** cl. 10. A. *kuhayate, -yitum,* to surprise, astonish; to excite wonder, to cheat, to deceive by trickery or jugglery, impose upon (related to *guh?*).

1. *kuha, as,* m. an epithet of Kuvera; a rogue, a cheat (in *a-kuha,* q. v.).

Kuhaka, as, ā, am, cheating, a cheat, a rogue, a juggler; (*as*), m. a frog; N. of a king of the serpent-race; (*am, ā*), n. f. juggling, deception, sleight-of-hand, legerdemain.—*Kuhaka-kāra, as, ī, am,* or *kuhaka-kāraka, as, ikā, am,* or *kuhaka-kārin, ī, iṇī, i,* practising jugglery or conjuring, cheating.—*Kuhaka-ćakita, as, ā, am,* afraid of a trick, suspicious, cautious, wary.—*Kuhaka-jīvin, ī, inī, i,* living by sleight-of-hand, a conjurer, a cheat, &c.—*Kuhaka-vṛitti, is,* f. juggling, conjuring, sleight-of-hand; hypocrisy.

Kuhana, as, ā, am, envious, hypocritical; (*as*), m. a mouse, a rat; a snake; N. of a man; (*ā*), f. hypocrisy; assumed and false sanctity; the interested performance of religious austerities; (*am*), n. a small earthen vessel; a glass vessel.

Kuhanikā, f. hypocrisy &c.; [cf. the preceding.]

कुह **2. kuha,** ind. (fr. 1. *ku*), Ved. where? *kuha ćid,* wherever, anywhere, somewhere, to any place.—*Kuhaćid-vid, t, t, t,* Ved. being everywhere.

Kuhayā, ind., Ved. where?—*Kuhayā-kṛiti, is, is, i,* Ved. where active?

कुहकस्वन **kuhaka-svana** or **kuhaka-svara, as,** m. (*kuhaka* being here an onomatopoetic word), a wild cock, Phasianus Gallus.

कुहर **kuhara, as,** m. (fr. *kuh* = *guh?*), N. of a serpent belonging to the Krodhavaśa race; (*am*), n. a cavity, hollow; a hole, rent; the ear; the throat or larynx; a guttural sound; proximity; copulation.

कुहरित **kuharita, am,** n. noise, a sound in general; especially the song or cry of the Kokila or Indian cuckoo; a sound uttered in copulation.

कुहलि **kuhali, is,** m. the leaf of the Piper Betel (commonly called Pān) with small pieces of the Areca-nut and Catechu and a little lime, which are chewed and eaten by the people of the East and especially offered to the persons present at a matrimonial ceremony.

कुहा **kuhā,** f., N. of a plant, also called Kaṭukī.—*Kuhā-vatī,* f. an epithet of the goddess Durgā.

कुहारीत **ku-hārīta, as,** m. (see 1. *ku*), N. of a man.

कुहु **kuhu, us,** f. the new moon; N. of a river; the cry of the Kokila; [cf. *kuhū.*]

कुहुकुहाय **kuhukuhāya** (fr. *kuhu-kuha* for *kuha-kuha,* where? where?), nom. A. *kuhukuhāyate,* to show one's admiration.

कुहू **kuhū, ūs,** f. (fr. *kuh* = *guh?*), the new moon, personified as a daughter of Aṅgiras; the first day of the first quarter on which the moon rises invisible; N. of one of the seven rivers of Plaksha-dvīpa; the cry or song of the Kokila or Indian cuckoo.—*Kuhū-kaṇṭha* or *kuhūka, as,* m. the Kokila or Indian cuckoo, κόκκυ.—*Kuhū-pāla, as,* m. the king of turtles, the tortoise supposed to uphold the world.—*Kuhū-mukha* or *kuhū-rava, as,* m. the Kokila or Indian cuckoo.

कुहूल **kuhūla, am,** n. a pit filled with stakes.

कुहेडिका **kuheḍikā** or **kuheḍī** or **kuhelikā,** f. a fog, a mist, haze, haziness.

कुह्वान **ku-hvāna, am,** n. (see 1. *ku*), a disagreeable noise.

कू **1. kū** or **ku,** cl. 2. P. *kauti, kavīti,* or cl. 1. A. *kavate,* or cl. 6. A. *kuvate,* or cl. 9. P. A. *kūnāti, -nīte,* or *kunāti, -nīte, ćukāva,* &c., to sound, make a noise, cry out; to move: Caus. *kāvayati:* Desid. *ćukūshati, -te:* Intens. *ćokūyate* or *kokūyate,* to cry aloud; [cf. Gr. κωκύω.]

कू **2. kū, ūs,** f. a female Piśāća or goblin.

कूकुद **kūkuda, as,** m. one who gives a girl in marriage with due ceremony and suitable decorations.

कूच **kūća, as,** m. a breast; the female breast, especially that of a young or unmarried woman; [cf. *kuća.*]

कूचका **kūćakā,** f. the milky juice of a bulbous plant; [? cf. *kūrćikā.*]

कूचक्र **kūćakra, as** or **am?** m. or n.? (for *ku-ćakra*), Ved. the female breast.

कूचवार **kūćavāra, as,** m. (?), N. of a region; also of a man.

कूचिका **kūćikā,** f. a small brush or hair-pencil; a key; [cf. *kūćī* and *kūrćikā.*]

कूचिदर्थिन् **kūćid-arthin, ī, inī, i** (for *kućid-ar°*), Ved. striving to get everywhere; (Sāy.) seeking (oblations) from any quarter.

कूची **kūćī,** f. a paint brush, a pencil; [cf. *kūćikā* and *kūrćikā.*]

कूच्छलिङ्ग **kūććhalinga, au,** m. du. = *kukundara,* q. v.

कूज् **kūj,** cl. 1. P. *kūjati, ćukūja, kūjitum,* to make any inarticulate or monotonous sound, to utter a cry as a bird, to coo as a pigeon, to caw as a crow, to warble; to moan, groan, &c.; to utter any sound in a low and indistinct voice; to fill with sounds &c.: Caus. *kūjayati:* Desid. *ćukūjishati:* Intens. *ćokūjyate, ćokūkti.*

Kūja, as, m. rumbling (as of the bowels &c.); cooing, murmuring, a warbling &c.

Kūjaka, as, ikā, am, cooing, warbling, sounding, &c.

Kūjat, an, antī, at, cooing, warbling, &c.

Kūjana, am, n. rumbling of the bowels; the uttering of any inarticulate sound, cooing, moaning; the rattling of wheels.

Kūjita, as, ā, am, uttered inarticulately, cooed, &c.; (*am*), n. the cry of a bird, cooing, warbling, &c.

Kūjin, ī, inī, i, making a rumbling sound in the bowels; warbling.

कूट् **kūṭ,** cl. 10. P. *kūṭayati,* to burn; to give pain, be distressed, to call, invite; to counsel, advise; A. *kūṭayate,* to avoid or decline giving, not to give; to render indistinct or unintelligible, to muddle, to render confused or foul; to be distressed; to despair; [cf. Eng. *heat, hot;* Old Iceland. *hiti, heitr;* Germ. *hitze, heiss.*]

कूट **kūṭa, as, am,** m. n. the bone of the forehead with its projections or prominences, a horn; the crown of the head; any prominence or projection (e. g. *aṃsa-kūṭa,* the hump of a buffalo; *akshi-kūṭa,* the prominence of the forehead above the eye); summit, the peak or summit of a mountain; summit, head, i. e. the highest, the most excellent, the first; a heap, a multitude (e. g. *abhra-kūṭa,* a multitude of clouds); a kind of vessel or implement; a hammer, an iron mallet; part of a plough, a ploughshare, the body of a plough; a trap for catching deer; a concealed weapon as a dagger in a wooden case, a sword-stick &c.; illusion, fraud, trick, deceit; a roguish scheme or plot; a knotty point, a puzzling question, an enigma, an obscure passage; untruth, falsehood, (or attributively) false, untrue; vile, low; uniform substance (as the ethereal element &c.); a water-jar; a kind of plant; (*as, ī*), m. f. a house, a dwelling [cf. *kuṭa* and *kuṭī*]; (*as*), m. an epithet of Agastya; (*as, ā, am*), Ved. not horned or cornuted, as an animal with incomplete continuations of the bone of the forehead; (*as*), m. an ox whose horns are broken.—*Kūṭa-kāra, as,* m. a rogue, a cheat, a false witness.—*Kūṭa-kāraka, as, ikā, am,* a rogue, a cheat, a false witness.—*Kūṭa-kṛit, t, t, t,* cheating, committing a fraud, bribing; (*t*), m. a Kāyastha or man of the writer-caste; an epithet of Śiva.—*Kūṭa-khaḍga, as,* m. a hidden sword, a sword-stick.—*Kūṭa-grantha,* title of a work supposed to be written by Vyāsa.—*Kūṭa-ććhadman, ā,* m. a rogue, a cheat.—*Kūṭa-tā,* f. or *kūṭa-tva, am,* n. falsehood, fraud.—*Kūṭa-tulā,* f. a false pair of scales.—*Kūṭa-dharma, as, ā, am,* (a country or house) where falsehood is considered a duty.—*Kūṭa-parva* or *kūṭa-pūrva, as,* m. fever occurring in an elephant from vitiation of the three humors; (more correctly *kūṭa-pūrva.*)—*Kūṭa-pālaka, as,* m. a bilious fever; a potter's kiln.—*Kūṭa-pāśa, as,* m. a trap.—*Kūṭa-bandha, as,* m. a trap.—*Kūṭa-māna, am,* n. a false measure or weight.—*Kūṭa-mudgara, as,* m. a concealed weapon similar to a hammer.—*Kūṭa-mohana, as,* m. an epithet of Skanda.—*Kūṭa-yantra, am,* n. a trap or snare for deer, birds, &c.—*Kūṭa-yuddha, am,* n. a treacherous or unfair battle; (*as, ā, am*), fighting treacherously.—*Kūṭa-yodhin, ī, inī, i,* fighting unfairly or treacherously.—*Kūṭa-raćanā,* f. a laid trap.—*Kūṭa-śas,* ind. in heaps, in multitudes, by crowds.—*Kūṭa-śālmali, is,* m. f. or *ikā,* f. a fabulous cotton-plant with sharp thorns, with which the wicked are tortured in the world of Yama; a species of the Simul silk-cotton tree.—*Kūṭa-śāsana, am,* n. a forged or false grant or decree.—*Kūṭa-śaila, as,* m., N. of a mountain.—*Kūṭa-sākshin, ī,* m. a false witness.—*Kūṭa-stha, as, ā, am,* standing at the top, keeping the highest position; standing in a multitude, standing in the midst; (in phil.) immovable, uniform, unchangeable, perpetually and universally the same, as the soul, spirit, space, ether, sound, &c.; (*am*), n. a sort of perfume, a species of dried shell-fish, commonly Nakhi; the soul. — *Kūṭastha-tā*, f. or *kūṭastha-tva*, *am*, n. unchangeableness, uniformity. — *Kūṭa-svarṇa*, *am*, n. alloyed or counterfeit gold. — *Kūṭāksha* (°*ṭa-ak*°), *as*, m. loaded or false dice. — *Kūṭāgāra* (°*ṭa-āg*°), *am*, n. an upper room, an apartment on the top of a house. — *Kūṭārtha* (°*ṭa-ar*°), *as*, m. ambiguity of meaning, fiction. — *Kūṭārtha-bhāshitā*, f., scil. *kathā*, a tale, a story, a fiction. — *Kūṭopāya* (°*ṭa-up*°), *as*, m. trick, fraud, stratagem.

Kūṭaka, *am*, n. elevation, prominence, projection; the body of a plough (i. e. the wood without the ploughshare and pole); a ploughshare; illusion, fraud, untruth, deceit; (*as*, *ā*, *am*), fraudulent, unfair; (*as*), m., N. of a mountain; a braid or tress of hair; a perfume; see *murā*. — *Kūṭakākhyāna* (°*ka-ākh*°), *am*, n. an invented tale.

कूटज *kūṭaja*, *as*, m. the plant Wrightia Antidysenterica; [cf. *kuṭaja*.]

कूड् *kūḍ*, cl. 6. P. *kūḍati*, *-ḍitum*, to eat; to graze; to become firm or fat or solid.

कूड्य *kūḍya*, *am*, n. a wall, = *kuḍya*.

कूण् *kūṇ*, cl. 10. P. A. *kūṇayati*, *-te*, *-yitum*, to draw together, contract, close.

Kūṇita, *as*, *ā*, *am*, contracted, shut, closed. — *Kūṇitekshaṇa* (°*ta-ik*°), *as*, m. a hawk.

कूणकुच्छ *kūṇakuććha*, *as*, m., N. of one of Śiva's attendants.

कूणि *kūṇi*, *is*, *is*, *i*, crooked-armed, having a curved or withered arm; [cf. *kunt*.]

कूणिका *kūṇikā*, f. the horn of any animal; the peg of a lute; [cf. *kalikā*.]

कूदर *kūdara*, *as*, m. the offspring of a Brāhman woman by a Ṛishi, begotten during menstruation.

कूदी *kūdī*, f., Ved. a fetter for the feet. — *Kūdī-maya*, *as*, *ī*, *am*, consisting of a fetter.

कूद्दाल *kūddāla*, *as*, m. mountain ebony, Bauhinia Variegata; [cf. *kuddāla*.]

कूप् *kūp*, cl. 10. P. *kūpayati*, *-yitum*, to be weak, to weaken.

कूप *kūpa*, *as*, m. (said to be fr. rt. 3. *ku*; according to others perhaps fr. 1. *ku* and *ap*; cf. *anūpa*, *dvīpa*), a hole, a hollow, a cave; a well; a post to which a boat or ship is moored; a mast (?); a tree or rock in the midst of a river; a leather oil vessel; (*ī*), f. a small well; the navel; a flask, a bottle; [cf. Gr. κύπη.] — *Kūpa-kaććhapa*, *as*, m. a tortoise in a well; (metaphorically) a man without experience, who has seen nothing of the world. — *Kūpa-kāra*, *as*, m. a well-digger. — *Kūpa-khā*, *ās*, m. (rt. *khan*), Ved. a well-digger. — *Kūpa-ja*, *as*, m. hair. — *Kūpa-jala*, *am*, n. well-water, spring-water. — *Kūpa-dardura* or *kūpa-maṇḍūka*, *as*, m. a frog in a well, applied to a person of no experience and enterprise, one who never leaves home. — *Kūpa-rājya*, *am*, n., N. of a country. — *Kūpānka* or *kūpānga* (°*pa-an*°), *as*, m. horripilation, erection of the hairs of the body. — *Kūpodaka* (°*pa-ud*°), *am*, n. well-water.

Kūpaka, *as*, m. a hole, a hollow, a cave; the hollow below the loins; a well, a temporary well, a hole dug for water in the dry bed of a rivulet; a stake &c. to which a boat is moored; the mast of a vessel; a rock or tree in the midst of a river; a funeral pile; a hole dug under a funeral pile; a leather oil vessel; (*ikā*), f. a stone or rock in the middle of a stream.

Kūpya, *as*, *ā*, *am*, being in a hole or well.

कूपद *kūpada*, *as*, m. = *kūkuda*, q. v.

कूपार *kūpāra*, *as*, m. the ocean, = *akūpāra*.

कूपुष *kūpusha*, *am*, n. the bladder.

कूबर *kūbara*, or in the later language generally *kūvara*, *as*, *ī*, *am*, m. f. n. the pole of a carriage or the wooden frame to which the yoke is fixed; (*ī*), f. a carriage covered with a cloth or blanket; (*as*), m. a hump-backed man; (*as*, *ī*, *am*), beautiful, agreeable, pleasing.

Kūbarin or *kūvarin*, *ī*, m. a carriage.

कूम *kūma*, *am*, n. a lake, a pond, a pool.

कूमनस् *kū-manas*, *ās*, *ās*, *as* (for *ku-manas*, see 1. *ku*), Ved. wicked-minded.

कूर *kūra*, *as*, m. boiled rice.

कूर्कुर *kūrkura*, *as*, m., N. of a demon who persecutes children (perhaps cough or some similar disease personified).

कूर्च *kūrća*, *as*, *am*, m. n. a bunch of anything, a bundle of grass &c. (often used as a seat); a handful of Kuśa grass or peacock's feathers; certain parts of the human body, as the hands, feet, neck, and the membrum virile; the upper part of the nose, the part between the eyebrows; the beard; the tip of the thumb and middle finger brought in contact so as to pinch &c.; deceit, fraud, circumvention; false praise, unmerited commendation either of one's self or another person, boasting, flattery; hypocrisy; hardness, solidity; the mystical syllable *hum*; (*as*), m. the head; a store-room. — *Kūrća-śiras*, *as*, n. the upper part of the palm of the hand and foot; the heel. — *Kūrća-śīrsha* or *kūrća-śīrshaka*, *as*, m., N. of a plant, a drug, commonly called Jīvaka, one of the eight principal medicaments. — *Kūrća-śekhara*, *as*, m. the cocoa-nut tree. — *Kūrćā-mukha*, *as*, m., N. of a Ṛishi.

Kūrćaka, *as*, m. a bushel; a brush for cleaning the teeth, a painter's brush &c.; certain parts of the human body [cf. the preceding]; (*ikā*), f. a painting brush or pencil; a key; a needle; a bud, a blossom; inspissated milk; (*am*), n. in *tri-kūrćaka*, scil. *śastra*, a three-edged sword.

Kūrćakin, *ī*, *inī*, *i*, stuffed, puffy.

कूर्चल *kūrćala*, *as*, m. (?) an animal teething for the second time.

कूर्द् *kūrd* and *kurd*, cl. 1. P. A. *kūrdati*, *-te*, *ćukūrde*, *kūrdishyate*, *akūrdishṭa*, *kūrditum*, to leap, jump; to play; [cf. Lat. *ludo*?].

Kūrda, *as*, m. a jump; N. of a Sāman.

Kūrdana, *am*, n. leaping; playing, sport, pastime; (*ī*), f. the day of full moon in the month Ćaitra; a festival in honour of Kāma-deva or the god of love, held on the day of full moon in the month Ćaitra.

कूर्प *kūrpa*, *am*, n. the space between the eyebrows; [cf. *kūrća*.]

कूर्पर *kūrpara*, *as*, *ā*, m. f. the elbow; the knee.

कूर्पास *kūrpāsa*, *as*, m. a cuirass or quilted jacket worn as armour.

Kūrpāsaka, *as*, *am*, m. n. a bodice, a jacket with short sleeves worn next the body, especially by women.

कूर्म *kūrma*, *as*, m. a tortoise, a turtle; the earth considered as a tortoise swimming on the waters; a particular gesticulation with the fingers; one of the outer winds of the body; N. of a serpent or Kādraveya king; the second incarnation of Vishṇu, his descent in the form of a tortoise to support the mountain Mandara at the churning of the ocean; N. of a son of Gṛitsa-mada, author of several hymns of the Ṛig-veda; (*ī*), f. a female tortoise; [cf. Gr. κλέμμυς, χέλυς, χελώνη.] — *Kūrma-ćakra*, *am*, n. an astrological diagram. — *Kūrma-pitta*, *am*, n. the bilious humor of a tortoise. — *Kūrma-purāṇa*, *am*, n. the Purāṇa of the tortoise incarnation (one of the incarnations of Vishṇu) or the fifteenth of the eighteen Purāṇas. — *Kūrma-pṛishṭha*, *am*, n. the back or shell of a tortoise; (*as*), m. globe-amaranth, Gomphrena Globosa. — *Kūrma-pṛishṭhaka*, *am*, n. the cover of a dish, a lid. — *Kūrmapṛishṭhāsthi* (°*ṭha-as*°), n. tortoise-shell. — *Kūrmapṛishṭhonnata* (°*ṭha-un*°), *as*, *ā*, *am*, raised or elevated like the back of a tortoise. — *Kūrma-rāja*, *as*, m. the king of turtles, the tortoise supposed to uphold the world. — *Kūrmāvatāra* (°*ma-av*°), *as*, m. the tortoise incarnation (of Vishṇu).

कूर्मि *kūrmi*. See *tuvi-kūrmi*.

कूल् 1. *kūl*, cl. 1. P. *kūlati*, *-litum*, to cover, hide, screen, protect; to enclose; to keep off, obstruct; [cf. Gr. κωλύω.]

Kūla, *am*, n. a declivity, slope; a shore, a bank; a heap, a mound; a pond or pool; the rear of an army; N. of a region; [cf. *aja-kūlā*, *anu-kūla*, *utkūla*, &c.; cf. also Hib. *cul*, 'custody, guard, defence, the back part of anything;' *col*, 'an impediment;' Lat. *collis*?]. — *Kūlan-kasha*, *as*, *ā*, *am*, carrying or tearing away the bank; (*as*), m. the ocean, the sea; the stream or current of a river; (*ā*), f. a river. — *Kūla-ćara*, *as*, *ī*, *am*, frequenting the banks of rivers, grazing there &c. — *Kūla-bhū*, *ūs*, f. a bank, the land upon the bank or shore. — *Kūlam-udruja*, *as*, *ā*, *am*, breaking down banks, as a river &c. — *Kūlam-udvaha*, *as*, *ā*, *am*, carrying or tearing away the bank, as a river &c. — *Kūla-vat*, *ān*, *atī*, *at*, furnished with shores; (*tī*), f. a river. — *Kūla-haṇḍaka*, *as*, m. an eddy.

Kūlaka, *as* or *am*, m. or n. a bank, shore, dyke; a mound of earth, a heap, a pile; (*as*), m. an ant-hill; (*am*), n. the plant Trichosanthes Dioeca.

Kūlin, *ī*, *inī*, *i*, furnished with banks or shores; (*inī*), f. a river.

Kūlya, *as*, *ā*, *am*, Ved. belonging to a bank or shore.

कूल् 2. *kūl* or *kūḍ*, cl. 10. P., Ved. *kūlayati*, *-yitum*, to burn, scorch.

कूलिक *kūlika*, *as*, m., N. of a prince; (*ā*), f. the bottom or lower part of the Indian lute.

कूवर *kūvara*. See *kūbara*.

कूवार *kūvāra*, *as*, m. the ocean. See *kūpāra* and *akūpāra*.

कूष्माण्ड *kūshmāṇḍa*, *as*, m. a kind of pumpkin-gourd, Benincasa Cerifera; a kind of spirit or imp, of which there exists a Gaṇa or class; a kind of spell or magical formula; (*ī*), f. a kind of plant [cf. *oshadhī*]; N. of the goddess Durgā; N. of several verses of the Yajur-veda.

Kūshmāṇḍaka, *as*, m. a kind of pumpkin-gourd, Benincasa Cerifera Savi; N. of one of Śiva's attendants.

Kūshmāṇḍinī, f., N. of a goddess; [cf. *kushmāṇḍa*.]

कूहना *kūhanā*, f. hypocrisy, affectation of religious zeal or austerity; [cf. *kuhanā*.]

कूहा *kūhā*, f. a fog, a mist, = *kujjhaṭikā*.

कृ 1. *kṛi*. The conjugational tenses are formed in the Veda according to four different methods, as follows: I) According to the rule for cl. 2, Pres. 2nd sing. P. *karshi*, du. *kṛithas*, pl. *kṛitha*; A. *kṛishe*; Impf. 2nd sing. P. *akar*, 3rd *akar* and *akat*; 3rd du. *akartām*; pl. *akarma*, *akarta*, *akran*; A. *akri*, *akṛithās*, *akrita*, *akrātām*, *akrata*; Impv. P. *kṛidhi*, *kṛitam*, *kṛita*; A. *kṛishva*, *kṛidhvam*: Leṭ, 2nd and 3rd sing. *kar*, pl. *karma*, *karta* and *kartana*, *kran*; A. 3rd sing. *kṛita*; 3rd pl. *kranta*: Pot. *kriyāma*; Part. nom. pl. m. *krantas*; A. *krāṇa*. II) According to the rule for cl. 1, Pres. P. *karasi*, *karati*, *karathas*, *karatas*, *karanti*; A. *karase*, *karate*, *karāmahe*; Impf. *akaram*, *akaras*, *akarat*; Impf. *kara*, *karatam*, *karatām*: Leṭ, *karam*, *karāṇi*, *karas*, *karat*, *karāma*, *karan*; A. *karāmahai*; Part.

karanti. III) According to the rule for cl. 5, Pres. P. kṛiṇomi, &c.; A. kṛiṇve, du. kṛiṇvaite; Impf. P. akṛiṇavam, &c., 2nd pl. akṛiṇuta and akṛiṇotana; A. 3rd sing. akṛiṇuta; Impv. P. kṛiṇu or kṛiṇuhi or kṛiṇutāt, kṛiṇotu; kṛiṇutam, kṛiṇutām; kṛiṇuta or kṛiṇota or kṛiṇotana; kṛiṇvantu; A. kṛiṇushva, kṛiṇutām, kṛiṇvāthām, kṛiṇudhvam: Leṭ, kṛiṇavas, kṛiṇavat and kṛiṇavāt, kṛiṇavāva, kṛiṇavāma, kṛiṇavātha, kṛiṇavatha, kṛiṇavan; A. kṛiṇavai, kṛiṇavase, kṛiṇavate, kṛiṇavāvahai, kṛiṇavāmahai, 3rd pl. kṛiṇavanta or kṛiṇavante or kṛiṇvata: Pot. A. kṛiṇvīta; Part. P. kṛiṇvat, A. kṛiṇvāna. IV) According to the rule for cl. 8, (this is the usual formation in the Brāhmaṇas, Sūtras, and in classical Sanskṛit), Pres. P. karomi (ep. kurmi), karoshi, &c., kurmas; A. kurve; Impf. P. akaravam; A. 3rd sing. akuruta; Impv. P. kuru, karotu (in the earlier language for 2nd and 3rd sing. kurutāt), kuruta or kurutana; A. kurushva, kurudhvam, kurvatām: Leṭ, P. karavāṇi, karavas, karavāt, &c.; A. karavai, kuruthās, karavāvahai (ep. karavāvahe), karavaithe, karavaite, karavāmahai (ep. karavāmahe): Pot. P. kuryām, A. kurvīya; Part. P. kurvat, A. kurvāṇa: Perf. P. ćakāra, ćakartha, &c.; A. ćakre, &c.; Part. P. ćakrivas (Acc. sing. Ved. ćakrusham); A. ćakrāṇa; 2nd Fut. karishyati; Leṭ, 2nd sing. karishyās; 1st Fut. kartā; Prec. kriyāsam; Aor. P., Ved. ćakaram, aćakriran, aćakrat; A. kṛishe; Class. akārshīt (poet. akārshīt); Pass. Aor. reflex. akāri and akṛita; Inf. kartum; Ved. kartave, kartavai, kartos; Ind. Part. kṛitvā, Ved. kṛitvī and kṛitvāya; to do, make, perform, accomplish, cause, effect, prepare, undertake; to do anything for the advantage or injury of another (with gen. or loc. of the person); to execute, carry out (as an order or command); to manufacture, prepare, work at, elaborate, build; to form, construct one thing out of another (with abl. or inst. of the thing); to compose, describe; to cultivate; to make a sound, utter, pronounce (often in comp. with the sounds phaṭ, phuṭ, bhāṇ, vashaṭ, svadhā, svāhā, him); to employ, use; to make use of (with inst.); to accomplish any period, bring to completion, spend (e. g. varshāṇi daśa ćakruḥ, they spent ten years; kshaṇaṃ kuru, wait a moment); to place, put, lay, bring, lead, to take hold of (with acc. or loc. or inst., e. g. ardhaṃ kṛi, to win over to one's own side or party; haste or pāṇau kṛi, to take by the hand, to marry; hṛidayena kṛi, to place in one's heart, love); to direct the thoughts, mind &c. (manaḥ or matim or buddhim or bhāvam &c.) towards any object, turn the attention to, resolve upon, determine on (with loc., dat., or inf. of the object, e. g. mā śoke manaḥ kṛithāḥ, do not turn your mind to grief; gamanāya matiṃ ćakre, he resolved upon going; alābuṃ srashṭuṃ ćakre, be resolved to create a gourd); to consider, turn in the mind, think; to make, to render (with two acc., e. g. ādityaṃ kāshṭhām akurvata, they made the sun their goal); to procure for another, bestow, grant; A. to procure for one's self, appropriate, assume; to give aid, help any one to perform an action; to make liable; to injure, violate (e. g. kanyāṃ kṛi, to violate a maiden); to appoint, institute; to give an order, commission; to cause to get rid of, free from (with abl.); to begin (e. g. ćakre śobhayitum purīm, he began to adorn the city); to proceed with, put in practice; to worship, sacrifice; (with numeral adverbs ending in dhā) to divide, separate, or break up into parts, e. g. dvidhā kṛi, to divide into two parts; sahasradhā kṛi, to break into a thousand pieces; (with adverbs ending in vat) to make like or similar, to consider equivalent, e. g. rājyaṃ tṛiṇavat kṛitvā, valuing the kingdom like a straw; (with adverbs ending in sāt) to reduce anything to, cause to become, make subject, e. g. bhasmasāt kṛi, to reduce to ashes; ātmasāt kṛi, to subject to one's self. The above senses of kṛi may be variously modified or almost infinitely extended according to the noun with which this root is connected, as in the following examples: sakhyaṃ kṛi, to contract friendship with; pūjāṃ kṛi, to honour; rājyaṃ kṛi, to reign; snehaṃ kṛi, to show affection; ājñāṃ or nideśaṃ or śāsanaṃ or kāmaṃ or yāćanāṃ or vaćaḥ or vaćanaṃ or vākyaṃ kṛi, to perform any one's command or wish or request &c.; dharmaṃ kṛi, to do one's duty; nakhāni kṛi, to clean one's nails; udakaṃ or salilaṃ kṛi, to offer a libation to the dead, to perform ablutions &c.; astrāṇi kṛi, to practice the use of weapons; darduraṃ kṛi, to play on the flute; daṇḍaṃ kṛi, to inflict punishment &c.; svaraṃ kṛi, to utter a sound; śabdaṃ kṛi, to make a noise; kālaṃ kṛi, to bring one's time to an end, i. e. to die; ćiraṃ kṛi, to be long in doing anything, to delay; manasi kṛi, to take to heart, to mind, to determine, resolve upon; manasā kṛi, to place in one's mind, think of, meditate; hṛidi kṛi, to place in the heart, remember; vaśe kṛi, to place in subjection, become master of; śirasā kṛi, to place on the head; mūrdhnā kṛi, to place on one's head, to obey, to honour: Caus. kārayati, -te, -yitum, to cause to act or do, to cause another to perform, to have anything made or done by another (with acc. or double acc., e. g. sabhāṃ kāritavān, he caused an assembly to be made; rāja-darśanaṃ māṃ kāraya, cause me to have an audience of the king; bāṇijyaṃ kārayed vaiśyam, he ought to cause the Vaiśya to engage in trade; or with acc. and inst., e. g. na śakshyāmi kinćit kārayitum tvayā, I shall not be able to have anything done by thee); to cause to manufacture or form or cultivate; to cause to place or put, to have anything placed, put upon, &c. (e. g. taṃ ćitra-paṭaṃ vāsa-gṛihe bhittāv akārayat, he had the picture placed on the wall in his house). Sometimes the Caus. of kṛi is used for the simple verb or without a causal signification (e. g. padaṃ kārayati, he pronounces a word &c.; mithyā kārayati, he pronounces wrongly; Kaikeyīm anu rājānaṃ kāraya, treat or deal with Kaikeyī as the king does): Desid. ćikīrshati, -te, to wish to make or do; to intend to do, to design, intend, begin, strive after; to wish to sacrifice or worship: Intens. ćarkarti, ćarikarti, ćarīkarti, ćarkarīti, ćarikarīti, ćarīkarīti, ćekrīyate, Ved. 3rd pl. karikrati, to do repeatedly; [cf. Hib. caraim, 'I perform, execute;' ceard, 'an art, trade, business, function;' sucridh, 'easy;' Cambro-Brit. creu, 'to form;' Island. gerdh, 'action;' Old Germ. karawan, 'to prepare;' Mod. Germ. gar, 'prepared (as food);' Lat. creo, cæremonia, ars (for cars); Gr. κραίνω, κρόνος.]

1. kṛit, t, t, t, making, doing, performing, accomplishing, effecting, manufacturing, acting; one who accomplishes or performs anything, an author; often occurring at the end of compounds, see su-kṛit, karma-kṛit, pāpa-kṛit, &c.; (t), m. an affix used to form nouns from roots; a noun formed with this affix. — Kṛid-anta, as, m. a word ending with a Kṛit affix (such a word would be called by Pāṇini simply kṛit). — Kṛil-lopa, as, m. the rejection of a Kṛit affix.

Kṛita, as, ā, am, done, made, accomplished, performed; prepared, made ready; obtained, gained, acquired; placed at hand; well done, proper, good. The preceding senses are mostly found in the Veda; the numerous other senses found in classical writers may be inferred from the meanings of the rt. kṛi above. The neuter of kṛita is used with saha or with the inst. alone in the sense of 'done with,' 'away with,' 'enough of,' 'no need of,' &c. (e. g. kṛitaṃ sandehena, away with doubt; kṛitam parihāsena, enough of joking). Kṛita is often found at the end of a compound, e. g. pūrva-kṛita, done formerly; janmāntara-kṛita, done in a former state of existence; (as), m., N. of one of the Viśva-devās; of a son of Vasu-deva; of a son of Sannati and pupil of Hiraṇya-nābha; of a son of Kṛita-ratha and father of Vibudha; of a son of Jaya and father of Haryavana; of a son of Cyavana and father of Upari-ćara; (am), n. deed, work, action; service done, kind action, benefit; consequence, result; aim, object, design; stake at a game; prize or booty gained in battle; N. of the die or of the side of a die marked with four points; (according to some) the collective name of the four dice in opposition to the fifth die, called kali; N. of the first of the four ages of the world (also called satya or 'the golden age') comprehending together with the morning and evening dawn 4,800 years of men, according to the Mahā-bhārata; but according to the Purāṇas 4,800 years of the gods, or 1,728000 years of men. — Kṛita-kapaṭa, as, ā, am, deceiving, beguiling, fraudulent. — Kṛita-kartavya, as, ā, am, one who has performed what was to be done, who has done his duty; having done or discharged one's duty. — Kṛita-karman, ā, ā, a, one who has done his work or duty; skilful, clever, able. — Kṛita-kalpa, as, ā, am, one who knows the customary rites. — Kṛita-kāma, as, ā, am, one whose desire is attained or fulfilled. — Kṛita-kārya, am, n. an attained object; (as, ā, am), one who has done his work or obtained his object; one who has no need of another person's aid (with inst.). — Kṛita-kāla, as, m. appointed time; (as, ā, am), fixed, settled as to time; sent, deposited &c. for a certain time; one who has accomplished a certain time, who has waited a certain time. — Kṛita-kūrććhaka, as, ā, am, tied up as a small bundle or brush. — Kṛita-kṛitya, am, n. what has been done and what is to be done; an attained object; (as, ā, am), having successfully accomplished a business; one who has accomplished or attained any object or purpose; contented, satisfied; clever. — Kṛitakṛitya-tā, f. or kṛitakṛitya-tva, am, n. the full discharge of any duty or realisation of any object, accomplishment, attainment, success. — Kṛita-koṭi, is, m., N. of a Kāśyapa; an epithet of Upavarsha. — Kṛita-kopa, as, ā, am, angry, indignant. — Kṛita-kautuka, as, ī, am, playful. — Kṛita-kraya, as, m. a purchaser, a buyer. — Kṛita-kriya, as, ā, am, one who has finished or accomplished any object in which he is engaged; one who has attained his end or object; one who has fulfilled his duty or performed a religious ceremony. — Kṛita-krudha, as, ā, am, angry, resentful. — Kṛita-kshaṇa, as, ā, am, one who is waiting for the exact moment, one who waits impatiently for a person or thing, (with prati or with the inf. or at the end of a comp., e. g. kṛita-kshaṇāham te gamanam prati, I am waiting impatiently for thy going; te bhūmiṃ gantuṃ kṛita-kshaṇāḥ, they are waiting for the time to proceed to the earth); (as), m., N. of a prince. — Kṛita-ghāta-yatna, as, ā, am, making efforts to slay, one who tries to kill. — Kṛita-ghna, as, ī, am, destroying past transactions or (benefits) done, unmindful of (services) rendered, recompensing evil for good, not acknowledging good offices or benefits received, ungrateful; defeating or rendering vain all previous measures. — Kṛitaghna-tā, f. or kṛitaghna-tva, am, n. ingratitude. — Kṛita-ćūḍa, as, m. a boy on whom the ceremony of tonsure has been performed. — Kṛita-ćetas, ās, m., N. of a Brāhman. — Kṛita-ććhidrā, f. the plant Luffa Acutangula. — Kṛita-janman, ā, ā, a, born, produced, generated. — Kṛita-jña, as, ā, am, remembering past transactions, mindful of former aid or favours, grateful; observing propriety, correct in conduct; (as), m. a dog; an epithet of Śiva. — Kṛitajña-tā, f. or kṛitajña-tva, am, n. gratitude. — Kṛitañ-jaya, as, m., N. of the seventeenth Vyāsa; also of a prince. — Kṛita-tanutrāṇa, as, ā, am, mailed, having covered one's self with armour. — Kṛita-tīrtha, as, m. one who has visited holy places &c., one who frequents them; a guide; an adviser, one fertile in expedients. — Kṛita-trā, f., N. of a plant, = trāyamāṇā. — Kṛita-tva, am, n. the state of being done or effected. — Kṛita-dāra, as, ā, am, married; [cf. dārakriyā.] — Kṛita-dāsa, as, m. one who offers himself as a servant for a certain time, a self-engaged servant, a hired servant. — Kṛita-dyuti, is, f., N. of the wife of king Citraketu. — Kṛita-dvishṭa, as, ā, am, Ved. angry with the

doings of another person. — *Krita-dhanvan, ā,* m., N. of a son of Kanaka. — *Krita-dhī, is, is, i,* prudent, considerate; learned, educated. — *Krita-dhvaṇsa, as, ā, am,* defeated, overpowered; injured, destroyed; destroying past transactions; [cf. *krita-ghna.*] — *Krita-dhvaja, as, ā, am,* Ved. furnished with banners; (*as*), m., N. of a prince, a son of Dharma-dhvaja. — *Krita-dhvasta, as, ā, am,* lost after being once possessed or acquired. — *Krita-nakha, as, ā, am,* one who has cleaned his nails.
— *Krita-nāśaka, as, ī, am,* ungrateful; [cf. *krita-ghna.*] — *Krita-nityakriya, as, ā, am,* having duly attended to the daily religious observances. — *Krita-nirṇejana, as,* m. a penitent, one who has performed penance or made expiation. — *Krita-niśćaya, as, ā, am,* one who has made a resolution, resolved, determined; confident, sure, certain. — *Krita-parva, am,* n.(?) the golden age of the world. — *Krita-paśćāttāpa, as, ā, am,* showing regret or penitence.
— *Krita-punkha, as, ā, am,* 'one who has fixed the feathers of his arrows,' skilled in archery. — *Krita-puṇya, as, ā, am,* accomplished in virtuous acts.
— *Krita-pūrva, as, ā, am,* done formerly. — *Krita-pūrva-nāśana, am,* n. forgetting past services, ingratitude; [cf. *krita-ghna.*] — *Krita-pūrvin, ī, iṇī, i,* one by whom anything was formerly done.
— *Krita-paurusha, as, ā, am,* behaving gallantly.
— *Krita-praṇāma, as, ā, am,* making obeisance, saluting. — *Krita-pratikrita, am,* n. assault and counter-assault; attack and resistance; retaliation for an assault. — *Krita-pratijña, as, ā, am,* fulfilling a promise or agreement. — *Krita-prayatna, as, ā, am,* making effort, active, industrious, persevering. — *Krita-phala, as, ā, am,* successful, fruitful; (*am*), n. result, consequence of an act; a poisonous substance; (*ā*), f., N. of a plant; [cf. *kola-śimbi.*] — *Krita-bandhu, us,* m., N. of a prince.
— *Krita-bāhu, us, us, u,* laying hands upon, touching. — *Krita-buddhi, is, is, i,* one who has made a resolution, a man of resolute or firm character; resolved; informed of one's duty, one who knows how religious rites ought to be conducted; learned, wise. — *Krita-brahman, ā, ā, a,* Ved. one who has performed his devotions; (a deity) towards whom devotion is made, (a sacrifice) in which prayers are duly offered. — *Krita-bhaya, as, ā, am,* alarmed, apprehensive. — *Krita-bhāva, as, ā, am,* one whose mind is directed towards anything, determined, resolved. — *Krita-bhūta-maitra, as, ī, am,* friendly to all. — *Krita-bhojana, as, ā, am,* one who has dined or made a meal. — *Krita-mangala, as, ā, am,* blessed, consecrated. — *Krita-mati, is, is, i,* one who has taken a resolution, one who has resolved upon anything. — *Krita-mandāra, as,* m., N. of a man. — *Krita-manyu, us, us, u,* angry, offended, indignant. — *Krita-mārga, as, ā, am,* having a road or path made; (*ā*), f., N. of a river. — *Krita-māla, as,* m. a species of animal; the tree Cassia Fistula.
— *Krita-mukha, as, ī, am,* skilled, clever, conversant. — *Krita-maitra, as, ā, am,* friendly. — *Krita-yajus, us, us, us,* Ved. one who has uttered the sacrificial formulas. — *Krita-yajña, as,* m., N. of a son of Ćyavana and father of Uparićara. — *Krita-yaśas, ās,* m., N. of a descendant of Angiras.
— *Krita-yuga, am,* n. the first of the four ages of the world; the golden age; see *krita* above.
— *Krita-yogya, as, ā, am,* joining in combat.
— *Krita-ratha, as,* m., N. of a grandson of Maru.
— *Krita-rava, as, ā, am,* sounding, singing.
— *Krita-ruć, k, k, k,* splendid, brilliant. — *Krita-rusha, as, ā, am,* angry, displeased. — *Krita-lakshaṇa, as, ā, am,* marked, stamped; branded; noted for good qualities, excellent, amiable, &c.; defined, discriminated; (*as*), m., N. of a man.
— *Krita-vat, ān, atī, at,* making, having done or made anything; one who holds the stake at a game.
— *Krita-varman, ā,* m., N. of several princes, especially of a son of Hridika, also of Kanaka or Dhanaka; N. of the father of the thirteenth Arhat of the present Avasarpiṇī. — *Krita-vāpa, as,* m. a penitent who has shaven his head and chin. — *Krita-vikāra* or *krita-vikriya, as, ā, am,* altered, changed.
— *Krita-vikrama, as, ā, am,* displaying valour, making vigorous efforts. — *Krita-vidya, as, ā, am,* one who has acquired knowledge, well informed, scientific, a philosopher. — *Krita-vivāha, as, ā, am,* married. — *Krita-vismaya, as, ā, am,* astonished, astonishing. — *Krita-vīrya, as, ā, am,* being strong or powerful; (*as*), m., N. of a prince, a son of Kanaka or Dhanaka and father of Arjuna. — *Krita-vega, as,* m., N. of a prince. — *Krita-vetana, as, ā, am,* one who receives wages, a hired servant or labourer. — *Krita-vedin, ī, inī, i,* grateful, observant of propriety, knowing what is correct; see *krita-jña.* — *Krita-vedhaka* or *krita-vedhana, as,* m. a plant, a sort of Ghosha with white flowers. — *Krita-vepathu, us, us, u,* trembling. — *Krita-veśa, as, ā, am,* attired, ornamented, decorated. — *Krita-vyadhana, as, ā, am,* Ved. having weapons, armed.
— *Krita-vyalīka, as, ā, am,* annoyed, vexed, irritated. — *Krita-vrata, as,* m., N. of a pupil of Loma-harshaṇa. — *Krita-śakti, is, is, i,* putting forth one's strength or courage. — *Krita-śastra-niśrama, as, ā, am,* exercised in arms. — *Krita-śilpa, as, ā, am,* one who has learned his art or is skilled in his own trade. — *Krita-śobha, as, ā, am,* splendid, brilliant; beautiful, beautified; dexterous, handy. — *Krita-śauća, as, ā, am,* purified, cleansed, freed from bodily impurities, released from conventional defilement &c. — *Krita-śrama, as, ā, am,* one who has made great exertions, painstaking, laborious; (*as*), m., N. of a Muni. — *Krita-saṃsarga, as, ā, am,* brought into contact, united.
— *Krita-saṇskāra, as, ā, am,* initiated, one who has undergone all the purificatory ceremonies. — *Krita-sankalpa, as, ā, am,* one who has made a resolution. — *Krita-sanketa, as, ā, am,* making an agreement or appointment. — *Krita-sanjña, as, ā, am,* one who never loses his self-consciousness, one who has presence of mind; aroused; restored to consciousness or animation; distinguished by appropriate marks, devices, &c. — *Krita-sannāha, as, ā, am,* cased in armour. — *Krita-sannidhāna, as, ā, am,* brought into contact, approximated. — *Krita-sambandha, as, ā, am,* connected, allied. — *Krita-sāpatnikā* or *krita-sāpatnī* or *krita-sāpatnikā* or *krita-sāpatnakā* or *krita-sapatnikā,* f. a woman whose husband has taken another wife; a superseded wife. — *Krita-sthiti, is, is, i,* abiding, staying, taking up an abode. — *Krita-sneha, as, ā, am,* showing affection, affectionate. — *Krita-smara, as,* m., N. of a mountain. — *Krita-svastyayana, as, ā, am,* blessed, commended to the protection of gods previous to any journey or undertaking. — *Krita-svećchāhāra* (°*sva-ićchā-āh*°), *as, ā, am,* feeding at pleasure. — *Krita-hasta* or *krita-hastaka, as, ā, am,* one who has exercised his hands; dexterous; skilled in archery; clever, skilful, dexterous. — *Krita-hasta-tā,* f. dexterity; the being skilled in archery.
— *Kritākrita* (°*ta-ak*°), *as, ā, am,* done and not done, done in part but not completed, done and omitted, prepared and not prepared, manufactured and not manufactured; (*am*), n. what has been done and what has not been done. — *Kritāgama* (°*ta-āg*°), *as, ā, am,* one who has made progress, advanced, proficient. — *Kritāgas* (°*ta-āg*°), *ās, ās, as,* one who has committed an offence, offending, criminal, sinful, in fault. — *Kritāgni* (°*ta-ag*°), *is,* m., N. of a son of Kanaka or Dhanaka. — *Kritāgni-kārya, as,* m. a Brāhman who has offered the usual fire-oblation. — *Kritānka* (°*ta-an*°), *as, ā, am,* marked, branded; numbered. — *Kritāñjali* (°*ta-añ*°), *is, is, i,* one who joins the hands in reverence or to solicit a favour (keeping the palms from touching as if to hold alms or an offering), standing in a reverent or respectful posture; (*is*), m. a shrub used in medicine, also in magical potions &c. — *Kritāñjaliputa, as, ā, am,* joining the palms of the hands for obeisance, also for holding water &c. — *Kritātman* (°*ta-āt*°), *ā, ā, a,* one whose spirit is disciplined, subdued, tranquil; of a self-governed spirit. — *Kritānati* (°*ta-ān*°), *is, is, i,* bending, bowing, paying homage or respect. — *Kritānukara* (°*ta-an*°), *as, ī, am,* imitating what has been done by another, following another's example, subservient, not independent.
— *Kritānukūlya* (°*ta-an*°), *as, ā, am,* compliant, kind, favouring. — *Kritānukrita* (°*ta-an*°), *am,* n. that which is done before and after. — *Kritānuvyādha* (°*ta-an*°), *as, ā, am,* mixed, combined, united.
— *Kritānusāra* (°*ta-an*°), *as,* m. established practice, usage, custom, rate. — *Kritānta* (°*ta-an*°), *as, ā, am,* causing an end, bringing to an end, leading to any decisive termination; whose end is action; (*as*), m. destiny, fate; the inevitable result of actions done in a past existence; a N. of Yama, the god of death, (he is son of Sūrya and regent of the dead); death personified; a demonstrated conclusion, a dogma, a proved or established doctrine; a sinful or inauspicious action; Saturday, 'closing the week,' considered as an unlucky day; (*ā*), f. a kind of perfume, [cf. *reṇukā.*]
— *Kritānta-janaka, as,* m. a N. of the sun, as father of Yama. — *Kritānna* (°*ta-an*°), *am,* n. prepared or cooked food; digested food, excrement; (*as, ā, am*), eating. — *Kritāpakāra* (°*ta-ap*°), *as, ā, am,* injured, wronged; discomfited, overpowered; doing wrong, offending. — *Kritāpakrita* (°*ta-ap*°), *as, ā, am,* done for and against. — *Kritāpadāna* (°*ta-ap*°), *as, ā, am,* completing a great or noble work.
— *Kritāparādha* (°*ta-ap*°), *as, ā, am,* guilty, culpable, an offender. — *Kritābhaya* (°*ta-abh*°), *as, ā, am,* saved from fear. — *Kritābharaṇa* (°*ta-ābh*°), *as, ā, am,* adorned, decorated. — *Kritābhisaraṇa-veśa* (°*ta-abh*°), *as, ā, am,* attired in the dress of a maiden who goes to meet her lover. — *Kritābhisheka* (°*ta-abh*°), *as, ā, am,* sprinkled, inaugurated; (*as*), m. a prince &c. who has been inaugurated. — *Kritābhyāsa* (°*ta-abh*°), *as, ā, am,* trained, exercised, practised. — *Kritāya* (°*ta-aya*), *as,* m. the die called Krita. — *Kritāyāsa* (°*ta-āy*°), *as, ā, am,* labouring, suffering. — *Kritārgha* (°*ta-ar*°), *as,* m., N. of the nineteenth Arhat of the past Utsarpiṇī. — *Kritārtanāda* (°*ta-ār*°), *as, ā, am,* making cries of pain.
— *Kritārtha* (°*ta-ar*°), *as, ā, am,* one who has attained an end or object, having accomplished a purpose or desire, successful; satisfied, contented; clever; (*as*), m. a various reading for *kritārgha.*
— *Kritārtha-tā,* f. or *kritārtha-tva, am,* n. accomplishment of an object, success. — *Kritārthī-krita, as, ā, am,* rendered successful. — *Kritārthī-bhūta, as, ā, am,* become successful. — *Kritālaka* (°*ta-al*°), *as,* m., N. of one of Śiva's attendants. — *Kritālaya* (°*ta-āl*°), *as, ā, am,* one who has taken up his abode in any place (often compounded with the name of a place or country, e. g. *svarga-kritālayah,* an inhabitant of heaven); (*as*), m. a frog. — *Kritāloka* (°*ta-āl*°), *as, ā, am,* supplied with light, lighted.
— *Kritāvadhāna* (°*ta-av*°), *as, ā, am,* careful, cautious, prudent, attentive. — *Kritāvadhi* (°*ta-av*°), *is, is, i,* fixed, appointed, agreed upon; bounded, limited. — *Kritāvamarsha* (°*ta-av*°), *as, ā, am,* effacing from recollection; intolerant. — *Kritāvaśyaka* (°*ta-āv*°), *as, ā, am,* having done all that is necessary. — *Kritāvasakthika* (°*ta-av*°), *as, ā, am,* seated on the hams with the knees tied together or the hips and knees surrounded by a cloth. — *Kritāvastha* (°*ta-av*°), *as, ā, am,* summoned, called; made present; fixed, settled. — *Kritāvāsa* (°*ta-āv*°), *as,* m. a lodging; (*as, ā, am*), lodging. — *Kritāśana* (°*ta-aś*°), *as, ā, am,* feeding upon. — *Kritāsana-parigraha* (°*ta-ās*°), *as, ā, am,* seated. — *Kritāskandana* (°*ta-ās*°), *as, ā, am,* assailing, attacking; effacing from recollection. — *Kritāstra* (°*ta-as*°), *as, ā, am,* one who has exercised himself in throwing arrows or other weapons, skilled in archery; armed; (*as*), m., N. of a warrior. — *Kritāstra-tā,* f. consummate skill or proficiency in the use of arms. — *Kritāspada* (°*ta-ās*°), *as, ā, am,* governed, ruled; supporting, resting on; residing in or on, taking up one's abode. — *Kritāhaka, as, ā, am* (fr. *krita* + *ahan*), having performed the daily ceremonies or devotions.
— *Kritāhāra* or *kritāhāraka* (°*ta-āh*°), *as, ā, am,* having eaten food, having made a meal. — *Kritāhvāna* (°*ta-āh*°), *as, ā, am,* summoned, called, chal-

lenged. — *Kṛitershya* (°*ta-īr*°), *as, ā, am,* envious, jealous. — *Kṛitoććhais* (°*ta-uć*°), ind. raised on high. — *Kṛitotsāha* (°*ta-ut*°), *as, ā, am,* making effort, striving. — *Kṛitodaka* (°*ta-ud*°), *as, ā, am,* one who has performed his ablutions. — *Kṛitodvāha* (°*ta-ud*°), *as, ā, am,* performing penance by standing with uplifted hands; married. — *Kṛitopakāra* (°*ta-up*°), *as, ā, am,* assisted, befriended; friendly, giving aid. — *Kṛitopaćāra* (°*ta-up*°), *as, ā, am,* served, waited upon. — *Kṛitopanāyana* (°*ta-up*°), *as,* m. a student who has been invested with the sacrificial cord. — *Kṛitopabhoga* (°*ta-up*°), *as, ā, am,* used, enjoyed. — *Kṛitaujas* (°*ta-oj*°), *ās,* m., N. of a son of Kanaka or Dhanaka.

Kṛitaka, as, ā, am, artificial, factitious, done artificially, made, prepared, not produced spontaneously; not natural, adopted (as a son); assumed, simulated, false; (*am*), ind. in a simulated manner; (*as*), m., N. of a son of Vasu-deva, also of a son of Cyavana.

Kṛitaya, nom. P. *kṛitayati, -yitum,* to take the die called Kṛita.

Kṛitānta, kṛitārtha. See under *kṛita* above.

1. *kṛiti, is,* f. (for 2. see col. 2), doing, making, performing, manufacturing, composing; action, activity; creation, work, literary work; magic; enchantment; an enchantress, a witch; a kind of Anushṭubh metre consisting of two Pādas of twelve syllables each and a third Pāda of eight syllables; another metre, a stanza of four lines with twenty syllables in each; a square number; N. of the wife of Saṃhrāda and mother of Pañća-jana; (*is*), m., N. of several persons. — *Kṛiti-sādhya-tva, am,* n. the state of being accomplished by exertion.

Kṛitin, ī, inī, i, expert; clever, skilful, knowing, wise, learned; good, virtuous; pure, pious; following, obeying, doing what is enjoined; one who has attained an object or accomplished a purpose, satisfied; (*ī*), m., N. of a son of Cyavana and father of Uparićara; N. of a son of Sannatimat.

Kṛite and *kṛitena,* ind. (originally loc. and inst. fr. *kṛita*), on account of, for the sake of, for (with gen. or in comp., e. g. *mama kṛite* or *mat-kṛite,* on my account, for me).

Kṛiteyuka, as, m., N. of a son of Raudrāśva.

Kṛitnu, us, us, u, working well, able to work, powerful; skilful, clever, an artificer or mechanic, an artist.

Kṛitya, as, ā, am, to be done or performed; practicable, feasible; right, proper to be done; one who may be seduced from allegiance or alliance, one who may be bribed or hired as an assassin, treacherous; (*as*), m., scil. *pratyaya,* the class of affixes forming the fut. pass. part. &c. (as *tavya, anīya, ya, elima,* &c.); a kind of evil spirit or ghost, either with or without the addition of *yaksha, mānusha, asura,* &c.; (*ā*), f. action, act, deed; magic; a female deity to whom sacrifices are offered for destructive and magical purposes; N. of a river; (*am*), n. what ought to be done; duty, office; purpose, end, object; what is proper or fit; motive, cause. — *Kṛitya-kalpa-taru, us,* m. title of a work on jurisprudence. — *Kṛitya-kalpa-latā,* f., N. of a work by Vāćaspati-miśra. — *Kṛitya-ćintāmaṇi, is,* m. title of a work by Śivarāma. — *Kṛitya-jña, as, ā, am,* who knows what is to be done, learned, wise. — *Kṛitya-tattva, am,* n. 'the true nature of duty or obligation,' title of a work. — *Kṛitya-tā,* f. seduction from allegiance or alliance. — *Kṛitya-ratnākara, as* or *am* (?), m. or n. (?), title of a work on jurisprudence. — *Kṛitya-vat, ān, atī, at,* having any business or request or object; busy, active. — *Kṛitya-vartman, a,* n. the right way, the manner in which any object is to be effected. — *Kṛitya-vid, t, t, t,* one who knows what ought to be done, knowing duty, learned, wise. — *Kṛitya-vidhi, is,* m. the way to do anything, a rule, a precept. — *Kṛityā-kṛit, t, t, t,* Ved. practising magic or sorcery, bewitching. — *Kṛityā-dūshaṇa, as, ī, am,* or *kṛityā-dūshi, is, is, i,* Ved. counteracting magic, destroying its effect. — *Kṛityā-rāvaṇa, as* or *am* (?), m. or n. (?), title of a work.

Kṛityaka, as, m. an injurer?; (*ā*), f. an enchantress, a witch, a woman who is the fatal cause of injury or destruction, the fatal destroyer, the bane.

Kṛitrima, as, ā, am, made artificially, factitious, artificial, the reverse of what is naturally or spontaneously produced; falsified, adopted (as a child); (*as*), m. incense, olibanum; an adopted son; (*am*), n. a kind of salt, the common Bit Noben, or Bit Lavan, obtained by cooking; a sort of perfume [cf. *jarādi*]; a kind of collyrium [cf. *rasāñjana*]. — *Kṛitrima-dhūpa, as,* m. incense, olibanum. — *Kṛitrima-dhūpaka, as,* m. compound perfume, containing ten or eighteen ingredients. — *Kṛitrima-putra, as,* m. an adopted son; one of the twelve kinds recognised in law, the son made. — *Kṛitrima-putraka, as,* m. a doll. — *Kṛitrima-bhūmi, is,* f. a made floor. — *Kṛitrima-mitra, as,* m. an acquired friend, one on whom benefits have been conferred, or from whom they have been received. — *Kṛitrima-vana, am,* n. a plantation, a park. — *Kṛitrima-śatru, us,* m. an acquired enemy. — *Kṛitrimo-dāsīna* (°*ma-ud*°), *as,* m. an acquired neutral.

Kṛitvan, ā, arī, a, Ved. causing, effecting; active, busy; practising magic or sorcery in order to bewitch.

Kṛitvas, ind. at the end of a numeral or numeral adjective, = fold, times (e. g. *daśa-kṛitvas,* ten times; *bahu-kṛitvas,* many times; *pañća-kṛitvas,* five-fold). In the earlier language *kṛitvas* is used as a separate word, but native grammarians regard it only as an affix, and it is so used in classical Sanskrit; it was perhaps originally an acc. plur. fr. a noun *kṛitu,* formed by the affix *tu* fr. the root 1. *kṛi;* [cf. also *kṛit* in *sakṛit.*]

Kṛitvā, ind. having made or done.

Kṛitvi, f., N. of a daughter of Śuka, wife of Aṇuha (Nīpa) and mother of Brahma-datta.

Kṛitvya, as, ā, am, Ved. one who is able to perform anything, strong, efficacious; having accomplished many deeds, exerting one's power.

Kriyamāṇa, as, ā, am, being done, made, &c.

कृ 2. *kṛi,* cl. 3. P., Ved. *ćakarti, akārīt,* Intens. *ćarkarti,* to make mention of, to praise, to speak highly of (with gen.); [cf. *kāru, kīri, kīrti.*]

कृ 3. *kṛi,* to injure &c. See 2. *kṝi.*

2. *kṛiti, is,* m. or f. (for 1. see col. 1), Ved. a kind of weapon, a sort of knife or a dagger; (*is*), f. hurt, hurting, injuring; waylaying. — *Kṛiti-kara, as,* m. epithet of Rāvaṇa. — *Kṛiti-mat, ān,* m. the founder of a race, realm, &c.; N. of a son of Yavīnara. — *Kṛiti-rāta, as,* m., N. of a prince; [cf. *kīrtti-rāta.*] — *Kṛiti-roman, ā,* m., N. of a son of Kṛitirāta.

कृक *kṛika, as,* m. the throat, the larynx.

कृकण *kṛikaṇa, as,* m. a kind of partridge, commonly Kaër, Perdix Sylvatica [cf. *kṛikara* and *krakara*]; a worm; N. of a man; N. of a place.

Kṛikaṇīya, as, ā, am, belonging or relating to a partridge.

Kṛikaṇeyu, us, m., N. of a son of Raudrāśva.

कृकदाशु *kṛikadāśu, us* or *ūs,* m., Ved. one who hurts or injures.

कृकर *kṛikara, as,* m. a kind of partridge, commonly Kaër, Perdix Sylvatica [cf. *kṛikaṇa* and *krakara*]; a kind of pepper, Piper Chaba; the fragrant oleander tree [cf. *karavīra*]; one of the five vital airs, that which assists in digestion; an epithet of Śiva.

कृकला *kṛikalā,* f. long pepper; [cf. *pippalī.*]

कृकलाश *kṛikalāśa* or *kṛikalāsa* or *kṛika-lāsaka, as,* m. a lizard, a chameleon. — *Kṛikalāsa-dīpikā,* f. title of a mystical work.

कृकवाकु *kṛikavāku, us,* m. a cock, a gallinaceous fowl; a peacock; a lizard, a chameleon; [with the first part of this word cf. Hib. *ceare,* 'a hen.'] — *Kṛikavāku-dhvaja, as,* m. an epithet of Kārttikeya.

कृकषा *kṛikashā,* f. a kind of bird; [cf. *kan-kaṇahārikā.*]

कृकाट *kṛikāṭa, am,* n., Ved. the joint of the neck.

Kṛikāṭaka, am, n. the neck; a part of a column; (*ikā*), f. the back of the neck; the raised and straight part of the neck.

कृकालिका *kṛikālikā,* f. a kind of bird.

कृकिन् *kṛikin, ī,* m., N. of a mythical king.

कृकुलास *kṛikulāsa, as,* m. a lizard, a chameleon; [cf. *kṛikalāsa.*]

कृच्छ्र *kṛiććhra, as, ā, am* (perhaps fr. rt. *kṛish* and connected with *kashṭa*), causing trouble or pain, painful, attended with pain or labour; being in a difficult or painful situation; bad, miserable, evil, wicked, sinful; (*am*), ind. miserably, painfully, laboriously, with difficulty; (*as* or *am*), m. n. difficulty, trouble, labour, hardship, distress, calamity, pain, evil, misery, danger, sin, (often in compounds, e. g. *vanavāsa-kṛiććhra,* the difficulties of living in a forest; *mūtra-kṛiććhra,* ischury; *artha-kṛiććhreshu,* in difficulties, in a miserable situation; *prāṇa-kṛiććhra,* danger of life); bodily mortification, austerity, penance, expiation; torment, torture; a particular kind of religious penance, according to some = *prājāpatya,* according to others = *sāntapana.* *Kṛiććhreṇa,* inst. with difficulty, with great exertion, painfully, laboriously, hardly, scarcely; *alpa-kṛiććhreṇa,* with little difficulty, easily. — *Kṛiććhra-karman, a,* n. a difficult act, difficulty, labour. — *Kṛiććhra-kāla, as,* m. a season of difficulty. — *Kṛiććhra-gata, as, ā, am,* undergoing trouble or misery, suffering pain; being in difficulties, distressed. — *Kṛiććhra-tā,* f. painful or dangerous state (especially in disease). — *Kṛiććhra-prāṇa, as, ā, am,* one whose life is in danger; breathing with difficulty; hardly supporting life. — *Kṛiććhra-mūtra-purisha-tva, am,* n. pain or difficulty in the evacuations. — *Kṛiććhra-sādhya, as, ā, am,* curable with difficulty. — *Kṛiććhrātikṛiććhra* (°*ra-at*°), *au,* m. du. the ordinary and extraordinary penance, penance; (*as*), m. sing. a particular kind of penance, taking no sustenance but water for three, nine, twelve, or twenty-one days. — *Kṛiććhrān-mukta, as, ā, am,* freed from trouble &c. — *Kṛiććhrāpta* (°*ra-āp*°) or *kṛiććhropanata* (°*ra-up*°), *as, ā, am,* gained with difficulty. — *Kṛiććhrāri* (°*ra-ari*), *is,* m., N. of a plant, a species of Vilva. — *Kṛiććhrārdha* (°*ra-ar*°), *as,* m. an inferior penance lasting only six days. — *Kṛiććhre-śrit, t, t, t,* Ved. undergoing danger; struggling with difficulties.

Kṛiććhrāya, nom. A. *kṛiććhrāyate, -yitum,* to feel pain; to have wicked designs.

Kṛiććhrin, ī, iṇī, i, encompassed with difficulties, being in trouble, feeling pain; angry.

कृड् *kṛiḍ,* cl. 6. P. *kṛiḍati,* to become thick or coarse; to become fat or gross, to become solid; to eat; (another form for *kūḍ.*)

कृणञ्ज *kṛiṇañja, as,* m. a kind of Chenopodium, = *kuṇañjara.*

कृणु *kṛiṇu, us,* m. a painter.

कृत् 2. *kṛit,* (for 1. *kṛit* see under rt. 1. *kṛi* at p. 246), cl. 6. P. *kṛintati, ćakarta, kartsyati* and *kartishyati, akartīt, kartitum,* to cut, cut in pieces, cut off, divide; to tear asunder, destroy: Caus. *kartayati,* to cut, divide, &c.: Desid. *ćikartishati* and *ćikṛitsati:* Intens. *ćarīkṛityate, ćarīkartti;* [cf. Lith. *kertu,* inf. *kirsti,* 'to cut;' Gr. κείρω, κάρσις; Slav. *korjû,* 'to split;' Lat. *curtus, culter;* Hib. *ceartaighim,* 'I prune, trim, cut;' *cuire,* 'a knife.']

Kṛitta, as, ā, am, cut, divided; desired, sought, wished for.

Kṛitti, is, f. skin, hide; a garment made of skin; the hide or skin on which the religious student sits, sleeps, &c., usually the skin of an antelope; the birch tree; the bark of the birch tree, used for writing upon, for making hooka pipes, &c.; one of the lunar mansions, the Pleiads; a house; [cf. Hib. *cart;* Lat. *cortex.*] — *Kṛitti-ratha, as,* m., N. of a prince. — *Kṛitti-vāsa, as,* m. or *kṛitti-vāsas, ās,* m. covered with a skin, an epithet of Rudra-Śiva; *(ās),* f. epithet of Durgā.

Kṛittikā, ās, f. pl., N. of a constellation, = the Pleiades, (originally the first, but in later times the third lunar mansion, having Agni as its regent; this constellation, containing six stars, is sometimes represented as a flame or as a kind of razor or knife; in mythology the six Kṛittikās are nymphs who became the nurses of the god of war, Kārttikeya); a vehicle, carriage, cart. — *Kṛittikāñji* (°*kā-añ*°), *is, is, i,* having a carriage as an emblem or sign. — *Kṛittikā-bhava, as,* m. 'being in the lunar mansion Kṛittikā,' an epithet of Candra, the moon. — *Kṛittikā-suta, as,* m. 'son of the Kṛittikās,' an epithet of Skanda or Kārttikeya; (the nymphs called Kṛittikās being his foster-mothers.)

Kṛintatra, am, n., Ved. a section, a shred, chip; a plough.

Kṛintana, am, n. cutting, cutting off, dividing.

कृत् 3. *kṛit,* cl. 7. P. *kṛiṇatti, ćakarta, kartishyati, kartitum,* to twist threads, to spin; to surround, encompass; attire.

Kṛitad-vasu, us, us, u, Ved. distributing goods (?).

Kṛitā, f., Ved. an abyss (?).

Kṛitsa, am, n. water; entire, whole; [cf. the next.]

Kṛitsna, as, ā, am (rarely used in pl.), all, whole, entire; *(am),* n. water; the flank or hip; the belly. — *Kṛitsna-tā,* f. totality, completeness. — *Kṛitsna-vid, t, t, t,* omniscient, knowing all things. — *Kṛitsna-śas,* ind. wholly, entirely, altogether. — *Kṛitsna-hṛidaya, am,* n. the whole heart. — *Kṛitsnāyata* (°*na-āy*°), *as, ā, am,* Ved. stretched out to its full length.

Kṛitsnaka, as, ā, am, all, every.

कृतान्त *kṛitānta, kṛitārtha.* See p. 247.

कृदन्त *kṛid-anta.* See under 1. *kṛit,* p. 246.

कृदर *kṛidara, am,* n., Ved. a store-room, a vessel; the lap; *(as),* m. a granary, a cupboard &c. for holding corn, grain, &c.

कृधु *kṛidhu, us, us, u,* or *kṛidhuka, as, ā, am,* Ved. shortened, mutilated, small, deficient. — *Kṛidhu-karṇa, as, ā, am,* Ved. having short ears (as a sort of imp); hearing badly.

कृन्तत्र *kṛintatra.* See under 2. *kṛit.*

कृप् 1. *kṛip, p,* f., Ved. (occurring only in inst.), beautiful appearance, beauty, splendor. — *Kṛipa-nīḷa* (for *kṛipā-*°), *as, ā, am,* Ved. one whose home is splendor, dwelling in splendor, epithet of Agni; (Sāy.) the support of sacred rites.

कृप् 2. *kṛip* (connected with rt. *krap*), cl. 1. A. *karpate,* to have pity or mercy on; cl. 10. P. *kṛipayati* or *kṛipāpayati, -yitum,* to be weak; to pity; to mourn, grieve, lament; [cf. Gr. ἔλπω.]

Kṛipa, as, m., N. of a man described in the Veda as a friend of Indra; *(as),* m. and *(ī),* f., N. of the son and daughter of the sage Śaradvat, (he performed severe penance and thereby alarmed the jealous Indra, who sent a nymph to tempt him, but without success; however, twin sons were born to the sage in a clump of grass (*śara-stambe*), who were found by king Śāntanu and out of pity (*kṛipā*) taken home and reared as his own; the daughter, Kṛipī, married Droṇa, and had by him a son called Aśvatthāman; the son, Kṛipa, became one of the privy council at Hastināpur, and is sometimes called Gautama, sometimes Śāradvata. According to the Hari-vaṇśa and Vishṇu-Purāṇa, Kṛipa and Kṛipī were only distant descendants of Śaradvat. According to others, Kṛipa = Vyāsa or = a son of Kṛishṇa.) — *Kṛipī-pati, is,* m. a N. of Droṇa as husband of Kṛipī. — *Kṛipī-putra* or *kṛipī-suta, as,* m., a N. of Aśvatthāman as son of Kṛipī.

Kṛipaṇa, as, ā or *ī, am,* inclined to grieve; pitiable, miserable, poor, wretched, feeble; low, vile; miserly, stingy; avaricious; arising from pity, caused by pity; *(am),* ind. miserably; *(as),* m. a worm; *(am),* n. wretchedness, misery; *sa-kṛipaṇam,* miserably, pitiably; [cf. *kārpaṇya.*] — *Kṛipaṇa-kāśin, ī, inī, i,* Ved. looking suppliantly, looking desirous; expressing a desire (?). — *Kṛipaṇa-tva, am,* n. misery; wretchedness; miserable condition. — *Kṛipaṇa-dhī, īs, īs, i,* little-minded. — *Kṛipaṇa-nindā,* f. 'censure of the miser,' title of a chapter of the Sārṅgadhara Paddhati. — *Kṛipaṇa-buddhi, is, is, i,* little-minded. — *Kṛipaṇa-vatsala, as, ā, am,* kind to the poor.

Kṛipaṇāya, nom. A. *kṛipaṇāyate,* to feel miserable.

Kṛipaṇin, ī, inī, i, miserable, one who is in misery.

Kṛipaṇya, nom. P. *kṛipaṇyati,* to wish, desire, be a suppliant for anything, pray for, obtain by entreaties; (in A. also *kṛipaṇate.*)

Kṛipaṇyu, us, us, u, Ved. one who praises.

Kṛipā, f. pity, tenderness, compassion; N. of a river. — *Kṛipā-dṛishṭi, is,* f. a look with favour, a kind look. — *Kṛipādvaita* (°*pā-ad*°), *as,* m. one of the Buddhas or deified saints of the Buddhists. — *Kṛipānvita* (°*pā-an*°), *as, ā, am,* or *kṛipā-maya, as, ī, am,* or *kṛipālu, us, us, u,* or *kṛipā-vat, ān, atī, at,* pitiful, merciful, compassionate, tender. — *Kṛipā-miśra, as,* m., N. of a son of Deva-miśra. — *Kṛipā-hīna, as, ā, am,* pitiless, unfeeling, unkind.

Kṛipāya, nom. A. *kṛipāyate, -yitum,* to mourn, grieve, lament, have pity.

कृपाण *kṛipāṇa, as,* m. (said to be fr. rt. *kṛip* for rt. *klṛip?*), a sword, a scymitar, a sacrificial knife; *(ī),* f. a pair of shears or scissors; a dagger.

Kṛipāṇaka, as, m. a sword, a scymitar; *(ikā),* f. a dagger, a knife.

कृपीट *kṛipīṭa, am,* n. (said to be fr. rt. 2. *kṛip*), underwood, wood, forest; fire-wood, wood, timber; water; the belly. — *Kṛipīṭa-pāla, as,* m. a rudder or large oar used as one; the ocean; air, wind. — *Kṛipīṭa-yoni, is,* m. fire.

कृमि *kṛimi, is,* or *krimi, is,* m. (said to be fr. rt. *kram;* cf. *krami*), a worm, an insect in general; a spider; an ant; lac, the red dye caused by insects; N. of a son of Uśīnara; N. of an Asura, the brother of Rāvaṇa; N. of a Nāga-rāja; *(is),* f., N. of the wife of Uśīnara and mother of Kṛimi; [cf. Lith. *kirminis, kirmele;* Russ. *ćervj;* Hib. *cruimh;* Cambro-Brit. *pryv;* Goth. *vaurms,* Them. *vaurmi* for *hvaurmi;* Lat. *vermi-s* for *quermi-s;* perhaps Gr. ἕλμινς for ἕρμινς.] — *Kṛimi-kaṇṭaka, am,* n. several plants efficacious in destroying worms, Ficus Glomerata; another plant, = *ćitrā* or *ćitrāṅga;* another plant, = *viḍaṅga.* — *Kṛimi-kara, as,* m. a kind of poisonous insect. — *Kṛimi-karṇa* or *kṛimi-karṇaka, as,* m. worms or lice generated in the external ear. — *Kṛimi-kośa* or *kṛimi-kosha, as,* m. the cocoon of a silkworm. — *Kṛimikośottha* (°*śa-ut*°), *as, ā, am,* silk, silken. — *Kṛimi-granthi, is,* m. a disease of the eyes, caused by insects generated at the roots of the eyelashes. — *Kṛimi-ghātin, ī, inī, i,* destroying worms; *(ī),* m. a medicinal drug, = *viḍaṅga* (?). — *Kṛimi-ghna, as, ī, am,* vermifuge, anthelmintic; *(as),* m. a shrub used in medicine as a vermifuge, commonly Bireng, Erycibe Paniculata, see *viḍaṅga;* the onion; the root of the jujube; the marking nut plant; *(ī),* f. turmeric. — *Kṛimi-ja, as, ā, am,* produced by worms; *(ā),* f. lac, a red dye produced by an insect, commonly called Lākshā; *(am),* n. Agallochum. — *Kṛimi-jagdha, am,* n. Agallochum. — *Kṛimi-jalaja, as,* m. a shell-fish, an animal living in a shell. — *Kṛimi-dantaka, as,* m. tooth-ache with decay of the teeth. — *Kṛimi-parvata, as,* m. an ant-hill. — *Kṛimi-bhaksha, as,* m., N. of a hell. — *Kṛimi-bhojana, as, ā, am,* one whose food consists of worms; *(as),* m., N. of a hell. — *Kṛimi-mat, ān, atī, at,* affected or covered with worms. — *Kṛimi-ripu, us,* m. an anthelmintic plant, = *viḍaṅga.* — *Kṛimi-roga, as,* m. disease caused by worms. — *Kṛimi-varṇa, as* or *am* (?), m. or n. (?), red cloth. — *Kṛimi-vāriruha, as,* m. a fish living in a shell. — *Kṛimi-vṛiksha, as,* m. a kind of plant, Koshāmra. — *Kṛimi-śaṅkha, as,* m. the fish living in the conch. — *Kṛimi-śatru, us,* m. an anthelmintic plant, Erythrina Fulgens, = *viḍaṅga.* — *Kṛimi-śātrava, as,* m. the plant Acacia Farnesiana. — *Kṛimi-śukti, is,* f. a bivalve shell, a muscle; the animal living in a bivalve shell; an oyster. — *Kṛimi-śaila* or *kṛimi-śailaka, as,* m. an ant or mole-hill; [cf. *kṛimi-parvata.*] — *Kṛimi-sarārī,* f. a kind of poisonous insect. — *Kṛimi-sena, as,* m., N. of a Yaksha. — *Kṛimi-hantṛi, tā, trī, tṛi,* or *kṛimi-hara, as, ī, am,* anthelmintic, vermifuge. — *Kṛimi-hā,* f. an anthelmintic plant, = *viḍaṅga.* — *Kṛimīśa* (°*mi-īśa*), *as,* m., N. of a hell.

Kṛimika, as, m. a small worm.

Kṛimiṇa, as, ā, am, having worms.

Kṛimin, ī, iṇī, i, affected with worms.

Kṛimila, as, ā, am, having worms, wormy; *(ā),* f. a fruitful woman, one bearing many children; N. of a town, called after Kṛimi. — *Kṛimilāśva* (°*la-aś*°), *as,* m., N. of a son of Bāhyāśva.

Kṛimilikā, f. linen cloth dyed with red colour.

Kṛimilaka, as, m. a white sort of kidney-bean; [cf. *vana-mudga.*]

कृमुक *kṛimuka, as,* m., Ved. a kind of tree; [cf. *kārmuka* and *kramuka.*]

कृव् *kṛiv* = 1. *kṛi,* cl. 5. *kṛiṇoti.* See p. 246.

कृवि *kṛivi, is,* m. (said to be fr. 1. *kṛi*), a loom (?); [cf. *krivi.*]

कृश् *kṛiś,* cl. 4. P. *kṛiśyati, ćakarśa, karśishyati, akṛiśat, karśitum,* to become lean or thin, to become emaciated or feeble; to wane (as the moon): Caus. *karśayati, -yitum,* to make thin or lean, to attenuate, emaciate, to keep short of food; [cf. perhaps Lat. *parco, parcus, parum, parvus, paucus;* Gr. παῦρος; Goth. *favai;* Eng. *few.*]

Kṛiśa, as, ā, am, lean, emaciated, thin, spare, weak, feeble; small, little, minute, insignificant, poor; *(as),* m., N. of a man, also of a Nāga; N. of a Ṛishi, author of a Ṛig-veda hymn; [cf. Hib. *creas,* 'narrow, straight;' *caile,* 'narrowness.'] — *Kṛiśa-gu, us, us, u,* Ved. one who has lean cattle. — *Kṛiśa-tā,* f. or *kṛiśa-tva, am,* n. leanness, thinness. — *Kṛiśa-śākha, as,* m., N. of a plant, = *parpaṭa.* — *Kṛiśāksha* (°*śa-ak*°), *as,* m., a spider. — *Kṛiśāṅga* (°*śa-aṅ*°), *as, ī, am,* emaciate, spare, thin; *(as),* m. an epithet of Śiva; *(ī),* f. a woman with a slender shape; a particular plant, commonly called Priyaṅgu. — *Kṛiśāśva* (°*śa-aś*°), *as,* m., N. of several persons; N. of an author of directions to players and dancers. — *Kṛiśāśvin, ī,* m. a pupil of Kṛiśāśva, a dancer, an actor, a tumbler. — *Kṛiśodara* (°*śa-ud*°), *as, ā, am,* thin-waisted.

Kṛiśikā, f. the plant Salvinia Cucculata.

कृशन *kṛiśana, am,* n., Ved. a pearl, mother-of-pearl; gold; form, shape; *(as, ā, am),* yielding or containing pearls; [cf. *ūrdhva-kṛiśana* and *kārśana.*] — *Kṛiśanā-vat, ān, atī, at,* Ved. decorated with pearls.

Kṛiśanin, ī, inī, i, Ved. decorated with pearls.

कृशर *kṛiśara, as, ā,* m. f. a dish composed of milk, sesamum, and rice; rice and peas boiled together with a few spices, commonly called Khichree; [cf. *kṛisara.*]

कृशला *kṛiśalā,* f. the hair of the head.

कृशाकु *kṛiśāku, us,* m. heating, grieving; (a various reading for *kṛiśānu.*)

कृशानु *kṛiśānu, us,* m. (fr. rt. *kṛiś* for *kṛish?*), Ved. 'bending the bow,' an epithet applied to a good archer, (generally connected with *astṛi*, 'an archer,' though sometimes used alone: some regard Kṛiśānu as a divine being, either similar in character to Rudra or this god himself; he is armed with the lightning and defends the 'heavenly' Soma from the hawk, who tries to steal and bear it from heaven to earth); a N. of Agni or fire; fire in general; N. of a plant, Plumbago Zeylanica; N. of an archer; N. of a Gandharva. — *Kṛiśānu-retas, ās,* m. an epithet of Śiva.

Kṛiśānuka, as, ī, am, containing the word Kṛiśānu, as an Anuvāka or Adhyāya.

कृष *kṛish,* cl. 1. P. *karshati, ćakarsha, karkshyati* and *krakshyati, akṛikshat, akārkshīt* and *akrākshīt, karshṭum* and *krashṭum,* to draw, attract, draw to one's self, drag, pull, pull to and fro, drag away, tear; to lead or conduct (as an army); to bend (a bow); to draw into one's power, become master of, overpower; to obtain; to take away anything from any one (with two acc., e.g. *akarshat tam rājyam,* he deprived him of the kingdom); cl. 6. P. A. *kṛishati, -te,* to draw or make furrows, to plough: Caus. *karshayati, -yitum,* to draw, to draw out, tear up, tear out; extract; to drag to and fro, cause pain, torture, torment; to draw or make furrows, to plough: Desid. *ćikṛikshati, -te:* Intens. *ćarīkṛishyate, ćarīkarshṭi* or *ćarīkrashṭi;* [cf. Lith. *karszu, pleszau;* Russ. *ćeshu;* Lat. *verro, vello;* Gr. κόρος, ἕλκω? Goth. *falh.*]

Karsha, karshaṇa, &c. See s. v. at p. 210.

Kṛishaka, as, ā, am, attractive, drawing, who or what draws furrows or ploughs; *(as),* m. a ploughman, husbandman, farmer; a ploughshare; an ox.

Kṛishāṇa, as, m. a ploughman, a husbandman.

Kṛishi, is, f. ploughing, cultivation of the soil; agriculture, husbandry; the cultivation of the soil personified. — *Kṛishi-karman, a,* n. agriculture, husbandry. — *Kṛishi-jīvin, ī,* m. a cultivator, a farmer. — *Kṛishi-phala, am,* n. agricultural produce or profit. — *Kṛishi-sevā,* f. agriculture.

Kṛishika, as, m. a cultivator of the soil, a husbandman; the ploughshare.

Kṛishīvala, as, ā, am, one who lives by husbandry or agriculture; *(as),* m. a husbandman.

Kṛishṭa, as, ā, am, ploughed or tilled, a field &c. — *Kṛishṭa-ja, as, ā, am,* grown in cultivated ground, cultivated. — *Kṛishṭa-paćya, as, ā, am,* ripening in cultivated ground, sown or ripening after ploughing, as rice &c.; cultivated. — *Kṛishṭa-pākya, as, ā, am,* ripening on cultivated ground; sown or ripening after ploughing. — *Kṛishṭa-phala, am,* n. the product of a harvest. — *Kṛishṭa-rādhi, is, is, i,* Ved. successful in agriculture. — *Kṛishṭopta* (°ṭa-up°), *as, ā, am,* sown on cultivated ground.

Kṛishṭi, ayas, f. pl., Ved. men, races of men, sometimes with the epithet *mānushīs;* (originally the word may have meant cultivated ground, then an inhabited land, next its inhabitants, and lastly any race of men; Indra and Agni have the N. *rājā kṛishṭīnām;* and *pañća kṛishṭayas,* 'the five races,' comprehends the whole human race, not only the Āryan tribes); according to native lexicographers the word means also ploughing, cultivating the soil; attracting, drawing; and *(is),* m. a teacher, a learned man or Paṇḍit. — *Kṛishṭi-prā; ās, ās, am,* Ved. pervading the human race. — *Kṛishṭi-han, hā, ghnī, ha,* Ved. subduing nations. — *Kṛishṭy-ojas, ās, ās, as,* Ved. overpowering men.

Kṛishya, as, ā, am, to be ploughed.

Krashṭavya, as, ā, am, to be drawn or drawn out.

कृषाणु *kṛishāṇu, us,* m. a N. of fire; (a wrong reading for *kṛiśānu.*)

कृष्कर *kṛishkara, as,* m. an epithet of Śiva; [cf. *kṛikara.*]

कृष्ण 1. *kṛishṇa, as, ā, am* (said to be fr. rt. *kṛish*), black, dark, dark-blue (opposed to *śveta, śukla, rohita,* and *aruṇa*); wicked, evil; *(as),* m. black, the colour, or dark-blue, which is often confounded with black by the Hindūs; the black antelope; a kind of beast of prey (described in the Veda as feeding on carrion and dead corpses); a crow; the Indian cuckoo or Kokila; the plant Carissa Carandas; the dark half of the lunar month from full to new moon [cf. *kṛishṇa-paksha* below]; the fourth or Kali-yuga; N. of one of the poets of the Ṛig-veda descended from Aṅgiras; N. of a celebrated Avatār of the god Vishṇu, or sometimes identified with Vishṇu himself, as distinct from his ten Avatārs or incarnations. (In the earlier legends he appears as a great hero and teacher; in the more recent he is deified, and is often represented as a young and amorous shepherd with flowing hair and a flute in his hand. The following are a few particulars of his birth and history as related in the Purāṇas &c.: Vasu-deva, who was a descendant of Yadu and Yayāti, had two wives, Rohiṇī and Devakī. The latter had eight sons, of whom the eighth was Kṛishṇa. Kaṇsa, king of Mathurā and cousin of Devakī, was informed by a prediction that one of these sons would kill him. He therefore kept Vasu-deva and his wife in confinement, and slew their first six children. The seventh was Bala-rāma, who was saved by being abstracted from the womb of Devakī and transferred to that of Rohiṇī. The eighth was Kṛishṇa, who was born with black skin and a peculiar mark on his breast. His father Vasu-deva managed to escape from Mathurā with the child, and favoured by the gods found a herdsman named Nanda, whose wife Yaśodā had just been delivered of a son, which Vasu-deva conveyed to Devakī, after substituting his own in its place. Nanda with his wife Yaśodā took the infant Kṛishṇa and settled first in Gokula or Vraja, and afterwards in Vṛindāvana, where Kṛishṇa and Bala-rāma grew up together, roaming in the woods and joining in the sports of the herdsmen's sons. Kṛishṇa as a youth contested the sovereignty of Indra, and was victorious over that god, who descended from heaven to praise Kṛishṇa, and made him lord over the cattle. Kṛishṇa is described as sporting constantly with the Gopīs or shepherdesses, of whom a thousand became his wives, though only eight are specified, Rādhā being the favourite. Kṛishṇa built and fortified a city called Dvāraka in Gujarāt, and thither transported the inhabitants of Mathurā after killing Kaṇsa. Kṛishṇa had various wives besides the Gopīs, and by Rukmiṇī had a son Pradyumna, who is usually identified with Kāma-deva; with Jainas, Kṛishṇa is one of the nine black Vasu-devas; with Buddhists he is the chief of the black demons, who are the enemies of Buddha and the white demons); N. of a king of the Nāgas; N. of an Asura or demon; N. of Arjuna, the most renowned of the Pāṇḍu princes (so named apparently from his colour as a child, see Mahā-bh. Virāṭa-parva 1389; the dual *kṛishṇau* = Kṛishṇa and Arjuna); N. of Vyāsa; of Kṛishṇa Hārīta; of a son of Śuka by Pīvarī, a teacher of the Yoga; N. of a pupil of Bharadvāja; of Dāśārha; of a son of Havirdhāna; of a son of Arjuna; of an adopted son of Asamañjas; of a chief of the Andhras; N. of the author of a commentary on the Mahā-bhārata; N. of a poet; N. of the author of a commentary on the Dāya-bhāga; N. of the son of Keśavārka and grandson of Jayāditya; N. of the father of Tānabhaṭṭa and uncle of Raṅganātha; N. of the father of Dāmodara and uncle of Malhaṇa; N. of the father of Prabhūjika and uncle of Vidyādhara; N. of the father of Madana; N. of the grammarian Rāma-ćandra; N. of the son of Vāruṇendra and father of Lakshmaṇa; N. of the father of Hīrabhaṭṭa, author of the commentary called Caraka-bhāshya, and of the work Sāhitya-sudhāsamudra; N. of a hell; *(ā),* f. a kind of poisonous insect; several plants, as Piper Longum, the Indigo plant; a grape; a kind of perfume [cf. *parpaṭī*]; an epithet of Draupadī; an epithet of Durgā; N. of one of the seven tongues of fire; N. of the river Kistna; *(ī),* f. night; *(am),* n. blackness, darkness; the black part of the eye; a kind of demon or spirit of darkness; black pepper; black Agallochum; iron; lead; antimony; blue vitriol; [cf. *kārshṇa,* &c.; cf. also Russ. *ćernyi,* 'black.'] — *Kṛishṇa-kanda, am,* n. the red lotus, Nymphæa Rubra. — *Kṛishṇa-karkaṭaka, as,* m. a kind of black crab. — *Kṛishṇa-karṇa, as, ā, am,* Ved. black-eared. — *Kṛishṇakarṇāmṛita* (°ṇa-am°), *am,* n., N. of a poem by Vilva-maṅgala. — *Kṛishṇa-karman, a,* n. making black; a peculiar manner of cauterising; *(ā, ā, a),* criminal, guilty. — *Kṛishṇa-kāka, as,* m. a raven. — *Kṛishṇa-kāpotī,* f. a kind of plant; [cf. *śveta-kāpotī, kṛishṇa-sarpā.*] — *Kṛishṇa-kāshṭha, am,* n. a black variety of Agallochum. — *Kṛishṇa-keli, is,* m. a plant, Mirabilis Jalapa. — *Kṛishṇa-kohala, as,* m. a gamester, a gambler. — *Kṛishṇa-krīḍita, am,* n., N. of a poem by Keśavārka celebrating the god Kṛishṇa. — *Kṛishṇa-khaṇḍa,* title of the fourth book of the Brahmavaivarta-purāṇa. — *Kṛishṇa-gaṅgā,* f., N. of a river, = *kṛishṇā, kṛishṇa-samudbhavā, kṛishṇaveṇyā.* — *Kṛishṇa-gati, is,* m. fire ('whose way is black'); [cf. *kṛishṇa-yāma, kṛishṇa-vartani,* &c.] — *Kṛishṇa-gandhā,* f. the tree Hyperanthera Moringa. — *Kṛishṇa-garbha, as, ā, am,* Ved. (clouds) having black cavities; *(ās),* f. pl. = according to Sāy. the pregnant wives of the Asura Kṛishṇa, but according to others = the waters contained in the black cavities of the clouds; *(as),* m., N. of a plant, = *kaṭphala.* — *Kṛishṇa-giri, is,* m., N. of a mountain; [cf. *kṛishṇāćala.*] — *Kṛishṇa-godhā,* f. a kind of poisonous insect. — *Kṛishṇa-grīva, as, ā, am,* Ved. black-necked. — *Kṛishṇa-ćaṇćuka, as,* m. a kind of pea; [cf. *ćaṇaka.*] — *Kṛishṇa-ćaturdaśī,* f. the fourteenth day in the dark half of the month. — *Kṛishṇa-ćanda, as,* m., N. of a copyist who lived about A. D. 1730, a son of Rāma-ćandra. — *Kṛishṇa-ćandra, as,* m., N. of a prince of the eighteenth century. — *Kṛishṇaćandra-devaśarman, ā,* m., N. of a logician who lived about A. D. 1736. — *Kṛishṇa-ćara, as, ā, am,* what formerly or in a former existence belonged to Kṛishṇa. — *Kṛishṇa-ćūḍā,* f. the plant Cæsalpinia Pulcherrima. — *Kṛishṇa-ćūḍikā,* f. the plant Abrus Precatorius. — *Kṛishṇa-ćūrṇa, am,* n. rust of iron, iron filings. — *Kṛishṇa-ććhavi, is,* m. fire? [cf. *kṛishṇārćis.*] — *Kṛishṇa-jaṇhas, ās, ās, as,* Ved. black-winged; (Sāy.) having a black path. — *Kṛishṇa-jaṭā,* f. a plant, Indian spikenard; [cf. *jaṭāmāṇsī.*] — *Kṛishṇa-janma-khaṇḍa,* N. of a part of the Brahmavaivarta-purāṇa. — *Kṛishṇa-janmāshṭamī* (°ma-ash°), f. the eighth day of the second half of the month Śrāvaṇa, the birthday of Kṛishṇa. — *Kṛishṇa-jī, is,* m., N. of a man. — *Kṛishṇa-jīraka, as,* m. Kalonji, a plant having a small black seed, which is used for medical and culinary purposes, Nigella Indica. — *Kṛishṇa-taṇḍulā,* f. a plant [cf. *karṇa-sphoṭā*], Piper Longum. — *Kṛishṇa-tarkālaṅkāra* (°ka-al°), *as,* m., N. of a scholiast. — *Kṛishṇa-tā,* f. or *kṛishṇa-tva, am,* n. blackness. — *Kṛishṇa-tāmra, am,* n. a kind of sandal-wood. — *Kṛishṇa-tāra, as,* m. a deer, an antelope ('black-eyed'). — *Kṛishṇa-tila, as,* m. black sesamum. — *Kṛishṇa-tīrtha, as,* m., N. of a teacher of Rāma-tīrtha. — *Kṛishṇa-tuṇḍa, as,* m. a kind of poisonous insect. — *Kṛishṇa-trivṛitā,* f., N. of a plant, a kind of Ipomœa, black Teōri. — *Kṛishṇa-datta, as,* m., N. of the author of a work on music. — *Kṛishṇa-danta, as, ā, am,* having black teeth; *(ā),* f. the tree Gmelina Arborea. — *Kṛishṇa-darśana, as,* m., N. of a pupil of Saṅkarāćārya. — *Kṛishṇa-daśana, as, ā, am,* having black or discoloured teeth. — *Kṛishṇa-dāsa, as,* m., N. of the author of the poem Camatkāra-ćandrikā; N. of the author of the work Caitanya-ćaritāmṛita; N. of the author of the poem Preta-tattva-nirūpaṇa; N. of a son of Harsha, author of the Vimalanātha-purāṇa. — *Kṛishṇa-deva, as,* m., N. of a son of Nārāyaṇa, author of the Prayoga-sāra; N. of a copyist, son of Paṇḍyāpurushottama-deva. — *Kṛishṇa-deha, as, ā, am,* black-bodied; *(as),* m. a large black bee.—*Kṛishṇa-daivajña, as,* m., N. of a man. —*Kṛishṇa-dvaipāyana, as,* m., a N. of Vyāsa, considered as the compiler of the Vedas and Purāṇas, (so named because of his dark complexion and because he was brought forth by Satyavatī on a dvīpa or island in the Ganges.)—*Kṛishṇa-dhattūra* or *kṛishṇa-dhattūraka, as,* m. a dark species of Datura or thorn-apple, Datura Fastuosa.—*Kṛishṇa-nagara, am,* n., N. of a small district called after a town situated in it.—*Kṛishṇa-paksha, as,* m. the dark half of the month, the fifteen days during which the moon is on the wane, the time from full moon to new moon; one who stands on the side of Kṛishṇa, an epithet of Arjuna.—*Kṛishṇa-pakshika, as,* m., N. of a king of the Nāgas.—*Kṛishṇa-pakshīya, as, ā, am,* pertaining to the wane of the moon.—*Kṛishṇa-pada, as,* m., N. of the author of the Prabodha-ćandrodaya; also of a scholiast on the Prakriyā-kaumudī.—*Kṛishṇa-padī,* f. a female with black feet.—*Kṛishṇa-parṇī,* f., N. of a plant, a kind of Ocimum; [cf. *kāla-tulasī.*]—*Kṛishṇa-pavi, is, is, i,* Ved. having black fellies, an epithet of Agni.—*Kṛishṇa-pāka* or *kṛishṇa-pāka-phala, as,* m. a tree bearing a small fruit, which, when ripe, is of a black colour, commonly Karinda or Karonda, Carissa Carandas; also called *kṛishṇa-phala, pāka-phala, pākakṛishṇa-phala,* &c.—*Kṛishṇa-pāṇḍura, as, ā, am,* greyish white.—*Kṛishṇa-piṅgala, as, ā, am,* dark-brown in colour; (*as*), m., N. of a man; (*ās*), m. pl. the descendants of this man; (*ā*), f. an epithet of the goddess Durgā.—*Kṛishṇa-piṇḍītaka, as,* m. a dark kind of Māyana, Vangueria Spinosa [cf. *varāha*]; also called *kṛishṇa-piṇḍīra.* —*Kṛishṇa-pippīlī,* f. a kind of black ant.—*Kṛishṇa-pilla, as,* m., N. of a poet.—*Kṛishṇapurushottamopanishad* (°*ma-up*°), *t,* f. title of an Upanishad belonging to the Atharva-veda.—*Kṛishṇa-pushpa, as,* m. a black kind of Datura or thorn-apple; (*ī*), f., N. of a plant [cf. *priyaṅgu*].—*Kṛishṇa-prut, t, t, t,* Ved. moving in darkness; (Sāy.) taking or imparting a black colour.—*Kṛishṇa-phala, as,* m. a fruit tree, the Karinda [cf. *kṛishṇa-pāka*]; (*ā*), f. the plant Vernonia Anthelmintica.—*Kṛishṇa-phala-pāka, as,* m. = *kṛishṇa-pāka.*—*Kṛishṇa-balaksha, as, ā, am,* black and white.—*Kṛishṇa-bhakti-ćandrikā,* f. title of a play.—*Kṛishṇa-bhaṭṭa, as,* m., N. of a grammarian; N. of a poet. —*Kṛishṇa-bhūma, as, ā, am,* having a black soil, furnished with black earth.—*Kṛishṇa-bhūmi, is,* f. a country with a dark soil, or black mould, blue clay, &c.—*Kṛishṇabhūmi-jā,* f. a species of grass, described as a nourishing food for cattle (growing in a black soil).—*Kṛishṇa-bhedī* or *ā,* f. a medicinal plant, = *kaṭu-rohiṇī.*—*Kṛishṇa-bhogin, ī,* m. a black kind of snake.—*Kṛishṇa-maṇḍala, am,* n. the black part of the eye.—*Kṛishṇa-matsya, as,* m. 'black-fish,' N. of a fish.—*Kṛishṇa-mallikā,* f. or *kṛishṇa-māluka, as,* m. a plant, = *mālūka, kṛishṇārjaka.*—*Kṛishṇa-mitra, as,* m., N. of the son of Rāma-sevaka, grandson of Devīdatta, author of the Mañjūshākuñćikā.—*Kṛishṇa-miśra, as,* m. the author of the Prabodha-ćandrodaya.—*Kṛishṇa-mukha, as, ī, am,* having a black mouth, having black nipples; (*as*), m., N. of an Asura; N. of a sect.—*Kṛishṇa-mudga, as,* m. a sort of pulse, Phaseolus, (*vāsanta, mādhava, surāshṭraja.*) —*Kṛishṇa-mūlī,* f. a plant, = *śārivā-viśesha.* —*Kṛishṇa-mṛiga, as,* m. the black antelope. —*Kṛishṇa-mṛittika, as, ā, am,* having black soil; (*ā*), f., N. of a Grāma.—*Kṛishṇa-mṛid, t,* f. black soil; a country with soil of a dark colour. —*Kṛishṇa-yajurveda, as,* m. the Black Yajur-veda.—*Kṛishṇa-yajurvedīya, as, ā, am,* belonging to the Black Yajur-veda.—*Kṛishṇa-yāma, as, ā, am,* Ved. having a black path; an epithet of Agni.—*Kṛishṇa-yoni, is, is, i,* Ved. = *kṛishṇa-garbha,* q. v.—*Kṛishṇa-rakta, as, ā, am,* of a dark-red colour.—*Kṛishṇa-ruhā,* f. a plant, = *jatukā.*—*Kṛishṇa-rūpya, as, ā, am,* = *kṛishṇa-ćara,* q. v.—*Kṛishṇa-lavaṇa, am,* n. a kind of black salt; a factitious salt, either that prepared by evaporation from saline soil, or the medicinal kind, called Bit Loben or Bit Noben, a muriate of soda with a portion of sulphur and iron. —*Kṛishṇa-līlā-taraṅgiṇī,* f. title of a poem by Nārāyaṇa-tīrtha.—*Kṛishṇa-loha, am,* n. the loadstone.—*Kṛishṇa-lohita, as, ā, am,* dark-red, of a purple colour.—*Kṛishṇa-vaktra, as,* m. the black-faced monkey.—*Kṛishṇa-varṇa, as, ā, am,* of a black colour, black or dark-blue; (*am*), n. the colour black.—*Kṛishṇa-vartani, is, is, i,* Ved. having a black path, epithet of Agni.—*Kṛishṇa-vartman, ā,* m. fire ('whose way is black'); the marking nut plant, Plumbago Zeylanica; an epithet of Rāhu or the personified ascending node; a man of evil conduct, a low man, an outcast, a profligate, a blackguard.—*Kṛishṇa-varvaraka, as,* m., N. of a plant, Varvara.—*Kṛishṇa-vallikā,* f., N. of a plant, = *jatukā.*—*Kṛishṇa-vallī,* f. a plant, a dark kind of Basil, Ocymum Pilosum; a kind of Sārivā. —*Kṛishṇa-vānara, as,* m. a black kind of monkey. —*Kṛishṇa-vinnā,* f., N. of a river.—*Kṛishṇa-vishāṇā,* f., Ved. the horns of the black antelope, whose inner sides are covered with dark hair. —*Kṛishṇa-vīja, as,* m. a red variety of the Moringa plant, Rakta-śigru; (*am*), n. a water melon. —*Kṛishṇa-vṛintā,* f. the trumpet flower, Bignonia Suaveolens; a leguminous plant, Glycine Debilis. —*Kṛishṇa-vṛintikā,* f. the tree Gmelina Arborea; see *gambhīrā.*—*Kṛishṇa-veṇā* or *ī,* f., N. of a river.—*Kṛishṇa-vyathis, is, is, is,* Ved. whose path is black (?), an epithet of Agni.—*Kṛishṇa-vrīhi, is,* m. a black sort of rice.—*Kṛishṇa-śakuni, is,* m. a crow.—*Kṛishṇa-śarman, ā,* m., N. of an author.—*Kṛishṇa-śāra, as,* m. = *kṛishṇa-sāra,* the spotted antelope.—*Kṛishṇa-śāli, is,* m. a sort of rice of a dark colour.—*Kṛishṇa-śigru, us,* m. a kind of Moringa; [cf. *śobhāñjana.*]—*Kṛishṇa-śimbikā,* f., N. of a plant, = *kākāṇḍī,* = *mahā-jyotishmatī.*—*Kṛishṇa-śimbī,* f. a sort of bean, Dolichus Virosus.—*Kṛishṇa-śṛiṅga, as,* m. a buffalo with black horns.—*Kṛishṇa-śrita* or *kṛishṇam-śrita, as, ā, am,* worshipping or devoted to Kṛishṇa.—*Kṛishṇa-sakha, as,* m. a friend or follower of Kṛishṇa, especially an epithet of Arjuna; (*ī*), f. cummin seed.—*Kṛishṇa-samudbhavā,* f., N. of a river, = *kṛishṇā, kṛishṇa-gaṅgā, kṛishṇa-veṇyā.*—*Kṛishṇa-saras, as,* n., N. of a lake. —*Kṛishṇa-sarpa, as,* m. a very poisonous snake, Cobra de Capello, Colubra Naga; (*ā*), f. a plant, = *kṛishṇa-kāpotī.*—*Kṛishṇa-sarshapa, as,* m. black mustard.—*Kṛishṇa-sāra, as, ā, am,* spotted black; (*as*), m. with and without *mṛiga,* the spotted antelope; several plants, a kind of Euphorbia; the plant Dalbergia Sisoo; another plant, Acacia Catechu; (*ā*), f. a kind of Euphorbia; the plant Dalbergia Sisoo.—*Kṛishṇa-sāraṅga, as, ā, am,* spotted black; (*as*), m. the spotted antelope.—*Kṛishṇa-sārathi, is,* m. having Kṛishṇa for a charioteer, an epithet of Arjuna; the tree Terminalia Arjuna. —*Kṛishṇa-sārvabhauma, as,* m., N. of a poet. —*Kṛishṇa-siṅha, as,* m., N. of the author of the work Trepanakriya-kathā.—*Kṛishṇa-sīta, as, ā, am,* Ved. drawing black furrows; (Sāy.) having a black path (as an epithet of fire).—*Kṛishṇa-sundara, as,* m., N. of a man; (*ās*), m. pl. the descendants of this man.—*Kṛishṇa-skandha, as,* m. a tree which bears black blossoms, the Tamāla tree; [cf. *kāla-skandha.*] —*Kṛishṇa-svasṛi, sā,* f. the sister of Kṛishṇa, an epithet of Durgā.—*Kṛishṇāgata* (°*ṇa-āg*°), *as, ā, am,* devoted to Kṛishṇa.—*Kṛishṇāguru* (°*ṇa-ag*°), *u,* n. a black variety of Agallochum or Aloe wood.—*Kṛishṇāćala* (°*ṇa-ać*°), *as,* m. an epithet of the mountain Raivata, part of the western portion of the Vindhya chain; it is also one of the nine principal mountains that separate the nine divisions or Varshas of the known world.—*Kṛishṇājina* (°*ṇa-aj*°), *am,* n., Ved the skin of the black antelope; (*as*), m., N. of a man ('covered with the skin of a black antelope'); (*ās*), m. pl. the descendants of this man.—*Kṛishṇājinin, ī, inī, i,* covered with the skin of a black antelope.—*Kṛishṇāñjanī,* f., N. of a plant, = *kālāñjanī.*—*Kṛishṇāñji* (°*ṇa-añ*°), *is, is, i,* Ved. having black marks.—*Kṛishṇātreya* (°*ṇa-āt*°), *as,* m., N. of a Muni.—*Kṛishṇādhvan* (°*ṇa-adh*°), *ā, ā, a,* Ved. having a black path (an epithet of Agni).—*Kṛishṇā-nadī,* f., N. of a river, probably the Kistna in the Dekhan. —*Kṛishṇānanda* (°*ṇa-ān*°), *as,* m., N. of a scholiast; N. of the author of the Tantra-sāra. —*Kṛishṇābhā* (°*ṇa-ābhā*), f., N. of a plant, = *kālāñjanī.*—*Kṛishṇāmisha* (°*ṇa-ām*°), *am,* n. iron; (probably only a various reading for *kṛishṇāyasa.*)—*Kṛishṇāyas, as,* or *kṛishṇāyasa* (°*ṇa-ay*°), *am,* n. iron, crude or black iron.—*Kṛishṇārćis* (°*ṇa-ar*°), *is,* m. fire; [cf. *kṛishṇa-ććhavi.*]—*Kṛishṇārjaka* (°*ṇa-ar*°), *as,* m. a black species of Basil, Ocimum Sanctum.—*Kṛishṇālankāra* (°*ṇa-al*°), *as,* m. title of a commentary.—*Kṛishṇālu* (°*ṇa-ālu*), *us,* m. a kind of ebony.—*Kṛishṇāvatāra* (°*ṇa-av*°), *as,* m. an Avatār of Kṛishṇa.—*Kṛishṇāvadāta, as, ā, am,* black and white.—*Kṛishṇāvāsa* (°*ṇa-āv*°), *as,* m. the holy fig tree, Ficus Religiosa, (the abode of Kṛishṇa.)—*Kṛishṇāśrita* (°*ṇa-āś*°), *as, ā, am,* devoted to or the votary of Kṛishṇa.—*Kṛishṇekshu* (°*ṇa-ik*°), *us,* m. a sort of sugar-cane.—*Kṛishṇaita* (°*ṇa-eta*), *as, ā, am,* Ved. spotted black.—*Kṛishṇodara* (°*ṇa-ud*°), *as,* m. a kind of snake.—*Kṛishṇodumbarikā* (°*ṇa-ud*°), f. Ficus Oppositifolia; [cf. *kākodumbara.*]—*Kṛishṇopanishad* (°*ṇa-up*°), *t,* f. title of an Upanishad in praise of the god Kṛishṇa, being a part of the Gopālopanishad.—*Kṛishṇoraga* (°*ṇa-ur*°), *as,* m. a kind of black snake.—*Kṛishṇo 'syākhareshṭhaka, as, ā, am,* containing the words *kṛishṇo 'syākhareshṭhaḥ* (as an Adhyāya or Anuvāka).

2. *kṛishṇa,* nom. P. *kṛishṇati,* to behave or act like Kṛishṇa.

Kṛishṇaka, as, ā, am, black, blackish; (*as*), m. a kind of plant, = *kṛishṇa-taṇḍulā.*

Kṛishṇala, as, am, m. n. the black berry of the plant Abrus Precatorius, used as a weight (the average weight being between one and two grains); a coin of about the same weight; (*ā*), f. a shrub bearing a small black and red berry, Abrus Precatorius.

Kṛishṇalaka, as, m. the black berry of the plant Abrus Precatorius or a coin of about the same weight.

Kṛishṇaśa, as, ā, am, Ved. blackish; (Sāy.) extremely black.

Kṛishṇāya, nom. A. *-yate, -yitum,* to make black; to behave like Kṛishṇa; [cf. Russ. *ćernjû.*]

Kṛishṇikā, f. black mustard.

Kṛishṇiman, ā, m. blackness.

Kṛishṇiya, as, m., Ved., N. of a man protected by the Aśvins.

Kṛishṇī-karaṇa, am, n. blackening, making black.—*Kṛishṇī-kṛita, as, ā, am,* blackened, made black.

Kṛishṇī-bhūta, as, ā, am, become black.

Kṛishṇeya, as, m., N. of a man.

कृष्य *kṛishya.* See under *kṛish.*

कृसर *kṛisara, as,* m. (said to be fr. rt. 1. *kṛī*), a dish consisting of sesamum and grain; a mixture of rice and peas with a few spices.

कॄ 1. *kṛī,* cl. 6. P. *kirati, ćakāra, karishyati* and *karīshyati, akārīt, karitum* and *karītum,* to pour out, scatter, throw, cast, disperse; to strew, pour over, fill with, cover with: Caus. *kārayati:* Desid. *ćikarishati:* Intens. *ćekīryate, ćākarti;* [cf. Gr. κεράω, κεράννυμι, κίρνημι.]

Kīrṇa, kīrṇi, &c. See s. v. at p. 231.

कॄ 2. *kṛī* (or sometimes written *kṛi*), cl. 5. and 9. P. A. *kṛiṇoti, -ṇute, kṛiṇāti, -ṇīte, ćakāra, ćakare* and *ćakre, karishyati, -te, akarishṭa, akarīshṭa, akīrshṭa, karitum, karītum, kartum,* to hurt, injure, kill.

कॄ 3. *kṛī,* cl. 10. A. *kārayate, -yitum,* to know, inform; (an incorrect form for *gṛī.*)

कृत् *krīt*, cl. 10. P. (sometimes A.) *kīrtayati, -te, -yitum*, Aor. *aćīkṛitat* or *aćikīrtat*, to mention, make mention of, tell, name, call, recite, repeat, relate, declare, communicate, commemorate, celebrate, praise, glorify; [cf. Lat. *celeber.*]

Kīrtana, am, n. mentioning, repeating, saying, telling, celebrating, praising; (*ā*), f. fame, glory.

Kīrtanīya, as, ā, am, to be mentioned, to be named or repeated, to be celebrated or praised.

Kīrtanya, as, ā, am, deserving to be mentioned, to be related.

Kīrtayat, an, antī, at, mentioning, relating, repeating, celebrating, praising.

Kīrtita, as, ā, am, said, asserted; mentioned, repeated; known, notorious; celebrated, praised.

Kīrtitavya, as, ā, am, to be mentioned or praised.

Kīrtenya, as, ā, am, Ved. deserving to be named or praised.

Kīrtti or *kīrti, is*, f. mention, making mention of, speech, report; good report, fame, renown, glory; Fame personified as daughter of Daksha and wife of Dharma; extension, expansion, diffusion; light, lustre; favour, approbation; sound; dirt, mud; one of the Mātṛikās or personified divine energies of Kṛishṇa. — *Kīrtti-kara, as, ī, am*, conferring fame. — *Kīrtti-dhara, as*, m., N. of a copyist. — *Kīrtti-pratāpa-bala-sahita, as, ā, am*, attended with fame, majesty, and power. — *Kīrtti-bhāj, k, k, k*, receiving fame, celebrated, famous; (*k*), m. an epithet of Droṇāćārya, the military preceptor of the Pāṇḍus and Kurus. — *Kīrtti-mat, ān, atī, at*, praised, famous, celebrated; (*ān*), m., N. of one of the Viśva-devās; a son of Uttāna-pāda and Sūnṛitā; also a son of Vasu-deva and Devakī; also a son of Aṅgiras. — *Kīrtti-maya, as, ī, am*, consisting of fame. — *Kīrtti-ratha, as*, m., N. of a prince of the Videhas, a son of Pratīndhaka; also called *Kṛitti-ratha* as son of Prasiddhaka. — *Kīrtti-rāta, as*, m., N. of a prince of the Videhas, a son of Mahāndhraka. — *Kīrtti-varman, ā*, m., N. of a prince. — *Kīrtti-vāsa, as*, m., N. of an author. — *Kīrtti-śesha, as*, m. death (the leaving behind of nothing but fame); [cf. *ālekhya-śesha, nāma-śesha, yaśaḥ-śesha.*] — *Kīrtti-sena, as*, m., N. of a nephew of Vāsuki, the serpent-king.

Kīrtya, as, ā, am, to be praised or celebrated.

क्लृप् *klṛip*, cl. 1. A. (and in Fut., Cond., and Aor. also P.) *kalpate, ćaklṛipe, kalpishyate* and *kalpsyati, akalpishṭa, aklṛipta* and *aklṛipat, kalpitum* and *kalptum*, to be well ordered or regulated, to be well managed; to succeed; to bear suitable relation to anything, to correspond, be adapted to, fit for, in accordance with, suitable to; to accommodate one's self to; to be favourable to, to subserve, to effect or obtain for one's self; to partake of, become possessed of; to fall to the share, be shared or partaken by (with loc., e. g. *yajño deveshu kalpatām*, let the sacrifice be shared by the gods); to become, to be; to happen, occur; to declare as right, decide in favour of (?); to prepare, arrange; to produce, cause, effect, create (with acc.): Caus. P. A. *kalpayati, -te*, Aor. *aćīklṛipat*, Ved. *ćāklṛipat, ćiklṛipāti*, &c., to set in order, arrange, distribute, dispose; to bring into suitable connection with, to cause any one (acc.) to partake of anything (inst.); to help any one in obtaining (dat.); to prepare, arrange, fit out, furnish with; to consider as fit; to fix, settle; to destine or design anything for; to declare as, consider as (with two acc., e. g. *mātaram enām kalpayantu*, let them consider her as their mother); to make, execute, bring about; to frame, form; to invent, compose (as a poem &c.); to perform (as a ceremony &c.); to pronounce a formula or verse which contains the word *klṛip*; to cut, pare, cut asunder (only in Prākṛit): Desid. *ćiklṛipsati* and *ćikalpishate*: Intens. *ćalī°* or *ćali°* or *ćalkalpyate, ćalkalpti*; [cf. Goth. *hilpa*; Eng. *help*; Germ. *helfe*; Lith. *gelbmi.*]

Klṛipta, as, ā, am, arranged, prepared, ready, at hand, in order, complete, right, perfect; made, done; formed, framed; caused, produced, effected, invented, contrived, created; fixed, settled, prescribed, appointed; ascertained, determined; cut, clipt, pared, shorn. — *Klṛipta-kīlā*, f. title-deed, lease of a house &c. — *Klṛipta-keśa-nakha-śmaśru, us, us, u*, having the hair, nails, and beard cut or clipt and arranged. — *Klṛipta-dhūpa, as*, m. frankincense, olibanum.

Klṛipti, is, f., Ved. accomplishment, success; distributing, arranging, making conformable; invention, contrivance; a term for certain formulas or verses containing the verb *klṛip*.

Klṛiptika, as, ā, am, bought, purchased.

केकय *kekaya, ās*, m. pl., N. of a warrior-tribe; (*as*), m. the chief of this tribe, a prince of the solar race; (*ī*), f. a princess of this tribe, wife of Daśa-ratha and mother of Bharata.

केकर *kekara, as, ī, am*, or *kekarāksha* (°*ra-ak*°), *as, ā, am*, squint-eyed; [cf. *kedara* and *ṭeraka.*]

केकल *kekala, as*, m. a dancer; (perhaps a various reading for *kelaka.*)

केका *kekā*, f. the cry of a peacock.

Kekāvala or *kekika, as*, m., or *kekin, ī*, m. a peacock.

केकेयी *kekeyī*, f. one of Daśa-ratha's three wives, the mother of Bharata; (a wrong form for *kaikeyī.*)

केचुक *kećuka, as, ā*, m. f. a plant with an esculent root, Colocasia Antiquorum; (*am*), n. the esculent root of this plant; [cf. *kaću, kaćvī, kemuka.*]

केणिका *keṇikā*, f. a tent.

केत *keta, as*, m. (connected with 2. *kā* or *kit=ćit?*), desire, wish, will, intention; summons, invitation; a house, an abode; apparition, form, shape; (Sāy.) wealth; atmosphere, sky. — *Keta-pū, ūs, ūs, u*, Ved. purifying the desire or will. — *Keta-vedas, ās, ās, as*, Ved. desirous, wishful; (Sāy.) knowing the wealth of another. — *Keta-sāp, p, p, p*, Ved. obeying the will (of another), obedient; (Sāy.) touching the sky.

Ketana, am, n. a summons, an invitation; a house, an abode; place, site, situation; the symbol of a goddess; the ensign of a warrior, a flag or banner (e. g. *vānara-ketana*, one who has a monkey as his ensign or arms; see also *makara-ketana*, &c.); a sign, a spot or mark; business, indispensable act.

Ketaya, nom. P. *ketayati, -yitum*, to summon, to call or invite; to counsel or advise; to fix or appoint a time; to hear.

Ketita, as, ā, am, called, summoned; dwelt, inhabited.

केतक *ketaka, as, ī*, m. f. the tree Pandanus Odoratissimus.

केतलिकीर्ति *ketali-kīrti, is*, m., N. of the author of the work Megha-mālā.

केतु *ketu, us*, m. (fr. *ki* for rt. 2. *ći*), bright appearance, clearness, brightness; a ray of light; day-time; apparition, form, shape; sign, mark, ensign, flag, banner; a chief, a leader, any eminent person; intellect, judgment, discernment; any unusual or striking phenomena, a comet, meteor, falling star; the dragon's tail or descending node considered in astronomy as the ninth of the planets, and in mythology as the body of the demon Saiṇhikeya, son of Siṇhikā, which was severed from the head or Rāhu by Vishṇu at the churning of the ocean, but was rendered immortal by having tasted the Amṛita; a pigmy race (see *ketu-gaṇa* below); disease; an enemy; N. of a son of Agni, supposed to be the author of a Ṛig-veda hymn; N. of a Dānava; N. of a son of Ṛishabha; also of a son of the fourth Manu; *aruṇāḥ ketavaḥ*, red apparitions, a class of superhuman spirits or demons, (a kind of sacrificial fire is called after them *agnir āruṇaketukaḥ.*) — *Ketu-gaṇa, ās*, m. pl. the dwarfish inhabitants of Kuśa-dvīpa, children of Jaimini. — *Ketu-graha, as*, m. the descending node. — *Ketu-tārā*, f. a comet. — *Ketu-dharman, ā*, m., N. of a man. — *Ketu-bha, as*, m. a cloud. — *Ketu-bhūta, as, ā, am*, being or become a banner. — *Ketu-mat, ān, atī, at*, endowed with brightness, clear; clear (as a sound), penetrating; (*ān*), m., N. of a Dānava; of a regent of the western part of the world, a son of Rajas; of a son of Kshema and father of Suketu; of a son of Kshema and father of Varsha-ketu; of a warrior; of a son of Dhanvantari; of Ambarīsha; N. of a mountain; N. of a palace of Sunandā, the wife of Vāsu-deva; (*tī*), f., N. of a metre consisting of two lines of twenty-one syllables each. — *Ketu-mālā*, f., N. of a Tīrtha; (*ās*), m. pl., N. of a people; (*am*), n. one of the nine great divisions of the known world, the western portion or Varsha of Jambu-dvīpa, called after a son of Agnīdhra; (*as*), m., N. of a boar. — *Ketumālin, ī*, or *ketumāli, is*, m., N. of a Dānava. — *Ketu-yashṭi, is*, f. a flag-staff. — *Ketu-ratna, am*, n. lapis lazuli. — *Ketu-vasana, as*, m. a flag. — *Ketu-vīrya, as*, m., N. of a Dānava. — *Ketu-śṛiṅga, as*, m., N. of a king.

केदर *kedara, as, ā, am*, squint-eyed; (*as*), m., N. of a plant; [cf. *kekara* and *ṭeraka.*]

केदार *kedāra, as*, m. a field, especially one under water, a meadow, a plain; a basin for water round the root of a tree, a bed in a garden or field; a mountain; a particular mountain; a particular place, the modern Kedār, part of the Himālaya mountains; an epithet of Śiva as worshipped in the Himālayas; N. of the author of a work entitled Abdhi. — *Kedāra-kaṭukā*, f., N. of a plant, = *kaṭukā*. — *Kedāra-kalpa, as*, m. a part of the Skanda-purāṇa. — *Kedāra-khaṇḍa, am*, n. a small dyke or mound, earth raised to keep out water; a part of the Skanda-purāṇa. — *Kedāra-ja, am*, n., N. of a plant. — *Kedāra-nātha, as*, m. an epithet of Śiva as worshipped in the Himālayas. — *Kedāra-bhaṭṭa, as*, m., N. of an author. — *Kedāra-malla, as*, m. an epithet of Madanapāla.

Kedāraka, as, m. a particular kind of rice, = *shashṭika*.

केन *kena*, ind. (inst. fr. 2. *ka*), by what? wherefore? whence?

केनती *kenatī*, f. an epithet of the wife of Kāma, the god of love; (a wrong form?).

केनव *kenava, as*, m., N. of a pupil of Śākapūrṇi.

केनार *kenāra, as*, m. the head; a skull; the temples, the upper part of the cheek; a joint; a division of hell, a hell compared to a potter's kiln.

केनिप *kenipa, as*, m., Ved. a sage, a wise man; [cf. *ākenipa.*]

केनिपात *kenipāta* or *kenipātaka, as*, m. the helm, a rudder, a large oar used as a rudder.

केनेषितोपनिषद् *keneshitopanishad* or *kenopanishad, t*, f. title of an Upanishad beginning with the word *keneshitam*.

केन्दु *kendu, us*, m. a kind of ebony.

Kenduka, as, m. another variety of ebony yielding a species of tar, Diospyros Glutinosa.

केन्द्र *kendra, am*, n. (a word borrowed from the Gr. κέντρον), the centre of a circle; the equation of the centre; the argument of a circle; the argument of an equation; the distance of a planet from the first point of its orbit in the fourth, seventh, or tenth degree; it is variously applied in composition, as *patana-kendram*, argument of the latitude; *dvitīya-kendram*, the distance of the higher apsis of a planet in any point of its orbit; *śighra-kendram*, commutation, the distance of the sun from a superior planet or of an inferior planet from the sun; *manda-kendram*, argument of anomaly.

केप् *kep*, cl. 1. A. *kepate*, to shake or tremble [cf. *kamp* and *vep*]; to go, move, approach [cf. *gep*].

केपि *kepi, is, is, i*, Ved. unclean; (or fr. rt. *kamp*), trembling, shaking (?).

केमद्रुम *kemadruma* in astronomy = the Gr. χρηματισμός.

केमुक *kemuka, as*, m., N. of a plant, = *kećuka*.

केयूर *keyūra, as, am*, m. n. a bracelet worn on the upper arm; (*as*), m. a kind of coitus. — *Keyūra-bala, as*, m., N. of a deity.

Keyūraka, as, m., N. of a Gandharva.

Keyūrin, ī, iṇī, i, decorated with a bracelet on the upper arm.

केरक *keraka, ās*, m. pl., N. of a people.

केरल *kerala, ās*, m. pl., N. of the inhabitants of Malabar; (*as*), m. sing. a king of the Keralas; N. of a son of Ākrīḍa, from whom the people of Kerala are derived; (*ī*), f. a kind of science; astronomical science; an astronomical S'āstra or treatise; a Hora or period of time equal to about one hour; (*am*), n. N. of the country inhabited by the Keralas. — *Keralotpatti* (°*la-ut*°), *is*, f., N. of a work.

Keralaka, ās, m. pl., N. of the inhabitants of Malabar.

केल् *kel* [cf. Prākṛit *kil* = *krīḍ*], cl. 1. P. *kelati*, to shake; to go or move, move about, be frolicsome, sport.

Kelaka, as, m. a dancer, a tumbler, one who walks or dances on the edge of a sword.

Kelāya, nom. P. *kelāyati, -yitum*, to sport, play.

Keli, is or *ī*, m. f. play, sport, amorous sport, pastime, amusement; (*is*), f. the earth. — *Keli-kalā*, f. amorous or sportive accents or address; sportive skill, wantonness; the Vīṇā or lute of Sarasvatī. — *Keli-kila, as*, m. the confidential companion of the hero of a drama, in general a sort of buffoon; one of S'iva's attendant demi-gods; (*ā*), f. an epithet of Rati the wife of Kāma-deva, the god of love. — *Keli-kīrṇa, as*, m. a camel. — *Keli-kuńćikā*, f. a wife's younger sister. — *Keli-kosha, as*, m. an actor, a dancer or tumbler. — *Keli-gṛiha* or *keli-niketana, am*, n. a pleasure-house, a private apartment. — *Keli-nāgara, as*, m. a sensualist, an enjoyer of worldly pleasures. — *Keli-para, as, ā, am*, wanton, sportive. — *Keli-maṇḍapa, as, am*, m. n. or *keli-mandira, am*, n. a pleasure-house, a play-room. — *Keli-mukha, as*, m. pastime, sport. — *Keli-ranga, as*, m. a pleasure-ground. — *Keli-raivataka, am*, n. title of a treatise. — *Keli-vṛiksha, as*, m. a species of the Kadamba, commonly called Kelikadamba (Nauclea Cordifolia), being abundant in the scene of Kṛishṇa's sports with the Gopīs. — *Keli-śayana, am*, n. a pleasure-couch, a sofa. — *Keli-śushi, is*, f. the earth. — *Keli-saćiva, as*, m. minister of the sports, master of the revels. — *Keli-sadana, am*, n. a pleasure-house, a play-room. — *Keli-sthalī*, f. a place of pleasure. — *Kelī-pika, as*, m. a cuckoo kept for pleasure. — *Kelī-vanī*, f. a pleasure-park, a pleasure-grove.

Kelika, as, ā, am, sporting, sportive; (*as*), m. the tree Jonesia Aśoka.

केल *kela* or *kelu*, a particular number.

केलास *kelāsa, as*, m. crystal.

केव् *kev*, cl. 1. A. *kevate, -vitum*, to serve, attend to.

केवट *kevaṭa, as*, m., Ved. a cave, a hollow.

केवर्त *kevarta, as*, m., Ved. a fisherman, = *kaivarta*, q. v.

केवल *kevala, as, ā* (or Ved. *ī*), *am*, exclusively one's own (not common to others); peculiar; alone, only, mere, sole, one, excluding others; not connected with anything else, isolated, abstract, absolute; simple, pure, uncompounded, unmingled, perfect in one's self, entire, whole, all; selfish, envious; (*am*), ind. only, merely, solely, entirely, wholly, absolutely, certainly; *na kevalam—api*, not only—but also; *kevalam—na tu*, only—but not; (*as*), m., N. of a prince, a son of Nara; (*ī*), f. the doctrine of the absolute unity of spirit; N. of a place; (*am*), n. the doctrine of the absolute unity of spirit; N. of a country. — *Kevala-jñānin, ī*, m., N. of the first Arhat of the last Utsarpiṇī. — *Kevala-tas*, ind. only. — *Kevala-tva, am*, n. the state of being alone. — *Kevala-dravya, am*, n. black pepper. — *Kevala-naiyāyika, as*, m. a mere logician, not versed in any other science. — *Kevala-vaiyākaraṇa, as*, m. a mere grammarian, one not versed in any other science. — *Kevalāgha* (°*la-agha*), *as, ā, am*, Ved. alone guilty. — *Kevalātman* (°*la-āt*°), *ā, ā, a*, one whose nature or essence is absolute unity. — *Kevalādin* (°*la-ād*°), *ī, inī, i*, eating by one's self alone or apart from others.

Kevalin, ī, inī, i, alone, one, only; devoted to the doctrine of the absolute unity of spirit; (*ī*), m. with Jainas, an Arhat.

केविका *kevikā* or *kevī*, f., N. of a flower, = *kavikā*, commonly *kevera*.

केश *keśa, as*, m. (said to be fr. rt. *kliś*), the hair of the head; the mane (of a horse or lion); a kind of perfume [cf. *hrīvera*]; an epithet of Varuṇa; of Vishṇu; N. of a Daitya; (*ī*), f. a lock of hair on the crown of the head; N. of several plants, the Indigo plant; another plant, Carpopogon Pruriens; an epithet of the goddess Durgā. — *Keśa-karman, a*, n. dressing or arranging the air of the head. — *Keśa-kalāpa, as*, m. a mass or quantity of hair, a head of hair. — *Keśa-kāra, as*, m. a sort of sugar-cane. — *Keśa-kārin, ī, iṇī, i*, dressing or arranging the hair of the head. — *Keśa-kīṭa, as*, m. a louse or other insect in the hair. — *Keśa-garbha, as*, m. a braid or tress of hair; an epithet of Varuṇa. — *Keśa-garbhaka, as*, m. a braid or tress of hair. — *Keśa-gṛihīta, as, ā, am*, pulled or seized by the hair. — *Keśa-graha, as*, m. or *keśa-grahaṇa, am*, n. pulling the hair. — *Keśa-ghna, am*, n. morbid baldness, falling of the hair. — *Keśa-ćūḍa, as, ā, am*, one who has dressed his hair in a tuft or top-knot. — *Keśa-ććhid, t*, m. a hair-dresser, a barber. — *Keśa-jāha, am*, n. the root of the hair. — *Keśa-dṛinhaṇa, as, ī, am*, Ved. serving for fastening the hair. — *Keśa-dhara, ās*, m. pl., N. of a people. — *Keśa-dhṛit, t*, f., N. of a plant, the root of sweet flag. — *Keśa-paksha, as*, m. much or ornamented hair, a tuft. — *Keśa-pankti, is*, f. a row or line of hair; a quantity of hair. — *Keśa-parṇī*, f. the plant Achyranthes Aspera; also *apāmārga*. — *Keśa-pāśa, as*, m. much or ornamented hair, a tuft; (*ī*), f. a lock of hair hanging down from the top of the head. — *Keśa-bandha, as*, m. a hair-band. — *Keśa-bhū, ūs*, m. the head. — *Keśa-bhūmi, is*, f. any place on which hair grows. — *Keśa-mārjaka, as, am*, m. n. (?) a comb. — *Keśa-marjana, am*, n. a comb; cleaning the hair. — *Keśa-mushṭi, is*, m. a handful of hair; N. of two plants, (also *visha-mushṭi* and *mahā-nimba*.) — *Keśa-raćanā*, f. arranging or dressing the hair. — *Keśa-rañjana* or *keśa-rāja, as*, m., N. of a vegetable, = *bhṛinga-rāja*. — *Keśa-ruhā*, f., N. of a plant, = *bhadra-dantikā*. — *Keśa-rūpā*, f., N. of a parasitical plant. — *Keśa-lunćaka, as, ā, am*, pulling the hair. — *Keśa-vat, ān, atī, at*, having a fine head of hair; having long hair; having a mane. — *Keśa-vapanīya, as*, m., N. of a festival. — *Keśa-vardhana, as, ī, am*, Ved. causing the hair to grow. — *Keśa-vardhinī*, f., N. of a plant, a kind of Sida. — *Keśa-veśa, as*, m. a tress or fillet of hair. — *Keśa-veshṭa, as*, m. the parting of the hair. — *Keśa-hantrī*, f., N. of a tree, = *śamī*. — *Keśa-hasta, as*, m. much or ornamented hair, a tuft. — *Keśā-keśi*, ind. hair to hair, head to head; pulling each other's hair. — *Keśāgra* (°*śa-ag*°), *am*, n. the top of a hair. — *Keśānta* (°*śa-an*°), *as*, m. the tip or end of a hair; long hair hanging down, a lock of hair, a tuft; cutting off the hair finally, as a religious ceremony performed upon Brāhmans at sixteen years of age, Kshatriyas at twenty-two, and Vaiśyas at twenty-four. — *Keśāntika, as, ā, am*, extending to the end of the hair as far as the forehead; relating to the ceremony of final tonsure. — *Keśāri* (°*śa-ari*), *is*, m. the plant Mesua Ferrea. — *Keśāruhā* (°*śa-ār*°), f., N. of a plant, = *saha-devī*. — *Keśārhā* (°*śa-ar*°), f., N. of a plant, = *mahānīlī*. — *Keśāvamarshaṇa* (°*śa-av*°), *am*, n. pulling the hair, especially amorously playing with it, rubbing it, &c. — *Keśoććaya* (°*śa-uć*°), *as*, m. much or handsome hair.

Keśaka, as, ā, am, skilful in dressing hair, bestowing care upon the hair.

Keśava, as, ā, am, having long or much or handsome hair; (*as*), m. an epithet of Vishṇu or Kṛishṇa; N. of the author of a lexicon called Kalpa-dru; the author of the Dvaita-pariśishṭa; the father of Govinda and Rućikara; N. of the father of Brāhma and uncle of Maheśvara; N. of the son of Viśvadhara and brother of Karināthа; N. of the father of Vopadeva; N. of a plant, = *punnāga*. — *Keśava-jātaka-paddhaty-udāharaṇa, am*, n. a commentary by Viśvanātha on the work Jātaka-paddhati. — *Keśava-jinanda-śarman, ā*, m., N. of an author. — *Keśava-dāsa, as*, m., N. of an author. — *Keśava-daivajña, as*, m., N. of an astronomer. — *Keśava-bhakti, is*, f. devotion to Kṛishṇa. — *Keśava-miśra, as*, m., N. of an author. — *Keśava-svāmin, ī*, m., N. of a grammarian. — *Keśavāyudha* (°*va-āy*°), *as*, m. the Mango tree; any of Kṛishṇa's weapons. — *Keśavārka* (°*va-ar*°), *as*, m., N. of the author of the poem Kṛishṇa-krīḍita, a son of Jayāditya and grandson of Rāṇiga; N. of the author of a work called Jātaka-paddhati; N. of the author of a work called Vivāha-vṛindāvana. — *Keśavālaya* (°*va-āl*°) or *keśavāvāla* (?) or *keśavāvāsa* (°*va-āv*°), *as*, m. the holy fig tree, Ficus Religiosa.

Keśi, is, m., N. of an Asura; [cf. *keśin*.]

Keśika, as, ī, am, having fine or luxuriant hair, relating to the hair; (*ā*), f. the plant Asparagus Racemosus.

Keśin, ī, inī, i, having fine or long hair, having a mane; epithet of Indra's and Agni's horses; epithet of Rudra; (*ī*), m. a lion; N. of a race; N. of an Asura slain by Kṛishṇa; an epithet of Kṛishṇa; N. of a son of Vasu-deva and Kauśalyā; (*inī*), f. the plant Chrysopogon Aciculatus; another plant, Nardostachys Jaṭāmāṃsī; an epithet of the goddess Durgā; N. of an Apsaras; N. of a daughter of the king of Vidarbha, wife of Sagara and mother of Asamañja; N. of the wife of Ajamīḍha (Suhotra) and mother of Jahnu; N. of the wife of Viśravas and mother of Rāvaṇa and Kumbhakarṇa; N. of a Rākshasī; N. of a servant of Damayantī. — *Keśi-nisūdana* or *keśi-mathana* or *keśi-sūdana, as*, m. or *keśi-han, ā*, m. &c. epithet of Kṛishṇa the slayer of the Asura Keśin.

Keśya, as, ā, am, being in or on the hair; suitable to the hair; (*as*), m., N. of a plant; (*am*), n. black Aloe wood.

केशट *keśaṭa, as*, m. a goat; a bug; a louse; N. of a tree, commonly Sonapat, = *śoṇaka*; the parching arrow of Kāma-deva, the god of love; a brother; an epithet of Vishṇu.

केशारुका *keśārukā*, f. = *kaśerukā*, the back-bone.

केसर *kesara* or *keśara, as, am*, m. n. (the former form being more usual in Vedic and the latter in classical literature), the hair; the mane (of a horse or lion); the filament of a lotus or of any vegetable; a fibre (as of a Mango fruit); (*am*), n.

the tail of the Bos Grunniens, used as a fan for driving away flies; (*as*), m., N. of several plants, Rottleria Tinctoria; Mimusops Elengi; Mesua Ferrea; (*am*), n. the flower of these plants; gold; sulphate of iron; N. of a metre consisting of four lines of eighteen syllables each; (*as, ā, am*), m. f. n. Asa Fœtida; [cf. Lat. *cæsaries;* Angl. Sax. *haer;* Eng. *hair;* Germ. *Haar.*] — *Kesara-grāma, as,* m., N. of a Grāma. — *Kesara-prābandhā,* f., Ved., N. of a woman. — *Kesara-vat, ān, atī, at,* having a mane. — *Kesara-vara, am,* n. saffron. — *Kesarāćala* (°*ra-ać*°), *as,* m. 'the filament mountain,' N. of the mountains situated round Meru, which is called 'the seed-vessel of the earth.' — *Kesarāmla* (°*ra-am*°), *as,* m. the citron.

Kesari, is, m., N. of the father of Hanumat.

Kesarin and *keśarin, ī, iṇī, i,* having a mane; (*ī*), m. a lion; a horse; N. of several plants, Rottleria Tinctoria; Mesua Ferrea; a citron tree; a variety of Moringa with red flowers (=*rakta-śigru*); N. of a man; of a monkey, husband of the mother of Hanumat. — *Kesari-suta, as,* m., N. of Hanumat.

केह्लदेव **kehla-deva,** *as,* m., N. of a man.

कै **kai,** cl. 1. P. *kāyati, ćakau, kāsyati, kātum,* to sound.

कैकय **kaikaya,** *as,* m. the king of the Kekayas; (*ās*), m. pl. the sons of this king; (*ī*), f. a daughter of this king.

Kaikeya, as, m. a descendant of Kekaya, who was prince of the Kekayas; a son of Śivi; Dṛishṭaketu, king of the Kekayas and father of the five Kaikeyas; (*ās*), m. pl. the Kekayas; (*ī*), f. a daughter of the prince of the Kekayas, one of the wives of Daśaratha, mother of Bharata; a shrew, a scold.

कैङ्कर्य **kainkarya,** *am,* n. (fr. *kin-kara*), the office of a servant or slave; service, servitude.

कैट **kaiṭa,** *as, ī, am* (fr. *kīṭa*), coming from an insect.

कैटज **kaiṭaja,** *as,* m. = *kuṭaja,* the plant Wrightia Antidysenterica.

कैटभ **kaiṭabha,** *as,* m., N. of an Asura slain by Vishṇu; title of a class of writings; (*ā* and *ī*), f. an epithet of Durgā. — *Kaiṭabha-jit, t,* m. or *kaiṭabha-han, ā,* m. or *kaiṭabhāri* (*bha-ari*), *is,* m. or *kaiṭabhārdana* (°*bha-ar*°), *as,* m. an epithet of Vishṇu.

कैटर्य **kaiṭarya,** *as,* m. a plant used in medicine, commonly Kayaphal; the Nimb tree; Mayana Vangueria Spinosa.

Kaiḍarya, as, m., N. of two plants, = *katphala* and *kaṭabhī.*

कैतक **kaitaka,** *as, ī, am* (fr. *ketaka*), coming from the plant Pandanus Odoratissimus; (*am*), n. the flower of the tree Pandanus Odoratissimus.

कैतव **kaitava,** *as,* m. (fr. *kitava*), a patronymic of Ulūka; (*am*), n. the stake in a game; gambling; deceit, fraud, cheating, roguery; the lapis lazuli. — *Kaitava-prayoga, as,* m. a trick, a device. — *Kaitava-vāda, as,* m. falsehood, evasion.

Kaitavaka, am, n. gambling.

Kaitaveya or *kaitavya, as,* m. a patronymic of Ulūka.

कैदार **kaidāra,** *as, ī, am* (fr. *kedāra*), being on or growing in a field or meadow, especially one under water; (*as*), m. rice, corn; (*am*), n. a multitude of fields.

Kaidāraka or *kaidārika* or *kaidārya, am,* n. a multitude of fields.

Kaidārya, as, ā, am, belonging to a field.

कैन्नर **kainnara,** *as, ī, am* (fr. *kin nara*), coming from Kinnara.

कैयट **kaiyaṭa** or *kaiyyaṭa, as,* m., N. of a son of Jaiyaṭa, author of a commentary on Patañjali's Mahā-bhāshya.

कैरलेय **kairaleya,** *as,* m. a king of the Keralas.

कैरव **kairava,** *as,* m. a gambler, a cheat, a rogue; an enemy; (*am*), n. the white esculent water-lily or lotus blossoming at night; (*ī*), f. moonshine, moonlight; N. of a plant, = *methikā.* — *Kairava-bandhu, us,* m. an epithet of the moon.

Kairavin, ī, m. the moon; (*iṇī*), f. a place or pond abounding in water-lilies, an assemblage of them. — *Kairaviṇī-khaṇḍa, am,* n. a multitude of spots filled with water-lilies.

कैराटक **kairāṭaka,** *as,* m. a species of vegetable poison, one of the fixed kinds.

कैरात **kairāta,** *as, ī, am* (fr. *kirāta*), relating or belonging to the Kirātas; (*as*), m. a prince of the Kirātas; a strong man; N. of a serpent; (*am*), n. the plant Agathotes Chirayta; a kind of sandal-wood.

Kairātaka, as, ī, am, belonging to the Kirāta people.

Kairātika, as, ā, am, Ved. belonging to the Kirātas.

कैराल **kairāla,** *am, ī,* n. f., N. of a plant, used as a remedy for worms; [cf. *viḍanga.*]

कैरिशि **kairiśi,** *is,* m. (fr. *kiriśi*), a patronymic of Sutvan.

कैर्मेदुर **kairmedura,** *as, am,* m. n. (?), N. of a place; (*as, ī, am*), coming from that place.

कैल **kaila,** *am,* n. sport, pleasure.

कैलकिल **kailakila,** an epithet of Yavana.

कैलावत **kailāvata,** *ās,* m. pl., N. of a people.

कैलास **kailāsa,** *as,* m., N. of the mountain Kailāsa, the fabulous residence of Kuvera and paradise of Śiva; it is placed by the Hindūs in the Himālaya range, and is regarded as one of the loftiest peaks to the north of the Mānasa lake. — *Kailāsa-nātha, as,* m. the sovereign of the Kailāsa mountain, i. e. the god Kuvera. — *Kailāsa-niketana, as,* m. an epithet of Kuvera or Śiva — *Kailāsa-paṇḍita, as,* m., N. of a copyist. — *Kailāsaukas* (°*sa-ok*°), *ās,* m. an epithet of Kuvera.

कैवर्त **kaivarta,** *as,* m. [cf. *kevarta*], a fisherman, born of a prostitute by a Kshatriya or of an Āyogava female by a Nishāda father; (*ī*), f. the wife of a fisherman; a kind of grass, Cyperus Rotundus; [cf. *paripela.*] — *Kaivarta-musta* or *kaivarta-mustaka, am,* n. the grass Cyperus Rotundus.

Kaivartaka, as, m. a fisherman.

Kaivartikā, f., N. of a plant, = *surangā, latā, vallī, daśaruhā,* &c.

Kaivarti-mustaka or *kaivartī-mustaka, am,* n. a fragrant kind of grass, Cyperus Rotundus.

कैवल **kaivala,** *am,* n. a kind of plant, used as a remedy for worms, = *kairāla.*

कैवल्य **kaivalya,** *am,* n. (fr. *kevala*), perfect isolation, abstraction, detachment from all other connections, detachment of the soul from matter or further transmigrations; becoming one with the Supreme; eternal happiness, emancipation, beatitude; exclusiveness, soleness, individuality, totality; (*as, ī, am*), connected with this state of mind. — *Kaivalya-tantra, am,* n., N. of a Tantra. — *Kaivalya-dīpikā,* f., N. of a commentary by Hemādri. — *Kaivalyāśrama* (°*ya-āś*°), *as,* m. a pupil of Govinda, author of a commentary on the poem Ānanda-laharī. — *Kaivalyendra* (°*ya-in*°), *as,* m., N. of the instructor of Rāyaṇendra. — *Kaivalyopanishad* (°*ya-up*°), *t,* f. title of an Upanishad.

कैशव **kaiśava,** *as, ī, am* (fr. *keśava*), belonging to Keśava, (Kṛishṇa or Vishṇu.)

कैशिक **kaiśika,** *as, ī, am* (fr. *keśa*), hair-like, fine as a hair; (*as*), m. love, passion, lust; N. of a subdivision of the Yādavas, descended from Kaiśika, who was son of Vidarbha and brother of Kratha; (*ī*), f., scil. *vṛitti,* one of the four varieties of dramatic style, the graceful style, suited especially to the passion of love; N. of a place or river; an epithet of Durgā; (*am*), n. a quantity of hair, a head of hair.

Kaiśina, as, ī, am (fr. *keśin*), connected with Keśin Dārbhya.

Kaiśya, am, n. (fr. *keśa*), the whole mass of hair, a head of hair, much or ornamented hair.

कैशोर **kaiśora,** *am,* n. (fr. *kiśora*), youth, boyhood, from the age of ten to that of fifteen. — *Kaiśoraka-vayas, as,* n. the age or life of a youth.

कैष्किन्ध **kaishkindha,** *as, ī, am,* coming from Kishkindhā.

को **ko,** a prefix in a number of words, as in *ko-jāgara, ko-mala, ko-vida,* &c., related to 1. *ku;* [cf. the prefixes *ka, kava, kā, kim, ku.*]

कोक **koka,** *as,* m. (an onomatopoetic word), a wolf; a cuckoo; the ruddy goose; a frog; a small lizard or chameleon; a kind of noxious parasitical animal; the wild date tree; an epithet of Vishṇu; N. of a man, a son of Soṇa; N. of a river. — *Koka-deva, as,* m. a pigeon. — *Koka-nakha, ās,* m. pl., N. of a people. — *Koka-bandhu, us,* m. the friend of the Ćakravāka or ruddy goose, an epithet of the sun. — *Koka-yātu, us,* m., Ved. a demon or ghost in the shape of a cuckoo. — *Koka-vāća, as,* m. a sort of animal living in caves, a fox (?). — *Koka-śāstra, am,* n., N. of a very indecent treatise on the art of love, ascribed to a Paṇḍit named Koka. — *Kokāgra* (°*ka-ag*°), *as,* m., N. of a plant, = *samashṭhila.*

कोकड **kokaḍa,** *as,* m. an animal of a brown colour, with a bushy tail, lurking in holes, perhaps a hare or fox.

कोकनद **kokanada,** *ās,* m. pl., N. of a people; (*am*), n. the red lotus; the red water-lily. — *Kokanada-ćhavi, is,* m. the colour of the red lotus; (*is, is, i*), of the colour of the red lotus.

कोकरक **kokaraka,** *ās,* m. pl., N. of a people.

कोकलिक **kokalika,** *as,* m., N. of a man.

कोकली **kokalī,** f., N. of a woman.

कोकामुख **kokāmukha,** *as* or *am,* m. or n. (?), N. of a Tīrtha.

कोकाह **kokāha,** *as,* m. a white horse; (perhaps a foreign word.)

कोकिल **kokila,** *as,* m. (an onomatopoetic word; but by some said to be fr. rt. *kuk*), the Kokila or Koil, the black or Indian cuckoo, Cuculus Indicus; a kind of mouse; a kind of poisonous insect; a firebrand, a lighted coal; N. of a poet; N. of a Rājaputra; (*ā*), f. the female of a Kokila, (the Kokila or Koil is frequently alluded to in Hindū poetry, and its musical cry is supposed to inspire pleasing and tender emotions.) — *Kokila-nayana, as,* m. a plant bearing a dark black flower, Capparis Spinosa; it is also applied to Barleria Longifolia; [cf. *kokilāksha.*] — *Kokila-maitrāvaruṇa, as, ī, am,* relating to the duties or office of the Maitrāvaruṇa priest at the Kaukilīshṭi; (*am*), n. title of a treatise. — *Kokila-hotra, as, ī, am,* relating to the duties or office of the Hotṛi priest at the Kaukilīshṭi; (*am*), n. title of a treatise. — *Kokilāksha* (°*la-ak*°), *as,* m. 'having eyes like those of the Koil,' the plant Asteracantha Longifolia or Capparis Spinosa. — *Kokilākshaka, as,* m. the same plant. — *Kokilā-māhātmya, am,* n. title of a part of the Skanda-purāṇa. — *Kokilāvāsa* (°*la-āv*°), *as,* m. the Mango tree; [cf. *āmra.*] — *Kokilekshu* (°*la-ik*°), *us,* m. the black variety of sugar-cane; [cf. *kṛishṇekshu.*] — *Kokileshṭā* (°*la-ish*°), f., N. of a plant, = *mahā-jambū.* — *Kokilotsava* (°*la-ut*°), *as,* m. the Mango tree.

Kokilaka, as or *am,* m. or n (?), N. of a metre of four lines, each containing seventeen syllables.

कोक्कट *kokkaṭa* = *konkaṭa*, q. v.

कोक्कोक *kokkvoka*, *as*, m., N. of the author of the Rati-rahasya.

कोङ्क *konka*, *ās*, m. pl., N. of a people.

कोङ्कट *konkaṭa*, *as*, m., N. of a scholiast on the Amara-kosha; (a various reading has *kokkaṭa*.)

कोङ्कण *konkaṇa*, *ās*, m. pl., N. of a people on the western shore of the Dekhan; (*am*), n. a kind of weapon; (*ā*), f. a female of the Konkaṇa people. — *Konkaṇā-vatī*, f., N. of a river. — *Konkaṇā-suta*, *as*, m. an epithet of Paraśu-rāma, the son of Konkaṇā.

Konkaṇaka, *ās*, m. pl., N. of a people on the western shore of the Dekhan.

कोङ्कार *kon-kāra*, *as*, m. the sound *kom*.

कोच *koća*, *as*, *ā*, *am* (fr. rt. *kuć*), drying, becoming dry; (*as*), m. drying up, desiccation, aridity; a man of mixed caste, the offspring of a fisherman by a female of the butcher tribe.

कोजागर *ko-jāgara*, *as*, m. a kind of festival, the night of full moon in the month Āśvina (September–October), celebrated with various games; (according to some authorities from *kaḥ* and *jāgara*, 'who is awake?' the exclamation of Lakshmī, who descending on this night, promised wealth to all that were awake; hence the night is spent in festivity and games of chance in honour of the goddess.)

कोञ्ज *koñja*, *as*, m. = *kauñća*, N. of a mountain.

कोट *koṭa*, *as*, m. (rt. *kuṭ*), a fort, a stronghold; a shed, a hut [cf. *kuṭa*, *kuṭī*]; crookedness, curvature; a beard. — *Koṭa-ćakra*, *am*, n. a sort of diagram.

Koṭaka, *as*, *ī*, *am*, who or what curves or bends; (*as*), m. a builder of sheds or huts, a thatcher, a carpenter; a mixed caste, the son of a mason and of the daughter of a potter.

Koṭara, *as*, *am*, m. n. the hollow of a tree; a cave in general; (*ī*), f. a naked woman; an epithet of the goddess Durgā. — *Koṭarā-vaṇa*, *am*, n. a wood in which there are hollow trees.

Koṭavī, f. a naked woman; a form of the goddess Durgā (represented naked).

Koṭi, *is* or *ī*, f. the curved end of a bow or of claws, &c.; the end or top of anything; the edge or point of a sword; the horns of the moon; the highest point, eminence, excellence; the highest number in the older system of numbers, viz. a Krore or ten millions; the complement of an arc to 90°; the side of a right-angled triangle; N. of a plant, Piring or Asparac, Medicago Esculenta, = *koṭi-varshā*. — *Koṭi-karṇa*, *as*, m., N. of a man. — *Koṭi-jit*, *t*, m. a conqueror of ten millions; an epithet of the poet Kālidāsa. — *Koṭi-jyā*, f. the cosine of an angle in a right-angled triangle. — *Koṭi-tīrtha*, *as*, m., N. of a Tīrtha. — *Koṭi-dvaya*, *am*, n. 'the two ends,' i. e. two alternatives. — *Koṭi-pātra*, *am*, n. a rudder or large oar used as one. — *Koṭi-pāla*, *as*, m. the guard of a stronghold? (a wrong reading for *koṭṭa-pāla*?). — *Koṭi-pura*, *am*, n., N. of a town. — *Koṭi-mat*, *ān*, *atī*, *at*, furnished with a point. — *Koṭi-varsha*, *am*, n., N. of a city, Vāṇapura or Devikote, on the Coromandel coast; (*ā*), f. a plant used medicinally, either Medicago Esculenta or Trigonella Corniculata. — *Koṭi-vedhin*, *ī*, *inī*, *i*, striking an edge or point, i. e. performing the most difficult things. — *Koṭi-śas*, ind. by tens of millions, in innumerable multitudes. — *Koṭi-śrī*, f. an epithet of the goddess Durgā. — *Koṭī-varsha*, *am*, n., N. of the town Vāṇapura on the Coromandel coast; (*ā*). f. the plant Medicago Esculenta or Trigonella Corniculata; [cf. *koṭi-varsha*.] — *Koṭīśvara* (°*ṭi-īś*°), *as*, m. the lord of ten millions, a millionaire.

Koṭika, *as*, *ā*, *am*, forming the highest point, top or summit of anything, placed in the highest position, e. g. *mānusha-koṭikā*, a princess; (*as*), m., scil. *maṇḍūka*, a frog; an insect, coccinella of various kinds; N. of the son of a prince. — *Koṭikāsya* (°*ka-ās*°), *as*, m., N. of a son of king Suratha.

Koṭira, *as*, m. the hair (collected on the forehead in the shape of a horn); an ichneumon, Viverra Ichneumon; an insect, coccinella of various kinds [cf. *koṭika*]; an epithet of Indra.

Koṭiśa, *as*, m. a harrow; N. of a Nāga.

Koṭīra, *as*, m. long entangled hair; a crest, a diadem.

Koṭīśa, *as*, m. a harrow; [cf. *koṭiśa*.]

कोट्ट *koṭṭa*, *as*, *am*, m. n. a fort, a castle, a stronghold; [cf. *koṭa*.]

कोट्टवी *koṭṭavī*, f. (fr. *ko-ārtava*?), a naked woman; an epithet of Durgā; the mother of Vāṇa, an Asura; [cf. *koṭavī*, *kauṭavī*, *koṭarī*.] — *Koṭṭavī-pura*, *am*, n., N. of the town Vāṇapura on the Coromandel coast; [cf. *koṭi-varsha* and *koṭī-varsha*.]

कोट्टार *koṭṭāra*, *as*, m. a fortified town, a stronghold; a pond; the stairs of a pond; a libertine; [cf. *koṭṭa*.]

कोठ *koṭha*, *as*, m. (fr. *kushṭha*), a species of leprosy with large round spots; ringworm, impetigo.

कोठर *koṭhara*, *as*, m., N. of a plant, = *ankoṭa*; [cf. *koṭara*.] — *Koṭhara-pushpī*, f. the plant Convolvulus Argenteus.

कोण *koṇa*, *as*, m. a corner, an angle (= *aśri*); an intermediate point of the compass; the quill or bow of a lute, a fiddle-stick, &c.; a sort of musical instrument, a stringed musical instrument; a drum-stick; the sharp edge of a sword; a stick, a staff, a club; a N. of Mangala, the planet Mars; a N. of the planet Saturn (in this sense fr. the Gr. κρόνος). — *Koṇa-kuṇa*, *as*, m. a bug; [cf. *kolakuṇa*, *utkuṇa*, *matkuṇa*.] — *Koṇa-vādin*, *ī*, m. an epithet of Siva. — *Koṇa-sprig-vritta*, *as* or *am*, m. or n. (?), a circle in contact with the angles of a figure; an exterior circle; one circumscribed. — *Koṇā-koṇi*, ind. from angle to angle, from one corner to the other, cornerwise, diagonally; athwart.

कोणि *koṇi*, *is*, *is*, *i*, having a crooked arm; [cf. *kuṇi*.]

कोणेरभट्ट *koṇera-bhaṭṭa*, *as*, m. a N. of a son of Vishṇu and father of Rudra-bhaṭṭa.

कोण्डभट्ट *koṇḍa-bhaṭṭa*, *as*, m., N. of a grammarian.

कोथ *kotha*, *as*, *ā*, *am* (fr. *kuth*), afflicted with pain, churned; (*as*), m. putrefaction, corruption; a sore; gangrene; a disease of the eyes, inflammation and ulceration of the angles of the eyelids; churning.

कोदण्ड *ko-daṇḍa*, *as*, *am*, m. n. a bow; (*as*), m. an eyebrow (shaped like a bow); a creeping plant; N. of a country.

Kodaṇḍin, *ī*, *inī*, *i*, armed with a bow; an epithet of Siva.

कोदार *kodāra*, *as*, *am*, m. n. (?), a kind of grain.

कोद्रव *kodrava*, *as*, m. a species of grain eaten by the poor, Paspalum Scrobiculatum.

कोनालक *konālaka*, *as*, *ā*, m. f. a kind of aquatic bird.

कोनालि *konāli*, *is*, m. or f. (?), a kind of plant.

कोन्तल *kontala*, *ās*, m. pl., N. of a people; [cf. *kuntala*.]

कोन्व *konva*, *as*, m., N. of a mountain; [cf. *kola*, *kollaka*, *kolagiri*, *kolvagireya*.]

कोन्वशिर *konvaśira*, *ās*, m. pl., N. of a degraded warrior-tribe.

कोप *kopa*, *as*, m. (fr. rt. *kup*), morbid irritation or disorder of the humours of the body; passion, wrath, anger, rage, (*sa-kopa*, enraged; *sa-kopam*, angrily.) — *Kopa-kāraṇa*, *am*, n. cause of anger. — 1. *kopa-krama*, *as*, m. one who goes to anger, an angry or passionate man. — *Kopa-jvalita*, *as*, *ā*, *am*, inflamed with wrath, enraged. — *Kopa-tas*, ind. through anger, angrily. — *Kopa-dīpta*, *as*, *ā*, *am*, incensed or inflamed with anger. — *Kopa-pada*, *am*, n. appearance of anger, pretended wrath. — *Kopa-parīta*, *as*, *ā*, *am*, affected by anger. — *Kopa-latā*, f., N. of a plant, = *karṇa-sphoṭā*. — *Kopa-vat*, *ān*, *atī*, *at*, angry; passionate; (*tī*), f., N. of a metre consisting of four lines of fourteen syllables each. — *Kopa-vaśa*, *as*, m. subjection to anger. — *Kopa-vega*, *as*, m. violence, impetuosity of passion; N. of a Ṛishi. — *Kopa-samanvita*, *as*, *ā*, *am*, affected by anger. — *Kopākula* (°*pa-āk*°), *as*, *ā*, *am*, furious, enraged. — *Kopā-kopi*, ind. in mutual anger, in reciprocal wrath. — *Kopāvishṭa* (°*pa-āv*°), *as*, *ā*, *am*, affected with anger.

Kopana, *as*, *ā*, *am*, inclined to passion, passionate, wrathful, angry; irritating, causing morbid irritation or disorder of the humours; (*as*), m., N. of an Asura; (*am*), n. irritating; becoming angry; (*ā*), f. a passionate woman.

Kopanaka, *am*, n. a kind of perfume; [cf. *ćoraka*.]

Kopayishṇu, *us*, *us*, *u*, intending to exasperate, inclined to make angry.

Kopita, *as*, *ā*, *am*, enraged, furious.

Kopin, *ī*, *inī*, *i*, angry, passionate, wrathful; (at the end of a compound) irritating, stirring up; (*ī*), m. a bird called the water-pigeon (*jala-pārāvata*).

कोपक्रम 2. *kopakrama* (*ka-up*°), *am*, n. Brahmā's creation; see 3. *ka*. (For 1. *kopa-krama* see under *kopa* above.)

कोपज्ञ *kopajña* (*ka-up*°), *am*, n. Brahmā's creation.

कोम *koma*, *am*, n. = *kloma*, q. v.

कोमल *ko-mala*, *as*, *ā*, *am* (fr. *ko* = *ku* and *mala* fr. rt. *mlai*, 'easily fading away?'), tender, soft (opposed to *karkaśa*); bland, sweet, low; pleasing, agreeable, beautiful; (*ā*), f., N. of a plant; (*am*), n. water. — *Komala-gīta* or *komala-gītaka*, *am*, n. a pleasing song. — *Komala-tā*, f. or *komala-tva*, *am*, n. softness, tenderness, agreeableness. — *Komala-svabhāva*, *as*, *ā*, *am*, tender-hearted.

Komalaka, *am*, n. the fibres of the stalk of a lotus.

कोमासिका *komāsikā*, f. a budding fruit; [cf. *jālikā*.]

कोम्य *komya*, *as*, *ā*, *am*, Ved. = *kāmya*, lovely (?).

कोयष्टि *ko-yashṭi*, *is*, or *koyashṭika*, *as*, m. the lapwing; a small white crane, commonly called a paddy-bird.

कोर *kora*, *as*, m. (said to be fr. rt. *kur*), a movable joint, as the fingers, the knee, &c.; amphiarthrosis; a bud (see the next).

Koraka, *as*, *am*, m. n. a bud, an unblown flower; the fibres of the stalk of a lotus; a species of perfume, commonly Cor (*ćora*); another perfume, a berry containing a resinous and fragrant substance; [cf. *kakkolaka*.]

Korakita, *as*, *ā*, *am*, covered with buds.

Korita, *as*, *ā*, *am*, budded, sprouted; ground, pounded, comminuted.

कोरङ्गी *korangī*, f. small cardamoms; [cf. *elā*.]

कोरदूष *kora-dūsha* or *koradūshaka*, *as*, m. a kind of grain eaten especially by the poor, Paspalum Scrobiculatum. See *kodrava*.

कोरली koralī or korilā, f., N. of a town.

कोल kola, as, m. a hog; a raft, a float, a boat; a kind of weapon; the breast, the hauoch, the hip or flank, the lap [cf. kroḍa]; an embrace, embracing; N. of a plant (= ćitra, ćitraka); the planet Sani or Saturn; N. of a son of Ākrīḍa; N. of a degraded warrior-tribe; an outcast, one of a tribe degraded by Sagara from the military order; a man of a mixed caste; a barbarian, a Kol, a tribe inhabiting the hills and forests in central India; (ā or ī), f. the jujube tree, Zizyphus Jujuba; (ā), f. Piper Longum, and Piper Chaba (ćavya); (am), n. the fruit of the jujube; black pepper; the weight of one Tola; [cf. Lith. kuilys, kiaule; Hib. cullach; Gr. χοῖρος.] — Kola-kanda, as, m. a sort of bulbous plant, used as a remedy for worms; [cf. krimi-ghna, pañjala, &c.] — Kola-karkaṭikā, f., N. of a plant, = madhu-kharjūrikā. — Kola-giri, is, m., N. of a mountain. — Kola-dala, am, n. a kind of perfume, = nakhī. — Kola-nāsikā, f., N. of a plant, = vanakiṇī. — Kola-puććha, as, m. a heron. — Kola-mūla, am, n. the root of long pepper. — Kola-vallī, f. the plant Pothos Officinalis, a plant with a pungent fruit resembling pepper, = gaja-pippalī; another plant, Piper Chaba (ćavya). — Kola-śimbī, f., N. of a plant, commonly called Ālakuśī, Carpopogon Pruriens; [cf. krita-phalā, khaṭvā, &c.] — Kolā-kolī, ind. with mutual embraces. — Kolāñća (°la-añ°), as, m. a N. of Kaliṅga, the Coromandel coast from Cuttack to Madras; but, according to some, this place is in Gangetic Hindūstan, with Kanouj for the capital. — Kolā-pura, am, n., N. of a town.

Kolaka, as, m., N. of two plants, = aṅkoṭha and bahu-vāra; (am), n. a kind of perfume, = kakkolaka; black pepper.

कोलकिल kolakila, as or am, m. or n. (?), N. of a town; (also read kilakila, kilinakila, kolikila.)

कोलकुण kolakuṇa, as, m. a bug; [cf. koṇakuṇa, utkuṇa, matkuṇa.]

कोलम्बक kolambaka, as, m. (fr. ko + lambaka?), the body of a lute, the whole of it except the strings.

कोलाहल kolāhala, as, am, m. n. (an onomatopoetic word), a loud and confused sound, an uproar, a great and indistinct noise (of men, animals, &c.); (as), m., N. of a personified mountain.

कोलि koli, is, is or ī, m. f. the jujube tree, Zizyphus Jujuba; [cf. karkandhu.] — Koli-sarpa, as, m., N. of a degraded warrior-tribe.

कोलिकिल kolikila, as or am, m. or n. (?), N. of a town (?); [cf. kolakila.]

कोलित kolita, as, m. an epithet of Maudgalyāyana.

कोलुह koluha, as, m., N. of a man.

कोलूक kolūka, as or am, m. or n. (?), N. of a country; also kolūta and śailūta; [cf. ulūka, ulūta, utūla, kulūṭa, kulūta, kaulūta.]

कोल्या kolyā, f. Piper Longum; [cf. kolā.]

कोल्लक kollaka, as, m., N. of a mountain; [cf. konva, konvaśira, kola, kolagiri, kolvagireya.] — Kolla-giri, is, m., N. of a mountain.

कोल्वगिरेय kolva-gireya, ās, m. pl., N. of a people.

कोविद ko-vida, as, ā, am (fr. ko and rt. vid, to know), experienced, skilled, learned, wise (with loc., gen., and at the end of comp., e. g. aśveshu or aśvānām or aśva-kovida, skilled in horses).

कोविदार ko-vidāra, as, m. a tree, Bauhinia Variegata; also one of the trees of paradise.

कोश kośa, as, am, m. n. (fr. rt. kuś or kush?, related to kukshi and koshṭha?; in the earlier literature generally spelt kośa; later books read both kośa and kosha), a cask, a vessel for holding liquids; (metaphorically) a cloud; a pail; a bucket; a drinking-vessel, a cup, a vessel in general; a box, a cupboard, a drawer, a trunk; the interior or inner part of a carriage; a sheath, a scabbard, &c.; a case, a covering, a cover; store-room, store, provisions; a treasury, the apartment where money or plate is kept; treasure, accumulated wealth, money; gold or silver, wrought or unwrought, as plate, jewellery, &c.; a kind of bandage (in surgery); a dictionary, lexicon, or vocabulary; a bud; the sheath or integument of a plant; a pod or any similar seed-vessel; a nutmeg, a nut-shell; the inner part of the fruit Artocarpus Integrifolia; the cocoon of a silk-worm; the vulva, the womb; the penis; a testicle or the scrotum; an egg; (in the Vedānta philosophy) a term for the three sheaths or succession of cases which make up the various frames of the body enveloping the soul, (these are, 1. the ānanda-mayaḥ kośaḥ or 'sheath of pleasure,' forming the kāraṇa-śarīra or 'causal frame;' 2. the vijñāna-mayaḥ or buddhi-mayaḥ or mano-mayaḥ or prāṇa-mayaḥ kośaḥ, 'the sheath of intellect or will or life,' forming the sūkshma-śarīra or 'subtile frame;' 3. the anna-mayaḥ kośaḥ, 'the sheath of nourishment,' forming the sthūla-śarīra or 'gross frame'); a ball or globe (e. g. sūtra-kosha, a ball of thread; netra-kosha, the eye-ball &c.); judicial trial, ordeal by fire, water, poison, the balance, heated balls of iron, boiling oil &c., attesting a deity with thrice-repeated drinking of the water in which some idol has been washed; the water used at an ordeal; an oath; (ā), f., N. of a river; (ī), f. a bud; a seed-vessel; the beard of corn; a shoe, a sandal; [cf. Hib. gucog, 'a bud, a sprout;' Gr. κόκκος.] — Kośa-kāra, as, m. one who makes scabbards, cases, boxes, &c.; the compiler of a dictionary, a lexicographer; the silk-worm or the insect while in its cocoon; a chrysalis or pupa; a variety of sugar-cane or sugar-cane in general. — Kośa-kāraka, as, m. a silk-worm. — Kośa-krit, t, m. a kind of sugar-cane. — Kośa-griha, am, n. a treasury; a room in which valuable garments, precious stones &c. are kept. — Kośa-grahaṇa, am, n. undergoing an ordeal. — Kośa-ćañću, us, m. the Indian crane. — Kośa-nāyaka, as, m. a chief over treasure, a treasurer; an epithet of Kuvera. — Kośa-pāla, as, m. the guardian of a treasure. — Kośa-peṭaka, as, am, m. n. a chest or strong box in which treasure is kept. — Kośa-phala, as, m. a kind of creeping plant [cf. ghoshaka]; (ā), f. a Cucurbitaceous plant, = pīta-ghoshā; the plant Cucumis Utilissimus, = trapushī; (am), n. a kind of perfume, a berry containing a waxy and fragrant substance; a nutmeg. — Kośa-bhūta, as, ā, am, treasured, stored, accumulated. — Kośa-vat, ān, atī, at, possessing treasures, rich, wealthy; (tī), f., N. of a kind of plant. — Kośa-vāsin, ī, inī, i, living in a shell, wrapped up in a sheath or shell, incased; (ī), m. any animal so incased, a chrysalis or pupa. — Kośa-vriddhi, is, f. swelled testicle, enlargement of the scrotum from hernia or hydrocele &c. — Kośa-reśman, a, n. a treasury. — Kośa-śāyikā, f. a clasp-knife or one lying in a sheath. — Kośa-śuddhi, is, f. purification by ordeal. — Kośa-skrit, t, m. a silk-worm. — Kośa-stha, as, ā, am, incased, sheathed, enveloped in a sheath or shell &c.; (as), m. any shelled insect or animal, as a snail &c.; a pupa or chrysalis; the silk-worm in its cocoon. — Kośa-hīna, as, ā, am, without treasure, deprived of riches, poor. — Kośāṅśa (°śa-aṅ°), as, m. part of a treasure, a portion of any one's wealth. — Kośāgāra (°śa-āg°), as, am, m. n. a treasure-house, store-room, treasury. — Kośāṅga (°śa-aṅ°), as, m. a kind of reed or grass, commonly Ikāḍa; [cf. utkaṭa.] — Kośādhipati (°śa-adh°), is, or kośādhīśa or kośādhyaksha (°śa-adh°), as, m. a superintendent of the treasury, a treasurer, a paymaster: an epithet of Kuvera. — Kośopaharaṇa (°śa-ap°), am, n. carrying off treasure. — Kośāmra (°śa-ām°), as, m., N. of a plant, = krimi-vriksha, sukeśaka, commonly kośāma; (am), n. the fruit of this plant, Vulg. keuḍā (= keurā? Sonneratia Apetala?).

Kośaka, as, m. an egg, a testicle.

Kośayī, f., Ved. a chest, a box; the interior of a carriage (?). According to Sāy. = kośa.

Kośikā, f. a drinking-vessel.

Kośin, ī, inī, i, incased (āma-kośin, having the cavity of the ear filled up); (ī), m. the mango tree; [cf. āmra.]

Kośilā, f. a kind of bean [cf. mudga-parṇī]; N. of a river.

कोशल kośala and kośalā. See under kosala.

कोशलिक kośalika, am, n. a bribe; (wrong reading for kauśalika, q. v.)

कोशातक kośātaka or koshātaka, as, m. (fr. kośa?), hair; (ī), f. several Cucurbitaceous plants, Trichosanthes Dioeca, Luffa Acutangula, and Luffa Pentandra; the fruits of these plants; a moonlight night.

कोशातकिन् kośātakin, ī, m. (fr. the preceding?), trade, business; a trader, a merchant; submarine fire.

कोश्य kośya, au or e (?), m. or n. (?), du., Ved. two lumps of flesh near the heart of a sacrificial horse.

कोष kosha with its compounds, see under kośa, for which kosha is only a later form.

कोषला koshalā, wrongly spelt for kosalā.

कोषातक koshātaka = kośātaka, q. v.

कोष्ठ koshṭha, as, m. (fr. rt. kush; probably related to kukshi and kośa), any one of the viscera of the body, as the stomach, heart, lungs, &c., but particularly the stomach; the belly, bowels, abdomen; an inner apartment; a granary, a place in which grain is kept, a store-room, a treasury; (am), n. a surrounding wall; a kind of vessel; the shell of anything; (as, ā, am), own. — Koshṭha-koṭi, is, m., N. of an attendant of Śiva. — Koshṭha-pāla, as, m. a municipal officer, a constable; a watch, a guard, the watch of a city; a storekeeper, a treasurer. — Koshṭha-vat, ān, m., N. of a mountain. — Koshṭha-śuddhi, is, f. dejection by stool, evacuation of the bowels. — Koshṭhāgāra (°ṭha-ag° or āg°), as, am, m. n. a store-room, a store; a treasury. — Koshṭhāgārika, as or ā (?), m. or f. (?), a kind of animal, any animal living in a shell. — Koshṭhāgārin, ī, m. a kind of poisonous insect. — Koshṭhāgni (°ṭha-ag°), is, m. the digestive faculty, the gastric juice. — Koshṭhi-pradīpa, as, m., N. of a work on astronomy.

Koshṭhaka, as or am, m. or n. (?), a granary, a treasury [cf. anna-koshṭhaka]; a surrounding wall; (am), n. a brick trough for watering cattle; N. of a town.

Koshṭhakī-kri, cl. 8. P. A. -karoti, -kurute, -kartum, to surround, enclose.

Koshṭhila, as, m., N. of a man.

Koshṭhya, as, ā, am, proceeding from the chest or interior of the body, emitted (as a sound) from the centre of the lungs.

कोष्ण koshṇa (kā-ush°), as, ā, am, moderately warm, tepid, warm; (am), n. warmth; [cf. kavoshṇa, kadushṇa.]

कोसल kosala, as, m. (in later books generally spelt kośala), N. of a country and the warrior-tribe inhabiting it, descendants of Māthava Videgha; (ā), f., N. of the capital of this country or Ayodhyā, the modern Oude. — Kosalātmajā (°la-āt°), f. the daughter of the king of the Kosalas, an epithet of a wife of Daśa-ratha, the mother of Rāma.

कोहड kohaḍa, as, m., N. of a man; [cf. kauhaḍa and kohala.]

कोहल kohala, as, ā, am (fr. ko+hala? cf. kutūhala), speaking indistinctly; (as), m. a kind of musical instrument; a sort of spirituous liquor; N. of a saint or Muni, the inventor or first teacher of the drama, also a writer on music.

Kohalīya, am, n. title of Kohala's work on music.

कोहित kohita, as, m., N. of a man.

कौकुट्टक kaukuṭṭaka, ās, m. pl., N. of a people; (variously written *kaukuntaka* and *kaukundaka*.)

कौकुर kaukura, ās, m. pl. (fr. kukura), N. of a people.

कौकुवादि kaukuvādi, is, m., N. of a man.

कौकूस्त kaukūsta, as, m., N. of a man.

कौकृत्य kaukṛitya, am, n. (fr. ku-kṛita or ku-kṛitya), evil doing, wickedness; repentance.

कौक्कुट kaukkuṭa, as, ī, am (fr. kukkuṭa), relating to a cock or domestic fowl, gallinaceous.

Kaukkuṭika, as, m. a poulterer, one who sells fowls; a kind of mendicant, one who walks with his eyes fixed on the ground for fear of treading upon insects &c.; a hypocrite.

Kaukkuṭi-kandala, as, m. a species of snake, the Boä or Bor.

कौक्ष kauksha, as, ī, am (fr. kukshi), abdominal, ventral.

Kauksheya, as, ī, am, being in the belly; being in a sheath.

Kauksheyaka, as, m. a sword; a scymitar.

कौङ्क kaunka, as, m. the country Kon-ka, = *konka, konkaṇa*.

Kaunkaṇa, ās, m. pl., N. of a people; the district of Kon-kan in the peninsula.

Kaunkiṇa, ās, m. pl. = *kaunkaṇa* above.

कौङ्कुम kaunkuma, as, ī, am (fr. kunkuma), relating to the saffron flower.

कौचवार्य kaućavārya, as, ā, am, coming from Kūćavāra.

कौञ्च kaunća, as, m., N. of a mountain, part of the Himālaya range; [cf. *krauńća*.]

कौञ्जर kauñjara, as, ī, am (fr. kuñjara), belonging to an elephant; (as), m., N. of a race.

कौञ्जायन kauñjāyana, ās, m. pl. (fr. kuñja), N. of a mountain-tribe, descended from Kuñja; (ī), f. a princess of this tribe; a female descendant of Kuñja; the wife of a Brāhman or any venerable personage.

Kauñjāyanya, as, m. a prince of the mountain-tribe called Kauñjāyana.

कौट 1. kauṭa, as, ī, am (fr. kuṭi), living in one's own house, independant, free; domestic, homely, home-born, home-bred; (as), m. = *kuṭaja*, the plant Wrightia Antidysenterica. — *Kauṭa-taksha, as*, m. an independant carpenter, one who works at home on his own account and not for the village or corporation.

कौट 2. kauṭa, as, ī, am (fr. kūṭa), snared, wired; fraudulent, dishonest; (am), n. fraud, falsehood. — *Kauṭa-sākshin, ī*, m. a false witness, = *kūṭa-sākshin*. — *Kauṭasākshya, am*, n. false evidence.

Kauṭakika, as, ā, am, one whose occupation is to catch animals in traps, caves, &c.; (as), m. a vender of the flesh of birds or beasts, a poacher, a butcher, &c.; [cf. *kauṭika*.]

Kauṭika, as, ī, am, one whose business is to catch animals in traps &c.; one who kills animals and sells their flesh for his own subsistence, a hunter, a poacher, a mountaineer, &c.; relating to a snare or trap; fraudulent, dishonest.

कौटज kauṭaja, as, ī, am (fr. kuṭaja), coming from the plant Wrightia Antidysenterica; (as), m. the plant Wrightia Antidysenterica. — *Kauṭaja-bhārika, as, ā, am*, carrying or bearing a load of Wrightia Antidysenterica.

Kauṭajika, as, ī, am, carrying a load of Wrightia Antidysenterica.

कौटभी kauṭabhī, f. an epithet of the goddess Durgā; [cf. *kaiṭabhī*.]

कौटल्य kauṭalya, as, m. an epithet of Cāṇakya; also called Vātsyāyana; [cf. *kauṭilya*.]

कौटवी kauṭavī, f. a naked woman; [cf. *koṭṭavī*.]

कौटिलिक kauṭilika, as, m. (fr. kuṭilikā), a hunter; a blacksmith.

कौटिल्य kauṭilya, as, m. (fr. kuṭila), an epithet of Cāṇakya [cf. *kauṭalya*]; N. of a grammarian; (am), n. crookedness, curvature, curliness of the hair; falsehood, fraudulent behaviour, dishonesty, deceit, insincerity; a kind of horse-radish.

कौटीर kauṭīra, as, ī, am, belonging to the plant Kuṭīra, made of it.

Kauṭīryā, f. an epithet of Durgā, 'living in a hut (?).'

कौटुम्ब kauṭumba, as, ī, am (fr. kuṭumba), necessary for the household; (am), n. family relationship.

Kauṭumbika, as, ī, am, belonging to a family, constituting a family; having relations; (as), m. the father or master of a family.

कौडविक kauḍavika, as, ī, am (fr. kuḍava), sown with a particular measure (a Kuḍava) of grain (as a field &c.), containing a Kuḍava.

कौडोदरि kauḍodari, is, m. (or kauṇḍodari fr. kuṇḍodara?), N. of a man.

कौड्य kauḍya, ās, m. pl., N. of a people.

कौणकुत्स्य kauṇakutsya, as, m., N. of a Brāhman; [cf. *kūṇa-kuććha*.]

कौणप kauṇapa, as, m. (fr. kuṇapa), 'feeding upon corpses,' a Rākshasa or goblin; N. of a Nāga (these beings are supposed to eat human flesh). — *Kauṇapa-danta, as*, m. an epithet of Bhīshma, uncle of the Pāṇḍus. — *Kauṇapāśana* (°pa-aś°), as, m., N. of a Nāga.

कौणिन्द kauṇinda, ās, m. pl., N. of a people; (as), m. sing. a prince of this people.

कौणेय kauṇeya, as, m. (fr. kuṇi?), Ved. a patronymic of Rajana.

कौण्डल kauṇḍala, as, ī, am (fr. kuṇḍala), furnished with rings.

कौण्डिन्य kauṇḍinya, as, m., N. of a Muni or divine sage; N. of a grammarian; a patronymic of the poet Jaya-deva.

कौण्डिल्यक kauṇḍilyaka, as, m. (or kauṇḍinyaka?), a kind of poisonous insect.

कौण्डोपरथ kauṇḍoparatha, ās, m. pl. (fr. kuṇḍoparatha), N. of a warrior-tribe.

Kauṇḍoparathīya, as, m. a prince of this tribe.

कौण्य kauṇya, am, n. (fr. kuṇi), distortion or paralysis of the hands; the being maimed or handless.

कौतुक kautuka, am, n. (fr. kutuka), curiosity, interest in anything, vehement desire for, wish, inclination; eagerness, vehemence, impatience; anything causing curiosity, admiration or interest, any singular or surprising object, a wonder; festivity, gaiety, a festival, a show, a solemn ceremony, especially the ceremony with the marriage-thread or ring preceding a marriage; the marriage-thread or ring; joy, pleasure, happiness, enjoyment; sport, pastime; public diversion; song, dance, show or spectacle; season of enjoyment; kind or friendly greeting, civility, salutation. — *Kautuka-kriyā*, f. a solemn ceremony, a marriage ceremony. — *Kautuka-gṛiha, am*, n. the house in which a marriage takes place. — *Kautuka-toraṇa, as, am*, m. n. a triumphal arch erected at certain festivals. — *Kautuka-maṅgala, am*, n. a solemn ceremony. — *Kautukāgāra* (°ka-ag° or āg°), *as, am*, m. n. a room for festivity, a room in which a marriage ceremony takes place.

Kautukita, as, ā, am, eagerly interested, eager.

Kautukin, ī, inī, i, festive, gay, jocose, a jester.

कौतूहल kautūhala, am, n. (fr. kutūhala), curiosity, interest in anything, vehement desire for anything, eagerness, vehemence; anything causing curiosity, any unusual phenomenon; a solemn ceremony. — *Kautūhala-para, as, ā, am*, curious, inquisitive. — *Kautūhalānvita* (°la-an°), *as, ā, am*, eager, vehement, curious.

कौतोमत kautomata, am, n. (fr. kutas+mata), N. of a Sūkta (?).

कौत्स kautsa, as, ī, am (fr. kutsa), composed by Kutsa; (am), n. a Sūkta or Sāman composed by Kutsa; (as), m. a patronymic from Kutsa; N. of a teacher; N. of a pupil of Vara-tantu; the son-in-law of Bhagīratha; a patronymic of Jaimini; N. of a degraded family. — *Kautsī-putra, as*, m., N. of a teacher.

कौथुम kauthuma, ās, m. pl. the pupils of Kuthumin.

कौदालिक kaudālika or kaudālīka, as, m. (fr. kudāla), a man of a mixed caste, the son of a fisherman by a woman of the washerman caste.

कौद्रविक kaudravika, am, n. (fr. kodrava), sochal salt.

Kaudravīṇa, as, ā, am, sown with Kodrava (as a field &c.).

कौनख्य kaunakhya, am, n. (fr. ku-nakhin), the condition of one who has a disease of the nails; ugliness of the nails. — *Kaunakhyādika* (°ya-ād°), *am*, n. neglect of personal decoration.

कौन्तिक kauntika, as, m. (fr. kunta), a spearman, a soldier armed with a spear.

कौन्ती kauntī, f. (fr. kunta or kunti), a sort of perfume, commonly *reṇuka*.

कौन्तेय kaunteya, as, m. (a patronymic fr. kuntī), a N. of Yudhishṭhira, Bhīma-sena, and Arjuna; N. of a tree = *arjuna*.

कौन्त्य kauntya, as, m. a king of the Kuntis.

कौन्द kaunda, as, ī, am (fr. kunda), relating to or coming from jasmine.

कौप kaupa, as, ī, am (fr. kūpa), coming from a well or cistern; (am), n. well-water.

Kaupīna, am, n. the pudenda; a privity, a privy part; a small piece of cloth worn over the privities by poor persons; a wrong or improper act, sin. — *Kaupīna-vat, ān, atī, at*, one who has only a piece of cloth over the privities.

Kaupya, as, ā, am, coming from a well or cistern.

कौपोदकी kaupodakī, f. the mace of Kṛishṇa, = *kaumodakī*; [also *kaupādakī*?].

कौब्ज्य kaubjya, am, n. (fr. kubja), crookedness, hump-backedness.

कौम kauma, am, n., N. of a Vedic treatise, so named from its author.

कौमार kaumāra, as, ī, am (fr. kumāra or kumārī), juvenile, youthful, girlish, belonging to a youth or young girl, maiden, maidenly, virgin, (*kaumārī bhāryā*, a virgin wife, one who has not had a husband previously; *kaumāraḥ patiḥ*, a man who marries a virgin; *kaumāram vratam*, a vow of abstinence); soft, tender; relating to the god of war or Sanat-kumāra, belonging or peculiar to them; (*ī*), f. one of the seven divine Mātṛis, the divine mothers or personified energies of the gods, the energy or *śakti* of Kumāra or Kārttikeya the god of war; a kind of bulbous plant, = *vārāhī-kanda*; (*am*), n. childhood, youth from birth to the age of five; maidenhood to the age of sixteen. — *Kaumāra-parvata, as*, m., N. of a mountain. — *Kaumāra-bhṛitya, am*, n. the rearing and education of children, a department of medical science; [cf. *kumāra-bhṛityā*.] — *Kaumārarājya, am*, n. (fr. *kumāra-rāja* = *rāja-kumāra, yuva-rāja*), the position of an heir-apparent; [cf. *yauvarājya*.].

Kaumāraka, am, n. childhood, the juvenile age.

Kaumārika, as, ī, am, endowed with girls; (*as*), m. a father of girls. — *Kaumārika-tantra, am*, n., N. of a Tantra.

कौमुद *kaumuda, as*, m. (fr. *kumuda*), the month Kārttika, October–November; (*ī*), f. moonlight, moonshine (from its causing the Kumudas to blossom); elucidation, (the word Kaumudī being metaphorically used like other words of similar import (*ćandrikā*) at the end of the title of grammatical commentaries and other explanatory works to imply that the book so designated throws much light on the subject of which it treats, e. g. *padārtha-kaumudī, prakriyā-k°, laghu-k°, vaishamya-k°, siddhānta-k°*); the day of full moon in the month Kārttika, sacred to the god Kārttikeya; the day of full moon in the month Āśvina; a festival in honour of Kārttikeya held on the full moon of the month Kārttika; a festival in general; N. of a metre consisting of two lines of twenty-four syllables each; N. of a river. — *Kaumudī-ćāra, as, am*, m. n. the day of full moon in the month Āśvina. — *Kaumudī-pati, is*, m. the moon. — *Kaumudī-vṛiksha, as*, m. the stick or stand of a lamp.

Kaumudika, as, ī, am, relating to a water-lily, abounding with them; (*ikā*), f., N. of a female friend of Umā.

कौमोदकी *kaumodakī*, f. (fr. *kumodaka*), N. of the club or mace of Vishṇu or Kṛishṇa, given to him by Varuṇa.

Kaumodī, f. the club or mace of Vishṇu or Kṛishṇa.

कौम्भ *kaumbha, as, ī, am* (fr. *kumbha*), put into a pot.

Kaumbhakāraka, made by a potter (?).

Kaumbhakāri, is, m. or *kaumbhakārya, as*, m. the son of a potter.

कौरम *kaurama, as*, m., N. of a man; (a various reading has *kauruma*.)

कौरयाण *kaurayāṇa, as*, m. (fr. *kurayāṇa*), a patronymic of Pāka-sthāman.

कौरव *kaurava, as, ī, am* (fr. *kuru*), belonging to the Kurus &c.; (*as*), m. a patronymic from Kuru; a descendant of Kuru; also *kauravaka*.

Kauravāyaṇi, is, or *kauraveya, as*, m. a patronymic from Kuru.

Kauravya, as, m. a patronymic from Kuru; a descendant of Kuru; N. of a Nāga, father of Ulūpī.

Kauravyāyaṇī, f. a female descendant of Kuru. — *Kauravyāyaṇī-putra, as*, m., N. of a teacher.

Kaurukatya, as, ā, am, belonging to the family of the Kurus and Katas.

Kaurukullaka, ās, m. pl., N. of a Buddhist sect.

Kaurupanćāla, as, ī, am, belonging to the race of the Kurus and Panćālas.

Kaurupathi, is, m. (fr. *kuru-patha*), N. of a teacher.

कौर्पर *kaurpara, as, ī, am* (fr. *kūrpara*), being at the elbow.

कौर्प्य *kaurpya, as*, m. (a word borrowed from the Gr. σκορπίος), the sign of the zodiac Scorpio.

कौर्म *kaurma, as, ī, am* (fr. *kūrma*), belonging or relating to a tortoise, connected with a tortoise, acting as one; belonging or relating to the Avatāra of Vishṇu as a tortoise; (*as*), m., N. of a Kalpa, the day of full moon of Brahmā; (*am*), n., scil. *purāṇam*, title of a Purāṇa on the subject of Vishṇu's descent as a tortoise. — *Kaurmopapurāṇa* (°*ma-up°*), *am*, n., N. of an Upa-purāṇa.

कौल *kaula, as, ī, am* (fr. *kula*), belonging or relating to a family, ancestral, extending over a whole family or race, sprung from a noble family, of a good family, well-born; (*as*), m. a worshipper of Sakti according to the left-hand ritual; (*am*), n. the doctrine and practices of the left-hand Sāktas. — *Kaulopanishad* (°*la-up°*), *t*, f. title of an Upanishad.

Kaulakeya, as, ī, am, sprung from a noble family, of a good family, well-born; (*as*), m. a bastard; (wrong form for *kaulaṭeya*.)

Kaulattha, as, ī, am (fr. *kulattha*), made or prepared with or consisting of Dolichos Uniflorus; (*am*), n. a drink prepared with Kulattha.

Kaulatthīna, as, ā, am, sown with Dolichos Uniflorus (as a field).

Kaulika, as, ī, am, belonging to a family or race, customary in a family, ancestral, heritable in the family; (*as*), m. a weaver; a heretic, an impostor; a follower of the left-hand Sākta ritual.

Kaulīna, as, ā, am, peculiar or belonging to a noble family; (*as*), m. the son of a female beggar; a follower of the left-hand Sākta ritual; (*am*), n. rumour, report; evil report, detraction; family scandal; combat of animals, of birds, snakes, &c.; cock-fighting, &c.; contention of animals as a species of gambling; a privity, a privy part, the pudenda; high birth, family descent; an improper act, a bad deed.

Kaulīnya, am, n. high birth, nobility; family honour; family trouble, family scandal.

Kauleya, as, ī, am, sprung from a noble family; of the left-hand Sākta sect; [cf. *kaula, kaulika, kaulīna*.]

Kauleyaka, as, ī, am, sprung from a noble family, of good parentage; pertaining to a family; (*as*), m. a dog (a domestic animal).

Kaulya, as, ā, am, sprung from a noble family, of good family or parentage; of the left-hand Sākta sect.

कौलटिनेय *kaulaṭineya, as, ī*, m. f. (fr. *kulaṭā*), the son or daughter of a female beggar; a bastard.

Kaulaṭeya, as, ī, m. f. the child of a female beggar; a bastard, the child of a disloyal wife.

Kaulaṭera, as, ā, m. f. a bastard, son or daughter of a disloyal wife; the child of a beggar.

कौलव *kaulava, as*, m., N. of the third Karaṇa or astronomical period.

कौलाल *kaulāla, as*, m., Ved. a potter, = *kulāla*; the son of a potter. — *Kaulāla-ćakra, am*, n. a potter's wheel.

Kaulālaka, as, ī, am, made by a potter, pertaining to a potter; (*am*), n. earthenware, porcelain.

कौलितर *kaulitara, as*, m., Ved. an epithet of the demon Sambara.

कौलिशिक *kauliśika, as, ī, am* (fr. *kuliśa*), resembling a thunderbolt.

कौलीक *kaulīka, as*, m., Ved. a kind of bird.

कौलीरा *kaulīrā*, f. (fr. *kulīra*), N. of a plant, = *karkaṭa-śṛiṅgī*.

कौलूत *kaulūta, as*, m. a king of the Kulūtas; (a various reading has *kaulūbha*.)

कौल्मलबर्हिष *kaulmalabarhisha, am*, n., N. of a Sāman called after Kulmala-barhisha.

कौल्माषी *kaulmāshī*, f. (fr. *kulmāsha*), a day of full moon on which Kulmāsha is eaten.

Kaulmāshīṇa, as, ā, am, sown with or fit for Kulmāsha (as a field).

कौवल *kauvala, am*, n. = *kuvala*, the fruit of the tree Zizyphus Jujuba.

कौवेर *kauvera, as, ī, am* (fr. *kuvera*), relating or belonging to Kuvera, coming from him; (*ī*), f., scil. *diś*, the region of Kuvera, the north quarter; the *śakti* or female energy of Kuvera; (*am*), n. a plant, a kind of Costus, Costus Speciosus.

कौश 1. *kauśa, as, ī, am* (fr. *kuśa*), made of Kuśa grass; (*am*), n., scil. *nagara*, the town of Kuśa, an epithet of Kānyakubja. — *Kauśāmbhas* (°*śa-am°*), *as*, n. Kuśa grass boiled in water.

Kauśya, as, ā, am, made of Kuśa grass.

कौश 2. *kauśa, as, ī, am* (fr. *kośa*), silken, silk.

1. *kauśika, as, ī, am*, being in a sheath or scabbard, sheathed, incased; silken, silk; (*as*), m. one who is versed in dictionaries; the compiler of a dictionary, a lexicographer; the fragrant substance bdellium; marrow; (*ā*), f. a drinking-vessel.

Kauśeya or *kausheya, as, ī, am*, silken, of silk; (*am*), n. silk, a silk cloth, a silk petticoat or trowsers, a woman's lower garments of silk.

कौशल *kauśala, am*, n. (fr. *kuśala*), well-being, welfare, good fortune, happiness, prosperity; skilfulness, cleverness, experience; (*ī*), f. friendly inquiry, greeting, salutation; a respectful present, a Nazr; (*ās*), m. pl., N. of a people.

Kauśalikā, f. a present, a respectful gift or offering.

Kauśalya, am, n. welfare, well-being, good fortune, prosperity; cleverness, experience; (*ā*), f. see *kausalya*.

कौशाम्ब *kauśāmba, am*, n. (fr. *kuśāmba*), N. of a realm; (*ī*), f., N. of an ancient city on the Ganges in the lower part of the Doab, in the vicinity of Kurrah; also *vatsa-pattana*.

Kauśāmbeya, as, m. a patronymic from Kuśāmba.

Kauśāmbya, as, m. the chief of Kauśambī.

कौशाश्वी *kauśāśvī*, f., N. of a town built by Kuśāśva.

कौशिक 2. *kauśika, as, ī, am* (fr. *kuśika*), of the family of Kuśika &c.; (*as*), m. a patronymic of Viśvā-mitra, who was the son or grandson of Kuśika; N. of a teacher, author of the Sūtras of the Atharva-veda; a brother of Paippalādi; N. of a grammarian; N. of one of Jarāsandha's generals; an epithet of Indra (as originally perhaps belonging to the Kuśikas or friendly to them); N. of a son of Vasudeva; N. of an Asura; an epithet of Śiva; N. of the plant Vatica Robusta [cf. *kuśika* and *aśva-karṇa*]; an ichneumon; an owl; love, passion; (*ī*), f., N. of a river in Bahar, commonly called Kosi or Koosa, created by Viśvā-mitra, or identified with Satyavatī, the sister of Viśvā-mitra; an epithet of the goddess Durgā; N. of a Buddhist female beggar or *pari-vrājikā*; (*as, ī, am*), coming from an owl. — *Kauśika-priya, as*, m. an epithet of Rāma. — *Kauśika-phala, as*, m. the cocoa-nut tree, (said to have been created by the sage Viśvā-mitra when endeavouring to form a human being in rivalry of Brahmā, the nut being the rudiment of the head.) — *Kauśikāṅguli, is*, m., N. of a teacher. — *Kauśikātmaja* (°*ka-āt°*), *as*, m. Indra's son, an epithet of Arjuna. — *Kauśikāyudha* (°*ka-āy°*), *am*, n. the bow of Indra, the rainbow. — *Kauśikārāti* (°*ka-ar°*), *is*, m. an enemy of owls, a crow; also *kauśikāri*, &c. — *Kauśikī-putra, as*, m., N. of a teacher. — *Kauśiky-oja, as*, m. (*oja* = *ojas*), N. of a tree, = *śākhoṭā*.

Kauśikāyani, is, m. (a patronymic fr. *kauśika*), N. of a teacher.

Kauśikin, inas, m. pl. the pupils of Kauśika.

कौशिकार *kauśikāra, as*, m. = *kośa-kāra*, q. v.

कौशिज *kauśija, ās*, m. pl., N. of a people.

कौशीतकी *kauśītakī* = *kaushītakī*, q. v.

कौशीधान्य *kauśīdhānya, am,* n. (fr. *kośī-dhānya*), a leguminous plant, pulse.

कौशीलव *kauśīlava* or *kauśīlavya, am,* n. (fr. *kuśīlava*), the profession of an actor, a dancer, &c.

कौशेय *kauśeya.* See under 2. *kauśa.*

कौश्य *kauśya.* See under 1. *kauśa.*

कौषारव *kaushārava, as,* m. (fr. *kushāru*), a patronymic of Maitreya.

कौषीतक *kaushītaka, as,* m. (fr. *kushītaka*), a patronymic of Kahoḍa; (*ī*), f. a patronymic of the wife of Agastya; N. of a school derived from Kushītaka; (*am*), n., N. of a work.

Kaushītaki, is, m. a patronymic from Kushītaka.

Kaushītakin, inas, m. pl. the pupils of Kaushītaka. — *Kaushītaki-brāhmaṇa, am,* n., N. of a Brāhmaṇa.

Kaushītakeya, as, m. a patronymic of a Kāśyapa; a patronymic of Kahoḍa.

कौषेय *kausheya.* See under 2. *kauśa.*

कौष्ठ *kaushṭha, as, ī, am* (fr. *koshṭha*), being in a store-room, &c.

Kaushṭhya, as, ā, am, being in the stomach or abdomen.

कौष्ठिल *kaushṭhila* in *Mahā-kaushṭhila, as,* m., N. of a Buddhist author.

कौष्य *kaushya, as,* m. a patronymic from Kosha.

कौसलक *kausalaka, ās,* m. pl. (fr. *kosala*), N. of a people; (sometimes spelt *kauśalaka.*)

Kausaleya, as, m. (fr. *kausalyā*), a metronymic of Rāma as son of Kausalyā.

Kausalya, as, ā, am (fr. *kosala*), belonging to the people of the Kosalas; (*as*), m. a prince of the Kosalas; (*ā*), f. the daughter of a prince of the Kosalas, the wife of Pūru and mother of Janamejaya; the wife of Satvat; the wife of Daśa-ratha and mother of Rāma; epithet of the mother of Dhṛita-rāshṭra; of the mother of Pāṇḍu. — *Kosalyā-nandana, as,* m. and *kosalyā-mātṛi, tā,* m. an epithet of Rāma.

Kausalyāyani, is, m. a metronymic of Rāma.

कौसिद *kausida, as, ī, am* (fr. *kusida*), relating or belonging to or coming from a Kusida, q. v.

कौसीद *kausīda, as, ī, am* (fr. *kusīda*), connected with or relating to a loan; usurious.

Kausīdya, am, n. sloth, indolence; the practice of usury.

कौसुम *kausuma, as, ī, am* (fr. *kusuma*), flowery, flowering; (*am*), n. the ashes of brass, used as a collyrium.

Kausumāyudha, as, ī, am (fr. *kusumāyudha*), relating to the god of love.

कौसुम्भ *kausumbha, as, ī, am* (fr. *kusumbha*), prepared with safflower; dyed with safflower, orange, red; (*as*), m. wild safflower.

कौसुरुबिन्द *kausurubinda, as, ī, am* (fr. *kusurubinda*), N. of a Daśa-rātra.

कौसृतिक *kausṛitika, as, ī, am* (fr. *ku-sṛiti*), following evil courses, fraudulent; a cheat, a knave; (*as*), m. a juggler, a conjurer.

कौस्तुभ *kaustubha, as,* m. (fr. *kustubha?*), N. of a celebrated jewel obtained with thirteen other precious things at the churning of the ocean and suspended on the breast of Kṛishṇa; a manner of joining the fingers; (*am*), n. a kind of oil (*sarsha-podbhava*). — *Kaustubha-lakshaṇa, as,* or *kaustubha-lakshaka, as,* m. or *kaustubha-vakshas, ās,* m. a N. of Vishṇu or Kṛishṇa.

कौस्थलपुर *kausthalapura, am,* n., N. of a town.

कौहलिय *kauhaliya* or *kauhalīya* (?), *ās,* m. pl., N. of a school called after Kohala.

Kauhalī-putra, as, m., N. of a grammarian.

क्नंस् *knaṇs,* cl. 1. 10. P. *knaṇsati, knaṇsayati,* to speak; to shine; [cf. *kuṇś, kuṇs, knas, kraṇś.*]

क्नथ् *knath,* cl. 1. P. *knathati, -thitum,* to hurt, injure; to kill.

क्नस् *knas,* cl. 4. P. *knasyati, -situm,* to be crooked (in mind or body); to shine: Caus. *knasayati, -yitum,* to shine; [cf. *kuṇś, kuṇs, knaṇs, kraṇś.*]

क्नु *knu* or *knū,* cl. 9. P. A. *knunāti, -nīte,* or *knūnāti, -nīte,* to sound, make a noise.

क्नूय् *knūy,* cl. 1. A. *knūyate, ćuknūye, knūyitum,* to be wet; to make a creaking sound; to stink: Caus. P. *knopayati, aćuknupat, -yitum,* to make wet.

Knūta, as, ā, am, stinking, noisy, wet (?).

Knūyitṛi, tā, trī, tṛi, stinking, emitting a stench.

क्मर् *kmar,* cl. 1. P. *kmarati,* to be crooked in person, to be crooked in mind, to be fraudulent or crafty; [cf. *hvṛi.*]

क्य *kya, am,* n., Ved. (according to Sāy. fr. 3. *ka = prajā-pati*), anything agreeable to Prajā-pati.

क्रंश् *kraṇś,* cl. 1. P. (?) *kraṇśati,* to illuminate; [cf. *knaṇs* and *knas.*]

क्रकच *krakaća, as, am,* m. n. (an onomatopoetic word), a saw; (*as*), m. the plant Capparis Aphylla, = *karīra;* N. of a part of hell; (*ā*), f. the tree Pandanus Odoratissimus, = *ketaka;* [cf. *krakara.*] — *Krakaća-ććhada, as,* m. the tree Pandanus Odoratissimus. — *Krakaća-pattra, as,* m. the teak tree. — *Krakaća-pād, t,* m. a lizard, a chameleon. — *Krakaća-prishṭhi,* f. a small fish with numerous small spines in the back, Cojus Cobojus.

क्रकण *krakaṇa, as,* m. a kind of partridge, commonly Kayar, Perdix Sylvatica; [cf. *kṛikaṇa* and *krakara.*]

क्रकर *krakara, as,* m. (an onomatopoetic word), a kind of partridge, Perdix Sylvatica; the plant Capparis Aphylla (see *karīra*); a saw; a poor man; disease; [cf. *krakaća.*]

क्रकुच्छन्द *krakuććhanda, as,* m., N. of a Buddha, a predecessor of Śākya-muni.

क्रक्षमाण *krakshamāṇa, as, ā, am* (a part. fr. an obsolete rt. *kraksh*), Ved. roaring, raving (?).

क्रतु *kratu, us,* m. (said to be fr. 1. *kṛi,* but perhaps rather fr. 2. *kṛi*), plan, design, intention, purpose; resolution, determination; desire, will (in this sense often occurring in the Vedic inst. case, *kratvā,* willingly, readily); power, ability, adequacy, efficiency, deliberation, consultation; intelligence, understanding (e. g. *bhadraḥ kratuḥ,* right judgment, good understanding; frequently found in conjunction with the almost synonymous word *daksha,* e. g. *daksha-kratū* or *kratu-dakshau,* ability and intelligence, intelligence and power); inspiration; enlightenment; a sacrificial rite or ceremony; sacrifice, offering, worship; an Aśvamedha sacrifice; (*Kratu,* as intelligence personified, is a son of Brahmā, and one of the Prajā-patis or ten principal Ṛishis or saints mentioned in Manu I. 35; he is said to be married to Kriyā and father of the 60,000 Vālikhilyas. or according to other authorities the husband of Haya-śirā); N. of one of the Viśva-devās; also of a son of Ūru and Āgneyī; N. of the author of a Dharma-śāstra; [cf. *a-kratu, adbhuta-kratu, abhi-kratu,* &c.; cf. also Gr. κράτος.] — *Kratu-karman, a,* n. a sacrificial ceremony. — *Kratu-ććhada, as,* m. one skilled (?) in sacrifice; a Jina; (in the latter sense a wrong form for *kraku-ććhanda.*) — *Kratu-jit, t,* m., N. of a man. — *Kratu-tulya, as, ā, am,* equal to an Aśvamedha in merit. — *Kratu-druh, -dhruk,* m. an enemy of sacrifices, an Asura. — *Kratu-dvish, ṭ,* m. hating sacrifices, an Asura, a Daitya or demon. — *Kratu-dhvaṇsin, ī,* m. an epithet of Śiva as 'destroyer of Daksha's sacrifice.' — *Kratu-pati, is,* m. the performer of a sacrifice. — *Kratu-paśu, us,* m. a sacrificial animal; a horse, especially one fit for an Aśvamedha. — *Kratu-pā, ās, ās, am,* Ved. watching one's sentiments or intentions. — *Kratu-purusha, as,* m. an epithet of Vishṇu. — *Kratu-prā, ās, ās, am,* or *kratu-prāvan, ā, ā, a,* Ved. becoming inspired or enlightened; (Sāy.) fulfilling religious rites. — *Kratu-phala, am,* n. the reward of a sacrifice, the object for which it is performed. — *Kratu-bhuj, k,* m. one who eats the sacrifice, a god, a deity. — *Kratu-mat, ān, atī, at,* Ved. intelligent, prudent, wise; inspired, enlightened; (Sāy.) having religious rites; (*ān*), m., N. of a son of Viśvā-mitra. — *Kratu-maya, as, ī, am,* endowed with intelligence. — *Kratu-rāj, ṭ,* m. the chief of sacrifices, the most excellent sacrifice. — *Kratu-rāja, as,* m. the chief of sacrifices, the Rājasūya sacrifice, performed by a monarch who has made all the princes of the world tributary to himself. — *Kratu-vikrayin, ī, iṇī, i,* or *kratu-vikrāyaka, as, ikā, am,* one who sells the possible benefits of a sacrifice performed by himself. — *Kratu-vid, t, t, t,* Ved. prudent, wise; causing inspiration, inspiring; (Sāy.) acquainted with religious rites; granting knowledge; (*t*), m., N. of a man. — *Kratu-sankhyā,* f., N. of the thirteenth of Kātyāyana's Pariśishṭas. — *Kratu-sangraha, as,* m. title of a Pariśishṭa of the Sāma-veda. — *Kratu-siddhi, is,* f. completion of a sacrifice, attainment of the object for which it is performed. — *Kratu-spriś, k, k, k,* causing intelligence or inspiration. — *Kratūttama* (°*tu-ut*°), *as,* m. the chief of sacrifices, the Rājasūya sacrifice. — *Kratvā-magha, as, ā, am,* Ved. giving readily.

Kratūya, nom. P., Ved. *kratūyati, -yitum,* to exert the intellect.

क्रथ् *krath,* cl. 1. P. *krathati, -thitum,* to hurt, kill; cl. 10. P. *krāthayati, -yitum,* to hurt, injure, kill (with gen. of the person); to amuse, to delight repeatedly; [cf. *knath* and *klath.*]

क्रथ *kratha, as,* m., N. of a race belonging to the Yādava people, derived from Kratha, a son of Vidarbha and brother of Kaiśika; N. of an Asura; [cf. the next.]

क्रथन *krathana, as,* m., N. of an Asura; N. of a Nāga, a son of Dhṛita-rāshṭra; N. of a monkey; (*am*), n. slaughter, killing; hemorrhage (?); snoring, stertor.

क्रथनक *krathanaka, as,* m., N. of a camel in the Pañća-tantra; (*am*), n. a black sort of Agallochum.

क्रन्द् *krand* or *krad,* cl. 1. P. A. *krandati, -te,* or *kradate, ćakranda, ćakrade, krandishyati, -te, akrandīt* (Ved. Aor. *akran*), *kranditum.* to neigh (as a horse); to roar (metaphorically applied to the clouds and to wind and water); to creak (as a wheel); to cry piteously, to weep, shed tears; to grieve, be confused with sorrow; to call out piteously to any one (with acc.); to cry out: Caus. *krandayati, -yitum,* to cause to roar or shake; to cause to weep or lament; to roar, rave: Desid. *ćikrandishati, -te:* Intens. *ćākrandyate, ćākranti,* Ved. *kanikranti* (part. *kanikradat, kanikradyamāna*), to neigh, roar, rave, cry out; to shake; to creak; [cf. Goth. *grêta,* 'to lament.']

Kranda, as, m., Ved. neighing; a cry, calling out.

Krandad-ishṭi, is, is, i, Ved. moving with a great noise or roaring, an epithet of Vāyu.

Krandana, as, m. a cat; (*am*), n. crying out, calling; mutual daring or defiance, challenging; weeping, lamenting, sobbing.

Krandanu, us, m., Ved. roaring, shaking.

Krandas, as, n., Ved. battle-cry; (*asī*), du. two

contending armies shouting defiance; (Sāy.) heaven and earth.

Krandita, as, ā, am, wept, called or cried out; (*am*), n. weeping, calling; mutual daring.

Krandya, am, n., Ved. neighing.

क्रप् krap, cl. 1. A. *krapate, ćakrape, krapishyate, akrapishṭa, krapitum,* to long for; to mourn; to lament, implore; to compassionate, pity; to go; [cf. *kṛip,* &c.]

क्रम् kram, cl. 1. P. A., 4. P. *krāmati* (ep. also *kramati*), *kramate* (ep. also *krāmate*), *krāmyati* and *kramyati* (?), *ćakrāma, ćakrame, kramitā, kramishyati* and *kraṃsyate, akramīt* and *akraṃsta, kramitum* (according to some also *krāntum*), to step, walk, go, go towards, approach (with acc.); to approach in order to ask for assistance (with loc., e. g. *tasmin krame,* I go to him for assistance); to go across, go over; to ascend; to have sexual intercourse with; to excel; to pervade, take possession of; to fill; to fulfil, accomplish; to undertake, strive after; A. to proceed well, to gain a footing, to succeed, have effect; (in gram.) to be liable to the peculiar arrangement of a Vedic text called Krama; to be doubled (as a letter or word) in connection with this arrangement; A. to read according to the Krama arrangement of a Vedic text: Caus. *kramayati, -yitum,* to cause to step; *kramayati* or *krāmayati,* to make liable to the peculiar arrangement called Krama; to double (a letter or word) in connection with this arrangement: Intens. *ćaṅkramyate* or *ćaṅkranti,* to step to and fro, to walk, wander about: Desid. *ćikramishati, ćikraṃsate;* [cf. Lat. *gra-dus, gra-dior, gran-dis;* Goth. *hlaupa,* 'to run;' Old Germ. *hlaufu, hloufu; laufu, loufu.*]

Krantṛi, tā, trī, tṛi, going, a goer, who or what goes.

Krama, as, m. a step; going, proceeding; course (e. g. *kāla-kramāt,* in course of time); passing; the foot; a position taken (by an animal &c.) before making a spring or attacking; uninterrupted or regular progress, order, series, regular arrangement, hereditary descent, succession (e. g. *varṇa-krameṇa,* in the order of the tribes or castes; *krameṇa,* in regular course, by degrees, according to order, rank, or series); method, manner (e. g. *yena krameṇa,* in which manner; *tad-anusaraṇa-krameṇa,* in a manner corresponding to that); an undertaking, enterprise, intention; a peculiar manner or method of reading and writing Vedic texts, i. e. 'progressing step by step,' so called because the reading proceeds from the first member (either word or letter) to the second, then the second is repeated and connected with the third, the third repeated and connected with the fourth, and so on, (this manner of reading or writing in relation to words is called *pada-krama;* in relation to conjunct consonants *varṇa-krama*); a term for the words or letters themselves when combined or arranged in this manner; power, strength. — *Krama-kāla, as,* m. the time of the Krama arrangement. — *Krama-ja, as, ā, am,* produced by the Krama arrangement. — *Krama-jit, t,* m., N. of a prince. — *Krama-jyā,* f. the sine of a planet; declination; [cf. *krānti-jyā.*] — *Krama-tas,* ind. gradually, successively, in order. — *Krama-trairāśika, as* or *am,* m. or n. (?), a particular method of applying the direct rule of three (opposed to *vyasta°* or *viloma-trairāśika*). — *Krama-pada, am,* n. the conjunction of words in the Krama reading, more usually written *pada-krama.* — *Krama-pāṭha, as,* m. the Krama reading, i. e. a peculiar 'step by step' arrangement of a Vedic text made to secure it from all possible error by, as it were, combining the Saṃhitā-pāṭha and the Pada-pāṭha, i. e. by giving the words both as connected and unconnected with following and preceding words; see under *krama* above. — *Krama-pūraka, as,* m., N. of a tree, = *vaka.* — *Krama-prāpta, as, ā, am,* obtained by succession or hereditary descent. — *Krama-bhaṅga, as,* m. interruption of order, irregularity. — *Krama-yoga, as,* m. succession, regular order, successive or methodical practice; (*ena*), ind. in regular manner. — *Krama-vat,* ind. in the manner of the Krama arrangement. — *Krama-varta, as* or *am,* m. or n. (?), N. of a district in Kaśmīra. — *Krama-śas,* ind. gradually, by degrees; regularly, seriatim. — *Krama-śāstra, am,* n. rules relating to the Krama arrangement. — *Krama-saṃhitā,* f. a collection of Vedic texts arranged according to the Krama method. — *Kramasaṃhitodāharaṇa* (°*tā-ud°*), *am,* n. an example from a Krama-saṃhitā. — *Krama-saṅgraha,* title of a treatise; [cf. *kṛita-dāsa.*] — *Krama-sandarbha-prabhāsa,* title of a chapter (*khaṇḍa*) in a particular work. — *Kramāgata* (°*ma-āg°*), *as, ā, am,* descended or inherited lineally, what comes from one's ancestors in regular succession, arrived in due course or succession. — *Kramāgata-tva, am,* n. hereditary succession or possession. — *Kramāditya* (°*ma-ād°*), *as,* m. an epithet of king Skanda-gupta. — *Kramādhyayana* (°*ma-adh°*), *am,* n. the Krama reading or arrangement; see *krama-pāṭha* above. — *Kramādhyāyin* (°*ma-adh°*), *ī,* m. one who reads the Krama arrangement of a Vedic text. — *Kramānuyāyin* (°*ma-an°*), *ī, inī, i,* following the methodical order. — *Kramānusāra* or *kramānvaya* (°*ma-an°*), *as,* m. regular order, due arrangement. — *Kramāyāta* (°*ma-āy°*), *as, ā, am,* descended or inherited lineally, coming from one's ancestors in regular succession; one who has acceded to the throne by succession; proceeding in regular order. — *Kramāvasāna* (°*ma-av°*), *am,* n. the end of a word in the Krama arrangement of a Vedic text. — *Kramokta* (°*ma-uk°*), *as, ā, am,* enjoined for the Krama arrangement. — *Kramodvega* (°*ma-ud°*), *as,* m. an ox.

Kramaka, as, ā, am, going, proceeding; orderly, methodical; (*as*), m. a student who goes through a regular course of study, one who proceeds methodically; one who reads or knows the Krama arrangement of a text.

Kramaṇa, as, m. a step; the foot; a horse; N. of a son of Bhajamāna; (*am*), n. stepping, walking, going; transgressing; proceeding; approaching or undertaking anything; treatment of words or letters according to the Krama arrangement, doubling letters, words, &c.

Kramaṇīya, as, ā, am, to be gone to, to be gone beyond.

Kramad-īśvara, as, m., N. of the author of the grammar called Saṅkshipta-sāra.

Kramamāṇa, as, ā, am, going, proceeding.

Kramika, as, ā, am, proceeding in a fixed order or methodically; successive.

Kramitṛi, tā, trī, tṛi, stepping, walking, going, who or what goes &c.

Kramya, as, ā, am, produced by the Krama arrangement, arising by the Krama.

Krā, ās, ās, am, (at the end of some compounds) stepping, going; [cf. *udadhi-krā, dadhi-krā.*]

Krānta, as, ā, am, gone, going, gone or going over or across; spread, extended; attacking, invading, gone to or against; overcome, surpassed; (*as*), m. a horse; (in astronomy) declination; (*ā*), f., N. of a plant, a kind of Solanum [cf. *bṛihatī*]; a species of the Atyashṭi metre [cf. *kāntā*]; (*am*), n. a step, (*Vishṇoḥ krāntam,* 'the step of Vishṇu,' N. of a Soma ceremony); a certain aspect in astronomy when the moon is in conjunction with a planet.

Krānti, is, f. going, proceeding, a step; overcoming, surpassing; attacking; declination of a planet; the sun's course on the globe, the ecliptic. — *Krānti-kaksha, as,* m. the course of the sun, the ecliptic. — *Krānti-kshetra, am,* n. a figure described by the ecliptic. — *Krānti-jyā,* f. the sine of the declination or of the ecliptic. — *Krānti-pāta, as,* m. the intersection of the ecliptic and equinoctial circles, the equinoctial points or nodes of the ecliptic. — *Krānti-pāta-gati, is,* f. motion of the nodes of the ecliptic, precession of the equinox. — *Krānti-bhāga, as,* m. the declination of a point of the ecliptic. — *Krānti-maṇḍala* or *krānti-vṛitta, am,* n. the ecliptic. — *Krānti-valaya, as,* m. the ecliptic; the space within the tropics.

Krāntu, us, m. a bird.

Krāmat, an, antī, at, going, proceeding over or across.

क्रमि krami, *is,* m. = *kṛimi,* a worm.

क्रमु kramu, *us,* m. the betel-nut tree, Areca Faufel or Catechu.

Kramuka, as, m., N. of several plants, the Areca or betel-nut tree, Areca Faufel or Catechu; the mulberry tree, Morus Indica (= *brahma-dāru*); another tree, a red sort of Lodhra (*paṭṭikā-lodhra*); a kind of fragrant grass, Bhadra-mustaka; the fruit of the cotton tree; (*ās*), m. pl., N. of a people; (*ī*), f. the betel-nut tree, Areca Faufel or Catechu. — *Kramuka-phala, am,* n. the Areca-nut.

क्रमेल kramela or *kramelaka, as,* m. the camel; [cf. Gr. κάμηλος; Lat. *camelus.*]

क्रय kraya, &c. See under rt. *krī.*

क्रयशीर्ष krayaśīrsha, *am,* n. = *kapi-śīrsha,* the coping of a wall.

क्रवण kravaṇa, *as,* m., Ved. a worshipper.

क्रविस् kravis, *is,* n., Ved. (or *kravi* in the comp. *a-kravi-hasta,* q. v.), raw flesh, carrion; [cf. Gr. κρέας; cf. also *krūra.*]

Kravishṇu, us, us, u, desirous of raw flesh.

Kravya, am, n. flesh, raw flesh, carrion; [cf. Lith. *krauja-s,* 'blood;' Russ. *krovj;* Hib. *cru;* Old Germ. *hreo;* Gr. κρέας; Lat. *cruor, cruentus, crūdus, caro.*] — *Kravya-ghātana, as,* m. a deer, an antelope; (killed for its flesh.) — *Kravya-bhuj, k, k, k,* carnivorous, eating carrion; (*k*), m. a Rākshasa. — *Kravya-bhojana, as, ā, am,* carnivorous. — *Kravya-mukha, as,* m. (?) having flesh in one's mouth, N. of a wolf in the Pañća-tantra. — *Kravya-vāhana, as, ī, am,* Ved. carrying corpses, an epithet of Agni (opposed to *havya-vāhana*). — *Kravyād* (°*ya-ad*), *t, t, t,* consuming flesh or corpses, epithet of the fire of the funeral pile, or Agni in one of his terrible forms; epithet of a Yātu-dhāna and other evil beings, imps, and goblins; N. of a Rakshas; a beast of prey, a carnivorous animal. — *Kravyāda* (°*ya-ada*), *as, ā, am,* carnivorous, an eater of flesh; (*as*), m. a goblin, a Rākshasa; a lion, a hawk; the fire of the funeral pile; N. of a people. — *Kravyāśin* (°*ya-āś°*), *ī, inī, i,* carnivorous; (*ī*), m. a demon; an anthropophagus.

क्रशय kraśaya (fr. *kṛiśa*), nom. P. *kraśayati, -yitum,* to emaciate, make thin or lean.

Kraśita, as, ā, am, emaciated, made thin or lean.

Kraśiman, ā, m. leanness, emaciation.

क्रष्टव्य krashṭavya. See rt. *kṛish,* p. 250.

क्राकचिक krākaćika, *as,* m. (fr. *krakaća*), a sawyer.

क्राथ krātha, *as,* m. (fr. rt. *krath*), killing, murder; N. of a prince; of a son of Dhṛita-rāshṭra; of a Nāga; of a monkey; a patronymic from Kratha; [cf. *krathana.*] — *Krātheśvara* (°*tha-iś°*) or *krodheśvara* (°*dha-iś°*), *as,* m., N. of a pupil of Āpastamba.

क्रान्त krānta, *krānti,* &c. See under *kram.*

क्रायक krāyaka. See under rt. *krī.*

क्रिमि krimi, *is,* m. a worm, an insect, &c., and the words derived and compounded with *krimi.* See under *kṛimi.*

क्रिय kriya, *as,* m. (a word borrowed from the Gr. κριός), the sign of the zodiac Aries.

क्रियमाण kriyamāṇa. See rt. 1. *kṛi.*

क्रिया kriyā, f. (fr. rt. 1. *kṛi*), doing, performing, performance; business; an act, action, undertaking; activity; work; labour; bodily action, exercise of the limbs; a literary work; medical treatment or practice; applying a remedy, cure (e. g. *samakriya-tva*, the being treated according to one and the same system of medicine; *vishamakriya-tva*, the being treated according to different methods); a religious rite or ceremony, sacrificial act, sacrifice; obsequies, rites performed immediately after death; purificatory rites, as ablution &c.; (religious action is sometimes personified as a daughter of Daksha and wife of Dharma, or a daughter of Kardama and wife of Kratu); judicial investigation by human means, as by witnesses, documents, &c., or by superhuman or ordeals of various kinds; (in grammar) action (as the general idea expressed by any verb); a verb, (according to later grammarians a verb is of two kinds, *sakarma-kriyā*, active, and *akarma-kriyā*, intransitive); a noun of action; native lexicographers give also the following meanings to *kriyā*,—atonement; disquisition; study; means, expedient; instrument, implement. — *Kriyā-kara, as*, m. one who performs an action, a student. — *Kriyā-kartṛi, tā*, m. the doer of an action, an agent. — *Kriyā-kalāpa, as*, m. title of a grammar; the great body of ceremonies enjoined in the Hindū laws, a number of actions of any kind; all the particulars or points of any business. — *Kriyā-kāra, as, ī, am*, one who does any act, an agent, a performer; (*as*), m. a beginner, a novice, a tyro, a student; an agreement. — *Kriyā-kaumudī*, f. title of a work by Govindānanda. — *Kriyā-tantra, am*, n. 'a Tantra of action,' one of the four classes of Tantras with Buddhists. — *Kriyā-dveshin, ī, iṇī, i*, one who is averse to the part of a lawsuit or judicial trial called *kriyā*, i. e. to witnesses, documents, ordeals, &c.; (*ī*), m. one of the five kinds of witnesses, he whose testimony is hurtful to the cause. — *Kriyā-dvaita, am*, n. efficient cause, as resigning all to God. — *Kriyā-nibandha*, title of a work. — *Kriyā-nirdeśa, as*, m. evidence. — *Kriyānurūpa* (°*yā-an*°), *as, ā, am*, conformable to the act, according to the action. — *Kriyānvita* (°*yā-an*°), *as, ā, am*, practising ritual observances. — *Kriyā-paṭu, us, us, u*, clever, dextrous. — *Kriyā-patha, as* or *am*, m. or n. (?), manner of medical treatment or application of remedies. — *Kriyā-pada, am*, n. a verb. — *Kriyā-para, as, ā, am*, attentive to or diligent in the performance of one's duties. — *Kriyāpavarga* (°*yā-ap*°), *as*, m. end of an affair, liberation from ceremonial acts. — *Kriyā-pāda, as*, m. the third division of a suit at law, witnesses, written documents and other proofs adduced by the complainants, the rejoinder of the plaintiff. — *Kriyā-prasaṅga, as*, m. course of proceeding. — *Kriyā-phala, am*, n. result or consequence of acts. — *Kriyābhyupagama* (°*yā-abh*°), *as*, m. special compact or agreement. — *Kriyāmbudhi* (°*yā-am*°), *is*, m. title of a work of Prāṇakṛishṇa. — *Kriyā-yoga, as*, m. the connection with an action or verb; the employment of expedients or instruments; the practical form of the Yoga system of philosophy, devotion by due performance of the duties of every day life, active devotion. — *Kriyāyoga-sāra, as*, m. a section of the Padma-purāṇa. — *Kriyā-lopa, as*, m. discontinuance or loss of any of the essential ceremonies of the Hindū religion. — *Kriyā-vat, ān, atī, at*, one who performs an action, active, busy, engaged in a business, understanding business, fit for it, possessed of worldly knowledge; performing ceremonies in the right manner, celebrating religious rites. — *Kriyā-vaśa, as, ā, am*, subject to the influence of acts; (*as*), m. necessity, necessary influence of acts done or to be done. — *Kriyāvasanna* (°*yā-av*°), *as, ā, am*, one who loses a lawsuit through the statements of the witnesses &c. — *Kriyā-vāćaka, as, ā, am*, or *kriyā-vāćin, ī, inī, i*, expressing an action (as a verbal noun). — *Kriyā-vādin, ī*, m. a plaintiff; one who states the arguments in a lawsuit. — *Kriyā-vidhi, is*, m. a rule of action; conduct of affairs, mode of performing any rite. — *Kriyāvidhi-jña, as, ā, am*, conversant with business, understanding the ritual &c. — *Kriyā-viśāla, am*, n. title of the thirteenth of the fourteen Pūrvas or most ancient Jaina writings. — *Kriyā-viśeshaṇa, am*, n. that which defines an action more closely; an adverb. — *Kriyā-śakti, is*, f. capability to act; the power of action. — *Kriyā-samabhihāra, as*, m. repetition of any act, doing anything repeatedly. — *Kriyā-sāra, as*, m. title of a work. — *Kriyā-sthānaka-vićāra, as*, m. title of a Jaina work. — *Kriyendriya* (°*yā-in*°), *as*, m. an organ of action, as the hand, foot, voice, organ of generation and that of excretion; also called *karmendriya*, q. v.

क्रिवि *krivi, is*, m., Ved. a leather bag, metaphorically 'a cloud;' N. of an Asura; a cistern, a well; the original name of the Pańćālas; [cf. *kraivya*.]

क्री 1. *krī*, cl. 9. P. A. *krīṇāti, krīṇīte, ćikrāya, ćikriye, kreshyati, -te, akraishīt, akreshṭa, kretum*, to buy, purchase (with inst. of the price, and abl. or gen. of the person from which anything is bought, e. g. *ka imam Indraṃ daśabhir dhenubhir mama krīṇāti*, who will buy this Indra of me for ten cows? *yam mātā-pitror antikāt* or *sakāśāt krīṇīyāt*, whom he may buy from his father and mother; *krīṇīshva tad daśabhiḥ suvarṇaiḥ*, buy that for ten suvarṇas); to barter or exchange; to win: Caus. *krāpayati, -yitum, aćikrapat*: Desid. *ćikrīshati, -te*: Intens. *ćekrīyate, ćekrayīti, ćekreti*; [cf. Hib. *creanaim*, 'I buy, I purchase;' Gr. πρίαμαι, πέρνημι; Lith. *prekis, perku* (?); Lat. *pretium*; Eng. *hire*.] — *Kry-ādi, ayas*, m. pl. the roots beginning with *krī*, i. e. those of the ninth class.

Kraya, as, m. buying, purchase. — *Kraya-krīta, as, ā, am*, bought, purchased. — *Kraya-dravya, am*, n. anything for which anything else is bought or exchanged. — *Kraya-lekhya, am*, n. deed of sale, conveyance, &c. — *Kraya-vikraya, au*, m. du. buying and selling, trade, traffic. — *Krayavikrayika, as*, m. a trader or merchant, a dealer. — *Krayavikrayin, ī, iṇī, i*, one who buys or sells, one who strikes a bargain. — *Krayāroha* (°*ya-ār*°), *as*, m. a market, a fair (where goods are piled up for sale).

Krayaṇa, am, n. buying, purchasing.

Krayaṇīya, as, ā, am, to be bought or purchased, purchasable.

Krayāṇaka, as, ikā, am, what is sold, fit to be sold.

Krayika, as, ā, am, buying, purchasing; (*as*), m. a trader, a dealer, a purchaser, a buyer.

Krayin, ī, iṇī, i, a buyer, a purchaser.

Krayya, as, ā, am, exhibited for sale, purchasable.

Krāyaka, as, m. a buyer or purchaser; a dealer, a trader.

2. *krī, īs, īs, i*, (at the end of some compounds) buying.

Krīta, as, ā, am, bought, purchased; (*as*), m. a son, one of the twelve kinds acknowledged by the ancient Hindū law, viz. one purchased from his natural parents. — *Krītānuśaya* (°*ta-an*°), *as*, m. repenting a purchase, returning a purchase upon the seller, admissible in some cases by law.

Krītaka, as, ā, am, acquired by purchase; (*as*), m. a son bought from his natural parents and adopted as male issue; also *krīta-putra* (?).

Kreṇi, is, m. and *kreṇī*, f. buying, purchasing, purchase.

Kretavya, as, ā, am, to be bought, purchasable.

Kretṛi, tā, m. a buyer, purchaser.

Kreya, as, ā, am, purchasable, to be bought. — *Kreya-da, as, ā, am*, one who exhibits anything for sale, a seller.

क्रीड् *krīḍ*, cl. 1. P. (ep. also A.) *krīḍati, ćikrīḍa, krīḍishyati, akrīḍīt, krīḍitum*, to play, sport, amuse one's self, frolic, gambol, dally, (used of men, animals, the wind and waves, &c.); to jest, joke with (with inst. or with *saha* and inst., e. g. *Droṇena* or *Droṇena saha krīḍati*, he sports with Droṇa): Caus. *krīḍayati, -yitum*, to cause to play, to allow to play: Desid. *ćikrīḍishati*: Intens. *ćekrīḍyate, ćekrīṭṭi*.

Krīḍa, as, ā, am, playing, sporting; (*as, ā*), m. f. sport, play, pastime, pleasure, amusement (often in compounds, e. g. *krīḍā-mudaḥ*, f. pl. the pleasures of play, or of amorous sport; *Kṛishṇa-krīḍā*, sport with Kṛishṇa; *jala-krīḍā*, playing about in water); disrespect shown by jest or joke. — *Krīḍā-kānana, am*, n. a pleasure-grove. — *Krīḍākūta* (°*ḍā-āk*°), *am*, n. sportive or wanton purpose or desire. — *Krīḍā-kopa, as*, m. assumed anger, anger in sport. — *Krīḍā-kautuka, am*, n. wanton curiosity; sport, play, pastime, enjoyment; lasciviousness, sexual intercourse. — *Krīḍā-khaṇḍa*, title of the second part of the Gaṇeśa-Purāṇa. — *Krīḍā-gṛiha, am*, n. a pleasure-house, a house for amusement. — *Krīḍā-ćaṅkramaṇa, am*, n. (?), N. of a place. — *Krīḍā-ćandra, as* or *am*, m. or n. (?), N. of a metre consisting of four lines of eighteen syllables each; N. of a poet. — *Krīḍā-nārī*, f. a harlot, a courtezan. — *Krīḍā-maya, as, ī, am*, consisting of play or sport. — *Krīḍā-mayūra, as*, m. a peacock kept for pleasure or amusement. — *Krīḍā-mṛiga, as*, m. any animal kept for pleasure, a toy-deer, a toy-animal of any kind. — *Krīḍā-ratna, am*, n. the gem of sports, copulation. — *Krīḍā-ratha, as*, m. a cart, a carriage used for amusements. — *Krīḍā-rasātala, am*, n. title of a work in the Sāhitya-darpaṇa. — *Krīḍā-vat, ān, atī, at*, sportive, playful. — *Krīḍā-vana, am*, n. a pleasure-garden, a park. — *Krīḍā-veśman, a*, n. a pleasure-house, a house for amusement. — *Krīḍā-śakunta, as*, m. a bird kept for pleasure or amusement. — *Krīḍā-śaila, as*, m. a pleasure-mountain, a pleasure-mound or hillock in a garden. — *Krīḍā-saras, as*, n. a pleasure-lake. — *Krīḍā-sthāna, am*, n. or *krīḍoddeśa* (°*ḍā-ud*°), *as*, m. a play-ground.

Krīḍaka, as, m. a player, one who sports.

Krīḍat, an, antī, at, playing, sporting, gamboling.

Krīḍana, am, n. playing, play, sporting, &c.

Krīḍanaka, as, ikā, am, playing, sporting; (*as, am*), m. or n. (?), a plaything, a toy for children. — *Krīḍanaka-tā*, f. the state of a plaything; *krīḍanakatayā*, after the manner of a plaything.

Krīḍanīya or *krīḍanīyaka, am*, n. a plaything, toy, a doll. — *Krīḍanīyaka-sannibha, as, ā, am*, like a toy or doll.

Krīḍamāna, as, ā, am, sporting, playing.

Krīḍi or *krīḷi, is, is, i*, Ved. playing, sporting; epithet of the winds.

Krīḍitṛi, tā, m. a player, one who sports.

Krīḍin, ī, inī, i, Ved. playing, sporting; epithet of the Maruts or winds; (*ī*), m., N. of a man.

Krīḍu or *krīḷu, us, us, u*, Ved. playing, effervescing (?); epithet of the Soma. — *Krīḍu-mat, ān, atī, at*, Ved. playing, playful; epithet of flame.

क्रुञ्च् 1. *kruńć*, cl. 1. P. *kruńćati, -ćitum*, to curve or make crooked; to be or become crooked, to move crookedly; to be or become small, to shrink; to make small, to lessen; to go towards, approach, arrive at; [cf. Hib. *cruinn*, 'rotundus.']

Krukta, as, ā, am, crooked, curved.

2. *kruńć, n*, m., Ved. a kind of snipe, a curlew.

Kruńća, as, m. a kind of snipe, a curlew; N. of a mountain; (*ā*), f. a female snipe or curlew; a kind of Vīṇā or lute.

Kruńćakīyā, f., N. of a place in India.

Krauńća, as, m. a curlew, heron, &c. See s. v.

क्रुड् *kruḍ*, cl. 6. P. *kruḍati, -ḍitum*, to sink, dive; to be or become thick; (another form for *bhṛiḍ*); [cf. *kūḍ* and *krūḍ*.]

क्रुध् 1. *krudh*, cl. 4. P. (rarely A.) *krudhyati, -te, ćukrodha, krotsyati, akrudhat, kroddhum*, to become angry, to be wrathful or angry with (with dat. or gen. or acc. or with *upari* and gen., e. g. *putrāya* or *putrasya* or *putram* or *putrasyopari ćukrodha*, he was angry with his son; Caus. *krodhayati, -yitum*, to make angry, provoke, irritate: Desid. *ćukrutsati*; Intens. *ćokrudhyate, ćokroddhi*;

[cf. Lith. *rus-tus*, 'angry;' *rus-tybė*, 'anger;' Lat. *crudelis* (?); Gr. κότος; Germ. *groll*; Hib. *corruidhe*, 'anger, wrath, motion;' *corruigh*, 'fury, resentment.']

Kruddha, as, ā, am, irritated, provoked, angry, wrathful; fierce, cruel; (*am*), n. anger.

2. *krudh, t*, f. or *krudhā*, f. anger, wrath, passion.

Krudhmin, ī, inī, i, Ved. wrathful, irritable.

Krudhyat, an, antī, at, being angry, feeling provoked.

Krodha, as, m. anger, wrath, passion; anger personified as a child of Lobha and Nikṛiti; or of death; or of Brahmā; N. of a Dānava; (*ā*), f., N. of a daughter of Daksha. — *Krodha-ja, as, ā, am*, proceeding from or engendered by wrath, (especially applicable to eight vices, hatred, envy, oppression, violence, &c.) — *Krodha-maya, as, ī, am*, a person of angry disposition; passionate, angry. — *Krodha-mūrćhita, as, ā, am*, overcome or infatuated with anger, passionate, angry; (*as*), m. a kind of perfume, commonly called Cor, = *ćora*. — *Krodha-varjita, as, ā, am*, free from wrath, mild, calm. — *Krodha-vardhana, as*, m., N. of a Dānava. — *Krodha-vaśa, as*, m. the power of anger; (*as, ā, am*), overpowered by anger, passionate, violent; N. of several kinds of evil spirits; (*as*), m., N. of a Rakshas; (*ā*), f., N. of a daughter of Daksha and wife of Kaśyapa. — *Krodhavaśa-ga, as, ā, am*, subject to anger, under the influence of anger. — *Krodha-samanvita, as, ā, am*, filled with anger. — *Krodha-hantṛi, tā*, m., N. of an Asura. — *Krodhānvita* (°*dha-an*°), *as, ā, am*, wrathful, angry. — *Krodhāmarsha-jihma-bhrū* (°*dha-am*°), *ūs, ūs, u*, bending the brow with anger and impatience. — *Krodhojjhita* (°*dha-uj*°), *as, ā, am*, free from wrath, composed, calm.

Krodhana, as, ā, am, inclined to wrath, passionate, angry; (*as*), m., N. of a son of Kauśika and pupil of Garga; also of a son of Ayuta and father of Devātithi; (*ā*), f. a passionate woman, a vixen; (*am*), n. the being angry, anger.

Krodhanīya, as, ā, am, anything which may produce anger, provocative; (*am*), n. an injury.

Krodhālu, us, us, u, passionate, violent.

Krodhin, ī, inī, i, passionate, angry; (*ī*), m. a buffalo; a dog; (*inī*), f. mystical name of the letter *r*.

Krodhishṭha, as, ā, am, very irate or wrathful.

क्रुन्थ् *krunth*, cl. 9. P. *kruthnāti, krunthitum*, to embrace, to cling or adhere to; to be distressed, to pain, injure, kill, suffer pain, be distressed; (another form for *kunth*.)

क्रुमु *krumu, us*, f., Ved., N. of a river, a tributary of the Indus.

क्रुमुक *krumuka, as*, m., Ved. a piece of wood or match used to catch the sacrificial fire when kindled by friction; [cf. *kṛmuka, kramuka*.]

क्रुश् *kruś*, cl. 1. P. (rarely A.) *krośati, -te, ćukrośa, krokshyati, akrukshat, kroshṭum*, to cry out, shriek, yell, bawl, call out, halloo; to exclaim; to cry, lament; to weep; to sound, make a singing noise (as the ear): Caus. *krośayati, -yitum*: Desid. *ćukrukshati*: Intens. *ćokruśyate, ćokruśīti*; [cf. Lith. *klykiu*, 'to cry;' *kryksztauju*; Hib. *cruisigh*, 'music, song;' Lat. *crocio, crocito*; Gr. κρώζω, κράζω, κραγγή; Goth. *krukya*.]

Kruśvan, ā, m. a jackal; [cf. *kroshṭu*.]

Krushṭa, as, ā, am, calling out, crying out, scolding; wept, cried; cried aloud, bawled; called at, abused; (*am*), n. crying, weeping, sobbing; noise, sound.

Krośa, as, m. a cry, a yell, a shriek, a shout, a call, calling out, a noise (e. g. *karṇa-krośa*, a noise in the ears); the range of the voice in calling or hallooing, a measure of distance, an Indian league, commonly called a Kos, = 1000 Daṇḍas, = 4000 Hastas, = ¼ Yojana; according to other authorities = 2000 Daṇḍas, = 8000 Hastas, = ½ Gavyūti; (*am*), n., N. of a Sāman. — *Krośa-tāla, as*, m. a large or double drum. — *Krośa-dhvani, is*, m. a large drum. — *Krośa-mātra-gata, as, ā, am*, gone the length of a Krośa. — *Krośa-mātra-sthita, as, ā, am*, standing at the distance of a Krośa. — *Krośa-yuga, am*, n. a measure of two Krośas, = 4000 yards or about 2½ miles; (this seems to correspond to the modern Krośa, but the standard varies.)

Krośat, an, antī, at, crying, calling out.

Krośana, as, ā, am, who or what cries; (*am*), n. crying.

Krośin, ī, inī, i, crying out, calling out, weeping (e. g. *ushṭra-krośin*, making sounds like a camel).

Kroshṭa, as, m., N. of a man.

Kroshṭu (*must* form strong cases and *may* form weak cases from *kroshṭṛi*, Gram. 128. *c*), a jackal; N. of a son of Yadu and father of Vṛijinīvat (in this last sense nom. sing. *kroshṭā* or *kroshṭus*). — *Kroshṭu-karṇa, as* or *am*, m. or n. (?), N. of a place. — *Kroshṭu-pāda, as*, m., N. of a man; (*ās*), m. pl. the descendants of this man. — *Kroshṭu-puććhikā* or *kroshṭu-puććhī*, f. the plant Hemionitis Cordifolia; [cf. *kroshṭuka-puććhikā* or *kroshṭu-vinnā*.] — *Kroshṭu-phala, as*, m. the tree Terminalia Catappa, = *inguda*. — *Kroshṭu-māna* and *kroshṭu-māya, as*, m., N. of two men; (*ās*), m. pl. the descendants of these men. — *Kroshṭu-vinnā*, f. a plant, either Chaculiya, Hemionitis Cordifolia (*priśni-parṇī*), or Ramvāsac; [cf. *śṛigāla-vinnā*.]

Kroshṭuka, as, m. a jackal; N. of a man, cf. *kraushṭuki*; (*ī*), f. a female jackal; a daughter of Krodha-vaśā and mother of the yellow apes. — *Kroshṭuka-puććhikā*, f. a plant, commonly Chaculiya, Hemionitis Cordifolia; or, according to some, Ramvāsac; [cf. *kroshṭu-vinnā*.] — *Kroshṭuka-māna, as*, m., N. of a man. — *Kroshṭuka-mekhalā*, f. the plant Hemionitis Cordifolia. — *Kroshṭuka-śiras, as*, n. a disease of the knee.

Kroshṭṛi, ṭā, m. (not used in the weakest cases, cf. *kroshṭu*), a jackal; N. of a son of Yadu and father of Vṛijinīvat; (*ṭrī*), f. the female of a jackal; a kind of Convolvulus; N. of another plant, [cf. *lāngalī*.] — *Kroshṭekshu, us*, m. (fr. *kroshṭā* = *kroshṭṛi* and *ikshu*?), a kind of sugar-cane, = *śvetekshu*.

क्रूड् *krūḍ*, cl. 10. P. *krūḍayati, -yitum*, to make thick; [cf. *kūḍ, kruḍ*.]

क्रूर *krūra, as, ā, am* (related to *kravis, kravya*), wounded, hurt, sore; bloody; raw; cruel, fierce, ferocious, hard-hearted; pitiless; hard, harsh, rough; formidable, terrible; inauspicious (opposed to *saumya* and *a-krūra*, and epithet of the first, third, fifth, seventh, ninth, and eleventh signs of the zodiac, which are supposed to have a malignant influence); mischievous, destructive; hard, solid; strong (as a bow, opposed to *manda*); hot, sharp, disagreeable; (*am*), ind. in a formidable manner; (*as, am*), m. n. boiled rice; (*as*), m. a hawk; a heron; two plants, red oleander, = *rakta-karavīra*, and another plant, = *bhūtānkuśa*; (*ā*), f., N. of a plant, = *rakta-punarnavā*; (*am*), n. a wound, a sore; blood-shedding, slaughter, cruelty, any horrible deed; any frightful apparition. — *Krūrakarma-kṛit, t, t, t*, perpetrating cruel actions; a rapacious animal. — *Krūra-karman, a*, n. a bloody or terrible deed; any hard or difficult labour; (*ā, ā, a*), performing bloody or terrible deeds, fierce, cruel, unrelenting; (*ā*), m., N. of a plant, = *kaṭutumbinī* = *kaṭutumbī* (?). — *Krūra-kṛit, t, t, t*, performing bloody or terrible deeds, fierce, cruel, unrelenting. — *Krūra-koshṭha, as*, m. torpid or costive bowels unaffected by strong purgatives; (*as, ā, am*), one whose bowels are torpid or costive. — *Krūra-gandha, as*, m. sulphur; (*ā*), f., N. of a tree, = *kanthārī*. — *Krūra-ćarita, as, ā, am*, cruel, ferocious, addicted to cruel practices. — *Krūra-tā*, f. or *krūra-tra, am*, n. cruelty, fierceness. — *Krūra-dantī*, f. an epithet of Durgā. — *Krūra-dṛiś, k, k, k*, evil-eyed, of terrible aspect, mischievous, villainous, cruel; (*k*), m. an epithet of the planet Śani or Saturn; also an epithet of the planet Mars. — *Krūra-dhūrta, as*, m. a kind of thorn-apple; [cf. *kṛishṇa-dhattūraka*.] — *Krūra-buddhi, is, is, i*, or *krūra-mānasa, as, ā, am*, cruel-minded. — *Krūra-rava, as*, m. a jackal (?). — *Krūra-rāvin, ī*, m. a raven. — *Krūra-loćana, as*, m. an epithet of the planet Saturn (of an evil or inauspicious aspect). — *Krūra-sarpa-vat*, ind. like an enraged serpent. — *Krūrākṛiti* (°*ra-āk*°), *is*, m. an epithet of Rāvaṇa, the ruler of Lankā. — *Krūrāksha* (°*ra-ak*°), *as*, m., N. of a minister of the owl-king Ari-mardana. — *Krūrāćāra* (°*ra-āć*°), *as, ā, am*, following cruel or savage practices. — *Krūrātman* (°*ra-āt*°), *ā*, m. an epithet of the planet Saturn; [cf. *krūra-dṛiś* and *krūra-loćana*.] — *Krūrāśaya* (°*ra-āś*°), *as, ā, am*, one whose bowels are torpid or costive; containing fierce animals (as a river &c.); of a terrible or fierce disposition. — *Krūropasaṃhata* (°*ra-up*°), *as, ā, am*, connected with cruelty.

क्रूर्च *krūrća, as, am*, m. n. the beard; [cf. *kūrća*.]

क्रेणि *kreṇi, kretavya*, &c. See rt. *krī*.

क्रैडिन *kraiḍina, as, ī, am* (fr. *krīḍin*, q. v.), Ved. belonging to the Maruts or winds.

Kraiḍinīyā, f., scil. *ishṭi*, the Ishṭi or sacrificial oblation, sacred to the Maruts.

क्रैव्य *kraivya, as*, m. (fr. *krivi*), a king of the Krivis.

क्रोञ्च *krońća*, &c. Cf. *krauñća*.

क्रोठिन् *krothin, ī*, m. (?), N. of a man.

क्रोड *kroḍa, as, am, ā*, m. n. f. (m. in the earlier language; n. in later works; also f. according to the lexicographers), the breast, the chest, the bosom, (at the end of compounds the fem. can only end in *ā*, e. g. *kalyāṇa-kroḍā*, a woman with a well-formed breast), the flank, the hollow above the hip; the lap; the interior of anything, the inner part, a cavity, a hollow [cf. *udara* and *garbha*]; (*as*), m. a hog; the esculent bulb of a kind of plant, = *vārāhī-kanda*, [cf. *kroḍa-kanyā*]; N. of Śani or the planet Saturn; (*ā*), f. a plant, = *kroḍa-ćūḍā*. — *Kroḍa-kanyā*, f. the esculent bulb of a kind of plant; [cf. *kroḍa*.] — *Kroḍa-ćūḍā*, f., N. of a plant, = *mahā-śrāvaṇikā*. — *Kroḍa-pattra, am*, n. a marginal writing omitted in its proper place, a postscript to a letter, a supplement, a codicil to a will. — *Kroḍa-parṇī*, f. a prickly nightshade, Solanum Jacquini, = *kaṇṭakārikā*. — *Kroḍa-pāda, as*, m. a turtle, a tortoise. — *Kroḍānka* (°*ḍa-an*°), *as*, m. a tortoise. — *Kroḍānghri* (°*ḍa-an*°), *is*, m. a turtle or tortoise. — *Kroḍī-mukha, as*, m. (?) a rhinoceros. — *Kroḍeshṭā* (°*ḍa-ish*°), f. a kind of grass, = *mustā*.

Kroḍī-kṛi, cl. 8. P. *-karoti, -kartum*, to fold to the breast, clasp to the bosom, clasp, embrace. — *Kroḍī-karaṇa, am*, n. folding to the breast, embracing. — *Kroḍī-kṛiti, is*, f. embracing, embrace.

Krauḍa, as, ī, am, fit for or belonging to a hog.

क्रोणकवर्ण *kroṇaka-varṇa, as*, m., N. of a man.

क्रोथ *krotha, as*, m. (fr. *kruth* for rt. *krunth*?), killing, slaying, murder; [cf. *krātha*.]

क्रोध *krodha*, &c. See under 1. *krudh*.

क्रोश *krośa, kroshṭu*. See under *kruś*.

क्रौञ्च *krauñća, as*, m. (fr. rt. *kruñć*, q. v.), a kind of curlew or heron (Ardea Jaculator); the emblem of the fifth Arhat of the present Avasarpiṇī; (*ī*), f. the female curlew; a daughter of Tāmrā and mother of the curlews; (*as*), m. a mountain, part of the Himālaya range, situated in the eastern part of the chain on the north of Asam; one of the Dvīpas or principal divisions of the world, surrounded by the sea of curds; N. of a Rakshas; N. of a pupil of Śāka-pūrṇi; (*am*), n., scil. *astra*, N. of a mystical weapon; N. of a Sāman; also of a particular Vedic formula. — *Krauñća-dāraṇa* or *krauñća-sūdana*, as, m. an epithet of the god of war, Kārttikeya, who tore asunder the mountain Krauńća. — *Krauńća-dvīpa*, *as*, m., N. of a Dvīpa, = *krauńća*. — *Krauńća-paksha*, *as*, *ā*, *am*, an epithet of horses, 'the flanks of which are similar to the wings of a curlew.' — *Krauńća-padā*, f., N. of a metre consisting of four lines of twenty-five syllables each. — *Krauńća-padī*, f., N. of a place. — *Krauńća-pura*, *as*, m., N. of a town. — *Krauńća-bandha*, *as*, m. a particular kind of knot. — *Krauńća-randhra*, *am*, n. the Krauńća pass, caused by the deity Kārttikeya and by Paraśu-rāma; see *krauńćāri* below. — *Krauńća-vat*, *ān*, m., N. of a mountain, = *krauńća*. — *Krauńćādana* (°*ća-ad*°), *am*, n. the fibres of the stalk of the lotus (*mṛiṇāla*); N. of several plants, = *gheńćulī*; another plant, = *ćińćoṭaka*; long pepper; (*ī*), f. the seed of the lotus. — *Krauńćāraṇya* (°*ća-ar*°), *am*, n., N. of a forest. — *Krauńćārāti* (°*ća-ar*°), *is*, m. an epithet of the deity Kārttikeya. — *Krauńćāri* (°*ća-ari*), *is*, m. an epithet of the deity Kārttikeya and of the hero and Avatāra Paraśu-rāma, who with his arrows made a pass or defile through the Krauńća mountain.

Krauńćiki-putra, *as*, m., N. of a teacher.

क्रौड **kraudā**. See under *kroḍa* last col.

क्रौर्य **kraurya**, *am*, n. (fr. *krūra*), cruelty, fierceness, anger; hard-heartedness; terribleness.

क्रौशशतिक **krauśaśatika**, *as*, *ī*, *am* (fr. *krośa* + *śata*), one who goes a hundred Krośas or leagues; one who deserves to be approached from a distance of a hundred Krośas or leagues (as a religious teacher &c.).

क्रौष्टिक **kraushṭika**, *as*, m. a wrong form for *kraushṭuki*, q. v.

क्रौष्टुकर्ण **kraushṭukarṇa**, *as*, *ī*, *am*, coming from Kroshṭu-karṇa.

क्रौष्टुकि **kraushṭuki**, *is*, m. (a patronymic fr. *kroshṭuka*), N. of a grammarian; N. of an astrologer; N. of a warrior-tribe belonging to the Trigarta-shashṭhas.

Kraushṭukīya, *as*, m. a prince of the warrior-tribe called Kraushṭuki.

क्र्यादि **kry-ādi**, a term of grammar to denote the roots of the ninth class of which *krī* is the first.

क्लथ् **klath**, cl. 1. P., Ved. *klathati*, *-thitum*, to turn round, revolve, to form into clots or lumps; to kill or hurt; [cf. Lat. *clades*.]

Klathana, *am*, n., Ved. turning round, forming into clots or lumps.

क्लदीवत् **kladīvat**, *ān*, *atī*, *at* (rt. *klid?*), Ved. wet, moist (?).

क्लन्द् **kland** or *klad* [cf. rt. *krand*], cl. 1. P. *klandati*, *ćaklanda*, *klandishyati*, *klanditum*, to call; to lament; to weep; cl. 1. A. *klandate* or *kladate* &c., to be confounded or troubled; to grieve; [cf. Hib. *glaodhaim*, 'I call, bawl, roar, shout;' Gr. κλάζω.]

Klanda, *as*, *ā*, *am* (fr. *kland* for *krand?*), Ved. crying, noisy (?).

क्लप् **klap**, cl. 10. P. *klāpayati*, *-yitum*, to speak barbarously; (another form for *klap*); [cf. Lith. *kalpu*, 'to speak.']

क्लम् **klam** [cf. rt. *śram*, the rt. *klam* seems principally confined to the later artificial poems], cl. 1. 4. P. *klāmati*, *klāmyati*, *ćaklāma*, *klamishyati*, *klamitum*, to be or become fatigued, to be weary or tired or exhausted; to be depressed; [cf. Gr. κάμνω; Lat. *lentus* for *clentus* (?); Germ. *lahm*; Old Germ. *lam*; Lith. *lumas*.]

Klama, *as*, m. fatigue, exhaustion, languor, weariness.

Klamatha, *as*, m. fatigue, exhaustion.

Klamathu, *us*, m. fatigue, languor.

Klamin, *ī*, *inī*, *i*, becoming tired, languishing, exhausted, weary. — *Klami-tā*, f. or *klami-tva*, *am*, n. exhaustion, langour, fatigue.

Klānta, *as*, *ā*, *am*, tired, fatigued, exhausted, languishing; wearied; depressed in spirits or exhausted; dried up, withering; thin, emaciated. — *Klānta-manas*, *ās*, *ās*, *as*, low-spirited, languid, melancholy. — *Klānta-vadana*, *as*, *ā*, *am*, having a weary face.

Klānti, *is*, f. fatigue, weariness. — *Klānti-ććhid*, *t*, *t*, *t*, relieving fatigue, refreshing, invigorating. — *Klānti-ććheda*, *as*, m. refreshing, restoring, removing fatigue.

क्लव् **klav**, cl. 1. A. *klavate*, to fear, be afraid: Caus. *klavayati*.

क्लिद् **klid**, cl. 4. P. *klidyati*, *ćikleda*, *kledishyati* and *kletsyati*, *aklidat*, *kleditum* and *klettum*, to be or become wet or damp: Caus. P. *kledayati*, *-yitum*, to bedew, wet, moisten: Desid. *ćikledishati*, *ćiklidishati*, *ćiklitsati*: Intens. *ćeklidyate*, *ćekletti*; [cf. Gr. κλύζω.]

Klinna, *as*, *ā*, *am*, moistened, wet; running (as an eye). — *Klinna-netra*, *as*, *ā*, *am*, having moist eyes, pitiful. — *Klinna-vartman*, *a*, n. excess of the lacrymal discharge, watering of the eyes. — *Klinna-hṛid*, *t*, *t*, *t*, tender-hearted. — *Klinnāksha* (°*na-ak*°), *as*, *ā*, *am*, having moist eyes, blear-eyed.

Kleda, *as*, m. wetness, dampness, moisture; running, discharge from a sore. — *Kleda-vat*, *ān*, *atī*, *at*, moist, flowing.

Kledaka, *as*, *ā*, *am*, wetting, moistening, making wet or moist; (*as*), m. phlegm in the stomach, excess of saliva.

Kledan, *ā*, m. the moon.

Kledana, *as*, *ī*, *am*, moistening, making wet; (*as*), m. phlegm, the phlegmatic or watery humor [cf. *kapha*]; a species of phlegm; (*am*), n. wetting, moistening; oozing, trickling.

Kledu, *us*, m. the moon; a morbid combination of the three humors of the body (*sannipāta*), complication of disorders.

Kledya, *as*, *ā*, *am*, to be moistened, to be wetted.

क्लिन्द् **klind**, cl. 1. P. A. *klindati*, *-te*, to lament; [cf. *krand* and *kland*.]

क्लिब **klib**, *p*, f. (?), Ved. accomplishment (fr. *klṛip?*); (Sāy.) the created world; (a various reading has *klṛib*.)

क्लिश् **kliś**, cl. 9. P. *kliśnāti*, *ćikleśa*, *kleśishyati* and *klekshyati*, *akleśit* and *aklikshat*, *kleśitum* and *kleshṭum*, to torment, torture, trouble, molest; to cause pain, afflict, distress; to suffer, feel pain, suffer distress; cl. 4. A. *kliśyate*, *ćikliśe*, *kleśishyate*, *akleśishṭa*, *kleśitum*, to be tormented or molested; to be afflicted, feel pain, suffer: Caus. P. A. *kleśayati*, *-te*, *-yitum*, to torment, molest: Desid. *ćiklikshati*, *ćikliśishati*, *ćikleśishati*, *ćikliśishate*, *ćikleśishate*: Intens. *ćekliśyate*, *ćekleshṭi*; [cf. Cambro-Brit. *glæsi*, 'to pain, to cause a pang, to suffer a pang.']

Kliśita or *klishṭa*, *as*, *ā*, *am*, molested, tormented, distressed, afflicted; wearied, hurt, injured; being in a bad condition, worn; put to shame; contradictory, inconsistent; connected with pain or suffering; (*am*), ind. in distress. — *Kliśita-vat*, *ān*, *atī*, *at*, suffering pain or distress. — *Klishṭa-vartman*, *a*, n. a disease of the eyelids; [cf. *klinna-vartman*.] — *Klishṭa-vṛitti*, *is*, *is*, *i*, leading a wretched life.

Kliśyamāna, *as*, *ā*, *am*, being distressed.

Klishṭi, *is*, f. affliction, calamity, distress; service.

Kleśa, *as*, m. pain, affliction, distress; pain from disease, anguish; wrath, anger; worldly occupation; care, trouble. — *Kleśa-kārin*, *ī*, *inī*, *i*, causing pain, afflicting. — *Kleśa-kshama*, *as*, *ā*, *am*, capable of enduring pain and trouble. — *Kleśa-da*, *as*, *ā*, *am*, distressing. — *Kleśa-nāśana*, *as*, *ā*, *am*, destroying or palliating trouble. — *Kleśa-prahāṇa*, *am*, n. termination of distress, especially of worldly cares and passions. — *Kleśa-bhāgin*, *ī*, *inī*, *i*, having trouble. — *Kleśa-bhāj*, *k*, *k*, *k*, having trouble. — *Kleśāpaha* (°*śa-ap*°), *as*, *ā*, *am*, allaying pain or suffering, consolatory, consoling; palliative; (*as*), m. a son.

Kleśaka, *as*, *ī*, *am*, giving pain, troublesome, annoying, afflicting.

Kleśita, *as*, *ā*, *am*, pained, distressed, afflicted.

Kleśin, *ī*, *inī*, *i*, connected with pain, causing pain or suffering; hurting, injuring.

Kleshṭṛi, *ṭā*, m. one who causes pain or suffering.

क्लीत **klīta**, *as*, m. a kind of poisonous insect.

क्लीतक **klītaka**, *am*, n. a kind of plant with a poisonous root, Glycyrrhiza Glabra ? (*Kāla-klītaka*, *am*, n. the Indigo plant.)

Klītakikā, f. the Indigo plant, Indigofera Indica.

क्लीतनक **klītanaka**, *am*, n. a kind of plant, = *ati-rasā*.

क्लीब् **klīb** or *klīv*, cl. 1. A. *klībate* or *klīvate*, *ćiklībe*, *klībishyate*, *klībitum* (according to some also *klīvāyate*), to be impotent, to behave like one who is impotent or like a eunuch; to be timorous, to be modest or unassuming.

Klība or *klīva*, *as*, *ā*, *am*, impotent, emasculated, a eunuch; unmanly, timorous, timid; weak, weak-minded, base; idle, slothful; a coward; of the neuter gender; (*as*, *am*), m. n. the neuter gender; [cf. Hib. *cailltean*, 'eunuch;' *caillte*, 'castrated;' *caillim*, 'I geld, castrate, destroy;' *cailleadh*, 'emasculation.'] — *Klība-tā*, f. or *klība-tva*, *am*, n. impotence, the being neuter. — *Klība-rūpa*, *as*, *ā*, *am*, Ved. similar to a eunuch. — *Klība-linga*, *am*, n. the neuter gender. — *Klīva-vat*, ind. like a base man, like a weak-minded, effeminate person.

Klaibya or *klaivya*, *am*, n. absence of virility, impotence, unmanly behaviour, unmanliness, weakness, timidity, cowardice; the neuter gender.

क्लु **klu**, cl. 1. A. *klavate*, to move.

क्लेश् **kleś**, cl. 1. A. *kleśate*, *ćikleśe*, *kleśitum*, to speak articulately; to impede or obstruct; to strike, kill; to distress.

क्लेश **kleśa**. See under rt. *kliś*.

क्लैतकिक **klaitakika**, *am*, n. a fermented liquor prepared from the root of the plant Klītaka (*klītakikā?*), wine, spirituous liquor.

क्लैब्य **klaibya** or *klaivya*. See under *klība*.

क्लोम **kloma**, *am*, n. or *kloman*, *ā*, *a*, m. n. (in the earlier language m.; in the later n.), the bladder; the lungs, the right lung; bile (?).

क्लोश **klośa**, *as*, m., Ved. = *krośa*, calling out to; (Sāy.) fear.

क्व **kva**, ind. (fr. 1. *ku*; according to Pāṇ. V. 3, 12, VII. 2, 104, formed first fr. *kim* and then fr. the substitute *ku* with affix *at*), where? in what place? whither? how? when? (rarely) how much less! [cf. *kutas*]; connected with the particles *id*, *svid*, *nu*, &c., in the same manner as 2. *ka*, q. v. (e. g. *kva nu te kshatriyāḥ śūrāḥ*, where now are those Kshatriya heroes?); *kva* appears to be used as a loc. of 2. *ka* in Manu X. 66. (e. g. *kva śreyastvam*, in whom is the preference?); *kva* with *bhū*, *as*, or *gata*, may denote, how is it with? what has become of? (e. g. *kva aham bhavāni*, what will become of me? *kva gatas tava mayy anurāgaḥ*, what has become of your affection for me?), or *kva* alone may have the same meaning (e. g. *kva sukham*, where is happiness? i. e. there is no such thing as happiness); *kva—kva* or *kutra—kva* implies excessive incongruity, where is this? where is that? how distant is this from that, how little does this agree with that (e. g. *kva sūrya-prabhavo vaṃśaḥ kva ća alpa-vishayā matiḥ*, how can my limited intellect describe the solar race?); *kvāpi* (*kva api*), anywhere, somewhere, to some place, to any place, in a certain place; sometimes; *kva ća*, anywhere, somewhere, at any time; *kva ća na*, anywhere (originally negative); *na kvaćana*, nowhere; *kva-ćid*, anywhere, somewhere, to any place, in a certain place; in a certain case, sometimes; at some time, once upon a time; *kvaćid—kvaćid*, here—there, here and there, in various places; now—then, now and then; *na kvaćid*, nowhere, never, by no means; *yatra kvāpi* or *yatra kvaća*, wherever, wheresoever, to whatsoever place, anywhere; *yatra kva-ćana*, to whatsoever place, hither and thither, anywhere; whenever, at any time, when, in any case or matter whatever; *yatra kva vātha—tatra tatrāpi*, wherever—there. — *Kva-janman, ā, ā, a*, where born? — *Kva-nivāsa, as, ā, am*, where dwelling?

Kvatya, as, ā, am, or *kvatyaka, as, ikā, am*, of or belonging to where or what place? being where?

क्वङ्गु *kvangu, us*, m. = *kangu*, a sort of Panic, Panicum Italicum.

क्वण् *kvaṇ*, cl. 1. P. *kvaṇati, ćakvāṇa, kvaṇitum*, to sound; to hum (as a bee); to make any sound; to tinkle: Caus. *kvaṇayati, -yitum*, to cause to sound, to make sound, to twang, to produce a sound with anything; e.g. *nūpuraiḥ*, with anklet ornaments; [cf. Lat. *cano;* Goth. *hana*, 'a cock.']

Kvaṇa, as, m. the sound or tone of any musical instrument; sound in general.

Kvaṇat, an, antī, at, sounding.

Kvaṇana, am, n. sounding, the sound of any musical instrument; (*as*), m. a small earthen pot or boiler.

Kvaṇita, as, ā, am, sounded, twanged (as a stringed instrument); (*am*), n. sound, twang.

Kvāṇa, as, m. the sound of a musical instrument; sound in general.

क्वथ् *kvath*, cl. 1. P. *kvathati, ćakvātha, kvathishyati, akvathīt, kvathitum*, to boil, stew, decoct, prepare by heat; to digest: Caus. *kvāthayati, -yitum*, to cause to boil, to boil, decoct.

Kvatha, as, m. a decoction, an extract.

Kvathana, am, n. boiling, decocting.

Kvathita, as, ā, am, boiled, decocted, stewed, digested.

Kvātha, as, m. a decoction, any solution or infusion prepared with a continued or gentle heat; the mixture of the materials for a decoction; pain, sorrow, calamity, distress. — *Kvāthodbhava* (°*tha-ud*°), *as, ā, am*, produced by boiling; (*am*), n. blue vitriol used as a collyrium.

क्वधःस्थ *kv-adhaḥ-stha, as, ā, am* (fr. 2. *ku-adhas-stha*), Ved. standing below on the earth.

क्वयि *kvayi, is*, m., Ved. a kind of bird.

क्वल *kvala, as* or *am*, m. or n. (?), Ved. a substance used for coagulating other substances.

क्वाचित्क *kvāćitka, as, ī, am* (fr. *kva-ćit*), met with somewhere or occasionally; rare, uncommon.

क्वाथि *kvāthi, is*, m., Ved. an epithet of Agastya.

क्वापि *kvāpi*, ind. somewhere, &c. See *kva*.

क्वेल् *kvel*, cl. 1. P. *kvelati*, to shake or move; (a less correct form for *kshvel*.)

क्शा *kśā*, a root forming, according to native grammarians, some tenses of *khyā* and *ćaksh* (e.g. the Fut. *kśāsyati;* Inf. *kśātum;* Aor. *akśāsīt, akśāsta;* Perf. *ćakśe*).

क्ष *ksha, as*, m. (fr. 4. *kshi*), destruction; loss, disappearance; destruction of the world; lightning; a field; the protector or cultivator of a field, a peasant, a husbandman; a demon or Rakshas; the fourth incarnation of Vishṇu as the man-lion or *nara-sinha*.

क्षज् *kshaj* or *kshañj*, cl. 1. A. *kshajate* or *kshañjate, ćakshañje, kshañjitum*, to go, approach; to give; cl. 10. P. *kshañjayati, -yitum*, to live in distress; to live in pain or want.

क्षण् *kshaṇ, kshaṇana*. See *kshan*.

क्षण *kshaṇa, as, am*, m. n. (said to be a corruption of *īkshaṇa*, a glance, and not used in the earlier literature; native lexicographers make this word m. only), any instantaneous point of time, an instant, the twinkling of an eye, a moment (e.g. *kshaṇam*, acc., or *kshaṇena*, inst. for an instant, in a moment; *kshaṇāt*, abl. after an instant, immediately, directly, at once; *kshaṇe kshaṇe*, every instant, every moment; *tat-kshaṇam*, that very moment, in that same moment, immediately; *tat-kshaṇāt*, immediately upon that); a moment regarded as a measure of time, equal to thirty Kalas or four minutes, or according to other authorities equal to $\frac{4}{5}$ or $\frac{24}{35}$ seconds; a leisure moment, a vacant instant, leisure, (*kshaṇam kṛi*, to have leisure for, wait patiently for; cf. *kṛita-kshaṇa*); a fit or suitable moment, an opportunity, (*kshaṇam kṛi* or *dā*, to give an opportunity); a festival; a certain day of the fortnight, as the full moon, change of the moon, &c.; dependance, servitude; the centre, the middle. — *Kshaṇa-kshepa, as*, m. a momentary delay. — *Kshaṇa-da, as*, m. an astrologer; (*ā*), f. night (giving leisure); turmeric; (*am*), n. night-blindness; water. — *Kshaṇadā-kara, as*, m. the moon. — *Kshaṇadā-ćara, as, ī, m*. f. a night-walker, a Rakshas, a fiend, a goblin. — *Kshaṇadāndhya* (°*da-ān*°), *am*, n. night-blindness, nyctalopis; [cf. *kshapāndhya, naktāndhya*.] — *Kshaṇa-drishṭa, as, ā, am*, momentarily visible, seen for an instant. — *Kshaṇa-dyuti, is*, f. momentary flash, lightning; [cf. *aćira-dyuti* and *kshaṇa-prabhā*.] — *Kshaṇa-niśvāsa, as*, m. a porpoise, the Gangetic porpoise. — *Kshaṇa-prakāśā*, f. lightning. — *Kshaṇa-prabha, as, ā, am*, gleaming or flashing for an instant; (*ā*), f. lightning. — *Kshaṇa-bhangura, as, ā, am*, perishing in an instant, transient, frail, perishable. — *Kshaṇa-bhūta, as, ā, am*, momentary, short-lived. — *Kshaṇa-mātram*, ind. for an instant merely, only for a moment. — *Kshaṇa-mātrānurāgin* (°*tra-an*°), *ī, iṇī, i*, one whose affection lasts only a moment. — *Kshaṇa-rāmin, ī*, m. a pigeon. — *Kshaṇa-vighna, am*, n. a momentary hindrance. — *Kshaṇa-vidhvansin, ī, inī, i*, collapsing or perishing in a moment; (*ī*), m. the name of a sect of atheistic philosophers who deny the continued identity of any part of nature, and maintain that the universe perishes and undergoes a new creation every instant. — *Kshaṇāntara* (°*ṇa-an*°), *am*, n. the interval of a moment; (*e*), ind. after a little while, the next moment, thereupon. — *Kshaṇārdha* (°*ṇa-ar*°), *am*, n. half the measure of time called Kshaṇa, half a moment, a small space of time.

Kshaṇika, as, ā, am, momentary, transient; (*ā*), f. lightning. — *Kshaṇika-tva, am*, n. momentary duration.

Kshaṇita, as, ā, am, having a leisure moment.

Kshaṇin, ī, inī, i, having a leisure moment; momentary, transient; (*inī*), f. the night; [cf. *kshaṇa-dā*.]

क्षणतु *kshaṇatu*, &c. See under rt. *kshan*.

क्षत्तृ *kshattṛi*. See under rt. *kshad*.

क्षत्र *kshatra, am, as*, n. m. (probably fr. rt. 1. *kshi;* the m. form does not appear to occur), dominion, supremacy, power, might (whether human or supernatural, in the Veda especially applied to the power of Varuṇa-Mitra and Indra); government, governing body, the military or reigning order (the members of which in the earliest times, as represented by the Vedic hymns, were generally called Rājanya, not Kshatriya; afterwards, when the difference between Brahman and Kshatra or the priestly and civil authorities became more distinct, the reigning or military caste accepted the title Kshatriya); a man of the second or Kshatriya caste, a warrior, a soldier (in this sense fancifully derived in Raghu. II. 53. fr. *kshatāt tra* fr. rt. *trai*, i.e. a preserver from injury); (*ī*), f. a woman of the second caste; the rank of a member of the reigning or military order, the authority of the second caste; wealth; water; the body; N. of a plant, = *tagara;* [cf. *tuvi-kshatra, deva-kshatra*, &c.] — *Kshatra-dharma, as*, m. the duty of a Kshatriya, bravery, military conduct. — *Kshatra-dharman, ā, ā, a*, having the duties of a soldier or of the second caste; (*ā*), m., N. of a prince. — *Kshatradharmānuga* (°*ma-an*°), *as, ā, am*, following or observing the duty of a soldier. — *Kshatra-dhṛiti, is*, f. the support of supreme power; N. of a particular part of the Rāja-sūya ceremony. — *Kshatra-pa, as*, m. a governor, a Satrap (a word found on coins). — *Kshatra-pati, is*, m., Ved. the possessor of dominion. — *Kshatra-bandhu, us, ūs* or *us, u*, one who belongs to the military order or second caste; (*us*), m. a member of the Kshatriya caste; a mere Kshatriya, i.e. a Kshatriya by birth but not by his actions (a term of abuse). — *Kshatrabandhu-vat*, ind. like a warrior. — *Kshatra-bhṛit, t, t, t*, Ved. one who holds or confers dominion. — *Kshatra-yoga, as*, m., Ved. union of the princely order. — *Kshatra-vat, ān, atī, at*, endowed with princely dignity. — *Kshatra-vani, is, is, i*, Ved. favourable to the princely order. — *Kshatra-vardhana, as, ī, am*, Ved. promoting dominion. — *Kshatra-vidyā*, f. the knowledge or science possessed by the Kshatriya or military order. — *Kshatra-vṛiksha, as*, m., N. of a tree, = *mućukunda*. — *Kshatra-vṛiddha, as*, m., N. of a prince. — *Kshatra-vṛiddhi, is*, m., N. of one of the sons of Manu Raućya. — *Kshatra-vṛidh, t*, m., N. of a prince, = *kshatra-vṛiddha*. — *Kshatra-veda, as*, m., the Veda of the Kshatriya or military order. — *Kshatra-śrī, īs, īs, i*, Ved. possessing sovereignty; (Sāy.) possessed of power. — *Kshatra-sava, as*, m., N. of a sacrificial ceremony. — *Kshatrāyatanīya, as, ā, am* (fr. *kshatra* + *āyatana*), Ved. based on the Kshatra or kingly power. — *Kshatropakshatra* (°*ra-up*°), *as*, m., N. of a prince. — *Kshatraujas* (°*ra-oj*°), *ās*, m., N. of a prince.

Kshatriṇa, as, m., N. of a man.

Kshatrin, ī, m. a man of the military order or second caste.

Kshatriya, as, ā, am, governing, endowed with sovereignty; (*as*), m. a member of the military or reigning order which in later time constituted the second caste; (*ā*), f. a woman of the military order or of the second caste; (*ī*), f. the wife of a man of the second caste; (*am*), n. the power or rank of this order. — *Kshatriya-jāti, is*, f. the military tribe or caste. — *Kshatriya-tā*, f. or *kshatriya-tva, am*, n. the order or rank of a Kshatriya. — *Kshatriya-dharma, as*, m. the duty or occupation of the warrior-tribe, war, government, &c. — *Kshatriya-dharman, ā, ā, a*, having the duties of a soldier or of the second caste. — *Kshatriya-prāya, as, ā, am*, mostly consisting of the military tribe. — *Kshatriya-mardana, as, ā, am*, destroying or destroyer of Kshatriyas. — *Kshatriya-rāja, as*, m. the chief of Kshatriyas. — *Kshatriyarshabha* (°*ya-ṛish*°), *as*, m. best of Kshatriyas. — *Kshatriya-hana, as*, m. one who destroys the military caste. — *Kshatriyāntakara* (°*ya-an*°), *as*, m. one who destroys the Kshatriyas.

Kshatriyakā or *ikā*, f. a woman belonging to the military or reigning order, a woman of the second caste.

Kshatriyāṇī, f. a woman belonging to the military caste; the wife of a man of the second caste.

क्षद् *kshad*, cl. 1. A., Ved. *kshadate, ćakshade*, to cut, dissect, cut to pieces, divide; to kill; to carve (meat), to distribute (food); to take (food), to consume, eat. (As a Sautra root *kshad* means 'to cover, protect, shelter.')

Kshattṛi, tā, m. one who cuts anything, one who carves or distributes; an attendant; a door-keeper, a porter; a charioteer, a coachman; [cf. *anu-kshatṛi*]; one who fights from a chariot; the son of a Sūdra man and a Kshatriya woman, or the son of a Kshatriya man and a Sūdra woman (called Ugra in Manu X. 9), or the son of a Sūdra man and Vaiśya woman (called Āyogava in Manu X. 12); the son of a female slave; (the proper employment of a Kshattṛi is said to be catching animals that live in holes); a N. of Vidura as the son of a female slave, his father being the celebrated Vyāsa (see Mahā-bh. I. 7381); an epithet of Brahmā; a fish.

Kshadat, an, antī, at, carving, dividing, tearing; eating.

Kshadana, am, n. the act of carving, dividing, tearing; eating.

Kshadman, a, n., Ved. a carving knife; pieces of food cut off or carved; (according to Schol.) water.

क्षन् *kshan* or *kshaṇ*, cl. 8. P. A. *kshaṇoti, -nute, ćakshāṇa, ćakshaṇe, kshaṇishyati, -te, akshaṇīt, kshaṇitum,* P. to hurt, injure, wound, break; A. to hurt one's self, be injured or wounded: Caus. *kshāṇayati, -yitum:* Desid. *ćikshaṇishati, -te:* Intens. *ćaṅkshaṇyate, ćaṅkshanti;* [cf. Gr. καίνω, κανῶ; καίνυται = *kshaṇute;* ξαίνω; perhaps also σίνομαι for ξίνομαι.]

Kshaṇatu, us, m. a wound or sore.

Kshaṇana, am, n. hurting, injuring; killing, slaughter.

Kshaṇanu, us, m. a wound, a sore.

Kshata, as, ā, am, wounded, hurt, hit, injured, broken, torn, rent, destroyed, impaired, violated; diminished, trodden or broken down; (*am*), n. a hurt, wound, sore, contusion. — *Kshata-kāsa, as,* m. a cough produced by an injury; [cf. *kshata-ja,* &c.] — *Kshata-ghna, as,* m., N. of a plant, commonly Kukuraśoṅkhā, Conyza Lacera; (*ā* or *ī*), f. a kind of insect; lac, the animal dye. — *Kshata-ja, as, ā, am,* produced by a wound or injury of any kind (e. g. *kāsa,* a kind of cough); (*am*), n. blood; pus, matter. — *Kshata-tejas, ās, ās, as,* dimmed, obscured (as light or power). — *Kshata-puṇya-leśa, as, ā, am,* having the stock of merit exhausted. — *Kshata-yoni, is,* f. a woman who has been violated, one no longer a virgin. — *Kshata-vikshata, as, ā, am,* mangled, covered with cuts and wounds. — *Kshata-vidhvaṇsin, ī,* m. a sort of pot-herb, Convolvulus Argenteus. — *Kshata-vṛitti, is,* f. destitution, the being without the means of support, living on what one can get. — *Kshata-vraṇa, as,* m. a sore produced by an injury. — *Kshata-vrata, as, ā, am,* a violator of a vow or religious engagement. — *Kshata-hara, am,* n. Agallochum or Aloe wood. — *Kshatāri* (°*ta-ari*), *is, is, i,* victorious, triumphant. — *Kshatottha* (°*ta-ut*°), *as, ā, am,* produced by injury. — *Kshatodara* (°*ta-ud*°), *am,* n. flux, dysentery. — *Kshatodbhava* (°*ta-ud*°), *as, ā, am,* produced by injury; (*am*), n. (?) blood; [cf. *kshata-ja.*] — *Kshataujas* (°*ta-oj*°), *ās, ās, as,* weakened, reduced, impaired.

Kshati, is, f. injury, hurt, a wound; destruction; damage, disadvantage.

क्षप् 1. *kshap,* cl. 1. P. A. *kshapati, -te,* to be abstinent, to fast, to do penance: Caus. *kshapayati, -yitum,* to regret sorrowfully, miss.

1. *kshapaṇa, as,* m. a Buddhist mendicant; (*as, ā, am*), shameless, impudent?; (*am*), n. abstinence, chastisement of the body, defilement, impurity.

Kshapaṇaka, as, m. a mendicant, especially a Buddhist mendicant, who wears no garments; also a Jaina mendicant; (*as*), m., N. of an author supposed to have lived at the court of king Vikramāditya.

क्षप् 2. *kshap,* cl. 10. P. *kshapayati, -yitum,* to send, throw, cast, direct, &c.; [cf. Goth. *skapa.*]

Kshapayat, an, antī, at, casting, sending.

Kshapita, as, ā, am, sent, cast, directed.

क्षप् 3. *kshap.* See Caus. of rt. 4. *kshi,* 'to destroy.'

4. *kshap, p,* f., Ved. night; a measure of time equivalent to a whole day of twenty-four hours; darkness; water; *kshapaḥ* or *kshapā,* ind. at night; [cf. Lat. *crepus-culum;* Gr. κνέφος, κνέφας.] — *Kshapotyaya* (°*pas-at*°), *as,* m. the end of night.

2. *kshapaṇa, as, ā, am,* destructive, one who destroys; (*am*), n. destroying, diminishing, suppressing, expelling.

Kshapā, f. night (Ved. only used in inst. pl. *kshapābhis*); turmeric. — *Kshapā-kara, as,* m. 'making the night,' the moon. — *Kshapā-ghana, as,* m. a dark cloud or dark nocturnal clouds. — *Kshapā-ćara, as,* m. a night-walker; a fiend, a goblin. — *Kshapāṭa* (°*pā-aṭa*), *as,* m. a night-walker; a Rākshasa, an imp or goblin. — *Kshapā-nātha, as,* m. the moon. — *Kshapānta* (°*pā-an*°), *as,* m. dawn, day-break. — *Kshapāndhya* (°*pā-an*°), *am,* n. night-blindness, nyctalopsis; [cf. *kshaṇadāndhya, naktāndhya.*] — *Kshapā-pati, is,* m. the moon; camphor. — *Kshapāha* (°*pā-ahan*), *am,* n. a day and night.

क्षपणी *kshapaṇī,* f. = *kshepaṇī,* an oar, a net.

क्षपण्यु *kshapaṇyu, us,* m. an offence, a transgression.

क्षम् 1. *ksham,* cl. 1. A., 4. P. *kshamate, kshāmyati* (ep. also 1. P. and Ved. 2. P. *kshamati, kshamiti*), *ćakshame, ćakshāma, kshamishyate, -ti,* and *kshaṇsyate, -ti, akshamishṭa, akshaṇsta, akshamat, kshamitum* and *kshantum,* to be patient or composed, to suppress anger, keep quiet; to submit to (with dat.); to bear patiently, endure, put up with, suffer; to pardon, forgive (with gen. or dat. of the person, e. g. *kshamasva tad me,* forgive me that); to allow, permit, suffer; to resist; to be competent or able to do anything (with inf.): Caus. *kshamayati, -te, -yitum,* to ask pardon for anything (with double acc., e. g. *tat kshamaye bhavantam,* I ask you to pardon that); to suffer or bear patiently: Desid. *ćikshamishate, -ti,* and *ćikshaṇsate, -ti:* Intens. *ćaṅkshamyate, ćaṅkshanti;* [cf. Goth. *hramja* (?); Angl. Sax. *hremman,* 'to hinder, disquiet.']

Kshantavya, as, ā, am, to be borne or endured, bearable, to be suffered or submitted to patiently, to be pardoned or forgiven.

Kshantṛi, tā, trī, tṛi, pardoning, bearing patiently, submissive.

2. *ksham,* f. (making *kshās* in the nom. case), Ved. the ground, the earth, χθών; [cf. χαμαί, &c.] — *Ksha-pāvat, ān,* m., Ved. an earth-protector, a ruler, a governor.

Kshama, as, ā, am, patient; enduring, suffering, bearing, submissive, resisting; adequate, competent, able, fit for (with inf. or at the end of a compound, *vayaṃ tyaktuṃ kshamāḥ,* we are able to quit; *gamana-kshama,* able to go); friendly; favourable; bearable, tolerable; fit, appropriate, becoming suitable, proper for (with gen. of the person, e. g. *kshamaṃ Kauravāṇām,* proper for the Kauravas; or with inf., e. g. *na sa kshamaḥ kopayitum,* he is not a fit object for anger); (*as*), m. a N. of Śiva, 'the patient;' (*ā*), f. patience, forbearance, indulgence; personified as a daughter of Daksha and wife of Pulaha; resistance; the earth; an epithet of Durgā; N. of a female shepherd; the tree Acacia Catechu (*khadira*); N. of a species of the Atijayatī metre [cf. *utpalinī*]; night (wrong form for *kshapā*); (*am*), n. propriety, fitness; [cf. Hib. *cam,* 'strong, stout, mighty; power, might;' *cama,* 'brave.'] — *Kshama-tā,* f. or *kshama-tva, am,* n. ability, fitness, capability. — *Kshamavat, ān, atī, at,* knowing what is proper or right. — *Kshamā-kalyāṇa, as,* m., N. of a pupil of Jinalābhasūri, who composed 1794 A. D. a commentary on the Jīva-vićāra. — *Kshamā-tala, am,* n. the earth. — *Kshamā-danśa, as,* m., N. of a tree, = *śigru.* — *Kshamānvita* (°*mā-an*°), *as, ā, am,* endowed with patience, patient, enduring, forgiving. — *Kshamā-pati, is,* m. lord of the earth, a king. — *Kshamāpanna* (°*mā-āp*°), *as, ā, am,* forbearing, patient. — *Kshamā-para, as, ā, am,* very patient, forbearing. — *Kshamā-bhuj, k, k, k,* patient; (*k*), m. a king, a prince. — *Kshamā-yukta, as, ā, am,* endowed with patience, patient, enduring. — *Kshamāvat, ān, atī, at,* patient, enduring, forbearing; (*atī*), f., N. of the wife of Nidhi-pati.

Kshamaṇīya, as, ā, am, to be suffered, to be patiently borne; to be pardoned.

Kshamā (inst. case of 2. *ksham*), on the earth, on the floor (included by Pāṇini among the indeclinables with *svar, divā,* &c.); [cf. Gr. χαμαί, χαμᾶ-ζε, χαμά-θεν; χθαμαλός.] — *Kshamā-ćara, as, ā, am,* Ved. being in the ground or under the earth.

Kshamāpaya, nom. P. A. *-payati, -te, -yitum,* to ask any one's (acc.) pardon, to beg forgiveness.

Kshamitavya, as, ā, am, to be endured, to be patiently borne, to be pardoned.

Kshamitṛi, tā, trī, tṛi, patient, enduring, forbearing, indulgent.

Kshamin, ī, iṇī, i, patient, enduring, forbearing, indulgent; capable, able.

Kshamya, as, ā, am, Ved. being in the earth, terrestrial; χθόνιος.

Kshānta, as, ā, am, borne, endured; patient, enduring; (*as*), m., N. of a man; of a hunter; epithet of Śiva [cf. *kshama*]; (*ā*), f. the earth, 'the patient one.'

Kshānti, is, f. patience, forbearance, endurance, indulgence, patient waiting for anything. — *Kshāntimat, ān, atī, at,* patient, enduring, indulgent. — *Kshānti-vādin, ī,* m., N. of a Ṛishi; N. of Śākya-muni in one of his former births.

Kshāntu, us, us, u, patient, enduring; (*us*), m. a father.

Kshāmya, as, ā, am, to be borne; to be pardoned or overlooked.

क्षमुद *kshamuda, as* or *am,* m. or n. (?), a particular number.

क्षम्प् *kshamp,* cl. 1. or 10. P. *kshampati* or *kshampayati, -yitum,* to suffer, bear; [cf. 1. *ksham.*]

क्षय *kshaya.* See under rt. 2. *kshi* and rt. 4. *kshi,* p. 266.

क्षयथु *kshayathu, us,* m. cough; (a wrong form for *kshavathu.*)

क्षयद्वीर *kshayad-vīra.* See under 1. *kshi.*

क्षर् *kshar,* cl. 1. P. *ksharati, ćakshāra, ksharishyati, akshārīt, ksharitum* (ep. cl. 1. A. *ksharate,* Ved. cl. 2. P. *kshariti,* Ved. inf. *ksharadhyai*), to flow, stream, glide; to flow away; to stream forth; pour out (either in active or neuter sense); to drop, distil, trickle, ooze, run; to melt away, wane, perish, be destroyed; to fall or slip from, to be deprived of (with abl.): Caus. *ksharayati, -yitum:* Desid. *ćiksharishati:* Intens. *ćāksharyate, ćāksharti;* [cf. Lat. *scateo?*].

Kshara, as, ā, am, melting away, perishable; (*as*), m. a cloud; (*am*), n. water; a body. — *Kshara-ja* or *kshare-ja, as, ā, am,* produced by distillation. — *Kshara-pattrā,* f., N. of a plant, = *droṇa-pushpī.* — *Kshara-bhāva, as, ā, am,* mutable, dissoluble.

Ksharaka, as, ikā, am, pouring forth.

Ksharaṇa, am, n. the act of flowing, trickling, distilling, dropping (e. g. *angulī-ksharaṇa,* perspiration of the fingers).

Ksharat, an, antī, at, flowing, running, trickling, oozing.

Ksharita, as, ā, am, dropped, liquefied, oozed, trickling, flowing.

Ksharin, ī, iṇī, i, flowing, dropping, trickling; (*ī*), m. the rainy season.

Kshāra, as, ā, am, caustic, biting, corrosive, acid, pungent, saline (according to some in these senses fr. rt. *kshai*), anything converted to alkali or ashes by distillation; (*as*), m. juice, essence; treacle, molasses; any corrosive or acid or saline substance, especially an alkali such as soda or potash; caustic alkali, one species of cautery; glass; a rogue, a cheat; (*am*),

n. a factitious or medicinal salt, commonly black salt [cf. *viḍ-lavaṇa* and *krishṇa-lavaṇa*]; water. – *Kshāra-kardama, as,* m. a pool of saline or acid mud; N. of a hell. – *Kshāra-karman, a,* n. applying caustic alkali (Lapis Infernalis) to proud flesh &c.; or applying acid remedies in general. – *Kshāra-kṛitya, as, ā, am,* to be treated with caustic alkali. – *Kshāra-taila, am,* n. oil cooked with alkaline ingredients. – *Kshāra-traya* or *kshāra-tritaya, am,* n. natron, saltpetre, and borax. – *Kshāra-dalā,* f. a kind of pot-herb, = *ćilli*. – *Kshāra-dru, us,* m. the tree Bignonia Suaveolens; [cf. *ghanṭā-pāṭali*.] – *Kshāra-nadī,* f. a river in hell, the water of which is alkaline. – *Kshāra-pattra, as* or *am,* m. or n. (?), or *kshāra-pattraka, as,* m. the pot-herb Chenopodium Album. – *Kshāra-pāla, as,* m., N. of a Ṛishi. – *Kshāra-bhūmi, is,* f. a saline soil. – *Kshāra-madhya, as,* m. the plant Achyranthes Aspera [cf. *apāmārga*]; its alkaline ashes make it useful in washing clothes. – *Kshāra-mṛittikā,* f. saline soil, especially an impure sulphate of soda. – *Kshāra-melaka, as,* m. an alkaline substance. – *Kshāra-meha, as,* m. a morbid state of the urine, in which its smell and taste resemble that of potash. – *Kshāra-rasa, as,* m. a saline or alkaline flavour. – *Kshāra-vṛiksha, as,* m. the tree Bignonia Suaveolens [cf. *kshāra-dru*]; any tree yielding abundant potash. – *Kshāra-śreshṭha, as,* m. the tree Butea Frondosa; also = *kshāra-vṛiksha; (am),* n. alkaline earth; [cf. *vajra-kshāra*.] – *Kshāra-shaṭka, am,* n. six kinds of trees distinguished by their juice, as the Butea Frondosa, Grislea Tomentosa, Achyranthes Aspera, Cowach, Ghanṭā-pāṭali, Coraya. – *Kshāra-samudra, as,* m. or *kshāra-sindhu, us,* m. the salt ocean. – *Kshāra-sūtra, am,* n. acid thread, applied to fistulas &c. – *Kshārāksha* (°*ra-ak*°), *as, ā, am,* having an artificial eye made of glass. – *Kshārāgada* (°*ra-ag*°), *as,* m. remedy prepared by extracting the alkaline particles from the ashes of plants. – *Kshāraćcha* (°*ra-aćcha*), *am,* n. sea-salt. – *Kshārāñjana* (°*ra-añ*°), *am,* n. an alkaline unguent. – *Kshārāmbu* (°*ra-am*°), *u,* n. or *kshāroda* (°*ra-uda*), *as,* m. or *kshārodaka* (°*ra-ud*°), *am,* n. an alkaline juice or fluid. – *Kshārāmbudhi* (°*ra-am*°), *kshārodadhi* (°*ra-ud*°), *is,* m. the salt ocean.

Kshāraka, as, m. alkali; a juice, essence; a blossom, a new-blown flower or a young fruit; a bud or a multitude of young buds; a cage or basket or net for birds or fish; a washerman.

Kshāraṇa, am, ā, n. f. accusing of unfaithfulness; *(am),* n. converting to alkali or ashes; distilling.

Kshāraya, nom. P. *kshārayati, -yitum,* to furnish or mix with acid substances; to torture a person with acid substances; to speak ill of a person; to abuse, accuse, calumniate.

Kshārikā, f. hunger.

Kshārita, as, ā, am, distilled from saline matter, strained through alkaline ashes &c.; calumniated, falsely accused (especially of adultery), accused of a crime, guilty.

क्षल् 1. *kshal,* cl. 1. P. *kshalati, -litum,* to flow; to collect; [cf. *kshar*.]

क्षल् 2. *kshal* (related to rt. *kshar*), cl. 10. P. *kshālayati, aćikshalat, -yitum,* to wash, wash off, purify, cleanse, clean, make clean; to wipe away; [cf. Lith. *skalauju,* 'to wash off;' *skalbju,* 'to wash;' Mod. Germ. *spüle?*].

Kshālana, am, n. washing, washing off, cleansing with water; sprinkling.

Kshālanīya or *kshālitavya, as, ā, am,* to be washed, to be cleansed with water.

Kshālayat, an, antī, at, washing, cleansing, sprinkling.

Kshālita, as, ā, am, cleansed, cleaned, washed.

क्षव *kshava.* See under rt. 1. *kshu.*

क्षाति *kshāti, is,* f. (fr. *kshai*), Ved. singeing, scorching, heat.

क्षात्त्र *kshāttra, am,* n. (fr. *kshattṛi*), Ved. a community or number of attendants or servants.

क्षात्र *kshātra, as, ī, am* (fr. *kshatra*), belonging or relating to or peculiar to the second or military tribe; *(am),* n. the second or military tribe; the dignity of a ruler or governor.

Kshātri, is, m. the son of a man of the second caste (by a woman of another caste?).

क्षान्त *kshānta,* &c. See under 1. *ksham.*

क्षाम *kshāma, as, ā, am* (fr. rt. *kshai*), scorched, singed; dried up, emaciated, wasted, fallen away, thin, slim, slender; weak, debilitated, infirm, slight. – *Kshāma-tā,* f. or *kshāma-tva, am,* n. emaciation, thinness, slenderness; debility. – *Kshāma-vat, ān, atī, at,* Ved. scorching, singeing, drying up; epithet of Agni; *(tī),* f., scil. *ishṭi,* N. of a particular sacrificial ceremony. – *Kshāmāsya* (°*ma-ās*°), *am,* n. any diet or any state of the body (as menstruation) incompatible with a particular medical treatment.

क्षामन् *kshāman, a,* n. (occurring only in nom., acc., loc. sing.), Ved. earth, soil, ground; [cf. 2. *ksham*.]

क्षामाप्रस्थ *kshāmā-prastha, as,* m., N. of a town.

क्षार *kshāra.* See under rt. *kshar,* p. 265.

क्षालन *kshālana,* &c. See under 2. *kshal.*

क्षास् *kshās,* nom. case of 2. *ksham,* q. v.

क्षि 1. *kshi,* cl. 1. P., Ved. *kshayati* (only the pres. seems to occur), to possess, have power over, rule, govern, be master of (with gen.).

Kshayat, an, antī, at, possessing, ruling, governing. – *Kshayad-vīra, as, ā, am,* Ved. ruling or governing men; an epithet of Indra, Rudra, and Pūshan; (Sāy. as if fr. 2. *kshi*), possessed of abiding or of going heroes such as sons &c.

1. *kshit, t, t, t,* ruling, a ruler, a governor, a sovereign, (used in comp., e. g. *mahī-kshit,* q. v.)

क्षि 2. *kshi,* cl. 2. 6. P., Ved. *ksheti, kshiyati, ćikshāya, ksheshyati, kshetum,* to abide, stay, dwell, reside (used especially of an undisturbed or secret residence); to inhabit; to remain; to be quiet; to go, move, approach: Caus. *kshayayati* or *kshepayati, -yitum,* to make a person live quietly; to pacify.

1. *kshaya, as,* m. (for 2. see under rt. 4. *kshi* below), an abode, residence, habitation, dwelling-place, seat, house [cf. *uru-kshaya*]; family, race; the house of Yama, god of death; dominion (?). – *Kshaya-taru, us,* m. the plant Bignonia Suaveolens.

1. *kshayaṇa, as, ā, am,* Ved. habitable (?); *(as),* m. a place with tranquil water; a bay, harbour (?); *(am),* n. a dwelling-place.

Kshayas, as, n. a dwelling-place, habitation.

3. *kshi, is,* f. abode, residence; going, moving.

2. *kshit, t, t, t,* dwelling, an inhabitant, (at the end of several compounds, e. g. *antariksha-kshit,* an inhabitant of the air &c.)

Kshitā, f. the earth.

1. *kshiti, is,* f. (for 2. see under rt. 4. *kshi* below), an abode, a dwelling, habitation, house, residence [cf. *uru-kshiti*]; the earth, the soil of the earth; *(ayas),* f. pl., Ved. settlements, colonies, races of men, nations, men in general; the families of the gods. – *Kshiti-kaṇa, as, ā,* m. f. a particle of earth, dust. – *Kshiti-kampa, as,* m. an earthquake. – *Kshiti-kshama, as,* m. the tree Mimosa Khayar; [cf. *khadira*.] – *Kshiti-kshit, t,* m. a ruler of the earth; a king, a prince. – *Kshiti-khaṇḍa, as,* m. a clod or lump of earth. – *Kshiti-garbha, as,* m., N. of a Bodhi-sattva. – *Kshiti-ja, as, ā, am,* earth-born, produced of or in the earth; *(as),* m. a tree; a kind of snail (= *bhū-nāga*); an earth-worm; N. of the planet Mars; an epithet of the demon Naraka; *(ā),* f. an epithet of Sītā, the wife of Rāma; *(am),* n., N. of a circle of the sky. – *Kshiti-jantu, us,* m. a kind of snail (= *bhū-nāga*); an earth-worm. – *Kshiti-tala, am,* n. the surface of the earth, the region below the earth. – *Kshiti-deva, as,* m. the 'earth-god,' an epithet of a king. – *Kshiti-devatā,* f. the deity of the earth, epithet of a Brāhman. – *Kshiti-dhara, as,* m. 'earth-supporter,' a mountain. – *Kshiti-dhārin, ī, iṇī, i,* carrying soil or earth. – *Kshiti-dhenu, us,* f. the earth considered as a milch-cow. – *Kshiti-nanda, as,* m., N. of a king. – *Kshiti-nāga, as,* m. a kind of snail (= *bhū-nāga*) or rather snail-shell; an earth-worm (?). – *Kshiti-nātha, as,* m. 'lord of the earth,' a king. – *Kshiti-pa, as,* m. 'earth-protector,' a king. – *Kshiti-pati, is,* m. lord of the earth, a king, a sovereign. – *Kshiti-pāla, as,* m. 'earth-protector,' a king, a prince. – *Kshiti-pīṭha, am,* n. the surface of the earth. – *Kshiti-putra, as,* m. a son of the earth, an epithet of Naraka. – *Kshiti-pratishṭha, as, ā, am,* dwelling or abiding on the earth. – *Kshiti-bhuj, k,* m. one who enjoys the earth, a king. – *Kshiti-bhṛit, t,* m. 'earth-supporter,' a mountain; a king. – *Kshiti-maṇḍala, am,* n. the earth, the globe. – *Kshiti-ruh, ṭ,* or *kshiti-ruha, as,* m. a plant, a tree. – *Kshiti-lava-bhuj, k,* m. one who possesses a small tract of the earth, a petty prince. – *Kshiti-vadarī,* f., N. of a plant, = *bhū-vadarī*. – *Kshiti-vardhana, as,* m. a corpse. – *Kshiti-vṛitti, is,* f. (patient) behaviour like that of the earth. – *Kshitivṛitti-mat, ān, atī, at,* patient like the earth. – *Kshiti-vyudāsa, as,* m. a cave within the earth. – *Kshiti-suta, as,* m. an epithet of the demon Naraka; also of the planet Mars; [cf. *kshiti-putra*.] – *Kshitīśa* (°*ti-īśa*), *as,* m. a ruler of the earth, a king. – *Kshitīśa-vanśāvalī-ćarita, am,* n. 'genealogy and history of the kings,' title of a work composed in the last century, being a family chronicle of the viceroys of a part of Bengal. – *Kshitīśvara* (°*ti-īś*°), *as,* m. a king. – *Kshity-aditi, is,* f. the Aditi of the earth, an epithet of Devakī, the mother of Kṛishṇa.

Kshitvan, ā, m. air, wind.

क्षि 4. *kshi,* cl. 1. 5. 9. P. *kshayati, kshiṇoti, kshiṇāti, ćikshāya, ksheshyati, akshaishīt, kshetum,* to destroy, corrupt, ruin, to make an end of; to kill, injure: Pass. *kshīyate,* to wane; to decrease; to be diminished, waste away, perish: Caus. *kshayayati* or *kshapayati* or Ved. *kshāpayati, -yitum,* to destroy, ruin, make an end of, finish; to weaken: Desid. *ćikshīshati*: Intens. *ćekshīyate, ćekshayīti, ćeksheti*; [cf. Gr. κτίννυμι?].

2. *kshaya, as,* m. (for 1. see under 2. *kshi* last col.), loss, waste, wane, diminution, destruction, decay wasting or wearing away; fall (as of prices, opposed to *vṛiddhi,* e. g. *kshayo vṛiddhiś ća paṇyānām,* the fall and rise in the price of commodities); removal; end, termination (e. g. *nidrā-kshaya,* the end of sleep; *dina-kshaye,* at the end of day; *jīvita-kshaye,* at the end of life; *kshayam yā* or *gam,* to become less, be diminished, go to destruction, come to an end, perish); consumption, pthisis pulmonalis; sickness in general; the destruction of the universe; (in algebra) a negative quality, a minus. – *Kshaya-kara, as, ī, am,* causing destruction or ruin, destructive, ruinous, terminating; liberating from existence. – *Kshaya-kāla, as,* m. the end of all things, the period of destruction. – *Kshaya-kāsa, as,* m. a consumptive or phthisical cough. – *Kshaya-kṛit, t, t, t,* or *kshayan-kara, as, ī, am,* causing ruin or loss; destructive. – *Kshaya-nāśinī,* f. the plant Celtis Orientalis, = *jīvantī* ('removing consumption'). – *Kshaya-paksha, as,* m. the dark fortnight, that of the moon's wane. – *Kshaya-yukti, is,* f. or *kshaya-yoga, as,* m. necessity or opportunity of destroying. – *Kshaya-roga, as,* m. consumption. – *Kshayarogi-tva, am,* n. or *kshayarogi-tā,* f. consumption. – *Kshaya-rogin, ī, iṇī, i,* consumptive. – *Kshaya-vāyu, us,* m. the wind that is to blow at

the end of the world. — *Kshaya-sampad, t,* f. total loss, ruin, destruction.

2. *kshayaṇa, as, ā, am,* destroying, annihilating, driving away, dispersing; (often at the end of compounds, e. g. *asura-kshayaṇa, piśāća-kshayaṇa,* &c.)

Kshayathu, us, m. consumption.

Kshayayitavya, as, ā, am, to be destroyed.

Kshayin, ī, iṇī, i, wasting, decaying, fragile; consumptive. — *Kshayi-tva, am,* n. fragility.

Kshayishṇu, us, us, u, destroying, wasting, decaying, perishing; perishable, fragile.

Kshayya, as, ā, am, perishable, decaying; [cf. *a-kshayya.*]

5. *kshi, is,* f. destruction; waste, loss.

Kshita, as, ā, am, wasted, decayed, exhausted; weakened; poor, miserable. — *Kshitāyus* (°*ta-āy*°), *us, us, us,* Ved. one whose life goes to an end, one whose life is forfeited.

2. *kshiti, is,* f. (for 1. see under rt. 2. *kshi* above), loss, destruction; wane; a period of the destruction of the universe, the end of the world; a kind of perfume = *roćanā*; (*is*), m., N. of a man.

Kshiyā, f. loss, waste, destruction; offence against the customs.

Kshīṇa, as, ā, am, diminished, wasted, expended, worn away; lost, destroyed; injured, broken, torn; subdued, suppressed; thin, emaciated, feeble; delicate, slender, poor, miserable. — *Kshīṇa-gati, is, is, i,* with slackened or diminished motion or progress. — *Kshīṇa-tamas, ās,* m., N. of a Vihāra. — *Kshīṇa-tā,* f. or *kshīṇa-tva, am,* n. the state of wasting away, diminution, decay; the state of being worn away or injured; emaciation, thinness; slenderness. — *Kshīṇa-dhana, as, ā, am,* impoverished. — *Kshīṇa-pāpa, as, ā, am,* one whose sins are destroyed; one who is purified after having suffered the consequences of sin. — *Kshīṇa-puṇya, as, ā, am,* one whose merit is lost; one who has enjoyed the fruits of merit and is doomed to labour for more in another birth. — *Kshīṇa-madhya, as, ā, am,* slender-waisted. — *Kshīṇa-vat, ān, atī, at,* wasted, decayed. — *Kshīṇa-vāsin, ī, inī, i,* inhabiting a dilapidated house; (*ī*), m. a dove or pigeon. — *Kshīṇa-vikrānta, as, ā, am,* one who has lost courage, destitute of prowess. — *Kshīṇa-vṛitti, is, is, i,* out of employ, having no means of subsistence or maintenance. — *Kshīṇa-śakti, is, is, i,* one whose strength is wasted, weak, impotent. — *Kshīṇa-śarīra, as, ā, am,* having a thin or emaciated body. — *Kshīṇa-sukṛita, as, ā, am,* having one's stock of merit exhausted. — *Kshīṇāṅga* (°*ṇa-aṅ*°), *as, ā, am,* having emaciated limbs. — *Kshīṇājya-karman* (°*ṇa-āj*°), *ā,* m. a Buddhist. — *Kshīṇāshṭa-karman* (°*ṇa-ash*°), *ā,* m. (with Jainas) an Arhat or inspired teacher.

Kshīyamāṇa, as, ā, am, perishing, wasting away, decaying.

Ksheya, as, ā, am, to be destroyed or removed.

क्षिण् *kshiṇ,* cl. 5. P. A. *kshiṇoti, -ṇute, ksheṇoti, -ṇute* (?), to kill, to hurt, = 4. *kshi.*

क्षिद्र *kshidra, as,* m. disease; the sun; a horn.

क्षिप 1. *kship,* cl. 6. P. A., 4. P. *kshipati, -te, kshipyati, ćikshepa, ćikshipe, kshepsyati, -te, akshaipsīt, akshipta, ksheptum,* to throw, cast, send, despatch; to put or place anything on or in (with loc.), pour on, scatter, strew; to fix or attach to; to throw away, cast away, get rid of; to reject, disdain; to lay (the blame) on; to strike, hit; to strike down, ruin, destroy; to utter abusive words, insult, revile, abuse, scold; A. to throw at each other, destroy one another: Caus. P. *kshepayati, -yitum,* to cause to cast &c.; to hurt, injure: Desid. *ćikshipsati, -te:* Intens. *ćekshipyate, ćekshepti;* [cf. Lat. *sipo, dissipo,* for *xipo;* Gr. ῥίπτω for κρίπτω; Cambro-Brit. *hipiaw,* 'to cast or dash suddenly;' Goth. *vairpa;* Germ. *werfe?*].

2. *kship, p,* f. (only used in nom. and inst. pl. *kshipas* and *kshipābhis*), Ved. the fingers.

Kshipa, as, ā, am, a thrower, striking, hitting; (*as*), m. throwing, casting, insulting, reviling; (*ā*), f. sending, casting, throwing, &c.; night; (a wrong form for *kshapā*.)

Kshipaka, as, m. an archer, a warrior.

Kshipaṇa, am, n. sending, despatching, throwing, casting; reviling, abusing.

Kshipaṇi, is, m. a stroke or blow with a whip; a missile weapon; (*is* or *ī*), f. an oar; a kind of net.

Kshipaṇu, us, m. an archer; a weapon; air, wind.

Kshipaṇyu, us, us, u (fr. *kshipaṇa?*), fragrant, sweet-smelling; diffusive, what may be sent or scattered; (*us*), m. the body; spring, the season of spring.

Kshipat, an, atī or *antī, at,* throwing, casting; abusing, reproaching.

Kshipati or *kshipasti, ī,* du., Ved. the arms.

Kshipta, as, ā, am, thrown, cast; sent, despatched, dismissed, &c.; (*ā*), f. night, (like *kshipā,* a wrong form for *kshapā*); (*am*), n. a wound caused by shooting or throwing. — *Kshipta-ćitta, as, ā, am,* distracted in mind, absent. — *Kshiptaćitta-tā,* f. absence of mind. — *Kshipta-deha, as, ā, am,* prostrating the body, lying down. — *Kshipta-bheshaja, as, ī, am,* Ved. healing wounds caused by missile weapons. — *Kshipta-yoni, is, is, i,* of despicable descent (?), such a man is not allowed to become a Ṛitvij. — *Kshipta-laguḍa, as, ā, am,* flinging the staff.

Kshipti, is, f. throwing; sending; solving a riddle; explaining or understanding a hidden meaning; the quantity to be added to the square of the least root multiplied by the multiplicator, to render it capable of yielding an exact square root; (in the latter sense also *kshiptikā*.)

Kshipnu (or *kshipnu?*), *us, us, u,* throwing, casting, throwing obstacles in the way; obstructive, scornful, or fond of abusing (?).

Kshipyat, an, antī, at, throwing, sending.

Kshipyamāṇa, as, ā, am, throwing, tossing; casting aside, throwing off; sending, directing; being thrown, &c.

Kshipra, as, ā, am (compar. *kshepīyas,* superl. *kshepishṭha*), springing, flying back with a spring, elastic (as a bow); quick, speedy, swift; (*as*), m., N. of a son of Kṛishṇa; (*am*), n. a measure of time equal to $\frac{1}{15}$ Muhūrta or 15 Etarhis; the part of the hand between the thumb and fore-finger and the corresponding part of the foot; (*am*), ind. quickly, immediately, directly; (*āt*), ind. shortly afterwards, thereupon; (*e*), ind. directly, immediately; [cf. Gr. κραιπνός.] — *Kshipra-kārin, ī, iṇī, i,* acting or working quickly, skilful. — *Kshipra-dhanvan, ā, ā, a,* Ved. armed with an elastic bow or one which flies back with a spring. — *Kshipra-pākin, ī, inī, i,* ripening quickly; (*ī*), m. the tree Hibiscus Populneoides; [cf. *gardabhāṇḍa.*] — *Kshipra-śyena, as,* m. a species of bird. — *Kshipra-sandhi, is,* m. a species of Sandhi produced by changing the first of two concurrent vowels to its semivowel; also the Svarita accent on a syllable formed by this kind of Sandhi; [cf. *kshaipra.*] — *Kshipra-hasta, as,* m., N. of a Rakshas (swift-handed).

Kshepa, as, m. throwing, casting, tossing; a throw, cast; a stroke of an oar &c.; sending, dismissing, striking down, depression; laying on (as paint &c.), besmearing; transgressing; passing away time; delay, procrastination, dilatoriness; insult, invective, abuse, reviling; disrespect, contempt; pride, haughtiness; a nosegay, a clump of flowers; (in arithmetic) an additive quantity, addendum.

Kshepaka, as, ā, am, a thrower, sender; inserted, interpolated; abusive, disrespectful; (*as*), m. a spurious or interpolated passage; an additive quantity, addendum; N. of a prince.

Kshepaṇa, am, n. the act of throwing, casting, shooting off (of an arrow &c.); sending, directing; sending away; passing away time, spending time; omitting; abusing; a sling; (*ī*), f. a sling or any instrument with which missiles are thrown; an oar; a kind of net.

Kshepaṇi, is, f. an oar; a net, a fishing-net.

Kshepaṇīya, as, ā, am, to be thrown or cast; (*am*), n. a sling, any instrument for casting missiles.

Kshepiman, ā, m. great velocity, speed.

Kshepishṭha, as, ā, am (see *kshipra*), quickest, speediest.

Kshepīyas, ān, asī, as (see *kshipra*), more quick, speedier.

Ksheptavya, as, ā, am, to be cast or thrown, to be reviled or abused.

Ksheptṛi, tā, trī, tṛi, a thrower, caster, sender.

Kshepya, as, ā, am, to be thrown; to be thrown round (as a garment).

क्षिया *kshiyā.* See under rt. 4. *kshi.*

क्षिल्लिका *kshillikā,* f., N. of the grandmother of king Ćakra-varman.

क्षिव् *kshiv,* cl. 1. 4. P. *kshevati, kshīvyati,* to eject from the mouth, spit, spit out, vomit; [cf. *shṭhiv* and *kshīv.*]

क्षी *kshī,* another form for 4. *kshi,* q. v.

क्षीज् *kshīj,* cl. 1. P. *kshījati, ćikshīja, kshījitum,* to sound inarticulately, to sigh or groan as in distress.

Kshījana, am, n. the whistling of hollow reeds or bamboos.

क्षीण *kshīṇa.* See under 4. *kshi* 1st col.

क्षीब् *kshīb* and *kshība.* See *kshīv, kshīva.*

क्षीर *kshīra, as, am,* m. n. (probably fr. *kshar,* but according to Uṇādi IV. 34. fr. *ghas*), milk, thickened milk; the milky juice or sap of plants; the resin of the plant Pinus Longifolia; water; (*as*), m., N. of a grammarian [cf. *kshīra-svāmin*]; (*ā*), f., N. of a plant [cf. *kākolī*]; (*ī*), f., N. of several plants containing a milky sap; a small shrub, Asclepia Rosea, also *dugdhikā*; a species of Mimosa, M. Kauki [cf. *kshīrikā*]; gigantic swallow-wort; Euphorbia &c. — *Kshīra-kaṅćukin, ī,* m., N. of a reed, Lipeocercis Serrata (*kshīrīśa*). — *Kshīra-kaṇṭha* or *kshīra-kaṇṭhaka, as,* m. an infant, a young child, 'having milk in its throat.' — *Kshīra-kanda, as, ā,* m. f. a kind of pot-herb, black Bhuincoōnra, Convolvulus Paniculatus; [cf. *kshīra-vidārī.*] — *Kshīra-kalambha,* see *kshairakalambhi.* — *Kshīra-kākolikā* or *kshīra-kākolī,* f. a drug, one of the eight principal medicaments of the Hindūs; it is a root from the Himālaya yielding a milky juice; [cf. *kākolī.*] — *Kshīra-kāṇḍaka, as,* m. the plant Tithymalus Antiquorum (*snuhī*), and Calotropis Gigantea (*arka*). — *Kshīra-kāshṭhā,* f., N. of a plant, = *vaṭī.* — *Kshīra-kīṭa, as,* m. an insect or animalcule generated by the fermentation of milk. — *Kshīra-kshava, as,* m., N. of a plant, = *dudgha-pāshāṇa.* — *Kshīra-kharjūra, as,* m. a species of Datura tree. — *Kshīra-garbha, as,* m., N. of a certain Brāhman who was born again as a flamingo. — *Kshīra-ghṛita, am,* n. purified butter mixed with milk. — *Kshīra-ja, am,* n. coagulated milk. — *Kshīra-taraṅgiṇī,* f. title of a grammar composed by Kshīra-svāmin. — *Kshīra-taila, am,* n. a kind of unguent prepared with milk, oil, &c. — *Kshīra-toyadhi, is,* m. the ocean of milk. — *Kshīra-da, as, ā, am,* milk-giving, what yields milk. — *Kshīra-dala, as,* m. the plant Calotropis Gigantea (= *arka*), the leaves &c. of which yield a milky juice. — *Kshīra-dātrī,* f. yielding milk as a cow. — *Kshīra-druma, as,* m. the tree Ficus Religiosa; [cf. *aśvattha.*] — *Kshīra-dhara, as,* m., N. of a king. — *Kshīra-dhātrī,* f. a wet-nurse. — *Kshīra-dhenu, us,* f. a milch-cow, symbolically represented by milk &c. offered as a gift to a Brāhman. — *Kshīra-nāśa, as,* m. the tree Trophis Aspera (= *śākhoṭa*). — *Kshīra-nidhi, is,* m. the ocean of milk. — *Kshīra-nīra, am,* n. milk and water; embracing, embrace (i. e. a union like the mixing of milk and water). — *Kshīra-pa, as, ā, am,* drinking milk, who or what drinks milk; epithet of a class of ascetics; an infant, a young child. — *Kshīra-parṇin, ī,* m. the plant Calotropis Gigantea; [cf. *arka* and *kshīra-dala.*] — *Kshīra-palāṇḍu, us,* m. a kind of onion. — *Kshīra-pāka, as, ā, am,* Ved. cooked in milk. — *Kshīra-pāṇa, ās,* m. pl. the milk-drinkers, an epithet of the Uśīnaras; (*am*), n. drinking milk; (*as, ī, am*), any vessel out of which milk is drunk. — *Kshīra-pāṇi, is,* m., N. of a physician. — *Kshīra-pāyin, ī, iṇī, i,* drinking or sucking milk; drinking or imbibing water repeatedly; (*iṇas*), m. pl. the milk-drinkers, an epithet of the Uśīnaras. — *Kshīra-bhṛita, as, ā, am,* supported by milk, receiving wages in the form of milk. — *Kshīra-maya, as, ī, am,* composed of milk. — *Kshīra-moćaka, as,* m. a kind of Moringa, M. Hyperanthera; [cf. *moćaka.*] — *Kshīra-moraṭa, as,* m. a kind of creeping plant; [cf. *sitadru, sudala, kshīraka.*] — *Kshīra-yashṭika, am,* n. a dish of liquorice and milk; (perhaps a wrong form for *kshīra-shashṭika?*). — *Kshīra-latā,* f. the plant Batatas Paniculata; [cf. *kshīra-vidārī.*] — *Kshīra-vat, ān, atī, at,* Ved. furnished with milk; (*tī*), f., N. of a river. — *Kshīra-vallī,* f. the dark Bhuincoönra, Convolvulus Paniculatus. — *Kshīra-vāri, is,* m. the sea of milk; [cf. *kshīroda.*] — *Kshīra-vāridhi, is,* m. the sea of milk. — *Kshīra-vikṛiti, is,* f. inspissated milk. — *Kshīra-vidārikā* or *kshīra-vidārī,* f. the plant Batatas Paniculata. — *Kshīra-vishāṇikā,* f. the plants Tragia Involucrata (= *vṛiśćikālī*) and *kshīra-kākolī.* — *Kshīra-vṛiksha, as,* m. the glomerous fig tree, Ficus Glomerata [cf. *udumbara*]; a common N. for the four trees *nyagrodha, udumbara, aśvattha,* and *madhūka.* — *Kshīra-vrata, as, ā, am,* living upon milk in consequence of a vow. — *Kshīra-śara, as,* m. cream, the surface or skim of milk, curds; [cf. *āmikshā.*] — *Kshīra-śīrsha, as,* m. the resin of the plant Pinus Longifolia; [cf. *śrī-vāsa.*] — *Kshīra-śukrā,* f. = *kshīra-vidārī* and *kshīra-kākolī.* — *Kshīra-śukla, as,* m. the plant Trapa Bispinosa [cf. *jala-kaṇṭaka*]; another plant, = *rājādanī;* (*ā*), f. the plant Batatas Paniculata. — *Kshīra-śrī, īs, īs, i,* Ved. mixed with milk. — *Kshīra-shashṭika, am,* n. Shashṭika rice cooked in milk. — *Kshīra-santānikā,* f. curds mixed with milk; (a various reading has °*santālikā.*) — *Kshīra-samudra, as,* m. the sea of milk in Śveta-dīpa. — *Kshīra-sarpis, is,* n. clarified butter mixed with milk. — *Kshīra-sāgara, as,* m. the ocean of milk; also N. of a place. — *Kshīrasāgara-sutā,* f. an epithet of Lakshmī as produced from the ocean of milk. — *Kshīra-sāra, as,* m. essence of milk, any product of milk, (in Hindī *pālajinu*), butter. — *Kshīra-sphaṭika, as,* m. a precious stone, described as a kind of milky crystal (opal or cat's eye?); [cf. *ākāśa-sphaṭika* and *taila-sphaṭika.*] — *Kshīra-svāmin, ī,* m., N. of a grammarian and commentator on the Amara-kosha. — *Kshīra-hrada, as,* m., N. of a man. — *Kshīrāda* (°*ra-ada*), *as,* m. an infant at the breast, a sucking child. — *Kshīrānnāda* (°*ra-anna-ada*), *as,* m. an infant which is both fed and suckled. — *Kshīrābdhi* (°*ra-abdhi*), *is,* m. the sea of milk, one of the seven seas surrounding the seven divisions of the terrestrial world. — *Kshīrābdhi-ja, as,* m. the moon; the Amṛita or any one of the precious objects produced at the churning of the ocean; an epithet of Śesha; an epithet of Tārkshya; (*ā*), f. an epithet of Lakshmī; (*am*), n. sea-salt, a pearl. — *Kshīrābdhi-tanayā,* f. or *kshīrābdhi-mānushī,* f. an epithet of Lakshmī as the daughter of the ocean of milk. — *Kshīrāhva* or *kshīrāhvaya* (°*ra-āh*°), *as,* m. the resin of the plant Pinus Longifolia. — *Kshīroda* (°*ra-uda*), *as, ā, am,* containing milk instead of water; (*as*), m. the sea of milk; the sea in general. — *Kshīroda-tanayā,* f. the daughter of the sea of milk; an epithet of Lakshmī. — *Kshīroda-tanayā-pati, is,* m. an epithet of Vishṇu. — *Kshīrodadhi* (°*ra-ud*°), *is,* m. the sea of milk. — *Kshīroda-nandana, as,* m. the son of the sea of milk, an epithet of the moon. — *Kshīroda-mathana, am,* n. the churning of the ocean of milk undertaken by the Devas and Asuras to obtain the Amṛita &c. — *Kshīrormi* (°*ra-ūr*°), *is,* m. a wave of milk, a wave of the sea of milk. — *Kshīraudana* (°*ra-od*°), *as,* m. rice boiled with milk.

Kshīraka, as, m., N. of a plant, = *kshīra-moraṭa.*

Kshīraya, nom. P. *kshīrayati, -yitum,* to have the appearance of milk, look like milk.

Kshīrasa, as, m. = *kshīra-sāra,* q. v.

Kshīrasya, nom. P. *kshīrasyati, -yitum,* to long for milk or for the breast.

Kshīrāvī or *kshīrāvikā,* f. a sort of Asclepias, A. Rosea, = *dugdhikā.*

Kshīrika, as, m. a kind of serpent; a kind of tree; (*ā*), f. a dish prepared with milk; a kind of Datura tree; [cf. *kshīra-kharjūra* and *piṇḍa-kharjūra.*]

Kshīrin, ī, iṇī, i, milky, yielding milk, abounding in milk, having plenty of milk; containing milky juice or sap (as a tree); (*ī*), m. a species of tree, the Udumbara (?); according to native lexicographers many plants have this epithet; (*iṇī*), f. a tree bearing an edible fruit, = Mimusops Kauki; a species of the moon-plant or acid Asclepias used in medicine.

Kshīriya, nom. P. *kshīriyati, -yitum,* to desire milk.

Kshīriśa, as, m. = *kshīra-kaṅćukin.*

Kshīreyī, f. an oblation of milk, rice, and sugar.

क्षीव् *kshīv,* cl. 1. 4. P. *kshīvati, kshevati* and *kshīvyati, -vitum,* to spit, sputter, eject from the mouth; to be drunk or intoxicated; [cf. *kshiv, kshev, kshīb, shṭhiv;* cf. also Hib. *siobhas,* 'rage, madness.']

Kshīva or *kshība, as, ā, am,* excited, drunk, intoxicated. — *Kshīva-tā,* f. or *kshīva-tva, am,* n. intoxication, drunkenness.

क्षु 1. *kshu,* cl. 2. P. *kshauti, ćukshāva, kshavishyati, akshāvīt, kshavitum,* to sneeze, to make any sound like sneezing; to cough: Caus. *kshāvayati:* Desid. of Caus. *ćukshāvayishati;* [cf. Lith. *czaudmi.*]

Kshava, as, m. sneezing, cough, catarrh; a black species of mustard, Sinapis Dichotoma; [cf. *rājikā.*] — *Kshava-kṛit, t, t, t,* anything which causes sneezing; making a sneeze, sneezing, coughing.

Kshavaka, as, m. the plant Achyranthes Aspera, = *apāmārga,* black mustard; (*am*), n. a kind of pot-herb; (*ikā*), f. a kind of Solanum; a species of rice; a woman.

Ksharathu, us, m. sneezing; catarrh; cough; irritation of the throat; sore throat.

Kshut, t, f. a sneeze, sneezing. — *Kshut-karī,* f., N. of a plant, commonly *kankālikā,* black mustard (?).

Kshuta, as, ā, am, one who has sneezed; sneezed upon; (as a less correct form for *kshṇuta*), sharp; (*as, ā, am*), m. f. n. a sneeze, sneezing, cough. — *Kshuta-vat, ān, atī, at,* sneezing. — *Kshutābhijanana* (°*ta-abh*°), *as,* m. black mustard; [cf. *kshudhābhijanana.*]

Kshutaka, as, m. black mustard.

Kshuti, is, f. sneezing.

Kshuvat, an, atī, at, sneezing, coughing, &c.

क्षु 2. *kshu,* n. (fr. *ghas?*), Ved. food. — *Kshu-mat, ān, atī, at,* Ved. abounding in food, nourishing, nutritious; strong; powerful, robust, valiant.

क्षुण *kshuṇa, as,* m. the soap-berry plant, Sapindus Saponaria; [cf. *arishṭa.*]

क्षुण्ण *kshuṇṇa.* See below under *kshud.*

क्षुद् *kshud,* cl. 7. P. A. and Ved. cl. 1. P. *kshuṇatti, kshunte, kshodati, ćukshoda, ćukshude, kshotsyati, -te, akshudat, akshautsīt, akshutta, kshottum,* to strike against, stamp or trample upon, pound; to bruise, crush, shiver, shatter, reduce to powder, dash to pieces, shake by stamping on; A. to move, to be agitated or shaken: Caus. P. *kshodayati, -yitum,* to crush, pound, comminute, pulverize, reduce to powder, diminish; shake or agitate by stamping; [cf. Gr. ξύω, ξέω for ξεύω, ξυστός, ξεστός; Lith. *skausti?*].

Kshuṇṇa, as, ā, am, pounded, bruised, crushed, stamped or trampled upon; broken to pieces, pulverized, shattered, pierced; violated (as a vow); exercised, practised, skilful; one versed in sacred science but unable to explain or teach it; defeated, overcome. — *Kshuṇṇa-manas, ās, ās, as,* contrite in heart, penitent.

Kshuṇṇaka, as, m. a kind of drum beaten at a funeral.

Kshuda, as, m. flour, meal.

Kshudra, as, ā, am (compar. *kshodīyas,* superl. *kshodishṭha*), minute, diminutive, tiny, very small, small, little, trifling; mean, low, vile, niggardly, base, avaricious; wicked; cruel; poor, indigent; (*as*), m. a small particle of rice; a bee or wasp; the plant Artocarpus Lacucha [cf. *lakuća* and *ḍahu*]; (*ās*), m. pl. a peculiar class of writings, see *kshudra-kalpa;* (*ā*), f. a woman maimed or crippled; a base or despicable woman; a whore, a harlot; a dancing girl; a quarrelsome woman; a bee, fly, gnat; several plants, Solanum Jacquini, = *vṛihatī;* also = *ćāngerikā;* also = *gavedhukā;* (*am*), n., Ved. a particle of dust, flour, meal; [cf. Lith. *kūdikis,* 'an infant;' Pers. كودك *kūdak,* 'small, a boy.'] — *Kshudra-kaṇṭakārī,* f. the plant Solanum Jacquini, = *agni-damanī.* — *Kshudra-kaṇṭakī,* f. a kind of Solanum, = *bṛihatī.* — *Kshudraka-mānasa, am,* n., N. of a lake. — *Kshudra-kambu, us,* m. a small shell. — *Kshudra-kalpa, as,* m. 'the smaller ritual,' title of a class of works. — *Kshudra-kāralikā,* f. (for *kshudra-karālikā?*), and *kshudra-kāravellī,* f. a kind of Cucurbitaceous plant. — *Kshudra-kuliśa, as,* m. a precious stone; [cf. *vaikrānta.*] — *Kshudra-kushṭha, am,* n. a mild form of leprosy, (comprising eleven varieties, whereas the *mahā-kushṭha* contains seven severe forms of leprosy.) — *Kshudra-kshura* and *kshudra-gokshuraka, as,* m. a variety of the plant Asteracantha Longifolia. — *Kshudra-ghaṇṭikā,* f. a tinkling ornament, a girdle of small bells. — *Kshudra-gholī,* f., N. of a plant, = *ćivīllikā.* — *Kshudra-ćaṅću, us,* f., N. of a plant. — *Kshudra-ćandana, am,* n. red sandal-wood. — *Kshudra-ćirbhiṭā,* f., N. of a plant, = *gopāla-karkaṭī.* — *Kshudra-ćūḍa, as,* m. a kind of small bird, commonly called *gosālika.* — *Kshudra-jantu, us,* m. any small animal; a kind of worm, Julus (*śata-padī*). — *Kshudra-jātīphala, am,* n. a kind of Myrobalan; [cf. *āmalaka.*] — *Kshudra-jīra, as,* m. small cummin. — *Kshudra-jīvā,* f., N. of a plant, = *jīvantī.* — *Kshudraṅ-ćara, as, ī, am,* following small or minute or trifling matters. — *Kshudra-taṇḍula, as,* m. a grain of rice. — *Kshudra-tā,* f. or *kshudra-tva, am,* n. minuteness, smallness; inferiority, insignificance; meanness. — *Kshudra-tulasī,* f. a kind of Ocimum, = *arjaka.* — *Kshudra-daṃśikā* or *kshudra-daṃśī,* f. a small gad-fly. — *Kshudra-durālabhā,* f., N. of a thorny plant much eaten by camels. — *Kshudra-duḥsparśā,* f. the plant Solanum Jacquini, = *agni-damanī.* — *Kshudra-dhātrī,* f., N. of a plant; [cf. *karkaṭa.*] — *Kshudra-dhānya, am,* n. shrivelled grain. — *Kshudra-nāsika, as, ī, am,* having a small nose. — *Kshudra-pakshika, as,* m. a small bird. — *Kshudra-pattrā,* f. a kind of wood-sorrel, Oxalis Monadelpha, = *ćāngerī;* (*ī*), f., N. of another plant, = *vaćā.* — *Kshudra-panasa, as,* m. the plant Artocarpus Lacucha (*lakuća*). — *Kshudra-parṇa, as,* m. a kind of Ocimum, = *arjaka.* — *Kshudra-pāshāṇa-bhedā* or *ī,* f., N. of a plant, = *ćatuh-pattrī, pārvatī, naga-bhū,* &c. — *Kshudra-pippalī,* f. wild pepper (= *vana-pippalī*). — *Kshudra-prishatī,* f., Ved. covered with small spots. — *Kshudra-potikā,* f., N. of a pot-herb. — *Kshudra-phalaka, as,* m., N. of a plant, = *jīvana,* Celtis Orientalis. — *Kshudra-phalā,* f., N. of several plants, Ardisia Solanacea, = *bhūmi-jambu,* and others. — *Kshudra-buddhi, is, is, i,* of little understanding, simple, silly, ignorant; (*is*), m., N. of a jackal in the Hitopadeśa. — *Kshudrabuddhi-nāman, ā, ā, a,* named Kshudra-buddhi. — *Kshudra-bhaṇṭākī,* f., N. of a plant, a kind of Solanum, = *bṛihatī;* [cf. *kshudra-kaṇṭakī.*] — *Kshudra-mīna, ās,* m. pl., N. of a people. — *Kshudra-mustā,* f. the plant Scirpus Kysoor; [cf. *kaseru.*] — *Kshudra-rasa, as,* m. honey; (*ā*), f. the plant Pongamia Glabra; [cf. *karañja.*] — *Kshudra-roga, as,* m. a minor disease, one of little importance; a name applied to various local diseases, especially exanthemas of different kinds; there are forty-four such diseases. — *Kshudrarogika, as, ā, am,* affected with such a disease. — *Kshudra-vanśā,* f., N. of a plant, Dioscorea, = *varāha-krāntā.* — *Kshudra-varvaṇā,* f. a small gad-fly; [cf. *varaṭā.*] — *Kshudra-vallī,* f., N. of a pot-herb; [cf. *mūla-poṭī.*] — *Kshudra-vārtākinī,* f. a kind of Solanum with white blossoms, = *śveta-kaṇṭakārī.* — *Kshudra-vārtākī,* f. a kind of Solanum, = *bṛihatī.* — *Kshudra-śaṅkha, as,* m. a small conch shell. — *Kshudra-śarkarā* or *kshudra-śarkarikā,* f. a kind of sugar-cane, = *yāvanāla-śarkarā.* — *Kshudra-śārdūla, as,* m. a kind of tiger, = *ćitra-vyāghra.* — *Kshudra-śīrsha, as,* m. the tree Celosia Cristata, = *mayūra-śikhā.* — *Kshudra-śukti, is,* m. a bivalve shell, = *jala-śukti.* — *Kshudra-śyāmā,* f., N. of a plant, = *kaṭabhī.* — *Kshudra-śleshmāntaka, as,* m., N. of a plant, = *bhūkarbudāraka.* — *Kshudra-śvāsa, as,* m. short breath. — *Kshudra-śvetā,* f., N. of a plant; [cf. *mahā-śvetā.*] — *Kshudra-sahā,* f. the plant Phaseolus Trilobus; the Coloquintida, = *indra-vāruṇī;* [cf. *mahā-sahā.*] — *Kshudra-suvarṇa, am,* n. bad gold, prince's metal. — *Kshudra-han, ā,* m. killing the wicked; an epithet of Śiva. — *Kshudra-hiṅgulikā,* f. a small species of prickly nightshade, Solanum Jacquini; [cf. *kaṇṭakārī.*] — *Kshudra-hiṅgulī,* f. = the preceding. — *Kshudrāgnimantha* (°*ra-ag*°), *as,* m. the plant Premna Spinosa used for kindling fire; [cf. *araṇi.*] — *Kshudrāñjana* (°*ra-añ*°), *am,* n. a kind of unguent applied to the eyes in certain diseases. — *Kshudrāṇḍa* (°*ra-aṇ*°), *as, ā, am,* born from minute eggs. — *Kshudrāṇḍa-matsya-saṅghāta, as,* m. small fry. — *Kshudrāntra* (°*ra-an*°), *am,* n. the small cavity of the heart. — *Kshudrāpāmārga* (°*ra-ap*°), *as,* m., N. of the plant Desmochæta Atropurpurea (= *raktāpāmārga*), a biennial plant. — *Kshudrāmalaka* (°*ra-ām*°), *am,* n. Myrobalan (*āmalaka*). — *Kshudrāmalaka-sañjña, as,* m., N. of a plant, = *karkaṭa.* — *Kshudrāmra* (°*ra-ām*°), *as,* m., N. of a plant, = *kośāmra.* — *Kshudrāmlapanasa* or *kshudrāmbupanasa* (°*ra-am*°), *as,* m. the plant Artocarpus Lacucha (*lakuća*). — *Kshudrāmlā* (°*ra-am*°), f. wood-sorrel, Oxalis Corniculata (= *amlaloṇikā*); another plant, = *śaśāṇḍulī.* — *Kshudrāmlikā* (°*ra-am*°), f. a kind of wood-sorrel or Oxalis, = *ćāṅgerī.* — *Kshudreṅgudī* (°*ra-iṅ*°), f., N. of a plant, = *yavāsa.* — *Kshudrervāru* (°*ra-ir*°), *us,* m., N. of a plant, = *gopāla-karkaṭī.* — *Kshudrodumbarikā* (°*ra-ud*°), f. the plant Ficus Oppositifolia; [cf. *kākodumbarikā.*] — *Kshudropodaka-nāmnī* (°*ra-up*°), f., N. of a pot-herb; [cf. *mūla-poṭī.*] — *Kshudropodakī* (°*ra-up*°), f., N. of a pot-herb, = *sūkshma-pattrā* and *maṇṭapī.* — *Kshudrolūka* (°*ra-ul*°), *as,* m. a small kind of owl.

Kshudraka, as, ikā, am, small, minute; (*as*), m. a species of plant; N. of a prince, a son of Prasenajit; title of a collection of Buddhist works, = *vinaya-kshudraka-vastu;* (*ās*), m. pl., N. of a people living by warfare, the Ὀξυδρακοι.

Kshudrula, as, ā, am, minute, small, unimportant (applied especially to animals and diseases).

Kshudrikā, f. a kind of gad-fly, = *danśa;* small bells employed for ornament; [cf. *kshudra-ghaṇṭikā.*]

Kshottṛi, tā, m. a pestle, any implement for grinding.

Kshoda, as, m. pounding, grinding; the stone or slab on which anything is ground or powdered, a mortar &c., any pounded or ground or pulverized substance, flour, meal, dust, a particle, a small piece or fragment. — *Kshoda-raja, as, ā, am,* ground to dust.

Kshodas, as, n., Ved. water in agitation, swell of the sea, rushing or stream of water.

Kshodita, as, ā, am, pounded, ground, comminuted; (*am*), n. powder, dust, flour, meal, any substance pulverized or ground.

Kshodiman, ā, m. minuteness, excessive smallness or inferiority.

Kshodishṭha, as, ā, am (superl. of *kshudra*), finely pounded, very small, very minute.

Kshodīyas, ān, asī, as (compar. of *kshudra*), more minute, very fine, very minute.

Kshodya, as, ā, am, to be stamped or trampled on or pounded.

क्षुध् 1. *kshudh,* cl. 4. P. *kshudhyati, ćukshodha, kshoddhum,* to feel hungry; to be hungry, hunger; [cf. Goth. *grêdôn,* 'to be hungry.']

2. *kshudh, t,* f. hunger. — *Kshut-kshāma, as, ā, am,* emaciated by hunger. — *Kshut-tṛiṭ-parīta, as, ā, am,* hungry and thirsty. — *Kshut-tṛiḍ-udbhava, as, ā, am,* beginning to feel hungry and thirsty. — *Kshut-tṛishānvita* (°*shā-an*°), *as, ā, am,* suffering from hunger and thirst. — *Kshut-tṛishṇopapīḍita* (°*ṇā-up*°), *as, ā, am,* hungry and thirsty. — *Kshut-parīta, as, ā, am,* overcome with hunger. — *Kshut-pipāsā-pariśrānta, as, ā, am,* wearied by hunger and thirst. — *Kshut-pipāsā-parītāṅga* (°*ta-aṅ*°), *as, ā, am,* one whose body is affected with hunger and thirst. — *Kshut-pipāsārta* (°*sā-ār*°), *as, ā, am,* afflicted with hunger and thirst. — *Kshut-pipāsita, as, ā, am,* hungry and thirsty. — *Kshut-pratīkāra, as,* m. allaying hunger, eating. — *Kshud-roga, as,* m. pain of hunger. — *Kshud-vat, ān, atī, at,* hungry. — *Kshun-nivṛitti, is,* f. cessation of hunger, appeasing of appetite.

Kshudhā, f. hunger; mystical N. of the letter *y.* — *Kshudhā-kara, as, ī, am,* causing hunger, increasing appetite. — *Kshudhā-kuśala, as,* m., N. of a tree, = *vilvāntara-vṛiksha.* — *Kshudhā-dhvansa, as,* m. allaying hunger. — *Kshudhānvita* (°*dhā-an*°), *as, ā, am,* afflicted with hunger. — *Kshudhā-pīḍita, as, ā, am,* hungry, starving. — *Kshudhābhijanana* (°*dhā-abh*°), *as,* m. black mustard; [cf. *kshutābhijanana.*] — *Kshudhā-māra, as,* m., Ved. death caused by starvation. — *Kshudhārta* (°*dhā-ār*°) or *kshudhārdita* (°*dhā-ar*°), *as, ā, am,* hungry, hungered. — *Kshudhāvishṭa* (°*dhā-āv*°), *as, ā, am,* affected by hunger. — *Kshudhā-śānti, is,* f. allaying hunger, satiety, satisfaction.

Kshudhālu, us, us, u, hungry.

Kshudhita, as, ā, am, hungry, hungered.

Kshodhuka, as, ikā, am, Ved. hungry.

क्षुधुन *kshudhuna, as,* m., N. of a savage and barbarous race.

क्षुप् *kshup,* a Sautra root (i. e. one used in grammatical Sūtras only), to depress, feel depressed.

क्षुप *kshupa, as,* m. [cf. *kshumpa*], a bush, a shrub; a small tree, one with short branches and roots; N. of an old king, a son of Prasandhi and father of Ikshvāku; N. of a son of Kṛishṇa from Satya-bhāmā; N. of a mountain westward from Dvārakā. — *Kshupa-ḍoḍamushṭi, is,* m., N. of a plant. — *Kshupālu* (°*pa-ālu*), *us,* m. a kind of bulbous plant, = *pānīyālu.*

Kshupaka, as, ā, m. f. a bush, a shrub.

क्षुभ् 1. *kshubh,* cl. 9. 4. P., 1. A. *kshubhnāti, kshubhyati, kshobhate, ćukshobha, ćukshubhe, kshobhishyati, -te, akshobhīt, akshubhat* and *akshobhishṭa, kshobhitum,* to shake, tremble, to be agitated or disturbed; to be unsteady; to stumble (literally or metaphorically): Caus. *kshobhayati, -yitum,* to agitate, cause to shake, disturb, stir up, excite: Desid. *ćukshubhishati, -te,* or *ćukshobhishati, -te:* Intens. *ćokshubhyate, ćokshobdhi;* [cf. Cambro-Brit. *hwbiau,* 'to make a sudden push;' Gr. κοῦφος; Mod. Germ. *schiebe.*]

Kshubdha, as, ā, am, agitated, shaken, tossed, stirred up; agitated (mentally), excited, disturbed; (*as*), m. the churning-stick; a kind of coitus. — *Kshubdha-tā,* f. agitation. — *Kshubdhārṇava* (°*dha-ar*°), *as,* m. a stormy ocean.

2. *kshubh, p,* f., Ved. a blow, a shake, a push.

Kshubhā, f. a kind of weapon.

Kshubhita, as, ā, am, agitated, tossed, set in motion; agitated (mentally), disturbed, anxious; frightened, alarmed, afraid; angry, enraged.

Kshobha, as, m. shaking, agitation, disturbance, tossing, trembling, emotion.

Kshobhaka, as, ā, am, shaking, causing agitation; (*as*), m., N. of a mountain in Kāmākhyā, a place sacred to the goddess Durgā.

Kshobhaṇa, as, ā, am, shaking, agitating, disturbing, causing emotion; (*as*), m., N. of one of the five arrows of the god of love.

Kshobhya, as, ā, am, to be shaken or agitated or disturbed.

क्षुमत् *kshu-mat.* See under 2. *kshu.*

क्षुमा *kshumā,* f., Ved. an epithet of an arrow, according to the scholiast 'causing to tremble' (for *kshubhā ?*); N. of several plants; linseed, Linum Usitatissimum; a sort of flax, Bengal San (*śaṇa*); the Indigo plant; a sort of creeper.

Kshauma, &c. See s. v., p. 271.

क्षुम्प् *kshump,* cl. 1. P. *kshumpati,* to go.

क्षुम्प *kshumpa, as,* m. [cf. *kshupa*], Ved. a bush, a shrub.

क्षुर् *kshur,* cl. 6. P. *kshurati, ćukshora, kshoritum,* to cut, dig, scratch; to make lines or furrows.

Kshura, as, m. (connected with the preceding, perhaps related to *kshar ?*; cf. Gr. ξυρόν), a razor; a razor-like barb or sharp blade attached to an arrow; N. of several plants, Asteracantha Longifolia; also Tribulus Lanuginosus, see *go-kshura;* also = *mahā-piṇḍitaka,* and Saccharum Sara (*śara*); the hoof of a cow &c.; a horse's hoof; the foot of a bedstead [cf. *khura*]; (*ī*), f. a knife, a dagger; (*as, ā, am*), Ved. (Sāy.) having claws. — *Kshura-karman, a,* n. the operation of shaving. — *Kshura-klṛipta, as, ā, am,* shaved. — *Kshura-kriyā,* f. the operation of shaving, the employment of a razor. — *Kshura-ćatushṭaya, am,* n. four things necessary for shaving. — *Kshura-dhāna, am,* n. a razor-case. — *Kshura-dhāra, as, ā, am,* razor-edged, sharp as a razor; any very sharp instrument for cutting. — *Kshura-dhārā,* f. the edge of a razor; N. of a hell. — *Kshuradhārābha* (°*ra-ābhā*), *as, ā, am,* sharp as a razor. — *Kshura-pattra, as,* m., N. of the plant Saccharum Sara (*śara*). — *Kshura-pattrikā,* f., N. of a pot-herb, = *pālankya.* — *Kshura-pavi, is, is, i,* Ved. sharp-angled, sharp-edged, very sharp; (*is*), m., N. of a sacrifice performed in one day (*ekāha*). — *Kshura-pra, as,* m. a razor shot as an arrow; a kind of arrow, one with a sharp horse-shoe-shaped head; a sort of hoe or weeding spade. — *Kshura-praga, am,* n. according to some authorities = *kshura-pra.* — *Kshura-bhāṇḍa, am,* n. a razor-case. — *Kshura-bhṛishṭi, is, is, i,* Ved. furnished with sharp angles. — *Kshura-mardin, ī,* m. a barber. — *Kshurāṅga* (°*ra-aṅ*°), *as,* m., N. of a plant; [cf. *go-kshuraka.*] — *Kshurārpaṇa* (°*ra-ar*°), *as,* m., N. of a mountain.

Kshuraka, as, m., N. of several plants, = Asteracantha Longifolia; also Tribulus Lanuginosus [cf. *go-kshura*]; also = *tilaka;* also another plant, = *bhūtāṅkuśa.*

Kshurikā, f. a small razor; a knife, a dagger; a sort of earthen vessel, a kind of pot-herb (= *pālankya*). — *Kshurikā-pattra, as,* m. the plant Saccharum Sara (*śara*). — *Kshurikopanishad* (°*kā-up*°), *t,* f. title of an Upanishad belonging to the Atharva-veda.

Kshurin, ī, m. a barber; (*iṇī*), f. the wife of a barber; a kind of yam, see *varāha-krāntā*.

Kshaura, &c. See s. v., p. 271.

क्षुलिक *kshulika, as*, m., N. of a prince.

क्षुल्ल *kshulla, as, ā, am* (fr. *kshudra?*), small, little, minute.—*Kshulla-tāta, as*, m. the younger brother of a father. — *Kshulla-tātaka, as*, m. the brother of a father.

Kshullaka, as, ā, am, little, small; low, vile, poor, indigent; wicked, malicious, abandoned; hard; young, youngest; pained, distressed; (*as*), m. a small shell; N. of a prince.

क्षुवत् *kshuvat*. See under rt. 1. *kshu*.

क्षेड *ksheḍa, ksheḍita*, = *kshveḍa, kshveḍita*.

क्षेत्र *kshetra, am*, n. (fr. 1. or 2. *kshi*), landed property, land, soil, a field (e. g. *kshetraṃ kṛi*, to cultivate the soil; *kshetrasya pati*, lord of the soil, N. for a kind of genius or tutelary deity regarded in the Veda as the guardian of cultivated fields); place, region, country; a sacred spot or district, a place of pilgrimage, as Benares &c.; an enclosed plot of ground, portion of space, superficies, circuit, circumference; fertile soil; the fertile womb, a wife; place of origin; department, sphere of action, the body considered as the field of the indwelling and working of the soul; a sign of the zodiac; (in geometry) a plane figure, as a triangle, circle, &c. enclosed by lines, any figure considered as having geometrical dimensions; a diagram; a house, town; [cf. *anya-kshetra, kuru-kshetra*, &c.; cf. also Goth. *haithi*, Them. *haithjo*; Germ. *Heide*.] —*Kshetra-kara, as, ī, am*, cultivating a field; a husbandman. — *Kshetra-karkaṭī*, f. a kind of gourd; [cf. *bālukī*.]—*Kshetrakarma-kṛit, t, t, t*, one who cultivates the soil, a husbandman.—*Kshetra-karman, a*, n. cultivation of the soil.—*Kshetra-gaṇita, am*, n. geometry.—*Kshetra-gata, as, ā, am*, geometrical.—*Kshetragatopapatti* (°*ta-up*°), *is*, f. geometrical proof.—*Kshetra-ćirbhiṭā*, f. a kind of gourd, = *ćirbhiṭā*.—*Kshetra-ja, as, ā, am*, produced in a field, as corn &c.; born from the body; (*as*), m., scil. *putra*, a son, the offspring of the wife by a kinsman or person duly appointed to raise up issue to the husband, (this is one of the twelve kinds of issue allowed by the old Hindū law); (*ā*), f., N. of several plants, = *śveta-kanṭakārī, śaśāṇḍulī, gomūtrikā, śilpikā, ćaṇikā*.—*Kshetra-jāta, as, ā, am*, begotten on the wife of another.—*Kshetra-jesha, as*, m., Ved. contest for landed property, acquisition of land. — *Kshetra-jña, as, ā, am*, knowing localities; familiar with the cultivation of the soil, a husbandman &c.; clever, dexterous, skilful, cunning; (*as*), m. 'knowing the body,' i. e. the soul, the conscious principle in the corporeal frame; a libertine, a whoremonger; a form of Śiva; N. of a prince; (*ā*), f. a girl fifteen years old who personates the goddess Durgā at a festival of this deity.—*Kshetra-tattva, am*, n. a part of the work Smṛiti-tattva.—*Kshetra-tara, am*, n., Ved. a spot very fit for cultivation or for habitation.—*Kshetra-tā*, f. the state of being a seat or residence, a seat, a place of residence.—*Kshetra-dūtī*, f. a kind of Solanum (*śveta-kanṭakārī*).—*Kshetra-devatā*, f. 'the deity of the fields,' epithet of a serpent in the Pañća-tantra.—*Kshetra-pati, is*, m. the owner of a field, a landowner, a landlord, a farmer; [cf. *kshaitrapata, kshaitrapatya*, p. 271, and *kshetrasya-pati* above.] — *Kshetra-pada, am*, n. a place sacred to a deity. — *Kshetra-parpaṭī*, f., N. of a shrub, Oldenlandia Biflora or another species. —*Kshetra-pāla, as*, m. a man employed to guard fields from depredation; a deity protecting the fields; an epithet of Śiva.—*Kshetra-phala, am*, n. (in geometry) the superficial contents of a figure. —*Kshetra-bhakti, is*, f. the division of a field. —*Kshetra-bhūmi, is*, f. cultivated land.—*Kshetra-yamānikā*, f., N. of a plant, = *vaćā*.—*Kshetra-raksha, as*, m. a man employed to guard fields from depredation.—*Kshetra-rāśi, is*, m. quantity represented by geometrical figures.—*Kshetra-ruhā*, f. a kind of gourd, = *bālukī*.—*Kshetra-vasudhā*, f. cultivated land.—*Kshetra-vid, t, t, t*, familiar with localities; experienced, clever, skilful; (*t*), m. a husbandman; a sage, one who possesses spiritual knowledge; the soul.—*Kshetra-vyavahāra, as*, m. drawing a figure in geometry; geometrical demonstration.—*Kshetra-sambhava, as*, m., N. of either of the shrubs Cañću and Bhiṇḍā; (*ā*), f. a kind of gourd, = *śaśāṇḍulī*.—*Kshetra-sambhūta, as*, m. a kind of grass, = *kundara*.—*Kshetra-sāti, is*, f., Ved. acquisition of field or land.—*Kshetra-sādhas, ās, ās, as*, Ved. arriving at or coming to a place. —*Kshetra-sīmā*, f. the boundary of a meadow or field or holy place.—*Kshetra-stha, as, ā, am*, residing at a sacred place.—*Kshetrājīva* (°*ra-āj*°), *as, ā, am*, one who gains a livelihood by cultivating the soil; a cultivator, a peasant.—*Kshetrādhidevatā* (°*ra-adh*°), f. the tutelary deity of any consecrated piece of ground.—*Kshetrādhipa* (°*ra-adh*°), *as*, m. = the preceding; the regent of a sign of the zodiac.—*Kshetrāmalakī*, the plant Flacourtia Cataphracta; [cf. *bhūmy-āmalakī*.]—*Kshetrā-sā, ās, ās, am*, Ved. acquiring or gaining land.—*Kshetrekshu* (°*ra-ik*°), *us*, m. a kind of grain, = *yāvanāla*. —*Kshetropeksha* (°*ra-up*°), *as*, m., N. of a son of Svaphalka.

Kshetrika, as, ī, am, having a field, relating to a field &c., agrarian; (*as*), m. the owner of a field, a farmer, a cultivator, a husband.

Kshetrin, ī, iṇī, i, owning a field, cultivating land, agricultural; (*ī*), m. an agriculturist, a husbandman, a cultivator; a husband; the soul.

Kshetriya, as, ā, am, relating to a field, belonging to land; curable in a future body, i. e. incurable in the present life; (*āṇi*), n. pl. the environs of any place; (*am*), n. a chronic or organic disease, an incurable one; meadow grass, herbage, pasturage; (*as*), m. a medicament, anything fit to be administered in medicine (?); an incurable disease; one who has carnal knowledge of other men's wives, an adulterer; physicking, operating.—*Kshetriya-nāśana, as, ī, am*, Ved. removing a chronic disease.

Kshetrīya, nom. P. *kshetrīyati*, to desire another man's wife.

क्षेद *ksheda, as*, m. (?) sorrowing, moaning (?).

क्षेप *kshepa, kshepaka, kshepaṇa, kshepaṇi*, &c. See under rt. *kship* at p. 267.

क्षेम *kshema, as, ā, am* (fr. 2. *kshi*), habitable, giving rest, giving ease or security or comfort; conferring happiness; at ease, prosperous, safe, secure, well, happy, right; (*as, am*), m. n. (Ved. always m.) basis, foundation; residence, place of rest; abiding at ease; safety, tranquillity, peace, rest, security, any secure, easy or comfortable state, well-being, weal, happiness (e. g. *kshemeṇa*, at ease, in security, safely; *ksheme—yoge*, Ved. both in rest and exertion —in enjoying and acquiring); preserving, protecting, keeping what is acquired; final emancipation, eternal happiness; (*as*), m. a kind of perfume (= *ćaṇḍā*); ease or prosperity personified as a son of Dharma and Śānti; also a son of Titikshā; N. of a prince, a son of Śući and father of Suvrata; N. of a son of the third Manu Sāvarṇa; N. of a kind of college or association [cf. *maṭha*]; the proper term (according to Manu II. 127) of civil address to a Vaiśya, asking him whether his property is secure; (*ā*), f., N. of an Apsaras; an epithet of Durgā; N. of another deity; a kind of perfume; (*am*), n., N. of one of the seven Varshas in Jambu-dvīpa.—*Kshema-kara, as, ā, am*, causing peace and security, conferring happiness or good fortune, propitious.—*Kshema-karṇa, as*, m., N. of a son of Maheśa, who composed, A. D. 1570, the work Rāga-mālā.—*Kshema-karman, ā, ā, a*, one whose work is peace and security, creating tranquillity and security; (*ā*), m., N. of a prince. —*Kshema-kāma, as, ā, am*, Ved. longing for rest. —*Kshema-kāra, as, ī, am*, granting peace and security, conferring happiness or good fortune, propitious, auspicious.—*Kshema-kutūhala, am*, n. title of a medical work of Kshema-śarman.—*Kshema-kṛit, t, t, t*, causing peace and security.—*Kshema-gupta, as*, m., N. of a king of Kāśmīra.—*Kshemankara, as, ī, am*, promoting well-being, causing peace and security, propitious, &c.; (*as*), m., N. of a king of Trigarta; N. of a mythical Buddha; N. of a son of Brahma-datta (Udayana); (*ī*), f. the Brāhmaṇī kite or Coromandel eagle, considered as a bird of good omen, Falco Ponticerianus; a form of the goddess Durgā; N. of another goddess; N. of a sister of Kshemaṅ-kara.—*Kshema-jit, t*, m., N. of a prince.—*Kshema-tara, as, ā, am*, better, happier.—*Kshema-darśin, ī*, m., N. of a prince of the Kosalas.—*Kshemadarśīya, as, ā, am*, relating to this prince.—*Kshema-dhanvan, ā*, m., N. of a prince, a son of Puṇḍarīka. — *Kshema-dharman, ā*, m., N. of a prince.—*Kshema-dhūrta, ās*, m. pl., N. of a people.—*Kshema-dhūrti, is*, m., N. of a warrior. — *Kshema-dhṛitvan, ā*, m., N. of a man with the patronymic Pauṇḍarīka.—*Kshema-phalā*, see *kshemā-phalā*.—*Kshema-bhūmi, is*, m., N. of a prince.—*Kshema-mūrti, is*, m., N. of a prince.—*Kshema-yuktam*, ind. both quietly and energetically; in rest and exertion.—*Kshema-rāja, as*, m., N. of a man.—*Kshema-vat, ān, atī, at*, accompanied with tranquillity and security; prosperous, happy; (*tī*), f., N. of a woman.—*Kshema-vṛiddhi, is*, m., N. of a general of the Śālvas. — *Kshema-śarman, ā*, m., N. of an author. —*Kshemāditya* (°*ma-ād*°), *as*, m., N. of a man. — *Kshemādhi* (°*ma-ādhi*), *is*, m., N. of a prince of Mithilā.—*Kshemā-phalā*, f. the tree Ficus Oppositifolia; [cf. *udumbara*.]—*Kshemāri* (°*ma-ari*), *is*, m., N. of a prince of Mithilā, = *kshemādhi*. — *Kshemārćis* (°*ma-ar*°), *is*, m. = *kshema-jit*. —*Kshemendra* (°*ma-in*°), *as*, m., N. of the author of a list of regents of Kāśmīra; N. of a lexicographer; also of the author of a Buddhist work. —*Kshemendra-prakāśa, as*, m., N. of a work by Kshemendra.

Kshemaka, as, m. a kind of perfume, = *ćaura*; N. of a Nāga; N. of a Rakshas; N. of an attendant of Śiva; N. of an old king; of a son of Alarka; of the last descendant of Parīkshit in the Kali-yuga; N. of a son of Nirāmitra.

Kshemayat, an, antī, at, Ved. resting; granting rest or an abode.

Kshemin, ī, iṇī, i, enjoying peace and security, safe, secure, happy, well.

Kshemya, as, ā, am, resting, at leisure, at ease; habitable, comfortable; healthy, salubrious; lucky, prosperous, thriving; giving peace and tranquillity; (*as*), m., N. of Śiva; N. of several princes, a son of Sunītha and father of Ketumat; of a son of Ugrāyudha and father of Suvīra; of a son of Śući and father of Suvrata; (*am*), n., Ved. resting.

क्षेय *ksheya*. See under rt. 4. *kshi*, p. 266.

क्षेव् *kshev*, cl. 1. P. *kshevati*, another form for *kshiv* or *kshīv*, 'to spit,' q. v.

क्षै *kshai*, cl. 1. P. *kshāyati, ćakshau, kshāsyati, kshātum*, to wane; to waste away, dry up, decline, become emaciated; [cf. 4. *kshi*.]

Kshāma, as, ā, am, wasted, dried up. See s. v.

क्षैण्य *kshaiṇya, am*, n. (fr. *kshīṇa*), destruction, wasting away; leanness, slenderness, emaciation.

क्षैत *kshaita, as*, m. (fr. 1. *kshiti*), Ved. the chief of a race, a prince.—*Kshaita-vat, ān, atī, at*, Ved. princely.

क्षैत्र *kshaitra, am*, n. (fr. *kshetra*), a multitude of fields &c.

Kshaitrajitya, am, n. (fr. *kshetra-jit*), Ved. acquisition of land, a victorious battle.

Kshaitrajña or *kshaitrajñya, am*, n. (fr. *kshetra-*

jña), spirituality, the nature of the soul; the knowledge of the soul &c.

Kshaitrapatya, as, ā, am (fr. *kshetra-pati*), Ved. belonging to the lord of the soil.

क्षैप्र *kshaipra, as, ī, am* (fr. *kshipra*), a term for a kind of Sandhi, produced by changing the first of two concurrent vowels to its semivowel; the Svarita accent on a syllable formed with this Sandhi; (*am*), n. quickness, speediness. — *Kshaipra-yukta, as, ā, am*, joined by the Kshaipra Sandhi. — *Kshaipra-varṇa, as, ā, am*, containing a semi-vowel.

क्षैरकलम्भि *kshairakalambhi, is*, m. (a patronymic fr. *kshīra-kalambha*), N. of a teacher.

क्षैरेय *kshaireya, as, ī, am* (fr. *kshīra*), prepared with milk, milky; (*ī*), f. milk and rice or any preparation of or dish prepared with milk.

क्षोट् *kshoṭ*, cl. 10. P. *kshoṭayati, -yitum*, to throw, cast; [cf. *khoṭ* and *khoḍ*.]

क्षोड *kshoḍa, as*, m. the post to which an elephant is fastened; [cf. *a-kshobha*.]

क्षोण *kshoṇa, as, ā, am*, Ved. immovable; or (*as*), m. a kind of lute; (perhaps the word is related to the following.)

क्षोणी *kshoṇī*, f., Ved. the earth; (*yau*), du. heaven and earth; (according to some the sing. of this word and sometimes the plur. may be used collectively, and the original meaning may be 'a multitude of men' or 'the people' (as opposed to the chief); the du. may then mean 'the two sets of people,' i. e. the inhabitants of heaven and earth; sometimes a form *kshoṇi* occurs); [cf. Gr. χθών.] — *Kshoṇī-maya, as, ī, am*, containing the earth in himself, 'the source of everything in the earth;' an epithet of Vishṇu in his fish-incarnation.

क्षोत्तृ *kshottṛi*. See under rt. *kshud*.

क्षोद *kshoda*. See under rt. *kshud*.

क्षोधुक *kshodhuka*. See under rt. 1. *kshudh*.

क्षोभ *kshobha, kshobhaṇa*, &c. See under rt. 1. *kshubh*.

क्षोम *kshoma, as, am*, m. n. (said to be fr. rt. *kshu*), a room on the top of a house; (*am*), n. wove silk; [cf. *kshauma*.]

क्षोमक *kshomaka, as*, m. a kind of perfume (*gaṇahāsaka*); [cf. *kshema* and *kshaumaka*.]

क्षौणी *kshauṇī, ī* or *is*, f. the earth; [cf. *kshoṇī*.] — *Kshauṇi-tala, am*, n. the surface of the earth. — *Kshauṇi-prāćīra, as*, m. the ocean. — *Kshauṇi-bhuj, k*, m. earth-possessor, a king; [cf. *kshiti-bhuj*.]

क्षौद्र *kshaudra, as*, m. (fr. *kshudra* and *kshudrā*), the tree Michelia Champaca (*ćampaka*); N. of a mixed caste, the son of a Vaideha and a Māgadhī; (*am*), n. smallness, minuteness; N. of a Sūtra of the Sāma-veda; honey, a species of honey; water. — *Kshaudra-ja, am*, n. wax. — *Kshaudra-dhātu, us*, m. a kind of mineral substance; [cf. *mā-kshika*.] — *Kshaudra-priya, as*, m. N. of a tree; [cf. *jala-madhūka*.] — *Kshaudra-meha, as*, m. the disease diabetes mellitus. — *Kshaudramehin, ī, inī, i*, affected with this disease.

Kshaudreya, am, n. wax.

क्षौद्रक्य *kshaudrakya, as, ī*, m. f. (fr. *kshudraka*), a prince or princess of the Kshudrakas, a man belonging to the Kshudrakas; (*as, ī, am*), small, minute.

Kshaudrakamālavī, f., scil. *senā*, the army of Kshudraka and Mālava.

क्षौम *kshauma, as, ī, am* (fr. *kshumā*), made of linen, linen, covered with linen; prepared from linseed (as oil); (*am*), n. linen cloth or garment; linseed; (*ī*), f. lin or flax, Linum Usitatissimum; (*as, am*), m. n. wove silk; an airy room on the top of a house; an apartment on the roof; the back of an edifice; a fortified place in front of a building; a building of a particular form; [cf. *kshoma*.]

Kshaumaka, as, ī, am, linen; (*as*), m. a particular perfume; [cf. *ćora*.]

क्षौर *kshaura, am*, n. (fr. *kshura*), shaving the head, shaving in general; (*ī*), f. a razor. — *Kshaura-karaṇa, am*, n. the operation of shaving.

Kshauraparya, as, ā, am (fr. *kshura-pavi*), formed out of razors and thunderbolts, very sharp, very hard.

Kshaurika, as, m. a barber, a shaver.

क्ष्णु *kshṇu*, cl. 2. P. *kshṇauti, ćukshṇāva, kshṇavitum*, to whet, sharpen.

Kshṇut, t, t, t, (at the end of compounds) sharp (e. g. *ubhayataḥ-kshṇut*, sharp on both sides).

Kshṇuta, as, ā, am, whetted, sharpened.

Kshṇotra, am, n., Ved. a grind-stone, a whet-stone.

क्ष्मा *kshmā*, f. (fr. rt. *ksham*), the earth, (Ved. only inst. sing. *kshmayā*); [cf. *kshamā*.] *Kshmā-ja, as*, m. 'earth-born,' the planet Mars. — *Kshmā-tala, am*, n. the surface of the earth. — *Kshmā-dhṛiti, is*, m. one who has to support the earth, a king. — *Kshmā-pa, as*, m. earth-protector, a king. — *Kshmā-pati, is*, m. lord of the earth, a king. — *Kshmā-pāla, as*, m. earth-protector, a king. — *Kshmā-bhuj, k*, m. possessor of the earth, a king. — *Kshmā-bhṛit, t*, m. supporter of the earth; a mountain; a king. — *Kshmā-vṛisha, as*, m. 'earth-bull,' i. e. a mighty king.

क्ष्माय् *kshmāy*, cl. 1. Ā. *kshmāyate, ćakshmāye, kshmāyitum*, to shake, tremble: Caus. *kshmāpayati, -yitum, aćikshmapat*, to cause to shake, to make tremble: Desid. *ćikshmāyishate*: Intens. *ćākshmāyyate, ćākshmāti* (?).

Kshmāyita, as, ā, am, shaken, made to tremble, trembling.

Kshmāyitṛi, tā, trī, tṛi, trembling, shaking.

क्ष्मील् *kshmīl*, cl. 1. P. *kshmīlati, ćikshmīla, kshmīlitum*, to wink, to twinkle, to close the eyelids; [cf. *mīl*.]

क्ष्रौम् *kshraum*, ind. a mystical exclamation.

क्ष्विङ्का *kshviṅkā*, f., Ved. a kind of bird.

क्ष्विड् *kshviḍ* or *kshvid*, cl. 1. P. *kshveḍati* or *kshvedati, -ḍitum* or *-ditum*, to utter an inarticulate sound, to hum, murmur, growl, roar, hiss, whiz, whistle; A. *kshveḍate* or *kshvedate*, or cl. 4. P. *kshvidyati*, to be wet or unctuous; to exude, discharge juice, emit sap: Caus. *kshveḍayati* or *-dayati, -yitum*, to sound inarticulately, hum, &c.

Kshviṇṇa, as, ā, am, sounded inarticulately; soft, unctuous.

Kshveḍa, as, ā, am (in some senses perhaps connected with rt. *kshvel*), curved, crooked, bending, bent; wicked, depraved; difficult to be approached; (*as*), m. singing or buzzing in the ear from hardening of the wax &c.; sound, noise; venom, poison; a Cucurbitaceous plant, Luffa Pentandra or Acutangula, = *pītaghoshā*; a mystical N. of the letter *m*; (*am*), n. the flower of the Ghosha plant; the fruit of a red kind of swallow-wort; (*ā*), f. the roaring of a lion, a war-whoop, a battle-cry; a bamboo rod or stake; a kind of Cucurbitaceous plant.

Kshveḍana, am, n. murmuring, hissing, whistling, sibilating; a hissing pronunciation.

Kshveḍita, as, am, m. n. humming, murmuring, growling; a growl, roar; a battle-cry, a war-whoop.

Kshveḍin, ī, inī, i, humming, murmuring.

क्ष्वेल् *kshvel*, cl. 1. P. *kshvelati*, &c., to leap, jump; to play; to go, move; to shake, tremble; [cf. Old Germ. *suillu, sual, suall*.]

Kshvelikā, f. or *kshvelita, as, am*, m. n. or *kshvelya, am*, n. play, jest, joke, trick.

ख

ख 1. *kha*, the second consonant of the alphabet, being the aspirate of the preceding consonant, and having the sound of *kh* in *inkhorn*. — *Kha-kāra, as*, m. the letter or sound *kha*.

ख 2. *kha, as*, m. the sun.

ख 3. *kha, am*, n. (fr. rt. *khan*), a cavity, hollow, cave, cavern, aperture; an aperture of the human body (of which there are nine, as the mouth, the two ears, the two eyes, the two nostrils, and the organs of excretion and generation); the glottis (in anatomy); an organ of sense; the hole made by an arrow, a wound; the hole in the nave of a wheel through which the axis runs; vacuity, empty space, air, ether, sky, heaven; the character in arithmetic which expresses nothing, a cypher; a dot, Anusvāra, represented by a circle (*vindu*); a city, a field; happiness, pleasure, auspiciousness [cf. *sukha* and *duḥkha*); understanding, knowledge; action; the tenth from any given constellation or the sun's entrance into it; talc; Brahma, the supreme spirit; (*ā*), f. a fountain, a well; [cf. Gr. χάος; Lat. *halo*.] — *Kha-kāminī*, f. the female of the Falco Cheela (*ćilla*); an epithet of Durgā (*ćarćikā*). — *Kha-kuntala, as*, m. an epithet of Śiva. — *Kha-kholka, as*, m. 'sky-meteor,' an epithet of the sun. — *Khakholkāditya* (°*ka-ād*°), *as*, m. a form of the sun. — *Kha-ga, as, ā, am*, moving in the air; (*as*), m. a bird; air, wind; the sun; a planet; a grasshopper; a deity; an arrow. — *Kha-gaṅgā*, f. the Gaṅgā (Ganges) of the sky. — *Kha-gaṇa, as*, m., N. of a prince, a son of Vajra-nābha. — *Kha-gati, is*, f. flight in the air; N. of a metre, [cf. *aśva-gati*.] — *Khaga-pati, is*, m. the chief of the birds, an epithet of Garuḍa, the vehicle of Vishṇu. — *Kha-gama, as, ā, am*, moving in the air, flying, an epithet of the Gandharvas and of missile weapons; (*as*), m. a bird; N. of a Brāhman. — *Kha-garbha, as*, m., N. of a mythical person with Buddhists — *Khaga-vaktra, as*, m. the tree Artocarpus Lacucha (*lakuća*). — *Khaga-vatī*, f. the earth. — *Khaga-śatru, us*, f. a plant, commonly called Chakuliya, Hemionitis Cordifolia; [cf. *priśni-parṇī*.] — *Khaga-sthāna, am*, n. the hollow of a tree; a bird's nest. — *Khagādhipa* (°*ga-adh*°), *as*, m. the chief of the birds, an epithet of Garuḍa. — *Khagāntaka* (°*ga-an*°), *as*, m. a hawk, a falcon (a destroyer of birds). — *Kha-gābhirāma* (°*ga-abh*°), *as*, m. an epithet of Śiva. — *Khagāsana* (°*ga-ās*°), *as*, m. an epithet of the mountain Udaya, the eastern mountain, on which the sun rises; an epithet of Vishṇu ('sitting on a bird,' i. e. on Garuḍa). — *Kha-guṇa, as, ā, am*, (in arithmetic or algebra) having a cypher as multiplier. — *Khagendra* (°*ga-in*°), *as*, m. the chief of the birds, an epithet of Garuḍa; N. of a prince. — *Khagendra-dhvaja, as*, m. an epithet of Vishṇu. — *Khageśvara* (°*ga-īś*°), *as*, m. the chief of the birds, epithet of Garuḍa. — *Kha-gola, as*, m. the vault or circle of the heaven, the celestial sphere. — *Khagola-vidyā*, f. knowledge of the celestial sphere, astronomy. — *Kha-ćamasa, as*, m. the moon ('the drinking-vessel in the sky'). — *Kha-ćara, as, ī, am*, moving in the air, flying; (*as*), m. a bird; a cloud; the wind; the sun; a Rakshas or demon; an aerial spirit; N. of a people. — *Kha-ćārin, ī, iṇī, i*, moving in the air, flying, an epithet of Skanda. — *Kha-jala, am*, n. 'air-water,' i. e. dew, rain, frost, hoar-frost. — *Kha-jit, t*, m. a Buddha, one of the seven teachers or saints of the Buddha sect. — *Kha-jyotis, is*, m. a shining flying insect, a fire-fly, &c. — *Kha-tamāla, as*, m. a cloud; smoke. — *Kha-tilaka, as*, m. the sun. — *Kha-dūra-vāsinī*, f., N. of one of the female deities or Śaktis with Buddhists. — *Kha-dyota, as*, m. a shining flying insect, a fire-fly, the sun; (*ā*), f., scil. *dvār*, the door which shines like a shining insect, an eye. — *Kha-dyotaka, as* or *am*, m. or n. (?), a kind of plant with a poisonous fruit. — *Kha-dyotana, as*, m. the sun. — *Kha-dhūpa, as*, m. a rocket, fire-work. — *Kha-parāga, as*, m. darkness. — *Kha-pushpa, am*, n. a flower in the sky, a term for any-thing impossible. — *Kha-bha, as* or *am*, m. or n. (?), a planet. — *Kha-bhrānti, is*, f. a kind of falcon, a kite; [cf. *ćilla*.] — *Kha-maṇi, is*, m. the jewel of the sky, the sun. — *Kha-milana, am*, n. sleepiness, lassitude, weariness. — *Kha-mūrti, is*, f. a celestial appearance or person. — *Khamūrti-mat, ān, atī, at*, having a divine or celestial person or form. — *Kha-mūli, is, ikā* or *ī*, f. an aquatic plant, Pistia Stratiotes (*kumbhikā*). — *Kha-valli*, f., N. of a parasitic plant, = *ākāśa-vallī*. — *Kha-vāri, i*, n. rain-water, dew, vapour, &c. — *Kha-vāshpa, as*, m. snow, hoar-frost, dew. — *Kha-śaya, as, ā, am*, resting or dwelling in the air. — *Kha-śarīra, am*, n. a celestial or immortal body. — *Khaśarīrin, ī, iṇī, i*, gifted with an etherial body, having a heavenly form. — *Kha-śvāsa, as*, m. wind, air. — *Kha-sama, as*, m. a Buddha or deified Bauddha saint. — *Kha-samuttha, as, ā, am*, produced in the sky. — *Kha-sambhava, as, ā, am*, produced in the sky, aerial, etherial; (*ā*), f. spikenard, = *ākāśa-māṅsī*. — *Kha-sarpaṇa, as*, m., N. of a Buddha or Bauddha saint; (*am*), n. gliding through the air. — *Kha-sindhu, us*, m. the moon. — *Kha-stanī*, f. the earth. — *Kha-sphaṭika, am*, n. aerial crystal, a N. for the sun and moon-gem, *sūrya-kānta* and *ćandra-kānta*; [cf. *ākāśa-sphaṭika*.] — *Kha-hara, as, ā, am*, (in arithmetic) having a cypher for its denominator (as a fraction). — *Khātman* (*kha-āt°*), *ā, ā, a*, having the air as one's nature. — *Khā-pagā* (*kha-āp°*), f. a stream in the air, an epithet of the Ganges. — *Khe-gamana, as*, m. a kind of galli-nule, = *kāla-kaṇṭha*. — *Khe-ćara, as, ī, am*, moving in the air, flying, aerial; (*as*), m. a bird; a Gan-dharva; a Rakshas; a Vidyādhara; an epithet of S'iva; a planet; quicksilver; (*ī*), f. a semi-divine female able to fly; an epithet of Durgā; (*am*), n. green vitriol. — *Khećara-tva, am*, n. capability of flying. — *Khe 'ṭa* (*khe-aṭa*), *as*, m. a planet; the ascend-ing node or Rāhu. — *Khe-paribhrama, as, ā, am*, flying about in the air. — *Khe-śaya, as, ā, am*, lying in the air. — *Kholka* (*kha-ulkā*), *as*, m. a meteor; a planet; [cf. *kha-kholka*.] — *Kholmuka* (*kha-ul°*), *as*, m. the planet Mars; [cf. *gaganol-muka*.]

खक्ख् *khakkh*, cl. 1. P. *khakkhati*, to laugh, to laugh at or deride; (also read *kakh*, q. v.); [cf. Goth. *hlaha*.]

खक्खट *khakkhaṭa, as, ā, am*, hard, solid; (also *kakkhaṭa*.)

खक्खर *khakkhara, as* or *am*, m. or n. (?), a beggar's staff; [cf. *hikkala*.]

खग *kha-ga*. See under 3. *kha*.

खगोड *khagoḍa, as*, m. Saccharum Spon-taneum, a kind of reed (for *khaggaḍa*?).

खग्गड *khaggaḍa, as*, m. a kind of reed, Saccharum Spontaneum, commonly *khāgḍā*.

खङ्कर *khaṅkara* or *khaṅkhara, as*, m. a curl, a lock of hair.

खङ्ख *khaṅkha, as*, m., N. of a minister of king Bālāditya.

खङ्खणा *khaṅkhaṇā* (an onomatopoetic word), the tinkling sound of a bell &c.

खङ्ग *khaṅga, as*, m. (for *khaḍga*?), Ved. a kind of animal.

खच् *khać*, cl. 1. 9. P. *khaćati* and *khać-nāti, ćakhāća, khaćitum*, to come forth, appear; to be born again; to cause prosperity; to purify; cl. 10. P. *khaćayati, -yitum*, to fasten, bind, set.

Khaćita, as, ā, am, fastened, joined; mixed, blended, combined; inlaid, set, studded, (used in comp., e. g. *maṇi-khaćita*, inlaid with jewels.)

खज् *khaj*, cl. 1. P. *khajati, ćakhāja, kha-jitum*, to churn or agitate.

Khaja, as, m. stirring, agitating, churning; contest, war (?); a churning-stick; a ladle, a spoon; (*ā*), f. a churning-stick, a ladle; the hand with the fingers extended; churning, stirring; killing, destroying. — *Khaja-kṛit, t, t, t*, or *khajan-kara, as, ī, am*, Ved. causing the tumult or din of battle.

Khajaka, as, m. a churning-stick; (*ikā*), f. a ladle or spoon.

Khajapa, am, n. ghee or clarified butter.

Khajāka, as, m. a bird; (*ā*), f. a ladle or spoon.

खञ्ज् 1. *khañj*, cl. 1. P. *khañjati, ća-khañja, khañjitum*, to limp, halt, walk lame; [cf. Gr. σκάζω; Germ. *hinke*.]

2. *khañj, khan, n, n*, probably = *khañja*, limping.

Khañja, as, ā, am, limping, lame, crippled; (*ā*), f. a metre consisting of 2 x 28 short syllables and 1 long and 30 short syllables and 1 long; another metre containing 30 short syllables + 1 long and 28 short syllables + 1 long; another metre containing 2 x 36 short syllables and 1 Amphimacer. — *Khañja-kheṭa* or *khañja-khela, as*, m. the wagtail. — *Khañ-ja-tā*, f. or *khañja-tva, am*, n. limping, lameness. — *Khañja-bāhu, us*, m., N. of a Daitya.

Khañjaka, as, ā, am, limping, lame.

Khañjana, as, m. a species of wagtail, Monta-cilla Alba; (*ā*), f. a kind of wagtail; mustard; (*am*), n. moving, going, going lamely. — *Khañjana-rata, am*, n. the secret pleasures of the Yatis, the cohabitation of saints. — *Khañjanākṛiti* (°*na-āk*°), *is*, f. a sort of wagtail.

Khañjanaka, as, m. a wagtail, Montacilla Alba; (*ikā*), f. a species of wagtail.

Khañjarīṭa or *khañjarīṭaka* or *khañjalekha, as*, m. the wagtail.

खञ्जार *khañjāra* and *khoñjāla, as*, m., N. of two persons.

खट् *khaṭ*, cl. 1. P. *khaṭati*, &c., to desire, wish, seek or inquire.

Khaṭa, as, m. (fr. rt. *khaṭ* above?), phlegm, the phlegmatic or watery humor [cf. *kapha*]; a blind well; an axe, a hatchet [cf. *ṭaṅka*]; a plough; a kind of blow or wound; the closed or doubled fist (as for striking &c.); grass; a coarse long grass of several species used to thatch houses [cf. *kaṭa* and *khaḍa*]; a fragrant kind of grass. — *Khaṭa-kaṭāhaka, as* or *am*, m. or n. (?), a spitting-box. — *Khaṭa-khādaka, as*, m. (?), an eater; a glass vessel; a jackal; an animal; a crow.

Khaṭaka, as, m. a go-between, a man whose business is to negociate marriages [cf. *ghaṭaka*]; the half-closed hand; the doubled fist of wrestlers or boxers. — *Khaṭakā-mukha, as* or *am*, m. or n. (?), a particular position of the hand in shooting; (*as*), m. a man in the attitude of shooting.

Khaṭikā, as, m. the hand half-closed, the fist; (*ā*), f. chalk [cf. *kakkhaṭī, kaṭhinī*, &c.]; the ex-ternal opening of the ear; the plant Andropogon Muricatus.

खटक्किका *khaṭakkikā*, f. a side door; [cf. *khaḍakkikā*.]

खटखटाय *khaṭakhaṭāya* (an onomatopoetic word), A. *-ṭāyate, -yitum*, to spring or issue forth with a noise.

खटिनी *khaṭinī* or *khaṭī*, f. chalk; (some books read *khaṭhinī*); [cf. *kaṭhinī, khaṭikā*.]

खटू *khaṭū* (?), an ornament worn on the wrist or ancle.

खट्ट् *khaṭṭ*, cl. 10. P. *khaṭṭayati, -yitum*, to cover, to screen.

खट्टन *khaṭṭana, as*, m. a dwarf [cf. *khaṭṭe-raka*]; (*as, ā, am*), dwarfish, short of stature.

खट्टा *khaṭṭā*, f. a bedstead; a kind of grass, Andropogon Serratus; (a wrong reading for *khaṭvā*.)

खट्टाश *khaṭṭāśa, as*, m. the civet or zebet cat, Viverra Zibetha; (*ī*), f. the same or (according to another authority) a different animal; (some write the word *khaṭṭāsa*.)

खट्टि *khaṭṭi, is, ī*, m. f. a bier, the bed on which the corpse is carried to the pile.

खट्टिक *khaṭṭika, as*, m. a butcher, a hunter, a fowler, one who lives by killing and selling game; the cream on the milk of a buffalo-cow; (*ā*), f. a small bedstead, a cot; a bier or bed on which the corpse is carried.

खट्टेरक *khaṭṭeraka, as, ā, am*, dwarfish, dwarf; [cf. *khaṭṭana*.]

खट्वा *khaṭvā*, f. (said to be fr. rt. *khaṭ*), a bedstead, a couch, a cot; a swing, a hammock; a kind of bandage; N. of a plant, = *kolaśimbī*. — *Kha-ṭvāṅga* (°*vā-aṅ*°), *as*, m. a club shaped like the foot of a bedstead,' i. e. a club or staff with a skull at the top considered as the weapon of S'iva and carried by ascetics and Yogis; wood from a funeral pile; N. of a king of the solar line, = Dilīpa; (*ī*), f., N. of a river. — *Khaṭvāṅga-dhāra, as*, m. or *khaṭvāṅga-bhṛit, t*, m. 'staff-bearer,' an epithet of S'iva. — *Khaṭvāṅga-vana, am*, n., N. of a forest. — *Kha-ṭvāṅgin, ī, inī, i*, having the staff described above; (*ī*), m. an epithet of S'iva. — *Khaṭvāpluta* (°*vā-āp*°) or *khaṭvārūḍha* (°*vā-ār*°), *as, ā, am*, mounted on a bed, lying on a bed: low, vile, abandoned, iniquitous; erring, going wrong; silly, stupid.

Khaṭvikā, f. a small bedstead.

खड् *khaḍ*, cl. 10. P. *khāḍayati, -yitum*, to divide, tear, break, break off a part or piece; [cf. *khaṇḍ*.]

Khaḍa, as, m. breaking, dividing; buttermilk boiled with acid vegetables and spices; (*as, am*), m. n. a kind of small grass, straw; (*as*), m., N. of a man. — *Khaḍonmattā* (°*ḍa-un*°), f., N. of a woman.

खडक्किका *khaḍakkikā*, f. a private or back door, a small or venetian door or window.

खडतू *khaḍatū, ūs*, m. a kind of ornament.

खडिका *khaḍikā* or *khaḍī*, f. chalk.

खडु *khaḍu, us*, or *khaḍū, ūs*, m. or f. a bier.

खड्ग *khaḍga, as*, m. (said to be fr. rt. *khaḍ* for *khaṇḍ*), a sword, a scymitar; a large sacrificial knife; the horn of a rhinoceros; a rhinoceros; one of the Buddhas or Buddhist saints, a Pratyeka-buddha, so called because he walks alone like a rhinoceros [cf. *eka-ćara* and *eka-ćārin*]; (*am*), n. iron. — *Khaḍga-kośa, as*, m. the sheath of a sword, a scabbard; a creeping plant, Scirpus Maximus. — *Khaḍga-ćarma-dhara, as*, m. a soldier armed with a sword and shield. — *Khaḍga-dṛih, -dhṛik, k, k*, grasping a scymitar. — *Khaḍga-dhara, as*, m. a swordsman. — *Khaḍga-dhenu, us*, f. a female rhinoceros; a small knife or sword, = *asi-dhenu*. — *Khaḍga-pattra, as*, m. a kind of creeper, Scirpus Maximus; N. of a mythical tree in hell bearing swords for leaves; (*am*), n. the blade of a sword. — *Khaḍga-pāṇi, is, is, i*, sword in hand. — *Khaḍga-pātra, am*, n. a vessel formed of buffalo's horns, a large salver or charger on which the sacrificial knife is laid. — *Khaḍga-pidhāna* or *khaḍga-pidhānaka, am*, n. a scabbard, the sheath of a sword. — *Khaḍga-putrikā*, f. a small sword, a knife. — *Khaḍga-prahāra, as*, m. a sword-cut. — *Khaḍga-phala, am*, n. a sword-blade. — *Khaḍga-māṅsa, as*, m. buffalo-beef. — *Khaḍga-lekhā*, f. a row of swords. — *Khaḍga-vat, ān, atī, at*, armed with a sword. — *Khaḍgāghāta* (°*ga-āgh*°), *as*, m. a sword-cut. — *Khaḍgādhāra* (°*ga-ādh*°), *as*, m. a sheath, a scabbard. — *Khaḍgābhihata* (°*ga-abh*°), *as, ā, am*, cut or struck with a sword. — *Khaḍgā-*

misha (°ga-ām°), am, n. buffalo's flesh. — Khaḍgāhva (°ga-āh°), as, m. a rhinoceros.

Khaḍgaṭa, as, m. a large kind of reed, Saccharum Spontaneum; [cf. bṛihat-kāśa.]

Khaḍgārīṭa or khaḍgārāṭa (?), as, m. a shield or the blade of a sword (?); one who observes a particular religious penance peculiar to Buddhists, viz. rubbing the feet backwards and forwards on the edge of a sword made red hot; [cf. asi-dhārā.]

Khaḍgika, as, m. a swordsman; a butcher, a vender of flesh meat; the cream of buffalo's milk; [cf. khaṭṭika.]

Khaḍgin, ī, inī, i, armed with a sword, a swordsman; (ī), m. a rhinoceros; N. of a Jina or Jaina saint. — Khaḍgi-māra, as, m. a kind of creeper, Scirpus Maximus, = khaḍga-kośa.

Khaḍgīka, am, n. a sickle, a small scythe.

खणखणाय khaṇakhaṇāya (an onomatopoetic word), A. khaṇakhaṇāyate, -yitum, to utter or give out any peculiar sound; to tick, tinkle, crack, &c.

Khaṇakhaṇāyamāna, as, ā, am, tinkling, &c.

खण्ड् khaṇḍ, cl. 1. A., 10. P. khaṇḍate, -ḍitum, khaṇḍayati, -yitum, to break, tear, break in pieces, crush, cut, divide; destroy, annihilate, defeat, conquer; disappoint, frustrate, interrupt, disturb, deceive, cheat.

Khaṇḍa, as, ā, am, broken, torn asunder, divided, having chasms, gaps, or breaks; deficient, defective, crippled; (as, am), m. n. a break, a gap, a chasm, a fissure, a fracture (e. g. kedāra-khaṇḍa, a gap or fracture in the embankment of a field); a piece, part, fragment, portion; a section of a work, part, chapter; a party, number, multitude, assemblage; a term in an equation; (as), m. treacle or molasses partially dried, candied sugar; a flaw in a jewel; N. of a people; (am), n. a kind of salt (viḍ-lavaṇa), black salt; a sort of sugar-cane; [cf. uttara-khaṇḍa, karka°, kāla°, kāśī°.] — Khaṇḍa-kaṭaka, as or am, m. or n. (?), title of an astronomical work composed by Brahma-gupta. — Khaṇḍa-kathā, f. a fragmentary tale; a tale or story divided into sections (?). — Khaṇḍa-karṇa, as, m. a kind of bulbous plant; sweet potato. — Khaṇḍa-kārya, am, n. a fragmentary poem; a poem interspersed with prose (?). — Khaṇḍa-giri, is, m., N. of a mountain. — Khaṇḍa-ja, as, m. a kind of sugar, treacle, molasses, = guḍa, yavāsa-śarkarā. — Khaṇḍajodbhavaja (°ja-ud°), as, m. a kind of candied sugar prepared from Khaṇḍaja. — Khaṇḍa-tā, f. the being divided, division. — Khaṇḍa-deva, as, m., N. of the author of a commentary on Jaimini's Nyāya-sūtras, called Bhāṭṭadīpikā; also of the Mīmāṃsā-Kaustubha. — Khaṇḍa-dravya, as, m., N. of a man. — Khaṇḍa-dhārā, f. shears, scissors; a kind of dance or air (?). — Khaṇḍa-pattra, am, n. a bundle of various leaves. — Khaṇḍa-paraśu, us, m. an epithet of Śiva as cutting his foes to pieces with his axe. — Khaṇḍa-parśu, us, m. a N. of Śiva; of Paraśu-rāma; of Rāhu; an elephant with a broken tusk; a spreader of unguents or fragrant powders &c.; a drug, commonly called Khaṇḍāmalaki (see khaṇḍāmalaka). — Khaṇḍa-pāṇi, is, m., N. of a prince. — Khaṇḍa-pāla, as, m. a confectioner, seller of sweetmeats (for khaṇḍa-pāna ?). — Khaṇḍa-pralaya, as, m. a partial destruction of the universe in which all the spheres beneath Svarga or heaven are dissolved in one common ruin; a quarrel; the dissolution of the bands of friendship or of society; (in the latter sense more correctly khaṇḍa-praṇaya.) — Khaṇḍa-praśasti, is, f., N. of a poem attributed to Hanumat; an older N. for the play Hanuman-nāṭaka. — Khaṇḍa-phaṇa, as, m. a kind of serpent. — Khaṇḍa-maṇḍala, am, n. a segment of a circle, part of a circle, an incomplete sphere; (as, ā, am), gibbous, not full or round — Khaṇḍa-maya, as, ī, am, consisting of pieces. — Khaṇḍa-modaka, as, m. a kind of sugar, granulated or candied (yavāsa-śarkarā). — Khaṇḍa-lavaṇa, am, n. a kind of salt (viḍ-lavaṇa), black salt. — Khaṇḍa-śarkarā, f. candied sugar or sugar in pieces. — Khaṇḍa-śas, ind. in pieces, by pieces, bit by bit, piece by piece, piece-meal; khaṇḍaśaḥ kṛi, to divide or cut into pieces; khaṇḍaśo bhū, to be divided, to be separated into pieces. — Khaṇḍa-śākhā, f., N. of a plant, = mahisha-vallī. — Khaṇḍa-śīlā, f. a loose woman, an unchaste wife. — Khaṇḍa-sara, as, m. a kind of sugar (yavāsa-śarkarā), candied sugar. — Khaṇḍābhra (°ḍa-abh°), am, n. scattered clouds; a bite, the impression of the teeth in amorous sport. — Khaṇḍāmalaka (°ḍa-ām°), am, n. myrobalan cut up into small pieces (to be used as a medicine). — Khaṇḍālī (°ḍa-ālī), f. a measure for oil; a pond; a woman whose husband has been guilty of infidelity.

Khaṇḍaka, as, ā, am, breaking to pieces, destroying, removing, rendering ineffectual; (as, am), m. n. a fragment, a part, a piece; (as), m. treacle or molasses partially dried, candied sugar; one who has no nails; pared or clipped finger-nails (?); N. of a metre, = āryā-gīti; a kind of dance or tune (?); [cf. khaṇḍa-dhārā.] — Khaṇḍakālu or khaṇḍakāluka (°ka-ālu), am, n. an esculent root, sweet potato.

Khaṇḍana, as, ā, am, breaking, dividing, cutting, reducing to pieces, destroying, annihilating, removing; (am), n. the act of breaking or cutting or dividing, hurting, injuring, injury; interrupting, disappointing, frustrating; cheating, deceiving; refuting (in argument); rebellion, opposition; discarding, dismissal. — Khaṇḍana-kāra, as, m. an epithet of Harsha. — Khaṇḍana-kṛit, t, m., N. of an author. — Khaṇḍana-khaṇḍakādya (°ka-ād°), am, n. title of a work on logic by Harsha. — Khaṇḍana-rata, as, ā, am, skilful in cutting or destroying, destructive.

Khaṇḍanīya or khaṇḍitavya, as, ā, am, to be broken or divided, frangible, fragile, brittle; destructible, refutable, &c.

Khaṇḍala or khaṇḍava, as, am, m. n. a piece, a part.

Khaṇḍika, as, m. a sugar-boiler, a sugar-baker (?); pease; the armpit; N. of a man; (ā), f. the pod of pease; a kind of air or tune in music.

Khaṇḍita, as, ā, am, cut, torn, broken in pieces, scattered, dispersed, destroyed; broken as allegiance, disobeyed against, rebelled; refuted, controverted; disappointed, betrayed, abandoned as a lover; (ā), f. a woman whose husband or lover has been guilty of infidelity. — Khaṇḍita-vigraha, as, ā, am, maimed, mutilated. — Khaṇḍita-vṛitta, as, ā, am, one whose manner of life is dissolute, an immoral man. — Khaṇḍitāśaṃsa (°ta-āś°), as, ā, am, disappointed, foiled, frustrated.

Khaṇḍin, ī, inī, i, consisting of pieces, in pieces or parts; divided, comminuted; (ī), m. a wild kind of kidney-bean, = Vana-mudga; a N. of Harsha; (inī), f. the earth.

Khaṇḍī-kṛi, cl. 8. P. A. -karoti, -kurute, -kartum, to divide or break into small pieces, to cut up, tear to pieces &c.

Khaṇḍīra, as, m. a kind of kidney-bean, Pīta-mudga.

Khaṇḍu = khaṇḍa, a kind of sugar (?).

Khaṇḍerāya, as, m., N. of an author.

Khaṇḍya, as, ā, am, to be broken or divided, fragile, destructible, &c.

खण्वखा khaṇvakhā, f. (an onomatopoetic word), Ved., N. of a frog.

खतमाल kha-tamāla, &c. See under 3. kha.

खत्त khatta, as, m., N. of an astronomer.

खद् khad, cl. 1. P. khadati, ćakhāda, akhadīt and akhādīt, &c., to be steady or firm, to strike, hurt, kill; to eat (?); [cf. Lat. clades.]

Khadira, as, m. the tree Acacia Catechu, having very hard wood, the resin of which is used in medicine, called Catechu, Khayar, Terra Japonica; an epithet of Indra; the moon; N. of a man; (ī), f. a sensitive plant, Mimosa Pudica; (sometimes also khadirā.) — Khadira-kuṇa, as, m. the fruit time of the Khadira tree. — Khadira-pattrikā or khadira-pattrī, f. a sensitive plant, a kind of Mimosa (khadirī). — Khadira-maya, as, ī, am, made of the wood of Khadira. — Khadira-vana, am, n. a Khadira forest. — Khadira-vaṇika, as, m., N. of a Buddhist Bhikshu. — Khadira-vat, ān, atī, at, overgrown with Khadira; (tī), f., N. of a region. — Khadira-varman, ā, m., N. of a king. — Khadira-svāmin, ī, m., N. of a scholiast. — Khadiropama (°ra-up°), am, n. a kind of Mimosa (kadara).

Khadiraka, as, m., N. of a mountain.

खदिका khadikā, ās, f. pl. fried or parched grain.

खदूरक khadūraka, as, m., N. of a man; (am), n. a dwarf.

खदूरवासिनी kha-dūra-vāsinī, &c. See under 3. kha.

खन् khan, cl. 1. P. A. khanati, -te, ćakhāna, ćakhne, khanishyati, -te, akhānīt and akhanīt, akhanishṭa, khanitum, to dig, dig up, delve, to turn up the soil, excavate, root up; to dig into the earth, bury: Caus. khānayati, -yitum, to cause to dig or dig up: Desid. ćikhanishati, -te: Intens. ćaṅkhanyate, ćākhāyate, ćaṅkhanti; [cf. Gr. χαίνω, χαυῶ; Old Germ. ginêm, ginôm; Mod. Germ. gähne; Angl. Sax. cina, cinan; Lat. cuniculus, canalis.]

Khana, as, ā, am, Ved. digging; rooting up.

Khanaka, as, ī, am, digging, digging up, dividing; a digger, excavator; (as), m. a miner; a house-breaker, a thief; a rat; N. of a friend of Vidura.

Khanat, an, antī, at, digging, digging up, excavating.

Khanana, am, n. the act of digging, excavating; digging into the earth, burying.

Khananīya, as, ā, am, to be digged, to be excavated.

Khani, is, is, i, Ved. digging or rooting up; (is or ī), f. a mine, especially of precious stones; a quarry, a cave. — Khani-netra or khanī-netra, as, m., N. of a prince with the epithet Karandhama.

Khanitṛi, tā, trī, tṛi, a digger, delver, excavator, ditcher.

Khanitra, am, n. an instrument for digging, a spade, shovel, hoe, pickaxe; (as), m., N. of a prince.

Khanitraka, am, n. or khanitrikā, f. a small shovel or scoop.

Khanitrima, as, ā, am, Ved. produced by digging.

Khanitvā, ind. having dug.

Khanya, as, ā, am, Ved. to be digged or excavated.

Khāta, as, ā, am, dug, dug up, excavated; torn, rent; (am), n. digging a hole; an excavation; a ditch, fosse, moat, well; a cavern; a square or oblong pond; (ā), f. an artificial pond; [cf. devakhāta, &c.] — Khāta-bhū, ūs, f. a moat, ditch. — Khāta-rūpa-kāra, as, m. a potter.

Khātaka, as, m. a digger, delver; a debtor [cf. khādaka]; (ikā), f. a ditch; (am), n. a moat, ditch.

Khāti, is, f. digging, excavating.

Khātra, am, n. a spade, shovel, hoe; a moat, a square or oblong pond; a wood; a thread; horror.

Khāna, as, m. digging. — Khānoduka (°na-ud°), as, m. the cocoa-nut tree.

Khānaka, as, ikā, am, one who digs, a digger.

Khāni, is, ī, f. a mine.

Khānika, am, n. an opening or hole in a wall, a breach.

Khānila, as, ā, am, a house-breaker; (sometimes read khānina.)

Khānya, as, ā, am, to be digged.

Kheya, as, ā, am, to be dug, to be excavated; (am), n. a ditch, a moat.

खनपान khanapāna, as, m., N. of a prince, a son of Aṅga and father of Divi-ratha.

खपराग kha-parāga. See under 3. kha.

खपुर *kha-pura, as,* m. (fr. 3. *kha* and *pura?*), flatulence; the betel-nut tree, Areca Faufel or Catechu; the tree Cyperus Pertenuis (*bhadra-mustaka*); a kind of perfume, = *vyāla-nakha;* (*am*), n. a city in the sky, epithet of Hiraṇya-pura, the city of the Kālakeyas; also N. of the city of Hariśćandra; a water-jar.

खपुष्प *kha-pushpa,* &c. See under 3. *kha.*

खम्ब् *khamb,* cl. 1. P. *khambati, -bitum,* to go or move.

खर *khara, as, ā, am,* hard, harsh, rough; sharp, pungent, acid (opposed to *mṛidu* and *ślakshṇa*); solid (opposed to *drava,* fluid); dense (as clouds); sharp, hot (as wind); hurtful, injurious; cutting (as a speech or word); sharp-edged; cruel; (*as*), m. a donkey, an ass, a mule; N. of several birds; an osprey, a heron, a crow; a thorny plant, a sort of prickly nightshade; a quadrangular mound of earth for receiving the sacrificial vessels; a Daitya or demon in general; epithet of the Asura Dhenuka; N. of a Rakshas slain by Rāma, a younger brother of Rāvaṇa; N. of an attendant of the Sun (= Dharma); N. of an attendant of Śiva; N. of a Rudra; (*ā*), f. a kind of grass, Andropogon Serratus; (*ī*), f. a she-ass. — *Khara-kāshṭhikā,* f. the plant Sida Cordifolia (*balā*). — *Khara-kuṭī,* f. a stable for asses, a donkey-stall (used as an abusive epithet); a barber's shop. — *Khara-ketu, us,* m., N. of a Rakshas. — *Khara-koṇa* or *khara-kvāṇa, as,* m. the francoline partridge. — *Khara-komala, as,* m. the month Jyeshṭha ('bracing yet mild'). — *Khara-gandha-nibhā* or *khara-gandhā,* f. the plant Hedysarum Lagopodioides, = *nāga-balā.* — *Khara-griha* or *khara-geha, am,* n. or *khara-graha, as,* m. a stable for asses. — *Khara-ghātana, as,* m. the tree Mesua Ferrea, commonly Nageśar. — *Khara-ććhada, as,* m., N. of several plants, a kind of reed or grass, Saccharum Cylindricum; another kind, commonly Okera; [cf. *ulūka, itkaṭa, kundara.*] — *Khara-jru, us, us, u,* Ved. sharp or quick in motion. — *Khara-ṇas, ās, ās, as,* or *khara-ṇasa, as, ā, am,* sharp-nosed; (*as*), m., N. of a man. — *Khara-tara, as, ā, am,* more sharp, very sharp. — *Khara-tvać, k,* f., N. of a plant, = *alambushā.* — *Khara-daṇḍa, am,* n. a lotus, Nymphæa Lotus. — *Khara-dalā,* f. opposite-leaved fig tree, Ficus Oppositifolia; [cf. *udumbara.*] — *Khara-dūshaṇa, as,* m. the thorn-apple, Datura Metel. — *Khara-dhāra, as, ā, am,* having a harsh edge or one full of notches like that of a saw. — *Khara-dhvansin, ī,* m. destroyer of the demon Khara, an epithet of Rāma. — *Khara-nakhara, as,* m., N. of a lion. — *Khara-narāya, as,* m., N. of a son of Śatānanda. — *Khara-nāda, as,* m. the braying of an ass. — *Khara-nādin, ī, inī, i,* braying like an ass; (*ī*), m., N. of a man; also of a Ṛishi; (*inī*), f. a kind of perfume, = *reṇukā* ('causing a donkey to bray?'). — *Khara-nāla, am,* n. a lotus. — *Khara-pa, as,* m., N. of a man; (*ās*), m. pl. the descendants of this man. — *Khara-pattra, as,* m., N. of several plants, a kind of Ocimum (*tulasī*) and Tectona Grandis; a kind of cane; also = *haridgarbha* and *maruvaka* (a kind of Ocimum); (*ī*), f., N. of two plants, Elephantopus Scaber (*gojihvā*) and Ficus Oppositifolia (*kākodumbarikā*). — *Khara-pattraka, as,* m., N. of a plant, = *tilaka.* — *Khara-pātra, am,* n. an iron pot or vessel. — *Khara-pādāḍhya* (°*da-āḍh°*), *as,* m. the elephant or wood-apple, Feronia Elephantum; [cf. *kapittha.*] — *Khara-pāla, as,* m. a wooden vessel; [cf. *khara-pātra.*] — *Khara-pushpa, as,* m. a plant, commonly Marūa, a kind of Ocimum, see *maruvaka;* (*ā* or *ikā*), f. a kind of Tulasi, Ocimum Gratissimum; also Varvara. — *Khara-priya, as,* m. a pigeon. — *Khara-majra, as, ā, am,* Ved. one whose strength is very intense. — *Khara-mañjari, is* or *ī,* f. the plant Achyranthes Aspera; [cf. *apāmārga.*] — *Khara-yāna, am,* n. a donkey-cart, any vehicle drawn by asses. — *Khara-raśmi, is,* m. the sun. — *Khara-roman* or *khara-loman, ā,* m., N. of one of the chiefs of the Nāga or serpent-race inhabiting hell. — *Khara-vallikā,* f., N. of a plant, commonly Goraksha Chākuliya, Hedysarum Lagopodioides; [cf. *nāga-balā.*] — *Khara-śabda, as,* m. an osprey; the braying of an ass. — *Khara-śāka, as,* m. the plant Clerodendrum Siphonanthus, = *bhārgī.* — *Khara-śāla, as, ā, am,* born or produced in a donkey-stall; (*ā*), f. a donkey-stable or stall. — *Khara-soṇi, is,* m. or *khara-sonda, as,* m. or *khara-solla, as,* m. an iron vessel. — *Khara-skandha, as,* m., N. of a tree, = *priyāla;* (*ā*), f. Phœnix Sylvestris, = *kharjūrī.* — *Khara-svarā,* f. wild jasmine, = *vana-mallikā.* — *Kharānśu* (°*ra-an°*), *us,* m. the sun. — *Khārā-garī,* f. a kind of grass, Andropogon Serratus. — *Kharāṇḍaka* (°*ra-aṇ°*), *as,* m., N. of one of Śiva's attendants. — *Kharābdānkuraka* (°*ra-abda-an°*), *am,* n. lapis lazuli. — *Kharāśvā* (°*ra-aś°?*), f. the plant Colosia Cristata, commonly *vanayamānī,* = *aja-gandhā, aja-modā, karavī.* — *Kharāhvā* (°*ra-āh°*), f., N. of a plant, = *aja-modā.* — *Kharin-dhama* or *kharin-dhaya, as, ā, am* (*kharin* = *kharīm* for *kharīm*), drinking ass's milk. — *Kharī-jangha, as,* m., N. of a man; (*ās*), m. pl. the descendants of this man. — *Kharī-vṛisha, as,* m. a jackass.

Kharikā, f. powdered musk.

खरटखरटाकृ *kharaṭa-kharaṭā-kṛi,* cl. 8. P. *-karoti, -kartum,* to make the sound *kharaṭa.*

खरालिक *kharālika, as,* m. a barber (*grāmaṇī*); a razor-case; an iron arrow (in this sense also *kharālaka*); a pillow.

खरु *kharu, us, us* or *ūs, u* (said to be fr. rt. *khan*), white; foolish, idiotic, a fool; harsh, cruel; desirous of improper or prohibited things; (*us*), m. a tooth; a horse; pride; love or Kāma, the deity of love; an epithet of Śiva; (*us*), f. a girl who chooses her own husband.

खरोस्ति *kharosti, is,* m. f. (?), N. of a place; (a various reading has *kharoshṭī.*)

खर्खोद *kharkhoda, as* or *am,* m. or n. (?), a kind of magic. — *Kharkhoda-vedin, ī, inī, i,* skilled in the Kharkhoda art, a conjurer (?).

खर्ज् *kharj,* cl. 1. P. *kharjati, ćakharja, kharjitum,* to creak (like a carriage-wheel); to worship, to treat with respect or courtesy; to pain, make uneasy; to cleanse, make clean; [cf. Hib. *cairtim* or *cartaim,* 'to cleanse.']

Khargalā, f., Ved. an owl or any similar night-bird.

Kharjikā, f. a relish, anything to provoke drinking; [cf. *kharju* and *kharjūra.*]

Kharju, us or *ūs,* f. scratching, itching, itch, scab, cutaneous eruption; a worm, a kind of insect; the wild datura tree. — *Kharjū-ghna, as,* m., N. of several plants, the thorn-apple; Calotropis Gigantea, Cassia Alata or Tora, = *ćakra-marda.*

Kharjura, am, n. silver; [cf. *kharjūra.*] — *Kharjura-karṇa, as,* m., N. of a man.

Kharjūra, as, m. the tree Phœnix Sylvestris, the date tree; a scorpion; N. of a man; (*ī*), f. the tree Phœnix Sylvestris; the wild date tree; (*am*), n. the fruit of the tree Phœnix Sylvestris; silver; yellow orpiment; (also *khala.*) — *Kharjūra-rasa, as,* m. the juice or extract of the wild date or Tāḍi, used to leaven bread, and as an intoxicating liquor.

Kharjūraka, as, m. a scorpion.

खर्द् *khard,* cl. 1. P. *khardati,* &c., to bite, to sting, to sting venomously.

खर्पर *kharpara, as,* m. a thief; a rogue, a cheat; the skull; the half of a skull; a beggar's bowl or dish; an umbrella or parasol; (*ī, am*), f. n. a kind of collyrium or application to the eyes. See *karpara.*

Kharparikā, f. or *kharparītuttha, am,* n. or *kharparīrasaka, am,* n. a kind of collyrium.

खर्पराल *kharparāla, as,* m., N. of a plant. See *kandarāla.*

खर्ब् *kharb,* cl. 1. P. *kharbati,* &c., to go, move; to go towards; [cf. Old Germ. *hwarb, hwarp, hwirbu,* &c.; Goth. *bi-hvairba,* 'to go round.']

खर्म *kharma, am,* n. virility, manliness; wove silk.

खर्व् *kharv,* cl. 1. P. *kharvati,* &c., to be proud or haughty; [cf. *garv.*]

खर्व *kharva* or *kharba, as, ā, am* (fr. rt. *kharb?*), mutilated, maimed, crippled, injured, imperfect; pressed down, low, dwarfish, short, little in size or stature; (*as*), m., N. of one of the nine Nidhis or treasures of Kuvera; the plant Trapa Bispinosa [cf. *kubjaka*]; (*as, am*), m. n. a large number, either 10,000,000,000, or 37 cyphers preceded by 1. — *Kharva-vāsin, ī, inī, i,* being or abiding in any mutilated object. — *Kharva-śākha, as, ā, am,* dwarfish, small, short.

Kharvaka, as, ikā, am, Ved. mutilated, imperfect, not full (as the moon).

खर्वट *kharvaṭa, as, am,* m. n. the capital of a district of four hundred villages, a market or country town; a village at the foot of a mountain; (a various reading for *karvaṭa.*)

खर्वुरा *kharvurā,* f., N. of a plant, = *taraḍī.*

खर्वूज *kharvūja, am,* n. the water-melon (fr. the Pers. خربوزه *kharbūza*).

खल् *khal,* cl. 1. P. *khalati, ćakhāla,* &c., to move, shake; to gather.

खल *khala, as, am,* m. n. a threshing-floor, a granary; earth, mould, or soil; place, site; sediment, dregs, the deposit of oil &c.; a mill; contest, battle; (*as, ā*), m. f. a wicked or mischievous person; low, base, inferior, cruel, mischief-making; (*as*), m. the sun; the plant Xanthochymus Pictorius, see *tamāla;* the datura plant, thorn-apple; (*ā*), f. N. of a daughter of Raudrāśva. — *Khala-kula, as,* m. = *kulattha,* Dolichos Uniflorus. — *Khala-ja, as, ā, am,* Ved. produced on a threshing-floor. — *Khalatā,* f. or *khala-tva am,* n. wickedness, villainy; filthiness. — *Khala-dhānya, am,* n. a threshing-floor; (also *khaladhāna, khaledhānya, khalādhāna.*) — *Khala-pū, ūs, ūs,* m. f. a sweeper, a cleaner, a Mehter or Ferash (originally 'one who cleans a threshing-floor'). — *Khala-prīti, is,* f. the friendship or favour of wicked or low persons. — *Khala-mūrti, is,* m. quicksilver. — *Khala-saṃsarga, as,* m. associating with bad company. — *Khalādhārā* (°*la-ādh°*), f. a kind of cockroach. — *Khale-dhānī* or *khale-bālī,* f. the post of a threshing-floor round which the oxen pass which tread out the grain. — *Khale-busam,* ind. at the time when the chaff is on the threshing-floor, at the threshing-time. — *Khale-yavam,* ind. at the time when barley is on the threshing-floor, at the barley threshing-time. — *Khale-vālī,* f. the post of a threshing-floor; [cf. *khale-dhānī.*] — *Khalokti* (°*la-uk°*), *is,* f. abuse, low or wicked language.

Khali, is, m. sediment of oil or oil-cake.

Khalin, ī, inī, i, having sediment &c.; (*ī*), m. an epithet of Śiva; (*inas*), m. pl., N. of a class of Dānavas; (*inī*), f. a multitude of threshing-floors; the plant Anthericum Tuberosum, = *tāla-parṇī,* = *tāla-mūlī.*

Khalina, as, ā, am, covered with sediment, covered with oil-dregs (?); (*as, am*), m. n. the bit of a bridle; see *khalīna;* [cf. Gr. χαλινός.]

Khalī-kṛi, cl. 8. P. A. *-karoti, -kurute, -kartum,* to reduce to sediment, to crush; to hurt, injure; to treat badly, scorn. — *Khalī-kāra, as,* m. or *khalī-kṛiti, is,* f. reducing to sediment; hurting, injuring; mischief, evil.

Khalīna, as, am, m. n. the bit of a bridle.

Khalya, as, ā, am, being on a threshing-floor, fit for one; fit for oil-cake &c.; (*ā*), f. a multitude of threshing-floors; N. of a woman.

Khalyakā, f., N. of a woman.

खलति khalati, is, is or ī, i (said to be fr. rt. khal), bald-headed, bald; [cf. kulva, khallița, &c.]
Khalatika, as, m., N. of a mountain; (am), n., N. of the forest situated near this mountain.

खलिश khaliśa, as, ā, m. f. a kind of fish, Trichopodus Colisa; or = kankatroța, Esox Kaukila; [cf. khalliśa, khaleśa, &c.]

खलु khalu, ind. (as a particle of asseveration or affirmation), indeed, verily, certainly, truly, yes; (as a continuative particle), now, now then, now further; (as a particle employed in syllogistic forms of speech), but now, = the Latin atqui. It occurs only once in the Ṛig-veda; oftener in the Brāhmaṇas and Buddhist compositions, especially when combined with other particles, thus atha khalu, u khalu, vai khalu, and khalu vai, = now then, now further. In later Sanskṛit khalu frequently does little more than lay stress on the word by which it is preceded, and is sometimes merely an expletive. According to native lexicographers khalu is also a particle of prohibition, endearment, conciliation, and inquiry. Na khalu, by no means, not at all, indeed not.

खलुज् kha-luj, k, m. (instead of kha-luk fr. luñć?), darkness.

खलुरेष khaluresha or khalureshaka, as, m. a kind of wild quadruped.

खलूरिका khalūrikā, f. a parade, a place for military exercise; [cf. khuralī.]

खलेश khaleśa or khaleśaya, as, m. a kind of fish, commonly Trichopodus Colisa; [cf. khaliśa and khaśeța.]

खल्ल् khall, cl. 1. A. khallate, &c., to shake, be loose; [cf. khal.]

खल्ल khalla, as, m. a little case or cap formed by rolling up paper &c. (used for holding any small articles of grocery &c.); a mill, a stone or vessel for grinding drugs; a kind of cloth or clothes; leather, leather garments; a leather water-bag; a canal, a cut, a creek, a trench, a deep hole; the Cātaka, a kind of cuckoo; (ī), f. shooting pain in the extremities.

खल्लातक khallātaka, as, m., N. of the first minister of king Bindusāra.

खल्लासर khallāsara, as or am, m. or n. (?), the tenth Yoga in astronomy.

खल्लिका khallikā, f. a frying-pan.

खल्लिट khallița or khallīța, as, ā, am, bald-headed, becoming morbidly bald; [cf. khalati.]

खल्लिश khalliśa, as, m. another form for khaliśa, q. v.

खल्व khalva, as, m., Ved. a kind of grain or leguminous plant.

खल्वट khalvața, as, m. a severe cough (?).

खल्वल khalvala, ās, m. pl., N. of a school.

खल्वाट khalvāța, as, ā, am, bald, bald-headed; [cf. khalati.]

खव् khav, cl. 9. P. khaunāti or khunāti, ćakhāva, &c., to cause prosperity, produce wealth, to purify; (another form for khać.)

खवल्ली kha-vallī, &c. See under 3. kha.

खश khaśa, as, m. a mountainous country in the north of India; a native of that country considered as a degraded Kshatriya; (ā), f., N. of a daughter of Daksha, one of the wives of Kaśyapa, the mother of the Yakshas and Rakshasas; a kind of perfume, = murā. (The word is sometimes spelt khasa.) — Khaśātmaja (°śā-āt°), as, m. a Rakshas.

खशय kha-śaya. See under 3. kha.

खशीर khaśīra, ās, m. pl., N. of a people; [cf. khāśīra.]

खशेट khaśeța, as, m. the Khaliśa, a kind of fish; [cf. khaleśa and khaliśa.]

खश्वास kha-śvāsa. See under 3. kha.

खष् khash, cl. 1. P. khashati, to hurt, injure, kill; [cf. kash.]

खष्प khashpa, am, n. (said to be fr. rt. khan), violence, oppression; anger, passion.

खस khasa, as, m. itch, scab, or any similar disease of the skin; [cf. also khaśa.]

खसकन्द khasakanda or khasagandha, as, m., N. of a plant, commonly called kshīra-kañćukī.

खसतिल khasatila, as, m. (kha-sa-tila?), poppy (khaskhasa).

खसम kha-sama, &c. See under 3. kha.

खसाक khasāka, ās, m. pl., N. of a people; (a various reading for khaśīra.)

खसात्मज khasātmaja. See under khaśa.

खसिन्धु kha-sindhu. See under 3. kha.

खसीक khasīka, ās, m. pl., N. of a people, = khasāka.

खसूचि khasūći, an expression of reproach at the end of a compound, e. g. vaiyākaraṇa-khasūći, one who has forgotten the grammar; (fr. kha and sūći?, 'one who pierces a needle into the air?').

खसृम khasṛima, as, m., N. of a Daitya, son of Vipraćitti and Siṃhikā.

खस्खस khaskhasa, as, m. poppy. — Khaskhasa-rasa, as, m. poppy-juice, opium.

खस्तनी kha-stanī. See under 3. kha.

खा khā, (at the end of some compounds) digging; [f. kūpa-khā and visa-khā.]

खागि khāgi, is, m. f. (?), N. of an Agra-hāra.

खाजिक khājika, as, m. fried or parched grain; [cf. khadikā.]

खाट् khāț, ind. (an onomatopoetic word), the sound made in clearing the throat; [cf. khāt.]

खाट khāța, as, ā, m. f. a bier, a cot or bedstead on which dead bodies are conveyed to the pile; [cf. khațțī.]
Khāți, is, f. a bier; a scar; caprice, whim.
Khāțikā, f. a bier; [cf. khațțikā.]

खाट्वाभारिक khāțvābhārika, as, ī, am (fr. khațvā-bhāra), or khāțvika, as, ī, am (fr. khațvā), laden with bedsteads.

खाडायन khāḍāyana, as, m. a patronymic from Khaḍa. — Khāḍāyana-bhakta, am, n. the district inhabited by the Khāḍāyanas.
Khāḍāyanin, inas, m. pl. the followers of Khāḍāyana.

खाड्ग khāḍga, as, ī, am (fr. khaḍga), belonging to a rhinoceros (as armour made of rhinoceros hide).

खाण्ड khāṇḍa, am, n. (fr. khaṇḍa), the state of having fractures, fissures, or gaps.
Khāṇḍava, as, m. (fr. khaṇḍu), sugar-candy, sugar-plums, sweetmeats; N. of a region; (am), n., N. of a forest in Kuru-kshetra, sacred to Indra and burnt by the god of fire, Agni with the assistance of Arjuna and Kṛishṇa (see Mahā-bh. I. 8207). — Khāṇḍava-prastha, as, m., N. of a town situated in the Khāṇḍava forest, founded by the Pāṇḍavas, = indra-prastha.
Khāṇḍavāyana, ās, m. pl., N. of a family of Brāhmans.
Khāṇḍavika, as, m. a confectioner; sugar-baker.
Khāṇḍika, as, m. (fr. khaṇḍa), a confectioner, a seller of sugar-plums or sweetmeats; (am), n. a mass or multitude of peas (fr. khaṇḍika).
Khāṇḍikīya, ās, m. pl. the followers of Khaṇḍika.
Khāṇḍikya, as, m., N. of a son of Amita-dhvaja or Mita-dhvaja; (am), n. the business of a confectioner (?).

खात् khāt, ind. (an onomatopoetic word), the sound made in clearing the throat; [cf. khāț.]

खात khāta, khāti, khātra. See rt. khan.

खात्मन् khātman. See under 3. kha.

खाद् khād, cl. 1. P. (ep. also A.) khādati, ćakhāda, khādishyati, akhādīt, khāditum, to chew, bite, eat, devour, feed, prey upon; to hurt: Caus. khādayati, -yitum, to cause or make to eat or devour; to eat: Desid. ćikhādishati: Intens. ćākhādyate, ćākhātti; [cf. Scot. cuid, 'food;' Hib. caithim, 'to eat.']
Khāda, as, ā, am, eating, devouring, (at the end of compounds, e. g. amitra-khāda, vṛitra-khāda, q. v.); (as), m. chewing, eating; food.
Khādaka, as, ikā, am, eating, consuming, devouring; an eater; a debtor; a borrower, one who borrows or uses; [cf. khātaka.]
Khādata-modatā, f. (fr. the two impv. khādata and modata), continual eating and being glad. — Khādata-vāmatā, f. (fr. the two impv. khādata and vāmata), continual eating and vomiting. — Khādatā-ćamatā or khādatā-ćāmatā, f. continual eating and washing the mouth.
Khādana, as, m. a tooth; (ā), f., N. of a wife of king Megha-vāhana; (am), n. chewing, eating; food, victuals.
Khādanīya, as, ā, am, eatable, edible, to be eaten.
Khādita, as, ā, am, eaten, devoured. — Khādita-vat, ān, atī, at, having eaten, eating, feeding.
Khāditavya, as, ā, am, to be eaten, what may be or must be eaten.
1. khādin, ī, inī, i, eating. (For 2. see under khādi.)
Khāduka, as, ī, am, mischievous, injurious, malignant.
Khādya, as, ā, am, eatable, edible, what may or must be eaten; (am), n. food, victuals. — Khādyā-khādhya (°ya-akh°), as, ā, am, fit or unfit for food.

खादि khādi, is, m., Ved. a brooch, bracelet, ring (worn on the hands or feet especially by the Maruts). — Khādi-hasta, as, ā, am, Ved. having the hands ornamented with bracelets or rings, epithet of the Maruts.
2. khādin, ī, inī, i, Ved. decorated with bracelets or rings (as the Maruts).

खादिर khādira, as, ī, am (fr. khadira), made of or coming from the tree Acacia Catechu; (as), m. Catechu extract prepared from the tree Acacia Catechu. — Khādira-gṛihya, am, n., N. of a literary work. — Khādira-sāra, as, m. Catechu, the resinous extract of the tree Acacia Catechu.

खादोअर्णस् khādoarṇas, ās, ās, as, Ved. tearing away the bank (as a river?).

खाधूया khādhūyā, f., N. of an Agra-hāra.

खान khāna, khānila, khānya. See rt. khan.

खापगा khāpagā. See under 3. kha.

खार khāra, as, or khāri, is, ī, m. f. a Khāri, a measure of grain = 16 Droṇas or about 3 bushels; it is also reckoned at 1½ Sūrpa or 3 Droṇas; also at 46 Gaunīs or 4096 Palas, or at 4 Droṇas; (ī), f. a scar. — Khārim-paća, as, ā, am, cooking a Khāri by measure; (a vessel &c.) in which a Khāri may be cooked. — Khārī-vāpa, as, ā, am, sown with a Khārī of grain (as a field &c.).

Khārika or khārika, as, ā, am, equal to or sown with a Khāri of grain (as a field &c.).

खार्कार khār-kāra, as, m. (khār an onomatopoetic word and kāra fr. 1. kṛi), the braying of an ass; [cf. khara.]

खार्गलि khārgali, is, m. (fr. khargalā or khṛigala), an epithet of Kapi; (a various reading has khārjali.)

खार्जूर khārjūra, as, ī, am (fr. kharjūra), coming from or made of the tree Phœnix Sylvestris.

खार्वा khārvā, f. (fr. kharva), the Tretā or second Yuga of the world.

खालत्य khālatya, am, n. (fr. khalati), Ved., or khālitya, am, n. morbid baldness.

खालिक khālika, as, ī, am (fr. khala), like a threshing-floor.

खाशि khāśi, is, m., N. of a country to the east of Bengal: the Cossya hills; (also khāśika); [cf. khaśa and khāshya.]

खाश्मरी khāśmarī, f. a plant, = kāśmarī.

खाष्य khāshya or (according to a various reading) khoshya, as or am, m. or n. (?), N. of a place; [cf. khaśa or khāśī.]

खासता khāsatā, f., N. of a place in Kāśmīra.

खासीर khāsīra, ās, m. pl., N. of a people; [cf. khaśīra.]

खिखि khikhi, is, f. a fox; (a various reading for kikhi.)

खिङ्खिर khinkhira, as, ī, m. f. a fox; (as), m. the foot of a bedstead (= khaṭvāṅga), one of Śiva's weapons; a kind of perfume, commonly Hāla.

खिट् khiṭ, cl. 1. P. kheṭati, &c., to be terrified or frightened, to fear, dread; to terrify, scare, startle, alarm, surprise.

Kheṭita, as, ā, am, terrified, scared, startled, frightened.

खिद् khid, cl. 6. P. khindati (Ved. khidati), ćikheda, akhaitsīt, khetsyati, khettum, to strike, press, press down; cl. 7. or 4. A. khintte or khinte and khidyate, to be pressed down or depressed, to suffer pain or misery, to be distressed, to be wearied, to feel tired or exhausted: Caus. khedayati, -yitum, to press down, molest, disturb, make tired or exhausted: Desid. ćikhitsati, -te: Intens. ćekhidyate, ćekhetti; [cf. Lith. zeidziu; Gr. κῆδος ?].

Khidira, as, m. an ascetic, a penitent; a pauper; the moon; an epithet of Indra.

Khidyamāna, as, ā, am, being depressed, suffering pain or distress.

Khidra, as, m. a poor man, a pauper; disease, sickness; (am), n., Ved. a press; (Sāy.) an instrument for splitting or dividing.

Khidvan, ā, arī, a, Ved. pressing upon, oppressing.

Khinna, as, ā, am, depressed, distressed, suffering pain or uneasiness; wearied, exhausted.

Kheda, as, m. lassitude, depression; exhaustion; pain; poverty; sorrow, affliction, distress; (ā), f., Ved. a hammer, mallet or similar implement belonging to Indra. — Khedānvita (°da-an°), as, ā, am, distressed, pained.

Khedana, am, n. lassitude, exhaustion, pain, sorrow, affliction, poverty, distress.

Khedayitavya, as, ā, am, to be depressed, to be made distressed.

Khedita, as, ā, am, disturbed, annoyed, harassed; afflicted, distressed, pained.

Kheditavya, as, ā, am, to be depressed or cast down, to be troubled.

Khedin, ī, inī, i, tiring, fatiguing, disturbing; (inī), f. a creeper, a creeping plant, Marsilea Quadrifolia (aśana-parṇī).

खिन्दक khindaka, as, or khindhi, is, m., N. of an Arabic astronomer, Alkindi.

खिरहिट्टी khirahiṭṭī, f., N. of a plant, = mahā-samaṅgā.

खिल khila, as, am, m. n. a piece of waste or uncultivated land situated between cultivated fields, a desert, bare soil, a vacant space, a space not filled up, a gap, that which serves to fill up a gap, a supplement (of a book &c.), an additional hymn appended to the regular collection; a compendium, a compilation (especially of hymns and prayers); remainder; emptiness, vacuity, vanity, anything vain, empty or fruitless; (as), m., N. of Brahmā, and of Vishṇu.

Khilī-kṛi, cl. 8. P. A. -karoti, -kurute, -kartum, to turn into a desert, to devastate, make impassable; to make vain or powerless.

Khilī-bhū, cl. 1. P. -bhavati, -vitum, to become a desert, become impassable or unfrequented, to be blocked up; to be frustrated.

Khilya, as, m., Ved. a piece of waste or uncultivated land situated between cultivated fields, a desert; a piece of rock in the earth, a mass, a heap, a lump, &c.

Khailika, as, ī, am, supplementary. See s. v.

खीर khīra, as, am, m. or n. (?), N. of a place.

खील khīla, as, m., Ved. = kīla, q. v.

खु khu, cl. 1. A. khavate, &c., to sound.

खुङ्खुणी khunkhuṇī, f. a kind of lute.

खुङ्गाह khungāha, as, m. a black horse.

खुज् khuj, cl. 1. P. khojati, to steal, rob; [cf. Lith. wagiù ?].

खुज्जाक khujjāka or (according to a various reading) khuñjāka, as, m. the plant Lipeocercis Serrata; [cf. deva-tāḍaka.]

खुड् khuḍ, cl. 10. P. khoḍayati, -yitum (another form for khuṇḍ below), to break in pieces, to divide, tear, rend, &c.

खुडक khuḍaka, as or am, m. or n. (?), the ankle-joint; [cf. khulaka.]

खुण्ड् khuṇḍ, cl. 1. A. khuṇḍate, to break in pieces; to limp, be lame; cl. 10. P. khuṇḍayati, -yitum, to break in pieces.

खुत्तीर्य khuttīrya, as, m., N. of a foreign astronomer.

खुद् khud, cl. 6. P., Ved. khudati, to sport wantonly or amorously: Intens. 3rd sing. Let, ćanīkhudat; [cf. khurd.]

खुनमुष khunamusha, as or am, m. or n. (?), N. of an Agra-hāra.

खुर् khur, cl. 6. P. khurati, ćukhora, khoritum, to cut, cut up, break in pieces; to scratch; [cf. kshur.]

खुर khura, as, m. (said to be fr. the last), a hoof, a horse's hoof, &c.; a sort of perfume, commonly called Nakhi, apparently a dried shell-fish shaped like a hoof [cf. koladala]; a razor; the foot of a bedstead [cf. kshura]. — Khura-kshepa, as, m. a kick with a hoof, kicking. — Khura-ṇas, ās, ās, as, or khura-ṇasa, as, ā, am, having a nose like a horse's hoof, flat-nosed. — Khura-padavī, f. a horse's foot-marks. — Khurāghāta (°ra-āgh°) or khurābhighāta (°ra-abh°), as, m. a kick, kicking (as of a horse).

Khuraka, as, m., N. of a plant, = tila; a kind of dance.

खुरप्र khurapra, as, m. an arrow with a semicircular head; (a wrong form for kshurapra.)

खुरली khuralī, f. military exercise, practising archery, &c.; [cf. khalūrikā.]

खुराक khurāka, as, m. an animal in general; (perhaps originally 'an animal with hoofs,' khura ?).

खुरालक khurālaka, as, m. an iron arrow.

खुरालिक khurālika, as, m. a razor-case; an iron arrow; a pillow; (a various reading for kharālika.)

खुरासान khurāsāna, Khurāsān.

खुर्द् khurd, cl. 1. A. khūrdate, to play, to sport, = kurd, gurd, q. v.

खुल्ल khulla, as, ā, am, small, little, low, mean, = kshudra and kshulla; (am), n. a kind of perfume, = khura. — Khulla-tāta, as, m. a father's younger brother; [cf. kshulla-tāta.]

Khullaka, as, ā, am, little, small, poor, indigent, low, vile; cruel, harsh; wicked, mischievous, malignant, = kshudraka.

खुल्लम khullama, as, m. a road.

खूर्द् khūrd = khurd, q. v.

खृगल khṛigala, as or am, m. or n. (?), Ved. a staff, a crutch (?); (Sāy.) a coat of mail.

खेखीरक khekhīraka, as, m. a hollow bamboo, a sounding reed or cane; [cf. kīćaka.]

खेगमन khe-gamana. See under 3. kha.

खेट् kheṭ, cl. 10. P. kheṭayati, -yitum, to eat, consume.

खेट kheṭa, as, m. a village, the residence of peasants and farmers; a small town, half a Pura; phlegm, the phlegmatic or watery humor of the body; a horse; the club of Bala-rāma; (am), n. grass; (as, am), m. n. hunting, the chase [cf. ā-kheṭa]; a shield; (as, ā, am), having a weapon or weapons, armed; vile, bad, low; (at the end of compounds expressing defectiveness or deterioration, e. g. nagara-kheṭam, a miserable town.) — Kheṭa-piṇḍa, as or am, m. or n. (?), a ball of phlegm, i. e. anything impossible.

Kheṭaka, as, m. a village, the residence of agricultural peasants, a small village; (as, am), m. n. a shield; the club of Bala-rāma (?). — Kheṭaka-pura, am, n., N. of a town.

Kheṭin, ī, m. a lecher, a libertine; [cf. nāgara fr. nagara.]

खेऽट khe'ṭa. See under 3. kha.

खेटिक kheṭika, as, m., N. of a man.

खेटित kheṭita. See under rt. khiṭ.

खेटिताल kheṭitāla, as, m. a minstrel, a family bard or piper, whose business is to awaken the master of the house with music and singing; [cf. vaitālika.]

खेड् kheḍ, cl. 10. P. kheḍayati, -yitum, to eat; [cf. kheṭ.]

खेड kheḍa, am, n. grass (?), in gandhakheḍa; [cf. khaṭa and kheṭa.]

खेडिताल kheḍitāla, as, m. a minstrel, a family bard or piper, &c., = kheṭitāla.

खेद kheda. See under rt. khid.

खेदि khedi, ayas, m. pl., Ved. rays (?).

खेपरिभ्रम khe-paribhrama. See under 3. kha.

खेमकर्ण khemakarṇa, as, m. (for kshemakarṇa ?), N. of a man.

खेय kheya. See under rt. khan, p. 273.

खेल् *khel*, cl. 1. P. *khelati*, &c., to shake, move to and fro, swing; to tremble: Caus. *khelayati*, *-yitum*, to cause to move to and fro, to swing, shake.

Khela, *as*, *ā*, *am*, moving, shaking, trembling, swinging; (*as*), m., N. of a man; (*ā*), f. sport, play. — *Khela-gati*, *is*, *is*, *i*, or *khela-gamana*, *as*, *ā*, *am*, having a stately walk. — *Khela-gāmin*, *ī*, *inī*, *i*, stately going.

Khelana, *am*, n. shaking; quivering motion (of the eyes); play, pastime, sport; (*ī*), f. a piece or man at drafts, chess, &c.

Khelāya, nom. P. *khelāyati*, *-yitum*, to play, sport.

Kheli, *is*, f. play, sport; an animal; a bird; the sun; an arrow; a song, a hymn.

खेलुद *kheluda*, *as* or *am*, m. or n. (?), a particular high number; [cf. *kalahu*.]

खेव् *khev*, cl. 1. A. *khevate*, to serve, wait upon; [cf. *kev* and *sev*.]

खेशय *khe-śaya*. See under 3. *kha*.

खेसर *khesara*, *as*, m. a mule; (a wrong form for *vesara* ?).

खै *khai*, cl. 1. P. *khāyati*, *ćakhau*, *khātum*, to make firm, be firm or steady; to strike, injure, hurt, kill; to dig; to mourn, to sorrow.

खैमखा *khaimakhā*, f., Ved., N. of a frog; [cf. *khanvakhā*.]

खैलिक *khailika*, *as*, *ī*, *am* (fr. *khila*), supplementary, additional, added afterwards.

खोङ्गाह *khongāha*, *as*, m. a white and brown horse; [cf. *khungāha*.]

खोट् *khoṭ*, cl. 1. P. *khoṭati*, to limp, to be lame or lamed; cl. 10. P. *khoṭayati*, *-yitum*, to throw; [cf. *khoḍ*, *khor*, *khol*, *kehoṭ*.]

Khoṭana, *am*, n. limping.

खोटि *khoṭi*, *is*, f. a cunning or scheming woman; (also read *khori*.)

खोटी *khoṭī*, f. the gum olibanum tree, Boswellia Thurifera; [cf. *pālankī*.]

खोड् *khoḍ*, cl. 1. P. *khoḍati*, to limp; to be or become lame; cl. 10. P. *khoḍayati*, *-yitum*, to throw or cast.

Khoḍa, *as*, *ā*, *am*, limping, lame.

खोडकशीर्ष *khoḍakaśīrsha* or *khoḍakaśīrshaka*, *am*, n. the arched roof of a house, the coping of a wall &c.; [cf. *kapi-śīrsha* and *kraya-śīrsha*.]

खोर् *khor*, cl. 1. P. *khorati*, to limp, to be lame; [cf. *khoṭ*, *khoḍ*, *khol*.]

Khora, *as*, *ā*, *am*, limping, lame.

खोल् *khol*, cl. 1. P. *kholati*, to limp, to be lame.

Khola, *as*, *ā*, *am*, limping, lame; (*am*), n. a helmet; [cf. Gr. χωλός.] — *Khola-śiras*, *ās*, *ās*, *as*, furnished with a helmet or armour for the head.

Kholaka, *as*, m. a helmet, armour for the head; an ant-hill; a pot, a saucepan; the shell of a betel-nut.

Kholi, *is*, f. a quiver.

खोल्क *kholka*, &c. See under 3. *kha*.

खोष्य *khoshya* or (according to a various reading) *khāshya*, *as* or *am*, m. or n. (?), N. of a place.

ख्या *khyā*, cl. 2. P. and in the non-conjugational tenses P. A. *khyāti*, *ćakhyau*, *ćakhye*, *khyāsyati*, *-te*, *akhyat*, *akhyata*, *khyātum*, (the original meaning of this root seems to have been 'to perceive, look, view, see,' and it has this sense in the Veda when combined with prepositions; the simple verb occurs only in Pass. and Caus.): Pass. *khyāyate*, to be known, be named: Caus. *khyāpayati*, *-yitum*, to make known, promulgate, proclaim; to relate, tell, say, declare, betray, denounce; to make well known or renowned, to praise: Desid. *ćikhyāsati*, *-te*: Intens. *ćākhyāyate*, *ćākhyāti* and *ćākhyeti*; [cf. Lat. *in-quam*, &c.]

Khyāta, *as*, *ā*, *am*, known, named, called, denominated; told; well known, celebrated, notorious, famous. — *Khyāta-garhaṇa* or *khyāta-garhita*, *as*, *ā*, *am*, having a bad name or evil report; notoriously vile, infamous.

Khyātavya, *as*, *ā*, *am*, to be styled or called or denominated; to be told; to be celebrated.

Khyāti, *is*, f. the being well known, renown, fame, glory, celebrity; a name, denomination, title; fame personified as a daughter of Daksha or as a daughter of Kardama and wife of Bhṛigu; the means of individual fruition, or the faculty of discriminating objects by appropriate designations and the like, opinion, knowledge; (*is*), m., N. of a son of the fourth Manu. — *Khyāti-kara* or *khyāti-janaka*, *as*, *ā*, *am*, causing renown, glorious. — *Khyāti-ghna*, *as*, *ī*, *am*, destroying reputation, disgraceful. — *Khyāti-bodha*, *as*, m. sense of honour. — *Khyāti-mat*, *ān*, *atī*, *at*, renowned.

Khyāpaka, *as*, *ā*, *am*, (at the end of a compound) making known, one who tells or declares, declaring; one who confesses; indicative.

Khyāpana, *am*, n. declaring, divulging; saying, avowing; confessing, public confession (of sins); making renowned, celebrating.

Khyāpya, *as*, *ā*, *am*, to be told or related.

ग

ग 1. *ga*, the third consonant of the alphabet, the soft guttural having the sound of *g* in *give*. — *Ga-kāra*, *as*, m. the letter or sound *ga*.

ग 2. *ga*, *as*, *ā*, *am* (fr. rt. *gam*) at the end of compounds, who or what goes, going, moving (e. g. *yāna-ga*, going in a carriage; *antariksha-ga*, moving through the air; *śighra-ga*, going quickly; *kāma-ga*, going where one lists; *anyastrī-ga*, one who goes to another's wife); staying, being, abiding in (e. g. *pañćama-ga*, abiding in or keeping the fifth place); relating to or standing in connection with anything; [cf. *a-ga*, *agra-ga*, *agre-ga*, &c.]

ग 3. *ga*, *as*, *ī*, *am* (fr. rt. *gai*) at the end of compounds, singing [cf. *ćhando-ga* and *sāma-ga*]; (*as*), m. a Gandharva or celestial musician; (*ā*), f. a song; (*am*), n. song, singing.

ग 4. *ga*, *as*, m. an epithet of the deity Gaṇeśa; [cf. the other letters of the alphabet, each of which is supposed to denote a deity.]

ग 5. *ga*, (used in works on prosody as an abbreviation of the word *guru* to denote) a long syllable.

गगण *gagaṇa*, *am*, n. (often spelt *gagana*; perhaps fr. *ga-gaṇa*, 'containing troops of moving beings?' said to be for *gamana* fr. rt. *gam*, to go), the atmosphere, air; the sky, heaven, the firmament; talc. — *Gagaṇa-kusuma*, *am*, n., see *gagaṇa-pushpa*. — *Gagaṇa-gañja*, *as*, m., N. of a Bodhi-sattva. — *Gagaṇa-gati*, *is*, *is*, *i*, moving in the air, an inhabitant of the sky. — *Gagaṇa-ćara*, *as*, m. moving in the air, a bird; [cf. *gagaṇe-ćara*.] — *Gagaṇa-dhvaja*, *as*, m. the sun; a cloud. — *Gagaṇa-pushpa*, *am*, n. a flower in the sky, i. e. any unreal or fanciful thing, an impossibility; [cf. *kha-pushpa*.] — *Gagaṇa-priya*, *as*, m., N. of a Dānava. — *Gagaṇa-mūrdhan*, *ā*, m., N. of a Dānava. — *Gagaṇa-vihārin*, *ī*, *iṇī*, *i*, moving or sporting in the sky; (*ī*), m. a heavenly luminary; the sun; a celestial being or divinity. — *Gagaṇa-sad*, *t*, *t*, *t*, abiding in the air; (*t*), m. an inhabitant of the air, a celestial being. — *Gagaṇa-stha* or *gagaṇa-sthita*, *as*, *ā*, *am*, situated or being in the sky. — *Gagaṇa-sparśana*, *as*, m. touching the sky; N. of one of the eight Maruts; air, wind. — *Gagaṇāgra* (°*ṇa-ag*°), *am*, n. the highest heavens, the summit or highest part of heaven. — *Gagaṇāṅganā* (°*ṇa-an*°), f., N. of a metre, containing four lines of twenty-five syllabic instants each. — *Gagaṇādhvaga* (°*ṇa-adh*°), *as*, m. the sun; a planet; a celestial spirit. — *Gagaṇāmbu* (°*ṇa-am*°), *u*, n. rain-water. — *Gagaṇe-ćara*, *as*, *ā*, *am*, going in the air; (*as*), m. a bird; a planet; a lunar mansion; a heavenly spirit; [cf. *gagaṇa-ćara*.] — *Gagaṇolmuka* (°*ṇa-ul*°), *as*, m. the planet Mars.

गगन *gagana*. See *gagaṇa* above.

गग्घ् *gaggh*, cl. 1. P. *gagghati*, to laugh, laugh at or deride; [cf. *kakh*.]

गग्नु *gagnu*, a various reading for *vagnu*, 'speech.'

गङ्गा *gangā*, f. (said to be fr. rt. *gam*, to go), the river Ganges; the Ganges personified and considered as the eldest daughter of Himavat and Menā, and wife of Śāntanu and mother of Bhīshma, or as one of the wives of Dharma; there is also a Gangā in the sky (*ākāśa-gangā*) and one under the earth; N. of the wife of Nīla-kaṇṭha and mother of Śankara; (*as*), m., N. of a son of Nārāyaṇa, who was the author of a commentary on the Vṛihad-araṇyaka-upanishad; he is also called Dviveda-ganga. — *Ganga-datta*, *as*, m. (the final *ā* being shortened), N. of a king of the frogs. — *Ganga-dāsa*, *as*, m., N. of a son of Poviya, called Jñānānanda, author of a commentary on the poem Khaṇḍa-praśasti. — *Gangā-kshetra*, *am*, n. the sacred district of the Gangā, i. e. the river Ganges and two Krośas on either of its banks; all dying within such limits go to heaven, whatever their crimes. — *Gangā-ćampū*, *ūs*, f. title of a work. — *Gangā-ćillī*, f. the black-headed gull, Larus Ridibundus; (fr. *gangā* and *ćillī*, a kite, considered by the Hindūs as a species of that bird, the Gangetic kite.) — *Gangā-ja*, *as*, m. the son of Gangā, an epithet of Bhīshma; and also of the deity Kārttikeya. — *Gangā-jala*, *am*, n. the water of the Ganges, the holy water by which it is customary to administer oaths. — *Gangāteya*, *as*, *ī*, *am*, going in the Ganges; (*as*), m. a shrimp or prawn; also *galāvila*. — *Gangā-tīra*, *am*, n. the bank of the Ganges. — *Gangā-tīrtha*, *am*, n., N. of a Tīrtha. — *Gangā-dāsa*, *as*, m., N. of the author of the Chando-mañjarī and of the Aćyuta-ćarita; N. of a copyist who lived about 1542; N. of the author of the work Chando-govinda. — *Gangāditya* (°*gā-ād*°), *as*, m. a form of the sun. — *Gangā-dvāra*, *am*, n. 'the door of the Ganges,' the place where the Ganges enters the plains; also called Haridvār. — *Gangādvāra-māhātmya*, *am*, n. title of a part of the Skanda-Purāṇa. — *Gangā-dhara*, *as*, m. 'Ganges-receiver,' 'Ganges-supporter,' the ocean; an epithet of Śiva, (according to the legend, the Ganges in its descent from heaven first alighted on the head of Śiva and continued for a long period entangled in his hair); N. of a man; N. of a lexicographer; N. of a commentator on the Śārīraka-sūtras; N. of a commentator on Bhāskara. — *Gangā-dhara-pura*, *am*, n., N. of a town. — *Gangādhara-bhaṭṭa*, *as*, m., N. of a scholiast. — *Gangādhara-mādhava*, *as*, m., N. of the father of Dādābhai. — *Gangādhara-rasa*, *as*, m. term for a particular prescription in medicine. — *Gangā-nāgarāja*, *as*, m., N. of a Nāga. — *Gangā-nātha*, *as*, m., N. of the founder of a sect. — *Gangā-pattrī*, f., N. of a plant, = *pattrī*, *su-gandhā*, *gandhapattrikā*. — *Gangā-pāra*, *am*, n. the opposite bank of the Ganges. — *Gangā-putra*, *as*, m. son of Gangā; an epithet of Bhīshma; a man of a mixed and vile caste, employed to remove dead bodies; a Brāhman who conducts pilgrims to the Ganges, especially at Benares. — *Gangā-bhṛit*, *t*, m. an epithet of Śiva; [cf. *gangā-dhara*.] — *Gangā-madhya*, *am*, n. the bed or stream of the Ganges. — *Gangā-māhātmya*, *am*, n. a poem or any composition in praise of the Ganges. — *Gangāmbu* (°*gā-am*°), *u*, n. or *gangāmbhas* (°*gā-am*°), *as*, n. pure rain-water, such as falls in the month Āśvina; Ganges-water. — *Gaṅgā-yamune*, du. f. the Ganges and Yamunā rivers. — *Gaṅgā-yātrā*, f. pilgrimage to the Ganges; carrying a sick person to the river side to die there. — *Gaṅgā-rāma*, *as*, m., N. of the father of Jaya-rāma and uncle of Rāma-ćandra. — *Gaṅgā-laharī*, f. title of a work ('the wave of the Ganges'). — *Gaṅgāvataraṇa-ćampū-prabandha*, title of a poem by Saṅkara-dīkshita. — *Gaṅgā-vākyāvalī* (°*ya-āv*°), f. title of a work on jurisprudence. — *Gaṅgā-vāsin*, *ī*, *inī*, *i*, dwelling on the Ganges. — *Gaṅgā-śoṇa*, *am*, n. the Ganges and the Sone. — *Gaṅgāshṭaka* (°*gā-ash*°), *am*, n. eight verses addressed to Gaṅgā. — *Gaṅgā-sāgara*, *as*, m. the mouth of the Ganges where it enters the ocean. — *Gaṅgā-suta*, *as*, m. son of Gaṅgā, epithet of the deity Kārttikeya; also of Bhīshma. — *Gaṅgā-stuti*, *is*, f. or *gaṅgā-stotra*, *am*, n. the praise of the Ganges. — *Gaṅgā-snāna*, *am*, n. bathing in the Ganges. — *Gaṅgā-hrada*, *as*, m., N. of a Tīrtha. — *Gaṅgeśa* (°*gā-īśa*), *as*, m., N. of the author of the Tattva-ćintāmaṇi. — *Gaṅgeśvara* (°*gā-īś*°), *as*, m., N. of an author. — *Gaṅgodaka* (°*gā-ud*°), *am*, n. Ganges-water. — *Gaṅgodbheda* (°*gā-ud*°), *as*, m. the source of the Ganges, a sacred place of pilgrimage.

Gaṅgakā or *gaṅgākā* or *gaṅgikā*, f. the Ganges.

Gaṅgin, *ī*, m., N. of a Nāga.

Gaṅgī-bhūta, *as*, *ā*, *am*, become (as sacred as) the Ganges.

गच्छ *gaććha*, *as*, m. (rt. *gam*), a tree; the period (number of terms) of a progression; (*ās*), m. pl., N. of a people: (a various reading for *kaććha* and *kaksha*); [cf. *a-ga*, *naga*, *a-gaććha*.]

Gaććhat, *an*, *antī*, *at*, going, &c.

गज् *gaj*, cl. 1. P. *gajati*, *jagāja*, *gajitum*, to sound, roar; to be drunk, to be confused or inebriated; cl. 10. P. *gājayati*, *-yitum*, to sound, roar.

Gaja, *as*, m. an elephant, one of the eight elephants of the quarters (= *dig-gaja*), and thus a symbolical term for the number 8; a measure of length, the Gaz, a yard, a measure of two cubits, = 1¾ or 2 Hastas; a place prepared for the building of a house; a mound of earth sloping on both sides, on which a house may be erected; a small hole in the ground for a fire, over which to prepare food or medicines; N. of an attendant on the sun; also of an Asura conquered by Śiva; (*ī*), f. a female elephant. — *Gaja-kanda*, *as*, m. a large esculent root, a sort of arum, = *hasti-kanda*. — *Gaja-karṇa*, *as*, m. 'elephant-ear,' N. of a Yaksha. — *Gaja-kūrmāśin* (°*ma-āś*°), *ī*, m. one who devours an elephant and a tortoise, an epithet of Garuḍa, the bird and vehicle of Vishṇu, (in allusion to his swallowing both those animals whilst engaged in a contest with each other.) — *Gaja-gati*, *is*, f. a stately gait like that of an elephant. — *Gaja-gāminī*, f. a woman of a stately elephant-like walk. — *Gaja-ćirbhaṭā*, f. a kind of cucumber, Cucumis Maderaspatanus, = *indra-vāruṇī*. — *Gaja-ćirbhiṭa*, *as*, m. the plant Cucumis Maderaspatanus; (*ā*), f. another kind of gourd, = *mahendra-vāruṇī*. — *Gaja-ććhāyā*, f. a portion of time proper for a Śrāddha (as long as the shadow of an elephant rests on the spot chosen for a ceremony?). — *Gaja-ḍhakkā*, f. a kettle-drum carried on an elephant. — *Gaja-tā*, f. a multitude of elephants. — *Gaja-turaṅga-vilasita*, *am*, n., N. of a metre; [cf. *ṛishabha-gaja-vilasita*.] — *Gaja-tva*, *am*, n. the state of an elephant. — *Gaja-daghna*, *as*, *ī*, *am*, as high or tall as an elephant. — *Gaja-danta*, *as*, m. an elephant's tusk; ivory; a bracket or pin projecting from a wall; an epithet of Gaṇeśa, (this deity being represented with an elephant's head.) — *Gajadanta-phalā*, f. a kind of pumpkin, = *ḍaṅgarī*. — *Gajadanta-maya*, *as*, *ī*, *am*, made of ivory. — *Gaja-dāna*, *am*, n. the liquor exuding from an elephant's temples. — *Gaja-dvayasa*, *as*, *ī*, *am*, as high as an elephant. — *Gaja-nāsā*, f. the trunk of an elephant. — *Gaja-pati*, *is*, m. the lord or keeper of elephants; a large stately elephant; a title given to kings; N. of an old king in the south of Jambu-dvīpa. — *Gaja-pādapa*, *as*, m. the plant Bignonia Suaveolens, = *sthalī*. — *Gaja-pippalī*, f. a plant bearing a seed which resembles pepper, Scindapsus Officinalis; [cf. *kari-pippalī*, &c.] — *Gaja-puṅgava*, *as*, m. a large and excellent elephant. — *Gaja-puṭa*, *as*, m. a small hole in the ground for a fire, over which to prepare food, medical decoctions, extracts, &c. — *Gaja-pura*, *am*, n. the town called after the elephant; another N. of Hāstina-pura; [cf. *gaja-sāhvaya*, *gajāhvaya*, *vāraṇa-sāhvaya*.] — *Gaja-pushpī*, f., N. of a flower. — *Gaja-priyā*, f. the gum olibanum tree, Boswellia Serrata. — *Gaja-bandhanī*, *am*, f. n. a post to which an elephant is bound. — *Gaja-bhakshaka*, *as*, m. the sacred fig tree, Ficus Religiosa, (the young branches of this tree being the elephants' favourite food.) — *Gaja-bhakshā* or *gaja-bhakshyā*, f. the gum olibanum tree; [cf. *gaja-priyā*.] — *Gaja-bhujaṅgama*, *au*, m. du. an elephant and a serpent. — *Gaja-maṇḍana*, *am*, n. the ornaments with which an elephant is decorated, especially the coloured lines on his head. — *Gaja-maṇḍalikā*, f. a ring or circle of elephants surrounding a car &c. — *Gaja-malla*, *as*, m., N. of a son of Karpūra and father of Kalyāṇa-malla. — *Gaja-māćala*, *as*, m. a lion; [cf. *kari-māćala*.] — *Gaja-mātra*, *as*, *ī*, *am*, as tall as an elephant. — *Gaja-muktā*, f. or *gaja-mauktika*, *am*, n. pearl supposed to be found in the projections (Kumbha) on the forehead of an elephant. — *Gaja-mukha*, *as*, m. 'elephant-faced,' an epithet of Gaṇeśa. — *Gaja-moṭana*, *as*, m. a lion; also *gaja-moćana* (?). — *Gaja-yāna-vid*, *t*, *t*, *t*, expert in managing an elephant. — *Gaja-yūtha*, *as*, m. a herd of elephants. — *Gaja-yodhin*, *ī*, *inī*, *i*, fighting on an elephant. — *Gaja-rāja*, *as*, m. a noble elephant. — *Gaja-vat*, *ān*, *atī*, *at*, furnished with elephants. — *Gaja-vadana*, *as*, m. 'elephant-faced,' an epithet of Gaṇeśa. — *Gaja-vara*, *as*, m. the choicest or best of elephants. — *Gaja-vallabhā*, f. the gum olibanum tree; another plant, = *giri-kadalī*. — *Gaja-vilasitā*, f. a sort of metre. — *Gaja-vīthi*, *is*, f. 'the course of the elephant,' or that division of the moon's course in the heavens which contains the signs Rohiṇī, Mṛiga-śiras, and Ārdrā, or (according to others) the signs Punar-vasu, Tishya, and Āślesha. — *Gaja-vraja*, *as*, *ā*, *am*, walking like an elephant; (*am*), n. the pace of an elephant; a troop of elephants. — *Gaja-śikshā*, f. the knowledge or science of elephants, elephant-lore. — *Gaja-śiras*, *ās*, m., N. of a Dānava. — *Gaja-śīrsha*, *as*, m., N. of a Nāga. — *Gaja-sāhvaya*, *am*, n. a famous city, Hāstina-pura, the capital of the Kurus; [cf. *gaja-pura*.] — *Gaja-skandha*, *as*, m. 'having shoulders like an elephant,' N. of a Dānava. — *Gaja-sthāna*, *as* or *am*, m. or n. (?), N. of a place. — *Gaja-snāna*, *am*, n. vain or unproductive efforts, efforts which resemble the ablution of elephants, which after squirting water over their bodies, end by throwing dust and rubbish. — *Gajākhya* (°*ja-ākh*°), *as*, m. the plant Cassia Alata or Tora, = *ćakra-marda*. — *Gajāgraṇī* (°*ja-ag*°), *īs*, m. the most excellent among the elephants, an epithet of Airāvata, the elephant of Indra. — *Gajājīva* (°*ja-āj*°), *as*, m. an elephant-keeper or driver, (originally 'one who gets his livelihood by elephants.') — *Gajāṇḍa* (°*ja-aṇ*°), *am*, n. a kind of carrot (*piṇḍa-mūla*). — *Gajādana*, a various reading for *gajāśana*, q. v. — *Gajādi-nāmā* (°*ja-ād*°), f., N. of a plant, = *gaja-pippalī*. — *Gajādhipati* (°*ja-adh*°), *is*, m. the prince of elephants, a noble elephant. — *Gajādhyaksha* (°*ja-adh*°), *as*, m. the master or superintendent of the elephants. — *Gajānana* (°*ja-ān*°), *as*, m. 'elephant-faced,' a N. of Gaṇeśa. — *Gajāpasada* (°*ja-ap*°), *as*, m. a common or low-born elephant. — *Gajāyur-veda* (°*ja-āy*°), *as*, m. a work on the treatment of elephants. — *Gajāri* (°*ja-ari*), *is*, m. a lion (the enemy of elephants); a particular tree. — *Gajārūḍha* (°*ja-ār*°), *as*, *ā*, *am*, riding on an elephant. — *Gajāroha* (°*ja-ār*°), *as*, m. an elephant-driver. — *Gajāśana* (°*ja-aś*°), *as*, m. the religious fig tree, = *aśvattha*; (*ā*), f. the gum olibanum tree, Boswellia Serrata; hemp (Cannabis Sativa, = *bhaṅgā*); the root of a lotus. — *Gajāsura-dveshin* (°*ja-as*°), *ī*, m. or *gajāsuhṛid* (°*ja-as*°), *t*, m. the enemy of the Asura Gaja, an epithet of Śiva. — *Gajāsya* (°*ja-ās*°), *as*, m. 'elephant-faced,' an epithet of Gaṇeśa; [cf. *gaja-vadana* and *gajānana*.] — *Gajāhva* (°*ja-āh*°), *am*, n. a N. of Hāstina-pura [cf. *gaja-pura*]; (*ā*), f. another N. of the plant Gaja-pippalī. — *Gajāhvaya* (°*ja-āh*°), *am*, n. = *gaja-pura*; (*ās*), m. pl. the inhabitants of Hāstina-pura. — *Gajekshaṇa* (°*ja-īk*°), *as*, m., N. of a Dānava. — *Gajendra* (°*ja-in*°), *as*, m. a chief among elephants, a large and noble elephant; Indra's elephant. — *Gajendra-karṇa*, *as*, m. an epithet of Śiva. — *Gajendra-nātha*, *as*, m. a very princely elephant. — *Gajendra-mokshaṇa*, *am*, n. title of a section of the Vāmana-Purāṇa; also said to be the title of a part of the Mahā-bhārata. — *Gajendra-vikrama*, *as*, *ā*, *am*, having the valour of an excellent elephant. — *Gajeshṭā* (°*ja-ish*°), f. the plant Batatas Paniculata, = *vidārī*. — *Gajodara* (°*ja-ud*°), *as*, m., N. of a Dānava. — *Gajoshaṇā* (°*ja-ush*°), f., N. of the plant Gaja-pippalī.

गजनवी *gajanavī* = غزنوى.

गञ्ज् *gañj*, cl. 1. P. *gañjati*, &c., to sound, give out a particular sound.

गञ्ज *gañja*, *as*, *am*, m. n. = گنج, a treasury, a jewel room, the place where plate &c. is preserved; (*as*, *ā*, *am*), m. f. n. a mine, a jewel mine; (*as*), m. a cowhouse or station of cowherds; a mart, a place where grain &c. is stored for sale; disrespect, contempt; (*ā*), f. a tavern, a drinking-vessel (especially one for intoxicating liquors); a hut, a hovel, the abode of low people; (? wrong reading for *Guñjā*) the plant Guñjā or Retti, Abrus Precatorius; [cf. *gagaṇa-gañja* and *dharma-gañja*.]

Gañjana, *as*, *ā*, *am*, contemning, conquering, excelling.

Gañjavara, *as*, m. a treasurer, = گنجور; a royal treasury (?).

Gañjikā, f. a tavern.

गञ्जाकिनी *gañjākinī*, f. anything made of hemp (?); perhaps *gṛiñjākinī* (?).

गड् *gaḍ*, cl. 1. P. *gaḍati*, *jagāḍa*, *gaḍitum*, to distil or drop, to run as a liquid; cl. 10. P. *gaḍayati*, *-yitum*, to cover, hide.

Gaḍa, *as*, m. a kind of fish, the young of the Ophiocephalus Lata; another species, Cyprinus Garra; a kind of gold-fish; a screen, a covering, a fence; a moat, a ditch; an impediment, an obstacle; a country, part of Malwa, Garha or Gara Mandala. — *Gaḍa-deśa-ja*, *am*, n. or *gaḍa-lavaṇa*, *am*, n. rock or fossil salt, especially that found in the district of Saṃvara (= *gaḍa*) in the province of Ajmere. — *Gaḍottha* (°*ḍa-ut*°), *am*, n. a kind of salt, = the preceding.

Gaḍaka, *as*, m. a kind of fish, = *gaḍa*.

गडयन्त *gaḍayanta*, *as*, m. or *gaḍayitnu*, *us*, m. [cf. *gardayitnu*], a cloud; [cf. *gaḍ* and *gaḍera*.]

गडि *gaḍi*, *is*, m. a young steer; a lazy ox.

गडु *gaḍu*, *us*, m. an excrescence on the neck, goitre or bronchocele; a hump on the back; a hump-backed or crooked man; a javelin, a spear; an earth-worm; a water-pot; any superfluous excrescence or continuation or addition (as to a poem). — *Gaḍu-kaṇṭha*, *as*, *ā*, *am*, having a goitre. — *Gaḍu-śiras*, *ās*, *ās*, *as*, having an excrescence on the head.

Gaḍuka, *as*, m. a water-pot; a finger-ring; N. of a man; (*ās*), m. pl. the descendants of this man.

Gaḍura, *as*, *ā*, *am*, hump-backed, crooked, bent.

Gaḍula, *as*, *ī*, *am*, hump-backed, crooked.

गडेर *gaḍera*, *as*, m. a cloud; [cf. *gaḍayanta*.]

गडोल *gaḍola*, *as*, m. (said to be fr. rt. *gaḍ*), raw sugar; a mouthful.

गड्डारिका *gaḍḍārikā*, f., N. of a river with a very strong current, of which the source and course are unknown; or (according to others) a single ewe going in front of a flock of sheeep.

गड्डुक *gaḍḍuka* or *gaḍḍūka*, *as*, m. a kind of water-jar, a golden vase; [cf. *gaḍu* and *gaḍuka*.]

गण् *gaṇ*, cl. 10. P. *gaṇayati*, *-yitum*, *ajagaṇat* or *ajīgaṇat*, to count, number, enumerate, sum up, add up, reckon, calculate, compute, take into account; collect into one series; to esteem, think worth, value at (with inst., e.g. *na gaṇayāmi tam tṛiṇena*, I do not value him at a straw); to consider, regard as, enumerate among (with loc.); to ascribe, attribute to (with loc.); to attend to, take notice of; (with a negative particle), not to care about, leave unnoticed (e.g. *na gaṇayati mṛityum*, he does not care for death).

Gaṇa, *as*, m. a flock, troop, multitude, number, tribe, series, class, &c. (of animate or inanimate beings), a body of followers or attendants; troops or classes of inferior deities (see *gaṇa-devatā*), especially certain troops of demi-gods considered as Śiva's attendants and under the special superintendence of the god Gaṇeśa (so called fr. *gaṇa-īśa*, 'lord of the troops,' but the word *gaṇa* may also denote a single attendant of Śiva); a N. of Gaṇeśa; a company, any assemblage, society, or association of men formed for the attainment of the same aims; (with Jainas) the nine assemblies of Ṛishis under the Arhat Vīra; a sect in philosophy or religion; a small body of troops, = 3 Gulmas or 27 chariots and as many elephants, 81 horses, and 135 foot; a series or group of asterisms or lunar mansions classed under three heads (that of the gods, that of men, and that of the Rākshasas or demons); (in arithmetic) a number; (in metre) a foot or four instants; (in grammar) a series of roots or words belonging to the same rule and called after the first word of the series (e.g. *ad-ādi*, the Gaṇa *ad* &c. or the whole series of roots of the 2nd class; *gargādi*, the Gaṇa *garga* &c. or the series of words commencing with *garga*); a kind of perfume, commonly Cor (*gaṇa-hāsaka*, *ćaura*, *ćaṇḍā*); N. of an author; [cf. *ahar-gaṇa*, *deva-gaṇa*, &c.] — *Gaṇa-karman*, *a*, n. a rite common to a whole class; [cf. *gaṇa-yajña*.] — *Gaṇa-kāra*, *as*, m. a classifier, one who arranges into classes, one who collects grammatical Gaṇas; an epithet of Bhīma-sena. — *Gaṇa-kāri*, *is*, m., N. of a man. — *Gaṇa-kumāra*, *as*, m., N. of the founder of a sect worshipping Haridrā-gaṇapati. — *Gaṇa-kṛitvas*, ind. for a whole series of times, for a number of times. — *Gaṇa-gati*, *is*, f. a particular high number; [cf. *gaṇanā-gati*.] — *Gaṇa-ćakraka*, *am*, n. a dinner eaten in common by a party of virtuous men. — *Gaṇa-ććhanda*, *as*, n. a metre measured by feet. — *Gaṇa-tā*, f. or *gaṇa-tva*, *am*, n. the forming a class or multitude or assemblage, the belonging to a party or faction; a cabal; collusion; classification; arithmetic; the office of an attendant of Śiva. — *Gaṇa-dāsa*, *as*, m., N. of a dancing-master. — *Gaṇa-dīkshā*, f. initiation of a number or class; performance of rites for a number of persons; initiation of a particular kind in which Gaṇeśa is especially worshipped. — *Gaṇa-dīkshin*, *ī*, *iṇī*, *i*, one who officiates for a number of persons or for various castes and people (as a priest); one who has been initiated into the worship of Gaṇeśa. — *Gaṇa-deva*, *as*, m., N. of a poet. — *Gaṇa-devatā*, *ās*, f. pl. troops of deities, deities who generally appear in classes, as the Ādityas, Viśvas, Vasus, Tushitas, Ābhāsvaras, Anilas, Mahārājikas, Sādhyas, and Rudras. — *Gaṇa-dravya*, *am*, n. public property, common stock; a variety of articles. — *Gaṇa-dvīpa*, *as*, m. a group of islands or the N. of a particular island (?). — *Gaṇa-dhara*, *as*, m. the head of a class or number, the teacher of a school; (with Jainas) the head of an assemblage of Ṛishis under the Arhat Vīra. — *Gaṇa-nātha*, *as*, m. an epithet of Śiva; the god Gaṇeśa. — *Gaṇa-nāyaka*, *as*, m. the leader or chief of the attendants of any god; the chief of Śiva's attendants, i.e. the god Gaṇeśa; the head of an assemblage; (*ikā*), f. an epithet of the deity Durgā. — *Gaṇa-pa*, *as*, m. = *gaṇeśa*. — *Gaṇa-pati*, *is*, m. the leader or chief of a class or troop or assemblage, an epithet of Bṛihaspati or Indra or Śiva; the god Gaṇeśa; N. of a king; N. of a scholiast on the Caura-pañćāśikā; N. of a poet. — *Gaṇapati-khaṇḍa*, *as*, *am*, m. n. title of a section of the Brahmavaivarta-Purāṇa. — *Gaṇapati-nātha*, *as*, m., N. of a man. — *Gaṇapati-pūjana*, *am*, n. the worship of Gaṇeśa. — *Gaṇapati-bhaṭṭa*, *as*, m., N. of the father of Govindānanda. — *Gaṇapati-stava-rāja*, *as*, m. title of a hymn in praise of Gaṇeśa. — *Gaṇapati-stotra*, *am*, n. prayers addressed to Gaṇeśa. — *Gaṇapaty-ārādhana*, *am*, n. a hymn in honour of Gaṇeśa, attributed to Kaṅkola. — *Gaṇa-parvata*, *as*, m. the mountain frequented by troops (of demi-gods, i.e. Kailāsa, this mountain being the residence of Śiva's attendants as well as of the Kinnaras and Yakshas, attendants of Kuvera). — *Gaṇa-pāṭha*, *as*, m. a collection of the Gaṇas or series of words (in grammar) which fall under the same grammatical rule. — *Gaṇa-pīṭhaka*, *am*, n. the breast or bosom. — *Gaṇa-puṅgava* or *gaṇa-pramukha*, *as*, m. the head of a tribe or class; also *gaṇa-pūjya*. — *Gaṇa-pūrva*, *as*, *ā*, *am*, one who can enumerate a series of ancestors. — *Gaṇa-bhartṛi*, *tā*, m. lord of the troops of deities or demi-gods, epithet of Śiva. — *Gaṇa-bhojana*, *am*, n. eating in common. — *Gaṇa-mukhya*, *as*, m. the chief of an assemblage. — *Gaṇa-yajña*, *as*, m. a rite common to all; [cf. *gaṇa-karman*.] — *Gaṇa-yāga*, *as*, m. worship of the troops or classes of deities. — *Gaṇa-ratna-kāra*, *as*, m. the author of the Pearls of Gaṇas, i.e. Vardhamāna. — *Gaṇa-ratna-mahodadhi*, *is*, m. 'the great ocean in which the Gaṇas form the pearls,' title of a collection of grammatical Gaṇas by Vardhamāna. — *Gaṇa-rājya*, *am*, n., N. of an empire in Dakshiṇāpatha. — *Gaṇa-rātra*, *as*, *am*, m. n. a series or multitude of nights. — *Gaṇa-rūpa*, *as*, m., N. of a plant, swallow-wort, Calotropis Gigantea, = *arka*. — *Gaṇa-rūpaka*, *as*, m. = *rājārka*. — *Gaṇa-rūpin*, *ī*, m. swallow-wort, the white sort. — *Gaṇa-vat*, *ān*, *atī*, *at*, consisting of a series or class &c.; followed by attendants; (*tī*), f., N. of the mother of Divodāsa or Dhanvantari. — *Gaṇavatī-suta*, *as*, m., N. of a sage and physician, also called Divodāsa or Dhanvantari or Kāśirāja. — *Gaṇa-vṛitta*, *am*, n. a kind of metre measured by metrical feet. — *Gaṇa-vyākhyāna*, *am*, n. 'explanation of the Gaṇas,' title of a literary work. — *Gaṇa-śas*, ind. by troops or classes. — *Gaṇa-śri*, *īs*, *īs*, *i*, Ved. associated in troops, associating. — *Gaṇa-hāsa* or *gaṇa-hāsaka*, *as*, m. a species of perfume, = *ćaṇḍā* &c. — *Gaṇāgraṇī* (°*ṇa-ag*°), *īs*, m. a N. of the god Gaṇeśa, leader of the troops of deities. — *Gaṇāćala* (°*ṇa-ać*°), *as*, m., a N. of the mountain Kailāsa as the residence of the Gaṇas or troops of demi-gods. — *Gaṇāćārya* (°*ṇa-āć*°), *as*, m. the teacher of a multitude, a teacher of the people. — *Gaṇādhipa* (°*ṇa-adh*°), *as*, m. a N. of Śiva; also of the god Gaṇeśa; the chief of a troop of soldiers, of a class of disciples, of a body of men or animals; (with Jainas) the chief of an assemblage of Ṛishis under the Arhat Vīra. — *Gaṇādhipati* (°*ṇa-adh*°), *is*, m. a N. of Śiva; also of the god Gaṇeśa. — *Gaṇānna* (°*ṇa-an*°), *am*, n. a mess, food prepared for a number of persons in common. — *Gaṇābhyantara* (°*ṇa-abh*°), *as*, *ā*, *am*, one of a troop or number; (*as*), m. a member of any religious association. — *Gaṇendra* (°*ṇa-in*°), *as*, m., N. of a Buddha. — *Gaṇeśa* (°*ṇa-īśa*), *as*, m. a N. of the god of wisdom and of obstacles, son of Śiva and Pārvatī, (or, according to one legend, of Pārvatī alone. Though Gaṇeśa causes obstacles he also removes them; hence he is invoked at the commencement of all undertakings and at the opening of all compositions with the words *namo Gaṇeśāya vighneśvarāya*, &c. He is represented as a short fat man, with a protuberant belly, frequently riding on a rat or attended by one, and to denote his sagacity has the head of an elephant, which however has only one tusk. The appellation *Gaṇeśa*, with other similar compounds, alludes to his office as chief of the various classes of subordinate gods, who are regarded as Śiva's attendants. He is said to have written down the Mahā-bhārata as dictated by Vyāsa); N. of Śiva; of a renowned astronomer of the sixteenth century; N. of a son of Rāmadeva, author of a commentary on the Nalodaya; N. of a son of Viśvanātha-dīkshita and grandson of Bhāvarāma-kṛishṇa, author of the commentary called Ćić-ćandrikā. — *Gaṇeśa-kumbha*, *as*, m., N. of a rocky cave in Orissa. — *Gaṇeśa-kusuma*, *as*, m. a kind of oleander with red flowers. — *Gaṇeśa-khaṇḍa*, *as*, *am*, m. n. the third book of the Brahmavaivarta-Purāṇa; title of a book of the Skanda-Purāṇa. — *Gaṇeśa-purāṇa*, *am*, n. title of an Upa-Purāṇa. — *Gaṇeśa-pūjā*, f. the worship of Gaṇeśa. — *Gaṇeśa-bhujaṅga-prayāta-stotra*, *am*, n. a hymn in praise of Gaṇeśa, attributed to Śaṅkarāćārya. — *Gaṇeśa-bhūshaṇa*, *am*, n. red lead. — *Gaṇeśa-miśra*, *as*, m., N. of a copyist of the last century. — *Gaṇeśa-sahasranāman*, *a*, n. a part of the Gaṇeśa-Purāṇa. — *Gaṇeśa-stava-rāja*, *as* or *am*, m. or n. (?), a part of the Bhavishya-Purāṇa. — *Gaṇeśa-stuti*, *is*, f. a hymn in honour of Gaṇeśa by Rāghava. — *Gaṇeśāna* (°*ṇa-īś*°), *as*, m. the god Gaṇeśa. — *Gaṇeśvara* (°*ṇa-īś*°), *as*, m. the chief of a troop, leader of a band &c.; N. of a being mentioned in the Hari-vaṅśa; the chief of the animals, i.e. the lion. — *Gaṇotsāha* (°*ṇa-ut*°), *as*, m. the rhinoceros ('avoiding assemblages?').

Gaṇaka, *as*, *ikā*, *am*, bought for a large sum; (*as*), m. one who reckons, an arithmetician; an astrologer, a calculator of nativities &c.; an assemblage of eight stars; (*ī*), f. the wife of an astrologer.

Gaṇatitha, *as*, *ī*, *am*, forming a troop or assemblage.

Gaṇana, *am*, *ā*, n. f. reckoning, counting, calculation; adding, collecting under one head; enumerating; considering, supposing, believing; regarding, taking notice of, consideration. — *Gaṇanā-gati*, *is*, f. a particular high number, = *gaṇa-gati*. — *Gaṇanā-pati*, *is*, m. an arithmetician; the master of prudent calculation, an epithet of Gaṇeśa. — *Gaṇanā-mahāmātra*, *as*, m. a minister of finance.

Gaṇanīya, *as*, *ā*, *am*, calculable, to be counted or reckoned, to be classed; numerable.

Gaṇi, *is*, m. one who is familiar with the sacred writings and the auxiliary sciences; (*is*), f. counting, enumerating. — *Gaṇi-piṭaka*, *am*, n. the twelve sacred writings of the Jainas collectively.

Gaṇikā, f. a harlot, a courtezan; a female elephant; N. of several plants, a sort of jasmine, Jasminum Auriculatum; another plant, Æschynomene Sesban, = *tarkārī*; another plant, commonly called Gaṇikārikā; counting, enumerating; apprehension.

Gaṇikārikā, f., N. of a small tree with a very fetid leaf, commonly Gaṇiyārī, or also Vaḍagaṇiyārī, the wood of which is used in attrition for the purpose of producing flame, Premna Spinosa; [cf. the last.]

Gaṇikāri, f. a plant similar to the preceding, commonly called Gaṇiyārī.

Gaṇita, *as*, *ā*, *am*, numbered, counted, reckoned, calculated; (*am*), n. reckoning, calculating, the science of computation (comprising arithmetic, algebra, and geometry, severally called *pāṭī-gaṇitam* or *vyakta-gaṇitam*, *vīja-gaṇitam*, and *rekhā-gaṇitam*); the astronomical or astrological part of a Jyotiḥ-śāstra, with exception of the portion treating of nativities; the sum of a progression, a sum in general. — *Gaṇita-kaumudī*, f. title of a commentary on the Līlāvatī. — *Gaṇita-tattva-ćintāmaṇi*, *is*, m. title of a commentary on Bhāskara's Sūrya-Siddhānta. — *Gaṇita-mālatī*, f. or *gaṇita-sāra*, *as*, m. titles of two mathematical works. — *Gaṇita-śāstra*, *am*, n. the book or science of computation; see above. — *Gaṇitādhyāya* (°*ta-adh*°), *as*, m. title of a chapter in the Brahma-Siddhānta. — *Gaṇitāmṛita-sāgarī* (°*ta-am*°), f. title of a commentary on the Līlāvatī.

Gaṇitavya, as, ā, am, to be counted or numbered, to be calculated.

Gaṇitin, ī, inī, i, one who has made a calculation.

Gaṇin, ī, m. a teacher ('having a class of pupils').

Gaṇī-bhūta, as, ā, am, included in any class or troop, calculated.

Gaṇeya, as, ā, am, numerable, calculable, what may be reckoned or counted.

Gaṇeru, us, m. the plant Pterospermum Acerifolium [cf. *karṇikāra*]; (*us*), f. a harlot, a whore; a female elephant.

Gaṇerukā, f. a bawd, a procuress, a female servant.

Gaṇeśa. See under *gaṇa,* p. 279.

Gaṇya, as, ā, am, calculable, to be counted or calculated; (at the end of compounds) belonging to a multitude or class or troop &c.

गण्ड् *gaṇḍ* (probably fr. *gaṇḍa,* the cheek), cl. 1. P. *gaṇḍati* (?), to affect the cheek, be rough as the cheek (?).

Gaṇḍa, as, m. the cheek, the whole side of the face including the temple; an elephant's cheek or temple; a bubble, a boil, a pimple; a goitre and other excrescences of the neck; a joint, a bone; the bladder; a mark, spot; part of a horse's trappings, a stud or button fixed as an ornament upon the harness; a rhinoceros [cf. *gaṇḍaka* and *gaṇḍāṅga*]; a hero [cf. *gaṇḍīra*]; the abrupt interchange of question and answer, as one of the characteristics of the dramatic composition, called Vīthī; the tenth Yoga or one of the twenty-seven portions of a circle on the plane of the ecliptic [cf. *yoga*]; an astronomical period; a pledge, deposit (?). In composition *gaṇḍa* may imply chief, best, excellent [cf. *gaṇḍa-grāma* and *gaṇḍa-mūrkha*]; (*ā*), f., N. of the female attendant of the seven sages; [cf. *gaḍu, gaṇḍi, gaṇḍu,* &c.] — *Gaṇḍa-kaṇḍu, us,* m., N. of a Yaksha. — *Gaṇḍa-kārī,* f., N. of two plants; [cf. *khadirī* and *varāha-krāntā.*] — *Gaṇḍa-kolī,* f., N. of a plant; [cf. *khadirī.*] — *Gaṇḍa-kusuma, am,* n. the juice that exudes from the elephant's temples during rut. — *Gaṇḍa-kūpa, as,* m. the peak or summit of a mountain. — *Gaṇḍa-gātra, am,* n. the fruit of the Anona Reticulata or Squamosa, commonly called Ātā or custard apple. — *Gaṇḍa-grāma, as,* m. any large or considerable village. — *Gaṇḍa-dūrvā,* f. a kind of Dūrvā grass. — *Gaṇḍa-deśa* or *gaṇḍa-pradeśa, as,* m. the region of the cheek, the cheek. — *Gaṇḍa-phalaka, am,* n. the cheek fancifully regarded as a seed-vessel. — *Gaṇḍa-bhitti, is,* f. a dimple in the cheek; the openings in the temples of an elephant, from which a juice exudes in the time of rut. — *Gaṇḍa-mālā,* f. or according to some also *gaṇḍa-māla, as,* m. inflammation of the glands of the neck &c. — *Gaṇḍa-mālikā,* f. a kind of Mimosa (*lajjālu*). — *Gaṇḍa-mālin, ī, inī, i,* having the glands of the neck inflamed. — *Gaṇḍa-mūrkha, as,* m. exceedingly foolish, very stupid. — *Gaṇḍa-vyūha, as,* m. title of a Buddhist Sūtra work. — *Gaṇḍa-śilā,* f. any large rock. — *Gaṇḍa-śaila, as,* m. a huge rock or rocky fragment thrown down by an earthquake, storm, &c.; the forehead. — *Gaṇḍa-sāhvayā,* f., N. of a river, = *gaṇḍakī* (?). — *Gaṇḍa-sthala, am, ī,* n. f. the cheek; the temples of an elephant. — *Gaṇḍāṅga* (°*ḍa-aṅ*°), *as,* m. a rhinoceros; [cf. *gaṇḍa* and *gaṇḍaka.*] — *Gaṇḍopadhāna* (°*ḍa-up*°), *am,* n. a pillow.

Gaṇḍaka, as, m. a rhinoceros [cf. *gaṇḍa* and *gaṇḍāṅga* above]; an obstacle or impediment; disjunction, separation; a mode of reckoning by fours, a peculiar manner of counting; a coin of the value of four cowries; a kind of science, astrological science or a part of it; a mark, spot; a kind of metre containing four lines of twenty syllables each; an epithet of the Videhas living on the river Gaṇḍakī; an epithet of Kāla, the brother of Prasena-jit; (*ī*), f., N. of the river Gaṇḍakī in the northern part of India; (*ā*), f. a lump, a ball. — *Gaṇḍaka-vatī,* f. another N. of the river Gaṇḍakī.

Gaṇḍalin, ī, m. an epithet of Śiva.

Gaṇḍārī, is, m. the plant Bauhinia Variegata, = *kovidāra.*

Gaṇḍālī, f. a bent grass with white blossoms, a white sort of Dūrvā (*sitā dūrvā*), Agrostis Linearis; also N. of two other plants, = *gaṇḍa-dūrvā, sarpākshī.*

Gaṇḍi, is, m. the trunk of a tree from the root to the beginning of the branches; goitre or bronchocele.

Gaṇḍikā, f. anything advanced beyond the first stage or commencement; a kind of beverage (in this sense also *gaṇḍikākāra?*); a declivity (?). This last sense appears probable in some names of places (e. g. in *apara-gaṇḍikā, pūrva-pūrṇānugaṇḍikā,* &c.), hence *anugaṇḍikā* may be the country bordering on a declivity.

Gaṇḍinī, f. an epithet of Durgā.

Gaṇḍīra, as, m. a kind of pot-herb, described as growing in watery ground, but according to some a species of cucumber; a hero, a champion [cf. *gaṇḍa*]; (*ī*), f. the plant Tithymalus Antiquorum, = *sohuṇḍa;* [cf. *gāṇḍīra.*]

Gaṇḍu, us, us, m. f. a pillow [cf. *gaṇḍopadhāna*]; (*ū, ūs*), f. a joint; a knot; a bone; oil. — *Gaṇḍūpada, as,* m. a kind of worm, an earth-worm; (*ī*), f. a small or female worm. — *Gaṇḍūpada-bhava, am,* n. lead.

Gaṇḍula, as, ā, am, bent, crooked; [cf. *gaḍula.*]

Gaṇḍūsha, as, ā, m. f. a mouthful, a handful; a handful of water, water &c. held in the hollowed palm of the hand for rincing the mouth &c.; filling the mouth, rincing it, &c.; the tip of an elephant's trunk; (*as*), m., N. of a son of Śūra and brother of Vasu-deva.

Gaṇḍola, as, am, m. n. raw sugar [cf. *gaḍola* and *guḍa*]; (*as*), m. a mouthful [cf. *gaṇḍūsha*].

गण्य *gaṇya.* See under rt. *gaṇ.*

गत् *gat, gata,* &c. See rt. *gam,* p. 282.

गद् *gad,* cl. 1. P. *gadati, jagāda, gadishyati, agādīt* or *agadīt, gaditum,* to speak articulately, speak, say, relate, tell anything to a person (with two acc.); to enumerate; to name, call; cl. 10. P. *gadayati, -yitum,* to thunder: Caus. *gādayati, -yitum:* Desid. *jigadishati,* to intend or wish to speak or tell: Intens. *jāgadyate, jāgatti;* [cf. Lith. *gadijos, zadas, zodis, giedmi;* Pol. *gadać;* Hib. *gadh.*]

Gada, as, m. speaking, speech; a sentence; N. of a son of Vasu-deva and younger brother of Kṛishṇa; disease, sickness; (*am*), n. poison; [cf. *a-gada.*] — *Gada-siṇha, as,* m., N. of an author. — *Gadākhya* (°*da-ākh*°), *am,* n., N. of a plant, = *kushṭha.* — *Gadāgada* (°*da-ag*°), *au,* m. du. the two Aśvins, physicians of Svarga. — *Gadāgraja* (°*da-ag*°), *as,* m. the elder brother of Gada, epithet of Kṛishṇa. — *Gadāgraṇī* (°*da-ag*°), *is,* m. the chief of all diseases, consumption. — *Gadāmbara* (°*da-am*°), *as,* m. a cloud. — *Gadārāti* (°*da-ar*°), *is,* m. a drug, a medicament ('the enemy of diseases'). — *Gadāhva* or *gadāhvaya* (°*da-āh*°), *am,* n. a kind of Costus, Costus Speciosus.

Gadayitnu, us, us, u, loquacious, talkative, talking much or idly; libidinous, desirous, lustful; (*us*), m. a bow; a N. of Kāma or Kandarpa, the god of love.

Gadā, f. a mace, club, bludgeon; the plant Bignonia Suaveolens; a particular constellation. — *Gadāgrapāṇi* (°*dā-ag*°), *is, is, i,* having a mace in the right hand. — *Gadā-dhara, as, ā, am,* bearing a club; (*as*), m. an epithet of Kṛishṇa [cf. *kaumodakī*]; N. of a physician; N. of the author of the work Vishaya-vićāra; N. of the father of Mukunda-priya and uncle of Rāmānanda &c. — *Gadādhara-bhaṭṭa, as,* m., N. of an author. — *Gadā-parvan, a,* n. title of a book of the Mahā-bhārata. — *Gadā-bhṛit, t, t, t,* a club-bearer, one who fights with a mace; an epithet of Kṛishṇa. — *Gadā-yuddha, am,* n. a fight with clubs or bludgeons. — *Gadāyudha* (°*dā-āy*°), *as, ā, am,* armed with a club. — *Gadāvasāna* (°*dā-av*°), *am,* n., N. of a place near Mathurā (where the mace thrown by Jarāsandha rested). — *Gadā-hasta, as, ā, am,* armed with a mace, mace-handed.

Gadita, as, ā, am, spoken, said, related; (*am*), n. speaking, speech. — *Gadita-vat, ān, atī, at,* having spoken, speaking.

Gadin, ī, inī, i, armed with a club, a mace-bearer; (*ī*), m. an epithet of Kṛishṇa. — *Gadi-siṇha, as,* m., N. of a grammarian.

Gadgada, as, ā, am, stammering, stuttering; (*am*), n. stammering; indistinct or convulsive utterance, as sobbing &c. — *Gadgada-tva, am,* n. stammering. — *Gadgada-dhvani, is,* m. low inarticulate expression of joy or grief. — *Gadgada-pada, am,* n. inarticulate speech. — *Gadgada-vāć, k,* f. inarticulate or convulsive speech, interrupted by sobbing &c. — *Gadgada-svara, as,* m. indistinct or stammering utterance; (*as, ā, am*), uttering stammering sounds; (*as*), m. a buffalo; N. of a Bodhi-sattva.

Gadgadita, as, ā, am, stammered.

Gadgadya, nom. P. *gadgadyati,* to stammer.

Gadya, as, ā, am, to be spoken or uttered; (*am*), n. prose, composition not metrical yet framed in accordance with harmony, elaborate prose composition.

गदाय *gadāya,* nom. A., Ved. *gadāyate, -yitum,* to become lazy or idle; [cf. *gaḍi.*]

गद्याणक *gadyāṇaka* or *gadyānaka* or *gadyālaka, am,* n. a weight, = 32 Guñjās or berries of the plant Abrus Precatorius, or = 64 such Guñjās with physicians.

गध् *gadh,* cl. 4. P. *gadhyati,* to be mixed.

Gadhya, as, ā, am, Ved. to be seized, to be gained as booty.

गन्तव्य *gantavya,* &c. See under rt. *gam.*

गन्दिका *gandikā,* f., N. of a place.

गन्ध् *gandh,* cl. 10. A. *gandhayate, -yitum,* to injure, hurt, kill; to move, to go; to ask or beg; [cf. *gandhana* and *gandhaya;* cf. also Lith. *gandinu.*]

गन्ध *gandha as,* m. (said to be fr. rt. *gandh*), smell, odour, (sometimes nine or ten kinds are enumerated, viz. *ishṭa, anishṭa, madhura, kaṭu, nirhārin, saṃhata, snigdha, rūksha, viśada, amla*); a fragrant substance, fragrance, scent, (in comp. = fragrant, see *gandhāmbu* &c.), a perfume; sulphur [cf. *gandhaka*]; pounded sandal-wood; myrrh [cf. *bala*]; the tree Hyperanthera Moringa; the mere smell of anything, a small quantity, a little; connection, relationship; a neighbour; pride, arrogance; an epithet of Śiva; (*ā*), f. the plant Curcuma Amhaldi or Zerumbet; the plant Desmodium Gangeticum, = *śāla-parṇī;* the bud of the plant Michelia Champaca; N. of a metre consisting of four lines with 17 + 18 + 17 + 18 syllables; (*am*), n. smell; black aloe-wood. — *Gandha-kanduka, as,* m. the plant Scirpus Kysoor, = *kaśeru.* — *Gandha-kārikā,* f. a female servant whose business is to prepare perfumes; a female artisan living in the house of another woman. — *Gandha-kālikā* or *gandha-kālī,* f., N. of the mother of the poet Vyāsa; N. of an Apsaras. — *Gandha-kāshṭha, am,* n. a fragrant wood, as sandal, aloe-wood, &c.; a species of sandal-wood (*śambara-ćandana*). — *Gandha-kuṭi,* f. a kind of perfume, commonly Mura; [cf. *gandha-kūṭī.*] — *Gandha-kusumā,* f. a kind of plant, = *gaṇikārī.* — *Gandha-kūṭī,* f. the hall of fragrances; (perhaps for *gandha-kuṭī.*) — *Gandha-kelikā,* f. musk; [cf. *gandha-ćelikā.*] — *Gandha-kokilā,* f. a kind of perfume. — *Gandha-kheḍa, am,* n. a kind of fragrant grass, Andropogon Schoenanthus; also *gandha-kheḍaka;* [cf. *gandha-tṛiṇa.*] — *Gandha-ga, as, ā, am,* taking a scent, smelling; redolent. — *Gandha-gaja, as,* m. 'scent-elephant,' an elephant of the best kind; [cf. *gandha-dvipa.*] — *Gandha-guṇa, as, ā, am,* having the property of odour. — *Gandha-ghrāṇa, am,* n. the smelling of any odour. — *Gandha-ćelikā*, f. musk. — *Gandha-jaṭilā*, f. the plant Acorus Calamus; [cf. *vaćā*.] — *Gandha-jala*, *am*, n. fragrant water. — *Gandha-jāta*, *am*, n. the leaf of the Laurus Cassia. — *Gandha-jña*, *ā*, f. the nose. — *Gandha-taṇḍula*, *as*, m. fragrant rice. — *Gandha-tūrya*, *am*, n. a musical instrument, one of a loud sound used in battle (a drum or trumpet). — *Gandha-tṛiṇa*, *am*, n. fragrant grass, Andropogon Schœnanthus. — *Gandha-taila*, *am*, n. a kind of oil prepared with fragrant substances. — *Gandha-tvać*, *k*, f. a kind of perfume, the fragrant bark of the tree Feronia Elephantum (*elavāluka*). — *Gandha-dalā*, f., N. of a plant, = *aja-modā*. — *Gandha-dāru*, *u*, n. aloe-wood. — *Gandha-dravya*, *am*, n. a fragrant substance. — *Gandha-dvipa*, *as*, m. an elephant of the best class, very much feared by other elephants (supposed to emit a peculiar smell). — *Gandha-dhārin*, *ī*, *iṇī*, *i*, bearing fragrances; (*ī*), m. an epithet of Śiva; [cf. *gandha-pālin*.] — *Gandha-dhūma-ja*, *as*, m. a kind of perfume; [cf. *svādu*.] — *Gandha-dhūli*, *is*, f. musk, the fragrant secretion of the musk deer. — *Gandha-nakula*, *as*, m. the musk rat of Bengal, Sorex Moschatus. — *Gandha-nākulī*, f., N. of a plant, possibly Ophioxylon Serpentinum. — *Gandha-nāman*, *ā*, m. a fragrant kind of basil with red flowers; also *gandha-nāmnī*, f.; [cf. *gandhāhvā*.] — *Gandha-nālikā* or *gandha-nālī*, f. the nose. — *Gandha-nilayā*, f. a kind of jasmine, J Zambac Floribus Multiplicatis; [cf. *nava-mallikā*.] — *Gandha-niśā*, f., N. of a plant, = *gandha-pattrā*. — *Gandha-pa*, *as*, *ā*, *am*, 'inhaling the odour,' epithet of a class of manes. — *Gandha-pattra*, *as*, m. several plants with fragrant leaves; a white sort of basil, Ocimum Gratissimum, = *śveta-pāṇā*; the plant Ægle Marmelos, = *vilva*; the orange tree; (*ā*), f. a kind of Curcuma; (*ī*), f., N. of several plants, = *ambashṭhā*, *aśva-gandhā*, *aja-modā*. — *Gandha-pattrikā*, f., N. of two plants, = *gandha-pattrā* and *aja-modā*. — *Gandha-parṇa*, *am*, n., N. of a plant, = *kāka-pushpa*. — *Gandha-palāśikā*, f. turmeric; [cf. *hari-drā*.] — *Gandha-palāśī*, f. the plant Curcuma Amhaldi or Zerumbet, = *śaṭī*. — *Gandha-pālin*, *ī*, *inī*, *i*, preserving fragrances; (*ī*), m. an epithet of Śiva. — *Gandha-pāshāṇa*, *as*, m. sulphur. — *Gandha-piṅgalā*, f., N. of a woman. — *Gandha-piśāćikā*, f. the smoke of burned fragrant resin, imp-like, from its dark colour or cloudy nature. — *Gandha-pītā*, f. a plant, = *gandha-pattrā*, a species of Zedoary. — *Gandha-pushpa*, *am*, n. a fragrant flower; flowers and sandal presented together at seasons of worship; (*as*), m. several plants with fragrant flowers, a kind of cane, Calamus Rotang [cf. *vetasa*]; another plant, Alangium Hexapetalum [cf. *aṅkoṭa*]; Sebesten, Cordia Myxa, = *bahu-vāra*; (*ā*), f. several plants, viz. the Indigo plant; Pandanus Odoratissimus [cf. *ketaka*]; the plant Premna Spinosa, = *gaṇikārī*. — *Gandha-pūtanā*, f. a kind of imp or goblin. — *Gandha-phaṇijjhaka*, *as*, m. a kind of Ocimum with red flowers. — *Gandha-phala*, *as*, m. several plants with fragrant fruits, viz. Feronia Elephantum, = *kapittha*; Ægle Marmelos, = *vilva*; another plant, = *tejah-phala*; (*ā*), f. several plants, = *priyaṅgu*, *methikā*, *vidārī*, *śallakī*; (*ī*), f., N. of a plant, = *priyaṅgu*; the bud of the plant Michelia Champaca. — *Gandha-baṇij*, *k*, f. a seller of perfumes. — *Gandha-bandhu*, *us*, m. the mango tree; [cf. *āmra*.] — *Gandha-bahula*, *as*, m. fragrant rice; (*ā*), f., N. of a plant, = *gorakshī*. — *Gandha-bhadrā*, f. a creeper, commonly Gandha-bhādāliyā, (Pœderia Fœtida?). — *Gandha-bhāṇḍa*, *as*, m. a tree, Hibiscus Populneoides; [cf. *gardabhāṇḍa*.] — *Gandha-māṅsī*, f. a kind of Indian spikenard, Valeriana; [cf. *jaṭā-māṅsī*.] — *Gandha-mātṛi*, *tā*, f. the earth (the quality of odour residing in the earth). — *Gandha-māda*, *as*, m., N. of a son of Svaphalka; also of a monkey who was an attendant of Rāma. — *Gandha-mādana*, *as*, *ī*, *am*, intoxicating with fragrance; (*as*), m. a large black bee; sulphur [cf. *gandha-modana*]; N. of a particular mountain, forming the division between Ilā-vṛita and Bhadrāśva or to the east of Meru, renowned for its fragrant forests; an epithet of Rāvaṇa, chief of the Rākshasas; N. of a monkey, an attendant of Śiva; (*ī*), f. spirituous liquor; a parasitical plant (*vandāka*), a kind of perfume, = *ćiḍā*; (*am*), n. the forest on the mountain Gandha-mādana. — *Gandha-mādin*, *ī*, *inī*, *i*, strong-scented, of intoxicating fragrance; (*inī*), f lac; a sort of perfume [cf. *purā*]; wine or spirituous liquor; [cf. the preceding.] — *Gandha-mārjāra*, *as*, m. the civet cat. — *Gandha-mālatī*, f. a kind of perfume. — *Gandha-mālinī*, f. a kind of perfume, = *murā*. — *Gandha-mālya*, *e*, n. du. fragrances and garlands; (*āni*), n. pl. fragrances and garlands; fragrant garlands. — *Gandha-muṇḍa*, *as*, m. a kind of creeper, Hibiscus Populneoides, = *gandha-bhāṇḍa* or *gardabhāṇḍa*. — *Gandha-mūla*, *as*, m. a plant with a fragrant and tuberous root, one of the Scitaminea, Alpinia Galanga, = *kulañjana*; (*ā*), f. the plant Curcuma Amhaldi or Zerumbet [cf. *śaṭī*]; the olibanum tree, = *śallakī*; (*ī*), f. the plant Curcuma Amhaldi or Zerumbet. — *Gandha-mūlaka*, *as*, m. the plant Curcuma Amhaldi or Zerumbet; (*ikā*), f. the same plant; another plant, = *mākandī*. — *Gandha-mūshika*, *as*, m. or *gandha-mūshī*, f. the musk rat or shrew, Sorex Moschatus. — *Gandha-mṛiga*, *as*, m. the civet cat; the name may also be applied to the musk deer. — *Gandha-maithuna*, *as*, m. a bull. — *Gandha-mojavāha*, *as*, m., N. of a son of Svaphalka, (incorrect for *gandha-māda*.) — *Gandha-modana*, *as*, m. sulphur. — *Gandha-mohinī*, f. the bud of the plant Michelia Campaca. — *Gandha-yukti*, *is*, f. the blending of fragrant substances, preparation of perfumes; title of the seventy-sixth Adhyāya of Varāhamihira's Bṛihaj-jātaka. — *Gandha-yuti*, *is*, f. mixture of fragrant substances. — *Gandha-rasa*, *as*, m. myrrh. — *Gandha-rasāṅgaka* (°*śa-an*°), *as*, m. turpentine, = *śri-veshṭa*. — *Gandha-rāja*, *as*, m. a kind of jasmine, = *mudgara*; another plant, = *kaṇa-guggulu*; (*ī*), f. a sort of perfume, commonly Nakhī; (*am*), n. sandal-wood; a kind of perfume; a kind of white flower. — *Gandha-lolupā*, f. a fly or gnat. — *Gandha-vat*, *ān*, *atī*, *at*, smelling, endowed with fragrance; scented, odoriferous; (*tī*), f. the earth (because it possesses the quality of smell); a kind of jasmine [cf. *nava-mallikā*]; wine or vinous liquor; a kind of perfume, = *murā*; an epithet of the mother of Vyāsa, also called Satya-vatī; N. of a city belonging to Varuṇa; N. of a river. — *Gandha-vadhū*, *ūs*, f. the plant Curcuma Amhaldi or Zerumbet; a kind of perfume, = *ćiḍā*. — *Gandha-valkala*, *am*, n. the cassia bark, Laurus Cassia; Sarsaparilla. — *Gandha-vallarī* or *gandha-vallī*, f., N. of a plant, = *saha-devī*. — *Gandha-vaha*, *as*, *ā*, *am*, bearing fragrances, epithet of the winds; (*as*), m. the wind; (*ā*), f. the nose. — *Gandha-vahala*, *am*, n. a kind of Ocimum, = *sitārjaka*. — *Gandha-vāha*, *as*, m. the wind; a deer, the musk deer; (*ā*), f. the nose. — *Gandha-vihvala*, *as*, m. wheat. — *Gandha-vijā*, f. a kind of grass, = *methikā*. — *Gandha-vṛikshaka*, *as*, m. the Sāl tree, Shorea Robusta. — *Gandha-vyākula*, *am*, n. a perfume, a fragrant berry, = *kakkola*. — *Gandha-śaṭī*, f. the tree Curcuma Amhaldi or Zerumbet. — *Gandha-śāka*, *am*, n. a kind of vegetable. — *Gandha-śāli*, *is*, m. a sweet-smelling kind of rice. — *Gandha-śuṇḍinī* or *gandhā-śuṇḍinī*, f. the musk rat or shrew. — *Gandha-śekhara*, *as*, m. musk. — *Gandha-sāra*, *as*, m. sandal; a kind of jasmine, = *mudgara*. — *Gandha-sāraṇa*, *as*, m. a kind of perfume, = *vṛihan-nakhī*. — *Gandha-sukhī* or *gandha-sūyī*, f. the musk shrew or small musk rat. — *Gandha-soma*, *am*, n. the white esculent water-lily. — *Gandha-hastin*, *ī*, m. 'the scent-elephant;' [cf. *gandha-dvipa*.] — *Gandha-hārikā*, f. a female servant who bears perfumes behind her mistress, a female artisan working in another person's house; [cf. *gandha-kārikā*.] — *Gandhākhu* (°*dha-ākhu*), *us*, m. the musk rat. — *Gandhājīva* (°*dha-āj*°), *as*, m. a vender of perfumes (one who makes a livelihood by them). — *Gandhāḍhya* (°*dha-āḍh*°), *as*, *ā*, *am*, rich in odour, fragrant; (*as*), m. the orange tree; (*ā*), f., N. of several plants, = *gandha-pattrā*; yellow jasmine, = *svarṇa-yūthī*; other plants, = *taruṇī*, *ārāma-śītalā*, *gandhālī*; (*am*), n. sandal-wood; a kind of perfume (= *javādi*). — *Gandhādhika* (°*dha-adh*°), *am*, n. a kind of perfume, = *tṛiṇa-kuṅkuma*. — *Gandhāpakarshaṇa* (°*dha-ap*°), *am*, n. removing smells. — *Gandhāmbu* (°*dha-am*°), *u*, n. fragrant water. — *Gandhāmlā* (°*dha-ām*°), f. the wild lemon tree. — *Gandhālā* (°*dha-āla* = *ālaya*?), f., N. of a plant, commonly Jiyatī, Celtis Orientalis. — *Gandhā-śuṇḍinī* = *gandha-śuṇḍinī*. — *Gandhāśman* (°*dha-aś*°), *ā*, m. sulphur. — *Gandhāshṭaka* (°*dha-ash*°), *am*, n. a mixture of eight fragrant substances varying according to the deities to whom they are offered (e. g. the eight articles, sandal, agallochum, camphor, saffron, valerian, and some fragrant grasses). — *Gandhāhvā* (°*dha-āh*°), f. = *gandha-nāmnī*. — *Gandhendriya* (°*dha-in*°), *am*, n. the organ of smell. — *Gandhebha* (°*dha-ibha*), *as*, m. 'the scent-elephant;' [cf. *gandha-dvipa*, *gandha-hastin*.] — *Gandhotu* or *gandhautu* (°*dha-otu*), *us*, m. the civet cat. — *Gandhotkaṭā* (°*dha-ut*°), f., N. of a plant, = *damanaka*. — *Gandhottamā* (°*dha-ut*°), f. spirituous or vinous liquor. — *Gandhoda* (°*dha-uda*), *am*, n. fragrant water. — *Gandhopajīvin* (°*dha-up*°), *ī*, *inī*, *i*, one who lives by perfumes, a seller of perfumes, a perfumer.

Gandhaka, *as*, m. sulphur; the Morunga tree, Hyperanthera Moringa, = *śobhāñjana*.

Gandhakīya, *as*, *ā*, *am*, relating to sulphur, treating of it.

Gandhaya, nom. P. *gandhayati*, *-yitum*, to make redolent or odoriferous.

Gandhālu, *us*, *us*, *u*, fragrant, perfumed.

Gandhi, *is*, *is*, *i*, (at the end of compounds) having the smell of, smelling of, perfumed with; having only the smell of, containing only a very small quantity; (*i*), n. a kind of perfume.

Gandhika, *as*, *ā*, *am*, having the smell of, smelling of [cf. *aja-gandhika*, *avi-g*°, *utpala-g*°]; having only the smell, having a very little of anything (e. g. *bhrātṛi-gandhika*, being brother only by name); (*as*), m. a seller of perfumes; sulphur.

Gandhin, *ī*, *inī*, *i*, having a smell, smelling, odoriferous; (*ī*), m. a bug; also the flying bug; the tree Xanthophyllum Virens; (*nī*), f. a kind of perfume, = *murā*. — *Gandhi-parṇa*, *as*, m., N. of a plant, = *sapta-ććhada*.

गन्धन *gandhana*, *am*, n. continued effort, perseverance; hurting, injury, killing; manifestation, information, intimation, informing against.

गन्धर्व *gandharva* or sometimes in post-Vedic writings *gandharba*, *as*, m. a Gandharva. Though in later times the Gandharvas are regarded as a class, yet in the Ṛig-veda rarely more than one is mentioned; he is commonly designated as the 'heavenly Gandharva' (*divyo Gandharvaḥ*), and sometimes named Viśvā-vasu; his habitation is the sky, or the region of the air and the heavenly waters; his especial duty is to guard the heavenly Soma, which the gods obtain through his intervention. It is obtained for the human race by Indra, who conquers the Gandharva and takes it by force. The heavenly Gandharva is supposed to be a good physician, because the Soma is considered as the best medicine; possibly, however, the word Soma originally denoted not the beverage so called, but the moon, and the heavenly Gandharva may have been the genius or tutelary deity of the moon. It is certain that the heavenly Gandharva and the Soma are sometimes identified. He is also regarded as one of the genii who regulate the course of the Sun's horses; he knows and makes known the secrets of heaven and divine truths generally. He is the parent of the first pair of human beings, Yama and Yamī, and has a peculiar mystical power over women and a right to possess them. For this reason he is invoked in marriage ceremonies. Exstatic states of mind and possession by evil spirits are supposed to be derived from the heavenly Gandharva. With Jainas he is an attendant of the seventeenth Arhat of the present Avasarpiṇī. The Gandharvas as a class have the same characteristic features as the one Gandharva; they live in the sky, guard the Soma, are governed by Varuṇa (just as the Apsarasas are governed by Soma), know the best medicines, regulate the course of the asterisms (in one passage of the Vājasaneyi-Saṃhitā twenty-seven being mentioned), follow after women and are desirous of intercourse with them. As soon as a girl becomes marriageable, she belongs to Soma, the Gandharvas, and Agni. The wives of the Gandharvas are the Apsarasas, and like them the Gandharvas are invoked in gambling with dice; they are also feared as evil beings together with the Rakshasas, Kimīdins, Piśāćas, &c., amulets being worn as a protection against them. In the Śatapatha-Brāhmaṇa they are called the preceptors of the Ṛishis. In epic poetry the Gandharvas are the celestial musicians or heavenly singers who form the orchestra at the banquets of the gods, and they belong together with the Apsarasas to Indra's heaven, sharing also in his battles. In the more systematic mythology the Gandharvas constitute one of the classes into which the higher creation is divided (e. g. gods, manes, Gandharvas; or gods, Asuras, Gandharvas, men, &c.). In one passage of the Taittirīya-Āraṇyaka eleven classes of Gandharvas are mentioned. The chief or leader of the Gandharvas is named Ćitra-ratha. They are sometimes called the creatures of Prajāpati or Brahmā. With Jainas the Gandharvas constitute one of the eight classes of the Vyantaras. The following meanings are also given to the word *gandharva*—a singer; the Koil or black cuckoo; the soul after death, and previous to its being born again (corresponding in some respects to the western notion of a ghost); a horse; the sun; a sage, a pious man; a kind of deer, according to some, the musk deer; (*ī*), f. Gandharvī, a daughter of Su-rabhi and mother of the race of horses; [cf. Gr. κένταυρος.] — *Gandharva-khaṇḍa*, one of the nine divisions of Bhārata-varsha. — *Gandharva-gṛihīta, as, ā, am*, Ved. possessed by a Gandharva. — *Gandharva-graha, as*, m. the being possessed by a Gandharva. — *Gandharva-nagara* or *gandharva-pura, am*, n. the city of the Gandharvas, an imaginary town in the sky, probably the result of the phenomenon called mirage. — *Gandharvanagarākāra* (°*ra-āk*°), *as, ā, am*, resembling the city of the Gandharvas. — *Gandharva-patnī*, f., Ved. the wife of a Gandharva, an Apsaras. — *Gandharva-rāja, as*, m. Ćitra-ratha, chief of the Gandharvas. — *Gandharvartu* (°*va-ṛitu*), *us*, m., Ved. the time or season of the Gandharvas. — *Gandharva-vidyā*, f. the science of the Gandharvas, music, dancing. — *Gandharva-vivāha, as*, m. one of the forms of marriage described in Manu III. 27, &c., viz. the form of the Gandharvas; it is described as a marriage proceeding entirely from love or the mutual inclination of a youth and maiden without ceremonies and without consulting relatives, and is allowable between persons of the second or military class. — *Gandharva-veda, as*, m. the Gandharva-veda, the science of music considered as a branch of the Sāma-veda. — *Gandharva-hasta* or *gandharva-hastaka, as*, m. the castor-oil tree, Palma Christi or Ricinus Communis, (the leaves being compared to the foot of a deer.)

गन्धार *gandhāra, ās*, m. pl., N. of a people [cf. *gāndhārī*]; (ī), f., N. of a Vidyā-devī; (a various reading has *gāndhārī*.)

Gandhāri, ayas, m. pl., N. of a people.

गन्धाली *gandhālī*, f. a wasp; a creeping plant, Pœderia Fœtida, commonly *gāndhālī* or *gandha-bhādālī*; [cf. *gandholī*.] — *Gandhālī-garbha, as*, m. small cardamoms (*sūkshmailā*).

गन्धोलि *gandholi, is*, f. the plant Curcuma Amhaldi or Zerumbet, = *śaṭī*; [cf. *gandholī* below.]

Gandholī, f [cf. *gandhālī* above], a wasp; the plant Pœderia Fœtida (= *bhadrā*), Cyperus Rotundus, a fragrant grass; the plant Curcuma Amhaldi or Zerumbet; dried ginger, = *śuṇṭhī*.

गभ *gabha, as*, m. (fr. *gabh*, = *gambh*, = *jambh*), Ved. a slit, anything split asunder, cleft; the vulva; [cf. *gabhasti, gabhīra, gambhīra*.]

गभस्तल *gabhastala, am*, n., N. of a hell; [cf. *gabhasti-mat*.]

गभस्ति *gabhasti, is, is*, m. f. (related to *gabha*; the original meaning may have been a fork), Ved. a particular part of a carriage, the shaft; the double-edged thunderbolt of Indra (?); the fore part of the arm, the hand; a ray of light, a sun-beam, a moon-beam, i. e. the hands of the sun or moon; (*is*), m. the sun; (*is*), f. an epithet of Svāhā, the wife of Agni. — *Gabhasti-nemi, is*, m. an epithet of Kṛishṇa. — *Gabhasti-pāṇi, is*, m. the sun, 'having rays for hands.' — *Gabhasti-pūta, as, ā, am*, Ved. purified with the hands. — *Gabhasti-mat, ān, atī, at*, shining, brilliant; (*ān*), m. the sun; N. of one of the nine divisions of Bhārata-varsha; (*at*), n. one of the seven divisions of Pātāla or the region below the earth. — *Gabhasti-hasta, as*, m. the sun; [cf. *gabhasti-pāṇi*.]

गभिषक् *gabhi-shak*, ind. (fr. *gabhi*, related to *gabha* and *saj* fr. rt. *sañj*), Ved. deeply down, far down or within; [cf. *ānushak*.]

गभीका *gabhīkā*, f., N. of a plant and its fruit.

गभीर *gabhīra* or *gambhīra, as, ā, am* (related to *gabha* and *gabhasti*, 'a deep cleft;' the Ṛig-veda generally uses *gabhīra* and only *gambhīra* at the beginning of a Pāda or quarter-verse; in post-Vedic writings *gambhīra* is the more usual form, but *gabhīra* occurs occasionally even in the latest writers), deep (opposed to *gādha* and *dīna*); deep in sound, deep-sounding, hollow in sound, hollow-toned (therefore enumerated in the Nighaṇṭu among the synonyms of *vāć*); profound, sagacious, grave, serious, solemn, earnest, secret, mysterious; dense, impervious; not to be penetrated, not to be investigated or explored, inscrutable, difficult to be perceived or understood; inexhaustible, continuous, uninterrupted (as time &c.). The deepness of a man's navel, of his voice, and of his character are sometimes praised together: when a man is said to have a deep navel, voice and character, he is said to be *tri-gambhīraḥ*; (*as*), m. (without the nasal), N. of a descendant of Āyu; (with the nasal), the lemon tree [cf. *jambhīra* and *jambīra*]; a lotus; a Mantra of the Ṛig-veda; (*ā*), f. hiccup, violent singultus; N. of a river; *gabhīra, am*, n. depth; [cf. Lith. *gillybe, gelme, gyle; gillus*: Slav. *glŭbok; glŭbina*.] — *Gambhīra-ćetas, ās, ās, as*, Ved. of profound mind. — *Gambhīra-tā*, f. or *gambhīra-tva, am*, n depth (of water); depth of sound; profoundness, earnestness, sagacity. — *Gambhīra-dhvani, is*, m. a deep sound, low note or tone. — *Gambhīra-nāda* or *gabhīra-śabda, as*, m. a deep or hollow sound, thundering, roaring. — *Gambhīra-nirghosha, as*, m., N. of a Nāga. — *Gambhīra-vedin, ī, inī, i* lit. deeply sagacious, restive (as an elephant). — *Gambhīra-vedha, as, ā, am*, very penetrating. — *Gambhīra-vepas* or *gabhīra-vepas, ās, ās, as*, Ved. moved deeply or inwardly, deeply excited. — *Gambhīra-śansa, as, ā, am*, Ved. ruling secretly or in a hidden manner; (Sāy.) whose praise is inexhaustible, an epithet of Varuṇa. — *Gambhīra-sattva-svara-nābhi, is, is, i*, having a deep character, voice, and navel. — *Gambhīra-svāmin, ī*, m. the inscrutable lord; N. of a figure representing Nārāyaṇa. — *Gambhīrārtha* (°*ra-ar*°), *as*, m. profound sense or meaning.

Gabhīrikā, f a large drum with a deep sound; a gong; [cf *gambhīraka*.]

Gambhīraka, as, ikā, am, lying deep; (with *dṛishṭi*), a particular disease of the eye, which causes the pupil to contract and the eye to sink in its socket; (*ikā*), f., N. of a river.

गभोलिक *gabholika, as*, m. a small round pillow, = *masūra*.

गम् 1. *gam*. The conjugational tenses are formed in the Veda according to four different methods, as follows: I) According to the rule for cl. 1, Pres. P. *gamati*; Pot. P. *gamet*; Impv. P. 1st sing. *gamāni*, &c. II) According to the rule for cl. 2, Pres. P. *ganti*; Pot. P. *gamyāt*; Impv. P. and sing. *gahi*, 3rd *gantu*; Impf. P. 2nd and 3rd sing. *agan*, 1st pl. *aganma*; 3rd pl. *agman*; Pres. Part. *gmat*. III) According to the rule for cl. 3, Pres. P. *jaganti*; Pot. P. *jagamyāt*; Impf. *ajagan*. IV) According to the rule for cl. 1, with substitution of *gaććh* for *gam* (this is the only formation used in classical Sanskṛit), Pres. P. *gaććhati*; Pot. *gaććhet*, &c. (the A. is often found in epic poetry): Perf. *jagama* or *jagāma*, *jagantha* or *jagamitha*, *jagāma*, 2nd du. *jagmathus*, 2nd pl. *jagma*; Perf. Part. *jaganvas* or *jagmivas*, f. *jagmushī*; 2nd Fut. *gamishyati*; 1st Fut. *gantā*; Aor. P. *agamat*, A. *agansta* and *agata*, *agansmahi* and *agasmahi*; Inf. *gantum*, Ved. *gantave*, *gantavai*, *gamadhyai*; Ind. Part. *gatvā*, Ved. *gatvī*, *gatvāya*; to go, move, go to or towards; to go away; to set out; to come; to go or pass as time (e. g. *kāle gaććhati*, time going on, in the course of time); to go towards, approach (with acc. or loc. or dat. or with *prati*), arrive at, fall to the share of; to go against with hostile intentions, attack; to approach carnally, have intercourse with a woman (with acc.); to go to any state or condition, to become (e. g. *mitratām gaććhati*, he goes to friendship, i. e. he becomes friendly); to undergo, partake of, participate in, receive, obtain; *pratīpam gam*, to go against, to oppose one's self to, resist a person (with gen.); *jānubhyām avanim gam*, to go to the earth with the knees, to kneel down; *dharaṇim mūrdhnā gam*, to go to the earth with the head, to bow, make a bow; *manasā gam* (or without *manasā*), to go with the mind, observe, perceive; understand, guess; *dosheṇa* or *doshato gam*, to approach with an accusation, to ascribe guilt to a person (acc.): Pass. *gamyate*, to be gone &c., to be understood, to be meant: Caus. *gamayati, -yitum*, to cause to go or come, lead or conduct towards; to send to (dat.); to bring to a place (acc.); to cause to go to any condition (acc.), cause to become; to spend time; to impart, grant; to cause to understand, to make clear or intelligible, explain; to convey an idea or meaning, denote; (causal of the causal) to cause a person (acc.) to go by means of another: Desid. P. A. *jigamishati, jigānsate*, to wish to go, to be going, to strive to approach; to wish to bring: Intens. *jangamyate, jangamīti*, Ved. *janganti* and *ganiganti*, to visit; [cf. Goth. *qvam*; Eng. *come*; Mod. Germ. *kommen*; Lat. *venio* for *guemio*.]

Gat, t, t, t, (at the end of a compound) going; [cf. *adhva-gat*.]

Gata, as, ā, am, gone, gone away, departed, departed from the world, deceased, dead; past (as time), gone by; disappeared; come, come forth from, come to, approached, arrived at, being in, situated in, contained in (with acc. or loc. or with *prati* and acc. or in a compound, e. g. *sabhām gata*, come to an assembly; *Kānyakubje gata*, gone to Kānya-kubja; *mṛigam prati gata*, directed towards the deer; *ratha-gata*, sitting or standing in a carriage; *ādya-gata, turya-gata, antya-gata*, taking the first, fourth, last place; *sarva-gata*, spread everywhere), gone to any state or condition, fallen into (with acc. or loc. or in compounds, e. g. *kshayam* or *kshaye gata*, gone to destruction; *āpad-gata*, fallen into misfortune); directed towards, belonging to; relating to, referring to, connected with (e. g. *putra-gataḥ snehaḥ*, love directed towards the son; *tvad-gata*, belonging to thee); frequented, visited; spread abroad, celebrated; known, understood; (*am*), n. going, motion, manner of going; the place where any one has gone; anything past or done, an event; diffusion, extension, celebration; manner. — *Gata-kalmasha, as, ā, am*, freed from crime. — *Gata-kāla, as,* m. past time. — *Gata-kīrtti, is, is, i,* deprived of reputation. — *Gata-klama, as, ā, am,* rested, refreshed. — *Gata-ćetana, as, ā, am,* deprived of sense or consciousness, senseless, void of understanding, fainted away. — *Gata-ćetas, ās, ās, as,* bereft of sense. — *Gata-jvara, as, ā, am,* free from fever or sickness, convalescent, recovered. — *Gata-toyada, as, ā, am,* cloudless, cleared up, fair. — *Gata-trapa, as, ā, am,* free from fear or shame, bold. — *Gata-dina, am,* n. or *gata-divasa, as,* m. the past day, yesterday; (*am*), ind. yesterday. — *Gata-nāsika, as, ā, am,* noseless. — *Gata-nidhana, am,* n., N. of a Sāman. — *Gata-pāpa, as, ā, am,* freed from sin or guilt. — *Gata-puṇya, as, ā, am,* devoid of holiness or religious merit. — *Gata-pratyāgata, as, ā, am,* gone away and returned; come back again after having gone away. — *Gata-prabha, as, ā, am,* bereft of splendor, dim, faded. — *Gata-prāṇa, as, ā, am,* lifeless, expired, dead. — *Gata-prāya, as, ā, am,* almost gone or vanished. — *Gata-bhartṛikā,* f. a widow. — *Gata-bhī, īs, īs, i,* free from fear. — *Gata-māya, as, ā, am,* without deceit, reformed, without compassion. — *Gata-rasa, as, ā, am,* anything which has lost its flavour or sap, dried, withered. — *Gata-rātri, is,* f. the past night, last night. — *Gata-lakshmīka, as, ā, am,* unfortunate, suffering losses; [cf. *gata-śrīka.*] — *Gata-vat, ān, atī, at,* going, passing, obtaining, falling into, feeling, entertaining. — *Gata-vayaska, as, ā, am,* advanced in life. — *Gata-varsha, as, am,* m. n. the past year. — *Gata-vitta* or *gata-vibhava, as, ā, am,* bereft of wealth, beggared, impoverished. — *Gata-vaira, as, ā, am,* at peace with, reconciled. — *Gata-vyatha, as, ā, am,* free from pain, unanxious. — *Gata-śaiśava, as, ā, am,* past infancy, above eight years of age. — *Gata-śrī, īs, īs, i,* Ved. one who has obtained fortune. — *Gata-śrīka, as, ā, am,* forsaken by fortune; unlucky. — *Gata-sankalpa, as, ā, am,* bereft of sense, foolish. — *Gata-sanga, as, ā, am,* free from attachment, detached from, dissevered; adverse or indifferent to. — *Gata-sattva, as, ā, am,* annihilated, lifeless, dead; base. — *Gata-sandeha, as, ā, am,* free from doubt. — *Gata-sannaka, as,* m. an elephant out of rut. — *Gata-sādhvasa, as, ā, am,* afraid. — *Gata-sauhṛida, as, ā, am,* bereft of friends; unkind, unfeeling, indifferent. — *Gatāksha* (°*ta-ak*°), *as, ā, am,* sightless, blind. — *Gatāgata* (°*ta-āg*°), *am,* n. going and coming, going to and fro, reiterated motion in general; the flight of a bird backward and forward; (in astron.) irregular course of the asterisms. — *Gatāgati* (°*ta-āg*°), *is,* f. going back to the place whence one came. — *Gatādhi* (°*ta-ādhi*), *is, is, i,* free from anxiety, happy. — *Gatādhvan* (°*ta-adh*°), *ā, ā, a,* one who has accomplished a journey, familiar with anything (loc.), conversant; (*ā*), f., scil. *paurṇamāsī,* the time immediately preceding new moon, when a small streak of the moon is still visible. — *Gatānugata* (°*ta-an*°), *am,* n. the following what precedes, following custom. — *Gatānugatika, as, ī, am,* following what precedes, following custom or the conduct of others, imitating, imitative, doing as others do. — *Gatānta* (°*ta-an*°), *as, ā, am,* one whose end has arrived. — *Gatāyāta* (°*ta-āy*°), *am,* n. coming and going. — *Gatāyus* (°*ta-āy*°), *us, us, us,* one whose vital power has vanished, decayed, decrepid, infirm, very old; dead. — *Gatārtavā* (°*ta-ār*°), f. a woman past her courses or past childbearing; a barren woman. — *Gatārtha* (°*ta-ar*°), *as, ā, am,* = *artha-gata,* unmeaning, nonsensical; poor, void of an object. — *Gatālīka* (°*ta-al*°), *as, ā, am,* real, true. — *Gatāsu* (°*ta-asu*), *us, us, u,* one whose breath has gone, expired, dead. — *Gatotsāha* (°*ta-ut*°), *as, ā, am,* dispirited. — *Gatodvega* (°*ta-ud*°), *as, ā, am,* comforted, freed from sorrow. — *Gataujas* (°*ta-oj*°), *ās, ās, as,* bereft of strength.

Gataka, am, n. going, motion.

Gati, is, f. going, moving, gait, carriage, deportment, motion in general; manner or power of going; going away; procession, march, passage, procedure, progress, movement, (e. g. *astra-gati,* the going or flying of arrows; *paraṃ gatiṃ gam,* to go the last way, i. e. to die; *daiva-gati,* the course of fate, fate, fortune; *kāryasya gatiḥ,* the progress or course of a poem); coming, arriving at, obtaining; path, way, course; the course of the asterisms; (in astron.) a certain division of the moon's path and the position of a planet in it; the diurnal motion of a planet in its orbit; issue, event; course of events, fortune; an issue, a running wound or sore; place of issue, origin, reason; event, possibility, an expedient, means; a means of success, way, or art, method of acting, stratagem; refuge, resource; remedy; the position (of a child at birth); state, condition, situation, proportion, mode of existence, nature; a happy issue, happiness (e. g. *anuttamā gatiḥ,* the incomparable course, the attainment of eternal bliss), transmigration, metempsychosis, the course or migration of the soul through several bodies, the condition of a person undergoing this migration; manner; knowledge, wisdom; (in gram.) a term for prepositions and some other adverbial prefixes (such as *alam* &c.) when immediately connected with the tenses of a verb or with verbal derivatives (see *karma-pravaćanīya*); a particular high number; (*gati* personified is a daughter of Deva-hūti and wife of Pulaha.) — *Gati-tālin, ī,* m., N. of an attendant of Skanda. — *Gati-bhanga, as,* m. stoppage, impediment to progress. — *Gati-mat, ān, atī, at,* possessed of motion, in motion, moving; having issues or sores; connected with a preposition &c.; [cf. *gati*] — *Gati-śakti, is,* f. the power of motion. — *Gati-hīna, as, ā, am,* forlorn, without resource or refuge. — *Gaty-anusāra, as,* m. following the way of another. — *Gaty-ūna, as, ā, am,* impassable, difficult of access, desert, helpless.

Gatika, am, n. going, motion; course; condition; refuge, asylum.

Gatilā, f. the not being different from one another, mutual agreement (?); N. of a river.

Gatīka, as, ā, am, passable; *a-gatīka,* impassable.

Gatvan. See *pūrva-gatvan.*

Gatvara, as, ā, am, going, moving, movable, locomotive, perishable.

Gatvā, ind. having gone, having gone to or attained.

Gantavya, as, ā, am, to be gone, to be gone to or attained; to be accomplished (as a way); to be approached, to be requested; to be undergone.

Gantu, us, m., Ved. a way, a course; a traveller, a way-farer.

Gantu-kāma, as, ā, am, wishing to go, on the point of departure, about to die.

Gantṛi, tā, trī, tṛi, who or what goes or moves, going, coming, approaching, arriving at (with acc. or loc.); going to a woman, having intercourse with one; (*trī*), f. a cart or car drawn by oxen. — *Gantri-ratha, as,* m. a car drawn by oxen; [cf. *maṭha.*]

2. *gam* (occurring only in gen. and abl. *gmas*), Ved. the earth; [cf. *ksham:* cf. also Gr. γῆ; Zend *zem;* Lith *zemie;* Slav. *zemlje;* Russ. *zemlu.*]

Gama, as, ā, am, (at the end of a comp.) going (e. g. *aran-gama, kāma-gama, kha-gama,* &c., q. v.); (*as*), m. going, moving; march, especially the march of an assailant; intercourse with a woman; a road; flightiness, superficiality, thoughtlessness; acting inconsiderately, looking at anything hastily or superficially; a game played with dice and men, as backgammon &c.; a similar reading in two texts (?), hasty or careless perusal, running over a book (?). — *Gamakāri-tva, am,* n. inconsiderateness, rashness.

Gamaka, as, ikā, am, leading to conviction (e. g. *hetu,* a convincing reason). — *Gamaka-tva, am,* n. or *gamaka-tā,* f. convincing proof.

Gamatha, as, m. a traveller; a road.

Gamana, am, n. going, manner of going, going away, departure, going to or approaching; march in general or the march of an assailant; intercourse with a woman, cohabitation; undergoing or obtaining, attaining; way, possibility. — *Gamana-vat, ān, atī, at,* furnished with motion, moving. — *Gamanārha* (°*na-ar*°), *as, ā, am,* to be sought, fit, suitable, desirable.

Gamanīya, as, ā, am, accessible, approachable, passable, attainable, what may be gone to or reached; intelligible, to be understood, what ought to be followed, to be practised or observed; relating to going &c (e. g. *gurustrī-gamanīya,* relating to intercourse with the wife of a teacher, or consisting in it, as a sin).

Gamayat, an, antī, at, causing or making to go.

Gamayitavya, as, ā, am, to be made to go, to be spent.

Gamayitṛi, tā, trī, tṛi, causing to arrive at, leading to.

Gamita, as, ā, am, caused to go, sent, brought, reduced, driven to.

Gamin, ī, inī, i, intending to go; (*ī*), m. a passenger.

Gamishṭha, as, ā, am, most ready to go, most willing to come; (a superlative fr. *gantṛi.*)

Gamya, as, ā, am, to be gone, to be gone to, approachable, accessible, passable, attainable; accessible to men (as a woman), fit for cohabitation; a man with whom a woman may have intercourse, libidinous, a voluptuary; easily brought under the influence of a drug or medicine, curable by it; to be perceived or understood, intelligible, perceptible; intended, meant; desirable, suitable, fit. — *Gamya-tā,* f. or *gamya-tva, am,* n. accessibility, perceptibility, the being intended or meant, being capable of attainment.

Gamyamāna, as, ā, am, being gone or gone to, being understood.

गमात्र *ga-mātra, as* or *am,* m. or n. (?), a particular number.

गम्ब् *gamb,* cl. 1. P. *gambati, -bitum,* to go or move.

गम्भन् *gambhan, a,* n., Ved., or *gambhara, am,* n., Ved. depth (as of water); water; [cf. *gahman* and *gabhīra.*]

गम्भारी *gambhārī* or *gambhārikā,* f. the tree Gmelina Arborea; also the flower, fruit, and root of this tree.

गम्भीर *gambhīra* and its compounds. See under *gabhīra.*

गय *gaya, as,* m. (said to be fr. rt. *gam* or *gai*), a house, household, family, goods and chattels, the contents of a house, property, wealth, a species of ox, the Gayal or Bos Gavæus; N. of a Ṛishi, son of Plati; also of a Rājarshi, performer of a celebrated sacrifice, (he was conquered by Māndhātṛi); a son of Amūrta-rajas; also of Āyus; also of a Manu; also of Havirdhāna and Dhishaṇā (Havirdhānī); also of Ūru and Āgneyī; of Vitatha; of Sudyumna; of Nakta and Druti; N. of the people living round Gayā and the district inhabited by them; N. of an Asura, who like the Rājarshi Gaya is connected with the town Gayā; one of the monkey followers of Rāma; N. of a mountain near Gayā; (*ās*), m. pl., Ved. the vital airs; (*ā*), f. Gayā, the city in Behār still so called and a place of pilgrimage, the residence of the saint of the same name; it was sanctified by the benediction of Vishṇu as a tribute to the piety of Gaya, the Rājarshi, or (according to another legend) to Gaya, the Asura, who was overwhelmed here with rocks by the gods; the Śrāddha should be performed once at least in the life of every Hindū to his progenitors at Gayā; N. of a river; [cf. *san-gaya* and *buddha-gayā.*] — *Gaya-dāsa, as,* m., N. of a physician. — *Gaya-śāta, as,* m., N. of a Buddhist patriarch. — *Gaya-śiras, as,* n., N. of a mountain near Gayā, a renowned place of pilgrimage. — *Gaya-sādhana, as, ī, am,* Ved. promoting domestic wealth or prosperity, an epithet of Soma. — *Gaya-sphāna, as, ā, am,* Ved. increasing domestic wealth, promoting the prosperity of a household; an epithet of Soma. — *Gayā-kāśyapa, as,* m., N. of a pupil of Śākya-siṃha. — *Gayā-dāsa, as,* m., N. of an author. — *Gayā-māhātmya, am,* n., N. of a section of the Vāyu-Purāṇa. — *Gayā-śikhara, as* or *am,* m. or n. (?), or *gayā-śiras, as,* n. or *gayā-śirsha, am,* n., N. of a mountain near Gayā, a renowned place of pilgrimage; [cf gaya-śiras.]

गर *gara, as, ī, am* (fr. 2. *gṛī*), swallowing; (*as*), m. any drink, beverage, fluid; a noxious or poisonous beverage; a factitious poison; an antidote; sickness, disease; probably a peculiar kind of disease attended with difficulty of swallowing (?), dysphagia (?); N. of a son of Uśīnara: (*am*), n. a kind of poison: the fifth of the eleven Karaṇas; sprinkling, wetting (?); (*ā*), f. swallowing: N. of a plant, = *devadāli-latā*; (*ī*), f. a kind of grass, Andropogon Serratus. — *Gara-gir, īr, īr, īr*, or *gara-gīrṇa, as, ā, am*, Ved. one who has swallowed a noxious draught, poisoned — *Garagīrṇin, ī*, m., N. of a Ṛishi. — *Gara-ghna, as, ī, am*, removing poison or the disease called Gara, an antidote; sanative, healthy; (*as*), m. a kind of basil, Ocimum Sanctum, = *kṛishṇārjaka*; another kind of Ocimum, = *varvara*; (*ī*), f a kind of fish, commonly Garaī, the young of the Ophiocephalus Lata. — *Gara-da, as, ā, am*, poisoning, a poisoner; unwholesome, occasioning sickness; (*am*), n. poison. — *Gara-dāna, am*, n. giving poison. — *Gara-vrata, as*, m. a peacock. — *Gara-han, ā*, m. the plant Ocimum Sanctum. — *Garātmaka* (°*ra-āt*°), *am*, n. the seed of the plant Sobhāñjana or Hyperanthera Moringa. — *Garādhikā* (*ra-adh*°), f. the insect called Lākshā or the red dye obtained from it.

Garaṇa, am, n. the act of swallowing; wetting, sprinkling. — *Garaṇa-vat, ān, atī, at*, occupied in swallowing.

Garala, as, am, m. n. poison; the venom of a snake or venom in general; (*am*), n. a bundle of grass or hay; a measure in general. — *Garalāri* (°*la-ari*), *is*, m. an emerald; [cf. *garuḍāṅkila, garuḍāśman, garuḍottīrṇa*.]

Garalin, ī, inī, i, venomous, poisonous.

Garita, as, ā, am, poisoned.

गरभ *garabha, as*, m. the fœtus or embryo, = *garbha*.

गरागरी *garāgarī*, f. a kind of grass, Andropogon Serratus, = *kharā, garī, agarī*.

गरिमन् *gariman, ā*, m. (fr. *guru*), heaviness, weight; one of the eight Siddhis or faculties of Śiva (making himself heavy at will); importance, dignity, venerableness; worth, excellence.

Garishṭha, as, ā, am (superl. fr. *guru*), heaviest, excessively heavy; very venerable; worst; (*as*), m., N. of a man; also of an Asura.

Garīyas, ān, asī, as (compar. fr. *guru*), heavier, very heavy, heaviest; weightier, greater; more precious or valuable, dearer; highly venerable; worse. — *Garīyas-tva, am*, n. weight, importance.

Garu = *guru* in *agaru*, q. v.

गरुड *garuḍa, as*, m. (said to be fr. rt. 2. *gṛī*, to swallow, because Garuḍa was perhaps originally identified with the all-consuming fire of the sun's rays), N. of a mythical bird, the chief of the feathered race, the enemy of the serpent-race, the vehicle of Vishṇu, and the son of Kaśyapa and Vinatā, and elder brother of Aruṇa; (shortly after his birth he frightened the gods by his brilliant lustre; they supposed him to be Agni, and requested his protection; when they discovered that he was Garuḍa, they praised him as the highest being, and called him fire and sun Aruṇa, the charioteer of the sun or the personified dawn, is said to be the younger brother of Garuḍa. In some legends Svāhā, the wife of Agni, takes the shape of a female Garuḍī, = *su-parṇī*. With Jainas, Garuḍa is an attendant of the sixteenth Arhat of the present Avasarpiṇī); a building shaped like Garuḍa; N. of a peculiar military array; N. of a son of Kṛishṇa; N. of a Kalpa, the fourteenth day of Brahmā. — *Garuḍa-dhvaja, as*, m. an epithet of Vishṇu or Kṛishṇa (whose symbol is Garuḍa) — *Garuḍa-purāṇa, am*, n., N. of the seventeenth Purāṇa; [cf. *gāruḍa*.] — *Garuḍa-ruta, am*, n. a species of metre, having four lines to the stanza and sixteen syllables to each line. — *Garuḍa-vegā*, f., N. of a plant. — *Garuḍāgraja* (°*ḍa-ag*°), *as*, m. having Garuḍa for his elder brother, an epithet of Aruṇa, the charioteer of the sun. — *Garuḍāṅka* (°*ḍa-aṅ*°), *as*, m. an epithet of Vishṇu or Kṛishṇa. — *Garuḍāṅkita* (°*ḍa-aṅ*°), *am*, n an emerald; [cf *garuḍāśman, garuḍottīrṇa, gāruḍa, gārutmata*.] — *Garuḍārdha* (°*ḍa-ar*°), *as*, m. (?), a kind of arrow. — *Garuḍāśman* (°*ḍa-aś*°), *ā*, m. an emerald. — *Garuḍottīrṇa* (*ḍa-ut*°), *am*, n. an emerald. — *Garuḍopanishad* (°*ḍa-up*°), *t*, f., N. of an Upanishad.

गरुत् *garut, t*, m. (said to be fr. 2. *gṛī*), the wing of a bird. — *Garut-mat, ān, atī, at* (in the Veda only found in connection with *su-parṇa*), feathered, winged; swallowing; (*ān*), m. the bird Garuḍa; a bird in general. — *Garud-yodhin, ī*, m. a quail.

गरुल *garula* = *garuḍa*.

गर्ग *garga, as*, m. (said to be fr. 2. *gṛī*), N. of an old sage, a descendant of Bharad-vāja and of Aṅgiras; N. of an astronomer; N. of a physician; N. of a son of king Vitatha; also of a grandson of this king; a bull; an earth-worm; (*ās*), m. pl. the descendants of Garga; (*ā*), f., N. of a woman; (*ī*), f., N. of a woman; [cf. *gārgī* and *gārgya*.] — *Garga-bhūmi, is*, m., N. of a prince; (also *bharga-bhūmi*.) — *Garga-śiras, ās*, m., N. of a Dānava. — *Garga-srotas, as*, n. Garga's stream, N. of a Tīrtha.

Gargiya, as, m. a descendant of Garga (?).

गर्गर *gargara, as*, m. (an onomatopoetic word), a whirlpool, an eddy [cf. Lat. *gurges*]; a kind of musical instrument; a kind of fish, Pimelodus Gagora; N. of a man; (*as, ī*), m. f. a churn; a vessel for holding water, a guglet.

Gargaraka, as, m. a kind of fish [cf. the preceding]; a kind of plant with a poisonous root.

Gargāṭa, as, m. a kind of fish, Pimelodus Gagora; [cf. the preceding.]

गर्ज् *garj*, cl. 1. 10. P. *garjati, jagarja, garjishyati, agarjīt, garjitum, garjayati, -yitum*, to emit a deep or full sound, to sound as distant thunder, to thunder; to roar, growl; to rave &c.; [cf. Lat. *garrio, gurges*; Old Germ. *kurran, krago, kragil, krachôn, gellan, kallôn, kallari*; Mod. Germ. *quarren, girren*.]

Garja, as, m. a (roaring) elephant; (*as, ā*), m. f. the roaring of elephants, the rumbling of clouds &c. — *Garjā-phala, as*, m., N. of a plant, = *vi-kaṇṭaka*.

Garjaka, as, m. a kind of fish, = *śāla* or *śālaja*, commonly *gajāḍa*.

Garjana, am, n. sound, noise; crying, roaring, the rumbling of clouds &c.; a grumbling noise, a growl, a grunt; passion, wrath; war, battle, conflict; excessive indignation, reproach, menace.

Garjanīya, as, ā, am, to be sounded or roared.

Garjan-megha, as, m. a thunder-cloud.

Garji, is, m. the muttering of clouds or distant thunder.

Garjita, as, ā, am, sounded, roared, bellowed; (*as*), m. a (roaring) elephant in rut; (*am*), n. the muttering of clouds or rolling of distant thunder.

Garjya, as, ā, am, to be roared or sounded.

गर्जर *garjara, am*, n. a carrot, Daucus Carota.

गर्त 1. *garta, as*, m., Ved. a high seat (?), a throne; the seat of a war-chariot, a chariot; a table for playing at dice; a house. — *Garta-sad, t, t, t*, Ved. sitting on a war-chariot. — *Gartāruh* (°*ta-ār*°), *k, k, k*, Ved. ascending a war-chariot; (Sāy.) entering a hall of justice.

गर्त 2. *garta, as, ā, am*, m. f. n. (said to be fr. rt. 2. *gṛī*, but perhaps a later form for *karta*), a hollow, a hole, a cave; a grave; (*as*), m. the hollow of the loins; a kind of disease; N. of a country, a part of Trigarta, in the north-west of India. — *Gartan-vat, ān, atī, al*, Ved. having holes or excavations. — *Garta-mit, t, t, t*, Ved. buried in a hole — *Gartāśraya* (°*ta-āś*°), *as*, m. any animal living in holes or under ground, a mouse, rat, &c. — *Garteśa* (°*ta-īśa*), *as*, m. the master of a cave. — *Garte-shṭhā, ās, ās, am*, being in a hole or grave.

Gartikā, f. a weaver's workshop (so called because a weaver sits at his loom with his feet in a hole below the level of the floor).

गर्द् *gard*, cl. 1. 10. P. *gardati, -ditum, gardayati, -yitum*, to sound, to roar, emit any sound.

Gardabha, as, m. (said to be fr. the last), an ass; a kind of perfume, = *gandha*, smell, odour; N. of a dynasty; (*ī*), f. a she-ass; an insect, a kind of beetle generated in cow-dung; N. of several plants, = *aparājitā, kaṭabhī, śveta-kaṇṭakārī*; a disease of the skin, an eruption of round, red, and painful spots; also *gardabhikā*; (*am*), n. the white esculent water-lily, Nymphæa Esculenta; a kind of plant used as a vermifuge; [cf. *viḍaṅga*]. — *Gardabha-gada, as*, m. a kind of disease of the skin; [cf. *gardabhikā, jāla-gardabha, jvālā-gardabhaka, pāshāṇa-gardabha*.] — *Gardabha-nādin, ī, inī, i*, Ved. braying like an ass. — *Gardabha-rūpa, as*, m. having the form of an ass, an epithet of Vikramāditya. — *Gardabha-śāka, as, ā* or *ī*, m. f. the plant Clerodendrum Siphonanthus. — *Gardabhākshu* (*bha-ak*°), *as*, m., N. of a descendant of Hiraṇya-kaśipu and son of Bali. — *Gardabhājina* (°*bha-aj*°), *am*, n. the skin or hide of an ass. — *Gardabhāṇḍa* (*bha-aṇ*°), *as*, m., N. of a tree, commonly Pārspīpal, Thespesia Populneoides; or also the tree Ficus Infectoria; an Adhyāya or Anuvāka, in which the word Gardabhāṇḍa occurs. — *Gardabhāṇḍaka, as*, m. the tree Thespesia Populneoides. — *Gardabhāṇḍīya, as*, m. an Adhyāya or Anuvāka, in which the word Gardabhāṇḍa occurs. — *Gardabhāhvaya* (°*bha-āh*°), *am*, n. the white esculent water-lily, Nymphæa Esculenta. — *Gardabhī-mukha, as*, m., N. of a preceptor. — *Gardabhī-vipīta, as*, m., N. of a man.

Gardabhaka, as, m. a kind of insect; (*ikā*), f. a cutaneous disease, a blotch, an eruption.

Gardabhi, is, m., N. of a man.

Gardabhin, ī, m., N. of a dynasty; [cf. *gardabha*.]

गर्दयित्नु *gardayitnu, us*, m. a cloud; [cf. *gadayat* and *gadayitnu*.]

गर्ध् *gardh*, another form of rt. *gṛidh*.

Gardha, as, m. desire, greediness, eagerness; a tree, commonly called Pārspīpal; [cf. *gardabhāṇḍa*.]

Gardhana or *gardhita, as, ā, am*, covetous, greedy.

Gardhin, ī, inī, i, desirous, greedy, covetous; pursuing or following with eagerness.

गर्ब् 1. *garb*, cl. 1. P. *garbati, -bitum*, to move, to go or approach, = *kharb, ćarb, gharb*, &c.

गर्ब् 2. *garb*. See *garv* and *garva*.

गर्भ *garbha, as*, m. (fr. *grabh* = *grah*, to conceive, said to be fr. 2. *gṛī*), the womb, the belly, the inside, the middle, the interior of anything; an inner apartment, a lying-in chamber; any interior chamber, the adytum of a temple &c.; a fœtus or embryo, a child, the brood or offspring of birds; the fruit (of plants); the offspring of the sky, i. e. the fogs and vapour drawn upwards by the rays of the sun during eight months and sent down again in the rainy season; the bed of a river (especially of the Ganges) when fullest, i. e. on the fourteenth day of the dark half of the month Bhadrā, or in the height of the rains, (the Garbha extends to this point, after which the Tīra or proper bank begins, and extends for 150 cubits; this space being holy ground); joining, union; the rough coat of the fruit of the

Jaka; the calyx of the lotus. (*Garbha* is often found at the end of compounds in the sense of having in the interior, containing, filled with; e. g. *jala-garbha, as, ā, am,* filled with water; *agni-garbha, as, ā, am,* containing fire); [cf. *amṛita-garbha, ardha-g°, kṛishṇa-g°, mūḍha-g°, viśva-g°, hiraṇya-g°:* cf. also Hib. *cilfin,* 'the belly;' Angl. Sax. *hrif;* Germ. *kalb* (?); Eng. *calf;* Gr. δελφός.] – *Garbha-kara, as, ī, am,* producing impregnation, procreative, fecundatory, impregnatory; (*as*), m. the plant Nageia Putrañjīva. – *Garbha-karaṇa, am,* n., Ved. anything which causes impregnation. – *Garbha-kāra, as, ā, am,* impregnating, fecundatory, procreative, producing impregnation; (*am*), n., N. of a ceremony. – *Garbha-kāla, as,* m. the time of impregnation; the time when the offspring of the sky, i. e. the vapour collected in the air [cf. *garbha* above], shows the first signs of life, 195 days or seven lunar months after its first conception. – *Garbha-kośa* or *garbha-kosha, as,* m. the uterus. – *Garbha-kleśa, as,* m. pains caused by the embryo, pains of childbirth. – *Garbha-kshaya, as,* m. loss of the embryo, miscarriage. – *Garbha-gṛiha, am,* n. an inner apartment, an inner chamber, a lying-in chamber; the sanctuary or adytum of a temple; (in compounds) a house containing anything (e. g. *śara-garbha-gṛiha,* a house containing arrows). – *Garbha-grahaṇa, am,* n. conception, impregnation. – *Garbha-ghātin, ī, inī, i,* killing the embryo, producing abortion; (*inī*), f. a poisonous plant, Methonica Superba. – *Garbha-ćalana, am,* n. quickening, the motion of the fœtus in the uterus. – *Garbha-ćyuta, as, ā, am,* fallen from the womb (as a child); miscarrying. – *Garbha-ćyuti, is,* f. falling from the womb, birth, delivery; miscarriage. – *Garbha-tā,* f. or *garbha-tva, am,* n. impregnation. – *Garbha-da, as, ā, am,* impregnating, procreative; (*as*), m. the tree Nageia Putrañjīva; (*ā*), f., N. of a shrub. – *Garbha-dātṛi, tā, trī, tṛi,* impregnating, procreative; (*ī*), f., N. of a shrub, = *garbha-dā, apatya-dā, putra-dā,* &c. – *Garbha-dāsa, as,* m. a slave by birth. – *Garbha-divasa, ās,* m. pl. certain days on which the vapours collected in the air show signs of life; [cf. *garbha-kāla.*] – *Garbha-druh, -dhruk, k, k,* destroying the fœtus, causing abortion. – *Garbha-dha, as, ā, am,* Ved. procreative, impregnatory. – *Garbha-dharā,* f. bearing a fœtus, pregnant. – *Garbha-dhāna, am,* n. impregnating. – *Garbha-dhāraṇa, am, ā,* n. f. gestation, impregnation, conception in the womb, pregnancy; N. of the twenty-second Adhyāya in Varāha-mihira's Bṛihat-saṃhitā. – *Garbha-dhārita, as, ā, am,* contained in the womb, conceived, borne. – *Garbha-dhi, is,* m., Ved. a breeding-place, a nest, cohabitation. – *Garbha-dhvaṅsa, as,* m. abortion. – *Garbha-nāḍī* or *garbha-nābhi-nāḍī,* f. the umbilical cord. – *Garbha-nud, t, t, t,* causing abortion; (*t*), m. the poisonous plant Methonica Superba. – *Garbha-parisrava, as,* m. secundines. – *Garbha-pākin, ī,* m. rice ripening in sixty days (during the latter period of the sky's pregnancy). – *Garbha-pāta, as,* m. miscarriage after the fourth month of pregnancy. – *Garbha-pātaka, as, ī, am,* causing miscarriage; (*as*), m. a red kind of Moringa. – *Garbha-pātana, as, ī, am,* causing miscarriage, producing abortion; (*as*), m., N. of a plant, = *rīṭhā-karañja;* (*ī*), f. the plant Methonica Superba; any plant or drug supposed to produce abortion; (*am*), n. producing abortion. – *Garbha-pātin, ī, inī, i,* causing miscarriage, producing abortion; (*inī*), f., N. of a plant, = *viśalyā.* – *Garbha-poshaṇa, am,* n. nourishing a fœtus, gestation. – *Garbha-bharman, a,* n. supporting a fœtus, gestation. – *Garbha-bhavana, am,* n. the sanctuary or adytum of a temple; [cf. *garbha-gṛiha.*] – *Garbha-bhāra, as,* m. the weight of the fœtus. – *Garbha-maṇḍapa, as,* m. an inner apartment, a bed-chamber. – *Garbha-māsa, as,* m. month of pregnancy. – *Garbha-moćana, am,* n. delivery, birth. – *Garbha-yoshā,* f. a pregnant woman, metaphorically the river Ganges overflowing its banks. – *Garbha-rakshaṇa, am,* n. protecting the fœtus, N. of a ceremony performed in the fourth month of gestation. – *Garbha-randhi, is,* f. complete cooking (?). – *Garbha-rasa, as, ā, am,* Ved. endowed with impregnating moisture. – *Garbha-rūpa* or *garbha-rūpaka, as, ā, am,* childish, juvenile; (*as*), m. a child, an infant, a youth. – *Garbha-lakshaṇa, as, ā, am,* observing the signs of the rainy season; (*am*), n. symptom of pregnancy; N. of the twenty-first Adhyāya of Varāha-mihira's Bṛihat-saṃhitā treating on the marks or signs of the rainy season. – *Garbha-lambhana, am,* n. a ceremony performed for the sake of facilitating conception. – *Garbha-vatī,* f. a pregnant female. – *Garbha-vasati, is,* f. or *garbha-vāsa, as,* m. the abode of the fœtus, the womb. – *Garbha-vāyu, us,* m. air in the womb. – *Garbha-vićyuti, is,* f. abortion in the beginning of pregnancy. – *Garbha-vipatti, is,* f. the death of the fœtus. – *Garbha-vedanā,* f. the pains of childbirth. – *Garbha-veśman, a,* n. the womb or a lying-in chamber. – *Garbha-vyākaraṇa, am,* n. the formation of the embryo, a part of the Sarīra section in medical works. – *Garbha-vyāpad, t,* f. the death of the fœtus. – *Garbha-vyūha, as,* m. a kind of battle array. – *Garbha-śanku, us,* m. a kind of vectis or instrument for extracting the dead fœtus. – *Garbha-śayyā,* f. the abode of the fœtus, the uterus. – *Garbha-sankramaṇa, am,* n. entering the womb. – *Garbha-samaya, as,* m. the time when the offspring of the sky, the vapour collected in the air, shows the first signs of life, 195 days or seven lunar months after its conception; [cf. *garbha-kāla.*] – *Garbha-sambhava, as,* m. or *garbha-sambhūti, is,* f. the production of a fœtus, the becoming pregnant. – *Garbha-subhaga* or *garbha-saubhāgya, as, ā, am,* blessing the fœtus. – *Garbha-sūtra, am,* n. title of a Buddhist Sūtra work. – *Garbha-stha, as, ā, am,* situated in the womb; central, internal, in the interior, within the centre of anything. – *Garbha-srāva, as,* m. abortion, miscarriage. – *Garbhasrāvin, ī, iṇī, i,* producing or occasioning abortion; (*ī*), m. the tree Phœnix Paludosa (*hintāla*). – *Garbhāgāra* (°*bha-āg*°), *am,* n. the uterus; an inner and private room, the female apartments, the lying-in chamber; the sanctuary of a temple, the chamber where the object of worship or the image of a deity is placed; [cf. *garbha-gṛiha.*] – *Garbhāṅka* (°*bha-an*°), *as,* m. interlude during an act. – *Garbhāda* (°*bha-ada*), *as, ā, am,* Ved. consuming the fœtus. – *Garbhādhāna* (°*bha-ādh*°), *am,* n. impregnation; a ceremony performed after menstruation to ensure or facilitate conception. – *Garbhāvakrānti* (°*bha-av*°), *is,* f. descent of the fœtus. – *Garbhāśankā* (°*bha-āś*°), f. suspicion of pregnancy. – *Garbhāśaya* (°*bha-āś*°), *as,* m. the womb, the uterus. – *Garbhāshṭama* (°*bha-ash*°), *as,* m. the eighth month of uterine gestation; the eighth year reckoning from conception. – *Garbhāspandana* (°*bha-asp*°), *am,* n. non-quickening of the fœtus. – *Garbhāsrāva* (°*bha-ās*°), *as,* m. miscarriage. – *Garbhe-tṛipta, as, ā, am,* contented in the womb, i. e. indolent. – *Garbheśvara* (°*bha-īś*°), *as,* m. a sovereign by birth. – *Garbheśvara-tā,* f. sovereignty attained by inheritance. – *Garbhotpatti* (°*bha-ut*°), *is,* f. the formation of the embryo. – *Garbhopaghāta* (°*bha-up*°), *as,* m. miscarriage of the embryo, (applied also to the sky.) – *Garbhopaghātinī* (°*bha-up*°), f. a cow (or female) miscarrying from unseasonable gestation. – *Garbhopanishad* (°*bha-up*°), *t,* f. title of an Upanishad.

Garbhaka, as, m. a chaplet of flowers &c. worn in the hair; (*am*), n. a period of two nights with the intermediate day.

Garbhita, as, ā, am, pregnant, full, filled.

Garbhin, ī, iṇī, i, pregnant, impregnated with (with acc. or inst.); (*iṇī*), f. pregnant, a pregnant woman or animal; compounded with names of animals (e. g. *go-garbhiṇī,* a pregnant cow). – *Garbhiṇī-vyākaraṇa, am,* n. or *garbhiṇī-vyākṛiti, is,* f. 'science of the progress of pregnancy,' a particular head or subject in medical works. – *Garbhiṇy-avekshaṇa, am,* n. midwifery, attendance and care of pregnant women and new-born infants.

गर्भाण्ड *garbhaṇḍa, as,* m. (fr. *garbha* and *aṇḍa?*), enlargement of the navel.

गर्मुटिका *garmuṭikā,* f. a species of rice; [cf. *garmuććhada.*]

गर्मुत् *garmut, t,* f. (said to be fr. rt. 2. *gṛī*), a kind of bee [cf. *gārmuta*]; a kind of grass; a creeper; a kind of reed (*naḍa*); according to some authorities the plant Vangueria Spinosa, commonly Mayanā; according to others Coix Barbata, commonly Gaḍagaḍa; gold.

गर्मुच्छद *garmuććhada, as,* m. and *garmūṭikā,* f. a kind of rice, commonly Māḍuyā, Eleusine Coracana; [cf. *garmuṭikā.*]

गर्मोटिका *garmoṭikā,* f. a species of reed, = *jaraḍī.*

गर्व् *garv* or *garb,* cl. 1. P., 10. A. *garvati, -vitum, garvayate, -yitum,* to be or become proud or haughty; [cf. Lith. *garbė,* 'honour, glory;' Old Germ. *gelban, gelf.*]

Garva or *garba, as,* m. pride, arrogance.

Garvara, as, ā, am, proud, haughty, arrogant.

Garvāya, nom. A. *garvāyate, -yitum,* to show pride or arrogance.

Garvita, as, ā, am, proud, haughty; conceited.

गर्वण *garvaṇa, as* or *am,* m. or n. (?), N. of a rock.

गर्वाट *garvāṭa, as,* m. a watchman, a door-keeper, a sort of village constable, a head-borough or beadle.

गर्ह् *garh,* cl. 1. 10. P. A. *garhati, -te, garhayati, -te, jagarha, jagarhe, garhishyate, agarhishṭa, garhitum,* to lodge a complaint before a person (dat.), accuse, charge with, reproach, blame, censure a person (acc.); to be sorry for, repent of: Desid. *jigarhishate, -ti:* Intens. *jāgarhyate, jāgarḍḍhi.*

Garhaṇa, am, ā, n. f. censuring, censure, blame, reproach; *garhaṇām yā,* to meet with reproach.

Garhaṇīya, as, ā, am, censurable, blamable, contemptible, vile, bad.

Garhā, f. abuse, censure, reproach.

Garhita, as, ā, am, blamed, censured; contemned, despised; contemptible, ignominious, forbidden, bad, vile.

Garhitavya, as, ā, am, to be censured, blamable.

Garhin, ī, iṇī, i, abusing, reproaching.

Garhya, as, ā, am, deserving reproach, contemptible, low, vile; (*as*), m., N. of a tree (?). – *Garhya-vādin, ī, inī, i,* speaking ill, speaking vilely or inaccurately.

गल् *gal,* cl. 1. P. *galati, jagāla, galishyati, agālīt, galitum,* to drip, drop, ooze, trickle, distil; to fall down or off; to vanish, perish, pass away; to eat, swallow [cf. 2. *gṛī*]: Caus. *gālayati, -yitum,* to cause to drop, to pour out; to filter, strain; to fuse, liquefy, dissolve, melt: A. *gālayate,* to flow; [cf. Old Germ. *qvall, quillu, qual,* and *quella,* 'a well.']

Gala, as, m. the throat, neck; resin, especially the resin of the plant Shorea Robusta; a kind of fish, a small kind of Cyprinus, a subgenus of that class or Cyprinus Garra; a kind of musical instrument; a reed, a large kind of the Saccharum Cylindricum; a rope [cf. *galyā*]; (*ā*), f. a kind of plant [cf. *alambushā;* cf. also Lat. *collum* (?); Germ. *hals.*] – *Gala-kambala, as,* m. a bull's dewlap. – *Gala-gaṇḍa, au,* m. du. neck and cheek, or neck and Adam's apple; (*as*), m. enlargement of the glands of the neck; goitre. – *Galagaṇḍin, ī, inī, i,* having a goitre. – *Gala-golin, ī, inī,* m. f. a kind of serpent. – *Gala-graha, as,* m. seizing by the throat, throttling, choaking; compression of the throat, a kind of disease; a fish-sauce prepared with salt, pepper, ghee, &c.; N. of certain days in the dark fortnight, viz. the fourth, seventh, eighth, ninth, thirteenth and three following days; a day on which a course of study is commenced, but immediately preceding a day on which study is prohibited; begun but immediately interrupted study; also *gala-grahaṇa, am,* n. — *Gala-ćarman, a,* n. the gullet, throat. — *Gala-dvāra, am,* n. the door of the throat, the mouth. — *Gala-mekhalā,* f. a string of beads worn round the neck, a necklace. — *Gala-vārtta, as, ā, am,* living by eating, a parasite. — *Gala-vidradhi, is,* m. tumor and abscess in the throat. — *Gala-vrata, as,* m. a peacock; [cf. *gara-vrata.*] — *Gala-śuṇḍikā,* f. the uvula; swelling of the glands of the neck; (*e*), du. the soft palate. — *Gala-śuṇḍī,* f. swelling of the glands of the neck. — *Gala-stanī,* f. a she-goat; (a species of the Bengal goat having small fleshy protuberances, resembling nipples, depending from the throat); [cf. *gale-stanī, ajāgala-stana, aja-gallikā.*] — *Gala-hasta, as,* m. the hand at the throat, seizing by the throat, collaring, throttling. — *Galahastaya,* nom. P. *-tayati,* to throttle, strangle. — *Gala-hastita, as, ā, am,* seized by the throat. — *Galāṅkura* (°*la-an*°), *as,* m. a disease of the throat, inflammation of the throat and enlargement of the tonsils. — *Gale-gaṇḍa, as,* m. a kind of bird, the Adjutant or Ardea Argala; (the name alludes to a pendulous fleshy purse hanging from the throat of this bird.) — *Gale-ćopaka, as, ikā, am,* moving the neck. — *Gale-stanī,* f. a she-goat; [cf. *gala-stanī.*] — *Galodbhava* (°*la-ud*°), *as,* m. the tuft of hair on the neck of a horse. — *Galaugha* (°*la-ogha*), *as,* m. tumor in the throat.

Galaka, as, m. the throat, the neck; a kind of fish, a small kind of Cyprinus.

Galat, an, antī, at, dropping, falling, oozing, trickling, flowing; melting.

Galana, as, ā, am, dropping, flowing; (*am*), n. dropping, oozing, trickling; melting, fusing; falling down or off; leaking.

Galanīya or *galitavya* or *galya, as, ā, am,* fusible, soluble, liquefiable, to be melted &c.

Galantikā or *galantī,* f. a small pitcher; a small water-jar with a hole in the bottom, from which the water drops upon a Liṅga or upon a Tulasi plant placed beneath.

Galita, as, ā, am, dropped, fallen; liquefied, melted; distilled, oozed, flowing; untied, loosed; lost, deprived; decayed, impaired. — *Galita-kushṭha, am,* n. advanced and incurable leprosy, when the fingers and toes fall off. — *Galita-danta, as, ā, am,* having the teeth decayed, toothless. — *Galita-nakha, as, ā* or *ī, am,* having the claws or nails fallen off. — *Galita-nakha-danta, as, ā, am,* one who has lost his claws and teeth. — *Galita-nayana, as, ā, am,* one who has lost his eyes, blind. — *Galita-pradīpa, as,* m. or *galita-pradīpikā,* f. title of a work, lit. 'the light of dropped words,' i. e. of certain words in a manuscript which occur several times and are given only once at full length.

Galitaka, as, m. a kind of dance, gesticulation.

Galyā, f. a multitude of throats; a quantity of a particular kind of grass or of ropes made of it.

गलानिल *galānila, as,* m. a prawn or shrimp; see *gaṅgāṭeya;* (also read *galānika* and *galāvila.*)

गलावल *galāvala, as,* m. a kind of tree.

गलि *gali, is,* m. a strong but lazy bull.

गलू *galū, ūs,* m. a sort of gem.

गलून *galūna, as,* m., N. of a minister.

गलोड्य *galoḍya* or *gāloḍya, as,* m.(?), N. of a plant; [cf. *giloḍya.*]

गल्द *galda, as, ā,* m. f., Ved. speech; straining; that which flows from a strainer (?).

गल्भ् *galbh,* cl. 1. A. *galbhate,* to be bold or confident; [cf. *garv;* cf. also Hib. *galbha,* 'rigour, hardness.']

Galbha, as, ā, am, bold, confident, audacious; proud, haughty, (*galbha* = *garbha* in *apa-galbha,* q. v.)

गल्ल *galla, as,* m. the part of the cheek near the corners of the mouth; the cheek. — *Galla-ćāturī,* f. a small round pillow to put underneath the cheek.

गल्लकी *gallakī,* f., N. of a river.

गल्वर्क *galvarka, as,* m. crystal; lapis lazuli (?), sapphire (?), emerald (?); a goblet, a vessel for drinking spirituous liquor.

गल्ह् *galh,* cl. 1. A. *galhate,* to blame, to censure or despise; [cf. *garh.*]

गव *gava* = *go,* a cow, cattle; used at the beginning of a compound before a word beginning with a vowel, see below; also at the end of a compound (e. g. *pańća-gavam,* five cows); (*as*), m. a ray of the sun. — *Gava-rāja, as,* m. a bull. — *Gavākriti* (°*va-āk*°), *is, is, i,* cow-shaped. — *Gavāksha* (°*va-ak*°), *as,* m. an air-hole, a loop-hole, a round window, a 'bull's eye,' &c.; the mesh of a shirt of mail; N. of a warrior; N. of a monkey-chief attached to Rāma, a son of Vaivasvata, the leader of the Go-lāṅgūlas; N. of a sea (n. in this sense?); (*ī*), f. a sort of cucumber, Cucumis Maderaspatanus or Coloquintida; the plant Trophis Aspera (*śākhoṭa*); the plant Clitoria Ternatea. — *Gavākshaka, as,* m. an air-hole, a loop-hole, a round window, a bull's eye. — *Gavāksha-jāla, am,* n. a lattice, a window of trellice-work. — *Gavākshita, as, ā, am,* furnished with windows, forming a lattice. — *Gavāgra* = *go-agra* = *go 'gra,* q. v. — *Gavādana* (°*va-ad*°), *am,* n. pasture or meadow grass; (*ī*), f. pasture or meadow grass, a hay-rack, a manger, a trough for holding grass &c. for feeding cattle; a species of cucumber, Cucumis Maderaspatanus, or (according to some) Cucumis Coloquintida; the plant Clitoria Ternatea. — *Gavāmṛita* (°*va-am*°), *am,* n. the beverage of immortality or nectar consisting of rays of light. — *Gavārtham* or *gavārthe* (°*va-ar*°), ind. for the sake of a cow. — *Gavārha* (°*va-ar*°), *as, ā, am,* of the value of a cow. — *Gavāvika* (°*va-av*°), *am,* n. cattle and sheep. — *Gavāśana* (°*va-aś*°), *as,* m. = *go-bhakshaka,* commonly *mući,* i. e. a worker in leather, a shoe-maker; an outcast. — *Gavāśira* (°*va-āś*°), *as, ā, am,* Ved. mixed with milk, as Soma. — *Gavāśva* (°*va-aś*°), *am,* n. cattle and horses; [cf. *go-aśva* and *go 'śva.*] — *Gavāhnika* (°*va-āh*°), *am,* n. the daily measure of food given to a cow. — *Gavendra* (°*va-in*°), *as,* m. an owner of kine. — *Gaveśa* or *gaveśvara* (°*va-īś*°), *as,* m. an owner of kine. — *Gavaiḍaka* (°*va-eḍ*°), *am* n. kine and sheep. — *Gavodgha* (°*va-ud*°), *as,* m. an excellent cow.

Gavaći, f. a Coloquintida, = *gavākshī.*

Gavaya, as, m. a species of ox, the Gayal, Bos Gavæus, erroneously classed by Hindū writers as a species of deer; a monkey-chief attached to Rāma, the son of Vaivasvata; (*ī*), f. the female Gayal.

Gavala, as, m. the wild buffalo; (*am*), n. buffalo's horn.

Gavāći, f. (fr. *go* and rt. *ańć*), a kind of fish, commonly *pāṅkālamāća,* Ophidium Punctatum or Macrognathus Pankalus.

Gavām-aya, as, m. or *gavām-ayana, am,* n. 'going of cows,' N. of a solemn ceremony; [cf. *go.*]

Gavām-pati, is, m. a guardian of cows, a cow-herd; the chief of cattle, a bull; the lord of rays, an epithet of the sun; also of Agni; N. of a Buddhist mendicant.

Gavālūka, as, m. the Gayal, Bos Gavæus; [cf. *gavaya.*]

Gavi-jāta, as, m., N. of a Muni. — *Gavi-putra, as,* m. an epithet of Vaiśravaṇa. — *Gavi-shṭhira, as,* m., N. of a Ṛishi of Atri's family; [cf. *gāvishṭhira* and *gāvishṭhirāyaṇa.*]

Gavinī, f. a herd of cows.

Gav-ish, ṭ, ṭ, ṭ, or *gav-isha, as, ā, am,* Ved. wishing for cows, desirous in general, eager, fervent. — *Gav-ishṭi, is, is, i,* Ved. wishing for cows; desiring fervently, eager, ardent; (*is*), f. desire, eagerness, ardour, fervour; desire for fighting, ardour of battle, battle. — *Gav-īśa* or *gav-īśvara, as,* m. an owner of kine.

Gavishṭha, as, m. the sun (either a superl. fr. *go,* 'a ray,' or fr. *gavi* + *stha,* 'standing in water'); N. of a Dānava.

Gavesha (either fr. *gava* + *ish,* or *go* + *esh*), nom. cl. 1. A. or 10. P. *gaveshate* or *gaveshayati, -yitum,* to desire ardently or fervently, to strive after; to seek, hunt after, search or inquire for. — *Gaveshaṇa, as, ā, am,* Ved. desiring ardently or fervently; desirous of combat; (*as*), m., N. of a Vṛishṇi; (*ā, am*), f. n. seeking after, searching for, inquiry, philosophical research. — *Gaveshaṇīya, as, ā, am,* to be desired or sought for. — *Gaveshita, as, ā, am,* eagerly desired, sought, inquired for. — *Gaveshin, ī, iṇī, i,* seeking; (*ī*), m., N. of a son of Citraka and brother of Pṛithu.

Gaveshṭhin, ī, m., N. of a Dānava.

1. *gavya,* nom. P., Ved. *gavyati,* to desire cattle or cows; especially in the part. *gavyat, an, antī, at,* wishing for or desirous of cattle or cows; ardently or fervently desiring, fervent; desirous of battle.

2. *gavya, as, ā, am,* consisting of cattle or cows, consisting of milk; coming from, of, or belonging to a cow, as milk, curds, &c. (e. g. *pańća-gavya, am,* n. five things coming from a cow,—milk, cheese, butter, urine, and dung); proper or fit for cattle; sacred to the cow, worshipping the cow; (*as*), m., N. of a people in the north of Madhyadeśa; (*am*), n. cattle, a herd of cows; pasture land; the milk of a cow; a bow-string; a colouring substance, a yellow pigment or dye; (*as, ā, am,* differing from the preceding only by its accent), belonging to cattle, consisting of cattle or cows, coming from cattle or cows; (*ā*), f. a multitude or herd of cows; a measure equal to 1 Gavyūti or 2 Krośas; a bow-string; a colouring substance, a yellow pigment or dye; [cf. *go-roćanā.*] — *Gavya-dṛiḍha, as* or *am,* m. or n. (?), a colouring substance, a yellow pigment or dye; [cf. the preceding.]

Gavyaya, as, ī, am, Ved. belonging to or coming from cattle.

Gavyayu, us, us, u, Ved. desirous of cattle.

Gavyā, f., Ved. desire for or delight in cows; desire, fervency; desire for what comes from a cow, i. e. for milk; desire of battle (generally used in the Ved. inst. *gavyā*).

Gavyu, us, us, u, Ved. delighting in cattle or cows; desiring cows or milk; fervent; desirous of battle.

Gavyūta, am, n. a measure of length equal to 2000 Daṇḍas or 1 Krośa, or to 4000 Daṇḍas or 2 Krośas; [cf. the following.]

Gavyūti, is, f. (fr. *go* and *yūti?* or *go* and *ūti?*), Ved. a pasture, a piece of pasture land, a district, place of residence; a measure of length equal to 4000 Daṇḍas or 2 Krośas.

गवल्गण *gavalgaṇa, as,* m., N. of a man, the father of Sańjaya; (also read *gavalgāṇa*); [cf. *gāvalgaṇi.*]

गवाषिका *gavāshikā,* f. the insect called Lākshā, and the red dye prepared from it; [cf. *gavādhikā.*]

गवीधुक *gavīdhuka, as, ā,* m. f., Ved. the grass Coix Barbata; [cf. *gavedhuka.*]

गवीनि *gavīni, ī,* or *gavīnī, yau,* or *gavīnikā, e,* f. du., Ved. a part of the belly near the pudenda; the groins (?).

गवेडु gaveḍu, us, m. a cloud; (us), f. or gaveḍukā, f. a kind of grass, Coix Barbata; [cf. the following.]

गवेधु gevedhu, us, f. the grass Coix Barbata.

Gavedhuka, as, m. a kind of serpent; (ā), f. a species of grass, Coix Barbata; according to some authorities also Hedysarum Lagopodioides [cf. gaveśakā]; (am), n. red chalk; [cf. gavīdhuka, gaveḍu, gaveruka.]

गवेरुक gaveruka, am, n. red chalk; [cf. gavedhuka, n.]

गवेशका gaveśakā, f. the plant Hedysarum Lagopodioides.

गह gah (connected with gāh), cl. 10. P. gahayati, -yitum, to be thick or impervious (?); to enter deeply into.

Gaha, as, m. a cave; a forest (?); [cf. dur-gaha.]

Gahana, as, ā, am, deep, dense, thick, impervious, impenetrable, inexplicable, hard to be understood, inaccessible; (am), n. an abyss, a depth; an inaccessible place, a hiding-place, a thicket, a wood, impenetrable darkness; a cave; pain, distress; [cf. gabhīra.] — Gahana-tva, am, n. density; imperviousness, impenetrability. — Gahana-vat, ān, atī, at, having hiding-places or thickets.

Gahanāya, nom. A. gahanāyate, -yitum, to have treacherous intentions towards another, (originally, to lie hid, lie in wait for a person in a secret place, lie in ambush.)

Gahīya, as, ā, am, relating to a cave or a thicket; deep, difficult of access, impervious.

Gahman, a, n., Ved. depth; [cf. gambhan.]

Gahvara, as, ā or ī, am (related to gabhīra and gahana), deep, impervious, impenetrable; (am), n. an abyss, a depth; water; a hiding-place, a thicket; a wood; an impenetrable secret, a riddle; a cave, cavern; hypocrisy; weeping; a deep sigh; (ī), an abyss, a cave, a cavern, a grotto, a recess in a rock or mountain &c.; (as), m. an arbour, a bower. — Gahvare-shṭha, as, ā, am, Ved. being at the bottom or lowest depths, being in the secret recesses.

Gahvarita, as, ā, am, being in a hiding-place, concealed.

गा 1. gā, cl. 1. or 2. A., 3. P. gāte, jigāti, jagau, agāt, gāsyati, gātum (Ved. gātave), (in classical Sanskrit only the aorist of the simple verb seems to occur), to go, go towards, to come, approach; to come into any state or condition, undergo, obtain: Pass. gīyate: Desid. jigāsati or jigishati(?): Intens. jegīyate: [cf. Gr. βίβημι, ἔβην; Old Germ. gâm, gâs, gât, &c.; Goth. ga-tvo; Eng. to go; Germ. gehen; Lith. gaju.]

2. gā, ās, ās, am, (at the end of compounds) going; [cf. a-gā, agre-gā, puro-gā, &c.]

1. gātu, us, m. (for 2. see col. 3), Ved. going, motion, unimpeded motion; free space for moving, place of abode; the earth; a refuge; way, course; egress, access; progress, increase, welfare; [cf. arishṭa-gātu and tura-gātu.] — Gātu-mat, ān, atī, at, Ved. spacious, commodious. — Gātu-vid, t, t, t, Ved. clearing the way for unimpeded motion or progress; finding or opening a way, promoting progress or welfare.

Gātuya or gātūya, nom. P., Ved. gātuyati or gātūyati, to desire unimpeded motion or free space for moving, to wish to obtain free progress.

Gātra, am, n. 'the instrument of moving,' a limb or member of the body; the body; the fore-quarter of an elephant (according to some also n. and f. in this meaning); (as), m., N. of a son of Vaśishṭha; (ā), f. earth. — Gātra-karśana, as, ā, am, emaciating the body. — Gātra-gupta, as, m., N. of a son of Kṛishṇa and Lakshmaṇā. — Gātra-bhangā, f. a kind of cowach, Mucuna Pruritus (= śūka-śimbī). — Gātra-mārjanī, f. a towel. — Gātra-yashṭi, is, m. a thin or slender body. — Gātra-ruha, am, n. the hairs on the body; [cf. anga-ruha.] — Gātra-latā, f. a flexuous or tender body. — Gātra-vat, ān, m., N. of a son of Kṛishṇa and Lakshmaṇā; (tī), f., N. of a daughter of Kṛishṇa and Lakshmaṇā. — Gātra-vinda, as, m., N. of a son of Kṛishṇa and Lakshmaṇā. — Gātra-vairūpyatā, f. deformity of the limbs. — Gātra-sankoćin, ī, m. the pole-cat, Viverra Putorius, (which draws up or contracts its body in order to spring.) — Gātra-samplava, as, m. a small bird, the diver, Pelicanus Fusicollis; [cf. plava.] — Gātra-sparśa, as, m. contact of the limbs. — Gātrānulepanī (°ra-an°), f. fragrant unguents &c. smeared upon the body, perfume for the person. — Gātrāvaraṇa (°ra-āv°), am, n. a shield. — Gātrotsādana (°ra-ut°), am, n. cleaning the person with perfumes &c.

Gātraka, am, n. the body.

Gātraya, nom. A. gātrayate, -yitum, to be loosened, or to loosen.

1. gāya, as, ā, am, going, striding; (am), n. going, motion; [cf. uru-gāya.]

गा 3. gā, ās, ās, am (fr. rt. gai), singing, at the end of a compound [cf. sāma-gā]; (ā), f. a song; a verse or metrical composition; [cf. gāthā.]

गागनायस gāganāyasa, am, n. (fr. gagana + ayas), meteoric iron (?).

गाङ्ग gānga, as, ī, am (fr. gangā), being in or on the Ganges, coming from or belonging or relating to the Ganges; (am), n., scil. ambu, rain-water of a peculiar kind (supposed to be from the heavenly Ganges); (as), m. a metronymic of Skanda or Kārttikeya; also of Bhīshma; (ī), f. an epithet of Durgā. — Gānga-deva, as, m., N. of a poet. — Gāngaugha (°ga-ogha), am, n. the current of the Ganges.

Gāngāyani, is, m. a metronymic of Bhīshma; also of Skanda or Kārttikeya; (Gangā was the first wife of S'antanu, and bore to him the hero Bhīshma, before his marriage with Satyavatī; she was also the receiver of the vivifying principle of Siva first cast into Agni, from which principle was generated Kārttikeya the god of war); also an epithet of Citra.

Gāngeya, as, ī, am, being in or on the Ganges; (as), m. a metronymic of Skanda; also of Bhīshma; the Hilsa or Illias fish, Clupanodon Ilisha [cf. illiśa]; the root of a kind of grass [cf. bhadra-mustā]; (am), n. the root of Scirpus Kysoor or Cyperus Hexastachyus Communis, = kaśeru.

Gāngya, as, ā, am, being on the Ganges; a metronymic from Gangā.

Gāngyāyani, is, m. a patronymic from Gāngya.

गाङ्गट gāngaṭa or gāngaṭaka or gāngaṭeya, as, m. a kind of prawn or shrimp; [cf. gangāṭeya.]

गाङ्गेरुकी gāngerukī, f. the plant Uraria Lagopodioides; (am), n. the seed of this plant.

गाङ्गेष्ठी gāngeshṭhī, f. the shrub Guilandina Bonducella.

गाञ्जिकाय gāñjikāya, as, m. a quail.

गाडव gāḍava, as, m. a cloud; [cf. gaveḍu.]

गाढ gāḍha. See under rt. gāh.

गाणगारि gāṇagāri, is, m., N. of a teacher; [cf. gaṇakāri.]

गाणपत gāṇapata, as, ī, am (fr. gaṇa-pati), relating to the leader of a troop or to the god Gaṇeśa.

Gāṇapatya, as (f. -tī), am, relating to the leader of a troop or to the god Gaṇeśa; (as), m. a worshipper of Gaṇeśa; (am), n. worship of him, chieftainship, presidency.

Gāṇika, as, ī, am (fr. gaṇa), familiar with the Gaṇas (in grammar).

Gāṇikya, am, n. (fr. gaṇikā), an assemblage of harlots.

Gāṇeśa, as, m. (fr. gaṇeśa), a worshipper of Gaṇeśa. — Gāṇeśopapurāṇa (°śa-up°), am, n., N. of an Upa-Purāṇa.

गाण्डिव gāṇḍiva. See under gāṇḍī next col.

गाण्डी gāṇḍī, f., N. of a plant, from which the bow Gāṇḍīva was made.

Gāṇḍiva or gāṇḍīva, as, am, m. n. the bow of Arjuna; presented by Soma to Varuṇa, by him to Agni, and by Agni to Arjuna, (also said to have belonged to Prajā-pati, Brahmā, and Siva); a bow in general. — Gāṇḍīva-dhanvan, ā, m. an epithet of Arjuna. — Gāṇḍīva-mukta, as, ā, am, discharged from the bow Gāṇḍīva.

Gāṇḍīvin, ī, m. an epithet of Arjuna; the tree Terminalia Arjuna; [cf. arjuna.]

गाण्डीर gāṇḍīra, as, ī, am, coming from the plant Gaṇḍīra.

गातव्य gātavya. See under rt. gai.

गातागतिक gātāgatika, as, ī, am (fr. gatāgata), caused by going and coming.

Gātānugatika, as, ī, am (fr. gatānugata), caused by following or imitating what precedes.

गातु 2. gātu, us, m. (fr. rt. gai), a song; a singer; a Gandharva or celestial chorister; the male Koïl or Indian cuckoo; a bee; N. of a descendant of Atri, author of a hymn of the Ṛig-veda; (us, us, u), angry, wrathful. (For 1. gātu see under 1. gā.)

Gātṛi, tā, trī, tṛi, a singer; angry; (tā), m. a Gandharva; the male Koïl or Indian cuckoo; a bee.

Gātha, as, m. (also am, n.?), singing, a song; (ā), f. a verse; (in the terminology of the Brāhmaṇas and liturgical books) a verse which is neither Ṛić, nor Sāman, nor Yajus, a religious verse, but not one belonging to the Vedas; a stanza; a song, a chant or verse to be chanted or sung; (with Buddhists) a metrical Sūtra; N. of the Āryā metre; also of a metre not enumerated in the regular treatises on prosody. — Gātha-pati, is, m., Ved. lord of songs. — Gāthā-kāra, as, m. an author of songs, hymns, verses; a singer, a reciter. — Gāthā-nī, īs, īs, i, Ved. leading the song, leading a choir. — Gāthāntara (°thā-an°), as, m., N. of a Kalpa, the fourth day in Brahmā's month.

Gāthaka, as, m. a singer, a musician; a chanter of the Purāṇas or sacred poems.

Gāthika, as, m. one who recites Gāthas, hymns or verses; (ā), f. a song, hymn.

Gāthin, ī, inī, i, familiar with or knowing songs or hymns, a singer; (ī), m., N. of a son of Kuśika and father of Viśvā-mitra; (inas), m. pl. the descendants of this man; (inī), f., N. of a metre, containing 12 + 18 + 12 + 20 or 32 + 29 syllabic instants; [cf. viṇā-gāthin.] — Gāthi-ja, as, m. the son of Gāthin, i. e. Viśvā-mitra.

Gāthina, as, m. a patronymic from Gāthin.

गात्र gātra. See col. 1. under rt. 1. gā.

गाथ gātha. See above.

गाद्गद्य gādgadya, am, n. (fr. gadgada), stammering.

गाध gādh [cf. gāh, to which this root is related], cl. 1. A. gādhate, jagādhe, gādhishyate, agādhishṭa, gādhitum, to stand firmly, to stay, remain; to set out; to seek, to search or inquire for, to desire; to compile, string or heap together.

Gādha, as, ā, am, any place offering firm standing-ground, fordable (as a river), not very deep, shallow; (am), n. ground for standing on in water, a shallow place, a ford (sometimes also m.); bottom, soundings; a place, site; desire of gain, cupidity, covetousness.

गाधि gādhi, is, m., N. of the father of Viśvā-mitra and king of Kānyakubja, also called gādhin; (ayas), m. pl. the descendants of Gādhi. — Gādhi-ja, as, m. Gādhi's son, a N. of Viśvā-mitra. Gādhin, ī, m. (a later form for gāthin, q. v.), = gādhi. — Gādhi-nagara, am, n. Gādhi's city, an epithet of Kānyakubja. — Gādhi-nandana, as, m. the son of Gādhi, an epithet of Viśvā-mitra; also gādhi-putra, as, m., gādhi-bhū, ūs, m., gādhi-

sūnu, us, m. — *Gādhi-pura, am,* n. Gādhi's city, an epithet of Kānyakubja; [cf. *gādhi-nagara.*]

Gādheya, as, m. a patronymic of Viśvā-mitra; (ī), f. a patronymic of Satyavatī.

गान *gāna, am,* n. (fr. *gai*), singing, a song; a sound; [cf. *araṇya-gāna, ūha-g°, ūhya-g°.*] — *Gāna-bandhu, us,* m. a friend of songs; N. of a man (?). — *Gāna-vidyā,* f. the science of vocal music.

Gānīya, as, ā, am, musical.

गानिनी *gānini,* f. Orris root [cf. *vacā*], a medicinal plant (supposed to be of use in clearing the voice; fr. *gāna ?*).

गान्तु *gāntu, us,* m. (fr. 1. *gam*), one who goes or moves, a goer, a traveller; a singer (in this sense a wrong form for 2. *gātu*).

Gāntrī, f. = *gantrī,* a carriage drawn by oxen.

गान्दम *gān-dama, as,* m. (*gān* = *gām,* acc. fr. *go*), N. of a man.

गान्दिक *gāndika, as, ī, am,* born in Gandikā.

गान्दिनी *gāndinī,* f., N. of a princess of Kāśi who was the wife of Svaphalka and mother of Akrūra (also called *gāndī*); an epithet of the river Ganges or the goddess Gaṅgā; (also read *gāndhinī.*) — *Gāndinī-suta, as,* m. a son of Gāndinī, epithet of Akrūra and of Bhīshma; [cf. *gāṅgeya.*]

Gāndī. See *gāndinī.*

गान्धर्व *gāndharva, as, ī, am* (fr. *gandharva*), belonging or relating to the Gandharvas (especially *gāndharvo vivāhaḥ* or *vidhiḥ,* the form of marriage called after the Gandharvas, that which requires only mutual agreement; see *gandharva-vivāha*); relating to the Gandharvas as heavenly choristers (e. g. *gāndharva-kalāḥ,* song, music, &c.; *gāndharvo vedaḥ* or *gāndharva-vedaḥ,* the Veda of music, musical science considered as an appendix of the Sāma-veda and ascribed to Bharata); (*as*), m. a singer in general; N. of a people in the north-east of Madhya-deśa; (ī), f. = *vāć,* speech, according to the legend that the gods gave speech to the Gandharvas and received from them the Soma in return; an epithet of the goddess Durgā; (*am*), n. the art of the Gandharvas, song, music, dance; N. of one of the nine sections of Bhārata-varsha; [cf. *gandharva-khaṇḍa.*] — *Gāndharva-ćitta, as, ā, am,* one whose mind is possessed by the Gandharvas; [cf. *gandharva-gṛihīta.*] — *Gāndharva-śālā,* f. music-hall, a concert-room.

Gāndharvika, as, m. a singer; (also read *gāndharvaka.*)

गान्धार *gāndhāra, as,* m. a prince of the Gāndhāris; the third of the seven primary notes of music; minium or red lead; (ī), f. a princess of the Gāndhāris (especially the wife of Dhṛita-rāshṭra); N. of a Vidyā-devī; N. of a Rāgiṇī (?); with Jainas, a divine being fulfilling the commands of the twenty-first Arhat of the present Avasarpiṇī; (*ās*), m. pl., N. of a people and their country, commonly called Kandahar, and lying between the north of India and Persia [cf. *gandhāra, gandhāri, gāndhāri*]; (ī), f., N. of two plants, Hedysarum Alhagi and Prickly Nightshade, = *yavāsa* and *dur-ālabhā;* (*am*), n. gum myrrh; [cf. *gandha-rasa.*] — *Gāndhāra-rāja, as,* m. the king of Gāndhāra, whose name was Su-bala.

Gāndhāraka, ās, m. pl. = *gāndhāra,* N. of a people.

Gāndhāri, ayas, m. pl., N. of a people; (*is*), m. a metronymic of Duryodhana; [cf. the following.]

Gāndhāreya, as, m. a metronymic of Duryodhana, the son of Dhṛita-rāshṭra.

गान्धिक *gāndhika, as,* m. (fr. *gandha*), a vender of perfumes, a perfumer; a scribe, a clerk; a kind of worm having a strong fetid smell, commonly *gāndhipokā,* a tree-bug; (*am*), n. fragrant wares, perfumes.

गान्धिनी *gāndhinī,* f. See under *gāndinī.*

गामिक *gāmika, as, ā, am* (fr. *gam,* used at the end of compounds), going, leading to (as a way).

Gāmin, ī, inī, i, going, moving on, or in, or towards, or in any peculiar manner, &c.; going to, having intercourse with; reaching to, extending to; coming to one's share, due; attaining, obtaining; directed towards; relating to; [cf. *agra-gāmin, anta-g°, anya-g°, āśu-g°, ṛitu-g°, kāma-g°.*]

Gāmuka, as, ā, am, going, locomotive.

गाम्भीर्य *gāmbhīrya, as, ā, am* (fr. *gambhīra*), being deep down, being in the depths; (*am*), n. deepness, depth (of water, sound, &c.); depth or profundity of character, earnestness, sagacity; the deep sound of the voice of a Jaina saint, like distant thunder or the muttering of clouds.

गाम्मन्य *gām-manya, as, ā, am,* thinking one's self a cow.

गाय 2. *gāya, as, ī, am* (fr. *gaya*), relating to Gaya, coming from him, &c. (For 1. *gāya* see under 1. *gā.*)

गाय 3. *gāya, am,* n. (fr. rt. *gai*), a song.

Gāyaka, as, ī, am, singing, one who sings; (*as*), m. a singer. — *Gāyaka-ćandra, as,* m., N. of a copyist who lived A. D. 1670.

Gāyat, an, antī, at, singing; (*antī*), f., N. of Gaya's wife.

Gāyatra, as, am, m. n. a song, hymn; (ī), f. an ancient metre of twenty-four syllables, variously arranged, but generally as a triplet of three divisions of eight syllables each; a hymn composed in the Gāyatrī metre; the Gāyatrī (i. e. Ṛig-veda III. 62, 10, *tat savitur vareṇyam bhargo devasya dhīmahi dhiyo yo naḥ praćodayāt.* This is a very sacred verse repeated by every Brāhman at his morning and evening devotions. From being addressed to Savitṛi or the Sun as generator, it is also called Sāvitrī. The Gāyatrī verse is personified as a goddess, the wife of Brahmā and mother of the four Vedas; and is often mentioned in connection with the Amṛita, both together constituting as it were the essence and type of sacred hymns in general. The Gāyatrī personified is also considered as the mother of the first three classes, in their capacity of twice born). According to the system of the Tāntrikas, a number of mystical verses are called Gāyatrīs, and each deity has one in particular; (*am*), n. a hymn composed and recited in the metre Gāyatrī; (*as, ī, am*), consisting in the Gāyatrī, connected with it, formed in accordance with it (e. g. in accordance with the number of syllables of a Gāyatrī verse &c.); (ī), f. the tree Acacia Catechu, = *khadira;* (*am*), n., N. of a Sāman. — *Gāyatra-kākubha, as,* m. a Pragātha beginning with a Gāyatrī and ending with a Kakubh. — *Gāyatra-ććhandas, ās, ās, as,* Ved. one to whom the Gāyatrī metre belongs or to whom it is sacred &c.; relating to the Gāyatrī metre. — *Gāyatra-pārśva, am,* n., N. of a Sāman. — *Gāyatra-bārhata, as,* m. a Pragātha beginning with a Gāyatrī and found where the Bṛihatī metre predominates. — *Gāyatra-vartani, is, is, i,* Ved. moving in Gāyatrī measures. — *Gāyatra-vepas, ās, ās, as,* Ved. inciting or inspiring to sing hymns. — *Gāyatrī-bhāshya, am,* n. title of a commentary on the Gāyatrī. — *Gāyatrī-mantra, as,* m. prayers connected with the Gāyatrī. — *Gāyatrī-vallabha, as,* m. a friend of the Gāyatrī, an epithet of Śiva. — *Gāyatrī-sāman, a,* n., N. of several verses of the Sāma-veda, recited in the Gāyatrī metre. — *Gāyatry-āsita, am,* n., N. of a Sāman.

Gāyatri, is, f. = *gāyatrī.*

Gāyatrin, ī, iṇī, i, one who sings hymns; (ī), m. the tree Acacia Catechu. — *Gāyatri-sāra, as,* m. Catechu, Terra Japonica; [cf. *khadira.*]

Gāyatrya, as, ā, am, epithet of a kind of Soma.

Gāyana, as, ī, am, singing, a singer; (*as*), m. a singer, a talker, a gossip; N. of an attendant of Skanda; (*am*), n. singing, song; professing or practising singing as a livelihood.

Gāyantikā, f. (fr. *gāyantī*), N. of a place on the Himālaya mountains.

गार *gāra, as,* m., N. of a Sāman, composed by Gara.

गारित्र *gāritra, am,* n. (fr. rt. 2. *gṛī*), rice, corn, grain.

गारुड *gāruḍa, as, ī, am* (fr. *garuḍa*), shaped like the bird Garuḍa, coming from or relating to Garuḍa; (ī), f., N. of a creeper [cf. *pātāla-garuḍī*]; (*am*), n. an emerald; gold; a Mantra or charm against poison. — *Gāruḍa-purāṇa, am,* n., N. of the seventeenth Purāṇa relating the birth of Garuḍa from Vinatā. It is doubtful whether a genuine Gāruḍa-Purāṇa exists.

Gāruḍika, as, m. a charmer, a dealer in antidotes.

गारुत्मत *gārutmata, as, ī, am* (fr. *garutmat*), shaped like the bird Garuḍa, sacred to Garuḍa &c.; (*am*), n. an emerald; [cf. *garuḍāṅkita,* &c.] — *Gārutmata-pattrikā,* f., N. of a plant; [cf. *pāćī* and *marakata-pattrī.*]

गार्ग *gārga, as, ī, am* (fr. *gārgya* below, which is derived fr. *garga*), coming from or connected with Gārgya; a contemptuous metronymic from Gārgī.

Gārgaka, as, ikā, am, belonging to Gārgya, worshipping Gārgya; (*am*), n. a multitude or assemblage of the descendants of Garga.

Gārgika, as, m. a metronymic from Gārgī, expressing contempt.

Gārgikā, f. descent from Garga, the relation to the school of Gārgya.

Gārgī, f. the wife of Gārgya; an epithet of Durgā. — *Gārgī-putra, as,* m. the son of Gārgī; N. of a teacher. — *Gārgīputrakāyaṇi* or *gārgīputrāyaṇi* or *gārgīputri, is,* m. a descendant of the son of Gārgī.

Gārgī-bhūta, as, ā, am, one who has become a Gārgya.

1. *gārgīya,* nom. P. *gārgīyati,* to act like a Gārgya; A. *gārgīyate,* to behave like a Gārgya.

2. *gārgīya, as, ā, am,* composed by Garga; coming from Gārgya; (*ās*), m. pl. the pupils of the descendants of Garga; the pupils of Gārgyāyaṇa.

Gārgeya, as, m. a metronymic from Gārgī.

Gārgya, as (f. *gī*), *am,* descended from Garga, as a son or daughter; (*as*), m., N. of several teachers of grammar, of the ritual, &c.; according to Durga, a Gārgya is the author of the Pada-pāṭha of the Sāma-veda; N. of a king of the Gandharvas; N. of a people. — *Gārgya-pariśishṭa, am,* n. title of a Pariśishṭa of the Atharva-veda.

Gārgyāyaṇa, as, m. a patronymic from Gārgya, N. of a teacher; (ī), f. = *gārgī.*

Gārgyāyaṇīya, ās, m. pl. the pupils of Gārgyāyaṇa.

गार्त्समद *gārtsamada, as,* m. a patronymic from Gṛitsa-mada; (*am*), n., N. of a Sāman.

गार्दभ *gārdabha, as, ī, am* (fr. *gardabha*), belonging to or coming from or relating to an ass; asinine.

Gārdabharathika, as, ī, am (fr. *gardabha-ratha*), fit for a donkey-cart.

गार्द्ध्य *gārddhya, am,* n. (fr. *gṛiddha,* rt. *gṛidh*), desire, greediness.

Gārdhra (or wrongly spelt *gārdha*), *as, ī, am* (fr. *gṛidhra*), derived from a vulture, vulturous, vulturine; rapacious, greedy (?); (*as*), m. an arrow; desire, greediness, cupidity (in the latter sense the word *gārdhra* is probably a wrong reading for *gārddhya*). — *Gārdhra-paksha,* or *gārdhra-pattra,* or *gārdhra-vājita,* or *gārdhra-rājita, as, ā, am* (?), or *gārdhra-vāsas, ās, ās, as,* decorated with vulture's feathers (especially an arrow so decorated); [cf. *gṛidhra-vāja* and *gṛidhra-vājita.*]

गार्भ *gārbha, as, ī, am* (fr. *garbha*), born from the womb; fetal, uterine; relating to or connected with gestation, also to conception (as any act or ceremony).

Gārbhika, as, ī, am, fetal, uterine; relating to or connected with gestation or the fœtus in the womb.

Gārbhiṇa, am, n. (fr. *garbhiṇī*), a number or assemblage of pregnant women.

Gārbhiṇya, am, n. an assemblage of pregnant women.

गार्मुत *gārmuta, am,* n. (fr. *garmut*), honey(?).

गार्ष्टेय *gārshṭeya, as, ī, am* (fr. *grishṭi*), Ved. born from a heifer.

गार्हपत *gārhapata, am,* n. (fr. *gṛiha-pati*), the position and dignity of a householder.

Gārhapatya, as, m., scil. *agni,* a sacred fire, perpetually maintained by a householder, received from his father and transmitted to his descendants, and from which fires for sacrificial purposes are lighted; the place where this sacred fire is kept; (*ās*), m. pl., N. of a class of manes; (*am*), n. the government of a family, position of a householder, a household. — *Gārhapatyāgāra* (°*ya-āg*°), *as,* m. the place in which the Gārhapatya fire is kept.

Gārhamedha, as, ī, am (fr. *gṛiha-medha*), fit or proper for a householder.

Gārhasthya, as, ā, am (fr. *gṛiha-stha*), fit for or incumbent on a householder; (*am*), n. the order or estate of a householder, of the father or mother of a family; household, domestic affairs, the house with its contents.

Gārhya, as, ā, am (fr. *gṛiha*), domestic.

गाल *gāla, as,* m. (fr. rt. *gal*), flowing, liquefying; dropping; a flux.

Gālana, am, n. straining fluids; fusing, liquefying, &c.

Gālava, as, m. the tree Symplocos Racemosa, the bark of which is used in dyeing, Lodh; a pale species of the same, = *śveta-lodhra;* also a kind of ebony, Diospyros Glutinosa [cf. *kenduka*]; N. of an old sage and preceptor, according to the Hari-vaṇśa a son, and according to the Mahā-bhārata a pupil of Viśvāmitra; N. of the author of a Dharma-śāstra; N. of a grammarian; (*ās*), m. pl. the descendants of Gālava.

Gālavi, a patronymic from Gālava.

Gāli, is, f. a curse, execration or imprecation. — *Gāli-pradāna, am,* n. cursing, reviling, abusing. — *Gāli-mat, ān, atī, at,* uttering curses or execrations.

Gālita, as, ā, am, distilled, strained, dropped, melted, fused.

Gālin, ī, inī, i, distilling, fusing, liquefying; abusing, abusive.

Gālinī, f. a particular gesticulation or position of the fingers.

गालोडय *gāloḍaya,* A. *-ḍayate, -yitum,* to examine, investigate.

Gāloḍita, am, n. examination, investigation.

गालोड्य *gāloḍya, am,* n. the seed of the lotus; [cf. *ankaloḍya, angaloḍya, galoḍya, giloḍya.*]

गावल्गणि *gāvalgaṇi, is,* m. (fr. *gavalgaṇa*), a patronymic of Sañjaya.

गाविष्ठिर *gāvishṭhira* and *gāvishṭhirāyaṇa,* two patronymics from Gavi-shṭhira.

गाह् *gāh,* cl. 1. A. (ep. also P.) *gāhate, -ti, jagāhe, gāhishyate, agāhishṭa, gāhitum* or *gāḍhum,* to dive into, bathe in, plunge into, penetrate, enter deeply into; roam, range, rove; to be absorbed in (with acc.); to hide one's self in: Caus. *gāhayati, -yitum, ajīgahat:* Desid. *jigāhishate* and *jighākshate:* Intens. *jāgāhyate* and *jāgāḍhi.*

Gāḍha, as, ā, am, dived into, bathed in, entered into; deeply entered, closely pressed together, tightly drawn, closely fastened, close, fast (opposed to *śithila*); thick, dense; deep (as sleep); strong, vehement, firm; (*am*), ind. excessively, much, very much, heavily, closely, firmly, strongly, &c. — *Gāḍha-karṇa, as,* m. an ear penetrated by sound, an attentive ear. — *Gāḍha-tā,* f. or *gāḍha-tva, am,* n. intensity, closeness; firmness, hardness; excess. — *Gāḍha-mushṭi, is, is, i,* close-fisted, avaricious, niggardly, miserly; (*is*), m. a scymitar, a large sacrificial knife. — *Gāḍha-śoka-prahāra, as, ā, am,* inflicting the keenest anguish. — *Gāḍhāngada* (°*ḍha-an*°), *as, ā, am,* having closely fitting bracelets. — *Gāḍhālingana* (°*ḍha-āl*°), *am,* n. a close embrace.

Gāḍhī-karaṇa, am, n. making stiff.

Gāha, as, ī, am, diving into, bathing; (*as*), m. depth, interior, innermost recess.

Gāhana, am, n. the act of diving into, plunging, bathing, penetrating.

Gāhanīya, as, ā, am, to be dived into or penetrated.

Gāhita, as, ā, am, bathed in, plunged into, immersed, entered deeply into, penetrated; shaken, agitated, destroyed.

Gāhitṛi, tā, trī, tṛi, one who plunges into water, a bather, diver; one who penetrates; shaking, agitating; destroying, a destroyer.

गिन्दुक *ginduka, as,* m. a ball for playing with; [cf. *genduka* and *kanduka.*]

गिर् 1. *gir, īr, īr, īr* (fr. 1. *gṛī*), Ved. addressing, invoking, praising; (*īr*), f. invocation, addressing with praise, praise, verse, song; speech, speaking, language, voice, words (e. g. *mānushīm giram kṛi,* to assume a human voice; *girām prabhavishṇuḥ,* 'lord of speech or words,' an epithet of Bṛihaspati, regent of the planet Jupiter); a N. of Sarasvatī, the goddess of speech; fame, celebrity; [cf. Hib. *gair,* 'an outcry, a shout;' Gr. γῆρυς.] — 1. *gir-īśa, as,* m. an epithet of Bṛihaspati; [cf. *gīsh-pati.*] — *Gir-vaṇas, ās, ās, as,* Ved. delighting in invocations, food of praise, an epithet of Indra and Agni. — *Gir-vaṇasyu, us, us, u,* Ved. fond of hymns or praise, an epithet of Indra. — *Gir-van, ā, ā, a,* Ved. addressed with many invocations, receiving much praise. — *Girva-vāh, ṭ, ṭ, ṭ,* Ved. bearing one who is addressed with many hymns. — *Gir-vāhas, ās, ās, as,* Ved. one to whom invocations are addressed, praised in song, an epithet of Indra &c. — *Gīḥ-pati* = *gīsh-pati.* — *Gī-ratha* (*gir-ra*°), *as,* m. 'the vehicle of words,' an epithet of Bṛihaspati. — *Gīr-devī,* f. the goddess of speech, Sarasvatī. — *Gīr-pati* = *gīsh-pati.* — *Gīr-latā,* f., N. of a plant, = *mahā-jyotishmatī.* — *Gīr-vāṇa, as,* m. a god, a deity ('whose arrow is speech;' or perhaps only a corruption fr. *gir-vaṇas.*) — *Gīrvāṇa-kusuma, am,* n. the flower of the gods, cloves. — *Gīsh-pati, is,* m. the lord of speech, a N. of Bṛihaspati, the regent of the planet Jupiter and preceptor of the gods; a Paṇḍit, a learned man. — *Gīs-tarā,* f. excellent speech, a good voice.

Girā, f. speech, speaking; voice. — *Girā-vṛidh, t, t, t,* Ved. delighting in being praised; (Sāy.) thriving by praise (as a god).

गिर् 2. *gir* (fr. 2. *gṛī*), swallowing, (at the end of compounds, e.g. in *gara-gir* and *muhur-gir.*)

1. *gira, as, ā, am,* swallowing.

Girita, as, ā, am, swallowed, eaten.

गिर 2. *gira,* at the end of an adverbial compound = *giri* (e. g. *anu-giram,* near the mountain).

गिरि *giri, is,* m. (said to be fr. rt. 2. *gṛī;* perhaps originally *gari* or *garu,* and related to *guru, gariman*), a hill, a mountain, a rock, an elevation, a rising-ground (in the foregoing senses often connected in the Veda with *parvata,* e. g. *parvato giriḥ,* explained by Sāy. as a mountain having many parts); a cloud (this last sense is often given to *giri* by the commentators on Vedic works); a term for the number eight, because of the eight mountains surrounding the mountain Meru; a wooden ball, with which children play [cf. *girika* and *giri-guḍa*]; a disease of the eyes; a peculiar defect in quicksilver; a honorific title given to one of the ten orders of the Das-nāmī Gosains; N. of a son of Svaphalka [cf. *giri-kshipa*]; (*is*), f. swallowing; a rat, a small rat, a mouse [cf. *girikā*]; (*is, is, i*), venerable, respectable, worshipful; [cf. Zend *gairi;* Slav. *gora;* Afghan. *ghur;* cf. also *garīyas, garishṭha, gariman.*] — *Giri-kaććhapa, as,* m. a kind of tortoise living in mountains. — *Giri-kaṇṭaka, as,* m. Indra's thunderbolt. — *Giri-kadamba* or *giri-kadambaka, as,* m. a species of the Kadamba tree, mountain Kadamba; [cf. *nīpa* and *dhārā-kadamba.*] — *Giri-kadalī,* f. the mountain or wild Kadalī. — *Giri-kandara, as,* m. a cave, a cavern. — *Giri-karṇā,* f. the plant Clitoria Ternatea; [cf. *a-parājitā.*] — *Giri-karṇikā,* f. the earth; the plant Clitoria Ternatea; a species of Kiṇihī with white blossoms. — *Giri-karṇī,* f. the plant Clitoria Ternatea [cf. the preceding]; another plant, Alhagi Maurorum = *kaććhurā.* — *Giri-kāṇa, as,* m. a blind or one-eyed man, one blind from a particular disease. — *Giri-kānana, am,* n. a mountain-grove. — *Giri-kūṭa, am,* n. the summit of a mountain. — *Giri-kshit, t, t, t,* Ved. living in mountains or on high, as Vishṇu; (*t*), m., N. of an Auććāmanyava; [cf. *gairikshita.*] — *Giri-kshipa, as,* m., N. of a son of Svaphalka; [cf. *arikshipa* and *giri.*] — *Giri-gangā,* f., N. of a river. — *Giri-guḍa, as,* m. a ball for playing with. — *Giri-guhā,* f. a mountain-cave. — *Giri-gairika-dhātu, us,* m. = *gairika,* red chalk. — *Giri-gairikadhātu-vat,* ind. like red chalk. — *Giri-ćara, as, ī, am,* Ved. living in or inhabiting mountains. — *Giri-ćārin, ī, iṇī, i,* living in mountains. — *Giri-ja, as, ā, am,* mountain-born, mountaineer; (*as*), m. the Mahwa tree, Bassia, = *madhūla;* N. of a man with the patronymic Bābhravya; (*ā*), f., N. of several plants, viz. a kind of lemon tree; a plant considered as a white species of Rasnā [cf. *rasnā*]; the shaddock or pumple-mouse, Citrus Decumana; also = *śveta-vuhnā, kshudra-pāshāṇa, giri-kadalī, kārī, trāyamāṇā;* a kind of jasmine, *mallikā;* a N. of the goddess Pārvatī, as the daughter of the personified Himālaya mountain; (*am*), n. talc; benzoin or gum benjamin; it is also confounded with another gum resin called styrax; red chalk; bitumen; iron. — *Girijā-kumāra, as,* m., N. of a pupil of Sankarāćārya. — *Girijā-pati, is,* m. an epithet of Siva, the husband of Pārvatī. — *Girijāmala* (°*ja-am*°), *am,* n. talc. — *Giri-jāla, am,* n. a range of mountains. — *Girijā-suta, as,* m., N. of the chief of a sect worshipping Gaṇeśa. — *Giri-jvara, as,* m. Indra's thunderbolt; [cf. *giri-kaṇṭaka.*] — *Giri-ṇaddha* or *giri-naddha, as, ā, am,* enclosed by a mountain. — *Giri-ṇitamba* or *giri-nitamba, as,* m. the declivity of a mountain. — *Giri-tra, as, ā, am,* Ved. ruling over mountains; epithet of Rudra-Siva. — *Giri-durga, as, ā, am,* or *am,* n. of difficult access in consequence of being surrounded by mountains; a hill-fort or any stronghold amongst mountains. — *Giri-dvāra, am,* n. a mountain-pass. — *Giri-dhara, as,* m., N. of a copyist of the seventeenth century. — *Giri-dhātu, us,* m. different kinds of earth or minerals in the interior of a mountain; red chalk. — *Giri-dhvaja, as,* m. Indra's thunderbolt; [cf. *giri-kaṇṭaka* and *giri-jvara.*] — *Giri-nagara, am,* n., N. of a town in Dakshiṇā-patha. — *Giri-nadī* or *giri-ṇadī,* f. a mountain-torrent. — *Giri-nandinī,* f. daughter of a mountain, a mountain-stream. — *Giri-nimnagā,* f. a mountain-torrent. — *Giri-nimba, as,* m., N. of a plant, = *mahārishṭa.* — *Giri-pīlu, us,* m., N. of a fruit tree, = *parusha.* — *Giri-pura, am,* n. mountain-town or N. of a town. — *Giri-pushpaka, am,* n. a fragrant resin, benzoin. — *Giri-prishṭha, am,* n. the top of a hill. — *Giri-prapāta, as,* m. the declivity of a mountain. — *Giri-prastha, as,* m. the table-land of a mountain. — *Giri-priya, as, ā, am,* fond of or frequenting mountains; (*ā*), f. the female of the Bos Grunniens. — *Giri-bāndhava, as,* m. a friend of the mountains, an epithet of Siva. — *Giri-budhna, as, ā, am,* Ved. resting on a mountain, produced on a hill; [cf. *adri-budhna.*] — *Giri-bhid, t, t, t,* breaking through the mountains, as a river; (*t*), f. the plant Plectranthus Scutellarioides. — *Giri-bhū, ūs, ūs, u,* mountain-born, mountaineer; (*ūs*), f., N.

of a plant, = *kshudra-pāshāṇa-bhedā*; a small stone (?); an epithet of Pārvatī, the wife of Śiva. — *Giri-bhraj, t, t, t,* Ved. breaking forth from mountains; (Sāy.) falling from the clouds. — *Giri-mallikā,* f. the plant Wrightia Antidysenterica; [cf. *kuṭa-ja.*] — *Giri-mātra, as, ā, am,* having the size or dimensions of a mountain. — *Giri-māna, as, ā, am,* having the extent or dimensions of a mountain; (*as*), m. a large and powerful elephant. — *Giri-māla* and *giri-mālaka, as,* m., N. of a tree. — *Giri-mṛid, t,* f. red chalk, mountain soil; [cf. *gairika.*] — *Girimṛid-bhava, am,* n. red chalk. — *Giri-meda, as,* m. a fetid Mimosa, = *ari-meda.* — *Giri-rāj, ṭ,* m. the king of the mountains, the Himavat (?). — *Giri-vāsin, ī, inī, i,* living on or in mountains, being or produced in them; (*ī*), m. a kind of bulbous plant, a large kind of Arum. — *Giri-vraja, as,* m., N. of the capital of Magadha. — *Giri-śa, as, ā, am,* or (*as*), m. inhabiting or frequenting mountains, an epithet of Rudra-Śiva. — *Giri-śanta, as, ā, am,* Ved. inhabiting or frequenting mountains. — *Giri-śaya, as, ā, am,* Ved. inhabiting mountains. — *Giri-śāla, as,* m. a kind of bird. — *Giri-śālinī,* f. the plant Clitoria Ternatea. — *Giri-śṛiṅga, as,* m. an epithet of Gaṇeśa; the peak of a mountain. — *Giri-shad, t, t, t,* sitting on mountains; an epithet of Rudra. — *Giri-shṭhā, ās, ās, am,* or *giri-shṭha, as, ā, am* (rt. *sthā*), inhabiting or frequenting mountains; epithet of the Maruts and of the Soma plant which is found in mountains. — *Giri-sarpa, as,* m. a kind of snake. — *Giri-sānu, u,* n. table-land. — *Giri-sāra, as,* m. iron; tin; an epithet of the Malaya mountains, situated in the south of India. — *Girisāra-maya, as, ī, am,* made of iron, iron. — *Giri-sutā,* f. the daughter of the mountain Himavat; an epithet of Pārvatī, the wife of Śiva. — *Giri-sena, as,* m., N. of a man. — *Giri-sravā,* f. a mountain-stream, a torrent. — *Giri-hvā,* f. another N. of the plant *giri-karṇikā,* Clitoria Ternatea. — *Girīndra* (°*ri-in*°), *as,* m. a prince among the mountains, a high mountain; a term for the number eight; [cf. *giri.*] — 2. *girīśa* (°*ri-īśa*), *as,* m. the prince of the mountains, a N. of the Himālaya, the snowy mountains on the north of Hindūstan, or the range personified; an epithet of Śiva; a N. of the eleventh Rudra: (for 1. *girīśa* see under 1. *gir.*) — *Giry-āhvā,* f. = *giri-hvā.*

Girika, as, m. the inhabitant of a mountain (?); a N. of Śiva; a ball for playing with [cf. *giri* and *giriyaka*]; N. of a chief of the Nāga or serpent-race; N. of a certain weaver in a Buddhist work; also called *ćaṇḍagirika*; (*ā*), f. a mouse, a small rat; N. of the wife of Vasu, daughter of the mountain Kolāhala and of the river Śaktimatī.

Giriyaka or *giriyākā* or *girīyaka, as,* m. a ball for playing with; [cf. *giri* and *giri-guḍa.*]

Giri-śa. See under *giri* above.

गिरित *girita.* See under 2. *gir.*

गिरीश 1. 2. *girīśa,* &c. See under 1. *gir* and under *giri* above.

गिल *gila, as, ā, am* (fr. 2. *gṝ*), who or what swallows; (*as*), m. the citron tree, = *jambīra.* — *Gila-gila, as, ā, am,* swallowing; [cf. *timiṅgila-gila.*] — *Gila-grāha, as,* m. a crocodile, a shark.

Gilat, an, atī or *antī, at,* swallowing, devouring.

Gilana, am, n. swallowing; also *giraṇa.*

Gilāyu, us, m. hard tumor in the throat.

Gili, is, f. swallowing, eating.

Gilita, as, ā, am, eaten, swallowed.

गिलोड्य *gilodya,* N. of a plant; [cf. *angalodya, galodya, gālodya.*]

गिष्णु *gishṇu, us,* m. (probably a corrupt form of *geshṇu*; rt. *gai*), a professional singer; a Brāhman versed in the Sāma-veda, a chanter of that Veda; an actor.

गीःपति *gīḥ-pati, gīsh-pati.* See 1. *gir.*

गीत *gīta, as, ā, am* (fr. rt. *gai*), sung, chanted, sounded, &c.; (*ā*), f. a song, a sacred song or poem, religious doctrines declared in metrical form by an inspired sage [cf. the titles Śiva-gītā, Rāma-gītā, Bhagavad-gītā, which last is also often called the Gītā]; N. of a metre; (*am*), n. singing, song either general or particular. — *Gīta-kaṇḍikā,* f. a Pariśishṭa of the Sāma-veda. — *Gīta-krama, as,* m. the arrangement of a song. — *Gīta-gaṅgādhara,* title of a poem by Kalyāṇa. — *Gīta-giriśa,* title of a poem by Rāma. — *Gīta-govinda, as,* m. Govinda (i.e. Kṛishṇa) celebrated in song; title of a lyrical drama by Jaya-deva, supposed to have been written about the twelfth or thirteenth century of our era; it is a mystical erotic poem, describing the loves of Kṛishṇa and the Gopīs, especially of Kṛishṇa and Rādhā, who is supposed to typify the human soul. — *Gīta-jña, as, ā, am,* versed in the art of singing, acquainted with songs. — *Gīta-priya, as, ā, am,* fond of songs; (*ā*), f., N. of one of the Mātṛis attending on Skanda. — *Gīta-modin, ī, inī, i,* gladdening with songs; (*ī*), m. a Kinnara or celestial chorister. — *Gīta-vādana, am,* n. the singing of a song. — *Gīta-śāstra, am,* n. the science of music. — *Gītāyana* (°*ta-ay*°), *am,* n. a procession accompanied with songs.

Gītaka, am, n. a song.

Gīti, is, f. song, singing; a kind of poetical metre, a form of the Āryā metre, in which the stanza consists of four lines of twelve and eighteen syllabic instants alternately. — *Gīti-viśesha, as,* m. a kind of song. — *Gīty-āryā,* f., N. of a metre of four lines of sixteen short syllables each.

Gītikā, f. a short song, a small hymn; N. of a metre consisting of four lines of twenty syllables each.

Gītin, ī, inī, i, one who recites in a singing manner.

Gīthā, f. a song.

गीरथ *gīratha,* &c. See under 1. *gir.*

गीर्ण 1. *gīrṇa, as, ā, am* (fr. 1. *gṝ*), praised.

1. *gīrṇi, is,* f. praise, applause; fame, celebrity.

गीर्ण 2. *gīrṇa, as, ā, am,* swallowed.

2. *gīrṇi, is,* f. swallowing.

Gīrvi, is, is, i, swallowing, devouring.

गु 1. *gu* (related to 1. *gā*), cl. 1. A. *gavate,* to go.

2. *gu,* (at the end of compounds) going; [cf. *adhri-gu, vanar-gu*; also *priyan-gu* and *śāci-gu* (?); cf. *gū* in *agre-gū.*]

गु 3. *gu,* cl. 1. A., Ved. *gavate, juguve, goshyate, agoshṭa, gotum,* (this verb seems only to occur in the reduplicated forms *joguve* and *joguvāna*), to speak articulately, to proclaim, to cause to sound: Caus. *gāvayati*: Desid. *jugūshate*: Intens. *jogūyate, jogoti,* to shout with joy; [cf. *jogū.*]

गु 4. *gu,* cl. 6. P. *guvati, jugāva, gushyati, agushīt, gutum* or *guvitum,* to void by stool, to void excrement.

गु 5. *gu* (at the end of an adj. comp.) = *go,* a cow, cattle, earth, ray, &c., see *go,* (e.g. *daśa-gu,* possessing ten cows; *sahasra-gu,* possessing 1000 cows; *ćalad-gu,* one under whom the earth trembles, &c.); [cf. *anu-gu, arishṭa-gu, ushṇa-gu, kṛiśa-gu,* &c.]

गुग्गुल *guggula, as,* m. or *guggulu, u, us,* n. m. (but always m. in the later language), a fragrant gum resin, bdellium or the exudation of the Amyris Agallochum, a perfume and medicament; sometimes with the epithet *saindhava* or *samudriya,* i. e. 'obtained near rivers or the sea,' (perhaps some other substance coming from rivers or the sea?); a species of Morunga with red flowers, Morunga Hyperanthera; (*ū, ūs*), f., N. of an Apsaras.

Gugguluka, as, ī, m. f. one who deals in bdellium.

गुङ्गु *guṅgu, us,* m., N. of a man; (*avas*), m. pl. the descendants of this man; (*ū, ūs*), f., Ved. (Sāy.) = *kuhū,* q. v.

गुच्छ *guććha, as,* m. (assimilated form fr. *gutsa*), a bundle, a bunch, a bunch of flowers, a cluster of blossoms, a clump (of grass &c.), a bunch of peacock's feathers, the plumage of a peacock; a pearl necklace of thirty-two or (according to others) of seventy strings [cf. *ardha-guććha*]; (*ī*), f. a kind of Bonduc or Karañja. — *Guććha-kaṇiśa, as,* m. a kind of corn, = *rāgin.* — *Guććha-karañja, as,* m. a kind of Karañja; [cf. *guććhi.*] — *Guććha-dantikā,* f. the plant Musa Sapientum, = *kadalī.* — *Guććha-pattra, as,* m. the palm tree; [cf. *tāla.*] — *Guććha-pushpa, as,* m., N. of a plant, = *sapta-ććhada*; (*ī*), f., N. of two plants, Grislea Tomentosa (*dhātakī*), and another plant = *śimṛiḍī.* — *Guććha-pushpaka, as,* m. two kinds of Karañja, the Rīṭhā-karañja and the Guććha-karañja. — *Guććha-phala, as,* m., N. of several plants, = *rīṭhā-karañja*; another plant, Strychnos Potatorum [cf. *kataka*]; another plant, = *rājādanī*; (*ā*), f., N. of several plants, Musa Sapientum, = *kadalī* or the plantain; the vine; the plant Solanum Indicum (*kāka-māćī*); the plant Solanum Jacquini (*agni-damanī*); a kind of leguminous plant, = *nishpāvī.* — *Guććha-badhrā,* f., N. of a plant, Guṇḍālā. — *Guććha-mūlikā,* f., N. of a plant, = *guṇḍāsinī.* — *Guććhārdha* (°*ćha-ar*°), *as,* m. a pearl necklace of twenty-four strings; a species of grass, Andropogon Schœnanthus. — *Guććhāhva-kanda* (°*ćha-āh*°), *as,* m. a kind of esculent root, = *gulanća-kanda.*

Guććhaka, as, m. a bunch, bundle, cluster of blossoms, clump of grass, the plumage of a peacock, a bunch of peacock's feathers; a pearl necklace of thirty-two strings; a kind of Karañja, = *rīṭhā-karañja*; (*am*), n. a kind of fragrant plant, = *granthi-parṇa.*

Guććhāla, as, m. a species of grass, Andropogon Schœnanthus.

गुज् *guj,* cl. 6. and 1 (?). P. *gujati* and *gojati* (?), *jugoja, gujitum*; oftener *guñj,* cl. 1. P. *guñjati, juguñja, guñjitum,* to sound inarticulately; to buz, hum.

Guñja, as, m. humming; a bunch, a bundle, a cluster of flowers, bunch of flowers, nosegay, = *guććha*; (*ā*), f. humming, a low murmuring sound; a kettle-drum; a small shrub, Abrus Precatorius, bearing a red and black berry, which forms the smallest of the jeweller's weights; either the berry which averages about 1 $\frac{5}{16}$ grains troy or the artificial weight called by this name, weighing about 2 $\frac{3}{16}$ grains; = $\frac{1}{5}$ Ādya-māshaka, = $\frac{1}{2}$ Māshaka, = 3 or 2 barley-corns, = 4 grains of rice, = 2 grains of wheat; (with physicians 7 Guñjās = 1 Māsha, with lawyers 7 $\frac{1}{2}$ Guñjās); a kind of plant with a poisonous root; a tavern; reflection, meditation. — *Guñja-kṛit, t,* m. 'making a humming,' a large black bee.

Guñjat, an, antī, at, buzzing, humming, making a low murmuring sound.

Guñjana, am, n. sounding low and deep, as buzzing, murmuring, &c.

Guñjikā, f. the seed of the plant Abrus Precatorius; [cf. *guñjā.*]

Guñjita, as, ā, am, uttered in a low tone, murmured, &c.; (*am*), n. sounding, murmuring, buzzing.

गुज्जरी *gujjarī,* f. one of the Rāgiṇīs; (for *gurjarī,* q. v.)

गुटिका *guṭikā,* f. a pill, a bolus, any small globe or ball; a small pustule; the cocoon of the silk-worm; a pill; a pearl; [cf. *guḍikā, gulikā, gulī, guḍa.*] — *Guṭikāñjana* (°*kā-añ*°), *am,* n. collyrium formed like a globe or ball. — *Guṭikā-mukha, as, ī, am,* furnished with a rounded orifice.

गुड् *guḍ,* cl. 6. P. *guḍati,* to defend, guard, preserve; [cf. *ghuḍ* and *guṇḍ.*]

Guḍa, as, m. (said to be from the last), a globe or ball; a ball for playing with; a bit, a mouthful, (rice kneaded in the shape of a ball?); sugar which forms itself into lumps, dry sugar; treacle, molasses, the first thickening of the juice of the sugar-cane by boiling; an elephant's trappings or armour (formed of small balls?); the cotton tree; the plant Tithymalus Antiquorum; another plant, = *kshīra-dāru;* (*ās*), m. pl., N. of a people in Madhya-deśa; (*ā*), f. a small ball, a pill; the plant Tithymalus Antiquorum; another plant, = *uśīrī;* (*ī*), f. the plant Tithymalus Antiquorum; [cf. *guḷa, gauḍa, gauḍika.*] — *Guḍa-karī*, f. (perhaps a corruption of *gurjarī* or *gujjarī*), one of the Rāgiṇīs or female personifications of the musical modes. — *Guḍa-tṛiṇa, am*, n. sugar-cane. — *Guḍa-tvać, k*, n. (?) the aromatic bark of the Laurus Cassia. — *Guḍa-tvaća, am*, n. the aromatic bark of the Laurus Cassia; mace. — *Guḍa-dāru, us, u*, m. n. sugar-cane. — *Guḍa-dhenu, us*, f. a milch-cow symbolically represented by sugar &c. and offered as a present to Brāhmans; sugar piled up for distribution at certain religious rites. — *Guḍa-pishṭa, am*, n. a sort of sweetmeat, flour or rice and sugar ground and boiled together. — *Guḍa-pushpa, as*, m. the plant Bassia Latifolia or another species of it, (the flowers being full of saccharine matter.) — *Guḍa-phala, as*, m. the tree Careya Arborea or Salvadora Persica; jujube; [cf. *gūḍha-phala.*] — *Guḍa-bhā*, f. a kind of sugar. — *Guḍa-miśra, am*, n. a sort of cake or sweetmeat, flour or rice and coarse sugar ground and boiled together. — *Guḍa-mūla, as*, m. a kind of amaranth, Amaranthus Polygamus; [cf. *alpa-mārisha.*] — *Guḍaliṇ-mat, ān, atī, at*, having a sugar-licker. — *Guḍa-lih, ṭ, ṭ, ṭ*, sugar-licking. — *Guḍa-vīja, as*, m. a kind of pease; [cf. *masūra.*] — *Guḍa-śarkarā*, f. sugar, refined sugar. — *Guḍa-śigru, us*, m. a red sort of Morunga; [cf. *śobhāñjana.*] — *Guḍa-śṛinga, am*, n. a cupola. — *Guḍa-harītakī*, f. myrobalan preserved in molasses. — *Guḍā-keśa, as*, m. whose hair forms tufts or matted locks (resembling in shape the leaves of the Euphorbia?), an epithet of the hero Arjuna; also of Śiva. — *Guḍāpūpikā* (°*ḍa-ap*°, scil. *paurṇamāsī*), f. a certain day of full moon, on which sweetmeats are eaten. — *Guḍāśaya* (°*ḍa-āś*°), *as*, m. a species of Pīlu growing in mountains; [cf. *akshoṭa.*] — *Guḍodaka* (°*ḍa-ud*°), *am*, n. water mixed with molasses; (*as, ā, am*), containing water instead of molasses. — *Guḍodbhavā* (°*ḍa-ud*°), f. sugar. — *Guḍaudana* (°*ḍa-od*°), *am*, n. boiled rice and coarse sugar.

Guḍaka, as, m. a ball [cf. *nābhi-guḍaka*]; a bit, a mouthful; a kind of drug prepared with treacle, a conserve; (*ikā*), f. a small ball, a pill; a kernel; (*am*), n. treacle, molasses.

Guḍala, am, n. a spirituous liquor distilled from molasses, a sort of rum.

Guḍera or *guḍeraka, as*, m. a bit, a mouthful.

गुडची *guḍaćī*, f. the shrub Cocculus Cordifolius; [cf. *guḍući* and *guḍūćī.*]

गुडाका *guḍākā*, f. sleep; sloth.

गुडाला *guḍālā*, f. a species of grass, = *gunḍālā.*

गुडुगुडायन *guḍuguḍāyana, as, ī, am*, rattling in the throat (as breath).

गुडुची *guḍućī*, f. the shrub Cocculus Cordifolius; [cf. *guḍaćī* and *guḍūćī.*]

गुडुह *guḍuha, ās*, m. pl., N. of a people in Madhya-deśa; (also read *guruha, guluha*, and *gulaha.*)

गुडूची *guḍūćī*, f. the shrub Cocculus Cordifolius; [cf. *guḍaćī* and *guḍućī.*]

गुण *guṇa, as*, m. (said to be fr. rt. *grah*), a single thread or strand of a cord or twine (e. g. *tri-guṇa*, consisting of three threads or strands), a string or thread, a rope in general; a garland; a bow-string; a sinew; the string of a musical instrument, a chord; (at the end of a compound after a numeral) fold, times, &c. (e. g. *tri-guṇa*, three-fold; *dvi-guṇa*, two-fold, double; *ćatur-guṇa*, four-fold; *sapta triguṇāni dināni*, twenty-one days; *mūlyāt pañćaguṇo daṇḍaḥ*, a fine five times more than the value; *dushṭo daśaguṇam*, ten times worse; *dviguṇatvam i*, to become double; *viśishṭo daśabhir guṇaiḥ*, of ten times higher value); a multiplier, a co-efficient (in arithmetic); division, subdivision, species, kind (e. g. *gandhasya guṇāḥ*, the different kinds of smell); a secondary element, a subordinate or unessential part of any action, an auxiliary act (e. g. *sarva-guṇa*, reaching to all subordinate parts, hence 'valid throughout'); a secondary dish (opposed to *anna*, i. e. rice or the chief dish), a side-dish; quality, the unessential part of anything (opposed to the substance); a quality, a peculiarity, an attribute or property in general, an attribute of the five elements, (each element has its own peculiar quality or qualities as well as organ of sense; thus 1. ether has *śabda* or sound for its Guṇa and the ear for its organ; 2. the air has tangibility and sound for its Guṇas and the skin for its organ; 3. fire or light has shape or colour, tangibility, and sound for its Guṇas, and the eye for its organ; 4. water has flavour, shape, tangibility, and sound for its Guṇas, and the tongue for its organ; 5. earth has the preceding Guṇas, with the addition of its own peculiar Guṇa of smell, and the nose for its organ); an ingredient or constituent of nature (according to the Sāṅkhya philosophy, which makes nature to consist in the equipoise of three Guṇas called *sattva, rajas*, and *tamas*, i. e. goodness, passion, and darkness, or virtue, foulness, and ignorance); a term for the number three (taken from the three qualities of the Sāṅkhya system); a property or characteristic of all created things (according to the Nyāya philosophy, which makes twenty-four Guṇas, viz. 1. *rūpa*, shape, colour; 2. *rasa*, savour; 3. *gandha*, odour; 4. *sparśa*, tangibility; 5. *saṅkhyā*, number; 6. *parimāṇa*, dimension; 7. *pṛithaktva*, severalty; 8. *saṃyoga*, conjunction; 9. *vibhāga*, disjunction; 10. *paratva*, remoteness; 11. *aparatva*, proximity; 12. *gurutva*, weight; 13. *dravatva*, fluidity; 14. *sneha*, viscidity; 15. *śabda*, sound; 16. *buddhi* or *jñāna*, understanding or knowledge; 17. *sukha*, pleasure; 18. *duḥkha*, pain; 19. *iććhā*, desire; 20. *dvesha*, aversion; 21. *prayatna*, effort; 22. *dharma*, merit or virtue; 23. *adharma*, demerit; 24. *saṃskāra*, faculty); an epithet; a good quality, virtue, merit, excellence, eminence, high degree, proper course of action in politics, (the six proper courses of action for a king in foreign politics are peace, war, march, halt, stratagem, and recourse to the protection of a mightier king; besides these the four Upāyas, or means of conquering an enemy, are sometimes called Guṇas; see *upāya*); the peculiar property of the letters which are pronounced with the *vāhya-prayatna* or external utterance, (these properties are eleven in all, viz. *vivāra*, expansion of the throat; *saṃvāra*, contraction; *śvāsa*, sighing; *nāda*, sounding; *ghosha*, soft sound or low murmur; *a-ghosha*, absence of that murmur; *alpa-prāṇa*, slight aspiration; *mahā-prāṇa*, strong aspiration; and the three accents); a secondary or subordinate gradation of a vowel (in opposition to the highest gradation or *vṛiddhi*), the vowels *a, e, o* (with *ar, al*); the merit of a composition in rhetoric, i. e. consistency of plan, elegance of expression, &c.; an organ of sense; a cook; an epithet of Bhīma [cf. *guṇa-kāra*]; (*ā*), f., N. of a grass, = *dūrvā;* a kind of perfume, = *māṅsa-rohiṇī;* N. of a princess; [cf. *gauṇa, nir-guṇa, vi-guṇa, sa-guṇa;* cf. also Hib. *gaoine*, 'goodness, honesty.'] — *Guṇa-karaṇḍa-vyūha, as*, m. title of a Buddhist work; [cf. *karaṇḍa-vyūha.*] — *Guṇa-karman, a*, n. an unessential secondary action; (in grammar) the secondary or less immediate object of an action. — *Guṇa-karma-vibhāga, as, ā, am*, distinguishing an action and an attribute; (*as*), m. separation of an action and an attribute. — *Guṇa-kāra, as, ī, am*, one who counts &c.; productive of good qualities, profitable; (*as*), m. one who prepares side-dishes or any secondary article of food, such as sweetmeats &c.; an epithet of Bhīma-sena, who performed the duties of a cook while the Pāṇḍava princes were servants to Virāṭa. — *Guṇa-kiraṇāvalī*, f., N. of a literary work. — *Guṇa-ketu, us*, m., N. of a Buddha. — *Guṇa-keśī*, f., N. of a daughter of Mātali, who was the charioteer of Indra. — *Guṇa-gāna, am*, n. praising the virtues of another, panegyric, praise. — *Guṇa-gṛidhnu, us, us, u*, desiring or possessing good qualities. — *Guṇa-gṛihya, as, ā, am*, capable of good qualities, admiring virtue, attached to merit. — *Guṇa-grahaṇa, am*, n. acknowledging or appreciating merit. — *Guṇa-grāma, as*, m. an assemblage of virtues or merits. — *Guṇa-grāhaka, as, ā, am*, or *guṇa-grāhin, ī, iṇī, i*, capable of appreciating merit; one who can appreciate good qualities. — *Guṇa-ghātin, ī, inī, i*, destroying merit, a detractor, a calumniator, envious, censorious. — *Guṇa-ćandra, as*, m., N. of a man; N. of a disciple of Deva-sūri, who was the author of a commentary called Tattva-prakāśaka-vṛitti. — *Guṇa-jña, as, ā, am*, one who knows how to appreciate men or things, knowing or judging of their merits. — *Guṇa-tas*, ind. according to the three chief qualities of all existing beings, from the side of the good qualities or virtues; according to property or quality; according to desert; according to the Guṇas or properties of the letters pronounced with the Vāhya-prayatna. — *Guṇa-tā*, f. subordination, dependence; virtue, excellence, the possession of good qualities; the possession of attributes or qualities in general; multiplication. — *Guṇa-traya* or *guṇa-tritaya, am*, n. the three constituent properties of nature, or *sattva, rajas*, and *tamas*. — *Guṇatrayābhāsa* (°*ya-ābh*°), *as*, m. life. — *Guṇa-tva, am*, n. the condition of a rope or string; subordination; excellence; the possession of qualities; multiplication. — *Guṇa-deva, as*, m., N. of a son of Guṇāḍhya. — *Guṇa-dosha, au*, m. pl. innocence and guilt, virtue and vice. — *Guṇa-dosha-parīkshaṇa, am*, n. test or investigation of merits and defects. — *Guṇa-dhara, as, ā, am*, possessing good qualities. — *Guṇa-dharma, as*, m. the virtue or duty incident to the possession of certain qualities, as clemency is the virtue and duty of royalty &c. — *Guṇa-padī*, f. having feet thin as cords. — *Guṇa-pūga, am*, n. great merit. — *Guṇa-prakarsha, as*, m. great merit, excellence. — *Guṇa-prabha, as*, m., N. of a Buddhist teacher. — *Guṇa-priya, as, ā, am*, attached to merit, fond of excellence. — *Guṇa-bhadra, as*, m., N. of the author of the Ātmānuśāsana; N. of a literary work. — *Guṇa-bhuj, k, k, k*, enjoying or endowed with qualities. — *Guṇa-bhedatas*, ind. according to the difference of quality &c. — *Guṇa-bhoktṛi, tā, trī, tṛi*, perceiving the properties of things. — *Guṇa-bhraṅśa, as*, m. the loss of all good qualities or merits. — *Guṇa-mati, is*, m., N. of a Buddhist teacher. — *Guṇa-maya, as, ī, am*, consisting of single threads; produced by or consisting of the three constituent properties of nature (see *guṇa*), resting on them, containing them, endowed with properties; possessed of merit or virtues. — *Guṇa-mahat, t*, n. great merit, superior qualities. — *Guṇa-yukta, as, ā, am*, possessed of virtues or properties. — *Guṇa-ratna, am*, n. the pearl of good qualities, title of a short collection of sentences by Bhava-bhūti. — *Guṇaratna-kośa-stotra, am*, n., N. of a hymn by Parāśara-bhaṭṭa. — *Guṇa-rāga, as*, m. delighting in the good qualities of others. — *Guṇa-rāja-prabhāsa, as*, m., N. of a Buddha. — *Guṇa-rāśi, is*, m. an epithet of Śiva; N. of a Buddha. — *Guṇa-lakshaṇa, am*, n. mark or indication of internal property. — *Guṇa-layanikā* or *guṇa-layanī*, f. a tent. — *Guṇa-lubdha, as, ā, am*, desirous of merit; attached to excellence; patronising merit. — *Guṇa-vaćana, am*, n. an attributive; an adjective. — *Guṇa-vat, ān, atī, at*, endowed with qualities; endowed with good qualities, with virtues or merits or excellences; excellent, perfect; (*ān*), m., N. of a son of Guṇavatī; (*tī*), f., N. of a daughter of Su-nābha, the wife of Sāmba and mother of Guṇa-vat. — *Guṇavat-tama, as, ā, am,* most excellent. — *Guṇavat-tara, as, ā, am,* more excellent, excellent. — *Guṇavat-tā,* f. or *guṇavat-tva, am,* n. the state of possessing qualities, the possession of good qualities, or of virtues; excellence. — *Guṇa-varṇana, am,* n. the describing the merits of another person. — *Guṇa-vartin, ī, inī, i,* being on the path of virtue. — *Guṇa-varman, ā,* m., N. of a man. — *Guṇa-vāćaka, as, ikā, am,* denoting a quality; (with *śabda*) an attributive noun, an adjective. — *Guṇa-vāda, as,* m. pointing out good qualities or merits. — *Guṇa-vidha, as, ā, am,* possessed of different qualities. — *Guṇa-vivećanā,* f. discernment in appreciating the merits of a person, a just sense of merit. — *Guṇa-viśesha, as,* m. a different property. — *Guṇa-vishṇu, us,* m., N. of a scholiast. — *Guṇa-vistara, as, ā, am,* abounding in excellent qualities. — *Guṇa-vriksha* or *guṇa-vrikshaka, as,* m. a mast or post to which a ship or boat is fastened. — *Guṇa-vritti, is,* f. a secondary or essential condition or relation (opposed to *mukhyā vrittiḥ*); character or style of qualities or merits. — *Guṇa-vaićitrya, am,* n. variety of qualities. — *Guṇa-vaiśeshya, am,* n. pre-eminence of merit or of any property. — *Guṇa-śata, am,* n. a hundred excellent qualities. — *Guṇa-śabda, as,* m. an adjective. — *Guṇa-śīla, as, ā, am,* virtuous. — *Guṇa-ślāghā,* f. encomium, praise. — *Guṇa-saṅkīrtana, am,* n. celebration of qualities. — *Guṇa-saṅkhyāna, am,* n. the theory of the three essential properties. — *Guṇa-saṅga, as,* m. association with properties or qualities. — *Guṇa-saṅgraha, as,* m. a collection of merits or properties; acknowledging or appreciating of merit. — *Guṇa-samudra, am,* n. an ocean of virtues. — *Guṇa-sampad, t,* f. great merit, perfection. — *Guṇa-sāgara, as, ā, am,* endowed with all good qualities; (*as*), m. an ocean of good qualities, one endowed with all virtues; an epithet of Brahmā; N. of a Buddha. — *Guṇa-stuti, is,* f. panegyric, encomium. — *Guṇa-sthāna-prakaraṇa, am,* n. title of a Buddhist and Jaina work. — *Guṇa-hīna, as, ā, am,* void of merit, free from properties; poor (as food). — *Guṇākara* (°*ṇa-āk*°), *as,* m. a mine or multitude of merits, one endowed with all virtues; a N. of Buddha Sākya-muni, the founder of the Buddhist religion; an epithet of Siva; N. of a poet; (*as, ā, am*), possessing all excellences. — *Guṇākshara* (°*ṇa-ak*°), probably for *ghuṇākshara,* q. v. — *Guṇāguṇa-jña* (°*ṇa-ag*°), *as, ā, am,* a judge of merit and demerit. — *Guṇāgradhara* (°*ṇa-ag*°), *as,* m., N. of a man. — *Guṇāḍhya* (°*ṇa-āḍh*°), *as, ā, am,* rich in virtues or excellences; (*as*), m., N. of a Brāhman, = Mālyavat in a former birth. — *Guṇātīta* (°*ṇa-at*°), *as, ā, am,* freed from or beyond all properties. — *Guṇātman* (°*ṇa-āt*°), *ā, ā, a,* having qualities. — *Guṇādhāra* (°*ṇa-ādh*°), *as,* m. a receptacle of virtues, i. e. a virtuous person. — *Guṇādhipa* (°*ṇa-adh*°), *as,* m., N. of a king. — *Guṇādhishṭhānaka* (°*ṇa-adhishṭhāna*), *am,* n. the region of the breast where the girdle is fastened. — *Guṇānurāga* (°*ṇa-an*°), *as,* m. delight or pleasure in the good qualities of others, approbation. — *Guṇānurodha* (°*ṇa-an*°), *as,* m. conformity or suitableness to good qualities &c. — *Guṇāntara* (°*ṇa-an*°), *am,* n. a different kind of merit, variety of property or quality. — *Guṇānvita* (°*ṇa-an*°), *as, ā, am,* having attributes or qualities; excellent, good, endowed with virtues. — *Guṇāpavāda* (°*ṇa-ap*°), *as,* m. detraction. — *Guṇābdhi* (°*ṇa-ab*°), *is,* m. a Buddha; [cf. *guṇa-sāgara.*] — *Guṇābhāsa* (°*ṇa-ābh*°), *as,* m. semblance of qualities. — *Guṇāyana* (°*ṇa-ay*°), *as, ī, am,* one who goes on the path of virtue. — *Guṇālaṅkrita* (°*ṇa-al*°), *as, ā, am,* adorned with virtues or good qualities. — *Guṇālābha* (°*ṇa-al*°), *as,* m. inefficiency. — *Guṇāśraya* (°*ṇa-āś*°), *as, ā, am,* virtuous, excellent, able, endowed with good qualities. — *Guṇeśa* (°*ṇa-īśa*), *as,* m. a lord of the three qualities; N. of a mountain. — *Guṇeśvara* (°*ṇa-īś*°), *as, ī, am,* having good qualities &c.; (*as*), m., N. of a mountain; according to some, Citrakūṭa or Chatarkot in Bundelcund. — *Guṇotkarsha* (°*ṇa-ut*°), *as,* m. excellence of merit, the being endowed with superior qualities. — *Guṇotkīrtana* (°*ṇa-ut*°), *am,* n. panegyric, eulogium. — *Guṇotkrishṭa* (°*ṇa-ut*°), *as, ā, am,* superior in merit or in good qualities. — *Guṇopeta* (°*ṇa-up*°), *as, ā, am,* endowed with good qualities, rich (as food). — *Guṇaugha* (°*ṇa-ogha*), *am,* n. superior or abundant merit.

Guṇaka, as, m. a calculator, a numerator, a reckoner; (in arithmetic) the multiplier; N. of a maker of garlands.

Guṇakarī, f. = *goṇḍakirī,* q. v.

Guṇana, am, n. multiplication; enumeration; describing, relating qualities, pointing out merits or virtues; (*ī*), f. examining books, studying, collating or correcting copies and determining the value of various readings.

Guṇanikā, f. determining the value of the various readings of a manuscript; dancing, the science or profession of dancing, acting, &c.; the prologue or introduction to a drama; a garland, a necklace; a cipher, the character in arithmetic which expresses nothing.

Guṇanīya, as, ā, am, to be advised, to be multiplied, to be enumerated; (*as*), m. practice, practising anything, but especially science or study; (*am*), n. the multiplicand.

Guṇaya, nom. P. *guṇayati, -yitum,* to multiply; to advise, invite.

Guṇala, as, m., N. of a son of Bhoja.

Guṇikā, f. a tumor, a swelling.

Guṇita, as, ā, am, mutiplied; heaped together, collected.

Guṇin, ī, inī, i, containing parts, consisting of parts; possessing qualities, an object, a thing, a noun substantive (as possessing qualities); endowed with good qualities or merits; auspicious; familiar with the merits of anything; (*ī*), m. a bow. — *Guṇi-gaṇa, as,* m. a number of virtuous persons. — *Guṇi-tā,* f. virtuousness, the state of possessing virtues or merits or good qualities. — *Guṇi-dvaidha, am,* n. equality of merit on both sides. — *Guṇi-liṅga, as, ā, am,* taking the same gender as a substantive. — *Guṇi-sarvasva, am,* n. title of a literary work.

Guṇī-bhūta, as, ā, am, made secondary or subordinate, deprived of the original meaning or importance; made or having become a merit or ornament; invested with attributes &c.; varied according to qualities; having a certain force or application (as a word &c.).

Guṇya, as, ā, am, endowed with virtues; to be enumerated; to be described, to be praised; to be multiplied, the multiplicand.

गुण्ठ् *guṇṭh* (connected with *guṇḍ* and *gudh*), cl. 10. P. *guṇṭhayati, -yitum,* to enclose or envelop, surround, hide, conceal; [cf. Old Pruss. *po-kuntu,* to protect; *kuns-t,* to guard: perhaps Lat. *cus-tos* for *cut-tos* or *cud-tos.*]

Guṇṭhana, am, n. concealing, covering, enclosing.

Guṇṭhita, as, ā, am, surrounded, covered with; pounded, ground, reduced to dust or powder; [cf. *guṇḍita.*]

गुण्ड् *guṇḍ* (connected with *guṇṭh* and *gudh*), cl. 10. P. *guṇḍayati, -yitum,* to cover, hide, conceal, protect; to pound, comminute.

Guṇḍa, as, m. a kind of fragrant grass, Scirpus Kysoor; [cf. *kaśeru;* cf. also *kāṇḍa-guṇḍa* and *guṇḍika.*] — *Guṇḍa-kanda, as,* m. the root of this grass. — *Guṇḍārośanikā* (°*ḍa-ar*° or *ār*°), f., N. of a plant, = *kāmpilya.*

Guṇḍaka, as, m. dust, powder; an oil vessel; a low pleasing tone; dirty flour or meal, = *malana* = *malina.*

Guṇḍana, am, n. concealing, covering, hiding; [cf. *guṇṭhana.*]

Guṇḍālā, f., N. of a plant, = *jalodbhūtā, guććha-bodhrā, jalāśayā;* a kind of grass, = *guṇḍāsinī.*

Guṇḍāsinī, f., N. of a grass; [cf. *guṇḍālā, gulālā, guććha-mūlikā, ćipiṭā,* &c.]

Guṇḍika, as, ā, m.f. flour, powder, meal.

Guṇḍita, as, ā, am, pounded, ground; covered with dust.

गुण्डिचा *guṇḍićā,* f., N. of the place where the image of Purushottama or Jagannāth is placed after being carried about at the Ratha-yātrā.

गुण्थ *guntha* (?), *as,* m. = *gavedhukā.*

Gunthaka (?), *am,* n. = *granthi-parṇa.*

गुण्य *guṇya.* See under *guṇa* last col.

गुत्स *gutsa, as,* m. (said to be fr. *gudh*), a bunch, a bundle, a cluster of blossoms, a nosegay; a clump of grass; a pearl necklace consisting of thirty-two strings; a plant or perfume, commonly Ganthiāla, = *granthi-parṇa;* [cf. *guććha.*] — *Gutsārdha* (°*sa-ar*°), *as,* m. a necklace or garland of twenty-four strings; [cf. *guććhārdha.*]

Gutsaka, as, m. a bundle, a bunch, a nosegay, a cluster of blossoms; a chowri, a cow-tail; a section of a work; [cf. *guććha* and *guććhaka.*] — *Gutsaka-pushpa, as,* m., N. of a plant, = *guććhaka-pushpa* = *sapta-ććhada.*

गुद् *gud,* cl. 1. A. *godate,* to play, sport; [cf. *gūrd* and *gudh.*]

Guda, as, am, m. n. (from the last?), an intestine, an entrail, the last of the large intestines, the rectum, the anus; (*ās*), f. pl. the bowels. — *Guda-kīla, as,* or *guda-kīlaka, as,* m. piles. — *Guda-graha, as,* m. constipation, flatulence, &c. — *Guda-pariṇaddha, as,* m., N. of a man; *Bakanakha-gudapariṇaddhāḥ,* the descendants of Bakanakha and Guda-pariṇaddha. — *Guda-pāka, as,* m. inflammation of the anus. — *Guda-bhraṅśa, as,* m. prolapsus ani. — *Guda-roga, as,* m. a disease of the last of the large intestines; piles (?). — *Guda-vartman, a,* n. the anus. — *Gudāṅkura* (°*da-an*°), *as,* m. piles. — *Gudāvarta* (°*da-āv*°), *as,* m. obstruction of the bowels. — *Gudodbhava* (°*da-ud*°), *as,* m. piles. — *Gudaushṭha* (°*da-osh*°), *as,* m. the opening of the anus.

गुध् *gudh,* cl. 4. P. *gudhyati,* to wrap up, envelop, cover, conceal, clothe [cf. *guṇṭh*]; cl. 9. P. *gudhnāti,* to be angry; cl. 1. A. *godhate,* to play, sport; [cf. Gr. κεύθω; Germ. *haut;* Old Germ. *hût;* Angl. Sax. *hyde, hyd;* Lat. *cutis?*].

Gudhita, as, ā, am, surrounded, enclosed.

Gudhera, as, ā, am, protecting, a protector, a defender; [cf. *guṇḍ.*]

गुन्दल *gundala, as,* m. the sound of a small oblong drum.

गुन्दाल *gundāla, as,* m. a kind of bird, a sort of pheasant; the bartavelle; see *ćakora;* (also read *gundrāla.*)

गुन्द्र् *gundr,* cl. 10. P. *gundrayati, -yitum,* to lie; (also read *kundr.*)

गुन्द्र *gundra, as,* m. a kind of grass, Saccharum Sara (*śara*); N. of a plant, = *paṭaraka, aććha, śriṅgaverāhva, mūlaka;* (*ā*), f., N. of several plants and roots, = *bhadra-mustaka,* the root of the grass Cyperus Pertenuis (also m. and n. in this sense); = *mustaka;* = *priyaṅgu;* = *kaivartī,* Cyperus Rotundus; = *erakā;* = *gavedhukā,* Coix Barbata.

Gundrāla, a kind of bird, a sort of pheasant.

गुप् 1. *gup,* cl. 4. P. *gupyati, jugopa, gopitum,* to become perplexed or confused.

गुप् 2. *gup, jugopa* and *gopayāñćakāra, gopsyati, gopishyati, gopāyishyati, agaupsīt, agopīt, agopāyīt, goptum, gopitum* and *gopāyitum,* to guard, defend, protect, preserve; to observe: Caus. or cl. 10. P. A. *gopayati, -te, ajūgupat, -yitum,* or *gopāyayati,* &c., to guard, preserve, protect, keep; to hide, conceal, keep secret; to speak, to shine: Desid. A. *jugupsate* (ep. also P.), *jugupishati, -te,* or *jugopishati, -te,* or *jugopāyishati, -te,* to seek to defend one's self from, be on one's guard, to beware of, to shun; to avoid, detest, spurn, despise; to feel offended or hurt: Desid. of Desid. *jugupsishate:* Intens. *jogupyate, jogopti.*

3. *gup, p, p, p,* defending, protecting, (in *dharma-gup,* defending justice, epithet of Vishṇu.)

Gupila, as, m. a king, a protector.

Gupta (and Ved. *gupita*), *as, ā, am,* protected, guarded, preserved; hidden, concealed, kept secret, secret; invisible, withdrawn from sight, (e. g. with *daṇḍa,* a secret fine, a fine secretly imposed); joined, combined; (*am*), ind. privately, secretly; (*as*), m. an appellation forming often the last member of the name of a Vaiśya or man of the third class; a Vaiśya with this appellation was the founder of the renowned Gupta dynasty, in which the names of the sovereigns generally end in *gupta* [cf. *ćandra-gupta, samudra-gupta, skanda-gupta*]; (*ā*), f. a married woman who withdraws from her lover's endearments; a kind of cowach, Mucuna Pruritus; N. of a woman, a Śākya princess. — *Gupta-kathā,* f. a confidential communication, a secret. — *Gupta-gati, is,* m. a spy or secret emissary; (*is*), f. going privately or secretly. — *Gupta-ćara, as, ī, am,* who or what goes secretly; (*as*), m. an epithet of Bala-rāma. — *Gupta-dāna, am,* n. a hidden gift or present. — *Gupta-dūta, as,* m. a secret messenger. — *Gupta-veśa, as,* m. a disguise, dress &c. used for concealment; (*e*), ind. in disguise. — *Gupta-sarasvatī,* f. title of a literary work. — *Gupta-sneha, as, ā, am,* one whose love is secret or invisible; (*as*), m. the plant Alangium Hexapetalum (*ankoṭa*), the oil of which is hidden. — *Guptārma* (°*ta-ur*°), *am,* n., N. of a place.

Guptaka, as, m. a preserver; N. of a Sauvīraka prince.

Gupti, is, f. preserving, protecting, protection; restraint, stoppage, check; concealing, hiding, concealment; a means of protection, fortification, a rampart; a prison; a hole in the ground, a cavern, a sink, a cellar, &c. (a place of concealment); a leak in a ship, or the well or lower deck of a boat (?); digging a hole in the ground.

Guptika, as, m., N. of a man.

Gopana, am, n. guarding, protecting, protection, preservation; hiding, concealment; reviling, abuse; flurry, hurry, alarm; light, lustre; the leaf of the Laurus Cassia, = *tamāla-pattra;* (*ā*), f. protection.

Gopanīya, as, ā, am, to be preserved or protected; to be prevented; to be concealed or hidden; secret, mysterious. — *Gopanīya-tā,* f. or *gopanīya-tva, am,* n. concealableness, fitness for being kept secret.

Gopayatya, as, ā, am, Ved. to be protected.

Gopāyaka, as, ī, am, a preserver, a cherisher, one who guards or protects.

Gopāyana, as, ā, am, preserving, protecting; (*am*), n. protecting, preserving, protection.

Gopāyita, as, ā, am, preserved, protected, cherished.

Gopāyitṛi, tā, m. a preserver, a protector.

Gopin, ī, inī, i, a protector, one who preserves or protects; (*inī*), f., N. of a creeping plant, Ichnocarpus Frutescens; [cf. *gopī* and *gopikā.*]

Gopila, as, ā, am, one who preserves or protects.

Gopishṭha, as, ā, am, Ved. superl. of *goptṛi.*

Goptavya, as, ā, am, to be protected or preserved.

Goptṛi, tā, trī, tṛi, a preserver, a protector, one who defends or cherishes; one who conceals anything.

Gopya, as, ā, am, to be protected or preserved; to be kept, to be taken care of; to be kept secret or hidden; to be cherished; (*as*), m. a servant, a slave; the son of a female slave; an assemblage of cowherdesses (? n.). — *Gopyādhi* (°*ya-ādhi*), *is,* m. a pledge which is not to be used but carefully preserved.

Gopyaka, as, m. a slave, a servant.

गुफ् *guph* or *gumph,* cl. 6. P. *guphati* or *gumphati, jugumpha, -phitum,* to string together, tie, string as a garland, wind round.

Gumpha, as, m. tying, stringing as a garland; a bracelet; a whisker, a mustachio.

Gumphana, am, n. winding (a garland &c.).

Gumphita or *guphita, as, ā, am,* tied, strung together; arranged, placed in order; also *gushpita.*

गुर् *gur* or *gūr,* cl. 6. A. *gurate, jugure, guritum,* to make effort or exertion; cl. 10. A. *gorayate* or *gūrayate,* &c., to make effort; to eat; cl. 4. A. *gūryate,* to hurt, go; Ved. also cl. 6. P. *gurati,* (not used without prepositions except in the part. *gūrta* and *gūrṇa,* = approved, welcome, agreeable; see under *gūr.*)

Guraṇa, am, n. effort, perseverance, great or continued exertion.

गुरु *guru, us, vī, u* (said to be fr. rt. 2. *gṛī,* compar. *garīyas,* superl. *garishṭha,* in Mahā-bh. VII. 5324, compar. *garīyastara*), heavy, weighty (opposed to *laghu*), heavy in the stomach (as food), difficult to digest; great, large, extended, long; (in prosody) long by nature or position (as a long vowel taken alone or a short vowel before two consonants; sometimes a long vowel followed by consonants is called *garīyas*); high in degree, vehement, violent, excessive, deep, much; difficult, hard; grievous; important, serious, momentous; valuable, highly prized; dear, beloved; haughty, proud (as a speech); venerable, respectable; best, excellent; (*us*), m. any venerable or respectable person, as a father, mother, or any relative older than one's self; a spiritual parent or preceptor from whom a youth receives the initiatory Mantra or prayer and who conducts the necessary ceremonies up to the period of investiture with the sacrificial thread or string; this person may be the natural parent or the religious preceptor; a religious teacher, one who explains the law and religion to his pupil, instructs him in the Śāstras &c.; a N. of Bṛihaspati or the planet Jupiter, who is considered as the Guru or preceptor of the gods; an epithet of Droṇa, the teacher of the Pāṇḍus; N. of a son of Sankṛiti; (*vī*), f. pregnant, a pregnant woman; the wife of a teacher; [cf. Gr. βαρύς; Lat. *gravis;* Goth. *kauriths;* Lith. *gieras.*] — *Guru-kāra, as,* m. worship, adoration. — *Guru-kārya, am,* n. a serious or momentous affair, the business or office of a spiritual teacher. — *Guru-kula, am,* n. the family of a spiritual preceptor or parent. — *Guru-kṛita, as, ā, am,* worshipped. — *Guru-kopa, as,* m. violent wrath. — *Guru-krama, as,* m. instruction handed down through a series of teachers, traditionary instruction. — *Guru-gata, as, ā, am,* being with or belonging to a spiritual teacher. — *Guru-gītā,* f. title of a section in the Skanda-Purāṇa relating to Gurus or spiritual preceptors. — *Guru-ghna, as, ī, am,* destroying or killing a spiritual teacher; (*as*), m. white mustard. — *Guru-jana, as,* m. any venerable or elder person, a father, mother, the elders of a family &c. — *Guru-tama, as, ā, am,* most important &c.; (*as*), m. the best teacher. — *Guru-tara, as, ā, am,* heavier, more important. — *Guru-talpa, as,* m. the bed of a teacher; the violation of a teacher's bed; a violator of his teacher's bed. — *Gurutalpa-ga, as,* m. a violator of his teacher's bed; the violation of it (?). — *Gurutalpa-vrata, am,* n. penance for intercourse with the wife of a Guru. — *Gurutalpābhigamana* (°*pa-abh*°), *am,* n. violation of a teacher's bed. — *Gurutalpin, ī, inī, i,* one who has criminal intercourse with his teacher's wife. — *Guru-tā,* f. weight, heaviness, burden, trouble; dignity; importance; the office of a teacher. — *Guru-tāpa, as,* m. excessive heat. — *Guru-tva, am,* n. weight, heaviness; burden, trouble; severity, hardness; greatness, magnitude; respectability, venerableness, sacredness; the office of a teacher. — *Gurutvaka, am,* n. heaviness. — *Guru-dakshiṇā,* f. a fee given to a spiritual preceptor. — *Guru-dāna, am,* n. a Guru's gift, a present to a religious teacher. — *Guru-dāsa, as,* m., N. of a teacher. — *Guru-dīkshā-tantra, am,* n., N. of a Tantra. — *Guru-daivata, as,* m. the eighth lunar constellation Pushya, (of which Bṛihaspati is the ruling deity.) — *Guru-pattrā,* f. the Tamarind tree; (*am*), n. tin. — *Guru-paripāṭī,* f. a series of Jaina sages. — *Guru-pāka, as, ā, am,* difficult of digestion. — *Guru-pūjā,* f. the ceremonies in propitiation of Bṛihaspati when a work is to be performed or undertaken; the worship of one's spiritual guide. — *Guru-pramoda, as,* m. happiness, delight. — *Guru-prasāda, as,* m. propitiousness or the favour of one's Guru; the product of a Guru's blessing, i. e. learning &c. — *Guru-priya, as, ā, am,* dear to a preceptor. — *Guru-bha, as,* m. the constellation of Bṛihaspati, i. e. the lunar mansion Pushya. — *Guru-bhāra, as,* m., N. of a son of Garuḍa. — *Guru-bhāva, as,* m. the condition of a spiritual preceptor, importance, consequence, weight. — *Guru-bhṛit, t, t, t,* Ved. bearing heavy things (as the earth). — *Guru-mat, ān, atī, at,* containing a vowel which is long by nature or position. — *Guru-mardala, as,* m. a kind of drum or tabor. — *Guru-ratna, am,* n. a topaz. — *Gurulaghu-tā,* f. (fr. *guru-laghu*), heaviness and lightness. — *Guru-lāghava, as,* m. (?) length and shortness of vowels; (*am*), n. great and small importance, relative importance or value. — *Guru-vat,* ind. like a Guru, as a Guru, as if to a Guru. — *Guruvad-vṛitti, is,* f. behaving to any one with as much respect as to a sacred teacher. — *Guru-varćo-ghna, as,* m. the lime or citron, = *limpāka.* — *Guru-varṇa, as,* m. a heavy vowel; [cf. *guru.*] — *Guru-vartin, ī, inī, i,* or *guru-vṛitta, as, ā, am,* treating parents or venerable persons with respect. — *Guru-vāra, as,* m. the day of Jupiter, Thursday. — *Guru-vṛitti, is, is, i,* long by nature. — *Guru-vyatha, as, ā, am,* heavily distressed. — *Guru-śinśapā,* f. the tree Dalbergia Sisu; [cf. *śinśapā.*] — *Guru-śikharin, ī,* m. epithet of the Himālaya (the venerable mountain). — *Guru-śishya-saṃvāda, as,* m. a philosophical dialogue by Caraṇa-dāsa. — *Guru-śuśrūshā,* f. service of a Guru. — *Guru-śokānala* (°*ka-an*°), *as,* m. the fire of heavy sorrow. — *Guru-sārā,* f., N. of a tree, = *śinśapā.* — *Guru-sevā,* f. obsequiousness to a spiritual preceptor. — *Guru-skandha, as,* m., N. of a large mountain. — *Guru-sthira, as, ā, am,* very firm. — *Guru-han, ā,* m. the murderer of a Guru or spiritual parent; (this is the worst of all criminals according to the Hindūs.) — *Gurv-akshara, am,* n. a long syllable. — *Gurv-anganā,* f. the wife of a Guru; any woman entitled to great respect. — *Gurv-artha, as,* m. a Guru's fee for instructing a pupil; (*am*), ind. for or on account of a Guru; (*as, ā, am*), important. — *Gurvartha-gahvara, as, ā, am,* deep in meaning.

Guruka, as, ī, am, a little heavy; (in prosody) long.

Gurviṇī, f. pregnant, a pregnant woman; N. of an irregular species of the Āryā metre.

गुरुण्टक *guruṇṭaka, as,* m. a kind of bird, a sort of peacock. See *tila-mayūra.*

गुरुह *guruha, ās,* m. pl., N. of a people in Madhya-deśa; [cf. *guḍuha, guluha, gulaha.*]

गुर्जर *gurjara, as,* m., N. of a district, Gurjara or Guzerat; (*ās*), m. pl. the people of Guzerat; (*ī*), f. one of the Rāgiṇīs or female personifications of music; [cf. *gujjarī.*]

गुर्द् *gurd* = *gūrd,* q. v.

गुर्व् *gurv,* cl. 1. P. *gūrvati, jugūrva,* &c., to raise; to endeavour, to aim or strive.

गुल *gula, as,* m. raw or unrefined sugar, molasses; the glans penis; the clitoris; (*ā*), f. the plant Tithymalus Antiquorum; (*ī*), f. a pill, a bolus, any small globular substance; small pox; [cf. *guḍa* and *gola.*]

Gulya, as, m. sweetness, a sweet or saccharine taste.

गुलञ्चकन्द *gulańćakanda, as,* m. an esculent root (Kanda), commonly Kult; [cf. *guććhāhva-kanda.*]

गुलह *gulaha, ās,* m. pl., N. of a people in Madhya-deśa; [cf. *guḍuha, guruha, guluha.*]

गुलिक *gulika, as,* m., N. of a hunter; *(ā),* f. = *guṭikā,* a ball; a pearl. — *Gulikā-krīḍā,* f. playing with a ball, bat and ball, golf, &c.

गुलिङ्क *gulinka, as,* m. = *kulinkaka,* a sparrow.

गुलुच्छ *guluććha* or *guluńća* or *guluńćha* or *guluńćhaka, as,* m. a bunch, a nosegay, a cluster of blossoms; [cf. *guććha, gutsa, gulańćakanda.*]

गुलुह *guluha, ās,* m. pl., N. of a people in Madhya-deśa; [cf. *guḍuha, guruha, gulaha.*]

गुल्गुलु *gulgulu, us, u,* m. n. bdellium; [cf. *guggulu.*]

गुल्फ *gulpha, as,* m. (said to be fr. rt. *gal*), the ancle; [cf. *vigulpha* and *kulpha.*] — *Gulpha-jāha, am,* n. the root of the ancle.

गुल्म *gulma, as, am,* m. n. a cluster or clump of trees, a thicket, a bush, a shrub; a troop or guard of soldiers, a body of troops, a division of an army, consisting of 45 foot, 27 horse, 9 chariots, and 9 elephants; or of 135 foot, 81 horse, 27 chariots, and 27 elephants; a fort, an intrenchment; disciplining an army, keeping it in a posture of defence; the spleen; a chronic enlargement of the spleen or as variously situated any glandular enlargement in the abdomen, as that of the mesenteric gland &c., so as to be perceived externally; a wharf or stairs, a Ghaṭ; *(ī),* f. a cluster or clump of trees, a multitude of thickets; Emblic Myrobalan; jujube; small cardamoms; a tent. — *Gulma-ketu, us,* m. a small sort of cane or reed, sorrel. — *Gulma-keśa, as, ā, am,* having bushy hair. — *Gulma-mūla, am,* n. fresh ginger. — *Gulma-vallī,* f. the plant Sarcostemma Viminale. — *Gulma-vāta, as,* m. or *gulmodara* (°*ma-ud*°), *am,* n. a disease of the spleen.

Gulmaka, as, m., N. of a son of the Brāhman Soma-śarman.

Gulmin, ī, inī, i, composed of different divisions (a force &c.); growing in a clump or cluster, clustered, bushy; having the spleen, affected by that disease; *(nī),* f. a spreading creeper or any creeping plant.

गुल्य *gulya.* See under *gula.*

गुवाक *guvāka, as,* m. the betel-nut tree, Areca Faufel or Catechu; [cf. *gūvāka.*]

गुष्पित *gushpita, as, ā, am,* Ved. interlaced, intwined, tied together &c.; [cf. *guph* and *gumph.*]

गुह 1. *guh,* cl. 1. P. A. *gūhati, -te, jugūha, juguhe, gūhishyati* or *ghokshyati, -te, agūhīt, aghukshat, agūḍha, aghukshata, agūhishi, aghukshi, gūhitum* or *goḍhum,* to cover, conceal, hide, hide away, keep secret; to cover with clothes: Caus. *gūhayati, -yitum, ajūguhat:* Desid. *jughukshati, -te,* to wish to conceal or hide away: Intens. *joguhyate, joguhīti* or *jogoḍhi.*

2. *guh, ghuṭ,* f., Ved. a hiding-place.

Guha, as, m. a N. of Skanda or Kārttikeya, the god of war (as reared in a secret place); an epithet of Śiva; of Vishṇu; N. of a king of the Nishādas, a friend of Rāma; a N. or title proper to persons of the writer-caste; a horse, a swift horse; *(ās),* m. pl., N. of a people in the south of India. — *Guha-gupta, as,* m., N. of a Bodhi-sattva. — *Guha-ćandra, as,* m., N. of a merchant. — *Guha-deva, as,* m., N. of a teacher. — *Guha-rāja, as,* m. a peculiar form or construction of a temple. — *Guha-śiva, as,* m., N. of a king of Kaliṅga. — *Guha-shashṭhī,* f. the sixth day in the former half of Mārgaśīrsha. — *Guha-sena, as,* m., N. of a merchant.

Guhad-aradya, as, ā, am, Ved. concealing or removing deficiencies.

Guhalu, us, m., N. of a man.

Guhā, f. a cave, a cavern, a hiding-place; a pit, a hole in the ground; the plant Hemionitis Cordifolia; another plant, = *śāla-parṇī; (ā),* ind. in a hiding-place, in secret, secretly (opposed to *āvis*). *Guhā dhā* or *guhā nidhā* or *guhā kri,* Ved. to conceal, remove. — *Guhā-gṛtha, am,* n. a cavern. — *Guhā-ćara, as, ī, am,* going in secret or secretly, going in the interior. — *Guhā-mukha, as, ī, am,* wide-mouthed, open-mouthed. — *Guhā-śaya, as, ā* or *ī, am,* lying in a secret place, being in the interior or in the heart; living in hiding-places or in caverns; *(as),* m. a tiger; an epithet of Vishṇu. — *Guhā-hita, as, ā, am,* being in a secret or hidden place, placed in the heart.

Guhina, am, n. a wood, a thicket.

Guhila, am, n. wealth, property; a wood (?); *(as),* m., N. of a prince.

Guhera, as, m. a guardian, a protector; a smith.

Guhya, as, ā, am, to be covered or concealed, to be hidden, to be kept hidden or secret, concealable, private; secret, solitary, retired; mysterious, mystical; *(am),* ind. secretly, privately; *(as),* m. hypocrisy; a tortoise; an epithet of Vishṇu; *(am),* n. a secret, a mystery; a privity, an organ of generation, &c.; the anus. — *Guhya-kālī,* f. 'the mysterious Durgā,' title of a poem in honour of this deity. — *Guhya-guru, us,* m. the mysterious Guru, an epithet of Śiva, this deity being considered as the especial teacher of the Tantras or Hindū mystical and magical works; [cf. *gṛihya-guru.*] — *Guhya-tantra, am,* n., N. of a Tantra. — *Guhya-dīpaka, as,* m. a flying insect which gives out light; the fire-fly. — *Guhya-nishyanda, as,* m. urine. — *Guhya-pati, is,* m. lord of the mysteries, an epithet of Vajra-dhara. — *Guhya-pidhāna, am,* n. a covering over the privities. — *Guhya-pushpa, as,* m. the tree with concealed blossoms, Ficus Religiosa; [cf. *aśvattha.*] — *Guhya-bhāshita, am,* n. secret speech, a Mantra, a mystical prayer or incantation; a secret. — *Guhya-maya, as, ī, am,* containing mysteries. — *Guhya-vija, as,* m. a kind of grass, = *bhū-tṛiṇa.* — *Guhyeśvarī* (°*ya-ī*°), f. the mysterious deity, i. e. Prajñā, the female energy of the Ādi-buddha.

Guhyaka, as, m. a N. of a class of demi-gods who like the Yakshas are attendants of Kuvera or the god of wealth, and guardians of his treasures; they may have received their name from living in mountain caverns. — *Guhyakādhipati* (°*ka-adh*°), *is,* m. or *guhyakādhipa, as,* m. or *guhyakeśvara* (°*ka-īś*°), *as,* m. an epithet of Kuvera, the deity of wealth.

Gūḍha (or Ved. *gūḷha*), *as, ā, am,* covered, hidden, concealed, invisible, secret, private; disguised; *(am),* n. a solitary or private place; a private part; a mystery. — *Gūḍha-ćāra, as, ī, am,* one who goes about secretly or unknown; *(as),* m. a secret emissary. — *Gūḍha-ćārin, ī, iṇī, i,* going about secretly or privately; *(ī),* m. a secret emissary, a spy. — *Gūḍha-ja, as, ā, am,* born privately; *(as),* m. the son of a concealed birth, born secretly of a woman whose husband is absent, the real father being unknown; (this is one of the twelve forms particularized in Hindū law, the child belonging to the husband of the disloyal wife); [cf. *gūḍhotpanna.*] — *Gūḍha-tā,* f. concealment, secrecy; *gūḍhatayā,* privately, secretly. — *Gūḍha-tva, am,* n. concealment, secrecy. — *Gūḍha-niḍa, as,* m. the wagtail. — *Gūḍha-pattra, as,* m. the plant Capparis Aphylla, = *karīra;* another plant, Alangium Hexapetalum, = *ankoṭha.* — *Gūḍha-patha, as,* m. a hidden path; the mind, intellect; a bye-path, a private way. — *Gūḍha-pād, t,* m. a snake. — *Gūḍha-pāda, as, ā, am,* having hidden feet; *(as),* m. a snake. — *Gūḍha-purusha, as,* m. a spy, a secret emissary, a disguised agent. — *Gūḍha-pushpaka, as,* m. the plant Mimusops Elengi, = *vakula.* — *Gūḍha-phala, as,* m. the jujube, = *badara.* — *Gūḍha-bhāshita, am,* n. secret intelligence, private communication. — *Gūḍha-mārga, as,* m. a subterranean passage, a bye-road or secret way; a defile. — *Gūḍha-maithuna, as,* m. a crow (copulating in secret). — *Gūḍha-varćas, ās,* m. a frog. — *Gūḍha-vallikā,* f. Alangium Hexapetalum, = *ankoṭha.* — *Gūḍha-sākshin, ī,* m. a concealed witness, one placed by the plaintiff so as to overhear what has been said by the defendant. — *Gūḍhāgūḍha-tā,* f. or *gūḍhāgūḍha-tva, am,* n. (fr. *gūḍha + agūḍha*), concealment and publicity. — *Gūḍhāṅga* (°*ḍha-an*°), *as,* m. a tortoise. — *Gūḍhāṅghri* (°*ḍha-an*°), *is,* m. a snake. — *Gūḍhārći* (°*ḍha-ar*°), *is, is, i,* of concealed glory. — *Gūḍhārtha-dīpikā* (°*ḍha-ar*°), f. 'light for the hidden meaning,' title of a commentary. — *Gūḍhotpanna* (°*ḍha-ut*°), *as, ā, am,* born secretly; *(as),* m. = *gūḍha-ja,* q. v.

Gūhana, am, n. concealing, hiding.

Gūhamāna, as, ā, am, hiding, concealing.

Gūhayitvā, ind. having concealed, having hidden or disguised.

Gūhitavya, as, ā, am, to be hidden or concealed, to be kept secret.

गुहेर *guhera.* See under rt. 1. *guh* last col.

गू 1. *gū,* cl. 6. P. *guvati,* to void by stool; (another form for 4. *gu.*)

Gūtha, as, am, m. n. feces, ordure. — *Gūtha-lakta, as,* m. a small bird, considered to be a species of the Mayna, Turdus Salica; [cf. *sālvika.*]

Gūna, as, ā, am, voided (as ordure).

गू 2. *gū* (fr. rt. 1. *gam*), going, (in *agre-gū,* q. v.)

गूढ *gūḍha.* See under rt. 1. *guh* last col.

गूर् *gūr* = *gur,* q. v.

Gūraṇa, am, n. = *guraṇa,* q. v.

Gūrṇa or *gūrta, as, ā, am,* Ved. approved, welcome, agreeable, thankful (Lat. *gratus*). — *Gūrta-manas, ās, ās, as,* Ved. with grateful mind; (Sāy.) with prepared mind. — *Gūrta-vaćas, ās, ās, as,* Ved. speaking agreeably. — *Gūrta-śravas, ās, ās, as,* Ved. of whom or of what one likes to hear or to speak. — *Gūrtā-vasu, us, us, u,* Ved. possessing agreeable things; (Sāy.) bestowing treasure.

Gūrti, is, f., Ved. approval, praise, a flattering expression.

गूर्द *gūrd* or *gurd,* cl. 1. A. *gūrdate* or *gurdate, jugūrde, gūrditum,* to play, sport; to jump, leap; cl. 10. P. *gūrdayati* or *gurdayati, -yitum,* to play, sport; to dwell, inhabit; [cf. *kūrd.*]

Gūrda, as, m. a jump; *Prajāpater gūrdaḥ* or *Prajāpateḥ kūrdaḥ,* N. of a Sāman.

गूर्ध *gūrdh,* cl. 10. P., Ved. *gūrdhayati, -yitum,* to praise.

गूवाक *gūvāka, as,* m. = *guvāka,* the betel-nut tree.

गूषणा *gūshaṇā,* f. the eye in a peacock's tail.

गूहन *gūhana,* &c. See under rt. *guh.*

गृ *gṛi,* cl. 1. P. *garati, jagāra, garishyati, agārshīt, gartum,* to sprinkle, moisten, wet; to grant: Caus. *gārayati:* Desid. *jigīrshati:* Intens. *jegrīyate, jargarti.*

गृज *gṛij* or *griñj* [cf. rt. *garj*], cl. 1. P. *garjati, jagarja, garjitum* or *griñjati, jagriñja, griñjitum,* to sound, roar, grumble, &c.

Griñja, N. of a plant, = *griñjana* (?).

Griñjana, as, m. garlic, or a small red variety of it; a turnip; the tops of hemp chewed to produce an inebriating effect, the Gāñja; *(am),* n. the bulb of a kind of onion; poisoned flesh, the meat of an animal destroyed by a poisoned arrow.

Griñjanaka, as, m. a kind of garlic.

गृञ्जिम *griñjima, as,* m., N. of a son of Sūra and brother of Vasu-deva.

गृणत् *gṛiṇat, gṛiṇishan.* See 1. *gṛī*, p. 296.

गृण्डिव *gṛiṇḍiva* or *gṛiṇḍīva, as,* m. a kind of jackal.

गृत्स *gṛitsa, as, ā, am* (fr. rt. *gṛidh?*), clever, dexterous; judicious, wise; a sharp fellow, a sharper; (*as*), m. the god of love, Kāma or Kandarpa. — *Gṛitsa-pati, is,* m., Ved. the chief of a number of sharpers. — *Gṛitsa-mati, is,* m., N. of a son of Su-hotra. — *Gṛitsa-mada, as,* m., N. of a son of Śaunaka, of the family of Bhṛigu; (according to a legend he was formerly a son of Śuna-hotra, of the family of Aṅgiras, but by Indra's will was transferred to the Bhṛigu family; he is the chief Ṛishi of the second Maṇḍala of the Ṛig-veda.)

गृध् *gṛidh,* cl. 4. P. *gṛidhyati, jagardha, gardhishyati, agṛidhat, gardhitum,* to endeavour to gain; to covet, desire, strive after greedily; be desirous of, be eager for, long for (with loc. or acc.), to be greedy: Caus. P. *gardhayati, -yitum,* to make desirous, make greedy, to be greedy; A. *gardhayate,* to deceive, cheat: Desid. *jigardhishati:* Intens. *jarīgṛidhyate, jarīgarddhi.*

Gṛiddha, as, ā, am, desirous of, eagerly longing for; [cf. Old Germ. *gir, kir:* Mod. Germ. *gier:* Eng. *greedy* (?): Goth. *gredags, gaurs:* Hib. *greadaim,* 'I burn;' *greadhnach,* 'joyful, glad;' *gradh,* 'love, charity; dear;' *graidhneog,* 'a beloved female,' &c.: Lith. *godus, gedu:* Slav. *glad,* 'hunger.']

Gṛidhu, us, us, u, desirous, lustful, libidinous; (*us*), m. the deity Kāma, god of love.

Gṛidhna, as, ā, am (? a wrong form for *gṛidhnu*), desirous (?).

Gṛidhnu, us, us, u, eager; greedily desirous of, greedy, covetous, cupidinous; [cf. Goth. *gairns, gairnja;* Lith. *godùs.*] — *Gṛidhnu-tā,* f. covetousness, greediness, extreme desire.

Gṛidhya, as, ā, am, to be desired or longed for; (*ā*), f. desire, greediness.

Gṛidhra, as, ā, am, desiring greedily or fervently; eager for, desirous, greedy, covetous; (*as, am*), m. n. a vulture; (*ī*), f. the female vulture; a daughter of Kaśyapa and Tāmrā and mother of the vultures: [cf. Old Germ. *gîr;* Mod. Germ. *geier.*] — *Gṛidhra-kūṭa, as,* m., N. of a mountain near Rāja-gṛiha. — *Gṛidhra-ćakra, au,* m. du. the vulture and the Cakra-vāka. — *Gṛidhra-jambūka, as,* m., N. of an attendant of Śiva. — *Gṛidhra-nakhī,* f. the jujube, Zizyphus Jujuba, = *koli;* another plant, Asteracantha Longifolia, = *kulika.* — *Gṛidhra-pati, is,* m. the lord of the vultures, an epithet of Jaṭāyu. — *Gṛidhra-pattra, as,* m., N. of an attendant of Skanda; (*ā*), f., N. of a plant, = *dhūmrā-pattrā.* — *Gṛidhra-mojāntaka, as,* m., N. of a son of Śvaphalka. — *Gṛidhra-yātu, us,* m., Ved. a Yātu or demon in the shape of a vulture. — *Gṛidhra-rāj, ṭ,* or *gṛidhra-rāja, as,* m. the king of the vultures, an epithet of Jaṭāyu. — *Gṛidhra-vaṭa, as* or *am,* m. or n. (?), N. of a Tīrtha. — *Gṛidhra-vāja* or *gṛidhra-vājita, as, ā, am,* furnished with vulture-feathers, as an arrow; [cf. *gārdhra-vājita.*] — *Gṛidhra-sad, t, t, t,* Ved. sitting on a vulture.

Gṛidhrāṇa, as, ā, am, similar to a vulture in greediness; (*ī*), f., N. of a plant, = *gṛidhra-pattrā.*

Gṛidhrikā, f. the mother of the vultures, a daughter of Kaśyapa and Tāmrā.

गृधू *gṛidhū, ūs,* m. air voided downwards [cf. *apāna*]; understanding, intellect, reason; bad, wicked (?).

गृध्रसी *gṛidhrasī,* f. lumbago; rheumatism affecting the loins.

गृभ् *gṛibh, p,* f. (fr. *grah*), Ved. grasping, seizing, grasp, hold.

Gṛibha, as, m., Ved. the place where anything is seized, handle, hold.

Gṛibhi, is, is, i, Ved. holding, containing, bearing.

Gṛibhīta, as, ā, am, Ved. grasped, seized; impregnated, bearing fruit. — *Gṛibhīta-tāti, is,* f., Ved. the being seized or grasped.

गृष्टि *gṛishṭi, is,* f. a cow which has had only one calf, a young cow; (in compounds with the names of other animals) any young female animal (e. g. *vāsitā-gṛishṭi,* a young female elephant); a kind of bulbous plant, = *vārāhī, varāha-kāntā, badarā;* Zizyphus Jujuba (?), Gmelinus Arborea, = *kāśmarī;* (*is*), m. a boar (various reading for *ghṛishṭi*).

Gṛishṭikā, f. a kind of plant.

Gṛishṭyā, f. young (as a cow).

गृह् *gṛih, ghṛiṭ, ṭ, ṭ* (fr. rt. *grah*), at the end of compounds, taking, holding, seizing, taking away, drawing away.

Gṛiha, am or *ās,* n. or m. pl. (in Ved. also m. sing.), a house, a habitation, a mansion; (*mṛinmayo gṛihaḥ,* 'the house of earth,' the grave; *gṛihās,* m. pl. a house as containing several rooms); the inhabitants of a house, a family (pl.); a wife (sing. or pl.); a sign of the zodiac (sing.); a name, an appellation (sing.); (*as*), m., Ved. an assistant, servant; [cf. *anti-gṛiha, devatā-gṛiha, bhūmi-gṛiha, śayyā-gṛiha, su-gṛiha;* cf. also Germ. *kirche* (?); Old Germ. *kiricha;* Island. *kyrkia;* Angl. Sax. *ciric* for *circ.*] — *Gṛiha-kaććhapa, as,* m. a small flat oblong stone, used for grinding condiments &c. (shaped like a tortoise); [cf. *gṛihāśman.*] — *Gṛiha-kanyā,* f. the plant Aloe Perfoliata, = *ghṛita-kumārī;* [cf. *kanyakā.*] — *Gṛiha-kapota* or *gṛiha-kapotaka, as,* m. a pigeon, a tame or domestic pigeon. — *Gṛiha-karaṇa, am,* n. household affairs, house-building. — *Gṛiha-kartṛi, tā,* m. a house-builder, a kind of sparrow. — *Gṛiha-karma-kara* or *gṛiha-karma-dāsa, as,* m. a domestic servant. — *Gṛiha-karman, a,* n. a domestic affair; a domestic rite, a ceremony relating to a house or household. — *Gṛiha-kalaha, as,* m. domestic dissension, intestine broils. — *Gṛiha-kāraka, as,* m. a house-builder, a mason, a carpenter, thatcher, &c. — *Gṛiha-kārin, ī,* m. a house-builder; a kind of wasp, commonly Kumirakyā. — *Gṛiha-kārya, am,* n. household affairs, domestic duties. — *Gṛiha-kukkuṭa, as,* m. a domestic cock. — *Gṛiha-kuliṅga, as,* m. a kind of bird; [cf. *kuliṅga.*] — *Gṛiha-kṛitya, am,* n. household matters or affairs, the affairs of a royal house, the ministry. — *Gṛiha-godhā* or *gṛiha-godhikā,* f. the small house-lizard; [cf. *āgāra-godhikā.*] — *Gṛihagolaka, as,* m. or *gṛihagolikā,* f. the small house-lizard. — *Gṛiha-ćaṭaka, as,* m. a house-sparrow. — *Gṛiha-ćulli,* f. two rooms contiguous to each other, but one facing west, the other east. — *Gṛiha-ććhidra, am,* n. a breach in a house, private or family dissensions or troubles. — *Gṛiha-ja* or *gṛiha-jāta, as, ā, am,* born in the house; (*as*), m. a slave born in the house. — *Gṛiha-jālikā,* f. deceit, disguise. — *Gṛiha-taṭī,* f. a terrace in front of a house, a threshold. — *Gṛiha-dāsa, as, ī,* m. f. a domestic slave. — *Gṛiha-dāha, as,* m. the burning of a house, a conflagration, arson. — *Gṛiha-dīpti, is,* f. the splendor or ornament of the house, a virtuous woman. — *Gṛiha-devatā* or *gṛiha-devī,* f. the goddess of a house. — *Gṛiha-druma, as,* m., N. of the plant Meḍhra-śṛiṅgī. — *Gṛiha-dvāra, as, am,* m. n. the door of a house. — *Gṛiha-dhūma, as,* m., N. of a plant; [cf. *āgāra-dhūma.*] — *Gṛiha-naraka, am,* n. a hell of a house. — *Gṛiha-nāśana, as,* m. a pigeon (destroying the walls of a house by building in and about it). — *Gṛiha-nīḍa, as,* m. 'having its nest in houses,' a sparrow. — *Gṛiha-pa, as,* m., Ved. the guardian of a house. — *Gṛiha-pati, is,* m. the master of a house, a householder; Ved. often an epithet of Agni; a man of the second class who after having finished his studies is married and settled; a householder of peculiar merit, giving alms and performing all the prescribed ceremonies &c.; one who has the precedence at a grand sacrifice; the maintenance of a sacred and perpetual fire; the virtue of a householder (i. e. hospitality &c.). — *Gṛiha-patin, ī,* m. used in the gen. pl. (*gṛihapatinām*) for the preceding. — *Gṛiha-patnī,* f., Ved. the mistress of a house, the wife of the householder. — *Gṛiha-pāla, as,* m. the guardian of a house, a house-dog. — *Gṛihapālāya,* nom. A. *-pālāyate, -yitum,* to resemble a house-dog. — *Gṛiha-potaka, as,* m. the site of a habitation, the ground on which it stands and which surrounds it. — *Gṛiha-praveśa, as,* m. or *gṛiha-praveśana, am,* n. solemn entrance into a house according to prescribed ceremonies. — *Gṛiha-praveśanīya, as, ā, am,* relating to the solemn entrance into a house. — *Gṛiha-bali, is,* m. a domestic oblation, the offering of the remnants of a meal to all creatures, such as animals, supernatural beings, and especially household deities. — *Gṛihabali-devatā,* f. the deity to whom a domestic oblation is offered. — *Gṛihabali-priya, as,* m. a kind of crane, Ardea Nivea. — *Gṛihabali-bhuj, k,* m. a sparrow; (according to other authorities), Ardea Nivea, or a crow. — *Gṛiha-bhaṅga, as,* m. an exile, one who is driven from his house; family decay; destroying a house, breaking into a house; failure, breaking up, ruin, destruction (of a family, firm or association). — *Gṛiha-bhañjana, am,* n. breaking down or destroying a house; causing the ruin or decay of a family. — *Gṛiha-bhartṛi, tā,* m. the master of a house. — *Gṛiha-bhitti, is,* f. the wall of a house. — *Gṛiha-bhūmi, is,* f. the site of a habitation. — *Gṛiha-bhedin, ī, inī, i,* prying into domestic affairs, causing family quarrels. — *Gṛiha-bhojin, ī, inī, i,* an inmate of the same house. — *Gṛiha-maṇi, is,* m. a lamp. — *Gṛiha-māćikā,* f. a bat. — *Gṛiha-mūḍha-dhī, is, īs, i,* bewildered with domestic cares. — *Gṛiha-mṛiga, as,* m. a dog. — *Gṛiha-megha, as,* m. a multitude of houses. — *Gṛiha-medha, as,* m. a domestic sacrifice; (*as, ā, am*), one who performs the domestic rites or is the object of them; connected with domestic rites or the duties of a householder; an epithet of a ray of the sun. — *Gṛihamedhin, ī, inī, i,* one who performs the domestic sacrifices or is the object of them, a religious man; (*ī*), m. the householder who performs the domestic rites, the married Brāhman who has a household, the Brāhman in the second period of his religious life; (*inī*), f. a housewife, the wife of a householder, natural sense or intelligence. — *Gṛihamedhīya* or *gṛihamedhya, as, ā, am,* relating to the Gṛiha-medha or Gṛiha-medhin. — *Gṛiha-yantra, am,* n. an apparatus to which on solemn occasions the flags of a house are fastened. — *Gṛiha-rakshā,* f. the guarding of a house. — *Gṛiha-randhra, am,* n. a breach in the wall of a house; private or family troubles or dissensions of an unpleasing nature; [cf. *gṛiha-ććhidra.*] — *Gṛiha-rāja, as,* m., Ved. the lord of the house, an epithet of Agni. — *Gṛiha-vat, ān, atī, at,* possessing a house, the possessor of a house. — *Gṛiha-vāṭikā* or *gṛiha-vāṭī,* f. a garden or grove near a house. — *Gṛiha-vāsa, as,* m. the living in a house, the office of a householder. — *Gṛiha-vāsin, ī, inī, i,* living in a house. — *Gṛiha-viććheda, as,* m. the extinction or destruction of a family or race. — *Gṛiha-vitta, as,* m. = *gṛiha-pati.* — *Gṛiha-vṛiksha-vāṭikā,* f. title of a literary work. — *Gṛiha-vyāpāra, as,* m. household affairs, domestic economy. — *Gṛiha-śuka, as,* m. a parrot kept in a house; a domestic poet. — *Gṛiha-śuddhi, is,* f. ceremonies for the purification of a house. — *Gṛiha-saṃveśaka, as,* m. a house-builder. — *Gṛiha-stha, as, ā, am,* living or staying in a house; (*as*), m. a householder, a Brāhman in the second period of his religious life, or one who after having finished his studies and after investiture with the sacred thread performs the duties of the master of a house and father of a family; (*ā*), f. a housewife. — *Gṛihastha-dharma, as,* m. the practice or duty of a householder. — *Gṛiha-sthāna, am,* n. a temporary residence. — *Gṛihasthāśrama* (°*stha-āś*°), *as,* m. the order of a householder.

— *Gṛiha-sthūṇa, am,* n. the pillar of a house. — *Gṛiha-han, ā, ghnī, a,* pernicious to a house or its inmates. — *Gṛihāksha* (°*ha-ak*°), *as,* m. a loop-hole, an eyelet-hole, a round or oblong window. — *Gṛihāgata* (°*ha-āg*°), *as, ā, am,* one who has come to a house; (*as*), m. a guest. — *Gṛihādhipa* (°*ha-adh*°), *as,* m. the Gṛihastha or householder; [cf. *gṛiha-stha.*] — *Gṛihānubaddha* (°*ha-an*°), *as, ā, am,* confined to the house. — *Gṛihābhipālin* (°*ha-abh*°), *ī, inī, i,* watching or taking care of the house; (*ī*), m. a watchman. — *Gṛihāmla* (°*ha-am*°), *am,* n. sour gruel made from the fermentation of rice-water. — *Gṛihāyanika* or *gṛihāyaṇika, as,* m. (fr. *gṛiha + ayana*), a householder; [cf. *gṛiha-stha.*] — *Gṛihārāma* (°*ha-ār*°), *as,* m. a garden, a grove &c. near a house and belonging to it. — *Gṛihārūḍha-ćetas* (°*ha-ār*°), *ās, ās, as,* devoted to home. — *Gṛihārtha* (°*ha-ar*°), *as,* m. household affairs, any household matter or care. — *Gṛihāvagrahaṇī* (°*ha-av*°), f. the threshold, raised ground or a terrace in front of the door. — *Gṛihārasthita* (°*ha-av*°), *as, ā, am,* dwelling or living in a house; situated or abiding in any dwelling-place. — *Gṛihāśayā* (°*ha-āś*°), f. the betel tree, Piper Betel. — *Gṛihāśman* (°*ha-aś*°), *ā,* m. a flat oblong stone upon which condiments are ground. — *Gṛihāśrama* (°*ha-āś*°), *as,* m. the order of a householder, the second stage in the religious life of a Brāhman. — *Gṛihāśramin, ī,* m. the Brāhman as a householder. — *Gṛihe-jñānin, ī, inī, i,* wise inside a house, inexperienced, stupid. — *Gṛihe-ruha, as, ā, am,* growing in a house. — *Gṛihe-vāsin, ī, inī, i,* Ved. living in a house. — *Gṛiheśa* (°*ha-īśa*), *as,* m. the regent of a sign of the zodiac. — *Gṛiheśvara* (°*ha-īś*°), *as,* m. the master of a house, a householder. — *Gṛihotpāta* (°*ha-ut*°), *as,* m. any domestic nuisance (as vermin &c.). — *Gṛihopakaraṇa* (°*ha-up*°), *am,* n. any domestic utensil.

Gṛihayāpya or *gṛihayāyya, as,* m. a householder, the master of a house or family.

Gṛihayālu, us, us, u, disposed to seize or to lay hold of.

Gṛihala, as, m., N. of a man.

Gṛihālikā, f. a small house-lizard; [cf. *gṛiha-golikā* and *gṛiholikā.*]

Gṛihin, ī, iṇī, i, possessing a house; (*ī*), m. the master of a house, a householder, the Brāhman as a householder [cf. *gṛiha-stha*]; (*iṇī*), f. the mistress of a house, a wife.

Gṛihī-bhū, cl. 1. P. *-bhavati, -vitum,* to become a house or habitation.

Gṛiholikā, f. a small house-lizard; [cf. *gṛiha-godhikā, gṛihālikā,* &c.]

1. *gṛihya, as, ā, am,* belonging to a house, domestic; N. of a series of ceremonies relating to family or domestic affairs (such as marriages, births, &c.) and treated of in a peculiar class of ritual works, called Gṛihya-sūtras (see below); domesticated, tame, living in houses (as animals); situated outside of, (originally 'adjoining the houses of a town;' e. g. *grāma-gṛihyā senā,* an army outside a village); (*as*), m. the inmate of a house, a domestic; a tame or domesticated animal; (*ā*), f. a suburb, a village adjoining to a city, or a small village attached to a larger. — *Gṛihya-kārikā,* f. the Sūtras of Āśvalāyana in metrical form. — *Gṛihya-guru, us,* m. an epithet of Śiva; (a wrong reading for *guhya-guru?*). — *Gṛihya-grantha, as,* m. a treatise on domestic ceremonies. — *Gṛihya-pariśishṭa, am,* n., N. of a Pariśishṭa. — *Gṛihya-saṅgraha, as,* m. title of a work on ritual ascribed to the son of Gobhila. — *Gṛihya-sūtra, am,* n. a class of ritual works containing directions for domestic rites and ceremonies, composed by Āśvalāyana, Gobhila, &c. — *Gṛihyāgni* (°*ya-ag*°), *is,* m. a sacred fire which it is incumbent on every Brāhman to keep up.

Gṛihyaka, as, ā, am, tame, domesticated, domestic; dependent, docile, not following one's own inclinations; (*as*), m. a tame or domesticated animal, whether a bird or beast.

गृहणी *gṛihaṇī,* f. sour gruel made from the fermentation of rice-water; [cf. *gṛihāmla.*]

गृहीत *gṛihīta.* See under rt. *grah.*

गृह्य 1. 2. 3. *gṛihya.* See last col. and under rt. *grah.*

गॄ 1. *gṛī,* cl. 9. P. A. *gṛiṇāti, gṛiṇīte, jagāra, garishyati* and *garīshyati, agārīt, garitum* and *garītum,* to utter a sound, call out to, invoke; to call; to announce, proclaim; to promulgate, relate; to mention with praise, praise, extol; [cf. Hib. *gairim;* Gr. γηρύω, γλῶσσα; Old Germ. *quar, quir,* &c.; Old Pruss. *gerbu,* 'to speak;' Angl. Sax. *gale;* Germ. *gal* in *Nachtigal;* Lat. *gallus?*].

Gṛiṇat, an, atī, at, praising, flattering; speaking.

Gṛiṇīshan, Ved. found only in the loc. *gṛiṇīshaṇi,* = in praise, with invocation; (Sāy.) to be praised.

गॄ 2. *gṛī,* cl. 6. P. *girati* and *gilati, jagāra* and *jagāla, garishyati* and *galishyati,* or *garīshyati* and *galīshyati, agārīt* and *agālīt, garitum* and *galitum,* or *garītum* and *galītum,* to swallow, devour, eat; to emit or eject from the mouth: Caus. *gārayati* and *gālayati:* Desid. *jigarishati* and *jigalishati:* Intens. *jegilyate, jāgarti;* [cf. Lith. *gerru,* 'to drink;' Lat. *glu-tio, gula;* Slav. *gr-lo;* Russ. *schora.*]

गॄ 3. *gṛī* or *kṛī,* cl. 10. A. *gārayate, -yitum,* to know, discern, make known, teach.

गेण्डु *geṇḍu, us,* m. or *geṇḍuka* or *geṇḍūka* or *genduka, as,* m. a ball for playing with; [cf. *kanduka* and *ginduka.*]

गेप् *gep,* cl. 1. A. *gepate,* to shake, tremble; [cf. *kep.*]

गेय *geya,* &c. See under *gai* next col.

गेल *gela* or *gelu,* a particular number.

गेव् *gev,* cl. 1. A. *gevate,* to serve, to gratify by service; [cf. *kev, khev, sev.*]

गेष् *gesh,* cl. 1. A. *geshate,* to seek, search, investigate; [cf. *gavesh.*]

गेष्ण *geshṇa,* &c. See under *gai.*

गेह *geha, am,* n. (corrupted fr. *gṛiha*), a house, a dwelling, a habitation. — *Geha-dāha, as,* m. the burning of a house, a conflagration. — *Geha-pati, is,* m. the master of a house, a householder, husband. — *Geha-bhū, ūs,* f. the site of a house, the ground on which it is built. — *Gehe-kshveḍin, ī, inī, i,* blustering at home, a house-hero, a coward. — *Gehe-dāhin, ī, inī, i,* scorching and burning at home, a house-hero. — *Gehe-dṛipta, as, ā, am,* overbearing at home. — *Gehe-dhṛishṭa, as, ā, am,* insolent at home. — *Gehe-nardin, ī, inī, i,* shouting defiance at home, a poltroon, a dunghill-cock. — *Gehe-mehin, ī, inī, i,* making water at home; a lazy, effeminate or indolent man. — *Gehe-vijitin, ī, inī, i,* victorious at home, a cowardly boaster. — *Gehe-vyāḍa, as,* m. fierce at home, a braggart, a boaster. — *Gehe-śūra, as,* m. a house-hero, a carpet-knight, a boasting coward. — *Gehopavana* (°*ha-up*°), *am,* n. a small forest near a house.

Gehin, ī, inī, i, having a house, domestic; (*ī*), m. a householder; (*inī*), f. a housewife, a wife.

Gehya, as, ā, am, Ved. domestic, being in a house; (*am*), n. domestic affairs; wealth.

गै *gai,* cl. 1. P. (rarely A.) *gāyati, jagau, gāsyati, agāsīt, gātum,* to sing, to speak or recite in a singing manner, (applied figuratively to the utterance of beings not endowed with human language, e. g. to gods, the earth, &c.); to relate in metrical language, to praise in song; to sing before (with acc.): Pass. *gīyate:* Caus. P. *gāpayati, -yitum,* to cause to sing or praise in song: Desid. *jigāsati:* Intens. *jegīyate, jāgeti, jāgāti;* [cf. Lith. *zaidziu.*]

Gātavya, as, ā, am, to be sung, what may be sung.

Gāyaka, gāyatrī, gīta, &c. See s. v.

Geya, as, ā, am, to be sung; singing, a singer; (*am*), n. song, singing, a song or chant. — *Geya-jña, as, ā, am,* skilful in song. — *Geya-rājan, ā,* m., N. of a Ćakra-vartin.

Geshṇa, as, m. a singer, a professional singer, an actor, a mime, a chanter of the Sāma-veda.

Geshṇu, us, m. a singer, an actor, a chanter of the Sāma-veda.

गैर *gaira, as, ī, am* (fr. *giri*), coming from mountains, grown on them, mountain-born, mountain, mountaineer; (*ī*), f., N. of a plant; [cf. *lāṅgalikī.*]

Gairāyaṇa, as, m. a patronymic from Giri.

Gairika, as, ī, am, mountain, mountain-born or produced; (*as, ā, am*), m. f. n. red chalk, sometimes used as a red ornament; (*am*), n. gold. — *Gairikāksha* (°*ka-ak*°), *as,* m., N. of a plant; [cf. *jalamadhūka.*]

Gairikshita, as, m. (fr. *giri-kshit*), a patronymic of Trasadasyu; also of the Yaskas.

Gaireya, as, ī, am, mountain-born, mountain; (*am*), n. bitumen, red chalk.

गैरकंवूल *gairakaṃvūla* or *gairikaṃvūla,* N. of the ninth Yoga.

गो *go, gaus,* m. f. (said to be fr. rt. 1. *gam*), an ox, a cow; cattle, kine, a herd of cattle (pl.); anything coming from or belonging to an ox or cow, as milk (generally pl.), flesh, skin, hide, leather, a strap of leather, a sinew, a bow-string; a particular day of the Abhiplava sacrifice, = *goshṭoma;* the herds of the sky, i. e. the stars; the sky; (pl.) rays of light (regarded as the herds of the sky, for which Indra fights with Vṛitra); the thunderbolt; water; the eye; an arrow; the hairs of the body; (the following are m. only), the sign Taurus of the zodiac; the sun; the moon; the sun's ray, called Sushumna; a kind of medicinal plant, = *ṛishabha;* a singer; a goer, a horse; a billion; N. of a Ṛishi; (the following are f. only), a region of the sky; the earth (as the milch-cow of kings); a mother; speech, Sarasvatī the goddess of speech; N. of the wife of Śuka, a daughter of the manes, called Sukālas; or N. of the daughter-in-law of Śuka; or N. of a daughter of Kakut-stha and wife of Yayāti; *gavām vratam,* N. of a Sāman; [cf. Gr. βοῦς; Lat. *bos;* Old Germ. *chua;* Mod. Germ. *kuh;* Eng. *cow;* Lett. *gohw;* cf. also Gr. γαῖα, γῆ; Goth. *gavi;* and Mod. Germ. *gau.*] — *Go-agra, as, ā, am,* Ved. headed by cows, having cows or milk &c. as the chief or most excellent part; (*am*), n. a multitude of cows; (according to native grammarians also *go 'gra* and *gavāgra.*) — *Go-ajana, as, ā, am,* Ved. anything (as a stick, goad, &c.) used for driving cattle. — *Go-argha, as, ā, am,* Ved. of the value of one cow. — *Go-arṇas, ās, ās, as,* Ved. flowing or streaming with milk (?). — *Go-aśra, am,* n. cattle and horses. — *Goaśvīya, am,* n., N. of a Sāman. — *Go-ṛijīka, as, ā, am,* Ved. prepared or mixed with milk. — *Go-opaśa, as, ā, am,* Ved. furnished with a twist or tuft of leather straps. — *Go-kaksha, as,* m., N. of a man. — *Go-kanṭa, as,* m. the plant Asteracantha Longifolia. — *Go-kaṇṭaka, as,* m. a road or spot trodden down by oxen or cows and so made difficult to be passed; the print of a cow's hoof, a spot so marked; a cow's hoof; the plant Asteracantha. — *Go-karṇa, as, ā, am,* having cow's ears, an epithet of certain men and demons; (*as*), m. a cow's ear; a kind of deer, Antilope Picta; a mule; a serpent; a kind of arrow; a span from the tip of the thumb to that of the ring finger; a place of pilgrimage on the Malabar coast, sacred to Śiva; Śiva as there worshipped; N. of one of the attendants of Śiva; of a king of Kaśmīra who erected a statue of Śiva, called after him Gokarṇeśvara; of a Muni; (*ā*), f., N. of one of the Mātṛis attendant on Skanda; (*ī*), f. the plant Sanseviera Zeylanica. — *Go-kāma, as, ā, am,* Ved. desirous of cattle. — *Go-kāmyā,* f. desire for cows. — *Go-kirāṭikā* (°*ra-aṭ*°?), f. a bird considered as one kind of the common Maina, Turdus Salica; also called Viṭ-sārikā. — *Go-kila* or *go-kīla*, *as*, m. a plough; a pestle. — *Go-kula*, *am*, n. a herd of kine, a multitude of cattle, a cow-house or station; a village or tract on the Jumnā, the residence of Nanda and of Kṛishṇa during his youth; the inhabitants of this station; N. of a certain sanctuary or holy place. — *Gokula-jit*, *t*, m., N. of an author of the seventeenth century. — *Gokula-nātha*, *as*, m., N. of the author of the work Padavākya-ratnākara; also of the work Rasa-mahārṇava. — *Gokula-stha*, *as*, m., N. of a sect of Vishṇu. — *Gokulika*, *as*, *ā*, *am*, one who gives help or gives no help (?) to a cow in the mud; squint-eyed; N. of a Buddhist sect. — *Gokulodbhavā* (*°la-ud°*), f. an epithet of Durgā. — *Go-kṛi*, cl. 8. P. *-karoti*, *-kartum*, to transform into a cow. — *Go-kṛita*, *am*, n. cow-dung. — *Go-kshīra*, *am*, n. cow's milk. — *Go-kshura* or *go-kshuraka*, *as*, m. (*kshura* = *khura*), the plant Asteracantha Longifolia; (*am*), n. a cow's hoof. — *Go-kshoḍaka*, *as*, m. a kind of bird. — *Go-khura*, *as*, m. = *go-kshura*, the plant Asteracantha Longifolia; another plant, Tribulus Lanuginosus; N. of a Dānava. — *Gokhuri*, *is*, m. = *go-kshura* = *go-khura*, the plant Asteracantha Longifolia. — *Go-grishṭi*, *is*, f. a young cow which has had only one calf. — *Go-goyuga*, *am*, n. a yoke of oxen or cows. — *Go-goshṭha*, *am*, n. a station for cattle; a stable for cows, a cattle-shed. — *Go-granthi*, *is*, m. dried cow-dung; a station for cows, a cow-yard, cow-house, &c.; N. of a plant, = *go-jihvikā*. — *Go-graha*, *as*, m. spoil, booty, capture of cattle. — *Go-grāsa*, *as*, m. the ceremony of presenting a mouthful of grass to a cow when performing an expiatory rite; the feeding like a cow. — *Go-ghāta*, *as*, m. or *go-ghātaka*, *as*, m. or *go-ghātin*, *ī*, m. a cow-killer. — *Go-ghāsa*, *as*, m. grass for a cow. — *Go-ghṛita*, *am*, n. melted butter coming from a cow; rain (i. e. the Ghṛita of the sky or earth). — *Go-ghna*, *as*, *ī*, *am*, noxious to kine; who or what kills kine; one for whom a cow is killed, a guest. — *Go-ghnata*, *ās*, m. pl., N. of a people. — *Go-ćandana*, *am*, n. a kind of sandal-wood [cf. *go-śīrsha*]; (*ā*), f. a poisonous sort of leech. — *Go-ćapalā*, f., N. of a daughter of Raudrāśva and Ghṛitāćī. — *Go-ćara*, *as*, *ā*, *am*, ranged or grazed over by cattle; frequented, visited, offering range or field or scope for action, within the range of, accessible, attainable, within the power of (e. g. *asmad-goćara*, within our power; *dṛishṭi-goćara*, perceptible, cognizable, worthy of observation or adoration; *dṛishṭy-agoćara*, not within range of the sight, invisible); ranging, circulating, passing current, having a particular meaning, prevalent; (*as*), m. the range of cattle, pasturage, range in general, field for action, an abode, dwelling-place, district, department, province; the range of the organs of sense, an object of sense, anything perceptible by the senses, especially the range of the eye, the horizon (e. g. *loćana-goćaraṃ yā*, to come within range of the eye, to become visible); the range of the planets from the Lagna or from each other. — *Goćara-phala* or *goćarādhyāya* (*°ra-adh°*), *as*, m., N. of the 104th Adhyāya of Varāha-mihira's Bṛihat-saṃhitā. — *Goćara-pīḍā*, f. inauspicious position of stars within the ecliptic. — *Goćarī-kṛi*, cl. 8. P. *-karoti*, *-kartum*, to place within the range, make current. — *Goćarī-kṛita*, *as*, *ā*, *am*, within the range of observation. — *Go-ćarman*, *a*, n. an ox-hide, a cow's hide; a particular measure of surface, a place large enough for the range of 100 cows, one bull, and their calves, (according to some authorities) 300 feet long by 10 broad; it is also defined as an extent of land sufficient to support a man for a year; (originally perhaps a piece of land large enough to be encompassed by straps of leather from a cow's hide.) — *Go-ćāraka*, *as*, m. a cowherd. — *Go-ćāraṇa*, *am*, n. the tending or feeding of cows. — *Go-ćārin*, *ī*, *iṇī*, *i*, going after cows, epithet of a class of Yatis; [cf. *mṛiga-ćārin*.] — *Go-jara*, *as*, m. an old ox or bull. — *Go-jala*, *am*, n. cow's urine. — *Go-jā*, *ās*, *ās*, *am*, Ved. produced by milk; (Sāy.) born amidst rays; (according to Mahī-dhara), born in the earth, the earth being identical with the elements. — *Go-jāgarika*, *as*, m. a kind of prickly nightshade [cf. *kaṇṭa-kāraka*]; (*am*), n. (?) a preparer of food, a baker [cf. *bhakshya-kāraka*]; happiness, fortune. — *Go-jāta*, *as*, *ā*, *am*, Ved. born in the starry sky, one whose home is the starry sky; (Sāy.) born in the middle region, an epithet of the gods. — *Gojā-parṇī*, f., N. of a plant, = *dugdha-phenī*. — *Go-jit*, *t*, *t*, *t*, Ved. conquering cattle, gaining cattle. — *Go-jihvā* or *go-jihvikā*, f. the plant Phlomis Esculenta or Elephantopus Scaber; or a kind of Hieracium, = *dārvikā*, or = *gavedhukā*; in Bengālī *gojiā* = Premna Esculenta. — *Go-taraṇi*, a kind of flower. — *Go-tallaja*, *as*, m. an excellent cow. — *Go-tīrtha*, *am*, n., N. of a Tīrtha. — *Go-tīrthaka*, *as*, m., scil. *ćheda*, an oblique cut applied to fistula of the rectum. — *Go-tra*, *am*, n. (rt. *trai*), protection or shelter for cows, a cow-pen, cow-shed, a stable for cattle, a stable in general, a hurdle, an enclosure; the family enclosed by the hurdle; family, race, lineage, kin, an affix used for forming patronymics; a name, an appellation, family name; (in Pāṇini's Sūtras), the grandson and his descendants if no older offspring of the same ancestor than this grandson lives (e. g. A. B. C. representing father, son, and grandson, then C. is called Gotra, if A. and B. are dead, otherwise he is called Yuvan); a caste, a tribe, a subdivision, a caste according to families, (in that of the Brāhman twenty-four Gotras are reckoned, supposed to be sprung from and named after celebrated teachers, as Śāṇḍilya, Kaśyapa, Gautama, Bharad-vāja, &c.); a multitude, increase; possession; a forest; a field; a road; a chattar, an umbrella or parasol; knowledge of futurity, inspiration; a genus, a class or species; (*as*), m. a mountain; (*ā*), f. a herd of kine; the earth; (a polysyllabic fem. in long *ī* shortens its final vowel before *gotra*, e. g. *Brāhmaṇi-gotrā*, a Brāhman woman only by name or birth?). — *Gotraka*, *am*, n. family, family name. — *Gotra-kartṛi*, *tā*, or *gotra-kārin*, *ī*, m. the founder of a family. — *Gotra-kīlā*, f. the earth; [cf. *aćala-kīlā* and *adri-kīlā*.] — *Gotra-ja*, *as*, *ā*, *am*, born in the same family, a relation (in law, the term is nearly equivalent to the 'Gentile' of Roman law, and is applied to kindred of the same general family, who are connected by offerings of food and water; hence it is opposed to the Bandhu or cognate kindred, who do not partake in the offerings to the common ancestors). — *Gotra-paṭa*, *as*, m. a genealogical table, pedigree. — *Gotra-pravara*, *as*, m. the oldest member of a family, founder of a family. — *Gotrapravara-darpaṇa*, *am*, n. title of a literary work. — *Gotra-bhid*, *t*, *t*, *t*, Ved. opening the cow-pens of the sky; (Sāy.) splitting the clouds or mountains (in the battle with the demon Vṛitra), an epithet of Indra and of the vehicle of Bṛihaspati; (*t*), m. Indra (as splitting the mountains with his thunderbolt [cf. *adri-bhid*], and as destroying families or names). — *Gotra-bhūmi*, *is*, f. (with Buddhists) 'family-range,' one of the periods in the life of a Śrāvaka. — *Gotra-riktha*, *e*, n. du. the family or family name and its inheritance; (*am*), n. family estate, patrimony. — *Gotra-vat*, *ān*, *atī*, *at*, belonging to a noble family. — *Gotra-vṛiksha*, *as*, m., N. of a plant; [cf. *dhanvana*.] — *Gotrākhyā* (*°ra-ākh°*), f. family name, patronymic. — *Gotrānta* (*°ra-an°*), *as*, m. destruction of families or of mountains; (scil. *śabda*) a patronymic, i. e. a word ending with a Gotra affix. — *Gotrika*, *as*, *ā*, *am*, relating to a family; *gotrikaṃ karma*, the consciousness of family descent, one of the four pure Karmans with Jainas. — *Go-tva*, *am*, n. the being a cow, the state of being an ox or cow. — 1. *go-da*, *as*, *ā*, *am*, giving cattle or cows; (*au*), m. du., N. of a village; (*ā*), f., N. of a river, commonly Godāvarī. — *Go-datra*, *as*, *ā*, *am*, Ved. giving cattle; an epithet of Indra. — *Go-danta*, *as*, m. a cow's tooth; yellow orpiment; a white fossil substance, apparently an earthy salt; N. of a Dānava; (*as*, *ā*, *am*), having cow's teeth; armed, armed with a coat of mail. — *Go-dari*, *is*, *is*, *i*, Ved. opening the stables of the sky; (Sāy.) splitting the clouds or mountains, epithet of Indra. — 2. *go-dā*, *ās*, *ās*, *am*, Ved. presenting with cattle or kine. — 1. *go-dāna*, *am*, n. presenting with cows, the gift of a cow; N. of the eastern continent; cutting (rt. *do*) of the hair (*go*), the ceremony of tonsure; see 2. *godāna*, s. v. — *Go-dāya*, *as*, *ā*, *am*, intending to present with cows. — *Go-dāraṇa*, *am*, n. a plough; a spade or hoe. — *Go-dāvarī*, f. 'granting water or kine,' N. of a river in Dakshiṇā-patha; [cf. 1. *go-dā*, *golā*, *saptagodāvara*.] — *Godāvarī-saṅgama*, *as*, m., N. of a place. — *Go-dugdha*, *am*, n. cow's milk. — *Go-dugdha-dā*, f. a kind of grass, = *ćaṇikā*. — *Go-duh*, *-dhuk*, *k*, m. f. a milkman or milkmaid; a cowherd; also *go-duha*, *as*, m. — *Go-doha*, *as*, m. the milking of cows. — *Go-dohana*, *am*, n. the time when cows are milked, or the time necessary for milking a cow; (*ī*), f. a milk-pail. — *Go-drava*, *am*, n. cow's urine. — *Go-dhana*, *am*, n. possession of cows, a herd of cows, a multitude or number of cattle, especially if considered as property, a station of cows; (*as*), m. a broad-pointed arrow. — *Go-dhara*, *as*, m., N. of a king of Kaśmīra. — *Go-dharma*, *as*, m. the law of cattle, ordinances relating to cattle. — *Go-dhas*, *ās*, m., N. of a Ṛishi of the family of Aṅgiras. — *Godha-sāman*, *a*, n., N. of a Sāman. — *Go-dhā*, *godhi*, see s. v. — *Go-dhāyas*, *ās*, *ās*, *as*, Ved. supporting or fostering cows. — *Go-dhuma* or *go-dhūma*, *as*, m. (as it were 'the smoke of the earth,' but derived in the Uṇādi-sūtras fr. *gudh*, to surround), wheat (generally plur.); the orange; a kind of medicinal plant; (*ī*), f., N. of a plant; [cf. *go-lomikā*.] — *Godhūmaka*, *as*, m. a kind of serpent. — *Godhūma-ćūrṇa*, *am*, n. wheat-flour. — *Godhūma-sambhava*, *am*, n. sour gruel made from wheat-flour, a sour paste. — *Go-dhūli*, *is*, m. 'dust of the earth,' a period of the day in the hot season when the sun is half risen; in the cold and dewy seasons, when the sun is full but mild; and in the three other seasons, sunset (originally a time at which mist seems to rise from the earth). — *Go-dhenu*, *us*, f. a milch-cow; [cf. *gaudhenuka*.] — *Go-dhra*, *as*, m. a mountain (bearing the earth). — *Go-nanda*, *as*, m., N. of a people in Dakshiṇā-patha; N. of an attendant of Śiva; (*ā*), f. an epithet of the wife of Śiva; (*ī*), f. the female of the Ardea Sibirica or Indian crane; [cf. the following.] — *Go-narda*, *as*, *ā*, *am*, bellowing like a bull, an epithet of Śiva; (*as*), m. the bird Ardea Sibirica or Indian crane; N. of a king of Kaśmīra; N. of a people in Dakshiṇā-patha; N. of a mountain; a various reading has *yomanta*; (*am*), n. the fragrant grass Cyperus Rotundus. — *Gonardīya*, *as*, *ā*, *am*, relating to the Gonardas; (*as*), m. an epithet of Patañjali, the founder of the Yoga philosophy; N. of a grammarian mentioned by Patañjali. — *Go-nasa*, *as*, m. a large kind of snake, by some considered to be the same as the Boa or Bor; a kind of gem; (*ā*), f. the mouth of a cow; (*ī*), f. a kind of plant; [cf. *go-nāsa*.] — *Go-nātha*, *as*, m. a bull; a herdsman. — *Go-nāya*, *as*, m. a cowherd. — *Go-nāsa*, *as*, *ā*, *am*, having a nose or snout like that of an ox; (*as*), m. a kind of snake; (*ā*), f. the projecting snout of a cow or ox; (*am*), n. a kind of gem, *vaikrānta-maṇi*; [cf. *go-nasa*.] — *Go-nishyanda*, *as*, n. cow's urine. — *Go-nyoghas*, *ās*, *ās*, *as*, Ved. streaming or flowing among milk; (Sāy.) having quantities of fluid streaming down. — *Go-pa*, *go-pī*, see s. v. — *Go-pati*, *is*, m. the lord of a herd of cows, a bull; the leader of a troop, a leader, a chief; the chief of herdsmen, i. e. Kṛishṇa or Vishṇu; the lord of the heavenly herds or stars or rays; the sun; Indra; the lord of the earth, a king; lord of the waters, an epithet of Varuṇa; a medicinal plant, = *ṛishabha*; an epithet of Śiva; N. of a Deva-gandharva; of a Dānava slain by Kṛishṇa; of a son of Śivi. — *Gopati-ćāpa*, *as*, m. the rainbow. — *Go-pa-tva*, *am*, n. the office or order of a herdsman. — *Go-patha*, *as*, m. or *gopatha-brāhmaṇa*, *am*, n. title of a Brāhmaṇa of the Atharva-veda. — *Go-paśu*, *us*, m. a sacrificial cow. — *Go-pāla*, *as*, m. a cowherd; a protector of the earth, a king; cowherd and king; the cowherd κατ' ἐξοχήν, i. e. Kṛishṇa; an epithet of S'iva; N. of an attendant of S'iva; N. of a Nāga; N. of a minister of king Bimbi-sāra, also of a king, and of a general of king Kīrti-varman; N. of a scholiast; N. of several other men; (ī), f., N. of one of the Mātṛis attending Skanda; N. of a Caṇḍālī; two plants, = *gopāla-karkaṭī* and *go-rakshī*. — *Go-pālaka, as*, m. a cowherd; an epithet of Kṛishṇa; an epithet of S'iva; N. of a son of king Caṇḍa-mahā-sena; (*ikā*), f. the wife of a cowherd; a kind of worm or fly found on dung-heaps. — *Gopāla-kaksha, as*, m., N. of a country and (in plur.) the inhabitants of this country. — *Gopāla-karkaṭī*, f. a kind of cucumber (in Hindī *goyālakāṅkarī, gurubhā*); [cf. *gopa-karkaṭikā*, &c.] — *Gopāla-keśava, as*, m., N. of a statue of Kṛishṇa, called after Gopāla-varman. — *Gopāla-tāpanīyopanishad* (°*ya-up*°), *t*, f. title of an Upanishad in honour of Kṛishṇa. — *Gopāla-dāsa, as*, m., N. of a physician; N. of a copyist. — *Gopāla-deva, as*, m., N. of a poet. — *Gopāla-pura, am*, n., N. of a town called after Gopāla-varman. — *Gopāla-prasāda, as*, m., N. of a teacher of Rāma-ćandra. — *Gopāla-maṭha, as*, m., N. of a college called after Gopāla-varman. — *Gopāla-yogin, ī*, m., N. of a man. — *Gopāla-varman, ā*, m., N. of a king of Kaśmīra. — *Gopāla-sarasvatī*, m., N. of a pupil of S'iva-rāma and teacher of Govindānanda. — *Gopāli, is*, m. an epithet of S'iva; N. of a man; [cf. *go-pāla*.] — *Gopāsh-ṭamī* (°*pa-ash*°), f. the eighth lunation of the light half of Kārttika, on which Kṛishṇa who had formerly been a keeper of calves became a cowherd; cows are especially to be worshipped on this day. — *Go-pitta, am*, n. ox-bile or the bile of cows from which the yellow orpiment called Go-roćanā, Roćanā or Roćanī, is supposed to be prepared; orpiment. — *Go-pīta, as*, m., N. of one of the four water wagtails, which are regarded as birds of augury. — *Go-pītha, as*, m. (rt. *pā*, to protect), protecting, preserving, protection; (*am*), n. a holy place, a place of pilgrimage; (*as*), m., Ved. (rt. *pā*, to drink), a draught of milk; (Sāy.) drinking of any fluid or juice; [cf. *soma-pītha*.] — *Go-pīthya, am*, n., Ved. protection; (Sāy.) protection of the earth. — *Gopī-nātha, as*, m., N. of a man; N. of a son of Mādhava. — *Go-pućcha, as, am*, m. n. a cow's tail; (*as*), m. a sort of monkey; a sort of necklace, one of two, or of four, or of thirty-four strings; a kind of drum. — *Go-puṭika, am*, n. a temple or edifice consecrated to S'iva's bull. — *Go-putra, as*, m. a young bull; a son of the sun, epithet of Karṇa. — *Go-pura, am*, n. a town-gate, a gate in general; the ornamented gateway of a temple; a kind of grass, Cyperus Rotundus, = *mustaka* [cf. *go-narda*]; (*as*), m., N. of a physician. — *Gopuraka, as*, m. the resin of the Boswellia Thurifera; [cf. *kunduruka*.] — *Go-purīsha, am*, n. cow-dung. — *Go-posha, as*, m., Ved. increase of herds. — *Go-prakāṇḍa, am*, n. a superior cow, excellent cattle. — *Go-praćāra, as*, m. pasturage for cows or oxen. — *Go-pratāra, as*, m. ox-ford, a ford for cattle; N. of a place of pilgrimage on the Sarayū; an epithet of S'iva, as leading cattle safely across the water (?). — *Go-pradāna, am*, n. gift of cattle. — *Go-praveśa-samaya, as*, m. the time when the cows come home, the evening twilight. — *Go-phaṇā*, f. a bandage hollowed out so as to fit the chin or nose &c.; a sling; also *gophaṇikā*. — *Go-baka, as*, m. Ardea Govina. — *Go-badha, as*, m. the killing of a cow. — *Go-bandhu, us, us, u*, Ved. having a cow as a relative; (Sāy.) having a cow as mother, an epithet of the Maruts; [cf. *go-mātṛi* and *pṛiśni-mātṛi*.] — *Go-bāla, as*, m. the hair of a cow. — *Gobālin, ī, inī, i*, covered with cow's hair; *gobālī gajas*, a kind of buffalo (?). — *Go-brāhmaṇa, am*, n. a cow and a Brāhman. — *Go-brāhmaṇa-manushya, ās*, m. cows, Brāhmans, and men. — *Go-bhaṭṭa, as*, m., N. of a poet. — *Go-bhaṇḍīra, as*, m. a kind of aquatic bird. — *Go-bhānu, us*, m., N. of a son of Vahni. — *Go-bhuj, k*, m. earth-possessor, a king. — *Go-bhṛit, t*, m. earth-supporter, a mountain. — *Go-makshikā*, f. a gad-fly (*daṇśa*). — *Go-magha, as, ā, am*, Ved. granting cattle or cows. — *Go-maṇḍala, am*, n. the orb of the earth, the globe. — *Go-mat, ān, atī, at*, possessing or containing cattle, cows, herds, &c.; rich in cattle; consisting of cattle; containing milk, mixed with milk; (*tī*), f., Ved. a place abounding in herds; N. of a river falling into the Indus; also of one falling into the Ganges; N. of a Vedic hymn, a prayer or formula, to be repeated during expiation for killing a cow; (*t*), n. possession of cattle, property consisting in herds. — *Go-matallikā*, f. a tractable and good cow. — *Go-mati, is*, f., N. of a river, = *go-matī*. — *Gomati-putra, as*, m., N. of a prince; (also read *gotamī-putra*.) — *Go-matsya, as*, m. a kind of fish living in rivers. — *Go-madhya-madhya* (?), *as, ā, am*, slender in the waist. — *Gomanta, as*, m., N. of a mountain; N. of a people (also *goghnata*); an owner of cattle; a herd of cattle; a multitude of cattle-owners. — *Go-manda, as*, m. = *gomanta* (?), N. of a mountain. — 1. *go-maya, as, ī, am*, bovine, consisting of cattle; defiled with cow-dung; (*as, am*), m. n. cow-dung. — 2. *gomaya* (for *gomayaya*), nom. P. *gomayati, -yitum*, to cover or smear with (cow-dung). — *Go-maya-ććhattra, am*, n. a mushroom, a fungus. — *Gomaya-ććhattrikā*, f. a kind of fungus or mushroom. — *Gomaya-priya, am*, n. the plant Andropogon Schœnanthus. — *Gomayāya*, nom. A. *gomayāyate, -yitum*, to be similar to cow-dung, to taste like cow-dung. — *Gomayotthā* (°*ya-ut*°), f. a kind of beetle found in cow-dung; a gad-fly. — *Gomayodbhava* (°*ya-ud*°), *as*, m. the plant Cathartocarpus Fistula; [cf. *āragbadha*.] — *Go-mahisha-dā*, f. granting cattle and buffaloes; N. of one of the Mātṛis attending on Skanda or Kārttikeya. — *Go-māṅsa, am*, n. the flesh of oxen, beef. — *Go-mātṛi, tā*, m., Ved. having a cow for mother, coming from a cow; an epithet of the Maruts; [cf. *pṛiśni-mātṛi*.] — *Go-māyu, us, us, u*, making sounds like cattle; (*us*), m. a kind of frog; a jackal; N. of a jackal; N. of a Gandharva or celestial musician; the bile or bilious humor of a cow. — *Gomāyu-bhaksha, ās*, m. pl., N. of a people (eating jackals). — *Go-mithuna, am*, n. a bull and a cow, a yoke or pair of cattle. — *Go-min, ī, inī, i*, rich in herds &c.; (ī), m. the owner of cattle or cows; a jackal; a worshipper, an attendant on a Buddha. — *Go-mīna, as*, m. a sort of fish, the bull-fish; [cf. *go-matsya*.] — *Go-mukha, as*, m. a crocodile, a shark; N. of a son of Mātali; also of a son of the treasurer of king Vatsa; also of one of S'iva's attendants; also of an attendant of the first Arhat of the present Avasarpiṇī; (*am*), n. a kind of musical instrument, (a sort of horn or trumpet?); a house built unevenly or crookedly, viz. with angles or projections; spreading unguents, plastering, smearing; (*as*), m. a hole in a wall of a peculiar shape made by thieves &c., a breach; (*am, ī*), n. f. a cloth-bag containing a rosary, the beads of which are counted by the hand, thrust inside; (ī), f. the chasm in the Himālaya mountains, through which the Ganges flows, erroneously conceived to be shaped like a cow's mouth; N. of a river in Rāḍha. — *Gomukha-vyāghra, as*, m. 'cow-faced tiger,' a wolf in sheep's clothing. — *Go-mūḍha, as, ā, am*, stupid as an ox. — *Go-mūtra, am*, n. cow's urine. — *Gomūtraka, as, ikā, am*, similar to the course of cow's urine; (*ikā*), f. a kind of grass, described as growing in corn-fields, of a reddish colour and eaten by cattle, commonly called Tāmbaḍu [cf. *kṛishṭa-bhūmijā, kshetra-jā, rakta-tṛiṇā*]; an artificial verse, the second half of which repeats nearly all the syllables of the first; a form of calculation. — *Go-mṛiga, as*, m., Ved. the Bos Gavæus. — *Go-meda, as*, m. a gem or precious stone brought from the Himālaya and the Indus, described as of four sorts, white, pale yellow, red, and dark-blue (perhaps varieties of agate); N. of a plant, = *kakkola*. — *Go-medaka, as*, m. a gem or precious stone [cf. the preceding]; a kind of poison, = *kākola*; smearing the body with unguents (= *pattraka*). — *Gomeda-sannibha, as*, m., N. of a plant, = *dugdha-pāshāṇa*; chalcedony or opal. — *Go-medha, as*, m. the offering or sacrifice of a cow; N. of the attendant of the twenty-second Arhat of the present Avasarpiṇī. — *Go-'mbhas, as*, n. (for *go-ambhas*), cow's urine; [cf. *go-mūtra*.] — *Go-yajña, as*, m. the sacrifice of a cow. — *Go-yāna, am*, n. a carriage drawn by oxen or cows, a cart in general. — *Go-yukta, as, ā, am*, drawn by oxen or cows. — *Go-yuga, am*, n. a yoke or pair of oxen, a pair of animals in general. — *Go-yuta, as, ā, am*, frequented by cattle; (*am*), n. a cattle-station, a hurdle for cattle. — *Go-raksh, ṭ, ṭ, ṭ*, or *k, k, k*, guarding or preserving cattle. — *Go-raksha, as, ā, am*, keeping or tending cattle; (*as*), m. a cowherd, a cowkeeper, the tender of kine: a Gorkha or inhabitant of Nepāl; an epithet of S'iva; N. of the author of a work entitled Goraksha-śataka; the orange; N. of a medicinal plant, = *ṛishabha*; (*am*), n. keeping or tending cattle; breeding cattle; the life of a herdsman; (ī), f., N. of several plants, = *gandha-bahulā, gopālī*, &c.; also = *goraksha-dugdhā*; a kind of cucumber, = *kumbha-tumbī*. — *Go-rakshaka, as, ikā, am*, guarding cattle; (*as*), m. a cowkeeper, one who tends cattle. — *Go-raksha-karkaṭī*, f. a kind of cucumber, = *ćirbhiṭā*. — *Goraksha-jambū, ūs*, f. wheat; the plant Uraria Lagopodioides; the fruit of the jujube. — *Go-rakshaṇa, am*, n. tending or taking charge of cattle. — *Go-raksha-taṇḍulā*, f. the plant Uraria Lagopodioides. — *Goraksha-tumbī*, f. = *kumbha-tumbī*, a kind of cucumber. — *Goraksha-dugdhā*, f. a small shrub, = *amṛitā, go-rakshī, jīvyā*, &c. — *Gorakshya, am*, n. tending cattle, the life of a herdsman. — *Go-ranku, us*, m. (?) a water-fowl; a chanter; a prisoner, any person or animal confined (?); a naked man, a mendicant &c. wandering about without clothes. — *Go-ratha, as*, m., N. of a mountain; of S'iva. — *Gorathaka, as*, m. a carriage drawn by cattle. — *Go-rabhasa, as, ā, am*, Ved. strengthened with milk; (Sāy.) endowed with strength, strengthening, an epithet of the Soma. — *Go-rambha, as*, m., N. of a man. — *Go-rava, am*, n. saffron. — *Go-rasa, as*, m. buttermilk; curdled or coagulated milk; cow-milk. — *Gorasa-ja, am*, n. buttermilk; curds. — *Go-rāja, as*, m. 'king of cattle,' a bull. — *Go-rāṭikā* or *gorāṭī* or *gorīkā*, f. = *go-kirāṭikā*, the bird Turdus Salica. — *Go-rula, am*, n. a measure of distance equal to two Kroś or Koś, (as far as the lowing of a cow may be heard.) — *Go-rudha* in *a-go-rudha*, q. v. — *Go-rūpa, as, ā, am*, Ved. cow-shaped. — *Go-roća, am*, n. yellow orpiment. — *Go-roćanā*, f. a bright yellow pigment prepared from the urine or bile of a cow, or vomited in the shape of scibulæ (?) by that animal; or (according to some) found in the head of a cow; it is employed in painting and dyeing, and is of especial use in marking the foreheads of the Hindūs with the Tilaka or sectarial mark; it is also used in medicine as a sedative, tonic, and anthelmintic remedy &c.; [cf. *roćanā*.] — *Go-lattikā*, f., Ved. a kind of animal. — *Go-lavaṇa, am*, n. the measure or quantity of salt given to a cow. — *Go-lāṅgula, as*, m. a kind of monkey described as of a black colour and having a tail like a cow; also *go-lāṅgūla, ī*, m. f.; (*ās*), m. pl., N. of a people (?). — *Golāṅgula-parivartana, as*, m., N. of a mountain near Rāja-gṛiha. — *Go-liha, as*, m., N. of a plant; [cf. *ghaṇṭā-pāṭali* and *go-līḍha*.] — *Golīgula*, a wrong reading for *golāṅgulu-parivartana*. — *Go-līḍha, as*, m., N. of plant, = *go-liha*. — *Go-loka, as, am*, m. n. 'cow-world,' a part of heaven, or (in the later mythology) the heaven of Kṛishṇa. — *Goloka-varṇana, am*, n., N. of a part of the Sadā-śiva-saṃhitā; N. of a part of the Skanda-Purāṇa. — *Go-lomikā*, f. a kind of small shrub, = *go-jā, go-dhūmī*, &c.; commonly *go-dhūmā* and *pāthari*. — *Go-lomī*, f., N. of several plants; a kind of bent grass, with white blossoms; also *śveta-dūrvā*; root of sweet flag; Orris root [cf. *vaćā, bhūta-keśa, go-lomikā*]; an excellent woman; a harlot (?). — *Go-vatsa, as*, m. a calf. — *Govatsādin* (°*sa-ad*°), *ī*, m. 'calf-eater,' a wolf. — *Go-vadha, as*, m. the killing of a cow; [cf. *go-badha*.] — *Go-vandanī*, f., N. of a plant bearing a fragrant seed [cf. *priyaṅgu*]; another plant, = *pīta-pushpa-*

daṇḍotpala or *gandha-vallī.* — *Go-vapusha, as, ā, am,* Ved. beautiful as a star or as light; (Sāy.) shaped like a cow. — *Go-vardhana, as,* m. a celebrated hill in Vṛindā-vana or the country about Mathurā; (this hill was lifted up and supported by Kṛishṇa upon one finger for seven days, to shelter the cowherds from a storm of rain sent by Indra to test Kṛishṇa's divinity); N. of a holy fig-tree in the country of the Bāhīkas; N. of a renowned author. — *Govardhana-dhara, as,* m. 'hill-supporter,' a N. of Kṛishṇa. — *Govardhanāćārya* (°*na-āć*°), *as,* m., N. of a poet. — *Govardhanānanda* (°*na-ān*°), *as,* m., N. of an author. — *Go-vallava, as,* m. a cowherd. — *Go-vaśā,* f. a barren cow. — *Go-vāṭa, as,* m. a hurdle for cattle. — *Go-vāsa, as,* m. the abode of cows, a cow-house, hurdle for cattle; (*as, ā, am*), covered with an ox-hide. — *Go-vāsana, as, ā, am,* covered with an ox-hide; (*as*), m., N. of a king of the Śivis. — *Go-vikarta, as,* or *go-vikarttṛi, tā,* m. the killer of a cow. — *Go-vid, t, t, t,* Ved. acquiring or procuring cows. — *Go-vinata, as,* m. (scil. *aśva-medha*), a form of the Aśva-medha. — *Go-vinda, as, ā, am,* obtaining cattle, finding cattle or cows; (*as*), m. a cow-keeper, the finder of cows, the searcher for cows, a chief-herdsman, an epithet of Bṛihaspati [cf. *gotra-bhid*], regent of Jupiter; one of the most usual appellations of Kṛishṇa or Vishṇu in that form; N. of the fourth month; N. of a prince; also of several teachers and authors; N. of a mountain. — *Govinda-kūṭa, as,* m., N. of a mountain. — *Govinda-gira, as,* m., N. of a son of Śiva-rāma-gira. — *Govinda-ćanda, as,* m., N. of a king of Pushpāvatī. — *Govinda-ćandra, as,* m., N. of a prince. — *Govinda-datta, as,* m., N. of a Brāhman. — *Govinda-deva, as,* m., N. of a man. — *Govinda-dvādaśī,* f. the twelfth day in the light half of the month Phālguna. — *Govinda-nātha, as,* m., N. of the preceptor of Saṅkarāćārya. — *Govinda-bhaṭṭa, as,* m., N. of an author. — *Govinda-rāja, as,* m., N. of an author. — *Govinda-rāma, as,* m., N. of a scholiast. — *Govinda-rāya, as,* m., N. of a lawyer; also of a poet. — *Govinda-sūri, is,* m., N. of a man. — *Govinda-svāmin, ī,* m., N. of a Brāhman. — *Govindānanda* (°*da-ān*°), *as,* m., N. of a scholiast. — *Govindārṇava* (°*da-ar*°), *as,* m. title of a work. — *Govindāshṭaka* (°*da-ash*°), *am,* n. 'the eight verses of Govinda,' title of a literary work. — *Go-vindu, us, us, u,* Ved. searching for cows or milk. — *Go-vish, ṭ,* f. cow-dung. — *Go-vishāṇa, as, am,* m. or n. (?), cow-horn. — *Go-vishāṇaka, as,* m. a kind of musical instrument, a sort of trumpet. — *Go-vishṭhā,* f. cow-dung. — *Go-visarga, as,* m. = *go-sarga,* day-break. — *Go-vīthī,* f. 'cow-path,' N. of that portion of the moon's path which contains the asterisms Bhadra-padā, Revatī, and Aśvinī, or (according to others) Hasta, Ćitrā, and Svātī. — *Go-vīrya, am,* n. the value or price received for milk &c. — *Go-vṛinda, am,* n. property in cattle, possession of flocks and herds, a herd, a drove of cattle. — *Go-vṛindāraka, as,* m. an excellent cow. — *Go-vṛisha, as,* m. a bull; an epithet of Śiva. — *Govṛisha-dhvaja, as,* m. an epithet of Śiva. — *Go-vṛisha-bha, as,* m. a bull. — *Govṛishabhāṅka* (°*bha-aṅ*°), *as,* m. an epithet of Śiva. — *Go-vaidya, as,* m. a cow-doctor, a quack doctor. — *Go-vyaććha, as, ā, am,* Ved. one who approaches a cow (in a bad sense). — *Go-vyāghra, am,* n. a cow and a tiger. — *Go-vyādhila, as,* m., N. of a man. — *Go-vraja, as,* m. a station for cattle, a cow-pen; N. of an attendant of Skanda; also of a Dānava. — *Go-vrata, as, ā, am,* or *govratin, ī, inī, i,* one who imitates a cow in frugality. — *Go-śakṛit, t,* n. cow-dung. — *Go-śata, am,* n. a present of 100 cows sent to a Brāhman. — *Go-śapha, as,* m. a cow's hoof. — *Go-śāla, am, ā,* n. f. a cow-stall, a cow-house; (*as, ā, am*), born in a cow-house; (*as*), m., N. of a Gauḍa prince. — *Gośāli, is,* m. (connected with the preceding?), N. of a man. — *Go-śirsha, as, ā, am,* shaped like a cow's head; (*as, am*), m. n. a kind of sandal-wood described as having the colour of brass and very fragrant; the head of a cow. — *Go-śīrshaka, as,* m., N. of a plant, = *droṇa-pushpī.* — *Go-śṛiṅga, am,* n. a cow's horn; N. of a Sāman (in this sense more correctly *gauśṛiṅga*); (*as*), m., N. of a plant, = *varvūra;* N. of a mountain. — *Gośṛiṅga-vratin, inas,* m. pl., N. of a sect. — *Go-śrīta, as, ā, am,* Ved. mixed with milk (as Soma). — *Go-śruti, is,* m., N. of a man with the patronymic Vaiyāghra-padya. — *Go 'śva* (*go-aś*°), *am,* n. oxen and horses; [cf. *gavāśva* and *goaśva.*] — *Go-shakhi* or *go-sakhi, is, is, i,* Ved. furnished with or possessing cattle; mixed with milk (as Soma). — *Go-shaḍgava, am,* n. three pairs of cattle. — *Go-shaṇi* and *go-sani, is, is, i,* Ved. acquiring or presenting with cattle. — *Go-shan, ā, ā, a,* or *go-shā, ās, ās, am,* Ved. acquiring or bestowing cattle. — *Go-shāti, is,* f., Ved. acquiring cattle, procuring cattle; fighting for the sake of cattle or booty. — *Go-shādi,* f. (fr. *go-sāda*), Ved. a kind of bird ('settling on cows'). — *Goshu-ćara, as, ī, am,* walking among cows. — *Goshu-yudh, t, t, t,* Ved. fighting for the sake of cattle or booty. — *Goshūktin, ī,* m. (fr. *go-sūkta*), N. of a Ṛishi. — *Go-shedhā* (*go-se*°), f., Ved. a kind of evil being. — *Go-shṭoma* (*go-st*°), *as,* m. a sort of liturgy, a ceremony lasting for one day and forming part of the Abhiplava which lasts six days. — *Go-shṭha* (*go-stha*), *as, am,* m. n. (in the later language the n. only occurs), an abode for cattle, a cow-house, cow-pen, a fold for cattle, any place where animals are kept, a stable; a station of cowherds; an epithet of Śiva (the refuge of men?); a purificatory Śrāddha for a family(?); N. of a Sāman; (*as*), m., N. of an author; (*ī*), f. an assembly, a meeting; society; association; family connections, but especially the dependant or junior branches; conversation, discourse, dialogue, dispute; a kind of dramatic composition or entertainment in one act. — *Goshṭha-ja, as, ā, am,* born in a cow-pen; (*as*), m., N. of a Brāhman. — *Goshṭha-pati, is,* m. a chief-herdsman. — *Goshṭha-vedikā,* f. a mound or altar in a cow-pen. — *Goshṭha-śva, as,* m. (*śva* fr. *śvan*), 'a dog in a cow-pen' which barks at every one; (the word is applied especially to a person who stays at home and slanders his neighbours); malignant, censorious, envious; (the word is also derived by native authorities from *goshṭha* and *aśva.*) — *Goshṭhāgāra* (°*ṭha-āg*°), *as, am,* m. n. a house in a cow-pen. — *Goshṭhādhyaksha* (°*ṭha-adh*°), *as,* m. a chief-herdsman. — *Goshṭhāna* (*go-sthā*°), *as, ā, am,* Ved. serving as an abode for cows; [cf. *go-sthāna.*] — *Goshṭhāshṭamī* (°*ṭha-ash*°), f. a particular festive day; [cf. *gopāshṭamī.*] — *Goshṭhi, is,* m. (= *goshṭhī?*), society, partnership, fellowship. — *Goshṭhika, as, ā, am,* relating to an assemblage or society. — *Goshṭhīka,* at the end of a compound = *goshṭhī,* partnership, fellowship. — *Goshṭhī-pati, is,* m. the chief person in an assembly, a president; the master of a family. — *Goshṭhe-kshveḍin, ī, inī, i,* bellowing in a cow-pen, a boasting coward. — *Goshṭhe-paṭu, us, us, u,* clever in a cow-pen, a vain boaster. — *Goshṭhe-paṇḍita, as, ā, am,* learned in a cow-pen, a vain boaster. — *Goshṭhe-pragalbha, as, ā, am,* enterprising in a cow-pen, a boasting coward. — *Goshṭhe-vijitin, ī, inī, i,* victorious in a cow-pen, a boasting coward. — *Goshṭhe-śaya, as, ā, am,* sleeping in a cow-pen or cow-stable. — *Goshṭhe-śūra, as,* m. a hero in a cow-pen, a boasting coward. — *Goshṭhya, as, ā, am,* Ved. relating to a cow-house, being in a cow-pen. — *Gosh-pada, am,* n. (fr. *gos,* gen. fr. *go* and *pada*), a cow's foot or hoof, the mark or impression of a cow's foot in the soil; a quantity of water sufficient to fill such an impression, a small puddle; a measure, as much as a cow's footstep will hold; a spot frequented by kine. — *Go-sakhi,* cf. *go-shakhi.* — *Go-saṅkhya, as,* m. one who counts the cows, a herdsman, a cowherd. — *Go-saṅkhyātṛi, tā,* m. 'counter of the cows,' a herdsman, a cowherd. — *Go-saṅga, as,* m. day-break, dawn; (a wrong reading for *go-sarga.*) — *Go-sattra, am,* n., Ved. a particular sacrifice. — *Go-sadṛiksha, as,* m. the Gayal, Bos Gavæus. — *Go-sani* = *go-shaṇi,* q. v. — *Go-sandāya, as, ā, am,* presenting with a cow; giving a cow. — *Go-sambhava, as, ā, am,* produced from or by a cow; (*ā*), f., N. of a plant, = *śveta-dūrvā;* [cf. *golosī.*] — *Go-sarga, as,* m. the time at which cows are usually let loose, day-break, dawn. — *Go-sarpa, as,* m. Lacerta Godica; [cf. *godhikā.*] — *Go-sava, as,* m. a kind of sacrificial ceremony lasting one day; the sacrifice of a cow, one of the great sacrifices of the Hindūs in former times, and not permitted in the present degenerate Kali age; see *go-medha.* — *Go-sahasra, am,* n. a thousand kine; (*ī*), f., N. of two holidays; the fifteenth day in the dark half of month Kārttika, and the fifteenth day in the dark half of month Jyaishṭha. — *Go-sūtrikā,* f. a rope fastened at both ends having separate halters for each ox or cow. — *Go-sevā,* f. attendance on a cow. — *Go-stana, as,* m. the udder of a cow; a cluster of blossoms, a nosegay &c.; a garland consisting of four or of thirty-four strings, a pearl necklace of four strings; (*ā*), f. a bunch of grape; (*ī*), f. a bunch of grape; N. of one of the Mātṛis attending on Skanda. — *Go-stoma* = *go-shṭoma.* — *Go-sthāna* or *go-sthānaka, am,* n. a station for cattle, a cow-stall, cow-house, cow-pen, a hurdle for cattle; [cf. *go-shṭhāna.*] — *Go-sphuraṇa, am,* n. a twitching of any particular part of the hide of a cow, as on being touched &c. — *Go-svāmin, ī,* m. the master or possessor of cows or of herds; a religious mendicant (commonly *gosain*); a honorary title affixed to proper names (e. g. *vopadeva-go-svāmin*); one who is master of his organs of sense (*go,* an organ?). — *Gosvāmi-sthāna, am,* n., N. of the peak of a mountain in the middle of the Himālaya. — *Go-hatyā,* f. the killing of a cow. — *Go-han, ā, ghnī, a,* Ved. killing cattle, a cow-killer. — *Go-hanna, am,* n. cow-dung; (incorrectly *gohalla.*) — *Go-hara, as,* m. or *go-haraṇa, am,* n. stealing cows; N. of a section of the fourth book of the Mahā-bhārata. — *Go-harītakī,* f. the tree Ægle Marmelos; [cf. *bilva.*] — *Go-hiṅsā,* f. hurting or injuring a cow. — *Go-hita, as, ā, am,* fit or proper for cattle; cherishing or protecting kine; (*as*), m. the tree Ægle Marmelos; N. of a creeping plant; [cf. *ghosha.*] — *Go-hiraṇya, am,* n. cows and gold.

Gokā, f. diminutive of *go,* a cow. — *Gokā-mukha, as,* m., N. of a mountain.

गोखा *gokhā,* f. a particular part of the body.

गोघ्नत *goghnata, ās,* m. pl., N. of a people.

गोच्छाल *goććhāla, as,* m., N. of a plant, also called Alambusha; the palm of the hand with the fingers extended (?).

गोजी *gojī,* f., N. of a plant with sharp leaves; (also *goji* if required by the metre.)

गोड *goḍa, as,* m. = *goṇḍa,* a fleshy navel; a lump of flesh on the navel; (also read *goḍu.*)

गोडनि *goḍani,* N. of a country; (a wrong reading for 1. *go-dāna.*)

गोडुम्ब *goḍumba, as,* m. the water-melon; (*ā*), f. a kind of cucumber, Cucumis Maderaspatanus; a coloquintida.

Goḍumbikā, f. Cucumis Maderaspatanus.

गोण *goṇa, as,* m. an ox (fr. the Pāli).

गोणिक *goṇika,* a kind of woollen clot (fr. the Pāli *goṇaka*).

गोणी *goṇī,* f. (at the end of an adj. comp. *goṇi*), a sack; the measure of a Droṇa; torn or ragged clothes; [cf. *gauṇika.*] — *Goṇī-tari,* f. a small sack.

गोण्ड *goṇḍa, as,* m. a fleshy navel; a person with a fleshy or prominent navel; a man of a low tribe, a mountaineer, especially inhabiting the eastern portion of the Vindhya range between the Narbadā and Kistna, giving name to the province of Gondvana. — *Goṇḍa-vana, am,* n. the Goṇḍa forest, N. of a country; (also *goṇḍuvāra.*)

गोण्डकिरी *goṇḍakirī* or *goṇḍākrī*, f., N. of a Rāgiṇī.

गोतम *gotama, as,* m., N. of a Rishi belonging to the family of Aṅgiras, with the patronymic Rāhūgaṇa, author of several hymns of the Vedas; N. of a lawyer; N. of a sage, the founder of the Nyāya philosophy; N. of the twentieth Vyāsa in the Vishṇu-Purāṇa; of a king of Potāla, son of Karṇika; (*ās*), m. pl. the descendants of Gotama. — *Gotama-stoma, as,* m., N. of an Ekāha sacrifice. — *Gotama-svāmin, ī,* m., N. of a Jaina saint; [cf. *gautama-svāmin.*] — *Gotamānvaya* (°*ma-an*°), *as,* m. a descendant of Gotama, epithet of Śākya-muni, the founder of the Buddhist religion. — *Gotamī-putra, as,* m., N. of a prince; (also *gomati-putra.*)

गोत्र *go-tra.* See under *go*, p. 297.

गोद 3. *goda, am* or *as,* n. m. the brain; [cf. 1. *go-da*, p. 297, and *gorda.*]

2. *godāna, am,* n. the part of the head close to the right ear: (for 1. *go-dāna* see under *go.*) — *Godāna-vidhi, is,* m. or *godāna-maṅgala, am,* n. a ceremony performed by anointing that part of the head of a youth of sixteen or eighteen years, when he has attained the age of puberty, and shortly before marriage.

Godānika = *gaudānika*, q. v.

गोदावरी *go-dāvarī.* See under *go*, p. 297.

गोधा *go-dhā*, f. (fr. *go* and rt. *dhā*), a sinew; a chord; a leathern fence wound round the left arm to prevent injury from the bow-string; an Iguana, either the Gosamp or the alligator, commonly Gosāpa. — *Godhā-padikā* or *godhā-padī*, f. the plant Cissus Pedata. — *Godhā-viṇākā*, f. a kind of stringed instrument. — *Godhā-skandha, as,* m. a kind of Mimosa; [cf. *viṭ-khadira.*]

Godhāya, nom. P. *godhāyati, -yitum,* to be curved as the leathern fence of archers.

Godhi, is, m. the forehead; the Gangetic alligator; an Iguana.

Godhikā, f. a kind of lizard or alligator, Lacerta Godica: [cf. *āgāra-godhikā* and *gṛiha-g*°.] — *Godhikātmaja* (°*kā-āt*°), *as,* m. a kind of lizard; [cf. *gaudhāra, gaudheya, gaudhera.*]

Godhinī, f. a kind of Solanum; [cf. *kshavikā.*]

गोधूम *go-dhūma, godhūmaka.* See under *go.*

गोधेर *godhera, as,* m. a guardian, a protector, a preserver; [cf. *guhera.*]

गोनाडीक *gonāḍīka, as,* m. a kind of plant; (other authorities have *gonāḍīća.*)

गोप *go-pa, as,* m. (fr. *go* and rt. *pā*), a cowherd, a herdsman, a milkman, considered as a man of mixed caste; the chief of a cow-pen or station; a protector, a guardian, a preserver, a cherisher, a helper, a friend or patron; the superintendent of several villages, the head of a district; a king; the chief herdsman, i. e. Kṛishṇa; N. of a Gandharva [cf. *go-pati*]; N. of a Buddhist Arhat; N. of a mountain; myrrh, = *gopa-rasa;* (*ā*), f. = *gopī*, the plant Ichnocarpus Frutescens; N. of one of the wives of Śākya-muni; (*ī*), f. the wife of a cowherd, see below; [cf. *go-pā, ahi-gopa, indra-g*°, *kula-g*°, *tridaśa-g*°, *surendra-g*°.] — *Gopa-kanyā*, f. the daughter of a cowherd; a nymph of Vṛindāvana; the plant Ichnocarpus Frutescens. — *Gopa-karkaṭikā*, f. = *gopāla-karkaṭī*. — *Gopa-ghoṇṭā*, f., N. of a plant, = *hastikolī*, commonly *śeyākula*, a wild sort of jujube, Zizyphus Nepeca or Zizyphus Œnoplia. — *Gopa-jīvin, ī,* m., N. of a mixed caste. — *Gopa-tā*, f. the office of a herdsman. — *Gopa-datta, as,* m., N. of a Buddhist author. — *Gopa-dala, as,* m. the betel-nut or areca tree. — *Gopa-badhū* or *gopa-vadhū, ūs,* f. a cowherd's wife; the plant Ichnocarpus Frutescens (*śārivā*); [cf. *gopa-kanyā.*] — *Gopa-badhūṭī*, f. the youthful wife of a cowherd. — *Gopa-bhadra, am,* n. the fibrous root of a water-lily (*śālūka*); (*ā*), f. the plant Gmelina Arborea, [cf. *kāśmarī*]; also *gopa-bhadrikā*. — *Gopa-rasa, as,* m. gum myrrh, myrrh; [cf. *go-pa* and *rasa.*] — *Gopa-rāshṭra, ās,* m. pl., N. of a people. — *Go-pariṇas, ās, ās, as,* Ved. abundantly furnished with cattle or milk. — *Gopa-vana, as,* m., N. of a Ṛishi of the family of Atri. — *Gopa-vallī*, f. the plant Ichnocarpus Frutescens (*anantā*); Sanseviera Zeylanica (*mūrvā*). — *Gopa-veśa* or *gopa-vesha, as, ā, am,* dressed as a herdsman. — *Gopāṭavika, as,* m. a cowherd (fr. *gopa*, a herd, and *āṭavika*, a forester?). — *Go-pāditya* (°*pa-ād*°), *as,* m., N. of a king of Kaśmīra; N. of a poet. — *Gopādhyaksha* (°*pa-adh*°), *as,* m. an overseer of herdsmen, the chief of herdsmen. — *Gopānasī* (°*pa-an*°), f. the wood of a thatch, a curved beam which supports it; the bamboo frame-work on which it rests. — *Gopendra* (°*pa-in*°), *as,* m. the chief of the herdsmen, an epithet of Kṛishṇa or Vishṇu. — *Gopeśa* (°*pa-īśa*), *as,* m. a chief herdsman, the keeper or owner of kine; an epithet of Kṛishṇa; also of Nanda, the foster-father of Kṛishṇa; also of Śākya-muni.

Gopaka, as, ā, am, one who guards or protects; (*as*), m. the superintendent of a district; myrrh; (*ikā*), f. the wife of a cowherd, a cowherdess; a protectress.

Go-pā, ās, m., Ved. a herdsman, a protector, a guardian; [cf. *go-pa, deva-gopā, vrāta-g*°, *vāyu-g*°, *saha-g*°, *su-g*°, *soma-g*°.] — *Gopā-jihva, as, ā, am,* Ved. one who has the tongue, i. e. the voice of a cowherd; (Sāy.) an epithet of Indra. — *Gopā-vat, ān, atī, at,* Ved. granting protection.

Gopī, f. a cowherd's wife (especially applied to the cowherdesses of Vṛindā-vana, the companions of Kṛishṇa's juvenile sports, who are considered sometimes as holy or celestial personages); a milkmaid; a protectress; nature, elementary nature; the plant Ichnocarpus Frutescens. — *Gopī-ćandana, am,* n. a species of white clay said to be brought from Dvārakā and used by Vishṇu's worshippers for smearing their face. — *Gopī-ćandanopanishad* (°*na-up*°), *t,* f. title of an Upanishad.

गोपन *gopana*, &c. See under rt. *gup.*

गोपालव *gopālava, ās,* m. pl., N. of a warrior-tribe; (for *gopālaka?*).

गोपुटा *gopuṭā*, f. large cardamoms; [cf. *puṭikā.*]

गोभिल *gobhila, as,* m., N. of an author of certain Gṛihya-sūtras and of grammatical Sūtras.

Gobhilīya, as, ā, am, relating to or proceeding from Gobhila.

गोमायु *go-māyu.* See under *go*, p. 298.

गोयीचन्द्र *goyīćandra, as,* m., N. of a scholiast of the Saṅkshipta-sāra; (for *gopī-ćandra?*).

गोरट *goraṭa, as,* m. a kind of Acacia; [cf. *dushkhadira.*]

गोरण *goraṇa, am,* n. effort, exertion, = *guraṇa.*

गोर्द *gorda* or *gordha, am,* n. the brain; [cf. *goda* and *godhi.*]

गोल *gola, as, ā, am,* m. f. n. (connected with *guḍa*, q. v.), a ball, a celestial or terrestrial globe; a circle, anything round or globular, a sphere, = *maṇḍala* [cf. *guḍa*]; (*as*), m. the tree Vangueria Spinosa; myrrh; a widow's bastard [cf. *kuṇḍa*]; the conjunction of all the planets or the presence of several in one sign; N. of a son of Ākrīḍa; (*ā*), f. a wooden ball with which children play; a large globular water-jar; red arsenic; ink; a woman's female friend; a N. of the goddess Durgā; N. of a river, = *golā* or *go-dāvarī;* [cf. *galagolin.*] — *Gola-grāma, as,* m., N. of a village situated on the Godāvarī; (the right reading may be *golā-grāma.*) — *Gola-yantra, am,* n. a kind of astronomical instrument. — *Golāṅka* (*gola-aṅ*°), *as,* m., N. of a man. — *Golādhyāya* (°*la-adh*°), *as,* m. title of a chapter of Bhāskara's Siddhānta-Śiromaṇi treating of the terrestrial and celestial globes.

Golaka, as, m. a ball or globe; a wooden ball for playing with, anything globular, a sphere &c.; a species of pease; gum myrrh; a globular water-jar; a widow's bastard; the conjunction of all the planets or the presence of several in one sign; N. of a pupil of Veda-mitra; (*am*), n. = *go-loka*, the heaven of Kṛishṇa.

गोलन्द *golanda, as,* m., N. of a man.

गोलास *golāsa, as,* m. a mushroom, a kind of fungus springing from cow-dung; [cf. *gomaya-ććhattrikā.*]

गोव *gova, as* or *am,* m. or n. (?), N. of a country; (also read *kuva.*)

गोवय *govaya*, nom. P. (a corruption fr. *gopaya*), *govayati, -yitum,* to keep back, to prevent from approaching.

गोवाल *govāla, as,* m., N. of a man; (perhaps a corruption fr. *go-pāla*); [cf. also *gobāla.*]

गोविचन्द्र *govićandra, as,* m., N. of a prince; (the names of the other princes of the same dynasty ending in *ćandra*, this word may be a comp. fr. *govi* and *ćandra*, *govi* being probably contracted fr. *go* and *avi.*)

गोविन्द *go-vinda.* See under *go*, p. 299.

गोशर्य *gośarya, as,* m., N. of a man.

गोशे *gośe*, ind. a word belonging to one of the provincial dialects, according to some also a Sanskṛit word; perhaps = *gose* (loc. of *gosa*), at day-break.

गोषक *goshaka, as,* m., N. of a Buddhist author.

गोष्ट् *gosht*, cl. 1. A. *goshṭate*, to assemble, to collect, to heap together; (probably a nom. fr. *goshṭha* and more correctly spelt *goshṭh.*)

गोष्ठ *go-shṭha.* See under *go*, p. 299.

गोस *gosa, as,* m. gum myrrh, myrrh, = *gopa-rasa;* the last watch of the night, early morning or day-break, = *go-sarga;* [cf. *gośe.*]

गोसगृह *gosa-gṛiha, am,* n. (?) the inner part of a house, an inner or sleeping-room, a bed-chamber.

गोसशश *gosaśaśa, as,* m. myrrh, = *gopa-rasa;* [cf. also *gosa* and *śaśa.*]

गोसिल *gosila, as,* m., N. of a man.

गोस्वलु *gosvalu, us,* m., N. of a pupil of Śākalya; [cf. *guhalu* and *gosila.*]

गोह *goha, as,* m. (fr. rt. *guh*), Ved. a hiding-place, a lair; a secret place for hiding refuse or filth.

Gohana, as, ā, am, covering, hiding; [cf. *avadya-gohana.*]

Gohira, am, n. the heel; ('hidden part?').

Gohya, as, ā, am, to be covered or concealed; to be kept secret; [cf. *a-gohya* and *guhya.*]

गौङ्गव *gauṅgava, am,* n. (fr. *guṅgu*), N. of several Sāmans.

गौञ्जिक *gauñjika, as,* m. (fr. *guñjā*), a goldsmith.

गौड *gauḍa, as, ī, am* (fr. *guḍa*), prepared from sugar or molasses; (*ī*), f. rum or spirit distilled from molasses; one of the Rāgiṇīs, the wife of the Rāga Megha; a style of poetry, the bold and spirited style; the Bengal dialect; (am), n. sweetmeats; (as), m., scil. deśa, or (am), n., scil. rāshṭra, the sugar country; N. of a country, 'the district of Gaur,' the central part of Bengal, extending from Vaṅga to the borders of Orissa, (the ruins of its capital called by the same name are still extensive); (ās), m. pl. the inhabitants of this country; (as), m., N. of a Rāga; N. of a lexicographer. — Gauḍa-deśa, as, m. the country Gauḍa. — Gauḍa-pāda, as, m., N. of a commentator on several Upanishads and on the Sāṅkhya-kārikā. — Gauḍa-pura, am, n., N. of a town. — Gauḍa-bhṛitya-pura, am, n., N. of a town. — Gauḍābhinanda or gauḍābhinandana (°ḍa-abh°), as, m., N. of a poet.

Gauḍaka, ās, m. pl., N. of a people living to the east of Madhya-deśa. — Gauḍaka-mṛiga, as, m. a wild horse; [cf. gaura-khara.]

Gauḍika, as, ī, am, relating to sugar or molasses, fit for the preparation of sugar, prepared with sugar or molasses; (am), n. rum.

Gauḍīya, as, ī, am, relating to Gauḍa or Bengal.

गौडन gauḍana = godana, q. v.

गौण gauṇa, as, ī, am (fr. guṇa), subordinate, secondary, unessential; metaphorical, figurative; secondary as applied to the month reckoned from full moon to full moon; having qualities, attributive, adjective; relating to multiplication or enumeration; gauṇam karma, the less immediate object of an action in a sentence. — Gauṇa-tva, am, n. the state of an adjective or subordinate word. — Gauṇa-paksha, as, m. the minor or weaker side of an argument &c.

1. gauṇika, as, ī, am, relating to the three qualities (of sattva, rajas, and tamas), having qualities, relating to or connected with qualities; subordinate.

Gauṇya, am, n. subordination; the state of being unessential &c.

गौणिक 2. gauṇika, as, ī, am (fr. goṇī), resembling a sack.

गौतम gautama, as, ī, am (fr. gotama), relating to Gotama (e. g. with pada-stobhāḥ, N. of a Sāman); (as), m., N. of Buddha or Śākya-muni the founder of the Buddhist religion; N. of a teacher of ritual; N. of a grammarian; of a legislator; a patronymic of Kuśri, of Aruṇa, of Uddālaka, of Śaradvat, of Śatānanda; the father of Ekata, Dvita, and Trita (Mahā-bh. IX. 2073); N. of the first pupil of the last Jina; a kind of poison, one of the fixed kinds; (ī), f. a patronymic of Kṛipī and other women; an epithet of Durgā; N. of a Rākshasī or female goblin; N. of a river, = gomatī; a kind of yellow pigment or dye, = go-roćanā; turmeric; (am), n., N. of a Sāman; fat; [cf. medas, and bhāradvāja, 'bone.'] — Gautama-sambhavā, f. an epithet of the river Godāvarī. — Gautama-saras, as, n., N. of a lake. — Gautama-svāmin, ī, m., N. of a Jaina teacher; [cf. gotama-svāmin.]

Gautamaka, as, m., N. of a king of the Nāgas.

Gautamī, a patronymic = gautama.

Gautamīya, as, ā, am, belonging to Gautama, coming from him &c.

गौतमस gautamasa, as, ī, am (fr. go-tamas?), epithet of two verses of the Sāma-veda.

गौदानिक gaudānika, as, ī, am, relating to the ceremony called Godāna (q. v.), performing it.

गौधार gaudhāra, as, m. (fr. godhā), an Iguana (considered as the offspring of the alligator on account of its smaller size and similar shape); also gaudheya and gaudhera.

Gaudheraka, as, m. a kind of small venomous animal.

गौधूम gaudhūma, as, ī, am (fr. go-dhūma), coming from wheat, made of it.

गौधूम्र gaudhūmra, a various reading for gautama, q. v.

गौपत्य gaupatya, am, n. (fr. go-pati), Ved. the possession of cattle.

Gaupavana, a patronymic from Gopa-vana; (am), n., N. of a Sāman.

Gaupāyana, as, m. a patronymic from Gopa.

Gaupika, as, m. (fr. gopikā), the son of a herdsman's wife.

Gaupuććha, as, ī, am (fr. go-puććha), like a cow's tail.

Gaupuććhika, as, ī, am, of or belonging to a cow's tail, bought for a cow's tail &c.

Gaumata, as, ī, am (fr. go-matī), being in the river Gomatī; (ī), f., N. of a river; (the latter being a wrong reading for gautamī.)

गौर gaura, as, ī, am (said to be fr. rt. 3. gu), white, yellowish, reddish, pale red; shining, brilliant, pure, clean, beautiful; (as), m. white, yellowish, &c. (the colour); a kind of buffalo, the Bos Gaurus, often classed with the Gavaya; white mustard, the seed of it used as a weight, = 3 Rāja-sarshapas [cf. gaura-sarshapa]; the plant Grislea Tomentosa (= dhava); the moon; the planet Jupiter; N. of a Yoga teacher, a son of Śuka and Pīvarī; an epithet of the saint Ćaitanya; (ī), f. the female of the Bos Gaurus; the Vāć or voice of the middle region of the air; turmeric, = rajanī, and N. of several other plants, = priyaṅgu, mañjishṭhā, &c.; a yellow pigment or dye, = go-roćanā; a girl eight years old, any young girl prior to menstruation, a maid, a virgin; the earth; 'the brilliant goddess,' N. of the goddess Pārvatī or daughter of Himālaya and wife of Śiva; N. of the wife of Varuṇa; N. of the mother of Śākya-muni [cf. māyā]; N. of one of the sixteen Vidyā-devīs; N. of the wife of Prasenajit (or Yuvanāśva), who incurring the curse of her husband was changed into the river Bāhu-dā; N. of the wife of Vi-rajas and mother of Su-dhāman; N. of a river; N. of a Rāgiṇī, the wife of the Rāga Mālava; N. of several metres, one consisting of four lines of twelve syllables each; another consisting of four lines of thirteen syllables each; another consisting of four lines of twenty-six long syllables each; (am), n. white mustard; the filament of a lotus; saffron; gold; [cf. Lat. gilvus; Lith. geltónas, giele; Russ. schiltyi; Germ. gelb?]. — Gaura-khara, as, m. a wild donkey; [cf. gauḍaka-mṛiga.] — Gaura-grīva, ās, m. pl., N. of a people in Madhya-deśa. — Gauragrīvīya, as, ī, am, belonging to this people. — Gaura-ćandra, as, m. an epithet of the saint Ćaitanya. — Gaura-jīraka, as, m. white cumin. — Gaura-tittiri, is, m. a kind of partridge. — Gaura-tvać, k, m. the plant Terminalia Catappa; [cf. iṅguda.] — Gaura-pṛishṭha, as, m., N. of a prince. — Gaura-mukha, as, m., N. of a pupil of Śamīka, a Purohita of king Ugra-sena. — Gaura-mṛiga, as, m., Ved. the Bos Gaurus. — Gaura-vāhana, as, m., N. of a prince. — Gaura-śāka, as, m., N. of a plant, a kind of Madhūka. — Gaura-śiras, ās, m., N. of a Muni. — Gaura-sarshapa, as, m. white mustard, Sinapis Glauca; the white mustard seed considered as a measure of weight. — Gaura-suvarṇa, am, n. a kind of vegetable; [cf. pattraśāka-viśesha, = kaṭu-śriṅgāla and gandha-śāka.] — Gaurāṅga (°ra-aṅ°), as, m. an epithet of the saint Ćaitanya; [cf. gaura and gaura-ćandra.] — Gaurājājī (°ra-aj°), f. white cumin. — Gaurārdraka (°ra-ār°), as, m. a kind of poison. — Gaurāvaskandin (°ra-av°), ī, m. an epithet of Indra. — Gaurāśva (°ra-aś°), as, m., N. of a prince. — Gaurāsya (°ra-ās°), as, m. a kind of black monkey with a white face. — Gaurāhika (°ra-ahi), as, m. a kind of serpent. — Gaurivīti, is, m. (for gaurī-v°), N. of a Ṛishi, a descendant of Śakti. — Gaurī-kalpa, as, m., N. of a Kalpa, the thirteenth day of the dark half in Brahmā's month. — Gaurī-kānta, as, m., N. of a commentator on the Tarka-bhāshā. — Gaurīkānta-sārvabhauma, as, m., N. of a commentary called Ānanda-laharītarī. — Gaurī-guru, us, m. the father of Gaurī, an epithet of the Himālaya. — Gaurī-ja, as, m. an epithet of Kārttikeya; (am), n. talc. — Gaurī-nātha, as, m. the husband of Gaurī, an epithet of Śiva. — Gaurī-paṭṭa, as, m. the horizontal plate of the Liṅga, typical of the female organ. — Gaurī-pati, is, m. the husband of Gaurī, an epithet of Śiva; N. of the father of the scholiast Vaṭeśvara. — Gaurī-putra, as, m. son of Gaurī, an epithet of the deity Kārttikeya. — Gaurī-pushpa, as, m., N. of a plant, = gaurī or priyaṅgu. — Gaurī-pūjā, f. the adoration of Gaurī, N. of a festival on the fourth day in the last half of month Māgha. — Gaurī-bhartṛi, tā, m. the husband of Gaurī, an epithet of Śiva. — Gaurī-mantra, as, m. a prayer to Gaurī. — Gaurī-lalita, am, n. yellow orpiment. — Gaurī-vara, as, m. the lover of Gaurī, an epithet of Śiva. — Gaurīvita, am, n. (fr. gauri-vīti, q.v.), N. of a Sāman. — Gaurī-vivāha, as, m. the marriage of Gaurī. — Gaurī-vrata, am, n. the vow of Gaurī, a kind of rite in honour of Gaurī. — Gaurīśa (°rī-īśa), as, m. the lord of Gaurī, an epithet of Śiva.

Gaurika, as, m. white mustard; a metronymic of Māndhāṭṛi; (ā), f. a virgin, a young girl, one eight years old or in whom menstruation has not yet commenced.

Gaurila, as, m. white mustard; iron or steel filings or dust.

गौरक्ष्य gaurakshya, am, n. (fr. go-raksha), the office of a herdsman, breeding cattle.

गौरव gaurava, as, ī, am (fr. guru), relating or belonging to a Guru or teacher; (am), n. weight, heaviness; length in prosody; importance, high value or estimation; cumbrousness; gravity, respectability, venerableness; dignity; respect shown to a person (e. g. mātṛi-gauravāt, out of respect for one's mother). — Gaurava-vat, ān, atī, at, important. — Gauravāsana (°va-ās°), am, n. a seat of honour. — Gauraverita (°va-īr°), as, ā, am, praised, famed, celebrated.

Gauravita, as, ā, am, highly esteemed or valued, venerable, respectable.

गौरि gauri, is, m., N. of a man.

गौरुतल्पिक gaurutalpika, as, m. (fr. guru-talpa), the violator of the bed of a Guru or religious preceptor.

गौलक्षणिक gaulakshaṇika, as, m. (fr. go-lakshaṇa), one who knows the good marks of a cow.

Gaulomana, as, ī, am (fr. go-loman), resembling cow's hair.

गौला gaulā, f. = gaurā = gaurī, N. of the daughter of Himālaya and wife of Śiva.

गौलिक gaulika, as, m., N. of a plant, = gauliha and gaulīḍha.

गौल्मिक gaulmika, as, m. (fr. gulma), a single soldier of a troop, one of a body of soldiers.

गौल्य gaulya, am, n. (fr. gula = guḍa), syrup; spirituous liquor.

गौशकटिक gauśakaṭika, as, ī, am (fr. go-śakaṭa), possessing a carriage drawn by oxen.

Gauśatika, as, ī, am (fr. go-śatam), possessing a hundred oxen or cows.

Gauśṛiṅga, am, n. (fr. go-śṛiṅga), N. of a Sāman.

Gaushūkta, am, n. (fr. goshūktin), N. of a Sāman.

Gaushūkti (fr. gaushūkta), N. of a man.

Gaushṭhīna, am, n. (fr. goshṭha), the site of an old and abandoned cow-pen.

Gausahasrika, as, ī, am (fr. go-sahasra), possessing a thousand cows.

ग्धि gdhi, is, f. (fr. ghas), Ved. eating, consuming; [cf. sagdhi.]

ग्ना gnā, f. (generally used in plur., but according to some in Ṛig-veda IV. 9, 4, the nom. sing. gnās occurs; the word seems to be derived from jñā rather than from jan, and to mean originally 'a wise female.' In the Nighaṇṭavas it is enumerated among the synonyms of vāć, 'the voice.' By Yāska in Nirukta III. 21. it is said to be derived from *gam*, 'to approach,' and to mean 'a female or woman' in general), Ved. a semi-divine or superhuman female, a kind of goddess or female genius; a woman. — *Gnā-vat, ān, atī, at*, Ved. (Sāy.) accompanied by women or wives. According to some the neut. may be *gnā-vas;* but Sāy. in Ṛig-veda II. 1, 5, considers *gnāvas* a nom. pl., and interprets it to mean 'words of praise.' — *Gnās-pati, is*, m., Ved. the husband of divine wives, or of a divine wife; (perhaps *gnās* is here a shortened genitive.) — *Gnās-patnī*, f. a divine wife, the wife of a deity; (Sāy.) a kind of female genius protecting women; (perhaps *gnās* is here the nominative in apposition to *patnī*, i. e. a divine female who is a wife.)

ग्रथ् 1. *grath* or *granth*, cl. 9. and 1. P. *grathnāti, granthati, jagrantha;* pl. *jagranthus* and *grethus; granthishyati, agranthīt, granthitum;* A. *grathnīte, granthate, agranthishṭa;* cl. 1. P. A. also *grathati, grathate;* to fasten, tie or string together; to wind round; to arrange, connect in a regular series; to string words together, compose, write (as a literary work); to set or strew with: Caus. P. *granthayati* and *grāthayati, -yitum;* [cf. Lat. *glut-en?*].

Grathana, am, n. coagulation, thickening, becoming obstructed or clogged with knotty lumps; (*ā*), f. tying, binding, stringing together.

Grathita, as, ā, am, strung, tied, bound, connected, tied together or in order, wound, arranged, classed, collected; set with, strewn with; artificially composed or put together (as the plot of a play); difficult to be unravelled, having knots, knotty, formed into lumps, coagulated, thickened, clogged; hardened; hurt, injured; seized, taken possession of; overcome; (*am*), n. a tumor with hard lumps or knots.

Grathna, as or *am*, m. or n. (?), a bunch, a tuft; (perhaps for *grantha*.)

Grantha, as, m. tying, binding, stringing together (literally or metaphorically); an artificial arrangement of words, a verse, composition, treatise, literary production, a book or composition in prose or verse, a section; the book or sacred scriptures of the Sikhs containing short moral poems by Nānak Shāh and others; a metre of thirty-two syllables; wealth, property; [cf. *uttara-grantha, nir-gr°, shaḍ-gr°.*] — *Grantha-karaṇa, am*, n. composing books or treatises, composition. — *Grantha-kartṛi, tā*, or *grantha-kāra, as*, m. a book-maker, the author of a book or treatise. — *Grantha-kuṭī* or *grantha-kūṭī*, f. a library; an office, a study. — *Grantha-kṛit, t*, m. the writer of a book, author or composer of a treatise. — *Grantha-vistara, as*, m. a multitude of scientific treatises. — *Grantha-vistāra, as*, m. diffuseness of style, voluminousness. — *Grantha-sandhi, is*, m. a section or chapter of a work.

Granthana, am, ā, n. f. stringing, tying or connecting together either as a chaplet or a book, arranging, composing.

1. *granthi, is*, m. a knot, a tie, the knot of a cord &c., a knot, bunch or protuberance of any kind (especially if produced by tying several things together), a knot tied in the end of a garment for keeping money &c.; the joint or knot of a reed or cane &c., a joint or articulation of the body; a complaint, knotting, i. e. swelling and hardening of the vessels as in varicocele; a knot tied closely and therefore difficult to be undone; N. of several plants and bulbous roots, = *granthi-parṇa, hitāvalī, bhadra-mustā, piṇḍālu;* [cf. *udara-g°, kaṭu-g°, kāla-g°*, &c.] — *Granthi-ćhedaka, as*, m. a purse-cutter, a cut-purse, pickpocket; [cf. *granthi-bheda.*] — *Granthi-tva, am*, n. state of becoming knotty; hardening. — *Granthi-dala, as*, m. a kind of perfume, = *ćoraka;* (*ā*), f., N. of a kind of bulbous root. — *Granthi-dūrvā*, f., N. of a plant, = *mālā-dūrvā.* — *Granthi-pattra, as*, m. a kind of perfume, = *ćoraka.* — *Granthi-parṇa, as*, m. a kind of perfume, = *ćoraka;* (*ā*), f. a kind of plant, = *jatukā;* (*ī*), f. a kind of Dūrvā grass, = *gaṇḍa-dūrvā;* (*am*), n. a kind of fragrant plant. — *Granthi-phala, as*, m., N. of several plants, = Feronia Elephantum, = *kapittha;* another plant, Vanguiera Spinosa, = *madana;* another plant, = *śākuruṇḍa.* — *Granthi-bandhana, am*, n. tying a knot; a ligament; tying together the garments of the bride and bridegroom at the marriage ceremony. — *Granthi-barhin, ī*, m., N. of a plant, = *granthi-parṇa.* — *Granthi-bheda, as*, m. a purse-cutter, cut-purse; [cf. *granthi-ćhedaka.*] — *Granthi-mat, ān, atī, at*, tied, bound; knotty, bulbous; (*ān*), m. the plant Heliotropium Indicum; [cf. *asthi-saṃhārī.*] — *Granthimat-phala, as*, m. the plant Artocarpus Lacucha (*lakuća*). — *Granthi-mūla, am*, n. garlic, = *griñjana;* (*ā*), f. a kind of Dūrvā grass, = *mālā-dūrvā.* — *Granthi-moćaka, as*, m. a cut-purse, thief.

Granthika, as, m. an astrologer (one who understands the joints or divisions of time, of the year, &c.; cf. *kāla-granthi*, 'a year'), a fortune-teller; a N. assumed by Nakula, the fourth son of Pāṇḍu, when he became master of the horse to king Virāṭa; a kind of disease of the outer ear; (*am*), n. (according to some) m., N. of the plant Capparis Aphylla; the root of long pepper; (*am*), n., N. of a plant, = *granthi-parṇa;* a kind of resin, bdellium; [cf. *guggulu.*]

Granthita, as, ā, am, strung, tied.

Granthin, ī, inī, i, one who reads books, bookish, well-read, learned; relating or belonging to a book, one who possesses many books.

Granthila, as, ā, am, knotted, knotty; (*as*), m., N. of several plants and roots, = Flacourtia Sapida; another plant, Capparis Aphylla; also = *taṇḍulīya-śāka* = *hitāvalī* = *piṇḍālu* = *vi-kaṇṭaka;* also = *ćoraka*, a kind of perfume; (*ā*), f., N. of several plants, = *gaṇḍa-dūrvā, mālā-dūrvā, bhadra-mustā;* (*am*), n. the root of long pepper; green or undried ginger, = *ārdraka.* — *Granthi-hara, as*, m. a counsellor, a minister (one who unravels the knots of business).

Granthīka, am, n. the root of long pepper, = *granthika.*

ग्रथ् 2. *grath* or *granth*, cl. 1. A. *grathate* and *granthate*, to be crooked (literally or metaphorically), to be wicked; to curve, bend or make crooked.

Grathin, ī, inī, i, false; (Sāy.) talkative, stringing (too many) words together.

2. *granthi, is*, m. crookedness, distortion; falsehood.

ग्रप्स् *graps*. See *glaps*.

ग्रभ् *grabh*. See *grah*.

ग्रस 1. *gras*, cl. 1. P. A. *grasati, -te, jagrāsa, jagrase, grasishyati, -te, agrasīt, agrasishṭa, grasitum*, to seize with the mouth, take into the mouth, swallow, devour, eat, consume; to swallow up, cause to disappear; to seize; to eclipse; to swallow or mouth or slur over words, pronounce indistinctly: Caus. P. *grāsayati, -yitum*, to cause to swallow, cause to devour; to consume, swallow, eat: Desid. *jigrasishate, -ti:* Intens. *jāgrasyate, jāgrasti;* [cf. Lat. *gra-men;* Germ. *gras, grasen;* Eng. *grass;* Gr. γραίνω.]

2. *gras, as, as, as*, (at the end of compounds) seizing with the mouth, devouring, swallowing (e. g. *piṇḍa-gras*, devouring a mouthful; see Gram. 164. *b*).

Grasana, am, n. swallowing, eating; taking, seizing; a kind of partial eclipse of the sun or moon.

Grasamāna, as, ā, am, swallowing, devouring; receiving, listening to anything eagerly.

Grasishṭha, as, ā, am, Ved. swallowing most, devouring very much; (Sāy. = *bhakshayitṛi-tama.*)

Grasishṇu, us, us, u, accustomed to swallow or devour or seize.

Grasta, as, ā, am, swallowed, eaten; taken, seized; involved in, affected by; possessed by (e. g. *graha-grasta*, seized or possessed by a demon; *dāridrya-grasta*, poverty-stricken); seized (as the sun or moon by Rāhu); eclipsed (e. g. *Rāhu-grasta*, q. v.); inarticulately pronounced, slurred, uttered with the omission of a letter or syllable. — *Grastāsta* (°*ta-as*°), *as, ā, am*, commenced and ended as an eclipse; (*am*), n. the setting of the sun or moon while eclipsed. — *Grastodaya* (°*ta-ud*°), *as*, m. the rising of the sun or moon while eclipsed.

Grasti, is, f. the act of swallowing or devouring.

Grasya, as, ā, am, to be swallowed, eaten or seized.

Grāsa, as, m. a mouthful or a quantity of anything equivalent to a mouthful, a lump of rice &c. of the size of a peacock's egg; food, nourishment; the erosion, the morsel bitten; the quantity eclipsed; the act of swallowing; the swallowing of the sun and moon (by Rāhu), an eclipse; slurring, uttering with the omission of a letter or syllable, a fault in the pronunciation of the gutturals; (in geom.) a piece cut out by the intersection of two circles. — *Grāsa-śalya, am*, n. any extraneous substance lodged in the throat. — *Grāsāććhādana* (°*sa-āć*°), *am*, n. bare subsistence, food and clothing.

Grāsī-kṛi, cl. 8. P. A. *-karoti, -kurute, -kartum*, to swallow, devour.

ग्रह् *grah* or *grabh* (the latter being the more ancient form used especially in the Ṛig-veda), cl. 9. P. A. *gṛihṇāti, gṛihṇīte* (Ved. *gṛibhṇāti, -ṇīte*); Impf. 1st sing. *agṛihṇām* (irreg. *agṛihṇam*), 2nd sing. Impv. P. *gṛihāṇa* (Ved. *gṛibhṇāna* and *gṛihṇāna*, other forms *gṛihṇāhi* and *gṛihṇīhi*, 3rd sing. *gṛihṇītāt*), *jagrāha* (Ved. Perf. *jagrabha*, 1st pl. *jagṛibhma*), *jagṛihe* (Ved. 3rd pl. *jagṛibhre*), *grahīshyati, -te, agrahīt, agrahīshṭa* (Ved. Aor. 1st sing. *agrabham*, 3rd sing. *agrabhīt*, 3rd pl. *agṛibhran, agṛibhīshata;* also 1st sing. *ajagrabham*), *grahītum*, to seize, take, receive, accept, take by the hand, adopt, catch, grasp, hold, lay hold of (e. g. *paksham grah*, to take a side, adopt a party; *pāṇim grah*, to take by the hand in the marriage ceremony, hence to marry); to seize, arrest, stop; to take captive, take prisoner, capture, imprison; to take possession of, gain over, captivate; to seize, overpower (especially said of diseases and demons and the punishments of Varuṇa); to seize, eclipse (the sun and moon being supposed by the Hindūs to be seized by Rāhu); to abstract, take away (by robbery); to lay the hand on, gain, win, obtain, receive, accept; to conceive; to acquire by purchase (with inst. of the price); to choose; to take up (as a fluid with any small vessel), to draw water; to catch, intercept; pluck, pick, gather; to collect a store of anything; to use, put on (as clothes &c.); to assume (as a shape); to place upon; to withdraw, draw back; to include; to take on one's self, undertake, undergo, begin; to receive hospitably (as a guest); to take back (as a divorced wife); to take into the mouth, mention, name [cf. *nāma-grahaṇa, nāma-grāham*, &c.]; to perceive with the organs of sense, observe, recognize; to receive into the mind, apprehend, understand, learn; to accept, admit, approve; to obey, follow; to take for, consider as; to take in a particular sense or meaning: Pass. *gṛihyate*, 1st Fut. *grahītā* and *grāhitā*, 2nd Fut. *grahīshyate* and *grāhishyate*, Aor. 3rd sing. *agrāhi*, 3rd du. *agrahīshātām* and *agrāhishātām:* Caus. P. *grāhayati, -yitum, ajigrahat*, to cause to take or seize or lay hold of; to give away a girl (acc.) in marriage to any one (acc.); to cause any one to be captured; to cause to take away; to make one take, to deliver over to; (with *āsanam* and acc.) to cause to take a seat, to bid any one sit down by the side of; to make any one choose; to cause a person to undertake or be occupied with (inst.); to make a person learn, to teach, make any one acquainted or familiar with (two acc.); to become familiar with: Desid. *jighṛikshati, -te*, to be about to seize or take; to be about to take away; to desire to take, to wish to perceive (with the organs of sense), to strive to apprehend or recognize: Intens. *jarigṛihyate, jāgrāḍhi* (Gram. 711): [cf. Zend *gerep, geurv;* Goth. *greipa;* Germ. *greife;* Lith. *grěbju, pagrěbju;* Slav. *grablja;* Hib. *grabaim*, 'I devour, stop, interrupt, disturb;' *gabhaim*, 'I take, receive, conceive;' Gr. γρῖφος, γρῖπος: cf. also Lat. *gero;* Pol. *garniać.*]

Gṛih, gṛiha, &c. See s. v. at p. 295.

Gṛihīta, as, ā, am, grasped, taken, seized, caught, held, laid hold of; obtained, acquired, gained; robbed; received, accepted, conceived; collected; agreed, promised; perceived, known, understood, ascertained, learnt, &c.; [cf. *grah* above.] — *Gṛihīta-khaḍga-ćarman, ā, ā, a,* grasping sword and shield. — *Gṛihīta-garbhā,* f. one who has conceived an embryo, a pregnant woman. — *Gṛihīta-ćetas, ās, ās, as,* one whose mind or heart is captivated. — *Gṛihīta-diś, k, k, k,* running away, flying; flown, escaped, retreated. — *Gṛihīta-deha, as, ā, am,* incarnate. — *Gṛihīta-nāman, ā, ā, a,* one who has received a name (e. g. *su-gṛihīta-nāman,* one who has received a good name, one named in accordance with the ordinances). — *Gṛihīta-vidya, as, ā, am,* one who has acquired knowledge, versed in science, learned, studied. — *Gṛihīta-vetana, as, ā, am,* one who has received his wages, paid, remunerated. — *Gṛihīta-śara-kārmuka, as, ā, am,* handling arrows and bows. — *Gṛihīta-śarāvāpa, as, ā, am,* taking a bow. — *Gṛihīta-hṛidaya, as, ā, am,* one whose heart is taken possession of or captivated; captivating the heart. — *Gṛihītāmisha* (°*ta-ām*°), *as, ā, am,* seizing prey. — *Gṛihītārtha* (°*ta-ar*°), *as, ā, am,* comprehending the sense or meaning. — *Gṛihītāstra* (°*ta-as*°), *as, ā, am,* one who has taken up arms.

Gṛihītavya, as, ā, am (an incorrect form for *grahītavya*), to be seized or taken; to be understood, meant.

Gṛihītin, ī, inī, i, seizing, one who has grasped.

Gṛihītṛi, tā, trī, tṛi (incorrect for *grahītṛi*), seizing, grasping, disposed to seize or take.

Gṛihītvā, ind. having taken.

Gṛihu, us, m., Ved. one who receives alms, a beggar.

Gṛihṇat, an, atī, at, taking, seizing, accepting.

2. *gṛihya, as, ā, am* (for 1. *gṛihya* see s. v. at p. 296), to be taken or received; to be seized, to be observed, perceptible, perceivable; to be acknowledged or admitted; to be adopted as faith or belief, to be trusted, to be relied on, to be honoured; taking the side of, adopting or choosing as best (e. g. *Arjuna-gṛihya,* taking the side or adhering to the party of Arjuna); dependant, subservient; (*as*), m. the anus.

3. *gṛihya,* irreg. ind. part. having taken, carrying along, together with, with.

Grabha, as, m., Ved. the taking possession of; one who lays hold of (?).

Grabhaṇa, am, n. seizing, that by which anything is seized (?). — *Grabhaṇa-vat, ān, atī, at,* Ved. anything furnished with a handle.

Grabhītṛi, tā, trī, tṛi, Ved. one who seizes; [cf. *grahītṛi.*]

Graha, as, ā, am, seizing, laying hold of, holding; taking, collecting, gathering; (*as*), m. one who seizes; the power that seizes and obscures the sun and moon and causes eclipses, especially Rāhu or the ascending node; a planet (as seizing or influencing the destinies of men in a supernatural manner; sometimes five planets are enumerated, viz. Mars, Mercury, Jupiter, Venus, and Saturn; sometimes seven, i. e. the preceding with Rāhu and Ketu or the ascending and descending nodes; sometimes nine, i. e. the sun and moon together with the preceding: the planets are either auspicious, *śubha-grahās, sad-grahās;* or inauspicious, *krūra-grahās, pāpa-grahās;* in the system of the Jainas the planets constitute one of the five classes of the Jyotishka); the place of a planet in the fixed zodiac, a N. for the number nine; N. of certain evil demons or spirits who seize or exercise a bad influence on the body and mind of man, (they cause insanity &c.; the Hindūs consider that it falls within the province of medical science to expel these demons; those which especially seize children and cause convulsions &c. are divided into nine classes, according to the number of the planets, cf. *pūtanā*); any state of mind which proceeds from magical influences and takes possession of the whole man; a crocodile, a shark; a house (= *gṛiha,* in *a-graha, khara-g°, graha-druma, graha-pati*); anything seized, spoil, booty, prey; as much as can be taken with a ladle, spoon &c. out of a larger vessel, a ladleful, spoonful, &c.; any ladle or vessel employed for taking up a portion of fluid out of a larger vessel, (especially applied to the vessels used for taking up the Soma; cf. *soma-graha*); the middle of a bow or that part which is grasped when the bow is used; grasp, seizing, laying hold of, the drawing up or taking up of water &c. [cf. *nīra-graha*]; seizure in general (e. g. *aṅga-graha,* spasm of the limbs), seizure of the sun or moon, eclipse; a movable point in the heavens; stealing, robbing; taking, receiving, reception, receipt; keeping back, obstructing; mention, nomination; apprehension, perception, intelligence, understanding; an organ or instrument of apprehension (of which according to the Upanishads there are eight, viz. Prāṇa, Vāć, Jihvā, Ćakshus, Śrotra, Manas, Hastau, and Tvać); insisting upon, tenacity, perseverance, purpose, design, favour, patronage; a N. of the fourth or fifth book of the Śatapatha-Brāhmaṇa; [cf. *guḍa-graha, śiro-gr°, hanu-gr°, hṛid-gr°.*] — *Graha-kallola, as,* m. the wave (or enemy?) of the planets, an epithet of Rāhu. — *Graha-gaṇa, as,* m. the whole number of planets taken collectively. — *Graha-gaṇita, am,* n. = *gaṇita,* the astronomical part of a Jyotiḥ-śāstra. — *Graha-ćintaka, as,* m. an astrologer. — *Graha-tā,* f. or *graha-tva, am,* n. state of being a planet. — *Graha-daśā,* f. the aspect of the planets. — *Graha-druma, as,* m. the creeper Gymnema Sylvestre, = *śāka-vṛiksha;* [cf. *gṛiha-druma.*] — *Graha-nāyaka, as,* m. the leader of the planets; the planet Saturn; the sun. — *Graha-nāśa* or *graha-nāśana, as,* m., N. of the plant Alstonia Scholaris, commonly *ćhātina.* — *Graha-nigraha, au,* m. du. favour and punishment. — *Graha-nemi, is,* m. the moon. — *Graha-pati, is,* m. the chief of the planets, the sun; the plant Calotropis Gigantea [cf. *arka*], = *gṛiha-pati.* — *Graha-pīḍana, am,* n. or *graha-pīḍā,* f. the pain or oppression caused by a planet; the obscurity caused by Rāhu, an eclipse; the influence of an unpropitious planet. — *Graha-pusha, as,* m. the sun (cherishing the planets with his light). — *Graha-pūjā,* f. worship of the sun and other planets. — *Graha-bhakti, is,* f. distribution among the planets, division of countries &c. with respect to the presiding planets; title of the sixteenth chapter in Varāha-mihira's Bṛihat-saṃhitā. — *Graha-bhīti-jit, t,* m., N. of a perfume ('conquering the fear of the demons'). — *Graha-bhojana, as,* m. a horse. — *Graha-maya, as, ī, am,* consisting of planets. — *Graha-mardana, am,* n. friction or opposition between the planets. — *Graha-yajña* or *graha-yāga, as,* m. worship or sacrifice offered to the planets. — *Grahayajña-tattva, am,* n. title of a part of the Smṛiti-tattva. — *Graha-yuti, is,* m. conjunction of the planets. — *Graha-yuddha, am,* n. strife or opposition of the planets; title of the seventeenth Adhyāya of Varāha-mihira's Bṛihat-saṃhitā. — *Graha-rāja, as,* m. the king of the planets; the sun; the moon; the planet Jupiter or its regent. — *Graha-lāghava, am,* n. title of an astronomical work of the sixteenth century. — *Graha-varsha, as,* m. a planetary year; title of the nineteenth Adhyāya of Varāha-mihira's Bṛihat-saṃhitā, which describes the good or evil fortune belonging to certain days, months or years ruled over by particular planets. — *Graha-vipra, as,* m. an astrologer. — *Graha-vimarda, as,* m. friction of the planets, opposition, = *graha-mardana.* — *Graha-śānti, is,* f. propitiation of the planets by sacrifices &c. — *Graha-śṛiṅgāṭaka, am,* n. triangular position of the planets with reference to each other; title of the twentieth Adhyāya in Varāha-mihira's Bṛihat-saṃhitā, treating also of many other positions of the planets. — *Graha-samāgama, as,* m. conjunction of the planets; also in the comp. *śaśi-graha-samāgama,* conjunction of the moon with asterisms or planets. — *Grahādhāra* (°*ha-ādh*°), *as,* m. the polar star as the fixed centre of the planets. — *Grahādhīna* (°*ha-adh*°), *as, ā, am,* subject to planetary influence. — *Grahāmaya* (°*ha-ām*°), *as,* m. epilepsy, convulsions, demoniacal possession, which is supposed to cause the complaint. — *Grahārāma-kutūhala* or *karaṇa-kutūhala, am,* n., N. of an astronomical work by Bhāskara. — *Grahāluńćana* (°*ha-āl*°), *am,* n. pouncing on prey, seizing and tearing it to pieces. — *Grahāvamardana* (°*ha-av*°), *am,* n. friction of the planets, opposition; [cf. *graha-mardana.*] — *Grahāśin* (°*ha-āś*°), *ī,* m. the plant Echites Scholaris; [cf. *graha-nāśa.*] — *Grahāśraya* (°*ha-āś*°), *as,* m. the polar star; [cf. *grahādhāra.*] — *Grahāhvaya* (°*ha-āh*°), *as,* m., N. of a plant; [cf. *bhūtāṅkuśa.*] — *Graheśa* (°*ha-īś*°), *as,* m. the chief of the planets, the sun.

Grahaka, as, m. a prisoner; [cf. *grāhaka.*]

Grahaṇa, as, ā, am, seizing, holding; (*am*), n. the hand; an organ of sense; a prisoner, captive; mentioning, naming, mention, a word mentioned (e. g. *vaćana-grahaṇa,* the word *vaćana*); seizing, holding, taking, catching, seizure; taking by the hand, marrying; receiving, acceptance; taking captive, captivating, overpowering, imprisonment; seizure of the sun or moon, eclipse; gaining, obtaining, purchasing; choosing; taking or drawing up; attraction; putting on; containing, enclosing; undertaking, undergoing; service; mentioning with praise, respect; perceiving, understanding, comprehension, the taking or receiving of instruction, or the acquirement of any science; acceptation, meaning; assent, agreement; inviting, calling, addressing; the taking up of sound, echo; an organ of sense; [cf. *kara-grahaṇa, keśa-g°, garbha-g°, ćakshur-g°, nāma-g°, pāṇi-g°, punar-g°.*] — *Grahaṇānta* (°*ṇa-an*°), *am,* n. close of study, acquirement of science &c. — *Grahaṇāntika* (°*ṇa-an*°), *am,* n. termination of holy study.

Grahaṇaka, am, n. containing, involving.

Grahaṇi, is or *ī,* f. an imaginary organ supposed to lie between the stomach and the intestines; the small intestines or that part of the alimentary canal where the bile assists digestion and from which vital warmth is diffused; diarrhœa, dysentery. — *Grahaṇī-dosha, as,* m. a morbid affection of the Grahaṇī, diarrhœa. — *Grahaṇī-pradosha, as,* m. a morbid affection of the Grahaṇī. — *Grahaṇī-ruj, k,* f. or *grahaṇī-roga, as,* m. a morbid affection of the Grahaṇī, diarrhœa. — *Grahaṇīrogin, ī, iṇī, i,* affected with diarrhœa. — *Grahaṇī-hara, am,* n. cloves.

Grahaṇīya, as, ā, am, acceptable, to be taken or received or understood. — *Grahaṇīya-tā,* f. or *grahaṇīya-tva, am,* n. acceptableness.

Grahayāyya, another form for *gṛihayāyya,* lord of a house, q. v.

Grahayālu, us, us, u, for *gṛihayālu,* taking, receiving, q. v.

Grahi, at the end of a compound in *phale-grahi,* q. v.

Grahila, as, ā, am, taking, accepting, acknowledging.

Grahishṇu, at the end of a compound in *phala-grahishṇu,* q. v.

Grahītavya, as, ā, am, to be taken or received, acceptable, to be accepted; to be taken up or drawn (as a fluid); to be apprehended or perceived, to be learned or acquired; (*am*), n. the being obliged to take or receive.

Grahītṛi, tā, trī, tṛi, a taker, seizer, accepter, receiver, purchaser; perceiver, perceiving, observant; taking, disposed to take; [cf. *pāṇi-grahītṛi* and *gṛihītṛi.*]

Grahya, as, ā, am, Ved. belonging to or fit for a Graha.

Grābha, as, m., Ved. one who seizes, what is seized; grasp, seizure.

Grāha, as, ī, am, seizing, holding, catching, taking, receiving, acceptance (e. g. *ṛiktha-grāha,* receiving inherited property; *yoshid-grāha,* taking a wife); [cf. *karṇa-grāha, gila-g°, dhanur-g°, pāṇi-g°, pārshṇi-g°,* &c.]; (*as*), m. a rapacious animal living in fresh or sea water; a crocodile, a shark, a serpent; (according to some the Gangetic alligator or Lacerta Gangetica, according to others the water elephant or hippopotamus); any large fish or marine animal; (*ī*), f. a female crocodile; (*as*), m. a prisoner; seizure, grasping, laying hold of; morbid affection, disease; beginning, undertaking; mentioning; [cf. *nāma-grāha;* cf. also *asad-grāha* and *svayaṃ-grāha.*] — *Grāha-vat, ān, atī, at,* containing or abounding with alligators &c.

Grāhaka, as, ikā, am, receiving, accepting, one who takes or seizes; a purchaser, buyer; containing, enclosing; perceiving, observing; taking away, persuading; (*as*), m. a police-officer, a constable, a bailiff; a hawk, a falcon [cf. Gr. γρύψ; Germ. *greif*]; a kind of vegetable, = *sitāvara;* N. of an attendant of Śiva.

Grāham, ind. part. taking, seizing, mentioning, (often at the end of compounds, e. g. *jīva-grāham,* taking alive; cf. also *nāma-grāham.*)

Grāhi, is, f., Ved. a female spirit of evil, seizing men and causing death and disease, (Sleep is described as her son); deprivation of sensation, a swoon, fainting fit. — *Grāhi-phala, am,* n. the tree Feronia Elephantum; [cf. *kapittha.*]

Grāhita, as, ā, am, made to take or seize.

Grāhin, ī, iṇī, i, seizing, taking, holding, laying hold of; catching, engaged in catching; picking, gathering; containing, holding; drawing, attracting, fascinating, alluring; gaining, obtaining, acquiring; choosing; searching through, scrutinizing; perceiving, observing; accepting, taking to heart; astringent; obstructing, binding, constipating; (*ī*), m. the plant Feronia Elephantum [cf. *kapittha*]; (*iṇī*), f. a small kind of Yavāśa; a kind of Hedysarum, = *kshudra-durālabhā, tāmra-mūlā.*

Grāhuka, as, ī, am, seizing, laying hold of.

Grāhya, as, ā, am, to be seized, taken, held; to be captured or imprisoned; to be carried away; to be picked or gathered, acceptable; to be received, accepted, gained; to be perceived, observed; to be taken in marriage; to be received in a friendly or hospitable manner; to be insisted upon; to be understood, perceivable; to be considered; to be understood in a particular sense, meant; to be accepted as a rule or law, to be acknowledged or assented to, to be attended to or obeyed, to be admitted in evidence; acceptable, agreeable; (*am*), n. a present; [cf. *dur-grāhya, sukha-grāhya, svayaṃ-grāhya.*] — *Grāhya-vāć, k, k, k,* uttering agreeable speech, praising.

Grāhyaka, as, ikā, am, to be perceived; to be discerned or distinguished.

ग्राम *grāma, as,* m. (said to be fr. rt. *gras* or fr. *grah*), an inhabited place, a village, a hamlet, an inhabited and unfortified place in the midst of fields and cultivated land, a municipal and fiscal division, a township (opposed to *araṇya,* and in later Sanskṛit also to *pura, nagara,* and *pattana*); the collective inhabitants of a place, a community, race; any number of men associated together, a troop, multitude, collection, especially a troop of soldiers; a number of tunes, a scale in music, a gamut; (at the end of a compound) a multitude, a class, a collection or number in general; [cf. *arishṭa-grāma, mahā-g°, śūra-g°, saṅgrāma;* cf. also Lith. *kiēma-s;* Hib. *gramaisg,* 'the mob;' *gramasgar,* 'a flock, company.'] — *Grāma-kaṇṭaka, as,* m. the village-pest or tale-bearer. — *Grāma-kāma, as, ā, am,* one who wishes to take possession of a village; desirous of villages; fond of living in villages. — *Grāma-kukkuṭa, as,* m. a village cock, a tame or domestic cock. — *Grāma-kumāra, as,* m. a village boy. — *Grāma-kulāla, as,* m. a village potter. — *Grāma-kūṭa, as,* m. the noblest man in a village, a Śūdra or man of the fourth tribe. — *Grāma-ga, as, ā, am,* or *grāma-gamin, ī, inī, i,* who or what goes to a village, (Pāṇ. II. 1, 24.) — *Grāma-gṛihya, as, ā, am,* being outside a village, (lit. adjoining the houses of a village.) — *Grāma-geya, as, ā, am,* to be sung in a village. — *Grāmageya-gāna, am,* n. one of the four books into which the Sāma-veda when arranged for chanting is distributed. — *Grāma-goduh, -dhuk,* m. the herdsman of a village. — *Grāma-ghāta, as,* m. plundering a village. — *Grāma-ghātin, ī, inī, i,* devastating or plundering a village. — *Grāma-ghoshin, ī, iṇī, i,* Ved. sounding among men or armies, as a drum. — *Grāmaṃ-gamin, ī, inī, i,* who or what goes to a village. — *Grāma-ćaryā,* f. the customs of social life, social intercourse. — *Grāma-ćaitya, as,* m. the sacred tree of a village. — *Grāma-ja, as, ā, am,* village-born, village-produced; rustic, village, grown in cultivated ground. — *Grāmaja-nishpāvī,* f. a kind of pulse. — *Grāma-jāta, as, ā, am,* rustic, village-born, produced in a village, grown in cultivated ground. — *Grāma-jāla, am,* n. a number of villages, a district. — *Grāmajālin, ī,* m. the governor of a province. — *Grāma-jit, t, t, t,* Ved. conquering or gaining villages; conquering troops; (Sāy.) either conquering villages or dispersing multitudes. — *Grāmaṇa, as, ī, am,* coming from a Grāma-ṇī. — *Grāma-ṇī, īs, īs, i* (for *grāma-nī*), the leader or chief of a village or community, the lord of the manor, the squire, the leader of a troop or army; a chief, a superintendent; best, pre-eminent, excellent; one who only thinks of enjoyment (?), the village barber (as the chief person of a village); a groom (?); N. of a Gandharva chief; N. of one of the attendants of Śiva; N. of certain beings who together with the Ṛishis, Gandharvas, Apsarasas, Nāgas, Yātu-dhānas, and Bālakhilyas are by some supposed to be attendant upon the Sun; N. of a place; (*īs*), f. a female peasant or villager; a whore, a harlot; the Indigo plant. — *Grāmaṇī-tva, am,* n. the position or condition of a chief or leader of a village. — *Grāmaṇīthya, am,* n. the station of the chief of a village or community. — *Grāmaṇī-putra, as,* m. the son of a harlot, a bastard. — *Grāmaṇīya, ās,* m. pl., N. of a people; (*am*), n. = *grāmaṇīthya.* — *Grāmaṇi-sava, as,* m., N. of an Ekāha sacrifice. — *Grāma-taksha, as,* m. a village carpenter. — *Grāma-tas,* ind. from the village. — *Grāma-tā,* f. or *grāma-tva, am,* n. a multitude of villages. — *Grāma-daśeśa* (*°śa-īśa*), *as,* or *grāmadaśādhipati* (*°śa-adh°*), *is,* m. the head of ten villages. — *Grāma-devatā,* f. the tutelary deity of a village. — *Grāma-druma, as,* m. a single tree in a village held sacred by the inhabitants. — *Grāma-dharā,* f. supporting a village or villages, N. of a rock. — *Grāma-dharma, as,* m. the observances or customs of a village. — *Grāma-nāpita, as,* m. the village barber. — *Grāma-nivāsin, ī, inī, i,* living in villages, tame. — *Grāma-pāla, as,* m. the guardian of a village. — *Grāma-putra, as,* m. a village boy. — *Grāma-preshya, as,* m. the messenger or servant of a community or village. — *Grāma-bāla-jana, as,* m. a young peasant. — *Grāma-bhṛita, as,* m. a village messenger or servant. — *Grāma-madgurikā,* f. a kind of fish, Silurus Singio (= *śṛiṅgī*); a riot, a fray, a village tumult; [cf. *grāma-yuddha.*] — *Grāma-mahishī,* f. a tame buffalo. — *Grāma-mukha, am,* n. a market town, a fair, a market. — *Grāma-mṛiga, as,* m. 'the village animal,' a dog. — *Grāma-maukhya,* head of a village; (probably incorrect for *grāma-saukhya,* see *grāma-sukha.*) — *Grāma-yājaka, as, ikā, am,* offering sacrifices for a whole village or community; (*as*), m. the village priest, one who conducts the ceremonies for any or all classes and is consequently considered as a degraded Brāhman; it also applies to the attendant of an idol. — *Grāma-yājin, ī, inī, i,* offering sacrifices for a whole village or community. — *Grāma-yuddha, am,* n. a riot, a fray, a village war. — *Grāma-rathyā,* f. a village street. — *Grāma-luṇṭana, am,* n. plundering or pillaging a village. — *Grāma-vat, ān, atī, at,* furnished with villages. — *Grāma-vāsa, as,* m. living in a village; a villager; [cf. *grāme-vāsa.*] — *Grāma-vāsin, ī, inī, i,* living in villages, tame; (*inas*), m. pl. the inhabitants of a village, the villagers; [cf. *grāme-vāsin* and *grāmya.*] — *Grāma-vāstavya, as,* m. the inhabitant of a village. — *Grāma-viśesha, as,* m. variety of the scales in music. — *Grāma-śata, am,* n. a hundred villages, a province. — *Grāmaśateśa* (*°ta-īśa*), *as,* m. or *grāmaśatādhipati* (*°ta-adh°*), *is,* m. or *grāmaśatādhyaksha* (*°ta-adh°*), *as,* m. the governor of a province. — *Grāma-saṅkara, as,* m. the common sewer or drain of a village. — *Grāma-saṅgha, as,* m. a village corporation, a municipality. — *Grāma-siṅha, as,* m. a dog. — *Grāma-sukha, am,* n. the pleasure of a villager; [cf. *grāmya-sukha.*] — *Grāma-stha, as, ā, am,* being or residing in a village, belonging to a village, rustic, &c.; (*as*), m. a villager. — *Grāma-hāsaka, as,* m. a sister's husband. — *Grāmāćāra* (*°ma-āć°*), *as,* m. village observances, customs, &c. — *Grāmādhāna* (*°ma-ādh°*), *am,* n. hunting; a village (?). — *Grāmādhikṛita* (*°ma-adh°*), *as,* or *grāmādhipati* (*°ma-adh°*), *is,* or *grāmādhyaksha* (*°ma-adh°*), *as,* or *grāmādhikārin* (*°ma-adh°*), *ī,* m. superintendent or chief of a village. — *Grāmānta* (*°ma-an°*), *as,* m. the border of a village; space near a village; (*e*), ind. in the neighbourhood of a village. — *Grāmāntara* (*°ma-an°*), *am,* n. another village. — *Grāmāntika, am,* n. the neighbourhood of a village. — *Grāmāntīya, as, ā, am,* situated in the neighbourhood of a village; (*am*), n. space near a village. — *Grāme-vāsa, as,* m. a village abode; a villager; [cf. *grāma-vāsa.*] — *Grāme-vāsin, ī, inī, i,* living in a village, tame; (*inas*), m. pl. the villagers. — *Grāmeśa* (*°ma-īśa*), *as,* m. the head man of a village. — *Grāmeśvara* (*°ma-īś°*), *as,* m. the head man or ruler over a village; the lord of the manor or squire. — *Grāmopādhyāya* (*°ma-up°*), *as,* m. the village priest.

Grāmaka, as, m. a village &c., see *grāma;* the collective department or range of celestial pleasures; N. of a town.

Grāmaya, nom. P. *grāmayati, -yitum,* to invite.

Grāmika, as, ī, am, village, rude, rustic; (in music) chromatic; (*as*), m. the head man of a village; a villager.

Grāmin, ī, iṇī, i, surrounded by a village community, pertaining to a village, rustic, rural, village; (*ī*), m. a villager, a peasant; the head man of a village; (*iṇī*), f. the Indigo plant. — *Grāmi-putra, as,* m. the son of a villager.

Grāmīṇa, as, ā, am, belonging to a village; produced in or peculiar to a village; vulgar, rude; (in music) chromatic; a villager, a rustic; (*as*), m. a dog; a hog; a crow; (*ā*), f. the Indigo plant; a kind of vegetable; [cf. *pālankya.*]

Grāmīya, as, ā, am, belonging to a village or to the same village community; produced in or derived from a village; (*as*), m. a villager.

Grāmīyaka, as, m. the member of a community, a villager.

Grāmeya, as, ī, am, village-born, a villager, a rustic.

Grāmeyaka, as, ikā, am, belonging to a village, a villager.

Grāmya, as, ā, am, relating to or used in a village, produced in a village; living in a village, a villager, rustic, homely, vulgar, clownish, rude; living in a village, i. e. among men, domesticated, tame (as an animal), cultivated (as a plant, opposed to *vanya* or *araṇya,* wild); allowed in a village, relating to the sensual pleasures of a village; relating to a musical scale; (*as*), m. a hog, a tame or village hog; (*ā*), f. the Indigo plant, and Phaseolus Radiata; [cf. *nishpāvī*]; (*am*), n. rustic or homely speech; the Prākṛit and the other dialects of India as contradistinguished from the Sanskṛit; food prepared in a village; sensual pleasure, sexual intercourse. — *Grāmya-kanda, as,* m. a kind of onion, = *sthala-kanda;* (perhaps rather *agrāmya-kanda.*) — *Grāmya-karkaṭī,* f. a kind of pumpkin-gourd, Benincasa Cerifera. — *Grāmya-karman, a,* n. the occupation of a villager, sensual pleasure and sexual intercourse. — *Grāmya-kuṅkuma, am,* n. a yellow dye, safflower, Carthamus Tinctorius. — *Grāmya-gaja, as,* m. a village-born or tame elephant. — *Grāmya-dharma, as,* m. the right of a villager or townsman (as opposed to the right of a recluse), sexual intercourse, copulation; the duties of a villager. — *Grāmyadharmin, ī, iṇī, i,* addicted to sexual intercourse, libidinous. — *Grāmya-paśu, us,* m. a domestic animal; (sometimes applied contemptuously to a man.) — *Grāmya-buddhi, is, is, i,* clownish, ignorant. — *Grāmya-madgurikā,* f. a kind of fish, Silurus Singio, = *grāma-madgurikā.* — *Grāmya-māṅsa, am,* n. the flesh of tame animals. — *Grāmya-mṛiga, as,* m. a dog; [cf. *grāma-mṛiga.*] — *Grāmya-rāśi, is,* m. a N. of several of the signs of the zodiac. — *Grāmya-vallabhā,* f. a kind of vegetable. — *Grāmya-vādin, ī,* m. the judge of a village, a village bailiff. — *Grāmya-śūkara, as,* m. a village hog, a tame hog, a pig. — *Grāmya-sukha, am,* n. the pleasure of a villager, sleeping, sexual intercourse. — *Grāmyāśva (°ya-aś°), as,* m. an ass. — *Grāmyehoparama (°ya-īhā-up°), as,* m. ceasing from sensual desires.

ग्रावन् *grāvan, ā,* m. (said to be fr. rt. *grah*), a stone for pressing out the Soma, (according to the commentators on the Brāhmaṇas there existed five such stones, but in earlier times probably only two were used); a stone or rock in general; a mountain; a cloud; also = *grāva-stut* below; (*ā, ā, a*), hard, solid. — *Grāva-grābha, as,* m., Ved. a person who uses the Soma stones. — *Grāva-rohaka, as,* m. the shrub Physalis Flexuosa; [cf. *aśva-gandhā.*] — *Grāva-stut, t,* m. he who praises the Soma stones; N. of one of the sixteen priests (called after the hymn addressed to the Soma stones). — *Grāva-stotrīya, as, ā, am,* relating or belonging to the praise of the Soma stones; (*am*), n. the duties of the Grāva-stut. — *Grāva-hasta, as, ā, am,* Ved. handling the Soma stones.

ग्रास *grāsa.* See under rt. *gras,* p. 302.

ग्राह *grāha.* See under rt. *grah,* p. 303.

ग्रीवा *grīvā,* f. (said to be fr. 2. *gṛī*), the back part of the neck, the nape, the tendon of the trapezium muscle, the neck (in the earlier literature always pl.), the neck-part of the hide of an animal; [cf. *asita-grīva, ṛiksha-g°, kambu-g°, kalmāsha-g°;* cf. also Lith. *galwà;* Russ. *glava* and *golova.*] — *Grīvāksha (°vā-ak°), as,* m., N. of a man. — *Grīvā-ghaṇṭā,* f. a bell hanging down from the neck of a horse. — *Grīvā-bila, am,* n. the hollow in the back part or nape of the neck.

Grīvālikā, f. the neck.

Grīvin, ī, iṇī, i, long-necked, handsome-necked; (*ī*), m. a camel.

Graiva, as, ī, am, being on or belonging to the neck, representing the neck, being on the neck; (*am*), n. a necklace, a close necklace or collar; a chain worn round the neck of an elephant.

Graiveya, as, ī, am, belonging to the neck; (*as, am*), m. n. a collar, a necklace; a chain on the neck of an elephant or horse.

Graiveyaka, as, am, m. n. an ornament of the neck, a chain worn round the neck of an elephant; (*ās*), m. pl. a class of deities (nine in number), who have their seat on the neck of the Loka-purusha or who form his necklace.

Graivya, as, ā, am, Ved. relating to the neck.

ग्रीष्म *grīshma, as, ā, am* (said to be fr. rt. *gras*), hot, warm; (*as*), m. the summer, the hot season, consisting of the months Śuci and Śukra or Jyeshṭha and Āshāḍha (from the middle of May to the middle of July); heat, warmth; N. of a man; (*ā*), f., N. of a tree [cf. *lodhra*]; (*ī*), f. the tree Jasminum Sambac; [cf. *nava-mallikā;* cf. also Hib. *gris,* 'fire;' *griosgaim,* 'I fry, boil;' *griosach,* 'burning embers;' Lith. *karsztas* and *karsztis.*] — *Grīshma-kāla, as,* m. the hot season (see above). — *Grīshmakālīna, as, ā, am,* pertaining to the hot season. — *Grīshma-ja, as, ā, am,* produced by heat, produced in the hot season; (*ā*), f. a kind of fruit-tree, Anona Reticulata; [cf. *lavanī.*] — *Grīshma-dhānya, am,* n. summer corn. — *Grīshma-pushpī,* f., N. of a plant, = *karuṇī.* — *Grīshma-bhava, as, ā, am,* produced by heat or in the hot season; (*ā*), f. Jasminum Sambac. — *Grīshma-sundaraka, as,* m. a kind of pot-herb, Erythræa Centaureoides, commonly called *gimā;* also the plant Pharnaceum Mollugo. — *Grīshma-hāsa, as,* m. the flocculent seeds, down, &c., blown about in the air in summer (compared from their white colour to 'the smiles of the season'). — *Grīshmodbhava (°ma-ud°), as, ā, am,* produced by heat or in the hot season; (*ā*), f. double jasmine, Jasminum Sambac.

Graishma, as, ī, am, relating to the summer, belonging to the hot weather, produced by heat or the hot season, sown in summer; (*ī*), f. Jasminum Sambac.

Graishmaka, as, ikā, am, sown in summer; to be paid in summer (as a debt).

Graishmika, as, ī, am, relating or belonging to summer, growing in summer.

ग्रुच् *gruć,* cl. 1. P. *groćati, jugroća, agrućat* and *agroćīt, groćitum,* to steal, rob; to go; [cf. *gluć.*]

ग्रैव *graiva.* See under *grīvā* last col.

ग्रैष्म *graishma.* See under *grīshma* above.

ग्लप् *glap.* Cf. *glai.*

ग्लप्स *glapsa, as, am,* m. n. a branch (?).

ग्लस् *glas,* cl. 1. A. *glasate,* = *gras,* to eat.

Glasta, as, ā, am, = *grasta,* eaten.

ग्लह् *glah,* cl. 1. A. *glahate, jaglahe, glahitum* and *glāḍhum,* to gamble, play with dice, win by gambling; (= rt. *grah*) to take, receive, accept.

Glaha, as, m. a dice-player, the stake in playing, a wager, bet; the prize or object fought for in a contest, the person aimed at; a die; a dice-box; cast of the dice, game at dice; gaming, playing with dice; contention; a chess-man; *glahaṃ div,* to play at dice.

Glahana, am, n., Ved. playing at dice, casting the dice.

ग्लान *glāna, glāni,* &c. See under rt. *glai.*

ग्लुच् *gluć,* cl. 1. P. *gloćati, jugloća, aglućat* and *aglоćīt, gloćitum,* to steal or rob; to go; [cf. *gruć* and *gluńć.*]

Glućuka, as, m., N. of a man.

ग्लुञ्च् *gluńć,* cl. 1. P. *gluńćati, jugluńća, agluńćat* and *agluńćīt, gluńćitum,* to go, move.

ग्लेप् *glep,* cl. 1. A. *glepate,* &c., to be poor or miserable; to shake, tremble; move.

ग्लेव् *glev,* cl. 1. A. *glevate,* to serve, worship, gratify by service or devotedness; [cf. *gev, khev, sev.*]

ग्लेष् *glesh,* cl. 1. A. *gleshate,* to seek, investigate; [cf. *gesh* and *garesh.*]

ग्लै *glai,* cl. 1. P. (ep. also A.) *glāyati, -te, jaglau, glāsyati, aglāsīt, glātum,* to feel aversion or dislike, to be averse or reluctant, be unwilling, disinclined to do anything (with inf., e. g. *glāyati bhoktum,* he dislikes to eat); to be languid or weary, to feel tired, to be exhausted, to fade away, lose one's strength, faint, despond, wane: Caus. P. *glāpayati* or *glapayati* (but the latter form never used with prepositions), to make unwilling or averse, to exhaust, tire; to injure; to cause to perish; (with or without *manas*) to make desponding; to become cast down or desponding.

Glapana, am, n. the act of wearying, making tired, exhaustion, relaxation.

Glātṛi, tā, trī, tṛi, one who is tired or exhausted.

Glāna, as, ā, am, wearied, languid, feeble, emaciated, exhausted by fatigue or disease; sick; (*am*), n. exhaustion, disease.

Glāni, is, f. unwillingness, displeasure, depression of mind, exhaustion, fatigue of body, lassitude, languor; debility; sickness.

Glānya, am, n. decrease of strength, languor.

Glāyat, an, antī, at, being exhausted, wearied, languid, faint.

Glāva, as, m., N. of a man (with the metronymic Maitreya).

Glāvin, ī, inī, i, displeased, averse, inactive.

Glāsnu, us, us, u, exhausted by fatigue or disease, languid, wearied; [cf. Lat. *lassus.*]

Gleya, as, ā, am, to be wearied or exhausted, exhaustible.

ग्लौ *glau, aus,* m. (said to be fr. rt. *glai*), Ved. a round lump, a wen-like excrescence; or (according to other authorities) certain arteries or vessels of the heart, or perhaps certain lumps, parts of the flesh of the sacrificial victim [perhaps related to *globus* and *glomus,* cf. also *guḍa* and *gola*]; the moon; camphor; the earth. *Glau-kṛi,* cl. 8. P. *-karoti, -kartum,* to transform into the moon. *Glau-as,* cl. 2. P. *-asti* and *glau-bhū,* cl. 1. P. *bhavati, -vitum,* to become (like) the moon.

ग्लौचुकायनक *glaućukāyanaka, as, ikā, am,* belonging to Glućukāyani [cf. *glućuka*], a worshipper of Glućukāyani; [cf. the Gr. Γλαυκανῖκαι.]

ग्व *gva* (at the end of a compound) in *atithi-gva, eta-gva, daśa-gva, nava-gva,* q. v.

ग्विन् *gvin.* Cf. *śata-gvin.*

घ

घ 1. *gha,* the fourth consonant of the Sanskrit alphabet, being the aspirate of the preceding letter, and having the sound of *gh* in *loghouse.* — *Gha-kāra, as,* m. the letter or sound *gha.*

घ 2. *gha,* ind. (a particle used to lay stress on a word), at least, surely, verily, indeed, (corresponding to the Gr. γε.) This word occurs often in the Ṛig-veda, elsewhere rarely; the final vowel is generally lengthened in the Saṃhitā, but the original form given in the Pada-pāṭha is always *gha;* it is connected with other particles (as *ćid, uta, id*), and appears often after pronouns at the beginning of a Pāda, after prepositions, and after the negative particle *na.* Frequently this particle occurs in the clause which depends on a conditional or relative sentence (e. g. *ā ghā gamad yadi śravat,* he will surely come when he hears).

घ 3. *gha, as, ā, am* (fr. rt. *han*), striking, killing [cf. *jīva-gha, tāḍa-gha, pāṇi-gha, rāja-gha*]; (*as*), m. a rattling, gurgling, or tinkling sound; a bell; (*ā*), f. striking, killing, a stroke; a tinkling ornament worn by women round the waist.

घ 4. *gha, as, ā, am* (fr. rt. *ghṛi*), wetting, sprinkling (?).

घंष् *ghaṅsh* and *ghaṇs,* cl. 1. A. *ghaṅshate, ghaṅsate,* to diffuse lustre or splendor; to flow; to stream.

घग्घ् *ghaggh* and *ghagh,* cl. 1. P. *ghagghati* and *ghaghati,* to laugh; laugh at; deride.

घट् *ghaṭ* or *ghaṇṭ,* cl. 1. A. *ghaṭate, jaghaṭe, ghaṭishyate, aghaṭishṭa, ghaṭitum,* to be intently occupied about anything, to be busy with, to strive or endeavour after, to exert one's self for (with loc., dat., acc., or inf., e. g. *asmākam arthe ghaṭatc,* he is occupied about our business; *tām trātuṃ ghaṭasva,* strive to rescue her); to reach, come to; to happen, take place, be possible: Caus. *ghaṭayati, -yitum,* to join together, connect, bring together, unite; to put on, place on, lay on (with loc.); to bring near, place near, procure; to effect, accomplish, produce, make, form, fashion; to impel; to exert one's self; to rub, graze, touch, move, agitate; *ghāṭayati, -yitum*, to hurt, injure; to unite or put together; to speak, shine.

Ghaṭa, as, ā, am, exerting one's self, intently occupied or busy with; (*as*), m. a jar, pitcher, jug, large earthen water-jar, ewer, watering-pot; an attribute of the nineteenth Arhat of the Jainas (?); the sign of the zodiac Aquarius; a measure equal to 1 Droṇa, or (according to other authorities) equal to 20 Droṇas; a part of a column; a peculiar form of a temple; an elephant's frontal sinus; a border; suspending the breath as a religious exercise [cf. *kumbha*]; (*ā*), f. effort, endeavour, an assembly; a number, a collection, an assemblage; a troop of elephants assembled for martial purposes; (*ī*), f. a small water-jar, a ewer (in this sense also *ghaṭi, is*, f.); a period of time = 24 minutes; the Gharī or Indian clock, a plate of iron or mixed metal on which the hours are struck; [cf. *kumbha* and *dur-ghaṭa*.] — *Ghaṭa-karpara, as*, m. the fragments of a pot; N. of the author of a highly artificial poem, which is also called *ghaṭa-karparam*, n., (according to other authorities the title of the poem is Yamaka-kāvya); the poet Ghaṭa-karpara appears among the nine gems of king Vikramāditya. — *Ghaṭa-kāra, as*, m. or *ghaṭa-kṛit, t*, m. a potter. — *Ghaṭa-graha, as, ā, am*, who or what takes a water-pot, a water-bearer. — *Ghaṭa-dāsī*, f. a bawd or procuress. — *Ghaṭa-prakshayaṇa, as*, m., N. of a man. — *Ghaṭa-bhava* = *ghaṭodbhava* (?). — *Ghaṭa-bhedanaka, as* or *am* (?), m. or n. (?), an instrument used in making pots. — *Ghaṭa-yoni, is*, m. an epithet of the sage Agastya, q. v. (born in a water-jar). — *Ghaṭa-rāja, as*, m. a large water-jar of baked clay. — *Ghaṭa-sṛiñjaya, ās*, m. pl., N. of a people. — *Ghaṭa-sthāpana, am*, n. placing a water-pot as a type of Durgā, an essential part of various Tāntrika ceremonies. — *Ghaṭāṭopa* (°*ṭa-āṭ*°), *as*, m. a covering for a carriage or any article of furniture. — *Ghaṭābha* (°*ṭa-ābhā*), *as*, m., N. of a Daitya. — *Ghaṭin-dhama, as, ā, am*, (*ghaṭin* = *ghaṭim* = *ghaṭīm*), one who blows into a jar or pot; (*as*), m. a potter. — *Ghaṭin-dhaya, as, ā, am*, one who drinks a pitcherful. — *Ghaṭī-kāra, as*, m. a potter. — *Ghaṭī-graha, as, ā, am*, who or what takes a small jar &c.; (*as*), m. a water-carrier. — *Ghaṭī-yantra, am*, n. (occasionally, to suit the metre, *ghaṭi-yantra*), the rope and bucket of a well, or any machine for raising water; [cf. *ara-ghaṭṭa* and *ara-ghaṭṭaka*.] — *Ghaṭotkaća* (°*ṭa-ut*°), *as*, m., N. of a Rākshasa, son of Bhīma or Bhīma-sena and of the Rākshasī Hiḍimbā, slain by Karṇa; N. of a Gupta king. — *Ghaṭotkaćāntaka* (°*ća-an*°), *as*, m. 'the slayer of Ghaṭotkaća,' epithet of Karṇa, natural brother of the Pāṇḍavas. — *Ghaṭodara* (°*ṭa-ud*°), *as*, m., N. of an attendant of Varuṇa, also of a Rākshasa and of a Daitya; [cf. *kumbhodara*.] — *Ghaṭodbhava* (°*ṭa-ud*°), *as*, m. an epithet of Agastya, q. v. — *Ghaṭodhnī* (°*ṭa-ūdh*°), f. a cow with a full udder; [see *ūdhas, pīnodhnī*, &c.; Gram. 778.]

Ghaṭaka, as, ikā, am, exerting one's self; forming a constituent part, constituting a substantial part; (*as*), m. a tree that produces fruit without apparent flowers; a match-maker, an agent, who ascertains or invents genealogies and negociates matrimonial alliances, a genealogist; [cf. *ghaṭa-dāsī*.]

Ghaṭana, am, ā, n. f. striving after, effort, exertion; motion; happening, occurring; accomplishment; making, effecting, forming, fashioning; joining, mixing, assembling, bringing together, bringing about.

Ghaṭayitavya, as, ā, am, to be joined or united; to be locked.

Ghaṭika, as, ā, am, crossing a river on a jar (?); (*as*), m. a waterman; (*ā*), f. a water-jar, a bucket, a pot; a period of time = 24 minutes [cf. *ghaṭī*]; (according to other authorities equal to 1 Muhūrta, i.e. 48 minutes, or = 1 Kalā); the ancle [cf. *ghuṭikā*]; (*am*), n. the hip, the posteriors.

Ghaṭita, as, ā, am, planned, devised, attempted; happened, occurred; joined, united, connected, contiguous, in contact with; produced, effected, exerted; made, made of. *Ghaṭita-tvāt*, from the taking place, because of the occurrence.

Ghaṭin, ī, m. the sign of the zodiac Aquarius.

घटरिका *ghaṭarikā*, in *ava-ghaṭarikā*, f. a kind of Vīṇā or Indian lute; [cf. *ghāṭarī*.]

घटिघट *ghaṭighaṭa, as*, m. an epithet of Śiva; [cf. *ghaṇṭa*.]

घट्ट *ghaṭṭ*, cl. 1. A. and 10. P. *ghaṭṭate, ghaṭṭayati, jaghaṭṭe, ghaṭṭitum*, to rub (the hands) over, touch, shake, cause to move; to stir round, stir about; to press down, to smooth; to touch with words, to speak of spitefully or malignantly.

Ghaṭṭa, as, m. a Ghaṭ, a quay or landing-place, steps on the side of a river &c. leading to the water's edge, a bathing-place; (*ā*), f. a kind of metre; (*ī*), f. a small or inferior landing-place, private stairs &c.; [cf. *ara-ghaṭṭa* and *ara-ghaṭṭaka*.] — *Ghaṭṭa-gā*, f., N. of a river. — *Ghaṭṭa-jīvin, ī*, m. a ferry-man (commonly Pāṭuni, the son of a washerman and of a Vaiśya woman); an attendant at a landing-place who takes care of the clothes of the bathers &c. — *Ghaṭṭānanda* (°*ṭṭā-ān*°), *as* or *am* (?), m. or n. (?), a kind of metre.

Ghaṭṭana, am, ā, n. f. pushing, touching, rubbing or striking together, going, moving, practice, business, means of living; stirring round or about.

Ghaṭṭitṛi, tā, trī, tṛi, one who exerts himself, (the sense of this word connects it with rt. *ghaṭ*.)

घण *ghaṇ*, cl. 8. P. A. *ghaṇoti, -ṇute*, &c., to shine; (a various reading for *ghṛiṇ*.)

घण्ट् *ghaṇṭ*, cl. 1. P. and 10. P. *ghaṇṭati* and *ghaṇṭayati*, &c., to speak; shine.

घण्ट *ghaṇṭa, as*, m. (said to be fr. rt. *han*, perhaps related to *ghaṭa* above), a N. of Śiva [cf. *a-ghaṇṭa, dhaṭin* or *ghaṭin* (?), *ghaṇṭin*, and *ćaṇḍika-ghaṇṭa*], a kind of dish [cf. *matsya-ghaṇṭa*]; a sort of sauce, vegetables made into a pulp and mixed with turmeric and mustard seeds and capsicums; (*ā*), f. a bell; also a plate of iron or mixed metal struck as a clock, (a form *ghaṇṭi* occurs in *kshudra-ghaṇṭī*, a small bell); N. of several plants, = *ghaṇṭā-pāṭali*; another plant, Sida Cordifolia and Rhombifolia; also Uraria Lagopodioides; also Achyranthes Aspera [cf. *apāmārga*]; (*ī*), f. a N. of Durgā, as having a clear voice (?). — *Ghaṇṭa-phalaka, as* or *am* (?), m. or n. (?), a shield with a ringing sound, or a shield furnished with small bells. (*Ghaṇṭa* = *ghaṇṭā*?). — *Ghaṇṭā-karṇa, as*, m. one who has ears as broad as a bell, or whose ears are decorated with bells; N. of an attendant of Skanda; also one of Śiva's attendants, who is supposed to preside over cutaneous complaints, and is worshipped for exemption from them in the month Caitra; N. of a Piśāća attendant on Kuvera. — *Ghaṇṭāgāra* (°*ṭā-āg*°), *am*, n. a belfry. — *Ghaṇṭā-tāḍa, as*, m. a bell-man, one who strikes a bell or Gharī. — *Ghaṇṭā-tāḍana, am*, n. striking a bell. — *Ghaṇṭā-nāda, as*, m. the sound of a bell &c. — *Ghaṇṭā-patha, as*, m. the chief road through a village, a highway, (i. e. the bell-road, or that by which elephants &c., decorated with tinkling ornaments, proceed); N. of Mallinātha's commentary on the Kirātārjunīya. — *Ghaṇṭā-pāṭali, is*, m., N. of a plant, commonly called Ghaṇṭāpārali, a species of the trumpet-flower with bell-shaped blossoms, Bignonia Suaveolens. — *Ghaṇṭābha* (°*ṭā-ābhā*), *as*, m., N. of a Daitya; (a various reading for *ghaṭābha*, q. v.) — *Ghaṇṭā-rava, as*, m. the sound of a bell; (*ā*), f. Crotolaria of various species. — *Ghaṇṭālī* (°*ṭā-ālī*), f., N. of several cucurbitaceous plants; [cf. *kośātakī*.] — *Ghaṇṭā-vat, ān, atī, at*, furnished with a bell or with bells. — *Ghaṇṭā-vādya, am*, n. the sound of a clock. — *Ghaṇṭā-vīja, am*, n. the tree Croton Jamalgota, commonly Jamālgoṭā; the nut of this tree. — *Ghaṇṭā-śabda, as*, m. bell-metal, brass; the sound of a bell. — *Ghaṇṭā-svana, as*, m. the sound of a bell or clock. — *Ghaṇṭeśvara* (°*ṭā-īś*°), *as*, m., N. of a son of Maṅgala (Mars) and Medhā. — *Ghaṇṭodara* (°*ṭa-ud*°), *as*, m., N. of an attendant of Varuṇa &c.; (a various reading for *ghaṭodara*, q. v.)

Ghaṇṭaka or *ghaṇṭāka, as*, m., N. of a plant, = *ghaṇṭā-pāṭali*.

Ghaṇṭikā, f. a small bell [cf. *kshudra-ghaṇṭikā*]; the uvula or soft palate.

Ghaṇṭin, ī, inī, i, furnished with bells, sounding like a bell; an epithet of Śiva; [cf. *ghaṇṭa*.] — *Ghaṇṭinī-vīja, am*, n. the tree Croton Jamalgota; [cf. *ghaṇṭā-vīja*.]

Ghaṇṭu, us, m. a string of bells tied on an elephant's chest &c. by way of ornament; heat, light, &c.; [cf. *nighaṇṭu*.]

Ghāṇṭika, as, m. a bell-ringer, a strolling ballad-singer who carries a bell; a bard who sings in chorus, and especially in honour of the gods, ringing a bell in presence of their images; the plant Datura Fastuosa.

घण्ड *ghaṇḍa, as*, m. a bee; [cf. *ghuṇḍa*.]

घतन *ghatana*. See *ghātana* under *ghāta*.

घन *ghana, as, ā, am* (fr. rt. *han*), who or what slays or strikes or crushes (in these senses Ved.); compact, solid, material, hard, firm; coarse, gross; viscid, thick, inspissated; full, densely packed; following closely or in uninterrupted series, uninterrupted, permanent, eternal; impenetrable; dark; deep (as sound); taken in the mass, collective, complete, all; very, much; auspicious, fortunate; (*as*), m. slaying; an iron club, mace, weapon shaped like a hammer (in these senses Ved.); any compact mass or substance; a cloud; talc; the bulbous root of the plant Cyperus Hexastychus Communis; phlegm [cf. *kapha*]; the body; the cube of a number (in arithmetic), a solid body or cube (in geometry); extension, diffusion; a collection, multitude, assemblage, mass, quantity; a method of reciting the Ṛig and Yajur-veda; (*ā*), f., N. of two plants, = *māsha-parṇī* and *rudra-jaṭā*; (*am*), n. a cymbal, a bell, a gong, &c.; any brazen or metallic instrument or plate which is struck as a clock &c.; iron; tin; skin, rind, bark, the fragrant bark of Laurus Cassia; a mode of dancing, neither quick nor slow. — *Ghana-kapha, as*, m. hail; [cf. *ghanopala*.] — *Ghana-kāla, as*, m. the rainy season. — *Ghana-garjita, am*, n. the roar of thunder, a deep loud roar. — *Ghana-golaka, as*, m. an alloy of gold and silver. — *Ghana-ghana, as*, m. the cube of a cube. — *Ghana-ghanaugha* (°*na-ogh*°), *as*, m. a gathering of dark clouds. — *Ghana-ćaya, as*, m. a collection of clouds, cumulus. — *Ghana-ććhada, as, ā, am*, involved in clouds. — *Ghana-jambāla, as*, m. a quantity of mire, a slough. — *Ghana-jāla, am*, n. a gathering of clouds. — *Ghana-jvālā*, f. lightning, a flash of lightning. — *Ghana-tā*, f. compactness. — *Ghana-tāla, as*, m. a kind of bird, = *sāraṅga*; [cf. also *ghana-tola*.] — *Ghana-timira, am*, n. the darkness of clouds, great darkness. — *Ghana-toya, as*, m. a particular sea having thick water; [cf. *ghanoda*.] — *Ghana-tola, as*, m. the bird Ćātaka. — *Ghana-tva, am*, n. or *ghana-tā*, f. compactness, firmness; thickness, coarseness, solidity. — *Ghana-druma, as*, m., N. of a plant; [cf. *vi-kaṇṭaka*.] — *Ghana-dhātu, us*, m. lymph. — *Ghana-dhvani, is, is, i*, roaring, who or what makes a roaring; (*is*), m. a deep and low tone, a roar; the muttering of thunder clouds. — *Ghana-nābhi, is*, m. smoke (being supposed to be a principal ingredient in clouds). — *Ghana-nīhāra, as*, m. thick hoar-frost or mist. — *Ghana-pattra, as*, m., N. of a plant, = *punar-navā*. — *Ghana-pada, am*, n. the cube root. — *Ghana-padavī*, f. the path of the clouds, the sky. — *Ghana-payodhara, as*, m. a firm breast. — *Ghana-pallava, as*, m. the plant Guilandina

Moringa; [cf. *śobhāñjana.*] — *Ghana-pāshaṇḍa*, *as*, m. a peacock, (this bird being supposed to delight in cloudy and rainy weather.) — *Ghana-phala*, *am*, n. (in geom.) the solid or cubical contents of a body or of an excavation compared to a cube; (*as*), m., N. of a plant; [cf. *vi-kaṇṭaka.*] — *Ghana-mala*, *am*, n. deep (thunder) and sin. — *Ghana-mūla*, *am*, n. (in arithm.) cube root; (*as*), m., N. of a plant; [cf. *moraṭa.*] — *Ghana-rava*, *as*, m. the roaring of clouds, thunder. — *Ghana-rasa*, *as*, m. a thick juice; extract, decoction; camphor; N. of two plants, = *moraṭa* and *pīlu-parṇī; (as* or *am*), m. n. the fluid of the clouds, water. — *Ghana-ruć*, *k*, *k*, *k*, shining like a cloud (with lightning), cloud-like. — *Ghana-rućira-kalāpa*, *as*, m. (a peacock) having a tail glistening like a cloud. — *Ghana-vara*, *am*, n. the face; [cf. *ghanottama.*] — *Ghana-varga*, *as*, m. the square of a cube; the sixth power. — *Ghana-vartman*, *a*, n. the path of the clouds, the sky, air. — *Ghana-vallikā*, f. lightning; (the creeper of the clouds.) — *Ghana-vallī*, f. lightning; N. of a plant, = *amṛita-savā*. — *Ghana-vāta*, *as*, m. a thick oppressive atmosphere or air (constituting a kind of hell); one of the regions of hell (?). — *Ghana-vāsa*, *as*, m. a kind of pumpkin-gourd; [cf. *kushmāṇḍa.*] — *Ghana-vāhana*, *as*, m. an epithet of Śiva, and also of Indra (who rides on the clouds). — *Ghana-vīthi*, *is*, f. the path of the clouds, the air; a line of clouds. — *Ghana-vyapāya*, *as*, m. the disappearance of the clouds; autumn. — *Ghana-vyūha*, *as*, m., N. of a Sūtra work. — *Ghana-śabda*, *as*, m. the noise of clouds, thunder. — *Ghana-śyāma*, *as*, *ā*, *am*, deep black, dark (as heavy clouds); (*as*), m. an epithet of Rāma, and also of Kṛishṇa; N. of a copyist of the last century, with the epithet Tripāṭhin. — *Ghana-saṃvṛitti*, *is*, f. profound secrecy. — *Ghana-samaya*, *as*, m. the rainy season. — *Ghana-sāra*, *as*, m. camphor; mercury, or some peculiar form of it (?); water; a kind of tree. — *Ghana-skandha*, *as*, m., N. of a plant; [cf. *kośāmra.*] — *Ghana-svana*, *as*, m. low thunder, the muttering of clouds; the plant Amaranthus Polygamus. — *Ghana-hasta-saṅkhyā*, f. (in geom.) the contents of an excavation; or of a solid alike in figure. — *Ghanākara* (°*na-āk*°), *as*, m. the rainy season. — *Ghanāgama* (°*na-āg*°), *as*, m. the approach of the clouds, the rainy season. — *Ghanāghana*, *as*, *ā*, *am*, fond of slaughter, easily striking down, fond of strife, mischievous, cruel; even, uniform, without spaces or interstices, compact; (*as*), m. an epithet of Indra; a vicious elephant, or one in rut; a thick or rainy cloud; mutual collision or contact; (*ā*), f. Solanum Indicum; [cf. *kāka-māćī.*] — *Ghanāñjana* (°*na-añ*°), *am*, n. gross ignorance. — *Ghanāñjanī* (°*na-añj*°), f. an epithet of Durgā. — *Ghanātyaya* (°*na-aty*°), *as*, m. the disappearance or departure of the clouds, the season succeeding the rains, autumn. — *Ghanānta* (°*na-anta*), *as*, m. the end of the rains, autumn. — *Ghanāmaya* (°*na-ām*°), *as*, m. the date tree, Phœnix Sylvestris; [cf. *kharjūra.*] — *Ghanāmala* (°*na-am*°), *as*, m. a kind of pot-herb, Chenopodium Album; [cf. *vāstūka.*] — *Ghanāmbu* (°*na-am*°), n. rain. — *Ghanāruṇa* (°*na-ar*°), *as*, *ā*, *am*, deep red. — *Ghanāruddha* (°*na-ār*°), *as*, *ā*, *am*, overspread with clouds. — *Ghanāvaruddha* (°*na-av*°), *as*, *ā*, *am*, 'the abode of clouds,' overspread with clouds. — *Ghanāśraya* (°*na-āś*°), *as*, m. ether, the atmosphere, the heavens, the firmament. — *Ghanottama* (°*na-ut*°), *am*, n. the face (the best part of the *ghana* or body); [cf. *ghana-vara.*] — *Ghanoda* (°*na-uda*), *as*, m. a particular sea having thick or viscid water; [cf. *ghana-toya.*] — *Ghanodadhi* (°*na-ud*°), *is*, m. the viscid sea (constituting a kind of hell); a division of hell (?). — *Ghanoparuddha* (°*na-up*°), *as*, *ā*, *am*, clouded, overcast. — *Ghanopala* (°*na-up*°), *as*, m. hail; [cf. *ghana-kapha.*] — *Ghanaugha* (°*na-ogha*), *as*, m. a gathering of clouds.

Ghanī-kṛi, cl. 8. P. *-karoti*, *-kartum*, to harden, thicken, solidify, congeal. — *Ghanī-kṛita*, *as*, *ā*, *am*, hardened, compacted, made solid or firm; congealed, thickened, condensed.

Ghanī-bhāva, *as*, m. the becoming hardened, compact or thick, thickening. — *Ghanī-bhūta*, *as*, *ā*, *am*, become thick, thickened, condensed, thick, congealed, inspissated, compact.

Ghanīya, nom. P. *ghanīyati*, *-yitum*, to long for solid food.

घम्ब् *ghamb*, cl. 1. A. *ghambate*, &c., to move, go.

घर् *ghar*, cl. 10. P. *ghārayati*, *-yitum*, to cover.

घरट्ट *gharaṭṭa*, *as*, m. a grindstone.

घर्घट *gharghaṭa*, *as*, m. a kind of fish, Pimelodus Gagora or Tengara; [cf. *gargara*, *gargaraka*, *gargāṭa.*]

घर्घर *gharghara*, *as*, *ā*, *am* (an onomatopoetic word implying an indistinct sound, especially in the throat), uttered with an indistinct gurgling or purring sound; (*as*), m. an indistinct murmur, a low murmuring or gurgling sound, the crackling of fire, rattling of a carriage, creaking, &c.; laughter, mirth; an owl; a fire of straw or chaff; a door, gate; a sliding or folding door or curtain (?); the pass of a mountain (?); the N. of a river, the Gogra or Ghogra; (*ā*), f. a bell hanging on the neck of a horse; (*ā*, *ī*), f. a bell used as an ornament; a girdle of small bells or tinkling ornaments worn by women; a kind of lute; (*as*, *ā*, *am*), m. f. n. one of the tones or notes in music. — *Gharghara-rava*, *as*, m. a tinkling sound, the sound of small bells.

Ghargharaka, *as*, m., N. of a river, = *gharghara; (ikā)*, f. bells used as an ornament; a short stick for striking several kinds of musical instruments; a kind of musical instrument; fried grain; N. of a river; an ornament of small bells.

Ghargharita, *am*, n. the grunting of a pig &c.

घर्घुर्घा *gharghurghā*, f. a sort of insect found in wood, = *yama-kīṭa;* [cf. *ghurghura.*]

घर्ब् *gharb*, cl. 1. P. *gharbati*, *-bitum*, to move, to go.

घर्म *gharma*, *as*, m. (fr. rt. *ghṛi* or *ghṛiṇ*), heat, warmth (of the sun as well as of fire), sunshine; the hot season, internal heat; sweat, perspiration; a cauldron, a boiler, saucepan, &c., especially the vessel in which the milk-offering to the Aśvins is boiled; a cavity in the earth shaped like a cauldron or boiler, an excavation; a crater; hot milk or any other hot beverage offered as an oblation, especially to the Aśvins; N. of a son of Anu and father of Ghṛita; *gharma-tanū*, du., N. of a Sāman; [cf. Gr. θέρμη; Zend *garĕma;* Goth. *varmja;* Germ. *warm.*] — *Gharma-ćarćikā*, f. eruptions caused by heat and suppressed perspiration. — *Gharma-ććheda*, *as*, m. cessation of the heat. — *Gharma-tapta*, *as*, *ā*, *am*, perspiring. — *Gharma-dīdhiti*, *is*, m. 'having warm rays,' the sun; [cf. *śītāṇśu.*] — *Gharma-dugha*, *as*, *ā*, *am*, or *gharma-duh*, *-dhuk*, *k*, *k*, Ved. giving warm milk or the substance used for the offering. — *Gharma-dyuti*, *is*, m. 'having warm radiance,' the sun. — *Gharma-payas*, *as*, n. perspiration; warm water. — *Gharma-pāvan*, *ā*, *arī*, *a*, Ved. drinking hot milk. — *Gharma-māsa*, *as*, m. a month of the hot season. — *Gharma-raśmi*, *is*, m. the sun; heat, radiance; [cf. *gharma-dīdhiti.*] — *Gharma-vat*, *ān*, *atī*, *at*, Ved. possessed of heat, an epithet of Indra. — *Gharma-vićarćikā*, f. cutaneous eruptions or pimples from heat and suppressed perspiration; [cf. *gharma-ćarćikā.*] — *Gharma-sad*, *t*, *t*, *t*, Ved. sitting near the fire or living in the heat (of the sky), an epithet of the manes. — *Gharma-stubh*, *p*, *p*, *p*, Ved. assuaging the heat, an epithet of the Maruts. — *Gharma-svaras*, *ās*, *ās*, *as*, Ved. breathing out heat; (Sāy.) sounding high or shrill (= *dīpta-dhvani*). — *Gharma-sveda*, *as*, *ā*, *am*, Ved. perspiring with heat, or one whose sweat is milk; (Sāy.) coming with splendor or showering down water or coming to the oblation. — *Gharmāṇśu* (°*ma-aṇśu*), *us*, m. the sun; [cf. *gharma-dīdhiti.*] — *Gharmānta* (°*ma-an*°), *as*, m. the end of the hot season, the beginning of the rainy season. — *Gharmānta-kāmukī*, f. a small white bird, a kind of crane; [cf. *valākā.*] — *Gharmāmbu* (°*ma-am*°), n. sweat, perspiration. — *Gharmāmbhas* (°*ma-am*°), *as*, n. perspiration. — *Gharmārta* (°*ma-ār*°), *as*, *ā*, *am*, suffering from heat. — *Gharmodaka* (°*ma-ud*°), *am*, n. warm water, perspiration.

Gharmin, *ī*, *iṇī*, *i*, Ved. one who has prepared the Gharma offering, engaged in preparing the Gharma.

Gharmya, *as*, *ā*, *am*, Ved. being in the Gharma or milk-vessel.

घर्ष *gharsha*, *gharshaṇa*, &c. See under rt. *ghṛish*, p. 309.

घस् *ghas* (according to Pāṇini II. 4, 37, a defective verb only used to supply certain tenses of *ad*, such as the Aor. and Desid.), cl. 2. and 1. P. *ghasti* and *ghasati:* Impf. 2nd sing. *aghas* or *aghat;* 2nd pl. *aghasta:* Perf. *jaghasa*, *jaghasitha*, *jaghāsa;* 3rd pl. *jakshus* (Part. Perf. *jakshivas*, fem. *jakshushī*); *aghasat*, *ghatsyati*, *ghastum*, to consume, devour, eat: Desid. *jighatsati*, to wish to consume or devour, wish to eat; [cf. rt. *jaksh* and *gras;* cf. also Gr. γαστήρ; Lat. *gustus.*]

Ghasa, *as*, m. the eater or devourer; N. of a kind of demon; also of a Rākshasa; [cf. *mahā-ghasa* and *pra-ghasa.*]

Ghasi, *is*, m., Ved. food, victuals; [cf. *ghāsi.*]

Ghasmara, *as*, *ā*, *am*, voracious, gluttonous; (*as*), m., N. of a deer (or a Brāhman changed into a deer).

Ghasra, *as*, *ā*, *am*, hurtful, injurious, mischievous, = *hiṇsra;* (*as*), m. a day [cf. *ghraṇsa*]; (*am*), n. saffron.

Ghāsa, *as*, m. food, meadow or pasture grass; [cf. *aśva-ghāsa* and *pūti-ghāsa.*] — *Ghāsa-kūṭa*, *am*, n. a hay-rick. — *Ghāsa-sthāna*, *am*, n. pasture, pasturage, food. — *Ghāse-ajra*, *as*, *ā*, *am*, Ved. impelling to consume, i. e. inviting or exciting appetite.

Ghāsaka, (at the end of an adj. comp.) food, victuals.

Ghāsi, *is*, m. fire or its deity (the all-consuming).

घाट *ghāṭa*, *as*, *ā*, m. f. the nape or back of the neck, the cervical ligament; (*as*), m. a pitcher, a pot (? for *ghaṭa*); [cf. *kara-ghāṭa.*] — *Ghāṭa-karkarī*, f. a kind of lute.

Ghāṭari, f. a kind of lute; [cf. *ghaṭarikā.*]

Ghāṭika, *as*, m. = *ghāṇṭika;* (*ā*), f. the nape or back of the neck; also incorrectly used for *ghaṭikā*, q. v.

घाटाल *ghāṭāla*, *as*, *ā*, *am* (a wrong form for *ghaṇṭāla*), bell-shaped (?).

घाण्टिक *ghāṇṭika*. See under *ghaṇṭā*.

घात *ghāta*, *as*, *ā*, *am* (fr. rt. *han*), killing; (*as*), m. a blow, a bruise, slaying, killing, murdering, slaughter; striking, wounding, hurting, destruction; an arrow; the product (of a sum in multiplication); [cf. *karma-ghāta* and *grāma-ghāta.*] — *Ghāta-kara*, *as*, *ī*, *am*, murderous, destructive. — *Ghāta-ćandra*, *as*, m. the moon when in an inauspicious mansion. — *Ghāta-tithi*, *is*, f. an inauspicious lunar day. — *Ghāta-nakshatra*, *am*, n. an inauspicious Nakshatra. — *Ghāta-vāra*, *as*, m. an inauspicious day of the week. — *Ghāta-sthāna*, *am*, n. a slaughter-house, a place of execution.

Ghātaka, *as*, *ī*, *am*, killing, a killer, a murderer; destroying, a destroyer (used at the end of comp.; cf. *viśvāsa-ghātaka*).

Ghātana or *ghatana*, *as*, *ā*, *am*, killing, a murderer, a killer; (*as*), m., N. of certain inhabitants of hell; (*ī*), f. a kind of club; (*am*), n. striking, slaying, killing, slaughter, immolating. — *Ghātana-sthāna*, *am*, n. a place of slaughter, a slaughter-house.

Ghātayat, *an*, *antī*, *at*, striking, hurting, killing.

Ghātavya, *as*, *ā*, *am*, to be killed, what may or ought to be killed &c., deserving death.

Ghāti, *is*, m. striking, killing in general; catching

or killing birds, fowling [cf. *ni-ghāti, ghāti-pakshin, ghāti-vihaga*]; (*is*), f. a bird-net. — *Ghāti-pakshin, ī,* m. or *ghāti-vihaga, as,* m. a hawk or falcon.

Ghātin, ī, inī, i, killing, murderous, who or what strikes or kills, a murderer; destroying, destructive, felonious; [cf. *andhaka-ghātin, amitra-gh°, ardhaka-gh°, kumāra-gh°,* &c.]

Ghātuka, as, ī, am, killing, tearing asunder, hurting, hurtful, mischievous; cruel, savage, violent, ferocious.

Ghātya, as, ā, am, to be killed, proper or fit to be killed.

घार *ghāra.* See under rt. *ghṛi.*

घार्तिक *ghārtika, as,* m. (fr. *ghṛita*), pulse ground and fried with clarified butter, a cake prepared with Ghṛita or clarified butter.

Ghārteya, ās, m. pl., N. of a warrior-tribe; (*as*), m. the prince of this tribe.

घास *ghāsa.* See under rt. *ghas.*

घिण्ण् *ghiṇṇ,* cl. 1. A. *ghiṇṇate, jighiṇṇe, ghiṇṇitum,* to take, grasp; [cf. *ghuṇṇ* and *ghṛiṇṇ.*]

घु 1. *ghu,* cl. 1. A. *ghavate,* &c., to utter a peculiar sound, to sound.

2. *ghu, us,* m. a kind of sound.

घुंष् *ghuṇsh,* cl. 1. A. *ghuṇshate,* &c., to diffuse lustre.

घुट् *ghuṭ,* cl. 6. P. *ghuṭati, jughoṭa, ghuṭitum,* to strike again or retaliate, to resist, oppose; to protect, preserve; cl. 1. A. *ghoṭate, jughuṭe, ghoṭishyate, aghuṭat* and *aghoṭishṭa, ghoṭitum,* to come back, to return; to barter, exchange.

Ghuṭa, as, m. or *ghuṭi, is,* f. or *ghuṭī,* f. the ancle.

Ghuṭika, as, ā, m. f. the ancle.

Ghuṇṭa, as, m. or *ghuṇṭaka, as,* m. or *ghuṇṭikā,* f. the ancle.

घुड् *ghuḍ,* cl. 6. P. *ghuḍati,* &c., to prevent, defend, protect.

घुण् *ghuṇ* (related to *ghūrṇ:* cf. *ghol*), cl. 1. A. *ghoṇate, jughuṇe, ghoṇitum,* &c., or cl. 6. P. *ghuṇati, jughoṇa,* &c., to move to and fro, stagger, shake.

Ghuṇa, as, m. a peculiar kind of insect found in timber; the pangolin or armadillo. — *Ghuṇa-kīṭuka, as,* m. = the preceding. — *Ghuṇa-vallabhā,* f., N. of a plant; [cf. *ati-vishā.*] — *Ghuṇākshara* (°*ṇa-ak*°), *am,* n. an incision in wood or in the leaf of a book caused by an insect or book-worm and resembling somewhat the form of a letter. — *Ghuṇākshara-nyāyena,* ind. in a fortuitous and unexpected manner, by a happy chance.

Ghuṇi, is, is, i, worm-eaten (?).

Ghuṇḍa, as, m. a large black bee.

घुण्टिक *ghuṇṭika, am,* n. cow-dung found in thickets.

घुण्ण् *ghuṇṇ,* cl. 1. A. *ghuṇṇate, jughuṇṇe, ghuṇṇitum,* to seize; [cf. *ghiṇṇ* and *ghṛiṇṇ.*]

घुर् *ghur,* cl. 6. P. *ghurati,* &c., to frighten with cries, to cry out through fear, utter cries of distress; to be frightful or terrible; to sound; [cf. *ghora.*]

Ghuraṇa, as, m. sound.

घुरघुराय *ghuraghurāya,* nom. A. *-ghurāyate,* to utter gurgling sounds, to wheeze, snort or grunt like a hog; [cf. *gharghara* and the next.]

घुर्घुर *ghurghura, as,* m. (an onomatopoetic word), a kind of worm, burrowing in the skin, guinea-worm, Dracunculus; (*ī*), f. the mole-cricket [cf. *mṛit-kirā*]; (*ā*), f. growling, as of a dog or cat.

Ghurghuraka, as, m. or (*ikā*), f. a gurgling or murmuring sound.

Ghurghurāya, nom. A. *ghurghurāyate,* to whistle, murmur, hum, &c.

घुलघुलारव *ghulaghulā-rava, as,* m. a kind of pigeon.

घुलञ्च *ghulañća, as,* m. Coix Barbata; [cf. *gavedhukā.*]

घुष् 1. *ghush,* cl. 1. P. *ghoshati, jughosha, ghoshishyati, aghoshīt* and *aghushat, ghoshitum,* to sound, make any sound or noise; to cry or proclaim aloud, call out, announce publicly, declare; to fill with cries; (according to some) to kill: Caus. *ghoshayati, -yitum, ajūghushat,* to proclaim aloud, call to, invite; to cause to proclaim aloud; to praise: Desid. *jughushishati* or *jughoshishati:* Intens. *joghushyate, joghoshṭi.*

Ghusha, as, ā, am, sounding.

Ghushita, as, ā, am, sounded, declared, proclaimed.

Ghushṭa, as, ā, am, sounded, proclaimed. — *Ghushṭānna* (°*ṭa-anna*), *am,* n. food given away by proclamation.

Ghushṭra, am, n. a cart, a carriage; (fr. *ghush,* in the sense 'to creak?').

Ghushya, as, ā, am, giving out sounds; to be proclaimed aloud.

Ghosha, as, m. indistinct noise, tumult; the confused cries of a multitude, battle-cry, cries of victory, cries of woe or distress, any cry or sound; an exclamation, the roar of animals; the sound of a drum or of a conch-shell, of the Soma stones, of a carriage, &c.; the whizzing or whir of a bow-string, crackling of fire, singing in the ear; roaring of a storm, of thunder, of water, &c.; the sound of the recital of prayers; rumour, report; a proclamation; (in grammar) the soft sound or low murmur heard in the articulation of the soft or sonant consonants *g, gh, j, jh, ḍ, ḍh, d, dh, b, bh, ṅ, ñ, ṇ, n, m, h, y, r, l, v,* the vowels, and Anusvāra, which with the Yamas of the first ten of the soft consonants make up altogether forty sounds, (the absence of this soft sound or murmur being called *a-ghosha,* q. v., and applied to *k, kh, ć, ćh, ṭ, ṭh, t, th, p, ph,* the sibilants, Visarga, the Jihvā-mūlīya, and the Upadhmānīya, which with the Yamas of the first ten consonants make up twenty-six sounds); a vowel; a station of herdsmen; a herdsman; a gnat, a musquito; a creeping plant bearing white or yellow flowers, Luffa Fœtida or a similar plant [cf. *ghoshaka*]; brass, bell-metal, tutenag, &c.; N. of a man; an epithet of Śiva; a son of Lambā, daughter of Daksha, and wife of Dharma; N. of an Arhat; N. of a prince of the Kāṇva dynasty (for *ghosha-vasu*); a common N. for a Kāyastha or one of the writer-caste, &c.; N. of a country; a station of herdsmen in general; (*ī*), f. a kind of fennel, Anethum Sowa, another plant = *karkaṭa-śṛiṅgī;* N. of a woman, said to be a daughter of Kakshīvat; [cf. *ātma-ghosha, indra-gh°, uććair-gh°, jyā-gh°, pad-gh°, madhu-gh°, mahā-gh°.*] — *Ghosha-kṛit, t,* m. a person making a noise. — *Ghosha-koṭi, is,* f., N. of the peak of a mountain. — *Ghosha-buddha, as, ā, am,* Ved. made attentive by the sound. — *Ghosha-mati, is,* m., N. of a man. — *Ghosha-vat, ān, atī, at,* sounding, making a noise; (in grammar) sonant, uttered with the soft articulation, see above; (*vān*), m., N. of a man; (*vatī*), f. a lute (*vīṇā*); a peculiar kind of lute or N. of a lute. — *Ghosha-varṇa, as,* m. a sonant letter. — *Ghosha-vasu, us,* m., N. of a prince of the Kāṇva dynasty.

Ghoshaka, as, m. a crier, a proclaimer (e. g. in *paṭaha-gh°,* q. v.); the creeping plant Luffa Fœtida or a similar plant. — *Ghoshakākṛiti* (°*ka-āk*°), *is,* m. a plant with white blossoms, similar to the Ghoshaka, and perhaps a species of it, commonly called Hātighosha.

Ghoshaṇa, as, ā, am, sounding; (*am, ā*), n. f. speaking loud, making a great noise; crying, proclaiming aloud.

Ghoshaṇīya, as, ā, am, to be proclaimed aloud, to be publicly announced.

Ghoshayitnu, us, m. a crier, a proclaimer, a herald; a Brāhman; the Koil or Indian cuckoo; a captive (?).

Ghoshi, is, is, i, Ved. (according to Sāy.) either 'accompanied with noise,' or 'to be proclaimed aloud;' but *ghoshi* might also be considered as the 3rd pers. sing. of the Aor. Pass. fr. rt. *ghush.*

Ghoshin, ī, iṇī, i, sounding, noisy; (in grammar) having the soft sound or articulation, sonant, (opposed to *a-ghosha*); [cf. *grāma-ghoshin.*]

घुष् 2. *ghush* = *ghṛish,* q. v.

घुसृण *ghusṛiṇa, am,* n. saffron.

घूक *ghūka, as,* m. an owl. — *Ghūkāri* (°*ka-ari*), *is,* m. a crow (enemy of the owl). — *Ghūkāvāsa* (°*ka-āv*°), *as,* m., N. of a tree; [cf. *śākhoṭa.*]

घूर् *ghūr,* cl. 4. A. *ghūryate,* &c., to kill, hurt, or injure; to become old, to decay.

घूर्ण् *ghūrṇ,* cl. 6. P. or 1. A. *ghūrṇati* or *ghūrṇate,* &c., to move to and fro, to shake, to be agitated, to tremble, roll about, cause to whirl, whirl, turn round: Caus. P. *ghūrṇayati, -yitum,* to cause to move to and fro or shake.

Ghūrṇa, as, ā, am, shaking, moving to and fro; (*as*), m. a kind of pot-herb, Chironia Centauroides; turning round, whirling, rolling, &c. — *Ghūrṇa-vāyu, us,* m. a whirlwind.

Ghūrṇana, am, ā, n. f. shaking, revolving, whirling, turning round.

Ghūrṇamāna, as, ā, am, being agitated, shaking, trembling, revolving, turning round.

Ghūrṇāyamāna, as, ā, am, whirling, revolving, rolling, tossing.

Ghūrṇi, is, f. rolling, revolving, going round or over.

Ghūrṇikā, f., N. of a woman.

Ghūrṇita, as, ā, am, rolling, turning, tossing.

Ghūrṇyamāna, as, ā, am, being agitated, set in motion, made to go round.

घृ *ghṛi,* cl. 1. 3. 10. P. *gharati, jigharti, ghārayati, jaghāra, gharishyati, aghārshīt, ghartum,* &c., to sprinkle, besprinkle, sprinkle over; to wet or moisten; to distil; cl. 3. P., 5. P. A. *jighasti, ghṛiṇoti, -ṇute,* or *gharṇoti, -ṇute,* to shine; to burn; [cf. *ghṛiṇ.*]

Ghāra, as, m. sprinkling, besprinkling, wetting; (*ī*), f. a kind of metre consisting of four lines of four syllables each.

Ghṛita, as, ā, am, sprinkled; illumined; (*am*), n. clarified butter or butter which has been boiled gently and allowed to cool; it is then used for culinary and religious purposes and is highly esteemed by the Hindūs; it is now commonly called Ghee (*ghi* or *ghī*); butter, fat, fat as an emblem of fertility, especially fluid grease; cream; rain or rather fertilizing rain, considered as the fat which drops from heaven, water; (*ā*), f. a kind of tree [cf. *ghṛita-maṇḍā*]; (*as*), m., N. of a son of Dharma, grandson of Anu and father of Duduha. — *Ghṛita-karañja, as,* m. a kind of Karañja, = *ghṛita-parṇaka, tapasvin, pra-kīrya, vi-roćana, vishāri.* — *Ghṛita-kumārī* or *ghṛita-kumārikā,* f. the plant Aloe Indica, (this plant being supposed to resemble a virgin in delicacy and elegance.) — *Ghṛita-kumbha, as,* m. a jar of ghee. — *Ghṛita-keśa, as, ā, am,* Ved. one whose locks are unctuous, dropping with butter. — *Ghṛita-kauśika, as,* m., N. of a religious teacher. — *Ghṛita-ćyutā,* f., N. of a river; [cf. *ghṛita-śćut.*] — *Ghṛita-dīdhiti, is,* m. fire, the deity of fire (as receiving the clarified butter offered in sacrifice); another reading has *dhṛita-dīdhiti.* — *Ghṛita-duh, -dhuk, k, k,* Ved. giving butter or cream. — *Ghṛita-dhārā,* f., N. of a river. — *Ghṛita-nirṇij, k, k, k,* Ved. having a garment of fat, covered with fat; (Sāy.) shining with butter mixed (with the Soma). — *Ghṛita-pa, as, ā, am,* drinking Ghṛita, epithet of a class of Ṛishis. — *Ghṛita-padī,* adj. f., Ved. (according to the Brāhmaṇas) one whose path is Ghṛita; or, perhaps, one whose foot (*pād*) drops with Ghṛita, an epithet of Iḷā. — *Ghṛita-parṇaka, as,* m. = *ghṛita-karañja;* [cf. *ghṛita-pūrṇaka.*] — *Ghṛita-paśu, us,* m. ghee or clarified butter made into or supposed to resemble an animal to be offered at a sacrifice, a sacrificial victim represented by ghee. — *Ghṛita-pāvan, ā, arī, a,* Ved. drinking butter &c. — *Ghṛita-pīta, as, ā, am,* = *pīta-ghṛita,* one who has drunk butter &c. — *Ghṛita-pū, ūs, ūs, u,* Ved. clarifying butter &c. — *Ghṛita-pūra, as,* m. a sweetmeat composed of flour, milk, cocoa-nut, and ghee, &c. — *Ghṛita-pūrṇaka, as,* m. a sweetmeat composed of flour, milk, cocoa-nut, and ghee, &c.; the tree Pongamia Glabra; [cf. *karañja;* cf. also *ghṛita-parṇaka.*] — *Ghṛita-prić, k, k, k,* Ved. sprinkling unctuous or fertilizing fluid; (Sāy.) accompanied with fertilizing fluid. — *Ghṛita-prishṭha, as, ā, am,* Ved. one whose back or surface consists of Ghṛita; especially an epithet of Agni or his horses; (Sāy.) having a brilliant form or shining body; (*as*), m., N. of a son of Priya-vrata by Barhishmatī, and sovereign of Krauñća-dvīpa, also a N. of fire. — *Ghṛita-pratīka, as, ā, am,* Ved. one whose form is brilliant with Ghṛita; an epithet of Agni and of Ushas. — *Ghṛita-prayas, ās, ās, as,* Ved. relishing Ghṛita; (Sāy.) receiving oblations of food mixed with Ghṛita. — *Ghṛita-prasatta, as, ā, am,* Ved. propitiated with Ghṛita; epithet of Agni. — *Ghṛita-prāśa, as,* m. swallowing ghee. — *Ghṛita-prāśana, am,* n. tasting or swallowing ghee. — *Ghṛita-prī, īs, īs, i,* Ved. satisfied with butter, an epithet of Agni. — *Ghṛita-prush, ṭ, ṭ, ṭ,* Ved. sprinkling fat &c., filling with Ghṛita, i. e. spreading welfare and gifts. — *Ghṛita-pluta, as, ā, am,* sprinkled or smeared with ghee. — *Ghṛita-bhṛishṭa, as, ā, am,* baked or stewed in grease. — *Ghṛita-maṇḍa, as,* m. the scum of melted butter, the fattiest part of grease; (*ā*), f. a kind of medicinal plant (the scum of its infusion resembling ghee); [cf. *kākolī.*] — *Ghṛita-maṇḍalikā,* f., N. of a plant, = *hansa-padī.* — *Ghṛitamaṇḍoda* (°*ḍa-uda*), *as,* m., N. of a lake on the mountain Mandara. — *Ghṛita-yoni, is, is, i,* Ved. an epithet of Agni, abiding or living in Ghṛita &c.; producing fertilizing rain or welfare and happiness generally; (Sāy.) whose source is Ghṛita. — *Ghṛita-raudhīya, ās,* m. pl. the Raudhīyas who are desirous of Ghṛita. — *Ghṛita-lekhanī,* f. a ladle for ghee. — *Ghṛita-lolīkṛita, as, ā, am,* mixed with ghee, steeped in it. — *Ghṛita-vat, ān, atī, at,* Ved. greasy, abounding in fat; mixed or smeared with butter; an epithet, especially of Agni and Soma; containing the word Ghṛita (as a verse); (*vat*), ind. like clarified butter. — *Ghṛita-vara, as,* m. a sweetmeat, or flour &c. baked with ghee and sugar. — *Ghṛita-vartani, is, is, i,* Ved. whose tracks are in Ghṛita or sprinkle Ghṛita, an epithet of the chariot of the Aśvins. — *Ghṛita-varti, is,* f. a wick fed with grease. — *Ghṛita-vikrayin, ī,* m. a vender of ghee. — *Ghṛita-vṛiddha, as, ā, am,* Ved. delighted with Ghṛita, nourished with it; an epithet of Agni. — *Ghṛita-vrata, as, ā, am,* living only upon Ghṛita. — *Ghṛita-śćut, t, t, t,* Ved. sprinkling ghee. — *Ghṛita-śćun-nidhana, am,* n., N. of a Sāman. — *Ghṛita-śćyut, t, t, t,* Ved. distilling ghee. — *Ghṛitaśćyun-nidhana, am,* n., N. of a Sāman. — *Ghṛita-śrī, īs, īs, i,* Ved. mixed with Ghṛita, mixing ghee; (Sāy.) having recourse to Ghṛita. — *Ghṛita-sad, t, t, t,* Ved. abiding in Ghṛita. — *Ghṛita-sthalā,* f., N. of an Apsaras; [cf. *ṛita-sthalā* and *kratu-sthalā.*] — *Ghṛita-snā, ās, ās, am,* Ved. dropping fat. — *Ghṛita-snu, us, us, u,* Ved. bathed in Ghṛita, sprinkling it; epithet of Mitrā-Varuṇa, and of heaven and earth; one whose surface consists of Ghṛita. — *Ghṛita-spriś, k, k, k,* who or what touches Ghṛita. — *Ghṛita-hrada, as, ā, am,* Ved. (a lake) consisting of Ghṛita. — *Ghṛitākta* (°*ta-ak*°), *as, ā, am,* anointed with clarified butter, smeared with Ghṛita. — *Ghṛitāći, is,* m., N. of a man, (derived fr. the following.) — *Ghṛitāćī* (°*ta* + rt. *ać*), adj. f. greasy, abounding in Ghṛita; filled with grease; sprinkling Ghṛita or fertilizing fluid, shining with it, (often with and without *juhū,* f. or the sacrificial ladle with which the Ghṛita is taken up, poured out, &c.); an epithet of Sarasvatī &c.; (*ī*), f. the night (considered as moist and dewy); a kind of serpent (shining like grease); N. of an Apsaras, loved by Bharad-vāja, or Vyāsa, or Viśvā-mitra; wife of Pra-mati and mother of Ruru; (according to other authorities) the wife of Raudrāśva or Kuśa-nābha. — *Ghṛitāćī-garbha-sambhavā,* f. large cardamoms. — *Ghṛitānna* (°*ta-an*°), *as, ā, am,* Ved. eating grease. — *Ghṛitābhyakta* (°*ta-abh*°), *as, ā, am,* smeared with ghee. — *Ghṛitārćis* (°*ta-ar*°), *is,* m. flaring or blazing fire. — *Ghṛitāvani* (°*ta-av*°), *is,* f. the spot on the sacrificial post which is smeared with Ghṛita. — *Ghṛitā-vṛidh, t, t, t,* Ved. delighted with butter; (Sāy.) increasing the Ghṛita. — *Ghṛitāsuti* (°*ta-ās*°), *is, is, i,* Ved. receiving the Ghṛita oblation, one whose food is Ghṛita; epithet of Mitrā-Varuṇa, Vishṇu, Indrā-Vishṇu. — *Ghṛitāhavana* (°*ta-āh*°), *as, ā, am,* Ved. one to whom the Ghṛita oblation belongs; epithet of Agni. — *Ghṛitāhuta* (°*ta-āh*°), *as, ā, am,* Ved. one to whom Ghṛita is offered. — *Ghṛitāhuti* (°*ta-āh*°), *is,* f. the Ghṛita oblation. — *Ghṛitāhva* (°*ta-āh*°), *as,* m. and *ghṛitāhvaya* (°*ta-āh*°), *as,* m. the resin of the tree Pinus Longifolia, turpentine. — *Ghṛitoda* (°*ta-uda*), *as, ā, am,* having Ghṛita as water; (*as*), m. the sea of Ghṛita surrounding Kuśa-dvīpa. — *Ghṛitodanka* (°*ta-ud*°), *as,* m. a leather vessel for holding ghee. — *Ghṛitaudana* (°*ta-od*°), *am,* n. rice sprinkled with Ghṛita.

Ghṛitin, ī, inī, i, containing Ghṛita.

Ghṛiteyu, us, m., N. of a son of Raudrāśva [cf. *ghṛitāćī*]; according to other authorities *kṛiteyu* or *kṛikaṇeyu.*

Ghṛitelī, f. a cock-roach; [cf. *tailapāyikā.*]

Ghṛitya, as, ā, am, Ved. consisting of Ghṛita.

घृङ् 1. *ghṛiṅ,* ind. an onomatopoetic sound. — *Ghṛiṅ-karikra, as, ā, am,* bleating, making the cry of a goat.

घृण 2. *ghṛiṇ* (allied to rt. *ghṛi*), cl. 8. P. A. *gharṇoti, -ṇute,* or *ghṛiṇoti, -ṇute,* to shine, burn.

Ghṛiṇa, as, m. heat, ardour, sunshine; (*ā*), f. a warm feeling towards others, compassion, tenderness, pity; reproach, blame, censure, aversion, contempt; [cf. *nir-ghṛiṇa* and *hṛiṇīyā.*] — *Ghṛiṇārćis* (°*ṇa-ar*°), *is,* m. fire.

Ghṛiṇālu, us, us, u, compassionate, pitiful.

Ghṛiṇi, is, m. heat, ardour, sunshine; a ray of the sun or moon, the sun; a wave, water; (*is, is, i*), displeasing, disagreeable. — *Ghṛiṇī-vat, ān, atī, at,* Ved. burning, shining; (*ān*), m. a kind of animal.

Ghṛiṇita, as, ā, am, pitied; reproached, abused, hated.

Ghṛiṇin, ī, inī, i, merciful, tender-hearted, compassionate; censorious, abusive. — *Ghṛiṇi-tva, am,* n. mercifulness, compassion, pity.

घृणावास *ghṛiṇāvāsa, as,* m. (probably for *ghana-vāsa*), a kind of pumpkin-gourd; [cf. *kushmāṇḍa.*]

घृण्ण् *ghṛiṇṇ,* cl. 1. A. *ghṛiṇṇate,* to seize; [cf. *ghiṇṇ* and *ghuṇṇ.*]

घृत्सतमस् *ghṛitsatamas, ās,* m., N. of a man (for *gṛitsa-tama?*).

घृत्समद् *ghṛitsamada,* a wrong form for *gṛitsa-mada.*

घृष् 1. *ghṛish* = *hṛish,* to be joyful.

Ghṛishu, us, us, u, Ved. lively, agile, mirthful, sportive.

1. *ghṛishvi, is, is, i,* Ved. lively, gay, merry, sportive; (Sāy.) crushing, (as if fr. 2. *ghṛish.*) — *Ghṛishvi-rādhas, ās, ās, as,* Ved. frolicsome with joy; (Sāy.) whose gifts touch each other or come closely together, (as if fr. 2. *ghṛish*); epithet of the Maruts.

घृष् 2. *ghṛish,* cl. 1. P. *gharshati, jagharsha, gharshishyati, gharshitum,* to rub, grind, brush, polish, furbish; crush, pound: Caus. P. *gharshayati, -yitum,* to rub, grind.

Gharsha, as, m. rubbing, grinding, friction, brushing.

Gharshaka, as, ā, am, rubbing; (*as*), m. a polisher.

Gharshaṇa, as, ā, am, rubbing, rubbing so as to make sore; (*um*), n. the act of grinding or rubbing, pounding, brushing, friction; (*ī*), f. turmeric. — *Gharshaṇāla* (°*ṇa-āla* = *ālaya*), *as,* m. a wooden roller or pestle for grinding.

Gharshaṇīya, as, ā, am, to be rubbed or cleaned.

Gharshita, as, ā, am, rubbed, ground, brushed.

Gharshin, ī, iṇī, i, grinding, rubbing.

Ghṛishṭa, as, ā, am, rubbed, ground, pounded; frayed, grazed, rubbed so as to be sore.

Ghṛishṭi, is, m. a hog [cf. *gṛishṭi* and 2. *ghṛishvi*]; (*is*), f. grinding, pounding; emulation, contest; N. of a plant, = *vārāhī,* Lycopodium Imbricatum; N. of another plant, Clitorea Ternatea; [cf. *vishṇu-krāntā.*]

2. *ghṛishvi, is,* m. a hog.

घृष्टिला *ghṛishṭhilā,* f., N. of a plant related to the plant Hemionitis Cordifolia; [cf. *priśni-parṇī.*]

घेञ्चुलिका *gheñćulikā* or *gheñćulī,* f., N. of an esculent root, Arum Oxicense, = *krauñćādana.*

घोङ्घ *ghongha, as,* m. intermediate space.

घोट *ghoṭa, as,* m. (said to be fr. rt. *ghuṭ*), a horse.

Ghoṭaka, as, m. a horse; (*ikā*), f. a mare; the plant Cucumis Utilissimus (*karkaṭī*); [cf. *turangī.*] — *Ghoṭaka-mukha, as,* m., N. of the author of the Kanyā-samprayuktakādhikaraṇa.

घोडाचोलिन् *ghoḍāćolin, ī,* m., N. of a man.

घोणस *ghoṇasa, as,* m. = *go-nasa,* a kind of serpent; (other authorities have *ghonasa.*)

घोणा *ghoṇā,* f. (corrupted fr. *ghrāṇā?*), the nose; the nose or nostrils of a horse.

Ghoṇin, ī, m. a hog (as having a large snout).

घोण्टा *ghoṇṭā,* f. the jujube, Zizyphus Jujuba, = *vadara, vadarī;* the betel-nut tree, see *guvāka;* a timber tree, Schrebera Swietenoides. — *Ghoṇṭā-phala, as,* m. a kind of plant.

घोनस *ghonasa, as,* m. a large kind of snake; [cf. *ghoṇasa.*]

घोर *ghora, as, ā, am* (said to be fr. rt. *han* with substitution of *ghur* for *han*), venerable, awful, sublime (in these senses Ved); terrific, frightful, terrible, horrible, dreadful, awful, violent, vehement; (*as*), m. the terrible, an epithet of Śiva; N. of an Aṅgirasa, a son of Aṅgiras; N. of Kutsa; (*ā*), f. the night; a kind of creeper, = *deva-dālī;* (scil. *gati*), N. of one of the seven stations of the planet Mercury; (*am*), n. venerableness; awfulness, horror; a horrible action, magic formulas and charms; poison; saffron; [cf. *dhīra* and *gaura.*] — *Ghora-ghushya, am,* n. brass; (a various reading for *ghora-pushpa*); [cf. *ghosha.*] — *Ghora-ćakshas, ās, ās, as,* Ved. of frightful appearance, having terrific eyes. — *Ghora-tara, as, ā, am,* more terrible, very awful. — *Ghora-tā,* f. or *ghora-tva, am,* n. horribleness, horror. — *Ghora-darśana, as, ā, am,* of horrible or frightful appearance, terrific; (*as*), m. an owl. — *Ghora-pushpa, am,* n. brass, bell-metal; [cf. *ghora-ghushya.*] — *Ghora-rāsana, as,* m. a jackal; (a wrong reading for *ghora-vāśana.*) — *Ghora-rāsin, ī,* m. a jackal (? for *ghora-vāśin*). — *Ghora-rūpa, as, ī, am,* frightful, hideous; (*am*), n. a hideous appearance. — *Ghora-rūpin, ī, iṇī, i,* frightful, horrible, hideous. — *Ghora-varpas, ās, ās, as,* Ved. of frightful or hideous appearance or shape; an epithet of the Maruts. — *Ghora-vāśana, as,* m. or *ghora-vāśin, ī,* m. a jackal; [cf. *ghora-rāsana.*] — *Ghora-sankāśa, as, ā, am,* dreadful, terrible. — *Ghora-svara, as, ā, am,* of dreadful sound. — *Ghorākṛiti* (°*ra-āk*°), *is, is, i,* frightful, hideous, of terrible aspect or form.

Ghoraka, ās, m. pl., N. of a people.

Ghaura, am, n. horror, horribleness; (*as*), m. a patronymic from Ghora.

घोल् *ghol* (substituted in Prākṛit for *ghuṇ=ghūrṇ*), cl. 10. P. *gholayati, -yitum,* to mix, to stir together into a semi-fluid substance; Bengālī *gholāite.*

Ghola, am, n. buttermilk; (*ī*), f. a kind of plant or vegetable; [cf. *araṇya-gholī, kshudra-gh°, vana-gh°.*]

Gholi, is, and *gholikā,* f. = *gholī.*

घोष *ghosha.* See under rt. 1. *ghush,* p. 308.

घोषातकी *ghoshātakī,* f., N. of a plant, = *śveta-ghoshā;* [cf. *hasti-ghoshātakī* and *kośātakī.*]

घौर *ghaura.* See above.

घ्न *ghna, as, ī, am* (fr. rt. *han,* and used at the end of compounds to express) killing, striking, a killer, destructive, destroying, removing; see *artha-ghna, jvara-ghna, śatru-ghna, go-ghna, daṇḍa-ghna;* (also to express) multiplied by; see *dvi-ćatur-ghna.* In a few compounds the fem. may end in *ā* [cf. *kula-ghnā*]; (*am*), n. killing, destruction.

Ghnat, an, atī, at (pres. part.), striking, beating, hurting, killing.

Ghnī = ghna, m., in *ahi-ghnī* and *śva-ghnī.*

Ghnya, used in a few compounds, see *a-ghnya* and *ati-ghnya.*

घ्रंस् *ghraṇs, n,* m., Ved. the heat of the sun.

Ghraṇsa, as, m., Ved. the heat of the sun, sunshine, brightness.

घ्रा *ghrā,* cl. 1. P., ep. also cl. 1. A. and 3. P. *jighrati, -te, ghrāti, jaghrau, ghrāsyati, aghrāt* and *aghrāsīt, ghrātum,* to smell, perceive odour, be eager for; to smell at, snuffle at; to kiss: Caus. P. *ghrāpayati, ajighrapat* and *ajighripat,* to cause to smell at: Desid. *jighrāsati:* Intens. *jeghrīyate, jāghreti* and *jāghrāti;* du. *jāghritas;* [cf. Lat. *fra-grare;* Hib. *gros,* 'a snout (?);' Germ. *riechen;* Old Germ. *riuhu;* Lith. *kwepju, kwapas;* Gr. ὄσφρωμα; ῥίς, ῥιν-ός.]

Ghrati, is, f. the nose (?).

Ghrāṇa, as, ā, am, smelled; (*as* or *am*), m. n. smell; smelling; (*am*), n. odour; (*as, ā, am*), m. f. n. the nose; (*as*), m., N. of a man. — *Ghrāṇa-ćakshus, us, us, us,* using the nose for eyes, blind. — *Ghrāṇa-ja, as, ā, am,* caused or effected by the nose. — *Ghrāṇa-tarpaṇa, as, ā, am,* pleasant to the nose, fragrant; (*am*), n. fragrance, odour; a fragrance, a perfume. — *Ghrāṇa-duḥkha-dā,* f., N. of a plant which causes sneezing (giving pain to the nose). — *Ghrāṇa-pāka, as,* m. a disease of the nose, = *nāsā-pāka,* q. v. — *Ghrāṇa-śravas, ās,* m., N. of one of the attendants of Skanda ('using the nose for ears' [cf. *ghrāṇa-ćakshus*] or 'renowned for his nose'). — *Ghrāṇendriya* (°*ṇa-in*°), *am,* n. the organ or sense of smell.

Ghrāta, as, ā, am, smelled, smelled at.

Ghrātavya, as, ā, am, to be smelled or smelled at; (*am*), n. odour.

Ghrāti, is, f. smell; smelling, snuffling at; the nose.

Ghrātṛi, tā, trī, tṛi, one who smells.

Ghrātvā, ind. having smelled.

Ghreya, as, ā, am, to be smelled, what may be smelled or snuffled at; (*am*), n. odour, smell.

ङ

ङ 1. *na,* the fifth consonant of the Sanskṛit alphabet, and the nasal of the first class. No real word in use begins with this letter; it is usually found as the first member of a compound consonant preceded by a vowel; the sound of *n* corresponds to that of *ng* in *song.* — *Na-kāra, as,* m. the letter or sound *na.*

ङ 2. *na, as,* m. an object of sense; desire, wish for any sensual object; an epithet of Śiva; (Bhairava.)

ङु *nu,* cl. 1. A. *navate, nunuve,* to sound: Desid. *nunūshate.*

च

च 1. *ća,* the twentieth letter of the alphabet, and first of the second or palatal class of consonants, having the simple sound of *ch* in *church.* — *Ca-kāra, as,* m. the letter or sound *ća.*

च 2. *ća,* ind. (a particle and conjunction usually translateable by) and, both, also, moreover, as well as. This conjunction, like the Lat. *que* and Gr. τε, is usually placed as an enclitic after the word which it connects with what precedes, and when used with the personal pronouns these must appear in their fuller accented forms (e. g. *tava ća mama ća,* both of thee and of me, not *te ća me ća*). It connects whole sentences as well as parts of sentences, and seems to have been originally placed after both the words or clauses which it joins together, for in the Ṛig-veda the double *ća* occurs much more frequently than the single (e. g. *ahaṃ ća tvaṃ ća,* I and thou). The double *ća* may also be used somewhat redundantly in classical Sanskṛit (e. g. *kva hariṇakānāṃ jīvitaṃ ćātilolaṃ kva ća vajra-sārāḥ śarās te,* where is both the frail existence of fawns and where are thy adamantine arrows?). In the later literature, however, the first *ća* is more usually omitted (e. g. *ahaṃ tvaṃ ća*), and when more than two things are enumerated only one *ća* is often found (e. g. *tejasā yaśasā lakshmyā sthityā ća parayā,* in glory, in fame, in beauty, and in high condition). Elsewhere, when more than two things are enumerated, *ća* is placed after some and omitted after others (e. g. *ṛiṇa-dātā ća vaidyaśća śrotriyo nadī,* both the payer of a debt and a physician [and] a Brāhman [and] a river). In the Veda and even in classical Sanskṛit, when the double *ća* would generally be used, the second may occasionally be omitted (e. g. *Indraśća Somaḥ,* both Indra [and] Soma; *dur-bhedyaśća āśu-sandheyaḥ,* both difficult to be divided [and] quickly to be united). Rarely *ća* may imply a reference to certain other words which are not expressed (e. g. *kamaṇḍalau ća karakaḥ,* the word *karaka* has the meaning 'pitcher' and other meanings).

Ca may be used for *vā* and is then translateable by 'either,' 'or' (e. g. *iha ćāmutra vā,* either here or hereafter; *strī vā pumān vā yaććānyat sattvam,* either a woman or a man or any other being); and when a negative particle is joined with *ća* the two may then be translated by 'neither,' 'nor.' Occasionally one *ća* or one *na* may be omitted (e. g. *na ća paribhoktuṃ naiva śaknomi hātum,* I am able neither to enjoy nor to abandon; *na pūrvāhṇe na ća parāhṇe,* neither in the forenoon nor in the afternoon).

Ca is often joined to the adverbs *eva, api, tathā, tathaiva,* &c., either with or without a negative particle (e. g. *vairiṇaṃ nopaseveta sahāyaṃ ćaiva vairiṇaḥ,* one ought not to serve either an enemy or the ally of an enemy). See *eva, api,* &c.

Ca sometimes = *eva,* even, indeed, certainly, just, &c. (e. g. *su-ćintitaṃ ćaushadhaṃ na nāma-mātreṇa karoty a-rogam,* even a well-devised remedy does not cure a disease by its mere name; *yāvanta eva te tārāṇśća sa,* as great as they [were] just so great was he).

Ca may occasionally be disjunctive and be translated by 'but,' 'on the contrary,' 'on the other hand,' 'yet,' 'nevertheless' (e. g. *varam ādyau na ćāntimaḥ,* better the two first but not the last; *śāntam idam āśrama-padaṃ sphurati ća bāhuḥ,* this hermitage is tranquil yet my arm throbs).

Ca—ća may be used to express immediate connection between two acts or their simultaneous occurrence (e. g. *mama ća muktaṃ tamasā mano manasijena dhanushi śaraśća niveśitaḥ,* no sooner is my mind freed from darkness than a shaft is fixed on his bow by the heart-born god).

Ca rarely = *ćet,* if (e. g. *jīvituṃ ćećchase,* if thou wishest to live).

Ca may be used as an expletive (e. g. *anyaiśća kratubhiśća,* and with other sacrifices). The native dictionaries assign to *ća* the following significations or forces:—conjunction (*anv-āćaya*), collective combination (*sam-āhāra*), mutual connection (*itaretara*), and aggregation (*sam-uććaya*). For the meaning of *ća* after an interrogative see 2. *ka,* 2. *kathā,* &c.; [cf. Gr. τε; Lat. *que, pe* (in *nempe,* &c.); Goth. *uh;* Zend *ća;* Old Pers. *ćā.*]

च 3. *ća, as, ā, am,* seedless; bad, vile, mischievous; (*as*), m. a thief; a tortoise; the moon; an epithet of Śiva.

चक् *ćak,* cl. 1. P. A. *ćakati, -te, ćaćāka, ćeke, aćakīt* and *aćākīt, ćakitum,* to be satiated, to be contented, to be satisfied; to repel, resist; to shine [cf. *kan* and 2. *kam*]: Caus. *ćakayati* and *ćākayati* (?).

Cakita, as, ā, am, shaking, trembling; fearful, timid; startled, frightened, afraid of. — *Cakita-ćakitam,* ind. with great alarm; (*am*), n. trembling, timidity, alarm; *sa-ćakitam,* tremblingly; (*ā*), f., N. of a metre consisting of four lines of sixteen syllables each. — *Cakita-hṛidaya, as, ā, am,* faint-hearted.

चकास् 1. *ćakās* [cf. rt. *kāś*], cl. 2. P. *ćakāsti,* 3rd pl. *ćakāsati,* Impf. 2nd sing. *aćakās* or *aćakat,* 3rd sing. *aćakāt,* Impv. 2nd sing. *ćakādhi* or *ćakāddhi,* Perf. *ćakāsāñ-ćakāra,* 1st Fut. *ćakāsitā,* Aor. *aćakāsīt,* to shine, to be bright: Caus. *ćakāsayati, -yitum,* Aor. *aćićakāsat* or *aćaćakāsat,* to cause to shine, make bright, illuminate: Desid. *ćićakāsishati.*

2. *ćakās, ās, ās, ās,* shining, brilliant.

Cakāsayat, an, antī, at, illuminating, beautifying.

Cakāsita, as, ā, am, illuminated, shining, splendid, beautiful.

चकोर *ćakora, as,* m. (said to be fr. rt. *ćak,* to be satisfied, i. e. with moon-beams), the bartavelle or Greek partridge, Perdix Rufa or Tetrao Rufus, (this bird is fabled to subsist upon moon-beams, hence 'an eye drinking the nectar of a moon-like face' is poetically called *ćakshuś-ćakora;* the eyes of the Cakora are said to turn red when it looks on poisoned food, see Schol. to Manu VII. 217); N. of a people; also of a prince; and of a mountain. — *Cakora-dṛiś, k, k, k,* having eyes like those of a partridge.

Cakoraka, as, m. the Greek partridge; [cf. the preceding.]

चक्क् *ćakk,* cl. 10. P. *ćakkayati, -yitum,* to suffer; to give or inflict pain.

चक्क *ćakka, as,* m., N. of a man.

चक्कल *ćakkala, as, ā, am,* round, circular.

चक्नस *ćaknasa, as,* m. (fr. rt. *knas*), crookedness, dishonesty.

चक्र *ćakra, am,* n. (fr. rt. *kram* or rt. 1. *kṛi?* reduplicated), the wheel of a carriage, the wheel of the Sun's chariot, or (metaphorically) the wheel of Time (in these senses sometimes *as,* m. in Ved.); a potter's wheel; a discus or sharp circular missile weapon (especially applied to the favourite weapon of Vishṇu); an oil-mill; a circle; any circle or ring (e. g. *kalāpa-ćakra,* the circle of a peacock's tail); a form of military array (in a circle); circular flight (of a bird &c.); a circle or depression of the body for mystical, astrological, or chiromantic purposes, (six of these are enumerated one above the other, viz. 1. *mūlā-dhāra,* the parts about the pubis; 2. *svādhishṭhāna,* the umbilical region; 3. *maṇi-pūram,* the pit of the stomach or epigastrium; 4. *anāhatam,* the root of the nose; 5. *vi-śuddham*, the hollow between the frontal sinuses; 6. *ājñākhyam*, the fontenelle or union of the coronal and sagittal sutures: various faculties and divinities are supposed to be present in these hollows); a general N. for a diagram of various circular forms used for astrological or astronomical purposes, a sphere or astronomical circle in general (e.g. *rāśi-ćakram*, the zodiac); a cycle, a cycle of years, the cycle of the seasons; the horizon; a particular constellation in the form of a hexagon; a troop, a multitude (in this sense m. and n.); an army, a host; a province, number of villages, region, district, circuit; range, department in general; section of a book; the wheel of a monarch's chariot rolling over his dominions, sovereignty; a realm; a whirlpool; the winding of a river; the convolutions or spiral marks of the Sāla-grāma or ammonite, a kind of petrified shell; the flower of the plant Tagara; N. of a particular plant or drug; a crooked or fraudulent device [cf. *ćakrikā*]; N. of a metre consisting of four lines of fourteen syllables each, = *ćakra-pāta;* the ruddy goose or Brāhmany duck, Anas Casarca (in this sense m.); N. of a people (m. pl.); N. of a man (m.); of a Nāga (m.); N. of one of the attendants of Skanda (m.); N. of a mountain (m.); (ī), f., Ved. a wheel; (ā), f., N. of two plants, = *karkaṭa-śriṅgī* and *nāgara-mustā*. At the end of an adj. comp. the f. will end in *ā;* [cf. *a-ćakra, uććā-ć°, eka-ć°, kāla-ć°, kū-ć°, daṇḍa-ć°, dharma-ć°, sa-ć°*, &c.; cf. also Gr. κύκλος.] — *Cakra-kāraka, am*, n. a kind of perfume, apparently a dried shell-fish, see *nakhī*. — *Cakra-kulyā*, f., N. of a plant [cf. *ćitra-parṇī*] said to be a species of fern, commonly Cākuliya (Hemionites Cordifolia). — *Cakra-gaja, as*, m., N. of a plant, = *ćakra-marda*. — *Cakra-gaṇḍu, us*, m. a round pillow. — *Cakra-gati, is*, f. rotation, revolution. — *Cakra-guććha, as*, m. the tree Jonesia Aśoca; [cf. *aśoka*.] — *Cakra-goptṛi, tā*, m. the protector of a wheel; (*tārau*), m. du. two men whose business is to preserve the wheels of a carriage from damage; [cf. *ćakra-raksha*.] — *Cakra-grahaṇa, am, ī*, n. f. (?) 'an army-holder,' a rampart, an intrenchment. — *Cakra-ćara, as, ā, am*, going in a circle, epithet of a class of superhuman beings; a juggler, = *ćakrāṭa* (?). — *Cakra-ćārin, ī, iṇī, i*, going in a circle, walking from one place to another. — *Cakra-ćūḍā-maṇi, is*, m. a round jewel in a coronet or diadem; a honorific title of Vopa-deva; N. of a man. — *Cakra-jīvaka, as*, m. or *ćakra-jīvin, ī*, m. a potter (who lives by his wheel). — *Cakra-talāmra* (°*tala-ām*°), *as*, m. a kind of mango tree. — *Cakra-tīrtha, am*, n., N. of a Tīrtha. — *Cakra-taila, am*, n. oil prepared from the plant Cakra (*ćakra-marda?*). — *Cakra-danshṭra, as*, m. a hog (having curved tusks). — *Cakra-datta, as*, m., N. of an author. — *Cakra-dantī*, f., N. of a plant; [cf. *dantī*.] • — *Cakradantī-vija, as*, m., N. of a plant, = *jaya-pāla* and *dantī-vija*. — *Cakra-dīpikā*, f., N. of a literary work. — *Cakra-dṛiś, k*, m., N. of an Asura. — *Cakra-deva, as*, m., N. of a warrior. — *Cakra-dvāra, as*, m., N. of a mountain. — *Cakra-dhanus, us*, m., N. of a Ṛishi. — *Cakra-dhara, as, ā, am*, bearing a wheel, having a wheel, a wheel-bearer; carrying a discus; driving in a carriage; (*as*), m. a N. of Vishṇu or Kṛishṇa (as holding a discus in one hand); a sovereign, ruler, the governor of a province, the owner of many villages; a village tumbler or juggler; a snake; N. of a man. — *Cakra-dharman, ā*, m., N. of a prince of the Vidyā-dharas. — *Cakra-dhāra* = *ćakra-dhara* above. — *Cakra-dhārā*, f. the periphery of a wheel. — *Cakra-nakha, as*, m. a kind of perfume, = *vyāghra-nakha*. — *Cakra-nadī* or *ćakra-ṇadī*, f., N. of a river. — *Cakra-nābhi, is*, f. the nave of a wheel. — *Cakra-nāman, ā*, m. a pyritic ore of iron, see *mākshika*. — *Cakra-nāyaka, as*, m. the leader of a troop; a kind of perfume, = *ćakra-nakha*. — *Cakra-nārāyaṇī-saṃhitā*, f., N. of a literary work. — *Cakra-nemi, is*, f., N. of one of the Mātṛis attending on Skanda. — *Cakra-padmāṭa, as*, m., N. of the plant Cassia Tora, = *ćakra-marda*. — *Cakra-parivyādha, as*, m. the plant Cathartocarpus Fistula; [cf. *āragbadha*.] — *Cakra-parṇī*, f. a plant, commonly Cākuliya, Hemionites Cordifolia; [cf. *ćakra-kulyā*.] — *Cakra-pāṇi, is*, m. an epithet of Vishṇu or Kṛishṇa (holding a discus in one hand); N. of an author; (sometimes *ćakra-pāṇin*.) — *Cakrapāṇi-datta, as*, m., N. of an author of a lexicon; [cf. *ćandrodaya*.] — *Cakra-pāta, as*, m. a kind of metre, = *ćakra*. — *Cakra-pāda* or *ćakra-pādaka, as*, m. a carriage (having wheels for feet); an elephant (having circular feet). — *Cakra-pāla, as*, m. the superintendent of a province; one who carries a discus; a circle; the horizon. — *Cakra-pura, am*, n., N. of a town built by Cakra-mardikā. — *Cakra-pushkariṇī*, f., N. of a sacred tank at Kāśī or Benares; [cf. *ćakra-tīrtha* and *maṇi-karṇikā*.] — *Cakra-phala, am*, n. a missile weapon, a kind of discus. — *Cakra-bāndhava, as*, m. the sun ('friend of the ruddy goose,' these birds being supposed to couple only in the day-time). — *Cakra-bāla* and *ćakra-vāla, as, am*, m. n. a ring, circle [cf. *bālī* and *vālaka*]; the horizon (usually n.); a mass, a multitude, a number, assemblage; (*as*), m. a mythical range of mountains supposed to encircle the orb of the earth like a wall and to be the limit of light and darkness (perhaps a bank of clouds shaped like mountains on the horizon); [cf. *ćakra-vāṭa* and *ćakra-vāḍa*.] — *Cakra-bāladhi, is*, m. a dog, 'having a curved tail.' — *Cakra-bhānu, us*, m., N. of a Brāhman. — *Cakra-bhṛit, t*, m. 'discus-bearer,' an epithet of Vishṇu. — *Cakra-bhedinī*, f. night ('dividing the ruddy geese,' the male and female of these birds being condemned to be separated at night); [cf. *ćakra-bāndhava*.] — *Cakra-bhrami, is*, m. f. (?) a grindstone. — *Cakra-bhrānti, is*, f. the whirling round of the wheels (of a chariot). — *Cakra-maṭha, as*, m., N. of a college built in a circular form by Cakra-varman. — *Cakra-maṇḍalin, ī*, m. a large snake, the Boa Constrictor, (the body of the snake or its spots being compared to a wheel.) — *Cakra-manda, as*, m., N. of a Nāga. — *Cakra-marda, as*, m. the plant Cassia Tora. — *Cakra-mardaka, as*, m. Cassia Tora; (*ikā*), f., N. of the wife of Lalitāditya. — *Cakram-āsaja, as, ā, am*, Ved. stopping the wheels (of the chariot). — *Cakra-mukha, as*, m. 'having a curved mouth,' a hog. — *Cakra-mushala, as, ā, am*, (a battle) carried on with the discus and club. — *Cakra-melaka, as* or *am* (?), m. or n., N. of a place in Kaśmīra. — *Cakra-mauli, is*, m., N. of a Rākshasa. — *Cakra-yāna, am*, n. any wheel-carriage. — *Cakra-yoga, as*, m. applying a splint or similar instrument by means of pulleys in case of dislocation of the thigh. — *Cakra-raksha, as*, m. = *ćakra-goptṛi*, q. v. — *Cakra-rada, as*, m. a hog, a boar ('having curved tusks'); [cf. *ćakra-mukha*.] — *Cakra-lakshaṇā*, f. the plant Cocculus Cordifolius, = *guḍūćī*. — *Cakra-latāmra, as*, m. a kind of mango tree; (another reading for *ćakra-talāmra*.) — *Cakra-vat, ān, atī, at*, furnished with wheels, wheeled; armed with a discus; circular, being in the form of a ring or circle; (*ān*), m. the proprietor of an oil-mill or one in which seeds are bruised; an epithet of Vishṇu; a sovereign, an emperor; N. of a mountain; (*vat*), ind. like a wheel, in rotation, going round or revolving like a wheel. — *Cakravarti-tā*, f. or *ćakravarti-tva, am*, n. the mark or state of a universal emperor; see the next. — *Cakra-vartin, ī*, m. a ruler the wheels of whose chariot roll everywhere without obstruction; an emperor, a sovereign of the world, a supreme ruler, the ruler of a Cakra or country described as extending from sea to sea, (twelve princes beginning with Bharata are especially considered as Cakra-vartins); (*ī, inī, i*), supreme, holding the highest rank; (*inī*), f. a fragrant plant, commonly Cakāvat [cf. *janī*]; the plant Nardostachys Jaṭāmāṇsī; another plant, = *alaktaka*. — *Cakra-varman, ā*, m., N. of a king of Kaśmīra; [cf. *ćākravarmaṇa*.] — *Cakra-vāka, as*, m. the ruddy goose, commonly called the Brāhmany duck, Anas Casarca; (*ī*), f. the female of this bird; [cf. *ćakra, ćakra-sāhvaya, ćakrāhva, ćakrāhvaya*, &c.] — *Cakravāka-bandhu, us*, m. the sun; [cf. *ćakra-bāndhava*.] — *Cakravāka-vati*, f. probably N. of a river (abounding in Cakra-vākas). — *Cakravākin, ī, inī, i*, filled with Cakra-vākas. — *Cakravākopakūjita* (°*ka-up*°), *as, ā, am*, made resonant with the cooing or cry of the Cakra-vāka. — *Cakra-vāṭa, as*, m. a limit, a boundary; a lamp-stand; engaging in an action; [cf. *ćakra-bāla*.] — *Cakra-vāḍa, as*, m. a fabulous range of mountains, see *ćakra-bāla; (am)*, n. a circle. — *Cakra-vāta, as*, m. a whirlwind, a hurricane, = *ćakra-vāla;* [cf. *ćakra-bāla*.] — *Cakra-vimala, as* or *am*, m. or n. (?), N. of a plant. — *Cakra-vṛiddhi, is*, f. interest upon interest; wages for transporting goods in a carriage. — *Cakra-vyūha, as*, m. any circular array of troops. — *Cakra-śata-pattra, as* or *am*, m. or n. (?), N. of a plant. — *Cakra-śreṇī*, f. = *aja-śriṅgī*, the plant Odina Pinnata, bearing a curved fruit. — *Cakra-saṃvara, as*, m., N. of a Buddha, = *vajra-ṭīka*. — *Cakra-saktha, as, ā, am*, having crooked thighs, bow-legged. — *Cakra-sañjña, am*, n. tin. — *Cakra-sāhvaya, as*, m. = *ćakra*, = *ćakra-vāka*, Anas Casarca. — *Cakra-sena, as*, m., N. of the son of Tārāćandra and father of Sinha. — *Cakra-svāmin, ī*, m. an epithet of Vishṇu; [cf. *ćakra-dhara*.] — *Cakra-hasta, as*, m. an epithet of Vishṇu ('discus-handed'). — *Cakra-hrada, as*, m., N. of a lake. — *Cakrākāra, as, ā, am*, or *ćakrākṛiti* (°*ra-āk*°), *is, is, i*, circular, round. — *Cakrāṅkī*, a various reading for *ćakrāṅkī*, q. v. — *Cakrāṅkitā* (°*ra-aṅ*°), f. a kind of plant. — *Cakrāṅkī*, f. a goose; [cf. *ćakrāṅga*.] — *Cakrāṅga* (°*ra-aṅ*°), *as*, m. a gander (having a curved neck); a carriage [cf. *ćakra-pāda*]; (*ī*), f. a goose; N. of several plants, = *kaṭu-rohiṇī;* N. of another plant, = Enhydra Heloncha (*hila-moćikā*); another plant, = *karkaṭa-śriṅgī;* another plant, Cocculus Tomentosus, = *vṛisha-parṇī* or *su-darśanā;* another plant, Rubia Munjista (*mañjishṭhā*); (*am*), n. a parasol. — *Cakrāṭa* (°*ra-aṭa*), *as*, m. a juggler, a snake-catcher, snake-charmer, one who exhibits snakes and pretends to cure their bites; a knave, a cheat, a rogue; a gold coin or certain weight of gold, a Dīnār. — *Cakrādhivāsin* (°*ra-adh*°), *ī*, m. the orange-tree. — *Cakrāyudha* (°*ra-āy*°), *as*, m. an epithet of Vishṇu or Kṛishṇa (whose weapon is the discus). — *Cakrāyodhya* (°*ra-ay*°), *as*, m., N. of a prince. — *Cakrāvarta* (°*ra-āv*°), *as*, m. turning round, whirling or rotatory motion. — *Cakrāhva* (°*ra-āh*°), *as*, m. = *ćakra-vāka*, Anas Casarca; = *ćakra-marda*, Cassia Tora; (*ā*), f. Cocculus Tomentosus; [cf. *ćakrāṅgā*.] — *Cakrāhvaya* (°*ra-āh*°), *as*, m. = *ćakrāhva*, Anas Casarca. — *Cakrīvat, ān, atī, at*, furnished with wheels, wheeled; (*ān*), m. an ass; N. of a king. — *Cakreśvara* (°*ra-iś*°), *as*, m. lord of the discus, an epithet of Vishṇu; (*ī*), f. a female deity peculiar to the Jainas, one of their Vidyā-devīs or goddesses of wisdom, executing the orders of the first Arhat.

Cakraka, as, ā, am, resembling a wheel or circle, wheel-shaped, circular; (*as*), m. a logical form or proposition, arguing in a circle; a kind of serpent; N. of a Ṛishi; (*ā*), f. a kind of plant having great curative properties.

Cakralā, f. a kind of Cyperus, = *uććaṭā*.

Cakrika, as, m. a discus-bearer; (*ā*), f. a heap, a troop; a crooked or fraudulent device; the knee (?).

Cakrin, ī, iṇī, i, having a wheel or wheels, wheeled; having or holding a discus, an epithet of Vishṇu or Kṛishṇa; driving in a carriage; circular; (*ī*), m. a potter; an oil-grinder; a sovereign of the world, an emperor, a Cakra-vartin; the governor of a province; a kind of juggler or tumbler who exhibits tricks with a discus or a wheel (?); one who offers sacrifices for a whole village (?); an informer; an ass; the ruddy goose, Anas Casarca; a crow; a snake; the plant Cassia Tora, = *ćakra-marda;* another plant, Dalbergia Ougeinensis; a kind of perfume; [cf. *sa-ćakrin*.]

Cakriya, as, ā, am, going in a carriage, being on a journey.

Cakrī-kṛi, cl. 8. P. A. *-karoti, -kurute, -kartum*, to make round or circular, to curve or bend (as a bow).

चक्राण *ćakrāṇa, as, ā, am* (fr. rt. 1. *kṛi*), having done, &c.

Cakri, is, is, i, Ved. doing, making, active, an agent; (*is*), m., N. of a man.

Cakru, us, m. a doer, a maker, an agent.

चक्ष् *ćaksh* (perhaps a reduplicated form of *kāś* = *kśā*, which according to some is the original root. According to Pāṇini the rt. *ćaksh* can only be used in the conjugational tenses and optionally in the Perf. In the non-conjugational tenses and optionally in the Perf. the rt. *khyā* is substituted), cl. 2. A. Pres. *ćashṭe*, Perf. *ćaćakshe*. Other forms are exceptionally found, e. g. 2nd sing. Pres. P. *ćakshi*, 2nd pl. Impv. P. (with *ā*) *ćakshata*, Impf. *aćaksham*, Aor. *aćaćaksham*, Inf. *ćashṭum*, Ved. Inf. *ćakshe*, to appear, become visible: to see, look at, perceive, observe; to speak, say, tell, inform; to eat, (a wrong form for *jaksh*): Pass. *ćakshyate*. The rt. *ćaksh* appears like *khyā*, to combine the two distinct meanings of seeing and speaking.

Cakshaṇa, am, n., Ved. appearing, becoming visible, appearance, aspect; speaking, saying; eating a relish to promote drinking, (a wrong form for *jakshaṇa?*); [cf. *viśva-ćakshaṇa*.]

Cakshaṇi, is, m., Ved. an illuminator, irradiating.

Cakshan, a, n., Ved. the eye, (du. *ćakshaṇī*, the eyes.)

Cakshas, ās, m. a teacher, a spiritual teacher, an instructor in sacred science; an epithet of Bṛihaspati, the teacher of the gods; (*as*), n. radiance, clearness; the act of seeing, being seen, (*ćakshase*, dat. = inf. to see, to be seen); look, sight, the eye; [cf. *apāka-ćakshas, īya-ć°, upāka-ć°, uru-ć°, ghora-ć°*, &c.]

Cakshu, us or *u*, m. or n. (?), Ved. the eye; (*us*), m., N. of a prince; N. of a river. — *Cakshu-pa, as*, m., N. of a prince; (a various reading has *ćākshusha*.)

Cakshus, us, us, us, seeing; (*us*), m., N. of a Marut; also of a Ṛishi with the patronymic Mānava; N. of a son of Anu; (*us*), f., N. of a river [cf. *ćakshu* and *su-ćakshus*]; (*us*), n. light, clearness; the act of seeing, faculty of seeing, sight, aspect, a look; the eye; often at the end of a compound (e. g. *ghrāṇa-ćakshus*, one who uses his nose for eyes; *ćāra-ćakshus*, one who sees by means of his spies; *dharma-ćakshus*, one who has an eye for justice); [cf. *a-ćakshus, aghora-ć°*, &c.; cf. also Zend *ćasman*.] — *Cakshuḥ-patha, as*, m. 'the path of the eyes,' the horizon, the range of sight (e. g. *ćakshuḥ-patham prāp*, to become visible; *ćakshuḥ-pathād apagam*, to vanish from the sight). — *Cakshuḥ-pīḍā*, f. pain of the eyes. — *Cakshuḥ-śravas, ās*, or *ćakshuḥ-śruti, is*, m. a snake (using its eyes for ears). — *Cakshuḥ-sāman, a*, n., N. of a Sāman (= *prajāpateḥ sāman*). — *Cakshur-indriya, am*, n. the sense of seeing. — *Cakshur-goćara, as, ā, am*, coming within range of the eye. — *Cakshur-grahaṇa, am*, n. morbid affection of the eyes. — *Cakshur-dā, ās, ās, am*, Ved. giving sight. — *Cakshur-dāna, am*, n. the ceremony of anointing the eyes of an image at the time of consecration. — *Cakshur-bhṛit, t, t, t*, promoting sight. — *Cakshur-mantra, as, ā, am*, Ved. bewitching with the eye. — *Cakshur-maya, as, ī, am*, resembling the eye. — *Cakshur-mala, am*, n. the excretion of the eyes. — *Cakshur-loka, as, ā, am*, seeing with the eyes. — *Cakshur-vanya, as, ā, am*, Ved. suffering from disease of the eyes. — *Cakshur-vardhanikā*, f., N. of a river. — *Cakshur-vahana, am*, n., N. of a plant, = *mesha-śṛingī*. — *Cakshur-vishaya, as*, m. the horizon, visibility; presence, sight, ken; an object of sight, any visible object. — *Cakshur-han, ā, -ghnī, a*, killing with a look. — *Cakshuś-ćit, t, t, t*, collecting the faculty of sight. — *Cakshush-kāma, as, ā, am*, Ved. wishing for the faculty of seeing. — *Cakshush-ṭas*, ind. away from the eye. — *Cakshush-pati, is*, m. the lord of the eyes. — *Cakshush-pā, ās, ās, am*, Ved. protecting the eye-sight. — *Cakshush-mat, ān, atī, at*, endowed with the faculty of seeing, seeing, furnished with eyes; representing the eye. — *Cakshushmat-tā*, f. the state of one who sees, the faculty of seeing. — *Cakshū-roga, as*, m. disease of the eye, ophthalmia.

Cakshusha, at the end of a compound = *ćakshus*, eye (e. g. *sa-ćakshusha*, having eyes); (*as*), m., N. of the father of Manu Cākshusha; (a wrong reading for *ćakshus?*)

Cakshushya, as, ā, am, pleasing or agreeable to the eyes, agreeable, pleasing, good-looking, beautiful; (*as*), m. a collyrium or application to the eyes, extracted from the Amomum Antorhiza; N. of the plant Pandanus Odoratissimus, = *ketaka*; another plant, Hyperanthera Moringa; (*ā*), f. a kind of collyrium, the calx of brass or a blue stone used thus; a pleasing or interesting woman; the plant Pandanus Odoratissimus; also of Glycine Labialis, and of Odina Pinnata; (*am*), n. two kinds of collyrium, = *kharparītuttha* and *sauvīrāñjana*; N. of a small shrub, = *prapauṇḍarīka*.

चघ् *ćagh*, cl. 5. P. *ćaghnoti*, &c., to smite or slay, to kill.

चङ्कुण *ćankuṇa, as*, m. (said to be fr. rt. *ćak*), a carriage, a tree; (*am*), n. any vehicle.

चङ्क्रमण *ćankramaṇa, as, ā, am* (fr. Intens. of rt. *kram*), going about, taking exercise; who or what goes slowly or crookedly; (*am*), n. going about, walking, proceeding, going tortuously or slowly.

Cankramā, f. going about, walking, going tortuously or slowly. — *Cankramā-vat, ān, atī, at*, who or what moves slowly or crookedly.

चङ्ग *ćanga, as, ā, am*, handsome, beautiful; dexterous, clever; sound, healthy; (*as*), m., N. of a man.

चचेण्डा *ćaćeṇḍā*, f., N. of a fruit-bearing creeper, = *bṛihat-phala, veśma-kūla, śveta-rājī*, commonly *ćićiḍā*.

चच्चपुट *ćaććapuṭa* or (according to another authority) *ćaććatpuṭa, as*, m. a kind of time in music.

चञ्च् *ćañć*, cl. 1. P. *ćañćati, ćaćañća, ćañćitum*, &c., to leap, jump; to go, move; to dangle; [cf. Hib. *ceangtha*, 'they go, travel;' *ceangastair*, 'walking, pacing;' Lat. *cunctari?*].

Cañća, as, m. a basket; (*ā*), f. anything made of cane, a mat, a stool &c. made of reeds or basket-work; a straw-man, a doll; a puppet of grass or reeds; a contemptuous epithet of a man.

Cañćat, an, antī, at, leaping, going, moving; dangling; unsteady, shaking.

Cañćatka, as, ā, am, leaping, jumping, trembling, moving.

Cañću, us, us, u, renowned, celebrated, known; clever [cf. *ćañću-tā, ćuñću, ćaṇa*, and *akshara-ćañću*]; (*us*), m. a deer; N. of several plants, the castor-oil plant, Ricinus Communis (*eraṇḍa*); also = *raktairaṇḍa* and *kshudra-ćañću*, = *gonāḍīka*; N. of a son of Harita; (*us*), f. a beak, bill; a kind of vegetable, = *ćañćū, ćañću-pattra*, &c. — *Cañću-tā*, f. celebrity, cleverness, activity; the state of a beak. — *Cañću-pattra, as*, m. a kind of vegetable, = *ćañću*, f. — *Cañću-puṭa, as, am*, m. n. the bill of a bird when shut. — *Cañću-prahāra, as*, m. a peck with the beak. — *Cañću-bhṛit, t*, m. 'having a beak,' a bird. — *Cañću-mat, ān, atī*, m. f. 'possessed of a beak,' a bird. — *Cañću-sūći, is*, m. the tailor-bird, Sylvia Sutoria; also *ćañćusūćika, as*, m.

Cañćukā, f. a beak, bill.

1. *ćañćura, as*, m. a kind of vegetable, = *ćañću*, f.; [cf. the following.]

Cañćū, ūs, f. a beak, the bill of a bird; a kind of vegetable. See *ćañću* above.

Cañćūka, ās, m. pl., N. of a people to the south-west of Madhya-deśa.

चञ्चरिन् *ćañćarin, ī*, m. or *ćañćarī*, f. or *ćañćarīka, as*, m. (fr. Intens. of rt. *ćar*), a bee. — *Cañćarīkāvalī* (°*ka-avalī*), f. a kind of metre consisting of four lines of thirteen syllables each.

2. *ćuñćura, as, ā, am*, going repeatedly, expert in, conversant with.

Cañćurī, īs, īs, i, constantly practising or engaged in.

Cañćūryamāṇa, as, ā, am, following evil practices, behaving ill, addicted to wickedness, wanton.

चञ्चल *ćañćala, as, ā, am* (fr. Intens. of rt. *ćal*), moving to and fro, movable, unsteady, shaking, trembling; unsteady, inconstant, inconsiderate, quivering, flickering, playing, moving irregularly; fickle; (*as*), m. the wind; a lover, a libertine, a lecher; (*ā*), f. lightning; long pepper; fortune, Lakshmī or the goddess of fortune; N. of a metre consisting of four lines of sixteen syllables each. — *Cañćala-tā*, f. or *ćañćala-tva, am*, n. movableness, unsteadiness, inconstancy, fickleness. — *Cañćala-hṛidaya, as, ā, am*, capricious, fickle, false-hearted. — *Cañćalākshikā* (°*la-akshi*), f., N. of a metre consisting of four lines of twelve syllables each. — *Cañćalākhya* (°*la-ākh*°), *as*, m. incense.

चञ्चु *ćañću*. See under rt. *ćañć*.

चञ्चुर *ćañćura*. See under *ćañć* and *ćañćarin*.

चञ्चुल *ćañćula, as*, m., N. of a man; (*ās*), m. pl. the descendants of this man.

चट् *ćaṭ* (fr. rt. *ćat* and *ćal* and *uć-ćaṭ*), cl. 1. P. *ćaṭati*, &c., to break, break off, fall off, separate; to rain; to cover; (in the last two senses a various reading for *kaṭ*): Caus. P. *ćāṭayati, -yitum*, to break, pierce; to kill, injure.

Caṭaka, as, m. a sparrow; N. of a poet; (*ās*), m. pl. a nickname of the pupils of Vaiśampāyana (also written *ćaraka*); (*ā*), f. a hen-sparrow; a young hen-sparrow; Turdus Macrourus, = *śyāmā*; the root of long pepper, = *ćaṭakā-śiras*; (*ikā*), f. a hen-sparrow; the root of long pepper. — *Caṭakā-śiras*, n. the root of long pepper. — *Caṭikā-śira, as*, m. or *ćaṭikā-śiras*, n. the root of long pepper.

Caṭana, am, n. cracking, splitting; falling off in small pieces.

Caṭu, us, u, m. n. kind or flattering discourse; a scream, screech; a devotional posture among ascetics; (*us*), m. the belly. — *Caṭu-grāma, as*, m., N. of a place. — *Caṭu-lālasa, as, ā, am*, pleased with or desirous of flattery.

Caṭula, as, ā, am, trembling, tremulous, moving, movable, shaking, unsteady; kind, fine, beautiful; (*ā*), f. lightning.

Caṭulola or *ćaṭullola, as, ā, am* (perhaps a corruption of *ćaṭula-lola*), moving gracefully; tremulous and beautiful, beautiful as a soft swimming eye &c.

चटचटा *ćaṭaćaṭā*, ind. an onomatopoetic word for the clashing of weapons, the crackling of fire, rattling of violent rain, &c.

Caṭaćaṭāya, A. *-yate*, to crackle, rattle, to make any sharp sound rapidly repeated.

Caṭaćaṭāyana, am, n. crackling, a rattling sound.

चण् *ćaṇ* [cf. rt. *ćan* and *vaṇ* and *van*], cl. 1. P. *ćaṇati*, &c., to sound, to give; to go, to injure, hurt, kill: Caus. *ćaṇayati* or *ćāṇayati, -yitum*, Aor. *aćīćaṇat* and *aćaćāṇat*.

चण *ćaṇa, as, ā, am*, (at the end of a compound) renowned, famous for, known [cf. *vidyā-ćaṇa* and *akshara-ćaṇa*]; (*as*), m. = *ćaṇaka*, the chick-pea. — *Caṇa-druma, as*, m., N. of a plant, = *kshudra-gokshura*; (also written *ćaṇi-druma*.) — *Caṇa-pattrī*, f., N. of a plant; [cf. *rudantī*.]

Caṇaka, as, m. the chick-pea (Cicer Arietinum); N. of a Muni, the father of Cāṇakya; (*akā*), f. linseed, Linum Usitatissimum (*atasī*), [cf. *ćaṇḍikā*]; (*ikā*), f. a kind of grass, = *kshetra-jā, go-dugdhā, su-nīlā, himā*. — *Caṇakātmaja* (°*ka-āt*°), *as*, m., N. of a sage, also called Cāṇakya or Vātsyāyana.

—*Caṇakāmlaka* (°*ka-amla*), *am*, n.=*ćaṇaka-lavaṇa*, pease with salt, sour pease.—*Caṇakāmla-vār*, *r*, n. acid drops of water on the leaves of the cicer.

चण्ड् ćaṇḍ, cl. 1. and 10. A. *ćaṇḍate* and *ćaṇḍayate*, *-yitum*, to be angry; to be wrathful or passionate; [cf. Goth. *hata*; Eng. *hate*; Germ. *hasse*; Lat. *odi?*].

Caṇḍa, *as*, *ā*, *am*, fierce, violent, impetuous, hot, warm, ardent with passion, passionate, wrathful, angry, cruel; active, quick; mischievous, evil; pungent, acrid; circumcised; *ćaṇḍam*, ind. violently, passionately, fiercely, in anger; (*as*), m. an evil being, a demon, (*ćaṇḍasya naptyaḥ*, the daughters of Caṇḍa, a class of female demons); an epithet of Śiva; also of Skanda; N. of a Daitya; of an attendant of Yama; or of Śiva; the tamarind tree; (*ā*), f. a N. of the goddess Durgā, applied especially to her incarnation for the purpose of destroying the Asura or demon called Mahisha, (this exploit forms the subject of a section of the Mārkaṇḍeya-Purāṇa, and is particularly celebrated in Bengal at the Durgā-pūjā, or festival held in honour of the goddess, towards the close of the year, about Oct.–Nov.); N. of one of the eight Nāyikās or Śaktis of Durgā; N. of a goddess fulfilling the orders of the twelfth Arhat of the present Ava-sarpiṇī; N. of a river; N. of several prickly plants, =*oshadhi*, Andropogon Aciculatus; Mucuna Pruritus (*kapi-kaććhu*); Salvinia Cucculata (*ākhu-karṇī*), =*śveta-dūrvā* and =*linginī*; a perfume, commonly Chor; (*ī*), f. a N. of Durgā; a passionate woman, a vixen; a term of endearment applied to a mistress; N. of the wife of Uddālaka; N. of a metre consisting of four lines of thirteen syllables each; (*am*), n. heat, warmth; passion, wrath; [cf. *a-ćaṇḍī*, *uć-ćaṇḍa*, *pra-ć*°, *ćāṇḍa*.] —*Caṇḍa-karman*, *ā*, m., N. of a Rākshasa. —*Caṇḍa-kolāhalā*, f. a kind of musical instrument. —*Caṇḍa-kauśika*, *as*, m., N. of a son of Kakshīvat; (*am*), n. (?) title of a drama.—*Caṇḍa-girika*, *as*, m., N. of a man.—*Caṇḍa-ghaṇṭā*, f., a N. of Durgā.—*Caṇḍa-tā*, f. and *ćaṇḍa-tva*, *am*, n. warmth, pungency; warmth of temper, passionateness.—*Caṇḍa-tuṇḍaka*, *as*, m., N. of a son of Garuḍa.—*Caṇḍa-dīdhiti*, *is*, m. 'having hot rays,' the sun; [cf. *ćaṇḍāṅśu*.]—*Caṇḍa-nāyikā*, f. an epithet of the goddess Durgā; N. of one of the eight Nāyikās or Śaktis of Durgā.—*Caṇḍa-bala*, *as*, m., N. of one of the monkey followers of Rāma. —*Caṇḍa-bhānu*, *us*, m., N. of a man.—*Caṇḍa-bhārgava*, *as*, m., N. of a Brāhman of the family of Cyavana.—*Caṇḍa-mahāvīra-tantra*, *as*, m. title of a Buddhist work, =*kallavīra-tantra*.—*Caṇḍa-mahāsena*, *as*, m., N. of a king of Ujjayinī.—*Caṇḍa-muṇḍā*, f. a form of Durgā; [cf. *ćarma-muṇḍa* and *ćāmuṇḍā*.]—*Caṇḍa-mṛiga*, *as*, m. a wild animal; epithet of a passionate man.—*Caṇḍa-rava*, *as*, m., N. of a jackal.—*Caṇḍa-rudrikā*, f. knowledge of mystical nature, acquired by worship of the Nāyikās.—*Caṇḍa-vat*, *ān*, *atī*, *at*, violent, warm, passionate; (*vatī*), f. an epithet of Durgā; N. of one of the eight Nāyikās or Śaktis of Durgā. —*Caṇḍa-varman*, *ā*, m., N. of a prince (probably a corruption of *ćandra-varman*).—*Caṇḍa-vikrama*, *as*, *ā*, *am*. of impetuous valour; (*as*), m., N. of a prince.—*Caṇḍa-vṛishṭi-prayāta*, *am*, n., N. of a metre of four lines of twenty-seven syllables each.—*Caṇḍa-vega*, *as*, *ā*, *am*, having an impetuous course or current, violent; (*as*), m., N. of a Gandharva chief.—*Caṇḍa-śakti*, *is*, m., N. of a Daitya. —*Caṇḍāṅśu* (°*ḍa-aṅ*°), *us*, m. the sun ('having hot rays;' cf. *ćaṇḍa-dīdhiti*).—*Caṇḍāditya-tīrtha* (°*ḍa-ād*°), *am*, n., N. of a Tīrtha.—*Caṇḍāśoka* (°*ḍa-aś*°), *as*, m., N. of a prince, also called Kāmāśoka, and as a protector of Buddhism, Dharmāśoka.—*Caṇḍī-kusuma*, *as*, m. red oleander; [cf. *rakta-karavīra*.]—*Caṇḍī-dāsa*, *as*, m., N. of the author of a commentary called Kāvya-prakāśa-ṭīkā. —*Caṇḍī-devī-śarman*, *ā*, m., N. of a scholiast. —*Caṇḍī-māhātmya*, *am*, n.=*ćaṇḍikā-māhātmya*. —*Caṇḍīśa* (°*ḍī-īśa*), *as*, m. the husband of Caṇḍī, Śiva.—*Caṇḍeśvara* (°*ḍā-īś*°), *as*, m. 'Caṇḍā's lord,' an epithet of Śiva; N. of a writer on jurisprudence; also of an astronomer.—*Caṇḍogrā* (°*ḍa-ug*°), f., N. of one of the eight Nāyikās or Śaktis of Durgā.

Caṇḍi, *is*, f.=*ćaṇḍī*, a N. of Durgā.

Caṇḍikā, f. a N. of Durgā; a N. of the Devī-māhātmya; Linum Usitatissimum; [cf. *umā*, *devī*, *haimavatī*, *ćaṇakā*.]—*Caṇḍika-ghaṇṭa*, *as*, m. (? fr. *ćaṇḍikā*+*ghaṇṭa*, q. v.), a N. of Śiva. —*Caṇḍikā-māhātmya*, *am*, n. a section of the Mārkaṇḍeya-Purāṇa.

Caṇḍin, *ī*, m., N. of an author; [cf. *ćāmuṇḍa*.]

Caṇḍiman, *ā*, m. passion, violence, cruelty; heat.

Caṇḍila, *as*, m., N. of Rudra; a barber; a kind of pot-herb [cf. *vāstūka*]; (*ā*), f., N. of a river.

Caṇḍī-kṛi, cl. 8. P. *-karoti*, *-kartum*, to enrage, make angry or violent.

चण्डात ćaṇḍāta, *as*, m. fragrant oleander, Nerium Odorum.

चण्डातक ćaṇḍātaka, *as*, *am*, m. n. (fr. *ćaṇḍa?*), a short petticoat.

चण्डाल ćaṇḍāla, *as*, m. (fr. *ćaṇḍa?*, cf. *ćāṇḍāla*), an outcast, a Caṇḍāla, the generic name for a man of the lowest and most despised of the mixed tribes, born from a Śūdra father and Brāhman mother.—*Caṇḍāla-kanda*, *as*, m. a kind of bulbous plant.—*Caṇḍāla-tā*, f. or *ćaṇḍāla-tva*, *am*, n. the state or condition of a Caṇḍāla.—*Caṇḍāla-vallakī*, f. the lute of the Caṇḍāla, a common lute.

Caṇḍālikā, f. the lute of the Caṇḍāla, a common or vulgar lute; an epithet of Durgā; a kind of plant. —*Caṇḍālikā-bandha*, *as*, m. a kind of knot.

चण्डु ćaṇḍu, *us*, m. a rat; a small monkey, Simia Erythræa.

चत् ćat, cl. 1. P. A. *ćatati*, *-te*, occurring only in pres. part. and past and fut. pass. part. (see below), Ved. to hide one's self; to go; to ask, beg, solicit [cf. *ćad*]: Caus. P. A. *ćātayati*, *-te*, *-yitum*, to cause to hide; to scare, frighten away; [cf. Gr. χατέω, χατίζω.]

Catat, *an*, *antī*, *at*, hiding one's self; (Sāy.) going, residing in, being in.

Catita, or Ved. *ćatta*, *as*, *ā*, *am*, bidden, made to disappear.

Catin, *ī*, *inī*, *i*, Ved. hiding one's self; (Sāy.) destroying enemies, frightening away.

Catya, *as*, *ā*, *am*, to be hiden &c.

Cātaka, *as*, m. See s. v.

Cātana, *as*, *ā*, *am*, driving away, removing [cf. *abhiśasti-ć*°, *amīva-ć*°, *arāya-ć*°]; (*am*), n., scil. *sūktam*, certain verses of the Atharva-veda, the object of which is to avert evil demons; (*as*), m., N. of the supposed Ṛishi of these verses of the Atharva-veda.

चतुर् ćatur, *ćatvāras* m. pl., *ćatasras* f. pl., *ćatvāri* n. pl. (said to be fr. rt. *ćat*), four. In Vedic Sanskṛit the inst., dat., abl., and loc. have the accent on the penultimate; in the latter language either on the penultimate or on the last syllable. A Vedic form of the gen. pl. fem. *ćatasṛiṇām* for *ćatasṛiṇām* occurs sometimes in Epic poetry; [cf. Gr. τέσσαρες, τέτταρες; Æol. πίσυρες; Goth. *fidvor*; Cambro-Brit. *pedwar*, *pedalr*; Lat. *quatuor*; Lith. *keturi*; Slav. *ćetyrje*; Hib. *ceathair*, *ceteora*; Zend *ćathru*.] —*Catuḥ-pañća*, *as*, *ā*, *am*, four or five; also *ćatuḥ-pañćan*.—*Catuḥpañćāśa*, *as*, *ī*, *am*, the 54th. —*Catuḥ-pañćāśat*, *t*, f., 54.—*Catuḥpañćāśad-adhika-śata*, *as*, *ī*, *am*, the 154th.—*Catuḥ-pattrī*, f., N. of a plant, =*kshudra-pāshāṇa-bhedī*. —*Catuḥ-parṇī*, f. a kind of sorrel (*kshudrāmlikā*). —*Catuḥ-pārśva*, *am*, n. the four sides of a square. —*Catuḥ-puṇḍra*, *as*, m., N. of a shrub, =*bhiṇḍā*. —*Catuḥ-phalā*, f. Uraria Lagopodioides (=*nāga-balā*).—*Catuḥ-śata*, *am*, n., 104; 400.—*Catuḥ-śata-tama*, *as*, *ī*, *am*, the 104th.—*Catuḥ-śāla*, *as*, *ā*, *am*, having four halls; built in a square; (*am*, *ā*), n. f. or *ćatuḥ-śālaka*, *am*, n. a square of four houses; a quadrangle enclosed by four buildings.—*Catuḥ-śriṅga*, *as*, *ā*, *am*, four-horned; (*as*), m., N. of a mountain.—*Catuḥ-śrotra*, *as*, *ā*, *am*, having four ears.—*Catuḥshashṭa*, *as*, *ī*, *am*, the 64th; having 64 added.—*Catuḥ-shashṭi*, *is*, f., 64; a N. for the Ṛig-veda which consists of 64 Adhyāyas; the 64 arts [cf. *kalā*].—*Catuḥshashṭi-tama*, *as*, *ī*, *am*, the 64th.—*Catuḥ-sana*, *as*, *ā*, *am*, containing the four sons of Brahmā, whose names begin with Sana (*sanaka*, *sananda*, *sanātana*, *sanatkumāra*).—*Catuḥsaptata*, *as*, *ī*, *am*, the 74th. —*Catuḥ-saptati*, *is*, f., 74.—*Catuḥsaptati-tama*, *as*, *ī*, *am*, the 74th.—*Catuḥ-sama*, *am*, n. an unguent of four ingredients, sandal, agallochum, saffron, and musk; (*as*, *ā*, *am*), one whose body has four smooth places.—*Catuḥ-sahasra*, *am*, n., 1004; 4000.—*Catuḥ-sīmā*, f. a border or boundary on all four sides.—*Catuḥ-srakti*, *is*, *is*, *i*, Ved. quadrangular.—*Catur-aṅśa*, *as*, m. a fourth part. —*Catur-aksha*, *as*, *ā*, *am*, Ved. having four eyes. —*Catur-akshara*, *am*, n. an aggregate or combination of four syllables; (*as*, *ā*, *am*), consisting of four syllables.—*Catur-aṅga*, *as*, *ā*, *am*, consisting of four members, quadripartite; (*ćatur-aṅgam balam*, an entire or complete army, comprising elephants, chariots, cavalry, and infantry); (*as*), m., N. of a son of Loma-pāda or Roma-pāda; the plant Cucumis Utilissimus [cf. *ghoṭikā*]; (*ā*), f., scil. *senā*, an entire army &c.; (*am*), n. an entire army &c.; a sort of chess.—*Caturaṅga-bala*, *am*, n. an entire army &c.; [cf. the preceding.]—*Caturaṅga-balādhyaksha* (°*la-adh*°), *as*, m. the commander-in-chief of a complete army.—*Caturaṅga-sainya*, *am*, n. an entire army; [cf. *ćatur-aṅga*.]—*Catur-aṅgin*, *ī*, *iṇī*, *i*, having four parts or members, quadripartite; (*iṇī*), f. a complete army.—*Catur-aṅgula*, *am*, n. the four fingers of the hand (without the thumb); four fingers broad, four inches; (*as*), m. the plant Cathartocarpus Fistula.—*Catur-adhyāyikā*, *am*, f. n. a collection of four Adhyāyas. —*Catur-anīka*, *as*, *ā*, *am*, Ved. having four faces, facing the four quarters.—*Catur-anugāna*, *am*, n., N. of a Sāman.—*Catur-anta*, *as*, *ā*, *am*, bordered on all four sides; (*ā*), f. the earth.—*Caturanteśa* (°*tā-īśa*), *as*, m. lord of the earth, a king.—*Catur-avatta*, *as*, *ā*, *am* (see *ava-d*°), divided into four parts; (*am*), n. division into four parts.—*Catur-avattin*, *ī*, *inī*, *i* (see *ava-d*°), one who is accustomed to offer the havis in four portions.—*Caturaśīta*, *as*, *ī*, *am*, [illegible] *Catur-aśīti*, *is*, f., 84.—*Catur-aśīti*-[illegible], *am*, the 84th.—*Catur-aśra* or *ćatur*-[illegible] *ćatur-asraka*, *as*, *ā*, *am*, four-cornered, quadrangular; regular; (*as*), m. a quadrangular figure; a square; (in astronomy) N. of the fourth and eighth lunar mansions; (*ās*), m. pl., N. of various Ketus.—*Catur-aśva*, *as*, m., N. of a prince. —*Catur-asraka*, *as*, m., N. of various postures in acting; see *ćatur-aśra*.—*Catur-aha*, *am*, n. a period of four days; (*as*), m. a Soma sacrifice lasting four days; [cf. *atri-ćatur-aha*.]—*Catur-ātman*, *ā*, *ā*, *a*, representing four persons; having four faces.—*Catur-ānana*, *as*, *ā*, *am*, having four faces; (*as*), m. an epithet of Brahmā.—*Catur-ānartana*, *am*, n. a dance by four, or in four divisions.—*Catur-iḍas-pada-stobha*, *am*, n., N. of a Sāman.—*Catur-uttara*, *as*, *ā*, *am*, increasing by four.—*Catur-ushaṇa*, *am*, n. the four hot spices, black pepper, long pepper, dry ginger, and the root of long pepper; [cf. *try-ūshaṇa* and *ćatur-jātaka*.]—*Catur-gati*, *is*, m. a tortoise (going on four feet).—*Catur-gava*, *am*, n. a carriage drawn by four oxen.—*Catur-guṇa*, *as*, *ā*, *am*, four times, four-fold, quadruple. —*Catur-gṛihīta*, *as*, *ā*, *am*, taken up (or ladled out, as a fluid) four times; (*am*), n. taking up (any fluid) four times.—*Catur-grāma*, *as* or *am* (?), m. or n. (?), N. of a country.—*Catur-jātaka*, *am*, n.=*ćāturjātaka*, =*kaṭu-ćāturjātaka*, q. v.—*Caturṇavata*, *as*, *ī*, *am*, with 94 added (e. g. *ćaturṇavatam śatam* = 194); [cf. *ćatur-navata*.]-

—*Catur-danshṭra, as,* m. 'having four tusks;' N. of Vishṇu; of one of the attendants of Skanda; of a Dānava.—*Catur-dat, an, antī, at,* four-toothed. —*Catur-danta, as,* m. 'having four tusks,' an epithet of Airāvata, the elephant of Indra; N. of an elephant mentioned in the Pañća-tantra.—*Caturdaśa, as, ī, am,* the fourteenth; consisting of fourteen; (*ī*), f., scil. *rātri,* the fourteenth day in a lunar fortnight. —*Caturdaśa-dhā,* ind. fourteen-fold. —*Catur-daśan, a,* pl. fourteen; [cf. Lat. *quatuordecim;* Lith. *keturólika.*]—*Caturdaśama, as, ī, am,* the fourteenth.—*Caturdaśa-mata-vireka, as,* m. title of a work by Śaṅkara.—*Caturdaśika, as* or *am,* m. or n. (?), a feast on the fourteenth day of a lunar fortnight.—*Catur-dārika, as* or *am,* m. or n. (?), N. of the fifth Lambaka in the Kathā-sarit-sāgara. —*Catur-dikshu* or *ćatur-diśam,* ind. towards the four quarters, on all sides, all around.—*Catur-dola, as, am,* m. n. a royal litter.—*Catur-dvīpa-ćakra-vartin, ī,* m. the sovereign of the four Dvīpas. —*Catur-dhā,* ind. in four parts, four-fold; [cf. Hib. *ceathardha;* Gr. τέτραχα.]—*Caturdhā-bhū,* cl. 1. P. *-bhavati, -vitum,* to be divided into four parts. —*Caturdhā-śānti, is,* f. a religious ceremony performed at the time of making the stated offerings to deceased ancestors.—*Caturnavata, as, ī, am,* the 94th.—*Catur-navati, is,* f., 94.—*Caturnavati-tama, as, ī, am,* the 94th.—*Catur-bāhu, us, us, u,* four-armed; an epithet of Vishṇu and Śiva; [cf. *ća-tur-bhuja.*]—*Catur-bhadra, am,* n. the aggregate of four objects of human wishes, viz. *dharma,* virtue; *kāma,* pleasure; *artha,* wealth; and *moksha,* final beatitude.—*Catur-bhāga, as,* m. the fourth part, a quarter.—*Catur-bhuja, am,* n. (generally in compounds), four arms; (*as, ā, am*), having four arms; quadrangular; (*as*), m. an epithet of Vishṇu or Kṛishṇa; a square; N. of a Dānava; N. of the instructor of Rāmānanda; N. of the father of Śiva-datta.—*Caturbhuja-bhaṭṭāćārya* (°*ṭa-āć*°), *as,* m., N. of an author.—*Catur-bhūyas, ān, asī, as,* containing four (syllables) more.—*Catur-mahārāja, ās,* m. pl. the four great kings or gods of the highest of the six Buddhist heavens.—*Caturmahārāja-kāyika, as, ā, am,* belonging to the group of the four great kings; epithet of a class of deities with Buddhists; also *ćaturmahārājika.*—*Catur-māsa, am,* n. a period of four months.—*Catur-mukha, am,* n. (in compounds), four faces; (*as, ī, am*), having four faces; (an arrow) having four points; (*as*), m. an epithet of Brahmā, of Vishṇu, Śiva, and of a Dānava; a preparation of mercury (?).—*Caturmukha-rasa, as,* m. a preparation of great curative power.—*Ca-tur-yuga, am,* n. the aggregate of the four Yugas or ages of the world, a Mahā-yuga or 4,320,000 years; (*as, ā, am*), drawn by four (oxen &c.); comprehending the four Yugas or ages of the world. —*Catur-yuj, k, k, k,* drawn by four (oxen &c.). —*Catur-vaktra, as,* m. 'four-faced,' N. of Brahmā; of a Dānava.—*Catur-vaya, as, ī, am,* Ved. four-fold. —*Catur-varga, as,* m. a collection of four things, the four objects of human pursuit collectively; see *ćatur-bhadra.* —*Caturvarga-ćintāmaṇi, is,* m. title of a work.—*Catur-varṇa, as* or *am,* m. or n. (?), the four classes or castes of Hindūs, viz. Brāhmans, Kshatriyas, Vaiśyas, and Śūdras; four principal colours; four letters.—*Caturvarṇa-maya, as, ī, am,* consisting of the four castes.—*Caturvarṇya, am,* n. the system of the four castes.—*Catur-var-shikā,* f., scil. *go,* a cow four years old.—*Catur-vāhin, ī,* m., scil. *ratha,* a carriage drawn by four (horses &c.).—*Caturviṇśa, as, ī, am,* the 24th; having 24 added (e. g. *ćaturviṇśam śatam,* 124); consisting of 24; (*as*), m., N. of a Stoma; (*am*), n., scil. *ahan,* N. of an Ekāha.—*Catur-viṇśati, is,* f., 24; the 24th year (e. g. *ā-ćaturviṇśateḥ,* to the 24th year); title of a work.—*Caturviṇśatika, as, ī, am,* consisting of 24.—*Caturviṇśati-tama, as, ī, am,* the 24th.—*Caturviṇśati-mata, am,* n. '24 sects,' title of a work.—*Caturviṇśatimata-vyākhyā,* f. a commentary by Bhaṭṭoji-dīkshita. —*Caturviṇśaty-avatāra-ćaritra, am,* n. 'history of 24 incarnations' by Narahara-dāsa.—*Caturviṇśā-kshara, as, ā, am,* containing 24 syllables.—*Catur-vidya, as, ā, am,* familiar with the four Vedas; (*as*), m. one who has studied the four Vedas.—*Catur-vidha, as, ā, am,* four-fold; of four sorts or kinds, in four ways.—*Catur-vīja, am,* n. the four kinds of seed, i. e. the seed of Kālājājī, Candra-śūra, Methikā, and Yavānikā.—*Catur-vīra, as, ā, am,* Ved. an epithet applied to a particular unguent; also to a Soma sacrifice which lasts four days.—*Catur-veda, ās,* m. pl., the four Vedas, viz. the Ṛig-veda, Yajur-veda, Sāma-veda, and Atharva-veda; (*as, ā, am*), containing the four Vedas; familiar with the four Vedas; (*ās*), m. pl. a class of manes.—*Catur-vedin, ī, inī, i,* familiar with the four Vedas. —*Catur-vyūha, as,* m. an epithet of Vishṇu; [cf. *nava-vyūha.*]—*Catur-hanu, us,* m. 'having four jaws,' N. of a Dānava.—*Catur-hasta, as, ā, am,* four-armed.—*Catur-hāyaṇa, as, ī, am,* four years old; (*ī*), f. a cow of four years.—*Catur-hotṛi, tā* or *tāras,* m. sing. or plur., N. of a certain liturgical section of Vedic works intended for recitation; containing the four chief priests.—*Catur-hotra, as,* m. comprehending the four chief priests.—*Caturho-traka, am,* n. the four chief priests; the duties of these priests.—*Catuśćatvāriṇśa, as, ī, am,* the 44th; having 44 added; containing 44; (*as*), m., N. of a Stoma.—*Catuś-ćatvāriṇśat, t,* f., 44.—*Catush-karṇa, as, ā, am,* four-eared; heard by four ears only; (*ī*), f., N. of one of the Mātṛis attendant on Skanda.—*Catushkarṇa-tā,* f. the state of being heard by only four ears, a secret.—*Catush-koṇa, as, ā, am,* square, quadrangular; (*as*), m. a quadrangular figure, a square, a tetragon.—*Catu-shṭoma, as,* m. (fr. *ćatur* and *stoma*), a Stoma consisting of four parts; (*as, ā, am*), connected with such a Stoma. —*Catush-patha, as, am,* m. n. a place where four roads meet, a cross-way; (*as*), m. a Brāhman (so called from the four *āśramās,* q. v.).—*Catushpatha-niketā* or *ćatushpatha-ratā,* f., N. of one of the Mātṛis attendant on Skanda.—*Catush-pada, as, ā, am,* having four feet; consisting of four Pādas; (in arithmetic or algebra) tetranomial; (*as*), m. an animal with four legs, a quadruped; (in astron.) a term for certain signs of the zodiac; N. of a particular Karaṇa; a kind of coitus; N. of a shrub; (*ā*), f. a metre containing 30 + 4 + 4 syllabic instants; (*am*), n. a conjunction of four Pādas.—*Catushpa-dikā,* f., N. of a metre containing 30 + 4 + 4 syllabic instants.—*Catush-pāṭī,* f. a river (winding four ways?).—*Catush-pāṭhī,* f. a school for Brāhmans in which the four Vedas are repeated.—*Catush-pāṇi, is, is, i,* four-handed; (*is*), m. an epithet of Vishṇu. —*Catush-pād, -pāt, -padī, -pat,* quadruped; having made four steps; consisting of four members, divided into four parts, consisting of four parts; (*-pāt*), m. a quadruped; anything which has four parts or members; a judicial procedure, consisting of four processes, plea, defence, rejoinder, and sentence; (*-padī*), f. a female quadruped; (*-pat*), n. the quadrupeds collectively, the animals.—*Catush-pāda, as, ī, am,* quadruped; divided into four parts, consisting of four parts; (*as*), m. a quadruped.—*Catush-pārśva, am,* n. the four sides of anything.—*Catu-stana, as, ā, am* (fr. *ćatuḥ-stana*), having four nipples.—*Catustriṇśa, as, ī, am,* the 34th; having 34 added; containing 34.—*Catustriṇśaj-jātaka-jña, as,* m. a Buddha.—*Catus-triṇśat, t,* f., 34. —*Catus-sama,* see *ćatuḥ-sama.*—*Catū-rājī,* f. (fr. *ćatur* + *rājan*), the four kings; N. of the luckiest or most desired termination of the game called Caturaṅga, by which one king gains the four thrones.—*Catū-rātra, as, ā, am* (fr. *ćatur* + *rātra*), lasting four days (lit. nights); (*as* or *am*), m. n., N. of a certain ceremony.

1. *ćatura, as, ā, am,* (at the end of some compounds) = *ćatur,* four; see *a-ć*°, *upa-ć*°, *tri-ć*°. (For 2. *ćatura* see next col.)

Caturtha, as, ī, am, fourth, the fourth; (*as*), m. the fourth letter in every class of consonants, i. e. *gh, jh, ḍh, dh, bh;* (*ī*), f., scil. *rātri,* the fourth day in a lunar fortnight; (scil. *vibhakti*), the termination of the fourth case, the fourth case, the dative case; (*as, ā, am*), constituting the fourth part; (*am*), n. a quarter; [cf. Lith. *ketwirtas;* Slav. *ćetvertyi, ćetvertaja;* Gr. τέταρτος; Lat. *quartus;* Goth. *fidvorda* (?); Germ. *vierter.*]—*Caturtha-karman, a,* n. the ceremonies performed on the fourth day of a marriage.—*Caturtha-kālam,* ind. at the fourth meal, at the evening of every second day of a person's fasting.—*Caturthakālika, as, ā, am,* one who passes three meals without eating and partakes only of the fourth.—*Caturtha-phala, am,* n. the second inequality or equation of a planet.—*Caturtha-bhakta, am,* n. consuming the fourth meal (after having passed three without eating).—*Caturtha-bhāj, k, k, k,* receiving the fourth part as a toll from one's subjects (as a king).—*Caturtha-svara, am,* n., N. of a Sāman. —*Caturthānśa* (°*tha-an*°), *as,* m. a quarter, a fourth part; (*as, ā, am*), receiving a quarter.—*Ca-turthāśrama* (°*tha-āś*°), *as,* m. the fourth order of a Brāhman's life.

Caturthaka, as, ā, am, the fourth; returning or repeated every four days as a fever, quartan; (*ikā*), f. a weight equal to four Karshas or one Pāla.

Caturya, nom. P. *ćaturyati,* to wish for four.

Catushka, as, ā, am, four, consisting of four, increased by four (e. g. *ćatushkam śatam* = 104 or four per cent; (*as*), m., N. of a man; (*ī*), f. a large four-sided pond or tank; a bed or musquito-curtain; (*am*), n. the number four; a collection of four; a cross-way; a quadrangular court-yard [cf. *ćatvara*]; a hall resting on four columns; a necklace of four strings.

Catushkikā, f. the number four.

Catushkin, ī, iṇī, i, having four (parts &c.) of anything.

Catushṭaya, as, ī, am, four-fold, consisting of four; (*am*), n. the number four, a collection of four, an aggregate of four, a quaternion; a square; a collection of Sūtras consisting of four sections; the first, fourth, seventh, and tenth signs of the zodiac; the centre of a circle.—*Catushṭaya-samāsa, ās,* m. pl. four classes of compounds, viz. Avyayī-bhāva, Tat-purusha, Dvandva, and Bahu-vrīhi.

Catus, ind. four times; [cf. Zend *ćathrus.*]

Catvara, am, n. a quadrangular place or court-yard, a place in which many ways meet; a levelled spot of ground prepared for a sacrifice.—*Catvara-vāsinī,* f., N. of one of the Mātṛis attendant on Skanda.

Catvāriṇśa, as, ī, am (fr. the next), the 40th; having 40 added; consisting of 40.

Catvāriṇśat, t, f. (said to be fr. *ćatvāri,* n. pl. + *daśat,* a decad), 40; [cf. Lat. *quadraginta;* Gr. τεσσαράκοντα.]

Catvāriṇśati, is, f. = the preceding (in *dvā-ćatvā-riṇśati*).

चतुर 2. *ćatura, as, ā, am* (said to be fr. rt. *ćat;* for 1. see under *ćatur* above), swift, quick; dexterous, clever, skilful, ingenious; charming, agreeable; visible, perceptible; (*as*), m. a round pillow, one for the cheek; (*am*), n. skilfulness, cleverness; an elephant's stable; [cf. *ćātura.*]—*Catura-tā,* f. cleverness, skilfulness, cunningness.

Caturaka, as, m., N. of a jackal; (*ikā*), f., N. of a woman.

चतुर्थ *ćaturtha.* See col. 2.

चतुल *ćatula, as, ā, am,* depositing, placing, fixing.

चत्वारिंशत् *ćatvāriṇśat.* See above.

चत्वाल *ćatvāla, as,* m. a hole in the ground &c. prepared for an oblation with fire, or for the sacrificial fire; the womb; Kuśa grass; [cf. *ćātvāla.*]

चद् *ćad,* cl. 1. P. A. *ćadati, -te,* to ask or beg, to solicit; [cf. *ćat.*]

चदिर *ćadira, as,* m. the moon; camphor; an elephant; a snake; [cf. *ćandira.*]

चन् 1. *ćan*, cl. 1. P. *ćanati*, to sound, utter a sound; cl. 1. P. or Caus. *ćanati* or *ćanayati*, *-yitum*, to hurt, injure, wound, kill.

चन् 2. *ćan* (related to rt. *kan*, only found in the Ved. Aor. 2nd du. *ćanishṭam*), to delight in anything, be satisfied with (with loc.), to love.

Canas, as, n., Ved. delight, satisfaction; (Sāy.) food; (only found connected with rt. *dhā*, in) *ćano dhā*, to delight in, be satisfied with, to find anything acceptable or agreeable (with acc. or loc.), to enjoy; (Sāy.) to grant food. — *Cano-dhā, ās, ās, am*, Ved. satisfied, gracious; (according to schol.) giving food. — *Cano-hita, as, ā, am*, Ved. made favourable or inclined to do anything, willing to do anything; (Sāy.) having food given to one's self.

Canasita, as, ā, am (fr. *ćanasya* below), Ved. delighted, satisfied, gracious. — *Canasita-vat, ān, atī, at*, Ved. containing the word *ćanasita*; agreeable (as speech or words).

Canasya, nom. P., Ved. *ćanasyati*, to delight in, be satisfied with; (Sāy.) to like; to eat.

Canishṭha, as, ā, am (superl. of rt. 2. *ćan*), Ved. very favourable, very gracious; very acceptable; (Sāy.) containing or granting much food.

चन *ćana* (originally for *ća+na*), ind. and not, also not, even not, not even; even, also, and. This particle is placed after the word to which it gives force; and in Vedic Sanskṛit is generally, but not always, found without any other negative particle, whereas in the later language another negative is usually added (e.g. *āpaś ćana pra minanti vratam vām*, not even the waters violate your ordinance; *nāha vivyāća pṛithivī ćanainam*, the earth even does not contain him). When *ćana* is added to the interrogatives *ka, katara, katama, kad, kim, katham, kadā, kutas, kva*, it makes them indefinite; see 2. *ka*, &c.

चन्द् *ćand* (originally *śćand?*), cl. 1. P. *ćandati*, to shine, to be bright; to gladden; (only the Ved. part. of the Intens. *ćaniśćadat* seems to occur); [cf. Lat. *candeo* and *candela*.]

Canda, as, m. the moon; N. of the author of the work Pṛithivī-rājarāsaka; [cf. *ćandra* below; cf. also Hib. *canu*, 'full moon.']

Candaka, as, ā, am, pleasing, joy-inspiring; (*as*), m. the moon, moonlight; a small silvery fish of a genus allied to the Zeus or Chanda; (a various reading has *ćandraka*.) — *Candaka-pushpa, am*, n. cloves; (a wrong form for *ćandana-pushpa*.)

Candana, as, am, m. n. sandal or Sirium Myrtifolium; either the tree, the wood, or the unctuous preparation of the wood held in high estimation as perfumes; anything which is the most excellent of its kind; (*am*), n. a kind of grass, = *bhadra-kālī*; red sandal-wood; (*as*), m., N. of a divine being with Buddhists; of a prince; of an ape; (*ā*), f. a kind of plant [cf. *ćandana-gopī* and *ćandana-śārivā*]; N. of a river; (*ī*), f., N. of a river; [cf. *ku-ćandana, pīta-ć°, rakta-ć°, śveta-ć°, hari-ć°*.] — *Candana-giri, is*, m. the Malaya mountain, part of the southern range of the Ghaṭs, where sandal-wood is found. — *Candana-gopī*, f. a kind of plant, = *śārivā-viśesha*; [cf. *ćandanā*.] — *Candana-dāsa, as*, m., N. of a merchant. — *Candana-pāla, as*, m., N. of a prince. — *Candana-pushpa, am*, n. cloves. — *Candana-maya, as, ī, am*, made of sandal-wood. — *Candana-vāri, i*, n. sandal-water. — *Candana-śārivā*, f., N. of a plant, a kind of Sārivā. — *Candana-sāra, as*, m. the most excellent sandal-wood; a kind of alkali (*vajra-kshāra*). — *Candanāgra* (°*na-ag*°), *as*, m., N. of a man. — *Candanāćala* (°*na-ać*°), *as*, m. or *ćandanādri* (°*na-ad*°), *is*, m. = *ćandana-giri*. — *Candanā-vatī*, f., N. of a river. — *Candanodaka* (°*na-ud*°), *am*, n. sandal-water. — *Candanodaka-dundubhi, is*, m. an epithet of Bhava.

Candanaka, as, m., N. of a man mentioned in the Mṛiććhakaṭika.

Candanin, ī, inī, i, rubbed with or smelling of sandal-wood, imbued with sandal.

Candanīyā, f. a kind of yellow pigment; [cf. *go-roćanā*.]

Candalā, f., N. of a woman; [cf. *ćandralā*.]

Candira, as, m. the moon; an elephant.

Candra, as, ā, am (originally *śćandra*; cf. *aśva-śćandra, puru-ść°*, &c.), Ved. glittering, shining (as gold), having the brilliancy or hue of light; (*as*), m. the moon (regarded as a planet), the moon personified or regarded as a deity; any eminent or illustrious person (at end of comp., e. g. *purusha-ćandra*, a moon of men, an excellent or eminent man, the moon being regarded as the most beautiful of the planets); a lovely or agreeable phenomenon of any kind, anything which gives pleasure; a spot similar to the moon; the eye in a peacock's tail; the symbol or mark of the Visarga; gold; a reddish kind of pearl; water; camphor; a particular plant, = *kāmpilla*; N. of a metre consisting of four lines of nineteen syllables each; N. of a Daitya, = Candra-varman, king of the Kāmbojas; also of a son of Viśva-gandhi and father of Yuvanāśva; N. of a grammarian; of a king; of one of the ancestors of the Gauḍa Brāhmans, and of several other men; one of the eighteen minor Dvīpas or divisions of the known continent; N. of one of the principal branches of the river Candra-bhāgā; N. of a mountain; (*ā*), f. a hall covered only at the top; an awning, a canopy; small cardamoms; Cocculus Cordifolius, = *guḍūćī*; (*ī*), f. Serratula Anthelmintica, = *vākućī*; (*am*), n. gold; a kind of sour rice-gruel, = *ćukra*; N. of a Sāman; [cf. *ardha-ćandra*.] — *Candra-kalā*, f. a digit or one-sixteenth of the moon's disc, (each digit is personified as a female divinity, and worshipped in Tantrika ceremonies); the crescent before or after the new moon; a kind of fish, = *vāćā* or *bāćā*, Pimelodus Vacha; title of a drama. — *Candra-kavi, is*, m., N. of a poet. — *Candra-kāṭuki, is*, m., N. of a man. — *Candra-kānta, as, ā, am*, lovely as the moon; (*as*), m. a fabulous gem, the moon-stone, supposed to be formed from the congelation of the rays of the moon and to dissolve under the influence of its light; a kind of crystal or jasper may perhaps be meant; (*am, as*), n. m. the white eatable water-lily, blossoming during the night; (*am*), n. sandal-wood; (*ā*), f. the wife of the moon; the night. — *Candra-kānti, is*, f. the brilliancy or lustre of the moon, moonlight. — *Candra-kālānala* (°*la-an*°), *am*, n. a kind of diagram. — *Candra-kīrtti, is*, m., N. of an author. — *Candra-kula, am*, n., N. of a town. — *Candra-kulyā*, f., N. of a river in Kaśmīra. — *Candra-ketu, us*, m., N. of a man; also of a son of Lakshmaṇa. — *Candra-kosha, as*, m. title of a lexicon. — *Candra-garbha, as*, m. title of a Buddhist Sūtra work. — *Candra-giri, is*, m., N. of a mountain; also of a prince. — *Candra-gupta, as*, m. 'moon-protected,' N. of a renowned king, the Σανδρο-κυπτος or Σανδρο-κοττος of the Greeks, who is supposed to have reigned at Pāṭali-putra, or the modern Patna, about 315 B.C., (he was installed by the Brāhman Cāṇakya after causing the death of Nanda, and was the founder of a new dynasty); N. of two kings of the Gupta dynasty; the registrar of Yama's court (in the latter sense a wrong form for *ćitra-gupta*). — *Candra-gomin, ī*, m., N. of a grammarian. — *Candra-gola, as*, m. the lunar orb or sphere. — *Candra-gola-stha, as*, m. 'dwelling in the lunar sphere,' a deceased progenitor, the manes. — *Candra-golikā*, f. moonlight. — *Candra-grahaṇa, am*, n. an eclipse of the moon. — *Candra-ćańćala, as, ā*, m. f. a small fish called Chanda, = *ćandraka*. — *Candra-ćūḍa, as*, m. an epithet of Śiva (whose diadem is a crescent), [cf. *ćandra-mauli, ćandra-śekhara*, &c.]; N. of an author. — *Candra-ćūḍāmaṇi, is*, m. title of a literary work. — *Candra-ćūḍāshṭaka* (°*ḍa-ash*°), *am*, n., N. of a hymn. — *Candra-ja, as*, m. the son of the moon, an epithet of Budha (Mercury). — *Candra-tāpana, as*, m., N. of a Dānava. — *Candra-dakshiṇa, as, ā, am*, Ved. offering anything bright (as gold &c.) in sacrifice. — *Candra-datta, as*, m., N. of an author. — *Candra-dāra, ās*, m. pl. the twenty-seven lunar mansions, which, in mythology, are so many nymphs, daughters of Daksha, and wedded to Candra or the moon. — *Candra-deva, as*, m., N. of a warrior; N. of a Brāhman of Kaśyapa's family; N. of a poet. — *Candra-dyuti, is*, m. sandal-wood; [cf. *ćandana*.] — *Candra-dhvaja-ketu, us*, m., N. of a Samādhi. — *Candra-nābha, as*, m., N. of a Dānava. — *Candra-nibha, as, ā, am*, like the moon, bright, handsome. — *Candra-nirṇij, k, k, k*, Ved. one who has a brilliant garment or appearance; (Sāy.) having a shape like the moon or whose form causes delight. — *Candra-pańćānga, am*, n. the luni-solar calendar. — *Candra-pāda, as*, m. a moon-beam, a ray of the moon. — *Candra-putra, as*, m. 'son of the moon,' a N. of Budha or Mercury. — *Candra-pura, as*, m., N. of a town; [cf. *ćāndrapura*.] — *Candra-pushpā*, f. a kind of solanum; [cf. *śveta-kaṇṭakārī*.] — *Candra-prakāśa, as*, m. title of a work. — *Candra-prabha, as*, m., N. of the Arhat of the present Ava-sarpiṇī; N. of a king; N. of several persons; (*ā*), f. moonlight; the plant Serratula Anthelmintica, = *vākućī*; a compound of various drugs used in jaundice, piles, &c.; N. of a woman. — *Candra-prabhāva, as, ā, am*, splendid as the moon. — *Candra-prabhāsvara-rāja, as*, m., N. of several Buddhas. — *Candra-priya, as*, m., N. of a prince. — *Candra-bālā*, f. large cardamoms. — *Candra-bāhu, us*, m., N. of an Asura. — *Candra-budhna, as, ā, am*, Ved. having a bright standing-ground; (Sāy.) the ground or cause of joy to all creatures. — *Candra-bha, as*, m., N. of an attendant of Skanda. — *Candra-bhāgā*, f., N. of a river, the Chenab, one of the five streams of the Pańjāb. — *Candra-bhāsa, as*, m. a sword; [cf. *ćandra-hāsa*.] — *Candra-bhūti, i*, n. silver. — *Candra-maṇi, is*, m. = *ćandra-kānta*, the moon-gem. — *Candra-maṇḍala, am*, n. the orb or disc of the moon; the lunar sphere; a halo round the moon. — *Candra-manas, ās*, m., N. of one of the ten horses of the moon. — *Candra-mas, ās*, m. (fr. *ćandra + mas*, derived fr. rt. *mā*), the moon, the deity of the moon; a month. — *Candra-mā*, f., N. of a river. — *Candra-mālā*, f., N. of a metre; N. of a river. — *Candra-mukha, as*, m. 'moon-faced,' N. of a man; (*ī*), f. a metre consisting of four lines of ten syllables each; a lovely woman, whose face is fair as the moon. — *Candra-mauli, is*, m. 'moon-crested,' an epithet of Śiva, (this deity being represented with a crescent on his forehead); [cf. *ćandra-ćūḍa*.] — *Candra-ratha, as, ā, am*, Ved. having a brilliant carriage. — *Candra-rāja, as*, m., N. of a minister of king Harsha. — *Candra-rekhā*, f. a digit of the moon. — *Candra-reṇu, us*, m. a plagiarist, a poetical thief (who has only the dust of the moon). — *Candra-lekha, as*, m., N. of a Rākshasa; (*ā*), f. a digit of the moon; the plant Serratula Anthelmintica, = *vākućī*; N. of a metre consisting of four lines of thirteen syllables each; N. of another metre of four lines of fifteen syllables each; N. of a daughter of the Nāga Su-śravas; also of the wife of Kshemagupta; N. of the daughter of king Vīra-siṇha, also called Śaśi-kalā. — *Candra-loka, am*, n. the sphere or heaven of the moon. — *Candra-loćana, as*, m., N. of a Dānava. — *Candra-lohaka* or *ćandra-lauha* or *ćandra-lauhaka, am*, n. silver. — *Candra-vaṇśa, as*, m. the race of the moon, the lunar race of kings or the second great line of Kshatriya or royal dynasties in India. (The progenitor of the lunar race of kings who reigned at ancient Delhi or Hāstina-pura was Soma the Moon, the child of the Ṛishi Atri and father of Budha. The latter married Iḷā, daughter of the solar king Ikshvāku, and had by her a son, Aila or Purūravas. This last had a son by Urvaśī, named Āyus, from whom came Nahusha, father of Yayāti. The latter had two sons, Puru and Yadu, from whom proceeded the two branches of the lunar line. In the line of Yadu was born Kṛishṇa and Bala-rāma; in that of Puru came Dushyanta, the hero of the Śakuntalā and father of the great

Bharata. Ninth from Bharata came Kuru, and fourteenth from him S'antanu, who had a son Vićitra-vīrya and a step-son Vyāsa. The latter married the two widows of his half-brother, and had by them Dhṛita-rāshṭra and Pāṇḍu, the wars of whose sons form the subject of the Mahā-bhārata); [cf. *sūrya-vanśa.*] — *Candravanśin, ī,* m. one of the lunar dynasty. — *Candra-vaktrā,* f., N. of a town. — *Candra-vat, ān, atī, at,* Ved. brilliant, golden, abounding in gold; illuminated by the moon; (*tī*), f., N. of a daughter of Su-nābha and wife of Gada; N. of a princess; the wife of a potter; N. of a town or district. — *Candra-vatsa, ās,* m., N. of a people. — *Candra-vadana, as, ā, am,* moon-faced, having a face fair as the moon. — *Candra-varṇa, as, ā, am,* Ved. of brilliant or bright colour. — *Candra-vartman, a,* n., N. of a metre consisting of four lines of twelve syllables each. — *Candra-varman, ā,* m., N. of a king of the Kāmbojas; also of a prince conquered by Samudra-gupta. — *Candra-vallarī,* f. a kind of Asclepias, = *soma-vallarī* or *brahmī-śāka.* — *Candra-vallī,* f., N. of several plants, = *pra-sāraṇī, mādhavī,* and *soma-latā.* — *Candra-vasā,* f., N. of a river. — *Candra-vindu, us,* m. the sign for the nasal ँ. — *Candra-vimala, as,* m., N. of a Samādhi (pure as the moon). — *Candra-vimala-sūrya-prabhāsa-śrī, is,* m., N. of a Buddha (the beauty of whom is spotless like the moon and brilliant as the sun). — *Candra-vihan-gama, as,* m. a kind of crane, Ardea Nivea. — *Candra-vrata, am,* n. a kind of vow or penance [cf. *ćāndrāyaṇa*]; a regal property or virtue. — *Candra-śarman, ā,* m., N. of a Brāhman. — *Candra-śālā,* f. an upper room, an apartment on the house-top; moonlight. — *Candra-śālikā,* f. a room on the top of a house. — *Candra-śilā,* f. a kind of gem, moon-stone [cf. *ćandra-kānta*]; N. of one of the Mātṛis attending on Skanda. — *Candra-śukla, as,* m., N. of one of the eight Upa-dvīpas in Jambu-dvīpa. — *Candra-śūra, am,* n. a kind of fruit, = *ćandrikā, kāravī,* &c., commonly *hālim,* Lepidium Sativum. — *Candra-śekhara, as,* m. an epithet of S'iva [cf. *ćandra-mauli*]; N. of a prince whose minister was the father of Viśva-nātha, the author of the Sāhitya-darpaṇa; or N. of that minister; N. of a commentator on Kālidāsa's S'akuntalā (perhaps identical with the minister of the same name); N. of the author of the play Madhurā-niruddha; N. of a mountain. — *Candraśekhara-ćampū-prabandha, as,* m. title of a work. — *Candra-śrī, īs,* m., N. of a prince. — *Candra-sañjña, as,* m. 'having any name of the moon,' camphor. — *Candra-sambhava, as,* m. son of the moon, i. e. Budha, the planet Mercury; (*ā*), f. small cardamoms. — *Candra-saras, as,* n. 'moon-lake,' N. of a lake. — *Candra-sālokya, am,* n. attainment of the lunar heaven. — *Candra-sinha, as,* m., N. of a king, son of Darpa-nārāyaṇa. — *Candra-suta, as,* m. = *ćandra-ja.* — *Candra-surasa, as,* m. the plant Vitex Negundo. — *Candra-sūrya, au,* m. du. moon and sun. — *Candra-sūrya-jihmīkara-prabha, as,* m., N. of a Buddha (whose splendor obscures moon and sun). — *Candra-sūrya-pradīpa, as,* m., N. of a Buddha (illuminating moon and sun). — *Candra-sena, as,* m., N. of a prince, son of Samudra-sena. — *Candra-han, ā,* m., N. of a Dānava. — *Candra-hanu, us,* and *ćandra-hantri, tā,* m., N. of a Dānava. — *Candra-hāsa, as,* m. a glittering scimitar ['deriding the moon;' cf. *ćandra-bhāsa*]; the sword of Rāvaṇa; N. of a prince; (*ā*), f. the plant Cocculus Cordifolius [cf. *guḍūćī*]; (*am*), n. silver. — *Candrākara* (*°ra-āk°*), *as,* m., N. of a man. — *Candrākṛiti* (*°ra-āk°*), *is, is, i,* moon-shaped; like the moon (in roundness, &c.). — *Candrāgra* (*°ra-ag°*), *as, ā, am,* Ved. having a brilliant beginning; (Sāy.) having joy or gold at the head or as the chief subject. — *Candrāngada* (*°ra-an°*), *as,* m., N. of a son of king Indra-sena. — *Candrātapa* (*°ra-āt°*), *as,* m. moonlight; an open hall, one only furnished with a roof; an awning. — *Candrātmaja* (*°ra-āt°*), *as,* m. the son of the moon, the planet Mercury. — *Candrānana* (*°ra-ān°*), *as, ā, am,* moon-faced; (*as*), m. an epithet of Skanda. — *Candrāpīḍa* (*°ra-āp°*), *as,* m. an epithet of S'iva; N. of a son of Janamejaya; of a king of Kaśmīra, the brother of Tārā-pīḍa; of a son of king Tārā-pīḍa. — *Candrābha-vaktra* (*°ra-ābh°*), *as, ā, am,* whose face is moon-like. — *Candrābhāsa* (*°ra-ābh°*), *as,* m. a false moon, an appearance in the sky like the real moon. — *Candrārka* (*°ra-ar°*), *au,* m. du. moon and sun; (*ī*), f. title of an astronomical work by Dina-kara. — *Candrārka-dīpa, as,* m., N. of a Buddha, = *ćandra-sūrya-pradīpa.* — *Candrārdha* (*°ra-ar°*), *as,* m. a half-moon. — *Candrārdha-kṛitaśekhara, as,* m. an ascetic who imitates the appearance of S'iva. — *Candrārdha-ćūḍāmaṇi, is,* m. or *ćandrārdha-mauli, is,* m. an epithet of S'iva. — *Candrāloka* (*°ra-āl°*), *as,* m. title of a work on rhetoric by Jaya-deva. — *Candrāvatī,* f., N. of a place of pilgrimage; N. of the wife of king Dharma-sena. — *Candrāvartā* (*°ra-āv°*), f. a metre consisting of four lines of fifteen syllables each. — *Candrāvalī* (*°ra-āv°*), f., N. of one of Kṛishṇa's female companions. — *Candrāvaloka* (*°ra-av°*), *as,* m., N. of a prince. — *Candrāśva* (*°ra-aś°*), *as,* m., N. of a son of Dhundhu-māra. — *Candrāspadā* (*°ra-ās°*), f., N. of a plant. — *Candrāhvaya* (*°ra-āh°*), *as,* m. camphor. — *Candreshṭā* (*°ra-ish°*), f. an assemblage of lotuses blossoming during the night (lit. 'loved by the moon'). — *Candrodaya* (*°ra-ud°*), *as,* m. moon-rise; an awning, a cloth or sheet spread over the large open courts of Hindū houses upon festive occasions; a mercurial preparation used in medicine; N. of a warrior on the side of the Pāṇḍavas; (*ā*), f. a medicine for the eyes. — *Candronmīlana* (*°ra-un°*), *am,* n. title of a work. — *Candropala* (*°ra-up°*), *as,* m. the moon-gem; [cf. *ćandra-kānta.*]

Candraka, as, m. the moon (generally at the end of adj. comp.); a spot similar to the moon; the eye in a peacock's tail; a finger-nail; a fish called Chanda; N. of a poet; of a minister; of an owl; (*ikā*), f. moonlight, moonshine, illumination, elucidation (used at the end of the title of some commentaries and original works to imply that the work so designated is intended to elucidate the subject of which it treats, e. g. *alankāra-ćandrikā, kātantra-ć°, kāvya-ć°,* &c.; cf. *kaumudī, dīpikā,* &c.); a kind of fish, = *ćandraka;* large or small cardamoms; N. of several plants, = *karṇa-sphoṭā, mallikā, śveta-kaṇṭakārī, methikā, ćandra-śūrā;* N. of a metre, = *utpalinī;* N. of a woman; N. of a river, = *ćandra-bhāgā;* (*am*), n. black pepper. — *Candraka-vat, ān,* m. a peacock. — *Candrikā-drava, as,* m. a kind of gem, the moon-stone (melting in the moonlight). — *Candrikā-pāyin, ī, inī, i,* drinking moonlight or the moon-beams; (*ī*), m. the bird Cakora. — *Candrikāmbuja* (*°kā-am°*), *am,* n. the white lotus, blossoming in the moonlight.

Candrakita, as, ā, am, furnished with brilliant spots similar to the moon.

Candrakin, ī, m. a peacock.

Candraṭa, as, m., N. of an ancient physician.

Candra-mas. See under *ćandra* above.

Candralā, f., N. of a woman.

Candrāya, nom. A. *ćandrāyate,* to play the part of the moon, to represent the moon.

Candrin, ī, iṇī, i, Ved. golden, possessing gold; (*ī*), m. the son of the moon, the planet Mercury.

Candrimā, f. (fr. *ćandra;* cf. *pūrṇimā*), moonlight.

Candrila, as, m. a barber; a N. of S'iva; a pot-herb, Chenopodium Album.

चन्द्रमह *ćandramaha, as,* m. a dog.

चप् *ćap,* cl. 1. P. *ćapati,* to caress, coax, soothe, or console; cl. 10. P. *ćapayati,* &c., to grind, pound, knead; to cheat.

चपट *ćapaṭa, as,* m. the palm with extended fingers; [cf. *ćapeṭa.*]

चपल *ćapala, as, ā, am* (said to be fr. rt. *ćup,* connected with rt. *kamp*), moving to and fro, shaking, trembling, tremulous, unsteady, agitated, wavering; wanton, fickle, inconstant, variable; inconsiderate, careless, thoughtless, ill-mannered, rude, impertinent; active, quick, swift, agile, expeditious; momentary, instantaneous; (*as*), m. a kind of animal (= *mūshika*); a fish; black mustard; quicksilver; a kind of perfume, = *ćoraka;* a kind of stone; N. of a prince; also of a superhuman being; (*ā*), f. lightning; long pepper; the tongue; a disloyal wife, a whore; spirituous liquor, especially the intoxicating drink made from hemp; the goddess Lakshmī or fortune; N. of two metres; one of the personifications of the fifth note in music. — *Capala-tā,* f. or *ćapala-tva, am,* n. trembling; fickleness, inconstancy, rudeness. — *Capalatāśaya* (*°tā-āś°*), *as,* m. indigestion, flatulence. — *Capalāṅga* (*°la-an°*), *as,* m. Delphinus Gangeticus. — *Capalā-jana, as,* m. a fickle or unsteady woman; the goddess of fortune. — *Capalātmaka* (*°la-āt°*), *as, ā, am,* of a fickle or inconstant nature.

Capalaka, as, ā, am, wanton, fickle, inconsiderate.

Capalāya, nom. A. *ćapalāyate,* to move to and fro, tremble, become unsteady, wanton.

चपेट *ćapeṭa, as,* m. a palm of the hand with the fingers extended; [cf. *ćapaṭa* and *ćarpaṭa.*] — *Capeṭāghāta* (*°ṭa-āgh°*), *as,* m. a blow or slap with the open hand.

Capeṭikā, f. a slap with the open hand.

चप्य *ćapya, am,* n., Ved. a kind of sacrificial vessel.

चम् *ćam,* cl. 1. P. *ćamati, ćaćāma, aćamīt, ćamitum,* Ved. cl. 5. P. *ćamnoti,* to sip, drink; to take anything into the mouth, as food, (generally applied to liquids, but occasionally used of solid food); to eat: Pass. Aor. *aćami* (used impersonally): Caus. *ćāmayati:* Desid. *ćićamishati:* Intens. *ćanćamyate* or *ćanćanti;* [cf. Hib. *toimhil,* 'eatings;' *toimhlim,* 'I eat, waste, spend, consume.']

Camara, as, ī, m. f. (fr. rt. *ćam,* in the sense of eating), a kind of deer, or rather the Bos Grunniens (erroneously classed by the Hindū writers amongst deer), highly valued for its bushy tail; (*as, am*), m. n. a chowrie or long brush, most usually made of the tail of the Yak or Bos Grunniens, and employed to whisk off insects, flies, &c.; it is also one of the insignia of royalty [cf. *ćāmara*]; a particular high number; (*as*), m., N. of a Daitya; (*ī*), f. a compound pedicle. — *Camara-puććha, am,* n. the tail of the Bos Grunniens; (*as*), m. a small animal with a bushy tail living in holes, a squirrel or perhaps fox (*kokaḍa*).

Camarika, as, m. a kind of ebony, Bauhinia Variegata, growing in clusters resembling a chowrie; [cf. *kovidāra.*]

Camasa, as, ī, m. f. a vessel used at sacrifices for drinking the juice of the Soma, a kind of flat dish, pan, or cup; (according to others) a kind of ladle or spoon, (according to the Brāhmaṇas and Scholiasts these vessels are generally of a square shape, made of wood and furnished with a handle, but sometimes also round or of other shapes); a cake made of barley, rice, or lentils, ground to meal; a sweetmeat, or flour, sesamum, &c., mixed up with sugar into a kind of cake; a plant, commonly Khetpāpara, Mollugo Pentaphylla; (*as*), m., N. of a man; also of a son of Ṛishabha; = *ćamasodbheda,* q. v. — *Camasādhvaryu* (*°sa-adh°*), *us,* m., Ved. the priest who manages the drinking-vessels. — *Camasodbheda* (*°sa-ud°*), *as,* m., N. of a place of pilgrimage, held sacred on account of the supposed bursting forth of the river Sarasvatī; also *ćamasodbhedana, am,* n.

Camasi, is, f. = *ćamasī,* a kind of cake.

Camasin, ī, m., N. of a man.

Camū, ūs, f., Ved. (loc. *ćamū* or *ćamvi;* du. *ćamvā;* pl. *ćamvas*), a vessel, a dish, (applied especially to the vessels or reservoirs into which the Soma is poured; these are generally two in number, and called *ćamvā,* Ved. du.), metaphorically the two grand receptacles of all living beings, or heaven and earth (*ćamvau*, du., Naigh. III. 30); a grave; an army; a squadron, a division of an army consisting of 129 elephants, as many cars, 2187 horse, and 3685 foot. — *Camū-ćara, as,* m. a soldier, a warrior. — *Camū-nātha* or *ćamū-pa, as,* m. the leader of an army, a general. — *Camū-pati, is,* m. a general of division, any general. — *Camū-shad, t, t, t,* Ved. lying on a dish. — *Camū-hara, as,* m., N. of one of the Viśve-devās.

चमक *ćamaka, as,* m., N. of a man.

चमकसूक्त *ćamaka-sūkta, am,* n., N. of several verses of the Vājasaneyi-saṃhitā, so called because the words *ća me* are repeated in them.

Camī-kāra, as, m. reciting the Camaka-sūkta.

Camī-kṛi, cl. 8. P., Ved. *-karoti, -kartum,* to recite the verses containing the words *ća me* over anything.

चमत् *ćamat,* ind. an interjection of surprise. — *Camat-karaṇa, am,* n. admiration; astonishing, producing wonder, causing surprise; festival, spectacle; high poetical composition. — *Camat-kāra, as,* m. admiration, astonishment, surprise; show, spectacle; row, riot, festive or angry turbulence; elaborate style or high poetical composition; N. of the tree Achyranthes Aspera; [cf. *apāmārga.*] — *Camat-kāra-ćandrikā,* f. title of a grammar; title of a Bengālī poem by Kṛishṇa-dāsa. — *Camatkāra-ćintā-maṇi, is,* m. title of a work. — *Camat-kārita, as, ā, am,* astonished. — *Camat-kārin, ī, iṇi, i,* astonishing, surprising, unusual. — *Camat-kṛita, as, ā, am,* astonished, surprised. — *Camat-kṛiti, is,* f. admiration, astonishment, surprise, &c.; [cf. *ćamat-kāra.*]

चमीकृ *ćamī-kṛi.* See under *ćamaka-sūkta.*

चमू *ćamū.* See under *ćam* above.

चमूरु *ćamūru, us,* m. a kind of deer; [cf. *samūru.*]

चम्प् *ćamp,* cl. 10. P. *ćampayati,* to go, move; (a various reading for *ćhamp.*)

Campa, as, m. (said to come fr. the last rt.), the plant Bauhinia Variegata, mountain ebony [cf. *kovidāra*]; N. of a son of Pṛithulāksha and founder of the town Campā; (*ā*), f., N. of a town in Aṅga, the modern Bhāgalpur or a place in its vicinity, founded by Campa, and the residence of Karṇa; also of Brahma-datta. — *Campa-karambhā,* f. a kind of plantain. — *Campa-kunda, as,* m. a kind of fish, commonly *ćānda-kuḍā.* — *Campa-kosha, as,* m. the Jāka or bread-fruit tree. — *Campādhipa* (°*pā-adh*°) or *ćampeśa* (°*pā-īśa*), *as,* m., N. of Karṇa, natural brother of the Pāṇḍus. — *Campā-vatī,* f., N. of a town; N. of the wife of Nidhi-pati. — *Campopalakshita* (°*pā-up*°), *as,* m. the district of Campā or Bhāgalpur; (*ās*), m. pl. the inhabitants of it.

Campaka, as, m. a tree bearing a yellow fragrant flower, Michelia Champaka; a kind of perfume; a variety of the jack or bread-fruit tree [cf. *ćampakālu*]; N. of the father of Kalhaṇa; N. of a man; N. of a country; (*ā*), f., N. of a town; (*am*), n. the flower of the Campaka tree; the fruit of a variety of the banana or plantain; commonly *ćāmpākalā.* — *Campaka-gandha, am,* n. a kind of incense. — *Campaka-ćaturdaśī,* f., N. of a festival, the fourteenth day in the light half of the month Jyaishṭha. — *Campaka-pura, am,* n., N. of a town. — *Campaka-prabhu, us,* m., N. of the father of Kalhaṇa. — *Campaka-mālā,* f., N. of a metre consisting of four lines of ten syllables each. — *Campaka-vatī,* f., N. of a wood in Magadha. — *Campakāraṇya* (°*ka-ar*°), *am,* n. the Campaka forest; N. of a place of pilgrimage. — *Campakā-vatī* or *ćampakāvalī* (°*ka-āv*°), f. = *ćampaka-vatī.* — *Campakolva* (°*ka-ul*°), *as,* m. the Jāka or bread-fruit tree.

Campakālu, us, m. the Jāka or Indian bread-fruit tree, Artocarpus Integrifolia; [cf. *ćampakolva, ćampālu, ćampaka.*]

Campālu, us, m. the Jāka or bread-fruit tree.

चम्पू *ćampū, ūs,* f. a kind of elaborate and highly artificial composition in which the same subject is continued through alternations in prose and verse (*gadya* and *padya*); [cf. *gaṅgā-ćampū* and *nala-ćampū.*]

चम्ब् *ćamb,* cl. 1. P. *ćambati,* &c., to go, to move.

चम्रिष *ćamrish,* f., Ved. (Sāy.) libations (contained) in the sacrificial ladles.

Camrisha, as, ā, am, Ved. contained in the sacrificial ladle.

चय् *ćay,* cl. 1. A. *ćayate,* &c., to go, go to or towards, move; [cf. Gr. κίω, κινέω; Lat. *cieo, cio, citus;* Hib. *cai,* 'a way, a road;' Lith. *koja,* 'foot;' *kettur-kojis,* 'quadruped.']

चय 1. *ćaya.* See under 1. *ći.*

चय 2. *ćaya.* See under 3. *ći.*

चर् *ćar,* cl. 1. P. (ep. also A.) *ćarati, -te, ćaćāra, ćere, ćarishyati, -te, aćārīt, ćaritum* (ep. *ćartum,* Ved. *ćaradhyai, ćaritave, ćarase*), to move one's self, go, walk, move, stir, drive (in a carriage &c.), roam about, walk about, wander, (in these senses applied to men, animals, water, ships, stars, &c.); to graze; to spread, be diffused; to be active; move or travel through, pervade, go along, follow; to behave, conduct one's self; to live, be, remain in any position, act; to be engaged in, occupied with, busy one's self with (with inst., e. g. *yajñena ćarati,* he is engaged in a sacrifice); to undertake, set about, undergo, observe, practise, do or act in general (e. g. *vratāni ćeruḥ,* they observed vows; and in this sense applied rather vaguely to express various ideas, e. g. *vighnam ćarati,* he puts a hindrance; *bhaiksham ćarati,* he begs; *vivādam ćarati,* he is engaged in a lawsuit; *mṛigayām ćarati,* he hunts; *sambandhāṅś ćarati,* he enters into connections; *mārgam ćaćāra vāṇaiḥ,* he made a way with arrows); to continue performing or being (with a part., e. g. *arćantaś ćeruḥ,* they continued worshipping; *svāminam avajñāya ćaret,* he may go on despising his master); to exercise the body with penance, e. g. *tapasā indriyāṇi ćaret,* he should exercise his organs with penance; (with or without *mithuna*) to perform the act of copulation, to have sexual intercourse with, have to do with; to make or render (with two acc., e. g. *narendraṃ satya-sthaṃ ćarāma,* let us make the king keep his word); to act as a spy; to consume, eat (e. g. *māṇsam ćaret,* let him eat flesh): Caus. *ćārayati, -yitum,* to cause to move or walk about; to pasture; to send, direct, turn, move; to cause to pervade; to drive away; to cause to practise or perform; to cause to copulate; to obtain knowledge of, acquaint one's self with (with acc.); to doubt [cf. *vi-ćar*]: Desid. *ćićarishati,* to wish to act or conduct one's self; to be willing to deal with, to have intercourse with: Intens. *ćarćarīti, ćañćūryate, ćañćurīti, ćañćūrti,* to move quickly or repeatedly, to walk about, pervade; to act wantonly or coquettishly; [cf. Lat. *curro, currus; properus* (?): Hib. *cara,* 'a leg or haunch;' *carachadh,* 'moving;' *carachd,* 'motion:' Gr. κύρω, κυρέω: Goth. *fara:* Germ. *fahren:* Old Germ. *hor-sc:* Eng. *horse:* Lith. *kieláuju, kielias, kielione:* Old Pers. *ćartanay.*]

Cara, as, ī, am, moving, walking, going; locomotive, any animal (so named as moving in contradistinction to plants); movable, trembling, shaking, unsteady; (at the end of comp.) going, walking, wandering, being, living [cf. *adhaś-ćara, anta-ćara, ap-ć*°, *upari-ć*°, *eka-ć*°, &c.]; following; performing, practising (e. g. *vrata-ćara,* practising vows). Sometimes *ćara* is placed at the end of a word as an affix in the sense of 'having been formerly,' e. g. *āḍhya-ćara,* one who has been rich formerly; *devadatta-ćara,* having been formerly possessed by Devadatta; (*as*), m. a spy, a secret emissary or agent; a wagtail; a kind of small shell, Cypræa Moneta [cf. *kaparda*]; a game played with dice and men similar to backgammon; the planet Mars; a cowrie; the seventh Karaṇa in astrology; the Karaṇas collectively; the difference of time between the rising of a heavenly body at Laṅkā or Ceylon, over which the first meridian passes, and that of its rising at any particular place; a term for particular lunar mansions and for a particular number of the signs of the zodiac. — *Cara-gṛiha, am,* n. a moving or varying sign of the zodiac, i. e. the first, fourth, seventh, and tenth. — *Cara-deva, as,* m., N. of a man. — *Cara-dravya, āṇi,* n. pl. movables, goods and chattels. — *Cara-pushṭa, as,* m. a mediator (lit. 'nourished by a spy'). — *Cara-bha, am,* n. a moving or varying sign of the zodiac, i. e. the first, fourth, seventh, and tenth; [cf. *ćara-gṛiha.*] — *Cara-bhavana, am,* n. a moving or varying sign of the zodiac; [cf. the preceding.] — *Cara-mūrti, is,* f. an idol which is carried about in procession. — 1. *ćarāćara* (°*ra-ać*°), *as, ā, am,* movable and immovable, locomotive and stationary, moving and fixed (as animals and plants); (*am*), n. the aggregate of all created things, whether animate or inanimate; the world; sky, atmosphere; heaven, paradise; (*ī*), f. a young woman.

Caraka, as, m. a wanderer, a wandering religious student; a spy or secret emissary; N. of a Muni and physician, (a legend relates that the serpent-king Śesha, who was himself the recipient of the Āyur-veda, once visited the earth, and finding it full of sickness and suffering became moved with pity, and determined to devise a scheme for alleviating disease; hence he became incarnate as the son of a Muni and was called Caraka because he had visited the earth as a kind of spy or *ćara;* he then composed a new book on medicine, based on older works of Agni-veśa and other pupils of Ātreya, which book was called after him); a kind of plant, cf. *parpaṭa;* (*am*), n. the title of the treatise on medicine written by Caraka; (*ās*), m. pl., N. of a branch of the Black Yajur-veda, the practices and rites enjoined by which are different in some respects from those in the Śatapatha-Brāhmaṇa; (*ī*), f. a kind of poisonous fish; N. of an evil spirit. — *Caraka-grantha, as,* m. Caraka's book. — *Caraka-tantra-vyākhyā,* f. title of a commentary by Harićandra. — *Caraka-bhāshya, am,* n. title of a commentary by an author named Kṛishṇa.

Caraṇa, as, m. a foot soldier; (*as, am*), m. n. a foot; a pillar, a support, a prop; the root of a tree; a single line of a verse, the fourth part of a stanza; (in prosody) a dactyl; a sect, a school, a branch of the Vedas; a race, a family; (*am*), n. moving, going round or about, wandering, roaming, grazing; course; acting, dealing, managing, conduct, performance; fixed or instituted observances for any class, age, or condition (as priesthood, manhood, &c.); behaving, conduct of life, good or moral conduct; practising, accomplishing; consuming, eating; a particular high number; [cf. *dvi-ćaraṇa, puraś-ćaraṇa, ratha-ć*°; cf. also Gr. and Lat. πέρνα, *perna;* Goth. *fairzna;* Germ. *Ferse;* Lith. *kulnis;* Hib. *cairine;* Lat. *crus?*]. — *Caraṇa-kamala* or *ćaraṇa-kisalaya, am,* n. a lotus-foot (lit. foot-lotus), a beautiful foot, the foot of a lover, of a deity, &c. — *Caraṇa-gata, as, ā, am,* fallen at one's feet, prostrate. — *Caraṇa-granthi, is,* m. the joint of the foot, the ancle. — *Caraṇa-dāsa, as,* m., N. of the author of the Gurušishya-saṃvāda and of the poems entitled Nāćiketūpākhyāna. — *Caraṇa-nyāsa, as,* m. the trace of a foot, foot-step. — *Caraṇa-pa, as,* m. a tree. — *Caraṇa-patana, am,* n. falling at the feet, prostration. — *Caraṇa-patita, as, ā, am,* fallen at the feet, prostrate. — *Caraṇa-padma, as* or *am,* m. n. a lotus (like) foot, the foot of a deity or lover. — *Caraṇa-parvan, a,* n. 'foot-joint,' the ancle. — *Caraṇa-pāta, as,* m. tread, trampling; foot-fall. — *Caraṇa-yuga, am,* n. both the feet; two lines of a stanza. — *Caraṇa-vyūha, as,* m. title of a treatise. — *Caraṇa-śuśrūshā,* f. prostration. — *Caraṇa-sevā,* f. service, devotion. — *Caraṇānamita* (°*ṇa-ān*°), *as, ā, am,* bent or bowed under the feet, trodden down. — *Caraṇā-*

bharaṇa (°*ṇa-ābh*°), *am*, n. an ornament for the feet. — *Caraṇāmṛita* (°*ṇa-am*°), *am*, n. 'foot-nectar,' the water in which the feet of a Brāhman or spiritual guide have been washed. — *Caraṇāyudha* (°*ṇa-āy*°), *as, ā, am*, having the feet for weapons; (*as*), m. a cock. — *Caraṇāravinda* (°*ṇa-ar*°), *am*, n. the lotus (like) foot (of a deity, lover, &c.). — *Caraṇārdha* (°*ṇa-ar*°), *am*, n. the half of the foot; half of the fourth of a stanza. — *Caraṇāskandana* (°*ṇa-ās*°), *am*, n. trampling, treading down with the feet. — *Caraṇodaka* (°*ṇa-ud*°), *am*, n. water in which the feet of a venerable Brāhman or spiritual teacher have been washed. — *Caraṇopaga* (°*ṇa-up*°), *as, ā, am*, in contact with the feet, at the feet.

Caraṇīya, nom. A., Ved. *ćaraṇīyate*, to follow, perform, be engaged in, carry on; (Sāy.) to desire to go.

1. *ćaraṇya*, nom. P. *ćaraṇyati*, to move.

2. *ćaraṇya, as, ā, am*, foot-like, like a foot.

Caraṇyu, us, us, u, Ved. moving, movable.

Carat, an, antī, at, going, moving, going on; proceeding, acting, practising.

Caratha, as, ā, am, Ved. moving, living; capable of moving, movable; (*as, am*), m. n. going, moving, wandering; movableness; liveliness, life; a going, a way.

2. *ćarāćara, as, ā, am* (fr. *ćar* reduplicated; for 1. see p. 317, col. 3), moving, locomotive, running; trembling, shaking, unsteady; wished, desired; (*am*), n., N. of a small shell; [cf. *kaparda.*]

Cari, is, m. an animal in general.

Carita, as, ā, am, gone, gone to, attained, practised; (*am*), n. going, moving, course; acting, doing, practice, behaviour, acts, deeds, practices, adventures, 'res gestæ;' story; nature; fixed institute, proper or peculiar observance; [cf. *uttara-rāma-ćarita, duś-ćarita, sać-ć°, saha-ć°, su-ć°.*] — *Carita-guṇatva, am*, n. (?) accompaniment, assistance; meritorious conduct. — *Carita-maya, as, ī, am*, (at the end of compounds) containing or relating deeds or adventures, made up of deeds. — *Carita-vrata, as, ā, am*, performing an act of devotion. — *Caritārtha* (°*ta-ar*°), *as, ā, am*, attaining one's object, successful in an undertaking, satisfied, effected, successful. — *Caritārtha-tva, am*, n. the attainment of an aim, successfulness, success. — *Caritārthaya*, nom. P. *ćaritārthayati*, to cause a person to attain his aim. — *Caritārthin, ī, inī, i*, desirous of success.

Caritavya, as, ā, am, to be gone, to be managed; to be followed or observed; to be practised or performed.

Caritin. Cf. *duś-ćaritin*.

Caritra, am, n. a foot, leg; going; acting, behaving, behaviour, habit, practice, acts, deeds, proceedings, exploits; instituted and peculiar observance or conduct; adventures, story, history or account of any one's deeds or exploits; nature, disposition; (*ā*), f. the tamarind tree; [cf. *ćāritra.*] — *Caritra-bandhaka, as*, m. a friendly pledge, one of unequal value to the loan. — *Caritra-vat, ān, atī, at*, experienced, familiar with customs.

Carishṇu, us, us, u, capable of moving, movable, locomotive, active, unsteady, wandering about; (*us*), m., N. of a son of Manu Sāvarṇa; also of a son of Kīrttimat and Dhenukā. — *Carishṇu-dhūma, as, ā, am*, Ved. having moving smoke, whose smoke goes everywhere.

Carītra, am, n. behaviour, conduct, practice; [cf. *ćaritra.*]

Cartavya, as, ā, am, to be practised &c.; [cf. *ćaritavya.*]

Carya, as, ā, am, to be gone; to be practised or performed &c.; (*ā*), f. going about, wandering, walking about, driving or going in a carriage; pervading, visiting; course; proceeding, behaviour; due and regular observance of all rites or customs, following the rules of studentship; practising religious austerities, wandering about as a mendicant; performing, practising, engaging in, practice, conduct [cf. *ku-ćaryā*]; behaviour, deportment, usage; eating; (*am*), n. going about, wandering, driving in a carriage &c.; proceeding, behaviour, conduct; [cf. *brahma-ćarya, bhikshā-ć°, bhaikshya-ć°.*] — *Caryāvatāra* (°*yā-av*°), *as*, m. title of a Buddhist work.

Cāra, as, m. a spy &c. See s. v.

चरट *ćaraṭa, as*, m. a wagtail; (*ī*), f. = *ćaraṇṭī, ćiriṇṭī, ćiraṇṭī.*

चरम *ćarama, as, ā, am*, m. pl. *ćarame* or *ćaramās*, (said to be fr. rt. *ćar*), last, hinder, ultimate, final; outermost; western, west; lowest, least; immediately following; (*as* or *am*), m. or n. (?), a particular high number; (*am*), ind. at last, at the end; *ćaramā kriyā*, the final ceremony, the funeral ceremony. — *Carama-kāla, as*, m. the last moments, the hour of death. — *Carama-kshmābhṛit, t*, m. the western mountain behind which the sun and moon are supposed to set. — *Carama-vaiyākaraṇa, as*, m. an ignorant grammarian. — *Carama-śairshika, as, ī, am*, having the head towards the west. — *Caramāćala* (°*ma-ać*°), *as*, m. or *ćaramādri* (°*ma-ad*°), *is*, m. = *ćarama-kshmābhṛit* above. — *Caramājā* (°*ma-ajā*), f., Ved. the last or smallest she-goat. — *Caramāvasthā* (°*ma-av*°), f. the last state.

Caramya, nom. P. *ćaramyati*, to be the last.

चरव्य *ćaravya*. See below under *ćaru*.

चरु *ćaru, us*, m. a kind of vessel in which a particular oblation is prepared, a saucepan, pot, kettle; a cloud; an oblation of rice, barley, and pulse, boiled with butter and milk for presentation to the gods or manes. — *Caru-ćelin, ī, inī, i*, having portions of offerings on the clothes (?); an epithet of Śiva; (perhaps a wrong form for *ćārućelin.*) — *Caru-vraṇa, as*, m. a kind of cake. — *Caru-śrapaṇa, am*, n. sprinkling an oblation of milk and ghee. — *Caru-sthālī*, f. the vessel in which an oblation is prepared, made either of clay or of udumbara-wood. — *Caru-homa, as*, m. an oblation of a meat-offering.

Caravya, as, ā, am, destined for the Caru oblation.

चर्करीत *ćarkarīta, am*, n. (fr. 1. *kṛi*, to do), a term used by Yāska and others for the intensive verb formed without the syllable *ya*.

चर्कृति *ćarkṛiti, is*, f. (fr. 2. *kṛi*), Ved. praising, mention, glory, praise.

Carkṛitya, as, ā, am, Ved. to be mentioned with praise, worthy of praise, renowned.

चर्घ् *ćargh*, cl. 1. P. *ćarghati*, &c., to go or move.

चर्च् *ćarć*, cl. 10. P. *ćarćayati*, to repeat (a word in reciting the Veda), to read, recite, study, peruse carefully, consider; cl. 1. or 6. P. *ćarćati*, &c., to speak, say, abuse, reprove, condemn, censure, menace; to injure or hurt, to inquire.

Carća, as, m. considering, deliberation, i. e. repeating over in thought; (*ā*), f. repetition of a word, recitation, incidental mention, popular talk, alternate recitation of a poem by two persons; reflection, consideration; the exercise of judgment or deliberation, inquiry, investigation; an epithet of the goddess Durgā; covering or cleansing the body with unguents, smearing with ointment; bribery (?).

Carćaka, as, ā, am, repeating, the repeater (of a word in the recitation of the Veda).

Carćana, am, n. repeating, repetition; covering the body with unguents.

Carćāya, nom. P. *ćarćāyate*, to undergo repetition, to be repeated.

Carći, is, f., Ved. repetition of words in recitation; (*is*), m., N. of a man.

Carćikā, f. deliberation, inquiry; cleaning the person with perfumes, an epithet of the goddess Durgā or Cāmuṇḍā; [cf. *gharma-ćarćikā* and *vi-ćarćikā.*]

Carćikya, am, n. anointing the body, an unguent, = *ćārćikya* and *ćarćā*.

Carćita, as, ā, am, perfumed, anointed, smeared with sandal &c., covered with anything; inquired into or after, investigated; sought, desired; (*am*), n. the being covered or anointed (with anything).

चर्चर *ćarćara, as, ā, am* (fr. rt. *ćar*), Ved. going; (*ī*), f. a kind of song; striking the hands to beat time; musical symphony; the recitation of scholars; festive cries or merriment, festive sport; a festival; flattery, dishonest praise; a kind of metre consisting of four lines of eighteen syllables each; curled or woolly hair.

Carćarikā, f. a kind of gesture, gesticulation.

Carćarīka, as, m. a pot-herb; decoration or curling of the hair [cf. *ćarćarī*]; a form of Śiva.

चर्चस् *ćarćas, ās*, m., N. of one of the nine treasures of Kuvera.

चर्तन *ćartana, as, ā, am* (fr. rt. *ćṛit*), Ved. stringing together; (*am*), n. a hook, a pin.

Cartya, as, ā, am, to be strung or tied in regular order; to be hurt or injured.

चर्तव्य *ćartavya*. See col. 1.

चर्पट *ćarpaṭa, as*, m. the open palm of the hand with fingers extended; a kind of plant, Mollugo Pentaphylla; a quantity of bubbles or specks (*sphāra-vipula*); (*ī*), f. a thin cake or biscuit of flour; [cf. *parpaṭī.*]

चर्पटि *ćarpaṭi, is*, m., N. of an author; (also read *ćarpaṭin.*)

चर्ब् *ćarb*, cl. 1. P. *ćarbati*, to go, move.

चर्भट *ćarbhaṭa, as*, m. a kind of cucumber, Cucumis Utilissimus [cf. *ervāru;* cf. also *ćirbhaṭī* and *ćirbhiṭā*]; (*ī*), f. = *ćarćarī*, the noise of merriment or festivity, cries of joy.

चर्म *ćarma, am*, n. (said to be fr. rt. *ćar*), Ved. a hide, a skin; a shield. See *ćarman* below.

Carmaṇya, am, n. (fr. the next), leather-work.

Carman, a, n. skin, leather, hide, bark, parchment, &c.; the hide of an antelope &c. used as a seat or bed by the religious student; a shield; [cf. *gala-ćarman, duś-ćarman*, &c.; cf. also Lat. *corium, calceus* (?); Hib. *croicionn;* Gr. πέλμα.] — *Carma-karaṇa, am*, n. working in skins or leather. — *Carma-kaśā* or *ćarma-kashā* or *ćarma-kasā*, f. 'skin-injurer,' a plant, commonly called Carmakashā or Carmaghās, Mimosa Abstergens; a particular kind of perfume. — *Carma-kāra, as*, m. a shoe-maker, a currier or worker in leather, the offspring of a Caṇḍāla woman by a man of the fisherman caste, or of a Vaideha female by a Nishāda; (*ī*), f. the wife of the preceding; N. of a plant, = *ćarma-kaśā*. — *Carma-kāraka, as*, m. a worker in leather. — *Carma-kārin, ī*, m. a currier, skinner, shoe-maker, worker in hides or leather. — *Carma-kārya, am*, n. working in leather or skins. — *Carma-kīla, as, am*, m. n. a wart; excrescences considered as a kind of hemorrhoids. — *Carma-kṛit, t*, m. a shoe-maker. — *Carma-khāṇḍika, ās*, m. pl., N. of a people; (perhaps for *ćarma-khaṇḍika?*); [cf. *ćarma-maṇḍala* and *ćarma-raṅga.*] — *Carma-grīva, as*, m., N. of one of the attendants of Śiva. — *Carma-ćaṭaka, as, ā*, m. f. or *ćarma-ćaṭikā*, f. or *ćarma-ćaṭī*, f. a bat. — *Carma-ćitraka, am*, n. white leprosy (*śveta-kushṭha*). — *Carma-ćela, as* or *am*, m. or n. (?), a garment with the hide turned outwards. — *Carma-ja, as, ā, am*, coming forth from the skin, produced by or from the skin; (*am*), n. the hairs of the body; blood. — *Carmaṇ-vat, ān, atī, at*, Ved. furnished with hide, covered with skin or leather; (*tī*), f. the plantain tree, Musa Sapientum [cf. *kadala*]; a river that flows through Bundelkhand into the Ganges, the modern Chambal. — *Carma-taraṅga, as*, m. a wrinkle, a fold of skin. — *Carma-tila, as, ā, am*, covered with pimples resembling the seeds of sesamum. — *Carma-daṇḍa, as*, m. 'a leather stick,' a whip. — *Carma-dala, am*, n. a form of leprosy or cutaneous disease. — *Carma-dūshikā*, f. a kind of leprosy with red spots, cutaneous disease. — *Carma-druma, as*, m., N. of a tree; [cf. *bhūrja.*] — *Carma-nāsikā*, f. 'a leather thong,' a whip. — *Carma-paṭṭikā*, f. a flat piece of leather for playing upon with dice, a leather backgammon board &c. — *Carma-pattrā,* f. a bat, the small house-bat. — *Carma-pādukā,* f. a leather shoe. — *Carma-prabhedikā,* f. a shoe-maker's awl. — *Carma-prasevaka, as, ikā,* m. f. a bellows. — *Carma-bandha, as,* m. a leather band or strap. — *Carma-maṇḍala, ās,* m. pl., N. of a people. — *Carma-maya, as, ī, am,* made of skin or leather, leathern, encased in leather. — *Carma-muṇḍā,* f. a form of the goddess Durgā, commonly *ćāmuṇḍā* and *ćaṇḍa-muṇḍā.* — *Carma-mna, as,* m., Ved. a tanner. — *Carma-yashṭi, is,* f. a whip; [cf. *ćarma-daṇḍa.*] — *Carma-ranga, as,* m., N. of a people in the north-west of Madhya-deśa; (*ā*), f., N. of a plant, = *āvartakī.* — *Carma-vat, ān, atī, at,* covered with hides or skins; (*ān*), m., N. of a warrior. — *Carma-vasana, as, ā, am,* clothed in skin; (*as*), m. an epithet of Śiva; [cf. *kṛitti-vāsas.*] — *Carma-vādya, am,* n. 'skin-instrument,' i. e. a drum, tabour, &c. — *Carma-vṛiksha, as,* m., N. of a tree; [cf. *ćarmin.*] — *Carma-sambhavā,* f. cardamoms. — *Carma-sāra, as,* m. lymph, serum. — *Carmāććhādita* (°*ma-āćć*h°), *as, ā, am,* covered with skin. — *Carmānta* (°*ma-an*°), *as,* m. a piece or strap of leather. — *Carmāmbhas* (°*ma-am*°), *as,* n. lymph, serum. — *Carmāvakartana* (°*ma-av*°), *am,* n. working in leather or skins. — *Carmāvakartin* (°*ma-av*°), *ī,* m. a worker in leather or skins, a shoe-maker, a man of the lowest caste. — *Carmāvakarttṛi* (°*ma-av*°), *tā,* m. a shoe-maker. — *Carmāvanaddha* (°*ma-av*°), *as, ā, am,* covered with skin, bound with leather, &c. — *Carmāvṛita* (°*ma-āv*°), *as, ā, am,* covered with skin or parchment. — *Carmāsi-mat* (°*ma-asi-*), *ān, atī, at,* possessed of shield and sword.

Carmaru, us, m. a shoe-maker, a worker in leather; [cf. *ćarmāra* and *ćarma-kāra.*]

Carmāra, as, m. a worker in leather, a shoe-maker.

Carmika, as, ā, am, armed with a shield, a shield-bearer.

Carmin, ī, iṇī, i, covered with skin or parchment, having a hide or skin; leather, leathern, made of leather, &c.; armed with a shield; (*ī*), m. a soldier armed with a shield, a shield-bearer; N. of a tree, the bark of which is used for writing upon, &c. [cf. *bhūrja*]; a plantain; N. of an attendant of Śiva.

चर्मरी *ćarmarī,* f., N. of a plant with a poisonous fruit.

चर्य *ćarya.* See p. 318, col. 1.

चर्व् *ćarv* [cf. *ćūrṇ*], cl. 1. 10. P. *ćarvati, ćarvayati,* &c., to bruise, crush, grind with the teeth, chew, champ, masticate; to eat; sup up, suck: Pass. *ćarvyate;* [cf. Hib. *carbad,* 'the jaw;' *carbal,* 'the palate of the mouth;' *creimim,* 'I gnaw;' *creim,* 'corrosion;' Lith. *kramtau.*]

Carvaṇa, as, ā, am, chewing; (*am*), n. chewing, masticating; sipping, tasting; food which must be chewed, solid food.

Carvaṇīya, as, ā, am, masticable, proper to be chewed.

Carvita, as, ā, am, chewed, eaten. — *Carvita-ćarvaṇa, am,* n. chewing the chewed; seeking happiness where others have sought it in vain; repetition of the same act, tautology, tedious reiteration. — *Carvita-pātra* or *ćarvita-pātraka, am,* n. a spitting-pot.

Carvya, as, ā, am, to be chewed, chewable; (*am*), n. solid food requiring mastication.

चर्वन् *ćarvan, ā,* m. a blow with the flat of the hand.

चर्षणि *ćarshaṇi, is, is, i* (said by some to be derived fr. *kṛish;* by other native commentators connected with rt. *ćaksh,* to see, and so probably derived by Yāska, who explains *ćarshaṇi* by *ćāyitṛi,* q. v.; other scholars connect it with rt. *ćar*), Ved. seeing, observing; discerning, moving, movable, running, going in a carriage, agile, active, swift; (*ayas*), f. pl. men, people, race, nation (e. g. *pañća ćarshaṇayas,* the five races of men, the five nations; cf. *kṛishṭi, kshiti, jana*); 'beings endowed with discernment,' N. of the children of Aryaman and Mātṛikā, who are regarded in the Bhāgavata-Purāṇa as the progenitors of the human race; (*ī*), f. a disloyal wife; N. of the wife of Varuṇa and mother of Bhṛigu; [cf. *vi-ć*° and *viśva-ć*°.] — *Carshaṇi-prā, ās, ās, am,* Ved. governing men or people or races of men, epithet of Indra. — *Carshaṇī-dhṛit, t, t, t,* Ved. supporting or protecting men or races of men; epithet of Indra, Mitra, Varuṇa, and the Viśve-devās. — *Carshaṇi-dhṛiti, is,* f., Ved. support or protection of men or races. — *Carshaṇi-sah, ṭ, ṭ, ṭ,* Ved. ruling over or overpowering men; (Sāy.) overpowering enemies.

चल् *ćal* [cf. *ćaṭ* and *ćar*], cl. 1. P. (sometimes A.) *ćalati, -te, ćaćāla, ćalishyati, aćālīt, ćalitum,* to move one's self, be moved; to stir, tremble, shake, quiver, throb, palpitate, be agitated; totter; to move on or forward, proceed, go away; to start off, set out, depart; to walk, march; to be moved from one's usual course, to be disturbed, become confused or disordered; to go astray; to turn away from the right course, swerve, deviate from (with abl., e. g. *ćalati dharmāt,* he swerves from virtue); fall off, leave off (with abl.); to sport about, frolic, play, wanton: Caus. P. *ćalayati* or *ćālayati, -te, -yitum,* to cause to move, to move, shake, jog, nudge, push, agitate, disturb; to turn off from, to cause to deviate, lead away from; cause to fall; drive away, remove or expel from; to cherish, foster, (wrong form for *bal*): Pass. of Caus. *ćālyate,* to be moved: Desid. *ćićalishati:* Intens. *ćañćalyate* or *ćāćalyate, ćāćalti;* [cf. Gr. κέλω, κέλλω, ὀκέλλω, κέλης; Lat. *celer, pro-cello, ex-cello, præcello; calco, calc-s, calcar;* Hib. *caill,* 'a path;' Germ. *falle;* Gr. πάλλω, πέλω; Lat. *pello.*]

Cala, as, ā, am, moving, trembling, tremulous, movable, shaking, loose, unfixed, unsteady, fickle, fluctuating, perishable, disturbed, confused; (*as*), m. agitation, shaking, trembling; wind; quicksilver; (*ā*), f. lightning; incense; fortune or Lakshmī the goddess of fortune; N. of a metre consisting of four lines of eighteen syllables each; [cf. *a-ćala, niśćala, ćāla.*] — *Cala-karṇa, as,* m. the true distance of a planet from the earth. — *Cala-kṛiti, is, is, i,* unsteady, wanton. — *Cala-ketu, us,* m. (in astron.) N. of a moving Ketu. — *Cala-ćañću, us,* m., N. of the Greek partridge, Perdix Rufa; [cf. *ćakora.*] — *Cala-ćitta, as, ā, am,* fickle-minded, inconstant; (*am*), n. fickleness, mutability. — *Calaćitta-tā,* f. or *ćalaćitta-tva, am,* n. fickleness of mind, unsteadiness, inconstancy, mutability, frivolity. — *Cala-tā,* f. or *ćala-tva, am,* n. shaking, trembling, a tremulous motion, pulsation. — *Cala-danta, as,* m. a loose tooth. — *Cala-dala, as,* m. the holy fig-tree, Ficus Religiosa; [cf. *aśvattha.*] — *Cala-pattra, as,* m. the Ficus Religiosa; [cf. *aśvattha.*] — *Cala-sandhi, is,* m. movable articulation of the bones, Diarthrosis. — 1. *ćalāćala* (°*la-ać*°), *as, ā, am,* movable and immovable, locomotive and stationary. — *Calātanka* (°*la+āt*°), *as,* m. rheumatism. — *Calātman* (°*la-āt*°), *ā, ā, a,* fickle-minded, inconstant. — *Calendriya* (°*la-in*°), *as, ā, am,* having unsteady organs, sensitive, sensual, not having subdued senses or passions. — *Caleshu* (°*la-ishu*), *us, us, u,* one whose arrow wavers or flies unsteadily.

Calat, an, antī, at, going, moving. — *Calat-padam,* ind. moving, walking. — *Calat-pūrṇimā,* f. a small fish called Chanda, = *ćandra-ćañćala.* — *Calad-anga* or *ćalad-angaka, as,* m. a fish, a sort of gilt-head, commonly Cengā, Ophiocephalus Aurantiacus.

Calana, as, ā, am, moving, movable, trembling, tremulous, shaking; (*as*), m. a foot; a deer, an antelope; (*ī*), f. a short petticoat worn by common women; the rope for tying an elephant; (*am*), n. a shaking motion, shaking, trembling; walking about, wandering, roaming; turning off from, leaving off.

Calanaka, as or *am,* m. or n. a short petticoat worn by women of low rank; (*ikā*), f. silken fringes.

Calanīya, as, ā, am, to be moved or shaken, movable.

Calamāna, as, ā, am, going, moving, proceeding, shaking, &c.

Calas, as, n. wood-sorrel.

2. *ćalāćala, as, ā, am* (fr. rt. *ćal* with reduplication), moving to and fro, movable, tremulous, unfixed, unsteady, shaking, loose; variable; (*as*), m. a cow.

Calita, as, ā, am, gone, departed, proceeded (often used like a past tense, e. g. *sa ćalitaḥ,* he started off, he departed); shaking, trembling.

Calitavya, as, ā, am, to be gone away; to be moved, movable.

Calu, us, m. (said to be fr. rt. *ćal*), water hastily taken up in the hollowed palm of the hand for rincing the mouth &c.; a handful or mouthful of water; [cf. *gaṇḍūsha.*]

Caluka, as, m. = the preceding; also a small pot, a gallipot, &c.; N. of a man; [cf. *ćuluka.*]

चलद्विष *ćaladvisha, as,* m. the Kokila or Indian cuckoo.

चलि *ćali, is,* m. a cover, a wrapper, a surtout; [cf. *ćola.*]

चवि *ćavi, is, ī,* f. or *ćavika, am, ā,* n. f. or *ćavyā, am,* f. n. a species of the pepper plant, Piper Chaba; Orris root.

चशाति *ćaśāti,* a wrong reading for *vaśāti,* q. v.

चष् *ćash,* cl. 1. P. A. *ćashati, -te,* to eat; to kill, hurt.

Cashaka, as, am, m. n. a vessel used for drinking spirits, a wine glass &c., any drinking-vessel; spirituous liquor; honey.

Cashoti, is, m. eating; killing; decay, infirmity.

Cashāla, as, am, m. n. a wooden ring on the top of a sacrificial post; an iron ring at the base of the post; (*as*), m. a hive. — *Cashāla-vat, ān, atī, at,* Ved. furnished with a Cashāla.

चष्ट *ćashṭa, as, ā, am* (past passive part. fr. *ćaksh ?*), spoken, asked.

चष्टान *ćashṭāna, as,* m., N. of a prince, (= Τιαστανος ?).

चह् *ćah* [cf. *ćap*], cl. 1. 10. P. *ćahati, aćahīt, ćahayati, -yitum,* to be wicked, commit wickedness; to cheat; to be proud; cl. 10. P. *ćahayati,* to grind, pound, knead; [cf. Hib. *cagnaim,* 'I chew, gnaw.']

चाकचिच्चा *ćākaćiććā,* f., N. of a plant, = *śveta-vuhnā.*

चाक्र *ćākra, as, ī, am* (fr. *ćakra*), carried on (as a battle) with the discus; circular, belonging to a wheel &c.; (*as*), m., N. of a man.

Cākravarmaṇa, as, m. (a patronymic fr. *ćakravarman*), N. of a grammarian.

Cākravākeya, as or *am* (?), m. or n.? (fr. *ćakravāka*), N. of a place.

Cākrāyaṇa, as, m. a patronymic of Ushasta.

Cākrika, as, ī, am, circular; belonging to a wheel or discus; relating to a company or circle; (*as*), m. a potter; an oil-maker; a proclaimer; a chorister, a bard who chants in chorus the praises of kings, heroes, gods, &c.; a coachman, a driver; (*ās*), m. pl. companions, followers.

Cākriṇa, as, m. the son of a potter or oil-maker.

Cākreya, as, ī, am, relating to a wheel or discus; (*as, am*), m. or n. (?), N. of a place.

चाक्षुष *ćākshusha, as, ī, am* (fr. *ćakshus*), consisting in sight, depending on or produced from it; belonging to the eye, visual, optical, perceptible by the eye, visible, seen; relating to Manu Cākshusha; *ćākshushī vidyā,* that magical science which gives the power of seeing anything; (*as*), m., N. of the sixth Manu who with five other Manus is a son of Manu Svāyambhuva, or according to other authorities a son of Viśva-karman and Ākṛiti, or a son of Cakshus; N. of a son of Ripu and Bṛihatī, (according to some he is called Cakshusha, and is father of Manu Cākshusha); N. of a son of Kaksheyu and brother of Sabhānara; also of a son of Anu and brother of Sabhānara; also of a son of Khanitra; (*ās*), m. pl., N. of a class of deities in the fourteenth Manvantara; (*am*), n. knowledge which depends on vision. — *Cākshusha-jñāna, am*, n. ocular evidence. — *Cākshusha-tva, am*, n. perceptibility by sight.

चाक्ष्म *ćākshma, as, ā, am* (fr. 1. *ksham*), Ved. forbearing, gracious.

चाङ्ग *ćāṅga, as*, m. (fr. *ćaṅga*), wood-sorrel; whiteness or beauty of the teeth.

Cāṅgerī, f. wood-sorrel, Oxalis Pusilla; [cf. *kućāṅgerī.*]

चाचपुट *ćāćapuṭa, as*, m. a kind of time in music; [cf. *ćaććapuṭa.*]

चाचलि *ćāćali, is, is, i* (fr. Intens. of rt. *ćal*), moving much or repeatedly; [cf. *vi-ćāćali* and *a-vić°.*]

चाञ्चल्य *ćāñćalya, am*, n. (fr. *ćañćala*), tremulousness, unsteadiness; transitoriness, fugitiveness, fidgetiness.

चाट *ćāṭa, as*, m. (fr. *ćaṭ* = *ćat?*), a cheat, a rogue, a speculator, one who makes away with or embezzles money &c. entrusted to him.

चाटकैर *ćāṭakaira, as*, m. (fr. *ćaṭaka* or *ćaṭakā*), a young sparrow.

चाटलिका *ćāṭalikā*, f., N. of a place.

चाटिग्राम *ćāṭigrāma, as*, m., N. of a place.

चाटु *ćāṭu, us, u*, m. n. (said to be fr. rt. *ćaṭ*), pleasing or grateful words or discourse, flattery, flattering, coaxing; distinct or clear speech; [cf. *ćaṭu.*] — *Cāṭu-kāra, as, ī, am*, speaking agreeably or kindly, flattering, complying with a request, humouring, complaisant; (*as*), m. a flatterer. — *Cāṭu-kārin, ī, iṇī, i*, speaking agreeably, flattering. — *Cāṭu-paṭu, us*, m. a jester, a buffoon, one who makes compliments (?). — *Cāṭu-lola, as, ā, am*, elegantly tremulous. — *Cāṭu-vaṭu, us*, m. a jester; [cf. *ćāṭu-paṭu.*] — *Cāṭu-śata, am*, n. repeated coaxing, a hundred entreaties. — *Cāṭūkti* (°*ṭu-ukti*), *is*, f. agreeable language, flattery, service.

Cāṭuka, as or *am* (?), m. or n. (?), pleasing or grateful discourse.

चाणकीन *ćāṇakīna, as, ā, am* (fr. *ćaṇaka*), fit for or sown with the chick-pea (a field &c.).

चाणक्य *ćāṇakya, as*, m. (a patronymic fr. *ćaṇaka*, N. of a Muni), N. of the sage Vātsyāyana; N. of a celebrated Brāhman also called Vishṇu-gupta, the reputed author of a work on morals and the principles of government. He is said to have destroyed the Nanda dynasty and to have made Candra-gupta (q. v.) king, whose minister he became. From the tone of his advice to princes he has been styled the Machiavelli of India; (*am*), n., scil. *śāstram*, the work of Cāṇakya, on morals and polity. — *Cāṇakya-mūlaka, am*, n. a kind of radish; [cf. *kauṭilya.*] — *Cāṇakya-śloka, ās*, m. pl. detached stanzas on morals and the principles of government, supposed to be written by the Brāhman Cāṇakya or compiled by him.

Cāṇaka, as, ī, am (an adj. formed fr. *ćāṇakya*), relating to Cāṇakya.

चाणूर *ćāṇūra, as*, m., N. of a prince; also of a wrestler in the service of Kaṃsa, slain by Kṛishṇa, and identified with the Daitya Varāha. — *Cāṇūra-sūdana, as*, m. an epithet of Kṛishṇa.

चाण्ड *ćāṇḍa, am*, n. (fr. *ćaṇḍa*), violence.

चाण्डाल *ćāṇḍāla, as*, m. = *ćaṇḍāla*, a name of an impure or degraded tribe, a Caṇḍāla, a Pariah, an outcast; (*ī*), f. a woman of the same tribe; N. of a plant, = *liṅginī.*

Cāṇḍālikā, f. a vulgar lute, the lute of the Caṇḍāla; a N. of Durgā; a kind of herb; [cf. *ćaṇḍālikā.*] — *Cāṇḍālikāśrama* (°*kā-āś*°), *as*, m. N. of the hermitage of Cāṇḍālikā.

चातक *ćātaka, as*, m. (said to be fr. rt. *ćat*), N. of the bird Cucolus Melanoleucus, according to the legend living only upon rain-drops; [cf. Lat. *cot-urnix.*] — *Cātakānandana* (°*ka-ān*°), *as*, m. the rainy season. — *Cātakāshṭaka* (°*ka-ash*°), *am*, n. the eight verses on the Cātaka bird.

चातन *ćātana*. See under rt. *ćat* at p. 313.

चातुर 1. *ćātura, as, ī, am* (fr. *ćatur*), relating to four; (a carriage &c.) drawn by four; (*ī*), f., N. of a poem by Nara-siṃha; (*am*), n. a carriage, a cart holding four people.

Cātuḥsāgarika, as, ī, am (fr. *ćatuḥ-sāgara*), belonging to the four oceans.

Cāturaksha, am, n. (fr. *ćatur-aksha*), four casts in playing at dice.

Cāturarthika, as, ī, am (fr. *ćatur-artha*), used in four particular senses or meanings.

Cāturāśramika, as, ī, am, or *ćāturāśramin, ī, iṇī, i* (fr. *ćatur-āśrama*), being in one of the four periods or orders [cf. *āśrama*] of life.

Cāturāśramya, am, n. the four periods of the life of a Brāhman collectively; the aggregate of the four orders of student, householder, ascetic, and mendicant.

Cāturjātaka, am, n. = *kaṭu-ćāturjātaka.*

Cāturthaka, as, ikā, am, quartan, appearing every fourth day; (*as*), m. a quartan ague.

Cāturthāhnika, as, ī, am (fr. *ćaturtha-ahan*), belonging to the fourth day.

Cāturthika, as, ī, am, belonging to the fourth or to the fourth day; (*as*), m. a quartan ague.

Cāturdaśa, as, ī, am (fr. *ćaturdaśī*), appearing on the fourteenth day of the half month.

Cāturdaśika, as, ī, am, reading the holy scriptures on the fourteenth day of the half month.

Cāturdaiva, as, ī, am (fr. *ćatur-deva*), sacred to four deities.

Cāturbhadra, am, n. (fr. *ćatur-bhadra*), an assemblage of four medicinal plants.

Cāturbhuji, is, m. a son of Catur-bhuja.

Cāturbhautika, as, ī, am (fr. *ćatur-bhūta*), consisting of four elements.

Cāturmahārājakāyika or *ćāturmahārājika* = *ćaturmahārājakāyika*; also an epithet of Vishṇu.

Cāturmāsa, as, ī, am (fr. *ćatur-māsa*), produced in four months.

Cāturmāsaka, as, ikā, am, or *ćāturmāsin, ī, inī, i*, one who performs the Cāturmāsya sacrifice.

Cāturmāsī, f., scil. *paurṇamāsī*, the day of full moon at the Cāturmāsya sacrifices.

Cāturmāsya, am, n., N. of three sacrifices belonging to the subdivision called Havir-yajña and performed (every four months) at the beginning of the three seasons, viz. the *vaiśvadevam* on the full moon in Phalguna, *varuṇa-praghāsāḥ* in Ashāḍha, and *sākamedhāḥ* in Kṛittikā; (*as, ā, am*), belonging to the Cāturmāsya sacrifice.

Cāturvarṇya, as, ā, am (fr. *ćatur-varṇa*), suited to the four tribes or castes, belonging to them (?); (*am*), n. the aggregate of the four original castes, viz. the Brāhman, Kshatriya, Vaiśya, and Śūdra.

Cāturviṃśika, as, ī, am (fr. *ćaturviṃśa*), belonging to the twenty-fourth day.

Cāturvidya, as, dī, am (fr. *ćatur-vidyā*), familiar with the four Vedas; (*am*), n. the four Vedas.

Cāturvidhya, am, n. (fr. *ćatur-vidha*), four kinds collectively.

Cāturvaidya, as, dī, am (fr. *ćatur-veda*), versed in or familiar with the four Vedas; (*am*), n. knowledge of the four Vedas.

Cāturhotṛika, as, ī, am (fr. *ćatur-hotṛi*), belonging to the Catur-hotṛi.

Cāturhotra, as, ī, am (fr. *ćatur-hotṛi*), conducted or performed by the four chief priests, viz. the Hotṛi, Adhvaryu, Udgātṛi, and Brahman; (*am*), n. a sacrifice performed by four priests; the office or duties of the four chief priests; the four chief priests collectively.

Cāturhotriya, as, ī, am (fr. *ćatur-hotṛi*), a sacrifice &c. at or in which the four chief priests are employed.

Cātushkāṇḍika, as, ī, am (fr. *ćatush-kāṇḍa*), divided into four parts.

Cātushṭaya, as, ī, am (fr. *ćatushṭaya*), knowing or familiar with the Catushṭaya.

Cātushprāśya, as, śī, am (fr. *ćatuḥ + prāśa*), enough for four persons to eat.

Cātvāriṃśa, am, n. (fr. *ćatvāriṃśat*), title of a Brāhmaṇa consisting of forty Adhyāyas.

Cātvāriṃśatka, as, ī, am, bought for forty.

चातुर 2. *ćātura, as, ī, am* (fr. 2. *ćatura*), clever, able, ingenious, shrewd, sagacious; speaking well or kindly, flattering; perceptible, visible; governing, ruling; (*as*), m. a small round pillow, see below; (*ī*), f. dexterity, ability, cleverness.

Cāturaka, as, ā, am, flattering; perceptible; governing; (*as*), m. a small round pillow for resting the cheek upon; [cf. *galla-ćāturī.*]

Cāturika, as, m. a charioteer, a coachman.

Cāturya, am, n. dexterity, cleverness, ability, shrewdness; amiableness.

चात्र *ćātra, am*, n. (sometimes read *ćatra*), a cylinder of catechu-wood twelve Aṅgulas long, tipped at both ends with iron and furnished with an iron bolt, (this and another piece of wood called Auvilī are used for producing the sacred fire.)

चात्वाल *ćātvāla, as* or *am*, m. or n. the hole formed in the ground by excavating the earth to construct the Uttara-vedi or north altar; (*as*), m. a hollow place dug in the ground to receive a burnt-offering; any hole in the ground; [cf. *ćatvāla.*] — *Cātvāla-vat, ān, atī, at*, (a sacrifice) at which the Cātvāla is excavated.

चान्दनिक *ćāndanika, as, ī, am* (fr. *ćandana*), made of or derived from sandal, perfumed with it, &c.

चान्द्र *ćāndra, as, ī, am* (fr. *ćandra*), lunar, relating to the moon, regulated by it, &c.; (*as*), m. a month, a lunar month (called Gauṇa, q. v., if reckoned from full moon to full moon, and Mukhya if reckoned from new moon to new moon); the light fortnight or half month, during which the moon is on the increase; the Candra-kānta or moon-gem; (*ās*), m. pl. the pupils of the grammarian Candra; (*ī*), f. moonlight; a kind of solanum [cf. *śveta-kaṇṭakārī*]; N. of a princess; (*am*), n., scil. *vratam*, the Cāndrāyaṇa penance, see below. — *Cāndra-māsa, as*, m. a lunar month; [cf. *ćāndra* above.] — *Cāndra-vatsara, as*, m. the lunar year. — *Cāndra-sūtra, am*, n., N. of a Sūtra work. — *Cāndrākhya* (°*ra-ākh*°), *am*, n. fresh ginger; [cf. *ćāndraka.*]

Cāndraka, am, n. dried ginger; [cf. *śuṇṭhī.*]

Cāndrapura, ās, m. pl. the inhabitants of Candrapura.

Cāndrabhāgā or *ī*, f. = *ćandra-bhāgā*, the Chenāb, a river in the Pañjāb.

Cāndramasa, as, ī, am (fr. *ćandramas*), lunar, relating or belonging to the moon; (*ī*), f., N. of the wife of Bṛihaspati; (*am*), n., N. of the fifth lunar mansion, the constellation Mṛiga-śiras; the stars in Orion. — *Cāndramasāyana, as*, or *ćāndramasāyani, is*, m. (fr. *ćandramas*), 'descendant of the moon,' a N. of Budha, regent of Mercury and son of the moon.

Cāndravratika, as, ī, am (fr. *ćandra-vrata*), acting in the manner of the moon, having the character of the moon.

Cāndrāyaṇa, am, n., scil. *vratam*, a religious observance or expiatory penance regulated by the moon's age, (it consists in diminishing the daily consumption of food every day by one mouthful for the dark half of the month, beginning with 15 at the full moon until the quantity is reduced to 0 at the new moon, and then increasing it in like manner during the fortnight of the moon's increase: if this penance begins with the full moon, it is called Pipīlikā-madhya, i. e. having the middle thin like an ant; if with the new moon, beginning with 0 and increasing to 15, it is called Yava-madhya or Yava-madhyama, i. e. having the middle thick like a barley-corn); (*ās*), m. pl., N. of various persons. —*Cāndrāyaṇa-bhakta, am,* n. the country inhabited by the Cāndrāyaṇas. — *Cāndrāyaṇa-vidhāna* or *ćāndrāyaṇa-vrata, am,* n. the penance called Cāndrāyaṇa.

Cāndrāyaṇika, as, ī, am, performing or a performer of the Cāndrāyaṇa, q. v.

चान्धनायन *ćāndhanāyana, as,* m., N. of an ancient preceptor.

चाप *ćāpa, as, am,* m. n. (perhaps fr. rt. *kap* = *kamp*), a bow; (in geometry) an arc or portion of a circle; the sign of the zodiac Sagittarius; a rainbow [cf. *indra-ćāpa* and *śakra-ćāpa*]; N. of a particular constellation; [cf. *dhanus.*] —*Cāpa-dāsī,* f., N. of a river. —*Cāpa-paṭa, as,* m. the tree Buchanania Latifolia (*piyāla*); [cf. *dhanu* and *paṭa.*]

Cāpin, ī, inī, i, armed with a bow; (*ī*), m. the sign of the zodiac Sagittarius.

चापल *ćāpala, am,* n. (fr. *ćapala*), fickleness, unsteadiness, mobility, quick movement, swiftness, transitoriness; agitation, tremour; inconsiderate conduct, impertinence, inconsiderateness. —*Cāpalāśraya* (°*la-āś*°), *am,* n. (?) unsteadiness.

Cāpalya, am, n. fickleness; unsteadiness, transitoriness; quickness, agitation, flurry; inconsiderate conduct, inconsiderateness.

चापाल *ćāpāla, as,* m., N. of a Buddhist Caitya.

चाबुका *ćābukā,* f. a small circular pillow.

चामर *ćāmara, am, ā* or *ī, as,* n. f. m. a chowrie, the bushy tail of the Bos Grunniens, used as a fly-flap or fan, and as one of the insignia of royalty; also used for a kind of streamer or plume on the heads of horses; (*am*), n., N. of a metre consisting of four lines of fifteen syllables each. —*Cāmara-grāha, as,* m. a person who carries a Cāmara. —*Cāmara-pushpa, as,* m., N. of several plants, Magnifera Indica [cf. *āmra*]; the betel-nut tree, Areca Faufel or Catechu [cf. *pūga*]; the Pandanus Odoratissimus [cf. *ketaka*]; a kind of grass, Saccharum Spontaneum [cf. *kāśa*]. —*Cāmara-pushpaka, as,* m. or *ćāmara-sāhvaya, as,* m. a kind of grass, Saccharum Spontaneum; [cf. *kāśa.*]

Cāmarika, as, m. a person who carries a Cāmara.

Cāmarin, ī, m. a horse (either from his bushy tail which he uses to whisk off flies or from his having a Cāmara as his crest; see above).

चामीकर *ćāmīkara, am,* n. gold; the thorn-apple. —*Cāmīkara-prakhya, as, ā, am,* like gold.

चामुण्डा *ćāmuṇḍā,* f. a form of Durgā; one of the seven Mātṛis; (*as*), m., N. of an author.

चाम्पिला *ćāmpilā,* f. a river.

चाम्पेय *ćāmpeya, as,* m. (fr. *ćampā*), N. of two trees, Michelia Champaka and Mesua Ferrea; a stamen or filament, especially of the lotus flower; a prince of Campā; N. of a son of Viśvā-mitra; (*as, am*), m. n. gold.

Cāmpeyuka, am, n. a stamen or filament.

चाम्य *ćāmya, am,* n. (fr. rt. *ćam*), food.

चाय *ćāy,* cl. 1. P. A. *ćāyati, -te,* to observe, discern, perceive; to worship, revere; [cf. 4. *ći.*]

Cāyamāna, as, m., Ved. a patronymic of Abhyāvartin.

Cāyitṛi, tā, trī, tṛi, Ved. observing, seeing.

Cāyu, us, us, u, Ved. showiog respect or reverence, honouring.

चार *ćāra, as,* m. (fr. rt. *ćar*), = *ćara,* a spy, scout, secret agent or emissary, messenger; going, motion, progression, course; wandering about, travelling; proceeding; performing, practising; binding, a bond, fetter; a prison, a house of confinement; the tree Buchanania Latifolia, = *piyāla;* (*am*), n. a factitious poison, (for *vāra*); [cf. Lat. *carcer.*] —*Cāra-kāṇḍa, am,* n. ascensional difference (in astronomy). —*Cāra-ćakshus, us, us, us,* 'spy-eyed,' i. e. a king or minister who uses spies as his eyes, one who employs spies or agents and sees through their medium; (*us*), n. espionage. —*Cāra-ćaṇa, as, ā, am,* graceful in gait or motion. —*Cāra-ćuñću, us, us, u,* graceful in walking, of graceful carriage. —*Cāra-jyā,* f. the sine of the ascensional difference. —*Cāra-patha, as,* m. a place where two roads meet. —*Cāra-bhaṭa, as,* m. a valorous warrior. —*Cāra-vāyu, us,* m. summer air, zephyr. —*Cārāntarita* (°*ra-an*°), *as,* m. a secret emissary or spy. —*Cārekshaṇa* (°*ra-ik*°), *as,* m. a statesman, a minister or king (who employs spies).

Cāraka, as, ikā, am, acting, setting to work, proceeding; composed by Caraka; (*as*), m. a spy, a secret agent or emissary; a driver, a herdsman, a leader; an associate, a companion; a groom, a horseman, a cavalier; a wandering Brāhmanical student; a fetter, a bond, a prison; the plant Buchanania Latifolia (= *ćāra*); N. of a man; (*ikā*), f. a female attendant; a cock-roach. —*Cāraka-trirātra, as,* m., N. of a festival.

Cārakiṇa, as, ā, am, fit for a wandering Brāhmanical student.

Cāraṇa, as, m. a wanderer, a pilgrim; a wandering actor or singer, an actor of note, a dancer, a mime, a bard, a herald; a celestial singer, a panegyrist of the gods; a reader of scripture; a spy; N. of a place. —*Cāraṇa-tva, am,* n. dancing (the art). —*Cāraṇa-dārā, ās,* f. pl. female dancers, actresses, &c. —*Cāraṇa-vidya* or *ćāraṇa-vaidya* or *ćāraṇā-vidya, ās,* m. pl., N. of a branch of the Atharva-veda.

Cāratha, as, ā, am, Ved. going, wandering or moving about, going in a carriage.

Cārayitvā, ind. having enjoined or prescribed, having caused to observe; having made to go &c.

Cārāyaṇa, as, ī, m. f. a patronymic from Cara; (*as*), m., N. of the author of the Sādhāraṇādhikaraṇa.

Cārāyaṇaka, as, ikā, am, derived from the Cārāyaṇas.

Cārāyaṇīya, ās, m. pl. the pupils of Cārāyaṇa.

Cārita, as, ā, am, caused to go; distilled, &c.

Cāritārthya, am, n. (fr. *ćaritārtha*), attainment of an object.

Cāritra, as, m., N. of a Marut; (*ā*), f. the tamarind tree; (*am*), n. proceeding, manner of acting, conduct; good conduct, behaviour; good name or character, reputation; peculiar observance or practice, peculiarity of customs or conditions; a ceremony. —*Cāritra-kavaća, as, ā, am,* cased in the armour of chastity. —*Cāritra-vatī,* f., N. of a Samādhi.

Cāritrya, am, n. becoming or honourable practices, moral conduct, instituted observance.

Cārin, ī, iṇī, i, (generally at the end of a comp.) moving, walking or wandering about, living, being (e. g. *pāda-ćārin,* going on foot; *nimeshāntara-ćārin,* going in an instant, arriving after a short interval &c.), [cf. *ambu-ćārin, eka-ć*°, *kha-ć*°, &c.]; acting, proceeding, doing, practising; living on; (*ī*), m. a foot soldier; (*iṇī*), f., N. of a plant, = *karuṇī.*

चारटिका *ćāraṭikā,* f. a kind of perfume, = *nalī.*

चारटी *ćāraṭī,* f., N. of two plants, = *padma-ćāriṇī* and *bhūmy-āmalī.*

चारभट *ćārabhaṭa, as,* m. a courageous man, a hero, a chief, a warrior; (*ī*), f. courage; [cf. *ārabhaṭa.*]

चारिवाच् *ćārivāć, k,* f., N. of a plant, = *karkaṭa-śṛiṅgī.*

चारु *ćāru, us, vī, u* (said to be fr. rt. *ćar,* perhaps connected with 2. *ćan*), agreeable, welcome, approved, esteemed, beloved, dear (with dat. or loc. of the person, e. g. *varuṇāya* or *varuṇe ćāruḥ,* dear to Varuṇa), pleasing, lovely, beautiful, pretty, elegant; (*us*), m. an epithet of Bṛihaspati; N. of a son of Kṛishṇa and Rukmiṇī; of a Cakra-vartin; (*vī*), f. a beautiful woman; splendor; moonlight; intelligence; N. of the wife of Kuvera; (*u*), n. a various reading for *vara,* saffron; [cf. Eng. *fair;* Brit. *kaer.*] —*Cāru-karṇa, as, ā* or *ī, am,* having beautiful ears. —*Cāru-keśarā,* f. a kind of grass, Cyperus, = *nāgara-mustā;* a kind of tree, = *taruṇī.* —*Cāru-garbha, as,* m., N. of a son of Kṛishṇa and Rukmiṇī. —*Cāru-giti, is,* f. a kind of metre, a sort of Gīti, containing 29 + 32 syllabic instants. —*Cāru-gupta, as,* m., N. of a son of Kṛishṇa and Rukmiṇī. —*Cāru-ghoṇa, as, ā, am,* handsome-nosed. —*Cāru-ćitra, as,* m., N. of a son of Dhṛita-rāshṭra. —*Cāru-tā,* f. or *ćāru-tva, ám,* n. loveliness, beauty. —*Cāru-datta, as,* m., N. of a Brāhman. —*Cārudatta-nāman, ā,* m. named Cāru-datta. —*Cāru-danta, as,* m. 'having beautiful teeth,' N. of a merchant's son. —*Cāru-darśana, as, ā, am,* good-looking. —*Cāru-deva, as,* m., N. of a man. —*Cāru-deshṇa, as,* m., N. of a son of Gaṇḍūsha; also of a son of Kṛishṇa by Rukmiṇī. —*Cāru-dhāman, ā,* m., N. of a plant. —*Cāru-dhāmā* or *ćāru-dhārā,* f. an epithet of Saćī, the wife of Indra. —*Cāru-dhishṇya, as,* m., N. of one of the Saptarshayas in the eleventh Manvantara. —*Cāru-nālaka, am,* n. a kind of lotus with red flowers. —*Cāru-netra, as, ā, am,* having beautiful eyes; (*ā*), f., N. of an Apsaras. —*Cāru-pada, as,* m., N. of a son of Namasyu. —*Cāru-parṇī,* f., N. of a plant, = *pra-sāraṇī.* —*Cāru-puṭa, as,* m. a particular time in music. —*Cāru-pratīka, as, ā, am,* Ved. of lovely appearance. —*Cāru-phalā,* f. a vine, a grape. —*Cāru-bāhu, us,* or *ćāru-bhadra, as,* m., N. of a son of Kṛishṇa by Rukmiṇī. —*Cāru-mat, ān, atī, at,* lovely, beautiful; (*ān*), m., N. of a Cakra-vartin; (*tī*), f., N. of a daughter of Kṛishṇa by Rukmiṇī. —*Cāru-mukha, as, ī, am,* handsome-faced, fair, beauteous; (*ī*), f., N. of a metre consisting of four lines of ten syllables each. —*Cāru-yaśas, ās,* m. 'of fair fame,' N. of a son of Kṛishṇa by Rukmiṇī; [cf. *ćāru.*] —*Cāru-ratha, as* or *am,* m. or n. (?), N. of a forest. —*Cāru-rāvā,* f. an epithet of Saćī, the wife of Indra. —*Cāru-loćana, as, ā, am,* lovely-eyed, having beautiful eyes; (*as*), m. a deer, antelope; (*ā*), f. a woman with fine eyes. —*Cāru-vaktra, as,* m. 'handsome-faced,' N. of one of Skanda's attendants. —*Cāru-vardhanā,* f. a woman. —*Cāru-vinda, as,* m., N. of a son of Kṛishṇa by Rukmiṇī. —*Cāru-veśa, as,* m. 'well-dressed,' = the preceding. —*Cāru-vratā,* f. a female who fasts for a whole month. —*Cāru-śilā,* f. 'beautiful stone,' a jewel, a gem. —*Cāru-śirsha, as,* m., N. of a man. —*Cāru-śila, as, ā, am,* of a lovely nature, beautiful. —*Cāru-śravas, ās,* m., N. of a son of Kṛishṇa by Rukmiṇī. —*Cāru-sarvāṅga-darśana* (°*ra-an*°), *as, ā, am,* having a beautiful appearance in all the limbs. —*Cāru-hāsin, ī, inī, i,* smiling sweetly; (*inī*), f., N. of a metre, containing 4 x 14 syllabic instants. —*Cārv-aṅgī,* f. a beautifully formed woman. —*Cārv-āghāṭa* or *ćārv-āghāta, as, ā, am,* destructive of beauty.

Cāruka, as, m. the seed of Saccharum Sara.

चार्चिक *ćārćika, as, ī, am* (fr. *ćarćā*), conversant with the repetitions (in the recitation of the Veda).

Cārćikya, am, n. perfuming the person, smearing it with sandal &c.; unguent; [cf. *ćarćikya.*]

चार्म *ćārma, as, ī, am* (fr. *ćarman*), made of hide or leather, leathern; covered with leather (as a car &c.); defended by a hide or skin; shielded, having a shield.

Cārmaṇa, as, ī, am, covered with skin or leather; (*am*), n. a multitude of hides or of shields &c.

Ćārmika, as, ī, am, leather, made of leather, belonging to the skin &c.

Ćārmikāyaṇi, is, m. a patronymic from Carm'n.

Ćārmiṇa, am, n. a number of men armed with shields.

चार्य ćārya, as, m., N. of a despised caste, the son of an outcast Vaiśya; (perhaps for aćārya.)

चार्वाक ćārvāka, as, m. (fr. ćāru + vāka), N. of a Rākshasa described in the Mahā-bh. Śānti-parva 1414, &c., as a friend of Duryodhana and an enemy of the Pāṇḍavas; (having taken the shape of a mendicant Brāhman, when Yudhishṭhira entered Hāstina-pura in triumph, he reviled him and the assembled Brāhmans, but was soon detected; and the real Brāhmans, filled with fury, killed him on the spot); N. of a sophistical philosopher who probably lived before the composition of the Rāmāyaṇa; see jāvāli. He was a sceptic in matters of Hindū faith, and considered by the orthodox as an atheist or materialist; according to some, the sceptical doctrines of the Indian materialists were handed down to Ćārvāka and his followers by Vāćas-pati or Bṛihaspati, and the aphorisms of Bṛihaspati (Bārhaspatya sūtras) are said to embody their opinions; (as, ī, am), derived from or composed by Ćārvāka. — Ćārvāka-darśana, am, n. the doctrine of Ćārvāka.

चाल ćāla, as, m. (fr. rt. ćal), the thatch or roof of a house; the blue jay; shaking, the being movable.

Ćālaka, as, m. a restive elephant.

Ćālana, am, n. causing to move or go, causing to pass through a sieve, sifting, shaking, moving to and fro, wagging (as the tail), loosening; muscular action; (ī), f. a sieve, a strainer.

Ćālanīya, as, ā, am, to be moved, capable of being moved.

Ćālya, as, ā, am, to be moved; to be loosened or shaken or led away from.

चालिक्य ćālikya, as, m. a patronymic.

चाष ćāsha, as, m. the blue jay, Coracias Indica; (according to some) a kingfisher.

Ćāsa, as, m. the blue jay, Coracias Indica; sugar-cane. — Ćāsa-vaktra, as, ā, am, having a face like that of a jay; (as), m., N. of one of the attendants of Skanda; (ās), m. pl. a class of demons or evil spirits.

चि 1. ći, cl. 5. P. A. ćinoti, -nute, ćikāya and ćićāya, ćikye and ćićye, ćeshyati, -te, aćaishīt, ćetum, to arrange in order, place in a line, heap up, pile up, construct (as a sacrificial altar, used in P. if the priests construct the altar for another, in A. if the sacrificer builds it for himself); to collect, gather together, accumulate, gain for one's self; to cover, inlay, set with (with inst., e. g. ratnaiḥ, with jewels): Caus. ćāyayati or ćāpayati, or ćayayati or ćapayati: Desid. ćikīshati and ćićīshati, to wish to pile up: Caus. of the Desid. ćićīshayati, to cause a person to wish to arrange in order or pile up: Intens. ćećīyate; [cf. Cambro-Brit. cai, 'collection;' Lat. cumulus; Pol. kupa; Germ. Haufen.]

1. ćaya, as, m. stacked wood; a mound of earth raised to form the foundation of a building; a rampart or mound of earth raised from the ditch of a fort; the gate of a fort; any edifice; a seat, a stool; a cover, a covering; a heap, pile, collection, a multitude, an assemblage, aggregation; the amount or augment by which each term increases, the common increase or difference of the terms; [cf. agni-ćaya; cf. also Cambro-Brit. cai, 'collection;' Hib. scea, 'plenty, abundance.']

Ćayana, am, n. the act of collecting, gathering, heaping up, aggregation; stacking wood; stacked wood; [cf. agni-ćayana.]

Ćayanīya, as, ā, am, to be collected or gathered, to be heaped up.

Ćićīshat, an, antī, at, wishing to gather or collect.

1. ćit, t, t, t, (at the end of compounds) piling up (e. g. agni-ćit, q. v.); forming a layer or stratum, piled up.

Ćita, as, ā, am, piled, heaped; collected, gathered, accumulated; covered, veiled, concealed; (ā), f. a layer, a pile of wood, a funeral pile, pyre; a heap, an assemblage, a multitude; (am), n. a building (e. g. pakveshṭaka-ćita, a building of burnt bricks). — Ćita-vistara, as, m. a kind of ornament. — Ćitāgni (°ta-ag°), is, m. the funeral fire. — Ćitā-ćūḍaka, am, n. a mark where a funeral pile has been, a mausoleum, a monument, &c. — Ćitaidha (°ta-edha), as, ā, am, Ved. belonging or referring to a funeral pile.

1. ćiti, is, f. a stratum, layer of wood or bricks &c.; a pile, a stack; a funeral pile; an oblong with quadrangular sides; collecting, gathering; a heap, a quantity, a multitude; N. of the eighth or tenth book of the Satapatha-Brāhmaṇa; [cf. amṛita-ćiti.] — Ćiti-vat, ān, atī, at, having a funeral pile.

Ćitikā, f. a stack, a pile; a funeral pile; a small chain worn as an ornament round the loins, a kind of girdle.

Ćitīka (at the end of an adj. comp. after a numeral) = ćiti, a layer (e. g. pańća-ćitīka, tri-ć°, eka-ć°).

Ćitya, as, ā, am, to be arranged in order or built up; (scil. agni, fire), placed or constructed upon a foundation or basis (as of stones &c.); (ā), f. piling up, building (an altar &c.); a funeral pile; (am), n. the place at which a corpse has been burnt and where a monument has been erected; a monument or any mark of the site of a funeral pile. — Ćityādhirohaṇa (°ya-adh°), am, n. burning with a husband's corpse. — Ćityārohaṇa (°ya-ār°), am, n. ascending the funeral pile.

1. ćinvat, an, atī, at, gathering, collecting.

Ćiti, is, f., Ved. gathering, collecting.

Ćetavya, as, ā, am, to be collected or gathered, to be piled up.

Ćeya, as, ā, am, to be piled up, to be gathered or collected.

चि 2. ći, cl. 3. P., Ved. ćiketi, Impf. aćiket, Impv. 2nd sing. ćikīhi, ćikāya; cl. 5. P. A. ćinoti, ćinute &c. like 1. ći, to observe, perceive; to fix the gaze upon; to be intent upon; to seek for, investigate; to make inquiries, search through.

2. ćit, t, t, t, observing, knowing (in ṛita-ćit).

2. ćinvat, an, atī, at, seeking for, searching for.

1. ćetṛi, tā, trī, tṛi, an observer, guardian.

चि 3. ći, cl. 1. A., Ved. ćayate, to detest, hate; to revenge, punish, take vengeance on.

2. ćaya, as, ā, am, revenging, punishing.

3. ćit, t, t, t, punishing (in ṛiṇa-ćit).

2. ćetṛi, tā, trī, tṛi, Ved. a revenger.

Ćetyā, f., Ved. revenge, punishment.

चि 4. ći, cl. 1. P. A. ćāyati, -te, to fear, be afraid of (with acc.); to respect, honour; to observe; [cf. ćāy.]

चिकरिषु ćikarishu, us, us, u (fr. Desid. of rt. 1. kṛī), desirous to cast or throw, wishing to pour out.

चिकर्तिषु ćikartishu, us, us, u (fr. Desid. of rt. 2. kṛit), desirous or intending to cut or cut off.

चिकित् ćikit, ćikiti, &c. See p. 323, col. 1.

चिकिन ćikina, as, ā, am, flat-nosed; (am), n. flat-nosedness; [cf. ćikka and ćipiṭa.]

चिकिल ćikila, as, m. mud, mire, a slough, a bog; [cf. ićikila and ćikhalla.]

चिकीर्षक ćikīrshaka, as, ā, am (fr. Desid. of rt. 1. kṛi), desirous of doing, meaning to do.

Ćikīrshat, an, antī, at, wishing or purposing to act or do.

Ćikīrshā, f. intention or desire to act, wish, will, design, purpose, desire of doing or performing anything.

Ćikīrshita, as, ā, am, intended to be done; wished, designed, purposed; (am), n. purpose, design, intention.

Ćikīrshu, us, us, u, wishing to act, desiring or intending to do or make or perform anything; wishing to practice; desirous for.

Ćikīrshya, as, ā, am, to be wished to be done, to be designed.

चिकुर ćikura, as, ā, am (perhaps a reduplicated form of rt. kṛī or of kar for ćar), inconsiderate, rash, punishing or injuring others without consideration; (as), m. the hair of the head, a lock of hair; a mountain; a kind of tree or plant; a snake, N. of a Nāga; a kind of bird; a musk-rat; [cf. ćikka and ćikkira; cf. also Gr. κίκιννος; Lat. cincinnus?]. — Ćikura-kalāpa or ćikura-paksha or ćikura-pāśa or ćikura-bhāra, as, m. or ćikura-raćanā, f. or ćikura-hasta or ćikuroććaya (°ra-uć°), as, m. a mass of hair, a tuft of hair.

Ćikūra, as, m. the hair, = ćikura.

चिक्क् ćikk, cl. 10. P. ćikkayati, -yitum, to feel pain; to give or inflict pain; [cf. ćakk and ćukk.]

चिक्क ćikka, as, ā, am, flat-nosed; (am), n. flat-nosedness; (as), m. the musk-rat; (according to other authorities ćika; cf. ćikura and ćikkira); (ā), f. a mouse; a betel-nut; [cf. ćikkaṇa.]

चिक्कण ćikkaṇa, as, ā, am (said to be fr. rt. 4. ćit), smooth, glossy; slippery; bland, emollient; unctuous, greasy; (as), m. the betel-nut tree; (am, ā or ī), n. f. the betel-nut; (ā), f. an excellent cow; (other authorities have ćikkiṇā.) — Ćikkaṇa-kantha, am, n., N. of a town; [cf. ćitkaṇa-kantha and ćihaṇa-kantha.] — Ćikkaṇa-tā, f. or ćikkaṇa-tva, am, n. smoothness, oiliness, greasiness, unctuousness.

चिक्कस ćikkasa, as, am, m. n. barley-meal.

चिक्किण ćikkiṇa, as, ā, am, glossy, shining, smooth; slippery; bland, emollient; unctuous, greasy; (ā), f. an excellent cow.

चिक्किर ćikkira, as, m. a small venomous animal (mūshika); [cf. ćikura, ćikka, ćhikkara.]

चिक्रंसा ćikraṃsā, f. (fr. Desid. of rt. kram), a wish to go, desire of approaching.

चिक्रीडिषा ćikrīḍishā, f. (fr. Desid. of rt. krīḍ), a wish or desire to play.

चिक्लिद ćiklida, as, m. (fr. rt. klid), the moon; (am), n. moisture, freshness; [cf. kledu.]

चिखल्ल ćikhalla, as, m. mud, mire, a slough; [cf. ićkila and ćikila.]

चिखादिषु ćikhādishu, us, us, u (fr. Desid. of rt. khād), wishing or desiring to eat.

चिङ्गट ćingaṭa, as, ī, m. f. or ćingaḍa, as, m. a shrimp or prawn; [cf. uććingaṭa.]

चिचिण्ड ćićiṇḍa, as, m. a sort of gourd, Trichosanthes Anguina.

चिचीकुची ćićīkući and ćićīkūćī. See ćićikūćī.

चिचीषत् ćićīshat. See under 1. ći, col. 1.

चिच्चिटिङ्ग ćiććiṭinga, as, m. a species of venomous insect; [cf. uććiṭinga.]

चिच्छित्सु ćiććhitsu, us, us, u (fr. rt. ćhid), wishing or intending to cut off.

चिच्छिल ćiććhila, ās, m. pl., N. of a people.

चिच्छुक ćić-ćhuka. See under 5. ćit.

चिञ्चा ćinćā, f. the tamarind tree or its

fruit. — *Ćinćāmla* (°*ćā-am*°) or *ćinćā-sāra*, *as*, m. an acid pot-herb, Rumex Vesicatorius.

चिञ्चाटक *ćinćāṭaka*, *as*, m. a various reading for *ćiñćoṭaka*.

चिञ्चिनी *ćinćinī*, f., N. of a town.

चिञ्ची *ćinćī*, f. the plant Abrus Precatorius; [cf. *kāka-ćinćā*.]

चिञ्चोटक *ćinćoṭaka*, *as*, m. a kind of plant, = *ankaloḍya* or *krauńćādana*.

चिट् *ćiṭ*, cl. 1. and 10. P. *ćeṭati* and *ćeṭayati*, &c., to send out or forth (as a messenger), to give orders to a servant; to be a servant.

Ceṭa, *as*, m. a servant, &c. See s. v.

चित् 1. 2. 3. *ćit*. See under rt. 1. 2. 3. *ći*.

चित् 4. *ćit* (= *kit*, which is by some regarded as a separate root; cf. *keta*, &c.; cf. also rt. *ćint*), cl. 1. 3. P. *ćetati*, *ćiketti*, *ćićeta* or *ćikela*, *ćikite* or *ćekite* or *ćićite* (Ved. 3rd pl. *ćikitre* or *ćikitrire*; Part. *ćikitāna* or *ćekitāna*), *ćetishyati*, *aćetīt*; Leṭ, *ćiketati* or *ćiketat*; *ćettum* or *ćetitum*, to perceive, fix the mind upon, attend to, be attentive, observe, notice, take notice of (with gen. or acc., e. g. *yajńasya* or *yajńam ćetati*, he takes notice of the sacrifice); to aim at, intend, design (with dat., e. g. *yudhaye ćiketati*, he intends fighting), to desire, long for (with acc.); to be anxious about, to care for; to resolve; to understand, comprehend, know, make known; to recover consciousness, become conscious; P. and A. to become perceptible, to appear; to be regarded as; to be known; Pass. Aor. *aćeti*: Caus. P. A. *ćitayati* Ved., and *ćetayati*, *-te*, *-yitum*, *ketayati*, *-yitum* (see *keta*, p. 252), to cause to attend, to make attentive, remind of; to cause to comprehend or understand, instruct, teach; to observe, perceive, be intent upon; to form an idea in the mind, be conscious of, understand, comprehend, think, reflect upon; to form a conception, have a right notion; to appear, be conspicuous, shine: Desid. P. A. *ćićitishati*, *ćićetishati*, *ćikitsati*, *-te*; Inf. *ćikitsitum*, to intend, have in view, aim at, desire, long for; to care for, be anxious about; to treat medically, heal, cure, attend as a physician (in these senses the form *ćikitsati* is usual); to wish to appear; to remove, destroy; to keep down, press down; to doubt: Caus. of the Desid. *ćikitsayati*, to cure, to heal; Intens. *ćećityate*, *ćećetti*; [cf. Lith. *kettu*.]

Cikit, *t*, *t*, *t*, Ved. understanding, knowing, experienced.

Cikita, *as*, m., N. of a man; [cf. *ćekita*.]

Cikitāna, *as*, m., N. of a man; [cf. *ćaikitāneya* and *ćekitāna*.]

Cikitāyana, *as*, m. a descendant of Cikita; [cf. *ćaikitāyana*.]

Cikiti, *is*, *is*, *i*, Ved. knowing, acquainted with, experienced.

Cikitu, *us*, *us*, *u*, Ved. understanding, knowing, experienced; (*us*), f. understanding, intellect.

Cikitvan, *ā*, m., Ved. understanding, intellect.

Cikitvas, *vān*. *ushī*, *vas*, one who has observed, observing, attending to, attentive, knowing, understanding, experienced, conversant with.

Cikitvit, ind., Ved. with intelligence, intelligently; with deliberation, deliberately; (Sāy.) making known (= *jńāpayantīm* in Ṛig-veda IV. 52, 4). — *Cikitvinmanas*, *ās*, *ās*, *as*, Ved. one whose mind is attentive; coming from an intelligent mind, well considered; (Sāy.) one who knows all hearts.

Cikitsaka, *as*, m. a physician, doctor, practiser in medicine.

Cikitsana, *am*, n. healing, practising medicine, medical attendance.

Cikitsā, f. the practice or science of medicine, healing, curing, administering or applying remedies; (in the system of medicine) one of the six sections, therapeutics. — *Cikitsā-kalikā*, f. title of a medical work by Tiśaṭa. — *Cikitsākalikā-ṭīkā*, f. a commentary on the last work by Candraṭa. — *Cikitsā-kaumudī*, f. title of a medical work by Kāśī-rāja. — *Cikitsā-tattva-jńāna*. *am*, n. title of a medical work by Dhanvantari. — *Cikitsā-darpaṇa*, *am*, n. title of a medical work by Divodāsa.

Cikitsita. *as*, *ā*, *am*, treated medically, remedied, healed, physicked, cured; (*am*), n. healing, remedying, medical attendance; pl. the chapters of the therapeutical section of medicine; (*as*), m., N. of a man.

Cikitsu, *us*, *us*, *u*, Ved. wise, cunning.

Cikitsya, *as*, *ā*, *am*, to be treated medically, to be cured, curable.

5. *ćit*, *t*, f. thought, intelligence, intellect, understanding, mind; the soul, heart. — *Cić-ćandrikā*, f. title of a commentary on the Prabodha-ćandrodaya by Gaṇeśa. — *Cić-ćhakti* (*ćit* + *śakti*), *is*, f. mental power, intellectual capacity. — *Cić-ćhuka* (*ćit-śu*°), *as*, m., N. of a scholiast on the Bhāgavata-Purāṇa; (*ī*), f. or *ćit-sukhī*, f. the commentary written by this scholiast. — *Cit-pati*, *is*, m., Ved. the lord of thought. — *Cit-pravṛitti*, *is*, f. thinking, reflection. — *Cit-svarūpa*, *am*, n. pure intelligence, an epithet of the Supreme. — *Cid-aćićchakti-yukta* (*-aćitśa*°), *as*, *ā*, *am*, having power over matter and spirit. — *Cid-ambara*, *as*, m., N. of the author of a law-book. — *Cid-asthi-mālā*, f. title of a commentary on a grammatical work. — *Cid-ātmaka*, *am*, n. consciousness, perception. — *Cid-ātman*, *ā*, m. the thinking principle, pure intelligence, spirit. — *Cid-ullāsa*, *as*, *ā*, *am*, gladdening the mind or heart. — *Cid-gagana-ćandrikā*, f. title of a literary work. — *Cid-rūpa*, *as*, *ā*, *am*, consisting of intelligence; wise, intelligent, of liberal or expansive mind; amiable, good-hearted; (*am*), n. pure intelligence, the Supreme Being as identified with intellect or intelligence. — *Cid-vilāsa*, *as*, m. a pupil of Śaṅkarāćārya. — *Cin-maya*, *as*, *ī*, *am*, spiritual, 'all intelligence,' as an epithet of the Deity; (*am*), n. pure intelligence. — *Cin-mātra*, *am*, n. pure intelligence.

2. *ćiti*, *is*, f. understanding; (*is*), m. the thinking mind.

Citta, *as*, *ā*, *am*, perceived, observed, considered; reflected upon; resolved; intended, aimed at, understood; visible, perceptible; (*am*), n. attending, observing; thinking, reflecting, imagining, thought; intention, aim, wish; the heart considered as the seat of intellect; the mind, the reasoning faculty; intellect, reason; reason personified; [cf. *a-ćitta*, *iha-ć*°, *ćala-ć*°, *pūrva-ć*°, *prāyaś-ć*°, &c.] — *Citta-kalita*, *as*. *ā*, *am*, anticipated, expected, calculated; known. — *Citta-garbhā*, f., Ved. visibly pregnant. — *Citta-ćārin*, *ī*, *iṇī*, *i*, proceeding or acting according to the wish of another (with gen.). — *Citta-janman*, *ā*, m. produced within the mind, love, the god of love; [cf. *ćitta-bhū*, *ćitta-yoni*, *manasi-ja*.] — *Citta-jńa*, *as*, *ā*, *am*, knowing the hearts, heart-searching. — *Cittajńa-tā*, f. knowledge of the heart. — *Citta-nāśa*, *as*, m. loss of conscience. — *Citta-nirvritti*, *is*, f. contentment of mind, happiness. — *Citta-pramāthin*, *ī*, *inī*, *i*, moving or touching the heart, exciting passion or love, afflicting the mind. — *Citta-praśama*, *as*, *ā*, *am*, satisfied in mind, composed, complacent, tranquil, content. — *Citta-prasanna-tā*, f. happiness of the mind, gaiety, joy. — *Citta-prasādana*, *am*, n. gladdening of the mind. — *Citta-bhara*, *as*, *ā*, *am*, being in the thoughts, felt, perceived. — *Citta-bheda*, *as*, m. inconsistency, contrariety of purpose or will. — *Citta-bhū*, *ūs*, m. love, the god of love. — *Citta-bhrama-ćikitsā*, f. 'medical treatment of mental derangement,' a chapter of the medical work Vaidya-vallabha. — *Citta-moha*, *as*, m. confusion or infatuation of mind — *Citta-yoni*, *is*, m. love; see *ćitta-janman*. — *Citta-rāga*, *as*, m. affection, passion, desire. — *Citta-vat*, *ān*, *atī*, *at*, endowed with understanding, reasonable; kind-hearted, amiable. — *Cittavat-kartṛika*, *as*, *ā*, *am*, (a root) employing an intelligent agent (e. g. *Deva-dattaḥ paćati*, Deva-datta cooks). — *Citta-vikāra*, *as*, m. change of thoughts or feelings, disturbance of mind. — *Citta-vikārin*, *ī*, *iṇī*, *i*, changing a person's character or feeling. — *Citta-vināśana*, *as*, *ā*, *am*, destroying the conscience. — *Citta-viplava*, *as*, m. disturbance of mind, madness, insanity. — *Citta-vibhrama*, *as*, m. derangement of mind, madness. — *Citta-viślesha*, *as*, m. parting of hearts, breach of friendship. — *Citta-vṛitti*, *is*, f. disposition of mind, feeling; inward purpose, emotion; thinking, imagining. — *Citta-vedanā*, f. anxiety, affliction. — *Citta-vaikalya*, *am*, n. bewilderment of mind, distraction, perplexity. — *Citta-saṃhati*, *is*, f. a multitude of thoughts or emotions, many minds. — *Citta-sankhya*, *as*, *ā*, *am*, pervading the heart, penetrating the soul, knowing the thoughts. — *Citta-samunnati*, *is*, f. pride of heart, arrogance, hauteur, haughtiness. — *Citta-stha* or *ćitta-sthita*, *as*, *ā*, *am*, fixed in the mind, being in the heart; (*as*), m., N. of a Samādhi. — *Citta-hārin*, *ī*, *iṇī*, *i*, stealing the heart, fascinating, agreeable, beautiful. — *Citta-hṛit*, *t*, *t*, *t*, fascinating, winning. — *Cittānuvartin* (°*ta-an*°), *ī*, *inī*, *i*, gratifying wishes, humouring. — *Cittāpahāraka* (°*ta-ap*°), *as*, *ikā*, *am*, or *ćittāpahārin* (°*ta-ap*°), *ī*, *iṇī*, *i*, heart-stealing, captivating, attractive. — *Cittābhoga* (°*ta-ābh*°), *as*, m. full consciousness, consciousness of pleasure or pain, the attention of the mind to its own sensations. — *Cittāsanga* (°*ta-ās*°), *as*, m. attachment, affection, love. — *Cittaikya* (°*ta-aik*°), *am*, n. unanimity, harmony, agreement. — *Cittonnati* (°*ta-un*°), *is*, f. pride of heart, arrogance.

1. *ćitti*, *is*, f. thinking, thought, reflection; understanding, wisdom; thoughts, devotion (in pl.); intention; a wise person; thought personified as the wife of Atharvan and mother of Dadhyać; [cf. *a-ćitti*, *pūrva-ćitti*, *prāyaś-ćitti*.]

Cittin, *ī*, *inī*, *i*, Ved. intelligent, wise.

Cittī-kṛi, cl. 8. P. A. *-karoti*, *-kurute*, *-kartum*, to make anything an object of thought or reflection.

Cittī-kṛita, *as*, *ā*, *am*, fixed in the mind.

Citra, *as*, *ā*, *am*, perceptible, visible, conspicuous, excellent, distinguished; bright, clear, bright-coloured; variegated, spotted, speckled; rough, agitated (as the sea, opposed to *sama*); clear, loud, perceptible (as a sound); various, different, manifold; strange, wonderful, surprising, (*kim atra ćitram*, what is there surprising in that? there is nothing strange in that); containing the word *ćitra*; (*as*), m. variety of colour; N. of several plants, viz. Plumbago Zeylanica, Ricinus Communis, Jonesia Aśoka; a form of Yama; N. of a king; of a descendant of Gaṅga and of Gauśra; of a son of Dhṛita-rāshṭra; of a king of Draviḍa; (*ā*), f. Spica Virginis, a star in the virgin's spike, a constellation; (according to the more ancient reckoning the twelfth, according to the new the fourteenth lunar mansion); a kind of snake; N. of several plants, viz. Anthericum Tuberosum or Salvinia Cucculata, Cucumis Maderaspatanus, a kind of cucumber; also = *dantī*; Ricinus Communis; the Myrobalan tree; also = *mṛigervāru* and *gaṇḍa-dūrvā*; Rubia Munjista; N. of a metre, a kind of Mātrāsamaka, containing 4 × 16 syllabic instants; another metre consisting of four lines of fifteen syllables each; another metre consisting of four lines of sixteen syllables each; worldly illusion, unreality; N. of an Apsaras; also of a sister of Kṛishṇa and wife of Arjuna, = *su-bhadrā*; also of a daughter of Gada, or (according to a various reading) of Kṛishṇa; also of a river; (*am*), n. anything bright or coloured which strikes the eyes; a brilliant ornament, an ornament; a bright or extraordinary appearance, a wonder; the ether, sky, heaven; a spot; a circular ornament, a sectarial mark on the forehead; white or spotted leprosy; a picture, painting, sketch, delineation; variety of colour; various modes of writing or arranging verses in the shape of mathematical or other fanciful figures, (this is done either by leaving out syllables which occur repeatedly, or by representing words in a shortened form); playing upon words, punning in the form of question and answer, facetious conversation, conundrums, riddles, &c.; [cf. *a-ćitra, dānu-ć°, vi-ć°, ćaitra;* cf. also Lith. *kytras.*] —*Ćitra-kaṇṭha, as,* m. 'having a speckled throat,' a pigeon. —*Ćitra-kathālāpa-sukha* (°*thā-āl*°), *as, ā, am,* happy in telling charming stories. —*Ćitra-kambala, as,* m. a variegated carpet; a painted cloth used as an elephant's housing. —*Ćitra-kara, as,* m. a painter; [cf. *ćitra-kāra* and *ćitra-kṛit.*] —*Ćitra-karṇa, as,* m. 'strange-ear,' N. of a camel. —*Ćitra-karman, a,* n. any extraordinary act, a wonderful deed; magic; ornamenting, decorating; painting, a painting, picture; (*ā*), m. working wonders, a magician; a painter; the tree Dalbergia Ougeinensis; [cf. *ćitra-kṛit.*] —*Ćitrakarma-vid, t,* m. skilled in the art of painting; a painter, a magician. —*Ćitra-kāya, as,* m. 'having a striped or speckled body,' a tiger, a leopard, panther. —*Ćitra-kāra, as,* m. a painter; [cf. *ćitra-kara.*] —*Ćitra-kuṇḍala, as,* m., N. of a son of Dhṛita-rāshṭra. —*Ćitra-kūṭa, as,* m. 'wonderful peak,' N. of a hill and district, the modern Chitrakote or Chatarcot (near Kampta), situated on the river Paisuni (Piśunī) about fifty miles S. E. of the town of Bandah in Bundelkhund, lat. 25. 12, long. 80. 47. It was the first habitation of Rāma and Lakshmaṇa in their exile after leaving Ayodhyā, and as the holiest spot of the worshippers of Rāma is crowded with temples and shrines; N. of a town. —*Ćitra-kṛit, t, t, t,* astonishing, surprising; (*t*), m. a painter; the tree Dalbergia Ougeinensis; [cf. *ćitra-karman.*] —*Ćitra-ketu, us,* m., N. of a son of Garuḍa; also of Vasishṭha; also of Lakshmaṇa; also of Devabhāga; also of a king of the Sūra-senas. —*Ćitra-kola, as,* m. a kind of lizard. —*Ćitra-kriyā,* f. painting. —*Ćitra-kshatra, as, ā, am,* Ved. one whose dominion is brilliant (as Agni); (Sāy.) having various power or one whose wealth is visible. —*Ćitra-ga, as, ā, am,* represented in a picture, painted. —*Ćitra-gata, as, ā, am,* coloured, variegated; represented in a picture, painted, delineated. —*Ćitra-gandha, am,* n. yellow orpiment. —*Ćitra-gupta, as,* m., N. of one of the beings recording the vices and virtues of mankind in Yama's world; N. of a mixed caste, a secretary or writer of a man of rank; a form of Yama; N. of the sixteenth Arhat of the future Utsarpiṇī. —*Ćitra-gṛiha, as,* m. a painted room, or one ornamented with pictures; [cf. *ćitra-śālā.*] —*Ćitra-go, aus, aus, u,* having a brindled cow. —*Ćitra-grīva, as,* m. 'speckled-neck,' N. of a pigeon-king. —*Ćitra-ćāpa, as,* m., N. of a son of Dhṛita-rāshṭra. —*Ćitra-jalpa, as,* m. talking on various things, talking incoherently. —*Ćitra-taṇḍula, am, ā,* n. f. a medicinal plant said to possess anthelmintic virtues; [cf. *viḍ-aṅga.*] —*Ćitra-tala, as, ā, am,* painted or variegated on the surface. —*Ćitra-tvać, k,* m. 'having curious bark,' the birch or bhūrja tree. —*Ćitra-daṇḍaka, as,* m. the cotton plant, Arum Campanulatum; [cf. *ola.*] —*Ćitra-darśana, as,* m., N. of a Brāhman changed into a bird ('having variegated eyes'). —*Ćitra-dīpa, as,* m. title of a philosophical work. —*Ćitra-dṛiśīka, as, ā, am,* Ved. looking brilliant or shining. —*Ćitra-deva, as,* m., N. of one of the attendants of Skanda; (*ī*), f., N. of a plant, = *mahendra-vāruṇī.* —*Ćitra-dharman, ā,* m., N. of a prince identified with the Asura Virūpāksha. —*Ćitra-dhā,* ind. in a manifold way. —*Ćitra-dhrajati, is, is, i,* Ved. making a bright line, an epithet of Agni; (Sāy.) having a wonderful course. —*Ćitra-dhvaja, as,* m., N. of a man. —*Ćitra-netrā,* f. a small bird called Maina, = *sārikā;* [cf. *ćitra-locanā* and *ćitrākshī.*] —*Ćitra-nyasta, as, ā, am,* represented in a picture, painted. —*Ćitra-paksha, as, ā, am,* having variegated wings; (*as*), m. the francoline partridge; N. of a demon causing head-ache. —*Ćitra-paṭa* or *ćitra-paṭṭa, as* or *am,* m. or n. (?), a painting, a picture. —*Ćitra-paṭṭa-gata, as, ā, am,* 'committed to a picture,' painted. —*Ćitra-pattrikā,* f., N. of a plant, = *kapittha-parṇī* and *droṇa-pushpī.* —*Ćitra-pattrī,* f., N. of an aquatic plant; [cf. *jala-pippalī.*] —*Ćitra-pada, as, ā, am,* divided into various parts; full of graceful words or expressions; (*ā*), f., N. of the plant Cissus Pedata [cf. *godhāpadī*]; N. of a metre consisting of four lines of eight syllables each; (*am*), n., N. of a metre consisting of four lines of twenty-three syllables each. —*Ćitrapada-kramam,* ind. at a good or brisk pace. —*Ćitra-parṇikā,* f., N. of a plant, commonly Ćākulīya, Hemionites Cordifolia; Bengal madder, Rubia Munjista, = *ati-guhā, ghṛishṭhilā, tri-parṇī, dīrgha-pattrā,* &c. —*Ćitra-parṇī,* f., N. of several plants, = *pṛiśni-parṇī, karṇa-sphoṭā, jala-pippalī, droṇa-pushpī;* also = Rubia Munjista. —*Ćitra-pāṭala, as* or *am,* m. or n. (?), N. of a plant. —*Ćitra-pādā,* f. a small bird commonly called Maina; [cf. *sārikā.*] —*Ćitra-piććhaka, as,* m. 'having a variegated tail,' a peacock. —*Ćitra-puṅkha, as,* m. 'having variegated feathers,' an arrow. —*Ćitra-pura, am,* n., N. of a town. —*Ćitra-pushpī,* f., N. of a shrub, = *ambashṭhā.* —*Ćitra-pṛishṭha, as,* m. 'speckled-back,' a sparrow. —*Ćitra-pratikṛiti, is,* f. a representation in colours, a painting, a picture. —*Ćitra-priya-katha, as, ā, am,* speaking very kindly. —*Ćitra-phala, as,* m. a kind of fish, commonly Chitala, Mystus Chitala; a kind of cucumber, Cucumis Sativus; (*ā*), f. a kind of fish, commonly Phalaī, = *phalakin, mahonmada, rāja-grīva,* Mystus Karpirat; N. of several plants, = *ćirbhiṭā, mṛigervāru, mahendra-vāruṇī, vārtākī, kaṇṭakārī;* (*ī*), f. the above fish. —*Ćitra-phalaka, am,* n. a tablet for painting, a picture, a painting; (*as*), m. a kind of fish; see above. —*Ćitra-barha, as,* m. 'having a variegated tail,' a peacock; N. of a son of Garuḍa. —*Ćitra-barhin, ī, iṇī, i,* having a variegated tail. —*Ćitra-barhis, is, is, is,* Ved. having a brilliant or shining litter (i. e. bed of stars), an epithet of Pūshan and the moon; (Sāy.) strewed with various grasses (as the ground). —*Ćitra-bāhu, us,* m., N. of a son of Dhṛita-rāshṭra. —*Ćitra-bhānu, us, us, u,* of variegated lustre, shining with light; epithet of Agni, Savitṛi, the Aśvins, &c.; (*us*), m. a N. of fire; of Śiva; the plant Plumbago Zeylanica; the sun; N. of the Calotropis Gigantea (= *arka*); the first year of the first cycle of Jupiter; an epithet of Bhairava, a form of Śiva; N. of the father of Vāṇa-bhaṭṭa, the author of the Kādambarī. —*Ćitra-bhūta, as, ā, am,* made into a picture, painted. —*Ćitra-bheshajā,* f. the tree Ficus Oppositifolia; [cf. *kākoḍumbara.*] —*Ćitra-maṇḍala, as,* m. a kind of snake. —*Ćitra-mahas, ās, ās, as,* Ved. having extraordinary abundance; (Sāy.) having conspicuous brightness or splendor. —*Ćitra-mṛiga, as,* m. the spotted antelope. —*Ćitra-mekhala, as,* m. 'girdled with spots,' a peacock. —*Ćitra-yajña, as,* m. title of a comedy by Vaidyanātha. —*Ćitra-yāna, as,* m., N. of a prince. —*Ćitra-yāma, as, ā, am,* Ved. having a splendid or brilliant course (as Agni). —*Ćitra-yodhin, ī, inī, i,* fighting in a wonderful manner or in various ways; (*ī*), m. an epithet of Arjuna; the tree Terminalia Arjuna. —*Ćitra-ratha, as, ā, am,* having a bright or splendid chariot (as Agni); (*as*), m. 'having a variegated car,' the sun; the king of the Gandharvas; N. of a snake-demon; of a Vidyā-dhara; of a son of Gada or (according to a various reading) of Kṛishṇa; of a king; of a king of the Aṅgas; of a descendant of Aṅga and son of Dharma-ratha; of a son of Ushadgu; of Vṛishṇi; of Gaya; of Su-pārśvaka; of Ukta; of a prince of Mṛittikāvatī; of a Sūta; and of others; (*ā*), f., N. of a river; [cf. *ćaitraratha.*] —*Ćitra-raśmi, is,* m., N. of a Marut ('having variegated rays'). —*Ćitra-rāti, is, is, i,* Ved. granting wonderful or excellent gifts, epithet of the Aśvins. —*Ćitra-rādhas, ās, ās, as,* Ved. bestowing excellent favour; (Sāy.) having wonderful wealth. —*Ćitra-repha, as,* m., N. of a son of Medhātithi, king of Śāka-dvīpa. —*Ćitra-latā,* f. the plant Rubia Munjista; [cf. *ćitra-parṇī.*] —*Ćitra-likhana, am,* n. 'variegated drawing,' painting. —*Ćitra-likhita, as, ā, am,* represented, delineated (as in a picture), painted; motionless, dumb (as a picture or statue). —*Ćitra-lekhaka, as,* m. a painter. —*Ćitra-lekhanikā,* f. a painter's brush. —*Ćitra-lekhā,* f. a picture, a portrait; N. of a metre of four lines of seventeen syllables each; another metre of the same sort; N. of a metre of four lines of eighteen syllables each; N. of an Apsaras born from Brahmā's hand, (she was a friend of Ūshā and skilful in painting); N. of a daughter of Kumbhāṇḍa, minister of king Vāṇa, also a friend of Ūshā. —*Ćitralekhā-dvitīyā,* f. having Ćitralekhā as a second, accompanied by Ćitralekhā. —*Ćitra-locanā,* f. 'having variegated eyes,' a small bird, commonly called Maina, = *sārikā;* [cf. *ćitra-netrā* and *ćitrākshī.*] —*Ćitra-vat, ān, atī, at,* decorated with paintings or ornaments; containing the word *ćitra;* (*tī*), f., N. of a metre of four lines of thirteen syllables each; N. of a daughter of Gada or (according to others) of Kṛishṇa. —*Ćitra-vadāla, as,* m. the sheat-fish, Silurus Pelorius, = *pāṭhīna.* —*Ćitra-vana, am,* n. 'wonderful wood,' N. of a wood near the Gaṇḍakī; [cf. *ćitraka.*] —*Ćitra-varman, ā,* m. 'having variegated arrows,' N. of a son of Dhṛita-rāshṭra; also of a king of the Kulūtas; N. of a king of Mathura and Ćampāvatī. —*Ćitra-varshin, ī, iṇī, i,* raining in an unusual manner. —*Ćitra-vallika, as,* m. a kind of sheat-fish, Silurus Boalis; [cf. *ćitra-vadāla.*] —*Ćitra-vallī,* f., N. of two plants, = *mṛigervāru* and *mahendra-vāruṇī.* —*Ćitra-vahā,* f., N. of a river. —*Ćitra-vāja, as, ā, am,* decorated with variegated feathers; possessed of excellent power; (Sāy.) making wonderful progress or having wonderful riches or strength; (*as*), m. a cock. —*Ćitra-vāṇa, as,* m., N. of a son of Dhṛita-rāshṭra. —*Ćitra-vāhana, as,* m., N. of a king of Maṇi-pūra. —*Ćitra-vićitra, as, ā, am,* variously coloured, variegated, multiform. —*Ćitra-vidyā,* f. the art of painting. —*Ćitra-vīrya, as,* m. a kind of Ricinus, = *raktairaṇḍa.* —*Ćitra-vṛitti, is,* f. any astonishing act or practice. —*Ćitra-vegika, as,* m. 'having wonderful velocity,' N. of a Nāga. —*Ćitra-veśa, as,* m. 'having a variegated dress,' an epithet of Śiva. —*Ćitra-śālā,* f. a painted room, or one decorated with pictures [cf. *ćitra-gṛiha*]; N. of a metre consisting of four lines of eighteen syllables each. —*Ćitraśikhaṇḍi-ja* or *ćitraśikhaṇḍi-prasūta, as,* m. epithet of Bṛihaspati or the planet Jupiter (regarded as the son of the Ćitraśikhaṇḍinas, but more properly of Aṅgiras). —*Ćitra-śikhaṇḍin, inas,* m. pl. 'having bright crests,' an epithet of the seven Ṛishis, Marīći, Atri, Aṅgiras, Pulastya, Pulaha, Kratu, and Vasishṭha, as represented in the seven principal stars of the Great Bear. —*Ćitra-śiras, ās,* m. 'having a variegated head,' a kind of venomous insect [cf. *ćitra-śīrshaka*]; N. of a Gandharva. —*Ćitra-śīrshaka, as,* m. a kind of venomous insect. —*Ćitra-śoćis, is, is, is,* Ved. shining brilliantly; epithet of Agni. —*Ćitra-śravas, ās, ās, as,* Ved. uttering loud cries, songs, &c.; worthy of loud praise; (Sāy.) having wonderful fame. —*Ćitra-śrī, is,* f. great beauty, the beauty of variegated colours. —*Ćitra-saṃstha, as, ā, am,* represented in a picture, delineated, painted; [cf. *ćitra-gata, ćitra-stha,* &c.] —*Ćitra-saṅga, as* or *am,* m. or n. (?), N. of a metre of four lines of sixteen syllables each. —*Ćitra-sarpa, as,* m. a kind of snake, the large speckled snake (Mālu-dhāna). —*Ćitra-sena, as, ā, am,* Ved. furnished with a brilliant spear; (Sāy.) having a bright weapon; (*as*), m., N. of a snake-demon; also of a leader of the Gandharvas who was a son of Viśvā-vasu; one of the judges or recorders of hell; N. of a son of Dhṛita-rāshṭra; of a son of Parīkshit; of a son of Sambara; of a son of Narishyanta; of a son of the thirteenth Manu; of a son of Gada; N. of an adversary of Kṛishṇa; of Jarā-sandha's general who is also called Ḍimbhaka; (*ā*), f., N. of an Apsaras; also of one of the Mātṛis attending on Skanda; N. of a river. —*Ćitrasena-bhaṭṭa, as,* m., N. of the author of a commentary entitled Piṅgala-ćhando-grantha-ṭīkā. —*Ćitra-stha, as, ā, am,* represented in a picture, painted; [cf. *ćitra-gata* and *ćitra-saṃstha.*] —*Ćitra-hasta, am,* n. a particular position of the hands in fighting. —*Ćitrākṛiti* (°*ra-āk*°), *is,* f a painted resemblance, portrait, picture. —*Ćitrāksha* (°*ra-ak*°), *as,* m. 'having variegated eyes,' N. of a son of Dhṛita-rāshṭra; also of a descendant of Parikshit; also of a Nāga-rāja; (ī), f. a kind of bird, commonly called Maina; [cf. *sārikā, ćitra-netrā, ćitra-locanā.*] — *Ćitrā-kshupa, as,* m., N. of a plant, = *droṇa-pushpī.* — *Ćitrāṅga* (°*ra-an*°), *as, ā, am,* having a variegated or spotted body, striped, painted; (*as*), m. a kind of snake; the plant Plumbago Zeylanica; another plant, = *rakta-ćitraka;* N. of a son of Dhṛita-rāshṭra; an epithet of Arjuna; N. given to various animals in fables; (*ī*), f. a kind of worm or ear-wig, Julus Cornifex; the plant Rubia Munjista; (*am*), n. vermilion; yellow orpiment. — *Ćitrāṅgada* (°*ra-an*°), *as, ā, am,* decorated with brilliant or variegated bracelets; (*as*), m., N. of a son of S'antanu; of a king of the Daśārṇas; of a Vidyā-dhara; of a Gandharva or chief of the Gandharvas; a judge and recorder of the deeds of men in Yama's kingdom or the lower regions; a secretary of a person of rank (?); (*ā*), f., N. of an Apsaras; a daughter of king Ćitravāhana, wife of Arjuna and mother of Babhru-vāhana. — *Ćitrāṅgada-sū, ūs,* f. the mother of Ćitrāṅgada, an epithet of Satyavatī, the mother of Vyāsa. — *Ćitrāṭīra, as,* m. (fr. *ćitrā* + ?), the moon; the forehead spotted with the blood of a goat slain in honour of the demon Ghaṇṭā-karṇa. — *Ćitrānna* (°*ra-an*°), *am,* n. variegated rice, rice dressed with coloured condiments. — *Ćitrāpūpa* (°*ra-ap*°), *as,* m. a kind of cake (lit. speckled cake, plum cake ?). — *Ćitrāmagha, as, ā, am,* Ved. bestowing brilliant gifts, an epithet of Ushas; (Sāy.) having wonderful wealth. — *Ćitrāyasa* (°*ra-ay*°), *am,* n. steel. — *Ćitrāyudha* (°*ra-āy*°), *as,* m., N. of a son of Dhṛita-rāshṭra. — *Ćitrāyus* (°*ra-āy*°), *us, us, us,* Ved. possessed of excellent vital power; (Sāy.) making wonderful progress or having excellent food. — *Ćitrārambha* (°*ra-ār*°), *as,* m. the outline of a picture, a sketch, drawing; (*as, ā, am*), represented in a picture. — *Ćitrārpita* (°*ra-ar*°), *as, ā, am,* committed to a picture, painted. — *Ćitrā-vasu, us, us, u,* Ved. rich in brilliant ornaments; decorated with shining stars, an epithet of the night. — *Ćitrāśva* (°*ra-as*°), *as,* m. 'having painted horses,' epithet of Satyavat as fond of painting horses. — *Ćitreśa* (°*rā-īśa*), *as,* m. lord of Ćitrā, i. e. the moon. — *Ćitrokti* (°*ra-uk*°), *is,* f. a marvellous voice or speech, a voice from heaven, the voice of an invisible speaker; a surprising tale; agreeable or eloquent discourse. — *Ćitroti* (°*ra-ūti*), *is, is, i,* Ved. one who gives excellent proofs of his love, one who bestows pleasure or happiness; (Sāy.) granting wonderful assistance. — *Ćitropalā* (°*ra-up*°), f., N. of a river. — *Ćitraudana* (°*ra-od*°), *am,* n. boiled rice coloured with turmeric &c.

Ćitraka, as, m. a painter; a tiger, a panther, the Chita or small hunting leopard; a kind of snake; the plant Plumbago Zeylanica; also Ricinus Communis or the castor-oil plant; N. of a son of Vṛishṇi or of Pṛiśni; N. of a son of Dhṛita-rāshṭra; also of a Nāga; (*ās*), m. pl., N. of a people; (*am*), n. a sectarial mark on the forehead; a particular manner of fighting; the fruit of the plant Plumbago Zeylanica; N. of a wood near the mountain Raivataka; [cf. *ćitra-vana.*]

Ćitraya, nom. P. *ćitrayati,* to make variegated, paint with various colours, decorate; to regard as a wonder.

Ćitrala, as, ā, am, variegated, spotted; (*as*), m. a variegated colour; (*ā*), f., N. of a plant, = *go-rakshī.*

Ćitrika, as, m. = *ćaitrika,* the month Ćaitra or Cheyt (March–April).

Ćitrita, as, ā, am, variegated, spotted, striped; painted.

Ćitrin, ī, iṇī, i, containing wonders, wonderful; variegated; having variegated (black and grey) hair; (*iṇyas*), f. pl. wonderful deeds; (*iṇī*), f., N. for a woman endowed with various talents and excellencies, one of the four divisions into which women are classed by erotic writers.

Ćitriya, as, ā, am, Ved. variegated (?), epithet of a species of Aśvattha; (*as*), m., N. of a man.

Ćitrī-karaṇa, am, n. and *ćitrī-kāra, as,* m. wondering, wonder, surprise.

Ćitrī-kṛi, cl. 8. P. A. *-karoti, -kurute, -kartum,* to feel wonder; to make a picture, change into a picture, paint, variegate, embellish.

Ćitrī-kṛita, as, ā, am, painted, variegated, embellished.

Ćitrīya, nom. A. *ćitrīyate, -yitum,* to wonder, be surprised; to become a wonder to any one (with gen.); to cause surprise.

Ćitrīyamāṇa, as, ā, am, becoming a wonder, causing wonder or astonishment.

Ćitrya, as, ā, am, Ved. brilliant; (Sāy.) to be honoured, to be thought highly of.

Ćekita, as, m., N. of a prince.

Ćekitāna, as, m. 'the intelligent one,' an epithet of S'iva; N. of a prince and ally of the Pāṇḍus.

Ćetaka, as, ī, am, causing to think, reminding; what thinks or feels, sentient; (*ī*), f. the yellow myrobalan, = *harītakī,* Terminalia Chebula; or = *jātī-phala,* Jasminum Grandiflorum.

Ćetana, as, ī, am, visible, conspicuous, distinguished, excellent; percipient, observing, conscious, sentient, intelligent; alive, living, feeling; (*as*), m. a living and sentient being, a man; self, soul, mind; (*ā*), f. consciousness, understanding, sense, intelligence, wisdom, reflection; (*am*), n. appearance; the thinking principle, the mind; [cf. *a-ćetana, niś-ć*°, *vi-ć*°, *sa-ć*°, *ćaitanya.*] — *Ćetana-tā,* f. or *ćetana-tva, am,* n. consciousness, the state or condition of an observing and conscious being. — *Ćetanāćetana* (°*na-ać*°), *as, ā, am,* animate and inanimate. — *Ćetanā-vat, ān, atī, at,* having consciousness, knowing, understanding, reasonable.

Ćetanakī, f. = *ćetakī.*

Ćetanīyā, f. a kind of medicinal herb, = *ṛiddhi.*

Ćetaya, as, ā, am, observing, conscious, sentient, living.

Ćetayamāna, as, ā, am, sentient, reflecting, conscious.

Ćetayāna, as, ā, am, understanding, having sense, sensible, conscious, sentient.

Ćetayitavya, as, ā, am, to be observed or thought.

Ćetayitṛi, tā, trī, tṛi, observing, perceiving, sentient.

Ćetas, as, n. bright appearance, Ved. (Sāy. a reverent mind); consciousness, intelligence, the sentient or thinking soul, heart, mind, intellect, the faculty of reasoning or understanding; will; [cf. *a-ćetas, dabhra-ć*°, *dhīra-ć*°, *nānā-ć*°, *laghu-ć*°, *vi-ć*°, *sa-ć*°, *su-ć*°.] — *Ćeto-bhava, as,* m. or *ćeto-bhū, ūs,* m. love, the deity of love. — *Ćeto-mat, ān, atī, at,* endowed with consciousness, living. — *Ćeto-vikāra, as,* m. disturbance of mind, emotion. — *Ćeto-vikārin, ī, iṇī, i,* disturbed in mind, moved.

Ćetasa at the end of an adv. comp. = *ćetas.*

Ćettṛi, tā, m., Ved. an observer, a guardian.

Ćetya, as, ā, am, Ved. observable, perceivable.

Ćaitanya, &c. See s. v.

चित् 6. *ćit,* an interjection. — *Ćit-kāra, as,* m. or *ćitkāra-śabda, as,* m. a cry, scream, bray. — *Ćitkāra-vat, ān, atī, at,* accompanied by cries or noise.

चित् 7. *ćit,* ind. a particle, = *ćid* below.

चित *ćita.* See p. 322, col. 2.

चित्कन्तकन्थ *ćitkana-kantha, am,* n., N. of a town; [cf. *ćikkaṇa-kantha.*]

चित्त *ćitta.* See p. 323, col. 2.

चित्ति 2. *ćitti, is,* f., Ved. (according to some commentaries) crackling, whizzing; (according to others) a sacrificial act; [cf. *ćit-kāra.*]

चित्य *ćitya.* See p. 322, col. 2.

चित्र *ćitra.* See p. 323, col. 3.

चिद् *ćid,* ind. [cf. 2. *ća* and *id*], an enclitic particle, requiring in the Veda a preceding simple verb to retain its accent. In the Pada-pāṭha *ćid* is considered as an independent word (*kaś ćid* &c. being always separated into two words). In later Sanskṛit it is generally a particle affixed to interrogative pronouns to render them indefinite. The use of *ćid* in Vedic Sanskṛit is principally to lay stress or emphasis on a preceding word or to extend or limit the sense. Hence it is often translateable by 'even,' 'indeed,' 'also,' 'at least,' 'just,' 'merely,' &c. (e. g. *devāś ćid,* the gods indeed; *ekasya ćid,* of one merely); or when preceded by a negative particle by 'not even' (e. g. *na devāś ćid,* not even the gods): but its force may often be expressed by merely laying an emphasis on the word by which it is preceded. Hence in Nirukta I. 4. it is said to be used *pūjāyām,* i. e. for enhancing the force of a word. It is also stated by Yāska to be a particle of comparison (*upamārthe*). The following Vedic uses of *ćid* may be noted; *yać ćid, yathā ćid,* = when indeed, as indeed; *ćid—ćid* or *ćid—ća* or *ćid—u,* = as well as—as; both—and.

Ćid is often joined to interrogative pronouns and adverbs (see 2. *ka, katama, katara, kad, kim, katham, kadā, kutas, kva,* &c.) to render them indefinite; especially in classical Sanskṛit, where the only other word after which it is found is *jātu,* q. v.

चिदम्बर *ćid-ambara.* See 5. *ćit,* p. 323.

चिन्त् *ćint,* cl. 10. P. *ćintayati, -yitum,* (according to some also cl. 1. P. *ćintati,* &c.), to think, have a thought or idea, reflect, consider; to think about, reflect upon, direct the thoughts towards any person or thing (with acc. or dat. or loc., or *prati* with acc., e. g. *anyonyaṃ ćintayatas,* they think of one another; *sutebhyas* or *suteshu* or *sutān prati ćintayan,* thinking about one's sons); to mind, take notice of, regard, turn the attention to; to find out, investigate; to take into consideration, treat of, speak of; to have an opinion about, consider as, esteem; [cf. Goth. *thagkja,* 'to think;' Lat. *censeo* ?].

Ćinta, as, m. (?) thought; [cf. *ćintā.*]

Ćintaka, as, ā, am, thinking of, reflecting on, considering, studying, conversant, familiar with; (used at the end of compounds, e. g. *daiva-ćintaka,* an astrologer; *vaṇśa-ćintaka,* a genealogist &c.)

Ćintana, am, n. thinking, thinking of, reflecting upon, anxious thought; (*pūrva-ćintana,* the former manner of thinking.)

Ćintanīya, as, ā, am, to be thought of or considered; to be meditated on; to be attended to; to be investigated or comprehended.

Ćintayat, an, antī, at, reflecting, considering, &c.

Ćintayāna, as, ā, am, reflecting, considering, meditating.

Ćintayitavya, as, ā, am, to be considered, to be reflected on.

Ćintayitvā, ind. having thought or considered; having mused or reflected.

Ćintā, f. thought, especially sad or sorrowful thought, care, anxiety; reflecting on, reflection, consideration, attention; recollection; N. of a woman. — *Ćintā-karman, a,* n. anxiety, troubled thoughts. — *Ćintā-kārin, ī, iṇī, i,* considering, regarding. — *Ćintākula* (°*tā-āk*°), *as, ā, am,* disturbed in thought, distracted by any idea. — *Ćintā-para, as, ā, am,* lost in thought, thoughtful, anxious. — *Ćintā-maṇi, is,* m. a fabulous gem, supposed to yield its possessor all desires; the philosopher's stone; a common title of various text-books, treatises, and commentaries (e. g. *abhidhāna-ćintāmaṇi, upamāna-ć*°, *kṛitya-ć*°, *janma-ć*°, *muhūrta-ć*°); N. of Brahmā; N. of a Buddha; of an author. — *Ćintāmaṇi-sāraṇikā* or *tithi-sāraṇikā,* f. title of a work on astrology by Daśabala. — *Ćintā-maya, as, ī, am,* consisting of thought or intelligence, produced by thoughts. — *Ćintā-vat, ān, atī, at,* thinking, thoughtful. — *Ćintā-veśman, a,* n. a council-house, council-room.

Ćintita, as, ā, am, thought, considered; reflecting, considering; (*ā*), f., N. of a woman; (*am*), n. thought, reflection, care, intention.

Ćintiti, is, f. or *ćintiyā,* f. thinking, consideration, reflection.

Ćintya, as, ā, am, to be considered or reflected; to be thought of or meditated upon; to be apprehended or conceived; to be deliberated about; uncertain, questionable; *(am),* n. the necessity of thinking about anything. — *Ćintya-dyota, ās,* m. pl. a class of deities (whose brightness is only to be apprehended by the imagination).

चिन्ति *ćinti, is,* m., N. of a man (?).

चिन्तिडी *ćintiḍī,* f. the tamarind tree; (a wrong form for *tintiḍī.*)

चिन्तोक्ति *ćintokti, is,* f. midnight cry or alarm; (a wrong form for *ćitrokti.*)

चिन्न *ćinna, as,* m. a kind of grain, Panicum Miliaceum; [cf. *ćina.*]

चिन्मय *ćinmaya.* See 5. *ćit,* p. 323.

चिन्वत् *ćinvat.* See p. 322, col. 2.

चिपट *ćipaṭa, as, ā, am,* flat-nosed; *(as),* m. rice or grain flattened; [cf. *ćipiṭa* and *ćipuṭa.*]

Ćipiṭa, as, ā, am, blunted, flattened, pressed flat, flat, flat-nosed; *(as),* m. a kind of poisonous insect; rice or grain flattened; *(ā),* f. a kind of grass; [cf. *gunḍāsinī.*] — *Ćipiṭa-grīva, as, ā, am,* short-necked. — *Ćipiṭa-nāsa* or *ćipiṭa-nāsika, as, ā, am,* flat-nosed; *(ās),* m. pl., N. of a people in the north of Madhya-deśa.

Ćipiṭaka, as, m. flattened rice.

Ćipiṭikā-vat, ān, atī, at, having the appearance of flattened grains of rice (?).

Ćipuṭa, as, m. flattened rice.

चिप्प *ćippa, am,* n. a kind of disease of the finger-nail; [cf. *ćipya.*]

चिप्पटजयापीड *ćippaṭa-jayāpīḍa, as,* m., N. of a king of Kaśmīra, (*ćippaṭa = ćipiṭa?*).

चिप्पिका *ćippikā,* f. a kind of bird (?); (a various reading for *ćhippikā.*)

चिप्य *ćipya, as,* m. a kind of worm [cf. *kipya*]; *(am),* n. a disease of the finger-nail, whitlow.

चिबुक *ćibuka.* See *ćivuka.*

चिमि *ćimi, is,* m. a parrot [cf. *ćiri*]; a kind of plant, from the fibres of which coarse cloth and ropes are made, = *paṭṭa-vṛiksha.*

Ćimika, as, m. a parrot.

चिर *ćira, as, ā, am* (fr. rt. 1. *ći,* or perhaps rather fr. rt. *ćar*), long, lasting a long time, existing from ancient times, old; *ćiram kālam,* during a long time; *ćirāt kālāt,* after a long time; *(am),* n. a long time, delay, putting off for too long a time (e. g. *gamana-ćiram,* delay in going; *kim ćireṇa,* wherefore delay? *kiyać-ćireṇa,* for how long a time? *a-ćirāt* or *a-ćiratas,* after no long time, soon, shortly; cf. *a-ćira*). Any of the oblique cases sing. of *ćira* may be used adverbially, e. g. *ćiram* or *ćireṇa* or *ćirāya* or *ćirāt* or *ćirasya* or *ćire,* = long, for a long time, after a long time, a long while ago, long since; at last, finally, too late. *Ćira* is also used adverbially at the beginning of comp. as in some of the following examples; [cf. Hib. *sir,* 'long.'] — *Ćira-kāra, as, ā, am,* or *ćira-kāri, is, is, i,* or *ćira-kārika, as, ā, am,* or *ćira-kārin, ī, iṇī, i,* working or acting slowly, dilatory, delaying. — *Ćira-kāri-tā,* f. or *ćirakāri-tva, am,* n. dilatoriness, slowness. — *Ćira-kāla, as,* m. a long period; *ćira-kālam* or *-lāya,* for a long time. — *Ćirakāla-pālita, as, ā, am,* protected for a long time. — *Ćirakālika* or *ćirakālina, as, ā, am,* of long standing, old, long-continued, chronic. — *Ćirakālopārjita* (°*la-up*°), *as, ā, am,* accumulated slowly or after a long time. — *Ćira-kīrtti, is,* m., N. of the founder of a religious sect. — *Ćira-kriya, as, ā, am,* dilatory, slow, tedious. — *Ćira-gata, as, ā, am,* long absent, long gone, gone a long while ago. — *Ćira-ćeshṭita, as, ā, am,* long sought for, of rare occurrence. — *Ćira-jāta, as, ā, am,* born long ago, old; (*tvattaś ćirajātaḥ* or *bhavataś ćirajātataraḥ,* older than thou.) — *Ćirajāmbā,* f., N. of the mother of Rudra-bhaṭṭa. — *Ćira-jīraka, as,* m., N. of a tree, = *jīraka.* — *Ćira-jīvin, ī, inī, i,* long-lived; an epithet of Mārkaṇḍeya, of Aśvatthāman, of Bali, Vyāsa, Hanumat, Vibhīshaṇa, Kṛipa, and Paraśu-rāma; (ī), m. a N. of Vishṇu; a crow; two plants, = *jīvaka* and *śālmali.* — *Ćirañ-jīva, as, ā, am,* long-lived; an epithet of Kāma-deva; *(as),* m. and *ćirañjīva-bhaṭṭāćārya, as,* m., N. of several authors. — *Ćirañ-jīvin, ī, inī, i,* long-lived; (ī), m. a N. of Vishṇu; a crow; two plants, = *jīvaka* and *śālmali.* — *Ćira-tā,* f. long duration. — *Ćira-divasam,* ind. for a long time. — *Ćira-nivishṭa, as, ā, am,* abiding long, anything which has rested for a long time. — *Ćira-pākin, ī, inī, i,* ripening late; (ī), m. the plant Feronia Elephantum; [cf. *kapittha.*] — *Ćira-pushpa, as, ā, am,* blossoming late; *(as),* m. the plant Mimusops Elengi; [cf. *vakula.*] — *Ćira-pravāsin, ī, inī, i,* dwelling long abroad, a long absentee. — *Ćira-mitra, am,* n. an old friend; a crony. — *Ćira-mehin, ī,* m. an ass. — *Ćira-moćana, am,* n., N. of a Tīrtha. — *Ćira-rātra, am,* n. a period of many nights, a long time, a long period; *ćira-rātram* or *-trāya,* &c., for a long time, after a long time, at last, finally, = *ćiram* above. — *Ćirarātroshita* (°*ra-ush*°), *as, ā, am,* having lodged for a long time. — *Ćira-roga, as,* m. a chronic disease. — *Ćira-labdha, as, ā, am,* obtained after a long time (as a son in old age). — *Ćira-loka-loka, as, ā, am,* whose world is a long-existing world; an epithet of the manes. — *Ćira-viproshita, as, ā, am,* long banished. — *Ćira-vilva, as,* m. the tree Pongamia Glabra; [cf. *karañja.*] — *Ćira-vṛitta, as, ā, am,* happened long since. — *Ćira-supta-buddhi, is, is, i,* one whose mind has been asleep a long time, long senseless or careless. — *Ćira-sūtā* or *ćira-sūtikā,* f. a cow that has borne many calves. — *Ćira-sevaka, as,* m. an old servant. — *Ćira-stha, as, ā, am,* or *ćira-sthāyin, ī, inī, i,* or *ćira-sthita, as, ā, am,* long continuing or enduring, lasting, of long continuance, left for a long time. — *Ćirasthāyi-tā,* f. long continuance, durability. — *Ćirād* (°*ra-ad*), *t, t, t,* eating for a long time; *(t),* m. an epithet of Garuḍa. — *Ćirāntaka* (°*ra-an*°), *as,* m., N. of a son of Garuḍa. — *Ćirāyusha* (°*ra-āy*°), *as, ā, am,* bestowing long life. — *Ćirāyus* (°*ra-āy*°), *us, us, us,* long-lived; *(us),* m. a deity, a divinity. — *Ćirārodha* (°*ra-ār*°), *as,* m. a long or protracted siege; blockade. — *Ćirāśrita* (°*ra-āś*°), *as, ā, am,* long maintained or protected; an old dependant. — *Ćirojjhita* (°*ra-uj*°), *as, ā, am,* long since abandoned or left. — *Ćirottha* (°*ra-ut*°), *as, ā, am,* existing a long time.

Ćiratna, as, ī, am, old, ancient, of long standing, long-lasting, long-enduring.

Ćirantana, as, ī, am, old, ancient, antiquated, of long standing.

Ćiraya, nom. P. A. *ćirayati, -te,* to act slowly, delay, to be absent a long while.

Ćirāya, nom. P. A. *ćirāyati, -te,* to delay, be slow, be absent for a long time.

चिरण्टी *ćiraṇṭī* or *ćiranṭhī,* f. a woman married or single who continues to reside after maturity in her father's house; a young woman; [cf. *ćaraṭī, ćaraṇṭī, ćiriṇṭī.*]

चिरतिक्त *ćiratikta, as,* m. a kind of gentian, Gentiana Cherayta, = *kirāta-tikta,* (in Beogālī *ćirātā.*)

चिरम्भण *ćirambhaṇa, as,* m. a kind of falcon or kite; [cf. *ćilla.*]

चिराटिका *ćirāṭikā,* f. (fr. *ćira?*), N. of a plant with white flowers, a kind of hogweed, Bœrhavia Erecta, = *ćaṭikā,* commonly *pāṭāḍī.*

चिरातिक्त *ćirātikta, as,* m. a sort of gentian, = *ćiratikta.*

चिरि 1. *ćiri, is,* m. (perhaps fr. the sound or imitative cry *ći*), a parrot; [cf. *kīra* and *ćimi.*] — *Ćiri-vilva, as,* m., N. of a tree, (perhaps = *ćira-vilva.*)

चिरि 2. *ćiri,* cl. 5. P. *ćiriṇoti,* &c., to hurt, injure, wound or kill; [cf. *jiri.*]

Ćirikā, f. a kind of weapon, = *ćilikā.*

चिरिण्टी *ćiriṇṭī,* f. = *ćiranṭī* above.

चिरु *ćiru, us,* m. the shoulder-joint.

चिर्भट *ćirbhaṭa, as* and *ī,* m. and f., Cucumis Utilissimus, = *karkaṭī;* also its fruit; [cf. *ćarbhaṭa.*]

Ćirbhiṭa, am, ā and *ikā,* n. f. a kind of gourd, different from the preceding; [cf. *indra-ćirbhiṭī, kshudra-ćirbhiṭā, kshetra-ć*°, *gaja-ć*°.]

चिल् *ćil,* cl. 6. P. *ćilati,* &c., to put on clothes; [cf. Hib. *ceilim,* 'I conceal, hide, cover;' *caille,* 'a veil, a cowl;' Lat. *celare;* Old Germ. *hilu, helm, heliu, heli;* Goth. *hulja;* Lat. *oc-culo.*]

चिलमीलिका *ćilamīlikā,* f. a kind of necklace; a luminous flying insect, a fire-fly; lightning.

चिलिका *ćilikā,* f. a kind of weapon, = *ćirikā.*

चिलिचिम *ćilićima, as,* m. a kind of sprat, Clupea Cultrata, commonly *vāliyā-gaḍaka* (*vāliyā,* Cyprinus Denticulatus, *gaḍaka,* a kind of golden trout); according to some authorities, a kind of prawn. Other forms of this word are *ćilićimi, ćillīcīma, ćilićimi, ćilimīnaka, ćilićima, ćillīćimi, ćilīma, ćelićima.*

चिलिमिनिका *ćiliminikā* and *ćilimīlikā,* a various reading for *ćilamīlikā,* q. v.

चिल्ल् *ćill,* cl. 1. P. *ćillati,* &c., to become loose; to be slack or flaccid; to play, sport, act wantonly; to indicate one's meaning (?).

Ćilla, as, ā, am, blear-eyed [cf. *ćulla* and *pilla*]; *(as),* m. a bleared or sore eye; the Bengal kite, Falco Cheela; (ī), f., cf. *ćilli;* [cf. *kuru-ćilla.*] — *Ćilla-bhakshyā,* f. a kind of vegetable perfume; see *haṭṭa-vilāsinī.* — *Ćillābha* (°*la-ābhā*), *as,* m. a petty thief, a shop-lifter, a pickpocket, &c.

Ćillaka, as or *ā,* m. or f. a particular animal; *(ā),* f. a cricket, = *ćīrikā* and *jhillikā.*

Ćilli, is, m. a species of bird of prey [cf. *ćilla*]; *(is),* f. a kind of plant [cf. *ćillī*]; (ī), f. a cricket [cf. *ćillakā*]; a kind of pot-herb.

Ćillikā, f. a kind of pot-herb.

चिवि *ćivi, is,* m. = *ćivuka,* the chin.

चिविट *ćiviṭa, as,* m. = *ćipiṭa,* flattened grain, rice, &c.

चिविल्लिका *ćivillikā,* f., N. of a small shrub, = *kshudra-gholī, madhu-māla-pattrikā, rakta-dalā.*

चिवुक *ćivuka* or *ćibuka, am,* n. the chin [cf. *ćubuka* and *ćhubuka*]; *(as),* m., N. of a tree, = *mućukunda;* *(ās),* m. pl., N. of a people.

चिश्चा *ćiśćā,* ind., Ved. an onomatopoetic word for a rattling sound.

चिहणकन्थ *ćihaṇa-kantha, am,* n., N. of a town.

चिहुर *ćihura, ās,* m. pl. = *ćikura,* the hair of the head.

चिह्न *ćihna, am,* n. a mark, spot, stain, stamp, sign, badge, symbol, symptom; a banner, a standard, insignia; a sign of the zodiac; aim, direction towards; [cf. *sa-ćihna.*] — *Ćihna-kārin, ī, iṇī, i,* making or leaving marks, marking, spotting; wounding, striking, killing; exciting fear, frightful, hideous. — *Ćihna-dhara, as,* m. bearing the signs or insignia (of office). — *Ćihna-dhāriṇī,* f. the plant Echites Frutescens, = *śyāmā-latā.* — *Ćihna-bhūta, as, ā, am,* become a mark, formed into a mark.

Cihnaya, nom. P. *ćihnayati*, *-yitum*, to mark, sign, stamp, spot.
Cihnita, *as*, *ā*, *am*, marked, signed, spotted, stained, stamped, designated; known.
Cihnī-kṛita, *as*, *ā*, *am*, marked, delineated.

चीक् *ćīk*, cl. 1. and 10. P. *ćīkati* and *ćīkayati*, to endure, suffer, to be patient; to be impatient; to touch.

चीचीकूची *ćīćīkūćī*, an onomatopoetic word for the chirping or warbling of birds.

चीडा *ćīḍā*, f. a kind of perfume.

चीणा *ćīṇa*, *ās*, m. pl. (for *ćīna*), N. of a country.

चीणक *ćīṇaka*, *as*, m. a kind of grain; [cf. *ćīna* and *ćīnaka*.]

चीति *ćīti*. See under 1. *ći*.

चीत्कार *ćīt-kāra*, *as*, m. crying, a cry, the braying of an ass, a noise.—*Cītkāra-vat*, *ān*, *atī*, *at*, accompanied with a noise or cry.

चीन *ćīna*, *ās*, m. pl., N. of a people, the inhabitants of China, the Chinese; (*as*), m. a kind of deer; Panicum Miliaceum; a sort of cloth; a thread; (*am*), n. a banner (perhaps made of deer skin), a standard; a kind of bandage for the corners of the eyes; lead.—*Cīna-karpūra*, *as*, m. a kind of camphor, also called *tushāra*, *dvīpa-karpūraja*.—*Cīna-ja*, *am*, n. steel.—*Cīna-nī*, *is*, m. a peach tree.—*Cīna-paṭṭa*, *am*, n. lead.—*Cīna-pati*, *is*, m., N. of a kingdom.—*Cīna-pishṭa*, *am*, n. minium or red lead; lead.—*Cīnapishṭa-maya*, *as*, *ī*, *am*, consisting of minium or representing it.—*Cīna-rāja-putra*, *as*, m. a pear tree.—*Cīna-vanga*, *am*, n. lead or more probably tutenag.—*Cīnānśuka* (°*na-an*°), *am*, n. China cloth, silk, a silken cloth.
Cīnaka, *as*, m. an inhabitant of China, Chinese; a kind of panic, Panicum Miliaceum; fennel, = *kangunī*; also = *ćīna-karpūra*.

चीनाककटी *ćīnākarkaṭī*, f. a kind of cucumber said to be found near Citra-kūṭa.

चीब् *ćīb* = *ćīv*, q. v.

चीभ् *ćībh* (a various reading for *bībh*), cl. 1. A. *ćībhate*, &c., to coax, commend, flatter; to boast, &c.

चीय् *ćīy* (another form for *ćīv*), cl. 1. P. A. *ćīyati*, *-te*, &c., to take, receive, wear.

चीर 1. *ćīra* = *ćira* in the adv. *a-ćīram*, quick, soon, shortly.

चीर 2. *ćīra*, *am*, n. (said to be fr. rt. 1. *ći*), a strip, a long narrow piece of bark or rind; a strip of cloth, clothes, a rag, tatter, old and torn cloth; the dress of a Buddhist priest; a kind of garland, a necklace of pearls consisting of four strings; a stripe, stroke, line; a manner of writing with strokes or lines; lead; a crest.—*Cīra-pattrikā*, f. a kind of vegetable, = *ćanću-śāka*.—*Cīra-parṇa*, *as*, m. the tree Shorea Robusta, = *śāla-vṛiksha*.—*Cīra-bhavantī*, f. the elder sister of a wife.—*Cīra-vāsas*, *ās*, *ās*, *as*, clothed in bark, dressed in rags or tatters; (*ās*), m. an epithet of Śiva; N. of a Yaksha; N. of a prince.
Cīraka, *as*, m. a manner of writing. See above.
Cīrita, *as*, *ā*, *am*, having strips or stripes, ragged, tattered.—*Cīrita-ććhadā*, f. a kind of vegetable; [cf. *pālankya*.]
Cīrin, *ī*, *iṇī*, *i*, clothed in bark, clothed in rags and tatters.

चीरल्लि *ćīralli*, *is*, m. or f. (?) a kind of large fish; (also read *ćīrilli* and *ćīrīlli*.)

चीरि *ćīri*, *is*, f. a veil or shade for covering the eyes.

चीरी *ćīrī* or *ćīrikā*, f. a cricket; the hem of an under garment.—*Cīrī-vāka*, *as*, m. a cricket.

चीरुक *ćīruka*, *am*, n. a kind of fruit, commonly *ćemura*; (*ā*), f. a cricket; [cf. *ćīrikā* and *ćīrī*.]

चीर्ण *ćīrṇa*, *as*, *ā*, *am* (rt. *ćar*), conversant, versed, learned; split, divided; (*am*), n. conduct.—*Cīrṇa-parṇa*, *as*, m., N. of two trees, = *nimba* and *kharjūra*.

चीलिका *ćīlikā*, f. a cricket; also *ćillakā*; [cf. *ćīrī*.]

चीव् *ćīv*, cl. 1. P. A. *ćīvati*, *-te*, &c., to take; to wear, cover; cl. 10. P. *ćīvayati*, *-yitum*, to shine; to speak; [cf. Hib. *cib*, 'the hand;' Cambro-Brit. *cipiaw*, 'to take;' Gr. σκεῦος.]

चीवर *ćīvara*, *am*, n. (said to be fr. 1. *ći*), the dress of a Buddhist mendicant or of any mendicant.—*Cīvara-gopaka*, *as*, m. a wardrobe-keeper, (a particular officer.)—*Cīvara-nivasana*, *ās*, m. pl., N. of a people.—*Cīvara-bhajaka*, *as*, m. a distributer of garments.
Cīvaraya, nom. A. *-yate*, *-yitum*, to collect rags, put on a tattered garment.
Cīvarin, *ī*, m. a Buddhist or Jaina mendicant.

चुकोपयिषु *ćukopayishu*, *us*, *us*, *u* (fr. Desid. of Caus. of rt. *kup*), wishing to make a person angry.

चुक्क् *ćukk*, cl. 10. P. *ćukkayati*, *-yitum*, to inflict or suffer pain.

चुक्कस *ćukkasa*, *as*, m. = *bukkasa*, a Cāṇḍāla.

चुक्कार *ćuk-kāra*, *as*, m. the roaring of a lion; (a various reading has *bukkāra*.)

चुक्र *ćukra*, *as*, *am*, m. n. (said to be fr. rt. *ćak*), vinegar made by the acetous fermentation of grain; acid seasoning; sourness; Indian sorrel, Rumex Vesicarius; (*ī*), f. = *ćāngerī*, Oxalis Pusilla; (*ā*), f. the tamarind tree.—*Cukra-phala*, *am*, n. the tamarind fruit.—*Cukra-vāstūka*, *am*, n. wood-sorrel.—*Cukra-vedhaka*, *am*, n. a kind of sour rice-gruel.—*Cukrāmla* (°*ra-am*°), *am*, n. vinegar made by the acetous fermentation of grain; (*ā*), f. a kind of wood-sorrel, = *amlaloṇikā*; a tamarind tree; a kind of sour rice-gruel.
Cukraka, *am*, n. a kind of wood-sorrel, Rumex Vesicarius, commonly *ćukāpālanga*; (*ikā*), f. wood-sorrel, = *kućāngerī*; a kind of sour rice-gruel; [cf. *amla-ćukrikā*.]
Cukriman, *ā*, m. sourness.

चुक्षा *ćukshā*, f. washing; [cf. *ćoksha* and *ćauksha*.]

चुक्षोभयिषु *ćukshobhayishu*, *us*, *us*, *u* (fr. Desid. of Caus. of rt. *kshubh*), intending or wishing to cause to shake.

चुचि *ćući*, *is*, m. the female breast, bosom.

चुचु *ćuću*, *us*, m. a kind of vegetable.
Cuććū, *ūs*, m. f. a kind of vegetable, = the preceding.

चुचुक *ćućuka*, *as*, *am*, m. n. the nipple of the breast, see *ćūćuka*; (*ās*), m. pl., N. of a people in Dakshiṇā-patha; [cf. *ćućupa*.]
Cućūka, *am*, n. a nipple; [cf. *ćūćuka*.]

चुचुप *ćućupa*, *ās*, m. pl., N. of a people; [cf. *ćućuka*.]

चुच्य् *ćućy*, cl. 1. P. *ćućyati*, &c., another form for *śućy*, q. v.

चुञ्चु *ćunću*, *us*, *us*, *u* (considered as an affix at the end of certain comp.), known, celebrated, renowned [cf. *akshara-ćunću*, *ćāra-ć*°, *ćanću*, *ćaṇa*]; (*us*), m. the musk-rat or shrew; a mixed caste, born of a Brāhman father by a Vaideha female, whose business is hunting; N. of a man.

चुञ्चुमायन *ćunćumāyana*, *am*, n. irritation or itching (of a wound).

चुञ्चुरी *ćunćurī*, f. a game, a kind of hazard played with tamarind seeds instead of dice; also *ćunćuli* and *ćunćulī*.

चुञ्चुल *ćunćula*, *as*, m., N. of a man; (*ās*), m. pl. his descendants.

चुट् *ćuṭ*, cl. 6. 10. P. *ćuṭati*, *ćoṭayati*, &c., to cut off, pierce, divide; cl. 1. and 10. P. *ćoṭati* and *ćoṭayati*, to wane, become small or low or shallow; [cf. *ćuṭṭ*, *ćuṇṭ*, *ćhuṭ*.]

चुट्ट् *ćuṭṭ*, cl. 10. P. *ćuṭṭayati*, &c., to become small or low or shallow as a river &c.; [cf. *puṭṭ*.]

चुड् *ćuḍ*, cl. 6. P. *ćuḍati*, &c., to conceal; [cf. *buḍ*.]

चुड्ड् *ćuḍḍ*, cl. 1. P. *ćuḍḍati*, &c., to dally, wanton, coquet, &c.; to hint one's meaning; to act (?); [cf. *ćull*.]

चुण् *ćuṇ*, cl. 6. P. *ćuṇati*, &c., to cut off, pierce, divide; [cf. Hib. *guinim*, 'I wound, prick, sting;' *guinneach*, 'sharp-pointed;' *gun-ta*, 'wounded.']

चुण्ट् *ćuṇṭ* [cf. rt. *ćuṭ* and *ćuṭṭ*], cl. 1. 10. P. *ćuṇṭati*, *ćuṇṭayati*, &c., to cut off, pierce, divide; cl. 1. P. *ćuṇṭati*, to become small.
Cuṇṭā and *ī*, f. a small well or reservoir near a well; [cf. *ćauṇṭya*, *ćūḍaka*, *ćūṭaka*.]

चुण्ठ् *ćuṇṭh*, cl. 10. P. *ćuṇṭhayati*, &c., to hurt, kill.

चुण्ड् *ćuṇḍ* [cf. rt. *ćuṭ* and *ćuṭṭ*], cl. 1. P. *ćuṇḍati*, &c., to become small; cl. 10. P. *ćuṇḍayati*, to cut off.
Cuṇḍhī, f. a small well. See *ćuṇṭā* above.

चुत् 1. *ćut*, a various reading for *ćyut*; [cf. *śćut*.]

चुत् 2. *ćut*, ind. an interjection.

चुत *ćuta*, *as*, m. and *ćuti*, *is*, f. the anus; [cf. *ćūta* and *ćyuti*.]

चुद् *ćud*, cl. 1. P. A., Ved. *ćodati*, *-te*, *aćodīt*, &c., to impel, incite, animate; to offer quickly (as the Soma); to hasten: Caus. P. (rarely A.) *ćodayati*, *-te*, *-yitum*, to urge on, drive, impel, incite, send, cause to move quickly, hasten, accelerate; to inspire, excite, animate; to direct (the eye) towards; to enjoin; to request, petition, ask, question, inquire after; to press or importune with a request; to help on, assist in the attainment of (with dat., e. g. *asmān śriye ćodaya*, help us on to fortune); to bring or offer quickly; to fix, settle, direct; to be quick; [cf. Gr. σπεύδω, σπουδάζω: Lat. *cudo*; *re-pudio*.]
Coda, *as*, m., Ved. an implement for driving horses, a goad or whip; (*as*, *ā*, *am*), animating, inspiring, promoting.—*Coda-pravṛiddha*, *as*, *ā*, *am*, Ved. exalted by the inspiring (draught of Soma), an epithet of Indra.
Codaka, *as*, *ā*, *am*, driving; (*as*), m. direction, invitation; (in grammar) = *pari-graha*, q. v.
Codana, *as*, *ā*, *am*, driving, impelling; (*am*), n. the act of driving, inviting, invitation, order, rule, precept; (*ā*), f. sending, commanding, directing; casting, throwing; enjoining, ordaining; a precept, sacred ordinance or commandment; (*ī*), f., N. of a plant, (a various reading for *rodanī*); [cf. *eka-ćodana*.]—*Codanā-guḍa*, *as*, m. a ball for playing with.
Codayat, *an*, *antī*, *at*, impelling, animating, inspiring.—*Codayan-mati* (°*yat-ma*°), *is*, *is*, *i*, Ved.

inspiring, promoting piety or devotion; (Sāy.) whose mind is inspiring.

Codayitṛi, tā, tṛī, tṛi, driving, impelling, animating, promoting.

Codas, as, n. = *ćodana.* See *a-ćodas.*

Codita, as, ā, am, impelled, urged; ordered, directed; thrown, cast; appointed; informed, apprised.

Coditṛi, tā, tṛī, tṛi, driving, impelling, animating, promoting.

Codishṭha, as, ā, am (superl. of preceding), Ved. impelling or animating much.

Codya, as, ā, am, to be driven or impelled; to be sent, thrown or directed; to be mentioned or communicated; (*am*), n. raising a question, objecting, asking a question; surprise, astonishment, wonder.

Codyamāna, as, ā, am, being urged or driven.

चुनन्द *ćunanda, as,* m., N. of a Bhikshu.

चुन्द् *ćund.* Cf. *bund.*

चुन्द *ćunda, as,* m., N. of a pupil of Śākyamuni; (*ī*), f. a procuress, a bawd.

चुप् 1. *ćup,* cl. 1. P. *ćopati, ćućopa, ćopishyati, ćopitum,* to move, stir; to move slowly, creep or steal along; [cf. Lith. *kopu;* Germ. *hüpfen;* Eng. *hop.*]

Copaka. Cf. *gale-ćopaka.*

Copana, as, ā, am, moving, stirring, moving slowly; (*am*), n. moving, moving slowly.

चुप् 2. *ćup* (a various reading for *ćhup*), cl. 6. P. *ćupati,* to touch.

चुप *ćupa, as,* m., N. of a man.

चुपुणीका *ćupuṇīkā,* f., Ved., N. of an *ishṭakā* or sacrificial brick.

चुबुक *ćubuka, am,* n. the chin; [cf. *ćibuka* and *ćhubuka.*]

चुब्र *ćubra, am,* n. (fr. 1. *ćumb?*), the face, the mouth.

चुमुरि *ćumuri, is,* m., Ved., N. of a hostile demon whom Indra, to favour Dabhīti, sent to sleep.

चुम्ब् 1. *ćumb,* cl. 1. P. *ćumbati, ćućumba, ćumbishyati, ćumbitum,* to kiss, touch with the mouth; touch softly or lightly, graze: Caus. P. *ćumbayati, -yitum,* to cause to kiss; [cf. Goth. *kukja;* Hib. *pogaim;* Lith. *bućioju;* Lett. *szkûpstit.*]

Cumba, as, ā, m. f. kissing, a kiss.

Cumbaka, as, ikā, am, a kisser, one who kisses much; a lecher; knavish, roguish, a rogue, a cheat; one who has read much, a superficial scholar who knows parts in a variety of books; (*as*), m. a loadstone; the upper part or middle of a balance.

Cumbat, an, antī, at, kissing.

Cumbana, am, n. kissing, a kiss. — *Cumbana-dāna, am,* n. giving a kiss, kissing.

Cumbita, as, ā, am, kissed, touched softly or lightly. — *Cumbita-vat, ān, atī, at,* one who has kissed; kissing.

Cumbin, ī, inī, i, kissing; touching closely or softly, grazing.

चुम्ब् 2. *ćumb,* cl. 10. P. *ćumbayati,* &c., to hurt, kill.

चुर् *ćur,* cl. 10. and (according to some) 1. P. *ćorayati, aćūćurat* &c., *ćorati* &c., to steal, rob; [cf. Gr. φωράω; Lat. *furari;* Hib. *coire,* 'trespass, offence,' &c.]

Curaṇa, am, n. stealing, thieving, robbing.

Curaṇya, nom. P. *ćuraṇyati,* to thieve, steal, rob.

Curā, f. stealing, theft; [cf. *ćaura.*]

Cora, as, m. a thief, a robber; N. of a plant, = *kṛishṇa-śaṭī;* a kind of perfume, = *ćoraka;* N. of a poet; (*ā*), f., N. of a plant, = *ćora-pushpī;* (*ī*), f. a female thief; [cf. *ćaura;* cf. also Gr. φώρ.] — *Cora-kaṇṭaka, as,* m. a kind of grass, the seeds of which stick in the clothes, commonly Chorkānta. — *Cora-pushpikā* or *ćora-pushpī,* f. the plant Chrysopogon Aciculatus. — *Cora-snāyu, us,* m. a plant, = *kāka-nāsā.*

Coraka, as, m. a thief; a kind of plant [cf. *pṛikkā* and *taskara*]; a kind of perfume.

Corikā, f. = *ćaurikā,* theft, robbery.

Corita, am, n. stealing, theft.

Corilaka, am, n. thieving, petty theft or larceny; anything stolen.

Caura, as, ī, m. f. a thief, a robber, a pilferer; a dishonest or unfair dealer, a usurper, any one who usurps a position or a title dishonestly; one who steals or captivates the heart; (at the end of a comp.) anything bad of its kind; N. of a plant, = *ćora-pushpikā,* used for the preparation of a perfume; a kind of perfume. — *Caura-karman, a,* n. theft, thievery. — *Caura-gata, as, ā, am,* stolen, robbed. — *Caura-tas,* ind. from robbers, from theft. — *Caura-dhvaja-baddhaka, as,* m. a term applied to a notorious thief. — *Caura-pańćāśikā,* f. 'the fifty stanzas of Caura,' title of an erotic poem by a poet named Sundara. — *Caura-pushpaushadhi* (°*pa-osh*°), *is,* f. = *ćora-pushpikā.* — *Caura-rūpa, as,* m. a clever thief. — *Caura-rūpin, ī, iṇī, i,* having the character of a thief. — *Caurasya-kula, am,* n. a gang of thieves. — *Caura-hṛita, as, ā, am,* taken by robbery, stolen. — *Caurāṇśā* (°*ra-aṇ*°), f., N. of a metre consisting of four lines of six syllables each. — *Caurāpahṛita* (°*ra-ap*°), *as, ā, am,* carried off, stolen.

Caurādika, as, ī, am (fr. *ćur-ādi*), belonging to the class of roots beginning with *ćur,* i. e. the tenth class.

Caurikā, f. (fr. *ćora* or *ćaura*), thievery, theft, robbing.

Caurikāka, as, m. 'a thief of a crow;' (perhaps a wrong form for *ćaura-kāka?* or *ćauri* may be = *ćauri* = *ćaurya?*).

Cauri, f. stealing, theft, = *ćaurya.*

Cauri-bhūta, as, ā, am, one who has become a thief or the prey of thieves.

Caurya, am, n. theft, robbery, thievery; trickery. — *Caurya-rata, am,* n. secret sexual enjoyment. — *Caurya-vṛitti, is,* f. the practice of theft or robbery. — *Cauryārjita* (°*ya-ar*°), *as, ā, am,* acquired by plunder or robbery.

Cauryaka, am, n. theft, stealing.

चुरी *ćurī,* f. a small well.

चुल् *ćul,* cl. 10. P. *ćolayati, -yitum,* to raise, elevate; to rise, increase; to dip, dive into; [cf. *bul.*]

चुलका *ćulakā,* f., N. of a river; (also read *ćulukā.*)

चुलुक *ćuluka, as,* m. deep mud or mire; a mouthful of water, the hand hollowed to hold water; a small vessel or pot, a gallipot &c.; N. of a man; (*ā*), f. = *ćulakā;* (*am*), n. water in which pulse has been steeped; [cf. *ćaluka.*]

Culukin, ī, m. a porpoise, sea-hog, or similar animal; [cf. *ulupin, ćullakī, ćulumpin.*]

चुलुम्प् *ćulump,* cl. 1. P. *ćulumpati,* &c., to swing, rock; to cut (?), to disappear, to be lost (?).

Culumpa, as, m. fondling or nursing children; (*ā*), f. a she-goat.

Culumpin or *ćulūpin, ī,* m. = *ćulukin,* a Gangetic porpoise, sea-hog, or similar animal.

चुल्ल् *ćull,* cl. 1. P. *ćullati,* &c., to play, sport, dally, wanton, coquet; to conjecture; manifest one's meaning (?).

चुल्ल *ćulla, as, ā, am,* blear-eyed; (*as*), m. a blear eye; [cf. *ćilla* and *pilla.*]

चुल्लक *ćullaka, as,* m. (for *ćuluka*), the palm of the hand hollowed as if to hold water.

Cullakī, f. a kind of water-pot; a porpoise, sea-hog [cf. *ćulukin*]; N. of a family; a sort of tribe or caste (?); the opposite bank of a river (?).

चुल्लि *ćulli, is,* f. a fire-place, chimney.

Cullī, f. a fire-place, chimney; a funeral pile; a large apartment or hall composed of three wings or divisions, one looking north, another east, and the third west.

चुश्च्यूषा *ćuśćyūshā,* f. (fr. *ćūsh*), sucking, sucking out.

चुस्त *ćusta, as, am,* m. n. the burnt exterior of roast meat; fried meat; chaff; rind.

चूचुक *ćūćuka, am,* n. (perhaps a reduplicated form of rt. *ćūsh* or fr. *ćūću,* imitative noise in sucking &c.), the nipple of the breast; (*as, ā, am*), stammering, a stammerer; [cf. *ćućuka;* cf. also Hib. *cioch,* 'the breast,' and Gr. θηλή, τίτθη, τιτθός; Germ. *zitze* in relation to rt. *dhe,* 'to drink,' and Lat. *papilla* in relation to rt. *pā.*]

चूड *ćūḍa, as,* m. a sort of knob or protuberance on a sacrificial brick (Ved.); the ceremony of tonsure as performed on a child; N. of a man with the patronymic Bhāgavitti; (*ā*), f. the hair on the top of the head, a single lock or tuft of hair left on the crown of the head after the ceremony of tonsure, a top-knot; the ceremony of tonsure (see *ćūḍā-karaṇa*); the crest of a cock or peacock; any crest, plume, diadem, &c.; the head; top, summit; an upper room, a room on the top of a house &c.; a kind of bracelet; a small well; a kind of metre; N. of a woman; [cf. *ćūla, ćoḍa, ćaula, uć-ćūḍa, tāmra-ćūḍa, pańća-ćūḍā;* cf. also *kūṭa* and Hib. *cuit,* 'the head.'] — *Cūḍā-karaṇa, am,* n. 'forming the crest,' i. e. shaving the head all but one lock, considered as a religious and purificatory rite; it should be performed in the first or third year; [cf. *ćaula.*] — *Cūḍā-karṇa, as,* m., N. of a mendicant. — *Cūḍā-karman, a,* n. the ceremony of forming the crest, the rite of tonsure; [cf. *ćūḍā-karaṇa.*] — *Cūḍā-paksha, as,* m., N. of a man (?). — *Cūḍā-pratigraha, as,* m., N. of a Caitya. — *Cūḍā-maṇi, is,* m. a jewel worn by men and women on the top of the head; a jewel worn in a crest or diadem; (often at the end of a comp.) the best or most excellent of a class, 'the gem' (e. g. *āćārya-ćakra-ćūḍāmaṇi,* 'the best of the whole circle of Āćāryas,' an epithet of Vopa-deva; *paṇḍita-ćūḍāmaṇi,* a chief among scholars); the seed of the Abrus Precatorius [cf. *guńjā*]; title of an astronomical work; title of a work on music. — *Cūḍāmaṇi-dhara, as,* m., N. of a serpent-demon. — *Cūḍā-ratna, am,* n. a jewel worn by men and women on the top of the head; [cf. *ćūḍā-maṇi.*] — *Cūḍā-lakshaṇa, am,* n. tonsure. — *Cūḍā-vat, ān, atī, at,* having a single lock of hair or tuft on the top of the head, crested, tufted. — *Cūḍā-vana, am,* n., N. of a mountain. — *Cūḍāvalambin* (°*ḍā-av*°), *ī, inī, i,* hanging down or reclining on the crest or summit.

Cūḍaka at the end of an adj. comp. = *ćūḍā,* tonsure; (*as*), m. a well; [cf. *ćūḍā, ćuṇṭā, ćūṭaka.*]

Cūḍāra, as, ā, am, = *ćūḍāla* (?), having one lock of hair on the top of the head.

Cūḍāraka, as, m., N. of a man; (*ās*), m. pl. his descendants.

Cūḍāla, as, ā, am, having a top-knot or single lock of hair on the crown of the head, crested; (*ā*), f. a kind of Cyperus, Kyllinga Monocephala, = *uć-ćaṭā,* = *nāgara-mustā* and *śveta-guńjā;* (*am*), n. the head.

Cūḍika, as, ā, am, having a lock or tuft of hair on the top of the head; (*ā*), f., N. of a metre; [cf. *ćūlikā.*]

Cūḍin, ī, inī, i, having a top-knot or tuft of hair on the crown of the head, crested, tufted. — *Cūḍi-kalā,* f., N. of a metre.

चूडाम्ल *ćūḍāmla, am,* n. vinegar prepared from fruits; [cf. *ćukrāmla.*]

चूण् ćūṇ, cl. 10. P. ćūṇayati, -yitum, to contract; to close or shrink.

चूत ćūta, as, m. the mango tree, Mangifera Indica; the anus; [cf. ćuta.]

Cūtaka, as, m. the mango tree; a small or shallow well; [cf. ćūḍaka.]

Cūti, is, f. the anus.

चूर् ćūr, cl. 4. A. ćūryate, ćućūre, ćūritum, to burn.

चूरी ćūrī, f. (a various reading for ćurī), a small well.

Cūrikā, f. = ćūrī, above.

चूरु ćūru, us, m. a kind of worm.

चूर्ण् ćūrṇ (perhaps more properly regarded as a nom. fr. ćūrṇa below), cl. 10. P. ćūrṇayati, -yitum, to reduce to powder or flour, to crumble, pulverize, grind, pound, knead, crush, bruise, split, crumple; [cf. Hib. coirneach, 'a part;' crinim, 'I gnaw, bite.']

Cūrṇa, as, am, m. n. (said to be connected in the first instance with rt. ćarv), powder, any minute particle of substance; flour; aromatic powder, pulvil, pounded sandal; pounded camphor; (as), m. chalk, lime. — Cūrṇa-kāra, as, m. a lime-burner, maker of lime, considered as a man of mixed caste. — Cūrṇa-kuntala, as, m. a lock of hair, a curl, curly hair. — Cūrṇa-khaṇḍa, as, am, m. n. a pebble, gravel, hardened fragments of earth or brick; limestone nodule, commonly known in India by the name of Concar or karkara. — Cūrṇa-tā, f. or ćūrṇa-tva, am, n. pulverulence, comminution, the state of dust or powder. — Cūrṇa-pada, am, n. a peculiar exercise or movement, walking backwards and forwards at various paces. — Cūrṇa-pārada, as, m. vermilion. — Cūrṇa-mushṭi, is, f. a handful of powder or perfume. — Cūrṇa-yoga, ās, m. pl. a fragrant compound, perfumed powder: [cf. vāsa-yoga.] — Cūrṇa-śas, ind. in powder, (ground) to powder (e. g. ćūrṇaśaḥ kṛi, to reduce to powder). — Cūrṇa-śākāṅka (°ka-aṅ°), as, m. a kind of vegetable; [cf. gaura-suvarṇa.]

Cūrṇaka, as, m. grain fried and pounded; a kind of grain belonging to the class called Shashṭika; (am), n. a fragrant powder; a kind of easy prose not abounding in compound words; expounding in prose the purport of a foregoing verse, giving the order or interpretation of the words; [cf. ćūrṇikā.]

Cūrṇana, am, n. rubbing, pounding, pulverizing.

Cūrṇi, is, f. (said by some to come fr. rt. ćar), a sum of 100 kapardas or cowries, i. e. the small shell Cypræa Moneta, used as a coin; (is or ī), f., N. of Patañjali's great commentary or Mahā-bhāshya, on the Sūtras of Pāṇini, perhaps so named because Patañjali notices every minute point of difficulty in Pāṇini's grammar [cf. eka-ćūrṇi]; a selection or picking out of an unanswerable argument; (ī), f., N. of a river near the Grāma Rāṇāghaṭṭa. — Cūrṇi-kṛit, t, m. an epithet of Patañjali, the author of the Mahā-bhāshya; an annotator, commentator in general.

Cūrṇikā, f. fried and pounded rice, or grain of any kind; a kind of cake; a sort of metre; a kind of easy prose; [cf. ćūrṇaka.]

Cūrṇita, as, ā, am, ground, pulverized, pounded, reduced to dust or powder; bruised, smashed.

Cūrṇin, ī, inī, i, made or mixed up with anything powdered or pounded, covered with it.

Cūrṇī-kṛi, cl. 8. P. A. -karoti, -kurute, -kartum, to reduce to dust or powder, pulverize, pound, grind, beat to pieces, bruise, smash. — Cūrṇī-kṛita, as, ā, am, pulverized, ground.

Cūrṇī-bhū, cl. 1. P. -bhavati, -bhavitum, to become dust or powder, fly off into minute particles. — Cūrṇī-bhavat, an, antī, at, becoming dust or pulverized, crumbling.

चूर्ति ćūrti, is, f. (fr. rt. ćar), going.

चूल ćūla, as, m. (= ćūḍa, q. v.), N. of a man; (ā), f. an upper room, a room on the top of a house; a crest, see ćūḍā; the top part or crest of a comet; [cf. uć-ćūla; cf. also Gr. σκόλλυς.]

Cūlikā, ās, m. pl., N. of a people; (ā), f. the crest or comb of a cock; the root of an elephant's ear; N. of a metre; a particular part or division of a drama, the body of a drama, the inferior personages of the drama collectively; title of a Jaina work forming one of the five parts of the Dṛishṭi-vāda; (am), n. cakes of flour fried with ghee. — Cūlikā-paiśāćī, f., N. of a particular dialect in the drama. — Cūlikopanishad (°kā-up°), t, f. title of an Upanishad.

Cūlin, ī, inī, i, having a crest (as a bird) or an ornament on the head; (ī), m., N. of a Ṛishi.

चूष् ćūsh, cl. 1. P. ćūshati, ćućūsha, ćūshishyati, ćūshitum, to suck, suck out: Pass. ćūshyate, to be sucked up or dried up (by internal inflammations &c.): Caus. ćūshayati, -yitum, to suck up; [cf. Lat. sugere, succus; Germ. saugen; Iceland. sūga.]

Cūshaṇīya, as, ā, am, capable of being sucked.

Cūshā, f. a leathern girth; a girdle; sucking (?); [cf. būshā.]

Cūshita, as, ā, am, sucked, sucked up.

Cūshya, as, ā, am, to be sucked, suckable; (am), n. anything that can be sucked.

Cosha, as, m. sucking, suction; burning (of the skin), heat, inflammation, dryness; drying up.

Coshaṇa, am, n. sucking, suction.

Coshya, as, ā, am, to be sucked out; [cf. ćūshya.]

चृत् ćṛit, cl. 6. P. ćṛitati, ćaćarta, ćartishyati or ćartsyati, ćartitum, to tie, connect together; to hurt, wound, kill; cl. 1. 10. P. ćartati, ćartayati, &c., to light, kindle; (a various reading for ćhṛid.)

चृप् ćṛip, cl. 1. 10. P. ćarpati, ćarpayati, &c., to light, kindle; (a various reading for ćhṛid.)

चेक ćeka, as or am (?), m. or n. (?), N. of a country.

चेकित ćekita, &c. See under 4. ćit.

चेक्रिय ćekriya, as, ā, am (fr. Intens. of rt. 1. kṛi), doing much or often, active, industrious.

चेच्चेत् ćeććet (ćet-ćet), ind. an interjection; hush! be quiet!

चेट ćeṭa, as, m. (fr. rt. ćiṭ), a servant, a slave, (garbha-ćeṭa, a slave by birth); (ī), f. a female servant or slave.

Ceṭaka, as, m. a servant, a slave, a minister who fulfils an appointed duty; a paramour; (ikā), f. a female slave or servant, a servant girl, a little maid-servant.

Ceḍa, as, m. (for ćeṭa above), a servant; (ī), f. a female servant or slave.

Ceḍaka, as, m. a servant; (ikā), f. a female servant.

चेत् ćet. See ćed below.

चेतक ćetaka. See p. 325, col. 2.

चेतव्य ćetavya. See p. 322, col. 2.

चेतस् ćetas, &c. See p. 325, col. 2.

चेतसक ćetasaka, ās, m. pl., N. of a place.

चेतिष्ठ ćetishṭha, as, ā, am, Ved. (superl. of ćitra, q. v.), very brilliant &c., especially an epithet of Agni.

चेतृ ćetṛi, ćetyā. See 2. and 3. ći, p. 322.

चेद् ćed (originally 2. ća + id), a compound particle, never found at the beginning of a sentence or verse. In the Veda it is sometimes used as a conjunction, like the simple ća, in the sense of 'and,' 'also,' 'even.' But in Vedic as well as classical Sanskṛit the most usual sense of ćed is 'if,' 'although,' 'provided that,' 'when,' and in these senses it may be joined with the present indicative (e. g. mahyam ćed dadāti tat, if he gives that to me); or with the future (e. g. trishṇāṃ ćet tyakshyati, if he shall abandon avarice); or with the conditional (e. g. vṛishṭiś ćed abhavishyat, if there should have been rain); or with the potential (e. g. gaććhec ćet, if he should go); or with the perfect (e. g. sa ćen mamāra, when he died); or with a participle (e. g. kartavyaṃ ćet priyam mahyam, if a kindness is to be done to me). It should be observed that in the Veda the verb which depends on ćed retains its accent.

The negative particle na may be prefixed to ćed either immediately or separated from it (e. g. na ćed vaćaḥ karishyati or na karishyati ćed vaćaḥ, if he should not make a speech); and frequently the negative no is used in connection with ćed, the verb being understood (e. g. dūram apasara no ćed dhantavyo 'si mayā, depart to a distance, if not, i. e. if thou departest not, thou art to be killed by me). Sometimes no ćed = api na, would that not! (e. g. no ćed evam kuryāt, would that he did not so!). Rarely yadi and ćed are joined together, when ćed may be translated by 'that is,' 'that is to say,' 'namely' (e. g. yadi ćed rājyam avāpsyati, if, that is, he shall obtain the kingdom). In the argumentative writings of native commentators ćed preceded by iti and followed by na is often placed at the end of an objector's statement (e. g. 'Ṛig-vedam adhyemi' ityādi vākyam pramāṇam iti ćen na, if it be urged that the text 'I peruse the Ṛig-veda' is a proof, no, it is not so). Atha ćed, but if; [cf. ned.]

चेदार ćedāra, as, m. (a wrong reading for vedāra), a lizard, a chameleon.

चेदि ćedi, ayas, m. pl., N. of a people who lived in Bandela-khaṇḍa (Bundelkhand) and were renowned in epic poetry for their attachment to ancient laws and institutions; their capital was Śuktimatī, and some of their kings were Vasu Upari-ćara, Su-bāhu, Dhṛishṭa-ketu, Dama-ghosha, Śiśu-pāla, &c.; their ancestor who was a son of Kaiśika or Uśika is also called Cedi; their country is supposed by some to be the same as the modern Chandail. — Cedi-pa, as, m. a prince of the Cedis. — Cedi-pati, is, m. a N. of Vasu Upari-ćara; a N. of Śiśu-pāla. — Cedi-bhūbhṛit, t, or ćedi-rāja, as, m. a N. of Śiśu-pāla, a king of the Cedayas slain by Kṛishṇa; see śiśu-pāla.

चेदिक ćedika, ās, m. pl., N. of a people living in the south-east of Madhya-deśa.

चेय ćeya. See 1. ći, p. 322, col. 2.

चेर ćera, N. of a kingdom in the south of India.

चेरु ćeru, us, us, u (rt. ćar), Ved. performing a holy work.

चेल् ćel, cl. 1. P. ćelati, to shake or tremble; to go or move; [cf. ćal, ćell, kel, khel, vel.]

चेल ćela, am, n. (fr. rt. ćil; according to the scholiasts also ćeli, f.), cloth, clothes, a garment, raiment; (at the end of a comp. ćela, as, ī, am, expresses) vile, wicked, bad (e. g. bhāryā-ćela, am, n. the garment or the mere outward appearance of a wife, a bad wife); [cf. ćaila; cf. also caille, 'a veil or cowl.'] — Cela-gaṅgā, f., N. of a river. — Cela-prakshālaka, as, m. a washerman. — Celāśaka (°la-āś°), as, m. a moth.

Celikā, f. a particular part of a woman's dress, a corset, a bodice, stays.

चेलक ćelaka, as, m., N. of a man.

चेलान ćelāna, as, m. a kind of cucumber, commonly ćelanā; [cf. the following.]

चेलाल ćelāla, as, m. a kind of cucumber, Cucumis Sativus.

चेलिचीम *ćelićīma* or *ćelīma* = *ćilicima*, q. v.

चेलुक *ćeluka, as,* m. a Buddhist novice.

चेल्ल् *ćell,* cl. 1. P. *ćellati,* a various reading for *ćel,* q. v.

चेवी *ćevī,* f. one of the Rāgiṇīs or female personifications of music.

चेष्ट् *ćeshṭ,* cl. 1. P. A. *ćeshṭati, -te, ći-ćeshṭe, ćeshṭishyate, ćeshṭitum,* to move the limbs, to move, stir, make effort, exert one's self, struggle, strive, endeavour, be active, be busy or occupied; to act, do, perform, prepare; to frequent: Caus. P. A. *ćeshṭayati, -te, -yitum,* to cause to move, set in motion, move, impel, drive; [cf. Lat. *quæro;* Cambro-Brit. *cais.*]

Ćeshṭa, am, n. moving the limbs, gesture; acting; (*ā*), f. moving any member of the body; gesture, action, activity; effort, endeavour, exertion, bodily effort; doing, performing, behaving, manner of existence; [cf. *karma-ćeshṭā, aćeshṭa-tā, niś-ćeshṭa.*] — *Ćeshṭā-nāśa, as,* m. the ceasing of every motion or action, destruction of the world. — *Ćeshṭā-nirūpaṇa, am,* n. observing a person's actions. — *Ćeshṭārha* (°*ṭā-ar*°), *as, ā, am,* worthy of effort. — *Ćeshṭā-vat, ān, atī, at,* having motion, full of activity, active.

Ćeshṭaka, as, ā, am, making effort or exertion; (*as*), m. a kind of coitus.

Ćeshṭana, as, ā, am, making effort, who or what acts or attempts any act; (*am*), n. motion; performing, doing; effort, exertion.

Ćeshṭamāna, as, ā, am, moving, stirring, struggling.

Ćeshṭayitṛi, tā, trī, tṛi, moving, impelling, causing to act.

Ćeshṭita, as, ā, am, done with effort, exerted, done, set in motion, &c.; (*am*), n. motion, gesture, act, function; doing, action, behaviour, manner of life.

Ćeshṭitavya, as, ā, am, to be acted; to be managed.

चैकित *ćaikita, as, ī, am,* an adjective derived fr. *ćaikitya.*

Ćaikitāna, as, m. a patronymic from Ćikitāna.

Ćaikitāneya, as, m. a patronymic from the preceding, or from Ćekitāna.

Ćaikitāyana, as, m. a patronymic of Dālbhya (fr. *ćikitāyana* or *ćekita*).

Ćaikitya, as, m. a patronymic from Ćekita.

चैकीर्षत *ćaikīrshata, as, ī, am,* = *ćikīrshat,* wishing to do &c.

चैटयत *ćaiṭayata, as,* m., N. of a man and his descendants. — *Ćaiṭayata-vidha, am,* n. the district inhabited by the Ćaiṭayatas.

Ćaiṭayatāyani, is, m. a patronymic from Ćaiṭayata.

चैतन्य *ćaitanya, am,* n. (fr. *ćetana*), intelligence, mental perception, feeling, consciousness, sense, sensation, soul, spirit, the deity considered as the essence of all being and source of all sensation; (*as*), m., N. of a modern reformer of the Vaishṇava faith, who is regarded in Bengal as an Ava-tāra of Kṛishṇa; he was born about 1484 A. D., and his life is described by Kṛishṇa-dāsa in a work named Ćaitanya-ćaraṇāmṛita or Ćaitanya-ćaritāmṛita. — *Ćaitanya-ćandrodaya* (°*ra-ud*°), *am,* n. 'the moonrise of Ćaitanya,' title of a play. — *Ćaitanya-yukta, as, ā, am,* endowed with consciousness, sentient. — *Ćaitanyāmṛita* (°*ya-am*°), *am,* n. title of a grammar.

चैतसिक *ćaitasika, as, ī, am* (fr. *ćetas*), relating to the mind or heart.

चैतिक *ćaitika, ās,* m. pl. (fr. 2. *ćaitya?*), N. of a Buddhist school.

चैत्त *ćaitta, as, ī, am* (fr. *ćitta*), mental, belonging to thought or intelligence.

Ćaittika, as, ī, am, mental, intellectual, belonging to thought.

चैत्य 1. *ćaitya, as,* m. (fr. 5. *ćit* or 2. *ćiti*), the individual soul.

चैत्य 2. *ćaitya, as, ā, am* (fr. *ćitā*), relating to a funeral pile or grave; (*as, am*), m. n. a monument, a tombstone, a column &c. erected in memory of some deceased person or on the site of a funeral pile; a pile of stones forming a landmark or boundary; a sacred tree, a religious fig-tree &c. growing in or near a village and held in veneration by the villagers; a place of sacrifice or religious worship, an altar, a shed kept for sacrifices &c.; a sacred building peculiar to the Jainas, a Jaina temple; a Jaina or Buddhist image; (*as*), m., N. of a mountain. — *Ćaitya-taru, us,* m. a fig-tree standing on a sacred spot. — *Ćaitya-dru, us,* m., N. of the Ficus Religiosa [cf. *aśvattha*]; a large tree in a village. — *Ćaitya-druma, as,* m. = *ćaitya-taru.* — *Ćaitya-pāla, as,* m. the guardian of a sanctuary. — *Ćaitya-mukha, as,* m. an hermit's water-pot. — *Ćaitya-yajña, as,* m. a sacrificial ceremony performed at monuments. — *Ćaitya-vat, ān, atī, at,* containing a sanctuary. — *Ćaitya-vṛiksha, as,* m. a fig-tree standing on a sacred spot; the tree Ficus Religiosa. — *Ćaitya-śaila, ās,* m. pl., N. of a Buddhist school; [cf. *ćaitika.*] — *Ćaitya-sthāna, am,* n. a place made sacred by a monument or a temple.

Ćaityaka, as, m., N. of one of the five mountains surrounding the town Giri-vraja.

चैत्र *ćaitra, as, ī, am* (fr. *ćitra* and *ćitrā*), made of the tree called Ćitra or Ćitrā; (*as*), m., N. of a spring month or the month in which the full moon stands in the constellation Ćitrā (March–April); N. of the sixth year in the cycle of Jupiter; a Buddhist or Jaina religious mendicant; a common N. for a man, used like Deva-datta as a general designation for any person; a metronymic (from Ćitrā) for the son of Budha and grandfather of Su-ratha; one of the seven ranges of mountains dividing the continent into divisions or Varshas; (*ī*), f., scil. *paurṇamāsī,* the day of full moon in the month Ćaitra and the sacrifice offered on that day; (*am*), n. a monument erected to the dead, a column or block of wood, a tree &c. so considered; [cf. 2. *ćaitya.*] — *Ćaitra-vatī,* f., N. of a river. — *Ćaitra-sakha, as,* m. the friend of the month Ćaitra, i. e. the god of love. — *Ćaitrāvalī* (°*ra-āv*°), f. the day of full moon in the month Ćaitra.

Ćaitraka, as, m. the month Ćaitra; (a patronymic fr. *ćitrā.*)

Ćaitrakūṭī, f. (fr. *ćitra-kūṭa*), title of a commentary on a grammatical work.

Ćaitraratha, as, ī, am (fr. *ćitra-ratha*), treating of the Gandharva Ćitra-ratha; (*as*), m. a patronymic from Ćitra-ratha; N. of a Dvyaha ceremony; a facetious expression for the pubes of a woman, 'Ćitra-ratha's wood;' (*ī*), f. a patronymic of a daughter of Śaśa-vindu; (*am*), n., scil. *vana,* the grove of the deity Kuvera cultivated by the Gandharva Ćitra-ratha.

Ćaitrarathi, is, m. a patronymic of Śaśa-vindu.

Ćaitrarathya, am, n. the grove of the deity Kuvera cultivated by the Gandharva Ćitra-ratha.

Ćaitravāhanī, f. (fr. *ćitra-vāhana*), a patronymic of Ćitrāṅgadā.

Ćaitrāyaṇa, a patronymic from Ćitra; N. of a place.

Ćaitri, is, m. the month Ćaitra; (a various reading for *ćaitrin.*)

Ćaitrika, as, m. and *ćaitrin, ī,* m. the month Ćaitra.

चैदिक *ćaidika, as, ā* or *ī, am* (fr. *ćedi*), an adjective derived fr. *ćedi.*

Ćaidya, as, ā, am, belonging to the Ćedis, a prince of the Ćedis; (*as*), m. a N. of Śiśu-pāla, son of Dama-ghosha and sovereign of Ćedi or Chandail, and adversary of Kṛishṇa; (*ās*), m. pl. the Ćedi people.

चैन्तित *ćaintita, as,* m. a metronymic from Cintitā.

चैल *ćaila, am,* n. = *ćela,* a piece of cloth, clothes, a garment; (*as*), m. a moth; (*as, ī, am*), cloth, made of cloth; bred in clothes (as insects, lice, &c.). — *Ćaila-dhāva, as,* m. a washerman. — *Ćailāśaka* (°*la-āś*°), *as,* m. a kind of goblin feeding on moths and lice.

Ćailaka, as, m. a Buddhist mendicant having only a piece of cloth round the middle of the body.

Ćailika, as, m. a piece of cloth.

चैलकि *ćailaki, is,* m. (fr. *ćelaka*), a patronymic of Jivala.

चोकुटि *ćokuṭi, is,* m., N. of a man.

चोक्ष *ćoksha, as, ā, am* (fr. *ćukshā?*), pure, clean; honest; clever, dexterous; pleasing, delightful, beautiful; sung (?); sharp, pungent, keen; [cf. *ćauksha.*]

चोच *ćoća, am,* n. the bark of Cinnamon Albiflorum or of another kind of cinnamon; bark, rind in general; skin, hide; the uneatable part of a fruit; the fruit of the fan-palm; the cocoa-nut; a banana or plantain.

Ćoćaka, am, n. the bark of Cinnamon Albiflorum or of another kind of cinnamon; bark, rind in general.

चोटी *ćoṭī,* f. a petticoat; [cf. *śāṭī.*]

चोड *ćoḍa, as,* m. = *ćūḍa,* a sort of knob or protuberance on a brick or tile; a bodice or jacket; (*ās*), m. pl., N. of a people [cf. *ćola*]; (*ā*), f., N. of a plant.

चोद *ćoda, ćodya.* See *ćud,* p. 327, col. 3.

चोपक *ćopaka.* See 1. *ćup,* p. 328, col. 1.

चोर *ćora,* &c. See rt. *ćur,* p. 328, col. 1.

चोल *ćola, as, ī,* m. f. a short jacket, a bodice; (*ās*), m. pl., N. of a people in southern India on the Coromandel coast, in the province now called Tañjora; (*as*), m. a prince of the Ćolas; the ancestor of this people is also called Ćola and was a son of Ā-krīḍa; (*am*), n. clothes, a garment. — *Ćolaṇḍuka* (°*la-uṇ*°), *as,* m. a diadem, a fillet for the head, a turban or tiara.

Ćolaka, as, m. a breastplate, a cuirass; N. of a people, = the preceding; (*am*), n. bark, rind.

Ćolakin, ī, m. a cuirassier, a soldier armed with a breastplate; the shoot of a bamboo; the orange tree; the wrist.

चोष *ćosha,* &c. See *ćūsh,* p. 329, col. 2.

चोस्क *ćoska, as,* m. a horse peculiar to the Indus district; a horse of a particular and good breed.

चौक्र्य *ćaukrya, am,* n. (fr. *ćukra*), sourness, acidity.

चौक्ष *ćauksha, as, ā, am* (fr. *ćukshā;* cf. *ćoksha*), pure, clean; honest (?); agreeable, pleasant.

चौड *ćauḍa, as, ī, am* (fr. *ćūḍā*), crested, relating to a crest; relating to tonsure; (*am*), n. the ceremony of tonsure; [cf. *ćaula.*] — *Ćauḍa-karman, a,* n. the rite of tonsure.

चौण *ćauṇa, ās,* m. pl., N. of a people in the west of Madhya-deśa.

चौण्ट्य *ćaunṭya, as, ā, am* (fr. *ćunṭī*), coming from a pond or well.

चौण्डपाचार्य *ćauṇḍapāćārya* (°*pa-āć*°), *as,* m., N. of a son of Ārya who was the author of a commentary called Prayoga-ratna-mālā.

चौदायनि *ćaudāyani, is,* m. a patronymic from Coda (?).

चौपयत *ćaupayata, as, tyā,* m. f. a patronymic from Copayat fr. rt. *ćup* (?). – *Caupayata-vidha, am,* n. the district inhabited by the Caupayatas.

Caupayatāyani, is, m. a patronymic from Caupayata.

चौपायन *ćaupāyana, as,* m. a patronymic from Cupa.

चौर *ćaura.* See p. 328, col. 2.

चौरोल *ćaurola, as* or *am* (?), m. or n. (?), N. of a metre.

चौल *ćaula, as, ī, am* (fr. *ćūlā* = *ćūḍā*), relating to a crest or top-knot &c.; *(am),* n. tonsure; [cf. Gr. σκόλλυς.] – *Caula-karman, a,* n. the ceremony of tonsure, cutting off all the hair from the head of a child three years old except one lock on the crown; [cf. *ćūḍā,* &c.]

चौलुक्य *ćaulukya, as,* m. (fr. *ćuluka*), a patronymic of Kumāra-pāla.

Cauluka, as, ī, am, an adjective derived from the last.

चौहित्थ *ćauhittha, as,* m., N. of a Paṇḍit.

च्यवन *ćyavana.* See below under 1. *ćyu.*

च्यु 1. *ćyu,* cl. 1. A. (ep. also P.) *ćyavate, -ti, ćućyuve, ćyoshyate, aćyoshṭa, ćyotum,* to move to and fro, shake about, move, stir, move from one's place, go away, retire from (with abl.); to fly from (the hand or the bow-string, as a spear or arrow); to fall off from, deviate from, abandon (duty &c.); to be deprived of, lose (with abl., e. g. *rājyāć ćyavate,* he loses the kingdom); to fall away, fade away, disappear, vanish, perish, wane, fail; to come forth from, come out of, flow out, drop from, trickle, stream forth from (in this sense cf. 2. *ćyut*); to fall down, fall, slip, slide; to sink down, sink (literally and metaphorically); to decrease; to cause to move or shake about; to bring about, create, make; to cause to go away, to make forget: Caus. P. *ćyāvayati,* (in the Pada-pāṭha *ćyavayati*), *-yitum,* to cause to move, excite, agitate; A. to move one's self, be shaken or moved; P. to loosen, to remove from a place, drive away, expel from, remove; to deprive a person of anything (with two acc., e. g. *devī na ćyāvayed rājānam prāṇān,* let not the goddess deprive the king of life); to cause to fall: Desid. of Caus. *ćićyāvayishati* and *ćućyāvayishati.*

Cyava. Cf. *bhuvana-ćyava.*

Cyavana, as, ā, am, causing to move, moving, shaking; *(as),* m., N. of a disease or of the demon causing it; N. of a Ṛishi who was a son of Bhṛigu and author of several hymns [cf. *ćyavāna,* which is the original form]; N. of an astronomer; also of one of the seven sages under Manu Svāroćisha; of a son of Mitrāyu; of Suhotra; of a physician; *(am),* n. moving, motion; departure from, deprivation, being deprived of; sinking, falling, perishing, dying; trickling, flowing; [cf. *dus-ćyavana.*] – *Cyavana-naghusha-saṃvāda, as,* m. an episode of the thirteenth book of the Mahā-bhārata. – *Cyavana-prāśa, as,* m., N. of an electuary (*ava-leha*). – *Cyavana-samāgama, as,* m. a chapter of the Padma-Purāṇa. – *Cyavanopākhyāna* (°*na-up*°), *am,* n. the story of Cyavana, a chapter of the Padma-Purāṇa.

Cyavas in *trishu-ćyavas,* q. v.

Cyavāna, as, m., N. of a Ṛishi restored to youth by the Aśvins; [cf. *ćyavana.*]

Cyāva in *dus-ćyāva,* q. v.

Cyāvana, as, ā, am, causing to move or fall; *(am),* n. expulsion, driving away; N. of a Sāman; *(as),* m. a patronymic from Cyavana.

Cyāvayitṛi, tā, trī, tṛi, one who causes to move or fall.

Cyāvita, as, ā, am, caused to fall, expelled.

1. *ćyut, t, t, t,* (at the end of compounds) shaking, causing to fall, removing, destroying; dropping, distilling; [cf. *aćyuta-ćyut, ṛiṇa-ć*°, *dhanva-ć*°, &c.]

Cyuta, as, ā, am, moved, shaken; deviated from, erred, strayed; deprived; removed, expelled, banished; fallen from, fallen off, broken, disordered; lost; fallen (e. g. *nabhaś-ćyuta,* fallen from the sky), dropped, oozed out; (in Rāmāyaṇa II. 91, 64, *madhu-ćyuta* is probably a wrong form for *madhu-ćyut.*) – *Cyuta-kūṭa, as,* m., N. of a country. – *Cyuta-pathaka, as,* m., N. of a pupil of Śākya-muni. – *Cyutāćāra* (°*ta-āć*°), *as, ā, am,* deviating from duty. – *Cyutādhikāra* (°*ta-adh*°), *as, ā, am,* dismissed from an office &c., deprived of a right. – *Cyutotsāha* (°*ta-ut*°), *as, ā, am,* one who has spent his energies, exhausted, incapable of effort.

Cyuti, is, f. quick motion; falling, a fall; falling from, deviating from (rectitude &c.); vanishing, perishing, dying; coming or streaming forth from; falling, gliding, dropping, dripping, oozing; the vulva; the anus; [cf. *ćuta, ćuti, ćūta.*]

Cyautna, as, ī, am, animating, inspiring, promoting; a mover, goer; oviparous; abandoned, wicked, void of virtue or purity; *(am),* n. shaking, concussion; enterprise, exertion, contrivance, management, strength.

च्यु 2. *ćyu* [cf. *ćyus*], cl. 10. P. *ćyāvayati, -yitum,* to laugh; to suffer, bear (?); [cf. Hib. *tibhim,* 'I laugh, joke.']

च्युत् 2. *ćyut,* cl. 1. P. *ćyotati, ćućyota, ćyotishyati, aćyutat* and *aćyotīt, ćyotitum,* to drop, sprinkle, flow, trickle, ooze, exude; to wet thoroughly, moisten; to fall down; to cause to drop or stream forth; [cf. *śćut, śćyut,* and 1. *ćyu* for 1. *ćyut;* cf. also Hib. *cioth,* 'a heavy shower;' *ciothmhar,* 'showery.']

Cyota, am, n. sprinkling, pouring, dropping, falling, dripping (as any unctuous substance), oozing, trickling, &c.; [cf. *śćyota.*]

च्युप *ćyupa, as,* m. (said to be fr. 1. *ćyu*), the face, mouth.

च्युस् *ćyus* [cf. 2. *ćyu* above], cl. 10. P. *ćyosayati, -yitum,* to laugh; to bear; to leave; to loose; to hurt, kill.

च्यूत *ćyūta, as,* m. (for *ćūta*), the anus.

च्यौत्न *ćyautna.* See under 1. *ćyu* above.

छ

छ 1. *ćha,* the seventh consonant of the Sanskṛit alphabet, being the aspirate of the preceding letter, and having the sound of *chh* in *church-hill.* – *Cha-kāra, as,* m. the letter or sound *ćhā.*

छ 2. *ćha, as,* m. (fr. rt. *ćho*), cutting, dividing; a part, a fragment.

छ 3. *ćha, as, ā, am* (perhaps connected with *ćho*), pure, clean; trembling, tremulous, unsteady; *(ā),* f. covering, concealing (in this sense connected with rt. *ćhad*); an infant, a child, any young animal (?); [cf. *ćhā.*]

छग *ćhaga, as, ā,* m. f. (said to be fr. rt. *ćho*), a goat; [cf. *ćhāga;* cf. also Germ. *Bock;* Angl. Sax. *bucca;* Old Germ. *boch, poch, pog;* Lat. *caper; hircus* (?); Hib. *gabhar.*]

Chagala, as, m. a goat; a N. of Atri; of a Muni; of a country; *(ā, ī),* f. a she-goat; a kind of convolvulus, see the next; *(am),* n. blue cloth or raiment; [cf. *ćhāgala.*] – *Chagalānghrī* (°*la-an*°) or *ćhagalāṇḍī* (°*la-aṇ*°), f. a plant, see the next. – *Chagalāntrikā* or *ćhagalāntrī* (°*la-an*°), f. the plant Argyreia Speciosa or Argentea; a wolf; [cf. *ajāntrī.*]

Chagalaka, as, m. a goat.

Chagalin, ī, m., N. of a preceptor who was himself a pupil of Kalāpin; [cf. *ćhāgaleyin.*]

छगण *ćhagaṇa, as, am,* m. n. dried cow-dung; [cf. *ćhāgaṇa.*]

छज्जू *ćhajjū, ūs,* m., N. of a man.

छटा *ćhaṭā,* f. a mass, lump, assemblage, number; a collection of rays of light, light, lustre, splendor; a straight or continuous line; [cf. *jaṭā.*] – *Chaṭā-phala, as,* m. the betel-nut tree, palmyra tree. – *Chaṭābhā* (°*ṭā-ābhā*), f. lightning.

छण्डक *ćhaṇḍaka,* a wrong form for *ćhandaka.*

छद् 1. *ćhad,* cl. 10. P. (ep. also A.) *ćhādayati, -te, -yitum* (also said to form *ćhandayati* and cl. 1. P. *ćhadati,* but these forms do not seem to occur; in the Aitareya-Brāhmaṇa a form *ćhadayati* is found), to cover, cover over, clothe, veil; to use anything as a cover, spread as a cover, cover one's self; to hide, conceal, keep secret; to protect: Desid. *ćiććhādayishati;* [cf. Hib. *scailim,* 'I shade, shelter;' *scailein,* 'a fan, umbrella,' &c.: Gr. σκιά, σκοτός: Goth. *scadus:* Lith. *skyda:* Germ. *Schild; schale:* Goth. *skal-ja:* Lat. *squāma; spolium.*]

Chattra, as, m. (often spelt *ćhatra*), a mushroom; N. of a kind of grass, = *bhū-triṇa;* a beehive of a conical or umbrella form; *(ā),* f., N. of several plants, viz. Anethum Sowa; also = *ati-ććhattra;* coriander; N. of a plant supposed to grow in Kaśmīra; the plant Rubia Munjista; a mushroom; *(am),* n. a parasol, an umbrella, called Chattar by the natives, and regarded as an ensign of royal or delegated power; N. of a constellation; concealing the faults of a teacher (this meaning is invented for the explanation of the word *ćhāttra*); [cf. *ati-ććhatra, ākṛiti-ććhattrā, gomaya-ććh*°.] – *Chattra-guććha, as,* m. the grass Scirpus Kysoor (*kaśeru*), = *gunḍa-triṇa.* – *Chattra-griha, am,* n. the room in which the parasol (or badge of royalty) is kept. – *Chattra-ćakra, am,* n. an astrological diagram. – *Chattra-dhāra, as, ī, am,* bearing a parasol or umbrella, having or possessing one; *(as),* m. the bearer of a parasol. – *Chattra-dhāraṇa, am,* n. carrying or using a parasol or umbrella; carrying one as a type of royal authority. – *Chattra-dhāra-tva, am,* n. the office of a parasol-bearer. – *Chattra-dhārin, ī, iṇī, i,* = *ćhatra-dhāra* above; *(ī),* m., N. of a son of Horila-siṃha. – *Chattra-pati, is,* or sometimes *ćhattra-pa, as,* m. 'lord of the umbrella or parasol,' title of an ancient king in Jambu-dvīpa, or of any king over whom a parasol is carried as a mark of dignity, (whence the title Satrap is probably derived.) – *Chattra-pattra, am,* n., N. of the plant Ketmia Mutabilis. – *Chattra-pushpaka, as,* m., N. of a plant, = *tilaka.* – *Chattra-bhanga, as,* m. breaking or destruction of the royal parasol, loss of dominion or empire, deposition, &c.; wilfulness, independence; a forlorn condition, widowhood. – *Chattra-yukti, is,* f. a chapter in king Bhoja's work called Yukti-kalpa-taru. – *Chattra-vat, ān, atī, at,* furnished with an umbrella; *(tī),* f., N. of a country or town. – *Chattrātiććhattra* (°*ra-at*°), *as, ā,* m. f. a fragrant grass described as growing in marshy ground, = *ćhattraka* and *ati-ććhattrā.* – *Chattrā-dhānya, am,* n. coriander.

Chattraka, as, m. a temple in honour of Śiva of a spherical or umbrella shape; a beehive of a conical form; the plant Asteracantha Longifolia; a mushroom; a kingfisher; *(ikā),* f. a mushroom.

Chattrāka, as, m., N. of a plant, = *jāla-varvūraka;* *(ī),* f., N. of a plant, = *rāsnā;* *(am),* n. a mushroom.

Chattrika, as, m. the bearer of a parasol.

Chattriṇa, as, m., N. of a man.

Chattrin, ī, iṇī, i, bearing or having a parasol or umbrella, belonging to one; *(ī),* m. a barber.

Chattvara, as, m. a house, a dwelling; a bower, an arbour.

2. *ćhad, t, t, t,* (in compounds) concealing, hiding; [cf. *dhāma-ććhad.*]

Chada, as, m. a cover, covering (e.g. *alpa-ććhada*, scantily covered or dressed; *ghana-ććhada*, concealed by clouds); a wing; a leaf; N. of two plants, = *granthi-parṇa* and = *tamāla*; [cf. Hib. *sgiath*, 'a wing.'] — *Chada-pattra*, *as*, m. the tree Symplocos Racemosa.

Chadana, *am*, n. a cover, covering, a sheath, a scabbard; a wing; a leaf; the leaf of Laurus Cassia.

Chadi = *ćhadis*, the roof of a carriage; a wing (?).

Chadis, *is*, n. (f.?), Ved. a cover, the roof of a carriage, the thatch or roof of a house.

Chadman, *a*, n. the thatch or roof of a house; external covering, a deceptive dress, disguise, masquerade; plea, pretext, pretence, trick, deceit; fraud, craft, dishonesty; [cf. Old Germ. *scerm*; Germ. *Schirm*.] — *Chadma-tāpasa*, *as*, m. a religious hypocrite, a false ascetic. — *Chadma-rūpeṇa*, ind. in disguise, incognito. — *Chadma-veśa*, *as*, m. a deceptive dress, disguise. — *Chadma-veśin*, *ī*, m. dressed in disguise, a player, a cheat.

Chadmikā, f. the plant Cocculus Cordifolius; [cf. *guḍūći*.]

Chadmin, *ī*, *inī*, *i*, (at the end of a comp.) disguised, in an assumed dress or garb (e.g. *Brāhmaṇa-ććhadmin*, disguised as a Brāhman).

Channa, *as*, *ā*, *am*, covered, clad, concealed, secret, clandestine, private, solitary.

Chāttra, *as*, m. a pupil, scholar, disciple, tyro, novice, (as carrying his teacher's umbrella or as concealing his faults?); (*am*), n. a kind of honey. — *Chāttra-gaṇḍa*, *as*, m. an indifferent poetical scholar knowing only the beginnings of verses. — *Chāttra-gomin*, *ī*, *inī*, *i*, any one attendant on a pupil. — *Chāttra-tā*, f. condition of a pupil, pupilage. — *Chāttra-darśana*, *am*, n. fresh butter prepared from milk one day old ('looked at by the pupils'). — *Chāttra-vyaṅsaka*, *as*, m. a knavish or roguish pupil.

Chāttraka, *am*, n. honey in the comb or hive.

Chāttrikya, *am*, n. the office of a parasol-bearer.

Chāda, *am*, n. thatch, a roof; (an incorrect form.)

Chādana, *as*, m. the plant Barleria Cærulea, = *nīlāmlāna*; (*ī*), f. hide, skin; (*am*), n. covering, a cover, screen; hiding, concealing; darkening; clothes; a leaf.

Chādayat, *an*, *antī*, *at*, covering, veiling, shrouding.

Chādita, *as*, *ā*, *am*, covered, hidden, concealed; cut, divided (?).

Chādin, *ī*, *inī*, *i*, (at the end of a comp.) hiding, covering.

Chādisheya, *as*, *ī*, *am* (fr. *ćhadis*), suitable for the roof of a carriage or for the thatch of a house.

Chādmika, *as*, *ī*, *am* (fr. *ćhadman*), fraudulent, dishonest; (*as*), m. a rogue.

Chādyamāna, *as*, *ā*, *am*, being covered.

छद् 3. *ćhad* or *ćhand*, cl. 10. P. A. *ćhadayati*, *-te*, *-yitum*, cl. 1. P. and 10. P. A., Ved. *ćhandati*, *ćhandayati*, *-te*, *ćaććhanda*, Aor. *aććhān*, *ćhantum*, to seem, appear, be considered or esteemed as; to seem good, please, be pleasant: A. *ćhandayate*, to be pleased with, delight in, approve of (with acc. or loc.); (Sāy.) to render celebrated or honoured: P. *ćhandayati*, to gratify a person (acc. or sometimes gen.) with anything (e.g. *vareṇa*, with a boon), to present.

4. *ćhad*, *t*, *t*, *t*, (in compounds) pleased with &c.; [cf. *kavi-ććhad*.]

Chanda, *as*, *ā*, *am*, pleasing, alluring, inviting; praising, a praiser; (*as*), m. appearance, look, shape; pleasure, delight, appetite, liking, fondness for, fancy, whim, predilection, desire, wish, subjection, will, free will, arbitrary choice; wilfulness, wilful conduct (e.g. *maććhandāt*, according to my wish or will, at my pleasure; *sva-ććhanda*, following one's own will, independent; *a-svaććhanda*, dependent; *sva-ććhandam*, according to one's own wish; *sva-ććhandāt*, willingly; *a-ććhandena*, against the will); meaning, intention, purport, opinion; poison; (*ena*), ind. at the will of, according to wish or will, at one's pleasure; [cf. *indra-ććhanda*, *kalāpa-ć°*, *deva-ć°*, *vijaya-ć°*, all meaning pearl-ornaments or necklaces of various kinds; cf. also Lat. *spons*, *sponte*.] — *Chanda-tas*, ind. at will, at pleasure, according to one's own wish or desire. — *Chandānuvartin*, *ī*, *inī*, *i*, indulging the humour, complying with the wishes. — *Chandānuvṛitta* (°*da-an*°), *am*, n. indulgence of whims, humouring, compliance.

Chandaka in *sarva-ććhandaka*, epithet of Nārāyaṇa, 'assuming every shape?;' (*as*), m., N. of the charioteer of Śākya-siṇha; [cf. *ćhaṇḍaka*.] — *Chandaka-nivartana*, 'the return of Chandaka,' N. of a Caitya. — *Chandaka-pātana* or *ćhanda-pātana*, *as*, m. a hypocrite, a pretended or false ascetic.

Chandana, *as*, *ā*, *am*, pleasing, charming.

Chandas, *as*, n. desire, longing for, delight, pleasure, wish, will; free will; meaning, intention, purport, object; a sacred hymn or verse as distinguished from the verses of the four Vedas, a verse which is neither Ṛić, nor Sāman, nor Yajus, nor Atharvaṇa, originally perhaps a hymn or verse used in incantations; the sacred text of the Vedic hymns; metre in general, supposed to consist of three or seven typical forms; metrical science, prosody. — *Chandaḥ-prakaraṇa*, *am*, n. a chapter on metre. — *Chandaḥ-praśasti* or *ćhanda-praśasti*, *is*, f. a work by Harsha. — *Chandaḥ-śāstra*, *am*, n. metrical science, a work on metre by Piṅgala. — *Chandaḥ-saṅgraha* and *ćhandaḥ-sāra*, *as*, m. a work giving a summary of metres. — *Chandaḥ-siddhi*, *is*, f. a chapter of the Kāvya-kalpa-latā-vṛitti-parimala. — *Chandaḥ-stut*, *t*, *t*, *t*, or *ćhandaḥ-stubh*, *p*, *p*, *p*, Ved. praising in hymns. — *Chandaś-ćūḍāmaṇi*, *is*, m. a work by Hema-ćandra. — *Chandas-kṛita*, *am*, n. any metrical part of the Vedas or other sacred compositions. — *Chandas-paksha*, *as*, *ā*, *am*, Ved. one whose wing is sacred song, (borne aloft on the wings of praise?). — *Chandas-vat*, *ān*, *atī*, *at*, Ved. pleasing, lovely. — *Chando-ga*, *as*, m. (rt. *gai*), a reciter or singer in metre, a chanter of the Sāma-veda, generally the same as the Udgātṛi priest. — *Chandoga-pariśishṭa*, *am*, n. title of a work by Kātyāyana giving a supplement to Gobhila's Sūtras. — *Chandoga-brāhmaṇa*, *am*, n. the Brāhmaṇa of the Udgātṛi priests attached to the Sāma-veda. Some authorities give eight of these Brāhmaṇas, the principal being called Prauḍha or Pañćaviṅśa, as consisting of twenty-five sections. — *Chandoga-māhaki*, *is*, m., N. of a preceptor. — *Chandoga-śākhā*, f. a branch of the Sāma-veda. — *Chāndoga-śruti*, *is*, f. the Veda of the Chandogas, the Sāma-veda. — *Chandogāhnika-paddhati* (°*ga-ah*°), title of a work by Rāma-kṛishṇa. — *Chando-govinda*, title of a work on metre by Gaṅgā-dāsa. — *Chando-deva*, *as*, m., N. of a man, = *mataṅga*. — *Chando-nāman*, *ā*, *ā*, *a*, Ved. having the name of metre, metrical. — *Chandonuvṛitta* (°*das-an*°), *am*, n. conforming to one's humour, humouring, indulgence. — *Chando-bhaṅga*, *as*, m. violation of the laws of metre. — *Chando-bhāshā*, f. the language of the Vedas (?). — *Chando-mañjari*, *is* or *ī*, f. title of a work on metre by Gaṅgā-dāsa. — *Chando-maya*, *as*, *ī*, *am*, Ved. consisting of or containing sacred hymns. — *Chando-māna*, *am*, n., Ved. the measure of metre, i.e. a syllable regarded as the metrical unit. — *Chando-mārtaṇḍa*, *as*, m. title of a work on metre. — *Chando-mālā*, f. title of a work on metre. — *Chando-ruṭ-stoma*, *as*, m., N. of a Shaḍaha rite. — *Chando-vićiti*, *is*, f. 'examination of metres,' title of a treatise on metre. — *Chando-vivṛiti*, *is*, f. 'explanation of metres,' title of Piṅgala's work on metre. — *Chando-vṛitta*, *am*, n. a metre in general, any metre.

Chandasya, *as*, *ā*, *am*, Ved. taking the form of hymns, metrical, fit for hymns, relating to the Vedic hymns; made or done according to one's wish.

Chandita, *as*, *ā*, *am*, gratified, pleased.

Chandu, *us*, *us*, *u*, Ved. pleasing, lovely.

Chandoma, *as*, m., N. of the eighth, ninth, and tenth day in a sacrificial ceremony which lasts twelve days (*dvādaśāha*). — *Chandoma-trikakud*, *t*, m., N. of a Soma ceremony lasting three days. — *Chandoma-daśāha*, *as*, m., N. of a Daśa-rātra. — *Chandoma-vat*, *ān*, *atī*, *at*, Ved. accompanied by a Chandoma.

छद् 5. *ćhad*, cl. 1. P. *ćhadati*, &c., to nourish, strengthen.

छद् 6. *ćhad*, cl. 1. and 10. P. *ćhandati* and *ćhandayati*, &c., to kindle; (a various reading for *ćhṛid*.)

छद्मट् *ćhadmaṭ*, ind. = *ćhambaṭ* (?).

छद्वर *ćhadvara*, *as*, m. a tooth (?); a bower; [cf. *ćhattvara*.]

छनच्छन् *ćhanaććhan*, ind. an imitative sound expressive of the noise of falling drops, of sobbing &c.; (according to some a reduplicated form of *ćhanat*.)

छन्न *ćhanna*. See col. 1.

छम् *ćham*, cl. 1. P. *ćhamati*, &c., to eat; [cf. *ćam*, *jam*, *jham*.]

छमच्छमिकारत्न *ćhamaććhamikā-ratna*, *as*, m., N. of a poet.

छमच्छमित *ćhamaććhamita*, *am*, n. (an onomatopoetic word with the termination of the past pass. part.), crackling, rattling.

छमण्ड *ćhamaṇḍa*, *as*, m. an orphan, a fatherless son; a single man, one who has no kinsmen; [cf. *ćhemaṇḍa*.]

छम्प् *ćhamp*, cl. 1. 10. P. *ćhampati*, *ćhampayati*, &c., to go, move.

छम्बट् *ćhambaṭ*, ind., Ved. (used with rt. *kṛi*, especially in sacrificial language), to make a failure, fail in obtaining or accomplishing.

छर्द् *ćhard*, cl. 10. P. *ćhardayati*, *-yitum*, to vomit, be sick; [cf. *ćhṛid*; cf. also Hib. *sceithim*, 'I vomit, spew;' Lat. *screo*.]

Charda, *as*, m. (a various reading for *ćhardi*), vomiting.

Chardana, *as*, m., N. of a plant (= *alambusha*); of a Rākshasa; another plant, = *nimba*; the plant Vangueria Spinosa; (*am*), n. vomiting, sickness; retching.

Chardi, *is*, f. sickness, vomiting. — *Chardi-ghna*, *as*, m. 'anti-emetic,' N. of a tree, = *nimba*.

Chardikā, f. sickness, vomiting; a plant, = *vishṇu-krāntā*. — *Chardikā-ripu*, *us*, m. small cardamoms ('anti-emetic').

1. *ćhardis*, *is*, f. n. vomiting. (For 2. *ćhardis* see below.)

Chardikā, f. vomiting, sickness.

छर्दापनिका *ćhardāpanikā*, f. a kind of cucumber, = *karkaṭī*; (a corruption of *ćhardāpanayikā*?).

छर्दिस् 2. *ćhardis*, *is*, n. (fr. 1. *ćhad*?), Ved. a fence, a secure place, secure residence; a house; [cf. *ćhadis*.] — *Chardish-pā*, *ās*, *ās*, *am*, Ved. protecting a house.

छल् *ćhal*, *ćhalayati*. See under *ćhala*.

छल *ćhala*, *as*, *am*, m. n. (probably fr. 1. *ćhad*), fraud, deceit, deception, sham, guise, disguise, pretence, pretext, delusion, illusion, semblance, counterfeit appearance, fiction, feint, circumvention, trick, stratagem; fallacy (e.g. *vāk-ćhalaiḥ*, with fallacious words); wickedness; design, device; intention; (*as*), m., N. of a son of Dala and descendant of Kuśa; *ćhalāt*, through deceit or fraud, deceitfully; *ćhalena*, deceitfully, illusively, under the disguise or pretext or pretence of; *upadā-ćhalena*, under pretence of gifts of honour, i.e. with feigned gifts; *rajaś-ćhalena*, under the semblance of dust; [cf. Lat. *scelus*.] — *Chala-kāraka*, *as*, *ā*, *am*, or *ćhala-*

kārin, *ī*, *iṇī*, *i*, practising fraud or deceit, fraudulent. — *Ćhala-tā*, f. fraud, deception, deceit.

Ćhalaka, *as*, *ikā*, *am*, delusive, deceptive, cheating.

Ćhalana, *am*, *ā*, n. f. deceiving, deluding, tricking, cheating, outwitting, feigning. — *Ćhalanā-para*, *as*, *ā*, *am*, deceitful, cunning, crafty.

Ćhalaya, nom. P. *ćhalayati*, *-yitum*, to deceive, cheat, delude, circumvent, outwit, feign.

Ćhalayat, *an*, *antī*, *at*, deceiving, cheating, deluding, outwitting.

Ćhalita, *as*, *ā*, *am*, deceived, cheated, deluded; feigned. — *Ćhalita-rāma*, *as*, m. 'Rāma the outwitted,' title of a play.

Ćhalin, *ī*, m. cheating, a cheat; a swindler.

छलिक *ćhalika*, *am*, n. a song consisting of four parts and recited with certain gestures or gesticulation; [cf. *ćhālikya*.]

छलितक *ćhalitaka*, *as*, m., N. of a man, the builder of a sanctuary which was called after him; (*am*), n. = *ćhalika* above.

छल्लि *ćhalli*, *is*, f. skin, bark, rind, = *ćhallī*; [cf. *ćhavi*.]

छल्लित *ćhallita* in *asthi-ććhallita*, elevation of a small portion of the bone.

छल्ली *ćhallī*, f. skin, bark, rind [cf. *ćhalli* and *ćhavi*]; a spreading creeper (*vīrudh*); a kind of flower; offspring, posterity.

छवि *ćhavi*, *is*, or *ćhavī*, f. (the latter only in Ved.; said to be fr. rt. *ćho*), skin, hide; hue, colour of the skin, colour in general; beauty, splendor, brilliance; light, lustre; [cf. *krishṇa-ććhavi*; cf. also Old Germ. *scieri*, 'lucid;' Hib. *sceimh*, 'beauty, bloom;' *sceimheach*, 'handsome.']

छविल्लाकर *ćhavillākara*, *as*, m., N. of an historian of Kaśmīra.

छष् *ćhash*, cl. 1. P. A. *ćhashati*, *-te*, to hurt, injure, kill.

छा *ćhā*, *ās*, m. a young animal; [cf. 2. *ćha*.]

छाग *ćhāga*, *as*, m. (said to be fr. rt. *ćho*), a goat; the sign of the zodiac Aries; N. of one of the attendants of Śiva; (*ī*), f. a she-goat; (*as*, *ī*, *am*), coming from or relating to a goat or she-goat. — *Ćhāga-bhojin*, *ī*, m. a wolf, ('goat-eater.') — *Ćhāga-maya*, *as*, *ī*, *am*, like a goat or she-goat. — *Ćhāga-mitra*, *as*, m., N. of a man. — *Ćhāga-mitrika*, *as*, *ā* or *ī*, *am*, relating to Ćhāga-mitra. — *Ćhāga-ratha*, *as*, m. Agni the god of fire (whose vehicle is the goat). — *Ćhāga-lakshaṇa*, *am*, n., N. of a Pariśishṭa attributed to Kātyāyana. — *Ćhāga-vāhana*, *as*, m. Agni the deity of fire.

Ćhāgala, *as*, *ī*, *am* (fr. *ćhagala*), coming from or relating to a goat or to a she-goat, caprigenous; born in Chagala; (*as*), m. a goat; a kind of fish, = *ćhāgalaka*; a patronymic from Chagala (when a descendant of Atri is to be designated); N. of a mountain. — *Ćhāgalāntrikā*, f. a kind of plant, = *ćhagalāntrikā*. — *Ćhāgalāntrī* (°*la-an*°), f. a wolf; also = *ćhagalāntrī*.

Ćhāgalaka, *as*, m. a kind of fish.

Ćhāgali, *is*, m. a metronymic from Chagalā and a patronymic from Chagala; a descendant of Atri; N. of a prince.

Ćhāgaleya, N. of a place; (*ās*), m. pl., N. of a school; (*as*), m., N. of the author of a law-book.

Ćhāgaleyin, *inas*, m. pl. the pupils of Chagalin; the Sūtras of the pupils of Chagalin.

Ćhāgikā, f. a she-goat.

Ćhāgeya, *ās*, m. pl., N. of a school.

Ćhāgyāyani, *is*, m. a patronymic from Ćhāga.

छागण *ćhāgaṇa*, *as*, m. a fire of dried cow-dung (*ćhagaṇa*).

छागलेय *ćhāgaleya*. See above.

छाछिका *ćhāćhikā*, f., N. of a Tīrtha.

छाटा *ćhāṭā*, f. title of a commentary on the Mugdha-bodha; [cf. *ćhaṭā*.]

छात *ćhāta*. See p. 334, col. 3.

छात्त्र *ćhāttra*. See p. 332, col. 1.

छाद *ćhāda*. See p. 332, col. 1.

छान्द *ćhānda*, *as*, *ī*, *am*, adj. fr. *ćhanda* or *ćhandas* (?).

छान्दड *ćhāndaḍa*, *as*, m., N. of a Brāhman.

छान्दस *ćhāndasa*, *as*, *ī*, *am* (fr. *ćhandas*), Vedic, having the sacred text of the Veda as (its) subject, peculiar to the Veda, relating or belonging to the Vedic hymns; studying the holy text of the Vedic hymns, a priest familiar with it; metrical, relating to poetical metre; (*as*), m. a priest conversant with the Veda or sacred hymns. — *Ćhāndasa-tva*, *am*, n. the being Vedic, the being metrical.

Ćhāndasaka, *am*, n. the being Vedic or metrical.

Ćhāndasīya, *as*, *ā*, *am*, metrical, familiar with metres, a metrical scholar.

Ćhāndoga, *as*, *ī*, *am* (fr. *ćhando-ga*), relating to the Chando-gas. — *Ćhāndoga-brāhmaṇa*, see *ćhandoga-brāhmaṇa*. — *Ćhāndoga-sūtra*, *am*, n. a Sūtra work of the Chando-gas.

Ćhāndogya, *am*, n. (fr. *ćhando-ga*), the doctrine of the Chando-gas or Udgātṛi priests contained in a Brāhmaṇa of the Sāma-veda; see *ćhandoga-brāhmaṇa*. — *Ćhāndogya-mantra-bhāshya*, *am*, n. a commentary by Guṇa-vishṇu on the prayers and texts in Gobhila's Gṛihya-sūtras. — *Ćhāndogyopanishad* (°*ya-up*°), *t*, f. title of the Upanishad attached to the Sāma-veda. — *Ćhāndogyopanishad-bhāshya*, *am*, n. a commentary on the above Upanishad by Saṅkarāćārya.

Ćhāndobhāsha, *as*, *ī*, *am* (fr. *ćhando-bhāshā*), relating to the language of the Vedas (?).

Ćhāndoma, *as*, *ī*, *am* (fr. *ćhandoma*), taken from the Chandomas.

Ćhāndomāna, *as*, *ī*, *am* (fr. *ćhando-māna*), relating to a syllable regarded as the measure of metre or metrical unity.

Ćhāndomika, *as*, *ī*, *am* (fr. *ćhandoma*), belonging to the Chandomas.

छाया *ćhāyā*, f. (said to be fr. rt. *ćho*, to cut off the light; perhaps a corruption of *ćhadyā* fr. rt. 1. *ćhad*), shade, shadow, dark shadow, a shady place, (in the Naighaṇṭuka III. 4. = a screened or covered place, i. e. a house); a reflected image, reflection; a shadowy fancy, hallucination; shading or blending of colours, play of light or colours, lustre, light, beauty; colour, the colour of the face, complexion, the features; a kind of metre consisting of four lines of nineteen syllables each; Shadow personified, and like Sañjñā wife of the Sun and mother of the planet Saturn; the sun; the shadow of a gnomon as indicating the sun's position; a screen, protection, nourishing, cherishing; a row, line, straight or continuous line; nightmare; a bribe; a N. of the goddess Durgā; (*am*), n. shade, shadow (at the end of a Tat-purusha compound); (*as*), m. one who grants shade. — *Ćhāyā-kara*, *as*, *ī*, *am*, causing shadow, shadowing, shading; (*as*), m. a parasol or umbrella-bearer; a species of metre. — *Ćhāyā-graha*, *as*, m. 'receiving the shadow or image,' a mirror, a sun-dial (?); [cf. *ćhāyā-yantra*.] — *Ćhāyāṅka* (°*yā-aṅ*°), *as*, m. the moon (containing the image of a hare or deer, i. e. marked like a hare or deer); [cf. *ćhāyā-bhṛit* and *ćhāyā-mṛiga-dhara*.] — *Ćhāyā-tanaya*, *as*, m. the son of Chāyā, an epithet of Saturn. — *Ćhāyā-taru*, *us*, m. a large umbrageous tree, (giving abundant shade or shelter.) — *Ćhāyātmaja* (°*yā-āt*°), *as*, m. the son of Chāyā, an epithet of Saturn. — *Ćhāyātman* (°*yā-āt*°), *ā*, m. a reflected image or form (lit. 'shadow-self,' the shadow or reflected image of one's own person). — *Ćhāyā-druma*, *as*, m. an umbrageous tree; see *ćhāyā-taru*. — *Ćhāyā-dvitīya*, *as*, *ā*, *am*, accompanied by one's shadow. — *Ćhāyā-patha*, *as*, m. ether, the atmosphere or firmament. — *Ćhāyā-purusha*, *as*, m. Purusha in the form of a shadow. — *Ćhāyā-bhinna*, *as*, *ā*, *am*, divided in radiance, reflecting light from various surfaces. — *Ćhāyā-bhṛit*, *t*, m. the moon; [cf. *ćhāyāṅka*.] — *Ćhāyā-maya*, *as*, *ī*, *am*, shadowy, casting a shadow, reflected. — *Ćhāyā-māna*, *am*, n. an instrument that measures a shadow. — *Ćhāyā-mitra*, *am*, n. a ćhattar or parasol (friend of the shade). — *Ćhāyā-mṛiga-dhara*, *as*, m. 'possessing the image of a deer,' the moon; [cf. *ćhāyāṅka*.] — *Ćhāyā-yantra*, *am*, n. 'shadow instrument,' a sun-dial. — *Ćhāyā-vat*, *ān*, *atī*, *at*, shadowy, possessing or granting shade. — *Ćhāyā-vyavahāra*, *as*, m. measuring or calculating the shadow cast by the sun on the dial. — *Ćhāyā-suta*, *as*, m. the son of Chāyā, an epithet of Saturn.

Ćhāyaka, *as*, *ikā*, *am*, Ved. shadowy (as a demon).

छालिक्य *ćhālikya*, *am*, n., N. of a kind of song; [cf. *ćhalika*.]

छि *ćhi*, *is*, m. abuse, reproach.

छिक्कन *ćhikkana*, *am*, n. (an onomatopoetic word with the affix of a noun of action), sneezing; (*ī*), f. the plant Artemisia Sternutatoria.

Ćhikkā, f. sneezing.

Ćhikkika, *as*, *ā*, *am*, sneezing, sternutatory; (*ā*), f. the plant Artemisia Sternutatoria.

छिक्कर *ćhikkara*, *as*, m. a kind of animal; (perhaps an incorrect form.)

छिक्कार *ćhikkāra*, *as*, m. a kind of antelope.

छित *ćhita*. See rt. *ćho*, p. 334.

छिद् 1. *ćhid*, cl. 7. P. A. *ćhinatti*, *ćhintte*, *ćiććheda*, *ćiććhide*, *ćhetsyati*, *-te*, *aććhidat* or *aććhaitsīt*, *aććhitta*, *ćhettum*, to cut, cut off, amputate, cut through, hew, chop, rend, split, pierce, separate, divide, unfasten; to take away, remove, deprive of; to interrupt, disturb; to destroy, annihilate, efface, blot out: Pass. *ćhidyate*, to be split, to be cut, to break, be torn, &c.: Caus. P. *ćhedayati*, *-yitum*; Aor. *aćiććhidat*, to cut off; to cause to cut off or through: Desid. *ćiććhitsati*, *-te*: Intens. *ćeććhidyate*, *ćeććhidīti*, *ćeććhetti*; [cf. Lat. *scindo*: Gr. σχίζω, σχίδη, σχέδη, σχινδαλμός, σκινδαλμός, σκίδνημι; σχάζω(?): Goth. *skcida*: Germ. *scheide*: Old Germ. *schite*; *splitar*: Mod. Germ. *splitter*: Hib. *scaithim*, 'I cut off, lop,' &c.]

Ćhitti, *is*, f. cutting, division; N. of a tree, = *karañja*.

Ćhittvara, *as*, *ā*, *am*, cutting or fit for cutting (as a weapon &c.), trenchant; hostile, inimical, a foe; roguish, fraudulent, knavish, a knave; [cf. *ćhattvara* and *ćhidura*.]

Ćhittvā, ind. having cut, amputated, divided.

2. *ćhid*, *t*, *t*, *t*, (at the end of a compound) cutting, cutting through, tearing asunder, splitting, piercing [cf. *ukha-ććhid*, *keśa-ććhid*, *paksha-ććhid*]; destroying, annihilating, removing [cf. *duḥkha-ććhid*]; (*t*), m. the divisor, denominator.

Ćhidaka, *am*, n. Indra's thunderbolt or diamond.

Ćhidā, f. cutting, dividing.

Ćhidi, *is*, *is*, *i*, cutting or tearing off, splitting; (*is*), f. an axe.

Ćhidira, *as*, m. an axe; a sword; fire; a rope, cord.

Ćhidura, *as*, *ā*, *am*, cutting, dividing, what cuts or divides; easily breaking; hostile, a foe; roguish, a knave; [cf. *ćhittvara*.]

Ćhidyamāna, *as*, *ā*, *am*, being cut, cut.

Ćhidra, *as*, *ā*, *am*, containing holes, pierced; (*am*), n. a hole, slit, incision, cleft, opening, fissure, crack, perforation, vacuity, interruption, (*ćhidram daiva-kṛitam*, the opening or hole made by nature, the cartilage of the ear, the pupil of the eye, &c.); defect, fault, blemish, flaw (moral or physical); a vulnerable or weak point, weak side, foible, imperfection, infirmity; (in astronomy) N. of the eighth house; [cf. *a-ććhidra, karṇa-ććh°, kṛita-ććh°, gṛiha-ććh°, niś-ćh°.*] — *Chidra-karṇa, as, ī, am,* having the ears bored or pierced. — *Chidra-tā,* f. the state of being perforated, the quality of being perforated or pervaded by everything. — *Chidra-darśana, as, ā, am,* exhibiting faults or deficiencies, (*a-ććhidradarśana,* faultless); (*as*), m., N. of a Cakra-vāka that had been a Brāhman in a former birth. — *Chidra-darśin, ī, inī, i,* observing faults or deficiencies, a captious critic; (*ī*), m., N. of a Cakra-vāka; see above. — *Chidra-vaidehī,* f. the plant Scindapsus Officinalis, = *gaja-pippalī.* — *Chidrātman* (°*ra-āt*°), *ā, ā, a,* one who exposes his weak points to attack. — *Chidrānusandhānin, ī, inī, i,* or *ćhidrānusārin* or *ćhidrānveshin* (°*ra-an*°), *ī, iṇī, i,* looking out for faults or flaws, picking holes, a censorious or captious critic. — *Chidrāntar* (°*ra-an*°), *aḥ,* m. 'internally hollow,' cane or reed. — *Chidrānveshaṇa* (°*ra-an*°), *am,* n. the searching for faults, picking holes; [cf. *ćhidrānusandhānin* above.] — *Chidrā-phala, am,* n. a kind of fruit; [cf. *māyā-phala.*]

Chidraya, nom. P. *ćhidrayati, -yitum,* to pierce, perforate, bore, make openings or holes, to perforate the ears for rings &c.

Chidrāpaya, nom. P. *-payati, -yitum,* to pierce, perforate.

Chidrita, as, ā, am, pierced, perforated, having holes, orifices or openings.

Chidrin, ī, iṇī, i, having holes, hollow.

Chidvara, as, ā, am, = *ćhittvara.*

Chindaka, as, m., N. of a family or race.

Chinna, as, ā, am, cut, divided, torn, broken, destroyed; decaying, declining, exhausted, tired; (*ā*), f. a whore, a harlot; the tree Cocculus Cordifolius, = *guḍūćī.* — *Chinna-karṇa, as, ī, am,* having the ears cut off. — *Chinna-keśa, as, ā, am,* having the hair cut, shorn, shaven. — *Chinna-granthinikā,* f. a kind of bulbous plant, = *tri-parṇikā.* — *Chinna-druma, as,* m. a riven tree. — *Chinna-dhanvan, ā,* m. a warrior whose bow has been cut or broken by his enemy's arrow. — *Chinna-nāsika, as, ā, am,* having the nose cut off, noseless. — *Chinna-nāsya, as, ā, am,* having the nose-rein (or cord passing through the nose) cut or broken. — *Chinna-paksha, as, ā, am,* having the wings clipped or torn off. — *Chinna-pattrī,* f., N. of a plant, = *ambashṭhā.* — *Chinna-bandhana, as, ā, am,* loosed from bonds, liberated. — *Chinna-bhinna, as, ā, am,* pierced through and through, cut up, destroyed, scattered. — *Chinna-bhūyishṭhadhūma, as, ā, am,* bursting through the thick smoke, scattering the mass of smoke. — *Chinna-masta* or *ćhinna-mastaka, as, ā, am,* decapitated; (*ā*), f. a headless form of Durgā. — *Chinna-mūla, as, ā, am,* cut up by the root. — *Chinna-ruha, as,* m., N. of a tree, = *tilaka;* (*ā*), f., N. of several plants, viz. Cocculus Cordifolius; incense, = *śallakī;* also = *svarṇa-ketakī.* — *Chinna-vat, ān, atī, at,* having cut or cut off. — *Chinna-veśikā,* f. the plant Clypea Hernandifolia, = *pāṭhā.* — *Chinna-śvāsa, as,* m. interrupted or irregular breathing, a kind of asthma; (*as, ā, am*), breathing at irregular intervals. — *Chinna-saṁśaya, as, ā, am,* one whose doubts are dispelled, freed from doubt; confirmed, confident. — *Chinnodbhavā* (°*na-ud*°), f. the plant Cocculus Cordifolius, = *guḍūćī.*

Chinnaka, as, ā, am, having a little cut off, incised; (Compar. *ćhinnaka-tara* = *ćhinnataraka.*)

Chettavya, as, ā, am, to be cut, to be cut off &c.

Chettṛi, tā, trī, tṛi, who or what cuts, a cutter, a wood-cutter; destroying, removing, solving, a resolver of (doubts &c.).

Cheda, as, ā, am, (at the end of comp.) cutting, cutting off [cf. *sthāṇu-ććheda*]; (*as*), m. a cutting or dividing, divisor, the denominator of a fraction; a distinguishing mark [cf. *bhakti-ććheda*]; a cut, a section, a piece, portion, a part cut off or broken off; an incision, cleft, slit; cutting, dividing, tearing off; solving, dissipating (doubt &c.); destruction, interruption, vanishing; cessation, deprivation, want, deficiency. — *Cheda-kara, as, ā* and *ī, am,* cutting; (*as*), m. a wood-cutter.

Chedaka, as, ikā, am, cutting off, dividing; the denominator of a fraction; [cf. *granthi-ććhedaka.*]

Chedana, as, ī, am, cutting asunder, splitting; destroying, solving, removing; (*am*), n. cutting, cutting off, amputation, dividing, tearing asunder, splitting; division; a section, a part, a portion; destruction, removing.

Chedanīya, as, ā, am, to be cut or divided, divisible.

Chedi, is, is, i, cutting off; breaking; (*is*), m. a carpenter.

Chedita, as, ā, am, cut, divided.

Cheditavya, as, ā, am, to be cut or divided, divisible.

Chedin, ī, inī, i, cutting off, tearing off or asunder; destroying, removing.

Chedya, as ā, am, to be cut or divided, divisible; to be cut off or amputated, to be split, to be mutilated; (*am*), n. amputation, excision; [cf. *kuḍya-ććhedya* and *pattra-ć°.*]

Chaidika, as, m. a ratan, a cane.

छिप्पिका *ćhippikā,* f. a kind of bird (?); [cf. *ćippikā.*]

छिलिहिण्ड *ćhilihiṇḍa, as,* m., N. of a plant, = *pātāla-garuḍa.*

छुच्छुन्दर *ćhuććhundara, as,* m. or (*i, is* or *ī*), f. the musk-rat or shrew.

छुच्छू *ćhuććhū, ūs,* f. or *ćhuććhū-piṅgalā,* f. a kind of animal.

छुट् *ćhuṭ* (a various reading for *ćuṭ*), cl. 6. 10. P. *ćhuṭati, ćhoṭayati,* &c., to cut; [cf. Hib. *sgoth,* 'a cut;' *sgothan,* 'a small flock.']

छुड् *ćhuḍ* (a various reading for *thuḍ*), cl. 6. P. *ćhuḍati,* &c., to cover.

छुड्ड *ćhuḍḍa, as,* m., N. of several men; (*ā*), f., N. of a woman.

छुद्र *ćhudra, am,* n. retaliation, counteraction, remedying; a ray.

छुप् *ćhup,* cl. 6. P. *ćhupati, ćuććhopa, ćhopsyati, aććhaupsīt, ćhoptum,* to touch.

Chupa, as, m. touch, touching; a small tree, a shrub, a bush; air, wind; war, combat.

छुबुक *ćhubuka, am,* n., Ved. the chin; [cf. *ćivuka* and *ćubuka.*]

छुर् *ćhur,* cl. 6. P. *ćhurati, ćuććhora, ćhuritum,* &c., to cut, engrave, incise, etch: Caus. *ćhurayati* and *ćhorayati, -yitum,* to inlay, veneer, to set with mosaic ornaments; [cf. *kshur;* cf. also Hib. *scuirim* or *sguirim,* 'I cease, desist,' cf. *ćheda;* Old Germ. *scar, sciru,* &c.; Mod. Germ. *Schere.*]

Churā, f. lime.

Churikā, f. a knife.

Churita, as, ā, am, cut, inlaid, set, coated, spread; blended, intermingled. — *Churitodara* (°*ta-ud*°), *as, ī, am,* pierced through the belly; transfixed.

Churī, f. a knife, = *kshurī.*

Chūrikā, f. = *ćhurikā* in *ćhūrikā-pattrī,* N. of a plant, = *śvetā,* Andropogon Aciculatus; the mouth of a cow; (other readings have *khurikā, sphurikā, sthurikā, sthūrikā.*)

Chūrī, f. = *ćhurī.*

Chorana, am, n. abandoning, leaving.

छृद् *ćhṛid,* cl. 7. P. *ćhṛiṇatti, ćaććharda, ćhardishyati* or *ćhartsyati, ćharditum,* to pour out; P. and A. *ćhṛiṇatti, ćhṛintte,* &c., to play, shine; to vomit; cl. 1. P. *ćhardati,* &c., to kindle: Caus. *ćhardayati,* to pour out; to spit out, eject, vomit; to cause to spit; to kindle: Desid. *ćiććhardishati, -te,* or *ćiććhṛitsati, -te:* Intens. *ćariććhṛidyate, ćariććhartti;* [cf. *ćhard;* cf. also Lat. *splendeo;* Lith. *spindziu, spindulys, skaistus, skaistas;* Germ. *glänzen?*].

छृप् *ćhṛip* (a various reading for *ćhṛid*), cl. 1. 10. P. *ćharpati, ćharpayati,* &c., to kindle, inflame.

छेक *ćheka, as, ā, am,* tame, domesticated (as a bird or beast); citizen, town-bred, shrewd, sharp, smart, trained in the acuteness and vice of towns; (with *anu-prāsa*), a kind of alliteration, repetition of two or more consonants in different words; (*as*), m. a bee. — *Chekokti* (°*ka-uk*°), *is,* f. indirect speech, insinuation, double entendre, hint.

Chekāla or *ćhekila, as, ā, am,* = *ćheka* above.

छेत्तव्य *ćhettavya.* See under 1. *ćhid.*

छेमण्ड *ćhemaṇḍa, as,* m. a fatherless child; [cf. *ćhamaṇḍa* and *kāćigha.*]

छेलु *ćhelu, us,* m. the plant Vernonia Anthelmintica.

छैदिक *ćhaidika.* See under 1. *ćhid.*

छो *ćho,* cl. 4. P. *ćhyati, ćaććhau, ćhāsyati, aććhāt* or *aććhāsīt, ćhātum,* to cut, divide, mow, reap: Caus. P. *ćhāyayati.*

Chāta or *ćhita, as, ā, am,* cut, divided, thin, feeble, emaciated.

छोज *ćhoja, as,* m., N. of a man.

छोटिका *ćhoṭikā,* f. snapping the thumb and forefinger together.

छोटिन् *ćhoṭin, ī,* m. (said to be fr. rt. *ćho*), a fisherman.

छोरण *ćhoraṇa.* See under rt. *ćhur.*

छोलङ्ग *ćholaṅga, as,* m. = *mātulu ga,* a citron, lime; [cf. *ambu-keśara.*]

छ्यु *ćhyu,* cl. 1. A. *ćhyavate,* &c., to go, move, approach.

ज

ज 1. *ja,* the third letter of the second or palatal class of consonants, having the sound of *j* in *jump.* — *Ja-kāra, as,* m. the letter or sound *ja.*

ज 2. *ja, as, ā, am* (fr. rt. *jan,* and used at the end of comp.), born from, descended from, a son or daughter of, produced or caused by, born in, produced in or at or upon, growing in, living at, being at [cf. *atri-dṛig-ja, dhṛitarāshṭra-ja, ātma-ja, aṇḍa-ja, kula-ja, vana-ja, sarasi-ja, agra-ja, avara-ja, eka-ja,* &c.]; prepared from, made of or with; belonging to, connected with, peculiar to [cf. *anna-ja* and *śakra-ja*]; (*as*), m. a father, progenitor; birth, production; [cf. *jā.*]

ज 3. *ja, as, ā, am* (connected with the preceding by some lexicographers, but the meanings appear to be artificial), speedy, swift; victorious, triumphant, conquering; eaten; (*as*), m. speed; enjoyment; light, lustre; poison; a Piśāća; a N. of Vishṇu; also of Śiva; (*ā*), f. a husband's brother's wife.

जंस् *jaṅs,* cl. 10. P. *jaṅsayati, -yitum,* to protect; to liberate.

जंह् *jaṅh,* Ved. only in Intens. *jaṅgahe,* to strike with the wings or feet, to kick; (Sāy. who derives this word from *grah*), to hold tight, hold fast.

Jaṅhas, as, n., Ved. flapping of the wings; (Sāy.) velocity, speed; [cf. *kṛishṇa-jaṅhas.*]

जक *jaka, as,* m., N. of a Brāhman.

जकुट *jakuṭa, as,* m. a dog; the Malaya

mountains; (*am*), n. a pair; (*as, am*), m. n. the egg-plant, Solanum Melongena, or its flower.

जक्ष् 1. *jaksh* (probably a reduplicated form of *ghas*, q. v.), cl. 2. P. *jakshiti*, 3rd pl. *jakshati* (Gram. 290. *b*); Impf. *ajakshīt* and *ajakshat* (Pāṇ. VII. 3, 98, 99), 3rd pl. *ajakshus; jajaksha, jakshishyati;* Aor. *ajakshīt*, 3rd pl. *ajakshishus; jakshitum* or *jagdhum*, (Pres. part. nom. sing. m. *jakshat*, Pāṇ. VII. 1, 78), to eat, consume, destroy; to wish to eat: Caus. *jakshayati, ajajakshat:* Desid. *jijakshishati:* Intens. *jājakshyate, jājashṭi.*

Jakshaṇa, am, n. eating, consuming.

Jakshi, is, f. eating, consuming.

Jakshivas, ān, ushī, at (perf. part. fr. rt. *ghas*), one who has eaten.

Jagdha, as, ā, am, eaten; (*am*), n. a place where a person has eaten. — *Jagdha-pāpman, ā, ā, a*, Ved. one whose sin or wickedness is consumed or blotted out.

Jagdhi, is, f. eating, consuming; food, victuals; [cf. *kalya-jagdhi.*]

जक्ष् 2. *jaksh* (reduplicated fr. rt. *has*), cl. 2. P., Ved. *jakshiti*, &c., to laugh.

जक्ष *jaksha, as*, m. a Prākṛit form for *yaksha.*

Jakshma, as, m. and *jakshman, ā*, m. two Prākṛit forms for *yakshman.*

जगत् *jagat, at, atī, at* (reduplicated form fr. rt. *gam*), moving, movable, locomotive, transitory; (*t*), n. that which moves or is alive, men and animals, or animals as opposed to men; (in the later language) the world, the earth, the universe; (*tī*), n. du. heaven and the lower world; *jaganti*, n. pl. the worlds; (*t*), m. air, wind; (*tī*), f. a female animal, a cow, (metaphorically 'milk, water'); the earth; the site of a house; people, mankind; the world, the universe; a particular metre consisting of four lines of twelve syllables each; a general name for any metre containing 4×12 syllables; a sacrificial brick named after the metre Jagatī; a field planted with Jambū. — *Jagać-ćakshus, us*, m. 'the eye of the universe,' the sun. — *Jagać-ćandrikā*, f., N. of a commentary by Bhaṭṭotpala on the work Vṛihaj-jātaka; (this commentary is also called Cintā-maṇi.) — *Jagać-ćhandas, ās, ās, as*, one to whom the metre Jagatī belongs, or to whom it is chiefly addressed &c. — *Jagaj-jīva, as*, m. living in the world, a living being. — *Jagaj-jīvana-dāsa, as*, m., N. of the author of three poems entitled Jñāna-prakāśa, Prathama-grantha, and Mahā-pralaya. — *Jagatī-dhara, as*, m. 'supporter of the world,' a mountain; N. of a Bodhi-sattva. — *Jagatī-pati, is*, m. 'lord of the earth,' a king. — *Jagatī-pāla, as*, m. 'earth-protector,' a king. — *Jagatī-bhartṛi, tā*, m. 'supporter of the earth,' king. — *Jagatī-bhuj, k*, m. one who enjoys or possesses the earth, a king. — *Jagatī-ruha, as*, m. 'growing on the earth,' a tree. — *Jagatī-varāha, am*, n., N. of a Sāman. — *Jagat-kartṛi, tā*, m. the creator of the world; Brahmā. — *Jagat-kāraṇa, am*, n. the cause of the universe. — *Jagat-kṛitsna, am*, n. the whole world, the universe. — *Jagat-kshaya, as*, m. the destruction of the world. — *Jagat-traya, am*, n. the three worlds, or heaven, earth, and the lower world (*pātāla*). — *Jagat-pati, is*, m. 'lord of the world,' an epithet of Śiva, also of Vishṇu or Kṛishṇa; a king. — *Jagat-prabhu, us*, m. 'lord of the world,' an epithet of Brahmā, of Śiva, of Vishṇu; an Arhat of the Jainas. — *Jagat-prasiddha, as, ā, am*, known throughout the world, notorious. — *Jagat-prāṇa, as*, m. the breath of the world, wind, air. — *Jagat-samagra, am*, n. the entire world, the universe. — *Jagat-sarva, am*, n. the whole world. — *Jagat-sākshin, ī*, m. the witness or spectator of the world, the sun. — *Jagat-sinha, as*, m., N. of a son of Māna-sinha and father of Mahā-sinha. — *Jagat-srashṭṛi, ṭā*, m. the creator of the world; Brahmā; Śiva. — *Jagat-svāmin, ī*, m. lord of the world, the supreme deity; N. of an image of the sun in Dvādaśādityāśrama; N. of Vishṇu. — *Jagad-anta, as*, m. the end of the world. — *Jagad-antaka, as*, m. the destroyer of the world. — *Jagadanta-kāntaka* (°*ka-an*°), *as*, m. destroying the destroyer of the world. — *Jagad-ambā*, f. the mother of the world, a N. of Durgā. — *Jagad-ātmaka, as, ā, am*, whose self is the world, identical with the world. — *Jagad-ātman, ā*, m. the soul of the world, the supreme spirit. — *Jagad-ādi-ja, as*, m. the first-born of the world, an epithet of Śiva. — *Jagad-ādhāra, as*, m. 'stay or supporter of the universe,' an epithet of Time; also of the Jina Vīra; air, wind. — *Jagad-ānanda, as, ā, am*, rejoicing the world. — *Jagad-āyu, us*, m. or *jagad-āyus, us*, m. the life-spring of the world, an epithet of the wind. — *Jagad-īśa, as*, m. 'lord of the universe,' an epithet of Vishṇu or Kṛishṇa, also of Śiva and Brahmā; N. of a man; N. of the author of a commentary entitled Anumāna-dīdhiti-ṭippanī. — *Jagad-īśvara, as*, m. the lord of the universe; an epithet of Śiva; a king; N. of the author of the play Hāsyārṇava. — *Jagad-uddhāra, as*, m. the salvation or deliverance of the world. — *Jagad-ekanātha, as*, m. the sole monarch of the world; an epithet of Raghu. — *Jagad-eka-pāvana, as, ī, am*, the sole purifier of the world. — *Jagad-guru, us*, m. the father of the world; an epithet of Brahmā, Vishṇu, Śiva, and Rāma (as an incarnation of Vishṇu). — *Jagad-gaurī*, f. an epithet of Manasādevī, the deified wife of the sage Jaratkāru and sister of the Nāgas or serpent-race. — *Jagad-ghātin, ī, inī, i*, destroying the world, destructive, hostile to mankind. — *Jagad-dīpa, as*, m. 'illuminator of the world,' an epithet of the sun. — *Jagad-dvīpa, as*, m. wrong reading for *jagad-vīja*, q. v. — *Jagad-dhara, as*, m. 'supporter or sustainer of the world,' N. of the author of a commentary on the plays Mālatī-mādhava and Veṇī-saṃhāra, a son of Ratna-dhara and grandson of Vidyā-dhara. — *Jagad-dhātṛi, tā*, m. 'maintainer of the world,' an epithet of Brahmā and of Vishṇu; (*trī*), f. 'fosterer of the world,' an epithet of Sarasvatī and Durgā. — *Jagad-bala, as*, m. 'the strength of the world,' or 'surrounding the world,' (fr. rt. *val*), wind, air. — *Jagad-yoni, is*, m. 'the womb or place of production of the world,' an epithet of Śiva, Vishṇu, Kṛishṇa, and Brahmā; (*is*), f. the mother of all living beings, the earth. — *Jagad-vandya, as*, m. 'to be praised or adored by the world,' an epithet of Kṛishṇa. — *Jagad-vahā*, f. 'bearer of all living beings,' the earth. — *Jagad-vināśa, as*, m. the destruction of the world, the expiration of a Yuga or period of the world's existence. — *Jagad-vīja, am*, n. seed or first principle of the world, epithet of Śiva. — *Jagan-nātha, as*, m. 'the lord of the world,' a N. of Vishṇu or Kṛishṇa; also of Rāma and of Dattātreya (both incarnations of Vishṇu); N. of a celebrated idol; also of a temple, and the surrounding district on the Coromandel coast near Cuttack in Orissa, where Vishṇu is especially worshipped as Jagan-nāth; (pilgrimages are made from all parts of India to the idol of Jagannātha there enshrined; see *jagannātha-kshetra* and *purushottama-kshetra*); N. of the author of a work entitled Rekhā-gaṇita; the author of the poem Bhāminī-vilāsa; N. of a son of Rudra who compiled at the end of the last century the work Vivāda-bhaṅgārṇava; (*au*), m. du. epithet of Vishṇu and Śiva; (*ā*), f. epithet of Durgā. — *Jagannātha-kshetra, am*, n. the shrine of Jagannātha and surrounding district, see above. — *Jagannātha-vallabha-nāṭaka, am*, n. title of a play. — *Jagan-nivāsa, as*, m. the abode of the world, an epithet of Vishṇu or Kṛishṇa; worldly existence. — *Jagan-maṇi, is*, m., N. of a copyist. — *Jagan-maya, as, ī, am*, containing the whole world. — *Jagan-mātṛi, tā*, f. 'mother of the world,' epithet of Durgā and Lakshmī.

Jaganvas, vān, gmushī, vat (perf. part.), one who has gone.

Jagmi, is, is, i, Ved. going, being in constant motion; going to, hastening towards (with acc. or loc.); (*is*), m. the wind, air.

Jagmivas, vān, mushī, vat, who or what has gone.

Jaṅgama, as, ā, am (fr. Intens. of rt. *gam*), moving, movable, locomotive, that which has motion as opposed to that which is stationary, living; a living being (= *jagat* in the earlier language); derived from living beings; [cf. Goth. *gagga;* Germ. *Gang.*] — *Jaṅgama-kuṭī*, f. a parasol, a ćhattar or umbrella ('movable house'). — *Jaṅgama-tva, am*, n. the state of having motion, movableness.

जगद *jagada, as*, m. an attendant, a guardian.

जगद्दल *jagaddala, as*, m., N. of a king of the Darads.

जगनु *jaganu* or *jagannu, us*, m. a living being, an animal; an insect; fire or its deity.

जगर *jagara, as*, m. armour, mail; [cf. *jāgara.*]

जगल *jagala, as, ā, am*, fraudulent, knavish; (*as*), m. a kind of intoxicating beverage, any fluid suitable for distillation; the plant Vangueria Spinosa, = *madana-vṛiksha;* armour, mail [cf. *jagara*]; (*am*), n. cow-dung.

जगुरि *jaguri, is, is, i* (fr. rt. *gam* or *gā*), Ved. leading, conducting.

जग्गिक *jaggika, as*, m., N. of a man.

जग्ध *jagdha.* See under 1. *jaksh.*

जग्मि *jagmi, jagmivas.* See under *jagat.*

जघन *jaghana, as, am*, m. n. in the later language always n. (probably a reduplicated form of rt. *han*, but by some connected with *jaṇh*), the hinder part, the buttock, the hip and loins, the pudenda, mons veneris; rear-guard, reserve of an army; [cf. *jaṅghā.*] — *Jaghana-kūpaka, au*, m. du. the hollow of the loins of a handsome woman. — *Jaghana-gaurava, am*, n. the weight of the hips. — *Jaghana-ćapalā*, f. a libidinous woman (moving the hips); a woman active in dancing; a species of the Āryā metre. — *Jaghana-tas*, ind. behind, on the hinder part, after; [cf. *agra-tas.*] — *Jaghanārdha* (°*na-ar*°), *as*, m. the hinder part (opposed to *pūrvārdha*); rear-guard, reserve of an army. — *Jaghane-phalā*, f. the opposite-leaved fig-tree, Ficus Oppositifolia.

Jaghanin, ī, inī, i, having stout hips or large buttocks.

Jaghanena, ind. behind, (with gen. or acc.) backwards, away from.

Jaghanya, as, ā, am, hindmost, hinder, last, latest, lowest, low, worst, vilest, vile, base, shortest, least, least important; of low origin or rank; (*as*), m. a Śūdra or man of the lowest class; N. of the attendant of Mālavya, who was one of the five princes born under particular constellations; (*am*), n. the penis; (*am* or *e*), ind. after, behind, last; *jaghanye kṛi*, to leave behind, turn the back on; [cf. Hib. *deaghanach*, 'last.'] — *Jaghanya-guṇa-vṛitti-stha, as, ā, am*, addicted to low pursuits, chiefly familiar with the lowest of the three Guṇas. — *Jaghanya-ćapalā*, f. a species of the Āryā metre; [cf. *jaghana-ćapalā.*] — *Jaghanya-ja, as, ā, am*, last born, youngest; low-born; (*as*), m. a younger brother; a Śūdra. — *Jaghanya-tara, as, ā, am*, lower, inferior. — *Jaghanya-tas*, ind. behind, at the back, after. — *Jaghanya-śayin, ī, inī, i*, lying down last, going to bed last.

जघन्वस् *jaghanvas, vān, ghnushī, vat* (fr. rt. *han*), who or what has killed.

Jaghni, is, is, i, striking, killing; (*is*), m. a weapon, offensive instrument.

Jaghnivas, vān, ghnushī, vat (perf. part.), = *jaghanvas* above.

Jaghnu, us, us, u, striking, beating, killing.

जघ्रि *jaghri, is, is, i* (reduplicated form fr. rt. *ghṛi*), Ved. pouring out, sprinkling about.

जङ्क्ष् *janksh*, cl. 1. P. *jankshati*, a various reading for *kshaj* or *kshañj*.

जङ्ग *janga, as,* m., N. of a man.

जङ्गपूग *jangapūga, as,* m. wickedness, sin (?).

जङ्गम *jangama.* See p. 335, col. 3.

जङ्गल *jangala, as, ā, am,* arid, sterile, desert; (*as*), m. a desert, waste or overgrown land, any arid or sterile region, any wild or uninhabited country, a jungle; (*as, am*), m. n. flesh, meat; [cf. *jāngala* and *jangula.*]

Jangāla, as, m. a land-mark, a limit, a boundary, a ridge of earth running along the edge of a field for collecting water and forming a passage over it, a balk.

Jangula, am, n. poison, venom.

जङ्गिड *jangiḍa, as,* m., N. of a plant which is worn as an amulet.

जङ्घ *jangha, as,* m. (said to be fr. rt. *jan,* or corrupted from *jangā* fr. rt. *gā,* to go, or fr. rt. *janh;* cf. *jaghana*), N. of a Rakshas; (*ā*), f. the shank or lower part of the leg from the ankle to the knee; (in the earlier language also) the upper part of the leg; a part of a bedstead; [cf. Old Germ. *scinkel;* Germ. *Schenkel.*] — *Janghā-kara, as, ī, am,* or *janghā-karika, as, ā, am,* active with the legs, running quickly, a runner. — *Janghā-kārika, as,* m. a runner, a courier, an express. — *Janghā-trāṇa, am,* n. armour or protection for the legs, cuisses or greaves. — *Janghā-bandhu, us,* m., N. of a man. — *Janghā-ratha, as,* m., N. of a man; (*ās*), m. pl. his descendants. — *Janghāri* (°*ghā-ari*), *is,* m., N. of a man.

Janghāla, as, ā, am, running swiftly, quick, rapid, going quickly; (*as*), m. a courier; a deer, an antelope.

Janghikā, f. a diminutive fr. *janghā.*

Janghila, as, ā, am, running swiftly, quick, rapid.

जज *jaj,* cl. 1. P. *jajati,* &c., to fight; [cf. *janj;* cf. also Hib. *fighim,* 'I fight;' Germ. *fechte;* Old Germ. *vihtu;* Lat. *pugno.*]

Jaja, as, m. a warrior. — *Jajaujas* (°*ja-oj*°), *as,* n. prowess, valour; [cf. *jājin.*]

जज्ज *jajja, as,* m., N. of a man.

Jajjala, as, m., N. of a man.

जज्ञि *jajñi, is, is, i* (reduplicated form fr. rt. *jan*), germinating, shooting.

जझ्झती *jajhjhatī, īs,* f. pl., Ved. (scil. *āpas*), dashing, splashing or rushing waters; (an onomatopoetic word formed like a pres. part. from a supposed rt. *jajhjh.*)

जञ्ज् *janj,* cl. 1. P. *janjati,* &c., = *jaj,* to fight; [cf. Lith. *žinczyju.*]

जञ्जणाभवत् *janjaṇā-bhavat, an, antī, at,* Ved. glittering, flashing.

जञ्जपूक *janjapūka, as, ā, am* (fr. Intens. of rt. *jap*), muttering prayers repeatedly, muttering incantations or charms; (*as*), m. an ascetic, a devotee, one who mutters prayers.

जट् *jaṭ* (probably a rt. derived fr. *jaṭa* below), cl. 1. P. *jaṭati,* &c., to clot, to form into a concrete mass, to become twisted together or entangled and matted as hair; [cf. *jhaṭ.*]

जट *jaṭa, as, ā, am* (fr. rt. *jan?*), wearing twisted or entangled locks of hair; (*ā*), f. the hair matted and twisted together as worn by the god Śiva and by ascetics and persons in mourning; the long tresses of hair twisted or braided together, and coiled in a knot over the head so as to project like a horn from the forehead, or at other times allowed to fall carelessly over the back and shoulders; a fibrous root, a root in general; N. of several plants, = *jaṭā-māṇsī;* Mucuna Pruritus, Flacourtia Cataphracta; Asparagus Racemosus; also = *rudra-jaṭā* [cf. *krishṇa-jaṭā*]; N. of a Pāṭha or arrangement of the Vedic text so called from a peculiar repetition and inversion of the words, (it is a still more artificial arrangement than the Krama-pāṭha, each pair of words being repeated three times and one repetition being in inverted order.) — *Jaṭā-kara, as, ā, am,* matting the hair. — *Jaṭā-ćīra* or *jaṭāṭīra, as,* m. a N. of Śiva. — *Jaṭā-jūṭa, as,* m. the long tresses of hair twisted on the top of the head; a quantity of twisted hair; Śiva's hair. — *Jaṭā-jvāla, as,* m. 'having a flame like a tuft,' a lamp. — *Jaṭā-ṭanka, as,* m. an epithet of Śiva; [cf. *kaṭankaṭa.*] — *Jaṭā-dhara, as, ā, am,* wearing twisted or matted hair; (*as*), m. any mendicant or ascetic wearing the Jaṭā; an epithet of Śiva; N. of one of the attendants of Skanda; N. of a Buddha; N. of a lexicographer; (*ās*), m. pl., N. of a people in the south of India. — *Jaṭā-dhārin, ī, iṇī, i,* wearing matted or braided hair. — *Jaṭā-pāṭha, as,* m. the Jaṭā reading or arrangement of the Vedic text, see above. — *Jaṭā-bandha, as,* m. the knot or coil of matted hair. — *Jaṭā-maṇḍala, am,* n. braided or twisted hair forming a coil on the top of the head. — *Jaṭā-māṇsī,* f. the plant Nardostachys Jaṭāmāṇsī. — *Jaṭā-mālin, ī,* m., N. of a form of Śiva, 'garlanded with matted hair.' — *Jaṭā-vat, ān, atī, at,* wearing the Jaṭā, wearing knotted or clotted hair; (*tī*), f. = *jaṭā-māṇsī.* — *Jaṭā-vallī,* f., N. of two plants, = *rudra-jaṭā* and *gandha-māṇsī.* — *Jaṭāsura* (°*ṭā-as*°), *as,* m., N. of a Rakshas killed by Bhīma-sena; (*ās*), m. pl., N. of a people living in the north-east of Madhya-deśa. — *Jaṭeśvara-tīrtha* (°*ṭā-īś*°), *am,* n., N. of a Tīrtha.

Jaṭāyu, us, and *jaṭāyus, us,* m., N. of a fabulous bird, the king of the vultures (*gridhra-rāja*), son of Aruṇa and Śyenī (or according to the Rāmāyaṇa, son of Garuḍa), and younger brother of Sampāti. (It is related in Chap. XX of the Araṇya-kāṇḍa of the Rāmāyaṇa, that whilst Rāma was on his way to Pańćavatī he met Jaṭāyus, who declared his intention of aiding Rāma, out of regard for his father Daśaratha. Accordingly when Rāvaṇa carried off Sītā, the semi-divine bird attempted to rescue her, but was defeated and mortally wounded by Rāvaṇa; Chap. LVI); bdellium, see *guggulu;* N. of a mountain.

Jaṭāla, as, ā, am, wearing a coil of twisted or clotted hair; (*as*), m. bdellium; a kind of Curcuma (*karćūra*); the plant Bignonia Suaveolens; the Indian fig-tree or *vaṭa;* (*ā*), f. = *jaṭā-māṇsī.*

Jaṭālaka, as, ikā, am, wearing knotted or matted hair.

Jaṭi, is, f. clotted or twisted hair, an assemblage, multitude; the waved-leaf fig-tree, Ficus Venosa (= *plaksha*); [cf. *jaṭī* and *dhurjaṭi.*]

Jaṭika, as, ā, am, wearing twisted or braided hair (= *jaṭin?*).

Jaṭin, ī, inī, i, wearing the Jaṭā, having twisted hair; (*ī*), m. an epithet of Śiva; N. of one of the attendants of Skanda; an elephant sixty years old; waved-leaf fig-tree (= *plaksha*).

Jaṭila, as, ā, am, wearing the Jaṭā, having clotted or entangled hair; complicated, twisted together, intermixed, confused; (*as*), m. a lion; a goat with certain marks; N. of a man; (*ā*), f., N. of a woman with the patronymic Gautamī said to have had seven husbands, mother-in-law of Rādhikā; N. of several plants, = *jaṭā-māṇsī;* long pepper; also = *uććaṭā;* = *vaćā,* Acorus Calamus; = *damanaka.* — *Jaṭila-sthala, am,* n., N. of a place.

Jaṭilaka, as, m., N. of a man; (*ās*), m. pl. the descendants of this man; (*ikā*), f., N. of a woman.

Jaṭilī-kri, cl. 8. P. A. *-karoti, -kurute, -kartum,* to twist together, form into a clotted mass, to braid; to complicate, interweave, wrap round.

Jaṭilī-bhāva, as, m. the being twisted together, complication, confusion.

Jaṭī, f. the waved-leaf fig-tree [cf. *jaṭi*]; also = *jaṭā-māṇsī.*

जटाटीर *jaṭāṭīra.* See *jaṭā-ćīra.*

जटुल *jaṭula, as,* m. a freckle, a mark; [cf. *jaḍula.*]

जठर *jaṭhara, as, ā, am* (said to be fr. rt. *jan*), hard, firm; old; bound, tied (?); yellowish (?); (*ās*), m. pl., N. of a people in the south-east of Madhya-deśa; (*as*), m., N. of a mountain; (*as, am*), m. n. the stomach, belly, abdomen, viscera, bowels; the womb; a hole, cavity; the interior of anything; the bosom; certain morbid affections of the bowels; Ved. course (?); [cf. Goth. *qvithrs,* Them. *qvithra;* Lat. *venter?*]. — *Jaṭhara-gada, as,* m. a morbid affection of the abdomen or bowels, dropsy (?). — *Jaṭhara-jvālā,* f. belly-ache, colic, enteritis. — *Jaṭhara-nud, t,* m. the plant Cathartocarpus Fistula; [cf. *āragbadha.*] — *Jaṭhara-yantraṇā* or *jaṭhara-yātanā,* f. pain endured by the child in the womb before birth. — *Jaṭhara-roga, as,* m. = *jaṭhara-gada* above. — *Jaṭhara-vyathā,* f. stomach-ache, colic. — *Jaṭhara-stha, as, ā, am,* or *jaṭhara-sthāyin, ī, inī, i,* or *jaṭhara-sthita, as, ā, am,* being in the belly, being in the womb. — *Jaṭharāgni* (°*ra-ag*°), *is,* m. the digestive fire of the stomach, the gastric juice [cf. *agni* and *jāṭhara*]; a N. of Agastya in a former birth; [cf. *dahrāgni.*] — *Jaṭharāmaya* (°*ra-ām*°), *as,* m. dropsy, water in the abdomen.

Jaṭharin, ī, iṇī, i, having a large belly; abdominal, = *udarin,* q. v.

Jaṭharī-krita, as, ā, am, contained in the belly; concealed in the bosom.

Jaṭhala, as, am, m. n. (?), Ved. = *jaṭhara;* (Sāy.) the cavity or receptacle of waters, the ocean.

जड *jaḍa, as, ā, am* (perhaps corrupted fr. rt. *jal,* cf. *jala*), cold, frigid, chilly; stiff; stunned, paralyzed, motionless, apathetic, senseless, stupid, idiotic, irrational, dumb; stunning, stupefying; (*as*), m. 'the stupid one,' an epithet of Su-mati who, though intelligent, simulated stupidity; cold, frost, winter; idiocy, fatuity, stupidity; dulness, apathy, sluggishness of mind or body; (*ā*), f. the plant Mucuna Pruritus; also the plant Flacourtia Cataphracta [cf. *jaṭā*]; (*am*), n. water [cf. *jala*]; lead; [cf. Hib. *fiod, fuar.*] — *Jaḍa-kriya, as, ā, am,* working slowly or stupidly, dilatory. — *Jaḍa-tā,* f. or *jaḍa-tva, am,* n. coldness, chilliness, frigidness, apathy, stupidity, stupefaction, despair. — *Jaḍa-dhī, īs, īs, i,* stupid, idiotic. — *Jaḍa-bharata, as,* m. 'the stupid Bharata,' N. of a man simulating stupidity; an idiot in general.

Jaḍiman, ā, m. frigidity, stupefaction, insensibility, stupidity, dulness.

Jaḍī-kri, cl. 8. P. *-karoti, -kartum,* to stun, stupify, benumb, congeal. — *Jaḍī-krita, as, ā, am,* stunned, rendered cold or torpid or insensible, stupefied, confounded, paralyzed.

Jaḍī-bhū, cl. 1. P. *-bhavati, -vitum,* to become insensible or stupid or frozen or rigid. — *Jaḍī-bhāva, as,* m. frigidity, coldness, apathy, stupidity. — *Jaḍī-bhūta, as, ā, am,* become torpid, stunned, stupefied, paralyzed, infatuated.

जडुल *jaḍula, as,* m. a freckle, a mark; [cf. *jaṭula* and *jatu-maṇi.*]

जतु *jatu, u,* n. (said to be fr. rt. *jan*), lac, a red dye or pigment formed by an insect analogous to cochineal, a kind of gum; (*ū, ūs*), f. a bat. — *Jatu-kārī,* f. or *jatu-krit, t,* f. a kind of fragrant tree, = *jatukā,* ('making lac,' the lac insect forming its nest in this tree.) — *Jatu-krishṇā,* f. = *parpaṭī.* — *Jatu-griha, am,* n. a house plastered with lac, resin, and other combustible substances, (such a house was built for the reception of the Pāṇḍava princes in Vāraṇāvata by Purоćana, at the instigation of Duryodhana, the object being to burn them alive when they were asleep after a festival. Warned, however, by Vidura, they discovered the dangerous character of their abode, and dug an underground passage by which to escape from the interior. Next having invited an outcaste woman with her five sons to a feast, they first stupefied them with wine, and then having burnt Purоćana in his own house, set fire to the house of lac and, leaving the charred bodies of the woman and her sons inside, escaped by the underground passage; see Mahā-bh. I. 5864.) — *Jatu-*

geha, am, n. = *jatu-gṛiha.* — *Jatu-putraka, as,* m. a man at chess or backgammon &c. (coloured with lac). — *Jatu-maṇi, is,* m. a mole, a natural mark on the body. — *Jatu-mukha, as,* m. a kind of rice. — *Jatu-rasa, as,* m. lac, the dye. — *Jatu-veśmadāha, as,* m. the conflagration of the house of lac. — *Jatu-veśman, a,* n. = *jatu-gṛiha,* q. v. — *Jatū-karṇa, as,* m., N. of a man; (a various reading for *jātūkarṇa.*) — *Jatv-aśmaka, am,* n. red arsenic; [cf. *śilā-jatu.*]

Jatuka, am, n. lac, see *jatu;* Asa Fœtida [cf. *jātukā*]; (*ā*), f. lac; a kind of fragrant plant or tree, = *jatu-kṛit, jatūkā, janī,* &c.; also = *parpaṭī;* a bat; [cf. *jatunī, jatūkā, aśma-jatuka.*]

Jatunī, f. a bat.

Jatūkā, f. a kind of fragrant plant; a bat.

जत्रु *jatru, us, u,* m. n. (said to be fr. rt. *jan;* in the earlier language m. and pl. only), the continuations of the vertebræ; (in later Sanskṛit) the collar-bone, clavicle; *ūrdhva-jatru,* the part of the body above the collar-bone.

Jatruka, am, n. the collar-bone, the clavicle.

जन् *jan,* cl. 1. 3. P. *janati, jajanti, jajāna, janishyati, janitum,* to generate, beget, (in these senses Ved.); cl. 4. A. *jāyate, jajñe, janishyate, ajanishṭa* and *ajani, janitum* (Ved. *janitos*), to be born or produced, to come into existence; to grow (as plants &c.); to be born again; to be, become, take place, happen; to be possible, applicable, suitable, &c.; to be born for or destined for anything (with acc., e. g. *tam lokam jāyate,* he is born for that world, Ved.): Caus. *janayati, -te, ajījanat, janayitum* (Ved. *janayitavai*), to generate, beget, bring forth, produce, create, cause, occasion; to cause to be born; to assign, procure: Desid. *jijanishati:* Intens. *jañjanyate* and *jājāyate, jañjanti, jājāti;* [cf. Gr. γίγνομαι; Lat. *gigno, genui,* (*g*)*nascor;* Hib. *genim,* 'I beget, generate;' Lith. *gemù;* Goth. *kin* in *keina, kain;* Germ. *Kind,* &c.]

Jana, as, m. a created being, a creature, a living being, man; a person or individual in general, (used collectively in sing. as well as in pl., e. g. *daivyo janaḥ* or *divyo janaḥ,* the gods collectively; often at the end of a compound, e. g. *preshya-jana,* a servant; *svajana-jana,* a relation; *dāsa-jana,* a slave; *sakhī-jana,* a female friend); people, race, tribe, subjects, nation (e. g. *pañca janāḥ,* the five races of men or nations; cf. *ćarshaṇi* and *krishṭi*); the person nearest to the speaker (hence *ayam janaḥ* = this person, these persons, often = I, I myself, we ourselves; cf. *hic homo*); a common person, one of the people; the world beyond the Mahar-loka, the heaven of deified mortals or the people living in it [cf. *jana-loka*]; N. of a man with the patronymic Śārkarākshya; (*ā*), f. birth, production; [cf. *antaḥpura-jana, itara-jana, kula-jana, guru-jana, tiro-jana,* &c.; cf. also Hib. *duine,* man either male or female; Goth. *qvinô;* Slav. *schena.*] — *Janaṃsaha, as, ā, am,* Ved. subduing all creatures, epithet of Indra. — *Jana-kalpa, as, ā, am,* containing ceremonial ordinances for mankind, (*janakalpā ṛićaḥ,* applied to several verses of the Atharva-veda); similar to mankind. — *Janan-gama, as,* m. a Ćaṇḍāla, a man of a low or degraded tribe; [cf. *jalan-gama.*] — *Jana-ćakshus, us,* n. the eye of all creatures, the sun; [cf. *jagać-ćakshus.*] — *Jana-tā,* f. a number of men, an assemblage of people, a community; people, subjects; mankind, manhood; birth, generation. — *Jana-traya, am,* n. three persons. — *Jana-trā,* f. (for *jala-trā?*), an umbrella, a parasol. — *Jana-deva, as,* m. a king. — *Janan-tapa, as,* m., N. of a man. — *Jana-pada, as,* m. a community, nation, people (sing. or pl.); the people (as opposed to the sovereign); an empire, an inhabited country; man, mankind; [cf. *jānapada.*] — *Janapadādhipa* (°*da-adh*°), *as,* m. the ruler of a people or empire, a prince, a king. — *Janapadāyuta* (°*da-āy*°), *as, ā, am,* crowded with people, populous. — *Janapadin, ī,* m. the ruler of an empire, a prince, king. — *Janapadeśvara* (°*da-īś*°), *as,* m. the lord of a country. — *Jana-pravāda, as,* m. 'the talk of men,' rumour, report. — *Jana-priya, as, ā, am,* fond of mankind; philanthropic; (*as*), m. an epithet of Siva; coriander-seed; the tree Morunga Hyperanthera, = *śobhāñjana.* — *Jana-bhaksha, as, ā, am,* Ved. devouring men; (Sāy.) loving men or to be loved by men. — *Jana-bhṛit, t, t, t,* Ved. supporting men. — *Jana-maraka, as,* m. 'men-killer,' an epidemic disease. — *Jana-maryādā,* f. popular observance, established usage. — *Janam-ejaya, as,* m. 'causing men to tremble,' N. of a celebrated king to whom Vaiśampāyana recited the Mahā-bhārata, (he was great-grandson to Arjuna, as being son and successor to Parikshit, who was son of Abhi-manyu, who was son of Arjuna); N. of a son of Kuru; of a son of Puru; of Purañ-jaya; of Soma-datta; of Su-mati; N. of a Nāga. — *Jana-mohin, ī, inī, i,* infatuating men. — *Jana-yopana, as, ā, am,* Ved. impeding or perplexing men, causing them to suffer; (Sāy.) gladdening men. — *Jana-rañjana, am,* n. gratifying the people, courting popular favour. — *Jana-rava, as,* m. rumour, report; calumny, scandal. — *Jana-rāj, ṭ,* or *jana-rājan, ā,* m., Ved. king of men, ruler of men. — *Jana-loka, as,* m. one of the seven Lokas or divisions of the universe, the fifth or next above Mahar-loka, where the sons of Brahmā and other pious men reside; [cf. *janas.*] — *Jana-vallabha, as, ā, am,* agreeable to men; a favourite with men, fond of men; (*as*), m., N. of a plant, = *śveta-rohita.* — *Jana-vāda, as,* m. 'the talk of men,' news, rumour, report, scandal; [cf. *jane-vāda* and *jano-vāda.*] — *Jana-vādin, ī,* m., Ved. a talker, newsmonger, gossip, tattler. — *Jana-vid, t, t, t,* possessing men. — *Jana-vyavahāra, as,* m. popular practice or usage. — *Jana-śrī, īs, īs, i,* Ved. coming or going to men; epithet of Pūshan. — *Jana-śruta, as, ā, am,* known among men; (*as*), m., N. of a man; (*ā*), f., N. of a woman. — *Jana-śruti, is,* f. rumour, news, tidings, intelligence. — *Jana-saṃsad, t,* f. an assembly of men. — *Jana-sankshaya, as,* m. destruction of men. — *Jana-sambādha, as, ā, am,* densely crowded with people (a place). — *Jana-stha, as, ā, am,* living or abiding among men. — *Jana-sthāna, am,* n. 'the resort of demons,' N. of a part of the Daṇḍaka forest in the Dakhin. — *Janasthāna-ruha, as, ā, am,* growing in Janasthāna. — *Janākīrṇa* (°*na-āk*°), *as, ā, am,* crowded with people. — *Janāćāra* (°*na-āć*°), *as,* m. popular usage or custom, propriety, decorum, good conduct. — *Janātiga* (°*na-at*°), *as, ā, am,* superhuman, superior. — *Janādhinātha* (°*na-adh*°), *as,* m. supreme lord of men, a king; an epithet of Vishṇu. — *Janādhipa* (°*na-adh*°), *as,* m. a ruler of men, a prince, a king. — *Janānta* (°*na-an*°), *as,* m. a place removed from men, an uninhabited place; a region; personal proximity; an epithet of Yama, the destroyer of men. — *Janāntika* (°*na-an*°), *am,* n. secret communication, whispering, speaking aside to another; (*am*), ind. (as a stage-direction) speaking aside, aside. — *Janāyana* (°*na-ay*°), *as, ā, am,* Ved. leading to men. — *Janārṇava* (°*na-ar*°), *as,* m. 'ocean of men,' a large concourse of people, a caravan. — *Janārtha-śabda* (°*na-ar*°), *as,* m. a family appellation, a gentile noun. — *Janārdana* (°*na-ar*°), *as,* m. an epithet of Vishṇu or Krishṇa (exciting or agitating men); N. of several men. — *Janārdana-vibudha, as,* m., N. of the author of a commentary called Bhāvārtha-dīpikā. — *Janāv* (°*na-av*), *aus,* m., Ved. a preserver or protector of mankind. — *Janāśana* (°*na-aś*°), *as,* m. 'man-eater,' a wolf. — *Janāśraya* (°*na-āś*°), *as,* m. an asylum or shelter for men, an inn, caravansary. — *Janā-shah* (in some forms *janā-sah*), *shāṭ, ṭ, ṭ,* Ved. subduing men. — *Janendra* (°*na-in*°), *as,* m. the prince or lord of men, a king. — *Jane-vāda, as,* m. rumour, report; [cf. *jana-vāda.*] — *Janeśa* or *janeśvara* (°*na-īś*°), *as,* m. lord of men, a king. — *Janeshṭa* (°*na-ish*°), *as, ā, am,* desired or praised by mankind; (*as*), m. a kind of jasmine (*mudgara*); (*ā*), f., N. of a fragrant plant, = *jatukā;* N. of a medicinal plant, = *vṛiddhi;* turmeric, = *haridrā;* the flower of Jasminum Grandiflorum, = *jāti-pushpa.* — *Janodāharaṇa* (°*na-ud*°), *am,* n. 'laudation of men,' glory, fame. — *Janau,* cf. *janāv.* — *Janaugha* (°*na-ogha*), *am,* n. a multitude of people, a crowd, a mob.

Janaka, as, ikā, am, generative, generating, begetting, producing, causing; (*as*), m. a father, a progenitor; N. of two kings of Videha or Mithilā, one a son of Mithi and father of Udāvasu, the other a son of Hrasva-roman and father of Rāma's wife Sītā, who is therefore called *Janaka-tanayā, Janaka-nandinī, Janaka-sutā,* and *Janakātmajā;* N. of a disciple of Bhagavat and of several others; (*ās*), m. pl. the descendants of Janaka; (*ikā*), f. a daughter-in-law [cf. *jani* and *janī*]; a mother. — *Janaka-kāṇa, as,* m. 'the one-eyed Janaka,' N. of a man. — *Janaka-ćandra, as,* m., N. of several persons. — *Janaka-tā,* f. or *janaka-tva, am,* n. generativeness, productiveness, paternity. — *Janaka-bhadra, as,* m., N. of a man. — *Janaka-rāja, as,* m., N. of a man. — *Janaka-saptarātra, as,* m., N. of a Saptāha. — *Janaka-siṇha, as,* m., N. of a man. — *Janakātmajā* (°*ka-āt*°), f., see above. — *Janakeśvara-tīrtha* (°*ka-īś*°), *am,* n., N. of a Tīrtha.

Janat, ind. a sacred exclamation used in religious ceremonies (like *om* &c.) without any definite meaning.

Janana, as, ī, am, generating, begetting, producing, causing; (*as*), m. a parent, progenitor, a creator; (*ī*), f. a mother; a queen-mother; a bat; lac; N. of several plants, = *janī, yūthikā, kaṭukā, mañjishṭhā;* tenderness, compassion; (*am*), n. birth, production, causation, coming into existence, life (e. g. *pūrve janane,* in a former birth, i. e. in a former life); race, lineage, family; [cf. *indra-janana* and *medhā-janana.*]

Janani, is, f. = *jananī,* a mother; birth; N. of a plant, = *janī.*

Jananīya, as, ā, am, to be produced, produced.

Janayat, an, antī, at, begetting, generating, engendering, producing.

Janayati, is, f., Ved. generation, engendering, production.

Janayanta, as, ā, am, generating, producing.

Janayitavya, as, ā, am, to be engendered, generated, produced.

Janayitṛi, tā, trī, tṛi, generating, begetting, producing, who or what produces; (*tā*), m. a progenitor, a father; (*trī*), f. a mother.

Janayishṇu, us, m. a progenitor.

Janar. See *janas* below.

Janas, as, n., Ved. race, class of beings; (Sāy.) generator, parent; (*as*) or *janar,* ind. (before soft letters generally *janar*), N. of one of the seven worlds or divisions of the universe; see *jana* and *jana-loka.* — *Jano-loka, as,* m. the world described above.

Jani, is, or *janī,* f. a woman, wife, mother; any female animal, (in the Veda perhaps metaphorically = the fingers, e. g. *janibhiḥ samiddha,* kindled by the fingers); the wife of a son or brother's son; birth, production; birthplace; a kind of fragrant plant; [cf. Hib. *gean,* 'a woman;' Goth. *qvêns, qveins;* Eng. *queen.*] — *Jani-kāma, as, ā, am,* Ved. wishing for a wife. — 1. *jani-tva* or *jani-tvana, am,* n. the state of a wife, wedlock, conjugal state. — *Jani-dā, ās, ās, am,* Ved. giving a wife. — *Jani-nīlikā,* f., N. of a plant, = *mahā-nīlī.* — *Jani-mat* or *jani-vat, ān, atī, at,* Ved. having a wife, relating to women.

Janika, as, ā, am, producing, generating.

Janita, as, ā, am, engendered, begotten; produced, occasioned; occurring. — *Janita-svana, as, ā, am,* making a noise, sounding. — *Janitodyama* (°*ta-ud*°), *as, ā, am,* making exertion, energetic.

Janitavya, as, ā, am, to be born or produced.

Janitṛi, tā, m. a father, progenitor; (*trī*), f. a mother; [cf. Lat. *genitor;* Gr. γενέτωρ, γενετήρ; Hib. *genteoir,* 'a begetter, sower, planter;' Lat. *genitrix;* Gr. γενέτειρα.]

Janitra, am, n., Ved. a birthplace, place of origin, home; origin, generative or procreative matter; N. of a Sāman; (*āṇi*), n. pl. parents, relatives.

2. *janitva, as, ā, am,*=*janitavya*, to be born or produced; (*as*), m. father; (*ā*), f. mother; (*au*), m. du. father and mother, parents.

Janiman, a, n. (said to be also m.), Ved. birth, generation, engenderment, production; offspring, descendants; a creature, being; gender, sex, genus, kind, race; [cf. Hib. *geineamhuin*, 'birth, conception.']

Janishṭha, as, ā, am, Ved. a superl. fr. *janitṛi*(?).

Janishya, as, ā, am, to be born or produced.

Janīna, as, ā, am, suitable for men.

Janīya, nom. P., Ved. *janīyati* or *janiyati*, to wish for a wife.

Janu, us, and *janū, ūs*, f. birth; [cf. *janus*.]

Janus, us, n. (Ved. Nom. m. *janūs*, Acc. *janusham*, Inst. *janushā*), birth, production, descent; nativity; birthplace; a creature, being; creation; genus, class, kind; *janushā*, ind., Ved. by birth, from birth (e. g. *janushāndha*, blind from birth), by nature, naturally, originally, essentially, necessarily, &c.

Jantu, us, m. a creature, a living being, man, person; people, mankind; any animal, (usually beings of the lowest organization, such as worms, insects, &c.); N. of a son of Somaka; [cf. *kshiti-jantu, kshudra-j°, jala-j°*.]—*Jantu-kambu, u*, n. any animal living in a shell, as a snail; a snail's shell. —*Jantu-ghna, as, ī, am*, killing worms; N. of several vermifuge plants; (*as*), m. the citron; (*ī*), f., N. of a plant,=*viḍanga*; (*am*), n.=*viḍanga*; Asa Fœtida.—*Jantu-nāśana, as, ī, am*, destroying worms; (*am*), n. Asa Fœtida.—*Jantu-pādapa, as*, m., N. of a tree,=*kośāmra*.—*Jantu-phala, as*, m. the glomerous fig-tree, Ficus Glomerata; [cf. *udumbara*.]—*Jantu-mat, ān, atī, at*, containing worms or insects.—*Janta-mārin, ī*, m. or (*ī*), f. 'destroying worms,' the citron.—*Jantu-hantrī*, f., N. of a vermifuge,=*viḍanga*.

Jantuka, as, m., N. of a man; (*ās*), m. pl. his descendants; (*ā*), f. lac, gum; a kind of Asa Fœtida; [cf. *jatukā*.]

Jantulā, f. the plant Saccharum Spontaneum.

Jantva, as, ā, am, Ved. to be born or produced.

Janma, am, n.=*janman*, birth.

Janman, a, n. birth, production, origin, (in comp.) born from (e. g. *śūdra-janman*, born from a Sūdra); existence, life (e. g. *dṛishṭādṛishṭa-janman*, present and future life); nativity; birthplace, home; a progenitor, father; natal star; (in astrology) N. of the first mansion or Nakshatra; a creature, being; people; the people of a household, kind, race (e. g. *ubhe janmanī* or *ubhayam janma*, both races or both kinds of living beings, i. e. gods and men or men and animals); nature, quality, custom, manner (e. g. *pratnena janmanā*, according to ancient custom); =*udaka*, water (?); [cf. *janiman, agra-janman, antya-j°, kaśmīra-j°, kāśmīra-j°, dvi-j°*, &c.; cf. also Lat. *ger-men*; Hib. *geanamhain*, 'engendering.'] —*Janma-kāla, as*, m. time or hour of birth. —*Janma-kīla, as*, m. 'pillar or stay of birth,' an epithet of Vishṇu.—*Janma-kṛit, t*, m. a progenitor, a father.—*Janma-kshetra, am*, n. birthplace. —*Janma-ćintāmaṇi, is*, m. title of a work on nativities.—*Janma-jyeshṭha, as, ā, am*, the eldest by birth, the first-born.—*Janma-tithi, is*, m. the lunar day on which a birth occurs, birthday.—*Janma-da, as*, m. 'a birth-giver,' a father, progenitor. —*Janma-dina, am*, n. or *janma-divasa, as*, m. a birthday.—*Janma-nakshatra, am*, n. the natal star, the constellation under which a person is born; [cf. *janma-rāśi* and *janmarksha*.]—*Janma-nāman, a*, n. the name received at birth (i. e. on the twelfth day after).—*Janma-pa, as*, m. the regent of a planet under which a person is born.—*Janma-pattra, am*, n. or *janma-pattrikā*, f. a horoscope, the paper or scroll on which are recorded the year, lunar day, configuration, and relative position of the planets &c., of the birth of a particular individual, a table of his fortunes throughout life.—*Janma-pādapa, as*, m. the tree under which a person is born, a family-tree.—*Janma-pratishṭhā*, f. birthplace; a mother.—*Janma-pradīpa, as*, m., N. of a work by Vi-budha.—*Janma-prabhṛiti*, ind. ever since birth.—*Janma-bhāj, k*, m. a creature, a living being (possessing birth).—*Janma-bhāshā*, f. mother-tongue. —*Janma-bhūmi, is*, f. birthplace, native country. —*Janma-bhṛit, t, t, t*, possessing birth, enjoying life.—*Janma-yoga, as*, m. a horoscope.—*Janma-rāśi, is*, m. or *janma-lagna, am*, n. the sign of the zodiac under which a person is born.—*Janma-rogin, ī, iṇī, i*, sickly from birth.—*Janmarksha* (°*ma-ṛik*°), *am*, n. the constellation under which a person is born; N. of the first Nakshatra.—*Janma-vat, ān, atī, at*, possessing birth, born, mortal, living. —*Janma-vartman, a*, n. 'the path of birth,' the vulva.—*Janma-vasudhā*, f. native country, home. —*Janma-vailakshaṇya, am*, n. acting in a manner contrary to or unbecoming one's birth.—*Janma-śayyā*, f. the bed on which a person is born.—*Janma-śodhana, am*, n. discharging the obligations derived from birth.—*Janma-sāphalya, am*, n. attainment of the object or end of existence.—*Janma-sthāna, am*, n. birthplace, native land, home; the womb.—*Janmādhipa* (°*ma-adh*°), *as*, m. lord of birth, an epithet of Siva; the regent of a constellation under which a person is born; [cf. *janma-pa*.] —*Janmāntara* (°*ma-an*°), *am*, n. another birth, another life; the preceding life; the future life; regeneration; the other world.—*Janmāntara-kṛita, as, ā, am*, committed in another birth.—*Janmāntarīya, as, ā, am*, belonging to or done in another life.—*Janmāndha* (°*ma-un*°), *as, ā, am*, blind from birth, born blind.—*Janmāshṭamī* (°*ma-ash*°), f. the birthday of Kṛishṇa, the eighth day in the dark half of the month Srāvaṇa or Bhādra, on which Kṛishṇa was born.—*Janmāspada* (°*ma-ās*°), *am*, n. birthplace; [cf. *bhavāspada*.]—*Janmeśa* (°*ma-īśa*), *as*, m. the regent of a constellation under which any one is born; [cf. *janma-pa*.]

Janmin, ī, m. a creature, a living being, a man, an animal.

Janmejaya. See *janam-ejaya* under *jana*.

Janya, as, ā, am, to be born or produced, producible; born, produced; (often at the end of a comp.) born from, arising or produced from, occasioned by; generating; (*as*), m. a father; (*am*), n. the body; a portent occurring at birth; (*as, ā, am*), belonging to a race or family; national; belonging to the same country; vulgar, common, belonging to or relating to men or to the people, fit for men; (*as*), m. the friend or attendant or companion of a bridegroom; a common man; (*ā*), f. the friend of a mother; the relation or companion of a bride, a bridesmaid; pleasure, happiness; affection; (*am*), n. people; a community, nation; fighting, war, combat; a market, a fair; rumour, report; censure, abuse.—*Janya-tā*, f. the state of anything that is to be born or produced.

Janyu, us, m. birth; a creature, an animal, a living and sentient being; fire; an epithet of Brahmā; N. of one of the seven sages of the fourth Manvantara.

Jāta, as, ā, am, born &c. See p. 344.

Jāyamāna, as, ā, am, being born, coming into life.

जनकरी *janakarī*, f. or *janakārin, ī*, m. a red substance called lac. See *alakta*.

जनमेजय *janam-ejaya*. See *jana*, p. 337.

जनान्तिक *janāntika*. See *jana*, p. 337.

जन्तु *jantu, janman*. See col. 1.

जप् *jap*, cl. 1. P. *japati, jajāpa, japishyati, ajapīt* and *ajāpīt, japitum*, to utter in a low voice or under-tone, to mutter, whisper, repeat internally, talk to one's self; to mutter prayers or incantations, whisper magical spells or charms; to pray to any one in a low voice (e. g. *Sivo japyate*, Siva is addressed with muttered prayers); to invoke or call upon in a low voice: Caus. *jāpayati, -yitum, ajījapat*: Desid. *jijapishati*: Intens. *jañjapyate, jañjapīti*; [cf. *jalp*.]

Japa, as, ā, am, muttering, whispering, uttering in a low voice [cf. *karṇe-japa*]; (*as*), m. muttering prayers, repeating in a murmuring tone passages from scripture, charms, names of a deity, &c.; counting silently the beads of a rosary, &c.; a muttered prayer or spell; [cf. *jāpa*.]—*Japa-tā*, f. the state of a mutterer or of one who mutters prayers.—*Japa-parāyaṇa, as, ā, am*, devoted to repetition of prayers, engaged in muttering prayers.—*Japa-mālā*, f. a rosary used for counting muttered prayers.—*Japa-yajña, as*, m. muttering prayers as a religious rite or sacrifice.—*Japa-homa, as*, m. a sacrifice which consists in muttering prayers.

Japat, an, antī, at, muttering prayers in a low tone.

Japana, am, n. the muttering or whispering of prayers or spells.

Japanīya, as, ā, am, to be uttered in a low voice, to be whispered, to be muttered or repeated inaudibly, to be meditated on.

Japita, as, ā, am, muttered, whispered.

Japitvā, ind. having muttered or repeated in a low tone.

Japin, ī, inī, i, uttering prayers in a low voice, muttering.

Japtavya, as, ā, am, to be muttered or whispered.

Japtvā, ind. having muttered or repeated inaudibly.

Japya, as, ā, am, to be repeated in an undertone, to be muttered or whispered; (*am, as*), n. m. a prayer to be uttered in a low voice, a muttered prayer; [cf. *jāpya, kiñ-japya, dhyāna-japya*.] —*Japyeśvara-tīrtha* (°*ya-īś*°), *am*, n., N. of a Tīrtha.

Japyaka, as, m., N. of a man.

जपा *japā*, f. the China rose, either the flower or plant; [cf. *javā*.]

जपिल *japila, as* or *am*, m. or n.(?), N. of a place.

जबारु *jabāru, us, us, u* (fr. *java?*), Ved. hastening, speedy.

जबाल *jabāla, as*, m., N. of a man; (*ā*), f., N. of a woman.

जभ् 1. *jabh* or *jambh*, cl. 1. A. *jabhate* or *jambhate*, &c., to snap at, seize with the mouth: Caus. P. *jambhayati, -yitum*, to crush, destroy: Intens. *jañjabhyate, jañjabhīti*, to open the jaws wide, snap at.

Jabdhṛi, dhā, dhrī, dhṛi, snatching at, seizing with the mouth.

Jambha, as, m. the jaws (generally used in plur.); the mouth, a tooth, an eye-tooth, tusk; one who crushes or devours, as a demon; N. of several demons; a leader of the demons in the war against the gods under Indra; N. of a son of Pra-hrāda; of a son of Hiraṇya-kaśipu; N. of the father-in-law of Hiraṇya-kaśipu; N. of the father of Sunda; the citron tree, =*jambhīra, jambhala, jambīra*; eating, food; biting asunder, opening by biting, explanation, interpretation; a quiver; a part, a portion; (*ā*), f. opening of the mouth; [cf. *antar-jambha, ka-j°, tapur-j°, tigma-j°, tṛishṭa-j°*, &c.; cf. also Gr. γαμφηλαί.] —*Jambha-kuṇḍa, am*, n., N. of a Tīrtha.—*Jambha-dvish, ṭ*, m. the enemy of Jambha, an epithet of Indra.—*Jambha-bhedin, ī*, m. the destroyer of Jambha, a N. of Indra.—*Jambha-suta, as, ā, am*, Ved. pressed with the jaws, chewed.—*Jambhāri* (°*bha-ari*), *is*, m. 'the enemy of Jambha,' Indra; Indra's thunderbolt; fire.

Jambhaka, as, ā, am, crushing, devouring; killing, destroying; biting asunder; explaining, interpreting; opening, expanding; yawning; (*as*), m., N. of a demon or of a despised tribe of men; N. of several evil spirits supposed to reside in various magical weapons; N. of a verse addressed to them; N. of a demon conquered by Kṛishṇa; N. of an attendant of Siva; a lime or citron; (*ā*), f. opening the mouth.

Jambhan=*jambha* in *tṛiṇa-jambhan*, &c.

1. *jambhana, as, ī, am*, Ved. crushing, destroying; one who crushes.

Jambhya, as, m., Ved. an incisor (tooth) or perhaps a grinder.

जभ् 2. *jabh* or *jambh*, cl. 1. P. *jabhati* or *jambhati*, a various reading for *yabh*, q.v. 2. *jambhana, am*, n. sexual intercourse.

जभ्य *jabhya, as*, m., Ved. a species of animal destructive to grain.

जम् 1. *jam*, cl. 1. P. *jamati, jajāma, jamitum*, to eat, consume; to go (?); to blaze (?); [cf. Hib. *diamanu*, 'food, sustenance;' *gion*, 'the mouth:' Old Germ. *gouma, kouma*, 'food;' *gaumo*, 'the palate:' Mod. Germ. *Gaumen.*]

Jamat, an, antī, at, Ved. blazing. — *Jamad-agni, is*, m., N. of a Ṛishi often mentioned together with Viśvā-mitra as an adversary of Vasishṭha, and according to some a descendant of Bhṛigu; in epic poetry a son of Bhārgava Ṛićīka and father of Paraśu-rāma.

Jamana, am, n. eating; food, victuals.

जम् 2. *jam*, Ved. (used in Inst. *jmā* and Abl. Gen. *jmas*), the earth; *jmā*, on earth; [cf. *gam* and *ksham.*]

जमज *jama-ja, as, ā, am*, = *yama-ja*, q. v.

जमदग्नि *jamad-agni*. See *jamat* above.

जम्पती *jampatī* (fr. *dampatī?*, but according to some *jam* is fr. *jāyā;* cf. Hib. *gamh;* Gr. *γάμος?*), m. du. wife and husband.

जम्बाल *jambāla, as, am*, m. n. mud, clay; an aquatic plant, Vallisneria; (*as*), m. a fragrant plant, Pandanus Odoratissimus.

Jambālinī, f. a river.

जम्बिर *jambira, as*, m. = *jambīra*, the citron tree.

Jambīra, as, m. the citron tree or common lime; a plant called by some a sort of basil with small leaves, a kind of Ocimum, = *maruvaka* or *prastha-pushpa;* (*am*), n. a citron; [cf. *jambhīra, jambha, jambhala.*]

Jambīraka, as, m. a kind of Ocimum.

जम्बु *jambu, us*, or *jambū, ūs*, f. (said to be fr. rt. 1. *jam*), a fruit tree, the rose apple, Eugenia Jambolana, or another species of Eugenia; (*ūs, u*), f. n. its fruit; (*us, u*), m. n., N. of a Dvīpa [cf. *jambu-dvīpa*]; N. of a fabulous river, said to flow from the mountain Meru and to be formed by the juice of the fruits of an immense Jambu tree on that mountain; [cf. *āḍhaka-jambu, kāka-j°, goraksha-j°.*] — *Jambu-dvīpa* or *jambū-dvīpa, as*, m., N. of one of the seven continents or rather large islands surrounding the mountain Meru; it is so named either from the Jambu trees abounding in it, or from an enormous Jambu tree on Mount Meru visible like a standard to the whole continent, and implies (according to the Purāṇas) the central division of the world, or the known world, including India; with Buddhists it is confined to India; with Jainas it is one of the five divisions of India. — *Jambu-dhvaja, as*, m. another N. for Jambu-dvīpa ('having the Jambu tree as its standard'); N. of a Nāga. — *Jambu-parvata, as*, m. another N. for Jambu-dvīpa. — *Jambu-prastha, as*, m., N. of a town. — *Jambu-mat, ān*, m. a mountain; a monkey; (*tī*), f. an Apsaras or heavenly nymph; [cf. *jāmbavat* and *jambu-vat.*] — *Jambu-māla, as*, m., N. of a man. — *Jambu-mālin, ī*, m., N. of a Rakshas. — *Jambu-rudra, as*, m., N. of a serpent-king. — *Jambu-vana-ja, am*, n. the white flower of the China rose. — *Jambu-sara, as*, m., N. of a town in Gurjara (Jumbooseer between Cambay and Baroch). — *Jambū-khaṇḍa, as, am*, m. n. another N. for Jambu-dvīpa. — *Jambūkhaṇḍa-vinirmāṇa-parvan, a*, n. the first six Adhyāyas of the sixth book of the Mahā-bhārata. — *Jambūnada-prabha, as*, m., N. of a future Buddha. — *Jambū-nadī*, f., N. of one of the seven arms of the heavenly Gaṅgā. — *Jambū-mārga, as, am*, m. n., N. of a Tīrtha (the way leading to the sacred Jambu on Meru). — *Jambū-svāmin, ī*, m., N. of the last Arhat of the Jainas. — *Jambv-oshṭha* = *jāmbavaushṭha*, q. v.

जम्बुक *jambuka, as*, m. a jackal; a low man; N. of one of the attendants of Skanda; an epithet of Varuṇa; the plant Eugenia (commonly called *golāpa jāma*); or perhaps a kind of Syonāka; (*ā*), f. a female jackal; [cf. *jambūka.*] — *Jambu-keśvara-tīrtha* (°*ka-īś*°), *am*, n., N. of a Tīrtha.

Jambūka, as, m. a jackal; a low man; N. of one of the attendants of Skanda; an epithet of Varuṇa; (*ā*), f. a kind of grape without stones, = *kākalī-drākshā;* [cf. *jambuka* and *gridhra-jambūka.*]

जम्बुल *jambula, as*, m. a kind of disease of the outer ear; the plant Eugenia Jambolana [cf. *jambu*]; another plant, Pandanus Odoratissimus; [cf. *ketaka;* cf. also *jambūla.*]

Jambūla, as, m. the plant Pandanus Odoratissimus; the plant Eugenia Jambolana [cf. *jambū*]; (*am*), n. jests addressed to the bridegroom by his female relatives and friends; [cf. the following.] — *Jambūla-mālikā*, f. a garland of Jambūla flowers; brightness of countenance in a bride and bridegroom; jesting compliments addressed to the bride and bridegroom by the female relatives of the bridegroom.

जम्भ *jambha*. See under 1. *jabh*, p. 338.

जम्भन *jambhana*. See under 1. and 2. *jabh*.

जम्भर *jambhara, as*, m. the lime or citron tree; [cf. the following.]

Jambhala, as, m. the lime or citron tree [cf. *jambīra*]; N. of a Jina or deified Jaina saint; N. of a man; (*ā*), f. a female Rākshasī, by meditating on whom women become pregnant. — *Jambhala-datta, as*, m., N. of the supposed author of the Vetāla-pañća-viṇśati.

Jambhin, ī, m. the lime or citron tree.

Jambhīra, as, m. the lime or citron tree, apparently of more than one species; a plant considered to be a kind of basil with small leaves; [cf. *jambīra.*]

जम्भलिका *jambhalikā*, f. a kind of song. (*Jambhālikā* appears to be incorrect.)

जम्व *jamva, as*, m. mud, mire.

जय *jaya, as, ā, am* (fr. rt. *ji*), conquering, winning, (used at the end of comp.; cf. *kṛitañ-jaya, dhanañ-j°, purañ-j°*, &c.); (*as*), m. conquest, victory, triumph, winning, being victorious (in battle, in playing with dice or in a lawsuit; *indriyāṇām jayaḥ*, victory over or restraint of the senses; *ātma-jaya*, self-restraint; *prāṇa-jaya*, victory over life, i. e. resigning it willingly; *rug-jaya*, healing of a disease); a verse or formula causing victory; the plant Premna Spinosa or Longifolia; a yellow variety of Phaseolus Mungo; N. of the third year of the sixth lustrum of the cycle of Jupiter; an epithet of the sun; a class of deities (pl.); N. of a son of Indra; of an attendant of Vishṇu; N. of a Nāga; of a Dānava; of a Ṛishi under the tenth Manu; of a son of Vatsara by Svar-vīthi; of a son of Viśvā-mitra; of a son of Purū-ravas and Urvaśī; N. of an ancient king; of the eleventh Ćakra-vartin in Bhārata; of a hero on the side of the Pāṇḍus; a N. assumed by Yudhi-shṭhira at the court of king Virāṭa; N. of several other persons; (*ā*), f., N. of several plants, viz. = *jayantī*, Sesbania Ægyptiaca, Premna Spinosa or Longifolia, Terminalia Chebula; also = *nīla-dūrvā, śāntā*, and *vi-jayā;* the third, eighth, or thirteenth lunar days of either half-month; a N. of Durgā; N. of a daughter of Daksha; of a wife of Śiva; of a confidential female attendant of Durgā and wife of Pushpa-danta; of a Buddhist deity; of the mother of the twelfth Arhat of the present Avasarpiṇī; of one of the seven kumārīs on the standard of Indra. — *Jaya-karaṇa, am*, n. obtaining a victory, conquering. — *Jaya-kāṅkshin, ī, iṇī, i*, desirous of victory. — *Jaya-kārin, ī, iṇī, i*, gaining a victory, victorious. — *Jaya-kṛit, t, t, t*, causing or granting victory. — *Jaya-kolāhala, as*, m. a shout of victory; a kind of dice; [cf. *jaya-putraka.*] — *Jaya-kshetra, am*, n., N. of a place. — *Jaya-gata, as, ā, am*, conquering, victorious. — *Jaya-garva, as*, m. pride of conquest, exultation. — *Jaya-gupta, as*, m., N. of a poet. — *Jaya-ghosha, as*, m. or *jaya-ghoshaṇa, am* or *ā*, n. f. a shouting to proclaim victory, a cry of victory. — *Jaya-ćandra, as*, m., N. of the author of the work Gośriṅga-svayambhū-ćaitya-bhaṭṭārakod-deśa; N. of a king of Gauḍa; of a king of Kānyakubja. — *Jaya-ćaryā*, f. a work on omens by Nara-hari. — *Jaya-ḍhakkā*, f. a large kettle-drum beaten as a sign of victory. — *Jaya-tīrtha, as*, m., N. of a scholiast. — *Jaya-da, as, ā, am*, granting victory; (*ā*), f., N. of a tutelary deity in the family of Vāma-deva. — *Jaya-datta, as*, m., N. of the son of Indra; of a Bodhi-sattva; of a certain king; of a minister of king Jayā-pīḍa; of a physician. — *Jaya-deva, as*, m., N. of the author of the Gīta-govinda; also of the Prasanna-rāghava-nāṭaka; also of the grammar entitled Īshat-tantra. — *Jaya-devaka, as*, m. = *jaya-deva*, N. of a Muhūrta. — *Jaya-dharman, ā*, m., N. of a hero on the side of the Kurus. — *Jaya-dhvaja, as*, m., N. of a son of Kārtavīrya Arjuna and father of Tāla-jaṅgha. — *Jaya-dhvani, is*, m. a shout or cry of victory. — *Jaya-nārāyaṇa, as*, m., N. of the author of the poem Kāśī-khaṇḍa. — *Jaya-nṛisiṇha, as*, m., N. of a deity. — *Jaya-pattra, am*, n. a written account of a victory, record of victory. — *Jaya-pāla, as*, m. 'guardian of victory,' an epithet of Brahmā, also of Vishṇu; a king; N. of several kings; the plant Croton Jamalgota. — *Jaya-putraka, as*, m. a kind of dice; [cf. *jaya-kolāhala* and *jatu-putraka.*] — *Jaya-pura, am*, n. 'town of victory,' N. of a fortress in Kaśmīra; also of a small state in Marwur. — *Jaya-prasthāna, am*, n. march to victory. — *Jaya-priya, as*, m., N. of a hero on the side of the Pāṇḍavas; (*ā*), f., N. of one of the Mātṛis in attendance on Skanda. — *Jaya-maṅgala, as*, m. a royal elephant; a remedy for fever, a febrifuge; N. of a commentator on the Bhaṭṭi-kāvya; (*ā*), f., N. of a commentary on the Bhaṭṭi-kāvya composed by Jaya-maṅgala; (*am*), n. a cheer of victory; [cf. *jayāśis.*] — *Jaya-mati, is*, m., N. of a Bodhi-sattva. — *Jaya-malī*, f., N. of several women; [cf. *jaya-vat.*] — *Jaya-mādhava, as*, m., N. of a poet. — *Jaya-yajña, as*, m. the Aśva-medha or sacrifice of a horse as a mark of dominion. — *Jaya-rāja, as*, m., N. of several men. — *Jaya-rāta, as*, m., N. of a warrior who took the side of the Kuru princes. — *Jaya-rāma, as*, m., N. of the author of the Nyāya-siddhānta-mālā; N. of several other men. — *Jaya-lakshmī, īs*, f. victory, the goddess of victory; N. of a woman. — *Jaya-lekha, as*, m. record of victory; [cf. *jaya-pattra.*] — *Jaya-vat, ān, atī, at*, victorious, triumphant; [cf. *jaya-matī* and *jayā-vatī.*] — *Jaya-vardhana, as*, m., N. of a poet. — *Jaya-varma-deva, as*, m., N. of a king. — *Jaya-vaha, as, ā, am*, conferring victory, victorious. — *Jaya-vādya, am*, n. a drum or other instrument sounded to proclaim victory. — *Jaya-vārāha-tīrtha, am*, n., N. of a Tīrtha. — *Jaya-vāhinī*, f., N. of the wife of Indra. — *Jaya-śabda, as*, m. a shout or song of victory, or the exclamation Jaya, Jaya repeated like the *Io* of the Greeks as in *Jaya-jaya deva hare*, &c. — *Jaya-śarman, ā*, m., N. of a poet. — *Jaya-śīla, as, ā, am*, victorious, triumphant. — *Jaya-śriṅga, am*, n. a horn blown to announce a victory. — *Jaya-śrī, īs*, f. victory, glory; the goddess of victory. — *Jaya-siṇha, as*, m., N. of several men; N. of a king of Kaśmīra; [cf. *jayā-siṇha.*] — *Jaya-sena, as*, m., N. of a king of Magadha; also of a son of Adīna or Ahīna; of a son of Sārvabhauma; N. of the father of the Āvantyau; also of the son of Mahendra-varman; N. of a Buddhist; (*ā*), f., N. of a female door-keeper; [cf. *jayat-sena.*] — *Jaya-skandha, as*, m., N. of a minister of king Yudhi-shṭhira. — *Jaya-stambha, as*, m. a trophy; a column erected to commemorate a victory. — *Jaya-svāmin, ī*, m. the lord of victory;

an epithet of Śiva; N. of a scholiast on the Chandoga-sūtras and of the author of a commentary on the Āśvalāyana-Brāhmaṇa. — *Jayasvāmi-pura, am,* n., N. of a town founded by Jushka. — *Jayā-kara* (°*ya-āk*°), *as,* m. 'a mine of victory,' N. of a man. — *Jayāditya* (°*ya-ād*°), *as,* m., N. of a king; N. of the author of the Kāśikā-vṛitti. — *Jayā-devī,* f., N. of a Buddhist deity [cf. *jayā*]; N. of a woman. — *Jayānanda* (°*ya-ān*°), *as,* m., N. of a man. — *Jayānanda-vāra, as,* m., N. of a man. — *Jayānīka* (°*ya-ān*°), *as,* m., N. of a warrior on the side of the Pāṇḍavas. — *Jayāntarāya* (°*ya-an*°), *as,* m. an impediment or hindrance to victory. — *Jayāpīḍa* (°*ya-āp*°), *as,* m., N. of a king of Kaśmīra. — *Jayā-bhaṭṭārikā,* f., N. of a place. — *Jayārava* (°*ya-ār*°), *as,* m. song of victory; [cf. *jaya-śabda.*] — *Jayāraghosha* (°*ya-av*°), *as,* m. proclamation of victory, cheering. — *Jayā-vatī,* f., N. of one of the Mātṛis attending on Skanda; [cf. *jaya-matī* and *jaya-vat.*] — *Jayāvaha* (°*ya-āv*°), *as, ā, am,* conferring victory, victorious; (*ā*), f. a kind of Croton; [cf. *bhadra-dantikā.*] — *Jayāśis* (°*ya-āś*°), *īs,* f. a prayer for victory; congratulations after a victory; cheer of victory. — *Jayāśraya* (°*ya-āś*°), *as, ā, am,* 'the asylum of victory,' favoured by victory; (*ā*), f. a kind of grass; [cf. *jaraḍī.*] — *Jayāśva* (°*ya-aś*°), *as,* m., N. of a hero on the side of the Pāṇḍavas. — *Jayā-sinha, as,* m., N. of a man. — *Jayāhvā* (°*ya-āh*°), f. = *jayāvahā,* q. v. — *Jayendra* (°*ya-in*°), *as,* m., N. of a king of Kaśmīra; also of another person; a vihāra built by the latter is called Jayendra-vihāra. — *Jayeśvara* (°*ya-īś*°), *as,* m., N. of a sanctuary built by Jayā-devī. — *Jayoddhura* (°*ya-ud*°), *as, ā, am,* exulting in victory. — *Jayollāsa-nidhi* (°*ya-ul*°), *is,* m. title of a work.

Jayaka, as, ā, am, victorious; (*as*), m., N. of a man.

Jayat, an, antī, at, conquering, defeating; excelling. — *Jayat-sena, as,* m., N. of a king of Magadha; of a son of Sārvabhauma; of Nadīna; a N. assumed by the fourth (?) son of Pāṇḍu; (*ā*), f., N. of one of the Mātṛis attending on Skanda; [cf. *jaya-sena.*] — *Jayad-bala, as,* m. a N. assumed by one of the youngest Pāṇḍu princes at the court of king Virāṭa. — *Jayad-ratha, as,* m., N. of a king of the Sindhus and Sauvīras fighting on the side of the Kuru princes; a son of Vṛihan-manas; a son of Vṛihat-karman; of Vṛihat-kāya; of the tenth Manu.

Jayana, am, n. conquering, subduing; armour for cavalry, elephants, &c.; (*ī*), f., N. of a daughter of Indra; [cf. *jayantī.*] — *Jayana-yuj, k, k, k,* caparisoned (as a war horse), victorious.

Jayanta, as, m., N. of a son of Indra; an epithet of Śiva; N. of a Rudra; N. of a son of Dharma by Marutvatī (he was a part of Vāsudeva and = *upendra*); a class of deities (with Jainas) forming a subdivision of the Anuttaras; the moon; the assumed N. of Bhīma at the court of king Virāṭa; N. of a minister of Daśa-ratha; also of a Gandharva, the father of Vikramāditya; of a king of Gauḍa; of a Brāhman of Kaśmīra; of an author of a grammatical work; N. of a mountain; (*ī*), f. a flag, a banner; the plant Sesbania Ægyptiaca, = *jīvantī;* blades of barley planted at the commencement of the Daśaharā and gathered at its close; a particular combination in astronomy, or the rising of the asterism Rohiṇī at midnight, on the eighth of the dark half of Śrāvaṇa, or in fact on the birthday of Kṛishṇa, which is then particularly sacred; an epithet of Durgā; of Dākshāyaṇī (the wife of Śiva) in Hastinā-pura; N. of the tutelary deity of Vasūdreka; N. of the daughter of Indra; N. of the wife of Ṛishabha received by him from Indra; N. of a river; N. of a country. — *Jayanta-pattra, am,* n. 'leaf of victory or triumph;' (in law) the sealed and written award of the judge in favour of either party; (in historical tradition) the label on the forehead of a horse turned loose for the Aśva-medha sacrifice. — *Jayanta-pura, am,* n., N. of a town. — *Jayanta-svāmin, ī,* m., N. of the author of a small treatise on the Vedic accent. — *Jayantī-purī,* f., N. of a town.

Jayitṛi, tā, trī, tṛi, a victor, conqueror, victorious.

Jayin, ī, inī, i, conquering, victorious, a conqueror; gaining the victory, winning in a suit at law; granting victory.

Jayishṇu, us, us, u, habitually victorious, victorious.

Jayus, us, us, us, Ved. victorious.

Jayya, as, ā, am, to be conquered or gained, conquerable, vulnerable.

जर *jara, as, ā, am* (fr. rt. 1. *jṛī*), becoming old or worn out, old; wearing out; causing old age, producing decay, consuming; (*as*), m. wearing out, wasting; (*ā*), f. the becoming old, old age; old age personified as a daughter of Death; decrepitude, the general debility consequent upon old age; digestion; a kind of date tree, = *kshīrikā;* N. of a Rākshasī worshipped for having united the two halves into which Jarā-sandha (q. v.) was divided at his birth; [cf. *vi-jara.*] — *Jarātura* (°*rā-āt*°), *as, ā, am,* infirm, decrepit, debilitated, old. — *Jarā-pariṇata, as, ā, am,* stooping, bent down with age or infirmity. — *Jarā-pushṭa, as,* m. = *jarā-sandha.* — *Jarā-bhīru, us,* m. love or the deity Kāma ('afraid of old age'). — *Jarā-mṛityu, ū,* m. du. old age and death; (*us, us, u*), one who dies from old age. — *Jarā-vat, ān, atī, at,* aged, old. — *Jarārasthā* (°*rā-av*°), f. state of old age, decrepitude. — *Jarā-sandha, as,* m., N. of a celebrated king and warrior, sovereign of Magadha and Cedi, son of Bṛihad-ratha, father-in-law to Kansa, and enemy of Kṛishṇa; he was slain in single combat by Bhīma; (according to a legend, he was born divided in two halves, which were put together by the Rākshasī Jarā, q. v.; he is also identified with the Dānava Vipracitti, and mentioned among the hundred sons of Dhṛita-rāshṭra.) — *Jarāsandha-jit, t,* m. 'conqueror of Jarā-sandha,' N. of Bhīma-sena, the second of the Pāṇḍu princes.

Jaraṭha, as, ā, am, old, decayed, infirm; bent, bowed down, drooping; hard, solid; hard-hearted, harsh, cruel; pale, yellowish-white (the colour of old leaves); (*as*), m. decrepitude, old age; [cf. Germ. *hart;* Goth. *hardus.*]

Jaraṇa, as, ā, am, old, decayed, infirm; solvent, promoting digestion; (*as, am*), m. n. several medicinal plants or drugs used for promoting digestion, = *jīraka,* cumin-seed; *kṛishṇa-jīraka,* Nigella Indica; = *kāsa-marda* and = *kushṭhaushadhi;* Asa Fœtida; a sort of salt, Bit-lobon or Bit-lavana; (*ā*), f. old age; the plant Nigella Indica; (*am*), n. old age, becoming old and infirm; one of the ten ways in which an eclipse is supposed to end. — *Jaraṇa-druma, as,* m. the tree Vatica Robusta.

1. *jaraṇā.* See under *jaraṇa* above.

Jaraṇḍa, as, ā, am, decayed, old.

Jaraṇyā, f., Ved. decrepitude.

Jarat, an, antī (or *atī ?*), *at,* old, ancient, advanced in years, infirm, decayed; (*an*), m. an old man; (*tī*), f. an old woman; [cf. Gr. γέρων; Hib. *gearait,* 'a saint, a holy man;' Germ. *krank ?*]. — *Jarat-kāru, us, us,* m. f., N. of an ancient Ṛishi of the family of Yāyāvara, and of his wife who was a sister of the serpent-prince Vāsuki, both being the parents of Āstīka; (*us*), m. the Vyāsa of the twenty-seventh Dvāpara. — *Jaratkāru-priyā,* f. the wife of Jarat-kāru exercising a peculiar power over serpents, see the preceding. — *Jarad-ashṭi, is, is, i,* Ved. reaching to a great age, very old; (*is*), f. longevity. — *Jarad-gava, as,* m. an old bull or ox; N. of a vulture; (*ī*), f. an old cow; [cf. *go-jara.*] — *Jaradgava-vīthi, is,* f. 'the course of the old bull,' N. of a part of the moon's path occupied by the constellations Vi-śākhā, Anu-rādhā, and Jyeshṭhā. — *Jarad-yoshā,* f. an old woman. — *Jarad-vish, ṭ, ṭ, ṭ,* Ved. (Sāy.) seizing on and devouring dry (wood) or consuming water (applied to Agni).

Jaratikā, f. an old woman.

Jaratin, ī, m., N. of a man.

Jaranta, as, m. an old man; a buffalo.

Jarayitṛi, tā, trī, tṛi, consuming, devouring.

Jarayu, us, us, u, becoming old; [cf. *a-jarayu.*]

Jaras, ā, f. (only *jaras* before vowel-terminations, Gram. 171), the becoming old, decay, decrepitude, old age; (*ā*), m., N. of a son of Kṛishṇa by Turī; N. of the hunter who wounded Kṛishṇa; [cf. Gr. γῆρας.]

Jarasa at the end of an adv. comp. = *jaras;* [cf. *ā-jarasam.*]

Jarasāna, as, m. a man.

1. *jarā,* f. old age &c. See under *jara,* col. 2.

Jarāyaṇi, is, m. = *jarā-sandha.*

Jarāyu, us, us, u, withering, dying away; (*u*), n. the slough or cast-off skin of a serpent; the membrane which envelopes the fetus, the outer skin of the embryo or chorion, (the inner or amnion is called *ulva*); after-birth, secundines; (*us*), m., N. of a plant, = *agni-jāra;* also = *jaṭāyu;* (*us*), f., N. of one of the Mātṛis attending on Skanda; [cf. *jyotir-jarāyu* and *nir-jarāyu.*] — *Jarāyu-ja, as, ā, am,* born from the womb, viviparous, born alive.

Jarita, as, ā, am, old, decayed; (*ā*), f., N. of a Sārṅgikā (or kind of bird), the mother of four sons at once by the Ṛishi Manda-pāla in the form of a male Sārṅgaka. — *Jaritāri* (°*ta-ari*), *is,* m., N. of the eldest son of Manda-pāla by Jaritā.

Jarin, ī, iṇī, i, old, ancient, infirm, decayed; (*ī*), m. an old man.

Jariman, ā, m., Ved. old age; decrepitude, death from old age.

1. *jarūtha, am,* n. skinniness, flesh flaccid with old age; flesh.

Jarjara, as, ā, am, old, infirm, decrepit, decayed; torn or broken in pieces, split up into small particles, divided in parts or pieces, broken; perforated, wounded, hurt; dull, hollow (as the sound of a broken vessel); (*am*), n. Indra's banner or emblem; = *saivala,* an aquatic plant. — *Jarjara-tva, am,* n. the being old or decayed or perforated &c. — *Jarjarānanā* (°*ra-ān*°), f., N. of one of the Mātṛis attending on Skanda.

Jarjarita, as, ā, am, torn in pieces, worn out.

Jarjarīka, as, ā, am, old, decayed; ragged, perforated, full of holes.

Jarjarī-kṛita, as, ā, am, wounded, disabled.

Jarṇa, as, ā, am, old, decayed; (*as*), m. the (waning) moon; a tree.

जरडी *jaraḍī,* f. a kind of grass; [cf. *garmoṭikā, jayāśrayā, sunālā.*]

जरणा 2. *jaraṇā,* f. (fr. 3. *jṛī*), Ved. roaring, crackling, sounding; (Sāy.) invoking, praising; [cf. 1. *jaraṇa,* col. 2.]

Jaraṇi-prā, ās, ās, am, Ved. moving on with noise; (Sāy.) increasing the wealth of the praiser.

Jaraṇīya, as, ā, am, to be addressed with praise or invoked.

Jaraṇyu, us, us, u, Ved. invoking aloud; (Sāy.) desiring praise.

Jaramāṇa, as, m., N. of a man.

2. *jarā,* f., Ved. crackling, roaring; invoking, greeting; praise; [cf. 1. *jarā* above.] — *Jarā-bodha, as, ā, am,* Ved. attending to invocation or praise. — *Jarābodhīya, am,* n., N. of several Sāmans.

Jaritṛi, tā, m., Ved. an invoker, singer, praiser, worshipper.

2. *jarūtha, as,* m., Ved. one who roars or makes a noise; N. of a demon conquered by Agni; (Sāy.) speaking harshly or to be invoked.

जर्च् *jarć,* cl. 1. 6. P. *jarćati,* &c., to say, speak; to reprove, abuse, blame; to threaten.

जर्छ् *jarćh,* cl. 1. 6. P. *jarććhati,* &c., to say, speak; to blame; [cf. *ćarć.*]

जर्ज् *jarj,* cl. 1. 6. P. *jarjati,* &c., to say; to blame, reprove; to kill or hurt (?).

Jarjita, as, ā, am, torn to pieces, wounded; (perhaps a wrong form for *jarjarita.*)

जर्जर *jarjara.* See above.

जर्झ् *jarjh,* cl. 1. 6. P. *jarjhati,* to say or speak; to blame; to threaten; [cf. *jarć.*]

जर्त *jarta, as,* m. = *jartu,* q. v.

जर्तिक *jartika, ās,* m. pl. = *bāhīka.*

जर्तिल *jartila, as,* m. wild sesamum.

जर्तु *jartu, us,* m. (said to be fr. rt. *jan*), the vulva; an elephant.

जर्त्स् *jarts,* cl. 1. P. *jartsati,* &c., to say, speak; to blame, censure, abuse; to protect.

जर्भरि *jarbhari, is, is, i* (fr. rt. *bhṛi?*), Ved. supporting (?). According to Sāy. *jarbharī* = *bhartārau,* supporters (epithet of the Aśvins).

जर्य *jarya, as, ā, am* (fr. rt. 1. *jṛī*), becoming old; [cf. *a-jarya.*]

जर्वर *jarvara, as,* m., N. of a priest assisting at a sacrifice by which the serpent-race overcame death.

जर्हिल *jarhila, as,* m. wild sesamum; [cf. *jartila.*]

जल् *jal,* cl. 1. P. *jalati,* &c., to be rich or wealthy; to cover, hide, or veil; to cover as with a net, encompass; to be sharp; to be cold, stiff, dull, dumb; cl. 10. P. *jālayati, -yitum,* to cover; [cf. Lat. *galea.*]

1. *jala, as, ā, am* (said to be fr. the preceding rt.; perhaps connected with *gal;* cf. *jaḍa*), cold, stupid, apathetic, idiotic; (*as*), m., N. of a man with the patronymic Jātukarṇya; (*ā*), f., N. of a river; (*am*), n. water, any fluid; a kind of fragrant medicinal plant, = *hrīvera;* the embryo or uterus of a cow; frigidity (moral, mental, or physical); [cf. Lat. *gelu;* Goth. *kalds;* Lith. *szala, szattas;* Russ. *cholodnyi;* Hib. *gil.*] — *Jala-kaṇṭaka, as,* m. a crocodile; 'water-thorn,' the plant Trapa Bispinosa. — *Jala-kapi, is,* m. the Gangetic porpoise, Delphinus Gangeticus ('water-monkey'). — *Jala-kapota, as,* m. 'water-pigeon,' N. of a particular species of bird. — *Jala-kara, as, ī, am,* making or pouring forth water; (*as*), m. rent or tax derived from water for fisheries &c. — *Jala-karaṅka, as,* m. a shell, a conch; a cocoa-nut; a cloud; a wave; a lotus. — *Jala-kalka, as,* m. 'water-sediment,' mud, mire. — *Jala-kalmasha, as,* m. the poison produced at the churning of the ocean. — *Jala-kāka, as,* m. 'a water-crow,' the diver bird. — *Jala-kāṅksha, as,* m. 'desirous of water,' an elephant; [cf. *jalākāṅksha.*] — *Jala-kāṅkshin, ī, iṇī, i,* desirous of water, fond of water; (*ī*), m. an elephant. — *Jala-kānta, as,* m. the wind ('the water-lover'). — *Jala-kāntāra, as,* m. a N. of Varuṇa ('whose grove or garden is water'). — *Jala-kāmuka, as,* m., N. of a plant, = *kuṭumbinī.* — *Jala-kirāṭa, as,* m. (*kirāṭa* for *kirāta?*), a shark or (according to some) a large alligator. — *Jala-kukkuṭa, as,* m. a water-fowl or other water-bird; (*ī*), f. the black-headed gull; [cf. *gaṅgāćillī.*] — *Jala-kukkubha, as,* m. a species of aquatic bird, = *koyashṭi.* — *Jala-kuntala, as,* m. 'water-hair,' N. of an aquatic plant, Blyxa Octandra; [cf. *jala-keśa.*] — *Jala-kubjaka, as,* m., N. of an aquatic plant, Trapa Bispinosa. — *Jala-kūpī,* f. a spring, well; pond, pool; whirlpool. — *Jala-kūrma, as,* m. the Gangetic porpoise. — *Jala-kṛit, t, t, t,* causing rain. — *Jala-ketu, us,* m., N. of a particular comet. — *Jala-keli, is, is,* m. f. playing or gamboling in water, splashing one another with water. — *Jalakeli-varṇana, am,* n. title of the third chapter of Hari-nātha's poem Rāma-vilāsa-kāvya. — *Jala-keśa, as,* m. 'water-hair,' the plant Blyxa Octandra; [cf. *jala-kuntala.*] — *Jala-kriyā,* f. a funeral ceremony, offering libations, presenting water to the manes of the deceased. — *Jala-krīḍā,* f. sporting or gamboling in water, bathing for pleasure or amusement; [cf. *jala-keli.*] — *Jala-khaga, as,* m. an aquatic bird. — *Jala-gandha, as, ā, am,* making the water fragrant (?) or turbid (?). — *Jala-gandhebha, as,* m. 'a scented elephant frequenting water,' N. of a species of animal. — *Jala-garbha, as,* m., N. of a son of Jala-vāhana, = Ānanda in a former birth. — *Jala-gulma, as,* m. a turtle, tortoise; a quadrangular tank, a piece of water; a whirlpool. — *Jalaṅ-ga, as, ā, am,* aquatic, frequenting water, going in water; (*as*), m. the colocynth (*mahākāla*). — *Jalaṅ-gama, as,* m. a Cāṇḍāla, an outcast; (a various reading for *janaṅ-gama.*) — *Jala-ćatvara, am,* n. a square tank. — *Jala-ćara, as, ī, am,* going in water, aquatic, amphibious; (*as*), m. an aquatic animal. — *Jalaćara-jīva, as,* m. a fisherman; (*ās*), m. pl. the inhabitants of the east coast. — *Jalaćarājīva* (°*ra-āj*°), *as,* m. a fisherman. — *Jala-ćārin, ī, iṇī, i,* living in or near water, frequenting water; (*ī*), m. an aquatic animal, a fish. — *Jala-ja, as, ā, am,* produced or born in water, living or growing in water; coming from or peculiar to water; (*as*), m. an aquatic animal, a fish; sea-salt, = *lonāra,* a collective N. for several signs of the zodiac; (*ā*), f. a kind of plant, = *klītaka;* (*as, am*), m. n. a shell; the conch-shell used as a trumpet; (*am*), n. a pearl, a shell or other product of the sea; the lotus (Nelumbium); N. of several other plants, = *hijjala, śaivala, vānīra, kupīlu.* — *Jalaja-kusuma, am,* n. 'water-flower,' the lotus. — *Jalaja-kusuma-yoni, is,* m. 'born from a lotus-flower,' a N. of Brahmā. — *Jalaja-dravya, am,* n. a pearl, a shell or other product of the sea. — *Jala-jantu, us,* m. a fish or any marine or aquatic or amphibious animal. — *Jala-jantukā,* f. a leech. — *Jala-janman, a,* n. 'water-born,' the lotus (Nelumbium). — *Jalajājīva* (°*ja-āj*°), *as,* m. a fisherman; (*ās*), m. pl. the inhabitants of the eastern coast; [cf. *jalaćara-jīva.*] — *Jalajāsana* (°*ja-ās*°), *as,* m. a N. of Brahmā (sitting on the lotus). — *Jala-jihva, as,* m. a crocodile ('having a cold tongue?'). — *Jala-jīvin, ī,* m. a fisherman. — *Jala-ḍimba, as,* m. a bivalve shell. — *Jala-taraṅga, as,* m. a wave; a metal cup filled with water producing harmonic notes like a musical glass. — *Jala-tā,* f. the state of water. — *Jala-tāḍana, am,* n. beating water, any fruitless action. — *Jala-tāpika, as,* m. the Hilsa or sable fish, Clupanodon Ilisha (also called *jala-tāpin*); another kind of fish, commonly Caöuchhi, Cyprinus Cachius. — *Jala-tāla, as,* m. the Ilisha or Hilsa fish. — *Jala-tiktikā,* f. Boswellia Murifera. — *Jala-turaga, as,* m. 'water-horse,' hippopotamus (?). — *Jala-trā,* f. 'water-guard,' an umbrella. — *Jala-trāsa, as,* m. hydrophobia. — *Jala-trāsin, ī, inī, i,* having hydrophobia, hydrophobic. — *Jala-da, as, ā, am,* giving or pouring forth water; (*as*), m. a cloud; a fragrant grass, Cyperus Rotundus [cf. *mustaka*]; (*ās*), m. pl., N. of a school of the Atharva-veda; N. of a Varsha in Sāka-dvīpa. — *Jalada-kshaya, as,* m. disappearance of the clouds, autumn. — *Jalada-paṅkti, is,* f. a line or long succession of clouds. — *Jala-dardura, as,* m. a water-pipe, a kind of musical instrument. — *Jalada-saṃhati, is,* f. the gathering of clouds, cloudiness. — *Jaladāgama* (°*da-āg*°), *as,* m. the arrival or approach of clouds, the rainy season. — *Jala-dāna, am,* n. the giving of water. — *Jaladābha* (°*da-ābha*), *as, ā, am,* cloud-like, dark, black. — *Jaladāśana* (°*da-aś*°), *as,* m. the tree Shorea Robusta, = *śāla.* — *Jala-deva, am,* n., scil. *bha* or *nakshatra,* the constellation Ashāḍhā, having the water as its deity. — *Jala-devatā,* f. a water-goddess, naiad. — *Jala-dravya, am,* n. a pearl, a shell or other product of the sea; [cf. *jalaja-dravya.*] — *Jala-droṇī,* f. a bucket. — *Jala-dvīpa, as,* m., N. of an island. — *Jala-dhara, as, ā, am,* holding or carrying or having water; (*as*), m. a cloud; the ocean; a kind of grass, Cyperus Rotundus; the plant Dalbergia Ougeinensis; N. of a metre containing 4 × 32 syllabic instants. — *Jaladhara-garjita-ghosha-susvara-nakshatra-rāja-saṅkusumitābhijña* (°*ta-abh*°), *as,* m., N. of a Buddha (having a voice musical as the sound of the thunder of the clouds and conversant with the appearance of the regents of the Nakshatras). — *Jaladhara-mālā,* f. a row of clouds; a metre consisting of four lines of twelve syllables each. — *Jala-dhāra, as,* m., N. of a mountain; N. of a Varsha in Sāka-dvīpa; (*ā*), f. a stream of water. — *Jaladhi, is,* m. the ocean; a large number, 100 billions. — *Jaladhi-gā,* f. 'going to the ocean,' a river. — *Jaladhi-jā,* f. 'ocean-born,' N. of the goddess Lakshmī (as one of the fourteen precious things recovered at the churning of the ocean). — *Jaladhi-rasana, as, ā, am,* 'ocean-girt,' an epithet of the earth. — *Jaladhi-sambhava, as, ā, am,* produced from the ocean, marine. — *Jala-nakula, as,* m. an otter. — *Jala-nara, as,* m. 'water-man,' merman, N. of a particular animal. — *Jala-nāḍī,* f. a water-course. — *Jala-nidhi, is,* m. 'treasure of water,' the ocean, sea. — *Jala-nirgama, as,* m. a drain, a water-course, a pipe along a wall or building for carrying off water, a water-fall, the descent of a spring &c. into a river below. — *Jala-nivaha, as,* m. a quantity of water. — *Jala-nīlikā* or *jala-nīlī,* f. the aquatic plant Blyxa Octandra. — *Jalan-dhama, as,* m., N. of one of the attendants of Skanda; also of a Dānava; (*ā*), f., N. of a daughter of Kṛishṇa by Satya-bhāmā. — *Jalan-dhara, as,* m. 'water-bearer,' N. of a man; N. of an Asura fabled to have been produced by the contact of a flash from Siva's eye with the ocean and adopted by the god of the waters; he is so called as having on a particular occasion caught the water which flowed from Brahmā's eye. — *Jalandhara-pura, am,* n., N. of a town. — *Jalandhara-vadha, as,* m. title of a chapter of the Liṅga-Purāṇa. — *Jala-pakshin, ī,* m. a water-bird. — *Jala-paṭala, am,* n. a sheet of water, a cloud. — *Jala-pati, is,* m. 'lord of the waters,' i. e. Varuṇa or the Hindū Neptune; the ocean. — *Jala-patha, as,* m. a sea voyage. — *Jala-paddhati, is,* f. a water-course, gutter, drain. — *Jala-pātra, am,* n. a drinking-vessel. — *Jala-pāda, as,* m. (for *jāla-pāda?*), N. of a frog-king. — *Jala-pāna, am,* n. the drinking of water; (in Bengal = refreshment, luncheon.) — *Jala-pārāvata, as,* m. 'an aquatic pigeon,' N. of a particular bird. — *Jala-pitta, am,* n. fire ('the bile of water'). — *Jala-pippalī,* f. an aquatic plant, Commelina Salicifolia, and another species. — *Jala-pippikā,* f. a fish. — *Jala-pushpa, am,* n. an aquatic flower. — *Jala-pūra, as,* m. the full bed or stream of a river, a full stream. — *Jala-pṛishṭhajā,* f. the plant Blyxa Octandra, or Pistia Stratiotes. — *Jala-prapāta, as,* m. a water-fall. — *Jala-pralaya, as,* m. destruction by water. — *Jala-prānta, as,* m. 'the water's edge,' shore, bank of a river. — *Jala-prāya, as, ā, am,* abounding with water; (*am*), n. a country abounding with water. — *Jala-priya as, ā, am,* fond of water, frequenting water; (*as*), m. the bird Cātaka, Cuculus Melanoleucus; a fish; (*ā*), f. an epithet of Dākshāyaṇī. — *Jala-plava, as,* m. an otter. — *Jala-plāvana, am,* n. immersion under water, an inundation, a deluge. — *Jala-phala, as,* m. the water-nut, Trapa Bispinosa. — *Jala-bandhaka, as,* m. 'water-barrier,' a dam, a dike, rocks or stones impeding a current. — *Jala-bandhu, us,* m. a fish ('friend of water'). — *Jala-bālaka* or *jala-vālaka, as,* m. an epithet of the Vindhya mountains; (*ikā*), f. lightning (surrounded by water, i. e. clouds?). — *Jala-bimba,* a kind of plant (?). — *Jala-budbuda, as, am,* m. n. a bubble of water. — *Jala-brahmī,* f. a kind of pot-herb, Hingcha Repens. — *Jala-bhājana, am,* n. a vessel for water, water-pot. — *Jala-bhīti, is,* f. hydrophobia. — *Jala-bhū, ūs, ūs, u,* aquatic, produced in or by water; (*ūs*), m. a cloud; N. of a plant, = *kanćaṭa.* — *Jala-bhūshaṇa, as,* m. wind ('decorating the water'). — *Jala-bhṛit, t,* m. a cloud ('water-bearing'). — *Jala-makshikā,* f. a water-insect. — *Jala-magna, as, ā, am,* immersed in water. — *Jala-madgu, us,* m. a kingfisher. — *Jala-madhūka, as,* m., N. of a plant, = *kīreshṭa, kshaudra-priya,* &c. — *Jala-mandira, am,* n. = *jala-yantra-gṛiha.* — *Jala-maya, as, ī, am,* formed of water, consisting of water, watery. — *Jala-masi, is,* m. 'water-ink,' a dark cloud. — *Jala-mātreṇa,* ind. by mere water. — *Jala-mārga, as,* m. a water-course, a drain or canal leading from a pond &c. — *Jala-mārjāra, as,* m. 'water-cat,' an otter. — *Jala-muć, k, k, k,* shedding water; (*k*), m.

a cloud. — *Jala-mūrti, is,* m. Śiva, of whom one form is water, (implying his presence in all matter.) — *Jala-mūrtikā,* f. hail (a form of water). — *Jala-moda, am,* n. 'delighting in water,' the fragrant root of Andropogon Muricatus, = *uśīra.* — *Jalambala* (?), *am,* n. a stream; collyrium. — *Jala-yantra, am,* n. a water-engine, a machine for raising water &c., any contrivance connected with that element; a water-clock, a clepsydra. — *Jala-yantraka, am,* n. a machine for raising water &c. — *Jalayantra-gṛiha* or *jalayantra-niketana* or *jalayantra-mandira, am,* n. a house or fabric erected in the midst of water; subterranean apartments constructed in the bank of a river to serve as a retreat in the hot season, a summer-house &c. — *Jala-yātrā,* f. a voyage. — *Jala-yāna, am,* n. 'a water vehicle,' a ship. — *Jala-raṅka, as,* m. or *jala-rañja, as,* m. a species of Vaka or crane (Ardea Nivea). — *Jala-raṅku, us,* m. a kind of gallinule. — *Jala-raṇḍa, as,* m. a whirlpool; a drop, drizzle, thin sprinkling of water; a snake; [cf. *jala-ruṇḍa.*] — *Jala-rasa, as,* m. sea-salt. — *Jala-rākshasī,* f. 'the water Rākshasī,' also called Su-rasā, a female demon described in Rāmāyaṇa V. 6. as the mother of the Nāgas; she placed herself in the way of Hanumat in his flight across the straits between the continent and Ceylon, and in order to prevent his crossing attempted to swallow him bodily. He escaped by reducing himself to the size of a thumb, darting through her huge body and coming out at her right ear. — *Jala-rāśi, is,* m. a sheet of water, a quantity of water; the ocean. — *Jala-ruṇḍa, as,* m. = *jala-raṇḍa.* — *Jala-ruh, ṭ,* m. 'growing in water,' a lotus (Nelumbium). — *Jala-ruha, as,* m. an aquatic animal; (*am*), n. the lotus (Nelumbium). — *Jala-rūpa, as,* m. the fish of Kāma-deva, = *makara.* — *Jala-latā,* f. 'water-creeper,' a wave, a billow. — *Jala-lava-muć, k, k, k,* discharging drops of water. — *Jala-lohita, as,* m. a Rākshasa (having water for blood). — *Jala-vat, ān, atī, at,* abounding in water. — *Jala-varaṇṭa, as,* m. a watery pustule. — *Jala-valkala, am,* n., N. of the aquatic plant Pistia Stratiotes. — *Jala-vallī,* f. the water-nut, Trapa Bispinosa. — *Jala-vādita, am,* n. water-music, a kind of music in which water is used. — *Jala-vādya, am,* n. a kind of musical instrument in which water is used. — *Jala-vāyasa, as,* m. 'a water-crow,' the diver bird. — *Jala-vālaka,* cf. *jala-bālaka.* — *Jala-vāsa, as,* m. residence in water; (*as, ā, am*), living or residing in water; (*as*), m. a kind of root, = *vishṇu-kanda*; (*am*), n. the root of Andropogon Muricatus, = *uśīra.* — *Jala-vāha, as, ā, am,* carrying water; (*as*), m. a water-bearer, a cloud. — *Jala-vāhaka, as,* m. a water-bearer or carrier. — *Jala-vāhana, as,* m. a water-carrier; N. of a physician, = Śākya-muni in a former birth; (*am*), n. flowing of water; (*ī*), f. a water-course, aqueduct. — *Jala-viḍāla, as,* m. an otter. — *Jala-vindu, us,* m. a drop of water; N. of a Tīrtha. — *Jalavinduja,* f. a kind of sugar. — *Jala-vilva, as,* m. the plant Pistia Stratiotes; a tortoise; a crab; a quadrangular pond. — *Jala-vishuva, am,* n. the autumnal equinox, the moment of the sun's entering Libra; a kind of circle or cycle. — *Jala-vihaṅgama, as,* m. a water-fowl. — *Jala-vīrya, as,* m., N. of a son of Bharata. — *Jala-vṛiśćika, as,* m. 'water-scorpion,' a prawn or shrimp. — *Jala-vetasa, as,* m. a kind of cane, = *vānīra.* — *Jala-vyatha* or *jala-vyadha, as,* m. a kind of fish, Esox Cancila. — *Jala-vyāla, as,* m. a water-snake; a marine monster. — *Jala-śaya* or *jala-śayana, as,* or *jala-śāyin, ī,* m. an epithet of Vishṇu, who is supposed to sleep, reposing on his serpent-couch above the waters, during the four months of the periodical rains; also during the intervals of the submersion of the world; [cf. *jale-śaya.*] — *Jalaśāyi-tīrtha, am,* n., N. of a Tīrtha. — *Jala-śukti, is,* f. a bivalve shell. — *Jala-śući, is, is, i,* cleansed by water, bathed, washed. — *Jala-śūka, am,* n. the plant Blyxa Octandra, a green moss-like substance growing on the surface of stagnant water, duckweed. — *Jala-śūkara, as,* m. a crocodile ('water-hog'). — *Jala-śosha, as,* m. drying up of water, drought. — *Jala-saṃsarga, as,* m. mixing with water, dilution. — *Jala-sandha, as,* m., N. of a prince, a son of Dhṛita-rāshṭra. — *Jala-samudra, as,* m. the sea of fresh water. — *Jala-samparka, as,* m. mixture or dilution with water. — *Jala-sarpiṇī,* f. 'water-glider,' a leech. — *Jala-sāt,* ind. to the state of water (e. g. *jalasāt kṛi,* to reduce to water; *jalasāt sampadyate,* it is turned into water). — *Jala-sikta, as, ā, am,* sprinkled with water, wetted. — *Jala-sūći, is,* m. the Gangetic porpoise, Delphinus Gangeticus; a crow; a fish, a small sort of pike, Esox Cancila; a leech; a water-nut, Trapa Bispinosa. — *Jala-seka, as,* m. sprinkling with water. — *Jala-stha, as, ā, am,* standing or abiding or situated in water; (*ā*), f. a kind of grass, = *gaṇḍa-dūrvā.* — *Jala-sthāna, am,* n. or *jala-sthāya, as,* m. a reservoir, a pond, a lake. — *Jala-ha, am,* n. a small water (or summer) house; [cf. *jalayantra-gṛiha.*] — *Jala-haraṇa, am,* n. a metre consisting of 4 × 32 syllabic instants. — *Jala-hastin, ī,* m. a water-elephant; hippopotamus (?). — *Jala-hāra, as, ī,* m. f. a water-carrier. — *Jala-hāriṇī,* f. a water-course, drain, a channel for water. — *Jala-hāsa* or *jala-hāsaka, as,* m. cuttle-fish bone, considered as the indurated foam of the sea. — *Jala-hrada, as,* m., N. of a man. — *Jalākara* (°*la-āk*°), *as,* m. a source of water, a spring, a fountain. — *Jalākā,* f. = *jalaukā,* a leech. — *Jalākāṅksha* (°*la-āk*°), *as,* m. = *jalakāṅksha,* an elephant. — *Jalākshi* (°*la-ak*°), f. an aquatic plant, Commelina Salicifolia. — *Jalākhu* (°*la-ākhu*), *us,* m. 'water-mole,' an otter. — *Jalāñćala* (°*la-añ*°), *am,* n. a spring, well; natural water-course; the plant Blyxa Octandra. — *Jalāñjali* (°*la-añ*°), *is,* f. a handful of water, or water held in the palms of the hand, as presented to the manes of a dead person &c. — *Jalāṭana* (°*la-aṭ*°), *as,* m. 'water-goer,' a heron; (*ī*), f. a leech. — *Jalāḍhya* (°*la-āḍh*°), *as, ā, am,* watery, marshy. — *Jalāṇuka* (°*la-aṇ*°), *am,* n. the fry of fish. — *Jalāntaka, as,* m. a shark or (according to some) a large alligator &c. — *Jalāṇḍaka* (°*la-aṇ*°), *am,* n. the fry of fish. — *Jalātmikā* (°*la-āt*°), f. a leech; a well (in the latter sense a various reading for *jalāmbikā*). — *Jalātyaya* (°*la-at*°), *as,* m. the passing away of the water (or clouds), autumn. — *Jalādarśa* (°*la-ād*°), *as,* m. a watery mirror, water reflecting any object like a mirror. — *Jalādhāra* (°*la-ādh*°), *as,* m. a pond, a lake, a reservoir, any receptacle of water. — *Jalādhidaivata* (°*la-adh*°), *am,* n., scil. *bha* or *nakshatra,* the constellation Ashāḍhā (having the water as its deity; cf. *jala-deva*); (*as*), m. an epithet of Varuṇa (?). — *Jalādhipa* (°*la-adh*°), *as,* or *jalādhipati* (°*la-adh*°), *is,* or *jalādhyaksha* (°*la-adh*°), *as,* m. an epithet of Varuṇa, lord of the waters. — *Jalānusāra* (°*la-an*°), *as,* m. going or acting like water. — *Jalāntaka* (°*la-an*°), *as,* m., N. of a son of Kṛishṇa by Satya-bhāmā; (*as, ā, am*), having water in the interior (*anta*); containing water. — *Jalāpasparśana* (°*la-ap*°), *am,* n. touching water, use of water. — *Jalābhisheka* (°*la-abh*°), *as,* m. sprinkling with water. — *Jalāmbara* (°*la-am*°), *as,* m., N. of a man, = Rāhala-bhadra in a former birth. — *Jalāmbikā* (°*la-am*°), f. a well; [cf. *jalātmikā.*] — *Jalāmbu-garbhā* (°*la-am*°), f., N. of a woman, = Gopā in a former birth. — *Jalāyukā* (°*la-āyu*) or 1. *jalālukā* or *jalālokā* or *jalāvukā* or *jalāsukā,* f. a leech (living in water). — *Jalārka* (°*la-ar*°), *as,* m. the sun reflected in water. — *Jalārṇava* (°*la-ar*°), *as,* m. the rainy season; the sea of fresh water. — *Jalārthin* (°*la-ar*°), *ī, inī, i,* desirous of water, thirsty. — *Jalārdra* (°*la-ār*°), *as, ā, am,* wet, charged with aqueous moisture; (*as, ā*), m. f. wet cloth or clothes. — *Jalālu* (°*la-ālu*), *us,* m. a kind of bulbous plant. — *Jalāvatāra* (°*la-av*°), *as,* m. a landing-place at a river's side. — *Jalāvarta* (°*la-āv*°), *as,* m. 'the turning round of water,' an eddy, a whirlpool. — *Jalāvila* (°*la-āv*°), *as, ā, am,* stained or soiled with water. — *Jalāśaya* (°*la-āś*°), *as, ā, am,* resting or lying in water; stupid, dull, apathetic, cold; (*as*), m. a pond, a tank, a lake, a reservoir or any piece of water; a fish; the water-nut, Trapa Bispinosa; (*ā*), f. a kind of plant, = *guṇḍālā*; (*am*), n. the root of Andropogon Muricatus. — *Jalāśayāntara* (°*ya-an*°), *am,* n. another lake. — *Jalāśayotsarga-tattva* (°*ya-ut*°), *am,* n. a part of the Smṛiti-tattva. — *Jalāśayotsarga-vidhi, is,* m. title of a work by Kamalākara-bhaṭṭa. — *Jalāśāyin* (°*la-āś*°), *ī, inī, i,* lying or sleeping in water as a penance. — *Jalāśraya* (°*la-āś*°), *as,* m. a piece of water, a pond, a lake; a water-house; (*ā*), f. a kind of crane; a kind of grass. — *Jalā-shah* or *jalā-sah, -shāṭ, ṭ, ṭ,* subduing water. — *Jalāshṭhīlā* (°*la-ash*°) or *ī,* f. a large square pond. — *Jalā-sāha, as, ā, am,* = *jalā-shah.* — *Jalāsukā,* f., see *jalāyukā.* — *Jalāhvaya* (°*la-āh*°), *am,* n. a lotus (Nelumbium). — *Jale-ćara, as, ī, am,* living or going in water; (*as*), m. an aquatic animal; a fish; any kind of water-fowl. — *Jaleććhayā,* f. the plant Heliotropium Indicum; [cf. *hasti-śuṇḍā.*] — *Jale-jāta, am,* n. a lotus (Nelumbium). — *Jalendra* (°*la-in*°), *as,* m. 'chief of waters,' the sea; the ocean of fresh water; Varuṇa, the regent of the waters; N. of a Jina or Jaina saint. — *Jalendhana* (°*la-in*°), *am,* n. submarine fire. — *Jalebha* (°*la-ibha*), *as,* m. a water-elephant; [cf. *jala-hastin.*] — *Jale-ruha, as,* m., N. of a king of Orissa; (*ā*), f., N. of a plant, = *kuṭumbinī.* — *Jale-vāha, as,* m. a diver (by caste or business). — *Jaleśa* (°*la-īśa*), *as,* m. the sea, ocean; lord of the waters, i. e. Varuṇa. — *Jale-śaya, as, ā, am,* resting or abiding in water; (*as*), m. an epithet of Vishṇu; a fish. — *Jaleśvara* (°*la-īś*°), *as,* m. 'lord of waters,' the sea, the ocean; the deity of the waters, i. e. Varuṇa; N. of a sanctuary. — *Jaloka, as,* m., N. of a king of Kaśmīra; (*ā*), f. a leech; see *jalaukas.* — *Jalokikā,* f. a leech; see *jalaukas.* — *Jaloććhvāsa* (°*la-uć*°), *as,* m. a drain or channel made for carrying off an excess of water, or a similar channel made naturally by the overflow of a river &c. — *Jalodara* (°*la-ud*°), *am,* n. 'water-belly,' dropsy. — *Jaloddhata-gati* (°*la-ud*°), *is,* f., N. of a metre consisting of four lines of twelve syllables each. — *Jalodbhava* (°*la-ud*°), *as, ā, am,* born or produced in water, aquatic, marine; (*as*), m. 'origin of the waters,' N. of a place; an aquatic animal; N. of a water-demon slain by Kaśyapa; (*ā*), f., N. of a plant, = *laghu-brāhmī,* benzoin. — *Jalodbhūta* (°*la-ud*°), *as, ā, am,* born in or produced from water; (*ā*), f., N. of a plant, = *guṇḍālā.* — *Jalonnāda* (°*la-un*°), *as,* m., N. of one of the attendants of Śiva. — *Jaloragī* (°*la-ur*°), f. 'water-snake,' a leech. — *Jalauka, as,* m. a leech; (*ā*), f. a leech; [cf. the next.] — *Jalaukas* (°*la-ok*°), *ās, ās, as,* living in water, an inhabitant of the water, an aquatic animal; (*ās*), m., N. of a king of Kaśmīra; (*ās*), f. a leech (said to be used in plur. only). — *Jalaukasa, as, ā, am,* m. f. n. a leech. — *Jalaugha* (°*la-ogha*), *as,* m. a quantity of water.

2\. *jala,* nom. P., Ved. *jalati,* to become water.

Jalaka, am, n. a conch, a shell.

Jalāya, nom. A. *-yate, -yitum,* to become water, appear as water.

2\. *jalāluka, am,* n. a lotus root; [cf. *jalāyukā.*]

Jalikā or *jalukā* or *jalūkā,* f. a leech.

Jaleyu, us, m., N. of a son of Raudrāśva.

Jalelā, f., N. of one of the Mātṛis attending on Skanda; (or perhaps for two words *jalā ilā.*)

जलालदीनाहकबरसाह m. = *jalālu 'ddīn akbar shāh.*

जलाष *jalāsha, as, ā, am,* Ved. mitigating, pacifying, appeasing, healing, comforting; (*am*), n. water; happiness, comfort. — *Jalāsha-bheshaja, as, ā, am,* Ved. possessed of healing medicines, an epithet of Rudra.

जल्प् *jalp* [cf. *jap* and *lap*], cl. 1. P. (ep. also A.) *jalpati, -te, jajalpa, jalpishyati, jalpitum,* to speak inarticulately, murmur; chatter, prattle, babble, wrangle; to speak, say; to address a person, speak with; to speak of or about (with acc.); to praise: Caus. P. *jalpayati, -yitum,* to cause to speak; [cf. Lith. *kalbu,* 'to speak;' *kalba,* 'speech:' Hib. *gaill,* 'speech.']

Jalpa, as, m. talk, speech; prate, babble, gossip, chatter, discourse; debate, disputation, wrangling discussion, an argument in which a disputant tries to assert his own opinion and to refute that of his adversary by overbearing reply or wrangling rejoinder; [cf. *ćitra-jalpa.*]

Jalpaka, as, ikā, am, a talker, chatterer, talkative, one who talks much or idly, garrulous.

Jalpana, as, ā, am, speaking, saying, talking; (*am*), n. talking, saying; chattering, prattling, garrulity.

Jalpāka, as, ī, am, a chatterer, talking much and foolishly, or improperly; [cf. *jalpaka.*]

Jalpi, is, f., Ved. inarticulate speech, murmuring; speaking in a low voice.

Jalpita, as, ā, am, said, told, spoken; (*am*), n. talk, babbling, gossip; talking.

Jalpitṛi, tā, trī, tṛi, or *jalpin, ī, inī, i*, a talker, speaker, chatterer; saying, speaking.

जल्लालदीन्द्र *jallāladīndra, as*, m. = *jalālu 'ddīn.*

जळ्हु *jaḷhu, us, us, u* (related to *jaḍa?*), Ved. deprived of splendor or without sacrificial fire.

जव *java, as*, m. (fr. rt. *ju* or *jū*), speed, quickness, velocity, rapidity, swiftness; (*as, ā, am*), swift, expeditious; (*ā*), f. the China rose, Hibiscus Rosa Sinensis; [cf. *japā.*] — *Java-yukta, as, ā, am*, possessed of fleetness. — *Java-vat, ān, atī, at*, quick, swift, fleet. — *Javādhika* (°*va-adh*°), *as, ā, am*, very quick, extremely swift; (*as*), m. a fleet horse, a courser. — *Javānila* (°*va-an*°), *as*, m. a strong wind, gale, hurricane. — *Javā-pushpa, as*, m. the China rose, the plant or its flower.

1. *javana, as, ī, am*, causing to hasten; quick, swift, fleet; (*as*), m. a courser, a fleet horse; a kind of deer; N. of one of the attendants of Skanda; (*ī*), f. a screen surrounding a tent, a Kanāt; N. of a plant; (*am*), n. speed, velocity; [cf. *dhī-javana.*]

Javanikā, f. a wall or screen of cloth surrounding a tent, an outer tent, &c.; a curtain, a screen in general; the sail of a boat; [cf. *yavanikā.*]

Javaniman, ā, m. quickness, speed, velocity.

Javas, as, n., Ved. quickness, velocity; [cf. *a-javas.*]

Javin, ī, inī, i, quick, fleet, expeditious; (*ī*), m. a horse, a camel.

Javina, as, ā, am, rapid, quick; (*as*), m. = *kokada.*

Javishṭha, as, ā, am, Ved. quickest, fleetest; (*as*), m., N. of a Dānava.

Javīyas, ān, asī, as, Ved. quicker, speedier.

जवन 2. *javana, as*, m., N. of a people whose country is by some thought to be identical with Ionia or Greece, = *yavana*, q. v.

जवनाल *javanāla, am*, n. a sort of grain, Andropogon Bicolor; [cf. *yavanāla.*]

जवस *javasa, as*, m. meadow or pasture grass; [cf. *yavasa.*]

जवादि *javādi, i*, n. a kind of perfume, = *kṛitrima, gandha-rāja.*

जवाल *javāla, as*, m., N. of a man.

जविपुला *ja-vipulā*, f. a kind of metre.

जष् *jash*, cl. 1. P. A. *jashati, -te*, &c., to kill, wound, hurt, injure; [cf. Hib. *gus*, 'death.']

जष *jasha, as*, m., Ved. a kind of aquatic animal; [cf. *jhasha.*]

जस् *jas*, cl. 1. A. P., cl. 4. P., Ved. *jasate, -ti, jasyati, jajāsa, jasitum*, to be exhausted or tired; cl. 4. P. to set free, release, liberate, let loose: Caus. P. *jāsayati, -yitum, ajījasat*, to exhaust, weaken, cause to expire; cl. 10. 1. P. *jāsayati, jasati*, &c., to hurt, injure; to strike, punish with blows; to slight or disregard, treat irreverently.

Jasu, us, f., Ved. exhaustion, weakness; a hiding-place, cover (?).

Jasuri, is, is, i, Ved. exhausted, weak; (*is*), m. Indra's thunderbolt.

Jasra, am, n. exhaustion, fatigue.

Jasvan, ā, arī, a, Ved. needy, poor, hungry; (Sāy.) causing to waste away, destroying; [cf. *a-jasra.*]

जस्सराज *jassa-rāja, as*, m., N. of a man.

जहक *jahaka, as, ā, am* (fr. rt. *hā*), abandoning, one who leaves or abandons; (*as*), m. time; a child; the slough of a snake; (*ā*), f. a kind of weasel or polecat.

Jahat, at, atī, at, leaving, quitting, foregoing. — *Jahat-svārthā*, f., scil. *lakshaṇā*, a particular figure of speech, a word losing its original meaning and taking a different sense; irony. — *Jahal-lakshaṇā*, f. = the preceding.

जहा *jahā*, f. a plant, commonly Muṇḍirī; also *kadamba-pushpī*, &c.

जहानक *jahānaka, as*, m. the period of the total destruction of the world; [cf. *jihānaka.*]

जहिजोड *jahi-joḍa, as, ā, am* (*jahi* impv. fr. rt. *han* and *joḍa*), one who is in the habit of hitting his chin.

Jahi-stambha, as, ā, am, one who is constantly striking against a post.

जहु *jahu, us*, m. a young animal; N. of a son of Pushpa-vat and descendant of Ṛishabha.

जह्नु *jahnu, us*, m., N. of an ancient king and sage who adopted the Gaṅgā as his daughter, (the river Ganges, when brought down from heaven by the austerities of Bhagīratha, was forced to flow over the earth and to follow him to the ocean, and thence to the lower regions, for the purpose of watering the ashes of Sagara's sons. In its course it inundated the sacrificial ground of Jahnu, who therefore drank up its waters, but consented at the prayer of Bhagīratha to discharge them from his ears. Hence the river is regarded as his daughter, and is called Jāhnavī); N. of a son of Aja-mīḍha, of a son of Su-hotra, of Kuru, and of Hotraka; N. of an ancestor of the Kuśikas; a N. of Vishṇu; (*avas*), m. pl. the descendants of Jahnu. — *Jahnu-kanyā*, f. or *jahnu-tanayā*, f. or *jahnu-sutā*, f. 'daughter of Jahnu,' N. of Gaṅgā or the Ganges.

Jahnāvī, f., Ved. the family of Jahnu.

जह्मन् *jahman, a*, n. water (?).

जह्ल *jahla, as*, m., N. of a man.

जा *jā, ās, ās, am* (fr. rt. *jan*, and used in Ved. for 2. *ja*, which appears rarely in the Veda), born, produced, &c. [cf. *agni-jā, agra-jā, adri-jā, indra-jā, go-jā*, &c.], see 2. *ja*; (*ās*), m. f., Ved. offspring, descendants; (*ā*), f. a race, tribe. — *Jās-pati, is*, m. (*jās* gen. fr. *jā!*), the father or head of a family or house. — *Jāspatya, am*, n., Ved. the state or condition of the father of a family.

जांहगिरि *jāṅhagiri, is*, m. = *jahāṅgīrī.*

जागत *jāgata, as, ī, am*, composed in the Jagatī metre, consisting of it, conforming to it; chiefly praised in the Jagatī metre (each deity having his own peculiar metre); (*am*), n. the Jagatī metre.

जागुड *jāguḍa, ās*, m. pl., N. of a people; (*as*), m., N. of their country, renowned for its saffron; (*am*), n. saffron.

जागृ *jāgṛi*, cl. 2. P. *jāgarti, jajāgāra* or *jāgarāñ-ćakāra, jāgarishyati, jāgaritum*, to be awake, to watch, be watchful, attentive, intent; to foresee, provide; to sit up during the night: Caus. *jāgarayati*, Aor. Ved. 2nd and 3rd sing. *ajīgar*, 2nd du. *jigṛitam*, 2nd pl. *jigṛita*, to awaken: Desid. *jijāgarishati*; [cf. Gr. ἐγείρω; Lat. *vigil, vigilo*; Old Germ. *wachar, wachem*; Goth. *waka.*]

Jāgara, as, ā, m. f. waking, wakefulness, vigilance; (*as, ā, am*), waking, awake; (*as*), m. a vision in a waking state; = *jagara*, mail, armour.

Jāgaraka, as, m. waking, awake.

Jāgaraṇa, as, ā, am, waking, remaining awake; (*am*), n. waking, watchfulness; keeping watch, sitting up at night as part of a religious ceremony.

Jāgarita, as, ā, am, one who has been long awake or is exhausted with sleeplessness; (*am*), n. waking.

Jāgaritṛi, tā, trī, tṛi, wakeful, awake, vigilant.

Jāgarin, ī, iṇī, i, wakeful, awake.

Jāgarishṇu, us, us, u, very wakeful or sleepless.

Jāgarūka, as, ā, am, wakeful, waking, sleepless, watchful.

Jāgartavya, as, ā, am, to be awake or awaked.

Jāgarti, is, f. waking, vigilance; keeping watch, watchfulness.

Jāgaryā, f. wakefulness, waking, watching.

Jāgṛitavya, as, ā, am, to be awake. See *jāgartavya.*

Jāgṛivi, is, is, i, Ved. watchful, attentive; awake; not extinguished, clear, bright (as fire); active, animating, exciting; (*is*), m. fire or its deity; a king.

Jāgrat, at, atī, at, watching, being awake. — *Jāgrat-svapna, au*, m. du. a state of waking and sleep; (*as*), m. Ved. dreaming in a waking state, day-dream, hallucination; (*as, ā, am*), occurring in a state of waking and sleep (?). — *Jāgrad-avasthā* or *jāgrad-daśā*, f. a state of wakefulness. — *Jāgrad-duḥshvapnya, am*, n., Ved. a disagreeable dream or vision while in a waking state.

Jāgriyā, f. waking, watching, wakefulness.

जाघनी *jāghanī*, f. (fr. *jaghana*), a tail; the thigh, leg.

जाङ्गल *jāṅgala, as, ī, am* (fr. *jaṅgala*), arid; sparingly grown with trees &c. but nevertheless fertile; rural, picturesque, diversified with hill, vale, wood, and water; found or existing in such a district; desert, covered with jungle; wild, not tame (as an animal &c.); savage, barbarous; (*as*), m. the francoline partridge; N. of a man; (*ās*), m. pl., N. of a people; (*ī*), f. the plant Mucuna Pruritus; (*am*), n. flesh; game, the flesh of deer &c.

Jāṅgali, is, m. a snake-catcher; [cf. *jāṅguli.*]

Jāṅgalika, as, m. a snake-charmer, = *jāṅgulika.*

Jāṅgula, am, n. poison, venom, = *jaṅgula*; the fruit of the Jālinī, a kind of cucumber; (*ī*), f. knowledge of poisons, the possession of charms or drugs and employment of them as antidotes; a pot-herb, Luffa Acutangula; an epithet of Durgā.

Jāṅguli, is, m. a snake-catcher, a dealer in antidotes, a conjuror.

Jāṅgulika, as, m. a snake-catcher, a snake-doctor, one who pretends by charms to cure the bite of snakes or other venomous animals, a dealer in antidotes &c.

जाङ्घनी *jāṅghanī*, f. (fr. *jaṅghā*), the thigh; (perhaps a wrong form for *jāghanī.*)

Jāṅghāprahatika or *jāṅghāprahṛitika, as, ī, am* (fr. *jaṅghā-prahata* or *-prahṛita*), produced by a blow with the leg.

Jāṅghālāyana, as, m. (fr. *jaṅghāla*), N. of a man.

Jāṅghi, a patronymic from Jaṅgha or metronymic from Jaṅghā.

Jāṅghika, as, ī, am (fr. *jaṅghā*), swift of foot, a courier; relating to or belonging to the leg; (*as*), m. a courier, a running footman, an express; a camel; a kind of antelope; [cf. *kapi-jāṅghikā.*]

जाजनाग *jājanāga, as*, m., N. of a man.

जाजमत् *jājamat, at, atī, at* (fr. Intens. of 1. *jam*, p. 339), excessively or repeatedly devouring.

जाजल *jājala, ās*, and *jājalin, inas*, m. pl., N. of a school of the Atharva-veda.

जाजलि *jājali, is*, m., N. of a preceptor.

जाजिन् *jājin, ī,* m. a warrior, a combatant; [cf. *jaj* and *jaja.*]

जाज्वल्यमान *jājvalyamāna, as, ā, am* (fr. Intens. of rt. *jval*), shining, flaming, blazing, resplendent, effulgent, dazzling.

जाटलि *jāṭali, is, ī,* m. f. the plant Bignonia Suaveolens; (other readings have *pāṭali* and *jhāṭali.*)

जाटालिका *jāṭālikā,* f. (fr. *jaṭāla* or *jaṭālaka*), N. of one of the Mātṛis attending on Skanda.

जाटिकायन *jāṭikāyana, as,* m. (fr. *jaṭika*), N. of the author of a hymn of the Atharva-veda.

जाठर *jāṭhara, as, ī, am* (fr. *jaṭhara*), stomachic, abdominal, visceral, being in the stomach or belly, relating to it, relating to the womb, e. g. *jāṭharo 'gniḥ,* the fire in the stomach, the digestive faculty, gastric juice, hunger; *(as),* m. 'offspring of the womb,' a child; N. of an attendant of Skanda.

Jāṭharya, am, n. morbid affection of the abdomen.

जाड्य *jāḍya, am,* n. (fr. *jaḍa*), coldness, frigidity; stiffness, inactivity, apathy, sluggishness, insensibility; absence of feeling in the tongue, tastelessness; dulness or coldness of intellect, stupidity, folly. — *Jāḍyāri* (°*ya-ari*), *is,* m. 'enemy of coldness,' the citron tree.

जात *jāta, as, ā, am* (fr. rt. *jan*), born, brought into existence, brought forth, engendered (e. g. *māsa-jāta,* born a month ago, one month old; *putro jātaḥ,* a son only by birth, not by qualities); grown, produced, arisen, caused, occasioned, appearing, appeared, apparent, manifest; happened; become, present; ready at hand, collected, stored up, possessed, felt, experienced, inspired with, affected by, (often at the beginning of an adjective compound, see examples below; also at the end of a comp., e. g. *putra-jāta,* having a son born; *śmaśru-jāta,* having a beard; *danta-jāta,* having teeth just growing); *(as),* m. male issue, a son; a living being (used of men and gods, but especially of the former); *(ās),* m. pl., N. of a race of the Haihayas; *(ā),* f. female offspring, a daughter; *jāte,* O daughter! *(am),* n. a living being, a creature; birth, production, origin; race, kind, sort, class, species; a multitude or collection of things forming a class (e. g. *karma-jātam,* the whole aggregate of actions; *sukha-jātam,* everything included under the name pleasure); individuality, specific condition; [cf. Gr. -γετος; Germ. *Kind;* Lith. *gentis.*] — *Jāta-karman, a,* n. a ceremony at the birth of a child when the navel string is divided, (it consists in touching the infant's tongue thrice with ghee after appropriate prayers); delivery of a new-born infant. — *Jāta-kalāpa, as, ā, am,* having a tail (as a peacock). — *Jāta-kāma, as, ā, am,* fallen in love. — *Jāta-kopa* or *jāta-krodha, as, ā, am,* enraged. — *Jāta-kautuka, as, ā, am,* delighted. — *Jāta-kautūhala, as, ā, am,* being eagerly desirous. — *Jāta-kshobha, as, ā, am,* agitated. — *Jāta-danta, as, ī, am,* (a child) that has a tooth or teeth growing; having teeth. — *Jāta-paksha, as, ā, am,* whose wings have grown, possessing wings. — *Jāta-pāśa, as, ā, am,* having fetters, fettered. — *Jāta-putrā,* f. a woman who has borne a son or sons. — *Jāta-pratyaya, as, ā, am,* inspired with confidence, confiding, believing. — *Jāta-bala, as, ā, am,* possessing strength, strong. — *Jāta-bhī, īs,* f. 'fearful,' N. of a woman. — *Jāta-manmatha, as, ā, am,* being in love, fallen in love, loving. — *Jāta-mātra, as, ā, am,* just born, merely born; *(am),* n. as soon as born, the instant of birth. — *Jāta-rajas, ās, ās, as,* having the catamenia. — *Jāta-rasa, as, ā, am,* having taste or flavour. — *Jāta-rūpa, as, ā, am,* embodied, having assumed a shape or form, beautiful, brilliant, golden (?); *(am),* n. the form in which a person is born, nakedness; gold; the thorn-apple. — *Jātarūpa-dhara, as, ā, am,* quite naked. — *Jātarūpa-parishkṛita, as, ā, am,* adorned with gold. — *Jātarūpa-maya, as, ī, am,* golden. — *Jātarūpa-śila, as,* m., N. of a golden mountain. — *Jāta-vat, ān, atī, at,* containing the word *jāta* or any other form derived from *jan.* — *Jāta-vāsa-gṛiha, am,* n. the room in which a child is born, the room of a lying-in woman. — *Jāta-vidyā,* f., Ved. a knowledge of what exists or of the origin and nature of all things. — *Jāta-vibhrama, as, ā, am,* flurried, precipitate. — *Jāta-viśvāsa, as, ā, am,* having the confidence excited. — *Jāta-vedas, ās,* m., Ved. an epithet of Agni; (the meaning is explained in five ways: 1. 'knowing all created beings;' 2. 'possessing all creatures or everything existent;' 3. 'known by created beings;' 4. 'possessing *vedas* = riches;' 5. 'possessing *vedas* = wisdom:' other derivations and explanations are found in the Brāhmaṇas, but the exact sense of this word seems to have been very early lost, and of the five explanations given above only the first two would seem to be admissible for the Vedic texts; in one passage a form *jāta-veda* seems to occur.) — *Jātavedasa, as, ī, am,* relating to Jāta-vedas; *(ī),* f. an epithet of Durgā. — *Jātavedasīya, as, ā, am,* belonging or relating to Jāta-vedas. — *Jāta-vepathu, us, us, u,* affected with tremor. — *Jāta-veśman, a,* n. the room in which a child is born, the room of a lying-in woman. — *Jāta-śmaśru, us, us, u,* one whose beard has grown. — *Jāta-śrama, as, ā, am,* wearied, exhausted. — *Jāta-saṃvṛiddha, as, ā, am,* born and grown up. — *Jāta-sankalpa, as, ā, am,* feeling a desire or passion for. — *Jāta-sādhvasa, as, ā, am,* afraid. — *Jāta-sena, as,* m., N. of a man. — *Jātasenya, as,* m. a patronymic from the last. — *Jāta-sneha, as, ā, am,* enamoured, feeling love or affection for. — *Jāta-spṛiha, as, ā, am,* desirous, wishing for. — *Jāta-harsha, as, ā, am,* rejoiced, glad. — *Jāta-hārda, as, ī, am,* feeling affection, becoming attached. — *Jātāgas* (°*ta-āg*°), *ās, ās, as,* offending, sinning, committing fault; also *jātāparādha, jāta-dosha,* &c. — *Jātāpatyā* (°*ta-ap*°), f. a mother, a woman who has borne a child. — *Jātāmarsha* (°*ta-am*°), *as, ā, am,* having the anger roused, vexed, enraged, put in a passion. — *Jātāśru* (°*ta-aś*°), *us, us, u,* weeping, shedding tears. — *Jāteshṭi* (°*ta-ish*°), *is,* f. rites or sacrifice performed at the birth of a child. — *Jātoksha* (°*ta-uk*°), *as,* m. a young bullock, an ox.

Jātaka, as, ā, am, born, produced; *(as),* m. a new-born child; a mendicant; *(am),* n. = *jāta-karman,* a ceremony performed after the birth of a child; nativity, astrological calculation of a nativity; (with Buddhists) a former birth of Śākya-muni and its history; an aggregate or a collection of similar things; [cf. *ćatur-jātaka.*] — *Jātaka-dhvani, is,* m. a leech. — *Jātaka-paddhati, is,* f., N. of a work on nativities by Ananta; another work by Keśava. — *Jātaka-muktāvalī,* f. title of an astrological work by Śiva-dāsa. — *Jātakāmbhonidhi* (°*ka-am*°), *is,* m. title of an astrological work by Bhadra-bāhu.

Jātāyana, as, m. a patronymic from Jāta.

Jāti, is, f. birth, production; the form of existence, whether as a man or animal, which is fixed by birth; position assigned by birth; rank; family, race, lineage; kind, sort, genus, species, class, tribe, caste; the character or peculiarities of a species, the genuine or true state of anything; reduction of fractions to a common denominator; false generalization; a futile answer, a self-confuting reply; a particular figure of speech in rhetoric; a class of metres; a manner of singing; a fire-place; N. of several plants, = Jasminum Grandiflorum; Emblica Officinalis; mace, nutmeg; [cf. *antya-jāti, eka-jāti, dvi-jāti;* cf. also Lat. *gens;* Lith. *pri-gentis.*] — *Jāti-kośa* or *jāti-kosha* or *jātī-kośa, am,* n. a nutmeg; *(ī),* f. the outer skin of the nutmeg. — *Jāti-tva, am,* n. or *jāti-tā,* f. distinction or nature of caste or tribe; special or generic property. — *Jāti-dharma, as,* m. the duty of caste, the law or usage of caste (e. g. sacred study is the caste-duty of the Brāhman, fighting of the Kshatriya, &c.); generic or specific property. — *Jāti-dhvaṇsa, as,* m. the loss of caste or its privileges. — *Jātin-dhara, as,* m., N. of a physician, = Suddhodana in a former birth. — *Jāti-pattrī* or *jātī-pattrī,* f. the outer skin of the nutmeg. — *Jāti-phala* or *jātī-phala, am,* n. a nutmeg; [cf. *kshudrajāti-phala.*] — *Jāti-brāhmaṇa, as,* m. a Brāhman by birth but not by knowledge. — *Jāti-bhraṇśa, as,* m. loss of rank or caste. — *Jāti-bhraṇśa-kara, as, ī, am,* causing loss of caste; forbidden, improper; *(am),* n. doing an act prohibited to a particular caste. — *Jāti-bhrashṭa, as, ā, am,* fallen from caste, outcast. — *Jāti-mat, ān, atī, at,* of high rank, obtaining a high position. — *Jāti-maha, as,* m. birthday-festival. — *Jāti-mātra, am,* n. mere birth, position in life obtained by mere birth; caste only, but not the performance of the especial duties; species, genus. — *Jātimātropajīvin* (°*ra-up*°), *ī, inī, i,* or *jātimātra-jīvin, ī, inī, i,* (a Brāhman) who lives only by his caste (without any sacerdotal acts). — *Jāti-mālā,* f. 'garland of the castes,' title of a work treating of the different castes. — *Jāti-lakshaṇa, am,* n. specific or generic distinction, characteristic, mark of tribe or caste. — *Jāti-vaćana, am,* n. the idea of species or genus. — *Jāti-vāćaka, as, ikā, am,* expressing genus, generic (as a name). — *Jāti-viveka, as,* m. title of a literary work. — *Jāti-vaira, am,* n. natural enmity, innate or instinctive hostility. — *Jāti-vailakshaṇya, am,* n. inconsistency, incompatibility, conduct or quality at variance with birth or tribe. — *Jāti-śabda, as,* m. a word expressing the idea of species or genus. — *Jāti-sampanna, as, ā, am,* sprung from a good family, belonging to a noble family. — *Jāti-sāra, as,* m. nutmeg. — *Jāti-smara, as, ā, am,* recollecting a former existence, remembering one's condition in a former life; N. of a Tīrtha. — *Jāti-smaraṇa, am,* n. recollection of a former existence. — *Jāti-svabhāva, as,* m. specific or generic character or nature. — *Jāti-hīna, as, ā, am,* of low birth or descent, void of caste, outcast, having a low position. — *Jātī-rasa, as,* m. gum myrrh. — *Jāty-andha, as, ā, am,* blind from birth, born blind.

Jātīya, as, ā, am (used at the end of a compound and by native grammarians considered as an affix), relating or belonging to any species, genus, tribe, order, family, race, &c. (e. g. *aśva-jātīya,* belonging to the horse-kind; *vṛiksha-jātīya,* belonging to trees); [cf. *vi-jātīya.*]

Jātīyaka, as, ā, am, = *jātīya;* (e. g. *evaṃ-jātīyaka,* of such a kind, of such a tribe or race.)

Jātya, as, ā, am, belonging to a family or caste; of the same family, related; sprung from a noble family, noble; well-born, legitimate, born of parents of the same caste, genuine (γνήσιος); best, excellent; pleasing, beautiful; (in mathematics) rectangular.

जातरूप *jāta-rūpa.* See col. 1.

जाति *jāti.* See col. 2.

जातु *jātu,* ind. (fr. *jan?;* cf. *janushā* under *janus*), at all, ever; possibly, perhaps; sometimes, some day, once, once upon a time (e. g. *kiṃ tena jātu jātena,* what is the use at all of him born?). *Jātu* is said to be used in connection with the potential in the sense of 'not allowing' (e. g. *jātu vṛishalaṃ yājayen na marshayāmi,* I suffer not that he should cause an outcast to sacrifice), or with a present indicative to express censure (e. g. *jātu yājayati vṛishalam,* ought he to cause an outcast to sacrifice?). In the Veda when *jātu* stands at the beginning of a sentence the verb which follows retains its accent. *Na jātu,* not at all, by no means, never; *api jātu,* perhaps, possibly; *jātu-ćit,* at some time or other, some day, one day. — *Jātū-shṭhira, as, ā, am,* Ved. eminently strong; (Sāy.) always strong; or *(as),* m., N. of a man.

जातुक *jātuka,* the plant from which the Asa Fœtida is obtained; *(am),* n. Asa Fœtida; [cf. *jatuka.*]

जातुधान *jātudhāna, as,* m. = *yātu-dhāna,* a Rākshasa, an imp, ogre or goblin.

जातुष *jātusha, as, ī, am* (fr. *jatu*), made of lac or gum, covered with lac or with any artificial form or condition of it; sticky, adhesive.

जातू *jātū*, Ved. (Sāy.) = *aśani*, a thunderbolt. — *Jātū-bharman, ā, ā, a*, Ved. (Sāy.) armed with the thunderbolt or nourishing created beings; [cf. *jātū* and *jāta*.]

जातूकर्ण *jātūkarṇa, as*, m. (fr. *jatū-karṇa?*), N. of an ancient preceptor; N. of a physician; and of the author of a law-book; an epithet of S'iva.

Jātūkarṇya, as, m., N. of several preceptors and grammarians; N. of the author of a law-book.

जान *jāna, am*, n. (fr. rt. *jan*), Ved. production, birth, origin, birthplace; (*as*), m. a patronymic of Vṛiśa.

Jānaka, as, m. (fr. *janaka*), a patronymic of Kratu-vid; also of Āya-sthūṇa; (*ī*), f. a patronymic of Sītā, the wife of Rāma; N. of a metre consisting of four lines of twenty-four syllables each. — *Jānakī-nātha* or *jānakīśa* (°*kī-īśa*), *as*, m. the husband of Sītā, i. e. Rāma. — *Jānakīnātha-śarman, ā*, m., N. of a man. — *Jānakī-rāghava, am*, n. title of a play.

Jānaki, is, m. a patronymic of Kratu-jit; also of Āya-sthūṇa.

Jānantapi, is, m. (fr. *janan-tapa*), a patronymic of Aty-arāti.

Jānapada, as, m. (fr. *jana-pada*), one who belongs to a country, a subject; (*as, ī, am*), living in the country, an inhabitant of the country (opposed to *paura*, inhabiting a town); a peasant, rustic, belonging to or suited for the inhabitants of the country; (*ā*), f. a popular expression; N. of a place; N. of an Apsaras.

Jānapadika, as, ī, am, relating to a country or to the subjects of a country.

Jānarājya, am, n. (fr. *jana-rājan*), Ved. sovereignty, supremacy.

Jānavādika or *jānevādika* or *jānovādika, as, ī, am* (fr. *jana-vāda, jane-vāda*, and *jano-vāda*), knowing the popular report.

Jānaśruti, is, m. a patronymic from Jana-śruta.

Jānaśruteya, as, m. (fr. *jana-śrutā* or *jāna-śruti*), a patronymic of Aupāvi.

Jānāyana, as, m. a patronymic from Jana.

Jānārdana, as, m. (fr. *janārdana*), a patronymic of Pra-dyumna.

1. *jānuka, as, ā, am* (fr. rt. *jan*), bringing forth. (For 2. *jānuka* see under *jānu* below.)

जानत् *jānat, an, atī, at* (fr. rt. 1. *jñā*), knowing, understanding, &c.

Jānanti, is, m., N. of a preceptor.

Jānāna, as, ā, am, knowing, understanding.

जानि *jāni* (at the end of an adj. comp. = *jani* or *jāna* for *jāyā*), a wife (e. g. *ananya-jāni*, having no other wife); [cf. *a-jāni, arundhatī-j°, dvi-j°*, &c.; cf. also Goth. *qvēns*.]

जानु *jānu, us, u*, m. n. (fr. rt. *jan?*), the knee; *jānubhyām avanīṃ gam*, to fall to the ground on one's knees; [cf. Lat. *genu*; Gr. γόνυ; Goth. *kniu*; Germ. *Knie*; Hib. *glun* (?); Slav. *koljena*; Lith. *kelis*.] — *Jānu-jangha, as*, m., N. of a king. — *Jānu-daghna, as, ī, am*, up to the knees. — *Jānuprahṛitika, as, ī, am*, produced by a blow with the knee; [cf. *jānghāprahṛitika*.] — *Jānu-phalaka* or *jānu-maṇḍala, am*, n. the knee-pan or patella. — *Jānu-vijānu, u*, n. contracting and extending the knees, a peculiar position in fighting. — *Jānu-sandhi, is*, m. the knee-joint.

2. *jānuka, as, ā, am*, at the end of an adj. comp. = *jānu*, the knee (e. g. *ūrdhva-jānuka*, having the knees raised).

जानेवादिक *jānevādika*. See *jānavādika*.

जान्धित *jāndhita, as, ā, am* (fr. *jana* and *dhita* = *hita?*), Ved. 'agreed upon by men,' customary, usual.

जान्य *jānya, as*, m. (fr. *jāni?*), N. of an ancient sage.

जाप *jāpa, as*, m. (fr. rt. *jap*), muttering, whispering, muttering prayers or telling beads, reciting passages of the Vedas &c. inaudibly; a prayer uttered in this manner; [cf. *karṇa-jāpa*.]

Jāpaka, as, ikā, am, muttering prayers, one who mutters prayers; relating to a muttered prayer; (*am*), n. a kind of fragrant wood; (a various reading has *jāyaka*.)

Jāpin, ī, inī, i, (at the end of an adj. comp.) reciting in a low voice.

Jāpya, as, ā, am, to be muttered, to be repeated in a low voice; (*am*), n. a prayer to be muttered inaudibly, the muttering of prayers &c.

जापन *jāpana, am*, n. (a Prākṛit form for *yāpana*), declining, rejection, dissent; dismissing, sending away; completing, finishing.

जाबाल 1. *jābāla, as*, m. (fr. *jabālā*), a metronymic of Mahā-śāla; also of Satya-kāma; the author of a law-book; also of a medicinal work; (*ās*), m. pl., N. of a school of the Yajur-veda. — *Jābālopanishad* (°*la-up*°), *t*, f., N. of an Upanishad belonging to the Atharva-veda.

Jābālāyana, as, m., N. of a preceptor.

Jābāli, is, m., N. of an ancient sage; also of the author of a law-book; N. of an infidel Brāhman who was one of the priests of king Daśa-ratha and after his death tried ineffectually to shake the resolution of Rāma and induce him to take the throne offered to him by his dutiful younger brother Bharata; (his speech, which is given in Rāmāyaṇa II. 108, contains doctrines very similar to those of the Cārvākas or materialists.)

Jābālin, inas, m. pl., N. of a school.

जाबाल 2. *jābāla, as*, m. (a corruption of *ajā-pāla*), a goat-herd.

जामदग्न *jāmadagna, as, ī, am* (fr. *jamad-agni*), derived from or produced by Jamad-agni; (*as*), m., N. of a Catur-aha ceremony.

Jāmadagniya and *jāmadagneya*, a patronymic from Jamad-agni.

Jāmadagnya, as, ā, am, belonging to Jamad-agni or to his son Jāmadagnya; a patronymic; (*as*), m., N. of a Catur-aha ceremony.

जामर्य *jāmarya, as, ā, am*, Ved. (Sāy.) from *jā-amarya*, making creatures immortal; but perhaps connected with a rt. *jam* for *ćam* and used as an epithet of milk.

जामल *jāmala* = *yāmala* in *kṛishṇa-jāmala* &c.

जामा *jāmā*, f. (fr. rt. *jan*), a daughter-in-law.

Jā-mātṛi, tā, m. ('the maker of [new] offspring,' or perhaps related to *jāmi* below), a daughter's husband, a son-in-law; a husband, a lord or master; a friend; the sunflower, Heliantus Annuus; [cf. *yāmātṛi*; cf. also Lat. *gener* (?); Gr. γαμβρός.] — *Jāmātṛi-tva, am*, n. the relationship of a daughter's husband.

Jāmātṛika, as, ā, am, coming from or belonging to a daughter's husband; (*as*), m. a daughter's husband.

Jāmi, is, is, i, Ved. related by blood, consanguineous, (rarely applied to a brother but often to a sister either with or without the word *svasṛi*); related like brother and sister; (in Vedic language the fingers are sometimes called *jāmayaḥ* or 'the sisters;' the *sapta jāmayaḥ* or 'seven sisters' are the seven Dhītayas or acts of devotion in the Soma worship); related in general, belonging to, peculiar to, customary, usual; (*is*), f. a sister, a virtuous and respectable woman; (more properly) a female relative of the head of a family, a daughter-in-law; N. of a deity; N. of an Apsaras; (*i*), n. blood-relationship, consanguinity, the relation of brother and sister, relation in general, descent; (in grammar and in the sacrificial language) tautology, repetition; water; [cf. *a-jāmi* and *deva-j°*.] — *Jāmi-kṛit, t, t, t*, Ved. creating relationship. — *Jāmi-tva, am*, n., Ved. consanguinity, relationship. — *Jāmi-vat*, ind., Ved. like a sister or brother. — *Jāmi-śaṇsa, as*, m., Ved. the curse pronounced by a brother or relation.

Jāmeya, as, m. a sister's son.

जामित्र *jāmitra, am*, n. (fr. the Gr. διάμετρον, in astronomy) the seventh lunar mansion.

जाम्बव *jāmbava, as, ī, am*, coming from or belonging to the Jambū tree; (*as*), m. = *jāmbavat*, q. v.; (*ī*), f., N. of a plant, = *nāga-damanī*; (*am*), n. the fruit of the Jambū tree, the rose-apple; gold; N. of a town. — *Jāmbavaushṭha* (°*va-osh*°), *am*, n. a cauterizing needle or probe; also *jāmbavoshṭha, jāmboshṭha, jāmbaushṭha*, and *jambv-oshṭha*.

Jāmbavaka, as or *am* (?), m. or n. (?), N. of a place.

Jāmbavat, ān, m. (for *jāmbava-vat?*), N. of the chief of the bears who, with the monkeys, was an ally of Rāma and therefore sometimes called a monkey; he was a son of Pitāmaha and father of Jāmbavatī who was wife of Kṛishṇa and mother of S'āmba; (*tī*), f., N. of the daughter of Jāmbavat, wife of Kṛishṇa and mother of S'āmba; N. of a plant, = *jambū*.

Jāmbuvat, ān, m. = *jāmbavat*; (*tī*), f. = *jāmbavatī*.

जाम्बीर *jāmbīra, am*, n. (fr. *jambīra*), a citron.

जाम्बील *jāmbīla, as*, m., Ved. the knee-bone, knee-pan; (said by some to be so called from its similarity to a citron, by others considered as a corruption fr. *jānu* and *bila*.)

जाम्बुक *jāmbuka, as, ī, am* (fr. *jambuka*), coming from or belonging to a jackal; *jāmbukaṃ vaćas*, a jackal's cry.

जाम्बूनद *jāmbūnada, as, ī, am* (fr. *jambū-nadī*), coming from or belonging to the river Jambū, epithet of a kind of gold; made of the gold called Jāmbūnada, golden; (*as*), m., N. of a son of Janam-ejaya; N. of a mountain; (*ī*), f., N. of a river; (*am*), n. gold from the Jambū river, any gold, a golden ornament; N. of a lake; the thorn-apple. — *Jāmbūnada-maya, as, ī, am*, made of the gold called Jāmbūnada, golden.

जाम्भ *jāmbha, as*, m. a patronymic from Jambha.

जायक *jāyaka, am*, n. a kind of yellow fragrant wood; [cf. *jāpaka* and *jāshaka*.]

जायद्रथ *jāyadratha, as, ī, am* (fr. *jayad-ratha*), belonging to Jayad-ratha.

Jāyantī-putra, as, m., N. of a preceptor.

Jāyanteya, as, m. a metronymic from Jayantī.

जायमान *jāyamāna*. See p. 338, col. 2.

जाया *jāyā*, f. (fr. rt. *jan*, to bring forth; cf. Manu IX. 8), a wife, one wedded lawfully or according to the ritual, a consort; (in astronomy) N. of the seventh mansion. — *Jāyā-ghna, as, ī, am*, a wife-murderer; (*as*), m. a mole or mark on the body indicative of the death of a wife. — *Jāyājīva* (°*yā-āj*°), *as*, m. a dancer, an actor (who gets a livelihood by his wife). — *Jāyā-tva, am*, n. the character or attributes of a wife. — *Jāyānujīvin* (°*yā-an*°), *ī*, m. an actor, a dancer, a mime; the husband of a harlot; a needy man, a pauper; a kind of crane, the Vaka or Ardea Nivea. — *Jāyā-pati, ī*, m. du. husband and wife.

जायान्य *jāyānya, as*, m., Ved. a kind of disease; [cf. *jāyenya*.]

जायिन् *jāyin, ī, inī, i* (fr. rt. 1. *ji*), conquering, subduing; (*ī*), m. a stanza repeated, the burden of a song; [cf. *dhruvaka*.]

Jāyu, us, us, u, victorious, striving to conquer or gain; (us), m. a medicine, medicament; a physician.

जायेन्य jāyenya, as, m., Ved. a kind of disease; [cf. jāyānyā.]

जार jāra, jāraka, &c. See p. 350, col. 3.

जारुधि jārudhi, is, m., N. of a mountain.

जारूथी jārūthī, f., N. of a river (?); [cf. jarūtha.]

जारूथ्य jārūthya or jāruthya. This word is generally found connected with aśva-medha, the horse sacrifice, but the meaning is doubtful.

Jāruttha, as, m. (is said to mean) a sacrifice in which three offerings are made, or in which the sun is thrice worshipped in his southern declination (?).

जार्तिक jārtika, ās, m. pl. a various reading for jartika.

जार्य jārya, as, ā, am, Ved. (according to Sāy.) 'to be praised' (as if fr. 3. jṛī); but perhaps rather (am), n. familiarity, intimacy, (fr. jāra.)

जार्यक jāryaka, as, m. a particular animal.

जाल jāla, am, n. (fr. rt. jal and connected with 1. jala), a net (for catching birds &c.); a web, a spider's web, cobweb, net-work, any reticulated or woven texture, a wire net, reticulated or chain-armour, a coat of mail, a helmet made of wire; a lattice, an eyelet or loophole, a window; a collection, multitude, assemblage; the membrane which unites the toes of many water-birds; the membrane between the fingers and toes of divine beings and godlike or heroic personages; a disease of the eyes in which the blood-vessels are filled with blood and look like net-work; an unblown flower; magic; conjuring, illusion, deception; pride, arrogance; (wrong reading for jāta), kind; (as), m. the tree Nauclea Cadamba, the young fruit of a gourd or cucumber; (ī), f. a small cucumber, Trichosanthes Dioeca, any medicament or drug. —Jāla-karman, a, n. the occupation of catching fish, fishing. —Jāla-kāraka, as, m. a web-maker, a spider, a net-maker. —Jāla-kīṭa, as, m., N. of an Udīćya-grāma. —Jāla-kshīrya, am, n. a kind of plant containing a poisonous juice. —Jāla-gardabha, as, m. a kind of pimple or boil; [cf. gardabha-gada, &c.] —Jāla-goṇikā, f. a kind of churning-vessel. —Jāla-daṇḍa, as, m., Ved. the pole of a net. —Jāla-padī, f., N. of a place. —Jāla-pād, t, m. a goose ('web-foot'). —Jāla-pāda, as, ī, am, having a web-like membrane between the toes, web-footed; (as), m. a web-footed bird; N. of a frog; of a magician. —Jāla-prāyā, f. armour, iron net-work, chain-armour. —Jāla-baddha, as, ā, am, caught in a net, snared. —Jāla-bhuja, as, ā, am, having the rudiments of a web-like membrane between the fingers. —Jāla-vat, ān, atī, at, furnished with a net or net-like texture, reticulated; covered with iron net-work or retiform armour; (according to some) cunning, deceptive. —Jāla-varvūraka, as, m., N. of a plant, a kind of Varvūra. —Jālāksha (°la-ak°), am, n. (?) a loophole, eyelethole, window.

Jālaka, am, n. a net, woven texture, web; multitude, assemblage; a lattice; an eyelet or loophole; a nest; a collection or bundle of buds, a germ, an unblown flower; a plantain, the fruit; illusion; pride; (as), m. a window, a lattice, a loop or eyelethole; N. of a tree; (ikā), f. a net (for catching birds &c.); chain-armour, armour; a spider; a leech; a kind of cloth or raiment, woollen cloth; plantain; iron; a widow, (perhaps so called from the net or braid worn by widows.) —Jālaka-mālin, ī, inī, i, veiled.

Jālāya, nom. A. jālāyate, to be like a net, to form a net-like enclosure.

Jālika, as, ī, am, one who uses nets to gain a livelihood, a fisherman, a fowler, birdcatcher, any hunter using nets; (as), m. a spider; the president of a district, governor of a province; a cheat, a rogue, a vagabond, a conjurer or juggler.

Jālin, ī, inī, i, having a net; retiform; having a window; illusory, deceptive; (inī), f., scil. piḍakā, a term applied to certain boils or pustules which make their appearance in the disease called Pra-meha; a painted room or one ornamented with pictures; = śveta-ghoshā, ghoshātakī, kośātakī, a species of melon or gourd (the rind of which is reticulated like a net).

Jālya, as, ā, am, liable to be caught in a net.

जालकि jālaki, ayas, m. pl., N. of a subdivision of the Trigarta people.

Jālakīya, as, m. a prince of the above people.

जालकिनी jālakinī, f. a sheep, an ewe.

जालन्धर jālandhara, as, m. (fr. jalandhara), N. of a country situated in the north-west of India, apparently part of Lahore, and perhaps the modern Jallindhar or Julinder; (ās), m. pl. its inhabitants. —Jālandharopākhyāna (°ra-up°), am, n. title of an episode of the Padma-Purāṇa.

Jālandharāyaṇa, a patronymic from Jalan-dhara.

Jālandharāyaṇaka, as, ikā, am, inhabited by the Jālandharāyaṇas.

Jālandhari, is, m., N. of a physician.

Jālahrada, as, m. a patronymic from Jala-hrada.

जालमानि jālamāni, is, m. a patronymic; (ayas), m. pl., N. of a subdivision of the Trigarta people.

Jālamānīya, as, m. a prince of the above people.

जालवाल jālavāla, as, m. a kind of fish, = vādāla.

जालाष jālāsha, am, n. (fr. jalāsha), Ved. a particular drug or anodyne with soothing qualities.

जालोर jālora, as, m., N. of an Agra-hāra.

जाल्म jālma, as, ī, am, cruel, harsh, severe; inconsiderate, rash, acting without thinking; (as, ī), m. f. a despised or contemptible person, a rogue; a wretch, a miscreant, a low man, one of a degraded tribe or occupation; one who reads or recites badly (Pāṇ. VI. 2, 158); [cf. Hib. galmha, 'hardness, hardihood, rigour, valour.']

Jālmaka, as, ikā, am, base, despised, contemptible, low.

जावड jāvaḍa, as, m., N. of a man; [cf. bhāvaḍa.]

जावत् jā-vat, ān, atī, at, Ved. possessing offspring, granting offspring; (Sāy.) received by praiseworthy persons (epithet of the Soma).

जावन्य jāvanya, am, n. (fr. javana), quickness, swiftness, rapidity.

जावालि jāvāli. See jābāli.

जाषक jāshaka, am, n. (a various reading for jāyaka), a kind of yellow fragrant wood.

जाष्कमद jāshkamada, as, m., Ved. a particular species of animal.

जासट jāsaṭa, as, m., N. of a man.

जास्पति jās-pati, jāspatya. See under jā at p. 343.

जाह jāha, am, n. (used at the end of a comp. and considered as an affix), the root or point of issue of certain parts of the body (e. g. oshṭha-jāha, the point of issue of the lips; cf. akshi-j°, karṇa-j°, keśa-j°, nakha-j°.)

जाहक jāhaka, as, m. a kind of animal; a polecat, a cat; Lemur Tardigradus; a leech; a bed, a cot.

जाहुष jāhusha, as, m., Ved., N. of a man protected by the Aśvins.

जाह्नव jāhnava, as, m. (fr. jahnu), a patronymic of Viśvā-mitra; also of Su-ratha; N. of a Catur-aha ceremony; (ī), f. the daughter of Jahnu, an epithet of the river Gaṅgā or Ganges. —Jāhnavī-phena-lekhā, f. a streak of the foam of the Ganges.

Jāhnavīya, as, ā, am, belonging or relating to the river Gaṅgā.

जि 1. ji, cl. 1. P. A. jayati, -te, jigāya, jigye, jeshyati, -te, ajaishīt, ajeshṭa, jetum (Ved. Inf. jetave and jishe), to win or acquire by conquest (or in gambling), to conquer, defeat, vanquish, overcome; excel, surpass; to vanquish in a game or in a suit at law; to convict; to conquer the passions; overcome a disease &c.; to expel from (with abl.); to be victorious, to gain the upper hand: Pass. jīyate: Caus. jāpayati, -yitum; Aor. ajījapat, to cause to conquer or win: Pass. of Caus. jāpyate, to be made to conquer: Desid. jigīshati, to wish to win, obtain, conquer, vanquish or excel &c., to vie with, emulate; to seek for prey: Intens. jejīyate, jejayīti, jejeti; [cf. Lith. galu, galybė; Hib. gar, 'profit, advantage, gain, good.']

Jaya, as, ā, am, conquering; (as), m. conquest, see s. v. at p. 339.

2. ji, is, is, i, victorious, conquering, a victor; (is), m. a Piśāća, a demon.

Jigīshat, an, antī, at, wishing or striving to overcome, emulous, ambitious, a warrior.

Jigīshamāṇa, as, ā, am, striving to win.

Jigīshā, f. desire of gaining or obtaining; desire of conquering or vanquishing or overpowering; military ardour; wish to excel, emulation, rivalry; eminence; usage, profession or habit of life.

Jigīshu, us, us, u, wishing to gain or obtain, seeking for; striving to conquer or overcome, or to excel, vying or contending with; (us), m., N. of a man. —Jigīshu-tā, f. desire of conquering, emulation.

Jigyu, us, us, u, Ved. victorious, triumphant.

Jit, t, t, t, (at the end of a comp.) winning, vanquishing, conquering, removing (e. g. śatru-jit, vanquishing enemies); [cf. ananta-jit, abhimāti-j°, aśva-j°, ugra-j°.] —1. jit-tama, as, ā, am, (at end of comp.) most victorious, first of conquerors; [cf. 2. jittama.]

Jita, as, ā, am, conquered, vanquished, subdued; surpassed, overcome, subject to, enslaved by (e. g. kāma-jita, under the dominion of lust); won, gained, obtained; (as), m. one of the attendants upon a Jina or Jaina saint; (a wrong form for a-jita.) —Jita-kāśi, is, m. the fist doubled. —Jita-kāśin, ī, inī, i, appearing victorious. —Jita-kopa or jita-krodha, as, ā, am, one who has subdued anger, imperturbable, not to be roused to wrath. —Jita-klama, as, ā, am, one who has overcome fatigue. —Jita-nemi, is, m. a staff made of the wood of the religious fig-tree (carried during the performance of certain vows). —Jita-manyu, us, us, u, one who has subdued his wrath; (as), m. an epithet of Vishṇu. —Jita-loka, as, ā, am, one who has conquered heaven, epithet of a class of manes. —Jita-vatī, f., N. of a daughter of Uśīnara. —Jita-vrata, as, m., N. of a son of Havir-dhāna. —Jita-śatru, us, us, u, one whose enemies are conquered, conquering foes, victorious, triumphant; (us), m., N. of a Buddha; the father of A-jita, the second Arhat of the present Ava-sarpiṇī. —Jita-śrama, as, m. one who has conquered toil, free from worldly cares, a stoic. —Jita-svarga, as, ā, am, one who has conquered or won heaven. —Jitākshara (°ta-ak°), as, ā, am, 'one who has mastered the letters,' reading well or readily. —Jitātman (°ta-āt°), ā, ā, a, self-subdued, void of passion; (ā), m., N. of one of the Viśve-devas. —Jitāmitra (°ta-am°), as, ā, am, one who has conquered an enemy, triumphant, victorious; (as), m. an epithet of Vishṇu. —Jitāri (°ta-ari), is, is, i, triumphant over an enemy; (is), m., N. of a son of Avikshit; a Buddha; N. of the father of Sam-bhava, the third Arhat of the present Ava-sarpiṇī. —Jitāhava (°ta-āh°), as, ā, am, one who has won a battle, victorious, triumphant. —Jitāhāra (°ta-āh°), as, ā, am, one who by abstraction is able to do without food. —Jitendriya (°ta-in°), as, ā, *am*, one who has conquered his passions or subdued the senses, calm, impassive, unmoved; (*as*), m. an ascetic, a sage; N. of a man. — *Jitendriya-tva, am*, n. subjugation of the senses or passions. — *Jitendriyāhva* (°*ya-āh*°), *as*, m., N. of a plant, = *kāma-vriddhi*.

Jiti, is, f. gaining, obtaining, a victory, conquest.

Jitya, as, ā, am, conquerable, vincible; (*ā*), f. victory, acquisition, gain; a ploughshare; (*as*), m. a harrow.

Jitvan, ā, arī, a, victorious; (*ā*), m., N. of a man.

Jitvara, as, ī, am, victorious, triumphant; (*ī*), f. 'Victrix,' N. of the city Benares.

Jitvā, ind. having conquered or excelled.

Jetavya, as, ā, am, to be conquered or overcome, conquerable, vincible; to be surpassed.

Jeya, as, ā, am, = *jetavya* above.

जिकण *jikaṇa, as*, m., N. of a lawyer.

जिगत्नु *jigatnu, us, us, u* (reduplicated form fr. rt. *gam*), going quickly, fleet; (*us*), m. breath, life.

Jigamishat, an, antī, at (fr. Desid. of rt. *gam*), wishing or endeavouring to go.

Jigamishā, f. wish to go or move, intention to go.

Jigamishu, us, us, u, wishing to go, intending or purposing to go.

जिगरिषु *jigarishu, us, us, u* (fr. Desid. of rt. 2. *grī*), wishing to swallow or devour, desirous of seizing.

Jigarti, is, m., Ved. a swallower, devourer; swallowing.

जिगीषा *jigīshā*. See p. 346, col. 3.

जिघत्नु *jighatnu, us, us, u* (fr. rt. *han*), Ved. endeavouring to hurt.

Jighāṅsaka, as, ikā, am (fr. Desid. of rt. *han*), wishing or endeavouring to kill, revengeful.

Jighāṅsā, f. wish or intention to strike, slay, or destroy; malice, revenge.

Jighāṅsin, ī, inī, i, intending to kill.

Jighāṅsīyas, ān, asī, as (compar. of the last), more intent on slaughter, very desirous of killing.

Jighāṅsu, us, us, u, intending or seeking to kill or slay, desirous of destroying, malicious, murderous, revengeful; (*us*), m. an unrelenting foe, an enemy.

जिघत्सत् *jighatsat, an, antī, at* (fr. Desid. of rt. *ghas*), wishing to eat, hungry.

Jighatsā, f. desire of eating, hunger, voracity.

Jighatsu, us, us, u, hungry, voracious; (*us*), f. an epithet of evil demons.

जिघृक्षत् *jighrikshat, an, antī, at*, or *jighrikshamāṇa, as, ā, am* (fr. Desid. of rt. *grah*), wishing or intending to take or seize, greedy, avaricious.

Jighrikshā, f. wish or intention to take or seize, greediness, covetousness.

Jighrikshu, us, us, u, wishing or intending to take or seize, covetous, avaricious; wishing to rob or deprive of; wishing to take up (a fluid); wishing to gather; wishing to learn.

जिघ्र *jighra, as, ā, am* (fr. rt. *ghrā*), smelling, a smeller; observing, conjecturing.

Jighrat, an, antī, at, smelling, smelling at.

जिङ्गशल्य *jingaśalya, as*, m. the tree Mimosa Catechu; [cf. *jihma-śalya*.]

जिङ्गिनी *jinginī*, f., N. of a plant, = *jhinginī, jhingī, pra-modinī, suniryāsā*.

जिङ्गी *jingī*, f. the plant Rubia Munjista.

जिजीविषा *jijīvishā*, f. (fr. Desid. of rt. *jīv*), desire to live.

Jijīvishu, us, us, u, wishing to live, desirous of life.

जिज्ञापयिषु *jijñāpayishu, us, us, u* (fr. Desid. of Caus. of 1. *jñā*), wishing to make known, seeking to inform, communicative.

Jijñāsaka, as, ā, am (fr. Desid. of 1. *jñā*), wishing to know, = *jijñāsu*.

Jijñāsana, am, n. desire of knowing or becoming acquainted with, examining.

Jijñāsanīya, as, ā, am, = *jijñāsya* below.

Jijñāsamāna, as, ā, am, desirous of knowing, inquiring, testing, investigating, proving.

Jijñāsā, f. desire of knowing or becoming acquainted with, inquiring; inquisitiveness; search, investigation, examination, test.

Jijñāsita, as, ā, am, investigated, asked, inquired, sought.

Jijñāsu, us, us, u, desirous of knowing, wishing to become acquainted with, inquiring, inquisitive, curious, examining.

Jijñāsya, as, ā, am, deserving of being inquired into, desirable to be known, worthy of being investigated; an object for inquiry, to be investigated or examined.

Jijñu, us, us, u, = *jijñāsu* (?).

जिडधन *jiḍadhana, as*, m., N. of a son of Paramānanda.

जित *jita*, &c. See under rt. 1. *ji*.

जित्तम 2. *jittama* or *jituma* or *jitma, as*, m. (a word borrowed fr. the Gr. δίδυμοι), the sign of the zodiac Gemini.

जिन *jina, as, ā, am* (fr. rt. 1. *ji*), victorious, triumphant; (*as*), m. 'the overcomer of all things,' a generic term applied to a Buddha or chief saint of the Bauddha sect in the same manner as to a Jaina saint; a N. applied to an Arhat who is a kind of sovereign pontiff or saint of the Jainas and regarded by them as superior to the gods of other sects; (twenty-four Jinas are supposed to flourish in each of the three Ava-sarpiṇīs or Jaina ages, past, present, and to come, making seventy-two in all; they are all born in Āryāvarta); N. of a Bodhi-sattva; an epithet of Vishṇu; any very old man; [cf. *jīna* and *jīrna*.] — *Jina-trāta* or *jina-datta* or *jina-putra, as*, or *jina-bandhu, us*, m., N. of various persons mentioned in Buddhist writings. — *Jina-dharma, as*, m., N. of a Jaina work. — *Jina-bhakti-sūri, is*, m., N. of a preceptor of Jina-lābha-sūri. — *Jina-mitra, as*, m., N. of one of the translators of the Lalita-vistara. — *Jina-lābha-sūri, is*, m., N. of a pupil of Jina-bhakti-sūri and preceptor of Kshamā-kalyāṇa. — *Jina-vaktra, as*, m., N. of a Buddha. — *Jina-śrī, īs*, m., N. of a king. — *Jina-sadman, a*, n. a Jaina temple or monastery. — *Jina-sena, as*, m., N. of the author of the work Trishashṭi-lakshaṇa-mahāpurāṇa-saṅgraha. — *Jinānkura* (°*na-an*°), *as*, m., N. of a Bodhi-sattva. — *Jinādhāra* (°*na-ādh*°), *as*, m., N. of a Bodhi-sattva. — *Jinendra* (°*na-in*°), *as*, m. a Jaina saint, a Buddha; N. of a grammarian. — *Jinendra-nyāsa, as*, m. title of the work of Jinendra-buddhi. — *Jinendra-buddhi* or *jinendra-bhūti, is*, m., N. of a writer on grammar. — *Jineśvara* (°*na-īś*°), *as*, m. an Arhat of the Jainas; N. of the twentieth Arhat of the past Ut-sarpiṇī. — *Jinottama* (°*na-ut*°), *as*, m. an Arhat of the Jainas. — *Jinorasa* (°*na-ur*°), *as*, m., N. of a Bodhi-sattva.

जिनयोनि *jina-yoni, is*, m. (for *ajina-yoni*, q. v.), a deer.

जिन्दुराज *jindu-rāja, as*, m., N. of a man.

जिन्व् *jinv* (connected with *jīv* and *jū*?), cl. 1. P., Ved. *jinvati, jijinva, jinvishyati, jinvitum*, to move one's self, be active or lively; to urge on, cause to move quickly, impel, incite, excite; to refresh, animate; to promote, help, favour; to help any one (acc.) to anything (dat.), cause to obtain, grant, confer; to please, satisfy, gladden, gratify, make happy or contented; to receive favourably (a request &c.): cl. 10. P. *jinvayati*, a various reading for *juñć*.

Jinva, as, ā, am, in *dhiyaṅ-jinva*, q. v.

जिम् *jim* [cf. *ćham, jam, jham*], cl. 1. P. *jemati*, &c., to eat.

Jemana, am, n. eating; food, victuals.

जिम्भ *jimbha*, perhaps for *jrimbha* in *jimbha-jihva-tā*, swelling of the tongue.

जिरण *jiraṇa, as*, m. = *jaraṇa, jīraka, jīraṇa*, cumin.

जिरि *jiri*, cl. 5. P. *jiriṇoti*, &c., to hurt, injure, wound, kill; [cf. *ćiri*; cf. also Hib. *gearaim*, 'I sharpen, whet, cut, bite.']

जिल्लिक *jillika, ās*, m. pl., N. of a people.

जिवाजिव *jivājiva, as*, m. a pheasant; [cf. *jīvaṅ-jīva*.]

जिव्रि *jivri, is, is, i* (fr. 1. *jrī*), Ved. old, worn out, decayed, decrepit; (*is*), m. time; a bird.

जिष् *jish*, cl. 1. P. *jeshati*, &c., to sprinkle; [cf. *vish* and *mish*.]

जिष्णु *jishṇu, us, us, u* (fr. rt. 1. *ji*), victorious, triumphant, gaining, winning; (with acc. or at end of comp.) vanquishing, conquering, excelling; (*us*), m. the sun; an epithet of Indra, of Vishṇu, and of Arjuna; N. of a Vasu; N. of a son of Manu Bhautya, N. of the father of Brahma-gupta; [cf. *parā-jishṇu*.]

जिहान *jihāna, as; ā, am* (fr. rt. *hā, jihīte*), going, going to, attaining, obtaining.

Jihānaka, as, m. the destruction of the world; [cf. *jahānaka*.]

जिहासा *jihāsā*, f. (fr. Desid. of rt. *hā, jahāti*), desire of abandoning or giving up.

Jihāsu, us, us, u, desirous of abandoning or giving up.

जिहीर्षा *jihīrshā*, f. (fr. Desid. of rt. *hri*), desire of seizing, taking, or robbing; wish to take away or remove.

Jihīrshu, us, us, u, wishing to seize, desirous of taking or carrying or removing, wishing to rob or appropriate.

Jihīrshya, as, ā, am, desirable to be taken away or brought near.

जिह्म *jihma, as, ā, am* (perhaps related to rt. *hvri*; but said to be fr. rt. *hā, jahāti*, and to denote originally quitting the upright direction or leaning out of the perpendicular), sloping, oblique, transverse, diagonal, athwart, squinting (as the eye), crooked, awry, not straight (opposed to *riju*), tortuous, going irregularly; (*jihmam i* or *gam*, to go crookedly, turn off from the right way); curved, bent; morally crooked, deceitful, deceptive, illusory, false, untrue, unfair, dishonest; slow, lazy; (*am*), n. falsehood, dishonesty; the plant Tabernæmontana Coronaria (*tagara*); [cf. Hib. *giomh*, 'a lock of hair, a fault.'] — *Jihma-ga, as, ā, am*, going tortuously or crookedly, moving slowly; (*as*), m. a snake. — *Jihma-gati, is, is, i*, going tortuously. — *Jihma-tā*, f. or *jihma-tva, am*, n. crookedness, curvature; dishonesty, falsehood. — *Jihma-bāra, as, ā, am*, Ved. having an aperture on one side; (Sāy.) having an opening below; having its door closed. — *Jihma-mīna, as*, m. appearing in the deceptive shape of a fish. — *Jihma-mohana, as*, m. a frog. — *Jihma-yodhin, ī, inī, i*, fighting unfairly; (*ī*), m. epithet of Bhīma, who in his great battle with Dur-yodhana struck him an unfair blow with his club on the thighs; (see Śalya-parva 3345.) — *Jihma-śalya, as*, m. the tree Acacia Catechu; [cf. *khadira*.] — *Jihma-śī, īs, īs, i*, Ved. lying crookedly or diagonally (on the ground &c.). — *Jihmāksha* (°*ma-ak*°), *as, ī, am*, crooked-eyed, squinting. — *Jihmāśin* (°*ma-aś*°), *ī*, m. 'eating crookedly,' N. of a man; (perhaps a wrong reading for *jihvāśin*.)

Jihmāya, nom. P., Ved. *-yati, -yitum*, to go crookedly or in crooked ways.

Jihmita, as, ā, am, bent, bowed, curved; turned away.

Jihmī-kṛi, cl. 8. P. *-karoti, -kartum*, to make crooked, bend. — *Jihmī-kara, as, ā, am*, making crooked or oblique, causing to bend; (metaphorically) obscuring. — *Jihmī-kṛita, as, ā, am*, made crooked, bent, bowed down (with fear &c.).

जिह्व *jihva, as*, m. (said to be fr. rt. 1. *ji*, perhaps fr. rt. *hve*; cf. 1. *juhū*), the tongue; (*ā*), f. the tongue; the tongue or tongues of Agni, i. e. various forms of flame, (sometimes three are mentioned, sometimes seven, the names of which are given as follows: *kālī, karālī, mano-javā, su-lohitā, sudhūmra-varṇā, sphuliṅginī, viśva-rūpī*; or are identified with the seven winds, *pra-vaha, ā-vaha, ud-vaha, sam-vaha, vi-vaha, pari-vaha*, and *ni-vaha*. The horses of Agni or *vahnayaḥ* are said to be *sapta-jihvāḥ*, having seven tongues); the root of the plant Tabernæmontana Coronaria; [cf. *jihma*; cf. also Lat. *lingua?*; Goth. *tuggô*; Germ. *Zunge*; Hib. *teanga?*]. — *Jihvā-kātya, as*, m., N. of a man, the voracious Kātya. — *Jihvāgra* (°*vā-ag*°), *am*, n. the tip of the tongue. — *Jihvā-tala, am*, n. the surface of the tongue. — *Jihvā-nirlekhana* and *jihvā-nirlekhanika, am*, n. scraping the tongue; a tongue-scraper; [cf. *jihvollekhana*.] — *Jihvā-pa, as*, m. ('drinking with the tongue'), a dog; a cat; a tiger; a panther, the hunting leopard; a bear. — *Jihvā-prathana, am*, n. expansion or too great flattening of the tongue (a defect in pronunciation). — *Jihvā-mala, am*, n. the fur of the tongue. — *Jihvā-mūla, am*, n. the root of the tongue. — *Jihvāmūlīya, as, ā, am*, belonging to or uttered from the root of the tongue, a term applied to the vowels *ṛi, ḷṛi*, the Visarga before *k, kh*, and the guttural class of consonants, but especially to the Visarga before *k, kh*. — *Jihvā-rada, as*, m. 'having a tongue-like beak,' a bird. — *Jihvā-lih, ṭ*, m. 'licking with the tongue,' a dog. — *Jihvā-laulya, am*, n. greediness. — *Jihvā-vat, ān*, m., N. of a preceptor. — *Jihvā-śata, am*, n. a hundred tongues. — *Jihvā-śalya, as*, m. = *jihma-śalya*, q. v. — *Jihvā-śodhana, am*, n. cleaning of the tongue. — *Jihvāsvāda* (°*vā-ās*°), *as*, m. 'tasting with the tongue,' licking, lapping. — *Jihvollekhana* (°*vā-ul*°), *am*, n. scraping the tongue; (*ī* and *ikā*), f. a tongue-scraper made of a thin piece of wood of the Mimusops Kauki or other trees.

Jihvaka at the end of an adj. comp. in *a-jihvakā*, f. tongueless.

Jihvala, as, ā, am, voracious, greedy.

Jihvikā, f. a diminutive fr. *jihvā*; [cf. *adho-jihvikā, ali-j*°, *upa-j*°, *prati-j*°.]

जिह्वु *jihvu, us*, m., N. of a man.

जी *jī*, in *kṛishṇa-jī* and *keśava-jī-nanda-śarman*, = the Bengālī *jī* (fr. *jīva*, life, soul?), sir, master, madam, attached to names and titles as a mark of endearment or respect.

जीत *jīta*, &c. See rt. 1. *jyā*, p. 352.

Jīti, is, f. fading away. See *a-jīti*.

Jīna, as, ā, am, old, aged; a leather bag.

जीमूत *jīmūta, as*, m. (said to be fr. rt. 1. *ji*), a cloud; a mountain; N. of the sun; N. of Indra; a nourisher, a sustainer; the plant Lipeocercis Serrata; also Luffa Fœtida or a similar plant; a kind of Cyperus; a kind of metre; N. of an ancient sage; of a certain wrestler; of a son of Vyoman. — *Jīmūta-kuṭa, as*, m. a small hill near a mountain. — *Jīmūta-ketu, us*, m. an epithet of Śiva; N. of a prince of the Vidyā-dharas. — *Jīmūta-mūla, am*, n. Curcuma Amhaldi or Zerumbet. — *Jīmūta-vāhana, as*, m. an epithet of Indra; N. of a son of king Śāli-vāhana; N. of a son of Jīmūta-ketu; N. of a lawyer, author of the Dāya-bhāga. — *Jīmūta-vāhin, ī*, m. smoke. — *Jīmūta-svana-sannibha, as, ā, am*, like the sound of a cloud. — *Jīmūtāshṭamī* (°*ta-ash*°), f., N. of a festival in honour of Jīmūta-vāhana, son of Śāli-vāhana, on the eighth day in the dark half of month Āśvina.

Jīmūtaka, as, m. the plant Lipeocercis Serrata.

जीर *jīra, as, ā, am* (said to be fr. rt. *jinv*), Ved. quick, speedy, lively, active, busy; driving, exciting; *go-jīra*, exciting (the milk of) the cows; (*as*), m. quick motion or movement (especially of the Soma stones); a sword, a scymitar, a sacrificial knife; Panicum Miliaceum; cumin-seed, (in this latter sense said to be fr. rt. *ju* or 1. *jṛī*.) — *Jīra-dānu, us, us, u*, Ved. dropping, trickling, drizzling, sprinkling or scattering in small drops; causing to flow abundantly; (Sāy.) 'granting a victorious disposition' (as if fr. rt. 1. *ji*). — *Jīrādhvara* (°*ra-adh*°), *as, ā, am*, Ved. having animated or vigorous rites; (Sāy.) free from injury or molestation. — *Jīrāśva* (°*ra-aś*°), *as, ā, am*, Ved. having lively or fleet horses.

Jīraka or *jīraṇa, as*, m. cumin-seed.

Jīri, is, m. f., Ved. quick or flowing water.

Jīrikā, f., N. of a plant, = *jīrṇa-pattrikā*.

जीर्ण *jīrṇa*. See under rt. 1. *jṛī*.

जीर्वि *jīrvi, is*, m. (said to be fr. rt. 1. *jṛī*), an axe; a cart; the body; an animal.

जीव् *jīv*, cl. 1. P. (poet. also A.) *jīvati, -te, jijīva, jīvishyati, jīvitum*, to live, be alive; to revive, return to life; to make a livelihood, live by (with inst.): Caus. P. (ep. also A.) *jīvayati, -te, -yitum*, to make alive, restore to life, vivify; to support life, to keep alive; to nourish, nurture, bring up; (a Causal form *jīvāpayati* occasionally occurs, meaning 'to restore to life'): Desid. *jijīvishati* (Ved. *jujyūshati* or *jijyūshati*), to wish to live, to seek a livelihood, wish to live by (with inst.); [cf. Lith. *gyvénu*, 'to live;' *gywas*, 'alive:' Slav. *schivû*, 'to live:' Goth. *qvivs*: Old Germ. *qech*: Angl. Sax. *cwic*: Eng. *quick*: Lat. *vivo*.]

Jīva, as, ā, am, living, existing, a living being; causing to live, vivifying; (*as*), m. the principle of life, the vital breath, the living or personal soul incorporated in the body and imparting to it life, motion, and sensation, (hence also called *jīvātman*; it is distinguished from the *paramātman* or supreme soul, q. v.); livelihood, profession, specific occupation; a kind of plant; an epithet of Bṛihaspati as regent of the planet Jupiter; or as regent of the Nakshatra Tishya or Pushya; the third lustrum in the cycle of Jupiter which lasts sixty years; N. of one of the eight Maruts; an epithet of Karṇa; (*as, am*), m. n. life, existence; (*ā*), f. the living or life-giving element, i. e. water; the earth; a bow-string; (in geometry) the chord of an arc, the sine of an arc; the tinkling of metallic ornaments; N. of two plants, = *jīvantī* and *vacā*; [cf. Lith. *gyvas*, 'alive;' Goth. *qvivs*; Lat. *vivus*; Gr. βίος; Hib. *beo*, 'living, alive.'] — *Jīva-gṛibh, -ghṛip, p, p*, Ved. taking alive, seizing beings alive. — *Jīva-graha, as*, m., Ved. filling (a cup) with the living Soma, i. e. with the plant in its unpressed state. — *Jīva-grāha, as*, m. a prisoner, one taken alive; *jīva-grāham grah*, to capture alive. — *Jīva-ghosha-svāmin, ī*, m., N. of a grammarian. — *Jīva-ja, as, ā, am*, born alive. — *Jīva-jīva* or *jīva-jīvaka, as*, m. a kind of bird; see the next. — *Jīvañ-jīva, as*, m. a kind of bird supposed to be a pheasant; the Chakor or Greek partridge; a kind of tree. — *Jīva-tokā*, f. a woman whose children are living. — *Jīva-tva, am*, n. the state of life or existence. — 1. *jīva-da, as, ā, am* (rt. *dā*), 'life-giving,' who or what gives life; (*as*), m. a physician, a practitioner of medicine. — 2. *jīva-da, as*, m. (rt. *do*), 'cutting off life,' an enemy. — *Jīva-daśā*, f. mortal existence. — *Jīva-dātrī*, f. 'life-giver,' a kind of medicinal plant, = *ṛiddhi*. — *Jīva-dāna, am*, n. 'giving life,' 'rescuing from sickness,' title of a manual of medicine composed by Cyavana. — *Jīva-dānu, us, us, u*, Ved. a wrong form for *jīra-dānu*, q. v. — *Jīva-dāman, ā*, m., N. of a prince. — *Jīva-dāyaka, as, ā, am*, 'life-giving.' — *Jīva-dhana, am*, n. 'living wealth,' property in living creatures, live stock, wealth in flocks and herds. — *Jīva-dhanya, as, ā, am*, 'supporting living beings;' (Sāy.) 'satiating living beings,' an epithet of Soma, and of Prajā-pati. — *Jīva-dhānī*, f. 'receptacle of living beings,' an epithet of the earth. — *Jīva-naś, k, k, k*, or *ṭ, ṭ, ṭ*, (a sacrifice &c.) where living beings are killed. — *Jīva-nātha, as*, m., N. of a writer on astronomy; N. of a physician. — *Jīva-nāya* or *jīva-nāyaka, as*, m., N. of a poet. — *Jīva-nāśam*, ind. with *naś*, to lose one's life, die, perish. — *Jīva-nikāya, as*, m. a being endowed with life. — *Jīva-netrī*, f., N. of a plant, = *saiṃhalī*. — *Jīva-pati, is*, * m. a living husband. — *Jīva-pattra, am*, n. a fresh leaf. — *Jīvapattra-pracāyikā*, f. gathering fresh leaves, a sort of game. — *Jīva-patnī*, f. a woman whose husband is alive. — *Jīva-pitṛi, tā, trī, tṛi*, or *jīva-pitṛika, as, ā, am*, a son or daughter whose father is still alive. — *Jīva-pīta-sarga, as, ā, am*, Ved. one whose rays are drunk by living beings; (Sāy.) one whose creation is enjoyed by all. — *Jīva-putra, as, ā* or *ī, am*, one whose sons or children are living; (*as*), m. a kind of plant. — *Jīva-putraka, as*, m. a tree, commonly Ingua; another plant bearing seeds used in rosaries, commonly Jiyaputa, Nageia Putranjiva. — *Jīvaputra-pracāyikā*, f. the gathering of the above plant, a sort of game. — *Jīva-purā*, f., Ved. the abode of living beings or men. — *Jīva-pushpa, am*, n. 'flower of life,' N. of a plant and metaphorically applied to the head; N. of two plants, = *damanaka* and *phaṇijjhaka*; (*ā*), f., N. of a plant, = *bṛihaj-jīvantī*. — *Jīva-priyā*, f. the tree Terminalia Chebula, = *harītakī*. — *Jīva-badha, as*, m. destruction of living beings. — *Jīva-barhis, is, is, is*, Ved. having a living, i.e. fresh bed of sacrificial grass. — *Jīva-bhadrā*, f a kind of plant, = *jīvantī*; a kind of medicinal plant, = *vṛiddhi*. — *Jīva-bhūta, as, ā, am*, become alive, endowed with life. — *Jīva-bhojana, as, ā, am*, Ved. giving enjoyment to living beings; (*am*), n. the pleasure or enjoyment of living beings. — *Jīva-mandira, am*, n. 'the mansion of the soul,' the body. — *Jīva-maya, as, ī, am*, animated, endowed with life. — *Jīva-miśra, as*, m., N. of an author. — *Jīva-yāja, as*, m., Ved. the sacrifice of living beings. — *Jīva-yoni, is, is, i*, enclosing a soul (as a body or a sentient being). — *Jīva-rakta, am*, n. living blood, menstrual blood. — *Jīva-rahita, as, ā, am*, lifeless. — *Jīva-loka, as*, m. the world or habitation of living beings (opposed to the world of deceased ancestors), living beings, mankind. — *Jīva-lauk̄ika, as, ā, am*, peculiar to the world of living beings or to men. — *Jīva-vat, ān, atī, at*, animated, living. — *Jīva-vallī*, f., N. of a plant. — *Jīva-vicāra, as*, m. title of a Jaina work. — *Jīvavicāra-prakaraṇa, am*, n. title of a Jaina work by Śānti-sūri. — *Jīva-vṛitti, is*, f. breeding or keeping cattle. — *Jīva-śaṃsa, as*, m., Ved. rule over living beings; (Sāy.) to be praised by living beings. — *Jīva-śarman, ā*, m., N. of an astronomer. — *Jīva-śāka, as*, m. a kind of pot-herb growing in Mālava — *Jīva-śuklā*, f. a kind of plant. — *Jīva-śesha, as, ā, am*, one to whom only life is left or who has escaped with his life and nothing more. — *Jīva-śoṇita, am*, n. living, i.e. healthy blood. — *Jīva-śreshṭhā*, f. a kind of medicinal plant. — *Jīva-saṅkramaṇa, am*, n. metempsychosis. — *Jīva-sañjña, as*, m., N. of a shrub, = *kāma-vṛiddhi*. — *Jīva-sādhana, am*, n. 'means of subsistence,' rice, grain. — *Jīva-sāphalya, am*, n. 'fruitfulness of life,' realisation of a life's wishes. — *Jīva-suta, as, ā, am*, one whose children are all alive. — *Jīva-sū, ūs*, f. the mother of living offspring. — *Jīva-sthāna, am*, n. a joint, an articulation. — *Jīvājīvādhāra* (°*va-ajīva-ādh*°), *as*, m. the world of organic beings and of inorganic matter. — *Jīvājīvādhāra-kshetra, am*, n. the material world, the

* having a living husband. Ṛig-patha 1.40.4

receptacle of inorganic beings and inorganic substances. — *Jīvātman* (°*va-āt*°), *ā*, m. the living or individual soul enshrined in the human body (distinguished from the *paramātman* or supreme soul), the vital principle or spirit, that principle of life which renders the body capable of motion or sensation; [cf. *jīva*.] — *Jīvādāna* (°*va-ād*°), *am*, n. abstracting living or healthy blood, bleeding. — *Jīvādhāna* (°*va-ādh*°), *am*, n. preservation of life. — *Jīvāntaka* (°*va-an*°), *as*, m. a fowler, a birdcatcher; a destroyer of life, a slayer, a murderer. — *Jīvābhigama-sūtra* (°*va-abh*°), *am*, n. title of a Jaina work. — *Jīvāśa* (°*va-āśa*), *as*, *ā*, *am*, hoping for life; (*ā*), f. hope of living. — *Jīvāstikāya* (°*va-as*°), *as*, m. (with Jainas) the category of 'soul.' — *Jīvendhana* (°*va-in*°), *am*, n. glowing fire-wood, burning wood. — *Jīvotsarga* (°*va-ut*°), *as*, m. abandonment of life, voluntary death. — *Jīvorṇā* (°*va-ūr*°), f. the wool of a living animal.

Jīvaka, *as*, *ā*, *am*, (at the end of a comp.) living, living by, making a livelihood by, causing to live, generating; one who lives a long time or for whom a long life is desired [cf. *āyush-mat*]; (*as*), m. a living being; a servant, slave, one who makes a livelihood by service; a mendicant, one who lives by begging; an usurer, one who lives by lending money at high interest; a snake-catcher, one whose business is to catch snakes and cure their bites &c.; a tree; N. of several plants, = Terminalia Tomentosa, Coccinia Grandis, a cucurbitaceous plant; a medicinal plant, commonly called by the same name Jīvaka and considered as one of the eight principal drugs classed together under the name Ashṭa-varga; N. of a man; (*ikā*), f. the living or life-giving element (i. e. water); living, means of living, livelihood; N. of a plant, = *jīvantī*; [cf. *aja-jīvaka*.]

Jīvat, *an*, *antī*, *at*, living, alive; *jīvann eva*, during life. — *Jīvat-tokā*, f. a woman whose children are living. — *Jīvat-pati*, *is*, or *jīvat-patnī*, f. a wife whose husband is alive. — *Jīvat-pitṛi*, *tā*, *trī*, *tṛi*, or *jīvat-pitṛika*, *as*, *ā*, *am*, a son or daughter whose father is alive; [cf. *jīva-pitṛi*.] — *Jīvatpitṛika-nirṇaya*, *as*, m. title of a work by Rāma-kṛishṇa. — *Jīvan-mukta*, *as*, m. a man purified by knowledge of Brahma and exonerated whilst living from future birth and all ritual ceremonies. — *Jīvan-mukti*, *is*, f. liberation in the present state of life. In the Vedānta system a secondary sort of liberation which conducts the soul after death to live with Brahma, not however divested of a subtile corporeal frame. — *Jīvanmukti-viveka*, *as*, m. title of a philosophical treatise. — *Jīvan-mṛita*, *as*, *ā*, *am*, at once alive and dead, dead while alive, (said of one whose character is lost or of a madman &c.)

Jīvatha, *as*, *ā*, *am*, long-lived; virtuous, pious; (*as*), m. life, existence, breath; a tortoise; a peacock; a cloud; virtue, piety.

Jīvana, *as*, *ī*, *am*, enlivening, vivifying, giving life; (*as*), m. a living being, an animal; wind; a son; a kind of drug, = *jīvaka*; N. of a plant, = *kshudra-phalaka*; N. of the author of the work Mānasa-nayana; (*ā*), f. a kind of medicinal plant; (*ī*), f., N. of several plants and drugs, = *jīvantī*, *kākolī*, a kind of jasmine &c.; (*am*), n. life, existence, living, livelihood, profession (often at the end of a comp., e. g. *mṛiga-jīvana*, living by hunting); enlivening, making alive; the life-giving element (water); butter made from new milk or milk one day old; marrow. — *Jīvana-tā*, f. life, mode of life. — *Jīvana-yoni*, *is*, m. source of life. — *Jīvana-vat*, *ān*, *atī*, *at*, possessed of or relating to life. — *Jīvana-viḍambana*, *am*, n. disappointment in life, living in vain. — *Jīvana-hetu*, *us*, m. object of life, cause of living. — *Jīvanāghāta* (°*na-āgh*°), *am*, n. 'that which destroys life,' poison. — *Jīvanānta* (°*na-an*°), *as*, m. end of life, death. — *Jīvanāvāsa* (°*na-āv*°), *as*, m. Varuṇa, the regent of water. — *Jīvanopāya* (°*na-up*°), *as*, m. livelihood, means of subsistence. — *Jīvanaushadha* (°*na-aush*°), *am*, n. an invigorating or life-giving medicine, a drug for reviving the dead; elixir vitæ.

Jīvanaka, *as*, *ikā*, *am*, enlivening; (*am*), n. food; (*ikā*), f. the tree Terminalia Chebula, = *harītakī*.

Jīvanasyā, f., Ved. desire of life.

Jīvanīya, *as*, *ā*, *am*, to be lived; supporting life, N. of a particular class of drugs; (*ā*), f. a kind of plant, = *jīvantī*; (*am*), n. a form of milk, milk fresh from the cow; water.

Jīvanta, *as*, *ī*, *am*, living, existent, long-lived; (*as*), m. life, existence; a medicament, a drug; a kind of pot-herb (*jīva-śāka*); N. of a man; (*ī*), f. a kind of medicinal plant, also eaten as a vegetable, = Pæderia Fœtida (?); also = *guḍūćī*, Cocculus Cordifolius and = *vandā*, a parasitical plant.

Jīvantika, *as*, m. a fowler, a birdcatcher; see *jīvāntaka*; (*ikā*), f. a parasitical plant, Epidendron Tesseloides, and other species; a plant Menispermum Glabrum; a kind of pot-herb.

Jīvamāna, *as*, *ā*, *am*, living, alive.

Jīvala, *as*, *ā*, *am*, full of life, animating; (*as*), m. a kind of plant; N. of a man; (*ā*), f. a kind of plant.

Jīvātu, *us*, f. life, existence; (*us*, *u*), m. n. victuals, food, boiled rice; a medicine for restoring life; [cf. Lat. *victus*.] — *Jīvātu-mat*, *ān*, *atī*, *at*, animated, living.

Jīvikā, see under *jīvaka*. — *Jīvikāpanna* (°*kā-āp*°), *as*, *ā*, *am*, having obtained subsistence. — *Jīvikā-prāpta*, *as*, *ā*, *am*, having obtained a livelihood.

Jīvita, *as*, *ā*, *am*, lived, lived through (as a period of time), living, alive, existent; revivified, returned to life; animated, enlivened; (*am*), n. a living being; living, life, existence; duration of life; livelihood, means of existence; [cf. Lith. *gywata*; Slav. *schivot*; Lat. *vita* for *vivita*.] — *Jīvita-kāla*, *as*, m. life-time, period or duration of life, a life. — *Jīvita-jñā*, f. an artery, a vessel of the body. — *Jīvita-nātha*, *as*, m. 'lord of life,' a husband. — *Jīvita-yopana*, *as*, *ā*, *am*, oppressing or molesting living beings. — *Jīvita-vyaya*, *as*, m. casting away life, sacrifice of life. — *Jīvita-saṃśaya*, *as*, m. risk of life, fear of death. — *Jīvita-hārin*, *ī*, *iṇī*, *i*, destroying life. — *Jīvitānta* (°*ta-an*°), *as*, m. end of life, death. — *Jīvitāntaka* (°*ta-an*°), *as*, m. putting an end to life, an epithet of Śiva. — *Jīvitāśā* (°*ta-āśā*), f. hope of life; love of life. — *Jīvitepsu* (°*ta-īp*°), *us*, *us*, *u*, seeking to save (one's) life. — *Jīviteśa* (°*ta-īśa*), *as*, *ā*, *am*, presiding over life; (*as*), m. 'the lord or master of existence,' a lover, a husband; an epithet of Yama the regent of death; the sun; the moon; a drug to revive the dead. — *Jīviteśvara* (°*ta-īś*°), *as*, m. 'lord of life,' an epithet of Śiva.

Jīvitavya, *as*, *ā*, *am*, to be lived, to be kept alive; (*am*), n. the possibility of living; possible return to life.

Jīvin, *ī*, *inī*, *i*, living, alive, animate; living upon or by; (*ī*), m. a living being. — *Jīvi-tva*, *am*, n. life, existence.

Jīvya, *am*, n. life; (*ā*), f. several plants, = *jīvantī*, *gokshura-dugdhā*; Terminalia Chebula, = *harītakī*. — *Jīvyopāya* (°*ya-up*°), *as*, m. means of existence, subsistence, livelihood.

जु *ju*, see 1. *jū*. The form of this root given in the Dhātu-pāṭha is *ju*, but the derivatives from it have the vowel long.

जुकुट *jukuṭa*, *as*, m. a dog [cf. *kukkuṭa*]; the Malaya range of mountains; (*am*), n. the egg-plant, Solanum Melongena; [cf. *jakuṭa*.]

जुगुपिषु *jugupishu*, *us*, *us*, *u* (fr. Desid. of rt. *gup*), intending or wishing to protect.

Jugupsana, *as*, *ā*, *am*, having a dislike, detesting; (*am*), n. censure, abuse, reproach, reviling, dislike, horror.

Jugupsā, f. censure; dislike, aversion, abhorrence, disgust.

Jugupsita, *as*, *ā*, *am*, reviled, blamed, censured, abused.

Jugupsu, *us*, *us*, *u*, having a dislike or disgust.

जुगुर्वणि *jugurvaṇi*, *is*, *is*, *i* (reduplicated form fr. rt. 1. *gṛī*), Ved. fond of praise, wishing to praise; (Sāy.) favouring the praiser.

जुङ्ग् *juṅg*, cl. 1. P. *juṅgati*, &c., to quit, abandon; to except, exclude; [cf. *yuṅg* and *vuṅg*.]

Juṅga, *as*, *ā*, m. f. or *juṅgaka*, *as*, m. a kind of plant, Argyreia Speciosa or Argentea.

Juṅgita, *as*, *ā*, *am*, deserted, injured, abandoned, outcast; (*as*), m. a man of a degraded caste, a Ćaṇḍāla &c.

जुञ्च् *juñć* (?), cl. 1. 10. P. *juñćati*, *juñćayati*, &c., to speak.

जुट् *juṭ*, cl. 6. P. *juṭati*, &c., a various reading for *juḍ*, to bind; [cf. *jaṭ*.]

Juṭaka, *am*, n. [cf. *jaṭā* and *jūṭaka*], a braid of hair, any knot or fillet of hair; (*ikā*), f. = *ćūḍā*, a tuft of hair on the top of the head; the matted hair of Śiva or of ascetics.

जुड् *juḍ*, cl. 6. P. *juḍati*, &c., to bind, to join together; cl. 10. P. *joḍayati*, &c., to send, cast or throw, direct; to grind or pound.

जुत् *jut*, cl. 1. A. *jotate*, to shine; [cf. *jyut*, *dyut*, *yut*.]

जुतुम *jutuma* and *juthuma*, two incorrect readings for *jituma*, q. v.

जुन् *jun*, cl. 6. P. *junati*, &c., to go; (a various reading has *juḍ*.)

जुमर् *jumara*, *as*, m., N. of a grammarian.

जुम्बक *jumbaka*, *as*, m., Ved., N. of Varuṇa.

जुर् 1. *jur* (related to 1. *jṛī*), cl. 6. 4. P., Ved. *jurati*, *jūryati*, *jujora* (?), &c., to decay, become old or decrepit, to grow old, perish; also *jūr*, cl. 4. A. *jūryate*, to grow old.

2. *jur*, *ūr*, m. an old man; [cf. 2. *jū*.]

Jurya, *as*, *ā*, *am*, becoming old; [cf. *a-jurya* and *jūrya*.]

Jūrṇa, *as*, *ā*, *am*, decayed, old. — *Jūrṇākhya* (°*ṇa-ākh*°), *as*, m. the plant Saccharum Cylindricum, commonly Ulū. — *Jūrṇāhvaya* (°*ṇa-āh*°), *as*, m. the plant Andropogon Saccharatus.

Jūrṇi, f., Ved., N. of a snake.

Jūrya, *as*, *ā*, *am*, Ved. becoming old, aged, weak, an old man.

जुर्व् *jurv*. See *jūrv*.

जुल् *jul*, cl. 10. P. *jolayati*, &c., to reduce to powder, grind.

जुवस् *juvas*. See under rt. *jū*.

जुष् 1. *jush*, cl. 6. A. (ep. also P.) *jushate*, -*ti*, *jujushe*, *joshishyate*, *ajoshishṭa*, *joshitum*, to be pleased or satisfied, to be propitiated or propitious; to be favourable; to like, be fond of, to have pleasure in, delight in (with acc. or gen.); to enjoy; to show one's self favourable towards (with acc.); to have pleasure in granting (with loc. of the person); to devote one's self to, practise, undergo, suffer; to delight in visiting, frequent, visit, inhabit, enter; happen to; to have pleasure in performing (with dat., e. g. *jushate karmaṇe*, he likes to engage in any act); to choose; to give pleasure to (with loc. of the person): Caus. *joshayati*, -*te*, -*yitum*, to like, be fond of, love, behave kindly towards (with acc.); fondle, cherish; to delight in, approve of, choose: Desid. *jujushishate* or *jujoshishate*: Intens. *jojushyate*, *jojoshṭi*; [cf. Zend *zaosha*, 'will, desire;' Hib. *gus*, 'a desire, inclination;' Goth. *kus*, 'to choose,' *kiusu*, *kaus*, *kusum*; Germ. *kiese*; Lat. *gus-tus*; Gr. γεύω, γεύομαι.]

2. *jush*, *ṭ*, *ṭ*, *ṭ*, liking, fond of, devoted to (with acc.); visiting, approaching; [cf. *sa-jush*.]

Jushāṇa, *as*, m., N. of a sacrificial formula containing the word *jushāṇa*, pres. part. of rt. 1. *jush*.

Jushṭa, *as*, *ā*, *am*, gratified, pleased, propitiated, propitious, favourable; liked, wished, loved, agreeable, usual; frequented, visited; served, obliged, worshipped, gratified by service; practised; furnished with, possessed of; (*am*), n. the crumbs or remnants of a meal or its leavings.

Jushṭi, is, f., Ved. love, service, favour, satisfaction.

Jushya, as, ā, am, to be served or worshipped.

Josha, joshaṇa, &c. See p. 351, col. 2.

जुष 3. *jush*, cl. 1. 10. P. *joshati, joshayati*, &c., to reason, think, conceive, imagine, investigate, examine; to injure, hurt, kill.

जुष्क *jushka, as*, m., N. of one of the three Turushka kings in Kaśmīra.—*Jushka-pura, am*, n., N. of a town founded by Jushka.

जुष्कक *jushkaka, as*, m.=*yūsha*, the water of boiled pulse, pease-soup, porridge, &c.

जुहु *juhu* = 2. *juhū* below.

जुहुराण *juhurāṇa, as*, m. (a corrupt form, said to be fr. rt. *hurćh*; or fr. rt. *hvṛi*), the moon; [cf. *juhūrāṇa* below.]

जुहुवाण *juhuvāṇa, as*, m. (fr. rt. *hu*; a corrupt form), fire, (also spelt *juhūvāṇa*); a sacrificing priest.

Juhuvāna, as, m. (perf. part. fr. rt. *hu*), fire; a tree; a hard-hearted man.

Juhūrāṇa, as, m. (a corrupt form), fire; a sacrificing priest; the moon.

जुहू 1. *juhū, ūs*, f. (fr. rt. *hve*), a tongue; especially the tongue or tongues of Agni, the flames; *sapta juhvaḥ*, the seven tongues of Agni; see *jihvā*. *Juhū* personified is the wife of Brahmā and goddess of speech; [cf. *sarasvatī*.]—*Juhū-vat, ān*, m. fire or its deity Agni.—*Juhv-āsya, as, ā, am*, Ved. tongue-mouthed, whose mouth consists of tongues or is full of them, an epithet of Agni.

जुहू 2. *juhū, ūs*, f. (fr. rt. *hu*), a wooden ladle or vessel of the shape of a semicircle or crescent, used for pouring the sacrificial butter into the fire; that part of the frame enshrining the supreme spirit which faces the east.

जुहोति *juhoti, is*, m. (fr. rt. *hu*), a technical name for those sacrificial ceremonies to which the verb *juhoti* and not *yajati* is applied.—*Juhoty-ādi, ayas*, m. pl. the roots beginning with *hu*, to sacrifice, i. e. the roots of the third class.

Juhvat, at, atī, at, sacrificing, offering oblations.

जु 1. *jū* (or according to the Dhātu-pāṭha *ju*), cl. 1. P. A., 9. P. *javati, -te, junāti*, &c., to press forwards, hurry on, move on quickly, be quick; to impel quickly, urge or drive on, incite; to excite, promote, animate, inspire.

Juvas, as, n., Ved. quickness, speed, liveliness.

2. *jū, ūs, ūs, u*, Ved. quick, speedy; (according to Sāy. *jūḥ* may also be the Nom. c. of *jur*, old); inciting, pressing, driving; (*ūs*), f. speed, expedition, velocity, going, motion; the atmosphere; a female demon or goblin; an epithet of the goddess Sarasvatī; a spot or mark on the forehead of horses and oxen; [cf. *kaśo-jū* and *mano-jū*.]

Jūta, as, ā, am, moved quickly, impelled, urged, pressed, (at the end of comp. in *adri-jūta, indra-j°, deva-j°*, &c., q. v.)

Jūti, is, f. going on, proceeding, moving; quickness, speed, velocity; flowing without obstruction or interruption; impulse, incitement, instigation, animation; inclination, impulse, energy.—*Jūti-mat, ān, atī, at*, Ved. impetuous, speedy.

जूक *jūka* (a word borrowed fr. the Gr. ζυγόν), the sign of the zodiac Libra.

जूट *jūṭa, as*, m. the matted hair of Śiva, the twisted or clotted hair of an ascetic; [cf. *jaṭā* and *ćūḍa*.]

Jūṭaka, am, n. twisted or braided hair; [cf. *jaṭā*.]

जूतिका *jūtikā*, f. a kind of camphor.

जूमरनन्दिन् *jūmara-nandin, ī*, m., N. of the author of a commentary on the grammar entitled Saṁkshipta-sāra.

जूर *jūr*, cl. 4. A. *jūryate*, &c., to hurt, injure, wound, kill; to be angry with (with dat.); to grow old. See rt. 1. *jur*, p. 349.

जूर्ण *jūrṇa, jūrya*. See rt. 1. *jur*, p. 349.

जूर्णि 1. *jūrṇi, is, is, i* (fr. *jur*=*gur*), Ved. skilfully praising, invoking.

जूर्व *jūrv* (connected with rt. *jvar*), cl. 1. P., Ved. *jūrvati*, &c., to consume by heat, singe, burn; to hurt, kill; [cf. Hib. *gearbaim*, 'I grieve, hurt, wound;' cf. also rt. *jval*.]

2. *jūrṇi, is*, f., Ved. glowing fire, a blaze, a fiery weapon; anger [cf. *jūr*]; speed (perhaps for *jūti*); fever [cf. *jvara*]; disease, sickness; the body; the sun; Brahmā.

Jūrṇin, ī, inī, i, Ved. surrounded by glowing fire, glowing.

Jūrti, is, f. fever; feverish or morbid heat; [cf. Hib. *gurt*, 'pain, trouble, fierceness.']

जूष *jūsh* (a various reading for *yūsh*), cl. 1. P. *jūshati*, &c., to kill, hurt.

Jūsha, am, n. the water of boiled pulse, pease-soup, porridge, &c.

Jūshaṇa, am, n. the plant Grislea Tomentosa, commonly Dhāiphula.

जृ *jṛi*, cl. 1. P. *jarati*, &c., to surpass, excel; make low, depress, humiliate; [cf. Germ. *kurz*; Scot. *gearr, goirid*, 'short.']

जृङ्गि *jṛingi, ayas*, or *jṛingin, iṇas*, m. pl., N. of a particular race or people.

जृभ *jṛibh* or *jṛimbh*, cl. 1. A. (poet. also P.) *jṛimbhate, -ti*, or *jarbhate, jajṛimbhe, jṛimbhishyate, jṛimbhitum*, to open the mouth, yawn, gape; to gape open, open (as a flower), burst open; fly back or recoil (as a bow); to unfold, spread, extend, expand, occupy a larger circuit; to spread (as sound); to feel at ease: Caus. *jṛimbhayati, -yitum*, to cause to gape or yawn, cause to expand or unfold; [cf. Old Germ. *chliupu*, 'to split;' Germ. *klaffe, kluft*; Goth. *graba*; Germ. *grabe*; Gr. γράφω; Hib. *grabhaim, grafain, grafan*; cf. also 1. *jabh*.]

Jṛimbha, as, ā, am, m. f. n. gaping, yawning; bursting open; blossoming, swelling, blowing, being puffed up; expansion, stretching, expanding; (*as*), m. a particular animal.—*Jṛimbhā-vat, ān, atī, at*, yawning, gaping.

Jṛimbhaka, as, m. a yawner, a sort of demon or spirit; N. of certain magical formularies for exorcising the evil spirits supposed to possess weapons; (*ikā*), f. gaping, yawning; (*am*), n. swelling.

Jṛimbhaṇa, as, ā, am, causing to gape or yawn; (*am*), n. gaping, yawning; stretching the limbs; bursting or gaping open, blossoming, blooming.

Jṛimbhamāṇa, as, ā, am, gaping, yawning; opening, blossoming, blowing.

Jṛimbhita, as, ā, am, opened, expanded; opened (as a flower), blown; enlarged, increased; done, exerted; (*am*), n. gaping, yawning; bursting, opening, expansion, unfolding; developing, coming into view, swelling; exertion; wish, active search for; a kind of coitus.

Jṛimbhin, ī, iṇī, i, yawning, gaping; expanding, blossoming; (*iṇī*), f. the plant Mimosa Octandra, =*elāparṇī*.

जृ 1. *jṛī*, cl. 4. 9. 1. P. *jīryati, jṛiṇāti, jarati, jajāra, jarishyati* and *jarīshyati, ajārīt* and *ajarat, jaritum* and *jarītum*, to grow old, become decrepit, decay, wear out, wither; to be consumed, perish; to break up or fall to pieces; to be dissolved or digested; (cl. 1. P.) to make old or decrepit; to cause to grow old; cl. 10. P. *jārayati, -yitum*, to become old: Caus. P. *jarayati, -yitum*, to make old, wear out, consume, cause to be consumed; to cause to be digested; to digest: Desid. *jijarishati, jijarīshati, jijīrshati*: Intens. *jejīryate, jājarti*; [cf. Hib. *crionaim*, 'I dry, wither;' *criona*, 'old, ancient:' Gr. γέρων, γεραιός, γραῦς, γῆρας: Lat. *grānum* for *gārnum*: Goth. *kaurn*: Germ. *Korn*: Lith. *girna*.]

Jara, jaratha, jaraṇa, jaras, &c. See p. 340.

Jāra, as, ā, am, Ved. becoming old; (*as*), m. a paramour, gallant, lover, (in the Veda applied to Agni or to the Sun as the paramour of the dawn); a confidential friend; (*ī*), f. a particular herb or medicament; a N. of Durgā; [cf. Goth. *hōrs*; Germ. *Hure*.]—*Jāra-garbha, as, ā, am*, pregnant by a paramour.—*Jāra-ja, as, ā, am*, a bastard, the child of a woman by her paramour.—*Jāra-jāta* or *jāra-jātaka, as, ā, am*, a bastard; (*as*), m. a plagiarist.—*Jāra-tā*, f. an intrigue, love-affair.—*Jāra-dvaya, am*, n. a couple of gallants.—*Jāra-bharā*, f. an adulteress.

Jāraka, as, ā, am, causing to decay; promoting digestion, digestive.

Jāraṇa, am, n. the act of causing to decay; promoting digestion; calcining or oxidizing metals; a condiment, a digester; (*ī*), f. a kind of cumin-seed.

Jāratineya, as, m. a metronymic from Jaratī; a patronymic from Jaratin.

Jāratkārava, as, m. a patronymic from Jaratkāru.

Jāradgava, as, ī, am (fr. *jarad-gava*), scil. *vīthi*, the path of the old ox, (according to Varāhamihira the portion of the moon's path occupied by the constellations Śravaṇā, Dhanishṭhā, and Śata-bhishaj, or according to other authorities that occupied by Vi-śākhā, Anu-rādhā, and Jyeshṭhā.)

Jāramāṇya, as, m. a patronymic from Jaramāṇa.

Jārāsandhi, is, m. (fr. *jarā-sandha*), a patronymic of Saha-deva.

Jāriṇī, f., Ved. a woman who has a paramour, enamoured.

Jāruja, as, ā, am,=*jarāyu-ja*.

Jīrṇa, as, ā, am, old, ancient; worn out, wasted, withered, decayed, ruined, in ruins; digested; (*as*), m. an old man; a tree; cumin-seed; (*ā*), f. large cumin-seed; (*am*), n. decrepitude, old age; benjamin.—*Jīrṇa-jvara* or *jīrṇāmaya-jvara, as*, m. a lingering fever with diminishing intensity.—*Jīrṇa-jvarin, ī, iṇī, i*, affected with the above fever.—*Jīrṇa-ṭīkā*, f. 'the ancient commentary,' title of an astronomical work.—*Jīrṇa-tā*, f. or *jīrṇa-tva, am*, n. old age; infirmity, decay.—*Jīrṇa-dāru, us*, m. the plant Convolvulus Argenteus.—*Jīrṇa-pattrikā*, f. 'having withered leaves,' N. of a plant, =*vaṅśa-pattrī*.—*Jīrṇa-parṇa, as, am*, m. n. 'having withered leaves,' the plant Nauclea Cadamba.—*Jīrṇa-phaṇjī*, f.=*jīrṇa-dāru*.—*Jīrṇa-budhna, as*, m. a kind of Lodhra.—*Jīrṇa-budhnaka, am*, n. a kind of Cyperus.—*Jīrṇa-vajra, am*, n. a gem, said to be a sort of diamond.—*Jīrṇa-vat, ān, atī, at*, old, decayed.—*Jīrṇa-vastra, am*, n. old, worn or tattered raiment; (*as, ā, am*), wearing old clothes.—*Jīrṇa-vāṭikā*, f. a ruined house.—*Jīrṇa-vradhnaka, as*, m. a fragrant grass, Cyperus Rotundus.—*Jīrṇoddhāra* (°*ṇa-ud°*), *as*, m. the repairing of what is worn out, renewal, repairs.—*Jīrṇoddhṛita* (°*ṇa-ud°*), *as, ā, am*, rescued from decay, repaired.—*Jīrṇodyāna* (°*ṇa-ud°*), *am*, n. a neglected garden.

Jīrṇaka, as, ā, am, almost dried up or withered.

Jīrṇi, is, is, i, decrepit with age; (*is*), f. old age, infirmity, decay; digestion.

जृ 2. *jṛī*, cl. 1. A., Ved. *jarate*, &c., to move, approach, come near.

जृ 3. *jṛī*, cl. 1. A., Ved. *jarate*, to crackle (as fire); to roar; to call out to, address, invoke, praise.

Jaraṇā, jaritṛi, jarūtha, &c. See s. v.

जेतव्य *jetavya*. See p. 347, col. 1.

जेतृ *jetṛi, tā, trī, tṛi* (fr. rt. 1. *ji*), victorious,

triumphant; surpassing, excelling; gaining; (*tā*), m. a victor, conqueror; N. of a Vedic poet who was son of Madhu-ćchandas; N. of a prince who had a garden near Srāvastī in which Sākya-muni promulgated his doctrines.—*Jeta-vana, am,* n. (for *jetṛi* + *vana*), the wood of Jetṛi, N. of a grove or garden near Srāvastī where Sākya-muni or Buddha promulgated his doctrines.—*Jetavanīya, ās,* m. pl. N. of a Buddhist school.—*Jeta-sāhvaya, as, ā, am,* called after Jetṛi.—*Jetārāma, as,* m. (for *jetṛi* + *ār°*), = *jeta-vana.*

Jetva, as, ā, am, Ved. to be gained or conquered.

Jeman, ā, ā, a, Ved. surpassing, excelling; (*ā*), m. excellence.

Jesha, as, m., Ved. winning, gaining, obtaining.

जेन्ताक *jentāka, as,* m. a dry hot bath or heated chamber for inducing perspiration in rheumatism, &c.

जेन्य *jenya, as, ā, am* (fr. *jana*), Ved. of noble origin (γενναῖος); genuine, true.—*Jenyā-vasu, us, us, u,* Ved. having genuine or true wealth, an epithet of the Aśvins; also of Indra and Agni; (Sāy.) having acquired wealth.

जेमन *jemana.* See under rt. *jim*, p. 347.

जेय *jeya.* See p. 347, col. 1.

जेलक *jelaka, as,* m., N. of a man.

जेष् *jesh,* cl. 1. A. *jeshate,* &c., to move, go.

जेष *jesha.* See above.

जेह् *jeh* (related to 1. *jabh* and *jṛibh*), cl. 1. A., Ved. *jehate, jijehe, jehishyate, jehitum,* to open the mouth, breathe heavily, gasp, gape, open wide, yawn; (Sāy.) to reach, go towards, strive after: Caus. *jehayati, ajijehat.*

Jehamāna, as, ā, am, gaping, opening wide; (Sāy.) going towards.

जै *jai,* cl. 1. P. *jāyati, jajau, jāsyati, jātum,* to wane, decline, fade away, perish; [cf. 1. *jyā.*]

जैगीषव्य *jaigīshavya, as,* m. (fr. *jigīshu*), N. of an ancient Ṛishi often named in connection with Asita Devala.—*Jaigīshavyeśvara* (°*ya-īś*°), *am,* n., N. of a Liṅga in Vārāṇasī.

जैत्र *jaitra, as, ī, am* (fr. rt. 1. *ji*), victorious, triumphant, leading to victory, overcoming, surpassing, superior; (*as*), m. a conqueror, victor; N. of a son of Dhṛita-rāshṭra; (*ī*), f. the plant Sesbania Ægyptiaca; (*am*), n. victory, triumph, superiority.—*Jaitra-ratha, as, ā, am,* having a triumphant car; (*as*), m. a victor, a conqueror, a hero; a triumphant car.

Jaitrāyaṇi, is, m. a patronymic from Jaitra.

जैन *jaina, as, ī, am* (fr. *jina*), relating to the Jinas; (*as*), m. a Jaina, a teacher of heterodox notions, the chief of which are the supremacy of certain Jinas or great saints over the gods of the Hindūs, a denial of the divine authority of the Vedas, and a disregard of the distinction of castes; N. of a prince of Kaśmīra.—*Jaina-taraṅgiṇī,* f. a history of Kaśmīra by Srīvara.—*Jaināśrama* (°*na-āś*°), *as,* m. a Jaina monastery.—*Jainendra* (°*na-in*°), *as,* m., N. of a grammarian.

Jainya, as, ā, am, relating to the Jainas (?).

जैपाल *jaipāla, as,* m. (= *jaya-pāla*), a plant, Croton Tiglium.

जैमन्त *jaimanta, as,* m., N. of a man.

Jaimantāyana, as, m. a patronymic from Jaimanta.

जैमिनि *jaimini, is,* m., N. of a celebrated saint and philosopher, the pupil of Vyāsa and founder of the Pūrva (or Karma) Mīmāṃsā school. He is said to have acted as Udgātṛi at the sacrifice of Janamejaya (Mahā-bh. I. 2046), and to have received the Sāma-veda from Vyāsa.

Jaiminīya, as, ā, am, relating to Jaimini; (*ās*), m. pl., N. of a school of the Sāma-veda.

जैमूत *jaimūta, as, ī, am* (fr. *jīmūta*), relating to Jīmūta.

जैयट *jaiyaṭa, as,* m., N. of the father of Kaiyaṭa; (sometimes spelt *jaigaṭa.*)

Jaiyyaṭa, as, m., N. of a physician.

जैव *jaiva, as, ī, am* (fr. *jīva*), relating to Jupiter.

Jaivantāyana, as, m. or *jaivantāyani, is,* m. or *jaivanti, is,* m. a patronymic from Jīvanta.

Jaivali, is, m. (fr. *jīvala*), a patronymic of Pravāhaṇa.

Jaivātṛika, as, ī, am, long-lived, one for whom long life is desired; thin, lean; (*as*), m. the moon; camphor (as a synonym of the moon); a peasant; a drug, medicament; a son; [cf. *jīvātu.*]

Jaivi, is, m. or *jaiveya, as,* m. a patronymic from Jīva.

जैष्णव *jaishṇava, as, ī, am* (fr. *jishṇu*), relating to a conqueror, relating to Arjuna.

जैह्म्य *jaihmya, am,* n. (fr. *jihma*), crookedness (moral or physical), deceit, falsehood.

जैह्व *jaihva, as, ī, am* (fr. *jihvā*), belonging or relating to the tongue, lying on the tongue.

Jaihvākāta, as, ī, am, an adj. derived fr. *jihvākātya.*

Jaihvya, am, n. the pleasure of taste (derived from the tongue), pleasure.

जोगू *jogū, ūs, ūs, u* (fr. rt. *gu*), Ved. praising.

जोङ्ग *joṅga* or *joṅgaka, am,* n. aloe wood, Agallochum.

जोङ्गट *joṅgaṭa, as,* m. longing, earnest wish, eager desire, the longing of a pregnant woman.

जोटिङ्ग *joṭiṅga, as,* m. an epithet of Siva; a devotee, an ascetic who subjects himself to the severest penances; the sacrificial cord (?).

जोड *joḍa,* the chin; [cf. *jahi-joḍa.*]

जोनराज *jona-rāja, as,* m., N. of the author of the Rāja-taraṅgiṇī.

जोन्नाला *jonnālā,* f. = *yavanāla,* the plant Andropogon Saccharatus; also *jontālā.*

जोल *jola,* N. of a mixed caste.

जोष *josha, as,* m. (fr. rt. 1. *jush*), satisfaction, approval, pleasure, enjoyment, felicity, happiness; (*josham ā,* Ved. to one's satisfaction, abundantly; *anu josham,* according to one's pleasure, willingly); (*am*), ind. according to one's wish or liking, happily, with ease, without effort; well; silently; *josham ās,* to remain quiet or silent; *josham āssva,* be thou quiet, keep thou silent; [cf. *a-josha.*]—*Josha-vāka, as,* m., Ved. unintelligible words, chattering nonsense; (Sāy.) words which ought to please but do not.

Joshaṇa, am, n. liking; satisfaction, approval; choosing; (*ā*), f. the expression of satisfaction by the word *jush.*

Joshayitavya, as, ā, am, to be made dear or agreeable, to be reflected upon or thought about, obscure, unintelligible (in words).

Joshayitṛi, tā, trī, tṛi, or *joshṭṛi, ṭā, ṭrī, ṭṛi,* loving, cherishing, fostering, taking care of; (Sāy.) serving.

Joshas in *vi-joshas, sa-joshas,* q. v.

Joshya, as, ā, am, Ved. delightful, agreeable, welcome, satisfactory.

जोषा *joshā,* f. = *yoshā,* a woman.

जोषिका *joshikā,* f. = *jālikā,* a cluster of young buds, a bud, a germ.

जोषित् *joshit* or *joshitā,* f. = *yoshit,* a woman.

जोहूत्र *johūtra, as, ā, am* (fr. *hve*), Ved. making a loud noise, neighing; calling out, challenging to battle, neighing (as a horse).

जौमर *jaumara, am,* n., scil. *vyā-karaṇa,* the grammar composed by Jumara.

जौलायनभक्त *jaulāyana-bhakta, am,* n. the district inhabited by the Jaulāyanas.

जौहोत्यादिक *jauhotyādika, as, ī, am* (fr. *juhoty-ādi*), belonging to the class of roots beginning with *hu,* i. e. to the third class.

ज्ञ 1. *jña* = *jñu* = *jānu,* the knee, in *ūrdhva-jña.* (For 2. *jña* see below.)

ज्ञा 1. *jñā,* cl. 9. P. A. *jānāti, jānīte, jajñau, jajñe, jñāsyati, -te, ajñāsīt, ajñāsta, jñātum,* [irreg. forms, *jānatha* for *jānītha* Mahā-bh. II. 842, *jānata* for *jānīta* II. 2397, *jijāhi* for *jājñāhi* = *jānīhi,* know thou, XIII. 4495, *abhy-anu-jānīthās* for *abhy-anv-ajānīthās* XIV. 1641, *jānamāna* pres. part.], to know, have knowledge, become acquainted with; to perceive, apprehend, understand, experience; to recognise; to ascertain, investigate; to know as, know or perceive that, regard or consider as (with acc. of the object and predicate, e. g. *tasya māṃ tanayāṃ jānīta,* know me to be his daughter); to be conversant or familiar with; to visit as a friend (Ved.); to acknowledge, approve, allow, permit; to recognise as one's own, take possession of; to act, engage in (with gen. of the instrument, e. g. *sarpisho* for *sarpishā jānīte,* he engages in sacrifice with clarified butter): Caus. *jñāpayati* or *jñapayati, -yitum,* Aor. *ajijñapat,* to make known, teach, make acquainted with, inform, announce, notify; to give information; A. to request, ask: Desid. A. *jijñāsate* (ep. also P.), to wish to know, &c.; to investigate, examine, wish to learn; to conjecture, suppose: Desid. of Caus. *jijñāpayishati* and *jijñapayishati* and *jñīpsati,* to wish to make known or inform: Pass. of Desid. of Caus. *jñīpsyate,* to be wished or intended to be informed: Intens. *jājñāyate, jājñāti, jājñeti;* [cf. Lat. *gna, gno,* in *gnārus,* (*g*)*nosco, cognosco, ignoro;* perhaps *gloria* for *gnoria:* Gr. γνω in γνῶθι, ἔγνων, γνῶσις; (γ)νοέω, (γ)νοῦς; γιγνώσκω: Old Germ. *chna, chnâta, chnât:* Eng. *know:* Goth. *kaun:* Old Germ. *chan:* Germ. *kann, kenne:* Lith. *zinnaù,* 'I know;' *zinne, sazinne:* Slav. *znajû:* Hib. *gnia,* 'knowledge;' *gnic; gno,* 'ingenious;' *gnas,* 'custom, use.']

2. *jña, as, ā, am,* who or what knows, a knower, knowing, familiar with (often in comp., e. g. *dharma-jña,* familiar with the law; *sarva-jña,* knowing everything); intelligent, wise; (*as*), m. a wise and learned man, especially one possessed of sacred learning or religious knowledge; the sentient soul; Budha who was first of the lunar line and regent of the planet Mercury; the planet Mars or its regent; an epithet of Brahmā; [cf. Lat. *beni-gnus, mali-gnus.*]—*Jña-tā,* f. (at the end of a comp.) knowledge of, familiarity with; intelligence.—*Jñanmanya, as, ā, am,* thinking one's self wise.

Jñaka, as, akā or *ikā,* m. f. a diminutive fr. 2. *jña.*

Jñapita, as, ā, am, made known, informed, taught, expounded.

Jñapta, as, ā, am, made known, = *jñapita.*

Jñapti, is, f. understanding, apprehension, the exercise of the intellectual faculty; promulgating, making known.

2. *jñā, ās, ās, am,* (at the end of a comp.) knowing, familiar with [cf. *ṛita-jñā, pada-jñā,* and 2. *jña*]; (*ā*), f. in epic poetry sometimes a shortened form of *ā-jñā,* the initial vowel of the latter being

irregularly elided after a preceding final e and o (e. g. te 'jñayā, by thy order, Mahā-bh. I. 3168).

Jñāta, as, ā, am, known, ascertained, comprehended, perceived, understood; āṃ jñātam, Ah! I know (lit. it is known).—Jñāta-nandana, as, m. an epithet of Vīra, the twenty-fourth Arhat of the present Ava-sarpiṇī.—Jñāta-mātre, ind. on its being ascertained merely.—Jñāta-siddhānta, as, m. a man completely versed in any science or Śāstra. —Jñātādharma-kathā (°ta-adh° or °tā-dha°?), f. title of one of the twelve sacred books of the Jainas.—Jñātānvaya (°ta-an°), as, m. 'of known lineage,' a name of Vardhamāna, the last Jina or Jaina pontiff.

Jñātaka, as, ā, am, known, &c. See jñāta.

Jñātala, as, m., N. of a man.

Jñātaleya, as, m. a patronymic from the last.

Jñātavya, as, ā, am, to be known or understood, to be investigated or inquired after; perceptible, conceivable; to be considered as.

Jñāti, is, m. a paternal relation, a kinsman in general, a father, a brother; a distant kinsman, one who does not participate in the oblations offered to deceased ancestors; (is), f., N. of a woman; (according to the Schol. jñāti is a paternal, and sam-bandhin a maternal relation; the original meaning of jñāti may be 'intimately acquainted;' cf. Gr. γνωτός, γνωτή; Goth. knôdi.)—Jñāti-karman, a, n. or jñāti-kārya, am, n. the act or duty of a kinsman.—Jñāti-tva, am, n. relationship, consanguinity.—Jñāti-dravya-vinākṛita, as, ā, am, deprived of relations and wealth.—Jñāti-putra, as, m. the son of a relative; an epithet of Pūrṇa.—Jñāti-bhāva, as, m. the condition of a kinsman, relationship, kin. —Jñāti-bheda, as, m. dissension among relatives. —Jñāti-mat, ān, atī, at, one who has near relations.—Jñāti-mukha, as, ā, am, Ved. having the appearance or character of a relative.—Jñāti-vid, t, t, t, one who has or makes near relations.

Jñātṛi, tā, trī, tṛi, knowing, wise, intelligent, a knower; (tā), m. an acquaintance; a bail, a surety; [cf. Gr. γνωστήρ.]—Jñātṛi-tva, am, n. or jñātṛi-tā, f. knowledge, information.

Jñāteya, am, n. relationship, affinity.

Jñātra, am, n., Ved. the faculty of perception, intelligence, knowledge.

Jñātvā, ind. having known, having ascertained, &c.

Jñāna, am, n. knowing, understanding, becoming acquainted with, knowledge; sacred or religious knowledge, especially that which is derived from meditation on the higher truths of religion and philosophy and which teaches man his own nature and how he may be reunited to the supreme spirit; knowledge about anything, cognizance, consciousness (e. g. tasya jñānāt, with his knowledge; a-jñānāt tasya, without his knowledge or cognizance; jñānād a-jñānād vā, knowingly or ignorantly; vigata-jñāna, one who has lost consciousness); conscience; organ of intelligence, sense.—Jñāna-kanda, as, m., N. of a pupil of Śaṅkarāćārya.—Jñāna-kāṇḍa, as, am, m. n. that inner or esoteric portion of the Veda which relates to true spiritual knowledge or the knowledge of the supreme spirit as distinguished from the knowledge of ceremonies; [cf. karma-kāṇḍa.]—Jñāna-kīrtti, is, m., N. of a Buddhist preceptor.—Jñāna-ketu, us, m. a mark of intelligence; (us, us, u), furnished with marks of intelligence.—Jñānaketu-dhvaja, as, m., N. of a divine being.—Jñāna-khaṇḍa, title of a part of the Siva-Purāṇa.—Jñāna-gamya, as, ā, am, attainable by the understanding.—Jñāna-garbha, as, m. 'filled with knowledge,' N. of a scholar; also of a Bodhisattva.—Jñāna-ćakshus, us, n. the eye of intelligence, inner eye, mind's eye, intellectual vision.—Jñāna-tattva, am, n. true knowledge, knowledge of God. —Jñāna-tapas, as, n. penance consisting in the cultivation of true knowledge.—Jñāna-tas, ind. knowingly, intuitively, designedly; jñānato 'jñānato vā, knowingly or unknowingly.—Jñāna-da, as, m. an imparter of knowledge.—Jñāna-datta, as, m. 'given by knowledge,' N. of a scholar.—Jñāna-darpaṇa, as, m. 'mirror of true knowledge,' a N. of Mañju-śrī.—Jñāna-dīpa, as, m. the lamp of knowledge, knowledge.—Jñāna-durbala, as, ā, am, deficient in knowledge, ignorant.—Jñāna-niśćaya, as, m. soundness of knowledge, certainty, ascertainment.—Jñāna-nishṭha, as, ā, am, engaged in cultivating true knowledge.—Jñānapata, as, ī, am, an adj. derived from the next.—Jñāna-pati, is, m. the lord of knowledge.—Jñāna-para, as, ā, am, versed in spiritual wisdom.—Jñāna-pāvana, as, ā, am, purifying knowledge, refining the understanding; (am), n., N. of a Tīrtha.—Jñāna-pūrva, as, ā, am, preceded by knowledge or wisdom.—Jñāna-prakāśa, as, m. title of a poem by Jagajjīvana-dāsa. —Jñāna-pradīpa, as, m. title of the second book of the Yoga-sāra-saṅgraha.—Jñāna-prabha, as, m., N. of a man; also of a Bodhi-sattva.—Jñāna-pravāda, am, n. title of one of the fourteen Pūrvas or older writings of the Jainas.—Jñāna-prasthāna, am, n. 'system or method of knowledge,' title of a Buddhist work.—Jñāna-bodhinī, f. 'awakening knowledge,' title of a philosophical treatise composed by Saṅkara.—Jñāna-bhāskara, as, m. 'sun of knowledge,' title of a medical compilation.—Jñāna-maṇḍapa, as, am, m. n. 'temple of knowledge,' N. of a temple.—Jñāna-maya, as, ī, am, consisting of knowledge, containing knowledge.—Jñāna-muktāvalī, f. 'necklace of knowledge,' title of an astronomical work.—Jñāna-mudra, as, ā, am, having the impress of wisdom, wise.—Jñāna-mūla, as, ā, am, founded on spiritual knowledge.—Jñāna-meru, us, m., N. of a man.—Jñāna-ratnāvalī, f. title of a book.—Jñāna-rāja, as, m. 'king of knowledge,' N. of the author of the Siddhānta-sundara. —Jñānarshi-bhāskarāćārya (°na-ṛish°, °ra-āć°), as, m., N. of an author.—Jñāna-lakshaṇa, am, ā, n. f. indication, sign, means of knowing or inferring; (in logic) sign or proof or characteristic of knowledge; subsequent derived from antecedent knowledge. —Jñāna-vajra, as, m., N. of a Buddhist author. —Jñāna-vat, ān, atī, at, endowed with knowledge or science, knowing, familiar with, intelligent, wise, learned, having spiritual knowledge; (ān), m., N. of a Bodhi-sattva.—Jñāna-varman, ā, m., N. of a poet.—Jñāna-vāpī, f. 'pool of divine knowledge,' N. of a Tīrtha.—Jñāna-vijñāna, am, n. sacred and miscellaneous knowledge; the Vedas with the supplementary branches of knowledge, medicine, arms, &c.—Jñāna-vibhūti-garbha, as, m. 'filled with superhuman knowledge,' N. of a Bodhi-sattva. —Jñāna-vilāsa-kāvya, am, n. title of a poem. —Jñāna-śakti, is, f. capacity of knowing.—Jñāna-śāstra, am, n. 'the science of knowing the future,' a manual of fortune-telling.—Jñāna-śreshṭha, as, ā, am, pre-eminent in wisdom.—Jñāna-hastika, as, m., N. of a man.—Jñānākara (°na-āk°), as, m. 'mine of knowledge,' N. of a son of Buddha Mahābhijñājñānābhibhū; N. of a Buddha.—Jñānātman (°na-āt°), ā, ā, a, all-wise. —Jñānānanda (°na-ān°), as, m. 'joy of knowledge,' N. of an author.—Jñānānutpāda (°na-an°), as, m. non-production of knowledge, folly, ignorance. —Jñānāmṛita (°na-am°), am, n. 'nectar of knowledge,' title of a grammar.—Jñānārṇava (°na-ar°), as, m. 'ocean of knowledge,' title of a manual of medicine composed by Yama-rāja; title of a prayer-book.—Jñānāvaraṇīya (°na-āv°), as, ā, am, to be covered or obstructed by knowledge, (an act which is considered) to be impeded by knowledge; also written jñānāvaraṇiya.—Jñānāvalokālaṅkāra (°na-avaloka-al°), as, m. title of a Buddhist work. —Jñānāvasthita (°na-av°), as, ā, am, engaged in cultivating wisdom.—Jñānendra-sarasvatī (°na-in°), m., N. of a scholiast on the Siddhānta-kaumudī. —Jñānendriya (°na-in°), am, n. an organ of perception or sensation, of which there are five, viz. the skin, tongue, eye, ear, and nose; see indriya. —Jñānoda-tīrtha (°na-ud°), am, n., N. of a Tīrtha; 'the Tīrtha of the waters of knowledge.' —Jñānolkā (°na-ul°), f. 'the meteor of knowledge,' N. of a Samādhi.

Jñānika, as, ā, am, at the end of comp. = jñāna.

Jñānin, ī, inī, i, endowed with knowledge or intelligence, intelligent, wise, a knower; (ī), f. an astrologer, a fortune-teller, a man prescient of future events; a sage, one possessing religious wisdom. —Jñāni-tva, am, n. prescience, fortune-telling.

Jñānīya, nom. P. jñānīyati, -yitum, to wish for knowledge.

Jñāpaka, as, ā, am, making or causing to know, teaching, designing, informing; (as), m. a teacher, an instructor; a commander, a master; a master of requests, an officer of the court of a Hindū prince; (am), n. a significant expression or one which gives some particular information, a precept, a rule, a name given to those rules of Pāṇini which imply or indicate some other grammatical laws than those which would follow from the mere words of the Jñāpaka rules themselves.—Jñāpaka-samuććaya, as, m. a work by Purushottama-deva giving a collection of the Jñāpaka rules contained in Pāṇini's grammar.

Jñāpana, am, n. making known, announcing, apprizing, informing, teaching, notification.

Jñāpanīya, as, ā, am, to be made known or announced.

Jñāpita, as, ā, am, made known, informed.

Jñāpti, is, f. making known, apprizing, informing.

Jñāpya, as, ā, am, to be made known or informed, to be told.

Jñās, m., Ved. a near relative; [cf. jñāti.]

Jñīpsyamāna, as, ā, am, being intended to be informed.

Jñeya, as, ā, am, cognizable, to be ascertained or investigated, to be learned or understood, to be perceived or inquired about; to be regarded as.—Jñeya-jña, as, ā, am, understanding what is to be understood; the mind.—Jñeya-tā, f. or jñeya-tva, am, n. perceptibility, intelligibleness.

ज्ञु jñu = jānu, the knee, in abhi-jñu, ūrdhva-jñu, &c.—Jñu-bādh, -bhāt, t, t, Ved. bending the knees; [cf. Gr. πρόχνυ.]

ज्मन् jman (fr. jam = gam), only occurring in the Ved. loc. jman, in (his) course or way; (Sāy.) in the sky; on the earth; [cf. uru-jman and pṛithu-jman.]—Jma-yā, ās, ās, am, Ved. going on or following a course; (Sāy.) on the earth (as if jmayā).

Jmāyat, an, antī, at (pres. part. of a nom. fr. jman), Ved. making a way or course; (Sāy.) going on or reaching the earth.

ज्या 1. jyā, cl. 9. P., 4. A. jināti, jīyate, jijyau, jijye, jyāsyati, -te, ajyāsīt, jyātum, to overpower, oppress, to deprive of property, &c., (in the Veda often connected with rt. han, e. g. jīyate hanti, 'he oppresses and kills;' and in the Brāhmaṇas applied to the oppressions of the Brāhmans and Vaiśyas by the Kshatriyas); (cl. 4. A.) to be oppressed, treated badly, deprived of property, &c.; (cl. 9. P.) to become old: Caus. jyāpayati, see jyāpaya below: Desid. P. jijyāsati, to wish to overpower or oppress: Intens. jejīyate, jājyāti; [cf. Gr. βιάω.]

Jīta or jīna, as, ā, am, oppressed, overpowered; become old. See also under jita, p. 348, col. 1.

Jya, as, ā, am, (at the end of a comp.) oppressing.

2. jyā, f. overpowering force or strength (βία, cf. parama-jyā); excessive demand, importunity.

Jyāna, am, n., Ved. oppression, tyrannizing over.

Jyāni, is, f. oppression; deprivation, loss; decay, infirmity, old age; quitting, abandoning; a river, a stream.

Jyāpaya, nom. P. jyāpayati, -yitum, to make old, to call a person old, (supposed to be a nom. fr. jya substituted for vṛiddha.)

Jyāyas, ān, asī, as (considered by grammarians to be a compar. of pra-śasya and vṛiddha, for which jya is substituted), superior, more excellent, greater, larger, stronger; elder, senior, elder born (opposed to kanīyas and aṇīyas); a master; most excellent; (in law) one who is of age and answerable for his own conduct. – *Jyāyas-vat, ān, atī, at,* Ved. having or acknowledging a senior or superior.

Jyāyasa, as, ī, am, Ved. greater in number (opposed to *kānīyasa*).

Jyāyishṭha, as, ā, am (irreg. superl.), the most excellent; noblest, first, best.

Jyeya, as, ā, am, to be oppressed, to be deprived of (property &c.); the most excellent, first, best.

Jyeshṭha, as, ā, am, the most excellent, noblest, pre-eminent; first, chief; best, greatest; eldest, very old, elder, senior, elder born; an elder brother; (*as*), m., N. of a month, for *jyaishṭha,* q. v.; N. of a man; (*ā*), f., N. of the sixteenth or (according to more modern reckoning) eighteenth lunar mansion sacred to Indra; the eighth year of a Jupiter cycle of twelve years; the middle finger; a small house-lizard; an epithet of the Gaṅgā; a kind of heroine; misfortune personified as a goddess and the elder sister of Lakshmī; (*ī*), f. a small house-lizard; (*am*), n. the most excellent, the first, the head; tin; (*am*), ind. most, extremely; [cf. Hib. *gast,* 'an old woman;' *giostaire,* 'an active old man;' *giostaireas,* 'old age.'] – *Jyeshṭha-ghnī,* f., Ved. = *jyeshṭhā,* the sixteenth lunar mansion. – *Jyeshṭha-tama, as, ā, am,* Ved. best of all; first of all; oldest of all. – *Jyeshṭha-tara, as, ā, am,* elder, an elder one. – *Jyeshṭha-tas,* ind., Ved. according to seniority, (reckoning) from the eldest. – *Jyeshṭha-tā,* f. or *jyeshṭha-tva, am,* n. superiority; primogeniture, seniority. – *Jyeshṭha-tāta, as,* m. a father's elder brother. – *Jyeshṭha-tāti, is,* f., Ved. superiority; superior. – *Jyeshṭha-pāla, as,* m., N. of a man. – *Jyeshṭha-pushkara, am,* n., N. of a renowned place of pilgrimage. – *Jyeshṭha-balā,* f., N. of a plant, a kind of Balā, = *mahā-balā, saha-devī.* – *Jyeshṭha-bhāryā,* f. an elder brother's wife, the elder, senior or chief wife. – *Jyeshṭha-rāj, ṭ,* m., Ved. a sovereign. – *Jyeshṭha-lalitā,* f. a particular vow to be observed in the month Jyeshṭha (Jyaishṭha). – *Jyeshṭha-varṇa, as,* m. one of the first caste, a Brāhman. – *Jyeshṭha-vṛitti, is, is, i,* behaving like the first-born or eldest brother; (*is*), f. the duties of seniority. – *Jyeshṭha-śvaśrū, ūs,* f. a wife's elder sister. – *Jyeshṭha-sāman, a,* n., N. of a Sāman; (*ā, ā, a*), a chanter of the Jyeshṭha-Sāman. – *Jyeshṭha-sāmika, as, ā, am,* an adj. derived from the last. – *Jyeshṭha-stoma, as,* m., N. of an Ekāha ceremony. – *Jyeshṭha-sthāna, am,* n., N. of a place of pilgrimage. – *Jyeshṭhāṅśa* (°*ṭha-aṅ*°), *as,* m. the eldest brother's share; the right of primogeniture or the right of the eldest son to a larger portion of the patrimonial property than his brothers,—a right formerly recognized but now obsolete; the best share. – *Jyeshṭhā-mūla* or *jyeshṭhā-mūlīya, as,* m. the month Jyaishṭha. – *Jyeshṭhāmbu* (°*ṭha-am*°), *us,* m. the scum of boiled rice or water in which grain has been washed. – *Jyeshṭhāśrama* (°*ṭha-āś*°), *as,* m. the most excellent order or period in the religious life of a Brāhman, viz. that of a householder; (*as, ā, am*), being in that period. – *Jyeshṭhāśramin, ī,* m. a Brāhman in the order of a householder. – *Jyeshṭheśvara* (°*ṭha-īś*°), *am,* n., N. of a Liṅga in Vārāṇasī.

Jyeshṭhilā, f., N. of a river.

Jyaishṭha, as, m., N. of a month (May–June), the month in which the full moon stands in the constellation Jyeshṭhā; (*ī*), f. the full moon in the month Jyaishṭha; a small house-lizard. – *Jyaishṭha-sāman,* a wrong form for *jyeshṭha-sāman,* q. v.

Jyaishṭhineya, as, ī, am, born from the elder or principal wife; *jyaishṭhineyo jyeshṭhaḥ,* the eldest son and at the same time the son of the father's first wife.

Jyaishṭhya, am, n. pre-eminence, sovereignty; precedence, priority of birth, primogeniture, seniority.

ज्या 3. **jyā,** f. (perhaps fr. rt. 1. *jyā*), the string of a bow, a bow-string; the chord of an arc, a sine in geometry; [cf. *adhi-jya, uj-jya,* &c.; cf. also Gr. βιός.] – *Jyā-kāra, as,* m., Ved. one who makes bow-strings. – *Jyā-ghosha, as,* m. the twang of a bow. – *Jyā-pāśa, as,* m. a bow-string. – *Jyā-piṇḍa* or *jyā-piṇḍaka,* a sine expressed in figures. – *Jyā-magha, as,* m., N. of the father of Vidarbha. – *Jyārdha* (*jyā-ar*°), *as,* m. the sine of an arc. – *Jyārdha-piṇḍa,* a sine expressed in figures. – *Jyā-vāja, as, ā, am,* Ved. having the elasticity of a bow-string; (Sāy.) a stout or strong bow (as if a substantive). – *Jyā-vāṇeya, ās,* m. pl., N. of a warrior-tribe; (*as*), m. a prince of this tribe. – *Jyā-hroḍa, as,* m. a peculiar kind of bow; (*au*), m. du., N. of a Sāman. – *Jyotpatti* (*jyā-ut*°), *is,* f. 'the calculation of the length of a chord,' derivation of (semi)-chords.

Jyakā, f. a bow-string; the chord of an arc in geometry.

Jyākā, f., Ved. a bow-string.

Jyāya, nom. A. *jyāyate,* to represent a bow-string.

ज्या 4. **jyā,** f. the earth; a mother.

ज्यु **jyu,** cl. 1. A. *jyavate,* &c., to go, approach.

ज्युत् **jyut** (for *dyut*), cl. 1. A. P. *jyotate, -ti,* to shine: Caus. P. *jyotayati, -yitum,* to shine upon, illuminate.

Jyuti, is, f. (for *dyuti*), light. – *Jyuti-mat, ān, atī, at,* shining, full of light.

Jyotā, f., Ved. 'the brilliant or shining one,' one of the mystical names of the cow.

Jyotisha, as, ī, am (fr. *jyotis*), relating to the heavenly bodies, astronomical, astrological; (*as*), m. an astronomer, astrologer; N. of certain magical formularies for exorcising the evil spirits supposed to possess weapons; (*am*), n. astronomy, astrology, the science of the course of the heavenly bodies and divisions of time resting thereon; N. of one of the six Vedāṅgas or of a short tract which gives only such a knowledge of the heavenly bodies as was required for fixing the days and hours of the Vedic sacrifices; (*ī*), f. a star, a planet, an asterism. – *Jyotisha-tattva, am,* n. or *jyotisha-ratnamālā,* f., N. of two works on astronomy. – *Jyotisha-vidyā,* f. astronomical science. – *Jyotisha-saṅgraha, as,* m. the whole science of astronomy. – *Jyotishī-mat, ān, atī, at,* Ved. shining, brilliant; (*ān*), m., N. of a particular sun or form of the sun.

Jyotishika, a wrong form for *jyautishika,* q. v.

Jyotishka, as, m. a luminary, a heavenly body; the luminaries regarded by the Jainas as a class of deities arranged under five heads, viz. sun, moon, the planets, fixed stars, and lunar mansions; the plant Premna Spinosa; the plant Plumbago Zeylanica; the seed of Trigonella Fœnum Græcum; N. of a Nāga; N. of a man; (*ā*), f., N. of a plant, = *jyotishmatī;* (*am*), n., N. of a luminous weapon with which Arjuna destroyed Tamas or darkness personified (see Mahā-bh. Droṇa-parva 1325); N. of the shining peak of the Meru.

Jyotis, is, n. light in various forms and under various aspects, as the light of the sun, of dawn, of fire, of lightning, &c.; brightness or clearness of the sky, daylight (opposed to Tamas); lightning; light appearing in three forms, viz. fire on the earth, ether or air in the intermediate region, and sun in the sky; a glance of the eye, the faculty of seeing, the eye; the heavenly bodies, the planets and stars (in this sense pl., e. g. *jyotishām ayanam,* the course of the heavenly bodies); sun and moon (in this sense du., e. g. *jyotishor upasargāḥ,* eclipses &c. of the sun and moon); the light of heaven, the celestial world; light as the divine principle of life or as the source of intelligence, intelligence; light as a type of freedom, of bliss and of victory, [cf. Lat. *lux* and Gr. φάος, φῶς]; N. of the Jyotishṭoma as applied to the first and sixth days of the Abhi-plava ceremony which lasts six days; N. of certain formularies containing the word *jyotis;* a kind of metre consisting of thirty-two short and sixteen long syllables; the science of the course of the heavenly bodies, &c., see *jyotisha;* a mystical term for the letter *r;* (*is*), m. fire; the sun; N. of the plant Trigonella Fœnum Græcum; N. of a son of Manu Svāroćisha; also of Marut; [cf. *ćitra-jyotis* and *dakshiṇā-j*°.] – *Jyotiḥ-śāstra, am,* n. the science of astronomy; a work upon astronomy. – *Jyotiḥ-sāman, a,* n., N. of a Sāman. – *Jyotiḥ-siddhānta, as,* m. title of an astronomical work. – *Jyotir-agra, as, ā, am,* Ved. preceded by light or life. – *Jyotirathyā,* f., N. of a river; (a wrong form for *jyotī-rathā.*) – *Jyotir-anīka, as, ā, am,* Ved. having a shining face or appearance. – *Jyotir-iṅga* or *jyotir-iṅgaṇa, as,* m. 'moving light,' a fire-fly. – *Jyotir-īśa* or *jyotir-īśvara, as,* m., N. of the author of the Dhūrta-samāgama. – *Jyotir-gaṇa, as,* m. the heavenly bodies collectively. – *Jyotir-jarāyu, us, us, u,* Ved. surrounded by a brilliant covering; (Sāy.) brilliant (among the clouds) like an embryo. – *Jyotir-jña, as,* m. 'star-knower,' an astrologer, one versed in astronomy. – *Jyotir-jvalanārći-śrī-garbha* (°*na-ar*°), *as,* m., N. of a Bodhi-sattva. – *Jyotir-dhāman, ā,* m., N. of one of the seven sages in the Manv-antara of Tāmasa. – *Jyotir-bhāsa-maṇi, is,* m. a kind of gem. – *Jyotir-bhāsin, ī, inī, i,* brilliant with light. – *Jyotir-maṇḍala, am,* n. the stellar sphere. – *Jyotir-maya, as, ī, am,* consisting of light, brilliant, abounding with stars, starry. – *Jyotirmālin, ī,* m. (for *-mālin?*), a fire-fly. – *Jyotir-mukha, as,* m., N. of one of the monkey-followers of Rāma. – *Jyotir-liṅga, am,* n., N. of several Liṅga temples. – *Jyotir-lekhāvalayin, ī, inī, i,* studded with rows of stars. – *Jyotir-loka, as,* m. the world of light. – *Jyotir-vid, t, t, t,* knowing the stars, an astronomer; creating light (in this sense rt. 3. *vid,* to find). – *Jyotir-vidyā,* f. the science of astronomy, astrology. – *Jyotir-vīja, am,* n. 'seed of light,' a fire-fly. – *Jyotir-hastā,* f. an epithet of Durgā. – *Jyotiś-ćakra, am,* n. 'circle of the luminaries,' the zodiac. – *Jyotish-kaṇa, as,* m. a spark of fire. – *Jyotish-kara, as,* m. 'light-causer,' a kind of flower. – *Jyotish-kalpa, as, ā, am,* like flame or fire, blazing, radiant. – *Jyotishkalpa-latā,* f. title of an astrological work. – *Jyotish-kṛi,* cl. 8. P. *-karoti, -kartum,* to make light, illumine. – *Jyotish-kṛit, t, t, t,* Ved. creating light. – *Jyotish-ṭama, as, ā, am,* diffusing the most brilliant light. – *Jyotishṭoma, as,* m. (fr. *jyotis-stoma*), a Soma ceremony considered as the typical form of a whole class of ceremonies; it consists of either four or seven subdivisions, viz. the Agni-shṭoma, Ukthya, Shoḍaśin, Ati-rātra, or in addition to these the Atyagni-shṭoma, Vāja-peya, and Aptor-yāma. – *Jyotish-ṭva, am,* n. luminousness, illumination; the condition of light. – *Jyotish-paksha, as, ā, am,* having brilliant wings. – *Jyotish-prabha, as,* m. 'brilliant with light,' N. of a kind of flower; N. of a Buddha; also of a Bodhi-sattva. – *Jyotish-mat, ān, atī, at,* luminous, brilliant, shining, belonging to the world of light, heavenly, celestial; *jyotishmatī trishṭup,* a form of the Trishṭubh metre, containing three Pādas of twelve syllables each and one Pāda of eight syllables; (*ān*), m. the sun; N. of one of the seven suns appearing at the destruction of the world; N. of the third foot of Brahmā; N. of a son of Manu Svāyambhuva; also of Manu Sāvarṇa; N. of a king of Kuśa-dvīpa; also of a son of Priya-vrata; N. of a mountain; (*tī*), f. the night (as illumined by the stars), heart-pea, Cardiospermum Halicacabum. – *Jyotis-sāt,* ind. to flame, to fire or light; *jyotissāt kṛi,* to light, illumine, set on fire. – *Jyotī-rata, as,* m., N. of a serpent-demon. – *Jyotī-ratha, as, ā, am,* whose chariot is light; (Sāy.) bearing fire or the oblation like a chariot; (*as*), m. the pole-star or in mythology Dhruva, son of Uttāna-pāda; a kind of serpent; (*ā*), f., N. of a river which joins the Soṇa or Sone. – *Jyotī-rasa, as,* m. a kind of gem. – *Jyotī-rūpa-svayambhū, ūs,* m. Svayambhū (Brahmā) in the form of light. – *Jyotī-rūpeśvara* (°*pa-īś*°), *am,* n., N. of a Liṅga.

Jyotsnā, f. a moonlight night; moonlight; light, splendor in general; N. of one of the bodies of Brahmā; N. of one of the sixteen Kalās of the moon; an epithet of Durgā; N. of two plants, =

jyotsnī and *ghoshātakī*. — *Jyotsnā-kālī*, f., N. of a daughter of the moon and wife of Pushkara who was a son of Varuṇa. — *Jyotsnā-priya*, *as*, m. 'a friend of the mooolight,' the bird Chakora or Greek partridge. — *Jyotsnā-vat*, *ān*, *atī*, *at*, illuminated by the moon, shining, brilliant. — *Jyotsnā-vriksha*, *as*, m. the tree or tripod of a lamp, a lamp-stand, candlestick. — *Jyotsneśa* (°*nā-īśa*), *as*, m. 'lord or husband of the moonlight,' the moon.

Jyotsnikā, f., N. of a plant, = *koshātakī*.

Jyotsnī, f. a moonlight night; a small cucumber, Trichosanthes Dioeca; a kind of perfume, = *reṇukā*; (a wrong form for *jyautsnī*.)

Jyautisha, *am*, n., N. of a Sāman.

Jyautishika, *as*, m. one who knows the Jyotisha, an astronomer, astrologer.

Jyautsna, *as*, *ī*, *am*, luminous especially with moonlight; (*as*), m. the time of moonlight, the light half of a month; (*ī*), f. a full moon night; N. of a plant, = *paṭolikā*.

Jyautsnikā, f. a moonlight night; (perhaps an incorrect form for *jyotsnikā*.)

ज्यो jyo, cl. 1. A. *jyavate*, &c., to advise, instruct, order; observe a vow or any religious obligation.

ज्योक् jyok, ind. long, for a long time, for a long while; *jyoktamām*, superl. ind. for the longest time, longest. — *Jyog-jīvātu*, *us*, f. long life; *jyok kṛi*, to be long about anything, delay.

ज्योडि jyoḍi, in names of plants. Cf. *kara-jyoḍi* and *hasta-j°*.

ज्योतयमानक jyotayamānaka, *as*, *ikā*, *am*, Ved. shining (?).

ज्योतिक jyotika, *as*, m., N. of a Nāga; (perhaps a wrong reading for *jyotishka*.)

ज्योतिस् jyotis, &c. See p. 353, col. 2.

ज्यौ jyau, *aus*, m. (a word borrowed fr. the Gr. Ζεύς), the planet Jupiter.

ज्रि 1. jri, cl. 1. P. *jrayati*, &c., to overpower, conquer; to go.

Jraya. Cf. *pṛithu-jraya*.

Jrayas, *as*, n., Ved. a plain, expanse, space; (Sāy.) speed; splendor; overpowering; [cf. Zend *zarajo*.]

Jrayasāna, *as*, *ā*, *am*, Ved. spreading, expanding, occupying space; (Sāy.) going.

2. *jri*, *is*, *is*, *i*, in *uru-jri*, q. v.

ज्रि 3. jri or *jrī* [cf. rt. 1. *jṝ*], cl. 1. 10. 9. P. *jrayati*, *jrāyayati*, *jriṇāti*, &c., to grow old, to be or become old or decayed.

ज्वर् jvar, cl. 1. P. *jvarati*, *jajvāra*, *jvarishyati*, *ajvārīt*, *jvaritum*, to be feverish, to be hot with fever or passion, to be diseased &c.: Caus. P. *jvarayati*, *-yitum*, to make feverish: Desid. *jijvarishati*: Intens. *jājvaryate*, *jājūrti*; [cf. Lat. *æ-ger*; Hib. *gurt*, 'pain, trouble, fierceness;' Germ. *schwer*; Old Germ. *swâr*, *swâri*; Germ. *quâlen*?].

Jūrṇa, *as*, *ā*, *am*. See rt. 1. *jur*, p. 349, col. 3.

Jvara, *as*, m. fever of different kinds (called after the different doshas or humors of the body which are supposed to be affected by them; fever is called the leader and king of all diseases); fever of the soul, mental pain, affliction, grief, trouble, sorrow, distress; (*ā*), f. fever; (*as*, *ā*, *am*), heated, raging (with fever, passion, &c.), excited, inflamed. — *Jvara-ghna*, *as*, *ī*, *am*, febrifuge, anti-febrile, dispelling fever or ague; (*as*), m. or according to some (*ī*), f. the plant Cocculus Cordifolius, = *guḍūćī*; the plant Chenopodium Album, = *vāstūka*. — *Jvara-ćikitsā*, f. medical treatment of fever. — *Jvara-nāśaka*, *as*, *ā*, *am*, febrifuge. — *Jvara-nirṇaya*, *as*, m., N. of a medical work. — *Jvara-pratīkāra*, *as*, m. cure of fever. — *Jvara-hantri*, *tā*, *trī*, *tri*, febrifuge; (*trī*), f. the plant Rubia Munjista. — *Jvarāgni* (°*ra-ag*°), *is*, m. feverish heat, the hot paroxysm in fever. — *Jvarāṅkuśa* (°*ra-an*°), *as*, m. a febrifuge; the plant Andropogon Jvarancusa; title of a work on medicine. — *Jvarāṅgī* (°*ra-an*°), f., N. of a plant, = *bhadra-dantikā*. — *Jvarāntaka* (°*ra-an*°), *as*, *ā*, *am*, febrifuge, dispelling fever; (*as*), m. the plant Cathartocarpus Fistula; a kind of Nimba growing in Nepal. — *Jvarānvita* (°*ra-an*°), *as*, *ā*, *am*, suffering from fever or ague. — *Jvarāpaha* (°*ra-ap*°), *as*, *ā*, *am*, febrifuge; (*ā*), f. a febrifuge, the plant Medicago Esculenta, = *villa-pattrī* (?).

Jvarita, *as*, *ā*, *am*, or *jvarin*, *ī*, *iṇī*, *i*, febrile, feverish, affected with fever.

Jvāra. See *nava-jvāra*.

ज्वल् jval, cl. 1. P. (ep. also A.) *jvalati*, *-te*, *jajvāla*, *jvalishyati*, *ajvālīt*, *jvalitum*, to burn brightly, blaze, flame, glow, shine; to burn (as a wound); to be ardent: Caus. P. *jvālayati* and *jvalayati*, *-yitum*, to set on fire, light, kindle, make radiant, illuminate: Desid. *jijvalishati*: Intens. *jājvalyate*, *jājvalti*, to flame violently, shine strongly, be brilliant; [cf. Hib. *gual-laim*, 'I blacken, burn;' *gual*, 'coal, coals, fire:' Germ. *Kohle*: Old Germ. *colo*: Eng. *coal*: Lith. *swelù*: Old Germ. *wallu*, *walm*, *wâli*.]

Jvala, *as*, *ā*, *am*, flaming, blazing, shining, brilliant; (*as*), m. flame, blaze, light. — *Jvala-mukhī*, f., N. of a tutelary deity in the family of Lomaśa; [cf. *jvālā-mukhī*.] — *Jvalānana* (°*la-ān*°), *as*, *ā*, *am*, having the face flaming. — *Jvalā-rāsabhakā-maya*, *as*, m. = *jāla-gardabha*.

Jvalakā, f. a large flame or blaze.

Jvalat, *an*, *antī*, *at*, burning, blazing; shining, radiant, brilliant. — *Jvalan-maṇi*, *is*, *is*, *i*, blazing with jewels; (*is*), m. a brilliant gem.

Jvalana, *as*, *ā*, *am*, inflammable, combustible, flaming, shining; (*as*), m. fire; a N. of the numeral 3; corrosive alkali; the plant Plumbago Zeylanica; (*ā*), f., N. of a daughter of Takshaka and wife of Ṛićeyu [cf. *jvālā*]; (*am*), n. burning, blazing. — *Jvalanāśman* (°*na-aś*°), *ā*, m. the sun-stone; [cf. *sūrya-kānta*.]

Jvalanīya, *as*, *ā*, *am*, fit to be burnt, combustible.

Jvalayat, *an*, *antī*, *at*, kindling, burning, illumining, blazing, radiant.

Jvalita, *as*, *ā*, *am*, kindled, burnt, blazing, flaming; (*triṇeshu jvalitaṃ tvayā*, you have lighted a fire in the grass, i. e. you have had easy work.) — *Jvalita-nayana*, *as*, *ā*, *am*, fiery-eyed, looking angrily or fiercely; also *jvalita-ćakshus*, *jvalita-netra*, &c. — *Jvalitānana* (°*ta-ān*°), *as*, *ā*, *am*, having the face flaming.

Jvalin, *ī*, *inī*, *i*, burning, flaming, shining; (*inī*), f. the plant Sanseviera Zeylanica, = *mūrvā*.

Jvāla, *as*, *ī*, *am*, burning, blazing; (*as*), m. light, flame, a torch; (*ā*), f. a blaze, flame, illumination; burnt rice; N. of a daughter of Takshaka and wife of Ṛiksha; [cf. Hib. *gual*, 'coal.'] — *Jvālā-khara-gada* and *jvālā-gardabhaka*, *as*, m. = *jāla-gardabha*. — *Jvālāgni* (°*la-ag*°), *is*, m. blazing fire, flame. — *Jvālā-jihva*, *as*, m. 'flame-tongued,' N. of fire; N. of an attendant of Skanda; of Śiva; of a Dānava. — *Jvālā-dhvaja*, *as*, m. 'flame-marked,' fire. — *Jvālā-mukha*, *as*, m. 'flame-mouthed,' a class of demons; (*ī*), f. a volcano; any place where subterranean fire or inflammable gas breaks forth, such places being held sacred by the Hindūs as indicating the presence of a form of Durgā; (a celebrated Jvālā-mukhī exists in the hills north-east of the Pañjāb to which pilgrimages are made; the soil abounds with carburetted hydrogen gas which takes fire upon coming in contact with the external air. According to the legend, the flame proceeds from the fire which the wife of Śiva created and in which she burned herself. Śiva finding that this flame was about to consume the world, buried it in the hollow of the mountain. According to another legend, the tongue of Pārvatī fell at this place. There is a similar volcanic region in Chinese Tartary where fire is produced by digging into the earth.) — *Jvālā-liṅga*, *am*, n. 'flame-liṅga,' N. of a temple of Śiva. — *Jvālā-vaktra*, *as*, m. 'flame-mouthed,' N. of an attendant of Śiva. — *Jvāleśvara* (°*la-īś*°), N. of a Tīrtha.

Jvālin, *ī*, *inī*, *i*, flaming, blazing; (*inī*), f. mystical name of the letter *v*.

झ

झ 1. jha, the ninth consonant of the Sanskrit alphabet and the aspirate of the preceding letter. — *Jha-kāra*, *as*, m. the letter or sound *jh*.

झ 2. jha, *as*, *ā*, *am*, asleep, sleeping; lost, destroyed; (*as*), m. a peculiar sound; playing a tune, beating time; a sound like the splashing of water or the clashing of symbols, jingling, clanking, &c.; wind accompanied by rain; a stray, a thing lost or mislaid; a N. of a chief of the Daityas or demons; an epithet of Bṛihaspati, the preceptor of the gods; (*ā*), f. the descent of a cascade, a water-fall.

झगझगाय jhagajhagāya, nom. A. *jhagajhagāyate*, to sparkle, flash.

झङ्कार jhan-kāra, *as*, m. or *jhan-kārita*, *am*, n. (fr. the imitative word *jham*), a low murmuring sound, as the buzzing or humming of bees &c.

झञ्झन jhañjhana, *am*, n. (onomatopoetic), an indistinct noise like the jingling and clanking of metal ornaments, any ringing or rattling sound.

Jhañjhā, f. the noise of the wind or of falling rain; wind, wind and rain, a hurricane, a gale; a clang or sharp clanking sound, jingling; raining in large drops; a stray, anything lost. — *Jhañjhānila* (°*jhā-an*°), *as*, m. wind with rain, a high wind in the rainy season, a typhoon or the sort of tempest frequent during the south-west monsoon. — *Jhañjhā-vāta*, *as*, m. wind with rain, a storm, a squall.

झट् jhaṭ, cl. 1. P. *jhaṭati*, &c., to become matted together or entangled (as hair), to become confused or intermixed.

Jhaṭā, f. the plant Flacourtia Cataphracta.

Jhaṭi, *is*, m. a small tree, a shrub, a bush.

Jhāṭa, *as*, m. an arbour, bower, place overgrown with creepers; a wood, a thicket; cleaning sores or wounds; (*ā* or *ī*), f. jasmine, Jasminum Auriculatum.

Jhāṭala, *as*, m. the tree Bignonia Suaveolens.

Jhāṭikā or *jhāṭīkā*, f. = *jhāṭā* above.

झटिति jhaṭiti, ind. (fr. *jhaṭ*, an onomatopoetic word with *iti*; cf. *paṭiti*), quickly, speedily, instantly; at once; on the spot.

झणझण jhaṇajhaṇa or *jhaṇajhaṇā* (an onomatopoetic word), the jingling or tinkling of ornaments; [cf. *ćhanaććhan* and *jhalajjhalā*.] — *Jhaṇa-jhaṇī-bhūta*, *as*, *ā*, *am*, rattling.

Jhaṇajhaṇāya, nom. A. *-yate*, &c., to jingle, tinkle.

Jhaṇajhaṇāyita, *am*, n. jingling, tinkling.

झणत्कार jhaṇat-kāra or *jhanat-kāra*, *as*, m. (fr. the imitative sound *jhaṇat* and *kāra*), the jingling, tinkling, or clinking of metallic ornaments.

झनज्झना jhanajjhanā, flapping noise.

झम् jham, cl. 1. P. *jhamati*, &c. = *ćham* and *jam*, to eat, consume.

झम्प jhampa, *as*, *ā*, m. f. a spring, a jump, jumping, springing, plunging. — *Jhampāśin* (°*pa-āś*°), *ī*, m. a kingfisher.

Jhampāka, *as*, m. or *jhampāru*, *us*, m. a monkey, an ape.

Jhampin, *ī*, m. 'a leaper,' an ape, a monkey.

झर jhara, *as*, *ā* or *ī*, m. f. a cascade, a water-fall; (*ī*), f. a river; [cf. *nir-jhara*.]

Jharat, *an*, *antī*, *at*, flowing or falling down; [cf. *kshar*.]

झर्च् jharć, cl. 6. P. *jharćati*, or *jharćh*, cl. 6. P. *jharćhati*, or *jharjh*, cl. 6. P. *jharjhati*, to speak; to blame, menace; injure.

झर्झर jharjhara, *as*, *ī*, m. f. (said to be fr.

the last), a sort of drum; (*as*), m. the Kali-yuga, the present Yuga or age of the world; N. of a Daitya, a son of Hiraṇyāksha; N. of a river; (*ā*), f. a whore [cf. *ṛććharā*]; (*am*), n. a sound as of splashing or dropping.

Jharjharaka, as, m. the fourth or present age of the world, the Kali-yuga.

Jharjharin, ī, iṇī, i, furnished with a drum; epithet of Śiva.

झर्झरीक *jharjharīka, as,* m. the body; a region, a country; a picture.

झलक्का *jhalakkā,* f. a large flame.

झलज्झला *jhalajjhalā,* f. an onomatopoetic word for the noise of falling drops, the flapping of an elephant's ears, or of flaccid breasts, &c.

झलरी *jhalarī,* f. = *jharjhara,* a sort of drum; a curl; [cf. *jhallarī.*]

झला *jhalā,* f. a girl, a daughter; sunshine, splendor, brilliant or glittering light; a cricket; [cf. *jhillī;* cf. also rt. *jval;* Hib. *gal,* 'heat;' *galla,* 'fairness, brightness, beauty;' *gallad,* 'a lass, a young girl.']

झलि *jhali, is,* f. the areca-nut.

झल्ल *jhalla, as,* m. a prize-fighter, a cudgel-player, a man of a tribe following the profession of a Jhalla; a designation of one of the degraded classes sprung from an outcast Kshatriya; (*ī*), f. a kind of drum.

झल्लक *jhallaka, am,* n. (fr. *jhalla,* imitative sound), cymbals; (*ī*), f. a kind of drum.

झल्लकण्ठ *jhallakaṇṭha, as,* m. a pigeon; [cf. *jhillī-kaṇṭha.*]

झल्लना *jhallanā,* f. a particular Prākṛit metre.

झल्लरी *jhallarī,* f. (fr. *jhalla,* imitative sound; cf. *jhalarī*), a kind of musical instrument, a sort of drum or cymbal; a curl, a lock of hair; moisture; purity; a ball &c. of perfumed substances used for cleaning the hair; [cf. *jhalarī* and *jhillarī.*]

झल्लिका *jhallikā,* f. a rag or cloth used for applying colour or perfumes; dirt rubbed off the body by the application of perfumes; light, splendor, lustre; [cf. *jhillikā.*]

झल्लीषक *jhallīshaka,* a sort of musical instrument.

झल्लोल *jhallola, as,* m. a ball or protuberance at the lower end of a spindle.

झष् *jhash,* cl. 1. P. A. *jhashati, -te,* &c., to take; to put on, wear, cover; (only P.) to hurt or kill.

Jhasha, as, m. a large fish, a fish in general; the sign of the zodiac Pisces; a forest, a thicket; a forest overgrown with grass; heat, warmth; (*ā*), f. the plant Uraria Lagopodioides; (*am*), n. a desert. — *Jhasha-ketana* or *jhasha-dhvaja, as,* m. a N. of Kandarpa or the god of love; love. — *Jhashāṅka* (°*sha-an*°), *as,* m. an epithet of Aniruddha or the son of Kāma. — *Jhashāśana* (°*sha-aś*°), *as,* m. the Gangetic porpoise, Delphinus Gangeticus. — *Jhashodarī* (°*sha-ud*°), f. an epithet of Satyavatī, the wife of Sāntanu and mother of Vyāsa.

झाङ्कृत *jhāṅ-kṛita, am,* n. (fr. *jhām,* imitative sound, and rt. 1. *kṛi*), a tinkling ornament worn round the toes or feet.

झाट *jhāṭa.* See under rt. *jhaṭ.*

झाटामला *jhāṭāmalā,* f. = *jhāṭā,* Jasminum Auriculatum; (according to others two separate words, *jhāṭā* and *amalā.*)

झाटास्त्रक *jhāṭāstraka, as,* m. the water melon.

झाबुक *jhābuka, as,* m. the tree Tamarix Indica (?); [cf. *jhāvuka.*]

झामक *jhāmaka, am,* n. a burnt or vitrified brick.

झामर *jhāmara, as,* m. a small whetstone, used chiefly by housewives for sharpening their spindles, needles, &c.

झार्झर *jhārjhara* or *jhārjharika, as,* m. (fr. *jharjhara*), a tabor-player, a drummer.

झालरी *jhālarī* [cf. *jhalarī*], a kind of drum or tabor.

झाला *jhālā,* f. = *jhalā,* q. v.

झालि *jhāli, is,* f. a sort of sour or unripe mango fried with salt, mustard, and Asa Fœtida.

झावु *jhāvu, us,* m. the tree Tamarix Indica; also *jhāvuka, as,* m. and *jhāvū, ūs,* m.

झिङ्गाक *jhingāka, as,* m. a sort of cucumber, Luffa Acutangula.

झिङ्गिनी *jhinginī,* f. a sort of cucumber, Luffa Acutangula; a torch, a firebrand.

Jhingī, f. a sort of cucumber, Luffa Acutangula.

झिज्झी *jhijjī,* f. = *jhillī,* a cricket; [cf. *jhiñjhī.*]

झिञ्झिम *jhiñjhima, as,* m. a forest on fire.

झिञ्झिरा *jhiñjhirā* and *jhiñjhirishṭā,* f., N. of a shrub.

झिञ्झी *jhiñjhī,* f. = *jhillī,* a cricket.

झिण्टी *jhiṇṭī,* f. a shrub, Barleria Cristata; *nīlā jhiṇṭī,* Barleria Cærulea.

झिरिका *jhirikā* or *jhirī* or *jhirīkā* or *jhirukā,* f. a cricket.

झिल्लरी *jhillarī,* f. = *jhallarī,* q. v.

झिल्लि *jhilli, is,* f. a cricket; a kind of musical instrument; membrane or parchment; [cf. *jhillī;* cf. also Lat. *gryllus;* Germ. *Grille.*]

Jhillikā, f. a cricket; a cricket's cry; the light of sunshine, strong light, splendor; the dirt which comes from the body in rubbing it with perfumes; a cloth or rag used for applying colour, unguents, &c.; a kind of skin or membrane, parchment. — *Jhillikā-gaṇa-nādita, as, ā, am,* resounding with a multitude of crickets.

Jhillī, f. a cricket; the wick of a lamp; a cloth or rag for applying unguents, colour, &c.; sunshine, light, lustre; rice burnt by cooking in a saucepan, &c.; a musical instrument, cymbals; parchment. — *Jhillī-kaṇṭha, as,* m. a domestic pigeon.

Jhillīka, as, m. a cricket; (*ā*), f. a cricket; sunshine; dirt taken off the body in rubbing it with perfumes.

Jhīrikā and *jhīrukā,* f. a cricket.

झिल्लिन् *jhillin, ī,* m., N. of a Vṛishṇi.

झु *jhu,* cl. 1. A. *jhavate,* &c., to go or move.

झुण्ट *jhuṇṭa, as,* m. a shrub, a bush.

झुमरि *jhumari* or *jhumeri, is,* f. one of the Rāgiṇīs or modes of music personified.

झुणि *jhuṇi, is,* f. a kind of betel-nut; a voice or communication from heaven boding ill-luck, evil omen; a thicket &c. (= *kaṭhina.*)

झूष् *jhūsh,* cl. 1. P. *jhūshati,* to hurt, kill; (a various reading for *yūsh.*)

झॄ *jhṝ* (another form of rt. 1. *jṝ*), cl. 4. 9. P. *jhīryati, jhṛiṇāti,* &c., to become old.

झोड *jhoḍa, as,* m. the betel-nut tree.

झौलिक *jhaulika,* a small bag for betel &c.

झ्यु *jhyu,* cl. 1. P. *jhyavati,* &c., to go or move.

ञ

ञ 1. *ña,* the nasal belonging to the palatal class of letters. It only really occurs in conjunction with palatal consonants; and when preceding *ć, ćh,* has much the sound of *n* in *inch;* when preceding *j, jh,* much the sound of *n* in *singe.* — *Ña-kāra, as,* m. the letter or sound *ñ.*

ञ 2. *ña, as,* m. a singer; any jingling or inarticulate sound; a heretic, an apostate; an ox; a N. of Śukra, regent of the planet Venus.

ट

ट 1. *ṭa,* the eleventh consonant of the Sanskṛit alphabet and first of the third class or cerebrals; it has much the sound of *t* in *true,* but properly pronounced by keeping back the tip of the tongue and slightly turning it upwards. — *Ṭa-kāra, as,* m. the letter or sound *ṭ.* — *Ṭa-varga, as,* m. the cerebral consonants collectively. — *Ṭavargīya, as, ā, am,* belonging to the cerebral class of consonants.

ट 2. *ṭa, as,* m. sound or an imitative sound like the twang of a bow-string &c.; a dwarf; a quarter, a fourth; (*ā*), f. the earth; an oath, confirming an assertion by ordeal &c; (*am*), n. a hollowed cocoa-nut.

टक्कदेश *ṭakka-deśa, as,* m. the country of the Ṭakkas; [cf. *ṭakva.*]

Ṭakkadeśīya, as, m. a kind of pot-herb, Chenopodium Album; [cf. *vāstūka.*]

टक्कर *ṭakkara, as,* m. the clapping of cymbals or a drum (?), a blow, knock, rap (?).

टक्किबुद्ध *ṭakkibuddha, as,* m., N. of a man.

टक्व *ṭakva, ās,* m. pl. = *bāhīka;* [cf. *ṭakka-deśa.*]

टक्वर *ṭakvara, as,* m. an epithet of Śiva.

टगर *ṭagara, as, ā, am,* squint-eyed [cf. *kekara* and *ṭeraka*]; (*as*), m. borax; wanton play or sport; wandering of the mind, confusion, perplexity; an object of sense.

टङ्क् *ṭank,* cl. 10. 1. P. *ṭankayati, ṭankati,* to bind, tie; cover.

Ṭanka, as, am, m. n. (according to some only m.; said to be fr. the preceding), a spade, hoe, hatchet, stone-cutter's chisel or similar instrument; a sword, scimitar, sacrificial hatchet or knife; a scabbard, the sheath of a sword (only m.); a peak or crag shaped like the edge of a hatchet, the edge or declivity of a hill, slope; a chasm, cleft; anger, wrath; pride, arrogance; a weight (of silver) equal to four Māshas or twenty-four Raktikās; the wood-apple or Feronia Elephantum, = *nīla-kapittha;* the fruit of the wood-apple (n. only); borax; a stamped coin; (*as, ā, am*), m. f. n. the leg. — *Ṭanka-ṭīka, as,* m. an epithet of Śiva. — *Ṭanka-pati, is,* m. the master of the mint. — *Ṭanka-vat, ān, atī, at,* having crags or declivities. — *Ṭanka-śālā,* f. a mint.

Ṭankaka, as, m. a stamped coin especially of silver, silver money. — *Ṭankaka-pati, is,* m. the master of a mint or superintendent of the silver coin. — *Ṭankaka-śālā,* f. a mint.

टङ्कण *ṭankaṇa, as,* m. borax; (*ās*), m. pl., N. of a people in the north-east of Madhya-deśa; (*am*), n. binding, tying. — *Ṭankaṇa-kshāra, as,* m. borax.

टङ्कानक *ṭaṅkānaka, as,* m. the mulberry, Morus Indica.

टङ्कार *ṭaṅ-kāra, as,* m. (fr. *ṭam,* imitative sound, and 1. *kāra*), howling, a howl, a cry, a sound, a clang, the twang of a bow-string &c.; fame, notoriety; surprise, wonder, [cf. *ṭāṅ-kāra*]; (ī), f., N. of a shrub, commonly called Ṭekārī.

Ṭaṅkārita, am, n. humming; (a various reading for *jhaṅkārita.*)

टङ्ग *ṭaṅga, as, am,* m. n. (another form of *ṭaṅka* above), a spade, a hoe; a sword, a peculiar kind of sword; a leg; (*as*), m. borax; a weight of four Māshās.

टङ्गण *ṭaṅgaṇa, as, am,* m. n. borax; [cf. *ṭaṅkaṇa.*]

टङ्गिनी *ṭaṅginī,* f. the plant Clypea Hernandifolia, commonly Ākanādi.

टट्टनी *ṭaṭṭanī,* f. a small house-lizard.

टट्टरी *ṭaṭṭarī,* f. a kind of musical instrument; a kettle-drum; a joke, a jest; a lie.

टट्टुर *ṭaṭṭura, as,* m. the sound of a drum; (a various reading for *dardura.*)

टण्डन *ṭaṇḍana, as,* m., N. of a prince.

टल् *ṭal,* cl. 1. P. *ṭalati, ṭaṭāla,* &c., to be confused, to be disturbed by fear or anxiety &c.

Ṭala or *ṭāla, as,* m. perturbation, confusion (?).

Ṭalana, am, n. anxiety, perturbation.

टाङ्क *ṭāṅka, am,* n. a spirituous liquor prepared from the fruit of the Feronia Elephantum or a similar tree.

टाङ्कर *ṭāṅkara, as,* m. a blackguard, a lecher, a libertine; [cf. *ṭāra.*]

टाङ्कार *ṭāṅ-kāra, as,* m. or *ṭāṅ-kṛita, am,* n. (fr. *ṭām,* imitative sound, and rt. 1. *kri*), a sound, a clang, a twang, &c.; [cf. *ṭaṅ-kāra* and *ḍāṅ-kṛiti.*]

टार *ṭāra, as,* m. a horse; a catamite.

टिक् *ṭik,* cl. 1. A. *ṭekate,* &c., to go or move; [cf. *ṭīk, tik, tīk.*]

टिका *ṭikā* in *svarga-grāma-ṭikā-viluṇṭhana,* the spoils of the poor villages of heaven (?).

टिक्क *ṭikka, as,* m., N. of a man.

टिटिभक *ṭiṭibhaka, as,* m. a bird, = *ṭiṭṭibha.*

टिटिल *ṭiṭila, am,* n. a large number, = 100 Nāga-balas.

टिट्टिभ *ṭiṭṭibha, as,* m. a kind of bird, Parra Jacana or Gœnsis; N. of a Daitya; also of a Dānava who was an enemy of Indra in the thirteenth Manvantara; (ī), f. the female of the bird Parra Jacana.

Ṭiṭṭibhaka, as, m. the bird Parra Jacana or Gœnsis.

टिण्टिणि *ṭiṇṭiṇi, is,* m., N. of a man.

टिण्टिणिका *ṭiṇṭiṇikā* or *ṭiṇṭiṇīkā,* f., N. of a plant.

टिण्डिश *ṭiṇḍiśa, as,* m. a kind of plant, = *tiṇḍiśa,* &c.

टिप् *ṭip,* cl. 10. P. *ṭepayati,* &c., to direct, send, throw, cast; (a various reading for *ḍip.*)

Ṭepana, am, n. sending, throwing.

टिप्पनी *ṭippanī,* f. (also spelt *ṭippaṇī*), a gloss, a comment, commentary.

टिरिटिरा *ṭiriṭirā,* f. (an onomatopoetic word), whispering.

टीक् *ṭīk* [cf. *ṭik*], cl. 1. A. *ṭīkate,* &c., to go or move; cl. 10. P. *ṭīkayati,* &c., to explain, make clear.

Ṭīkā, f. any commentary, but especially a commentary on another commentary (e.g. the commentary by Ānanda-giri on Śaṅkara's Upanishad-bhāshya is called *bhāshya-ṭīkā.*

टु *ṭu, us,* m. gold; one who changes his shape at will, a proteus; Kāma or the god of love.

टुण्टुक *ṭuṇṭuka, as, ā, am,* small, little, low, vile; cruel, harsh; (*as*), m. the tree Colosanthes Indica; the bird Sylvia Sutoria; (*ā*), f. a plant, commonly Aknidhi; [cf. *ṭaṅginī.*]

टुनाका *ṭunākā,* f. the plant Curculigo Orchioides.

टुल्ल *ṭulla, as,* m., N. of a man.

टेपन *ṭepana.* See rt. *ṭip,* last col.

टेर *ṭera, as, ā, am,* squinting.—*Ṭerāksha* (°*ra-ak*°), *as, ī, am,* squint-eyed.

Ṭeraka, as, ā, am, squinting.

टोटक *ṭoṭaka,* a kind of metre consisting of four lines of twelve syllables each.

टोडरक्ष्मापति *ṭoḍara-kshmāpati, is,* m. or *ṭoḍaramalla* or *ṭoḍarendra, as,* m., N. of a minister of Akbar Shāh and author of the Ṭoḍarānanda.

टोतला *ṭotalā,* f., N. of a deity.

टोदलतन्त्र *ṭodala-tantra, am,* n., N. of a Tantra.

टौक् *ṭauk,* cl. 1. A. *ṭaukate,* &c., to go, approach; (various reading for *ḍhauk.*)

ट्वल् *ṭval,* cl. 1. P. *ṭvalati,* &c., to be disturbed or confused.

ठ

ठ 1. *ṭha,* the twelfth consonant and aspirate of the preceding letter.—*Ṭha-kāra, as,* m. the letter or sound *ṭh.*—*Ṭhakārāya* (fr. the last), nom. P. *ṭhakārāyati:* Desid. *ṭiṭhakārāyishati.*

ठ 2. *ṭha, as,* m. a loud noise; an imitative sound as of a golden pitcher rolling down steps; the disk of the sun or moon, a circle, a globe; a cypher; a place frequented or held sacred by all; an object of sense; an idol, a deity; an epithet of Śiva.

ठक्कन *ṭhakkana, as,* m., N. of a prince; (various readings have *ḍhakkana* and *thakkana.*)

ठक्कुर *ṭhakkura, as,* m. an idol, a deity, an object of reverence or worship; an honorific title after the name of a distinguished person; (sometimes written Thākur or popularly Tagore.)

ठठम् *ṭhaṭham,* ind. an imitative sound. See 2. *ṭha.*

ठार *ṭhāra, as,* m. rime, hoar-frost.

ठालिनी *ṭhālinī,* f. a girdle.

ठिण्ठा *ṭhiṇṭhā,* f., N. of a woman.

ड

ड 1. *ḍa,* the third letter of the cerebral class of consonants, having much the sound of *d* in *drum,* but properly pronounced by keeping back the tip of the tongue and slightly turning it upwards. In Bengal *ḍ* is often confounded in pronunciation with a hard *r.*—*Ḍa-kāra, as,* m. the letter or sound *ḍ.*

ड 2. *ḍa, as,* m. a sound; a kind of drum or tabor; fear; submarine fire; an epithet of Śiva; (*ā*), f. a Ḍākinī, i.e. a kind of female imp or goblin; a basket &c. carried by means of a sling.

डक्कारी *ḍakkārī,* f. the lute of the Čaṇḍālas.

डङ्गर *ḍaṅgara, as,* m. = *ḍiṅgara,* throwing, casting; (ī), f. a kind of gourd; (also *ḍaṅgarī,* &c.)

डप् *ḍap,* cl. 10. A. *ḍāpayate,* &c., to collect, accumulate, heap together.

डम् *ḍam,* cl. 1. P. *ḍamati,* &c., to sound.

डम *ḍama, as,* m. a despised mixed caste (commonly Ḍom), the son of a Čāṇḍālī and a Leṭa, employed to clear away filth &c.

डमर *ḍamara, as, ā,* m. f. a riot, tumult, affray, a conflict without weapons; terrifying an enemy by shouts and gestures; petty or predatory warfare carried on by detachments or between villages and not kings; (*am*), n. flight, rout, running away through fear; [cf. *ḍāmara.*]

डमरिन् *ḍamarin, ī,* m. (?) a sort of drum, = the next.

Ḍamaru, us, m. a musical instrument, a sort of small drum shaped like an hour-glass and held in one hand; anything surprising, any strange occurrence &c.

Ḍamaruka, am, n. a kind of drum.

डम्प् *ḍamp,* cl. 10. A. *ḍampayate,* &c. (a various reading for *ḍap*), to heap together.

डम्ब् *ḍamb,* cl. 10. P. *ḍambayati,* &c., to throw, cast, send; order.

डम्बर *ḍambara, as,* m., N. of one of the attendants of Skanda; an assemblage, collection, mass; (*as, ā, am*), famous, renowned.

डम्भ् *ḍambh,* cl. 10. A. *ḍambhayate,* &c. (various reading for *ḍap*), to collect.

डयन *ḍayana.* See rt. *ḍī,* p. 357, col. 1.

डलक *ḍalaka* or *ḍallaka, am,* n. a sling, a basket, a Ḍūlī carried on men's shoulders by means of a stick and ropes like the beam and strings of a balance, (presents of fruit, sweetmeats, &c., are usually sent in this manner); (*as*), m., N. of a man.

डलन *ḍalana* or *ḍallana, as,* m., N. of a scholiast on the medical work of Su-śruta.

डवित्थ *ḍavittha, as,* m., N. of a man; a wooden antelope (?); [cf. *ḍittha.*]

डहु *ḍahu, us,* or *ū, ūs,* m. the plant Artocarpus Lacucha.

डाकिनी *ḍākinī,* f. a kind of female imp or evil being attending Kālī and feeding on human flesh; N. of a place; [cf. *śākinī.*]—*Ḍākinī-tva, am,* n. the condition of a female demon.

डाङ्कृति *ḍāṅ-kṛiti, is,* f. (fr. *ḍām,* imitative sound, and 1. *kṛiti*), a sound, the clang of a bell, ding-dong, &c.; [cf. *ṭāṅ-kāra.*]

डाङ्गरी *ḍāṅgarī,* f. = *ḍaṅgarī,* q. v.

डामर *ḍāmara, as,* m. affray, riot, conflict without weapons &c. [cf. *ḍamara*]; rout, uproar, the bustle and confusion of festivity or strife; any surprising thing, sight, or occurrence; a N. common to six Tantras, viz. the Yoga-ḍāmara, Śiva-ḍ°, Durgā-ḍ°, Sārasvata-ḍ°, Brahma-ḍ°, and Gandharva-ḍ°; N. of one of the attendants of Śiva; N. of a race or mixed caste; (*as, ā, am*), riotous; [cf. *uḍ-ḍāmara.*]—*Ḍāmara-tva, am,* n. the state of one who excites awe.

डालिम *ḍālima, as,* m. = *dāḍima,* a pomegranate.

डाहल *ḍāhala, as,* m., N. of a people and their country.

डाहुक *ḍāhuka, as,* m. a gallinule; [cf. *dātyūha.*]

डिक्करी *ḍikkarī*, f. a young woman; (wrong form for *ḍikkarī*.)

डिङ्गर *ḍingara*, *as*, m. a servant, a slave; a rogue, a cheat; a low or depraved man; a fat man; throwing, flinging; invective, insult (?).

डिडका *ḍiḍakā*, f. perhaps a wrong form for *ḍimbhakā*.

डिडिम *ḍiḍima* or *ḍiḍimāṇaka*, a kind of bird; [cf. *ṭiṭṭibha*.]

डिण्डिक *ḍiṇḍika*, *as*, m., N. of a mouse whose story is told in the Mahā-bh. Udyoga-parva 5440.

डिण्डिम *ḍiṇḍima*, *as*, m. a musical instrument, a kind of small drum or tabor; a plant bearing a small fruit, Carissa Carandas. — *Ḍiṇḍimeśvara-tīrtha* (°*ma-īś*°), *am*, n., N. of a Tīrtha.

डिण्डिर *ḍiṇḍira*, *as*, m. cuttle-fish bone considered to be the foam of the sea; [cf. *hiṇḍira* and *ḍiṇḍīra*.] — *Ḍiṇḍira-modaka*, *am*, n. garlic.

डिण्डिश *ḍiṇḍiśa*, *as*, m. = *ṭiṇḍiśa* = *tiṇḍiśa*.

डिण्डीर *ḍiṇḍīra*, *as*, m. cuttle-fish bone held to be the foam of the sea; [cf. *ḍiṇḍira*.]

डित्थ *ḍittha*, *as*, m., N. of a man; a wooden elephant; a good-looking dark-coloured young man who is conversant with every branch of learning; [cf. *ḍavittha*.]

डिप् *ḍip* or *ḍimp* or *ḍimbh*, cl. 10. A. *ḍepayate* or *ḍimpayate* or *ḍimbhayate*, to collect, heap together; *ḍip*, cl. 4. 6. 10. P. *ḍipyati*, *ḍipati*, *ḍepayati*, to throw, cast, send or order; to direct; also *ḍimb*, cl. 10. A. *ḍimbayate*; [cf. rt. *ṭip*.]

डिम् *ḍim* (a Sautra root or one not occurring in the Dhātu-pāṭha), to hurt, injure.

डिम *ḍima*, *as*, m. a dramatic entertainment, dramatic exhibition of battle or siege, such as the Tripura-dāha, in which the destruction of the three cities of Tripura by Śiva is dramatised; a kind of mixed caste.

डिम्ब *ḍimba*, *as*, m. affray, riot, conflict without weapons, mutual defiance, petty and predatory war, &c. [cf. *ḍamara*]; sound or noise occasioned by terror; an egg; a chrysalis; the embryo in the first stage of its existence; a new-born child, any young animal; the bladder, the spleen, the lungs; the uterus; a globe or ball. — *Ḍimba-yuddha*, *am*, n. or *ḍimbāhava* (°*ba-āh*°), *as*, m. petty warfare, affray, skirmish, riot, &c.

डिम्बिका *ḍimbikā*, f. a libidinous woman; a bubble; a kind of water-fly; = *śoṇaka*, Calosanthes Indica.

डिम्भ् *ḍimbh* or *ḍimb*. See rt. *ḍip* above.

डिम्भ *ḍimbha*, *as*, m. a new-born child, any young animal; a fool, an idiot, a blockhead; (*ā*), f. an infant. — *Ḍimbha-ćakra*, *am*, n. a mystical circle; a diagram for telling fortunes.

Ḍimbhaka, *as*, *ikā*, m. f. a new-born child, young animal; (*as*), m., N. of a general of Jarā-sandha, younger brother of Haṃsa and son of Brahma-datta.

डी *ḍī*, cl. 1. 4. A. *ḍayate*, *ḍīyate*, *ḍiḍye*, *ḍayishyate*, *aḍayishṭa*, *ḍayitum*, to fly, pass through the air; to go: Caus. P. *ḍāyayati*, *-yitum*, *aḍiḍayat*: Desid. *ḍiḍayishate*: Intens. *ḍeḍīyate*, *ḍeḍayīti* or *ḍeḍeti*.

Ḍayana, *am*, n. flying in the air, the flight of a bird; a car or litter carried upon men's shoulders, a palanquin, a Dūlī.

Ḍayamāna, *as*, *ā*, *am*, flying, passing through the air.

Ḍītara, *as*, *ā*, *am*, Ved. following one another quickly.

Ḍīna, *as*, *ā*, *am*, flown, flying; (*am*), n. flying, the flight of a bird. — *Ḍīna-ḍīnaka*, *as*, m. flying reiteratedly. — *Ḍīnāvaḍīna* (°*na-av*°), *am*, n. flying up and down; flying badly.

डुडुभ *ḍuḍubha* or *ḍuḍuma*, *as*, m. or *ḍuṇḍu*, *us*, f. or *ḍuṇḍubha*, *as*, m. a kind of snake (Amphisbæna) or lizard.

Ḍauṇḍubha, *as*, *ī*, *am*, of or belonging to an Amphisbæna.

डुण्डुल *ḍuṇḍula*, *as*, m. a small owl.

डुन्दुक *ḍunduka*, *as*, m. a gallinule, = *ḍāhuka*.

डुलि *ḍuli*, *is*, f. a small turtle, a female turtle, = *duli*, *kamaṭhī*.

डुलिका *ḍulikā*, f. a kind of wagtail.

डुली *ḍulī*, f. a kind of pot-herb, = *ćillī*.

डोडी *ḍoḍī*, f. a sort of shrub, = *jīvantī*, *jīvanī*, &c.; [cf. *kshupaḍoḍa-mushṭi*.]

डोम *ḍoma*, *as*, m. a man of low caste, a Ḍom; [cf. *ḍama*, *ḍomba*; cf. also the N. for the Gypsies, *Rom*.]

डोम्ब *ḍomba*, *as*, m. a man of low caste obtaining a livelihood by singing and music &c.; N. of a man.

डोर *ḍora* or *ḍoraka*, *am*, n. a fillet of thread or cord tied round the arm or wrist; the string for tying a packet or parcel.

डोरडी *ḍoraḍī*, f. a kind of Solanum, = *vṛihatī*.

डौण्डुभ *ḍauṇḍubha* (scil. *rūpa*), the form of an Amphisbæna. See under *ḍuḍubha*.

ड्वल् *ḍval*, Caus. P. *ḍvālayati*, &c., to mix; [cf. rt. *ṭval*.]

ढ

ढ 1. *ḍha*, the aspirate of the preceding letter; its use as an initial letter is very limited, and several of the words in which it occurs can scarcely be regarded as pure Sanskrit. — *Ḍha-kāra*, *as*, m. the letter or sound *ḍh*.

ढ 2. *ḍha*, *as*, m. an imitative sound; a large drum; a dog's tail; a dog; a serpent; void of qualities (?).

ढक्क *ḍhakka*, *as*, m., N. of a city or district (commonly *ḍhākā* or *ḍhakka*; the word is said also to signify a large sacred building); (*ā*), f. a large or double drum, a Ḍhāk; coveting; disappearance.

ढक्कन *ḍhakkana*, *as*, m., N. of a man; (also written *ṭakkana*, *ḍhakkama*, *thakkana*.)

ढक्कारी *ḍhakkārī*, f. an epithet of the goddess Tāriṇī or Tārā, a Tāntrika form of Durgā.

ढङ्क *ḍhaṅka*, *as*, m., N. of a mountain.

ढण्ठी *ḍhaṇṭhī*, *is*, f. = *vākya-viśesha*.

ढामरा *ḍhāmarā*, f. a goose.

ढाल *ḍhāla*, *am*, n. a shield.

Ḍhālin, *ī*, m. a warrior armed with a shield, a shield-bearer.

ढुण्ढ् *ḍhuṇḍh*, *ḍhuṇḍhati* (properly a Sautra root not occurring in the Dhātu-pāṭha), to search, seek.

Ḍhuṇḍhana, *am*, n. seeking, investigating.

Ḍhuṇḍhi, *is*, m. an epithet of Gaṇeśa. — *Ḍhuṇḍhi-rāja*, *as*, m., N. of an author who was the father of Bāla-Kṛishṇa and uncle of Saṅkara-dīkshita.

Ḍhuṇḍhita, *as*, *ā*, *am*, sought, inquired.

ढेङ्क *ḍheṅka*, *as*, m. a kind of bird.

ढोल *ḍhola*, *as*, m. a large drum or tabor.

ढौक् *ḍhauk*, cl. 1. A. *ḍhaukate*, *ḍuḍhauke*, *ḍhaukishyate*, *aḍhaukishṭa*, *ḍhaukitum*, to go, move, approach: Caus. *ḍhaukayati*, *-yitum*, *aḍuḍhaukat*, to bring near, cause to approach, offer: Desid. *ḍuḍhaukishate*: Intens. *ḍoḍhaukyate*.

Ḍhaukana, *am*, n. offering; a present, a bribe.

ण

ण 1. *ṇa*, the nasal *ṇ* belonging to the third or cerebral class of consonants. — *Ṇa-kāra*, *as*, m. the letter or sound *ṇ*.

ण 2. *ṇa*, *as*, m. knowledge; certainty, ascertainment; ornament; a water or summer-house; a bad man; a N. of Vindu-deva, said to be a Jaina deity; an epithet of Śiva; the sound of negation; gift, giving.

णद् *ṇad*, *ṇam*, *ṇaś*, &c. Many roots which really begin with the dental *n* are written in native grammars and the Dhātu-pāṭha with the cerebral *ṇ* to show that the nasal is liable to be cerebralized when preceded by prepositions like *pra*, *pari*, &c. These roots will be found in the present Dictionary under the dental *n*. See *nad*, *nam*, *naś*, &c.

ण्य *ṇya*, *as*, m., N. of an ocean in Brahma-loka.

त

त 1. *ta*, the first consonant of the fourth or dental class, the sound of which is more dental than the English *t*. — *Ta-kāra*, *as*, m. the letter or sound *t*. — *Ta-varga*, *as*, m. the dental class of letters. — *Tavargīya*, *as*, *ā*, *am*, belonging to the dental class.

त 2. *ta*, the base of the third personal pronoun in all the cases except the nom. sing. masc. and fem. See *tad*, p. 360.

त 3. *ta*, *as*, m. a tail; any tail except that of the Bos Gaurus; the tail of a jackal; the breast; the womb; the hip or flank; a warrior; a thief; a wicked man; an outcast, a barbarian or Mleććha; a Buddha; a jewel; nectar, the food of the immortals; (*ā*, *am*), f. n. passing, crossing; virtue, sanctity; (*ā*), f., N. of Lakshmī.

तंस् *taṃs*, cl. 1. A., Ved. *taṃsate*, *tatasre*, &c., to shake, move to and fro; to pour out (metaphorically a wish); to request: Caus. P. *taṃsayati*, *-yitum*, to move to and fro, shake; cl. 1. 10. P. *taṃsati*, *taṃsayati*, to decorate; [cf. Old Pruss. *teisint*, 'to honour;' *teisi*, 'honour.']

तंसु *taṃsu*, *us*, m., N. of a prince of the lunar race, a son of Matināra (or Rantināra); in some places he is called Taṃsu-rodha.

तक् *tak*, cl. 1. 2. P., Ved. *takati*, *takti*, *tatāka*, *takishyati*, *atakīt* and *atākīt*, *takitum*, to fly (as an arrow or bird), fly at, rush or pounce upon; to laugh at or deride; to bear.

Takavāna, *as*, *ā*, *am*, Ved. rushing, darting along, moving quickly; (Sāy.) shaking, moving with difficulty.

Taku, *us*, *us*, *u*, Ved. rushing, moving quickly; (Sāy.) approaching.

Takta, *as*, *ā*, *am*, Ved. rushing or darting along.

1. *takman*, *ā*, m., Ved. (especially in the Atharva-veda), a kind of disease, or probably a whole class of diseases, accompanied by eruptions of the skin. — *Takma-nāśana*, *as*, *ī*, *am*, Ved. removing the disease called Takman.

Takya, *as*, *ā*, *am*, to be borne or endured; laughable, ridiculous.

Takva, *as*, *ā*, *am*, Ved. quick (?).

Takvan, *ā*, *arī*, *a*, Ved. rushing, darting, pouncing on; (*ā*), m. a bird, especially a bird of prey; (Sāy.)

a fleet horse; a thief. — *Takva-vī, īs,* m., Ved. a bird, bird of prey, or a particular bird. — *Takvavīya, as,* m., Ved. rapid flight, rush.

तक **taka,** *as, ā, at* (fr. *tad* with *ak* inserted after *t*), that.

तकरी **takarī,** f., Ved. a particular part of the pudenda of a woman.

तकिल **takila,** *as, ā, am,* fraudulent, crafty, a rogue or cheat; (*ā*), f. a medicament, drug; a kind of plant.

तक्कोल **takkola,** the tree Pimenta Acris, commonly called Kaṅkola.

तक्मन् 2. **takman,** *a,* n. = *tokman* = *apatya,* offspring, a child; [cf. Gr. τέκνον; cf. also 1. *takman* under rt. *tak,* p. 357, col. 3.]

तक्र **takra,** *am,* n. (fr. rt. 1. *tañć*), buttermilk which is half water; (according to others) with a fourth or three parts of water. — *Takra-kūrćikā,* f. inspissated buttermilk. — *Takra-bhid, t,* n. (?) the fruit of Feronia Elephantum. — *Takra-māṇsa, am,* n. meat fried with ghee, turmeric, Asa Fœtida, &c., and eaten with buttermilk. — *Takra-sāra, am,* n. fresh butter. — *Takrāṭa* (°*ra-aṭa*), *as,* m. a churning-stick; [cf. *dadhi-ćāra.*]

तक्ष् 1. **taksh,** cl. 1. 5. P. (sometimes A.) *takshati, -te, takshṇoti, -ṇute, tatakshа, -she, takshishyati* or *takshyati, -te, atakshīt, takshitum* or *tashṭum,* to form by cutting, plane, chisel, pare, chip, chop, slice, split; to cut, wound; to make thin; to fashion, form (out of wood &c.), to make, create in general; to form in the mind, invent; to make one's own, appropriate; to cover; to skin, peel: Caus. *takshayati, -yitum, atatakshat:* Desid. *titakshishati* or *titakshati* (?): Intens. *tātakshyate, tātashṭi;* [cf. Lith. *taszau:* Russ. *tesatj:* Pol. *ćiesla:* Lat. *tignum:* Old Pruss. *tikint,* 'to make;' *tikinnimai, teikusna:* Gr. τίκτω, τέκνον, τεύχω, τάσσω.]

2. **taksh,** *ṭ, ṭ, ṭ,* (at the end of a comp.) paring, cutting, forming by cutting, working; [cf. *kāshṭha-taksh.*]

Taksha, as, ā, am, cutting off, cutting through; (*as*), m. (at the end of a comp.) = *takshan,* a carpenter [cf. *kauṭa-taksha* and *grāma-t°*]; N. of a serpent-demon; N. of a son of Bharata; N. of a son of Vṛika.

Takshaka, as, m. a cutter, one who cuts off, a wood-cutter, a carpenter; the divine architect or artist Viśva-karman; the Sūtra-dhāra or manager and chief actor in the prelude of a drama; one of the principal Nāgas or serpents of Pātāla; N. of a son of Prasena-jit and father of Bṛihad-bala; N. of a particular tree.

Takshakīyā, f., N. of a place.

Takshaṇa, am, n. cutting, paring, peeling, planing; (*ī*), f. a carpenter's adze or similar instrument for cutting, an axe &c; (*as*), m. a cutter, an abrader; (in mathem.) the divisor employed in certain computations.

Takshan, ā, m. (Ved. acc. *takshāṇam* or *takshaṇam*), a wood-cutter, a carpenter; N. of a preceptor; [cf. Gr. τέκτων.] — *Taksha-śilā,* f., N. of a city of the Gandhāras, the Τάξιλα of Ptolemy in the Pañjāb; (*ās*), m. pl. the inhabitants of this city. — *Taksha-śilā-vatī,* f., N. of a district. — *Takshāyaskāra* (°*sha-ay*°), *am,* n. a carpenter and a blacksmith.

Takshitṛi, tā, trī, tṛi, one who cuts, pares, &c.; a cutter.

Takshya, as, ā, am, to be formed or fashioned.

तगडवल्ली **tagaḍa-vallī,** f. (*tagaḍa* = *tagara*), the shrub Cassia Auriculata.

तगर **tagara,** *am,* n. the shrub Tabernæmontana Coronaria and a fragrn t powder prepared from it; N. of a town; (*as*), m. a thorny shrub, Vangueria Spinosa; another plant, commonly Tagara-mūla; [cf. *kāla-parṇa, kaṭu-ććhada, madana-vṛiksha.*] — *Tagara-pādikā, am,* f. n. or *tagara-pādī,* f. the plant Tabernæmontana Coronaria and its powder. — *Tagara-śikhin, ī,* m., N. of a man.

Tagarika, as, ī, m. f. a seller of Tagara powder.

तङ्क् **tank,** cl. 1. P. *tankati, tatanka, tankitum,* to live in distress, be in poverty or pain; to go (?); [cf. Hib. *teicheamh,* 'a going, passage;' *tochamhlaim,* 'I march;' *tochar,* 'a causeway, pavement;' *toichim,* 'going, departing:' Lith. *tekù,* 'I run;' *tākas,* 'a path;' *tekūnas,* 'a runner:' Slav. *takŭ,* 'I run.']

1. *tanka, as,* m. grief produced by separation from a beloved object; fear, terror; [cf. *ā-tanka, tapas-tanka.*]

तङ्क 2. **tanka,** *as, am,* m. n. (for *ṭanka*), an axe, a stone-cutter's chisel.

तङ्ग् **tang,** cl. 1. P. *tangati,* &c., to go, move; to stumble; to shake, tremble; [cf. Hib. *tagaidh,* 'advance;' *tigim,* 'I come, go.']

तङ्गण **tangaṇa,** *ās,* m. pl., N. of a people in the upper part of the valley of the Sarayū.

तङ्गल्व **tangalva,** *as,* m., Ved., N. of an evil spirit.

तच्छील **taććhīla.** See *tad,* p. 360, col. 1.

तज्ज **taj-ja,** *taj-jaya,* &c. See *tad,* p. 360.

तज्वी **tajvī,** f. = *hingu-pattrī.*

तञ्च् 1. **tañć** or **tañj,** cl. 7. P. *tanakti, tatañća, tankshyati* and *tañćishyati, atānkshīt* and *atañćīt, tanktum* and *tañćitum,* to contract, shrink: Caus. *tañćayati, -yitum:* Desid. *titankshati* or *titañćishati:* Intens. *tātaćyate, tātankti.*

तञ्च् 2. **tañć,** cl. 1. P. *tañćati,* &c., to go.

तञ्ज् **tañj,** a various reading for 1. *tañć* above.

तट् **taṭ,** cl. 1. P. *taṭati,* &c., to rumble, groan; to be raised or elevated, rise; cl. 10. P. *tāṭayati,* to beat, strike; (a various reading for *tad*); [cf. Lith. *tesiu,* 'to raise.']

Taṭa, as, ā, m. f. a slope, an acclivity, declivity, precipice; the sky or horizon (as appearing to slope); (*as, ā* or *ī, am*), m. f. n. a shore or bank; a term applied to certain parts of the human body which have, as it were, sloping sides (e. g. *śroṇi-taṭa, stana-taṭa,* q. v.); (*am*), n. a field; [cf. *a-taṭa, ut-taṭa, pura-taṭī.*] — *Taṭa-stha, as, ā, am,* situated on a declivity, or on a bank or shore; standing near; indifferent, not partaking of or engaging in, alien, neuter; (*as*), m. an indifferent person, one neither a friend nor a foe; (*am*), n. that property which is distinct from the nature of anything and yet is the faculty by which it is known, spiritual essence unconnected with bodily wants or passions.

Taṭaka, am, n. a shore or bank.

Taṭāka, as, am, m. n. a pond deep enough for the lotus and other aquatic flowers.

Taṭinī, f. a river (as having a bank). — *Taṭinī-pati, is,* m. 'the lord of the rivers,' the ocean.

Taṭya, as, ā, am, living on hills or slopes, epithet of Śiva.

तटतट **taṭataṭa** (an onomatopoetic word to express a particular noise), rumbling, thundering, &c.

तड् **taḍ,** cl. 10. P. *tāḍayati, -yitum, atītaḍat* (redupl. perf. *tatāḍa*), to beat, strike, hit, knock; to strike with arrows, wound, punish; to strike a musical instrument; (in astronomy) to strike against, touch, partially obscure or eclipse; (in arithmetic) to multiply; to speak; to shine; [cf. Hib. *tathaim,* 'I kill, destroy;' *tathog,* 'a clash, a slap.']

Taḍit, t, f., Ved. (in Ṛig-veda *taḷit*), lightning; *taḷit* or *taḷitas,* ind. closely, near, (as it were striking against.) — *Taḍit-kumāra, ās,* m. pl. (with Jainas) N. of a class of deities belonging to the Bhavana-patis. — *Taḍit-prabhā,* f., N. of one of the Mātṛis attendant on Skanda. — *Taḍit-vat, ān, atī, at,* having lightning, emitting lightning, flashing; (*ān*), m. a cloud, a kind of Cyperus, = *mustaka.* — *Taḍid-garbha, as,* m. a cloud, 'containing lightning.' — *Taḍin-maya, as, ī, am,* consisting of lightning, flashing like lightning. — *Taḍin-mālāvalambin* (°*lā-av*°), *ī, inī, i,* having garlands of lightning hanging down. — *Taḍil-latā,* f. forked lightning. — *Taḍil-lekhā,* f. a line or streak of lightning.

तडग **taḍaga,** *as,* m. = *taḍāga,* a pool, lake.

तडाक **taḍāka,** *as,* m. (said to be fr. rt. *taḍ*), = *taḍāga,* a pond or pool deep enough for the lotus; (*ā*), f. a blow; a bank, a shore; splendor, lightning (?); [cf. *taṭāka.*]

Taḍākin, ī, inī, i, having pools or lakes.

Taḍāga, as, am, m. n. a pond or pool deep enough for the growth of the lotus &c.; a tank; a trap for catching deer. — *Taḍāga-vat, ān, atī, at,* having pools or lakes; (*ān*), m., scil. *deśa,* a district.

तडाघात **taḍāghāta,** *as,* m. a blow from an elephant's uplifted trunk; probably a wrong form for *tāḍāghāta* (*tāḍa-āghāta*).

तडित् **taḍit.** See *taḍ,* col. 2.

तण्ड् **taṇḍ** (connected with *taḍ*), cl. 1. A. *taṇḍate,* &c., to beat.

तण्ड **taṇḍa,** *as,* m., N. of a man.

तण्डक **taṇḍaka,** *as, am,* m. n. complete performance or preparation; decoration; the upright post of a house; composition abounding in compound words; (*as*), m. a juggler, a cheat; the trunk of a tree; froth, foam; a wagtail; [cf. *tāṇḍaka.*]

तण्डि **taṇḍi,** *is,* m., N. of a man; also of a Ṛishi in the Kṛita-yuga who saw and praised Śiva.

तण्डिन् **taṇḍin,** *ī,* m., N. of the author of a work on prosody quoted by Piṅgala.

तण्डु **taṇḍu,** *us,* m., N. of one of Śiva's door-keepers and one of the original teachers of the arts of dancing and mimicry.

तण्डुरीण **taṇḍurīṇa,** *as,* m. one not a citizen, a barbarian; a fool, a blockhead; the water in which rice has been soaked or steeped.

तण्डुल **taṇḍula,** *as, am,* m. n. (said to be fr. *taḍ,* cf. *taṇḍ*), grain after threshing and winnowing, especially rice; rice used as a weight; (*as, ā*), m. f. a vermifuge plant or its seed [cf. *taṇḍulu, viḍanga*]; (*as*), m. a pot-herb, a sort of amaranth, = *taṇḍulīya;* (*ā*), f. a kind of plant, = *odanāhvayā, odanikā, mahā-samangā;* a sort of Sida; (*ī*), f., N. of several plants, = *yava-tiktā, śaśāṇḍulī, taṇḍulīya.* — *Taṇḍula-kaṇa, as,* m. a grain of rice. — *Taṇḍula-deva, as,* m., N. of a poet of Kaśmīra. — *Taṇḍula-phalā,* f. long pepper. — *Taṇḍulāmbu* (°*la-am*°), *u,* n. rice-water or gruel. — *Taṇḍulottha* (°*la-ut*°), *am,* n. or *taṇḍulodaka* (°*la-ud*°), *am,* n. water in which rice has been boiled, rice-gruel. — *Taṇḍulaugha* (°*la-ogha*), *as,* m. a prickly sort of bamboo, Bambusa Spinosa; a heap of grain.

Taṇḍulika, as, m. a kind of pot-herb, Amaranthus Polygonoides.

Taṇḍulīya, as, m. a kind of pot-herb, Amaranthus Polygonoides; a vermifuge plant [cf. *viḍanga*]; a mineral, iron pyrites.

Taṇḍulīyaka, as, m. Amaranthus Polygonoides; a vermifuge seed; [cf. *viḍanga.*]

Taṇḍulu, us, m. a plant the seeds of which are used as a vermifuge; [cf. *viḍanga.*]

Taṇḍulera, as, m. Amaranthus Polygonoides.

तण्डूलिकाश्रम **taṇḍūlikāśrama** (°*ka-āś*°), *as,* m., N. of a hermitage, Mahā-bh. Vana-parva 4084.

तत् 1. **tat** for *tad,* that. See *tad,* p. 360.

तत् 2. *tat*, 2. *tata*. See rt. 3. *tan*, p. 361.

तत 1. *tata, as*, m. (connected with *tāta*, said to be fr. rt. 3. *tan*), Ved. father (a familiar expression corresponding to *nanā*, mother). — *Tata-tata, as*, m. father of fathers. — *Tatā-maha, as*, m., Ved. a grandfather; [cf. *pra-tatāmaha*.]

ततत्व *tatatva, am*, n. slow time in music; [cf. *tattva*.]

ततनुष्टि *tatanushṭi, is, is, i* (fr. rt. 3. *tan?*), Ved. fond of ornaments.

ततम *tatama, as, ā, at* (fr. *tad*), that one (of many).

Tatara, as, ā, at, that one (of two).

ततस् *tatas*, ind. (fr. the pronom. base 2. *ta*; correlative of *yatas*, and often used for the abl. cases *tasmāt, tasyāḥ*, &c., of the pronoun *tad*, but oftener as an adverb), from that place, thence; in that place, there, thither (e. g. *tata ā-yāhi*, come from that place); thereupon, then, after that, afterwards (e. g. *tataḥ kim*, what happened then?); from that, in consequence of that; for that reason, therefore, consequently; beyond that, besides that, further, moreover. *Tatas-tatas*, from that and that place, here and there, hither and thither, from all sides, to every place, everywhere. *Tatas tatas*, (in dramatic poetry) what then? what took place after that? *yato-yatas—tatas-tatas*, from whatever place—to that place; wherever—there; *itas-tatas*, from this place and that, here and there, hither and thither, see s. v.; *yatas-tatas*, from which place soever, from any one whatever; *tataḥ kshaṇāt*, immediately afterwards; *tataḥ param*, thereupon, afterwards; *tataḥ paśćāt*, after that; *tataḥ-prabhṛiti*, thenceforth, thenceforward, from that time forward; *tato 'nyatas*, to some other place, i. e. to another place than that; [cf. Gr. τότε, τόθεν; Slav. *ot-tądă*.] — *Tato-bhavat, ān*, m. His Highness from there, His Highness there, Your Honour there; [cf. *tatra-bhavat* and *atra-bhavat*.]

Tatastya, as, ā, am, coming from that, proceeding thence; of or belonging to that, &c.

तति 1. *tati* (fr. the pronom. base 2. *ta*), pl. (in nom. and acc. without termination), so many. (For 2. *tati* see p. 361, col. 2.)

Tatitha, as, ī, am (correlative of *yatitha*), so maniest, that one of a number; e. g. *tatithī samā*, that year (out of a number of years).

Tatidhā, ind., Ved. in so many parts, of such a number.

ततुरि *taturi, is, is, i* (fr. rt. *tṛī*), preserving, cherishing, conquering; an epithet of Agni and Indra.

ततृपि *tatṛipi* for *tātṛipi*, q. v.

तत्कर *tat-kara, tat-kāla, tat-kriya*, &c. These and other similar compounds will be found under *tad*, p. 360, col. 1.

तत्त्व *tattva, am*, n. (fr. *tad*), the state of being that, true state, real state, truth, reality, opposed to what is illusory or fallacious; essential nature; the real nature of the human soul as being one and the same with the supreme spirit pervading the universe; (in philosophy) truth, reality, a true principle, first principle, (the number of these first principles varies according to the different systems; the Sāṅkhya phil. has twenty-five Tattvas, viz. A-vyakta or 'the undiscrete;' Buddhi, 'intellect;' Ahaṅ-kāra, 'individuality;' the five Tan-mātras or 'subtile elements;' the five Mahā-bhūtas or 'gross elements;' the eleven organs, including Manas or 'mind;' and, lastly, Purusha or 'soul:' hence *tattva* is sometimes a term for 'twenty-five.' The Māheśvaras admit only five Tattvas, viz. the five elements. In the Vedānta phil. *tattva* is regarded as made up of *tad* and *tvam*, 'this—thou,' and called *mahā-vākya*, 'the great word,' by which the identity of the whole world with the one eternal Brahma is expressed); an element or elementary property; the essence or substance of anything, sum and substance; slow time in music, a musical instrument; (*ena*), ind. according to the true state or nature of anything, in truth, truly, really, accurately. — *Tattva-kaumudī*, f. 'moonlight of the Tattvas,' or *sāṅkhya-tattvakaumudī*, title of a commentary on the Sāṅkhya-kārikā. — *Tattva-ćandra, as*, m. 'the moon of truth,' title of a commentary on the grammar Prakriyā-kaumudī. — *Tattva-ćintāmaṇi, is*, m. title of a philosophical work by Gaṅgeśa. — *Tattva-jña, as, ā, am*, or *tattva-jñānin, ī, inī, i*, knowing the truth or true nature of anything; acquainted with the true principles of philosophy, understanding the principles of a science thoroughly; (*as*), m. a Brāhman. — *Tattva-jñāna, am*, n. knowledge of the truth; a thorough knowledge of the principles of a science, insight into the true principles of philosophy. — *Tattva-tas*, ind. truly, really, actually, accurately, according to the truth, fully. — *Tattva-tā*, f. truth, reality. — *Tattva-darśa, as*, m. 'perceiving truth,' N. of one of the seven Ṛishis under Manu Deva-sāvarṇi. — *Tattva-darśin, ī*, m. 'perceiving truth,' N. of one of the sons of Manu Raivata; N. of a Brāhman. — *Tattva-dīpana, am*, n. 'light of the Tattvas,' title of a work. — *Tattva-nikasha-grāvan, ā*, m. the touchstone of principle. — *Tattva-nyāsa, as*, m. 'the imposition of truth or of the true principles,' N. of a ceremony performed in honour of Vishṇu; it consists in the application of mystical letters and other marks to the different parts of the body while certain prayers are recited. — *Tattva-prakāśa, as*, m. 'light of the true principles,' title of a philosophical commentary. — *Tattva-bodhinī*, f. 'revealing truth,' title of a commentary on the Siddhānta-kaumudī by Jñānendra-sarasvatī. — *Tattva-bhāva, as*, m. true being or nature. — *Tattva-vat, ān, atī, at*, possessing truth or the reality of things. — *Tattva-vid, t, t, t*, knowing the truth or first principles, knowing things as they are. — *Tattva-vindu, us*, m. 'drop of truth,' title of a philosophical treatise. — *Tattva-vivitsā*, f. desire of knowing the truth or God. — *Tattva-viveka, as*, m. or *siddhānta-tattvaviveka*, 'sifting of established truths,' title of an astronomical work. — *Tattvaviveka-dīpana, am*, n. 'light of the investigation of truth,' title of a philosophical work. — *Tattva-sańćaya, as*, m. 'collection of truths,' title of a Buddhist work. — *Tattva-satya-śāstra, am*, n. title of a work by Guṇa-prabha. — *Tattva-samāsa, as*, m. 'compendium of the Tattvas or principles,' the title of the Sāṅkhya-sūtras ascribed to Kapila. — *Tattvābhiyoga* (°*va-abh*°), *as*, m. a positive charge or declaration. — *Tattvārtha* (°*va-ar*°), *as*, m. the exact truth, reality, truth. — *Tattvārtha-kaumudī* (°*va-ar*°), f. the title of a commentary by Govindānanda on the Prāyaśćitta-viveka. — *Tattvārtha-vid, t, t, t*, knowing the exact truth, knowing the reality. — *Tattvārtha-sūtra* (°*va-ar*°), *am*, n. title of a Jaina work. — *Tattvāvabodha* (°*va-av*°), *as*, m. perception of truth.

तत्र *tatra*, ind. (fr. the pronom. base 2. *ta*; correlative of *yatra*, and often used for the loc. cases *tasmin, tasyām*, &c., of the pronoun *tad*, but oftener as an adverb), in that place, there, yonder, thither, to that place; in that, therein; on that occasion, in that case, under those circumstances, then; therefore; *tatra tatra*, in that and that place, here and there, hither and thither, to every place; *yatra tatra*, indiscriminately; [cf. Goth. *thathrô*.] — *Tatra-bhavat, ān, atī, at*, 'Your Honour there,' venerable, respectable, reverend; a respectful title given in dramatic language to absent persons; [cf. *atra-bhavat*.] — *Tatra-stha, as, ā, am*, there standing, dwelling there, situated there, belonging to that place, a by-stander. — *Tatrāpi* (°*tra-api*), ind. there also, even there, nevertheless.

Tatratya, as, ā, am, produced there or in that place, relating to that place, of that place, being there.

तत्व *tatva*, a less correct form for *tattva*.

तथा *tathā*, ind. (fr. the pronom. base 2. *ta* and correlative of *yathā*), in that manner, so, thus, (the correlative standing in the preceding clause, e. g. *yathā priyaṃ tathā 'stu*, as is agreeable so let it be; or in the subsequent clause, e. g. *tathā prayatnam ātishṭhed yathā na pīḍayed ātmānam*, he should so make effort as that he may not injure himself.) *Yathā-tathā*, in whatever way, in any way; by all means. *Yathā-yathā—tathā-tathā*, in whatever manner—in that manner; in whatever degree—in that degree; the more—the more, (*yathā yathā purushaḥ śāstraṃ samadhi-gaććhati tathā tathā vi-jānāti*, the more a man studies a book the more he understands it.)

Tathā followed by *iti* is also used as a particle of assent, agreement, or promise, to express 'so be it,' 'yes,' 'so it shall be,' &c. (e. g. *tathety uktvā*, having said, 'so be it' or 'yes;' *tatheti prati-jñāya*, having promised, 'so it shall be'); also in forms of adjuration (e. g. *yathā 'ham anyaṃ na ćintaye tathā 'yam patatāṃ kshudraḥ parāsuḥ*, as surely as I do not think on any other man, so surely let this wretch fall dead).

Tathā is frequently used as a conjunction to express 'so also,' 'in like manner,' 'and also' (e. g. *sukhaṃ seved duḥkhaṃ tathā*, let him make use of prosperity and also adversity). *Tathā hi*, for so, for thus (it has been said), for instance; *tathā ća*, and likewise; and so it has been said; (this and the preceding are often used in introducing quotations.) *Tathāpi* (*tathā-api*), even thus, even so, nevertheless, yet, still, notwithstanding; *yadyapi—tathāpi*, even if—yet; although—nevertheless. *Tathaiva* (*tathā-eva*), even so, even thus, exactly so, in like manner. — *Tathā-kṛita, as, ā, am*, thus done or made. — *Tathā-kratu, us, us, u*, so intending, having such an aim. — *Tathā-gata, as, ā, am*, being in such a state or condition; of such a quality or nature; (*as*), m. a Buddha; a Jina; N. of a prince. — *Tathāgata-kūpa, as*, m. 'the well of the Tathā-gata,' N. of a well. — *Tathāgata-garbha, as*, m. title of a Buddhist Sūtra work; N. of a Bodhi-sattva. — *Tathāgata-guṇa-jñānāćintya-vishayāvatāra-nirdeśa* (°*na-aćintya-vishaya-av*°), *as*, m. title of a Buddhist Sūtra work; direction (*nir-deśa*) how to attain (*ava-tāra*) to the inconceivable subject (*aćintya-vishaya*) of the qualities (*guṇa*) and to the knowledge (*jñāna*) of a Tathā-gata. — *Tathāgata-gupta, as*, m., N. of a man; N. of a king. — *Tathāgata-guhyaka, am*, n. 'the mystery of a Tathā-gata,' title of one of the nine works highly revered by the Buddhists of Nepal. — *Tathāgata-bhadra, as*, m., N. of a pupil of Nāgārjuna. — *Tathā-guṇa, as, ā, am*, endowed with such qualities. — *Tathā-tā*, f. or *tathā-tva, am*, n. such a state of things, such a condition; true state of things, true nature; the being so; the case or circumstances being admitted to be as stated. — *Tathā-prabhāva, as, ā, am*, having such power. — *Tathā-bhāvin, ī, inī, i*, of such a nature; about to be so or of such a kind. — *Tathā-bhūta, as, ā, am*, of such qualities, of such a kind or nature. — *Tathā-mukha, as, ī, am*, 'so-facing,' turning the face in the same direction. — *Tathāyata* (°*thā-āy*°), *as, ā, am*, 'so-directed,' turned towards the same point. — *Tathā-rāja, as*, m. a Buddha or Jina; [cf. *tathā-gata*.] — *Tathā-rūpa, as, ā, am*, or *tathā-rūpin, ī, iṇī, i*, of such a form, thus shaped, so formed, looking thus. — *Tathā-vādin, ī, inī, i*, professing to be so and so. — *Tathā-vidha, as, ā, am*, of such a sort or kind, being in such a condition or state, of such qualities; (*am*), ind. thus, in this manner; likewise, equally. — *Tathā-vidheya, as, ā, am*, relating to such a sort or kind, being of such a kind or nature. — *Tathā-vrata, as, ā, am*, observing such conduct or practices, so acting. — *Tathā-śīla, as, ā, am*, behaving or conducting one's self thus. — *Tathāstu* (°*thā-as*°), ind. so be it. — *Tathā-svara, as, ā, am*, uttered with the same accent. — *Tatheti*, see *tathā* followed by *iti* above. — *Tathaiva* (°*thā-eva*), ind., see *tathā* above. — *Tathotsāha* (°*thā-ut*°), *as, ā, am*, making so great efforts.

Tathya, as, ā, am, 'being really so,' true, real, genuine; (*am*), n. truth, reality; *tathyena* or *tathyatas,* ind. according to truth. — *Tathya-vādin, ī, inī, i,* speaking the truth.

तथ्य *tathya.* See above.

तद् *tad, sas, sā, tad* or *tat,* (the actual base of this pronoun in all the cases except the nom. sing. m. and f. is *ta,* but the neut. *tad* represents the base in compounds and in the derivative *tadīya.* In the Veda the nom. and acc. du. m. may be *tā* as well as *tau,* the nom. plur. n. *tā* as well as *tāni,* and the inst. plur. m. or n. *tebhis* as well as *tais*), he, she, it, that, this, (often occurring as a correlative of the relative pronoun *ya,* 'who, which,' the relative generally standing in the preceding clause, e. g. *yasya buddhiḥ sa balavān,* of whom there is intellect he is strong, see Gram. 799.)

Tad is sometimes used, for the sake of emphasis, in connection with the first and second personal pronouns, with other demonstratives and with relatives like the Lat. *ille* (e. g. *so 'ham,* I that very person, I myself; *te vayam,* we those very persons; *tāv imau,* those very two; *tad etad,* that very thing; *yat tat kāraṇam,* that very reason which; *yā sā śrīḥ,* that very fortune which).

Tad is repeated in the sense of 'this and that,' 'this or that,' 'various,' 'different' (e. g. *taṃ taṃ deśaṃ jagāma,* he went to this and that place; *tāsu tāsu yonishu,* in different or various birth-places).

Tad is used in connection with a relative pronoun in the sense of 'whosoever,' 'whichsoever,' 'every' (e. g. *yasmins tasmin kule,* in any family whatever). Sometimes both the demonstrative and the relative are repeated (e. g. *yadyat karma para-vaśaṃ tat-tad varjayet,* whatever action depends on another, that he should avoid).

Tad, n., may be used to signify 'this world' [cf. *idam*]; also to denote 'the supreme spirit or Brahma' (opposed to *tvam*).

Tad, ind. there, thither, in that place, to that spot (e. g. *tamāṃsi yatra gaććhanti tat kravyādo ajīgamam,* where dark shades prevail there I caused the flesh-eaters to go); then, at that time, in that case (e. g. *yadi māṃ na vihātum iććhasi tat kim-artham panthāḥ samupa-diśyate,* if thou dost not wish to leave me why is the road pointed out?); thus, in this manner, with regard to that, in connection with that (often so used in the Brāhmaṇas, e. g. *tad etau ślokau bhavataḥ,* with reference to that there are these two verses); on that account, for that reason, therefore, consequently (in this sense commonly used in classical Sanskṛit, e. g. *yad—tad* or *yena—tad,* because—therefore); now, so also, equally, in like manner (often connecting two sentences or clauses in the Brāhmaṇas). *Tad api,* and also, and equally; nevertheless, notwithstanding (*yady api—tad api,* even if—nevertheless); *tad yathā,* in such a manner as follows, as here follows, namely; *taććāpi,* and also, and likewise; [cf. Lith. *tas, ta,* 'this;' Goth. *tha* (the base of the article), masc. *sa,* fem. *sô;* Gr. ὁ, ἡ, τό; Slav. *t'; ta, to;* Lat. *is-te, is-ta, is-tud, tam, tum, tunc;* Hib. *so* 'this,' *se* 'he,' *si* 'she.'] — *Taććhīla* (*tad-śī°*), *as, ā, am,* having an inclination for that, accustomed to that; [cf. *tāććhīlika* and *tāććhīlya.*] — *Taj-ja* (*tad-ja*), *as, ā, am,* 'produced at that moment,' immediate, instantaneous. — *Taj-jaya* (*tad-ja°*), *as,* m. the conquest of that. — *Taj-ja-lān* (*tad-ja-la-an*), *n, n, n,* produced, absorbed, and breathing in that. — *Taj-jña* (*tad-jña*), *as, ā, am,* knowing that, knowing, experienced in or familiar with; (*as*), m. a knowing or intelligent man, (in this and other compounds *tad* often loses its meaning and becomes redundant; cf. *tat-para, tad-bhāva,* &c.) — *Tat-kara, as, ā, am,* performing a particular work or service, serving, obeying, a servant. — *Tat-kartavya, as, ā, am,* proper or necessary to be done with reference to present circumstances; [cf. *iti-kartavya.*] — *Tat-kāla, as,* m. that time (opposed to *etat-kāla,* this time); present time, time being, the time referred to or spoken of, the same time, the time when an act occurs; (*am*), ind. at that time, at a certain time; directly, immediately; (*as, ā, am*), happening at the same time or immediately; [cf. *tātkālika.*] — *Tatkāla-dhī, īs, īs, i,* wise or intelligent for the time being, having presence of mind, &c. — *Tatkāla-lavaṇa, am,* n. a kind of salt prepared artificially, = *viḍ-lavaṇa.* — *Tatkālotpanna-dhī* (*°la-ut°*), *īs, īs, i,* possessed of presence of mind. — *Tat-kulīna, as, ā, am,* belonging to that family or caste. — *Tat-kriya, as, ā, am,* performing a particular work or service; working without hire or wages. — *Tat-kshaṇa, as,* m. time present, time being; the same moment; a measure of time, = 120 Kshaṇas, = $\frac{1}{60}$ Lava; (*am* or *āt*), ind. at the same moment, immediately, directly. — *Tatkshaṇa-bhaṅgura, as, ā, am,* vanishing immediately, transient. — *Tat-tṛitīya, as, ā, am,* doing that for the third time. — *Tat-pada, am,* n. the place or position of that; the word *tad;* (*as*), m. the tree Ficus Religiosa. — *Tat-para, as, ā, am,* following that or thereupon, coming after, inferior; having that as one's highest object or aim, totally devoted or addicted to anything, attending to anything closely, eagerly engaged in (with loc. or in composition); diligent; (*as*), m. the thirtieth part of the twinkling of the eye; (with reference to the redundant use of *tad* cf. *taj-jña, tad-gata, tad-bhāva, tātparya.*) — *Tatpara-tā,* f. or *tatpara-tva, am,* n. entire devotion or addiction to; the state of following after or behind, inferiority. — *Tat-parāyaṇa, as, ā, am,* attached or addicted to any particular thing or person. — *Tat-purusha, as,* m. the original or supreme spirit; the servant or attendant of him; a class of compounds in which the last member is defined or qualified by the first without losing its original independance, i. e. continues the principal member of the compound and preserves its original grammatical character whether as a noun, adjective, or participle, whereas in a Bahu-vrīhi compound the last member loses its independance as well as its original grammatical character and serves together with the first member only to qualify or define *another word;* the Karma-dhāraya and Dvigu compounds are considered as subdivisions of the Tat-purusha class. The word *tat-purusha,* 'his servant,' is itself an example of this class of compounds. The stock example is *divya-kusumam,* 'heavenly flower,' which belongs to the Karma-dhāraya subdivision. — *Tat-pūrva, as, ā, am,* occurring or happening for the first time; prior, former. — *Tatpūrva-saṅga, as, ā, am,* then first restrained. — *Tat-prakāra, as, ā, am,* of that kind, of that sort. — *Tat-prathama, as, ā, am,* doing that for the first time. — *Tat-prabhāte,* ind. early on the next morning. — *Tat-phala, as, ā, am,* having that as a fruit or reward; having as a result or consequence; (*as*), m. the white water-lily; a kind of medicinal plant (*kushṭha*); a kind of perfume (= *ćaura*). — *Tat-samanantaram,* ind. immediately upon that or afterwards; [cf. *tad-anantaram.*] — *Tat-sādhu-kārin, ī, iṇī, i,* accomplishing or performing that. — *Tat-stha, as, ā, am,* being on or in that, connected with that; (*as*), m. a particular mode of multiplication. — *Tad-atipāta, as, ā, am,* transgressing that, going beyond the bounds. — *Tad-anantara, as, ā, am,* nearest or next to that; (*am*), ind. immediately upon that, thereupon, then (*prāk—tad-anantaram,* first—afterwards; *prathamam—tad-anantaram—tṛitīyam—ataḥ param,* first—afterwards—thirdly—further; [cf. *tat-samanantaram.*] — *Tad-anu,* ind. after that, afterwards. — *Tad-anusaraṇa-krameṇa,* ind. in a manner conformably to that, subsequently to that. — *Tad-anta, as, ā, am,* coming to an end or perishing in that, ending thus, thus terminating. — *Tad-anna, as, ā, am,* Ved. accustomed to that food. — *Tad-anyat,* ind. other than that, different from that. — *Tad-apas, ās, ās, as,* Ved. doing that work, having that occupation, accustomed to do that; (*as*), ind. in the usual way. — *Tad-artha, as, ā, am,* destined or intended for that, on that account, with that object; having that meaning; (*am*), ind. on that account, with that object, for that end, therefore; [cf. *tādarthya.*] — *Tad-arthīya, as, ā, am,* destined or intended for that, undertaken for that end. — *Tad-arpaṇa, am,* n. delivery of that, delivering or returning any article. — *Tad-arha, as, ā, am,* meriting that. — *Tad-avadhi, is,* m. that limit, that period; (*i*), ind. so far, up to that period; from that time. — *Tad-avastha, as, ā, am,* so situated, thus circumstanced, in that condition. — *Tad-ākāra, as, ā, am,* having that appearance or aspect. — *Tad-āmukha, am,* n. commencement, beginning. — *Tad-id-artha, as, ā, am,* Ved. intent on that particular object. — *Tad-ekaćitta, as, ā, am,* having all the thoughts fixed on that (person or thing). — *Tadevopanishad* (*tad-eva-up°*), *t,* f. title of an Upanishad beginning with the words *tad eva.* — *Tad-okas, ās, ās, as,* Ved. rejoicing or delighting in that, at home in it; (Sāy.) having that as one's dwelling-place. — *Tad-ojas, ās, ās, as,* Ved. endowed with such strength. — *Tad-gata, as, ā, am,* gone to that, directed towards that, devoted to, intent on; (*as*), m.(?) the continued multiplication of four or more like quantities; [cf. *taj-jña, tat-para, tad-bhāva.*] — *Tad-guṇa, as,* m. the quality of that (person or thing), quality or virtue of anything; (*as, ā, am*), possessing these qualities; (*as*), m. a figure of speech in rhetoric, transferring the qualities of one thing to another. — *Tadguṇa-saṃvijñāna, as, ā, am,* a term applied to those Bahu-vrīhi compounds in which the qualities implied in the name are perceived along with the thing itself (e. g. *Dīrgha-karṇam ā-naya,* bring *Dīrgha-karṇa,* 'long-ear,' where the long ears accompany and mark the individual. An example of the *a-tadguṇa-saṃvijñāna* would be *dṛishṭa-sāgaram ā-naya,* bring the man who has seen the ocean). — *Tad-dina, am,* n. that day; (*am*), ind. during the day, every day, day by day, on a certain day. — *Tad-duḥkha, am,* n. that grief, grief for that or of that. — *Tad-dvitīya, as, ā, am,* doing that for the second time. — *Tad-dhana, as, ā, am,* miserly, niggardly. — *Tad-dharman, ā, ā, a,* having that business, accomplishing that business; [cf. *tāddharmya.*] — *Tad-dharmin, ī, iṇī, i,* obeying the laws of him or that. — *Tad-dhita, as, ā, am* (fr. *tad-hita*), good for that, salutary; (*am*), n. the welfare of any one; (*as*), m., scil. *pratyayaḥ,* an affix which forms nouns from other nouns, (whereas a Kṛit affix forms nouns from roots); a noun formed by a Taddhita affix, a derivative noun. — *Tad-bala, as, ā,* m. f. a kind of arrow. — *Tad-bhāva, as,* m. the becoming that, becoming (in general), e. g. *abhūta-tadbhāva,* the becoming what one was not formerly. — *Tad-bhinna, as, ā, am,* different or distinct from that. — *Tad-rasa, as,* m. the spirit thereof. — *Tad-rāja, as,* m., scil. *pratyayaḥ,* an affix added to a proper name to form from it the name of a king or chief (e. g. fr. *aṅga* is formed *āṅga,* 'king of the Aṅgas,' by the Tad-rāja affix *aṅ*). — *Tad-rūpa, as, ā, am,* thus shaped, so formed. — *Tadryańć, aṅ, drīćī, ak* (fr. *tad,* with *adri* substituted for *ad,* and rt. *ańć*), extending thither; [cf. *devadryańć,* &c.] — *Tad-vaćaḥ-pratīta, as, ā, am,* believing his words. — *Tad-vat, ān, atī, at,* having or containing that, possessed of that; (*vat*), ind. like that, in that manner, thus; in like manner, equally, likewise, also; (*yadvat—tadvat* or *yathā—tadvat,* as—so.) — *Tadvat-tā,* f. conformity, agreement. — *Tad-vaśa, as, ā, am,* Ved. longing for or desiring that. — *Tad-vāćaka, as, ikā, am,* signifying that. — *Tad-vid, t, t, t,* knowing that, familiar with that; knowing the truth, a knowing man. — *Tad-vidya, as, ā, am,* possessing a knowledge of that. — *Tad-vidha, as, ā, am,* of that kind, corresponding to that, conformable to that. — *Tadvidhatva, am,* n. correspondence or conformity with that. — *Tad-vishaya* or *tad-vishayaka, as, ā, am,* having that for its object, attending to that business, relating to that. — *Tan-na,* ind. not that, not so. — *Tan-nāśa, as,* m. destruction of that. — *Tan-madhya-stha, as, ā, am,* situated in the midst of that. — *Tan-madhyāt,* ind. from the midst thereof, from amongst them. — *Tan-maya, as, ī, am,* made up of that, having the nature of that, absorbed or contained in or identical with that, become one with. — *Tanmaya-tā,* f. or *tanmaya-tva, am,* n. the being contained in or identical with that. — *Tan-maraṇa, am,* n. his death. — *Tan-mātra, as, ā, am,* only so much or so little; consisting of rudimentary atoms or elementary matter; (*am*), n. merely that, only a trifle; that in which its own peculiar property resides without any change or variety, i. e. a subtile element or a rudiment of elementary matter, (of these there are five, viz. *śabda-t°, sparśa-t°, rūpa-t°, rasa-t°,* and *gandha-t°,* from which the five Mahā-bhūtas or grosser elements are produced. In this sense also according to some *tan-mātrā,* f.) — *Tanmātra-tā,* f. or *tanmātra-tva, am,* n. the state of a Tanmātra. — *Tanmātra-sarga, as,* m. (in the Sāṅkhya phil.) the rudimental creation. — *Tan-mātrika, as, ā, am,* consisting of rudimentary atoms or elementary matter. — *Tan-mānin, ī, inī, i,* implying the doing of that which the base indicates (?), (e. g. the nominal *aghāya,* to act wickedly, is a *tan-mānin.*) — *Tal-lakshaṇa* (*tad-la°*), *am,* n. the mark of him, a particular high number.

Tadā, ind. at that time, then; in that case; (sometimes used rather redundantly in epic poetry, e. g. *tato 'ntarīkshago vāćaṃ vyā-jahāra Nalaṃ tadā,* upon that the bird addressed words to Nala then); *yadā tadā,* at any time whatsoever; *tadā prabhṛiti,* from that time forward; *yad—tadā* or *yatra—tadā* or *yadā—tadā* or *yadi—tadā,* when —then; if—then, &c.; *yatas—tadā,* from the time when—then, i. e. ever since; *yarhy eva—tadaiva,* at what time—at that very time, i. e. at the very time when. — *Tadā-tva, am,* n. 'the state of then,' that time, present time, time being, present state or circumstances, (usually in connection with *āyati,* future time.)

Tadānīm, ind. at that time, then [cf. *idānīm*]; *yadā—tadānīm,* when—then. — *Tadānīn-tana, as, ī, am,* of that time, belonging to that time. — *Tadānīn-dugdha, as, ā, am,* Ved. milked at that time or at the time spoken of, just milked.

Tadīya, as, ā, am, belonging to him or her or that or them; his, hers, its, theirs; such (e. g. *ćintayā tadīyayā,* with a thought such as that). — *Tadīya-saṅga, as,* m. meeting with her, union with her.

तन् 1. *tan* (= *stan*), cl. 4. P., Ved. *tanyati,* to resound, sound aloud, roar; [cf. Gr. τόνος; Lat. *tonare;* Angl. Sax. *thunor;* Eng. *thunder.*]

Tanayitnu, us, us, u, Ved. roaring, thundering; [cf. *stanayitnu, tanyatā, tanyatu, tanyu.*]

तन् 2. *tan,* cl. 1. and 10. P. *tanati* and *tānayati,* &c., to confide, believe or have faith in; to aid, assist; to be harmless; to pain or afflict with disease (?); [cf. rt. 1. *ćan* and *van.*]

तन् 3. *tan,* cl. 8. P. A. *tanoti, tanute, tatāna* (2nd sing. *tatantha* or *tenitha*), *tene, tanishyati, -te, atānīt* and *atanīt, atata* and *atanishṭa, tanitum,* to extend, stretch, spread, be diffused over, shine (as light), extend towards, reach to; protract, prolong, lengthen out, augment; to lengthen, be lengthened out, be protracted, continue, endure, last; to stretch (a cord), extend or bend (a bow), spread or spin out, weave; to emboss, chase; to prepare (a way for); direct one's way towards; to propagate, be propagated; to accomplish, perform (as a ceremony), to sacrifice; to compose (a literary work); to bestow, grant, cause, prepare: Pass. *tanyate* or *tāyate,* to be extended; to increase, &c.: Caus. *tānayati, -yitum, atītanat:* Desid. *titanishati, titaṃsati, titāṃsati:* Intens. *tantanyate, tantanīti, tantanti;* [cf. Gr. τάνυμαι, τείνω: Lat. *tendo, tenuis, tener:* Goth. *thanja:* Russ. *tonju:* Lith. *tempju:* Hib. *tana,* 'thin, slender, lean;' *tanaighim,* 'I make thin.'] — *Tan-ādi, ayas,* m. pl., scil. *dhātavas,* the roots beginning with *tan,* i. e. the eighth class of roots.

2. *tat, t, t, t,* at the end of a comp.; [cf. *pari-tat.*] (For 1. *tat* see p. 358, col. 3.)

2. *tata, as, ā, am* (for 1. see p. 359), extended, stretched, spread, diffused, expanded; spreading or reaching over, extending to; covered over, concealed; protracted, continued; bent (as a bow); spreading, wide, &c.; (*as*), m. wind, air; (*am*), n. any stringed musical instrument; a kind of metre consisting of four lines of twelve syllables each. — *Tata-ćihna, as, ā, am,* having marks drawn along, distinctly marked. — *Tata-pattrī,* f. the plantain tree, Musa Sapientum; [cf. *kadala.*]

2. *tati, is,* f. (for 1. see p. 359, col. 1), a series, a line, a row or range; a number, a crowd, a troop; a sacrificial act, a ceremony; [cf. *tanti.*]

4. *tan* (probably f., but occurring only in dat., inst., and abl.), Ved. continuation, diffusion, propagation, offspring, posterity, descendants; (*tanve tane ća,* for one's own person and one's children); *tanā* (inst. used as an adv.), in uninterrupted succession or series, one after another, continually.

Tana, as, m., Ved. a descendant; (*ā, am*), f. n. offspring, a descendant, posterity.

Tanaya, as, ā, am, Ved. propagating or extending a family, belonging to one's own family; (*tokaṃ tanayam,* a child which propagates the family); (*as*), m. a male descendant, a son; N. of one of the seven sages in the eleventh Manv-antara with the patronymic Vāsishṭha; (in astrology) N. of the fifth lunar mansion; (*au*), m. du. a son and a daughter; (*ā*), f. a daughter; N. of a plant, = *ćakra-kulyā;* (*am*), n. posterity, family, race, offspring, child, descendant; (according to the scholiasts *tanaya* is a grandchild and *toka* a child); (*ās*), m. pl., N. of a people. — *Tanaya-bhavana, as,* m. (in astrology) N. of the fifth lunar mansion.

Tanayī-kṛita, as, ā, am, made a son.

Tanas, as, n., Ved. offspring, posterity.

Tanman, ā, m. (fr. *tanu* below), thinness, slenderness, minuteness; (*a*), n. the liver.

Tanishṭha, as, ā, am (superl. of *tanu*), thinnest, very thin, smallest, least; very minute or delicate.

Tanīyas, ān, asī, as (compar. of *tanu*), thinner, more minute, smaller, less, very thin, &c.

Tanu, us, us or *vī* or *ūs, u,* thin, slender, slim, attenuated, emaciated, small, minute; delicate, fine, having minute interstices (as a web); little, unimportant; shallow (as a river); spare; (*us*), m., N. of a certain Ṛishi with a very emaciated body [cf. *tānavya*]; (*us* or *tanū, ūs*), f. (the latter form only being used in the earlier language), the body, the person (applied also to gods); one's own person, self (often used in the Veda like a reflexive pronoun, e. g. *yajasva tanvam,* worship thy own person or thyself; cf. *ātman*); outward form or manifestation; nature, form, or character of anything; appearance; (*us*), f. the skin; N. of the first lunar mansion; (*vī*), f. a delicate or slender or graceful woman; N. of one of the wives of Kṛishṇa; a kind of plant [cf. *śāla-parṇī*]; a stanza of four lines and twenty-four syllables in each; [cf. Gr. ταvυ-; Lat. *tenuis;* Old Germ. *dunni;* Germ. *dünn;* Hib. *tana;* Eng. *thin.*] — *Tanu-kūpa, as,* m. a pore of the skin, (lit. well of the skin.) — *Tanu-kshīra, as,* m. the tree Spondias Magnifera; [cf. *āmrātaka.*] — *Tanu-gṛiha, am,* n. (in astrology) N. of the first lunar mansion. — *Tanu-ććhad, t, t, t,* or *tanu-ććhada, as, ā, am,* covering the body, protecting, clothing; (*t*), f. or (*das*), m. armour, attire. — *Tanu-ććhāya, as,* m. a kind of Acacia, = *jāla-varvūraka.* — *Tanu-ja, as,* m. a son; (*ā*), f. a daughter; [cf. *tanū-ja* and *ātma-ja.*] — *Tanuja-tva, am,* n. sonship. — *Tanu-tara, as, ā, am,* thinner, more minute; [cf. *tanīyas.*] — *Tanu-tā,* f. thinness, tenuity, extenuation, littleness, diminutiveness. — *Tanu-tyaj, k, k, k,* giving up one's person, dying; risking one's life, facing death with courage; [cf. *tanū-tyaj.*] — *Tanu-tyāga, as,* m. giving up one's own self, risking one's life; (*as, ā, am*), giving scantily, spending little, niggardly, sparing. — *Tanu-tra, am,* n. armour, mail ('protecting the body'). — *Tanutra-vat, ān, atī, at,* having armour, defended. — *Tanu-trāṇa, am,* n. ('protection for the body'), armour, mail. — *Tanu-tva, am,* n. thinness. — *Tanu-tvać, k,* n. (?) the cinnamon tree; the plant Cassia Senna. — *Tanu-tvaćā,* f. the plant Premna Spinosa; [cf. *kshudrāgni-mantha.*] — *Tanu-pattra, as,* m. the tree Terminalia Catappa [cf. *inguda*], commonly Hingaṇabeṭa; leafy orpiment. — *Tanu-bhava, as,* m. a son; [cf. *tanū-ja* and *tanūdbhava.*] — *Tanu-bhastrā,* f. the nose ('the bellows of the body'). — *Tanu-bhāva, as,* m. thinness. — *Tanu-bhūmi, is,* f. 'the stage of personality,' one of the periods in the life of a Buddhist Srāvaka. — *Tanu-bhṛit, t,* m. any being furnished with a body, especially a human being. — *Tanu-mat, ān, atī, at,* embodied, corporeal. — *Tanu-madhya, as, ā, am,* having a slender or elegant waist; (*ā*), f., N. of a metre of four lines, each consisting of two short syllables between four long ones (— — ◡ ◡ — —); [cf. *tanu-śiras.*] — *Tanu-madhyama, as, ā, am,* slender-waisted. — *Tanu-rasa, as,* m. perspiration, sweat. — *Tanu-ruh, ṭ,* or *tanu-ruha, am,* n. the hair or down of the body; [cf. *tanū-ruha.*] — *Tanu-vāta, as,* m. a very thin or rarefied atmosphere (constituting a kind of hell; opposed to *ghana-vāta,* q. v.); according to others, a peculiar division of hell. — *Tanu-vāra, am,* n. (fr. *tanu* and *vāra* fr. rt. *vṛi,* to cover, protect), armour, mail. — *Tanuvāra-bhasa, as,* m. (?) a man in armour, a warrior. — *Tanu-vīja, as,* m. the jujube; [cf. *rāja-badara.*] — *Tanu-vraṇa, as,* m. a pimple, a pustule, a boil, elephantiasis. — *Tanu-śarīra, as, ā, am,* having a delicate body, delicately formed. — *Tanu-śiras, ās, ās, as,* 'having a small head,' N. of a subdivision of the Ushṇih metre, consisting of three Pādas of eleven, eleven, and six syllables; [cf. *tanu-madhyā.*] — *Tanu-sańćāriṇī,* f. a young woman, a girl, one ten years old ('moving the body coquettishly?'). — *Tanu-hrada, as,* m. the anus, the rectum; [cf. *tanū-hrada.*] — *Tanū-ja, as, ā, am,* produced or born on or from the body; belonging to the person; (*as*), m. a son; N. of a Sādhya; (*ā*), f. a daughter; [cf. *tanu-ja.*] — *Tanū-jani, is,* m. a son. — *Tanū-janman, ā,* m. a son. — *Tanūjāṅga* (°*ja-aṅ°*), *am,* n. a wing, the feathers ('member produced on the body'); [cf. *tanū-ruha.*] — *Tanū-tala, as,* m. a measure of length equal to the arms extended, a fathom. — *Tanū-tyaj, k, k, k,* Ved. giving up one's person, risking one's life, rash, foolhardy. — *Tanū-dūshi, is, is, i,* Ved. destroying the person. — *Tanū-devatā,* f. a form of fire deified. — *Tanū-deśa, as,* m. a region or part of the body. — *Tanūdbhava* (°*nu-ud°*), *as,* m. a son; [cf. *tanu-bhava.*] — *Tanūna* (°*nu-ūna*), *as,* m. 'the bodiless one,' the wind. — *Tanū-napa, am,* n. clarified butter, ghee; (this word owes its existence to a wrong derivation of the following word from *tanūnapa-ad,* 'eating the clarified butter.') — *Tanū-napāt, t,* m. one of the sacred names of Fire, 'the son or descendant of himself,' so called because fire need not necessarily be derived from other fire, but is sometimes self-generated as in the lightning or by the attrition of the Araṇis, q. v.; (for a fanciful derivation see the preceding. Agni appears chiefly as Tanū-napāt in some verses of the Āprī hymns; see *ā-prī*); the plant Plumbago Zeylanica. — *Tanūnapāt-vat, ān, atī, at,* containing the word *tanū-napāt.* — *Tanū-naptṛi, tā,* m., Ved. = *tanū-napāt;* [cf. *tānūnaptra.*] — *Tanū-pā, ās, ās, am,* Ved. protecting the person, preserving the life. — *Tanū-pāna, as, ī, am,* Ved. protecting the person or life; (*am*), n. protection of the person. — *Tanū-pāvan, ā, arī, a,* Ved. protecting the person or life. — *Tanū-prishṭha, as,* m., N. of a Soma sacrifice. — *Tanū-bala, am,* n., Ved. the strength of the body, one's own strength. — *Tanū-ruć, k, k, k,* Ved. brilliant in person (as Agni); brilliant with arms (?). — *Tanū-ruha, as, am,* m. n. the hair of the body; the wing or feathers of a bird; (*as*), m. a son; [cf. *tanu-ruha, tanu-ja, tanu-jāṅga.*] — *Tanūrja* (°*nu-ūr°*), *as,* m., N. of a son of the third Manu. — *Tanū-vaśin, ī, inī, i,* Ved. having power over the body, an epithet of Agni. — *Tanū-*

śubhra, as, ā, am, Ved. decorating the person, adorning the body. — *Tanū-havis, is,* n., N. of three oblations offered to the three tanūs or forms (of Agni). — *Tanū-hrada, as,* m. the anus, the rectum; [cf. *tanu-hrada.*] — *Tanv-aṅga, as, ā, am,* having slender limbs, delicate, slim; (*ī*), f. a delicate or slender woman; (*as*), m., N. of a man.

Tanuka, as, ā, am, thin, small; (*as*), m., N. of several plants, Grislea Tomentosa, Terminalia Bellerica; the cinnamon tree; (*ā*), f. the tree Diospyros Embryopteris.

Tanula, as, ā, am, spread, expanded.

Tanus, us, n. the body.

Tanū, ūs, f. the body. See *tanu,* p. 361, col. 2.

Tanū-kṛi, cl. 8. P. A. *-karoti, -kurute, -kartum,* to make thin or fine, to attenuate, diminish, emaciate; to pare. — *Tanū-karaṇa, am,* n. making thin, attenuation, diminishing, weakening. — *Tanū-kṛit, t, t, t,* Ved. shaping or forming the person, preserving the life; (Sāy.) forming offspring, granting children. — *Tanū-kṛita, as, ā, am,* made delicate or thin, pared. — *Tanū-kṛitha, as* or *am,* m. or n. (?), Ved. preservation of the person; (Sāy.) on account of his son (in loc. case).

Tanti, is, f. a thread, cord, line, string; a series, a line, row; expansion, extension; N. of a woman; (*is*), m. a weaver. — *Tanti-pāla* or *tanti-pālaka, as,* m. 'a guardian of the rows (of calves),' a N. assumed by Saha-deva when living with king Virāṭa; (also applied to Nakula.)

Tantī, f. a leading cow (i. e. one going at the head of the Tantayas or lines of calves).

Tantu, us, m. a thread, cord, wire, string, line, the warp of a web; N. of the Supreme Being; a cobweb; a filament, fibre, sprig; a line of descendants, propagation of offspring, issue, race; a shark [cf. *tantuṇa* and *tantu-nāga*]; N. of a man; [cf. *kāshṭha-tantu, vara-t°, sapta-t°.*] — *Tantu-kāshṭha, am,* n. a piece of fibrous wood, or a brush used by weavers for cleaning the threads of the woof; [cf. *tantra-kāshṭha.*] — *Tantu-kīṭa, as,* m. a silk-worm. — *Tantu-nāga, as,* m. a shark. — *Tantu-niryāsa, as,* m. the palmyra tree [cf. *tāla*]; (fr. *tantu,* a thread, and *nir-yāsa,* exudation, alluding to the stringy or adhesive nature of this tree.) — *Tantu-parvan, a,* n. 'the festival of the thread,' the anniversary of the day of full moon in the month Śrāvaṇa, when Kṛishṇa was invested with the Brāhmanical cord. — *Tantu-bha, as,* m. mustard-seed, Sinapis Dichotoma, also *tantuka;* a calf. — *Tantu-mat, ān,* m. an epithet of Agni, perhaps 'uninterrupted like a thread;' (*tī*), f., N. of the mother of Murāri. — *Tantu-vardhana, as,* m. 'increasing a race,' a N. of Vishṇu; also of Śiva. — *Tantu-vādya, am,* n. a stringed musical instrument in general. — *Tantu-vāna, am,* n. weaving. — *Tantu-vāpa, as,* m. a weaver; a loom; weaving. — *Tantu-vāya, as,* m. a weaver; a spider; weaving; [cf. *tantra-vāya.*] — *Tantuvāya-daṇḍa, as,* m. a loom. — *Tantu-vigrahā,* f. the banana or plantain, Musa Sapientum. — *Tantu-śālā,* f. a weaver's shop. — *Tantu-santata, as, ā, am,* woven, sewn; (*am*), n. wove cloth. — *Tantu-santati, is,* f. or *tantu-santāna, as,* m. sewing, weaving. — *Tantu-sāra* or *tantu-sāraka, as,* m. the areca or betel-nut tree (as having a fibrous pith). — *Tantv-agra, am,* n. the end of a thread.

Tantuka, as, m. (at the end of an adj. comp.), a thread, a rope; a kind of serpent; mustard-seed, Sinapis Dichotoma, = *tantu-bha;* (*ī*), f. a vein or any tubular vessel.

Tantuṇa, as, m. a shark.

Tantura or *tantula, am,* n. the filaments or fibrous root of a lotus; (*as*), m. = *taṇḍula.*

Tantra, am, n. an implement of weaving, a loom; a thread; the warp or threads extended lengthwise in a loom; an uninterrupted series (e. g. *deha-tantra,* assuming a series of bodies); posterity; the leading or principal action of a ceremony, characteristic or prevalent features, the regular order of ceremonies or rites, system, framework, ritual; chief or essential part, main point; principal doctrine, rule, theory; model, typical form, science; a scientific work; any scientific chapter of a work (especially the first section of a Jyotiḥ-śāstra or treatise on astronomy); a religious treatise teaching magical and mystical formularies for the worship of the deities, or the attainment of superhuman power; it is mostly in the form of a dialogue between Śiva and Durgā, who are the peculiar gods of the Tāntrikas, (these works are very numerous, and their authority, in many parts of India, seems to have superseded that of the Vedas: they are said to comprise five subjects, viz. 1. the creation, 2. the destruction of the world, 3. the worship of the gods, 4. the attainment of all objects, especially of six superhuman faculties, 5. the four modes of union with the supreme spirit by meditation; a variety of subjects are, however, introduced into many of them, whilst some are limited to a single topic, as the mode of breathing in certain rites, the language of birds, beasts, &c.); a cause which leads to two or more results; the cause of more than one effect; a medicament, a drug; a chief remedy or 'charm' considered as producing medicinal effects; a spell; oath or ordeal; raiment, vesture; supporting a family; necessary or indispensable act or provision; the right way of doing anything; royal retinue, a court, train; an army; providing for the security and prosperity of a kingdom; a realm, a country; subservience, service, dependance; decoration, hanging with trophies, garlands, &c.; heap, multitude; wealth; a house; happiness, felicity; (*as*), m. a weaver (?); (*tantrī, īs* or *ī*), f. any string, cord, or rope; a bow-string; the wire or string of a lute; (metaphorically) the strings of the heart; any tubular vessel of the body, a sinew; a tail; the plant Cocculus Cordifolius [cf. *tantrikā* and *tantraka*]; a young woman or girl with peculiar qualities; N. of a river. *Tantreṇa,* ind. in such a way as to hold good or remain. — *Tantra-kāshṭha, am,* n. a fibrous stick or brush used by weavers for cleaning the threads of the woof; [cf. *tantu-kāshṭha.*] — *Tantra-kaumudī,* f., *tantra-gandharva, tantra-garbha, tantra-ćūḍāmaṇi,* titles of different Tantra works. — *Tantra-tā,* f. or *tantra-tva, am,* n. arranging into a system; dependance, subservience; the quality or character of a Tantra; comprehending several rites in one, performance of one ceremony, or penance in lieu of a number. — *Tantra-prakāśa, as,* m. title of a literary work. — *Tantra-pradīpa, as,* m. title of a commentary on the Dhātu-pāṭha. — *Tantra-bheda,* title of a Tantra. — *Tantra-ratna, am,* n. title of a work by Pārtha-sārathi. — *Tantra-rāja, as,* m. title of a work. — *Tantra-vāpa, as,* m. a weaver; (*as, am*), m. n. a loom, weaving; [cf. the next.] — *Tantra-vāya, as,* m. a weaver; a spider; [cf. *tantu-vāya.*] — *Tantra-vārttika* = *mīmānsā-tantra-vārttika.* — *Tantra-sāra, as,* m. 'the essence of the Tantras,' title of a compilation. — *Tantra-hṛidaya, am,* n. title of a Tantra work. — *Tantrī-mukha, as,* m. a peculiar position of the hand.

Tantraka, as, ikā, am, new and unbleached (as cloth), recently from the loom; (at the end of a comp.) = *tantra;* (*ikā*), f. the plant Cocculus Cordifolius; [cf. *tantrī.*]

Tantraṇa, am, n. (fr. *tantraya*), maintenance of order, discipline.

Tantraya (fr. *tantra*), nom. P. *tantrayati,* to perform or go through in order; to maintain by discipline, keep in order; A. *tantrayate,* to support a family.

Tantrāyin, ī, iṇī, i, Ved. drawing out a thread; going continuously (as the sun).

Tantrin, ī, iṇī, i, having threads, made of threads, spun, wove; chorded, having chords or wires (as an instrument); having a Tantra, following one; (*ī*), m. a musician; a soldier.

1. *tandra, am,* n., Ved. a series, a row.

Tanvat, an, atī, at, stretching, extending.

तनक *tanaka, as* or *am,* m. or n. (?), a reward; (perhaps a wrong reading for *vetanaka.*)

तनबाल *tanabāla, ās,* m. pl., N. of a people; [cf. *tālavana.*]

तनयित्नु *tanayitnu.* See 1. *tan,* p. 361.

तनु *tanu.* See p. 361, col. 2.

तनोनु *tanonu,* a kind of rice (= *shashṭika*).

तन्तस्य *tantasya,* nom. P. *tantasyati,* to grieve, be distressed; to afflict; [cf. rt. *tans.*]

तन्ति *tanti, tantu, tantra,* &c. See col. 1.

तन्त्रा *tantrā,* f. a wrong form for *tandrā.*

तन्त्रि *tantri, is,* f. another form for *tantrī,* see col. 2; (also a wrong form for *tandri.*) — *Tantri-pālaka, as,* m. an epithet of Jayad-ratha.

तन्त्रिज *tantrija, as,* m., N. of a son of Kanavaka; (another reading has *tandrija.*)

तन्त्रित *tantrita, tantri-tā,* wrong forms for *tandrita, tandri-tā.*

तन्त्रिपाल *tantripāla, as,* m. a N. assumed by Saha-deva [cf. *tanti-pāla*]; N. of a son of Kanavaka; (another reading has *tandripāla.*)

तन्त्रिल्लक *tantrillaka, as,* m., N. of a man.

तन्त्री *tantrī.* See col. 2.

तन्त्वग्र *tantv-agra.* See *tantu,* col. 1.

तन्द् *tand,* cl. 1. A., Ved. *tandate,* &c., to relax, give away, become relaxed, to grow fatigued; (Sāy.) to make languid or fatigued.

2. *tandra, as, ā, am,* tired, fatigued; lazy; (*ā*), f. lassitude, exhaustion, weariness, syncope; sleepiness, sluggishness. (For 1. *tandra* see col. 2.)

Tandraya (fr. the preceding), nom. A. *tandrayate,* to grow fatigued.

Tandrayu, us, us, u, Ved. fatigued, lazy.

Tandrāya, another form for *tandraya.*

Tandrālu, us, us, u, tired, wearied, sleepy, overcome with sleep or fatigue, slothful, sluggish.

Tandri, is (?) and *ī, īs* or *ī,* m. (?), f. sleepiness, drowsiness, fatigue, lassitude; fainting, exhaustion. — *Tandri-ja* or *tandri-pāla, as,* m., N. of a son of Kanavaka; [cf. *tantri-pāla.*]

Tandrikā, f. sloth, sleepiness.

Tandrita, only in *a-tandrita, as, ā, am,* indefatigable, unremitting; [cf. *a-tanda* and *tantrita.*]

Tandrin, ī, iṇī, i, weary, lazy. — *Tandri-tā,* f. lassitude, exhaustion, weariness, sleepiness.

तन्द्र् *tandr* (a Sautra root), to be disturbed in mind, become bewildered, be exhausted or fatigued.

तन्द्र 1. and 2. *tandra.* See above and col. 2.

तन्द्रवाय *tandravāya,* a wrong form for *tantra-vāya,* q. v.

तन्नी *tannī,* f. or *tanni, is* (?), f. the plant Hemionitis Cordifolia.

तन्मय *tan-maya.* See p. 361, col. 1.

तन्मात्र *tan-mātra.* See p. 361, col. 1.

तन्यता *tanyatā,* f., Ved. or *tanyatu, us,* m., Ved. (fr. rt. 1. *tan*), roaring, thundering, thunder; wind; night; a musical instrument (?).

Tanyu, us, us, u, Ved. making a roaring sound, epithet of the winds.

तन्लीक *tanlīka* (?), an areca seller, a designation of one of the inferior castes of Hindūs.

तन्व *tanva, as,* m., N. of a man; [cf. *tānva.*]

तन्वङ्ग *tanv-aṅga.* See col. 1.

तन्वत् *tanvat.* See col. 2.

तन्विन् *tanvin, ī,* m., N. of a son of Manu Tāmasa.

तप् 1. *tap* [cf. 2. *pat*], cl. 4. A. *tapyate*, &c., to rule, govern.

तप् 2. *tap*, cl. 1. P. (rarely A.) *tapati*, *-te*, *tatāpa*, *tapsyati* (ep. also *tapishyati*), *atāpsīt*, *taptum*, to give out heat, be hot; to shine; to heat, make hot or warm; to shine upon; to be burnt; to burn, to consume or destroy by heat; to suffer pain; to cause pain or distress; to injure, hurt, damage, spoil; to torment one's self, mortify the body, undergo penance, (often with *tapas*, e. g. *tapas tatāpa*, he performed penance); cl. 4. P. *tapyati* (rarely used), to warm one's self, become hot: Pass. *tapyate*, to be heated, to suffer or feel pain; to be injured or hurt; to suffer pain voluntarily, undergo severe penances, (often with *tapas*, e. g. *tapas tapyāmahe*, we undergo penance): Caus. P. A. *tāpayati*, *-te*, *-yitum*, to make warm or hot; to burn, consume by heat, cause pain, trouble, distress; to torment one's self, undergo penance: Desid. *titapsati*, *-te*: Intens. *tātapyate*, *tātapti*, to feel violent pain, suffer torment, be in great anxiety or distress; [cf. Lat. *tepeo*: Gr. τέφρα, rt. ταφ, θάπτω: Russ. *tepl*, 'warm;' *teplota*, 'warmth:' Hib. *tebhot*, 'intense heat:' Old Germ. *damf*: Lat. *tempus*?].

3. *tap*, *p*, *p*, *p*, warming one's self; [cf. *agni-tap*.]

Tapa, *as*, *ā*, *am*, warming; burning, consuming by heat [cf. *lalāṭan-tapa*]; causing pain or trouble, distressing [cf. *janan-tapa* and *paran-tapa*]; (*as*), m. heat, warmth, fire [cf. *ā-tapa*]; the sun; the hot season; religious austerity, penance, mortification (= *tapas*); a peculiar form of fire which generated the seven mothers of Skanda; N. of one of the attendants of Śiva; (*ā*), f., N. of one of the eight deities of the Bodhi-druma; [cf. *a-tapa* and *tāpa*.] — *Tapa-ruj*, *k*, f. the pain of penance. — *Tapātmaka* (°*pa-āt*°), *as*, *ikā*, *am*, practising austerities. — *Tapātyaya* (°*pa-at*°), *as*, m. the end of the heat, the beginning of the rainy season. — *Tapānta* (°*pa-an*°), *as*, m. the end of the heat, the beginning of the rainy season.

Tapat, *an*, *antī*, *at*, heating or warming; performing penance &c. — *Tapatām-pati*, *is*, m. 'the chief of burners,' the sun.

Tapatī, f. 'the warming one,' N. of a daughter of the Sun and of his wife Chāyā, married to Saṃvaraṇa and mother of Kuru; N. of a river, commonly called Taptī; [cf. *tāpatya*.]

Tapana, *as*, *ā*, *am*, warming, burning, shining, an epithet of the sun; causing pain or distress; (*as*), m. the sun; N. of a divine being (perhaps the sun) who fights with Garuḍa; N. of one of the five fires in the Svāhā-kāra; N. of a Rakshas; a N. of Agastya; heat, burning, the hot season; N. of a burning hell; N. of several plants, viz. Semecarpus Anacardium [cf. *arush-kara*]: Calotropis Gigantea (*arka*), the white variety of it; Premna Spinosa (*kshudrāgni-mantha*); Cassia Senna; the sun-stone [cf. *sūrya-kānta*, *tapana-maṇi*, *tapanopala*]; (*ī*), f. heat; the root of Bignonia Suaveolens; N. of a river, = *tāpī* and *tapanātmajā*, according to some authorities = *godāvarī*; (*am*), n. the being hot, burning; pining, grieving, mental distress; [cf. *rāma-tapana*, 'the distress of Rāma,' N. of an Upanishad; *tripurā-t*°, *gopāla-t*°; cf. also *tāpana*.] — *Tapana-kara*, *as*, m. a ray, a sunbeam. — *Tapana-ććhada*, *as*, m. the sunflower, = *āditya-pattra*. — *Tapana-tanaya*, *as*, m. 'the son of the Sun,' a N. of Karṇa; (*ā*), f. 'the daughter of the Sun,' the Yamunā river; the Taptī river [cf. *tapanātmajā*]; N. of a tree; [cf. *śamī*.] — *Tapana-maṇi*, *is*, m. the sun-stone; [cf. *sūrya-kānta*.] — *Tapanāṇśu* (°*na-aṇ*°), *us*, m. a ray of the sun, a sunbeam. — *Tapanātmajā* (°*na-ātma-jā*), f. 'the daughter of the Sun,' N. of a river, = *tapanī* and *tāpī*, according to some authorities = *godāvarī* [cf. *tapanī* and *tapana*], and *yamunā*. — *Tapaneshṭa* (°*na-ish*°), *am*, n. copper ('loved by the rays of the sun,' i. e. easily heated or coloured by them). — *Tapanopala* (°*na-up*°), *as*, m. the sun-stone; [cf. *sūrya-kānta*.]

Tapanīya, *as*, *ā*, *am*, to be heated; to be suffered or practised as penance; (*am*), n. gold purified with fire, gold in general; a sort of rice. — *Tapanīya-maya*, *as*, *ī*, *am*, consisting of purified gold, golden.

Tapanīyaka, *am*, n. gold.

Tapantaka, *as*, m., N. of a man.

Tapas, *as*, n. warmth, heat, fire, (*pañća tapāṇsi*, the five fires to which an ascetic is exposed in the hot season, viz. four fires lighted in the several quarters and the sun burning from above); pain, suffering; religious austerity, penance, mortification, the practice of mental or personal self-denial or the infliction of bodily tortures; the meditation connected with such a practice; moral virtue, merit; special observance or duty of any particular caste (e. g. the Tapas of a Brāhman is sacred learning; of a Kshatriya, the protection of subjects; of a Vaiśya, giving alms to Brāhmans; of a Śūdra, service; and of a Ṛishi or saint, feeding upon herbs and roots); a particular month of the cold season intervening between winter and spring (= Māgha or January-February, the month of religious austerities; cf. *tapasya*); one of the seven worlds, the region above the Jana-loka, inhabited by saints or devotees after death [cf. *tapo-loka*]; (in astrology) the ninth lunar mansion, = *dharma*; N. of a long period of time, a Kalpa; (*ās*, *as*), m. n. the cold or dewy season (= *śiśira*); the winter (= *himartu*); the hot season. — *Tapaḥ-kara*, *as*, *ā*, *am*, undergoing religious austerities or penance &c.; (*as*), m. a kind of fish, Polynemus Risua or Paradiseus, (this fish is also called Tapasyā-matsya); [cf. *tapas-vin*.] — *Tapaḥ-kriśa*, *as*, *ā*, *am* emaciated by austerities. — *Tapaḥ-kleśa-saha*, *as*, *ā*, *am*, patient of austerities, enduring the pain of penance. — *Tapaḥ-prabhāva*, *as*, m. the efficacy of devotion. — *Tapaḥ-śīla*, *as*, *ā*, *am*, inclined to religious austerities. — *Tapaḥ-samādhi*, *is*, m. the practice of penance. — *Tapaḥ-sādhya*, *as*, *ā*, *am*, to be accomplished by penance. — *Tapaḥ-siddha*, *as*, *ā*, *am*, accomplished by penance. — *Tapaḥ-sthalī*, f. 'the seat of religious austerity or piety,' a N. of Benares. — *Tapaś-ćaraṇa*, *am*, n. or *tapaś-ćaryā*, f. the practice of penance. — *Tapaś-ćit*, *t*, *t*, *t*, accumulating religious merit by austerities; (*tas*), m. pl., N. of a class of deities; *tapaśćitām ayanam*, N. of a religious ceremony which lasts several days. — *Tapaso-mūrti*, *is*, m., N. of one of the seven sages in the twelfth Manv-antara; [cf. *tapo-mūrti*.] — *Tapas-taksha*, *as*, m. 'destroying religious penance,' an epithet of Indra as disturbing the austerities of ascetics lest they should acquire too great power; (other authorities explain the word 'emaciating himself by his devotions;' and others read *tapas-tanka*, 'afraid of austerities' or 'the axe of austerities.') — *Tapas-tīrtha*, *am*, n., N. of a place of pilgrimage. — *Tapas-pati*, *is*, m. the lord of penance. — *Tapas-vat*, *ān*, *atī*, *at*, Ved. burning, hot; ascetic, devout; [cf. *tapo-vat*.] — *Tapasvi-tā*, f. devout austerity, religious penance, bodily mortification. — *Tapas-vin*, *ī*, *inī*, *i*, distressed, wretched, poor, miserable, pitiable; practising austerities, devout; a mendicant, a pauper; an ascetic, a religious man engaged in the practice of rigorous and devout penance; (*ī*), m., N. of a son of Manu Ćākshusha and Naḍvalā; N. of one of the seven sages of the twelfth Manv-antara; an epithet of Nārada; the mango fish, Polynemus Risua [cf. *tapaḥ-kara*]; N. of a tree, a kind of Karañja (*ghṛita-karañja*); (*inī*), f. a female devotee, a woman leading a religious life; a poor wretched woman; spikenard, Valeriana Jaṭāmānsi; another plant, Helleborus Niger, = *kaṭu-rohiṇī*; also = *mahā-śrāvaṇikā*. — *Tapasvi-pattra*, *as*, m., N. of a plant, = *damanaka*; [cf. *tapo-dhana*.] — *Tapo-jā*, *ās*, *ās*, *am*, Ved. born from heat; one who practises religious austerities. — *Tapo-da*, *as*, *ā*, *am*, granting piety; (*am*), n., N. of a Tīrtha in Magadha. — *Tapo-dāna*, *am*, n., N. of a Tīrtha. — *Tapo-dhana*, *as*, *ā*, *am*, rich in religious penance; ascetic, pious; a very treasure of mortifications and austerities, a devotee, an ascetic, performing religious penance; consisting in religious penance; granting religious merit or piety; (*as*), m., N. of a son of Manu Tāmasa; N. of a plant, = *damanaka*, commonly *davanā*, Artemisia [cf. *tapasvi-pattra*]; (*ā*), f. the plant Sphæranthus Mollis, = *muṇḍīrī*, commonly *muṇḍī*. — *Tapo-dharma*, *as*, m., N. of a son of the thirteenth Manu. — *Tapo-dhāman*, *a*, n. 'the abode of penance,' N. of a place of pilgrimage. — *Tapo-dhṛiti*, *is*, m., N. of one of the seven sages of the twelfth Manv-antara. — *Tapo-nitya*, *as*, *ā*, *am*, devoting one's self uninterruptedly to religious austerities or penance; (*as*), m., N. of a man with the patronymic Pauruśishṭi. — *Tapo-nidhi*, *is*, m. a treasury of religious austerities and penance, a very treasure of merit derived from self-mortification, an eminently pious man. — *Tapo-nishṭha*, *as*, *ā*, *am*, performing penance, practising austerities. — *Tapo-'nubhāva* (°*pas-an*°), *as*, m. the influence of religious penance. — *Tapo-bala*, *am*, n. the power acquired by religious austerities. — *Tapo-bhanga*, *as*, m. interruption of religious penance. — *Tapo-bhṛit*, *t*, *t*, *t*, undergoing penance, ascetic, pious; an ascetic, a pious man. — *Tapo-maya*, *as*, *ī*, *am*, consisting in religious penance, containing it; practising austerities, devout. — *Tapo-mūrti*, *is*, f. an incarnation of religious austerity or penance; an ascetic; (*is*), m., N. of one of the seven sages of the twelfth Manv-antara; [cf. *tapaso-mūrti*.] — *Tapo-mūla*, *as*, *ā*, *am*, founded on religious austerity or penance; (*as*), m., N. of a son of Manu Tāmasa. — *Tapo-yukta*, *as*, *ā*, *am*, employed in penitential exercises, ascetic, pious. — *Tapo-rati*, *is*, *is*, *i*, rejoicing in religious austerity; (*is*), m., N. of a son of Manu Tāmasa. — *Tapo-ravi*, *is*, m. 'the sun of the ascetics,' N. of one of the seven sages in the twelfth Manv-antara. — *Tapo-rāja*, *as*, m. 'king of penance,' the moon. — *Tapo-rāśi*, *is*, m. 'a heap of religious austerities;' an ascetic. — *Tapo-loka*, *as*, m. one of the seven worlds, that which is situated above the Jana-loka; [cf. *tapas*.] — *Tapo-vaṭa*, *as*, m. 'enclosure or district of religious penance,' a N. applied to Brahmāvarta, i. e. the holy land situated in central India. — *Tapo-vat*, *ān*, *atī*, *at*, ascetic, pious; [cf. *tapas-vat*.] — *Tapo-vana*, *as*, m. 'penance-grove,' a sacred grove in which ascetics perform their religious austerities. — *Tapo-vāsa*, *as*, m. a place of religious austerity. — *Tapo-viśesha*, *as*, m. excellence of devotion. — *Tapo-vṛiddha*, *as*, *ā*, *am*, rich in religious austerity or penance, very ascetic or pious. — *Tapo-vrāta*, *as*, m. a multitude of penances. — *Tapo-'śana* (°*pas-aś*°), *as*, *ā*, *am*, one whose food is religious austerity; (*as*), m., N. of one of the seven sages of the twelfth Manv-antara; also of a son of Manu Tāmasa.

Tapasīvan, *ā*, *arī*, *a*, causing pain (?).

1. *tapasya*, nom. P. *tapasyati*, to undergo religious austerities, do penance.

2. *tapasya*, *as*, *ā*, *am*, produced by heat; (*as*), m. the month Phālguna (February-March), the second month of the season intervening between winter and spring; a N. of Arjuna; N. of a son of Manu Tāmasa; (*ā*), f. devout austerity, religious penance; (*am*), n. devout austerity, mortification, religious penance; the flower of Jasminum Multiflorum or Pubescens (*kunda-pushpa*). — *Tapasyā-matsya*, the mango fish; [cf. under *tapaḥ-kara*.]

Tapita, *as*, *ā*, *am*, heated, burnt, refined.

Tapishṭha, *as*, *ā*, *am* (fr. 2. *tap* with the superl. affix), Ved. extremely hot, burning; [cf. *tapīyas*.]

Tapishṇu, *us*, *us*, *u*, warming, heating, burning.

Tapīyas, *ān*, *asī*, *as* (fr. 2. *tap* with the compar. affix), extremely ascetic, most devoted to religious austerities.

Tapu, *us*, *us*, *u*, Ved. burning hot.

Tapushi, *is*, *is*, *i*, Ved. burning.

Tapushī, f. the heat of anger or wrath.

Tapus, *us*, *us*, *us*, Ved. burning hot; (*us*), m. fire; the sun; an enemy (who causes pain); (*us*), n. heat, pain. — *Tapur-agra*, *as*, *ā*, *am*, Ved. having a burning point or extremity (as a spear). — *Tapur-jambha*, *as*, *ā*, *am*, Ved. having burning jaws, an epithet of Agni. — *Tapur-mūrdhan*, *ā*, *ā*, *a*, Ved.

having a burning head, an epithet of Agni; (*ā*), m., N. of an author of a hymn of the Ṛig-veda who was a son of Bṛihaspati. — *Tapur-vadha, as, ā, am*, Ved. having burning weapons. — *Tapush-pā, ās, ās, am*, Ved. (Sāy.) protecting from pain; (perhaps rather) drinking warm (beverages).

Tapta, as, ā, am, heated, inflamed, burnt; hot; red-hot; fused, melted, molten; burnished; scorched by pain or sorrow, distressed, afflicted; inflamed with anger, incensed; undergone or performed (as penance). — *Tapta-kumbha, as*, m. a heated or red-hot jar; N. of a particular hell; (*as, ā, am*), having hot jars. — *Tapta-kūpa*, 'hot-well,' N. of a hell; (perhaps a wrong reading for the preceding.) — *Tapta-kṛicchra, as, am*, m. n. a sort of penance which consists in drinking hot water, milk, and ghee for three days each, and inhaling hot air for three days. — *Tapta-tapas, ās*, m. one who has performed penance, an ascetic. — *Tapta-pāshāṇa-kuṇḍa, am*, n. 'a pit filled with burning stones,' N. of a hell. — *Tapta-bāluka, as, ā, am*, having hot or burning gravel; (*as*), m., N. of a hell. — *Tapta-rūpa* or *tapta-rūpaka, am*, n. silver. — *Tapta-lomaśa*, green vitriol. — *Tapta-loha, am*, n. 'glowing iron,' N. of a hell. — *Tapta-śūrmi* or *tapta-sūrmi, is*, f. 'a red-hot iron statue,' N. of a hell in which the wicked are made to embrace red-hot images. — *Taptaśūrmi-kuṇḍa, am*, n., N. of a hell. — *Tapta-surā-kuṇḍa, as*, m. 'a jar or hole filled with burning spirituous liquor,' N. of a hell. — *Tapta-hema-maya, as, ī, am*, like or consisting of melted gold. — *Taptānna* (°*ta-an*°), *am*, n. hot food, hot rice. — *Taptāyana* (°*ta-ay*°), *as, ī, am*, Ved. serving as a dwelling-place for the distressed (as the earth).

Taptavya, as, ā, am, to be performed as a religious penance.

Taptṛi, tā, trī, tṛi, making warm or hot, heating, a heater.

Taptvā, ind. having heated, having performed penance.

Tapya, as, ā, am, performing religious austerity, doing penance.

Tapyati, is, f., Ved. heat.

Tapyatu, us, us, u, Ved. hot, glowing.

Tapsyat, an, atī or *antī, at*, practising or intending to practise austerities.

तपश *tapaśa, as*, m. the moon; [cf. the following.]

तपस *tapasa, as*, m. (said to be fr. 2. *tap*), the moon; a bird; [cf. the preceding.]

तबलाकृति *tabalākṛiti, is*, f. (fr. *tabala?* and *ākṛiti*), N. of a kind of creeping plant.

तम् *tam*, cl. 4. P. (rarely A.) *tāmyati, tāmyate, tatāma, tamitum*, to gasp for breath (as one suffocating), choke, be suffocated, breathe with difficulty; to faint away; to be exhausted, perish; to be distressed in body or mind; to be disturbed or perplexed; to stop, become immovable or stiff; to wish, desire: Caus. *tamayati, -yitum*, to suffocate, deprive of breath; [cf. Lat. *temere, tabeo* (?); Old Germ. *damf*; Russ. *tomlju*.]

1. *tama, as*, m. darkness &c., = *tamas* in its various meanings; also = *tamāla*; (*ā*), f. night, = *tamāla*, Phyllanthus Emblica; (*am*), n. darkness, gloom; the point of the foot. — *Tamāhvaya* (°*ma-āh*°), a kind of plant, = *tāliśa-pattra*.

Tamaka, as, m. oppression (of the chest), a kind of asthma; [cf. *pra-tamaka*.]

Tamakā, f. = *tamā, tamālakā*, °*kī, tamālī, tamālinī*, Phyllanthus Emblica.

Tamata, as, ā, am, desirous, cupidinous, longing or hankering after; wished, desired.

Tamana, am, n. the becoming breathless.

Tamas, as, n. darkness, gloom; the darkness of hell, hell itself or a peculiar division of hell; the obscuration of the sun or moon in eclipses, darkness personified as Rāhu or the ascending node; mental darkness, illusion, error (constituting one of the five forms of *a-vidyā* in the Sāṅkhya phil.), sin, sorrow; (in the Sāṅkhya phil.) darkness or ignorance as one of the three qualities or constituents of everything in creation, the other two being *sattva* and *rajas*, see *guṇa*; as an inherent quality of nature *tamas* is heavy and obstructive, and predominates in earth and water, whence they fall and tend downwards; in living beings it is the cause of ignorance, illusion, lust, anger, pride, sorrow, dulness, and stolidity; (*as*), m., N. of a descendant of Gṛitsa-mada, a son of Śravas and father of Pra-kāśa; N. of a son of Pṛithu-śravas and father of Uśanas; [cf. Lith. *tamsa*, 'darkness;' *tamsus*, 'obscure:' Russ. *temnyi*, 'dark;' *temno-ta*, 'darkness:' Hib. *teim*, 'dark, obscure;' *teimhen*, 'darkness;' *teimheal*, 'an eclipse, darkness:' Old Germ. *demar*: Old Sax. *thim*: Angl. Sax. *dim*: Lat. *tenebræ?*]. — *Tamaḥ-prabhā* or *tama-prabhā*, f., or *tama-prabha* or *tamaḥ-prabha, as*, m. a hell, one of the lowermost divisions of the infernal regions. — *Tamaḥ-praveśa, as*, m. groping in the dark; mental perplexity or aberration. — *Tamaḥ-sthita, am*, n. 'situated in darkness,' N. of a hell, one of the lowest divisions of hell. — *Tamasā-kṛita, as, ā, am*, or *tamas-kalpa, as, ā, am*, like darkness, black, gloomy. — *Tamas-kāṇḍa, as*, m. or *tamas-tati, is*, f. great or spreading darkness. — *Tamas-vat, ān, atī, at*, having darkness, dark, gloomy; (*tī*), f. night. — *Tamas-vin, ī, inī, i*, dark, gloomy; (*nī*), f. night; turmeric. — *Tamo-gā, ās, ās, am*, Ved. roaming in the darkness, concealing himself in darkness, an epithet of Śushṇa. — *Tamo-gu, us*, m. an epithet of Rāhu, the personified ascending node, the causer of darkness. — *Tamo-guṇa, as*, m. the quality of darkness or ignorance; see above under *tamas*. — *Tamoguṇin, ī, inī, i*, having the quality of *tamas* predominant in the temperament, irascible, ignorant, proud, &c. — *Tamo-ghna, as, ī, am*, destroying darkness; (*as*), m. the sun; the moon; fire; an epithet of Vishṇu; an epithet of Śiva; a Buddha. — *Tamo-jyotis, is*, m. 'light in darkness,' a fire-fly. — *Tamo-darśana*, bilious fever. — *Tamo-nud, t, t, t*, dispersing darkness; (*t*), m. a shining body; the sun; the moon; fire; a lamp; light. — *Tamo-nuda, as, ā, am*, dispersing darkness; (*as*), m. the sun; the moon. — *Tamo-'ntakṛit* (°*mas-an*°), *t, t, t*, making an end of darkness; (*t*), m., N. of one of the attendants of Skanda. — *Tamo-'ntya* (°*mas-an*°), *as*, m. one of the ten ways in which an eclipse may happen. — *Tamo-'paha* (°*mas-ap*°), *as, ā, am*, removing darkness physical or moral, illumining, enlightening; (*as*), m. the sun; the moon; fire; a Buddha. — *Tamo-bhid, t, t, t*, dispersing darkness; (*t*), m. a fire-fly. — *Tamo-bhūta, as, ā, am*, 'become darkness,' dark, covered with darkness; ignorant. — *Tamo-maṇi, is*, m. 'the jewel of darkness,' a kind of gem; a fire-fly. — *Tamo-maya, as, ī, am*, consisting or composed of darkness, derived from it, covered with it; (*as*), m. the mind enveloped with darkness, vexation, anger, one of the five forms of *a-vidyā* in the Sāṅkhya phil. — *Tamo-'ri* (°*mas-ari*), *is*, m. the enemy of darkness, the sun. — *Tamo-vat, ān, atī, at*, dark, gloomy; [cf. *tamas-vat*.] — *Tamo-vikāra, as*, m. disease, sickness, (as a modification of the Guṇa *tamas*.) — *Tamo-vṛita, as, ā, am*, obscured, clouded; overcome with or influenced by rage, fear, &c., or any of the effects of the property of darkness. — *Tamo-vṛidh, t, t, t*, Ved. rejoicing or delighting in darkness; (Sāy.) growing in the darkness, increasing by the darkness. — *Tamo-han, ā, -ghnī, a*, Ved. striking down or dispersing darkness. — *Tamo-hara, as, ā, am*, removing darkness, illuminating; (*as*), m. the moon.

Tamasa, as, ī, am, dark-coloured; (*as*), m. darkness; a well; (*ā*), f., N. of a river, the Tamasā or Tonse, falling into the Ganges below Pratishṭhāna; (*am*), n. darkness (at end of comp., cf. *andha-t*°, *ava-t*°, *rī-t*°, *san-t*°); a city.

Tamaska, as, ā, am, at the end of an adj. comp. = *tamas*; [cf. *nis-tamaska*.]

Tamāla, as, m., N. of a tree with a very dark bark (but white blossoms), Xanthochymus Pictorius; N. of various other plants, = *varuṇa* and *kṛishṇa-khadira*; (*as*), m. the sectarial mark made with sandal (or perhaps the juice of the Tamāla fruit) upon the forehead; a sword, a scymitar or large sacrificial knife; (*ī*), f., N. of several plants, = *tāmra-vallī*; Phyllanthus Emblica; also = *varuṇa*; (*as, am*), m. n. the bark of the bamboo; (*am*), n. the leaf of the Laurus Cassia, = *pattraka* = *tamāla-pattra*. — *Tamāla-pattra, am*, n. the leaf of the Xanthochymus Pictorius; the leaf of the Laurus Cassia, Malabathron; a sectarial mark on the forehead; the tree Xanthochymus Pictorius. — *Tamālapattra-ćandana-gandha, as*, m., N. of a Buddha.

Tamālaka, as, am, m. n. the tree Xanthochymus Pictorius; the bark of a bamboo; (*ikā*), f., N. of two plants, = *tāmra-vallī* and *bhūmy-āmalī*, Phyllanthus Emblica; N. of a place, = *tāma-lipta* [cf. *tamālinī*]; N. of a woman; (*am*), n. the leaf of the Laurus Cassia; a sort of pot-herb, Marsilea Dentata.

Tamālinī, f. a place overgrown with Tamāla trees; N. of a country, = *tāma-lipta*; N. of a plant, = *bhūmy-āmalī*, Phyllanthus Emblica.

Tamisra, am, n. darkness, a dark night; darkness of mind, illusion; anger, wrath; (*ā*), f. a dark night, or one during the wane of the moon; great or extensive darkness, the night of new moon, any night; (*as*), m. the dark half of the month, from the full to the change; [cf. *su-tamisra, tāmisra, tamishīći*.] — *Tamisra-paksha, as*, m. the fortnight of the moon's wane, the time from full moon to new moon.

तम 2. *tama* (for 1. see under rt. *tam*, col. 1), a Taddhita affix, the termination of the superlative degree, used also as an independent word in the sense of *ishṭa-tama*, most desired, and sometimes added adverbially in the form *tamām*; [cf. *tāra-tamya*.]

तमङ्ग *tamaṅga, as*, m. a platform, stage.

Tamaṅgaka, as, m. the flat and projecting roof of a house, a sort of balcony or terrace.

तमर *tamara, am*, n. tin; lead (?).

तमराज *tamarāja, as*, m. a kind of sugar.

तमाल *tamāla*. See col. 2.

तमाह्वय *tamāhvaya*. See 1. *tama*, col. 1.

तमि *tami, is*, or *tamī*, f. the night; turmeric; [cf. 1. *tama* and *tamas*.]

तमिषीचि *tamishīći, is, is, i* (fr. rt. *tam?*), Ved. oppressing, stunning, afflicting, confusing, disturbing; (Sāy.) powerful, strong.

तमिस्र *tamisra*. See above.

तमुष्टुहीय *tamushṭuhīya, as, ā, am*, N. of a Sūkta beginning with the words *tam u shṭuhi*.

तमोलिप्ती *tamoliptī*, f., N. of a country, the district of Tumlook in Bengal, = *tāma-lipta*, commonly called *tamoluka*.

तम्पा *tampā*, f. a cow; [cf. *tambā*.]

तम्ब् *tamb*, cl. 1. P. *tambati*, &c., to go.

तम्बा *tambā*, f. a cow; [cf. *tampā*.]

तम्बीर *tambīra* or *tamvīra*, in astrology = ثموبر, the fourteenth Yoga.

तम्र *tamra, as, ā, am* (fr. rt. *tam*), Ved. oppressing, darkening; (Sāy.) causing to languish.

तय् *tay*, cl. 1. A. *tayate, teye, tayitum*, to go, move; to guard, preserve.

Taya, as, ā, am, who or what protects; (*as*), m. protection.

तर 1. *tara*, a Taddhita affix, the termination of the comparative degree, sometimes added adverbially in the form *tarām*; [cf. *kashṭa-tara*, &c.]

तर 2. tara, *as, ī, am* (fr. rt. *tṛī*), who or what passes over or beyond, crossing; surpassing; conquering, overpowering; excelling; to be crossed, to be overcome [cf. *dus-tara* and *dush-ṭara*]; (*as*), m. passing over, crossing, passage; freight; a road (?); a ferry-boat, raft (?); a tree (?); a sort of magical spell against the evil spirits supposed to possess certain weapons; N. of a man; (for *tarī* see *tari* next col.) — *Tara-paṇya*, *am*, n. ferriage, freight, the price or fare paid at a ferry. — *Tara-paṇyika*, *as*, m. one who receives the ferriage or freight. — *Tara-sthāna*, *am*, n. a landing-place, a wharf or stairs.

1. *taraṅga*, *as*, m. (perhaps fr. *taram* + *ga*), a wave; a name given to sections of certain literary works (especially when the title contains such a word as 'sea,' 'river,' &c., e. g. of the Kathā-sarit-sāgara and Rāja-taraṅgiṇī); a jumping motion, a leap, a jump, the gallop of a horse, waving, moving to and fro; cloth or clothes; [cf. *ut-taraṅga* and *ćarma-taraṅga*.] — *Taraṅga-bhīru*, *us*, m., N. of a son of the fourteenth Manu. — *Taraṅgāpatrastu* (°*ga-ap*°), *as, ā, am*, a little afraid of waves (Pāṇ. II. 1, 38).

2. *taraṅga*, nom. P. *taraṅgati*, *-gitum*, to move like a billow, wave, move to and fro.

Taraṅgaka, *as*, m. a wave; [cf. *nārī-taraṅgaka*.]

Taraṅgita, *as, ā, am*, wavy, billowy, tossing with waves; overflowing; (*am*), n. waving, moving to and fro.

Taraṅgin, *ī, iṇī, i*, wavy, moving like a billow, moving restlessly to and fro, unsteady; (*iṇī*), f. a river; (sometimes at the end of the title of a literary work, e. g. *kshīra-taraṅgiṇī*, *rāja-t*°.)

Taraṇa, *as*, m. a raft, a boat; Svarga or paradise (the final landing-place); (*am*), n. crossing over, passing, going across, carrying over, transporting; conquering, overcoming; an oar; (for *taraṇī* see under *taraṇi* below; cf. also *su-taraṇa*.)

Taraṇi, *is, is* or *ī, i*, Ved. passing through, pervading (space &c., said of the sun); moving forwards, quick, untired, energetic; bringing or carrying over, saving, helping, benevolent; (*is*), m. the sun; the plant Calotropis Gigantea [cf. *arka*]; a ray of light; (*is* or *ī*), f. a float, a raft, a boat, ferry-boat; the plant Aloe Perfoliata or Hibiscus Mutabilis; (according to others = *taraṇī-vallī*), a kind of rose, Rosa Glandulifera; [cf. *go-taraṇi*.] — *Taraṇi-tva*, *am*, n., Ved. quickness, eagerness, zeal. — *Taraṇi-dhanya*, *as*, m. an epithet of Śiva. — *Taraṇi-peṭaka*, *as*, m. an oval bowl or bason of wood for baling a boat. — *Taraṇī-ratna*, *am*, n. a ruby ('a sun-jewel'). — *Taraṇī-vallī*, f. a kind of rose, Rosa Glandulifera.

Taraṇīya, *as, ā, am*, to be crossed or passed over.

Taraṇḍa, *as, ā* or *ī, am*, m. f. n. a boat, a vessel; (*as, am*), m. n. a raft or float made of bamboos &c. tied together and sometimes floated upon jars or hollow gourds inverted; the float of a fishing line; an oar; (*as*), m., N. of a country; [cf. the following.] — *Taraṇḍa-pādā*, f. a boat, a ship.

Taraṇḍaka, *am*, n., N. of a Tīrtha.

Taraṇya (fr. *taraṇa*), nom. P. *taraṇyati*, &c., to cross over.

Tarat, *an, antī, at*, crossing, passing over. — *Tarad-dveshas*, *ās, ās, as*, Ved. conquering or overpowering enemies, an epithet of Indra.

Taratsamandīya, *am*, n., scil. *sūktam*, the Sūkta beginning with the words *tarat sa mandī*.

Tarad, *t*, f. a raft, a float; a kind of duck.

Taranta, *as*, m. the ocean; a hard shower, a torrent of rain; a frog; N. of a man with the patronymic Vaidadaśvi; (*ī*), f. a boat, ship.

Tarantuka, *am*, n., N. of a Tīrtha; [cf. *taraṇḍaka*.]

Tarala, *as, ā, am*, moving to and fro, trembling, tremulous; fickle, splendid, glittering, sparkling, luminous; unsteady, vain; liquid, liquefied; libidinous, lecherous, wanton; hollow; (*as*), m. the central gem of a necklace; a necklace; iron; a level surface (= *tala*); bottom, depth, lower or under part; the thorn-apple; N. of a poet; (*ā*), f. rice-gruel; wine, vinous or spirituous liquor; a bee; (*ās*), m. pl., N. of a race. — *Tarala-tā*, f. or *tarala-tva*, *am*, n. tremulousness, unsteadiness, sprightliness. — *Tarala-nayanī*, f. a woman having tremulous or rolling eyes; N. of a metre consisting of four lines of twelve short syllables each. — *Tarala-lekhā*, f., N. of a woman. — *Tarala-loćanā*, f. a woman with tremulous eyes.

Taralaya, nom. P. *taralayati*, *-yitum*, to cause to tremble, impart a tremulous motion; to wave, flutter, move to and fro.

Taralāya, nom. A. *taralāyate*, &c., to tremble, move to and fro.

Taralāyita, *as, ā, am*, caused to tremble, made tremulous, agitated, waving to and fro, undulating; (*as*), m. a large wave, surf; (*as* or *am*), m. or n. (?), fickleness.

Taralikā, f., N. of a woman.

Taralita, *as, ā, am*, shaking, dangling, moving to and fro, undulating, trembling, tremulous. — *Taralita-hāra*, *as, ā, am*, having a tremulous garland.

Taras, *as*, n. rapid progress, speed, velocity; strength, energy, efficacy; a bank; a float, a raft; a ferry, a place of crossing; a symbolical N. of Stoma; (*ās, ās, as*), Ved. pervading, quick, energetic; *tarasā*, ind. speedily, quickly, directly, energetically. — *Taras-mat*, *ān*, m., N. of a son of the fourteenth Manu. — *Taras-vat*, *ān, atī, at*, Ved. quick, swift (e. g. *taras-vatyas*, 'the swift ones,' i. e. the rivers); valiant, energetic, an epithet of Indra. — *Taras-vin*, *ī, inī, i*, Ved. quick, swift, strong, violent, energetic, courageous, bold; (*ī*), m. a courier, an express, a runner; a hero; air, wind; an epithet of Garuḍa, the bird of Vishṇu.

Tarasa, *am*, n. meat, flesh. — *Tarasa-maya*, *as, ī, am*, consisting of meat.

Tarasāna, *as*, m. a boat.

Tarāndhu or *tarālu*, *us*, m. a large flat-bottomed boat.

Tari, *is*, f. a boat, ship; a clothes-basket; the end of a cloth; (*ī, is* or *ī*), f. a boat; a clothes-basket; the hem of a garment; a small wooden baling-vessel; a club; smoke. — *Tari-ratha*, *as*, m. an oar, a paddle.

Tarika, *as*, m. a ferry-man; a float, a raft, a boat; (*ā*), f. a boat; cream.

Tarikin, *ī*, m. a ferry-man.

Taritavya or *tarītavya* or *tartavya*, *as, ā, am*, to be crossed or passed over, to be carried over or across.

Taritṛi or *tarītṛi*, *tā, trī, tṛi*, who or what crosses, passes or carries over; (*trī*), f. a boat, a raft.

Taritra, *am*, n. a boat, a ship.

Tarin, *ī, iṇī, i*, who or what crosses; crossing; (*iṇī*), f. a boat.

Tarīyas, *ān, asī, as*, Ved. easily passing through or pervading; (Sāy.) easy to be passed through.

Tarīsha, *as*, m. a raft, a float, a boat; the ocean; a fit or competent person; a fine shape or form; decorating, ornamenting; practice, business, profession; heaven or paradise; (*ī*), f., N. of a daughter of Indra.

Tarishan (occurring only as a loc. or Vedic inf. *tarishaṇi*), Ved. passing through, going across.

1. *taru*, *us, us, u*, = *taraṇi*, Ved. passing through; (Sāy.) rapid motion, velocity; a wooden ladle for taking up the Soma; [cf. 2. *taru* next col.]

Tarutṛi, *tā, trī, tṛi*, Ved. overcoming, conquering, a conqueror; impelling, causing to be quick; [cf. *tarītṛi*.]

Tarutra, *as, ā, am*, Ved. carrying across; overcoming, conquering.

Tarusha, *as*, m., Ved. a conqueror, overcomer; (*ī*), f. victory.

Tarushya (fr. the next), nom. P. *tarushyati*, &c., Ved. to attack, overcome, conquer.

Tarus, *us*, n., Ved. battle; superiority; (Sāy.) overcoming.

Tarūshas, *ās, ās, as*, Ved. (Sāy.) overcoming, conquering, saving, protecting; (*as*), n. rescue (?).

तरक्ष taraksha, *as*, m. or *tarakshu*, *us*, m. or *tarakshuka*, *as*, m. a hyena, or perhaps a tiger (?).

तरङ्ग taraṅga. See col. 1.

तरट taraṭa, a kind of medicinal plant, commonly *ṭāṁkalā*; [cf. *taradī*.]

तरत्सल taratsala, *as*, m. conflagration of chaff; (perhaps a wrong reading.)

तरदी taradī, f., N. of a thorny plant (= *tāradī, tīvrā, kharvurā, rakta-vījakā*; some read also *taraṭī* and *tāraṭī*).

तरन्तुक tarantuka. See col. 1.

तरबालिका tarabālikā, f. a kind of sword, = *karabālikā*; [cf. *taravāri*.]

तरम्बुज tarambuja, *am*, n. a water-melon, (most probably borrowed from the Persian تربز); [cf. also *kharvūja*.]

तरल tarala. See col. 1.

तरवट taravaṭa, the plant Cassia Auriculata.

तरवारि taravāri, *is*, m. a sword, a scymitar; [cf. *tarabālikā*.]

तरवी taravī, in astrology = تربيع, quadrature.

तरस् taras, tarasā, &c. See col. 2.

तरसन्ती tarasantī, f. (fr. rt. *tras*), Ved. the female of a deer.

तराम् tarām, an adverbial form of 1. *tara*.

तरिता taritā, f. (perhaps fr. rt. *tṛī*), the fore-finger; garlic, or perhaps hemp; a form of Durgā; [cf. *tāriṇī*.] — *Taritā-dhāraṇā-yantra* and *taritā-pūjā-yantra*, *am*, n. mystic diagrams given in the Tantra-sāra.

तरु 2. taru, *us*, m. (said to be fr. rt. *tṛī*; for 1. *taru* see col. 2), a tree; N. of a son of Manu Ćākshusha; (*taru* in the sense of 'tree' does not appear to occur in the Veda or Manu; it is perhaps a modern derivation fr. *dru*; but according to Sāy. it is used in Ṛig-veda V. 44, 5, in the sense of 'wooden ladle;' cf. 1. *taru*, col. 2); [cf. Lat. *termes*.] — *Taru-khaṇḍa*, *as, am*, m. n. an assemblage of trees; (also *taru-shaṇḍa*.) — *Taru-ććhāyā*, f. the shade of a tree. — *Taru-ja*, *as, ā, am*, produced by a tree (as a flower, fruit, &c.). — *Taru-jīvana*, *am*, n. the root of a tree, i. e. the vital organ of a tree. — *Taru-tala*, *as*, m. the part under the branches of a tree, the ground about its root, the foot of a tree. — *Taru-tā*, f. the state of a tree, the being a tree. — *Taru-tūlikā* or (according to another reading) *taru-dūlikā*, f. the flying fox (suspended like a balance from the branches of a tree); [cf. *vātuli*.] — *Taru-nakha*, *as*, m. a thorn, ('a tree-nail.') — *Taru-paṅkti*, *is*, f. a row of trees, an avenue. — *Taru-bhuj*, *k*, m. a kind of parasitical plant, Vanda Roxburghii; [cf. *taru-ruhā, taru-rohiṇī, taru-sthā*.] — *Taru-mahiman*, *ā*, m. a section in the Vṛikshāyur-veda which treats of the future rewards of those who plant trees. — *Taru-mṛiga*, *as*, m. 'a tree-animal,' a monkey, an ape. — *Taru-rāga*, *as* or *am*, m. or n. (?), a sprout; a bud, a blossom. — *Taru-rāja*, *as*, m. 'the king of trees,' the palmyra-tree; [cf. *tṛiṇa-rāja*.] — *Taru-rājan*, *ā*, m. 'the king of the trees,' an epithet of the Pārijāta. — *Taru-ruhā*, f. and *taru-rohiṇī*, f. 'growing on trees,' a parasitical plant, = *taru-bhuj*. — *Taru-vara*, *as*, m. an excellent tree, the best of trees, an epithet of the Pārijāta. — *Taru-vallī*, f. a kind of plant; [cf. *parpaṭī*.] — *Taru-viṭapa*, *as*, m. a branch or sprout. — *Taru-śāyin*, *ī*, m. a bird ('sleeping on trees'). — *Taru-śreshṭha*, *as*, m. the best of trees. — *Taru-shaṇḍa*, *as*, m. a group of trees. — *Taru-sāra*, *as*, m. 'essence of trees,' camphor. — *Taru-stha*, *as*, *ā*, *am*, staying or being in a tree; (*ā*), f. a parasitical plant.

Taruśa, *as*, *ā*, *am*, abounding in trees.

तरुकूणि *tarukūṇi*, *is*, m. a sort of bird, = *vāgguda*.

तरुक्ष *taruksha*, *as*, m., N. of a man; [cf. *tārukshāyaṇi*, *tārukshya*, *taluksha*.]

तरुण *taruṇa*, *as*, *ī*, *am* (said to be fr. rt. *tṛī*), young, tender, juvenile; new, fresh; a young man, one of the virile age; fresh, lively, vivid; risen only a short time ago (as the sun), not yet high in the sky; (*as*), m. the castor-oil plant, Ricinus Communis; large cumin seed, = *kubja-pushpa*, the blossom of Achyranthes Aspera; N. of one of the Saptarshayas in the eleventh Manv-antara; N. of a Gandharva; N. of a particular section in a mystical Tantra work treating of various stages in the life of the Tāntrika; (*ī*), f. a young woman, a girl from about sixteen years of age; N. of several plants; a kind of pot-herb, Aloe Perfoliata; also = *taraṇī*, Rosa Glandulifera; also = *dantī*, a kind of flower, = *sahā*, *kumārī*, *gandhāḍhyā*, *ćāru-keśarā*, &c.; a kind of perfume, commonly *ćiḍā*; (*am*), n. cartilage [cf. *taruṇāsthi* below]; a sprout; [cf. *taluna*; cf. also Gr. τέρην, τέρεινα; Old Germ. *diorna*, 'maiden;' Old Island. *therna*.] — *Taruṇa-jvara*, *as*, m. a fever that lasts a week. — *Taruṇa-dadhi*, *i*, n. coagulated milk five days old. — *Taruṇa-piṭikā*, f. red arsenic. — *Taruṇābhāsa* (°*ṇa-ābh*°), *as*, m. a kind of cucumber. — *Taruṇāsthi* (°*ṇa-as*°), *i*, n. 'soft-bone;' cartilage, gristle. — *Taruṇi-kaṭāksha-māla*, *as*, m., N. of a plant, = *tilaka*. — *Taruṇī-gaṇa*, *as*, m. a number of young women. — *Taruṇī-jana*, *as*, m. a young woman.

Taruṇaka, *as*, m., N. of a serpent-demon; (*am*), n. a sprout.

Taruṇāya, nom. P. -*yati*, &c., to bring forth; A. *taruṇāyate*, &c., to become or remain young or fresh.

Taruṇiman, *ā*, m. youth, juvenility.

तरूट *tarūṭa*, *as*, m. the root of the lotus.

तरूणक *tarūṇaka*, *am*, n. (probably a wrong reading for *taruṇaka*), Ved. a sprout.

तर्क् *tark*, cl. 10. P. (ep. also A.) *tarkayati*, -*te*, *tarkayāmāsa*, *tarkayitum*, to suppose, conjecture, guess, suspect, make a guess, infer, express an opinion, try to discover or ascertain, reason, speculate about; to consider or regard as (with two acc.); to reflect, think of, recollect, have in one's mind, intend; to ascertain; to shine, to speak; [cf. Lat. *torqueo*, *torques*, *torcular*, *torvus*; Goth. *threihan*; Angl. Sax. *thringan*; Old Germ. *drayan*; Mod. Germ. *drehen*; Goth. *thagkyan*; Lith. *tikiu*?].

Tarka, *as*, m. supposition, conjecture; reasoning, speculation, inquiry, meditation, discussion; doubt; the science of logic, logic; a system of doctrine founded on speculation or free thinking, a philosophical system (especially one of the six, viz. Pūrva-mīmāṃsā, Uttara-mīmāṃsā, Nyāya, Vaiśeshika, Sāṅkhya, and Yoga); a name of the number six; (in logic) confutation, reduction to absurdity, a conclusion opposed to or disproving the premises; wish, desire; supplying an ellipsis; cause, motive; (*ā*), f. speculation, reasoning. — *Tarka-kārikā*, f., N. of a work setting forth the principles of the Vaiśeshika phil. by Jīva-rāja Dīkshita. — *Tarka-kaumudī*, f., N. of an elementary work on the Vaiśeshika system. — *Tarka-grantha*, *as*, m. a treatise on reasoning, manual of logic. — *Tarka-ćandrikā*, f., N. of an elementary exposition of the Nyāya philosophy. — *Tarka-jvālā*, f. 'the flame of speculation,' N. of a Buddhist work. — *Tarka-dīpikā*, f., N. of a commentary on the Tarka-sangraha. — *Tarka-prakāśa*, *as*, m. = *tarka-bhāshā-prakāśa*. — *Tarka-pradīpa*, *as*, m., N. of a manual of Vaiśeshika principles by Koṇḍa-bhaṭṭa. — *Tarka-bhāshā* or *tarkānubhāshā* (°*ka-an*°) or *tarka-paribhāshā*, f., N. of a manual of the Nyāya phil. — *Tarkabhāshā-prakāśa*, *as*, m. or *tarkabhāshā-prakāśikā*, f. or *tarkabhāshā-bhāva*, *as*, m. or *tarkabhāshā-sāra-mañjarī*, f., N. of certain commentaries on this work. — *Tarka-mañjarī*, f., N. of a commentary on the Tarka-kārikā by the author of the original work. — *Tarka-mudrā*, f. a particular position of the hand. — *Tarka-yukta*, *as*, *ā*, *am*, conjectured, suspected. — *Tarka-ratna*, *am*, n., N. of a Vaiśeshika disquisition by Koṇḍa-bhaṭṭa. — *Tarka-vāg-īśa*, *us*, m., N. of several writers on the Nyāya phil. — *Tarka-vidyā*, f. the science of reasoning or logic, a logical treatise. — *Tarka-śāstra*, *am*, n. the science of reasoning, logic; a philosophical work. — *Tarka-sangraha*, *as*, m., N. of a manual of the Vaiśeshika branch of the Nyāya phil. by Annam-bhaṭṭa. — *Tarkasangraha-dīpikā*, f., N. of a commentary on the preceding by the same author. — *Tarkābhāsa* (°*ka-ābh*°), *as*, m. apparent reasoning, fallacy in drawing conclusions, incompatibility of conclusion and premises. — *Tarkāmṛita* (°*ka-am*°), *am*, n., N. of an elementary work on the Vaiśeshika doctrine by Jagad-īśa Tarkālankāra Bhaṭṭāćārya. — *Tarkāmṛita-ćashaka*, N. of a commentary on the preceding work by Gangārāma Jaḍī. — *Tarkāmṛita-taranginī*, f., N. of a commentary on the Tarkāmṛita by Mukunda Bhaṭṭa Gāḍegila.

Tarkaka, *as*, *ā*, *am*, inquiring, inquisitive, investigating; (*as*), m. a suppliant, a petitioner, an asker, an inquirer; a logician.

Tarkaṇa, *am*, n. conjecturing, reasoning, speculating.

Tarkaṇīya, *as*, *ā*, *am*, to be suspected, to be an object of the suspicion of others (with gen.); causing suspicion.

Tarkayat, *an*, *antī*, *at*, conjecturing, expecting, anticipating, doubting, &c.

Tarkārī, f. the tree Sesbania Ægyptiaca, a kind of gourd.

Tarkiṇa or *tarkila*, *as*, m. the tree Cassia Tora, = *ćakra-marda*.

Tarkita, *as*, *ā*, *am*, investigated, examined, doubted, discussed, &c.; (*am*), n. conjecture, supposition.

Tarkin, *ī*, *iṇī*, *i*, conjecturing, supposing; reasoning, skilled in speculation or philosophy; (*ī*), m. a logician, disputant, reasoner.

Tarkuka, *as*, m. a suppliant, beggar; [cf. *tarkaka*.]

Tarkya, *as*, *ā*, *am*, to be imagined or supposed, capable of investigation or reasoning.

तर्कु *tarku*, *us*, *us*, m. f. (said to be fr. rt. *kṛit*, with transposition of the consonants), a spindle, an iron pin upon which the cotton is first drawn out and which serves as the distaff, the cotton being next transferred from it to the wheel; [cf. Gr. ἄ-τρακτος.] — *Tarku-piṇḍa*, *as*, m. a ball of clay &c. at the lower end of a spindle to assist in giving it a rotatory motion. — *Tarku-pīṭha*, *as*, *ī*, m. f. or *tarku-pāṭhī*, f. a ball at the lower end of a spindle. — *Tarku-lāsaka*, *as*, m. a concave shell or saucer which serves to hold the lower end of the spindle when whirled round. — *Tarku-śāṇa*, *as*, m. a small whetstone for sharpening spindles, &c.

Tarkuṭa, *am*, n. drawing out the cotton upon the distaff or upon the wheel; spinning; (*ī*), f. a spindle, a distaff.

तर्क्षु *tarkshu*, *us*, m. = *tarakshu*, a hyena.

तर्क्ष्य *tarkshya*, *as*, m. nitre, saltpetre.

तर्ज् *tarj*, cl. 1. P. (ep. also A.) *tarjati*, -*te*, *tatarja*, *tarjitum*, to threaten, menace; to blame, censure, reprove; Caus. P. (ep. also A.) *tarjayati*, -*te*, -*yitum*, to threaten; to scold, censure; to frighten, terrify; to deride, mock; [cf. Old Germ. *trug*, *druk*, *triugu*, *driuku*, 'to cheat:' Angl. Sax. *threagan*, 'to chide;' *thracian*, *thraec*: Old Germ. *dravyan*: Mod. Germ. *drohen*.]

Tarjana, *am*, n. threatening, blaming, censuring; pointing at in ridicule or contempt; putting to shame, surpassing; wrath, anger; (*ā*), f. threatening, censuring; (*ī*), f. the fore-finger (as used for threatening).

Tarjanīya, *as*, *ā*, *am*, to be threatened, reprehensible.

Tarjita, *as*, *ā*, *am*, threatened, blamed, reviled; shamed, disgraced; (*am*), n. threatening, menace.

तर्जिक *tarjika*, *ās*, m. pl., N. of a country or people, perhaps to the north-west of India or Bokhara, the country of the Tājiks; (also *tāyika* or *tājika*.)

तर्ण *tarṇa* or *tarṇaka*, *as*, m. (perhaps corrupted fr. *taruṇa*), a calf.

तर्णि *tarṇi*, *is*, m. (fr. rt. *tṛī*), a float, a raft; the sun.

तर्तरीक *tartarīka*, *as*, *ā*, *am* (fr. Intens. of rt. *tṛī*), being in the habit of passing or crossing over, a passenger; (*am*), n. a boat, a raft, a vessel.

Tartarya, *as*, *ā*, *am*. See *taritarya*, p. 365, col. 2.

तर्द् *tard* (connected with rt. *tṛid*), cl. 1. P. *tardati*, &c., to kill, injure, hurt; cut through; [cf. rt. *tṛid*.]

Tarda, *as*, m., Ved. a species of bird; [cf. Lat. *turdus*.]

Tardū, *ūs*, m. f.? (fr. rt. *tṛid*, but said to be fr. rt. *tṛī*), a wooden ladle.

Tardman, *a*, n., Ved. a hole, an opening, a cleft.

तर्पण *tarpaṇa*, *as*, *ī*, *am* (fr. rt. *tṛip*), satisfying, satiating, pleasing, refreshing [cf. *ghrāṇa-tarpaṇa*]; (*as*, *am*), m. n. a kind of plant; (*ī*), f., N. of a plant, = *guru-skandha*, *śleshmaṇā*; (*am*), n. the becoming satisfied or satiated, the act of satiating, refreshing, pleasing; satisfaction given or received; the state of being pleased; satiety, fulness; pleasure; a religious rite, libation, presenting libations of water to the manes of the deceased or to the Pitṛis collectively, also to the gods, either generally or individually; gladdening; satiating the eyes, i. e. filling them with oil &c.; food; fuel used on sacrificial occasions or for lighting a sacrificial fire; a kind of sweetmeat (?). — *Tarpaṇa-vidhi*, *is*, m. a chapter of the Smṛity-artha-sāra by Srīdhara-svāmin on funeral ceremonies &c. — *Tarpaṇećchu* (°*ṇa-ić*°), *us*, *us*, *u*, desirous of satisfaction or of receiving after death the presentation of water called Tarpaṇa; (*us*), m. an epithet of Bhīshma.

Tarpaṇīya, *as*, *ā*, *am*, to be satiated or satisfied.

Tarpayitavya, *as*, *ā*, *am*, to be satiated or refreshed.

Tarpayitvā, ind. having satisfied.

Tarpita, *as*, *ā*, *am*, pleased, gratified, satisfied.

Tarpin, *ī*, *iṇī*, *i*, gratifying, giving pleasure or satisfaction; offering oblations to the manes, one who does so; (*iṇī*), f. the plant Hibiscus Mutabilis (*padma-ćāriṇī*).

तर्फितृ *tarphitṛi*, *tā*, *trī*, *tṛi* (fr. rt. *tṛiph*), a killer, injurer.

तर्ब् *tarb*, cl. 1. P. *tarbati*, &c., to go or move.

तर्बट *tarbaṭa*, *as*, m. a year; the plant Cassia Tora, = *ćakra-marda*.

तर्मन् *tarman*, *a*, n. (perhaps fr. rt. *tṛī*), the top or end of the sacrificial post; [cf. *su-tarman*; cf. also Gr. τέρμα; Lat. *terminus*.]

तर्य *tarya*, *as*, m. (fr. rt. *tṛī*), Ved. (Sāy.) N. of a man.

1. *tarsha*, *as*, m. a raft or float; the ocean; the sun; [cf. *taraṇi*.]

तर्ष 2. *tarsha*, *as*, m. (fr. rt. *tṛish*), thirst; wish, desire; Desire personified as a son of Arka (the sun) and Vāsanā.

Tarshaṇa, *am*, n. thirsting, thirst; desiring, wish, desire.

Tarsham, ind. thirsting, being thirsty.

Tarshita, as, ā, am, thirsting, athirst, thirsty; desiring, wishing for; [cf. *trishita*.]

Tarshula, as, ā, am, wishing, desiring; in *a-tarshula*, without desire.

Tarshyā-vat, ān, atī, at, Ved. thirsty.

तर्हण *tarhaṇa, as, ī, am* (fr. rt. *tṛih*), Ved. injuring, crushing, bruising; [cf. *dasyu-tarhaṇa*.]

तर्हि *tarhi*, ind. (fr. the pronom. base 2. *ta*), at that time, then, at that moment, in that case; in the mean time; (this word occurs in the Veda, but is rarely found in the earlier epic poetry); *yadā—tarhi*, when—then; *yadi—tarhi, yatra—tarhi, ćed—tarhi*, if—then; [cf. *etarhi, karhi, yarhi*.]

तल् *tal*, cl. 1. 10. P. *talati, tālayati*, &c., to be full or complete; to fix, found; to establish; to be fixed; to accomplish a vow; (according to others a Sautra root.)

तल *tala, as, am*, m. n. (perhaps fr. rt. *stṛi*), surface, a level surface, the flat roof of a house; (often used in composition with only a slight alteration of the sense of the word to which it is added, but explained by lexicographers to mean 'essential nature,' e.g. *mahī-tala*, the very earth, the surface of the earth, earth itself; *nabhas-tala*, the sky, heaven); the inner side or palm of the hand with extended fingers (in *pāṇi-tala*, &c.); the sole of the foot (in *pāda-tala*); the fore-arm; a span; a slap or clap with the hand, (*anyonyasya talān daduḥ*, they slapped each other with the palms of the hands); depth, lowness, inferiority of position, the under part, the part underneath, lower part, base, bottom; a hole, a pit, a chasm; *tale*, ind. at the bottom, under, beneath; (*am, ā*), n. f. a leathern fence worn by archers on the left arm [cf. *tala-tra* and *tala-trāṇa*]; (*as*), m. an epithet of Śiva [cf. *tāla* and *a-tala*]; the palmyra-tree, = *tāla*; the hilt or haft or handle of a sword &c.; pressing the strings of a lute with the left hand; a division of hell; (*am*), n. a wood; a pond; cause, origin, motive, the root or seed of events; [cf. *a-tala, jihvā-t°, dharaṇī-t°, ni-t°, pra-t°, mahā-t°, rasā-t°, vi-t°, su-t°*; cf. also Hib. *talamh*, 'the world, earth;' Lat. *tellus*.] — *Tala-ghāta, as*, m. a slap with the palm of the hand. — *Tala-tas*, ind. from the bottom. — *Tala-tāla, as*, m. clapping the hands; [cf. *tāla-śabda*.] — *Tala-tra* or *tala-trāṇa, am*, n. (hand or arm-guard), the leathern glove of an archer. — *Talatra-vat, ān, atī, at*, wearing a leathern glove (as an archer). — *Tala-prahāra, as*, m. a slap or blow with the palm of the hand or with a claw. — *Tala-mukha-hasta, as*, m. a particular position of the hand with the palm expanded. — *Tala-yukta, as, ā, am*, furnished with a handle or haft. — *Tala-yuddha, am*, n. a fight carried on with the palms of the hands, a fight. — *Tala-loka, as*, m. the lower regions, nether world; [cf. *talātala, rasātala, a-tala*.] — *Tala-sāraka, am*, n. a martingale, a strap passing between the fore-legs of a horse; a kind of trough or vessel from which horses are fed (?). — *Tala-stha* or *tala-sthita, as, ā, am*, remaining beneath. — *Tala-hṛidaya, am*, n. the centre of the sole of the foot. — *Talāṅguli* (°*la-aṅ*°), *is*, f. a toe. — *Talāći*, f. (fr. *tala* and rt. *aṅć*), a mat, one made of reeds or bamboos. — *Talātala* (°*la-at*°), *am*, n. the fourth of the seven divisions of the infernal regions; [cf. *a-tala, mahā-t°, rasā-t°, vi-t°, su-t°*.] — *Talekshaṇa* (°*la-ik*°), *as*, m. a hog ('looking downwards'). — *Talottama* (°*la-ut*°), *as, am*, m. n. (?), cover, site (?). — *Talodara* (°*la-ud*°), *as, ā* or *ī, am*, having a protuberant belly or one that hangs down (?); (*ī*), f. a mistress or wife. — *Talodā* (°*la-ud*), f. a river ('whose water flows downwards').

Talaka, am, n. a large pond; [cf. *talla*.]

Talakoṭa, a kind of plant.

Talikā, f. a martingale; [cf. *tala-sāraka*.]

1. *talita, as, ā, am*, fixed, placed, having a bottom; [cf. 2. *talita* next col.]

Talin, ī, inī, i, wearing the leathern fence called Tala (as an archer).

तलमीन *tala-mīna*, a various reading for *nala-mīna*, q. v.

तलव *talava, am*, n., Ved. a musician. — *Talava-kāra, ās*, m. pl., N. of a school of the Sāma-veda. — *Talavakāropanishad* (°*ra-up*°), *t*, f. = *kenopanishad*.

तलवारण *talavāraṇa, am*, n. a sword; [cf. *taravāri*; Beng. *talvār*; Hind. تلوار.]

तलाशा *talāśā*, f., Ved. a kind of tree.

तलित 2. *talita, am*, n. fried meat. (For 1. *talita* see col. 1, under *tala*.)

तलिन *talina, as, ā, am* (said to be fr. rt. *tal*), thin, spare, meagre, delicate; small, little; clear, clean; separate, having spaces or interstices; below, situated under or beneath [cf. *tala*]; (*am*), n. a bed, a couch or cot; (a various reading for *talima*.)

तलिम *talima, am*, n. ground prepared for the site of a dwelling &c. (*kuṭṭima*); a bed, a couch or cot [cf. *talina* and *talpa*]; an awning; a scymitar, a large sacrificial sword or knife.

तलीद्य *talīdya*, Ved. a particular part of the body.

तलुक्ष *taluksha, as*, m., N. of a man; [cf. *taruksha*.]

तलुन *taluna, as, ī, am* (for *taruṇa*, q. v.), young; (*as*), m. a youth; air, wind; (*ī*), f. a girl, a young woman.

तल्क *talka, am*, n. a wood, a forest; [cf. *tala*.]

तल्प *talpa, as, am*, m. n. (in the earlier language m., in the later n.; perhaps fr. rt. *stṛi*, but according to others fr. rt. *tal* or fr. rt. *tṛip*), a couch, bed, sofa; a wife; the seat of a carriage; an upper story, a room on the top of a house, a turret, a tower or keep; (in the Atharva-veda XIII. 1, 17, *talpā* occurs.) — *Talpa-kīṭa, as*, m. 'a bed-insect,' a bug. — *Talpa-ga*, see under *guru*. — *Talpa-giri, is*, m., N. of a mountain. — *Talpa-ja, as, ā, am*, brought forth in or on a marriage-bed; born of a wife (as a son by an appointed substitute). — *Talpa-śīvan, ā, arī, a*, or *talpe-śaya, as, ā, am*, Ved. resting on a couch.

Talpaka, as, m. a maker of beds or sofas.

Talpana, am, n. (fr. a nom. formed fr. *talpa*), an elephant's back, the exterior muscles of the back.

Talpī-kṛita, as, ā, am, made into a bed or couch.

Talpya, as, ā, am, Ved. belonging to a bed; worthy of a couch or sofa; born in a marriage-bed.

तल्ल *talla, as*, m. a reservoir, a large pond, a tank or Talao; (*ī*), f. a young woman; N. of the wife of Varuṇa; a boat; (*am*), n. a pit, a hole; [cf. *tala* and *talaka*.]

तल्लक्षण *tal-lakshaṇa*. See under *tad*, p. 361.

तल्लज *tallaja, as*, m. excellence, happiness; (also attributively) excellent, happy; used in apposition as an epithet (e.g. *kumārī-tallaja*, an excellent maiden; *go-tallaja*, the best of cows.)

तल्लह *tallaha*(?), *as*, m. a dog.

तल्लिका *tallikā*, f. a key; [cf. *tālī*.]

तल्व *talva, am*, n. scent arising from the rubbing of fragrant substances.

तवक *tavaka, as, ā, am*, thine; (perhaps an incorrect form for *tāvaka*.)

तवक्षीर *tavakshīra* (a corruption of *tvakkshīra*), *am*, n. manna of bamboo (commonly Tabāshīr); a N. applied to a kind of extract of wheat, barley, rice, &c., (or, according to some, a kind of milk and water), = *payaḥ-kshīra, yava-ja, yavajodbhava* (commonly Toshākshīra); (*ī*), f. a kind of Curcuma (*gandha-pattrā*). — *Tavakshīry-ekapattrikā*, the single-leaved Tavakshīrī, turmeric, Curcuma Zedoaria.

तवर *tavara*, a particular high number.

तवराज *tavarāja, as*, m. a sort of sugar prepared from a species of Hedysarum (*yavāsa-śarkarā*). — *Tavarājodbhava-khaṇḍa* (°*ja-ud*°), *as*, m. a sort of hard sugar prepared from the preceding.

तवस् *tavas, ās, ās, as* (fr. rt. 2. *tu*), Ved. strong, powerful, courageous, efficacious, energetic; an epithet of Rudra, the Maruts, Indra, Parjanya, Agni, Pūshan; (*ās*), m. power, strength, courage; [cf. *pra-tavas*.] — *Tavas-vat, ān, atī, at*, Ved. powerful, strong, an epithet of Soma.

Tavasya, am, n., Ved. strength, efficacy; courage; (Sāy.) an oblation which increases the strength.

Tavāgā (fr. *tavā*, a derivative of rt. 2. *tu*, and *go*?), an epithet of a bull; (but in the Pada-pāṭha this word is not considered as a compound, and by Sāy. it is said to mean) of great strength.

Tavisha, as, ā, am, Ved. powerful, strong, energetic, efficacious; courageous; (*as*), m. the ocean, sea; heaven, paradise; (*ī*), f. power, strength, violence, courage, (inst. plur. *tavishībhis*, powerfully, violently); the earth; a river; N. of a daughter of Indra; (*am*), n. power, strength. — *Tavishī-mat, ān, atī, at*, Ved. powerful, violent, epithet of the winds. — *Tavishī-vat, ān, atī, at*, Ved. powerful, strong, an epithet of Indra.

Tavishīya, nom. P., Ved. *tavishīyati*, &c., to be strong or violent or courageous, to make effort; (Sāy.) to wish for power or strength; [cf. *tavishya*.]

Tavishīyu, us, us, u, Ved. spirited (as a horse); violent, epithet of the Maruts; (Sāy.) evincing strength.

Tavishya, nom. A., Ved. *tavishyate*, &c., to be strong or violent, have courage.

Tavishyā, f., Ved. violence, force.

Tavīyas or *tavyas, ān, asī, as* (compar. of *tavas*), stronger, very strong, powerful, rich; (generally found in the phrase *tavasas tavīyān*, stronger than the strong.)

Tavīsha, as, m. the ocean; heaven; gold; (*ī*), f., N. of a daughter of Indra; [cf. *tavisha*.]

1. *tavya, as, ā, am*, Ved. powerful, strong, grown strong. (For 2. *tavya* see below.)

तवारिसाण *tavārisāṇa*, N. of a place.

तविपुला *ta-vipulā*, f. a particular metre.

तव्य 2. *tavya*, a *kṛit* affix by means of which the future passive participle is formed from roots.

तश्ली *taślī*, f. in astron., trigon. = تثليث.

तष्ट *tashṭa, as, ā, am* (fr. rt. *taksh*), pared, hewn, cut, chiseled, split, made thin; fashioned.

Tashṭṛi, ṭā, m. a carpenter, a builder, a builder of chariots; a N. of Viśva-karman, the architect of the gods; N. of one of the twelve Ādityas; [cf. *trashṭṛi*.]

तस् *tas*, cl. 4. P. *tasyati*, &c., to fade away, become exhausted, perish, wane; to throw down; to cast upwards, reject, cast; [cf. rt. *taṅs* and Eng. *toss*.]

तसर *tasara, am, as*, n. m.(?), (fr. rt. *taṅs*?), Ved. a shuttle.

तसीर *tasīra*, in astron. = *tāsīra*, = تسير.

तस्कर *taskara, as*, m. (said to be derived fr. *atas* and rt. *kṛi*; according to others fr. *tad* and rt. *kṛi*), a thief, a robber; (at the end of a comp.) anything bad or contemptible [cf. *ćaura*]; (in astron.) N. of certain Ketus; a kind of pot-herb, Trigonella Corniculata; a tree, Vangueria Spinosa [cf. *madana*]; the ear; (*ī*), f. a passionate woman; N. of several plants, a sort of Mimosa, = *taskara-snāyu*, Leea Hirta, &c. — *Taskara-tā*, f. or *taskara-tva*, *am*, n. thievishness, thieving, theft; catching by means of the ear, hearing. — *Taskara-vat*, ind. like a thief. — *Taskara-snāyu*, *us*, m. the plant Leea Hirta.

तस्तुव *tastuva*, *am*, n., Ved. an antidote against poison (?).

तस्थु *tasthu*, *us*, *us*, *u* (fr. the weakest cases of *tasthivas*, perf. part. of rt. *sthā*), stationary, immovable, motionless.

तस्दी *tasdī*, in astron., hexagon, = تسدیس.

तस्मात् *tasmāt*, ind. (abl. of the pronom. base 2. *ta*), from that, on that account, therefore, (correlative to *yasmāt* and *yad.*)

ताक्षक *tākshaka*, *as*, *ī*, *am* (fr. *takshakīyā*), relating or belonging to Takshakīyā.

Tākshaṇya, *as*, m. (fr. *takshan*), the son of a woodcutter or carpenter.

Tākshaśila, *as*, *ī*, *am*, coming or produced from Takshaśilā.

Tākshṇa, *as*, *ī*, *am* (fr. *takshan*), fit for a carpenter; (*as*), m. the son of a carpenter.

ताच्छब्द्य *tāćchabdya*, *am*, n. (fr. *taććhabda* [*tad* + *śabda*], having that name or the name of that), the being called or named after that.

ताच्छीलिक *tāćchīlika*, *as*, *ī*, *am* (fr. *taććhīla* or *tāćchīlya*), a N. given to an affix when it denotes 'having a particular inclination or custom.'

Tāćchīlya, *am*, n. the being accustomed to that, doing anything regularly, consuetude.

ताजक् *tājak*. See *tājat*.

ताजक *tājaka* and *tājika*, *am*, n., N. of certain astronomical books translated from the Arabic and Persian (e.g. *tājika-jyotir-maṇi*, *tājaka-paddhati*, *tājaka-śāstra*, *tājaka-sāra-sudhā-nidhi*, *viśvanātha-tājaka*, &c.).

ताजत् *tājat* or sometimes *tājak*, ind., Ved. suddenly, abruptly, (opposed to *ćiram*.) — *Tājad-bhaṅga*, *as*, m., Ved. a species of very fragile wood; [cf. *kovidāra*.]

ताजिक *tājika* or *tājīka*, N. of a district; also = *tājaka*, q. v.

ताटङ्क *tāṭanka*, *as*, m. an ornament for the ear, a large sort of ear-ring; [cf. *tāḍanka*.]

ताटस्थ्य *tāṭasthya*, *am*, n. (fr. *taṭa-stha*, a by-stander), proximity; indifference, disregard, exemption from attachment or aversion, neutrality.

ताड *tāḍa*, *as*, *ā*, *am* (fr. rt. *taḍ*), beating, striking; (*as*), m. a blow, thump, knock, beating, whipping, chastisement; sound, noise; a handful of grass, corn, &c., a sheaf; a mountain; a kind of grass, Andropogon Serratus, = *devatāḍa*; [cf. *tāḍi* next col.] — *Tāḍa-gha*, *as*, *ā*, *am*, beating with a whip or strokes of any kind; (*as*), m. a blacksmith (?). — *Tāḍa-ghāta*, *as*, m. an artificer who beats or hammers, a smith. — *Tāḍa-vakra*, N. of a district.

Tāḍakā, f., N. of a Yakshiṇī or female fiend, daughter of Su-ketu, wife of Sunda, and mother of Mārīća, (she was changed into a Rākshasī by Agastya, whose devotions she had disturbed, and was afterwards killed by Rāma, see Rāmāyaṇa I. 28); the large dark-green pumpkin. — *Tāḍakā-phala*, *am*, n. large cardamoms.

Tāḍakāyana, *as*, m., N. of a Ṛishi.

Tāḍana, *as*, *ā*, *am*, beating, whipping, striking, hitting, hurting; (*am*), n. the act of striking, beating, thumping, whipping, chastising, a stroke, blow; (in astron.) touching, partial eclipse; (*ā*), f. striking; (*ī*), f. a whip.

Tāḍanīya, *as*, *ā*, *am*, to be beaten, punishable.

Tāḍayitṛi, *tā*, *trī*, *tṛi*, a striker, beater, thumper, who or what beats or strikes.

Tāḍayitvā, ind. having beaten or struck.

Tāḍita, *as*, *ā*, *am*, struck, beaten, chastised.

Tāḍula, *as*, *ā*, *am*, beating, who or what beats or strikes, punishing with blows.

Tāḍya, *as*, *ā*, *am*, to be beaten or chastised or punished, punishable.

Tāḍyamāna, *as*, *ā*, *am*, being beaten or struck; suffering blows, undergoing a beating; (*as*), m. a musical instrument which is struck (as a drum &c.).

ताडङ्क *tāḍanka*, *as*, m. or *tāḍapattra*, *am*, n. a kind of ear-ring or ornament of the ear; [cf. *tāṭanka*.]

ताडाग *tāḍāga*, *as*, *ī*, *am* (fr. *taḍāga*), being in tanks, coming from ponds (as water &c.).

ताडि *tāḍi*, *is* or *ī*, f. (for *tālī*), a kind of palm, Corypha Taliera; (*ī*), f. a kind of ornament.

ताण्ड *tāṇḍa*, *as*, m. (fr. *taṇḍa* or *taṇḍā*), N. of an old sage; (*am*), n., N. of a Brāhmaṇa.

Tāṇḍaka, *am*, n., N. of a Brāhmaṇa.

ताण्डव *tāṇḍava*, *as*, *am*, m. n. dancing, especially with violent gesticulation, and particularly applied to the frantic dance of the god Śiva and his votaries; (in prosody) a tribrach or foot of three short syllables; a sort of grass, Saccharum Procerum. — *Tāṇḍava-tālika*, *as*, m. an epithet of Nandin the door-keeper of Śiva. — *Tāṇḍava-priya*, *as*, m. an epithet of Śiva ('fond of the Tāṇḍava dance'). — *Tāṇḍava-brāhmaṇa*, perhaps a wrong reading for *tāṇḍaka-brāhmaṇa*.

Tāṇḍavita, *as*, *ā*, *am*, moving round in a wild dance; dancing; fluttering; frowning.

Tāṇḍi, *i*, n., N. of a manual of the art of dancing; the science of dancing.

Tāṇḍin, *ī*, m., N. of a writer on prosody; (*inas*), m. pl., N. of a Vedic school founded by a pupil of Vaiśampāyana. — *Tāṇḍi-brāhmaṇa*, *am*, n., N. of a Brāhmaṇa belonging to this school.

Tāṇḍya, *as*, m., N. of a preceptor; (*am*), n., N. of a Brāhmaṇa belonging to the Sāma-veda, to which there is a commentary by Sāyaṇa.

Tāṇḍyāyanī, f. a patronymic from Tāṇḍya.

तात् *tāt*, ind. (an obsolete abl. fr. the pronom. base 2. *ta*), Ved. thus, in this way.

तात *tāta*, *as*, *ā*, *am* (said to be fr. rt. 3. *tan*), venerable, reverend, respectable, dear; (*as*), m. a father; a term of affection or endearment addressed to any person, but especially to a junior or inferior, as to a child or pupil (e.g. *he tāta*, O child!); any person for whom one feels pity; [cf. Lat. *tata*: Gr. τέττα: Boh. *tata*, 'father:' Lith. *tėta*, *tėtis*, 'daddy;' *teta*, 'aunt:' Old Germ. *toto*: Low Germ. *teite*, 'daddy, dad.'] — *Tāta-gu*, *us*, *us*, *u*, agreeable to a father, paternal, fatherly, relating or belonging to a father; (*us*), m. a paternal uncle. — *Tāta-janayitrī*, *tryau*, f. du. father and mother, parents. — *Tāta-tulya*, *as*, *ā*, *am*, like a father, paternal; (*as*), m. a paternal uncle or the most respectable of a man's male relations.

Tātala, *as*, m. a fatherly relative, one who may be considered as a father; an iron club or spike; sickness, disease; cooking or maturing; heat, physical or morbid; (*as*, *ā*, *am*), hot.

Tāti, *is*, m. offspring, a son.

Tātya, *as*, *ā*, *am*, Ved. paternal, fatherly.

तातन *tātana*, *as*, m. a wagtail.

तातृपि *tātṛipi*, *is*, *is*, *i* (fr. Intens. of rt. *tṛip*), Ved. satisfying, delighting much.

तातृषाण *tātṛishāṇa*, *as*, *ā*, *am* (perf. part. fr. rt. 1. *tṛish*), Ved. thirsting, very thirsty.

तात्कर्म्य *tātkarmya*, *am*, n. (fr. *tat-karman*), sameness of occupation.

तात्कालिक *tātkālika*, *as*, *ā* or *ī*, *am* (fr. *tat-kāla*), 'lasting that time,' lasting equally long, happening at that time, simultaneous, contemporary, instantly appearing; happening immediately or without delay; relating to any particular moment of time.

Tātkālya, *am*, n. simultaneousness.

तात्तलि *tāttali*, *is*, m., N. of a man.

तात्त्विक *tāttvika*, *as*, *ī*, *am* (fr. *tattva*), accordant with reality, real, true, essential.

तात्पर्य *tātparya*, *am*, n. (fr. *tat-para*), aim, reference to any object (with loc.), object, purpose, intent, design; meaning, scope, purport; explanation; *tātparyatas* or *tātparyeṇa*, ind. with this intention, with this aim or object. — *Tātparya-pariśuddhi*, *is*, f., N. of a work by Udayana. — *Tātparya-bodhinī*, f., N. of a commentary on a philosophical work called Citra-dīpa. — *Tātparyārtha* (°*ya-ar*°), *as*, m. the meaning or purpose of a sentence.

Tātparyaka, *as*, *ikā*, *am*, aiming at, intending, meaning.

तात्य *tātya*. See under *tāta*, col. 2.

तात्स्तोम्य *tātstomya*, *am*, n. (fr. *tat-stoma*), sameness of praise.

तात्स्थ्य *tātsthya*, *am*, n. (fr. *tat-stha*), the residing in that, the being contained in.

ताथाभाव्य *tāthābhāvya*, *as*, *ā*, *am* (fr. *tathā-bhāva*), a N. for the Svarita accent at the end of the first member of a compound when an Udātta syllable immediately follows, (the low-sounding vowel in such a position cannot strictly be called either Svarita or Anudātta-tara, and a new name is therefore given to it; this may often happen in the case of two separate words, but the vowel is then called Anudātta-tara.)

तादर्थिक *tādarthika*, *as*, *ī*, *am* (fr. *tad-artha* or *tādarthya*), destined or intended for that.

Tādarthya, *am*, n. the being destined or intended for that, the having that or the same object, identity of aim, object; relation to; sameness or precision of meaning.

तादात्म्य *tādātmya*, *am*, n. (fr. *tad-ātman*), sameness of nature or character, identity, unity.

तादीत्ना *tādītnā*, ind. (fr. *tadī* = *tadi*, a correlative of *yadi*, and affix *tnā*?), Ved. at that time.

तादुरी *tādurī*, f., Ved. epithet of a frog (explained by Durga as either *taraṇa-śīlā*, able to swim, or *tāvad udaram*, consisting only of a belly; perhaps a wrong reading for *tādurī*, as if fr. rt. *taḍ*; cf. also *dardura*, 'a frog').

तादृक्ष *tā-dṛiksha*, *as*, *ī*, *am* (fr. the pronom. base 2. *ta* and *dṛiksha* fr. rt. *dṛiś*), such like, such a one, like that, like him, &c.

Tā-dṛiś, *k*, *k*, *k* (Ved. nom. m. f. *tādṛiṅ*), like that, such like, like him or it, &c.; (*k*), ind. in such a manner. — *Tādṛig-guṇa*, *as*, *ā*, *am*, of such qualities. — *Tādṛig-rūpa*, *as*, *ā*, *am*, of such a shape or form. — *Tādṛig-vidha*, *as*, *ā*, *am*, of such a kind, of such qualities, being in this situation.

Tā-dṛiśa, *as*, *ī*, *am*, such like, such a one; *yādṛiśas tādṛiśas*, anybody whosoever; [cf. Prāk. *tārisa*; Gr. τηλίκος; Dor. ταλίκος; Slav. *tolik*; Lat. *talis*.]

ताद्धर्म्य *tāddharmya*, *am*, n. (fr. *tad-dharman*), sameness of law, analogy.

ताद्धित *tāddhita*, *as*, *ī*, *am* (fr. *tad-dhita*), formed with a Taddhita affix.

ताद्रूप्य *tādrūpya*, *am*, n. (fr. *tad-rūpa*), oneness or sameness of form, figure, &c.

तान *tāna*, *as*, m. (fr. rt. 3. *tan*), a thread, a fibre; a tone, a protracted tone, the key-note (in music); a monotonous tone (in reciting, also called Eka-śruti); (*am*), n. expanse, extension; an object of sense; [cf. Gr. τόνος.] — *Tāna-karman*, *a*, n.

tuning the voice previously to singing; running over the notes to catch the key.

तानव tānava, am, n. (fr. tanu), thinness, spareness, meagreness, smallness. — Tānava-kṛit, t, t, t, diminishing, causing thinness.

Tānavya, as, m. a patronymic from Tanu; (the fem. is tānavyāyanī.)

तानूनपात tānūnapāta, as, ī, am (fr. tanū-napāt), relating to Tanū-napāt, addressed to that form of Agni.

Tānūnaptra, am, n. (fr. tanū-naptṛi), a ceremony in which Tanū-napāt is invoked and the oblation touched by the sacrificer and the priests as a form of adjuration; (as, ī, am), used or employed in this ceremony, (as clarified butter &c.)

तानूर tānūra, as, m. a whirlpool; [cf. tālūra.]

तान्त tānta, as, ā, am (fr. rt. tam), wearied, fatigued, distressed; languid, languishing; faded, withered, blighted; a mystical N. of the letter d. — Tānta-nayana, as, ā, am, having languid or languishing eyes.

तान्तव tāntava, as, ī, am (fr. tantu), made of thread; (am), n. spinning, weaving; a web; a woven cloth.

Tāntavya, as, m. a patronymic from Tantu; (the fem. is tāntavyāyanī.)

Tāntuvāyya, as, m. (fr. tantu-vāya), the son of a weaver.

तान्त्र tāntra, as, ī, am (fr. tantra; rt. 3. tan), stringed, having wires or strings (as a musical instrument); relating to the Tantras &c.; (am), n. the music of a stringed instrument.

Tāntrika, as, ī, am, completely versed in any science or system, a scholar; a philosopher; relating to the Tantras, taught or contained in them, following them, &c.; tāntrikī sañjñā, a technical name; (as), m. a follower of the Tantra doctrine or mystical system of the Tantras.

तान्दन tāndana (?), as, m. wind.

तान्व tānva, as, ī, am (fr. tanū), Ved. belonging to one's own body or person, personal; (as), m. a patronymic from Tanva; (am), n., N. of a Sāman called after Tanva; (as, ā, am), forming the warp of a web, woven, spun; (Sāy.) a cloth for filtering the Soma; (perhaps for tanva by a metrical lengthening of the first syllable.)

Tānvaṅga, as, m. a patronymic from Tanv-aṅga.

ताप tāpa, as, m. (fr. rt. 2. tap), heat, glow, burning, torment, pain (mental or physical); fever; sorrow, affliction, distress; (ī), f., N. of the Taptī or Surat river; N. of the Yamunā or Jumnā river; [cf. paścāt-tāpa.] — Tāpa-hara, as, ī, am, removing heat; cooling; consoling, alleviating distress; (ī), f. a dish, a sort of soup of pulse and grain, first fried with ghee and turmeric and afterwards boiled with salt and sugar. — Tāpī-ja or tāpī-samudbhava, as, ā, am, produced near or occurring near the river Taptī; pyrites or another kind of mineral substance; a kind of gem. — Tāpeśvara-tīrtha (°pa-īś°), am, n., N. of a Tīrtha. — Tāpy-uttha-sañjñaka, am, n. = tāpya below.

Tāpaka, as, ā, am, heating, burning, inflaming; (as), m. fever, morbid heat.

Tāpatya, as, ā, am, relating to Tapatī (q. v.), treating of her; a metronymic from Tapatī, epithet of Kuru, also of Arjuna.

Tāpana, as, ī, am, burning, inflaming, heating, distressing [cf. indra-t° and candra-t°]; (as), m. the sun; the hot season; the sun-stone [cf. sūrya-kānta]; N. of one of the arrows of the god of love; (am), n. burning; distressing, chastising; a division of hell; gold; [cf. tapana.]

Tāpanīya, as, ā, am (fr. tapanīya), golden, made of gold; (ās), m. pl., N. of a school of the Vājasaneyi-saṃhitā or White Yajur-veda. — Tāpanīyopanishad (°ya-up°), t, f., N. of an Upanishad.

Tāpayāna, as, ā, am, warming, burning, illuminating.

Tāpayishṇu, us, us, u, Ved. heating, burning, causing pain.

Tāpaścita, am, n. (fr. tapaś-cit), N. of a sacrificial ceremony of long continuance; (as, ī, am), an epithet of the sacrificial fire used at this ceremony.

Tāpasa, as, ī, am (fr. tapas), performing penance, a practiser of austerities; devout; a hermit; a devotee, an ascetic; relating to religious penance or to an ascetic; (as), m., N. or epithet of a Hotṛi; a kind of crane, Ardea Nivea, = vaka; a kind of sugar-cane; a kind of plant, = damanaka; (ī), f., N. of two plants, viz. Curcuma Zedoaria and Jaṭāmāṃsī; (am), n. the leaf of the Laurus Cassia, = tamāla-pattra; [cf. tāpasa-ja.] — Tāpasa-ja, am, n. the leaf of the Laurus Cassia. — Tāpasa-taru, us, m. or tāpasa-druma, as, m. the tree of the ascetics, Terminalia Catappa [cf. iṅguda] or Putranjiva Roxburghii. — Tāpasadruma-sannibhā, f. a kind of plant, = garbha-dātrī. — Tāpasa-pattrī, f. the plant Artemisia Indica. — Tāpasa-priya, as, ā, am, dear to ascetics; (as), m. the tree Buchanania Latifolia, = priyāla; (ā), f. a kind of sugar-cane; a grape; Ganitrus Sphærica; Chironia Sapida, = rudrāksha. — Tāpasa-vriksha, as, m. = tāpasa-taru. — Tāpasādhyushita (°sa-adh°), as, ā, am, inhabited by hermits. — Tāpasāraṇya (°sa-ar°), am, n. a wood of hermits. — Tāpaseshṭa (°sa-ish°), as, m. the tree Buchanania Latifolia.

Tāpasya, am, n. asceticism, the condition of a devotee, penance.

Tāpāyana, ās, m. pl., N. of a school of the Vājasaneyi-saṃhitā or White Yajur-veda.

Tāpika in jala-tāpika, q. v.

Tāpita, as, ā, am, heated, inflamed, distressed, pained.

Tāpin, ī, inī, i, oppressed by heat, morbid, suffering from disease (moral or physical); anything heated or glowing; (ī), m. one of the deified saints of the Buddhists; (inī), f. a N. of the letter v; [cf. jala-tāpika.]

Tāpya, as, am, m. n. or tāpyaka, am, n. a mineral substance, sulphuret of iron.

तापिच्छ tāpiccha or tāpiñcha, as, m. the plant Xanthochymus Pictorius; [cf. tamāla.]

Tāpiñja, as, m. the plant Xanthochymus Pictorius; (am), n. = tāpīja, tāpya, sulphuret of iron.

तापिलट tāpilaṭa or tāpīlaṭa or tāpīlaṭa-deśa, as, m., N. of a country.

तापीमाहात्म्य tāpī-māhātmya, am, n., N. of a part of the Skanda-Purāṇa.

तावरिसाणु tābarisāṇu, N. of a country.

ताबुव tābuva, am, n., Ved. an antidote against poison.

ताम tāma, as, m. (fr. rt. tam), an object of terror; fault, defect, vice; anxiety, distress, desire.

तामर tāmara, am, n. water; ghee or oiled butter.

तामरस tāmarasa, am, n. a red-coloured lotus; gold; copper [cf. tāmra]; a metre consisting of four lines of twelve syllables each; (as), m. a kind of crane, Ardea Sibirica; (ī), f. a lotus pond.

तामलकी tāmalakī, f. the tree Flacourtia Cataphracta.

तामलिप्त tāmalipta, ās, m. pl., N. of a people in the south of Bengal; (am, ī), n. f., N. of the city and district inhabited by this people, the modern Tumlook or Tamoluk in the district of Midnapore; (also called tamoliptī, tāmralipta, dāmalipta; cf. also tamālikā and tamālinī.)

तामस tāmasa, as, ī, am (fr. tamas), dark; of or belonging to darkness; affected by or appertaining to the third quality or that of darkness (vice, ignorance, &c.); ignorant, vicious, malignant; relating to Manu Tāmasa; (as), m. a malignant or mischievous person, a villain, an incendiary; a snake; an owl; N. of the fourth Manu; N. of one of the attendants of Śiva; (ī), f. night; sleep; an epithet of Durgā; N. of a river, = jaṭāmāṃsī (in this sense a wrong reading for tāpasī); (am), n. darkness [cf. andha-tāmasa]; tāmasī tanūs, the form assumed by the Deity for the destruction of the world; tāmasī śaktis, the faculty of Tamas. — Tāmasa-kīlaka, as, m., N. of certain astronomical Ketus. — Tāmasa-guṇa, as, m. the quality of darkness; see guṇa. — Tāmasa-līna, as, ā, am, (in the Sāṅkhya phil.) one of the forms of a-tushṭi, dissatisfaction. — Tāmasa-vana, am, n. 'the dark wood,' N. of a forest.

Tāmasika, as, ī, am, dark, obscure, of or belonging to the quality of darkness, derived from it, teaching lessons so characterized, &c.

तामि tāmi, is or ī, f. (fr. rt. tam), restraining or keeping in the breath until it produces exhaustion; (also said to = tamī, night.)

तामिस्र tāmisra (fr. tamisra), scil. paksha, the dark half of the month, the time from full moon to new moon; (as), m. a Rākshasa (as going about in the dark); indignation at being disappointed or slighted, anger, one of the five forms of Avidyā in the Sāṅkhya system; a division of hell, that of deep gloom.

तामु tāmu, us, m., Ved. a praiser; (a various reading has stāmu.)

ताम्बली tāmbalī, f., N. of a kind of plant.

ताम्बूल tāmbūla, am, ī, n. f. (said to be fr. rt. tam), betel, Piper Betel, or rather its pungent and aromatic leaf, which together with the areca-nut and catechu and sometimes caustic lime and spices is eaten or chewed very generally by the natives of the east, acting as a carminative and antacid tonic, It is called Pān (fr. parṇa, 'a leaf,' the name betel being connected with vīṭikā, q. v.), and is presented to guests and visitors, and sometimes sent to relations and friends at family festivals, inclosed in gold or silver paper; (am), n. the areca-nut; (as), m. Bengal Saṇa or Crotolaria Juncea. — Tāmbūla-karaṅka, as, m. the Pān-dān or betel-box, (this box generally resembling a Karaṅka or hollowed cocoa-nut.) — Tāmbūla-da or tāmbūla-dāyaka or tāmbūla-dhara, as, m. the betel-bearer (who attended on kings and great men). — Tāmbūla-pattra, am, n. betel-leaf; (as), m. the Dioscorea Globosa; [cf. piṇḍālu.] — Tāmbūla-peṭikā, f. a betel-box. — Tāmbūla-bhakshaṇa, am, n. the eating of betel-leaf. — Tāmbūla-rāga, as, m. a kind of pulse, Ervum lens. — Tāmbūla-vallikā or tāmbūla-vallī, f. the betel plant (Piper Betel) bearing a pungent leaf; see above. — Tāmbūla-vāhaka, as, m. or tāmbūla-vāhin, ī, m. a betel-bearer, a servant attached to men of rank to prepare the Pān and carry the betel-box. — Tāmbūlākta (°la-ak°), as, ā, am, smeared with the juice of chewed betel. — Tāmbūlādhikāra (°la-adh°), as, m. the office of carrying the betel-box for persons of rank.

Tāmbūlika, as, m. a seller of betel.

Tāmbūlin, ī, inī, i, relating or belonging to betel, having betel, giving it, &c.; (ī), m. the Pān-bearer, a servant who prepares and furnishes the Pān; a seller of betel.

ताम्य tāmya, am, n. (?) = kloman.

ताम्यत् tāmyat, an, antī, at (fr. rt. tam), distressing, afflicting, annoying.

ताम्र tāmra, as, ā, am (said to be fr. rt. tam), of a coppery red colour, (tāmrā tvac, the fourth of the seven skins or membranes with which an embryo is covered); (*as*), m. a kind of leprosy with large red spots; N. of a man [cf. *tāmrāyaṇa*]; N. of an island [cf. *tāmra-dvīpa*]; (*ā*), f., N. of several plants, viz. = *mañjishṭhā*, Rubia Munjista, = *rakta-guñjā*, Abrus Precatorius, = *saiṇhalī;* N. of a daughter of Daksha, one of the wives of Kaśyapa, and mother of various birds; N. of a river; (*am*), n. a dark or coppery red; copper; a kind of sandal, represented as of a dark-red colour and smelling like a lotus; Ved. form, figure; (*as, ī, am*), made of copper; (*ī*), f. a copper or metallic cup of prescribed capacity and perforated by a small hole at the bottom, (when placed in a vessel of water it answers the purpose of a clepsydra, and the water gradually filling it marks the time that has elapsed); [cf. Hib. *umha*, 'copper.'] — *Tāmra-kaṇṭaka, as* or *am*, m. or n. (?), a kind of Acacia. — *Tāmra-karṇī*, f., N. of the female of one of the elephants of the quarters called Añjana; also of the elephant Śesha. — *Tāmra-kāra, as*, m. a brazier, a copper-smith. — *Tāmra-kili, is*, m. a small worm of a red colour; [cf. *tāmra-kṛimi.*] — *Tāmra-kuṭṭa, as, ī*, m. f. a brazier or copper-smith. — *Tāmra-kuṭṭaka, as*, m. = the last; tobacco(?). — *Tāmra-kuṇḍa, am*, n. a copper bason or other vessel; probably N. of a place. — *Tāmra-kūṭa, as, am*, m. n. a kind of plant, tobacco (?). — *Tāmra-kṛimi, is*, m. the lady-bird; cochineal. — *Tāmra-garbha, am*, n. blue vitriol or sulphate of copper. — *Tāmra-ćakshus, us*, m. a kind of pigeon. — *Tāmra-ćūḍa, as, ā, am*, red-crested; (*as*), m. a cock [cf. *tāmra-śikhin*]; a kind of plant (*kukkura-dru*); a particular position of the hand [cf. *tāmraćūḍaka*]; N. of a Pari-vrājaka; (*ā*), f., N. of one of the Mātṛis attending on Skanda. — *Tāmraćūḍaka, as*, m. (scil. *hasta*), a kind of theatrical gesticulation or motion of the hands. — *Tāmraćūḍa-bhairava, as*, m. a peculiar form of Bhairava. — *Tāmraćūḍādi-kathana* (°*ḍa-ād*°), *am*, n. 'explanation of the Tāmra-ćūḍa gesticulation &c.,' N. of a section of the Mantra-mahodadhi by Mahī-dhara — *Tāmrajāksha* (°*ja-ak*°), *as*, m., N. of a son of Kṛishṇa and Satya-bhāmā. — *Tāmra-tanu, us, us, u*, having a ruddy or fair complexion, copper-coloured. — *Tāmra-tuṇḍa, as*, m. a sort of monkey. — *Tāmra-trapuja*, brass. — *Tāmra-tva, am*, n. dark-red or copper colour, redness. — *Tāmra-dugdhā*, f. a species of plant, = *goraksha-dugdhā*. — *Tāmra-dru, us*, m. red sandal-wood. — *Tāmra-dvīpa, as*, m. the island Ceylon. — *Tāmra-dhātu, us*, m. red chalk. — *Tāmra-dhūmra, as, ā, am*, Ved. dark-red, coppery red. — *Tāmra-dhvaja, as*, m., N. of a man. — *Tāmra-netra, as, ā, am*, red-eyed. — *Tāmra-pakshā*, f., N. of a daughter of Kṛishṇa. — *Tāmra-pakshin, ī*, m., N. of a son of Kṛishṇa. — *Tāmra-paṭṭa, as*, m. a copper plate on which Hindū grants of land &c. are frequently inscribed; [cf. *tāmra-śāsana.*] — *Tāmra-pattra, am*, n. a copper plate; (*as*), m. a kind of pot-herb, = *jīva-śāka*. — *Tāmra-pattraka*, N. of the two plants Bauhinia Tomentosa and Capparis Aphylla. — *Tāmra-parṇa, am*, n., N. of a district renowned for a temple of Śiva, the ancient Taprobane; Ceylon; (*ī*), f. the plant Rubia Munjista (*mañjishṭhā*); a kind of pond or lake; N. of a river rising in Malaya and of the district in its vicinity, (the river is celebrated for its pearls); N. of a town in Ceylon, after which the whole island is by some called Tāmra-parṇī; [cf. *tāmra-dvīpa.*] — *Tāmraparṇīya, as*, m. (fr. the last), an inhabitant of Ceylon, especially a Buddhist. — *Tāmra-pallava, as*, m. the Aśoka tree. — *Tāmra-pākin, ī*, m. the tree Thespesia Populneoides and Hibiscus Populneoides. — *Tāmra-pātra, am*, n. a copper vessel. — *Tāmra-pādī*, f. a kind of plant related to the Mimosa Pudica, = *haṇsa-padī*. — *Tāmra-pushpa, am*, n. a copper-coloured or red flower; (*as*), m. the plant Bauhinia Variegata or a kind of ebony (*rakta-kāñćana*); another plant, Kæmpferia Rotunda (*bhūmi-ćampaka*); (*ī*), f., N. of several plants having red flowers, viz. Bignonia Suaveolens, Grislea Tomentosa, Ipomœa Turpethum (*tri-vṛit*); [cf. *tāmra-pushpikā.*] — *Tāmra-pushpaka, as*, m. Bauhinia Variegata or a kind of ebony; (*ikā*), f., N. of several plants, viz. = Bignonia Suaveolens, Grislea Tomentosa, also = Marāṭhī *rakta-niśottarā*. — *Tāmra-phala, as*, m. the tree Alangium Hexapetalum. — *Tāmra-phalaka, am*, n. a copper plate. — *Tāmra-maya, as, ī, am*, consisting of copper, coppery. — *Tāmra-māraṇa, am*, n. the decomposition of copper and its application as a remedy. — *Tāmra-mukha, as, ī, am*, copper-faced, fair-complexioned; (*as*), m. a European. — *Tāmra-mūlā* and *ī*, f., N. of several plants, Rubia Munjista, Alhagi Maurorum, Mimosa Pudica. — *Tāmra-mṛiga, as*, m. the red deer. — *Tāmra-rasāyanī*, f. a species of plant with a milky juice, = *tāmra-dugdhā*. — *Tāmra-lipta, ās*, m. pl., N. of a people near the western mouth of the Ganges; (*as*), m., N. of a Ṛishi; (*ā* or *ī*), f., N. of the capital of the Tāmra-liptas; [cf. *tāmaliptī.*] — *Tāmraliptaka, ās*, m. pl., N. of a people near the western mouth of the Ganges; (*ikā*), f., N. of the capital of this people, = *tāmra-liptā*. — *Tāmra-varṇa, as, ī, am*, copper-coloured, dark-red; (*as*), m. a kind of grass, = *pallivāha;* N. of one of the nine divisions of Bhārata-varsha; (*ā*), f. the China rose; (*ī*), f. the blossom of sesamum. — *Tāmra-varṇaka, as*, m. = *tāmra-varṇa*. — *Tāmra-vallī*, f. the plant Rubia Munjista; a medicinal plant used as an emollient in affections of the mouth and fauces; also called *tamālī, tālī, sūkshma-vallī*, &c. — *Tāmra-vīja, as*, m. a kind of vetch, Dolichos Uniflorus (*kulattha*). — *Tāmra-vṛiksha, as*, m. the plant Dolichos Uniflorus; a red sort of sandal-wood. — *Tāmra-vṛinta, as*, m. the plant Dolichos Uniflorus; (*ā*), f. another kind of Dolichos. — *Tāmra-śāṭīya, ās*, m. pl. 'having red vestments,' N. of a Buddhist school. — *Tāmra-śāsana, am*, n. an edict or grant &c. inscribed on copper; [cf. *tāmra-paṭṭa.*] — *Tāmra-śikhin, ī*, m. 'having a red crest,' a cock; [cf. *tāmra-ćūḍa.*] — *Tāmra-sāgara, as*, m., N. of an ocean. — *Tāmra-sāra, am*, n. a red kind of sandal, Pterospermum Santolinum. — *Tāmra-sāraka, as*, m. a sort of Khadira with red flowers; (*am*), n. red sandal-wood. — *Tāmra-sena, as*, m., N. of a king. — *Tāmrāksha* (°*ra-ak*°), *as, ī, am*, red-eyed; (*as*), m. a crow; the Indian cuckoo. — *Tāmrākhya* (°*ra-ākh*°), *as, ā, am*, N. of a kind of pearl, so called either because reddish in colour or because found in the river Tāmra-parṇī. — *Tāmrābha* (°*ra-ābh*°), *am*, n. red saunders. — *Tāmrāri* (°*ra-ari*), *is*, m. 'the copper-coloured enemy,' N. of a hostile people. — *Tāmrāruṇa* (°*ra-ar*°), *as*, m. a coppery red dawn; (*ā*), f., N. of a river; (*am*), n., N. of a Tīrtha. — *Tāmrārdha* (°*ra-ar*°), *am*, n. mixed or bell-metal. — *Tāmrā-vatī*, f., N. of a river. — *Tāmropajīvin* (°*ra-up*°), *ī*, m. a copper-smith. — *Tāmroshṭha* and *tāmraushṭha* (°*ra-osh*°), *au*, m. du. red lips; (*as, ā, am*), having red lips; (*as*), m., N. of a Yaksha.

Tāmraka, am, n. copper; (*ikā*), f. = *tāmrī*, the plant Abrus Precatorius, = *guñjā*.

Tāmrāyaṇa, as, m., N. of a pupil of Yājñavalkya; (also read *tāmrāyaṇi*.)

Tāmrika, as, ī, am, coppery, made of copper, &c.; (*as*), m. a brazier, a copper-smith; (for *tāmrikā* see *tāmraka*.)

Tāmriman, ā, m. redness, dark-red, copper colour, the colour of copper.

Tāmrī-kṛi, cl. 8. P. A. *-karoti, -kurute, -kartum*, to die red or a dark-red or coppery.

Tāmrya, am, n. a dark-red colour, redness.

ताम्राकु *tāmrāku, us*, m., N. of an Upa-dvīpa.

ताय् *tāy* [cf. rt. 3. *tan, trai, tay*], cl. 1. A. *tāyate, tatāye, tāyishyate, atāyi* and *atāyishṭa, tāyitum*, to spread, extend, proceed in a continuous stream or line; to cherish, protect.

Tāyana, am, n. proceeding or succeeding well; increase, growth.

ताय *tāya*, ? in Gaṇa to Pāṇ. VI. 1, 203.

तायादर *tāyādara*, ? Atharva-veda VI. 72, 2.

तायिक *tāyika, ās*, m. pl., N. of a country; the inhabitants of this country, = *tarjika*.

तायु *tāyu, us*, m. [cf. *stāyu;* Gr. τητάω], Ved. a thief.

तार *tāra, as, ā, am* (fr. rt. *tṛi*, or in the senses 'shining,' 'star,' &c., for *stāra* fr. rt. *stṛi*, to scatter rays of light, or according to others fr. rt. 2. *as*, cf. *astra*), all-pervading, all-conquering, a protector; an epithet of Rudra and Vishṇu; high (as a note in music), soprano; loud, shrill; a loud or shrill note, a high tone or note (in music); shining, radiant, radiating; clean, clear; good, excellent, well flavoured, &c.; (*as*), m. descent to a river, a bank [cf. *tīra* and *tīrtha*]; crossing, passing over, &c.; the clearness or transparency of a pearl, a clear or beautiful pearl; the (saving) mystical syllable *om* (*praṇava*); a mystical monosyllable in the Tantras; N. of a Daitya slain by Vishṇu; N. of one of Rāma's monkey generals, who was a son of Bṛihas-pati, and whose wife is called Tārā; N. of Maṇi-rāma, a commentator on the Bhāminī-vilāsa; (*as, ā, am*), m. f. n. a star in general, a fixed star, asterism, &c. [cf. *tṛi* and *stṛi*]; (*ā*), f. a star, planet, a kind of meteor, perhaps a falling star; the pupil of the eye, (according to some also m. and n.); N. of one of the eight Siddhis in the Sāṅkhya phil.; a kind of perfume; N. of the wife of Bṛihas-pati who was carried off by Soma; of a form of Dākshāyaṇī worshipped on the mountain Kishkindha, protectress of the Gṛitsa-madas; of the wife of Buddha Amogha-siddha; of one of the Jaina Śaktis; of a female monkey in the Rāmāyaṇa, daughter of Su-sheṇa, wife of Bālin and mother of Aṅgada; N. of the wife of Tāra; (*am*), n. silver; (*as, am*), m. n. camphor; (*am, ā*), n. f. a pearl; [cf. Zend *stārĕ;* Gr. ἀστήρ, ἄστρον; Goth. *stairno;* Lat. *aster, astrum, stella* for *sterula.*] — *Tāra-ja, as* or *am*, m. or n. (?), a kind of mineral substance. — *Tāra-taṇḍula, as*, m. a kind of Sorghum (*dhavala-yāvanāla*). — *Tāra-tama, as, ā, am*, very loud. — *Tāra-tāra, am*, n., N. of one of the eight Siddhis in the Sāṅkhya phil.; [cf. *tāra* and *tārā.*] — *Tāra-nātha, as*, m. (for *tārā-n*°), N. of a renowned Tibetian who lived in the beginning of the seventeenth century and wrote a history of Buddhism. — *Tāra-nāda, as*, m. a loud or shrill sound or cry. — *Tāra-patana, am*, n. the falling of a meteor, a falling star. — *Tāra-pāla, as*, m., N. of a lexicographer. — *Tāra-pushpa, as*, m. jasmine. — *Tāra-mākshika, am*, n. a kind of mineral substance, = *tāra-ja*. — *Tāra-mūla* and *tāra-mūlaka, am*, n., N. of a place. — *Tāra-vimalā*, f. a sort of mineral said to be of the colour of silver. — *Tāra-śuddhi-kara, am*, n. ('what refines silver'), lead. — *Tāra-sāra, as*, m., N. of an Upanishad. — *Tāra-svara, as, ā, am*, having a loud or shrill sound. — *Tārā-kavaća, am*, n., N. of a chapter in the Tantra-sāra by Kṛishṇānanda; see *kavaća*. — *Tārā-kāruṇya, am*, n. 'the compassion of Tārā,' N. of a chapter in the Rāmāyaṇa. — *Tārāksha* (°*rā-ak*°), *as, ī, am*, star-eyed, one whose eyes are stars; (*as*), m., N. of a Daitya, = *tārakāksha*, uncle of Dhūmrāksha and king of the Nishadhas. — *Tārā-graha*, 'star-planet,' i. e. one of the five lesser planets exclusive of the sun and moon. — *Tārā-ćakra, am*, n., N. of a mystical circle. — *Tārā-ćandra, as*, m., N. of a scholiast and of a king. — *Tārā-ććhāya, as, ā, am*, reflecting the stars. — *Tārādhipa, as*, m. or *tārādhipati* (°*rā-adh*°), *is*, m. 'ruler of the stars,' the moon. — *Tārādhīśa* (°*rā-adh*°), *as*, m., N. of a prince. — *Tārā-pajjhaṭikā*, f., N. of a hymn written by Saṅkarāćārya. — *Tārā-pati, is*, m. 'lord of the stars,' the moon; a N. of Bṛihas-pati as husband of Tārā; N. of Śiva; of the monkey Bālin; of a prince. — *Tārā-patha, as*, m. the path of the stars, the atmosphere, the firmament, heaven or sky; N. of a country. — *Tārāpaharaṇa* (°*rā-ap*°), *am*, n., N. of a chapter in the Brahmavaivarta-Purāṇa. — *Tārāpīḍa* (°*rā-āp*°), *as*, m. the moon ('having a chaplet of stars'); N. of several princes. — *Tārā-pramāṇa*, *am*, n. sidereal measure, sidereal time. — *Tārābha* (°*ra* or °*rā-ābha*), *as*, m. quicksilver, ('looking like silver or bright as the stars.') — *Tārā-bhūshā*, f. 'decorated with stars,' an epithet of the night. — *Tārābhra* (°*rā-abh*°), *as*, m. camphor. — *Tārā-maṇḍala*, *am*, n. the starry region, the sphere of the stars, the zodiac; the pupil of the eye; (*as*), m. a Śiva temple of a particular form or decorated in a peculiar manner. — *Tārā-mantra*, *as*, m., N. of a chapter in the Mantra-mahodadhi. — *Tārā-maya*, *as*, *ī*, *am*, consisting of stars. — *Tārā-mṛiga*, *as*, m. the star-antelope, the Nakshatra Mṛiga-śirsha. — *Tārāri* (°*ra-ari*), *is*, m. a pyritic ore of iron; see *viḍ-mākshika*. — *Tārā-rūpa*, *as*, *ā*, *am*, star-shaped, star-like. — *Tārā-vatī*, f., N. of a form of Durgā; of a daughter of Kakut-stha and Mano-māthinī, wife of king Candra-śekhara; of the wife of Dharma-dhvaja, who was a king of Kāñćana-pura. — *Tārā-varsha*, *am*, n. 'star-rain,' falling stars. — *Tārāvalī* (°*rā-āv*°), f., N. of a daughter of the Yaksha prince Maṇi-bhadra. — *Tārā-vākya*, *am*, n. 'the speech of Tārā,' N. of a chapter in the fourth book of the Rāmāyaṇa. — *Tārā-vilāpa*, *as*, m. 'the lamentation of Tārā,' N. of a chapter in the fourth book of the Rāmāyaṇa. — *Tārā-sthāna*, *am*, n. the place in the gamut for the treble notes, those of the higher octave. — *Tārendra* (°*rā-in*°), *as*, m. 'the prince of the stars,' N. of an author.

Tāraka, *as*, *ikā*, *am*, one who causes or enables to pass or go over, carrying over; rescuing; one who helps another through a difficulty &c.; a protector, a preserver (e.g. *tārakam brahma*, 'the saving prayer,' N. of a particular prayer which saves or liberates); belonging to the stars; (*as*), m. a pilot, a helmsman or steersman; a N. of Śiva; N. of a Daitya conquered by Indra with the assistance of Kārttikeya or Skanda; (Tāraka is also enumerated among the nine enemies of Vishṇu); N. of a friend of Sīmanta; (*ās*), m. pl. the children of Tāraka; (*as*, *am*), m. n. a float, a raft; (*akā*), f. a star; a meteor, a falling star, &c., (with Jainas constituting one of the five divisions of the Jyotishkas); a sort of coloquintida; N. of a daughter of Sunda; of the wife of Bṛihas-pati, usually called Tārā; also = *laghu-vṛindārana*; (*ikā*), f. the juice of palms, = *tāla-rasa*, commonly *tāḍī*; (*ā*, *am*), f. n. the pupil of the eye; the eye; (*am*), n., N. of a metre of four lines of thirteen syllables each. — *Tāraka-jaya*, *as*, m. 'conquest of Tāraka,' N. of a chapter in the Padma-Purāṇa. — *Tāraka-jit*, *t*, m. 'conqueror of Tāraka,' epithet of Skanda. — *Tāraka-tīrtha*, *am*, n., N. of a Tīrtha. — *Tāraka-vadha*, *as*, m. 'the killing of Tāraka,' N. of a chapter in the Śiva-Purāṇa. — *Tārakāksha* (°*kā-ak*°), *as*, *ī*, *am*, having stars for eyes; (*as*), m., N. of a Daitya, a son of Tāraka. — *Tārakākhya* (°*ka-ākh*°), *as*, m., N. of a Daitya, a son of Tāraka. — *Tārakāntaka* (°*ka-an*°), *as*, m. 'destroying Tāraka,' an epithet of Skanda. — *Tārakā-maya*, *as*, *ī*, *am* (*tārakā* = *tārā*), on account of Tārā, by reason of Tārā, (generally used as an epithet of either Saṅgrāma or Yuddha or Samara, i.e. the war waged by gods and demons for the rescue of Tārā, the wife of Bṛihas-pati, who had been carried off by Soma); a N. of Śiva, as taking part in that fight. — *Tārakā-māna*, *am*, n. sidereal measure, sidereal time. — *Tārakāri* (°*ka-ari*), *is*, m. 'the enemy of Tāraka,' an epithet of Skanda. — *Tārakopanishad* (°*ka-up*°), *t*, f. 'the saving or liberating Upanishad,' N. of an Upanishad.

Tārakāyaṇa, *as*, m. a patronymic from Tāraka.

Tārakita, *as*, *ā*, *am*, starry, star-spangled.

Tārakin, *ī*, *iṇī*, *i*, starry; (*iṇī*), f. night.

Tāraṇa, *as*, *ī*, *am*, who or what causes or enables to cross; helping over a difficulty &c.; liberating, saving; (*as*), m. a N. of Śiva and of Vishṇu; a raft, a float; (*am*), n. crossing, reaching the opposite shore, safe passage; conquering; carrying or conveying across, the act of saving or liberating; a sort of sacrificial vessel (?); N. of a Sāman; N. of the third year of the fourth Jupiter cycle.

Tāraṇi, *is*, f. = *taraṇi*, a boat, ship.

Tāraṇeya, *as*, m. a patronymic of Yāja and Upa-yāja.

Tārayitṛi, *tā*, *trī*, *tṛi*, a liberator, promoter, promoting, liberating.

Tārāyaṇa, *as*, m. the tree of salvation, the holy fig-tree.

Tārika, *am*, n. fare, freight, toll for passage.

Tārikā, f. See under *tāraka*, col. 1.

Tārita, *as*, *ā*, *am*, made to cross, conveyed across, saved.

Tārin, *ī*, *iṇī*, *i*, enabling or causing to get over or across, saving; (*iṇī*), f. a form of Durgā, = *dvitīyā śaktiḥ*; N. of a kind of goddess with Buddhists. — *Tāriṇī-tantra*, *am*, n., N. of a section of the Śakti-ratnākara.

Tāreya, *as*, m. a metronymic of the monkey Aṅgada; [cf. *tārā*.]

Tārya, *as*, *ā*, *am*, to be crossed, passable, to be carried across, to be ferried over, to be conquered or defeated; (*am*), n. fare, freight, toll.

तारक्षति tārakshati, *tārakshiti*, and *tirikshati*, N. of a district to the west of Madhya-deśa.

तारतम्य tāratamya, *am*, n. (an abstract noun from *tara* + *tama*, the affixes of the comparative and superlative degrees), gradation, proportion, the state or condition of more or less; dependance of larger numbers on smaller in a progressive series; (*ena*), ind. in different degrees, in various gradations.

तारदी tāradī, f. a kind of plant, = *taradī*; also read *tāraṭī* (*taraṭī*).

तारल tārala, *as*, *ī*, *am* (= *tarala*), unsteady; libidinous, dissipated, a lecher.

Tāralya, *am*, n. tremulousness, unsteadiness, libidinousness, wantonness.

ताराज् tā-rāj, *ṭ*, f., N. of a kind of Virāj metre.

तारिक tārika, tārin. See under *tāra* above.

तारीष tārīsha, an incorrect form for *tāvīsha*, q.v.

तारुक्षायणि tārukshāyaṇi, a patronymic from Tarukshа.

Tārukshya, *as*, m. a patronymic from Taruksha; (the fem. is *tārukshyāyaṇī*.)

तारुण tāruṇa, *as*, *ī*, *am* (fr. *taruṇa*), youthful, young, adolescent.

Tāruṇya, *am*, n. youth, youthfulness.

तार्कव tārkava, *as*, *ī*, *am* (fr. *tarku*), spun, woven, made with a spindle, belonging to a spindle.

तार्किक tārkika, *as*, *ī*, *am* (fr. *tarka*), related or belonging to the science of reasoning or logic, belonging to philosophy; (*as*), m. a dialectician, a logician, a philosopher, a sophist, a follower of one of the six schools of Hindū philosophy.

तार्क्ष tārksha, *as*, m. a kind of bird; a kind of plant; a N. of Kaśyapa; a wrong reading for *tārkshya*, i.e. Garuḍa; (*ī*), f. a sort of creeping plant, = *pātāla-garuḍī*. — *Tārksha-ja* = *tārkshya-ja*, q.v. — *Tārksha-putra* or *tārksha-suta*, *as*, m. 'the son of Tārksha or Kaśyapa,' i.e. Garuḍa.

Tārkshāka, a patronymic from Tṛikshāka.

Tārkshya, *as*, m. (a patronymic fr. *tṛiksha*), N. of a mythical being, described either as a horse or bird, and originally one of the personifications of the sun, which was represented under these forms; (the most ancient representation seems to have been that of the horse: in Mahā-bh. I. 2548, Tārkshya, Arishṭa-nemi, Garuḍa, Aruṇa, and Āruṇi are described as children of Kaśyapa and Vinatā; Tārkshya is also called Garuḍāgra-ja, the elder brother of Garuḍa: in Mahā-bh. III. 12660, mention is made of a Muni called Arishṭa-nemi Tārkshya, but in the epic and later literature Tārkshya is generally identified with Garuḍa, the bird and vehicle of Vishṇu and destroyer of the race of snakes); a N. of Garuḍa; a N. of Śiva; a Vedic hymn supposed to be composed by Arishṭa-nemi Tārkshya; a horse in general; a car, a chariot; a bird in general; N. of a race; a snake; the tree Vatica Robusta [cf. *tārkshya-prasava*]; a sort of antidote; gold; (*ī*), f. a wild creeper; (*am*), n. a kind of drug; a sort of collyrium. — *Tārkshya-ja* and *tārksha-ja*, *am*, n. a sort of collyrium. — *Tārkshya-dhvaja*, *as*, m. an epithet of Vishṇu (whose symbol is Garuḍa). — *Tārkshya-nāyaka*, *as*, m. 'the leader or chief of the birds,' an epithet of Garuḍa. — *Tārkshya-nāśaka*, *as*, m. 'destroyer of birds,' the bird Falco Calidus. — *Tārkshya-prasava*, *as*, m. the tree Vatica Robusta; [cf. *aśva-karṇa* and *tārkshya*.] — *Tārkshya-śaila*, *am*, n. a substance prepared from the calx of brass or from the Amomum Anthorrhiza, and used as a medical application to the eyes; [cf. *rasāñjana*.] — *Tārkshya-sāman*, *a*, n., N. of a Sāman.

Tārkshyāyaṇa, *as*, m. a patronymic from Tārkshya. — *Tārkshyāyaṇa-bhakta*, *am*, n. the district inhabited by the Tārkshyāyaṇas.

तार्ण tārṇa, *as*, *ī*, *am* (fr. *tṛiṇa*), made of grass; levied from grass (as a tax); (*as*, *ī*), m. f. a patronymic from Tṛiṇa.

Tārṇaka, *as*, *ī*, *am*, an adjective derived from Tṛiṇakīyā.

Tārṇakarṇa, a patronymic from Tṛiṇa-karṇa.

Tārṇavindavīya, *as*, *ā*, *am*, sacred to Tṛiṇa-vindu.

Tārṇāyana, a patronymic from Tṛiṇa.

तार्तीय tārtīya, *as*, *ā* or *ī* (?), *am* (fr. *tṛitīya*), belonging to the third; the third; (*am*), n. a third part. — *Tārtīyasavana* or *tārtīyasavanika*, *as*, *ī*, *am* (fr. *tṛitīya-savana*), belonging to the third Savana; [cf. *tri-shavaṇa*.] — *Tārtīyāhnika*, *as*, *ī*, *am* (fr. *tṛitīya* + *ahan*), belonging to the third day.

Tārtīyaka, belonging to the third, third.

Tārtīyīka, *as*, *ā*, *am*, the third.

तार्प्य tārpya, *am*, n., Ved. a garment made of a particular vegetable substance; (according to Sāy. derived fr. *tṛipā*, a kind of plant.)

तार्य tārya. See col. 2.

तार्ष्टघ tārshṭagha, *as*, m. (fr. *trishṭagha*?), a kind of tree; (*as*, *ī*, *am*), coming from or belonging to this tree.

ताल tāla, *as*, m. (fr. rt. *taḍ* or *tal*), the palmyra-tree or fan-palm, Borassus Flabelliformis, from the juice of which a sort of sugar or by fermentation a spirituous liquor is prepared; a measure of height (i.e. the palm-tree so considered, e.g. *prāsādo bahu-tāla-samutsedhaḥ*, a palace many palm-trees in height); a banner formed of the palm [cf. *tāla-ketu*, *tāla-dhvaja*, *tāla-bhṛit*, *tāla-lakshman*, *tālāṅka*]; slapping or clapping the hands together or against the opposite arm; clapping or flapping in general; the flapping of the ears of an elephant; beating time in music, musical time or measure; a musical instrument of bell-metal or brass, a sort of cymbal played with a stick; (in prosody) a trochee; an epithet of Śiva [cf. *tala*]; a short span, one measured by the thumb and middle finger; the open hand with the fingers extended, the palm; the hilt of a sword or sacrificial knife; a lock, a bolt; (*ās*), m. pl., N. of a people [cf. *apara-tāla* and *tāla-vana*]; (*as*, *am*), m. n. a division of hell [cf. *tala*]; = *haritāla*, yellow orpiment; (*ī*), f. the tree Corypha Taliera; a species of the mountain-palm; Corypha Umbraculifera; Flacourtia Cataphracta; Curculigo Orchioides; the spirituous juice of the palm, the common toddy; a fragrant earth, = *tuvarī*; a sort of key or instrument for opening a door, = *prati-tālī*; a sort of metre consisting of four lines of three long syllables each; (*am*), n. the fruit or nut of the palmyra-palm; orpiment; the throne of Durgā [cf. *manas-tāla*]; (*as, ī, am*), made of the palmyra-tree or of the palm-wood; [cf. *ucća-tāla, ut-t°, eka-t°, kara-t°, kāma-t°, krośa-t°*, &c.] — *Tāla-ketu, us*, m. 'having the palm-tree as a banner,' an epithet of Bhīshma; N. of an adversary of Kṛishṇa, slain by the latter; N. of a Dānava who was a younger brother of Pātāla-ketu. — *Tāla-kshīra, am*, n. an extract, = *tavakshīra.* — *Tāla-kshīraka, am*, n. the exudation of the palm. — *Tāla-garbha, as* or *am*, m. or n. (?), the fermented exudation of the palm-tree. — *Tāla-ćara, ās*, m. pl., N. of a race. — *Tāla-jaṅgha, as, ā, am*, having legs as long as a palm-tree; (*ās*), m. pl., N. of a warrior-tribe; (*as*), m. the prince of this tribe; N. of the ancestor of the Tāla-jaṅghas who was a descendant of Śaryāti; N. of a son of Jaya-dhvaja; of a Rakshas; of a Daitya. — *Tāla-jaṭā*, f. the fibres of the palm-tree under the outer bark. — *Tāla-dhvaja, as*, m. 'having the palm-tree as a banner,' a N. of Bala-rāma [cf. *tāla-bhṛit, tāla-lakshman, tālāṅka*]; N. of a mountain; (*ā*), f., N. of a town; (*ī*), f., N. of a river. — *Tāla-navamī*, f. the ninth day of the light half of the month Bhādra, sacred to Durgā. — *Tāla-pattra, am*, n. the palm-leaf, an oblong piece of the leaf used to write on with an iron stile; Trigonella Fœnum Græcum; a hollow cylinder of gold (or a palm-leaf used as a substitute) with or without a ring attached and thrust through the lobe of the ear as an ornament; (*ī*), f., N. of several plants, = *raṇḍā*, Salvinia Cucullata; Anethum Graveolens; Curculigo Orchioides. — *Tāla-parṇa, am, ī*, n. f. a kind of vegetable perfume, see *murā*; (*ī*), f. a sort of anise, Anethum Graveolens (*madhurikā*). — *Tāla-pushpaka, am*, n. a medicinal application to the eyes (= *pra-pauṇḍarīka*). — *Tāla-pralamba, am*, n. the fibres growing on the cocoa-nut and other palms under the outer rind, and from which a sort of cordage called coir is prepared, = *tāla-jaṭā.* — *Tāla-baddha* or *tāla-śuddha, as, ā, am*, measured, rhythmical, regulated by measure or musical time. — *Tāla-bhaṭa, as*, m., N. of a warrior. — *Tāla-bhṛit, t*, m. 'bearer of the palm-tree,' a N. of Bala-rāma; [cf. *tāla-dhvaja.*] — *Tāla-maya, as, ī, am*, made of the palm. — *Tāla-mardaka, as*, m. a kind of musical instrument. — *Tāla-mardala, as*, m. a cymbal. — *Tāla-mātra, as, ā, am*, of the measure of a palm-tree, as big as a palm; (*am*), ind. only a moment, i. e. one beat. — *Tāla-mūlikā* or *tāla-mūlī*, f. Curculigo Orchioides. — *Tāla-yantra, am*, n. a particular surgical instrument, a small pair of pincers; a lock, a lock and key. — *Tāla-rećanaka, as*, m. a dancer, actor; (a various reading has *tāla-većanaka.*) — *Tāla-lakshman, ā*, m. a N. of Bala-rāma; [cf. *tāla-dhvaja.*] — *Tāla-vana, am*, n. a grove of palmyra-trees; (*ās*), m. pl., N. of a race. — *Tāla-vṛinta, am*, n. a palm-leaf used as a fan, a fan in general; (*as*), m. a kind of Soma plant. — *Tāla-vṛintaka, am*, n. a fan. — *Tālavṛinta-nivāsin, ī*, m., N. of a scholiast. — *Tāla-većanaka*, see *tāla-rećanaka.* — *Tāla-śabda, as*, m. the noise caused by the falling of the fruit of the palm; clapping the hands; [cf. *tala-tāla.*] — *Tālākhyā* (°*la-ākh*°), f. = *tāla-parṇī*, a sort of vegetable perfume (*murā*). — *Tālāṅka* (°*la-aṅ*°), *as*, m. a N. of Bala-rāma [cf. *tāla-dhvaja*]; a N. of Śiva [cf. *tālin*]; a man marked with every fortunate spot or sign &c.; the leaf of a palm used for writing, the leaf of a book; a book; a saw; a sort of vegetable. — *Tālādhyāya* (°*la-adh*°), *as*, m., N. of the sixth book of the Saṅgīta-darpaṇa, treating of musical instruments. — *Tālāvaćara* (°*la-av*°), *as*, m. a dancer, an actor; (also read *tālāvaćaraṇa* and, less correctly, *tālārdha-ćaraṇa.*) — *Tāli-pattra, am*, n. = *tālīśa-pattra.* — *Tālīśa* (°*li-īśa*), *am*, n. or *tālīśa-pattra, am*, n. the tree Flacourtia Cataphracta, the leaves of which are used in medicine.

Tālaka, as, m. a kind of poisonous insect; N. of a teacher; of a prince; (*ikā*), f. the open palm of the hand [cf. *tālika*]; N. of two plants, = *tāla-mūlī* and *tāmra-vallī*; (*ī*), f. toddy or the fermented exudation of the palm; (*am*), n. = *tāla, hari-tāla*, yellow orpiment; a fragrant earth; a bolt, a latch, a kind of lock for fastening a door; a kind of ornament. — *Tālakābha* (°*ka-ābh*°), *as, ā, am*, ('like orpiment'), green; (*as*), m. green, the colour.

Tāli, is, f. Corypha Taliera; Flacourtia Cataphracta; [cf. *tāḍi*, and *tālī* under *tāla*, p. 371.]

Tālika, as, m. the open palm of the hand; clapping the hands; a tie, seal, string or cover for binding a letter, or parcel of papers, or the leaves of a manuscript; N. of a preceptor; [cf. *tālikā* under *tālaka.*]

Tālita, am, n. dyed or coloured cloth; a string, a tie; any musical instrument. — *Tālita-nagara, am*, n., N. of a town.

Tālin, ī, inī, i, 'furnished with cymbals,' an epithet of Śiva; (*inas*), m. pl. the pupils of Tala.

Tālī, compounded as a *gati* (q. v.) with the roots *as, bhū*, and *kṛi*; see also *tālī* under *tāla*, p. 371.

Tālīyaka, as or *am*, m. or n. (?), a cymbal.

तालकट *tālakaṭa* or *tālikaṭa* or *tālākaṭa, as*, m., N. of a country.

ताल्व्य *tālavya.* See under *tālu* below.

तालित *tālita.* See above.

तालिश *tāliśa, as*, m. a mountain.

तालीश *tālīśa, am*, n., N. of a tree or its leaf. — *Tālīśa-pattra, am*, n. the leaf of this tree; Flacourtia Cataphracta.

तालु *tālu, u*, n. (rarely used as masc.; said to be fr. rt. *tṛī*), the palate. — *Tālu-kaṇṭaka, as*, or *am*, m. or n. (?), a disease of the palate with children. — *Tālu-jihva, as*, m. a crocodile; the uvula. — *Tālu-pāka, as*, m. suppuration or abscess in the palate. — *Tālu-pāta* or *tālu-piḍaka, as*, m. a particular disease of the palate with children. — *Tālu-puppuṭa, as*, m. an indolent swelling of the palate. — *Tālu-mūla, am*, n. the root or back part of the palate. — *Tālu-viśoshaṇa, am*, n. the drying of the palate (through much talking &c.). — *Tālu-śosha, as*, m. morbid dryness of the palate. — *Tālu-sthāna, as, ā, am*, palatal.

Tālavya, as, ā, am, relating to the palate, palatal; (the palatal letters are formed by the contact of the tongue and the palate; they are *i, e, ai, ć, ćh, j, jh, ñ, y*, and *ś.*) — *Tālavya-varṇa, as*, m. a palatal letter.

Tāluka, am, n. the palate; a disease of the palate; *tālakā, e*, f. du. the two arteries of the palate.

Tālukin. See *kāka-tālukin.*

Tālūshaka = *tālu*, the palate.

तालुक्ष्य *tālukshya, as*, m. a patronymic from Taluksha; (the fem. is *tālukshyāyaṇī.*)

तालुन *tāluna*, adj. formed fr. *taluna.*

तालूर *tālūra, as*, m. a whirlpool, an eddy; (also written *tālura*; cf. *tānūra.*)

ताल्प *tālpa, as, ī, am* (fr. *talpa*), = *talpya*, offspring of the marriage-bed.

तावक *tāvaka* (fr. *tava*), *as, ī, am*, thy, thine.

Tāvakīna, as, ā or *ī* (?), *am*, thine.

तावत् *tāvat, ān, atī, at* (fr. the pronom. base 2. *ta*; correlative of *yāvat*), so great, so large, so much, so far, so long, so many, such (e. g. *tāvantas taṇḍulāḥ*, so many rice-grains; *yāvatā kshaṇena tāvatā*, after what time, in that time; *yāvanti tasya dvīpasya vastūni tāvanty upanetavyāni*, whatever are the commodities of that island, so many are to be brought); *tāvatā*, ind. in the mean time, during that time; to that extent; *tāvat*, ind. so much, so greatly, to such an extent, in such a number, so far, so long, in that time (correlatively to *yāvat*, e. g. *yāvat—tāvat*, as long as—so long; when—then; *yāvat trayas te jīveyus tāvan nānyaṃ samāćaret*, as long as those three live, so long he must perform no other duty), meanwhile, in the mean time, (often connected with *yāvat* and a negative, e. g. *tāvać ćhobate mūrkho yāvat kinćin na bhāshate*, so long a fool shines as long as he says nothing; or with omission of the negative, e. g. *śoshayishyāmy ātmānaṃ tāvad yāvan me prāptum brāhmaṇyam*, so long I will emaciate myself as long as, i. e. until I have obtained the state of a Brāhman); at once, now, just, (often connected rather redundantly with an imperative or with a potential or the verb *arh*, e. g. *gaććha tāvat* or *gaććhes tāvat*, go now; *tat tāvad vākyaṃ kshantum arhasi*, deign now to pardon that speech); indeed, really, truly, well, (as an emphatic particle, or to express assent, e. g. *dṛiḍhas tāvad bandhaḥ*, the knot is tight I must admit; *gatā tāvat*, she is indeed gone; sometimes connected in this sense with the particle *eva*, e. g. *vikrayas tāvad eva saḥ*, it is really a sale.) *Na tāvat*, not at all; not yet (e. g. *na tāvad dṛiśyate sūryaḥ*, the sun is not yet visible); *itas tāvat*, away then I just come hither; *mā tāvat*, by no means, God forbid! *yāvat—dvis-tāvat*, as long—twice so long. According to the lexicographers *tāvat* may imply measure, limitation, totality, restriction, surprise, emphasis, &c.; [cf. Lat. *tantus* fr. *tavantus*; Gr. τόσος, τῆμος.] — *Tāvaććhata* (°*vat-śa*°), *as, ī, am*, a measure containing so many hundreds. — *Tāvać-ćhas* (*tāvat-śas*), ind., Ved. in so many ways, so manifoldly. — *Tāvat-kālam*, ind. for so long a period, for such a time. — *Tāvat-kṛitvas*, ind. so many times. — *Tāvat-phala, as, ā, am*, having such results. — *Tāvad-guṇa, as, ā, am*, having so many qualities. — *Tāvad-dvayasa, as, ī, am*, measuring so much, so long, &c. — *Tāvad-dhā*, ind. in that number, in such a number; so many times, so often. — *Tāvad-varsha, as, ā, am*, so many years old. — *Tāvad-vyakta*, (in alg.) a known number annexed to an unknown quantity. — *Tāvan-mātra, as, ī, am*, just so much, just so many. — *Tāvan-māna, as, ā, am*, measuring so much.

Tāvatika, as, ā, am, bought for so much, worth so much, of so great value; [cf. *tāvatka.*]

Tāvatitha, as, ī, am, the so manieth, such a one (of a number).

Tāvatka, as, ā, am, bought for so much, worth so much, of so much value, &c.; [cf. *tāvatika.*]

तावर *tāvara, am*, n. a bow-string.

ताविष *tāvisha, as, ī*, m. f. the ocean; heaven or paradise; gold; [cf. *tavisha.*]

Tāvisha, as, m. the ocean; heaven or paradise; gold; (*ī*), f. a river; the earth; N. of a daughter of Indra; N. of a daughter of the moon (?); [cf. *tavisha.*]

तावुरि *tāvuri, is*, m. (borrowed fr. the Gr. ταῦρος), the sign of the Zodiac Taurus.

तासीर *tāsīra* = *tasīra*, q. v.

तास्कर्य *tāskarya, am*, n. (fr. *taskara*), theft, robbery, larceny.

तास्यन्द्र *tāsyandra* or *tāsvindra, am*, n., N. of a Sāman.

ति *ti* = *iti* in the Śatapatha-Brāhmaṇa.

तिक् *tik*, cl. 1. A. *tekate*, &c., to go or move [cf. rt. *tīk*]; cl. 5. P. *tiknoti*, &c., to go or move; to assail, assault; to wound; to seek to injure or kill; to challenge; [cf. rt. *tig* and *stigh.*]

तिक *tika, as*, m., N. of a man. — *Tika-kitava, ās*, m. pl. the descendants of Tika and Kitava.

Tikīya, as, ā, am, an adj. derived from Tika.

तिक्त *tikta.* See rt. *tij*, p. 373, col. 1.

तिग् *tig*, cl. 5. P. *tignoti*, &c., to go or move; to assail, assault; to seek to injure or kill; [cf. rt. *tik.*]

तिगल *tigala* (?), *as*, m., N. of a man.

तिग्म *tigma.* See next page, col. 2.

तिघ् *tigh*, cl. 5. P. *tighnoti*, &c., to strike; to hurt or kill.

तिङ्गुद *tinguda, as*, m. (a wrong reading for *tinduka*), N. of a plant.

तिज् *tij*, cl. 1. P. A., Ved. *tejati, -te*, Ved. Inf. *tejase*, to be or become sharp; to sharpen: Caus. P. *tejayati, -yitum*, to sharpen, whet; to stir up, excite, incite, urge on: Desid. A. *titikshate*, to desire to become sharp or firm, to resist, oppose, to bear with firmness, suffer with courage or patience, endure, bear: Intens. Ved. *tetikte*; [cf. Zend *tigh-ra*, 'pointed, peaked;' *tigh-ri*, 'an arrow:' Gr. *στίζ-ω, στίγ-μα, στιγ-μή, στικ-τό-ς*: Lat. *di-sting-u-o* (δια-στίζω), *in-stinc-tu-s, in-stiga-re, sti-mulu-s* for *stig-mulu-s, sti-lu-s* for *stig-lu-s*: Goth. *us-stiggan*, 'to sting;' *têka*, 'to touch;' *stiggqvan, stik-s, stak-s*: Old Germ. *sting-u, stihhu*, 'I sting;' *stachila*, 'a prickle;' *stihhil*, 'a stile:' Angl. Sax. *stician*, 'to sting:' Lith. *tékinu*, 'I whet;' *tékėlis*, 'a large whetstone:' Russ. *točū*, 'I whet;' *točilo*, 'a whet-stone:' Cambro-Brit. *teg*, 'clear, fair, beautiful, pretty, bland.']

Tikta, as, ā, am, bitter (as sharpening the appetite), pungent; fragrant; *(as)*, m. a bitter taste; one of the six modifications of flavour *(rasa)*; bitterness, pungency; fragrance, perfume; N. of several plants, viz. Wrightia Antidysenterica (= *kuṭaja*); Capparis Trifoliata (= *varuṇa*); Agathotes Chirayta (= *kirāta-tikta*); Melia Azadirachta; Terminalia Catappa (= *ingudī*); a bitter sort of cucumber, Trichosanthes Cucumerina (?); a kind of salt; *(ā)*, f., N. of several plants, viz. Helleborus Niger (= *kaṭu-rohiṇī*); Clypea Hernandifolia (= *pāṭhā*); Artemisia Sternutatoria; *(am)*, n. a medicinal plant, Mollugo Pentaphylla. — *Tikta-kandakā*, f. Curcuma Zedoaria. — *Tikta-gandhā* or *tikta-gandhikā*, f. mustard, Lycopodium Imbricatum. — *Tikta-guñjā*, f. Pongamia Glabra, = *karañja*. — *Tikta-ghṛita, am*, n. a mixture of Ghṛita with bitter herbs &c. — *Tikta-taṇḍulā*, f. long pepper. — *Tikta-tuṇḍī*, f. = *kaṭu-tuṇḍī*. — *Tikta-tumbī*, f. = *kaṭu-tumbī*, a bitter gourd. — *Tikta-dugdhā*, f., N. of several plants, = *kshīriṇī, aja-śṛingī, svarṇa-kshīrī*. — *Tikta-dhātu, us*, m. bile. — *Tikta-pattra, as*, m. a cucurbitaceous plant, Momordica Mixta. — *Tikta-parvan, ā*, f., N. of several plants, viz. Cocculus Cordifolius; Hingcha (= *hilamoći*) Repens; Panicum Dactylon, = *madhu-yashṭi*; liquorice. — *Tikta-pushpā*, f. Clypea Hernandifolia; Bignonia Suaveolens. — *Tikta-phala, as*, m. Strychnos Potatorum [cf. *kataka*]; *(ā)*, f., N. of several plants, = *yava-tiktā, vārtākī, shaḍ-bhujā*. — *Tikta-bhadraka, as*, m. a kind of cucumber, Trichosanthes Dioica. — *Tikta-marića, as*, m. Strychnos Potatorum; [cf. *kataka*.] — *Tikta-yavā*, f., N. of a plant, = *śankhinī*. — *Tikta-rohiṇikā* or *tikta-rohiṇī*, f. a medicinal plant, = *kaṭu-rohiṇī*. — *Tikta-vallī*, f. the plant Sanseviera Roxburghiana. — *Tikta-vījā*, f. a kind of cucumber, = *kaṭu-tumbī*. — *Tikta-śāka, as*, m. 'bitter herbs or greens,' N. of several plants, viz. Capparis Trifoliata; Acacia Catechu, a kind of Mimosa [cf. *khadira*]; = *pattra-sundara*. — *Tikta-sāra, as*, m. the plant Acacia Catechu; *(am)*, n. a kind of fragrant grass. — *Tiktākhyā* (°*ta-ākh*°), f. the plant Tikta-tuṇḍī. — *Tiktāngā* (°*ta-an*°), f. a kind of creeper, = *pātāla-garuḍī*. — *Tiktāmṛitā* (°*ta-am*°), f. Menispermum Glabrum. — *Tiktāyana* (°*ta-ay*°), *as, ī, am*, Ved. possessing the heat or radiance of fire.

Tiktuka, as, ā, am, bitter; anything having a bitter flavour; *(as)*, m., N. of several plants, viz. Trichosanthes Dioica; Agathotes Chirayta; a sort of Acacia Catechu; Terminalia Catappa [cf. *kirāta-tiktaka*]; *(ā)*, f. a kind of gourd (*kaṭu-tumbī*); Cardiospermum Halicacabum, = *karañja-vallī*; *(ikā)*, f. a kind of gourd (*kaṭu-tumbī*); [cf. *jala-tiktikā*.]

Tigita, as, ā, am, Ved. sharp, pointed.

Tigma, as, ā, am, sharp, pointed (as a weapon or as flame or a ray of light); violent; hot; pungent, acrid; scorching; fiery, passionate, hasty; *(as)*, m., N. of a prince; *(am)*, n. heat; a pungent or hot flavour, the heat of spices, pungency; [cf. *tīkshṇa*; cf. also Hib. *time*, 'heat, warmth.'] — *Tigma-kara, as*, m. 'hot-rayed,' the sun; [cf. *tigma-dīdhiti, tigma-raśmi, tigmānśu*.] — *Tigma-ketu, us*, m., N. of a son of Svar-vīthi and Vatsara. — *Tigma-ga, as, ā, am*, going or flying swiftly. — *Tigma-jambha, as, ā, am*, Ved. having sharp teeth, an epithet of Agni. — *Tigma-tā*, f. or *tigma-tva, am*, n. sharpness, pungency; heat; passion, petulance. — *Tigma-tejas, ās, ās, as*, Ved. sharp-edged, sharp-pointed; penetrating, pervading; of a violent character. — *Tigma-dīdhiti, is*, m. the sun; [cf. *tigma-kara*.] — *Tigma-bhrishṭi, is, is, i*, Ved. sharp-pointed, a N. of Agni. — *Tigma-yātanā*, f. acute pain, agony, torment. — *Tigma-raśmi, is*, m. the sun; [cf. *tigma-kara*.] — *Tigma-ruć, k, k, k*, shining brightly, hot; *(k)*, m. the sun. — *Tigma-vat, ān, atī, at*, Ved. containing the word *tigma*. — *Tigma-śṛinga, as, ā, am*, Ved. having sharp horns. — *Tigma-śoćis, is, is, is*, Ved. having sharp rays, epithet of Agni. — *Tigma-heti, is, is, i*, Ved. having sharp weapons (or flames); forming a sharp weapon (as the horns of Agni). — *Tigmānśu* (°*ma-an*°), *us, us, u*, having sharp rays or warm beams; *(us)*, m. the sun; fire; an epithet of Śiva. — *Tigmātman* (°*ma-āt*°), *ā*, m., N. of a prince, son of Urva. — *Tigmānīka* (°*ma-an*°), *as, ā, am*, Ved. sharp-pointed; (Sāy.) sharp-mouthed. — *Tigmāyudha* (°*ma-āy*°), *as, ā, am*, Ved. having or casting or forming sharp weapons. — *Tigmeshu* (°*ma-ishu*), *us, us, u*, Ved. having sharp arrows.

Titiksha, as, m. (fr. Desid. of rt. *tij*), N. of a man; *(ā)*, f. endurance, patience, resignation, suffering, forbearance; Patience personified as a daughter of Daksha and wife of Dharma and mother of Kshema.

Titikshita, as, ā, am, borne, endured, suffered.

Titikshu, us, us, u, bearing, enduring patiently, patient, resigned, forbearing; *(us)*, m., N. of a son of Mahā-manas and descendant of Janam-ejaya.

तिजिल *tijila, as*, m. (said to be fr. rt. *tij*), the moon; a Rakshas.

तिटिभ *tiṭibha*, a particular high number; (also read *tiṭilambha*.)

तिणिस *tiṇisa, as*, m. = *tiniśa*, q. v.

तिण्टी *tiṇṭī*, f. a plant, commonly Teori, Convolvulus Turpethum (= *tri-vṛit*).

तितउ *tita-u, us, u*, m. n. (said to be fr. rt. 3. *tan* by a kind of reduplication, cf. *τιταίνω*; but perhaps fr. rt. *tans*), a sieve, a cribble; a parasol; [cf. *ćālanī*.]

तितनिषु *titanishu, us, us, u* (fr. Desid. of rt. 3. *tan*), desirous of extending or enlarging.

तितिक्ष *titiksha*. See above.

तितिभ *titibha, as*, m. an insect, cochineal.

तितिरि *titiri, is*, m. = *tittiri*, a partridge.

तितिल *titila, am*, n. a sort of sweetmeat made of sesamum ground and baked with sugar; one of the seven Karaṇas or astronomical periods; a bowl or bucket, = *nandaka*.

तितीर्षा *titīrshā*, f. (fr. Desid. of rt. *tṛī*), desire of crossing over, wish to pass, wish to be freed from mundane existence, desire of final emancipation.

Titīrshu, us, us, u, desirous of crossing; wishing to attain; desirous of emancipation from existence.

तित्तिड *tittiḍa* and *tittiḍīka*, incorrect forms for *tintiḍa* and *tintiḍīka*.

तित्तिर *tittira, as*, m. = *tittiri*, col. 3; *(ās)*, m. pl., N. of a race.

तित्तिरि *tittiri, is*, m. (said to be fr. rt. *tṛī*, but perhaps an onomatopoetic word fr. the cry *titti*), the francoline partridge; N. of a Muni, pupil of Yāska, and said to be the first teacher of the Taittirīya or Black Yajur-veda; (according to a legend the pupils of Vaiśampāyana became partridges in order to pick up the Veda which was vomited forth in a tangible shape by Yājñavalkya; cf. *taittirīya*); N. of a Nāga; [cf. Gr. *τέτριξ, τέτραξ, τετράων, τετράζω*; Old Island. *thid-r*, 'a kind of hen;' Lith. *tetĕrva*, 'black grouse;' Boh. *tetrev*.]

Tittirika, as, m. the francoline partridge.

Tittirika, as, ā, am, variegated like a partridge (*tittiri*) or made of Croton Tiglium (*tittirī-phala*).

Tittirī-phala (*tittirī* = *tittiri* ?), Croton Tiglium.

तिथ *titha, as*, m. (said to be fr. rt. *tij*), fire; love; time; autumn.

तिथि *tithi, is, ī*, m. f. (said to be fr. rt. *at*), a lunar day, the thirtieth part of a whole lunation, (the auspicious Tithis are Nandā, Bhadrā, Vi-jayā, Pūrṇā); the number 15; [cf. *janma-tithi*.] — *Tithi-kshaya, as*, m. the day of new moon; the day or space in which a Tithi begins or ends without one sunrising; the difference between the solar and lunar days in a Yuga. — *Tithi-tattva, am*, n., N. of the seventh section of the Smṛiti-tattva, treating of lunar holidays, by Raghu-nandana. — *Tithitattva-ṭīkā*, f., N. of the commentary on the preceding work by Kāśī-rāma. — *Tithi-dāna, am*, n., N. of a chapter of the second part of the Bhavishya-Purāṇa, treating of the observance of various ceremonies. — *Tithi-dvaita, am*, n., N. of a chapter of the Purāṇa-sarva-sva by Halāyudha. — *Tithi-niyama, as*, m., N. of a chapter of the Tantra-sāra, or compendium of Tantra doctrine, by Krishṇānanda. — *Tithi-nirṇaya* and *tithinirṇaya-sankshepa, as*, m., N. of two astronomical works. — *Tithi-pati, is*, m. = *tithīśa*. — *Tithi-pattrī*, f. an almanack. — *Tithi-pālana, am*, n. observance of the rites appointed for the several lunar days. — *Tithi-prakaraṇa, am*, n., N. of a chapter of the Cintā-maṇiḥ Sāraṇikā or Tithi-sāraṇikā, treating of astronomical periods and constellations, by Daśa-bala; N. of a chapter of the Jyotisha-ratna-mālā, an astronomical work by Śrī-pati. — *Tithi-praṇī, is*, m. 'the leader of the lunar days,' the moon; [cf. *dina-praṇī*.] — *Tithi-vāra-yoga, ās*, m. pl., N. of a chapter of the Purāṇa-sarva-sva. — *Tithi-viveka, as*, m., N. of a chapter of the Saṃskāra-tattva by Raghu-nandana, treating of the Indian sacraments. — *Tithi-vṛiddhi, is*, f. that day or space in which a Tithi commences before or with one sunrise and ends after or at the next, thus completed under two suns. — *Tithīśa* (°*thi-īśa*), *as*, m. the regent of a lunar day. — *Tithy-anta-nirṇaya, as*, m., N. of a chapter of the Smṛity-artha-sāra by Śrī-dhara-svāmin, treating of the Indian ceremonies. — *Tithy-ardha, as, am*, m. n. half a Tithi, = *karaṇa*.

तिनाशक *tināśaka, as*, m. a tree, = *tiniśa*.

तिनिका *tinikā*, f. Holcus Sorghum.

तिनिश *tiniśa, as*, m. the tree Dalbergia Ougeinensis; [cf. *tiṇisa* and *timiśa*.]

तिन्तिड *tintiḍa, as*, m. the tamarind tree, Tamarindus Indica; acid seasoning, sour sauce, especially a sauce made of the fruit of the tamarind tree; an inauspicious period, the evil aspect of planets (?); *(ī)*, f. the Indian tamarind tree; a sour sauce, especially one made of the fruit of the tamarind tree; Emblic Myrobalan. — *Tintiḍi-dyūta, am*, n. a kind of game, a sort of odd or even played with tamarind seeds.

Tintiḍikā, f. the tamarind tree.

Tintiḍīka, as, ā, am, m. f. n. the tamarind tree; *(am)*, n. the fruit of the tamarind; a sour sauce, especially one made of the fruit of the tamarind tree.

Tintilī or *tintilikā* or *tintīlikā*, f. the tamarind tree.

तिन्दिश *tindiśa*, *as*, m. a kind of plant, = *ṭinḍiśa*.

तिन्दु *tindu*, *us*, m. a species of ebony, from the fruit of which is obtained a kind of resin used in India as pitch for caulking vessels &c., Diospyros Glutinosa; also Strychnos Nux Vomica.

Tinduka, *as*, m. the tree Diospyros Embryopteris or Diospyros Glutinosa; (*ī*), f. the resinous fruit of this tree; (*am*), n. the fruit of this tree; a Karsha, a kind of measure or weight (= the weight of the Tinduka fruit).

Tinduki, *is*, f. or *tindula*, *as*, m. the tree Diospyros Embryopteris.

Tindukinī, f. the senna plant, = *ārartakī*.

तिन्दुविल्व *tinduvilva*, *am*, n., N. of the birthplace of the Lyric poet Jaya-deva.

तिप् *tip*, cl. 1. P. *tepati*, &c., to sprinkle, to distil or drop, to ooze or leak.

तिम् *tim*, cl. 4. P. *timyati*, *titema*, &c., to be or become wet or damp &c.; to become pacified or quiet: Intens. *tetimyate*; [cf. rt. *tim* and *stim*.]

Timita, *as*, *ā*, *am*, moistened, moist, wet, damp; quiet; unmoved, unshaken; steady, fixed.

तिमि *timi*, *is*, or sometimes *tima*, *as*, m. (said to be fr. rt. *tam*), a kind of whale or fabulous fish of an enormous size, said to be 100 Yojanas long; a fish in general; the figure of a fish produced by drawing two lines, one intersecting the other at right angles; the ocean; N. of a son of Dūrva and father of Bṛihad-ratha; (*is*, *ī*), f. a fish; N. of a daughter of Daksha who was the wife of Kaśyapa and mother of the sea-monsters. — *Timi-kosha* or *timi-koshaka*, *as*, m. the ocean ('the receptacle of great fish'). — *Timin-gila*, *as*, m. 'swallowing even the Timi,' a large fabulous fish; (*ās*), m. pl., N. of a people in Dakshiṇā-patha; (*as*), m. a prince of this people. — *Timingila-gila*, *as*, m. a large fabulous fish ('swallowing even the Timin-gila'). — *Timi-ja*, *as*, *ā*, *am*, coming or derived from the Timi, a sort of pearl. — *Timi-timin-gila*, *as*, m. a large fabulous fish. — *Timi-dhvaja*, *as*, *ā*, *am*, 'having a Timi depicted in his banner,' epithet of the Asura Śambara, prince of Vaijayanta; (*as*), m., N. of a man.

तिमित *timita*. See under rt. *tim* above.

तिमिर *timira*, *as*, *ā*, *am* (said to be fr. rt. *tim*, but rather related to *tamas* fr. rt. *tam*), dark, gloomy; (*am*), n. darkness; darkness of the eyes, blindness; a class of morbid affections of the eyes seated in the *paṭala* or coats of the eye; gutta serena, total blindness from affection of the optic nerve; iron-rust; a sort of aquatic plant [cf. *timīra* and *timisha*]; (*am*, *ā*), n. f., N. of two towns. — *Timira-nud*, *t*, *t*, *t*, dispelling darkness; (*t*), m. the sun; the moon. — *Timira-pratishedha*, *am*, n., N. of a chapter of the Uttara-tantra or sixth book of the Ashṭāṅga-hṛidaya-saṃhitā by Vāg-bhaṭa, treating of medicine. — *Timira-maya*, *as*, *ī*, *am*, consisting of darkness; (*as*), m. an epithet of Rāhu (who creates darkness), or an eclipse in general. — *Timira-ripu*, *us*, m. 'the enemy of darkness,' the sun. — *Timirāri* (°*ra-ari*), *is*, m. 'the enemy of darkness,' the sun. — *Timirodghāṭa* (°*ra-ud*°), N. of a treatise in verse connected with the Śaiva dogmas.

Timiraya, nom. P. *timirayati*, *-yitum*, to obscure, darken, eclipse.

Timirāya, nom. A. *timirāyate*, &c., to appear dark, to darken.

Timirin, *ī*, m. the cochineal insect.

तिमिरि *timiri*, a kind of fish (not the *timi*).

तिमिर्घ *timirgha*, *as*, m., N. of a man with the patronymic Daureśruta.

तिमिश *timiśa*, probably a wrong reading for *tiniśa*.

तिमिष *timisha*, *as*, m. a kind of pumpkin-gourd, Benincasa Cerifera; a water-melon (*nāṭāmra*).

तिमीर *timīra*, *as*, m. a kind of tree; [cf. *timira*.]

तिरय *tiraya*. See next col.

तिरश्च् *tiraść*, &c. See under *tiryañć*.

तिरस् *tiras*, ind. (fr. rt. *tṝ*, the *as* being probably the ablative termination), through (with acc. in Ved., e. g. *tiraḥ pavitram*, through the strainer; *tiras tamāṇsi darśataḥ*, discernible through the darkness); across, beyond, over (e. g. *nadīm tiras*, across the river; *rajāṇsi tiras*, over the world; *te nas tiro viśvāni duritā nayanti*, they lead us over all difficulties); without (i. e. in such a manner as to pass by or leave on one side); apart from, on one side of, aside, secretly from, 'clam' (with acc., e. g. *tiras ćittāni*, without the knowledge; *tiro raśam*, against the will; or sometimes with abl., e. g. *manushyebhyas tiras*, on one side of the men); crookedly, obliquely, awry; transversely, indirectly, badly, secretly, covertly; [cf. Lat. *trans*: Goth. *thairh*: Germ. *durch*: Hib. *tar*, *tair*, 'beyond, over, across, through; bad;' *tri*, 'through, by:' Lith. *tiēs*: Zend *tarō*.] — *Tiras-kara*, *as*, *ī*, *am*, leaving on one side, passing by, surpassing, excelling. — *Tiras-karin*, *ī*, *iṇī*, m. f. a curtain, veil; an outer tent, kanāt, wall, or screen of cloth surrounding the principal tent; a kind of magical veil rendering the wearer invisible. — *Tiras-kāra*, *as*, m. placing aside, concealment, disappearance; disrespect, abuse, reproach, censure, disgrace, disdain. — *Tiras-kāriṇī*, f. a curtain, = *tiras-kariṇī*. — *Tiras-kudya* or *tiras-prākāra*, *as*, *ā*, *am*, looking through a wall. — *Tiras-kṛi* or *tiraḥ kṛi*, cl. 8. P. *-karoti*, *-kartum*, to put on one side, set aside, remove, cover, conceal; to pass by, surpass, excel, conquer; to blame, reproach, abuse, treat disrespectfully, contemn, despise; [according to Pāṇini I. IV. 71, 72, *tiras* must be a *gati* (q. v.), in the sense of 'covering,' 'concealing,' but an option is allowed in its connection with rt. 1. *kṛi*.] — *Tiras-kṛita*, *as*, *ā*, *am*, concealed, hidden, veiled, vanished, disappeared; censured, reviled, abused, reproached, scorned. — *Tiras-kṛitya* (or *tiraḥ kṛitvā*), ind. having concealed. — *Tiras-kriyā*, f. concealment, disappearance; disrespect, reproach, contempt. — *Tiro-ahnya* or *tiro-'hnya*, *as*, *ā*, *am* (the former form occurring in the Veda, the latter in the Brāhmaṇas and later writings), more than one day old, prepared the day before yesterday. — *Tiro-gata*, *as*, *ā*, *am*, disappeared, vanished, out of sight. — *Tiro-janam*, ind., Ved. apart from men. — 1. *tiro-dhā* or *tiro dhā*, cl. 3. P. A. *dadhāti*, *dhatte*, *dhātum*, to place on one side, set aside, remove out of the way, cover, conceal, hide; to hide one's self from (with abl.), disappear; to overpower, conquer: Pass. *tiro-dhīyate* or *tiro dhīyate*, to be hidden, to vanish, disappear. — 2. *tiro-dhā*, f., Ved. concealment, secrecy. — *Tiro-dhātavya*, *as*, *ā*, *am*, to be covered or concealed, to be closed. — *Tiro-dhāna*, *am*, n. disappearance, vanishing, the being hidden or the act of hiding, concealing, &c.; a covering, a sheath, a veil, a cloth or cloak, anything which conceals from sight. — *Tiro-bhavitṛi*, *tā*, *trī*, *tṛi*, disappearing. — *Tiro-bhāva*, *as*, m. disappearance, (opposed to *āvir-bhāva* and *prādur-bhāva*.) — *Tiro-bhū*, cl. 1. P. *tiro-bhavati*, *-vitum*, to be set on one side, disappear, vanish, hide one's self: Caus. *tiro-bhāvayati* or *tiro bhāvayati*, *-yitum*, to cause to disappear, dispel. — *Tiro-varsha*, *as*, *ā*, *am*, protected from rain. — *Tiro-hita*, *as*, *ā*, *am*, covered, concealed, hidden, removed or withdrawn from sight. — *Tirohita-tā*, f. disappearance, the becoming invisible; *tirohitatām gam*, to disappear.

Tiraya, nom. P. *tirayati*, *-yitum*, to keep hidden or concealed, to prevent from appearing, hinder, stop, restrain; to conquer.

Tirasya, nom. P. *tirasyati*, &c., to disappear.

Tirohaya, nom. P. *tirohayati*, *-yitum*, to hide, conceal.

Tiro-'hnya. See *tiro-ahnya*, col. 2.

तिरस्कर *tiras-kara*, *tiras-kṛi*, &c. See under *tiras*, col. 2.

तिरिजिह्विक *tirijihvika*, *as* or *am*, m. or n. (?), Erythrina Crista Galli (?).

तिरिटि *tiriṭi*, *is*, or *tiriṭa*, *as* (?), m. the joint of the sugar-cane.

तिरिणीकण्ट *tiriṇīkaṇṭa* = *tirijihvika*.

तिरिन्दिर *tirindira*, *as*, m., Ved., N. of a man.

तिरिम *tirima* or *tiriya*, *as*, m. a sort of rice; [cf. *tīrya*.]

तिरीट *tirīṭa*, *am*, n. (said to be fr. rt. *tṝ*, perhaps for *tirī-tra*, or a wrong form for *kirīṭa*), a kind of head-dress, a tiara, a diadem; gold; (*as*), m. the tree Symplocos Racemosa.

Tirīṭaka, *as*, m. a kind of bird.

Tirīṭin, *ī*, *inī*, *i*, Ved. furnished with a head-dress.

तिरो *tiro* for *tiras*. See under *tiras*.

तिरोहित *tiro-hita*. See under *tiras*.

तिर्पिरिक *tirpirika*, *am*, n. = *tilpilika*.

तिर्पिलि *tirpili*, *is*, m., N. of an author.

तिर्य *tirya*, *as*, *ā*, *am*, = *tilya*, Ved. prepared from the seeds of sesamum (?); [cf. *tiriya*.]

तिर्यग *tiryaga* for *tiryag-ga*. See *tiryañć*.

तिर्यञ्च् *tiryañć* or *tiryać*, *an*, *tiraśćī*, or according to Vopa-deva also *tiryañćī*, *ak* (fr. *tiras* and rt. *añć*), going or lying crosswise or transversely or obliquely, oblique, transverse (opposed to *anv-añć*), horizontal (opposed to *ūrdhva*, vertical); going across; crossing over, traversing; moving tortuously, going crookedly or awry; curved, crooked; meandering; lying in the middle or between; (*an*, *ak*), m. n. an animal (going horizontally, as opposed to man who walks erect), a brute, an amphibious animal; a bird; (with Jainas) plants, the organic world; (*tiraśćī* or *tiryañćī*), f. the female of an animal or of any beast or bird; (*ak*), ind., Ved. across, obliquely, transversely, horizontally, sideways; *tiraśćā*, ind. across, obliquely. — *Tiraśći-rāji*, *is*, *is*, *i* (*tiraśći* loc. case of *tiryañć*), Ved. striped across (as a serpent). — *Tiryak-kāram* or *tiryak-kṛitya*, ind. having laid aside (after the completion of any work), having placed on one side. — *Tiryak-kshipta*, *as*, *ā*, *am*, placed obliquely or across; a form of dislocation when a part of the joint is forced outwards. — *Tiryak-tā*, f. or *tiryak-tva*, *am*, n. the state of going across or obliquely; the state of a beast or animal, animal nature; measurement across, breadth. — *Tiryak-pātana*, *am*, n., N. of a part of the Ānanda-kanda, treating of medicine. — *Tiryak-pramāṇa*, *am*, n. measurement across, breadth; *purastāt-tiryak-pramāṇa*, breadth in front; *paśćāt-t*°, breadth behind. — *Tiryak-prekshaṇa*, *as*, *ā*, *am*, looking obliquely or askance; (*am*), n. a squint, oblique glance, side look. — *Tiryak-prekshin*, *ī*, *iṇī*, *i*, looking obliquely or sideways. — *Tiryak-sūtra*, *am*, n. a cross-line. — *Tiryak-srotas*, *as*, n. 'the horizontal stream of life,' the animal creation; (*ās*), m. 'hurrying the stream of life horizontal,' i. e. the animal world; an animal, a beast or bird; [cf.

arvāk-srotas, avāk-srotas, ūrdhva-srotas.] — *Tiryag-antara, am,* n. intermediate space measured across, breadth. — *Tiryag-ayana, am,* n. the horizontal course, the annual revolution of the sun, (opposed to its diurnal revolution, in which it rises and sets vertically.) — *Tiryag-āgata, as, ā, am,* lying across (a particular position of the child at birth). — *Tiryag-īksha, as, ā, am,* looking obliquely; [cf. *tiryak-prekshaṇa.*] — *Tiryag-īśa, as,* m. 'the lord of the animals,' an epithet of Kṛishṇa. — *Tiryag-ga* (or sometimes *tirya-ga*), *as, ā, am,* going obliquely, going across or horizontally [cf. *pratīpa-ga, adho-mukha, ūrdhva-ga*]; an animal; going towards the north or south, (opposed to *pūrva-mukhī* and *paśćān-mukhī.*) — *Tiryag-gata, as, ā, am,* going horizontally, (opposed to man who walks erect.) — *Tiryag-gati, is,* f. the course of an animal, transmigration of animals. — *Tiryag-gama, as, ā, am,* going sideways or obliquely. — *Tiryag-gamana, am,* n. motion sideways or across, (opposed to *ūrdhva-g°* and *adho-g°.*) — *Tiryag-guṇana, am,* n. oblique multiplication. — *Tiryag-ja, as, ā, am,* born from an animal, having an animal as father or mother. — *Tiryag-jana, as,* m. an animal. — *Tiryag-jāti, is, is, i,* belonging to the race of animals or to the brute creation, born as an animal; (*is*), f. the brute kind. — *Tiryag-jyā,* f. an oblique chord. — *Tiryag-diś, k,* f. the region or part of the universe which lies horizontally, (opposed to *ūrdhva* and *adhas.*) — *Tiryag-dhāra, as, ā, am,* having curved or oblique edges. — *Tiryag-nāsa* or *tiryan-nāsa, as, ā, am,* crooked-nosed, wry-nosed. — *Tiryag-yavodara* (*°va-ud°*), *am,* n. a barleycorn. — *Tiryag-yāna, as,* m. 'going crookedly,' a crab. — *Tiryag-yona, as,* m. an animal (as a bird &c.); [cf. *tairyagyona.*] — *Tiryag-yoni, is, is, i,* born of or as an animal; (*is*), f. the womb of an animal, the animal creation or race, organic nature (including plants). — *Tiryagyony-anvaya, as, ā, am,* of the animal race; (*as*), m. the race of animals, birds, &c. — *Tiryag-viddha, as, ā, am,* pierced obliquely (as a vein in bleeding by an unskilful operator). — *Tiryan-niraya, as,* m. the hell of animals or animal nature as a punishment for evil deeds.

Tiraśća, am, n., Ved. the cross-board of a bed-stead. — *Tiraśćāṅgirasa* (*°ća-āṅ°*), *as,* m. the Āṅgirasa Tiraśća; [cf. *tiraśći.*]

Tiraśćatā, ind., Ved. across, transversely, through.

Tiraśćathā, ind., Ved. aside, secretly.

Tiraśći, m., Ved., N. of a Ṛishi, descendant of Aṅgiras. — *Tiraśći-nidhana, am,* n., N. of a Sāman.

Tiraśćīna, as, ā, am, lying across, oblique, transverse, sideways, awry, horizontal; irregular; *ā-tiraśćīnam,* a little across. — *Tiraśćīna-nidhana, am,* n., Ved., N. of a Sāman. — *Tiraśćīna-priśni, is, is, i,* Ved. spotted across. — *Tiraśćīna-vaṇśa, as,* m., Ved. a bee-hive.

तिल् 1. *til,* cl. 1. P. *telati,* &c., to go or move; [cf. rt. *till.*]

तिल् 2. *til* (probably an artificial rt. fr. *tila* below), cl. 6. 10. P. *tilati, telayati,* &c., to be unctuous or greasy; to oil or anoint.

Tila, as, m. the sesamum plant (Sesamum Indicum) which bears an oily seed; the seed of this plant (much used in Oriental cookery); a mole or spot compared to a seed of sesamum; a small particle or portion as much as a sesamum-seed [cf. *kṛishṇa-tila* and *ćarma-tila*]; (*ās*), m. pl., N. of a chapter of the Purāṇa-sarva-sva. — *Tila-kaṭa, am,* n. the farina of sesamum. — *Tila-kalka, as,* m. dough made of ground sesamum. — *Tilakalka-ja, as* or *am,* m. or n. (?), oil-cake made of the sediment of ground sesamum. — *Tila-kālaka, as,* m. a mole, a dark spot under the skin; a disease of the penis in which the fleshy parts become black and die off; (*as, ā, am*), having a mole or mark. — *Tila-kiṭṭa, am,* n. the caky sediment of sesamum after the oil is pressed out. — *Tila-khali, is* or *ī,* f. oil-cake made from sesamum. — *Tila-gañji-tīrtha, am,* n., N. of a place mentioned in the Rasika-ramaṇa by Raghu-nātha. — *Tila-grāma, as,* m., N. of a Grāma or township. — *Tila-ćitra-pattraka, as,* m. a kind of bulbous plant. — *Tila-ćūrṇa, am,* n. sesamum ground and pounded. — *Tila-taṇḍulaka, am,* n. an embrace (as agreeable as rice mixed with sesamum). — *Tila-tejā,* f. a kind of plant. — *Tila-taila, am,* n. sesamum-oil. — *Tiladeśvara-tīrtha* (*°da-īś°*), *am,* n., N. of a Tīrtha; [cf. *tilakeśvara-tīrtha.*] — *Tila-dvādaśī,* f. a festival occurring on the twelfth day of a particular month. — *Tila-dhenu, us,* f. sesamum made up in the shape of a cow for the purpose of being presented to Brāhmans &c. — *Tiladhenu-dāna, am,* n., N. of a chapter of the Vāraha-Purāṇa. — *Tilan-tuda, as, ā, am,* bruising sesamum-seed, a sesamum-grinder, one who extracts oil out of sesamum-seed; [cf. *tila-pīḍa.*] — *Tila-parṇa, as,* m. turpentine; (*ī*), f. the sandal tree, Pterocarpus Santalinus; frankincense; turpentine; (*am*), n. the leaf of the Tila tree; sandal-wood. — *Tila-parṇikā,* f. or *tila-parṇika* or *tila-parṇaka, am,* n. red sanders, sandal-wood. — *Tila-piććaṭa, am,* n. (*piććaṭa = pishṭaka*), a sort of sweetmeat made chiefly of ground sesamum. — *Tila-piñja, as,* m. barren sesamum, bearing no blossom or yielding a seed which gives no oil; white sesamum; [cf. *tila-peja, tilpiñja, taila-piñja.*] — *Tila-pīḍa, as,* m. = *tilan-tuda;* [cf. *taila-pīḍa.*] — *Tila-pushpaka,* Terminalia Bellerica (*vibhītaka*). — *Tila-peja, as,* m. barren sesamum; [cf. *tila-piñja.*] — *Tila-bhāra, ās,* m. pl., N. of a race. — *Tila-bhāvinī,* f. jasmine. — *Tila-bhṛishṭa, am,* n. fried sesamum-seed. — *Tila-maya, as, ī, am,* made of or prepared from sesamum, abounding with sesamum. — *Tila-mayūra, as,* m. a species of peacock. — *Tila-miśra, as, ā, am,* mixed with sesamum. — *Tila-rasa, as,* m. sesamum-oil. — *Tila-vatsa, as, ā, am,* Ved. having sesamum-seed (as it were) for children. — *Tila-vratin, ī, inī, i,* eating only sesamum-seeds in consequence of a vow. — *Tila-śas,* ind. in pieces as small as sesamum-seeds. — *Tila-sambaddha, as, ā, am,* mixed with sesamum-oil. — *Tila-sneha, as,* m. oil, especially of sesamum. — *Tila-homa, am,* n. burnt-offering of sesamum. — *Tilāṅkita-dala* (*°la-aṅ°*), *as,* m. a kind of bulbous plant, = *taila-kanda.* — *Tilāḍhaka?* (*°la-āḍh°*), N. of a monastery; (also read *tilaṭaka, tilaḍhāka, tila-śākya.*) — *Tilānna* (*°la-an°*), *am,* n. rice with sesamum-seeds. — *Tilāpatyā* (*°la-ap°*), f. a plant bearing a small pungent seed, Nigella Indica. — *Tilāmbu* (*°la-am°*), *u,* n. water with sesamum. — *Tilottamā* (*°la-ut°*), f., N. of an Apsaras; a form of Dākshāyaṇī; N. of a woman. — *Tilodaka* (*°la-ud°*), *am,* n. sesamum-seeds and water (as an oblation). — *Tilaudana* (*°la-od°*), *am,* n. a dish of milk, rice, and sesamum.

Tilaka, as, m. a species of tree with beautiful flowers, (so called either because it is similar in some way to the sesamum plant, or because it is used as an ornament like the mark on the forehead); a plant growing near water; a freckle, a natural mark under the skin (compared to a seed of sesamum); a kind of eruption of the skin; (*as, am*), m. n. a mark or marks made with coloured earths, sandal-wood, or unguents, upon the forehead and between the eyebrows, either as an ornament or a sectarial distinction; the ornament of anything (used in comp. to express greatness or distinction, e. g. *trailokya-tilaka,* the ornament of the three worlds, i. e. a distinguished personage); (*as*), m. the burden of a song, = *dhruvaka;* a species of horse; N. of a son of Pra-dyota; N. of a prince of Kampanā; (*ā*), f. a kind of necklace; (*am*), n. the bladder; the lungs; black sochal salt, a factitious salt containing sulphur and iron &c.; a disease, the appearance of dark spots on the skin, unattended with inflammation; alliteration; a kind of metre consisting of four lines of six syllables each; [cf. *ūrdhva-tilakin, eṇa-tilaka, kha-t°, vasanta-t°.*] — *Tilaka-rāja, as,* m., N. of a man. — *Tilaka-vrata, am,* n., N. of a chapter of the second part of the Bhavishya-Purāṇa, treating of ceremonies. — *Tilaka-siṇha, as,* m., N. of a man. — *Tilakāśraya* (*°ka-āś°*), *as,* m. the forehead ('the receptacle of the Tilaka'). — *Tilakeśvara-tīrtha* (*°ka-īś°*), *am,* n., N. of a Tīrtha; [cf. *tiladeśvara-tīrtha.*]

Tilakaka, as, m., N. of a man.

Tilakāya, nom. A. *tilakāyate,* &c., to form the Tilaka mark on the forehead, to ornament.

Tilakita, as, ā, am, marked with the Tilaka, ornamented; freckled, spotted.

Tilakin, ī, inī, i, marked with the Tilaka; freckled, spotted.

Tilu, an adj. derived by Sāy. fr. *tila,* and meaning 'fertile,' 'rich;' [cf. *tilvila* below.]

Tilpiñja, as, m., Ved. = *tila-piñja,* q. v.

Tilya, as, ā, am, suited for the cultivation of sesamum, grown with sesamum; (*am*), n. a field of sesamum.

Tilva or *tilvaka, as,* m. the tree Symplocus Racemosa, = *iṅgudī,* Terminalia Catappa.

Tilvila, as, ā, am, Ved. having a fertile soil, prolific, rich; [cf. *ibhya-tilvila* and *dhānya-t°.*]

Tilvilāya, nom. A. *tilvilāyate,* &c., Ved. to be fertile or rich, to cause fertility of soil.

तिलकनिज *tilakanija, ās,* m. pl., N. of a race.

तिलिङ्ग *tiliṅga,* N. of a place mentioned in the Kāka-rudra-saṃvāda.

तिलिङ्गिल *tiliṅgila, ās,* m. pl., N. of a people; (also *timiṅgila, tileṅgala.*)

तिलित्स *tilitsa* or *tiliććha, as,* m. a large snake; (according to some = Gokhura; according to others = the Boa or Boa Constrictor.)

तिल्पिलिक *tilpilika, am,* n. = *tirpirika.*

तिल्ल् *till,* cl. 1. P. *tillati,* &c., to go or move; (a various reading for 1. *til.*)

तिव्य *tivya, as,* m., N. of a Brāhman.

तिष्ठत् *tishṭhat, an, antī, at* (pres. part. fr. rt. *sthā*), staying, remaining, abiding, standing, being, &c. — *Tishṭhad-gu,* ind. (*gu* fr. *go*), at milking-time (when the cows stand to be milked), after sunset. — *Tishṭhad-dhoma* (*°at-ho°*), *as, ā, am,* Ved. (a sacrifice) at which the oblation is offered standing, (opposed to *upavishṭa-homa.*)

तिष्य *tishya, as,* m., N. of a mythical being who like Kṛiśānu is a kind of heavenly archer; an asterism regarded as shaped like an arrow and containing three stars, of which δ Cancri is one, (it is the sixth Nakshatra of the old or eighth of the new order, and is also called Pushya and Sidhya); the month Pausha (December–January); a common N. of men, 'born under the asterism Tishya' [cf. *upa-tishya*]; (*ā*), f. Terminalia Tomentosa; Emblica Officinalis; Emblic Myrobalan; (*as, am*), m. n. the Kali-yuga, the fourth or present age; (*as, ā, am*), auspicious, fortunate, lucky (?). — *Tishya-ketu, us,* m. an epithet of Siva. — *Tishya-punarvasīya, as, ā, am,* relating to the asterisms Tishya and Punar-vasu. — *Tishya-pushpā,* f. Emblic Myrobalan (*āmalakī*). — *Tishya-phalā,* f. Emblic Myrobalan. — *Tishya-rakshitā,* f., N. of the first wife of Aśoka.

Tishyaka, as, m. the month Pausha.

तिसृ *tisṛi, tisras,* f. pl. three; see *tri.* — *Tisṛi-dhanva, am,* n., Ved. a bow with three arrows.

Tisṛikā, f., N. of a Grāma.

Tisrā, f. the grass Andropogon Aciculatus.

तिहन् *tihan, ā,* m. sickness; a good disposition; rice; a bow.

तीक् *tīk,* cl. 1. A. *tīkate,* &c., to go or move; [cf. rt. *tik.*]

तीक्ष्ण *tīkshṇa, as, ā, am* (fr. rt. *tij;* cf. the similar word *tigma,* which is more used than *tīkshṇa* in the older literature), sharp (in all senses), hot, pungent, warm, fiery; acid (= *khara-ushṇa*); virulent, harsh, rough, rude, cross; injurious, noxious, unfriendly, unpropitious, inauspicious (e. g. *tīkshṇāni nakshatrāṇi*, the inauspicious Nakshatras, viz. Mūla, Ārdrā, Jyeshṭhā, Ā-śleshā); sharp, keen; intelligent; zealous, vehement, active, eager, energetic, quick; devoted, self-abandoning; devout, ascetic, a devotee, zealot; (*as*), m. nitre; the resin of Boswellia Thurifera, = *śveta-kuśa* or *śveta-darbha;* long pepper; black pepper; black mustard; Moringa Pterygosperma, horse-radish tree; Dalbergia Sissoo (*śinśapā*), marjoram; Asa Fœtida; Galmei; N. of a Nāga; N. of a man; (*ā*), f., N. of several plants, = *vaćā*, = *sarpa-kankālikā* (wrongly translated 'the cast skin of a snake'); Mucuna Pruritus, = *mahā-jyotishmatī*, = *atyamla-parṇī;* Cardiospermum Halicacabum; black mustard; a mystical name of the letter *p;* (*am*), n. iron; steel; any weapon; anything sharp (as sharp language, &c.); heat, pungency; haste; sea-salt, nitre; poison, = *mushkaka;* the tree Bignonia Suaveolens or (according to others) the scrotum or testicles; Piper Chaba; war, battle; plague, pestilence, epidemic destruction; death, dying; [cf. *a-tīkshṇa* and *su-tīkshṇa.*] — *Tīkshṇa-kaṇṭaka, as*, m., N. of several plants, viz. thorn-apple; Capparis Aphylla; Terminalia Catappa; Acacia Arabica; Euphorbia Tortilis; (*ā*), f. a kind of plant, = *kanthārī.* — *Tīkshṇa-kanda, as*, m. 'pungent root,' the onion. — *Tīkshṇa-karma-kṛit, t, t, t*, acting in a sharp or clever manner, active, energetic. — *Tīkshṇa-karman, ā, ā, a*, 'sharp in action,' active, energetic, zealous, brisk; (*a*), n. a clever work. — *Tīkshṇa-kalka, as*, m. coriander. — *Tīkshṇa-kāntā*, f. a form of Ćaṇḍikā. — *Tīkshṇa-gandha, as*, m. 'having a pungent smell,' N. of two plants, = *śobhāñjana* and *phaṇijjhaka;* the resin of the Boswellia Thurifera; (*ā*), f., N. of several plants, = *śobhāñjana, rājikā, vaćā, śveta-vaćā, kanthārī, jīvantī;* small cardamoms. — *Tīkshṇa-gandhaka, as*, m. = *śobhāñjana.* — *Tīkshṇa-taṇḍulā*, f. long pepper. — *Tīkshṇa-tara, as, ā, am*, sharper, &c. — *Tīkshṇa-tā*, f. or *tīkshṇa-tva, am*, n. warmth, heat, sharpness, pungency. — *Tīkshṇa-tuṇḍa, as, ā, am*, having a sharp beak (as a bird). — *Tīkshṇa-taila, am*, n. 'pungent oil,' the resin of the Shorea Robusta; the milky juice of the Euphorbia Lactea; spirituous or vinous liquor. — *Tīkshṇa-daṇshṭra, as, ā, am*, having sharp teeth or tusks; (*as*), m. a tiger. — *Tīkshṇa-daṇshṭraka, as*, m. a leopard. — *Tīkshṇa-dhāra, as, ā, am*, sharp-edged, sharp; (*as*), m. a sword. — *Tīkshṇa-pattra, as*, m. 'having pungent leaves,' coriander; the plant Terminalia Catappa; a species of sugar-cane. — *Tīkshṇa-pushpa, am*, n. 'pungent flower,' cloves; (*ā*), f. Pandanus Odoratissimus; the clove tree. — *Tīkshṇa-priya* = *tīkshṇa-śūka*, barley. — *Tīkshṇa-phala, as*, m. 'having pungent fruit,' coriander; black mustard. — *Tīkshṇa-buddhi, is, is, i*, sharp-witted, sagacious, acute. — *Tīkshṇa-mañjarī*, f. the betel plant. — *Tīkshṇa-mukha, as, ī, am*, sharp-mouthed. — *Tīkshṇa-mūla, as*, m. 'having a pungent root,' Moringa Pterygosperma; Alpinia Galanga. — *Tīkshṇa-raśmi, is, is, i*, having hot rays (as the sun). — *Tīkshṇa-rasa, as*, m. 'pungent liquid,' saltpetre. — *Tīkshṇa-loha, as*, m. 'sharp iron,' steel. — *Tīkshṇa-visha, as, ā, am*, having virulent poison. — *Tīkshṇa-vṛishaṇa, as*, m. 'having strong testicles,' N. of a bull. — *Tīkshṇa-vega, as, ā, am*, possessing great velocity; (*as*), m., N. of a Rakshas. — *Tīkshṇa-śūka, as*, m. 'having sharp awns,' barley. — *Tīkshṇa-śṛiṅga, as, ā* or *ī, am*, having sharp horns. — *Tīkshṇa-sāra, as*, m. Dalbergia Sissoo (= *śinśapā*); Bassia Latifolia; iron. — *Tīkshṇāṇśu* (°*ṇa-aṇ*°), *us, us, u*, having hot rays; (*us*), m. the sun; fire. — *Tīkshṇāṇśu-tanaya, as*, m. 'the son of the sun,' the planet Saturn. — *Tīkshṇāgni* (°*ṇa-ag*°), *is*, m. 'acid gastric juice,' heartburn, dyspepsia. — *Tīkshṇāgra* (°*ṇa-ag*°), *as, ā, am*, sharp-pointed; (*as*), m. Zingiber Zerumbet. — *Tīkshṇāyasa* (°*ṇa + ayasa* for *ayas*, q. v.), *am*, n. 'sharp iron,' steel; (*as, ī, am*), made of steel, sharp. — *Tīkshṇeshu* (°*ṇa-ishu*), *us, us, u*, having sharp arrows. — *Tīkshṇopāya* (°*ṇa-up*°), *as*, m. forcible means, a strong measure.

Tīkshṇaka, as, m. = *mushkaka*, Bignonia Suaveolens or (according to others) the scrotum or testicles; black mustard; long pepper.

Tīkshṇishṭha, as, ā, am, sharpest, &c.

Tīkshṇīyas, ān, asī, as, sharper, &c.

तीम् *tīm*, cl. 4. P. *tīmyati*, &c., to be wet or moist; [cf. rt. *tim.*]

तीर् *tīr*, cl. 10. P., to accomplish, (better regarded as a nominal verb; see under *tīra* below.)

तीर *tīra, am*, n. (fr. rt. *tṛī*), a shore, a bank; margin, brink, edge; the brim of a vessel; a sort of arrow [cf. the Pers. تير]; (*as*), m. tin [cf. *tīvra*]; (*ī*), f. a kind of arrow, three-fourths of which consists of reed and a fourth part of iron. — *Tīra-graha, ās*, m. pl., N. of a race. — *Tīra-ja, as, ā, am*, growing or standing near a shore; (*as*), m. a tree near a shore. — *Tīra-bhukti, is*, m., N. of a country, the modern Tirhut, a province in the east of central Hindūstan, lying to the north of Bahar (fr. *tīra*, a bank, and *bhukti*, here signifying a limit; being bounded on the east by Bhaugulpore, on the west by Sarun, on the south by the Ganges, and on the north by the skirts of the Himālaya mountains); [cf. *tri-bhukti.*] — *Tīra-ruha, as, ā, am*, growing on a bank; (*as*), m. a tree growing on a bank. — *Tīra-stha, as, ā, am*, situated on a bank or shore. — *Tīrāntara* (°*ra-an*°), *am*, n. the opposite bank or shore.

Tīraya, nom. P. *tīrayati, -yitum*, to get through, cross over, to finish, accomplish, complete successfully.

Tīrita, as, ā, am, finished, settled, completed, adjudged, decided according to evidence; (*am*), n. completion of any act or affair; corrupt or improper non-infliction of a sentence.

तीरण *tīraṇa*, a kind of plant, = *karañjikā.*

तीराट *tīrāṭa, as*, m. = *tirīṭa*, Symplocos Racemosa.

तीरु *tīru*, perhaps a wrong reading for *bhīru.*

तीर्ण *tīrṇa, as, ā, am.* See under rt. *tṛī.*

तीर्त्वा *tīrtvā*, ind. See under rt. *tṛī.*

तीर्थ *tīrtha, as, am*, m. n. (fr. rt. *tṛī*, the masc. is only exceptionally used in epic poetry), a passage, way, road, ford; especially a Ghāt or the stairs of a landing-place, a descent into a river, a bathing-place, a holy place, a shrine or sacred place of pilgrimage, as Benares &c., especially particular spots along the course of sacred streams, as the Ganges &c., or in the vicinity of sacred springs; any piece of water; (in sacrificial language) the path to the altar between the Ćātvāla and Utkara; a channel, a canal, watercourse; the usual way, the usual or right manner (e. g. *tīrthena* or *tīrthatas*, in right order, in the usual way; *a-tīrthena*, in a wrong way); the right place, the right moment; a sacred place, a sacred moment, opportunity; a sacrifice; advice, instruction, counsel; a counsellor, an adviser; a sacred preceptor, a Guru; an opportunity, a means, an expedient; certain lines or parts of the hand sacred to the deities &c. (as the root of the two smaller fingers, to Prajāpati; the tops of the fingers, to the gods; the space between the thumb and finger, to the manes; the root of the thumb, to Brahma or to the Veda; *saumyan tīrtham* = the middle of the hand); an object of veneration, a sacred object; a worthy object or person, a fit recipient, (sometimes at the end of names, e. g. *ānanda-tīrtha, jaya-t*°, &c.); a Brāhman; a minister; a N. given to certain officers (eighteen or fifteen in number) who are in close attendance on a king; pudendum muliebre; menstrual courses of a woman; a school of philosophy (= *darśana*), a sect; ascertainment of disease; fire. — *Tīrtha-kamaṇḍalu, us, u*, m. n. a pot with water from a sacred bathing-place. — *Tīrtha-kara, as, ā* or *ī, am*, 'creating a passage (through life, or through the circuit of life);' (*as*), m. an epithet of Vishṇu; one of the synonyms of an Arhat or sanctified teacher of the Jaina sect; (with Buddhists) an ascetic ('bathing in holy waters'). — *Tīrtha-kāka, as*, m. a crow at a sacred bathing-place, i. e. one not in his own proper place. — *Tīrtha-kāśikā*, f., N. of a work by Gaṅgā-dhara. — *Tīrtha-kīrtti, is, is, i*, one whose mere fame makes holy. — *Tīrtha-kṛit, t*, m. = *tīrtha-kara*, a Jaina Arhat. — *Tīrtha-gopāla, am*, n., N. of a place of pilgrimage. — *Tīrthan-kara, as*, m. = *tīrtha-kara*, a Jaina Arhat. — *Tīrtha-ćintā-maṇi, is*, m. f., N. of a chapter of the Saṃskāra-tattva by Raghu-nandana, treating of the Indian sacraments. — *Tīrtha-tama, am*, n. (fr. *tīrtha* with the affix of the superl.), a more sacred place of pilgrimage; an object of the highest sanctity. — *Tīrtha-deva, as*, m. an epithet of Śiva. — *Tīrtha-dhvāṅksha, as*, m. 'a crow at a place of pilgrimage,' a contemptuous epithet; [cf. *tīrtha-kāka.*] — *Tīrtha-pati, is*, m., N. of the chief of a sect. — *Tīrtha-pād, pāt, padī, pat*, 'one whose feet are sacred or sanctify,' an epithet of Kṛishṇa. — *Tīrtha-pādīya, as*, m. an adherent of Kṛishṇa. — *Tīrtha-bhūta, as, ā, am*, rendered holy, sacred. — *Tīrtha-mahā-hrada, as*, m., N. of a shrine or place of pilgrimage. — *Tīrtha-mahiman, ā*, m., N. of a chapter of the Sūdra-dharma-tattva, treating of the duties of the Sūdras. — *Tīrtha-māhātmya, am*, n., N. of a chapter of the Purāṇa-sarva-sva by Halāyudha. — *Tīrtha-yātrā*, f. a visit to any sacred shrine or bathing-place, a pilgrimage; N. of a chapter of the Śiva-Purāṇa. — *Tīrthayātrā-tattva, am*, n., N. of a part of the Smṛiti-tattva by Raghunandana. — *Tīrthayātrā-parvan, a*, n., N. of a section of the third book of the Mahā-bhārata (ch. 80–156). — *Tīrtha-yātrin, ī, iṇī, i*, going to a place of pilgrimage. — *Tīrtha-rājī*, f. 'a line of sacred bathing-places,' epithet of Benares. — *Tīrtha-vat, ān, atī, at*, having descents to the water, abounding in sacred bathing-places; (*atī*), f., N. of a river. — *Tīrtha-vāka, as*, m. the hair of the head. — *Tīrtha-vāyasa, as*, m. a crow at a Tīrtha; see *tīrtha-kāka.* — *Tīrtha-vāsin, ī, inī, i*, dwelling at a place of pilgrimage. — *Tīrtha-vidhi, is*, m. the rites observed at a place of pilgrimage. — *Tīrtha-śilā*, f. the stone steps leading to a bathing-place. — *Tīrtha-śravas, ās, ās, as*, one whose mere fame is sacred or sanctifies. — *Tīrtha-śrāddha-prayoga, as*, m., N. of a chapter of the Srāddha-ćintā-maṇi by Śiva-rāma, treating of funeral ceremonies. — *Tīrtha-seni, is*, f., N. of one of the Mātṛis attending on Skanda. — *Tīrtha-sevin, ī, inī, i*, visiting shrines, a pilgrim; (*ī*), m. a kind of crane, Ardea Nivea. — *Tīrtha-saukhya, am*, n. title of a particular work or of a part of a work.

Tīrthaka, as, ā, am, holy, sacred, venerable; (*as*), m. an ascetic Brāhman; N. of a Nāga.

Tīrthika, as, m. an ascetic Brāhman (visiting holy shrines or bathing-places), a pilgrim.

Tīrthī-kṛi, cl. 8. P. A. *-karoti, -kurute, -kartum*, to make sacred. — *Tīrthī-karaṇa, am*, n. the act of rendering sacred; (*as, ī, am*), sanctifying.

Tīrthī-bhūta, as, ā, am, become sacred.

Tīrthya, as, ā, am, relating to a ford or to a sacred bathing-place, &c.; (*as*), m. an ascetic; [cf. *tairthya.*]

तीव् *tīv*, cl. 1. P. *tīvati*, &c., to be large or strong, to be fat or corpulent; [cf. rt. *nīv.*]

तीवर *tīvara, as*, m. (said to be fr. rt. *tīr*), the ocean; a hunter, the adulterine offspring of a Rājaputrī by a Kshatriya; one who lives by killing and selling game; a fisherman (?); (ī), f. the wife of a hunter or of a fisherman.

तीव्र *tīvra, as, ā, am* (said to be fr. rt. *tij;* probably connected with rt. *tīv* and rt. 2. *tu*), strong, severe, violent, intense, fierce, ardent, impetuous, sharp, keen, acute, poignant, pungent, sour; hot, warm; flashing, pervading; much, exceeding, excessive, endless, unbounded, unlimited; horrible, dreadful; (*as*), m. sharpness, &c.; a hunter (?); an epithet of Śiva; (*ā*), f., N. of several plants, viz. Helleborus Niger; black mustard; a sort of Dūrvā or bent grass, = *gaṇḍa-dūrvā;* basil, = *taraḍi,* = *mahā-jyotishmatī;* N. of a river, the Padma-vatī, in the east of Bengal; (*am*), n. heat, pungency; a shore [cf. *tīra*]; tin [cf. *tīra*]; iron, steel [cf. *tīkshṇa*]; (*am*), ind. violently, impetuously, sharply, fiercely; much, excessively. — *Tīvra-kanda* or (according to a various reading) *tīvra-kaṇṭha, as,* m. a pungent kind of Arum. — *Tīvra-gati, is, is, i,* moving rapidly, quick, swift. — *Tīvra-gandhā,* f. cumin-seed or Ptychotis Ajowan. — *Tīvra-jvālā,* f. Grislea Tomentosa; [cf. *agni-jvālā* and *vahni-śikhā.*] — *Tīvra-tā,* f. violence, sharpness, heat, pungency. — *Tīvra-dāru, us,* m. a species of tree. — *Tīvra-paurusha, am,* n. daring heroism, such as the storming of a fortress. — *Tīvra-rosha-samāvishṭa, as, ā, am,* filled with fierce anger. — *Tīvra-vedanā,* f. excessive pain, agony, the pain of damnation. — *Tīvra-śoka-samāvishṭa, as, ā, am,* filled with excessive sorrow. — *Tīvra-śokārta* (°*ka-ār*°), *as, ā, am,* afflicted with poignant grief. — *Tīvra-sava, as,* m., N. of an Ekāha sacrifice. — *Tīvra-sut, t, t, t,* Ved. pressed out of a sour or fermenting substance; (Sāy. *tīvra-suta, as, ā, am*), whose expressed juice is sharp or pungent; (*t*), m., N. of an Ekāha sacrifice. — *Tīvrānanda* (°*ra-ān*°), *as,* m. 'having intense joy,' an epithet of Śiva. — *Tīvrānta* (°*ra-an*°), *as, ā, am,* Ved. becoming strong or sharp at the close (i. e. by a process of fermentation); having a sure or excessive result.

Tīvraya, nom. P. *-yati, -yitum,* to make sharp, strengthen.

तीसट *tīsaṭa, as,* m., N. of a writer on medicine.

तु 1. *tu,* the base of some of the cases of the 2nd personal pronoun; [cf. *tva.*]

तु 2. *tu,* cl. 2. P., Ved. *tavīti* and *tauti, tūtāva, totum* and *tavitum,* to have authority or power, to be strong; to attain; to thrive or increase, to fill, become full; to go or move; to injure, hurt, kill: Caus., Ved. (only used in aor. *tūtot*), to make strong or efficient, make valid, accomplish; [cf. Zend *tav,* 'to be able;' *tavan,* 'powerful:' Pers. توان *tuvān,* 'power;' توانم *tuvānam,* 'I can:' Gr. τύλος, τύλη, τυλόω, ταῦς: Lat. *tumor, tumere, tumidus, tumulus* (?), *tuber, tueri, totus:* Umbr. Osc. *tauta, tota, touta,* 'town;' *tut-icus,* 'townish:' Goth. *thiuda, thiuth, thiuthyan:* Angl. Sax. *thū-ma,* 'the thumb;' *theod,* 'people:' Old Germ. *dū-mo,* 'the thumb:' Slav. *ty-ti,* 'to grow fat;' *tu-kŭ,* 'fat:' Lith. *tau-ka-i,* 'fat;' *tunk-u,* 'I become fat:' Old Pruss. *tau-ta,* 'land, country:' Cambro-Brit. *tyv-u,* 'to increase.']

तु 3. *tu,* ind. (a particle, perhaps connected with the pronom. base 2. *ta,* or with the Vedic pronoun *tva;* never found at the beginning of a sentence or verse, and causing the verb with which it is constructed to retain its accent). As a particle implying 'earnest entreaty' or 'urgent request' it is often used in the Veda, like Lat. *dum,* with an imperative, and may be translated by 'pray!' 'I beg,' 'do' (e. g. *ā tvetā,* come here, do); or it may be rendered by 'well,' 'now then,' 'now,' 'just.' As an adversative particle it is equivalent to 'but,' 'on the contrary,' 'on the other hand' (e. g. *na ćhinatti janayati tu,* he does not destroy but he produces). The sense 'but' is most common in later Sanskṛit. *Tu* is sometimes, however, used for *ća,* 'and' (e. g. *ā samudrāt pūrvād ā samudrāt tu paśćimāt,* to the eastern sea and to the western sea); and even for *vā,* 'or' (e. g. *ushṭra-yānaṃ samāruhya khara-yānaṃ tu,* having ascended a camel-carriage or one drawn by donkeys). Sometimes it appears to be incorrectly written for *nu* (e. g. *kin tu* for *kin nu*). Occasionally it seems to be used for *tadā* after *ćet* (e. g. *tāṃ ćed na ditseyam pramathyainām hareyus tu,* if I were not willing to give her then they would take her by force). Not unfrequently *tu* is used as an expletive to fill out a verse or prevent the blending of vowels (e. g. *īrshyī ghṛiṇī tv a-santushṭaḥ,* &c., an envious man, one over-compassionate, a discontented man, &c.). *Tu—tu,* although—yet; *api-tu,* moreover; *kin tu,* but, nevertheless, notwithstanding; *paran tu,* moreover, but, nevertheless; *na tv eva tu,* but by no means. According to lexicographers *tu* implies disjunction, mutual opposition, alternative, asseveration, emphasis, conjunction, &c.

तुःखार *tuḥkhāra, ās,* m. pl. (probably = *tukhāra*), N. of a race of people; (*as*), m. a man of this race.

तुक् *tuk.* See 1. *tuć* below.

तुकज्योतिर्विद् *tuka-jyotir-vid, t,* m., N. of an astronomer.

तुकाक्षीरी *tukākshīrī,* f. = *tugākshīrī,* the manna of bamboos.

तुक्क *tukka, as,* m., N. of a man.

तुखार *tukhāra, ās,* m. pl., N. of a non-Hindū people to the north-west of Madhya-deśa; (often written *tushāra*); [cf. *tuḥkhāra.*]

तुगा *tugā,* f. the so-called Tabāshīr (fr. *tvak-kshīrā*), a white secretion found sometimes in the joints of bamboos, the manna of bamboos. — *Tugā-kshīrī,* f. a peculiar kind of bamboo manna; [cf. *tukā-kshīrī.*]

तुग्र *tugra, as,* m., N. of the father of Bhujyu who was protected by the Aśvins; N. of an enemy of Indra, conquered by the latter.

Tugriya, Ved. = *tugrya.*

Tugrya, as, m., Ved. a patronymic of Bhujyu; N. of a man or of a race; (*ā*), f. water. — *Tugryā-vridh, t, t, t,* Ved. delighting in the Tugryas; epithet of Indra and of Soma; (Sāy.) increasing water, increasing with water.

तुग्वन् *tugvan, a,* n., Ved. = *tīrtha,* q. v.

तुङ्ग *tunga.* See under rt. 2. *tuj* next col.

तुच् 1. *tuć* or 1. *tuj, k,* f., Ved. offspring, children, propagation; [cf. *toka* and *tokman.*]

Tuji, is, f., Ved. propagation, begetting children; (*is*), m., Ved., N. of a man protected by Indra.

तुच् 2. *tuć* in *ā-tuć* (q. v.), growing dusk.

तुच्छ *tuććha, as, ā, am* (probably for *tusha*), empty, void, vain, light; small, little, trifling; abandoned, deserted; low, mean, insignificant, contemptible; miserable, poor; worthless; (*ā*), f. the Indigo plant, = *tutthā;* (*am*), n. chaff; [cf. Lith. *tuszćias,* 'empty.'] — *Tuććha-tva, am,* n. emptiness, meanness, inanity, vanity. — *Tuććha-dru, us,* m. ('the sapless tree'), the castor-oil tree, Ricinus Communis. — *Tuććha-dhānya* or *tuććha-dhānyaka, am,* n. straw, chaff.

Tuććhaka, as, ā, am, void, empty, &c., = *tuććha.*

Tuććhaya, nom. P. *tuććhayati,* &c., to make empty or poor.

Tuććhī-kṛi, cl. 8. P. A. *-karoti, -kurute, -kartum,* to consider as vain or idle, to despise, contemn.

Tuććhya, as, ā, am, Ved. void, empty, vain.

तुज् 1. *tuj.* See 1. *tuć* above.

तुज् 2. *tuj* or *tuñj,* cl. 1. 6. P., Ved. *tojati, tujati, tutoja, tojitum,* or cl. 1. P. *tuñjati, tutuñja, tuñjitum,* Ved. Inf. *tujase,* to strike, hit; impel, push; to press out, emit; to stir up, urge on, instigate, incite; wave to and fro; to hasten; Ved. reach, extend, project; to kill or hurt; to guard, protect, to be strong; to clothe; to live: Pass. *tujyate,* &c., to be struck, to be vexed, &c.: Caus. *tujayati, -yitum,* Ved. to promote, instigate; to move quickly, spring, run [cf. *tūtujāna*]; *tuñjayati* or *tojayati, -yitum,* to hurt, to injure or kill; to be strong or vigorous; to give or take; to dwell, abide; to shine, speak; [cf. *tūtuji.*]

Tunga, as, ā, am, high, elevated, prominent, erect, lofty; long; vaulted; chief, principal; strong, passionate [cf. *ut-tunga*]; (*as*), m. an elevation, height, culmination, altitude; a mountain; top, highest point, peak, vertex; the superior apsis or aphelion of a planet; (metaphorically) a throne; a wise man; a rhinoceros; the planet Mercury; the tree Rottleria Tinctoria; the cocoa-nut; N. of a man; (*ā*), f., N. of a tree [cf. *śamī*]; also = *tugā,* bamboo manna; N. of a metre consisting of four lines of eight syllables each; N. of a river in the Mysore territory; (*ī*), f. a kind of Ocimum (*varvarā*); turmeric; night; (*am*), n. the stamina of the lotus blossom; [cf. Lith. *tunkū,* 'to grow fat:' Russ. *tućnyĭ,* 'fat:' Hib. *tonngo,* 'a billowy sea;' *tonnghail, tonnta,* 'waved.'] — *Tunga-kūṭa, as* or *am,* m. or n. (?), N. of a place of pilgrimage. — *Tunga-tā,* f. or *tunga-tva, am,* n. altitude, loftiness, height, passionateness. — *Tunga-dhanvan, ā,* m., N. of a king of Suhma. — *Tunga-nābha, as,* m. a particular species of poisonous insect. — *Tunga-nāsikā* or *ī,* f. a woman having a prominent nose. — *Tunga-prastha, as,* m., N. of a mountain. — *Tunga-bala, as,* m., N. of a warrior. — *Tunga-bha, am,* n. the lunar mansion in which a planet reaches its apsis, the apsis of a planet. — *Tunga-bhadra, as,* m. a restive elephant or one in rut; (*ā*), f., N. of a river in the Mysore territory, commonly called Tumbudra, formed by the junction of the Tunga and Bhadra rivers. — *Tunga-mukha, as,* m. a rhinoceros, ('having a prominent snout.') — *Tunga-vīja, as* or *am,* m. or n. (?), quicksilver, ('forming long seed-like balls.') — *Tunga-veṇā,* f., N. of a river in the Dekhan. — *Tunga-śekhara, as,* m. the top of a mountain. — *Tunga-śaila, as,* m. 'the high mountain,' N. of a mountain with a temple of Śiva. — *Tungī-nāsa, as,* m. a kind of poisonous insect. — *Tungī-pati, is,* m. the moon, ('lord of night.') — *Tungīśa* (°*gī-īśa*), *as,* m. the moon; the sun; an epithet of Śiva; N. of Krishṇa. — *Tungeśvara* (°*ga-īś*°), *as,* m. 'lord of the mountains,' an epithet of Śiva; a temple of Śiva; [cf. *giriśa* and *girīśa.*]

Tungaka, as, m. the tree Rottleria Tinctoria; (*am*), n., N. of a sacred forest.

Tungin, ī, inī, i, high, lofty; (*ī*), m. a planet at the apex of its orbit or of its position with regard to others considered astrologically; (*inī*), f., N. of a plant, = *mahā-śatāvarī.*

3. *tuj, k* (?), f., Ved. shock, impulse; pressure; assault; (*k, k, k*), pressing, urging on, impelling.

Tujya, as, ā, am, Ved. to be struck or pushed, to be impelled.

Tuñja, as, m., Ved. shock, assault; a Daitya, a demon; a thunderbolt; giving; (*as, ā, am*), noxious, mischievous.

तुजि *tuji.* See under 1. *tuć,* col. 2.

तुञ्जीन *tuñjīna, as,* m., N. of several kings of Kaśmīra.

तुट् *tuṭ,* cl. 6. P. *tuṭati, tutoṭa, tuṭitum,* to dispute, quarrel, wrangle; to hurt or injure: Caus. P. *toṭayati,* &c., a wrong reading for *troṭayati.*

तुटितुट *tuṭituṭa, as,* m. a N. of Śiva.

तुटुम *tuṭuma, as,* m. a mouse or rat.

तुड् *tuḍ*, cl. 1. 6. P. *toḍati, tuḍati, tutoḍa, toḍitum* or *tuḍitum*, to tear, split, break, cut, pull to pieces; to push; to injure, hurt or kill; to bring near.

तुड्ड् *tuḍḍ*, cl. 1. P. *tuḍḍati*, &c., to disrespect, disregard, contemn; [cf. rt. *tūḍ* and *toḍ*.]

तुण् *tuṇ*, cl. 6. P. *tuṇati, tutoṇa, toṇitum*, to curve, bend or make crooked; to be crooked or curved; to act fraudulently.

तुणि *tuṇi, is*, m. = *kuṇi* = *tunna*, the tree Cedula Toona.

तुणिक *tuṇika* (*tūṇika?*), *as*, m., N. of a tree, = *nandī-vṛiksha*.

तुण्ड् *tuṇḍ*, cl. 1. A. *tuṇḍate*, &c., = *tuḍ*.

Tuṇḍa, am, n. (according to some also *as*, m.), a beak, snout (of a hog &c.), trunk (of an elephant), mouth, face; the point of an instrument; (*as*), m. a N. of Śiva; of a Rakshas or demon; [cf. *asthi-t°, kaṅka-t°, kāka-t°*, &c.] — *Tuṇḍa-deva, as*, m., N. of a race or of a particular class of men. — *Tuṇḍa-deva-bhakta, am*, n. the district inhabited by the Tuṇḍa-devas.

Tuṇḍaka = *tuṇḍa* above.

Tuṇḍakerikā, f. = *tuṇḍikerī*, the cotton plant.

Tuṇḍakerī, f. a cucurbitaceous plant, Momordica Monadelpha.

Tuṇḍi, is, m. a beak, the mouth, the face; (*is*), f. the navel, a prominent navel [cf. *tundi*]; emphysema or distention of the navel (in infants); a kind of gourd or cucumber, = *īrvāru, kushmāṇḍa*; [cf. *tuṇḍī* in *kaṭu-tuṇḍī, tikta-t°*.]

Tuṇḍika, as, ā, am, furnished with a trunk or snout; (*ā*), f. the navel [cf. *tundikā*]; the plant Momordica Monadelpha; [cf. *kaṭu-tuṇḍikā* and *kāka-t°*.]

Tuṇḍikera, ās, m. pl., N. of a race; (*as*), m. the prince of this race; (*ī*), f. the cotton plant; a kind of cucumber, Momordica Monadelpha; a large boil or swelling on the palate.

Tuṇḍikerikā, f. Momordica Monadelpha.

Tuṇḍikerin, ī, m. a species of poisonous insect.

Tuṇḍikeśī, f. a sort of gourd, Momordica Monadelpha.

Tuṇḍićela, am, n. a particular kind of costly garment.

Tuṇḍibha, as, ā, am, having a prominent or elevated navel; [cf. *tundibha*.]

Tuṇḍila, as, ā, am, talkative; speaking harshly or severely; loquacious; having a prominent or elevated navel; [cf. *tundila*.]

तुण्डेल *tuṇḍela, as*, m., Ved., N. of a kind of evil spirit or goblin.

तुतात *tutāta, as*, m., N. of the founder of a philosophical system; [cf. *tautātika*.]

तुतुर्वणि *tuturvaṇi, is, is, i* (fr. rt. 1. *tur*), Ved. striving to bring near or obtain; (Sāy.) acting with alacrity, acting speedily; [cf. *jugurvaṇi* and *śuśukvani*.]

तुत्थ *tuttha, as*, m. (said to be fr. rt. 1. *tud*), fire; (*ā*), f. the Indigo plant; small cardamoms; (*am*), n. blue vitriol, sulphate of copper, especially considered as an ointment or medical application to the eyes; a collyrium extracted from the Amomum Zanthorrhiza; a stone, a rock. — *Tutthāñjana* (°*tha-añ*°), *am*, n. blue vitriol as an ointment or medicinal application to the eyes.

Tutthaka, am, n. blue vitriol.

Tutthaya (originally 'to cover with blue vitriol?'), nom. P. *tutthayati, -yitum*, to screen, veil, cover; to spread.

तुथ *tutha*, Ved. occurring in certain formularies, (explained in commentaries by *brahma-rūpa*, 'having the shape or form of Brahma.')

तुद् 1. *tud*, cl. 6. P. A. *tudati, -te, tutoda, tutude, totsyati, -te, atautsīt, atutta, tottum*, to strike, hit, push; to goad, prick; to bruise; to pain, wound, sting, vex, harass, tease, torture, torment: Caus. *todayati, -yitum, atūtudat*, to push &c.: Desid. *tututsati, -te*: Intens. *totudyate, totottí*; [cf. rt. *tund, tottra, toda*; Gr. Τυδ-εύ-ς, Τύδ-α-ς, Τυνδ-άρη-ς, Τυνδ-άρεο-ς, Τυνδ-άρεω-ς, Τυνδάρ-ιχο-ς; Lat. *tund-o, tud-es, tud-i-tare, dea Pertunda, tussis*; Goth. *staut-an*; Old Germ. *stoz-an*; Mod. Germ. *stoss-en*; Angl. Sax. *a-stintan*, 'to blunt:' the initial *s* is original, and dropped in Sanskrit.]

2. *tud, t, t, t*, (at the end of a comp.) striking, pricking, goading.

Tuda, as, ā, am, (at the end of a comp.) striking, pricking, stinging, paining, tormenting [cf. *tilan-tuda* and *arun-tuda*, 'striking a wound']; (*as*), m., N. of a man. — *Tud-ādi*, the grammatical designation of the sixth class of roots or those of which *tud* is the first.

Tunna, as, ā, am, struck, hit; pricked; goaded, tormented, hurt, vexed, injured; cut, broken, cut down &c.; (*as*), m. the Toon or Tuna tree, the wood of which bears some resemblance to mahogany and is used for furniture &c.; Cedrela Toona. — *Tunna-vāya, as*, m. a tailor. — *Tunna-sevanī*, f. the suture of a wound (in surgery); a suture of the skull.

तुन *tuna, as, am*, m. n. (?), Ved. a various reading (in the Sāma-veda) for *tana*, posterity.

तुन्द् *tund*, cl. 1. P. *tundati*, &c., to be busy, active; to search, seek; [cf. rt. *trand*.]

तुन्द *tunda, am*, n. (said to be fr. rt. 1. *tud*), a protuberant belly, the belly, abdomen; (*as, ī*), m. f. the navel. — *Tunda-kūpikā* or *tunda-kūpī*, f. the cavity of the navel. — *Tunda-parimārja, as, ā, am*, one who is in the habit of stroking his belly (in the literal sense). — *Tunda-parimṛija, as, ā, am*, one who is in the habit of rubbing his belly (metaphorically), a lazy man, a sloth, a sluggard. — *Tunda-vat, ān, atī, at*, corpulent, fat.

Tundi, is, i, f. n. the belly; (*is*), f. the navel; (*is*), m., N. of a Gandharva.

Tundika, as, ā, am, having a large or prominent navel or belly, fat, corpulent; (*ā*), f. the navel.

Tundikara, as, m. the navel.

Tundita, as, ā, am, or *tundin, ī, inī, i*, or *tundibha* or *tundila, as, ā, am*, having a large or prominent belly or navel; gorbellied, corpulent. — *Tundila-phalā*, f. Cucumis Utilissimus.

तुन्न *tunna*. See under rt. 1. *tud* above.

तुप् *tup* or *tuph* or *tump* or *tumph*, cl. 1. 6. P. *topati, tupati, tophati, tuphati, tumpati, tumphati*, &c., (in the last two the form in cl. 1. will only differ from that in cl. 6. by the accent), to injure, hurt, wound; kill; *tump*, cl. 10. P. *tumpayati*, &c., a various reading for *tumb*, q. v.; [cf. Gr. τύπ-τ-ω, τύπο-ς, τυπή, τύμ-μα, τυπά(δ)ς, τύμπ-ανο-ν; Lat. *stupeo*; Old Germ. *stumpf, stumb-alon, stumph*; Old Island. *stúf-r*.]

तुवरी *tubarī*, f. = *tumbarī*, coriander; a bitch.

तुभ् *tubh*, cl. 1. A., 4. 9. P. *tobhate, tubhyati, tubhnāti, tutobha, tutubhe, tobhitum*, to push, to kill, hurt, injure in any manner; [cf. *stubh*; Goth. *thiubs*; Angl. Sax. *theof*.]

तुभ *tubha, as*, m. = *stubha*, a goat.

तुमल *tumala*, a various reading for *tumula*, q. v.

तुमिञ्ज *tumiñja, as*, m., N. of a man.

तुमुर *tumura, as, am*, m. n. mingled combat; [cf. *tumula*.]

तुमुल *tumula, as, ā, am*, tumultuous, noisy; excited, perplexed, confused; (*as, am*), m. n. uproar, tumult, tumultuous sound, clang, clatter, tumultuous or confused combat, melée, confusion; (*as*), m. Beleric Myrobalan, Terminalia Bellerica; (sometimes read *tumala* and *tumūla*); [cf. Lat. *tumultus*.] — *Tumula-yuddha, am*, n. a tumultuous conflict.

तुम्प् *tump* and *tumph*. See rt. *tup*.

तुम्ब् *tumb*, cl. 1. P. *tumbati*, &c., to distress, trouble, torment; to hurt, kill; cl. 10. P. *tumbayati*, &c., to trouble; or (according to a various reading) to be invisible.

तुम्ब *tumba, as*, m. a kind of long gourd, Lagenaria Vulgaris; (*ā*), f. Lagenaria Vulgaris; a milk-pail or vessel used in milking; a milch-cow; (*ī*), f. Lagenaria Vulgaris; Asteracantha Longifolia; (*am*), n. the fruit of Lagenaria Vulgaris; [cf. *kaṭu-tumbī, kumbha-t°, goraksha-t°*.] — *Tumba-vana, as* or *am*, m. n. (?), N. of a country. — *Tumba-vīṇa, as*, m. 'having a Tumba or gourd for a lute,' a N. of Śiva. — *Tumbī-pushpa, am*, n. the flower of the Lagenaria Vulgaris.

Tumbaka, as, m. the gourd Lagenaria Vulgaris; (*am*), n. the fruit of this gourd.

Tumbi, is, or *tumbikā*, f. a long white gourd, Lagenaria Vulgaris.

Tumbinī, f. = *kaṭu-tumbī*.

Tumbuka, as, m. the plant, and (*am*), n. the fruit, of Lagenaria Vulgaris.

तुम्बर *tumbara, as* or *am*, m. or n. (?), a kind of plant; (*ī*), f. = *tuvarī*, a sort of earth, = *tubarī*, a bitch.

तुम्बरु *tumbaru, us*, m., N. of a Gandharva; (perhaps a wrong reading for *tumburu*.)

तुम्बुम *tumbuma, ās*, m. pl., N. of a race or people; [cf. *tumbura*.]

तुम्बुर *tumbura, ās*, m. pl., N. of a race; (*ī*), f. coriander; a bitch; [cf. *tumbarī*.]

तुम्बुरु *tumburu, us*, m., N. of a pupil of Kalāpin; N. of a Gandharva; N. of the attendant of the fifth Arhat of the present Ava-sarpiṇī; (*u*), n. the fruit of Diospyros Embryopteris; coriander; (according to others *us, u*), m. n. the plant and seed of Diospyros Embryopteris.

तुम्र *tumra, as, ā, am* [cf. *tumura* above], Ved. big, strong, powerful; wild; (Sāy.) energetic (= *preraka*); destroying or defeating adversaries; see *tūtuma*; [cf. Lat. *tumidus*.]

तुर् 1. *tur* (connected with rts. *tṛī, tvar*, and *tūr*), cl. 6. P. A., Ved. *turati, -te*, &c., to hurry, hasten, press forwards, run; overcome; injure; cl. 3. P., Ved. *tutorti*: Caus. *turayati, -yitum*, to run: Desid., Ved. *tūtūrshati*: Intens. A., Ved. in the part. *tarturāṇa*, running forwards; [cf. rt. *tvar*; Gr. τύρ-βη, τύρ-βα, τυρβάζω, τυρβασία, Τυρ-μ-ίδαι; Lat. *turba, turbare, turb-idu-s, turma*; Angl. Sax. *thrym*, 'multitude, mass, troop;' Goth. *thaurp*; Old Germ. *dorf*, 'conference, assembly, meeting;' Old Island. *thyrpaz*, 'to congregate.']

2. *tur, tūr, tūr, tūr*, Ved. running a race, hastening, fighting, conquering, a warrior; [cf. *ap-tur, āji-tur*, &c.]

1. *tura, as, ā, am* (for 2. 3. *tura* see p. 379, col. 1), Ved. furthering, promoting, a promoter; quick, willing, prompt; (*am*), ind. quickly. — *Tura-ga, as*, m. 'going quickly,' a horse; the mind, thought; (*ī*), f. a mare, = *aśra-gandhā*, the plant Physalis Flexuosa; [cf. *turan-ga* and *turan-gama*.] — *Turaga-gandhā*, f. = *tura-gī*, Physalis Flexuosa; [cf. *turanga-gandhā*.] — *Turaga-dānava* or *turaga-daitya, as*, m. 'horse-

titan' or 'Dānava in the shape of a horse,' an epithet of Keśin. — *Turaga-nīla-tāla, as*, m. a kind of gesture with the hand. — *Turaga-priya, as* or *am*, m. or n. (?), barley, 'liked by horses;' [cf. *turanga-priya.*] — *Turaga-brahma-ćaryaka, am*, n. the sexual restraint of horses, i. e. compulsory celibacy, leading a life of continence, in consequence merely of being without female society. — *Turaga-medha, as*, m. a horse-sacrifice, = *aśva-medha*. — *Turaga-raksha, as*, m. 'horse-guardian,' a groom, an equery. — *Turaga-līlaka, as*, m. a particular time in music. — *Turaga-vadana* or *turagānana* (°*ga-ān*°), *ās*, m. pl. 'horse-faced,' N. of a race in the north of Madhya-deśa. — *Tura-gātu, us, us, u*, Ved. going quickly. — *Turagāroha* (°*ga-ār*°), *as*, m. 'one mounted on a horse,' a horseman. — *Turagin, ī, iṇī, i*, equestrian, riding, mounted or carried on a horse; (*ī*), m. a horseman, a cavalier. — *Turagīya*, an adj. derived fr. *tura-ga* in *khara-turagīya-samparka, as*, m. sexual intercourse between asses and horses. — *Turagopaćāraka* (°*ga-up*°), *as*, m. 'attending to horses,' a groom, an equery. — *Turan-ga, as*, m. 'going quickly,' a horse; a N. of the number seven (because of the seven horses of the sun); the mind considered as the seat of feeling as well as of intellect, the heart; (*ī*), f. a mare, = *tura-gī*, Physalis Flexuosa, = *ghoṭikā*, Cucumis Utilissimus; [cf. *tura-ga* and *turan-gama.*] — *Turan-gaka, as*, m. the plant Luffa Fœtida; (*ikā*), f. a kind of cucurbitaceous plant, = *deva-dālī*, the large dark-green pumpkin. — *Turanga-gandhā*, f. = *turaga-gandhā*. — *Turanga-dvishaṇī*, f. (for *-dveshaṇī*), a she-buffalo. — *Turanga-nātha, as*, m., N. of the chief of a sect. — *Turanga-priya, as*, m. = *turaga-priya*, barley. — *Turan-gama, as*, m. a horse; (*ī*), f. a mare; [cf. *tura-ga* and *turan-ga.*] — *Turangama-śālā*, f. a horse-stable. — *Turanga-medha, as*, m. a horse-sacrifice, = *aśva-medha*. — *Turanga-yāyin, ī, inī, i*, going on horseback. — *Turanga-vaktra* or *turanga-vadana, as*, m. 'horse-faced,' a Kinnara or chorister of Indra's heaven. — *Turanga-sādin, ī*, m. a horseman, a horse-soldier. — *Turanga-skandha, as*, m. a troop of horses. — *Turanga-sthāna, am*, n. a horse-stable. — *Turangāri* (°*ga-ari*), *is*, m. 'enemy of the horse,' a buffalo; fragrant oleander (*karavīra*). — *Turangārūḍha* (°*ga-ār*°), *as, ā, am*, mounted on horseback; (*as*), m. a horseman. — *Turangin, ī*, m. a horseman, a rider, a groom; [cf. *turagin.*] — *Tura-yā, ās, ās, am*, Ved. going quickly.

Turaṇa, as, ā, am, Ved. quick, swift, energetic; (*am*), n. haste.

Turaṇya, nom. P., Ved. *turaṇyati*, &c., to be quick or swift; to make haste, to accelerate.

Turaṇya-sad, t, t, t, Ved. dwelling among the quick or active.

Turaṇyu, us, us, u, Ved. quick, swift, energetic, zealous.

Turas-peya, am, n., Ved. anything drunk quickly (?).

1. *turi*, f., Ved. overpowering strength, superior power. (For 2. *turi* see col. 2.)

Turyā, f., Ved. overpowering or superior strength.

तुर 2. **tura**, *as, ā, am* (fr. rt. 2. *tu*; for 1. *tura* see p. 378, col. 3), Ved. strong, powerful, excelling, surpassing, overpowering; an epithet of Indra, of the Maruts, Ādityas, &c.; possessed of property; rich; abundant, abounding; (*as*), m., N. of a preceptor and priest with the patronymic Kāvasheya. — *Turā-shāh, -shāṭ, ṭ, ṭ*, overpowering the mighty or overpowering quickly, epithet of Indra and of Vishṇu; (*ṭ*), m. a N. of Indra.

Turāyaṇa, as, m. (a patronymic fr. 2. *tura*), N. of a man; (*am*), n., N. of a particular sacrifice or vow, = *paurṇamāsa-vikāra*, a modification of the full moon sacrifice; N. of a Sattra; (*as, ā, am*), m. f. n. attachment to any object or pursuit; attached to any object or pursuit (?); [cf. *parāyaṇa.*]

तुर 3. **tura**, *as, ā, am*, Ved. hurt, wounded; (according to Sāy. = *ā-tura*, q. v.)

तुरकिन् **turakin**, *ī, iṇī, i*, Turkish; [cf. *turushka.*]

तुरक्व **turakva**, N. of a people, 'the Turks;' [cf. *turushka.*]

तुरग **tura-ga**, *turanga*. See 1. *tura*, p. 378.

तुरष्क **turashka**, N. of a country and people mentioned in the Srī-shavāyaṇa or part of the Romaka-siddhānta.

तुराषाह् **turā-shāh**. See 2. *tura*, col. 1.

तुरी 2. **turī**, f. (or *turi, is*, in the first sense; cf. *tuli*), the fibrous stick used by weavers to clean and separate the threads of the woof; a painter's brush; a shuttle; N. of a wife of Kṛishṇa (or Vasudeva) and mother of Jaras. (For 1. *turī* see col. 1.)

तुरीप **turīpa**, *am*, n., Ved. seminal fluid; (*as*), m. an epithet of Tvashṭṛi, 'spermatic.'

तुरीय 1. **turīya**, P., Ved. *turīyati*, &c., to go or move; [cf. rt. 1. *tur* and *turaṇya.*]

तुरीय 2. **turīya**, *as, ā, am*, Ved. fourth, a fourth; consisting of four parts; whose power extends on all four sides, mighty; (*am*), n. the fourth state of the soul (according to the Vedānta phil.), that state in which it has become one with Brahma or the universal spirit; (*as, ā, am*), (with a different accent), a fourth, constituting the fourth part; (*am*), n. a fourth part, a quarter; [cf. *turya* and *ćaturtha.*] — *Turīya-bhāga, as*, m. a fourth part or share. — *Turīya-bhāj, k, k, k*, a sharer of a fourth. — *Turīya-varṇa, as, ā, am*, belonging to the fourth caste; (*as*), m. the fourth caste or tribe, a Sūdra. — *Turīyānśa* (°*ya-an*°), *as*, m. a fourth part or share, a quarter. — *Turīyātīta* (°*ya-at*°), N. of an Upanishad. — *Turīyārdha* (°*ya-ar*°), *am*, n. one half of a fourth, an eighth part.

Turīyaka, as, ā, am, a fourth (part).

Turya, as, ā, am, = 2. *turīya*, fourth, a fourth; (*am*), n. the fourth state of the soul, in which it becomes one with Brahma, a quarter; (*as, ā, am*), being in the above state; the fourth (part). — *Turya-vah* or *-vāh, ṭ*, f. *turyauhī*, Ved. an ox or cow four years old.

तुरुष्क **turushka**, *ās*, m. pl., N. of a race, the Indo-Scythian race or Turks; (*as*), m. the country of this race, Turan or Turkestan; a prince of this race; (*as, am*), m. n. olibanum, Indian incense, the resin of the Boswellia Serrata; the resin of the Pinus Longifolia; [cf. *yāvana.*]

तुर्फरि **turphari**, Ved. (fr. rt. *tṛiph*), according to Yāska = *kshipra-hantṛi*, striking quickly; (according to Sāy., *turpharī*, du. = killers of the enemy.)

Turpharītu, us, us, u, Ved. according to Yāska = *hantṛi*, striking; (according to Sāy., *turpharītū*, du. = *tarphitārau* = *śatrūṇām hantārau.*)

तुर्य **turya**. See above under 2. *turīya*.

तुर्या **turyā**, f. See col. 1.

तुर्व् **turv** [cf. rt. 1. *tur*], cl. 1. P., Ved. *tūrvati, tutūrva, tūrvitum*, to overpower, overcome, excel; to cause to overpower or conquer, help to victory; to save; to strike, to hurt, kill, injure; [cf. *tūrvayāṇa* and *tūrvi.*]

Turvaṇi, is, is, i (fr. rt. 1. *tur*), Ved. overpowering, excelling, victorious; (Sāy.) acting quickly, serving quickly, moving quickly; injuring or destroying enemies.

Turvan, a, n., Ved. (only used in the dat. *turvaṇe*), conquering, defeating, injuring.

तुर्वश **turvaśa**, *as*, m. (also written *turvasu*), Ved., N. of a hero and ancestor of the Āryan race, often mentioned in the Ṛig-veda and probably related to the Kaṇvas; he is generally mentioned together with his brother Yadu; N. of a whole race; [cf. *turvasu* and *taurvaśa.*]

तुर्वसु **turvasu**, *us*, m. (a later form of *turvaśa*), N. of a son of Yayāti and Devayānī and brother of Yadu.

तुर्वीति **turvīti**, *is*, m., Ved., N. of a man or of a race.

तुल् **tul** [cf. rt. *tūl*], cl. 10. P. A. (according to Vopa-deva also cl. 1. P.) *tolayati* or *tulayati, -te*, (the form *tolayati* is rarely used in the metaphorical sense), *tolati, atūtulat, -yitum*, to lift up, raise; to determine the weight of anything by lifting it; to weigh, poise, measure; to compare by weighing and examining; to ponder, weigh in the mind, consider; to examine with distrust, suspect; to make equal in weight, to equal, compare one thing with another (with inst., e. g. *na brāhmaṇais tulaye bhūtam anyat*, I do not compare any other being with Brāhmans); to counterpoise, counterbalance, outweigh, weigh against, equal in weight, match, be equal to (with acc.); to possess in the same degree, to attain, reach; [cf. rt. *dul*: Old Lat. *tul-o, te-tul-i*: Lat. *tul-i, lātus* (for *tlātus*), *tollere, toll-o, tolleno, tolerare, tolūtim*: Gr. τλῆ-ναι, τάλα-ς, πολύ-τλᾱ-ς, ταλα-ό-ς, τλή-μων, τάλ-αντο-ν, ἀ-τάλαντο-ς, τάλ-αρο-ς, τελα-μών, τόλ-μα, τολμά-ω, Τάν-ταλο-ς: Goth. *thul-an*, 'to tolerate;' *us-thul-ain-s*, 'patience:' Angl. Sax. *tholian, thyl-dian, athylgian*: Old Germ. *dol-an*: Germ. *duld-en*: Slav. *tul-ŭ*, 'a quiver.']

Tulana, am, n. lifting, raising; weighing, measuring; rating, assessing, taxing; a particular high number.

Tulayitvā, ind. having weighed, having counterpoised, having made equal or like, &c.

Tulā, f. a balance, especially a fine balance, the beam of a balance, goldsmith's or assay scales; a measure, a weight, (*tulayā dhṛi*, to hold in a balance, to weigh); the balance as an ordeal; weighing; resemblance, likeness, equality, similarity; the sign of the zodiac Libra; the seventh sign in a circle divided like a zodiac; a measure or weight of gold and silver = 100 Palas or about 145 ounces troy; a kind of vessel; sloping beams or timbers in the roof of a house; [cf. *bhāra-tulā* and *tulopatulā.*] — *Tulā-koṭi, is, ī*, m. f. an ornament on the feet or toes of women; a particular weight; a hundred millions, = *arbuda*. — *Tulā-kośa* or *tulā-kosha, as*, m. a place where a balance or pair of scales is kept; ordeal by weighing; see *tulā-parīkshā*. — *Tulākośa-rahasya, am*, n. a mystical rite which consists in weighing seeds and thence calculating the fertility of the soil. — *Tulā-dāna, am*, n. the gift to a Brāhman of as much gold, silver, &c., as equals the weight of the body. — *Tulā-dhaṭa, as*, m. the scale or cup of a balance; an oar, a paddle. — *Tulā-dhara, as*, m. 'holding a pair of scales,' the sign of the zodiac Libra, the sun. — *Tulā-dhāra, as, ā, am*, 'holding a pair of scales;' trading, trafficking, a trader, a dealer; (*as*), m. the string of a balance; the beam; the sign of the zodiac Libra; N. of a merchant. — *Tulā-paddhati*, N. of a book by Kamalākara-bhaṭṭa. — *Tulā-parīkshā*, f. ordeal by the balance, (the weight of the accused being first taken, certain prayers and ceremonies are performed, after which he is weighed again; if lighter, he is innocent; if heavier, or as at first, guilty.) — *Tulā-purusha, as*, m. 'a weighed man,' or gold, jewels, and other ornaments equal to a man's weight, an offering of such extent constituting one of the sixteen pious gifts; a kind of penance. — *Tulāpurusha-dāna, am*, n. gift of gold or valuables to an amount equivalent to the weight of the donor. — *Tulā-pragraha* or *tulā-pragrāha, as*, m. the string of a balance. — *Tulā-māna, am*, n. measure by weight. — *Tulā-yashṭi, is*, m. or f. (?), the beam of a balance. — *Tulā-vat, ān, atī, at*, furnished with or possessed of a balance. — *Tulā-vīja, am*, n. the Guñjā or berry of the Abrus Precatorius, from which the goldsmith's or jeweller's weight in India is taken; the berry weighs about $1\frac{5}{16}$ grain troy, the factitious weight about $2\frac{3}{16}$.

—*Tulā-sūtra, am,* n. the string of a balance. —*Tulopatulā* (°*lā-up*°), f. a supporting beam or prop in the roof of a house (?).

Tulita, as, ā, am, made equal or like, equalled, compared (with inst., e. g. *śaśāṅkena tulita,* compared with the moon); weighed, counterpoised.

Tulya, as, ā, am, equal to, of the same kind or class, well matched, similar, comparable, equally valuable or precious, like, resembling (with gen. or inst., e. g. *tulya etasya,* equal to him; *prāṇais tulyā,* a woman as dear as life; or with the crude form in comp., e. g. *amṛita-tulya,* similar to the immortals or to nectar; *etat-tulya,* equal to this man); fit for (with inst.); even, same; indifferent; (*am*), ind. equally, similarly, in like manner; (*as*), m., N. of a Gandharva. —*Tulya-tā,* f. or *tulya-tva, am,* n. equality, likeness, sameness, resemblance (with inst., e. g. *vayasā tulyatā,* equality in age); equality of place, conjunction (in astronomy); *dṛik-tulyatā,* conformity with any observed place. —*Tulya-tejas, ās, ās, as,* equal in splendor. —*Tulya-darśana, as, ā, am,* regarding with equal or indifferent eyes. —*Tulya-pāna, am,* n. drinking together, compotation. —*Tulya-bala, as, ā, am,* of equal strength. —*Tulya-bhāvanā,* f. (in arithm. or algebra) combination of like or analogous sets of magnitude. —*Tulya-mūlya, as, ā, am,* of equal value. —*Tulya-yogitā,* f. 'combination of equal actions or qualities,' a figure in rhetoric. —*Tulya-rūpa, as, ā* or *ī, am,* of like or equal form; like, similar, analogous. —*Tulya-lakshaṇā,* f. a particular figure in rhetoric. —*Tulya-vaṅśa, as, ā, am,* equal in race, of equal race. —*Tulya-vikrama, as, ā, am,* of equal prowess. —*Tulya-vīrya, as, ā, am,* of equal strength. —*Tulya-vṛitti, is, is, i,* following the same or similar occupation. —*Tulya-śas,* ind. in equal parts. —*Tulya-śuddhi, is,* f. equal subtraction, transposition (in arithmetic). —*Tulya-śodhana, am,* n. reducing an equation by removing the like magnitudes on both sides. —*Tulyākṛiti* (°*ya-āk*°), *is, is, i,* of the same form, alike. —*Tulyātulya, as, ā, am,* similar and dissimilar, like and unlike. —*Tulyānumāna* (°*ya-an*°), *am,* n. like inference, a parallel case. —*Tulyodyoga* (°*ya-ud*°), *as, ā, am,* equal in labours or exertions.

तुलकुचि ***tulakuċi, is,*** **m., N. of a prince.**

तुलभ ***tulabha, ās,*** **m. pl., N. of a warrior-** tribe.

Tulabhīya, as, m. a prince of the above tribe.

तुलसारिणी ***tulasāriṇī,*** **f. = *tūṇa*, a quiver.**

तुलसी ***tulasī*** **or *tulasikā,* f. holy basil,** a small shrub said to have been produced from the hair of the goddess Tulasī and held in veneration by the worshippers of Vishṇu (Ocymum Sanctum); N. of a deity. —*Tulasī-dveshā,* f. a kind of plant, = *varvarī.* —*Tulasī-pattra, am,* n. a Tulasī leaf, hence a very small gift. —*Tulasī-vivāha, as,* m. the marriage of an image of Vishṇu with the holy basil, a festival on the twelfth day in the first half of the month Kārttika. —*Tulasī-vṛindāvana, as,* m. a small altar, a square pedestal before the gate of a Hindū house on which the sacred basil is planted.

तुलि ***tuli, is,*** **or *tulī,* f. a fibrous stick or** brush used by weavers for cleaning the threads of the woof; a painter's brush used for that purpose; [cf. *tūlī, tūli, tūlikā, turī.*] —*Tuli-phalā,* f. the Simul or silk-cotton tree; [cf. *tūli-phalā.*]

Tulinī (= *tūlinī*), f. the Simul or silk-cotton tree.

तुलिका ***tulikā,*** **f. a small bird said to re-**semble the wagtail.

तुल्य ***tulya.*** **See above.**

तुवर ***tuvara, as, ā, am,*** **astringent; beard-**less; (*as, am*), m. n. an astringent taste; (*as*), m. a sort of grain, = *tuvara-yāvanāla;* (*ī*), f. = *āḍhakī,* a kind of lentil, Cajanus Indicus; a fragrant earth; alum; [cf. *tūvara.*] —*Tuvara-yāvanāla, as,* m. a sort of grain, = *kashāya-yāvanāla,* &c. —*Tuvarī-śimba, as,* m. a kind of plant, Cassia Tora, = *ċakra-mardaka.*

Tuvaraka, as, m. a sort of grain (?); N. of a tree growing in the countries bordering on the western ocean; (*ikā*), f. Cajanus Indicus; a sort of earth; alum.

तुवि ***tuvi*** **(fr. rt. 2. *tu*), = *bahu*, much, many,** great, strong, excessive, very, (only used in the Ved. compounds enumerated below); (*is*), f. = *tumbī,* a long gourd. —*Tuvi-kūrmi, is, is, i,* or *tuvi-kūrmin, ī, iṇī, i,* Ved. powerful in working, efficacious; (Sāy.) doing many and various deeds; epithet of Indra. —*Tuvi-kratu, us, us, u,* Ved. of a strong will; (Sāy.) doing many deeds; having much knowledge; epithet of Indra. —*Tuvi-ksha, as, ā, am,* Ved. epithet of Indra's bow, (according to Sāy. and the Nirukta = *bahu-vikshepa* or *mahā-vikshepa*), 'throwing far,' perhaps 'very destructive,' (*ksha* being then fr. rt. 4. *kshi.*) —*Tuvi-kshatra, as, ā, am,* Ved. ruling powerfully, (according to Mahī-dhara) preserving from many injuries, epithet of Aditi. —*Tuvi-gra, as, ā, am,* Ved. swallowing much; (Sāy.) sounding loudly; going quickly. —*Tuvi-grābha, as, ā, am,* Ved. seizing powerfully. —*Tuvi-gri, is, is, i,* Ved. swallowing much or greedily; (Sāy.) having a full throat or to be praised by many. —*Tuvi-grīva, as, ā, am,* Ved. having a powerful or firm or erect neck, having many throats, swallowing or consuming much, all-embracing. —*Tuvi-jāta, as, ā, am,* Ved. of strong or powerful nature, powerful; born for many, born for the protection of many; (Sāy.) born with many (qualities), from whom many are born; epithet of the gods Indra, Varuṇa, Varuṇa-Mitra, &c. —*Tuvi-deshṇa, as, ā, am,* Ved. granting excellent gifts, epithet of Indra; (Sāy.) giving much. —*Tuvi-dyumna, as, ā, am,* Ved. very glorious, powerful, wealthy; epithet of Indra, and of the Maruts. —*Tuvi-nṛimṇa, as, ā, am,* Ved. very manly or valiant or courageous; epithet of Indra. —*Tuvi-prati, is, is, i,* Ved. (Sāy.) visiting many, approaching many; withstanding many, (perhaps rather) resisting powerfully; [cf. *a-prati.*] —*Tuvi-bādha, as, ā, am,* Ved. killing many. —*Tuvi-brahman, ā, ā, a,* Ved. very devoted or pious. —*Tuvi-manyu, us, us, u,* Ved. very zealous, very furious. —*Tuvi-mātra, as, ā, am,* Ved. making or creating much, very efficacious, measuring many (?). —*Tuvi-mraksha, as, ā, am,* Ved. injuring greatly, destructive; (Sāy.) destroying much (timber). —*Tuvi-rādhas, ās, ās, as,* Ved. granting in abundance; (Sāy.) opulent, having great wealth. —*Tuvi-vāja, as, ā, am,* Ved. having much food or strength, strengthening, abounding with food. —*Tuvi-śagma, as, ā, am,* Ved. able to do much; (Sāy.) having much enjoyment or pleasure. —*Tuvi-shma, as, ā, am,* Ved. high-spirited; (Sāy.) of great power, very strong, epithet of Indra and of Indra-Varuṇa. —*Tuvi-śravas, ās, ās, as,* Ved. highly renowned, having great fame. —*Tuviśravas-tama, as, ā, am,* having very great fame, an epithet of Agni. —*Tuvishṭama, as, ā, am,* Ved. strongest, most powerful, most valid. —*Tuvish-mat, ān, atī, at,* Ved. powerful, mighty, efficacious. —*Tuvi-shvaṇas* (°*vi-sv*°), *ās, ās, as,* or *tuvi-shvaṇi, is, is, i,* or *tuvi-shvan, ā, ā, a,* Ved. loud-sounding, roaring. —*Tuvi-magha, as, ā, am,* Ved. giving abundantly; (Sāy.) having great riches, epithet of Indra, and of the Maruts. —*Tuvi-rava, as, ā, am,* Ved. making a terrible noise (in battle &c.). —*Tuvi-ravat, ān, atī, at,* Ved. making a great noise (?); (Sāy.) possessed of many praisers, (either for *tuvirava-vat,* or *ravān* may be an irregular nom. case of the part. *ravat.*) —*Tuvy-ojas, ās, ās, as,* Ved. very strong or powerful.

तुश 1. *tuś,* cl. 1. A., Ved. *tośate,* &c., to drip, trickle; sprinkle; (Sāy.) to be struck; to be pressed out or extracted; to be drunk; [cf. *tośa* and *tośas.*]

तुश 2. *tuś* (for *tush?*), cl. 1. A., Ved. *tośate,* &c., to quiet, pacify, appease, satisfy.

तुष *tush* [cf. rt. 1. *jush*], cl. 4. P. (ep. also A.) *tushyati, -te, tutosha, tokshyati, atushat, toshṭum,* to become tranquil or calm or quiet; to be contented or satisfied, to be pleased or delighted with anything or any person (with inst., gen., loc. or *prati* after the acc., e. g. *dattena tushyati,* he is satisfied with the gift; *tasya* or *tena* or *tasmin* or *tam prati tushyāmi,* I am pleased with him); to satisfy, please (with acc., e. g. *sā patiṃ na tutosha,* she did not please her husband): Caus. P. *toshayati, -yitum,* to make satisfied, satisfy, please, gratify, gladden, quiet, calm, appease, pacify; to gratify any one with anything (with acc. of the person and inst. of the thing, e. g. *toshaya Haraṃ tapasā,* gratify Śiva with penance; *ātmānam toshayati,* he satisfies himself, he becomes satisfied): Desid. *tutukshati:* Intens. *totushyate, totoshṭi;* [cf. *tūshṇīm;* cf. also Lith. *tësziju,* 'to recreate, to refresh;' Lat. *taceo;* Goth. *thahan.*]

Tushita, ās, m. pl. a class of subordinate deities, thirty-six in number (sometimes reckoned as twelve in number and identified with the twelve Ādityas); N. of twelve sons of Bhaga-vat; (*as*), m. a N. of Vishṇu (one of the Ādityas); (*ā*), f., N. of the wife of Veda-śiras and mother of the god Vibhu. —*Tushita-kāyika, as, ā, am,* belonging to the body or class of the Tushitas.

Tushṭa, as, ā, am, satisfied, contented, pleased, glad, &c. —*Tushṭa-dhī, dhīs, dhīs, dhi,* pleased in mind, satisfied.

Tushṭi, is, f. satisfaction, gratification, contentment, pleasure; acquiescence, indifference to everything but that possessed, (the Sāṅkhya phil. reckons nine kinds of Tushṭi); Contentment personified as a daughter of Daksha and mother of Santosha or Muda; N. of a daughter of Kaśyapa; of a deity sprung from the Kalās of Prakṛiti and wife of Ananta; of a Mātṛikā; of one of the Kalās of the moon. —*Tushṭi-kara, as, ā* or *ī, am,* causing satisfaction, pleasing, gratifying, satisfying. —*Tushṭi-janana, as, ī, am,* or *tushṭi-da, as, ā, am,* giving or producing satisfaction, affording pleasure, gratifying. —*Tushṭi-mat, ān, atī, at,* pleased, gratified; (*ān*), m., N. of a prince, a son of Ugra-sena.

Tushṭvā, ind. having pleased or satisfied.

Tushya, as, ā, am, to be satisfied or gratified, easily satisfied; an epithet of Śiva.

Tosha, toshita, &c. See s. v.

तुष ***tusha, as,*** **m. (perhaps connected with** *tvaċ*), the husk or chaff of grain, of corn, rice, &c. [cf. *a-tusha, ut-tusha, nis-tusha, tuċċha*]; Beleric Myrobalan, Terminalia Bellerica. —*Tusha-graha, as,* m. Agni or fire ('seizing the husk'). —*Tusha-ja, as, ā, am,* produced from husk or chaff. —*Tushaja-ka, as,* m., N. of a Śūdra. —*Tusha-dhānya, am,* n. a leguminous plant; N. of a place. —*Tusha-vana, as* or *am,* m. or n. (?), N. of a place; (a various reading has *tumva-vana.*) —*Tusha-sāra, as,* m. (= *tusha-graha*), Agni or fire. —*Tushāgni* (°*sha-ag*°), *is,* m. or *tushānala* (°*sha-an*°), *as,* m. a conflagration of chaff or of the husk of corn; a capital punishment which consists in twisting dry straw &c. round the limbs of a criminal and setting it on fire. —*Tushāmbu* (°*sha-am*°), *u,* n. sour rice or barley-gruel. —*Tushottha* (°*sha-ut*°), *as,* m. or *tushodaka* (°*sha-ud*°), *am,* n. sour rice-gruel or barley-gruel, ('made from husk.')

तुषस्प ***tushaspa, as,*** **m., N. of a man.**

तुषार ***tushāra, as, ā, am*** **(said to be fr. rt.** *tush*), cold, frigid, frosty, dewy; (*as*), m. frost, cold; ice, snow, mist, dew, thin rain; N. of a place mentioned in the Śrī-shavāyaṇa or part of the Romaka-siddhānta; (*ās*), m. pl., N. of a race; [cf. *tuhina;* cf. also Angl. Sax. *thystre, thystrian, theodre, theosterlic.*] —*Tushāra-kaṇa, as,* m. a dew-drop, an icicle, hoar frost. — *Tushāra-kāla, as,* m. winter, the cold season. — *Tushāra-kiraṇa, as,* m. the moon ('having cold rays'). — *Tushāra-giri, is,* m. the snowy mountain, the Himālaya. — *Tushāra-gaura, as, ī, am,* white as snow, white with snow; camphor. — *Tushāra-raśmi, is,* m. the moon; [cf. *tushāra-kiraṇa.*] — *Tushārādri* (°*ra-ad*°), *is,* m. or *tushāra-parvata* or *tushāra-śaila, as,* m. the Himālaya mountain.

तुषित *tushita, tushṭi,* &c. See under rt. *tush.*

तुष्टु *tushṭu, us,* m. a jewel worn in the ears.

तुस् *tus,* cl. 1. P. *tosati,* &c., to sound.

तुस *tusa, as,* m. the husk of corn or rice, = *tusha,* q. v.

तुस्त *tusta, as, am,* m. n. dust; husk; (a various reading for *busta*); [cf. *tūsta;* Angl. Sax. and Eng. *dust.*]

तुह् *tuh,* cl. 1. P. *tohati,* &c., to hurt, pain, kill.

तुहर *tuhara, as,* m., N. of one of the attendants of Skanda; (also written *tuhāra.*)

तुहिन *tuhina, as, ā, am* (said to be fr. rt. *tuh*), cold, frigid, frosty; (*am*), n. mist, dew, snow, frost, cold; moonlight, moonshine; camphor; (*ā*), f., N. of a tree, = *śuka-nāsa;* [cf. *tushāra;* Hib. *deigh,* 'ice.'] — *Tuhina-kaṇa, as,* m. a dew-drop; snow-flake. — *Tuhina-kiraṇa, as,* m. 'cold-rayed,' the moon. — *Tuhinakiraṇa-putra, as,* m. the son of the moon, the planet Mercury. — *Tuhina-gu, us,* m. 'having cold rays,' the moon. — *Tuhina-dyuti, is,* m. or *tuhina-raśmi, is,* m. 'cold-rayed,' the moon. — *Tuhina-śarkarā,* f. a piece of ice, ice. — *Tuhina-śaila, as,* m. a snowy mountain, a snowy peak, the Himālaya. — *Tuhināṅśu* (°*na-aṅ*°), *us,* m. 'cold-rayed,' the moon; camphor. — *Tuhināṅśu-taila, am,* n. oil of camphor. — *Tuhināćala* (°*na-ać*°), *as,* m. or *tuhinādri* (°*na-ad*°), *is,* m. a snow mountain, a snowy peak, the Himālaya.

तुहुण्ड *tuhuṇḍa, as,* m., N. of a Dānava; of a son of Dhṛita-rāshṭra.

तूख *tūkha, as,* m., N. of a man.

तूड् *tūḍ* (= *tuḍ*), cl. 1. P. *tūḍati,* &c., to split; to slight, disrespect.

तूण् *tūṇ* [cf. *kūṇ* and *ćūṇ*], cl. 10. P. *tūṇayati, -yitum,* to shrink, contract, close as the eyelids, wink; A. *tūṇayate,* to fill, fill up.

तूण *tūṇa, as, ī,* m. f. (this word appears to be connected with the preceding root, which may perhaps be formed from it), a quiver; (*ī*), f. an internal disease by which the anus and the bladder become painfully affected; the Indigo plant; [cf. Slav. *tūl,* 'quiver.'] — *Tūṇa-dhāra, as,* m. a quiver-bearer (a kind of officer). — *Tūṇa-mukha, am,* n. the mouth or opening of a quiver. — *Tūṇa-vat, ān, atī, at,* furnished with a quiver.

Tūṇi, is, m. a quiver [cf. *tūṇa* and *tūṇī*]; N. of a prince, father of Yugan-dhara.

Tūṇika or *tūṇīka, as,* m., N. of a tree, = *nandī-vṛiksha.*

Tūṇin, ī, inī, i, having a quiver, quivered; (*ī*), m., N. of a tree, = *nandī-vṛiksha.*

Tūṇīra, as, am, m. n. a quiver. — *Tūṇīra-vat, ān, atī, at,* provided with a quiver.

तूणक *tūṇaka, as,* m. a kind of metre consisting of four lines of fifteen syllables each.

तूणव *tūṇava, as,* m., Ved. a wind instrument, a flute (?). — *Tūṇava-dhma, as,* m., Ved. a flute-player (?).

तूणिक *tūṇika, tūṇīka.* See above.

तूतक *tūtaka, am,* n. = *tuttha,* blue vitriol.

तूतुजान *tūtujāna, as, ā, am* (fr. rt. 2. *tuj*), Ved. hastening, quick, eager, ardent.

Tūtuji, is, is, i, Ved. quick, swift; (a various reading has *tūtujit.*)

तूतुम *tūtumu, as, ā, am,* Ved. granting much (?); (Sāy.) quick, active; [cf. *tumra.*]

तूद *tūda, as,* m. = *tūla-vṛiksha,* the cotton tree; also = توت, the mulberry tree; Thespesia Populneoides; (*ī*), f., N. of a district.

तूपर *tūpara, as, ā, am,* Ved. hornless, (often applied to a goat, and sometimes used alone to denote 'a hornless goat.')

तूबर *tūbara,* see *tūvara; tūbarikā, tubarī,* and *tūbarikā,* f. = *tubarikā,* a kind of earth.

तूय *tūya, as, ā, am* (fr. rt. 2. *tu*), Ved. strong, powerful; (Sāy.) quick, not delaying; (*am*), n. water; (*am*), ind. quickly, swiftly.

तूर् 1. *tūr* [cf. rt. 1. *tur* and *tvar*], cl. 4. A. *tūryate,* &c., to go quickly, make haste; to kill, hurt, injure.

तूर् 2. *tūr, r, r, r* (fr. *tvar*), hastening; a courier; (*r*), f. speed, swift motion, swiftness; [cf. 2. *tur.*]

तूर *tūra, am,* n. = 1. *tūrya,* any musical instrument; (*ī*), f. a thorn-apple; [cf. *ardha-tūra.*]

तूर्घ्न *tūrghna, am,* n., N. of the northern part of Kuru-kshetra.

तूर्ण *tūrṇa, as, ā, am* (fr. rt. *turv* and *tvar*), quick, expeditious; fleet; (*am*), n. rapidity, quickness; (*am*), ind. quick, swift, quickly, speedily, in haste; [cf. Hib. *tonn,* 'quick.'] — *Tūrṇa-vani,* quickly honouring or serving, (a word made by Yāska to explain the etymology of *turvaṇi,* q. v.) — *Tūrṇodita* (°*ṇa-ud*°), *as, ā, am,* spoken quickly, uttered rapidly.

Tūrṇaka, as or *am,* m. or n. (?), a sort of rice which ripens quickly.

Tūrṇi, is, is, i, Ved. quick, swift, expeditious; clever, zealous; (*is*), m. f. speed, velocity, expedition; (*is*), m. the mind; a Śloka; dirt, excrement. — *Tūrṇy-artha, as, ā, am,* Ved. pursuing an object with zeal, eager to accomplish a purpose; (Sāy.) going quickly.

Tūrta, as, ā, am, Ved. quick, speedy.

तूर्णाश *tūrṇāśa, am,* n., Ved. water; a waterfall (?).

तूर्य 1. *tūrya, am,* n., Ved. an abstract noun of 2. *tur,* occurring at the end of comp. [cf. *ap-tūrya* under *apta,* &c.]; (*as, am*), m. n. a musical instrument, of which four kinds are sometimes reckoned, (wind instruments, stringed instruments, &c.); *sa-tūrya,* accompanied by music; *sa-tūryam,* with music; [cf. *mangala-t*°, *mṛityu-t*°, *yāma-t*°, *taurya.*] — *Tūrya-khaṇḍa, as,* m. a musical instrument, a sort of tabor. — *Tūrya-maya, as, ī, am,* representing music, musical. — *Tūryaugha* (°*ya-ogha*), *as,* m. a band of instruments.

तूर्य 2. *tūrya, as, ā, am* (for *turya*), a fourth, a quarter.

तूर्वयाण *tūrvayāṇa, as, ā, am* (fr. rt. *turv*), Ved. overpowering; (Sāy.) going quickly, having a rapid course (as if *tūrva-yāna*); (*as*), m., N. of a man.

Tūrvi, is, is, i, Ved. excelling, superior; (Sāy.) quick, rapid.

तूल् *tūl* [cf. *tul*], cl. 1. P. and according to some cl. 10. P. A. *tūlati, tūlayati, -te,* &c., to ascertain quantity or weight; to weigh, measure; to fill; [cf. rt. *tūṇ.*]

तूल *tūla, am,* n. a tuft of grass or reeds &c.; the panicle of a flower or plant; (*as, am*), m. n. cotton; (*am*), n. the mulberry, Morus Indica; the thorn-apple; the sky, air, atmosphere; (*ā*), f. the cotton tree; the wick of a lamp, cotton twisted into that form for applying unguents &c.; (*ī*), f. cotton; the wick of a lamp; a weaver's fibrous stick or brush, a painter's brush &c.; the Indigo plant; [cf. *indra-tūla* &c.] — *Tūla-kārmuka* or *tūla-ćāpa, am,* n. or *tūla-dhanus, us,* n. 'cotton-bow,' i. e. a bow or similarly shaped instrument used for cleaning cotton. — *Tūla-nālī* or *tūla-nālikā,* f. 'cotton-tube,' i. e. a thick roll of cotton which is drawn out in spinning. — *Tūla-piću, us,* m. = *tūla* or *piću,* cotton. — *Tūla-mūla,* N. of a district on the Candra-bhāgā. — *Tūla-vṛiksha, as,* m. the cotton tree. — *Tūla-śarkarā,* f. a pod or seed of the cotton plant, any seed yielding a similar substance. — *Tūla-sećana, am,* n. the act of spinning ('sprinkling or moistening the cotton').

Tūlaka, am, n. cotton.

Tūli, is, f. a painter's brush or pencil or a fibrous stick so used and for other purposes; [cf. *tūlī* under *tūla.*] — *Tūli-phalā,* f. the silk-cotton tree.

Tūlikā, f. a pencil, a brush, a painter's brush or stick with a fibrous extremity used as one; a wick or twist of cotton either for a lamp or for applying unguents, a whisk of any soft substance, &c.; a kind of probing-rod; a mattress or quilt filled with cotton, a bed, a down or cotton bed; an ingot mould.

Tūlinī, f. the silk-cotton tree; a kind of bulbous plant, = *lakshmaṇā-kanda.*

तूवर *tūvara, as, ā, am,* = *tuvara,* astringent; (*as*), m. an astringent taste; a bull without horns [cf. *tūpara*] though of an age to have them; a beardless man; a eunuch; (*ī*), f. a fragrant earth, = *tuvarī.*

Tūvaraka, as, ā, am, unmanly; a eunuch; (used as a taunt or abusive epithet.)

Tūvarikā, f. = *tuvarikā,* a kind of earth.

तूष् *tūsh* (= *tush*), cl. 1. P. *tūshati,* &c., to be satisfied or pleased; to satisfy.

तूष *tūsha, as, am,* m. n., Ved. a lappet, the border or fringe of a garment.

तूष्णीम् *tūshṇīm,* ind. (fr. rt. *tush* with the termination *nīm,* as in *idānīm, tadānīm,* &c.; cf. *josham* fr. rt. 1. *jush*), silent, in silence, silently, quietly, still, softly, without speaking, without noise. — *Tūshṇīm-śansa, as,* m., Ved. silent recitation, certain formulas or verses to be recited; [cf. Russ. *tishina,* 'silence, tranquillity:' Lith. *tylà,* 'silence;' *tylù,* 'to be silent:' Hib. *tosd,* 'silence, taciturnity;' *tosdadh,* 'silencing, confutation.'] — *Tūshṇīm-śīla, as, ā, am,* silent, taciturn. — *Tūshṇīn-gangam,* ind. (a place) where the Ganges flows silently. — *Tūshṇīm-bhāva, as,* m. the being silent, silence, taciturnity; (rarely spelt *tushṇī-bhāva.*) — *Tūshṇīm-bhūta, as, ā, am,* being silent, silent. — *Tūshṇīm-bhūya, as, ā, am,* become silent. — *Tūshṇī-śīla* = *tūshṇīm-śīla,* (perhaps a wrong reading.)

Tūshṇīka, as, ā, am, silent, taciturn; (*am* or *ām*), ind. silently, quickly.

तूस्त *tūsta, am,* n. (said to be fr. rt. *tus*), a braid of hair, matted or clotted hair; dust; sin; an atom, any very minute or delicate substance.

तृ *tṛi, tā,* m. (for *stṛi*), Ved. a star; [cf. *tāra.*]

तृंह् *triṇh.* See rt. *triḥ,* p. 383, col. 2.

Triṇhaṇa, am, n. crushing, bruising, hurting, killing.

Triṇhaṇīya, as, ā, am, to be crushed, killed, &c.

Tṛiḍha, as, ā, am, crushed, bruised, hurt, injured, &c. See under rt. *tṛih*, p. 383.

तृक्वन् *tṛikvan, ā*, m., Ved. a thief; (also read *trikvan* and *ṛikvan*.)

तृक्ष् *tṛiksh*, cl. 1. P. *tṛikshati*, &c., to go, move or approach; [cf. rt. *stṛiksh*: Gr. τρέχω: Goth. *thragjan*, 'to run;' *treihan*, 'to urge:' Hib. *teilg*, 'to go;' *teilgin*, 'a shock.']

तृक्ष *tṛiksha, as*, m. or *tṛikshas, as*, n., Ved. strength (?), [cf. *tvakshas*]; (*as*), m. a kind of tree (?); N. of a man.

तृक्षाक *tṛikshāka, as*, m., N. of a man.

तृक्षि *tṛikshi, is*, m., N. of a man with the patronymic Trāsadasyava.

तृख *tṛikha, am*, n. nutmeg.

तृच *tṛića* or *trića, as, am*, m. n. (fr. *tri-ṛić*), a strophe consisting of three verses; [cf. *try-ṛić*.] — *Tṛića-klṛipta, as, ā, am*, Ved. arranged in strophes of three verses each.

तृढ *tṛiḍha*. See above.

तृण् *tṛiṇ* (according to some, a rt. formed from the conjugational base of rt. *tṛid*), cl. 8. P. A. *tṛiṇoti, -ṇute*, or *tarṇoti, -ṇute*, &c., to eat (especially grass), to graze; [cf. *tṛiṇa*.]

तृण *tṛiṇa, am*, n. (according to the lexicographers also *as*, m.; perhaps connected with the preceding rt. or fr. rt. *stṛi*, to spread, or rt. *tṝi*, to pierce, cf. *taru*; but according to native authorities fr. rt. *tṛih*; according to the conjecture of others, *tṛiṇa* is for *tṛiṇṇa* fr. rt. *tṛid*), grass, a herb or any gramineous plant, a blade of grass, a bamboo, a reed, (often a symbol of minuteness and worthlessness); straw, grass or reeds for roofing a house [cf. rt. *jval*]; (*as*), m., N. of a man; N. of a prince, a son of Uśīnara; [cf. Goth. *thaurnus*; Angl. Sax. *thorn*; Germ. *dorn*; Russ. *tern*, 'thorn;' Hib. *dreas, dris*, 'a briar, bramble.'] — *Tṛiṇa-karṇa, as*, m., N. of a man; (*ās*), m. pl. the descendants of this man. — *Tṛiṇa-kāṇḍa, am*, n. a heap or quantity of grass. — *Tṛiṇa-kuṅkuma, am*, n. a sort of perfume. — *Tṛiṇa-kuṭī*, f. or *tṛiṇa-kuṭīraka, am*, n. a hut of grass or straw. — *Tṛiṇa-kūṭa, as, am*, m. n. a heap of grass. — *Tṛiṇa-kūrma, as*, m. a long gourd, Cucurbita Lagenaria (= *tumbī*). — *Tṛiṇa-ketakī*, f. a kind of Tabāshīr (*tavakshīra*). — *Tṛiṇa-ketu, us*, or *tṛiṇa-ketuka, as*, m. a bamboo; [cf. *tṛiṇa-dhvaja*.] — *Tṛiṇa-gaḍa, as*, m. a sort of sea crab, = *uć-ćiṅgaṭa*. — *Tṛiṇa-gandhā*, f. Batatas Paniculata, = *vidārī*; [cf. *ikshu-gandhā*.] — *Tṛiṇa-godhā*, f. a kind of newt, a chameleon, a worm, = *ćitra-kola* and *kṛikalāsa*. — *Tṛiṇa-gaura, am*, n. a sort of perfume, = *tṛiṇa-kuṅkuma*. — *Tṛiṇa-granthi, is*, f., N. of a plant, = *svarṇa-jīvantī*. — *Tṛiṇa-grāhin, ī*, m. sapphire, = *nīla-maṇi*; another gem, commonly *kāphura-dānā*, amber, &c., or any gem which being rubbed becomes electrically attractive. — *Tṛiṇa-ćara, as* or *am*, m. or n. (?), a kind of gem, = *go-meda*. — *Tṛiṇa-jambhan, ā, ā, a*, grass-toothed, having teeth like grass, &c., graminivorous, feeding on grass. — *Tṛiṇa-jalāyukā* or *tṛiṇa-jalūkā*, f. a caterpillar. — *Tṛiṇa-jāti, is*, m. the vegetable kingdom. — *Tṛiṇa-jyotis*, a particular kind of shining plant. — 1. *tṛiṇa-tā*, f. or *tṛiṇa-tva, am*, n. the aggregate properties of grass or herbage, the state or condition of grass, gramineousness; (for 2. *tṛiṇatā* see col. 3.) — *Tṛiṇa-duh, -dhuk*, m. = *baḍavāgni*. — *Tṛiṇa-druma, as*, m. a palm-tree, any of the various species, as the palmyra, cocoa-nut, date, &c.; [cf. *tṛiṇa-vṛiksha*.] — *Tṛiṇa-dhānya, am*, n. grain growing wild or without cultivation; [cf. *tṛiṇānna*.] — *Tṛiṇa-dhvaja, as*, m. a bamboo; [cf. *tṛiṇa-ketu*.] — *Tṛiṇa-nimba, as*, m. a kind of Nimba growing in Nepal (*nepāla-nimba*); Agathotes Chirayta (*kirāta-tikta*). — *Tṛiṇa-pa, as*, m., N. of a Gandharva. — *Tṛiṇa-pańća-mūla, am*, n. an aggregate of five roots of gramineous plants, viz. of rice, sugar-cane, Darbha, Scirpus Kysoor (*ka-śeru*), and a cane similar to Saccharum Sara (= *śara*). — *Tṛiṇa-pattrikā*, f. a kind of sugar-cane (*ikshu-darbhā*). — *Tṛiṇa-pattrī*, f. a kind of grass, = *gunḍāśinī*. — *Tṛiṇa-padī*, f. having legs as thin as blades of grass. — *Tṛiṇa-pāṇi, is*, m., N. of a Ṛishi. — *Tṛiṇa-pīḍa, am*, n. pressing as close as grass, hand to hand fighting, close quarters. — *Tṛiṇa-pushpa, am*, n. a kind of perfume, = *tṛiṇa-kuṅkuma*; (*ī*), f. a kind of plant, = *sindūra-pushpī*. — *Tṛiṇa-pūlaka* = *tṛiṇa-pūlī* (?). — *Tṛiṇa-pūlī*, f. a mat, a seat made of reeds or basket-work. — *Tṛiṇa-prāya, as, ā, am*, worth a straw, worthless. — *Tṛiṇa-maṇi, is*, m. 'straw-attracting gem,' a sort of gem, apparently amber; [cf. *tṛiṇa-grāhin*.] — *Tṛiṇa-maya, as, ī, am*, consisting or made of grass, grassy. — *Tṛiṇa-mushṭi, is*, f. a handful of grass. — *Tṛiṇa-rāj, ṭ*, m. 'the king of the grasses,' the vine-palm. — *Tṛiṇa-rāja, as*, m. 'the king of the grasses,' the palm or the palmyra-tree, Borassus Flabelliformis; the cocoa-nut tree; bamboo; sugar-cane. — *Tṛiṇa-rājan, ā*, m. 'the king of the grasses,' the vine-palm. — *Tṛiṇa-vat, ān, atī, at*, abounding in grass, grassy. — *Tṛiṇa-valva-ja, as* or *am*, m. or n. (?), Saccharum Cylindricum; (*ā*), f. = *valva-jā*. — *Tṛiṇa-vindu, us*, m., N. of an ancient sage and prince; [cf. *tārṇavindavīya*.] — *Tṛiṇavindu-saras, as*, m., N. of a lake. — *Tṛiṇa-vistara, as*, m. a heap of grass. — *Tṛiṇa-vīja* or *tṛiṇa-vījaka* or *tṛiṇavījottama* (°*ja-ut*°), *as*, m. a kind of grain, = *śyāmāka*. — *Tṛiṇa-vṛiksha, as*, m. the fan-palm; the date tree; the cocoa-nut tree; the areca-nut tree; Pandanus Odoratissimus; [cf. *tṛiṇa-druma*.] — *Tṛiṇa-śīta, am*, n. a kind of fragrant grass, Andropogon Serratus; (*ā*), f. a kind of aquatic plant, = *jala-pippalī*. — *Tṛiṇa-śūnya, as*, m. Jasminum Sambac; the fruit of Pandanus Odoratissimus. — *Tṛiṇa-śūlī*, f. a kind of plant. — *Tṛiṇa-śoṇita, am*, n. a kind of perfume, = *tṛiṇa-kuṅkuma*; [cf. *tṛiṇāsṛij*.] — *Tṛiṇa-śoshaka, as*, m. a kind of serpent. — *Tṛiṇa-śauṇḍikā*, f. a kind of Achyranthes. — *Tṛiṇa-shaṭpada, as*, m. a wasp ('an insect with six feet infesting grass'). — *Tṛiṇa-sārā*, f. the plantain or banana, Musa Sapientum. — *Tṛiṇa-siṅha, as*, m. an axe ('a reed lion'). — *Tṛiṇa-somāṅgiras* (°*ma-aṅ*°), *ās*, m., N. of one of the seven sacrificial priests of Yama. — *Tṛiṇa-skanda, as*, m., Ved., N. of a man; (Sāy.) trembling or fading away like grass. — *Tṛiṇa-harmya, as*, m. a house or upper room of grass or straw. — *Tṛiṇāṅkhripa* (°*ṇa-aṅ*°), *as*, m. a kind of grass, = *manthānaka-tṛiṇa*; (also read *tṛiṇāṅghripa*.) — *Tṛiṇāgni* (°*ṇa-ag*°), *is*, m. a grass fire, i. e. one quickly extinguished; conflagration of straw or chaff; burning a criminal wrapped up in straw. — *Tṛiṇāńjana* (°*ṇa-ań*°), *as*, m. a chameleon, a lizard. — *Tṛiṇāṭavī* (°*ṇa-aṭ*°), f. a forest abounding in grass. — *Tṛiṇāḍhya* (°*ṇa-āḍh*°), *as*, m. a kind of grass, = *parvata-tṛiṇa*; [cf. *pat-trāḍhya*.] — *Tṛiṇānna* (°*ṇa-an*°), *am*, n. rice growing wild; [cf. *tṛiṇa-dhānya*.] — *Tṛiṇāmla* (°*ṇa-am*°), *am*, n. a kind of grass, = *lavaṇa-tṛiṇa*. — *Tṛiṇāri* (°*ṇa-ari*), *is*, m. a kind of Mollugo, (a common weed.) — *Tṛiṇāvarta* (°*ṇa-āv*°), *as*, m., N. of a man. — *Tṛiṇāvarta-vadha, as*, m., N. of a chapter of the Gaṇeśa-khaṇḍa or third part of the Brahmavaivarta-Purāṇa. — *Tṛiṇā-valli-tīrtha*, N. of a place mentioned in the Rasika-ramaṇa by Raghu-nātha. — *Tṛiṇāsṛij* (°*ṇa-as*°), *k*, n. a kind of perfume, = *tṛiṇa-kuṅkuma, tṛiṇa-śoṇita*. — *Tṛiṇekshu* (°*ṇa-ik*°), *us*, m. a kind of long grass, Saccharum Cylindricum. — *Tṛiṇendra* (°*ṇa-in*°), *as*, m. 'prince of the grasses,' the palmyra-palm (= *tāla*); [cf. *tṛiṇa-rāja*.] — *Tṛiṇottama* (°*ṇa-ut*°), *as*, m. 'best of grasses,' a kind of Andropogon (*ukhar-vala*). — *Tṛiṇottha* (°*ṇa-ut*°), *as*, m. a kind of perfume, = *tṛiṇa-kuṅkuma*. — *Tṛiṇodaka* (°*ṇa-ud*°), *am*, n. grass and water. — *Tṛiṇodbhava* (°*ṇa-ud*°), *as*, m. rice &c. growing wild or without cultivation; a kind of perfume, = *tṛiṇottha*. — *Tṛiṇolapa* (°*ṇa-ul*°), *am*, n. grass and shrubs. — *Tṛiṇolkā* (°*ṇa-ul*°), f. a torch of hay; a fire-brand made of a wisp of straw. — *Tṛiṇaukas* (°*ṇa-ok*°), *as*, n. a hut, a house of straw or mats. — *Tṛiṇaushadha* (°*ṇa-osh*°), *am*, n. the fragrant bark of Feronia Elephantum (= *elavāluka*).

Tṛiṇaka, am, n. grass, a worthless blade of grass; (*as*), m., N. of a man.

Tṛiṇakīyā, f. a grassy place.

Tṛiṇasa, as, ā, am, grassy, abounding in grass, &c.

Tṛiṇī-kṛi, cl. 8. P. *-karoti, -kartum*, to make straw of, to make light of. — *Tṛiṇī-kṛitya*, having esteemed as lightly as straw.

Tṛiṇiya, as, ā, am, relating to grass (?).

Tṛiṇyā, f. a heap or quantity of grass or straw.

तृणता 2. *tṛiṇatā*, f. (for 1. see under *tṛiṇa*, col. 1), a bow, = *tṛiṇatā*.

तृणमत्कृण *tṛiṇamatkṛiṇa* or *tṛiṇamatkuṇa, as*, m. a bail or surety, security, warranty; (the right reading may be *ṛiṇamatkuṇa*.)

तृणाङ्कु *tṛiṇāṅku, us*, m., N. of an ancient sage.

तृणामल्ल *tṛiṇāmalla*, N. of a temple; (also read *triṇāmalla* and *trimalla* and *tṛiṇāvallī-tīrtha*.)

तृण्ण *tṛiṇṇa*. See under rt. *tṛid* below.

तृत *tṛita* = *trita*, q. v.

तृतीय *tṛitīya, as, ā, am* (fr. *tri*), the third; forming or constituting the third part; (*as*), m., scil. *varṇa*, the third consonant of a Varga (i. e. *g, j, ḍ, d, b*); (*ā*), f., scil. *tithi*, the third day in a half month; scil. *vibhakti*, the terminations of the third case, the third case, the instrumental; (*am*), n. a third part; (*am* or *ena*), ind. at or for the third time, thirdly; [cf. Zend *thri-tya*; Lith. *tre-ćia-s* of *tretias*; Lat. *ter-tius*; Gr. τρίτος; Goth. *thri-dya*; Slav. *tre-tii*; Scot. *tri-teamh*; Hib. *triugha*.] — *Tṛitīya-tā*, f. 'thirdness,' the condition of the third consonant of a Varga. — *Tṛitīya-prakṛiti, is*, f. ('the third nature'), a eunuch; the neuter gender. — *Tṛitīya-savana, am*, n., Ved. the third Soma offering (in the evening). — *Tṛitīya-savanīya, as, ā, am*, belonging to the third Soma offering. — *Tṛitīya-svara, am*, n., N. of a Sāman. — *Tṛitīyāṅśa* (°*ya-aṅ*°), *as*, m. a third part; (*as, ā, am*), receiving a third as one's share. — *Tṛitīyā-prakṛiti, is*, f. a eunuch; a hermaphrodite; the neuter gender, = *tṛitīya-prakṛiti*. — *Tṛitīyā-samāsa, as*, m. a compound word (Tat-purusha), the former member of which would stand in the instrumental case, if separated from the latter.

Tṛitīyaka, as, ikā, am, recurring every third day, tertian (as fever &c.); occurring for the third time; the third; (*ikā*), f. = *tṛitīyā*, the third day in a half month. — *Tṛitīyaka-jvara, as*, m. tertian ague.

Tṛitīyā-kṛi, cl. 8. P. A. *-karoti, -kurute, -kartum*, to plough for the third time. — *Tṛitīyā-kṛita, as, ā, am*, thrice ploughed (as a field).

Tṛitīyin, ī, inī, i, holding the third place or rank; having or receiving a third as one's share.

तृत्सु *tṛitsu, us*, m., *avas*, m. pl., Ved., N. of a Vedic race or family; (Sāy.) injurious, an enemy.

तृद् *tṛid* [cf. rt. *tard*], cl. 7. P. A. *tṛi-ṇatti, tṛintte* or *tṛinte, tatarda, tatṛide, tardishyati, -te*, and *tartsyati, -te, atṛidat* and *atardīt, atṛitta, tarditum*, to cleave; to split open; to pierce, cut through; to let out, set free; to kill, destroy, injure; to disregard; to eat (?); to give; cl. 1. P. *tardati*, to kill, injure: Caus. *tardayati, -yitum, atatardat* and *atītṛidat*: Desid. *titardishati, -te*, and *titṛitsati, -te*: Intens. *tarītṛidyate, tarītartti*.

Tṛiṇṇa, as, ā, am, split, pierced, cut, injured, &c.

Tṛidila, as, ā, am, Ved. having holes, porous; (Sāy.) splitting, cleaving.

तृप् 1. *tṛip*, cl. 4. 5. 6. P. *tṛipyati*, *tṛipnoti* (Ved. *tṛipṇoti*), *tṛipati* or *tṛimpati*, *tatarpa*; *tarpishyati*, *tarpsyati*, *trapsyati*; *atṛipat*, *atarpīt*, *atārpsīt*, *atrāpsīt*; *tarptum*, *traptum*, *tarpitum*; to satisfy one's self, to become satiated or satisfied, to be pleased or satisfied or contented (with gen., inst., or loc., e. g. *nāgnis tṛipyati kāshṭhānām*, fire is not satisfied with wood; *tṛipyati phalaiḥ*, he is satisfied with fruits); to enjoy; to satisfy, satiate, please; cl. 1. P. *tarpati*, &c., to light up, kindle (i. e. satiate a fire with fuel): Caus. P. A. *tarpayati*, *-te*, *-yitum*, Aor. *atītṛipat* and *atatarpat*, to gladden, exhilarate; to satiate, refresh, satisfy; A. to become satiated or satisfied; P. to light, kindle: Desid. *titṛipsati*, *titarpishati*, to wish to satiate one's self, to desire to satisfy: Desid. of the Caus. *titarpayishati*, to wish to satiate or refresh or satisfy: Intens. *tarītṛipyate*, *tarītarpti* and *tarītrapti*; [cf. *tṛimp*, *tṛiph*, *tṛimph*: Gr. τέρπω, τρέφω (?): Old Pruss. *en-terpo*, 'to be useful:' Lith. *tarpstu*, 'to increase, to prosper;' *tarpà*, 'increase:' Goth. *tharf*, 'to satisfy, to be useful:' Old Germ. *trôstyan*: Angl. Sax. *thearf*: Hib. *tropadh*, 'heavy, grave;' *tromaighim* = *tarpayāmi*; *tormach*, 'increase, augmentation;' *torp*, 'bulk;' *tormad*, 'pregnant, big.']

2. *tṛip*, at the end of a comp. in *a-sutṛip* and *paśu-tṛip*.

Tṛipa. See *a-tṛipa*.

Tṛipat, ind., Ved. with pleasure or enjoyment, to one's satisfaction; (*t*), m. a parasol; the moon.

Tṛipala, *as*, *ā*, *am* (said by some to be fr. rt. *trap*), Ved. quick, restless, hasty, anxious; pleased, glad; (*ā*), f. a creeper or creeping plant; [cf. *tṛipra*.] — *Tṛipala-prabharman*, *ā*, *ā*, *a*, Ved. pressing quickly forwards, acting quickly.

Tṛipā, f. a kind of plant; [cf. *tārpya*.]

Tṛipāya (fr. *tṛipat*), nom. A. *tṛipāyate*, &c.

Tṛipta, *as*, *ā*, *am*, satiated, satisfied, contented; (*am*), n. the becoming satiated, satisfaction. — *Tṛiptānśu* (°*ta-an*°), *us*, *us*, *u*, Ved. having well nourished shoots or members, epithet of the Soma plant. — *Tṛiptātman* (°*ta-āt*°), *ā*, *ā*, *a*, having a contented mind, contented, satisfied, tranquil.

Tṛiptāya, nom. A. *tṛiptāyate*, &c., to be or become satiated or satisfied.

Tṛipti, *is*, f. satisfaction, contentment; satiety, disgust; hilarity, pleasure, gratification; Ved. water; [cf. *ati-tṛipti*.] — *Tṛipti-da*, *as*, *ā*, *am*, giving satisfaction, pleasing. — *Tṛipti-dīpa*, *as*, m., N. of a work. — *Tṛipti-mat*, *ān*, *atī*, *at*, satisfied, feeling satisfaction.

Tṛiptin, *ī*, *inī*, *i*, satiated, satisfied.

Tṛipra, *as*, *ā*, *am*, restless, hasty, anxious; pleased, contented, (compar. *trapīyas*, superl. *trapishṭha*); (*as*), m. an oblation of ghee or boiled butter. — *Tṛipra-danśin*, *ī*, *inī*, *i*, Ved. biting hastily.

Tṛiprālu, *us*, *us*, *u*, having ghee, but not liking it or not blending with it.

तृपु *tṛipu*, *us*, m., Ved. a thief; [cf. *tripu*.]

तृफ् *tṛiph*, cl. 6. P. *tṛiphati*, &c., = 1. *tṛip*, to satisfy, gratify, please; to be contented or pleased; to kill, hurt. See *tarphitṛi*.

तृफला *tṛiphalā*, f. = *tri-phalā*, the three myrobalans.

तृफू *tṛiphū*, *ūs*, f. a serpent in general, the serpent race.

तृमदण्डिक *tṛimadaṇḍika* (?), *as*, m., N. of a man.

तृम्प् *tṛimp* or *tṛimph*, cl. 6. P. *tṛimpati* or *tṛimphati*, &c., = 1. *tṛip*, to be pleased or satisfied; to content, please.

Tṛimphaṇa, *am*, n. pleasing.

Tṛimphaṇīya, *as*, *ā*, *am*, to be pleased, &c.

तृष् 1. *tṛish*, cl. 4. P. *tṛishyati*, *tatarsha* (Ved. 3rd pl. *tātṛishus*, part. *tātṛishāṇa*), *atarshat*, *tarshitum*, to be thirsty, to thirst; to thirst for (metaphorically), desire, long for: Caus. *tarshayati*, *-yitum*, to cause to thirst; [cf. Zend *tarshna*, 'thirst:' Goth. *thars*, 'to become dry;' *thairsa*, *thars*, *thaursum*; *thaursus*, 'dry;' *thaurstei*, 'thirst;' *thaursyan*, 'to thirst;' *ga-thaursan-s*, 'dry:' Angl. Sax. *thurst*, *thyrr*: Old Germ. *darran*, 'to become dry:' Germ. *durst*: Gr. τέρσ-ο-μαι, τερσαίνω, ταρσός, ταρσ-ιά, τρασ-ιά: Lat. *torreo* for *torseo*, *tos-tum* from *tors-tum*, *torris*, *torrens*: Lith. *trôksztu*, 'to thirst;' *trôszkulis*, 'thirst:' Hib. *tart* (*tar-t*), 'thirst, drought;' *tartmhar*, 'thirsty, dry.']

2. *tṛish*, *ṭ*, f. thirst; thirst after (metaphorically), wish, strong desire; Desire personified as a daughter of the god of Love (Kāma).

Tṛishā, f. thirst; strong desire or wish; Desire personified as a daughter of Kāma; a poisonous plant, Methonica Superba (*lāṅgalikī*). — *Tṛishā-bhū*, *ūs*, f. the bladder (whence thirst exists or arises). — *Tṛishā-roga*, *as*, m. 'morbid thirst,' N. of a particular disease. — *Tṛishārta* (°*shā-ār*°), *as*, *ā*, *am*, suffering from thirst, thirsty; affected by desire. — *Tṛishā-ha*, *am*, n. water (destroying or quenching thirst); (*ā*), f. a kind of anise, = *madhurikā*.

Tṛishāṇa, *as*, *ā*, *am*, (Ved. part.) being thirsty.

Tṛishita, *as*, *ā*, *am*, thirsty, thirsting (physically or metaphorically); (*am*), n. thirst, desire. — *Tṛishitottarā* (°*ta-ut*°), f., N. of a plant, = *aśanaparṇī*.

Tṛishitvā or *tarshitvā*, ind. having become thirsty.

Tṛishu, *us*, *us*, *u*, Ved. greedy, libidinous, thirsting for, eagerly desirous; rushing violently, quick. — *Tṛishu-ćyavas*, *ās*, *ās*, *as*, Ved. moving rapidly or quickly. — *Tṛishu-ćyut*, *t*, *t*, *t*, Ved. quickly issuing, rapidly moving.

Tṛishṇaka, *as*, *ā*, *am*, said to = *tṛishṇaj*.

Tṛishṇaj, *k*, *k*, *k*, thirsty (physically or metaphorically), desiring, longing for, cupidinous; [cf. *a-tṛishṇaj*.]

Tṛishṇā, f. (in the Veda the accent is on the first syllable, in later Sanskrit on the last), thirst, strong wish, desire, avidity; (Tṛishṇā and Lobha are sometimes personified as the parents of Dambha; or Tṛishṇā is variously regarded as a daughter of Death, or of Pāpīyas, or as generated by Vedanā and generating Upādāna); [cf. *ati-tṛishṇa*.] — *Tṛishṇā-kshaya*, *as*, m. cessation of desire, tranquillity of mind, resignation, patience, content. — *Tṛishṇā-ghna*, *as*, *ī*, *am*, quenching the thirst. — *Tṛishṇāmaya* (°*ṇā-ām*°), *as*, *ā*, *am*, ill with thirst. — *Tṛishṇā-māra*, *as*, m., Ved. dying of thirst. — *Tṛishṇāri* (°*ṇā-ari*), *is*, m. 'enemy of thirst,' a kind of plant (= *parpaṭa*).

Tṛishṇālu, *us*, *us*, *u*, thirsting much, very thirsty.

Tṛishyat, *an*, *antī*, *at*, thirsting, athirst; desiring.

Tṛishyā, f., Ved. thirst. — *Tṛishyā-vat*, *ān*, *atī*, *at*, Ved. thirsty; [cf. *tarshyā-vat*.]

तृषम *tṛishama* = *trishama*, q. v.

तृष्ट *tṛishṭa*, *as*, *ā*, *am*, Ved. rough, harsh; pungent; rugged; hoarse. — *Tṛishṭa-jambha*, *as*, *ā*, *am*, Ved. having rough or uneven teeth. — *Tṛishṭa-danśman*, *ā*, *ā*, *a*, Ved. biting roughly. — *Tṛishṭa-dhūma*, *as*, *ā*, *am*, Ved. having pungent breath, epithet of a snake. — *Tṛishṭa-vandana*, *as*, *ā*, *am*, Ved. one whose praise is distasteful. — *Tṛishṭāmā* (°*ṭa-am*°), f., Ved., N. of a river.

Tṛishṭikā, f., Ved. rough, disagreeable, epithet of a woman.

तृह् *tṛih* or *tṛiṅh*, cl. 6. 7. P. *tṛihati* or *tṛiṇhati*, *tṛiṇeḍhi*, *tatarha*, *tarhishyati* and *tarkshyati*, *atarhīt* and *atṛikshat*, *tarhitum* and *tarḍhum*, to dash to pieces, crush, bruise; to hurt, injure, strike, kill: Caus. *tarhayati*: Desid. *titarhishati*, *titṛikshati*, *titṛiṅhishati*: Intens. *tarītṛihyate*, *tarītarḍhi*: [cf. perhaps Goth. *thrascan*; Angl. Sax. *therscan* old desid.]

Tṛiḍha, *as*, *ā*, *am* (Ved. *tṛilha*), crushed, bruised, hurt, injured, wounded, killed.

Tṛiḍhvā or *tarhitvā*, ind. having killed, &c.

तृ *tṛī*, cl. 1. P. (ep. also A., Ved. also cl. 6.) *tarati*, *-te*, *tatāra* (2nd sing. *teritha*, 3rd du. *teratus*, 3rd pl. *terus*), *tarishyati* or *tarīshyati*, *atārīt*, *taritum* or *tarītum* or *tartum*; [the following are Vedic forms, some of them occurring also in epic poetry; *tirati* when preceded by prep.; *titarti*, part. *titrat*; *tīryati*, *-te*; *turyāt*, *tuturyāt*; Aor. *tārishat*, *atārima*, *tarīt*; *tarushema* in Ṛig-veda VII. 48, 2, Pāṇ. III. 1, 85, *tarushanta*, *tarushante*; *titirus*, part. *titirvas*; gen. *tatarushas*; inf. *taradhyai*]; to pass across or over, cross over (a river), sail across, navigate; to float, swim; to move on rapidly; to get through, attain an end or aim; to pervade; to come to the end of; to live through (a definite period); to fulfil, accomplish, perform; to surpass, overcome, overpower, subdue, destroy, become master of; to acquire, gain; to escape (with acc.); to be saved or rescued; to escape from a danger (with abl.); to carry through or over, transport, save, liberate from; to strive or contend together, to compete: Caus. P. *tārayati*, *-yitum*, to carry or lead over or across; to cause to arrive at; to rescue, save, liberate [cf. rt. *trai*]: Desid. *titīrshati*, *titarishati*, *titarīshati*, to wish to cross: Intens. *tetīryate*, *tātarīti* or *tātarti* (Ved. pres. part. *tarītrat*), to pass completely through, make a way through, pervade; [cf. 1. *tur*, *tul*, *turv*; *tara* at p. 365; Zend *tarō*, 'over:' Gr. τερ-έ-ω, τέρ-ε-τρο-ν, τέρ-θρο-ν, τέρ-μα, τέρμων, τέρμ-ιο-ς, τερμιό-ει-ς, τείρ-ω, τρύ-ω, τρί-βω, τρύ-χ-ω, τέρ-ην, τι-τρά-ω, τι-τραίν-ω, τέρ-α-ς, τορ-ό-ς, τόρ-ο-ς, τόρ-νο-ς, τορ-ύνη, τορ-εύ-ω, τρῦ-μα, τρῶ-μα, τρῆ-μα, τέλος, τέλλω ('to rise'), τηρέω (caus.), τρυτάνη; perhaps also Τάρας, Τρο-ία, Τροιζήν, τελέω, τέλειος, τελευτή, τᾶλις, θραύ-ω, τραῦ-μα, θλά-ω, θλίβ-ω: Lat. *ter-mo*, *ter-men*, *ter-minu-s*, *ter-o*, *ter-e(t)-s*, *ter-e-bra*, *trib-ula*, *tribulare*, *trīti-cu-m*, *in-tra-re*, *peni-tra-re*, *ex-tra-re*, *trans*: Umbr. *termnu*, *traf* = *trans*: Osc. *teremenniû*: Sabin. *terentum*, *Terentius*, *tur-unda*, *tru-à*, 'a ladle;' *trāme(t)-s*, *Tras-im-enu-s*, 'the opposite, ulterior:' Goth. *thair-ko*, 'a hole;' *thairh*: Old Germ. *durh*: Eng. *through*: Old Island. *thrö-m*, 'margin:' Old Germ. *dru-m*, 'limit, border:' Angl. Sax. *thrā-v-an*: Old Germ. *drā-y-an*, 'to turn, whirl;' *thearl*, *thearm*, *thirel*, *thirlian*, *thole*, *tholian*, *thaelian*, *for-thyldian*: Slav. *trê-ti*, *try-ti*, 'to rub:' Lith. *trìn-ti*, 'to rub, file, polish, bore;' *til-tas*, 'a bridge;' *tolùs*, 'long, distant:' Hib. *toir*, 'a pursuit;' *tor*, 'a pursuer;' *toramh*, 'pursuit;' *toras*, 'a journey;' *teirin*, 'a descent;' *tearnadh*, 'descending;' *tarradh*, 'protection;' *tarthadoir*, 'a saviour.']

Tarūtṛi = *tarutṛi*, at p. 365, by Pāṇ. VII. 2, 34.

Tīrṇa, *as*, *ā*, *am*, crossed, passed over; spread, expanded; surpassed, excelled; (*ā*), f., N. of a metre consisting of four lines of four long syllables each. — *Tīrṇa-padī*, f. a species of plant, = *tāla-mūlī*.

Tīrtvā, ind. having passed, crossed over, &c.

तेग *tega*, *as*, m., Ved. only occurring in Vājasaneyi-saṃhitā XXV. 1, where the sense is doubtful.

तेज् *tej* (probably connected with rt. *tij*), cl. 1. P. *tejati*, &c., to guard, cherish, defend, protect.

तेज *teja*, *as*, m. (fr. rt. *tij*), sharpness, pungency; sharpness (of a weapon); brilliancy; spirit; N. of a man. — *Teja-pattra*, *as*, m. the leaf of Laurus Cassia. — *Teja-vat*, *ān*, *atī*, *at*, sharp, &c.; see *tejo-vat*. — *Teja-sinha*, *as*, m., N. of a king, a descendant of Paramāra, mentioned in the Rāja-taraṅgiṇī by Kalhaṇa.

Tejana, *am*, n. sharpening; kindling, inflammation;

enlightening, rendering bright, making splendid or polished; whetting; a point, the point of an arrow; a reed, a bamboo, the shaft of an arrow; the reed Saccharum Sara; (*ī*), f. a number of reeds, straw, &c., twisted or matted together, a mat; a tuft; a tuft of hair on the head (of a horse); N. of a plant, = *mūrvā*, Sanseviera Roxburghiana; also = *jyotish-matī*, Cardiospermum Halicacabum.

Tejanaka, *as*, m. a kind of reed, Saccharum Sara (= *śara*).

Tejala, *as*, m. the francoline partridge (= *ka-piñjala*).

Tejas, *as*, n. sharpness; the sharp edge (of a knife &c.); the point or top of a flame or of a ray &c.; glow, glare, fierce or scorching heat, radiance, splendor, brilliance, lustre, light, fire; clearness of the eyes; the clear or bright appearance of the human body (in health), beauty; the heating and strengthening faculty of the human frame seated in the *pitta*; the bile; bilious humor &c.; fiery energy, ardour, power, might, spirit, strength, efficacy, male energy, semen virile, vital power; the brain; marrow; the essential nature or value of anything, essence; violence, mettle, fierceness, severity, energetic opposition; impatience, inability to bear or put up with; spiritual or moral or magical power; virtue; influence, effect, consequence, majesty, fame, dignity, glory, authority; a brave man; a venerable or dignified person, a splendid object, a renowned person, a person of consequence; fresh butter; gold; [cf. *a-tejas*, *agni-t°*, *ugra-t°*, *tigma-t°*, &c.; cf. also Hib. *teas*, 'warmth, fervour.'] — *Tejaḥ-prabha*, *as*, *ā*, *am*, gleaming with lustre, flashing with brilliance (as a weapon). — *Tejaḥ-phala*, *as*, m. a kind of plant, = *bahu-phala*, &c. — *Tejaḥ-sambhava*, *as*, m. = *rasa*, lymph; [cf. *agni-sambhava*.] — *Tejaḥ-siṇha*, *as*, m., N. of an astronomer. — *Tejaḥ-sena*, *as*, m., N. of a man. — *Tejas-ka*, *as*, *ā*, *am*, splendid, radiant, glorious, famous. — *Tejas-kara*, *as*, *ā* or *ī*, *am*, irradiating, illuminating, granting strength or vital power. — *Tejas-kāma*, *as*, *ā*, *am*, longing for manly strength or vital power, desiring influence or authority or dignity. — *Tejas-timira*, *e*, n. du. light and darkness. — *Tejas-tejas*, *ās*, m. whose essence is light, who is light of lights. — *Tejas-tva*, *am*, n. the nature or essence of light, brightness, &c. — *Tejas-vat*, *ān*, *atī*, *at*, having a sharp edge (as a weapon); sharp, pungent; splendid, bright; energetic, spirited; (*tī*), f., N. of a princess; [cf. *tejo-vat*.] — *Tejasvi-tā*, f. or *tejasvi-tva*, *am*, n. energetic behaviour or nature, energy, brilliancy, splendor. — *Tejas-vin*, *ī*, *inī*, *i*, brilliant, splendid, bright; powerful, energetic, strong, sound, inspiring respect, dignified, noble; famous, glorious, illustrious, celebrated; violent; lawful; haughty; granting strength &c.; (*ī*), m., N. of a son of Indra; (*inī*), f. = *jyotish-matī*, Cardiospermum Halicacabum. — *Tejasvi-praśaṇsā*, f., N. of a chapter of Śārṅga-dhara's anthology called Śārṅga-dhara-paddhati. — *Tejo-nātha-tīrtha*, *am*, n. the Tīrtha of the lord of light (the Sun?). — *Tejo-nidhi*, *is*, *is*, *i*, 'a treasury of glory,' abounding in glory. — *Tejo-bala-samanvita* or *tejo-bala-samāyukta*, *as*, *ā*, *am*, endowed with spirit and strength. — *Tejo-bhaṅga*, *as*, m. destruction of dignity, disgrace. — *Tejo-maṇḍala*, *am*, n. a disk or halo of light. — *Tejo-mantha*, *as*, m. the tree Premna Spinosa, (the friction of the wood engendering flame); [cf. *agni-mantha*.] — *Tejo-maya*, *as*, *ī*, *am*, consisting of splendor or light, shining, brilliant, luminous, glorious; full of energy or ardour. — *Tejo-mūrti*, *is*, *is*, *i*, whose form is light, consisting totally of light. — *Tejo-rāśi*, *is*, m. a heap or mass of splendor, i. e. all splendor. — *Tejo-rūpa*, *as*, *ā*, *am*, whose form is light, consisting wholly of splendor; (*am*), n. Brahma, the supreme spirit; the nature of light. — *Tejo-vat*, *ān*, *atī*, *at*, sharp, pungent; bright, splendid; energetic; (*tī*), f. = *ćavya*, Piper Chaba; Scindapsus Officinalis, = *gaja-pippalī*, = *mahā-jyotishmatī*; a kind of medicinal root, commonly called Tejo-bala; N. of a princess; [cf. *tejas-vat*.] — *Tejo-vid*, *t*, *t*, *t*, Ved. possessing splendor or light. — *Tejo-vindūpanishad* (°*du-up*°), *t*, f. 'a drop or particle of light,' N. of an Upanishad. — *Tejo-vīja*, *am*, n. marrow. — *Tejo-vṛiksha*, *as*, m. = *kshudrāgni-mantha*. — *Tejo-vṛitta*, *am*, n. noble or dignified behaviour; superior brilliancy or power. — *Tejo-vṛiddhi*, *is*, f. increase of glory or dignity. — *Tejo-hrāsa*, *as*, m. loss of dignity or lustre. — *Tejohvā* (°*jas-āh*°?), f. = *tejasvinī*, = *tejinī*.

Tejasa, *am*, n. = *tejas*, power &c. (at the end of a compound).

Tejasya, *as*, *ā*, *am*, Ved. splendid, conspicuous.

Tejita, *as*, *ā*, *am*. sharpened, whetted, polished, burnished; excited, invigorated, stimulated.

Tejinī, f. a sort of medicinal plant, commonly called Tejo-bala; Sanseviera Zeylanica.

Tejishṭha, *as*, *ā*, *am* (superl. of *tigma* or *tikshṇa*), Ved. very sharp or pointed, very bright, splendid, shining; vigorous, powerful, violent.

Tejīyas, *ān*, *asī*, *as*, Ved. very bright, radiant, splendid; very powerful or vigorous; a man of high dignity or influence.

Tejeyu, *us*, m., N. of a son of Raudrāśva.

तेजाउर *tejāura*, N. of a place mentioned in the poem Rasika-ramaṇa by Raghu-nātha.

तेदनी *tedanī*, f., Ved. blood or clotted blood.

तेन 1. *tena*, *as*, m. a note or cadence introductory to a song &c.

तेन 2. *tena*, ind. (Inst. sing. of the pronom. base 2. *ta*), in that direction, there (correlative to *yena*, in which direction, where); in that manner, thus, so (correlative to *yena*, in what manner); on that account, for that reason, therefore, in consequence of; so with regard to (with acc.); *tena hi*, therefore, now then.

तेप् *tep*, cl. 1. A. *tepate*, &c., to sprinkle, distil, ooze, drop; to shake, tremble; to shine.

तेम *tema*, *as*, m. (fr. rt. *tim*), the becoming wet, wet, damp, moisture; [cf. *stema*.]

Temana, *am*, n. wetting, moistening, moisture; a sauce, condiment; (*ī*), f. a sort of chimney, a fire-place.

तेर *tera* (?), *am*, n. the mouth.

तेल *tela*, *as*, m. a particular high number.

तेलु *telu*, *us*, m., N. of a race.

तेव् *tev*, cl. 1. A. *tevate*, &c., to play, sport; to weep, lament; [cf. *div* and *dev*.]

Tevana, *am*, n. play, sport, pastime; a garden, a pleasure-garden or play-ground.

तैकायन *taikāyana*, *as*, m. and *taikāyani*, *is*, m. two patronymics from Tika.

Taikāyanīya, *as*, m. a descendant or a pupil of Taikāyani.

तैक्ष्णायन *taikshṇāyana*, *as*, m. a patronymic from Tikshṇa.

तैक्ष्ण्य *taikshṇya*, *am*, n. (fr. *tīkshṇa*), sharpness (of a knife &c.), acuteness, heat, pungency, acerbity, fierceness, severity, vehemence, violence, cruelty.

तैग्म्य *taigmya*, *am*, n. (fr. *tigma*), sharpness, pungency, &c.

तैजनित्वच् *taijanitvać*, *k*, f. (?), a sort of Vīṇā.

तैजस *taijasa*, *as*, *ī*, *am* (fr. *tejas*), bright, luminous, brilliant, consisting of light or fire, fiery, splendid; consisting of any shining substance such as metal, metallic; the gastric juice as coloured by digested food; passionate, energetic, vigorous, powerful, intense; (*as*), m. 'the bright one,' i. e. the highly refined or subtle essence (in the Vedānta phil.); (*ī*), f. Scindapsus Officinalis; (*am*), n. any metal; ghee or oiled butter; intensity; vigour, energy; N. of a Tīrtha. — *Taijasāvartanī* or *taijasāvartinī* (°*sa-āv*°), f. a crucible.

तैतल *taitala*, *as*, m., N. of a man.

Taitalāyani, *is*, m. a patronymic from Taitala.

तैतिक्ष *taitiksha*, *as*, *ī*, *am* (fr. *titikshā*), patient; (this word is also an adj. fr. *taitikshya*.)

Taitikshava, *as*, m. a patronymic from Titikshu.

Taitikshya, *as*, m. a patronymic from Titiksha.

तैतिर *taitira*, *as*, m. = *tittiri*, a partridge; (probably a wrong reading for *taittira*.)

तैतिल *taitila*, *as*, m. a rhinoceros; a god; = *kaliṅga*; (*am*), n., N. of the fourth astronomical period called Karaṇas.

Taitili, *is*, m., N. of a man.

तैत्तिर *taittira*, *as*, *ī*, *am* (fr. *tittiri*), produced or coming from a partridge; sprung from the sage Tittiri; (*as*), m. = *tittiri*, a partridge; a rhinoceros; (*am*), n. a flock of partridges.

Taittiri, *is*, m., N. of an ancient sage who was an elder brother of Vaiśampāyana; N. of a son of Kapota-roman and father of Punar-vasu.

Taittirika, *as*, m. one who catches partridges.

Taittirīya, *ās*, m. pl. the pupils of Tittiri, the followers of the Taittirīya school of the Yajur-veda; or the Yajur-veda itself, according to the version of this school; see *taittirīya-saṃhitā*. — *Taittirīya-ćaraṇa*, *as*, *am*. m. n. the school or sect of the Taittirīyas. — *Taittirīya-prātiśākhya*, *am*, n. the Prātiśākhya of the Taittirīyas. — *Taittirīya-brāhmaṇa*, *am*, n. a Brāhmaṇa of the Taittirīya Yajur-veda. — *Taittirīya-śikshā*, f. the pronunciation of letters, accents, &c., according to the Taittirīyas. — *Taittirīya-saṃhitā*, f. the collection of the hymns &c. of the dark or black Yajur-veda; (this, the more ancient version of the Yajur-veda, was called Taittirīya, as handed down by Tittiri, the pupil of Yāska, the pupil of Vaiśampāyana; the more modern or bright Yajur-veda being attributed to Yājñavalkya, of the family of the Vājasaneyins: the legend relates that the Yajus in its original form was first taught by the sage Vaiśampāyana to twenty-seven pupils, Yājñavalkya being deputed by him to teach it to others; subsequently the sage being offended with Yājñavalkya, bade him relinquish the Veda committed to him, which he instantly disgorged in a tangible form; whereupon the other disciples of Vaiśampāyana receiving his command to pick it up, assumed the form of partridges for that purpose, and swallowed the texts, which were soiled, and hence named 'black,' the other name *taittirīya* having reference to the partridges. Yājñavalkya then had recourse to the Sun, and from that deity received a new revelation of the Yajus, which is sometimes called 'white,' and sometimes from the patronymic of Yājñavalkya, Vājasaneyin.) — *Taittirīyāraṇyaka* (°*ya-ār*°), *am*, n. the Āraṇyaka of the Taittirīyas. — *Taittirīyopanishad* (°*ya-up*°), *t*, f. the Upanishad of the Taittirīyas.

Taittirīyaka, *as*, *ā*, *am*, belonging to the Taittirīya version of the Yajur-veda; (*ās*), m. pl. = *taittirīyās*, i. e. the followers of the Taittirīya school of the Yajur-veda. — *Taittirīyakopanishad* (°*ka-up*°), *t*, f. the Upanishad of the Taittirīyas mentioned in the Sarva-darśana-saṅgraha.

तैन्तिडीक *taintiḍīka*, *as*, *ī*, *am* (fr. *tintiḍīka*), prepared with a sour sauce of tamarinds.

तैन्दुक *tainduka*, *as*, *ī*, *am* (fr. *tinduka*), derived from or belonging to the tree Diospyros Embryopteris.

तैभ *taibha*, *am*, n., N. of a Sāman.

तैमात *taimāta, as,* m., Ved. a kind of serpent.

तैमिर *taimira, as,* m. (fr. *timira*), scil. *roga,* darkness or dimness of the eyes, a disease of the eyes; [cf. *timira.*]

Taimirika, as, ī, am, affected by this disease.

तैर *taira, as,* m. or *tairaṇa, as,* m. or *tairaṇī,* f., N. of a plant, = *ku-nīlī, rāga-da.*

तैरभुक्त *tairabhukta, as, ī, am,* derived from or a native of Tīra-bhukti.

तैरश्च *tairaśća, as, ī, am,* derived from or composed by Tiraśćī (as a Sāman or Sūkta).

Tairaśćya, am, n., N. of a Sāman.

तैरोविराम *tairovirāma, as,* m. (fr. *tiras* + *virāma*), 'extending beyond a pause' or 'having a pause between,' i. e. the dependent Svarita in a compound when the Udātta upon which it depends stands on the last syllable of the first member of the compound.

तैरोव्यञ्जन *tairovyañjana, as,* m. (fr. *tiras* + *vy°*), 'extending beyond the consonant' or 'having a consonant between,' the dependent Svarita when separated from the Udātta syllable of the same word by one or more consonants, i. e. a circumflex accent between which and the preceding acute vowel one or more consonants intervene.

तैरोऽह्न्य *tairo'hnya* = *tiro-'hnya,* q. v.

तैर्थ *tairtha, as, ī, am* (fr. *tīrtha*), relating to a sacred bathing-place or shrine, coming from it, &c.

Tairthaka, as, &c., an adj. fr. *tīrtha.*

Tairthika, as, ī, am, coming or derived from a holy place of pilgrimage; visiting the holy shrines or bathing-places; sacred, holy; (*am*), n. water from a sacred bathing-place, holy water; (*as*), m. an ascetic; [cf. *tīrthika.*]

Tairthya, am, n. abstract noun fr. *tīrtha.*

तैर्यगयनिक *tairyagayanika, as, ī, am* (fr. *tiryag-ayana*), measured by the revolution of the sun, as a year, (opposed to *sāvanaḥ saṃvatsaraḥ.*)

तैर्यग्योन *tairyagyona, as, ī, am,* or *tairyagyoni, is, is, i,* or *tairyagyonya, as, ā, am* (fr. *tiryag-yoni*), of animal origin, relating to the animals, an animal, &c.

तैल *taila, am,* n. (fr. *tila*), oil expressed from sesamum, mustard, &c.; oil in general, (often compounded with the name of the plant from which the oil is extracted); storax, gum benzoin, incense; [cf. *tīkshṇa-taila.*] — *Taila-kanda, as,* m. a kind of bulbous plant. — *Taila-kalka-ja, as,* m. oil-cake; [cf. *tilakalka-ja.*] — *Taila-kalpanā,* f., N. of a chapter in the Sārṅga-dhara-saṃhitā or medical work by Sārṅga-dhara, son of Dāmodara. — *Taila-kāra, as,* m. an oil manufacturer. — *Taila-kiṭṭa, am,* n. oil-cake, a cake made of oily seed; [cf. *tila-kiṭṭa.*] — *Taila-kīṭa, as,* m. a kind of insect, = *tailinī, dardru-nāśinī,* &c. — *Taila-ćaurikā,* f. a cock-roach ('stealing oil'). — *Taila-tva, am,* n. oiliness, oily state. — *Taila-droṇī,* f. a tub or bath filled with oil. — *Taila-paka, as,* m. (*paka* fr. *pa,* drinking), a kind of bird; an 'oil-drinking' beetle, a cock-roach; [cf. *taila-pā.*] — *Taila-parṇaka, am,* n. a kind of fragrant grass, = *granthi-parṇa;* sandal-wood. — *Tailaparṇika, as,* m. a kind of sandal-wood. — *Taila-parṇī,* f. sandal; turpentine; incense; [cf. *tila-parṇa* and *tila-parṇī.*] — *Taila-pā* or *taila-pāyikā,* f. a kind of beetle or cock-roach; [cf. *taila-paka.*] — *Taila-pāyin, ī,* m. a kind of cock-roach; a sword ('drinking oil,' i. e. anointed with oil?); (*inī*), f. a kind of cock-roach. — *Taila-piñja* = *tila-piñja,* white sesamum. — *Taila-pipīlikā,* f. the small red ant. — *Taila-pīta, as, ā, am,* = *pīta-taila,* one who has drunk oil. — *Taila-phala, as,* m. the sesamum plant; Terminalia Catappa (= *iṅgudī*); Terminalia Bellerica. — *Taila-bhāvinī,* f. = *tila-bhāvinī,* jasmine. — *Taila-mālī,* f. a wick, the cotton of a lamp. — *Tailam-pātā,* f. the pouring of sesamum-seeds into fire [cf. *śyainam-pātā*]; oblation to fire; (*as, ā, am*), mixed with oil &c. — *Taila-yantra, am,* n. an oil-mill. — *Taila-vallī,* f. a kind of plant, = *laghu-śatāvarī* (Asparagus). — *Taila-vīja,* Semecarpus Anacardium. — *Taila-sādhana, am,* n. a fragrant substance or perfume, civet? (= *kakkolaka*). — *Taila-spandā,* f., N. of several plants, = *śveta-gokarṇī; kākolī;* Cucurbita Pepo. — *Taila-sphaṭika, as,* m. a sort of gem, amber(?). — *Tailākara* (°*la-āk*°), *as,* m. seeds &c. from which oil is expressed. — *Tailāguru* (°*la-ag*°), *u,* n. a sort of Agallochum. — *Tailāṭī* (°*la-aṭi*), f. a wasp. — *Tailābhyaṅga* (°*la-abh*°), *as,* m. anointing the body with oil. — *Tailāmbukā* (°*la-am*°), f. = *taila-pāyikā,* a sort of cock-roach.

Tailaka, am, n. a small quantity of oil.

Tailika, as, m. an oilman, an oil manufacturer.

Tailin, ī, inī, i, relating or belonging to oil, oily, &c.; (*ī*), m. an oilman, an oil-grinder or preparer; (*inī*), f. the wick or cotton of a lamp; a kind of insect found in oil (= *taila-kīṭa*). — *Taili-śālā,* f. an oil-mill.

Tailīna, as, ā, am, grown with sesamum; (*am*), n. a field of sesamum.

तैलक्य *tailakya, am,* n. (fr. *tilaka*), putting the Tilaka-mark on the forehead (?).

तैलङ्ग *tailaṅga, as,* m. the country along the coast south of Orissa as far as Madras, the modern Carnatic.

तैलवक *tailavaka, as,* &c., inhabited by the Telus.

तैल्वक *tailvaka, as,* &c. (fr. *tilvaka*), coming from or made of the Tilvaka tree, the plant Symplocos Racemosa.

तैव्रक *taivraka, as,* &c., inhabited by the Tīvras.

तैव्रदारव *taivradārava, as, ī, am,* made of or coming from the tree Tīvra-dāru.

तैष *taisha, as, ī, am* (fr. *tishya*), relating to the asterism Tishya; (*as*), m., N. of a month (December–January), the month in which the full moon stands in the asterism Tishya, = *pausha* and *sahasya;* (*ī*), f., scil. *tithi* or *rātri,* the day of full moon in month Taisha.

तोक *toka, am,* n. (connected with 1. *tuć* and 1. *tuj,* and said by some to be fr. rt. 2. *tu*), offspring, children, race, male or female offspring, a child, (in the Ṛig-veda *toka* is never used in pl.; it is often joined with *tanaya*); a new-born child; the offspring of any animal (in comp., e. g. *varāha-toka,* a young boar); [cf. *tvaksh, stoka, taksh;* Gr. τέκνον, τίκτω, ἔτεκον, τοκός; Angl. Sax. *thegn, thegen;* Old Germ. *degan,* 'servant.'] — *Toka-vat, ān, atī, at,* Ved. connected with offspring, having children. — *Toka-sāti, is,* f., Ved. the acquisition of offspring.

Tokma, as, m. and (in the earlier language) *tokman, a,* n. a young green blade of corn, especially of barley, green or unripe barley; (*as*), m. green colour; (*am*), n. the wax of the ear; a cloud.

तोटक *toṭaka, as,* m. a kind of poisonous insect; N. of a pupil of Saṅkarāćārya; (*am*), n. a particular metre (each line of the stanza containing twelve syllables); according to some also a kind of drama, (probably a Prākṛit form for *troṭaka.*)

तोड् *toḍ,* cl. 1. A. *toḍate,* &c., to treat with disrespect; to despise; [cf. *tuḍḍ, tūḍ, rauḍ.*]

तोडन *toḍana, am,* n. (fr. rt. *tuḍ*), splitting (?).

तोडलतन्त्र *toḍala-tantra, am,* n., N. of a Tantra.

तोतल *totala, as,* m., N. of a writer on medicine; (*ā*), f., N. of a goddess; [cf. *trotala.*]

तोतस् *totas,* ind., Ved. (according to Mahī-dhara), a wife; or = *tvayi.*

तोत्तायन *tottāyana, ās,* m. pl., N. of a branch of the Atharva-veda, (also read *tottāyanīya, tauta,* and *tauttāyana.*)

तोत्त्र *tottra* or *totra, am,* n. (fr. rt. 1. *tud*), a stick or bamboo with a sharp iron head used for guiding an elephant; a goad or pike for driving cattle. — *Totra-vetra, am,* n. a rod or wand borne by Vishṇu.

Toda, as, m. guiding or driving (horses &c.); 'the instigator and exciter' (of all nature), an epithet of the Sun; sharp, shooting or pricking pain; pain, anguish, vexation, torture, disease, uneasiness either of body or mind; (*as*), m., Ved. a sacrificer; *gotamasya todaḥ,* N. of a Sāman. — *Toda-parṇī,* f. 'prick-leaf,' N. of a plant enumerated among the Ku-dhānyas.

Todana, am, n. a stick used for guiding or driving cattle &c., a goad; stinging; pain, affliction from disease &c.; (*as, am*), m. n., N. of a tree and its fruit, (in Marāṭhī *laghukāṅkaḍa.*)

तोमर *tomara, as, am,* m. n. an iron club or crow; a lance, a javelin; a kind of metre consisting of four lines of nine syllables each; N. of a man; (*ās*), m. pl., N. of a race. — *Tomara-graha, as,* m. a warrior armed with a club or lance; throwing a lance. — *Tomara-dhara, as,* m. a warrior armed with a club or lance; fire.

तोमराण *tomarāṇa, as,* m., N. of a man; [cf. *toramāṇa.*]

तोमरिका *tomarikā,* f. = *tuvarikā,* a fragrant earth.

तोय *toya, am,* n. (perhaps fr. rt. 2. *tu*), water; the regent of the Nakshatra Āshāḍhā; (*toyam kṛi,* to make an offering of water to a deceased person, with gen.); (*ā*), f., N. of a river; [cf. Slav. *tayati,* 'to melt.'] — *Toya-karman, a,* n. a religious ceremony performed with water, ablutions of various parts of the body, oblations of water offered to a deceased person. — *Toya-kāma, as, ā, am,* fond of water; (*as*), m. a sort of cane growing in or near water, Calamus Fasciculatus. — *Toya-kumbha,* Blyxa Saivala. — *Toya-kṛićchra, as, am,* m. n. a sort of penance, drinking nothing but water for a fixed period. — *Toya-kṛit, t, t, t,* causing water or rain. — *Toya-krīḍā,* f. sport or pastime in water, splashing about in water or besprinkling one another: [cf. *jala-krīḍā.*] — *Toya-garbha,* the cocoa-nut ('containing water'). — *Toya-ćara, as, ā, am,* moving in water; (*as*), m. an aquatic animal. — *Toya-ja, as ā, am,* born or living in water. — *Toya-ḍimba* or *-ḍimbha* or *-ḍimbhaka, as,* m. hail. — *Toya-da, as, ā, am,* giving water; (*as*), m. a cloud; a kind of Cyperus, = *mustaka;* (*am*), n. ghee or oiled butter. — *Toyadātyaya* (°*da-at*°), *as,* m. the departure of the clouds, the autumn. — *Toya-dāna, am,* n. a kind of gesticulation mentioned in the Purāṇa-sarva-sva by Halāyudha. — *Toya-dhara, as, ā* or *ī, am,* bearing or containing water; (*as*), m. a cloud; a kind of medicinal plant, = *su-nishaṇṇa;* a kind of Cyperus, = *mustā.* — *Toya-dhāra, as, ā, am,* bearing or containing water; (*as*), m. a stream of water. — *Toya-dhi, is,* m. 'the receptacle of waters,' the ocean. — *Toyadhi-priya, am,* n. cloves, ('fond of the sea,' i. e. produced in maritime countries.) — *Toya-nidhi, is,* m. 'a treasure-house of water,' the ocean. — *Toya-nīvī,* f. 'girdled by the ocean,' an epithet of the earth. — *Toya-pāshāṇa-ja-mala, am,* n. calamine, oxide of zinc. — *Toya-pippali,* f. the plant Jussiæa Repens. — *Toya-pushpī* or *toya-prashṭhā,* f. trumpet-flower, Bignonia Suaveolens. — *Toya-prasādana, as, ā, am,* purifying water; (*am*), n. the tree or the nut of the tree Strychnos Potatorum, the clearing-nut, (this nut being rubbed upon the inside of a water-jar occasions the precipitation of the impurities of the water poured into it.) — *Toyaprasādana-phala, am,* n. the nut of the tree Strychnos Potatorum; [cf. the preceding.] — *Toya-phalā,* f. Cucumis Utilissimus (= *irvāru*). — *Toya-maya, as, ī, am,* formed or consisting of water. — *Toya-mala, am,* n. sea foam. — *Toya-muć, k,* m. a cloud (' discharging water'). — *Toya-yantra, am,* n. a water-clock, a clepsydra; [cf. *jala-yantra.*] — *Toya-rasa, as,* m. water, moisture. — *Toya-rāj, ṭ,* m. 'the king of the waters,' an epithet of the ocean. — *Toya-rāśi, is,* m. 'a heap of water,' a pond, a lake. — *Toya-vat, ān, atī, at,* 'having water,' surrounded by water; (*atī*), f., N. of a plant, = *amṛita-vallī,* Cocculus Cordifolius. — *Toya-vallikā,* f. Cocculus Cordifolius. — *Toya-vallī,* f. a kind of gourd, Momordica Charantia; [cf. *kāravella.*] — *Toya-vṛiksha, as,* m. the plant Blyxa Saivala. — *Toya-vṛitti* = *toyāpāmārga.* — *Toya-velā,* f. the margin of the water, the water's edge, the shore. — *Toya-vyatikara, as,* m. blending or union of the waters (of two rivers). — *Toya-śuktikā,* f. a bivalve shell, an oyster. — *Toya-śūka,* Blyxa Saivala. — *Toya-sarpikā,* f. a frog. — *Toya-sūćaka, as,* m. a frog. — *Toyādhāra* (°*ya-ādh*°), *as,* m. a water reservoir, a lake. — *Toyādhi-vāsini* (°*ya-adh*°), f. trumpet-flower, Bignonia Suaveolens; [cf. *ambu-vāsinī* and *ambu-vāsī.*] — *Toyāpāmārga* (°*ya-ap*°), *as,* m. Achyranthes Aquatica. — *Toyālaya* (°*ya-āl*°), *as,* m. ocean, sea; N. of a constellation. — *Toyāśaya* (°*ya-āś*°), *as,* m. a water reservoir, a cistern, a lake, a river. — *Toyotsarga* (°*ya-ut*°), *as,* m. the pouring out or discharge of water, raining. — *Toyotsarga-stanita-mukhara, as, ā, am,* noisy with rain and thunder. — *Toyodbhavā* (°*ya-ud*°), f. Achyranthes Aquatica.

तोरण *toraṇa, as, am,* m. n. (perhaps fr. rt. 1. *tur,* to press forwards, i. e. through a passage), an arch, a gate, an arched doorway, a portal, the ornamented arch of a door or gateway; any temporary and ornamental arch; decoration of the gate-post (with boughs of trees, garlands, &c.); an outer door; a mound or elevated place near a bathing-place; a triangle supporting a large balance; (*am*), n. the neck, the throat; (*as*), m. an epithet of Siva. — *Toraṇa-māla, as* or *am,* m. or n. (?), N. of a place of pilgrimage. — *Toraṇa-vat, ān, atī, at,* arched, having ornamental arches.

तोरमाण *toramāṇa, as,* m., N. of a prince; [cf. *tomarāṇa.*]

तोरश्रवस् *tora-śravas, ās,* m., N. of a Ṛishi with the patronymic Āṅgirasa; [cf. *taura-śravasa.*]

तोल *tola, as, ā, am* (fr. rt. *tul*), poising one's self, e. g. *ghana-tola,* (a bird) poising itself in the clouds; (*as, am*), m. n. weighing, weight or quantity measured by the balance; a Tola, a weight of gold or silver, (reckoned in books at 16 Māshas or 5 Rettis or 6¼ grains each, and weighing therefore 105 grains troy: in practice it is calculated at 12 Māshas, jeweller's weight, and weighs nearly double or 210 grains; but actually it is of the same weight as the Sicca or 179⅝ grains.)

Tolaka, as, am, m. n. a kind of weight, = *tola.*

Tolana, am, n. raising, lifting up, weighing.

Tolayitvā, ind. having lifted up, having weighed.

Tolya, as, ā, am, to be raised, to be weighed.

तोश *tośa, as, ā, am,* or *taśas, ās, ās, as* (fr. rt. 1. *tuś*), Ved. distilling, trickling, granting.

तोष *tosha, as,* m. (fr. rt. *tush*), satisfaction, gratification, contentment, pleasure, joy, happiness; Contentment personified as a son of Bhaga-vat and one of the twelve Tushitas.

Toshaka, as, ikā, am, gratifying, causing pleasure or happiness.

Toshaṇa, as, ī, am, satisfying, gratifying, making contented, appeasing, pleasing; (*am*), n. the act of satisfying, satisfaction, gratification, pleasing, delighting; (*ī*), f. an epithet of Durgā.

Toshaṇīya or *toshayitavya, as, ā, am,* to be satisfied or gratified or made contented, to be pleased.

Toshita, as, ā, am, pleased, satisfied, gratified, appeased.

Toshin, ī, iṇī, i, (at the end of a comp.) satisfied or contented with, pleased with, liking; gladdening, satisfying, making contented.

Toshya, as, ā, am, to be made satisfied or contented, to be pleased or delighted.

तोषल *toshala* or *tosala, ās,* m. pl., N. of a race (?).

तौक्षायण *taukshāyaṇa,* adj. from Tuksha.

तौक्षिक *taukshika, as,* m. (a word borrowed fr. the Gr. τοξότης), the sign of the zodiac Sagittarius.

तौग्र्य *taugrya, as,* m., Ved. the son of Tugra, a patronymic of Bhujyu.

तौच्छ्य *tauććhya, am,* n. (abstract noun fr. *tuććha*), emptiness, meanness, worthlessness.

तौण्डिकेर *tauṇḍikera, ās,* m. pl., N. of a race; [cf. *taṇḍikera.*]

तौत *tauta,* another form for *tottāyana.*

तौतातिक *tautātika, as, ī, am,* composed by Tutāta, (according to a scholiast) = Kaumārilam Śāstram.

तौतिक *tautika, as,* m. the pearl-oyster; (*am*), n. a pearl.

तौत्तायन *tauttāyana,* another form for *tottāyana.*

तौद *tauda, am,* n. (fr. *tuda* or *toda*), N. of a Sāman; (*ī*), f., Ved., N. of a plant (?).

तौदादिक *taudādika, as, ī, am* (fr. *tud* + *ādi*), belonging to the class of roots which begins with *tud,* i. e. to the sixth class.

1. *taudeya, as,* m. a patronymic from Tuda.

तौदिय *taudiya, as,* m., N. of a Brāhman.

तौदेय 2. *taudeya, as, ī, am,* produced in or coming from the district called Tūdī, q. v.

तौम्बुरविन् *taumburavin, iṇas,* m. pl. the pupils of Tumburu.

तौर *taura, as, ī, am,* relating to Tura; (*am*), n., scil. *ayana,* N. of a Sat-tra ceremony.

तौरयाण *taurayāṇa, as, ā, am,* Ved. = *tūrṇayāna,* hastening.

तौरश्रवस *tauraśravasa, am,* n. (fr. *tora-śravas*), N. of two Sāmans.

तौरायणिक *taurāyaṇika, as, ī, am,* performing the sacrifice or vow Turāyaṇa.

तौर्य *taurya, am,* n. (fr. *tūrya*), the sound of musical instruments, music, harmony, &c. — *Taurya-trika, am,* n. triple symphony or harmony, i. e. union of song, dance, and instrumental music.

तौर्वश *taurvaśa, as, ī, am* (fr. *turvaśa*), epithet of a peculiar species of horse.

तौल *taula, am,* n. a balance, = *tulā.*

1. *taulika* in *daśa-taulika,* having the weight of 10 Tulās.

Taulin, ī, m. (fr. *tulā*), one who holds a balance, a weigher; the sign of the zodiac Libra.

Taulya, am, n. weight; equality, similarity, likeness.

तौलिक 2. *taulika, as,* m. (fr. *tūlikā*), a painter; [cf. the next.]

Taulikika, as, m. a painter.

तौल्वलि *taulvali, is,* m. (fr. *tulvala?*), N. of a preceptor; *ajā-taulvali,* Taulvali fond of goats.

Taulvalāyana, as, m. a patronymic from Taulvali.

तौवरक *tauvaraka, as, ī, am,* derived or coming from the plant Tuvaraka.

तौविलिका *tauvilikā,* f., Ved. a kind of animal (?).

तौषार *taushāra, as, ī, am* (fr. *tushāra*), snowy, dewy; (*am*), n. snow, cold.

त्मन् *tman, ā,* m. = *ātman* (acc. *tmanam* and *tmānam,* dat. *tmane,* loc. *tmani;* the initial *ā* is also rarely dropped in epic poetry after *e* or *o*), Ved. the vital breath; one's own person, self. *Tman* is also used in Ved. for *tmanā* at the end of a Pāda.

Tmanā, ind., Ved. Although according to the unanimous interpretation of the native scholiasts and grammarians (cf. Pāṇ. VI. 4, 141) this word stands for *ātmanā,* 'by itself, myself, himself, one's self,' &c., yet it has evidently in many cases lost its original meaning and is used as an emphatic particle in the same way as the Greek μέν and μήν; it may then be translated by 'yet,' 'really,' 'indeed,' 'even,' 'at least,' 'certainly,' 'also;' (*tmanā* usually lays stress on a preceding and more rarely on a following word); *uta tmanā, tmanā ća,* and also, and certainly; *iva tmanā* or *na tmanā,* just as; *adha tmanā,* then certainly, even.

Tmanyā, ind., Ved. (in certain Āprī hymns) = *tmanā.*

त्मूत *tmūta, as, ā, am* (perhaps for *tyūta* fr. rt. *tiv*), Ved. soaked with fat.

त्य *tya.* See *tyad.*

त्यगल *tyagala, as,* m., N. of an author; (also read *tigala.*)

त्यग्नायि *tyagnāyi,* Ved., N. of a Sāman.

त्यज् 1. *tyaj,* cl. 1. P. *tyajati, tatyāja* (Ved. *tityāja*), *tyakshyati* (rarely *tyajishyati*), *atyākshīt, tyaktum,* to leave, abandon, quit; to leave a place, go away from; to let go, dismiss, discharge; to shoot off; to give up, surrender, resign, part from, renounce (e. g. *tanum* or *deham* or *kalevaram tyaj,* to abandon the body, die; *prāṇān* or *śvāsam* or *jīvitam tyaj,* to give up breath or life, die, risk one's life); to shun, avoid; to get rid of, free one's self from, lose; to distribute, give away, give, offer (as a sacrifice or oblation to a deity); to set aside, leave unnoticed, disregard; to except: Pass. *tyajyate,* to be abandoned by, to become deprived of, lose, get rid of (with inst., e. g. *dhanena tyajyate,* he loses his riches): Caus. *tyājayati, -yitum,* Aor. *atityajat,* to cause to leave or abandon or quit, to deprive a person of anything (with two acc., e. g. *tyājayati mām gṛiham,* he causes me to quit the house; or with acc. and inst., e. g. *atityajat tam prāṇaiḥ,* he caused him to lose his life); to expel, turn out; to quit; to cause anything not to be noticed: Desid. *tityakshati:* Intens. *tātyajyate, tātyakti;* [cf. Hib. *treigim,* 'I leave, forsake;' *treigthe,* 'forsaken,' = *tyakta; treigean,* 'leaving, forsaking, abandonment,' = *tyajana; treigtheoir,* 'a deserter, forsaker,' = *tyaktṛi.*]

Tyakta, as, ā, am, left, resigned, forsaken, abandoned, deserted, left alone, &c. — *Tyakta-jīvita* or *tyakta-prāṇa, as, ā, am,* ready to abandon life; willing to run all hazards, having relinquished all expectation of life as men on the forlorn hope. — *Tyakta-lajja, as, ā, am,* abandoning shame, shameless. — *Tyakta-vat, ān, atī, at,* having left, leaving, abandoning, &c. — *Tyakta-vidhi, is, is, i,* transgressing rules. — *Tyakta-śrī, īs, īs, i,* abandoned by fortune. — *Tyaktāgni* (°*ta-ag*°), *is,* m. a Brāhman who has given up his household fire, one who neglects essential ceremonies.

Tyaktavya, as, ā, am, to be left or abandoned or released, to be left to one's fate; to be removed or kept back; to be given up or sacrificed.

Tyaktu-kāma, as, ā, am, wishing to leave.

Tyaktṛi, tā, trī, tṛi, resigning, leaving, abandoning, giving up, sacrificing; an abandoner, forsaker.

Tyaktrā, ind. having left, abandoned, surrendered, &c.; leaving aside, disregarding, with exception of.

2. *tyaj, k, k, k,* (at the end of a comp.) leaving, abandoning, giving up, dying, risking one's life; [cf. *tanu-t*°.]

Tyajana, am, n. leaving, quitting, abandoning; giving; excepting, exclusion.

Tyajanīya, as, ā, am, to be left or abandoned, to be avoided, to be excepted, &c.

Tyajas, as, n., Ved. abandonment; difficulty, danger; alienation, estrangement, dislike, anger, aversion, envy; (Sāy.) a weapon or instrument causing abandonment; (*ās, ās, as*), m. f. n., Ved. offspring, a descendant.

Tyāga, as, m. leaving, letting go, abandoning, forsaking, parting from, deserting, renouncing, separation; discharging; dismissing; giving up, resigning; gift, donation, distribution; sacrificing one's life; liberality, generosity, prodigality; secretion, excretion; a sage, one who separates himself from the world; [cf. *ātma-t*°, *tanu-t*°, *deha-t*°.] — *Tyāga-pattra, am,* n. a bill of divorcement. — *Tyāga-maya, as, ī, am,* consisting only in giving or in donation. — *Tyāga-yuta, as, ā, am,* liberal. — *Tyāga-śīla, as, ā, am,* disposed to give away, generous, liberal. — *Tyāgaśīla-tā,* f. or *tyāgaśīla-tva, am,* n. generosity.

Tyāgin, ī, inī, i, leaving, abandoning, renouncing; giving up, resigning; sacrificing; liberal; (*ī*), m. an abandoner, (often applied to the religious ascetic who abandons terrestrial objects, thoughts, &c.); a giver, a donor; a hero. — *Tyāgi-tā,* f. or *tyāgi-tva, am,* n. liberality, generosity.

Tyāgima, as, ā, am, left, abandoned.

Tyājaka, as, ikā, am, one who leaves, abandons, expels; leaving, abandoning, &c.

Tyājita, as, ā, am, made to quit or abandon; caused to be disregarded.

Tyājya, as, ā, am, to be left or abandoned or quitted, to be avoided or shunned, to be expelled, to be removed; to be given up or relinquished or abstained from; to be sacrificed; to be excepted; (*am*), n. part of an asterism or its duration considered as unlucky.

त्यद् **tyad, syas, syā, tyad** (a pronoun composed of the base of the demonstrative pron. *ta* and the relative *ya,* and not found in the later language), Ved. that, that person or thing, (often used like the article in other languages, e. g. *tyad vasu Paṇīnām vidas,* thou didst find that wealth, i. e. the wealth of the Paṇis); it is sometimes strengthened by *ćid* and often occurs in connection with other demonstratives; (*tyad*), ind., Ved. indeed, namely, as it is known, (always preceded by the particle *ha,* e. g. *tvam ha tyad Indra Kutsam āvas,* thou indeed, O Indra, didst help Kutsa); [cf. Old Germ. *dër* fr. *dĭar,* f. *diu,* acc. *dia* = *tyām,* nom. pl. m. *die* = *tye,* f. *dio* = *tyās,* n. *diu* = *tyāni:* to *syā* belongs Old Germ. *siu,* acc. *sia:* Lith. and Slav. *szis, sy,* = *syas; szi, si,* = *syā.*]

Tyatra, ind., Ved. at that place, there.

Tyatratya, as, ā, am, Ved. existing or being there.

Tyada, as, m. a son of that person; (*am*), ind. (at the end of an adv. comp.) = *tyad.*

Tyadāyani, is, m. a son of that person.

Tyā-dṛiś, k, k, k, and *tyā-dṛiśa, as, ī, am,* such a one as that.

त 1. **tra, as, ā, am** (fr. rt. *trai*), protecting (in comp.; see *aṇsa-t*°, *anguli-t*°, *ātapa-t*°, *kaṭi-t*°, &c.).

त 2. **tra** = *tri,* three, in *dvi-tra,* q. v.

त्रंस् **traṇs,** cl. 1. 10. P. *traṇsati, traṇsayati,* &c., to speak or shine.

त्रख् **trakh,** cl. 1. P. *trakhati,* &c., to go, move.

त्रङ्क् **trank,** cl. 1. A. *trankate,* &c., to go, move.

त्रङ्ख् **trankh** or **trang,** cl. 1. P. *trankhati* or *trangati,* &c., to go or move, (a various reading for *tvang*); [cf. Hib. *tairgim,* 'I escape;' *tairgeadh,* 'going, passing.']

त्रङ्ग **tranga, as, ā,** m. f. a kind of town or N. of a town; the city of Hari-śćandra supposed to be suspended in the air; [cf. *dranka, dranga,* &c.]

त्रद **trada, as,** m. (fr. rt. *tṛid*), Ved. splitting, one who cleaves or opens; a creator; (Sāy.) = *tardayitṛi,* a killer or injurer (of enemies).

त्रन्द् **trand,** cl. 1. P. *trandati,* &c., to act, perform functions; to endeavour, strive; to be busy.

त्रप् **trap,** cl. 1. A. *trapate, trepe, trapishyate* and *trapsyate, atrapishṭa* and *atrapta, trapitum* and *traptum,* to become perplexed or embarrassed, to be ashamed, be modest: Caus. *trapayati* and *trāpayati, -yitum,* to make perplexed or ashamed: Desid. *titrapishate* and *titrapsate:* Intens. *tātrapyate, tātrapti;* [cf. Gr. τρέπω, ἐν-τρέπω; Lat. *turpis,* probably also *trepidus,* = Ved. *tṛipra,* 'hastening;' Lith. *trôpiyu,* 'to throw;' Slav. *trepet,* 'trembling;' probably Goth. *dreiban;* Angl. Sax. *drif-an, dref-an.*]

Trapa, as, ā, m. f. (more commonly *ā,* f.), perplexity, embarrassment, bashfulness, shame, modesty; (*ā*), f. an unchaste woman (a shame to her family); family, race; fame, celebrity; [cf. Gr. ἐν-τροπή.] — *Trapā-nirasta, as, ā, am,* shameless, impudent. — *Trapānvita* (°*pā-an*°), *as, ā, am,* modest, bashful, ashamed. — *Trapā-bhara, as, ā, am,* overcome with shame. — *Trapā-yukta, as, ā, am,* bashful, modest. — *Trapā-raṇḍā,* f. a harlot. — *Trapā-vat, ān, atī, at,* modest, ashamed. — *Trapā-hīna, as, ā, am,* shameless, immodest, impudent.

Trapamāṇa, as, ā, am, being ashamed.

Trapita, as, ā, am, modest, bashful, ashamed.

Trapu, u, n. tin; lead; (tin is said to be called *trapu* from its contracting just before melting; cf. *lajjālu,* as a N. of the sensitive plant.) — *Trapu-karkaṭī,* f. a kind of cucumber, = *trapusī.* — *Trapu-karṇin, ī, inī, i,* having tin ear-ornaments; (*ī*), m. an epithet of Bhava-nandin.

Trapula, am, n. tin, lead.

Trapusha, as, m., N. of a merchant; a cucumber or melon; (*ī*), f. = *trapusī;* (*am*), n. cucumber, the fruit of the Trapushī; tin.

Trapus, us, n. tin; [cf. *trāpusha.*]

Trapusa, am, n. cucumber, the fruit of the Trapusī; tin; (*ī*), f. coloquintida and other sorts of cucumber, = *mahendra-vāruṇī, karkaṭī, pīta-pushpā.*

त्रपाक **trapāka, as,** m., N. of a barbarous tribe.

त्रपिष्ठ **trapishṭha, as, ā, am** (superl. of *tṛipra*), highly satisfied, much pleased or contented.

Trapīyas, ān, asī, as (compar. of *tṛipra*), more satisfied, highly pleased.

त्रपुटी **trapuṭī,** f. small cardamoms; [cf. also *tri-puṭā* and *tri-puṭī.*]

त्रपुस् **trapus.** See under rt. *trap* above.

त्रप्र **trapra, am,** n. (a various reading for *vapra*), lead.

त्रप्स्य **trapsya, am,** n. (said to be fr. rt. *tṛip*), thin or diluted curds; (according to some authorities written *drapsya* and *drapsa.*)

त्रय **traya, as, ī, am** (fr. *tri*), triple, threefold, consisting of three, divided into three parts, of three kinds, treble; (*ī*), f., scil. *vidyā,* the threefold knowledge, the triple science (i. e. sacred revelation in its threefold form of hymn, sacrificial formula, and song, afterwards represented by the Ṛig, Yajur, and Sāma Vedas), the three Vedas collectively (omitting the Atharvan, which is not of equal authority); a triad, three collectively, a triplet, three, (e. g. *śata-trayī,* 300); a matron, a married woman whose husband and children are living; intellect, understanding; N. of a plant (Conyza Serratula), = *soma-rājin;* (*am*), n. a triad, three collectively, three, τριάς. — *Trayī-tanu, us,* m. an epithet of the Sun (having the three Vedas for a body, either as celebrated in the Vedas or because the Sāma-veda and portions of the other Vedas are said to have proceeded from the Sun); an epithet of Śiva. — *Trayī-dharma, as,* m. the duty enjoined by the Vedas (i. e. the forms of sacrifice &c. prescribed by them). — *Trayī-maya, as, ī, am,* consisting of the three Vedas, containing them, resting on them, &c. — *Trayī-mukha, as,* m. a Brāhman ('having the three Vedas in his mouth'). — *Trayī-vida, as, ā, am,* Ved. knowing the triple science; [cf. *trayī* and *traivida.*]

Trayas, nom. pl. of *tri,* three, (used in comp. with a following decad, except *aśīti* which takes *tri.* The other decads, except ten, twenty, and thirty, may also take *tri* for + 3.) — *Trayaḥ-pańćāśat, t,* f. fifty-three; [cf. *tri-pańćāśat.*] — *Trayaḥ-shashṭi, is,* f. sixty-three; [cf. *tri-shashṭi.*] — *Trayaḥ-saptati, is,* f. seventy-three; [cf. *tri-saptati.*] — *Trayaś-ćatvāriṇśa, as, ī, am,* the forty-third. — *Trayaś-ćatvāriṇśat, t,* f. forty-three; [cf. *tri-ćatvāriṇśat.*] — *Trayas-triṇśa, as, ī, am,* the thirty-third; joined with thirty-three (e. g. *trayastriṇśam śatam,* 133); consisting of thirty-three; celebrated with the Stoma which consists of thirty-three parts or syllables, containing that Stoma, &c. — *Trayas-triṇśat, t,* f. thirty-three. — *Trayas-triṇśati, is,* f., Ved. thirty-three. — *Trayastriṇśa-pati, is,* m. the chief of the thirty-three gods, an epithet of Indra. — *Trayastriṇśa-stoma, as, ā, am,* Ved. containing the Trayastriṇśa-stoma. — *Trayas-triṇśin, ī, inī, i,* containing thirty-three. — *Trayo-daśa, as, ī, am,* the thirteenth; joined with thirteen or having thirteen added (e. g. *trayodaśam śatam,* 113); consisting of thirteen; (*ī*), f. the thirteenth day of the lunar fortnight; a kind of gesticulation mentioned in the Purāṇa-sarva-sva. — *Trayodaśaka,* consisting of thirteen; (*am*), n. the number thirteen. — *Trayodaśa-dhā,* ind. into or in thirteen parts. — *Trayo-daśan, a,* m. f. n. pl. thirteen; [Gr. τρισ-καί-δεκα for τρεῖς-°; cf. Lat. *tredecim* for *tres-decem;* Lith. *trylika* fr. *trydika.*] — *Trayodaśama, as, ī, am,* the thirteenth. — *Trayodaśa-vidha, as, ā, am,* of thirteen kinds. — *Trayodaśika,* happening on the thirteenth day of the half-moon. — *Trayo-daśin, ī, inī, i,* Ved. containing thirteen. — *Trayo-navati, is,* f. ninety-three; [cf. *tri-navati.*] — *Trayoviṇśa, as, ī, am,* the twenty-third; consisting of twenty-three. — *Trayo-viṇśati, is,* f. twenty-three. — *Trayo-viṇśatika, as, ī, am,* consisting of twenty-three. — *Trayoviṇśati-tama, as, ī, am,* the twenty-third. — *Trayoviṇśati-dhā,* ind. in twenty-three parts, in twenty-three ways, &c.

त्रययाय्य **trayayāyya, as, ā, am,** Ved. (according to Sāy.) = *trātavya,* to be protected.

त्रयोदशन् **trayo-daśan.** See *trayas* above.

त्रय्यारुण **trayyāruṇa, as,** m., N. of a prince, a son of Tri-dhanvan; a son of Uru-kshaya; N. of the Vyāsa in the fifteenth Dvāpara.

त्रवाडिलघु *travāḍi-laghu, us,* m., N. of the father of Mahī-dhara.

त्रस् 1. *tras,* cl. 10. P. *trāsayati, -yitum,* to take, seize; to hold; to oppose, prevent, forbid.

त्रस् 2. *tras,* cl. 1. and 4. P. (ep. also A.) *trasati, trasyati, tatrāsa* (3rd pl. *tatrasus* and *tresus*), *trasishyati, atrāsīt* and *atrasīt, trasitum,* to tremble, quiver, quake, or start with fear; to be agitated, be afraid of; to fear, dread (with abl. or gen. and more rarely with inst., e. g. *tasmāt* or *tasya trasyati,* he fears that or is afraid of him); to run away, run: Caus. *trāsayati, -yitum,* to cause to tremble, terrify, to frighten, scare, agitate, set in motion: Desid. *titrasishati:* Intens. *tātrasyate, tātrasti;* [cf. Zend *tareś, tars-ti:* Gr. τρέω for τρεσιyω, ταρταρίζω, τρήρων for τρεσρων, τρέ-μω, τάρβος, ταράσσω, θάλασσα, ὀ-τρηρός, ὀ-τραλέος: Lat. *tristis* = *trasta; tremo; terreo* fr. *terseo* for *treseo* = Caus. *trāsayāmi:* Goth. *thlahsyan:* Russ. *tryasu,* 'to shake;' *tryasu-sy,* 'I tremble:' Lett. *trisseht,* 'to tremble:' Hib. *tor,* 'fear, dread.']

Trasa, as, ā, am, movable, moving, locomotive; (*am*), n. the collective body of moving or living beings; animals; animals and men, (opposed to *sthāvara,* cf. *jagat;* under *trasa* are sometimes reckoned gods, men, and the inhabitants of the lower regions); (*as*), m. the heart ('the quivering one'); (*am*), n. a forest, a wood. — *Trasa-dasyu, us,* m. 'before whom evil beings tremble,' N. of a prince, (celebrated for his liberality and favoured by the gods; he bears the patronymic Paurukutsya or Paurukutsi or Paurukutsa, and is supposed to be the author of certain Ṛig-veda hymns; in the Bhāgavata-Purāṇa *Trasad-dasyu,* which is probably the original form, is identified with Mām-dhātṛi and regarded as the father of Puru-kutsa; the meaning of the name may be 'frightening evil beings;' cf. *jamad-agni, taraddveshas, bharad-vāja,* &c.) — *Trasa-reṇu, us,* m.f. an atom, the mote or atom of dust which is seen moving in a sun-beam, especially considered as an ideal weight either of the lowest denomination or equal to three or (according to some) thirty invisible atoms; (*us*), f., N. of one of the wives of the Sun.

Trasana, am, n. in *hasti-trasanāni,* the moving ornaments of an elephant (?).

Trasara, as, m. a shuttle; weaving; = *tasara.*

Trasura, as, ā, am, trembling, timid, fearful.

Trasta, as, ā, am, frighted, alarmed; timid, trembling, fearful; quick. — *Trasta-rūpa, as, ā, am,* terrified, fearful.

Trasnu, us, us, u, fearful, timid, timorous.

Trasyat, an, antī, at, fearing, apprehending.

Trāsa, as, ā, am, moving, movable, locomotive; frightening; (*as*), m. fear, terror, anxiety; terrifying, frightening, causing alarm, (often in comp., e. g. *trāsārtham,* ind. in order to frighten); a flaw or defect in a jewel. — *Trāsa-kara, as, ī, am,* causing fear, fearful, alarming. — *Trāsa-dāyin, ī, inī, i,* causing alarm, fear-exciting.

Trāsadasyava, as, m. a patronymic from Trasad-dasyu; (*am*), n., N. of a Sāman.

Trāsana, as, ī, am, terrifying, alarming, frightening (with gen.), making anxious; (*as*), m. epithet of Śiva; (*am*), n. the act of frightening or alarming; a means of frightening, cause of alarm, fright.

Trāsanīya, as, ā, am, to be dreaded, frightened, &c.

Trāsita, as, ā, am, frightened, scared, alarmed.

Trāsin, ī, inī, i, fearful, timid, afraid.

त्रा 1. *trā* (by native authorities written *trai,* q. v.), cl. 1. A. *trāyate,* &c., to protect, &c. See rt. *trai,* p. 394.

2. *trā, ās,* m., Ved. a protector, a defender; [cf. 1. *tra.*]

Trāṇa, as, ā, am, preserved, saved, guarded, protected; (*am*), n. protecting, preserving; protection, a preservative, defence; shelter, help, (often in comp., e. g. *ārta-trāṇāya,* for the protection of the distressed; *ātma-trāṇa,* self-defence); protection for the body, armour; (*ā*), f., N. of a plant, = *trāyamāṇā;* [cf. Hib. *troiath,* 'a helmet.'] — *Trāṇa-kartṛi, tā,* or *trāṇa-kārin, ī,* m. a preserver, protector, saviour, deliverer.

Trāta, as, ā, am, preserved, rescued, guarded, protected; (*as*), m., N. of a man; (*am*), n. preserving, protection.

Trātavya, as, ā, am, to be guarded or protected.

Trātṛi, tā, trī, tṛi, a protector, saviour, guardian, defender; protecting, defending.

Trātra, am, n. defence, protection.

Trātvā, ind. having preserved or rescued.

Trāman, a, n., Ved. protection; [cf. *su-trāman.*]

Trāyat, an, antī, at, preserving, defending, protecting; (*antī*), f. a protectress; a medicinal plant; [cf. *trāyamāṇā.*]

Trāyantikā, f. a medicinal plant.

Trāyamāṇa, as, ā, am, preserving, defending, a preserver; (*ā*), f., N. of a medicinal plant; also *trāyamāṇikā,* f.; [cf. *krita-trā.*]

Trāhi (2nd sing. impv. of rt. *trai*), save! deliver! to the rescue!

त्रापुष *trāpusha, as, ī, am* (fr. *trapu*), made of tin [cf. *jātusha*]; silver (produced from tin).

त्रापुस *trāpusa, as, ī, am,* sprung or coming from the plant Trapusī.

त्रायोदश *trāyodaśa, as, ī, am* (fr. *trayodaśī*), relating &c. to the thirteenth day of a half-moon.

त्रि *tri, trayas* m. pl., *tisras* f. pl., *trīṇi* n. pl. (said to be fr. rt. *tṛī;* in Ved. *trī* occurs for *trīṇi* and *trīṇām* for *trayāṇām*), three; [cf. Gr. τρεῖς, τρί-α, τρί-το-ς, τρί-ς, τρισσό-ς: Zend *thri, thri-tya, thris:* Lat. *tres, tri-a, ter-tiu-s, ter:* Goth. *threis, thriya, thri-dya:* Angl. Sax. *threo, thry, thri:* Slav. *triye, tre-tii,* 'third:' Lith. *trys,* 'three;' *tré-ćza-s,* 'third:' to *tisras* belong Old Hib. *teora,* Cambro-Brit. f. *tair,* Armor. *teir.*] — *Tri-kakud, t, t, t,* having three peaks or points or horns &c.; (*t*), m., N. of a mountain in the Himālaya [cf. *tri-kūṭa* and *su-vela*]; an epithet of Kṛishṇa or Vishṇu; N. of a son of Śuci and father of Dharma-sārathi; a kind of ritual observance; the highest, chief. — *Tri-kakuda, as, ā, am,* having three peaks or humps &c. — *Tri-kakubh, p, p, p,* Ved. having three peaks or points; an epithet of Indra's thunderbolt or of Indra himself; (*p*), m., N. of a mountain; a kind of ritual observance; [cf. *tri-kakud.*] — *Tri-kaṭa, as,* m., N. of a plant (Ruellia Longifolia), = *go-kshuraka;* [cf. *tri-kaṇṭa.*] — *Tri-kaṭu, u,* n. or *tri-kaṭuka, am,* n. the aggregate of three spices, viz. black and long pepper and dry ginger; [cf. *kaṭu-traya.*] — *Tri-kaṇṭa, am,* n. the three thorny plants, a collective N. of three kinds of Solanum, viz. *bṛihatī, agni-damanī,* and *duhsparśā;* (*as, ā, am*), having three thorns; (*as*), m., N. of a plant, = *go-kshuraka* or *pattra-gupta;* a kind of fish. — *Tri-kaṇṭaka, as,* m., N. of a plant, = *go-kshuraka;* a kind of poisonous insect; a kind of fish (Silurus); a kind of weapon. — *Tri-kadruka, ās,* m. pl., Ved. probably a N. of three peculiar Soma-vessels [cf. *kadru*], or perhaps a N. of an oblation consisting of three offerings of the Soma (which is of a dark-brown colour); the first three days of the Abhi-plava festival which lasts six days, (respectively called Jyotis, Go, and Āyus.) — *Trikadrukīya, as, ā, am,* containing the word *tri-kadruka.* — *Tri-karṇa, as, ī, am,* having three ears. — *Tri-karman,* (at the beginning of a comp.) the three chief duties of a Brāhman, viz. sacrifice, study of the Vedas, and liberality (e. g. *tri-karma-krit,* performing these three duties); (*ā, ā, a*), engaging in these three actions. — *Tri-karsha, am,* n. = *tri-kārshika.* — *Tri-kalā,* f., N. of a female deity produced by the union of three gods for the destruction of Andhaka. — *Tri-kāṇḍa, as, ā, am,* consisting of three parts or divisions; forty-eight cubits long; (*as* or *am*), m. or n. (?), a work consisting of three parts, especially the dictionary of Amara-siṃha, also called Amara-kosha. — *Trikāṇḍa-ćintā-maṇi, is,* m. or *trikāṇḍa-viveka, as,* m., N. of commentaries on this work. — *Trikāṇḍa-mandana,* N. of a work. — *Trikāṇḍa-śesha, as,* m. a vocabulary in three chapters supplementary to the Amara-kosha by Purushottama. — *Tri-kāya, as, ā, am,* having three bodies; (*as*), m., N. of Buddha or of a Buddha. — *Tri-kārshika, am,* n. the three contracting (*kārshika* fr. rt. *krish*) substances, dry ginger, Ativishā, and Mustā; [cf. *tri-karsha, danta-karshaṇa.*] — *Tri-kāla, am,* n. the three times, viz. past, present, and future time; morning, noon, and evening; the present, past, and future tenses of a verb; (*am*), ind. three times, thrice; (*as, ā, am*), connected with or relating to the three times (past, present, and future). — *Trikāla-jña, as, ā, am,* knowing the three times, omniscient; (*as*), m. a divine sage; a deity; a N. of Buddha, the founder of the Buddhist religion. — *Trikāla-darśin, ī, inī, i,* seeing (or knowing) the past, present, and future, omniscient; (*ī*), m. a Ṛishi or divine sage; N. of Buddha. — *Trikāla-vid, t, t, t,* knowing the three times; (*t*), m. a Buddha; (with Jainas) an Arhat. — *Tri-kuṇḍīśvara* (°*ḍa-īś*°?), *am,* n., N. of a Tantra. — *Tri-kūṭa, as, ā, am,* having three peaks or humps or elevations &c.; (*as*), m., N. of several mountains, = *tri-kakud* and *su-vela;* a mountain in Ceylon on the top of which Laṅkā, the capital of Rāvaṇa, was situated; (*am*), n. sea-salt prepared by evaporation. — *Trikūṭa-lavaṇa, am,* n. a peculiar kind of salt (= *droṇi-lavaṇa*). — *Trikūṭa-vat, ān,* m., N. of a mountain. — *Tri-kūrćaka, am,* n. a sort of knife with three edges. — *Trikaika* (°*ka-eka*), Ved., N. of an Ekāha; [cf. *eka-trika.*] — *Tri-koṇa, as, ā, am* (borrowed fr. the Gr. τρίγωνον), triangular, forming a triangle; (*as, ā*), m. f. Trapa Bispinosa; (*am*), n. (in astron.) N. of the fifth and ninth mansion [cf. *tri-koṇa-bhavana* and *tri-trikoṇa*]; the vulva; [cf. *tri-bhuj.*] — *Trikoṇa-kuṇḍa, am,* n., N. of a mystical vessel in the form of a diagram. — *Trikoṇa-phala, am,* n. Trapa Bispinosa. — *Trikoṇa-bhavana, am,* n. (in astron.) N. of the fifth and ninth mansion. — *Tri-krama, as,* m. (according to the Prātiśākhyas) a Krama word composed of three words or members, the middle one of which is a single vowel. — *Tri-kshāra, am,* n. the three burning or acrid substances, viz. natron, saltpetre, and borax. — *Tri-kshura,* N. of a plant, = *kokilāksha.* — *Tri-kha, am,* n. a cucumber ('having three cavities'). — *Tri-khaṭva, am, ī,* n. f. three beds collectively. — *Tri-khaṇḍa,* the earth as divided into three portions. — *Tri-kharva, ās,* m. pl., Ved., N. of a particular school of theologians. — *Tri-gaṅga, am,* n., N. of a Tīrtha; [cf. *sapta-gaṅga.*] — *Tri-gaṇa, as,* m. the aggregate of the three objects of existence, viz. virtue (*dharma*), pleasure or the 'dulce' (*kāma*), and wealth or the 'utile' (*artha*); [cf. *tri-varga.*] — *Tri-gata, as, ā, am,* tripled; gone or done in three ways; (*am*), n. the expression of different senses by the same word. — *Tri-gandhaka, am,* n. = *tri-jātaka.* — *Tri-gambhīra,* see under *gabhīra.* — *Tri-garta, ās,* m. pl., N. of a people inhabiting the modern Lahore; (*as*), m. a prince of the Tri-gartas; the country of the Tri-gartas; a particular method of calculation; (*ā*), f. a lascivious woman, a wanton; a woman in general; a kind of cricket (= *ghurguri, ghurgurikā*); a pearl. — *Trigartaka, ās,* m. pl. = *tri-garta.* — *Trigarta-rāja, as,* and *trigarta-rājan, ā,* m. king of Tri-garta. — *Tri-gartika, as,* m. the country of the Tri-gartas. — *Tri-guṇa, ās,* m. pl. the three qualities or constituents of nature and every existing thing, i. e. *sat-tva, rajas,* and *tamas;* (*as, ā, am*), consisting of three threads or strings; threefold, three times repeated, thrice, triple, treble (e. g. *sapta triguṇāni dināni,* three times seven days); containing the three Guṇas or properties; (*am*), ind. in three ways, three times, thrice. — *Triguṇā-karṇa, as, ī, am,* whose ears have two slits dividing them into three parts (as a mark of distinction). — *Triguṇā-kṛita, as, ā, am,* thrice ploughed (a field &c.). — *Tri-grāmī,* f. an assemblage of three villages, N. of a place. — *Tri-grāhin, ī, iṇī, i,* extending to the length of three (padyās). — *Tri-ćakshus, us,* m. 'triocular,' 'three-eyed,' an epithet of Kṛishṇa (more properly of S'iva). — *Tri-ćatuḥ-karṇa,* the third and fourth hypotenuses. — *Tri-ćatura, ās, ās, āṇi,* pl. three or four. — *Tri-ćaturdaśa, au,* &c., du. the thirteenth and fourteenth. — *Tričatvāriṅśa, as, ī, am* (fr. the next), the forty-third. — *Tri-ćatvāriṅśat, t,* f. forty-three. — *Tri-ćaritra* (?), *am,* n. three kinds of characters, (perhaps a wrong reading for *strī-ćaritra;* cf. *tri-gūḍha.*) — *Tri-ćit, t, t, t,* consisting of three layers or seats of sacrificial grass. — *Tri-ćīvara, am,* n. the three vestments of the Buddhist ascetic. — *Trijagaj-jananī,* f. the mother of the three worlds, an epithet of Pārvatī. — *Tri-jagat, t,* n. or *tri-jagatī,* f. the triple world, i.e. heaven, the intermediate region, and earth, or heaven, earth, and the lower world. — *Trijagan-mohinī,* f. confounding the minds of the (inhabitants of the) three worlds, a form of Durgā (?). — *Tri-jaṭa, as, ā, am,* wearing three braids of hair; (*as*), m. an epithet of S'iva; N. of a Brāhman; (*ā*), f., N. of a Rākshasī who was friendly to Sītā; N. of a tree, = *vilva,* Ægle Marmelos. — *Trijaṭā-svapna-darśana, am,* n. 'the dream of Tri-jaṭā,' N. of a chapter in the fifth book of the Rāmāyaṇa. — *Tri-jāta* or *tri-jātaka, am,* n. three spices collectively, viz. mace, cardamoms, and Laurus Cassia (cinnamon). — *Tri-jīvā,* f. the sine of three signs or ninety degrees, a radius. — *Tri-jyā,* f. = the preceding. — *Tri-ṇata, as, ā, am* (fr. *tri-nata*), bent in three places, epithet of a bow; (*ā*), f. a bow; [cf. *triṇatā.*] — *Tri-ṇayana, as,* m. [cf. *tri-nayana*], 'three-eyed,' an epithet of S'iva. — *Tri-ṇavan* or *tri-ṇava* (fr. *tri* + *navan*), consisting of three times nine or twenty-seven parts, connected with the Tri-ṇava Stoma; three times nine, i.e. twenty-seven; *triṇava-sāhasra,* twenty-seven thousand; [cf. *tri-saptan.*] — *Tri-ṇāćiketa, as, ā, am,* one who has thrice kindled the fire called Nāćiketa; (*as*), m. an epithet of Nārāyaṇa (perhaps as worshipped with this fire); (according to Kullūka Bhaṭṭa on Manu III. 185, *tri-ṇāćiketa* means either 'a part of the Adhvaryu or Yajur-veda,' or 'a vow connected with it,' or 'one who performs this vow.') — *Tri-ṇāman, ā, ā, a,* Ved. having three names, epithet of a deity, perhaps of Agni. — *Tri-ṇītā,* f. a wife, ('thrice married,' according to the belief that a girl belongs to Soma, Gandharva and Agni, before she obtains a human husband.) — *Tri-taksha, am, ī,* n. f. (fr. *tri-takshan*), an association of three carpenters. — *Tri-tas,* ind. on three sides, from every side. — *Tri-tā,* f. or *tri-tva, am,* n. a triad, a trinity, an assemblage of three. — *Tri-trikoṇa, am,* n. (in astronomy) N. of the ninth mansion; [cf. *tri-koṇa* and *trikoṇa-bhavana.*] — *Tri-daṇḍa, am,* n. the three staves of a mendicant Brāhman who has resigned the world, (these staves are tied together so as to form one); triple subjection of words, thoughts, and acts; the state of a religious ascetic; (*ī*), f., N. of a literary work. — *Tri-daṇḍaka, am,* n. the three staves of a mendicant Brāhman described above. — *Tridaṇḍa-dhāraṇa, am,* n. carrying three staves tied together. — *Tri-daṇḍin, ī,* m. a wandering mendicant or devotee who has resigned worldly pursuits and carries three long bamboo staves tied together in his right hand; the religious man who has obtained a command over his words, thoughts, and actions, or mind, body, and speech; [cf. *eka-daṇḍin.*] — *Tri-dat, an, atī, at,* having three teeth. — *Tri-dalā,* f. a creeping plant, Cissus Pedata. — *Tri-dalikā* or (according to some) *tri-dālikā,* f., N. of a plant, = *ćarma-kashā.* — *Tri-daśa, ās,* m. pl. (fr. *tri-daśan*), three times ten, i.e. thirty; the three times ten or thirty deities, i.e. in round numbers a N. for the thirty-three deities, not including Brahmā, Vishṇu, and S'iva, viz. the twelve Ādityas, eight Vasus, eleven Rudras, and two Aśvins; (*as, ā, am*), divine; (*as*), m. a god, a deity, an immortal; (*am*), n. the residence of the thirty-three deities, i.e. heaven. — *Tridaśa-guru, us,* m. 'the preceptor of the gods,' i.e. Bṛihas-pati, regent of the planet Jupiter. — *Tridaśa-gopa* or *tridaśa-gopaka, as,* m. a fire-fly, = *indra-gopa,* q. v. — *Tridaśa-tva, am,* n. the state or condition of a god, divinity, divine nature. — *Tridaśa-dīrghikā,* f. 'the heavenly lake,' epithet of the Gaṅgā. — *Tridaśa-nadī,* f. the heavenly river, the Gaṅgā. — *Tridaśa-pati, is,* m. the chief of the gods, Indra. — *Tridaśapati-śastra, am,* n. Indra's weapon, the thunderbolt. — *Tridaśa-pratipaksha, as,* m. an adversary of the gods. — *Tridaśa-mañjarī,* f. = *tulasī,* basil. — *Tridaśa-vadhū, ūs,* f. or *tridaśa-vanitā,* f. a nymph of Indra's heaven, an Apsaras, a goddess. — *Tridaśa-śreshṭha, as,* m. 'the best of the thirty-three deities,' a N. of Agni; of Brahmā. — *Tridaśa-sarshapa, as,* m. = *deva-sarshapa.* — *Tridaśāṅkuśa* (°*śa-an*°), *as,* m. the thunderbolt ('divine goad'). — *Tridaśāćārya* (°*śa-āć*°), *as,* m. = *tridaśa-guru* above. — *Tridaśādhipati* (°*śa-adh*°), *is,* m. 'lord of the thirty-three deities,' a N. of S'iva. — *Tridaśāyana* (°*śa-ay*°), *as,* m. 'the refuge of the deities,' i.e. to whom the deities resort, an epithet of Nārāyaṇa; [cf. *brahmāyaṇa* and *lokāyana.*] — *Tridaśāyudha* (°*śa-āy*°), *am,* n. 'the divine bow,' the rainbow; a thunderbolt. — *Tridaśāri* (°*śa-ari*), *is,* m. 'enemy of the gods,' an Asura, a demon, a Titan. — *Tridaśāri-rājan, ā,* m. 'king of the demons,' a N. of Rāvaṇa. — *Tridaśālaya* (°*śa-āl*°), *as,* m. the residence of the gods, Svarga, Indra's heaven or paradise, the mountain Su-meru; an inhabitant of the divine world, a god. — *Tridaśāvāsa* (°*śa-āv*°), *as,* m. the residence of the gods, heaven. — *Tridaśāhāra* (°*śa-āh*°), *as,* m. the food of the gods, i.e. Amṛita or ambrosia. — *Tridaśī-bhūta, as, ā, am,* become divine or immortal. — *Tridaśendra* (°*śa-in*°) or *tridaśeśa* (°*śa-īś*°), *as,* m. 'the chief of the thirty-three deities,' epithet of Indra; of S'iva; of Brahmā, &c. — *Tridaśeśa-dvish, ṭ,* m. epithet of Rāvaṇa or any demon. — *Tridaśeśvara* (°*śa-īś*°) = *tridaśendra;* (*ī*), f., N. of Durgā. — *Tridaśeśvara-dvish* = *tridaśeśa-dvish.* — *Tri-dālikā,* f. for *tri-dalikā,* q. v. — *Tri-dina, am,* n. three days collectively. — *Tridina-spṛiś, k,* m. conjunction or concurrence of three lunations with one solar day. — *Tri-diva, am,* n. the space within the third sky, i.e. the innermost or most sacred part of the sky, heaven; the sky, atmosphere; paradise; (*ā*), f., N. of a river; cardamoms. — *Tridivādhīśa* (°*va-adh*°) or *tridiveśa* (°*va-īś*°) or *tridiveśvara* (°*va-īś*°), *as,* m. 'the lord of Tri-diva or heaven,' an epithet of Indra; a god, a deity. — *Tridivodbhavā* (°*va-ud*°), f. small cardamoms. — *Tridivaukas* (°*va-ok*°), *ās,* m. an inhabitant of Tri-diva, a celestial, a god. — *Tri-dṛiś, k,* m. 'triocular,' 'three-eyed,' an epithet of S'iva. — *Tri-dosha, am,* n. disorder of the three humors of the body, vitiation of the bile, blood, and phlegm. — *Tridosha-ghna, as, ī, am,* correcting the vitiated state of the three humors. — *Tridosha-ja, as,* m. disease &c. proceeding from disorder of the three humors of the body. — *Tri-dhanvan, ā,* m., N. of a prince or father of Trayyāruṇa. — *Tri-dhā,* ind. adv. in three ways, in three parts, in three places, triply, trebly; *tridhā-kṛi,* to do in three ways, to make threefold. — *Tri-dhātu, us, us, u,* consisting of three elements or ingredients, triple, threefold, thrice repeated (used like *triplex* in Lat. to denote excessive), tripartite; (Sāy.) causing the well-being of the three humors; (*us*), m. a N. of Gaṇeśa; (*u*), n. the aggregate of three minerals or of the three humors; the triple world. — *Tridhātu-śṛiṅga, as,* m., Ved. having a tripartite horn, having horns or flames of three colours, red, white, and black (with smoke), an epithet of Agni. — *Tridhā-tva, am,* n. the state of being threefold or in three parts, tripartition. — *Tri-dhāman, a,* n. probably = *tri-diva;* (*ā, ā, a*), belonging or relating to the three worlds or regions; having three residences, &c.; (*ā*), m. an epithet of Vishṇu; N. of Vyāsa (= Vishṇu) in the tenth Dvāpara; an epithet of S'iva; Agni or fire; death. — *Tridhā-mūrti, is,* f. a girl three years of age representing the deity Durgā at her festivals. — *Tri-dhāraka, as,* m. 'having three edges,' the plants Scirpus Kysoor and Euphorbia Antiquorum. — *Tri-dhāra-snuhī,* f., N. of a plant, = *dhārā-snuhī, try-aśra.* — *Tri-nagarī,* f. the three cities. — *Tri-nayana, as, ā, am,* triocular, three-eyed; (*as*), m. an epithet of Rudra-S'iva; (*ā*), f. epithet of Durgā; [cf. *tri-ṇayana.*] — *Tri-navata, as, ī, am* (fr. *tri-navati*), the ninety-third. — *Tri-navati, is,* f. ninety-three. — *Trinavati-tama, as, ī, am,* the ninety-third. — *Tri-nāka, am,* n., Ved. = *tri-diva.* — *Tri-nābha, as, ā, am,* having three navels or centres or central points; whose navel supports the three worlds. — *Tri-nābhi, is, is, i,* = *tri-nābha.* — *Tri-nidhana, am,* n., N. of a Sāman (generally in connection with the names *āgneyam, āyasyam,* and *tvāshṭri-sāma*). — *Tri-nishka, as, ā, am,* = *tri-naishkika,* worth three Nishkas. — *Tri-netra, as, ī, am,* triocular; (*as*), m. an epithet of Rudra-S'iva; N. of a prince; (*ī*), f. = *vārāhī-kanda,* the root of Yam (Dioscorea). — *Trinetra-ćūḍā-maṇi, is,* m. 'the crest of the three-eyed,' i.e. the moon (worn by S'iva as his crest). — *Tri-paksha, am,* n. a period of three fortnights or six weeks. — *Tri-paććhas,* ind. adv. (*tri* + *pad* + *śas*), by three Pādas. — *Tripañćāśa, as, ī, am* (fr. *tri-pañćāśat*), the fifty-third; containing or consisting of fifty-three. — *Tri-pañćāśat, t,* f. fifty-three; [cf. *trayaḥ-pañćāśat* under *trayas.*] — *Tripañćāśat-tama, as, ī, am,* the fifty-third. — *Tri-paṭu, u,* n. the three saline substances, stone-salt (= *saindhava*), Viḍ-lavaṇa, and black salt (= *kāća*). — *Tri-patāka, as, ā, am,* (with *hasta*) the hand with three fingers stretched out or erect; (with *lalāṭa*) the forehead marked naturally with three horizontal lines or wrinkles. — *Tri-paṭī,* f., N. of a place of pilgrimage. — *Tri-pattra, as,* m. three-leaved, trifoliate, the plant Ægle Marmelos (= *vilva*); (*am*), n. = *ćaṇḍāla-kanda,* a kind of bulbous plant. — *Tri-pattraka, as,* m. the Kiṅśuka tree, Butea Frondosa. — *Tri-patha, am,* n. the three paths or ways, viz. the sky, atmosphere, and earth, or the sky, earth, and lower world; a place where three roads meet; (*ā*), f. epithet of Mathurā. — *Tripatha-gā* or *tri-patha-gāminī,* f. 'flowing through heaven, earth, and the lower regions,' an epithet of the Gaṅgā. — *Tri-pad* or *tri-pād, -pāt, -pāt* or *-padī, -pat,* Ved. 'three-footed,' 'tripod,' epithet of Vishṇu (as pacing the universe in three steps; cf. *tri-vikrama*); epithet of Fever personified as a demon or evil spirit and represented with three feet and three hands, (probably symbolizing the cold, hot, and sweating stages of fever); having three steps; containing three Pādas; trinomial; (*t*), m., N. of a Daitya; (*-padī*), f. the girth of an elephant; the plant Cissus Pedata (= *godhā-padhī*); a kind of mètre in Prākṛit; (according to Pāṇ. IV. 1, 9, the f. must be *tri-padā* when agreeing with *ṛić,* e.g. *tripadā ṛik,* a verse containing three Pādas, cf. the next.) — *Tri-pada, as, ā, am,* three-footed; having three divisions (as a stanza); containing a measure of three feet; containing three words; (*ā*), f., N. of a plant, = *haṅsa-padī;* (*am*), n. a tripod; three words. — *Tri-padikā,* f. a stand with three feet. — *Tri-panna, as,* m., N. of one of the ten horses of the moon. — *Tri-parikrānta, as, ā, am,* one who walks thrice round the sacred fire or who circumambulates the three sacred fires. — *Tri-parṇa, as, ī, am,* three-leaved, trefoil; (*as*), m. Butea Frondosa; (*ā*), f. wild hemp; (*ī*), f., N. of several plants, Desmodium Gangeticum, = *śāla-parṇī,* wild cotton, wild hemp, = *pṛiśni-parṇī-bheda* and *vana-kārpāsī,* Sanseviera Ceylanica; a kind of bulbous plant, = *tri-parṇikā.* — *Tri-parṇikā,* f., N. of several plants, a kind of bulbous plant (= *bṛihat-pattrā,* &c.); Carpopogon Pruriens; Alhagi Maurorum. — *Tri-paryāya, as, ā, am,* Ved. having three folds or plaits. — *Tri-paśu, us, us, u,* having three victims. — *Tri-pastya, as,* m., Ved. 'having three dwellings,' an epithet of Agni. — *Tri-pājasya, as, ā, am,* Ved. having three flanks or sides; (Sāy.) having three breasts (or seasons). — *Tri-pāṭa, as,* m. intersection of a prolonged side and perpendicular (in a quadrangular figure); the figure formed by such intersection. — *Tripāṭhin, ī, inī, i* (fr. *tri-pāṭha*), familiar with the three Pāṭhas, (probably with the *saṃhitā, pada,* and *krama-pāṭha,* q. v.) — *Tri-pāṇa, as, ī, am* (probably a Prākrit form for *tri-parṇa* or *traiparṇa*), made of the plant Tri-parṇī. — *Tri-pād,* see *tri-pad.* — *Tri-pāda, as,* m. a constellation or asterism of which three-fourths are included under one sign of the zodiac; a stand with three feet? ; (ī), f. a kind of Mimosa. — *Tri-pādaka, as, ikā, am,* three-footed; (*ikā*), f., N. of a plant, = *haṇsa-padī,* a kind of Mimosa. — *Tri-piṭaka, am,* n. the three baskets or collections of writings, a collective N. for the three classes of Buddhist writings, viz. Sūtra-piṭaka, Vinaya-piṭaka, and Abhi-dharma-piṭaka. — *Tri-piṇḍī,* f. the three sacrificial cakes (mentioned in Manu III. 215). — *Tri-piba, as, ā, am,* drinking with three members of the body (as with the two pendent ears and tongue); (*as*), m. a long-eared goat. — *Tri-pishṭapa, am,* n. = *tri-diva,* the residence of the thirty-three gods, Indra's heaven; paradise; the sky, ether; [cf. *tri-vishṭapa.*] — *Tri-pishṭapa-sad, t,* m. an inhabitant of heaven, a deity. — *Tri-puṭa, as, ī, am,* triangular; (*as*), m. pulse, pease of three kinds; a kind of vetch, Cicer Arietinum; the palm of the hand; a measure, = *hasta-bheda,* a cubit; a bank or shore; (*ā*), f. Convolvulus Turpethum; Arabian jasmine; small cardamoms; a form of Durgā; (ī), f. Convolvulus Turpethum; small cardamoms; [cf. *karāla-tri-puṭā.*] — *Tripuṭaka, as, ā, am,* triangular; (*as*), m. a triangle; a species of pulse. — *Tripuṭā-pūjā-yantra, am,* n., N. of a kind of mystical diagram described in the Tantra-sāra by Kṛishṇānanda. — *Tri-puṭā-mantra, ās,* m. pl., N. of a chapter of the Tantra-sāra. — *Tripuṭā-stotra, am,* n., N. of a chapter of the Tantra-sāra. — *Tripuṭin, ī,* m. or *tripuṭī-phala, as,* m. the castor-oil plant, Ricinus Communis. — *Tri-puṇḍra* or *tri-puṇḍhra* or *tri-puṇḍraka, am,* n. a mark consisting of three lines on the forehead, the back, heart, and shoulders, or three curved horizontal marks made across the forehead with cow-dung, ashes, &c., which are worn especially by the followers of Śiva or Śakti, and are indispensable in proceeding to worship the former; (*as, ā, am*), having three horizontal marks. — *Tri-pur,* f. (in pl. *tri-puras*) = *tri-pura.* — *Tri-pura, am,* n. three strong cities collectively, a triple fortification; (in epic poetry) three strong cities of gold, silver, and iron, in the sky, air, and earth, built by Maya for a celebrated Asura or demon, and burnt by Śiva; (*as*), m., N. of the above Asura and king of Tri-pura; a form of Śiva; (*ā*), f., N. of a town; a form of Durgā (= *tri-puṭā* ?); (ī), f., N. of a town, = *ćedi-nagarī;* N. of a country to the south-east of Madhya-deśa, the modern Tipparah; (*ā* or *ī* ?), N. of an Upanishad. — *Tripura-kumāra, as,* m., N. of a pupil of Saṅkarāćārya mentioned in the Saṅkara-vijaya by Anantānanda-giri. — *Tripura-ghna, as,* or *tripura-jit, t,* or *tripura-dahana,* or *tripura-dāha, as,* m., N. of Śiva as destroyer of Tri-pura. — *Tripura-dāha, as,* m. 'burning of Tri-pura,' N. of the 3rd chapter of the Pātāla-khaṇḍa of the Padma-Purāṇa. — *Tripura-bhairavī,* f. a form of Durgā. — *Tripura-mallikā,* f. a medicinal plant, apparently a kind of jasmine; [cf. *tri-puṭā.*] — *Tripura-vadha, as,* m. 'slaughter of Tri-pura,' N. of the 7th chapter of the Uttara-khaṇḍa of the Śiva-Purāṇa. — *Tripura-vijaya, as,* m. 'conquest of Tri-pura,' N. of the 70th chapter of the Liṅga-Purāṇa. — *Tripura-hara, as,* m., N. of the 71st chapter of the Liṅga-Purāṇa. — *Tripurādhāraṇa-yantra* (°*na-ādh*°), *am,* n., N. of a mystical diagram given in the Tantra-sāra. — *Tripurādhipati* (°*ra-adh*°), *is,* m., N. of Maya, builder of the city of Tri-pura. — *Tripurāntaka* or *tripurānta-kara* (°*ra-an*°), *as,* m., N. of Śiva as destroyer of Tri-pura. — *Tripurā-nyāsa, as,* m., N. of a chapter of the Tantra-sāra. — *Tripurā-bhairavī,* f. a form of Durgā. — *Tripurābhairavī-pūjā-yantra, am,* n., N. of a mystical diagram given in the Tantra-sāra. — *Tripurāri* (°*ra-ar*°), *is,* m. 'the enemy of Tri-pura,' a N. of Śiva. — *Tripurārṇava* (°*ra-ar*°), *as,* m., N. of a literary work. — *Tripurārdana* (°*ra-ar*°), *as,* m. = *tripurāntaka.* — *Tripurī-prakaraṇa, am,* n., N. of a work, probably by Saṅkara, containing the elements of the Vedānta phil. — *Tri-purusha, as, ā, am,* having the length of three men; having three assistants; (*am*), ind. through three males, i. e. through three generations of men, or father, grandfather, and great-grandfather. — *Tri-purushāgata* (°*sha-āg*°), *as, ā, am,* inherited through three generations. — *Tripureśa* (°*ra-īś*°), *as,* m. 'lord of Tri-pura,' N. of Śiva. — *Tripureśādri* (°*śa-ad*°), *is,* m., N. of a mountain. — *Tripureśvara* (°*ra-īś*°), N. of a town or district, or of a sacred place. — *Tripuropākhyāna* (°*rā-up*°), *am,* n. 'the story of Tri-pura,' N. of the 52–54th chapters of the Jñāna-khaṇḍa or second part of the Śiva-Purāṇa. — *Tri-pushā,* f. Convolvulus Turpethum, = *kṛishṇa-tri-vṛit;* [cf. *tri-puṭā.*] — *Tri-pushkara, ās,* m. pl. 'the three lakes,' N. of certain holy bathing-places; (*as, ā, am*), decorated with three lotus flowers. — *Tri-pṛishṭha, as,* m. (with Jainas) N. of the first of the black Vāsu-devas; a N. of Vishṇu, as 'living above the three worlds,' or as 'existing independently of the three qualities of nature;' epithet of the Soma, as having three elevations or surfaces, found in three places (?), having three hymns (?), having three vessels (?), having three waters (used in its preparation ?), having three oblations (?), having three filtering cloths (?), or press, filter, and vessel for holding the Soma (?). (The above are the conjectures of various scholars, but according to Sāy. the word means) 'mixed with cream, thickened with milk,' &c.; (*am*), n. the highest part of the three heavens, the highest heaven. — *Tri-paurusha, as, ī, am,* extending or belonging to three persons or three generations of men; offered to three (as the funeral cake &c.), inherited from three (as an estate &c.); [cf. *trai-purusha.*] — *Tri-prasruta, as, ā, am,* epithet of a rutting elephant, i. e. 'having three streams of fluid flowing from the forehead.' — *Tri-plaksha, ās,* m. pl. 'the three fig-trees,' a place near the Yamunā in the neighbourhood of which the Dṛishad-vatī disappears. — *Tri-phala, as, ā, am,* having three fruits; (*ā*), f. the three myrobalans, the fruits of Terminalia Chebula, T. Bellerica, and Phyllanthus Emblica; the three fragrant fruits, nutmeg, areca-nut, and cloves; the three sweet fruits, grape, pomegranate, and date. — *Triphalādi-varga* (°*la-ād*°), *as,* m., N. of a chapter of the Śabda-ćandrikā or medical lexicon by Ćakra-pāṇi-datta. — *Tri-bandhana, as,* m., N. of the son of Aruṇa and father of Tri-śaṅku. — *Tri-bandhu, us,* m. the friend of the three worlds or regions; (Sāy.) binding together or supporting the three worlds, (said of Indra.) — *Tri-bandhura, as, ā, am,* Ved. having three uneven poles or seats, (said of the chariot of the Aśvins.) — *Tri-barhis, is, is, is,* Ved. having three seats of sacrificial grass. — *Tri-balī,* f. three folds of skin or corrugations over the navel (of a woman; this peculiarity is regarded as a beauty); the anus. — *Tri-balīka, as,* m., N. of Rāma, 'having three folds in the neck;' (*am*), n. the anus. — *Tri-bāhu, us, us, u,* 'three-armed,' epithet of a kind of spirit or demon; (*us*), m. a technical term in fighting. — *Tri-bulika, am,* n. the anus. — *Tri-bha, am,* n. three signs of the zodiac, the quadrant of a circle, ninety degrees; (*as, ā, am*), containing three signs of the zodiac. — *Tri-bhaṅga, as, ā, am,* having three curves or bends (as have many images of Kṛishṇa); (ī), f., N. of a metre consisting of 4 × 32 syllabic instants. — *Tribha-jīvā,* f. and *tri-bha-jyā,* f. = *tri-jīvā* and *tri-jyā.* — *Tri-bhaṇḍī,* f. Convolvulus Turpethum. — *Tri-bhadra, am,* n. copulation, cohabitation. — *Tribha-maurvikā,* f. = *tri-jyā.* — *Tri-bhāga, as,* m. the third part; the third part of a sign of the zodiac. — *Tri-bhānu, us,* m., N. of a descendant of Yayāti and father of Karan-dhama. — *Tri-bhāshya-ratna, am,* n., N. of a commentary on the Taittirīya-Prātiśākhya. — *Tri-bhukti* = *tīra-bhukti* (?). — *Tri-bhuj, k, k, k,* Ved. threefold. — *Tri-bhuja, as, ā, am,* having three arms, triangular; (*as*), m. a triangle. — *Tri-bhuvana, am,* n. the three worlds, i. e. sky, atmosphere, and earth, or heaven, earth, and the lower region; (*as*), m., N. of a prince. — *Tribhuvana-guru, us,* m. 'master of the three worlds,' epithet of Śiva. — *Tribhuvana-pati, is,* m. 'lord of the three worlds,' epithet of Vishṇu. — *Tribhuvaneśvara* (°*na-īś*°), *as,* m. 'lord of the three worlds,' epithet of Indra. — *Tribhuvaneśvara-liṅga, am,* n., N. of a Liṅga temple. — *Tribhona-lagna* (°*bha-ūn*°), *am,* n. that part of the ecliptic which does not reach the eastern point by three signs or ninety degrees, i. e. the highest point of the ecliptic above the horizon. — *Tri-maṇḍalā,* f., scil. *lūtā,* a kind of poisonous spider. — *Tri-mala, as, am,* m. n. (?) the three narcotic plants, Mustā, Ćitraka, Viḍaṅga; the threefold illusion. — *Tri-madhu, u,* n. the three sweet substances, sugar, honey, and ghee; (*us*), m. one who knows or recites the three verses of Ṛig-veda I. 90, 6–8, which begin with *madhu.* — *Tri-madhura, am,* n. the three sweet substances, sugar, honey, and ghee. — *Tri-malla,* N. of a place of pilgrimage. — *Tri-mātṛi, tā,* m., Ved. 'having three mothers;' (Sāy.) the maker or creator of the three worlds. — *Tri-mārga,* (at the beginning of a comp.) the three paths; (ī), f. three ways or paths; the meeting of three roads; [cf. *tri-patha.*] — *Trimārga-gā,* f. flowing by three ways; [cf. *tripatha-gā.*] — *Tri-mukuṭa, as,* m. a mountain with three peaks; N. of a mountain, = *tri-kūṭa.* — *Tri-mukha, as, ī, am,* three-faced, having three faces, having three mouths; (*as*), m., N. of the third Arhat of the present Ava-sarpiṇī; (*ā*), f. an epithet of Māyā or the mother of Śākya-muni. — *Tri-muni,* ind. produced by the three Munis or sages, (as the grammar of Pāṇini, Kātyāyana, and Patañjali.) — *Tri-mūrti, is, is, i,* having or assuming three forms or shapes, (as Brahmā, Vishṇu, and Śiva); (*is*), m. a Buddha, a Jina; (*is*), f. (?) the Hindū triad, the united form of the above three gods. — *Tri-mūrdha, as, ā, am,* three-headed. — *Tri-mūrdhan, ā,* m. 'three-headed,' N. of a Rākshasa. — *Triy-ambaka, as,* m. = *try-ambaka,* 'triocular,' 'three-eyed,' N. of Śiva. — *Tri-yava, as, ā, am,* containing or weighing three barleycorns; (*am*), n. a retti (= *raktikā*) or weight of three barley-corns, = *kṛishṇala.* — *Triy-avi* = *try-avi.* — *Tri-yashṭi, is,* m. a species of plant, = *kshetra-parpaṭī.* — *Tri-yāna, am,* n. (with Buddhists) the three vehicles (leading to welfare). — *Tri-yāma, as, ā, am,* containing (as the night) three Yāmas or watches, i. e. about nine hours; (*ā*), f. night, (*ahas-triyāmam,* day and night); turmeric; a convolvulus with dark flowers; the Indigo plant; the river Yamunā. — *Tri-yāmaka, am,* n. sin ('the impeder of the three objects of life ?'). — *Tri-yuga, am,* n. a space of time containing three periods or ages; (*as*), m. 'appearing in the three Yugas,' epithet of Kṛishṇa. — *Tri-yoni, is,* f. a lawsuit in which a person engages from anger, covetousness, or infatuation. — *Triyyṛića* = *try-ṛića* = *tṛića,* a strophe consisting of three verses. — *Tri-ratna, am,* n. the three gems, viz. Buddha, the law, and the congregation. — *Tri-rasaka, am,* n. a spirituous liquor ('having a triple flavour'). — *Tri-rātra, am,* n. three nights collectively, or the duration of three nights or days; (*am*), ind. for three nights or days, during three days; (*āt* or *eṇa*), ind. after three days; (*as, ā, am*), lasting three days; (*as*), m. a festival which lasts three days; [cf. *try-aha.*] — *Tri-rāśi-pa, as, ā, am,* governing three signs of the zodiac. — *Tri-rūpa, as, ā, am,* of three colours. — *Tri-rekha, as,* m. 'having three lines,' a conch, a muscle-shell, a shell marked with three lines. — *Tri-lavaṇa, am,* n. the three salts, = *tri-paṭu,* q. v. — *Tri-liṅga, as, ā, am,* possessing the three Guṇas; having three genders, (often = 'an adjective'); the Sanskṛit form for Telinga (called so fr. three Liṅgas). — *Tri-liṅgaka, as,* &c., having three genders, an adjective. — *Tri-liṅgī,* f. the three grammatical genders. — *Tri-loka, am,* n. the three worlds, i. e. sky, atmosphere, and earth, or heaven, earth, and the lower region; (*as*), m. an inhabitant of the three worlds; (*ī*), f. the universe, the aggregate of the three worlds. — *Triloka-nātha, as,* m. 'lord of the three worlds,' an epithet of Indra. — *Triloka-rakshin, ī,* m. guardian of the three worlds. — *Trilokātman* (°*ka-āt*°), *ā,* m. 'soul of the three worlds,' epithet of Śiva. — *Trilokī-nātha, as,* m. an epithet of Vishṇu. — *Trilokeśa* (°*ka-īś*°), *as,* m. 'lord of the three worlds,' an epithet of the Sun. — *Tri-locana, as, ā* or *ī, am,* 'tri-ocular,' 'three-eyed,' epithet of Śiva; (*as*), m., N. of a poet; of a grammarian; of a prince &c.; (*ā*), f. a disloyal wife, unchaste woman; (with Buddhists) N. of a deity; (*ī*), f. an epithet of Durgā. — *Trilocana-tīrtha, am,* n., N. of a Tīrtha. — *Trilocana-dāsa, as,* m., N. of a grammarian. — *Trilocaneśvara-tīrtha* (°*na-īś*°), *am,* n., N. of a Tīrtha. — *Tri-lohaka, am,* n. the three metals, i. e. gold, silver, and copper. — *Tri-lauha, as, ī, am,* made of the above three metals. — *Tri-vat, ān, atī, at,* containing the word *tri.* — *Tri-vatsa, as, ā, am,* Ved. three years old (as an ox or cow). — *Tri-vandhura,* see *tri-bandhura.* — *Tri-varga, as,* m. an aggregate of three things or substances &c.; the three objects or pursuits of life, viz. religion or virtue (*dharma*), pleasure (*kāma*), and wealth (*artha*); the three conditions of a king or kingdom, viz. progress (*vṛiddhi*), remaining stationary (*sthāna*), and decline (*kshaya*); the three qualities of nature, viz. *sat-tva, rajas,* and *tamas,* see under *guṇa;* the three higher castes or tribes; the three myrobalans; the three spices &c.; propriety, good behaviour. — *Trivarga-cintana, am,* n., N. of a chapter of the Purāṇa-sarva-sva. — *Trivarga-pārīṇa, as, ā, am,* having passed through the three conditions or attained the three objects of life. — *Tri-varṇa, am,* n. three colours; (*as, ā, am*), three-coloured (Ved.). — *Tri-varṇaka, am,* n. a kind of plant, = *go-kshuraka;* the three myrobalans [cf. *tri-phalā*]; the three spices; [cf. *tri-kaṭu.*] — *Trivarṇa-kṛit, t,* m. the chameleon. — *Tri-vartu, us, us, u,* Ved. threefold; [cf. *tri-vṛit.*] — *Trivartma-gā,* f. 'flowing by three paths,' an epithet of the Gaṅgā; [cf. *tripatha-gā.*] — *Tri-vartman, a,* n. three paths; (*ā, ā, a*), going by three paths (Ved.). — *Tri-varsha, am,* n. a period of three years; (*as, ā, am*), three years old. — *Tri-varshikā,* f. a three-year-old heifer. — *Tri-varshīya, as, ā, am,* triennial, lasting for three years, used for three years. — *Tri-vali, ī,* n. f. the three folds or wrinkles across the belly; [cf. *tri-balī.*] — *Tri-vāra, as,* m., N. of a son of Garuḍa; (*am*), ind. three times, thrice. — *Tri-vikrama, am,* n. the three steps (of Vishṇu), three strides; (*as*), m. 'one who makes three steps or strides,' an epithet of Vishṇu, who paced the three worlds in three steps in his Vāmana or dwarf Avatār, see *bali;* N. of a Brāhman; of an astronomer; of a jurist; of a medical author. — *Trivikrama-tīrtha, am,* n., N. of a Tīrtha. — *Trivikrama-deva, as,* m., N. of an author. — *Trivikrama-bhaṭṭa, as,* m., N. of the author of the Damayantī-kathā. — *Trivikramācārya* (°*ma-āc*°), *as,* m., N. of an astronomer. — *Tri-vidya, as,* m. an epithet of Śiva, 'familiar with or containing the three Vedas;' (*ā*), f. three branches of knowledge, especially that of the three Vedas. — *Tri-vidha, as, ā, am,* of three kinds, threefold, triple, in three ways. — *Tri-vidhā,* ind. (?), in three parts, triply (?). — *Tri-vinata, as, ā, am,* bowing in the presence of three, viz. gods, Brāhmans, and preceptors; bent in three places, curved in three parts of the body (?). — *Tri-vishṭapa, am,* n. = *tri-pishṭapa,* the world of Indra, i. e. heaven or paradise; the three worlds. — *Trivishṭapa-sad, t,* m. an inhabitant of heaven, a deity. — *Tri-vista, as, ā, am,* = *tri-vaistika,* worth three Vistas. — *Tri-vīja, as,* m. a kind of grain; [cf. *śyāmāka.*] — *Tri-vṛit, t, t, t,* threefold, triple, tri-form; consisting of three parts or folds &c.; (with *stoma*) a threefold hymn of praise, (i. e. a particular recitation, in which first the first three Ṛiks of each Tṛica of the eleventh hymn of the ninth Maṇḍala of the Ṛig-veda are sung together, then the second Ṛiks, and lastly the third; hence this Stoma consists of 3 × 3 or 9 verses); connected with the Trivṛit-stoma; (*t*), m. a triple cord consisting of three strings; a girdle &c. of three strings; an amulet of three strings; (*t*), f. a plant of valuable purgative properties, commonly called Teori, and distinguished into two species, white and black (Convolvulus Turpethum); also called *tri-vṛitā;* [cf. *try-āvṛit.*] — *Tri-vṛitā,* f.; see the preceding. — *Trivṛit-karaṇa, as, ī, am,* combining three things; (*am*), n. making a combination of three things; combining earth, water, and fire, in the proportion of half of one with a quarter of each of the others. — *Tri-vṛitti, is,* f. truth (?); [cf. *try-akshara.*] — *Trivṛit-parṇī,* f., N. of a pot-herb, Hincha Repens; [cf. *hila-moci.*] — *Tri-vṛinta, as,* m. (?) the plant Butea Frondosa. — *Trivṛintikā,* f. the plant Ipomœa Turpethum. — *Tri-vṛisha, as,* m., N. of a Muni; [cf. the next.] — *Tri-vṛishan, ā,* m., N. of the father of Try-aruṇa [cf. *trai-vṛishṇa*]; N. of the Vyāsa of the twelfth Dvāpara. — *Tri-veṇī,* f. 'triple-braid,' the place (now called Allahabad) where the Gaṅgā joins with the Yamunā or Jumnā and is supposed to receive underground the Sarasvatī; N. of the Gaṅgā. — *Tri-veṇu, us,* m. a particular part of a carriage; (*us, us, u*), epithet of a carriage, (according to some) furnished with three banners. — *Tri-veda,* (at the beginning of a comp.) the three Vedas, viz. Ṛig, Yajus, and Sāman; (*as, ā, am*), familiar with the three Vedas. — *Tri-vedin, ī, inī, i,* familiar or acquainted with the three Vedas. — *Tri-vedī,* f. the three Vedas collectively. — *Tri-velā,* f. the plant Ipomœa Turpethum. — *Tri-śakti, is,* f., N. of a female deity, = *tri-kalā.* — *Tri-śaṅku, us,* m., N. of a sage; N. of a prince of the solar race, king of Ayodhyā, (according to the Rāmāyaṇa he was a son of Pṛithu, and was a pious prince who aspired to celebrate a great sacrifice whereby to ascend to heaven in his mortal body; he first requested the sage Vasishṭha to officiate for him, but being refused he then applied to the sage's hundred sons, by whom he was cursed and degraded to the condition of a Cāṇḍāla; in this emergency he had recourse to Viśvā-mitra, who undertook the sacrifice and invited all the gods to be present; they, however, declined, upon which the enraged Viśvā-mitra, by his own power, transported Tri-śaṅku to the skies, whither he had no sooner arrived than he was hurled down again headforemost by the gods; but, being arrested in his downward course by Viśvā-mitra, remained suspended with his head towards the earth, forming a constellation in the southern hemisphere: according to the Hari-vaṃśa and Vāyu-Purāṇa he was a son of Trayyāruṇa: according to the Bhāgavata-Purāṇa, a son of Tri-bandhana: and he is sometimes described as a wicked prince, guilty of three Śaṅkus or heinous crimes); a cat, the civet-cat; a bird, the Cātaka, Cuculus Melanoleucos; a grasshopper; a fire-fly. — *Triśaṅku-ja, as,* m. 'the son of Tri-śaṅku,' epithet of Hari-ścandra. — *Triśaṅku-yājin, ī,* m. 'sacrificing for Tri-śaṅku,' epithet of Viśvā-mitra. — *Tri-śata, am,* n., 103, 300; (*as, ī, am*), the 300th; consisting of 300; (*ās*), m. pl., 300. — *Tri-śataka, as, ikā, am,* consisting of 300. — *Triśata-tama, as, ī, am,* the 300th; the 103rd. — *Tri-śatī,* f. the aggregate of 300 (e. g. *paśūnām tri-śatī,* 300 cattle). — *Tri-śaraṇa, am,* n. (with Buddhists) the three places of refuge, Buddha, the Law, and the Assembly; (*as*), m. a Buddha. — *Tri-śarkarā,* f. three kinds of sugar, viz. *guḍotpannā, himotthā,* and *madhurā;* [cf. *tri-sitā.*] — *Tri-śalā,* f., N. of the mother of the twenty-fourth Arhat of the present Avasarpiṇī. — *Triśalākā-purusha-carita, am,* n., N. of a work by Hema-candra. — *Tri-śas,* ind. by threes, by three at a time. — *Tri-śākha, as, ī, am,* having three branches. — *Triśākha-pattra, as,* m. the plant Ægle Marmelos. — *Tri-śāṇa, as, ī, am,* worth three Śāṇas. — *Tri-śānu, us,* m. a various reading for *tri-bhānu.* — *Tri-śāla, as, ā, am,* or *tri-śālaka, as, ā, am,* consisting of three halls or rooms; (*am*), n. a house with three halls. — *Tri-śikha, as, ā, am,* three-crested, three-headed, having the shape of a trident; (*as*), m. the plant Ægle Marmelos; the son of Rāvaṇa, a demon with three heads; N. of Indra in the Manv-antara of Tāmasa; (*ī*), f., N. of an Upanishad; (*am*), n. a trident, a three-pronged spear; a crest, a tiara with three points. — *Tri-śikhara, as, ā, am,* having three tops or peaks; (*as*), m. (with *śaila*) N. of a mountain. — *Triśikhi-dalā,* f. a kind of bulbous plant. — *Tri-śikhin, ī, inī, i,* three-crested, three-headed. — *Tri-śira, as, ā, am,* having three points; (*as*), m., N. of a Rākshasa; (*ā*), f. the root of Bignonia Suaveolens. — *Tri-śiras, ās, ās, as,* three-headed, having three points or tops; (*ās*), m. epithet of Tvashṭṛi Viśva-rūpa; Fever personified as a demon with three heads [cf. *tri-pad* and *tri-pād*]; N. of an Asura killed by Vishṇu; N. of a Rākshasa killed by Rāma; an epithet of Kuvera. — *Tri-śīrsha, as, ā, am,* 'three-headed,' an epithet of Śiva. — *Tri-śīrshaka, as, ā, am,* three-headed; (*am*), n. a trident, a three-pointed or three-pronged spear. — *Tri-śīrshan, ā, ā, a,* Ved. three-headed. — *Tri-śukra, as, ā, am,* Ved. white or bright in three places. — *Tri-śukriya, as, ā, am,* Ved. triply illuminated. — *Tri-śuc, k, k, k,* Ved. triply shining or splendid, shining in three ways. — *Tri-śūla, am,* n. a trident, a three-pointed pike or spear, especially the weapon of Śiva; (*as, ā, am*), 'bearing the trident,' epithet of Śiva; N. of a mountain. — *Triśūla-khāta, am,* n., N. of a Tīrtha, ('digged with the trident.') — *Triśūla-gaṅgā,* f., N. of a river. — *Triśūlāṅka* (°*la-aṅ*°), *as,* m. 'trident-marked,' a N. of Śiva; of a teacher. — *Tri-śūlin, ī, inī, i,* 'armed with the trident;' (*ī*), m. epithet of Śiva; (*inī*), f. epithet of Durgā. — *Tri-śṛiṅga, as, ā, am,* having three horns or peaks; (*as*), m. a hill with three peaks; N. of a mountain; a triangle. — *Triśṛiṅgin, ī, iṇī, i,* having three horns; (*ī*), m. a sort of fish, commonly Rohi, Cyprinus Rohita. — *Tri-śoka, as, ā, am,* Ved. = *tri-śuc* (?); (*as*), m., N. of a Ṛishi. — *Tri-shaṃyukta, as, ā, am* (for *tri-sam*°), triply connected. — *Tri-shaṃvatsara, as, ā, am* (for *tri-sam*°), lasting three years. — *Tri-shatya, as, ā, am* (for *tri-satya*), Ved. trebly true (in thought, word, and deed). — *Tri-shadhastha, as, ā, am,* Ved. being in three places. — *Tri-shandhi, is, is, i* (for *tri-san*°), Ved. composed of three parts or members; (*is*), m., N. of a demon in the Atharva-veda, generally associated with Arbudi; (*i*), n., N. of a Sāman. — *Tri-shapta* or *tri-sapta* (fr. *tri* + *saptan*), Ved. three times seven, twenty-one; an indefinite number. — *Tri-shaptīya, as,* m. adj., N. of the first verse of the Atharva-veda, beginning with the words *ye tri-shaptās,* &c. — *Tri-shavaṇa* or *tri-savana, as, ā, am,* containing three oblations; (*as*), m., N. of an ancient sage; *tri-shavaṇam* or *trishavaṇa-snānam,* the three ablutions to be performed daily, i. e. at dawn, noon, and sunset. — *Trishavaṇa-snāyin, ī,* m. a man performing regularly the prescribed ablutions morning, noon, and evening. — *Trishashṭa, as, ī, am,* the sixty-third. — *Tri-shashṭi, is,* m. sixty-three; [cf. *trayaḥ-shashṭi.*] — *Trishashṭi-tama, as, ī, am,* the sixty-third. — *Trishashṭi-dhā,* ind. in sixty-three parts, sixty-three-fold. — *Trishashṭi-śalākāpurusha-carita, am,* n., N. of a work. — *Trishṭup-chandas, ās, ās, as,* Ved. having the metre Tri-shṭubh. — *Tri-shṭubh, p,* f. (for *tri-stubh* fr. *tri* + *stubh,* to praise; or possibly the word may come fr. *stubh,* to stop, because the voice is obliged to pause three times; according to Yāska, the prefix *tri* may be fr. rt. *tṝ,* to denote the rapidity of the metre, cf. *jagatī;* or fr. *tri,* three, + *stubh,* to praise, because the metre is in praise of the *vajra* or thunderbolt, which has three edges); N. of a Vedic metre consisting of four Pādas of eleven syllables each; (in the later metrical system) N. of every metre consisting of four times eleven syllables (e. g. the Indra-vajrā and Upendra-vajrā metres); [cf. *traishṭubha.*] — *Tri-shṭoma, as, ā, am* (for *tri-stoma*), Ved. containing three Stomas; (*as*), m., N. of an Ekāha. — *Tri-shṭha, as, ā, am* (for *tri-stha*), Ved. standing on three (wheels), situated in three places; (*as*), m., N. of a man. — *Tri-shṭhin, ī, inī, i* (for *tri-sthin*), Ved. standing on triply divided ground. — *Tri-saṃvatsara*, see under *tri-shaṃvatsara.* — *Tri-satya*, see under *tri-shatya.* — *Tri-sandhi, is, is, i*, see *tri-shandhi*; (*is*), f. a kind of mallow. — *Tri-sandhika, as, ā, am*, occurring or happening at the three periods or divisions of the day, (probably a wrong reading for *trisandhyika.*) — *Tri-sandhya, am*, n. the three periods or divisions of the day, viz. dawn, noon, and evening or sunset; (*ā*), f., N. of a goddess; a form of Durgā; a kind of mallow; (*ā* or *ī*), f. the three periods of the day; (*am*), ind. at the time of the three Sandhyās; (*as, ā, am*), relating to the three periods of the day. — *Tri-sandhya-kusumā*, f. a kind of mallow. — *Tri-saptata, as, ī, am* (fr. the following), the seventy-third. — *Tri-saptati, is*, f. seventy-three; [cf. *trayaḥ-saptati.*] — *Trisaptati-tama, as, ī, am*, the seventy-third. — *Tri-saptan* or *tri-sapta*, three times seven, twenty-one [cf. *tri-shapta*]; *trisapta-kṛitvas*, ind. twenty-one times. — *Tri-sama, as, ā, am*, (in geom.) having three equal sides; (*am*), n. an aggregate of equal parts of three substances, viz. yellow myrobalan, ginger, and molasses; *trisama-ćaturaśra, am*, n. a quadrangle having three equal sides. — *Tri-sara, as, am*, m. n. a dish of sesamum, rice, &c., = *kṛiśara* or *kṛisara.* — *Tri-sarga, as*, m. the triple product of the three qualities of nature. — *Tri-savana* = *tri-shavaṇa*, q. v. — *Tri-sādhana, as, ā, am*, triply composed, having three component parts. — *Tri-sāman, ā, ā, a*, singing three Sāmans or the Sāman called Triḥ-sāman. — *Tri-sāmā*, f., N. of a river. — *Tri-sāmya, am*, n. equilibrium of the three (qualities). — *Tri-sāhasra, as, ī, am*, Ved. consisting of 3000. — *Tri-sitā*, f. = *tri-śarkarā*, three kinds of white sugar, viz. *guḍot-pannā, madhu-jā*, and *himotthā.* — *Tri-sītya, as, ā, am*, thrice ploughed (as a field &c.). — *Tri-sugandhi* or *tri-sugandhika, am*, n. = *tri-jāta*, the three fragrant substances or spices. — *Tri-suparṇa, as*, m. a N. of certain hymns of the Ṛig and Yajur Vedas; (*as, ā, am*), or *tri-suparṇaka, as, ikā, am*, familiar or conversant with the above hymns of the Veda; [cf. *tri-sauparṇa.*] — *Tri-suvarćaka, as, ā, am*, having a threefold excellent splendor. — *Tri-saugandhya, am*, n. = *tri-sugandhi.* — *Tri-sauparṇa, as, ī, am*, relating to the part of the Vedas called Tri-suparṇa; N. of a particular religious vow or observance. — *Tri-sauvarṇa, am*, n. perhaps a wrong reading for *tri-suparṇa.* — *Tri-skandhaka*, N. of a Sūtra work. — *Tri-stana, as, ā* or *ī, am*, milked from three nipples (Ved.); having three breasts. — *Tri-stobha-yukta, as, ā, am*, having three pauses or three rhythms or three divisions (?). — *Tri-sthalī*, f. the three (sacred) places. — *Tristhalī-setu*, N. of a work. — *Tri-sthāna, am*, n. a sacred spot celebrated for a junction of three streams of the Ganges; (*as, ā, am*), reaching through the three worlds. — *Tri-srotas, ās, ās, as*, having three streams; (*ās*), f. an epithet of the Ganges [cf. *tri-patha-gā, tri-mārga-gā, tri-vartma-gā*]; N. of another river. — *Tri-srotasī*, f., N. of a river. — *Tri-halya, as, ā, am*, thrice ploughed (as a field &c.). — *Tri-hāyaṇa, as, ī, am*, three years old; appearing in three ages of the world; (*ī*), f. a three-year-old heifer. — *Trishu* (*tri-ish°*), *us, us, u*, or *trishuka, as, ā, am*, furnished with three arrows. — *Trishṭaka* (*tri-ish°*), *as, ā, am*, Ved. furnished with three Ishṭakās or sacrificial bricks. — *Try-anśa, as, am*, m. or n. (?), three shares or portions, three-fourths; a third part, the third part of a sign of the zodiac (= *dṛikkāṇa*, q. v.). — *Tryanśa-nātha, as*, m. the regent of a Dṛikkāṇa. — *Try-aksha, as, ī, am*, triocular; (*as*), m. an epithet of Rudra-Śiva; also of a Daitya or Dānava. — *Tryakshaka, as*, m. an epithet of Śiva. — *Try-akshan, ā, ā, a*, triocular; (*ā*), m. epithet of Rudra. — *Tryaksha-patnī*, f. an epithet of Pārvatī. — *Try-akshara, as, ā, am*, consisting of three sounds or letters or syllables, triliteral; (*am*), n. a word or song consisting of three letters or syllables (e. g. *satyam* or *sa + ti + am*); (*as*), m. a genealogist; the Ghaṭaka or matchmaker; [cf. *ghaṭaka* and *khaṭaka.*] — *Try-ankaṭa, am*, n. or *try-angaṭa, as*, m. a sling or three strings like those of a balance suspended to either end of a pole for carrying burdens; a sort of collyrium; (*as*), m. a N. of Śiva. — *Try-anga, āni*, n. pl., Ved. three portions of the sacrificial victim supposed to belong to the Sv-ishṭa-kṛit, q. v., viz. the upper part of the right fore-foot, a part of the left thigh, and a part of the bowels. — *Try-angula, as, ā, am*, Ved. three fingers long or broad or deep &c. — *Tryangya, as, ā, am*, Ved. belonging to the Try-angas. — *Try-añjana, am*, n. the three kinds of collyrium, or Kālāñjana, Push-pāñjana, and Rasāñjana. — *Try-añjala, am*, n. and *try-añjali, i*, n. three handfuls. — *Try-adhipati, is*, m. 'the lord of the three qualities,' (i. e. *sat-tva, rajas*, and *tamas*; cf. *guṇa*), an epithet of Kṛishṇa or Vishṇu. — *Try-adhishṭhāna, as, ā, am*, having three stations, situated in three places. — *Try-adhīśa, as*, m. = *try-adhipati*, q. v. — *Try-adhva-gā*, f. a N. of the Ganges, 'going or flowing through the three worlds.' — *Try-anīka, as, ā, am*, Ved. having three faces, followed by three hosts; (Sāy.) having the three properties of heat, rain, and cold. — *Try-anta, am*, n., N. of a Sāman. — *Try-abda, am*, n. a period of three years; (*am*), ind. during three years; (*as, ā, am*), three years old. — *Try-ambaka, as*, m. a N. of Śiva (Rudra) as triocular or uttering the three (Vedas) or uttering the three mystical letters (?), or as having three wives or sisters (as if fr. *tri + ambā*); N. of one of the eleven Rudras; the sacrificial ceremony in which the Try-ambakās or cakes sacred to Rudra Try-ambaka are offered; N. of a mountain; (*ā*), f. an epithet of Pārvatī; (*am*), n., N. of a Linga. — *Tryambaka-māhātmya, am*, n. 'the glory of Try-ambaka,' N. of a part of the Padma-Purāṇa. — *Tryambaka-sakha, as*, m. 'the friend of Try-ambaka,' an epithet of Kuvera, the god of wealth. — *Try-aruṇa, as*, m., N. of a man with the patronymic Traivṛishṇa. — *Try-arusha, as, ī, am*, Ved. marked red in three places. — *Try-avara, as, ā, am*, having three who are inferior, three at the least; (*am*), ind. at least three times, (see Manu XI. 80.) — *Try-avi, is, ī*, m. f., Ved. a calf eighteen months old. — *Tryaśīta, as, ī, am* (fr. *try-aśīti*), the eighty-third. — *Try-aśīti, is*, f. eighty-three. — *Tryaśīti-tama, as, ī, am*, the eighty-third. — *Try-aśra, as, ā, am*, triangular; (*as*), m., N. of a plant, = *tridhāra-snuhī*; (*am*), n. a triangle. — *Tryaśra-kuṇḍa, am*, n., N. of a mystical diagram. — *Try-ashṭaka, as, ā, am*, containing three Ashṭakās; (*am*), n. a kind of vessel. — *Try-ashṭan* or *try-ashṭa*, three times eight, twenty-four; *try-ashṭa-varsha*, twenty-four years old. — *Try-asra*, see *try-aśra.* — *Try-aha, am*, n. a period of three days; *try-aham*, ind. during three days; *try-ahāt* or *try-ahena*, ind. after three days; (*as, ā, am*), lasting three days; (*as*), m., Ved. a festival lasting three days. — *Tryaha-sparśa, as*, m. or *tryaha-spṛiśa, am*, n. the meeting of part of three lunar days in one solar day, (the first lunar day ending just after midnight and the third beginning a little before the next midnight.) — *Tryahīna, as, ā, am*, Ved. lasting three days. — *Tryahaihika* (°*ha-aih*°), *as, ī, am*, having provision sufficient for three days, providing for three days. — *Try-ahna, as, ā, am*, happening or occurring after three days. — *Tryākshāyaṇa, as*, m. (fr. *try-aksha*), a worshipper of Śiva (?). — *Tryā-kshāyaṇa-bhakta, am*, n. a district inhabited by worshippers of Śiva. — *Try-āyusha, am*, n., Ved. threefold vital power or period of life; (according to Mahī-dhara) the threefold period of life, consisting of childhood, youth, and old age. — *Tryāruṇi, is*, m. (fr. *try-aruṇa*), N. of the Vyāsa in the fifteenth Dvāpara; N. of a mountain. — *Try-ārsheya, as, ī, am*, containing three lines or families of Ṛishis; (*ās*), m. pl. an aggregate of three persons, viz. blind, deaf, and dumb. — *Try-ālikhita, as, ā, am*, Ved. scratched or marked in three places. — *Tryālikhita-vat, ān, atī, at*, consisting of bricks marked in three places. — *Try-āvṛit, t, t, t*, Ved. carried on in three periods, consisting of three series. — *Try-āśir, ir*, m., Ved. mixed with three products of milk; (according to Sāy.) mixed with Dadhi, Saktu, and Payas, (said of the Soma.) — *Tryāhika, as, ī, am* (fr. *try-aha*), produced or performed &c. in three days; tertian; returning after the third day, quartan (as a fever); having provisions for three days. — *Try-uttari-bhāva, as*, m. progression by three. — *Try-udāya, am*, n., Ved. the threefold going to the altar, i. e. in the three daily oblations; (Sāy.) having three goings to the altar (as the Soma). — *Try-udhan, ā*, m., Ved. three-uddered, (according to Sāy.) said of the year as having three seasons. — *Try-ushaṇa* or *try-ūshaṇa, am*, n. the three spices collectively, i. e. black pepper, long pepper, and dry ginger. — *Try-ṛića, am*, n. = *tṛića*, a strophe consisting of three verses. — *Try-eta, as*, m., *tryeṇī* or *tryenī*, f., *am*, n., Ved. variegated or spotted in three places.

Trinśa, as, ī, am (fr. *trinśat*), the thirtieth, constituting the thirtieth part; joined with thirty (e. g. *trinśaṃ śatam*, 130); consisting of thirty (as a Stoma); connected with the Trinśa-stoma; $\frac{1}{30}$ of a sign of the zodiac, a degree. — *Trinśānśa* or *trinśānśaka* (°*śa-an*°), *as*, m. a thirtieth part, $\frac{1}{30}$ of a sign of the zodiac, a degree.

Trinśaka, as, ā, am, = *trinśa*, consisting of thirty parts, divided into thirty; bought for thirty, worth thirty; (*am*), n. a collection or aggregate of thirty.

Trinśat, t, f. (fr. *tri* and *śat* = *daśat*), thirty, the number thirty. — *Trinśać-ćhata, am*, n., 130.

Trinśati, is, f. = *trinśat*, thirty; [cf. *trayas-trinśati, pañća-t°, sapta-t°.*]

Trinśatka, am, n. an aggregate or collection of thirty.

Trinśat-tama, as, ī, am, the thirtieth.

Trinśat-pattra, am, n. the white esculent water-lily, Nymphæa Esculenta.

Trinśad-vinśa, ās, m. pl. about twenty or thirty, between twenty and thirty.

Trinśin, ī, inī, i, containing thirty, consisting of thirty.

Trika, as, ā, am, triple, threefold; trine, forming a triad; trebly repeated, happening the third time; (with or without *śata*) three out of every hundred, three per cent; (*as*), m., N. of two plants, = *go-kshuraka* and Trapa Bispinosa [cf. *tri-kaṇṭaka*]; (*ā*), f. a triangular frame or bar across the mouth of a well over which passes the rope of the bucket; a wooden frame at the mouth of a well, or the upper part of the well; a frame at the bottom of a well on which the masonry rests; the cover or lid of a well; (*am*), n. the aggregate of three, a triad [cf. *taurya-trika*]; a place where three roads meet; the lower part of the spine or regio sacra; the part about the hips; the part between the shoulder-blades; the three mystical words pronounced before the Gāyatrī [cf. *vyāhṛiti*]; the three spices, three myrobalans &c. collectively. — *Trika-sthāna, am*, n. the region at the lower part of the spine. — *Trikāgni-kāla* (°*ka-ag*°), *as*, m. an epithet of Rudra.

Trita, as, m., Ved. (in the Atharva-veda also *trita*), N. of a Vedic deity; (he is generally associated with the Maruts, Vāyu, and Indra; and fights like the latter with Tvāshṭra, Vṛitra, and other demons: he is also called Āptya, q. v., either as produced in water by Agni, whence he is sometimes called 'a son of the water,' or as son of the Ṛishi Āpta. In some passages of the Taittirīya-Saṃhitā he is regarded as bestowing long life; while elsewhere he is supposed to reside in the remotest regions of the world, whence the idea of wishing to remove calamity to Trita or to the remotest place possible; cf. Ṛig-veda VIII. 47, 14. In some passages of the

Veda, Indian commentators explain Trita by *tri-sthāna*, 'reaching through the triple world,' as an epithet of Indra or Vāyu. In later myths Trita is described as a Ṛishi, by whom several hymns of the Ṛig-veda were composed. Sāyaṇa in his introduction to Ṛig-veda I. 105, relates that there were three Ṛishis, named Ekata, Dvita, and Trita, who lived in a desert country; being parched with thirst, they looked about for a well, and having found one, Trita entered it to draw water, when the other two, desirous of obtaining his property, threw him into the well and closed up the mouth with a wheel; shut up in the well, Trita composed a hymn to the gods, and managed, in a marvellous manner, to perform the Soma sacrifice, that he might drink the Soma himself before death, or offer it to the deities in the hope of being extricated by them: his preparation of the Soma is described in the Mahā-bh. Śalya-parva 2095, and he is elsewhere celebrated as an offerer of the Soma. In various other epic legends, Ekata, Dvita, and Trita are described as three brothers, sons of Gautama or of Prajā-pati, = Brahmā. According to the Bhāgavata-Purāṇa, Trita is one of the twelve sons of Manu and Naḍvalā. Some identify the Vedic *Trita* with the Vedic *Traitana*, and with *Thraetana* the Zend form of *Feridun*. His connection with water points to a comparison with the Gr. Τρίτων, τριτο-γενής, Τριτωνίς, Τριτο-πάτορες, &c.) (*Trita* seems also to mean) a class of deities, 'the third ones,' i. e. those who live in the sky (?); the priest who prepares the Soma.

Tritaya, as, ā, am, consisting of three parts; (*am*), n. a collection of three, τριάς.

Tris, ind. thrice, three times, at three places; (followed by gutturals and palatals there may be the optional substitution of *sh* for Visarga, e. g. *trish karoti* or *triḥ karoti*, he does thrice.) — *Triḥ-plaksha* = *tri-plaksha*, q. v. — *Triḥ-sāman, a*, n., N. of a Sāman. — *Triḥ-snāna, am*, n. bathing thrice every day. — *Trir-aśri, is, is, i*, Ved. having three edges, three-cornered. — *Tris-tāvā*, f. (fr. *tris-tāvat*), three times the usual size, (only used with *vedi*.)

त्रिगूढ *trigūḍha, am*, n. the dancing or acting of a man in female attire, (evidently a wrong form for *strī-gūḍha*); [cf. *tri-ćaritra*.]

त्रिङ्ख् *trinkh*, cl. 1. P. *trinkhati*, &c., to go, move.

त्रिचरित्र *tr̥ićaritra*, a wrong reading for *strī-ćaritra*; [cf. *trigūḍha*.]

त्रिण *triṇa, am*, n. = *tr̥iṇa*, grass.

त्रिणाक *tri-ṇāka* = *tri-nāka*, p. 389, col. 3.

त्रिपु *tripu, us*, m., Ved. a thief.

त्रिभुक्ति *tribhukti* (?) for *tīra-bhukti*, q. v.

त्रियूह *triyūha, as*, m. (probably a foreign word), a chesnut-coloured horse; [cf. *ukanāha, urāha, kiyāha, kokāha*, &c.]

त्रिल्लक *trillaka* and *trillasena, as*, m., N. of two men.

त्रिषम *trishama*, Ved. = *hrasva*, short (?).

त्रिस् *tris*. See above.

त्रीणि *trīṇi*, n. pl. three. See *tri*.

त्रीशट *trīśaṭa, as*, m. [cf. *tīsaṭa*], N. of the author of a medical work.

त्रुट् *truṭ*, cl. 6. 4. P. *truṭati, truṭyati, tutroṭa, truṭitum*, to be torn or split, to tear, break, burst, snap, fall asunder: Caus. P. A. *troṭayati, -te, -yitum*, to tear, break, cut, divide.

Truṭi, is, f. (or *truṭī*, f.?), cutting, breaking, a tear, split; a small part, an atom or a visible atom composed of three subtler elementary particles; a very minute space of time, a moment, equal to $\frac{1}{2}$ Lava, = $\frac{1}{4}$ Kshaṇa, = $\frac{1}{30}$ Kāshṭhā, = $\frac{1}{450}$ Kalā, = $\frac{1}{4500}$ Nālikā, = $\frac{1}{9000}$ Muhūrta, (or = $\frac{1}{100}$ Vedha, = $\frac{1}{300}$ Lava, = $\frac{1}{900}$ Nimesha, = $\frac{1}{2700}$ Kshaṇa, = $\frac{1}{13500}$ Kāshṭhā, = $\frac{1}{202500}$ Laghu, = $\frac{1}{3037500}$ Nāḍikā, = $\frac{1}{6075000}$ Muhūrta); small cardamoms (Alpinia Cardamomum), cardamoms from Guzerat; a sort of tree; doubt, uncertainty; breaking (a promise); loss, destruction; N. of one of the Mātṛis attending on Skanda. — *Truṭi-vīja, as*, m. Arum Colocasia (= *kaću*), an esculent root. — *Truṭi-śas*, ind. in short spaces of time. — *Truṭy-avayava, as*, m. one half of a Truṭi.

Truṭita, as, ā, am, cut, broken, divided, hurt, wounded, chapped, chafed. — *Truṭita-vat, ān, atī, at*, having cut or broken, &c.

Troṭi, is, f. the beak or bill of a bird; the mouth of a fish; a kind of bird; a kind of pike (Esox Kankila); a medicinal plant. — *Troṭi-hasta, as*, m. a bird ('having a beak for hands').

त्रुड् *truḍ*, Ved. = *truṭ*, q. v.

त्रुप् *trup* or *truph* or *trump* or *trumph*, cl. 1. P. *tropati* or *trophati* or *trumpati* or *trumphati*, &c., to hurt, injure, kill; [cf. Gr. θρύπτω, τρύφος: Lith. *truppù*, 'to be worn away by friction;' *trumpas*, 'short;' *trumpinu*, 'to shorten.']

त्रेता *tretā*, f. (fr. *traya*, which is fr. *tri*, p. 388), a triad, a collection or assemblage of three, a triplet; the three sacred fires collectively (i. e. the southern, household, and sacrificial fires; often called *agni-tretā*, see *agni-traya*); trey, i. e. a throw at dice or the side of a die marked with three spots or points; (with or without *yuga*) the second Yuga or silver age of the Hindūs which consists of 1,296,000 years. — *Tretāgni* (°*tā-ag*°), *is*, m. one who has preserved the three sacred fires; the three fires collectively (= *agni-tretā*).

Tretinī, f., Ved. the threefold flame of the three fires of the altar.

Tre-dhā, ind. = *tri-dhā*, triply, in three parts, in three ways, in three places. — *Tredhā-vihita*, divided into three parts. — *Tredhā-sthita, as, ā, am*, existing in three states.

Trainśa, am, n. (fr. *trinśat*), scil. *brāhmaṇa*, the Brāhmaṇa consisting of thirty Adhyāyas.

Trainśika, as, ā, am, consisting of thirty.

Traikakuda, as, ī, am, Ved. coming from the mountain Tri-kakud.

Traikakubha, am, n. (fr. *tri-kakubh*), N. of a Sāman.

Traikaṇṭaka, as, ī, am, coming from or made of the plant Tri-kaṇṭaka.

Traikāla-jña, probably a wrong reading for *traikālya-jña*; [cf. *tri-kāla-jña*.]

Traikālika, as, ī, am (fr. *tri-kāla*), relating to the three times, i. e. past, present, and future.

Traikālya, am, n. the three times; past, present, and future time; sunrise, noon, and sunset; tripartition; an aggregate of three, a triad.

Traikuntaka, am, n.? (fr. *tri-kunta*), a kind of ornament.

Traigarta, as, ī, am, belonging to the Trigartas; (*as*), m. a prince of the Trigartas; (*ī*), f. a princess of the Trigartas; (*ās*), m. pl. the Trigartas.

Traigartaka, belonging to the Trigartas.

Traiguṇika, as, ī, am (fr. *tri-guṇa*), relating or belonging to three qualities, repeated three times, triple, relating to thrice, threefold, &c.

Traiguṇya, am, n. the state of consisting of three threads, qualities, &c.; triplicity, tripleness, a triad, the triad of qualities, the three Guṇas or properties collectively (i. e. Sat-tva, Rajas, and Tamas; cf. *guṇa*).

Traićīvarika, as, ī, am (fr. *tri-ćīvara*), possessing three mendicant garments.

Traita, am, n. (fr. *tretā*), Ved. a triad, a collection of three, the aggregate of three, triplicity; (fr. *trita*), N. of a Sāman.

Traitana, as, m., Ved., N. of a Vedic deity or supernatural being, thought by some to be connected with Trita, q. v.; (according to Sāy.) N. of a Dāsa.

Traidaśika, as, ī, am (fr. *tridaśa*), relating to the thirty-three gods; sacred to the gods, belonging to them, divine; (*am*), n. the part of the hand sacred to the gods.

Traidha, as, ī, am (fr. *tri-dhā* or *tre-dhā*), threefold, triple; (*am*), ind. = *tri-dhā* or *tre-dhā*, triply, in a triple manner, in three ways.

Traidhātavī, f. (scil. *ishṭi*), N. of a particular closing ceremony, (fr. *tri-dhātu*.)

Traidhātavīya, am, n. (scil. *karman*), N. of a particular closing rite.

Traidhātuka, am, n. the three worlds.

Traidhātva, as, m. a patronymic of Try-aruṇa.

Trainishkika, as, ī, am, three Nishkas worth.

Traipatha, am, n. (fr. *tri-patha*), a peculiar manner of sitting (generally with *āsana*).

Traipada, am, n. (fr. *tri-pada*), three quarters (of a Yojana).

Traipārāyaṇika, as, ī, am, performing the Pārāyaṇa three times.

Traipishṭapa, as, ī, am, relating to Tri-pishṭapa, q. v.

Traipura, as, ī, am, relating to Tri-pura; (*ās*), m. pl. the inhabitants of the three cities of the Asura named Tri-pura, q. v.; the inhabitants of Tri-purā or Tri-purī or the Ćedis; (*as*), m. a prince of Tri-pura.

Traipurīya, N. of an Upanishad.

Traipurusha, as, ī, am (fr. *tri-purusha*), extending through three male generations, or father, grandfather, and great-grandfather.

Traiphala, as, ī, am (fr. *tri-phalā*), coming from or belonging to the three myrobalans &c.

Traibali, is, m. (fr. *tri-bali* or *tri-balī*), N. of a man.

Traibhāvya, am, n. (fr. *tri-bhāva*), threefold nature or manner.

Traimātura, as, ī, am (fr. *tri-mātṛi*), having three mothers.

Traimāsika, as, ī, am (fr. *tri-māsa*), three months old, lasting three months, occurring every three months, quarterly.

Traimāsya, am, n. a period of three months.

Traiyambaka, as, ī, am, relating or belonging to Try-ambaka (e. g. *apūpa*, cake sacred to Try-ambaka). — *Traiyambaka-mantra, am*, n., N. of the twenty-third chapter of the Śāradā-tilaka by Lakshmaṇa.

Traiyāruṇa, as, m., N. of a Muni.

Trairāśika, as, ā or *ī, am* (fr. *tri-rāśi*), relating to three numbers or to the three signs of the zodiac; *trairāśikam* or *trairāśika-gaṇitam*, the rule of three in arithmetic, (this is of two kinds, viz. *krama-trairāśika*, rule of three direct; *vyasta-* or *viloma-trairāśika*, rule of three inverse.)

Trairūpya, am, n. (fr. *tri-rūpa*), tripleness of form, threefold change of form; three forms or ways.

Trailāṭa (fr. *tri-lāṭa*?), a sort of horse-fly.

Trailinga, as, ī, am (fr. *tri-linga*), having three genders.

Trailoka, as, m. (fr. *tri-loka*), 'the ruler of the three worlds,' epithet of Indra.

Trailokya, am, n. the three worlds, see *tri-loka*; (*as*), m., N. of a man. — *Trailokya-kartṛi, tā*, m. 'creator of the three worlds,' epithet of Śiva. — *Trailokya-ḍambara*, N. of a medical work. — *Trailokya-dīpikā*, f., N. of a Jaina work. — *Trailokya-devī*, f., N. of the wife of king Yaśas-kara. — *Trailokya-nātha, as*, m. 'lord of the three worlds,' epithet of Rāma as an incarnation of Vishṇu. — *Trailokya-prakāśa, as*, m., N. of an astronomical work. — *Trailokya-prabhava, as*, m., N. of Vishṇu. — *Trailokya-bhaya-kāraka, as, ā, am*, causing fear to the three worlds. — *Trailokya-rāja, as*, m. 'king of the three worlds,' N. of a powerful man. — *Trailokya-rājya, am*, n. the sovereignty of the three worlds. — *Trailokya-vikramin, ī*, m., N. of a Bodhi-sattva (striding through the three worlds). — *Trailokya-vijayā*, f. a sort of hemp from which an intoxicating infusion &c. is prepared. — *Trailokya-sāgara, as,* m., N. of a work. — *Trailokya-sāra, am,* n., N. of a work. — *Trailoćana, as, ī, am* (fr. *tri-loćana*), relating to Śiva.

Traivaṇi, is, m., N. of a teacher.

Traivargika, as, ī, am (fr. *tri-varga*), relating to the three objects of life [cf. *tri-varga*], directed towards or devoted to them.

Traivargya, as, ā, am, belonging to the Tri-varga. See *traivargika* above.

Traivarṇika, as, ī, am (fr. *tri-varṇa*), relating or belonging to the first three castes; (*as*), m. a member of the first three castes.

Traivarshika, as, ī, am (fr. *tri-varsha*), triennial, three years old, lasting three years, &c.

Traivārshika, as, ī, am, sufficient for three years, lasting three years.

Traivikrama, as, &c. (fr. *tri-vikrama*), belonging to Vishṇu; (*am*), n. the three strides or steps (of Vishṇu).

Traivida, a various reading for *trayī-vida,* q. v.

Traividya, am, n. (fr. *tri-vidyā* and *tri-vidya*), the three sciences; the three Vedas (Ṛig, Yajus, and Sāman); study or knowledge of the three Vedas; the three duties of teaching the Veda, sacrificing, and donation; a particular Vrata or religious observance; a collection or assembly of Brāhmans who are familiar with the three Vedas; (*as, ā, am*), familiar with the three Vedas.

Traividhya, am, n. (fr. *tri-vidha*), the state of being of three kinds, threefoldness, triplicity, tripleness, three ways or kinds.

Traivishṭapa or *traivishṭapeya, as,* m. an inhabitant of Tri-vishṭapa, a god.

Traivṛita, as, ī, am (fr. *tri-vṛit*), coming from the plant Ipomœa Turpethum.

Traivṛishṇa, as, m. a patronymic of Try-aruṇa.

Traivedika, as, ī, am (fr. *tri-veda*), relating to the three Vedas.

Traiśankava, as, m. (fr. *tri-śanku*), a patronymic of Hari-śćandra.

Traiśāṇa, as, ī, am, = *triśāṇa,* worth three Śāṇas.

Traiśāmba, as, m., N. of the father of Karandhama; (various readings have *tribhānu, triśānu, triśāri, traisānu.*)

Traiśīrsha, as, ā, am (fr. *tri-śīrshan*), relating to the three-headed Viśva-rūpa.

Traiśoka, am, n. (fr. *tri-śoka*), N. of a Sāman.

Traishṭubha, as, ī, am, relating to or written in the metre Tri-shṭubh; (*am*), n. the Tri-shṭubh stanza or metre; (Sāy.) the atmosphere or intermediate region consisting of rain, clouds, and lightning. (In the Brāhmaṇas the three chief metres Gāyatrī, Tri-shṭubh, and Jagatī are often identified with the sky, atmosphere, and earth.)

Traisānu, us, m., N. of the father of Karandhama.

Traisrotasa, as, ī, am (fr. *tri-srotas*), belonging to the Ganges.

Traisvarya, am, n. (fr. *tri-svara*), the three accents collectively.

Traihāyaṇa, am, n. (fr. *tri-hāyaṇa*), Ved. a period or age of three years.

त्रै *trai* (by some modern scholars written *trā,* q. v.), cl. 1. A. *trāyate* (3rd sing. Pres. ep. *trāti;* 2nd sing. Impv. Ved. *trāsva,* ep. *trāhi, trātu*), *tatre, trāsyate* (ep. *trāsyati*), *atrāsta, trātum,* to protect, preserve, cherish, defend, rescue from, (in the earlier language with abl. and gen., in the later only with abl.)

Trāṇa, trāta, &c. For these and other derivatives of the rt. *trai* see 1. *trā,* p. 388, col. 1.

त्रैगुण्य *traiguṇya, am,* n. See p. 393, col. 2.

त्रोटक *troṭaka, as,* m. [cf. *toṭaka*], a kind of poisonous insect; N. of a pupil of Śankarāćārya; (*ī*), f. a Rāgiṇī or one of the female personifications of music; (*am*), n. a minor drama, such as the Vikramorvaśī; angry speech.

त्रोटि *troṭi.* See p. 393, col. 2.

त्रोतल *trotala, am,* n. f., N. of a Tantra. — *Trotalottara* (°*la-ut*°), *am,* n., N. of a Tantra.

त्रोत्र *trotra, am,* n. (said to be fr. rt. *trai* above), a weapon, a goad; a kind of disease.

त्रौक् *trauk,* cl. 1. A. *traukate,* &c., to go, move.

त्र्यंश *try-aṅśa.* For compounds with *try* for *tri* see under *tri.*

त्व 1. *tva,* base of some cases of the second personal pronoun (in some of the cases the base is *tu,* Nom. sing. *tvam,* Acc. *tvā* and *tvām,* Abl. *tvat* or *tvad;* in Ved. *tvā* occurs for *tvayā, tubhya* for *tubhyam, tve* for *tvayi;* at the beginning of a compound *tvat* or *tvad,* and in the Vedas *tvā* is used), thou, you; [cf. Lat. *tu;* Lith. *tù;* Hib. *tu;* Goth. *thu;* Slav. *ty;* Gr. τούν, τύ, σύ.] — *Tvan-kāra, as,* m. the expression 'thou,' addressing with 'thou' (disrespectfully). — *Tvan-kṛi,* cl. 8. P. *-karoti, -kurute, -kartum,* to address with 'thou.' — *Tvat-ka, as, ā, am* (a familiar diminutive), thine, your. — *Tvat-kṛita, as, ā, am,* made or composed by thee; made like you. — *Tvat-tana,* 'your sphere or department,' you. — *Tvat-sangama, as,* m. union with thee. — *Tvad-anya, as, ā, at,* other than thee. — *Tvad-artham* or *tvad-arthe,* ind. on thy account, about thee, respecting thee. — *Tvad-gṛiha, am,* n. thy house. — *Tvad-bhaya, am,* n. dread of thee. — *Tvad-bhū,* cl. 1. P. *-bhavati, -vitum,* to become thou, to become like you. — *Tvad-yoni, is, is, i,* Ved. produced or proceeding from thee. — *Tvad-vidha, as, ā, am,* similar to thee, like thee, of thy kind. — *Tvad-viyoga, as,* m. separation from thee. — *Tvan-maya, as, ī, am,* produced from thee, consisting of thee. — *Tva-yata, as, ā, am,* Ved. given by thee. — *Tvān-kāma, as, ā, am,* Ved. longing for thee. — *Tvā-datta* or *tvā-dāta, as, ā, am,* Ved. given by thee; (Sāy. *tvā-dāta,* purified by thee.) — *Tvā-dūta, as, ā, am,* Ved. having thee as a messenger. — *Tvā-dṛiś, k, k, k,* or *tvā-dṛiśa, as, ī, am,* similar to thee, one of thy kind. — *Tvā-nid, t, t, t,* Ved. blaming thee. — *Tvā-vat, ān, atī, at,* Ved. similar to thee; as rich, mighty, great, &c., as you; worthy of thee. — *Tvā-vasu, us, us, u,* Ved. having thee as a possession; (Sāy.) having thee as a pervading attribute. — *Tvā-vṛidha, as, ā, am,* Ved. having thee as patron, favoured by thee. — *Tveshita, as, ā, am* (*tva* or *tvā* + *ishita*), Ved. sent by thee. — *Tvota, as, ā, am* (*tva* or *tvā* + *ūta*), Ved. helped or protected or loved by thee. — *Tvoti, is, is, i* (*tva* or *tvā* + *ūti*), Ved. enjoying thy protection or help or love.

2. *tva, as, ā,* m. f. thy, your, yours.

Tvakat, a familiar diminutive from *tvad,* e. g. in *tvakat-pitṛika;* [cf. *tvat-ka* above.]

Tvadīya, as, ā, am, thine, your, yours.

Tvadrik, ind. towards thee, directed towards thee; (Sāy. = *tvad-abhimukha.*)

Tvāyat, an, antī, at (part. fr. a nom. derived fr. 1. *tva*), Ved. longing for thee, seeking thee, loving thee.

Tvāyā (fr. the same nom.; used as an inst.), Ved., out of love towards thee, for thee.

Tvāyu, us, us, u, Ved. longing for thee, loving thee.

त्व 3. *tva, as, ā, at,* Ved. pron. one, several, other, different; *tva—tva,* one—the other; *tvad,* ind. partly; *tvad—tvad,* partly—partly.

त्वक्ष् *tvaksh,* cl. 1. P. *tvakshati, tatvaksha, tvakshitum* and *tvashṭum,* to create, produce, generate, effect, to work (Ved.); to pare, make thin, peel, skin; to cover; [cf. rt. *taksh, takman, toka:* Zend *thwakhsh, tash,* 'to cut;' *tasha,* 'a hatchet;' *tas-ta,* 'a cup, bowl;' *tuć,* 'to produce, create:' Gr. τεκ, ἔ-τεκ-ον, τίκ-τ-ω, τοκεύ-ς, τόκ-ος, τέκ-μαρ, τεκμήρ-ιο-ν, Τέκμησσα, τόξο-ν, τόσσαις, τέχ-νη, τέκ-τ-ων, τυκ, τυχ, τυγχάν-ω, ἔ-τυχ-ο-ν, τύχ-η, τεύχ-ω, τε-τύκ-οντο, τύκ-ο-ς, Τεῦκ-ρο-ς: Lat. *tig-nu-m, tē-lu-m, tē-mo, tex-o, tex-tor, tex-tura, tē-la:* Goth. *theik-an,* 'to thrive:' Old Sax. *thigg-yu:* Old Germ. *dig-yu,* 'I obtain;' *deh-s-a,* 'a mattock, trowel;' *deh-sen,* 'to break flax;' *dihsel,* 'a shaft:' Lith. *tek-ý-s,* 'a ram;' *tenk-ù,* 'to fall to one's share;' *tink-ù,* 'to be fit;' *tinka-s,* 'it happens;' *tik-ra-s,* 'right, orderly;' *tikỳ-ti,* 'to take aim;' *taszý-ti,* 'to cut timber;' *taisy-ti,* 'to prepare:' Slav. *tŭk-ña-ti,* 'to fix;' *tŭk-a-ti,* 'to weave;' *tes-a-ti,* 'to cut;' *těz-a-ti,* 'to obtain:' Boh. *tesar,* 'a smith.']

Tvakshas, as, n., Ved. efficiency, energy, vigour; (Sāy.) foe-destroying might.

Tvakshīyas, ān, asī, as, Ved. very vigorous, very invigorating; [cf. Zend *thwakhshista.*]

Tvashṭa, as, ā, am, pared, peeled, made thin.

Tvashṭi, is, f. carpentry, the profession of a carpenter.

Tvashṭṛi, ṭā, m. a carpenter, builder, workman, maker of carriages, &c. [cf. *tashṭṛi*]; N. of a god, sometimes identified with the later deity Viśva-karman, (he is the builder and architect κατ' ἐξοχήν and the Vulcan of the Hindūs; hence in the Veda he has the epithets *su-pāṇi, su-gabhasti, sv-apas, su-kṛit, viśva-rūpa, puru-rūpa,* &c.: he makes the various implements of the gods, especially the thunderbolt of Indra, and is said to have taught the Ṛibhus who are also skilful workmen: he is sometimes regarded as the creator himself, and as forming the bodies of men and animals is invoked for the sake of offspring, especially in the Āprī hymns; elsewhere he is associated with other similar deities, e. g. Dhātṛi, Savitṛi, Prajā-pati, and Pūshan; as Indra is accompanied by the Vasus, Rudra by the Rudras, so Tvashṭṛi is surrounded by the divine females called Gnās, Janayas, Devānām Patnyaḥ, who may be regarded as the recipients of his generative energy; he has a son Viśva-rūpa or Tri-śiras, a daughter Saraṇyū (or Sureṇu, Svareṇu, Sañjñā), wife of Vivasvat, the children of whom are the Aśvins, and Vāyu is called his son-in-law: Indra overpowers Tvashṭṛi and recovers the Soma, which, according to the Brāhmaṇas, was concealed by the latter because Indra had killed his son Viśva-rūpa: Tvashṭṛi is the deity of the Nakshatra Ćitrā, regent of the fifth Yuga or of the fifth cycle of Jupiter; and is also a form of the sun, the N. being derived by Yāska in Nirukta VIII. 13. fr. the rt. *tvish,* 'to shine,' and being applied in Ṛig-veda I. 84, 15, to one of the Ādityas; it is also in the sense 'shining,' 'brilliant,' applied to Agni and to Vāyu as well as to the Rudras); N. of a prince, a son of Manasyu (Bhauvana). — *Tvashṭṛi-mat* or *tvashṭī-mat, ān, atī, at,* Ved. connected with or accompanied by Tvashṭṛi.

Tvāshṭī, f. (? for *tvāshṭrī*), N. of Durgā.

Tvāshṭra, as, ī, am, belonging to or coming from Tvashṭṛi; (with *yuga*) the fifth Jupiter cycle, the regent of which is Tvashṭṛi; (with *putra*) the son of Tvashṭṛi; (*as*), m. the son of Tvashṭṛi, i. e. Viśva-rūpa (also identified with Vṛitra), and Ābhūti; (*ī*), f. the daughter of Tvashṭṛi, patronymic of Saraṇyū (or Sureṇu, Svareṇu, Sañjñā), who was wife of Vivasvat; the asterism Ćitrā, the regent of which is Tvashṭṛi; a small car; *tvāshṭryas,* f. pl. the daughters of Tvashṭrī, certain divine female beings; (*am*), n. the power or energy of Tvashṭṛi, creative power; (with *bha* or *nakshatra*) the asterism Ćitrā [cf. *tvashṭṛi*]; a kind of eclipse.

त्वगेल *tvagela, am,* n. probably = *elavālu,* the bark of Feronia Elephantum.

त्वङ्ग् *tvang,* cl. 1. P. *tvangati,* &c., to go, move, tremble, wave; to jump, leap, gallop.

त्वच् 1. *tvać,* cl. 6. P. *tvaćati,* &c., to cover, (a root artificially formed to furnish an etymology for 2. *tvać*); [cf. Lat. *tego;* Old Germ. *dekiu,* 'to cover;' Lith. *dengiù.*]

Tvakka at end of adj. comp., e. g. *sāndra-tvakka,* covered with thick armour-like skin.

2. *tvać, k*, f. skin (as of men, serpents, &c.); hide (as of a goat, cow, &c.); a cow's hide (used in pressing out the Soma); bark, rind, peel; any surface or covering (as turf of the earth); a cover, horse-cloth; (Ved.) the black cover, = darkness; a protecting cover or guard, mail, a shield; a leather bag; Cassia bark; cinnamon, the cinnamon tree; mystical N. of the letter *ya*. — *Tvak-kaṇḍura, as*, m. skin-wound, a sore. — *Tvak-kshīrā, ī*, f. manna of bamboo (commonly Tabāshīr); [cf. *tavakshīra*.] — *Tvak-ćhada, as*, m. the grass Lipeocercis Serrata. — *Tvak-ćheda, as*, m. a skin-wound, flesh-wound, cut, scratch; circumcision. — *Tvak-ćhedana, am*, n. cutting the skin; see *tvak-ćheda*. — *Tvak-taraṅgaka, as*, m. 'skin-wave,' a wrinkle. — *Tvak-tra, am*, n. 'protection for the skin,' armour. — *Tvak-pattra, am*, n. Cassia (the plant and bark); (*ī*), f. = *kāravī, hingu-pattrī*, the leaf of the Asa Fœtida (?), = *tamāla-pattra*, the leaf of the Laurus Cassia, Malabathron. — *Tvak-pariputana, am*, n. peeling of the skin, desquamation. — *Tvak-pāka, as*, m. inflammation of the skin, N. of a particular disease. — *Tvak-pārushya, am*, n. roughness of the skin. — *Tvak-pushpa, am*, n. 'skin-sprout,' erection of the hairs of the skin, horripilation; (*am, ī*), n. f. blotch, scab, cutaneous eruption, &c. — *Tvak-pushpikā*, f. scab, blotch. — *Tvak-sāra, as, ā, am*, having an excellent or sound skin; (*as*), m. a bamboo; Cassia (the plant and the bark); Bignonia Indica; (*ā*), f. Tabāshīr; [cf. *tvak-kshīrā*.] — *Tvak-sāra-bhedinī*, f. a kind of plant, = *kshudra-ćańću*. — *Tvak-sugandha, as*, m. an orange ('having fragrant peel'); (*ā*), f. the fragrant bark of Feronia Elephantum (= *elavāluka*). — *Tvak-svādvī*, f. a kind of cinnamon ('having sweet bark'). — *Tvag-ankura, as*, m. = *tvak-pushpa* above. — *Tvag-asthi-mātra-śesha, as, ā, am*, with mere skin and bone left, reduced to a skeleton. — *Tvagā-kshīrī*, f. = *tugā-kshīrī*, = *tvak-kshīrā, ī*. — *Tvag-indriya, am*, n. the sense or organ of touch. — *Tvag-gandha, as*, m. an orange; [cf. *tvak-sugandha*.] — *Tvag-ja, as, ā, am*, produced on or issuing from the skin; (*am*), n. the hairs on the body; blood. — *Tvag-dosha, as*, m. disease of the skin, leprosy. — *Tvag-doshāpahā* (°*sha-apahā*), f. Vernonia Anthelminthica ('destroying leprosy'). — *Tvag-doshāri* (°*sha-ari*), *is*, m. a kind of bulbous plant ('the enemy of leprosy'), = *hasti-kanda*. — *Tvagdoshin, ī, iṇī, i*, affected with skin disease or with leprosy. — *Tvag-bheda, as*, m. 'breaking of the skin,' a flesh-wound, a scratch. — *Tvag-bhedaka, as*, m. one who cuts the skin, a stabber, scratcher, one who draws blood from the skin. — *Tvag-roga, as*, m. any cutaneous disease; leprosy &c. — *Tvag-vat, ān, atī, at*, furnished with skin or bark. — *Tvan-maya, as, ī, am*, made of bark or skin. — *Tvan-mala, am*, n. the hairs of the body. — *Tvaći-sāra, as*, m. (*tvaći* loc. of 2. *tvać*), = *tvak-sāra*, a bamboo. — *Tvaći-sugandhā*, f. small cardamoms.

Tvaća at the end of a comp. = 2. *tvać*; cf. *sa-t°*, *sūrya-t°*, *hiranya-t°*; (*am*), n. skin; bark, rind; cinnamon, the cinnamon tree, Cassia bark; (*ā*), f. skin; [cf. *guḍa-tvaća* and *tanu-tvaćā*.] — *Tvaćā-pattra, am*, n. = *tvak-pattra*, Cassia bark.

Tvaćana, am, n. covering with a skin or hide; skinning.

Tvaćaya, nom. P. *tvaćayati*, &c., to cover with a skin or hide; to tear off the skin, to skin.

Tvaćasya, as, ā, am, Ved. being in the skin.

Tvaćishṭha, as, ā, am (superl. of *tvag-vat*, Pāṇ. V. 3, 65), having the best skin, having an excellent skin; bark &c.

Tvaći-sāra. See under 2. *tvać* above.

Tvaćīyus, ān, asī, as (compar. of *tvag-vat*, Pāṇ. V. 3, 65), having a more excellent or an excellent skin; bark &c.; [cf. *tvaćishṭha*.]

Tvaćya, as, ā, am, conducive to the healthiness of the skin.

Tvāća, as, ī, am, cuticular, relating to the skin, contagious, derived from touch. — *Tvāća-pratyaksha, am*, n. ascertainment of objects by contact.

त्वञ्च् *tvańć* = *tańć*, cl. 1. P. *tvańćati*, &c., to go, move; cl. 7. P. *tvanakti*, &c., to contract.

त्वत् *tvat* or (according to the proper form of the base) *tvad*. See 1. *tva*, p. 394.

त्वर् *tvar*, cl. 1. A. *tvarate* (ep. also P. *tvarati*), *tatvare, tvaritum*, to hurry, make haste, go or move with speed, do anything quickly or precipitately: Caus. *tvarayati, -yitum*, Aor. *atatvarat*, to cause to hasten, quicken, urge forward, accelerate: Desid. *titvarishati*: Intens. *tātvaryate, totūrti*; [cf. *tur, tṛī*: Gr. θόρνυμι, θοῦρος, θρύσκω; perhaps ἀ-θύρω, τύρβη, θόρυβος: Lat. *turba*: perhaps Angl. Sax. *a-thwerian*, 'to move, shake:' Hib. *tuairim*, 'to go round, move in a circle.']

Tūrṇa = *tvarita*. See p. 381, col. 2.

Tvaraṇa, as, ā, am, making haste; (*am*), n. making haste, speed, velocity.

Tvaranīya, as, ā, am, to be hastened or accelerated.

Tvarā, f. haste, speed, velocity. — *Tvarānvita* (°*rā-an°*), *as, ā, am*, possessed of haste, swift, quick. — *Tvarā-yukta, as, ā, am*, hasty, impetuous, quick, expeditious. — *Tvarāroha* (°*rā-ār°*), *as*, m. a pigeon ('ascending quickly'). — *Tvarā-vat, ān, atī, at*, quick, expeditious.

Tvarāyasya, nom. P. *tvarāyasyati*, &c., to make haste.

Tvari, is, f. haste, speed.

Tvarita, as, ā, am, hastening, quick, swift, speedy, expeditious; (*am*), n. despatch, haste; (*am*), ind. quickly, swiftly; hastily, in haste, fast, speedily; (*ā*), f. a form of Durgā; a magical formula called after her. — *Tvarita-gati, is*, f. swift motion; a species of the Paṅkti metre. — *Tvarita-prayoga, as*, m., N. of a chapter of the Tantra-sāra. — *Tvaritā-mantra, as*, m., N. of a chapter of the Śāradā-tilaka. — *Tvaritā-yantra, am*, n., N. of a mystical diagram. — *Tvaritodita* (°*ta-ud°*), *as, ā, am*, spoken quickly, uttered rapidly, hurried.

Tvaritaka, as, ā, m. f. a sort of rice ripening before the usual time.

त्वरायण *tvarāyaṇa, as, ā, am*, m. f. n. (a various reading for *parāyaṇa*), adherence, attachment; (according to some only *am*, n.)

त्वष्ट *tvashṭa, tvashṭṛi*, &c. See under rt. *tvaksh*, p. 394.

त्वाच *tvāća*. See col. 1.

त्वादृश् *tvā-dṛiś*. See 1. *tva*, p. 394.

त्वायत् *tvāyat*. See under 1. *tva*, p. 394.

त्विष् 1. *tvish*, cl. 1. P. A. *tveshati, -te, titvesha, titvishe* (part. *titvishāṇa*), *tvekshyati, -te, atvikshat, atvikshata* (Ved. forms *atvishus, atvishanta, atitvishanta*), *tveshṭum*, Ved. inf. *tvishe*, to be violently agitated or moved; to be excited; to be troubled or perplexed; to excite, instigate; to shine, glitter, sparkle; to be brilliant, to blaze: Caus. *tveshayati, -yitum*, Aor. *atitvishat*: Desid. *titvikshati, -te*: Intens. *tetvishyate, tetveshṭi*.

2. *tvish, t*, f. violent agitation or quivering motion of any kind, vehemence, violence, fury, perplexity; light, brilliance, glitter, any shining colour, splendor, beauty; authority, weight, consideration; speech; wish, desire; custom, practice, usage; [cf. *aćala-t°* and *vāta-t°*.]

Tvishā, f. light, splendor; N. of a daughter of Kaśyapa. — *Tvishām-īśa, as*, or *tvishām-pati, is*, m. 'the lord of rays,' the sun.

Tvishi, is, f., Ved. vehemence, impetuousity, energy, internal power; (Sāy.) splendor, light, ray, brilliancy, beauty. — *Tvishi-mat* and (Ved.) *tvishīmat, ān, atī, at*, vehemently excited, vehement, energetic; brilliant, beautiful, N. of Rudra.

Tvesha, as, ī, am, Ved. vehement, impetuous; inspiring awe, causing fear, awful; (Sāy.) brilliant, bright, glittering, epithet of Rudra and the Maruts, shining. — *Tvesha-dyumna, as, ā, am*, Ved. having vehement energy, impetuous; (Sāy.) possessed of brilliant reputation. — *Tvesha-nṛimṇa, as, ā, am*, Ved. having impetuous energy or courage; (Sāy.) of brilliant power. — *Tvesha-pratīka, as, ā, am*, Ved. having a brilliant appearance, having an awful aspect, having the aspect of great power; (Sāy.) bright-pointed (as a shaft). — *Tvesha-yāma, as, ā, am*, Ved. impetuous in course, rushing impetuously; (Sāy.) 'having a brilliant course,' epithet of the Maruts. — *Tvesha-ratha, as, ā, am*, Ved. having rushing chariots; (Sāy.) having brilliant chariots. — *Tvesha-sandṛiś, k, k, k*, Ved. of a splendid aspect, similar to flame; 'looking awful,' epithet of the Maruts, of Indra, &c.

Tveshatha, as, m., Ved. fury, violence; (Sāy.) radiance.

Tveshas, as, n., Ved. force, energy, impulse; (Sāy.) brilliant energy.

Tveshya, as, ā, am, agitating, terrifying, awful, inspiring awe, any terrible object; (Sāy.) shining, brilliant, epithet of Rudra.

Tvatshīrathi, is, m. a patronymic of Kuśika.

त्वोत *tvota, tvoti*. See 1. *tva*, p. 394.

त्सर् *tsar*, cl. 1. P. *tsarati, tatsāra, tsarishyati, atsārīt* and *atsār, tsaritum*, Ved. to go or approach stealthily, to creep, crawl, creep on, steal upon, sneak, to obtain by sneaking; to proceed crookedly or fraudulently.

Tsaru, us, m. any creeping or crawling animal or a particular animal of this kind; the stalk of a leaf &c.; the hilt or handle of a sword and similar weapons. — *Tsaru-mārga, as*, m. sword-exercise, sword-fight.

Tsārin, ī, iṇī, i, Ved. creeping, sneaking, approaching stealthily or secretly; crooked; (Sāy.) very fearful, very much alarmed.

Tsāruka, as, ā, am, skilful in handling a sword, skilled in sword-exercise.

थ

थ 1. *tha*, the second consonant of the dental class and the aspirate of the preceding letter, having much the sound of *th* in *ant-hill*, but more dental. — *Tha-kāra, as*, m. the letter or sound *th*.

2. *tha, as*, m. a mountain; a protector, preserver; a sign of danger; a kind of disease; eating; (*am*), n. preserving, preservation; fear, terror; auspiciousness; a prayer for the welfare of another.

थक्कन *thakkana, as*, m., N. of a man; (also read *ḍhakkana* and *ḍhakkama*.)

थक्कियक *thakkiyaka, as*, m., N. of a man.

थक्रिय *thakriya, as*, m., N. of a man.

थर्व् *tharv* (said to be = rt. *ćar*), cl. 1. P. *tharvati*, &c., to go, move.

थल्योरक *thalyoraka, as*, m., N. of a village.

थुड् *thuḍ*, cl. 6. P. *thuḍati*, &c., to cover, screen; to clothe; to hide; [cf. rt. *sthuḍ*.] *Thoḍana, am*, n. covering, clothing, wrapping up.

थुत्कार *thut-kāra, as*, m. the making of the sound *thut*, the sound made in spitting.

थुथु *thuthu* (an onomatopoetic word), the sound heard in eating.

Thuthu-kṛit, t, m. the making the imitative sound *thuthu*; a kind of bird (= Marāṭhī *holā*).

थुर्व् *thurv*, cl. 1. P. *thūrvati, tuthūrva*, &c., to hurt, injure; [cf. rt. *turv*.]

थूत्कार *thūt-kāra, as*, m. the making of

the sound *thūt*, the sound made in spitting; [cf. *thut-kāra.*] — *Thūt-kṛita, am*, n. the sound *thūt* made in spitting.

थूथू *thūthū*, imitative sound of spitting; (according to others *thuthu.*)

थैथै *thaithai*, imitative sound of a musical instrument.

द

द 1. *da*, the eighteenth consonant of the alphabet and the third letter of the fourth or dental class, the sound of which is more dental than the English *d.* — *Da-kāra, as*, m. the letter or sound *d.*

द 2. *da, as, ā, am* (fr. rt. 1. *dā*, to give), giving, a giver, donor; presenting, favouring with, granting, a granter; causing, (often at the end of comp., e. g. *vāri-da*, giving water; *anna-da*, granting food &c.; exceptionally compounded with the receiver of the gift, e. g. *pitṛi-da*, giving to the father); (*as*), m. a gift, anything given; (*am, ā*), n. f. a gift, donation.

द 3. *da, as, ā, am* (fr. rt. 3. *dā* for *do*, to cut), cutting off, destroying, breaking, &c., (generally at the end of comp.); (*as, ā*), m. f. the act of cutting off, dividing.

द 4. *da, as, ā, am* (fr. rt. 4. *dā*, to bind), binding, (generally at the end of comp.; cf. *riśya-da.*)

द 5. *da, as, ā, am* (fr. rt. 7. *dā*, to purify), cleaning, cleansing.

द 6. *da, as*, m. a mountain; (*ā*), f. heat, pain, repentance; (*am*), n. a wife; [cf. *dam-patī.*]

दंश् 1. *daṇś*, cl. 1. 10. P. *daṇśati, daṇśayati*, &c., to speak or shine.

दंश् 2. *daṇś*, cl. 1. P. (ep. also A.) *daśati, -te, dadaṇśa, daṅkshyati* (ep. also *daṇśishyati*), *adāṅkshit, daṇshṭum*, to bite, sting; to see [? cf. rt. *daṇs*]: Caus. P. *daṇśayati, -yitum*, Aor. *adadaṅkshat*, to cause to bite; to bite: Desid. *didaṅkshati*: Intens. *dandaśyate, dandaṇshṭi, dandashṭi*: Caus. of Intens. *dandaśayati*, to cause to bite violently; [cf. Gr. δάκνω, δάκος, δδαγμός, ὀδάζω, ὀδακτάζω, ὀδαξέω, &c., δάκρυ; Lat. *lacruma*, perhaps *lacero*; Goth. *tahyan*, 'dilacerate,' *tagr*; Angl. Sax. *taeher, tux, tusk, tang*; Old Germ. *zanga, zangar*; Cambro-Brit. *danhezu*, 'to bite;' Hib. *dan-t*, 'a morsel, portion, share;' Russ. *desnà*, 'ginger.']

Daṇśa, as, m. biting, stinging; cutting, dividing, tearing; the sting of a snake; a bite, the spot bitten; pungency; fault, defect (in a jewel &c.); a tooth; a gad-fly; armour, a coat of mail; a joint, limb; N. of an Asura; (*ī*), f. a small gad-fly; [cf. *kshamā-d°* and *vṛisha-d°.*] — *Daṇśa-nāśinī*, f. ('healing irritation of the skin?'), a kind of insect, = *taila-kīṭa*; [cf. *dardru-nāśinī.*] — *Daṇśa-bhīru, us*, m. or *daṇśa-bhīruka, as*, m. 'afraid of the gad-fly,' a buffalo. — *Daṇśa-mūla, as*, m. 'having a pungent root,' the plant Hyperanthera Moringa or a sort of horse-radish, = *śigru*. — *Daṇśa-vadana, as*, m. 'having a sharp beak,' a heron.

Daṇśaka, as, ā or *ikā, am*, biting, stinging; (*as*), m. a dog; gad-fly, common fly; N. of a prince of Kampana; (*ikā*), f. a kind of gad-fly.

Daṇśana, am, n. the act of biting, stinging; armour, mail.

Daṇśita, as, ā, am, bitten, stung; (fr. *daṇśa*), armed, mailed; protected; fitting closely (like armour), standing closely together, crowded; (*am*), n. a bite; [cf. *pari-daṇśita.*]

Daṇśin, ī, inī, i, biting, stinging [cf. *tripra-daṇśin*]; (*ī*), m. a dog; a gad-fly, a wasp.

Daṇśuka, as, ā, am, Ved. biting, stinging.

Daṇśera, as, ā, am (more correctly *daśera*, q. v.), biting, mordacious; noxious, mischievous.

Daṇśman, a, n., Ved. a bite; the place bitten.

Daṇshṭṛi, ṭā, ṭrī, ṭṛi, Ved. a biter, biting, stinging.

Daṇshṭra, as, ā, m. f. (in the later language usually f.), a large tooth, tusk, fang, (often at the end of comp.; cf. *ayo-d°, ashṭa-d°, tīkshṇa-d°*, &c.) — *Daṇshṭrā-karāla, as, ā, am*, having terrible tusks. — *Daṇshṭrā-nivāsin, ī*, m., N. of a Yakshas. — *Daṇshṭrāyudha* (°*rā-āy*°), *as, ā, am*, using tusks as weapons; (*as*), m. a wild boar. — *Daṇshṭrā-sena, as*, m., N. of a Buddhist scholar.

Daṇshṭrāla, as, ā, am, tusked, having large tusks; (*as*), m., N. of a Rākshasa.

Daṇshṭrika, as, ā, am, tusked, having tusks; (*ā*), f. = *dāḍhikā*, a beard (?); a kind of plant; [cf. *nakuleshṭā.*]

Daṇshṭrin, ī, iṇī, i, tusked, having tusks or large teeth; biting or wounding with the teeth; carnivorous; (*ī*), m. any animal with tusks; a wild boar; a hyena; a snake.

Daṇshṭvā, ind. having bitten.

Dashṭa, as, ā, am, bitten, &c. See p. 406, col. 1.

दंस् *daṇs* (connected with rt. *das*, q. v.; perhaps only a various reading for rt. 1. and 2. *daṇś*, col. 1, or a Prākṛit form of rt. 1. *dṛiś*), cl. 1. P. 10. A. *daṇsati, daṇsayate* or *dāsayate*, &c., to bite; to destroy, overpower; to see, (*daṇsati*?); cl. 10. P. *daṇsayati*, &c., to speak or to shine.

Daṇsana, am, ā, n. f. (Ved. inst. *daṇsanā*), a surprising or wonderful deed or operation, marvellous power; an action, work, deed; armour, mail, (in the latter meaning only a various reading for *daṇśana*); [cf. *dasma* and *dasra.*] — *Daṇsanā-vat, ān, atī, at*, Ved. having wonderful power; (Sāy.) abounding in marvellous deeds.

Daṇsayitṛi, tā, m. a destroyer, (a word formed to explain *dasra.*)

Daṇsas, as, n., Ved. = *daṇsana*, a surprising action or deed (applied especially to the wonderful actions of the Aśvins, by which these deities protected their human friends); [cf. *puru-d°* and *su-d°.*]

Daṇsi, is, m. f. (?), Ved. = *karman*, act, deed.

Daṇsishṭha, as, ā, am (superl. of *daṇsu* or *dasra*), Ved. of very wonderful strength, performing marvellous deeds, eminent in action, epithet of the Aśvins and of Indra.

Daṇsu, us, us, u, Ved. of wonderful strength; (according to Sāy., loc. of *dam* = *daṇseshu* or *karma-vatsu*); (*u*), ind. in a wonderful way, wonderfully. — *Daṇsu-jūta, as, ā, am*, Ved. wonderfully quick; (Sāy.) borne along by well-trained horses (as if fr. rt. 1. *dam*). — *Daṇsu-patnī*, f., Ved. having a powerful lord or master; (Sāy.) having the Asuras as good masters (as if fr. *dam* + *su* + *patnī*, *su* = *sushṭhu*); in Ṛig-veda VI. 3, 7, *dam* is regarded as a separate word.

दंह् *daṇh*, cl. 10. P. *daṇhayati*, &c., to shine, burn; [cf. rt. 1. *dah.*]

दक *daka, am*, n. = *udaka* (the initial vowel being dropped), water. — *Daka-lāvaṇika, as, ī, am* (fr. *daka* + *lavaṇa*), prepared with water and salt. — *Dakodara* (°*ka-ud*°), *am*, n. (instead of *udakodara*, cf. *udakodarin*), a watery or dropsical belly.

दक्ष् *daksh*, cl. 1. P. A. *dakshati, -te, dadaksha, dakshitum*, Ved. to act to the satisfaction of another (with dat. in P.); to be competent, be able, be strong or powerful (A.); to grow, increase; to do or act quickly, go, move; to hurt, kill: Caus. P. *dakshayati, -yitum*, Aor. *adadakshat*, to make able or strong.

Daksha, as, ā, am, able, fit, competent, suitable, adroit, expert, clever, judicious, dexterous [cf. Gr. δεξιός]; intelligent, upright, honest; (*as*), m. epithet of Soma (as heightening or strengthening the intellectual faculties; according to Sāy. = *vriddha*); epithet of Śiva; epithet of the Ganges (as satisfying or suiting all); ability, power, fitness; capacity, intellectual ability, mental power, talent; strength of will, energy, will, disposition; (in the Veda *daksha* and *kratu*, i. e. energy and intelligence, are often joined together as the chief two faculties of the mind, cf. *kratu*); bad disposition, evil design; N. of an Āditya; a creative power associated with Aditi, and therefore sometimes identified with Prajā-pati; (his daughter is called Kṛittikā: in the Post-vedic literature Daksha is the subject of numerous legends, which relate his history differently; he is there generally called the son of Brahmā, and placed among the Prajā-patis or at their head as 'the lord of all creatures,' being born from Brahmā's right thumb, as his wife was from the left, see Manu IX. 128: in other legends he is said to be the son of the ten Pra-ćetasas or of Pra-ćetas alone, whence his patronymic Prāćetasa; he is variously stated to have had fifty, sixty, forty-four, and a less number of daughters, of whom twenty-seven became the wives of the Moon, forming the lunar asterisms, and thirteen or, according to others, seventeen or only eight the wives of Kaśyapa, becoming by this latter the mothers of gods, demons, men, and animals: Daksha on one occasion celebrated a great sacrifice to obtain a son, but omitted to invite Śiva who, according to one legend, was his son-in-law, (Śiva's wife being Satī, a form of Durgā, daughter of Daksha); this irritated the god, who interrupted the sacrifice and decapitated his father-in-law, see *dakshādhvara-dhvaṇśa-kṛit*: Daksha is sometimes regarded as an Avatār of Brahmā himself, and is even in one legend identified with Vishṇu); N. of a son of Garuḍa; N. of a man with the patronymic Pārvati; of a Muni and legislator; of a prince or a son of Uśīnara; of one of the five Brāhmans of Kānya-kubja, from whom the Brāhmans of Bengal are said to have sprung; (according to the lexicographers also) the bull of Śiva; a cock; a kind of plant; a name of Agni or fire; a general lover, one attached to many mistresses; (*ā*), f. the earth; [cf. *atūrta-daksha, dīna-d°*, &c.: cf. also *dakshiṇa*; Gr. δεξιός, δεξιτερός; Lat. *dex-ter, dextimus*; Goth. *taihsvs*; Angl. Sax. *teso*; Old Germ. *zeso*; Hib. *deas*, 'right, southern.'] — *Daksha-kanyā*, f. 'daughter of Daksha,' (especially) epithet of Durgā, the wife of Śiva. — *Daksha-kratu, us, us, u*, Ved. having a strong will or intelligence, having a clear understanding. — *Daksha-jā*, f. 'daughter of Daksha,' the goddess Durgā; a lunar asterism; [cf. *daksha.*] — *Dakshajā-pati, is*, m. 'the husband of the daughters of Daksha,' an epithet of the Moon; also of Śiva. — *Daksha-tā*, f. or *daksha-tva, am*, n. dexterity, cleverness, ability. — *Daksha-tāti, is*, f., Ved. mental power or capacity. — *Daksha-nidhana, am*, n., N. of a Sāman. — *Daksha-pati, is*, m., Ved. lord of the faculties, lord of power or might; protector of the sacrifice. — *Daksha-pitṛi, tā, trī, tṛi*, Ved. having Daksha as father or progenitor, (the m. pl. may be either *daksha-pitaras* or *-pitāras*); preserving, possessing or granting abilities. — *Daksha-makha-mathana, am*, n. 'destruction of Daksha's sacrifice,' N. of the ninety-seventh and ninety-eighth chapters of the Liṅga-Purāṇa. — *Daksha-yajña, as*, m. the sacrifice celebrated by Daksha. — *Daksha-yajña-bhanga, as*, m. the interruption of Daksha's sacrifice. — *Dakshayajña-vidhvaṇsa, as*, m. 'destruction of Daksha's sacrifice,' N. of the fifteenth chapter of the Kūrma-Purāṇa. — *Dakshayajña-vidhvaṇsana, am*, n., N. of the fifth chapter of the Sṛishṭi-khaṇḍa of the Padma-Purāṇa. — *Dakshaya-jña-vināśinī*, f. 'destroyer of the sacrifice of Daksha,' an epithet of Durgā. — *Daksha-vihitā*, f. (scil. *gāthā*), a hymn or song arranged by Daksha. — *Daksha-vṛidh, t, t, t*, Ved. rejoicing in power or energy &c. — *Daksha-śāpa, as*, m. 'the curse of Daksha,' N. of the thirty-third chapter of the Svarga-khaṇḍa or third part of the Padma-Purāṇa. — *Daksha-sādhana, as, ā, am*, Ved. effective of energy, inspiring courage. — *Daksha-sāvarṇi, is*, m., N. of the ninth Manu. — *Daksha-suta, as*, m. the son of Daksha (?); (*ā*), f. a daughter of Daksha, a lunar asterism or one of the wives of the Moon. — *Dakshādhvara-dhvaṇśa-kṛit*

(°ksha-adh°), t, m. 'disturber of the sacrifice of Daksha,' a N. of S'iva; (Daksha having instituted a sacrifice to which he invited all the gods except his son-in-law S'iva and his wife Satī, the latter went unbid, and being received contemptuously, threw herself into the fire; upon which an emanation or incarnation of S'iva was produced, named Vīra-bhadra, who attacked Daksha, and a general affray ensued in which the gods and Ṛishis took the part of Daksha, but were wounded and dispersed: Daksha himself was decapitated, but was restored to life by S'iva at the prayer of the gods; the decapitated head, however, was not to be found, and the head of a ram had therefore to be substituted for the one lost.) — *Dakshes'vara-linga* (°ksha-īś°), *am*, n., N. of a Linga.

Dakshas, ās, ās, as, Ved. = *daksha*, able, strong, dexterous, &c.

Dakshāyya, as, ā, am, Ved. to be satisfied or pleased; (Sāy.) increaser of all; to be honoured, to be augmented (by oblations); (*as*), m. a vulture; an epithet of Garuḍa or the bird of Vishṇu.

Dakshiṇa, as, ā, am (according to Pāṇ. I. 1, 34, and VII. 1, 16, can only be declined as a pronominal when it denotes relative position, i. e. 'situated on the right hand' or 'southern,' and even in this sense can be optionally declined like *s'iva* in abl. loc. sing. m. n. and nom. voc. pl. m.; but *dakshiṇāyām dis'i*, for the loc. f. in Hari-vaṇśa 12390, is against the rule), able, competent, clever, skilful, dexterous [cf. *daksha*]; right (not left; probably applied to the right hand, foot, &c., as the cleverest or most skilful), situated on the right side, (opposed to *savya, vāma; dakshiṇam pari*, to walk round a person with the right side towards him; *dakshiṇam kṛi*, to place on the right side, to turn the right side towards a person as a mark of respect); south, southern (as being on the right side of a person looking towards the east), situated to the south, turned or directed southward, (*dakshiṇā dis'*, the south, the southern quarter or point of the compass; *dakshiṇasyām dis'i*, in the southern quarter; *dakshiṇa āmnāyas*, the southern sacred text, one of the holy texts of the Tāntrikas); straightforward, candid, sincere, upright, honest, impartial; pleasing, amiable, compliant; submissive, dependent, subject; (*as*), m. the right (hand or arm); the right hand horse, the horse on the right side of the pole of a carriage; an epithet of S'iva; (*as, am*), m. n. the right side; *savyam dakshiṇam eva ća*, to the left and to the right; the south, the country of the south, the Dekhan; (*ā*), f., scil. *go*, a prolific cow, 'able to calve and give milk,' a good milch-cow; a present to Brāhmans or young virgins (consisting originally of a cow, and given upon solemn or sacrificial occasions); property so acquired [cf. Manu VIII. 349]; Donation to Brāhmans personified as a goddess, (generally mentioned together with Brahmaṇas-pati, Soma, Indra, &c., and said to be the authoress of Ṛig-veda X. 107; sometimes regarded as a daughter of Prajā-pati, or as the wife of Sacrifice personified, or as born from Kṛishṇa's right side, or as the wife of Rući); wages or remuneration in general; a fee, gift, donation (e. g. *prāṇa-dakshiṇā*, the gift of life); offering, oblation in general; completion of any rite, fixing or establishing any act or place; scil. *dis'*, the south; the southern quarter, the southern point of the compass, the Dekhan; a form or figure of Durgā, in which the right side is said to be advanced; (*am*), n. the right hand or highest doctrine of the Sāktas; *dakshiṇā* or *dakshiṇena*, ind. on the right, on the right side of (with acc. and gen.); on the south, southward; *dakshiṇena kṛi*, to place on the right, to leave on the right; *dakshiṇāt*, ind. on the right, from the south, southward; *dakshiṇe*, ind. on the right, on the south, southward; [cf. Lith. *dészinè*, f. 'the right hand,' = perhaps Russ. *yug*, 'south;' *yushnyĭ*, 'southern.'] — *Dakshiṇa-kālikā*, f. a form of Durgā worshipped by the Tāntrikas. — *Dakshiṇa-tas*, ind. from the right, to the right hand; from the south, southward, southerly; *dakshiṇataḥ kṛi*, to turn the right side towards a person (as a mark of respect); to stand on the right side of any one and so assist him; *dakshiṇataḥ purastāt* or *dakshiṇataḥ puraḥ*, to the south-east, on the south-east. — *Dakshiṇatas-kaparda* or *dakshiṇā-kaparda, ās*, m. pl., Ved. 'wearing the hair knotted or braided on the right side of the head,' epithet of the Vasishṭhas. — *Dakshiṇa-trā*, ind., Ved. on the right side. — *Dakshiṇa-tva, am*, n. uprightness, honesty. — *Dakshiṇa-dhurīṇa, as, ā, am*, harnessed on the right side of the pole of a carriage. — *Dakshiṇa-patha*, a wrong reading for *dakshiṇā-patha*, q. v. — *Dakshiṇa-pas'ćāt*, ind. to the south-west, on the south-west. — *Dakshiṇa-pas'ćārdha* (°ća-ar°), *as*, m. the south-western side. — *Dakshiṇa-pas'ćima, as, ā, am*, south-western. — *Dakshiṇa-pānćālaka, as, ikā, am*, relating to the southern Panćālas. — *Dakshiṇa-pūrva, as, ā, am*, south-eastern; (*ā*), f., scil. *dis'*, the south-east quarter; (*eṇa*), ind. to the south-east of (with acc.). — *Dakshiṇa-prānć, ān, āćī, āk*, south-eastern; *dakshiṇa-prāćī*, f. the south-east quarter. — *Dakshiṇa-bhāga, as*, m. the southern hemisphere. — *Dakshiṇa-mānasa*, N. of a place of pilgrimage. — *Dakshiṇa-māruta, as*, m. the south wind. — *Dakshiṇa-sad* or *dakshiṇā-sad, t, t, t*, sitting or remaining seated on the right or southern side. — *Dakshiṇa-stha, as, ā, am*, standing upon the right, to the south, &c.; (*as*), m. a charioteer (as standing on the right of his master; cf. *savye-shṭha*). — *Dakshiṇā-kaparda*, see *dakshiṇatas-kaparda*. — *Dakshiṇā-kāla, as*, m. the time of (receiving) the sacrificial gift or fee. — *Dakshiṇāgni* (°ṇa-ag°), *is*, m. the southern fire of the altar, a sacred fire placed towards the south, (in the Brāhmaṇas generally called Anvāhārya-paćana.) — *Dakshiṇāgra* (°ṇā-agra), *as, ā, am*, pointing to the south, having the head or point turned towards the south. — *Dakshiṇāćala* (°ṇa-ać°), *as*, m. the southern mountain, the Malaya range. — *Dakshiṇāćāra* (°ṇa-āć°), *as, ā, am*, honest or upright in conduct, well-behaved; a worshipper of S'akti according to the purer or right hand ritual. — *Dakshiṇāćārin, ī, iṇī, i*, a worshipper of S'akti according to the purer or right hand ritual; a follower of the right hand Sākta system. — *Dakshiṇā-jyotis, is, is, is*, Ved. brilliant by the sacrificial gift. — *Dakshiṇānć* (°ṇa-anć), *ān, āćī, āk*, turned to the south, southward. — *Dakshiṇātyaya* (°ṇa-at°), *as*, m. one who goes beyond the south, a dweller in the south. — *Dakshiṇā-dvāra, as, ā, am*; having the door on the south. — *Dakshiṇāntikā* (°ṇa-an°), f. a kind of metre. — *Dakshiṇā-patha, as*, m. the path or road of the Dakshiṇā, i. e. of the cow constituting the sacrificial fee (situated between the S'ālā and the Sadas); the southern region or country, the Dekhan. — *Dakshiṇāpatha-gāmin, ī, inī, i*, going to the south, living in the south. — *Dakshiṇāpatha-janman, ā*, m. born in the south, a southern; (*-janmānas*), m. pl., N. of the Andhakas, Guhas, Pulindas, Savaras, Ćućukas, and Madrapas, all outcast or barbarous tribes. — *Dakshiṇā-pathika, as, ā, am*, belonging to the southern region. — *Dakshiṇāpara* (°ṇa-ap°), *as, ā, am*, south-western. — *Dakshiṇā-pravaṇa, as, ā, am*, shelving or inclining to the south. — *Dakshiṇā-prashṭi, is*, m., Ved. the horse harnessed on the right side of the yoke-horses (*yugya*); [cf. Gr. δεξιόσειρος.] — *Dakshiṇā-bandha, as*, m. (in the Sāṅkhya phil.) N. of one of the three states of bondage, the bondage of ritual observance; [cf. *dākshiṇa* and *dākshiṇika*.] — *Dakshiṇābhimukha* (°ṇā-abh°), *as, ā, am*, facing southwards, directed southwards, flowing southwards. — *Dakshiṇābhimukha-sthita, as, ā, am*, standing with the face southwards. — *Dakshiṇā-mukha, as, ī, am*, turning the face to the right or to the south, facing south. — *Dakshiṇāmūrti, is*, m. one of the forms of S'iva with the Tāntrikas; N. of an author. — *Dakshiṇāmūrti-prayoga, as*, m., N. of a chapter of the Tantra-sāra. — *Dakshiṇāmūrti-mantra, as*, m., N. of a chapter of the S'āradātilaka by Lakshmaṇa. — *Dakshiṇāmūrti-saṃhitā*, f., N. of a chapter of the Tantra-sāra. — *Dakshiṇāmūrty-upanishad, t*, f., N. of an Upanishad. — *Dakshiṇāyana* (°ṇa-ay°), *am*, n. the sun's progress south of the equator, the winter's solstice, the half-year in which the sun moves from north to south; *dakshiṇāyanam anuyā*, to follow the southward way, to go to Yama's quarter, i. e. to die; (*as, ā, am*), situated in the sun's course from north to south (said of certain asterisms). — *Dakshiṇā-yugya, as*, m. the right yoke-horse. — *Dakshiṇāraṇya* (°ṇa-ar°), *am*, n. the southern forest, N. of a particular forest (probably in the Dekhan). — *Dakshiṇārus* (°ṇa-ar°), *us, us, us*, wounded on the right side. — *Dakshiṇārdha* (°ṇa-ar°), *as*, m. the right side, the southern side. — *Dakshiṇārdhya, as, ā, am* (fr. the preceding), Ved. situated on the right, being on the southern side. — *Dakshiṇārha* (°ṇā-ar°), *as, ā, am*, deserving a fee, meriting a reward, worthy of a gift. — *Dakshiṇā-vat, ān, atī, at* (fr. *dakshiṇa* with lengthening of the final), Ved. able, competent, strong, fit, effective; (fr. *dakshiṇā*), giving sacrificial presents, offering large remuneration, abounding in presents, possessed of a gift, having ample rewards, piously disposed. — *Dakshiṇāvarta* (°ṇā-āv°), *as, ā, am*, turning to the right, turned towards the south; *dakshiṇāvarta ādityas*, the sun in his course from the north to the south; (*as*), m. the southern country, the Dekhan, a conch-shell with the valve opening to the right. — *Dakshiṇāvartaka* (°ṇā-āv°), *as, ikā, am*, turning to the right, turned towards the south; (*akī*), f., N. of a plant or shrub (= *vṛis'ći-kālī*); a line of bees. — *Dakshiṇā-vah, -vāṭ*, Ved. 'being borne to the right or to the south of the (Āhavanīya) fire,' epithet of the sacrificial ladle. — *Dakshiṇāvṛit* (°ṇā-āv°), *t, t, t*, Ved. turned towards the right, going round on the right. — *Dakshiṇās'ā* (°ṇa-ās'ā), f. the southern quarter, the south. — *Dakshiṇās'ā-pati, is*, m. 'the lord of the south,' epithet of Yama. — *Dakshiṇās'ā-rati, is*, m. (? *rati* for *pati*), an epithet of Agastya. — *Dakshiṇā-sad*, see *dakshiṇa-sad*. — *Dakshiṇetara* (°ṇa-it°), different from the right, other than the right, the left. — *Dakshiṇerman* (°ṇa-īrman = 2. *īrma*), *ā, ā, a*, wounded on the right side or right fore leg (as a deer). (In any other sense this compound takes the form *dakshiṇerma, as, ā, am*, e. g. *dakshiṇermam s'akaṭam*, a cart broken on the right side.) — *Dakshiṇottara* (°ṇa-ut°), *as, ā, am*, situated on the right and left, lying to the south and north, turned to the south and north. — *Dakshiṇottara-vritta*, the meridian line. — *Dakshiṇottarin* (°ṇa-ut°), *ī, iṇī, i*, Ved. being above on the right side, overhanging on the right side.

Dakshiṇā, dakshiṇena, dakshiṇe. See col. 1, under *dakshiṇa*.

Dakshiṇāhi, ind. far on the right, far in the south (with abl.).

Dakshiṇit, t, ind., Ved. on the right hand, to the right; [cf. *pra-dakshiṇit*.]

Dakshiṇī-kṛi, cl. 5. P. A. *-karoti, -kurute, -kartum*, to place on the right hand, to turn the right side towards any one (acc.), to walk round a person with the right side turned towards him (as a mark of respect). — *Dakshiṇī-kṛitya*, ind. having walked round in the above manner.

Dakshiṇīya, as, ā, am, worthy of the sacrificial fee, meriting a reward, fit for a sacrificial donation, worthy to be honoured with presents; [cf. *ā-dakshiṇīya* and *dakshiṇya*.]

Dakshiṇya, as, ā, am, Ved. = *dakshiṇīya*, meriting a sacrificial reward &c.; [cf. *dākshiṇya*.]

दक्षि **dakshi** or **dakshin** (fr. 1. *dah*), Ved. burning, blazing; (according to Sāy. = *dhakshi*), thou burnest. (In Ṛig-veda I. 141, 8, *dakshi* = *dahati*.)

दक्षिण *dakshiṇa*. See col. 1.

दगार्गल *dagārgala, am*, n. (fr. *da* = *uda* + 2. *ga* + *argala*), examining the soil in searching for wells or rules for doing so.

दगु *dagu, us,* m., N. of a man; [cf. *dāga-ryāyani.*]

दग्ध *dagdha, as, ā, am* (fr. rt. 1. *dah*), burnt, scorched, consumed by fire; (metaphorically) tormented, tortured, pained, consumed by grief, distressed; burnt by the fire of the gastric juice (as the stomach; cf. *jaṭharāgni*), famished; dry; tasteless, insipid; inauspicious; cunning (= *vi-dagdha*); (*ā*), f. the quarter where the sun remains overhead (?); a lunar day or Tithi on which it is unlucky to do anything and religious rites are prohibited; a species of plant, = *dagdhikā, dagdha-ruhā;* (*am*), n. burning, cauterizing (e. g. *agni-dagdha,* actual cautery; *kshāra-dagdha,* potential cautery, in surgery; *tvag-dagdha,* cauterizing of the skin); a species of fragrant grass, = *rohisha.* — *Dagdha-kāka, as,* m. 'a black or inauspicious crow,' a raven, or perhaps the carrion crow. — *Dagdha-tithi,* N. of a chapter of the Purāṇa-sarva-sva. — *Dagdha-mandira-sāra, as, ā, am,* one who has burned the best of mansions. — *Dagdha-maraṇa, as,* m., N. of an author. — *Dagdha-yoni, is, is, i,* having its source or origin destroyed. — *Dagdha-ratha, as,* m. = *ćitra-ratha,* N. of the chief of the Gandharvas. — *Dagdha-ruha, as,* m. 'growing in ashes,' N. of a tree, = *tilaka;* (*ā*), f., N. of a plant, = *dagdhā, dagdhikā, bhasma-rohā,* &c. — *Dagdha-varṇaka,* 'black-coloured (?),' a species of grass, = *dagdha, rohisha.* — *Dagdhākshara* (°*dha-ak*°), N. of certain letters regarded as inauspicious in poems. — *Dagdheshṭakā* (°*dha-ish*°), f. a burnt or vitrified brick. — *Dagdhodara* (°*dha-ud*°), *as, ā, am,* 'having a burnt or starving stomach,' starving; (*am*), n. 'a burnt stomach,' i. e. an empty or craving stomach.

Dagdhavya, as, ā, am, to be burnt or consumed by fire, inflammable.

Dagdhikā, f. scorched rice; N. of a plant, = *dagdhā.*

Dagdhṛi, dhā, dhṛī, dhṛi, a burner, consuming by fire, one who burns, a consumer.

Dagdhvā, ind. having burnt, having consumed.

दघ् *dagh,* cl. 4. P. *daghyati,* &c., Ved. to move, go, flow, reach, attain; to go away; (with *paśćā* or *paśćāt*) to lag behind, fall short of [cf. *a-paśćā-daghvan*]; cl. 5. P. *dagh-noti,* &c., to hurt, kill; to go, to leap; to protect; [cf. rt. *dangh* below; cf. also Gr. ταχύς, δέχομαι; Goth. *tekan,* 'to take;' Angl. Sax. *taengan,* 'to hasten;' Lat. *tango.*]

Daghna, as, ī, am (at the end of a comp.; regarded by native grammarians as an affix), reaching to, as high as; [cf. *ā-daghna, upastha-daghna, ūru-daghna, jānu-daghna,* &c.]

Dagh-van in *apaśćā-daghvan,* q. v.

दंक्ष्णु *dankshṇu, us, us, u* (fr. rt. 2. *danś*), Ved. biting, mordaceous.

दङ्घ् *dangh,* cl. 1. P. *danghati,* &c., to quit, abandon; to cherish, protect; [cf. rt. *dagh* above.]

दच्छद *daććhada.* See under *dat,* p. 399.

दण्ड् *daṇḍ,* cl. 10. P. *daṇḍayati, -yitum,* to punish, &c. (rather to be regarded as a nom. fr. *daṇḍa* below).

Daṇḍa, as, am, m. n. (fr. rt. 1. *dam,* but connected with the preceding; the neut. is rare), a stick, staff, rod, pole, cudgel, mace, club or club-shaped weapon; a sceptre; a blow with a stick, &c.; the staff given to a twice-born man at initiation or at investiture with the sacred thread, (this staff was of different lengths, the longest belonging to the Brāhmans, see Manu II. 45–47); the penis; the trunk of an elephant; an arm or leg (generally in comp. with a word signifying 'arm,' &c.; see *dor-daṇḍa, bāhu-daṇḍa*); a stalk, the stem of a tree [cf. *ud-d*° and *khara-d*°]; the handle of anything (as of a ladle, sauce-pan, fly-flap, parasol, &c.), the staff or pole of a banner or of a tent; the beam of a plough; the oar of a boat; the cross-bar or bridge of a lute or other stringed instrument which holds the strings; a churning-stick (said to be neut. only, cf. *daṇḍāhata*); a pole as a measure of length, = 4 Hastas, = 96 finger-breadths; a particular measure of time, = 60 Vi-kalās, = 360 breaths, = $\frac{1}{60}$ part of the day and night, = 24 minutes [cf. *nāḍikā*]; the stick with which an instrument is played; a particular appearance in the sky similar to a staff or rod; a particular planet, = *graha-bheda;* a particular constellation; a form of military array, a long line or column of troops [cf. *daṇḍa-vyūha*]; an uninterrupted row or series, a line [cf. *daṇḍa-pāta* and *daṇḍaka*]; a staff or sceptre as a symbol of power and sovereignty; application of power or physical force (e. g. *rājā nityam udyata-daṇḍaḥ syāt,* a king should always hold his sceptre erect, i. e. prepared to use his power; *daṇḍodyama,* raising the sceptre, exertion of power; *nyasta-daṇḍa,* laying aside the sceptre, resigning power); assault, attack, violence, (in this sense *daṇḍa* is one of the four Upāyas; *sāman,* 'negotiation,' *dāna,* 'bribery,' and *bheda,* 'sowing dissension,' constituting the other three, see *upāya*); power over, control, restraint (e. g. *mano-d*°, *vāg-d*°, *kāya-d*°, restraint of thoughts, words, and bodily actions, see Manu XII. 10; cf. *tri-daṇḍin*); power or physical force embodied, an army (e. g. *kosha-daṇḍau,* du. treasure and army); the rod as a symbol of judicial authority and punishment; punishment in general; corporal chastisement; fine, mulct, amercement; imprisonment; capital punishment, putting to death; reprimand; (Punishment personified is a son of Dharma and Kriyā; sometimes = Yama or = Śiva); standing upright or erect; N. of one of the attendants of the sun; N. of a man; N. of a prince slain by Arjuna (brother of Daṇḍa-dhara and identified with the Asura Krodha-hantṛi); N. of a son of Ikshvāku; (according to lexicographers *daṇḍa* also means) pride; a horse, a corner, an angle (?); (*ā*), f. Hedysarum Lagopodioides, = *nāga-balā;* [cf. *ćarma-d*°, *jāla-d*°, &c.] — *Daṇḍa-kandaka, as,* m. a species of bulbous plant, = *dharaṇī-kanda.* — *Daṇḍa-kartṛi, tā,* m. a punisher, chastiser. — *Daṇḍa-karman, a,* n. 'application of the rod,' infliction of punishment, chastisement. — *Daṇḍa-kala,* a kind of metre. — *Daṇḍa-kāka, as,* m. a raven; (perhaps for *dagdha-kāka,* q. v.) — *Daṇḍa-kāshṭha, am,* n. a wooden staff or pole. — *Daṇḍa-kuśa, ās,* m. pl. a various reading for the next. — *Daṇḍa-kūla, ās,* m. pl., N. of a people. — *Daṇḍa-ketu, us,* m., N. of a man. — *Daṇḍa-gaurī,* f., N. of an Apsaras. — *Daṇḍa-grahaṇa, am,* n. assumption of the (pilgrim's) staff, becoming a mendicant or ascetic. — *Daṇḍa-grāha, as,* m. a staff-bearer, (probably) N. of a man. — *Daṇḍa-ghna, as, ī, am,* striking with a stick, one who commits an assault. — *Daṇḍa-ćakra, as,* m. 'the discus of punishment,' N. of a mythical weapon; a division of an army; [cf. *daṇḍānīka.*] — *Daṇḍa-ććhadana, am,* n. a room in which utensils of various kinds are kept. — *Daṇḍa-jita, as, ā, am,* subdued by punishment. — *Daṇḍa-ḍhakkā,* f. a sort of kettle-drum, upon which the hours are struck. — *Daṇḍa-tāmrī,* f. = *tāmrī,* p. 370, col. 1. — *Daṇḍa-tva, am,* n. the state of a staff, stick, &c. — *Daṇḍa-dāsa, as,* m. 'a slave from a fine not paid,' i. e. one who has become a slave from non-payment of a debt. — *Daṇḍa-deva-kula, am,* n. 'temple of punishment,' a court of justice. — *Daṇḍa-dhara, as, ā, am,* a staff-bearer, having or carrying a staff or sceptre, having oars (as a ship); exercising judicial power, chastising, punishing, having authority to punish; (*as*), m. a king; a magistrate, judge, the supreme judge; a N. of Yama; a mendicant carrying a staff; a potter. — *Daṇḍadharādhipa* (°*ra-adh*°), *as,* m. 'the prince of sceptre-bearers,' a plenipotentiary, a king. — *Daṇḍa-dhāra, as, ā, am,* bearing the sceptre, exercising judicial power; (*as*), m. a king; a judge; an epithet of Yama; N. of a prince slain by Arjuna (brother of Daṇḍa and identified with the Asura Krodha-vardhana, enumerated among the sons of Dhṛita-rāshṭra in Mahā-bh. I. 2738); (*ās*), m. pl., N. of a barbarous people. — *Daṇḍa-dhāraṇa, am,* n. the carrying a staff (as by the Brahma-ćārin); following the order of a mendicant; chastising, punishment. — *Daṇḍa-dhārin, ī, iṇī, i,* carrying the rod, chastening, punishing. — *Daṇḍa-dhṛish, k, k, k,* carrying the staff or rod, exercising authority. — *Daṇḍa-nāyaka, as,* m. 'one who applies the rod,' a judge, magistrate, a head police-officer; a leader of a column, leader of an army, general, commander-in-chief; N. of one of the attendants of the sun. — *Daṇḍanāyaka-purusha, as,* m. a policeman, police-officer, constable, beadle. — *Daṇḍa-nipātana, am,* n. applying the rod, chastising, punishing; [cf. *daṇḍa-pātana.*] — *Daṇḍa-nīti, is,* f. application of the rod, administration of justice, judicature, the doctrine of the right administration of justice; the rule of inflicting punishment, the system of civil and military administration taught by Cāṇakya and others, polity, ethics, system of morals; an epithet of Durgā. — *Daṇḍanīti-mat, ān, atī, at,* familiar with the administration of justice. — *Daṇḍa-netṛi, tā,* m. 'one who applies the rod,' a punisher, an inflicter of punishment, a judge; *adhi-daṇḍanetṛi,* the supreme chastiser, i. e. Yama. — *Daṇḍanetṛi-tva, am,* n. the office of a judge, administration of justice. — *Daṇḍa-pa, as,* m., N. of a man. — *Daṇḍa-pakshaka, as,* m. a particular gesture or motion of the hands. — *Daṇḍa-pānśula* (?), *as,* m. a porter, a warder or door-keeper. — *Daṇḍa-pāṇi, is, is, i,* staff-handed, bearing a staff or rod; (*is*), m. an epithet of Yama; N. of a leader of two of the troops of the god Śiva in Kāśī (identified with the Yaksha Hari-keśa); N. of the father of Go-pā, the wife of Śākya-muni; N. of a prince, grandfather of Kshemaka; [cf. *khaṇḍa-pāṇi.*] — *Daṇḍa-pāṇi-vara-pradāna, am,* n., N. of the forty-fourth chapter of the Jñāna-khaṇḍa or second part of the Skanda-Purāṇa. — *Daṇḍa-pāta, as,* m. 'the falling of the stick' [cf. *dāṇḍa-pātā*]; dropping one line in a manuscript. — *Daṇḍa-pātana, am,* n. applying the rod, punishing, punishment; [cf. *daṇḍa-nipātana.*] — *Daṇḍa-pātin, ī, inī, i,* 'letting fall the stick or rod,' punishing, chastising, fining, mulcting. — *Daṇḍa-pārushya, am,* n. 'stick-assault,' actual violence, assault and battery (as a title of jurisprudence); cruel or harsh infliction of punishment, (one of the seven vices of kings and rulers.) — *Daṇḍa-pāla* or *daṇḍa-pālaka, as,* m. 'superintendent of punishment or of the administration of justice,' a head magistrate or judge; a door-keeper, a porter; a kind of fish (= *ardha-śaphara, śakula;* commonly *dāṇḍikā*). — *Daṇḍapāla-tā,* f. the administration of justice. — *Daṇḍa-pāśaka* or *daṇḍa-pāśika, as,* m. 'holding the fetters or noose of punishment,' a head police-officer, policeman; a hangman, an executioner. — *Daṇḍa-pāsika* (?) = *paurika,* q. v. — *Daṇḍa-piṅgalaka, ās,* m., N. of a people to the north of Madhya-deśa. — *Daṇḍa-poṇa, am,* n. (*poṇa* = *pavana*), a strainer or filtering machine with a handle. — *Daṇḍa-praṇayana, am,* n. 'infliction of punishment,' N. of a chapter of the Purāṇa-sarva-sva by Halāyudha. — *Daṇḍa-praṇāma, as,* m. a stiff bow, bowing without bending the body like a stick. — *Daṇḍa-badha, as,* m. 'death by punishment,' capital punishment. — *Daṇḍa-bāladhi, is,* m. an elephant ('having a tail like a stick'). — *Daṇḍa-bāhu, us, us, u,* 'stick-armed,' carrying a stick or staff; (*us*), m., N. of one of the attendants of Skanda. — *Daṇḍa-bhaṅga, as,* m. 'omission of punishment,' non-execution of a sentence, reprieve, escape. — *Daṇḍa-bhaya, am,* n. fear of the rod. — *Daṇḍa-bhīti, is,* f. dread of punishment. — *Daṇḍa-bhṛit, t, t, t,* carrying a staff or stick; (*t*), m. a potter. — *Daṇḍa-māṇava* or *daṇḍa-mānava, as,* m. 'a staff-man,' a staff-bearer, an ascetic, one who bears a staff; a chief or leader. — *Daṇḍa-mātaṅga,* Tabernæmontana Coronaria (= *piṇḍa-tagara*). — *Daṇḍa-mukha, as,* m. the leader of an army, a general, a commander-in-chief; [cf. *daṇḍa-nāyaka.*] — *Daṇḍa-yātrā,* f. a solemn or festive procession, moving in state or with attendants, especially a bridal procession; warlike expedition, subjection or conquest of a region or quarter (= *dig-vijaya*). — *Daṇḍa-yāma, as,* m. a day; an epithet of Yama; of Agastya; (also written *daṇḍā-yāma.*) — *Daṇḍa-yoga, as,* m. infliction of punishment. — *Daṇḍa-leśa, am,* n. a small fine. — 1. *daṇḍa-vat, ān, atī, at,* having a stick, carrying a staff; furnished with a handle; having a large army. — 2. *daṇḍa-vat,* ind. like a stick, erect or upright as a stick; prostrate, falling or lying prostrate; *daṇḍa-vat praṇamya,* bowing like a stick; [cf. *daṇḍa-praṇāma.*] — *Daṇḍa-vādin, ī, inī, i,* uttering a reprimand, rebuking, censuring, threatening with punishment or castigation; (*ī*), m. a door-keeper, warder; [cf. *daṇḍa-vāsin.*] — *Daṇḍa-vārksha, am,* n. a particular posture, a mode of sitting. — *Daṇḍa-vāsika, as,* m. a door-keeper. — *Daṇḍa-vāsin, ī,* m. a door-keeper, warder, chamberlain; the magistrate or head of a village. — *Daṇḍa-vāhin, ī,* m. a police-officer. — *Daṇḍa-vikalpa, as,* m. 'alternative of punishment,' discretionary punishment or fine. — *Daṇḍa-vidhi, is,* m. criminal law; rule or mode of punishment. — *Daṇḍa-viśesha, as,* m. kind or degree of punishment. — *Daṇḍa-vishkambha, as,* m. a post or a stake to which is fastened the string that works the churning-stick. — *Daṇḍa-vīrya, as,* m., N. of a prince. — *Daṇḍa-vṛikshaka, as,* m. the plant Tithymalus Antiquorum (= *snuhī*). — *Daṇḍa-vyūha, as,* m. drawing up or arraying an army in long lines or columns. — *Daṇḍa-vrata-dhara, as, ā, am,* exercising judicial power, decreeing punishment, punishing. — *Daṇḍa-śarman, ā,* m., N. of a prince; (also read *datta-śarman.*) — *Daṇḍa-śāstra, am,* n. the criminal law. — *Daṇḍa-saṅkhyā,* f., N. of a chapter of the Purāṇa-sarva-sva. — *Daṇḍa-sena, as,* m., N. of a prince, son of Vishvak-sena. — *Daṇḍa-hasta, as,* m. 'staff-handed,' 'a staff-bearer;' epithet of the god of death; a door-keeper, warder; (*as, ā* or *ī*), m. f. the plant Tabernæmontana Coronaria; (*am*), n. the flower of this plant. — *Daṇḍākhya* (°*ḍa-ākh*°), *as, ā, am,* called after a staff; having the name Daṇḍa; (*am*), n., N. of a place of pilgrimage; a hall with two wings, one of which faces towards the north, the other towards the east. — *Daṇḍāghāta* (°*ḍa-āgh*°), *as,* m. a blow with a stick or staff. — *Daṇḍājina* (°*ḍa-aj*°), *am,* n. 'staff and skin' (as mere outer signs of devotion); hypocrisy, deceit, fraud, cheating, roguery; [cf. *dāṇḍājinika.*] — *Daṇḍājñā* (°*ḍa-āj*°), f. judicial sentence. — *Daṇḍā-daṇḍi,* ind. 'stick against stick' in fighting, single-stick, cudgelling, fighting with sticks and staves. — *Daṇḍādhipa, as,* or *daṇḍādhipati* (°*ḍa-adh*°), *is,* m. a superior judge, supreme magistrate. — *Daṇḍānīka* (°*ḍa-an*°), *am,* n. a division of an army, a detachment; [cf. *daṇḍa-ćakra.*] — *Daṇḍāpatānaka* (°*ḍa-ap*°), *as,* m. tetanus, lock-jaw, spasm. — *Daṇḍāmitrā* (°*ḍa-am*°), f., N. of a place; [cf. *dattāmitra* or *dattāmitrā.*] — *Daṇḍā-yāma* = *daṇḍa-yāma.* — *Daṇḍārta* (°*ḍa-ār*°), N. of a sacred bathing-place. — *Daṇḍārha* (°*ḍa-ar*°), *as, ā, am,* deserving punishment. — *Daṇḍālasikā* (°*ḍa-al*°), f. the cholera. — *Daṇḍāśrama* (°*ḍa-āś*°), *as,* m. the order of the staff, condition of a pilgrim. — *Daṇḍāśramin* (°*ḍa-āś*°), *ī,* m. assuming the pilgrim's staff, a devotee. — *Daṇḍāsana* (°*ḍa-as*° or *-ās*°), *am,* n. a sort of arrow. — *Daṇḍāstra* (°*ḍa-as*°), *am,* n. the stick-weapon or 'the weapon of punishment,' N. of a fabulous weapon. — *Daṇḍāhata* (°*ḍa-āh*°), *am,* n. 'struck with the churning-stick,' buttermilk. — *Daṇḍotpala* (°*ḍa-ut*°), *am,* n. a species of plant (commonly Ḍānipolā and Ḍānakuni) with yellow, red, and white flowers; (according to some, the one with white flowers is called Daṇḍotpalā.)

Daṇḍaka, as, am, m. n. a stick, staff, handle, staff of a banner &c., see *daṇḍa;* a species of plant; a line, row, uninterrupted series; a sort of metre the stanza of which may extend from 27 × 4 to 999 × 4 syllables; N. of a work; (*as, ā, am*), m. f. n., N. of a district in the Dekhan between the Nermadā and Godavarī rivers, which in the time of Rāma-ćandra was a forest and celebrated as a place of pilgrimage; (*ās*), m. pl. the above district and its inhabitants; (*as*), m., N. of a prince who was son of Ikshvāku and connected with the Daṇḍaka district; N. of a man; (*ikā*), f. a stick, a staff; a row, line, series; a rope; a string of pearls; [cf. *yashṭi.*] — *Daṇḍakāraṇya* (°*ka-ar*°), *am,* n. the Daṇḍaka forest, see above; N. of a part of the Skanda-Purāṇa. — *Daṇḍakāraṇya-prasthāna, am,* n., N. of a part of the Abhirāma-maṇi-nāṭaka. — *Daṇḍakālasaka* (°*ka-al*°), *as,* m., N. of a man.

Daṇḍana, as, m., Ved. a cane? (*am*), n. beating, punishing, chastising, inflicting punishment (e. g. *adharma-daṇḍana,* unjust punishment).

Daṇḍanīya, as, ā, am, punishable, to be chastised, deserving punishment, liable to a fine.

Daṇḍaya, nom. P. *daṇḍayati, -yitum,* to punish, chastise, to fine, amerce (with acc. of the person and of the punishment inflicted).

Daṇḍāya, nom. A. *daṇḍāyate,* &c., (common in Bengālī for) to stand erect.

Daṇḍāyamāna, as, ā, am, (common in Bengālī for) standing erect.

Daṇḍika, as, ā, am, carrying a stick, punishing, one who chastises; (*as*), m. a staff-bearer, mace-bearer [cf. *dāṇḍika*]; a fish, Cyprinus Dankena, commonly called Ḍānikaṇā Māća; (*ā*), f., see *daṇḍaka.*

Daṇḍita, as, ā, am, punished, chastised, amerced, sentenced, mulcted, fined.

Daṇḍin, ī, inī, i, having or bearing a staff or stick [cf. *tri-daṇḍin*]; (*ī*), m. a Brāhman of the fourth order or in the fourth stage of his life; a religious mendicant or Bhikshu carrying a staff; N. of a particular order of mendicants deriving their origin from Śaṅkarāćārya; a Jaina ascetic; a door-keeper, warder, porter; an oarsman, boatman; a N. of Yama; of Mañju-śrī; of a son of Dhṛita-rāshṭra; of the author of the Kāvyādarśa; of the author of the Daśa-kumāra-ćarita; a species of plant; [cf. *damanaka.*] — *Daṇḍi-mat, ān, atī, at,* possessing staff-bearers, having club-bearers. — *Daṇḍi-muṇḍa, as,* m. 'carrying a staff and having the head shaved,' epithet of Śiva. — *Daṇḍimuṇḍīśvara* (? for *daṇḍimuṇḍeśvara*), a form of Śiva; N. of a Muni.

Daṇḍiman, ā, m. (abstract noun fr. *daṇḍa*), the state or condition of a staff, rod, &c.

Daṇḍya, as, ā, am, to be punished, punishable, deserving punishment, to be fined (with acc. of the punishment inflicted, or in comp., e. g. *sarva-sva-daṇḍya,* to be fined in all one's property).

दण्डरी *daṇḍarī,* f. = *ḍaṅgarī,* a species of cucumber.

दण्डार *daṇḍāra, as,* m. a carriage, vehicle; a raft, boat; a potter's wheel; a bow or any other instrument for shooting arrows or darts; an elephant in rut, a furious or intoxicated elephant.

दत् *dat* (perhaps fr. rt. *ad,* to eat, the initial being dropped, as in *khādana,* a tooth, fr. rt. *khād* and φαγόνες fr. φαγ; or according to others fr. rt. 3. *dā,* to cut), optionally substituted for *danta,* a tooth, in the acc. pl. and remaining weak and middle cases (Pāṇ. VI. 1, 63; Vopa-deva III. 39); the form *dat* occurs frequently at the end of compounds, the nom. case ending in *an* as in pres. participles; [cf. *ubhayato-dat, su-dat, a-dat,* &c.] — *Daććhada, as,* m. 'the covering of the teeth,' the lip, (chiefly in comp., see *dashṭa-daććhada*); [cf. *danta-ććhada.*] — *Dat-vat, ān, atī, at,* Ved. furnished with teeth, biting; *dat-vatī rajjuḥ,* 'a rope with teeth,' = a serpent or snake.

Datka in *adatka,* q. v.

दत्त 1. *datta, as, ā, am* (fr. rt. 1. *dā,* to give; cf. 1. *dad*), given, granted, presented, made over, assigned; placed, extended, stretched forth; (*as*), m. a given son, i. e. a son given away by his natural parents to persons engaging to adopt him [cf. *dattaka* and *datrima*]; a common N. or title of a man of the Vaiśya or third tribe, (generally in comp. with a preceding word, e. g. *vasu-datta, deva-datta,* &c., but *datta* sometimes stands alone, at present the title is common to the Kāyastha or writer class); N. of a man, brother of Dur-vāsas; of a son of Atri, = *dattātreya;* (with Jainas) N. of a son of Agni-siṅha and the seventh black Vāsu-deva; of a son of Rājādhideya Śūra; one of the seven sages in the second Manv-antara; (*ā*), f., N. of several women; (*am*), n. a gift, a donation. — *Datta-tīrtha-kṛit, t,* m., N. of the eighth Arhat of the past Ut-sarpiṇī. — *Datta-nṛityopahāra* (°*ya-up*°), *as, ā, am,* complimented with a dance. — *Datta-prāṇa, as, ā, am,* one who has given up or sacrificed life. — *Datta-bhujaṅga-stotra, am,* n. and *datta-mahiman, ā,* m., N. of two works of Śaṅkarāćārya. — *Datta-mārga, as, ā, am,* given way to, having the road ceded. — *Datta-vat, ān, atī, at,* one who has given. — *Datta-vara, as, ā, am,* allowed to choose a boon; granted as a boon. — *Datta-śatru, us,* or *datta-śarman, ā,* m., N. of a son of Rājādhideya Śūra. — *Datta-śulkā,* f. a bride for whom a sum of money or dowry has been paid. — *Datta-hasta, as, ā, am,* having a hand given for support, supported. — *Dattātman* (°*ta-āt*°), *ā, ā, a,* one who has given himself, self-given; (with *putra*) an orphan or a son deserted by his parents who gives himself to persons disposed to adopt him as their child; (*ā*), m., N. of one of the Viśve Devās. — *Dattātreya* (°*ta-āt*°), *as,* m., N. of a sage, son of Atri and Anasūyā, who favoured Arjuna Kārtavīrya, (see Mahā-bh. Śānti-parva 1751; according to one legend, Atri performed a very severe penance by which the three gods Brahmā, Vishṇu, and Śiva were propitiated and became in portions of themselves severally his sons Soma, Datta, and Dur-vāsas); N. of an author mentioned in the Ānanda-laharī or Saundarya-laharī by Śaṅkara. — *Dattātreyāshṭottara-śata-nāma-stotra, am,* n., N. of a chapter of the Brahmāṇḍa-Purāṇa. — *Dattātreyīya, am,* n. the story of Dattātreya. — *Dattādatta* (°*ta-ad*°), *as, ā, am,* given and received. — *Dattādara* (°*ta-ād*°), *as, ā, am,* showing respect, respectful; treated with respect. — *Dattānapakarman* (°*ta-an*°), *a,* n. non-resumption of gifts. — *Dattāpahṛita* (°*ta-ap*°), *as, ā, am,* given and taken again. — *Dattāpradānika* (°*ta-a-pr*°), *as, ā, am,* relating to the non-delivery of a gift; (*am*), n. non-delivery or resumption of gifts, one of the eighteen titles of law. — *Dattāmitra* (°*ta-am*°), *as,* m., N. of a prince of the Sauvīras; (*as, ā*), m. f., N. of a district; [cf. *daṇḍāmitrā.*] — *Dattāravadhāna* (°*ta-av*°), *as, ā, am,* attentive. — *Dattāsana* (°*ta-ās*°), *as, ā, am,* having a seat given, requested to sit. — *Dattairaṇḍa-pallaka* (°*ta-er*°), N. of a district in the Dekhan. — *Dattopanishad* (°*ta-up*°), *t,* f., N. of an Upanishad; (also written *śrīmad-dattopanishad,* q. v.)

Dattaka, as, m. (scil. *putra*), a son given away by his natural parents to persons engaging to adopt him; one of the twelve heirs acknowledged by the old Hindū law; N. of the father of Māgha; N. of the author of the Vaiśikādhikaraṇa; a familiar diminutive of the names of persons ending with *datta.* — *Dattaka-ćandrikā* and *dattaka-mīmāṅsā,* f., N. of two legal works.

Datti, is, f. a gift, donation, offering.

Dattika, dattiya, and *dattila, as,* m. familiar diminutives of the names of persons ending in *datta.*

Datteya, as, m., N. of Indra.

दत्त 2. *datta, as, ā, am* (fr. 5. *dā*), preserved, guarded, protected.

दत्तोलि *dattoli, is,* m., N. of a son of Pulastya, one of the seven sages in the second Manv-antara.

दत्र *datra.* See below under rt. 1. *dad.*

दद् 1. *dad,* a reduplicated form substituted for rt. 1. *dā,* to give, before certain affixes and terminations (Pāṇ. VI. 4, 126; VII. 4, 46; VIII. 2, 38), and by some grammarians given as a separate rt.: cl. 1. A. *dadate*, &c., to give, (see rt. 1. *dā*.)

Datra, am, n. (perhaps more correctly *dattra*), Ved. gift, donation; [cf. *a-datrayā* and *go-datra*.] — *Datra-vat, ān, atī, at*, Ved. rich in gifts, giving abundantly.

Datrima, as, ā, am, received by gift, produced or effected by gifts; (*as*), m. a slave or a son received by gift; (see Manu VIII. 415; IX. 141.)

2. *dad*, giving, in *āyur-dad*.

Dada, as, ā, am, giving; [cf. *abhayan-dada*.]

Dadat, at, atī, at (pres. part. of rt. 1. *dā*), giving, presenting.

Dadana, am, n. gift, giving, donation.

Dadi, is, is, i, Ved. giving, bestowing, distributing (with acc.); [cf. Pāṇ. II. 3, 69.]

Dadiṭṛi, tā, trī, tṛi, Ved. a giver, giving; (according to others) a preserver, preserving; a possessor; [cf. 5. *dā*.]

Dadivas, vān, dushī, vas, who or what has given.

ददद *dadada*, an onomatopoetic word for the roaring of thunder.

ददरि *dadari*, N. of a river. — *Dadari-saṅgama*, N. of a place mentioned in the Rasika-ramaṇa by Raghu-nātha.

ददाश्वस् *dadāśvas, vān, ushī, vas* (perf. part. fr. rt. 1. *dāś*), worshipping, serving the gods, giving, having given or bestowed.

ददृक्षेण्य *dadṛikshenya, as, ā, am* (fr. rt. 1. *dṛiś*), Ved. worth seeing, worthy to be seen, (Pāṇ. III. 4, 14; according to some *didṛikshenya*, q. v., is the only correct form.)

Dadṛiśāna-pavi, is, m., Ved. having the track of the wheels visible; epithet of Agni; (Sāy.) having a thunderbolt or weapon visible.

Dadṛiśivas or *dadṛiśvas, vān, ushī, vas*, having seen, having looked at.

ददृत् *dadṛit, t, t, t* (reduplicated form fr. rt. *dṛī*), tearing, splitting, bursting out.

Dadru, us, or *ū, ūs*, m. f. [cf. *dardru*], a cutaneous eruption or rash, herpes; a kind of leprosy, (or according to others) a ringworm; a tortoise. — *Dadru-ghna* or *dadrū-ghna, as, ī, am*, destroying or removing cutaneous eruptions; (*as*), m. ringworm-shrub, Cassia Tora or Alata; Psoralea Corylifolia, (commonly Hākuć; the seeds are used as a remedy for cutaneous diseases.)

Dadruka, as, m. cutaneous eruption or scab, leprosy.

Dadruṇa or *dadrūṇa, as, ā, am*, or *dadru-rogin, ī, iṇī, i*, herpetic, afflicted with cutaneous diseases or ringworm; [cf. *dardru-rogin*.]

दध् *dadh* (reduplicated form substituted for rt. 1. *dhā* before certain affixes and terminations; also given as a distinct rt.), cl. 1. A. *dadhate*, &c., to hold, possess, retain; to give, present, assign, make over; (see rt. 1. *dhā*.)

Dadha, as, ā, am, holding, having, possessing, giving; [cf. *ilā-d°*.]

Dadhat, at, atī, at (pres. part. of rt. 1. *dhā*), having, holding, possessing.

Dadhāna, as, ā, am (pres. part.), having, holding, possessing.

1. *dadhi, is, is, i*, Ved. presenting, giving; preserving, keeping (with acc.); holding, having, possessing, bearing; (*i*), n. a house, an abode.

दधन् *dadhan*, substituted for 2. *dadhi* below, in the weakest cases (e. g. inst. *dadhnā*, dat. *dadhne*, abl. gen. *dadhnas*, loc. *dadhni* or *dadhani*). — *Dadhan-vat, ān, atī, at*, Ved. containing coagulated milk.

दधि 2. *dadhi, i*, n. (perhaps a reduplicated form fr. rt. *dhe*, to drink; cf. *dadhan* above), milk thickened or coagulated spontaneously by heat, thick sour milk, commonly called *dahī*, (it is a general article of food in high estimation among the Hindūs, and regarded as a remedy or preventive of many disorders; it differs from curds in not having the whey separated from it); turpentine, the resin of the Shorea Robusta; [cf. Goth. *daddyan*, 'to suckle.'] — *Dadhi-karṇa, as*, m., N. of a Nāga; N. of a cat in the Pańća-tantra. — *Dadhi-kulyā*, f. a stream of coagulated milk. — *Dadhi-kūrćikā*, f. a mixture of boiled and coagulated milk; see *kūrćaka*. — *Dadhi-kra, as*, m., N. of a man; [cf. the following.] — *Dadhi-krā, ās*, m., Ved., N. of a mythical being often mentioned in the Veda, and the actual subject of Ṛig-veda IV. 38, 39, 40; VII. 44; (he is described as a kind of divine horse, and probably, like Tārkshya, is a personification of the morning Sun; sometimes he is considered as a creation of heaven and earth, sometimes of Mitra-Varuṇa, and is invoked in the morning, together with Agni, Ushas, and the Aśvins; the N. is probably derived fr. 2. *dadhi* and rt. 1. *kṛī*, to scatter, in allusion to the rising sun spreading dew and hoar frost like milk, but Mahī-dhara and Yāska explain it as if fr. 1. *dadhi* and rt. *kram*, i. e. one who bears his rider and advances, see Nirukta II. 27: in Nigh. I. 14, *dadhi-krā* is given as one of the synonyms of *aśva*, a horse.) — *Dadhi-krāvan, ā*, m., Ved. = *dadhi-krā*. — *Dadhi-gharma, as*, m., Ved. a warm beverage made of inspissated milk. — *Dadhi-ćāra, as*, m. the churning-stick. — *Dadhi-ja, as, ā, am*, produced from thickened or coagulated milk; (*am*), n. fresh butter. — *Dadhi-drapsa, as*, m., Ved. a drop or globule of thickened milk. — *Dadhi-dhenu, us*, f. a quantity of thickened milk representing or equivalent to a cow given as an offering to the priests at a sacrifice; N. of the 105th chapter of the Varāha-Purāṇa. — *Dadhidhenu-vidhi, is*, m., N. of the 168th chapter of the second part of the Bhavishya-Purāṇa. — *Dadhi-nadī*, f., N. of a river. — *Dadhi-parṇa, as*, m., N. of a saint. — *Dadhi-puććha, as*, m., N. of a jackal. — *Dadhi-pushpikā*, f. the plant Clitoria Ternatea, = *aparājitā*. — *Dadhi-pushpī*, f., N. of a plant, = *kolaśimbī*. — *Dadhi-pūraṇa, as*, m., N. of a Nāga. — *Dadhi-pūrva-mukha, as*, m. = *dadhi-mukha*, N. of a monkey, ('in whose name the word *mukha* is preceded by *dadhi*.') — *Dadhi-phala, as*, m. the elephant or wood-apple, Feronia Elephantum, (the fruit having the acid taste of coagulated milk.) — *Dadhi-bhāṇḍa, am*, n. a vessel for holding coagulated milk, a pail. — *Dadhi-maṇḍa, as*, m. the liquid part of curdled milk, whey. — *Dadhi-maṇḍoda* (°*ḍa-uda*), *as*, m. the sea of whey. — *Dadhi-manthana, am*, n. the churning of coagulated milk. — *Dadhi-mukha, as*, m. a kind of serpent, N. of a Nāga; N. of a monkey, brother-in-law of Su-grīva; N. of a Yaska. — *Dadhimukha-śrāva, as*, m., N. of the fifty-seventh chapter of the Sundara-kāṇḍa of the Rāmāyaṇa. — *Dadhi-vaktra, as*, m., N. of a monkey, brother-in-law of Su-grīva. — *Dadhi-vat, ān, atī, at*, Ved. having coagulated milk, prepared with thick sour milk. — *Dadhi-varga, as*, m., N. of a chapter in the medical work called Bhāva-prakāśa. — *Dadhi-vāmana-prayoga, as*, m., N. of a chapter of the Tantra-sāra. — *Dadhivāmana-mantra, ās*, m. pl., N. of a chapter of the Tantra-sāra. — *Dadhi-vāri, is, is, i*, containing coagulated milk for water (as a sea). — *Dadhi-vāhana, as*, m., N. of a prince, son of Aṅga and father of Divi-ratha. — *Dadhi-vidarbha, ās*, m. pl., N. of a people; (various reading for *dasī-vidarbha*.) — *Dadhi-śoṇa, as*, m. a monkey. — *Dadhi-saktu, avas*, m. pl. barley-meal mixed with thickened milk. — *Dadhi-sambhara, as, ā, am*, prepared or produced from thickened milk. — *Dadhi-sara, as*, m. the skim of coagulated milk. — *Dadhi-sāra, as*, m. fresh butter. — *Dadhi-skanda, as*, m., N. of a Tīrtha. — *Dadhi-sneha, as*, m. the oily skim of coagulated milk. — *Dadhi-sveda, as*, m. buttermilk. — *Dadhy-ańć, aṅ*, m. (acc. *dadhyańćam*, inst. *dadhīćā*, &c.), Ved., N. of a Ṛishi or of a mythical being, called in Ṛig-veda I. 80, 16, and 117, 22, son of Atharvan; (the N. properly denotes 'sprinkling or bestowing thick milk' [cf. *ghṛitāćī*]; and the legends concerning him were probably originally connected with those of Dadhi-krā; he is described as having the head of a horse given to him by the Aśvins, with which he taught them the Madhu-vidyā and revealed to them where the Soma of Tvashṭṛi was concealed; according to Ṛig-veda I. 84, 13, Indra slew ninety times nine Vṛitras with his bones converted into a thunderbolt; a portion of the latter part of the Yajur-veda is ascribed to Dadhy-ańć, and he and his father are regarded as the first founders of sacrifice.) — *Dadhy-anna, am*, n. rice prepared with *dadhi*. — *Dadhy-ākara, as*, m. the sea of inspissated milk. — *Dadhy-āśir, īr, īr, īr*, Ved. mixed with coagulated milk (as Soma). — *Dadhy-āhva* or *dadhy-āhvaya, as*, m. the resin of the Pinus Longifolia. — *Dadhy-uttara* or *dadhyuttaraka, am*, n. the skim of curdled milk, whey. — *Dadhy-uda, as, ā, am*, = *dadhi-vāri* above. — *Dadhy-odana, as*, m. boiled rice mixed with coagulated milk.

Dadhika (at the end of adj. comp.) = *dadhi*.

Dadhittha, as, m. the wood-apple, Feronia Elephantum, the wood of which is not allowed to be used in sacrifices; [cf. *dadhi-phala, kapittha, dādittha*.] — *Dadhittha-rasa, as*, m. or *dadhitthākhya* (°*tha-ākh*°), *as, am*, m. n. the resin of the above tree.

Dadhishāyya, as, m. clarified butter; [cf. *didhishāyya*.]

Dadhisya, nom. P. *dadhisyati*, &c., to wish for thick milk; [cf. *dadhīya* and *dadhyasya* below.]

Dadhīća, as, m. (a later and corrupt form of *dadhy-ańć*, col. 2), the N. of a Ṛishi or sage celebrated for having devoted himself to death that the gods might be armed with his bones, (his story is told in Mahā-bh. III. 8695; the gods being oppressed by the Kālakeya Asuras, solicited from the sage his bones, and with them Tvashṭṛi fabricated the thunderbolt with which Indra slew Vṛitra and routed the Asuras; the Saras-vatī receives his generative energy, from which springs Sāras-vata.) — *Dadhīća-kshupa-saṃvāda, as*, m., N. of the thirty-fifth chapter of the Liṅga-Purāṇa.

Dadhīći, is, m. = *dadhīća*. — *Dadhīćy-asthi*, n. Dadhīći's bones, the thunderbolt; the diamond, (the latter being regarded as similar in nature to the thunderbolt.)

Dadhīya, nom. P. *dadhīyati*, &c., to like sour curds.

Dadhyasya, nom. P. *dadhyasyati*, &c., to long for thick or coagulated milk; [cf. *dadhisya* and *dadhīya*.]

Dadhyānī, f., N. of a medicinal plant, = *sudarśanā*.

दधृष् *dadhṛish, k, k, k*, m. f. n. (reduplicated form of rt. *dhṛish*), Ved. firm, strong, bold. — *Dadhṛik*, ind. firmly, strongly, boldly; (according to some, this word is to be referred to rt. *dṛiṅh*.)

Dadhṛisha, as, ā, am, Ved. courageous, bold, fighting bravely.

Dadhṛishvaṇi, is, is, i, = *dadhṛisha*.

दध्न *dadhna, as*, m. an epithet of Yama.

दध्यञ्च् *dadhy-ańć*, &c. See bottom of col. 2.

दन् 1. *dan*, Ved., explained by Sāyaṇa as a participle fr. rt. 1. *dā* = *dadat* or *dātṛi*, giving, bestowing; modern scholars connect this word with *pati* and explain *patir-dam* as a transposition of *dam-pati*, q. v.

दन् 2. *dan*, considered by some as a Vedic root, from which they derive the Desid. *didāṅsate* (referred by Pāṇ. III. 1, 6, to rt. *dān*, q. v.) and other forms; the meaning is said to be straight, to straighten; to correct. (In Ṛig-veda I. 174, 2, *danas* is said by Yāska to = *dāna-manasas*, liberal-minded, disposed to give, see Nirukta VI. 31; but according to Sāy., *danas* = *adamayas*, thou hast humbled, or by transposition of the letters *ana-das*.)

दनायुस् *danāyus, us,* f., N. of one of the daughters of Daksha, married to Kaśyapa; (*ūs*), m. (?), N. of the supposed father (?) of the Dānavas; [cf. *danu*.]

दनीध्वंस *danīdhvaṇsa*, an adj. formed fr. Intens. of rt. *dhvaṇs*.

दनु *danu, us,* f., N. of one of the daughters of Daksha, wife of Kaśyapa, and mother of the demons called Dānavas, the Titans of Hindū mythology; the number of these Dānavas is stated to be 40 in Mahā-bh. I. 252, but 100 &c. are reckoned in other places; (*us*), m., N. of a son of Śrī, also called Dānava; (he was originally very handsome, but having offended Indra, was changed by him into a deformed monster; see *kabandha*.) — *Danu-ja, as,* or *danu-sambhava, as,* or *danu-sūnu, us,* m. a son of Danu, a Dānava. — *Danuja-dvish, ṭ,* or *danujāri* (°*ja-ari*), *is,* m. an enemy of the Dānavas, a god, a deity.

Danusha, as, m. (?) a Rākshasa.

दन्त *danta, as,* m. (for etym. see *dat*, p. 399, col. 2), a tooth, tusk, fang; an elephant's tusk, ivory; the point of an arrow; the peak of a mountain, the side or ridge of a mountain; (*ī*), f. a medicinal plant yielding a pungent oil, commonly Danti, Croton Polyandrum or Croton Tiglium [cf. *danta-mūlikā* and *dantinī*]; at the end of an adj. comp. the fem. of *danta* may end in *ā* or *ī*; [cf. *ibha-dantā, kuḍmala-dantī, krūra-dantī,* &c.: cf. also Zend *dañt-an*, 'tooth;' Gr. ὀ-δούς, ὀ-δοντ, Æol. pl. ἔδοντες; Lat. *dens;* Lith. *dant-i-s;* Goth. *tunth-u-s;* Angl. Sax. *todh;* Old Germ. *zant, zand, zan;* Cambro-Brit. *dant;* Hib. *dead*.] — *Danta-karshaṇa, as, ī, am,* contracting the teeth, i. e. setting them on edge; (*as*), m. the common lime, Citrus Acida. — *Danta-kāra, as,* m. an artist who works in ivory. — *Danta-kāshṭha, am,* n. a piece of stick or small twig of particular trees used as a tooth-brush or chewed to cleanse the teeth; cleaning the teeth in this manner; (*as*), m., N. of various trees, the wood of which is used for cleaning the teeth; Flacourtia Sapida (= *vi-kaṅkata*); Asclepias Gigantea; Ficus Indica (= *vaṭa*); Acacia Catechu; Pongamia Glabra; Terminalia Alata; [cf. *danta-dhāvana*.] — *Danta-kāshṭhaka, as,* m. the shrub Tabernæmontana Coronaria (= *āhulya*). — *Dantakāshṭhā-bhakshaṇa* (°*ṭha-a-bh*°), *am,* n., N. of the 128th chapter of the Vārāha-Purāṇa. — *Danta-kumāra, as,* m., N. of a man. — *Danta-krūram,* ind. cruelly or fearfully on the teeth, fearfully with or by the teeth (e. g. to seize or strike a person in this manner). — *Dantagrāhi-tā,* f. the state of causing injury to the teeth. — *Danta-grāhin, ī, iṇī, i,* injuring the teeth, causing them to decay &c. — *Danta-gharsha, as,* m. chattering or grinding of the teeth; [cf. *danta-saṅgharsha* and *danta-harsha*.] — *Danta-ghāta, as,* m. 'a blow with the teeth,' a bite [cf. *danta-vighāta*]; N. of a man. — *Danta-ćāla, as,* m. looseness of the teeth. — *Danta-ććhada, as,* m. 'the covering of the teeth,' a lip [cf. *dać-ćhada* and *daśana-ććhada*]; (*ā*), f. Momordica Monadelpha. — *Dantaććhadopamā* (°*da-up*°), f. Momordica Monadelpha, (to the red fruit of which the lips are often compared.) — *Danta-jāta* = *jāta-danta, as, ā, am,* 'having teeth,' a child who is teething or whose teeth are just appearing; (*a-dantajāta*, having no teeth.) — *Danta-jāha, am,* n. the root of a tooth. — *Danta-darśana, am,* n. showing the teeth (as a dog does). — *Danta-dhāvana, am,* n. cleaning or washing the teeth; a tooth-brush or fibrous stick for cleaning the teeth, or a piece of wood chewed for that purpose [cf. *danta-kāshṭha*]; (*as*), m., N. of various trees, the wood of which is used for cleaning the teeth, Acacia Catechu, Mimusops Elengi (= *vakula*); N. of a chapter of the Purāṇa-sarva-sva by Halāyudha. — *Dantadhāvanaka, as,* m. a species of tree. — *Dantadhāvana-prakaraṇa, am,* n., N. of a chapter of the Parāśara-smṛiti-vyākhyā by Mādhava. — *Dantadhāvana-vidhi, is,* m., N. of a chapter of the Smṛiti-kaumudī. — *Danta-pattra, am,* n. a kind of ear-ring. — *Danta-pattraka, am,* n. a kind of jasmine (= *kunda*), Jasminum Pubescens, (the petals or leaves of the flower resembling teeth in colour and shape, and are often so compared in poetry.) — *Danta-pavana, am,* n. a dentifrice, or a small piece of wood taken to clean the teeth; [cf. *danta-kāshṭha* and *danta-dhāvana*.] — *Danta-pāta, as,* m. the falling out of the teeth. — *Danta-pālī,* f. the gum. — *Danta-puppuṭa* or *danta-puppuṭaka, as,* m. gum-boil. — *Danta-pura, am,* n. 'the town of Buddha's tooth,' N. of the capital of the Kaliṅgas. — *Danta-pushpa, as,* m. the plant Strychnos Potatorum, the flower of which is compared to a tooth; (*am*), n. the fruit of the above plant. — *Danta-prakshālana, am,* n. cleaning the teeth; any instrument or means for cleaning the teeth; [cf. *danta-kāshṭha, danta-dhāvana, danta-pavana*.] — *Danta-phala, us,* m. Feronia Elephantum, = *kapittha* [cf. *dadhi-phala*]; (*ā*), f. long pepper; (*am*), n. = *danta-pushpa*, q. v. — *Danta-bhaṅga, as,* m. fracture of the teeth. — *Danta-bhāga, as,* m. the fore part of an elephant's head (where the tusks appear); part of a tooth. — *Danta-maya, as, ī, am,* made of ivory. — *Danta-mala, am,* n. the tartar of the teeth, any impurity of the teeth. — *Danta-māṇsa, am,* n. the gums. — *Danta-mūla, am,* n. the root of a tooth, the gums; a gum-boil. — *Danta-mūlikā,* f. = *dantī*, Croton Polyandrum or Croton Tiglium. — *Dantamūlīya, as, ā, am,* belonging to the root of the teeth, as the dental letters; *dantamūlīyas ta-kāra-vargas*, the class of letters beginning with *ta* which are uttered from the root of the teeth. — *Danta-rajas, as,* n. the tartar of the teeth, impurity of the teeth. — *Danta-roga, as,* m. disease of the teeth, tooth-ache. — *Dantarogin, ī, iṇī, i,* affected with tooth-ache. — *Danta-lekhaka, as,* m. one who makes a livelihood by painting or marking the teeth. — *Danta-loka, as,* m., N. of a mountain in Gāndhāra. — *Danta-vaktra, as,* m., N. of a prince of the Karūshas (described as a Dānava or Asura; more correctly *danta-vakra*). — *Danta-vat, ān, atī, at,* having teeth, toothed. — *Danta-valka, am,* n. the enamel of the teeth. — *Danta-vastra, am,* n. (according to some also *as,* m.), 'teeth-covering,' i. e. the lip. — *Danta-vāsas, ās* (?), *as,* m. (?) n. the lip; see the preceding. — *Danta-vighāta, as,* m. = *danta-ghāta*, a bite. — *Danta-vīja, as, ā,* m. f. and *danta-vījaka, as,* m. pomegranate; (*ā*), f. a kind of cucumber. — *Danta-vīṇā,* f. 'a tooth-guitar,' a kind of jew's-harp; (*danta-vīṇāṃ vādayat*, playing this instrument; in Pañća-tantra 94. 4, = making a chattering with the teeth.) — *Danta-veshṭa, as,* m. the gums; (*au*), m. du. the gums of the upper and lower jaw; a ring round the tusk of an elephant (?); tumor of the gums; see the next. — *Danta-veshṭaka, as,* m. tumor of the gums (internal abscess accompanied with loosening of the teeth), gum-boil. — *Danta-vaidarbha, as,* m. loosening of the teeth through external injury. — *Danta-vyasana, am,* n. fracture or decay of the teeth or of a tusk. — *Danta-śanku, u,* n. a pair of forceps or pincers for drawing teeth. — *Danta-śaṭa, as,* m. a wrong form for *danta-śaṭha*. — *Danta-śaṭha, as, ā, am,* 'bad for the teeth,' acid; (*as*), m. sourness, acidity; N. of several trees with acid fruits; common lime (Citrus Acida), elephant or wood-apple, Feronia Elephantum, Averrhoa Carambola (Acida), Citrus Aurantium; (*ā*), f. wood-sorrel, Oxalis Pusilla, = *kshudrāmlikā;* (*am*), n. the fruits of the above trees. — *Danta-śarkarā,* f. tartar or concretion of the teeth. — *Danta-śāṇa, am,* n. a dentifrice composed chiefly of the powdered fruit of the myrobalan and green sulphate of iron. — *Danta-śirā,* f. a back or double tooth (= *māḍhī*); the gum. — *Danta-śuddhi, is,* f. cleaning the teeth. — *Danta-śūla, as, am,* m. n. tooth-ache. — *Danta-śodhanī,* f. 'tooth-cleanser,' a tooth-pick. — *Danta-śopha, as,* m. swelling of the gum. — *Danta-śliṣhṭa* or *danta-sakta, as, ā, am,* entangled in or between the teeth. — *Danta-saṅgharsha, as,* m. rubbing the teeth together, gnashing the teeth; [cf. *danta-gharsha* and *danta-harsha*.] — *Danta-harsha, as,* m. morbid sensitiveness of the teeth, intolerance of any rough or acid substances; chattering of the teeth; [cf. *danta-gharsha* and *danta-saṅgharsha*.] — *Danta-harshaka* or *danta-harshaṇa, as,* m. 'making the teeth sensitive, setting them on edge,' the lime tree, Citrus Acida. — *Danta-hīna, as, ā, am,* toothless. — *Dantāgra* (°*ta-ag*°), *am,* n. the top or point of a tooth. — *Dantāghāta* (°*ta-āgh*°), *as,* m. 'tooth-blow' or 'tooth-wound,' a bite; the citron or lime tree. — *Dantāghātin, ī, inī, i,* struck with the teeth, bitten, remaining between the teeth. — *Dantāda* (°*ta-ad*°), *as, ā, am,* corroding the teeth. — *Dantā-danti,* ind. tooth against tooth, i. e. biting one another. — *Dantāntara* (°*ta-an*°), *am,* n. the space between the teeth. — *Dantāntarādhishṭhita* (°*ra-adh*°), *as, ā, am,* sticking between the teeth. — *Dantāyudha* (°*ta-āy*°), *as,* m. a wild boar, a hog ('having tusks for weapons'). — *Dantārbuda* (°*ta-ar*°), *as, am,* m. n. gum-boil, ulceration of the gums. — *Dantālaya* (°*ta-āl*°), *as,* m. 'the abode of the teeth,' i. e. the mouth. — *Dantālikā* or *dantālī* (°*ta-āl*°), f. a horse's bridle or bit; [cf. 1. *āli*.] — *Dantoććhishṭa* (°*ta-uć*°), *am,* n. the remains of food lodged between the teeth. — *Dantodbheda* (°*ta-ud*°), *as,* m. appearance of the teeth, dentition. — *Dantolūkhalika, as, ā, am,* or *dantolūkhalin* (°*ta-ul*°), *ī, inī, i,* 'one who uses his teeth as a mortar,' one who grinds his grain between the teeth, i. e. eats it before being ground, an anchorite. — *Dantoshṭhaka* (°*ta-osh*°), *as, ā, am,* one who attends to or takes care of his teeth and lips.

Dantaka = *danta*, a tooth &c. (at the end of a comp., cf. *a-dantaka, kṛimi-d*°, *śyāva-d*°); (*as*), m. a jagged peak or projection in a rock or mountain; a bracket, a pin or shelf projecting from a wall; (*as, ā, am*), paying attention to one's teeth.

Dantāvala or *dantābala, as,* m. an elephant (? for *danta-vala* = *dantin*).

Danti, is, m. (probably) an epithet of Gaṇeśa; [cf. *eka-danta*.]

Dantikā or *dantijā* = *dantī* below; [cf. *guććha-dantikā*.]

Dantin, ī, inī, i, having teeth, toothed, tusked; (*ī*), m. an elephant; a mountain; (*inī*), f. = *dantī* below. — *Danti-danta, as,* m. an elephant's tusk, ivory. — *Dantidanta-maya, as, ī, am,* made of ivory. — *Danti-mada, as,* m. the juice flowing from the temples of a rutting elephant.

Dantila, as, m., N. of a man.

Dantī, f. the plant Croton Polyandrum; see above under *danta;* [cf. *dantikā* and *dantijā*.] — *Dantī-vīja, am,* n. a strongly purgative nut, the fruit of the Croton.

Dantura, as, ā, am, having long or projecting teeth; jagged, notched, serrated, uneven; waving, undulatory; rising (as hair), bristling. — *Dantura-ććhada, as,* m. the lime tree ('having prickly leaves').

Danturaka, as, ā, am, having prominent teeth; (*ās*), m. pl., N. of a people living to the east of Madhya-deśa.

Danturita, as, ā, am, having prominent teeth, toothed, notched, bristling.

Dantūla, as, ā, am, having teeth, furnished with teeth.

Dantya, as, ā, am, dental, of or belonging to the teeth, produced on the teeth; suitable to the teeth; [cf. *a-d*°.] — *Dantyoshṭhya* or *dantyaushṭhya* (°*ya-osh*°), *as, ā, am,* denti-labial.

दन्तकूर *dantakūra*, N. of a place.

दन्दश *dandaśa, as,* m. (fr. Intens. of rt. 2. *daṅś*), a tooth.

Dandaśūka, as, ā, am, mordacious, biting, mischievous, malignant, venomous; (*as*), m. a snake, serpent; a particular kind of serpent; N. of a hell infested by serpents: a Rākshasa, a demon or goblin.

दन्द्रम *dandrama, as, ā, am* (fr. Intens. of rt. *dram*), going tortuously or slowly (?).

Dandramaṇa, am, n. the act of going tortuously; (*as, ā, am*), who or what goes tortuously.

दन्व् *danv,* cl. 1. P. *danvati,* &c., to go or move; [cf. 1. *du, dhanv, dhāv;* Gr. δονέω = Caus. *danvayāmi.*]

दफारवाह्लीक *daphārabāhlīka,* N. of a place mentioned in the Romaka-siddhānta.

दभ् *dabh* (connected with rt. *dambh,* q. v.), cl. 1. 5. P. *dabhati, dabhnoti,* &c., to hurt, injure, destroy; to go; cl. 10. P. *dābhayati* or *dambhayati,* &c., to send, impel, order, command; [cf. Gr. θάμβος, ἔταφον, τέθηπα; Old Germ. *tepyan* or *depyan.*]

Dabdhi, is, f., Ved. injury, hurt, damage.

Dabha, as, ā, am, Ved. injuring, hurting; (*as*), m. deception, deceiving, (only occurring in dat. case, *dabhāya* used for inf.; cf. *a-dabha, dambha, dūḍabha.*)

Dabhīti, is, is, i, Ved. injuring, an enemy; (*is*), m., N. of a being protected by the Aśvins and especially by Indra.

Dabhya, as, ā, am, Ved. to be hurt or injured, to be deceived.

Dabhra, as, ā, am, little, small, deficient; (*as*), m. the sea, ocean; (*am*), ind. a little, slightly. — *Dabhra-ćetas, ās, ās, as,* or *dabhra-buddhi, is, is, i,* little-minded, weak-minded.

दम् 1. *dam,* cl. 4. P. *dāmyati, dadāma, damitum,* to be tamed or subdued; to be tranquillized; to tame, subdue, conquer, subject, control, restrain; to quiet, pacify: Pass. *damyate* (Aor. *adami*): Caus. P. A. *damayati, -te,* &c., to subdue, overpower, conquer; [cf. Gr. δάμνημι, δαμνάω, δαμνάζω, δάμ-αρ, δαμάλη-ς, δμώς, δαμάω = Caus. *damayāmi;* Lat. *domare, damnum, damnare;* Goth. *tamyan,* 'to tame,' *ga-timan;* Angl. Sax. *tam, tamyan;* Old Germ. *zami, zam;* Mod. Germ. *zahm, ziemen.*]

2. *dam* (in comp.) = *dama,* a house. — *Dampati, is,* m., Ved. the master or lord of the house, a master or lord in general; (*ī*), du. wife and husband; (in this case the compound is by modern scholars explained as = 'the two masters;' but according to Sāy. and others *dam* is here = *jāyā,* a wife; cf. Gr. δεσπότης.)

Dama, as, am, m. n., Ved. house, home, (properly 'domain,' the place of the husband's dominion); the inmates of a house [cf. Gr. δόμος, δέμω; Lat. *domus;* Goth. *timryan;* Angl. Sax. *timber, timbrian*]; (*as, ā, am*), (at the end of comp.) taming, subduing, see *arin-dama;* (*as*), m., N. of several men; of a Maharshi; of one of the three sons of Bhīma, king of Vidarbha; taming, subduing; self-command, self-restraint, self-control, endurance of painful austerities, temperance, subduing the passions; punishing, punishment, chastisement, fine, mulct, a N. of Prajā-pati (?); mud, mire (?). — *Dama-kartṛi, tā,* m. a ruler. — *Damaghosha, as,* m. a prince of the lunar race, king of Ćedi, father of Śiśu-pāla. — *Damaghosha-suta, as,* m., N. of Śiśu-pāla, the enemy of Kṛishṇa. — *Damamaya, as, ī, am,* consisting of self-control. — *Damasvasṛi, ā,* f. 'the sister of Dama,' a N. of Damayantī.

Damaka, as, ā, am, taming, a tamer, subduer.

Damatha, as, am, m. n. self-restraint, self-control, taming, subduing, endurance of rigorous austerities, subduing the senses, suppressing the passions; punishment, punishing, chastising.

Damathu, us, m. self-restraint, self-subjugation; self-denial, subjection; punishment, punishing.

Damana, as, ī, am, taming, subduing, overpowering, (at the end of a comp., e. g. *śatru-d°*); tranquil, passionless, a philosopher; (*as*), m. a subduer, a tamer of horses, a charioteer; N. of a son of Vasu-deva and Rohiṇī; of a Brahmarshi; of a son of Bharad-vāja; of an old king; of a son of Bhīma, king of Vidarbha; the flower Artemisia Indica, commonly called Donā; (*ī*), f., N. of a plant, = *agni-damanī,* Solanum Jacquini; (*am*), n. taming, subduing, subjugation, restraining, chastising, punishing, self-restraint.

Damanaka, as, m., N. of a man; N. of a jackal; Artemisia Indica, = *damana;* N. of a metre consisting of four lines of six short syllables each; N. of another metre of four lines of ten short syllables and one long.

Damanīya, as, ā, am, tamable, to be restrained or subdued.

Damanya, Nom. P. *damanyati,* &c., Ved. to subdue, overpower, conquer.

Damayat, an, antī, at, subduing, taming, restraining, chastising.

Damayantikā, f., N. of a woman.

Damayantī, f. ('subduing men'), N. of a beautiful woman who was the daughter of Bhīma, king of Vidarbha, and wife of Nala, whose story forms the subject of a celebrated episode of the Mahā-bhārata; (according to some) = Śākya-muni in a former birth; a kind of cucumber, see *bhadra-mallikā.* — *Damayantī-kathā,* f. 'the story of Damayantī,' N. of a song. — *Damayantī-kāvya, am,* n. 'poem of Damayantī,' N. of a work.

Damayitṛi, tā, trī, tṛi, a tamer, subduer, subduing; a punisher, chastiser; epithet of Vishṇu and of Śiva.

Damāya, Nom. P. *damāyati,* &c., Ved. to restrain or control one's self; to subdue, overpower.

Damita, as, ā, am (or *dānta,* q. v.), tamed, subdued, patient of every suffering or exaction or privation.

Damitṛi, tā, trī, tṛi, Ved. a tamer, subduer.

Damitvā or *dāntvā,* ind. having subdued or tamed.

Damin, ī, inī, i, tamed, subdued, subduing the passions; taming, subduing, a tamer; (*i*), n., N. of a Tīrtha.

Damunas, ās, m., N. of Agni, the god of fire.

Damūnas, ās, ās, as, Ved. belonging to the house or family, devoted to the house or family; a friend of the house; epithet of Agni, Savitṛi, Indra, &c.; (Sāy.) of subdued mind, docile. In Ṛig-veda V. 42, 12, the pl. is regarded by Sāy. as an epithet of the Ṛibhus.

1. *damya, as, ā, am* (fut. pass. part.), to be tamed, tamable, to be subjected or controlled; to be punished, punishable; (*as*), m. a young bullock; a steer that has to be tamed. — *Damya-sārathi, is,* m. 'the guide of those who have to be restrained,' an epithet of Buddha.

2. *damya, as, ā, am* (fr. *dama*), Ved. being in a house, being at home, homely.

दमावन्दु *damāvandu,* N. of a place mentioned in the Romaka-siddhānta.

दम्पति *dam-pati.* See under 2. *dam,* col. 1.

दम्भ् *dambh* (connected with rt. *dabh,* q. v.), cl. 1. 5. P. *dabhati, dabhnoti, dadambha* or *dadābha* or *debha* (pl. *dadambhus* or *debhus*), *dambhishyati, adambhīt, dambhitum,* Ved. inf. *ā-dabhe,* to seek to injure, to hurt, injure, cause damage; to act deceitfully, cheat, impose upon, trick, deceive: Caus. P. A. *dambhayati, -te, -yitum,* Aor. *adadambhat,* to destroy, strike down; A. to collect, gather, arrange, string: Desid. *didambhishati, dhipsati, dhīpsati,* Ved. *dipsati* or *dīpsati,* to wish to hurt or injure, desire to destroy; to have the power to deceive or destroy: Intens. *dādabhyate, dādambdhi.*

Dambha, as, m. deceit, fraud, cheating, trickery, feigning hypocrisy, sanctimony; arrogance, ostentation, pride; sin, wickedness; Deceit personified as a son of A-dharma and Mṛishā; an epithet of Śiva; Indra's thunderbolt. — *Dambha-ćaryā,* f. deceit, hypocrisy. — *Dambhodbhava* (°*bha-ud*°), *as,* m., N. of a king whose story is told in Mahā-bh. Udyoga-parva 3473, (he fought with two hermits but was worsted.)

Dambhaka, as, ikā, am, (at the end of comp.) cheating, deceiving, deluding; [cf. *kāma-d°.*]

Dambhana, as, ā, am, (at the end of comp.) injuring, damaging, subduing [cf. *amitra-dambhana, sapatna-d°*]; (*as*), m. cheating, deceiving, deceit.

Dambhin, ī, inī, i, acting deceitfully, hypocritical, wicked, proud; (*ī*), m. a hypocrite, a deceiver, an impostor.

Dambholi, is, m. Indra's thunderbolt.

दम्य *damya.* See col. 2.

दय् *day* [cf. rt. 3. *dā*], cl. 1. A. *dayate, dayāṅ-ćakre, dayitum,* to divide, impart, allot, grant, give, (according to Pāṇ. II. 3, 52, requiring the gen. case); to partake, possess; to divide asunder, destroy, kill, hurt; to take part in, be interested in, sympathise with, have pity on, love, protect (with acc. or gen.); to repent; to go, move: Intens. *dandayyate* and *dādayyate;* [cf. Gr. δαίομαι, δαίνυμι, δαΐς: Hib. *deidh,* f. 'desire, longing;' *deidh,* m. 'a protector, defender;' *deide,* 'obedience, submission.']

Dayamāna, as, ā, am, dividing, having pity on, preserving, protecting.

Dayā, f. taking interest in, sympathy, compassion, pity, mercy, tenderness, love, clemency, pity for (with loc. or gen., e. g. *mayi* or *mama dayām kuru,* take pity on me); Pity personified as a daughter of Daksha, wife of Dharma, and mother of Abhaya. (According to some, the form *daya, as,* m. occurs; and according to others, *daya* may be used as an adj. meaning 'compassionate;' cf. *a-daya, nir-d°, sa-d°.*) — *Dayā-kara, as, ā* or *ī, am,* showing pity or compassion, sympathising, kind; (*as*), m. an epithet of Śiva. — *Dayā-kūrća, as,* m. a Buddha or a form of Buddha, the founder of the Buddhist religion. — *Dayā-kṛit, t, t, t,* pitiful, compassionate. — *Dayā-nidhi, is,* m. a treasure of mercy, a very compassionate person. — *Dayānvita* (°*yā-an*°) or *dayā-yukta, as, ā, am,* full of pity, pitiful, compassionate, benevolent. — *Dayā-rāma, as,* m., N. of several men. — *Dayā-vat, ān, atī, at,* pitiful, merciful, tender, compassionate, taking pity on (with loc. or gen.). — *Dayā-vīra, as,* m. a hero in compassion, a very merciful man. — *Dayā-śaṅkara, as,* m., N. of a man. — *Dayā-śīla, as, ā, am,* tender-hearted, compassionate. — *Dayormi* (°*yā-ūr*°), *is, is, i,* having compassion for (its) waves.

Dayālu, us, us, u, or *dayāluka, as, ā, am,* pitiful, merciful, compassionate, kind, tender, taking pity on (with loc.). — *Dayālu-tā,* f. or *dayālu-tva, am,* n. pitifulness, tenderness, compassionateness, pity for (with loc.).

Dayita, as, ā, am, desired, cherished, beloved, dear; (*as*), m. 'the loved one,' a husband, a lover; (*ā*), f. a wife or mistress, a woman. — *Dayitādhīna* (°*tā-adh*°), *as, ā, am,* subject to a wife, hen-pecked.

Dayitnu, us, us, u, Ved. pitiful, compassionate.

दर *dara, as, ā, am* (fr. rt. *dṛī;* at the end of comp.) cleaving, rending, splitting, cutting open, opening, breaking [cf. *puran-d°*]; (*as, am*), m. f. n. a hole in the ground, a cave, cavity; a conch-shell; (*ī*), f. a natural or artificial excavation in a mountain, a cave, a cavern, a grotto, &c.; a valley; (*as*), m. a stream [cf. *asṛig-d°*]; fear, terror, dread, despair; (*as, ā, am*), little, small; (*am*), ind. a little. — *Dara-kaṇṭikā,* f. the plant Asparagus Racemosa (= *śatāvarī*). — *Dara-timira, am,* n. the darkness of fear. — *Dara-manthara, as, ā, am,* a little slow. — *Dara-mukulita, as, ā, am,* a little budded — *Dara-vidalita, as, ā, am,* slightly burst or opened. — *Dara-vrīḍā,* f. slight shame. — *Dara-ślatha, as, ā, am,* a little loose. — *Darī-bhū, ūs,* f. a cavern, a hollow. — *Darī-bhṛit, t,* m. 'having caves,' a mountain. — *Darī-mukha, am,* n. a mouth like a cave; a cave like a mouth; the opening of a cave; *(as, ī, am),* having a mouth as large as a cave; *(as),* m., N. of a monkey. — *Darī-vat, ān, atī, at,* containing caves, cavernous, abounding in caves. — *Darendra* (°*ra-in*°), *as,* m. Vishṇu's conch.

Daraṇa, am, n. the act of cleaving, rending, splitting, tearing, breaking; breaking off, falling away.

Daraṇi, is, is, m. f. breaking; an eddy; a current; breakers, surf.

Daratha, as, m. a cavity, cave; running away, taking flight; spreading over the country for forage.

Darad, t, m., N. of a people; *(t),* f. the heart; a bank, mound; a mountain; a precipice; terror, fear.

Darada, ās, m. pl. a country bordering on Kaśmīr, the mountains about Kaśmīr and above Peshāwar; the inhabitants of this country; *(as),* m. the king or chief of the Daradas; *(as),* m. fear, terror; *(am),* n. red lead.

Dari, is, is, i, splitting, rending, opening [cf. *go-d*°]; *(is),* m., N. of a Nāga; *(is),* f. a cave. (For *darī* see under *dara.*)

Darita, as, ā, am, frightened, terrified, timid; torn, rent, divided.

Dartṛi, tā, trī, tṛi, or *dartnu, us, us, u,* Ved. a breaker, render, splitting, breaking, one who splits, breaks, or opens.

Dardara, as, ā, am, cracked, broken, burst, flawed, slightly broken; *(as),* m. a mountain ('containing caves'); N. of a mountain (also *dardura*); a kind of drum. — *Dardarāmra* (°*ra-ām*°), *as,* m. a sort of sauce or condiment (= *mināmrịṇa*).

Dardarīka, as, m. a frog; a cloud; a kind of musical instrument; *(am),* n. any musical instrument; [cf. *darvarīka.*]

Dardura, as, m. (perhaps an onomatopoetic word), a frog [cf. *dārdura* and *dārdurika*]; a sort of musical instrument, a pipe or flute; the sound of a drum; a cloud; a sort of rice; a mountain; N. of a mountain in the south (sometimes associated with the mountain Malaya); N. of a man; of a gamester; *(ā* or *ī),* f. a N. of Durgā; *(am),* n. an assemblage of villages, a district, a province. — *Dardura-ćchadā,* f. or *dardura-parṇī,* f., N. of a plant, = *brāhmī.* — *Dardura-puṭa, as,* m. the mouth or extremity of a pipe.

Darduraka, as, m., N. of a gamester; [cf. *darodara* and *durodara.*]

Dardū, ūs, or *dardru, us,* or *dardrū, ūs,* m. (according to some fr. *daridrā*), = *dadru,* cutaneous and herpetic eruptions, especially a kind of leprosy. — *Dardru-ghna, as,* m. = *dadru-ghna,* the shrub Cassia Tora; Psoralea Corylifolia. — *Dardru-nāśinī,* f. a kind of insect, = *tailinī.* — *Dardru-rogin* or *dardrū-rogin, ī, iṇī, i,* afflicted with cutaneous eruptions, herpetic.

Dardruṇa or *dardrūṇa, as, ā, am,* having cutaneous eruptions, herpetic.

दरिद्रा *daridrā* (reduplicated form of rt. 1. *drā;* according to some, an old Intens. form; perhaps connected with rt. *dṛī*), cl. 2. P. *daridrāti* (*daridrivas, daridritas,* 3rd pl. *daridrati*), *daridrāñ-ćakāra* or *dadaridrau, daridrishyati, adaridrīt* and *adaridrāsīt, daridritum,* to be poor or needy, to be in distress.

Daridra, as, ā, am, poor, needy, indigent, distressed, a poor person, beggar; (Ved.) unsteady, roving, strolling. — *Daridra-tā,* f. or *daridra-tva, am,* n. poverty, indigence, penury. — *Daridra-nindā,* f., N. of the twenty-fifth chapter of the Śārṅgadhara-paddhati.

Daridrāṇa, am, n. the state of being poor, poverty.

Daridrāyaka, as, ā or *ikā, am,* poor, needy.

Daridrita, as, ā, am, impoverished, distressed.

Daridritṛī, tā, trī, tṛi, poor, distressed, needy.

दरोदर *darodara, as,* m. = *durodara,* a gamester [cf. *dardura* and *darduraka*]; a stake at play; *(am),* n. gambling, playing at dice; a die, dice.

दर्दर *dardara, dardarīka, dardura.* See last col.

दर्प *darpa, as,* m. (fr. rt. 3. *dṛip* or 2. *dṛip;* according to some, also *am,* n.), pride, arrogance, haughtiness, insolence, rashness, temerity; vanity, conceit; sullenness, sulkiness; Pride &c. personified as a son of Śrī, or of A-dharma and Śrī, or of Dharma and Lakshmī, or of Unnati; heat; musk; [cf. *ati-d*° and *sa-d*°.] — *Darpa-ćchid, t, t, t,* destroying pride, humbling. — *Darpa-da, as,* m., N. of Śiva. — *Darpa-dhmāta, as, ā, am,* puffed up or swelling with pride. — *Darpa-nārāyaṇa, as,* m., N. of a king. — *Darpa-pattraka, as,* m. a kind of grass; [cf. *darbha-pattra.*] — *Darpa-pūrṇa, as, ā, am,* full of pride. — *Darpa-sāra, as,* m., N. of a man. — *Darpa-ha* or *darpa-hara, as, ā, am,* pride-destroying, humbling, humiliating. — *Darpa-han, ā,* m., N. of Śiva. — *Darpārambha* (°*pa-ār*°), *as,* m. beginning of pride, incipient pride, conceit. — *Darpopaśānti* (°*pa-up*°), *is,* f. allaying pride, conciliating or subduing arrogance.

Darpaka, as, ā, am, making proud, inflaming, exciting, an inflamer; *(as),* m. a N. of Kāma-deva, god of love.

Darpaṇa, as, m. 'causing vanity or pride,' a looking-glass, mirror, (sometimes occurring at the end of comp. or titles of books, e. g. *karṇa-d*°, *jñāna-d*°, *sāhitya-d*°, q. v.); a N. of Śiva [cf. *darpa-da*]; N. of a mountain inhabited by Kuvera and of a river rising there; *(am),* n. the eye; kindling, inflaming.

Darpita, as, ā, am, made proud, arrogant; inflamed. — *Darpita-pura, am,* n., N. of a town.

Darpin, ī, iṇī, i, proud, arrogant, insolent.

दर्भ *darbha, as,* m. (fr. rt. 1. *dṛibh;* said to be fr. rt. *dṛī*), a bundle of grass, tuft or bunch of grass; N. of various kinds of grass used at sacrificial ceremonies, especially of the Kuśa grass, Poa Cynosuroides; Saccharum Spontaneum; Saccharum Cylindricum; (the first kind or Kuśa grass was held very sacred; it was used to strew the ground in preparing for a sacrifice, the officiating Brāhmans being purified by sitting on it; under the name Darbha it was even addressed as a deity; its various sanctifying qualities are described in Manu II. 43, III. 208, IV. 36, &c.; cf. *kuśa, kāśa, muñja, valva-ja, śara*); N. of a man; [cf. Old Germ. *zurba, zurft;* Mod. Germ. *torf;* Eng. *turf.*] — *Darbha-kusuma, as,* m. a kind of insect (= *darbha-pushpa*). — *Darbha-ćīra, am,* n. a dress of Kuśa grass. — *Darbha-taruṇaka, am,* n., Ved. a young shoot of Kuśa grass. — *Darbha-pattra, as,* m. a kind of grass, Saccharum Spontaneum (= *kāśa*). — *Darbha-puñjīla* = *darbha-piñjūla, am,* n., Ved. a bunch or bundle of Kuśa grass. — *Darbha-pushpa, as,* m. a kind of serpent; a kind of insect, 'similar to the Darbha flower;' [cf. *darbha-kusuma.*] — *Darbha-maya, as, ī, am,* made of Kuśa or Darbha grass. — *Darbha-mushṭi, is,* m. f. a handful of Kuśa grass. — *Darbha-saṃstara, as,* m. a bed of Darbha grass. — *Darbha-stamba, as,* m. a cluster or bunch of Kuśa grass. — *Darbhāhvaya* (°*bha-āh*°), *as,* m. a kind of grass; [cf. *muñja.*]

Darbhara, as, m. (?), a kind of bird, = *lāvā,* Perdix Chinensis.

Darbhi, is, m. or *darbhin, ī,* m., N. of a man.

दर्भट *darbhaṭa, am,* n. a private apartment or house, a retired room; [cf. *dārvaṭa.*]

Darvaṭa, as, m. a door-keeper, warder, village constable, police officer; [cf. *garvāṭa.*]

दर्म *darma, as,* or *darman, ā,* m. (fr. rt. *dṛī*), Ved. a destroyer, demolisher; a tearer.

दर्यक *daryaka, as,* m., N. of a man.

दर्व *darva, as,* m. (said to be fr. rt. *dṛī*), a ladle, spoon (at the end of comp., e.g. *pūrṇa-d*°, q.v.); the hood of a snake [cf. *darvi* below]; a Rākshasa, an imp, goblin; a mischievous man, a rapacious animal, &c.; *(ās),* m. pl., N. of a people [cf. *dārva*]; *(ā),* f., N. of a wife of Uśīnara; (sometimes written *darbā;* cf. *dārvan.*)

Darvi or *darbi, is,* f. (in later Sanskṛit also *darvī* or *darbī,* f.; acc. in Ved. *darvyam* or *darvim*), a ladle, spoon; the expanded hood of a snake; *(ī),* f., N. of a country. — *Darvi-homa* or *darvī-homa, as,* m. an oblation made with a ladle; [cf. *dārvi-haumika.*] — *Darvihomin,* relating to the preceding oblation. — *Darvī-kara, as,* m. (scil. *sarpa*), a class of snakes with expanded hoods, of which twenty-six species are enumerated. — *Darvī-saṅkramaṇa, am,* n., N. of a Tīrtha.

Darvikā or *darbīkā, as, ā,* m. f. a ladle, a spoon; *(ā),* f. a pot-herb; a kind of collyrium; [cf. *dārvikā.*]

दर्वट *darvaṭa.* See above.

दर्वरीक *darvarīka, as,* m. a kind of musical instrument; air, wind; an epithet of Indra; [cf. *dardarīka.*]

दर्वि *darvi* or *darvī.* See above.

दर्विदा *darvidā,* f., Ved. a species of bird, (according to Mahī-dhara) = *kāshṭha-kuṭṭa,* a sort of woodpecker; (perhaps corrupted fr. *dāru-vidha;* cf. *dārvāghāṭa.*)

दर्श *darśa, as, ā, am* (fr. rt. 1. *dṛiś*), looking at, viewing, seeing, perceiving, showing, having a view, (generally at the end of comp., see *arasāna-d*°, *ādīnava-d*°, *ātma-d*°, *tattva-d*°); *(as),* m. sight, view, seeing, appearance, (generally at the end of comp., see *priya-d*°, *dur-d*°); the moon when only just becoming visible, the new moon; day of new moon; the festival of new moon; half monthly sacrifice (performed at the change of the moon by persons maintaining a perpetual fire); New Moon or Day of New Moon, personified as a son of Dhātṛi and Sinīvalī. — *Darśa-pa, as, ā, am,* drinking the new moon oblation. — *Darśa-pūrṇa-māsau,* m. du. new and full moon, the days and the ceremonies which precede all other ceremonies. — *Darśa-yāga, as,* m. a sacrifice or ceremony on the day of new moon. — *Darśa-yāminī,* f. the night of new moon on which it rises hardly visible. — *Darśa-vipad, t,* m. the moon ('as having the misfortune to be hardly visible when new').

Darśaka, as, ā or *ikā, am,* seeing, looking at, a spectator; examining, searching; who or what shows or displays or explains or makes clear; *(as),* m. a door-keeper, a warder; a shower, exhibiter, discoverer, one who points out; a skilful man, one conversant with any science or art; *(ās),* m. pl., N. of a people.

Darśata, as, ā, am, Ved. visible, striking the eye, beautiful; conspicuous; *(as),* m. the sun; the moon. — *Darśata-śrī, īs, īs, i,* Ved. of conspicuous beauty.

Darśana, as, ā, am, seeing, looking, (at the end of comp., e. g. *tulya-d*°, *deva-d*°, *dharma-d*°); showing, exhibiting, demonstrating, teaching; *(ī),* f. epithet of Durgā, 'as showing the way or leading;' *(am),* n. seeing, observing, looking; sight, vision, observation; inspection, examination; perception; the being or becoming visible; the act of showing [cf. *danta-d*°]; exhibition; appearance, aspect, semblance, colour; visiting, visiting a sacred shrine, worshipping in the presence of an image; going into the presence of (e. g. *darśanaṃ kṛi,* to visit, to go into any one's presence; cf. *puṇya-darśana*); a view or theory prescribed in a system or book (e. g. *Śāstra-darśanāt*, in the manner prescribed in the Śāstras); experiencing; seeing in the mind, mental or spiritual vision, foreseeing, divining; contemplating; a vision, a dream; apprehension, judgment; discernment, understanding, intellect; knowledge, religious knowledge; opinion; intention; doctrine, demonstration, a Śāstra, a N. applied to the six recognized systems of philosophy (viz. 1. Pūrva-mīmāṃsā, usually called Mīmāṃsā by Jaimini; 2. Uttara-mīmāṃsā, usually called Vedānta by Vyāsa or Bādarāyaṇa; 3. Nyāya by Gotama; 4. Vaiśeshika by Kaṇāda; 5. Sāṅkhya by Kapila; 6. Yoga by Patañjali; cf. *tarka*); virtue, moral merit; the eye; a mirror [cf. *ā-d°*]; a sacrifice, oblation [cf. *danta-d°*]; (*ī*), f. a kind of insect (= *taila-kīṭa*). — *Darśana-patha, as,* m. 'the path of the sight,' the range of sight or view, horizon. — *Darśana-pāla, as,* m., N. of a man. — *Darśana-pratibhū, ūs,* m. bail or surety for appearance. — *Darśana-prātibhāvya, am,* n. surety for appearance, bail. — *Darśana-bhūmi, is,* f. the region or range of perception; (with Buddhists) one of the periods in the life of a Śrāvaka. — *Darśana-lālasa, as, ā, am,* longing to see, ardently desirous of beholding. — *Darśanepsu* (°*na-īp°*), *us, us, u,* anxious to see. — *Darśanojjvalā* (°*na-uj°*), f. 'of brilliant aspect,' great white jasmine. — *Darśanopanishad* (°*na-up°*), *t,* f., N. of an Upanishad.

Darśanīya, as, ā, am, visible, to be seen; observable, perceptible, conspicuous; worthy of being seen, good-looking, beautiful, agreeable, handsome; to be made to appear before a court of justice, to be produced in court; (*as*), m. Asclepias Gigantea. — *Darśanīya-tama, as, ā, am,* most worthy of being seen, very beautiful. — *Darśanīya-mānin, ī, inī, i,* thinking one's self good-looking, vain, conceited.

Darśayitu-kāma, as, ā, am, wishing to show.

Darśayitṛi, tā, trī, tṛi, showing, exhibiting, displaying, a shower, exhibiter, director, instructor, showman, guide; (*tā*), m. a warder, usher, door-keeper.

Darśayitvā, ind. having shown or exhibited, having made manifest.

Darśayishyat, an, antī, at, intending or proposing to show or explain.

Darśita, as, ā, am, shown, displayed, exhibited, exposed to view; explained; seen, understood; visible, apparent. — *Darśita-vat, ān, atī, at,* having shown or explained or taught.

Darśin, ī, inī, i, (at the end of comp.) seeing, a spectator, looking, looking at, inspecting, observing, examining, perceiving, apprehending; knowing, understanding; seeing or knowing (the hymns of the Veda); experiencing, looking, appearing, having an aspect; causing to see, showing, exhibiting, teaching, causing to experience or suffer; [cf. *anīći-d°*, *amogha-d°*, *kshema-d°*, *pāpa-d°*, &c.] — *Darśitva, am,* n. the state of seeing &c.

Darśivas, ān, m. (perf. part. fr. rt. 1. *dṛiś* without reduplication; always at the end of comp., and usually at the end of a verse), a seer, one who has seen, one who sees or knows or understands (e. g. *Arjuna-darśivān*, one who has seen Arjuna; cf. *dīrgha-d°*.)

Darśya, as, ā, am, Ved. worthy of being shown or exhibited; worthy of being seen, conspicuous.

दल् *dal* (connected with rt. *dṛī*), cl. 1. P. *dalati, dadāla, adālīt, dalitum,* to burst open, split, crack, to be divided, to fly open, open in chinks, open (as a bud or blossom), expand, blossom: Caus. *dalayati* and *dālayati, -yitum,* to cause to burst, to split or tear or open, tear asunder; to cut, divide, split, pierce; to wither; [cf. Lith. *dalis,* 'a part;' *dallykas,* 'a fragment;' *daliyu,* 'to divide:' Goth. *dails,* 'a part:' Old Germ. *tail, teil; tīlōn, tīligōn* = Caus. *dalayāmi*: Lat. *dolo*: Hib. *dail,* 'a share;' *dailim,* 'I deal out;' *duil,* 'partition;' *duillean,* 'a spear.']

Dala, am, n. (according to lexicographers also *as,* m.), a piece torn or split off; a part, a portion, a fragment, a rent, side [cf. *ashṭa-dala*]; a degree; a half, the half (e. g. *ahar-dala,* mid-day); a sheath, scabbard; a small shoot, blade, petal, leaf (i. e. what unfolds itself; often occurring at the end of names of plants, the fem. being *dalā*; cf. *udumbara-d°*, *karkaśa-d°*, *kāma-khaḍga-d°*, *kshāra-d°*); the blade of anything (as of a knife &c.); a clump, lump, heap, quantity; a detachment, body of men; dividing, tearing, cutting, splitting, &c.; an adulteration or alloy; (*as*), m., N. of a prince; (*ī*), f., see *dali* below; [cf. Hib. *duille,* 'a leaf.'] — *Dala-kapāṭa, as,* m. a folded petal or leaf. — *Dala-komala* = *kamala,* the lotus (Nelumbium). — *Dala-kosha, as,* m. 'having young shoots incased in sheaths,' a sort of jasmine (J. Pubescens). — *Dala-ja, am,* n. 'produced by small bees' or 'produced from young shoots,' a kind of honey; [cf. *dāla*.] — *Dala-taru, us,* m. = *tāḍī,* a kind of palm, Corypha Taliera. — *Dala-nirmoka, as,* m. a kind of birch (lit. 'leaf-shedding'), the bark of which is used for hookahs &c. (= *bhūrja-pattra*). — *Dala-pati, is,* m., N. of a prince. — *Dala-pushpā, ī,* f. a fragrant plant, the leaves of which surround the flower, Pandanus Odoratissimus (= *ketakī*). — *Dala-mālinī,* f. a kind of cabbage. — *Dalaśas,* ind. in pieces or fragments (e. g. *dalaśo yā,* to go or fall to pieces). — *Dala-śālinī,* f. a species of pot-herb (= *kańćuka-śāka*). — *Dala-sāyasī* (?), f. white basil. — *Dala-sāriṇī,* f. = *kemuka,* a species of pot-herb, (probably) = *dala-śālinī*. — *Dala-sūći, is,* m. a thorn. — *Dala-snasā,* f. the fibre or vein of a leaf. — *Dalākhya* (°*la-ākh°*), *as,* m., N. of a particular constellation (subdivisions of which are Ahi and Mālā). — *Dalāgra-lohita, as* or *am,* m. or n. (?), a sort of spinage. — *Dalāḍhaka* (°*la-āḍh°*), *as,* m., N. of several plants, Pistia Stratiotes (= *pṛiśnī*); a kind of jasmine (= *kunda*); wild sesamum; Mesua Ferrea (commonly Nageśar); Acacia Sirissa (= *śirīsha*); red chalk (= *gaurika*); foam (= *phena*); cuttle-fish bone; a moat, a ditch; a Śūdra; the head man of a village (?), the driver of an elephant (?); an elephant's ear; a hurricane, a high wind. — *Dalāḍhya* (°*la-āḍh°*), *as,* m. mud, especially on the banks of a river; [cf. *dalāḍhaka*.] — *Dalāmala* (°*la-am°*), *am,* n., N. of several plants, = *damanaka* and *maruvaka*; Vangueria Spinosa and Artemisia. — *Dalāmla* (°*la-am°*), *am,* n. sorrel. — *Dalī-kṛita, as, ā, am,* divided, bisected, halved. — *Dale-gandhi, is,* m. ('fragrance in the leaf'), N. of a plant, Echites Scholaris; [cf. *sapta-parṇa*.] — *Dalodbhava* (°*la-ud°*), *am,* n. a kind of honey; [cf. *dala-ja* and *dāla*.]

Dalat, an, antī, at, splitting, bursting open, rending; being torn or cut. — *Dalad-dhṛidaya, as, ā, am* (*dalat* + *hṛidaya*), broken-hearted, cut to the heart, &c.

Dalana, as, ī, am, splitting, tearing asunder or in two, breaking to pieces, cutting, dividing; (*ī*), f. a clod of earth [cf. *dali*]; (*am*), n. bursting; tearing, rending, breaking, crushing, cutting to pieces, grinding.

Dalanīya, as, ā, am, to be broken or destroyed or trodden down.

Dali, is, f. (according to some also *dalī*), a clod of clay or earth; [cf. *dalanī* and *dalana*.]

Dalika, am, n. timber, a piece of wood.

Dalita, as, ā, am, burst, split, broken, torn, rent; torn asunder, cut to pieces, wounded; opened, unfolded, expanded, blown, full blown; divided in two, bisected, halved; divided into degrees, distributed; driven asunder, scattered; trodden down; crushed; destroyed; manifested.

Dalin, ī, inī, i, having pieces, leaves, &c.

Dalmi, is, m. Indra's thunderbolt; an epithet of Indra; [cf. *darma, darmin, dālmi*.] — *Dalmi-mat, ān, atī, at,* having a thunderbolt.

दलप *dalapa, as,* m. a weapon; a sacred or religious book (= *śāstra* for *śastra*); gold.

दल्भ *dalbha, as,* m. a wheel; fraud, dishonesty, sin; N. of a Ṛishi; [cf. Hib. *dalbh,* 'falsehood.']

Dalbhya, as, m., N. of an ancient preceptor.

दव *dava, as,* m. (fr. rt. 2. *du*), fire, burning, heat; fever, pain; a wood on fire, a forest conflagration; a wood, a forest; [cf. *dāva*; cf. also Cambro-Brit. *daiv,* 'burning.'] — *Dava-dagdhaka, as* or *am,* m. or n. (?), a kind of grass (= *rohisha*). — *Dava-dahana, as,* m. the fire in a burning forest. — *Davāgni* (°*va-ag°*), *is,* or *davānala* (°*va-an°*), *as,* m. a wood on fire, a forest conflagration; [cf. *dāvāgni*.]

Davathu, us, m. fire, heat; pain, anxiety, vexation, distress; inflammation of the eye.

दवय *davaya* (fr. *dava,* substituted for *dūra* in the same manner as in *davīyas, davishṭha*), Nom. P. *davayati, -yitum,* to make distant, remove.

Davayat, an, antī, at, removing, making distant, distancing, placing at a distance.

Davishṭha, as, ā, am (superl. fr. *dūra*), very remote, very distant.

Davīyas, ān, asī, as (compar. fr. *dūra*), more or very remote, more distant.

दश् *daś.* See 2. *daṃś,* p. 396, col. 1.

दशन् *daśan, a,* m. f. n. pl. (said to be fr. rt. 2. *daṃś*), ten; [cf. Gr. δέκα; Lat. *decem*; Goth. *taihun* for *tihun*; Armor. *dek*; Hib. *déagh, deich*; Lith. *deszimtis, deszim-ts, deszim-t*; Slav. *desya-ty*.] — *Daśa-kaṇṭha* or *daśa-kandhara, as, ā, am,* ten-necked; (*as*), m. an epithet of Rāvaṇa. — *Daśa-kaṇṭha-jit, t,* m. or *daśakaṇṭhāri* (°*ṭha-ari*), *is,* m. an epithet of Rāma. — *Daśa-kanyā-tīrtha, am,* n. 'the Tīrtha of the ten virgins,' N. of a Tīrtha. — *Daśa-karman, āṇi,* n. pl. the ten ceremonies prescribed to the three twice-born classes. — *Daśa-karma-paddhati, is,* f., N. of a work on the ten ceremonies. — *Daśa-kāma-ja-vyasana, am,* n. ten vices (see Manu VII. 47) arising from love of pleasure, viz. hunting, gambling, sleeping by day, fault-finding, lust, drunkenness, dancing, singing, playing, and useless travel. — *Daśa-kumāra-ćarita, am,* n. 'the adventures of the ten princes,' N. of a book of stories by Daṇḍin. — *Daśa-kshiti-garbha, as* or *am,* m. or n. (?), N. of a Buddhist Sūtra work. — *Daśa-kshīra, as, ā, am,* mixed with ten parts of milk; (*am*), n. a compound of ten parts of milk mixed with one part of some other substance. — *Daśa-gaṇī,* f. ten classes collectively. — *Daśa-gītikā,* f., N. of an astronomical work, i. e. 'the ten poems of Ārya-bhaṭṭa.' — *Daśa-guṇa, as, ā, am,* ten-fold, ten times larger, ten times more; (*am*), ind. ten times, ten-fold. — *Daśa-grāma, am,* n. a district or collection of ten villages. — *Daśagrāma-pati, is,* m. a magistrate or chief of ten villages. — *Daśagrāmin, ī,* m. the head man of ten villages. — *Daśa-grāmī,* f. a collection of ten villages; a municipality or corporation of ten villages. — *Daśa-grīva, as, ā, am,* ten-necked; (*as*), m., N. of a demon; of an enemy of Vṛisha, who is the Indra of the eleventh Manv-antara; an epithet of Rāvaṇa; N. of a son of Dama-ghosha. — *Daśa-gva, as, ā, am,* Ved. going in ten ways, one who observes a ten-days rite or conducts sacrifices for ten months; going to completion in ten months; a N. applied to the Maruts; also to the family of the Aṅgirasas. — *Daśa-gvin, ī, inī, i,* ten-fold, going ten ways; (Sāy.) going for ten (leagues). — *Daśa-jyoti* and *daśa-jyotis, is,* m., N. of a son of Su-bhrāj. — *Daśa-daśin* or *daśan-daśin* or *daśā-daśin, ī, inī, i,* Ved. consisting of repeated decads. — *Daśa-diś, k,* f. the ten quarters of the heavens (including that overhead and underneath). — *Daśa-dyu, us,* m., Ved. (according to Sāy.) N. of a person. — *Daśa-dhanus, us,* m., N. of one of the ancestors of Śākya-muni. — *Daśa-dhā,* ind. in ten parts, into ten parts, ten-fold, in ten ways. — *Daśa-pa, as,* m. a chief of ten villages; [cf. *daśagrāma-pati*.] — *Daśa-paśu, us, us, u,* Ved. prepared or intended for ten oxen. — *Daśa-pādī,* f., N. of a grammatical work. — *Daśa-pāramitā-dhara, as, ā, am,* possessing the ten Pāramitās or perfections; (*as*), m. a Buddha or Buddhist saint. — *Daśa-pārśva, ās,* m. pl., N. of a people.

— *Daśa-piṇḍa-śrāddha, am,* n. a funereal ceremony in which a Piṇḍa or ball of rice is offered by the next of kin to a person deceased, increasing the number daily for ten successive days until they amount to ten. — *Daśa-pura, am,* n. a district or part of Malwa or Bandelkhand; (perhaps) N. of a town, Decapolis; a fragrant grass, a species of Cyperus Rotundus. — *Daśa-purusham,* ind. for ten persons or male progenitors, i. e. through a series of ten ancestors. — *Daśapurusham-rājya, am,* n. a kingdom inherited through a series of ten ancestors. — *Daśa-pūra, am,* n. a fragrant grass (= *daśa-pura*). — *Daśa-pūrusham* = *daśa-purusham* above. — *Daśa-pūrva-ratha, as,* m. a periphrasis for the name Daśa-ratha ('*ratha* preceded by *daśa*'). — *Daśa-pūrvin, ī,* m., N. of seven saints of the Jainas. — *Daśa-peya, as,* m., Ved. 'to be quaffed by ten,' N. of a Soma oblation forming part of the Rāja-sūya. — *Daśa-pramati, is, is, i* (?), Ved. receiving excessive honour in the ten regions or spreading over the ten regions. — *Daśa-bandha, as,* m. a tenth part, a fine equivalent to the tenth part. — *Daśa-bala, as, ā, am,* possessing ten powers; (*as*), m. an epithet of Buddha. — *Daśabala-kāśyapa, as,* m., N. of one of the first five pupils of Śākya-muni. — *Daśa-bāhu, us, us, u,* ten-armed; (*us*), m. an epithet of Śiva. — *Daśabhakti-pañća-stuti, is,* f., N. of a collection of Jaina prayers. — *Daśa-bhujā,* f. 'the ten-armed,' a form of Durgā. — *Daśa-bhūmi-ga, as, ā, am,* traversing the ten worlds; (*as*), m. Buddha, the founder of the Buddhist religion, a Buddha or the generic name of the sanctified teachers of that religion. — *Daśa-bhūmīśa* (°*mi-īśa*), *as,* m. 'lord of the ten worlds,' a N. of Buddha or a Buddha. — *Daśabhūmīśvara* (°*mi-īś*°), N. of a Buddhist Sūtra work. — *Daśa-mahā-vidyā,* f. an epithet of Durgā ('possessing the ten great sciences'). — *Daśa-māla, am, ī,* n. f. a collection of ten garlands. — *Daśa-mālika, ās,* m. pl., N. of a people. — *Daśa-māsya, as, ā, am,* ten months old, as the child in the womb just before birth; (with *aśva*), a horse let loose for ten months. — *Daśa-mukha, āni,* n. pl. ten mouths or faces; (*as, ī, am*), having ten faces; (*as*), m. an epithet of Rāvaṇa. — *Daśamukha-ripu, us,* or *daśamukhān-taka* (°*kha-an*°), *as,* m. 'the enemy of Rāvaṇa,' an epithet of Rāma. — *Daśa-mūtraka, am,* n. the urine of ten (i. e. of the elephant, buffalo, camel, cow, goat, sheep, horse, donkey, man, and woman). — *Daśa-mūla, am,* n. a tonic medicine prepared from the roots of ten plants, viz. Tri-kaṇṭaka, the two Vṛihatīs, Pṛithak-parṇī, Vidāri-gandhā, Vilva, Agni-mantha, Tuṇṭuka, Pāṭalā, and Kāśmarī; [cf. *dvipañća-mūla.*] — *Daśa-yojana-vistīrṇa, as, ā, am,* ten Yojanas broad. — *Daśa-ratha, as, ā, am,* having ten chariots; (*as*), m., N. of several princes, among whom the most renowned is the father of Rāma, (he was a descendant of Ikshvāku and sovereign of Ayodhyā or Oude); N. of an older Daśaratha, son of Mūlaka, and ancestor of the above, (also written *śata-ratha*); N. of a son of Navaratha and father of Śakuni; N. of a son of Su-yaśas and father of Saṅgata; N. of an ancestor of Buddha; (*am*), n. the body (?). — *Daśaratha-tattva, am,* n., N. of a work. — *Daśaratha-yajñārambha* (°*ña-ār*°), *as,* m., N. of the fourteenth chapter of the Pātāla-khaṇḍa or fourth part of the Padma-Purāṇa. — *Daśaratha-vijaya, as,* m., N. of the twelfth chapter of the Pātāla-khaṇḍa of the Padma-Purāṇa. — *Daśa-raśmi-śata, as,* m. 'possessed of a thousand rays,' an epithet of the sun; [cf. *daśaśata-raśmi.*] — *Daśa-rātra, as,* m. a period of ten days and nights; (*as, ā, am*), Ved. lasting ten days; (*as*), m., Ved. any ceremony that lasts ten days; a particular ceremony lasting ten days (forming the chief part of the Dvādaśāha). — *Daśarātra-parvan, a,* n., N. of a Sāman. — *Daśa-rūpaka, am,* n., N. of a rhetorical work. — *Daśarūpaka-ṭīkā,* f., N. of a commentary on the preceding work by Pāṇi. — *Daśa-rūpa-bhṛit, t, t, t,* taking ten forms, appearing in ten shapes; (*t*), m. an epithet of Vishṇu (with reference to his ten Avatāras). — *Daśarća* (°*śa-ṛića*), *as,* m., Ved. a strophe of ten verses. — *Daśarshabha* (°*śa-ṛish*°), *as, ā, am,* Ved. consisting of ten bulls. — *Daśa-lakshaṇa, am,* n. ten marks or attributes. — *Daśa-lakshaṇaka, as, ikā, am,* having ten forms or characteristics, ten-fold. — *Daśa-vaktra, as, ā, am,* having ten mouths; (*as*), m. a particular magical formula against the evil spirits supposed to possess certain weapons. — *Daśa-vadana, as,* m. 'the ten-faced,' an epithet of Rāvaṇa. — *Daśa-varman, ā,* m., N. of a prince. — *Daśa-varsha, as, ā, am,* ten years old. — *Daśa-vājin, ī,* m. the moon 'whose car is drawn by ten horses.' — *Daśa-vārshika, as, ī, am,* happening after ten years. — *Daśa-vidha, as, ā, am,* of ten kinds, ten-fold. — *Daśa-vīra, as, ā, am,* Ved. granting ten men. — *Daśa-vṛiksha, as,* m., Ved. a species of tree. — *Daśa-vraja, as,* m., N. of a man. — *Daśa-śata, am,* n. ten hundred, a thousand; one hundred and ten; (*ī*), f. a thousand; (*as, ī, am*), Ved. containing ten hundred. — *Daśa-śata-kara-dhārin, ī,* m. 'having a thousand rays,' the sun. — *Daśaśata-tama, as, ī, am,* the one hundred and tenth. — *Daśaśata-nayana, as, ā* or *ī, am,* having a thousand eyes; (*as*), m. an epithet of Indra. — *Daśaśata-raśmi, is, is, i,* having a thousand rays; (*is*), m. the sun; [cf. *daśa-raśmi-śata.*] — *Daśaśatāksha* (°*ta-ak*°), *as, ī, am,* having a thousand eyes; (*as*), m. an epithet of Indra. — *Daśaśatāṅghri* (°*ta-an*°), *is, is, i,* having a thousand feet; (*is*), f. a species of plant, = *śatāvarī.* — *Daśa-śipra, as,* m., N. of a man. — *Daśa-śiras, ās, ās, as,* ten-headed; (*ās*), m. an epithet of Rāvaṇa; N. of a mountain. — *Daśa-śīrsha, as, ā, am,* ten-headed; (*as*), m. an epithet of Rāvaṇa; a kind of magical formula against the evil spirits supposed to possess weapons. — *Daśa-ślokī,* f. 'a collection of ten Ślokas,' N. of a summary of the Vedānta system by Śaṅkarāćārya; also of another similar summary by Nimbārka. — *Daśa-saptā,* f., Ved., N. of a Vishṭuti of the Saptadaśa-stoma (in which the verses of a Tṛića are repeated in the following order, 11123, 12223, 1222333). — *Daśa-sāhasra, am,* n., 10,000; (*as, ī, am*), consisting of 10,000, forming 10,000. — *Daśa-sāhasrika, as, ī, am,* consisting of 10,000. — *Daśa-stobha, am,* n., N. of a Sāman. — *Daśa-harā,* f. an epithet of Gaṅgā or the Ganges, 'as taking away ten sins;' a festival in honour of Gaṅgā (vulgarly called Dusrah) on the tenth day of the month Jyaishṭha, but now held in honour of Durgā in the month Āśvin. — *Daśa-hotṛi, tā,* m., Ved. a particular Mantra in which the ten sacrificial vessels are mentioned; (*tā, tṛī, tṛi*), connected with the Mantra Daśa-hotṛi. — *Daśāṅśa* (°*śa-aṅśa*), *as* or *am,* m. or n. (?), ten parts, the tenth part, ten-fold amount of anything (?). — *Daśāksha* (°*śa-ak*°), *as, ī, am,* ten-eyed; (*as*), m. a kind of magical formula against the evil spirits supposed to possess weapons. — *Daśākshara* (°*śa-ak*°), *as, ā, am,* Ved. containing ten syllables. — *Daśāṅgula* (°*śa-an*°), *as,* &c., ten fingers long; (*am*), n. a water-melon. — *Daśādhipati* (°*śa-adh*°), *is,* m. a decurion or commander of ten men. — *Daśānana* (°*śa-ān*°), *as, ā* or *ī, am,* ten-faced; (*as*), m. an epithet of Rāvaṇa. — *Daśānugāna* (°*śa-an*°), *am,* n., N. of a Sāman. — *Daśārdha* (°*śa-ar*°), *ās, ās, āni,* pl. half of ten, five. — *Daśārdha-saṅkhya, as, ā, am,* five in number. — *Daśārha* (°*śa-ar*°), *as,* m. 'worthy of ten (?),' an epithet applied to a Buddha; an epithet of Kṛishṇa; (*ās*), or *daśārhakās,* m. pl., N. of a warrior-tribe descended from Daśārha of the family of Yadu; (*ī*), f. a princess of the Daśārhas. — *Daśāvatāra* (°*śa-av*°), *as,* m. an epithet of Vishṇu (the deity, of whom there are ten descents from heaven); N. of the fifty-sixth chapter of the Bhavishya-Purāṇa. — *Daśāvara* (°*śa-av*°), *as, ā, am,* consisting of ten at least; (*as*), m., N. of an evil spirit. — *Daśāśva* (°*śa-aś*°), *as, ā, am,* possessing ten horses, driving ten horses; (*as*), m. the moon; N. of a son of Ikshvāku. — *Daśāśvamedha* (°*śa-aś*°), *am,* n., N. of a Tīrtha, the Tīrtha of the ten horse-sacrifices. — *Daśāsya* (°*śa-ās*°), *as, ā, am,* having ten mouths, ten-faced; (*as*), m. an epithet of Rāvaṇa. — *Daśāsya-jit, t,* m. 'conqueror of the ten-faced,' an epithet of Rāma. — *Daśāha* (°*śa-aha*), *as, ā, am,* lasting ten days; (*as*), m. a period of ten days; a kind of ceremonial observance; [cf. *daśa-rātra.*] — *Daśendra* (°*śa-in*°), *as,* &c., having the ten Indrāṇīs as a deity (schol. to Pāṇ. I. 2, 49). — *Daśendriya* (°*śa-in*°), *āni,* n. pl. the ten organs of perception and action, viz. the skin, eye, tongue, nose, ear, larynx, hand, foot, anus, and pudendum; see *indriya.* — *Daśeśa* (°*śa-īś*°), *as,* m. a superintendent of ten villages. — *Daśaikādaśika* (°*śa-ek*°), *as, ī, am,* one who lends ten and receives eleven in return, i. e. one who lends money for ten per cent. — *Daśoṇi* (°*śa-oṇi*), *is,* m., N. of a person protected by Indra; of an Asura; (Sāy.) offering many oblations; (according to some) an oblation giving ten-fold reward. — *Daśoṇya, as,* m., N. of a man. — *Daśopanishad-bhāshya* (°*śa-up*°), *am,* n., N. of a commentary by Ānanda Tīrtha.

Daśa (at the end of comp.) = *daśan* above; [cf. *tri-daśa, dvi-daśa, nir-daśa.*] *Daśa* (at the end of comp.) may also stand for *daśā,* p. 406, col. 1.

Daśaka, as, ā, am, consisting of ten, having ten, having ten parts, ten-fold; (with *śata*), ten in a hundred, ten from a hundred, ten per cent; (*am*), n. an aggregate of ten, a decad. — *Daśaka-māsika, as, ā, am,* hired for ten months.

Daśat, t, f. a collection or aggregate of ten, a decad; (m. f. n.?), consisting of ten, divided into ten parts; [cf. *dāśat* and *pañćat.*]

Daśataya, as, ī, am, consisting of ten parts, ten-fold; (*yyas*), f. pl., scil. *śākhās* or *ṛićas,* the texts of the ten-fold Ṛig-veda, i. e. of the Ṛig-veda divided into ten Maṇḍalas; (*ī*), f., N. of a commentary; [cf. *dāśataya.*]

Daśati, is, f. (probably for original *daśatī*), a collection or aggregate of ten, a decad; N. of the subdivisions of a Prapāṭhaka of the first part of the Sāma-veda, usually containing ten verses, (in this sense the crude form *daśati* without Visarga is used, probably as a weakened form of *daśatī*); = a hundred in connection with *daśan* (e. g. *daśatīr daśa* in Mahā-bh. I. 1081).

Daśama, as, ī, am, the tenth, the tenth part, the tenth day, N. of an Ekāha, the last day of the Daśa-rātra belonging to the Dvādaśāha; (*ī*), f., scil. *tithi,* the tenth day of the half moon; the tenth decad or last stage of human life, the last ten years of a century; (*am*), n. a tenth part; (*am*), ind. at or for the tenth time; [cf. Lat. *decimus;* Scot. *deicheamh;* Hib. *deachmad.*] — *Daśama-bhāva, as,* m. the culminating point, or that point in which the meridian crosses a given circle. — *Daśamīn-gata* or *daśamī-stha, as, ā, am,* arrived at the tenth decad of life, above ninety years old.

Daśamin, ī, inī, i, between ninety and one hundred years, very old or aged.

Daśin, ī, inī, i, having ten, divided into ten parts; (*inī*), f. a decad; (*ī*), m. a superintendent of ten villages.

दशन *daśana, as, am,* m. n. (fr. rt. *daś* or 2. *daṅś*), a tooth; biting; (*as*), m. the peak of a mountain; (*am*), n. armour, mail; [cf. *daṅśana.*] — *Daśana-ććhada, as,* m. 'teeth-covering,' the lip. — *Daśana-pada, am,* n. 'teeth-mark,' a bite. — *Daśana-vāsas, as,* n. 'the covering of the teeth,' the lip. — *Daśana-vīja, am,* n. (?) the pomegranate. — *Daśanāṅśu* (°*na-aṅ*°), *us,* m. whiteness or brightness of the teeth. — *Daśanāṅka* (°*na-an*°), *as,* m. 'teeth-mark,' a bite. — *Daśanāḍhyā* (°*na-āḍh*°), f. a kind of sorrel (= *ćukrikā*). — *Daśanoććhishṭa* (°*na-uć*°), *as,* m. 'remainder or leavings of the teeth,' a kiss; a sigh; a lip.

Daśera, as, ā, am, biting, mordacious, injuring; hurtful, attacking or killing any one when asleep; (*as*), m. a mischievous or venomous animal, a beast of prey, &c.

Daśeraka or *daseraka, ās,* m. pl., N. of a people, = *maru;* a young camel; [cf. *dāśera, dāśeraka, dāsera, dāseraka.*]

Dashṭa, as, ā, am, bitten, stung; pressed together. — *Dashṭa-daććhada, as, ā, am*, biting the lips.

दशमान *daśamāna* or *daśamānika, ās*, m. pl., N. of a people; (also written *deśamānika*.)

दशस्य *daśasya* (fr. *daśas*, probably an old form for *yaśas*, = Lat. *decus*; cf. rt. 1. *dāś*), Nom. P. *daśasyati*, &c., Ved. to render service, serve, worship, favour, oblige, aid (with acc.); to do service or favour to any one (with dat.); to grant, accord; [cf. *namasya*; *dāśaspatya*.]

Daśasyā, f. occurring only in Ved. inst. *daśasyā*, at the pleasure of, according to the liking, in order to please; (Sāy.) by desire of giving or granting.

दशा *daśā*, f. (said to be fr. rt. *daś* or 2. *daṅś*), the threads or fringe projecting at the end of a piece of woven cloth, the fringe of a garment (e. g. *apa-daśaṃ vāsas*, a fringeless garment), the loose ends of any piece of cloth or garment, the skirt or edge or hem of a garment, (according to some in these senses also m. pl., but in most passages where the pl. *daśās* occurs the gender may be f.); the wick of a lamp; 'the wick of life,' state or condition of life; age, period or time of life (as youth, manhood, &c.); period in general; state, condition, circumstances; state or condition of mind; the result of actions, fate; (in astrology) the aspect or position of the planets (at birth &c.), the fate of men as depending on the position of the planets; the mind, understanding. — *Daśākarsha, as*, or *daśākarshin* (°*śā-āk*° or °*śā-ka*°), *ī*, m. 'wick-drawing,' a lamp. — *Daśānta* (°*śā-an*°), *as*, m. the end of a wick, the end of life. — *Daśāpanna* (°*śā-āp*°), *as, ā, am*, being in a particular state or condition. — *Daśā-pavitra, am*, n. a fringed filtering cloth for straining the Soma. — *Daśā-pāka, as*, m. the fulfilment of fate. — *Daśā-phala, am*, n. result of circumstances or of condition of life. — *Daśāruhā* (°*śā-ār*°), f, N. of a particular species of plant, = *kaivartikā*, (probably so called as sticking or attaching itself to clothes.) — *Daśā-lakshaṇa, am*, n., N. of a chapter of the Purāṇa-sarva-sva. — *Daśā-viśesha, as*, m. any particular state or condition, existing circumstances. — *Daśendhana* (°*śā-in*°), *as*, m. 'wick-kindling,' a lamp.

दशानिक *daśānika, as*, m. = *dantī*, Croton Polyandrum or Croton Tiglium.

दशामय *daśāmaya, as*, m. (fr. *daśā* or *da-śan* + *āmaya*?), an epithet of Śiva.

दशार्ण *daśārṇa, ās*, m. pl. (said to be fr. *daśan* + *ṛiṇa*, 'having ten forts'), N. of a people living south-east of Madhya-deśa in the centre of Hindūstān; (*as*), m. the king of the Daśārṇas; the region of the Daśārṇas; (*ā*), f., N. of a river rising in the Vindhya hills, the ancient Dosarene (?).

Daśārṇaka, a wrong form for *dāśārṇaka*, q. v.

Daśārṇeya, us, m., N. of a son of Raudrāśva.

दशार्ह *daśārha*. See p. 405, col. 2.

दशीविदर्भ *daśīvidarbha, ās*, m. pl., N. of a people; [cf. *dadhi-vidarbha*.]

दशेर *daśera*. See *daśana*, p. 405, col. 3.

दशोनसि *daśonasi, is*, m., Ved. a kind of serpent.

दष्ट *dashṭa*. See above at top of this col.

दस् *das* (connected with rt. *daṅs*, p. 396, col. 2), cl. 4. P. *dasyati, dadāsa*, &c., Ved. to suffer want, to waste away, perish, become exhausted, to be ruined; to throw up, toss [cf. rt. *tas*; Eng. *toss*]; cl. 1. 10. P. *daṅsati, daṅsayati*, &c. (see rt. *daṅs*), to bite, destroy, overpower; to see; to shine: Caus. P. *dasayati, dāsayati, -yitum*, to cause to waste away, exhaust.

Dasa, as, m., Ved. = *dasyu*, q. v.

Dasana, am, n. wasting, perishing, destroying; throwing, tossing; dismissing.

Dasamāna, as, ā, am, Ved. wasting away, becoming exhausted.

Dasta, as, ā, am, wasted, lost, destroyed; thrown, tossed; sent away, dismissed.

Dasma, as, ā, am, destroying, destructive, overcoming enemies, worthy to be seen, beautiful, accomplishing wonderful deeds, wonderful, extraordinary; (*as*), m. an epithet of Agni; of Indra; of Pūshan; of Varuṇa; (*ās*), m. pl. an epithet of the Maruts; of the horses of Agni. According to the lexicographers *dasma, as*, m., may also mean 'a sacrificer' or 'institutor of a sacrifice;' 'fire;' 'a thief,' 'a rogue;' [cf. *daṅsana*.] — *Dasma-varćas, ās, ās, as*, Ved. of wonderful appearance; (Sāy.) whose glory is worthy of being seen or whose power is destructive; (*ās*), m. an epithet of Indra; of Pūshan; (*asas*), m. pl. an epithet of the Maruts.

Dasmat, ān, atī, at, Ved. wonderful, extraordinary; (Sāy.) worthy of being seen, desirable, acceptable. According to Sāy. on Ṛig-veda I. 74. 4, the form *dasmat* is for *dasmam*.

Dasmya, as, ā, am, Ved. wonderful, extraordinary; (Sāy.) beautiful.

Dasyu, us, m. (probably connected with *dāsa*), 'destroyer (of the good),' N. of a class of evil beings or demons, enemies of god and men, and especially of Indra and Agni; (many of the demons defeated by Indra have the general name Dasyu, e. g. Vṛitra, Sambara, Sushṇa, Cumuri, &c.; and these Dasyus are not only spirits of darkness like the Rākshasas, but have other characteristics which bring them into closer relationship to men living in the world: sometimes a general distinction is drawn between man, i. e. *manu, āyu, nṛi*, and the Dasyus, the latter being called *a-mānusha*, or the Dasyu is contrasted as an *an-ārya* with the pious and respectable man or *ārya*; or rarely *dasyu* means 'a barbarian or savage,' as contrasted with 'a civilized man'); any cruel or mischievous man, an enemy, thief, robber, oppressor, bandit, ruffian, violator, perpetrator of injustice; (according to Manu) a barbarian, an outcast or a Hindū who has become so by neglect of the essential rites. — *Dasyu-jīvin, ī, inī, i*, living the life of a robber or barbarian. — *Dasyu-jūta, as, ā, am*, Ved. instigated by Dasyus or by wicked men. — *Dasyu-tarhaṇa, as, ī, am*, Ved. crushing the Dasyus; killing or injuring the Dasyus. — *Dasyu-sāt*, ind. into the hands of the Dasyus, a prey to robbers. — *Dasyu-hatya, am*, n., Ved. a fight with the Dasyus or with wicked men. — *Dasyu-han, ā, ghnī, a*, Ved. destroying the Dasyus or the wicked; (*ā*), m. an epithet of Indra; of Agni; of Manyu. — *Dasyuhan-tama, as*, m. (superl. of the preceding), an epithet of Budha, who was son of Tārā and Soma.

Dasra, as, ā, am, Ved. destroying, destructive, overcoming enemies, accomplishing wonderful deeds, giving marvellous aid; worthy to be seen, handsome, beautiful; (*as*), m., N. of Pūshan; N. of one of the two Aśvins (the other being called Nāsatya); an ass; a robber, thief, &c., see *dasyu*; (*au*, Ved. *ā*), m. du., N. or epithet of the Aśvins, said to be so called as 'destroying diseases or enemies,' (occurring usually in the nom. and voc.); a N. of Indra-Vishṇu; the numeral two; (*ās*), m. pl. an epithet of the Maruts; (*am*), n. the cold season, hoar frost. In Sūrya-siddhānta VIII. 9, *dasrādīnām* must be translated 'of the Nakshatra Aśvinī, &c.,' see *dasra-devatā*; [cf. *daṅsana, daṅsas, daṅsa, daṅsishṭha*.] — *Dasra-devatā*, f. the lunar constellation Aśvinī. — *Dasra-sū, ūs*, f. 'the mother of the Aśvins,' N. of Sañjñā or the wife of the Sun.

Dāsita, as, ā, am, = *dasta* above.

दसाराम *dasārāma, as*, m., N. of a man.

दह् 1. *dah* (the original form of this rt. was probably *dagh*), cl. 1. P. *dahati* (ep. *dahate*), *dadāha, dhakshyati* (ep. *dahishyati*), *dhakshyate, dagdhum* (Ved. inf. *dagdhos*; other Vedic forms are *dakshi, adhāk, dhāk*; part. *dhakshat* or *dakshat*), to burn, consume by fire, scorch, roast; (in surgery) to cauterize; to consume, destroy completely; to torment, torture, pain, distress, disturb, grieve: Pass. *dahyate* (ep. also *dahyati*), to be burnt, to burn, to be in flames; to be consumed by fire; to be inflamed; to be consumed by internal heat or by grief, to suffer pain, be distressed, be vexed; to be destroyed &c.; (also transitive) to burn: Caus. *dāhayati, -yitum*, Aor. *adīdahat*, to cause to burn or to be burned &c.; to cause to roast or to be cooked: Desid. *didhakshati* (ep. *-te*), to wish to burn, to be about to consume or destroy, &c. [cf. *didhakshā* and *didhakshu*]: Caus. of Desid. *didhakshayati, -yitum*, to cause to desire to burn or to be about to burn: Intens. *dandahīti, dandahyate, dandagdhi* (also 2nd sing. impv.), to burn completely, destroy completely; (A.) to be burnt completely, be entirely consumed by fire or grief; [cf. Hib. *daghaim; daighim, daghte*, 'burnt,' = *dagdha*; *dvighir*, 'flame:' Lith. *degù*, 'I am hot;' *deginù*, 'I burn:' Old Germ. *tāh-t* or *dāh-t*, 'a wick,' fr. Caus.: Goth. *dag-s*, 'the day:' Angl. Sax. *daeg*: Mod. Germ. *tag*: Eng. *day*: perhaps Gr. *τήγανον*: Lat. *lig-nu-m* for *dig-nu-m*.]

2. *dah, dhak, k, k*, burning (at the end of comp.; cf. *uśa-dhak*).

Dahat, an, antī, at, burning, scorching.

Dahati, is, m., N. of one of the attendants on Skanda.

Dahadahā, f., N. of one of the Mātṛis attending on Skanda.

Dahana, as, ī, am, burning, consuming by fire, scorching, destroying [cf. *tripura-d*°]; destructive, injurious, mischievous; (*as*), m. fire, a N. of Agni the god of fire; the numeral three; one of the five forms of fire in the Svāhā-kāra; N. of one of the eleven Rudras; of one of the attendants of Skanda; a bad man; a pigeon; lead-wort, Plumbago Zeylanica (= *ćitraka*); the marking-nut, Anacardium Officinarum (= *bhallātaka*); (*ī*), f. fire; (*am*), n. burning, cauterizing, consuming by fire; sour gruel. — *Dahana-ketana, as*, m. 'the mark of burning,' smoke. — *Dahana-priyā*, f. 'the beloved of fire,' N. of Svāhā or the wife of Agni. — *Dahanarksha* (°*na-ṛiksha*), *am*, n. 'the burning constellation,' the constellation Kṛittikā. — *Dahanāguru* (°*na-ag*°), *us*, m., N. of a species of the plant Agallochum. — *Dahanārāti* (°*na-ar*°), *is*, m. 'enemy of fire,' water. — *Dahanopakaraṇa* (°*na-up*°), *am*, n. the means for cauterizing. — *Dahanopala* (°*na-up*°), *as*, m. 'fire-stone,' the sun-gem, a crystal lens; (also read *dahanopama*; cf. *sūrya-kānta*.) — *Dahanolkā* (°*na-ul*°), f. a firebrand.

Dahanīya, as, ā, am, to be burnt, burnable, combustible. — *Dahanīya-tā*, f. or *dahanīya-tva, am*, n. combustibility.

Dahyamāna, as, ā, am, being burnt.

दहर *dahara, as, ā, am* (said to be fr. rt. 1. *dah*, probably another form of *dahra*, which is for *dabhra*; see *dahra* below), small, fine, thin, subtile, short; young in age, (opposed to *vṛiddha*); the cavity of the heart, the heart; (*as*), m. a child, infant; a younger brother; a young animal; a rat, mouse. — *Dahara-prishṭha, am*, n., N. of a section of the Taittirīya-saṃhitā; [cf. *mahā-prishṭha*.] — *Dahara-sūtra, am*, n., N. of a Buddhist Sūtra work.

Daharaka = *dahara* above.

Dahra, as, ā, am, small, fine, thin; the cavity of the heart; the heart itself; (*as*), m. fire; a forest conflagration, a wood on fire. — *Dahra-tas*, ind. from the cavity of the heart. — *Dahrāgni* (°*ra-ag*°), *is*, m., N. of Agastya in a former birth.

दहियक *dahiyaka, as*, m. (?), N. of a particular kind of bird.

दह्र *dahra*. See above under *dahara*.

दा 1. *dā* (many of the forms of this rt. are to be referred to the base *dad*, which is sometimes regarded as a separate rt.; cf. 1. *dad*), cl. 3. P. A. *dadāti, datte*, 1st pl. *dadmas*, 2nd pl. *dattha*,

3rd pl. dadati (3rd pl. A. dadate); Impf. adadāt, adatta (3rd du. adattām, 3rd pl. adadus, A. adadata); Pot. dadyāt, dadīta (1st pl. A. dadīmahi, 3rd pl. dadīran); Impv. dadātu, dattām (2nd sing. dehi, A. datsva, 3rd du. dattām, 2nd pl. datta, 3rd pl. dadatu); Perf. dadau, dade (2nd sing. daditha or dadātha, 2nd du. dadathus, 2nd pl. dada, 3rd pl. dadus, 3rd du. A. dadāte, part. dadivas, gen. dadushas); Fut. dātā, dāsyati, -te; Aor. adāt, adita (3rd pl. P. adus, 1st sing. A. adishi, 3rd pl. adishata); Prec. deyāt, dāsīshṭa; (Ved. forms are Pres. 3rd sing. dāti, 1st pl. dadmasi; Impf. 2nd pl. adadāta, adattana, 2nd sing. dadās, 3rd sing. dadāt, 2nd pl. dadāta; Impv. dātu, 2nd sing. daddhi; Perf. 3rd pl. A. with pra, dadrire, part. dadāvat, dadvat; Aor. dāt, 3rd du. dātām, 2nd pl. dāta, 3rd pl. dus, 3rd sing. A. adadishṭa, adadishṭa, 2nd sing. Let dadas. Ep. forms fr. 1. dad are 1st sing. Pres. dadmi, 3rd sing. dadati, -te, 3rd pl. dadanti, -te; Impf. 3rd sing. adadat; Impv. 2nd sing. dada, A. dadasva; Perf. 3rd sing. dadade, 3rd du. dadadāte, 3rd pl. dadadire); dātum, Ved. inf. dātave, dātavai, dātos, dai in parā-dai; to give, bestow, grant, yield, impart, present, offer (usually with acc. of the thing and dat. gen. or loc. of the person, e. g. tat tasmai or tasya or tasmin dehi, give that to him); to deliver over, hand over; to give back, restore, return; to pay (e. g. ṛiṇam dā, to pay a debt; daṇḍam dā, to pay a fine); to give away, give up, cede, sacrifice, devote, surrender (e. g. prāṇān or jīvitam dā, to give one's life; ātmānam dā, to sacrifice one's self; ātmānam khedāya dā, to give one's self up to grief); to give in marriage (with or without bhāryām, e. g. dadau kanyām tasmai bhāryām, he gave the maiden to him as wife; yasmai pitā tām dadyāt, to whomsoever a father may marry her); to communicate knowledge or advice, to teach (e. g. vidyām dā, to impart knowledge); to sell (with inst. of the price, e. g. gavām sahasreṇa dā, to sell for a thousand cows); to permit, allow (e. g. vāshpo na dadāti tām drashṭum, tears do not allow her to see); to place, put, apply (e. g. padam bhasma-ćaye dadau, he placed his foot on a heap of ashes). The root dā may sometimes yield senses equivalent to 'to do,' 'make,' 'cause,' 'perform,' 'bring about,' 'accomplish;' and the meanings of this root may be variously modified according to the nouns with which it is connected, as in the following examples: śokam dā, to cause grief; vratam dā, to accomplish a vow; śrāddham dā, to perform the Śrāddha; sanjñām dā, to make a sign; panthānam or mārgam dā, to give up the road, stand out of the way, allow to pass; avakāśam dā, to give room or space, allow to enter; yuddham or saṅgrāmam dā, to give battle, fight with; ājñām or ādeśam dā, to give an order, to command; sandeśam dā, to give information; varam dā, to grant a boon; āśisho dā, to grant or utter blessings; prati-vaćas or prati-vaćanam or praty-uttaram dā, to give an answer; śabdam dā, to make a noise, call out; vāćam dā (with dat.), to address a speech to; satyam vaća dā, to speak the truth; samayam dā, to propose an agreement; śāpam dā, to utter a curse or oath; āliṅganam dā, to embrace; jhampam dā, to give a spring, to jump; anuyātrām dā, to accompany; talam or talān dā, to slap with the palms of the hands, to shake hands; tala-prahāram dā, to strike with the palm &c.; tālam dā, to beat time with the hands; saṅketakam dā, to make an appointment with any one; prayogam dā, to give a dramatic representation; vṛitim dā, to inclose or fence in; darśanam or dṛishṭim dā, to show one's self, become visible, appear; dṛishṭim or dṛiśam or akshi or ćakshur dā (with loc.), to fix the eyes on, look at; nigaḍāni dā, to put on fetters; pāvakam dā, to set on fire; śāram dā, to move a chess-man; argalam dā, to draw a bolt, to bar; padam dā, to direct the steps; karṇam dā, to give ear, listen; mano dā, to direct the mind to anything, think upon. In some passages of the Veda the base dad (A. dadate) yields senses equivalent to 'to receive,' 'carry,' 'convey,' 'bear,' 'hold,' 'keep,' 'preserve,' to which some refer the part. datta, preserved; [cf. 5. dā.] Caus. P. dāpayati, -yitum, adīdapat, to cause to give or to be given, to cause to bestow, present, &c. (with two acc.); to cause to be offered; to oblige to pay, make pay; to force to restore or return, to make surrender or deliver; to procure; to cause to do or perform or accomplish; to cause to put or apply, cause to be put on; to cause to speak or utter: Desid. P. A. ditsati, -te, (Ved.) didāsati, to wish to give &c., to be ready to bestow &c.: Intens. dedīyate, dādāti; [cf. rts. dās, rā, lā: Zend dā, 'to give;' dā-tar, dā-ta, 'giver;' dā-na, dā-thra, 'present:' Gr. δίδωμι = dadāmi, δο-τήρ, δω-τήρ, δῶ-τι-ς, δό-τι-ς, δῶ-ρο-ν, δάνος, δαπάνη from the Caus. dāpayati: Lat. dă-re, dă-tor, dō-s, dō-nu-m: Slav. da-mĭ = dad-mi; da-rŭ, 'present;' da-nĭ, 'tax:' Lith. dů-mi = dad-mi, dů-ti-s, dů-ni-s, 'a gift:' Hib. daighim or dailim fr. daidim, 'I give:' Cambro-Brit. dodi, 'to give:' Angl. Sax. tidhe, tidhian.]

2. dā, ās, m., Ved. a giver; (at the end of comp.) giving, granting; [cf. an-aśva-dā, aśva-dā, āyur-dā, &c.]

Dāka, as, m. a giver, donor, one who makes presents, especially to Brāhmans; the institutor of a sacrifice who employs and pays the officiating priests.

1. dāta, Ved., said by some to = datta, 'given,' in tvā-dāta, q. v.; but the form dāta according to native authorities can only belong to 3. dā or 7. dā.

Dātavya, as, ā, am, to be given or bestowed; to be paid, payable; to be restored or returned; to be communicated or taught; to be given in marriage; to be placed upon or applied.

1. dāti, is, f. giving. See dāti-vāra under 2. dāti, p. 408, col. 1.

Dātu-kāma, as, ā, am (fr. dātum inf. of 1. √dā + kāma), wishing to bestow, desirous of giving.

1. dātṛi, tā, trī, tṛi, giving, bestowing, imparting, communicating, liberal; a giver, donor, imparter, lender, creditor, payer; teacher; [cf. kanyā-d°, brahma-d°, ṛiṇa-d°; Gr. δωτήρ, δοτήρ; Lat. dator.] — Dātṛi-tā, f. or dātṛi-tva, am, n. the state of being a giver, liberality. — Dātṛi-nirūpaṇa, am, n., N. of a chapter of the Purāṇa-sarva-sva. — Dātṛi-pura, am, n., N. of a town.

Dātva, as, m. a giver, donor; (am), n. a sacrificial ceremony; the performance of a sacrifice.

Dāda, as, m. (fr. base dad), a gift, donation, oblation, giving. — Dāda-da, as, m. a donor, giver of a gift.

Dādin, ī, inī, i, giving, a giver.

1. dāna, as, m., Ved. a giver, giving; an offering, (according to Sāy. = datta or deya-bhūta, but thought by modern scholars to be the epithet of a horse); (am), n. giving, presenting; giving in marriage (e. g. kanyā-d°, q. v.); giving up, sacrificing (e. g. prāṇa-d°, q. v.); delivering, distributing; communicating, imparting, teaching, giving instruction (e. g. brahma-d°, q. v.); a gift, present, donation (e. g. dānam dā, to offer a gift; cf. Lat. donum); special gift, oblation (e. g. udaka-d°, q. v.); adding, addition; liberality; bribery (one of the four means by which a king overpowers his enemies; cf. upāya); the fragrant fluid that flows from the temples of an elephant in rut (more probably connected with rt. 3. dā; see 2. dāna, p. 408, col. 1); a kind of honey, (perhaps for dāla.) — Dāna-kalpa-taru, us, m., N. of a work mentioned in the Saṃskāra-tattva by Raghunandana. — Dāna-kāma, as, ā, am, Ved. fond of giving, liberal. — Dāna-kulyā, f. the flow of fluid from an elephant's temples. — Dāna-kusumāñjali (°ma-añ°), N. of a poem. — Dāna-kaumudī, f., N. of the second part of the Kriyā-kaumudī. — Dāna-ćyuta, as, m., N. of a man. — Dāna-tas, ind. through gifts, by liberality. — Dāna-darpaṇa, N. of a work mentioned in the Saṃskāra-tattva. — Dāna-dharma, as, m. alms-giving, charitable acts, charity; the rules or practice of alms-giving. — Dānadharma-vidhi, is, m. 'the rules for alms-giving &c.,' N. of a chapter of the Skanda-Purāṇa. — Dāna-pati, is, m. 'a master of liberality,' an exceedingly liberal or munificent man; an epithet of A-krūra, who was kinsman of Kṛishṇa; N. of a Daitya. — Dāna-pattra, am, n. a deed of gift or conveyance. — Dāna-paddhati, is, f., N. of a work on the sixteen chief oblations. — Dāna-pātra, am, n. 'an object of charity, one who deserves a gift,' N. of a chapter of the Purāṇa-sarva-sva. — Dāna-pratibhāvya, am, n. security for payment of a debt &c. — Dāna-bhinna, as, ā, am, divided or made hostile by bribes. — Dāna-yogya, as, ā, am, worthy of a gift, meriting a donation. — Dāna-vajra, as, &c., 'whose thunderbolt is liberality,' an epithet of the Vaiśyas or men of the third tribe. — Dāna-vat, ān, atī, at, having gifts, presenting gifts, liberal. — Dāna-vidhi, is, m., N. of a chapter of the Skanda-Purāṇa. — Dāna-vīra, as, m. 'a hero in liberality,' an exceedingly liberal man. — Dāna-vyatyāsa, as, m. 'perversion of gifts,' gift under error, giving to the wrong person. — Dāna-vrata, as, ā, am, devoted to liberality or benevolence; (ās), m. pl. the inhabitants of Śāka-dvīpa. — Dāna-śīla, as, ā, am, liberally disposed, liberal, generous, charitable, munificent; (as), m., N. of one of the translators of the Lalita-vistara in Tibetian. — Dāna-śūra, as, m. 'a hero in liberality,' N. of a Bodhi-sattva (= Śākya-muni in a former birth; cf. dāna-vīra). — Dāna-śauṇḍa, as, ī, am, 'intoxicated with giving,' exceedingly liberal. — Dāna-sāgara, as, m. 'the ocean of gifts,' N. of a work by Malamāsa mentioned in the Saṃskāra-tattva by Raghu-nandana. — Dāna-stuti, is, f. 'praise of liberality,' N. of a kind of hymn. — Dāna-hīna, as, ā, am, deprived of gifts. — Dāna-hemādri (°ma-ad°), N. of a work on oblations written under the patronage of Hemādri. — Dānādhikāra (°na-adh°), as, m., N. of a short Buddhist work on alms-giving.

Dānaka, am, n. a mean, paltry, or miserable gift.

Dānika, (at the end of comp.) relating or referring to a gift, liberality, giving instruction, &c. (e. g. adhyayana-d°, consisting in the giving of instruction or in reading; cf. vara-d° and udaka-d°).

Dānin, ī, inī, i, giving, liberal, benevolent; having gifts; [cf. agra-d°.]

Dānīya, as, ā, am, due, bestowable, worthy or fit to be given; receiving gifts or oblations; (am), n. a thing to be given, gift, donation.

1. dānu, us, us, u, Ved. liberal; a donor, giver; prosperity, contentment; air, wind.

Dāpana, am, n. (fr. the Caus.), forcing or obliging to give or pay, causing to restore.

Dāpanīya, as, ā, am, to be made to give or pay, liable to be amerced, subject to the payment of a fine (with acc. of the sum paid); to be caused to be given.

Dāpayitavya, as, ā, am, to be forced or obliged to give or pay.

Dāpayitvā, ind. having caused or compelled to give or pay, having fined.

1. dāpita, as, ā, am, caused to be given, condemned to pay, fined; adjudged, to be paid by way of fine; assigned, awarded, entitled to receive a fine, any one to whom a fine is to be paid.

Dāpya, as, ā, am, = dāpanīya above.

1. dāman, ā, m. (for 2. and 3. dāman see p. 408, col. 2), Ved. a giver, donor; (a), n. giving, a gift; [cf. a-d° and su-d°.] — 1. dāman-vat, ān, atī, at, furnished with gifts; [cf. 2. dāman-vat under 3. dāman, p. 408, col. 2.]

1. dāya, as, ā, am [cf. 2. dāya, p. 408, col. 2], giving, presenting [cf. śata-d°]; (as), m. a gift, present, donation; a special gift, a nuptial present, that which a bride and bridegroom receive on their marriage; alms to a student at his initiation &c.; delivering, delivery, handing over; (for other meanings given by same under 1. dāya see 2. dāya, p. 408, col. 2.)

1. dāyaka, as, ikā, am, giving, bestowing, presenting, granting; effecting; a giver, donor (e. g. visha-d°, uttara-d°, manoratha-d°, kānti-d°,

jīva-d°, q. v.); placing upon, arranging. — *Dāyaka-tā*, f. the state of a giver, giving.

Dāyita, as, ā, am, probably a wrong reading for *dāpita*, q. v.

1. *dāyitṛi*, incorrect form for 1. *dātṛi*, p. 407, col. 2.

Dāyin, ī, inī, i, (at the end of comp.) giving, presenting, granting, paying, owing; communicating; causing, effecting; [cf. *a-d°, udaka-d°, ṛishabha-d°*.]

1. *dāru, us, us, u* (for 2. *dāru* see p. 410, col. 1), liberal, munificent, giving, communicating, compassionate; a giver, donor; an artist (in this sense perhaps to be referred to rt. *dṛī*).

Dāvan, Ved., occurring only in dat. *dāvane*, for the giving, in order to give or present; in order to receive; (*ā, ā, a*), giving, granting, (usually at the end of comp.; cf. *aśva-d°* and *śata-d°*.)

दा 3. *dā*, cl. 2. 4. P. *dāti, dyati, dātum*, to cut, divide; [according to native authorities the proper form of this rt. is *do*, q. v.; cf. rts. *dāy, dal*: Gr. δαί-ο-μαι, δαί(τ)-ς, δαιτύ-ς, δαί-τη, δαι-τρό-ς, δαί-νυ-μι, δαί-νυ-μαι, δαι-τυ-μών, δαΐζω, δατέ-ο-μαι, δα-σ-μό-ς, δάπτω (Caus.), δεῖπνον: Lat. *daps*: Cambro-Brit. *de*, 'to part;' *dead*, 'a parting.']

2. *dāta, as, ā, am*, cut, divided; reaped; (see Pāṇ. VIII. 4, 46.)

2. *dāti, is*, f. cutting, destroying; distribution. — *Dāti-vāra, as, ā, am*, Ved. (Sāy.) splitting the clouds or yielding water or giving strength or giving riches, (as if fr. 1. *dā*; see 1. *dāti*, p. 407, col. 2.)

Dātu, u, n., Ved. a part, division, allotted portion or task; (at the end of an adj. comp. after a numeral = fold, e. g. *sahasra-dātu*, thousand-fold.)

2. *dātṛi, tā, trī, tṛi* (for 1. *dātṛi* see p. 407, col. 2), Ved. cutting off, mowing; cropping (grass); a cutter.

Dātra, am, n., Ved. anything allotted or fallen to one's share, share, possession; an instrument for cutting or chopping wood &c., a sort of sickle or large knife, a bill-hook or hatchet with a curved point, commonly called a Dā.

2. *dāna, as*, m. (for 1. *dāna* see p. 407, col. 2), Ved. distribution (especially of food); a meal; a sacrificial meal; distributing, communicating, liberality; part, share, possession; a distributer; (*am*), n. cutting off, dividing; pasture; the fluid flowing from an elephant's temples when in rut; [cf. 1. *dāna*.] — *Dānāpnas* (°*na-ap°*), *ās, ās, as*, Ved. having abundant shares (or gifts, fr. 1. *dāna*). — *Dānaukas* (°*na-ok°*), *ās*, m., Ved. delighting in the sacrificial meal; (Sāy.) 'the abode of liberality, munificent,' epithet of Indra, (as if fr. 1. *dāna*.)

Dānava, as, ī, m. f. a class of demons, a giant, a Titan; (according to a later conception the Dānavas, who are implacable enemies of the Devas, are children of Danu and Kaśyapa, see *danu*, p. 401; the Daityas and Dānavas are often identified, and both of them are called Asuras); (*as, ī, am*), belonging to the Dānavas, peculiar to the Dānavas, &c. — *Dānava-guru, us*, m. 'the preceptor of the Dānavas,' N. of the regent of the planet Venus. — *Dānava-pati, is*, m. the king of the Dānavas. — *Dānava-pūjita, as, ā, am*, worshipped by the Dānavas; (*as*), m. the regent of the planet Venus. — *Dānava-priyā*, f. the betel plant. — *Dānava-sūdana, as, ā, am*, destroying the Dānavas. — *Dānavāri* (°*va-ari*), *is*, m. an enemy of the Dānavas; an epithet of Indra; of Śiva; (*ayas*), m. pl. the gods. — *Dānavendra* (°*va-in°*), *as*, m. the chief of the Dānavas.

Dānaveya, as, m. a Dānava or demon.

2. *dānu, us, us, u* (for 1. see p. 407, col. 3), valiant; a victor, conqueror, destroyer; (*us*), m. a class of demons; (*u*), n. a fluid, a drop, dew; [cf. *ārdra-d°, jīra-d°*.] — *Dānu-ćitra, as, ā, am*, Ved. shining with dew, brilliant with moisture; (Sāy.) wonderfully destructive, wonderfully liberal, marvellous by gifts, (as if fr. 1. *dā*.) — *Dānu-da, as, ā, am*, Ved. giving drops, trickling. — *Dānunas-patī*, m. du. (fr. the gen. sing. of 2. *dānu*), Ved. 'the lords of dew,' epithet of Mitra-varuṇa and of the Aśvins; (Sāy.) lords of munificence, (as if fr. 1. *dā*.) — *Dānu-pinva, as*, &c., Ved. swelling with drops. — *Dānu-mat, ān, atī, at*, Ved. having many oblations; liquid, fluid, trickling; (Sāy.) malignant, injurious; having gifts, liberal, suited to a giver, (as if fr. 1. *dā*.)

2. *dāman, ā, ā*, m. f. (for 1. *dāman* see p. 407, col. 3; for 3. *dāman* see below), an allotment, share.

2. *dāya, as*, m. [cf. 1. *dāya*, p. 407, col. 3], share, portion, separate property, inheritance, patrimony (e. g. *dāyād upāgata*, fallen to one's share by inheritance); a part (in *śata-d°*, q. v.); distributing, dividing, breaking; loss, destruction; irony; place, site, (some of the meanings here given as connected with rt. 3. *dā* may perhaps be referred to rt. 1. *dā*; cf. 1. *dāya*.) — *Dāya-kāla, as*, m. the time of dividing an inheritance. — *Dāya-krama-saṅgraha, as*, m., N. of a work on the law of inheritance. — *Dāya-tattva, am*, n., N. of a part of the Smṛiti-tattva. — *Dāyatattva-kṛit, t*, m., N. of an author mentioned in the Mitrodaya by Mitra-miśra. — *Dāya-bandhu, us*, m. 'a friend or partner in the inheritance,' a brother. — *Dāya-bhāga, as*, m. partition or portioning of inheritance, division of property among heirs, apportioning, inheritance; N. of a work on the law of inheritance. — *Dāyabhāga-ṭīkā*, f., N. of a commentary on the Dāya-bhāga by Kṛishṇa. — *Dāyabhāga-tattva, am*, n., N. of a work by Raghu-nandana. — *Dāya-vibhāga, as*, m. portioning of inheritance, division of property amongst heirs, portion. — *Dāyāda* (°*ya-āda*), *as*, m. 'the receiver of a portion or heritage,' an heir, claimant, candidate, pretender (with gen. or loc. of thing); a son, a kinsman near or remote, a distant descendant; (*ā, ī*), f. an heiress, daughter. — *Dāyāda-vat, ān, atī, at*, having an heir. — *Dāyādya, am*, n. inheritance. — *Dāyādya-tā*, f. the state of being an inheritor or near relation, near relationship, affinity. — *Dāyāpavartana* (°*ya-ap°*), *am*, n. forfeiture of property, privation. — *Dāyārha* (°*ya-ar°*), *as, ā, am*, claimable or claiming inheritance.

2. *dāyaka, as*, m. a heir, inheritor, kinsman.

Dāyādava, as, m. an inheritor, heir, kinsman (?).

1. *dita, as, ā, am*, cut, torn, divided.

1. *dina, as, ā, am* (for 2. *dina* see p. 412, col. 3), cut, split, destroyed.

दा 4. *dā*, cl. 4. P. *dyati, dātum*, to bind; (this root does not occur separately, and is not given in the Dhātu-pāṭha); [cf. Gr. δέ-ω, δί-δη-μι, δέ-σι-ς, δε-τή, δε-σ-μό-ς, διά-δη-μα; Angl. Sax. *ti-an*, 'to tie.']

Dāma (at the end of comp.) = 3. *dāman* below; [cf. *ud-d°* and *srag-d°*.]

3. *dāman, a*, n. (said to be also *ā*, f.), a string, cord, thread, rope, fetter, fillet; a girdle; a chaplet, wreath or garland for the forehead; a large bandage; a particular constellation. The word *dāman* may be used at the end of an adj. comp., e. g. *uru-dāman*, having a large garland; and according to Pāṇini IV. 1, 27, when a numeral precedes, the fem. must end in *ī*, e. g. *dvi-dāmnī*, having two cords: it also occurs at the end of proper names, e. g. *śiśā-d°*, q. v.; [cf. Gr. κρή-δεμνον.] — *Dāma-kaṇṭha, as, ā* or *ī, am*, having a rope round the neck; (*as*), m., N. of a man; (*ās*), m. pl. the descendants of this man. — *Dāma-granthi, is*, m. a name assumed by Nakula; [cf. *granthika*.] — *Dāma-ćandra, as*, m., N. of a man. — *Dāma-jāta-śrī, īs*, m., N. of a prince (occurring only on coins). — 2. *dāman-vat, ān, atī, at* (for 1. see p. 407, col. 3), furnished with cords &c. — *Dāma-siṅha, as*, m., N. of a prince. — *Dāmāñćana* (°*ma-añ°*), *am*, n. a foot-rope for horses &c.; (also *dāmāñćala, am*, n.) — *Dāmādy-upākhyāna* (°*ma-ād°*), *am*, n., N. of the fourteenth chapter of the Vāsishṭha-rāmāyaṇa, commonly called Yoga-vāsishṭha. — *Dāmodara* (°*ma-ud°*), *as*, m., N. of Kṛishṇa or Vishṇu ('having a cord round the belly,' Yaśodā his foster-mother having in vain passed a rope round his body, whilst a child, to keep him in confinement); N. of the twelfth month; of the ninth Arhat of the past Ut-sarpiṇī; of two kings of Kaśmīra; of a poet in the Bhoja-prabandha by Ballāla; of the editor of the drama called Mahā-nāṭaka; of the author of a medical work; of the father of Malhaṇa and of several other men; of a river. — *Dāmodara-gupta, as*, m., N. of a poet. — *Dāmodara-datta, as*, m., N. of the father of Padma-nātha-datta. — *Dāmodara-deva, as*, m., N. of a poet. — *Dāmodara-paddhati, is*, f., N. of an astronomical work. — *Dāmodarāraṇya* (°*ra-ar°*), *am*, n. 'Kṛishṇa's wood,' N. of a forest. — *Dāmoshṇīsha* (°*ma-ush°*), *as*, m., N. of an old sage; (also read *dāmoshṇīva* and *dāmoshṇīśa*.) — *Dāmoshṇīshi, is*, m. a patronymic from Dāmoshṇīsha. — *Dāmoshṇīshya, as*, m. a patronymic from Dāmoshṇīshi.

Dāmanī, f. [cf. *dāmana*, p. 409, col. 3], a multitude of ropes or strings for tying cattle (especially calves).

Dāmanīka, as, ā, am, at the end of an adj. comp. = *dāmanī* above.

Dāmā, f. a string, cord, &c., = 3. *dāman*, col. 2.

2. *dita, as, ā, am*, bound; [cf. *sam-dita*.]

दा 5. *dā*, cl. 1. A. *dayate, dātum*, to protect, defend, guard; (according to native authorities the proper form of this rt. is *de*, q. v.)

Datta, as, ā, am, protected, defended.

6. *dā, ās*, f. protection, defence.

दा 7. *dā*, cl. 1. P. *dāyati, dātum*, to clean, purify; (according to native authorities the proper form of this rt. is *dai*, q. v.)

8. *dā, ās*, f. cleansing, purifying.

3. *dāta, as, ā, am* [cf. *ava-dāta*], cleansed, cleaned, washed, purified; (see Pāṇ. VII. 4, 46.)

3. *dāna, am*, n. purification; [cf. 1. *ava-dāna*.]

दाक *dāka*. See under. rt. 1. *dā*.

दाक्ष *dāksha, as, ī, am* (fr. *daksha*), relating to Daksha; relating to Dākshi; (*as*), m. or (*am*), n. the south; *dākshasyāyanam* (°*ya-ay°*) = *dakshiṇāyanam*, the progress of the sun towards the south; the winter solstice; the sacrifice performed at this time; (*ās*), m. pl., N. of the disciples of a particular school.

Dākshaka, as, &c., inhabited by the Dākshis; (*am*), n. a multitude of the descendants of Daksha.

Dākshāyaṇa, as, ī, am, coming from the Daksha family, of or relating to Daksha; (*as*), m. a son or distant descendant of Daksha; a particular kind of sacrifice [cf. *dākshāyaṇa-yajña*]; (*ī*), f., N. of any of the daughters of Daksha; of Aditi; of Diti; of Kadrū; of Vi-natā; of the nymph and asterism Rohiṇī; of Su-rasā, mother of the Nāgas; of Jayā and Vi-jayā; of Svadhā; of Durgā, wife of Śiva; of the wife of Dharma, mentioned in the Vāmana-Purāṇa; N. of the plant Croton Polyandrum, = *dantī*; (*yas*), f. pl. the twenty-seven lunar mansions considered mythologically as the daughters of Daksha and wives of the Moon; (*am*), n. the posterity of Daksha; gold or a gold ornament (as an ear-ring &c.); = *dākshasyāyanam*, the winter solstice; the sacrifice performed at this time. — *Dākshāyaṇa-bhakta, am*, n. the district inhabited by the Dākshas. — *Dākshāyaṇa-yajña, as*, m., N. of a kind of sacrifice said to be a modification of the Darśapaurṇamāsa (extending through fifteen instead of thirty years). — *Dākshāyaṇayajñika, as, ā, am*, or *dākshāyaṇayajñin, ī, inī, i*, belonging to the Dākshāyaṇa sacrifice. — *Dākshāyaṇī-pa, as*, or *dākshāyaṇī-pati, is*, m. 'husband of Dākshāyaṇī,' epithet of the Moon; of Śiva. — *Dākshāyaṇī-ramaṇa, as*, m. 'delighting in Dākshāyaṇī,' epithet of the Moon. — *Dākshāyaṇy-agni-praveśa, as*, m., N. of the tenth chapter of the Uttara-khaṇḍa of the Śiva-Purāṇa.

Dākshāyaṇin, ī, inī, i, having gold, wearing golden ornaments; (*ī*), m. a Brāhman student wearing golden ear-rings.

Dākshāyaṇya, as, m. the son of the Dākshāyaṇī Aditi, the sun.

Dākshāyiṇī, f. wrong form for *dākshāyaṇī* above.

Dākshi, is, m. a son of Daksha; (*ī*), f. a daughter

of Daksha. — *Dākshi-kanthā*, f., N. of a village in the north of India in the country of the Vāhlikas or Balkh. — *Dākshikanthīya, as, ā, am*, produced or born in Dākshi-kanthā, relating to Dākshi-kanthā. — *Dākshi-karsha, as*, m., N. of a village. — *Dākshikārshuka, as, ī, am*, coming from or relating to Dākshi-karsha. — *Dākshi-kūla, am*, n., N. of a village. — *Dākshi-grāma, as*, m., N. of a village. — *Dākshigrāmīya, as, ā, am*, coming from or relating to Dākshi-grāma. — *Dākshi-nagara, am*, n., N. of a town. — *Dākshi-palada* and *dākshi-prastha, as*, m., N. of places. — *Dākshi-hrada, as*, m., N. of a lake. — *Dākshihradīya, as, ā, am*, relating to the above lake. — *Dākshī-putra, as*, m. 'the son of Dākshī,' Pāṇini.

Dākcheya, as, m. 'the son of Dākshī,' a metronymic of Pāṇini; (*ī*), f. 'the daughter of Dākshī (?).'

Dākshya, am, n. cleverness, dexterity, skill, ability, capability, fitness; probity, integrity.

दाक्षाय्य *dākshāyya, as*, m. a vulture; [cf. *dakshāyya*.]

दाक्षिण *dākshiṇa, as, ī, am* (fr. *dakshiṇā*), belonging or relating to a sacrificial gift or to a gift in general; relating or belonging to the south; (*am*), n. a collection of sacrificial gifts; (*āni*), n. pl., N. of a Kāṇḍa in the Taittirīya-saṃhitā. — *Dākshiṇaśāla, as*, &c. (fr. *dakshiṇa* + *śālā*), relating to a hall or room situated to the south.

Dākshiṇātya, as, ā, am (fr. *dakshiṇā*, ind.), southerly, southern, belonging to or produced in the south; belonging to or living in the Dekhan, situated in the Dekhan; *dākshiṇātyā bhāshā*, the language spoken in the south; (*as*), m., N. of a preceptor mentioned in the Ānanda-laharī; the cocoanut; (*as, am*), m. or n. (?), the south; (*ās*), m. pl. the inhabitants of the Dekhan; N. of several preceptors mentioned in the Kāma-sūtra by Vātsyāyana.

Dākshiṇika, as, ī, am (fr. *dakshiṇā*), connected with a sacrificial gift.

Dākshiṇīya = *dakshiṇīya*.

1. *dākshiṇya, as*, &c. (fr. *dakshiṇā*), belonging or relating to a sacrificial gift; meriting a sacrificial gift or reward.

2. *dākshiṇya, am*, n. (fr. *dakshiṇa*), civility, courtesy, politeness, conciliatory conduct, propitiation, kindness, obsequiousness, concord, harmony, agreement; honesty, sincerity, candour; cleverness, talent; (probably) the ritual of the right-hand Sāktas (?); N. of a Tantra.

दागव्यायनि *dāgavyāyani*, a patronymic from Dagu.

दाडक *dāḍaka, as*, m. a tooth, tusk; [cf. *dāḍhā*.]

दाडिम *dāḍima, as, ī, am*, m. f. n. (said to be fr. rt. *dal*), the pomegranate tree, (according to some the m. f. applies to the tree, and the n. to the fruit); small cardamoms; (*as, ī, am*), being on the pomegranate tree. — *Dāḍima-pattraka, as*, m. or *dāḍima-pushpa* or *dāḍima-pushpaka, as*, m. the plant Soymida Febrifuga or Amoora Rohitaka (= *rohitaka*). — *Dāḍima-priya, as*, m. 'fond of pomegranates,' a parrot. — *Dāḍima-bhakshaṇa, as*, m. 'eating pomegranates,' a parrot. — *Dāḍimī-vat, ān, atī, at*, planted with pomegranate trees. — *Dāḍimī-sāra, as*, m. = *dāḍima*, the pomegranate tree.

Dāḍimba, as, m. = *dāḍima*, the pomegranate tree.

दाडी *dāḍī*, f. a kind of plant and its fruit; [cf. *doḍī* and *dālī*.]

दाढा *dāḍhā*, f. = *daṃshṭrā*, a large tooth, tusk; wish, desire; a number, multitude.

Dāḍhikā, f. = *daṃshṭrikā*, the beard, the whiskers; (Manu VIII. 283.)

दाण्ड *dāṇḍa, as, ī, am*, relating to a stick or staff, relating to punishment, &c.; (*ā*), f. a particular game with sticks. — *Dāṇḍagrāhika, as*, m. a patronymic from Daṇḍa-graha. — *Dāṇḍapātā*, f. (fr. *daṇḍa-pāta*), scil. *tithi*, a particular festival, the day of full moon in the month Phālguna, on which sticks are thrown; [cf. *tailampātā* and *śyainampātā*.] — *Dāṇḍapāyana, as*, m. a patronymic from Daṇḍa-pa. — *Dāṇḍamāthika, as, ī, am* (fr. *daṇḍa-mātha*), churning with a straight stick or staff. — *Dāṇḍājinika, as, ī, am* (fr. *daṇḍājina*), carrying a staff and hide as mere outward signs of religion; (*as*), m. a cheat, rogue, an hypocrite.

Dāṇḍaki, is, m. a patronymic from Daṇḍaka; (*ayas*), m. pl., N. of a race belonging to the Tri-gartas.

Dāṇḍakīya, as, m. a prince of the Dāṇḍakis.

Dāṇḍāyana, as, m. a patronymic from Daṇḍa (?). — *Dāṇḍāyanasthalaka, as, ī, am*, relating to or coming from Dāṇḍāyana-sthalī. — *Dāṇḍāyana-sthalī*, f., N. of a village.

Dāṇḍika, as, ī, am, inflicting punishment, punishing; (*as*), m. a chastiser, punisher.

Dāṇḍikya, am, n. punishing, the state of being a punisher (?).

Dāṇḍin, inas, m. pl., N. of the disciples of the school of Daṇḍa.

Dāṇḍināyana, as, m. a patronymic from Daṇḍin.

दात *dāta, ās*, m. pl., N. of a school of the Atharva-veda.

दातृ *dātṛi*. See p. 407, col. 2; p. 408, col. 1.

दात्तामित्रीय *dāttāmitrīya, as, ā, am*, relating to or coming from Dattāmitra or Dattāmitrā.

Dātteya, as, m. a metronymic from Dattā, q. v.

दात्यूह *dātyūha, as*, m. a gallinule; the Cātaka, a sort of cuckoo, Cuculus Melanoleucus; a cloud (the water of which the Cātaka is said to drink).

Dātyūhaka, as, m. a familiar diminutive of *dātyūha*, a little gallinule.

Dātyauha, as, m. (according to Pāṇ. VII. 3, 1, fr. *ditya-vāh*), a gallinule; (*as, ī, am*), relating to or produced in the vehicle of a demon (?).

दाद *dāda, dādin*, &c. See p. 407, col. 2.

दादाभाइ *dādābhāi*, N. of the author of the Kiraṇāvalī (a commentary on the Indian astronomical work Sūrya-siddhānta).

दाधिक *dādhika, as, ī, am* (fr. *dadhi*), made of or from Dadhi or coagulated milk; mixed with it, sprinkled with it; carrying about or selling coagulated milk; eating anything with coagulated milk; (*am*), n. a kind of broth or gruel made of coagulated milk mixed with other substances.

Dādhikra, as, ī, am, Ved. relating to Dadhi-krā.

दाधित्थ *dādhittha, as, ī, am* (fr. *dadhittha*), coming from or belonging to the Feronia Elephantum; (*am*), n. the resin of this tree.

दाधीच *dādhīća, as*, m. (fr. *dadhyańć*), Ved. a patronymic of Cyavana.

दाधृवि *dādhṛivi, is, is, i* (fr. rt. *dhṛi*), Ved. holding, bearing.

दाधृषि *dādhṛishi, is, is, i* (fr. the Intens. of rt. *dhṛish*), Ved. courageous, bold; overbearing, overpowering.

दान् *dān*, cl. 1. P. A. or cl. 10. P. *dānayati*, &c., to cut off: Desid. P. A. *dīdaṃsati, -te*, to straighten, make straight; to be straight; (this verb is by some regarded as a nominal fr. 2. *dāna*; cf. 2. *dan*.)

दान *dāna*, &c. See under rts. 1. and 3. *dā*.

दानव *dānava*. See ~~dānu.~~ dānu

दान्त 1. *dānta, as, ā, am* (fr. rt. 1. *dam*), tamed, broken in, subdued, daunted, bridled, restrained; tame, mild; patient of privations or austerity, &c.; resigned; liberal (fr. rt. 1. *dā*?); (*as*), m. a tamed ox or steer; a donor, giver (fr. rt. 1. *dā*); N. of a plant, = *damanaka*, = *vada*, = *vaṭa*, Ficus Indica; N. of a son of Bhīma, king of Vidarbha; (*ās*), m. pl., N. of a school of the Atharva-veda; (*ā*), f., N. of an Apsaras.

Dānti, is, f. self-restraint; the patient endurance of religious austerities or privations; subjection, humiliation.

Dāntvā, ind. having subdued, tamed, &c.

दान्त 2. *dānta, as, ī, am* (fr. *danta*), dental, made of ivory; 'completed by Danta (?),' epithet of a well situated on the northern or southern bank of the river Vipāśā; (see Pāṇ. IV. 2, 74, Schol.)

Dāntika, as, ī, am, made of ivory.

दाभी *dābhī*, f. (fr. rt. *dabh*?), Ved. hurting, injuring (?).

Dābhya, as, ā, am, to be disturbed or obstructed; to be governed or ruled.

दामचरित *dāma-ćarita* or *śrī-dāma-ćarita* or *-ćaritra, am*, n. 'the adventures of Srī-dāman' (or Srī-dāma?), N. of a drama in five acts.

दामन *dāmana, as, ī, am* (fr. *damana*), relating to the Dona or Artemisia flower. — *Dāmana-parvan, a*, n. the fourteenth of the light half of the month Caitra, a festival on which Artemisia flowers are gathered.

Dāmani, is, m. a patronymic from Damana; (*ayas*), m. pl., N. of a warrior-tribe.

Dāmanīya, as, m. (fr. *dāmani*), a prince of the Dāmanis.

दामलिप्त *dāmalipta, am*, n., N. of a town or country, the modern district of Tumlook, = *tāmalipta*; [cf. *tāmralipta*.]

दामोद *dāmoda, ās*, m. pl., N. of a school of the Atharva-veda.

दाम्पत्य *dāmpatya, am*, n. (fr. *dam-pati*), matrimony, the marriage-state, the matrimonial or conjugal relation.

दाम्भिक *dāmbhika, as, ī, am* (fr. *dambha*, q. v.), deceitful, hypocritical; proud, imperious, ostentatious; sanctimonious; (*as*), m. a cheat; a hypocrite; a kind of crane, Ardea Nivea.

दाय् *dāy* (a form of rt. 1. *dā*, given by some grammarians; cf. *ā-dāyamāna* under 1. *ā-dā*), cl. 1. A. *dāyate*, &c., to give.

दाय *dāya*. See under rts. 1. *dā* at p. 407, col. 3, and 3. *dā* at p. 408, col. 2.

दार *dāra, as*, m. (fr. rt. *dṛi*), a rent, cleft, gap, hole; a ploughed field; a wife, (usually occurring in the m. pl. *ās* or in comp.: an exceptional form *dārā*, f. sing., occurs in one or two passages; and in Pańćatantra I. 450, the neut. pl. *dārāṇi*); *dārān kṛi*, to take a wife, marry; [cf. *kṛita-d*°.] — *Dāra-karman, a*, n. or *dāra-kriyā*, f. taking a wife, marrying, marriage; [cf. *dāra-parigraha*.] — *Dāra-gava, am*, n. wife and cows. — *Dāra-grahaṇa, am*, n. 'taking a wife,' marriage. — *Dāra-parigraha, as*, m. 'taking a wife,' marriage. — *Dāraparigrahin, ī, iṇī, i*, 'taking a wife,' marrying. — *Dāra-lakshaṇa, am*, n. a characteristic sign or decisive mark of wife-hood. — *Dāra-saṅgraha, as*, m. 'taking a wife,' marrying, marriage. — *Dārāṇukramaṇa* (°*ra-an*°), *am*, n., N. of a chapter of the Purāṇa-sarva-sva. — *Dārādhīna* (°*ra-adh*°), *as, ā, am*, dependent on a wife, in the power of a wife. — *Dāropasaṅgraha* (°*ra-up*°), *as*, m. 'taking a wife,' marrying, marriage.

Dāraka, as, ikā, am, breaking, tearing, splitting; (*as*), m. a boy, son, child, infant; a young animal; a village hog; the charioteer of Krishṇa; (*ikā*), f. a rent, cleft, gap, chap; a daughter; a harlot; (*au*), m. du. a boy and a girl. — *Dārakāćārya* (°*ka-āć*°), *as*, m. 'a preceptor of boys,' a schoolmaster. — *Dārikā-dāna, am*, n. the gift of a daughter in marriage.

Dāraṇa, as, ī, am, tearing, splitting, tearing asunder; (*ī*), f. an epithet of Durgā; (*am*), n. the act of tearing, rending, dividing; opening, bursting, flying open; a means of opening; the clearing-nut plant, Strychnos Potatorum; [cf. kataka.]

Dārava, as, ī, am (fr. 2. dāru below), wooden, made of wood, coming from or relating to wood.

Dāri, is, is, i, tearing, causing to burst, splitting [cf. veṇu-d°]; (is), f. cutting, tearing, dividing.

Dārita, as, ā, am, torn, rent, divided.

Dārin, ī, iṇī, i, tearing, splitting; (ī), m. (fr. dāra), a husband; a polygamist.

Dārī, f. a cleft, gap; a chap.

2. *dāru*, us, us or vī, u (for 1. dāru see p. 408, col. 1), tearing, rending; a tearer, breaker, destroyer; (us), m., Ved. 'the destroyer of cities,' an epithet of Indra; (us, u), m. n. (usually n.), a piece of wood, wood, timber; a block; a lever; a bolt; (u), n. a sort of pine, Pinus Devadāru; ore, metal in its natural state; [cf. taru, dru; Zend dāuru, 'wood;' Gr. δόρυ, δούρατα for δόρϝατα, δορῆιος, δούρ-ειο-ς, δουράτ-εο-ς; Goth. triu, 'tree;' Old Sax. trio, 'timber;' Eng. tree; Slav. drěvo, 'tree;' Russ. dérevo, drova; Lith. dervà; Hib. doireach, 'woody.'] — *Dāru-kaććha*, as, am, m. n. (?), N. of a district. — *Dārukaććhaka*, relating to the above district. — *Dāru-kadalī*, f. a wild uneatable plantain (= vana-kadalī). — *Dāru-karṇin*, ī, m. 'having wooden ear-rings,' a N. of Bhavila. — *Dāru-gandhā*, f. a kind of perfume (commonly ćiḍā). — *Dāru-garbhā*, f. a wooden puppet, a doll. — *Dāru-ja*, as, ā, am, produced from wood, made of wood, wooden; (as), m. a kind of drum. — *Dāru-tīrtha*, am, n., N. of a Tīrtha. — *Dāru-niśā*, f. Curcuma Zanthorrhizon (= dārvī). — *Dāru-pattrī*, f. a plant, = hiṅgu-pattrī. — *Dāru-pātra*, am, n. a wooden vessel. — *Dāru-pītā*, f. a plant, = dārvī. — *Dāru-putrikā* or dāru-putrī, f. a wooden doll or puppet. — *Dāru-phala*, as, am, m. n. (?), Pistachio (tree and nut). — *Dāru-maya*, as, ī, am, wooden, made of wood (e. g. dāru-mayī yoshā or strī or nārī, 'a wooden woman,' a doll). — *Dāru-mukhyāhvayā* or dāru-mukhyāhvā (°ya-āh°), f. a lizard. — *Dāru-yantra*, am, n. a wooden puppet moved by strings. — *Dāru-varman*, ā, m., N. of a man. — *Dāru-vaha*, as, ā, am, bearing or carrying timber. — *Dāru-sitā*, f. cinnamon in sticks. — *Dāru-strī*, f. a wooden doll; [cf. dāru-maya.] — *Dāru-haridrā*, f. a species of Curcuma, = dārvī. — *Dāru-hastaka*, as, m. a wooden spoon or ladle. — *Dārv-āghāṭa*, as, m. or dārv-āghāta, as, m. the woodpecker. — *Dārv-āhāra*, as, m. a collector of wood.

Dāruka, as, m., N. of Kṛishṇa's charioteer, who was son of Satyaka; N. of an incarnation of Śiva; (ā), f. a wooden figure; a doll, puppet; (am), n. a sort of pine, Pinus Devadāru. — *Dārukā-vana*, am, n., N. of a wood containing a famous Liṅga. — *Dārukeśvara-tīrtha* (°ka or °kā-īś°), am, n., N. of a Tīrtha.

Dāruki, is, m., N. of Pra-dyumna's charioteer, who was son of Dāruka.

Dāruṇa, as, ā or rarely ī, am (perhaps not directly fr. rt. dṛī, but rather fr. 2. dāru above), hard, harsh (opposed to mṛidu), rough, sharp, severe (as speech); cruel, pitiless, heart-rending; terrible, terrific, frightful, dreadful, fearful, grievous; shocking, atrocious, dire; agonising, painful; intense, violent, severe, great; (as, am), m. n. harshness, severity, hard-heartedness, cruelty, horror, horribleness; (as), m., N. of the plant Plumbago Zeylanica (= ćitraka). *Dāruṇa* at the beginning of comp. or before a verb expresses excellence or superiority; [cf. kāshṭha and see dāruṇādhyāpaka below.] — *Dāruṇa-karman*, a, n. violent treatment (as of diseases). — *Dāruṇa-tā*, f. harshness, roughness, frightfulness, direness, severity, intensity. — *Dāruṇa-vapus*, us, us, us, of frightful shape. — *Dāruṇā-kṛiti* (°ṇa-āk°), is, is, i, of terrible or dreadful form. — *Dāruṇātman* (°ṇa-āt°), ā, ā, a, hard-hearted, cruel. — *Dāruṇādhyāpaka* (°ṇa-adh°), as, m. an energetic or indefatigable teacher; [cf. dāruṇa above.]

Dāruṇaka, am, n. 'harshness,' N. of a particular disease affecting the roots of the hair.

Dāruṇāya, Nom. A. dāruṇāyate, &c., to act harshly or cruelly, to be unmerciful.

Dāruṇya, am, n. harshness (as of a sound &c.); cruelty, dreadfulness, direness, severity, &c.

Dārva, as, ī, am, wooden, made of wood; (ās), m. pl., N. of a people to the north-east of Madhya-deśa, generally associated with the Abhi-sāras; (ī), f., N. of several plants, = dāru-haridrā, dāru-niśā, Curcuma Aromatica or Curcuma Xanthorrhiza; a particular species of collyrium extracted from an infusion of the Curcuma Xanthorrhiza; a species of pine, = deva-dāru; turmerick; a species of pot-herb, Go-jihvā. — *Dārvī-pattrikā*, f., N. of a plant, = go-jihvā. — *Dārvī-kvāthodbhava* (°tha-ud°), am, n. a particular kind of collyrium prepared from an infusion of Curcuma Aromatica or Curcuma Xanthorrhiza.

Dārvaka, as, ī, am, relating to or coming from Dārva.

Dārvikā, f. a sort of collyrium prepared from an infusion of Curcuma Aromatica; N. of a plant, = go-jihvā.

दारक dāraka, dāraṇa, &c. See p. 409, col. 3.

दारद dārada, as, ī, am, coming from the country of the Darads, (a various reading has darada); (ās), m. pl., N. of a people, (probably only a wrong form for darada); (as), m. a kind of poison brought from the above country; quicksilver; the ocean; (as, am), m. n. vermilion.

दारबलिभुज् dāra-bali-bhuj, incorrect form for dvāra-bali-bhuj, q. v.

दारित dārita, &c. See col. 1.

दारिद्र dāridra, am, n. (fr. daridra), poverty, indigence, (perhaps a wrong form for dāridrya below.)

Dāridrya, am, n. poverty, indigence.

दारु dāru. See col. 1. and p. 408, col. 1.

दारुण dāruṇa. See col. 1.

दारोदर dārodara, as, ī, am (fr. darodara), connected with gambling.

दार्घसत्त्र dārghasattra, as, ī, am (fr. dīrgha-sattra), connected with a long continued sacrifice, performing such a sacrifice.

दार्ढच्युत dārḍhaćyuta, as, m. (fr. dṛiḍha-ćyuta), a patronymic, (also read dauryāćyuta); (am), n., N. of a Sāman.

दार्ढ्य dārḍhya, am, n. (fr. dṛiḍha), hardness, fixedness, tightness, stability; strength, energy; confirmation, corroboration.

दार्तेय dārteya, as, ī, am, leathern, made of leather; (as), m. a patronymic from Dṛiti, q. v.

दार्दुर dārdura, as, ī, am (fr. dardura), relating to a cloud, frog, &c.; (am), n. a conch-shell or muscle, the valve of which opens to the right; lac; water.

Dārdurika, as, ā, am, belonging to a frog, &c.

दार्भ dārbha, as, ī, am (fr. darbha), made of Darbha grass.

Dārbhāyaṇa, as, m. a patronymic from Darbha; (see Pāṇ. IV. 1, 102.)

Dārbhi, is, m. a patronymic from Darbha; (see Pāṇ. IV. 1, 102.)

Dārbhya, as, m., Ved. a patronymic from Darbha, applied to Syāvāśva; [cf. dālbhya.]

दार्व dārva. See above.

दार्वट dārvaṭa, am, n. (fr. the Pers. دربار), a court or council-house; [cf. darbhaṭa.]

दार्वण्ड dārvaṇḍa, as, m. a peacock.

दार्वन् dārvan, ā, m., N. of a son of Uśī-nara; [cf. darvā.]

दार्वाघाट dārv-āghāṭa. See 2. dāru, col. 1.

दार्वीहौमिक dārvīhaumika, as, ī, am (fr. darvī-homa), relating to an oblation made with a ladle.

दार्श dārśa, as, ī, am (fr. darśa), relating to the new moon or the new moon sacrifice; (as), m., scil. yajña, the new moon sacrifice.

Dārśanika, as, ī, am (fr. darśana), seeing far; familiar with the Darśanas or philosophical systems.

Dārśapaurṇamāsika, as, ī, am (fr. darśa-pūrṇa-māsa), belonging to the Darśa-pūrṇa-māsa sacrifice.

Dārśika, as, ī, am, or dārśya, as, ā, am, relating to the new moon or the new moon sacrifice.

दार्षद dārshada, as, ī, am (fr. dṛishad), ground on a flat stone (as meal &c.); stony, of stone, mineral.

दार्षद्वत dārshadvata, am, n. (fr. dṛishad-vatī), N. of a Sattra.

दार्ष्टान्त dārshṭānta, as, ī, am (fr. dṛishṭānta), explained by an example or simile or case in point; illustrated by metaphor or figure.

Dārshṭāntika, as, ī, am, explained by an illustration or simile; illustrated, any thing which is the subject of an illustration or simile; suitable to be used in illustration; one who uses an example or simile as a proof.

दाल dāla, am, n. a sort of wild or unprepared honey, (according to some produced by a peculiar kind of small bee; see dala-ja); (ā), f. = dālikā, deva-dālikā, colocynth; (ī), f. a kind of plant, = deva-dālī; (as), m. a sort of grain, = Paspalum Frumentaceum.

दालकि dālaki, is, m., N. of a pupil of Saka-pūrṇi.

दालन dālana, am, n. (fr. rt. dal), crumbling or decay (of the teeth), tooth-ache.

दालभ्य dālabhya, a wrong form for Dālbhya, q. v.

दालव dālava, as, m. a sort of poison.

दालिका dālikā, f. = dālā, deva-dālikā, colocynth.

दालिम dālima, as, m. the pomegranate; [cf. dāḍima.]

दाल्भ dālbha, as, ī, am (fr. dālbhya below), relating to or coming from Dālbhya.

Dālbhi, is, m. (fr. dalbha), a patronymic of Vaka.

Dālbhya, as, m. (fr. dalbha), a patronymic of Keśin; of Caikitāyana; N. of a grammarian. — *Dālbhya-ghosha*, as, m., N. of an ancient sage. — *Dālbhya-pariśishṭa*, am, n., N. of a poetical work.

Dālbhyaka, as, m., N. of an ancient sage.

दाल्मायणि dālmāyaṇi, probably a wrong form for dālbhāyani or dārbhāyaṇi.

दाल्मि dālmi, is, m., N. of Indra; [cf. dalmi.]

दाव dāva, as, m. (fr. rt. 2. du), a forest conflagration, a forest on fire; fire in general, heat; a forest; [cf. antar-d° and dava.] — *Dāva-dahana-jvālā-kalāpa*, the mass or sheet of flame arising from the conflagration of a forest. — *Dāvadahanajvālā-kalāpāya*, Nom. A. -yate, &c., to resemble the sheet of flame of a burning forest. — *Dāva-pa*, as, m., Ved. one who keeps watch over a forest on fire. — *Dāva-latā*, f. a creeper in a burning wood. — *Dāva-vivarjita*, as, ā, am, free from fire. — *Dāva-su*, us, m., N. of an Aṅgirasa. — *Dāvasu-nidhana*, am, n., N. of a Sāman. — *Dāvāgni* (°va-ag°), is, or dāvānala (°va-an°), as, m. a forest on fire, a forest conflagration, fire in a wood; [cf. davāgni.]

दाविक dāvika, as, &c. (fr. devikā), coming from the river Devikā; (Pāṇ. VII. 3, 1.)

Dāvikakūla (fr. devikā-kūla), see Pāṇ. VII. 3, 1.

दाश् 1. dāś (apparently occurring only in Ṛig-veda), cl. 1. P. A. dāśati, -te, (rarely cl. 2. 5. P.) dāshṭi, dāśnoti, (according to Vopa-deva also) cl. 10. A. dāśayate, dadāśa, (Ved. forms are dadāśati, dadāśat, part. dāśivas and dāśvas, dat. sing. dāśushe or dadāśushe), dāśitum, Ved. to honour or serve a god (dat. or acc.) with any offering (inst.); to offer any thing (acc.), make an oblation; to grant, give, bestow [cf. rt. dās]; cl. 5. dāśnoti, &c., to hurt, injure, kill [cf. rts. dās and das]: Caus. P. dāśayati, -yitum, Aor. adadāśat, to offer: Desid. didāśishati, -te: Intens. dādāśyate, dādāshṭi.

2. dāś, worshipping, making oblations (?); [cf. dū-ḍāś.]

Dāśa, as, m. [cf. dāsa with which daśa is interchanged], Ved. presenting oblations, honouring the gods with offerings [cf. puro-ḍāśa]; a fisherman, ferryman, boatman, mariner; the son of a Nishāda by a woman of the Āyogava caste; a servant, = 1. dāsa, col. 2; (ī), f. a fisherwoman; a female slave. – Dāśa-nandinī or dāsa-nandinī, f. 'the fisherman's daughter,' epithet of Satya-vatī, who was the mother of the poet Vyāsa.

Dāśaka, (probably) a fisherman, (occurring only in dāśaka-putra.)

Dāśu, us, us, u, giving, &c.; see a-d°. – Dāśv-adhvara, Ved. presenting oblations, honouring the gods with sacrifices; (Sāy.) the oblation of the giver of the sacrifice.

Dāśuri, is, is, i, Ved. making oblations or offerings.

Dāśeya or dāśeya, as, m. (fr. dāśī), the son of a fisherman's wife; (ī), f. 'the daughter of a fisherman's wife,' epithet of Satya-vatī, mother of Vyāsa.

Dāśera, as, m. a fisherman; a camel.

Dāśeraka, as, m. a fisherman; (ās), m. pl., N. of a people, = maru-bhū; [cf. daśeraka.]

Dāśva, as, ā, am (corrupted fr. dāśvas), liberal, giving, a giver, donor.

Dāśvas (rarely dāśivas), vān, ushī, vas, Ved. honouring or serving the gods with offerings, bestowing, offering, giving, granting (with acc. or compounded with the thing given). In the Ṛig-veda dāśvas is often a general expression for a faithful worshipper of the gods or a religious and pious man, especially when connected with marta, martya, and jana.

दाशत् dāśat, wrong form for daśat.

दाशतय dāśataya, as, ī, am (fr. daśataya), belonging to the Ṛig-veda which consists of ten divisions or Maṇḍalas.

दाशपुर dāśapura, as, ī, am (fr. daśa-pura), coming from Daśa-pura; (am), n. a fragrant grass related to the Cyperus Rotundus; (also dāśapūra.)

Dāśaphalī, f. (fr. daśa-phala), N. of a plant.

Dāśaratha, as, ī, am (fr. daśa-ratha), belonging to Daśa-ratha, coming from Daśa-ratha, a descendant of Daśa-ratha; (as), m. a patronymic of Rāma.

Dāśarathi, is, m. 'descendant of Daśa-ratha,' a patronymic of Rāma; of Lakshmaṇa, the younger brother of Rāma; of Catur-aṅga; (with Jainas) N. of the eighth Black Vāsu-deva; (ī), m. du. Rāma and Lakshmaṇa.

Dāśarājña, am, n. (fr. daśan + rājan), Ved. 'the fight with ten kings,' a famous battle fought by Su-dās.

Dāśarūpya (fr. daśan + rūpa), N. of a Grāma.

Dāśavāja, am, n. (fr. daśan + vāja); in kautsam dāśavājam, N. of a Sāman; [cf. pāñcavāja.]

Dāśaśiras, n. (perhaps for dāśaśīrasa fr. daśa-śiras), N. of a Sāman.

Dāśārṇa, as, ī, am (fr. daśārṇa), containing the word Daśārṇa, treating of it (as an anu-vāka or adhyāya); (as), m. a prince of the Daśārṇas; (ās), m. pl. = daśārṇa, N. of a people. – Dāśārṇa-rāja, as, m. or dāśārṇeśa (°ṇa-īśa), as, m. a king of the Daśārṇas.

Dāśārṇaka, as, ikā, am, coming from or relating to or belonging to the Daśārṇas.

Dāśārha, as, ī, am (fr. daśārha, q. v.), containing the word Daśārha, treating of it (as an adhyāya or anu-vāka); belonging to Daśārha, i. e. to Kṛishṇa; (as), m. a prince of the Daśārhas; an epithet of Kṛishṇa; a Daśārha king of Mathurā; (ī), f. a princess of the Daśārhas; (ās), m. pl. = the Daśārhas.

Dāśārhaka, ās, m. pl. = daśārhās above.

Dāśāśvamedha, ās, m. pl. (perhaps a wrong reading for daśāśvamedhās), ten horse-sacrifices.

Dāśaudanika, as, ī, am (fr. daśan + odana), N. of a particular sacrificial rite; (ī), f. the offering made to the priests at this rite; [cf. pañcaudanika.]

दाशमेय dāśameya. See dāsameya.

दाशर्म dāśarma, as, m., N. of a man.

दाशस्पत्य dāśaspatya, am, n. (fr. daśas or dāśas? + pati; cf. daśasya and rt. 1. dāś), N. of a Sāman, (perhaps 'the lord of pious oblations.')

दाशिवस् dāśivas, dāśvas. See col. 1.

दाशुर dāśura or dāśūra, as, m., N. of a man.

दाशेय dāśeya, dāśera. See col. 1.

दास् dās (generally occurring in connection with the prep. abhi, connected with rts. 1. dāś, das, daṅś, daṇs), cl. 1. P. A. dāsati, -te, dadāsa, -se, dāsitā, &c., to give; cl. 5. P. dāsnoti, &c., Ved. to hurt, injure, wound, kill; [cf. perhaps Gr. ληΐη, ληΐς, ληΐζομαι, ληϊστής, the d being changed into l, as in rt. lā fr. rt. dā; probably also Gr. λά-τρο-ν, λά-τρις; Lat. la-tro.]

1. dāsa, as, m. a general N. applied in the Veda to certain evil beings or demons, hostile to the human race and to Indra, (those defeated by Indra have also special names, e. g. Namuci, Pipru, Sambara, Varcin, &c.); a savage, a barbarian, (opposed in the Veda to ārya, &c.; cf. dasyu); a slave, servant, (in this sense occurring at the end of the names of Sūdras and Kāya-sthas; cf. also kāli-dāsa); one to whom gifts may be made; = dāśa, a fisherman, boatman; (ī), f. a female servant or slave, servant-maid; whore, harlot, (in this sense having the accent on the first syllable); N. of a plant, = nīlā jhiṇṭī, = kāka-jaṅghā, = nīlāmlāna; an altar; N. of a river; (as, ī, am), belonging to the Dāsas, i. e. to demons, barbarians, &c.; consisting of the Dāsas, &c.; [cf. Gr. δοῦλος derived in a similar manner from δοῦν, 'to give or serve.'] – Dāsa-jana, as, m. a slave; = dāsī, a female servant. – Dāsa-jīvana, am, n. 'slave-life,' the work or business of a slave. – Dāsa-tā, f. or dāsa-tva, am, n. the condition of a slave, slavery, servitude. – Dāsa-dāsī, f. the female slave of a slave. – Dāsa-nandinī = dāśa-nandinī, q. v. – Dāsa-patnī, f., Ved. having the demons as masters, being in the power of the demons; (Sāy.) having Dāsa, i. e. the destroyer, or Vṛitra as husband; [cf. Gr. δέσποινα.] – Dāsa-pravarga, as, ā, am, Ved. (according to Sāy.) having a multitude of servants, having a large number of slaves; [cf. pra-varga.] – Dāsa-bhārya, am, n. servants and wives. – Dāsa-bhāva, as, m. the condition of a slave, slavery, servitude. – Dāsa-mitra, as, m. 'friend of a slave,' N. of a man. – Dāsamitrāyaṇa, as, or dāsamitri, is, m. a patronymic from Dāsa-mitra. – Dāsamitrāyaṇa-bhakta or dāsamitri-bhakta, am, n., N. of the district inhabited by the Dāsamitrāyaṇas or Dāsamitris. – Dāsamitrika, as, ā or ī, am, relating to or coming from Dāsa-mitra. – Dāsa-mithuna, am, n., Ved. a couple of slaves or servants. – Dāsa-varga, as, m. the whole collection of slaves, all the servants. – Dāsa-veśa, as, m., Ved. (according to Sāy.) the destruction of the demons. – Dāsa-śarman, ā, m., N. of a scholiast on the Srauta-sūtras of Sāṅkhāyana. – Dāsasya-kula, am, n. (see Pāṇ. VI. 3, 21), the common people, low people, the mob. – Dāsānudāsa (°sa-an°), as, m. a slave of a slave, a servant of servants; (sometimes applied by a humble speaker to himself.) – Dāsī-kṛi, cl. 8. P. A. -karoti, -kurute, -kartum, to make any one a slave or a female slave; to enslave. – Dāsī-kṛita, as, ā, am, made a slave. – Dāsī-tva, am, n. the state of a female slave. – Dāsī-dāna-vidhi, is, m. 'the rules for giving female slaves,' N. of the 146th chapter of the Bhavishyottara-Purāṇa or second part of the Bhavishya-Purāṇa. – Dāsī-dāsa, am, n. female slaves and slaves, female servants and servants. – Dāsī-putra, as, m. 'the son of a female slave' (used as an abusive expression), = a low wretch, a miscreant. – Dāsī-māṇavaka, am, n. female slaves and boys. – Dāsī-śrotriya, as, m. a Brāhman (conversant with the Vedas) who goes after a female slave. – Dāsī-sabha, am, n. an assembly of female slaves or servants. – Dāsī-suta, as, m. the son of a female slave. – Dāsyāḥ-putra, as, m. the son of a female slave; (ī), f. the daughter of a female slave; [cf. dāsī-putra.] – Dāsyāḥ-sadṛiśī, f. behaving like a female slave. – Dāsyāḥ-suta, as, m. = dāsī-suta, q. v.

Dāsaka, as, m., N. of a man; of a son of Bhajamāna.

Dāsakāyana, as, m. a patronymic from Dāsaka.

Dāsanu, us, m., Ved., N. of a semi-divine being associated with Kṛiśānu.

Dāsāya, Nom. P. A. dāsāyati, -te, &c., to become a slave.

Dāsāyana, as, m. the son of a slave or of a man called Dāsa.

Dāsikā, f. a female slave or servant.

Dāsī, f. See under 1. dāsa, col. 2.

Dāsīka for dāsī, at the end of comp. (e. g. triṇśad-dāsīka, having thirty female slaves).

1. dāseya, as, m. (fr. dāsī), the son of a female slave, a slave, servant, = dāśeya, q. v.; (as, ī, am), born of a slave.

Dāsera, as, m. (fr. dāsī), the son of a female slave, a slave, servant, = dāśera, q. v.

Dāseraka, as, m. = dāsera; (ās), m. pl., N. of a people to the north of Madhya-deśa, = daśeraka, q. v.

Dāsya, am, n. servitude, slavery, service. – Dāsya-yoga, as, m. servitude, slavery. – Dāsya-vṛitti, is, f. the business of a slave or servant.

Dāsvat, ān, atī, at, Ved. disposed to give, giving, liberal.

दास 2. dāsa, as, m. (said to be fr. rt. daṇs, q. v.), a knowing man; a knower of the universal spirit.

दास 3. dāsa, as, m. = dāśa, a fisherman, &c.

दासनीय dāsanīya for dāsamīya, q. v.

दासपूर dāsapūra, am, n. = dāśapūra, q. v.

दासमीय dāsamīya, ās, m. pl., N. of a people; [cf. dāsameya.]

दासमेय dāsameya, ās, m. pl., N. of a people to the north of Madhya-deśa; (also written dāśameya; cf. dāsamīya.)

दाससरस् dāsasaras, as, n., N. of a Sāman; (also read dāsaśiras.)

दासित dāsita. See under rt. das.

दाह dāha, as, m. (fr. rt. 1. dah), burning, combustion, conflagration; glowing redness (as of the sky; cf. dig-dāha); cauterizing, cautery (in surgery); the sensation of burning, internal heat; the heat of a fever, feverish or morbid heat [cf. antar-d°, gṛiha-d°, geha-d°]; (ās), m. pl., N. of a people; (a various reading for vaideha, q. v.) – Dāha-kāshṭha, am, n. a kind of Agallochum used as a perfume; [cf. dāhāgura.] – Dāha-jvara, as, m. inflammatory fever. – Dāha-maya, as, ī, am, consisting in burning or heat. – Dāhamaya-tva, am,

n. the state of consisting in burning, &c. — *Dāha-vat, ān, atī, at,* burning, heated, on fire. — *Dāha-śara, as,* m. or *dāha-saras, as,* n. or *dāha-sthala, am,* n. a place where dead bodies are burnt. — *Dāha-haraṇa, as, ā* or *ī, am,* removing heat; (*am*), n. the root of Andropogon Muricatus, (a fragrant grass, the root of which when woven into screens and kept wet tempers the hot winds, = *vīraṇa-mūla.*) — *Dā-hāguru* (°*ha-ag*°), *u,* n. = *dāha-kāshṭha,* q. v. — *Dāhātmaka* (°*ha-āt*°), *as, ikā, am,* of an inflammable nature, easily kindled or burning, combustible. — *Dāhādhikāra* (°*ha-adh*°), *as,* m., N. of a chapter of a medical work by Vṛinda on cauterizing, &c.

Dāhaka, as, ikā, am, burning, kindling, setting on fire; causing heat or combustion; incendiary, inflammatory; cauterizing, caustic; (*as*), m. the plant Plumbago Zeylanica (= *ćitraka* = *rakta-ći-traka*).

Dāhana, am, n. (fr. the Caus.), causing to burn, burning, inflaming, reducing to ashes; cauterizing. — *Dāhanāguru* for *dahanāguru,* q. v.

Dāhanīya, as, ā, am, to be burnt, combustible.

Dāhin, ī, inī, i, burning, setting on fire, burning hot; tormenting, paining; [cf. *gehe-d*°.]

Dāhuka, as, ā, am, burning, inflaming.

Dāhya, as, ā, am, to be burnt, inflammable, combustible.

दिकम् *dikam,* ind. given by some as an indeclinable under the Gaṇa *ćādi.*

दिक्क *dikka, as,* m. = *karabha,* a young elephant?; (also read *dhikka* and *vikka.*)

दिक्कन्या *dik-kanyā,* 2. *dik-kara, dik-karikā, dik-karin,* &c. See under the compounds of 2. *diś.*

दिक्कर 1. *dikkara, as,* m. (for 2. see p. 414, col. 3), a youth; (*ī*), f. a young woman; [cf. *ḍikkarī.*]

दिगन्त *dig-anta, dig-antara, dig-ambara.* See under the compounds of 2. *diś.*

दिग्ध *digdha, as, ā, am* (fr. rt. 1. *dih*), smeared, anointed, plastered; soiled, polluted, defiled; (*as*), m. oil, ointment, unguent, oily substance; a name of fire; a poisoned arrow; a tale true or false. — *Digdha-saha-śaya, as, ā, am,* lying in the midst of mud (?). — *Digdha-hasta, as, ā, am,* having the hands smeared or soiled. — *Digdhāṅga* (°*dha-aṅ*°), *as, ī, am,* having the limbs anointed.

दिङ्क *dinka, as,* m. a nit, the egg of a louse or bug (= *utkuṇa-ḍimbha*).

दिङ्नाग *diṅ-nāga, diṅ-maṇḍala, diṅ-mā-taṅga.* See under the compounds of 2. *diś.*

दिण्डि *diṇḍi, is,* m. or *diṇḍan, ā,* m., N. of one of the attendants of Skanda; [cf. *ḍhuṇḍhi.*]

दिण्डीय *diṇḍiya, as,* m., N. of a man.

दिण्डीर *diṇḍīra, as,* m. cuttle-fish bone held to be indurated sea-foam; (also read *hiṇḍīra;* cf. *ḍiṇḍīra.*)

दित *dita.* See under rt. 3. *dā* at p. 408, col. 2, and 4. *dā* at p. 408, col. 3.

दिति *diti, is,* f. (fr. rt. 3. *dā* or *do*), cutting, splitting, dividing; distributing, liberality, (in this sense also fr. rt. 1. *dā*); Liberality personified; (*is*), f., N. of a divine female, (probably a N. formed to answer to A-diti, as Sura to A-sura, and without any distinct character: in epic poetry Diti is a daughter of Daksha and wife of Kaśyapa; the race of Daityas or implacable enemies of the gods are described as her progeny or derived from her through her son Hiraṇya-kaśipu; but the Vishṇu-Purāṇa I. 21, describes Indra as dividing the embryo in the womb of Diti, through fear of his future enemies, and forming the forty-nine Maruts from the divided pieces); (*is*), m., N. of a king; a king. — *Diti-ja, as,* m. 'a son of Diti,' a Daitya, an enemy of the gods. — *Ditijārāti* (°*ja-ar*°), *is,* m. 'the enemy of the Daityas,' an epithet of Vishṇu. — *Diti-tanaya* or *diti-nandana* or *diti-suta, as,* m. 'a son of Diti,' a Daitya. — *Diti-rūpa-rākshasī-vadha, as,* m., N. of the twenty-first chapter of the Krīḍā-khaṇḍa or second part of the Gaṇeśa-Purāṇa. — *Diti-śoka-praśama, as,* m., N. of the sixth chapter of the Bhūmi-khaṇḍa or second part of the Padma-Purāṇa. — *Diti-sambodhana, am,* n., N. of the ninth chapter of the Bhūmi-khaṇḍa.

Ditya, as, m. 'a son of Diti,' a Daitya; (a wrong form for *daitya.*)

दित्यवह् *ditya-vah* or *ditya-vāh, -vāṭ,* m. (inst. *dityauhā*), *dityauhī,* f. (*ditya* probably a corruption of *dvitīya*), Ved. a two-year-old steer or cow; [cf. *turya-vah* and *dātyauha.*]

Dityauhī. See above under *ditya-vah.*

दित्सा *ditsā,* f. (fr. the Desid. of rt. 1. *dā*), desire or intention of giving.

Ditsu, us, us, u, ready or wishing to give, willing to grant (with acc.); ready to perform (e. g. *śrād-dham,* the funeral ceremony; cf. *a-ditsu*).

Ditsya, as, ā, am, what one is willing to give or ready to grant.

Diditsu, us, us, u, = *ditsu,* ready or wishing to give away; (an irregular form with double reduplication.)

दिदम्भिषु *didambhishu, us, us, u* (fr. the Desid. of rt. *dambh*), intending or wishing to deceive; [cf. *dhipsu* and *dipsu.*]

दिदिवि *didivi, is, i,* m. n. heaven, the sky. See *didīvi.*

दिदीवि *didīvi, is,* m. boiled rice.

दिदृक्षमाण *didṛikshamāṇa, as, ā, am* (fr. the Desid. of rt. 1. *dṛiś*), wishing to see.

Didṛikshā, f. desire of seeing, wish to see. — *Di-dṛikshā-vat, ān, atī, at,* having a desire to see.

Didṛikshu, us, us, u, desirous of seeing (with acc.); wishing or desiring to examine, desirous of inspecting.

Didṛikshenya or *didṛiksheya, as, ā, am,* Ved. what one likes or wishes to see, conspicuous, attracting.

दिदेविषत् *didevishat, an, antī, at* (fr. the Desid. of rt. 2. *div*), wishing to play or sport.

दिद्दा *diddā,* f., N. of a princess of Kaśmīra. — *Diddā-kshema, as,* m. 'having affection for Diddā,' an epithet of Kshema-gupta. — *Diddā-pāla, as,* m., N. of a man. — *Diddā-pura, am,* n., N. of a town built by Diddā. — *Diddā-svāmin, ī,* m., N. of a temple built by Diddā.

दिद्यु *didyu, us,* m. (fr. 2. *div* or 2. *dī* or 1. *dyut?*), Ved. a missile weapon, arrow; (Sāy.) a shining weapon; the sky, heaven.

Didyut, t, f., Ved. an arrow, a missile (especially the missiles of the gods and the thunderbolt of Indra); N. of an Apsaras; (*t, t, t*), shining, blazing, bright, (in this last sense derived by some fr. rt. 3. *dyut.*)

दिद्योतिषु *didyotishu, us, us, u* (fr. the Desid. of rt. 3. *dyut*), wishing to shine.

दिधक्ष् *didhaksh, k, k, k* (fr. the Desid. of rt. 1. *dah*), wishing or intending to burn.

Didhakshamāṇa, as, ā, am, wishing to burn.

Didhakshayat, an, antī, at, desiring to burn.

Didhakshā, f. desire or wish to burn or consume by fire.

Didhakshu, us, us, u, intending to burn or destroy, desirous of burning.

दिधि *didhi, is,* f. (fr. rt. 1. *dhā*), firmness, stability, fixed state of mind or being; (probably a wrong form.)

दिधिक्ष् *didhiksh, k, k, k* (fr. the Desid. of rt. 1. *dih*), intending to smear.

दिधिषाय्य *didhishāyya, as,* m. (fr. the Desid. of rt. 1. *dhā*), 'to be tried to be gained,' an epithet of Agni; (Sāy.) a supporter; (*as*), m. a pretended friend (?); [cf. *dadhishāyya,* which is by some considered as another reading.]

Didhishu, us, us, u, Ved. wishing or trying to gain or obtain; (*us*), m. a suitor; a husband; the second husband of a woman twice married; (*us* or *didhishū, ūs*), f. a virgin widow remarried; an elder sister unmarried having a younger married sister; [cf. *agre-d*° and *edidhishuḥ-pati.*] — *Di-dhishū-pati, is,* m. the husband of a woman remarried.

Didhīshū, f. = *didhishū.*

दिन 1. *dina.* See rt. 3. *dā,* p. 408, col. 2.

दिन 2. *dina, as, am,* m. n. (probably for *divana* and related to 3. *div* fr. rt. 2. *div,* said to be fr. rt. *do*), a day; [cf. *dur-d*°, *puru-d*°, *madh-yan-d*°, *su-d*°; cf. also Lith. *diena,* f. 'a day;' Slav. *deny,* 'a day;' Lat. *peren-dinus, peren-dina-tio, peren* = *para;* perhaps Goth. *sin-teins,* 'daily,' *sin* = *sam.*] — *Dina-kara, as, ī, am,* making day or light; (*ī*), f., scil. *ṭīkā,* N. of a commentary on the Bhāshā-pariććheda; (*as*), m. the sun; N. of the author of the work Ćandrārkī. — *Dinakara-tanaya, as,* m. 'the son of the Sun,' the planet Saturn. — *Dinakara-deva, as,* m., N. of a poet. — *Dinakarātmajā* (°*ra-āt*°), f. 'the daughter of the Sun,' an epithet of the Yamunā or Jumnā river. — *Dina-kartṛi, tā,* m. or *dina-kṛit, t,* m. 'the day-maker,' the sun. — *Dina-keśara* or *dina-kesara* or *dina-keśava, as,* m. 'the hair of the day,' the darkness. — *Dina-kshaya, as,* m. 'the decline of day,' the evening, = *tithi-kshaya;* N. of a chapter in the Purāṇa-sarva-sva. — *Dina-jyotis, is,* n. 'day-light,' sunshine. — *Dina-duḥkhita, as, ā, am,* afflicted by day, sorrowing by day; (*as*), m. the bird Ćakra-vāka, the ruddy goose. — *Dina-nakta, am,* n. day and night. — *Dina-pati, is,* m. 'the lord of the day,' the sun. — *Dina-praṇī, īs,* m. 'the bringer of day,' the sun; [cf. *tithi-praṇī.*] — *Dina-ban-dhu, us,* m. 'the friend of the day,' the sun. — *Dina-bala, as,* m. 'the strength of the day,' N. of the fifth, sixth, seventh, eighth, eleventh, and twelfth signs of the zodiac collectively. — *Dina-maṇi, is,* m. 'the jewel of day,' the sun. — *Dina-mala, am,* n. 'day-refuse (?),' a month. — *Dina-mūrdhan, ā,* m. 'the head of the day,' the eastern mountain behind which the sun is supposed to rise; [cf. *udaya.*] — *Dina-ratna, am,* n. 'the jewel of the day,' the sun. — *Dina-rāśi, is,* m. 'the sum or collective amount of days,' i. e. the number of solar days which have elapsed from one given point of time to another. — *Dina-vyāsa-dala, am,* n. 'half-diameter or radius of the sky,' i. e. the radius of a circle made by an asterism in its daily revolution. — *Dināṅśa* (°*na-aṅśa*), *as,* m. 'any portion of a day,' i. e. a watch, an hour, morning, forenoon, afternoon, &c. — *Dināgama* (°*na-āg*°), *as,* m. day-break. — *Di-nāṇḍa* (°*na-aṇḍa?*), *am,* n. 'day-egg,' i. e. darkness, (the egg or embryo whence day proceeds.) — *Dinātyaya* (°*na-at*°), *as,* m. 'the decline of day,' evening. — *Dinādi* (°*na-ādi*), *is,* m. 'day-break,' dawn. — *Dinādhīśa* (°*na-adh*°), *as,* m. 'the lord of day,' the sun. — *Dinānta* (°*na-an*°), *as,* m. 'end of day,' sun-set, evening. — *Dināntaka* (°*na-an*°), *as,* m. 'day-destroyer,' darkness. — *Di-nārambha* (°*na-ār*°), *as,* m. 'day-break,' morning. — *Dinārdha* (°*na-ar*°), *as,* m. 'the half of the day,' noon. — *Dināvasāna* (°*na-av*°), *am,* n. 'close of day,' evening. — *Dināstra* (°*na-as*°), *am,* n. 'day-missile,' N. of a magical formula. — *Dinī-kṛi,* cl. 8. P. A. *-karoti, -kurute, -kartum,* to reduce to days. — *Dineśa* (°*na-īśa*), *as,* m. 'the lord of day,' the sun; the regent of a day. — *Dineśātmaja* (°*śa-āt*°), *as,* m. 'the son of the Sun,' the planet Mercury. — *Dineśvara* (°*na-iś*°), *as,* m. 'the lord of the day,' the sun. — *Dinaika* (°*na-eka*), *as,* m. one day.

Dinikā, f. a day's wages, hire for a day or by the day.

दिन्नाग्राम *dinnā-grāma, as,* m., N. of a village of the Khāśakas.

दिन्व् *dinv*, cl. 1. P. *dinvati*, &c., to be glad, to gladden; to please, to be pleased; [cf. *dhinv* and *jinv*.]

दिप् *dip*, cl. 1. A. *depate*, &c., to drop; (various reading for *tip*.)

दिप्सु *dipsu, us, us, u* (fr. the Desid. of rt. *dabh*), Ved. intending to hurt or injure; [cf. *dhipsu* and *didambhishu*.]

दिम्प् *dimp*, cl. 10. A. *dimpayate*, &c., to accumulate, order, direct; [cf. *dip*.]

दिम्भ् *dimbh*, cl. 10. A. *dimbhayate*, &c., to accumulate; P. *dimbhayati*, &c., to order, command, direct; to incite.

दिय *diya, as, ā, am*, Ved. to be given, deserving of a gift, (according to Durga on Nirukta III. 15 = *deya* or *dānārha*.)

दिर् *dir* (fr. rt. *dṛī*), 'a fracture' in *kalaśa-dir*, q. v.

दिरिपक *diripaka, as, am,* m. or n. (?), a ball for playing with.

दिलीप *dilī-pa, as,* m. (said to be fr. *dili*, a name for the ancient Hāstina-pura or modern Delhi, + *pa*, a protector), N. of a king and ancestor of Rāma, son of Aṅśu-mat and father of Bhagīratha; [cf. *dailīpi*.] — *Dilīpa-ćarita, am,* n., N. of the fifth chapter of the Pātāla-khaṇḍa or fourth part of the Padma-Purāṇa. — *Dilīpa-rāj, ṭ,* m. the king of Dilīpa. — *Dilīpa-vara-lābha, as,* m., N. of the sixth chapter of the Pātāla-khaṇḍa.

दिलीर *dilīra, as,* m. = *śilīndhraka*, a mushroom.

दिल्ह *dilha, as,* m., N. of a man; [cf. *dihlā*.]

दिव् 1. *div*, cl. 1. P. *devati*, cl. 10. P. *devayati, -yitum*, to cause to lament, to pain, vex; to ask, beseech, beg; A. (*-te*), to suffer pain, lament, wail, mourn audibly.

दिव् 2. *div*, cl. 4. P. *dīvyati, dideva* (2nd sing. *didevitha*, part. *didivas*, or according to Vopa-deva *dudyūvas*), *devishyati, adevīt, devitum* (Ind. part. *devitvā* or *dyūtvā*), to shine (perhaps originally to shoot forth as a ray of light), to be bright or splendid [cf. 3. *div*, 2. *dī, dīp, dev*, 1. *dyut*]; to cast, throw; to cast dice, play with dice, gamble (with inst., e. g. *akshair dīvyati*, he plays with dice: but with gen. of the stake played for, e. g. *śatasya dīvyati*, he plays for a hundred; or sometimes with inst., e. g. *tena dhanena dīvyāmi tvayā*, I will play with thee for this money; or even with dat. or in the Brāhmaṇas with acc., e. g. *gām dīvyeyus*, they may play for a cow); to lay a wager, make a bet (with dat. of the thing betted upon); to play, sport, joke; to trifle with, make sport of, play upon, rally (with acc.); to play with, squander, make light of (as property &c. with gen.); to sell; to buy (?); to have free play or scope; to praise (e. g. *Brāhmaṇam dīvyati*, he praises the Brāhman; cf. *paṇate*, he bets; *paṇāyati*, he praises); to be glad, rejoice; to be mad or drunk with pride, passion, &c.; to be sleepy; to wish for, desire to gain; to go; [cf. rt. 1. *dyu*]: Caus. *devayati, -yitum, adīdivat*, to cause to play with dice: Desid. *didevishati* and *dudyūshati*: Caus. of the Desid. *dudyūshayati*, &c., to cause any one to wish to play: Intens. *dedivīti, dedeti, dedīvyate*; [cf. *dyūta*, 'play:' probably Lat. *ludo, jocus*; *Jupiter, Jovis*, for *Dyupiter, Dyovis*: Lith. *yūkas*, 'joke;' *yūkoyu*, 'I joke:' perhaps also Lith. *żibu*, 'I shine.']

3. *div, dyaus*, m. f. (in the Veda usually m., rarely f., but in later Sanskṛit only f. In the Veda the acc. sing. is *dyām* and *divam*; inst. *divā*; dat. *dyave*, Mahā-bh. I. 3934, and *dive*; abl. and gen. *dyos* and *divas*; loc. *dyavi* and *divi*: nom., acc., voc. du. *dyāvā*, and in Ṛig-veda IV. 56, 5, *dyavī*, cf. *dyāvā-pṛithivī*, heaven and earth: nom. pl. *dyāvas*; acc. *dyūn*; inst. *dyubhis*. According to native grammarians the base of this noun is both *div* and *dyo*, the nom. and voc. sing. being formed from *dyo* as *gaus* fr. *go*, the base *div* remaining before vowel terminations, and the form *dyu* being used before terminations beginning with consonants and at the beginning of a comp., see 3. *dyu*; Vopa-deva gives the acc. *dyām* as well as *divam*. In Mahā-bh. VIII. 4658, the base *dyo* occurs in the comp. *dyo-salileshu*; cf. *dyo*); heaven, the sky, air, atmosphere (e. g. *dyaur bhūmir āpaśća*, air, earth, and water); the place where the Soma is produced (apparently used in this sense in the Sāma-veda); day, the day (generally in pl., see 3. *dyu*, except in such forms as *divā*, by day; *dive dive, dyavi dyavi*, daily, every day; *ahar-dive*, &c.); daylight, light, brightness, brilliancy, glow (generally in inst. pl., e. g. *pari-bhūshati dyubhis*, he adorns with splendor); fire, the glow of fire; [in the Veda 'the Sky' is generally regarded as a masculine deity, being called in certain passages *dyaush-pitṛi* or 'the universal father, the Earth being regarded as 'the mother;' while the daughter of 'the Sky' is Ushas or the dawn. In Vedic cosmology there are three Skies, an upper, a middle, and a lower. As a feminine personification, Dyaus is the daughter of Prajā-pati. The inst. c. *divā*, 'by day,' 'the day,' is often used in comp. or as a subst.; so also *divam* acc., *divas* gen., and *divi* loc. are used in comp. as in the examples given below; cf. *eka-dyu*; cf. also *dyo, di-na, a-dya, deva*: Zend *dīv*, 'to shine;' *daēva*, 'demon:' Gr. Ζεύς = *dyaus*; Διός = *divas*; ἔν-δι-ο-ς, εὐ-δί-α, δία-λος, δέελο-ς, δῆλος, Διώνη, πρῴ-ζος, χθι-ζός, ἤδη, δέ-α-το, δο-ά-σσα-το: Lat. *Diov-i-s, Jovis, Ju-piter, deu-s, dīvu-s, sub-dio, Diana, die-s, bi-du-u-m, nū-diu-s, inter-diū, nun-dinæ, jam, dum, dudum*: Old Iceland. *tīvar*, 'gods, heroes:' Old Germ. *Zio*: Lith. *deva-s*, 'god;' *dënà*, 'day:' Slav. *dĭ-nă*, 'day.'] — *Divaḥ-śyenī*, f. epithet of particular sacrifices or oblations. — *Divan-gama, as, ā, am*, going or rising or leading to heaven. — *Divas-pati, is,* m. 'the lord of heaven,' epithet of Indra; also of Nahusha and of Vishṇu; N. of the Indra of the thirteenth Manv-antara. — *Divā-kara, as,* m. 'the day-maker,' the sun; N. of one of the sons of Garuḍa, (often mentioned with Niśā-kara, who is another son of Garuḍa); a crow [cf. *divāṭana*]; a flower, the sun-flower, Calotropis Gigantea [cf. *arka*]; N. of a prince, (also read *divārka*); of the founder of the Sūrya-bhakta sect; of a poet; of a pupil of Śaṅkarāćārya, and of several other men. — *Divākara-vatsa, as,* m., N. of the author of the Kakshyā-stotra hymn. — *Divākara-suta, as,* m. 'the son of the Sun,' the planet Saturn; (*ā*), f. 'the daughter of the Sun,' an epithet of the river Yamunā. — *Divā-kīrtti, is,* m. a man of low or impure caste, a Caṇḍāla; a barber; an owl; (the barber not being allowed to operate at night; or *divākīrtti* may be fr. *divā* + *akīrtti*, the Caṇḍāla and owl only coming abroad by night.) — *Divā-kīrtya, as, ā, am*, to be recited or pronounced at day-time; (*am*), n., N. of certain recitations and songs; furnished with a recitation which must be performed at day-time; (*as*), m. a Caṇḍāla; [cf. the preceding.] — *Divā-kṛita, as, ā, am*, done by day. — *Divā-ćara, as, ā, am*, or *divā-ćārin, ī, iṇī, i*, going about by day (as certain animals). — *Divāṭana* (°*vā-aṭ*°), *as, ā, am*, wandering about by day; (*as*), m. a crow. — *Divā-tana, as, ī, am*, or *divā-tara, as, ā, am*, Ved. daily, diurnal, of or belonging to the day. — *Divā-niśam*, ind. day and night. — *Divāndha* (°*vā-an*°), *as, ā, am*, blind by day; (*as*), m. an owl; (*ā*), f. a kind of bird (= *valgulā*). — *Divāndhakī*, f. the musk-rat. — *Divā-pushṭa, as,* m. the sun ('nourished by the day,' appearing in its full splendor in day-time). — *Divā-pradīpa, as,* m. 'a lamp by day,' i. e. an obscure man. — *Divā-bhīta, as, ā, am*, timid by day; (*as*), m. an owl; a thief or house-breaker; the white lotus, or perhaps any such flower (the petals of which open at night and close in the day-time). — *Divā-bhīti, is,* m. 'having fear by day,' an owl. — *Divā-bhūta, as, ā, am*, turned into day, become bright as the day. — *Divā-maṇi, is,* m. 'the jewel of the day,' the sun. — *Divā-madhya, am,* n. midday, noon. — *Divā-manya, as, ā, am*, thinking one's self the day. — *Divā-maithunin, ī, inī, i*, cohabiting by day. — *Divā-rātram*, ind. day and night. — *Divā-rātri, is,* f. day or night. — *Divārka* (°*vā-ar*°), *as,* m., N. of a prince. — *Divāvasāna* (°*va-av*°), *am,* n. the end of day, close of day. — *Divā-vasu, us, us, u*, Ved. eminent or excellent by day; (Sāy.) having splendid oblations. — *Divā-śaya, as, ā, am*, sleeping by day. — *Divāśaya-tā*, f. sleeping in the day-time. — *Divā-sanćara, as, ā, am*, = *divā-ćara*, walking about by day. — *Divā-supta, as, ā, am*, asleep by day. — *Divā-svapana, am,* n. sleeping by day. — *Divā-svapna, as,* m. sleep by day (considered as noxious). — *Divā-svāpa, as,* m. sleep by day; (*as, ā, am*), sleeping by day; (*ā*), f. a kind of bird (= *valgulā*). — *Divi-kshaya, as, ā, am*, living in the sky. — *Divi-kshit, t, t, t*, Ved. living in the sky or in heaven. — *Divi-gata, as, ā, am*, being in the sky or in heaven. — *Divi-ćara, as, ā, am*, or *divi-ćārin, ī, iṇī, i*, moving in the sky, celestial, an inhabitant of the sky. — *Divi-ja, as, ā, am*, born in heaven, of heavenly origin, heavenly, celestial; (*as*), m. 'an inhabitant of the sky,' a deity, a god. — *Divi-jā, ās, ās, am*, Ved. born or produced in the sky. — *Divi-jāta, as, ā, am*, born or produced in the sky or heaven; (*as*), m., N. of a son of Purū-ravas. — *Div-it, t, t, t*, Ved. going to the sky. — *Divit-mat, ān, atī, at*, Ved. going in or to the sky, heavenly; (Sāy.) = *dīpti-mat*, shining; (*-matā*), ind. turned towards heaven; [cf. *it-van*.] — *Divi-yaj, ṭ, ṭ, ṭ*, Ved. offering oblation or worship to heaven. — *Divi-yoni, is, is, i*, born in the sky, Ved. having origin in heaven. — *Divi-ratha, as,* m., N. of a son of Bhumanyu; also of Dadhivāhana; also of Khanapāna (who like Dadhi-vāhana is the grandfather of Dharma-ratha; cf. *diva-ratha*). — *Divi-śrit, t, t, t.* (rt. *śri*), Ved. taking up one's abode in heaven. — *Divi-shad, t, t, t*, Ved. living in the sky; (*t*), m. an inhabitant of the sky, a deity. — *Divi-shṭambha, as, ā, am*, Ved. resting on the sky. — *Div-ishṭi, is,* f., Ved. 'eagerness or ardour for heaven,' devotion, practising devotion, any religious rite, sacrifice; [cf. *gavishṭi*.] — *Divi-shṭha, as, ā, am*, situated or dwelling in heaven, heavenly, celestial. — *Divi-sad* and *divi-stha*, see *divi-shad* and *divi-shṭha*. — *Divi-spṛiś, k, k, k*, or *divi-spṛiśat, an, atī* or *antī, at*, touching or reaching the sky or heaven, pervading the sky; [cf. *diva-spṛiś*.] — *Divo-jā, ās, ās, am*, produced in heaven. — *Divo-dāsa, as,* m. 'slave of heaven,' N. of a man with the surname Bharad-vāja (celebrated in the Ṛig-veda for his liberality, and the assistance rendered to him by Indra and the Aśvins against Śambara; his father is called in the Veda Vadhryaśva, but in the later literature Bhadhrasva or Badhryāśva or Bahvaśva &c., and his son is Mitrayu or Mitrāyu); N. of the father of Su-dās; N. of a king of Kāśi or Benares with the surname Dhanvantari, founder of the Indian school of medicine &c.; N. of several other men; [cf. *daivodāsi*.] — *Divodāseśvara-liṅga* (°*sa-īś*°), *am,* n., N. of a Liṅga mentioned in the Skanda-Purāṇa. — *Divodāsopākhyāna* (°*sa-up*°), *am,* n. 'the episode of Divo-dāsa,' N. of the twenty-third chapter of the Svarga-khaṇḍa or third part of the Padma-Purāṇa. — *Divo-duh, dhuk, k, k*, Ved. milking from the sky. — *Divo-ruć, k, k, k*, Ved. shining from heaven.

Diva, am, n. = 3. *div*, heaven, sky, atmosphere; paradise; a day; a wood, thicket; (often at the end of comp.; cf. *ahar-d*°, *tri-d*°, *naktan-d*°; cf.

also Lat. *divum, sub-divo.*) — *Diva-kshas, ās, ās, as* (*kshas* fr. rt. 2. *kshi*), Ved. living in heaven, heavenly; (*ās*), m. epithet of Indra; [cf. *dyu-ksha.*] — *Diva-darśa, ās*, m. pl., N. of a school of the Atharva-veda. — *Diva-ratha*, wrong reading for *divi-ratha*, q. v. — *Divas-prithivyau*, f. du. heaven and earth. — *Diva-spriś, k, k, k*, Ved. touching or reaching the sky, pervading the sky; (*k*), m. an epithet of Krishṇa. — *Divokas, ās*, m. an inhabitant of heaven, a deity; the Ćātaka; [cf. *divaukas.*] — *Divodbhava* (°*va-ud*°), *as, ā, am*, born or produced in heaven or the sky, of heavenly origin; (*ā*), f. cardamoms. — *Divolkā* (°*va-ul*°), f. 'firebrand in the sky,' a meteor; [cf. *divyolkā.*] — *Divaukas* (°*va-ok*°), *ās*, m. an inhabitant of heaven, a deity; the Ćātaka, Cuculus Melanoleucus; a deer; a bee; an elephant; [cf. *divokas.*] — *Divaukasa, as*, m. an inhabitant of heaven, a deity.

Divan, ā, m. a day; [cf. *prati-d*°.]

Divasa, as, am, m. n. the sky, heaven; a day (generally *as*, m.); [cf. Lat. *dies;* Old Germ. *zies-tac;* Angl. Sax. *tiwes-daeg;* Eng. *tues-day;* perhaps also Cambro-Brit. *diev* and Hib. *dia*, 'day.'] — *Divasa-kara, as*, m. or *divasa-krit, t*, m. 'the day-maker,' the sun. — *Divasa-ćara, as, ā, am*, going about in the day-time, (opposed to *niśā-ćara.*) — *Divasa-nātha, as*, m. 'the lord of day,' the sun. — *Divasa-bhartri, tā*, m. 'the supporter of day,' the sun. — *Divasa-mukha, am*, n. 'the beginning of day,' day-break, dawn. — *Divasa-mudrā*, f. 'day's coin,' a day's wages. — *Divasa-vigama, as*, m. the departure of day. — *Divasātyaya* (°*sa-at*°), *as*, m. 'the passing away of day,' evening. — *Divasāntara* (°*sa-an*°), *as, ā, am*, only one day old. — *Divasāvasāna* (°*sa-av*°), *am*, n. 'the close of day,' evening. — *Divaseśvara* (°*sa-īś*°), *as*, m. 'the lord of day,' the sun.

Divā, ind. by day, see 3. *div*, p. 413, col. 2; *a-divā*, not by day.

Divi, is, m. the blue jay, = *kikīdivi.*

Divī, f. a species of insect, = *upa-jihvā, upadīkā.*

1. *divya*, Nom. P. *divyati*, &c., to long for heaven.

2. *divya, as, ā, am*, divine, heavenly, celestial, (opposed to *pārthiva, kshamya, bhauma*, &c.); supernatural, wonderful, brilliant (as heaven); charming, beautiful, agreeable; (*as*), m. barley; a fragrant resin, bdellium; a kind of animal (= *dhanvina*); N. of a prince; (*ā*), f., N. of several plants, Emblica Officinalis (= *harītakī*), Terminalia Chebula, Asparagus Racemosus (= *śatāvarī*); cumin-seed (= *mahā-medā, brāhmī, sthūla-jīraka*); a kind of perfume (= *śveta-dūrvā, surā*); N. of an Apsaras; (*am*), n. divine or celestial nature, divinity; the celestial regions, the sky, heaven; an ordeal, (of which ten kinds are enumerated, viz. 1. Tulā, cf. *tulā-parīkshā;* 2. Agni, 'touching fire;' 3. Jala, 'immersion in water;' 4. Visha, 'poison;' 5. Kośa, q. v.; 6. Taṇḍula, 'chewing rice-grains and ejecting them,' if they appear dry or blood-stained, they are a proof of guilt; 7. Tapta-māsha, 'taking a Māsha weight of gold out of heated oil;' 8. Phāla, 'holding a hot plough-share;' 9. Dharmādharma, 'drawing concealed images of Virtue and Vice out of a vessel filled with earth;' 10. Tulasī, 'holding the leaves of holy basil and after repeating a form of oath swallowing them'); an oath, adjuration, solemn declaration or promise; cloves; a sort of sandal; N. of a grammar. — *Divya-kaṭa, am*, n., N. of a town. — *Divya-kānana-darśana, as, ā, am*, in aspect like to a celestial grove. — *Divya-kārin, ī*, m. undergoing an ordeal, taking an oath. — *Divya-kuṇḍa, am*, n. 'the heavenly lake,' N. of a lake on the mountain Kshobhaka in Kāma-rūpa. — *Divya-gandha, as, ā, am*, having a divine odour; (*as*), m. sulphur; (*ā*), f. large cardamoms; a kind of vegetable, = *mahā-ćanću;* (*am*), n. cloves. — *Divya-gāyana, as*, m. a divine songster, a Gandharva or heavenly minstrel. — *Divya-ćakshus, us*, n. a divine eye, prophetic or supernatural vision, the faculty of seeing what is invisible by the human eye; (*us, us, us*), having divine or prophetic visions, heavenly-eyed; blind, i. e. using the mental instead of the physical eye; (*us*), m. a monkey; a kind of perfume. — *Divya-jñāna, am*, n. supernatural knowledge. — *Divya-tattva, am*, n. 'heavenly truth,' N. of a work. — *Divya-tā*, f. heavenliness, heavenly or divine nature. — *Divya-tejas, ās*, f. 'having heavenly splendor,' a kind of plant; [cf. *brāhmī.*] — *Divya-darśana-viśruta, as, ā, am*, renowned for a divine aspect. — *Divya-darśin, ī, inī, i*, having a divine vision. — *Divya-driś, k, k, k*, 'seeing heavenly things,' observing heavenly phenomena; (*k*), m. an astrologer. — *Divya-deha, as*, m. a celestial body. — *Divya-dohada, am*, n. divine desire, the object of a deity's desire; (*as, ā, am*), fit for an offering or oblation. — *Divya-dharmin, ī, iṇī, i*, having a divine nature. — *Divya-nadī*, f. a heavenly stream. — *Divya-nārī*, f. a divine female, an Apsaras. — *Divya-pañćāmrita* (°*ća-am*°), *am*, n. 'the five divine ambrosias,' viz. ghee, milk, coagulated milk, honey, and sugar. — *Divya-pāṭala*, 'having a heavenly pale-red colour,' a kind of plant. — *Divya-pushpa, as*, m. fragrant oleander, = *karavīra;* (*ā*), f. a kind of plant (= *mahā-droṇā*). — *Divyapushpikā*, f. a kind of Calotropis (= *lohita-varṇārka-vriksha*). — *Divya-prabhāva, as, ā, am*, having celestial power. — *Divya-praśna, as*, m. inquiry into celestial phenomena, augury. — *Divya-māna, as*, m. measuring the time according to the days and years of the gods. — *Divya-mānusha, as*, m. a demi-god, a being half divine and half human, a semi-divine being; (*as, ā, am*), divine and human. — *Divya-yamunā*, f. 'the heavenly Jumnā,' N. of a river in Kāma-rūpa. — *Divya-ratna, am*, n. 'the heavenly gem,' the fabulous gem Ćintā-maṇi. — *Divya-ratha, as*, m. 'a heavenly car,' the car or vehicle of any deity. — *Divya-rasa, as*, m. 'the divine fluid,' quicksilver. — *Divya-latā*, f. 'the divine creeper,' N. of the plant Sanseviera Zeylanica (= *mūrvā*). — *Divya-vastra, as, ā, am*, 'having heavenly clothes,' clothed in celestial raiment, divinely dressed; (*as*), m. a plant, commonly Sūrya-śobhā, a sort of sun-flower. — *Divya-vākya, am*, n. a celestial voice. — *Divya-śrotra, am*, n. 'a heavenly ear,' an ear which hears everything. — *Divya-sānu, us*, m. 'divine eminence,' N. of one of the Viśve-Devās. — *Divya-sāra, as*, m. 'having divine juice or resin,' N. of the tree Shorea Robusta. — *Divya-strī*, f. a divine female, an Apsaras. — *Divyāṅśu* (°*ya-aṅśu*), *us*, m. the sun, 'having heavenly rays.' — *Divyāṅganā* (°*ya-an*°), f. a divine woman. — *Divyā-divya* (°*ya-a-div*°), *as, ā, am*, divine and not divine, partly human, partly divine; (*ā*), f. a demi-goddess (as Sītā, heroine of the Rāmāyaṇa). — *Divyāvadāna* (°*ya-av*°), *am*, n. 'heavenly achievements,' N. of a Buddhist collection of legends. — *Divyodaka* (°*ya-ud*°), *am*, n. 'heavenly water,' rain-water, dew, &c. — *Divyopapāduka* (°*ya-up*°), *as, ī, am*, divinely born, of heavenly birth or origin, celestial, divine. — *Divyaugha* (°*ya-ogha*), *as*, m. 'having divine energy,' N. of particular forms of Śiva (worshipped by the Tāntrikas).

Divyaka, as, m. a kind of serpent; another species of animal, = *dhanvina;* [cf. 2. *divya.*]

Divyelaka, as, m. a kind of serpent (= *divyaka?*).

Dīv (acc. *dyuvam*, dat. *dīve* and *dyuve*), Ved. gambling, gaming, playing with dice.

Dīvana, am, n. gambling, playing with dice; [cf. *devana.*]

Dīvi, is, m. the blue jay; [cf. *divi*, col. 1.]

Dīvyat, an, antī, at, playing, sporting, gambling.

Dīvyamāna, as, ā, am, playing, sporting; throwing, darting, shooting.

दिविर *divira, as*, m., N. of a man. — *Divira-kiśora, as*, m., N. of a poet.

दिश् 1. *diś*, cl. 3. and in later Sanskrit cl. 6. P. (rarely A.) *dideshṭi, diśati, -te, dideśa, didiśe, dekshyati, -te, adikshat, adikshata* (Ved. *adishṭa*), *deshṭum*, to point out, show, exhibit, produce, bring forward (as a witness in a court of justice); to assign; to bestow upon (with gen.); grant, give, deliver; to pay (tribute); to direct, order, command (with inf.); to point to, denote: Pass. *diśyate:* Caus. *deśayati, -yitum, adīdiśat*, to show, point out, assign; to teach, communicate, tell, inform; to direct, order, command, govern; to confer: Desid. *didikshati, -te*, to wish to show, &c.: Intens. *dediśyate, dedeshṭi*, (A.) to exhibit exceedingly, show, show one's self, &c.; (P.) to order or direct urgently; [cf. Zend *diś;* Gr. δείκ-νυ-μι, δείκελος, δεῖξ-ις, δεῖγμα, δίκ-η, δικ-εῖν, δίκτυον, δειδίσκομαι, δίσκος; Lat. *in-dic-are, ju-dex, causi-dic-us, dic-ere;* Goth. *teih-an, taikns, taiknyan;* Angl. Sax. *tihian, tihhan, taccan, tácn, tácen, tier* for *tihher, tiid, tid;* Old Germ. *zeig-ōn, zīt* for *zig-ti, zeinyan;* probably also Lith. *źénklas*, 'a sign.']

2. *diś, k*, f. direction pointed at, point of the compass, quarter of the sky, cardinal point, quarter, region, place, space, part (e. g. *diśi diśi*, in all directions, in every quarter; *digbhyas*, from all regions or quarters; *diśodiśas*, hither and thither: the four chief quarters or cardinal points are *prāći*, east; *dakshiṇā*, south; *pratīći*, west; and *udīći*, north: sometimes five are enumerated, i. e. the preceding four with *dhruvā*, q. v.: sometimes six or seven are given, but oftener eight, i. e. the four cardinal and the four intermediate quarters, S.E., S.W., N.W., and N.E., cf. *upa-diś:* or sometimes ten, viz. the preceding eight with *tiryak*, horizontally, and *ūrdhvam*, perpendicularly, or *adhas*, underneath, and *ūrdhvam*, overhead: *diśo daśa*, towards the ten quarters, i. e. in all directions; *diśām patis*, 'the lord of the quarters,' is a N. of Soma and Rudra in the Veda, cf. *dik-pati* below; in Vishṇu-Purāṇa I. VIII. the collective *diśas*, 'the regions or quarters,' is mentioned as one of the wives of the eight manifestations of Rudra); the numeral ten; side, party, people; a foreign or distant quarter or region, cf. *dig-āgata;* a hint, reference; precept, order, manner; manner of thinking, point of view, method of considering a subject; the mark of a bite; N. of a river. — *Dik-kanyā*, f. a region of the sky considered as a virgin or mistress. — 2. *dik-kara, as*, m. = *aruṇa*, q. v. = *śambhu*, q. v.; (*as, ī, am*), juvenile, youthful; [cf. 1. *dikkara* at p. 412, col. 1.] — *Dik-kara-vāsinī*, f., N. of a goddess; [cf. *dik-kāminī* and *dik-sundarī.*] — *Dikkarikā*, f. (fr. the next), N. of a river. — *Dik-karin, ī*, m. 'elephant of the quarter,' an elephant of one of the eight quarters or points, i. e. a mythical elephant standing in one of the four or eight regions of the sky and supporting with the others the earth; [cf. *dig-ibha, dig-gaja, dig-dantin, dig-vāraṇa, diṅ-nāga, diṅ-mātaṅga, diśā-gaja.*] — *Dik-kāntā*, f. or *dik-kāminī*, f. = *dik-kanyā*. — *Dik-kumāra, ās*, m. pl. the youths of the quarters; (with Jainas) a class of deities belonging to the Bhavanādhīśas. — *Dik-ćakra, am*, n. the circuit of the quarters of the compass, the horizon; the compass, the whole world; [cf. *diṅ-maṇḍala.*] — *Dik-taṭa, as*, m. the horizon, the line of the horizon. — *Dik-tas*, ind. from the regions of the sky. — *Dik-pati, is*, or *dik-pāla, as*, m. the regent or guardian of a quarter of the world, (the guardian of the eight points are Indra of the east, Agni of the south-east, Yama of the south, Nirṛiti of the south-west, Varuṇa of the west, Vāyu or Marut of the north-west, Kuvera of the north, Īśāna or Śiva of the north-east; these are generally regarded as identical with the regents of the quarters, but other lists substitute Sūrya 'the sun' and Ćandra or Soma 'the moon' for Nirṛiti and Īśāna, and others again give the sun and moon and the six planets; cf. Manu V. 96, VII. 303.) — *Dik-patha, as*, m. 'the path of the horizon,' the surrounding region or quarter. — *Dik-pravibhāga, as*, m. a point, direction, quarter; [cf. *dig-bhāga* and *dig-vibhāga.*] — *Dik-śūla, am*, n. 'stake of the sky,' any inauspicious planetary conjunction as for the sun and Venus to be in the west, &c.; N. of particular days on which it is not allowed to travel in certain directions. — *Dikśūla-lakshaṇa, āni*, n. pl., N. of a chapter of the

Purāṇa-sarva-sva. — Dik-sama, as, ā, am, having the same direction. — Dik-sundarī, f. = dik-kanyā. — Dik-srakti, is, is, i, having the angles or corners towards the four cardinal points. — Dik-svāmin, ī, m. = dik-pati. — Dig-anta, as, m. the end of the horizon or of space, remote distance; (as, ā, am), being at the end of the horizon or in the remote distance. — Dig-antara, am, n. another region, a distant quarter, a foreign country; space, the atmosphere. — Dig-ambara, as, ā, am, 'sky-clothed,' having only the sky or atmosphere for raiment, clad by the regions of space, unclad, unclothed, stark naked; (as), m. a naked mendicant (especially of the Jaina or Bauddha sect; cf. 1. kshapaṇa); a mendicant or ascetic in general; an epithet of Śiva; also of Skanda; darkness; (ī), f. an epithet of Durgā; [cf. dig-vastra and dig-vāsas.] — Dig-ambaraka, as, m. a naked mendicant (especially of the Jaina sect). — Digambara-tva, am, n. entire nakedness. — Dig-āgata, as, ā, am, come from a distant region or country. — Dig-ibha, as, m. = dik-karin, q. v. — Dig-īśvara, as, m. = dik-pati, q. v. — Dig-gaja, as, m. = dik-karin, q. v. — Dig-grahaṇa, am, n. observation of and fixing the quarters of the compass. — Dig-jaya, as, m. the conquest of various countries in all directions; [cf. dig-vijaya.] — Dig-dantin, ī, m. = dik-karin, q. v. — Dig-darśana, am, n. the act of looking to every side, a general survey. — Dig-darśin, ī, inī, i, looking round on all sides, taking a general view. — Dig-dāha, as, m. preternatural redness of the horizon, as if on fire; (also called diśāṃ dāhas.) — Dig-devatā, f. the deity of a quarter, = dik-pati, q. v. — Dig-deśa, as, m. the country in various directions, various regions, distant countries. — Dig-daivata, am, n. = dig-devatā, q. v. — Dig-nāga, see diṅ-nāga. — Dig-bhāga, as, m. a point, direction, quarter; dig-bhāgeshu, loc. pl. in all directions; [cf. dik-pravibhāga and dig-vibhāga.] — Dig-bhrama, as, m. or dig-bhramaṇa, am, n. a wandering about in every direction. — Dig-maṇḍala, see diṅ-maṇḍala. — Dig-lābha, as, m. profit or gain in a distant region. — Dig-vastra, as, ā, am, or dig-vāsas, ās, ās, as, = dig-ambara. — Dig-vāraṇa, as, m. = dik-karin. — Dig-vijaya, as, m. 'the subjugation of various countries in all directions,' N. of a part of the Mahā-bhārata (Sabhā-parva 983, describing the victories of the four younger Pāṇḍavas and the subjugation of all the neighbouring princes of India under their eldest brother Yudhi-shṭhira, which led to his performance of the Rāja-sūya sacrifice); N. of a work by Saṅkarāčārya showing the superiority of the Vedānta over the other systems of philosophy. — Digvijaya-krama, as, m. invasion of various countries, going forth to conquer the whole world. — Dig-vidik-stha, as, ā, am, situated towards the cardinal and intermediate points, encompassing. — Dig-vidhāna, am, n., N. of a chapter of the Tantra-sāra. — Dig-vibhāga, as, m. = dig-bhāga, q. v. — Dig-vibhāvita, as, ā, am, celebrated or known in all quarters. — Dig-vilokana, am, n. looking vacantly towards the sky, gazing vacantly in the air. — Dig-vyāpin, ī, inī, i, spreading through all space or every quarter. — Diṅ-nāga, as, m. = dik-karin; N. of a Buddhist author; (also read dig-nāga.) — Diṅ-maṇḍala, am, n. the circle of the quarters of the compass, the horizon, the compass, all regions or quarters; [cf. dik-čakra; also read dig-m°.] — Diṅ-mātaṅga, as, m. = dik-karin, q. v. — Diṅ-mārga, as, m. a country road, a road to a distant country. — Diṅ-mukha, as, ī, am, facing any point or quarter; (am), n. 'face of the sky,' any quarter or part of the heavens, (diṅ-mukheshu, loc. pl. in all regions); a place. — Diṅ-mūḍha, as, ā, am, confused about the quarters of the compass, not able to find out the bearings of any place; anything or place about the direction of which one is doubtful. — Diṅ-moha, as, m. perplexity about the quarters of the compass or the exact situation and bearings of any place, mistaking the way or direction. — Diśo-daṇḍa, as, m. (diśo for diśas, gen. case), 'the staff of a quarter of the sky,' a particular appearance in the sky; [cf. daṇḍa.] — Diśo-bhāga, as, ā, am, one who runs away or takes to his heels.

Diśa, am, ind. = 2. diś, at the end of adv. comp. (Pāṇ. V. 4, 107).

Diśas, ās, f. a region, quarter, &c.; [cf. 2. diś.]

Diśā, f. direction, region, quarter or point of the compass; N. of a wife of Rudra; [cf. antara-d° and avāntara-d°.] — Diśā-gaja, as, m. = dik-karin, q. v. — Diśā-čakshus, us, m. 'sky-vision,' N. of a son of Garuḍa. — Diśā-pāla, as, m. 'the guardian of a quarter,' the elephant of a quarter; [cf. dik-pāla and dik-karin.]

Diśya, as, ā, am, relating or belonging to the quarters of the sky or to the horizon; situated towards any particular point, lying in a particular tract or quarter, bearing in a particular direction or towards a particular point of the compass [cf. pūrva-d°]; N. of a particular kind of brick used in constructing an altar.

Dishṭa, as, ā, am, shown, pointed out, appointed, assigned (e. g. dishṭā gatis, 'the assigned way,' i. e. death); delineated, described, referred to; directed, ordered, prescribed, advised, enjoined; fixed, settled; resigned to destiny or fate; (am), n. allotment, assignment, appointment, decree; assigned place or portion, fate, destiny, good or ill luck; direction, order, command, aim, object; (as), m. time; a sort of Curcuma [cf. dāru-haridrā]; N. of one of the sons of Manu Vaivasvata. — Dishṭānta (°ṭa-an°), as, m. 'the appointed end' or 'the end of one's appointed life,' death, dying.

Dishṭi, is, f. pointing out, assigning, allotting, prescribing, assignment, direction, injunction, instruction, precept, order, command; auspicious juncture, good fortune, happiness; a sort of measure of length; (tyā), ind. an expression of joy or congratulation, thank heaven! how fortunate! mayest thou be fortunate! hail! I congratulate you! bravo! auspiciously, fortunately, luckily; [cf. ku-d°.]

दिष्णु dishṇu, us, us, u (for deshṇu fr. rt. 1. dā), giving, one who gives, a giver, donor.

दिह् 1. dih, cl. 2. P. A. degdhi, digdhe, dideha, didihe, dhekshyati, -te, adhikshat, adhikshata, adigdha, degdhum, to anoint, smear, plaster, spread over; to soil; pollute, defile; to increase, augment, accumulate: Caus. dehayati, -yitum, Aor. adīdihat: Desid. didhikshati, -te, Ved. dhikshate, to wish to anoint or to anoint one's self: Intens. dedihyate, dedegdhi: [cf. Gr. τεῖχος, τοῖχος, θιγγάνω; Lat. tingere, probably fingere, figulus; Goth. deigan, ga-dikis, daigs; Angl. Sax. dic, deag, tigel, tigul; Old Germ. ziagal, zehom = Caus. dehayāmi.]

2. dih, dhik, f. smearing, anointing, soiling, pollution.

दिह्ला dihlā, f., N. of a woman; [cf. dilha.]

दी 1. dī [cf. rt. ḍī], cl. 4. P. dīyati, &c., Ved. to poise one's self in the air, soar, fly, (also used of the motions of deities, especially of the Aśvins and their vehicle): Intens. dedīyate, Ved. inf. of Intens. dedīyitavai, to hasten or fly away; [cf. Gr. δίνη, δινέω; perhaps δίω, δίεμαι.]

दी 2. dī (an anomalous reduplicated rt. sometimes given in the form dīdī or dīdi; cf. rt. 1. dhī and dīdhī), cl. 3. P. 3rd pl. dīdyati, adīdet, 2nd impv. dīdihi or dīdīhi, dīdiyus, dīdāya, dīdayati, dīdayat, Ved. to shine, be bright (especially used of fire), to shine forth, excel; to shine upon, bestow by shining; to seem or appear good or eminent, to please, be admired; [cf. 2. div, dīp: Gr. δέατο, δέατο; perhaps δῆλος.]

Dīti, is, f. splendor, brightness; [cf. su-d°.]

Dīdi, is, is, i, or dīdī, is, is, i, shining. — Didy-agni, m. du., Ved. (according to Sāy.) 'having bright fires,' 'bright with sacrificial fires,' epithet of the Aśvins.

Dīditi, is, f. splendor, brightness; [cf. su-d°.]

Dīdivi, is, is, i (said to be fr. rt. 2. div), shining; risen, ascended (as a star); (is), m. epithet of Agni; of Bṛihas-pati, the planet Jupiter; heaven [cf. didivi]; (is, ī), m. n. or (is, is), m. f. boiled rice, food; final emancipation.

दी 3. dī, cl. 4. A. dīyate, didīye, dāsyate, adāsta, dātum, to decay, waste away, be ruined; to waste, diminish: Caus. dāpayati, -yitum: Desid. didīshate, didāsate.

4. dī, is, f. decay, ruin, wasting, destruction. — Dīda, as, ā, am, causing destruction, destroying.

Dīna, as, ā, am, scarce, scanty (Ved.); poor, indigent, needy, afflicted, distressed, ruined, miserable, wretched, dejected, downcast, melancholy; frightened, afraid, timid [cf. pari-d°]; (am), n. distress, wretchedness [cf. dainya]; the plant Tabernæmontana Coronaria; (am), ind. miserably; (ā), f. the female of a mouse or shrew. — Dīna-četana, as, ā, am, 'distressed or dejected in mind,' distressed, dejected. — Dīna-tā, f. scarcity, rarity (Ved.); wretchedness, distress, weakness. — Dīna-daksha, as, ā, am, of weak understanding. — Dīna-dāsa, as, m. a name applied to a Śūdra. — Dīna-dhī, īs, īs, i, 'having melancholy thoughts,' dejected, helpless. — Dīna-manas, ās, ās, as, or dīna-mānasa, as, ā, am, 'afflicted in mind,' distressed, dejected, downcast. — Dīna-mukha, as, ī, am, 'having a dejected countenance,' of melancholy aspect. — Dīna-ločana, as, m. a cat. — Dīna-vatsala, as, ā, am, kind to the poor. — Dīna-vadana = dīna-mukha. — Dīna-varṇa, as, ā, am, 'having a bad colour,' discoloured. — Dīnānukampana (°na-an°), as, ā, am, 'compassionating the poor,' kind to the poor.

Dīnaka, as, ā, am, wretched, distressed; (am), ind. in a wretched manner, miserably.

दीक्ष् dīksh (a rt. formed fr. the Desid. of rt. daksh, and signifying originally 'to wish to make one's self fit or competent'), cl. 1. A. dīkshate, didīkshe, dīkshishyate, dīkshitum, to prepare or consecrate one's self for the performance of a sacred rite, especially of the Soma offering; to dedicate one's self; to sacrifice, perform a sacrifice; to shave one's head, to be shaved; to introduce or initiate a pupil, invest with the sacred thread; to instruct in the rules or principles of religious observances; to practise self-restraint, to announce the performance of a vow: Caus. dīkshayati or dīkshāpayati, &c., to prepare, make ready, consecrate, initiate; to determine: Desid. didīkshishate.

Dīkshaka, as, m. a priest, a spiritual guide.

Dīkshaṇa, am, n. preparing or consecrating one's self, consecration; initiating; causing one's self to be consecrated.

Dīkshaṇīya, as, ā, am, to be consecrated or initiated; (fr. dīkshaṇa) relating or belonging to Dīkshaṇa or initiation, &c.; (ā), f. a particular rite or sacrifice, that preceded by the Dīkshā; [cf. dīkshaṇīyeshṭi and adhvara-dīkshaṇīyā.] — Dīkshaṇīyeshṭi (°ya-ish°), is, f. the sacrifice of consecration or initiation, = dīkshaṇīyā.

Dīkshayitṛi, tā, trī, tṛi, consecrating, a consecrator, one who initiates.

Dīkshā, f. preparation or consecration for a religious ceremony; a ceremony preliminary to a sacrifice, initiation, dedication; receiving the initiatory Mantra; undertaking religious observances for the attainment of a certain object, religious rites for a special purpose; sacrificing, offering oblations, dedicating one's self to a particular object (as to battle) or to a person (as to a god), self-devotion; Initiation personified as the wife of Soma or of Rudra Ugra (one of the eight manifestations of Rudra) or of Rudra Vāma-deva. — Dīkshā-krama-ratna, am, n. 'the jewel of the regular order of initiation,' N. of a work treating of initiation. — Dīkshā-tattva, am, n. 'the essence of initiation,' N. of another work on consecration or initiation. — Dīkshānta (°shā-an°), as, m. 'the end of a Dīkshā,' = ava-bhṛitha, a supplementary sacrifice made to atone for any defects in a preceding one. — Dīkshā-pati, is, m., Ved. 'the lord of consecration,' i. e. the Soma. — *Dīkshā-pāla, as,* m., Ved. 'guardian of initiation,' epithet of Agni and Vishṇu. — *Dīkshā-phala, am,* n. 'the fruit of initiation,' N. of a chapter of the Purāṇa-sarva-sva. — *Dīkshā-maya, as, ī, am,* consisting in initiation.

Dīkshita, as, ā, am, initiated, consecrated; prepared for a sacrifice; one who has received initiation or by whom the preparatory ceremonies have been observed; performed (as the Dīkshā ceremony); prepared for, made ready for, ready, &c.; *dīkshitam kṛi,* to initiate a person, instruct any one in rules or principles; (*as*), m. a priest engaged in a Dīkshā or in a particular sacrifice; a pupil, (often at the end of a name, especially of a Brāhman, after the name of another person, to denote his initiation by that person or his being a pupil of that person, e. g. *bhaṭṭoji-d°, bhānuji-d°, apyaya-d°,* &c., and the preceding name is sometimes omitted, leaving Dīkshita to stand alone.) — *Dīkshita-vasana, am,* n., Ved. the garment of an initiated person. — *Dīkshita-vimita, am,* n. a temporary dwelling erected for a person about to be initiated; [cf. *prāćīna-vanśa.*] — *Dīkshita-vrata, am,* n. the vow of an initiated person.

Dīkshitāyanī, f., N. of the wife of Dīkshita Yajña-datta.

Dīkshitṛi, tā, m. a consecrator, a spiritual father, one who initiates, the communicator of the initiatory Mantra or prayer.

Dīkshin, ī, iṇī, i, (at the end of a comp.) being initiated, one who has been initiated; [cf. *gaṇa-d°.*]

दीदी *dīdī* or *dīdi.* See rt. 2. *dī,* p. 415.

दीधी 1. *dīdhī* (connected with rt. 2. *dī*), cl. 2. A. *dīdhīte* (3rd pl. *dīdhyate*), &c., Caus. *dīdhayati,* &c., to shine, to be bright, to seem, appear.

1. *dīdhiti, is,* f. brightness, splendor, light; a ray [cf. *amṛita-d°*]; a finger, (connected by Vedic commentators with rt. 1. *dhā* or 3. *dhī*); N. of a commentary on the Tattva-ćintā-maṇi by Śiromaṇi treating of the Nyāya doctrines. — *Dīdhiti-mat, ān, atī, at,* having splendor, shining, brilliant; (*ān*), m. the sun.

Dīdhyāna, as, ā, am, shining, brilliant.

दीधी 2. *dīdhī* (a reduplicated form of 1. *dhī* and connected with rt. *dhyai*), cl. 2. A. *dīdhīte,* &c., to perceive, think, reflect upon, be intent upon; wish, desire.

2. *dīdhiti, is,* f., Ved. religious reflection, devotion; divine inspiration; prayer; religious rites; (Sāy.) a son-in-law (= *dhartṛi, jāmātṛi,* connected with 1. *dhā*).

दीन *dīna, as, ā, am.* See p. 415, col. 3.

दीनार *dīnāra, as,* m. (fr. the Gr. δηνάριον, = *denarius,* said to be fr. rt. 3. *dī*), a coin, a gold coin; a weight of gold (variously stated as 2 Kāshṭhas, 1 Pala of 32 Rettis or the large Pala of 108 Su-varṇas); a gold ornament; a seal.

दीप् *dīp,* cl. 4. A. (ep. also P.) *dīpyate, -ti, didīpe, dīpishyate, adīpi* or *adīpishṭa, dīpitum,* to blaze, burn with a bright flame, shine, be bright or luminous; to burn, glow, be inflamed or excited (as with anger); to be illustrious: Caus. *dīpayati, -yitum,* Aor. *adidīpat* or *adīdipat,* to kindle, set on fire, inflame; illuminate, irradiate, make bright, make illustrious; excite, raise: Desid. *didīpishate:* Intens. *dedīpyate, dedīpti,* to be very bright, to shine intensely; to blaze fiercely, be all on fire or in flames; [cf. *tap, div,* 2. *dī,* 1. *dīdhī;* Lith. *žibbu,* 'to shine;' Lat. *limpidus?*].

Dīpa, as, m. a light, lamp, lantern; [cf. *jagad-d°.*] — *Dīpa-kiṭṭa, am,* n. 'the sediment of a lamp,' lamp-black, soot. — *Dīpa-kūpī,* f. 'lamp-well,' the wick of a lamp. — *Dīpa-khaṭvā,* f. a bedstead upon which the sun shines, (perhaps for *dīpa-kh°.*) — *Dīpa-kharī,* f. the wick of a lamp. — *Dīpaṅ-kara, as,* m. 'light-maker,' N. of a Buddha. — *Dīpaṅkara-jñāna, as,* m. 'having the knowledge of a Buddha,' N. of a man. — *Dīpa-dāna, am,* n. 'giving light,' N. of a chapter of the Purāṇa-sarva-sva. — *Dīpa-dāna-vidhi, is,* m., N. of the 115th chapter of the Bhavishyottara-Purāṇa or second part of the Bhavishya-Purāṇa. — *Dīpa-dhvaja, as, am,* m. n. 'lamp-sign,' lamp-black, the condensed smoke or soot of a lamp. — *Dīpa-nirvāṇa-gandha, as,* m. the smell of an extinguished lamp. — *Dīpa-pādapa, as,* m. 'a lamp-tree,' a candlestick, lamp-stand; [cf. *dīpa-vṛiksha.*] — *Dīpa-pushpa, as,* m. 'lamp-flower,' N. of the plant Michelia Champaka (= *ćampaka*). — *Dīpa-bhājana, am,* n. 'vessel of light,' a lamp. — *Dīpa-mālā,* f. a row of lamps; an illumination; [cf. *dīpālī* and *dīpāvali.*] — *Dīpamālikotsava* (°*ka-ut*°), *as,* m. 'the feast of illumination,' N. of the 125th chapter of the Bhavishyottara-Purāṇa; [cf. *dīpālī.*] — *Dīpa-māhātmya, am,* n. 'the glory of the Dīpa,' N. of a chapter of the Bhavishya-Purāṇa. — *Dīpa-vat, ān, atī, at,* 'containing lights,' illuminating, making bright; (*atī*), f., N. of a river in Kāmākhyā. — *Dīpa-vṛiksha, as,* m. 'lamp-tree,' the stand or stem of a lamp, a candlestick; a light; a lantern; Pinus Longifolia or Deodora (= *deva-dāru*). — *Dīpa-śatru, us,* m. 'the enemy of a lamp,' a moth. — *Dīpa-śikhā,* f. the flame of a lamp; lamp-black (especially as used for darkening the eyelashes, &c.). — *Dīpa-śṛiṅkhalā,* f. a row or string of lamps. — *Dīpānvita* (°*pa-an*°), *ā,* f., scil. *tithi,* 'furnished with lamps,' N. of the Dīwālī festival; (see the next.) — *Dīpārādhana* (°*pa-ār*°), *am,* n. worshipping an idol by waving a light before it. — *Dīpālī* (°*pa-ālī*), f. 'a row of lamps,' the day of new moon in the month Āśvina or Kārttika (September–October), on which day there is a festival with nocturnal illuminations in honour of Kārttikeya; (this festival or feast of lights is commonly called Dīwālī.) — *Dīpāvali* (°*pa-āv*°), *is,* f. 'a row of lamps,' a nocturnal illumination, the Dīwālī festival; (see the preceding.) — *Dīpotsava* (°*pa-ut*°), *as,* m. the festival of lights; (see the preceding.)

Dīpaka, as, ā or *ikā, am,* kindling, inflaming; illuminating, making bright or luminous, illustrating, beautifying, making illustrious; exciting, rendering intense (as a feeling &c.); stimulating, tonic, exciting appetite, digestive; skilful in managing a lamp; (*as*), m. a light, lamp; N. of two plants promoting digestion, Ptychotis Ajowan (= *yavānī*) and Celosia Cristata [cf. *dīpya*]; a bird of prey, falcon; N. of a Rāga; an epithet of Kāma ('the inflamer'); N. of a son of Garuḍa; of a man; of a poet; (*ikā*), f. a light, lamp, lantern; moonlight; the plant Ptychotis Ajowan; the root of Calmus; N. of one of the Rāgiṇīs or female personifications of the musical modes; 'the illustrator,' in which sense often at the end of the titles of books, see *gūḍhārtha-d°, trailokya-d°;* (*am*), n. saffron; a figure of rhetoric (dilating upon an idea or accumulating expressions to strengthen it; various kinds of this figure are given, as *kāraka-dīpaka, mālā-dīpaka,* &c.); a kind of metre containing 4 × 10 syllabic instants. — *Dīpikā-taila, am,* n. the oil of the plant Ptychotis Ajowan. — *Dīpikā-prakāśa, as,* m. (also called Nīla-kaṇṭhī), 'the illuminator of the illustrator,' N. of a commentary on the Tarka-dīpikā by Nīla-kaṇṭha. — *Dīpikā-vivaraṇa, am,* n. 'explanation of the Dīpikā,' N. of a lost commentary on the Pūrva-mīmāṇsārtha-saṅgraha by Nṛi-siṇha.

Dīpana, as, ī, am, kindling, inflaming, setting on fire, burning, causing light or heat; digestive, tonic, stimulating [cf. *agni-d°* and *anala-d°*]; N. of several plants with digestive properties, = *mayūra-śikhā,* = *śāliṅća-śāka;* Cassia Sophora (= *kāsamarda*); an onion; (*ī*), f., N. of several plants, = Ptychotis Ajowan, = *pāṭhā,* = *methikā;* N. of a chapter of the Tantra-sāra or of a mystical formula therein described; (*am*), n. the act of kindling or setting on fire, inflaming; lighting, illuminating, making bright [cf. *tattva-d°*]; kindling the digestive fire, promoting digestion; a digestive, stimulant, tonic; saffron; the root of the plant Tabernæmontana Coronaria.

Dīpanīya, as, ā, am, to be lighted or set on fire; inflammable; to be excited or stimulated; relating to tonic medicines, serving to promote digestion; (*as*), m. an aromatic seed, Ptychotis Ajowan; (*am*), n. a stimulating drug, a digestive.

Dīpayat, an, antī, at, setting on fire, inflaming; illuminating.

Dīpita, as, ā, am, set on fire, inflamed; excited; illuminated, irradiated; manifested.

Dīpitṛi, tā, trī, tṛi, an illuminator, enlightener; irradiating, shining.

Dīpin, ī, inī, i, kindling, setting on fire, inflaming; illuminating, shining.

Dīpta, as, ā, am, blazing, flaming, being in flames, flashing, radiant, illuminated, luminous, bright, glittering; glowing, hot; burning, burnt; (as a term of augury) irradiated by the sun, exposed to the glare of sunshine, (this is considered inauspicious, the opposite expression being *śānta,* q. v.); situated on the inauspicious side, inauspicious in general; clear, shrill? (opposed to *pūrṇa,* q. v., as a term of augury); (*as*), m. a lion (from its bright colour); a lime, a citron tree (from its golden colour); a particular disease, inflammation of the nose; (*ā*), f., N. of several plants with bright red flowers, Methonica Superba, Cardiospermum Halicacabum (= *jyotishmatī*), = *sātalā;* red arsenic; (*am*), n. Asa Fœtida; gold. — *Dīpta-kiraṇa, as, ā, am,* 'having glowing rays,' epithet of the Sun. — *Dīpta-kīrtti, is,* m. 'of splendid renown,' epithet of Skanda. — *Dīpta-ketu, us,* m. 'bright-bannered,' N. of a king; of a son of Manu Dakshasāvarṇi. — *Dīpta-jihvā,* f. 'red-tongued,' a fox. — *Dīpta-tapas, ās, ās, as,* fervent in devotion, of glowing piety. — *Dīpta-tejas, ās, ās, as,* brilliant or radiant with glory. — *Dīpta-piṅgala, as,* m. 'bright and yellowish,' a lion. — *Dīpta-pushpā,* f. 'having bright flowers,' the plant Tragia Involucrata (the flowers of which are of a bright greenish colour). — *Dīpta-rasa, as,* m. 'having a yellow liquid,' an earth-worm. — *Dīpta-roman, ā,* m. 'red-haired,' N. of one of the Viśve-Devās. — *Dīpta-loćana, as,* m. 'bright-eyed,' 'having glittering eyes,' a cat. — *Dīpta-loha, as,* m. 'the shining metal,' brass, bell-metal. — *Dīpta-varṇa, as,* m. 'red-coloured,' epithet of Skanda. — *Dīpta-śakti, is,* m. 'having a glittering spear,' epithet of Skanda. — *Dīptānśu* (°*ta-an*°), *us, us, u,* having burning rays; (*us*), m. the sun. — *Dīptāksha* (°*ta-ak*°), *as, ī, am,* having glittering eyes, bright-eyed; (*as*), m. a cat; a peacock; N. of a minister of the king of the owls, Ari-mardana; (*ās*), m. pl., N. of a people. — *Dīptāgni* (°*ta-ag*°), *is,* m. blazing fire; (*is, is, i*), set on fire, kindled (as fire); having the gastric fire well kindled, i. e. digesting well; (*is*), m. an epithet of Agastya; [cf. *dahrāgni* and *satyāgni.*] — *Dīptāgni-tā,* f. goodness of digestion; [cf. the preceding.] — *Dīptāṅga* (°*ta-aṅ*°), *as,* m. 'having a brilliant body,' a peacock. — *Dīptātman* (°*ta-āt*°), *ā, ā, a,* having a flaming or fiery nature. — *Dīptānala-dyuti* (°*ta-an*°), *is, is, i,* having the brilliancy of glowing fire. — *Dīptoda* (°*ta-uda*), *am,* n. 'having brilliant water,' N. of a Tīrtha. — *Dīptopala* (°*ta-up*°), *as,* m. 'the flaming stone,' the sun gem (= *sūrya-kānta*); a crystalline lens. — *Dīptaujas* (°*ta-oj*°), *ās, ās, as,* glowing with energy.

Dīptaka, as, m. a kind of disease of the nose [cf. *dīpta*]; (*am*), n. gold.

Dīpti, is, f. brightness, brilliancy, splendor, light, glow, lustre; clearness, brilliancy of beauty (in a woman), extreme loveliness; the flash-like flight of an arrow; lac; brass, bell-metal; (*is*), m. (?), N. of one of the Viśve-Devās. — *Dīpti-kara, as, ā* or *ī, am,* irradiating, illuminating. — *Dīpti-mat, ān, atī, at,* having brightness, splendid, brilliant, lustrous, radiant, shining, blazing, flaming; (*ān*), m., N. of a son of Kṛishṇa.

Dīptika, as, m. a species of plant; [cf. *dugdha-pashāṇa.*] — *Dīptikeśvara-tīrtha* (°*ka* or °*kā-īś*°), *am*, n. 'the Tīrtha of the lord of Dīptika or Dīptikā (?),' N. of a Tīrtha mentioned in the S'iva-Purāṇa.

Dīpya, as, ā, am, to be kindled or inflamed, inflammable; to be stimulated; promotiog digestion, digestive; (*as*), m. the plants Celosia Cristata, Ptychotis Ajowan; cumin-seed; (*am*), n. white cumin-seed.

Dīpyaka, as, am, m. n. (?), N. of several plants, cumin, Ptychotis Ajowan, Celosia Cristata, Apium Involucratum; (*as*), m. a figure of rhetoric; [cf. *dīpaka.*]

Dīpyamāna, as, ā, am, shining, blazing, glowing, radiant.

Dīpra, as, ā, am, shining, brilliant, radiant, luminous, irradiating; (*as*), m. fire. — *Dīprāstra-dhara* (°*ra-as*°), *as, ā, am*, armed with shining weapons, well accoutred.

दीर्घ *dīrgha, as, ā, am* (fr. rt. *dṛih*, originally *dargh;* compar. *drāghīyas* or *dīrgha-tara;* superl. *drāghishṭha* or *dīrgha-tama*), long (as space or time), reaching far, lasting long; long (as the quantity of a vowel); lofty, high, tall; deep; (*as*), m. a long vowel; a camel; N. of several plants, = Saccharum Sara (= *śara*) or a similar kind of grass (= *utkaṭa*), = *rāma-śara;* Shorea Robusta (= *latā-śāla*); the fifth, sixth, seventh, and eighth sign of the zodiac; a mystical N. of the letter *a;* N. of a prince of Magadha; (*ā*), f. a long lake or oblong tank [cf. *dīrghikā*]; a plant related to the Hemionitis Cordifolia (= *dīrgha-pattrā*); a mystical N. of the letter *n;* (*am*), n., N. of a Sāman; (*am*), ind. for a long time, long; far; deeply; [cf. Zend *darĕgha:* Gr. δολιχός, ἐν-δελεχής: Russ. *dolog*, 'long;' *dolga* = *dīrghā:* Lith. *ilga-s, d* being dropped; *isz-drykens, isz-drykẽlis*, 'grown long:' perhaps Lat. *longus;* Germ. *lang.*] — *Dīrgha-kaṇā*, f. white cumin. — *Dīrgha-kaṇṭaka* or *dīrgha-kaṇṭa, as*, m. 'long-thorned,' N. of a plant (= *varvūra*). — *Dīrgha-kaṇṭha, as*, m. 'long-necked,' N. of a Dānava; (variously read *dīrgha-bāhu.*) — *Dīrghakaṇṭhaka, as*, m. 'long-necked,' a sort of crane, the Vaka, Ardea Nivea. — *Dīrgha-kandaka, am*, n. 'having long bulbs,' a kind of radish (= *mūlaka*); (*ikā*), f. Curculigo Orchioides (= *mushalī*). — *Dīrgha-kandhara, as*, m. 'long-necked,' a sort of crane, Ardea Nivea. — *Dīrgha-karṇa, as*, m. 'long-ear,' N. of a cat. — *Dīrgha-kāṇḍa, as*, m. 'having long joints,' N. of a kind of grass, Scirpus Kysoor (= *kaśeru*); (*ā*), f. a parasitical plant (= *pātāla-garuḍī*). — *Dīrgha-kāya, as, ā, am*, having a long body, tall. — *Dīrgha-kāla, am*, n. a long time, a long period. — *Dīrghakāla-jīvin, ī, inī, i*, long-lived. — *Dīrgha-kāshṭha, am*, n. a long piece of timber, a spar, a beam. — *Dīrgha-kīla, as*, m. or *dīrghakīlaka, as*, m. 'having a long stem,' the tree Alangium Hexapetalum (= *aṅkoṭa*). — *Dīrgha-kūraka, am*, n. 'long rice,' a kind of rice (= *rājānna*). — *Dīrgha-keśa, as, ā, am*, long-haired; (*as*), m. a bear; (*ās*), m. pl., N. of a people to the north-east of Madhya-deśa. — *Dīrgha-kośā* or *dīrgha-koshī* or *dīrgha-koshikā* or *dīrgha-kośikā*, f. a kind of muscle shell, a cockle. — *Dīrgha-gati, is*, m. 'making long journeys,' a camel. — *Dīrgha-gāmin, ī, inī, i*, going far, flying far (as an arrow). — *Dīrgha-granthi, is*, m. 'having long knots or joints,' Scindapsus Officinalis (= *gaja-pippalī*). — *Dīrgha-grīva, as, ā, am*, long-necked; (*as*), m. a camel; a kind of curlew (= *nīla-krauńća*); (*ās*), m. pl., N. of a people in the north-east of Madhya-deśa. — *Dīrgha-ghāṭika, as*, m. 'long-necked,' a camel. — *Dīrgha-ćańću, us*, m. 'long-beaked,' a kind of bird, = Marāṭhī *rukhauḍā;* [cf. *dīrgha-śira.*] — *Dīrgha-ćaturaśra, as, ā, am*, shaped like an oblong square or parallelogram. — *Dīrgha-ććhada, as, ā, am*, long-leaved; (*as*), m. the tree Tectona Grandis; sugar-cane. — *Dīrgha-jaṅgala, as*, m. a kind of fish (commonly *bhangāna*). — *Dīrgha-jaṅgha, as, ā, am*, long-legged, spindle-shanked; (*as*), m. a camel; a crane, Ardea Nivea; N. of a Yaksha. — *Dīrgha-jānuka, as*, m. 'long-kneed,' Ardea Sibirica. — *Dīrgha-jihva, as, ā, am*, long-tongued; (*as*), m. a snake; N. of a Dānava; (*ā*), f., N. of a Rākshasī; one of the Mātṛis attending on Skanda; (*ī*), f., Ved., N. of an evil spirit. — *Dīrgha-jihvya, as, ā, am*, Ved. long-tongued. — *Dīrgha-jīva, as*, m. long life. — *Dīrghajīvi-tā*, f. longevity. — *Dīrgha-jīvin, ī, inī, i*, long-lived, living long. — *Dīrgha-tanu, us, vī, u*, 'having a long body,' tall, long; (*vī*), f. 'long and narrow,' N. of a plant. — *Dīrgha-tantu, us, us, u*, Ved. forming a long thread or row. — *Dīrghatapa-ākhyāna, am*, n. 'the story of the long penance,' N. of a chapter of the S'iva-Purāṇa. — *Dīrghatapaḥ-svarga-gamana, am*, n. 'going to heaven by long penance,' N. of a chapter of the S'iva-Purāṇa. — *Dīrgha-tapas, ās, ās, as*, performing long penances; (*ās*), m., N. of a son of Kāśya and grandfather or father of Dhanvantari; also of a Muni in Kāmpilya, epithet of the sage Gautama. — *Dīrgha-tama, as, ā, am*, the longest, farthest; (*am*), ind. for the longest time. — *Dīrgha-tamas, ās*, m., N. of a Ṛishi with the patronymic Aućathya and metronymic Māmateya, author of some hymns of the Ṛig-veda; (he was the father of Kakshī-vat, and was born blind through a curse pronounced on him by Bṛihas-pati; in some Purāṇas he is described as the father of Dhanvantari, and has by Su-deshṇā, wife of Bali, five sons, viz. Aṅga, Baṅga, Kaliṅga, Puṇḍra, and Suhma); *dīrghatamaso 'rkaḥ* or *vratam*, N. of a Sāman; (*asas*), m. pl. the descendants of Dīrghatamas; [cf. *dīrgha-tapas* and *dairghatamasa.*] — *Dīrgha-tara, as, ā, am*, longer, farther. — *Dīrgha-taru, us*, m. 'the high tree,' the Tāl or palm tree. — *Dīrgha-tā*, f. or *dīrgha-tva, am*, n. length, longness. — *Dīrgha-timishā*, f. a kind of cucumber, Cucumis Utilissimus; [cf. *timisha.*] — *Dīrgha-tuṇḍā*, f. 'long-snouted,' the musk-rat. — *Dīrgha-tṛiṇa, as*, m. 'long grass,' a species of grass (= *pallivāha*). — *Dīrgha-daṇḍa, as*, m. 'having a long stem,' the palm tree; the castor-oil tree, Ricinus Communis; (*ī*), f. a kind of small shrub (= *go-rakshī*). — *Dīrghadaṇḍaka, as*, m. = *dīrgha-daṇḍa*, Ricinus Communis. — *Dīrghadarśi-tā*, f. or *dīrgha-darśi-tva, am*, n. the faculty of seeing far, long-sightedness, far-sightedness, providence. — *Dīrgha-darśin, ī, inī, i*, far-seeing, long-sighted, fore-casting, provident, sagacious, wise; (*ī*), m. a bear; a vulture; N. of a monkey; [cf. *dūra-darśin.*] — *Dīrghadarśi-vas, vān*, m. a far-seeing man, one who is long-sighted. — *Dīrgha-dṛishṭi, is, is, i*, far-seeing, far-sighted, provident, shrewd, deep; (*is*), m. a sagacious or penetrating man. — *Dīrgha-dru, us*, m. 'the high tree,' the palm tree. — *Dīrgha-druma, as*, m. 'lofty-tree,' Bombax Heptaphyllum (= *śālmali*). — *Dīrgha-dveshin, ī, iṇī, i*, cherishing long hatred or an old grudge, implacable. — *Dīrgha-nakha, as, ā, am*, having long nails; (*as*), m., N. of a man; (*ī*), f., N. of the tree Diospyros Embryopteris. — *Dīrgha-nāda, as, ā, am*, 'long-sounding,' sounding or crying to a long distance, making a long-continued noise; (*as*), m. a dog; a cock; a conch-shell. — *Dīrgha-nāla, as*, m. 'having a long stalk,' N. of several kinds of grass, = *vṛitta-guṇḍa* and *yāvanāla;* (*am*), n. = *dīrgha-rohishaka*. — *Dīrgha-nidrā*, f. long sleep; death. — *Dīrgha-niśvasya*, ind. sighing or having sighed deeply, having fetched a long drawn breath. — *Dīrgha-niśvāsa, as*, m. a long or deep drawn breath, a sigh. — *Dīrgha-nītha, as*, m., N. of a man. — *Dīrgha-paksha, as*, m. 'long-winged,' the fork-tailed shrike. — *Dīrgha-paṭolikā*, f. a kind of cucurbitaceous plant ('having a long fruit'). — *Dīrgha-pattra, as, ā* or *ī, am*, long-leaved; (*as*), m. a kind of sugar-cane; the palm tree, = *rāja-palāṇḍu*, = *vishṇu-kanda*, = *hari-darbha*, = *kundara*, = *kupīlu;* (*ā*), f. a kind of plant related to the Hemionitis Cordifolia, = *hrasva-jambu*, = *gandha-pattrā;* Pandanus Odoratissimus, = *ḍoḍi;* (*ī*), f. = *palāśī*, = *mahā-ćańću*. — *Dīrghapattraka, as*, m., N. of several plants, = a kind of sugar-cane, a kind of garlic (= *rakta-lasuna*); Ricinus Communis, Barringtonia Acutangula (= *hijjala*); a kind of reed (= *vetasa*), = *karīra*, Capparis Aphylla, = *jalaja-madhūka;* (*ikā*), f. Desmodium Gangeticum (= *śāla-parṇī*); Aloe Indica (= *ghṛita-kumārī*), = *palāśī*. — *Dīrgha-pad* or *dīrgha-pād, -pāt, -padī, -pat*, long-footed, long-legged; (*t*), m. a heron. — *Dīrgha-parṇa, as, ā* or *ī, am*, long-leaved; (*ī*), f. a species of plant related to the Hemionitis Cordifolia. — *Dīrgha-parvan, ā*, m. 'having long knots or joints,' sugar-cane. — *Dīrgha-pallava, as, ā* or *ī, am*, having long shoots or tendrils; (*as*), m. Crotolaria Juncea (= *śaṇa*). — *Dīrgha-pavana, as, ā, am*, long-winded; (*as*), m. an elephant; [cf. *dīrgha-māruta.*] — *Dīrgha-pāṭha, as*, m. 'the long reading,' a peculiar manner of reading or writing the Vājasaneyi-saṃhitā in which the letters are often doubled. — *Dīrgha-pāda, as, ā, am*, long-footed, long-legged; (*as*), m. a heron; [cf. *dīrgha-pad.*] — *Dīrgha-pādapa, as*, m. 'the lofty tree,' the cocoa-nut tree; the areca-nut tree. — *Dīrgha-pṛishṭha, as, ā, am*, long-backed; (*as*), m. a snake. — *Dīrgha-prajña, as, ā, am*, having a far-seeing mind; (*as*), m., N. of a king. — *Dīrgha-prayajyu, us, us, u*, Ved. persevering in offerings and sacrifices; (*ū*), m. du. epithet of Vishṇu-Varuṇa as receiving constant offerings. — *Dīrgha-prayatna, as*, m. persevering effort. — *Dīrgha-prasadman, ā, ā, a*, Ved. inhabiting an extensive district; (Sāy.) having extensive sacrificial halls, epithet of the earth. — *Dīrgha-phala, as, ā, am*, having long fruit; (*as*), m., N. of several plants, Cathartocarpus (Cassia) Fistula; Butea Frondosa; Asclepias Gigantea; (*ā*), f. = *jatukā*, a vine with reddish grapes, = *mesha-śṛiṅgī*, a kind of cucumber. — *Dīrghaphalaka, as*, m., N. of a plant, = *agastya*. — *Dīrgha-bālā*, f. 'long-tailed,' the bos grunniens; [cf. *ćamara* and *ćāmara.*] — *Dīrgha-bāhu, us, us, u*, long-armed; (*us*), m., N. of one of the attendants on S'iva; of a Dānava, (also read *dīrgha-kaṇṭha*); of a son of Dhṛita-rāshṭra; of a son of Dilīpa and father of Raghu; of a grandson of Dilīpa. — *Dīrgha-bāhu-garvita, as, ā, am*, proud of having long arms; (*as*), m., N. of a demon. — *Dīrgha-bhuja, as, ā, am*, long-armed; (*as*), m., N. of one of the attendants on S'iva. — *Dīrgha-māruta, as, ī, am*, long-winded; (*as*), m. an elephant; [cf. *dīrgha-pavana.*] — *Dīrgha-mukha, as, ī, am*, long-mouthed, long-beaked, long-faced; (*as*), m., N. of a Yaksha (?); (*ī*), f. the musk-rat. — *Dīrgha-mūla, am*, n. 'long-root,' the root of Andropogon Muricatus; (*as, ā, am*), having long roots; (*as*), m., N. of several plants, = *moraṭa*, a kind of Vilva tree; (*ā*), f. Desmodium Gangeticum; Ichnocarpus Frutescens; (*ī*), f. Alhagi Maurorum; Leea Hirta; Solanum Indicum. — *Dīrghamūlaka, am*, n. a kind of radish; (*ikā*), f. Desmodium Gangeticum. — *Dīrgha-yajña, as, ā, am*, performing a long sacrifice; (*as*), m., N. of a king of Ayodhyā. — *Dīrgha-yaśas, ās, ās, as*, Ved. renowned far and wide; having abundant food. — *Dīrgha-yātha, as*, m. (?), Ved. a long course or journey; (*as, ā, am*), having a long course. — *Dīrgha-yāma, as, ā, am*, having long watches (as the night). — *Dīrgha-raṅgā*, f. 'having a lasting colour,' turmeric. — *Dīrgha-rata, as*, m. 'long in copulation,' a dog; [cf. *dīrgha-surata.*] — *Dīrgha-rada, as*, m. 'long-tusked,' a hog. — *Dīrgha-rasana, as*, m. 'long-tongued,' a serpent. — *Dīrgha-rāgā*, f. = *dīrgha-raṅgā*. — *Dīrgha-rātram*, ind. (*rātra* for *rātri*, see Gram. 778), for a long night, for a long time or period. — *Dīrgha-rāva, as, ī, am*, making a long-continued noise, yelling, howling, = *dīrgha-nāda;* (*as*), m., N. of a jackal. — *Dīrgha-rūpa, as, ā, am*, having a long form, having the form of a long vowel. — *Dīrgha-rogin, ī, iṇī, i*, long ill, long sick. — *Dīrgha-roma, as*, m., N. of a son of Dhṛita-rāshṭra. — *Dīrgha-roman, ā, ā, a*, long-haired; (*ā*), m. a bear; N. of one of the attendants on S'iva. — *Dīrgha-rohishaka, am*, n. a kind of fragrant grass. — *Dīrgha-loćana, as, ā, am*, long-eyed; (*as*), m., N. of a son of Dhṛita-rāshṭra. — *Dīrgha-lohita-yashṭikā*, f. 'having a long red stem,' red sugar-cane.

— *Dīrgha-vanśa, as, ā, am,* having a long reed; having a long lineage, being of an ancient family; *(as),* m. a kind of sugar-cane; [cf. *nala.*] — *Dīrgha-vaktra, as,* m. 'long-faced,' an elephant. — *Dīrgha-vaććhikā* or *dīrgha-varćhikā,* f. (*vaććhikā* probably = *vatsa,* a young animal), an alligator, a kind of crocodile. — *Dīrgha-vat,* ind. like a long vowel. — *Dīrgha-varṇa, as,* m. a long vowel. — *Dīrgha-vartman, a,* n. a long road, a long journey. — *Dīrgha-varshābhū, ūs,* f., N. of a plant, = *śveta-punar-navā.* — *Dīrgha-vriksha, as,* m. 'the lofty tree,' the palm tree. — *Dīrgha-vrinta, as,* m. 'long-stalked,' the tree Calosanthes Indica; *(ā),* f., N. of a plant, = *indra-ćirbhiṭī.* — *Dīrgha-vrintaka, as,* m. 'long-stalked,' Calosanthes Indica; a variety of it; *(ikā),* f. Mimosa Octandra. — *Dīrgha-śara, as,* m. 'having a long reed,' Andropogon Bicolor. — *Dīrgha-śākha, as, ā, am,* having long branches; *(as),* m. Shorea Robusta; a sort of hemp. — *Dīrghaśākhikā,* f., N. of a shrub, = *nīlāmlī.* — *Dīrgha-śimbika, as,* m. 'having a long pod,' a kind of plant, = *kshara.* — *Dīrgha-śira, as,* m. (*śira* = *śiras*), 'having a long head or beak,' a kind of bird, = Marāṭhī *rukhauḍā;* [cf. *dīrgha-ćańću.*] — *Dīrgha-śūkaka, am,* n. 'having long awns or beards,' a sort of rice. — *Dīrgha-śmaśru, us, us, u,* Ved. long-bearded. — *Dīrgha-śravas, ās, ās, as,* Ved. renowned far and wide; *(ās),* m., N. of a son of Dīrgha-tamas; of another man. — *Dīrgha-śrut, t, t, t,* Ved. 'long-hearing,' hearing from afar; audible or perceptible from afar or at a long distance; renowned far and wide, heard of everywhere. — *Dīrghaśrut-tama, as, ā, am,* Ved. being audible at a long distance. — *Dīrgha-saktha, as, ā, am* (*saktha* for *sakthi;* see Gram. 778), long-thighed, spindle-legged. — *Dīrgha-sattra, am,* n. 'a long-continued Soma sacrifice,' N. of a place of pilgrimage. — *Dīrghasattrin, ī, iṇī, i,* occupied with a long-continued Soma rite. — *Dīrgha-sandhya, as, ā, am,* performing long prayers or rites at the different twilights. — *Dīrghasandhya-tva, am,* n. long-continued observance of the twilight rites, the continued repetition of the twilight prayer. — *Dīrgha-sasya, as,* m. 'having long fruits,' the tree Diospyros Embryopteris. — *Dīrgha-surata, as,* m. = *dīrgha-rata.* — *Dīrgha-sūtra, as, ā, am,* 'spinning a long yarn,' working slowly, procrastinating, slow, dilatory, tedious. — *Dīrghasūtra-tā,* f. or *dīrghasūtra-tva, am,* n. procrastination, dilatoriness, irresolution, tediousness. — *Dīrghasūtrin, ī, iṇī, i,* = *dīrgha-sūtra,* dilatory, irresolute, procrastinating. — *Dīrgha-skandha, as,* m. 'long-stemmed,' the palm tree. — *Dīrgha-svara, as,* m. a long vowel; a long note, a minim or semibreve. — *Dīrghākāra* (°*gha-āk*°), *as, ā, am,* long-formed, oblong. — *Dīrghāgama* (°*gha-āg*°), *as,* m., N. of a Buddhist work. — *Dīrghāṅghri* (°*gha-aṅ*°), *is,* m. 'having long roots,' Desmodium Gangeticum. — *Dīrghā-dhi, is, īs, i,* Ved. having a far-seeing mind; (Sāy.) making long prayers or oblations. — *Dīrghādhva* (°*gha-adh*°), *as,* m.(?), a long way, a long journey. — *Dīrghādhva-ga, as, ā, am,* going long journeys; *(as),* m. a camel; a letter-carrier, messenger, courier or express. — *Dīrghāpāṅga* (°*gha-ap*°), *as, ā, am,* having long outer corners (of the eyes). — *Dīrghāpekshin* (°*gha-ap*°), *ī, iṇī, i,* regarding from afar, very regardful or considerate. — *Dīrghāpsas* (°*gha-ap*°), *ās, ās, as,* Ved. long-shaped, having a long fore part (as a waggon). — *Dīrghāmaya* (°*gha-ām*°), *as, ā, am,* long ill, long sick, affected with a chronic disease. — *Dīrghāyu* (°*gha-āy*°), *us, us, u,* long-lived, wished to be long-lived. — *Dīrghāyu-tva, am,* n. long-livedness; [cf. *dīrghāyush-tva.*] — *Dīrghāyudha* (°*gha-āy*°), *as,* m.(?), a long weapon, spear, a javelin; *(as, ā, am),* having long weapons; *(as),* m. a hog. — *Dīrghāyu-śoćis, is, is, is,* Ved. having a long-lived splendor, i. e. one which lasts through a long life. — *Dīrghāyush-tva, am,* n. long-livedness, a long life; [cf. *dīrghāyu-tva.*] — *Dīrghāyushya, as,* m., N. of a tree, = *śveta-mandāraka;* *(am),* n. long-livedness. — *Dīrghāyus* (°*gha-āy*°), *us, us, us,* long-lived [cf. *āyush-mat*]; *(us),* m. a crow; N. of two trees, = *jīvaka* and *śālmali,* Bombax Heptaphyllum; an epithet of Mārkaṇḍeya; [cf. *dīrghāyu.*] — *Dīrghāraṇya* (°*gha-ar*°), *am,* n., Ved. a long tract of wild or desert country. — *Dīrghālarka* (°*gha-al*°), *as,* m., N. of a tree, = *śveta-mandāraka.* — *Dīrghāsya* (°*gha-ās*°), *as, ā, am,* long-faced; *(ās),* m., N. of a people to the north-east of Madhya-deśa. — *Dīrghāhan* (°*gha-ah*°), *ā, hnī, a,* having long days. — *Dīrghī-kṛi,* cl. 8. P. A. *-karoti, -kurute, -kartum,* to lengthen, prolong; to lead away to a distant place. — *Dīrghī-bhāra, as,* m. the becoming long, the lengthening (of a vowel). — *Dīrghī-bhū,* cl. 1. P. *-bhavati,* &c., to become long, lengthen. — *Dīrghī-bhūta, as, ā, am,* become long, lengthened. — *Dīrgherrāru* (°*gha-ir*°), *us,* m. a kind of cucumber (= *ḍaṅgarī*). — *Dīrghoććhvāsa* (°*gha-uć*°), *am,* n. 'having a long breath,' epithet of the body.

Dīrghikā, f. a long or oblong lake or pond; [cf. *tridaśa-d*°.]

दीर्ण *dīrṇa, as, ā, am* (fr. rt. *dṛī*), torn, rent, sundered; frightened, afraid.

दीव् *dīv, dīvi, dīvyat,* &c. See under rt. 2. *div* at p. 414, col. 2.

दु 1. *du* (the original form of this rt. was probably *dū*), cl. 1. P. *davati, dudāva* (2nd sing. *dudavitha,* 1st du. *duduviva*), *dotā, doshyati, adāvīt, adaushīt, dotum,* to go, move: Caus. *dāvayati,* &c., to cause to go; [cf. rt. 1. *dru.*]

Dūta. See p. 426, col. 2.

1. *dūna, as, ā, am,* gone; going, moving. — *Dūna-vat, ān, atī, at,* having gone.

दु 2. *du* (also written *dū,* see 1. *dū*), cl. 5. P. 4. A. *dunoti, dūyate* (ep. also *dūyati*), *dudāva, doshyati, adaushīt, dotum,* to be burnt, be consumed with internal heat, be consumed by pain or sorrow, to be agitated or disturbed, to be distressed; (cl. 5. P.) to burn, consume with fire; to cause pain by internal heat or fever; to cause anxiety or sorrow or distress; to afflict: Caus. P. *dāvayati, -yitum,* Aor. *adūdavat,* to burn, cause pain: Desid. *dudūshati:* Intens. *dodūyate, dodoti;* [cf. Lith. *dowyu,* 'I vex,' = Caus. *dāvayāmi;* Gr. ὀ-δύνη, ὀ-δυνάω, δαίω, δεδαυμένος, δαυλός, probably δυή; Lat. *doleo* fr. *doreo;* Angl. Sax. *tynan;* Hib. *leirim,* 'I pain,' probably = Caus. *dāvayāmi.*]

Dut, t, f. pain, anxiety, uneasiness. — *Dud-da, as, ā, am,* or *dud-dādin, ī, inī, i,* giving or causing pain, cruel, wicked.

Duta, as, ā, am (?), pained, afflicted.

Dunvat, ān, atī, at, afflicting, causing pain or sorrow, injuring.

2. *dūna.* See under 1. *dū,* p. 426, col. 1.

दुः *duḥ,* euphonically substituted for *dus* in *duḥkha* (see the next) and in comps. like *duḥ-prajña, duḥ-śansa,* &c. See under *dus* at p. 424.

दुःख *duḥkha, am,* n. (more properly written *dush-kha,* and said to be fr. *dus* + *kha,* q. v.; cf. *duḥ* above and *su-kha;* the word *duḥkha* does not occur in the earliest literature), uneasiness, unhappiness, pain, sorrow, affliction, distress, misery, anguish, agony; difficulty, trouble; *(as),* m. Unhappiness or Pain personified as son of Naraka and Vedanā; *(as, ā, am),* painful, disagreeable, unpleasant, uncomfortable, uneasy, difficult; *(am),* ind. difficultly, scarcely, hardly; *(ena),* ind. with difficulty; difficultly; *(āt),* ind. with difficulty, hardly; [cf. Hib. *diuic,* 'pain, sorrow, grief;' perhaps *doilghe,* 'sore, hard;' *doilgheas,* 'sorrow.'] — *Duḥkha-kara, as, ī, am,* causing pain; afflicting, occasioning sorrow or trouble. — *Duḥkha-ćārin, ī, iṇī, i,* going with pain, distressed. — *Duḥkha-ććhinna, as, ā, am,* cut with difficulty, tough, hard; pierced by sorrow, pained, distressed. — *Duḥkha-ććhedya, as, ā, am,* to be cut with difficulty, hard to be divided, tough, hard; to be conquered or overcome with difficulty; to be pierced or pained by affliction, &c. — *Duḥkha-jāta, as, ā, am,* suffering pain, feeling pain, distressed. — *Duḥkha-jīvin, ī, inī, i,* living in pain or distress. — *Duḥkha-tara, am,* n. greater pain, a greater evil; a very great evil; *(as, ā, am),* more painful or disagreeable; *(am),* ind. more painfully or disagreeably. — *Duḥkha-tā,* f. unhappiness, misery, pain, discomfort, painful state. — *Duḥkha-dagdha, as, ā, am,* burnt or tormented by affliction, pained, distressed. — *Duḥkha-duḥkhena,* ind. with great difficulty. — *Duḥkha-dohyā,* f. (a cow) difficult to be milked. — *Duḥkha-nivaha, as, ā, am,* difficult to be borne. — *Duḥkha-parītāṅga* (°*ta-aṅ*°), *as, ā, am,* whose limbs are surrounded or filled with pain. — *Duḥkha-parītātman* (°*ta-āt*°), *ā, ā, a,* whose soul is affected with anguish. — *Duḥkha-prāya* or *duḥkha-bahula, as, ā, am,* full of trouble, suffering excessively, abounding with distress or trouble, &c. — *Duḥkha-bhāgin, ī, inī, i,* having pain as one's portion, suffering pain, unhappy. — *Duḥkha-maya, as, ī, am,* consisting in suffering, one whose nature is made up of suffering. — *Duḥkhamaya-tva, am,* n. a condition made up of suffering. — *Duḥkha-moksha, as,* m. deliverance from pain. — *Duḥkha-yoga, as,* m. occurrence or presence of trouble or pain, &c. — *Duḥkha-labdhikā,* f. 'gained with difficulty,' N. of a princess. — *Duḥkha-labhya, as, ā, am,* to be obtained or effected with difficulty, hardly procurable. — *Duḥkha-loka, as,* m. 'the world of pain,' = *saṃsāra* or the world as a scene of constant suffering and transmigration. — *Duḥkha-vyābhāshita, as, ā, am,* pronounced with difficulty. — *Duḥkha-śīla, as, ā, am,* of a difficult temper, i. e. hard to manage, bad-tempered, irritable. — *Duḥkha-śīla-tva, am,* n. irritability of temper. — *Duḥkha-śoka-samanvita, as, ā, am,* filled with pain and sorrow. — *Duḥkha-saṃyoga, as,* m. occurrence or presence of pain, distress, &c. — *Duḥkha-saṃvardhita, as, ā, am,* reared with difficulty. — *Duḥkha-saṃsthiti, is, is, i,* in a wretched condition, poor, miserable. — *Duḥkha-saṃsparśa, as, ā, am,* = *duḥkha-sparśa.* — *Duḥkha-sańćāra, as, ā, am,* passing unhappily (as time). — *Duḥkha-samāyukta, as, ā, am,* accompanied with pain, affected by anguish. — *Duḥkha-sāgara, as,* m. 'an ocean of trouble or pain,' great sorrow; the world. — *Duḥkha-sparśa, as, ā, am,* unpleasant or hard to the touch. — *Duḥkha-han, ā, ghnī, a,* removing pain. — *Duḥkhā-kara, as, ā* or *ī, am,* causing pain, afflicting. — *Duḥkhā-kṛi,* cl. 8. P. *-karoti, -kartum,* to cause pain to any one (with acc.); to distress. — *Duḥkhāćāra* (°*kha-āć*°), *as, ā, am,* of a difficult temper or disposition; hard to manage. — *Duḥkhātīta* (°*kha-at*°), *as, ā, am,* freed or escaped from pain. — *Duḥkhānta* (°*kha-an*°), *as,* m. 'the end of pain or trouble' (with the Māheśvaras), final emancipation or the acquisition of superhuman powers and freedom of will. — *Duḥkhānvita* (°*kha-an*°), *as, ā, am,* accompanied with pain, filled with grief, pained, afflicted, distressed. — *Duḥkhārta* (°*kha-ār*°), *as, ā, am,* afflicted by pain, pained, distressed. — *Duḥkhālīḍha* (°*kha-āl*°), *as, ā, am,* consumed with grief. — *Duḥkhopeta* (°*kha-up*°), *as, ā, am,* affected by pain, suffering distress, &c.

Duḥkhaya, Nom. P. *duḥkhayati, -yitum,* to pain, cause pain, afflict, distress; (also given as a rt. of the 10th cl. and even cl. 1. *duḥkhati,* &c.)

Duḥkhāya, Nom. A. *duḥkhāyate,* &c., to feel pain, be distressed.

Duḥkhita, as, ā, am, pained, suffering pain, distressed, afflicted, unhappy, poor, indigent; *(am),* n. pain, distress, trouble. — *Duḥkhita-ćitta, as, ā, am,* afflicted at heart, grieved in mind.

Duḥkhin, ī, inī, i, having pain, pained, sorrowing, afflicted, grieved; difficult, painful.

Duḥkhīya, Nom. P. *duḥkhīyati,* &c., to feel pain, be distressed.

Duḥkhya, Nom. P. *duḥkhyati,* &c., to cause pain.

दुःप° duḥ-pa°, duḥ-pra°, duḥ-prā°, duḥ-pre°, &c. See the comp. under dus at p. 424.

दुःफालिकुत्थ duḥphālikuttha (a word said to be borrowed fr. the Arabic), N. of the twelfth Yoga (in astrology).

दुःश° duḥ-śa°, duḥ-sha°, duḥ-sa°. See the comp. under dus at p. 424.

दुःसाधिन् duḥ-sādhin. See 1. dur, col. 3.

दुकूल dukūla, as, m. (said to be fr. rt. 2. du), a species of plant; (am), n. woven silk, very fine cloth or raiment made of the inner bark of this plant, (opposed to valkala; also read dugūla.)

दुग्ध dugdha, as, ā, am (fr. rt. 2. duh), milked; milked out, extracted, sucked out so as to be impoverished; milked together, collected, filled, full; (am), n. milk, the milky juice of plants, sap [cf. go-raksha-d°]; milking, (in dugdha-bandhaka); (ī), f. a medicinal plant, a kind of Asclepias, = kshīrāvikā, = dugdha-pāshāṇa. — Dugdha-kūpikā, f. a sort of cake made of ground rice and mixed with milk &c. ('having a milk-well?'). — Dugdha-tā, f. or dugdha-tva, am, n. milkiness, milky nature. — Dugdha-tālīya, am, n. (fr. dugdha and tāla?), the froth of milk, syllabub; the skim of milk or cream; milk and mangoes, mango fool. — Dugdha-dā, f. giving milk, milk-giver, milch. — Dugdha-pāćana, am, n. a kind of salt (= vajraka); a vessel for boiling milk. — Dugdha-pātra, am, n. a milk-pan. — Dugdha-pāyin, ī, inī, i, drinking milk. — Dugdha-pāshāṇa, as, m. a species of plant, = dugdha-pāshāṇaka, dugdhāśman, dugdhī; kshīrin, kshīra-kshava, gomedha-sannibha, dīptika, vajrābha. — Dugdha-pućchī, f. a kind of plant, = niśā, bhangā, sevakālu, commonly dugdha-peyā. — Dugdha-poshya, as, ā, am, a suckling, a child &c. living on its mother's milk. — Dugdha-phena, as, m. the froth or skim of milk, syllabub, cream; (ī), f. a small medicinal shrub, = gojā-parṇī, payaḥ-phenī, payasvinī, phena-dugdha, lūtārī. — Dugdha-bandhaka, as or am, m. or n. (?), the post to which a cow is fastened before being milked. — Dugdha-vatī, f. giving milk. — Dugdha-vījā, f. rice mixed with milk. — Dugdha-samudra, as, m. the sea of milk. — Dugdhāksha (°dha-ak°), as, m. 'having milk-white eyes,' a particular kind of precious stone (opal?). — Dugdhāgra (°dha-ag°), am, n. the upper part, surface or skim of milk, cream. — Dugdhābdhi (°dha-ab°), is, m. the sea of milk. — Dugdhābdhi-tanayā, f. 'the daughter of the sea of milk,' epithet of the goddess Lakshmī. — Dugdhāmbudhi (°dha-am°), is, m. the sea of milk. — Dugdhāmra (°dha-am°) = dugdha-tālīya, q.v. — Dugdhāśman (°dha-aś°), ā, m. = dugdha-pāshāṇa, q. v.

Dugdhikā, f. a sort of Asclepias, A. Rosea, = kshīrāvī, = uttamā; (the Hindī derivative Dūdhi is also applied to Euphorbia Hirta and Thymifolia.)

Dugdhin, ī, inī, i, having milk, milky, milch.

Dugdhinikā, f. a species of plant, = raktāpāmārga or a red kind of Achyranthes Aspera.

Dugdhvā, ind. having milked; having pressed or squeezed out.

Dugha, as, ā, am, (at the end of a comp.) milking; yielding, granting; (ā), f. a milch-cow; [cf. kāma-d°, gharma-d°, droṇa-d°.]

दुच्छक duććhaka, as, m. a kind of perfume, = gandha-kuṭī, = vihārādyavakāśaka (?).

दुच्छुना duććhunā, f. (fr. dus + śuna?), Ved. misfortune, calamity; injury, evil, often personified as a malicious being or evil spirit; [cf. a-duććhuna.]

Duććhunāya, Nom. A. duććhunāyate, &c., Ved. to wish to injure or hurt, to be evil disposed.

दुडि duḍi, is, f. = duli, a small tortoise; a female tortoise.

दुण्डुक duṇḍuka, as, ā, am, fraudulent, dishonest, bad-hearted.

दुण्डुभ duṇḍubha, as, ā, am, = ḍuṇḍubha, a kind of lizard without feet; a kind of snake described as not venomous, = rājila; [cf. dundubha.]

Duṇḍubhi, is, m. f. a species of venomous animal; a kind of snake; [cf. dundubhikā.]

दुत्थोत्थदवीर dutthotthadavīra, (in astrology) N. of the thirteenth Yoga.

दुद duda, as, m., N. of a mountain.

दुदुह duduha, as, m. (fr. rt. 2. duh?), N. of a prince, father of Pra-ćetas.

दुद्द dud-da. See dut, rt. 2. du, p. 418.

दुद्यूषु dudyūshu, us, us, u (fr. the Desid. of rt. 2. div), wishing to play, wishing to brandish.

दुद्रुम dudruma, as, m. (said to be fr. du = dus + druma), a green onion; [cf. dur-druma.]

दुधि dudhi, is, is, i (fr. rt. 1. dhū?), Ved. violent, impetuous, injurious; [cf. dudhita and dudhra.]

Dudhita, as, ā, am, Ved. troubled, perplexed, turbid.

Dudhūshat, an, atī, at (fr. the Desid.), trying, wishing or endeavouring to shake.

Dudhra, as, ā, am, Ved. = dudhi, powerful, violent, impetuous, terrible; (Sāy.) restraining wicked enemies. — Dudhra-kṛit, t, t, t, Ved. doing dreadful acts, rendering excited, exciting, impetuous, boisterous; (ās), m. pl. epithet of the Maruts. — Dudhra-vāć, k, k, k, Ved. speaking in an excited or uncontrolled manner.

दुधुक्षु dudhukshu, us, us, u (fr. the Desid. of rt. 2. duh), wishing or intending to milk.

दुन्दम dundama, as, m. a sort of drum, = dundubhi below.

दुन्दु dundu, us, m. (an onomatopoetic word), a sort of drum; an epithet of Vasu-deva who was the father of Kṛishṇa; [cf. ānaka-d°.]

दुन्दुभ dundubha, as, m. a species of water-snake described as not venomous [cf. duṇḍubha and duṇḍubhi]; an epithet of Śiva; (ās), m. pl., N. of a Vedic school, = dundubhi, a kind of drum (occurring in the comp. ānaka-d°).

दुन्दुभि dundubhi, is, m. (fr. dundu, imitative sound), a sort of large kettle-drum; a sort of poison; N. of the fifty-sixth year in the Jupiter cycle of sixty years; an epithet of Varuṇa; Kṛishṇa; N. of an Asura; of a Rakshas; of a son of Andhaka and grandson of Anu; of a man considered as a son of Śiva; (is), f. a drum; a particular throw of the dice in gambling; twice three dots or spots on a die or a pair of dice with three spots on each; (ī), f. 'a kettle-drum,' N. of a Gandharvī; [cf. karṇa-d°.] — Dundubhi-grīva, as, ā, am, having a neck like a kettle-drum (an ox). — Dundubhi-nirhrāda, as, m. 'having the sound of a kettle-drum,' N. of a Dānava. — Dundubhi-vadha, as, m., N. of the eighty-ninth chapter of the Gaṇeśa-Purāṇa. — Dundubhi-svana, as, m. 'emitting the sound of a kettle-drum,' a kind of magical formula or spell against the evil spirits supposed to possess weapons. — Dundubhi-svara, as, m. 'sounding like a kettle-drum,' N. of a man. — Dundubhisvara-rāja, as, m., N. of several Buddhas. — Dundubhīśvara (°bhi-īś°), as, m., N. of a Buddha.

Dundubhika, as, m. a kind of venomous insect.

Dundubhya, only in the comp. ćakra-dundubhya (scil. mantra), Ved. 'relating to Cakra and Dundubhi.'

दुन्दुमा dundumā, f. (an onomatopoetic word), a particular sound, sound in general.

Dundumāya, Nom. A. dundumāyate, -yitum, to sound.

Dundumāyita, as, ā, am, sounded; (am), n. a particular sound, sound.

दुन्दुमार dundumāra, as, m. a sort of red worm; the smoke of a house; a cat, = dhundhumāra.

दुन्वत् dunvat. See rt. 2. du, p. 418, col. 2.

दुफार duphāra, N. of a place mentioned in the Romaka-siddhānta.

दुमेल dumela, am, n. a particular high number.

दुम्मदुमाक dummadumāka, as, m., N. of a Grāma.

दुर् 1. dur, f., Ved. (occurring only in nom. and acc. pl. duras), = dvār, a door; (at the end of a comp. the form dura is used, see 2. dura.) — Duḥ-sādhin, ī, m. a door-keeper.

दुर् 2. dur, ind. a prefix substituted for dus, q. v., at the beginning of a compound before vowels and soft consonants; (for the comps. beginning duḥ, duś, dush, dus, see under dus.) — Dur-aksha, as, m. (fr. 2. aksha), a loaded or fraudulent die or dice; (as, ī, am), (fr. 4. aksha), weak-eyed. — Dur-atikrama, as, ā, am, difficult to be surpassed or overcome, difficult to be conquered, unconquerable; difficult of performance or accomplishment, insurmountable; difficult to be escaped from, inevitable; (as), m., N. of a Brāhman regarded as a son of Śiva. — Dur-atyaya, as, ā, am, difficult to be passed or surpassed, hard to be overcome; difficult to be escaped from; difficult to be attained; difficult to be passed through or fathomed. — Dur-atyayānukramaṇa (°ya-an°), as, ā, am, whose ways are past finding out (God). — Dur-atyetu, us, us, u, Ved. difficult to be overcome &c., = the preceding. — Dur-adṛishṭa, am, n. bad luck, ill fate, misfortune. — Dur-admanī, f., Ved. bad or noxious food. — Dur-adhiga, as, ā, am, difficult to be attained &c., see the next. — Dur-adhigama, as, ā, am, difficult to be attained or reached, unattainable, hard to be traversed; not to be overcome, insurmountable; difficult to be read through or studied. — Dur-adhishṭhita, as, ā, am, badly managed or executed; (am), n. improper residence at a place. — Dur-adhīta, as, ā, am, badly read or learnt, studied with difficulty. — Dur-adhyaya, as, ā, am, difficult of attainment; difficult of perusal, hard to be studied. — Dur-adhyayana, am, n. reading or studying badly or with difficulty. — Dur-adhyavasāya, as, m. a bad or foolish undertaking; (wrongly read durādhyavasāya.) — Dur-adhva, as, m. a bad road. — Dur-anupālana, as, ā, am, difficult to be kept or preserved. — Dur-anubodha, as, ā, am, difficult to be recollected. — Dur-anushṭhita, as, ā, am, badly done or performed. — Dur-anushṭheya, as, ā, am, difficult to be accomplished. — Dur-anta, as, ā, am, whose end is difficult to be reached, having no end, infinite; ending ill, ending in misery, having a bad end, miserable, unhappy. — Dur-antaka = the preceding; (as), m. epithet of Śiva. — Duranta-kṛit, t, t, t, doing what is endless, (perhaps) suffering endless pains. — Duranta-moha, as, ā, am, whose infatuation has a bad ending or has no end. — Duranta-vīrya, as, ā, am, possessed of endless energy. — Duranta-śakti, is, is, i, having endless power. — Dur-anvaya, as, ā, am, difficult to be passed along (as a road &c.), difficult to be followed; difficult to be carried out, hard to be comprehended or attained; (as), m. a false concord (in gram.); a consequence wrongly deduced from given premises. — Dur-anveshya, as, ā, am, difficult to be searched. — Dur-apaćāra, as, ā, am, difficult to be displeased or offended. — *Dur-abhigraha, as, ā, am,* difficult to be laid hold of; (*as*), m. Achyranthes Aspera [cf. *apāmārga*]; (*ā*), f. Mucuna Pruritus; Alhagi Maurorum. — *Dur-abhimānin, ī, inī, i,* badly or disagreeably proud. — *Dur-avagama, as, ā, am,* difficult to be understood, incomprehensible. — *Dur-avagraha, as, ā, am,* difficult to be kept back or restrained; disagreeable. — *Duravagraha-vādin, ī, inī, i,* speaking disagreeably. — *Dur-avagrāhya, as, ā, am,* difficult to be apprehended or reached. — *Dur-avabodha, as, ā, am,* difficult to be understood, unintelligible. — *Duravabodha-tā,* f. unintelligibleness. — *Dur-avaroha, as, ā, am,* difficult to be descended. — *Dur-avavada, am,* adj. n. difficult to be spoken against or censured. — *Dur-avasita, as, ā, am,* difficult to be conceived (?). — *Dur-avastha, as, ā, am,* badly situated, poorly circumstanced; (*ā*), f. bad situation, miserable condition, evil case. — *Dur-avāpa, as, ā, am,* difficult to be reached, gained, attained or obtained; difficult to be acquired; difficult to be fulfilled. — *Dur-avekshita, am,* n. an improper look, a forbidden glance. — *Dur-ahna, as,* m. a bad day; [cf. *dur-dina.*] — *Dur-ākṛiti, is, is, i,* badly formed; deformed, disfigured, misshapen. — *Dur-ākranda, am,* ind. crying miserably; [cf. *dur-ākrośa.*] — *Dur-ākrama, as, ā, am,* difficult to be ascended or passed; hard to be approached, attacked or assailed; invincible. — *Dur-ākramaṇa, am,* n. unfair attack; difficult approach. — *Dur-ākrānta, as, ā, am,* unjustly attacked; difficult of access. — *Dur-ākrośa, as,* m. a miserable cry; (*am*), ind. crying miserably; [cf. *dur-ākranda.*] — *Dur-āgata, as, ā, am,* badly come, arrived with difficulty, unhappily arrived; (*as*), m., N. of a man. — *Dur-āgama, as,* m. bad income, improper gain, illegal accession (of property &c.). — *Dur-āgraha, as, ā, am,* obstinate retention of an opinion, wicked or foolish obstinacy, pertinacity, head-strongness. — *Dur-āćara, as, ā, am,* difficult to be practised, hard to be performed; difficult to be treated or cured, incurable. — *Dur-āćaritu, am,* n. bad practice or performance, bad treatment. — *Dur-āćāra, as,* m. bad behaviour, ill conduct, bad manners, wickedness; (*as, ā, am*), difficult to be practised or managed; ill-conducted, badly behaved; addicted to evil practices, wicked, depraved, profligate. — *Dur-āḍhya, as, ā, am,* not rich or opulent, not abounding. — *Dur-āḍhyankara, as, ī, am,* difficult to be made rich. — *Dur-āḍhyambhuva, as, ā, am,* difficult to become rich; (*am*), n. becoming rich with difficulty. — *Durātma-tā,* f. (fr. the following), mean-spiritedness, baseness, wickedness. — *Dur-ātman, ā, ā, a,* bad-hearted, evil-natured, mean-spirited, ill-conditioned, low, vile, wicked, bad; (*ā*), m. a rascal, scoundrel, villain, wretch. — *Durātma-vat, ān, atī, at,* = the preceding. — *Dur-ādāna, as, ā, am,* Ved. difficult to be laid hold of or apprehended. — *Dur-ādeya, as, ā, am,* difficult to be taken away or seized. — *Dur-ādhana, as,* m., N. of one of the 100 sons of Dhṛita-rāshṭra; (probably a wrong form for *dur-ādhara.*) — *Dur-ādhara, as, ā, am,* difficult to be withstood, not to be restrained, irresistible; difficult to be subdued or overpowered; (*as*), m., N. of one of the 100 sons of Dhṛita-rāshṭra; [cf. the preceding.] — *Dur-ādharsha, as, ā, am,* difficult to be attacked, not to be assailed, unassailable, hard to be approached or attacked; not to be assaulted or molested with impunity, dangerous; intractable, haughty; (*as*), m. white mustard; (*ā*), f. a kind of plant (= *kuṭumbinī*); [cf. *dur-dharsha* and *dush-pradharsha.*] — *Dur-ādhāra, as,* m. 'not to be confined, illimitable,' epithet of Śiva. — *Dur-ādhi, is, is, i,* painful, distressing. — *Dur-ādhī, īs, is, i* (rt. *dhyai*), Ved. intending or meditating evil, malignant. — *Dur-ānama, as, ā, am,* difficult to be bent, hard to bend (as a bow). — *Dur-āpa, as, ā, am,* difficult to be obtained, difficult of attainment; difficult to be approached; hard to be overcome; (*as*), m., N. of a Dānava. — *Dur-āpana, as, ā, am,* Ved. difficult to be attained, difficult to be overtaken. — *Dur-āpādana, as, ā, am,* difficult to be accomplished, hard to be brought about. — *Dur-āpūra, as, ā, am,* difficult to be filled or fulfilled or satisfied. — *Dur-ābādha, as, ā, am,* not to be molested, not to be assaulted with impunity; (*as*), m. epithet of Śiva. — *Dur-āmnāya, as, ā, am,* difficult to be handed down. — *Dur-āyya, as, ā, am,* Ved. difficult to be attained; (probably for *dur-āpyu.*) — *Dur-ārakshya, as, ā, am,* difficult to be protected; [cf. *ā-rakshya.*] — *Dur-ārādhya, as, ā, am,* difficult to be won over or propitiated, hard to be conciliated, difficult to be worshipped. — *Dur-āri-han, ā,* m. (fr. *dur-ari-han*), 'killing wicked enemies,' epithet of Vishṇu. — *Dur-āruha, as, ā, am,* difficult to be ascended or mounted; (*as*), m. a cocoa-nut tree; Ægle Marmelos (= *vilva*); (*ā*), f. Phœnix Sylvestris (= *kharjūrī*). — *Dur-ārūḍha, as, ā, am,* ascended with difficulty. — *Dur-āroha, as, ā, am,* difficult of ascent; (*as*), m. the palm tree, the date tree; (*ā*), f. the silk-cotton tree (= *śālmalī*; = *śrī-vallī*). — *Dur-ārohaṇīya, as, ā, am,* difficult to be ascended. — *Dur-ālakshya, as, ā, am,* difficult to be observed or perceived; [cf. 1. *ā-lakshya.*] — *Durālakshya-tama, as, ā, am,* most difficult to be perceived. — *Dur-ālabha* or *dur-ālamba, as, ā, am,* difficult to be laid hold of or handled, unfit to be touched; difficult of attainment; (*ā*), f. the prickly Alhagi Maurorum; [cf. *kshudra-d°.*] — *Dur-ālāpa, as,* m. a curse; imprecation; abuse, scurrilous or abusive language. — *Dur-āloka, as, ā, am,* difficult to be perceived; not to be looked at, painfully bright, dazzling; (*as*), m. dazzling splendor. — *Dur-āvarta, as, ā, am,* difficult to be turned (from an opinion &c.). — *Dur-āvaha, as, ā, am,* difficult to be brought, difficult to be led towards. — *Dur-āvāra, as, ā, am,* difficult to be covered or surrounded; difficult to be shut in or kept together; hard to be filled up; difficult to be restrained or stopped or kept back. — *Dur-ārya, as, ā, am* (perhaps for *dur-arya* fr. rt. *av*), Ved. displeasing. — 1. *dur-āśa, as,* m., N. of an Ekāha; [cf. *dur-ṇaśa, dū-ṇaśa, dū-ṇāśa.*] — 2. *dur-āśa, as, ā, am,* having bad expectations; (*ā*), f. bad hope or expectation. — *Dur-āśaya, as,* m. a bad resting-place or asylum; (*as, ā, am*), having a bad place of rest or refuge, having a difficult shelter or asylum; having evil thoughts or designs, evil-minded, malicious. — *Dur-āśir, īr, īr, īr,* Ved. badly mixed (as Soma). — *Dur-āsa, as, ā, am,* difficult to be driven out or expelled. — *Dur-āsada, as, ā, am,* difficult of access or attainment, difficult to be approached; difficult to be met with or found; hard to be borne; unequaled, unparalleled, unrivaled; (*as*), m. epithet of Śiva; mystical N. of a sword. — *Durāsada-jaya, as,* m., N. of the forty-second chapter of the Krīḍā-khaṇḍa or second part of the Gaṇeśa-Purāṇa. — *Durāsadopākhyāna* (°*da-up*°), *am,* n., N. of the fortieth chapter of the Krīḍā-khaṇḍa or second part of the Gaṇeśa-Purāṇa. — *Dur-āsaha, as, ā, am,* difficult to be accomplished. — *Dur-āsita, am,* n. bad or unbecoming manner of sitting. — *Dur-āhā,* ind. (opposed to and formed like *sv-āhā*), Ved. ill luck, misfortune. — *Dur-i,* cl. 1. A. *dur-ayate* or *dul-ayate,* &c., to go badly, to go wrong? (this verb is given by grammarians, but seems only to occur in its derivatives). — *Dur-ita, am,* n. bad course, difficulty, danger, damage; evil ways, evil, sin, Evil or Sin personified; (*as, ā, am*), difficult, bad; sinful, wicked; [cf. *dur-iti, dur-gata, dur-gati.*] — *Durita-kshaya, as,* m., N. of a son of Mahā-vīrya and father of Trayyāruṇi. — *Durita-damanī,* f., N. of a tree. — *Duritāri* (°*ta-ari*), *is,* f. 'the enemy of sin,' N. of a female deity of the Jainas (accompanying the third Arhat of the present Ava-sarpiṇī). — *Dur-iti, is,* f., Ved. bad course; difficulty, distress, trouble; [cf. *dur-ita* and *dur-gati.*] — 1. *dur-ishṭa, am,* n. (*ishṭa* fr. rt. 3. *ish*), 'bad wish,' curse, malediction, imprecation, a spell for the injury of another person; [cf. *dur-ishaṇā.*] — 2. *dur-ishṭa, as, ā, am* (*ishṭa* fr. rt. *yaj*), badly sacrificed, defective in a sacrifice, (opposed to *sv-ishṭa.*) — *Durishṭa-kṛit, t, t, t,* performing a magic spell to injure another. — *Dur-ishṭi, is,* f., Ved. defect or failure in a sacrifice. — *Durishṭha, as, ā, am* (superl. fr. 2. *dur*), very bad, very wicked; (*am*), n. great crime, extreme wickedness. — *Dur-īśa, as,* m. a bad master. — *Dur-ishaṇā,* f. (*īshaṇā* being a wrong form for *eshaṇā*), 'bad wish,' curse, cursing, imprecation; an evil eye; [cf. 1. *dur-ishṭa.*] — *Dur-ukta, as, ā, am,* badly spoken, uttered wrongly, harshly or injuriously spoken, harshly addressed; (*am*), n. injurious speech, reproach, hard or harsh words, rough or offensive words. — *Dur-ukti, is,* f. harsh or injurious speech, offensive speech; personified as a daughter of Krodha and Hiṃsā and sister and wife of Kali, (their children are Bhaya and Mṛityu.) — *Dur-uććheda, as, ā, am,* difficult to be extirpated or destroyed. — 1. *dur-uttara, as, ā, am* (see 1. *ut-tara,* p. 149), unanswerable. — 2. *dur-uttara, as, ā, am* (see *ut-tṛī,* p. 150), difficult to be crossed, hard to pass, difficult to be come out of or escaped from. — *Dur-utsaha* or *dur-utsāha, as, ā, am,* difficult to be borne; difficult to be resisted, irresistible. — *Dur-udaya, as, ā, am,* rising into view or appearing with difficulty, not easily manifested. — *Dur-udāhara, as, ā, am,* difficult to be articulated or pronounced. — *Dur-udvaha, as, ā, am,* difficult to be borne or suffered; unbearable, burthensome. — *Dur-upakrama, as, ā, am,* difficult of access or approach; difficult of cure. — *Dur-upaćāra, as, ā, am,* difficult of approach; unmanageable; difficult of cure. — *Dur-upalaksha, as, ā, am,* difficult to be perceived. — *Dur-upasarpin, ī, iṇī, i,* approaching incautiously. — *Dur-upasthāna, as, ā, am,* difficult of approach, unapproachable, unattainable. — *Dur-upāya, as,* m. a bad expedient. — *Dur-ūha, as, ā, am,* difficult to be inferred or perceived or understood; abstruse. — *Durūha-tā,* f. abstruseness. — *Dur-eva, as, ā, am,* Ved. evil-affected, ill-disposed, malignant; (Sāy.) going badly, having evil ways; difficult to be approached, unassailable; (*as*), m. a wicked person, a criminal. — *Dur-okam,* ind., Ved. unwillingly, reluctantly. — *Dur-osha, as, ā, am,* Ved. slow, lazy [cf. *osham*]; (Sāy.) difficult to be burnt; dwelling in houses; [cf. Zend *dūraosha.*] — *Dur-oshas, ās, ās, as,* Ved. slow, lazy; whose anger is difficult to be overcome. — *Dur-ga, as, ā, am,* difficult of access or approach, almost impassable or inaccessible, impervious, impermeable; difficult of attainment, unattainable; difficult to be understood; (*as*), m. bdellium; N. of an Asura (supposed to have been slain by the goddess Durgā, according to some she received her name from him); N. of a man; of a grammarian and lexicographer and commentator on Yāska's Nirukta; an abridged form for *durgādāsa, durga-gupta, durga-siṃha,* &c.; (*ā*), f., N. of two rivers; 'the inaccessible goddess,' N. of the daughter of Hima-vat and wife of Śiva, (also called Umā, Pārvatī, &c., and mother of Kārttikeya and Gaṇeśa; in her character of Durgā she is a goddess of terrific form and irascible temper, particularly worshipped at the Durgā-pūjā held in Bengal in the month of Aśvin or about October); N. of a princess; the indigo plant; a creeping shrub, Clitoria Ternatea; a singing bird, = *śyāmā*; (*am*), n. a difficult or narrow passage over a stream or a mountain or through a wood &c., a defile, narrow pass, gorge; a place difficult of access, a citadel, fort, fortress, stronghold, castle, crag, Droog or hill-fort, (in the sense of 'an inaccessible place' often at the end of a compound after a word indicating that by which the difficulty is caused, see *giri-d°, dhanva-d°, vāri-d°*); rough ground, roughness; difficulty, adversity, distress, danger. — *Durga-karman, a,* n. fortification; difficult work. — *Durga-kāraka, as, ikā, am,* building a fort; making difficult or impassable; (*as*), m. the Bhojpatra or birch tree. — *Durga-gupta, as,* m. (for *durgā-g°*), N. of a grammarian. — *Durga-ghāta, as* or *am,* m. or n. (?), N. of a fort. — *Durga-ghnā,* f. 'remover of difficulties,' epithet of Durgā. — *Durga-ṭīkā,* f. 'Durga's commentary' on Yāska's Nirukta &c.; (according to some authorities

Durga = Durga-gupta; according to others = Durga-siṇha.) — *Dur-gata, as, ā, am,* 'one whose affairs go badly,' unfortunate, in bad circumstances, poor, indigent, in trouble; distressed; suffering pain or affliction; [cf. *dur-ita.*] — *Durgata-tā,* f. ill luck, bad circumstances, distress, poverty, misery. — *Durga-taraṇī,* f. 'conveying over difficulties,' an epithet of Sāvitrī. — *Durga-tā,* f. impassableness, difficulty of being crossed. — *Dur-gati, is,* f. bad circumstances, misfortune, poverty, straits, indigence, want; a difficult path or situation; hell. — *Durgati-nāśinī,* f. 'removing distress,' an epithet of Durgā. — *Durga-nivāsin, ī, inī, i,* dwelling in a fortress or stronghold. — *Dur-gandha, as,* m. a bad smell, bad odour, stink; *(as, ā, am),* ill-smelling, ill-scented; *(as),* m. any ill-smelling substance; the mango tree (= *āmra*), an onion; *(am),* n. sochal-salt. — *Durgandha-tā,* f. badness of smell, stink. — *Durgandhi, is, is, i,* or *durgandhin, ī, inī, i,* ill-smelling, stinking. — *Durga-pati, is,* m. or *durga-pāla, as,* m. the commandant or governor of a fortress. — *Durga-pura, am,* n. a fortified town, citadel. — *Durga-pushpī,* f., N. of a plant (commonly *keśa-pushṭā*). — *Dur-gama, as, ā, am,* difficult to be traversed or travelled over, difficult of access or approach, impassable, inaccessible, impervious, unattainable, difficult of attainment, difficult to be understood; *(as, am),* m. n. a difficult situation; *(as),* m., N. of a son of Vasu-deva and Pauravī; also of Dhṛita. — *Dur-gamanīya, as, ā, am,* difficult to be traversed, hard to be passed, impassable. — *Durga-mārga, as,* m. a difficult pass or way, a defile. — *Durgamāśu-bodhinī* (°*ma-āś*°), f., N. of a commentary by Mālaṅka on the Mālatī-mādhava. — *Dur-gala, as,* m., N. of a people. — *Durga-laṅghana, as, ī, am,* making one's way through difficult places, surmounting or overcoming difficulties; *(as),* m. a camel. — *Durga-vākya-prabodha, as,* m. 'knowledge of difficult words,' N. of a grammatical work. — *Durga-vyasana, am,* n. defect in a fortress (e. g. its being ill-guarded &c.). — *Durga-śaila, as,* m. 'an inaccessible mountain,' N. of a mountain. — *Durga-saṅćara* or *durga-saṅćāra, as,* m. difficult passage, defile passing through an almost impervious or inaccessible place; a bridge, pontoon, or contrivance for passing a river, defile, &c. — *Durga-sampad, t,* f. excellence or perfection of a fortress. — *Durga-siṇha, as,* m. (for *durgā-s*°), N. of a king: of a grammarian; of an astronomer; *(ī),* f., N. of Durga-siṇha's commentary on the Kātantra; [cf. *durga-ṭīkā.*] — *Durga-sena, as,* m., N. of an author. — *Dur-gaha, as, ā, am* (rt. *gāh*), Ved. difficult to be entered or passed through or fathomed; *(āni),* n. pl. impassable or dangerous places, intolerable evils, dangers; *(as),* m., N. of a man; [cf. *daurgaha.*] — *Durgākramaṇa* (°*ga-āk*°), *am,* n. the taking of a fort. — *Dur-gāḍha, as, ā, am,* difficult to be fathomed or investigated; [cf. *dur-gādha* and *dur-gāhya.*] — *Durgā-datta, as,* m., N. of the author of the Vṛitta-muktāvalī (a modern work on Prākṛit prosody). — *Durgā-dāsa, as,* m., N. of a commentator on the grammar and collection of roots by Vopa-deva (this commentary is called the Dhātu-dīpikā); N. of a physician; of a prince. — *Dur-gādha, as, ā, am,* unfathomable. — *Durgādhikārin* (°*ga-adh*°), *ī,* m. or *durgādhyaksha* (°*ga-adh*°), *as,* m. the governor of a fortress. — *Durgā-navamī,* f. the ninth day of the light half of the month Kārttika (sacred to Durgā and the first day of the Treta-yuga). — *Durgāntarātithi* (°*ra-at*°), *is, is, i,* guest of the interior of a stronghold, a prisoner. — *Durgā-pūjā,* f. the festival in honour of the goddess Durgā, held in Bengal in the month Aśvin or about October; N. of a chapter of the Purāṇa-sarva-sva. — *Durgāpūjā-prakaraṇa, am,* n., N. of a chapter of the Purāṇa-sarva-sva. — *Durgā-prayoga, as,* m., N. of a chapter of the Tantra-sāra. — *Durgā-bhakti-taraṅgiṇī,* f., N. of a work on the worship of Durgā. — *Durgā-manu, us,* m., N. of the eleventh chapter of the Śāradātilaka by Lakshmaṇa. — *Durgā-mahattva, am,* n. 'the greatness of Durgā,' N. of a work. — *Durgā-māhātmya, am,* n. = *devī-māhātmya.* — *Durgā-yantra, am,* n., N. of a mystical diagram in the Tantra-sāra. — *Durgārādhana-māhātmya* (°*gā-ār*°), *am,* n., N. of the fourteenth chapter of the Śakti-ratnākara treating of the mystical worship of Durgā. — *Durgārohaṇa* (°*ga-ār*°), *as, ā, am,* difficult to be ascended. — *Durgāvarodha* (°*ga-av*°), *as,* m. investing or besieging a fortress. — *Durgā-vākya, am,* n., N. of the 118th chapter of the Krīḍā-khaṇḍa or second part of the Gaṇeśa-Purāṇa. — *Durgā-vilāsa, as,* m., N. of a poem. — *Durgāśrayaṇa* (°*ga-āś*°), *am,* n. taking refuge in a fortress. — *Durgā-stuti, is,* f. 'praise of Durgā,' N. of a chapter of the Purāṇa-sarva-sva. — *Durgā-stotra, am,* n., N. of the sixty-third chapter of the Prakṛiti-khaṇḍa or second part of the Brahma-vaivarta-Purāṇa. — *Dur-gāhya, as, ā, am,* difficult to be fathomed or forded, unfathomable; [cf. *dur-gāḍha.*] — *Durgāhya-tva, am,* n. unfathomableness. — *Durgāhva* (°*gā-āh*°), *as,* m. bdellium. — *Durgi, is,* f. = *durgā.* — *Dur-gribhi, is, is, i,* Ved. difficult to be seized or laid hold of. — *Dur-gribhi-śvan, ā,* m. (Sāy.) whose pervasion of space is difficult to be apprehended. — *Durgribhīya* (fr. the preceding), Nom. A. *durgribhīyate,* &c., Ved. to be difficult to seize or lay hold of. — *Durgotsava* (°*gā-ut*°), *as,* m. 'festival of Durgā,' N. of a treatise; N. of a chapter of the Tithi-tattva-ṭīkā by Kāśī-rāma. — *Durgotsava-tattva, am,* n., N. of a work by Raghu-nandana. — *Dur-goshṭhī,* f. evil association, secret alliance, conspiracy. — *Dur-graha, as,* m. seizing badly; a spasm, cramp; an evil demon (causing diseases); *(as, ā, am),* difficult to be conquered or gained; difficult to be obtained or accomplished; hard to be understood. — *Dur-grāhya, as, ā, am,* difficult to be seized, hard to be caught or laid hold of; difficult to be imprisoned; difficult to be gained or obtained; difficult to be understood or investigated. — *Durgrāhya-tva, am,* n. the state of being difficult to be seized, &c. — *Durgrāhya-hṛidaya, as, ā, am,* whose heart is difficult to be gained. — *Dur-ghaṭa, as, ā, am,* difficult to be accomplished, difficult, impossible, unattainable; *(as* or *am),* m. or n. (?), N. of a work. — *Durghaṭa-ghāṭana,* 'removing difficulties,' N. of a commentary on the Saṅkshipta-sāra. — *Durghaṭa-tva, am,* n. the state of being difficult to be accomplished. — *Durghaṭa-vṛitti, is,* f., N. of a commentary. — *Dur-ghaṇa, as, ā, am,* too crowded or closely packed. — *Dur-ghosha, as, ā, am,* uttering a harsh or disagreeable sound, harsh-sounding, roaring, bellowing; *(as),* m. a harsh or disagreeable cry; a bear. — *Dur-jana, as,* m. a bad man, a wicked wretch, a mischievous person, a scoundrel, a villain; *(as, ā, am),* bad, wicked, vile; malicious, mischief-making. — *Durjana-tā,* f. or *durjana-tva, am,* n. wickedness, villainy. — *Durjana-dūshita-manas, ās, ās, as,* having a mind corrupted by the wicked. — *Durjana-nindā,* f. 'censure of the wicked,' N. of the twenty-second chapter of the Śārṅgadhara-paddhati. — *Durjana-mukha-ćapeṭikā,* f. 'a box on the ear for perverse men,' N. of a controversial work. — *Durjanāya,* Nom. A. *durjanāyate,* &c., to become a wicked man, to become wicked. — *Dur-jaya, as, ā, am,* difficult to be subdued or overcome, hard to win or conquer, invincible; difficult to be obtained; *(as),* m., N. of a Dānava; of an assemblage of Dānavas; of a Rakshas; of several heroes; *(ā),* f., N. of a place. — *Dur-jayanta, as,* m., N. of a mountain. — *Dur-jara, as, ā, am,* difficult to be made old, ever youthful; difficult of digestion, indigestible, hard; difficult to be enjoyed; *(as* or *am),* m. or n. (?), N. of a place. — *Dur-jāta, as, ā, am,* badly or inauspiciously born or produced, wretched, unhappy; bad-natured, bad; of a bad kind; not genuine, false; *(am),* n. misfortune, calamity; disparity, impropriety. — *Dur-jāti, is,* f. misfortune; ill condition; *(is, is, i),* bad-natured, vile, wicked; low, outcast. — *Dur-jātīya, as, ā, am,* bad-natured, vile. — *Dur-jīva, as, ā, am,* difficult to live; *(am),* n. a difficult life. — *Dur-jñāna, as, ā, am,* difficult to be known. — *Durjñāna-tva, am,* n. the state of being difficult to be known. — *Dur-jñeya, as, ā, am,* difficult to be known or understood, hard to be discovered; *(as),* m. an epithet of Śiva. — *Dur-ṇaya, as,* m. bad conduct, impropriety, impolicy, &c. (see *dur-naya*). — *Dur-ṇaśa, as, ā, am,* Ved. unattainable, inaccessible; [cf. *dū-ṇaśa* and *dū-ṇāśa.*] — *Dur-ṇashṭa, as, ā, am,* unattained. — *Durṇāma-ćātana, as, ā, am,* Ved. driving away or averting the demons called Dur-ṇāman. — *Dur-ṇāman, ā, mnī, a,* having a bad name; *(ā),* m., N. of certain demons hostile to man and causing diseases &c.; (according to a scholiast) N. of a worm; [cf. *dur-nāman.*] — *Durṇāma-han, ā, ghnī, a,* Ved. destroying the demons called Dur-ṇāman. — *Dur-ṇihitaishin* (°*ta-esh*°), *ī, iṇī, i,* tracing out what is badly kept. — *Dur-ṇīta, as, ā, am,* ill-behaved, ill-governed; impolitic; untoward, froward; *(am),* n. misconduct, impolicy; [cf. *dur-nīta.*] — *Dur-ṇīti, is,* f. bad policy, misconduct, injustice, maladministration; [cf. *dur-nīti.*] — *Dur-datta, as, ā, am,* badly given. — *Dur-dama, as, ā, am,* difficult to be subdued; *(as),* m., N. of a son of Vasu-deva and Rohiṇī; of a prince, son of Bhadra-śreṇya; of a Brāhman. — *Dur-damana, as, ā, am,* difficult to be subdued; *(as),* m., N. of a prince, son of Śatānīka. — *Dur-damya, as, ā, am,* difficult to be subdued, untamable, indomitable, obstinate. — *Dur-darśa, as, ā, am,* difficult to be seen; disagreeable or painful to the sight, dazzling; [cf. *dur-driśa.*] — *Durdarśa-tā,* f. the state of being disagreeable to the sight, loathsomeness. — *Durdarśatāya,* Nom. A. *durdarśatāyate,* &c., to have a bad or disgusting appearance. — *Dur-darśana, as, ā, am,* difficult to be seen; disagreeable to the sight, looking badly. — *Dur-daśā,* f. a bad situation, misfortune, calamity. — *Dur-dānta, as, ā, am,* badly tamed, untamable, intractable, difficult or hard to be restrained or disciplined; *(as),* m. a calf; strife, quarrel. — *Dur-dina, am,* n. a rainy or cloudy day, a wet day, bad weather, rainy weather, a cloud, a shower; *(as, ā, am),* cloudy, rainy, clouded, overcast, lowering, dark. — *Durdina-grasta-bhāskara, as, ā, am,* having the sun obscured by dark clouds. — *Durdināya,* Nom. A. *durdināyate,* &c., to become covered with clouds, to be cloudy. — *Dur-divasa, as,* m. a dark or rainy day; [cf. *dur-dina.*] — *Dur-duhā,* f. difficult to be milked (a cow). — *Dur-driś, k, k, k,* seeing badly. — *Dur-driśa, as, ā, am,* difficult to be seen or looked at or met with; disagreeable to the sight, disgusting; [cf. *dur-darśa.*] — *Dur-driśika, as, ā, am,* Ved. having a bad aspect, looking bad or ill. — *Dur-drishṭa, as, ā, am,* ill-seen (literally or figuratively), ill-examined, imperfectly investigated; looked at with an evil eye. — *Dur-daiva, am,* n. hard fate, bad luck, unlucky destiny, misfortune. — *Durdaiva-vat, ān, atī, at,* unlucky, pursued or overtaken by misfortune, unhappy. — *Dur-dyūta, am,* n. a bad or unfair game. — *Durdyūta-devin, ī, inī, i,* playing a bad or unfair game. — *Dur-druma, as,* m. a green onion. — *Dur-dhara, as, ā, am,* difficult to be carried, borne, or suffered; irresistible, hard to be obstructed or restrained; difficult to be accomplished [cf. *aṅkuśa-d*°]; difficult to be kept in mind or recollected; *(as),* m. quicksilver; N. of two plants, = *ṛishabha* and *bhallātaka;* a kind of hell; N. of a son of Dhṛita-rāshṭra [cf. *dur-dharsha*]; of one of Śambara's generals; N. of Mahisha. — *Durdharā-yogādhyāya* (°*ga-adh*°), *as,* m., N. of a chapter of the Mīna-rāja-jātaka, an astrological work attributed to Yavaneśvara. — *Dur-dharītu* or *dur-dhartu, us, us, u,* Ved. irresistible, unrestrainable. — *Dur-dharma, as, ā, am,* having or obeying bad laws. — *Dur-dharsha, as, ā, am,* difficult to be laid hold of or assaulted, secure from assault, not to be touched or violated, inviolable, difficult of attainment or approach, difficult to be mastered or overpowered; inaccessible; dangerous; haughty, distant; fearful, dreadful, awful; *(as),* m., N. of a son of Dhṛita-rāshṭra [cf. *dur-dhara*]; of a mountain in Kuśa-dvīpa; *(ā),* f., N. of two plants, = *nāga-damanī,* = *kanthārī;* [cf.

dur-ādharsha and *dush-pradarsha.*] — *Durdharsha-kumāra-bhūta, as,* m. 'who has become a youth of inviolable (sanctity),' N. of a Bodhi-sattva. — *Dur-dharshaṇa* = *dur-dharsha,* q. v. — *Durdharsha-tā,* f. or *durdharsha-tva, am,* n. difficulty of being touched or of being conquered, intangibility, inviolability. — *Dur-dhā, ās,* f. bad order, derangement; [cf. *dur-dhita.*] — *Dur-dhārya, as, ā, am,* difficult to be borne or suffered; (with *manasā,* difficult to be kept in mind or recollection.) — *Dur-dhita, as, ā, am,* Ved. badly placed or arranged, loosely arranged, not in order, untidy. — *Dur-dhī, īs, īs, i,* weak-minded, stupid, silly; [cf. *dūḍhī.*] — *Dur-dhur, ūr, ūr, ūr,* Ved. unfitted for drawing vehicles; (Sāy.) difficult to be restrained. — *Dur-naya, as,* m. bad conduct, imprudent or impolitic behaviour, injustice; (often incorrectly written *dur-ṇaya,* but cf. *dur-ṇāman* and *durṇihitaishin.*) — *Dur-nāmaka, am,* n. 'having a bad name,' hemorrhoids, piles. — *Dur-nāman, ā,* m., N. of a Yaksha; N. of a chapter of the Brahma-Purāṇa; (*ā* and *mnī*), f. a cockle, scollop, kind of muscle; (*a*), n. piles or hemorrhoids; [cf. *dur-ṇāman.*] — *Durnāmāri* (°*ma-ari*), *i,* n. 'enemy of hemorrhoids, i. e. destroying them,' the bulbous root of Amorphophallus Campanulatus. — *Dur-nigraha, as, ā, am,* difficult of restraint, irrepressible, ungovernable. — *Dur-nimita, as, ā, am,* badly or carelessly put to the ground (as the feet). — *Dur-nimitta, am,* n. a bad omen; a bad pretext. — *Dur-niyantu, us, us, u,* Ved. difficult to be checked or held back; (Sāy. in one passage) bad restrainer (as if gen. c. of *niyantṛi*). — *Dur-nirīksha, as, ā, am,* difficult to be looked at or seen. — *Dur-nirīkshya, as, ā, am,* difficult or hard to be looked at, scarcely visible. — *Dur-nivartya, as, ā, am,* difficult to be turned back (as a flying army). — *Dur-nivāra* or *dur-nivārya, as, ā, am,* unrestrainable, difficult to be kept back, stopped, checked, hindered or contradicted, difficult to suppress, irrepressible; invincible, unconquerable. — *Durnivāra-tva, am,* n. irrepressibleness, unrestrainableness. — *Dur-nivṛitta, as, ā, am,* difficult to be returned from. — *Dur-nishkramaṇa* or *dur-nishprapatana* or *dur-niḥsaraṇa, am,* n. coming out or escaping with difficulty, difficult escape. — *Dur-nīta, as, ā, am,* badly managed, ill-conducted, ill-governed, improperly or unjustly decided, wrong; (*am*), n. a bad act, misconduct, imprudent conduct, impolicy; ill luck; [cf. *dur-naya* and *dush-praṇīta.*] — *Durnīta-bhāva, as,* m. bad behaviour, misconduct, imprudent conduct. — *Dur-nīti, is,* f. maladministration, impolicy, &c.; see *dur-ṇīti.* — *Dur-nṛipa, as,* m. a bad king. — *Dur-baddha, as, ā, am,* badly fastened. — *Durbala, as, ā, am,* of little strength, weak, feeble, thin, emaciated, impotent, scanty; (*as*), m. circumcised, having the glans penis void of prepuce, (also written *dur-vala*); a kind of bird, = *bhāṇḍika,* (also written *dur-vala;* cf. *durbalika*); (*ā*), f. a species of plant (= *ambu-śirīshikā*). — *Durbala-tā,* f. weakness, feebleness, thinness. — *Durbalāgni* (°*la-ag*°), *is, is, i,* having a weak digestion. — *Durbalāgni-tā,* f. weakness of digestion. — *Durbalāyāsa* (°*la-āy*°), *as, ā, am,* 'weak of effort,' ineffective. — *Durbalika* or *durvalika, as,* m. a kind of bird, = *dur-bala.* — *Durbalīyas, ān, asī, as,* weaker, feeble. — *Durbalendriya* (°*la-in*°), *as, ā, am,* having feeble (i. e. unrestrained) organs of sense. — *Dur-bāla, as, ā, am,* bald-headed, red-haired; void of prepuce; (various reading for *dur-bala.*) — *Dur-biriṇa, as, ā, am,* Ved. bristly, rough (as a beard). — *Dur-buddhi, is,* f. weak-mindedness, silliness; (*is, is, i*), weak-minded, silly, foolish; perverse, evil-minded, badly disposed; ignorant. — *Dur-budha, as, ā, am,* little-minded, weak-minded, silly. — *Dur-bodha, as, ā, am,* difficult to be understood, unintelligible, unfathomable. — *Dur-brāhmaṇa, as,* m. a bad Brāhman. — *Dur-bhaksha* or *dur-bhakshya, as, ā, am,* to be eaten with difficulty. — *Dur-bhaga, as, ā, am,* difficult to be gained or obtained; unfortunate, unlucky; (*ā*), f. a wife disliked by her husband; a bad or ill-tempered woman, a shrew; (personified) = Old Age, daughter of Time; [cf. *daurbhāgya* and *daurbhagineya.*] — *Durbhaga-tva, am,* n. the being unlucky or unfortunate, ill luck, ill fortune. — *Dur-bhagna, as, ā, am,* badly broken. — *Dur-bhaṅga, as, ā, am,* difficult to be broken, difficult to be loosened. — *Dur-bhara, as, ā, am,* difficult to be borne, insupportable, burdensome, troublesome; hard to be maintained or supported. — *Dur-bhāgya, as, ā, am,* unfortunate, unlucky; (*am*), n. ill luck. — *Dur-bhāvanā,* f. an evil thought; bad inclination. — *Dur-bhāvya, as, ā, am,* difficult to be kept in the memory or to be imagined. — *Dur-bhāshita, as, ā, am,* badly spoken or uttered. — *Dur-bhāshin, ī, iṇī, i,* speaking ill, abusing, insulting. — *Dur-bhiksha, am,* n. scarcity of provisions, dearth, famine; want in general; (also wrongly read *dur-bhikshya.*) — *Durbhiksha-tva, am,* n. a state of famine, scarcity of food. — *Durbhiksha-vyasana, am,* n. the horrors of famine. — *Durbhikshavyasanin, ī, inī, i,* afflicted by famine. — *Dur-bhida, as, ā, am,* difficult to be broken or torn asunder or destroyed. — *Dur-bhishajya, am,* n., Ved. difficult cure. — *Dur-bhūta, am,* n., Ved. ill luck, bad fortune; damage. — *Dur-bhṛiti, is,* f., Ved. scanty maintenance or subsistence. — *Dur-bheda* or *dur-bhedya, as, ā, am,* difficult to be broken or divided or torn asunder, not easily disunited or separated, firm. — *Dur-bhrātṛi, tā,* m. a bad brother; [cf. *daurbhrātra.*] — *Dur-makha,* see *a-durmakha.* — *Dur-maṅgala, as, ā, am,* inauspicious. — *Dur-mati, is,* f., Ved. bad disposition of mind, evil intention, envy, hatred; (*is, is, i*), weak-minded, silly, ignorant, simple; a blockhead; evil-minded, malicious, wicked; (*is*), m., N. of a demon; N. of the fifty-fifth year of the cycle of Jupiter which lasts sixty years. — *Durmati-kṛita, as, ā, am,* done unadvisedly or through bad advice. — *Dur-mada, as,* m. a mad conception or imagination or illusion; (*as, ā, am*), drunken, fierce, ferocious, seized by a mad illusion, infatuated; (*as*), m., N. of one of the 100 sons of Dhṛita-rāshṭra; of a son of Dhṛita and father of Pra-ćetas; of a son of Bhadra-sena and father of Dhanaka; N. of a son of Vasu-deva and Rohiṇī or Pauravī. — *Durmada-vīra-mānin, ī, inī, i,* fancying (one's self) a hero in (one's) foolish pride. — *Durmadāndha* (°*da-an*°), *as, ā, am,* 'blinded by mad illusion,' besotted. — *Dur-manas, as,* n. bad disposition or perversity of mind, evil intention; (*ās, ās, as*), distressed or troubled in mind, depressed in spirit, discouraged, sad, melancholy, meditating sorrowfully; [cf. Zend *dus-mananh;* Gr. δυσ-μενής.] — *Durmanāya,* Nom. A. *durmanāyate,* &c., to be or become troubled in mind or sad, to meditate sorrowfully. — *Dur-manushya, as,* m. a wicked man, a bad or mischievous man. — *Dur-mantu, us, us, u,* Ved. difficult to be understood. — *Dur-mantra, as,* m. or *dur-mantraṇā,* f. bad advice, evil or bad counsel. — *Dur-mantrita, as, ā, am,* imprudently advised; (*am*), n. an imprudent advice. — *Dur-mantrin, ī,* m. an evil adviser, a bad counsellor or minister; an unlucky minister; (*ī, iṇī, i*), having bad counsellors or ministers. — *Dur-manman, ā, ā, a,* Ved. badly disposed, evil-minded. — *Dur-mara, as, ā, am,* not easily dying, dying hardly, tenacious of life; (*am*), n. difficult death, dying with difficulty, a hard death; (*ā*), f. a kind of grass, = *dūrvā,* = *śveta-dūrvā.* — *Dur-maraṇa, am,* n. any violent or unnatural death. — *Durmara-tva, am,* n. the state of dying with difficulty, a hard death. — *Dur-marāyu, us, us, u,* Ved. not to be killed or made to die easily, not easy to be destroyed. — *Dur-maryāda, as, ā, am,* having evil ways or courses, wicked. — *Durmaryāda-tā,* f. misconduct, wickedness. — *Dur-marsha, as, ā, am,* Ved. unbearable, insupportable, not to be suffered; not to be forgotten; obstinate, angry, hostile; (*as*), m. an epithet of the Asura Bali. — *Dur-marshaṇa, as, ā, am,* difficult to be endured or borne, hard to be managed; (*as*), m. an epithet of Vishṇu; N. of one of the 100 sons of Dhṛita-rāshṭra; of a son of Sṛiñjaya. — *Dur-marshita, as, ā, am,* instigated to enmity, made hostile, stirred up. — *Dur-mallikā* or *dur-mallī,* f. a minor drama, a comedy, a farce. — *Dur-mātsarya, am,* n. evil envy. — *Dur-māyin, ī, inī, i,* or *dur-māyu, us, us, u,* Ved. using bad arts; (Sāy.) using bad weapons. — *Dur-mitra, as, ā, am,* Ved. unfriendly; (*as*), m., N. of an author of a Ṛig-veda hymn; of a prince; (*ā*), f., N. of a woman. — *Dur-mitriya, as, ā, am,* Ved. unfriendly. — *Dur-milā,* f., N. of two kinds of metre, one consisting of 4 × 32 syllabic instants, the other consisting of 4 × 8 anapests. — *Durmilikā,* f., N. of a metre consisting of 4 × 32 syllabic instants. — *Dur-mukha, as, ī, am,* having a bad countenance or an ugly face, hideous; foul-mouthed, abusive, scurrilous; (*as*), m. a horse; N. of a prince of the Pańćālas; of one of the 100 sons of Dhṛita-rāshṭra; of an astronomer; of an ascetic; of a Rakshas; of one of the principal Nāgas or serpents; N. of a Yaksha; of a monkey; of a general of the Asura Mahisha; N. of the twenty-ninth year of the cycle of Jupiter which consists of sixty years; [cf. *daurmukhi.*] — *Dur-muhūrta, as, am,* m. n. an inauspicious hour or moment. — *Dur-mūlya, as, ā, am,* high-priced, dear; (*am*), n. anything of high price or value. — *Dur-medha, as, ā, am,* or more correctly *dur-medhas, ās, ās, as,* dull-witted, simple-minded, silly, stupid, ignorant, uninformed. — *Dur-medha-tva, am,* n. dulness or weakness of intellect, foolishness, stupidity. — *Dur-medhāvin, ī, inī, i,* = *dur-medha* above. — *Dur-maitra, as,* &c., unfriendly, hostile, an enemy. — *Dur-moća, as, ā, am,* hard to unloose. — *Dur-moha, as* or *ā,* m. or f., N. of a tree, = *kāka-tuṇḍī.* — *Dur-yavana, am,* ind. the bad Yavanas. — *Dur-yaśas, as,* n. ill repute, dishonour, disgrace. — *Dur-yāman, ā,* m. 'going badly,' N. of a prince; (also read *dur-dama.*) — *Dur-yuj, k, k, k,* Ved. difficult to be yoked. — *Dur-yoga, as,* m. bad contrivance, clumsy artifice, bad or inauspicious conjunction. — *Dur-yodha, as, ā, am,* difficult to be conquered. — *Dur-yodhana, as, ā, am,* difficult to be conquered, invincible; (*as*), m., N. of the eldest of the Kuru princes and leader in the war against his cousins the Pāṇḍavas and Kṛishṇa, described in the Mahā-bhārata; N. of a son of Su-durjaya; [cf. *su-yodhana.*] — *Duryodhana-tā,* f. the state of being difficult to be conquered, invincibility, difficulty of being attacked. — *Duryodhana-vīrya-jñāna-mudrā,* f. 'the mark of the knowledge of invincible heroism,' a peculiar position of the hands. — *Dur-yoni, is, is, i,* of low or impure origin. — *Dur-lakshaṇa, as, ā, am,* badly marked. — *Dur-lakshya, as, ā, am,* difficult to be observed, hardly visible. — *Dur-laṅghana* or *dur-laṅghya, as, ā, am,* difficult to be surmounted or transgressed, insurmountable, not to be overcome. — *Durlaṅghana-śakti, is,* f. of insurmountable power. — *Dur-labha, as, ā, am,* difficult to be obtained, hard to be attained, difficult of attainment or accomplishment, difficult to be found or met with, scarce, rare; excellent, eminent; dear, beloved; difficult (with an inf., e. g. *ratho durlabhaḥ samārodhum,* a chariot difficult to be mounted); (*as*), m. a kind of plant, = Curcuma Amhaldi or Zerumbet, = *karbura, kaććhura;* N. of a man; (*ā*), f., N. of two plants, = *śveta-kaṇṭa-kārī* and *dur-ālabhā.* — *Dur-labhaka, as,* m., N. of a king of Kaśmīra, also called Pratāpāditya. — *Durlabha-tara, as, ā, am,* extremely difficult of attainment, more hard to be obtained. — *Durlabha-tva, am,* n. difficulty of attainment, scarceness, rarity. — *Durlabha-vardhana, as,* m., N. of a king of Kaśmīra. — *Durlabha-svāmin, ī,* m., N. of a temple built by Durlabha-vardhana. — *Dur-lalita* or *durlalitaka, as, ā, am,* ill-bred, ill-mannered, uncivil; spoilt, wayward, naughty; (*am*), n. ill-breeding, waywardness, rudeness. — *Dur-lasita, as, ā, am,* ill-mannered; (various reading for *dur-lalita;* cf. *dur-vilasita.*) — *Dur-lābha, as, ā, am,* difficult to be obtained, = *dur-labha.* — *Dur-lekhya, am,* n. a false or forged document. — *Dur-vaća, as, ā, am,* difficult to be uttered, hard to be spoken, difficult to be explained, not to be spoken about; anything about which it is difficult or disagreeable to speak; speaking ill or improperly, abusing; (*am*), n. abuse, censure; evil or unlucky speech. — *Dur-vaćana, am*, n. a harsh expression, abusive language. — *Dur-vaćas, as*, n. evil speech, bad language, insult, abuse; (*ās, ās, as*), using bad or abusive language; difficult to be explained or answered; [cf. *dur-vaća*.] — *Durvaćas-tva, am*, n. bad or abusive language; difficulty of being answered. — *Dur-vadaka, as, ā, am*, speaking or uttering badly or indistinctly, uttering incoherently, stammering. — *Dur-varāha, as*, m., Ved. a wild hog (?). — *Dur-varṇa, as, ā, am*, of a bad or inferior colour, bad-coloured; of a bad or low species or class; (*am*), n. silver, (opposed to *su-varṇa*, gold); the fragrant bark of Feronia Elephantum (commonly Elabāluka). — *Dur-varṇaka, am*, n. silver. — *Dur-vartu, us, us, u*, Ved. difficult to be kept back or restrained, irresistible. — *Dur-vala*, see *dur-bala*. — *Dur-vasa, as, ā, am*, difficult to be inhabited or resided in; difficult to be passed or spent (as time). — *Dur-vasati, is*, f. a difficult dwelling, painful residence. — *Dur-vaha, as, ā, am*, difficult to be borne or supported. — *Dur-vākya, am*, n. harsh or abusive language. — *Durvāg-bhava, as*, m. the being abusive, abusiveness, the use of bad language. — *Dur-vāć, k*, f. evil speech, bad words, abuse; inelegant language or utterance; (*k, k, k*), having a bad voice, speaking ill, using bad language. — *Dur-vāćya, as, ā, am*, difficult to be uttered or spoken; abusive, harsh (as words); (*am*), n. any harsh or bad or ill-omened speech, inauspicious news; censure, abuse. — *Dur-vāda, as*, m. calumnious report, slander, defamation, calumny; (*as, ā, am*), one who speaks badly or incorrectly or ungrammatically, one who utters abusive or unbecoming language. — *Dur-vānta, as, ā, am*, one who has vomited badly or on whom an emetic has not had the desired effect. — *Dur-vāra* or *dur-vāraṇa* or *dur-vāraṇīya, as, ā, am*, difficult to be restrained or stopped, not to be repressed or checked, irresistible. — *Durvāra-tva, am*, n. irrepressibleness, unrestrainableness. — *Dur-vārita, as, ā, am*, badly restrained or obstructed. — *Dur-vārttā*, f. bad news, sad intelligence. — *Dur-vārya* = *dur-vāra* above. — *Durvārya-tā*, f. unrestrainableness, irrepressibleness. — *Dur-vāsanā*, f. bad inclination, evil propensity; a chimera. — *Dur-vāsas, ās, ās, as*, badly clad, ill-dressed, unclothed, denuded, naked; (*ās*), m., N. of a Ṛishi or saint (who was a son of Atri by Anasūyā and an incarnation of a portion of Śiva; he became notorious for his irascible temperament). — *Durvāseśvara-liṅga* (°*sa-īś*°), *am*, n., N. of a Liṅga; N. of the eighty-fifth chapter of the Kāśī-khaṇḍa of the Skanda-Purāṇa. — *Durvāso-darpa-bhaṅga, as*, m. 'the humbling of the pride of Dur-vāsas,' N. of the fiftieth chapter of the Kṛishṇa-khaṇḍa of the Brahma-vaivarta-Purāṇa. — *Durvāsopanishad* (°*sa-up*°), *t*, f. 'the mystical doctrine of Dur-vāsa (?),' N. of the thirty-fourth to the forty-first chapters of the Jñāna-khaṇḍa of the Śiva-Purāṇa. — *Durvāso-matatantra, am*, n., N. of a work mentioned in the commentary to the Ānanda-laharī or 'wave of pleasure' by Gaurī-kānta-sārva-bhauma. — *Durvāso-vākya, am*, n., N. of the ninety-ninth chapter of the Uttara-kāṇḍa of the Rāmāyaṇa. — *Durvāso-śāpa-kathana, am*, n. 'the tale of the curse of Dur-vāsas,' N. of the thirty-eighth chapter of the Uttara-khaṇḍa or fifth part of the Padma-Purāṇa. — *Dur-vāhita, am*, n. a heavy load or burden. — *Dur-vikatthana, as, ā, am*, boasting in an arrogant or offensive manner. — *Dur-vigāha, as, ā, am*, difficult to be fathomed or penetrated or reached, unfathomable; (*as*), m., N. of one of the 100 sons of Dhṛita-rāshṭra. — *Dur-vigāhya, as, ā, am*, = *dur-vigāha* above. — *Dur-vićintya, as, ā, am*, difficult to be imagined, inconceivable, inscrutable. — *Dur-vićeshṭa, as, ā, am*, behaving badly, ill-behaved, misconducted. — *Dur-vijñāna, am*, n. comprehending or understanding with difficulty; (*as, ā, am*), difficult to be understood or comprehended; having an evil mind. — *Dur-vijñeya, as, ā, am*, difficult to be understood or perceived, unintelligible. — *Dur-vitarka* or *durvitarkya, as, ā, am*, difficult to be reasoned about or discussed, difficult to be understood. — *Dur-vida, as, ā, am*, difficult to be known or discovered. — *Dur-vidagdha, as, ā, am*, 'badly burned,' i. e. imperfectly skilled, unskilled, raw, scantily versed, stupid, silly; wholly ignorant; foolishly puffed up. — *Dur-vidatra, as, ā, am*, Ved. ill-disposed, envious, ungracious. — *Dur-vidya, as, ā, am*, uninformed, uneducated. — *Dur-vidvas, vān, dushī, vas*, Ved. evil-minded, ill-disposed, malignant. — *Dur-vidha, as, ā, am* ('acting badly,' 'of a bad nature'), mean, low, base; wicked, malevolent; poor, badly circumstanced, pauper, indigent; stupid, foolish, silly, (? for *dur-vidya*.) — *Dur-vidhi, is*, m. 'bad fate,' bad luck, misfortune. — *Dur-vinaya, as*, m. imprudent conduct, bad behaviour. — *Dur-vinīta, as, ā, am*, ill-conducted, badly behaved, badly educated, ill-mannered, unrefined, mean, wicked; stubborn, obstinate, restive (as a horse); (*as*), m. a wicked wretch, reprobate, ruffian; N. of a sage (associated with Dur-vāsas, Kaṇva, Kātyāyana). — *Durvinītaka* = *dur-vinīta*. — *Dur-vipāka, as*, m. a bad end or result, evil consequences of acts done either in this or a former birth. — *Dur-vibhāga, ās*, m. pl. 'difficult to be disunited,' N. of a people. — *Dur-vibhāvya, as, ā, am*, difficult to be conceived, incomprehensible, inconceivable. — *Dur-vibhāsha, as, ā, am*, difficult to be pronounced or uttered; (*am*), n. harsh or offensive words, abuse. — *Dur-vimoćana, as, ā, am*, difficult to be set free or liberated; (*as*), m., N. of one of the 100 sons of Dhṛita-rāshṭra. — *Dur-viroćana, as*, m. 'shining badly (?),' N. of one of the 100 sons of Dhṛita-rāshṭra. — *Dur-vilasita, am*, n. a rude or ill-mannered trick, rudeness, naughtiness, a wayward act; [cf. *dur-lasita*.] — *Dur-vivaktṛi, tā, trī, tṛi*, declaring badly, answering wrongly. — *Dur-vivāha, as*, m. a bad marriage, mesalliance. — *Dur-viśa, as, ā, am*, hard to be entered, difficult to be trod or walked upon. — *Dur-visha, as, ā, am*, bad-tempered (?); ill-natured, malignant; (*as*), m. an epithet of Śiva. — *Dur-vishaha, as, ā, am*, difficult to be borne or supported, intolerable, insupportable, difficult to be subdued or overcome, irresistible; difficult to be performed; (*as*), m. an epithet of Śiva; N. of one of the 100 sons of Dhṛita-rāshṭra; (also read *dur-visaha*; cf. *duḥ-shaha, duḥ-saha, dush-prasaha*.) — *Dur-vishahya, as, ā, am*, = *dur-vishaha*. — *Dur-vṛitta, am*, n. bad conduct, misconduct, ill-behaviour, mean practices; (*as, ā, am*), behaving badly, misbehaved, vile, wicked, criminal, leading a low or infamous life, following disreputable habits or business, cheating, roguish, a cheat, rogue, blackguard. — *Dur-vṛitti, is*, f. bad circumstances, distress, misery, want, indigence; disreputable conduct, bad practices; fraud. — *Dur-vṛishṭi, is*, f. insufficient rain, drought, dryness, aridity. — 1. *dur-veda, as, ā, am* (rt. 1. *vid*), having bad or little knowledge, unlearned; difficult to be known. — 2. *dur-veda, as, ā, am* (rt. 3. *vid*), difficult to be found. — *Dur-vyavasthāpaka, as, ā, am*, deciding badly, giving a bad or unfavourable judgment. — *Dur-vyavahāra, as*, m. a wrong judgment (in law). — *Dur-vyāhṛita, as, ā, am*, spoken badly or ill; (*am*), n. a bad or unfit expression. — *Dur-vrajita, as*, m. a bad or improper gait, bad manner of going. — *Dur-vrata, as, ā, am*, disobedient, not conforming to rules; [cf. *daurvratya*.] — *Dur-haṇa* or *dur-hana, as, ā, am*, Ved. difficult to be killed, difficult to be destroyed or overcome, hard to be overpowered, irresistible; (*ṇā*), f., Ved. ill luck, misfortune. — *Durhaṇāyat, an, antī, at*, or *durhaṇāyu, us, us, u*, Ved. seeking to destroy, intending injury, meditating evil or damage. — *Durhaṇā-vat, ān, atī, at*, Ved. fatal, pernicious. — *Dur-hanu, us, us, u*, Ved. having deformed jaws. — *Dur-hana*, see *dur-haṇa*. — *Dur-hārd, t, t, t*, Ved. ill-disposed; [cf. *dur-hṛid* and *daurhārda*.] — *Dur-hita, as, ā, am*, Ved. unfriendly, hostile, troublesome. — *Dur-huta, am*, n. a badly offered sacrifice. — *Dur-hṛiṇāyat, an, antī, at*, or *durhṛiṇāyu, us, us, u*, Ved. whose fury is difficult to restrain or be borne. — *Dur-hṛid, t, t, t*, bad-hearted, hard-hearted, ill-disposed, inimical; (*t*), m. an enemy; [cf. *dur-hārd* and *daurhārda*.] — *Dur-hṛidaya, as, ā, am*, evil-minded, bad-hearted; [cf. *daur-hṛidaya*.] — *Dur-hṛishīka, as, ā, am*, having defective organs of sense, badly restraining the senses; [cf. *durbalendriya* and *dur-bala*.]

Durasya (probably connected with 2. *dur*), Nom. P. *durasyati*, &c., Ved. to wish to hurt, desire to injure.

Durasyu, us, us, u, Ved. wishing to do harm, desirous of inflicting injury.

दुर 1. *dura, as, ā, am*, Ved. (according to Sāy. fr. rt. 1. *dā*), a giver, granter; (perhaps rather to be derived fr. rt. *dṛī*, one who opens, unlocks.)

दुर 2. *dura* = 1. *dur* (occurring only in *śata-dura*, q. v.). — *Dura-dabhna, as, ā, am*, Ved. deceiving or illuding doors, i. e. not to be kept in or restrained by bolts and bars.

Duroṇa, am, n., Ved. residence, dwelling, home. — *Duroṇa-sad, t, t, t*, Ved. residing in a house.

Duroṇāyu, us, us, u, Ved. fond of the house; (Sāy.) frequenting the sacrificial hall.

Durya, as, ā, am, Ved. belonging to the door or house; (*ās*), m. or f. pl. a residence; (perhaps 'the posts of the door;' cf. Lat. *fores*.)

Duryoṇa, am, n., Ved. a residence, dwelling-place, = *duroṇa* (?); Sāy. = *saṅgrāma*, battle, or (*dus* + *yoni*) = *Duryoni*, N. of a king.

दुराक *durāka, as*, m., N. of a barbarous tribe.

दुरु *duru, us*, m., N. of a mountain.

दुरुःफ *duruḥpha*, (in astrology) N. of the fifteenth Yoga; (also read *durapha* and *durupha*.)

दुरुधरा *durudharā*, f. (a word borrowed fr. the Gr. δορυφορία), a peculiar position of the moon.

दुरोदर *durodara, as*, m. (probably for *darodara*, q. v., and connected with rt. *dṛī*; according to others perhaps fr. *duras*, acc. pl. of 1. *dur*, q. v., + *dara*, piercing or breaking the doors; cf. *dura-dabhna* under 2. *dura*), one who plays at dice, a gamester; a dice-box; a stake; (*am*), n. (according to a commentator also *as*, m.), playing, gaming, a game at dice.

Durdara, as, ā, am (probably for *dardara*, q. v.), tearing; distressing; a kind of drug, = *ṛishabha*; [cf. *dardura* and *dur-dhara*.]

दुर्ग *dur-ga, dur-gā*, &c. See p. 420, col. 3.

दुर्गि *durgi* = *dur-gā*, q. v.

दुर्दुरूट *durdurūṭa* or *durduruṭa, as*, m. (said to be fr. 2. *dur*, 'vile,' repeated), an expression of reproach; an atheist, = *karaṭa*.

Durdhurūṭa or *durdhuruṭa, as*, m. a pupil who does not obey his teacher without exercising his own judgment.

दुर्द्रिता *durdritā*, f. a kind of creeping plant.

दुर्व् *durv*, cl. 1. P. *dūrvati*, &c., to hurt, injure, kill; [cf. rt. *dhurv*.]

दुर्वारि *durvāri, ayas*, m. pl., N. of a tribe of the Kāmbojas.

दुर्वासस् *dur-vāsas*. See col. 1.

दुल् *dul*, cl. 10. P. *dolayati*, &c., to swing, heave upwards, raise, throw up, whirl, shake to and fro, cause to oscillate or vibrate, excite; [cf. *tul, dola, dolāya*.]

Dulā, f., Ved. 'shaking,' N. of an Ishṭakā or sacrificial brick.

दुलयते *dul-ayate* = *dur-ayate*. See *dur-i*, p. 420, col. 2.

दुलि *duli, is*, m., N. of a Muni or saint; (*is, ī*), f. a small or female tortoise; [cf. *dauleya*.]

दुलिदुह *duliduha, as*, m., N. of a prince; of a son of An-amitra and father of Dilīpa.

दुवन्य *duvanya* (perhaps fr. rt. 1. *du*), Ved. worshipping. — *Duvanya-sad, t, t, t*, Ved. (Sāy.) dwelling among worshippers, abiding with the devout; [cf. *duvas* below.]

Duvas, as, n., Ved. worship, honour, reverence; (Sāy.) wealth; (*ās, ās, as*), active, moving restlessly. — *Duvas-kṛi*, cl. 8. P. A. *-karoti, -kurute, -kartum*, to worship. — *Duvas-vat, ān, atī, at*, Ved. worshipping; enjoying or receiving worship. — *Duvo-dhā*, cl. 3. P. A. *-dadhāti, -dhatte, -dhātum*, to worship.

Duvasana, as, ā, am, active, moving; (Sāy.) adorable, worthy of worship.

1. *duvasya*, Nom. P. *duvasyati*, &c., Ved. to honour, worship, celebrate, acknowledge, reward; to present with, give as a reward.

2. *duvasya, as, ā, am*, Ved. (according to Sāy.) worthy of worship or honour.

Duvasyu, us, us, u, Ved. honouring, worshipping, respectful.

Duvoyā, f., Ved. worship; (only occurring in inst. *duvoyā*, in worship.)

Duvoyu, us, us, u, Ved. honouring, worshipping; (*u*), ind. reverently; out of acknowledgment.

दुश् *duś*, euphonically substituted for *dus* in comp. like *duś-ćakshas*. See bottom of col. 3.

दुश्चिक्य *duśćikya, am*, n. (in astrology) N. of the third lunar mansion.

दुष् 1. *dush*, euphonically substituted for *dus* in *dush-kara* &c. See p. 425, col. 1.

दुष् 2. *dush*, cl. 4. P. (ep. also A.) *dushyati, -te, dudosha, dokshyati, adushat* (according to Vopa-deva also *adukshat*), *doshṭum*, to become bad or corrupted, to be ruined, to perish, suffer damage, to be soiled; to be or become depraved or defiled or impure, to be violated (as a woman), to be contaminated by a crime, to sin, to commit a mistake, to be wrong; to be faithless or unchaste (as a wife): Caus. *dūshayati* (ep. also *-te*), *-yitum*, to corrupt, spoil, make bad, cause to perish, hurt, destroy, lay waste, to make unclean or impure, to soil, defile, contaminate, vitiate, taint; to dishonour or violate (as a girl or the wife of another); to cause evil or misfortune (in astrology); to corrupt the morals, deprave, demoralize; to adulterate; to falsify; to rescind, abrogate, annul, retract; to object, refute, disprove; to find fault with, speak ill of, accuse, blame, abuse, contemn; (it is to be observed that *dūshyate*, Pass. of the Caus., may often more correctly be read where *dushyate* is given in the printed editions of epic poems, the sense of *dūshyate* being the same; according to Pāṇ. VI. 4, 91, another form of the Caus., viz. *doshayati*, &c., is optionally used in speaking of moral corruption, e. g. *kāmo dūshayati* or *doshayati ćittam*, lust corrupts the mind.)

Dushṭa, as, ā, am, become bad, spoiled, corrupted, reduced to a bad state, injured, damaged, ruined, spoiled, vitiated, contaminated, diseased, tainted, infected, degraded; depraved; violated; corrupt, vicious, wicked; bad, evil; faulty, guilty, convicted, culpable; having evil intentions, ill-affected; roguish, low, vile; worthless; painful; (*ā*), f. a bad woman, a harlot, an unchaste woman; (*am*), n. sin, an offence, crime, guilt; a kind of Costus, Costus Speciosus, = *kushṭha*. — *Dushṭa-gaja, as*, m. a vicious elephant. — *Dushṭa-ćaritra, as, ā, am*, ill-conducted. — *Dushṭa-ćārin, ī, iṇī, i*, practising evil deeds, wicked, criminal. — *Dushṭa-ćetas, ās, ās, as*, evil-minded, malevolent, bad-hearted. — *Dushṭa-tā*, f. or *dushṭa-tva, am*, n. badness, wickedness; perversity, falsehood; contamination, defilement, violation. — *Dushṭa-dhī, īs, īs, i*, or *dushṭa-buddhi, is, is, i*, having bad thoughts, evil-minded, evil-affected. — *Dushṭa-bhāva, as, ā, am*, evil-natured, of a wicked or depraved nature, innately bad or wicked. — *Dushṭabhāva-tā*, f. wickedness, innate depravity. — *Dushṭa-mati, is, is, i*, evil-minded, wicked, depraved. — *Dushṭa-mānasa, as, ī, am*, evil-minded, depraved in mind. — *Dushṭa-vāć, k, k, k*, speaking evil, uttering bad language. — *Dushṭa-vṛisha, as*, m. a bad or vicious ox, a strong but stubborn ox which refuses to draw. — *Dushṭa-vraṇa, as*, m. a dull boil or sore, an obstinate tumor; a sinus. — *Dushṭātman* (°*ṭa-āt*°), *ā, ā, a*, of a bad nature, evil-minded, wicked. — *Dushṭānvita* (°*ṭa-an*°), *as, ā, am*, defiled, rendered impure.

Dushṭi, is, f. corruption, corruptness, depravity.

Dushṭiya, Nom. P. *dushṭīyati*, &c., to become bad or corrupted (?).

दुष्ट *dushṭa*. See col. 1.

दुष्टु *dushṭhu*. See p. 425, col. 2.

दुष्यन्त *dushyanta*. See p. 425, col. 3.

दुस् *dus*, ind. (related to rt. 2. *dush*, and reckoned by Pāṇini among the Upa-sargas), a particle and prefix to nouns and rarely to verbs, implying evil, bad, badly, wicked, wickedly, difficult, hard, with difficulty, slight, inferior, &c., and sometimes equivalent to the English prefix *in-* or *un-*; [cf. rt. 2. *dush*; rt. 1. *drish*: Zend *dush, dus-mananh, dush-i-ti*: Gr. δυς, e. g. δυσ-μενής: Goth. *tus* in *tuz-veryan*: Old Germ. *zur-*: Hib. *do, do-dhail*, 'bad luck;' *do-dhuine*, 'a bad man;' *do-dheanta*, 'hard to be done;' *do-bhasuighte*, 'immortal.'] *Dus* becomes *dur*, q. v., before vowels and soft consonants; becomes *dū*, q. v., before *r*; remains unchanged before *t, th* (not however in the earlier language where *s* becomes *sh* and the following *t, th* are changed to *ṭ, ṭh*); becomes *dush* and rarely *duḥ* before *k, kh* [cf. *duḥ-kha*], *p, ph*; becomes *duḥ* and rarely *dus, duś, dush* before *s, ś*, and *sh*. Those compounds in which *dus* becomes *dur* and *dū* will be found under *dur* and *dū* respectively. The other compounds formed with *dus* are as follow. — *Duḥ-paća, duḥ-patana, duḥ-pattra, duḥ-prajña*, &c., see *dush-paća*, &c., p. 425, col. 2. — *Duḥ-śaṇsa, as, ā, am*, Ved. wishing evil, malevolent, malicious, wicked. — *Duḥ-śaka* or *duḥ-śakta, as, ā, am*, or *duḥ-śakti, is, is, i*, having no power, possessed of little power, powerless. — *Duḥ-śala, as*, m., N. of one of the 100 sons of Dhṛita-rāshṭra; (*ā*), f., N. of the only daughter of Dhṛita-rāshṭra, (she was the wife of king Jayad-ratha.) — *Duḥ-śasta, as, ā, am*, badly recited; (*am*), n. a bad recitation. — *Duḥ-śāka, am*, ind. the luckless Śakas (see Pāṇ. II. 1, 6). — *Duḥ-śāsa, as, ā, am*, difficult to be controlled. — *Duḥ-śāsana, as, ā, am*, difficult to be governed, intractable, difficult to be managed; (*as*), m., N. of one of the 100 sons of Dhṛita-rāshṭra. — *Duḥ-śāsu, us, us, u*, Ved. wishing evil, malevolent. — *Duḥ-śīma, as, ā, am*, Ved. = *dush-prāpa*, difficult to be attained; (*as*), m., N. of a man?; [cf. *su-śīma*.] — *Duḥ-śīla, as, ā, am*, badly disposed, ill-behaved, reprobate, abandoned. — *Duḥśīla-tā*, f. bad behaviour, badness of disposition. — *Duḥ-śṛiṅgī*, f. a disloyal wife. — *Duḥ-śeva, as, ā, am*, Ved. 'badly propitious,' envious; (Sāy.) difficult to serve (as if *seva*); delighting in evil. — *Duḥ-śodha, as, ā, am*, difficult to be cleaned. — *Duḥ-śosha, as, ā, am*, difficult to be dried. — *Duḥ-śruta, as, ā, am*, badly or wrongly heard. — *Duḥ-shanta, as*, m., N. of the father of Bharata; [cf. *dauḥshanti*; later forms are *dushmanta, dushyanta, dushranta, duḥshranta*.] — *Duḥ-shama, as, ā, am*, unlike, uneven; adverse, unlucky, unfortunate; wrong; (*am*), ind. unevenly, improperly; at a wrong time; (*ā*), f. (with Jainas) N. of two spokes in the wheel of time, viz. the fifth in the Ava-sarpiṇī, and the second in the Ut-sarpiṇī; [cf. *duḥ-sama*.] — *Duḥshama-sushamā*, f. 'both unfortunate and fortunate' (but with a preponderance of misfortune), N. of two spokes in the Jaina wheel of time, viz. the fourth in the Ava-sarpiṇī, and the third in the Ut-sarpiṇī. — *Duḥ-shaha, as, ā, am*, Ved. difficult to be borne, irresistible; [cf. *duḥ-saha*.] — *Duḥ-shupta, as, ā, am*, sleeping badly, having bad dreams. — *Duḥ-shṭutu* and *duḥ-shṭuti*, see *du-shṭuta, du-shṭuti*, p. 425, col. 2. — *Duḥ-shvapnya, am*, n., Ved. 'causing bad dreams,' evil dream, pain; (Sāy.) poverty; [cf. *jāgra-d*°, *svapna-d*°, *dauḥ-shvapnya, duḥ-svapna*.] — *Duḥ-saṃlakshya, as, ā, am*, difficult to be observed or recognised. — *Duḥ-saṃskāra, as*, m. a bad custom or practice. — *Duḥ-saktha, as, ā, am*, or *duḥ-sakthi, is, is, i*, having deformed thighs. — *Duḥ-saṅga, as*, m. bad inclination, evil attachment. — *Duḥ-sañćāra, as, ā, am*, difficult to be passed. — *Duḥ-sañćintya, as, ā, am*, difficult to be conceived or imagined. — *Duḥ-sattva, am*, n. an evil being, noxious creature, ferocious animal. — *Duḥsattva-vat, ān, atī, at*, filled with or infested by evil beings or ferocious animals. — *Duḥ-santushṭa, as, ā, am*, unsatisfied, discontented. — *Duḥ-sandhāna* or *duḥ-sandheya, as, ā, am*, difficult to be joined together or united or reconciled. — *Duḥ-sama, as, ā, am*, unequal, uneven, unlucky, unfit, improper, evil, bad, unseasonable; [cf. *duḥ-shama*.] — *Duḥ-samatikrama, as, ā, am*, difficult to be surmounted, insurmountable. — *Duḥ-samīkshya, as, ā, am*, difficult to be observed or perceived. — *Duḥ-sampāda* or *duḥ-sampādya, as, ā, am*, difficult to be reached or attained. — *Duḥ-saha, as, ā, am*, difficult to be borne, unbearable, irresistible; (*as*), m., N. of one of the 100 sons of Dhṛita-rāshṭra; of a son of Puru-kutsa and father of Sam-bhūti; of an evil demon; (*ā*), f. an epithet of Śrī; N. of a shrub (= *nāga-damanī*); [cf. *duḥ-shaha, dur-vishaha, dush-prasaha*.] — *Duḥ-sahāya, as, ā, am*, having evil companions or associates. — *Duḥ-sākshin, ī*, m. a false witness. — *Duḥ-sādhya, as, ā, am*, difficult to be accomplished; difficult to be managed; difficult to be cured; difficult to be conquered. — *Duḥ-sevya, as, ā, am*, difficult to be used or dealt with, hard to be managed, intractable. — *Duḥ-strī*, f. a bad woman. — *Duḥ-stha, as, ā, am*, 'standing badly,' badly fixed, unsteady, disquieted; badly circumstanced, suffering pain or affliction, distressed, unhappy; unwell, ill, badly situated, ill-conditioned, poor, miserable; ignorant, unwise, a fool; (*am*), ind. badly, ill, unwell; in bad circumstances. — *Duḥ-sthita, as, ā, am*, = *duḥ-stha* above; (*am*), n. an improper manner of standing. — *Duḥ-sthiti, is*, f. instability, unsteadiness; ill condition, bad fortune, unhappiness. — *Duḥ-stheya, as, ā, am*, difficult to be stood; (*am*), n. difficult standing or position. — *Duḥ-snāna, am*, n. defective or inauspicious ablution. — *Duḥ-sparśa, as, ā, am*, difficult or unfit to be touched or laid hold of, unpleasant to the touch; (*as*), m. the prickly plant Alhagi Maurorum (= *latā-karañja*); (*ā*), f., N. of several plants, Solanum Jacquini [cf. *kshudra-ḍ*°]; Alhagi Maurorum, Mucuna Pruritus, Cassyta Filiformis. — *Duḥ-spriśa, as, ā, am*, difficult to be touched; [cf. *duḥ-sparśa*.] — *Duḥ-sprishṭa* or *du-sprishṭa, am*, n. slight contact, the slight action of the tongue which produces the sounds *y, r, l, v*; (*as*), m. a sound produced by this slight motion of the tongue. — *Duḥ-sphoṭa, as*, m. 'difficult to be burst,' a sort of weapon. — *Duḥ-svana, as, ā, am*, sounding badly, cacophonous. — *Duḥ-svapna, as*, m. a bad dream. — *Duḥsvapna-darśana, as, ā, am*, seeing a bad dream. — *Duḥsvapna-nāśa, as*, m. the removal of bad dreams. — *Duḥsvapna-nāśana, as, ā, am*, removing bad dreams. — *Duḥsvapna-pratibodhana, as, ā, am*, difficult to be awakened from sleep. — *Duḥsvapnopaśānti* (°*na-up*°), *is*, f. the cessation of a bad dream. — *Duś-ćakshas, ās, ās, as*, Ved. evil-eyed. — *Duś-ćar*, cl. 1. P. *-ćarati, -ritum*, to act wrongly or badly towards (with acc. of person), to behave badly. — *Duś-ćara, as*, *ā, am*, difficult to be gone to or approached, unattainable, inaccessible, difficult to be passed or spent (as time); difficult to be performed or accomplished; going with trouble or difficulty; acting ill, behaving wickedly; (*as*), m. a bear (as moving slowly); a bivalve shell. — *Duśćara-ćārin, ī, iṇī, i*, practising very difficult penance. — *Duśćara-tva, am*, n. inaccessibility, difficulty of being approached or practised. — *Duś-ćarita, as, ā, am*, misbehaving, wicked, abandoned; (*am*), n. misbehaviour, misdoing, ill-conduct, wickedness; (*āni*), n. pl. (with Buddhists) the ten chief sins, viz. murder, theft, adultery, lying, calumny, lewdness, evil speech, covetousness, envy, heresy. — *Duśćaritin, ī, inī, i*, performing wicked actions. — *Duś-ćarman, ā, ā, a*, affected with disease of the skin, leprous; a circumcised man, one whose prepuce is naturally or artificially wanting; [cf. *dauśćarmya*.] — *Duś-ćāritra, as, ā, am*, or *duś-ćārin, ī, iṇī, i*, badly conducted, misbehaving. — *Duś-ćikitsa, as, ā, am*, difficult to be cured, incurable. — *Duś-ćikitsā*, f. (in medic.) wrong treatment. — *Duś-ćikitsita* or *duś-ćikitsya, as, ā, am*, difficult to be cured. — *Duśćikitsya-tama, as, ā, am*, most difficult to be cured. — *Duśćikitsya-tva, am*, n. difficulty of being cured, incurableness. — *Duś-ćit, t, t, t*, Ved. thinking evil. — *Duś-ćintya, as, ā, am*, difficult to be thought about or understood. — *Duś-ćeshṭita, as, ā, am*, misbehaving, doing or designing evil; (*am*), n. evil purpose or action, misconduct, error. — *Duś-ćyavana* or *duś-ćyāva* or *duś-ćyāvana, as, ā, am*, difficult to be felled or brought to the ground, unshaken, unmovable; (*as*), m. an epithet of Indra; (another etymology for the latter meaning is based upon the legend, that Indra having raised his arm to hurl his thunderbolt at Cyavana, had it fixed in that position by the curse of the saint.) — *Duś-ćhada, as, ā, am*, 'covering badly,' forming a bad garment; difficult to be clothed, hardly covered, tattered. — *Duś-ćhid, t, t, t*, difficult to be cut or destroyed. — *Duś-ćhinna, as, ā, am*, badly cut or separated, badly extracted. — *Dush-kara, as, ā* or *ī, am*, difficult or hard to be done or performed or accomplished; difficult to be reached or attained; difficult, arduous (with inf., e. g. *dushkaraṃ kartum*, difficult to perform); difficult to be borne or supported; doing badly or with difficulty, acting badly, wicked, bad; (*am*), n. difficult or painful act, a difficult task, a difficulty; atmosphere, ether; the tree of plenty? (*am*), ind. hardly, scarcely (with following *yadi*). — *Dushkarakāri-tā*, f. the state of experiencing difficulties. — *Dushkara-kārin, ī, iṇī, i*, experiencing difficulties, suffering what is hard to be borne. — *Dushkara-ćaryā*, f. 'the performance of difficulties,' N. of the seventeenth chapter of the Lalita-vistara which describes Śākya-muni as the performer of difficult tasks. — *Dush-karaṇa, am*, n. anything difficult to be done or performed, a difficult task. — *Dush-karṇa, as*, m., N. of one of the 100 sons of Dhṛita-rāshṭra; (also read *duḥ-karṇa*.) — *Dush-karman, a*, n. evil act, crime, wickedness, sin; any difficult or painful act; (*ā, ā, a*), acting wickedly, wicked, criminal. — *Dush-kalevara, as, am*, m. n. 'the bad or miserable body,' i. e. the body considered as the seat of diseases &c. — *Dush-kāyastha-kula, am*, n. the miserable writer-caste. — *Dush-kāla, as*, m. 'bad or all-destroying time,' an epithet of Śiva. — *Dush-kīrtti, is, is, i*, dishonourable. — *Dush-kula, am*, n. a low family or race; (*as, ā, am*), of a low family, low-born; [cf. *daushkulu, daushkuleya, daushkulya*.] — *Dush-kula-tā*, f. lowness of origin, meanness of birth or family. — *Dushkulīna, as, ā, am*, of a low or degraded family or race, low-born; (*as*), m. a sort of perfume, commonly called Chora. — *Dush-kṛit, t, t, t*, Ved. an evil-doer, offender, wicked, criminal. — *Dush-kṛita, as, ā, am*, done wrongly or wickedly, done with difficulty or pain, badly organized, badly applied (e. g. *dushkṛitā pūjā*, badly applied worship); (*am*), n. evil action, misdeed, sin, crime, guilt. — *Dushkṛita-karman, ā, ā, a*, acting wickedly, wicked, reprobate, a criminal; (*a*), n. a wicked deed, wickedness. — *Dushkṛita-vahishkṛita, as, ā, am*, free from sin. — *Dushkṛitātman* (°*ta-āt*°), *ā, ā, a*, evil-minded, wicked, base. — *Dush-kṛiti, is, is, i*, or *dushkṛitin, ī, inī, i*, acting wickedly, an evil-doer. — *Dush-krishṭa, as, ā, am*, Ved. badly ploughed, ill-cultivated. — *Dush-krama, as, ā, am*, difficult of access; going ill; ill-arranged, unmethodical. — *Dush-kriyā*, f. evil act, a misdemeanour. — *Dush-krīta, as, ā, am*, badly purchased, bought too dearly. — *Dush-kha*, see *duḥkha* at p. 418, col. 2. — *Dush-khadira, as*, m. a tree related to the Acacia Catechu (= *khadira*). — *Dush-ṭanu, us, vī, u*, Ved. having an ugly body, having an odious form. — *Dush-ṭara, as, ā, am*, Ved. difficult to be crossed or passed, hard to be overcome, unconquerable, invincible, irresistible; not to be subdued; not to be surpassed or excelled; difficult to be endured; [cf. the later form *dus-tara*.] — *Dush-ṭaritu, us, us, u*, Ved. = *dush-ṭara*; (*us*), m. epithet of Indra; N. of a man. — *Du-shṭuta, am*, n. (for *duḥ-shṭuta*), Ved. faulty recitation of the Stotra. — *Du-shṭuti, is*, f. (for *duḥ-shṭuti*), Ved. a faulty or bad hymn. — *Dushṭhu, us, us, u* (for *duḥ-sthu*), 'standing badly,' ill-behaved, depraved; (*u*), ind. ill, bad; improperly, incorrectly; [cf. *daushṭhava* and *sushṭhu*.] — *Dush-paća, as, ā, am*, difficult to be digested. — *Dush-patana, am*, n. falling badly, (formed to explain *apa-bhranśa*.) — *Dush-pattra, as*, m. a kind of perfume, commonly called Chora; (also read *duḥ-pattra*.) — *Dush-pada, as, ā, am*, Ved. (according to Sāy. = *dush-prapadana*), not to be reached or overtaken. — *Dush-parājaya, as, ā, am*, difficult to be conquered; (*as*), m., N. of one of the 100 sons of Dhṛita-rāshṭra. — *Dush-parigraha, as, ā, am*, difficult to be seized or kept. — *Dush-pariṇāma, as, ā, am*, difficult to be finished or ended. — *Dush-parihantu, us, us, u*, Ved. difficult to be destroyed or disturbed. — *Dush-parīkshya, as, ā, am*, difficult to be investigated or examined. — *Dushparśa*, see *duḥ-sparśa*. — *Dush-pāna, as, ā, am*, difficult to be drunk. — *Dush-pāra, as, ā, am*, difficult to be crossed or passed over; difficult to be accomplished or performed. — *Dush-pārshṇigraha, as, ā, am*, having a dangerous enemy in the rear; (also read *duḥ-pārshṇi-grāha*.) — *Dush-pīta, as, ā, am*, badly drunk. — *Dush-putra, as*, m. a bad son. — *Dush-purusha, as*, m. a bad man; (also read *duḥ-purusha*; cf. *daushpurushya*.) — *Dush-pūra, as, ā, am*, difficult to be filled or satiated or satisfied. — *Dush-prakampa* or *dush-prakampya, as, ā, am*, difficult to be shaken or agitated, immovable. — *Dush-prakāśa, as, ā, am*, 'lighting badly,' obscure, dark. — *Dush-prakṛiti, is, is, i*, evil-natured, bad-tempered. — *Dush-prajas, ās, ās, as* (*prajas* = *prajā*), having bad offspring. — *Dush-prajña, as, ā, am*, having a weak intellect, weak-minded, stupid; [cf. *duḥprajña*.] — *Dushprajña-tva, am*, n. stupidity. — *Dush-prajñāna, am*, n. want of understanding, weak intellect; (*as, ā, am*), Ved. weak in intellect, stupid. — *Dush-praṇīta, as, ā, am*, badly led, badly conducted or trained, ill-managed; (*am*), n. imprudent or impolitic conduct; ill luck, evil fortune; [cf. *dur-nīta*.] — *Dush-pratara, as, ā, am*, difficult to be passed over or crossed. — *Dush-pratigraha, as, ā, am*, difficult to be taken or laid hold of. — *Dush-prativāraṇa, as, ā, am*, difficult to be warded off or averted. — *Dush-pratīvīkshaṇīya* or *dush-pratīvīkshya, as, ā, am*, difficult to be looked at, one whose glance is unbearable. — *Dush-pradharsha, as, ā, am*, not to be assailed or meddled with; difficult to be attacked; secure from assaults, intangible, not to be touched; (*as*), m., N. of one of the 100 sons of Dhṛita-rāshṭra; (*ā*), f., N. of two prickly plants which cannot be touched, = *kharjūrī*, Phœnix Sylvestris; = *dur-ālabhā*, Alhagi Maurorum; [cf. *dur-ādharsha* and *dur-dharsha*.] — *Dush-pradharshaṇa, as, ī, am*, = *dush-pradharsha*; (*as*), m., N. of one of the 100 sons of Dhṛita-rāshṭra; (*ī*), f., N. of the plant Melongena Incurva; [cf. *vārtākī*.] — *Dush-pradharshiṇī*, f. (wrong form for *dush-pradharshaṇī*, according to some) = *kaṇṭakārī*, = *bṛihatī*. — *Dush-pradhṛishya, as, ā, am*, = *dush-pradharsha*. — *Dush-prapadana, as, ā, am*, difficult to be overtaken or attained. — *Dush-pramaya, as, ā, am*, difficult to be measured, immeasurable. — *Dush-pralambha, as, ā, am*, difficult to be deceived; (according to others) difficult of attainment. — *Dush-pravāda, as*, m. calumnious report, slander, defamation. — *Dush-pravṛitti, is*, f. bad news, sad intelligence. — *Dush-praveśa, as, ā, am*, difficult to be entered; (*ā*), f. a kind of tree, = *kanthārī*. — *Dush-prasaha, as, ā, am*, difficult to be borne or supported or suffered, hard to endure or resist, irresistible; terrible, frightful; (*as*), m., N. of a Jaina teacher; [cf. *dush-prasāha, dur-vishaha, duḥ-saha, duḥ-shaha*.] — *Dush-prasāda* or *dush-prasādana, as, ā, am*, difficult to be propitiated or conciliated or appeased. — *Dush-prasādhana* (perhaps wrongly read for *dush-prasādana*) or *dush-prasādhya, as, ā, am*, difficult to be managed or dealt with (as a bad-tempered man). — *Dush-prasāha, as, ā, am*, = *dush-prasaha*. — *Dush-praharsha, as*, m. 'bad rejoicing,' N. of one of the 100 sons of Dhṛita-rāshṭra. — *Dush-prāpa* or *dush-prāpaṇa* or *dush-prāpya, as, ā, am*, difficult of attainment, hard to attain, difficult to be reached, unattainable, remote. — *Dush-prāvī, īs, īs, i*, Ved. difficult of access, unfavourable, unfriendly. — *Dush-prīti, is*, f. displeasure. — *Dush-preksha* or *dush-prekshaṇīya* or *dush-prekshya, as, ā, am*, difficult to be looked at, disagreeable to the sight. — *Dushmanta, as*, m. another form for *dushyanta* below; [cf. *daushmanta, daushmanti, sushmanta*.] — *Dushyanta, as*, m. (a later form for *duḥ-shanta*, q. v.), N. of a prince of the lunar line or descendant of Puru, husband of Śakuntalā and father of Bharata; [cf. *daushyanta* and *daushyanti*.] — *Dushvanta, as*, m. another form for *dushyanta*, q.v.; [cf. *daushvanti* and *duḥ-shvanta*.] — *Dushvapnya, as, ā, am*, Ved. = *duḥ-shvapnya*, q. v. — *Dus-tapa, as, ā, am*, difficult to be endured (as a penance). — *Dus-tara, as, ā, am*, or *dus-taraṇa, as, ī, am*, or *dus-taraṇīya*, or *dus-tāra, as, ā, am*, or *dus-tīrṇa, as, ā, am*, difficult to be crossed or passed over, hard to be traversed, impassable, hard to be subdued, invincible; [cf. the older form *dush-ṭara*.] — *Dus-tarka, as*, m. false reasoning, bad reasoning, wrong argument. — *Dustarkā-mūla, as, ā, am*, founded on false or wrong reasoning. — *Dus-tarkya, as, ā, am*, difficult to be supposed or reasoned about. — *Dus-tosha, as, ā, am*, difficult to be satisfied. — *Dus-tyaja* or *dus-tyājya, as, ā, am*, difficult to be relinquished or quitted. — *Dustha, dusthita, dusprishṭa*, see *duḥ-stha, duḥ-sprishṭa*.

दुस्सथ *dussatha, as*, m. a cock; a dog; (perhaps for *duḥ-saktha*.)

दुस्सनि *dussani, is*, m., N. of a man.

दुह् 1. *duh* (connected with rt. *tuh*), cl. 1. P. *dohati, dudoha, aduhat*, and *adohīt*, to hurt, pain, give pain, distress, torment.

दुह् 2. *duh* (the original form of this rt. was probably *dugh*, cf. *dugha*), cl. 2. P. A. *dogdhi, dugdhe* (2nd sing. *dhokshi, dhukshe*); Impf. P. *adhok* (1st du. *aduhva*); Impv. P. *dogdhu* (2nd sing. *dugdhi*, A. *dhukshva*), *dudoha, duduhe* (3rd pl. P. *duduhus*; Bhāg.-Purāṇa V. 15, 9, *dudūhus*), *dhokshyati, -te, adhukshat, adhukshata*, and *adugdha*: (Vedic and irregular forms are, *dogdhe; dhukshasva; duhām*; 3rd sing. *duhe*; 3rd pl. *duhre, duhate*, and *duhrate; aduhran; dohat; duhus; dhukshan, dhukshata; duhīyat*; part. *duhāna* and *dughāna*); Inf. *dogdhum*, Ved. *dogdhos, dohase*, to milk; to milk out, squeeze out; to extract (as the juice of the Soma); to draw anything out of another thing (with two acc., e. g. *prāṇān duhann ivātmānam*, as it were drawing the life out of himself); to make a profit or extract gain out of anything (with acc.); to enjoy; to give milk (A., in this sense also cl. 4. *duhyati, -te*); to yield milk or any desired object (A.), to grant desires (A.): Pass. *duhyate*, Aor. *adohi*, to be milked, to be drawn or extracted from: Caus. P. *dohayati* (rarely *-te*), *-yitum*, Aor. *adūduhat*, to cause to milk or to be milked, to cause to yield milk or any desired object; to milk, milk out from, extract: Desid. *dudhukshati, -te*, to wish to milk, to wish to milk out or enjoy [cf. *dudhukshu*]: Intens. *doduhyate, dodogdhi*; [cf. Goth. *tiuhan*; Them. *tuh, tiuha, tauh, tuhum*, 'to draw:' Angl. Sax. *tucian, teon, teoge*: Old Germ. *ziuhan, ziug (gaziug), zaugyan*: Mod. Germ. *ziehen*: Lat. *duc-ere*: Hib. *diugaim*, 'I drink off;' *diughailfainn*, 'sucking:' Scot. *deoghail*, 'to suckle.']

3. *duh, dhuk, k, k*, (at the end of a comp.) milking, yielding milk; yielding, granting (e. g. *kāma-d°, go-d°, gharma-d°, ghṛita-d°*, q. v.).

Duha, as, ā, am, (at the end of a comp.) milking; yielding, granting (e. g. *kāma-d°, go-d°*; cf. *dur-duhā*).

Duhat, an, atī, at, milking; yielding, granting, parting with.

Duhitṛi, tā, f. a daughter (either as drawing milk from the mother or as milking the cows, 'the milk-maid of the family'); [cf. Zend *dugh-dhar*; Gr. θυγ-ά-τηρ; Goth. *dauh-tar*; Old Germ. *toh-tar*; Slav. *dush-ti*; Lith. *duk-tē* for *dukter*; the original form must have been *dhugh-atar*.] — *Duhituḥ-pati, is*, m. a daughter's husband, son-in-law. — *Duhitṛi-tva, am*, n. the state of being a daughter, the condition of a daughter. — *Duhitṛi-pati, is*, m. a daughter's husband. — *Duhitṛi-mat, ān, atī, at*, having a daughter, possessing a daughter.

Duhya, as, ā, am, to be milked, milkable.

दुह्यु *duhyu*, a wrong form for *druhyu*.

दू 1. *dū*, generally written *du*. See 2. *du*, p. 418, col. 2.

Dū, ūs, ūs, u, burning with eagerness (?) in *a-dū*; (*ūs*), f. pain, distress. — *Dū-da, as, ā, am*, giving pain, afflicting, harassing.

1. *dūtaka, as*, m. a N. of Agni in the form of a forest conflagration; [cf. *dava* and *dāva*.]

2. *dūna, as, ā, am* (for 1. *dūna* see under rt. 1. *du* at p. 418), burnt, inflamed; pained, afflicted, distressed, fatigued; agitated. — *Dūna-mānasa, as, ā, am*, distressed in mind.

दू 2. *dū* at the beginning of some comps. = *dur* for *dus*, as in the following examples. — *Dū-ḍabha* or *dū-ḷabha, as, ā, am* (fr. *dur* for *dus + labha*), difficult to be deceived, not to be deceived. — *Dū-ḍāś, ṭ, ṭ, ṭ* (fr. *dur* for *dus + dāś*), not offering oblations, not worshipping. — *Dū-ḍāśa, as, ā, am*, Ved. = the preceding. — *Dū-ḍhī, īs, īs, i* (fr. *dur* for *dus + dhī*), Ved. of an evil disposition. — *Dū-ḍhya, as, ā, am*, incorrect form for the preceding. — *Dū-ṇaśa, as, ā, am* (fr. *dus + naś*), Ved. unattainable, inaccessible; [cf. *dur-āśa, dur-ṇaśa, dū-ṇāśa*.] — *Dū-ṇāśa, as, ā, am* (fr. *dus + nāśa*, attainment), Ved. unattainable, inaccessible [cf. *dur-ṇaśa*]; (*as*), m., N. of an Ekāha; (*as, ā, am*), (fr. *nāśa*, destruction), imperishable, not to be destroyed, not ceasing, perpetual. — *Dū-rakta, as, ā, am*, badly coloured or dyed. — *Dū-rakshya, as, ā, am*, difficult to be guarded or preserved. — *Dū-rāḍha, as, ā, am*, difficult to be accomplished. — *Dū-rūḍha, as, ā, am*, badly grown; badly or imperfectly cicatrized. — *Dūrūḍha-tva, am*, n. the state of being badly grown; bad or imperfect cicatrization. — *Dū-roha, as, ā, am*, ascending or climbing with difficulty. — *Dū-rohaṇa, as, ā, am*, difficult to be ascended; (*am*), n., N. of a difficult ritual recitation in which a verse is recited in seven ways, (first only one Pāda, then one half of the verse, then three Pādas, then the whole verse, then three Pādas again, then one half of the verse, and then one Pāda again.) — *Dūrohaṇīya, as, ā, am*, recited or recitable in the manner described above.

दूत *dūta, as*, m. (probably fr. rt. 1. *du*, to go; cf. *dūra*), a messenger, carrier of intelligence, envoy, ambassador, go-between, negotiator, cf. *agni-d°, tvā-d°, yama-d°*; (*ī* or *dūti, is*), f. a female messenger, confidante, procuress, go-between, &c. [cf. *kāma-d°*]; a kind of bird; [cf. *sārikā*.] — *Dūta-karman, a*, n. business or duty of a messenger. — *Dūta-ghnī*, f. 'the killer of messengers,' a plant resembling the Kadamba, = *kadamba-pushpī*. — *Dūta-tva, am*, n. the office of an ambassador, condition of an envoy. — *Dūta-mukha, as, ī, am*, 'having an ambassador as mouth,' speaking by an ambassador. — *Dūta-moćana, am*, n. 'the liberating of a messenger,' N. of the fifty-sixth chapter of the Krīḍā-khaṇḍa or second part of the Gaṇeśa-Purāṇa. — *Dūta-lakshaṇa, am*, n. 'the characteristic mark of a messenger,' N. of a chapter of the Purāṇa-sarva-sva. — *Dūtāṅgada* (°*ta-an*°), *am*, n. 'Aṅgada as messenger,' N. of a play. — *Dūtī-tva, am*, n. the office of a confidante, condition or function of a procuress. — *Dūtī-lakshaṇa, am*, n. 'the characteristic of go-betweens,' N. of a chapter of the Purāṇa-sarva-sva. — *Dūty-upahāsa, as*, m. 'the joking of go-betweens,' N. of the 109th chapter of the Sārṅgadhara-paddhati.

2. *dūtaka, as*, m. (for 1. see col. 1. under rt. 1. *dū*), a messenger, ambassador [cf. *deva-d°*]; (*ikā*), f. a female messenger, go-between, &c.; a gadding, gossiping, mischief-making woman; [cf. *kāma-d°*.]

Dūtikā, f. = *dūtikā* under 2. *dūtaka* above.

Dūtya, am, n. the rank or employment or office of an ambassador; an embassy, a message; [cf. *dautya*.]

दून *dūna*. See col. 1. and rt. 1. *du* at p. 418.

दूप्र *dūpra, as, ā, am*, strong.

दूर् *dūr*, N. of the Prāṇa or vital breath regarded as a deity.

दूर *dūra, as, ā, am* (probably connected with *dūta* and rt. 1. *du*, but said to be fr. rt. *i* with prefix *dur* and affix *ra*, the rt. being then dropped, see Uṇ.-sūt. II. 20; compar. *davīyas*, superl. *davishṭha*, q. v.), distant, far from (with abl. or gen.); remote, long (e. g. *gatvā dūram adhvānam*, having gone a long journey), a long way off; (*am*), n. distance, farness, remoteness, a long way, a long distance. The various cases of *dūra* are used adverbially, as follow: (*am*), ind. far, to a distance, far away, far or distant from (with abl. or gen., e. g. *grāmāt* or *grāmasya dūram*, far from the village), to a great height, aloft, high above; to a great depth below, far below, deeply; highly, in a high degree; *dūram kṛi*, to make distant, distance, surpass, exceed; (*eṇa*), ind. far, in a distant place, far from afar, by far, by a long way; (*āt*), ind. from a distance, from afar, far from (with abl., e. g. *dūrād āvasathāt*, far from the fire-temple), afar, in a remote degree; a long way back, from a remote period; (*e*), ind. in a distant place, far, far away. — *Dūra-ādiś, k, k, k* (for *dūre-ādiś*), Ved. announcing or proclaiming to a distance. — *Dūra-ādhī, īs, īs, i* (for *dūre-ādhī*), whose thoughts are in the distance or far away. — *Dūra-upabdas* (for *dūre-up°*), Ved. sounding to a distance; (perhaps ind.) — *Dūra-ga, as, ā, am*, going far or to a distance, receding, being far, remote. — *Dūra-gata, as, ā, am*, gone far away. — *Dūra-gāmin, ī, inī, i*, going far; (*ī*), m. an arrow. — *Dūra-gṛiha, as, ā, am*, whose house is distant. — *Dūra-grahaṇa, am*, n. seizing or perceiving objects from afar (a supernatural faculty). — *Dūraṅ-karaṇa, as, ī, am*, making far, making distant, removing. — *Dūraṅ-gata, as, ā, am*, gone to a distance, far removed, distant. — *Dūraṅ-gama, as, ā, am*, going far away or to a distance; (*ā*), f., scil. *bhūmi*, one of the ten stages in the life of a Srāvaka. — *Dūra-ćara, as, ā, am*, going to a distance, walking far off. — *Dūra-ja, as, ā, am*, born in a distant place, a native of a distant place. — *Dūra-tara, as, ā, am*, farther; (*e*), ind. at some distance from, far from (with abl.). — *Dūra-tas*, ind. from afar, from a distance, at a distance from, aloof from, far off, afar, far, at a distance; [cf. *a-d°*.] — *Dūra-tā*, f. or *dūra-tva, am*, n. remoteness, distance, farness. — *Dūra-darśana, as, ā, am*, far-seeing; to be seen only from afar; (*am*), n. long-sightedness; foresight; (*as*), m. a vulture. — *Dūra-darśin, ī, inī, i*, far-seeing, long-sighted; (*ī*), m. a vulture, N. of a vulture who was prime-minister of Citra-varṇa; a Pandit, learned man, doctor, teacher; a prophet, seer, sage; [cf. *dīrgha-d°*.] — *Dūra-dṛiś, k, k, k*, far-seeing, long-sighted; (*k*), m. a vulture; a learned man. — *Dūra-dṛishṭi, is*, f. far-sightedness, long-sightedness; foresight, discernment. — *Dūra-pāta, as*, m. a long flight; falling from a great height; (*as, ā, am*), shooting from afar, discharging (missiles) from a distance; [cf. *dūrāp°*.] — *Dūra-pātana, am*, n. the act of shooting to a distance, discharging (missiles) from afar. — *Dūrapāti-tā*, f. or *dūrapāti-tva, am*, n. state or property of taking a long flight. — *Dūra-pātin, ī, inī, i*, flying far, having a long flight, flying a long way; one whose (arrows) fly far, discharging (missiles) to a distance; [cf. *dūrāp°* and *dūreshu-p°*.] — *Dūra-pātra, as, ā, am*, having a wide channel or bed (as a river). — *Dūra-pāra, as, ā, am*, having the opposite shore far off (as a river); very broad; difficult to be crossed, hard of attainment; (*as*), m. a broad river which is difficult to be crossed; (*ā*), f. epithet of the Ganges; [cf. *dush-pāra*.] — *Dūra-bandhu, us, us, u*, having one's kinsmen distant, banished from wife and kindred. — *Dūra-bhāj, k, k, k*, possessing distance, distant. — *Dūra-bhāva, as*, m. farness, remoteness, distance. — *Dūra-bhinna, as, ā, am*, struck or wounded from a distance; wounded deeply. — *Dūra-bheda, as*, m. striking from a distance. — *Dūra-mūla, as*, m. a kind of grass, Saccharum Munjia (= *muñja*). — *Dūram-bhavishṇu, us, us, u*, and *dūram-bhāvuka, as, ā, am*, being far away, proceeding to a distance. — *Dūra-yāyin, ī, inī, i*, going far. — *Dūra-vartin, ī, inī, i*, being in the distance, far removed. — *Dūra-vastraka, as, ā, am*, having the clothes removed, naked. — *Dūra-vāsin, ī, inī, i*, residing in a distant land, outlandish. — *Dūra-vidāritānana* (°*ta-ān*°), *as, ā, am*, having the mouth stretched widely open. — *Dūra-vibhinna, as, ā, am*, 'far-separated,' unconnected by the ties of nature. — *Dūra-vilambin, ī, inī, i*, hanging far down. — *Dūra-vedhin, ī, inī, i*, piercing or striking from afar, missile, projectile (as weapons &c.). — *Dūra-saṃstha, as, ā, am*, being in the distance, remote, distant. — *Dūra-saṃsthāna, am*, n. residing or residence at a distance. — *Dūra-sūrya, as, ā, am*, having the sun distant. — *Dūra-stha, as, ā, am*, or *dūra-sthita, as, ā, am*, or *dūra-sthāyin, ī, inī, i*, situated at a distance, standing afar off, remote, far off. — *Dūrastha-tva, am*, n. the state of being remote. — *Dūra-svarga, as, ā, am*, having heaven distant. — *Dūrād-āgata, as, ā, am*, come from a distance. — *Dūrāntara* (°*ra-an*°), *am*, n. a wide space, a long interval. — *Dūrāntarita* (°*ra-an*°), *as, ā, am*, separated by a wide space. — *Dūrāpāta* (°*ra-āp*°), *as*, m. shooting from afar, discharging from a distance; [cf. *dūra-p°*.] — *Dūrāpātin* (°*ra-āp*°), *ī, inī, i*, shooting or discharging (missiles) from afar; [cf. *dūra-p°*.] — *Dūrāplāva* (°*ra-āp*°), *as, ā, am*, jumping or leaping far. — *Dūrārūḍha* (°*ra-ār*°), *as, ā, am*, mounted high, advanced or reaching far, intense. — *Dūrārtha* (°*ra-ar*°), *as*, m. remote or recondite object. — *Dūrāvasthita* (°*ra-av*°), *as, ā, am*, standing or being afar off. — *Dūrī-karaṇa, am*, n. the act of making distant, removing, placing at a distance. — *Dūrī-kṛi*, cl. 8. P. A. *-karoti, -kurute, -kartum*, to make distant, remove to a distance, expel, banish, distance, exceed, excel. — *Dūrī-kṛita, as, ā, am*, made distant, removed, placed to a distance or afar off. — *Dūrī-bhū*, cl. 1. P. *-bhavati, -bhavitum*, to become distant, move away, retire, go back. — *Dūrī-bhūta, as, ā, am,* become distant, removed, remote, far off. — *Dūre-anta, as, ā, am,* Ved. ending in the remote distance, boundless; (*e*), f. du. epithet of heaven and earth. — *Dūre-amitra, as, ā, am,* Ved. whose enemies are far away. — *Dūre-artha, as, ā, am,* Ved. whose aim is far off; (Sāy.) going far or widely sought. — *Dūre-gavyūti, is, is, i,* Ved. whose range or sphere reaches to a distance or is in the distance. — *Dūre-ćara, as, ā, am,* going or travelling far, being far away, distant, remote. — *Dūre-tya, as, ā, am* (fr. *dūre* with affix *tya,* Pāṇ. IV. 2. 104), being far off, being distant, come from afar. — *Dūre-dṛiś, k, k, k,* Ved. visible in remote places, far-seeing. — *Dūre-bhā, ās, ās, am,* Ved. shining to a distance. — *Dūre-yama, as, ā, am,* one from whom Yama the god of death is distant, one from whom he is far removed. — *Dūreritekshaṇa* (°*ra-īrita-īksh*°), *as, ā, am,* 'one who sends his glances far apart,' squinting, squint-eyed. — *Dūre-vadha, as, ā, am,* Ved. far-striking, hitting at a distance. — *Dūre-śravas, ās, ās, as,* far-renowned; (*ās*), m., see *daureśravasa.* — *Dūre-śruta,* see *daureśruta.* — *Dūreshupātin* (°*ra-ish*°), *ī, inī, i,* discharging or shooting arrows to a distance; [cf. *dūra-pātin.*] — *Dūre-heti, is, is, i,* whose arrows or missile weapons fly to a distance. — *Dūronnamita* (°*ra-un*°), *as, ā, am,* raised aloft, stretched far out.

Dūraka, as, ā, am, remote, distant, &c., = *dūra.*

दूरक्त *dū-rakta, dū-rakshya, dū-roha,* &c. See 2. *dū,* p. 426, col. 1.

दूर्य *dūrya, am,* n. feces, ordure; a kind of Curcuma (= *śaṭī*).

दूर्व *dūrva, as,* m., N. of a prince who was son of Nṛipañ-jaya and father of Ṭimi.

दूर्वा *dūrvā,* f. (said to be fr. rt. *durv*), bent grass, panic grass, commonly Panicum Dactylon; [cf. *ali-d*°, *gaṇḍā-d*°, *granthi-d*°.] — *Dūrvā-kāṇḍa, am,* n. a quantity or heap of Dūrvā grass. — *Dūrvākshī* (°*vā-ak*°), f., N. of the wife of Vṛika. — *Dūrvā-vaṇa* or *dūrvā-vana, am,* n. a thicket of Dūrvā grass. — *Dūrvā-vat, ān, atī, at,* intertwined or joined with Dūrvā grass. — *Dūrvāshṭamī* (°*vā-ash*°), f., N. of a festival on the eighth day of the light half of the month Bhādra on which the Dūrvā is worshipped as a deity. — *Dūrvā-soma, as,* m. a species of Soma plant. — *Dūrveshṭakā* (°*vā-ish*°), f. Dūrvā grass used like bricks in erecting an altar.

दूर्श *dūrśa, am,* n., Ved. a kind of woven cloth or vesture; [cf. *dūśya* and *dūshya.*]

दूलास *dūlāsa, as,* m.(?), a bow.

दूलिका *dūlikā* and *dūlī,* f. the indigo plant; [cf. *tūlī, dolā, taru-dūlikā.*]

दूश्य *dūśya, am,* n. = *dūshya,* a tent.

दूष *dūsha, as, ā, am* (fr. the Caus. of rt. 2. *dush*), defiling, polluting, contaminating, corrupting, (generally at the end of comp.; cf. *kora-d*° and *paṅkti-d*°.)

Dūshaka, as, ikā, am, making bad, corrupting, polluting, contaminating, vitiating, spoiling, violating, dishonouring, disgracing, seducing, making mischief, hurting [cf. *ćarma-dūshikā*]; committing an offence against, offending, trespassing; disfiguring; acting against a command or precept; an offender, a seducer, corrupter, any infamous or wicked person; sinful, wicked (as an action); *Vedānām dūshakas,* one who vitiates or is a disparager of the Vedas; (*ikā*), f. a pencil or paint-brush; impurity or secretion of the eyes, rheum of the eyes [cf. *dūshikā*]; a kind of rice.

Dūshaṇa, as, ī, am, corrupting, spoiling, ruining, destroying, vitiating, contaminating, dishonouring, violating; offending against; counteracting [cf. *arāti-d*°, *kṛityā-d*°, *khara-d*°, *visha-d*°]; (*as*), m., N. of a Rakshas or Rākshasa who was one of the generals of Rāvaṇa; of a Daitya slain by Śiva; (*ā*), f., N. of a deity, the wife of Bhauvana and mother of Tvashṭṛi; (*am*), n. the act of spoiling or corrupting, ruining, vitiating, contaminating, hurting; violating (a contract), breaking (an agreement), dishonouring or violating a woman; slighting, speaking ill of any one, abusing, finding fault, censuring, disparaging, blaming, detracting, throwing doubts upon, criticising, objecting, refuting, rendering suspected; objection, adverse argument; fault, defect, offence, guilt, sin, blame; [cf. *artha-d*° and *dosha.*] — *Dūshaṇāri* (°*ṇa-ari*), *is,* m. 'the enemy of Dūshaṇa,' epithet of Rāma. — *Dūshaṇāvaha* (°*ṇa-āv*°), *as, ā, am,* occasioning guilt.

Dūshaṇīya, as, ā, am, corruptible, liable to be vitiated, &c., = *dūshya.*

Dūshayat, an, antī, at, making bad, corrupting, defiling, &c.

Dūshayāṇa, as, ā, am, vitiating, defiling, spoiling.

Dūshayitṛi, tā, trī, tṛi, or *dūshayitnu, us, us, u,* a corrupter, one who dishonours or deflowers or violates (a girl).

Dūshi, is, is, i, (at the end of comp.) corrupting, ruining, destroying [cf. *arāti-d*°, *ātma-d*°, *kṛityā-d*°]; (*is*), f., Ved. a poisonous substance; (*is, ī*), f. = *dūshikā, dūshīkā,* the rheum of the eyes. — *Dūshī-visha, am,* n. a vegetable poison that ceases to act because it has become old or decomposed (*dūshita*). — *Dūshīvishāri* (°*sha-ari*), *is,* m. a kind of antidote. — *Dūshy-udara, am,* n. a disease of the abdomen caused by poisonous substances. — *Dūshyudarin, ī, iṇī, i,* affected with the above disease.

Dūshita, as, ā, am, corrupted, spoiled, contaminated; violated, hurt, injured; demoralized; disgraced; blamed, censured; calumniated, falsely accused, often at the end of comp., see *manyu-d*°, *śatrūpajāpa-d*°; (*ā*), f. a girl who has been violated or deflowered.

Dūshin, ī, iṇī, i, corrupting, contaminating, violating.

Dūshikā, f. the secretion or rheum of the eyes; [cf. *dūshikā* under *dūshaka, dūshi.*]

Dūshya, as, ā, am, corruptible, liable to be corrupted or defiled or contaminated; liable to be ruined, to be seduced or dishonoured, deserving censure, condemnable; reprehensible, culpable, contemptible, vile, bad; (*as*), m. a wicked man; (*am*), n. matter, pus, poison; (*am*), n. clothes or a kind of cloth; cotton, calico; a tent (in this sense perhaps for *dūśya*; cf. *dūrśa*); (*ā*), f. an elephant's leathern girth; [cf. *ćūshā* and *kakshyā.*] — *Dūshya-yukta, as, ā, am,* associated with a vile rascal.

Dūshyat, an, antī, at, offending, insulting (for *dūshayat* ?).

दूस *dūsa, am,* n. (considered as an affix), milk, (occurring in *avi-dūsa,* q. v.)

दृ *dṛi,* cl. 6. A. *driyate,* &c., to honour, worship, (only occurring with prep. *ā*; cf. *ā-dṛi* at p. 120, col. 1.)

Dṛita, respected, honoured; (*ā*), f. cumin.

दृंह *dṛiṅh* (connected and sometimes identified with rt. *dṛih*), cl. 1. P. *dṛiṅhati, dadṛiṅha, dṛiṅhitum,* to make firm, fix, strengthen, confirm; to make fast, fasten; to fortify; cl. 1. A. *dṛiṅhate,* to be firm or fixed; to grow, increase: Caus. *dṛiṅhayati, -yitum*: Desid. *didṛiṅhishati*: Intens. *darīdṛiṅhyate.*

Dṛiṅha in *bhūmi-dṛiṅha,* q. v.

Dṛiṅhaṇa, am, n., Ved. making firm or fast, strengthening, fastening, fortifying; means of strengthening; [cf. *keśa-d*°.]

Dṛiṅhita, as, ā, am, made firm or fast, fixed, strengthened, fortified; grown, increased.

Dṛiṅhitṛi, tā, trī, tṛi, Ved. one who makes firm, a strengthener.

Dṛiḍha or Ved. *dṛiḷha, as, ā, am,* fixed, firm, hard, strong, solid, massive; firmly fastened, shut fast; tough; difficult to be bent (as a bow), compact; tight, close, dense, without interstices, (opposed to *bhinna*); durable; confirmed, established; not giving way, stubborn; certain, sure, not subject to vacillations; secure; reliable; steady, persevering; great, intense, excessive, severe, violent, mighty, powerful, important; (in mathematics) reduced to the last term or smallest number by a common divisor; (*as*), m. a term in music; N. of a son of the thirteenth Manu; of one of the sons of Dhṛita-rāshṭra; (*ā*), f., N. of a Buddhist goddess, 'the goddess of the earth;' (*am*), n. anything fixed or firm or solid; a stronghold, fortress; iron; (*am*), ind. firmly, fast, much, in a high degree, excessively; thoroughly, very well. — *Dṛiḍha-kaṇṭaka, as,* m. 'having hard thorns,' a kind of plant, = *kshudra-phalaka,* commonly *dhalāṅkaḍā*; (*ā*), f. the wild date tree, Phœnix Sylvestris. — *Dṛiḍha-kāṇḍa, as,* m. 'having a strong stem,' a bamboo; (*ā*), f. a kind of creeping plant, = *pātāla-garuḍī*; (*am*), n. a kind of fragrant grass (= *dīrgha-rohishaka*). — *Dṛiḍha-kārin, ī, iṇī, i,* 'acting firmly,' resolute, persevering, determined. — *Dṛiḍha-krodha, as, ā, am,* having violent anger. — *Dṛiḍha-kshatra, as,* m. 'having strong prowess,' N. of one of the 100 sons of Dhṛita-rāshṭra. — *Dṛiḍha-kshurā,* f. 'having hard blades,' a kind of grass, = *valva-jā.* — *Dṛiḍha-gātrikā,* f. 'having hard particles,' granulated sugar. — *Dṛiḍha-granthi, is,* m. 'having hard knots,' a bamboo. — *Dṛiḍha-grāhin, ī, iṇī, i,* seizing firmly, i. e. pursuing an object with untiring energy. — *Dṛiḍha-ććhada, as,* m. 'having hard leaves,' a kind of fragrant grass, = *dīrgha-rohishaka.* — *Dṛiḍha-ćyuta* or *dṛiḷha-ćyuta* or *dṛiḍhāćyuta, as,* m., N. of a son of Agastya or author of a hymn of the Ṛig-veda; [cf. *dārḍha-ćyuta.*] — *Dṛiḍha-jñāna, am,* n. certain knowledge, firm conviction. — *Dṛiḍha-tara, as, ā, am,* firmer, harder. — *Dṛiḍha-taru, us,* m. 'the strong tree,' Grislea Tomentosa (= *dhava*). — *Dṛiḍha-tā,* f. or *dṛiḍha-tva, am,* n. firmness, hardness, solidity, strength; steadiness, perseverance. — *Dṛiḍha-tṛiṇa, as,* m. 'the strong grass,' a kind of grass, Saccharum Munjia; (*ā*), f. a kind of grass, = *valva-jā.* — *Dṛiḍha-toraṇārgala, as, ā, am,* having the bars of the gates firmly fastened. — *Dṛiḍha-tvać, k,* m. 'having tough bark,' a kind of reed, = *yāvanālaśara.* — *Dṛiḍha-daṅśaka, as,* m. 'having strong teeth or a hard biter,' a shark. — *Dṛiḍha-dasyu, us,* m., N. of an old sage, also named Idhma-vāha, (son of Dṛiḍha-ćyuta; cf. *dṛiḍhasyu.*) — *Dṛiḍha-dvāra, as, ā, am,* having strong gates, having the gates well-secured. — *Dṛiḍha-dhana, as,* m. 'having secure wealth,' an epithet of Śākya-muni. — *Dṛiḍha-dhanus, us,* m. 'having a strong bow,' N. of a prince who was an ancestor of Śākya-muni; (also read *dṛiḍha-hanu, dṛiḍhāśva.*) — *Dṛiḍha-dhanvan, ā, ā, a,* having a strong bow; (*ā*), m. a good archer; (perhaps) N. of a man. — *Dṛiḍha-dhanvin, ī, inī, i,* having a strong bow, a strong or sure archer; (perhaps) furnished with strong archers. — *Dṛiḍha-dhur, ūr, ūr, ūr,* having a strong pole or beam; able to bear a weight or load. — *Dṛiḍha-nābha, as,* m., N. of a spell or formula for restraining magical weapons. — *Dṛiḍha-niśćaya, as, ā, am,* 'having a fixed determination,' certain, confirmed, corroborated, undoubted. — *Dṛiḍha-nīra, as,* m. 'having strong juice,' the cocoa-nut tree. — *Dṛiḍha-netra, as,* m. 'strong-eyed,' N. of one of the sons of Viśvā-mitra. — *Dṛiḍha-nemi, is,* m. 'having a strong circle or wheel (?),' N. of a prince who was a son of Satya-dhṛiti. — *Dṛiḍha-pattra, as,* m. 'having strong leaves,' a bamboo; (*ī*), f. a kind of grass, = *valva-jā.* — *Dṛiḍha-pāda, as,* m. 'firm on the feet,' epithet of Brahmā; (*ā*), f. a kind of plant, = *yava-tiktā*; (*ī*), f. Flacourtia Cataphracta. — *Dṛiḍha-pratijña, as, ā, am,* keeping a promise, firm to a promise, faithful to an agreement. — *Dṛiḍha-pratyaya, as,* m. firm confidence. — *Dṛiḍha-praroha, as,* m. 'growing strongly,' the holy fig-tree (= *plaksha*). — *Dṛiḍhaprahāri-tā,* f. hard striking &c. — *Dṛiḍha-prahārin, ī, iṇī, i,* striking hard, hitting strongly or firmly, shooting surely. — *Dṛiḍha-phala, as,* m. 'having a hard fruit,' the cocoa-nut. — *Dṛiḍha-baddha, as, ā, am,* firmly bound, tied tightly. — *Dṛiḍha-bandhana-baddha, as, ā, am,* caught fast in a snare. — *Dṛiḍha-bandhinī,* f. 'winding closely round a tree or stem,' a kind of creeper, Echites Frutescens (= *śyāmā*). — *Dṛiḍha-bala, as,* m., N. of a medical author. — *Dṛiḍha-bhakti, is, is, i,* 'firm in devotion,' faithful, devoted. — *Dṛiḍha-mati, is, is, i,* firm-minded, strong-willed, firm, devoted. — *Dṛiḍha-manyu, us, us, u,* violent in anger or grief. — *Dṛiḍha-mushṭi, is, is, i,* 'having a hard fist,' close-fisted, one whose hand is difficult to be opened; one who does not open his hand, miserly, niggardly; (*is*), m. a sword, any weapon furnished with a hilt or handle; [cf. *gāḍha-mushṭi.*] — *Dṛiḍhamushṭi-tā,* f. firmness or tightness of grasp. — *Dṛiḍha-mūla, as,* m. 'having a hard root,' the cocoa-nut; a kind of grass, Saccharum Munjia (= *muñja*); another kind of grass (= *manthānaka*). — *Dṛiḍha-rangā,* f. 'having a fast colour,' a sort of white substance, = *sphaṭī,* commonly *phaṭkirī* (sulphate of alumine?). — *Dṛiḍha-ratha, as,* m. 'having a strong chariot,' N. of one of the 100 sons of Dhṛita-rāshṭra; of a son of Jayad-ratha and father of Viśva-jit; (with Jainas) N. of the father of the tenth Arhat of the present Ava-sarpiṇī. — *Dṛiḍharathāśraya* (°*tha-āś*°), *as,* m. 'having a firm chariot-seat,' N. of one of the 100 sons of Dhṛita-rāshṭra. — *Dṛiḍha-ruci,* 'of great glory,' N. of a Varsha. — *Dṛiḍha-latā,* f. 'having strong branches,' a kind of plant, = *pātāla-garuḍī.* — *Dṛiḍha-loman, ā, ā, a,* coarse-haired, having coarse bristles; (*ā*), m. a wild hog; coarse hair, bristles. — *Dṛiḍha-vajra, as,* m. 'having a strong thunderbolt,' N. of a king of the Asuras. — *Dṛiḍha-varman, ā,* m. 'having strong armour,' N. of one of the 100 sons of Dhṛita-rāshṭra. — *Dṛiḍha-valkala, as,* m. 'having a hard bark,' Artocarpus Locucha (= *lakuca*); the areca-palm (= *pūga*). — *Dṛiḍha-valkā,* f. 'hard-barked,' a kind of plant, = *amba-shṭhā.* — *Dṛiḍha-vikrama, as, ā, am,* having great fortitude. — *Dṛiḍha-vīja, as,* m. 'having hard seeds,' Cassia Tora (= *cakra-marda*); Zizyphus Jujuba, = *varvūra,* a kind of plant. — *Dṛiḍha-vṛiksha, as,* m. 'the firm tree,' the cocoa-nut. — *Dṛiḍha-vedhana, am,* n. piercing strongly, striking firmly. — *Dṛiḍha-vairin, ī,* m. a relentless foe. — *Dṛiḍha-vrata, as, ā, am,* 'having firm vows,' strictly observing religious vows or obligations, firm in religious austerity, having a firm resolution, persevering, persistent, strict, firm, faithful, (sometimes used in comp., e. g. *bhartṛi-dṛiḍha-vratā,* q. v.) — *Dṛiḍha-śaktika, as, ā, am,* of great power or great strength of will. — *Dṛiḍha-sandha, as,* m. 'firm or faithful to engagements,' N. of one of the 100 sons of Dhṛita-rāshṭra. — *Dṛiḍha-sandhi, is, is, i,* firmly united, closely joined or allied; strong-knit, thick-set; close, compact, without interstices, well fixed. — *Dṛiḍha-sūtrikā,* f. 'having strong fibres,' a plant from the fibres of which bow-strings are made, Sanseviera Zeylanica; [cf. *mūrvā.*] — *Dṛiḍha-sena, as,* m. 'possessing a strong army,' N. of a prince. — *Dṛiḍha-sauhṛida, as, ī, am,* firm in friendship, constant. — *Dṛiḍha-skandha, as,* m. 'strong-stemmed,' a plant, a sort of Mimusops (= *kshīrikā*). — *Dṛiḍha-sthūṇa, as, ā, am,* having firm posts or columns. — *Dṛiḍha-hanu, us,* m. 'possessing strong jaws,' N. of a prince; [cf. *dṛiḍha-dhanus.*] — *Dṛiḍha-hasta, as,* m. 'strong-handed,' N. of one of the 100 sons of Dhṛita-rāshṭra. — *Dṛiḍhāksha* (°*ḍha-ak*°), *as,* m. 'strong-eyed,' N. of a prince. — *Dṛiḍhānga* (°*ḍha-an*°), *as, ā, am,* firm-bodied, hard-limbed, stout, stalwart; (*am*), n. a diamond. — *Dṛiḍhānutāpa, as, ā, am,* deeply penitent. — *Dṛiḍhāyu* or *dṛiḍhāyus* (°*ḍha-āy*°), *us,* m. 'having a firm life,' N. of a prince; of a son of Purū-ravas and Urvaśī; N. of one of the seven sages of the south; of a son of the third Manu Sāvarṇa. — *Dṛiḍhāyudha* (°*ḍha-āy*°), *as, ā, am,* having strong weapons; (*as*), m. epithet of Śiva; N. of one of the 100 sons of Dhṛita-rāshṭra. — *Dṛiḍhārti* (°*ḍha-ar*°), *is,* f. the strong end of a bow; great pain. — *Dṛiḍhāśva* (°*ḍha-aś*°), *as,* m. 'having a strong horse,' N. of a son of Dhundhu-māra; of a son of Kāśya. — *Dṛiḍhī-karaṇa, am,* n. or *dṛiḍhī-kāra, as,* m. making strong or firm, fixing firmly, corroboration, confirmation. — *Dṛiḍhī-kṛi,* cl. 8. P. A. *-karoti, -kurute, -kartum,* to make firm or fast; to fix, fasten, make strong, strengthen; to fasten tightly together; to corroborate, confirm. — *Dṛiḍhī-bhū,* cl. 1. P. *-bhavati, -bhavitum,* to become strong or fixed. — *Dṛiḍheshudhi* (°*ḍha-ish*°), *is,* m. 'having a strong quiver,' N. of a prince.

Dṛiḍhaya, Nom. P. *dṛiḍhayati, -yitum,* to make firm, to fasten, confirm, strengthen, fortify, intensify; [cf. *draḍhaya.*]

Dṛiḍhavya, as, m., N. of a Ṛishi; (a wrong form for *dṛiḍhāyu,* q. v.)

Dṛiḍhasyu, us, m., N. of an ancient sage, also called Idhma-vāha; [cf. *dṛiḍha-dasyu.*]

Dṛiḍheyu, us, m., N. of one of the seven sages of the west.

दृक *dṛika, am,* n. a hole, opening.

दृकाण *dṛikāṇa* or *dṛikkāṇa* or *drekkāṇa* or *dreshkāṇa, as,* m. (fr. the Gr. δέκανος), the third part of a sign of the zodiac or a demi-god presiding over it.

दृक्कर्ण *dṛik-karṇa, dṛik-karma,* &c. See under 2. *dṛiś,* p. 429, col. 1.

दृक्ष *dṛiksha, as, ī, am,* looking, appearing, having any aspect or appearance; (occurring in comp. with certain pronominal bases, see *amū-d*°, *ī-d*°, *kī-d*°, *tā-d*°; cf. 2. *dṛiś* and *dṛiśa.*)

दृगध्यक्ष *dṛig-adhyaksha.* See under 2. *dṛiś,* p. 429, col. 1.

दृग्भू *dṛigbhū, ūs,* f. a thunderbolt; the sun, a serpent; [cf. *dṛinbhū, dṛimbhū, dṛinphū, dṛimphū.*]

दृङ्नीरज *dṛin-nīraja, dṛin-maṇḍala.* See under 2. *dṛiś,* p. 429, col. 1.

दृडक *dṛiḍaka, as,* m. a fire-place or hole made in the ground for cooking (?).

दृढ *dṛiḍha.* See under rt. *dṛinh* at p. 427.

दृति *dṛiti, is,* m. (said to be fr. rt. *dṛī*; cf. *kṛitti* fr. rt. 2. *kṛit*), a skin of leather, a leather bag for holding water and other fluids; a cloud (Ved.); skin, hide; a pair of bellows; a fish; N. of a man with the patronymic Aindroti or Aindrota; [cf. *dārteya*; cf. also rt. *dṛī*; Gr. δέρ-ω, δείρ-ω, δέρ-μα; Angl. Sax. *teld,* 'a tent;' Old Germ. *gi-zelt* = Mod. Germ. *zelt,* 'a tent.'] — *Dṛiti-dhāraka, as,* m. a kind of plant, = *ānandī,* commonly *āka-napātā.* — *Dṛiti-hari, is, is, i,* carrying a leather skin or leather bags (as cattle); (*is*), m. a dog. — *Dṛiti-hāra, as, ā, am,* carrying a leather skin or bag; (*as*), m. a carrier of skins or bags, a water-carrier, &c.

दृध्र *dṛidhra, as, ā, am* (fr. rt. *dhṛi*), Ved. seizing or fastening tightly.

दृन् *drin,* ind. an interjection; (probably an artificial word made to explain *drinbhū,* q. v.)

दृन्फू *dṛinphū* or *dṛinbhū, ūs,* m. (said to be fr. rt. *dṛimph* or *dṛimp,* q. v.), a thunderbolt; the sun; f. a snake in general; a wheel; [cf. *dṛig-bhū, dṛimphū, dṛimbhū,* and see Gram. 126. *c.*]

दृप् 1. *dṛip* or *dṛiph* (connected with rt. *dṛimp* next col.), cl. 6. P. *dṛipati, dṛiphati, dṛimphati,* &c., to pain, inflict pain, torture.

दृप् 2. *dṛip,* cl. 1. 10. P. *darpati* and *darpayati,* &c., to light, kindle, inflame.

दृप् 3. *dṛip,* cl. 4. P. *dṛipyati, dadarpa, darpitā, darptā, draptā, drapsyati, adṛipat, adrāpsīt* or *adārpsīt, adarpīt, darpitum, darptum* and *draptum,* to be mad; to be foolish; to be extravagant or wild; to be arrogant or insolent; to be vain or proud; to be wildly delighted: Caus. *darpayati, -yitum,* to make mad or proud or arrogant; [cf. rt. *tṛip*; Gr. δόρπος.]

Dṛipta, as, ā, am, mad, wild, proud, arrogant. — *Dṛipta-bālāki, is,* m., Ved., N. of a man with the patronymic Gārgya.

Dṛipyat, an, antī, at, being proud or arrogant.

Dṛipra, as, ā, am, proud, arrogant; strong, powerful.

दृभ् 1. *dṛibh,* cl. 6. 1. 10. P. *dṛibhati, darbhati, darbhayati, dadarbha,* &c., to string together, arrange, tie, fasten.

Darbha, as, m. See p. 403, col. 2.

1. *dṛibdha, as, ā, am,* strung, tied, connected.

Dṛibdhi, is, f. stringing together, arranging.

दृभ् 2. *dṛibh,* cl. 1. 10. P. *darbhati* and *darbhayati,* &c., to fear, be afraid.

2. *dṛibdha, as, ā, am,* afraid, frightened.

दृभीक *dṛibhīka, as,* m. (fancifully derived by Sāyaṇa fr. rt. *dṛī* with 2. *bhī,* 'fear,' and 1. *kṛi*), Ved., N. of a demon slain by Indra.

दृमिचण्डेश्वर *dṛimicaṇḍeśvara,* N. of a Linga; (said to be a various reading for *kṛimi-caṇḍeśvara.*)

दृम्प् *dṛimp* or *dṛimph* or *dṛinph,* cl. 6. P. *dṛimpati* or *dṛimphati,* to pain, inflict pain, torture.

Dṛimphū or *dṛimbhū, ūs,* f. (said to be fr. the preceding rt.), a snake in general; [cf. *dṛinphū, dṛinbhū, dṛigbhū.*]

दृळ्ह *dṛiḷha.* See *dṛiḍha,* p. 427, col. 2.

दृवन् *dṛivan, ā,* &c., or *as, ā, am* (according to Mahī-dh. fr. rt. *dṛī*), Ved. piercing (as an arrow).

दृश् 1. *dṛiś* (this rt. forms the Pres., Impf., Pot., and Impv. fr. a rt. *paś,* said to be a weakened form of rt. *spaś*), cl. 1. P. *paśyati, dadarśa* (rarely *dadṛiśe,* 2nd sing. P. *dadarśitha* or *dadrashṭha,* Ved. *dadṛikshe,* part. *dadṛiśvas* or *dadṛiśivas* or *darśivas,* q. v.), *drashṭā, drakshyati, adarśat, adrākshīt* (Vedic forms *adrāk, adṛikshata, adṛiśram*), *drashṭum,* Ved. inf. *dṛiśe, dṛiśaye,* to see, look at, view, behold, be a spectator; regard, consider; to perceive; visit, wait upon; to see with the mind, learn, know, understand; to notice, inspect; to discover, examine, search, investigate, decide; to see by divine intuition (as the hymns of the Veda, which were said to be 'seen' by the Ṛishis); to look on while anything occurs which cannot be prevented: Pass. *dṛiśyate* (rarely with P. terminations *dṛiśyati*), to be seen, to become visible, appear in sight, be manifested; to appear like, look like, look; to be found, to occur (as in a book); to be regarded or considered: Caus. P. A. *darśayati, -te, -yitum,* Aor. *adīdṛiśat, adadarśat,* to cause any one (acc. or gen. or dat. or also according to grammarians inst.) to see anything (acc.); to show; to point out, prove, demonstrate; to make visible; to produce (as in a court of justice); to pay; (A.) to show one's self, appear, show one's self to any one (acc. or gen. or inst.), show anything belonging to one's self: Desid. A. *didṛikshate,* &c., to wish to see, desire to see: Intens. *darīdṛiśyate, dardarshṭi*; [cf. Gr. δέρκ-ω, ἔ-δρακ-ο-ν, δέ-δορκ-α, δράκοι, ὑπό-δραξ, ὑπό-δρα, δράκων: Goth. *ga-tarh-yan*: Angl. Sax. *torht*: Old Germ. *zorht-yan,* 'to manifest:' Hib. *dearcaim,* 'I see;' *dreach,* 'form, looking-glass:' Lith. *zerkolas,* 'a mirror:' Russ. *serkolo*: Old Pruss. *en-deirit,* 'to consider.']

2. *dṛiś, k, k, k,* (at the end of comp.) one who

sees or views; seeing, viewing; a seer, overseer, superintendent; seeing with the mind, discerning, knowing, looking like [cf. *ī-d°, tā-d°, kī-d°*]; (*k*), f. seeing, viewing, perceiving; sight, view, the eye; the aspect of a planet, the place in which a planet is observed; [cf. *dṛishṭi, a-d°, ahar-d°, tri-d°*, &c.] — *Dṛik-karṇa, as,* m. 'whose eyes are his ears,' a snake, (in the opinion of the Hindūs the snake has no visible external ear); [cf. *dṛik-śruti.*] — *Dṛik-karman, a,* n. an operation by which any planet of a certain latitude (*vi-kshepa*) is referred to a point on the ecliptic, the operation for apparent longitude. — *Dṛik-krodha, as,* m. the wrathfulness of the aspect (of a planet &c.). — *Dṛik-kshaya, as,* m. decay of sight, growing dim-sighted. — *Dṛik-kshepa, as,* m. the sine of the zenith-distance of the highest or central point of the ecliptic at a given time. — *Dṛik-tulya, as, ā, am,* according or coincident with an observed spot (in astron.). — *Dṛiktulya-tā,* f. coincidence or accordance (of a planet) with its observed place. — *Dṛik-patha, as,* m. 'the path of the sight,' the range of the sight; *dṛik-patham i,* to appear, become visible. — *Dṛik-pāta, as,* m. the letting fall a glance, a look; a downward glance. — *Dṛik-prasādā,* f. a blue stone used for a collyrium and the collyrium prepared from it (= *kulatthā, kulatthāñjana*). — *Dṛik-priyā,* f. 'delight of the sight,' beauty, splendor. — *Dṛik-śakti, is,* f. the power of sight, the faculty of perception (comprehending, according to the Māheśvaras, *darśana, śravaṇa, manana, vi-jñāna,* and *sarva-jña-tva*). — *Dṛik-śruti, is,* m. 'hearing with the eyes,' a snake. — *Dṛig-adhyaksha, as,* m. 'ruler of the sight,' the sun. — *Dṛig-gati, is,* or *dṛiggati-jyā* or *dṛig-gati-jīvā,* f. the cosine of the zenith-distance or the sine of the highest or central point of the ecliptic at a given time. — *Dṛig-gočara, as,* m. the range of sight. — *Dṛig-gola, as,* m. = *dṛiṅ-maṇḍala.* — *Dṛig-jala, am,* n. 'eye-water,' tears. — *Dṛig-jyā,* f. the sine of the zenith-distance or the cosine of the altitude. — *Dṛig-bhakti, is,* f. a look of love, an amorous glance. — *Dṛig-ruj, k,* f. disease of the eye. — *Dṛig-lambana, am,* n. vertical parallax. — *Dṛig-visha, as, ā, am,* having poison in the eyes, poisoning by the mere look; (*as*), m. a Nāga or serpent; [cf. *dṛishṭi-visha.*] — *Dṛig-vṛitta, am,* n. a vertical circle. — *Dṛiṅ-nīraja, as, ā, am,* one whose eyes are like the lotus. — *Dṛiṅ-maṇḍala, am,* n. a small circle on the axis of the earth within the greater circles of the armillary sphere, accompanying each planetary circle or orbit.

Dṛiśa, as, m. seeing, looking [cf. *ī-d°, kī-d°, tā-d°*, &c.]; (*ā*), f. the eye; (*am*), ind. = 2. *dṛiś,* at the end of adv. comp. — *Dṛiśākāṅkshya* (°*śā-āk°*), *am,* n. 'the desire of the eye,' a lotus, a species of Nelumbium. — *Dṛiśopama* (°*śā-up°*), *am,* n. 'resembling the eye,' the white lotus, Nelumbium Speciosum.

Dṛiśati, is, f., Ved. looking.

Dṛiśāna, as, ā, am, Ved. seeing; (*as*), m. a ruler, a Loka-pāla or protector of the world, a god presiding over one of the quarters; N. of a Ṛishi with the patronymic Bhārgava; a spiritual teacher; a Brāhman; N. of a demon, also called Vi-ročana; (*am*), n. light, brightness.

Dṛiśālū (?), *us,* m. the sun.

Dṛiśi, is, f. seeing, viewing; (the dat. *dṛiśaye* being used in the Veda as an infinitive; cf. 1. *dṛiś*); (*is, ī*), f. the eye; a Śāstra.

Dṛiśika, as, ā, am, Ved. worthy of regard, conspicuous; (*am*), n. the becoming manifest, appearance; (*ā*), f. appearance; [cf. *čitra-d°* and *dur-d°*.]

Dṛiśenya, as, ā, am, Ved. visible, conspicuous.

1. *dṛiśya, as, ā, am,* to be seen, visible; to be looked at; to be looked at with pleasure, beautiful, pleasing; (*as*), m. (in arithmetic) a given or known quantity or number; (*am*), n., N. of a town; [cf. *a-d°.*] — *Dṛiśya-tā,* f. or *dṛiśya-tva, am,* n. visibility, vision, sight. — *Dṛiśya-pura,* N. of a town, = 1. *dṛiśya,* q.v. — *Dṛiśya-sthāpita, as, ā, am,* anything placed so as to be visible. — *Dṛiśyādṛiśya* (°*ya-ad°*), *as, ā, am,* visible and invisible; (*ā*), f. an epithet of Sinībālī.

2. *dṛiśya,* ind. (ep. for *dṛishṭvā*), having seen.

Dṛiśvan, ā, varī, a, (at the end of comp.) seeing, a seer; conversant with.

Dṛishṭa, as, ā, am, seen, looked at, beheld, perceived, viewed, observed, noticed; visible, apparent, observable; considered, regarded; treated of; appearing, manifested; occurring, found; experienced, suffered, endured; seen in the mind, devised, imagined, learned, known; understood; foreseen; allotted, destined; declared, fixed, determined, decided, approved of, acknowledged, valid; *dṛishṭam bhayam,* a really seen or obvious danger or calamity; (*am*), n. perception, observation. — *Dṛishṭa-karman, ā, ā, a,* one whose actions are seen or proved, tried by practice. — *Dṛishṭa-kashṭa, as, ā, am,* one who has experienced calamity or suffered misery. — *Dṛishṭa-kūṭa, am,* n. a riddle, an enigma. — *Dṛishṭa-tva, am,* n. the state of having been looked at or examined or read (e. g. *Śāstra-dṛishṭatvāt,* because the Śāstras have been examined). — *Dṛishṭa-duḥkha, as, ā, am,* having seen or experienced misfortune. — *Dṛishṭa-dosha, as, ā, am,* found out or detected in a fault, one whose faults are apparent or manifest, regarded as guilty; found out, exposed, detected. — *Dṛishṭa-nashṭa, as, ā, am,* seen and (immediately afterwards) lost to view, appeared and disappeared. — *Dṛishṭa-pūrva, as, ā, am,* seen before. — *Dṛishṭa-pratyaya, as, ā, am,* having confidence manifested. — *Dṛishṭa-bhakti, is, is, i,* whose service has been beheld. — *Dṛishṭa-rajas, ās,* f. a girl arrived at puberty ('who has experienced the menstrual discharges;' cf. *rajas*). — *Dṛishṭa-vat, ān, atī, at,* having seen or beheld. — *Dṛishṭa-vīrya* or *dṛishṭa-sāra, as, ā, am,* one whose strength has been proved or experienced. — *Dṛishṭa-vyatikara, as, ā, am,* one who has seen or experienced a misfortune, one who foresees evil. — *Dṛishṭādṛishṭa* (°*ṭa-ad°*), *as, ā, am,* one who has seen what has not been seen, seen for the first time; seen and not seen. — *Dṛishṭānta* (°*ṭa-an°*), *as, am,* m. n. 'the end or aim of what is seen,' or 'of what is in view,' an example, comparison, illustration, parable, allegory, type; a Śāstra; science; a particular high number; death, dying; [cf. *dishṭānta.*] — *Dṛishṭānta-śataka, am,* n. a hundred examples. — *Dṛishṭāntita, as, ā, am* (fr. *dṛishṭānta*), adduced as an example or comparison, chosen as an illustration. — *Dṛishṭārtha* (°*ṭa-ar°*), *as, ā, am,* having the aim or object apparent, having the scope or meaning obvious, practical, (opposed to *a-dṛishṭārtha,* 'speculative,' and applied to the Upa-vedas which are practical sciences); one who discerns the meaning of anything or has a clear idea about it; one who sees the state of the case. — *Dṛishṭārtha-tattva-jña, as, ā, am,* knowing the true state or circumstances of a case.

Dṛishṭi, is, f. seeing, viewing; seeing with the mental eye; knowing; sight, the faculty of seeing; the eye, look, the sight of the eye, the pupil; (in astrol.) aspect of the stars (e. g. *śubha-d°*, q. v.); the mind's eye, intellect, wisdom, knowledge; consideration, regard; view, notion; (with Buddhists generally) 'a wrong view.' — *Dṛishṭi-kṛit, t,* or *dṛishṭi-kṛita, am,* n. 'suitable to the faculty of seeing,' the plant Hibiscus Mutabilis. — *Dṛishṭi-kshepa, as,* m. 'throwing the sight,' a glance, look. — *Dṛishṭi-guṇa, am,* n. 'an object for the sight,' a mark for archers &c., a target, butt. — *Dṛishṭi-guru, us,* m. 'the lord or master of sight,' an epithet of Śiva. — *Dṛishṭi-gočara, as,* m. the range or compass of the sight; (*as, ā, am*), within the range of sight, in sight, visible. — *Dṛishṭi-nipāta, as,* m. 'falling of the sight,' looking at or on, a look, a glance. — *Dṛishṭi-pa, as, ā, am,* drinking with the eyes. — *Dṛishṭi-patha, as,* or *dṛishṭi-pathin, -panthās,* m. the path or range of sight. — *Dṛishṭi-pāta, as,* m. 'falling of the sight,' a look, a glance. — *Dṛishṭi-pūta, as, ā, am,* purified or kept pure by the sight, i.e. watched that no impropriety is committed or impurity contracted. — *Dṛishṭi-prasāda, as,* m. the favour of a look. — *Dṛishṭi-phala, am,* n. 'the results or consequences of the aspect of the planets,' N. of the seventeenth or eighteenth Adhyāya in Varāha-mihira's Bṛihat-saṃhitā. — *Dṛishṭi-bandhu, us,* m. 'the friend of sight,' a fire-fly. — *Dṛishṭi-maṇḍala, am,* n. the circle or circuit of the sight. — *Dṛishṭi-mat, ān, atī, at,* having eyes or intellect, wise, a connaisseur. — *Dṛishṭi-vāṇa, as,* m. 'eye-arrow,' a glance, leer. — *Dṛishṭi-vāda, as,* m., N. of the last of the twelve sacred writings of the Jainas. — *Dṛishṭi-vikshepa, as,* m. 'casting the eye obliquely,' an oblique look, a side glance, leer. — *Dṛishṭi-vidyā,* f. the science of vision, optics. — *Dṛishṭi-vibhrama, as,* m. 'the wandering of the eye,' a coquettish or amorous glance. — *Dṛishṭi-visha, as, ā, am,* 'having poison in the eyes,' poisoning by the mere look; (*as*), m. a snake.

Dṛishṭin, ī, inī, i, having an insight into or familiar with anything; having the looks or thoughts directed upon anything.

Dṛishṭvā, ind. having seen, having beheld.

दृशद् *dṛiśad, dṛiśad-vatī,* = *dṛishad, dṛishad-vatī* below.

दृषद् *dṛishad, t,* f. (said to be fr. rt. *dṛī*), a rock, large stone, mill-stone, flat stone for grinding condiments upon, the lower mill-stone on which the upper or Upalā rests [cf. *upalā*]; a sacrificial vessel. — *Dṛishadi-māshaka, as,* m. (with the eastern people) a tax raised from mill-stones. — *Dṛishad-upala, am,* n. a grindstone for grinding condiments. — *Dṛishad-vat, ān, atī, at,* having stones or rocks, stony, rocky; (*ān*), m., N. of the father of Varāṅgī who was the wife of Saṃyāti; (*atī*), f., N. of a river which flows into the Saras-vatī, forming the eastern boundary of the Āryāvarta or holy land of the Hindūs, and running to the north-east of Delhi, (also read *dṛiśad-vatī*); N. of several women, (also written *dṛiśad-vatī*); the mother of Ashṭaka and wife of Viśvā-mitra; the mother of Pratardana and wife of Divodāsa; the mother of Śivi Auśīnara and wife of Nṛipa; the mother of Prasena-jit with the epithet Haimavatī (probably as N. of a river); an epithet of Durgā.

Dṛishada = *dṛishad* in comp. (as in *dṛishadolūkhala* (°*da-ul°*), Hari-v. 6509).

Dṛishadya, Nom. A. *dṛishadyate, dṛishadyitā, dṛishaditā,* to be stony (?), Schol. to Pāṇ. VI. 4, 50.

दृष्काण *dṛishkāṇa* (?) = *dṛikāṇa.*

दृष्ट *dṛishṭa.* See col. 2.

दृष्या *dṛishyā,* f. = *dūshyā,* the girdle of an elephant.

दृह *dṛih* (connected with rt. *dṛiṇh*), cl. 1. P. *darhati, dṛiṇhati, dadarha, darhishyati, darhitum,* to fix, fasten, make firm or strong, make immovable; (A.) to be fixed or fastened; to be firm; to grow, increase, prosper: Caus. *dṛiṇhayati,* &c., to make firm, to fix; to keep, hold fast; to become fixed or strong, be firm.

Dṛihita or *dṛiṇhita, as, ā, am,* grown, increased.

दॄ *dṛī,* cl. 9. P. *dṛiṇāti, dadāra* (3rd du. *dadaratus* or *dadratus,* 3rd pl. *dadarus* or *dadrus*), *dartā, darishyati* and *darīshyati, adārīt, daritum* or *darītum,* to burst, break or burst asunder, split open; to cause to burst, tear, rend, divide, sunder, pull to pieces: Pass. *dīryate* (ep. also *dīryati*), to be split, burst, break open; to separate, be dispersed or scattered (as soldiers in a battle); to be afraid, to fear: Caus. P. *darayati, -yitum,* to split, tear, pull to pieces, break open; (in the later language) *dārayati, -te,* &c., to tear asunder, divide by splitting or digging; cause to run away, disperse, scatter: Desid. *didirshati, didarishati, didarīshati:* Intens. *dedīryate, dardarīti* (1st sing. *dardarīmi,* 2nd *dardarshi*), 2nd sing. Impv. P. *dardṛihi* (according to Sāy. also *dādṛihi*), 3rd sing. *dardartu;* 2nd sing. Aor. *adardar, dardar, dard,* 2nd du. *adardṛitam,* 3rd pl. *adardirus,* to rend or tear in pieces, split, &c.

दे de [cf. rt. 5. dā], cl. 1. A. dayate, digye, dāsyate, adita, dātum, to preserve, protect; to cherish, take compassion on: Pass. dīyate: Caus. dāpayati, &c.: Desid. ditsate: Intens. dedīyate, dādeti.

देउलिय deūliya, N. of a Grāma.

देङ्गपाल denga-pāla, as, m., N. of a man.

देदीप्यमान dedīpyamāna, as, ā, am (fr. the Intens. of rt. dīp), shining intensely, glowing, blazing.

देय deya, as, ā, am (fr. rt. 1. dā), to be given or presented, to be granted or allowed; fit or proper for a gift; to be shown; to be given in matrimony; to be delivered; to be returned; to be paid (as a debt, wages, taxes, &c.); to be placed, put, applied, laid; (am), n. a gift, oblation; water (?); [cf. a-d° and bala-d°.] — Deya-dharma, as, m. 'the duty of giving,' charity, beneficence.

देव dev (related to rt. 1. div), cl. 1. A. devate, dideve, devitum, to throw, cast; to sport, play, gamble; to lament; to shine.

1. devana, am, n. (fr. the above rt. or fr. rt. 1. div), lamentation, wailing, grief, sorrow. (For 2. devana see p. 433, col. 3.)

देव deva, as, ī, am (fr. rt. 2. div), divine, celestial, heavenly, (applied in the Veda to devotion, prayer, the human mind, &c., as standing in some relationship to the supernatural world or as being of high excellence, but in the later language occurring rarely as an adjective); (as), m. an inhabitant of heaven, a deity, god, (sometimes applied even to evil beings if superhuman; the gods are often reckoned as thirty-three in number, or eleven for each of the three worlds, cf. tri-daśa; in the Brāhmaṇas they are distributed under three heads, viz. eight Vasus, eleven Rudras, and twelve Ādityas, to which the two Aśvins must be added to make up the number thirty-three; the expression viśve devās, which meant originally 'all the gods,' became the name of a peculiar class of deities, to which the third oblation had to be offered; the Jainas divide the gods into four classes, viz. Bhavanādhīśa, Vyantara, Jyotishka, and Vaimānika); a N. of Indra, the giver of rain; a cloud; the twenty-second Arhat of the future Jaina Ut-sarpiṇī; one occupied with divine things, a god on the earth, a divine man, a Brāhman, a priest; a god among men, a king, prince [cf. kshiti-deva]; a title of honour, 'His Majesty,' 'His Honour,' &c.; a husband's brother, cf. devṛi and devara; a familiar abbreviation of the name Deva-datta. Deva is often found at the end of names of Brāhmans, and at the end of a comp. it may mean 'having as one's deity' (e.g. Purushottama-deva, having Vishṇu as one's deity); at the beginning of a comp. it may mean 'divine.' According to some lexicographers, deva is said to have the following additional meanings, —a fool, a dolt; a child; a man following any particular line or business; a spear-man, a lancer; emulation, wish to excel or overcome; sport, play; (ā), f., N. of two plants, Hibiscus Mutabilis (= padma-ćāriṇī) and Marsilea Quadrifolia (= aśana-parṇī); (ī), f. a female deity, goddess; a N. of Sarasvatī; of Durgā [cf. mahā-deva]; of Sāvitrī; of Ushas; of the nymph Urvaśī; of a nymph beloved by the Sun; of the mother of the eighteenth Arhat of the present Ava-sarpiṇī; a queen, one who has been consecrated as well as the king (in theatrical language chiefly); the daughter of a king, a princess; a respectful epithet or title applied to a lady of the first rank; a kind of bird [cf. śyāmā]; N. of several plants, Sanseviera Roxburghiana, Medicago Esculenta, Trigonella Corniculata, = linginī, = bandhyā, = karkoṭakī, = śāli-parṇī, = mahā-droṇī, = pāṭhā, = nāgara-mustā, = mṛigervāru, = harītakī, = atasī; (am), n. an organ of sense; [cf. Old Pruss. deiwas; Lith. diewas, 'a god;' Lat. deus; Gr. θεός; Hib. dia, 'a god.'] — Deva-ṛishabha, as, m. 'a bull among the gods,' N. of a son of Dharma and Bhānu. — Deva-ṛishi, is, m. 'a Ṛishi among the gods, a divine saint,' an epithet of Nārada; [cf. devarshi and deva-brahman.] — Deva-kanyakā or deva-kanyā, f. a celestial or divine maiden, a nymph. — Deva-kardama, as, m. 'divine paste,' a fragrant paste of sandal, agallochum, camphor, and safflower. — Devakarma-kṛit, t, t, t, doing religious acts, offering oblations or worship to the gods. — Deva-karman, a, n. a religious act or rite or oblation to the gods, worship of the gods; [cf. deva-kārya and deva-kṛitya.] — Deva-kalaśa, as, m., N. of a man. — Deva-kavaća, as, am, m. n. divine armour. — Deva-kāñćana, as, m. (?), 'divine gold,' the tree Bauhinia Purpurea. — Devakātmajā (°ka-āt°), f. 'the daughter of Devaka,' i.e. the mother of Kṛishṇa. — Deva-kāma, as, ā, am, Ved. loving the gods, pious. — Deva-kārya, am, n. = deva-karman, worship of or oblation to the gods, a religious rite in general, anything relating to or coming from the gods, a divine command. — Deva-kāshṭha, am, n. 'divine wood,' a kind of pine, Pinus Devadāru. — Deva-kirī, f. (fr. rt. 2. kṛi), N. of a Rāgiṇī regarded as wife of Megha-rāga; [cf. deva-giri, deśa-karī, goṇḍa-kirī.] — Deva-kilvisha, as, m., Ved. an offence against the gods. — Deva-kīrtti, is, m., N. of an astronomer. — Deva-kuṭa, am, n. 'the house of the gods,' a temple. — Deva-kuṇḍa, am, n. a natural spring. — Deva-kuru, avas, m. pl., N. of a people and the district inhabited by them, (usually associated with the name Uttara-kuru.) — Deva-kurumbā, f., N. of a plant, = mahā-droṇā. — Deva-kula, am, n. = prāsāda, a temple; [cf. daṇḍa-d°.] — Deva-kulyā, f. 'the river of the gods,' personified as a daughter of Pūrṇiman and grand-daughter of Marīći; N. of the wife of Ud-gītha. — Deva-kusuma, am, n. 'the flower of the gods,' cloves. — Deva-kūṭa, 'the divine peak,' N. of a mountain; N. of Adam's Peak. — Deva-kṛita, as, ā, am, Ved. made or done or performed by the gods. — Deva-kṛitya, am, n. a religious act directed to the gods; anything relating to the gods, a divine command. — Deva-kośa, as, m., Ved. divine cask or receptacle. — Deva-kshatra, am, n. divine dominion; (as, ā, am), Ved. under the dominion of the gods; (as), m., N. of a prince who was a son of Deva-rāta. — Deva-kshetra, am, n., Ved. the domain of the gods. — Deva-kshema, as, m., N. of the author of the Vijñāna-kāya; [cf. deva-śarman.] — Deva-khāta, as, ā, am, 'dug by the gods,' i.e. hollow by nature; (am), n. a cave or natural hollow among mountains; a natural pond or reservoir. — Devakhātaka, am, n. a natural pond or one in front of a temple; a natural cavern, a grotto. — Devakhāta-vila, am, n. 'a chasm dug by the gods,' a cavern, a chasm, a natural receptacle of water or reservoir. — Deva-gaṇa, as, m. a troop or class of gods. — Devagaṇa-deva, as, m., N. of a poet. — Deva-gaṇikā, f. 'a divine courtezan,' an Apsaras. — Devagaṇeśvara (°ṇa-īś°), as, m. 'lord of the troop of gods,' an epithet of Indra. — Deva-gandharva, ās, m. pl. the divine Gandharvas (superior to the human Gandharvas; cf. manushya-gandharva); (as), m. an epithet of Nārada; (am), n. a mode of singing; [cf. ćhālikya and deva-gāndhāra.] — Deva-gandhā, f. 'having divine fragrance,' a kind of fragrant medicinal plant (= mahā-modā). — Deva-garjana, am, n. 'celestial roaring,' thunder. — Deva-garbha, as, m. a divine child, the offspring of a god [cf. deva-śiśu]; (ā), f., N. of a river in Kuśa-dvīpa. — Deva-gāndhāra, as or am, m. or n. a peculiar mode of singing, a kind of song [cf. ćhālikya]; (ī), f. one of the Rāgiṇīs or female personifications of the modes of music, who was wife of Śrī-rāga. — Deva-gāyana, as, m. 'a songster of the gods,' a celestial chorister, a Gandharva. — Deva-giri, is, m. 'the divine hill,' N. of a mountain, (periphrastically expressed in Meghadūta 43. as deva-pūrvo giris, and according to a commentator so called because thought to be the domicile of Kārttikeya); N. of the town Daulatābād which is situated between mountains. — Deva-girī, f. (girī fr. rt. 1. gṛī), N. of a Rāgiṇī or one of the female personifications of the modes of music; (according to some) the wife of Vasanta-rāga; (according to others) the wife of Nāga-dhvani who was a son of Hiṇḍola-rāga; (according to others) the wife of Naṭa-kalyāṇa; [cf. deva-kirī.] — Deva-gupta, as, ā, am, guarded or protected by a god or by gods; (as), m., N. of a man. — Deva-guru, us, m. 'the father of the gods,' an epithet of Kaśyapa; 'the preceptor of the gods,' an epithet of Bṛihas-pati. — Deva-guhī, f., N. of a place on the river Sarasvatī. — Deva-guhya, am, n. a secret only known by the gods; [cf. deva-rahasya.] — Deva-gṛiha, am, n. 'the house of the gods,' a celestial or planetary sphere; a temple, chapel, oratory; the palace of a king. — Deva-gopā, ās, ās, am, Ved. 'having the gods for guardians,' guarded by the gods; (ā), f. a divine protectress. — Deva-graha, as, m. a class of demons who cause harmless madness. — Devaṅ-gama, as, ā, am, Ved. going to the gods. — Deva-ćakra, as, m. a divine wheel, a circle of the gods; a peculiar kind of magical circle. — Deva-ćarita, am, n. the course of action or practices of the gods. — Deva-ćaryā, f. worship or service of the gods. — Devaćaryopaśobhita (°yā-up°), as, ā, am, beautified by the service of the gods (as an hermitage). — Deva-ćikitsaka, as, m. a divine physician; (au), m. du. the two Aśvins or sons of Aśvinī who were considered physicians of heaven; see aśvin. — Deva-ććhanda, as, m. a garland or necklace of pearls &c. (composed of 100 or 103 or 81 or 108 strings). — Deva-ććhanda-prāsāda, as, m. a temple consecrated to a god. — Deva-ććhandas, as, n. or deva-ććhandasa, am, n. a divine metre. — Deva-ja, as, ā, am, god-born, born or produced by gods [cf. deva-jā]; (as), m., N. of a prince who was a son of Saṃyama. — Deva-jagdha or devajagdhaka, am, n. a kind of fragrant grass, = kat-tṛiṇa. — Deva-jana, as, m., Ved. the gods collectively, a troop or collection of deities, any collection of superhuman beings (as of serpents; cf. daivajana and itara-jana). — Deva-jā, ās, ās, am, Ved. born or produced by gods; [cf. deva-ja.] — Deva-jāta, as, ā, am, Ved. = deva-jā; (am), n. a class or race of gods. — Deva-jāmi, is, is, i, Ved. peculiar to the gods; (is), f. a sister of the gods. — Deva-jushṭa, as, ā, am, Ved. agreeable to the gods. — Deva-jūta, as, ā, am, Ved. incited by the gods, inspired; gained by the gods. — Deva-tara, as, m., N. of a man; [cf. deva-taras.] — Deva-taratha, as, m., N. of a teacher. — Deva-taras, ās, m., N. of a teacher (with the patronymic Śāvasāyana); [cf. daivatarasa.] — Deva-taru, us, m. 'the tree of the gods,' the divine tree, the holy fig-tree; one of the trees of Svarga or paradise, the tree of plenty, (a general N. for the five trees mandāra, pārijātaka, santāna, kalpa-vṛiksha, and hari-ćandana); the old tree of a village, held sacred by the villagers and usually the place of their assembling; [cf. 2. ćaitya and dyu-taru.] — Deva-tā, f. the state or nature of a deity, divine dignity or power, divinity; a deity or divine being, a god; the image of a deity; an idol; an organ of sense; (ā), ind., Ved. in the nature of a god; among the gods, to the gods; [cf. a-d° and gṛiha-d°.] — Devatāgāra (°tā-āg°) or devatā-gṛiha, am, n. 'the house of the gods,' a temple, chapel. — Devatā-jit, t, m. 'the conqueror of a deity,' N. of a son of Sumati and grandson of Bharata. — Deva-tāḍa, as, m. a kind of grass, Lipeocercis Serrata, (also deva-tāḍī, f. and deva-tāḍaka, as, m.); (as), m. = ghoshaka, Luffa Fœtida or a similar plant; fire; an epithet of Rāhu; [cf. tāḍa and deva-dālī.] — Deva-tāt, f. (occurring only in dat. and loc.), Ved. divine service. — Deva-tāti, is, f., Ved. = deva-tāt, divine service; divinity, the gods collectively. — Devatātmā (°tā-āt°), f. the mother of the gods; [cf. devātmā.] — Devatādhipa (°tā-adh°), as, m. 'the ruler or chief of the gods,' an epithet of Indra. — Devatādhyāya (°tā-adh°), am, n., scil. brāhmaṇa, N. of a Brāhmaṇa. — Devatānukrama (°tā-an°), as, m. or devatānukramaṇī, f. an index of the deities to which the hymns of the Vedas are addressed. — *Devatā-pratimā*, f. the image of a god, an idol. — *Devatābhyarćana* (°*tā-abh*°), *am*, n. the act of worshipping an idol, worship of a deity. — *Devatābhyarćana-para, as, ā, am*, devoted to the worship of a deity. — *Devatā-maya, as, ī, am*, containing all the gods, made up of all the deities. — *Devatā-mithuna, am*, n. the cohabitation of deities. — *Devatāyatana* (°*tā-āy*°), *am*, n. or *devatālaya* (°*tā-āl*°), *as*, m. or *devatā-veśman, a*, n. the dwelling or sanctuary of a god, a temple, chapel. — *Devatā-snāna, am*, n. the ablution of an idol. — *Deva-tīrtha, am*, n. 'the Tīrtha of the gods,' N. of a bathing-place; the right moment for the (worship of the) gods; the part of the hands sacred to the gods, i. e. the tips of the fingers. — *Deva-tta, as, ā, am* (*tta* = *datta*, Gram. 533. *a*), Ved. given by the gods. — *Deva-trā*, ind., Ved. among the gods, to the gods. — *Deva-tva, am*, n. the state of a deity, divinity, the abstract attribute of divine being, divine dignity; identification with a deity, deification. — *Deva-datta, as, ā, am*, given by the gods, god-given, granted by the gods; (*as*), m., N. of the conch-shell of Arjuna; one of the vital airs, that which is exhaled in yawning; a common N. for men, (often used in grammatical and other examples and then equivalent to 'any one,' 'a certain person, &c.'); N. of a cousin of Śākya-muni; of a son of Uru-śravas and father of Agniveśya; of a son of the Brāhman Govinda-datta; of a son of Hari-datta; of a son of the king Jaya-datta; of the author of a commentary; of a Nāga; of a Grāma of the Bāhīkas; (*ā*), f., N. of the mother of Deva-datta who was the cousin of Śākya-muni. — *Devadattaka, ās*, m. pl. the band led by Deva-datta. — *Devadattāgraja* (°*ta-ag*°), *as*, m. 'the elder brother of Deva-datta,' an epithet of Śākya-muni. — *Deva-dattīya, ās*, m. pl. the pupils of Deva-datta. — *Deva-dantin, ī*, m. an epithet of Śiva? (see Kathā-sarit-s. III. 5). — *Deva-darśa, as*, m., N. of a teacher of the Atharva-veda. — *Deva-darśana, as, ā, am*, seeing the gods, visiting them, familiar with them; (*as*), m. an epithet of Nārada. — *Deva-darśin, ī, inī, i*, seeing the gods, having intercourse with them; (*inas*), m. pl., N. of a school of the Atharva-veda. — *Deva-dānī*, f. a species of creeper, = *ghoshakākṛiti*. — *Deva-dāru, us*, m. a species of pine, Pinus Deodora or Deodar; (in Bengal it is usually applied to the Uvaria Longifolia, and in the peninsula to another tree, Erythrosylon Sideroxyloides.) — *Devadāru-maya, as, ī, am*, made of the wood of the Deva-dāru tree. — *Deva-dālikā* or *deva-dālī*, f. a kind of cucurbitaceous plant; [cf. *dālikā* and *mahā-kāla*.] — *Deva-dāsa, as*, m. a servant of a god or of the gods (especially slaves or servants who serve in a temple or Buddhist monastery); N. of the son of a merchant who was the brother of Śārṅga-dhara's mother; N. of the son of a Kāli-dāsa; (*ī*), f. a courtezan (especially one employed as a dancer &c. in a temple); the wild citron tree (= *vana-vīja-pūraka*; cf. *deva-dūtī*). — *Deva-dāsa-deva, as*, m., N. of a poet, (perhaps the brother of Śārṅga-dhara's mother.) — *Deva-dīpa, as*, m. 'the lamp of the gods,' 'the divine light,' the eye; [cf. *daiva-dīpa* and *deha-dīpa*.] — *Deva-dundubhi, is*, m. a divine or celestial drum; holy basil with red flowers; an epithet of Indra. — *Deva-dūta* or *deva-dūtaka, as*, m. a messenger of the gods, a divine envoy, an angel; (*ī*), f. a female messenger of the gods, the wild citron tree. — *Deva-deva, as*, m. ('the god of the gods'), 'the chief of the gods,' epithet of Brahmā; of Rudra or Śiva; of Kṛishṇa or Vishṇu; of Gaṇeśa; (*ās*), m. pl. epithet of the Brāhmans. — *Devadeveśa* (°*va-īś*°), *as*, m. 'the lord among the chiefs of the gods,' epithet of Śiva; [cf. *deveśa*.] — *Deva-dyumna, as*, m., N. of a son of Devatā-jit and father of Parameshṭhin. — *Deva-droṇī*, f. an idol procession, a procession with idols, (originally perhaps 'the ablution of idols;' cf. *droṇi*.) — *Devadryańć* (fr. *deva* and rt. *ańć*), *aṅ, drīćī, ak*, 'turned towards or approaching the gods,' adoring a deity. — *Deva-dharma, as*, m. a religious duty or office. — *Deva-dhānī*, f. 'the residence of the gods,' N. of Indra's city on the Mānasottara, to the east of Meru. — *Deva-dhānya, am*, n. 'god's grain,' a sort of grain cultivated in many parts of Hindūstān, Andropogon Saccharatus, Andropogon or Holcus Sorghum (commonly *dedhān, jo-ār*). — *Deva-dhūpa, as*, m. a fragrant resin or bdellium used for incense. — *Deva-nakshatra, as*, m., N. of a prince, (a various reading for *deva-kshatra*); (*am*), n., N. of the first fourteen Nakshatras on the southern quarter, (opposed to the Yama-nakshatras on the northern.) — *Deva-nadī*, f. 'the divine river,' epithet of several sacred rivers. — *Deva-nandin, ī*, m., N. of one of Indra's door-keepers. — *Deva-nala, as*, m. a kind of reed, Arundo Bengalensis; [cf. *deva-nāla*.] — *Deva-nāgarī*, f. 'the divine city writing,' N. of the character in which Sanskrit is usually written, (probably from its having originated in some city.) — *Deva-nātha, as*, m. 'the lord of the gods,' an epithet of Śiva. — *Deva-nābha, as*, m., N. of a man. — *Deva-nāma, a*, n. the N. of a god. — *Deva-nāman, ā*, m. 'having divine names,' N. of the seven Varshas in Kuśa-dvīpa. — *Deva-nāyaka, as*, m., N. of a man. — *Deva-nāla, as*, m. = *deva-nala*, q. v. — *Deva-nikāya, as, ā, am*, living with the gods or in heaven; (*as*), m. the residence of a divinity, a paradise, heaven. — *Deva-nid, t, t, t*, Ved. hating the gods, a god-hater. — *Deva-nindaka, as*, m. a reviler of the gods, a heretic, an unbeliever, atheism. — *Deva-nindā*, f. reviling the gods, infidelity, heresy, atheism. — *Deva-nirmita, as, ā, am*, 'god-made,' god-created, natural. — *Deva-nītha, as*, m. a formula consisting of seventeen Pādas. — *Deva-pańćarātra, as*, m., N. of a Pańćāha. — *Deva-pati, is*, m. 'the lord of the gods,' an epithet of Indra; (*ayas*), m. pl. the most excellent of the gods. — *Devapati-mantrin, ī*, m. 'Indra's counsellor,' an epithet of Bṛihas-pati, the planet Jupiter. — *Deva-patnī*, f. having a god as husband; (*ī*), f. the wife of a deity; sweet potato (= *madhv-āluka*). — *Deva-patha, as*, m. the way of the gods, the celestial path or way, heaven, the firmament; N. of a place of pilgrimage. — *Devapatha-tīrtha, am*, n. 'the Tīrtha of the way to heaven,' N. of a particular Tīrtha. — *Devapathīya, as, ā, am*, relating to or coming from Deva-patha above. — *Deva-pada* or *deva-pāda, am*, n. the foot of a god or king, the royal presence, a honorific term for a king, = 'His Majesty.' — *Deva-parishad, t*, f. an assembly of deities. — *Deva-parṇa, am*, n. 'the divine leaf,' N. of a medicinal plant (= *sura-parṇa*). — *Deva-pallī-paṭṭana, as* or *am*, m. or n. (?), N. of a place. — *Deva-paśu, us*, m. any animal consecrated to a deity. — *Deva-pātra, am*, n. 'cup of the gods,' a divine drink. — *Deva-pāda*, see *deva-pada*. — *Deva-pāna, as, ā, am*, Ved. constituting the beverage of the gods, drunk by the gods. — *Deva-pāla, as*, m. 'god-defender,' N. of several princes; N. of a mountain. — *Deva-pālita, as*, m. 'god-protected,' N. of a man. — *Deva-pīyu, us, us, u*, Ved. reviling or despising the gods. — *Deva-putra, as*, m. the son of a god; (*ī* or *ikā*), f. a kind of plant, = *pṛikkā*; (*as, ā, am*), having gods as children. — *Devaputra-māra, as*, m., N. of one of the four Buddhist Māras. — *Deva-pur, ūr*, f., Ved. 'the city of the gods,' a divine fortress, the residence of Indra. — *Deva-pura, am*, n. 'the city of the gods,' the residence of Indra (= *amara-vatī*). — *Deva-purā*, f., Ved. a divine fortress, a stronghold of the gods. — *Deva-pūjaka, as*, m. a worshipper of the gods. — *Deva-pūjā*, f. worship of the gods. — *Deva-pūjya, as*, m. 'to be honoured by the gods,' an epithet of Bṛihas-pati, the planet Jupiter. — *Deva-pratikṛiti, is*, f. or *deva-pratimā*, f. the image of a deity, an idol. — *Deva-pratishṭhā-tattva, am*, n., N. of a work. — *Deva-prayāga, as*, m. 'the divine place of sacrifice,' N. of a sacred bathing-place. — *Deva-praśna, as*, m. enquiring of the gods, consulting the deities, fortune-telling, astrology; [cf. *daiva-praśna*.] — *Deva-prasāda, as*, m. 'having the divine favour,' N. of a man. — *Deva-prasūta, as, ā, am*, Ved. produced by the gods. — *Deva-prastha, as*, m., N. of the city of Sena-vindu. — *Deva-priya, as, ā, am*, 'dear to the gods,' an epithet of Śiva; (*as*), m., N. of two plants, = *pīta-bhṛiṅga-rāja* and *vaka-pushpa*. — *Deva-psarastama, as, ā, am*, Ved. very pleasing to the gods or propitiatory of the gods. — *Deva-badhū, ūs*, f. the wife of a god. — *Deva-bandhu, us, us, u*, Ved. related to the gods; (*us*), m., N. of a Ṛishi. — *Deva-balā*, f. 'having divine strength,' N. of a plant, a kind of Balā, = *mahā-balā, jyeshṭha-balā, saha-devī*. — *Deva-bali, is*, m. an oblation to the gods; (also read *deva-vali*, q. v.) — *Deva-bāhu, us*, m. 'the arm of the gods,' N. of an ancient Ṛishi; of a son of Hṛidīka. — *Deva-bodha, as*, m. 'having the knowledge of the gods,' N. of a commentator on the Mahā-bhārata. — *Deva-bodhi, is*, m. 'god-inspired,' N. of a poet. — *Devabodhi-sattva, as*, m., N. of a Buddhist saint. — *Deva-brahman, ā*, m. 'a Brāhman among the gods,' an epithet of Nārada; [cf. *deva-ṛishi*.] — *Deva-brāhmaṇa, as*, m. a Brāhman esteemed by the gods, a venerable Brāhman. — *Devabrāhmaṇa-nindaka, as*, m. a despiser of the gods and Brāhmans. — *Deva-bhakta, as, ā, am*, Ved. distributed by the gods. — *Deva-bhakti, is*, f. the service of the gods, religion, piety. — *Deva-bhavana, am*, n. 'the residence of the gods,' heaven, paradise; a temple; the holy fig-tree (= *aśvattha*). — *Deva-bhāga, as*, m. 'the portion or allotment of the gods,' the northern hemisphere, (opposed to *asura-bhāga*, the southern hemisphere); N. of a teacher with the epithet Śrauta or Śrautarsha; N. of a son of Śūra and brother of Vasu-deva. — *Deva-bhīti, is*, f. fear of the gods. — *Deva-bhū, ūs*, m. a divine being, a god, a deity; Svarga or paradise. — *Deva-bhūta, as, ā, am*, become a god. — *Deva-bhūti, is*, m., N. of the last prince of the Suṅga dynasty; (*is*), f. the Gaṅgā of the sky. — *Deva-bhūmi, is*, m. 'having a divine domain,' = *deva-bhūti*. — *Deva-bhūya, am*, n. divinity, godhead; inferior deification or identification with a deity. — *Deva-bhojya, am*, n. 'the food of the gods,' Amṛita, nectar. — *Deva-bhrāj, ṭ*, m. 'shining like a god,' N. of a son of Mahya, son of Vivas-vat (i. e. of the Sun). — *Deva-mańjara, am*, n. the jewel of Vishṇu or Kṛishṇa suspended on his breast; [cf. *kaustubha*.] — *Deva-maṇi, is*, m., Ved. a divine amulet; the jewel on Kṛishṇa's breast; a twist of hair on a horse's neck; N. of a drug belonging to the Ashṭa-varga (= *mahā-medā*); an epithet of Śiva. — *Deva-mata, as*, m. 'god-approved,' N. of a Ṛishi; [cf. *daivamati*.] — *Deva-maya, as, ī, am*, containing the gods, made up of all the gods. — *Deva-malimluć, k*, m., N. of an Asura. — *Deva-māta, as*, m., N. of a man. — *Deva-mātṛi, tā*, f. 'the mother of the gods,' an epithet of Aditi (= *dākshāyaṇī*). — *Deva-mātṛika, as, ā, am*, fostered or watered by the clouds (or by Indra, the giver of rain), as corn, land, &c., deprived of every other kind of water ('having the clouds as foster-mother;' cf. *nadī-mātṛika*.) — *Deva-mādana, as, ā, am*, Ved. 'gladdening or inspiring the gods,' an epithet of Soma. — *Deva-māna, am*, n. the residence of the gods, dwelling of the gods. — *Deva-mānaka, as*, m. = *deva-maṇi*. — *Deva-māyā*, f. an illusion created by a god or gods. — *Deva-mārga, as*, m. 'the way of the gods,' (according to commentators a facetious expression for the penis or anus.) — *Deva-māsa, as*, m. 'the divine month or month of the gods,' the eighth month of pregnancy. — *Deva-mitra, as, ā, am*, having the gods as friends; (*as*), m., N. of an ancient preceptor with the epithet Śākalya; of the father of Vishṇu-putra of the family of Vatsa [cf. *daivamitri*]; (*ā*), f., N. of one of the Mātṛis attending on Skanda. — *Deva-mithuna, am*, n., Ved. cohabitation of the gods. — *Deva-miśra, as*, m., N. of a man. — *Deva-mīḍha, as*, m., N. of a Yādava, grandfather of Vasu-deva; of a descendant of Nimi and Jaraka. — *Deva-mīḍhusha, as*, m. the grandfather of Vasu-deva. — *Deva-muni, is*, m. a heavenly or divine Muni; N. of a son of Irammada and author of a hymn of the Ṛig-veda. — *Deva-yaj, k, k, k*, or *ī, ī, ī* (?), making oblations or sacrifices to the gods, a worshipper of the gods. — *Deva-yajana, as, ī, am,* Ved. worshipping the gods, making oblations to them; serving for an oblation or constituting an oblation to the gods; (*am*), n. the place where a sacrifice is performed. — *Deva-yaji, is, is, i,* worshipping the gods, making oblations or sacrificing to them; (*is*), m. a worshipper of the gods; a Muni. — *Deva-yajña, as,* m. a sacrifice to the superior gods performed by oblations to Fire or through Fire to the other gods; the Homa or burnt sacrifice (one of the five great sacrifices mentioned in Manu III. 84, 85); N. of a man. — *Deva-yajya, am,* n. or *deva-yajyā,* f. (inst. *-yajyā*), Ved. worshipping the gods, a sacrifice. — *Deva-yā, ās, ās, am,* Ved. going to the gods, desirous of them, honouring them. — *Deva-yājin, ī, inī, i,* making sacrifices to the gods; (*ī*), m., N. of one of the attendants of Skanda; N. of a Dānava. — *Deva-yājñika, as,* m., N. of an author, = *yājñika-deva.* — *Deva-yātu, us,* m. 'a heavenly Yātu,' N. of a class of Yātus; (also read *deva-yāta;* cf. *daiva-yātaka* and *daivayātavaka.*) — *Deva-yātrā,* f. an idol procession, any sacred festival when the images of gods are carried in procession. — *Devayātrin, ī,* m., N. of a Dānava; [cf. *deva-yājin.*] — *Deva-yāna, as, ī, am,* Ved. going to the gods, following them; serving as a way to the gods (especially applied to the paths by which the gods descend from heaven, and sacrifices ascend to them), the ways leading to the gods; (*am*), n. the car or vehicle of a god; (*ī*), f., N. of a daughter of Uśanas or wife of Yayāti and mother of Yadu and Turvasu. — *Deva-yāvan, ā, varī, a,* Ved. going to the gods. — *Deva-yukta, as, ā, am,* Ved. yoked by the gods (as horses). — *Deva-yuga, am,* n. 'the age of the gods,' the first age of the world; any age or period of the gods comprising the four ages of mankind, (two of these ages or Yugas form a day and night of Brahmā; cf. *kṛita-yuga.*) — *Deva-yoni, is,* m. f. the place of origin of a god, a divine birthplace; epithet of the wood used for kindling fire; (*is, is, i*), of divine origin; (*is*), m. a being of divine origin; a superhuman being, a demi-god or demon. — *Deva-yoshā,* f. the wife of a god. — *Deva-rakshita, as, ā, am,* guarded by a god or by the gods; (*as*), m., N. of a son of Devaka; of a prince of the Kośalas; (*ā*), f., N. of a daughter of Devaka and one of the wives of Vasu-deva. — *Deva-rata, as, ā, am,* Ved. delighting in the gods, pious. — *Deva-ratha, as,* m. the car or vehicle of a deity, a car for carrying the images of the gods in a procession [cf. *dairaratha*]; N. of a man. — *Devarathāhnya, am,* n. a day's journey for the chariot of a god (of the Sun). — *Deva-rahasya, am,* n. a secret of the gods, divine mystery; [cf. *deva-guhya.*] — *Deva-rāj, ṭ,* m. 'the king of the gods,' an epithet of Indra; of Nahusha. — *Deva-rāja, as,* m. a divine ruler; king of the gods; an epithet of Indra; of a king; of a Ṛishi; of a Buddha; of a commentator on the Naighaṇṭuka; (the full name is *devarāja-yajvan,* q. v.; cf. *daivarājaka* and *daivarājika.*) — *Deva-rājan, ā,* m. a prince of a Brāhmanical family. — *Devarāja-yajvan, ā,* m., N. of a commentator on the three chapters of Vedic synonyms, usually called the Naighaṇṭuka portion of the Nighaṇṭus, incompletely explained by Yāska; N. of the grandfather of this commentator. — *Devarāja-samadyuti, is, is, i,* equal in glory to the king of the gods. — *Deva-rājya, am,* n. sovereignty over the gods; [cf. *daivarājya.*] — *Deva-rāta, as, ā, am,* 'god-given;' (*as*), m. the N. given to Sunaḥ-śepha after being received into the family of Viśvā-mitra; (*ās*), m. pl. the descendants of Sunaḥ-śepha; N. of a king who was the son of Su-ketu and descendant of Nimi; N. of a king who was the son of Karambhi; an epithet of Parikshit [cf. *dairarāti*]; a sort of crane. — *Deva-rāshṭra, am,* n. the empire of the gods; N. of an empire in the Dekhan. — *Deva-rūpin, ī, iṇī, i* (fr. *deva-rūpa*), of divine form, godlike. — *Devarshi* (*deva-ṛishi*), *is,* m. a Ṛishi, a saint of the celestial class, as Nārada, Atri, Marīći, Bharad-vāja, Pulastya, Pulaha, Kratu, Bhṛigu, Vasishṭha, Pra-ćetas, Bharata, Kaṇāda, and others. — *Devarshi-tva, am,* n. state or rank of a divine Ṛishi. — *Devarshi-varya, as,* m. chief of sages. — *Deva-latā,* f. double jasmine (= *nava-mallikā*). — *Deva-lāṅgulikā,* f., N. of a plant; [cf. *vriśćikālī.*] — *Deva-liṅga, am,* n. the image or statue of a deity. — *Deva-lekhā,* f., N. of a princess. — *Deva-loka, as,* m. the particular sphere or heaven of any divinity; heaven or paradise; any one of the seven superior worlds (from the earth to the highest or Satya-loka, in opposition to those below the earth; *deva-loke gata,* gone to the world of the gods, one who has died). — *Deva-vaktra, am,* n. 'the mouth of the gods,' an epithet of fire or its deity Agni (as eating or consuming the oblations made to the gods). — 1. *deva-vat, ān, atī, at,* guarded by the gods, surrounded by them, (also read *devā-vat*); (*ān*), m., N. of the grandfather of Su-dās; of a son of A-krūra; of Devaka who was a son of Āhuka; of the twelfth Manu; [cf. *deva-vāyu.*] — 2. *deva-vat,* ind. like a god. — *Deva-vadha, as,* m., Ved. a weapon of the gods. — *Deva-vadhū, ūs,* f. the wife of a god. — *Deva-vanda, as, ā, am,* Ved. praising the gods. — *Deva-vara, as,* m. a superior or supreme deity; (*am*), n. a divine boon or blessing. — *Deva-vartman, a,* n. 'the path of the gods,' the atmosphere. — *Deva-vardhaki, is,* m. 'the builder or architect of the gods,' an epithet of Viśva-karman or of Tvashṭṛi the carpenter of the gods. — *Deva-vardhana, as,* m., N. of a son of Devaka. — *Deva-varman, a,* n. the armour of the gods, divine armour. — *Deva-varsha, as* or *am,* m. or n. (?), N. of a Varsha in the Dvīpa Sālmala. — *Deva-vallabha, as,* m. the tree Rottlera Tinctoria. — *Deva-vāṇī,* f. a divine voice, a voice from heaven. — *Deva-vāta, as, ā, am,* Ved. agreeable to the gods; (*as*), m., N. of a Bhārata; [cf. *daivavāta.*] — *Deva-vāyu, us,* m., N. of the son of the twelfth Manu; [cf. 1. *deva-vat.*] — *Deva-vāhana, as, ā, am,* Ved. carrying the gods (as a horse). — *Deva-vid, t, t, t,* knowing the gods. — *Deva-vidyā,* f. the doctrine or science of the gods, divine science; (according to a commentator = *nirukta,* q. v.) — *Deva-vibhāga, as,* m. the division or quarter of the gods, the northern hemisphere; [cf. *deva-bhāga.*] — *Deva-viś, ṭ,* or *deva-viśā,* f., Ved. a divine person, a deity, the gods collectively. — *Deva-vī, īs, īs, i,* Ved. gratifying the gods. — *Devavī-tama, as, ā, am,* Ved. very much liked by the gods. — *Deva-vīti, is,* f., Ved. a feast or meal or enjoyment prepared for the gods; N. of one of the nine daughters of Meru and wife of one of the nine sons of Agnīdhra. — *Deva-vṛiksha, as,* m. 'the divine tree,' a common N. of the Mandāra and other fabulous trees of heaven or paradise; the tree Alstonia Scholaris; a plant yielding a fragrant resin, bdellium (= *guggulu*). — *Deva-vṛitti, is,* m. the commentary of Deva (= *Purushottama-deva*) on the Uṇādi-sūtras. — *Deva-vyaćas, ās, ās, as,* Ved. affording space for the gods, receiving the gods. — *Deva-vrata, am,* n. a religious observance; any religious obligation or vow; the favourite food of the gods; (*as, ā, am*), devoted to the gods, religious; (*as*), m. an epithet of Bhīshma; of Kārttikeya. — *Deva-vratin, ī, inī, i,* obeying the divine commands, serving the gods. — *Deva-śakti, is,* m. 'having the power of a god,' 'having divine strength,' N. of a king. — *Devaśata-bhāshya, am,* n., N. of a work mentioned in the Sūdra-dharma-tattva by Kamalākara. — *Deva-śatru, us,* m. an enemy of the gods; an Asura; a Rakshas; (*us, us, u*), Ved. having the gods as enemies. — *Deva-śarman, ā,* m., N. of several persons; of an old sage; of a Buddhist author, (wrongly written *deva-sarman*); of a minister of Jayāpīḍa who was king of Kāśmīra; [cf. *daiva-śarmi.*] — *Deva-śas,* ind., Ved. deity after deity. — *Deva-śilpin, ī,* m. 'the artist of the gods,' an epithet of Tvashṭṛi. — *Deva-śiśu, us,* m. the child of a god; [cf. *deva-garbha.*] — *Deva-śishṭa, as, ā, am,* Ved. taught or directed by the gods. — *Deva-śunī,* f., Ved. 'the divine female dog,' an epithet of Saramā. — *Deva-śūra, as,* m. 'the divine hero,' N. of a man. — *Deva-śekhara, as,* m. 'the diadem of the gods,' a kind of plant, = *damanaka.* — *Deva-śesha, am,* n. the remnants of a sacrifice offered to the gods. — *Deva-śravas, ās,* m., N. of a Bhārata; of a son of Yama and author of hymns of the Ṛig-veda. — *Deva-śrī, īs, īs, i,* Ved. approaching the gods, worshipping. — *Devaśrī-garbha, as,* m., N. of a Bodhi-sattva. — *Deva-śrut, t, t, t,* Ved. audible to the gods, heard by the gods. — *Deva-śruta, as,* m. (with Jainas) N. of the sixth Arhat of the future Ut-sarpiṇī; a god (= *īśvara*); N. of Nārada; a sacred treatise or branch of scripture. — *Deva-śrū, ūs, ūs, u,* Ved. known to the gods. — *Deva-śreṇī,* f. the plant Sanseviera Zeylanica (= *mūrvā*). — *Deva-śreshṭha, as,* m., N. of a son of the twelfth Manu. — *Deva-sakha, as,* m., Ved. a friend or companion of the gods. — *Deva-saṅgīta-yonin, ī, inī, i,* 'furnishing sources of amusement or entertainment to the gods,' N. of the Nāradas who appear as messengers. — *Deva-sattra, am,* n. a festival or sacrifice of long continuance in honour of the gods. — *Deva-sattva, as, ā, am,* having the nature of a god, godlike. — *Deva-sad, t, t, t,* Ved. living among the gods. — *Deva-sadana, as, ā, am,* Ved. serving as a seat or residence for the gods. — *Deva-sadman, a,* n. the seat or residence of a god. — *Deva-sandha, as, ā, am,* connected with the gods, divine. — *Deva-sannidhi, is,* m. presence of the gods. — *Deva-sabhā,* f. an assembly of the gods; a gambling-house; [cf. the next.] — *Devasabhya, as,* m. the keeper of a gambling-house; a gambler; a frequenter of gambling-houses or clubs; an attendant on a deity. — *Deva-sarasa, am,* n. 'the pool of the gods,' N. of a place. — *Deva-sarshapa, as,* m. 'divine mustard,' a kind of mustard. — *Deva-saha, as,* m. 'the strength of the gods,' N. of a mountain; (*ā*), f. a kind of plant, = *saha-devī, daṇḍotpalā,* = *bhikshā-sūtra* (or *bhikshu-sūtra?*). — *Deva-sāt,* ind. to a god or gods, to the nature of a deity; *devasād-bhū,* to become changed into a god. — *Deva-sāyujya, am,* n. conjunction with the gods, reception among the gods, absorption into or identification with a deity; inferior deification, the state or being of the inferior gods. — *Deva-sāvarṇi, is,* m., N. of the thirteenth Manu. — *Deva-siṅha, as,* m. 'the lion of the gods,' an epithet of Śiva. — *Deva-sunda, as,* m., N. of a lake. — *Deva-sumati, is,* f. the favour of the gods. — *Deva-sumanas,* 'divine flower,' a species of flower. — *Deva-sushi, is,* m. a tube or cavity which leads to the gods; (the heart has five, viz. *prāṇa, vyāna, apāna, samāna,* and *udāna.*) — *Deva-sū, ūs, ūs, u,* Ved. an epithet applied to eight deities, viz. Agni gṛiha-pati, Soma vanas-pati, Savitṛi satya-prasava, Rudra paśu-pati, Bṛihas-pati vāćas-pati, Indra jyeshṭha, Mitra satya, and Varuṇa dharma-pati. — *Deva-sūda, am,* n., N. of a village. — *Deva-sūri, is,* m., N. of a preceptor. — *Deva-sṛishṭa, as, ā, am,* let go or discharged by a god; caused or created by the gods; (*ā*), f. an intoxicating drink, a kind of spirituous liquor. — *Deva-sena, as,* m., N. of a king of Śrāvastī; of Pauṇḍra-vardhana; of a Buddhist Arhat; (*ā*), f. an army or host of celestials; N. of a daughter of Prajā-pati or niece of Indra and wife of Skanda who is the leader of the hosts of heaven, (she is worshipped by the race of Jātukārṇya); N. of a daughter of Indra. — *Deva-senā-pati, is,* m. 'the commander of the hosts of heaven,' an epithet of Skanda. — *Devasenā-priya, as,* m. 'the beloved of Deva-senā,' epithet of Skanda. — *Deva-stut, t, t, t,* Ved. praising the gods. — *Deva-strī,* f. the wife of a deity. — *Deva-sthāna, as,* m., N. of an ancient Ṛishi [cf. *daivasthāni*]; (*am*), n., N. of a Sāman. — *Devasyatvaka, as, ā, am,* containing the words *devasya tvā* (as an Adhyāya or Anu-vāka). — *Deva-sva, am,* n. the property of the gods, property applicable to religious purposes or endowments &c. — *Devasvāpaharaṇa* (°*sva-ap*°), *am,* n. 'plunder of sacred property,' sacrilege. — *Deva-svāmin, ī,* m. 'the lord of the gods,' N. of several Brāhmans; N. of an astrologer; of a commentator on the Āpastamba. — *Deva-havis, is,* n., Ved. an oblation to the gods. — *Deva-havya, am,* n. an oblation to the gods; (*as*), m., N. of an ancient Ṛishi. — *Deva-hiṅsaka, as,* m. an enemy of the gods. — *Deva-hita, as, ā, am,* Ved. arranged or appointed or settled by the gods. — *Deva-hiti, is,* f., Ved. divine ordinance or arrangement. — *Deva-hū, ūs, ūs, u,* Ved. invoking the gods, devoted to the gods; (*ūs*), m., N. of a man; (*ūs*), f., scil. *dvār,* N. of the northern aperture of the human body, i. e. of the left ear (which is turned northwards if the face is directed towards the east; cf. *pitṛi-hū*). — *Deva-hū-tama, as, ā, am,* most devoted to the gods; very pious. — *Deva-hūti, is* or *ī,* f., Ved. invocation of the gods; N. of a magical formula with which the gods are invoked; N. of a daughter of Manu Svayam-bhū and wife of Kardama. — *Deva-hūya, am,* n., Ved. = *deva-hūti,* invocation of the gods. — *Deva-heḍana* or *deva-heḷana, am,* n., Ved. disregarding the gods, an offence against them. — *Deva-heti, is,* f., Ved. the weapon of a god, a divine weapon. — *Deva-hotra, as,* m., N. of the father of Yogeśvara, a partial incarnation (*anśa*) of Hari. — *Deva-hrada, am,* n. 'the divine lake,' N. of a sacred bathing-place. — *Devānśa* (°*va-an*°), *am,* n. a portion of a god, a partial incarnation of a god. — *Devākrīḍa* (°*va-āk*°), *as,* m. the playing-place or pleasure-grove of the gods. — *Devāgāra* (°*va-ag*° or -*āg*°), *as, am,* m. n. 'the dwelling of a god,' a temple. — *Devāṅga* (°*va-an*°), *as,* m., N. of an emanation from the body of the god Sadāśiva, (said to be the inventor of the art of weaving.) — *Devāṅga-ćaritra, am,* n. 'the adventures or story of Devāṅga,' N. of a book. — *Devāṅganā* (°*va-an*°), f. a divine female, courtezan of Svarga. — *Devājīva, as,* m. or *devājīvin* (°*va-āj*°), *ī,* m. an attendant upon an idol, a low Brāhman, subsisting by attendance upon an image and upon the offerings made to it. — *Devāńć* (°*va-ańć*), *āṅ, āćī, āk,* Ved. approaching the gods; directed towards them; worshipping them. — *Devāñjana* (°*va-añ*°), *am,* n., Ved. divine unguent or ointment. — *Devāṭa* (°*va-aṭa* or -*āṭa*), *as,* m., N. of a sacred bathing-place; [cf. *patnyāṭa.*] — *Devātithi* (°*va-at*°), *is,* m. 'the guest of the gods,' N. of a descendant of Kaṇva and author of a hymn of the Ṛig-veda; of a prince or son of A-krodhana or Krodhana by Karambhā; (also read *deva-tithi.*) — *Devātideva* (°*va-at*°), *as,* m., a god surpassing or excelling all other gods; epithet of Vishṇu; of Śākya-muni. — *Devātman* (°*va-āt*°), *ā,* m. the divine soul; the holy fig-tree or Ficus Religiosa; (*ā, ā, a*), being of divine nature, containing a divinity; one with or identified with a deity; belonging to a deity, consecrated, sacred. — *Devātma-śakti, is,* f. the power of the divine soul. — *Devātmā* (°*va-āt*°), f. the mother of the gods; [cf. *deva-tātmā.*] — *Devādhideva* (°*va-adh*°), *as,* m. a god over all other gods, an Arhat of the Jainas. — *Devādhipa* (°*va-adh*°), *as,* m. 'the king of the gods,' an epithet of Indra; N. of a king identified with the Asura Nikumbha. — *Devānām-priya, as, ā, am,* 'the beloved of the gods,' simple, foolish; (*as*), m. a fool, an idiot; a goat; an ascetic, one who relinquishes or abandons the world; [cf. the Prākṛit N. of a Buddhist king, *Devānam-piyatissa.*] — *Devānīka* (°*va-an*°), *am,* n. an army of celestials; (*as*), m., N. of a prince who was the son of Kshema-dhanvan; of a son of the eleventh Manu; of a mountain. — *Devānukrama, as,* m. 'the series of the gods, enumeration of the gods in order,' N. of a work supposed to be written by Śaunaka, (serving as an index to the deities to whom hymns are addressed.) — *Devānućara, as,* or *devānuyāyin* (°*va-an*°), *ī,* m. a follower or attendant of a god. — *Devānta* (°*va-an*°), *as,* m., N. of a son of Hṛidīka. — *Devāntaka* (°*va-an*°), *as,* m., N. of a Rakshas; of a Daitya. — *Devāntaka-vadha, as,* m. 'the destruction of Devāntaka,' N. of the seventy-first chapter of the Krīḍā-khaṇḍa or second part of the Gaṇeśa-Purāṇa. — *Devāndhas* (°*va-an*°), *as,* n. divine food, ambrosia. — *Devānna* (°*va-an*°), *am,* n. divine food, ambrosia; rice or food that has been first presented to an idol. — *Devāpi* (°*va-āpi*), *is,* m. 'the friend of the gods,' N. of a Ṛishi who was son of Ṛishṭi-sheṇa; (according to a later legend he is a son of king Pratīpa, resigns his kingdom, retires to the woods, becomes a Brāhman, and is supposed to be still alive near the Su-meru mountain; cf. *daivāpa.*) — *Devābhishṭa* (°*va-abh*°), *as, ā, am,* desired by the gods, sacred or dedicated to a deity; (*ā*), f. betel, piper betel (= *tāmbūlī*). — *Devāyatana* (°*va-āy*°), *am,* n. 'the dwelling of a god,' a temple; [cf. *devatāyatana.*] — *Devāyudha* (°*va-āy*°), *am,* n. 'the weapon of a god,' a divine weapon, Indra's bow, the rainbow. — *Devāyusha* (°*va-āy*°), *am,* n. the life-time of a god. — *Devāraṇya* (°*va-ar*°), *am,* n. a divine grove, the forest of the gods. — *Devārādhana* (°*va-ār*°), *am,* n. or *devārādhanā,* f. worship of the gods. — *Devāri* (°*va-ari*), *is,* m. 'an enemy of the gods,' an Asura. — *Devārćaka* (°*va-ar*°), *as,* m. a worshipper of the gods. — *Devārćana* (°*va-ar*°), *am,* n. or *devārćanā,* f. the worship of the gods; idolatry. — *Devārpaṇa* (°*va-ar*°), *as, ā, am,* received among the gods, considered as a god. — *Devārya* (°*va-ār*°), *as,* m., N. of the last Arhat of the present Ava-sarpiṇī. — *Devārha* (°*va-ar*°), *as, ā, am,* worthy of the gods, divine; (*as*), m. a kind of medicinal plant; (*ā*), f. a species of plant, = *deva-balā,* = *saha-devī.* — *Devālaya* (°*va-āl*°), *as,* m. 'the residence of the gods,' heaven; a temple. — *Devā-vat, ān, atī, at,* = *deva-vat,* q. v. — *Devāvatāra* (°*va-av*°), *as,* m. 'the place of descent of a god (?),' N. of a place. — *Devāvasatha* (°*va-āv*°), *as,* m. 'the habitation of a deity,' a temple. — *Devāvāsa* (°*va-āv*°), *as,* m. 'the residence of a god or gods,' a temple; an epithet of the tree Ficus Religiosa. — *Devāvī* (°*va-avī*), *īs, īs, i,* Ved. gladdening or satisfying the gods, agreeable to the gods. — *Devā-vṛidh, t, t, t,* Ved. gladdening or satisfying the gods; (*t*), m., N. of a mountain; (also read *devā-vṛidha.*) — *Devā-vṛidha, as,* m., N. of a prince who was father of Babhru [cf. *daivāvṛidha*]; of a mountain; [cf. *devā-vṛidh.*] — *Devāśva* (°*va-aś*°), *as,* m. the horse of a god, a divine horse; Indra's horse Uććaiḥ-śravas. — *Devāsura* (°*va-as*°), *ās,* m. pl. the gods and the Asuras; [cf. *daivāsura.*] — *Devāsura-guru, us,* m. 'the preceptor of the gods and Asuras,' epithet of Śiva. — *Devāsura-namaskṛita, as,* m. 'worshipped by the gods and Asuras,' epithet of Śiva. — *Devāsura-mahāmātra, as,* m. 'the chief of the gods and Asuras,' epithet of Śiva. — *Devāsura-mahāśraya* (°*hā-āś*°), *as,* m. 'the great refuge of the gods and Asuras,' epithet of Śiva. — *Devāsura-maheśvara* (°*hā-īś*°), *as,* m. 'the great lord of the gods and Asuras,' epithet of Śiva. — *Devāsura-yuddha, am,* n. the battle between the gods and Asuras. — *Devāsura-vara-prada, as,* m. 'conferring boons on the gods and Asuras,' epithet of Śiva. — *Devāsura-saṅgrāma, as,* m. the war between the gods and Asuras. — *Devāsureśvara* (°*ra-īś*°), *as,* m. 'the lord of the gods and Asuras,' epithet of Śiva. — *Devāhāra* (°*va-āh*°), *as,* m. 'food of the gods,' divine food, ambrosia. — *Devāhvaya* (°*va-āh*°), *as,* m. 'called Deva,' N. of a prince. — *Devī-dāsa, as,* m. (for *devī-d*°), 'the slave of the goddess,' N. of a man; N. of a commentator on the Mugdha-bodha. — *Devī-koṭa, as,* m. = *śoṇita-pura,* N. of a town (the city of Vāṇa, probably Devicotta on the Coromandel coast). — *Devī-garbha-gṛiha, as,* m. 'a house containing an image of the goddess Durgā,' a shrine of the goddess Durgā. — *Devī-gṛiha, am,* n. a temple of the goddess (Durgā); the apartment of a queen. — *Devī-tantra, am,* n. 'the Tantra of the goddess (Durgā),' N. of a Tantra. — *Devī-tva, am,* n. 'the state of being a goddess,' the rank of a goddess; the rank of a queen. — *Devī-datta, as,* m., N. of the father of Rāmasevaka and grandfather of Kṛishṇa-mitra. — *Devīn-dhiyaka, as, ā, am,* containing the words *devīṃ dhiyā* (as an Anu-vāka or Adhyāya). — *Devī-pāda-dvaya, am,* n. 'the two feet of the goddess, i. e. of Durgā,' N. of a holy bathing-place. — *Devī-purāṇa, am,* n., N. of an Upa-Purāṇa. — *Devī-bhavana, am,* n. the temple of the goddess (Durgā). — *Devī-bhāgavata-purāṇa, am,* n., N. of a Purāṇa. — *Devī-mahādeva, am,* n., N. of a play. — *Devī-mahiman, ā,* m., N. of a work, (perhaps = the following.) — *Devī-māhātmya, am,* n. 'the majesty of Durgā,' N. of a section of the Mārkaṇḍeya-Purāṇa. — *Devīr-āpasaka, as, ā, am,* containing the words *devīr āpaḥ* (as an Anu-vāka or Adhyāya). — *Devī-sūkta, am,* n. 'the hymn of the goddess,' N. of a hymn to Durgā. — *Devej* (°*va-ij*), *ṭ, ṭ, ṭ,* sacrificing to the gods, worshipping them. — *Devejya* (°*va-ij*°), *as,* m. 'the preceptor of the gods,' an epithet of Bṛihaspati, the planet Jupiter. — *Deveddha* (°*va-iddha*), *as, ā, am,* Ved. kindled by the gods. — *Devendra* (°*va-in*°), *as,* m. 'the chief of the gods,' an epithet of Indra; of Śiva; N. of a man. — *Devendra-buddhi, is,* m. 'having the intellect of the chief of the gods,' N. of a learned Buddhist. — *Devendra-samaya, as,* m., N. of a Buddhist work; of a part of the Suvarṇa-prabhāsa. — *Deveśa* (°*va-īśa*), *as,* m. 'the chief of the gods,' an epithet of Brahmā; of Vishṇu; of Śiva; of Indra; (*ī*), f. 'the queen of the gods,' epithet of Durgā; of Devakī who was mother of Kṛishṇa. — *Deveśa-tīrtha, am,* n. 'the Tīrtha of the chief of the gods,' N. of a Tīrtha. — *Deve-śaya, as, ā, am,* 'resting or reposing on a god,' epithet of Vishṇu. — *Deveśvara* (°*va-īś*°), *as,* m. 'the sovereign of the gods,' an epithet of Śiva; N. of an author. — *Deveśvara-paṇḍita, as,* m., N. of a poet. — *Deveshita* (°*va-ish*°), *as, ā, am,* Ved. sent or impelled by the gods. — *Deveshṭa* (°*va-ish*°), *as, ā, am,* wished by the gods, acceptable to the gods; (*as, ā*), m. f. a sort of drug (reckoned among the Ashṭa-varga, = *mahā-medā*); bdellium; (*ā*), f. the wild lime tree (= *vana-vijapūraka*). — *Devainasa* (°*va-en*°), *am,* n., Ved. the curse of the gods. — *Devodyāna* (°*va-ud*°), *am,* n. 'the grove of the gods,' a sacred grove, a garden near a temple or consecrated to a deity. — *Devopāsaka* (°*va-up*°), *as,* m. a worshipper of the gods. — *Devaukas* (°*va-ok*°), *as,* n. 'the residence of the gods,' the mountain Meru. — *Devy-āgama, as,* m. 'the arrival of the goddess,' N. of a work. — *Devy-upanishad, t,* f., N. of an Upanishad.

Devaka, as, ikā, am, who or what sports or plays; divine, celestial, godlike, &c.; (*as*), m. a god, deity, (at the end of an adj. comp.); N. of a man; of a Gandharva; of a prince, son of Āhuka and father of Devakī who was mother of Kṛishṇa; of a son of Yudhi-shṭhira and Yaudheyī or Pauravī [cf. *devikā*]; a familiar diminutive for Deva-datta, q. v.; (*ās*), m. pl., N. of the inhabitants of a Varsha in Krauńća-dvīpa; (*ikā*), f. a diminutive of Devī; N. of a class of goddesses of an inferior order; (*ās*), f. pl. the oblations made to the aforesaid goddesses (viz. to Anu-matī, Rākā, Sinīvālī, Kuhū, and to Dhātṛi); N. of the wife of Yudhi-shṭhira and mother of Yaudheya; of a river; of a country [? cf. *dāvika*]; the thorn-apple (= *dhustūrā*); (*akā*), f. a familiar diminutive for Deva-dattā, q. v.; (*akī*), f., N. of a daughter of Devaka, (she was the wife of Vasu-deva and mother of Kṛishṇa); N. of Aditi; of Dākshāyaṇī. — *Devakī-nandana* or *devakī-nandana* or *devakī-putra, as,* m. or *devakī-sūnu, us,* m. 'the son of Devakī,' an epithet of Kṛishṇa. — *Devakī-mātṛi, tā,* f. the mother of Devakī.

Devakīya, as, ā, am, divine, godlike, belonging or relating to a divinity; [cf. *devakya.*]

Devakya, as, ā, am, divine, godlike; corresponding to the number of the gods; (*ā*), f. epithet of the metre Anushṭubh; [cf. *devakīya.*]

Devatya, as, ā, am, (at the end of an adj. comp.) having as one's deity; sacred to a deity [cf. *eka-d*°, *kiṃ-d*°, *daivatya*]; (*ā*), f., Ved. (perhaps) N. of a particular species of animal.

Devan, ā, m. a husband's brother; [cf. *devṛi.*]

2. *devana, as,* m. (for 1. see rt. *dev,* p. 430, col. 1), a die, dice for gambling; (*ā*), f. sport, wanton sport or pastime; service; (*am*), n. shining, splendor,

lustre, beauty; gaming, gambling, a game at dice; sport, play, pastime; a play or pleasure-ground, a garden; a lotus; praise; emulation, desire to excel or overcome; affair, business, profession; going, motion.

Devayat, an, antī, at (from a Nom. *devaya*), Ved. following the gods, serving the gods, religious; desirous of divinity (?); shining (?); [cf. *a-d°* and *devāyat.*]

Devayu, us, ū, u, Ved. loving the gods, devoted to the gods, pious, virtuous, righteous; frequenting sacred festivals; (*us*), m. a deity; [cf. *a-d°.*]

Devara or *devaraka, as,* m. a husband's brother, especially his younger brother; a beloved person; a husband; [cf. Lith. *dëweris;* Gr. δαήρ; Lat. *levir* for *devir;* Slav. *dever;* Angl. Sax. *tacur, taeor;* Old Germ. *zeihur.*]

Devala, as, m. an attendant upon an idol; a Brāhman of an inferior order who subsists upon the offerings made to the idols he attends, and who conducts various ceremonies for hire; a holy or virtuous man; N. of a descendant of Kaśyapa, author of the hymns of the ninth Maṇḍala of the Ṛig-veda; an epithet of Asita, (according to other authorities a son of Asita); N. of an astronomer; of a legislator; of the son of Pratyūsha; of the elder brother of Dhaumya; of the husband of Eka-parṇā; of the father of Sannati who was wife of Brahma-datta; of the grandfather of Pāṇini; of a son of Kṛiśāśva by Dhishaṇā, wrongly identified with Nārada, with whom Asita Devala is sometimes associated.

Devalaka, as, m. the attendant on an idol. See the preceding.

Devāyat = *devayat* above.

Devālā, f. one of the female personifications of music.

Devika, as, ī, am, appertaining to or derived from a deity, divine; (*as*), m. a familiar diminutive of Deva-datta; (*ā*), f., see under *devaka.*

Devitṛi, tā, m. a dice-player, gamester, dicer.

Devitvā, ind. having played.

Devin, ī, inī, i, gambling, a gambler, gamester.

Deviya, as, m. a familiar diminutive of Deva-datta.

Devila, as, ā, am, appertaining to a deity, divine; virtuous, pious, just; (*as*), m. a familiar diminutive of Deva-datta.

Devīka for *devī,* a queen &c. (at the end of an adj. comp.; cf. *sa-d°.*) — *Devīka-vaća, am,* n. 'the prayer of Durgā,' N. of a mystical book treating of the worship of Durgā.

Devṛi, ā, m. a husband's brother, especially his younger brother; the husband of a woman previously married. — *Devṛi-kāma, as, ā, am,* loving the brother of one's husband.

Devya, am, n., Ved. divine dignity or power, rank, godhead.

देवकड *devakaḍa, as* or *am,* m. or n. (?), N. of a Grāma.

देवट *devaṭa, as,* m. (said to be fr. rt. *dev,* q. v.), an artist, artisan.

देवट्टी *devaṭṭī,* f. a sort of gull, Larus Ridibundus (= *gangāćillī*).

देश *deśa, as,* m. (fr. rt. 1. *diś*), any place or spot shown or pointed out; place or spot in general, region, country (whether inhabited or uninhabited, e. g. *deśam āvas* or *nivis,* to settle in a place; *ātmīya-deśa,* one's own country); a province, part, department, side, portion; an institute, ordinance; *deśa* occurs at the end of some comps., the fem. ending in *ā;* [cf. *a-d°, eka-d°, vi-d°,* &c.] — *Deśa-kāla, au,* m. du. place and time. — *Deśa-kālajña, as, ā, am,* knowing the (proper) place and time. — *Deśa-kāla-vid, t, t, t,* knowing place and time. — *Deśa-kāla-vibhāga, as,* m. apportioning of place and time. — *Deśa-kāla-vyavasthita, as, ā, am,* regulated by place and time. — *Deśa-ja* or *deśa-jāta, as, ā, am,* 'country-born,' native, indigenous; born in the right place; produced in the right country (as a horse, elephant, &c.); of genuine descent; genuine; [cf. *deśya.*] — *Deśa-jña, as, ā, am,* knowing the district, familiar with places. — *Deśa-dṛishṭa, as, ā, am,* seen or experienced in a country; customary in a country; considered locally, judged as to place. — *Deśa-dharma, as,* m. local law, local rights or customs, the law or usage of any country. — *Deśa-nirṇaya, as,* m. 'description of countries,' N. of a work. — *Deśa-bhāshā,* f. the dialect of a country. — *Deśa-bhramaṇa, am,* n. wandering about, peregrination, tour. — *Deśa-rāja-ćarita, am,* n. 'history of native princes,' N. of a work. — *Deśa-rūpa, am,* n. 'the being in the right place,' conformity with place, propriety, fitness. — *Deśa-vāsin, ī, inī, i,* residing in a country. — *Deśa-vṛitta, am,* n. a circle depending upon its relative position with regard to the spot from which it is observed. — *Deśa-vyavahāra, as,* m. local usage, custom of the country. — *Deśa-stha, as, ā, am,* situated or living in a country. — *Deśāćāra* (°*śa-āć°*), *as,* m. local usage or custom. — *Deśātithi* (°*śa-at°*), *is,* m. 'a guest in a country,' a foreigner. — *Deśāntara* (°*śa-an°*), *am,* n. another country, abroad, foreign parts; longitude or difference of longitude; the distance from the chief meridian. — *Deśāntara-phala, am,* n. the equation for difference of meridian. — *Deśāntara-bhāṇḍānayana* (°*ḍa-ān°*), *am,* n. importing wares from foreign countries. — *Deśāntarin, ī, iṇī, i,* belonging to another country, foreign, a foreigner. — *Deśāpeksha* (°*śa-ap°*), *as, ā, am,* spying or inspecting a land.

Deśaka, as, ikā, am, who or what shows, points out, describes, directs, teaches, &c.; a shower, indicator; (*as*), m. a ruler, governor; a guide, instructor.

Deśanā, f. direction, command, instruction, doctrine.

Deśika, as, ā, am, familiar with a place, a guide; (*as*), m. a Guru or spiritual teacher; a traveller, stranger, sojourner; [cf. *daiśika.*]

Deśita, as, ā, am, directed, commanded; shown, pointed out; advised, instructed.

Deśin, ī, inī, i, showing, pointing out, instructing, guiding; of or belonging to a country; (*inī*), f. the index or fore-finger.

Deśī, f., scil. *bhāshā,* the dialect of a country; N. of a Rāgiṇī, (according to Hanu-mat) wife of the Rāga Dīpaka. — *Deśī-kosha, as,* m. a vocabulary of the dialect of a country.

Deśīya, as, ā, am, peculiar or belonging to a country or province, provincial, native; (at the end of a comp.) inhabiting any country (e. g. *Māgadha-deśīyas,* an inhabitant of Magadha); bordering upon, contiguous, not very distant from, almost (in this sense regarded by Indian grammarians as an affix, see *pañća-varshaka-d°, paṭu-d°,* &c.). — *Deśīya-bhāshā,* f. the dialect of a country, native dialect. — *Deśīya-varāḍī,* N. of a Rāga ?; (also read *deśī-varāḍī.*)

Deśya, as, ā, am, to be pointed out, to be ordered or proved; being in a place or on the spot, present at any transaction (and so witnessing it); belonging to or being in a country, local, provincial, inhabiting or coming from a country, (often at the end of a comp., e. g. *nānā-d°,* coming from various countries; *tad-d°,* inhabiting the same country); born in or belonging to one's own country, native; born at the right place or in the right country, of genuine descent; genuine [cf. *deśa-ja*]; contiguous, not far from, almost [cf. *deśīya* above, and see *ṛitusti-d°, śiśu-d°, paṭu-d°,* &c.]; (*as*), m. an eye-witness of anything, one who was on the spot; the inhabitant of a country; (*am*), n. the proposition, the statement or exhibition of a question or argument; the fact or thing to be proved or substantiated; [cf. *a-d°.*] — *Deśya-bhikshu, us,* m. a native mendicant.

Deshṭavya, as, ā, am, to be pointed out or shown or declared.

Deshṭṛi, tā, ṭrī, ṭṛi, one who shows or directs or points out, an indicator; (*ṭrī*), f., N. of a divine female (= *dharmādy-upadeśa-kartrī*).

Deshṭra, am, n., Ved. direction, order; promise.

देशकारी *deśakārī,* f., N. of a Rāgiṇī or musical mode, (according to Hanu-mat) the wife of the Rāga Megha; [cf. *deva-kirī.*]

देशाख *deśākha* and *deśāga, as,* m., N. of a Rāga; (*ī*), f., N. of a Rāgiṇī.

देष्ठ *deshṭha, as, ā, am* (superl. fr. 1. *dā*), Ved. giving the most, most liberal, greatest giver.

Deshṇa, am, n., Ved. giving, a gift; [cf. *kumāra-d°, ćāru-d°, turi-d°.*]

1. *deshṇu, us, us, u,* liberal, giving, a donor.

देष्णु 2. *deshṇu, us, us, u* (fr. 3. *dā* or 4. *dā ?*), difficult of subjection, intractable, ungovernable.

देष्णु 3. *deshṇu, us,* m. (fr. rt. 7. *dā*), a washerman.

देह *deha, as, am,* m. n. (fr. rt. 1. *dih,* because it defiles or perhaps rather because it envelopes the soul), the body; (*ī*), f. a mound, bank, rampart, surrounding wall; [cf. Goth. *leik,* 'dead body;' Old Germ. *līh;* Mod. Germ. *leiche.*] — *Deha-kara, as,* m. 'the former of the body,' a father. — *Deha-kartṛi, tā,* m. 'creating the bodies, i. e. body and life,' an epithet of the Sun; a father. — *Deha-kṛit, t, t, t,* forming the body; (*t*), m. a father; epithet of Śiva. — *Deha-kosha, as,* m. the covering of the body; skin, epidermis; a feather, wing; [cf. *deha-dhi.*] — *Deha-kshaya, as,* m. decay of the body, sickness, disease. — *Deha-gata, as, ā, am,* 'gone into a body,' incarnate. — *Deha-grahaṇa, am,* n. assuming a body or visible form. — *Deha-ćyuta, as, ā, am,* separated or detached from the body (as excrement or the spirit). — *Deha-ja, as,* m. 'born of the body,' a son. — *Deha-tantra, as, ā, am,* see *tantra,* p. 362, col. 1. — *Deha-tyāga, as,* m. resigning or relinquishing the body, dying; death in general, voluntary death. — *Deha-da, as,* m. 'what gives a body or life (?),' quicksilver (= *pāra-da*). — *Deha-dīpa, as,* m. 'lamp of the body,' the eye. — *Deha-dharma, as,* m. the function or law of the body. — *Deha-dhāraka, am,* n. 'supporter of the body,' a bone. — *Deha-dhāraṇa, am,* n. 'supporting the body,' living, life (e. g. *pūrvasmin deha-dhāraṇe,* in a former life or existence). — *Deha-dhi, is,* m. 'sustaining the body,' a wing; [cf. *deha-kosha.*] — *Deha-dhṛish, k,* m. 'carrying or sustaining the body,' air, wind; (*dhṛik* is by some derived fr. rt. *dhṛi* or *dṛih.*) — *Deha-bhṝj, k, k, k,* possessed of a body, corporeal; (*k*), m. a being possessed of a body or of life, especially a man. — *Deha-bhuj, k,* m. 'possessed of a body,' an epithet of Śiva. — *Deha-bhṛit, t, t, t,* 'carrying a body,' embodied, corporeal; (*t*), m. a living being, especially a man; an epithet of Śiva; life, vitality. — *Deha-mātrāvaśeshita* (°*tra-av°*), *as, ā, am,* destitute of all except the body, having merely the body left. — *Deha-mānin, ī, inī, i,* proud of the body. — *Deham-bhara, as, ā, am,* intent upon nourishing the body, minding only one's own body, an epicure, gluttonous. — *Deha-yātrā,* f. 'departure of the body,' dying, death; nourishment, food, prolonging bodily life. — *Deha-lakshaṇa, am,* n. a mole, spot or mark upon the body. — *Deha-vat, ān, atī, at,* furnished with a body, embodied; (*ān*), m. a living being, a man; the soul. — *Deha-vāyu, us,* m. an air of the body, a vital air; [cf. *apāna, udāna, prāṇa, vyāna, samāna.*] — *Deha-visarjana, am,* n. quitting the body, death. — *Deha-śanku, us,* m. (according to a commentator) a column or pillar of stone. — *Deha-sańćāriṇī,* f. a daughter. — *Deha-sāra, as,* m. 'essence of the body,' marrow. — *Deha-svabhāva, as,* m. bodily temperament. — *Dehātma-vāda, as,* m. materialism; see the next. — *Dehātma-vādin* (°*ha-āt°*), *ī, inī, i,* one who asserts that the body and soul are one, a materialist, a Ćārvāka. — *Dehāntara* (°*ha-an°*), *am,* n. another body, another embodied state (in the doctrine of metempsychosis). — *Dehāntara-prāpti, is,* f. 'obtaining another body,' transmigration. — *Dehāvaraṇa* (°*ha-āv°*), *am,* n. 'screen for the body,' armour; dress. — *Deheśvara* (°*ha-īś°*), *as,* m. 'lord of the body,' the soul. — *Dehod-*

bhava or *dehodbhūta* (°*ha-ud*°), *as, ā, am*, born in the body, innate.

Dehalā, f. spirituous liquor.

Dehali, is, or *dehalī*, f. the threshold of a door, the sill or lower part of the wooden frame of a door or a raised terrace in front of it. — *Dehalī-mukta-pushpa, am*, n. a flower dropped on the threshold.

Dehikā, f. a sort of ant or insect which throws up the earth; [cf. *ud-dehikā*.]

Dehin, ī, inī, i, having a body, corporeal, embodied; (*ī*), m. living, a living being, especially a man; the spirit, soul (enveloped in the body); (*inī*), f. the earth.

दै **dai**, cl. 1. P. *dāyati*, &c., to purify, cleanse; to protect; [cf. rts. 5. *dā* and *de*.]

दैक्ष **daiksha**, *as, ī, am* (fr. *dīkshā*), relating to initiation, inauguration, &c.

दैतेय **daiteya**, *as*, m. (fr. *diti*), a son of Diti, an Asura, an enemy of the gods, (especially) epithet of Rāhu; (*as, ī, am*), proceeding from or belonging to the Daiteyas.

Daitya, as, m. a son of Diti, a demon; (*as, ā, am*), belonging or relating to the Daityas; (*ā*), f. a kind of fragrant plant (=*murā*); a perfume; a drug (=*ćaṇḍaushadhi*); spirituous liquor. — *Daitya-guru, us*, m. 'the preceptor of the Daityas,' an epithet of Sukra, the regent of the planet Venus. — *Daitya-dānava-mardana, as*, m. 'subduer or crusher of Daityas and Dānavas,' a title of Indra. — *Daitya-deva, as*, m. 'the god of the Daityas,' an epithet of Varuṇa, deity of the waters; Air or Wind personified. — *Daitya-dvīpa, as*, m. 'refuge or protector of the Daityas(?),' N. of a son of Garuḍa. — *Daitya-nisūdana, as*, m. 'the destroyer of the Daityas,' an epithet of Vishṇu. — *Daitya-pa, as*, or *daitya-pati, is*, m. 'the prince of the Daityas,' epithet of Bali. — *Daitya-purodhas, ās*, or *daitya-purohita*, or *daitya-pūjya, as*, m. 'family priest of the Daityas, to be honoured by them,' epithet of Sukra, regent of Venus. — *Daitya-mātṛi, tā*, f. 'mother of the Daityas,' epithet of Diti. — *Daitya-medaja, as*, m. 'produced from the marrow of a Daitya,' a kind of bdellium (=*bhūmija-guggulu*); (*ā*), f. the earth (supposed to be produced from the Meda or marrow of the Daityas Madhu and Kaiṭabha). — *Daitya-yuga, am*, n. an age of the demons (consisting of 12000 divine years or the sum of the four Yugas or ages of man). — *Daitya-senā*, f., N. of a daughter of Prajā-pati and sister of Deva-senā. — *Daityāri* (°*ya-ari*), *is*, m. 'enemy of the Daityas,' an epithet of Vishṇu; a god in general. — *Daityāhorātra* (°*ya-ah*°), *as*, m. a day and night of the demons (being a year of mortals). — *Daityejya* (°*ya-ij*°), *as*, m. 'preceptor of the Daityas,' an epithet of Sukra who is the regent of Venus; [cf. *daitya-guru*.] — *Daityendra* (°*ya-in*°), *as*, m. 'a prince of the Daityas,' an epithet of Pātāla-ketu. — *Daityendra-pūjya, as*, m. 'to be honoured by the chief of the Daityas,' an epithet of Sukra, regent of Venus.

दैधिषव्य **daidhishavya**, *as*, m. (fr. *didhishū*), the son of a woman by her second husband (?).

दैन 1. **daina**, *as, ī, am* (fr. *dina*), relating to a day, diurnal, daily.

Dainandina, as, ī, am, happening daily, diurnal, quotidian. — *Dainandina-pralaya, as*, n. destruction of the world after the lapse of fifteen years of Brahmā's age.

Dainika, as, ī, am, diurnal, relating daily to a day; (*ī*), f. a day's hire or wages.

दैन्य 2. **daina** or **dainya**, *am*, n. (fr. *dīna*), wretchedness, feebleness, weakness, affliction, sorrow, grief, depression, low-spiritedness; poverty, humbleness, a poor and pitiable state, miserable state; meanness, covetousness.

दैनार **daināra**, *as, ī, am* (fr. *dīnāra*), bought with a Dīnār, of the value of a Dīnār.

दैप **daipa**, *as, ī, am* (fr. *dīpa*), relating or belonging to a lamp.

दैयांपाति **daiyāmpāti**, *is*, m., Ved. a patronymic from Dyāmpāta, q. v.

दैर्घ **dairgha**, *am*, n. (fr. *dīrgha*), length. — *Dairghatama, as*, m. (fr. *dīrgha-tama*), a patronymic of Dhanvantari. — *Dairghatamasa, as, ī, am*, relating to Dīrgha-tamas; (*as*), m. a patronymic from Dīrgha-tamas. — *Dairghavaratra, as*, m. (fr. *dīrgha-varatrā*), scil. *kūpa*, a well in which a long rope is used. — *Dairgha-śravasa, as, ī, am*, relating to Dīrgha-śravas.

Dairghya, am, n. length, longness. — *Dairghya-saṃyuta, as, ā, am*, possessing length, lengthy.

दैलीपि **dailīpi**, *is*, m. a patronymic from Dilīpa, q. v.

दैव **daiva**, *as, ī, am* (fr. *deva*; only the fem. *daivī* occurs in the Ṛig-veda), of or belonging to a deity or divinity, coming from the gods, divine, celestial; royal; (*as*), m. (with or without *vivāha*), one of the forms of marriage, the gift of a daughter at a sacrifice to the officiating priest; a patronymic of Atharvan; (*am*), n. a deity [cf. *kula-d*°]; a religious offering or rite, an oblation to the gods; divine power, destiny, fortune, chance, fate, accident (e.g. *daivāt*, ind. by chance, accidentally); the part of the hands sacred to the gods, i.e. the tips of the fingers [cf. *tīrtha*]; (*ī*), f. a division of medicine, the medical use of charms, prayers, &c.; [cf. *a-d*°.] — *Daiva-karman, a*, n. offering oblations to the gods, worship of the gods, a religious rite. — *Daiva-kṛita, as, ā, am*, caused by destiny, fated; formed by nature, natural. — *Daiva-kovida, as, ā, am*, acquainted with the destinies of men; (*as, ā*), m. f. a fatalist, astrologer, fortune-teller. — *Daiva-gati, is*, f. course of destiny, fortune. — *Daiva-ćintaka, as, ā, am*, 'reflecting on fate or the destiny of men,' an epithet of Siva; (*as*), m. an astrologer, a fatalist. — *Daiva-ćintana, am*, n. or *daiva-ćintā*, f. fatalism, reliance on fate; foretelling fate by astrology (?). — *Daiva-jña, as, ā, am*, acquainted with fate, knowing the destinies of men, foretelling, prophetic; (*as*), m. an astrologer; (*ā*), f. a female fortune-teller. — *Daivajña-tva, am*, n. fatalism, astrology. — *Daivajña-vilāsa, as*, m., N. of a work. — *Daivajña-sanmuni, is*, m., N. of an astrologer. — *Daiva-tantra, as, ā, am*, subject to fate. — *Daiva-tas*, ind. by fate or destiny, through fortune, by chance. — 1. *daiva-datta, as, ā, am*, granted by fate or fortune; (for 2. see col. 3.) — *Daiva-dīpa, as*, m. 'the heavenly lamp,' the eye; [cf. *deva-dīpa* and *deha-dīpa*.] — *Daiva-dur-vipāka, as*, m. 'the hard or cruel ripening of destiny,' hardness of fortune, unpropitiousness of fate. — *Daiva-dosha, as*, m. the fault or evil result of destiny; badness of fate. — *Daiva-para, as, ā, am*, trusting to fate, believing in predestination, a fatalist; fated, willed, predestined. — *Daiva-praśna, as*, m. inquiring of fate, fortune-telling, astrology; (according to the lexicographers) a supernatural and prophetic voice heard at night; [cf. *upa-śruti* and *deva-praśna*.] — *Daiva-yuga, as*, m. an age of the gods or immortals; [cf. *daitya-yuga*.] — *Daiva-yoga, as*, m. a fortuitous combination, the occurrence of any unforeseen event, the intervention of destiny, fortune, chance; (*ena*) or (*āt*), ind. through the influence of fortune, by chance, accidentally. — *Daiva-rakshita, as, ā, am*, guarded by destiny. — *Daiva-ratha, as*, m. a divine chariot; (perhaps wrongly for *deva-ratha*.) — *Daiva-rājya, am*, n. dominion over the gods; [cf. *deva-rājya*.] — *Daiva-lekhaka, as*, m. a fortune-teller, an astrologer. — *Daiva-laukika, as, ī, am*, celestial and worldly. — *Daiva-vaśa, as, am*, m. n. the will or power of destiny; *daiva-vaśāt*, by chance, by accident, fatally. — *Daiva-vāṇī*, f. a voice from heaven. — *Daiva-vid, t, t, t*, knowing the destiny of man, acquainted with astrology, an astrologer. — *Daiva-sampanna, as, ā, am*, favoured by destiny. — *Daivasampanna-tā*, f. the state of being favoured by destiny. — *Daiva-hata, as, ā, am*, stricken by destiny, fate-stricken. — *Daiva-hataka, as, ā, am*, beaten or struck by destiny; (*am*), n. a blow of destiny; [cf. *daivopahataka*.] — *Daivātyaya* (°*va-at*°), *as*, m. danger or evil resulting from unusual natural phenomena. — *Daivādhīna* (°*va-adh*°), *as, ā, am*, depending on fate, subject to fate. — *Daivānurodhin* (°*va-an*°), *ī, inī, i*, subject or obedient to the gods. — *Daivāyatta* (°*va-āy*°), *as, ā, am*, dependant upon destiny. — *Daivāhorātra* (°*va-ah*°), *as*, m. a day of the gods, the human year; [cf. *daityāhorātra*.] — *Daivoḍhā* (°*va-ūḍhā*), f. a woman married according to the Daiva ritual; [cf. above.] — *Daivodyāna* (°*va-ud*°), *am*, n. a divine grove, a grove or garden of the gods. — *Daivopahata* or *daivopahataka* (°*va-up*°), *as, ā, am*, struck by fate, ill-fated, unfortunate, unlucky.

Daivaka (at the end of an adj. comp.)=*daiva*, a deity, &c.; (*ī*), f.=*devakī*, N. of the mother of Kṛishṇa. — *Daivakī-nandana, as*, m. 'the son of Daivakī' or 'Devakī's joy,' epithet of Kṛishṇa; (also read *devakī-nandana*.)

Daivata, as, ī, am (fr. *devatā*), of or relating to a god or to the gods, especially relating to the peculiar deity honoured by any religious rite or a hymn &c., belonging to such a deity, divine; (*as, am*), m. n. (usually n.), a god, a deity, (often collectively) the deities, especially as celebrated in any hymn, a number of gods; an idol; (at the end of an adj. comp.) having as one's deity, worshipping as one's deity. — *Daivata-kāṇḍa* or *daivata, am*, n. that part (books 7–12) of Yāska's Nirukta in which the names or epithets of deities collected in the fifth Adhyāya of the Nighaṇṭus are explained. — *Daivata-pati, is*, m. 'the prince of the gods,' an epithet of Indra. — *Daivata-para, as, ā, am*, a worshipper of the gods. — *Daivata-pratimā*, f. the image of a deity.

Daivatya, as, ā, am (fr. *devatā*), having as one's deity, addressed to some deity, sacred to a deity; [cf. *devatya*.]

Daivalaka, as, m. the servant or worshipper of an evil spirit, an attendant on an idol (?); [cf. *devalaka*.]

Daivāt, ind. by chance, by accident, fatally. See *daiva*.

Daivātitha, as, ī, am (fr. *devātithi*), relating to Devātithi.

Daivika, as, ī, am, peculiar to the gods, relating to the deities, divine, deific; performed in honour of the gods; (*am*), n. an inevitable accident.

Daivin, ī, m. an astrologer.

Daivya, as, vī or *vyā, am*, divine; (*am*), n. divine power or effect; fortune, fate.

दैवजन **daivajana**, *as, ī, am* (fr. *deva-jana*), Ved. belonging to the gods collectively.

दैवदत्त 2. **daivadatta**, *as, ī, am* (fr. *deva-datta*; for 1. see under *daiva*, col. 2), being in the village Deva-datta; (*ās*), m. pl. the disciples of Deva-datta.

Daivadattika, as, ā or *ī, am*, relating to Deva-datta.

दैवदर्शनिन् **daivadarśanin**, *inas*, m. pl. the adherents or disciples of Deva-darśana.

दैवदारव **daivadārava**, *as, ī, am* (fr. *deva-dāru*), made of the tree Deva-dāru, being upon it.

दैवयातक **daivayātaka**, *as, ī, am* (fr. *deva-yāta*), inhabited by the Deva-yātas.

दैवयातवक **daivayātavaka**, *as, ī, am* (fr. *deva-yātu*), inhabited by the Deva-yātus.

दैवयानेय **daivayāneya**, *as*, m. (fr. *deva-yānī*), a patronymic from Deva-yānī.

दैवराति **daivarāti**, *is*, m. (fr. *deva-rāta*), a descendant of Deva-rāta; a patronymic of Janaka; a N. of Yājñavalkya.

दैववात **daivavāta**, *as, ī, am* (fr. *deva-vāta*), relating to Deva-vāta; (*as*), m. an epithet of Sṛiñjaya.

दैवाकरि *daivākari, is,* m. (fr. *divākara*), 'the son of the Sun,' a patronymic of Yama and Sani or the planet Saturn; (*ī*), f. 'the daughter of the Sun,' an epithet of Yamunā or the river Jumnā.

दैवादिक *daivādika, as, ī, am* (fr. *div-ādi*), belonging to the class of roots which begins with *div*, i. e. to the fourth class.

दैवावृध *daivāvṛidha, as,* m. (fr. *devā-vṛidha*), a patronymic of Babhru.

दैवासुर *daivāsura, as, ī, am* (fr. *deva-asura*), relating to the gods and Asuras; (with *vaira*) the natural enmity perpetually subsisting between the gods and Asuras; containing the word *devāsura* (as an Adhyāya or Anu-vāka; cf. *devāsura*).

दैवोदास *daivodāsa, as, ī, am,* relating to Divo-dāsa; (*as*), m. a patronymic from Divo-dāsa. — *Daivodāsi, is,* m. a patronymic of Pratardana, and of Paruććhepa.

दैशिक *daiśika, as, ī, am* (fr. *deśa*), belonging or relating to a place, local, provincial; relating or having reference to space; belonging to a country, national; produced in any place or country; acquainted with any place or country; teaching, directing, showing, pointing out [cf. *deśika* and *deśya*]; (*as*), m. a guide; a teacher.

दैष्टिक *daishṭika, as, ī, am* (fr. *dishṭa*), fated, predestined; (*as*), m. a predestinarian, a fatalist. — *Daishṭika-tā,* f. or *daishṭika-tva, am,* n. fatalism, predestinarianism.

दैहिक *daihika, as, ī, am* (fr. *deha*), corporeal, bodily.

Daihya, as, ā, am, being in the body; (*as*), m. the soul (enclosed by the body).

दो *do* (sometimes written *dā,* see 3. *dā,* p. 408, col. 1), cl. 4. 2. P. *dyati, dāti, dadau, dāsyati, adāsīt* and *adāt, dātum,* to cut, divide; to reap, mow; to untie, loosen: Pass. *dīyate* and *dāyate,* Aor. 3rd sing. *adāyi*: Desid. *ditsati* and *didāsati*: Intens. *dedīyate* and *dādāyate.*

दोग *doga, as,* m. a bull (?).

दोग्धव्य *dogdhavya, as, ā, am* (fr. rt. 2. *duh*), to be milked.

Dogdhu-kāma, as, ā, am (fr. the inf. *dogdhum + kāma*), wishing to milk.

Dogdhṛi, dhā, dhṛi, dhṛi, a milker, who or what milks; one who performs anything from interested motives or who makes profit out of (with acc.); yielding milk or desirable objects of any kind; (*dhā*), m. a cowherd; a calf; a poet, panegyrist, one who writes verses for hire or reward; (*dhrī*), f. a cow which yields milk; a wet-nurse who has much milk; a female who yields or grants anything (with acc.).

Dogha, as, ā, am, Ved. milking; (*as*), m. milking.

दोडी *doḍī,* f. a species of plant and its fruit; [cf. *doḍi* and *dāḍī.*]

दोदुल्यमान *dodulyamāna, as, ā, am* (fr. the Intens. of rt. *dul*), swinging backwards and forwards, being swung repeatedly or violently.

दोध *dodha, as,* m. (fr. *dogdhṛi?*), a calf.

दोधक *dodhaka* or *dodhaka-vṛitta, am,* n. a kind of metre consisting of four lines of eleven syllables each.

दोधूयमान *dodhūyamāna, as, ā, am* (fr. the Intens. of rt. 1. *dhū*), shaking or trembling violently.

दोमन् *doman, a,* n. (fr. rt. 2. *du*), pain, inconvenience, (occurring only in *a-doma-da,* q. v.)

दोरक *doraka, as, ikā,* m. f. a string for fastening the wires of a lute.

दोल *dola, as,* m. (fr. rt. *dul*), swinging, rocking, oscillating; a festival on the fourteenth of the month Phālguna (February-March) when figures of the juvenile Krishṇa are swung in an ornamental swing; a swing, litter; a peculiar position of the closed hand; (*ā*), f. a litter, a swinging cradle or cot or hammock, a dooly, palanquin, sedan, a swing, swinging; fluctuation, incertitude, doubt; the indigo plant. — *Dolākula-dhī* (°*lā-āk*°), *īs, īs, i,* or *dolā-ćala-ćittavṛitti, is, is, i,* whose mind is agitated like a swing. — *Dolādhirūḍha* (°*lā-adh*°), *as, ā, am,* mounted on a swing; restless, disquieted. — *Dolā-yātrā,* f. 'the swing festival,' N. of a festival in honour of Krishṇa when figures of him and his consort Rādhā are carried about in a litter or swung in an ornamental swing.

Dolāya, Nom. A. *dolāyate,* &c., to swing, rock about like a swing, shake, toss, move to and fro, fluctuate, oscillate, be unsteady.

Dolāyamāna, as, ā, am, oscillating, swinging, rocking, tossing, being swung backwards and forwards; vacillating, wavering; perplexed, doubting. — *Dolāyamāna-mati, is, is, i,* wavering in mind, with a wavering mind.

Dolāyita, as, ā, am, swinging about, oscillating, moving to and fro, rocking. — *Dolāyita-śravaṇa-kuṇḍala, as, ā, am,* whose ear-rings swing to and fro.

Dolikā, f. a litter, swing; a cradle.

Dolita, as, ā, am, swung, shaken, rocked, tossed backwards and forwards.

दोष *dosha, as,* m. (fr. rt. 1. *dush*), fault, vice, defect, deficiency, want, blemish, blame, accusation, reproach (with rt. *gam,* to accuse, e. g. *dosheṇa mām gaććhati,* he accuses me); a bad or noxious quality; badness, wickedness, sinfulness; offence, transgression, sin, guilt, crime; damage, harm, detriment; bad consequence, detrimental effect (e. g. *mātṛi-doshāt,* q. v.); morbid affection, morbid element, disease; disorder of the three humors of the human body, defect in the functions of *vāyu* or wind, *pitta* or bile, and *śleshman* or phlegm (e. g. *tridosha-kṛit,* causing disorder of the three humors); a N. applied to the three fluid elements or humors themselves (as causing diseases when in a state of derangement); evening, dusk, darkness, Evening personified as one of the eight Vasus and husband of Night; refutation; a calf; (1. *doshā*), f. evening, darkness, night; Night personified (regarded with Prabhā as wife of Pushpārṇa and mother of Pradosha or Evening, Niśītha or Midnight, and Vyushṭa or Day-break); *doshām,* ind. in the evening; *doshā,* old inst. in the evening, at dusk, at night; [cf. *anna-d*°, *tvag-d*°, *doshas, pra-dosha, prati-dosham.*] — *Dosha-kara, as, ī, am,* or *dosha-kārin, ī, iṇī, i,* or *dosha-kṛit, t, t, t,* causing evil or harm, hurtful. — *Dosha-kalpana, am,* n. attributing blame, reprehending, condemning. — *Dosha-grasta, as, ā, am,* involved in guilt, convicted, guilty. — *Dosha-grāhin, ī, iṇī, i,* fault-finding, censorious, vituperative, malicious, malignant; [cf. *guṇa-grāhin.*] — *Dosha-ghna, as, ī, am,* removing vitiation or disease of the humors. — *Dosha-jña, as, ā, am,* acquainted with what is noxious or dangerous, discerning sins, understanding diseases, knowing faults, &c.; (*as*), m. a physician; a Pandit, teacher, discerning man. — *Dosha-tas,* ind. from a fault or defect; *doshato brū,* to accuse of a fault. — *Dosha-traya, am,* n. vitiation of the three humors, or wind, bile, and phlegm; any combination of three defects. — *Doshatraya-hara, as, ā, am,* removing vitiation of the three humors. — *Dosha-tva, am,* n. faultiness, deficiency. — *Dosha-dṛishṭi, is,* f. looking at faults, fault-finding. — *Dosha-prasaṅga, as,* m. attaching blame, attribution of blame, censure, condemnation. — *Dosha-bala-pravṛitta, as, ā, am,* proceeding from the influence of bad humors (a disease). — *Dosha-bhāj, k, k, k,* possessing faults, wrong, faulty, doing wrong, being defective or to blame. — *Dosha-bhīti, is,* f. fear of offence. — *Dosha-bheda, as,* m. a peculiar modification of disease of the three humors. — *Dosha-vat, ān, atī, at,* having faults, faulty, defective, blemished, deficient; guilty of an offence; detrimental, connected with crime or guilt, sinful, wicked; noxious, dangerous. — *Dosha-śamana, as, ā, am,* allaying disorder of the humors. — *Dosha-sthāna, am,* n. the seat of disorder of the humors. — *Dosha-hara, as, ā, am,* removing disease of the humors. — *Doshākara* (°*sha-āk*°), *as, ā* or *ī, am,* 'a mine of faults,' full of defects, faulty; (°*shā-ka*°), *as,* m. 'the night-maker,' epithet of the Moon. — *Doshā-kleśī,* f. 'fading in the evening,' a kind of plant (= *vana-varvarikā*). — *Doshākshara* (°*sha-ak*°), *as,* m. 'a word of blame,' accusation, censure. — *Doshā-tana, as, ī, am* (fr. *doshā,* ind.), nocturnal, at evening, nightly. — *Doshā-tilaka, as,* m. 'the ornament of the night,' a lamp. — *Doshānuvāda* (°*sha-an*°), *as,* m. talking over faults, tale-bearing. — *Doshā-bhūta, as, ā, am,* having become night, turned into night. — *Doshā-manya, as, ā, am,* considering one's self as night, regarding as night; [cf. *divā-manya.*] — *Doshāropa* (°*sha-ār*°), *as,* m. imputing fault, accusation. — *Doshā-vastṛi, tā,* m. (generally occurring in loc. *doshā-vastar*), Ved. 'illuminating the darkness or shining in the evening,' an epithet of Agni; (Sāy.) by night and day. — *Doshāsya* (°*shā-ās*°), *as,* m. 'the face of the night,' a lamp. — *Doshaikadṛiś* (°*sha-ek*°), *k, k, k,* seeing only defects, fault-finding, censorious, malevolent. — *Doshoććhrāya* (°*sha-uć*°), or *doshopaćaya* (°*sha-up*°), *as,* m. the rise or undue accumulation of vitiated humors.

Doshaka, as, m. a calf.

Doshaṇa, am, n. imputation of a crime, accusation.

Doshala, as, ā, am, of a faulty nature, defective, corrupt.

Doshas, as, n. evening, darkness.

Doshika, as, ī, am, faulty, defective, bad; (*as*), m. sickness, disease.

Doshin, ī, iṇī, i, becoming defiled or impure or contaminated; faulty, defective; criminal, wicked, bad.

दोषन् *doshan,* m. n. (defective; substituted for *dos,* q. v., in certain cases), the fore-arm, the lower part of the fore-foot of an animal, the arm in general. — *Doshaṇi-śrish, ṭ, ṭ, ṭ,* leaning or hanging on the arm.

Doshaṇya, as, ā, am, Ved. belonging to the arm, seated in the arm (as a disease).

2. *doshā,* f. the arm. (For 1. *doshā* see col. 2.)

Dos, s, m. n. (nom. sing. *dos,* du. m. *doshau,* n. *doshī,* acc. pl. *doshas* or *doshṇas,* inst. sing. *doshā* or *doshṇā,* du. *dorbhyām,* loc. pl. *doḥshu,* Gram. 166. *d*), the fore-arm, the arm; the part of an arc defining its sine; the side of a triangle or square, [cf. *bāhu* and *bhuja.*] — *Doḥ-sahasra-bhṛit, t,* m. 'thousand-armed,' N. of a king also called Kārtavīrya. — *Dor-āndolana, am,* n. swinging the arm. — *Dor-gaḍu, us, us, u,* having a crippled arm, crooked-armed. — *Dor-graha, as, ā, am,* 'seizing with the arms,' strong, powerful; (*as*), m. pain in the arm. — *Dor-jyā,* f. the sine of the base. — *Dor-daṇḍa, as,* m. the arm; [cf. *daṇḍa.*] — *Dor-nikartana, am,* n. amputation of the arm. — *Dor-madhya, am,* n. the middle of the arm. — *Dor-mūla, am,* n. 'the root of the arm,' the armpit. — *Dosh-mat, ān, atī, at,* having arms. — *Do-stha* (for *doḥ-stha*), placed on the arm; (*as*), m. 'standing near the arm,' a servant [cf. *pārśva-stha*]; service; a player, one who plays or sports; play, sport.

दोह *doha, as,* m. (fr. rt. 2. *duh*), milking; milk; a milk-pail; making profit out of anything, satisfaction, success. — *Doha-kāma, as, ā, am,* Ved. desirous of being milked. — *Doha-ja, am,* n. 'produced by milking,' milk. — *Dohadohīya, am,* n. (fr. *doha-doha*), N. of a Sāman. — *Dohāpanaya* (°*ha-ap*°), *as,* m. milk.

Dohana, as, ā, am, milking, a milker; giving or yielding milk or other desirable objects; (*ī*), f. a milk-vessel, milk-pail; (*am*), n. milking, the result of milking; a milk-pail; [cf. *go-d*°.]

Dohanīya, as, ā, am, proper to be milked.

Dohas, as, n., Ved. milking; (the dat. *dohase* is used as an inf. of rt. 2. *duh.*)

Dohita, as, ā, am, made to yield milk, milked.
Dohin, ī, inī, i, milking; giving milk, granting or yielding desirable objects; a milker.
Dohīyas, ān, asī, as, giving much milk, yielding abundance of milk.
Dohya, as, ā, am, to be milked, milkable; *(as),* m. (?) a cow; [cf. *duhya, duḥkha-d°, sukha-d°.*]

दोहडिका *dohaḍikā,* f. a kind of Prākrit metre consisting of thirty-five syllables, (commonly called *dohā.*)

दोहद *dohada, as, am,* m. n. (a Prākrit form for *daurhṛida;* cf. *dauhṛida*), the longing of a pregnant woman, that craving after particular objects which is regarded as a sign of impregnation; (sometimes) the desired object itself; pregnancy; the desire of plants at budding time to be touched by the foot of a beautiful girl, (poetically imagined to cause the production of blossoms); violent or morbid desire, desire in general, wish; a kind of incense used as a manure. — *Dohada-lakshaṇa, am,* n. 'having longing desire as its mark,' the fetus, the embryo, (sometimes confounded with the womb itself); the period of passing from one season of life to another (as from childhood to youth, from youth to manhood). — *Dohada-vatī,* f. or *dohadānvitā* (°*da-an*°), f. 'possessing the desire of a pregnant woman,' a pregnant woman longing for anything; [cf. *dohala* and *divya-dohada.*]
Dohadin, ī, inī, i, eagerly longing for, desirous of, craving after.
Dohala, as, m. = *dohada,* longing, wish, desire, craving after; (ī), f. the Aśoka tree. — *Dohala-vatī* = *dohada-vatī.*

दौःशलेय *dauḥśaleya, as,* m. probably a metronymic from Duḥ-śalā.

दौःशासनि *dauḥśāsani, is,* m. (fr. *duḥ-śāsana*), a patronymic from Duḥ-śāsana.

दौःशील्य *dauḥśīlya, am,* n. (fr. *duḥ-śīla*), bad inclination or custom, bad character, badness of disposition, wickedness.

दौःष्वप्न्य *dauḥshvapnya, am,* n. (fr. *dush-svapna*), Ved. evil dreams; [cf. *duḥ-shvapnya.*]

दौःसाधिक *dauḥsādhika, as,* m. (the first syllable fr. *dvār?*), a door-keeper, a warder, a porter; a beadle; the superintendent of a village; [cf. *duḥ-sādhin.*]

दौःस्त्र *dauḥstra, am,* n. (fr. *duḥ-strī*), discord or wrangling contention between women.

दौकूल *daukūla* or *daukūlaka, as, ī, am* (fr. *dukūla*), covered with fine silk, see *dukūla; (am),* n. cloth made of Dukūla, silk cloth.
Daugūla = *daukūla* above.

दौत्य *dautya, am,* n. (fr. *dūta*), the state of a messenger, an embassy or message, mission; the office of a messenger; function of an ambassador.

दौरात्म्य *daurātmya, am,* n. (fr. *dur-ātman*), evil-mindedness, badness of soul, wickedness, depravity, mischievousness.

दौरित *daurita, am,* n. (fr. *dur-ita*), mischief.

दौरुधर *daurudhara, as, ī, am,* relating to the lunar mansion called Durudhara, q. v.

दौरेश्रवस *daureśravasa, as,* m. (fr. *dūre-śravas*), a patronymic of the priest of the serpents called Pṛithu-śravas.
Daureśruta, as, m. (fr. *dūre-śruta*), a patronymic of the serpent-priest Timirgha.

दौर्ग *daurga, as, ī, am* (fr. *dur-ga*), relating to Durga or Durgā.
Daurgasiṅha, as, ī, am, belonging to or composed by Durga-siṅha.
Daurgāyaṇa, as, m. a patronymic from Durga.
Daurgya, am, n. difficulty, inaccessibility.

दौर्गत्य *daurgatya, am,* n. (fr. *dur-gata*), misfortune, bad circumstances, want, wretchedness, distress.

दौर्गन्धि *daurgandhi, is,* m. or *daurgandhya, am,* n. (fr. *dur-gandha*), bad or disagreeable smell, badness of smell, fetor.

दौर्जन *daurjana, as, ī, am* (fr. *dur-jana*), consisting of wicked men.
Daurjanya, am, n. wickedness, maliciousness, depravity, vileness.

दौर्जीवित्य *daurjīvitya, am,* n. (fr. *dur-jīvita*), a miserable life, a wretched state of existence.

दौर्बल *daurbala* or *daurbalya, am,* n. (fr. *dur-bala*), impotency, feebleness, weakness, debility.

दौर्भागिणेय *daurbhāgiṇeya, as,* m. (fr. *dur-bhagā*), the son of a woman disliked by her husband; (ī), f. the daughter of such a woman.
Daurbhāgya, am, n. ill luck, misfortune, bad condition; the unhappiness of a woman resulting from the dislike of her husband.

दौर्भ्रात्र *daurbhrātra, am,* n. (fr. *dur-bhrātṛi*), a bad understanding between brothers.

दौर्मद्य *daurmadya, am,* n. (fr. *dur-mada*), a drunken brawl, a fight, battle.

दौर्मनस्य *daurmanasya, am,* n. (fr. *dur-manas*), evil-mindedness, evil disposition; mental pain, discomposure of mind, affliction, distress; despair.

दौर्मन्त्र्य *daurmantrya, am,* n. (fr. *dur-mantra*), bad consultation or counsel, evil advice.

दौर्मित्रि *daurmitri, is,* f. a metronymic from Dur-mitrā, q. v.

दौर्मुखि *daurmukhi, is,* m. a patronymic from Dur-mukha.

दौर्योधन *dauryodhana, as, ī, am* (fr. *dur-yodhana*), belonging or relating to Dur-yodhana &c.
Dauryodhani, is, m. a patronymic from Dur-yodhana, q. v.

दौर्लभ्य *daurlabhya, am,* n. (fr. *dur-labha*), difficulty of attainment, rarity, scarceness.

दौर्वचस्य *daurvaćasya, am,* n. (fr. *dur-vaćas*), evil speech, bad language.

दौर्वास *daurvāsa* or *daurvāsasa, as, ī, am* (fr. *dur-vāsas*), belonging to or composed by Dur-vāsas; *(am),* n., scil. *purāṇam,* N. of an Upa-Purāṇa.

दौर्विण *daurviṇa, am,* n. (fr. *dūrvā*), the sap or juice of bent grass; a clean leaf.

दौर्व्रत्य *daurvratya, am,* n. (fr. *dur-vrata*), Ved. disobedience, ill conduct.

दौर्हार्द *daurhārda, am,* n. (fr. *dur-hṛid*), badness of heart; hard-heartedness; evil disposition of mind, enmity.
Daurhṛida, am, n. evil disposition of mind, enmity; the longing of pregnant women, (perhaps originally the disgust felt by pregnant women for certain things); longing, desire.
Daurhṛidaya, am, n. evil disposition of mind, enmity.

दौलेय *dauleya, as,* m. (fr. *duli*), a turtle or tortoise.

दौल्मि *daulmi, is,* m. an epithet of Indra; [cf. *dalmi* and *dālmi.*]

दौवारिक *dauvārika, as,* m. (fr. *dvār* or *dvāra*), a door-keeper, warder, porter; the door-keeper of paradise (?).

दौवालिक *dauvālika, ās,* m. pl., N. of a people.

दौश्चर्म्य *dauśćarmya, am,* n. (fr. *duś-ćarman*), a disease of the skin, a defect in the generative organs (supposed to be a disease of the prepuce or paraphimosis).

दौश्चर्य *dauśćarya, am,* n. (fr. *duś-ćara*), acting wickedly, evil conduct, wickedness; a bad deed.

दौष्क *daushka, as, ī, am* (fr. *dos*), one who swims or crosses a stream by the help of his arms.

दौष्कुल *daushkula* or *daushkuleya, as, ī, am* (fr. *dush-kula*), sprung from a bad or low or contemptible family or race.
Daushkulya, as, ā, am, sprung from a bad or low family; *(am),* n. lowness of origin, low extraction.

दौष्कृत्य *daushkṛitya, am,* n. (fr. *dush-kṛita*), bad conduct, badness of conduct, wickedness.

दौष्ट्य *daushṭya, am,* n. (fr. *dushṭa*), depravity, badness, wickedness.

दौष्ठव *daushṭhava, am,* n. (fr. *du-shṭhu*), badness, wickedness.

दौष्मन्त *daushmanta, as,* or *daushmanti, is,* m. (fr. *dush-manta*), 'the son of Dush-manta,' a patronymic of Bharata, the first sole monarch of India.
Daushyanta, as, ī, am, relating to Dushyanta.
Daushyanti or *daushvanti* or *dauḥshanti, is,* m. a patronymic of Bharata.

दौहित्र *dauhitra, as,* m. (fr. *duhitṛi*), a daughter's son; a term applied to a rhinoceros; (ī), f. a daughter's daughter; *(am),* n. sesamum-seed; ghee from a brownish cow (?). — *Dauhitra-vat, ān, atī, at,* having or possessing a daughter's son.
Dauhitraka, as, ī, am, relating to a daughter's son.
Dauhitrāyaṇa, as, m. the son of a daughter's son.

दौहृद *dauhṛida, am,* n. (see *daurhṛida*), the longing or desire of pregnant women for certain things, pregnancy; [cf. *dohada.*]
Dauhṛidinī, f. a woman who has the longing which attends pregnancy, a pregnant woman.

द्य *dya.* See *a-dya.*

द्यस् *dyas.* See *sa-dyas.*

द्या *dyā,* f. = *jyā,* the sinew of a bow, a bow-string; (in Satapatha-Br. XIV. 6, 8, 2, *u-dya* = *uj-jya.*)

द्याम्पात *dyāmpāta, as,* m. (fr. *dyām,* acc. sing. of *dyo,* + *pāta*), N. of a man; [cf. *dayāmpāti.*]

द्यावा *dyāvā* (according to Sāy., Ṛig-veda VII. 65, 2) = *dyāvā-pṛithivī,* du. heaven and earth. — *Dyāvā-kshame* or *dyāvā-kshāmā* or *dyāvā-pṛithivī* or *dyāvā-pṛithivyau* or *dyāvā-bhūmī* or *dyāvā-bhūmyau,* f. du. (the comp. consisting of two Vedic duals which may even be separated by intermediate words), heaven and earth. — *Dyāvā-pṛithivī-vat, ān, atī, at,* Ved. connected with heaven and earth.
Dyāvāpṛithivīya or *dyāvāpṛithivya, as, ā, am,* relating to heaven and earth, sacred to them.

द्यु 1. *dyu,* cl. 2. P. *dyauti, dudyāva, dyoshyati, adyaushīt, dyotum,* to advance towards or against, approach, assail, attack; [cf. *didyu,* rt. 2. *div.*]
1. *dyut, t, t, t,* (at the end of a comp.) advancing against, assaulting.

द्यु 2. *dyu,* sharpness, in *a-dyu,* q. v.

द्यु 3. *dyu, us,* m. (connected with 3. *div,* q. v.), a N. of Agni or fire; *(u),* n. a day, brightness; heaven, sky, ether, paradise; *dyu* is the form of 3. *div,* used before terminations beginning with consonants and in comp., see 3. div; dyubhis = upa-dyubhis, in the course of days, in the course of time; [cf. Lat. nu-diu-s; Hib. an-diu, 'to-day.'] — Dyu-ksha, as, ā, am (fr. dyu and ksha = 3. kshi?), Ved. heavenly, celestial; light, brilliant; (as), m. epithet of Varuṇa; of Aryaman; of Indra; of Agni; of Soma. — Dyuksha-vaćas, ās, ās, as, Ved. uttering heavenly words. — Dyu-ga, as, m. 'going in the sky,' a bird; [cf. khe-ćara.] — Dyu-gaṇa, as, m. a given term of days (as a month &c.). — Dyu-gat, ind. (gat fr. rt. gam), Ved. pervading the sky, going through the sky; (according to Naigh. II. 15), quickly. — Dyu-ćara, as, ā, am, 'going or moving in heaven,' an inhabitant of heaven. — Dyu-jaya, as, m. conquering or gaining heaven; attainment of heaven. — Dyu-taru, us, m. the tree of heaven; [cf. deva-taru.] — Dyu-dala, as or am, m. or n. (?), 'dividing of the sky,' noon. — Dyu-dhuni, is, f. 'the river of heaven,' the Ganges. — Dyu-nadī, f. 'the river of heaven,' the Ganges. — Dyunadī-sangama, as, m. 'the confluence of the river of the sky,' N. of a place of pilgrimage mentioned in the Rasika-ramaṇa by Raghu-nātha. — Dyu-nirāsa, as, m. 'heavenly abode,' heaven; an inhabitant of heaven, a deity. — Dyunirāsa-bhūya, am, n. the becoming a deity. — Dyu-nivāsin, ī, m. 'an inhabitant of heaven,' a deity; a pious person. — Dyu-niś, au, f. du. or dyu-niśa, am, n. or dyu-niśe, n. du. day and night; dyu-niśam or dyu-niśi, for a day and night, by day and night. — Dyu-pati, is, m. 'the lord of heaven,' the sun; an epithet of Indra. — Dyu-patha, as, m. 'the path of heaven,' the upper part of the sky. — Dyu-maṇi, is, m. 'the jewel of the sky,' the sun; an epithet of Śiva. — Dyu-mat, ān, atī, at, Ved. bright, light, brilliant; clear, loud, heard from afar; serene; brisk, energetic, strong; excellent, conspicuous; (ān), m. an epithet of Agni; of Soma; of Brahmā; of the chariot of the gods; N. of a son of Vasishṭha; of Divo-dāsa (= Pra-tardana); of Manu Svāroćisha; (at), ind. clearly, brightly. — Dyumat-sena, as, m., N. of a prince of Śālva, father of Satya-vat. — Dyumad-gāman, ā, m., Ved. one who sings distinctly (rt. gai) or one who walks (rt. gam) within the sacred enclosure. — Dyu-maya, as, ī, am, light, clear; (ī), f., N. of a daughter of Tvashṭṛi and wife of the Sun. — Dyu-mārga, as, m. the path of the sky or air. — Dyu-yoshit, t, f. 'a heavenly woman,' an Apsaras. — Dyu-loka, as, m. the heavenly world; [cf. pṛithivī-loka, antariksha-loka, dyaur-loka.] — Dyu-shad, t, m. (fr. dyu-sad), an inhabitant of heaven, a god, deity; a planet. — Dyu-sad = dyu-shad. — Dyu-sadman, ā, m. 'an inhabitant of heaven,' a god. — Dyu-saras, n. the lake of heaven. — Dyu-sarit, t, f. or dyu-sindhu, us, f. 'the river of heaven,' the Ganges.

Dyumna, am, n. splendor, glory, majesty; clearness or serenity of mind, enthusiasm, inspiration; energy, ability, strength, power; wealth, property, substance; N. of a Sāman; (Sāy.) sacrificial offering, oblation; (as), m., N. of an author of a Ṛig-veda hymn; of a son of Manu and Naḍvalā; [cf. abhishṭi-d°, indra-d°, ṛita-d°, turi-d°.] — Dyumna-vat, ān, atī, at, Ved. inspired, sounding clearly; having wealth, rich, powerful; (Sāy.) accompanied by oblations. — Dyumna-vardhana, as, ā, am, Ved. increasing strength. — Dyumna-śravas, ās, ās, as, Ved. producing a strong or clear sound; (Sāy.) having splendid food or offerings. — Dyumna-sah or dyumna-sāh, ṭ, ṭ, ṭ, Ved. bearing or bringing strength; (Sāy.) carrying off or taking away wealth. — Dyumna-sāti, is, f., Ved. receiving inspiration or power; (Sāy.) obtaining food or glory. — Dyumna-hūti, is, f., Ved. inspired invocation; (Sāy.) invocation characterized by oblations or accompanied by offerings. — Dyumnodā, ās, ās, am (fr. dyumnas = dyumna? and dā), Ved. granting splendor.

Dyumnin, ī, inī, i, Ved. majestic; strong, spiritual; inspired, courageous; (Sāy.) having wealth, having food or oblations; (ī), m., N. of a son of Vasishṭha and author of a hymn of the Ṛig-veda.

Dyuran, ā, m. the sun; heaven.

Dyus, a contraction of divas, the gen. sing. of 3. div, day; [cf. adhare-dyus, anyatare-d°, apare-d°.]

Dyo, aus, f. (considered by native grammarians as another form of the base 3. div, forming in the nom. dyaus, as gaus fr. go, and used in a few comp.), the sky, heaven, paradise, &c.; see 3. div. — Dyo-kāra, as, m. 'a maker of brightness,' a goldsmith (?), a N. applied to some sort of handicraft. — Dyo-bhūmi, is, m. 'moving between heaven and earth (?),' a bird; (ī), f. du. heaven and earth. — Dyo-shad, t, m. (fr. dyo + sad), 'sitting in heaven,' a deity, a celestial. — Dyaur-dā, ās, ās, am (dyaur for dyaus, nom. of dyo), giving heaven. — Dyaur-loka, as, m. (dyaur for dyaus, nom. of dyo), the heavenly world. — Dyau-saṃśita, as, ā, am, Ved. impelled or incited by heaven.

द्युक dyuka, as, m. an owl. — Dyukāri (°ka-ari), is, m. 'the owl's enemy,' a crow; (wrong forms for dyūka and dyūkāri.)

द्युत 1. dyut, occurring in the Atharva-veda, and said to mean 'to be broken, to break;' it occurs IV. 12, 2, XII. 3, 22, in the past part. dyutta, as, ā, am, broken: Caus. dyotayati, -yitum, to break.

द्युत 2. dyut, cl. 1. A. dyotate, didyute (Pāṇ. VII. 4, 67; part. didyutāna), dyotishyate, adyotishṭa and adyutat (Ved. adyaut, adidyutat), dyotitum, to shine, to be bright or brilliant: Caus. P. dyotayati, &c., Aor. adidyutat, to make bright or brilliant, illuminate, irradiate; to cause to appear or become manifest, to enlighten, cause to understand; to express, mean: Desid. didyutishate and didyotishate: Intens. dedyutyate, dedyotti, Ved. Intens. davidyotti, davidyot, 3rd pl. davidyutati, part. davidyutat; [cf. rt. jyut, which is probably derived fr. dyut with change of d to j.]

3. dyut, t, f., Ved. shining, splendor, a ray of light.

Dyutad-yāman, ā, ā, a, Ved. having a shining or brilliant path.

Dyutāna, as, m., N. of a Ṛishi with the patronymic Māruta or Māruti, who is author of a hymn of the Ṛig-veda; N. of the hymn ascribed to him.

Dyuti, is, f. splendor, brightness, brilliancy, lustre, beauty; light, a ray of light; majesty, dignity; Splendor personified as a deity; (is), m., N. of one of the Saptarshis under the reign of Manu Meru-sāvarṇa IV; of a son of Manu Tāmasa. — Dyuti-kara, as, ī, am, producing splendor, illuminating, shining, handsome; (as), m. the polar star or (in mythology) the divine sage Dhruva. — Dyuti-mat, ān, atī, at, resplendent, bright, brilliant; majestic, dignified; (ān), m., N. of a prince of the Madras and father-in-law of Saha-deva; of a prince of the Śālvas and father of Ṛićīka; of a son of Madirāśva and father of Su-vīra; of a son of Priya-vrata and king of Krauñća-dvīpa; of a son of Prāṇa (or Pāṇḍu); of one of the seven sages under the first Manu Meru-sāvarṇa or under Manu Dakshasāvarṇi; N. of a son of Manu Svayam-bhuva; N. of a mountain. — Dyuti-mati, is, is, i, of brilliant understanding, clear-minded.

Dyutita, as, ā, am, illuminated, enlightened, shining; [cf. dyotita.]

Dyutitvā or dyotitvā, ind. (Pāṇ. I. 2, 26), having become bright or brilliant.

Dyutilā, f. the plant Hemionitis Cordifolia.

Dyota, as, m. light, lustre, brilliance; sunshine; heat; [cf. kha-d° and ćintya-d°.]

Dyotaka, as, ā, am, shining; illuminating [cf. kha-d°]; making clear, explaining; meaning, significant, expressing, expressive of. — Dyotaka-tva, am, n. the power or faculty of expressing, expressiveness.

Dyotana, as, ā or ī, am, shining, bright, brilliant; illuminating, enlightening [cf. kha-d°]; explaining, meaning; (as), m. a lamp; N. of a prince; (am), n. shining; illumination; making manifest, explaining, showing; sight, seeing.

Dyotanaka, as, ikā, am, making manifest, explaining; (ikā), f. explanation.

Dyotani, is, f., Ved. splendor, brightness.

Dyotamāna, as, ā, am, shining, being bright, brilliant.

Dyotayamāna, as, ā, am, illuminating, enlightening, irradiating.

Dyotita, as, ā, am, shone upon, illustrated, illuminated, &c., = dyutita, q. v. — Dyotita-prabha, as, ā, am, resplendent.

Dyotin, ī, inī, i, shining, brilliant, splendid.

Dyotis, is, n. light, brightness; a star. — Dyotir-ingaṇa, as, m. a shining insect, fire-fly. — Dyotish-patha, as, m. 'the path of the stars,' the upper part of the sky; (also read jyotish-patha.)

Dyotya, as, ā, am, to be made clear or expressed or explained.

Dyauta, am, n., N. of a Sāman.

Dyautāna, am, n. (fr. dyutāna), N. of a Sāman.

Dyauttra, am, n. light, splendor; forked lightning.

द्युत dyuta, am, n. (in astrology) N. of the seventh mansion; (also read dyuna or dyūna, q. v.)

द्युन dyuna = dyuta and 2 dyūna.

द्यू dyū, ūs, ūs, u (fr. rt. 2. div), playing, sporting with, delighting in, (used at the end of a comp., see aksha-d°, eka-d°, kama-d°); going after, (explained by some native commentators as derived fr. 1. dyu.)

Dyūta, as, am (past part. pass. of 2. div), gambled; (as, am), m. n. play, gaming, gambling, playing with dice or any inanimate object; (figuratively) a battle or fight (the end of a battle being as uncertain as that of a game); the prize won, that which is gained in battle; [cf. aksha-d°.] — Dyūta-kara, as, m. a gambler. — Dyūta-kāra or dyūta-kāraka, as, m. the keeper of a gaming-house; a gambler. — Dyūta-kṛit, t, m. a gambler. — Dyūta-krīḍā, f. playing at dice, gambling. — Dyūta-tā, f. gambling, gaming, playing with dice. — Dyūta-parvan, a, n., N. of a section of the Sabhā-parva of the Mahā-bhārata, comprising Adhyāyas 45–69. — Dyūta-pūrṇimā, f. or dyūta-paurṇamī (or more correctly -paurṇimī), f. the day of full moon in the month Kārttika (October–November), the night of which is spent in games of chance in honour of Lakshmī, goddess of fortune. — Dyūta-pratipad, t, f. the first day of the bright half of the month Kārttika kept as a festival and celebrated by gambling. — Dyūta-priya, as, ā, am, fond of gambling. — Dyūta-bhūmi, is, f. gambling-ground, playing-place. — Dyūta-viśesha, ās, m. pl. 'the different sorts of play,' N. of a chapter in the Kāma-sūtra by Vātsyāyana. — Dyūta-vīja, am, n. a cowrie, a small shell used as a coin and in playing. — Dyūta-vṛitti, is, m. a gambler by profession or the keeper of a gaming-house. — Dyūta-vaitaṇsika, as, m. one who lives by exhibiting fights between animals (?). — Dyūta-sabhā, f. a gaming-house, assembly of gamblers. — Dyūta-samāja, as, m. an assembly of gamblers, a gaming-house. — Dyūta-samāhraya-prakaraṇa, am, n. 'a treatise on the lawsuits arising from gambling,' N. of a chapter of the legal work Su-bodhinī by Viśveśvara. — Dyūtādhikārin (°ta-adh°), ī, m. the keeper of a gaming-house.

Dyūtvā, ind. having played or gambled.

द्यून 1. dyūna, as, ā, am (past part. pass. of 1. div or of 2. div, but not in the sense 'to gamble'), lamenting, sorrowful; playing (but not with dice); [cf. pari-dyūna.]

द्यून 2. dyūna, am, n. the seventh mansion or sign of the zodiac reckoning from that which the sun enters; [also dyūnaka in comp.; cf. dyuta and dyuna.]

द्यै 1. dyai, cl. 1. P. dyāyati, dadyau, &c., to despise, reprove, treat with contempt; to disfigure.

2. dyai, ind. fie! for shame!

द्यो *dyo.* See p. 438, col. 2.

द्योत *dyota, dyotita,* &c. See p. 438, cols. 2, 3.

द्यौष्पितृ *dyaush-pitṛi.* See 3. *div,* p. 413.

द्रकट *drakaṭa* or *dragaḍa, as,* m. a kettle-drum with which sleepers are awakened.

द्रङ्क्षण *drankshaṇa, am,* n. a measure or weight, = *tolaka.*

द्रङ्ग *dranga, as, ā,* m. f. a town, city; [cf. *udranga* and *tranga.*]

द्रढय *draḍhaya* (fr. *dṛiḍha*), Nom. P. *draḍhayati, -yitum,* to make firm, fasten, tighten; confirm, corroborate, affirm, assert; [cf. *dṛiḍhaya.*]

Draḍhika, as, m., N. of a man.

Draḍhiman, ā, m. firmness, hardness; heaviness; affirmation, assertion.

Draḍhishṭha, as, ā, am, (superl.) very hard, hardest, firmest, tightest.

Draḍhīyas, ān, asī, as, (compar.) harder, firmer, hardest.

द्रधस् *dradhas, as,* n., Ved. a garment (?).

द्रप्स *drapsa, as, ā, am* (fr. rt. 2. *dru* or rt. 2. *drā?*), dripping, falling in drops, flowing as liquid; (*as*), m. (according to some only used as a subst.), a drop (as of Soma &c.); a drop of fire, i. e. a spark, (the moon is considered in the Veda as a bright drop; cf. *indu*); diluted sour milk, thin coagulated milk, diluted curds; [cf. *trapsya;* Angl. Sax. *dropa;* Old Germ. *trofo, trauf, traufi.*] — *Drapsa-vat, ān, atī, at,* Ved. sprinkled with drops, besprinkled.

Drapsin, ī, inī, i, Ved. dripping, falling in drops, flowing thickly; distilling; gushing (as rain &c.).

Drapsya, am, n. thin coagulated milk, diluted sour milk, diluted curds.

द्रबुद्ध *drabuddha, as* or *am,* m. or n. (?), a particular high number.

द्रम् *dram,* cl. 1. P. *dramati, dadrāma, dramishyati, dramitum,* to run, go, move, run about: Caus. *dramayati, -yitum:* Desid. *didramishati:* Intens. *dandramyate* or *dandranti,* to run to and fro; [cf. rt. 2. *dru;* Gr. δρέμ-ω, ἔ-δραμ-ο-ν, δέ-δρομ-α, δρόμος.]

द्रमिट *dramiṭa* or *dramita, as,* m., N. of a serpent-king.

द्रमिल *dramila, as,* m., N. of a country; of a lexicographer [cf. *drimila*]; (*ās*), m. pl., N. of a school.

द्रम्म *dramma* (fr. Gr. δραχμή), a drachma.

द्रव *drava, as, ā, am* (fr. rt. 2. *dru*), running (as a horse); flowing, fluid; dropping, dripping, distilling, oozing; liquid; fused, liquefied, melted; (*as*), m. going, motion, quick motion, walking about; flight, retreat; play, sport, amusement; the act of dropping, distilling, trickling, exudation; fusion, fluid condition of a substance, liquefaction, fluidity; a liquid substance; juice, essence; decoction. — *Drava-ja, as,* m. a treacle. — *Drava-tā,* f. or *drava-tva,* or *dravatvaka, am,* n. fluidity, fusibility, fusion, natural or artificial fluid condition of a substance, wetness, distillation; ductility. — *Drava-dravya, am,* n. a fluid substance. — *Drava-rasā,* f. 'having fluid essence,' lac; gum; extract. — *Dravādhāra* (°*va-ādh*°), *as,* m. 'fluid-holder,' a small vessel or receiver. — *Dravī-karaṇa, am,* n. liquefying, melting. — *Dravī-kṛi,* cl. 8. P. *-karoti, -kartum,* to liquefy, dissolve, melt. — *Dravī-kṛita, as, ā, am,* liquefied, melted. — *Dravī-bhū,* cl. 1. P. *-bhavati, -bhavitum,* to become fluid. — *Dravī-bhūta, as, ā, am,* become fluid, liquefied, melted, fused. — *Dravetara* (°*va-it*°), *as, ā, am,* other than fluid, hard, solid, congealed. — *Dravottara* (°*va-ut*°), *as, ā, am,* chiefly fluid, very fluid.

Dravaka, as, ā, am, running.

Dravaṇa, as, ā, am, running, going; flowing, dropping, exuding; heat.

Dravat, an, antī, at, running, flowing, going; trickling, oozing; (*antī*), f. a river in general; the plant Anthericum Tuberosum; (*at*), ind. quickly, speedily. — *Dravać-ćakra, as, ā, am* (for *dravat-ćakra*), having rapid wheels. — *Dravat-pattrī,* f. a kind of plant (= *śimṛiḍi*). — *Dravat-pāṇi, ayas,* m. pl., Ved. 'swift of foot,' epithet of the horses of the Aśvins; (*ī*), m. du. 'possessed of quick-footed horses,' (Sāy.) 'having nimble hands (to seize the oblation),' epithet of the Aśvins. — *Dravad-aśva, as, ā, am,* Ved. drawn by swift horses (as a carriage).

Dravatya, Nom. P. *dravatyati,* &c., to become fluid.

Dravamāṇa, as, ā, am, flowing, fluid, melted.

Dravara, as, ā, am, Ved. running quickly.

Dravasya (fr. an unused *dravas*), Nom. P. *dravasyati, -yitum,* to harass one's self, take great pains; to attend upon or serve any person.

Dravi, is, m., Ved. a smelter, one who melts metal.

Draviṇa, am, n. (thought by some to be connected with 4. *dru*), any valuable possession, property, substance, goods, wealth, gold, money; thing, matter, material; that of which anything consists; substantiality; strength, power; N. of a Sāman; (*as*), m., N. of a son of Vasu Dhara (or Dhava); of a son of Pṛithu; of a mountain; (*ās*), m. pl. wealth (in Bhāg.-Purāṇa V. 14, 12); the inhabitants of a Varsha in Krauńća-dvīpa. — *Draviṇa-nāśana, as,* m. 'destroying vigour,' the plant Hyperanthera Moringa (= *śobhāñjana*). — *Draviṇa-vat, ān, atī, at,* possessing goods or property, rich; strong, powerful. — *Draviṇādhipati* (°*ṇa-adh*°), *is,* m. or *draviṇeśvara* (°*ṇa-īś*°), *as,* m. 'lord of wealth,' an epithet of Kuvera.

Draviṇaka, as, m., N. of a son of Vasu Agni; [cf. *draviṇa.*]

Draviṇas, as, n., Ved. property, possession, goods, substance; (*ās*), m., N. of a son of Pṛithu; (according to Sāy. on Ṛig-veda III. 7, 10, *draviṇas* is for *draviṇa,* and means 'moving, ever moving,' as applied to Agni.) — *Draviṇas-vat, ān, atī, at,* Ved. possessed of goods or wealth, procuring wealth. — *Draviṇo-da, as, ā, am,* or *draviṇo-dā, ās, ās, am,* or *draviṇo-das,* granting wealth or any desired good; (*as* or *ās*), m. an epithet of Agni; of Tvashṭṛi. — *Draviṇo-vid, t, t, t,* Ved. = *draviṇo-da.*

Draviṇasyu, us, us, u, Ved. desiring goods or wealth; (Sāy.) desiring sacrificial offerings; (*us*), m. an epithet of Agni.

Dravitṛi, tā, trī, tṛi, Ved. a runner, running.

Dravitnu, us, us, u, Ved. running, making haste.

1. *dravya, am,* n. (thought by some to be connected with 4. *dru*), a substance, thing, object; the ingredients or materials of anything; medicinal substance or drug; the receptacle or substratum of properties &c., elementary substance (nine kinds of which are reckoned in the Nyāya philosophy, viz. *pṛithivī,* earth; *ap,* water; *tejas,* fire; *vāyu,* air; *ākāśa,* ether; *kāla,* time; *diś,* space; *ātman,* soul; and *manas,* mind: the Jainas recognize only six, viz. *jīva, dharma, a-dharma, pudgala, kāla,* and *ākāśa*); an object possessed, a possession, wealth, property, goods, wares, chattels, money; a fit object; (according to lexicographers *dravya* may also mean) bell-metal, brass; ointment; anointing, plastering; spirituous liquor; modesty, propriety; a stake, wager. — *Dravya-gaṇa, as,* m. a class of similar substances (in medicine &c.). — *Dravya-guṇa, as,* m. 'the quality of medicinal substances,' N. of a chapter of the Purāṇa-sarva-sva by Halāyudha. — *Dravya-tas,* ind. in substance, according to substance, &c. — *Dravya-tva, am,* n. substantiality, substance. — *Dravya-dvaita, am,* n. duality of substance, instrumental cause (?). — *Dravya-niśćaya, as,* m. 'enquiry into the (elementary) substances,' N. of a chapter of Bhaṭṭotpala's commentary to Varāha-mihira's Bṛihat-saṃhitā. — *Dravya-parigraha, as,* m. the possession of property or wealth. — *Dravya-pūjā,* f. 'adoration of substance,' N. of a chapter of the Purāṇa-sarva-sva. — *Dravya-prakarsha, as,* m. the excellence of a matter. — *Dravya-prakṛiti, is,* f. the nature of a matter. — *Dravya-prayojana, am,* n. use or employment of any article. — *Dravya-maya, as, ī, am,* material, substantial; having or holding any substance; consisting of wealth. — *Dravya-yajña, as,* m. offering oblations, material sacrifice, &c. — *Dravya-vat, ān, atī, at,* having property, possessed of substance, rich, wealthy; inherent in the substance. — *Dravya-vardhana, as,* m. 'wealth-increaser,' N. of an author of a work on augury. — *Dravya-vāćaka,* a substantive. — *Dravya-vṛiddhi, is,* f. increase of wealth. — *Dravya-śuddhi, is,* f. cleansing of soiled or defiled articles, purification of inanimate objects; N. of a work. — *Dravyaśuddhi-dīpikā,* f., N. of a commentary on the Dravya-śuddhi by Purushottama. — *Dravya-saṃskāra, as,* m. consecration of articles for sacrifice, purification or cleansing of soiled or defiled articles. — *Dravya-sańćaya, as,* m. accumulation of property, a store of worldly goods. — *Dravya-sāra-sangraha, as,* m. 'collection of the essence of substances,' N. of a philosophical work. — *Dravya-siddhi, is,* f. acquirement of property or wealth; effecting an object by means of wealth. — *Dravya-hasta, as, ā, am,* holding anything in the hand. — *Dravyātmaka* (°*ya-āt*°), *as, ā, am,* substantial, containing a substance. — *Dravyātma-kāryasiddhi, is,* f. effecting one's object by means of wealth. — *Dravyāntara* (°*ya-an*°), *am,* n. another thing. — *Dravyārjana* (°*ya-ar*°), *am,* n. acquiring property, gain or acquisition of wealth. — *Dravyaugha* (°*ya-ogha*), *as,* m. a stream of wealth, abundance of property.

Dravyaka, as, m. = *dravya-vāhaka,* a carrier or taker of anything.

द्रविड *draviḍa, as,* m., N. of a people and district on the east coast of the Dekhan, (the people are regarded as degraded Kshatriyas; the name is said to be derived from Draviḍa son of Vṛishabha-svāmin); (*ī*), f., N. of a Rāginī.

द्रव्य 2. *dravya, as, ā, am* (fr. 4. *dru*), derived from or relating to a tree; (*am*), n. lac, the animal dye; extract, gum, resin. (For 1. *dravya* see col. 2.)

द्रष्टव्य *drashṭavya, as, ā, am* (fr. rt. 1. *dṛiś*), to be seen, visible, apparent; to be perceived or recognized, perceptible; to be understood; to be examined or investigated; to be regarded or considered as.

Drashṭu-kāma, as, ā, am (*drashṭu* for *drashṭum,* inf. of rt. 1. *dṛiś*), wishing to see, desirous of seeing.

Drashṭu-manas, ās, ās, as, having a mind to see, wishing to see.

Drashṭu-śakya, as, ā, am, able to be seen.

Drashṭṛi, ṭā, ṭrī, ṭṛi, a seer, spectator; one who examines or investigates or decides in a court of law, a judge; appearing, any person or thing that appears. — *Drashṭṛi-tva, am,* n. the faculty of seeing.

द्रह *draha, as,* m. a deep lake.

द्रह्यत् *drahyat* (fr. rt. *dṛih*), ind., Ved. firmly, strongly.

द्रा 1. *drā* or *drai,* q. v., cl. 4. 2. P. *drāyati, drāti,* &c., to sleep.

द्रा 2. *drā* (connected with rts. 2. *dru* and *dram*), cl. 2. P. *drāti, dadrau, drāsyati, drātum,* to run, make haste; run away, fly; to be ashamed or spoiled: Caus. P. *drāpayati, -yitum, adidrapat,* to cause to run: Intens. *dādrāyate, dādrāti, dādreti;* Old Intens. *daridrāti,* see *daridrā;* [cf. rt. 2. *dru,* rt. *dram:* Gr. ἀπο-δρᾶ-ναι, δι-δρά-σκ-ω, δρα-σ-μό-ς, ἄ-δρα-σ-το-ς; δρᾶ-π-έτη-ς fr. Caus. *drā-p-aya-ti.*]

Drāk, ind. (fr. rt. 2. *drā* + *ańć*), quickly, speedily, instantly, immediately, shortly, soon. — *Drāg-bhṛitaka, am,* n. water just drawn from the well.

Drāṇa, as, ā, am, flown, run away.

द्राक्षा *drākshā,* f. a vine, grape; (*as, ī,*

am), made of grapes; [cf. Hib. dearc, 'a berry;' perhaps Old Germ. *drûbo; Mod. Germ. traube;* Lat. *racemus* with dropped *d.*] — *Drākshā-prastha, as,* m., N. of a town. — *Drākshā-mat, ān, atī, at,* furnished with grapes. — *Drākshā-rasa, as,* m. grape-juice, wine. — *Drākshā-latā,* f. a vine, vine-tendril.

द्राख् *drākh,* cl. 1. P. *drākhati,* &c., to become dry or arid; to be able or competent or sufficient; to adorn; to prohibit or prevent; [cf. rts. *dhrākh* and 1. *trish;* Old Germ. *truk-an;* Angl. Sax. *drig, dryg, drī;* Old Iceland. *thurka,* 'to dry.']

द्राघ् *drāgh,* cl. 1. A. *drāghate,* &c. (probably a Nom. fr. *dīrgha,* but regarded as a separate rt.), to be able or competent; to stretch, lengthen; to exert one's self; to be tired or fatigued; to tire, vex, torment; to roam about, stroll.

Drāghaya (fr. *dīrgha*), Nom. P. *drāghayati,* &c., to lengthen, extend, stretch; to tarry, delay, to be slow or dilatory.

Drāghita, as, ā, am, lengthened, made long.

Drāghiman, ā, m. length; a degree of longitude. — *Drāghima-vat, ān, atī, at,* long, lengthy.

Drāghishṭha, as, ā, am (superl. fr. *dīrgha*), longest, very long.

Drāghīyas, ān, asī, as (compar. fr. *dīrgha*), longer, very or exceedingly long.

Drāghman, ā, m., Ved. = *drāghiman.*

द्राङ्क्ष् *drāṅksh,* cl. 1. P. *drāṅkshati,* &c., to utter a discordant sound; to croak, to caw &c. (as a bird); to desire, wish, long for; [cf. *dhrāṅksh.*]

द्राङ्गवध *drāṅgavadha, as,* m., N. of a man.

द्राड् *drāḍ,* cl. 1. A. *drāḍate,* &c., to divide, split, pierce, pull to pieces, &c.; to go to pieces; [cf. *dhrāḍ.*]

द्राप *drāpa, as,* m. mud, mire; heaven, sky; a fool, blockhead, an idiot; a N. of Śiva with his hair twisted or matted; a small shell, Cypræa Moneta.

द्रापि 1. *drāpi, is,* m., Ved. a mantle, garment.

द्रापि 2. *drāpi, is,* m. (according to Mahīdhara fr. the Caus. of rt. 2. *drā*), Ved. 'one who causes to run,' epithet of Rudra.

द्रामिल *drāmila, as,* m. (fr. *dramila*), 'born in Dramila,' N. of the Muni Ćāṇakya; (also *dromiṇa.*)

द्रायुध *drāyudha* (?), a peculiar species of horse.

द्राव *drāva, as,* m. (fr. 2. *dru*), flight, retreat; speed, going quickly; running, flowing; fusing, liquefaction; heat. — *Drāva-kara, am,* n. a kind of borax, a flux.

Drāvaka, as, ā, am (fr. the Caus.), causing to run; solvent; captivating, enchanting; cunning; (*as*), m. a flux to assist the fusion of metals; a kind of stone, a loadstone; a thief; a wit, wag, sharp or clever man; a libertine, a lecher; a kind of Rasa or sentiment; (*ikā*), f. saliva (as 'flowing'); (*am*), n. bee's wax (as 'melting'); a drug employed in diseases of the spleen. — *Drāvaka-kanda, as,* m. a kind of bulbous plant (= *taila-kanda*).

Drāvaṇa, as, ā, am, putting to flight, causing to run or retreat; fusing; (*am*), n. the act of causing to fly or retreat, putting to flight; fusing, distilling; the fruit of Strychnos Potatorum, used for purifying water; the clearing-nut.

Drāvayat-sakha, as, ā, am, Ved. causing a companion to go quickly; carrying a rider quickly away.

Drāvayāṇa, as, ā, am (part. fr. the Caus.), putting to flight, causing to run.

Drāvayitnu, us, us, u, Ved. causing to run or to make haste.

Drāvita, as, ā, am, made to run or fly, put to flight, chased, driven away; melted, liquefied; softened.

Drāvya, as, ā, am, to be made to run, to be set in motion, to be put to flight; fusible, liquefiable, to be made fluid.

द्राविड *drāviḍa, as, ī, am,* Drāviḍian, belonging to the Draviḍas, a Draviḍa; (*ās*), m. pl. the Draviḍa people and their country (properly the coast of Coromandel from Madras to Cape Comorin, or the country in which Tamul is spoken); (*as*), m. a Brāhman of Drāviḍa or rather of the south, (the name is applied to a class of Brāhmanical tribes called the five Drāviḍa Brāhmans, comprehending all those of the peninsula, i. e. Drāviḍa, Karṇāta, Gujerāta, Mahārāshṭra or Marāṭha, and Telinga); a patronymic from Draviḍa; N. of a scholiast of the Amara-kosha; a particular number; Curcuma Zedoaria (= *vedha-mukhya,* = *karćūra*); (*ī*), f. cardamoms.

Drāviḍaka, as, m. zedoary, Curcuma Zedoaria; (*am*), n. black salt (= *viḍ-lavaṇa*). — *Drāviḍa-bhūtika, as,* m. Curcuma Zedoaria.

द्राविणोदस *drāviṇodasa, as, ī, am* (fr. *draviṇo-das*), Ved. coming from or belonging to those who present gifts, i. e. from sacrificers; relating to Draviṇo-das, i. e. Agni.

द्रावित *drāvita.* See under *drāva,* col. 1.

द्राह् *drāh,* cl. 1. A. *drāhate,* &c., to wake; to deposit, pledge, put or cast down.

द्राह्यायण *drāhyāyaṇa, as,* m., N. of an author of certain Kalpa-sūtras. — *Drāhyāyaṇa-sūtra, am,* n. the Sūtras of Drāhyāyaṇa. — *Drāhyāyaṇa-sūtra-bhāshya, am,* n., N. of a commentary on the preceding work by Dhanvin.

Drāhyāyaṇaka, am, n. the Sūtras of Drāhyāyaṇa.

Drāhyāyaṇi, is, m. a patronymic from Drāhyāyaṇa.

Drāhyāyaṇīya, as, ā, am, relating to Drāhyāyaṇa, composed by him.

द्रिमिल *drimila, as,* m., N. of a lexicographer; (various reading for *dramila,* q. v.)

द्रु 1. *dru,* cl. 5. P. *druṇoti,* &c., to hurt, injure, wound or kill; to repent; to go; [cf. Old Germ. *drug, ga-driuzit, ar-driuzit.*]

द्रु 2. *dru* (connected with rts. 1. *drā* and *dram*), cl. 1. P. (in the poetry of the later language also A.) *dravati, -te, dudrāva, dudruve, droshyati, -te, adudruvat* (Ved. *adudrot, dudravat*), *drotum,* to run, make haste, run away, retreat, fly; to run up to, rush, attack, assault quickly (with acc.); to move, go; to become fluid, dissolve, melt; to distil or ooze; to drop: Caus. P. (ep. also A.) *drāvayati* (*-te*), Aor. *adudravat* or *adidravat,* &c., to cause to run or flow; to cause to run away, put to flight; to make fluid, melt; Ved. A. *dravayate,* &c., to run, flow: Desid. *dudrūshati;* Desid. of Caus. *dudrāvayishati* or *didrāvayishati:* Intens. *dodrūyate, dodroti;* [cf. Goth. *drib,* 'to drive,' fr. *drāvayati:* Angl. Sax. *driopan, dropa:* Old Germ. *trofo, trauf, traufi, triufan:* Lith. *drebo,* 'I tremble;' *drimba,* 'it drops;' *pa-dribbà,* 'running of the eyes:' Hib. *driogaim,* 'I trickle;' *drabh,* 'a chariot:' probably Germ. *tau,* 'dew,' from original *trau,* 'the river Drau:' probably also Lat. *gruere* in *in-gruere* and *ruere.*]

3. *dru, us, us, u,* at the end of a comp., cf. *mita-d°, raghu-d°, śata-d°;* (*us*), f. going, motion.

Druta, as, ā, am, quick, speedy, swift; quickly pronounced and therefore indistinct; flown, escaped, run or running away; scattered, diffused; liquid, dissolved, melted, fluid; (*as*), m. a scorpion; a tree [cf. *druṇa* and *druma*]; (*am*), ind. quickly, rapidly, instantly, immediately, without delay. — *Druta-tara, as, ā, am,* quicker, swifter; (*am*), ind. very quickly, as quickly as possible. — *Drutatara-gati, is, is, i,* having a very swift course, quicker in motion. — *Druta-tva, am,* n. melting, fusion. — *Druta-pada, as, ā, am,* quick of step, going quickly; (*am*), ind. a quick pace or step, quickly; (*am*), n. a kind of metre consisting of four lines of twelve syllables each. — *Druta-bodha, as,* m. 'quick understanding,' N. of a grammar. — *Drutabodhikā,* f., N. of a modern commentary on the Raghu-vaṅśa. — *Druta-madhyā,* f. 'quick in the middle,' a kind of metre consisting of two lines of twenty-three syllables each. — *Druta-varāha-kula, am,* n. a herd of flying boars. — *Druta-vikrama, as, ā, am,* having a quick step. — *Druta-vilambita, as, ā, am,* quick and slow alternately; (*am*), n. or *druta-vilambitaka, am,* n. a kind of metre consisting of four lines of twelve syllables each.

Druti, is, f., N. of the wife of Nakta and mother of Gaya.

द्रु 4. *dru, us, u,* m. n. = *dāru* (said to be fr. rt. *dṛī*), wood, any implement made of wood, as a cup or an oar; (*us*), m. (said to be fr. rt. 2. *dru,* to go or grow), a tree; a branch; [cf. 2. *dāru;* Zend *dru, dāuru,* 'wood, spear;' Gr. δρῦ-ς, δρῦ-μά, δρῦ-μό-ς, δρυ-τόμο-ς, δέν-δρε-ο-ν, δρία, δόρυ, δούρειος, δουράτ-εο-ς, δρύτη, δροίτη; Goth. *triu, triv-ein-s,* 'wooden;' Old Sax. *trio,* 'wood, tree;' Eng. *tree;* Slav. *drĕvo,* 'tree;' Lith. *derva.*] — *Dru-kilima, am,* n. a tree, a sort of pine, Pinus Deva-dāru; [cf. *kilima.*] — *Dru-ghaṇa* or *dru-ghana, as,* m. a wooden mace, mallet, hammer; an iron weapon made like a carpenter's hammer; an axe, a hatchet; a kind of plant [cf. *bhūmi-ćampaka*]; an epithet of Brahmā. — *Dru-ghnī,* f. a hatchet for cutting wood. — *Dru-ṇasa, as, ī, am,* 'having a nose like a tree,' large-nosed. — *Dru-ṇaha* or *dru-naha, as,* m. a scabbard, the sheath of a sword. — *Dru-pada, am,* n., Ved. a pillar or post of wood, a pillar in general; (*as*), m., N. of a king of the Pāñćālas, he was the son of Pṛishata and was father of Dhṛishṭa-dyumna, of Śikhaṇḍin, of Śikhaṇḍinī, and of Kṛishṇā the wife of the Pāṇḍu princes, hence called Draupadī; (*ā*), f., N. of a Ṛić; (*ī*), f. having large feet. — *Drupadātmajā* (°*da-āt*°), f. 'daughter of Dru-pada,' an epithet of Kṛishṇā or Draupadī, sometimes identified with Umā. — *Drupadāditya* (°*da-ād*°), *as,* m. a form of the Sun. — *Dru-padī,* f. a splay-footed female. — *Dru-mat, ān, atī, at,* furnished with wood. — *Dru-shad, t, t, t,* or *dru-shadvan, ā, varī, a* (fr. *dru-sad*), Ved. sitting in or on a piece of wood or a tree. — *Dru-sallaka, as,* m. a kind of tree. — *Drv-anna, as, ā, am,* Ved. one whose food is wood.

Druma, as, m. (said by some to be for *druhma* fr. rt. *dṛih*), a tree in general; a tree of Svarga or paradise; N. of a prince of the Kim-purushas; a prince of the Yakshas; (*ā*), f., N. of a river. — *Druma-kinnara-prabha, as,* m., N. of a prince of the Gandharvas. — *Druma-kinnara-rāja, as,* m., N. of Druma who was king of the Kin-naras. — *Druma-kinnararāja-paripṛićchā,* f. 'the questioning of Druma, king of the Kin-naras,' N. of a Buddhist work. — *Druma-nakha, as,* m. 'tree-nail,' a thorn. — *Druma-maya, as, ī, am,* made of wood, wooden. — *Druma-ratna-śākhā-prabha, as,* m., N. of a prince of the Kin-naras. — *Druma-vat, ān, atī, at,* overgrown with trees, woody. — *Druma-valka, as* or *am,* m. or n. (?), the bark of a tree. — *Druma-vyādhi, is,* m. 'tree-disease,' lac, resin. — *Druma-śīrsha, am,* n. 'tree-head,' a sort of decoration on the upper part of a building or wall. — *Druma-śreshṭha, as,* m. 'the best of trees,' epithet of the palm tree (= *tāla*). — *Druma-shaṇḍa, am,* n. an assemblage of trees; [cf. *taru-shaṇḍa* and *taru-khaṇḍa.*] — *Druma-sena, as,* m., N. of a king (identified with the Asura Gavishṭha). — *Drumāmaya* (°*ma-ām*°), *as,* m. 'tree-disease,' lac, the animal dye, resin; [cf. *druma-vyādhi.*] — *Drumāri* (°*ma-ari*), *is,* m. 'the enemy of trees,' an epithet of the elephant. — *Drumālaya* (°*ma-āl*°), *as,* m. a place of shelter or dwelling in trees. — *Drumāśraya* (°*ma-āś*°), *as, ā, am,* seeking shelter or dwelling in trees; (*as*), m. a lizard, chameleon. — *Drumeśvara* (°*ma-īś*°), *as,* m. 'the king of trees,' an epithet of the Pārijāta; the palm tree; an epithet of the Moon. — *Drumotpala* (°*ma-ut*°), *as,* m. the tree Pterospermum Acerifolium (= *karṇi-kāra*).

Drumara, as, m. a thorn.
Drumāya, Nom. A. *drumāyate*, &c., to pass or be counted or considered as a tree.
Druminī, f. (fr. *drumin* derived fr. *druma*), an assemblage of trees, a forest.
Drumila, as, m., N. of a Dānava who was prince of Saubha &c.; [cf. *dramila* and *drimila*.]
Druvaya, as, m., Ved. a wooden vessel, the wooden part of a drum; (*as, am*), m. n. a measure.

द्रुड् *druḍ*, cl. 1. and 6. P. *droḍati* and *druḍati*, &c., to sink, perish; [cf. rt. *drūḍ*.]

द्रुण् *druṇ*, cl. 6. P. *druṇati*, &c., to make crooked or curved, to bend; to go, move, approach; to hurt, injure, kill.
Druṇa, as, m. a scorpion; a bee; a rogue, cheat; (*ī*), f. a small or female tortoise; an oval vessel or basin of wood &c. (shaped like a boat and used for pouring or baling out water; cf. *droṇa* and *droṇī*); a bucket, a basket; a centipede; (*ā*), f. a bow-string; (*am*), n. a bow; a sword, scimitar; [cf. *dru-ṇaha*.]
Druṇi, is, f. = *druṇī, droṇī*, an oval water-basin of wood or stone &c.; a bucket, basket.

द्रुम्म् *drumm*, cl. 1. P. *drummati*, &c., Ved. to go.

द्रुह् 1. *druh*, cl. 4. P. (ep. also A.) *druhyati, dudroha, drohishyati, dhrokshyati, adruhat, drohitum, drogdhum* and *droḍhum*, to hurt, seek to hurt or injure or grieve, seek to do harm, to plot revengefully or maliciously, to contrive, machinate or meditate mischief (with dat., but also with gen., loc., acc.); to bear malice or hatred: Caus. *drohayati, -yitum*: Desid. *dudrohishati, dudruhishati, dudhrukshati*; [cf. rt. 1. *drū*: Goth. *driugan, dulgs*: Angl. Sax. *trucyan*: Old Germ. *triugan, drawyan*: Lett. *draudeht*, 'to menace:' Lat. *trux, atrox*: Hib. *driuch*, 'anger;' *droch*, 'evil.']
Drugdha, as, ā, am, injured, plotted against; an injurer; (*am*), n. offence, injury.
2. *druh, dhruk*, or (according to the grammarians) *dhruṭ*, (at the end of a comp.) injuring, having injured, hurting, acting as an enemy against; (in the older language often also in its uncompounded state) one who hurts or injures, an evil or hostile being or spirit; (*k*), f. injury, damage. — *Druhan-tara, as, ā, am*, Ved. conquering one who injures or an evil spirit.
Druhā, f., Ved. (according to Sāy. inst. sing. of 2. *druh*), injury, damage.
Druhu, us, us, u, Ved. = 2. *druh*, injuring, hurting.
Druhya, as, m., N. of a man; (*ās*), m. pl. his descendants.
Druhyat, an, antī, at, injuring, hurting, attacking, assailing, defying; tyrannizing over, oppressing.
Druhyu, avas, m. pl., N. of a people; (in epic poetry Druhyu is with Yadu a son of Yayāti, sometimes wrongly written *duhyu*.)
Druhvan, ā, varī, a, Ved. hurting, injuring; [cf. *a-d°*.]
Drogdhavya, as, ā, am, to be injured or hurt.
Drogdhri, dhā, dhrī, dhri, an injurer, one who seeks to hurt, malevolent.
Drogha, as, m. injury, damage; [cf. *a-d°*.] — *Drogha-mitra, as*, m., Ved. a mischievous friend. — *Drogha-vaćas, ās, ās, as*, or *drogha-vāć, k, k, k*, Ved. using injurious or malicious words; [cf. *a-d°*.]
Droha, as, m. injury, insidious wounding, hostile action, mischief, malice, perfidy, treachery, trespass; wrong, offence; rebellion; [cf. *a-d°*.] — *Droha-ćintana, am*, n. injurious design, malice prepense; the wish or thought or attempt to injure. — *Droha-buddhi, is, is, i*, maliciously minded, malevolent, one whose mind is set on mischief. — *Droha-vritti, is, is, i*, malicious, wicked; [cf. *a-d°*.] — *Drohāṭa* (°*ha-aṭa* or -*āṭa*), *as*, m. a false man; a religious impostor, an impostor; a hunter, deer-killer; a sort of metre, the Doha or stanza of Hindī poetry.
Drohita, as, ā, am (adj. fr. *droha* above), hostile, maliciously inclined.
Drohin, ī, iṇī, i, hurting, harming, injuring, endeavouring to hurt, malignant, malicious; rebellious.

द्रुह *druha, as*, m. a son; a lake [cf. *draha*]; (*ī*), f. a daughter.

द्रुहण *druhaṇa* or *druhiṇa, as*, m. (said to be either fr. rt. 1. *druh* or = *dru-ghaṇa*), an epithet of Brahmā; of Śiva.

द्रू 1. *drū*, cl. 9. P. *drūṇāti*, &c., to raise the arm or hand in order to strike, &c.; cl. 5. P. *drūṇoti*, &c., to hurt, injure, wound, kill; to go, move.

द्रू 2. *drū, ūs*, m. f.? (said to be fr. rt. 2. *dru*), gold; taking any shape at will.

द्रूघण *drū-ghaṇa, as*, m. = *dru-ghana*, a sort of hatchet, an iron club; an epithet of Brahmā.

द्रूण *drūṇa, as*, m. = *druṇa*, a scorpion; (*am*), n. a bow.

द्रूड् *drūḍ* or *drūḷ*, cl. 1. P. *drūḷati*, &c., Ved. to go; [cf. rt. *druḍ*.]

द्रेक् *drek* [cf. rt. *dhrek*], cl. 1. A. *drekate*, &c., to sound; to manifest joy or high spirits by noise; to grow, increase.

द्रेक्क *drekka* or *drekkāṇa* or *dreshkāṇa* = *drikāṇa*, q. v. — *Dreshkāṇādhyāya* (°*ṇa-adh*°), *as*, m. 'the chapter on the Drikāṇas,' N. of a chapter of the Brihaj-jātaka by Varāha-mihira.

द्रेश्य *dreśya, as, ā, am* (probably fr. a form *driś* for rt. 1. *driś*), visible, = *driśya*.

द्रै *drai*, cl. 1. P. *drāyati*, &c., to sleep; [cf. 1. *drā*; cf. also Gr. δαρθ-άν-ω, ἔ-δραθ-ο-ν; Lat. *dor-mi-o*; Slav. *drě-m-a-ti*, 'to sleep;' Old Sax. *drom*; Eng. *dream*; Mod. Germ. *traum*.]

द्रोण *droṇa, am*, n. (said to be fr. rt. 2. *dru*), a wooden vessel or cup, a bucket, a tub; a trough; a Soma vessel; (*as, am*), m. n. a measure of capacity, = 4 Āḍhakas, = 16 Pushkalas, = 128 Kuńćis, = 1024 Mushṭis, or = 200 Palas, = $\frac{1}{20}$ Kumbha, or = $\frac{1}{16}$ Khārī, = 4 Āḍhakas, or = 2 Āḍhakas, = $\frac{1}{2}$ Śūrpa, = 64 Śeras, or = 32 Śeras; a measure for measuring fields, as much land as is sown with a droṇa of corn; (*as*), m. a lake or large piece of water of 400 poles length; a cloud abounding in water; a peculiar kind of cloud (from which the rain streams forth as from a bucket); a raven, or perhaps the carrion-crow [cf. *droṇa-kāka*]; a scorpion [cf. *druṇa*]; a small tree bearing white flowers, commonly Ghalaghasiyā and Halakasiyā; N. of a man; N. of a Brāhman said to have been generated by Bharad-vāja in a bucket or wooden vessel, (he was called Droṇāćārya as military preceptor of both the Kuru and Pāṇḍu princes; afterwards he became king of a part of Pāńćāla and general of the Kurus against the Pāṇḍu princes; he was husband of Kripī and father of Aśvatthāman); N. of one of the four sons of Maṇḍa-pāla and Jaritā (who were born as birds); N. of one of the eight Vasus (whose children by Abhi-mati were Harsha, Śoka, and Bhaya); N. of a Brāhman; N. of a mountain; (*ā*), f. a kind of shrub [cf. *droṇa-pushpī*]; N. of a daughter of Siṅha-hanu; (*ī*), f. any oval vessel made of wood &c. (shaped like a boat and used for holding or pouring out water, as a bathing-tub, a baling-vessel, a basin, bucket, a watering-pot, &c.); a trough or trough-like rack for feeding cattle; a measure of capacity, = 2 Śūrpas, = 128 Śeras; the hollow of two mountains, the valley or chasm between them; N. of two plants, the indigo plant and a sort of coloquintida (= *indra-ćirbhiṭī*); N. of a country; of a river; a kind of salt brought from Droṇī; [cf. *droṇī-lavaṇa, droṇija, droṇeya*; cf. also Zend *draona*.] — *Droṇa-kalaśa, as*, m. a large wooden vessel for the Soma. — *Droṇa-kāka* or *droṇa-kākala, as*, m. a raven; [cf. *droṇa*.] — *Droṇa-kshīrā*, f. a cow yielding a droṇa of milk. — *Droṇa-gandhikā*, f. a kind of plant. — *Droṇa-ghā*, f. (corrupted fr. *droṇa-dughā*), = *droṇa-dughā*, a cow yielding a droṇa of milk. — *Droṇa-ćit, t, t, t*, Ved. arranged in the form of a droṇa. — *Droṇa-dugdhā* or *droṇa-dughā*, f. a cow yielding a droṇa, i. e. much milk. — *Droṇa-padī*, f. having feet like a droṇa (oval-shaped?). — *Droṇa-parṇī*, f. the tree Musa Sapientum. — *Droṇa-parvan, a*, n. 'the Droṇa section,' N. of the seventh book of the Mahā-bhārata. — *Droṇa-pushpī*, f. a kind of small shrub (= *kumbha-yoni, kurumbā, kurumbikā, kharva-pattrā, ćitra-pattrikā, ćitrākshupa, su-pushpā*, commonly *gūmā*); another plant (= *go-śīrshaka*, commonly *ghalaghasiyā*). — *Droṇa-maya, as, ī, am*, full of droṇas, consisting only of a droṇa. — *Droṇa-mānā*, f. = *droṇa-dugdhā*, q. v. — *Droṇa-mukha, am*, n. the capital of a district, the chief of 400 villages; the end of a valley; (also read *droṇī-mukha*.) — *Droṇa-megha, as*, m. a peculiar kind of cloud from which the rain streams forth as from a watering-pot; [cf. *droṇa*.] — *Droṇam-paća, as, ā, am*, 'one who cooks a droṇa,' i. e. liberal in entertaining. — *Droṇa-vrishṭi, is*, f. a peculiar kind of rain streaming forth from a cloud as from a droṇa; [cf. *droṇa* and *droṇa-megha*.] — *Droṇa-śarma-pada, am*, n., N. of a Tīrtha. — *Droṇa-sāć, k, k, k*, Ved. fixed on or belonging to a droṇa. — *Droṇa-siṅha, as*, m., N. of a prince of the Vallabhī dynasty. — *Droṇa-stūpa, as*, m., N. of a Stūpa (said to be so called as containing a droṇa holding certain relics of Śākya-muni). — *Droṇāćārya* (°*ṇa-āć*°), *as*, m., N. of Droṇa, son of Bharad-vāja, as Āćārya or teacher of the Kuru and Pāṇḍu princes. — *Droṇāsa* (°*ṇa-āsa*), *as*, m. 'whose mouth is shaped like a droṇa (?),' N. of a demon who causes diseases; (*āsa* = *āsan?*, perhaps = *dīrgha-nāsa*; cf. *dru-ṇasa*.) — *Droṇāhāva* (°*ṇa-āh*°), *as, ā, am*, Ved. using the box of a chariot for a droṇa. — *Droṇī-ja, am*, n. = *droṇī-lavaṇa*. — *Droṇī-dala, as*, m. Pandanus Odoratissimus. — *Droṇī-padī*, f. = *droṇa-padī*. — *Droṇī-mukha, as*, m. = *droṇa-mukha*. — *Droṇī-lavaṇa, am*, n. a kind of salt coming from Droṇī. — *Droṇodana* (°*ṇa-od*°), *as*, m., N. of a son of Siṅha-hanu and uncle of Śākya-muni. — *Droṇy-aśva, as, ā, am*, Ved. having clouds (*droṇī*) for horses; (Sāy.) quickly pervading. — *Droṇy-āmaya, as*, m. a disease of the interior of the body, (the body being compared to a hollow droṇī.)
Droṇaka, ās, m. pl. 'the inhabitants of a valley,' N. of a people.
Droṇi, is, f. [cf. *droṇī* under *droṇa* above], any oval vessel made of wood &c. in the shape of a boat and used for holding and pouring out water, as a tub, bucket, baling-vessel, watering-pot, &c.; N. of a country.
Droṇikā, f. a tub, bucket, trough, &c.; (metaphorically) the tongue bent in the form of a droṇa (by which the sound *sh* is produced); the indigo plant.
Droṇeya, am, n. = *droṇī-lavaṇa*.
Droṇya, as, ā, am, Ved. belonging to a bucket, tub, trough, rack, &c.
Drauṇa, as, ī, am, containing a droṇa.
Drauṇāyana, as, m. or *drauṇāyani, is*, m. a patronymic of Aśvatthāman son of Droṇa.
Drauṇi, is, m. a patronymic of Aśvatthāman; of Vyāsa in a future Dvāpara.
Drauṇika, as, ī, am, containing a droṇa; sown with a droṇa of grain (as a field); (*ī*), f. a vessel holding a droṇa by measure.
Drauṇī, f. (a wrong form for *droṇī*), a trough, tub, &c.

द्रोमिण *dromiṇa, as*, m. = *drāmila*, q. v.

द्रौघण *draughaṇa, as, ī, am*, an adj. formed fr. *dru-ghaṇa*, q. v.

द्रौपद *draupada, as*, m. (fr. *dru-pada*), in *draupadāditya*, a form of the Sun; (*ī*), f. a patronymic of Krishṇā, wife of the Pāṇḍu princes. — *Draupadī-ja, as*, m. (for *draupadī-ja*), a son of Draupadī. — *Draupadī-pramātha, as*, m. the forcible abduction of Draupadī; [cf. *draupadī-haraṇa.*] — *Draupadī-vastrāharaṇa* (°*ra-āh*°), *am*, n. 'the seizure of Draupadī's garments,' N. of a poem by an unknown author on the story told in Sabhā-p. 2186. — *Draupadī-haraṇa, am*, n. 'forcible abduction of Draupadī,' N. of a section of the Mahā-bh. Vana-p. 15492.

Draupadeya, as, m. a patronymic of any of the five sons of the five Pāṇḍu princes, viz. of Prativindhya, son of Yudhi-shṭhira; of Suta-soma, son of Bhīma; of S'ruta-kīrtti or S'ruta-karman, son of Arjuna; of S'atānīka, son of Nakula; and of S'ruta-sena, son of Saha-deva.

द्रौह्य *drauhya, as*, m. (fr. *druhya*), a patronymic from Druhya.

Drauhyava, as, m. a patronymic from Druhyu.

द्व *dva*. See *dvā* and *dvi*.

Dvaka, au, du. (fem. *dvake* or *dvike*), Ved. two and two, two by two.

द्वन्द *dvanda, am*, n. (fr. *dvandva*), a pair, a couple; (*as*), m. a clock or plate on which the hours are struck.

द्वन्द्व *dvandva, am*, n. (a reduplicated form fr. *dva*), a pair, brace, couple; a couple of animals of different sexes, male and female; any two things taken together, any pair of qualities or conditions which are the opposite of one another (e. g. heat and cold, happiness and misery, &c.); strife, contention, bickering, dispute, quarrel, contest, fight; a fight between two persons, a duel; doubt, uncertainty; a stronghold, fortress; a secret; using sacrificial vessels? (*as*), m. (rarely n.) a form of compound or grammatical combination (*samāsa*) uniting two or more words which if uncompounded would be in the same case and connected by the conjunction 'and,' (this form of compound was called *dvandva* as originally combining couples or pairs of things, e. g. *Rāma-lakshmaṇau*, Rāma and Lakshmaṇa; *pāṇi-pādam*, hand and foot); (*as*), m., N. of several Ekāhas; the sign of the zodiac Gemini; a species of disease, a complication of two disorders, a compound affection of two humors [cf. *nir-d*°]; (*am* or *ena*), ind. two by two. — *Dvandva-ćara, as, ā, am*, going about or living in couples; (*as*), m. the ruddy goose, Anas Casarca. — *Dvandva-ćārin, ī, iṇī, i*, living in couples; (*ī*), m. the ruddy goose. — *Dvandva-ja, as, ā, am*, produced or proceeding from morbid affection of two humors; proceeding from a pair &c.; arising from a quarrel, occasioned by a dispute. — *Dvandva-duḥkha, am*, n. pain arising from alternations (as of heat and cold, pleasure and pain, &c.). — *Dvandva-bhāva, as*, m. antagonism, discord. — *Dvandva-bhinna, am*, n. separation of the sexes. — *Dvandva-bhūta, as, ā, am*, become doubtful, hesitating, irresolute. — *Dvandva-moha, as*, m. trouble excited by doubt. — *Dvandva-yuddha, am*, n. a duel, single combat. — *Dvandvayuddha-varṇana, am*, n. 'description of the single combat,' N. of the forty-first chapter of the Krīḍā-khaṇḍa or second part of the Gaṇeśa-Purāṇa. — *Dvandva-yodhin, ī, inī, i*, fighting in couples or by single combat. — *Dvandva-śas*, ind. two by two, in couples. — *Dvandva-sahishṇu-tva, am*, n. ability of supporting opposites (as happiness and misery &c.). — *Dvandvātīta* (°*va-at*°), *as, ā, am*, gone beyond or freed from pairs of opposite worldly affections. — *Dvandvī-bhūta, as, ā, am*, engaged in single combat or close fighting.

Dvandvin, ī, inī, i, forming a couple; opposed to one another; contradictory, quarrelsome, antagonistic.

द्वय *dvaya, as, ī, am* (fr. *dva*; in S'iśupāla-b. III. 57. *dvaye* nom. pl. m. occurs), twofold, double, of two kinds or sorts; (*ī*), f. a pair; (*am*), n. a pair, couple, two things, both, a brace (chiefly used at end of comps., e. g. *go-dvayam*, a couple of oxen); the masc. and fem. gender (in grammar); twofold nature, untruthfulness. — *Dvaya-vādin, ī, inī, i*, double-tongued, insincere. — *Dvaya-hīna, as, ā, am*, destitute of both (masc. and fem.) genders, i. e. neuter. — *Dvayāgni* (°*ya-ag*°), *is*, m. a kind of tree, = *pāṭhin, hrasvāgni*, commonly *rāṅćitā*, Plumbago Zeylanica. — *Dvayātiga* (°*ya-at*°), *as, ā, am*, one who has passed beyond or overcome the two bad qualities, passion and ignorance, or who has surmounted the several pairs of affection which disturb the mind; (*as*), m. a saint, a holy or virtuous man. — *Dvayātmaka* (°*ya-āt*°), *as, ā, am*, having a twofold nature, appearing in a twofold manner.

Dvayat, dvayas. See *a-d*°.

Dvayāvin, ī, inī, i, Ved. false, dishonest.

Dvayu, us, us, u, Ved. false, dishonest; [cf. *a-d*°.]

द्वर *dvara, as, ā, am*, or *dvari, is, is, i*, or *dvarin, ī, iṇī, i* (fr. rt. *dvṛi*), Ved. obstructing.

द्वा *dvā*, old nom. du. m. fr. *dva* = *dvi*, two (in comp. before other numerals and before *ja* and *para*). — *Dvāćatvāriṅśa, as, ī, am*, the 42nd. — *Dvā-ćatvāriṅśat, t*, or *dvā-ćatvāriṅśati, is*, f., 42. — *Dvā-ja, as*, m. a son of two fathers, (formed to explain one derivation of *bhara-dvāja*, which is however more properly deduced from *bharat* and *vāja*.) — *Dvātriṅśa, as, ī, am*, the 32nd; consisting of 32. — *Dvā-triṅśat, t*, f., 32. — *Dvātriṅśad-aksharin, ī*, m. a book or composition written in S'lokas (consisting of 32 syllables). — *Dvātriṅśad-rātra, am*, n., scil. *sattram*, a sacrifice lasting 32 days. — *Dvātriṅśal-lakshaṇopeta* (°*ṇa-up*°), *as, ā, am*, 'having 32 auspicious marks or spots upon the body,' illustrious, great. — *Dvātriṅśikā*, f. occurring in the compound *Bharaṭaka-dvātriṅśikā*, q. v. — *Dvādaśa, as, ī, am*, the 12th (e. g. *dvādaśo bhāgaḥ*, the 12th part); consisting of 12, divided into 12 parts; accompanied by or increased by 12; (*ī*), f., scil. *rātri* or *tithi*, the 12th day of the half month; (*am*), n. a collection or aggregate of 12; [cf. Gr. δώ-δεκα; Lat. *duo-decim*; Hib. *da-deug*; Hindūst. *bā-rah* through change of *d* into *r*; Lith. *dwy-lika* through change of *d* into *l*; Goth. *tva-lif* through change of the guttural into the labial; Eng. *twelve*; Mod. Germ. *zwö-lf*.] — *Dvādaśaka, as, ī, am*, the 12th; containing 12, consisting of 12, amounting to 12; (*am*), n. the aggregate of 12. — *Dvādaśa-kapāla, as, ī, am*, having 12 skulls. — *Dvādaśa-kara, as, ā, am*, possessed of 12 hands or rays; (*as*), m. an epithet of Kārttikeya; of Bṛihas-pati. — *Dvādaśa-gava, as, ī, am*, having 12 oxen or cows. — *Dvādaśa-tā*, f. or *dvādaśa-tva, am*, n. the aggregate of 12. — *Dvādaśa-dhā*, ind. into or in 12 parts or ways, twelvefold. — *Dvādaśan, a*, m. f. n. pl., 12. — *Dvādaśa-pattraka, am*, n., N. of a Yoga or particular religious observance in which the 12 syllables *oṃ namo bhagavate vāsudevāya* are connected with the 12 signs of the zodiac and with the 12 months. — *Dvādaśa-bhuja, as, ā, am*, having 12 arms; (*as*), m., N. of one of Skanda's attendants. — *Dvādaśama, as, ī, am*, the 12th; [cf. *dvādaśa*.] — *Dvādaśa-mahā-vākya-vivaraṇa, am*, n. 'the explanation of the 12 great words,' N. of a philosophical work by Vaikuṇṭha-purī. — *Dvādaśa-mūla, as*, m. 'having 12 roots or sources (?),' an epithet of Vishṇu. — *Dvādaśa-rātra, am*, n. a period of 12 nights (or days); (*as, ā, am*), lasting 12 nights (or days). — *Dvādaśarća* (°*śa-ṛića*), *as, ā, am*, containing 12 verses (Ṛićs). — *Dvādaśa-liṅgodbhava* (°*ga-ud*°), *am*, n. 'the origin of the 12 Liṅgas,' N. of a chapter of the Vrata-prakāśa by Viśva-nātha. — *Dvādaśa-loćana, as, ā, am*, twelve-eyed; (*as*), m. an epithet of Kārttikeya. — *Dvādaśa-vārshika, as, ī, am*, 12 years old or lasting 12 years. — *Dvādaśavārshika-vrata, am*, n. a vow for 12 years. — *Dvādaśa-vidha, as, ā, am*, twelvefold. — *Dvādaśa-śata, am*, n., 112. — *Dvādaśaśata-tama, as, ī, am*, the 112th. — *Dvādaśa-sāhasra, as, ī, am*, consisting of 12000 (years). — *Dvādaśāṅśu* (°*śa-aṅ*°), *us, us, u*, having 12 rays; (*us*), m. an epithet of Bṛihaspati; the planet Jupiter over which Bṛihas-pati presides; [cf. *dvādaśa-kara* and *dvā-daśārćis*.] — *Dvādaśākṛiti* (°*śa-āk*°), *is, is, i*, having 12 shapes. — *Dvādaśāksha* (°*śa-ak*°), *as, ī, am*, twelve-eyed; (*as*), m. an epithet of Kārttikeya; N. of one of the attendants of Kārttikeya; a Buddha; [cf. *dvādaśākhya*.] — *Dvādaśākshara* (°*śa-aksh*°), *as, ā, am*, containing 12 syllables; [cf. *dvādaśa-pattraka*.] — *Dvādaśākshara-mantra, am*, n. a prayer of 12 syllables addressed to Vishṇu (viz. *oṃ namo bhagavate vāsudevāya*). — *Dvādaśākhya* (°*śa-ākh*°), *as*, m. a Buddha; [cf. *dvādaśāksha*.] — *Dvādaśāṅgī* (°*śa-aṅ*°), f. the collective sacred writings of the Jainas (consisting of 12 parts). — *Dvādaśāṅgula* (°*śa-aṅ*°), *as*, m. a measure of 12 fingers. — *Dvādaśātman* (°*śa-āt*°), *ā, ā, a*, appearing in 12 forms; (*ā*), m. or *dvādaśātmaka, as*, m. the sun (as identified with the 12 Ādityas or the sun in each month of the year). — *Dvādaśāditya-tīrtha* (°*śa-ād*°), *am*, n., N. of a sacred bathing-place. — *Dvādaśādityāśrama* (°*śa-āditya-āś*°), *as*, m., N. of a sacred hermitage. — *Dvādaśādhyāyī* (°*śa-adh*°), f., N. of Jaimini's Mīmāṅsā consisting of 12 Adhyāyas. — *Dvādaśānyika* (°*śa-an*°), *as, ā, am*, one who has made 12 mistakes in reading. — *Dvādaśāyus* (°*śa-āy*°), *us*, m. 'whose life lasts 12 years,' a dog. — *Dvādaśāra* (°*śa-ara*), *as, ā, am*, Ved. having 12 spokes (as the wheel or cycle of the year). — *Dvādaśāratni* (°*śa-ar*°), *is, is, i*, being 12 cubits long. — *Dvādaśārćis* (°*śa-ar*°), *is, is, is*, containing 12 rays; (*is*), m. an epithet of Bṛihas-pati or the planet Jupiter; [cf. *dvādaśa-kara* and *dvādaśāṅśu*.] — *Dvādaśāśra* or (less correctly) *dvādaśāsra, am*, n. or *dvādaśāśri, is*, f. or *dvādaśāsri* (°*śa-aś*°), f. a dodecagon, a dodecagonal figure. — *Dvādaśāha* (°*śa-aha*), *as*, m. a period of 12 days; (*as, ā, am*), lasting 12 days; (*as*), m. a particular ceremony lasting 12 days; [cf. *bharata-d*°.] — *Dvādaśāhika, as, ī, am* (fr. *dvādaśan* + *ahan*), relating to or coming from a period of 12 days. — *Dvādaśika*, taking place or happening on the 12th day or on the 12th day of a half month. — *Dvādaśin, ī, inī, i*, consisting of 12, divided into 12. — *Dvādaśī-tīrtha, am*, n., N. of a sacred bathing-place mentioned in the S'iva-Purāṇa. — *Dvādaśī-vrata, am*, n. a peculiar religious observance on the 12th day of a half month. — *Dvānavata, as, ī, am*, the 92nd. — *Dvā-navati, is*, f. = *dvi-navati*, 92. — *Dvāpańćāśa, as, ī, am*, the 52nd; accompanied by 52, increased by 52. — *Dvā-pańćāśat, t*, f., 52. — *Dvāpara, as, am*, m. n. that die or side of a die which is marked with two spots or points; the Die personified; 'the age with the number two,' N. of the third of the four Yugas or ages of the world, comprising 2400 years, (the Yuga itself = 2000, each twilight = 200 years); the Age personified as a god; doubt, uncertainty. — *Dvāviṅśa, as, ī, am*, the 22nd; consisting of 22. — *Dvā-viṅśati, is*, f., 22. — *Dvāviṅśati-tama, as, ī, am*, the 22nd. — *Dvāviṅśati-dhā*, in 22 parts or ways, twenty-two-fold. — *Dvāviṅśati-śata, am*, n., 122. — *Dvāviṅśatiśata-tama, as, ī, am*, the 122nd. — *Dvāshashṭa, as, ī, am*, the 62nd; accompanied by or joined with 62; [cf. *dvi-shashṭi*.] — *Dvāshashṭi, is*, f., 62. — *Dvāshashṭi-tama, as, ī, am*, the 62nd. — *Dvāsaptata, as, ī, am*, the 72nd. — *Dvāsaptati, is*, f., 72; [cf. *dvi-s*°.]

द्वादशन् *dvā-daśan*. See *dvā*, col. 2.

द्वार् *dvār, r*, f. (said to be fr. rt. *dvṛi*), Ved. a gate, door, entrance; access, way; expedient, means, opportunity; *dvārā*, inst. c., at the end of a comp. = by means of, by; [cf. 1. *dur*, 2. *dura*; Zend *dvara-m*, 'gate, palace;' Gr. θύρα, θύρ-ε-τρο-ν, θύρασι, θυρί-ς, θυρ-εό-ς, θαιρό-ς; Lat. *for-ē-s, foris, foras*; Umbr. *vero*, 'gate,' for *dvero*; perhaps also πύλη and *porta*, *d* being dropped and *v* changed into *p*, as in Zend *aspa* = ἵππος from Sanskrit *aśva*; Goth. *daur*; Angl. Sax. *duru, dyr*; Old Germ. *tor*; Slav. *dverĭ*, 'gate, door;' Lith. *dùr-ys*, 'door;' Hib. *dor, doras*, 'a door, gate.'] — *Dvāḥ-stha* or *dvā-stha* or *dvāḥ-sthita* or *dvā-sthita, as, ā, am*, standing at the gate or door; (*as*), m. a door-keeper, porter, warder. — *Dvār-vat, ān, atī, at*, having many doors; (*atī*), f. = *dvāra-vatī*, q. v.

Dvāra, am, n. a door, gate, gateway, passage, entrance, opening (cf. *vaktra-dvāra* and *sahasra-d°;* the body is sometimes called *nava-dvāram puram,* a city with nine gates or openings); a way, means, medium, vehicle, (the Māheśvaras hold that there are six Dvāras or means of obtaining a wished-for object); (*eṇa*), ind. 'by means of, by; with regard to, according to; (*ī*), f. a door; [cf. *a-d°.*] — *Dvāra-kaṇṭaka, as,* m. 'door-thorn,' the bolt of a door; a door, gate. — *Dvāra-kapāṭa, as* or *am,* m. or n. (?), the leaf or fold of a door, the panel of a door. — *Dvāra-tā,* f. a gate, door, an entrance, way, access. — *Dvāra-darśin, ī,* m. 'watching the door,' a door-keeper. — *Dvāra-dātu* (?), *us,* m. a species of tree, = *vara-dātu, bhūmi-saha.* — *Dvāra-dāru, us,* m. (?), 'having wood fit for a door,' the tree Tectona Grandis, teak. — *Dvāra-nāyaka, as,* m. or *dvāra-pa, as,* m. a door-keeper, porter, warder. — *Dvāra-paṭṭa, as,* m. the panel or surface of a door; the curtain of a door. — *Dvāra-pati, is,* m. a door-keeper, warder; N. of a kingdom (?). — *Dvāra-pāla, as,* m. a door-keeper, warder; an epithet of various Yakshas and of sacred places connected with them. — *Dvāra-pālaka, as,* m. a door-keeper; (*ikā*), f. a metronymic from Dvāra-pālī. — *Dvāra-piṇḍī,* f. the threshold of a door. — *Dvāra-pidhāna* or *dvārāpidhāna* (°*ra-ap°*), *as,* m. the bolt of a door. — *Dvāra-bali-bhuj, k,* m. 'eating the offering (of food) scattered before the door,' the bird Ardea Nivea; a crow; a sparrow. — *Dvāra-bāhu, us,* m. 'door-arm,' a door-post, jamb. — *Dvāra-mahima-varṇana, am,* n. 'description of the glory of the dvāra,' N. of the 127th chapter of the Krīḍā-khaṇḍa or second part of the Gaṇeśa-Purāṇa. — *Dvāra-yantra, am,* n. 'door-implement or door-restrainer,' a lock, bolt. — *Dvāra-vat, ān, atī, at,* having many doors; (*atī*), f., N. of the capital of Kṛishṇa; [cf. *dvārakā* and *dvār-vatī.*] — *Dvāravatī-nirmāṇa, am,* n. 'the construction of Dvāra-vatī,' N. of the 116th Adhyāya of the Vārāha-Purāṇa. — *Dvāra-vartman, a,* n. a gateway. — *Dvāra-vṛitta, am,* n. black pepper. — *Dvāra-śākhā,* f. the leaf of a door, division of a door. — *Dvāra-stambha, as,* m. a door-post. — *Dvāra-stha, as, ā, am,* standing at the door; (*as*), m. a door-keeper, porter. — *Dvārādhipa* or *dvārādhyaksha* (°*ra-adh°*), *as,* m. 'superintendent of the door,' a door-keeper, porter, warder, chamberlain. — *Dvārābhimānin* (°*ra-abh°*), *ī, inī, i,* assuming the character of the (sacrificial) doors. — *Dvārā-vatī,* f. = *dvāra-vatī,* q. v.

Dvāraka = *dvāra* above; (*ā* or *ikā*), f. 'the city with many gates,' N. of the capital of Kṛishṇa (on the western point of Guzerāt, supposed to have been submerged by the sea). — *Dvārakā-dāsa, as,* m. 'slave of Dvārakā,' N. of a man. — *Dvārakā-praveśa, as,* m. 'the entrance into Dvārakā,' N. of the 103rd chapter of the Kṛishṇa-khaṇḍa or fourth part of the Brahma-vaivarta-Purāṇa. — *Dvārakā-māhātmya, am,* n. 'the glory of Dvārakā,' N. of a part of the Skanda-Purāṇa. — *Dvārakārambha* (°*kā-ār°*), *as,* m. 'the commencement of Dvārakā,' N. of the 102nd chapter of the Kṛishṇa-khaṇḍa of the Brahma-vaivarta-Purāṇa. — *Dvārakeśa* (°*kā-īśa*), *as,* m. 'the lord of Dvārakā,' an epithet of Kṛishṇa.

Dvārika, as, m. a door-keeper, warder; N. of one of the eighteen attendants of the Sun; (*ikā*), f., see *dvāraka.*

Dvārin, ī, m. a door-keeper, porter, warder.

Dvārya, as, ā, am, belonging to a door, being at a door; (*ā*), f., scil. *sthūṇā,* a door-post.

द्वि *dvi, dvau,* m. du., *dve,* f. n. du. (the old dual form is *dvā,* q. v., from the original base *dva*), two, both. In native lexicons *dvayos* = 'in two genders,' i. e. in the masc. and fem. gender; [the original form was *dva,* as shown in nom. du. *dvau:* Zend *dva,* 'two;' *bi-* in comp., e. g. *bi-tya,* 'the second:' Gr. δύο, δύω, δυάκις, δοιοί, δί-πυλος, δὶς for δϝὶς, 'twice;' δεύ-τερο-ς from *dva-tara-s;* δοιή, 'doubt;' δί-α, δίζω, δισσός, 'double;' δώ-δεκα: Lat. *duo, bis* for *dvis; bi-* in comp., e. g. *bi-farius; ve-* in comp., e. g. *ve-sanus; dis-* in comp., e. g. *displicere; bi-ni, du-plex, du-b-ius, du-ellum, be-llum:* Umbr. *du-r,* 'two:' Goth. *tvai, tvōs,* f., *tva,* n., *tweiflyan, tvi-standan, dis-dailyan:* Angl. Sax. *twa, twi, tweogan:* Old Germ. *zer* or *zar* in comp.: Slav. *dŭva:* Lith. *dù, dvì,* f. 'two:' Hib. *da, do, di.*] — *Dvi-ka, as, ā, am,* having two *k*s in one's name; (*as*), m. a crow (= *kāka*); the ruddy goose, Anas Casarca (= *koka, ćakra-vāka*). — *Dvi-kakāra, as,* m. the bird with the two *k*s in its name, the crow (= *kāka*). — *Dvi-kakud, t,* or *dvika-pṛishṭha, as,* m. the camel ('two-humped,' 'two-backed'). — *Dvi-kara, as, ā* or *ī, am,* doing two things, making two or twofold. — *Dvi-kāṇḍa, as, ī, am,* consisting of two parts, (but the fem. is in *ā* if measure is denoted, Pāṇ. IV. 1, 23.) — *Dvi-kārshāpaṇa* or *dvi-kārshāpaṇika, as, ī, am,* worth two Kārshāpaṇas. — *Dvi-kubja, as, ā, am,* having two humps. — *Dvi-khaṇḍikā,* f. a couplet. — *Dvi-khārika, as, ā, am,* worth two Khārīs. — *Dvi-khura, as, ā, am,* cloven-hoofed, cloven-footed. — *Dvi-gat, t,* m., N. of a Bhārgava. — *Dvi-gu, us,* m., scil. *samāsā,* a compound word in which the first member of the compound is a numeral; (the word *dvi-gu,* 'having two cows or worth two cows,' is itself an example of this class of compounds, a single example often serving in native grammatical terminology as the name for the whole class.) — *Dvi-guṇa, as, ā, am,* double, twofold, of two kinds, twice as much or as large; multiplied by two, doubled. — *Dviguṇa-tva, am,* n. the state of being twofold, duplication. — *Dviguṇā-karṇa, as, ā, am,* having an ear divided into two parts by a slit (as a mark to distinguish cattle). — *Dviguṇā-kṛi,* cl. 8. P. A. *-karoti, -kurute, -kartum,* to plough twice. — *Dviguṇā-kṛita, as, ā, am,* twice ploughed; (also read *dviguṇī-kṛita.*) — *Dviguṇita, as, ā, am,* doubled, double, multiplied by two; folded, invested, enveloped. — *Dviguṇī-kṛita, as, ā, am,* doubled, increased. — *Dviguṇī-bhūta, as, ā, am,* doubled, augmented. — *Dvi-ćakra, as,* m., N. of a Dānava. — *Dvi-ćaturaśraka* or *-asraka, as,* m., N. of a particular gesture or posture. — *Dvi-ćatur-ghna, as, ī, am,* multiplied by two and four. — *Dvićatvāriṇśa, as, ī, am,* the 42nd. — *Dvi-ćatvāriṇśat, t,* f., 42; [cf. *dvā-ćatvāriṇśat.*] — *Dvićatvāriṇśika, as,* &c., consisting of 42. — *Dvi-ćaraṇa, as, ā, am,* two-legged, having two legs, bipedal. — *Dvi-ććhinna, as, ā, am,* cut into two, bisected. — *Dvi-ja, as, ā, am,* twice-born; (*as*), m. a man of any one of the first three classes, a Brāhman, Kshatriya, or Vaiśya (whose investiture with the Yajñopavīta or sacrificial cord at the age of puberty constitutes religiously and metaphorically their second birth, see *upa-naya,* p. 164, col. 3); a Brāhman; any oviparous animal (as a bird, a snake, a fish, &c., born first in the shell and next produced from it); a tooth (which falls out and grows again); coriander seed (= *tumburu*); (*ā*), f. a kind of fragrant plant, = *reṇukā;* Clerodendrum Siphonanthus (= *bhārgī*); kundur or gum olibanum (= *pālankī*); [cf. *dvi-jā.*] — *Dvija-kutsita, as,* m. 'the tree despised by the Brāhmans,' Cordia Latifolia and Myxa (= *śleshmāntaka*). — *Dvija-ketu, us,* m. a kind of citron. — *Dvija-ććhattra, am,* n., N. of a place. — *Dvija-jetṛi, tā,* m., N. of a Brāhman. — *Dvija-tva, am,* n. 'the state of being twice-born,' the condition or rank of a Brāhman. — *Dvija-dāsa, as,* m. 'the slave of the twice-born,' a servant of the first three classes, a Sūdra. — *Dvija-deva, as,* m. 'a god among the twice-born,' a Brāhman. — *Dvijadeva-deva, as,* m. 'a god among the Brāhmans,' a very pious or excellent Brāhman. — *Dvija-nishevita, as, ā, am,* inhabited by birds. — *Dvi-janman, ā, ā, a,* having a double birth or birthplace, having two natures; regenerate; oviparous; (*ā*), m. a member of the first three classes, especially a Brāhman; a bird, any oviparous animal; a tooth; [cf. *dvi-ja* and *dvi-jāti.*] — *Dvija-pati, is,* m. 'lord of the twice-born' (i. e. according to some 'lord of the Brāhmans;' but according to others the moon is said to be 'the chief of the twice-born,' as produced in the first instance from the eye of Atri and again from the ocean of milk at its churning by the gods and demons); the moon; [cf. *dvija-rāja, dvijeśa, dvijeśvara.*] — *Dvija-prapā,* f. the trench round the foot of a tree into which water is poured; a trough near a well for watering birds, cattle, &c. — *Dvija-priya, as, ā, am,* dear to a man of the first three classes, especially to a Brāhman; (*ā*), f. the Soma plant, Asclepias Acida. — *Dvija-bandhu, us,* m. 'a mere twice-born man,' i. e. a member of the first three classes not invested with the sacred string, or one merely called a Dvi-ja, but not so in fact; [cf. *kshatra-bandhu.*] — *Dvija-bruva, as,* m. 'merely called twice-born,' i. e. a Brāhman merely by name or by birth and not by observance of spiritual duties. — *Dvija-malla, as,* m., N. of a man. — *Dvija-mukhya, as,* m. 'the most excellent among the twice-born,' a Brāhman. — *Dvija-rāja, as,* m. 'the king of the twice-born,' the moon [cf. *dvija-pati*]; 'the king of the birds,' an epithet of Garuḍa; 'the king of the serpents,' an epithet of Ananta (as a synonym of the moon); camphor. — *Dvijarshabha* (°*ja-ṛish°*), *as,* m. 'the bull among the twice-born,' i. e. the best of the twice-born, a Brāhman. — *Dvija-lingin, ī, inī, i,* wearing the insignia of a Brāhman; (*ī*), m. a Kshatriya or man of the military tribe; an impostor, a pretended Brāhman who wears the distinguishing badge of that tribe without belonging to it. — *Dvija-vara, as,* m. 'the best among the twice-born,' a Brāhman. — *Dvija-varya, as,* m. an excellent or superior Brāhman. — *Dvija-vāhana, as,* m. 'whose vehicle is the bird (Garuḍa),' epithet of Kṛishṇa or Vishṇu. — *Dvija-vraṇa, as,* m. gum-boil, tooth-ache (= *dantārbuda*). — *Dvija-śapta, as,* m. 'the pulse cursed by the Brāhmans,' i. e. prohibited on some occasions, Dolichos Catjang (= *rāja-māsha*); (also read *dvija-sapta.*) — *Dvija-śuśrūshā,* f. service of the twice-born, service done to the first three classes, especially to the Brāhmans by the fourth or Sūdras. — *Dvija-śreshṭha* or *dvija-sattama, as,* m. 'the best of the twice-born,' a Brāhman. — *Dvija-sevaka, as,* m. 'a servant of the twice-born,' a servant of the first three classes, a Sūdra or man of the fourth and servile class; [cf. *dvijopāsaka.*] — *Dvija-sevā,* f. 'the service of the twice-born,' service of the first three classes, especially of the Brāhmans by the fourth or Sūdras. — *Dvija-sneha, as,* m. 'the favourite of Brāhmans,' N. of the Butea Frondosa. — *Dvi-jā, ās, ās, am,* Ved. twice-born, doubly born; [cf. *dvi-ja.*] — *Dvijāgrya* (°*ja-ag°*), *as,* m. 'chief of the twice-born,' a Brāhman. — *Dvijāngikā* and *dvijāngī* (°*ja-an°*), f. a kind of medicinal plant, = *kaṭukā.* — *Dvi-jāti, is, is, i,* twice-born; (*is*), m. a man of either of the first three classes, especially a Brāhman; any oviparous animal (as a bird, snake, &c.); [cf. *dvi-ja* and *dvi-janman.*] — *Dvijāti-jana-vatsala, as, ā, am,* friendly to the Brāhman race. — *Dvijāti-mukhya, as,* m. 'the chief among the twice-born,' a Brāhman. — *Dvijāti-sāt,* ind. as a present for Brāhmans. — *Dvijātīya, as, ā, am,* relating to the first three or twice-born classes; of twofold nature, of mixed origin or breed, mongrel; (*as*), m. a mule. — *Dvi-jāni, is, is, i,* Ved. having two wives. — *Dvijānuloma* (°*ja-an°*), *am,* n. the regular order or series of the first three twice-born classes. — *Dvijāyanī,* f. the thread or cord worn over the shoulder and marking the first three twice-born classes. — *Dvijālaya* (°*ja-āl°*), *as,* m. 'the residence of birds,' the hollow trunk of a tree; the residence of Brāhmans. — *Dvi-jihva, as, ā, am,* two-tongued, double-tongued (literally or figuratively), insincere; (*as*), m. a peculiar disease of the tongue; a snake; an informer, a rogue, scoundrel, bad man; a thief; N. of a Rakshas; (also read *dvi-jihba.*) — *Dvijihva-tā,* f. 'the state of having two tongues,' insincerity, dishonesty. — *Dvijendraka* (°*ja-in°*), *as,* m. = *dvija-ketu,* q. v. — *Dvijeśa* (°*ja-īś°*), *as,* m. 'lord of the twice-born,' the moon; [cf. *dvija-pati, dvija-rāja, dvijeśvara.*] — *Dvijeśvara* (°*ja-iś°*), *as,* m. 'the lord of the twice-born,' epithet of the Moon, see *dvija-pati*; of Śiva. — *Dvijottama* (°*ja-ut*°), *as*, m. 'servant of the twice-born,' best of the twice-born, a Brāhman. — *Dvijopāsaka* (°*ja-up*°), *as*, m. 'servant of the twice-born,' a servant of the first three classes, a Śūdra; [cf. *dvija-sevaka*.] — *Dvi-jyā*, f. the sine or chord of an arc. — *Dvijyā-mārga*, *am*, n. a horizontal line. — *Dvi-ṭha*, *as*, m., N. of the symbol Visarga (as having two points); N. of Svāhā, wife of Agni. — 1. *dvi-tā*, f. = *dvi-tva* below; [cf. p. 445, col. 3.] — *Dvi-tra*, *ās*, *ās*, *āṇi*, pl. two or three. — *Dvi-tri-ćatura*, *as*, &c., happening two or three or four times; (*am*), ind. twice or thrice or four times. — *Dvi-tva*, *am*, n. doubleness, the number two, a pair, couple; duality; the dual; reduplication (of a letter or word). — *Dvidaṇḍi*, ind. (fr. *dvi-daṇḍa*), with two sticks, stick against stick, single-stick, quarter-staff. — *Dvidaṇḍin*, *ī*, m. 'carrying two staves,' a kind of mendicant. — *Dvi-dat*, *an*, *atī*, *at*, having two teeth (as a mark of age); [cf. Lat. *bi-dens*.] — *Dvi-danta*, *as*, *ī*, *am*, having two teeth. — *Dvi-dala*, *as*, *ā*, *am*, 'having two parts,' split in two, two-leafed; (*ā*), f. Bauhinia Tomentosa. — *Dvi-daśa*, *ās*, m. pl. twenty, two tens. — *Dvi-dāmnī*, f. (a cow) tied with two ropes. — *Dvi-diva*, *as*, *ā*, *am*, lasting two days; (*as*), m. a ceremony or festival that lasts two days. — *Dvi-devata*, *as*, *ā*, *am*, belonging to or sacred to two deities; (*am*), n. the constellation Viśākhā; (also read *dvi-daivatyā*.) — *Dvi-devatya*, *as*, *ā*, *am*, relating or belonging to two deities. — *Dvi-deha*, *as*, m. 'two-bodied, double-bodied,' epithet of the god Gaṇeśa (having the head of an elephant with the figure of a man; cf. *dvi-śarīra* and *dvi-dhātu*). — *Dvi-daivatyā*, f. the constellation Viśākhā (Indra and Agni jointly presiding over this asterism; cf. *dvi-devata*). — *Dvi-dha*, *as*, *ā*, *am*, divided in two, split asunder. — *Dvi-dhā*, ind. in a twofold manner, in two parts, of two kinds or sorts, in two ways, in two directions, divided; [cf. Gr. δίχα, διχθά, δισσός.] — *Dvidhā-karaṇa*, *am*, n. the act of making twofold, dividing into two parts, splitting, arranging in two ways, &c. — *Dvidhākāra* (°*dhā-āk*°), *as*, *ā*, *am*, of a twofold form, in a twofold manner. — *Dvidhā-gati*, *is*, m. 'going in two ways or by water and land,' a crab; a crocodile. — *Dvi-dhātu*, *us*, *us*, *u*, having two natures or two roots &c.; (*as*), m. an epithet of Gaṇeśa; [cf. *dvi-deha*.] — *Dvidhātmaka* (°*dhā-āt*°), *am*, n. a nutmeg (as being of two kinds?). — *Dvidhā-lekhya*, *as*, *ā*, *am*, to be written in two ways; (*as*), m. the tree Phœnix Paludosa (= *hintāla*), the marshy date tree. — *Dvi-nagnaka*, *as*, m. a circumcised man, one having no prepuce. — *Dvinavata*, *as*, *ī*, *am* (fr. the following), the 92nd. — *Dvi-navati*, *is*, f., 92. — *Dvinavati-tama*, *as*, *ī*, *am*, the 92nd. — *Dvi-nāman*, *ā*, *mnī*, *a*, having two names. — *Dvi-nidhana*, *am*, n., N. of a Sāman. — *Dvi-nishka*, *as*, *ā*, *am*, or *dvinaishkika*, *as*, *ī*, *am*, bought &c. with two Nishkas. — *Dvi-pa*, *as*, m. 'drinking twice,' an elephant, (the elephant imbibing fluids by his trunk and thence conveying them into his mouth); the tree Mesua Ferrea; [cf. *gandha-d*° and *dvi-pāyin*.] — *Dvipańćamūlī*, f. = *daśa-mūla*, q. v. — *Dvipańćāśa*, *as*, *ī*, *am* (fr. *dvi-pańćāśat*), the 52nd. — *Dvi-pańćāśat*, *t*, f., 52. — *Dvipańćāśat-tama*, *as*, *ī*, *am*, the 52nd. — *Dvi-paṇya*, *as*, *ā*, *am*, worth two Paṇas. — *Dvi-pattraka*, *as* or *am*, m. or n. (?), a kind of bulbous plant (= *ćaṇḍāla-kanda*). — *Dvi-patha*, *am*, n. a cross-way, a place where two roads meet; (*ā*), f. a kind of metre. — *Dvi-pad* or *dvi-pād*, *-pāt*, *-pāt* or *-padī*, *-pat*, two-footed, bipedal; (*pāt*), m. a biped, a man; a god; a demon; a bird; (*pat*), n. men collectively; (*t*, *t*, *t*), consisting of two Padas; m. a metre of two Padas; (*padī*), f. a kind of Prākṛit metre; [cf. Lat. *bi-pes*; Gr. δί-πους.] (According to Pāṇ. IV. 1, 9, the fem. must be *dvi-padā* when agreeing with *ṛić*, e.g. *dvi-padā ṛik*, 'a verse containing two Pādas,' but *dvi-padī strī*, 'a woman with two feet.') — *Dvi-pada*, *as*, *ā*, *am*, two-footed, bipedal; containing two Padas; (*as*), m. a biped, (contemptuously) a man; (*ā*), f., scil. *ṛić*, a verse consisting of two Padas; a kind of Prākṛit metre; (in mathem.) binomial; containing two words; a peculiar sign of the zodiac; (*ā*), f. a kind of jasmine [cf. *dvi-puṭī*]; (*am*), n. a combination of two words. — *Dvipada-pati*, *is*, m. 'the lord of bipeds,' a king, prince. — *Dvipada-rāśi*, *is*, f. any one of the signs Gemini, Libra, Aquarius, Virgo, and half of Sagittarius. — *Dvipadāntara* or *dvipadābhyāsa* (°*da-an*°, °*da-abh*°), *am*, n., N. of a Sāman. — *Dvi-padikā*, f. double amount (?); a kind of Prākṛit metre (= *dvi-padī*); a peculiar manner of singing. — *Dvipa-mada*, *as*, m. the juice exuding from the elephant's temples. — *Dvi-parṇa*, *as*, *ī*, *am*, two-leaved, opposite-leaved; (*ī*), f. wild jew's thorn (= *vana-kolī*). — *Dvipāt-tva*, *am*, n. or *dvipāt-tā*, f. two-footedness, the state of a biped; bipartiteness. — *Dvi-pātra*, *am*, n. a couple of vessels. — *Dvi-pād*, see *dvi-pad*. — *Dvi-pāda*, *as*, *ī*, *am*, two-footed, bipedal, a biped. — *Dvi-pādya*, *as*, *ā*, *am*, worth double; bought &c. with two quarters, double; (*as*, *am*), m. n. a double penalty, an amercement of twice the common amount. — *Dvi-pāyin*, *ī*, m. 'drinking twice,' an elephant; [cf. *dvi-pa*.] — *Dvipāsya* (°*pa-ās*°), *as*, m. 'having the face of an elephant,' an epithet of Gaṇeśa. — *Dvi-puṭa*, *as*, *ī*, *am*, folded double, having two folds; (*ī*), f. a kind of jasmine. — *Dvi-purusha*, *as*, *ā* or *ī*, *am*, having the length of two men; (*as*, *ā*, *am*), worth two men, Pāṇ. IV. 1, 24; (*am*), ind. through two generations. — *Dvi-pṛishṭha*, *as*, m. (with Jainas) the second black Vāsu-deva. — *Dvipendra* (°*pa-in*°), *as*, m. 'prince of elephants,' a large elephant. — *Dvipendra-dāna*, *am*, n. or *dvipendra-mada*, *as*, m. the liquor flowing from the temples of a large elephant in rut. — *Dvi-pratika*, *as*, *ī*, *am*, bought &c. with two Kārshāpaṇas. — *Dvi-bandhu*, *us*, m. 'having two friends (?),' Ved., N. of a man. — *Dvi-barha-jman*, *ā*, m., Ved. having a double course; (Sāy.) whose course is spread through two. — *Dvi-barhas*, *ās*, m., Ved. doubly close or thick, strong; doubled (as opposed to single); (Sāy.) mighty in two places, mightily expanded in the two worlds; (the form *dvi-barhās* appears also as neut. and as an adverb.) — *Dvi-bāhu*, *us*, *us*, *u*, two-armed. — *Dvi-bāhuka*, *as*, m. 'the two-armed one,' N. of one of the attendants of Śiva. — *Dvi-bhuja*, *as*, *ā*, *am*, two-armed; (*as*), m. an angle. — *Dvi-bhūma*, *as*, *ā*, *am*, having two floors. — *Dvi-maya*, *as*, *ī*, *am*, made or consisting of two (parts). — *Dvi-mātṛi*, *tā*, *trī*, *tṛi*, Ved. having two mothers; (Sāy.) the measurer of the two worlds. — *Dvimātṛi-ja*, *as*, *ā*, *am*, having two mothers, born from two mothers, born in two ways, having different mothers (thus Gaṇeśa was the son of Pārvatī, but according to one legend was formed of the scurf and impurities of her body; cf. *dvaimātura*). — *Dvi-mātra* or *dvimātrika*, *as*, *ā*, *am*, containing two syllabic instants (as a long vowel). — *Dvi-mārgī*, f. a cross-way, a place where two roads meet. — *Dvi-māshya*, *as*, *ā*, *am*, worth two Māshas. — *Dvi-mīḍha*, *as*, m., N. of a son of Hastin (Bṛihat) and grandson of Su-hotra. — *Dvi-mukha*, *as*, *ā*, *am*, two-faced, having two mouths; (*as*), m. a sort of snake; (*as*), m. a kind of serpent, Amphisbœna, a kind of worm (= *kṛimi*); (*ā*), f. a leech; a small water-jar with two mouths (= *karkarī*). — *Dvimukhāhi* (°*kha-ahi*), *is*, m. 'a snake with two mouths,' a peculiar kind of serpent (= *ahiraṇī*). — *Dvimukhoraga* (°*kha-ur*°), *as*, m. a kind of serpent; see above. — *Dvi-muni*, ind. produced by two sages; [cf. *tri-muni*.] — *Dvi-musali* or *dvi-mushali*, ind. with two clubs or maces, club against club (in fighting). — *Dvi-mūrdha*, *as*, *ī*, *am*, two-headed. — *Dvi-mūrdhan*, *ā*, *ā*, *a*, two-headed, bicipital; (*ā*), m., N. of an Asura. — *Dvi-yamunam*, ind., N. of a place. — *Dvi-yodha*, *as*, m. 'fighting with two,' epithet of the charioteer of Kṛishṇa; (*ī*), f. a kind of metre consisting of four lines of six syllables each. — *Dvi-ra*, *as*, m. a bee; [cf. *dvi-repha*.] — *Dvi-rada*, *as*, *ā*, *am*, two-toothed, two-tusked; (*as*), m. an elephant. — *Dvirada-karāgra* (°*ra-ag*°), *am*, n. the tip of an elephant's trunk. — *Dviradāntaka* (°*da-an*°), *as*, m. 'destroyer of the elephant,' the lion. — *Dviradārāti* (°*da-ar*°), *is*, m. 'enemy of the elephant,' N. of the fabulous animal Śarabha. — *Dviradāśana* (°*da-aś*°), *as*, m. 'food of the elephant,' epithet of the Ficus Religiosa. — *Dvi-rasana*, *as*, *ā*, *am*, double-tongued, having a forked tongue; (*as*), m. a snake in general. — *Dvi-rāja*, *am*, n., Ved. the battle between the two kings. — *Dvi-rātra*, *as*, *ā*, *am*, lasting two nights; (*as*), m. a period of two nights or days. — *Dvirātrīṇa*, *as*, *ā*, *am*, lasting two nights; to be accomplished in two nights. — *Dvi-rūpa*, *as*, *ā*, *am*, biform, of two forms, twofold; bicolour; bipartite; having a different shape; spelt or written in two ways; (*as*), m. variety of interpretation or reading; a word that may be correctly spelt in two ways. — *Dvirūpa-kosha*, 'the treasury of words written in two ways,' a dictionary of words spelt in two ways. — *Dvirūpa-tā*, f. doubleness of form, a double form or manner of expression. — *Dvi-retas*, *ās*, *ās*, *as*, doubly impregnating (as the male ass which impregnates the she-ass and mare); receiving double impregnation (as a mare which is impregnated by the horse and male ass). — *Dvi-repha*, *as*, m. the insect with two *r*s in its name (= *bhramara*), a large black bee. — *Dvirepha-gaṇa-sammitā*, f. 'resembling a multitude of bees,' a kind of rose. — *Dvirepha-mālā*, f. or *dvirepha-vṛinda*, *as*, m. a flight or swarm of bees. — *Dvi-lakshaṇa*, *as*, *ā*, *am*, twofold, of two kinds. — *Dvi-laya*, 'double-time (?),' a term in music. — *Dvi-vaktra*, *as*, *ā*, *am*, having two mouths, two-faced; (*as*), m., N. of a Dānava. — *Dvi-vaćana*, *am*, n. or *dvi-vaćas*, *as*, n. the dual, the terminations of the dual. — *Dvivaćanānta* (°*na-an*°), *as*, m. a dual termination. — *Dvi-vajraka*, *as*, m. a column with sixteen angles or sides. — *Dvi-varṇa*, *as*, *ā*, *am*, two-coloured, bicolour; (*am*), n. doubling of a consonant. — *Dvivarṇa-ratha*, *as*, m. 'having a bicolour chariot,' N. of one of the ancestors of Śākya-muni. — *Dvi-varsha*, *as*, *ā*, *am*, two years old &c.; (*ā*), f. a cow two years old. — *Dvi-varshaka*, *as*, *ikā*, *am*, or *dvivarshīṇa*, or *dvi-vārshika*, *as*, *ī*, *am*, biennial, two years old, of two years standing. — *Dvi-vāhikā*, f. a swing, a swinging cot, a litter. — *Dvi-vinśatikīna*, *as*, *ā*, *am*, worth twice twenty. — *Dvi-vida*, *as*, m., N. of a monkey (slain by Vishṇu, or Vishṇu in the form of Kṛishṇa or of Bala-rāma; but according to other legends an ally of Rāma and, like Mainda, a son of the Aśvins). — *Dvividāri* (°*da-ari*), *is*, m. 'the enemy of Dvivida,' an epithet of Vishṇu. — *Dvi-vidha*, *as*, *ā*, *am*, of two sorts, biform, of two kinds or ways, bipartite. — *Dvi-vindu*, *us*, m. 'consisting of two points,' the symbol Visarga. — *Dvi-vista*, *as*, *ā*, *am*, or *dvi-vaistika*, *as*, *ī*, *am*, worth two Vistas. — *Dvi-veda*, *as*, *ā*, *am*, or *dvivedin*, *ī*, *inī*, *i*, studying two Vedas, familiar with two Vedas. — *Dviveda-gaṅga*, *as*, m., N. of a commentator. — *Dvi-veśarā*, f. a kind of light carriage drawn by mules. — *Dvi-śata*, *am*, n., 200; 102; (*as*, *ī*, *am*), the 200th; consisting of 200, containing 200. — *Dviśataka*, worth 200, bought for 200. — *Dviśata-tama*, *as*, *ī*, *am*, the 200th. — *Dvi-śatikā*, f. an aggregate or amount of 200. — *Dviśatya*, *as*, *ā*, *am*, = *dviśataka*. — *Dvi-śapha*, *as*, *ā*, *am*, cloven-footed, bisulcous; (*as*), m. any cloven-footed animal. — *Dvi-śarīra*, *as*, m. 'two-bodied, double-bodied,' epithet of Gaṇeśa; [cf. *dvi-deha*.] — *Dvi-śavas*, *ās*, *ās*, *as*, Ved. having twofold strength. — *Dvi-śas*, ind. two by two, in couples, by pairs. — *Dvi-śāṇa* or *dvi-śāṇya*, *as*, *ā*, *am*, worth two Śāṇas; [cf. *draiśāṇa*.] — *Dvi-śāla*, *as*, *ā*, *am*, containing two rooms (as a house). — *Dvi-śīrsha* or *dvi-śīrshaka*, *as*, *ā*, *am*, two-headed, bicipital; (*as*), m. an epithet of Agni. — *Dvi-śūrpa* or *dviśaurpika*, *as*, *ī*, *am*, worth two Śūrpas or winnowing baskets. — *Dvi-śṛiṅgikā*, f., N. of a plant, = *meḍhra-valli*. — *Dvi-śṛiṅgin*, *ī*, *iṇī*, *i*, two-horned; (*ī*), f. a sort of fish, commonly called Marmaka. — *Dvi-shaṃhita*, *as*, *ā*, *am* (fr. *dvi* + *saṃh*°), twice folded (as a skin). — *Dvi-shandhi* or *dvi-sandhi*, *is*, *is*, *i*, admitting a twofold Sandhi. — *Dvi-shash*, *ṭ*, m. f. n. pl. twice six, twelve. — *Dvi-shashṭa*, *as*, *ī*, *am*, the 62nd.

— *Dvi-shashṭi, is,* f., 62; [cf. *dvā-shashṭi.*] — *Dvi-shashṭi-tama, as, ī, am,* the 62nd. — *Dvi-shāshṭika, as, ī, am,* consisting of 62; worth 62, &c. — *Dvi-shāhasra, as, ī, am,* Ved. = *dvi-sāhasra,* q. v. — *Dvi-shūkta, as, ā, am,* having two Sūktas. — *Dvi-shṭha, as, ā, am,* staying in two places. — *Dvishṭha-tā,* f. the state of staying in two places. — *Dvi-sandhi,* see *dvi-shandhi.* — *Dvisaptata, as, ī, am,* the 72nd. — *Dvi-saptati, is,* f., 72; [cf. *dvā-saptati.*] — *Dvisaptati-tama, as, ī, am,* the 72nd. — *Dvisapta-dhā,* ind. into or in 14 parts, in 14 ways. — *Dvisaptāha* (°*ta-aha*), *as,* m. a fortnight. — *Dvi-sama, as, ā, am,* consisting of two equal portions, having two equal sides. — *Dvisama-tribhuja, as,* m. an isosceles triangle. — *Dvi-sahasra, am,* n., 2000; (*as,* &c.), worth 2000. — *Dvisahasrāksha* (°*ra-ak*°), *as, ī, am,* having 2000 eyes; (*as*), m. 'the two-thousand-eyed one,' the great serpent Śesha who is regarded as sovereign of the serpent-race and who formed the couch of Vishṇu. — *Dvi-sāṃvatsarika, as, ī, am,* lasting two years or intended for two years. — *Dvisāptatika, as, ī, am,* having the value of 72. — *Dvi-sāhasra* or *dvi-shāhasra, as, ī, am,* having the value of 2000, consisting of 2000. — *Dvi-sītya, as, ā, am,* twice furrowed, twice ploughed (first lengthways and then across). — *Dvi-suvarṇa* or *dvisauvarṇika, as,* &c., worth two Su-varṇas. — *Dvi-stana, as, ā, am,* two-breasted, two-uddered. — *Dvi-svabhāva, as, ā, am,* having a double nature, of two characters. — *Dvi-han, ā,* m. 'striking twice or with tusks and teeth,' an elephant. — *Dvi-halya, as, ā, am,* twice ploughed; [cf. *dvi-sītya.*] — *Dvi-hāyana, as, ī, am,* two years old; (*ī*), f. a cow two years old. — *Dvi-hiṅkāra, am,* n., N. of a Sāman. — *Dvi-hīna, as, ā, am,* destitute of both genders (i. e. of the masc. and fem.), neuter; (*am*), n. the neuter gender. — *Dvi-hṛidaya, ā,* f. 'having two hearts,' a pregnant woman. — *Dvi-hotṛi, tā,* m. 'a double Hotṛi,' epithet of Agni. — *Dviḍa* (*dvi-iḍa*), *am,* n., N. of a Sāman. — *Dvīndriya* (*dvi-in*°), *am,* n. two organs of sense; (*as, ā, am*), having two organs of sense (touch and taste). — *Dvīndriya-grāhya, as, ā, am,* perceptible by two senses (by sight and touch &c.). — *Dvīpa,* see col. 3. — *Dvy-aṃśa, as* or *am,* m. or n. (?), two parts. — *Dvy-aksha, as, ī, am,* two-eyed, binocular. — *Dvy-akshara, as, ā, am,* two-syllabled, dissyllabic; (*am*), n. a dissyllable, a word of two syllables. — *Dvy-agra, as, ā, am,* two-pointed, ending in two extremities. — *Dvy-aṅgula, am,* n. two fingers' length; (*as, ā, am*), measuring two fingers. — *Dvy-añjala, am,* n. or *dvy-añjali,* n. two Añjalis or handfuls; (*as, ī, am*), measuring &c. two Añjalis or handfuls. — *Dvy-aṇuka, am,* n. the aggregation or combination of two atoms, (the first step in the formation of substances when they become perceptible.) — *Dvy-anya, as, ā, am,* accompanied &c. by two others; (*am*), n. two others collectively. — *Dvy-artha, as, ā, am,* having two senses or interpretations, ambiguous, equivocal; having two objects; (*as*), m. double meaning, double entendre. — *Dvy-aśīta, as, ī, am,* the 82nd. — *Dvy-aśīti, is,* f., 82. — *Dvyaśīti-tama, as, ī, am,* the 82nd. — *Dvy-ashṭa, am,* n. copper. — *Dvyashṭa-sahasra, am,* n., 16000. — *Dvy-aha, as,* m. a period of two days (loc. *dvy-ahni*); (*as, ā, am*), lasting two days; (*as*), m. a ceremony or festival lasting two days. — *Dvyahīna, as, ā, am,* of or belonging to two days, relating to a ceremony which lasts two days. — *Dvy-ātmaka, as, ā, am,* having a double nature, comprising two, being two; (*ās*), m. pl. the signs of the zodiac Gemini, Virgo, Sagittarius, and Pisces. — *Dvy-āmushyāyaṇa, as,* m. descended from two persons, standing in the relationship of an Āmushyāyaṇa to two people; a son of two fathers, a boy who remains heir to his father though adopted by another. — *Dvy-āyusha, am,* n. a double life, two lives. — *Dvyāhika, as, ī, am* (fr. *dvy-aha*), returning the third day, produced &c. in two days. — *Dvy-udātta, as, ā, am,* doubly accented; (*am*), n. a word so accented. — *Dvy-ṛića, as,* m., Ved. a strophe consisting of two verses. — *Dvy-ekāntara* (°*ka-an*°), *as, ā, am,* having two or one between, separated by one or two, one or two off. — *Dvyoga, as, ā, am* (for *dvi-yoga*), drawn by two pairs (as a carriage). — *Dvy-opaśa, as, ā, am,* having two superfluous (syllables &c.); having two appendages.

Dvika, as, ā, am, consisting of two, twofold, a pair; the second; happening the second time; increased by two (e. g. *dvikaṃ śatam,* 102, i. e. two per cent).

Dvita, as, m., N. of an Āptya (supposed to be the author of a Ṛig-veda hymn; in epic poetry, Ekata, Dvita, and Trita are children of Gautama or of Brahmā or Prajā-pati); N. of a descendant of Atri; [cf. *trita.*] — *Dvita-vana, as,* m., N. of a man; [cf. *dvaitavana.*]

Dvitaya, as, ā, am, consisting of two, divided into two parts, twofold, double; *dvitaye* or *dvitayās,* m. pl. two, both (e. g. *te dvitaye,* these two or these two classes of things); (*am*), n. a pair, two.

Dvitīya, as, ā, am, second, the second; forming the half or second part of anything; (*as*), m. the second person, the second in a family, i. e. a son; a companion, fellow, partner (e. g. *Kṛishṇa-dvitīya,* accompanied by Kṛishṇa; cf. *a-dv*°, *dhanur-dv*°, *ćhāyā-dv*°); the second letter (in a class), the hard or aspirated consonant in each of the five classes; (*ā*), f. a female companion, a wife ('a second self'); the second day of a half month; (scil. *vibhakti*) the second case, the accusative, the terminations of this case, a word standing in this case; (with *bhāga*) the second half; (*am*), n. the half; (*am*), ind. for the second time, a second time, again. — *Dvitīya-tā,* f. or *dvitīya-tva, am,* n. the state of being second, the condition or quality or rank of a second. — *Dvitīya-triphalā,* f. the second set of three fruits, viz. the grape, the date, and the gambhārī. — *Dvitīya-vat, ān, atī, at,* having as a second or companion. — *Dvitīya-vayas, ās, ās, as,* having arrived at the second period of life. — *Dvitīya-svara, am,* n., N. of a Sāman. — *Dvitīyā-kṛi,* cl. 8. P. A. *-karoti, -kurute, -kartum,* to plough twice. — *Dvitīyā-kṛita, as, ā, am,* twice ploughed (as a field). — *Dvitīyābhā* (°*ya-ābhā*), f. a scitamineous plant, Curcuma Xanthorrhiza (= *dāru-haridrā*).

Dvitīyaka, as, ā or *ikā* (?), *am,* the second, happening the second time; returning every second day; [cf. *dvaitīyaka.*]

Dvitīyika, as, ā, am, second.

Dvitīyin, ī, inī, i, standing in the second place or rank; [cf. *tritīyin.*]

Dvis, ind. twice; [cf. Gr. δίς; Zend *bis;* Lat. *bis, dis-* in *dis-cedo* &c.; probably also Goth. prefix *mis-* and *missa-* in *missa-dēths, missaleiks.*] — *Dviḥ-svara, as, ā, am,* doubly accented. — *Dvir-aṃsaka, as, ā, am,* having two shoulders. — *Dvir-abhyasta, as, ā, am,* twice repeated. — *Dvir-abhyasākūpāra* (°*sa-ak*°), *am,* n., N. of a Sāman. — *Dvir-aśana, am,* n. eating twice a day. — *Dvir-āgamana, am,* n. 'twice coming,' the ceremony of the second entrance or approach of the bride to her husband's house after a visit to that of her father. — *Dvir-āpa, as,* m. 'drinking twice, i. e. with trunk and mouth,' the elephant; [cf. *dvipa.*] — *Dvir-āvṛitti, is,* f. repetition of an act. — *Dvir-āshāḍha, as,* m. an intercalary Āshāḍha month. — *Dvir-iḍa, as, ā, am,* containing the word *iḍa* twice. — *Dvir-ukta, as, ā, am,* twice spoken, twice said, repeated, doubled, reduplicated; said or told in two ways; (*am*), n. repetition. — *Dvir-ukti, is,* f. saying twice, repetition, tautology; (in grammar) repetition of a syllable; twofold way of expression or of spelling a word; variety of narration, telling anything in two ways. — *Dvirukti-prakriyā,* f., N. of a chapter of the Madhya-siddhānta-kaumudī by Varada-rāja. — *Dvir-udātta, as, ā, am,* doubly accented. — *Dvir-ūḍhā,* f. a woman who has been twice married. — *Dvir-bhāva, as,* m. doubling, reduplication. — *Dvir-vaćana, am,* n. repetition, reduplication. — *Dvis-tāvā,* f. (fr. *dvis* + *tāvat*), exceeding twice the usual measure; (only used with *vedi;* cf. *tris-tāvā.*)

Dve-dhā (fr. *dvaya;* cf. *tre-dhā*) = *dvi-dhā,* in two parts, into two parts, in a twofold way, twice; [cf. *dvaidha* and *dvaidham.*]

द्विता 2. *dvitā,* ind. (a particle of affirmation or emphasis = the Greek δή, δῆτα, and occurring only in the Ṛig-veda), Ved. indeed, certainly, exactly, really, precisely, surely, especially; (native commentators derive the word from *dvi* and translate it 'in two ways, twofold,' &c.; cf. 1. *dvi-tā,* p. 444, col. 1.)

द्विष् 1. *dvish,* cl. 2. P. A. *dveshṭi, dvishṭe, didvesha, dvekshyati, dveshṭum* (Ved. *dveshṭos*), to hate, show hatred against (with acc., dat., or gen.), to dislike, be hostile or unfriendly: Pass. *dvishyate:* Caus. *dveshayati, -yitum,* Aor. *adidvishat:* Desid. *didvikshati, -te:* Intens. *dedvishyate, dedveshṭi, dedvishīti;* [cf. rt. 2. *dush, dus; dvis,* implying division: Zend *ḍbish,* 'to hate:' Gr. base ὀδυς, ὀδ-ώδυσ-ται, ὠδυσ-ά-μην, ὀδυσσά-μενο-ς, ὠδυσίη, 'Οδυσ-εύ-ς; perhaps also μισέω = Caus. *dveshayāmi, d* being dropped and *v* changed to *m.*]

2. *dvish, ṭ, ṭ, ṭ,* hostile, hating, disliking; (*ṭ*), m. an enemy, a foe; (*ṭ*), f., Ved. hostility, dislike, hatred. — *Dviṭ-sevā,* f. service of a foe, secret agreement with an enemy; treachery. — *Dviṭsevin, ī, inī, i,* serving an enemy, having a secret understanding with an enemy, traitor.

Dvisha, as, ā, am, (at the end of a comp.) hostile, hating; (*as*), m. an enemy; [cf. *anṛita-d*°, *ṛishi-d*°, *brahma-d*°.] — *Dvisha-tā,* f. hostility, enmity, hostile behaviour, hating. — *Dvishan-tapa, as, ā, am,* punishing or harassing an enemy, revenging, retaliating.

Dvishat, an, atī, at, hating or detesting, hostile, inimical, unfriendly; (*an*), m. an enemy, foe. — *Dvishatī-tāpa, as, ā, am* (?), vexing or harassing an enemy.

1. *dvishṭa, as, ā, am* (for 2. see below), hated, disliked, odious; hostile.

Dvesha, as, m. (opposed to *rāga, kāma, iććhā*), hatred, hate, dislike, abhorrence; repugnance; malignity, enmity; [cf. *a-d*° and *tulasī-d*°.]

Dveshaṇa, as, ā, am, hating, disliking, inimical, hostile; (*as*), m. an enemy; (*am*), n. hate, hatred against (with gen.), enmity, dislike.

Dveshaṇīya, as, ā, am, to be hated.

Dveshas, as, n., Ved. dislike, hatred, hostility; a mischievous man, an enemy; [cf. *a-d*°, *tarad-d*°, *rakshas.*] — *Dvesho-yut, t, t, t,* Ved. removing hostility, remover of sin; (Sāy.) filled with hatred.

Dveshin, ī, iṇī, i, hating, disliking, hostile, inimical; (*ī*), m. a hater, foe, an enemy; [cf. *kriyā-d*° and *gajāsura-d*°.] — *Dveshi-dvesha-para, as, ā, am,* filled with hatred towards enemies.

Dveshṭṛi, ṭā, ṭrī, ṭṛi, one who hates, a hater, disliking, hating, inimical, an enemy, foe. — *Dveshṭṛi-tva, am,* n. hatred, hostility.

Dveshya, as, ā, am, to be hated; disagreeable, hateful, odious, detestable; (*as*), m. an enemy, a foe. — *Dveshya-tā,* f. aversion, dislike, disfavour; odiousness, detestableness.

द्विषण्डिक *dvishaṇḍika, as,* m. a garment which protects from wind and cold; (the right reading is perhaps *dvikhaṇḍika* fr. *dvi-khaṇḍa.*)

द्विषदा *dvishadā,* f. Polianthes Tuberosa.

द्विषा *dvishā,* f. cardamoms.

द्विष्ट 2. *dvishṭa, am,* n. (for *dvy-ashṭa*), copper. (For 1. *dvishṭa* see above.)

द्वीप *dvīpa, as, am,* m. n. (fr. *dvi* + *ap,* water), an island, peninsula, any land surrounded by water, a sandbank; a place of refuge, shelter, protector, a protector; a division of the terrestrial world (of which according to different authorities there are seven or four or nine or thirteen and which are situated round the mountain Meru like the leaves encircling a lotus flower; each Dvīpa is separated from the next by a distinct circumambient ocean: the seven Dvīpas, reckoning from the central one, are Jambu, Plaksha or Go-medaka, Śālmalī, Kuśa, Krauñća, Śāka, and Pushkara: according to Mahā-bhārata, Bhīshma-parva 208, there are four Dvīpas, viz. Bhadrāśva, Ketu-māla, Jambu-dvīpa, and Uttarāḥ kuravas. In Vishṇu-Purāṇa II. 3. nine Dvīpas are enumerated, which are sometimes joined with the above-named four, so as to make thirteen in all); a tiger's skin?; (according to some) cubebs; [cf. *dvīpa-sambhava.*] — *Dvīpa-karpūraka* or *dvīpa-karpūraja* (?), *as*, m. camphor from China. — *Dvīpa-kumāra, ās*, m. pl. (with Jainas) N. of a class of deities belonging to the Bhavana-patis. — *Dvīpa-kharjūra* or *dvīpa-ja, am*, n. a kind of fruit tree, = *mahā-pārevata.* — *Dvīpa-ćhandtra*, N. of a place mentioned in the Tarka-bhāshā-prakāśikā by Ćinna-bhaṭṭa. — *Dvīpa-vat, ān, atī, at*, abounding in islands; (*ān*), m. the ocean; a river; (*tī*), f. a river; the earth. — *Dvīpa-śatru, us*, m. Asparagus Racemosus (= *śatāvarī*; cf. the right form *dvīpi-śatru* and *dvīpikā*). — *Dvīpa-śreshṭha, as, am*, m. n. best of islands. — *Dvīpa-sambhava, as*, m. the largest sort of raisin [cf. *dvīpya*]; Vernonia Anthelminthica; (*ā*), f. a kind of date.

Dvīpikā, f. Asparagus Racemosus; [cf. *dvīpa-śatru* and *dvīpya.*]

Dvīpin, ī, inī, i, having islands; having spots like islands; (*ī*), m. a tiger, an ounce or panther, leopard; (*inī*), f. a kind of plant, = *vaṭa-pattrī.* — *Dvīpi-karṇi, is*, m. 'having the ear of a tiger,' N. of a king; [cf. *manda-karṇi.*] — *Dvīpi-nakha, as*, m. a kind of perfume; [cf. *vyāghra-nakha* and *vyāla-nakha.*] — *Dvīpi-śatru, us*, m. the plant Asparagus Racemosus.

Dvīpya, as, ā, am, living on an island, an islander; (*as*), m. the largest sort of raisin, cubebs; a sort of crow; N. of Vyāsa [cf. *dvaipāyana*]; (*ā*), f. Asparagus Racemosus; [cf. *dvīpikā* and *dvīpi-śatru.*]

द्वृ *dvṛi*, cl. 1. P. *dvarati*, &c., to obstruct; to cover; to disregard; to appropriate.

द्वेधा *dve-dhā*. See p. 445, col. 3.

द्वेष *dvesha*. See p. 445, col. 3.

द्वेसत *dvesata, as, ā, am*, having the same length above and below the navel; (also read *dvayasata.*)

द्वैगत *dvaigata, am*, n. (fr. *dvi-gat*), Ved., N. of a Sāman.

द्वैगुणिक *dvaiguṇika, as, ī, am* (fr. *dvi-guṇa*), one who requires the double or cent per cent interest; (*as*), m. an usurer, money-lender.

Dvaiguṇya, am, n. the double, double amount, double value or measure, double the amount; duality; doubling; the possession of two out of the three qualities.

द्वैजात *dvaijāta, as, ī, am* (fr. *dvi-jāti*), belonging to the twice-born, consisting of twice-born men, belonging to one of the three higher classes.

द्वैत *dvaita, am*, n. (fr. 1. *dvi-tā*), duality, the state of being doubled, duplicity, dualism in philosophy, the assertion of two principles (as of spirit and matter, God and the universe, &c.); doubt. — *Dvaita-nirṇaya, as*, m. 'the decision or discussion of duality,' N. of a philosophical work by Vaćaspati-miśra. — *Dvaita-pariśishṭa, am*, n. 'the remainder of discussions on duality,' N. of a work by Keśava. — *Dvaita-bhṛita, ās*, m. pl., N. of a philosophical school. — *Dvaita-vādin, ī*, m. 'an assertor of dualism,' a philosopher who asserts the two principles or the existence of the soul as separate from the Supreme Being. — *Dvaita-viveka, as*, m. 'discrimination of duality,' N. of a part of the Pañćadaśī by Bhāratī-tīrtha. — *Dvaita-vaitathyopanishad* (°*ya-up*°), *t*, f., N. of an Upanishad.

Dvaitavana, as, m. (fr. *dvita-vana*), Ved. a patronymic of the king Dhvasan; (*as, ī, am*), belonging or relating to Dhvasan Dvaitavana.

Dvaitīyaka, as, ī, am, returning every second day, second; [cf. *dvitīyaka.*]

द्वैध *dvaidha, as, ī, am* (fr. *dvi-dhā*), twofold, double; (*am*), n. duality, duplicity, double existence or nature, twofold form or state, a double resource, secondary array or reserve; division or separation into two parts; disunion, diversity, difference, variance, contest, conflict, a duel; doubt, uncertainty; a dilemma; contradiction, dispute; (*am*), ind. in two parts, into two portions; in two ways, doubly. — *Dvaidhā-karaṇa, am*, n. making into two, separating into two parts, disuniting. — *Dvaidhi-kṛita, as, ā, am*, separated, made twofold, divided into two, sundered; brought into a dilemma. — *Dvaidhi-bhāva, as*, m. twofold form or state, a double state, duality, duplicity, double nature, the nature or property of being two or distinct; separation into two, difference; contest, dispute, doubt, dilemma, uncertainty; sowing dissension or causing the separation of allies, dividing an army into two detachments, making peace with one and waging war with another (one of the six kinds of military tactics); falsehood. — *Dvaidhi-bhū*, cl. 1. P. *-bhavati, -bhavitum*, to become separated or divided into two parts, to be disunited. — *Dvaidhi-bhūta, as, ā, am*, separated into two, divided, disunited.

Dvaidhya, am, n. 'the state of being twofold,' double nature, duplicity; diversity, variance, discrepancy; falsehood.

द्वैप *dvaipa, as, ī, am* (fr. *dvīpa*), being or living on an island, an islander; occurring on an island; (fr. *dvīpin*), belonging to a tiger or panther, made of a tiger's skin, covered with it; (*as*), m. a car covered or hung with a tiger's skin.

Dvaipaka, as, ī, am, living on an island, an islander.

Dvaipāyana, as, m. (fr. *dvīpa*), 'the island-born,' N. of Vyāsa, author or compiler of the Vedas and Purāṇas, (the place of his nativity being a small island in the Ganges); (*as, ī, am*), relating to Dvaipāyana.

Dvaipya, as, ā or *-pī, am* (fr. *dvīpa*), of or relating to an island or peninsula, the inhabitant of an island or of the coast, an islander.

द्वैपक्ष *dvaipaksha, am*, n. (fr. *dvi-paksha*), two factions or parties.

द्वैपद *dvaipada, as*, m. (fr. *dvi-pada*), a combination or compound of two words. — *Dvaipada-śas*, ind. in a compound or combination of two words.

Dvaipadika, as, ī, am (fr. *dvi-padā*), familiar with the Dvi-padā.

द्वैपराक *dvaiparāka, as*, m. (fr. *dvi-parāka*), N. of a Tri-rātra.

द्वैपारायणिक *dvaipārāyaṇika, as, ī, am*, one who performs the Pārāyaṇa twice.

द्वैभाव्य *dvaibhāvya, am*, n. double nature, division or separation into two.

द्वैमातुर *dvaimātura, as, ī, am* (fr. *dvi-mātṛi*), having two mothers, i. e. a natural mother and a step-mother; having another mother, having two different mothers (as two brothers); (*as*), m. an epithet of Gaṇeśa [cf. *dvimātṛi-ja*]; of Jarāsandha.

Dvaimātṛika, as, ī, am, nourished by rain and rivers (as a country); cf. *devamātṛika* and *nadī-matṛika*).

द्वैमित्रि *dvaimitri, is, is, i* (fr. *dvi-mitra*), born of two friends.

द्वैयह्निक *dvaiyahnika, as, ī, am* (fr. *dvi-ahan*), of or belonging to two days.

द्वैयोग्य *dvaiyogya, am*, n. (fr. *dvi-yoga*), a combination of two.

द्वैरथ *dvairatha, am*, n. (fr. *dvi-ratha*), 'chariot-duel,' a single combat in chariots, single combat in general; (*as, ī, am*), relating to a single combat in chariots; (*as*), m. an adversary.

द्वैराज्य *dvairājya, am*, n. (fr. *dvi-rājan*), a dominion divided between two princes.

द्वैरात्रिक *dvairātrika, as, ī, am* (fr. *dvi-rātra*), of or belonging to a period of two nights.

द्वैवर्षिक *dvaivarshika, as, ī, am* (fr. *dvi-varsha*), biennial, happening after two years.

द्वैविध्य *dvaividhya, am*, n. (fr. *dvi-vidha*), the state of being twofold, duality, twofold manner or character, duplicity, diversity, variance.

द्वैशाण *dvaiśāṇa, as, ī, am*, worth two Śāṇas; [cf. *dvi-śāṇa* and *dviśāṇya.*]

द्वैषणीया *dvaishaṇīyā*, f. (fr. *dveshaṇīya*), a sort of betel pepper.

द्वैसमिक *dvaisamika, as, ī, am* (fr. *dvi-samā*), two years old.

द्वैहायन *dvaihāyana, am*, n. (fr. *dvi-hāyana*), the age of two years, the state of being two years old.

द्व्यंश *dvy-aṇśa*, for this and other comps. beginning with *dvy* see under *dvi*, p. 445, col. 1.

ध

ध 1. *dha*, the nineteenth consonant of the alphabet and the fourth of the fourth or dental class, being the aspirate of *d* and pronounced like *dh* in *madhouse.* — *Dha-kāra, as*, m. the letter or sound *dh.*

ध 2. *dha, as, ā, am* (fr. rt. 1. *dhā*), placing, putting; holding, containing, possessing, having; causing, &c.; (*as*), m. an epithet of Brahmā; epithet of Kuvera; virtue, moral merit; (*ā*), f., N. of the residence of Kṛishṇa; (*am*), n. wealth, property.

धक् 1. *dhak*, ind. (probably fr. rt. 1. *dah*), an exclamation of wrath.

धक् 2. *dhak*, see *uśa-dhak*; cf. 2. *dah.*

धक्वित् *dhakit*, ind. = *dhik*, q. v.

धक्क् *dhakk*, cl. 10. P. *dhakkayati*, &c., to destroy or annihilate.

धट *dhaṭa, as*, m. (probably a Prākṛit form of *dhartṛi*, derived from the nom. sing. *dhartā* and rt. *dhṛi*, like *bhaṭ, bhāṭa, bhāṭaka, bhāṭi* fr. rt. *bhṛi*; cf. *tulā-dhaṭa* and *tulayā dhṛi* under *tulā*), a balance, the scale of a balance, a pair of scales; the sign of the zodiac Libra; ordeal by the balance; (*ī*), f. old cloth or raiment; a piece of cloth worn over the privities. — *Dhaṭī-dāna, am*, n. giving old cloth to a woman after impregnation.

धटक *dhaṭaka, as*, m. a kind of weight equal to 14 Vallas or 42 Raktikās.

धटिन् *dhaṭin, ī*, m. an epithet of Śiva, (perhaps a wrong reading for *ghaṭin*; cf. *ghaṇṭa, ghaṇṭin, ghaṭīghaṭa*); (*inī*), f. a cotton cloth or string fastened round the loins; [cf. *dhaṭī* under *dhaṭa.*]

धटोत्कच *dhaṭotkaća, as*, m., N. of a man; (probably for *ghaṭotkaća.*)

धडि *dhaḍi*, m., N. of a man.

धण् *dhaṇ*, cl. 1. P. *dhaṇati*, &c., to sound; [cf. rt. 1. *dhan, dhvaṇ*, 2. *dhran, dhraṇ.*]

धत्तूर *dhattūra, as,* m. or *dhattūraka, as, ā,* m. f. the white thorn-apple, Datura Alba; [cf. *dhustūra.*]

धन् 1. *dhan,* cl. 1. P. *dhanati,* &c., to sound; [cf. rt. 2. *dhvan* and *dhaṇ.*]

धन् 2. *dhan* (related to rt. *dhanv*), cl. 3. P. *dadhanti,* &c., Ved. to cause to move or run, to put in motion; to bear fruit, produce crops of grain, &c.: Caus. P. A. *dhanayati, -te, -yitum,* to cause to move or run, to put in motion; to move, run.

Dhana, am, n. (connected with 2. *dhan,* but said to be fr. rt. 1. *dhā*), the reward given to a victor in a combat, spoil taken from an enemy, booty, prey; a gift; the prize or thing won in a game, (*dhanam bhṛi,* to carry off the prize, to carry off booty); a contest or struggle for any prize, a match; anything valuable; property of any description, wealth, treasure, riches, money, gold, chattels, wealth in cattle or herds, abounding in anything, possessions in general [cf. *strī-dh°, dhānya-dh°, vidyā-dh°*]; a valued object, an object of affection or endearment, capital (opposed to *vṛiddhi,* interest); surplus, residue, the affirmative quantity or plus (in arithmetic, opposed to *ṛiṇa, kshaya, vyaya, hāni*); (in astrology) N. of the second mansion; [cf. probably Gr. εὐ-θενής.] — *Dhana-kāma* or *dhana-kāmya, as, ā, am,* desirous of money, avaricious, covetous. — *Dhana-keli, is, is, i,* sporting with riches or treasures; (*as*), m. an epithet of Kuvera. — *Dhana-krītī* (according to some also *dhana-krītā*), f. a woman bought with money. — *Dhana-kshaya, as,* m. loss of money or property; 'one who has lost his money,' N. of a man. — *Dhana-garva, as,* m. 'one who has pride in riches, purse-proud,' N. of a man. — *Dhana-garvita, as, ā, am,* proud of riches, purse-proud. — *Dhana-gupta, as, ā, am* (for *gupta-dhana*), one who guards his property carefully; (*as*), m., N. of a merchant's son. — *Dhanagupta-tā,* f. careful guarding of property. — *Dhana-ććhū, ūs,* m. the numidian crane (said to = *kareṭavyā,* but the name suggests an analogy to the Dhaneśa of the spoken dialects or the Indian Buceros). — *Dhana-ćyuta, as, ā, am,* fallen from affluence, reduced to poverty, poor. — *Dhana-jāta, as, ā, am,* arising from wealth, produced by wealth; (*āni*), n. pl. all kinds of valuable objects or possessions. — *Dhana-jit, t, t, t,* Ved. conquering booty, victorious in a fight; acquiring treasures; (*t*), m., N. of an Ekāha. — *Dhanañ-jaya, as, ā, am,* Ved. conquering booty, victorious in battle; wealth-acquiring; (*as*), m. an epithet of Soma; a N. of fire; a particular vital air which is supposed to nourish the body; the plant Plumbago Zeylanica; N. of a Brāhman; an epithet of Arjuna, third son of Pāṇḍu; the plant Terminalia Arjuna; N. of a serpent-demon; of a Vyāsa; of a king of Kaliṅga; of a king of Kausthala-pura; of a merchant; of a lexicographer; of the author of the Dharma-pradīpa; (*ās*), m. pl. the descendants of the Brāhman Dhanañ-jaya. — *Dhanañjaya-nighaṇṭu, us,* m. 'the vocabulary of Dhanañ-jaya,' N. of a dictionary mentioned in the commentary Prauḍha-manoramā by Bhaṭṭoji-dīkshita. — *Dhanañjaya-vijaya, as,* m. 'the victory of Dhanañ-jaya (or Arjuna),' N. of a drama. — *Dhanañjaya-saṅgraha, as,* m., N. of a work mentioned in the Saṃskāra-tattva by Raghu-nandana. — *Dhana-tama, am,* n., scil. *dāyam,* an exceedingly rich donation. — *Dhana-tṛishṇā,* f. thirst for riches, covetousness. — *Dhana-tyaj, k, k, k,* resigning wealth. — *Dhana-da, as, ā, am,* giving money or property, granting wealth, munificent, wealth-yielding, liberal, tributary; (*as*), m. an epithet of Kuvera, god of riches; N. of a Guhyaka or a being attending on Kuvera; N. of a mountain; the plant Barringtonia Acutangula (= *hijjala*); (*ā*), f., N. of one of the Mātṛis attending on Skanda; of a Tantra deity; [cf. *dhana-dā.*] — *Dhana-daṇḍa, as,* m. fine, amercement. — *Dhanada-tīrtha, am,* n., N. of a Tīrtha mentioned in the Revā-māhātmya. — *Dhana-datta, as,* m. 'wealth-given,' N. of several persons. — *Dhanada-deva, as,* m. = *dhana-deva,* N. of a poet. — *Dhana-darpa, as,* m. pride of wealth. — *Dhanada-stotra, am,* n. 'praise of the liberal,' N. of a small work. — *Dhana-dā, ās, ās, am,* Ved. giving rewards, granting spoil; granting riches or treasures; [cf. *dhana-da.*] — *Dhanadākshī* (°*da-akshi*), f. a kind of tree, = *kuverākshī, latā-karañja.* — *Dhanadānuja* (°*da-an°*), *as,* m. the younger brother of Kuvera, an epithet of Rāvaṇa. — *Dhanadā-pūjā-yantra, am,* n., N. of a mystical diagram given in the Tantra-sāra. — *Dhanadā-mantra, ās,* m. pl., N. of a particular prayer mentioned in the Tantra-sāra. — *Dhana-dāyin, ī, inī, i,* granting treasures; (*ī*), m. an epithet of Agni. — *Dhanadāvāsa* (°*da-āv°*), *as,* m. the residence of Kuvera, epithet of the mountain Kailāsa. — *Dhana-deva, as,* m., N. of a man, = *dhanada-deva,* N. of a poet. — *Dhanadeśvara* (°*da-īś°*), *as,* m. 'lord of wealth-givers,' an epithet of Kuvera. — *Dhanadeśvara-tīrtha, am,* n., N. of a place of pilgrimage. — *Dhana-dhānī,* f. a receptacle for valuable articles, a treasury, storehouse. — *Dhana-dhānya, am,* n., N. of a spell for restraining certain magical weapons. — *Dhanadhānyādhika* (°*ya-adh°*), *as, ā, am,* rich in money and grain. — *Dhanan-dadā,* f. 'granting treasures,' one of the Saktis or female personifications of divine power peculiar to the Buddhas. — *Dhana-pati, is,* m. 'the lord of riches or treasures,' epithet of Indra, and especially of Kuvera. — *Dhana-pāla, as,* m., Ved. a guardian of treasure, a treasurer; N. of a merchant; of a poet; of a lexicographer. — *Dhana-piśāćikā* or *dhana-piśāćī,* f. avarice, thirst for wealth. — *Dhana-priya, as, ā, am,* fond of wealth; (*ā*), f. the plant Ardisia Solanacea (= *kāka-jambū*). — *Dhana-bhaksha, as,* m., Ved. enjoying a reward, enjoyment of booty or wealth; (Sāy.) desirous of distributing wealth or possessing wealth (in cattle &c.). — *Dhana-mada, as, ā, am,* proud, inflated with the pride of wealth, purse-proud; (*as*), m. pride or intoxication of wealth. — *Dhana-mitra, as,* m. 'having wealth as a friend,' N. of a merchant. — *Dhana-mūla, am,* n. principal, capital; (*as, ā, am*), proceeding from wealth, founded on wealth. — *Dhana-mohana, as,* m., N. of a merchant's son. — *Dhanarća* (°*na-ṛića?*), *as, ā, am,* Ved. perhaps incorrectly for *dhanarja* (°*na-ṛija*), striving after a reward (?). — *Dhanarṇa* (°*na-ṛiṇa*), *am,* n. positive and negative quantities (in mathematics). — *Dhana-lubdha, as, ā, am,* or *dhana-lobhin, ī, inī, i,* 'greedy of wealth,' avaricious, covetous, miserly, mercenary. — *Dhana-lobha, as,* m. 'desire of wealth,' covetousness, avarice. — *Dhana-vat, ān, atī, at,* wealthy, opulent, rich; (*atī*), f. the constellation Dhanishṭhā; N. of a merchant's daughter; [cf. probably Lat. *dives.*] — *Dhana-vibhāga, as,* m. distribution of property. — *Dhana-vṛiddhi, is,* f. increase of property. — *Dhana-vyaya, as,* m. 'the spending of money,' expenditure, extravagance. — *Dhana-sañćaya, as,* m. collection of riches. — *Dhanasañćayin, ī, inī, i,* rich; one who has amassed wealth; (*ī*), m. a rich man. — *Dhana-sani, is, is, i,* Ved. granting a reward, giving riches. — *Dhana-sampatti, is,* f. accumulation of wealth. — *Dhana-sā, ās, ās, am,* Ved. granting a reward, distributing gifts or treasures; acquiring or conquering booty. — *Dhana-sāti, is,* f., Ved. acquisition of wealth or treasure. — *Dhana-sū, ūs,* m. 'producing wealth,' the fork-tailed shrike. — *Dhana-stha, as, ā, am,* 'living in wealth,' rich, wealthy. — *Dhana-sthāna, am,* n. a receptacle for riches, a treasury. — *Dhanasthānādhikārin* (°*na-adh°*), *ī,* m. the superintendant of a treasury, a treasurer. — *Dhana-spṛit, t,* m., Ved. carrying away or conquering booty; (Sāy.) gratifying with wealth; epithet of Agni; of Indra. — *Dhana-hara, as, ā* or *ī, am,* carrying off wealth, stealing property, a thief; receiving property, inheriting, an heir; (*ī*), f. a kind of perfume commonly called Chora. — *Dhana-harin* or *dhana-hārin, ī, iṇī, i,* stealing property, a thief; inheriting property, an heir. — *Dhana-hīna, as, ā, am,* deprived of wealth; reduced to poverty, poor. — *Dhana-hṛit, t, t, t,* a stealer of property, a thief; (*t*), m. f. n. (?), a kind of bulbous plant (= *ćaṇḍāla-kanda*). — *Dhanāgama* (°*na-āg°*), *as,* m. accession of wealth, gain. — *Dhanāḍhya* (°*na-āḍh°*), *as, ā, am,* opulent, wealthy. — *Dhanādāna* (°*na-ād°*), *am,* n. acceptance of money. — *Dhanādhana-nibandhana* (°*na-adh°*), *as, ā, am,* contingent on the possession or non-possession of wealth. — *Dhanādhāra* (°*na-ādh°*), *as,* m. a treasury, storehouse. — *Dhanādhikāra* (°*na-adh°*), *as,* m. title or right to property. — *Dhanādhikārin* (°*na-adh°*), *ī, iṇī,* m. f. an heir, an heiress, one who has a right or title to property; (*ī*), m. a treasurer; a collector. — *Dhanādhikṛita* (°*na-adh°*), *as,* m. 'any one placed over treasures,' a treasurer. — *Dhanādhigoptṛi* (°*na-adh°*), *tā,* m. 'the guardian of treasure,' an epithet of Kuvera. — *Dhanādhipa, as,* or *dhanādhipati* (°*na-adh°*), *is,* m. 'the lord of treasure,' an epithet of Kuvera; a treasurer. — *Dhanādhipatya* (°*na-adh°*), *am,* n. the dominion or superintendance over treasure. — *Dhanādhyaksha* (°*na-adh°*), *as,* m. an overseer of treasure, a treasurer; an epithet of Kuvera; of Śiva; [cf. *koshādhyaksha.*] — *Dhanāndha* (°*na-an°*), *as, ā, am,* blinded by riches. — *Dhanāpahāra* (°*na-ap°*), *as,* m. 'taking away of property,' fine, amercement; plunder. — *Dhanāyus* (°*na-āy°*), *us,* m., N. of a son of Dṛiḍhāyus. — *Dhanārgha* (°*na-ar°*), *as, ā, am,* Ved. deserving a reward, worthy of wealth. — *Dhanārćita* (°*na-ar°*), *as, ā, am,* wealthy, opulent. — *Dhanārjana* (°*na-ar°*), *am,* n. acquisition of property or of wealth. — *Dhanārthin* (°*na-ar°*), *ī, inī, i,* desiring wealth, wealth-seeking, a seeker of riches, covetous, miserly. — *Dhanāśā* (°*na-āśā*), f. longing after wealth, desire of riches. — *Dhaneśa* (°*na-īśa*), *as,* m. the lord of treasure, a rich man; an epithet of Kuvera; N. of the teacher of Vopa-deva. — *Dhaneśvara* (°*na-īś°*), *as,* m. 'lord of treasure,' an epithet of Kuvera; N. of a Brāhman; of a teacher of Vopa-deva; (*ī*), f. a female possessor of riches; the wife of Kuvera. — *Dhanaiśvarya* (°*na-aiś°*), *am,* n. the dominion over treasure. — *Dhanaishin* (°*na-esh°*), *ī, iṇī, i,* longing for riches, wishing or claiming property; (*ī*), m. a creditor who claims his money. — *Dhanopaćaya* (°*na-up°*), *as,* m. accumulation of wealth. — *Dhanoshman* (°*na-ush°* or *-ūsh°*), *ā,* m. burning desire for wealth or treasure.

Dhanaka, as, m. avarice, covetousness, desire for riches; N. of a Yādava, son of Dur-dama or Dur-mada; of another man.

Dhanāya, Nom. P. *dhanāyati,* &c., to wish for wealth, long for riches, be desirous of anything (with gen.).

Dhanāyā, f. the desire of obtaining riches, covetousness.

Dhanika, as, ā, am, rich, wealthy, opulent; pious, virtuous, excellent; (*as*), m. a wealthy man; a money-lender, a creditor, owner; a husband; coriander; N. of a poet; (*ikā*), f. a virtuous or excellent woman; a wife, young woman; a tree, see *priyaṅgu.*

Dhanin, ī, inī, i, possessing wealth or treasures, opulent, wealthy, rich, well off; (*ī*), m. a rich man; a creditor; the possessor of anything; N. of a messenger of the Kapas, Mahā-bh. Anuśāsana-p. 7333.

Dhanishṭha, as, ā, am, very rich; (superl. of 2. *dhan*), Ved. very swift; (*ā*), f. the more modern N. of the Nakshatra Śravishṭhā or twenty-third lunar mansion, (it comprises four stars, apparently α, β, γ, and δ Delphini, and is figured by a drum or tabor.)

Dhanikā, f. = *dhanikā,* f. a young woman.

Dhanīya, Nom. P. *dhanīyati,* &c., to wish for riches.

Dhanīyaka or *dhaneyaka, am,* n. coriander seed, = *dhanyāka.*

1. *dhanū, ūs,* m. a store of grain. (For 2. *dhanū* see p. 448, col. 1.)

Dhaneyu, us, m., N. of a son of Raudrāśva.

Dhanya, as, ā, am, bringing wealth, bestowing

opulence (Ved.); opulent, wealthy, rich; fortunate, happy, blest, lucky, auspicious; good; virtuous; (*as*), m. a fortunate or virtuous man; an infidel, atheist; N. of a spell for using or restraining magical weapons; N. of a man; (*ā*), f. a nurse; Emblic Myrobalan; coriander; (*am*), n. treasure, wealth; coriander. — *Dhanya-tā*, f. or *dhanya-tra*, *am*, n. good fortune, fortunate condition, good luck; opulence. — *Dhanyam-manya*, *as*, *ā*, *am*, considering one's self happy, thinking one's self fortunate. — *Dhanya-vāda*, *as*, m. thanksgiving, thankfulness, thanks, praise, applause. — *Dhanya-stotra*, *am*, n. 'the praise of the blessed,' N. of a short philosophical poem ascribed to Saṁkarāćārya.

Dhanyaka, *as*, m., N. of a man.

Dhanyāka, *am*, n. a plant bearing a small pungent seed used by the Hindūs as a condiment, Coriandrum Sativum.

धनस्यक *dhanasyaka*, *as*, m. the plant Asteracantha Longifolia (= *go-kshura*).

धनाश्री *dhanāśrī*, *īs* (?), f., N. of a Rāgiṇī; (according to Hanu-mat, the third wife of Śrī-rāga.)

धनु *dhanu*, *us*, m. or 2. *dhanū*, *ūs*, f. (fr. *dhan* = rt. *han*, to kill, or according to some fr. rt. *tan*, to stretch; the full form is *dhanus* below), a bow; a measure of four Hastas or cubits; the sign of the zodiac Sagittarius; a kind of tree, = *piyāla*, Semecarpus Anacardium; (*us*), f. a dry sandbank, a sandy shore; [cf. *dhanus*, *dhanvan*; Gr. θίς, θινός.] — *Dhanu-ketakī*, f. a kind of flower. — *Dhanu-gupta*, *as*, m., N. of a tree. — *Dhanu-rāja*, *as*, m., N. of one of the ancestors of Śākya-muni. — 1. *dhanv-antara*, *am*, n. (for 2. see under *dhanvan*, col. 2), an extent or distance of a Dhanu or four Hastas.

Dhanusha, *as*, m., N. of a Ṛishi.

Dhanushka (at the end of an adj. comp.) = *dhanus*, a bow [cf. *sa-dh°*]; (*am*), n. a small bow.

Dhanus, *us*, m. n. (generally n.), a bow; a measure of length equal to four Hastas or = $\frac{1}{2000}$ Gavyūti; (*us*), n. an arc or part of a circle; an arc or quadrant for obtaining by observation the altitude of the sun and the zenith-distance; the sign of the zodiac Sagittarius; a kind of tree, = *piyāla*; a desert, arid land; (*us*, *us*, *us*), armed with a bow; (*us*), m. a N. of Śiva. — *Dhanuḥ-kāṇḍa*, *am*, n. a bow and arrow. — *Dhanuḥ-khaṇḍa*, *am*, n. a portion of a bow; the stick or any other part of a bow. — *Dhanuḥ-paṭa*, *as*, m. the Piyal tree, Buchanania Latifolia; (also read *dhanush-paṭa*.) — *Dhanuḥ-śata*, *am*, n., 100 Dhanus or 400 Hastas or cubits. — *Dhanuḥ-śākhā*, f. = *dhanur-guṇa*, q. v. — *Dhanuḥ-śālā*, f. the place where bows are kept, bow-room. — *Dhanuḥ-śreṇī*, f., N. of two plants, = *dhanur-guṇā* or *dhanu-śreṇī* and *mahendra-vāruṇī*. — *Dhanuḥ-stambha*, *as*, m. (?), a kind of spasmodic contraction of the body. — *Dhanur-ākāra*, *as*, *ā*, *am*, or *dhanur-ākṛiti*, *is*, *is*, *i*, bow-shaped, formed like a bow, curved, bent. — *Dhanur-guṇa*, *as*, m. a bow-string; (*ā*), f. a plant from the leaves of which a tough thread is extracted of which bow-strings were formerly made; Sanseviera Zeylanica, S. Roxburghiana. — *Dhanur-graha*, *as*, *ā*, *am*, bearing a bow, an archer; (*as*), m., N. of one of the 100 sons of Dhṛita-rāshṭra [cf. *dhanur-dhara*]; the art of managing a bow. — *Dhanur-grāha*, *as*, *ā*, *am*, 'bearing a bow,' an archer. — *Dhanur-jyā*, f. a bow-string. — *Dhanurjyā-tala-śabda*, *as*, m. the mere twanging noise of the bow-string. — *Dhanur-durga* = *dhanva-durga* under *dhanvan*, col. 2. — *Dhanur-druma*, *as*, m. the bamboo used for bows. — *Dhanur-dvitīya*, *as*, *ā*, *am*, furnished with a bow. — *Dhanur-dhara*, *as*, *ā*, *am*, bearing a bow, armed with a bow, an archer, a bowyer; (*as*), m. the sign of the zodiac Sagittarius; N. of one of the 100 sons of Dhṛita-rāshṭra. — *Dhanur-dhārin*, *ī*, m. or *dhanur-bhṛit*, *t*, m. an archer, a bowyer. — *Dhanur-madhya*, *am*, n. the middle part of a bow (= *lastaka*). — *Dhanur-maha*, *as*, m. a festival or ceremony performed at the consecration of a bow; (a various reading has *dhanur-makha*.) — *Dhanur-mārga*, *as*, m. a line curved like a bow, a curve. — *Dhanur-mālā*, f. a plant from the leaves of which bow-strings were made; [cf. *dhanur-guṇā*.] — *Dhanur-yāsa*, *as*, m. the plant Hedysarum Alhagi (= *dhanvayāsa*). — *Dhanur-latā*, f. the moon-plant (= *soma-vallī*). — *Dhanur-vaktra*, *as*, m., N. of one of Skanda's attendants; (probably a wrong form for *dhanur-vakra*.) — *Dhanur-vāta*, *as*, m. a kind of disease. — *Dhanur-vidyā*, f. the science of archery, skill in archery. — *Dhanur-vṛiksha*, *as*, m., N. of several plants used for making bows, as the bamboo, Ficus Religiosa, Semecarpus Anacardium; a measure of four cubits; an arc, a portion of the circumference of a circle; [cf. *dhanu* and *dhanus*.] — *Dhanur-veda*, *as*, m. 'knowledge of archery, the science of archery,' N. of a treatise on archery (regarded as an Upa-veda connected with the Yajur-veda and ascribed to Viśvā-mitra or according to others to Bhṛigu). — *Dhanurveda-para* or *dhanurveda-parāyaṇa*, *as*, *ā*, *am*, devoted to the science of archery. — *Dhanur-vedin*, *ī*, *inī*, *i*, versed in the Dhanur-veda; (*ī*), m. epithet of Śiva. — *Dhanur-hasta*, *as*, *ā*, *am*, bow in hand, bearing a bow: — *Dhanushāksha* (°*shā-ak*°), *as*, m. (*dhanushā* probably inst. c. of *dhanus*), N. of a Ṛishi. — *Dhanush-kara*, *as*, m. a bow-maker; (*as*, *ā*, *am*), carrying a bow in the hand, armed with a bow, an archer, bowyer; (*ī*), f. a kind of plant; (also read *dhānush-kari*.) — *Dhanush-kāra*, *as*, or *dhanush-kṛit*, *t*, m. a bow-maker. — *Dhanush-paṭa*, *as*, m. a kind of tree, = *piyāla*. — *Dhanush-pāṇi*, *is*, *is*, *i*, 'bow-handed,' armed with a bow, an archer. — *Dhanush-mat*, *ān*, *atī*, *at*, furnished or armed with a bow, bearing a bow, an archer, bowman, bowyer; (*ān*), m., N. of a mountain to the north of Madhya-deśa; (*atī*), f., N. of the tutelary deity in the family of Vyāghra-pād. — *Dhanushmat-tā*, f. archery.

धन्य *dhanya*. See p. 447, col. 3.

धन्व् *dhanv*, cl. 1. P. A. (allied to rts. *dhav* and *dhāv* and 2. *dhan*), Ved. *dhanvati*, *-te*, *dadhanve*, &c., to run; to flow; to cause to run or flow.

Dhanutri, *tā*, *trī*, *tṛi* (fr. rt. *dhanv* or 2. *dhan*), Ved. running, flowing, flowing quickly; (Sāy.) enriching by crops of grain; causing to flow.

धन्व *dhanva*, *am*, n. (a curtailed form of *dhanvan* below; said to be fr. rt. *dhanv*), a bow, (in the classical language almost always at the end of an adj. comp.; cf. *priya-dh°*); (*as*), m., N. of a man. — *Dhanva-dhi*, *is*, m. a bow-case, anything in which a bow is kept.

Dhanvan, *a*, n. a bow, (in the later language generally at the end of a comp.; cf. *avatata-dh°*, *asthi-dh°*, *ugra-dh°*, *kṛita-dh°*, *kshipra-dh°*, *kshema-dh°*, &c.); (*ā*, *a*), m. n. (in the earlier language n. only), a dry soil, a country scantily supplied with water, a desert, a waste; a firm spot, land, ground, shore; the plant Alhagi Maurorum which grows in a dry soil; (Sāy.) the sky, rain-water; [cf. Gr. θέναρ: Old Germ. *ten-ar*: Angl. Sax. *denu*, 'valley:' Mod. Germ. *tenne*, 'thrashing-floor;' *duene*, 'down.'] — *Dhanva-ćara*, *as*, *ā*, *am*, Ved. going in a desert land; (Sāy.) going like an archer or warrior armed with a bow. — *Dhanva-ćyut*, *t*, *t*, *t*, Ved. agitating or moving the soil; (Sāy.) flowing with rain-water. — *Dhanva-ja*, *as*, *ā*, *am*, growing on dry soil, produced on waste or barren land. — *Dhanva-taru*, *us*, m. a kind of Soma plant. — *Dhanva-durga*, *am*, n. inaccessible by reason of a surrounding desert. — 2. *dhanvan-tara*, *as*, m. (for 1. see col. 1) = *dhanvan-tari*, a N. of Śiva. — *Dhanvan-tari*, *is*, m. (for *dhanvani-tari*), 'moving in a curve,' N. of a form of the Sun; of a deity to whom oblations were offered in the north-east quarter, (the deity Dhanvantari was honoured with morning and evening oblations along with Soma, Vanas-pati, Agni-Soma, Indra-Agni, Heaven and Earth, Indra, the Viśve-devās, and Brahmā); the physician of the gods (who was produced at the churning of the ocean, holding a cup of Amṛita in his hands; author of the Āyur-veda); a celebrated physician also called Divo-dāsa, king of Kāśi, (said to be the same as the preceding in another existence, and considered to be the founder of the Hindū school of medicine; also read *dhānvantari*); N. of the author of a medical dictionary (perhaps the same as the Dhanvantari mentioned among the nine gems of the court of Vikramāditya). — *Dhanvantari-grastā*, f. 'the plant eaten by Dhanvantari,' Helleborus Niger, a medicinal plant; [cf. *kaṭukī*.] — *Dhanvantari-darpa-bhaṅga*, *as*, m. 'the breaking of Dhanvantari's pride,' N. of the fifty-second chapter of the Kṛishṇa-khaṇḍa of the Brahma-vaivarta-Purāṇa. — *Dhanvantari-nighaṇṭu*, *us*, m. the vocabulary of Dhanvantari. — *Dhanvantari-yajña*, *as*, m. the sacrifice of Dhanvantari. — *Dhanvantarīya*, *as*, *ā*, *am*, composed by Dhanvantari; (also read *dhānvantarīya*.) — *Dhanva-yavāsa* or *dhanvayavāsaka* or *dhanva-yāsa*, *as*, m. Alhagi Maurorum. — *Dhanvā-sah* or *dhanvā-sāh*, *ṭ*, *ṭ*, *ṭ*, Ved. skilled in archery.

Dhanvanya, *as*, *ā*, *am*, Ved. being in dry soil or barren land.

Dhanvāyana, bearing bows (?), in *bhīma-dhanvāyanī*. See *bhīma-dhanvāyana*.

Dhanvāyin or *dhanvāvin*, *ī*, *inī*, *i*, Ved. carrying or bearing a bow.

Dhanvin, *ī*, *inī*, *i*, armed with a bow, an archer, a bowman, (at the end of comp., e.g. *ishu-dh°*, furnished with arrow and bow); cunning, shrewd, a wag, wit, sharp or shrewd fellow; (*ī*), m. the sign of the zodiac Sagittarius; an epithet of Śiva; of Vishṇu; of Arjuna; N. of a son of Manu Tāmasa; N. of a commentator on the Drāhyāyaṇa-sūtras; several plants, Terminalia Arjuna, Mimusops Elengi (= *vakula*); Alhagi Maurorum. — *Dhanvi-bhāshya*, *am*, n. the commentary of Dhanvin.

धन्वङ्ग *dhanvaṅga* or *dhanvana*, *as*, m. a fruit tree called in the modern languages of India 'Dhāmani, Dhāmana, Dhāminī, and Dhunin;' (*am*), n. the fruit of this tree. — *Dhanvana-ććhada*, *as*, m. the tree Grewia Asiatica; (also read *dhanvaga*; cf. *dhānvana*.)

धन्वन्तरि *dhanvan-tari*. See col. 2.

धन्विन *dhanvina*, *as*, m. a kind of animal.

धम *dhama*, *as*, *ā* or *ī*, *am* (fr. rt. *dhmā*), blowing (fire, a trumpet, tube, &c.); smelting, fusing, melting, (generally at the end of a comp.; cf. *karan-dh°*, *jalan-dh°*, *ghaṭin-dh°*); (*as*), m. the moon; an epithet of Kṛishṇa; of Yama; of Brahma, the supreme spirit.

Dhamaka, *as*, m. 'a blower,' a blacksmith (as blowing the forge).

Dhamadhama, *as*, m. (fr. *dhmā* with reduplication), 'the blower,' N. of a demon that causes disease; N. of one of the attendants of Śiva; (*ā*), f., N. of one of the Mātṛis attending on Skanda; (*ā*), ind. blowing repeatedly or the sort of sound made by blowing with a bellows or a trumpet.

Dhamana, *as*, *ā*, *am*, blowing (a bellows or wind instrument, trumpet, &c.); cruel; (*as*), m. a kind of reed, Arundo Tibialis or Karka (= *naḍa*, *nala*); a particular high number.

Dhamani, *is*, and in the later language also *dhamanī*, f. a reed, a pipe, (perhaps also) the act of blowing (a wind instrument); a tube or canal of the human body; any tubular vessel, as a vein, nerve, &c., (in the Hindū medical system there are twenty-four chief tubular vessels, which starting from the heart carry the *rasa* or chyle through the body; according to another system the starting-point of these vessels is the navel, whence they branch out and perform various functions); the throat, neck; (*ī*), f. a sort of perfume (= *haṭṭa-vilāsinī* and *nalikā*); turmeric (= *haridrā*); another plant, = *pṛiśni-parṇī*;

(*is*), f., N. of the mother of Vātāpi and Ilvala, and wife of Hrāda.

Dhamanīla, as, ā, am, full-veined, large-veined, having prominent veins.

Dhamara or *dhamātra* (also read *dhemātra*), a particular high number.

Dhami, is, is, i, blowing, puffing; (*is*), f. the act of blowing.

Dhamita, as, ā, am, Ved. blown, kindled.

Dhamyat, an, antī, at, or *dhamyamāna, as, ā, am*, being blown; being melted.

धम्मट dhammaṭa, *as*, m., N. of a man.

धम्मल dhammala, *as*, m. the breast ornamented with gold or jewels; [cf. *dhammilla*.]

धम्मिका dhammikā, f., N. of a woman.

धम्मिल्ल dhammilla, *as*, m. the braided and ornamented hair of a woman tied round the head and intermixed with flowers, pearls, &c.

Dhammillaka = *dhammilla* at end of comp. (e. g. *srasta-dhammillakā vadhūs*, a woman with loosened braided hair).

धय dhaya, *as, ā* or *ī, am* (fr. rt. *dhe*), drinking, sipping, sucking, (often at the end of a comp., e. g. *āsyan-dhaya, ghaṭīn-dh°, stanan-dh°*, &c.); (*ā*), f. a little girl (?).

धर dhara, *as, ā* or *ī, am* (fr. rt. *dhṛi*), holding, bearing, carrying; wearing; possessing, having, possessed of, containing, keeping, sustaining, preserving, observing, (often compounded with its object; cf. *anśu-dh°, aksha-dh°, aśruti-dh°, asṛig-dh°, kaksha-dh°*, &c.); (*as*), m. a mountain [cf. *kshiti-dh°, bhū-dh°, mahī-dh°*]; a flock of cotton; a frivolous or dissolute man (= *viṭa*), N. of one of the Vasus; of a hero on the side of the Pāṇḍavas; of the king of the tortoises; of the father of Padma-prabha, the sixth Arhat of the present Ava-sarpiṇī; (*ā*), f. 'the bearer, supporter,' the earth, the ground; the uterus or womb; a vein or tubular vessel of the body; marrow; a mass of gold or heap of valuables (representing the earth and given to Brāhmans); N. of one of the wives of Kaśyapa, mother of the land and water-birds, (probably = the Earth.) — *Dhara-paṭṭa* or *dhara-sena, as*, m., N. of a prince of the Ballabhī or Vallabhī dynasty. — *Dhara-saṃstha, as, ā, am*, equal to a mountain, huge as a mountain, &c. — *Dharā-kadamba, as*, m. the Kadamba tree, Nauclea Cadamba; [cf. *dhārā-kadamba*.] — *Dharātmaja* (°*rā-āt*°), *as*, m. 'son of the earth,' the planet Mars or its regent. — *Dharā-dhara, as, ā, am*, 'bearing or sustaining the earth, prop of the earth,' an epithet of Vishṇu or Kṛishṇa; (*as*), m. a mountain. — *Dharādhārā* (°*rā-ādh*°?), f. the earth. — *Dharādhipa* (°*rā-adh*°), *as*, m. 'sovereign of the earth,' a king. — *Dharāntara-ćara, as, ā, am*, walking in the interior of the earth; (probably a wrong reading for *dhārāntara-ćara*, q. v.) — *Dharā-pati, is*, m. 'lord of the earth,' an epithet of Vishṇu. — *Dharā-putra, as*, m. 'son of the earth,' the planet Mars. — *Dharā-bhuj, k*, m. 'enjoying or possessing the earth,' a king. — *Dharā-bhṛit, t*, m. 'sustaining the earth,' a mountain. — *Dharāmara* (°*rā-am*°), *as*, m. 'a god or immortal on the earth,' a Brāhman. — *Dharā-śaya, as, ī, am*, sleeping on the earth, lying on the ground. — *Dharā-sūnu, us*, m. 'son of the earth,' the planet Mars. — *Dharoddhāra* (°*rā-ud*°), *as*, m. deliverance of the world. — *Dharopastha* (°*rā-up*°), *as*, m. surface of the earth.

Dharaṇa, as, ī, am, bearing, holding; preserving; (*as*), m. a dike, a bank, a ridge of land answering the purpose of a bridge &c., the side of a mountain; the world; the sun; the female breast; rice, corn; the Himālaya considered as king of mountains; N. of a king of the Nāgas; (*ī* or *dharaṇi, is*), f. the earth, the soil, the ground, the Earth personified as the wife of Dhruva; a tubular vessel of the body, a vein; a kind of bulbous plant, an esculent root, = *dhāraṇīyā, dhīra-pattrī, kandālu, kandāḍhya, daṇḍa-kandaka, vana-kanda, su-kandaka;* the silk-cotton tree, = *śālmali;* a beam or rafter for a roof; N. of a dictionary (generally called *dharaṇi* or *dharaṇi-kośa*); (*am*), n. the act of holding, seizing, possessing, keeping, bearing, supporting, support; bringing, procuring; a support, fastening, prop, stay; security; a sort of weight variously reckoned as = 10 Palas, = 16 silver Māshakas, = 1 silver Purāṇa, = $\frac{1}{10}$ Śatamāna, = 19 Nishpāvas, = ⅜ Karsha, = $\frac{1}{10}$ Pala, = 24 Raktikās; a particular high number. — *Dharaṇa-priyā*, f., N. of the goddess executing the commands of the nineteenth Arhat. — *Dharaṇi-goṇiga, as*, m., N. of a man. — *Dharaṇi-ja, as*, m. 'the son of the earth,' an epithet of Aṅgiras or the planet Mars. — *Dharaṇi-dhara, as*, m. 'the bearer of the earth,' an epithet of Vishṇu; [cf. *dharaṇī-dhara*.] — *Dharaṇi-maṇḍa*, N. of a place. — *Dharaṇi-stha, as, ā, am*, being or staying on earth. — *Dharaṇī-kanda, as*, m. an esculent root or bulb (= *dharaṇī*). — *Dharaṇī-kīlaka, as*, m. a mountain. — *Dharaṇī-tala, am*, n. the surface of the earth. — *Dharaṇī-talaśrī, īs*, m., N. of a king of the Kin-naras. — *Dharaṇī-dhara, as, ī, am*, 'bearing or sustaining the earth,' epithet of the mythical elephants which are fabled to support the earth; (*as*), m. epithet of Śesha; of Vishṇu or Kṛishṇa; of Śiva; a mountain; a tortoise; a king; N. of several persons; of a man of the family of Maunin and son of Maheśvara; of the father of Śaśi-dhara; of the father of Vāsu-deva and grandfather of the author Hari-nātha; of the father of Dayā-śaṅkara; of a scholiast on Manu; of a Bodhi-sattva; (sometimes read *dharaṇi-dhara* or *dharaṇīn-dhara*.) — *Dharaṇī-dhṛit, t*, m. 'supporting the earth,' an epithet of Śesha. — *Dharaṇī-pati, is*, m. 'lord of the earth,' a king. — *Dharaṇī-pūra, as*, m. the ocean (as 'surrounding the earth'). — *Dharaṇi-plava, as*, m. the ocean ('in which the earth floats'). — *Dharaṇī-bhṛit, t, t, t*, bearing or supporting the earth; (*t*), m. a mountain; a king; (also read *dharaṇi-bhṛit*.) — *Dharaṇī-maṇḍala, am*, n. 'the sphere of the earth,' the globe. — *Dharaṇī-ruha, as*, m. 'growing on the earth,' a tree; [cf. *kshiti-ruh* and *kshiti-ruha*.] — *Dharaṇīśvara* (°*ṇi-īś*°), *as*, m. 'lord of the earth,' an epithet of Śiva. — *Dharaṇīśvara-rāja, as*, m. 'king of the lords of the earth,' N. of a Bodhi-sattva. — *Dharaṇī-suta, as*, m. 'son of the earth,' an epithet of Aṅgiras or the planet Mars; (*ā*), f. 'the daughter of the earth,' an epithet of Sītā, wife of Rāma (as produced from the soil by Janaka when he was ploughing a spot to prepare it for a sacrifice).

Dharaṇi, is. See above under *dharaṇa*.

Dharaṇīya, as, ā, am, to be held or kept, to be borne or carried; supportable.

Dharini, is, m. (?), N. of an Agastya.

Dharitri, f. a female bearer, supporter; the earth.

Dhariman, ā, m. a balance, a pair of scales, a weight; form, figure, semblance; [cf. *dharīman*.] — *Dharima-meya, as, ā, am*, measurable by weight.

Dharīman = *dharman* (only occurring in the loc. *dharīmaṇi*), Ved. according to custom or law or precept; (Sāy.) containing the essence of the earth (as an altar); a vessel for holding anything.

1. *dharuṇa, as, ā, am* (for 2. see p. 451, col. 3), Ved. carrying, holding, supporting, one who supports or keeps; (*as*), m. the supposed author of a hymn of the Ṛig-veda; an epithet of Brahmā; heaven, paradise; water; opinion, conception; (*as, ī, am*), containing in one's self, spacious; a place where anything is preserved or kept; (*am*), n. a basis, foundation, support, prop, stay; the firm soil of the earth; anything that is undermost or innermost; a receptacle, reservoir; water. — *Dharuṇa-hvara, as, ā, am*, Ved. trembling in its innermost foundations? (Sāy.) obstructing the flow of waters.

Dharṇasa, as, ā, am, or *dharṇasi* or *dharṇi, is, is, i*, Ved. bearing, supporting, sustaining; a supporter; strong, energetic, powerful, able; full of spirit (as Soma); firm, durable; (*dharṇasi* in Naigh. II. 9. is one of the synonyms of *bala*, strength.)

Dhartavya, as, ā, am, to be upheld or supported; to be held, had or possessed; to be placed or fixed.

Dhartṛi, tā, trī, tṛi, holding, bearing, supporting; (*tā*), m. a bearer, supporter, preserver.

Dhartra, am, n. a prop, a stay; a house; a sacrifice; virtue, moral merit.

1. *dharma, as, am*, m. n. (rarely n.; the older form which occurs in the Ṛig-veda is *dharman*, q. v.; for 2. *dharma* see p. 451, col. 3), that which is to be held fast or kept, ordinance, statute, law, usage, practice, custom, the customary observances of caste, sect, &c.; religion, piety; prescribed course of conduct, duty, (thus 'giving alms' &c. is the *dharma* of the householder, 'administering justice' of a king, 'piety' of a Brāhman, 'courage' of a Kshatriya); right, justice, equity, anything right, proper, or just; virtue, morality, morals, merit, good works; nature, character, the peculiar state or condition of anything; an essential or characteristic quality, mark, peculiarity; manner, resemblance; any sacrifice; a peculiar kind of sacrifice; an Upanishad; religious abstraction, devotion (= *yoga*); associating with the virtuous; a bow; a drinker of Soma juice; Right, Justice, Law, or Virtue personified (as born from the right breast of Brahmā, and having Śama, Kāma, and Harsha as his offspring); or personified as a Bull; or personified as a Dove; a N. of Yama (the Hindū Pluto, ruler of the lower regions, god of justice, and judge of the dead); one of the attendants of the god of the Sun; Justice or Virtue identified with Vishṇu; also identified with Prajā-pati, and said to be son-in-law of Daksha; N. of the fifteenth Arhat of the present Ava-sarpiṇī, descended from Ikshvāku, son of Bhānu and Su-vratā; N. of a son of Anu and father of Ghṛita; of a son of Gāndhāra and father of Dhṛita; of a son of Haihaya and father of Netra; of a son of Pṛithu-śravas and father of Uśanas; of a son of Su-vrata; of a son of Dīrgha-tapas; of a prince of Kaśmīra; of a lexicographer; (in astrology) N. of the ninth mansion; *dharmāt* or *dharmeṇa*, ind. according to right, rightly, justly, according to rule, according to the nature of anything. — *Dharma-kathaka, as*, m. a propounder of the law. — *Dharma-kathā*, f. a discourse upon law, &c. — *Dharma-karman, a*, n. a work of duty or piety; any virtuous or pious action. — *Dharma-kāma, as, ā, am*, loving justice, observing right or duty; (*as*), m., N. of a son of the demon Pāpīyas; of a god of the Bodhi tree. — *Dharma-kāmārtha-sambaddha* (°*ma-ar*°), *as, ā, am*, joined with or containing virtue, pleasure, and wealth. — *Dharma-kāya, as*, m. 'the body of law or of abstract existence,' epithet of one of the three bodies of a Buddha; (*as*), m. a Buddha; a Jina or Jaina saint; an epithet of Avalokiteśvara. — *Dharma-kāra, as*, m. a doer or observer of the law; N. of a person. — *Dharma-kāraṇa, am*, n. cause of virtue. — *Dharma-kārya, am*, n. any act of duty or religion (as digging a well, building a temple, &c.); pious act, good work, virtuous conduct. — *Dharma-kīrtti, is*, m. 'glory of religion,' N. of a poet; of a logician; of a king mentioned in the twenty-first chapter of the Vṛihan-nāradīya-Purāṇa. — *Dharma-kīla, as*, m. royal edict or order, decree, grant. — *Dharma-kīlaka, as*, m. the command of a Brāhman. — *Dharma-kūpa, as*, m. 'the holy well,' N. of a Tīrtha. — 1. *dharma-kṛit, t, t, t* (for 2. see under *dharman*), fulfilling duty, one who acts justly or practises virtue. — *Dharma-kṛitya, am*, n. fulfilment of duty, virtue; any moral or religious observance. — *Dharma-ketu, us*, m. 'having justice for a banner or symbol,' N. of a son of Su-ketu and father of Satya-ketu; N. of a Buddha; of a Jaina deified saint. — *Dharma-kośa* or *dharma-kosha, as*, m. the treasury of law or duties; the collective body of laws or duties. — *Dharmakośa-vyākhyā*, f. 'the explanation of the treasury of law,' N. of a Buddhist work. — *Dharma-kriyā*, f. observance of duties, acting according to law, righteous conduct, any religious act or pious work. — *Dharma-kshetra, am*, n. the department or province of the law; a plain in the north-west of India near Delhi (the scene of the

great battle between the Kurus and Pāṇḍus, commonly called Kuru-kshetra); (*as*), m. a man of piety and virtue. — *Dharma-gañja, as,* m. 'treasury of law or religion,' N. of a library. — *Dharma-gavesha, as,* m. 'seeking virtue &c.,' N. of a man. — *Dharma-gahanābhyudgata-rāja* (°*na-abh*°), *as,* m. 'a prince who has threaded the labyrinth of the law,' N. of a Buddha. — *Dharma-gupta, as,* m. 'protected by the law,' N. of several persons; (*ās*), m. pl., N. of a Buddhist school. — *Dharmagupta-miśra, as,* m., N. of an author mentioned in the Saṅkshepa-śaṅkara-jaya by Mādhava. — *Dharma-grantha, as,* m. book of the law, sacred scriptures. — *Dharma-grahaṇa, am,* n. observance of moral or religious precepts, accepting or following the law. — *Dharma-ghaṭa, as,* m. a jar of fragrant water offered daily in the month Vaiśākha. — *Dharma-ghna, as, ī, am,* 'destroying law or right,' contrary to law or duty, immoral, unlawful; (*as*), m. (?), the plant Terminalia Bellerica (so called because the seeds are used as dice). — *Dharma-ćakra, am,* n. 'the wheel or circle of religion or law,' (an expression used to denote the vast range of Dharma); a kind of mythical weapon; (*as*), m. 'having the wheel of Dharma,' a Buddha. — *Dharmaćakra-bhṛit, t,* m. 'holding the wheel of Dharma,' a Buddha or Jaina. — *Dharma-ćaraṇa, am,* n. or *dharma-ćaryā,* f. observance of the law, performance of duty. — *Dharma-ćārin, ī, iṇī, i,* observing the law, fulfilling one's duties, practising virtue, virtuous, dutiful, moral; (*ī*), m., N. of a Buddhist deity; epithet of Śiva; (*iṇī*), f. a female helpmate in the fulfilment of duties, especially a wife, an honest wife, a virtuous woman. — *Dharma-ćintaka, as, ā, am,* reflecting on the law, studying duty, familiar with it. — *Dharma-ćintana, am,* n. or *dharma-ćintā,* f. pondering on the law or duty, study of virtue, consideration of moral duties, virtuous reflection. — *Dharma-ćinti, is, is, i,* reflecting on the law or duty; an epithet of Śākya-muni; (perhaps wrongly for *dharma-ćintin.*) — *Dharma-ja, as, ā, am,* produced by a sense of duty; (*as*), m. 'son of Dharma, judge of the dead,' an epithet of Yudhi-shṭhira. — *Dharma-jijñāsā,* f. 'inquiry into the law,' N. of a Pariśishṭa ascribed to Kātyāyana. — *Dharma-jīvana, as, ā, am,* living by fulfilment of prescribed duties, a Brāhman who lives according to the rules of his class, one who practises the outward acts of the law. — *Dharma-jña, as, ā, am,* knowing the law or what is right, knowing one's duty, conversant with virtue. — *Dharma-jñāna, am,* n. knowledge of moral, legal, and religious duty. — *Dharma-tattva, am,* n., N. of a Mīmāṇsā work by Kamalākara. — *Dharmatattva-vid, t, t, t,* knowing the truths of law or religion. — *Dharma-tas,* ind. according to law or to rule, rightly, justly, religiously, righteously, virtuously; from a virtuous motive. — *Dharma-tīrtha, am,* n. 'the holy Tīrtha,' N. of a sacred place of pilgrimage. — *Dharma-tyāga, as,* m. abandonment of religion, apostacy. — *Dharma-trāta, as,* m. 'protected by the law,' N. of a Buddhist author. — *Dharma-tva, am,* n. religion, virtue, righteousness, morality, piety; inherent nature, peculiar property. — *Dharma-da, as, ā, am,* giving or granting virtue; (*as*), m., N. of one of the attendants of Skanda. — *Dharma-datta, as,* m. 'given by religion,' N. of a writer on rhetoric. — *Dharma-darśana, am,* n. seeing or knowing duty or the law. — *Dharma-dāna, am,* n. a gift made from a sense of duty (without regard to self-interest). — *Dharma-dāra, ās,* m. pl. a lawful wife; [cf. *dharma-patnī.*] — *Dharma-dāsa, as,* m. 'the slave of duty,' N. of a poet, author of the Vidagdha-mukha-maṇḍana. — *Dharma-dinnā,* f. 'given by religion,' (*dinna* in Pāli = *datta*), N. of a female. — *Dharma-dīpikā,* f., N. of a work. — *Dharma-dughā,* f. a cow milked for the fulfilment of religious duty. — *Dharma-dṛiḍhābhedya-sunilambha* (°*dha-abh*°), *as,* m., N. of a king of the Garuḍas. — *Dharma-dṛiś, k, k, k,* seeing the right, regarding piety. — *Dharma-dravī,* f. 'having law or virtue for its waters,' the Ganges. — *Dharma-drohin, ī, iṇī, i,* violating the law or right; (*ī*), m. a Rākshasa. — *Dharma-dveshin, ī,* m. the plant Terminalia Bellerica; see *dharma-ghna.* — *Dharma-dhara, as,* m. 'supporter of the law,' N. of a king of the Kin-naras. — *Dharma-dhātu, us,* m. 'the element of law or of existence,' one of the eighteen Dhātus of the Buddhists; a Buddha ('whose Dhātu is Dharma'). — *Dharmadhātu-vāg-īśvara, as,* m., N. of a deity. — *Dharma-dhṛit, t, t, t,* Ved. observing the law. — *Dharma-dhṛish, k,* m. (*dhṛik* is also referred to rt. *dhṛi* or to rt. *dṛih*), 'supporter of the law or right,' N. of a son of Śva-phalka; [cf. *dharma-bhṛit.*] — *Dharma-dhvaja, as, ā, am,* 'whose banner is virtue,' one who hangs out the flag of religion for selfish purposes, one who makes a livelihood by assumed devotion, a religious hypocrite or impostor; (*as*), m., N. of the Sun; of a king of Mithilā, son of Kuśa-dhvaja and father of Amita-dhvaja and Kṛita-dhvaja; N. of a brother of Kuśa-dhvaja; of a king of Kaṅkana-pura. — *Dharma-dhvajin, ī, inī, i,* 'hoisting the flag or colours of religion,' a religious hypocrite or impostor, one who makes a livelihood by assumed devotion. — *Dharma-nada, am,* n., N. of a sacred lake; (according to a legend, a metamorphosis of the god Dharma.) — *Dharma-nandana, as,* m. 'Dharma's joy, a son of the god Dharma,' properly an epithet of Yudhi-shṭhira, but applied in Bhāg.-Purāṇa I. 9, 12, to all the sons of Pāṇḍu; [cf. *dharma-ja, dharma-putra, dharma-suta.*] — *Dharma-nandin, ī,* m., N. of a Buddhist who translated certain sacred writings into Chinese. — *Dharma-nātha, as,* m. legal protector, rightful lord. — *Dharma-nābha, as,* m. 'the centre of the law,' an epithet of Vishṇu; N. of a king. — *Dharma-nibandha, as,* m. attachment to virtue or religion, piety, virtue. — *Dharma-nibandhin, ī, inī, i,* pious, attached to virtue, engaged in religious duties, holy. — *Dharma-niveśa, as,* m. religious devotion. — *Dharma-nishpatti, is,* f. fulfilment or discharge of duty, moral or religious observance. — *Dharma-netra, as,* m. 'law-eyed,' N. of a grandson of Dhṛita-rāshṭra; of a son of Taṇsu and father of Dush-manta (Dushyanta). — *Dharma-paṭṭa, as,* m. the band of law or duty. — *Dharma-pati, is,* m., Ved. the lord or guardian of order and law. — *Dharma-pattana, am,* n. 'the city of the law,' epithet of the city of Śrāvantī [cf. *dharma-paṭṭana*]; pepper. — *Dharma-pattra, am,* n. the plant Ficus Glomerata. — *Dharma-patnī,* f. a lawful wife, a man's first wife, a wife of the same caste with her husband and married conformably to the established law. — *Dharma-patha, as,* m. the way of duty or virtue, virtuous course; N. of a merchant. — *Dharma-pathin, -panthās,* m. the way of duty or virtue. — *Dharma-para, as, ā, am,* intent on virtue, devoted to duty; pious, righteous. — *Dharma-pāṭhaka, as,* m. a teacher of law, a lawyer. — *Dharma-pāla, as,* m. 'protector or guardian of the law,' metaphorical expression for 'punishment' or for 'a sword;' N. of a minister of king Daśa-ratha; of a learned Buddhist; of a prince. — *Dharma-pālaka, as, ikā, am,* observing the law, dutiful. — *Dharma-pāśa, as,* m. 'the noose of the god of justice,' N. of a mythical weapon. — *Dharma-pīṭha,* 'the seat of law,' N. of a place in Vārāṇasī. — *Dharma-pīḍā,* f. an offence against the law, transgressing the law or right. — *Dharma-putra, as,* m. a lawful son, a son begot from a sense of duty (not from sensual pleasure); 'son of the god Dharma,' epithet of Yudhi-shṭhira; (*au*), m. du. epithet of the Ṛishis Nara and Nārāyaṇa. — *Dharma-pura, am,* n. 'the city of the law,' N. of a town situated on the Narmadā river. — *Dharma-purāṇa, am,* n. 'the Purāṇa of law,' N. of a work. — *Dharma-praćāra, as,* m. 'the course of law or right,' metaphorical expression for 'a sword.' — *Dharma-pradīpa, as,* m. 'light of the law,' N. of a work composed by Dhanañ-jaya. — *Dharmapradīpa-vyākhyāna, am,* n. 'the explanation of the lamp of law,' N. of a commentary to the preceding work. — *Dharma-pradhāna, as, ā, am,* eminent in piety. — *Dharma-prabhāsa, as,* m. 'illuminator of the law,' N. of a Buddha. — *Dharma-pravaktṛi, tā,* m. a teacher or expounder of the law. — *Dharma-pravaćana, am,* n. enunciation of the law, the act of propounding the law. — *Dharma-prastha, as,* m. 'the table-land of the god Dharma,' N. of a place. — *Dharma-priya, as,* m. 'a friend of the law,' N. of a Buddhist scholar. — *Dharma-bala, as,* m. 'the strength of law,' N. of a man. — *Dharma-bāṇijika, as,* m. one who tries to make a profit out of his virtue like a merchant. — *Dharma-buddhi, is, is, i,* virtuously-minded, virtuous; (*is*), m., N. of a king. — *Dharma-bhaginī,* f. a lawful sister, a female that has the rights of a sister; 'a sister in respect of religion,' i. e. as belonging to the same religion; [cf. *dharma-bhrātṛi.*] — *Dharma-bhāgin, ī, inī, i,* possessed of religion or virtue; (*inī*), f. a virtuous wife. — *Dharma-bhāṇaka, as,* m. 'an expounder of the law;' a lecturer, a public reader of the Mahā-bhārata and other sacred works which are read aloud and explained to large assemblies of Hindūs at particular seasons. — *Dharma-bhikshuka, as,* m. a mendicant from virtuous motives. — *Dharma-bhīruka, as, ā, am,* tremblingly alive to duty. — *Dharma-bhṛit, t,* m. 'a supporter of law, a maintainer of justice,' (often an epithet of a king); a virtuous person; N. of a son of Śva-phalka. — *Dharma-bhṛita, as,* m., N. of one of the sons of the thirteenth Manu. — *Dharma-bhrātṛi, tā,* m. 'a brother in respect of religion,' a fellow religious student, any one regarded as a brother from discharging the same religious duties; [cf. *dharma-bhaginī.*] — *Dharma-mati, is,* m. 'virtuous-minded,' N. of a prince; of a god; of the Bodhi tree. — *Dharma-maya, as, ī, am,* consisting of law or virtue, made up or replete with virtue, moral, righteous. — *Dharma-mahāmātra, as,* m. a minister in matters of religion. — *Dharma-mātra, as, ā, am,* depending only on custom. — *Dharma-mārga, as,* m. the path of virtue. — *Dharma-mitra, as,* m., N. of a Buddhist. — *Dharma-mīmāṇsā-saṅgraha, as,* m. 'an abridgment of the inquiry into Dharma,' N. of a Mīmāṇsā work by Kṛishṇa-deva. — *Dharma-mūla, am,* n. the foundation of Hindū law and religion; the Vedas. — *Dharma-meghā,* f., N. of one of the ten Bhūmis with Buddhists. — *Dharma-yuga, am,* n. 'the age of religion,' the Kṛita-yuga. — *Dharma-yuj, k, k, k,* righteous, pious, just. — *Dharma-rakshitā,* f., N. of a female. — *Dharma-rati, is, is, i,* 'delighting in justice or virtue,' N. of one of the sons of the demon Pāpīyas. — *Dharma-ratna, am,* n. 'gem of the law,' N. of a work. — *Dharma-ratha, as,* m. 'whose chariot is dharma,' N. of a son of Sagara; of Divi-ratha. — *Dharma-rāj, ṭ,* m. 'the king of justice,' epithet of Yama; of Yudhi-shṭhira; of a king of the herons, son of Kaśyapa and an Apsaras. — *Dharma-rāja, as,* m. 'king of justice,' an epithet of Yama; an epithet of Yudhi-shṭhira; a king in general; a Buddha. — *Dharmarāja-tā,* f. the rank or title of Dharma-rāja. — *Dharmarāja-dīkshita, as,* m., N. of the author of the Vedānta-paribhāshā. — *Dharma-rājan, ā,* m. 'king of justice,' epithet of Yudhi-shṭhira. — *Dharmarāja-purogama, as, ā, am,* having Yudhi-shṭhira for a leader; headed by Yudhi-shṭhira. — *Dharma-rājikā,* f. a Stūpa. — *Dharma-ruci, is,* m., N. of a god of the Bodhi tree; N. of a man. — *Dharma-rodhin, ī, inī, i,* opposed to law or virtue, illegal, immoral. — *Dharma-lakshaṇa, am,* n. an essential mark or characteristic of ethics or law, as place, time, &c. — *Dharma-lopa, as,* m. irreligion. — *Dharma-vat, ān, atī, at,* endowed with virtue, virtuous, pious, upright, just, lawful; accompanied by Dharma; (*atī*), f., N. of a Mudrā; N. of a queen. — *Dharma-vatsala, as, ā, am,* tenderly alive to duty, loving piety. — *Dharma-vartin, ī, inī, i,* 'abiding in duty,' righteous. — *Dharma-vardhana, as, ā, am,* 'increasing right or virtue,' an epithet of Śiva; (*as*), m., N. of a king of Śrāvastī; of a poet; (*am*), n., N. of a town. — *Dharma-varman, a,* n. 'shield or armour of justice or virtue,' epithet of Kṛishṇa. — *Dharma-vāda, as,* m. discussion or argument about law or duty.

— *Dharma-vādin, ī, inī, i,* discussing the law or duty. — *Dharma-vāsara, as,* m. 'day of religious duties,' the day of full moon, peculiar sacrifices being performed on this day. — *Dharma-vāhana, as,* m. 'whose vehicle is the bull, considered as a personification of virtue,' an epithet of Śiva. — *Dharma-vāhya, as, ā, am,* 'outside the law,' contrary to what is right. — *Dharma-vićāra-saṅgraha, as,* m., N. of an abridgment of the Mīmāṇsā-sūtras by the Muni Jaimini. — *Dharma-vid, t, t, t,* acquainted with the law, duty-knowing, endued with a sense of justice, virtuous, pious, moral. — *Dharma-vidyā,* f. knowledge of the law or right; [cf. *dhārmavidya.*] — *Dharma-vidhi, is,* m. legal precept or injunction. — *Dharma-viplava, as,* m. 'confusion or violation of duty,' immorality, wickedness. — *Dharma-vivardhana, as,* m. 'promoter of law or right,' epithet of a son of Aśoka, = *kunāla.* — *Dharma-viveka, as,* m. investigation of right or virtue. — *Dharma-viveka-vākya, am,* n., N. of a short poem ascribed to Halāyudha. — *Dharma-vivećana, am,* n. judicial investigation. — *Dharma-vṛitti, is,* f. 'explanation of the law,' N. of a chapter of the Śārṅgadhara-paddhati. — *Dharma-vṛiddha, as,* m. 'advanced in virtue,' N. of a son of Sva-phalka; [cf. *dharma-dhṛish* and *dharma-bhṛit.*] — *Dharma-vaitaṇsika, as,* m. one who gives away money unlawfully acquired in the hope of appearing generous. — *Dharma-vyādha, as,* m. 'the hunter versed in law,' N. of a Brāhman changed into a hunter in consequence of a curse; of a Brāhman-killer (born as a hunter from the body of Vasu, king of Kaśmīra). — *Dharma-śarīra, am,* n. 'religious or sacred relic,' a term applied to certain small Buddhist Stūpas. — *Dharma-śarman, ā,* m., N. of a preceptor. — *Dharma-śālā,* f. a court of justice, a tribunal; a charitable institution, a hospital. — *Dharma-śāsana* or *dharma-śāstra, am,* n. 'a law-book,' a code of laws, the body or code of Hindū law, jurisprudence, any work on the subject. — *Dharma-śīla, as, ā, am,* of a virtuous disposition, virtuous, just, pious; (*ā*), f., N. of a female. — *Dharma-śreshṭhin, ī,* m., N. of a Buddhist Arhat. — *Dharma-saṃśrita, as, ā, am,* 'following or seeking virtue,' virtuous, just, pious. — *Dharma-saṃhitā,* f. a code or collection of law, especially the work of some saint or divine person (as Manu, Yājñavalkya, &c.). — *Dharma-saṅga, as,* m. addiction to justice or virtue; hypocrisy. — *Dharma-saṅgīti, is,* f. a discussion about the law; (with Buddhists) a council; N. of a work. — *Dharma-saṅgraha, as,* m. 'collection of laws, legal compilation,' N. of a Buddhist work on law. — *Dharma-santāna-sū, ūs, ūs, u,* producing virtuous offspring or actions. — *Dharma-sabhā,* f. a court of justice, tribunal. — *Dharma-sahāya, as,* m. a companion in the fulfilment of religious duties. — *Dharma-sādhana, am,* n. 'means of performing duty,' any act or virtue essential to a system of duties. — *Dharma-sārathi, is,* m., N. of a son of Tri-kakud. — *Dharma-sāvarṇi, is,* m., N. of the eleventh Manu. — *Dharma-siṇha, as,* m., N. of a man. — *Dharma-suta, as,* m. 'the son of the god Dharma,' an epithet of Yudhi-shṭhira. — *Dharma-sū, ūs, ūs, u,* Ved. promoting order or justice; (*ūs*), m. the fork-tailed shrike. — *Dharma-sūtra, am,* n. a Sūtra work treating on law and custom; (*as*), m., N. of a son of Su-vrata. — *Dharma-setu, us,* m. 'barrier of justice,' epithet of Śiva; N. of a son of Āryaka. — *Dharma-sena, as,* m., N. of a king. — *Dharma-skandha, as,* m. 'collection of laws,' N. of a work by Śāriputra and Maudgalyāyana. — *Dharma-stha, as,* m. 'abiding in the law,' a judge. — *Dharma-sthala, am,* n. 'the place of justice,' N. of a town. — *Dharma-sthavira, as,* m. 'firm in law,' N. of a man. — *Dharma-svāmin, ī,* m. 'the lord of law and right,' epithet of Buddha; N. of a sanctuary built by Dharma, king of Kaśmīra. — *Dharma-hantṛi, tā, trī, tṛi,* transgressing the law or justice. — *Dharmākara* (°*ma-āk*°), *as,* m. 'mine of virtue or law,' N. of a disciple of Buddha Lokeśvara-rāja; of the ninety-ninth Buddha; of a Buddhist translator. — *Dharmāgama* (°*ma-āg*°), *as,* m. a law-book. — *Dharmāṅgada* (°*ma-aṅ*°), *as,* m., N. of a man; of a prince, son of Priyaṅ-kara. — *Dharmāṅgā* (°*ma-aṅ*°), f. a heron. — *Dharmāćārya* (°*ma-āć*°), *as,* m. a teacher of law or of customs. — *Dharmāćārya-stuti, is,* f. 'praise of the teacher of the law,' N. of a work. — *Dharmātmaja* (°*ma-āt*°), *as,* m. 'the son of Dharma,' an epithet of Yudhi-shṭhira. — *Dharmātma-tā,* f. pious-mindedness, justice, virtue. — *Dharmātman* (°*ma-āt*°), *ā, ā, a,* just, virtuous, pious-minded, virtuously-minded, of a virtuous disposition, pious, fulfilling duties; (*ā*), m. a saint, a pious or virtuous person; an epithet of Kumāra-pāla. — *Dharmāditya* (°*ma-ād*°), *as,* m., N. of a Buddhist king. — *Dharmādharma* (°*ma-adh*°), *au,* m. du. right and wrong, justice and injustice. — *Dharmādharma-parīkshā,* f. or *-parīkshaṇa, am,* n. 'test of right and wrong,' a kind of ordeal by drawing lots or slips of black and white paper. — *Dharmādharma-senā-hanana, am,* n., N. of the 120th chapter of the Krīḍā-khaṇḍa of the Gaṇeśa-Purāṇa. — *Dharmādhikaraṇa* (°*ma-adh*°), *am,* n. administration of the laws; a court of justice; (*as*), m. a judge, magistrate. — *Dharmādhikaraṇa-sthāna, am,* n. a court of justice. — *Dharmādhikaraṇika, as,* m. or *dharmādhikaraṇin, ī,* m. 'presiding over justice,' a judge, an administrator of the law. — *Dharmādhikāra* (°*ma-adh*°), *as,* m. administration of justice, the office of a judge; N. of a work. — *Dharmādhikārin, ī,* m. or *dharmādhikṛita, as,* m. a chief officer of justice, an administrator of the law, lord-chief-justice, magistrate, a judge. — *Dharmādhishṭhāna* (°*ma-adh*°), *am,* n. a court of justice. — *Dharmādhyaksha* (°*ma-adh*°), *as,* m. 'overseer of justice,' minister of justice, a magistrate, a judge. — *Dharmādhvan* (°*ma-adh*°), *ā,* m. the way of justice or virtue. — *Dharmānushṭhāna* (°*ma-an*°), *am,* n. virtuous or moral conduct, acting according to law. — *Dharmānusāra* (°*ma-an*°), *as,* m. conformity to law or virtue, course or practice of duty. — *Dharmānusmṛity-upasthāna, am,* n., N. of a Buddhist Āgama. — *Dharmāndhu* (°*ma-an*°), *us,* m. 'the well of Dharma, the holy well,' N. of a Tīrtha. — *Dharmāpeta* (°*ma-ap*°), *as, ā, am,* departing from virtue, wicked, immoral, unrighteous; (*am*), n. injustice, immorality, vice. — *Dharmābhimanas* (°*ma-abh*°), *ās, ās, as,* directing the mind to virtue or religion, virtuous. — *Dharmābhisheka-kriyā* (°*ma-abh*°), f. any ablution prescribed as a religious duty. — *Dharmāmbhodhi* (°*ma-am*°), *is,* m. 'the ocean of laws,' N. of a work. — *Dharmāyatana* (°*ma-āy*°), *am,* n. knowledge of *dharma* by means of *manas* (?). — *Dharmāraṇya* (°*ma-ar*°), *am,* n. 'grove of religion,' a sacred grove, a wood inhabited by hermits or ascetics; N. of a sacred forest in Madhya-deśa, into which Dharma is said to have retired; N. of a town founded by Amūrta-rajas. — *Dharmārtha-kāma-moksha* (°*ma-ar*°), *ās,* m. pl. religious merit, wealth, pleasure, and final emancipation, (the four ends or objects of existence.) — *Dharmārtha-darśin, ī, inī, i,* having an eye to duty and interest or to religion and wealth. — *Dharmārtha-pratibaddha-tā,* f. attachment to duty and interest or to religion and wealth. — *Dharmārtham,* ind. for religious purposes; according to right or duty, in a just manner, according to prescript. — *Dharmārthīya, as, ā, am* (fr. *dharma-artha*), relating to law or duty. — *Dharmālīka* (°*ma-al*°), *as, ā, am,* having a false character. — *Dharmāloka-mukha* (°*ma-āl*°), *am,* n. introduction to the understanding of the *dharma* of Śākya-muni. — *Dharmāśoka* (°*ma-aś*°), *as,* m. the Aśoka of justice,' epithet of king Aśoka, grandson of Ćandra-gupta, (after he had adopted the Buddhist faith.) — *Dharmāśrita* (°*ma-āś*°), *as, ā, am,* seeking virtue, just, virtuous. — *Dharmāsana* (°*ma-ās*°), *am,* n. the throne of justice, judgment-seat, the bench. — *Dharmāsana-gata, as, ā, am,* seated on the judgment-seat. — *Dharmāstikāya* (°*ma-as*°), *as,* m. (with Jainas) the category or predicament of virtue. — *Dharmendra* (°*ma-in*°), *as,* m. 'lord of justice,' epithet of Yama. — *Dharmepsu* (°*ma-īp*°), *us, us, u,* wishing to acquire religious merit. — *Dharmeśa* (°*ma-īśa*), *as,* m. 'lord of justice,' epithet of Yama. — *Dharmeśvara* (°*ma-īś*°), *as,* m. 'lord of justice,' epithet of Yama; N. of a Buddhist deity; of a commentator on Yājñavalkya. — *Dharmeśvara-tīrtha, am,* n. 'the Tīrtha of the lord of justice,' N. of a place of pilgrimage. — *Dharmeśvara-liṅga, am,* n. 'the Liṅga of the lord of justice,' N. of a place of pilgrimage. — *Dharmoććaya* (°*ma-uć*°), *as,* m. 'collection of law,' N. of a place (in which Śākya-muni is said to have instructed the deities called Tushitas). — *Dharmottara* (°*ma-ut*°), *as,* m. 'chiefly characterized by virtue,' N. of a Buddhist teacher. — *Dharmottarīya, ās,* m. pl. the disciples of Dharmottara. — *Dharmopadeśa* (°*ma-up*°), *as,* m. instruction in law or duty, a discourse on religion, moral or religious instruction; the laws, the collective body of laws. — *Dharmopadeśaka* (°*ma-up*°), *as,* m. a teacher of the law, a Guru or spiritual preceptor. — *Dharmopadeśanā* (°*ma-up*°), f. instruction in the law, advice relating to it. — *Dharmopadha* (°*ma-up*°), *as, ā, am,* making a pretence of religion, hypocritical. — *Dharmopeta* (°*ma-up*°), *as, ā, am,* endowed with virtues, virtuous, moral.

2. *dharma,* Nom. P. *dharmati,* &c., to become law. (For 1. *dharma* see p. 449, col. 3.)

Dharmaka (at the end of an adj. comp.) = 1. *dharma;* (*as*), m., N. of a man.

Dharman, ā, m., Ved. bearer, maintainer, supporter, arranger; N. of a son of Bṛihad-rāja and father of Kṛitañ-jaya; (*a*), n. (the older form for the later *dharma;* and even in the later language used as a substitute for *dharma* at the end of adj. comps.), support, prop; (Sāy.) religious rite (Ved.); law, order, custom; religion, duty; mode, manner; quality, characteristic mark, natural order [cf. *kshatra-dh*°, *kshema-dh*°, *jaya-dh*°, &c.]; *dharmaṇā,* inst. sing. or *dharmabhis,* inst. pl., Ved. in order, according to rule, regularly, naturally. — 2. *dharma-kṛit, t,* m., Ved. 'a maintainer of order or a performer of religious rites,' epithet of Indra; (for 1. see p. 449, col. 3.)

Dharmayu, us, us, u, righteous, virtuous.

Dharmāya, Nom. P. A. *dharmāyati, -te,* &c., to become law.

Dharmin, ī, iṇī, i, virtuous, religious, pious, just; obeying the law, knowing one's duties, having duties; endowed with any peculiar property or faculty; (often at the end of comp.) subject to particular laws (e. g. *vināśa-dh*°, q. v.); having the peculiar qualities or properties or nature of anything, having anything as a characteristic mark [cf. *eka-dh*°]; following the habits of any person; (*ī*), m., N. of the fourteenth Vyāsa; (*iṇī*), f. a kind of perfume; [cf. *dhārmiṇeya.*] — *Dharmi-tva, am,* n. virtuousness, justice, devotion to one's duties, virtue.

Dharmishṭha, as, ā, am (superl. of *dharmin*), very pious or virtuous; completely according to law, completely harmonizing or agreeing with law or virtue, lawful. — *Dharmishṭha-tā,* f. great virtuousness, righteousness.

Dharmīyas, ān, asī, as (compar. of *dharmin*), more virtuous &c.; very pious or moral &c.

Dharmeyu, us, m., N. of a son of Raudrāśva.

Dharmya, as, ā, am, lawful, legal, conformable to justice or law or custom or morality, consistent with duty; usual; just, righteous; legitimate; endowed with particular qualities (e. g. *tad-dharmya,* endowed with those qualities); suitable to any person or thing (with gen.). — *Dharmya-vivāha, as,* m. legal marriage (of which there are various kinds described in Manu III. 22).

धरुण 2. *dharuṇa, as,* m. (fr. rt. *dhe?*), Ved. a sucking calf; (for 1. *dharuṇa* see p. 449, col. 2; cf. *dhāru.*)

धर्कट *dharkaṭa, as,* m., N. of a teacher.

धर्बक *dharbaka, as,* m., N. of a son of Ajāta-śatru.

धर्म *dharma.* See p. 449, col. 3; p. 451, col. 3.

धर्मण *dharmaṇa, as,* m. a kind of snake; a kind of tree.

धर्मीपुत्र *dharmīputra, as,* m. an actor, a player; (also read *dhātri-putra.*)

धर्ष *dharsha, as,* m. (fr. rt. *dhṛish*), boldness, insolence, overbearing conduct, daringness, impudence, licentiousness, pride, arrogance; impatience; violation (of a woman); injury, wrong, insult; restraint; a eunuch; [cf. *dharsha-vara.*] — *Dharsha-kāriṇī,* f. a violated virgin. — *Dharsha-vara, as,* m. a eunuch superintending the women's apartments; (probably wrong reading for *varsha-dhara.*)

Dharshaka, as, ā, am, attacking, assailing, assaulting, violating, overbearing; seducing; *(as),* m. a seducer, adulterer; a dancer, actor; mime, mummer.

Dharshaṇa, as, ā, am, offending, hurting, injuring, assaulting; *(am, ā),* n. f. assault, affront, insult, outrage; offence; violation, rape, seduction; bad treatment; overbearingness; contempt, disrespect, contumely, abuse; arrogance; copulation; *(ī),* f. or *(is),* f. a wanton or unchaste woman, a harlot.

Dharshaṇīya, as, ā, am, liable to be attacked or assaulted, easily assailable or conquerable, violable.

Dharshita, as, ā, am, violated; overpowered, overcome, smitten, ill-treated; *(am),* n. contumely, pride, insolence; copulation, cohabitation; *(ā),* f. an unchaste woman.

Dharshin, ī, iṇī, i, attacking, assaulting, ill-treating, treating badly; audacious, overbearing; proud, arrogant; cohabiting; *(iṇī),* f. a disloyal or unchaste woman, a harlot; [cf. *dharshaṇī.*]

धलण्ड *dhalaṇḍa, as,* m. a kind of small thorny tree, commonly called Dhala-āṅkaḍā.

धलिल *dhalila,* N. of a valley in which the capital of Udyāna is said to have been situated.

धव् *dhav* (connected with rts. 1. *dhāv* and *dhanv*), cl. 1. A. *dhavate,* &c., Ved. to run, flow; [cf. Gr. θέ-ω, θεύσομαι, θοός, βοη-θέ-ω, νω-θής.]

धव 1. *dhava, as,* m. the plant Grislea Tomentosa (= *madhura-tvaća*).

धव 2. *dhava, as,* m. (said by some to be fr. rt. 1. *dhū!*), a man; a husband [cf. *sa-dhavā* and *vi-dhavā*]; a possessor, master, lord; a rogue, a cheat; N. of a Vasu (probably incorrect for *dhara*).

धवनी *dhavanī,* f. a kind of plant, Desmodium Gangeticum or a similar species.

धवर *dhavara, am,* n. a particular high number.

धवल *dhavala, as, ā, am* (said to be fr. rt. 2. *dhāv*), white, dazzling white, of a shining white colour; handsome, beautiful; *(as),* m. white (the colour); an old bull, an excellent ox; a kind of camphor (= *ćīna-karpūra*); the plant Grislea Tomentosa (= *dhava*); N. of one of the elephants of the quarters; N. of a Rāga or mode of music, (according to Bharata, the eighth son of Hiodola-rāga); *(ā* or *ī),* f. a white cow; *(ī),* f. a kind of disease (perhaps only whiteness of the hair); N. of a river; *(am),* n. white pepper; a kind of metre consisting of 4 × 18 short syllables and 1 long (= *dhavalāṅka;* cf. *udaya-dh°*). — *Dhavala-giri, is,* m. 'the white or snowy mountain' (commonly *dhoula-giri* or *dola-gir*), N. of one of the highest peaks of the great snowy range of the Himālayas, lat. 29. 11, long. 82. 59. — *Dhavala-gṛiha, am,* n. a house whitened with chunam or stucco, a palace. — *Dhavala-tva, am,* n. whiteness. — *Dhavala-paksha, as,* m. 'white-winged,' a goose; the light half of the month, the fortnight of the moon's increase. — *Dhavala-purāṇa-samuććaya, as,* m., N. of a work. — *Dhavala-mṛittikā,* f. 'white earth,' chalk. — *Dhavala-yāvanāla, as,* m. white Yāvanāla. — *Dhavalāṅka* (°*la-aṅ*°), *am,* n. = *dhavala,* a species of the Ati-dhṛiti metre. — *Dhavalī-kṛita, as, ā, am,* made white, whitened, whited. — *Dhavalī-bhūta, as, ā, am,* become white. — *Dhavalotpala* (°*la-ut*°), *am,* n. the white esculent water-lily.

Dhavalita, as, ā, am, made dazzling white, whitened, white.

Dhavaliman, ā, m. whiteness, white colour, white.

धवाणक *dhavāṇaka, as,* m. (fr. rt. 1. *dhū*), air, wind.

Dhavitavya, as, ā, am, Ved. to be fanned.

Dhavitra, am, n. a Paṅkhā or fan (made of antelope's skin or leather, and used especially for blowing a sacrificial fire).

धा 1. *dhā,* cl. 3. P. A. *dadhāti, dhatte* (1st pl. *dadhmas,* 2nd *dhattha,* 3rd *dadhati;* 1st sing. A. *dadhe,* 2nd *dhatse,* 3rd *dhatte,* 2nd du. *dadhāthe,* 3rd du. *dadhāte,* 3rd pl. *dadhate*); Impf. *adadhāt, adhatta* (2nd du. P. *adhattam,* 2nd pl. *adhatta,* 3rd pl. *adadhus;* 2nd sing. A. *adhatthās,* 3rd pl. *adadhata*); Pot. *dadhyāt, dadhīta;* Impv. *dadhātu, dhattām* (2nd sing. *dhehi,* 2nd du. *dhattam,* 3rd du. *dhattām,* 2nd pl. *dhatta,* 3rd pl. *dadhatu;* 2nd sing. A. *dhatsva,* 2nd pl. *dhaddhvam,* 3rd pl. *dadhatām*); Perf. *dadhau, dadhe* (2nd sing. *dadhitha* or *dadhātha,* 1st pl. *dadhima,* 2nd pl. *dadha,* 3rd pl. *dadhus;* 3rd pl. A. *dadhire*); Fut. *dhātā; dhāsyati, -te;* Aor. *adhāt, adhita* (3rd pl. A. *adhishata*); Prec. *dheyāt, dhāsīshṭa;* (Ved. forms are, Pres. 1st pl. P. *dadhmasi,* 3rd pl. *dadhanti,* 2nd sing. A. *dadhase,* 3rd sing. *dadhe* or *dadhate,* 3rd du. *dadhete,* 2nd pl. *dadhidhve;* Impf. 2nd sing. P. *dadhas,* 3rd sing. *dadhat, dadhāt,* 1st pl. *dadhāma,* 3rd pl. *dadhan;* Leṭ, Impf. 2nd du. P. *dadhathas;* Pot. 1st sing. *dheyām,* 2nd sing. *dhāyīs,* 1st pl. *dhema,* 2nd pl. *dhetana;* Impv. 3rd sing. *dhātu,* 2nd pl. *dhāta, dhattana, dadhāta, dadhātana,* 3rd pl. *dhāntu, dadhantu,* 2nd sing. A. *dhishva;* Perf. 2nd sing. A. *dhishe,* 3rd pl. *dadhre, dhire;* Aor. 1st sing. P. *dhām,* 2nd sing. *dhās,* 3rd sing. *dhāt,* with *prati* also *dhat,* 3rd pl. *dhus;* 1st pl. A. *adhīmahi, dhīmahi,* see under 1. *dhī;* Leṭ, Aor. 3rd sing. P. *dhāti,* 2nd du. P. *dhāsathas,* A. *dhethe, dhaithe,* 1st pl. A. *dhāmahe,* 2nd pl. P. *dhāsatha,* 3rd pl. *dhāsus*); *dhātum* (Ved. inf. *dhātave, dhātavai, dhātos, dhai* in *vayo-dhai, dhām* in *prati-dhām, dhiyadhyai*), to put, place, set, lay; put in, lay on or upon (with loc., e. g. *teshu daṇḍam dadhāti,* he lays the stick on them, i. e. punishes them); to place in any state or condition; to bring, convey, lead towards (Ved.); to cause to obtain, cause (Ved.); to fix upon, direct towards (with dat. or loc.), fix or direct the mind (*manas* or *matim*), fix the thoughts or attention (*samādhim*) on (dat. or loc.), make up the mind to do anything (dat., loc., or inf.), to resolve upon; to bestow anything (acc.) upon a person (loc., dat., gen.), grant, confer, present, give; to put in possession; to appoint, fix, constitute; to make, render, produce, generate; to cause, create; to perform, do, undertake; to hold, take hold of, seize; to keep, preserve; to bear, wear, put on (clothes); to sustain, support, maintain; to accept, take, receive, obtain, get; to conceive (in the womb); to take possession of, assume, have, possess; to show, exhibit (A.); to incur, undergo: Pass. *dhīyate,* to be put or placed or laid; to be arranged; to be contained in; to be fixed (as the thoughts), to resolve (e. g. *me dhīyate matis,* my opinion or resolution is): Caus. *dhāpayati, -yitum,* Aor. *adīdhipat,* generally with prepositions [cf. *antar-dhā, api-dhā, abhi-dhā, ava-dhā,* &c.]: Desid. *dhitsati, -te* (Ved. *didhishati*), to wish to give or present (Ved.); to wish to place or put; to wish to obtain, strive to gain, &c.: Intens. *dedhīyate, dādhāti;* [cf. Zend *dā,* 'to put, make;' *dā-ta-m,* 'law;' *dā-man,* 'creature:' Gr. τί-θη-μι, θέ-μα, θέ-σι-ς, θε-σ-μό-ς, θέ-μι-ς, θεμός, θε-μέ-λιο-ν, θέ-με-θλο-ν, θής, θῆσσα, θή-κη, θῶκος, θᾶκος: Lat. *fămulus, familia, -do* in *ab-do, con-do, per-do, ven-do, pessum-do, cre-do* = *śrad-dadhāmi:* Osc. *faa-ma,* 'house (?),' *famel* = *familia:* Goth. *ga-dêd-s, dê-ths,* 'deed,' in *missa-dêths,* 'a crime;' *dôm-s,* 'judgment:' Angl. Sax. *don,* 'to do;' *dema,* 'a judge;' *dom,* 'judgment:' Old Sax. *dō-m,* 'I do,' — *dadhāmi:* Old Germ. *tō-m,* 'I do:' Old Eng. *-de* in *ask-e-de* = 'ask-did:' Mod. Germ. *-te* in *such-te:* Lith. *de-mi, de-du,* 'I put:' Slav. *de-yun,* 'I do;' *de-lo,* 'work:' Hib. *deanaim,* 'I do;' *dan,* 'work.']

2. *dhā, ās, ās, am,* (at the end of an adj. comp.) placing; holding; containing, having; causing, &c., see *kiye-dhā, ćano-dhā, dhāma-dhā, dhiyan-dhā,* &c.; *(ās),* m. a placer; a holder, container, possessor, &c.; a N. of Brahmā; of Bṛihas-pati; *(ās),* f. the act of placing or holding, &c., (at the end of comp., cf. *tiro-dhā* and *dur-dhā.*) The affix *dhā* after numerals is thought by some to be an old inst. from this *dhā;* [cf. the use of 1. *dhātu* after numerals.]

Dhāka, as, m. an ox; a receptacle, reservoir (= *ā-dhāra* or according to another reading *ā-hāra*); food, boiled rice; a post.

1. *dhātu, us,* m. (for 2. *dhātu* see p. 453, col. 3), that which is placed or laid, a deposit, layer (Ved.); a constituent or essential part, an ingredient, (thus *guṇa,* string, is the *dhātu* of a rope made of several strings); part, portion, (sometimes used at the end of an adj. comp. like the English 'fold,' see *tri-dhātu, sapta-dh°*); an element, primary or elementary substance, primitive matter (of which five are usually reckoned or with Brahma six, thus enumerated by Yājñavalkya III. 145: 1. *Brahma,* the eternal spirit; 2. *kha* or *ākāśa,* ether; 3. *anila,* air; 4. *tejas,* fire; 5. *jala,* water; 6. *bhū,* earth: the Buddhists substitute *Vijñāna* for *Brahma:* the eighteen elements or *dhātu-lokas* of the southern Buddhists are the five organs of sense with *manas,* the six qualities observed by these, and six ideas produced by these six qualities); constituent element or essential ingredient of the body, primary or essential fluid or juice, a secretion, (the number of which is variously given as seven or ten; these Dhātus are distinct from the five elements of which the body also consists, and are sometimes regarded as Rasas, i. e. secretions or fluids; they are chyle, blood, flesh, fat, bone, marrow, and semen, to which must be added hair, skin, and sinews, if ten are reckoned); a humor or affection of the body (viz. phlegm, wind, and bile); a bone; (according to some) any one of the five organs of sense; any one of the five properties or qualities of the elements observed by the organs of sense (viz. sound, tangibility, colour, flavour, smell, see under *guṇa*); a primary element of the earth or of mountains, a mineral, fossil, metal, ore; a fluid mineral of a red colour; the primary element of words, a verbal root; [cf. *upa-dh°, kāma-dh°, giri-dh°,* &c.] — *Dhātu-kāya, as,* m. 'body of elements,' N. of a Buddhist work by Pūrṇa. — *Dhātu-kāśīśa* or *dhātu-kāsīsa, am,* n. red sulphate of iron. — *Dhātu-kuśala, as, ā, am,* skilled in metals, a metallurgist, mineralogist. — *Dhātu-kriyā,* f. metallurgy, mineralogy. — *Dhātu-kshaya, as,* m. waste of the bodily humors, any mortal disease. — *Dhātukshaya-kāsa, as,* m. a consumptive cough. — *Dhātu-garbha, as,* m. a receptacle for Buddhist relics, a dagop, (according to some *da-gop* = *dhātu-gopa.*) — *Dhātu-grāhin, ī,* m. calamine. — *Dhātu-ghoshā,* f., N. of a work on the verbal roots. — *Dhātu-ghna, am,* n. sour gruel prepared from the fermentation of rice-water. — *Dhātu-ćandrikā,* f. 'elucidation of roots,' N. of a grammatical work by Kavi-ćandra. — *Dhātu-ja* = *dhātuka,* bitumen. — *Dhātu-dīpikā,* f. 'elucidation of roots,' N. of a commentary by Durgā-dāsa on Vopa-deva's collection of roots. — *Dhātu-drāvaka,* 'dissolving metals,' borax, tinkal. — *Dhātu-nāśana, am,* n. 'destroying the humors,' sour gruel; [cf. *dhātu-ghna.*] — *Dhātu-nyāya-mañjūshā,* f., N. of

a work on the radicals.—*Dhātu-pa, as,* m. the alimentary juice or chyle, the chief of the seven elementary ingredients of the body.—*Dhātu-pāṭha, as,* m. 'recital of roots,' a list or collection of roots compiled and arranged according to Pāṇini's system, (the most important and well-known Dhātu-pāṭha is ascribed to Pāṇini himself.)—*Dhātu-pārāyaṇa* or *dhātu-pārāyaṇīya, am,* n., N. of a work on verbal roots.—*Dhātu-pushṭi, is,* f. nutrition of the bodily humors.—*Dhātu-pushpī* and *dhātu-pushpikā,* f. a plant, = *dhātri-pushpī.*—*Dhātu-pradīpa, as,* m., N. of a commentary by Maitreya-rakshita on the Dhātu-pāṭha.—*Dhātupradīpa-dīpikā* or *dhātupradīpa-ṭīkā,* f., N. of a commentary on the preceding work.—*Dhātu-bhṛit, t,* m. 'bearing metals,' a mountain; (*t, t, t*), promoting the elementary juices or secretions, robust.—*Dhātu-mañjarī,* f., N. of a commentary by Kāśī-nātha on the Dhātu-pāṭha.—*Dhātu-mat, ān, atī, at,* containing or possessing elements or elementary substances, abounding in minerals or metals.—*Dhātu-mat-tā,* f. richness in metals &c.—*Dhātu-maya, as, ī, am,* consisting of or abounding in metals, metallic.—*Dhātu-mala, am,* n. impure excretion from the essential fluids of the body; lead (the most impure of metals).—*Dhātu-mākshika, am,* n. a mineral substance, sulphuret of iron.—*Dhātu-mārin, ī,* m. 'dissolving metals,' sulphur; (*iṇī*), f. borax.—*Dhātu-ratna-mālā,* f., N. of a medical work by Deva-datta.—*Dhātu-ratnāvalī,* f. 'a necklace or string of roots,' N. of a metrical collection of roots by Rādhā-kṛishṇa.—*Dhātu-rājaka, am,* n. 'the chief of the essential fluids of the body,' semen, the seminal fluid.—*Dhātu-lakshaṇa, am,* n., N. of a work.—*Dhātu-vallabha, am,* n. 'friend of metals,' borax (used as a flux).—*Dhātu-vāda, as,* m. metallurgy, mineralogy.—*Dhātuvādin, ī,* m. an assayer, miner, mineralogist, metallurgist.—*Dhātu-vikāra, as,* m. = *dhātu-kshaya.*—*Dhātu-vish, ṭ,* f. = *dhātu-mala,* lead.—*Dhātu-vṛitti, is,* f. a commentary on the roots.—*Dhātu-vairin, ī,* m. 'enemy of metals,' sulphur.—*Dhātu-śekhara, am,* n. 'chief of minerals,' green sulphate of iron or green vitriol.—*Dhātu-śodhana* or *dhātu-sambhava,* lead.—*Dhātu-sāmya, am,* n. equilibrium of the bodily humors, good health.—*Dhātu-han,* 'killing metals,' sulphur.—*Dhātūpala* (°*tu-up*°), *as,* m. 'the stone among metals,' chalk.—*Dhātv-artha, as,* m. 'having the sense of a root,' i. e. a verb.

Dhātuka (at the end of comp.) = *dhātu;* bitumen.

Dhātṛi, tā, m. one who places or lays, a founder [cf. Lat. *con-ditor*], maker, creator, originator, author; orderer, arranger; bearer, supporter, maintainer, preserver; N. of a divine being who is the creator, arranger, maintainer, and manager of all things, (strictly perhaps without any distinct and definite place in the Hindū mythological system, but rather the personification of the various ideas and functions inherent in the rt. 1. *dhā;* he is not mentioned in the older hymns of the Ṛig-veda, but is invoked in the tenth Maṇḍala, and agrees in many points with Tvashṭṛi and Prajā-pati; he is described as promoting generation, presiding over matrimony and domestic life, preserving health, curing diseases and broken limbs, granting riches, ordering times and seasons, &c.; not only is he associated with Tvashṭri and Prajā-pati, but with Savitṛi and Bṛihas-pati; sometimes with Mitra, Vishṇu, and Aryaman, and occasionally identified with Prajā-pati: in one Brāhmaṇa Dhātṛi and Aryaman are declared to be the first-born children of Aditi: in epic poetry Dhātṛi is one of the twelve Ādityas, and in post-vedic mythology the name Dhātṛi is applicable to Prajā-pati and to Brahmā as 'creator and maintainer of the world;' in the Bhagavad-gītā it is applied to Kṛishṇa in the same sense; elsewhere Dhātṛi and Vidhātṛi are associated as sons of Brahmā, the goddess Lakshmī being then their sister, and in another place as children of Bhṛigu and Khyāti); one of the seven sages of the fourth Manv-antara; one of the forty-nine winds; the paramour of a married woman, an adulterer; N. of the forty-fourth year in the cycle of Jupiter.—*Dhātṛi-putra, as,* m. 'Brahmā's son,' especially an epithet of Sanat-kumāra.—*Dhātṛi-pushpikā* or *dhātṛi-pushpī,* f. Grislea Tomentosa.—*Dhātṛi-bharaṇa, am,* n. Brahmā's heaven.

Dhātra, am, n. a vessel for holding anything, a receptacle; (*as, ī, am*), belonging to Dhātṛi.

Dhātrī, f. See under 2. *dhātu,* col. 3.

Dhāna, as, ā, am (at the end of comp.), containing [cf. *uda-dh*°]; (*am*), n. a receptacle, reservoir, seat, (at the end of comp., see *agni-dh*°, *aila-dh*°, &c.); (*ī*), f. a receptacle, anything which holds or contains, a place where anything is kept, seat, (at the end of comp., see *aṅgāra-dh*°, *khale-dh*°, *jīva-dh*°, *matsya-dh*°, &c.); the site of a habitation, N. of a tree (= *pīlu*); coriander; N. of a river; (*ās*), f. pl. corn, grain; fried barley or rice; grain fried and reduced to powder; coriander, Coriandrum Sativum (= *dhanyāka*); a bud, shoot.—*Dhānā-ćūrṇa, am,* n. the meal or flour of fried barley or rice &c.—*Dhānāntarvat* (°*nā-an*°), *ān,* m., N. of a Gandharva.—*Dhānā-pūpa, as,* m. a cake of fried barley &c.—*Dhānā-bharjana, am,* n. the frying or parching of grain.—*Dhānā-mushṭi, is,* f. a handful of grain.—*Dhānā-vat, ān, atī, at,* Ved. accompanied by grain (as the Soma).—*Dhānā-soma, as,* m., Ved. Soma with grain.

Dhānaka, am, n. = *dhanyāka,* coriander.

Dhānākā, ās, f. pl. grain, corn; fried barley or parched rice; (*am*), n., N. of a Sāman.

Dhānī, f. See under *dhāna* above.

Dhāneya or *dhāneyaka, am,* n. = *dhanyāka, dhānyāka,* coriander; Coriandrum Sativum.

Dhānya, as, ā, am, consisting of grain or corn, made of grain, &c.; (*am*), n. grain, corn in general, rice (Oryza Sativa); a measure equal to four sesamum-seeds; coriander; Cyperus Rotundus (= *paripela*); (*ā*), f. coriander.—*Dhānya-kartana, am,* n. 'the cutting of corn,' N. of a chapter of the Purāṇa-sarva-sva.—*Dhānya-kalka, am,* n. bran; chaff; straw.—*Dhānya-kosha, as,* m. a granary, storehouse of corn or rice.—*Dhānya-koshṭhaka, am,* n. a granary, a basket or cupboard or small shed of matting &c. for keeping rice, &c.—*Dhānya-kshetra, am,* n. a corn-field, rice-field.—*Dhānya-ćamasa, as,* m. rice flattened by threshing after it has been steeped and fried in the husk.—*Dhānya-tilvila, as, ā, am,* Ved. abounding in corn.—*Dhānya-tvać, k,* f. the husk of corn or rice.—*Dhānya-da, as, ā, am,* giving or distributing rice.—*Dhānya-dhana, am,* n. property in grain; *dhānya-dhanatas,* on account of possessing grain &c.—*Dhānya-dhenu, us,* f. a heap of rice (like a cow) to be presented to Brāhmans.—*Dhānya-parvata-dāna-vidhi, is,* m. 'rules for giving heaps of grain,' N. of the 156th chapter of the Bhavishyottara-Purāṇa.—*Dhānya-maya, as, ī, am,* abounding with rice, made of grain.—*Dhānya-mātṛi, tā,* m. a measurer of corn.—*Dhānya-māya, as,* m. a corn-chandler, corn-dealer, &c.—*Dhānya-rāja, as,* m. 'the prince of grains,' barley.—*Dhānya-ropaṇa, am,* n. 'the planting of corn or rice,' N. of a chapter of the Purāṇa-sarva-sva.—*Dhānya-vat, ān, atī, at,* abounding in grain, rich in corn.—*Dhānya-vani* (?), a heap of grain.—*Dhānya-vapana, am,* n. 'the sowing of corn or rice,' N. of a chapter of the Purāṇa-sarva-sva.—*Dhānya-vardhana, am,* n. lending grain at interest, usury with grain, receiving an usurious return for a load of seed-corn supplied to peasants.—*Dhānya-vīja, am,* n. coriander.—*Dhānya-vīra, as,* m. 'the chief of grain,' a sort of pulse, Phaseolus Max. (= *māsha*).—*Dhānya-śīrshaka, am,* n. the ear or spike of corn.—*Dhānya-śūka, am,* n. the awn or beard of corn.—*Dhānya-śaila-dāna, am,* n. 'the giving of a heap of corn or rice,' N. of the eighty-second chapter of the Matsya-Purāṇa.—*Dhānya-sangraha, as,* m. a store or magazine of grain.—*Dhānya-sāra, as,* m. 'the essence of grain,' threshed corn.—*Dhānyā-kṛit, t, t, t,* Ved. preparing corn; (Sāy.) a cultivator of grain.—*Dhānyāćala* (°*ya-ać*°), *as,* m. a pile of grain for presentation to Brāhmans.—*Dhānyāda* (°*ya-ada*), *as, ā, am,* eating corn, feeding on corn.—*Dhānyāmla* (°*ya-am*°), *am,* n. sour gruel made of the fermentation of rice-water.—*Dhānyāri* (°*ya-ari*), *is,* m. 'enemy of corn,' a mouse, rat.—*Dhānyārtha* (°*ya-ar*°), *as,* m. wealth in rice or grain.—*Dhānyāsthi* (°*ya-as*°), *i,* n. 'the kernel of grain,' threshed corn.—*Dhānyottama* (°*ya-ut*°), *as,* m. the best of grain, rice.

Dhānyaka (at the end of an adj. comp. for *dhānya*), grain, corn; (*as*), m., N. of a man; (*am*), n. = *dhānya, dhānyāka, dhanyāka,* coriander.

Dhānyāka, am, n. = *dhānyaka,* coriander.

Dhāma, am, n. = *dhāman,* abode, &c.; (*ās*), m., N. of a class of superhuman beings.

Dhāman, a, n. a dwelling-place, house, abode, home, residence; domain; site, especially the site of the sacred fire and the Soma; (in the sacrificial formulas and in the Brāhmaṇas generally with *priya,* e. g. *priyam dhāma,* favourite residence, also = any favourite thing or person); the inmates of a house, the members of a family, domestics; a class; a troop, host, race; the body; law, rule (Ved.); state or condition; manner, fashion, mode, form, tone (Ved.); effect, power, strength, ability, faculty; majesty, dignity, glory, light, splendor, radiance, brilliancy [cf. *dhyāman*]; (Sāy.) property, wealth; a band, fetter, (wrong reading for 3. *dāman*); (*ā*), m., N. of one of the Saptarshis in the fourth Manv-antara; [cf. Gr. *θέ-μα;* Lat. *do-mu-s;* Osc. *faa-ma;* Hib. *dai-m,* 'a house, church, people;' Old Germ. *do-m;* Angl. Sax. and Eng. *dom* = Mod. Germ. *thum* as affix of abstract nouns; Slav. *do-mŭ.*]—*Dhāma-keśin, ī, inī, i,* 'having rays for hair,' epithet of the Sun.—*Dhāma-ććhad, t,* m., Ved. 'covering his residence or changing his abode,' epithet of Agni as giver of rain, (also applied to the Vashaṭ-kāra); N. of a verse in the Vājasaneyi-saṃhitā containing the word *dhāma-ććhad* (18. 76).—*Dhāma-dhā, ās,* m., Ved. the causer of order, a creator; (Sāy.) a bearer, supporter.—*Dhāma-nidhi, is,* m. 'treasure of splendor,' the sun.—*Dhāma-bhāj, k, k, k,* Ved. possessing sites or seats.—*Dhāma-vat, ān, atī, at,* splendid, luminous, eminent, exalted, illustrious, heroic.—*Dhāma-śas,* ind., Ved. according to (their) several abodes, in (their) several places, according to order.—*Dhāma-sāć, k, k, k,* attached to or keeping a particular place; (Sāy.) possessing splendor or riches.

Dhāya, as, ā, am, or *dhāyaka, as, ikā, am,* having, possessing, holding, &c.

1. *dhāyas, as,* n. sustaining, supporting, bearing. (For 2. *dhāyas* see p. 454, col. 1.)

1. *dhāyu, us, us, u,* Ved. liberal; (Sāy.) possessing power, supporting. (For 2. *dhāyu* see p. 454, col. 1.)

Dhāyya, as, m., Ved. a Puro-hita or family priest?; (*ā*), f., scil. *ṛić,* an additional verse inserted in certain hymns.

1. *dhāsi, is,* f., Ved. a dwelling-place, seat, home; (Sāy.) a holder, bearer, maintainer; food.

धाटी *dhāṭī,* f. assault, assaulting or confronting an enemy.

धाणक *dhāṇaka, as,* m. (said to be fr. rt. 1. *dhā*), a weight of gold, a gold coin, part of a Dīnāra [cf. *dhānaka*]; (*ikā*), f., Ved. pudendum muliebre (?).

धातकि *dhātaki, is,* m., N. of one of the two sons of Vītihotra Praiyavrata, king of a Varsha of Pushkara-dvīpa; (*ī*), f. the plant Grislea Tomentosa.

धातु 2. *dhātu, us, us, u* (fr. rt. *dhe;* for 1. *dhātu* see p. 452, col. 3), Ved. to be drunk or sucked in?; (Sāy.) sustainer, supporter, (fr. rt. 1. *dhā*); (*us*), m. anything to be drunk or sucked, milk, &c.; (*us*), f. a milch cow.

Dhātrikā, f. the plant Emblica Officinalis.

Dhātrī, f. a wet-nurse, foster-mother, nurse, mother; the earth; Emblica Myrobalan, Emblica Officinalis.—*Dhātrī-putra, as,* m. the son of a nurse, a foster-brother; an actor; (a various reading for *dharmi-putra.*)—*Dhātrī-phala, am,* n. the fruit of the Emblic Myrobalan.

Dhātreyikā, f. a foster-sister, (sometimes employed as a sort of confidante); a nurse, foster-mother, wet-nurse (according to some).

Dhātreyī, f. the daughter of a nurse, a foster-sister, (sometimes employed as a sort of confidante); a wet-nurse (according to some).

2. *dhāyas, ās, ās, as* (for 1. *dhāyas* see p. 453, col. 3), Ved. nourishing, fostering, sustaining, (often in comp., e. g. *ari-dh°, kāru-dh°, go-dh°, bhūri-dh°*, &c.); drinking, sipping; the act of fostering, nourishing, satiating, (used only in dat. *dhāyase* in the sense of an infinitive.)

2. *dhāyu, us, us, u* (for 1. *dhāyu* see p. 453, col. 3), Ved. feeding, eating, fond of eating; (Sāy.) holding, supporting, (as if fr. rt. 1. *dhā*.)

Dhāru, us, us, u, Ved. drinking, sucking, a drinker, sucker.

2. *dhāsi, is*, m. (for 1. *dhāsi* see p. 453, col. 3), Ved. a milk-beverage, a drink; nourishment in general.

Dhāsyu, us, us, u, Ved. desirous of drinking or of eating.

धातृ *dhātṛi*. See p. 453, col. 1.

धात्री *dhātrī*. See 2. *dhātu*, p. 453, col. 3.

धानक *dhānaka*, a copper coin worth about twopence.

धानद *dhānada, as, ī, am* (fr. *dhana-da*), relating to Dhana-da, i. e. Kuvera, 'giver of riches.'

धानुर्दण्डिक *dhānurdaṇḍika, as, ī, am* (fr. *dhanus* and *daṇḍa*), living by bow and club.

धानुष्क *dhānushka, as, ī, am* (fr. *dhanus*), armed with a bow, one who carries a bow, a bowyer, bowman, archer; (*ā*), f. the plant Achyranthes Aspera (= *apāmārga*).

Dhānushkari, N. of a plant; (probably a wrong reading for *dhanushkarī*.)

Dhānushya, as, m. 'suitable for bows,' a bamboo.

धान्त *dhānta* (or *dhvānta?*), a mystical name of the letter *n*.

धान्धा *dhāndhā*, f. small cardamoms.

धान्व *dhānva, as*, m. (probably fr. *dhanvan*), a patronymic of Asita, chief of the Asuras; (also read *dhānvana*.)

धान्वन 1. *dhānvana, as, ī, am* (fr. *dhanvan*), situated in a desert.

धान्वन 2. *dhānvana, as, ī, am* (fr. *dhanvana*), made of the wood of the tree Dhanvana (as bows).

धान्वन्तर *dhānvantara, as, ī, am*, or *dhānvantarīya*, or *dhānvantarya*, &c. (fr. *dhanvantari*), relating to or proceeding from Dhanvantari; sacred to the sun.

धान्वपत *dhānvapata, as, ī, am* (fr. *dhanva-pati*), relating to or proceeding from Dhanva-pati.

धामक *dhāmaka, as*, m. a sort of weight (= *māshaka*).

धामन् *dhāman*. See p. 453, col. 3.

धामनिका *dhāmanikā*, f. (fr. *dhamanī*), the plant Solanum Jacquini.

धामनी *dhāmanī*, f. the plant Hemionitis Cordifolia; any tubular vessel of the body; [cf. *dhamanī*.]

धामार्गव *dhāmārgava, as*, m. a sort of plant (= *ghoshaka*) with white flowers, Luffa Fœtida or a similar plant; Achyranthes Aspera.

धार *dhāra, as, ā, am* (fr. rt. *dhṛi*, but in some of its senses apparently connected with rt. 1. *dhāv*), holding, bearing, supporting, containing, (at the end of a comp., see *asṛig-dh°, karṇa-dh°, jala-dh°, tulā-dh°*); continuing, streaming down in a continuous line, raining hard, flowing, dripping, (in these senses said to be connected with rt. 1. *dhāv*); (*as*), m. 'a supporter, holder,' epithet of Vishṇu; a sudden and violent shower of rain; snow, hail; frost (?); a deep place, depth; debt; a boundary, limit, line; a sort of stone; (*ā*), f. the flowing or dropping of any fluid, (said to be connected with rt. 1. *dhāv*); a stream or current of water, a line of descending fluid; a water-course, a torrent, a flood, a hard shower falling in large drops or in hail, a shower, the dripping of any liquid, a drop, (often at the end of a comp., cf. *asṛig-dh°*); a leak, a hole in a pitcher &c. letting out the water; the pace of a horse (of which five are enumerated, cf. *dhorita, valgita, pluta, ut-tejita, ut-terita*); the margin or border of anything, the sharp edge of a sword or any cutting instrument, the edge of anything, (often at the end of a comp.; cf. *ardha-dh°, asi-dh°, kshura-dh°, khaṇḍa-dh°, khara-dh°*); the edge of a mountain or precipice; the circumference or periphery of a wheel; a garden-wall, fence, hedge; any continuous line or series, the line of a family; the van or front line of an army [cf. *dhārāṅkura*]; the tip of the ear, ear-lap; the highest point, excellence, pre-eminence; a multitude; fame; night; turmeric; likeness; custom, usage (?); N. of a town; of a sacred bathing-place; (*am*), n. rain-water (?). — *Dhāra-pūta, as, ā, am*, Ved. purified with streams of water; clear as water (?). — *Dhāra-vāka, as, ā, am*, Ved. (Sāy.) sustaining or reciting praises. — *Dhārā-kadamba* or *dhārā-kadambaka, as*, m. a kind of Kadamba tree; N. of a poet. — *Dhārā-gṛiha, am*, n. a bath-room with flowing water, shower-bath. — *Dhārāgra* (°*rā-ag°*), *am*, n. the broad-edged head of an arrow. — *Dhārāṅkura* (°*rā-aṅ°*), *as*, m. a drop of rain; hail; advancing before the line of an army to defy the enemy. — *Dhārāṅga* (°*rā-aṅ°*), *as*, m. a sacred bathing-place; a sword, scimitar. — *Dhārāṭa* (°*rā-aṭa*), *as*, m. the Cātaka bird; a horse; a cloud; a furious elephant or one in rut (when juice exudes from his temples). — *Dhārā-dhara, as*, m. 'containing showers,' a cloud; 'having an edge,' a sword. — *Dhārādhirūḍha* (°*rā-adh°*), *as, ā, am*, elevated to the highest point, raised to the highest pitch. — *Dhārā-dhvani, is*, m. the sound of falling rain or flowing water. — *Dhārā-nipāta* or *dhārā-pāta, as*, m. a fall of rain, pelting shower; a stream of water. — *Dhārāntara-ćara* (°*rā-an°*), *as, ā, am*, moving among the showers; flying amid the clouds (as the Cātakabird). — *Dhārā-phala, as*, m., N. of a tree with prickly fruits (= *madana*). — *Dhārā-yantra, am*, n. 'machine for sprinkling water,' a fountain; a watering-can, a sprinkling vase or ewer, a sort of censer. — *Dhārā-vat, ān, atī, at*, having an edge, edged; (*atī*), f., N. of a town. — *Dhārā-vani, is*, m. wind, air. — *Dhārā-vara, ās*, m. pl. 'fond of showers,' epithet of the Maruts; (Sāy.) covering (the sky) with showers or preventing the stability of stationary objects, i. e. moving them. — *Dhārā-varsha, as, am*, m. n. a stream or torrent of rain, a hard shower. — *Dhārā-visha, as*, m. 'having a poisoned edge,' a crooked sword, a scimitar, sabre. — *Dhārāśru* (°*rā-aś°*), *u*, n. a flood of tears. — *Dhārā-sampāta, as*, m. a hard shower, a heavy fall of rain. — *Dhārāsāra* (°*rā-ās°*), *as*, m. a heavy downfall of rain, a hard shower. — *Dhārā-snuhī*, f., N. of a plant (= *tridhāra-snuhī*). — *Dhāroshṇa* (°*rā-ush°*), *as, ā, am*, warm from the cow (as milk).

Dhāraka, as, ā, am, holding, containing, possessing, bearing, carrying, (at the end of a comp., see *kula-dh°, deha-dh°, nāma-dh°*); (*as*), m. a receptacle or vessel of any kind, a trunk or box (for holding clothes &c.), a water-pot; (*ā*), f. the vulva of a female.

Dhāraṇa, as, ī, am, holding, bearing, carrying, keeping, sustaining, preserving, maintaining, protecting; possessing, having, assuming; keeping in remembrance; (*as*), m., N. of a son of Kaśyapa; of a prince of the Candra-vatsas; (*au*), m. du. the two female breasts; (*ā*), f. the act of holding, supporting, bearing, maintaining, preserving, keeping, holding fast, keeping back; keeping in remembrance, retaining in the mind, a good memory; memory; keeping the mind collected, holding the breath suspended and all the natural wants restrained; steady or immovable abstraction of mind; fortitude, firmness, steadiness, resolution; continuance in rectitude, keeping in the right way; fixed precept or injunction, a settled rule, certainty, conclusion; understanding, intellect; conviction; (*ās*), f. pl. the four days following the eighth day in the light half of month Jyaishṭha; (*ī*), f. any tubular vessel of the body; a mystical verse or charm or collection of such verses among the Buddhists; a row or line, (wrong reading for *dhoraṇī*); N. of a daughter of Svadhā [cf. *dhāriṇī*]; (*am*), n. the act of holding, bearing, upholding, supporting, sustaining; possessing, possession; containing; keeping, maintaining; observing, holding fast; keeping in the memory; immovable abstraction of the mind; restraining; (in grammar) keeping back, i. e. pronouncing imperfectly; [cf. *anka-dh°, asu-dh°, garbha-dh°, ćhattra-dh°, daṇḍa-dh°, deha-dh°*, &c.] — *Dhāraṇa-pātra, am*, n. a receptacle for the sieve (?) of a Buddhist mendicant; a vessel for holding anything. — *Dhāraṇa-yantra, am*, n., N. of certain amulets. — *Dhāraṇā-maya, as, ī, am*, depending on or connected with abstraction of the mind. — *Dhāraṇā-yoga, as*, m. deep devotion. — *Dhāraṇā-vat, ān, atī, at*, possessing memory, connected with memory. — *Dhāraṇī-mati, is*, m. (?), N. of a Samādhi. — *Dhāraṇī-mukha-sarva-jagat-praṇidhi-sandhāraṇa-garbha, as*, m., N. of a Bodhi-sattva. — *Dhāraṇī-rāja, as*, m., N. of a Buddhist work.

Dhāraṇaka, as, ā, am, holding, containing; (*as*), m. a debtor.

Dhāraṇīya, as, ā, am, to be held or retained, to be maintained, borne, sustained, possessed, &c.; to be adhered to; (*ā*), f. = *dharaṇī-kanda*, q. v.

Dhāraya, as, ā, am, holding, possessing, having, keeping.

Dhārayat, an, antī, at, having, possessing; holding as doctrine, believing, maintaining, asserting, professing; acquainted with, versed in. — *Dhārayat-kavi, is, is, i*, Ved. supporting or cherishing sages; (Sāy.) supporting or bearing water. — *Dhārayat-kshiti, is, is, i*, Ved. bearing or sustaining creatures; (Sāy.) one who has prepared ground (for an altar). — *Dhārayad-vat, ān, atī, at*, Ved. 'possessing the quality of sustaining or supporting,' an epithet of the Ādityas.

Dhārayāṇa, as, ā, am, bearing, holding, supporting, containing, &c.

Dhārayitavya, as, ā, am, to be borne, to be kept or retained; to be perceived or understood.

Dhārayitṛi, tā, trī, tṛi, a holder, bearer; holding, keeping, keeping back, restraining; (*ī*), f. = *dharitrī*, the earth.

Dhārayishṇu, us, us, u, capable of holding, bearing, maintaining, sustaining. — *Dhārayishṇu-tā*, f. capability of bearing or supporting, patience.

Dhārayu, us, us, u, Ved. flowing, streaming, dropping.

Dhārā, f. See under *dhāra*, col. 1.

Dhāri, is, is, i, holding, maintaining, carrying, bearing.

Dhārikā, f. a division of time, = 6 Kshaṇas, = ½ Muhūrta.

Dhārita, as, ā, am (fr. the Caus.), borne, supported, maintained; (*am*), n. a horse's trot; (wrong reading for *dhorita, dhauritaka*.)

Dhārin, ī, iṇī, i, carrying, bearing, wearing, having, holding, keeping, possessing; sustaining, maintaining, preserving, keeping in one's memory, observing [cf. *jaṭā-dh°, daṇḍa-dh°, dhanur-dh°*]; having an edge, edged; (*ī*), m., N. of a tree [cf. *pīlu*]; (*iṇī*), f. the earth; Bombax Heptaphyllum (= *śālmalī*); N. of a daughter of Svadhā [cf. *dhāraṇī*]; (*iṇyas*), f. pl. a collective N. of the seventy-four wives of the gods; (with Jainas) N. of a deity who executes the commands of the eighteenth Arhat of the present Ava-sarpiṇī; N. of the wife of Agni-mitra.

Dhārya, as, ā, am, to be held or maintained,

to be borne or carried, bearable; to be imposed (as a punishment); to be worn; to be suffered, supportable; to be upheld or preserved; to be contained; to be kept or detained; to be kept in the memory; to be directed steadily towards; to be kept back or restrained [cf. *a-dhārya* and *dur-dh°*]; (*as* or *am*), m. or n. (?), Ved. water; (*am*), n. clothes, garments. — *Dhārya-tva, am*, n. the being held or borne or worn; capability or fitness for the same.

Dhāryamāṇa, as, ā, am, being held, borne, maintained, &c. — *Dhāryamāṇa-tva, am*, n. possessions, property.

धार्तराष्ट्र *dhārtarāshṭra, as, ī, am*, belonging to Dhṛita-rāshṭra; (*as*), m. a son of Dhṛita-rāshṭra, especially a patronymic of Dur-yodhana who was his eldest son; a kind of snake [cf. *dhṛita-rāshṭra*]; (fr. *dhṛita-rāshṭrī*), a sort of goose with black legs and bill. — *Dhārtarāshṭra-padī*, f., N. of a plant.

Dhārtarāshṭri, is, m. a patronymic from Dhṛita-rāshṭra.

धार्तेय *dhārteya, ās*, m. pl. (perhaps fr. *dhṛita*), N. of a warlike tribe; (*as*), m. a prince of this tribe.

धार्म *dhārma, as, ī, am* (fr. *dharma*), relating to justice or virtue, belonging to Dharma or the god of justice.

Dhārmapata, as, ī, am, relating to Dharma-pati.

Dhārmapattana, am, n. (fr. *dharma-pattana*), black pepper.

Dhārmavidya, as, ā, am (fr. *dharma-vidyā*), knowing the law, familiar with it, a lawyer, a jurist.

Dhārmika, as, ī, am, righteous, just, fulfilling or performing duties, virtuous, religious, pious; resting on right, conformable to justice. — *Dhārmika-tā*, f. or *dhārmika-tva* or *dhārmikya, am*, n. righteousness, justice, virtuousness.

Dhārmiṇa, am, n. an assemblage of virtuous men.

Dhārmiṇeya, as, m. a metronymic from Dharmiṇī.

Dhārmyāyaṇa, as, m. a patronymic from Dharmya.

धार्ष्ट *dhārshṭa, as, ī, am*, or *dhārshṭika, as, ī, am* (fr. *dhṛishṭa*, rt. *dhṛish*), proceeding or descended from Dhṛishṭa.

Dhārshṭadyumna, as, m. or *dhārshṭadyumni, is*, m. a patronymic from Dhṛishṭa-dyumna.

Dhārshṭya, am, n. violence, boldness, daringness, audacity, arrogance, impudence, rudeness.

Dhārshṇaka, as, ī, am (fr. *dhṛishṇu*), descended from Dhṛishṇu; (the more correct form would be *dhārshṇava*.)

धाव् 1. *dhāv* (connected with rts. *dhav* and *dhanv*), cl. 1. P. and sometimes A. *dhāvati, -te, dadhāva, -e, dhāvishyati, -te, adhāvīt, adhāvishṭa, dhāvitum*, to flow, stream or flow forth, flow towards; to give milk (as a cow); to run, proceed quickly, advance, run away, run towards, advance against; to rush against, assault; run a race; run away, flee; to go, move, glide: Caus. *dhāvayati*, &c., Aor. *adīdhavat*, to cause to run, make run, drive, impel, push on; *dhāvayati rathena*, he drives in a chariot: Desid. *didhāvishati, -te*: Intens. *dādhāvyate*: [cf. Gr. θέ-ω, θεύσομαι, θο-ό-ς, θοάζ-ω, βοη-θό-ος; Hib. *deifir*, 'haste.']

1. *dhāraka, as, ā, am*, running, flowing, going quickly, running in advance, expeditious; (*as*), m., N. of an author in the pay of king Śrī-harsha; (also read *Bhāsaka*; he is said to have composed the Ratnāvalī for Śrī-harsha.)

Dhāvat, an, antī, at, running, going quickly, running away.

1. *dhāvana, am*, n. running, galloping, flowing, moving; attack, assault; (*as*), m., N. of a spell for using or restraining magical weapons.

Dhāvamāna, as, ā, am, running, going quickly.

1. *dhāvita, as, ā, am*, running, running off or away; running towards, advanced against.

Dhāvitṛi, tā, m. a runner; running.

Dhāvin, ī, inī, i, running, going quickly.

धाव् 2. *dhāv*, cl. 1. P. A. *dhāvati, -te, dadhāva, -e, dhāvishyati, -te, adhāvīt, adhāvishṭa, dhāvitum*, to rub, rub off, cleanse, clean, wash, purify, polish, brighten, make pure or bright; A. to rub one's self with anything, to rub into one's person: Caus. *dhāvayati*, &c., Aor. *adīdhavat*, to cleanse, wash: Desid. *didhāvishati, -te*: Intens. *dādhāvyate*; [cf. probably Goth. *daupya* = Old Sax. *dopyu* = Mod. Germ. *taufe*, 'I baptize,' = Caus. *dhāvayāmi*.]

Dhāva, as, ā, am, cleansing, washing, making bright, polishing, (at the end of an adj. comp.; cf. *ćaila-dh°* and *asi-dh°*.)

Dhāvaka, as, ā, am, washing, cleansing; (*as*), m. a washerman, a dhobī.

2. *dhāvana, am*, n. rubbing off, washing off, cleansing, purifying; rubbing with anything, (in comp., e. g. *mīna-dhāvana-toya, manaḥśilā-ćandana-dh°*, q. v.)

Dhāvani, is, ī, f. a sort of creeping plant, Hedysarum Lagopodioides.

Dhāvanikā, f. a kind of prickly nightshade, = *kaṇṭa-kārikā*.

2. *dhāvita, as, ā, am*, purified, cleansed, clean.

Dhauta, as, ā, am, cleansed, &c. See p. 460, col. 2.

धावल्य *dhāvalya, am*, n. (fr. *dhavala*), whiteness, white (the colour).

धासस् *dhāsas, ās*, m., Ved. a mountain.

धि 1. *dhi* (allied to rt. 1. *dhā*), cl. 6. P. *dhiyati, didhāya, dheshyati, adhaishīt, dhetum*, to have, hold, keep, possess.

2. *dhi, is*, m. (fr. rt. 1. *dhā*), what holds, contains or preserves; any receptacle, (only at the end of a comp., e. g. *ambu-dhi, ambho-dhi, ishu-dhi, utsa-dhi, uda-dhi, jala-dhi*, &c.)

1. *dhita, as, ā, am* (earlier form of *hita* fr. rt. 1. *dhā*), put, placed, arranged, given, caused; resolved; [cf. *dur-dh°* and *nema-dh°*.]

Dhitāvan, ā, m., Ved. abounding in gifts (?). (According to Sāy. Ṛig-veda III. 27, 2, *dhitāvānam* = *dhita-vānam* = *nihita-dhanam*, laying up or granting wealth; III. 40, 3, = *nihita-havishkam*, [a sacrifice] in which oblations are offered.)

Dhiti in *nema-dh°, mitra-dh°*, &c., q. v.

धि 3. *dhi* or *dhinv*, cl. 5. P. *dhinoti, didhinva, dhinvitum*, to satisfy (Ved.); to delight, please.

2. *dhita, as, ā, am*, satisfied, pleased.

धि 4. *dhi* sometimes = 2. *adhi*, as *pi* = *api* and *va* = *ava*.

धिक् *dhik*, ind. (said to be connected with rt. 1. *dih*), an interjection of reproach, menace or displeasure, = fie! shame! out upon! what a pity! &c.; (generally followed by the acc., sometimes by the nom. or voc., and rarely by the gen., e. g. *dhik tvām*, shame upon thee! *dhig iyam daridratā*, shame upon this poverty!) — *Dhik-pārushya, am*, n. abuse, reproach, excessive reviling. — *Dhig-daṇḍa, as*, m. reprimand, censure.

Dhik-kṛi, cl. 8. P. *-karoti, -kartum*, to reproach, censure, reprimand, curse (with acc.). — *Dhik-kāra, as*, m. or *dhik-kriyā*, f. reproach, contempt, censure, disrespect. — *Dhik-kṛita, as, ā, am*, reproached, reviled, censured, condemned, cursed; (*am*), n. a reproach, contempt, curse.

धिक्ष् *dhiksh* (perhaps a Desid. form of rt. 1. *dah*, cf. rt. *dhuksh*), cl. 1. A. *dhikshate*, &c., to kindle; to live; to be weary or harassed.

धिग्वण *dhigvaṇa, as*, m. (perhaps a Prākṛit form of *dhik-varṇa*), a man of a low or mixed caste, sprung from a Brāhman and a female of the tribe called Āyogava.

Dhitsya, as, ā, am, to be wished to be placed, &c.; desirable to be given or created, &c.

धित 1. and 2. *dhita*. See col. 2.

धिन्व् *dhinv*. See rt. 3. *dhi*, col. 2.

धिप्सु *dhipsu, us, us, u* (fr. Desid. of rt. *dambh*), wishing to trick or deceive, deceptive.

धियञ्जिन्व *dhiyañ-jinva, dhiyāya, dhiyā-vasu*. See p. 456, col. 1.

धिष् 1. *dhish* (thought by some to be an abbreviated form of a Vedic Desid. *didhish* derived fr. rt. 1. *dhā*; connected with rt. 1. *dhī*), cl. 3. P. *didheshṭi*, &c., to sound, emit a sound; to praise, celebrate by hymns (?).

2. *dhish*, f. (only occurring in inst. *dhishā* and probably connected with rt. 1. *dhī*), fixing the mind, attention (?), intelligence (?), devotion; (Sāy.) = *dhishaṇā*, knowledge, understanding; action; praise, hymn.

Dhishaṇa, as, m. (said to be fr. *dhish* substituted for rt. *dhṛish*), 'the intelligent one,' N. of Bṛihas-pati, preceptor of the gods and regent of the planet Jupiter, the planet Jupiter itself [cf. *dhishaṇādhipa* and *dhī-mat*]; any Guru or spiritual preceptor; epithet of a Nārāyaṇa; N. of an astronomer; of an evil spirit or demon; (*ā*), f. a sort of Soma-vessel, a cup, goblet, bowl; a Soma press; (according to some commentators) the Soma juice itself and its effects; (metaphorically *dhishaṇe*, f. du. the two cups or bowls, i. e. the two worlds or heaven and earth; and *dhishaṇās*, f. pl. the three worlds or heaven, earth, and the intermediate atmosphere); a female divinity presiding over prosperity and gain, (sometimes reckoned among the wives of the gods); = *vāć*, speech, praise, hymn; = 2. *dhī*, intelligence, intellect, understanding, knowledge; N. of the wife of Havir-dhāna, daughter of Agni; of the wife of Kṛiśāśva and mother of Veda-śira, Devala, Vayuna, and Manu; (*am*), n. a dwelling-place, abode, seat, site, resting-place [cf. *dhishṇya*]; understanding, intellect. — *Dhishaṇādhipa, as*, m. 'lord of the planet Jupiter,' epithet of Bṛihas-pati.

Dhishaṇya, an adj. formed by Yāska (Nir. VIII. 3) to explain *dhishṇya*.

Dhishaṇyat, an, antī, at (fr. a Nom. *dhishaṇya* which only occurs in the part.), attentive, devout (?); (Sāy.) desiring to praise.

Dhishṭya, as, ā, am, placed on a fire-altar (?); (wrong reading for *dhishṇya*, q. v.)

Dhishṭhya, am, n. site, seat, place, (wrong reading for *dhishṇya*, q. v.); (*as*), m. fire; the planet Venus (?). — *Dhishṭhya-pa, as*, m. world-protector.

Dhishṇiya for *dhishṇya*, q. v.

Dhishṇīya, as, ā, am, Ved. intended for or belonging to the Dhishṇyas, i. e. certain receptacles or places for fire.

Dhishṇya, as, ā, am, Ved. only perceptible by the mind; (Sāy. = *dhārshṭya-yukta*), endowed with fortitude; intelligent, thoughtful, devout, pious; (Sāy.) to be praised or meditated upon; worthy of a high station; placed upon the heaps of earth used for side-altars; see below. In Ṛig-veda III. 22, 3, Sāy. explains *dhishṇyā* by *prāṇās* = the divinities presiding over the vital airs; (*as*), m. a place for the sacrificial fire, a sort of inferior or side-altar, (generally a heap of earth covered with sand on which the fire is placed, and of which eight are enumerated, cf. *āgnīdhrīya, mārjālīya*, &c.); an epithet of Uśanas, the planet Venus; power, strength; (*am*), n. a site, seat, place, abode, spot, region, house; a star, asterism, (looking like the fire on the side-altars); a meteor.

धी 1. *dhī* (sometimes given in the reduplicated form *dīdhī*; the later forms of *dhī* are 1. *dhā, dhyā, dhyai*, q. v., with which such Vedic forms as *dhīmahi* are connected by native commentators), cl. 2. A. *dīdhīte*, &c., to shine, appear (see *dīdhī*); cl. 1. P. (fr. rt. *dhyai*), *dhyāyati*, &c. (see *dhyai*), to perceive, think, reflect; to wish, desire. (A root *dhī*, cl. 4. A. *dhīyate*, &c., which is properly Pass. of rt. 1. *dhā*, is given in the Dhātu-pāṭha and is said to have the following senses,—to contain, hold; to slight, disregard; to accomplish; to propitiate.)

Dhiyasāna, *as*, *ā*, *am*, reflecting, meditating upon, fixing the mind upon.

Dhiyāya (fr. 2. *dhī*), Nom. A. *dhiyāyate*, &c., Ved. to fix the mind upon; to be devout, practise devotion; (Sāy.) to wish for praise.

Dhiyāyu, *us*, *us*, *u* (fr. the preceding), Ved. reflecting, devout, pious; (Sāy.) wishing to understand.

2. *dhī*, *īs*, f. thought, idea, notion, intention; understanding, wisdom, intellect, intelligence, intellectual power, mind; knowledge, science, art; religious reflection, devotion, prayer; a religious rite, sacrifice; Intelligence personified (as the wife of Rudra in the form Manyu); (in astrology) the fifth house from the Lagna; (*iyas*), f. pl. Holy Thoughts personified; [cf. *itthā-dhī*, *udāra-dhī*, *dur-dhī*, *dūḍhī*, *su-dhī*, &c.] — *Dhiyañ-jinva*, *as*, *ā*, *am*, Ved. exciting pious reflection or promoting devotion; (Sāy.) to be propitiated by pious rites; (*ā*), m. du. epithet of the Aśvins. — *Dhiyan-dhā*, *ās*, *ās*, *am*, Ved. reflecting, devout, pious, wise; (Sāy.) celebrating sacred rites. — *Dhiyā-jur*, *ūr*, *ūr*, *ūr*, Ved. worn out or grown old in the performance of religious duties. — *Dhiyām-pati*, *is*, m. 'lord of the thoughts,' the soul; an epithet of Mañju-ghosha. — *Dhiyā-vasu*, *us*, *us*, *u*, Ved. abounding in devotion, very devout; (Sāy.) recompensing religious rites by wealth. — *Dhī-javana*, *as*, *ā*, *am*, or *dhī-jū*, *ūs*, *ūs*, *u*, Ved. infusing spirit, inspiring; (Sāy.) rapid as thought. — *Dhīndriya* (*dhī-in°*), *as*, m. an organ of perception (= *buddhīndriya* and opposed to *karmendriya*, see *indriya*). — *Dhī-mat*, *ān*, *atī*, *at*, possessed of understanding, endowed with intelligence, intellectual, intelligent, wise, learned, sensible; (*ān*), m. an epithet of Bṛihas-pati, preceptor of the gods; N. of a son of Virāj; of a son of Purū-ravas. — *Dhī-mantrin*, *ī*, m. a minister for counsel (as distinguished fr. *karma-mantrin*, a minister for action). — *Dhī-maraṇa*, *as*, m. (with preceding *miśra*), N. of a man. — *Dhī-raṇa*, *as*, *ā*, *am*, Ved. delighting in devotion; (Sāy.) whose speech is with praise, a devout worshipper. — *Dhī-rāja*, *as*, m., N. of one of the attendants of Śiva. — *Dhī-vat*, *ān*, *atī*, *at*, Ved. intelligent, pious, religious. — *Dhī-śakti*, *is*, f. power of the mind, mental or intellectual faculty (as attention, comprehension, &c.). — *Dhī-sakha*, *as*, m. a wise counsellor, an adviser, mentor, minister; a tutor or friendly adviser. — *Dhī-saćiva*, *as*, m. a minister for counsel, a counsellor, minister; a wise or prudent adviser. — *Dhī-harā*, f. a kind of sweet gourd.

1. *dhīta*, *as*, *ā*, *am*, reflected on, thought about.

1. *dhīti*, *is*, f. (for 2. *dhīti* see col. 2), Ved. thought, notion, reflection, idea; devotion, prayer; (*ayas*), f. pl. understanding, wisdom; (Sāy.) the fingers.

Dhītika, *as*, m., N. of a Buddhist patriarch.

1. *dhīdā*, f. (for 2. *dhīdā* see col. 2), understanding, intellect.

Dhīvan, *ā*, *varī*, *a*, Ved. clever, skilful; (*ā*), m. an artizan, artificer, a worker in brass; a fisherman; [cf. the next.]

Dhīvara, *as*, m. a fisherman, fisher; (*ī*), f. a fisherman's wife; a sort of harpoon for catching fish; a receptacle for fish, a fish-basket; (*am*), n. iron; [cf. *tīvra*.]

Dhīvaraka, *as*, m. a fisherman, fisher.

धीक्ष् *dhīksh* (perhaps Desid. of rt. 1. *dih*), cl. 1. A. *dhīkshate*, &c., Ved. to wish to anoint.

धीत 2. *dhīta*, *as*, *ā*, *am* (fr. rt. *dhe*), drunk, sucked, sucked in, sucked out. — *Dhīta-rasa*, *as*, *ā*, *am*, having the juice sucked out or extracted.

2. *dhīti*, *is*, f. (for 1. *dhīti* see col. 1), drinking; (according to the commentators), thirst.

धीदा 2. *dhīdā*, f. (probably a Prākrit form for *duhitā*), a daughter, a virgin, a maiden. (For 1. *dhīdā* see col. 1.)

धीन *dhīna*, *am*, n. iron (?).

धीर *dhīra*, *as*, *ā*, *am* (fr. rt. *dhṛi*, but said to be fr. rt. 1. *dhā* and certainly connected with this latter rt.), steady, holding firmly, steadfast, enduring, durable, lasting, constant, continual; firm, determined, resolute, persevering, persistent; strong, energetic, courageous; brave, bold, daring, headstrong, self-controlled, strong-minded, self-possessed, composed, calm, collected; sedate, grave, solemn, sober; deep, grave, hollow, low, dull (as sound); emitting a long or prolonged sound; lazy, dull, slow; gentle, soft (as a breeze); well-conducted, well-behaved, well-bred; (fr. 1. *dhā* = 1. *dhī*), intelligent, wise, prudent; sensible, learned, skilful, clever, shrewd; (*as*), m. the ocean, sea; 'the wise one,' epithet of a Buddha; of Bali; of several men; a species of medicinal plant, = *ṛishabha*; (*ā*), f. a woman who, although jealous of a husband or lover, suppresses all expression of resentment in his presence; an intoxicating beverage; N. of several medicinal plants, = *kākolī*, = *mahā-jyotishmatī*, = *kshīra-kākolī*, *śveta-vaćā*, *medā*, Rosa Glandulifera; (*am*), n. saffron; (*am*), ind. firmly, steadily, resolutely, steadfastly. — *Dhīra-govinda-śarman*, *ā*, m., N. of the author of the modern work Ātharvaṇa-rahasya. — *Dhīra-ćetas*, *ās*, *ās*, *as*, strong-minded, self-possessed, courageous. — *Dhīra-tā*, f. or *dhīra-tva*, *am*, n. firmness, fortitude, energy, courage; suppression; the female property of suppressing violent expression of jealousy; refusal. — *Dhīra-dhvani*, *is*, m. a deep sound. — *Dhīra-pattrī*, f. a kind of bulbous plant (= *dharaṇī-kanda*). — *Dhīra-praśaṇsā*, f. 'the praise of the firm or of the wise,' N. of the thirteenth chapter of the Śārṅgadhara-paddhati. — *Dhīra-praśānta*, *as*, m. the hero of a poem or play who is both brave and calm or mild (?). — *Dhīra-lalita*, *as*, m. the hero of a poem or play who is firm and brave but reckless and sportive at the same time; (*ā*), f., N. of a metre consisting of four lines of sixteen syllables each. — *Dhīra-skandha*, *as*, m. 'strong-shouldered,' a buffalo. — *Dhīrādhīrā* (°*ra-adh*°), f. a mistress or wife who having cause for jealousy pursues a middle course between suppression and expression of resentment, a jealous woman who alternately expresses and conceals her jealousy. — *Dhīreśa-miśra* (°*ra-īśa-m*°), *as*, m., N. of a man. — *Dhīreśvara* (°*ra-īś*°), *as*, m., N. of the father of Jyotir-īśvara, author of the Dhūrta-samāgama. — *Dhīrodātta* (°*ra-ud*°), *as*, m. the hero of a poem or play who is brave and noble-minded. — *Dhīroddhata* (°*ra-ud*°), *as*, m. the hero of a poem or play who is brave but haughty. — *Dhīroshṇin* (°*ra-ush*°), *ī*, m., N. of one of the Viśve-devās.

Dhīrāvī, f., N. of a plant (= *pītaśiṇśapā*).

Dhīrya, *as*, *ā*, *am* (fr. 1. *dhā* = 1. *dhī*), Ved. intelligent, wise, clever; (*am*), n. intelligence, prudence.

धीलटी *dhīlaṭī*, f. (probably a Prākrit form for *duhitṛi*), a daughter.

धीवर *dhīvara*. See col. 1.

धु 1. *dhu* = rt. 1. *dhū*, to shake, q. v.

2. *dhu*, *us*, f. shaking, trembling.

Dhuta, *as*, *ā*, *am*, shaken, agitated, moved quickly to and fro; abandoned, deserted, left. — *Dhuta-pāpa*, *as*, *ā*, *am*, purified from sin.

Dhuna, *as*, *ā*, *am*, shaking. See col. 3.

Dhunana, *am*, n. shaking, agitation.

Dhunāna, *as*, *ā*, *am*, shaking, agitating.

Dhuni, *is*, *is*, *i*. See col. 3.

Dhunvat, *an*, *atī*, *at*, shaking, agitating.

Dhunvāna, *as*, *ā*, *am*, shaking, agitating.

Dhuvana, *as*, m., Ved. fire; (*am*), n. shaking, agitation; place of execution.

Dhuvitra, *am*, n. a sort of fan (made of deer-skin and especially used to kindle or excite a sacrificial fire); [cf. *dhavitra*.]

धुक *dhuka*, *as*, *ā*, m. f. a kind of plant (commonly Bhuyabora or Rānabora, *bora* = *badara*).

धुक्ष् *dhuksh*, cl. 1. A. *dhukshate*, &c., to kindle; to be weary; to live.

धुङ्क्षा *dhuṅkshā*, f., Ved. a kind of bird.

धुन *dhuna*, *as*, *ā*, *am* (variously derived fr. rt. 2. *dhvan* or rt. 1. *dhu*), Ved. sounding, roaring; shaking, agitating, (only in comp.) — *Dhuneti* (°*na-iti*), *is*, *is*, *i*, having a roaring or blustering course; having an agitating or destructive course.

Dhunaya (fr. *dhuni* below), Nom. P. A. *dhunayati*, *-te*, &c., Ved. to sound, roar, to flow with a roaring noise; to flow.

Dhuni, *is*, *is*, *i*, Ved. sounding, roaring, blustering; (Sāy.) shaking, agitating, causing to tremble, (fr. rt. 1. *dhu*); (*is*), m. epithet of the Soma; N. of a demon slain by Indra; (*is* or *dhunī*), f. a river [cf. *nadī*]; (*ayas*), m. pl. 'the agitators,' an epithet of the Maruts. — *Dhuni-mat*, *ān*, *atī*, *at*, Ved. roaring, sounding; (Sāy.) agitated, trembling. — *Dhuni-vrata*, *as*, *ā*, *am*, Ved. habitually roaring or blustering; (Sāy.) whose function is the agitation or shaking (of trees &c.). — *Dhunī-nātha*, *as*, m. 'lord of the rivers,' the ocean.

धुन्धु *dhundhu*, *us*, m., N. of an Asura slain by Kuvalāśva (or Kuvalayāśva), father of Sunda; (a various reading for *Cuñću* who was a descendant of Tri-śaṅku.) — *Dhundhu-māra*, *as*, m. 'the slayer of Dhundhu,' epithet of Kuvalāśva (Kuvalayāśva), a son of Tri-śaṅku and father of Yuvanāśva; a house-lizard (? = *gṛihātika*); an insect, coccinella (= *indra-gopa*, *śakra-gopa*); a kind of plant (= *gṛiha-dhūma*); the smoke of a house (?), cf. *dundu-māra*. — *Dhundhumāropākhyāna* (°*ra-up*°), *am*, n. 'the episode of Dhundhu-māra,' N. of the seventeenth chapter of the Svarga-khaṇḍa or third part of the Padma-Purāṇa.

धुर् *dhur*, *ūr*, f. (fr. rt. *dhṛi*?, in Mahā-bh. Anuśāsana-p. 2876. *dhur* is masc.), that part of a yoke which rests on the shoulder; a yoke; a burden, load (literally and metaphorically); the peg or pin at both ends of an axle for fastening the nave of the wheel; the foremost part of the pole, where the yoke is fixed; the pole itself, the shaft, the foremost or highest place, the top, the place of honour; a finger; N. of six verses of the Bahish-pavamāna which are to be sung in a peculiar manner; (some lexicographers add the following meanings) agitation, trembling; reflection, recollection; a spark of fire; a part, a portion; wealth; a N. of the Ganges; *dhuri*, ind. at the head of, = *agre*; [cf. *dhūr*, *dur-dhur*, *dṛiḍha-dhur*.] — *Dhuran-dhara*, *as*, *ī*, *am*, bearing the yoke, bearing a burden, fit to be harnessed; bearing a burden with patience, (figuratively) laden with good qualities or with weighty duties, &c.; (*as*), m. a beast of burden; a man of business; a chief, leader; an epithet of Śiva; (*ās*), m. pl., N. of a people; N. of a Rakshas; the tree Grislea Tomentosa. — *Dhur-gata*, *dhur-vaha*, *dhur-voḍhṛi*, incorrect forms for *dhūr-gata*, *dhūr-vaha*, *dhūr-voḍhṛi*; see under 2. *dhūr*, p. 458, col. 2.

Dhura, *as*, m. at end of comp. = *dhur*, a yoke, pole; burden; pin at the end of an axle &c.; (1. *dhurā*), f. a burden, load. — *Dhurā-vaha*, *as*, *ā*, *am*, bearing a burden (= *dhūr-vaha*).

Dhuriṇa, *as*, *ā*, *am*, fit to be harnessed; bearing a burden or able to bear one, laden with, abounding with (qualities, duties, &c.); (*as*), m. a beast of burden; a man of business; a leader, chief; [cf. *uttara-dh°*, *eka-dh°*, *dakshiṇa-dh°*, *sarva-dh°*.]

Dhurīya, *as*, *ā*, *am*, able to bear a burden, fit

for a load, suited to a burden; charged with important duties; (*as*), m. a beast of burden; a man of business or one entrusted with weighty affairs.

Dhurya or (sometimes wrongly spelt) *dhūrya*, *as*, *ā*, *am*, fit to be harnessed, fit for a burden, able to bear one, &c.; standing at the head, holding the first place, foremost, best; a leader; (*as*), m. a beast of burden, a horse or bullock attached to the shaft, shafter; a leader, chief (e.g. *kula-dhurya*, the chief or leader of a family); a minister, a chargé d'affaires; a kind of medicinal plant, = *ṛishabha*; (*am*), n. the fore-part of the pole.

धुरा 2. *dhurā*, ind. (for 1. see *dhura*, p. 456, col. 3), violently, hurtfully, (perhaps fr. rt. *dhurv* or *dhūrv*.)

धुर्व् *dhurv* [cf. rt. *dhūrv*], cl. 1. P. *dhurvati*, &c., to hurt, kill.

धुवका *dhuvakā*, f. the introductory stanza of a song, forming afterwards the burden of each verse; [cf. *dhruvakā*.]

धुशुल्या *dhuśulyā*(?), f., N. of a river.

धुस्तुर *dhustura* or *dhustūra*, *as*, m. the thorn-apple, Datura Fastuosa; [cf. *dhattūra*.]

धू 1. *dhū*, cl. 5. P. A. *dhūnoti*, *dhūnute*, (in the later language also) *dhunoti*, *dhunute*; cl. 6. P. *dhuvati*; cl. 9. P. A. *dhunāti*, *dhunīte*, *dudhāva*, *dudhuve*, *dhoshyati* and *dhavishyati*, *-te*, *adhāvīt* and *adhaushīt*, (cl. 6. Aor. *adhuvīt*), *adhoshṭa* and *adhavishṭa*, *dhotum* and *dhavitum*, to shake, shake off, remove; to agitate, cause to tremble; to treat (a person) roughly, hurt, injure; to blow away, destroy; to kindle, excite, fan (a fire &c.); to shake off from one's self, liberate one's self from (A.); to strive against, resist: Pass. *dhūyate*: Caus. *dhāvayati* and *dhūnayati*, *-yitum*, to shake: Desid. *dudhūshati*, *-te*: Intens. *dodhūyate*, *dodhoti*, *dodhavīti*, to shake or agitate violently, shake in a threatening manner, shake out, shake down from; to be shaken violently, totter exceedingly (A.); [cf. Zend *dun-man*, 'mist, fog:' Gr. θύ-ω, θύ-ν-ω, θυά-ω, θυά-ζω, θῦ-νο-ς, θύ-ελλα, θυά-(δ)-ς, θυι-ά-ς, θυ-μό-ς, θῦ-μα, θυ-σία, θύ-ος, θυή-εις, θύ-μο-ν: Lat. *fū-mu-s*, *sub-fi-o*, *sub-fi-men*: Goth. *daun-s*, 'smell:' Old Iceland. *du-s-t* = Eng. *dust*: Old Germ. *tun-s-t*, 'storm;' *tou-m*, 'smoke:' Slav. *du-na-ti*, 'to breathe;' *dy-mŭ*, 'smoke;' *du-chŭ*, 'breath;' *du-sha*, 'soul:' Lith. *dū-mai*, 'smoke;' *du-ma-s*, *dū-mà*, 'thought, mind.']

2. *dhū*, *ūs*, f. shaking, agitating.

Dhūka, *as*, m. air or wind; a rogue, cheat; time; a kind of plant (= *vakula*).

Dhūta, *as*, *ā*, *am*, shaken, shaken off, removed, agitated; fanned, rinsed, cleansed (in this sense said to be an old form for *dhauta*, q. v.); deserted, abandoned; reproached, reviled; judged, discriminated; (*am*), n. (?), good behaviour; (*ā*), f. a wife. — *Dhūta-kalmasha*, *as*, *ā*, *am*, one whose sins are shaken off, free from sin, pure. — *Dhūta-pāpa*, *as*, *ā*, *am*, one who has shaken off his sins; removing or destroying sin; (*ā*), f., N. of a river; of the daughter of the ascetic Veda-śiras. — *Dhūtapāpa-tīrtha*, *am*, n., N. of a Tīrtha. — *Dhūtapāpeśvara-tīrtha* (°*pa-īś*°), *am*, n., N. of a sacred bathing-place. — *Dhūta-pāpman*, *ā*, *ā*, *a*, = *dhūta-pāpa*, q. v.

Dhūti, *is*, m., Ved. 'a shaker, agitator,' N. of an Āditya; (*is*), f. shaking, moving to and fro, fanning; (*ayas*), m. pl. epithet of the Maruts.

Dhūtvā, ind. having shaken or shaken off; having agitated.

Dhūna, *as*, *ā*, *am*, shaken, agitated; distressed by heat or thirst.

Dhūnana, *as*, m. wind; (*am*), n. the act of shaking, agitation.

Dhūnaya (fr. *dhūna*), Nom. P. A. *dhūnayati*, *-te*, &c. (generally considered as the Caus. of rt. 1. *dhū*), to shake, agitate, move to and fro.

Dhūni, *is*, f. shaking, agitating.

Dhūpa, *as*, m. (by native authorities derived fr. a rt. *dhūp*, q. v.), incense, frankincense, perfume, aromatic vapour or smoke, the vapour proceeding from fragrant gum or resin, (often in pl. *dhūpās*); fragrant powder; [cf. *kṛitrima-dh*°, *kḷipta-dh*°, *kha-dh*°, &c.] — *Dhūpa-dāna*, *am*, n. 'the giving of incense,' N. of a chapter of the Purāṇa-sarva-sva by Halāyudha. — *Dhūpa-dhūpita*, *as*, *ā*, *am*, made fragrant or fumigated with incense. — *Dhūpa-pātra*, *am*, n. a vessel for incense, censer; a perfume box. — *Dhūpa-vṛiksha* or *dhūpavṛikshaka*, *as*, m. 'incense-tree,' a species of pine, Pinus Longifolia. — *Dhūpāguru* (°*pa-ag*°), *u*, n. a kind of Agallochum used for incense. — *Dhūpāṅga* (°*pa-aṅ*°), *as*, m. turpentine. — *Dhūpārha* (°*pa-ar*°), *am*, n. a black kind of Agallochum used or fit for incense.

Dhūpaka, *as*, m. = *dhūpa* in *kṛitrima-dh*° and other adj. comp.; a preparer of perfumes or incense, a perfumer [cf. *dhūpika*].

Dhūpana, *am*, n. (fr. *dhūpaya*), incensing, fumigation, perfuming; perfume, incense, the aromatic vapour produced from gums or resins. — *Dhūpanāṅga* (°*na-aṅ*°), *as*, m. = *dhūpāṅga*, turpentine (?).

Dhūpaya (fr. *dhūpa*, but native authorities recognise a rt. *dhūp*, q. v.), Nom. P. *dhūpayati*, *-yitum*, to fumigate, perfume, incense, make fragrant; (in astron.) to obscure with mist, to be about to eclipse; to speak; to shine; [cf. Gr. τύφ-ω, τῦφ-ο-ς, τυφ-ών, τυφώς, τυφεδών, Τυμφρηστός (?), τυφλό-ς, τυφεδανός, τυφεδών: Old Germ. *dimpf-en*, 'to smoke:' Lith. *dump-iù*, 'I fan or blow a fire;' *dùmp-les*, 'bellows.']

Dhūpāya (fr. *dhūpa*, but native authorities give a rt. *dhūp*, q. v.), Nom. P. *dhūpāyati*, *-yitum*, to fumigate, perfume with incense; [cf. *dhūpaya*.]

Dhūpāyita, *as*, *ā*, *am*, incensed, perfumed, fumigated, scented with incense; vexed, pained.

Dhūpi, *is*, m., Ved., N. of a class of divine beings presiding over rain (?).

Dhūpika, *as*, m. a preparer of perfumes or incense, a perfumer; [cf. *dhūpaka*.]

Dhūpita, *as*, *ā*, *am*, scented, perfumed, incensed; suffering pain or fatigue.

Dhūpya, *am*, n. (?), the claw of a particular animal which when burned emits a fragrant perfume; [cf. Pers. *nākhuni khwush*.]

Dhūma, *as*, m. (connected by some with rt. 1. *dhmā*), smoke, vapour, incense; mist, haze; breath (Ved.); a cloud; (in medic.) smoke as a sternutatory in five forms; = *go-dhūma*, = *śilārasa*, a kind of incense; a place prepared for the building of a house; N. of a man; (*ā*), f. a kind of plant (= *dhīrāvī*); [cf. *go-dh*°, *ćarishṇu-dh*°, *trishṭa-dh*°: cf. also rt. 1. *dhmā*; Gr. θῦ-μό-ς; Lat. *fū-mu-s*; Old Germ. *daum*, *toum*, 'fume;' Lith. *dū-mai*, 'smoke;' Slav. *dŭ-mŭ*, 'smoke;' Hib. *dluimh*, 'cloud, darkness.'] — *Dhūma-ketana*, *as*, *ā*, *am*, 'smoke-marked,' whose ensign or mark is smoke; (*as*), m. fire or its deity; a meteor, a comet; Ketu or the personified descending node. — *Dhūma-ketu*, *us*, *us*, *u*, Ved. 'whose sign is smoke,' known or to be known from smoke; (*us*), m. fire; a comet or falling star, the personified descending node; N. of a son of Kṛiśāśva by Arćis; of Tṛiṇa-vindu by Alambushā. — *Dhūma-gandhi*, *is*, *is*, *i*, Ved. smelling of smoke. — *Dhūma-gandhika*, *am*, n. a kind of grass (= *rohisha-tṛiṇa*). — *Dhūma-jāṅgaja* (*dhūma-ja-aṅ*°), *am*, n. ammoniac. — *Dhūma-jāla*, *am*, n. a multitude or mass of clouds or smoke. — *Dhūma-darśin*, *ī*, *inī*, *i*, Ved. seeing smoke or vapour (as a person affected with a peculiar disease of the eye). — *Dhūma-dhvaja*, *as*, m. 'whose banner or symbol is smoke,' fire. — *Dhūma-pa*, *as*, *ā*, *am*, drinking or inhaling only smoke; [cf. *dhūma-prāśa*.] — *Dhūma-patha*, *as*, m. 'the way of smoke,' sacrifice; seeking salvation by works; [cf. *dhūma-vartman*.] — *Dhūma-pāna*, *am*, n. inhaling smoke or vapour; smoking tobacco. — *Dhūmapāna-vidhi*, *is*, m. 'the rule of inhaling smoke,' N. of the twenty-eighth chapter of the Sārṅgadhara-saṃhitā. — *Dhūma-prabhā*, f., N. of one of the seventeen divisions of hell where smoke takes the place of light. — *Dhūma-prāśa*, *as*, *ā*, *am*, 'smoke-eating,' feeding only on smoke, as a hermit; [cf. *dhūma-pa*.] — *Dhūma-maṅgaja*, various reading for *dhūma-jāṅgaja*, q. v. — *Dhūma-maya*, *as*, *ī*, *am*, consisting of smoke or vapour, smoky. — *Dhūma-mahishī*, f. fog, mist. — *Dhūma-yoni*, *is*, m. 'engendered from smoke or vapour,' a cloud. — *Dhūma-vat*, *ān*, *atī*, *at*, smoky; smoking, steaming; containing the word *dhūma*. — *Dhūmavat-tva*, *am*, n. smokiness. — *Dhūma-varćas*, *ās*, m., N. of a man. — *Dhūma-varṇa*, *as*, m. 'smoke-coloured,' N. of a king of the serpents. — *Dhūma-vartman*, *a*, n. 'the path of smoke,' sacrifice; seeking salvation by works. — *Dhūma-śikha*, *as*, *ā*, *am*, 'smoke-crested' (said of flame or a tongue of fire). — *Dhūma-saṃhati*, *is*, f. a quantity of smoke, a mass or cloud of smoke. — *Dhūmākāra* (°*ma-āk*°), *as*, *ā*, *am*, having the form or appearance of smoke. — *Dhūmāksha* (°*ma-ak*°), *as*, *ī*, *am*, Ved. having dim, dark or troubled (?) eyes. — *Dhūmāṅga* (°*ma-aṅ*°) = *śiṅśapā*. — *Dhūmābha* (°*ma-ābha*), *as*, *ā*, *am*, of a smoky appearance or colour, of a purple colour; (*as*), m. purple. — *Dhūmā-vatī*, f., N. of a place of pilgrimage. — *Dhūmāvatī-mantra*, *as*, m. or *dhūmāvatī-manu*, *us*, m., N. of certain magical formulas. — *Dhūmāvali* (°*ma-āv*°), *is*, f. a wreath or cloud of smoke. — *Dhūmottha* (°*ma-ut*°), *am*, n. = *vajra-kshāra*, ammoniac; [cf. *dhūma-jāṅgaja*.] — *Dhūmodgāra* (°*ma-ud*°), *as*, m. 'the issuing of smoke or vapour,' N. of a kind of disease. — *Dhūmopahata* (°*ma-up*°), *as*, *ā*, *am*, 'smoke-struck,' suffocated with smoke. — *Dhūmorṇā* (°*ma-ūr*°), f., N. of the wife of Yama; of the wife of Mārkaṇḍeya; [cf. *dhūmrorṇā*.] — *Dhūmorṇā-pati*, *is*, m. 'husband of Dhūmorṇā,' epithet of Yama, ruler of the dead.

Dhūmaka, *as*, *ā*, *am*, = *dhūma* at the end of a comp.; (*ikā*), f. smoke, vapour, fog. — *Dhūmaka-pushpā*, f. a species of plant (compared to smoke).

Dhūmaya (fr. *dhūma*), Nom. P. *dhūmayati*, &c., to cover with smoke, obscure with mist: Pass. *dhūmyate*, &c., to be obscured with vapour or mist; to be about to be eclipsed, to be darkened; [cf. *dhūmāya*.]

Dhūmala, *as*, *ā*, *am*, smoke-coloured, of a smoky hue, brownish red, of a purple colour; (*as*), m. a colour compounded of black and red, purple; a kind of musical instrument.

Dhūmasa, *as*, m. the plant Tectona Grandis; (*ī*), f. a sort of cake made of pulse steeped in water and dried in the sun.

Dhūmāya (fr. *dhūma*), Nom. P. A. *dhūmāyati*, *-te*, *-yitum*, to smoke, be covered or obscured with smoke, to steam: Caus. P. *dhūmāyayati*, *-yitum*, to cause to smoke or to be covered with smoke, mist, vapour, &c.

Dhūmāyana, *am*, n. smoking, steaming; (in medic.) heat, fever, feverishness.

Dhūmāyita, *am*, n. the act of smoking.

Dhūmikā. See *dhūmaka*.

Dhūmita, *as*, *ā*, *am*, obscured with smoke, mist, &c., darkened; (*ā*), f., scil. *diś*, that quarter towards which the sun turns first.

Dhūmin, *ī*, *inī*, *i*, smoking, steaming; (*inī*), f., N. of one of the seven tongues of Agni; of the wife of Aja-mīḍha; of another woman.

Dhūmyamāna, *as*, *ā*, *am*, being obscured with mist &c., being obscured.

Dhūmyā, f. thick smoke, a volume or cloud of smoke. — *Dhūmyāṭa* (°*yā-aṭa*), *as*, m. the fork-tailed shrike.

Dhūmra, *as*, *ā*, *am*, smoky, smoke-coloured, grey; (according to the lexicographers) dark-red or the colour of fire seen through smoke; of a deep purple colour, purple; (metaphorically) dark, lurid, obscured; (*as*), m. a mixture of red and black; purple (the colour); incense (= *turushka*); N. of one of Skanda's attendants; of a Dānava; of a Muni; of a monkey or bear [cf. *dhūmrāyaṇa* and *dhaumrāyaṇa*]; an epithet of Śiva; of Parāśara; (in astrology) N. of the twenty-eighth Yoga; (*ā*), f. a kind of gourd (= *śaśāṇḍulī*); epithet of Durgā; of the mother of Vasu-dhara; (*am*), n. sin, vice, wickedness; [cf. *tāmra-dh°*.] — *Dhūmra-ketu, us,* m. 'grey-bannered,' N. of a son of Bharata; of Tṛiṇa-vindu. — *Dhūmra-keśa, as,* m. 'dark-haired,' N. of a son of Pṛithu and Arćis; of a son of Kriśāśva and Arćis [cf. *dhūma-ketu*]; of a son of Danu. — *Dhūmra-giri, is,* m. 'the smoky mountain,' N. of a mountain. — *Dhūmra-dhī, īs, īs, i,* 'whose intellect is dim' or 'whose devotion is obscured,' devoted to works. — *Dhūmra-nīkāśa, as, ā, am,* Ved. of a deep dark-red colour. — *Dhūmra-pattrā,* f. 'having grey or dark-red leaves,' N. of a shrub (= *dhūmrāhvā, su-labhā, svayam-bhuvā, gṛidhra-pattrā, gridhrāṇī, kṛimi-ghnī, śrīmalāpahā*). — *Dhūmra-mūlikā,* f. 'having a grey or dark-red root,' a kind of grass (= *śūlī*). — *Dhūmra-ruć, k, k, k,* of a purple hue, of a deep-red colour. — *Dhūmra-rohita, as, ā, am,* Ved. dark-red, deep purple. — *Dhūmra-loćana, as,* m. 'dark-eyed,' a pigeon; N. of a general of the Asura Sumbha. — *Dhūmra-lohita, as, ā, am,* dark-red, deep purple. — *Dhūmra-varṇa, as, ā, am,* smoky-coloured, dark-red, deep purple; (*as*), m. incense; N. of a son of Aja-mīḍha and Dhūminī; N. of a mountain; (*ā*), f., N. of one of the seven tongues of Fire; flame. — *Dhūmra-varṇaka, as,* m. 'the dark-coloured one,' a kind of animal living in caves, a fox; [cf. *kokaḍa*.] — *Dhūmravarṇā-manu,* N. of a magical formula. — *Dhūmra-śūka, as,* m. 'having grey bristles,' a camel; (also read *dhūmra-śūla*.) — *Dhūmra-saṃrakta-loćana, as, ā, am,* having dark-red or greyish-red eyes. — *Dhūmrāksha* (°*ra-ak*°), *as, ī, am,* grey-eyed; (*as*), m., N. of a Rakshas; of a son of Hema-ćandra, grandson of Tṛiṇa-vindu [cf. *dhūmrāśva*]; of a king of the Nishadhas. — *Dhūmrākshi* (°*ra-ak*°), *is,* m. a pearl of a bad colour. — *Dhūmrāṭa* (°*ra-aṭa*), *as,* m. the fork-tailed shrike; [cf. *dhūmyāṭa*.] — *Dhūmrānika* (°*ra-an*°), *as,* m., N. of one of the seven sons of Medhātithi and a Varsha called after him. — *Dhūmrābha* (°*ra-ābha*), *as,* m. air, wind, atmosphere (sometimes of a smoky or dark-red hue?). — *Dhūmrāśva* (°*ra-aś*°), *as,* m. 'having dark horses,' N. of a son of Su-ćandra (son of Hema-ćandra) and father of Sṛiñjaya; [cf. *dhūmrāksha*.] — *Dhūmrāhvā* (°*ra-āh*°), f. = *dhūmra-pattrā*. — *Dhūmrorṇā* (°*ra-ūr*°), f. = *dhūmorṇā* (?).

Dhūmraka, as, m. 'the grey animal,' a camel; (*ikā*), f. the plant Dalbergia Sissoo (= *śiṇśapā*).

Dhūmrāyaṇa, as, m. (fr. *dhūmra*), a patronymic from Dhūmra; [cf. *dhaumrāyaṇa*.]

Dhūmriman, ā, m., Ved. dark-red (the colour), darkness of colour; obscurity.

Dhūyamāna, as, ā, am, being shaken or agitated or fanned.

Dhūli, is, m. f. or *dhūlī,* f. (perhaps connected with rt. *dhvas* or *dhvaṇs,* cf. *dhūsara*), dust; powder; [cf. *gandha-dh°, go-dh°*]; a particular number. — *Dhūli-kuṭṭima, am,* n. or *dhūli-kedāra, as,* m. a mound, rampart of earth. — *Dhūli-guććhaka, as,* m. the red fragrant vegetable powder thrown about at the spring festival called the Holi. — *Dhūli-dhūmra, as, ā, am,* dark-red or dark with dust. — *Dhūli-dhvaja, as,* m. 'dust-marked,' 'whose sign is dust,' air or wind. — *Dhūli-pushpikā,* f. the plant Pandanus Odoratissimus; [cf. *ketakī*.] — *Dhūli-maya, as, ī, am,* covered with dust. — *Dhūli-mushṭi, is,* m. f. a handful of dust. — *Dhūlimushṭi-prakshepa, as,* m. the throwing of handfuls of dust. — *Dhūli-kadamba* or *dhūlī-kadambaka* or *dhūli-kadamba* or *dhūli-kadambaka, as,* m. the plant Dalbergia Ougeinensis (= *tiniśa*); a species of the Kadamba tree, Nauclea Cordifolia (= *nīpa*); Capparis Trifoliata (= *varuṇa*). — *Dhūlī-paṭala, as,* m. a cloud of dust.

Dhūlikā, f. fog, mist, (from its dust-like appearance.)

धूण *dhūṇa, as* or *am,* m. or n. (?), the resin of the Shorea Robusta; [cf. *dhūnaka*.]

Dhūnaka, as, m. the resin of the Shorea Robusta or resin in general; [cf. *dhūrṇa* and *dhūṇa*.]

धूप् *dhūp,* cl. 1. P. *dhūpāyati,* &c., cl. 10. P. *dhūpayati,* &c. See *dhūpaya* and *dhūpāya,* p. 457, col. 2.

Dhūpa. See p. 457, col. 2.

धूम *dhūma, dhūmra.* See p. 457, cols. 2, 3.

धूर् 1. *dhūr* (connected with rt. *dhūrv*), cl. 4. A. *dhūryate,* &c., to hurt or kill; to move or approach.

धूर् 2. *dhūr* for *dhur* (q. v.) at the beginning of a comp. — *Dhūr-gata, as, ā, am,* standing on or going along the pole or fore-part of a chariot; standing at the head, taking the first place, preceding, foremost. — *Dhūr-jaṭi, is,* m., in one place also *dhūr-jaṭin, ī,* m. (fr. *dhur* and *jaṭi* = *jaṭā*), 'whose matted locks are like a burden,' an epithet of Rudra-Śiva; N. of a medical author. — *Dhūr-dhara, as, ā, am,* bearing a load or burden, managing affairs; (*as*), m. a beast of burden; [cf. *dhuran-dhara*.] — *Dhūr-vat, ān, atī, at,* having a load, laden. — *Dhūr-vaha, as, ā, am,* bearing a load, carrying a burden; managing affairs; (*as*), m. a beast of burden. — *Dhūr-voḍhṛi, ḍhā, ḍhrī, ḍhṛi,* bearing a load, the carrier of a burden. — *Dhūr-shad, t, t, t,* Ved. standing under the yoke, drawing a load; resting on the yoke; moving, promoting. — *Dhūr-shāh, ṭ, ṭ, ṭ,* Ved. bearing the yoke.

Dhūrya, as, ā, am, for *dhurya,* q. v.

धूर्ण *dhūrṇa* = *dhūṇa* = *dhūnaka.*

धूर्त *dhūrta.* See under rt. *dhūrv* below.

धूर्व् *dhūrv* (connected with rts. *dhurv, dhvṛi, dhūr, hvṛi*), cl. 1. P. *dhūrvati, dudhūrva, dhūrvishyati, adhūrvīt, dhūrvitum,* Ved. to bend, cause to fall, hurt, injure: Desid. *dudhūrshati,* to wish to hurt.

Dhūrta, as, ā, am, cunning, crafty, dishonest, knavish, fraudulent, subtle; mischievous, injurious; (*as*), m. a rogue, cheat, swindler; a gamester; (in amatory language) a gay deceiver, a lover or gallant; the thorn-apple, Datura [cf. *kitava* and *krūra-dhūrta*]; a kind of perfume [cf. *ćoraka*]; (*ā*), f. a sort of nightshade; (*am*), n. rust or iron-filings; black salt (= *khaṇḍa-lavaṇa;* cf. *kshema-dhūrta*). — *Dhūrta-kitava, as,* m. a gamester. — *Dhūrta-kṛit, t,* m. = *dhūrta,* dishonest, a knave, rogue, cheat; (*t*), m. thorn-apple. — *Dhūrta-ćarita, am,* n. 'the actions of rogues,' N. of a work. — *Dhūrta-jantu, us,* m. 'the cunning creature,' man. — *Dhūrta-tā,* f. or *dhūrta-tva, am,* n. knavery, craftiness, roguery, knavishness, shrewdness. — *Dhūrta-traya, am,* n. three rogues, a trio of swindlers. — *Dhūrta-nartaka, am,* n. 'rogues as actors,' N. of a comedy by Sāma-rāja. — *Dhūrta-pralāpa, as,* m. the talk or confabulation of rogues. — *Dhūrta-maṇḍala, as,* m. a party of rogues or gamblers. — *Dhūrta-mānushā,* f., N. of a plant (= *rāsnā*). — *Dhūrta-raćanā,* f. a cunning plot, roguery. — *Dhūrta-rāja, as,* m. the chief of rogues. — *Dhūrta-samāgama, am,* n. 'assemblage of rogues,' N. of a comedy by Jyotir-Īśvara. — *Dhūrta-svāmin, ī,* m. 'lord of the rogues,' N. of a commentator on Āpastamba.

Dhūrtaka, as, ā, am, cunning, a cheat, a rogue; (*as*), m. a jackal; N. of a Nāga.

Dhūrti, is, f., Ved. injury, damage.

Dhūrtila in *aksha-dh°,* q. v.

Dhūrvan, a, n., Ved. causing to fall, bending.

धूर्वा *dhūrvā,* f., Ved. = *dūrvā,* q. v.

धूर्वी *dhūrvī,* f. the fore-part or pole of a carriage, = *dhur,* q. v.

धूलक *dhūlaka, am,* n. poison.

धूलि *dhūli.* See col. 1.

धूश् *dhūś* or *dhūsh* or *dhūs* (perhaps a Prākṛit form of *dhṛish* for *hṛish*), cl. 10. P. *dhūśayati, dhūshayati, dhūsayati,* &c., to make splendid or elegant; to embellish.

धूषर *dhūshara,* a wrong spelling for *dhūsara* below.

धूसर *dhūsara, as, ā, am* (fr. rt. *dhvas* for *dhvaṇs,* cf. *dhvasira;* but said to be fr. rt. 1. *dhū* and connected with *dhūli,* q. v.), of a dusty or greyish or dusty-white colour, grey; (*as*), m. grey (the colour); a jackass, a donkey; a camel; a pigeon; an oilman; anything of a grey tint; (*ā*), f., N. of a small shrub, = *pāṇḍura-phalī;* (*ī*), f., N. of a Kinnarī or female chorister of heaven. — *Dhūsara-ććhadā,* f. a kind of plant, = *śveta-vuhnā.* — *Dhūsara-tva, am,* n. grey colour, paleness; (also read *dhūshara-tva*.) — *Dhūsara-pattrikā,* f. the plant Tragia Involucrata [cf. *ushṭra-dhūsara, puććhikā*]; a kind of Heliotropium (= *hasti-śuṇḍī*).

Dhūsaraka, as, m., N. of a jackal.

Dhūsarita, as, ā, am, made grey, greyish.

धूस्तूर *dhūstūra, as,* m. = *dhustūra,* the thorn-apple, Datura Metel and Fastuosa.

धृ *dhṛi* (allied to rt. *bhṛi,* which is probably the more ancient form), cl. 1. P. A. *dharati, -te, dadhāra* (Ved. *dādhāra*), *dadhre* (part. *dadhrāṇa*), *dharishyati, -te, adhārshīt, adhṛita, dhartum,* and more commonly cl. 10. (identical with Caus. but with the same senses as cl. 1.) *dhārayati, -te,* Pot. *dhārayet, -ta* (Mahā-bh. Anuśāsana-p. 5007. *dhārayīta*), *dhārayāmāsa, dhārayishyati, -te, adīdharat, -ta* (Vedic forms *dīdharat, didhṛitam, didhṛita, ni-dīdhar*), *dhārayitum,* to hold, bear, carry; hold up, support, sustain, maintain; carry on; to hold in, hold back, keep back, restrain, stop, detain, curb, resist; to hold in one's possession, keep, possess, have; to keep, retain (in one's service); to hold fast, preserve; to hold, contain; to lay hold of, seize, recover; to hold, observe, practise; to wear, use (as clothes &c.); to bear, undergo, suffer; to hold out, hold on, endure, continue, continue to live; (A.) to hold one's place, stand firm, remain; to fix, place, deposit; to destine for, assign or present anything (acc.) to any person (dat.); to allot, assign, confer; (A.) to destine a person (acc.) to anything (dat.); (cl. 10.) to owe anything (acc.) to any person (dat. or gen.); to weigh in a balance; to prolong (in pronunciation); to cite, quote. The above meanings of *dhṛi* (cl. 1. or more frequently cl. 10. identified with Caus.) may be variously extended by connecting it with various nouns, e. g. *garbhaṃ dhṛi,* to conceive, to become pregnant, (in this sense the older language uses rt. *bhṛi*); *daṇḍaṃ dhṛi,* to carry a stick, use force, chastise (with loc. of the pers.); *damaṃ dhṛi,* to punish (with loc. of the pers.); *ātmānaṃ* or *jīvitaṃ* or *prāṇān* or *śarīraṃ* or *gātraṃ* or *dehaṃ dhṛi,* to maintain the soul, preserve the vital spirits, body, &c., to continue to live, survive; *mano* or *mānasaṃ* or *matiṃ* or *ćittaṃ* or *buddhiṃ dhṛi,* to fix the mind, direct the thoughts or attention upon, resolve; *vrataṃ dhṛi,* to observe or keep a vow, &c. [cf. *dhṛita-vrata*]; *tapo dhṛi,* to undergo or perform penance; *dhāraṇāṃ dhṛi,* to practise self-control; *tulayā dhṛi* (or without *tulayā*), to hold in a balance, weigh, measure; *śirasā* or *mūrdhni dhṛi,* to bear on the head, honour highly; *manasā dhṛi* (or without *manasā*), to bear in mind, recollect, remember; *samaye dhṛi,* to bring to an agreement, cause to make a compact; *antare dhṛi,* to deposit anything as surety, to give bail, to pledge: Pass. or cl. 6. A. *dhriyate* (ep. also *dhriyati*), to be firm or fixed, to be supported or maintained, to be preserved; to exist, live, continue to live, remain alive, survive; to remain, continue; to undertake, resolve upon (with dat. or acc. of the thing or with inf.): Caus. *dhārayati, -te* (with the meanings of cl. 1. and cl. 10.): Pass. of Caus. *dhāryate,* to be held or supported, to be maintained or preserved; to continue to live (with inst., e. g. *tena na dhāryate*, it is not lived by him): Desid. *didhīrshati, -te, didharishate, didhārayishati*, to wish to hold or keep, to try to support or maintain, &c.: Intens. *dedhrīyate, dardharti* (Ved. *dādharti*), to hold very fast, lay hold of firmly, bear firmly, &c.; [cf. 1. *dharma, dhīra, dhruva, dhur, dhurya;* Zend *dar*, 'to hold;' Gr. θρῆ-σα-σθαι, θρᾶ-ν-ος, θρῆν-υ-ς, θρόνο-ς, θέρ-μα, θέλ-ω, ἐ-θέλ-ω; Lat. *frē-tu-s, frē-nu-m, fir-mu-s, for-ma;* Angl. Sax. *drag-an, dreog-an;* Old Germ. *trag-an;* Mod. Germ. *trag-en.*]

Dhṛik (at end of comp., and only occurring in nom. sing. *dhṛik*, and more probably to be referred to rt. *dhṛish* or to rt. *dṛih*), bearing, carrying, supporting, sustaining, suffering, wearing, possessing, having, &c.; [cf. *kāla-rūpa-dh°, śakti-dh°, śarīra-dh°.*]

Dhṛit, t, t, t (at end of comp.), a holder, bearer, possessor; bearing, carrying, possessing, having, observing, &c.; [cf. *ćarshaṇī-dh°, dharaṇī-dh°, dharma-dh°, nitya-dh°.*]

Dhṛita, as, ā, am, held, borne, carried, maintained, supported; contained; possessed; kept, retained, detained; laid hold of, seized, grasped, griped; worn, used; observed, practised; weighed; placed, deposited; holding, bearing, continuing, enduring, existing, standing; intent upon, i. e. resolved or determined to do anything (with dat. or loc., e. g. *jaye dhṛitas*, resolved on victory); firm, prepared, ready; (*as*), m., N. of a son of the thirteenth Manu; of a descendant of Druhyu and son of Dharma [cf. *dhārteya*]; (*am*), n. a peculiar manner of fighting; (*am*), ind. firmly, slowly, solemnly. — *Dhṛita-kanaka-māla, as, ā, am*, wearing a golden collar or wreath. — *Dhṛita-kārmukeshu* (°*ka-ishu*), *us, us, u*, armed with bow and arrows. — *Dhṛita-daksha, as, ā, am*, Ved. of enduring intelligence; (Sāy.) of enduring strength, possessing vigour. — *Dhṛita-daṇḍa, as, ā, am*, carrying the stick, inflicting punishment; one on whom punishment has been inflicted. — *Dhṛita-dīdhiti, is*, m. 'constant in splendor,' fire; [cf. *ghṛita-dīdhiti.*] — *Dhṛita-devā*, f., N. of a daughter of Devaka. — *Dhṛita-paṭa, as, ā, am*, covered or overspread with a cloth &c. — *Dhṛita-matī*, f., N. of a river; (wrong form for *dhṛiti-matī.*) — *Dhṛita-rājan, ā*, m., N. of a man; [cf. *dhārtarajña.*] — *Dhṛita-rāshṭra, as, ā, am*, whose empire is firm or who holds the kingdom; (*as*), m. a good king; N. of a Nāga, also called Airāvata; of a Deva-gandharva, sometimes identified with king Dhṛita-rāshṭra; of a son of the Daitya Bali; of a king of Kāśī; (according to the Mahā-bhārata) N. of the eldest son of Vyāsa by the widow of Vićitra-vīrya, (he was brother of Pāṇḍu and Vidura, and as the first-born was entitled to the throne of Hāstina-pura, but being born blind, he at first renounced the sovereignty in favour of Pāṇḍu; afterwards, on the retirement of Pāṇḍu to the woods, Dhṛita-rāshṭra was called to undertake the government, which he did with the assistance of Bhīshma as his regent; he was husband of Gāndhārī and father of 100 sons, the eldest of whom was named Dur-yodhana; he is sometimes identified with Dhṛita-rāshṭra and with Haṇsa, two chiefs of the Gandharvas); N. of a son of Janam-ejaya; a kind of bird, perhaps a sort of goose; (*ās*), m. pl. the sons of Dhṛita-rāshṭra, whose names are enumerated in Mahā-bh. Ādi-p. 4540; (*ī*), f., N. of a daughter of Tāmrā, mother of the geese and other water-birds, = *haṇsa-patnī*, = *haṇsa-padī;* [cf. *dhārtarāshṭra* and *dhārtarāshṭri.*] — *Dhṛita-rāshṭra-ja, as*, m. 'sprung from Dhṛita-rāshṭra,' epithet of any son of Dhṛita-rāshṭra. — *Dhṛita-varman, ā*, m. 'bearing armour or mail, mailed,' N. of a warrior on the side of the Kurus. — *Dhṛita-vrata, as, ā, am*, Ved. of fixed law or order; keeping vows or engagements, devoted, attached, faithful; (Sāy.) accepting pious acts, performing religious rites; (*as*), m. epithet of Varuṇa; of Indra; of Rudra; of Savitṛi; of Agni; of a son of Dhṛiti; (*ās*), m. pl. epithet of the Ādityas. — *Dhṛita-śarīra, as, ā, am*, continuing to live or exist, existing. — *Dhṛita-śrī, īs*, f., N. of a metre consisting of four lines of twenty-one syllables each. — *Dhṛita-sandhi, is*, m. 'keeping agreements or compacts,' N. of a son of Su-sandhi and father of Bharata. — *Dhṛita-siṇha, as*, m. a various reading for *dhṛiti-siṇha*, q. v. — *Dhṛita-heti, is, is, i*, 'bearing weapons,' armed. — *Dhṛitātman* (°*ta-āt*°), *ā, ā, a*, firm-minded, self-possessed, steady, calm, collected. — *Dhṛitāmbhas* (°*ta-am*°), *ās, ās, as*, containing water. — *Dhṛiteshudhi* (°*ta-ish*°), *is, is, i*, carrying a quiver.

Dhṛitaka, as, m., N. of a Buddhist patriarch.

Dhṛita-vat, ān, atī, at, having taken or conveyed or held or resolved; (*atī*), f., N. of a river.

Dhṛiti, is, f. holding, holding fast, laying hold of, seizing, having, possessing; supporting, maintaining; firmness (e. g. *dhṛitim kṛi*, to show firmness, stand firm); constancy, steadiness, steadfastness, fortitude, energy, resolution; strong will, self-command; will, command (Ved.); satisfaction, happiness, pleasure, contentment; N. of certain evening oblations offered at the Aśva-medha; a sacrifice, offering; N. of a Vedic metre of seventy-two syllables; (in the later language) any metre consisting of 4 × 18 syllables; a metre composed of the Upendra-vajrā and Indra-vajrā; N. of one of the astrological Yogas; Resolution or Satisfaction personified as a daughter of Daksha and wife of Dharma, (regarded as one of the Vasu-patnīs or as a form of Dākshāyaṇī in Piṇḍāraka); N. of one of the sixteen Kalās of the Moon; N. of a goddess, daughter of a Kalā of Prakṛiti and wife of Kapila; N. of the wife of Rudra-manu; N. of the thirteenth of the sixteen Mātṛikās; (*is*), m., N. of one of the Viśve-Devās; of a preceptor, Dhṛiti Aindrota; of a son of Vi-jaya and father of Dhṛita-vrata; of a son of Vīta-havya and father of Bahulāśva; of a son of Babhru; [cf. *a-dh°* and *kshmā-dh°.*] — *Dhṛiti-paripūrṇa, as*, m., N. of a Bodhi-sattva. — *Dhṛiti-mat, ān, atī, at*, steadfast, firm, steady, calm, determined, resolute; satisfied, content; (*ān*), m., N. of a form of Agni; of a son of Manu Raivata; of Manu Sāvarṇa; of one of the Saptarshis in the thirteenth Manv-antara; of a son of Kīrtti-mat, son of Aṅgiras; of a son of Yavīnara; of a Brāhman; (*atī*), f., N. of a river, also read *dhṛita-vatī;* (*at*), n., N. of a Varsha in Kuśa-dvīpa. — *Dhṛitimat-tā*, f. steadfastness, steadiness, calmness, &c. — *Dhṛiti-maya, as, ī, am*, consisting of steadfastness or constancy; consisting of contentment. — *Dhṛiti-mush, ṭ, ṭ, ṭ*, 'fortitude-stealing,' who or what robs one of one's steadfastness, discomposing, agitating. — *Dhṛiti-siṇha, as*, m., N. of a man said to have assisted Purushottama in composing the Hārāvalī; (also read *dhṛita-siṇha.*)

Dhṛitvan, ā, m. an epithet of Vishṇu; of Brahmā; a clever man; virtue, morality; the sea; the sky [cf. *kshema-dh°*]; (*arī*), f. the earth.

Dhṛitvā, ind. having held, having laid hold of or seized; having taken, &c.

धृज् *dhṛij* or *dhṛiñj* (connected with rts. *dhraj* and *dhrij*), cl. 1. P. *dharjati, dhṛiñjati*, &c., to go, move.

धृष् *dhṛish*, cl. 1. 5. P. *dharshati, dhṛishṇoti, dadharsha* (part. *dadhṛishvas*), *dharshishyati, adharshīt* (Vedic forms *dadharshīt, dadharshat, dadharshati*), *dharshitum*, to be bold or courageous; to be confident or presumptuous, to be proud or overbearing; to be impudent or impatient; to have courage to do anything, to dare, venture (with inf., e. g. *dhṛishṇumaḥ prashṭum*, we dare to ask); to dare to attack, &c. (with acc. of the person); to insult, overbear, treat with indignity: Pass. *dhṛishyate*, to be attacked or insulted, to be subdued or overpowered: Caus. *dharshayati, -yitum*, Aor. *adadharshat* or *adīdhṛishat*, to dare to attack, to overbear, insult, treat with indignity, violate (a woman); offend, injure; assail, overpower, overcome, conquer, destroy; (A.) to surpass (?): Desid. *didharshishati:* Intens. *darīdhṛishyate, darīdharshṭi;* [cf. Zend *daresh*, 'to dare;' *darshi*, 'strong:' Gr. θρασ-ύ-ς, θρά-σος, θάρσ-ος, θαρσ-έ-ω, θαῤῥέω, θαρσ-ύνω, Θερσ-ίτη-ς: Lat. *fortis:* Goth. *ga-daurs-an*, 'to dare:' Slav. *drīz-a-ti, drīz-na-ti*, 'to dare:' Lith. *dras-ù-s*, 'courageous;' *dras-à*, 'courage:' Hib. *das-achd*, 'fierceness.']

Dhṛishaj, k, k, k (?), Ved. assailing, attacking, destroying.

Dhṛishat, an, atī or *antī, at*, pres. part., Ved. bold, daring, courageous, confident; (*atā*), ind. boldly, courageously. — *Dhṛishad-varṇa, as, ā, am*, Ved. of a brave race, heroic. — *Dhṛishad-vin, ī, inī, i*, Ved. bold, courageous. — *Dhṛishan-manas, ās, ās, as*, Ved. brave-hearted.

Dhṛishita, as, ā, am, bold, courageous, brave, daring.

Dhṛishu, us, us, u, bold, proud; clever; (*us*), m. a heap, multitude.

Dhṛishṭa, as, ā, am, bold, daring, courageous, confident; insolent, impudent, rude, saucy, shameless; forward, intrusive, presumptuous; profligate, abandoned; obtained?; (*as*), m. a faithless husband; N. of a son of Manu Vaivasvata, (also read *dhṛishṇu;* cf. *dhārshṭa*); of a son of Kunti; of a son of Bhajamāna; (*as*), m., N. of a spell for using or restraining magical weapons; (*ā*), f. a disloyal or unchaste woman; (*am*), ind. boldly, courageously, fearlessly; (it is said that *dhṛishṭa* may be used at the end of a comp. to give a bad sense to the word with which it is compounded); [cf. Angl. Sax. *thriste;* Swed. *dristig;* Old Iceland. *dreiss;* Mod. Germ. *dreist.*] — *Dhṛishṭa-ketu, us*, m., N. of a king of Ćedi; of a king of Videhā or Mithilā, son of Su-dhṛiti; of a son of Satya-dhṛiti; of a son of Su-kumāra; of the father of Su-kumāra; of a son of Dhṛishṭa-dyumna; of a king of the Kaikayas; of a son of Manu. — *Dhṛishṭa-tama, as, ā, am*, very bold or daring, most confident or courageous. — *Dhṛishṭa-tā*, f. or *dhṛishṭa-tva, am*, n. boldness, courage, impudence. — *Dhṛishṭa-dyumna, as*, m., N. of a son of Dru-pada (killed by Aśvatthāman while asleep). — *Dhṛishṭa-dhī, īs*, or *dhṛishṭa-buddhi, is*, m. 'bold-minded,' N. of a man. — *Dhṛishṭa-parākrama, as, ā, am*, of daring valour. — *Dhṛishṭa-mānin, ī, inī, i*, having a high opinion of one's self. — *Dhṛishṭa-ratha, as*, m., N. of a prince. — *Dhṛishṭa-śarman, ā*, m., N. of a son of Śvaphalka. — *Dhṛishṭokta* (°*ṭa-uk*°), *as*, m., N. of a son of Arjuna Kārttavīrya; (also read *dhṛishṇokta.*)

Dhṛishṭaka, as, m., N. of a prince.

Dhṛishṭi, is, is, i, Ved. (according to Mahīdhara) bold; (*is*), m. a pair of tongs; N. of a son of Hiraṇya-kaśipu; of a minister of king Daśa-ratha; (*is*), f. boldness.

Dhṛishṇa, as, &c., a wrong reading for *dhṛishṭa*, q. v. — *Dhṛishṇokta* (°*ṇa-uk*°), *as*, &c., a wrong reading for *dhṛishṭokta*, q. v.

Dhṛishṇaj, k, k, k, bold, confident; impudent, shameless.

Dhṛishṇi, is, m. a ray of light.

Dhṛishṇu, us, us, u, courageous, bold, confident, valiant; impudent, shameless; strong, powerful, (applied in the Veda to Indra, Soma, the Maruts, and the horses of Indra); (*u*), ind. in a bold or confident or powerful way; firmly, strongly; with force [cf. *dadhṛik*]; (*us*), m., N. of a son of Manu Vaivasvata [cf. *dhṛishṭa*]; of a son of Manu Sāvarṇa; of a son of Kavi; of a son of Kukura; *Kaśyapasya dhṛishṇu*, N. of a Sāman. — *Dhṛishṇu-tva, am*, n. boldness, confidence. — *Dhṛishṇu-sheṇa, as, ā, am*, Ved. having an overpowering weapon; (Sāy.) having a conquering or overpowering host, leading a valiant army (as a drum). — *Dhṛishṇv-ojas, ās, ās, as*, Ved. of overpowering strength, endowed with resistless might, (applied to Indra and the Maruts.)

Dhṛishṇuka, as, m., N. of a prince; [cf. *dhṛishṭaka.*]

Dhṛishṇuyā, ind., Ved. in a bold or powerful manner, firmly.

Dhṛishya, as, ā, am, assailable, to be attacked; conquerable.

धृषद् *dhṛishad,* Ved. = *dṛishad,* q. v.

धॄ *dhṝ,* cl. 9. P. *dhṛiṇāti,* &c., to be old, grow old; (various reading for rt. 1. *jṝ.*)

धे *dhe,* cl. 1. P. *dhayati, dadhau, dhāsyati, adhāt, adhāsīt, adadhat,* Prec. *dheyāt, dhātum,* to suck, drink, to suck in, drink in, absorb; appropriate; to suck out, draw away, take away: Caus. *dhāpayati, -yitum,* to give suck, suckle, nourish: Desid. *dhitsati,* to wish to suck; [cf. *dadhi, dhātri,* 2. *dhāyas, dhāru,* 2. *dhāsi:* Zend *daenu,* 'female:' Gr. θῆ-σθαι, θη-λή, θη-λώ, θηλα-μών, τήθη, τι-θή-νη, τί-τθη, τί-τθο-ς, θῆ-λυ-ς, γαλα-θη-νό-ς, Τη-θύ-ς, Θέ-τι-ς: Lat. *fī-liu-s, fīli-a, fē-lā-re, fē-mina:* Umbr. *fe-liu* = *filius:* Goth. *dadd-ya* = Old Germ. *tā-u,* 'I suck;' *tila,* 'female breast;' *tuta, tutta* = Eng. *teat:* Slav. *doya,* 'to suck;' *dollica,* 'nurse;' *dě-te,* 'child;' *dě-va,* 'virgin:' Hib. *daif,* 'drink.']

Dhena, as, m. the ocean, a male river; (*ā*), f., Ved. a milch cow; a mare (?); a river; speech; voice; N. of the wife of Bṛihas-pati; (*ās*), f. pl. any beverage made of milk; [cf. *dhenu, go.*] (In Ṛig-veda I. 2, 3, *dhenā* may possibly be an epithet of the horses of Vāyu.)

Dhenu, us, f. a milch cow, a cow that has lately calved, (sometimes compounded with the names of other animals to denote the female of a species, see *khaḍga-dh°, go-dh°, vaḍava-dh°*); the earth [cf. *go*]; a gift, offering, present to Brāhmans, (properly a milch cow so presented, but applied also to) any gift supposed to be formed in the shape of a cow or to be offered in its stead, (in this sense *dhenu* is generally at the end of a compound, e. g. *ghṛita-dh°,* an offering of ghee; *jala-dh°,* an oblation of water; cf. *lavaṇa-dh°, ratna-dh°, suvarṇa-dh°:* occasionally it is uncompounded, e. g. *tilānām dhenuḥ,* an offering of sesamum-seeds); (*avas*), f. pl. any beverage made of milk; (*u*), n., N. of a Sāman. (*Dhenu* at the end of a comp. may form a diminutive, the female being weaker than the male; cf. *asi-dh°, khaḍga-dh°, patrī, putrikā.*) — *Dhenu-go-duha, am,* n. cow and milker. — *Dhenu-dugdha, am,* n. cow's milk; a kind of gourd, = *ćirbhiṭa.* — *Dhenudugdha-kara, as,* m. carrot, Daucus Carota. — *Dhenu-makshikā,* f. a horse-fly, gad-fly. — *Dhenu-mat, ān, atī, at,* Ved. possessing cows, rich in cattle; containing or giving nourishing beverage; containing the word *dhenu;* (*atī*), f., N. of the wife of Deva-dyumna. — *Dhenum-bhavyā,* f. (probably) about to become a milch cow.

Dhenuka, as, m., N. of an Asura or demon in the shape of a donkey (killed by Kṛishṇa or according to other authorities by Rāma); a kind of coitus [cf. *dhainuka*]; (*ā*), f. a milch cow; a gift, offering, see *dhenu* above; a female animal in general (as a she-elephant, a woman, &c., see *dhenu* above); also used like *dhenu* at the end of comps. to form diminutives (e. g. *asi-dh°,* a knife, from *asi,* a sword); a vein which when cut bleeds only at intervals; N. of the wife of Kīrtti-mat who was a son of Aṅgiras; (*am*), n., N. of a place of pilgrimage. — *Dhenuka-vadha, as,* m. 'the killing of Dhenuka,' N. of the twenty-third chapter of the Kṛishṇa-khaṇḍa or fourth part of the Brahma-vaivarta-Purāṇa. — *Dhenuka-sūdana, as,* m. 'the slayer of Dhenuka,' an epithet of Kṛishṇa. — *Dhenukā-dugdha, am,* n. cow's milk; N. of a plant, = *dhenu-dugdha.* — *Dhenukāri* (°*ka-ari*), *is,* m. 'enemy of Dhenuka,' an epithet of Kṛishṇa; a kind of small tree, = Nagesar.

Dhenushṭarī, f. (fr. *dhenus,* nom. case of *dhenu,* with the comparative affix), a milch cow ceasing to give milk.

Dhenushyā, f. a cow whose milk has been pledged; a cow tied up to be milked (?).

Dhenushyita, as, ā, am, (probably) one who has pledged the milk of his cows and therefore cannot make use of it himself.

Dhenāka in *bahu-dh°,* q. v.

Dhainuka, am, n. a herd of cows; a kind of coitus.

धेमात्र *dhemātra,* a particular high number; (a various reading for *dhamātra.*)

धेय *dheya, as, ā, am* (fr. rt. 1. *dhā*), to be held or taken &c.; to be created; what is created or produced; (at the end of comps. the neut. is considered as an affix, Pāṇ. V. 4, 36, vārt.; cf. *nāma-dheya, bhāga-dh°, mitra-dh°, rūpa-dh°.*)

Dheshṭha, as, ā, am, Ved. giving the most; (Sāy.) the best supporter, firmest stay.

धैर्य 1. *dhairya, am,* n. (fr. *dhīra*), firmness, durability, steadiness, stability, strength, consistency, constancy; calmness; gravity; patience; fortitude, courage; inflexibility; precision of diction; (Ved.) intelligence, forethought. — *Dhairya-kalita, as, ā, am,* assuming firmness or composure, endowed with calmness. — *Dhairya-dhvaṇsa, as,* m. failure of courage. — *Dhairya-mitra, as,* m., N. of a poet. — *Dhairya-vat, ān, atī, at,* possessed of firmness or patience, firm, steady. — *Dhairya-vṛitti, is, is, i,* of steady conduct, steadily behaved.

धैवत *dhaivata, as,* m. the sixth note of the gamut.

धैवत्य *dhaivatya, am,* n. (fr. *dhīvan,* Pāṇ. VI. 4, 174), cleverness, skilfulness (?).

धैवर *dhaivara, as, ī, am* (fr. *dhīvara*), belonging or relating to a fisherman.

धोईकवि *dhoī-kavi, is,* m., N. of a poet mentioned in the Śārṅgadhara-paddhati; [cf. *dhoyin.*]

धोड *dhoḍa, as,* m. a sort of snake, commonly Dhora, a kind of water-snake.

धोयिन् *dhoyin, ī,* m. or *dhoyī, is,* m., N. of a poet.

धोर् *dhor,* cl. 1. P. *dhorati, dudhora, dhoritum,* to run well, to trot, to be quick or alert, to have good paces: Caus. *dhorayati, -yitum,* Aor. *adudhorat.*

Dhoraṇa, am, n. a vehicle in general, any means of conveyance (as a horse, an elephant, a car, &c.); a horse's trot; going well or quickly; (*ī*), f. or (*dhoraṇi, is*), f. an uninterrupted series; tradition.

Dhorita or *dhoritaka, am,* n. a horse's trot; [cf. *dhauritaka.*]

धौत *dhauta, as, ā, am* (fr. rt. 2. *dhāv*), washed, cleansed, cleaned, purified, washed off; polished, brightened, whetted; white, bright, silvered, shining; (*am*), n. silver. — *Dhauta-kaṭa, as,* m. a bag of coarse cloth, a sack made of a kind of matting. — *Dhauta-koshaja* or *dhauta-kausheya* or *dhauta-kauśeya, am,* n. bleached or purified silk (= *pattrorṇa*). — *Dhauta-khaṇḍī,* f. sugar-candy. — *Dhauta-balī,* f. = *dhautāñjalī,* (probably rather *dhautāñjanī,* q. v.) — *Dhauta-mūlaka, as,* m., N. of a prince of the Cīnas. — *Dhauta-śila, am,* n. 'bright stone,' crystal, rock-crystal. — *Dhautāñjanī,* f. a sort of collyrium, = *tryaṅkaṭa* or *tryaṅgaṭa.* — *Dhautāpāṅga, as, ā, am,* having the corners of the eyes brightened.

धौतय *dhautaya, as* or *am,* m. or n. (?), a kind of salt (= *saindhava*).

धौतरी *dhautarī,* f. (fr. rt. 1. *dhū*), Ved. (according to Sāy.) shaking, agitating, causing to tremble.

धौति *dhauti, is,* f. (fr. rt. 1. *dhāv*), Ved. a spring, well; river, rivulet.

धौन्धुमार *dhaundhumāra, as, ī, am,* treating of Dhundhu-māra (as an episode).

Dhaundhumāri, is, m. a patronymic from Dhundhu-māra.

धौमक *dhaumaka, as,* m. (fr. *dhūma*), N. of a district.

Dhaumata, myrrh.

Dhaumatāyana, as, m. a patronymic (?).

Dhaumatāyanaka, as, m. a patronymic from Dhaumatāyana.

Dhaumāyana, as, m. a patronymic from Dhūma.

Dhaumīya, as, ī, am, smoky.

Dhaumya, as, m. a patronymic from Dhūma; N. of an ancient Ṛishi; a son of Vyāghra-pāda; a younger brother of Devala and family priest of the Pāṇḍavas; a pupil of Vālmīki. — *Dhaumya-śikshā,* f. 'the science of Dhaumya,' N. of a chapter of the Purāṇa-sarva-sva.

Dhaumra, as, m., N. of an ancient Ṛishi; N. of a class of demons; (*am*), n. grey (the colour), greyness; a place for building prepared in a peculiar way; [cf. *dhūma.*]

Dhaumrāyaṇa, as, m. a patronymic from Dhūmra; [cf. *dhūmrāyaṇa.*]

धौर *dhaura, as,* m. Grislea Tomentosa. — *Dhaurāditya-tīrtha* (°*ra-ād*°), *am,* n., N. of a Tīrtha.

धौरितक *dhauritaka, am,* n. a horse's trot; [cf. *dhorita* and *dhoritaka.*]

धौरेय *dhaureya* or *dhaureyaka, as, ī, am* (fr. *dhur*), fit to be harnessed, fit for a burden, capable of drawing or bearing a load (either a vehicle or beast, &c.); (*as*), m. a beast of burden: a horse.

धौर्तक *dhaurtaka, am,* n. (fr. *dhūrta*), roguery, knavery, fraud.

Dhaurtika, as, ī, am, cheating, dishonest, roguish, knavish, fraudulent, &c.; (*am*), n. fraud, dishonesty.

Dhaurteya, ās, m. pl., N. of a warlike tribe; (*as*), m. a prince of this tribe.

Dhaurtya, am, n. fraud, dishonesty.

धौर्य *dhaurya, am,* n. a horse's trot, = *dhorita,* &c.

धौवकि *dhauvaki, is,* m. (fr. *dhuvakā*), a metronymic from Dhuvakā.

ध्मा 1. *dhmā,* cl. 1. P. *dhamati, dadhmau, dhmāsyati* (ep. *dhamishyati*), *adhmāsīt, dhmātum,* to blow (as wind or breath), breathe out, exhale; to blow (a conch-shell, trumpet, or any wind instrument), to produce sound by blowing; to blow a fire, excite fire by blowing; to excite sparks; to manufacture by blowing, melt, smelt; to blow away from one's self, cast, throw: Pass. *dhmāyate,* ep. and Ved. *dhamyate, dhmāyati,* to be blown, to be melted, &c.: Caus. *dhmāpayati,* &c., to cause to blow or melt, to consume by fire, burn: Desid. *didhmāsati:* Intens. *dedhmīyate, dādhmāti* (*dādhmāyate*), to be blown violently; [cf. Lat. *flāre;* Old Germ. *blayan, blāhan, blāsan,* 'blow;' Gr. σμώ-νη, σμώ-ς?].

Dhma, as, ā, am, blowing; [cf. *tāṇava-dh°* and *śaṅkha-dh°.*]

2. *dhmā, ās,* m. (?), blowing. — *Dhmā-kāra, as,* m. a blacksmith, a smith.

Dhmāta, as, ā, am, blown (as a wind instrument), blown into, blown up, inflated, blown by a bellows (a fire &c.), inflamed, puffed, excited.

Dhmātavya, as, ā, am, to be blown, to be excited or kindled.

Dhmātṛi, tā, m., Ved. a blower, smelter (of metal); (*tṛi*), n. a contrivance for blowing or melting.

Dhmāna, am, n. blowing, puffing, swelling.

Dhmāpita, as, ā, am (fr. the Caus.), reduced to ashes, burnt to cinder.

Dhmāyat, an, antī, at, or *dhmāyamāna, as, ā, am,* being blown; being melted, &c.

ध्माङ्क्ष् *dhmāṅksh* (various reading for *dhvāṅksh*), cl. 1. P. *dhmāṅkshati,* &c., to crow or caw; to desire; [cf. *dhrāksh.*]

Dhmānksha, as, m. a crow, &c.; (wrong form for *dhvānksha,* q. v.)

ध्मामन् *dhmāman, ā,* m. wrong reading for *dhyāman,* col. 2.

ध्या *dhyā, dhyāta, dhyāna.* See under rt. *dhyai* below.

ध्याम *dhyāma, as, ā, am,* dark-coloured, black; *(am),* n. a fragrant grass in general or a particular kind of it; the plant Artemisia Indica (= *damanaka*). — *Dhyāmī-karaṇa, am,* n. making dark-coloured, blackening. — *Dhyāmī-kṛita, as, ā, am,* made dark-coloured, blackened.

Dhyāmaka, am, n. a particular kind of grass (= *rohisha*).

ध्युषिताश्व *dhyushitāśva, as,* m., N. of a prince; (a various reading for *vyushitāśva.*)

ध्यै *dhyai* [cf. the older form 1. *dhī*], cl. 1. P. (ep. also A.) *dhyāyati* (ep. also *dhyāti,* 2nd sing. Impv. *dhyāhi*), Pot. *dhyāyet, dadhyau, dhyātā, dhyāsyati, adhyāsīt, dhyātum,* to think of, have in mind, imagine, contemplate, ponder, meditate, think on, meditate on, reflect upon (with or without *manasā* or *manasi* or *ćetasā* or *dhiyā*), to call to mind, recollect: Caus. *dhyāpayati, -yitum:* Desid. *didhyāsati:* Intens. *dādhyāyate, dādhyāti, dādhyeti;* [cf. Gr. θέα, θεά-ο-μαι, related to *dhyai,* as Lat. *vid-ere* to Sanskrit *vid,* 'to know;' or as Zend *budh,* 'to see,' to Sanskrit *budh,* 'to know.']

Dhyā, ās, f. thinking, thought, meditation.

Dhyāta, as, ā, am, thought of, meditated on.

Dhyātavya, as, ā, am, to be thought of or reflected upon.

Dhyātṛi, tā, trī, tṛi, one who reflects upon or meditates; a thinker, reflector.

Dhyātra, am, n. thought, reflection.

Dhyātvā, ind. having thought of or reflected, having pondered or recollected, &c.

Dhyāna, am, n. meditation, thought, reflection, especially profound and abstract religious contemplation; divine intuition or discernment; mental representation of the personal attributes of a deity; *(as),* m., N. of the eleventh day in the light half in Brahmā's month. — *Dhyāna-gamya, as, ā, am,* attainable by meditation or reflection. — *Dhyāna-goćara, as,* m., N. of a class of Buddhist deities; [cf. *dhyānāvaćara.*] — *Dhyāna-japya, ās,* m. pl., N. of a race. — *Dhyāna-tatpara, as, ā, am,* lost in thought, absorbed in meditation, reflecting, meditative. — *Dhyāna-dīpa, as,* m. 'the lamp of meditation,' N. of a work. — *Dhyāna-dyuti, is,* m., N. of a man. — *Dhyāna-nishṭha, as, ā, am,* engaged in meditation, contemplative, lost in thought. — *Dhyāna-para, as, ā, am,* = *dhyāna-tatpara.* — *Dhyāna-pāramitā,* f., see *pāramitā.* — *Dhyāna-phala, am,* n. 'the fruit of meditation,' N. of a chapter of the Purāṇa-sarva-sva by Halāyudha. — *Dhyāna-bhanga, as,* m. interruption of thought or meditation. — *Dhyāna-maya, as, ī, am,* consisting of reflection or meditation. — *Dhyāna-mātra, am,* n. mere reflection, thought alone. — *Dhyāna-mudrā,* f. the prescribed attitude in which to meditate on the deity. — *Dhyāna-yoga, as,* m. profound meditation, the performance of religious abstraction, (also explained as a Dvandva, meditation and abstraction); N. of a kind of magic mentioned in the Yoga-ratna-mālā, 'destroying one's enemies by images formed in the mind.' — *Dhyāna-lakshaṇa, am,* n. 'the mark of meditation,' N. of a chapter of the Purāṇa-sarva-sva. — *Dhyāna-vat, ān, atī, at,* occupied in or intent on religious meditation. — *Dhyāna-vindūpanishad* (°*du-up*°), *t,* f., N. of an Upanishad belonging to the Atharva-veda. — *Dhyāna-stha, as, ā, am,* absorbed in meditation; lost in thought. — *Dhyānāvaćara* (°*na-av*°), *ās,* m. pl., N. of a class of Buddhist deities; [cf. *dhyāna-goćara.*]

Dhyānika, as, ā, am, proceeding from religious meditation, sought or obtained by pious contemplation.

Dhyānin, ī, inī, i, contemplative, engaged in religious meditation, meditating.

Dhyāni-buddha, as, m. (probably fr. *dhyāni,* patronymic fr. *dhyāna;* cf. *mānushi-buddha*), a spiritual or mental Buddha, an incorporeal Buddha resulting from meditation, (their number is given as five or six or ten or more.)

Dhyāni-bodhi-sattva, as, m. (with Buddhists) an incorporeal son of a Dhyāni-buddha.

Dhyānīya, as, ā, am (according to Vopa-deva 26. 25, fut. pass. part.), to be meditated upon.

Dhyāman, ā, m. measure; light; *(a),* n. meditation.

Dhyāyat, an, antī, at, thinking of, considering, reflecting, meditating upon; supposing, imagining.

Dhyāyamāna, as, ā, am, being reflected on, being meditated upon.

Dhyeya, as, ā, am, to be meditated upon, to be pondered or contemplated; fit for meditation; to be imagined.

ध्र *dhra, as, ī, am* (fr. rt. *dhṛi*), = *dhara* (at the end of some comps., e. g. *aṇsa-dhrī, mahīdhra,* q. v.).

ध्रज *dhraj* or *dhrañj,* cl. 1. P. *dhrajati* or *dhrañjati* or *dhriñjati,* &c., Ved. to move, go, glide (as a bird &c.); [cf. rt. *dhṛij, dhrij, dhvaj, dhvañj.*]

Dhrajas, as, n. (?), Ved. = *dhraji* below.

Dhraji, is, f., Ved. the gliding course or motion of the wind, &c. — *Dhraji-mat, ān, atī, at,* Ved. gliding, moving.

Dhrāji, is, f., Ved. the gliding course of the wind, &c.; impulse; whirlwind, gale.

ध्रण *dhraṇ,* cl. 1. P. *dhraṇati,* &c., to sound (as a drum or other instrument); [cf. rt. *dhaṇ,* 2. *dhvan,* 3. *dhārā;* Gr. θρέ-ο-μαι, θρό-ο-ς, θρῆ-νο-ς, θρῦ-λο-ς, θρύλλος, θόρυ-βο-ς, τεν-θρη-δών, ἀν-θρη-δών, τον-θρύ-ς, τον-θορύζω; Goth. *drun-yu-s,* 'voice;' Angl. Sax. *dran,* 'a drone;' Mod. Germ. *drönen.*]

ध्रस *dhras,* cl. 9. and 10. P. *dhrasnāti, dhrāsayati, -yitum,* to glean; to throw or toss up, cast upward; [cf. *uddhras.*]

ध्रा *dhrā,* cl. 2. and 1. P. *dhrāti* or *dhrati, dhrayati,* &c., Ved. to go, (Naigh. II. 14.)

ध्राख *dhrākh,* cl. 1. P. *dhrākhati,* &c., to be dry or arid, &c., = rt. *drākh.*

ध्राघ *dhrāgh,* cl. 1. A. *dhrāghate,* &c., to be able or competent, &c., = rt. *drāgh.*

ध्राङ्क्ष *dhrānksh* [cf. rt. *dhmānksh, dhvānksh, drānksh*], cl. 1. P. *dhrānkshati,* &c., to utter the sound of birds, to crow, caw, &c.; to desire.

ध्राड *dhrāḍ,* cl. 1. A. *dhrāḍate,* &c., to divide, split, &c., = rt. *drāḍ.*

Dhrāḍi, is, m. gathering or plucking flowers.

ध्रि *dhri* (fr. rt. *dhṛi*) in *a-dhri,* q. v.

Dhriyamāṇa, as, ā, am, being held or sustained; being withheld or checked or suppressed, &c.

ध्रिज *dhrij,* cl. 1. P. *dhrejati,* &c., to go or move, &c., = rt. *dhraj.*

Dhrija in *a-dhrija, as, ā, am,* unrestrainable.

ध्रु 1. *dhru* (connected with rt. *dhṛi*), cl. 1. 6. P. *dhravati, dhruvati, dudhrāva,* &c., to be firm or fixed, to stand firm; to go, move; to ascertain, know with certainty; to kill: Caus. *dhrāvayati:* Desid. *dudhrūshati, dudhruvishati:* Intens. *dodhrūyate;* [cf. Lith. *drūtas,* 'firm;' Goth. *trauа,* 'I trust,' = Caus.]

Dhruti, is, f., Ved. (Sāy.) fixed destiny, settled course of fate; (according to modern scholars) misleading, leading astray, corrupting, seduction, (fr. rt. *dhvṛi.*)

Dhruva, as, ā, am, fixed, firm, remaining fixed in one place, firmly fixed, fast, immovable, stable, enduring, constant, lasting, permanent, continual, perpetual, eternal, invariable, unchangeable, inevitable; certain, sure, well-ascertained; firm, strong, fixed, settled (as a day); fixed (in astrology, as a *karaṇa,* q. v.; the fixed Karaṇas are four, viz. Śakuni, Nāga, Ćatushpada, and Kiṇstughna or Kintu-ghna (?): the seven A-dhruvāṇi are given under *karaṇa:* some of the Nakshatras are also called Dhruvāṇi, see *nakshatra*); fixed (in anatomy, as certain members or organs of the body which cannot be severed without causing death, those which are separable being called *a-dhruva,* q. v.); tenacious, retentive (e. g. *dhruvā smṛitiḥ,* a retentive memory); *(as),* m. the polar star or the north pole itself (personified in mythology as son of Uttāna-pāda and grandson of the first Manu); the pole of any great circle (especially either of the celestial poles); polar longitude, the distance of a planet from the beginning of the sidereal zodiac; a constant arc; N. of one of the twenty-seven astronomical Yogas or the Yoga star of the twelfth lunar asterism (supposed to = β Leonis?); a knot (?); the trunk of a lopped tree or pollard, a post, stake; the Indian fig-tree; the tip or point of the nose (?); a sort of bird, = *śarāri,* (perhaps incorrectly for *smarāri,* meaning Śiva); the introductory stanza of a poem or song ('the constantly recurring verse,' which is repeated as a kind of burden or chorus); time, epoch, era, any fixed period from which dates are computed; an epithet of Brahmā; of Vishṇu [cf. *dhruvākshara*]; of Śiva; N. of one of the serpents supporting the earth; N. of one of the Vasus; of a son of Vasu-deva and Rohiṇī; of an Āngirasa, supposed to be the author of a Ṛig-veda hymn (Ṛig-veda X. 173); of a son of Nahusha; of a hero on the side of the Pāṇḍus; of a son of Ranti-nāra (or Ranti-bhāra); *(ā),* f. the largest of the three sacrificial ladles (made in the shape of the Indian fig-leaf and of the wood of the Flacourtia Sapida?); the plant Desmodium Gangeticum; the plant Sanseviera Zeylanica, a small tree from the fibres of which bow-strings are made (= *mūrvā*); a virtuous woman; a cow which stands quiet when milked; scil. *diś,* the point of the heavens directly under the feet, the point of the lower hemisphere directly opposite to the zenith; *(am),* n. 'the enduring sound,' a sound heard or supposed to be heard after the Abhinidhāna, probably the mere prolongation of the preceding sound; heaven, sky, atmosphere; *(am),* ind. certainly, surely, assuredly; eternally; *(āya),* ind. for ever. (According to grammarians, *dhruva* at the end of a comp. may give a bad sense to the word with which it is compounded, Pāṇ. II. 1, 53); [cf. Hib. *dearbh,* 'sure, true;' Goth. *triggvs;* Angl. Sax. *treowe, for-truwyan;* Old Germ. *triu, triuwi, ga-triu, ga-triuwi, ga-triwi,* = Mod. Germ. *treu, treue, ge-treu,* = Eng. *true, trusty.*] — *Dhruva-ketu, us,* m. a kind of meteor. — *Dhruva-kshit, t, t, t,* Ved. resting firmly, abiding fixedly; abiding in the fixed (sacrifice). — *Dhruva-kshiti, is, is, i,* Ved. having a firm position or abode. — *Dhruva-kshema, as, ā, am,* Ved. abiding in fixed habitations, having enduring mansions; firmly fixed. — *Dhruva-gati, is,* f. a firm position; *(is, is, i),* going firmly. — *Dhruva-ćarita, am,* n., N. of the twelfth and thirteenth chapters of the Svarga-khaṇḍa or third part of the Padma-Purāṇa; N. of the sixty-second chapter of the Linga-Purāṇa; of a chapter of the Purāṇa-sarva-sva. — *Dhruva-ćyut, t, t, t,* Ved. causing to fall or shaking the immovable (mountains). — *Dhruva-tārā,* f. or *dhruva-tāraka, am,* n. the polar star. — *Dhruva-paṭu, us,* m., N. of a king of Vallabhī or Ballabhī; [cf. *dhruva-sena.*] — *Dhruva-yoni, is, is, i,* Ved. having a firm resting-place. — *Dhruva-ratnā,* f., N. of one of the Mātṛis attending on Skanda. — *Dhruva-lakshaṇa, am,* n. 'the mark of recurring stanzas,' N. of a chapter of the Purāṇa-sarva-sva. — *Dhruva-sad, t, t, t,* Ved. resting on firm ground, abiding in a firm place. — *Dhruva-sandhi, is,* m., N. of a prince, son of Su-sandhi or Su-shandhi and father of Bharata. — *Dhruva-siddhi, is,* m. 'through whom convalescence is sure,' N. of a physician at the court of Agni-mitra. — *Dhruva-sena, as,* m., N. of two Ballabhī princes; [cf. *dhruva-paṭu.*] — *Dhruvākshara* (°*va-aksh*°), *as,* m. 'fixed and eternal,' epithet of Vishṇu. — *Dhruvāvarta* (°*va-āv*°), *as,* m. the point on the crown of the head from which the hairs radiate. — *Dhruvāśva* (°*va-aś*°), *as,* m., N. of a prince.

Dhruvaka, as, m. polar longitude; the trunk of a lopped tree; a post, pale, stake; the introductory or recurring stanza of a song, see *dhruva;* N. of one of the attendants of Skanda; (*ā*), f. the introductory stanza and burden of a song [cf. *dhuvakā*]; N. of a woman.

Dhruvase (an infinitive form from *dhruvas* which may be derived from *dhruva*), Ved. in order to rest; (Sāy.) for a firm seat.

Dhruvi, is, is, i, Ved. firmly fixed, firm.

Dhrauva, as, ī, am, belonging to Dhruva or the polar star; being in the ladle called Dhruvā.

Dhrauvya, am, n. fixedness, firmness, immovableness, uninterrupted rest; duration; certainty, necessity; (*as,* &c.), conferring duration or fixedness.

ध्रु 2. *dhru* (said to be fr. rt. *dhvṛi*) in *a-smṛita-dhru,* not disappointing desire; (Sāy.) not remembering injury.

Dhrut in *varuṇa-dhrut,* q. v.

ध्रुव् *dhruv,* cl. 6. P. *dhruvati,* &c., to stand firm; to go, move; (various reading for rt. 1. *dhru.*)

ध्रू *dhrū,* cl. 6. P. *dhruvati,* &c., = rt. 1. *dhru* and *dhruv.*

ध्रेक् *dhrek,* cl. 1. A. *dhrekate,* &c., to sound; to grow or increase; to be exhilarated or elevated with joy; to manifest elevation or hilarity by noise; [cf. *drek.*]

ध्रै *dhrai,* cl. 1. P. *dhrāyati,* &c., to be satisfied or pleased; [cf. probably Gr. τρέφ-ω = Caus. *dhrāpayāmi,* θρέψις, τρόφις, ταρφύς.]

ध्वंस् *dhvaṇs* (sometimes written *dhvas*), cl. 1. A. *dhvaṇsate* (ep. also *-ti*), *dadhvaṇse, dhvaṇsishyate, adhvaṇsishṭa, adhvasat, dhvaṇsitum,* to fall down, fall to pieces, fall to dust, be reduced to powder, decay, to be ruined; perish; to become eclipsed; to scatter or sprinkle over, cover with; to be covered or sprinkled with dust; (the imperative *dhvaṇsa, dhvaṇsata,* = 'be gone,' 'away with you,' 'vanish'): Pass. *dhvasyate,* to be destroyed, perish, &c.: Caus. *dhvaṇsayati,* to cause to fall, fell, throw down, cause to perish, destroy; to interrupt; *dhvasayati,* &c., Ved. to scatter, disperse (darkness &c.): Desid. *didhvaṇsishate:* Intens. *danīdhvasyate* and *danīdhvaṇsti, danīdhvaṇsiti;* [cf. Goth. *drus,* 'to fall;' *drausya* = 'I fall,' = Caus. *dhvaṇsayāmi:* Old Germ. *troryu,* 'I gush.']

Dhvaṇsa, as, m. falling down, perishing, destruction, demolition; vanishing, ceasing to exist, loss, ruin; (*ī*), f. a mote in a sun-beam.

Dhvaṇsaka, as, ā, am (at the end of a comp.), destroying, causing to fall or perish, removing.

Dhvaṇsana, as, ā, am, causing to fall, destroying, demolishing, ruining; scattering, dispersing; sprinkling; (*am*), n. perishing, dying; loss, destruction, ruin; falling; going.

Dhvaṇsanīya, as, ā, am, liable to destruction, capable of being ruined.

Dhvaṇsayitvā, ind. having destroyed; having interrupted.

Dhvaṇsi, is, m. $\frac{1}{100}$ part of a Muhūrta.

Dhvaṇsita, as, ā, am, caused to fall, destroyed, demolished, ruined, lost.

Dhvaṇsin, ī, inī, i, falling, perishing, being destroyed, decaying; causing to fall, destroying, destructive; (*ī*), m. a Pīlu tree (said to grow in mountainous districts).

ध्वज् 1. *dhvaj* or *dhvañj,* cl. 1. P. *dhvajati, dhvañjati,* &c., to go, move; [cf. perhaps Lat. *vagus, vagari.*]

2. *dhvaj* = *dhvaja* in *kṛita-dh*°, Ṛig-veda VII. 83. 2.

Dhvaja, as, rarely *am,* n. (connected with rt. 1. *dhvaj* and perhaps with rt. 1. *dhū*), a banner, standard, flag-staff, flag, ensign, pennon; (metaphorically) a distinguished or eminent personage (e. g. *kula-dhvaja,* the head or ornament of a family); a mark, emblem, sign, symbol, characteristic mark [cf. *kajjala-dh*°, *dharma-dh*°, *dhūma-dh*°, *dhūli-dh*°, *vṛishabha-dh*°, &c.]; the attribute of a deity; the sign of any trade; the sign of a distillery or of a tavern [cf. *surā-dh*°]; the business there carried on; the penis &c., the organ of generation (of any animal, male or female); a skull carried on a staff as a mark of ascetics and Yogis; a house situated to the east of any object; a place prepared in a peculiar way for building; (in prosody) an iambic; (in Vedic grammar) N. of a peculiar kind of Krama-pāṭha; (in astronomy) N. of a Yoga; N. of a Grāma situated towards the north; (*as*), m. one who prepares or sells spirituous liquors; (according to some) pride, hypocrisy. — *Dhvaja-gṛiha, am,* n. a room in which banners are kept or from which flags wave. — *Dhvaja-grīva, as,* m. 'having a neck erect as a banner,' N. of a Rakshas. — *Dhvaja-druma, as,* m. the palm tree (used for making flag-staffs, = *tāla*). — *Dhvaja-navamī,* f., N. of a particular festival. — *Dhvaja-paṭa, as,* m. 'banner-cloth,' the cloth of the flag, a flag. — *Dhvaja-praharaṇa, as,* m. 'striking banners or flags,' air, wind, gale. — *Dhvaja-bhaṅga* or *dhvaja-pāta, as,* m. 'fall or impotence of the male organ,' inability to procreate children; fracture or fall of a banner. — *Dhvaja-yantra, am,* n. 'banner-instrument,' any contrivance to which a flag-staff is fastened. — *Dhvaja-yashṭi, is,* f. a flag-staff. — *Dhvaja-rājin, ī, inī, i,* displaying flags or ensigns. — *Dhvaja-vat, ān, atī, at,* decorated or adorned with flags; having a mark or sign, bearing the mark of a criminal, branded; (*ān*), m. an ensign, a standard-bearer; a distiller, a vendor of spirituous liquors; a Brāhman who having slain another carries the skull of the murdered man with him to places of pilgrimage by way of penance; (*atī*), f., N. of a divine female; N. of a divine attendant of a Bodhi-sattva. — *Dhvaja-stambha, as,* m. a flag-staff. — *Dhvajāṇśuka* (°*ja-aṇ*°), *am,* n. 'banner-cloth,' a flag. — *Dhvajāgra-keyūra* (°*ja-ag*°), *am,* n. 'the ring on the top of a standard,' N. of a kind of abstract contemplation (among Buddhists). — *Dhvajāgra-niśā-maṇi* (°*ja-ag*°), *is,* m. 'the moon (night-jewel) of the standard-top,' N. for a peculiar method of numeration. — *Dhvajāgra-vatī* (°*ja-ag*°), f. 'furnished with a standard-top,' N. for a mode of reckoning. — *Dhvajāroha,* probably a wrong reading for *gajāroha,* q. v. — *Dhvajāhṛita* (°*ja-āh*°), *as, ā, am,* robbed or taken possession of at the standard, i. e. on the battle-field. — *Dhvajī-karaṇa, am,* n. raising a standard, hoisting a flag; making anything a plea, setting up as a claim or right. — *Dhvajī-kṛi,* cl. 8. P. A. *-karoti, -kurute, -kartum,* to set up a standard, hoist a flag; to use as a mark, sign, or pretext. — *Dhvajī-kṛitya,* ind. having raised a standard; having made a plea or pretext. — *Dhvajoććhrāya* (°*ja-uć*°), *as,* m. erecting a banner; erection of the male organ. — *Dhvajotthāna* (°*ja-ut*°), *am,* n. 'erection of a flag,' a festival in honour of Indra, the twelfth day of the light half of the month Bhādra.

Dhvajika in *dharma-dhvajika,* a hypocrite who only makes a pretence of religion; [cf. *dharma-dhvaja.*]

Dhvajin, ī, inī, i, furnished with or bearing a flag, carrying a flag or standard, hoisting an ensign; (at end of comp.) having as a mark or sign; (*ī*), m. a standard-bearer; one having an emblem or sign; a distiller or vendor of spirituous liquors; a car, chariot, carriage; a mountain; a snake; a peacock; a horse; a Brāhman; (*inī*), f. 'a bannered host,' an army. — *Dhvajinī-pati, is,* m. the leader of an army.

ध्वञ्ज् *dhvañj.* See rt. 1. *dhvaj,* col. 1.

ध्वण् *dhvaṇ* (connected with rt. 2. *dhvan*), cl. 1. P. *dhvaṇati,* &c., to sound.

ध्वन् 1. *dhvan* (related to rt. *dhvaṇs*), Ved. to become covered or shut up, cover one's self, &c.: Caus. *dhvanayati, -yitum,* to envelope, wrap up.

1. *dhvānta, as, ā, am* (for 2. see under 2. *dhvan* below), covered, enveloped, dark; (*am*), n. darkness, night. — *Dhvānta-ćitta, as,* m. 'perceived in the dark(?),' a fire-fly; (also read *dhvānta-vitta.*) — *Dhvānta-jāla, am,* n. 'the net of darkness or the cover of night,' a veil(?). — *Dhvānta-śātrava, as,* m. 'enemy of darkness,' N. of the tree Cassia Fistula; the sun or any luminary. — *Dhvāntārāti* (°*ta-ar*°), *is,* m. 'enemy of darkness,' the sun or any luminary. — *Dhvāntonmesha* (°*ta-un*°), *as,* m. 'flashing or twinkling in the darkness,' a fire-fly.

ध्वन् 2. *dhvan* (connected with rts. *dhvaṇ* and *dhran*), cl. 1. P. *dhvanati, dadhvāna, dhvanitum,* to sound, produce a sound, utter sounds, buzz, roar, echo, reverberate: Caus. P. *dhvanayati* and *dhvānayati,* &c., to sound, cause to sound; [cf. Goth. *drun-yu-s,* 'sound;' Angl. Sax. *dyn-an, dyne.*]

Dhvana, as, m., N. of a wind; sound, tone; N. of a man. — *Dhvana-modin, ī,* m. 'delighting by its sound,' the humble-bee.

Dhvanat, an, antī, at, sounding, making a noise.

Dhvanana, am, n. sounding; hinting at.

Dhvanayat, an, antī, at, causing to sound or resound, resounding, echoing with; (*an*), m., N. of a wind.

Dhvani, is, m. sound, echo, noise; tone, tune; thunder; the sound of a drum; an inarticulate sound, a mere empty sound without reality; a word; allusion, hint, figurative allusion, implied meaning, poetical style; N. of a work. — *Dhvani-kāra, as,* or *dhvani-kṛit, t,* m. the author of the work called Dhvani. — *Dhvani-graha, as,* m. 'apprehending sounds,' the ear; hearing. — *Dhvani-tva, am,* n. figurative allusion, poetical style. — *Dhvani-nātha, as,* m., N. of a man. — *Dhvani-nālā,* f., N. of several musical instruments, = *kāhalā,* a sort of trumpet; the Vīṇā or lute; a pipe, fife. — *Dhvani-bodhaka* or *dhvani-bodhana, as* or *am,* m. or n.(?), N. of the grass Rohisha. — *Dhvani-vikāra, as,* m. a change of voice (caused by fright or grief, &c.). — *Dhvany-artha, as,* m. the meaning or truth implied.

Dhvanita, as, ā, am, sounded, making a noise (as a drum); alluded to, implied, figuratively or rhetorically expressed; (*am*), n. sound, thunder.

Dhvanya, as, m., Ved., N. of a man.

Dhvāna, as, m. humming, murmuring, one of the seven kinds of speech or *vāćaḥ sthānāni,* (a degree louder than *upāṇśu,* q. v.); sound or tone in general.

Dhvānita, as, ā, am, caused to sound, made resonant.

2. *dhvānta, as,* m., Ved., N. of a wind. (For 1. *dhvānta* see under 1. *dhvan* above.)

ध्वस् *dhvas.* See rt. *dhvaṇs,* col. 1.

Dhvas, dhvat (fr. rt. *dhvaṇs*), (at the end of certain comps.) causing to fall, throwing down.

Dhvasan, ā, m., Ved., N. of a king of the Matsyas.

Dhvasani, is, m., Ved. the sprinkler; sprinkling, scattering (as a cloud).

Dhvasanti, is, m., N. of a man.

Dhvasira, as, ā, am, Ved. sprinkled, spattered, covered; (Sāy.) destroyed; [cf. *dhūsara.*]

Dhvasta, as, ā, am, fallen; destroyed, perished, hurt, lost; covered, eclipsed, disappeared. — *Dhvastāksha* (°*ta-aksha*), *as, ī, am,* having the eyes sunk (as in death).

Dhvasti, is, f. ceasing, destruction, cessation (of all the consequences of actions), one of the four states to which the Yogin attains.

Dhvasman, ā, m., Ved. polluting, darkening; (Sāy.) destroying, destructive; causing destruction. — *Dhvasman-vat, ān, atī, at,* Ved. covered?; (Sāy.) whose faults or imperfections are destroyed; (*at*), n. (according to Yāska) water.

Dhvasra, as, ā, am, Ved. sprinkling, spattering; scattering, liberal; (Sāy.) destructive; (*as*), m., N. of a king.

ध्वाक्षा *dhvākshā,* f., N. of a plant and its fruit.

ध्वाङ्क्ष् *dhvāṅksh* [cf. rts. *dhmāṅksh* and *dhrāṅksh*], cl. 1. P. *dhvāṅkshati,* &c., to utter the cry of birds, to caw, croak, crow, &c.; to desire.

Dhvāṅksha, as, m. a crow; (according to some) any aquatic bird, as a crane, gull, &c., feeding on fish, = Ardea Nivea; (sometimes used at the end of a comp. to express contempt, e. g. *tīrtha-dhvāṅksha,* a crow at a sacred bathing-place, i. e. a man in the wrong place); a beggar (on account of his insatiableness); an impudent fellow; N. of one of the Nāgas (= *takshaka*); a house?; (in astronomy) N. of a Yoga; (*ī*), f. a kind of plant, = *kākolī, kakkolikā, laghu-kāvalī;* [cf. Hib. *duis,* 'a crow.'] — *Dhvāṅksha-jaṅghā,* f., N. of a plant, = *kāka-jaṅghā.* — *Dhvāṅksha-jambū, ūs,* f. = *kāka-jambū.* — *Dhvāṅksha-tuṇḍa-phala,* a kind of plant the fruit of which resembles the beak of a crow, (commonly called Thora-śvetakāvalī.) — *Dhvāṅksha-tuṇḍā, ī,* f. = *dhvāṅksha-tuṇḍa-phala;* (*ī*), f. = *kāka-nāsā.* — *Dhvāṅksha-dantī* or *dhvāṅksha-nakhī,* f. = *kāka-tuṇḍī.* — *Dhvāṅksha-nāman, ā* or *a,* m. or n. (?), a dark species of Uḍumbara; (*nāmnī*), f. = *kākodumbarikā.* — *Dhvāṅksha-nāśinī,* f. = *hapushā* (?). — *Dhvāṅksha-nāsā,* f. and *dhvāṅksha-nāsikā,* f. = *kāka-nāsā.* — *Dhvāṅksha-pushṭa, as,* m. the Kokila or Indian cuckoo, = *kāka-pushṭa.* — *Dhvāṅksha-māćī,* f. = *kāka-māćī,* = *laghu-kāvalī.* — *Dhvāṅksha-rāvin, ī, iṇī, i,* cawing like a crow, having a voice like a crow. — *Dhvāṅksha-vallī,* f. = *kāka-nāsā,* = *dhvāṅksha-dantī,* = *karañja.* — *Dhvāṅkshādanī* (°*sha-ad*°), f. = *dhvāṅksha-dantī.* — *Dhvāṅkshārāti* (°*sha-ar*°), *is,* m. 'enemy of crows,' an owl.

Dhvāṅkshikā, f. = *kākolī.*

Dhvāṅksholikā or *dhvāṅksholī,* f. a medicinal plant, = *kākolī.*

ध्वान्त *dhvānta.* For 1. and 2. *dhvānta* see p. 462, col. 3.

ध्वृ *dhvṛi* (connected with rts. *hvṛi* and *dhūrv*), cl. 1. P. *dhvarati, dadhvāra, dhvarishyati, adhvārshīt* (3rd du. Aor. A. *adhvarishātām* or *adhvṛishātām*); Prec. *dhvarishishṭa* or *dhvṛishīshṭa, dhvartum,* to bend, make crooked, cause to fall, fell; to kill: Caus. *dhvārayati, -yitum:* Desid. *dudhvūrshati, dudhvarishati:* Intens. *dādhvaryate;* [cf. *a-dhvara,* 2. *dhru;* probably Angl. Sax. *thwer, thweorh, thwir, thwur, dwelian, dol, dweorg, for-dwilman;* Old Germ. *dwer-an, ga-dwor, twar-ōn, dwerh;* Goth. *dvals;* Gr. θόλο-ς, θάλ-α-μο-ς.]

Dhvaras, ās, m. f., Ved. 'destructive, hurtful, injurious,' N. of certain female demons or noxious beings.

Dhvarya, as, ā, am, to be bent, made crooked, &c.

Dhvṛit, t, t, t (at the end of a comp.), causing to fall, felling, killing.

ध्वृण *dhvraṇ,* cl. 1. P. *dhvraṇati,* &c., to sound; (a various reading for *dhraṇ.*)

न

न 1. *na,* the twentieth consonant of the alphabet, and the fifth letter of the fourth or dental class, having much the sound of the English *n* in *tenth.* — *Na-kāra, as,* m. the letter or sound *na.*

न 2. *na,* ind. a particle of negation equivalent to 'not,' 'no,' 'nor,' 'neither' [cf. *no, nanu, na-hi, na-tarām*], and in the Veda a particle of comparison; it is used as a negative particle in wishing, requesting, and commanding (e. g. *na mā garan nadyaḥ,* let not the waters swallow me; *nāvamanyeta kañćana,* let him not despise any one), but not in prohibition before an imperative, and not before the aorist when it has lost its augment and stands for an imperative (in both which cases *mā,* q. v., is used). When joined with the potential, *na* may often have the sense of 'that not,' 'lest,' 'for fear lest' (e. g. *na tvām śapet,* lest he should curse thee). In argumentative writings *na* often comes at the end of a hypothetical argument in the sense 'not so' (e. g. *nanu na kiñćin mānam iti ćen na,* now if it be said that there is no proof, not so). Two *nas* are not unfrequently used in the same sentence to intensify an affirmation (e. g. *na khalu na tat karishyāmi,* I will most certainly do that; *na tu jātu na,* most assuredly), or any other negative particle may be joined with *na* with the same effect (e. g. *nādaṇḍyo 'sti,* he is not to go unpunished, i. e. he must certainly be punished). When a negation has to be repeated in successive clauses of a sentence or in successive sentences, *na* may be simply repeated or may be strengthened by one of the particles *uta, ća, api, ćāpi, vā, athavā* (e. g. *nāham asyāraṇyasya devatā na ćāpy asya gireḥ,* I am not the deity of this forest nor of this mountain), or the negative is not expressed in the second clause but represented by *vā* or *api vā* or *ća* standing alone (e. g. *na hṛishyati glāyati vā,* he neither rejoices nor desponds), or two clauses may have the negative particle and not a third (e. g. *na deveshu na Yaksheshu mānusheshv api ćānyeshu tādṛig rūpavatī dṛishṭapūrvā,* neither among gods nor Yakshas nor other mortals has so beautiful a female been before seen). *Na* is sometimes placed before round or collective numbers to denote a deficiency, the deficient number being prefixed in the inst. or abl. case (e. g. *ekayā* or *ekena na viṅśatiḥ,* not twenty by one, i. e. nineteen; *pañćabhir na ćatvāri śatāni,* 395). When *na* is the negative of the simple idea expressed by a word, it may be regarded as compounded with it, and is then identical with 3. *a,* q. v. (e. g. *na-vidvas,* unwise; *nādhīta,* unread; *na-kiñćana,* q. v.) *Na* is often joined with other particles, e. g. *na ća, na ćāpi, nāpi, nota, na vā, naiva, na ćaiva, nāpi ća, na tu, na tveva, na tveva tu, na ćet* (see *ćed*), *na khalu, na ha* (after this last a verb is said to retain its accent if used in the future with an imperative sense, Pāṇ. VIII. 1, 31). *Na* is frequently used in early Vedic composition as a particle of comparison = 'like,' 'as,' 'as it were' (e. g. *tvā nāvaṃ na dhīmahi,* we meditate on thee like a boat; cf. 3. *a,* which also in a few instances = 'like'); it is also found in this sense in the later artificial poems; [cf. Lat. *ne, non;* Gr. νη in νη-κερδής, νη-κηδής; Lith. *ne;* Slav. *ne;* Goth. *ni, ne, nei;* Angl. Sax. *na;* Old Germ. *ni;* Hib. *ni.*]

न 3. *na, as,* m. a N. of Buddha; binding, tying, a band; one who is praised; a N. of Gaṇeśa (= *dvi-randa?*); a jewel, pearl; war; giving, a gift; welfare, prosperity; (*ā*), f. the navel; a musical instrument; knowledge; (*as, ā, am*), thin, spare; vacant, empty; identical, same, like; unvexed, unwearied; undivided, unbroken.

न 4. *na,* (in prosody) a tribrach or foot of three short syllables.

नंश् *naṅś,* the base of many forms of rt. 2. *naś,* q. v.

Naṅśa, as, m. (?), Ved. (according to Sāy.) = *nāśana,* removal, removing, destruction; (but perhaps fr. rt. 1. *naś*), acquisition.

Naṅśana, am, n. (?), destruction, in *svapna-n*°, q. v.

Naṅśuka, as, ī, am, injurious, destructive; going astray, being lost; small, minute.

Naṅshṭavya, as, ā, am, destructible, to be injured or killed.

Naṅshṭri, ṭā, ṭrī, ṭṛi, a destroyer, destructive; perishing, being lost.

नःक्षुद्र *naḥ-kshudra.* See under 3. *nas.*

नक् *nak,* ind. (probably fr. rt. 2. *naś*), Ved. night; [cf. 1. *nakta,* 2. *niś, niśā.*]

1. *nakta, am,* n., *ā,* f. (in the Veda *naktā* is regarded as f. du.), night; eating only at night as a sort of penance; a species of poisonous plant, = *kalikāru;* (*as*), m., N. of a son of Pṛithu; of Pṛithu-sheṇa and Ākūtī; (*am*), ind. by night, at night; [cf. 2. *niś, niśā;* Zend *nakhturu* or *nakhtru,* 'nocturnal;' Gr. νύξ, νύκτωρ, νύκτερο-ς, νυκτερ-ινό-ς, νύχιο-ς, νυκτερί-ς; Lat. *nox, noctu, nocturnu-s, noctua;* Goth. *nahts;* Angl. Sax. *naht, niht;* Mod. Germ. *nacht;* Eng. *night;* Slav. *noshtĭ;* Russ. *noćyi;* Lith. *nakti-s;* Hib. *noehd.*] — *Nakta-ćārin, ī, iṇī, i,* going or moving about at night; (*ī*), m. an owl; a cat; a thief; a goblin, a Rakshas; (also read *naktañ-ćārin,* which is the better form.) — *Naktañ-ćara, as, ī, am,* going or walking about at night; (*as*), m. any creature or animal that goes about at night; a nocturnal fiend, a goblin, demon, evil spirit, Rakshas; a thief; the bdellium tree, see *guggula;* (*ī*), f. a female demon. — *Naktañćareśvara* (°*ra-iś*°), *as,* m. the lord of the night-rovers or goblins. — *Naktañ-ćaryā,* f. walking or moving about at night, wandering by night. — *Naktañ-ćārin, ī, iṇī, i,* walking about at night, (opposed to *divā-ćārin, divā-ćara*); (*ī*), m. a cat; [cf. *nakta-ćārin.*] — *Naktañ-jāta, as, ā, am,* Ved. grown or produced at night. — *Naktan-dina, am,* n. night and day; (*am*), ind. by night and day. — *Naktan-divam,* ind. by night and day. — *Nakta-bhojana, am,* n. 'eating at night,' supper. — *Nakta-mukhā,* f. evening, night; (a wrong reading for *nakta-mushā.*) — *Naktam-prabhava, as, ā, am,* produced at night; (also read *nakta-prabhava.*) — *Nakta-vrata, am,* n. fasting by day and eating at night; any religious rite or obligation observed at night. — *Naktāndha* (°*ta-an*°), *as, ā, am,* blind at night. — *Naktāndhya* (°*ta-an*°), *am,* n. blindness at night. — *Naktoshāsā* (°*ta-ush*°), f. du., Ved. night and morning.

Naktan, a, n., Ved. night.

Naktam, ind. by night, at night. See under 1. *nakta* above.

Naktayā, ind., Ved. at night.

Nakti, is, f., Ved. night; [cf. Lith. *nakti-s,* 'night.']

नक *naka, as,* m., N. of a son of Dāruka; (*am*), n. in *Bharad-vājasya nakam,* N. of a Sāman.

नकिञ्चन *na-kiñćana, as, ā, am,* having nothing, very poor, beggarly; [cf. *a-kiñćana.*]

Na-kim, ind. not, not at all; [cf. *na-kīm* and *mā-kīm.*]

Na-kis, ind. (*kis* is said to be an old nom. sing. m. of *ki,* see *kim* and cf. Lat. *quis*), Ved. not, not at all, never, (a little stronger than in the simple *na*); no one, nobody; (also written *na-kir.*)

Na-kīm, ind., Ved. not, not at all, never; [cf. *na-kim* and *mā-kīm.*]

नकुच *nakuća, as,* m. a various reading for *lakuća,* q. v.

नकुट *nakuṭa, am,* n. the nose; [cf. *nar-kuṭaka.*]

नकुल *nakula, as, ā, am* (fr. *na-kula,* without a family?), rejected from a family or race (?), disgraced (?), coloured like the ichneumon?; (*as*), m. the Bengal mungoose or Viverra Ichneumon (similar to the polecat and hostile to mice and serpents, from the poison of which it protects itself by a medicinal plant, cf. *gandha-n*° and *jala-n*°); a son; N. of a Vedic poet with the patronymic Vāma-deva or Vāma-devya or Vaiśvāmitra; N. of a Sāman (*Nakulasya Vāmadevasya prenkhas*); N. of a son of Pāṇḍu or rather of the Aśvins by Pāṇḍu's wife Mādrī, he was twin-brother of Saha-deva, and fourth of the five Pāṇḍu princes; N. of a physician mentioned in the Brahma-vaivarta-Purāṇa, author of a work on horses; an epithet of Śiva; (*ī*), f. a female ichneumon; several plants, Salmalia Malabarica, = *kukkuṭī*; Nardostachys Jatamansi, = *jaṭāmāṇsī*; saffron, = *śankhinī*; a mystical N. of the letter *h* [cf. *nakulīśa*]; (*ā*), f. an epithet of the wife of Śiva; (also read *a-kulā*, q. v.) — *Nakula-tva, am*, n. the state or condition of an ichneumon. — *Nakulāḍhyā* (°*la-āḍh*°), f. a plant (= *gandha-nākulī*). — *Nakulāndha-tā* (°*la-an*°), f. or *nakulāndhya, am*, n. a kind of disease of the eye in which the eye becomes like that of an ichneumon and all objects have a variegated appearance; [cf. *nākulāndhya*.] — *Nakulīśa* (°*lī-īśa*), *as*, or (according to others) *nakuleśa* (°*la-īśa*), *as*, m. a form of Bhairava regarded as an attendant on or emanation from Śiva; the letter *h* used mystically in the Tantras; [cf. *nakulī*.] — *Nakulīśa-yoga-pārāyaṇa, am*, n., N. of a Yoga work. — *Nakuleshṭā* or *nakuleshṭakā* (°*la-ish*°), f. 'liked by the ichneumon,' a plant, = *nākulī, gandha-nākulī*, (the mungoose if wounded in a conflict with a poisonous snake is supposed to prevent the effects of the venom by the use of this plant.)

Nakulaka, as or *am*, m. or n. (?), an ornament shaped like an ichneumon.

नक्क् *nakk*, cl. 10. P. *nakkayati*, &c., to destroy, kill, annihilate.

नक्त 2. *nakta* or *nakla* (?), *am*, n. (for 1. *nakta* see p. 463, col. 3), = نقل, N. of the fifth Yoga (in astronomy).

नक्तक *naktaka, as*, m. dirty or ragged cloth; a rag, wiper, handkerchief, &c.; (a various reading for *laktaka*.)

नक्तमाल *naktamāla* or *naktamālaka, as*, m. the tree Pongamia Glabra or Dalbergia Arborea or Galedupa Arborea.

नक्र *nakra, as*, m. (derived in Pāṇ. VI. 3, 75, fr. *na-kra*), a crocodile, an alligator [cf. *nākra*]; the sign of the zodiac Scorpio; (*am, ā*), n. f. the nose; (according to others) a peculiar disease of the nose (= *nāsā-jvara, āhaka-jvara*); (*am*), n. the upper timber of a door-frame; (*ā*), f. a swarm of bees or wasps. — *Nakra-rāj, ṭ*, or *nakra-rāja, as*, or *nakra-hāraka, as*, m. 'king of the Nakras, seizer of the Nakras,' a shark or any other large sea animal.

नक्ष् *naksh* (connected with rt. 1. *naś*, cf. *inaksh*), cl. 1. P. A. *nakshati, -te*, &c., Ved. to come near, come to, approach, visit, meet with, attain, gain, obtain; [cf. Lat. *nanciscor, nactum*.]

Nakshat, an, antī, at, approaching. — *Nakshad-dābha, as, ā, am*, Ved. striking down any one that approaches; (*as*), m. an epithet of Indra.

Nakshatra, am, n. (fr. the above rt. in the sense of 'coming or ascending;' derived by some fr. *naksha* = *nakta* + *tra*, i.e. guarding the night, but this would not apply to the sun; also by some fr. *na* + *kshatra*, decaying?), a star in general (also applied to the sun), a constellation, an asterism in the moon's path, a lunar mansion, of which, according to the earlier reckoning, twenty-seven are enumerated, but in the later astrology more usually twenty-eight, distinct in name, figure, and number of stars, (the usual names are as follow: 1. Śravishṭhā or Dhanishṭhā; 2. Śata-bhishaj; 3. Pūrva-Bhādrapadā; 4. Uttara-Bhādrapadā; 5. Revatī; 6. Aśvinī; 7. Bharaṇī; 8. Kṛittikā; 9. Rohiṇī or Brāhmī; 10. Mṛiga-śiras or Āgrahāyaṇī; 11. Ārdrā; 12. Punar-vasū or Yāmakau; 13. Pushya or Sidhya; 14. Āśleshā; 15. Maghā; 16. Pūrva-Phalgunī; 17. Uttara-Phalgunī; 18. Hasta; 19. Ćitrā; 20. Svātī; 21. Viśākhā or Rādhā; 22. Anurādhā; 23. Jyeshṭhā; 24. Mūla; 25. Pūrvā Ashāḍhā; 26. Uttarā Ashāḍhā; 27. Abhijit; 28. Śravaṇa. In the Taittirīya-Brāhmaṇa, Śravishṭhās is given for 1; Pūrve Proshṭha-padās for 3; Uttare Proshṭha-padās for 4; Aśva-yujau for 6; Apabharaṇīs or Bharaṇīs for 7; Kṛittikās for 8; Invakās or Mṛiga-śīrsham for 10; Bāhū and Ārdrā for 11; Tishyas for 13; Āśleshās or Āśreshās for 14; Maghās for 15; Pūrve Phalgunī or Phalgunīs for 16; Uttare Phalgunī for 17; Nishṭyā or in the Taittirīya-Saṃhitā also Svātī for 20; Viśākhe for 21; Anurādhās for 22; Rohiṇī or Jyeshṭha-ghnī or Jyeshṭhā for 23; Mūla-barhaṇī or in the Taittirīya-Saṃhitā also Vićṛitau for 24; Pūrvā Ashāḍhās for 25; Uttarā Ashāḍhās or Abhijit for 26; Śroṇā for 27: the names of the months Māgha, Phālguna, Ćaitra, Vaiśākha, Jyeshṭha, Āshāḍha, Śrāvaṇa, Bhādra, Āśvina, Kārttika, Mārgaśīrsha, and Pausha were derived from the names of the corresponding twelve lunar mansions; according to some, certain Nakshatras are called *dhruvāṇi*, fixed, viz. Rohiṇī and the three double asterisms Uttara-Phalgunī, Uttarā Ashāḍhā, and Uttara-Bhādrapadā. In the Vedas the asterisms are considered to be the abodes of the gods or the visible forms of pious persons after death, see Sāyaṇa on Ṛig-veda I. 50, 2; in the later mythology the lunar mansions are regarded as the wives of the moon and daughters of Daksha; according to the Jainas, the sun, moon, Grahas or planets, Nakshatras, and Tārās or stars form the Jyotishkas); a pearl; [cf. *deva-n*° and *yama-n*°.] — *Nakshatra-kalpa, as*, m., N. of a Pari-śishṭa belonging to the Atharva-veda and treating of the lunar mansions. — *Nakshatra-kānti-vistāra, as*, m. 'spreading brilliance (like that) of the Nakshatras or constellations,' the white Yāvanāla flower. — *Nakshatra-kūrma-ćāra, as*, m., N. of a chapter of Bhaṭṭotpala's commentary to Varāha-mihira's Bṛihat-Saṃhitā. — *Nakshatrakūrma-vibhāga, as*, m. distribution of countries supposed to be under the dominion of the different lunar mansions. — *Nakshatra-graha-yuty-adhikāra, as*, m. 'the chapter of the conjunction of asterisms and planets,' N. of a chapter of the Sūrya-siddhānta. — *Nakshatra-ćakra, am*, n. a particular diagram for astrological calculations; the sphere of the fixed stars; the lunar asterisms collectively. — *Nakshatra-ćintāmaṇi, is*, m. 'Nakshatra gem' (see *ćintā-maṇi*), N. of a work on lunar mansions. — *Nakshatra-jā, ās*, m., Ved. 'star-born,' son of the stars. — *Nakshatra-tārā-rājāditya* (°*ja-ād*°), *as*, m. the sun as king of the stars and lunar asterisms; (with Buddhists) N. of a particular kind of religious meditation. — *Nakshatra-darśa, as*, m., Ved. 'star-gazer,' one who looks at the stars. — *Nakshatra-dāna-vidhi, is*, m. 'rules about the Nakshatra offering,' N. of the 153rd chapter of the Bhavishyottara-Purāṇa. — *Nakshatra-dohada-śāntika, am*, n., N. of a chapter of the Purāṇa-sarva-sva. — *Nakshatra-nātha, as*, m. 'lord of the lunar mansions,' the moon. — *Nakshatra-nirṇaya, as*, m. 'determination of the Nakshatras,' N. of a chapter of the Tantra-sāra; N. of a chapter of the Purāṇa-sarva-sva. — *Nakshatra-nemi, is*, m. the pole star; the moon; an epithet of Vishṇu; (*is*), f. the last of the asterisms, Revatī, containing thirty-two stars. — *Nakshatra-nyāsa, as*, m., N. of a chapter of the Purāṇa-sarva-sva. — *Nakshatra-pa, as*, m. 'protector or lord of the lunar asterisms,' the moon. — *Nakshatra-patha, as*, m. 'the path of the Nakshatras or stars,' the starry sky. — *Nakshatra-pāṭhaka, as*, m. 'reader of the stars,' an astrologer. — *Nakshatra-purusha, as*, m. (in astrology) the figure of a man's body on the limbs of which the various lunar asterisms are distributed (e.g. Mūla on the feet, Jyeshṭhā on the neck, &c., cf. *kāla-purusha*; in this sense also written *nakshatra-purushaka*); a ceremony in which such a figure is worshipped; N. of the eightieth chapter of the Vāmana-Purāṇa. — *Nakshatrapurusha-vrata, am*, n. 'the vow Nakshatra-purusha,' N. of the fifty-third chapter of the Matsya-Purāṇa. — *Nakshatra-pūjita, as, ā, am*, 'star-honoured,' favoured by the constellations. — *Nakshatra-prakaraṇa, am*, n. 'the Nakshatra chapter,' N. of the second chapter of the Ćintā-maṇi Sāraṇikā by Daśa-bala. — *Nakshatra-phala, am*, n. 'the result obtained from the observation or influence of the lunar mansions,' N. of a work on the lunar mansions. — *Nakshatra-bhakti, is*, f. 'distribution of the Nakshatras or explanation of the relation in which they stand to each other,' N. of the fifteenth Adhyāya of Varāha-mihira's Bṛihat-Saṃhitā; [cf. *nakshatra-vyūha*.] — *Nakshatra-mārga, as*, m. the path of the Nakshatras. — *Nakshatra-mālā*, f. a ring or group of stars; the table of the asterisms in the moon's path, the asterisms collectively; a necklace containing twenty-seven pearls; a kind of dance. — *Nakshatra-yājaka, as, ā, am*, offering oblations to the lunar mansions; [cf. *graha-yajña*.] — *Nakshatra-yoga, as*, m. the conjunction of the moon with the lunar mansions. — *Nakshatra-yogin, ī, inī, i*, connected with the lunar mansions; (*inyas*), f. pl. the chief stars in the lunar asterisms. — *Nakshatra-rāja, as*, m. 'the king of the asterisms,' the moon; N. of a Bodhi-sattva. — *Nakshatrarāja-vikrīḍita, am*, n. 'moon-sport,' N. of a particular kind of abstract contemplation. — *Nakshatra-loka, as*, m. the starry region, the firmament; (*ās*), m. pl. the world of the Nakshatras. — *Nakshatra-vartman, a*, n. 'the path of the Nakshatras,' the sky. — *Nakshatra-vidyā*, f. 'star-knowledge,' astronomy. — *Nakshatra-vīthī*, f. the path of the Nakshatras. — *Nakshatra-vṛishṭi, is*, f. 'star-shower,' falling or shooting stars. — *Nakshatra-vyūha, as*, m. = *nakshatra-bhakti*, q. v. — *Nakshatra-śavas, ās, ās, as*, Ved. equal to the Nakshatras in number?; (Sāy.) going to the gods. — *Nakshatra-śuddhi-prakaraṇa, am*, n., N. of the first chapter of the Vivāha-vṛindāvana by Keśavārka, a work on the different lunar mansions regarded as favourable or unfavourable to marriage. — *Nakshatra-samuććaya, as*, m. 'the assemblage of the Nakshatras,' N. of an astrological work by Lalla-vārāha-suta. — *Nakshatra-sūćaka, as*, m. 'star-indicator,' an astrologer. — *Nakshatreśa* (°*ra-īśa*), *as*, m. 'lord of the Nakshatras,' the moon. — *Nakshatreshṭakā* (°*ra-ish*°), f., Ved., N. of certain sacrificial bricks. — *Nakshatreshṭi* (°*ra-ish*°), *is*, f. a sacrifice or oblation to the asterisms.

Nakshatrin, ī, m. 'bearing the stars (?),' an epithet of Vishṇu.

Nakshatriya, as, ā, am, belonging or relating to the Nakshatras or to the stars in general, containing a number equal to that of the Nakshatras, i. e. twenty-seven.

Nakshya, as, ā, am, to be approached or attained.

नख् *nakh* or *nankh*, cl. 4. and 1. P. *nakhyati, nakhati* and *nankhati*, &c., Ved. to move, go.

नख *nakha, as, am*, m. n. (said to be fr. rt. 1. *nah*, perhaps fr. *nagh* for rt. *angh* = *ank*, to move in a curve; in Pāṇ. VI. 3, 75, derived fr. *na* + *kha*), a nail of a finger or of a toe, a claw, talon, the spur of a cock; an expression for the number twenty; (*as*), m. a part, portion; (*am, ī*), n. f. a particular perfume, a dried substance of a brown colour and of the shape of a nail, apparently a dried shell-fish (= *śukti*) used as a perfume, see *dhūpya*; (*ī*), f. a vegetable perfume different from the above though known by the same name, *nakhī*; [cf. Lith. *naga-s*, 'nail;' Slav. *nogŭ-tĭ* = Russ. *nogotĭ*; Gr. ὄ-νυξ; Lat. *unguis, ungula*; Old Germ. *nagal*; Angl. Sax. *naegel*; Hib. *ionga*, perhaps for *nionga*.] — *Nakha-kuṭṭa, as*, m. 'a nail-cutter,' a barber. — *Nakha-khādin, ī, inī, i*, 'eating the nails,' biting the nails. — *Nakha-guććha-phalā*, f. = *nakha-nishpāva*. — *Nakha-ćheda, as*, m. nail-paring, nail-cutting. — *Nakha-jāha, am*, n. the root of a nail. — *Nakha-dāraṇa, as*, m. 'tearing with the nails,' a falcon, a hawk. — *Nakha-nikṛintana, as* or *am*,

m. or n. (?), a pair of nail-scissors. — *Nakha-nishpāra, as,* m. or *nakha-nishpārikā* or *nakha-nishpārī,* f. a kind of pulse. — *Nakha-pada, am,* n. the mark of a finger-nail, a scratch. — *Nakha-parṇī,* f. a species of plant (= *vriśćikā*). — *Nakha-puñja-phalā,* f. = *nakha-nishpāva.* — *Nakha-pushpī,* f. a species of grass (= *prikkā*). — *Nakha-pūrvikā* or *nakha-phalinī,* f. = *nakha-nishpāva.* — *Nakha-bhinna, as, ā, am,* 'nail-divided,' scratched or torn off with a nail. — *Nakha-muća, as,* m. 'nail-looser,' a bow. — *Nakham-paća, as, ā, am,* nail-scalding, nail-scorching. — *Nakha-rajanī,* f. a species of plant and its fruit. — *Nakha-rañjanī,* f. a nail-parer. — *Nakha-lekhaka, as,* m. a nail-painter. — *Nakha-lekhā,* f. a scratch; nail-painting. — *Nakha-vilekha, as,* m. a scratch; nail-painting (?). — *Nakha-visha, as, ā, am,* having venom in the nails or claws. — *Nakha-vishkira, as, ā, am,* tearing or rending with the claws; *(as),* m. a bird of prey. — *Nakha-vriksha, as,* m. a species of plant (= *nīla-vriksha*). — *Nakha-vraṇa, am,* n. 'nail-wound,' a scratch. — *Nakha-śankha, as,* m. a small shell. — *Nakhāṇśu* (°*kha-an*°), *us,* m. elegance or brightness of the finger-nails. — *Nakhāṅka* (°*kha-aṅ*°), *am,* n. 'nail-mark,' a scratch; a sort of perfume (= *vyāghra-nakhī*). — *Nakhāṅga* (°*kha-aṅ*°), *am,* n. a kind of perfume (= *nalī*). — *Nakhā-nakhi,* ind. nail against nail, (a fight with) mutual scratching, scratching one another. — *Nakhāyudha* (°*kha-āy*°), *as, ā, am,* 'claw-armed,' using the nails or claws as weapons; *(as),* m. an animal which uses its claws as weapons, any beast or bird having talons; a tiger; a lion; a cock; a monkey, &c. — *Nakhāyudha-tva, am,* n. the state of being claw-armed or of using claws as weapons. — *Nakhāri* (°*kha-ari*), *is,* m., N. of one of the attendants of Śiva. — *Nakhāli, is,* m. or *nakhālikā* (°*kha-āl*°), f. a small shell; [cf. *nakha-śankha.*] — *Nakhāśin* (°*kha-āś*°), *ī,* m. 'eating with claws,' an owl (as using its claws in feeding).

Nakhaka, as, m., N. of a Nāga-rāja.

Nakhara, as, ā, am, shaped like a claw, any pointed and curved instrument (as a knife, sword, &c.); *(as, ā, am),* m. f. n. a finger-nail, claw; *(ī),* f. a kind of perfume (= *nakhī,* = *kshudra-nakhī*). — *Nakharāyudha* (°*ra-āy*°), *as, ā, am,* 'claw-armed,' using claws as weapons; *(as),* m. a lion, tiger, any beast of prey; a cock. — *Nakharāhva* (°*ra-āh*°), *as,* m. fragrant oleander (= *kara-vīra*).

Nakhālu, us, m. = *nakha-vriksha,* q. v.

Nakhin, ī, inī, i, having nails, armed with claws or talons, clawed; thorny, prickly; *(ī),* m. an animal or a beast with claws, especially the lion.

नग *na-ga, as,* m. (fr. *na-ga,* not moving, or said to be fr. rt. 1. *dah* through change of *d* into *n,* Uṇādi-s. V. 61), a mountain; a symbolical expression for the number seven (because of the seven principal mountains; cf. *kula-parvata*); a tree; a plant in general; a serpent; the sun; *(as, ā, am),* not moving, immovable; [cf. *a-ga.*] — *Naga-ja, as, ā, am,* mountain, mountaineer; *(as),* m. 'mountain-born,' an elephant; *(ā),* f. a species of plant (= *kshudra-pāshāṇa-bhedā*). — *Naga-nadī,* f. 'mountain-river,' N. of a river. — *Naga-nandinī,* f. an epithet of the goddess Durgā ('daughter of the mountain,' Durgā being in one of her characters the daughter of the personified Himālaya). — *Naga-pati, is,* m. 'chief of mountains,' the Himālaya range of mountains. — *Naga-bhid, t,* m. 'rock-splitter' or 'tree-splitter,' a species of plant (= *pāshāṇa-bhedana*), Plectanthrus Scutellaroides; an axe; a crow; Indra. — *Naga-bhū, ūs, ūs, u,* 'mountain-born,' mountain, mountaineer; *(ūs),* m. a species of plant, = *kshudra-pāshāṇa-bhedā,* (more probably fem. like *naga-jā.*) — *Naga-mūrdhan, ā,* m. the crest or brow of a mountain. — *Naga-randhra-kara, as,* m. 'rending the mountains,' an epithet of Kārttikeya. — *Naga-vat, ān, atī, at,* possessing mountains, abounding in trees. — *Naga-vāhana, as,* m. 'whose vehicle is a mountain, mountain-borne,' an epithet of Śiva. — *Naga-svarūpiṇī,* f. a kind of metre consisting of four lines of eight syllables each. — *Nagāgra* (°*ga-ag*°), *am,* n. the summit or top of a mountain. — *Nagāṭana* (°*ga-aṭ*°), *as,* m. 'moving about on trees,' a monkey. — *Nagādhipa* (°*ga-adh*°), *as,* m. 'chief of mountains,' the Himālaya. — *Nagādhirāja* (°*ga-adh*°), *as,* m. = the preceding. — *Nagāri* (°*ga-ari*), *is,* m., N. of a man. — *Nagāvāsa* (°*ga-āv*°), *as,* m. 'living on trees,' a peacock. — *Nagāśraya* (°*ga-āś*°), *as, ā, am,* living in or frequenting mountains; *(as),* m. a species of bulbous plant growing on mountains (= *hasti-kanda*). — *Nagāhvaya* (°*ga-āh*°), *as,* m., N. of a man. — *Nagendra* (°*ga-in*°), *as,* m. 'chief of mountains,' the Himālaya, Kailāsa. — *Nageśa* (°*ga-īśa*), *as,* m. 'chief of mountains,' N. of a particular mountain. — *Nagoććhrāya* (°*ga-uć*°), *as,* m. heighth or elevation of a mountain. — *Nagaukas* (°*ga-ok*°), *ās,* m. 'inhabiting a mountain or tree;' a lion; the fabulous animal Śarabha; a bird in general; a crow; [cf. *agaukas.*]

नगणा *nagaṇā,* f. a plant, Cardiospermum Halicacabum; (also read *nagnā.*)

नगर *nagara, am, ī* (fr. *na-ga?*), n. f. a town, city, (often appended to the names of cities in India or standing alone as a name.) According to Pāṇ. VIII. 4, 39, the initial *n* cannot be cerebralized [cf. *giri-nagara*]; at the end of adj. comps. the fem. may end in *ā* (e. g. *sa-grāma-nagarā medinī,* the earth with its villages and cities). — *Nagara-kāka, as,* m. 'a crow in a town,' an expression of contempt; [cf. *nagara-vāyasa.*] — *Nagara-koṭi,* N. of a place; N. of a town at the foot of the Himālaya, Nagar-kot. — *Nagara-ghāta, as, ā, am,* town-destroying; *(as),* m. an elephant. — *Nagara-ghātaka, as,* m. the destroyer of a city. — *Nagara-jana, as,* m. towns-folk; a citizen. — *Nagara-dvāra, am,* n. the gate of a town, city-gate. — *Nagara-dhana-vihāra, as,* m., N. of a Buddhist monastery. — *Nagara-pati, is,* m. the chief of a town. — *Nagara-pura, am,* n., N. of a town. — *Nagara-pradakshiṇā,* f. carrying an idol round a city in procession; [cf. *pradakshiṇā.*] — *Nagara-prānta, as,* m. the outskirts of a town. — *Nagara-mardin, ī,* m. 'town-crusher,' N. of a man. — *Nagara-mālin, ī, inī, i,* garlanded with cities. — *Nagara-mustā,* f. = *nagarotthā;* [cf. *nāgara-mustā.*] — *Nagara-rakshā,* f. superintendence or government of a town. — *Nagararakshādhikrita* (°*kshā-adh*°), *as, ā, am,* appointed to the government of a town. — *Nagara-rakshin, ī,* m. the governor or superintendent of a town, civic-guard, town-watchman. — *Nagara-vāyasa, as,* m. = *nagara-kāka.* — *Nagara-vāsin, ī, inī, i,* inhabiting towns, dwelling in cities, citizen. — *Nagara-vāhya, as, ā, am,* situated without the town. — *Nagara-sammita, as, ā, am,* equal to a town. — *Nagara-stha, as, ā, am,* city-dwelling; a resident in a city, a townsman, citizen, burgess. — *Nagara-svarūpiṇī,* f. a species of the Anu-shṭubh metre. — *Nagara-hāra, as* or *am,* m. or n. (?), 'town-taking,' N. of a kingdom. — *Nagarādhikrita* (°*ra-adh*°), *as,* m. the superintendent or governor of a town. — *Nagarādhipa* (°*ra-adh*°), *as,* m. or *nagarādhipati, is,* m. the chief magistrate of a town, head police-officer. — *Nagarādhyaksha* (°*ra-adh*°), *as,* m. the overseer or superintendent of a town. — *Nagarābhyāśa* (°*ra-abh*°), *as,* m. the neighbourhood of a city. — *Nagarī-nirodha, as,* m., N. of the sixty-third chapter of the Krīḍā-khaṇḍa or second part of the Gaṇeśa-Purāṇa. — *Nagarī-yukti, is,* f., N. of a chapter of the Yukti-kalpa-taru ascribed to king Bhoja. — *Nagarī-rakshin, ī,* m. = *nagara-rakshin.* — *Nagarī-raka, as,* m. 'town-crane,' a crow. — *Nagarotthā* (°*ra-utthā*), f. a species of plant, = *nagara-mustā;* [cf. *nāgarotthā.*] — *Nagaropānta* (°*ra-up*°), *am,* n. suburb, skirts of a town. — *Nagaraukas* (°*ra-ok*°), *ās,* m. the inhabitant of a town, townsman. — *Nagaraushadhi* (°*ra-osh*°), *is,* f. the plantain, Musa Sapientum (= *kadalī*).

Nagarāya, Nom. P. *nagarāyate,* &c., to have the appearance of a town, look like a town.

Nagarin, ī, m., N. of a man.

Nagarīya, as, ā, am, belonging to a town, civic, city, urban.

नग्न *nagna.* See under rt. *naj* below.

नग्नहु *nagnahu, us,* m. or *nagnahū, ūs,* m. ferment, a drug used for fermenting spirituous liquor.

नग्ना 1. *nagnā,* f. (for 2. *nagnā* see *nagna* below), Ved. speech; (a various reading for *nanā,* q. v.)

नघमार *nagha-māra, as,* m. (fr. *nagha,* a disease? and *māra*), Ved. an expression for the plant *kushṭha.*

Naghā-risha, as, ā, am, Ved. an epithet of plants.

नघुष *naghusha, as,* m. = *nahusha,* q. v.

नङ्ख् *naṅkh.* See rt. *nakh,* p. 464, col. 3.

नङ्ग *naṅga, as,* m. a lover, paramour.

नचिकेतस् *na-ćiketas, ās,* or *na-ćiketa, as,* m., N. of a son of Vājaśravasa; [cf. *nāćiketa.*]

नचिर *na-ćira, as, ā, am,* not long (in time), not of long duration; *(am),* ind. not long, for a short time; *(eṇa* or *āt* or *āya),* ind. in no long time, in a short time, quickly, speedily, shortly, soon; [cf. *a-ćira* and *māćiram.*]

नच्युत *na-ćyuta* = *a-ćyuta,* q. v.

नज् *naj* (allied to rt. *laj* = *lajj,* of which it appears to be another form only found in the past pass. part. *nagna* below), cl. 1. A. *najate,* &c., to be ashamed, be modest or bashful.

Nagna, as, ā, am, naked, nude, bare; uncultivated, uninhabited, desolate; *(as),* m. a naked mendicant; a N. of Śiva; a hypocrite (whose nakedness is a mere pretence); a Buddhist mendicant, = *kshapaṇaka;* a bard accompanying an army; (2. *nagnā*), f. a naked, wanton woman; a girl before menstruation (and therefore allowed to go naked; cf. *nagnikā*); the plant Cardiospermum Halicacabum; [cf. *nagaṇā,* 1. *nagnā* above; Lith. *nŏga-s,* 'naked;' Russ. *nagii;* Slav. *nago-ta,* 'nakedness;' Goth. *naqvaths;* Old Iceland. *nakt-r;* Angl. Sax. *nacud, nacod, genacyan;* Old Germ. *nachat;* Mod. Germ. *nackt;* Hib. *nochd;* Lat. *nudus.*] — *Nagnankaraṇa, as, ī, am,* making naked. — *Nagna-jit, t,* m., N. of a prince of the Gandhāras, father of one of Krishṇa's wives; N. of an author of a work on architecture; of a poet. — *Nagna-tā,* f. or *nagnatva, am,* n. nakedness, nudity. — *Nagnam-bhavishṇu, us, us, u,* or *nagnam-bhāvuka, as, ā, am,* becoming naked, uncovering one's self in a shameless manner. — *Nagna-vritti, is,* f. 'the mendicant's commentary,' N. of a commentary on the Uṇādi-sūtras. — *Nagna-vrata-dhara, as,* m. 'observing the vow of a naked mendicant,' epithet of Śiva. — *Nagnāṭa* or *nagnāṭaka* (°*na-aṭ*°), *as,* m. a man who wanders about naked, especially a Buddhist or Jaina religious mendicant. — *Nagnī-karaṇa, am,* n. making naked, undressing, stripping. — *Nagnī-kri,* cl. 8. P. A. *-karoti, -kurute, -kartum,* to render naked, to convert into a naked mendicant. — *Nagnī-krita, as, ā, am,* made naked, undressed, stripped; converted into a naked mendicant.

Nagnaka, as, ikā, am, naked, wanton; *(as),* m. a naked mendicant, especially a Buddhist or Jaina ascetic; a bard; *(ikā),* f. a naked or wanton woman; a girl before menstruation.

Nagnikā, f. a naked woman; a girl before menstruation or about ten years old.

नञ् *nañ,* ind. (in grammar) the technical term for the negative particle *na,* q. v., negation. — *Nañ-artha-nirṇaya, as,* m. 'inquiry into the meaning of the negative particle,' N. of a chapter of the grammatical work Vaiyākaraṇa-bhūshaṇa-sāra by Koṇḍa-bhaṭṭa. — *Nañ-vāda-ṭippaṇī,* f. 'commentary to the chapter of negation,' N. of a grammatical work by Raghu-deva.

नट् naṭ (a corrupted form of the original rt. nṛit), cl. 1. P. naṭati, nanāṭa, naṭish-yati, &c., to dance, to dance or perform as an actor, to act; to injure by any deceptive trick; cl. 10. P. nāṭayati, &c., to represent anything (acc.) dramatically or by pantomime; to act; to drop or fall; to injure; to speak or shine.

Naṭa, as, m. (said to be fr. rt. nam, Uṇādi-s. IV. 104), a dancer, mime, actor, &c.; (in modern times) N. for a particular caste, the son of a degraded Kshatriya by a woman of the second caste; the tree Calosanthes Indica [cf. kuṭannaṭa]; Jonesia Asoka (= aśoka); a sort of reed, Arundo Tibialis, or latterly called Arundo Karka (= kishku-parvan); a subordinate mode of music; N. of a man who with his brother Bhaṭa built a Vihāra; (ā), f. a species of shrub, Cæsalpina Banducella; (ī), f. an actress, a dancer, a Nauch girl; a courtezan, harlot; a species of fragrant plant (= nalī); red arsenic; N. of a Rāgiṇī. — Naṭa-gati, is, f. a kind of metre consisting of four times fourteen syllables. — Naṭa-ćaryā, f. the performance of an actor. — Naṭa-tā, f. the office or state of a player, condition of an actor. — Naṭa-nārāyaṇa, as, m. a Rāga or mode of music, (according to some) the sixth, (or according to others) a subdivision of that called Dīpaka or of Megha. — Naṭa-pattrikā, f. Solanum Melongena. — Naṭa-parṇa, am, n. the skin (?). — Naṭa-bhaṭika-vihāra, as, m. 'the temple of Naṭa and Bhaṭa,' N. of a temple on the mountain Uru-muṇḍa. — Naṭa-bhūshaṇa, am, n. 'actor's ornament or pigment,' orpiment. — Naṭa-maṇḍana, am, n. 'actor's ornament,' yellow orpiment. — Naṭa-ranga, as, m. 'actor's stage, a theatrical stage,' a metaphorical N. for anything illusory. — Naṭa-vaṭu, us, m. (vaṭu said to be fr. rt. vaṭ), the son of an actor, a young actor. — Naṭa-vara, as, m. a chief dancer or actor. — Naṭa-śreshṭha, as, m. a chief or excellent dancer or actor. — Naṭa-sañjñaka, as, m. yellow orpiment; an actor, a dancer, &c.; [cf. naṭa-bhūshaṇa and naṭa-maṇḍana.] — Naṭa-sūtra, am, n. rules or directions for actors. — Naṭāntikā (°ṭa-an°), f. shame, modesty; (also read naṭāndhikā.) — Naṭī-suta, as, m. the son of a dancing girl. — Naṭeśvara (°ṭa-īś°), as, m. 'the lord of dancers,' an epithet of Śiva.

Naṭaka, as, m. an actor. — Naṭaka-melaka, am, n. 'the company of actors,' N. of a comedy.

Naṭana, am, n. (derived fr. nartana), the act of dancing or representing dramatically, pantomime, &c.; a dance.

Naṭita, am, n. acting, representation.

Naṭī, f. an actress, &c. See under naṭa above.

Naṭyā, f. a company of actors.

नट्टपट्टग्राम naṭṭa-paṭṭa-grāma, as, m., N. of a village.

नड् naḍ (connected with rt. naṭ = nṛit), cl. 10. P. nāḍayati, &c., to fall.

Naḍa, as, am, m. n. (the n. does not seem to occur), a species of reed, Arundo Tibialis or Karka; (Ved. written naḷa; cf. nala); (as), m. a particular tribe whose employment is making a sort of glass bracelets; N. of a prince with the patronymic Naishidha; (according to the commentator) = Nala Naishadha; N. of a Nāga; [cf. Lith. néndrė, 'a reed.'] — Naḍa-prāya, as, ā, am, abounding in reeds. — Naḍa-bhakta, am, n. a place abounding in reeds. — Naḍa-maya, as, ī, am, consisting of reeds, made of reeds. — Naḍa-mīna, as, m. a small fish, a species of sprat frequenting reedy places (= nala-mīna). — Naḍa-vana, am, n. a thicket of reeds; N. of a place. — Naḍa-saṃhati, is, f. a collection or quantity of reeds. — Naḍāgāra (°ḍa-āg°), am, n. a hut of reeds. — Naḍā-giri, is, m., N. of an elephant.

Naḍaka, as, am, m. n. (?), the hollow of a bone.

Naḍakīya, as, ā, am, abounding in reeds (as a field &c.).

Naḍaśa, as, ī, am, covered with reeds.

Naḍinī, f. a quantity of reeds, a reed bed.

Naḍila, as, ā, am, reedy, covered with reeds.

Naḍyā, f. a quantity of reeds, a bed of reeds.

Naḍvat, ān, atī, at (naḍ for naḍa), covered with reeds, abounding in reeds.

Naḍvala, as, ā, am (naḍ for naḍa), abounding in reeds, reedy; (am), n. a quantity of reeds, a reed bed; (ā), f. a quantity of reeds; N. of the wife of Manu Ćākshusha; (also written navalā; cf. nāḍvaleya.)

Naḍvā-bhā, ūs, f. a house or hut of reeds (?).

नडह naḍaha, as, ā, am, lovely, beautiful, desirable.

नत् nat, t, t, t (fr. rt. nam), bowing, bowing one's self, (at the end of comp.)

Nata, as, ā, am, bent, bowed, inclined, inclining; depressed, sunk; crooked, curved; (am), n. the zenith-distance at meridian transit; hour-angle or the distance of any planet from the meridian; (as), m. the plant Tabernæmontana Coronaria (= tagara, tagara-pādī). — Nata-kandhara, as, ā, am, 'bowing the neck,' bowing. — Nata-jyā, f. the sign of the hour-angle. — Nata-druma, as, m. = lātā-śāla (?). — Nata-nāḍī or nata-nāḍikā, f. hour-angle or the distance in time of any planet from the meridian; any hour of birth after noon or before midnight. — Nata-nāsika, as, ā, am, having a depressed or flattened nose, flat-nosed. — Nata-bhāga, as, m. (in astronomy) zenith-distance. — Nata-bhrū, ūs, ūs, u, bending the brow, frowning. — Nata-mukha, as, ī, am, bending down the face, looking down. — Nata-mūrdhan, ā, ā, a, bending or hanging down the head. — Natāṃśa (°ta-aṃ°), as, m. (in astronomy) zenith-distance. — Natānga (°ta-an°), as, ī, am, bowing the limbs, bending the body, bent, curved, bowed, stooping; (ī), f. a woman. — Natonnata-bhrū (°ta-un°), ūs, ūs, u, depressing and elevating the eye-brows, frowning.

Nati, is, f. bending, bowing, stooping; curvature, crookedness; a bow, a courtesy, modest behaviour; (in grammar) the change of a dental letter to a cerebral; parallax in latitude.

नतमंहस् na-tam-aṃhas, the beginning of a particular holy text.

नतराम् natarām, ind. (fr. na with the affix of the compar.), Ved. a strong negative particle equivalent to 'not at all,' 'never.'

नद् nad (allied to rt. nard), cl. 1. P. (ep. rarely A.) nadati (-te), nanāda, nadishyati, anadīt and anādīt, naditum, to vibrate; to sound, resound, thunder (as a cloud); to roar, shout, cry, speak (often with the acc. of words denoting sound, e. g. śabdam, svanam, nādam, nādān, ravān, &c., thus nadanto bhairavān nādān, uttering frightful cries): Caus. P. nadayati, -yitum, to cause to vibrate or shake (Ved.); nādayati, -te, &c., to cause to sound or resound, fill with noise, make resonant: Intens. nānadīti, nānadyate, to vibrate or shake violently (Ved.); to make a tremulous sound, to cry, roar (especially used of the lion), howl; to sound violently; [cf. rts. vad, nard; Cambro-Brit. nadu, 'to cry.']

Nada, as, m., Ved. who or what sounds or makes a noise; a horse; a cloud (which thunders); a praiser; N. of a verse of the Ṛig-veda beginning with nadam (Ṛig-veda VIII. 58, 2); a river (the personification of which is male, as the Brahma-putra, Sone, Indus, &c.); any flowing water; (ī), f. a torrent, a river (the common personification of rivers being female); a kind of metre consisting of four lines of fourteen syllables each; (in grammar) a N. for crude bases ending in ī or ū, if like nadī they are invariably feminine (and not like grāma-ṇī which is both masc. and fem., see Pāṇini I. 4, 3). At the end of an adverbial compound nada becomes nadam and nadī becomes nadi [cf. upa-nadam, upa-nadi, and see Pāṇini V. 4, 110]. — Nada-nadī-pati, is, m. 'lord of the male and female (personified) rivers,' the ocean, sea. — Nada-rāja, as, m. 'king of the rivers,' the Sindhu, father of Śrī. — Nadī-kadamba, as, m., N. of a plant. — Nadī-kānta, as, m. 'lover of the rivers,' the ocean; a small tree, Vitex Negundo; another sort of tree, Baringtonia Acutangula; (ā), f. 'beloved by rivers,' the rose-apple, Eugenia Jambolana; a shrub, Leea Hirta; a species of creeper. — Nadī-kāśyapa, as, m., N. of a contemporary of Śākya-muni. — Nadī-kūla, am, n. the bank or shore of a river. — Nadīkūla-priya, as, m. 'fond of river-banks,' a species of reed, Calamus Rotang. — Nadī-ja, as, ā, am, river-born, water-born, aquatic; (as), m. 'son of the river,' an epithet of Bhīshma; several plants, Terminalia Arjuna; a species of reed (= yāvanāla-śara); Baringtonia Acutangula; a species of grain (= nadī-nishpāva); antimony; (ā), f. Premna Spinosa or Longifolia; (am), n. a lotus. — Nadī-jña, as, ā, am, knowing the course of rivers. — Nadī-tara, as, ī, am, crossing a river. — Nadītara-sthāna or nadītara-sthala, am, n. 'a place for crossing a river,' a landing-place, ferry, Ghāt. — Nadī-tīra, am, n. the bank of a river. — Nadī-datta, as, m., N. of a Bodhi-sattva. — Nadī-doha, as, m. a river-toll or tribute. — Nadī-dhara, as, ā, am, 'bearing the river Ganges,' an epithet of Śiva. — Nadīna (°dī-ina), as, m. 'lord of the rivers,' the ocean; Varuṇa, the god of the ocean; N. of a son of Saha-deva and father of Jagat-sena. — Nadī-nishpāva, as, m. a species of grain (= kaṭu-nishpāva). — Nadī-panka, as, am, m. n. 'river-mud,' the marshy bank of a river. — Nadī-pati, is, m. 'lord of the rivers,' an epithet of the ocean; (metaphorically) the water of the ocean, sea-water (Ved.). — Nadī-pūra, as, m. a river which has overflown its banks. — Nadī-bhava, am, n. river-salt. — Nadī-mātṛika, as, ā, am, nourished or watered by rivers (as land, rice, &c.); well-irrigated, possessing rivers. — Nadī-mukha, am, n. the mouth of a river; a kind of grain; [cf. nandī-mukha.] — Nadī-raya, as, m. the stream or current of a river. — Nadī-vanka, as, m. the bend or arm of a river. — Nadī-vaṭa, as, m. a species of tree (= vaṭi). — Nadī-vṛit, t, t, t, Ved. stream-obstructing. — Nadī-vega, as, m. the stream or flow of a river. — Nadī-velā, f. the current or tide of a river. — Nadīśa (°dī-īśa), as, m. 'lord of the rivers,' the ocean. — Nadī-shṇa, as, ā, am (fr. nadī + sna), bathing &c. in rivers; knowing the dangerous spots in rivers or their depth, course, &c.; (hence) versed in, experienced, clever in general. — Nadī-sarja, as, m. the tree Terminalia Arjuna. — Nady-ambu-jīvana, as, ā, am, deriving its sustenance from river-water. — Nady-āmra, as, m. a species of plant (= samashṭhilā).

Nadat, an, antī, at, sounding, resounding, making a noise or cry, roaring.

Nadathu, us, m. noise, sound; roaring; crying; din.

Nadana, as, ā, am (formed by Yāska to explain nada), sounding (as water).

Nadaniman, ā (?), m., Ved. sounding, humming, murmuring.

Nadanu, us, m., Ved. noise, roaring, sounding; the sound of approbation; thunder (?); a cloud; a lion; (according to the Naighaṇṭuka) = saṅgrāma, war, battle; (Sāy.) = na-danu, not giving. — Nadanu-mat, ān, atī, at, Ved. possessed of sound, loud-sounding, roaring.

Nadi, is, m., Ved. a crier, caller, one who calls out; (Sāy.) praise.

Nadikā, f. in ku-nadikā, an insignificant rivulet.

Nadeyī, f. the plant Premna Herbacea; (wrong form for nādeyī?).

Nadya, as, ā, am, connected with a river.

नदाल nadāla, am, n. a potsherd, the fragment of a broken pitcher, &c.

नदी *nadī*. See rt. *nad*, p. 466, col. 2.

नदृश्य *na-dṛiśya, as, ā, am*, not to be seen, invisible. — *Nadṛiśya-tva, am*, n. invisibility.

नद्ध *naddha, as, ā, am* (fr. rt. 1. *nah*), bound, tied, bound on, bound round, put on, fastened, joined, connected; covered, inlaid, embroidered, interwoven; (*am*), n. a tie, fastening, band, bond, knot. — *Naddha-vimoksha, as*, m. deliverance from fastenings or fetters.

Naddhi, is, f. binding, fastening; [cf. *barsa-n°*.]

Naddhrī, f. a strip of leather, a leather thong.

ननन्दृ *nanandṛi* or *nanāndṛi, ā*, f. (said to be fr. rt. *nand*), a husband's sister, a sister-in-law. — *Nanāndṛi-pati* or *nanānduḥ-pati, is*, m. the husband of a husband's sister.

नना *nanā*, f., Ved. a familiar expression for 'mother,' corresponding to *tata*, q. v.; (according to the Naighaṇṭuka I. 11) = *vāć*, speech.

ननु *na-nu*, ind. (fr. 2. *na* + *nu*), a strong negative particle = 'not at all' (Ved.); a particle of interrogation = the Latin *nonne*, 'not?' 'is not?' 'are not?' 'does he not?' often a particle of affirmation = 'is it not so?' i. e. 'it certainly must be so,' hence = 'certainly,' 'assuredly,' or with an imperative = 'pray,' 'do,' 'just,' 'well,' 'do now,' &c., or sometimes with an interrogative pronoun (e. g. *nanu ko bhavān*, pray who art thou?); in argumentative writings often a mere inceptive particle = 'now then,' 'but then,' 'but' (e. g. *nanu na kińćin mānam iti ćen na*, now if it be said that there is no proof, not so); *nanv astu tathāpi*, 'well, be it so, nevertheless;' *nanu ća*, 'and (is it) not so?' 'is not then?' 'there can be no doubt.' According to native lexicographers *nanu* is also a vocative particle = 'ho,' 'hallo;' a particle implying kindness, conciliation, &c., = 'pray,' 'good friend;' a responsive particle; a particle of reproach, perplexity, &c.

नन्तृ *nantṛi, tā, trī, tṛi* (fr. rt. *nam*), bending, bowing, stooping; (in grammar) Ved. changing a dental to a cerebral.

Nantarya, as, ā, am, to be bent or bowed, to be saluted, to be revered or honoured.

Nantva, as, ā, am, Ved. to be bent or bowed, to be humbled.

नन्द् *nand* (thought by some to be for *nanad*, a reduplicated form of rt. *nad*, to utter sounds of approbation; the initial *n* is never cerebralized), cl. 1. P. (ep. also A.) *nandati (-te)*, *nananda, nandishyati, anandīt, nanditum*, to be pleased or satisfied with, to be contented with, be glad of anything (with inst., rarely abl.): Caus. *nandayati, -yitum*, Aor. *ananandat*, to make glad, gladden: Desid. *ninandishati*: Intens. *nānandyate, nānanti*.

Nanda, as, m. happiness, pleasure, joy, felicity, prosperity; a flute eleven inches long; N. of one of the two drums of Yudhi-shṭhira; of one of the nine inestimable gems or treasures of Kuvera; an epithet of Vishṇu; N. of one of Skanda's attendants; of a Buddhist deity, (also read *nandana*); of a Nāga [cf. *nandaka*]; of a Nāga-rāja; of an attendant on Daksha; of a son of king Dhṛita-rāshṭra [cf. *nandaka*]; of a brother of Śākya-muni [cf. *nandaka*]; of a son of Vasu-deva; of a cowherd who was the foster-father of Kṛishṇa and apparently also of Durgā; of a leader of the Sātvatas; of a king of Pāṭali-putra, cut off by the machinations of Ćandragupta's minister Ćāṇakya, and founder of the Nanda dynasty; of a Buddhist writer on law [cf. *nanda-paṇḍita*]; of a mountain [cf. *nandi-giri*]; (*ā*), f. Delight, Felicity (personified as the wife of Harsha, cf. *nandi*), prosperity, happiness, joy; a small earthen water-jar [cf. *nandikā*]; a husband's sister [cf. *nanāndṛi*]; N. of one of the seven or five small Kumārīs or staffs of Indra's standard, (according to a commentator *nandā* and *upa-nandā*); the first, sixth, or eleventh day of the fortnight, considered as three auspicious Tithis [cf. *nandikā*]; an epithet of Gaurī; a form of Dākshāyaṇī; N. of an Apsaras, (also read *kāmyā*); of the eldest daughter of Vibhīshaṇa; N. of a girl connected with Śākya-muni, (also read *nandī*); of the mother of the tenth Arhat of the present Ava-sarpiṇī; N. of a wife of Gopāla-varman; of a river flowing near Kuvera's city Alakā, (often mentioned with *apara-nandā*; cf. *nandā-tīrtha*); (*ī*), f. the tree Cedrela Toona [cf. *nandī-vṛiksha*]; an epithet of Durgā; N. of Indra's residence, = *amarā-vatī*; [cf. *ā-n°, alaka-n°, go-n°*.] — *Nanda-kiśora, as*, m., N. of the author of a supplement to Vopa-deva's Mugdha-bodha. — *Nanda-gopa, as*, m. the cowherd Nanda. — *Nandagopa-kumāra, as*, m. 'son of the cowherd Nanda,' epithet of Kṛishṇa. — *Nanda-gopitā*, f., N. of a plant, see *rāsnā*. — *Nanda-nandana, as*, m. 'the foster-son of the cowherd Nanda,' epithet of Kṛishṇa. — *Nanda-nandanī*, f. 'daughter of the cowherd Nanda,' epithet of Durgā. — *Nanda-paṇḍita, as*, m., N. of a writer on jurisprudence. — *Nanda-padra*, N. of a town. — *Nanda-pāla, as*, m. 'guardian of the treasure Nanda,' epithet of Varuṇa. — *Nanda-putrī*, f. 'daughter of the cowherd Nanda,' epithet of Durgā. — *Nanda-putrotsava* (°*ra-ut*°), *as*, m., N. of the ninth chapter of the Kṛishṇa-khaṇḍa or fourth part of the Brahma-vaivarta-Purāṇa. — *Nanda-prayāga, as*, m., N. of a place mentioned in the Rasika-ramaṇa by Raghu-nātha (at the confluence of two rivers containing the word *nanda* in their names). — *Nanda-balā*, f., N. of a girl connected with Śākya-muni. — *Nanda-mitra, as*, m., N. of a man. — *Nanda-vardhana, as*, m. 'joy-increaser,' N. of a poet mentioned in the Śārṅgadhara-paddhati. — *Nanda-śarman, ā*, m., N. of an author. — *Nandā-tīrtha, am*, n., N. of a Tīrtha (the river Nandā?). — *Nandātmaja* (°*da-āt*°), *as*, m. 'son of the cowherd Nanda,' epithet of Kṛishṇa; (*ā*), f. 'daughter of the cowherd Nanda,' epithet of Durgā. — *Nandā-purāṇa, am*, n. 'the Purāṇa treating of Nandā,' N. of an Upa-Purāṇa. — *Nandā-prāćī-māhātmya, am*, n., N. of the eighteenth chapter of the Sṛishṭi-khaṇḍa or first part of the Padma-Purāṇa. — *Nandāśrama* (°*da-āś*°), *as*, m., N. of a hermitage. — *Nandā-hrada-tīrtha, am*, n., N. of a sacred bathing-place. — *Nandī-pura, am*, n., N. of a town mentioned in the Kathārṇava. — *Nandī-vṛiksha, as*, m., N. of several plants, = *nandi-vṛiksha*, Cedrela Toona; = *mesha-śṛiṅgī*, Thespesia Populneoides; = *sthālī*. — *Nandī-saras, as*, n., N. of Indra's lake.

Nandaka, as, ā, am, rejoicing, making happy or glad, causing pleasure, gladdening; rejoicing or delighting in; rejoicing a family; joyful; (*as*), m. a frog (= *nandana*); N. of Kṛishṇa's sword; of a Nāga [cf. *nanda*]; of one of Skanda's attendants; of a son of king Dhṛita-rāshṭra [cf. *nanda*]; of a Śākya [cf. *nanda*]; of a bull; of a village; (according to some also) happiness, pleasure (= *ānanda*); N. of the foster-father of Kṛishṇa, = *nanda*; (*ikā*), f. a small water-jar [cf. *nandā*]; N. of three auspicious Tithis, the first, sixth, and eleventh, (according to the Tithi-tattva) the sixth Tithi [cf. *nandā*]; N. of Indra's pleasure-ground.

Nandaki, is, m. (fr. *nand*?), long pepper.

Nandakin, ī, m. 'the possessor of Nandaka,' an epithet of Kṛishṇa-Vishṇu.

Nandathu, us, m. happiness, joy, felicity, prosperity.

Nandana, as, ā, am, delighting, rejoicing, gladdening, pleasing, making glad or happy; (*as*), m. 'rejoicing (a father),' a son; 'the rejoicer,' an epithet of Vishṇu; an epithet of Śiva; a frog [cf. *nandaka*]; a species of plant with a poisonous fruit, (according to commentators also f.); N. of one of Skanda's attendants; of a Siddha; of a Buddhist deity, (also read *nanda*); of the seventh of the nine white Jaina Balas; of a mountain; of the twenty-sixth year in a Jupiter cycle of sixty years; of a particular form of temple; (*ā*), f. 'rejoicing (a mother),' a daughter; (*am*), n. a grove or garden frequented by the gods, especially Indra's pleasure-ground or elysium [cf. *nāndana*]; N. of a sword (= *asi-ratna*, cf. *nandaka*); N. of a species of the Dhṛiti metre (four times eighteen syllables); rejoicing, gladdening; joy, felicity; [cf. Hib. *naoidhin*, 'an infant.'] — *Nandana-kānana, am*, n. 'the divine pleasure-grove,' N. of a wood mentioned in the Rasika-ramaṇa by Raghu-nātha. — *Nandana-ja, am*, n. 'produced in elysium,' yellow sandal-wood. — *Nandana-mālā*, f. 'joy-causing garland,' N. of a garland worn by Kṛishṇa. — *Nandana-vana, am*, n. the pleasure-grove of the gods; [cf. *nandana*, n.]

Nandanaka, as, m. (at the end of a comp.) a son.

Nandanta, as, ī, am, delighting, making happy; (*as*), m. a son; a friend; a king, a prince; (*ī*), f. a daughter; [cf. *nandayanta*.]

Nandayat, an, antī, at, rejoicing, delighting, making glad.

Nandayanta, as, ī, am, making happy, rejoicing, delighting; (also read *nandanta*.)

Nandāyanīya, as, m., N. of a pupil of Bāshkali.

Nandi, is, m. (for *nandī* see under *nanda*), 'the happy one,' epithet of Vishṇu; of Śiva; N. of an attendant of Śiva [cf. *nandin* and *nandikeśvara*]; N. of a man; of a Gandharva; (according to some also) the speaker of the prologue or prelude to a drama or one who pronounces the benediction, see *nāndī, nāndin*; (*is, i*), m. n. gambling, gaming; (*is*), f. joy, delight, pleasure, happiness, prosperity, welfare, (in these senses said to be also m. n.); Joy personified as a daughter of Heaven or as the wife of Kāma and mother of Harsha. — *Nandi-kuṇḍa, as, am*, m. n., N. of a sacred bathing-place. — *Nandi-kshetra, am*, n., N. of a district frequented by the gods. — *Nandi-giri, is*, m., N. of a mountain; [cf. *nandi-devī*.] — *Nandigiri-māhātmya, am*, n. 'the glory of Nandi-giri,' N. of a work. — *Nandi-gupta, as*, m., N. of a prince of Kaśmīra. — *Nandi-grāma, as*, m., N. of a village (near the modern Daulatābād, where Bharata resided during Rāma's banishment). — *Nandigrāma-darśana, am*, n. 'description of the village Nandi-grāma,' the twenty-ninth chapter of the Pātāla-khaṇḍa of the Padma-Purāṇa. — *Nandi-ghosha, as*, m. cry of joy (= *vandi-ghosha*); the proclamation of a panegyrist or herald; the chariot of Arjuna. — *Nandi-taru, us*, m. = *dhava*, the tree Grislea Tomentosa. — *Nandi-tūrya, am*, n. a musical instrument played on joyful occasions. — *Nandi-deva, as*, m., N. of a man; (*ī*), ? the common N. of one of the loftiest Himalayan peaks. — *Nandi-purāṇa, am*, n. 'the Purāṇa of Nandi,' N. of part of the Kedāra-kalpa. — *Nandi-mukha* = *nandī-mukha*, a species of rice [cf. *nadī-mukha*]; N. of a man. — *Nandimukha-sughosha, as*, m., N. of a man. — *Nandimukhasughoshāvadāna* (°*sha-av*°), N. of a Buddhist work. — *Nandi-rudra, as*, m., N. of Śiva in a joyful or serene form. — *Nandi-vardhana, as, ā, am*, increasing pleasure, promoting happiness; (*as*), m. an epithet of Śiva; a son [cf. *nandana*]; a friend; the end of a half month, i. e. the day of full moon or new moon; N. of a particular form of temple (= *nandin*); N. of a prince, son of Udāvasu or of Janaka, (in this sense also read *nandi-vardha*); N. of a place. — *Nandi-vāralaka, as*, m. a species of fish. — *Nandi-vṛiksha* or *nandi-vṛikshaka, as*, m. the tree Cedrela Toona; [cf. *nandī-vṛiksha*.] — *Nandi-vega, ās*, m. pl., N. of a people. — *Nandi-sheṇa* or *nandi-sena, as*, m., N. of one of Skanda's attendants. — *Nandisheṇeśvara* (°*ṇa-īś*°), *am*, n., N. of a Liṅga. — *Nandī-mukha, as*, m. (*nandī* for *nandi*?), 'having joy on the face,' an epithet of Śiva; a species of aquatic bird; a species of rice [cf. *nandi-mukha, nadī-mukha, nāndī-mukhī*]; (*ās*), m. pl. a class of manes or deceased ancestors who are worshipped on festival occasions [cf. *nāndī-mukha*]; (*ī*), f. sleep (in which the face shows joy), drowsiness; a species of the Ati-śakvarī metre; (more correctly *nāndī-mukha*.) — *Nandīśa* (°*di-īśa*), *as*, m., N. of one of Śiva's attendants [cf. *nandi, nandin*]; N. of Śiva; a kind of time in music (= *nandīśvara*). — *Nandīśvara* (°*di-iś*°), *as*, m. 'lord of joy,' an epithet of Śiva; N. of Nandin, the leader of Śiva's attendants; N. of one of Kuvera's attendants; N. of a place held sacred by the Jainas; a kind of time in music (= *nandīśa*). — *Nandīśvara-purāṇa* = *nandi-purāṇa*. — *Nandīśvara-yogopākhyāna* (°*ga-up*°), *am*, n., N. of the thirty-first and thirty-second chapters of the Uttara-khaṇḍa of the Śiva-Purāṇa. — *Nandīśvarotpatti* (°*di-īś*°, °*ra-ut*°), *is*, f. 'the birth of Śiva,' N. of the forty-second chapter of the Liṅga-Purāṇa. — *Nandy-āvarta*, *as*, m. a particular kind of diagram [cf. *nandikāvarta*]; a sort of palace or temple built in the shape of the above diagram or in the form of a quadrangle without a western gate, (in this sense also *am*, n.); a species of large fish; a kind of tree; the shrub Tabernæmontana Coronaria (= *tagara*, = *bhagavad-druma*), probably the sacred fig-tree; a species of shell called so because of its convolutions (*āvarta*). — *Nandy-upapurāṇa*, *am*, n. = *nandi-purāṇa*. — *Nandy-upākhyāna*, *am*, n. 'the episode of Nandi,' N. of the forty-fifth to the fiftieth chapter of the Uttara-khaṇḍa of the Śiva-Purāṇa.

Nandika, *as*, m. the Tūn tree (Cedrela Toona), the wood of which resembles mahogany and is used for furniture &c. [cf. *nandi, nandi-vṛiksha*]; N. of one of Śiva's attendants; N. of a pupil of Śākyamuni, chief of the village Uru-vilvā. — *Nandikāćārya-tantra* (°*ka-āć*°), N. of a medical work. — *Nandikāvarta* (°*ka-āv*°), *as*, m. a kind of diagram (= *nandy-āvarta*); a species of plant. — *Nandikeśa* (°*ka-īśa*), *as*, m., N. of a temple or holy place. — *Nandikeśa-liṅga*, *am*, n., N. of the thirty-ninth chapter of the Śiva-Purāṇa. — *Nandikeśvara* (°*ka-iś*°), *as*, m., N. of one of Śiva's chief attendants [cf. *nandin, nandi*]; N. of an author. — *Nandikeśvara-kāśikā*, f., N. of a Vedānta work by Nandikeśvara treating of the first of Pāṇini's grammatical aphorisms as containing the dogmas of the Vedānta belief. — *Nandikeśvara-tīrtha*, *am*, n., N. of a sacred bathing-place mentioned in the Śiva-Purāṇa. — *Nandikeśvara-purāṇa*, *am*, n., N. of an Upa-Purāṇa. — *Nandikeśvara-saṃhitā*, f., N. of a work mentioned in the Tantra-sāra. — *Nandikeśvarābhisheka* (°*ra-abh*°), *as*, m., N. of the forty-third and forty-fourth chapters of the Liṅga-Purāṇa. — *Nandikeśvarotpatti* (°*ra-ut*°), *is*, f., N. of the twenty-first chapter of the Uttara-khaṇḍa of the Śiva-Purāṇa.

Nandin, *ī*, *inī*, *i* (at the end of a comp.), rejoicing, gladdening; happy, delighted; delighting in, liking; making happy, gladdening; (*ī*), m. 'rejoicing (a father),' a son; the speaker of the prelude or benediction at the opening of a drama [cf. *nāndin*]; N. of several plants, the Indian fig-tree, Thespesia Populneoides, Phaseolus Radiatus; N. of a particular form of temple [cf. *nandi-vardhana*]; N. of a being attending on Śiva and (commonly) of the bull on which he rides [cf. *nandi, nandīśa, nandikeśvara*]; N. of a Buddhist saint and teacher; (*inī*), f. 'rejoicing (a mother),' a daughter; a husband's sister (= *nanāndṛi*); holy basil (= *tulasī*); Nardostachys Jatamansi (= *jaṭāmāṃsī*); a kind of perfume (= *reṇukā*); a fabulous cow, daughter of Surabhi, related to the cow of plenty, and the property of the sage Vasishṭha; an epithet or a form of Durgā; an epithet of Gaṅgā or the Ganges; N. of one of the Mātṛis attending on Skanda; of a place; of a river (also called Vala-jā). — *Nandinī-tanaya* or *nandinī-suta*, *as*, m. 'son of Nandinī,' epithet of Vyāḍi. — *Nandinī-tīrtha*, *am*, n., N. of a sacred bathing-place.

Nandī, f. See under *nanda* and *nandi*.

Nandya (fr. *nanda*), Nom. P. *nandyati*, &c., to be glad, to rejoice.

नन्दलाल *nandalāla*, *as*, m., N. of a man.

नन्दीक *nandīka*, *as*, m. (?), a cock.

नन्दीट *nandīṭa*, *as*, m. a bald-headed man.

नन्नम *nannama* (fr. rt. *nam*) in *ku-n*°, q. v.

Nannamyamāna, *as*, *ā*, *am* (fr. the Intens.), bending or bowing very low.

नपराजित् *na-parājit*, *t*, m. 'having no conquerer,' 'not overpowered (?),' an epithet of Śiva.

नपात् *napāt* and *naptṛi*, *tā*, m. (in Uṇādi-s. II. 96. derived fr. *na* + rt. *pat*, 'to fall;' in Pāṇini VI. 3, 75, fr. *na* + *pāt* fr. rt. 3. *pā*, 'to protect,' according to which latter derivation *napāt*, *naptṛi* are for *na-pātṛi*, 'not the protector,' allied to *na-pitṛi*, 'not the father;' but a more probable derivation is fr. rt. 1. *nabh*, an older form of rt. 1. *nah*, 'to connect,' a descendant being 'the connecting relative;' in the earlier Vedic language the strong cases are formed fr. *napāt*, the weak fr. *naptṛi*, e. g. acc. sing. *napātam*, dat. sing. *naptre*; in the later Sanskṛit all the cases come fr. *naptṛi*), a descendant, offspring in general, a son, &c. (Ved.); a grandson, a son's son, (in the later language restricted to this meaning); N. of one of the Viśve-devās; (according to Mahī-dhara on Vājasaneyi-saṃhitā XIX. 56. *napātaḥ* = *deva-yāna-pathaḥ*, the path of the gods; according to Sāyaṇa on Ṛig-veda X. 15, 3, *napātaḥ* = *vināśābhāvaḥ*); (*tī*), f., Ved. a daughter; a granddaughter, (in Atharva-veda IX. 1, 3, *naptī*); *naptī* and *naptyā*, f. du. = (in Sāma-veda) 'the two pieces of wood for pressing out the Soma,' or = 'heaven and earth;' or in Ṛig-veda IX. 9, 1, = 'the hands;' *naptyaḥ*, f. pl. in Ṛig-veda I. 50, 9, = 'the female horses of the chariot,' i. e. 'the daughters of the chariot,' (according to Sāy. so called 'because with them the chariot does not fall'); in Ṛig-veda IX. 14, 5, *naptyaḥ* is said to = 'rays' or 'fingers;' horses as 'granddaughters of the chariot;' the fingers, the hands; (*trī*), f. a granddaughter, (*naptrī*, f., and not *naptī*, is the only form used in classical Sanskṛit); [cf. *tanū-napāt, pra-napāt*: Zend *naptar, napat*, 'descendant;' *napt-i*, 'kindred;' *naptya*, 'a family:' Gr. ἀ-νεψιό-ς for ἀ-νεπτιό-ς, quasi *con-nepot-iu-s*, νέπ-ο-δες: Lat. *nepō(t)-s*, f. *nept-i-s*: Old Iceland. *nefi*, 'brother;' *nift*, 'sister:' Old Germ. *nefo*, 'grandson, cousin;' *niftila*, 'female cousin:' Goth. *nithyi-s*, m. 'cousin;' *nith-yō*, f. 'a female cousin:' Slav. *netii*, 'a brother's son:' Boh. *neti*, base *neter*, 'a female cousin.']

Napātka, *as*, *ā*, *am*, relating or belonging to a grandson; (applied to a particular sacrificial fire, = *tṛitīyo 'gnis*.)

Naptṛikā, f. a species of bird.

नपुंस् *na-puṃs*, *-pumān*, m. not a man, a eunuch.

Na-puṃsa, *as*, m. not a male, a eunuch.

Na-puṃsaka, *as*, *am*, m. n. neither man nor woman, a hermaphrodite; a eunuch, an impotent or imbecile man, a coward; (*am*), n. a word in the neuter gender; the neuter gender. — *Napuṃsaka-pāda*, *as*, m., N. of the eighth chapter of Durgādāsa's commentary on Vopa-deva's Mugdha-bodha, called Su-bodhā. — *Napuṃsaka-liṅga-saṅgraha*, *as*, m., N. of a chapter of the grammatical work Nāma-liṅgānuśāsana by Amara-siṃha.

नप्तृ *naptṛi*, *naptī*, *naptrī*. See *napāt* above.

नभ् 1. *nabh*, cl. 1. A. *nabhate*, &c., Ved. to burst, to be torn or rent asunder; to hurt, injure, destroy, (*nebhe* occurs in Bhaṭṭi-kāvya XIV. 33); cl. 4. 9. P. *nabhyati*, *nabhnāti*, &c., to hurt, injure: Caus. P. *nabhayati*, *-yitum*, to cause to burst, tear open.

2. *nabh*, *p*, f., Ved. (according to Sāy.) hurt, injury, destruction.

Nabhanu, *us*, m. and *ū*, *ūs*, f., Ved. a spring, river, (water which bursts forth.)

1. *nabhanya*, *as*, *ā*, *am* (fr. *nabhana*), Ved. bursting out, breaking or coming forth (as a hymn or as a horse). According to Sāy. = 'being in the sky,' 'ethereal;' 'injuring,' 'destroying;' 'a hymn.' (For 2. *nabhanya* see under *nabha* below.)

Nabhanva, *as*, m., Ved. a river; (according to modern scholars the form is *nabhanu*.)

नभ *nabha*, *as*, m. (said to be fr. rt. 1. *nah* with affix *bha*, but rather fr. *nabh* an older form of 1. *nah*, 'to bind,' 'connect,' as 'connecting heaven and earth;' according to others fr. rt. 1. *nabh*, 'to rend asunder or be broken up into clouds'), = *nabhas*, the sky, atmosphere; the month Śrāvaṇa (July–August); N. of a son of Manu Svāroćisha or of the third Manu (mentioned together with Nabhasya); N. of one of the seven sages of the sixth Manvantara; N. of a demon, son of Vipra-ćitti by Siṃhikā; N. of a son of Nala (Nishadha) and father of Puṇḍarīka [cf. *nabhas*]; (*ā*), f. a spitting-pot (for *nabhās?*); N. of the city of the Sun; [cf. Zend *nap-ta*, 'moist, wet;' Gr. νέφ-ος, νεφ-έλη, ξυν-νέ-νοφε, νεφό-ω, probably δνόφος, ἰο-δνεφής, γνόφος; Lat. *nūb-ē-s*, *nūbilu-s*, *nebula*, probably *Neptū-nu-s*, *nimbu-s* for *nembu-s*; Old Iceland. *nifl-heim-r*; Old Germ. *nib-ul*; Mod. Germ. *neb-el*; Angl. Sax. *ge-nip*, 'a cloud;' Slav. *neb-o*, base *neb-es*, 'sky;' Lith. *debes-i-s*, 'a cloud,' through change of *n* into *d*, as in *dewyni*, 'nine;' Hib. *neamh*, 'heaven;' Cambro-Brit. *nev*, 'heaven.'] — *Nabha-ga*, *as*, m. 'going on the sky,' N. of a son of Manu Vaivasvata; [cf. *nabhāga*, *nābhāga*.]

2. *nabhanya*, *as*, *ā*, *am*, Ved. (according to Sāy.) being in the sky, ethereal, heavenly; (see col. 2.)

Nabhas, *as*, n. fog, vapour; a cloud; sky, atmosphere, ether or heaven; ether as one of the five elements; N. of a month in the rainy season (= *śrāvaṇa*) or July–August, (according to lexicographers in this sense m.); period of life, age; the vapour or fluidity of the Soma (Ved.); water (Ved.); the sun (according to Nir. II. 14); (*ās*), m. a cloud, the rains or the rainy season; the nose, smell; the fibres in the root of a lotus or a rope made of lotus fibres; a spitting-pot; N. of a prince, son of Nala and father of Puṇḍarīka; (*asī*), n. du. both worlds, heaven and earth. — *Nabhaḥ-ketana*, *am*, n. 'sky-banner,' the sun. — *Nabhaḥ-krānta*, *as*, or *nabhaḥ-krāntin*, *ī*, m. 'going in the sky' (from the lion-like shape of certain clouds), a lion. — *Nabhaḥ-pāntha*, *as*, m. 'sky-traveller,' the sun. — *Nabhaḥ-prabheda*, *as*, m., N. of a descendant of Vi-rūpa and author of a Ṛig-veda hymn (X. 112). — *Nabhaḥ-prāṇa*, *as*, m. 'sky-breath,' air, wind; [cf. *kha-śvāsa*, *nabhaḥ-śvāsa*.] — *Nabhaḥ-śrit*, *t*, *t*, *t*, reaching to the sky, attaining heaven. — *Nabhaḥ-śvāsa*, *as*, m. 'sky-breath,' air, wind; [cf. *nabhaḥ-prāṇa*.] — *Nabhaḥ-sad*, *t*, m. 'inhabiting the sky,' a god; a star. — *Nabhaḥ-saras*, *as*, n. 'sky-lake,' the clouds. — *Nabhaḥ-sarit*, f. 'sky-river,' the milky-way (= *deva-patha*); the celestial Ganges. — *Nabhaḥ-stha*, *as*, *ā*, *am*, 'situated in heaven,' celestial, aerial, heavenly, ethereal. — *Nabhaḥ-sthala*, *as*, m. 'whose residence is the sky,' an epithet of Śiva; (*ī*), f. the sky. — *Nabhaḥ-sthita*, *as*, *ā*, *am*, abiding in heaven or in the sky; (*as*), m. a division of the infernal regions, a hell. — *Nabhaḥ-spriś*, *k*, *k*, *k*, or *nabhaḥ-spriśa*, *as*, *ā*, *am*, Ved. 'sky-touching,' reaching to the sky. — *Nabhaś-ćakshus*, *us*, m. 'eye of the sky,' the sun. — *Nabhaś-ćamasa*, *as*, m. 'drinking vessel of heaven,' the moon; a variegated cake (= *ćitra-pūpa*); magic, conjuring. — *Nabhaś-ćara*, *as*, *ī*, *am*, 'sky-going,' going in the air; (*as*), m. an inhabitant of heaven, a god; a Vidyā-dhara or demigod so called. — *Nabhas-tala*, *am*, n. 'the bottom of the clouds,' the lower region of the sky, nether sky; the sky, atmosphere; (in astronomy) N. of the tenth solar mansion. — *Nabhas-maya*, *as*, *ī*, *am*, Ved. vaporous, vapory, filled with vapour, exhaling vapour, misty, hazy; (Sāy.) bright as the sun. — 1. *nabhas-vat*, *ān*, *atī*, *at*, vaporous, filled with vapour, misty, cloudy; young; (*ān*), m. air, wind; (*atī*), f., N. of the wife of Antar-dhāna and mother of Havir-dhāna. — 2. *nabhas-vat*, ind. like vapour. — *Nabho-ga*, *as*, *am*, m. n. (?), a star; (*as*), m.,

N. of one of the seven sages of the tenth Manv-antara.—*Nabho-gaja, as,* m. 'an elephant in the sky,' a cloud.—*Nabho-gati, is,* f. going through the sky, going in the air, soaring, flying.—*Nabho-jā, ās, ās, am,* Ved. produced from vapour.—*Nabho-jū, ūs, ūs, u,* Ved. impelling the clouds; (Sāy.) pervading or traversing the sky.—*Nabho-ḍa, as,* m., N. of one of the Viśve-devās.—*Nabho-duha,* 'milking the sky;' or *nabho-dvīpa,* 'sky-island;' or *nabho-dhūma,* 'sky-smoke;' or *nabho-dhvaja, as,* m. 'sky-banner,' a cloud.—*Nabho-drishṭi, is, is, i,* blind; looking up to heaven.—*Nabho-nadī,* f. 'sky-river,' the celestial Ganges.—*Nabho-maṇi, is,* m. 'sky-jewel,' the sun.—*Nabho-maṇḍala, am,* n. 'sky-circle,' the firmament; the atmosphere.—*Nabhomaṇḍala-dīpa, as,* m. 'light of the sky,' the moon.—*Nabho 'mbu-pa, as,* m. 'drinking the water of the sky or rain-water,' the bird Cātaka, Cuculus Melanoleucus.—*Nabho-yoni, is,* m. 'whose birthplace is the sky,' epithet of Śiva.—*Nabho-rajas, as,* n. 'sky-dust (?),' darkness.—*Nabho-rūpa, as, ā, am,* Ved. having the form or colour of the clouds, dark-coloured.—*Nabho-reṇu, us,* f. fog, mist, vapour.—*Nabho-laya, as,* m. 'having its abode in the sky,' smoke.—*Nabho-lih, ṭ, ṭ, ṭ,* 'sky-licking,' lofty, towering, rising to the clouds.—*Nabho-rata, as,* m. 'the expanse of the sky,' the atmosphere.—*Nabho-vid, t, t, t,* knowing or possessing heaven or the sky.—*Nabho-vīthī,* f. 'sky-road,' the path of the sun.—*Nabhaukas* (*nabha* for *nabhas* + *okas*), inhabiting the atmosphere or heaven.

Nabhasa, as, ā, am, Ved. vapourish, vapoury, filled with vapour, misty; (*as*), m. heaven, air, atmosphere; the rainy season; the ocean; N. of one of the seven sages in the tenth Manv-antara; of a Dānava; (also read *rabhasa.*)—*Nabhasaṅ-gama, as,* m. 'sky-goer,' a bird.

Nabhasya, as, ā, am, vapoury, filled with vapour, misty, foggy; (*as*), m., N. of a month of the rainy season (=Bhādra, August–September); N. of a son of Manu Svāroćisha or of the third Manu [cf. *nabha*]; epithet of Śiva.

Nabhāka, as, m., N. of a Vedic Ṛishi by whom three hymns of the Ṛig-veda (VIII. 39–41) are supposed to have been composed, see *nābhāka;* (*am*), n. (said to be = *nabhas* and to be derived fr. 2. *na* + rt. 1. *bhā* + aff. *āka*), darkness; a cloud; the sky.—*Nabhāka-vat* in Ṛig-veda VIII. 40 = the hymn of Nabhāka.

1. *nabhya, as, ā, am,* foggy, misty, cloudy.

नभाग *nabhāga, as,* m., N. of a son of Manu Vaivasvata; [cf. *nabha-ga, nābhāga.*]

नभि *nabhi, is,* m. (?), a wheel.

नभीत *na-bhīta, as, ā, am,* not afraid, undaunted, dauntless.—*Nabhīta-vat,* ind. in a fearless manner, fearlessly.

नभ्य 2. *nabhya, am,* n. (said to be fr. *nabha* for *nābhi*), Ved. the centre part of a wheel, the nave; the middle.—*Nabhya-stha, as, ā, am,* standing in the middle; belonging to the nave of a wheel, fit for a nave; *nabhyaṃ tailam,* oil for greasing the nave of a wheel.

नभ्राज् *na-bhrāj, ṭ,* m. 'not shining,' a dark cloud.

नम *nam,* cl. 1. P. A. *namati, -te* (the Ātmane-pada being generally used in the intransitive sense), *nanāma, neme* (2nd sing. *nemitha* or *nanantha,* ep. 3rd pl. A. *ava-nanāmire,* Ved. 1st sing. P. *nānāma*), *nantā, naṇsyati, namishyati, anaṇsīt, anaṇsta* (Ved., Aor. 3rd sing. *anān;* Leṭ, 1st sing. *naṇsai,* Ṛig-veda III. 33. 10), *nantum* (Ved. inf. *ni-name*), to bow to, make or pay obeisance to (with dat., gen., and acc.); to bow, bow down, subject or submit one's self; to bend; to be bent or curved; to sink; (in grammar) to change a dental letter into a cerebral; to sound: Pass. *namyate:* Caus. *namayati* and (with prep.) *nāmayati, -yitum,* Aor. *anīnamat,* to cause to bow, bend, curve, make curved, (with *dhanus* or *ćāpam*) to bend a bow; to cause to sink or decline; to ward off; to turn away from; (in grammar) to change a dental into a cerebral: Desid. *ninaṇsati:* Intens. *nannamīti, nannanti, nannamyate,* to bow, be bent, bend very low; [cf. Zend *nemanh* = *namas, nim-ata,* 'grass:' Gr. νέμ-ω, νέμ-ο-μαι, νωμά-ω, νομ-ή, νέμ-η-σι-ς, νεμ-έ-τωρ, νομ-εύ-ς, νέμ-ε-σι-ς, νόμο-ς, νομίζ-ω, νόμισ-μα, νέμ-ος, Νε-μέα, νομ-ό-ς: Lat. *Nūma, Nūm-i-tor, nūm-e-ru-s, Numerius, nĕm-us:* Goth. and Angl. Sax. *nim-an,* 'to take,' originally 'to subdue:' Old Germ. *nām-a,* 'prey:' Lith. *náma-s,* 'a house;' *nūm-a-s,* 'gain:' Lett. *nom-a,* 'interest:' probably Hib. *naomh,* 'a saint, sacred;' *naomhachd,* 'holiness.']

Namat, an, antī, at, bending, bowing, stooping.

Namata, as, ā, am, bent, bowed, crooked, curved; (*as*), m. a master, lord (?); an actor, mime; smoke; a cloud; (*am*), n. felt, woollen stuff; [cf. *nāmatika,* 1. *navata.*]

Namana, as, m. one who causes to bend or bow; (*am*), n. bowing down, sinking; [cf. *griha-n°.*]

Namanīya, as, ā, am, to be bowed down to, one to whom one must pay obeisance, venerable.

Namayat, an, antī, at, bending, causing to bow down, inclining.

Namayishṇu, us, us, u, Ved. bowing, bending.

Namas, as, n. (often treated as an indeclinable interjection or exclamation), bowing, bending, making a bow, a bow, salutation, reverential salutation, paying honour (in gesture or words); adoration, obeisance (performed by joining the palms and inclining the head; often used in connection with the N. of a deity in the dat., e. g. *Rāmāya namas,* salutation or glory or reverence to Rāma); food (Ved.); giving, presenting, a gift, present; a thunderbolt (Ved.); an inarticulate cry (said to be m.?).—*Nama-ukti, is,* f., Ved. uttering a salutation, paying homage or obeisance.—*Namas-kartṛi, tā, trī, tṛi,* worshipping or adoring (the gods); a worshipper, pious.—*Namas-kāra, as,* m. uttering the interjection or exclamation *namas,* bowing, respectful or reverential address or salutation, adoration, obeisance; a sort of poison; (*ī*), f. a sensitive plant.—*Namaskāra-vat, ān, atī, at,* Ved. containing the Namas-kāra.—*Namas-kārya, as, ā, am,* to be bowed down to, one to whom one must pay obeisance, before whom one must say *namas;* to be worshipped.—*Namas-kṛi,* cl. 8. P. *-karoti, -kartum,* to utter the exclamation *namas* (sometimes with dat., loc., and acc.).—*Namas-kṛita, as, ā, am,* worshipped, reverenced, adored.—*Namas-kṛitya* or *namas-kṛitvā,* ind. having saluted reverentially.—*Namas-kriyā,* f. reverential salutation, bowing, worshipping, adoration.—*Namas-vat, ān, atī, at,* Ved. paying adoration or homage, worshipping, adoring; inspiring veneration; (Sāy.) abounding in food.—*Namas-vin, ī, inī, i,* paying homage, worshipping, reverential, respectful.—*Namo-guru, us,* m. a spiritual teacher.—*Namo-vāka, as,* m., Ved. uttering the *namas* or obeisance in general.—*Namo-vṛikti, is,* f., Ved. reverential cleansing (of the Barhis).—*Namo-vṛidh, t, t, t,* Ved. honoured by adoration; (Sāy.) food-augmenting, increasing food; (*ā*), m. du. 'delighting in adoration,' epithet of Mitra-Varuṇa.

Namasa, as, ā, am, favourable, kindly disposed; (*as*), m. agreement (?).

Namasāna, as, ā, am, Ved. paying obeisance, worshipping.

Namasita, as, ā, am (probably corrupted from *namasyita*), reverenced, respected, worshipped.

1. *namasya* (fr. *namas*), Nom. P. (ep. also A.) *namasyati* (*-te*), &c., to pay homage, make obeisance, worship (with acc.); to act humbly or deferentially.

2. *namasya, as, ā, am,* to be worshipped or adored, one to whom obeisance must be made, venerable, respectable, entitled to salutation or civility; reverential, respectful, humble; (*ā*), f. reverence, respect, worship, adoration.

3. *namasya,* ind. having paid homage, having worshipped.

Namasyat, an, antī, at, saluting reverentially, making obeisance, bowing to, paying adoration.

Namasyita, as, ā, am, reverenced, respected, worshipped; [cf. *namasita.*]

Namasyu, us, us, u, Ved. paying homage, making obeisance, worshipping; (*us*), m., N. of a son of Pravīra, descendant of Puru.

Namita, as, ā, am, bowed, bent down, making salutation or obeisance.

Namya, as, ā, am, to be bowed down to, venerable; changeable to a cerebral letter; (*ā*), f. the night (Ved.).

Namra, as, ā, am, bowing, bowing down, inclining, (*mūrdhnā namraḥ,* bowing the head, lit. with the head); bent, bowed, inclined; curved, crooked; hanging down; sunk; making obeisance; lowly, submissive, reverential, humble; worshipping, adoring; devoted to; (*ā*), m. du., Ved. epithet of two verses addressed to Agni.—*Namra-tā,* f. or *namra-tva, am,* n. the state of being bowed or bent, bowing, bowing or hanging down, obeisance, adoration, respect, devotion; submissiveness, humbleness, humility, meekness; condescension.—*Namra-prakṛiti, is, is, i,* of a gentle or submissive disposition.—*Namra-mukha, as, ī, am,* having the face bent down, looking down.—*Namra-mūrti, is, is, i,* having the form bent, stooping, bowed.—*Namrāṅga* (°*ra-aṅ*°), *as, ī, am,* bowing or bending the body, bowed, bent, stooping.—*Namrī-kṛita, as, ā, am,* bowed down, bent down, humbled.

Namraka, as, ā, am, bowed down, bent, stooping; (*as*), m. a species of reed (= *vetasa*).

Namrita, as, ā, am, bent down, bowed down, made to sink.

नमात्र *na-mātra, as, am,* m. n. (?), a particular high number; [cf. *nahi-mātra.*]

नमि *nami* = *nemi,* q. v.

नमी *namī,* m., Ved., N. of a Ṛishi; (according to Sāy. on Ṛig-veda I. 53. 7), foe-prostrating (applied to the thunderbolt).

नमुच *namuća, as,* m., N. of an ancient sage; (also read *unmuću, pramuću, muću, unmuća, vimuća.*)

नमुचि *na-mući, is,* m. 'not loosing the heavenly waters' (i. e. confining the clouds and preventing the flow of rain), N. of a demon vanquished and slain by Indra and the Aśvins; N. of the god of love.—*Namući-dvish, ṭ,* 'enemy of Namući;' or *Namući-sūdana, as,* 'destroyer of Namući;' or *Namući-han, ā,* m. 'killer of Namući,' epithets of Indra.

नमुर *na-mura, as, am,* m. n. (?), Ved. not dying (?).

नमेरु *nameru, us,* m. the tree Eleocarpus Ganitrus (= *rudrāksha,* = *sura-punnāga*).

नमैय *namaiya, as,* m., N. of a poet.

नम्ब् *namb,* cl. 1. P. *nambati,* &c., to go, move.

नम्र *namra.* See above.

नय् 1. *nay,* cl. 1. A. *nayate, neye, nayitum,* to go, move; to protect; [cf. rt. 1. *nī.*]

नय *naya, as,* m. (fr. rt. 1. *nī*), guiding, leading, directing, managing; manner of conducting one's self, behaviour, conduct, course of conduct, way of life, management; prudent conduct or behaviour, good management; prudence, reason; polity, policy, political wisdom, state-policy, political economy, statesmanship, civil administration, government; any work on policy or political economy; Prudence or Policy personified as a son of Dharma and Kriyā; plan, design; leading thought, maxim, principle; opinion, system, course, method; philosophical system; the philosophical part of the Veda(?); a kind of game; a sort of dice or men for playing this game [cf. *naya-pīṭhī*]; a move in this game (?); N. of a son of the thirteenth Manu; (*as, ā, am*), = *netṛi*, leading, guiding, conducting; a leader, guide; = *nyāya*, fit, right, proper. — *Naya-kovida, as, ā, am*, skilled in policy, prudent. — *Naya-ga, as, ā, am*, following a system. — *Naya-ćakshus, us, us, us*, having political foresight, wise, prudent. — *Naya-jā*, f., N. of the wife of king Brahma-dāsa, father of Nārāyaṇa, who composed the Praśnārṇava. — *Naya-jña, as, ā, am*, knowing polity, prudent; knowing any system, a follower of any system. — *Naya-netṛi, tā*, m. a master in policy or politics. — *Naya-pāla, as*, m. 'protector of policy,' N. of a man; of a king. — *Naya-pīṭhī*, f. the board or cloth on which dice or men are moved in play. — *Naya-prayoga, as*, m. policy, political wisdom or address. — *Naya-loćana, am*, n. 'the eye of policy,' N. of a work. — *Naya-vat, ān, atī, at*, familiar with policy, versed in polity, prudent; containing any form of rt. 1. *nī* (as a Ṛik). — *Naya-vid, t, t, t*, or *naya-viśārada, as, ā, am*, m. knowing polity, skilled in policy, a politician, statesman. — *Naya-śālin, ī, inī, i*, possessing political wisdom, endowed with prudence. — *Naya-śāstra, am*, n. any work on policy or political economy, the doctrine of polity. — *Naya-sāra, as*, m. 'essence of polity,' N. of a treatise. — *Naya-siddhi, is*, f. political success, accomplishing anything by good management.

Nayaka, as, ā, am, a skilful manager, clever in policy or political administration.

Nayat, an, antī, at, leading, guiding; tending or conducing to; informing, certifying, giving evidence, obtaining.

Nayana, as, m., N. of a man; (*ā* or *ī*), f. the pupil of the eye; (*am*), n. leading, guiding, conducting, managing; governing, directing, ruling; leading or bringing to, drawing; (with *kālasya*), passing or spending (time); attaining, obtaining; 'the guiding or leading organ,' the eye. — *Nayana-goćara, as, ā, am*, perceptible by the eye, within the range of vision, visible, apparent. — *Nayana-ććhada, as*, m. 'eye-covering,' an eyelid. — *Nayana-jala, am*, n. 'eye-water,' tears. — *Nayana-patha, as*, m. range or field of sight. — *Nayana-puṭa, as, am*, m. n. (?), the eyelid. — *Nayana-vāri, i*, n. 'eye-water,' tears. — *Nayana-vishaya, as*, m. 'field of vision, range of sight,' the horizon. — *Nayana-salila, am*, n. 'eye-water,' tears. — *Nayanāñjana* (°*na-añ*°), *am*, n. any ointment for the eye. — *Nayanānanda* (°*na-ān*°) or *nayanānanda-śarman, ā*, m., N. of a commentator on the Amara-kosha. — *Nayanāmoshin* (°*na-ām*°), *ī, inī, i*, 'sight-stealing,' blinding. — *Nayanotsava* (°*na-ut*°), *as, ā, am*, 'eye-festival,' any lovely or desired object; a lamp. — *Nayanoda* (°*na-uda*), *am*, n. eye-water; [cf. *nayana-salila*.] — *Nayanopānta* (°*na-up*°), *as*, m. the outer angle or corner of the eye, the canthus. — *Nayanaushadha* (°*na-osh*°), *am*, n. 'eye-medicament,' green sulphate of iron or that salt in a state of partial decomposition by exposure to the atmosphere (used as a collyrium).

Nayitavya, as, ā, am, to be conducted or brought.

Nayishṭha, as, ā, am, Ved. leading in the best manner.

नयुत *nayuta, as, am*, m. n. (?), 100,000 millions.

नय्यग्रोध *nayyagrodha, as, ī, am* (fr. *nyagrodha*), Ved. relating to or produced from the sacred fig-tree; (also read *naiyagrodha*.)

नर *nara, as*, m. (for etymology see the simple form *nṛi*), a man, a male, a person; a man or piece at chess, draughts, &c.; the pin or gnomon of a sun-dial; (in grammar) person, personal termination [cf. *purusha*]; a sort of measure, a man's length; the original or eternal Man, the divine imperishable spirit pervading the universe (always associated with Nārāyaṇa which as a patronymic from Nara = 'son of the original Man;' in Manu Nara is apparently identified with Nārāyaṇa, see I. 10, where the waters are called Nārā as produced from Nara or the eternal spirit [according to Kullūka = Paramātman, Brahman], which spirit is thence also called Nārāyaṇa as 'having his first place of motion on the waters;' but in the more systematic mythology Nara and Nārāyaṇa are distinct, the former being regarded as a sage or patriarch, 'the best of men' or 'chief man,' while the latter is a god; in epic poetry they are the sons of Dharma by Mūrti or A-hiṅsā and are emanations of Vishṇu, Arjuna being identified with Nara, and Kṛishṇa with Nārāyaṇa; in some places Nara and Nārāyaṇa are called *devau*, 'the two gods,' or *pūrva-devau*, 'the two original gods,' or *ṛishī*, 'the two sages,' or *purāṇāv ṛishi-sattamau*, 'the two most ancient and best of sages,' or *tāpasau*, 'the two ascetics,' or *mahā-munī*, 'the two great Munis'); (*ās*), m. pl., N. of certain mythical beings allied to the Gandharvas and Kin-naras, qq. vv. (thought by some to be a kind of centaur, half horse, half man); N. of one of the ten horses of the moon; N. of a son of Manu Tāmasa; of a son of Viśvā-mitra; N. of a son of Gaya and father of Virāj; of a son of Su-dhṛiti and father of Kevala; N. of a son of Bhavan-manyu (Manyu) and father of Saṅkṛiti; N. of two kings of Kaśmīra; (*ī*), f. a woman, = *nārī*; (*am*), n. a kind of fragrant grass, = *rāma-karpūra*; [cf. Gr. ἀνήρ; Lat. *Nero, Neriene*; probably Hib. *naoi*, 'a man,' but see *nṛi*.] — *Nara-kapāla, as, am*, m. n. a man's skull. — *Nara-kīlaka, as*, m. the murderer of his spiritual preceptor. — *Nara-keśarin, ī*, m. 'man-lion,' 'half man, half lion,' Vishṇu in his fourth Ava-tāra; [cf. *nara-siṅha*.] — *Nara-grāha, as*, m. 'man-crocodile,' 'half man, half crocodile,' N. of a kind of Kirāta. — *Nara-tā*, f. or *nara-tva, am*, n. humanity, manhood, human condition. — *Nara-troṭakāćārya* (°*ka-āć*°), *as*, m., N. of a man. — *Nara-datta, as*, m., N. of a Brāhman, a nephew of the Ṛishi Asita; (*ā*), f., N. of a goddess executing the commands of the twentieth Arhat of the present Ava-sarpiṇī; one of the sixteen Vidyā-devīs. — *Nara-deva, as*, m. 'a god among men,' a sovereign, king. — *Naradeva-tva, am*, n. kingship, royalty, kingly rank. — *Naradeva-deva, as*, m. a god among the gods of men or kings. — *Naradeva-putra, as*, m. the son of a man and a god. — *Nara-dvish, ṭ*, m. 'enemy of men,' a Rakshas. — *Nara-nagara, am*, n., N. of a town. — *Nara-nātha, as*, m. 'protector of men,' a king, a prince. — *Naranātha-mārga, as*, m. 'king's road, royal road,' the chief road, high street. — *Naranāthāsana* (°*tha-ās*°), *am*, n. the throne or dignity of a king. — *Nara-nāyaka, as*, m. 'leader of men,' a king, a prince. — *Nara-nārāyaṇa, as*, m. an epithet of Kṛishṇa; (*au*), m. du. Kṛishṇa and Arjuna, see *nara* above. — *Naran-dhi, is*, m. 'man-containing,' the world, (a word given by Mahī-dhara to explain the etymology of *narandhisha* below.) — *Naran-dhisha, as*, m., Ved. 'observing men (?),' an epithet of Vishṇu; of Pūshan; (according to Mahī-dhara on Vājasaneyi-s. VIII. 55. this comp. is either *narandhi-sha*, 'destroying the world,' see *naran-dhi* above, or *na-randhisha*, 'not injuring,' i. e. 'a protector;' in XXII. 20. he explains *naran-dhisha* by 'man-praising.') — *Nara-pati, is*, m. 'lord of men,' a king, sovereign; N. of one of the four mythical kings of Jambu-dvīpa. — *Narapati-jaya-ćaryā*, f., N. of a work. — *Narapati-patha, as*, m. 'king's road,' the chief road, high street. — *Narapati-vijaya, as*, m., N. of a work. — *Nara-paśu, us*, m. 'man-beast,' a brute in human form, a beast-like man. — *Nara-pāla, as*, m. 'protector of men,' a king, a prince. — *Nara-puṅgava, as*, m. an excellent hero. — *Nara-priya, as, ā, am*, favourable or friendly to mankind; (*as*), m. a species of tree (= *nīla-vṛiksha*). — *Nara-bali, is*, m. a human sacrifice; [cf. *nara-medha, purusha-medha*.] — *Nara-brahma-deva, as*, m., N. of a king. — *Nara-bhuj, k, k, k*, man-eating, cannibal. — *Nara-bhū, ūs*, f. or *nara-bhūmi, is*, f. 'the land of men, birthplace of men,' Bhārata-varsha, i. e. India or the central part of the known continent. — *Nara-māṇikā* or *nara-māninī*, f. a man-like woman, a woman with a beard; [cf. *nara-mālinī*.] — *Nara-mālā*, f. a string or girdle of skulls. — *Nara-mālinī*, f. = *nara-māninī* (of which it is probably a corruption). — *Nara-mūrćhana, am*, n., N. of the eighty-ninth chapter of the Pātāla-khaṇḍa of the Padma-Purāṇa. — *Nara-medha, as*, m. a human sacrifice, the sacrifice of a man; [cf. *nṛi-bali, purusha-medha*.] — *Naram-manya, as, ā, am*, considered as a man, passing for a man. — *Nara-yantra, am*, n. 'instrument with a gnomon,' a sun-dial. — *Nara-yāna, am*, n. a carriage drawn by men; (in Pañća-tantra III. 248. *nara-yāṇa* with cerebral *ṇ* = 'a man-vehicle, a man serving as a vehicle for carrying another.') — *Nara-ratha, as*, m. a wrong form for *nava-ratha*. — *Nara-rāja, as*, m. 'king of men,' a king. — *Nararājya, am*, n. 'empire over men,' kingship, royalty, kingdom. — *Nara-rūpa, as, ī, am*, formed like a man, man-like; (*am*), n. the form of a man, human form. — *Nara-rūpin, ī, iṇī, i*, having the human form. — *Nararshabha* (°*ra-ṛish*°), *as*, m. 'man-bull,' chief of men, a prince. — *Nara-loka, as*, m. the world of men, the earth; mortals, men. — *Naraloka-pāla, as*, m. 'protector of men,' a king. — *Naraloka-vīra, as*, m. 'a hero among men,' a human hero. — *Nara-vat*, ind. like a man. — *Nara-vara, as*, m. an excellent or illustrious man. — *Naravara-vṛishabha, as*, m. an excellent hero (like a bull). — *Naravarottama* (°*ra-ut*°), *as*, m. the best of excellent men. — *Nara-varman, ā*, m., N. of a prince of Mālava in the twelfth century. — *Nara-vāhana, as, ā, am*, borne or carried by men, drawn by men; (*as*), m. an epithet of Kuvera; N. of a prince, successor of Sāli-vāhana; of a prince of the Darvābhisāras; of a minister of king Kshema-gupta. — *Naravāhana-janana, am*, n., N. of the fourth section of the Kathā-sarit-sāgara by Soma-deva. — *Naravāhana-datta, as*, m., N. of a son of king Udayana. — *Nara-vāhin, ī, inī, i*, carried or drawn by men (as a vehicle). — *Nara-vishvaṇa, as*, m. 'man-devourer,' a Rakshas, an imp or goblin. — *Nara-vīra, as*, m. 'a hero of a man,' an heroic man, a hero or brave man. — *Naravīra-loka, as*, m. the bravest of men; mankind in general. — *Nara-vyāghra* or *nara-śārdūla, as*, m. 'man-tiger,' an eminent man; the most illustrious of men. — *Nara-śṛiṅga, am*, n. 'man's horn,' i. e. anything chimerical or impossible. — *Nara-śreshṭha, as*, m. the best of men. — *Nara-saṃsarga, as*, m. intercourse of men, human society. — *Nara-sakha, as*, m. 'friend of Nara,' an epithet of Nārāyaṇa. — *Nara-saṅghārāma* (°*gha-ār*°), *as*, m. (?), N. of a Buddhist monastery. — *Nara-sāra, as*, m. a particular substance or article of commerce, sal ammoniac (?). — *Nara-siṅha, as*, m. 'man-lion,' a lion among men, a great warrior, a man of eminence or power, a chief; 'the lion-headed man' or Vishṇu in his fourth Ava-tāra when he descended to fight with Hiraṇya-kaśipu; N. of the father of king Bhairava; of several authors and princes; [cf. *nāra-siṅha, nṛi-siṅha, nara-hari*.] — *Narasiṅha-deva, as*, m. 'a god among the men-lions,' N. of several princes. — *Narasiṅha-dvādaśī-vrata, am*, n., N. of a particular ceremony performed in the month Phālguna; N. of the forty-second chapter of the Vārāha-Purāṇa. — *Narasiṅha-paṇḍita, as*, m., N. of an author. — *Narasiṅha-pārijāta*, N. of a work by Nara-siṅha. — *Narasiṅha-purāṇa, am*, n., N. of a Purāṇa. — *Narasiṅha-manu*, N. of the sixteenth chapter of the S'āradā-tilaka by Lakshmaṇa. — *Narasiṅha-yantra, am*, n., N. of a mystical diagram described in the Tantra-sāra. — *Narasiṅha-sarasvatī*, m., N. of a commentator on the Vedānta-sāra. — *Narasiṅha-sahasra-nāmāni*, n. pl. 'the thousand names of the man-lion,' i. e. of Vishṇu, N. of a work. — *Nara-skandha, as*, m. a multitude or body of men. — *Nara-haya, am*, n. (with *yuddha*), a fight between man and horse; [cf. *devāsura*.] — *Nara-hari, is*, m. Vishṇu as 'the man-lion' in his fourth Ava-tāra [cf. nara-sinha]; N. of a man. — Narahari-deva, as, m., N. of a prince. — Narāṅga (°ra-an°), as, am, m. n. 'male-member,' the penis; (as), m. eruption on the face. — Narāći (°ra + āći fr. anć), f., Ved. a species of plant (?); N. of a wife of Kṛishṇa; a kind of metre, (see under nārāća.) — Narādhama (°ra-adh°), as, m. a low or vile man, a wretch. — Narādhāra (°ra-ādh°), as, m. 'asylum or receptacle of men,' an epithet of Śiva; (ā), f. the earth. — Narādhipa (°ra-adh°), as, m. 'lord of men,' a prince, king, monarch; the tree Cathartocarpus Fistula; [cf. rāja-vṛiksha.] — Narādhipati (°ra-adh°), is, m. 'lord of men,' a king, a prince. — Narānta (°ra-an°), as, m., N. of a son of Hṛidīka. — Narāntaka (°ra-an°), as, m. 'man-destroyer,' death; N. of a Rākshasa, son of Rāvaṇa. — Narāntaka-nigraha-varṇana, am, n. 'description of the subjugation of Narāntaka,' N. of the fifty-ninth chapter of the Krīḍā-khaṇḍa of the Gaṇeśa-Purāṇa. — Narāntaka-nirgama, as, m. 'the coming forth of Narāntaka,' N. of the fifty-seventh chapter of the Krīḍā-khaṇḍa of the Gaṇeśa-Purāṇa. — Narāyaṇa (°ra-ay°), as, m. = nārāyaṇa, a N. of Vishṇu, &c. — Narāśa (°ra-āśa), as, m. 'man-eater,' a Rakshas, an imp or demon. — Narāśansa (°ra-āś°), as, m., Ved. 'the desire of men, desired of men (?),' a mystical N. of Agni (invoked in the Āprī hymns with Tanū-napāt, another mystical epithet of Fire, or taking the place of Tanū-napāt in these hymns, see ā-prī). — Narāśana (°ra-aś°), as, m. 'man-eater,' a Rakshas or demon. — Naretara (°ra-it°), as, m. a being differing from men; a higher being than a man; a lower being, an animal, a beast-like man. — Narendra (°ra-in°), as, m. 'lord of men,' a king, a prince, an anointed sovereign; a physician, a dealer in antidotes; a juggler (?); a conveyer of news or intelligence (?); N. of a man; a species of tree (= narādhipa); a kind of metre consisting of four lines of twenty-one syllables each. — Narendra-tva, am, n. kingship, royalty. — Narendra-druma, as, m. the tree Narendra. — Narendra-putra, as, m. a prince. — Narendra-mārga, as, m. the king's high-road, a royal or main road, high street. — Narendra-svāmin, ī, m., N. of a temple or holy place built by and called after Narendrāditya. — Narendrāćārya (°ra-āć°), as, m., N. of a grammarian. — Narendrāditya (°ra-ād°), as, m., N. of two princes of Kaśmīra. — Narendrāhva (°ra-āh°), as, am, m. n. (?), a kind of Aloë (= kāshṭhā-guru). — Nareśa or nareśvara (°ra-īś°), as, m. 'lord of men,' a king, a prince. — Nareśvara-viveka, as, m., N. of a Śaiva work by Parameshṭhin. — Nareshṭhā, ās, ās, am, Ved. serving as a standing-place for men?; (Sāy.) resting on conducting (wheels). — Narottama (°ra-ut°), as, m. 'best of men,' an epithet of Vishṇu; of Buddha; N. of a scholiast of the Adhyātma-rāmāyaṇa.

Narya, as, ā, am, Ved. manly, human, (often with apas, a manly deed, a heroic deed); strong, powerful; suitable or agreeable to men (as food); (as), m. a man, a person; an epithet of Indra; of Agni Gārhapatya; N. of a man; (ā), m. du., scil. nbhā śansā, the two objects of desire, i. e. heaven and earth [cf. narāśansa]; (ās), m. pl. epithet of the Maruts; (am), n. a manly act, manly deed; a gift for men. — Naryāpas (°ya-ap°), ās, ās, as, Ved. performing manly deeds; (Sāy.) performing deeds agreeable or suitable to men.

नरक naraka, as, am, m. n. (said to be fr. rt. nṛī), hell, the place of torment (distinguished fr. pātāla, the lower regions, q. v.), including a number of places of torture of various descriptions, generally said to be twenty-one in number [cf. nāraka]; (Hell is sometimes personified as a son of Anṛita and Nirṛiti or Nikṛiti); (as), m., N. of a demon, a son of Bhūmi or Earth (therefore called Bhauma, haunting Prāg-jyotisha and slain there by Kṛishṇa); N. of a man; N. of a district; of a place of pilgrimage. — Naraka-kuṇḍa, am, n. a pit or abyss in hell wherein the wicked are tormented, (eighty-six such are enumerated). — Naraka-jit, t, m. 'vanquisher of the demon Naraka,' epithet of Vishṇu-Kṛishṇa. — Naraka-devatā, f. 'the deity of hell,' Nirṛiti; Misfortune personified as a goddess. — Naraka-bhūmi, is, f. a division of hell, (of which seven are enumerated.) — Naraka-rūpin, ī, iṇī, i, 'hell-formed,' hellish. — Naraka-varga, as, m. 'the hell chapter,' N. of a chapter of Amara-sinha's Nāma-linganuśāsana. — Naraka-varṇana, am, n. 'description of hell,' N. of a chapter of the Revā-māhātmya. — Naraka-stha, as, ā, am, living or being in hell; (ā), f. the river of hell, Vaitaraṇī. — Naraka-svarga-prāpti-prakāra-varṇana, am, n. 'description of the mode of obtaining heaven and hell,' N. of the eighth chapter of the Māgha-māhātmya. — Narakāntaka (°ka-an°), as, m. 'destroyer of the demon Naraka,' an epithet of Kṛishṇa-Vishṇu. — Narakāmaya (°ka-ām°), as, m. the soul after death; a ghost or spirit. — Narakāri (°ka-ari), is, m. 'enemy of the demon Naraka,' an epithet of Kṛishṇa-Vishṇu. — Narakāvāsa (°ka-āv°), as, m. 'one whose abode is hell,' an inhabitant of hell. — Narakaukas (°ka-ok°), ās, m. an inhabitant of hell.

Narakāya, Nom. A. narakāyate, &c., to represent a hell; to resemble or be similar to hell.

नरङ्ग naranga, as, m. pimples on the face (= varaṇḍaka); (am), n. the penis; (wrong form for narānga, see col. 1.)

नरद narada, as or am, m. or n. (?), a particular substance or article of commerce, a kind of perfume? [cf. nalada]; (as), m., N. of a Brāhman.

Naradika, as, ī, am, dealing in the substance called Narada.

नरायण narāyaṇa, narendra. See col. 1.

नरिष्टा narishṭā, f., Ved. joking, chattering; sport, pastime; [cf. narma, narman.]

नरिष्यत् na-rishyat, an, m., N. of a son of Manu Vaivasvata.

Narishyanta, as, m., N. of a son of Marutta.

नरीय narīya, as, m., N. of a son of Bhanga-kāra; (also read nāreya.)

नरुण naruṇa, as, m. (fr. rt. nṛī), Ved. (according to a commentator) a leader.

नर्कुटक narkuṭaka, am, n. a nose [cf. nakuṭa]; a kind of metre consisting of four lines of seventeen syllables each; [cf. nardaṭaka.]

नर्त narta, as, ā, am (fr. rt. nṛit, the initial n of which is not liable to become ṇ), dancing; (as), m. dancing, dance.

Nartaka, as, m. a dancer, a player of any description; an actor, gesticulator, mime, mummer; a bard, herald; an elephant; a peacock; a species of reed [cf. poṭagala]; (ī), f. a female dancer, actress, singing girl; a female elephant; a peahen; a kind of perfume (= nalikā; cf. naṭī); (as, ā, am, fr. the Caus.), causing to dance; (as), m. a dancing-master.

Nartana, as, m. a dancer; (am), n. the act of dancing, gesticulating, acting, performing on the stage; [cf. nartanā-gṛiha.] — Nartana-priya, as, ā, am, fond of dancing; (as), m. a peacock. — Nartana-śālā, f. or nartanāgāra (°na-ag° or -āg°), am, n. or nartanā-gṛiha, am, n. a dancing-room. — Nartana-sthāna, am, n. a dancing-place.

Nartayitṛi, tā, m. 'one who causes to dance,' a dancing-master.

Nartita, as, ā, am, danced; made to dance; dandled; dancing.

Nartin, ī, inī, i, dancing; [cf. vanśa-n°.]

Nartū, ūs, f. a female dancer or actress.

नर्द nard (connected with rt. nad), cl. 1. P. (ep. also A.) nardati (-te), nanarda, narditā, nardishyati, anardīt, narditum, to bellow, roar, shriek, sound; to go, move; [cf. probably Hib. nuail-im, 'I roar, howl;' nuail, 'roaring, howling.']

Narda, as, ā, am, bellowing, roaring, sounding; [cf. go-n°.]

Nardat, an, antī, at, roaring, sounding; praising aloud; proclaiming.

Nardana, as, m. 'one who roars,' N. of a Nāga-rāja; (am), n. sounding, roaring, making a noise; celebrating, praising aloud.

Nardanīya, as, ā, am, to be sounded; to be celebrated or praised aloud.

Nardamāna, as, ā, am, shouting, roaring.

Nardita, as, ā, am, roared, sounded, bellowed; celebrated, loudly praised; (am), n. sound, roar, bellow, bellowing; (as), m. a kind of die or a throw at dice, the chief die, (commonly nādi or nāndi, perhaps 'an ace,' cf. vṛisha, a N. for the chief die in Nala VII. 6.)

Nardin, ī, inī, i, sounding, roaring, making a noise; [cf. gehe-n°.]

नर्दटक nardaṭaka, am, n. a kind of metre consisting of four lines of seventeen syllables each; (wrongly written nardhaṭaka; cf. narkuṭaka.)

नर्दबुद nardabuda or **nardavuda**, as, m., Ved. an epithet of Indra.

नर्धटक nardhaṭaka, wrong form for nardaṭaka.

नर्ब् narb, cl. 1. P. narbati, &c., to go, move; [cf. rt. namb.]

नर्म narma, as, m., Ved. sport, pastime; [cf. narishṭā.]

Narmaṭha, as, m. a jester; a rake, lecher, libertine; sport, amusement; coition; the nipple; the chin.

Narman, a, n. sport, play, amusement, pastime; diversion; jest, joke, (narmāṇi kṛi, to joke); wit, humour; (aṇā), ind. in jest, by way of jest. — Narma-kīla, as, m. a husband. — Narma-garbha, as, m. a secret lover. — Narma-da, as, ā, am, delighting, making happy, giving or causing pleasure; (as); m. a jester; the associate or companion of a person's sports or amusements; N. of the son of Lāḍana; (ā), f. the Narma-dā or modern Nerbudda river, which, rising in the Vindhya mountains, runs westward to the gulf of Cambay, (personified as the wife of Puru-kutsa and mother of Trasa-dasyu); a sister of the Uragas or serpents; a daughter of the Soma-pas; a species of plant (see pṛikkā). — Narmadā-taṭa-deśa, as, m., N. of a district mentioned in the Ratna-kosha. — Narmadā-tīra-gamana, am, n., N. of the seventeenth chapter of the Uttara-kāṇḍa of the Rāmāyaṇa. — Narmadā-tīrtha, am, n. a sacred bathing-place on the Narma-dā; [cf. nārmada.] — Narmadā-māhātmya, am, n. 'the glory of Narma-dā,' N. of the 173rd–181st chapter of the Matsya-Purāṇa. — Narmadeśvara (°dā-īś°), as, m. a form of Śiva. — Narmadeśvara-tīrtha, am, n., N. of several sacred bathing-places. — Narmadeśvara-māhātmya, am, n. 'the glory of Śiva,' N. of a chapter of the Śiva-Purāṇa. — Narmadeśvara-linga, am, n., N. of the ninety-second chapter of the Skanda-Purāṇa. — Narma-dyuti, is, is, i, bright with joy, cheerful, happy, merry; (is), f. enjoyment of a joke or any amusement. — Narma-vatī, f., N. of a comedy. — Narma-saćiva, as, m. 'amusement-companion,' an associate or promoter of the amusements of a prince or man of rank. — Narma-sāćivya, am, n. superintendence of a prince's amusements. — Narma-suhṛid, t, m. = narma-saćiva. — Narma-sphūrja, as, m. happiness or amusement ending in alarm (?). — Narma-sphoṭa, as, m. slight or inferior amusement (?).

Narmaya, Nom. P. narmayati, &c., to make happy or gladden by jests or sports, exhilarate by jesting and wit.

नर्मट narmaṭa, as, m. a potsherd; the sun.

नर्मरा narmarā, f. a cavity, a valley; a

bellows; an old woman past menstruation; a species of plant (= *saralā*).

नर्य *narya*. See p. 471, col. 1.

नल् *nal*, cl. 1. P. *nalati*, &c., to smell; to pain (?); to bind (?); cl. 10. P. *nālayati*, &c., to speak or shine; to bind or confine, (the two meanings 'smelling' and 'binding' have probably arisen from a confusion between *gandhe* and *bandhe* in the Dhātu-pāṭha.)

नल *nala*, *as*, m. (for *naḍa*, q.v.), a species of reed, Amphidonax Karka, eight to twelve feet high [cf. *naḍa*, *nāla*, *deva-nala*]; N. of a king of the Nishadhas or of the country called Nishadha, son of Vīra-sena and husband of Damayantī and hero of the celebrated tale called Nala and Damayantī; a son of Nishadha and father of Nabha or Nabhas; a descendant of the latter Nala, son of Su-dhanvan and father of Uktha [cf. *naḍa*]; N. of a son of Yadu; N. of a monkey-chief, son of Tvashṭṛi or Viśvakarman, who made a bridge for Rāma from the continent to Laṅkā; N. of a Daitya; N. of a medical author; (in astrology) N. of a particular form of constellation in which all the planets or stars are grouped in double mansions; a deified progenitor, wrongly written for *nalva*; (*ī*), f. a kind of fragrant substance, a perfume (= *naṭī*); red arsenic, = *manaḥ-śilā*, *kunaṭī*; (*am*), n. the blossom of Nelumbium Speciosum (?); smell, odour; [cf. rt. *nal*.] — *Nala-kānana*, *ās*, m. pl., N. of a people, (this word may perhaps be separated into *nalaka-ānana*; also read *nala-kālaka*, *nabha-kānana*.) — *Nala-kīla*, *as*, m. the knee. — *Nala-kūbara* and *nala-kūvara*, *as*, m., N. of a son of Kuvera. — *Nala-ćampū*, *ūs*, f., N. of a work by Tri-vikrama-bhaṭṭa, also called Damayantī-kathā, describing the fortunes of Nala and Damayantī in a highly artificial mixed style, half prose, half verse; [cf. *ćampū*.] — *Nala-da*, *am*, *ā*, n. f. Indian spikenard, Nardostachys Jatamansi (= *jaṭāmāṅsī*); (*am*), n. the root of Andropogon Muricatus (= *uśīra*); the honey or nectar of a flower; (*ā*), f., N. of a daughter of Raudrāśva. — *Nala-paṭṭikā*, f. a sort of mat made with reeds, a coarse mat. — *Nala-pura*, *am*, n., N. of a town. — *Nala-mīna*, *as*, m. a species of sprat or (according to some) a shrimp or prawn; (also read *tala-mīna*.) — *Nala-setu*, *us*, m. 'Nala's bridge,' the causeway constructed by the monkey Nala, (a name given to the rocks between Ramisseram and Ceylon, commonly called Adam's bridge.) — *Naleśvara-tīrtha* (°*la-is*°), *am*, n., N. of a sacred bathing-place. — *Nalottama* (°*la-ut*°), *as*, m. a species of reed (= *deva-nala*). — *Nalodaya* (°*la-ud*°), *as*, m. 'Nala's rise,' N. of an artificial poem ascribed to Kāli-dāsa and describing the restoration of the fallen Nala to prosperity and power. — *Nalopakhyāna* (°*la-up*°), *am*, n. 'the story of Nala (and Damayantī),' N. of a celebrated episode of the Mahā-bhārata.

Nalaka, *am*, n. a bone (hollow like a reed), any long bone of the body; the tibia; the radius of the arm; (*ikā*), f. a kind of fragrant substance (= *nalī*, commonly *pavāri* or *panṭhāri*); the leguminous plant Dolichos Lablab; the plant Polianthes Tuberosa; Dæmia Extensa.

Nalakinī, f. (fr. an unused *nalakin*), the knee-cap or knee-pan; the leg.

Naladika, *as*, *ī*, *am*, dealing in Indian spikenard.

Nalita, *as*, m. a species of vegetable, (commonly *nālitā*.)

Nalina, *am*, n. (connected with *nala*, its stalk being hollow like that of a reed), a lotus flower or water-lily, Nelumbium Speciosum or Nymphæa Nelumbo; the indigo plant; water; (*ī*), f. a lotus, Nelumbium Speciosum, the flexible stalk of the water-lily; an assemblage of the Nelumbium Speciosum or of lotus flowers; a pond in which the lotus grows or may grow, a place abounding in lotuses, (*nalinī* is to *nalina* as *abjinī* to *abja*, *pankajinī* to *pankaja*, and *padminī* to *padma*); the Ganges of heaven or rather an arm of it; a mystical N. of one of the nostrils (= *nalikā*); a kind of fragrant substance; the fermented and intoxicating juice of the cocoa-nut; N. of the wife of Aja-mīḍha and mother of Nīla; (*as*), m. the Indian crane (as a synonym of *pushkara*); a species of shrub (= *kṛishṇa-pāka-phala*). — *Nalina-dala*, *am*, n. a leaf of the lotus flower; [cf. *nalinī-dala*, *nava-nalina-dalāya*.] — *Nalinī-khaṇḍa*, *am*, n. an assemblage of the Nelumbium Speciosum. — *Nalinī-dala*, *am*, n. a leaf of the lotus plant; [cf. *nalina-dala*.] — *Nalinī-nandana*, *am*, n. 'the divine garden near the Nalinī (?),' N. of a garden of Kuvera. — *Nalinī-padma-kosha*, *as*, m., N. of a particular position of the hands in dancing. — *Nalinī-ruha*, *as*, *ā*, *am*, what comes forth or has come forth from a Nelumbium Speciosum; (*as*), m. an epithet of Brahmā; (*am*), n. the fibres of the stalk of Nelumbium Speciosum. — *Naline-śaya*, *as*, m. (*naline*, loc. sing.), 'reclining on a lotus,' an epithet of Vishṇu.

Nalinika at the end of comp. = *nalinī*, q. v.

नल्ल *nalla*, wrongly for *nalva*.

नल्व *nalva*, *as*, m. a furlong, a measure of distance = 400 or 104 (?) cubits; (wrongly read *nalla*, *nala*.) — *Nalva-vartmaga*, *as*, *ā*, *am*, going the distance of a Nalva; (*ā*), f. a spreading plant; the orange tree (= *kākāngī* for *nāranga?*).

नव 1. *nava*, *as*, *ā*, *am* (probably connected with the particle 1. *nu*, q. v., or less probably with *nu* for prep. *anu*, or by some derived fr. rt. 4. *nu*, to praise), new, fresh, recent, young, modern; (*as*), m. a crow; a species of plant (= *rakta-punar-navā*); N. of a son of Uśīnara and Navā; (*ā*), f., N. of a wife of Uśīnara and mother of Nava; (*am*), ind. recently, newly, lately, a short time ago, not long since, just, (the crude *nava* is prefixed to a past pass. part. in this sense, see *nava-baddha*); [for 2. *nava* see p. 473, col. 1: cf. Zend *nava*: Gr. νέο-ς for νέϝο-ς, νεός, νειός, νε-αρό-ς, νε-ᾶν, νεᾶν-ία-ς, νέ-αξ, νε-οσσό-ς, νε-οττ-ία, νε-οχ-μό-ς, νε-βρό-ς, νέ-ατο-ς, νεί-αιρα, νει-ό-ν: Lat. *novu-s*, *Noviu-s*, *nov-īciu-s*, *nov-āli-s*, *nov-ellu-s*, *nov-āre*, *nov-er-ca*, *nū-nt-iu-s*, *de-nuo*, *nū-per*: Osk. *Nuv-la*, *Nuceria*: Goth. *niu-yi-s*, 'new;' *niuyi-tha*, 'newness:' Angl. Sax. *niwe*, *neow*, *niwa*: Lith. *naú-ye-s*, 'new;' *nauyô-ka-s*, 'a novice:' Slav. *nov-ŭ*, 'new:' Hib. *nua*, *nuadh*.] — *Nava-kārikā*, f. a bride, a woman newly married, (probably wrong reading for *nava-varikā*); a new Kārikā or comment. — *Nava-kālikā*, f. (fem. of *nava-kālaka*), a young woman, either one recently married or one in whom menstruation has lately commenced. — *Nava-kṛit*, wrongly for *nava-gat*. — *Nava-gat*, *t*, *t*, *t*, Ved. first-born (?). — 1. *nava-graha*, *as*, *ā*, *am* (for 2. see under *navan*), lately caught; [cf. *nava-baddha*.] — *Nava-ćhāttra*, *as*, m. a new scholar, a student, novice. — *Nava-ja*, *as*, *ā*, *am*, recently born, lately produced, new, young (e. g. *nava-jaḥ śaśī*, the new moon or the moon just becoming visible). — *Nava-jā*, *ās*, *ās*, *am*, Ved. lately produced, new, young. — *Nava-jāta*, *as*, *ā*, *am*, Ved. born anew, new-born, fresh, new. — *Nava-tara*, *as*, *ā*, *am* (compar.), newer, younger, fresher, &c.; [cf. *navīyas*.] — *Nava-tā*, f. or *nava-tva*, *am*, n. freshness, novelty. — *Nava-dala*, *am*, n. the fresh leaf of a lotus flower, any young leaf. — *Nava-dvīpa*, *as*, m. 'the new island,' N. of a place now called Nuddea, sixty miles from Calcutta, in the district of Burdwan on the right bank of the Bhāgīrathī or great western branch of the Ganges at the point where it is joined by the Jellinghee. — *Nava-nagara*, *am*, n. 'the new town,' N. of a town. — *Nava-nalina-dalāya* (fr. *nava-nalina-dala*), Nom. A. *nava-nalina-dalāyate*, &c., to resemble the leaf of a fresh lotus blossom. — *Navanalinadalāyamāna*, *as*, *ā*, *am*, resembling the leaf of a fresh lotus flower. — *Nava-nī*, *is*, f. or *nava-nīta*, *am*, n. fresh butter. — *Navanītaka*, *am*, n. clarified butter. — *Navanīta-dhenu*, *us*, f. a quantity of butter presented to Brāhmans, see *dhenu*. — *Nava-parṇādi-bhakshaṇa*, *am*, n. 'eating of new leaves &c.,' N. of a chapter of the Purāṇa-sarva-sva. — *Nava-pallava*, *am*, n. a new shoot, young sprout. — *Nava-prasūtā*, f. a woman who has lately brought forth (a child). — *Nava-prāśana*, *as*, m. eating of new rice or new barley. — *Nava-phalikā*, f. a bride, a newly-married woman; a girl in whom menstruation has recently begun. — *Nava-baddha*, *as*, *ā*, *am*, lately caught, recently bound. — *Nava-mallikā*, f. Arabian jasmine, Jasminum Sambac; (also read *nava-mālikā*.) — *Nava-mālikā*, f. many-flowered Nykanthes, Jasminum Sambac (= *nava-mallikā*); N. of a daughter of Dharma-vardhana, king of Śrāvastī. — *Nava-mālinī*, f. a kind of metre consisting of four lines of twelve syllables each. — *Nava-megha*, *as*, m. a new cloud or one just appearing. — *Nava-yajña*, *as*, m. sacrifice or oblation of the first-fruits of the harvest; [cf. *nāvayajñika*, *navaśasyeshṭi*, *nava-śasya*.] — *Nava-yauvana*, *am*, n. fresh or incipient youth, bloom of youth, prime; (*as*, *ā*, *am*), being in the bloom of youth; (*ā*), f. a young woman. — *Navayauvana-vat*, *ān*, *atī*, *at*, blooming with the freshness of youth. — *Nava-raktaka*, *am*, n. a newly-dyed garment. — *Nava-rajas*, *ās*, f. a girl who has only recently menstruated. — *Nava-vadhū*, *ūs*, f. a bride, a newly-married woman; a daughter-in-law. — *Nava-varikā*, f. a newly-married woman; [cf. *nava-kārikā*.] — *Nava-vastra*, *am*, n. new cloth. — *Nava-vāstva*, *as*, m., Ved., N. of a man or of an evil spirit. — *Nava-śaśi-bhṛit*, *t*, m. 'bearing the new moon (on his brow),' an epithet of Śiva. — *Nava-śasya*, *am*, n. the first-fruits of the year's harvest, the grain first matured. — *Navaśasyeshṭi* (°*ya-ish*°), *is*, f. 'sacrifice of first-fruits,' a sacrifice performed on eating the first matured rice or grain of the year; (wrongly written *navasasyeshṭi*; cf. *nava-yajña*.) — *Nava-śrāddha*, *am*, n. the first series of Śrāddhas collectively, or funeral offerings on the first, third, fifth, seventh, ninth, and eleventh days after a person's demise. — *Nava-sanghārāma* (°*gha-ār*°), *as*, m., N. of a monastery. — *Nava-sū*, *ūs*, f., Ved. a cow that has recently calved. — *Nava-sūtikā*, f. a milch cow; a woman recently delivered. — *Navāṅkura* (°*va-aṅ*°), N. of a work. — *Navānna* (°*va-an*°), *am*, n. new rice, new grain, the first-fruits; the grain first ripened, rice or grain recently matured; a ceremony observed on first eating the new rice, &c. — *Navānna-bhakshaṇa*, *am*, n. 'eating of new grain,' N. of a chapter of the Purāṇa-sarva-sva. — *Navānna-sthālī-pākamantra*, *ās*, m. pl., N. of a work. — *Navānneshṭi* (°*na-ish*°), *is*, f. sacrifice of the first-fruits, see *navaśasyeshṭi*. — *Navāmbara* (°*va-am*°), *am*, n. new and unbleached cloth. — *Navāmbu* (°*va-am*°), n. fresh water. — *Navārma* (°*va-ar*°), *am*, n., N. of a place. — *Navāha* (°*va-aha*), *as*, m. a new day, the first day of a fortnight. — *Navī-karaṇa*, *am*, n. making new, doing anew, renewing. — *Navī-kṛi*, cl. 8. P. A. *-karoti*, *-kurute*, *-kartum*, to make new, renew, restaurate, revive. — *Navī-kṛita*, *as*, *ā*, *am*, done or made anew, renewed, revived. — *Navī-bhāva*, *as*, m. becoming young or new, renovation. — *Navī-bhūta*, *as*, *ā*, *am*, become new, renewed, revived. — *Navetara* (°*va-it*°), *as*, *ā*, *am*, 'other than new,' old. — *Navoḍhā* (°*va-ūḍhā*), f. a newly-married woman, a bride. — *Navoddhṛita* (°*va-ud*°), *am*, n. fresh butter; [cf. *nava-nīta*.]

1. *navaka*, *as*, *ikā*, *am*, = 1. *nava*, col. 2.

Navishṭha, *as*, *ā*, *am*, Ved. the newest, youngest, last; (*am*), ind. (?), at last.

Navīna, *as*, *ā*, *am*, = 1. *nava*, new, fresh, recent, modern. — *Navīna-ćandra*, *as*, m. the new moon. — *Navīna-mata-vićāra*, *as*, m. 'inquiring into new opinions,' N. of a philosophical work by Hari-rāma. — *Navīna-vedāntin*, *ī*, m. a modern Vedānta philosopher.

Navīyas or *navyas*, *ān*, *asī*, *as* (compar. of 1. *nava*), Ved. new, fresh, young, recent, who has done anything or shown himself recently; very new; (*as*), ind. recently, lately; (*ase* or *asā*), ind. anew.

1. *navya*, *as*, *ā*, *am*, Ved. new, fresh, young; (*as*), m. a species of plant, = *rakta-punar-navā*;

[cf. Lith. nauya-s; Goth. niuyi-s.] — *Navya-mata-vićāra*, as, m.=navīna-mata-vićāra. — *Navya-vat*, ind. like new, ever new (?).

Navyas. See navīyas, p. 472, col. 3.

नव 2. *nava*, as, m. (fr. rt. 4. nu), praise; panegyric, celebration. (For 1. nava see p. 472, col. 2.)

Navana, am, n. the act of praising, laudation.

Navishṭi, is, f., Ved. a song of praise, hymn; (Sāy.) a new sacrifice or oblation, (as if fr. 1. nava.)

2. *navya*, as, ā, am, Ved. to be praised, praiseworthy, laudable, deserving of praise. — Navya-vardhamāna, as, m., N. of an author.

नवत 1. *navata*, as, m. (for 2. see col. 2), an elephant's painted or variegated housings; woollen cloth; a cover, blanket, wrapper.

नवन् *navan*, m. f. n. pl. (said to be fr. rt. 4. nu), nine; [cf. Zend navan, 'nine;' Gr. ἐννέα, ἔνα-το-ς, ἔννα-το-ς, εἴνατο-ς, ἐννά-κις, ἐνάκις, εἰνάκις, ἐνα-κόσιοι, ἐννα-κόσιοι, ἐνενή-κοντα, ἐννή-κοντα: Lat. novem, nōnu-s, nov-iens, nōnā-ginta, non-genti: Goth. niun, 'nine;' niun-da, 'the ninth:' Angl. Sax. nigan, 'nine:' Old Germ. niun: Mod. Germ. neun: Old Pruss. nevīn-ts, 'the ninth:' Slav. devan-tĭ, 'nine:' Lith. devyn-i, 'nine,' n changed into d as in debes-i-s, 'a cloud,' from Sanskrit nabhas; devin-ta-s, 'the ninth:' Hib. naoi, 'nine:' Cambro-Brit. naw, 'nine.'] — Navakāṇḍikā-bhāshya, am, n. 'commentary of nine sections,' N. of a commentary on Kātyāyana's Srāddha-sūtras by Nīlāsura. — Nava-kṛitvas, ind., 9 times. — 2. nava-graha, ās, m. pl. the 9 planets, or sun, moon, five planets, and the ascending and descending nodes. — Navagraha-mantra, ās, m. pl. 'hymns or prayers to the 9 planets (?),' N. of a work. — Navagraha-śānti, is, f. propitiation of the 9 planets. — Nava-gva, as, ā, am, Ved. ninefold, consisting of 9; (ās), m. pl., N. of a mythological family often associated with that of Angiras and described as sharing in Indra's battles, regulating the worship of the gods, &c.; (as), m. one of the family called Nava-gvas; [cf. daśa-gva, daśagvin.] — Navaćatvārinśa, as, ī, am (fr. the following), the 49th. — Nava-ćatvārinśat, t, f., 49. — Nava-tantu, us, m., N. of a son of Viśvā-mitra. — Navatrinśa, as, ī, am (fr. the following), the 39th. — Nava-trinśat, t, f., 39. — Nava-daśa, as, ī, am (fr. the following), the 19th; consisting of 19. — Nava-daśan, a, m. f. n. pl., 19. — Nava-dīdhiti, is, m. 'nine-rayed,' Mars, the planet or its deified regent; [cf. navārćis.] — Nava-durgā, f. Durgā in her 9 forms (viz. kumārikā, tri-mūrti, kalyāṇī, rohiṇī, kālī, ćaṇḍikā, śāmbhavī, durgā, bhadrā). — Nava-dolā, f. a litter borne by 9 men. — Nava-dvāra, as, ā, am, 'nine-doored,' having 9 gates; an epithet of the body, which has 9 apertures or outlets, as the nostrils, ears, mouth, &c.; [cf. nava-mukha.] — Nava-dhā, ind. divided into 9 parts, ninefold, in 9 ways, 9 times. — Nava-navati, is, f., 99; (in the Veda the number 99 is used for any large number.) — Navanavati-tama, as, ī, am, the 99th. — Nava-pańćāśa, as, ī, am (fr. the following), the 59th. — Nava-pańćāśat, t, f., 59. — Nava-pad, -pāt, -padī, -pat, Ved. having 9 feet, consisting of 9 feet. — Nava-bhāga, as, m. the 9th part, especially of an asterism or of a lunar mansion; [cf. navānśa.] — Nava-mukha, as, ī, am, having 9 apertures or openings; [cf. nava-dvāra.] — Nava-ranga, am, n. gift to five and acceptance by four persons of the best Kāyastha families (?). — Navaranga-kula, as, ā, am, having the privilege of marrying into 9 distinct families (?). — Nava-ratna, am, n., 9 precious gems, viz. a pearl, ruby, topaz, diamond, emerald, lapis lazuli, coral, sapphire, and one called Go-meda, (these 9 jewels are supposed to be related to the 9 planets); the 9 jewels, i. e. the 9 men of letters at the court of Vikramāditya were Dhanvantari, Kshapaṇaka, Amara-sinha, Sanku, Vetāla-bhaṭṭa, Ghaṭa-karpara, Kāli-dāsa, Vararući, and Varāha-mihira; N. of a collection of 9 verses. — Nava-ratha, as, m., N. of a son of Bhīma-ratha and father of Daśa-ratha. — Nava-rātra, as, m. or navarātrika, am, n. a period of 9 days; a Soma sacrifice with 9 Sutyā days; 9 days in the middle of the Gavām-ayana; (am), n. the period of 9 days from the first of the light half of month Āśvina to the 9th, devoted to the worship of Durgā. — Nava-rāśika, the rule of proportion with 9 terms comprising four proportions. — Navarća (°va-ṛića), as, ā, am, Ved. consisting of 9 verses. — Navavinśa, as, ī, am (fr. the following), the 29th. — Nava-vinśati, is, f., 29. — Nava-vidha, as, ā, am, ninefold, consisting of 9 parts. — Nava-vyūha, as, m. an epithet of Vishṇu; [cf. ćatur-vyūha.] — Nava-śakti, is, m. 'having 9 faculties,' an epithet of Siva or Vishṇu. — Nava-śata, am, n., 109. — Navaśata-tama, as, ī, am, the 109th. — Nava-śas, ind., 9 by 9, by nines. — Nava-śāyaka, as, m. a N. given to any of 9 inferior classes, viz. cowherd, gardener, oilman, weaver, confectioner, water-carrier, potter, blacksmith, and barber. — Nava-shaṭka, as, ā, am, consisting of 9 × 6 (strings &c.). — Nava-shashṭi, is, f., 69. — Navashashṭi-tama, as, ī, am, the 69th. — Nava-saptati, is, f., 79. — Navasaptati-tama, as, ī, am, the 79th. — Nava-saptadaśa, as, m., N. of an Atirātra ('containing 9 Saptadaśa-stotras'). — Nava-sāhasānka-ćarita, am, n. 'the 9 or the new (fr. 1. nava) deeds of king Sāhasānka,' N. of a Campū composed by Srī-harsha. — Navāṇśa or navāṇśaka (°va-āṇ°), as, m. a 9th, a 9th part, especially of an asterism or lunar mansion; [cf. nava-bhāga.] — Navāṇśaka-pa, as, m. the regent of a Navāṇśaka. — Navāṇśa-nātha, as, m. the regent of a Navāṇśa. — Navāngā (°va-an°), f. a species of plant (= karkaṭa-śṛingī). — Navāyasa (°va-āy°), am, n. a medicinal preparation of iron, containing 9 parts of iron. — Navārćis (°va-ar°), is, m. 'nine-rayed,' the planet Mars or its deified personification. — Navāśīti (°va-aś°), is, f., 89. — Navāśīti-tama, as, ī, am, the 89th. — Navāha (°va-aha), as, m. a period of 9 days; a Soma sacrifice with 9 Sutyā days; 9 days in the middle of the Gavām-ayana; [cf. nava-rātra.]

3. *nava*=navan, nine, in tri-ṇava, q. v.

2. *navaka*, as, ā, am, consisting of 9; (am), n. the aggregate of nine, nine.

2. *navata*, as, ī, am, the 90th; [cf. eka-n°, ćatur-ṇ°, ćatur-n°, tri-ṇ°, dvā-n°, dvi-n°.]

Navati, is (according to lexicographers also navatī), f., 90. — Navati-tama, as, ī, am, the 90th. — Navati-dhanus, us, m., N. of an ancestor of Sākya-muni. — Navati-dhā, ind. ninetyfold. — Navati-ratha, as, m., N. of an ancestor of Sākya-muni. — Navati-śas, ind. by nineties, ninety by ninety.

Navatika, f. (fr. navati), a paint-brush containing 90 hairs.

Navama, as, ī, am, the 9th; (ā), f., scil. tithi, the 9th day of a lunar half month. — Navamāṇśa (°ma-aṇ°), as, m.=navāṇśa, q. v.

Navamaka, as, ikā, am, the 9th.

Navin, ī, inī, i, consisting of 9, composed of 9.

नवपत्त्रिका *nava-pattrikā*, f. (fr. 1. or 2. nava?), a particular sport described in the Kāma-sūtra by Vātsyāyana.

नवर *navara*, a particular number.

नवरम् *navaram*, ind. only.

नविपुला *na-vipulā*, f. a kind of metre.

नवेदस् *novedas*, ās, ās, as, Ved. cognizant, observing, perceiving; appreciating; an observer; appreciator (with gen. of the object); [cf. ko-vida.]

नव्य 1. and 2. *navya*. See p. 472, col. 3; and col. 1. of this page.

नश् 1. *naś* (related to rt. naksh; cf. rt. 1. aś), cl. 1. P. A. naśati, -te, Aor. ānaṭ or ānak, &c. (Pāṇ. VI. 4, 73, but these forms may be referred to rt. 1. aś), Ved. to reach, attain, obtain; to meet with, find: Caus. naśayati, &c., to cause to obtain or meet with; [cf. Lat. nanciscor.]

1. *naśa* in dū-ṇaśa, dur-ṇaśa, q. v.; [cf. 1. nāśa.]

नश् 2. *naś*, cl. 1. 4. (more usually cl. 4.) P. naśati, naśyati (ep. also -te), nanāśa (3rd pl. neśus), naśitā, nanshṭā (according to Vopa-deva also nangdhā), naśishyati, nankshyati, anaśat, aneśat, naśitum, nanshṭum, to be lost, disappear, to become invisible, to vanish; to perish, be destroyed, wane; to escape, run away; to come to nothing, be frustrated, be unsuccessful: Caus. nāśayati (ep. also A. nāśayate), -yitum, Aor. anīnaśat, to cause to disappear, make invisible; to cause to perish, suffer to perish, destroy, efface; to violate, deflower; to cause to be lost, to lose; to forget; to extinguish (as a fire); to drive away, cause to fly away; to disappear (in mā vyāghrā ninaśur vanāt, let not the tigers disappear from the forest, Mahā-bh. Udyoga-p. 862): Desid. ninaśishati, ninankshati: Intens. nānaśyate, nānanshṭi; [cf. Zend naśu, 'a corpse;' naś-ista, 'very destructive:' Gr. νέκ-υ-ς, νέκυ-ια, νεκ-ρό-ς, probably νόσο-ς, νοῦσο-ς for νοξο-ς, like συν for ξυν: Lat. nex, necare, noc-ēre, noxa, per-nicies, ve-ne-nu-m for venec-nu-m: Goth. nau-s, navi-s, 'a corpse,' for nag-u-s or nah-u-s.]

3. *naś*, k, k, k, or ṭ, ṭ, ṭ, disappearing; perishing; [cf. jīva-n°.]

2. *naśa*, as, m. destruction; perishing; [cf. 2. nāśa.]

Naśana, am, n. disappearing, vanishing; perishing; escaping.

Naśitṛi, tā, trī, tṛi, one who disappears; perishing, being lost; destroying, a destroyer; [cf. nanshṭṛi.]

Naśyat, an, antī, at, perishing, decaying, being destroyed; waning, wasting. — Naśyat-prasūti, is, is, i, whose offspring perishes; (is), f. a woman who brings forth a dead child. — Naśyatprasūtikā, f. a female bearing a dead child.

Naśvara, as, ī, am, perishing, perishable; destructible; transitory, evanescent, subject to decay; destructive, mischievous. — Naśvara-tva, am, n. perishableness, transitoriness; destructiveness.

Nashṭa, as, ā, am, lost, disappeared, disappearing; vanished, invisible, lost sight of; perished, destroyed, ruined, spoiled, wasted, annihilated, dead; run away, fled; depraved, debauched; deprived of (at the beginning of a comp.). — Nashṭa-ćandra, as, m., N. of the fourth day in both halves of the month Bhādra. — Nashṭa-ćetana, as, ā, am, one who has lost consciousness, unconscious, fainted, insensible, swooning away, losing one's senses. — Nashṭa-ćeshṭa, as, ā, am, one who has lost the power of motion; unconscious, fainted, insensible. — Nashṭaćeshṭa-tā, f. unconsciousness, insensibility, fainting, swooning. — Nashṭa-janman, a, n. 'the lost nativity,' subsequent calculation or casting of a lost nativity. — Nashṭa-jātaka, am, n.=nashṭa-janman; N. of the thirteenth Adhyāya in Varāha-mihira's Laghu-jātaka. — Nashṭa-dṛishṭi, is, is, i, one who has lost his sight, blind. — Nashṭa-mati, is, is, i, one who has lost his intellects. — Nashṭa-mārgaṇa, am, n. seeking any lost object. — Nashṭa-rājya, am, n., N. of a district to the north-east of Madhya-deśa. — Nashṭa-rūpa, as, ā, am, one whose form is lost or no more seen; (ā), f., scil. anushṭubh, a variety of the Anu-shṭubh. — Nashṭa-visha, as, ā, am, Ved. (a snake &c.) that has lost (its) venom. — Nashṭa-vīja, as, ā, am, destitute of the seminal secretion, without the power of procreating, impotent. — Nashṭa-vedana, as, ī, am, finding a lost object. — Nashṭa-samsmṛiti, is, is, i, one who has lost his memory, unmindful, forgetful. — Nashṭa-sanjña, as, ā, am, one who has lost his consciousness. — Nashṭa-smṛiti, is, is, i, one who has lost his memory, forgetful. — Nashṭāgni (°ṭa-ag°), is, m. a Brāhman or householder whose fire has been extinguished or who has lost his consecrated fire. — Nashṭātankam (°ṭa-āt°), ind. without anxiety or fear. — *Nashṭātman* (°*ṭa-āt*°), *ā, ā, a,* deprived of mind or sense. — *Nashṭāpti-sūtra* (°*ṭa-āp*°), *am,* n. booty, plunder. — *Nashṭārtha* (°*ṭa-ar*°), *as, ā, am,* one who has lost his property, reduced to poverty. — *Nashṭāśaṅka* (°*ṭa-āś*°), *as, ā, am,* destitute of fear, fearless, dauntless. — *Nashṭāsu* (°*ṭa-asu*), *us, us, u,* Ved. one whose vital spirits have disappeared. — *Nashṭendu-kalā* (°*ṭa-in*°), f. the day of new moon when it rises invisible. — *Nashṭendriya* (°*ṭa-in*°), *as, ā, am,* one who has lost his organs of sense, deprived of one's senses. — *Nashṭaishin* (°*ṭa-esh*°), *ī, iṇī, i,* seeking any lost object. — *Nashṭaishya, am,* n. the act of seeking what has been lost.

Nashṭi, is, f. loss, destruction, ruin.

नशाक *naśāka, as,* m. a species of crow.

नष्ट *nashṭa.* See p. 473, col. 3.

नस् 1. *nas* (the alternative form for *asmān* acc. pl., for *asmabhyam* dat. pl., and for *asmākam* gen. pl. of the first personal pronoun *asmad,* q. v.); us, to us, of us; (*nas* is an enclitic and has no accent.)

नस् 2. *nas,* cl. 1. A. *nasate, nese, nasitā,* &c., Ved. to approach, to go towards, to join; to copulate (especially as husband and wife); (said to mean also) to be crooked or curved; to bend; to be fraudulent; [cf. Gr. νέ-ο-μαι, νίσ-σ-ο-μαι, νόσ-το-ς, probably also ναίω for νασ-y-ω, ἔ-νασ-σα, ἐ-νάσ-θη-ν.]

नस् 3. *nas,* f. (probably fr. rt. *snā,* to bathe, or *snu,* to flow, the initial *s* being dropped; cf. *nau; nas* is defective in nom. voc. sing. du. and pl., acc. sing. du., but may be optionally substituted for *nāsikā,* q. v., in the acc. pl. and remaining cases, e. g. *nasas* or *nāsikās, nasā* or *nāsikayā, nobhyām* or *nāsikābhyām;* only the weak cases *nasā, nasi, nasos,* however, appear to occur), the nose; [cf. *nāsā, nāsikā;* Lat. *nasus, naris.*] — *Naḥ-kshudra, as, ā, am,* small-nosed. — *Nastaḥ-karman, a,* n. 'the putting into the nose,' taking snuff. — *Nas-tas,* ind. from the nose, into the nose. — *Nasy-ota, as, ā, am* (fr. *nasi* loc. sing. + *ota*), led by a string through the septum of the nose, fastened by the nose, furnished with a nose-ring; an ox or other animal led by a string through the septum of the nose. — *Nas-vat, ān, atī, at,* Ved. having a nose.

Nasa (at the end of an adj. comp.) = 3. *nas,* the nose, see *un-n*°, *urū-ṇ*°, *kumbhi-n*°, *khara-ṇ*°, *go-n*°, *dru-ṇ*°, &c.; (*ā*), f. the nose.

Nasi, the nose (?), in *kumbhī-n*°, q. v.

Nasta, as, m. the nose; (*ā*), f. a hole bored in the septum of the nose, cf. *nastaka, nastita;* (*am*), n. a sternutatory, snuff. — *Nasta-karaṇa, am,* n. a kind of instrument used by the Bhikshus for injecting the nose. — *Nasta-tas,* ind. (perhaps only = *nas-tas* with reduplicated affix *tas*), from the nose, out of the nose. — *Nastota* (°*ta-ota*), *as,* m. an ox led by a string through his nose; (also read *nasy-ota;* see under 3. *nas.*)

Nastaka, as, m. a hole bored in the septum or bridge of the nose of cattle for draught.

Nastita, as, ā, am, nozzled, having a hole bored in the septum of the nose, an ox or any other draught animal with a string through its nose, (the sort of rein usually employed in India.)

Nasya, as, ā, am, belonging or relating to the nose, nasal, in the nose; (*ā*), f. the nose; the string through the nose of an animal [cf. *nāsya*]; (*am*), n. the hairs in the nose; a sternutatory, snuff. — *Nasya-vidhi, is,* m. 'rules about sternutatories,' N. of the twenty-seventh chapter of the medical work Sārṅgadhara-saṃhitā.

नसंविद् *na-saṃvid, t,* f. unconsciousness; forgetfulness.

नसुकर *na-sukara, as, ā* or *ī, am,* not easy to be done.

नह 1. *nah,* cl. 4. P. A. *nahyati, -te, nanāha, nehe, naddhā, natsyati, -te, anātsīt, anaddha, naddhum,* to bind, tie, bind on, bind round, put on, gird round, bind together; A. to put on one's self, dress, put on armour, arm one's self: Caus. *nāhayati, -yitum,* Aor. *anīnahat,* to cause to bind or tie together, to cause to put on: Desid. *ninatsati, -te:* Intens. *nānahyate, nānaddhi;* [cf. Gr. νέ-ω, νή-θ-ω, νῆ-μα, νῆ-σι-ς, νῆ-τρο-ν, νέ-ω, Intens. νη-νέ-ω, νη-έ-ω: Lat. *ne-o, ne-men, ne-tu-s, nec-t-o, nexu-s:* Old Germ. *nā-an, nāw-an, nāh-an,* 'to sew;' *nā-dal,* 'needle;' *nah,* 'near:' Goth. *nethla,* 'a needle;' *nēhva,* 'near:' Angl. Sax. *naedl,* 'needle;' *neah, neh-st, nearra:* Eng. *nigh:* Mod. Germ. *näh-en, nad-el, nah, nach, ge-nug:* Hib. *nasgaim,* 'I bind;' *nas,* 'a tie.']

2. *nah, t,* f., Ved. a bond, tie; [cf. *akshā-n*°.]

Naha in *dru-ṇaha,* q. v.

Nahana, am, n., Ved. a bolt, a nail or connecting beam in a wall.

Nahyamāna, as, ā, am, being bound, tied, or fettered.

नहि *na-hi,* ind. for not, surely not, certainly not, by no means, not at all; *na-nahi,* certainly not; (*nahi* is sometimes strengthened in the Veda by other particles, e. g. *nahy aṅga, nahī nu, nahī sma.*) — *Nahi-mātra, as* or *am,* m. or n. (?), a particular high number; [cf. *na-mātra.*]

नहुस् *nahus, us,* m. a man, one who does not belong to one's own immediate community, a neighbour [cf. *nābhi;* Mod. Germ. *nahe*]; (collectively) the neighbourhood.

Nahusha, as, m., Ved. = *nahus,* a man; N. of a son of Manu and author of a Ṛig-veda hymn; N. of an ancient king, one of the lunar race, son of Āyus and grandson of Purū-ravas, father of Yayāti, who took possession of Indra's throne in heaven for a time, but was afterwards deposed and changed into a serpent; (according to others) a son of Ambarīsha, father of Nābhāga; N. of a serpent-demon; N. of a Marut; an epithet of Kṛishṇa-Vishṇu; [cf. *naghusha, nāhusha, nāhushi.*] — *Nahusha-ċarita, am,* n. 'the life of Nahusha,' N. of the 112th chapter of the Bhūmi-khaṇḍa of the Padma-Purāṇa. — *Nahushākhya* (°*sha-ākh*°), *am,* n. the plant Tabernæmontana Coronaria (= *tagara-pushpa*). — *Nahushātmaja* (°*sha-āt*°), *as,* m., N. of a king, the son of Nahusha, also called Yayāti.

Nahushṭara, as, ā, am, Ved. nearer (?), nearer than a neighbour.

Nahushya, as, ā, am, Ved. belonging to a descendant of Nahus, belonging to a man in general, human; (*as*), m. a man.

ना *nā,* ind. = *na,* no, not.

नाक *nāka, as,* m. (said to be fr. *na* + *a-ka,* where there is no unhappiness), heaven, the vault or ceiling of heaven, the upper sky, the firmament, sky, atmosphere, ether, paradise, (often in the Veda with *divo,* gen. of 3. *div,* or with *uttama* or *tritīya;* cf. *tri-nāka, tri-diva:* in Vājasaneyi-saṃhitā XVII. 67, the scale upwards is given as follows, 1. *Pṛithivī,* earth; 2. *Antarīksha,* atmosphere; 3. *Div,* sky; 4. *Divo-nāka,* upper sky; 5. *Svar-jyotis,* heaven of light or sphere of the luminaries); the sun (?); N. of a Maudgalya; N. of a mythical weapon of Arjuna; (*as, ā, am*), 'painless (?),' N. of a dynasty. — *Nāka-ċara, as, ā, am,* walking in the sky (as the Pitṛis). — *Nāka-nātha, as,* m. or *nāka-nāthaka, as,* m. 'guardian of the sky,' an epithet of Indra. — *Nāka-nāyaka, as,* m. 'chief of the sky,' an epithet of Indra. — *Nākanāyaka-purohita, as,* m. 'Indra's chief priest,' an epithet of Bṛihas-pati. — *Nāka-pāla, as,* m. guardian or lord of the sky. — *Nāka-pṛishṭha, am,* n. 'sky-ceiling,' the upper sky, the uppermost heaven. — *Nāka-pṛishṭhya, as, ā, am,* being in the highest heaven. — *Nāka-loka, as,* m. the heavenly world. — *Nāka-vanitā,* f. 'a nymph of heaven,' an Apsaras. — *Nāka-sad, t, t, t,* resting in the firmament, inhabiting the sky; (*t*), m. an inhabitant of heaven, a deity; (*as*), m. pl., N. of nine Ekāhas; (*t*), f., N. of an Ishṭakā. — *Nākāpagā* (°*ka-āp*°), f. the river of heaven, the heavenly Gaṅgā. — *Nākeśa* (°*ka-īśa*), *as,* m. 'the lord of the sky,' an epithet of Indra. — *Nākeśvara* (°*ka-īś*°), *as,* m. 'the lord of heaven,' a god. — *Nākaukas* (°*ka-ok*°), *ās,* m. 'whose dwelling is the sky,' an inhabitant of heaven, a god.

Nākin, ī, m. a deity, god (as dwelling in Nāka). — *Nāki-nātha, as,* m. 'chief of the gods,' an epithet of Indra.

नाकु *nāku, us,* m. (said to be fr. rt. *nam*), an ant-hill or mole-hill, a burrow; a mountain; N. of a Muni or saint. — *Nāku-sadman, ā,* m. a snake.

नाकुल *nākula, as, ī, am* (fr. *nakula*), relating or belonging to an ichneumon, ichneumon-like, similar to an ichneumon; (*as*), m. a patronymic from Nakula [cf. *nākuli*]; (*ās*), m. pl., N. of a people; (*ī*), f. the ichneumon plant, a particular plant supposed to furnish the ichneumon or mungoose with an antidote when bitten in a conflict with a snake [cf. *gandha-nākulī, nakuleshṭā*]; a sort of pepper, Piper Chaba (= *ċavya*); the root of the Seemul tree (= *kukkuṭī-kanda*) and several other plants, as *yava-tiktā, śveta-kaṇṭa-kārī, sarpa-gandhā.* — *Nākulāndhya* (°*la-an*°), *am,* n. 'ichneumon blindness,' a kind of weakness of sight.

Nākuli, is, m. a descendant of Nakula, a patronymic of Satānīka.

नाक्र *nākra, as,* m., Ved. an aquatic animal; [cf. *nakra.*]

नाक्षत्र *nākshatra, as, ī, am* (fr. *nakshatra*), belonging to the constellations or lunar asterisms, starry, sidereal; (*am*), n. a month computed by the moon's passage through the twenty-seven mansions, or one of thirty days of sixty Ghaṭis each.

Nākshatrika, as, ī, am, relating or belonging to the lunar asterisms, sidereal; (*as*), m. a month of twenty-seven days, each day being the period of the moon's passage through a lunar asterism; (*ī*), f. the state or condition to which a person is subjected agreeably to the asterism presiding over his nativity.

नाग *nāga, as,* m. (perhaps for original *snāga;* Angl. Sax. *snaca;* Eng. *snake;* or connected with *naga,* a mountain, or *nagna,* naked; said to be fr. rt. 1. *dah* through change of *d* into *n*), a snake in general, especially the spectacle-snake or cobra capella, Coluber; a Nāga or fabulous serpent-demon so called, having a human face with the tail of a serpent, (the race of these beings is said to have sprung from Kadrū, wife of Kaśyapa [or from Su-rasā], in order to people Pātāla, one of the regions below the earth, their city is called Bhoga-vatī); an elephant; a shark (= *tantu-nāga*); a cruel or tyrannical person; (at the end of a comp.) 'an elephant of a man,' any great or pre-eminent person; N. of several plants, the small tree with fragrant blossoms, Mesua Roxburghii [cf. *nāga-kesara*]; Rottlera Tinctoria (= *pun-nāga*); a Cyperus (= *mustaka*); Piper Betel; a poisonous plant (see *nāga-stokaka*); a cloud; a peg or nail projecting from a wall to hang anything upon; one of the five airs of the body, that which is expelled by eructation; N. of the number seven, (probably to be referred to seven mythical serpents, but eight principal Nāgas are mentioned); N. of a Sādhya; of a Buddhist teacher; of a king of Āryāvarta, contemporary of Samudragupta; N. of a dynasty consisting of nine or seven princes; N. of several men; N. of a mountain; of a district; (*ī*), f. a female Nāga; a female elephant; (*am*), n. tin; lead; one of the astronomical periods called Karaṇas, (it is one of those termed *dhruva,* q. v., or invariable, and corresponds to the last half of Amāvāsya or new moon); the effects of that period on anything done or happening during it; (*as, ī, am*), formed or consisting of snakes, serpentine, snaky; relating to serpents or serpent-demons;

elephantine, belonging to or resembling an elephant; (*ā*), f., N. of a woman; [cf. *kshiti-n°.*] — *Nāga-kanda, as,* m. a kind of bulbous plant (= *hasti-kanda*). — *Nāga-kanyakā,* f. a serpent-virgin. — *Nāga-karṇa, as,* m. a kind of Ricinus (= *rak-tairaṇḍa, hasti-karṇa*). — *Nāga-kiñjalka, am,* n. the blossom of Mesua Roxburghii. — *Nāga-kumāra, as,* m. a prince of the serpent-demons; N. of a class of deities among the Bhavanādhīśas guarding the treasures of Kuvera. — *Nāga-keśa, as,* m., N. of a minister of king Nageśa. — *Nāga-keśara* or *nāga-kesara, as,* m. a small tree with fragrant blossoms (commonly Nageśar), Mesua Roxburghii or Ferrea; (*am*), n. the blossom of this tree. — *Nāga-khaṇḍa,* N. of one of the nine divisions of Bhārata-varsha. — *Nāga-gandhā,* f. a species of bulbous plant (= *nākulī* or *sarpa-gandhā*). — *Nāga-garbha, am,* n. red lead. — *Nāga-ćūḍa, as,* m. 'snake-crested' or 'whose top-knot consists of snakes,' an epithet of Śiva. — *Nāga-ćhattrā,* f. a kind of plant, Tiaridium Indicum. — *Nāga-ja, as, ā, am,* produced by or born from a Nāga, &c.; (*am*), n. red lead; tin. — *Nāga-jihvā,* f. 'snake-tongue,' a species of plant, Asclepias Pseudosarsa; (see *śārivā.*) — *Nāga-jihvikā,* f. red arsenic. — *Nāga-jīvana, am,* n. tin. — *Nāgajīvana-śatru, us,* m. 'enemy of tin,' orpiment. — *Nāga-tīrtha, am,* n., N. of a Tīrtha. — *Nāga-datta, as, ā, am,* given by Nāgas or serpents; (*as*), m., N. of one of the 100 sons of Dhṛita-rāshṭra; N. of a man related to Śākya-muni; of a king of Āryāvarta, contemporary of Samudra-gupta. — *Nāga-danta, as,* m. elephant's tusk or ivory, the tooth or tusk of an elephant; a shelf, peg, or bracket projecting from a wall and used to hang things upon; (*ā*), f., N. of an Apsaras; (*ī*), f. a species of sun-flower, Heliotropium Indicum; a harlot. — *Nāgadantaka, as,* m. ivory; a wooden peg or bracket projecting from a wall, a shelf; (*ikā*), f. a plant, commonly called Rāma-dūti, Tragia Involucrata. — *Nāga-damanī,* f. a particular plant (= *jambū, jāmbavatī, vṛikkā*). — *Nāga-dalopama* (°*la-up*°), *am,* n. the tree Xylocarpus Granatum. — *Nāga-dāśaka, as,* m., N. of a prince. — *Nāga-dentikā,* f. the betel plant. — *Nāga-deva, as,* m., N. of an author. — *Nāga-dru, us,* m. a species of Euphorbia used in offerings to the snake-goddess Manasā (= *samanta-dugdha*). — *Nāga-dvīpa, as,* m., N. of a Dvīpa in Jambū-khaṇḍa or Bhārata-varsha. — *Nāga-nakshatra, am,* n., N. of the three asterisms forming the Nāga-vīthi (?). — *Nāga-nātha, as,* m. the king of the serpents, a serpent-chief; (*am*), n., N. of a Liṅga sacred to Śiva; (also called *nāganāthesa-liṅga.*) — *Nāga-nābha, as,* m., N. of a man. — *Nāga-nāmaka, am,* n. tin. — *Nāga-nāman, ā,* m. holy basil (= *tulasī*). — *Nāga-nāyaka, as,* m. the leader or chief of the Nāgas or snakes. — *Nāga-nāsā,* f. the trunk or proboscis of an elephant. — *Nāganāsorū* (°*sā-ūrū*), *ūs,* f. a woman whose thighs taper like the trunk of an elephant; [cf. *karabhorū,* p. 205, col. 2.] — *Nāga-niryūha, as,* m. = *niryūha* and *nāga-danta,* a large pin or bracket projecting from a wall like a shelf. — *Nāga-pańćamī,* f. a particular festival, the fifth day in the light half of month Śrāvaṇa; the fifth day in the dark half of month Āshāḍha. — *Nāga-pati, is,* m. a serpent-chief. — *Nāga-pat-trā,* f. = *nāga-damanī.* — *Nāga-pattrī,* f. a species of plant (= *lakshmaṇā*). — *Nāga-pada, as,* m. a kind of coitus. — *Nāga-parṇī,* f. the betel plant. — *Nāga-pāla, as,* m., N. of a man; a prince of Sāśikya. — *Nāga-pāśa, as,* m. a sort of magical noose or lasso used in battle to entangle an enemy; 'the serpent-noose,' an epithet of the weapon of Varuṇa, regent of the waters; a kind of coitus. — *Nāga-pāśaka, as,* m. a kind of coitus. — *Nāga-pura, as,* m. 'elephant's town,' ancient Delhi (= *gaja-pura, hāstina-pura*). — *Nāga-pushpa, as,* m. several plants, = Rottlera Tinctoria (= *pun-nāga*); Mesua Roxburghii (= *nāga-kesara*); Michelia Champaka (= *ćampaka*); (*am*), n. the blossom of this plant; (*ī*), f. = *nāga-damanī.* — *Nāgapushpa-phalā,* f. the plant Benincasa Cerifera (= *kush-māṇḍī*). — *Nāga-pushpikā,* f. yellow jasmine (= *svarṇa-yūthī*). — *Nāga-phala, as,* m. the plant Trichosanthes Dioeca; (*ā*), f. a various reading for *nāga-balā.* — *Nāga-badhū, ūs,* f. a female elephant. — *Nāga-bandhaka, as,* m. an elephant-catcher. — *Nāga-bandhu, us,* m. 'elephant-friend, liked by elephants,' the holy fig-tree, Ficus Religiosa (= *aśvattha*). — *Nāga-bala, as,* m. 'having the strength of an elephant,' an epithet of Bhīma; (*ā*), f. the plant Uraria Lagopodioides; (*am*), n. a particular high number. — *Nāga-buddha, as,* m. or *nāga-bodhi, is,* m., N. of a Buddhist teacher. — *Nāga-buddhi, is,* m., N. of a medical author. — *Nāga-bodha, as,* m., N. of an author. — *Nāga-bhaginī,* f. 'serpent's sister,' N. of the goddess Manasā; [cf. *nāga-mātṛi.*] — *Nāga-bhid, t,* m. 'elephant-destroyer,' a species of snake, Amphisbæna; (also written *nāga-bhṛit,* = *ḍuṇḍu.*) — *Nāga-bhūshaṇa, as, ā, am,* 'decorated with serpents,' an epithet of Śiva; [cf. *nāga-ćūḍa.*] — *Nāga-bhoga, as,* m. a species of serpent. — *Nāga-maṇḍalika, as,* m. a snake-keeper; a snake-catcher. — *Nāga-matī,* f. the plant Ocimum Sanctum. — *Nāga-maya, as, ī, am,* consisting of or in elephants. — *Nāga-malla, as,* m. 'an athlete among the elephants,' an epithet of Indra's elephant Airāvata. — *Nāga-mātṛi, tā,* f. 'mother of serpent-demons,' an epithet of Su-rasā; an epithet of the goddess Manasā (supposed to preside over snakes); red arsenic. — *Nāga-māra, as,* m. a species of pot-herb, also Keśa-rāja. — *Nāga-mudra, as,* m., N. of a Buddhist Sthavira (= *nāga-sena*). — *Nāga-yashṭi, is,* f. or *nāga-yashṭikā,* f. a graduated pole or post for showing the depth of water in a newly dug pond, a boring-rod or stick driven into the earth. — *Nāga-rakta, am,* n. red lead. — *Nāga-raṅga, as,* m. the orange, (usually applied to the Silhet orange, Citrus Aurantium.) — *Nāga-raṭṭa, as,* m. a various reading for *nāga-vaṭṭa,* q. v. — *Nāga-rāj, ṭ,* m. a serpent-king, a chief of the Nāgas. — *Nāga-rāja, as,* m. 'king of the serpents,' an epithet of Ananta or of Vāsuki, chief of the serpents; a king among the elephants, a large elephant. — *Nāgarāja-kara, as,* m. the trunk of the king of elephants. — *Nāga-rājan, ā,* m. a serpent-king. — *Nāga-ruka, as,* m. = *nāga-raṅga,* the orange-tree. — *Nāga-reṇu, us,* m. red lead. — *Nāga-latā,* f. the penis; N. of a woman. — *Nāga-lekhā,* f., N. of a woman. — *Nāga-loka, as,* m. the Nāga world or one of the regions below the earth, otherwise called Pātāla, the world of the serpent-demons, the abode of serpents or the race of serpents collectively. — *Nāga-vaṭṭa, as,* m., N. of a man; [cf. *nāga-raṭṭa.*] — *Nāga-vat, ān, atī, at,* consisting of snakes; possessed of elephants. — *Nā-ga-vadhū,* see *nāga-badhū.* — *Nāga-vana, am,* n. 'serpent-wood,' N. of a place. — *Nāga-vartman, ā,* m., N. of a Tīrtha. — *Nāga-vallarī* or *nāga-valli, is, ī,* or *nāga-vallikā,* f. Piper Betel, the betel plant. — *Nāga-vārika, as,* m. a royal elephant; an elephant-driver or keeper; a peacock; an epithet of Garuḍa, the bird of Vishṇu; the chief person in a court or assembly. — *Nāga-vāsa, as,* m. 'abode of snakes,' N. of a lake supposed to have been formed originally by the valley of Nepal. — *Nāga-vīthi,* f. a row of serpents; the serpents' path, that part of the moon's path which contains the asterisms Svāti or (according to others) Aśvinī, Bharaṇī, and Kṛittikā; N. of a daughter of Yāmī who was the daughter of Daksha and wife of Dharma; of a daughter of Kaśyapa by Yāminī. — *Nāga-vṛiksha, as,* m. a species of tree. — *Nāga-śata, as,* m., N. of a mountain. — *Nāga-śrī, is,* f., N. of a queen. — *Nāga-sam-bhava, am,* n. minium or red lead. — *Nāga-sam-bhūta,* 'produced from serpents,' epithet of a sort of pearl. — *Nāga-sāhvaya, as, ā, am,* called after elephants, (generally with *nagara* = 'elephant's town,' i. e. Hāstina-pura.) — *Nāga-sugandhā,* f. the ichneumon plant (= *su-gandhā, sarpa-sugandhā, bhujaṅgākshī;* cf. *nākulī*). — *Nāga-sena, as,* m., N. of a Buddhist Sthavira; a king of Āryāvarta and contemporary of Samudra-gupta. — *Nāga-stokaka, am,* n. a species of poisonous plant. — *Nāga-sthala,* N. of a village near Mathurā. — *Nāga-sphotā* or rather *nāga-sphoṭā,* f. two plants (= *dantī* and *nāga-dantī*). — *Nāga-svarūpiṇī,* f. a kind of metre consisting of four lines of eight syllables each. — *Nāga-hanu, us,* m. a kind of perfume (= *nakha*). — *Nāga-hantrī,* f. a species of plant (= *bandhyā-karko-ṭakī;* cf. *nāgārāti*). — *Nāga-hrada, am,* n. a lake inhabited by snakes or serpent-demons. — *Nā-gākhya* (°*ga-ākh*°), *as,* m. = *nāga-kesara,* Mesua Roxburghii. — *Nāgāṅga, am,* n. Hāstina-pura. — *Nā-gāṅganā* (°*ga-aṅ*°), f. a female elephant; the proboscis of an elephant; [cf. *nāgāñjanā.*] — *Nāgāń-ćalā* (°*ga-ań*°), f. = *nāga-yashṭi,* q. v. — *Nāgāñ-janā,* f. the female of an elephant (= *nāga-yashṭi,* q. v.). — *Nāgādhipa* (°*ga-adh*°), *as,* m. 'the serpent-prince,' an epithet of Śesha. — *Nāgādhipati* (°*ga-adh*°), *is,* m. 'serpent-chief,' an epithet of Virūḍhaka. — *Nāgādhirāja* (°*ga-adh*°), *as,* m. the king or chief of the elephants. — *Nāgānanda* (°*ga-ān*°), *as* or *am,* m. n. (?), or *nāgānanda-nā-ṭaka, am,* n., N. of a play ascribed to king Harsha. — *Nāgāntaka* (°*ga-an*°), *as,* m. 'destroyer of serpents,' an epithet of Garuḍa, the bird of Vishṇu. — *Nāgābhibhu, us,* or *-bhū* (°*ga-abh*°), *ūs,* m., N. of a Buddha. — *Nāgārāti* (°*ga-ar*°), *is,* m. a species of plant (= *bandhyā-karkoṭakī;* cf. *nāga-hantrī*). — *Nāgāri* (°*ga-ari*), *is,* m. 'enemy of serpents,' epithet of Garuḍa. — *Nāgārūḍha* (°*ga-ār*°), *as, ā, am,* mounted or riding upon an elephant. — *Nāgār-juna* (°*ga-ar*°), *as,* m., N. of an ancient Buddhist teacher of the rank of a Bodhi-sattva, said to be the author of the Yoga-ratna-mālā or Āśćarya-ratna-mālā; (*ī*), f., N. of a rock-cavern. — *Nāgālābu* (°*ga-al*°), *us,* f. a species of gourd (= *kumbha-tumbī*). — *Nāgāśana* (°*ga-aś*°), *as,* m. 'snake-eater,' a peacock; an epithet of Garuḍa. — *Nā-gāhva* (°*ga-āh*°), *am,* n. 'the town called after elephants,' Hāstina-pura; (*ā*), f. a species of bulbous plant (= *lakshmaṇā;* cf. *nāga-pattrī*). — *Nāgāh-vaya* (°*ga-āh*°), *as,* m. a species of plant; an epithet of Tathāgata-bhadra. — *Nāgendra* (°*ga-in*°), *as,* m. a serpent-prince, serpent-chief; (*ī*), f., N. of a river. — *Nāgeśa* (°*ga-īśa*), *as,* m., N. of a prince; an epithet of Patañjali; *Nāgeśa* or *Nāgeśa-bhaṭṭa,* N. of a grammarian, see *Nāgojī;* (*am*), n., N. of a Liṅga in Dārukā-vana. — *Nāgeśvara* (°*ga-īś*°), *as,* m., N. of a man; (*ī*), f., N. of the deity Manasā; (*am*), n., N. of a Liṅga. — *Nāgeśvara-tīrtha, am,* n., N. of several sacred bathing-places. — *Nāgodara* (°*ga-ud*°), *as,* m., N. of a medical author; (*am*), n. a medical term for a peculiar disease of pregnancy, dissolution of the fetus in the womb; a breast-plate, a cuirass. — *Nāgodbheda* (°*ga-ud*°), *as,* m., N. of a sacred spot where the river Saras-vatī re-appears.

Nāgaka, as, m., N. of a man.

Nāgin, ī, inī, i, having serpents, covered with or surrounded by serpents; snaky.

Nāgoda, am, n. armour for the front of the body; [cf. *nāgodara* above.]

नागपैय *nāgapaiya, as,* m., N. of a poet mentioned in the Śārṅgadhara-paddhati.

नागम्मा *nāgammā,* f., N. of a female poet.

नागर *nāgara, as, ī, am* (fr. *nagara*), town-born, town-bred, city, citizen; relating or belonging to a town, civic; spoken in a town or city; polite, civil; clever, sharp, knowing; bad, vile; nameless; (*as*), m. a citizen; = *paura,* a term for a prince engaged in war under certain circumstances and (in astrology) applied to a planet in a state of opposition to other planets; a husband's brother; an orange; a lecturer; denial of knowledge; hardship, toil, fatigue; desire of final beatitude; (*ī*), f. the Nāgarī or Deva-nāgarī (q. v.) character in which Sanskrit is commonly written; a species of Euphorbia (= *snuhī*); a clever or crafty or intriguing woman; (*am*), n. dry ginger; the root of Cyperus Pertenuis; a sort of coitus. — *Nāgara-khaṇḍa, as,* m., N. of a section of the Skanda-Purāṇa. — *Nāgara-ghana, as,* m. or *nāgara-mustā,*

f. a species of grass, Cyperus. — *Nāgarāhva* (°*ra-āh*°), *am*, n. dry ginger. — *Nāgarotthā* (°*ra-ut*°), f. = *nāgara-mustā*, q. v.

Nāgaraka, *as*, *ī*, *am*, living in a town, (opposed to *āraṇyaka*); clever, cunning; (*as*), m. a citizen; the chief of the police or of a town; an artist; a thief, (a various reading for *nāgarika*); (*am*), n. dry ginger; [cf. *nāgara*.]

Nāgarika, *as*, *ī*, *am*, town-born, town-bred; living in or inhabiting a town; produced from a town; polite; clever, cunning; (*as*), m. a citizen, the chief of a town, superintendant of police; (*am*), n. the toll raised from a town. — *Nāgarika-puṛq*, *am*, n., N. of a town. — *Nāgarika-bala*, *am*, n. the guard of a police-officer.

Nāgareyaka, *as*, *ī*, *am*, city, citizen.

Nāgarya, *am*, n. town-life, shrewdness.

नागरमर्दि *nāgaramardi*, *is*, m. (fr. *nagara-mardin*), a patronymic from Nagara-mardin.

नागरीट *nāgarīṭa*, *as*, m. a libertine, rake, blackguard; (probably for *nāgavīṭa* below.)

Nāgavīṭa, *as*, m. a rake; intriguer, match-maker.

नागशुण्डी *nāgaśuṇḍī*, f. a species of gourd; (also read *nāmaśuṇḍī*.)

नागुली *nāgulī*, f., N. of a town.

नागोजी *nāgojī* or *nāgoji* or *nāgoji-bhaṭṭa*, *as*, m., N. of a modern grammarian, also called *nāgeśa-bhaṭṭa*, author of a Vivaraṇa or interpretation of Kaiyaṭa's commentary on Patañjali, of a grammar called Paribhāshendu-śekhara, &c.

नाग्नजित *nāgnajita*, *as*, m. (fr. *nagna-jit*), a descendant of Nagna-jit; (*ī*), f., N. of one of the wives of Kṛishṇa; (wrongly spelt *nagnajitī*.)

नाचिक *nāćika*, *as*, m., N. of a son of Viśvā-mitra.

नाचिकेत *nāćiketa*, *as*, *ī*, *am* (fr. *na-ćiketa*, q. v.), relating to Na-ćiketa or Na-ćiketas; (*as*), m. a synonym of fire, (wrongly written *nāćiketu*); N. of an ancient sage, son of Uddālaki; [cf. *na-ćiketa*, *tri-ṇāćiketa*.]

नाचीन *nāćīna*, *ās*, m. pl., N. of a people.

नाज्जक *nājjaka*, *as*, m., N. of a man.

नाट *nāṭa*, *as*, *am*, m. n. (fr. rt. *naṭ*), dancing, acting, a dance; (*as*), m., N. of a Nāga-rāja; (*ās*), m. pl., N. of a people, = *karṇāṭaka*, the Carnatic; (*ī*), f., scil. *bhāshā*, the language spoken by the Nāṭas. — *Nāṭāmra* (°*ṭa-am*°), *as*, m. the water-melon, Cucurbita Citrullus.

Nāṭaka, *as*, *ī*, *am*, dancing, acting; (*am*), n. a play, drama; the first of the ten pieces of dramatic compositions of the first order; (*as*), m. an actor, dancer, mime; N. of a mountain in Kāmākhyā; (*ikā*), f. a kind of play, see below; (*akī*), f. the court of Indra. — *Nāṭaka-prapanća*, *as*, m. course or arrangement of a drama. — *Nāṭaka-ratna-kosha*, *as*, m. 'treasure of jewels of plays,' N. of a work. — *Nāṭaka-vidhi*, *is*, m. mimic art, dramatic action. — *Nāṭakāvatāra* (°*ka-av*°), *as*, m., N. of a work.

Nāṭakīya, *as*, *ā*, *am*, dramatic.

Nāṭakeya, *ās*, m. pl., N. of a people.

Nāṭāra, *as*, m. (fr. *naṭī*), the son of an actress; [cf. *nāṭera*, *nāṭeya*.]

Nāṭikā, f. a short or light comedy, the first of the Upa-rūpakas or dramas of the second order.

Nāṭitaka, *am*, n. a mimic representation, a gesture.

Nāṭeya, *as*, m. the son of an actress or dancing-girl.

Nāṭera, *as*, m. = *nāṭeya*; [cf. *nāṭāra*.]

Nāṭya, *am*, n. dancing, mimic or dramatic representation, a play; action on the stage, the science or art of dancing or acting, scenic art, the union of song, pantomime dance and instrumental music; the costume of an actor; (*as*), m. an actor, mime. — *Nāṭya-darpaṇa*, *am*, n. 'mirror of acting,' N. of a work. — *Nāṭya-dharmikā* or *nāṭya-dharmī*, f. the rules of dramatic representation. — *Nāṭya-priya*, *as*, m. 'fond of dancing,' an epithet of Śiva. — *Nāṭya-loćana-kāra*, *as*, m., N. of a work on acting. — *Nāṭya-varga*, *as*, m., N. of a chapter of the Nāma-liṅgānuśāsana by Amara-siṃha. — *Nāṭya-śālā*, f. a room or building for dramatic exhibitions, a theatre, a dancing-room, (according to some it should be built near the gate of a palace.) — *Nāṭya-śāstra*, *am*, n. any book on dancing or dramatic representation. — *Nāṭyāćārya* (°*ya-āć*°), *as*, m. a dancing-master. — *Nāṭyokti* (°*ya-uk*°), *is*, f. dramatic phraseology.

नाड *nāḍa*, *am*, n. = *nāla*.

नाडपित् *nāḍapit*, Ved., N. of a place.

नाडायन *nāḍāyana*, *as*, m. (fr. *naḍa*), a patronymic from Naḍa.

Nāḍāyanaka, relating to Nāḍāyana.

नाडि *nāḍi*, *is*, or *nāḍī*, f. (fr. *naḍa*, q. v.), the tubular stalk or culm of any plant; the hollow stalk of a lotus, &c.; any tubular organ of the body (as an artery, vein, intestine, &c.); any pipe or tube, a flute; a fistulous sore, fistula, sinus [cf. *nāḍī-vraṇa*]; the pulse either at the hand or feet, &c.; a measure of time = $\frac{1}{60}$ of a sidereal day or $\frac{1}{2}$ Muhūrta; a period or hour of twenty-four minutes; the box of a wheel (Ved.); a sort of bent grass; a juggling trick, deception. — *Nāḍi-ćīra*, *am*, n. a small reed or tube round which the woof is wound, (it is then used as a shuttle.) — *Nāḍin-dhama*, *as*, *ā*, *am*, causing movement of the intestines (as fright), terrifying; (*as*), m. a goldsmith; (also read *nāḍīn-dhama*.) — *Nāḍin-dhaya*, *as*, *ī*, *am*, drinking or sucking through a tube. — *Nāḍi-pattra*, *am*, n. an esculent root, Arum Colocasia. — *Nāḍi-maṇḍala*, *am*, n. the celestial equator. — *Nāḍī-kalāpaka*, *as*, m. a species of plant (= *gaṇḍinī* in Hindī). — *Nāḍī-ćaraṇa*, *as*, m. 'whose feet or legs are like stalks,' a bird. — *Nāḍī-jaṅgha*, *as*, m. 'having stalk-like legs,' a crow; N. of a fabulous crane; N. of a holy teacher or saint; [cf. *nālī-jaṅgha*.] — *Nāḍī-taraṅga*, *as*, m. = *kākola*; a sort of poison; an astrologer; a ravisher, debaucher (= *rata-hiṇḍaka*; cf. *nārī-taraṅgaka*). — *Nāḍī-tikta*, *as*, m. a species of Nimba growing in Nepal (= *nepāla-nimba*). — *Nāḍī-datta*, *as*, m. = *nāḍikā-datta*, q. v. — *Nāḍī-deha*, *as*, m. 'thin-bodied like a tube or stalk,' N. of one of the attendants of Śiva (= *bhṛiṅgin*; cf. *nāḍī-vigraha*). — *Nāḍī-nakshatra*, *am*, n. the planet of a person's nativity (= *janma-nakshatra*). — *Nāḍīn-dhama* = *nāḍin-dhama*, q. v. — *Nāḍī-parīkshā*, f. feeling the pulse; N. of a medical work. — *Nāḍī-prakāśa*, *as*, m., N. of a pharmaceutical work commented on by Saṅkara-sena. — *Nāḍī-maya*, *as*, *ī*, *am*, abounding with blood-vessels. — *Nāḍī-yantra*, *am*, n. any tubular instrument. — *Nāḍī-vigraha*, *as*, m., N. of Bhṛiṅgin, one of Śiva's chief attendants; [cf. *nāḍī-deha*.] — *Nāḍī-vraṇa*, *as*, m. an ulcer, a fistula, fistulous sore, sinus. — *Nāḍī-śāka*, *as*, m. a species of vegetable (= *nāḍīka*). — *Nāḍī-śuddhi*, *is*, f., N. of a Yoga work. — *Nāḍī-saṅkhyā*, f., N. of a chapter of the Purāṇa-sarva-sva. — *Nāḍī-sanćāra*, *as*, m., N. of the forty-second chapter of the Jñāna-khaṇḍa of the Śiva-Purāṇa. — *Nāḍī-sneha*, *as*, m. a N. of Bhṛiṅgin; see *nāḍī-vigraha*. — *Nāḍī-hiṅgu*, *u*, n. = *hiṅgu-nāḍikā*, the resin of the plant Gardenia Gummifera?; (*us*), m. a plant (= *vanśa-pattrī*).

Nāḍika, *am*, n. the plant Ocimum Sanctum (= *kāla-śāka*); (*ā*), f. a hollow stalk or stalk in general; any tubular organ of the body (as an artery, vein, intestine, &c.); a fistulous sore; a ray of the sun (supposed to be hollow); an Indian hour or twenty-four minutes = $\frac{1}{60}$ of a sidereal day = $\frac{1}{2}$ Muhūrta; a measure of length = $\frac{1}{2}$ Daṇḍa, (also read *nārikā*); a piece of metal on which the hours are struck, an Indian clock, a gong. — *Nāḍikā-datta*, *as*, m., N. of an author mentioned in the Saṃskāra-tattva by Raghu-nandana; [cf. *nāḍī-datta*.]

Nāḍīka, *as*, m. a species of pot-herb (= commonly *pāṭśāk*); Corchorus Olitorius; (*ā*), f. the wind-pipe or throat.

नाडिकेल *nāḍikela* or *nāḍīkela*, *as*, m. = *nārikela*, the cocoa-nut palm.

नाडीच *nāḍīća*, *as*, m. an esculent root, Colocasia Antiquorum.

नाड्लेय *nāḍvaleya*, *as*, m. a metronymic from Naḍvalā.

नाणक *nāṇaka*, *am*, n. a coin or anything stamped with an impression. — *Nāṇaka-parīkshā*, f. 'the testing of coin,' assaying. — *Nāṇaka-parīkshin*, *ī*, m. 'coin-tester,' an assayer, assay-master.

नातिचिर *nāti-ćira*, *as*, *ā*, *am*, not very long (in time), of no long duration; (*āt* or *e*), ind. in no very long time, soon.

नातिदूर *nāti-dūra* (*na-ati-d*°), *as*, *ā*, *am*, not very distant; (*e*), ind. not far from (with abl. or gen.); (*am*), ind. not very far, no great distance, not far away. — *Nātidūra-nirīkshin*, *ī*, *iṇī*, *i*, not seeing very far, not far-sighted.

नातिभिन्न *nāti-bhinna* (*na-ati-bh*°), *as*, *ā*, *am*, not very different from (with abl.).

नातिवाद *nātivāda* (*na-at*°), *as*, m. avoiding opprobrious or abusive language, abstaining from reproof.

नात्र *nātra*, *am*, n. (for *nāntra*), praise, eulogium; surprise, wonder; (*as*), m. Śiva; a sage.

नाथ् *nāth* (allied to rt. *nādh* and generally identified with it), cl. 1. P. *nāthati*, *nanātha*, *nāthitā*, *nāthishyati*, *anāthīt*, *nāthitum*, to ask, solicit, beg for anything (with dat. or gen. of the object or with two acc.); to have power; to be master; to harass, destroy (?); to be sick or ill (?); (in the Veda only the part. *nāthita* and *nādhamāna* fr. *nādh* appear to occur); [cf. rt. *nādh*; Old Germ. *nōt*, 'necessity;' Mod. Germ. *noth*; Angl. Sax. *nead*, *neod* = Eng. *need*; Goth. *nauthyan*, 'to force.']

Nātha, *am*, n. refuge, help; (*as*), m. a protector, patron, master, leader, ruler, lord, (often at the end of a comp., see *jīvita-n*°, *parjanya-n*°, *ku-n*°; and often used at the end of names of gods and men, see *govinda-n*°, *jagan-n*°, *trailokya-n*°); a husband [cf. *a-n*°]; a possessor [cf. *sa-nātha*, possessed of]; a rope passed through the nose of a draft ox [cf. *nātha-hari*]; N. of an author; [cf. *a-n*°, *ku-n*°, *govinda-n*°.] — *Nātha-kāma*, *as*, *ā*, *am*, Ved. seeking for help or protection, seeking a refuge. — *Nātha-kumāra*, *as*, m., N. of a poet mentioned in the Sārṅgadhara-paddhati. — *Nātha-tva*, *am*, n. the office or dignity of a protector or patron, protectorship, patronage. — *Nātha-vat*, *ān*, *atī*, *at*, having a patron or protector, having a master, dependant, subservient, subject; (*atī*), f. having a husband. — *Nātha-vid*, *t*, *t*, *t*, or *nātha-vindu*, *us*, *us*, *u*, Ved. possessing or granting protection. — *Nātha-hari*, *is*, *is*, *i*, carrying a master, any animal bridled by the nose. — *Nātha-hāra*, *as*, *ī*, *am*, taking or carrying a master, &c.

Nāthamāna, *as*, *ā*, *am*, Ved. seeking help, asking, begging.

Nāthāya, Nom. P. *nāthāyati*, *-yitum*, to become a protector or patron, to grant a request.

Nāthita, *as*, *ā*, *am*, one who needs help, needy, oppressed.

Nāthin, *ī*, *inī*, *i*, having a protector or master.

नाद *nāda*, *as*, m. (fr. rt. *nad*), a loud sound, cry, sounding, roaring, bellowing, crying, a sound or tone in general, (sometimes at the end of an adj. comp., e. g. *dāruṇa-nāda*, *as*, *ā*, *am*, sounding dreadfully); (in the Yoga) the nasal sound represented by a semicircle and used as an abbreviation or hieroglyphic in mystical words; one who praises. — *Nāda-tā*, f. the quality of sounding.

—*Nāda-purāṇa, am,* n., N. of a Purāṇa treating of musical sounds. —*Nāda-vat, ān, atī, at,* pronounced with sound (as letters), sonant. —*Nāda-vindūpanishad* (°*du-up*°), *t,* f., N. of an Upanishad.

Nādi, is, is, i, sounding, roaring.

Nādin, ī, inī, i, who or what sounds, sounding, resonant, sounding aloud, pronounced with sound (as a letter); roaring, bellowing, braying, (often at the end of a comp.; cf. *khara-n°, gardabha-n°*); (*ī*), m., N. of a Dānava; of a Brāhman metamorphosed into an antelope.

नादर *nādara* (*na-ād°*), *as,* m. disrespect, disregard, inattention.

नादिक *nādika,* N. of a country.

नादिग *nādiga, as,* m., N. of a man.

नादेय 1. *nādeya, as, ī, am* (fr. *nadī*), coming from or belonging to a river, river-born, fluvial, fluviatic, aquatic, marine; (*as*), m. the reed Saccharum Spontaneum (=*kāśa*); Calamus Rotang (=*vānīra*); (*ī*), f. several plants, a species of reed growing usually near water, Calamus Fasciculatus (=*ambu-vetasa,=jala-vānīra*); the orange-tree (=*bhūmi-jambūka, bhūmi-jambū,* or *bhū-jambū*); Sesbania Ægyptiaca (=*jayā*); the China rose (=*japā, javā,=vyangushṭha,=agni-mantha, kāka-jambū*); (*am*), n. rock-salt (=*saindhava*); antimony (=*sauvīrāñjana*).

Nādya, as, ā, am, coming from a river, fluvial, river-born.

नादेय 2. *nādeya* (for *na ādeya*), not to be taken, &c.

नाध् *nādh* (=*nāth,* q. v.), cl. 1. A. *nādhate, nanādhe, nādhishyate, nādhitum,* to ask, beg for, crave, &c. See rt. *nāth.*

Nādhamāna, as, ā, am, Ved. seeking help, asking, begging.

Nādhas, as, n. (probably=*nātha*), Ved. refuge, help.

नान *nāna, as,* m., N. of a man.

नानद *nānada, am,* n. (fr. rt. *nad*), N. of a Sāman; [cf. *nānanda.*]

नानन्द *nānanda, am,* n. (fr. rt. *nand*), scil. *indrasya,* N. of a Sāman; [cf. *nānada.*]

नानर्दमान *nānardamāna, as, ā, am* (fr. the Intens. of rt. *nard*), sounding loudly, roaring lustily.

नाना *nānā,* ind. (probably a reduplication of the negative particle *na* or of the pronominal affix *na* in *a-na* &c.), in different or various ways, in different places, manifoldly, differently, variously; distinctly, separately; (when used as an adj. at the beginning of a comp.=) of different kinds, of different classes, various, sundry, different, manifold, diverse; (according to Pāṇ. II. 3, 32)=*vinā,* without (with gen., abl., inst.). —*Nānā-kanda, as,* m. a species of bulbous plant (=*piṇḍālu*). —*Nānākāra* (°*nā-āk°*), *as, ā, am,* of different forms or manifold kinds, multiform, various. —*Nānā-kāram,* ind. having done variously. —*Nānā-graha, as,* m. taking separately, (used to explain *ava-graha.*) —*Nānā-jātīya, as, ā, am,* of various kinds or sorts, belonging to different classes, &c. —*Nānātma-vādin, ī, inī, i,* maintaining the Sāṅkhya doctrine that each individual being has a soul distinct from the universal spirit. —*Nānātyaya* (°*nā-at°*), *as, ā, am,* of different kinds, manifold. —*Nānā-tva, am,* n. variety, diversity, difference, manifoldness, (opposed to *eka-tva, aikya.*) —*Nānā-dānāni,* n. pl. 'various presents,' N. of a chapter of the Purāṇa-sarva-sva. —*Nānā-deśya, as, ā, am,* belonging to or coming from different districts or countries. —*Nānā-dharman, ā, ā, a,* Ved. having different customs or characteristics. —*Nānā-dhātu-śata, am,* n. a hundred various minerals. —*Nānādhātu-samākīrṇa, as, ā, am,* filled with various minerals. —*Nānā-dhī, is, īs, i,* Ved. having different intentions. —*Nānā-dhvani, is,* m. a musical instrument of more than one tone. —*Nānā-nāma-nirūpaṇa, am,* n., N. of the tenth chapter of the Krīḍā-khaṇḍa of the Gaṇeśa-Purāṇa. —*Nānā-pakshi-gaṇākīrṇa* (°*ṇa-āk°*), *as, ā, am,* filled with flocks of various birds. —*Nānāpakshi-nishevita, as, ā, am,* frequented by various birds. —*Nānā-pada, am,* n., Ved. a different or separate or independent word. —*Nānāpada-stha, as,* m., Ved. (an accent) standing on distinct words or on a separate word (?). —*Nānā-prabhṛiti, is, is, i,* Ved. beginning differently, (opposed to *nānodarka.*) —*Nānā-bhaṭṭa, as,* m., N. of the great-grandfather of Raṅga-nātha, a commentator on Kāli-dāsa's Vikramorvaśī. —*Nānā-mṛiga-gaṇa, ās,* m. pl. flocks of various animals. —*Nānā-ratham,* ind., Ved. in many chariots, in various cars. —*Nānā-rasa, as, ā, am,* of different flavours, variously flavoured. —*Nānā-rāga, as, ā, am,* variegated, of many colours. —*Nānā-rūpa, āṇi,* n. pl. various forms, different shapes; (*as, ā, am*), of different forms or shapes, of various kinds, multiform, various. —*Nānārūpa-tā,* f., Ved. multiformity, diversity of form, variousness. —*Nānārtha* (°*nā-ar°*), *as, ā, am,* having a different aim or object, containing something else (as a new sentence or thing); having different meanings (as a word). —*Nānārtha-kosha, as,* m. a dictionary which contains words with different meanings. —*Nānārtha-dhvani-mañjarī,* f. 'a cluster or nosegay of words with different meanings,' N. of a dictionary by an anonymous author. —*Nānārtha-ratna-tilaka,* N. of a dictionary,=*anekārtha-tilaka.* —*Nānārtharatna-mālā,* f. 'necklace of words of different meanings,' N. of a glossary. —*Nānārtha-saṅgraha, as,* m. 'collection of words with different meanings,' N. of a dictionary by Ajaya-pāla. —*Nānā-varṇa, ās,* m. pl. different colours; (*as, ā, am*), many-coloured, variegated. —*Nānā-vidha, as, ā, am,* of various sorts, of sundry kinds, in various ways, multiform, manifold. —*Nānā-vīrya, as, ā, am,* having different effects, having manifold efficacy. —*Nānāvīrya-tā,* f., Ved. the state of having manifold efficacy. —*Nānā-sūrya, as, ā, am,* Ved. illuminated by different suns.

Nānānam, ind., Ved.=*nānā,* differently, separately, &c.

नानान्द्र *nānāndra, as,* m. (fr. *nanāndṛi*), a husband's sister's son, a sister-in-law's son.

नानुष्ठेय *nānushṭheya* (*na-an°*), *as, ā, am,* not to be performed, improper, unusual, not right.

नानू *nānū, ūs,* m., N. of a man.

नान्त *nānta* (*na-an°*), *as, ā, am,*=*an-anta,* endless.

नान्तरीयक *nāntarīyaka* (*na-an°*), *as, ā, am,* inseparable, invariably connected.

नान्त्र *nāntra, am,* n. (fr. rt. *nam*), praise, eulogy; [cf. *nātra.*]

नान्द *nānda, as, ī, am* (fr. *nanda*), relating to Nanda.

नान्दन *nāndana, am,* n. (fr. rt. *nand* or *nandana*), Ved. a pleasure-garden, a paradise, elysium; [cf. *nandana.*]

नान्दिन् *nāndin, ī,* m. the speaker of the benediction before the commencement of a play.

नान्दी *nāndī,* f. (fr. rt. *nand*), joy, satisfaction; prosperity; eulogium or praise of a deity, or a prayer recited in benedictory verses at the opening of a religious ceremony or of a drama, (generally a kind of blessing pronounced as a prologue to a Nāṭaka or play; cf. *nandi.*) —*Nāndī-kara, as,* m. the speaker of the benediction at the opening of a drama; (also with the vowel *ī* made short, *nāndi-kara.*) —*Nāndī-ninūda, as,* m. a shout of joy. —*Nāndī-paṭa, as,* m.=*nāndī-mukha,* the lid or cover of a well. —*Nāndī-pura, am,* n., N. of a town in the East. —*Nāndīpuraka, as,* &c., coming from or relating to the town Nāndī-pura. —*Nāndī-mukha, as, ī, am,* (with *pitaras* or *pitṛi-gaṇas*) the class of manes of deceased progenitors to whom the Nāndī-mukha Śrāddha is offered; (*am*), n. (with or without *śrāddha*) a Śrāddha or commemorative offering to the manes preliminary to any joyous occasion, as initiation, marriage, &c., in which nine balls of meat are offered to the deceased father, paternal grandfather, and great-grandfather; to the maternal grandfather, great-grandfather, and great-great-grandfather; and to the mother, paternal grandmother, and paternal great-grandmother; (*as*), m.=*nāndī-paṭa,* the lid or cover of a well; (*ī*), f. a female ancestor sharing in the above Śrāddha; a kind of grain reckoned among the Ku-dhānyas; a kind of metre consisting of four lines of fourteen syllables each; [cf. *nandī-mukha.*] —*Nāndī-rava, as,* m. a cry of joy. —*Nāndī-vādin, ī,* m. the speaker of the prologue or introduction to a drama; a drummer, one who beats a drum at festivals. —*Nāndī-śrāddha, am,* n.=*nāndī-mukham śrāddham,* q. v.

Nāndīka, as, m. a post in a door-way set up for good luck; (also read as du. *nāndīkau.*)

नान्दुक *nānduka, as,* m., N. of a man.

नापि *nāpi* (*na-api*), ind. not even. See *na.*

नापित *nāpita, as,* m. (according to some a corruption of *snāpitṛi,* one who bathes), a barber, a shaver; (*ī*), f. the wife of a barber; [cf. *vaptṛi.*] —*Nāpita-vāstu, u,* n. a barber's dwelling. —*Nāpitavāstuka, as, ī, am,* belonging to or coming from the dwelling of a barber. —*Nāpita-śālā* or *nāpita-śālikā,* f. a barber's shop.

Nāpitāyani, is, m. the son or offspring of a barber.

Nāpitya, as, m. the son of a barber; (*am*), n. the trade or business of a barber.

नाभ् *nābh, p,* f. (fr. rt. 1. *nabh*), Ved. an opening, aperture, mouth (?); a rent (?); (Sāy.) destructive, obstructing.

नाभ *nābha.* See p. 478, col. 1.

नाभक *nābhaka, as,* m. a myrobalan, Terminalia Chebula.

नाभस *nābhasa, as, ī, am* (fr. *nabhas*), celestial, heavenly, appearing in the sky; (with *yoga*) N. of certain constellations, (according to Bhaṭṭotpala there are thirty-two, divided into four classes, viz. three Āśraya-yogas, two Dala-yogas, twenty Ākṛiti-yogas, and seven Saṅkhyā-yogas.) —*Nābhasa-yogādhyāya* (°*ga-adh°*), *as,* m., N. of the twelfth chapter of the Bṛihaj-jātaka, an astrological work by Varāha-mihira.

नाभाक *nābhāka, as, ī, am* (fr. *nabhāka*), belonging to or composed by Nabhāka; (*as*), m. (like *nabhāka*), Ved., N. of a Ṛishi of the Kaṇva family.

नाभाग *nābhāga, as,* m. (fr. *nabha-ga*), N. of a son of Manu Vaivasvata; a patronymic of Ambarīsha [cf. *nābhāgi*]; a son of Manu and father of Ambarīsha, &c.; a son of Nabha-ga or Nabhāga and father of Ambarīsha; a son of Śruta and father of Ambarīsha; of a son of Nedishṭha or Arishṭa or Dishṭa and father of Bhalandana; of a son of Yayāti, grandson of Ambarīsha, and father of Aja; [cf. *nabhāga, nābhā-nedishṭha.*] —*Nābhāga-dishṭa, as,* m., N. of a son of Manu Vaivasvata; [cf. *nābhā-nedishṭha, nābhāga, dishṭa.*] —*Nābhāga-dheya,* perhaps=*nābhāga-bhāgadheya,* one who has the same lot or destiny as Nābhāga. —*Nābhāga-nedishṭha, as,* m. and *nābhāgārishṭa* (°*ga-ar°*), *as,* m., N. of a son of Manu Vaivasvata; [cf. *nābhāga, arishṭa.*]

Nābhāgi, is, m. a patronymic of Ambarīsha.

नाभि *nābhi, is,* or *nābhī,* f. (according to

lexicographers also m.; probably fr. *nabh*, an older form of rt. 1. *nah*, to bind, connect), the navel; any navel-like cavity; the nave of a wheel (e.g. *tri-nābhi ćakram*, a three-naved wheel, a wheel with a triple nave or centre, Ṛig-veda I. 164, 2); the centre, focus, central point, middle, point of junction or that which holds the parts of anything together, point of concentration, chief point, chief, head, (hence *nābhir nṛipa-maṇḍalasya* in Raghu-v. XVIII. 19 = the chief of the circle of kings); the close connection of relations, near relationship, community of race or family; home; a near relation; musk (= *mṛiga-nābhi*); (*is*), m. a sovereign, a lord paramount; a chief; a Kshatriya or Hindū of the regal and military tribe; N. of a grandson of Priya-vrata [cf. *nābhi-gupta*, *nābhi-varsha*], son of Agnīdhra and father of Ṛishabha; of the father of Ṛishabha, first Arhat of the present Ava-sarpiṇī; [cf. *nābha*, 2. *nabhya*, *anya-n°*, *ghana-n°*, &c.: cf. also Gr. ὀμφ-αλό-ς, ὄμφαξ: Lat. *umb-il-icu-s*, *umbo:* Old Germ. *nab-a*, 'nave;' *nabulo*, 'navel:' Angl. Sax. *nafu*, *nafela:* Mod. Germ. *nabe*, *nabel:* Lett. *nabba*, 'navel:' Lith. *namba*, 'navel.'] — *Nābhā-nedishṭha*, *as*, m. (*nābhā* loc. sing. for *nābhau*), N. of a son of Manu Vaivasvata and author of two Ṛig-veda hymns, (Ṛig-veda X. 61, 62.) — *Nābhānedishṭha*, *as*, *ī*, *am*, or *nābhānedishṭhīya*, *as*, *ā*, *am*, relating to or composed by Nābhā-nedishṭha; (*am*), n., scil. *sūktam*, N. of a Vedic hymn. — *Nābhi-kaṇṭaka*, *as*, m. ruptured or protruded navel (= commonly *goṇḍa*). — *Nābhi-guḍaka*, *as*, m. a protruding or ruptured navel. — *Nābhi-gupta*, *as*, m. (?), 'protected by Nābhi,' N. of a Varsha in Kuśa-dvīpa, (the king of Kuśa-dvīpa was Hiraṇya-retas, a son of Priya-vrata, who divided the seven Varshas of his Dvīpa among his seven sons; Nābhi was probably the N. of one of these seven sons; cf. *nābhi-varsha*.) — *Nābhi-golaka*, *as*, m. a protruding or ruptured navel (= *nābhi-guḍaka*). — *Nābhi-ććhedana*, *am*, n. cutting or separating the umbilical cord. — *Nābhi-ja*, *as*, m. or *nābhi-janman*, *ā*, m. an epithet of Brahmā, (this deity appearing on the lotus which sprang from the navel of Vishṇu.) — *Nābhi-dvāra*, *am*, n. the aperture of the navel. — *Nābhi-nāḍi*, f. or *nābhi-nālā*, f. or *nābhi-nāla*, *am*, n. the umbilical cord; [cf. *garbha-nāḍī*.] — *Nābhi-bhū*, *ūs*, m. 'born from the navel,' an epithet of Brahmā; [cf. *nābhi-ja*.] — *Nābhi-mūla*, *am*, n. the part of the body immediately under the navel. — *Nābhi-vardhana*, *am*, n. division of the umbilical cord; rupture of the navel, umbilical hernia; corpulency. — *Nābhi-varsha*, *as*, *am*, m. n. the Varsha governed by Nābhi, son of Āgnīdhra (= *Bhārata-varsha*). — *Nābhy-āvarta*, *as*, m. the cavity of the navel.

Nābha (substituted for *nābhi* at the end of an adj. comp.), the navel (e.g. *abja-nābha*, *as*, m. 'lotus-naveled,' an epithet of Vishṇu; cf. *un-n°*, *ūrṇa-n°*, *kañja-n°*, *kāla-n°*); the nave of a wheel; the centre or central point of anything; (*as*), m. an epithet of Śiva; N. of a son of Śruta and father of Sindhu-dvīpa.

Nābhika, *as*, *ā*, *am*, (at the end of an adj. comp.) = *nābhi* (e.g. *shaṇ-nābhika*, having six naves); (*ā*), f. a cavity shaped like a navel; a species of plant, Achyranthes Atropurpurea (= *kaṭabhi*). — *Nābhika-pura*, *am*, n., N. of a town of the Uttara-kurus.

Nābhila, *as*, *ā*, *am*, relating to or coming from a navel; [cf. *nābhila*.]

Nābhila, *am*, n. the groin of a woman; a prominent or ruptured navel; the cavity of the navel; pain.

Nābheya, *as*, m. a patronymic of Ṛishabha, first Arhat of the Jainas.

Nābhya, *as*, *ā*, *am*, proceeding from the navel, being in the navel, umbilical, of or relating to the navel; (*as*), m. an epithet of Śiva; [cf. *nābha*.]

नाभिजात *nābhijāta* (*na-abhijāta*), *as*, *ā*, *am*, not well-born, not noble, low-bred, ignoble.

नाभिमान *nābhimāna* (*na-abh°*), *as*, m. absence of pride, humbleness.

नाम *nāma*, ind. See under *nāman* below.

नामतिक *nāmatika*, *as*, *ī*, *am* (fr. *namata*), dressed in woollen cloth.

नामधेय *nāma-dheya*. See under *nāman*.

नामन् *nāman*, *a*, n. (fr. rt. 1. *jñā*, the initial *j* being lost; said to be fr. rt. *mnā*), a mark by which anything is known, sign, token (Ved.); form, manner, mode, character, personal character, nature, species (Ved.); name, appellation, (especially a personal name, as opposed to *gotra*, a family name); merely the name (as opposed to the reality); (in grammar) appellative, common name for a class of objects, noun, word (e.g. *megha-nāman*, [every] noun or word denoting cloud); substance, essence, (in the Mīmāṃsā phil. opposed to *guṇa*, accidental quality); water (according to Naigh. I. 11); *nāmnā vać* or *nāma grah*, to address by name, mention or call upon by name; *nāma kṛi* or *nāma dā* or *nāma dhā* or *nāmnā kṛi* or *nāmnā vi-dhā*, to give a name, to name, call (e.g. *Sāvitrīti nāmāsyāś ćakruḥ*, they called her name Sāvitrī; *Lakshmaṇam iti nāma kṛitavān*, he named him Lakshmaṇa; *tāṃ Duḥkha-labdhikāṃ nāmnā ćakāra*, he called her Duḥkha-labdhikā). *Nāman* often occurs at the end of an adj. comp., in which case the fem. is generally *nāmnī* (e.g. *Vishṇu-śarma-nāmā paṇḍitaḥ*, a sage named Vishṇu-śarman; *nadī-nāmnī kanyā*, a girl with the name of a river); but the fem. may be also *nāmā* from *nāman* and *nāmā* from a base *nāma*, which is rarely substituted for *nāman* at the end of a comp. (*Nāma*, acc. sing. used as an adverb =) namely, by name (e.g. *Mādhavo nāma Brāhmaṇaḥ*, a Brāhman, Mādhava by name); indeed, certainly, forsooth, really, of course, even, probably, possibly, perhaps, agreed, granted, granting (e.g. *astu nāma sa dhanī me kiñćid dadhāti*, granting [which I doubt] that this rich man will offer me something). *Nāma* as an emphatic particle may have some of the above senses, but is often untranslatable by any single equivalent English word. It is frequently placed after interrogative pronouns (e.g. *kiṃ nāma*, *kathaṃ nāma*, *kadā nāma*, *ko nāma*), when it may be translated by 'then,' 'indeed,' &c.; *api nāma* at the beginning of a sentence = perhaps, probably, would that! oh that! of course; *mā nāma* = may it not be that, perhaps, but I hope not; *nanu nāma*, certainly, evidently; after an imperative *nāma* = I care not, no matter, if you like, &c. According to native lexicographers *nāma* implies certainty, possibility, anger, reproach, consent, promise, recollection, surprise, pretence, &c.; [cf. Zend *nāman:* Gr. ὄνομα(τ), ἀν-ώνυ-μο-ς, νώνυμν-ο-ι, ὀνομαίνω, ὀνομάζω: Lat. *co-gnō-men*, *i-gnō-min-ia*, *nō-men*, *nōmin-ā-re*, *nam*, *quis-nam*, *quem-nam* = Sanskṛit *kaṃ nāma*, *nem-pe* = Sanskṛit *nāma api:* Umbr. *nume*, *nome*, dat. sing. *nomn-e:* Goth. *namō*, gen. sing. *namin-s*, *namn-yan*, *ga-namn-yan*, 'to name:' Mod. Germ. *namen*, *nāme:* Angl. Sax. *nāma*, *nemn-an:* Eng. *name:* Slav. *i-man*, 'name;' *imen-ova-ti*, 'to name:' Scot. *ainm*, 'name:' Cambro-Brit. *enr*, 'name.'] — *Nāma-karaṇa*, *as*, m. a nominal affix; (*am*), n. giving a name, naming a child after birth. — *Nāma-karman*, *a*, n. the ceremony of naming a child after birth. — *Nāma-graha*, *as*, m. or *nāma-grahaṇa*, *am*, n. or (Ved.) *nāma-grāha*, *as*, m. addressing or mentioning by name. — *Nāma-grāham*, ind., Ved. by mentioning the name, by naming. — *Nāma-tas*, ind., see col. 3. — *Nāma-deva*, *as*, m., N. of a man. — *Nāma-dvādaśī*, f. a religious ceremony, worshipping Durgā daily under one of her twelve appellations (Gaurī, Kālī, Umā, Bhadrā, Durgā, Kānti, Sarasvatī, Maṅgalā, Vaishṇavī, Lakshmī, Śivā, and Nārāyaṇī). — *Nāma-dha*, *as*, or *nāma-dhā*, *ās*, m., Ved. one who gives a name, a name-giver. — *Nāma-dhātu*, *us*, m. a verbal base derived from a noun, a nominal verb. — *Nāma-dhāraka*, *as*, *ā*, *am*, bearing only the name, being anything only by name (e.g. *purusho nāma-dhārakaḥ*, one who is a man only in name). — *Nāma-dheya*, *am*, n. a name, a title, an appellation, (sometimes at the end of a comp., e.g. *kin-n°*, see under *kim*; *pun-n°*, see under *puns*); the ceremony of giving a name to a child. — *Nāmadheya-karaṇa*, *am*, n. giving a name, naming. — *Nāmadheya-tas*, ind. by name. — *Nāma-nāmika*, *as*, m. an epithet of Vishṇu. — *Nāma-nidhāna*, *am*, n. 'a collection of nouns,' N. of a glossary. — *Nāma-niyata-praveśa*, *as*, m., N. of a Samādhi. — *Nāma-nirdeśa*, *as*, m. pointing out by name. — *Nāma-pārāyaṇa*, *am*, n. 'a complete collection of nouns,' N. of a glossary. — *Nāma-mātra*, *am*, n. the mere name, a mere name; (*as*, *ā*, *am*), having only the name; (*eṇa*), ind. by the mere name, merely, nominally. — *Nāmamātrāvaśeshita* (°*ra-av°*), *as*, *ā*, *am*, having only the name left. — *Nāma-mālā*, f. a vocabulary, nomenclature; N. of a Prākṛit glossary of synonyms. — *Nāma-mudrā*, f. a seal-ring, signet-ring with a name (engraved on it). — *Nāma-yajña*, *as*, m. a sacrifice only in name. — *Nāma-liṅga*, *am*, n. 'the gender of nouns,' N. of a work treating thereof. — *Nāmaliṅgānuśāsana* (°*ga-an°*), *am*, n. the rules of gender or lessons on the gender of nouns. — *Nāma-varjita*, *as*, *ā*, *am*, destitute of name, nameless, stupid. — *Nāma-vāćaka*, *as*, *ikā*, *am*, expressing a name; (in grammar) a proper name. — *Nāma-vidhi*, *is*, m. 'name-rule,' N. of the twenty-third chapter of the Jñāna-khaṇḍa of the Śiva-Purāṇa. — *Nāma-vismṛiti*, *is*, f. forgetting the name (of any one). — *Nāma-śesha*, *as*, *ā*, *am*, having only the name left, deceased, dead; (*as*), m. name as the only thing left, dying, death; [cf. *ālekhya-śesha*, *kīrtti-śesha*.] — *Nāma-saṅkīrtana*, *am*, n. 'name-glorification,' N. of the fourteenth chapter of the Jñāna-khaṇḍa of the Śiva-Purāṇa. — *Nāma-saṅgraha*, *as*, m. a collection of words (exclusive of verbs). — *Nāma-sāroddhāra* (°*ra-ud°*), *as*, m., N. of a commentary on Hema-ćandra's Abhidhāna-ćintā-maṇi. — *Nāmākhyātika* (°*ma-ākh°*), *as*, *ā*, *am*, relating to nouns and verbs. — *Nāmāṅka* (°*ma-aṅ°*), *as*, *ā*, *am*, marked with a name. — *Nāmāṅka-śobhita* (°*ma-aṅ°*), *as*, *ā*, *am*, adorned with the mark of the name or with name and cipher. — *Nāmādeśam* (°*ma-ād°*), ind. by announcing one's name. — *Nāmānuśāsana* (°*ma-an°*), *am*, n. 'the rules about nouns,' N. of a lexicographical work. — *Nāmāparādha* (°*ma-ap°*), *as*, m. abusing (a respectable person) by name, calling names. — *Nāmārtha-nirṇaya* (°*ma-ar°*), *as*, m. 'inquiry into the bases of nouns,' N. of a chapter of the Vaiyākaraṇa-bhūshaṇa-sāra by Koṇḍa-bhaṭṭa. — *Nāmāvali* (°*ma-āv°*), *is*, f. a list of names (especially of a god). — *Nāmāshṭami-vidhāna* (°*ma-ash°*), *am*, n., N. of the twenty-fourth chapter of the Jñāna-khaṇḍa of the Śiva-Purāṇa.

Nāmaka, *as*, *ikā*, *am*, (at the end of an adj. comp.) = *nāman*, e.g. *kṛita-nāmaka*, one to whom a name has been given, having a name, named; [cf. *a-n°*, *añjana-n°*.]

Nāma-tas, ind. by name, namely, with the name, with respect to the name; (in Bhāgavata-Purāṇa V. 12, 8, used for the abl. c. of *nāman*); *nāmatas* is sometimes redundantly joined with *nāma* (e.g. *Bāhuko nāma nāmataḥ*, namely Bāhuka by name); *nāmataḥ kṛi*, to give a name, to name, call.

Nāma-thā, ind., Ved. by name.

Nāmika, *as*, *ā*, *am*, relating to a name or to a noun.

नामि *nāmi*, *is*, m. an epithet of Vishṇu.

नामित *nāmita*, *as*, *ā*, *am* (fr. rt. *nam*), bent, bent down, bowed.

Nāmin, *ī*, *inī*, *i*, bending; (in grammar) changing a dental to a cerebral, a N. given to all the vowels except *a* and *ā*; [cf. *bhāvin*.]

Nāmya, *as*, *ā*, *am*, to be bent (as a bow &c.), bendable, pliable, pliant.

नाम्ब nāmba, as, m., Ved. a species of grain, (also read āmba); (as, ī, am), consisting of Nāmba.

नाय nāya, as, m. (fr. rt. 1. nī), a leader, guide, driver (e.g. in aśva-n°, go-n°); perhaps N. of a man; = naya, guiding, directing (morally or physically); policy; means, expedient.

Nāyaka, as, ikā, am, guiding, leading, conducting; (as), m. a guide, leader, conductor [cf. ku-n°]; a chief, lord, head; pre-eminent, principal; (with or without sainyasya) a general, a commander; (in erotic or dramatic poetry) the lover or hero in a drama &c., a husband; the central gem of a necklace; a paradigm or example (in grammar); an epithet of Śākya-muni; N. of a Brāhman; (ikā), f. a mistress; a wife; the heroine in a drama &c., a noble lady; an inferior form or Śakti of Durgā, (of which there are eight, viz. Ugra-ćaṇḍā, Pra-ćaṇḍā, Caṇḍogrā, Caṇḍa-nāyikā, Ati-ćaṇḍā, Cāmuṇḍā, Caṇḍā, and Caṇḍā-vatī; cf. kula-n°.) — Nāyaka-tva, am, n. leadership, headship, chieftainship. — Nāyaka-ratna, am, n., N. of a commentary on Pārtha-sārathi's Nyāya-ratna-mālā by Rāmānuja. — Nāyakādhipa (°ka-adh°), as, m. the chief of leaders, a king, sovereign, prince.

Nāyin, ī, inī, i, leading, conducting; [cf. ayuta-n°.]

नार nāra, as, ī, am (fr. nara), proceeding from men, relating or belonging to men, human, mortal; spiritual (?); (as), m. a man (?); a calf; (as or, according to some, am, ā), m. n. f. water, (probably only a form invented to explain nārāyaṇa; cf. nīra, νάω, νηρός, Νηρεύς); (am), n. a multitude or assemblage of men; dry ginger; (ī), f. a woman, a wife, (in the older language also with short i, nari); a female or any object regarded as feminine; a kind of metre consisting of four lines of three long syllables each; N. of a daughter of Meru; (yas), f. pl. a sacrifice, oblation (Ved.). — Nāra-kīṭa, as, m. a species of worm (= aśma-kīṭa); a deceiver, one who disappoints expectations excited by himself. — Nāra-jīvana, am, n. gold. — Nārī-kavaća, as, m. 'having women for armour,' an epithet of Mūlaka, king of the solar line and son of Aśmaka. — Nārī-tīrtha, āni, n. pl. 'bathing-places of women,' N. of five sacred bathing-places. — Nārī-dūshaṇa, am, n. a woman's vice, any great fault in women, (six are usually reckoned, viz. drinking spirits, keeping bad company, quitting a husband, rambling abroad, sleeping and dwelling in a strange house.) — Nārī-nātha, as, ā, am, having a woman for possessor or owner (e.g. nārī-nātham gṛiham, a house having a woman for its possessor). — Nārī-parāyaṇa, as, ā, am, devoted to women. — Nārī-prasanga, as, m. libertinism, lechery. — Nārī-maya, as, ī, am, consisting of women. — Nārī-mukha, as, m., N. of a people to the south-east of Madhya-deśa. — Nārī-yāna, am, n. a woman's conveyance, a litter, &c. — Nārī-ratna, am, n. a jewel of a woman, an excellent woman. — Nārī-vākya, am, n. the word of a wife. — Nārīshṭā (°rī-ish°), f. 'dear to women,' Arabian jasmine. — Nārī-shṭha, as, ā, am, accompanying women (?), fond of them (?).

Nārāyaṇa, as, m. (fr. nara, q. v.; sometimes derived fr. nāra + ayana), 'son of Nara or the original man,' patronymic of the personified Purusha or first living being, author of the Purusha hymn; he is often associated with Nara or the original man, and identified with Brahmā (in Manu I. 9, 11) and with Vishṇu or Kṛishṇa; in Hari-vaṅśa 4601 Urvaśī is described as springing from his thigh; elsewhere he is regarded as a Kāśyapa or Āngirasa [cf. mahā-n°, ardha-n°]; chief of the Sādhyas; the eighth of the nine black Vāsu-devas (with Jainas); the Purusha hymn, composed by Nārāyaṇa (Ṛig-veda X. 90); N. of the second month, reckoning from Mārgaśīrsha; N. of a son of Ajāmila; of Bhūmi-mitra; of Nara-hari; N. of several men, authors and commentators; a mystical N. of the letter ā; (as, ī, am), relating or belonging to Nārāyaṇa or Kṛishṇa, (the warriors in Kṛishṇa's army are called Nārāyaṇāḥ in Udyoga-parva 147); (with kshetra) a term applied to the ground on the banks of the Ganges for a distance of four Hastas or cubits from the water; (with taila) a sort of oil to which efficacy is ascribed in medicine; (ī), f. epithet of Lakshmī, the goddess of prosperity and wife of Vishṇu; epithet of Durgā; epithet and patronymic of Indra-senā, wife of Mudgala; epithet of the Ganges or of the Gaṇḍakī (?); the plant Asparagus Racemosus. — Nārāyaṇa-kaṇṭha, as, m., N. of an author. — Nārāyaṇa-kalpa, as, m., N. of a work. — Nārāyaṇa-kshetra, am, n. four cubits on either side of the Ganges; see above. — Nārāyaṇa-gītā, f., N. of a work containing the principles of the sect founded by Rāmānanda. — Nārāyaṇa-gupta, as, m., N. of a Gupta prince. — Nārāyaṇa-ćakravartin, ī, m., N. of a grammarian. — Nārāyaṇa-tāra, as, m., N. of an author; (also read nārāyaṇa-tārā.) — Nārāyaṇa-tīrtha, as, m., N. of an author; (am), n., N. of a bathing-place. — Nārāyaṇa-taila, am, n. an oil expressed from various plants of great reputed efficacy in many complaints. — Nārāyaṇa-dāsa-siddha, as, m., N. of an author. — Nārāyaṇa-deva, as, m. the god Nārāyaṇa; N. of an author. — Nārāyaṇa-daiva-vid, t, m., N. of a man. — Nārāyaṇa-paṇḍita, as, m., N. of a learned man. — Nārāyaṇa-priya, as, m. 'the friend of Nārāyaṇa,' an epithet of Śiva; yellow sandal-wood (= pīta-ćandana). — Nārāyaṇa-bali, is, m. 'an oblation to Nārāyaṇa,' N. of a peculiar funeral ceremony. — Nārāyaṇa-bhaṭṭa, as, m., N. of an author. — Nārāyaṇa-maya, as, ī, am, consisting of or in Nārāyaṇa. — Nārāyaṇa-varman, a, n. 'armour of Nārāyaṇa,' N. of a poem in praise of Kṛishṇa, forming part of the sixth book of the Bhāgavata-Purāṇa. — Nārāyaṇa-śrī-garbha, as, m., N. of a Bodhisattva. — Nārāyaṇa-saras, as, n. Nārāyaṇa's lake. — Nārāyaṇa-sarasvatī, īs, m., N. of a commentator. — Nārāyaṇa-sūri, is, m., N. of a man. — Nārāyaṇāśrama (°ṇa-āś°), as, m. Nārāyaṇa's hermitage; N. of the author of the commentary Bheda-dhikkāra-satkriyā. — Nārāyaṇāstra (°ṇa-as°), am, n. 'weapon of Nārāyaṇa,' a mystical weapon. — Nārāyaṇendra (°ṇa-in°), as, m., N. of a commentator. — Nārāyaṇopanishad (°ṇa-up°), t, f. the Upanishad treating of Nārāyaṇa. — Nārāyaṇopādhyāya (°ṇa-up°), as, m., N. of an author.

Nārāyaṇi, is, m., N. of a son of Viśvā-mitra.

Nārāyaṇīya, as, ā, am, referring or relating to Nārāyaṇa, treating of him; (ā), f., scil. upanishad, N. of an Upanishad. — Nārāyaṇīya-tantra, am, n., N. of a Tantra.

Nārika, as, ī, am, watery, aqueous; spiritual; (nārikā wrong reading for nāḍikā.)

Nārika at the end of an adj. comp. = nārī; (am), n. (in the Sāṅkhya phil.) one of the nine kinds of Tushṭi.

Nāreya, as, m. (fr. nārī), N. of a son of Bhaṅga-kāra.

नारक nāraka, as, ī, am (fr. naraka), relating to hell, happening in hell, being or abiding in hell, hellish, infernal, (nārakī nirvṛitiḥ, the death suffered in hell); (as), m. an inhabitant of the infernal regions; hell or the infernal regions.

Nārakika, as, ī, am, hellish, infernal; (as), m. an inhabitant of hell.

Nārakin, ī, iṇī, i, hellish, infernal, being in hell, condemned to or deserving hell; (ī), m. an inhabitant of hell.

Nārakīya, as, ā, am, hellish; (as), m. an inhabitant of hell.

नारङ्ग nāranga, as, m. (said to be fr. rt. nṛī, but probably a corruption of nāga-ranga, q. v.), the orange-tree; the juice of the pepper plant; a libertine, a catamite; a living being, an animal; a twin, one of twins; (am), n. a carrot, Daucus Carota (= garjara). — Nāranga-pattraka, as, m. yellow carrot.

नारद nārada, as, m. (etymology uncertain), N. of a Ṛishi or rather Devarshi (i. e. Ṛishi among the gods) regarded in the Veda as a descendant of Kaṇva and author of certain hymns of the Ṛig-veda (VIII. 13, IX. 104, 105), often associated in the later mythology with Parvata, (he appears on the earth, like Mercury, as a messenger from the gods to men or vice versâ, and is reckoned among the ten Prajā-patis as a son of Brahmā (Manu I. 35), from whose forehead he is said to have been produced; in the modern mythology he is a friend of Kṛishṇa and is regarded as inventor of the Vīṇā or lute; in epic poetry he is occasionally called a Deva-gandharva, 'divine Gandharva,' or a Gandharva-rājan, 'king of the Gandharvas,' or simply Gandharva); N. of a son of Viśvā-mitra; of an author; of a mountain; (ā), f. a species of sugar-cane, = ikshu-mūla; (as, ī, am), relating to Nārada, composed by him, &c. — Nārada-pañća-rātra, am, n., N. of a work. — Nārada-purāṇa, am, n., N. of a Purāṇa. — Nāradapurāṇa-sūćana, am, n., N. of the sixty-fifth chapter of the Vārāha-Purāṇa. — Nārada-prakaraṇa, am, n. 'Nārada chapter,' N. of the 129th chapter of the Kṛishṇa-khaṇḍa or fourth section of the Brahma-vaivarta-Purāṇa. — Nārada-vākya, am, n. 'speech of Nārada,' N. of the sixty-seventh chapter of the Uttara-kāṇḍa or seventh section of the Rāmāyaṇa. — Nārada-saṃhitā, f., N. of a musical work. — Nārada-sanatkumāra-vāda, as, m. 'discourse of Nārada and Sanatkumāra,' N. of the 103rd chapter of the Uttara-khaṇḍa of the Padma-Purāṇa. — Nārada-samāgama, as, m. 'arrival of Nārada,' N. of the twenty-first chapter of the Uttara-kāṇḍa of the Rāmāyaṇa. — Nāradeśvara-tīrtha (°da-īś°), am, n., N. of a sacred bathing-place. — Nāradopadeśa (°da-up°), as, m. 'the advice of Nārada,' N. of the first chapter of the Krīḍā-khaṇḍa of the Gaṇeśa-Purāṇa.

Nāradin, ī, m., N. of a son of Viśvā-mitra.

Nāradīya, as, ā, am, relating to Nārada, composed by Nārada, &c.; (am), n. (with or without purāṇa), N. of a Purāṇa. — Nāradīya-mahā-sthāna, am, n., N. of a place. — Nāradīyopapurāṇa (°ya-up°), am, n., N. of an Upa-Purāṇa.

Nāradīyaka, as, ī, am, relating to or proceeding from Nārada; (am), n., N. of a Purāṇa.

नारद्वसव nāradvasava (?), am, n., N. of a Sāman.

नारसिंह nārasinha, as, ī, am (fr. nara-sinha), referring or belonging to Vishṇu in his man-lion Ava-tāra or incarnation; (as), m., N. of Vishṇu; of a man; of a town. — Nārasinha-tantra, am, n., N. of a Tantra. — Nārasinha-purāṇa, am, n., N. of a Purāṇa. — Nārasinhopapurāṇa (°ha-up°), am, n., N. of an Upa-Purāṇa.

नाराच nārāća, as, m. an iron arrow, an arrow in general; a water-elephant (= jalebha, ambu-hastin); a bad or cloudy day (?); a species of the Dhṛiti metre, also called Narāća, consisting of 4 times 8 Iambics; (nārāćī or nārāćikā), f. a goldsmith's scales, a fine or assay balance.

नारायण nārāyaṇa. See col. 1.

नाराशंस nārāśansa, as, ī, am (fr. narā-śansa), Ved. laudatory or eulogistic praise of a man or men, (hence a tale or legend which eulogizes a liberal patron is called Nārāśansī or Nārāśansam); sacred to or belonging to Agni-narāśansa, relating to him, containing him, (applied to certain Soma libations, at which Narāśansa's name is mentioned; applied also to the Pitṛis because reference is made to them at these libations.)

नाराशर्य nārāśarya, as, m., N. of a man; (also read pārāśarya.)

नारिकेर nārikera or nārikela, as, m. or nārikelī, is and ī, f. the cocoa-nut tree, the cocoa-nut. — Nārikela-dvīpa, as, m., N. of an island.

नारिङ्गकन्द *nāriṅga-kanda, as* or *am*, m. or n. (?), the yellow carrot; [cf. *nāraṅga-pattraka.*]

नारी *nārī*, f. See *nāra*, p. 479, col. 1.

नारीकेल *nārīkela, as, ī*, m. f. the cocoa-nut; (*ī*), f. fermented liquor made from the water or milk of the cocoa-nut.

नारीच *nārīća, am*, n. an esculent root (= commonly *nālitā*), Corchorus Capsularis; [cf. *nāḍikā.*]

नारीतरङ्गक *nārī-taraṅgaka, as*, m. a libertine, a catamite; [cf. *nāḍi-taraṅga.*]

नारुन्तुद *nāruntuda* (*na-ar°*), *as, ā, am*, not causing wounds, not hurting.

नार्तिक *nārtika, as, ī, am* (fr. *narta*), relating to or connected with dancing (?).

नार्पत्य *nārpatya, as, ā, am* (fr. *nṛi-pati*), kingly, relating to royalty.

नार्मत *nārmata, as*, m. (fr. *nṛi-mat*), a patronymic.

नार्मद *nārmada, as*, m. (fr. *narma-dā*), a metronymic from Narma-dā.

नार्मर *nārmara, as*, m. (fr. *nṛi-mara*), Ved. 'man-slayer,' N. of a demon.

नार्मिण *nārmiṇa, as, ī, am* (perhaps fr. *narmin* or *narmiṇa*, which may be a N. derived fr. *narma* or *narman*), Ved. (Sāy.) delightful, joyful (= *narma-vat*).

नार्मेध *nārmedha, am*, n. (fr. *nṛi-medha*), Ved., N. of a Sāman.

नार्य *nārya, as*, m. (fr. *narya*), Ved. probably N. of a person.

नार्यङ्ग *nāryaṅga, as*, m. = *nāraṅga*, the orange-tree.

नार्यतिक्त *nārya-tikta* = *anārya-tikta*, Agathotes Chirayta (= *kirāta-tikta*).

नार्षद *nārshada, as*, m. (fr. *nṛi-shad*), Ved. a patronymic of Kaṇva; N. of a demon (?).

नाल *nāla, as, ā, am* (fr. *nala*), consisting of reeds, made of a reed or reeds; (*ā* or *ī, am*), f. n. a hollow or tubular stalk, especially the stalk of the lotus [cf. *khara-n°*], of a pot-herb, &c.; (*am*), n. any pipe or tube or tubular vessel of the body, the windpipe, urethra, &c.; a handle; = *tāla, āla*, yellow orpiment; (*ā*), f., N. of a river; (*ī*), f. an instrument for perforating an elephant's ear; a piece of metal on which the hours are struck (= *ghaṭī*); a period of twenty-four minutes; a lotus flower. — *Nāla-vaṅśa, as*, m. = *nala*, a reed.

Nālaka for *nāla* in *ćāru-nālaka*, q. v.

Nālakinī = *nālikinī*, q. v.

Nālāyita, as, ā, am (fr. an unused Nom. *nālāya*), representing the handle (of an axe).

Nāli, is, f. = *nāḍi*, any tubular vessel of the body.

Nālika, as, m. a buffalo; (*ā*), f. a stalk, the stalk of a lotus, a tube, see *gandha-n°, kapāla-n°;* a species of pot-herb (= *nālitā*); a species of plant (= *ćarma-kashā*); an instrument for piercing an elephant's ear; = *nāḍī*, a period of twenty-four minutes; (*am*), n. a lotus flower [cf. *nālīka*]; myrrh; a kind of wind instrument, (perhaps) a flute; a peculiar manner of sitting.

Nālinī, f. (fr. an unused form *nālin*, which is derived fr. *nāla*), a mystical N. of one nostril.

Nālīka, as, m. an arrow (= *nārāća*, but in the epic poetry different from it); a dart, a javelin, a pike; body, limb (?); a lotus; the fibrous stalk of the lotus; (*am*), n. an assemblage of lotus flowers.

Nālīkinī, f. (fr. an unused form *nālīkin*, which is derived fr. *nālīka*), a multitude or assemblage of lotus flowers, a lotus lake.

नालन्द *nālanda*, N. of a village near Rāja-gṛiha containing a celebrated Buddhist monastery.

Nālandara, N. of a Buddhist monastery.

नालिकेर *nālikera, as*, m. the cocoa-nut tree, the cocoa-nut; N. of a district to the south-east of Madhya-deśa.

Nālikela, am, n. the cocoa-nut; (various reading for *nālikera.*)

नालिजङ्घ *nāli-jaṅgha, as*, m. a raven or the carrion-crow; [cf. *nāḍi-jaṅgha.*]

नालिता *nālitā*, f. an esculent root, Arum Colocasia.

नालीप *nālīpa, as*, m. = *kadambaka;* perhaps for *kaḍambaka*, the stalk of a pot-herb.

नालीव्रण *nālī-vraṇa, as*, m. a fistulous or sinous sore (= *nāḍī-vraṇa*).

नाव 1. *nāva, as*, m. (fr. rt. 4. *nu*), Ved. a shout of joy or triumph.

नाव 2. *nāva* = 2. *nau*, q. v., a boat, a ship, in Dvigu comps. after numerals and *ardha* (e. g. *dvi-nāvam*, two boats; *ardha-n°*, q. v., Pāṇ. V. 4, 99, 100). — *Nāvāja* (°*va-aja*), *as*, m., Ved. the steerer of a boat, a sailor. — *Nāvopajīvana* (°*va-up°*), *as*, m. a sailor.

Nāvika, as, ī, am, belonging to a vessel, ship, boat, &c.; (*as*), m. (said to be fr. rt. *nud*), the helmsman of a vessel, the steersman, pilot; a passenger on board ship, a navigator, a sailor; (*am*), n., N. of a Sāman.

Nāvin, ī, m. a boatman, shipman, sailor.

1. *nāvya*, Nom. P. *nāvyati*, &c., to wish for a ship.

2. *nāvya, as, ā, am*, navigable; belonging to a boat; attainable or accessible by a boat or ship; (*ā*), f., Ved. a navigable river.

नावनीत *nāvanīta, as, ī, am* (fr. *nava-nīta*), mild.

नावमिक *nāvamika, as, ī, am* (fr. *navama*), the ninth.

नावयज्ञिक *nāvayajñika* (fr. *nava-yajña*), with *kāla*, the time of offering the first-fruits &c. of the harvest.

नावाकार *nāvākāra, nāvāroha*. See 2. *nau*.

नाव्य 3. *nāvya, am*, n. (fr. 1. *nava*), newness, novelty.

नाश 1. *nāśa, as*, m. (fr. rt. 1. *naś*), Ved. attainment, obtaining; [cf. *dū-ṇāśa.*]

नाश 2. *nāśa, as*, m. (fr. rt. 2. *naś*), disappearance; destruction, annihilation, ruin, loss; death; misfortune; abandonment, desertion; flight, retreat; (in arithmetic) elimination; [cf. *karma-n°, graha-n°, ćitta-n°, dū-ṇāśa.*] — *Nāśa-tas*, ind. = *nāśāt*, from death.

Nāśaka, as, ā, am, destroying, destructive, annihilating, causing to perish; [cf. *ku-n°, kṛita-n°.*]

Nāśana, as, ī, am, destroying, annihilating, causing to be lost, causing to perish, removing, (commonly in comp. with the object; cf. *duḥsvapna-n°*); (*am*), n. destruction, removing, removal, expulsion; ruin, perishing; forgetting.

Nāśanīya, as, ā, am, liable to be destroyed, destructible.

Nāśayat, an, antī, at, destroying, annihilating, removing.

Nāśayitṛi, tā, trī, tṛi, Ved. a destroyer, remover, a remover.

Nāśita, as, ā, am, destroyed, ruined, suffered to perish, lost.

Nāśin, ī, inī, i, destructive, destroying, a destroyer; removing; perishing, perishable, being lost or destroyed; [cf. *anartha-n°, kushṭha-n°, ksharya-n°.*]

Nāśī, f., N. of a river near Benares.

Nāśuka, as, ā, am, Ved. disappearing, perishing, being lost.

Nāśya, as, ā, am, liable to be destroyed, destructible.

Nāshṭika, as, ī, am (fr. *nashṭa*), belonging or relating to anything lost; (*as*), m. the owner of anything lost, the former owner of a lost chattel.

Nāshṭrā, f., Ved. danger, destruction; an evil spirit, a demon.

नास् 1. *nās*, cl. 1. A. *nāsate, nanāse, nāsitum*, to sound.

नास् 2. *nās*, Ved. the nose, in *nāsā*, du. (Ṛig-veda II. 39, 6); [cf. 3. *nas.*]

Nāsā, f. (said by some to be fr. rt. *snā* = rt. *snu*), the nose, (originally perhaps *nāsā*, sing. = a nostril; *nāse*, du. = the two nostrils or the nose); a proboscis, the trunk of an elephant [cf. *gaja-n°*]; a piece of wood over a door projecting like a nose, the upper timber of a door [cf. *nakra*]; the plant Gendarussa Vulgaris (= *vāsaka*); [cf. Lat. *nāsus*, *nāris* for *nāsis;* Old Germ. *nāsa;* Angl. Sax. *nase;* Mod. Germ. *nase;* Slav. *nosŭ;* Lith. *nosis;* Gr. *νῆσος*; Hib. *neas*, 'a promontory,' *ness* in Dunge-ness.] — *Nāsāgra* (°*sā-ag°*), *as*, m. the point or tip of the nose. — *Nāsā-ćhidra, am*, n. a nostril. — *Nāsā-ćhinnī*, f. a species of bird with a divided beak (= *pūrṇikā*). — *Nāsā-jvara, as*, m. a kind of disease of the nose (= *nakra*). — *Nāsā-dakshiṇāvarta* (°*ṇa-āv°*), *as*, m. wearing the nose-ring in the right nostril by rich women who have children (?). — *Nāsā-dāru*, n. = *nāsā*, a piece of wood over a door projecting like a nose; the upper timber of a door-frame. — *Nāsā-nāha, as*, m. thickening of the membrane of the nose, stoppage of the nostrils. — *Nāsāntika, as, ā, am* (fr. *nāsā-anta*), reaching to the nose; [cf. *keśāntika.*] — *Nāsā-pariśosha, as*, m. heat and dryness of the nose. — *Nāsā-parisrāva, as*, m. 'nose-flow,' running at the nose, a running cold. — *Nāsā-pāka, as*, m. a kind of disease of the nose attended with inflammation. — *Nāsā-puṭa, as*, m. 'nose-cup,' the outside of the nostril, the nostril. — *Nāsāpuṭa-maryādā*, f. the septum of the nose. — *Nāsā-pratīnāha, as*, m. = *nāsā-nāha*, thickening of the membrane of the nose, stoppage of the nostrils. — *Nāsā-rakta-pitta, am*, n. bleeding of the nose. — *Nāsā-randhra, am*, n. 'nose-aperture,' the nostril. — *Nāsārśas* (°*sā-ar°*), *ās*, m. polypus of the nose. — *Nāsā-vaṅśa, as*, m. the bridge of the nose. — *Nāsā-vāmāvarta* (°*ma-āv°*), *as*, m. wearing the nose-ring in the left nostril, a mark of sorrow or distress. — *Nāsā-vivara, as*, m. 'nose-cavity,' a nostril. — *Nāsā-śosha, as*, m. dryness of the nostrils. — *Nāsā-saṃvedana, as*, m. Momordica Charantia (= *kāṇḍira-latā*). — *Nāsā-srāva, as*, m. = *nāsā-parisrāva*, 'nose-flow,' running at the nose, a running cold.

Nāsālu, us, m. a tree, commonly Kāyaphal. See *kaṭphala*, p. 196, col. 1.

Nāsikā, f. the nose, (originally *nāsikā*, sing. = a nostril; *nāsike*, du. = the two nostrils or the nose); the trunk of an elephant; a proboscis; any nose-shaped object [cf. *ćarma-n°*]; a projection, the upper timber of a door; an epithet of the nymph Aśvinī; [cf. *a-nāsika, kāka-nāsikā, ćarma-n°.*] — *Nāsika-tryambaka-tīrtha, am*, n., N. of a sacred bathing-place mentioned in the Rasika-ramaṇa. — *Nāsikan-dhama, as, ā, am* (*nāsikam* for acc. sing. *nāsikām*), blowing or breathing through the nose, snoring, &c. — *Nāsikan-dhaya, as, ī, am* (*nāsikam* for acc. sing. *nāsikām*), drinking through the nose. — *Nāsika-vat, ān, atī, at* (for *nāsikā-vat*), Ved. having a nose. — *Nāsikāgra* (°*ka-ag°*), *am*, n. the tip of the nose. — *Nāsikā-pāka, as*, m. = *nāsā-pāka*, a kind of disease or inflammation of the nose. — *Nāsikā-puṭa, as*, m. = *nāsā-puṭa*, 'nose-cup,' the outside of the nostril, the nostril. — *Nāsikā-mala, am*, n. the mucus of the nose, snot.

Nāsikya, as, ā, am, being in the nose; uttered through the nose, nasal; *(as),* m. any nasal sound; a peculiar nasal sound related to the so-called Yamas; *(ās),* m. pl., N. of a people in Dakshiṇā-patha; *(au),* du. = *nāsatyau,* the two sons of Aśvinī, the Aśvins; *(am),* n. the nose; N. of a town.

Nāsikyaka, am, n. the nose.

Nāsya, am, n. a nose-cord, the rein of a draught-ox passed through the septum of the nostrils; (perhaps collectively) noses, a multitude of noses (?); [cf. *nasya.*]

नासत्य *nāsatya, as,* m. (derived by native commentators fr. *na + a-satya,* 'not untrue,' or fr. *nāsā* + affix *tya,* or still more improbably fr. *nā,* nom. of *nṛi = netṛi + satya*), N. of one of the Aśvins, the other being then called Dasra; *(au),* m. du. the common N. of the two Aśvins, see *aśvinau;* *(ā),* f. the constellation Aśvinī; *(as, ā, am),* referring or relating to the Nāsatyas; [cf. Zend *nāonhaitya.*]

नासमौजस *nāsamaujasa (na-as°), as,* m., N. of the brother of Asamaujas and son of Kambala-barhisha.

नासिका *nāsikā.* See p. 480, col. 3.

नासीर *nāsīra, am,* n. advancing or skirmishing in front of an army, leaving the line and defying or challenging the enemy by shouts and gestures; *(as),* m. the van or a champion who advances before the line; (also read *nāśira.*)

नास्ति *nāsti (na-asti),* ind. non-existence, not so, it is not. — *Nāsti-tā,* f. or *nāsti-tva, am,* n. non-existence. — *Nāsti-vāda, as,* m. "assertion of 'it is not' or of non-existence," infidelity.

Nāstika, as, ī, am, atheistical, unbelieving, infidel, an unbeliever, applied by the orthodox Hindūs to any one who denies the divine authority of the Vedas and a future life, or doubts the legends of the Purāṇas; [cf. *āstika.*] — *Nāstika-tā,* f. or *nāstika-tva, am,* n. or *nāstikya, am,* n. infidelity, disbelief, atheism, denial of the deity, of a future state, of the authority of the Vedas, &c.; Buddhism, heresy, &c. — *Nāstika-mata, am,* n. an atheistical opinion.

नास्तिद *nāstida* or (according to others) *nāstitada, as,* m. the mango tree (= *āmra*).

नाह *nāha, as,* m. (fr. rt. 1. *nah*), binding, confinement; a trap, a snare for catching deer &c.; obstruction in any organ or secretion of the body, as costiveness &c.

नाहल *nāhala, as,* m. a man of a barbarous or outcast tribe; *(ās),* m. pl., N. of a non-Āryan people (= *mlećcha*).

नाहुष 1. *nāhusha, as, ī, am* (fr. *nahus*), Ved. neighbouring, being in the vicinity, neighbourly?; (Say.) human, belonging to men; *(as),* m. a neighbour.

नाहुष 2. *nāhusha, as,* m. (fr. *nahusha*), a patronymic of Yayāti; N. of a serpent-demon; [cf. *nahusha.*]

Nāhushi, is, m. a patronymic of Yayāti.

नि *ni* (an indeclinable prefix to verbs and nouns, used as a preposition except in one passage in Atharva-veda X. 8, 7, where it stands alone as an adverb), in, into, within; down, under, back; on, upon. As a prefix to nouns *ni* appears sometimes to be a curtailed form of *nis* in its sense of 'without,' 'deprived of' (e. g. in *ni-kilvisha, ni-khila,* q. v.), but the idea of negation in such compounds may possibly be derived from the meanings 'down,' 'downwards,' 'back,' which properly belong to *ni;* occasionally, however, *ni* is inaccurately written for *niḥ* (= *nis*), as in *ni-śabda* for *niḥ-śabda;* according to native lexicographers the senses in which *ni* may be used are expressed by the following Sanskṛit words, *kshepa, bhṛitārtha, nityārtha, dāna, san-nidhāna, upa-rama, sam-śraya, ā-śraya, rāśi, moksha, antar-bhāva, adho-bhāva, bandhana, kauśala, ni-veśa, vi-ny-āsa;* [*ni* is thought by some to be for primitive *ani;* cf. *an-tar, an-tarā;* Gr. ἐν, ἐνί, εἰν, εἰς, ἐς for ἐν-ς, ἐν-τό-ς, ἔν-δο-ν, ἔσ-ω, ἔνεροι, ἔνερ-θε, ὑπ-ένερ-θε, ἐνέρ-τερο-ς, ἔν-τερο-ν; Lat. *en-do, in-du, in, in-ter, in-trā, in-ter-ior, in-tumu-s, in-tus;* Umbr. *en, an-der;* Osk. *an-ter;* Goth. *in, inna, innuma, inna-thrō, un-dar;* Mod. Germ. *nieder;* Angl. Sax. *in, nidhan.*]

निंस *niṅs* (thought by some to be a contraction of *ninaṅs,* old Desid. of rt. *nam*), cl. 2. A. *niṅste* (2nd sing. *niṅsse,* 2nd sing. Impv. *niṅssva*), *niniṅse, niṅsitum,* &c., Ved. to touch, kiss, salute. (After *pra* the initial *n* is optionally cerebralized, cf. *pra-ṇiṅsitavya, pra-niṅsitavya, pari-ṇiṅsaka;* cf. also rt. *niksh.*)

निः *niḥ,* euphonically substituted for *nis,* q. v., before *ś, sh, s,* and rarely before *k, kh, p, ph.*

निःक° *niḥ-ka°, niḥ-kā°,* &c. See under *nish-ka°, nish-kā°,* &c.

निःक्षत्र *niḥ-kshatra* or *niḥ-kshatriya, as, ā, am,* destitute of the military tribe, having no warrior-caste.

निःक्षिप् *niḥ-kship,* probably for *ni-kship,* q. v.

Niḥ-kshipta, as, ā, am, thrown or sent away; spent (as time), passed.

Niḥ-kshipya, ind. having thrown or sent away; having spent (as time); having wiped away (as tears).

Niḥ-kshepa, as, m. throwing, sending, putting away; spending, passing (time); wiping away (as tears).

निःप° *niḥ-pa°* and *niḥ-pha°.* See under *nish-pa°* and *nish-pha°.*

निःशंसय *niḥ-śaṅsaya,* wrongly spelt for *niḥ-saṃśaya.*

निःशङ्क *niḥ-śaṅka, as, ā, am,* free from fear, fearless, without misgiving or apprehension, having no cares, free from risk; *(am),* ind. fearlessly, without fear or care, without anxiety. — *Niḥśaṅka-supta, as, ā, am,* sleeping without care, sleeping calmly and securely.

Niḥ-śaṅkita, as, ā, am, free from fear or care, free from risk, secure.

निःशब्द *niḥ-śabda, as, ā, am,* noiseless, soundless, not making a noise; *(as, am),* m. n. (?), soundlessness, silence, a calm; *(am),* ind. without noise, noiselessly; [cf. *ni-śabda.*]

निःशम *niḥ-śama, as,* m. uneasiness, discomposure, anxiety.

निःशयान *niḥ-śayāna, as, ā, am,* not sleeping, not lying down.

निःशरण *niḥ-śaraṇa, as, ā, am,* without protection or refuge, defenceless, unprotected.

निःशर्कर *niḥ-śarkara, as, ā, am,* free from stones or pebbles (as a bathing-place).

निःशलाक *niḥ-śalāka, as, ā, am,* free from talking birds (as parrots, jays, or crows); solitary, private.

निःशल्य *niḥ-śalya, as, ā, am,* freed from an arrow; free from spikes or thorns; *(am),* ind. without an arrow; unthorny; without pain or difficulty; without reluctance, willingly.

निःशस् *niḥ-śas,* f., Ved. refusing, declining; (Sāy.) disinclination, absence of wish or desire, dislike (= *niḥ-śaṅsana*).

निःशस्त्र *niḥ-śastra, as, ā, am,* without arms, unarmed, weaponless.

निःशास् *niḥ-śās (nis-ś°),* cl. 2. P. *-śāsti, -śāsitum,* Ved. to order off or away; to expel.

निःशिष् *niḥ-śish (nis-ś°),* Caus. *-śeshayati, -yitum,* to take away or destroy completely, consume entirely, annihilate; (also regarded as a Nom. fr. *niḥ-śesha.*)

Niḥ-śesha, as, ā, am, having no remainder, without remainder, completely spent, complete, entire, whole, (often in the sense of an adverb at the beginning of a comp. before a participle, e. g. *niḥ-śesha-bhagna,* completely broken); *(am* or *eṇa),* ind. completely, totally; *niḥśesham kṛi,* to destroy or consume completely; [cf. *a-śesha.*] — *Niḥśesha-tas,* ind. without remainder, completely, totally. — *Niḥśesha-tā,* f. complete destruction.

Niḥ-śeshaṇa, as, ā, am, = *niḥ-śesha.*

Niḥ-śeshita, as, ā, am, having nothing left, completely consumed or finished, destroyed, annihilated; (wrongly read *ni-śeshita.*)

निःशुक्र *niḥ-śukra, as, ā, am,* Ved. without brilliancy; without virile energy, impotent.

निःशूक *niḥ-śūka, as,* m. beardless rice without any awn.

निःशेष *niḥ-śesha.* See *niḥ-śish* above.

निःशोक *niḥ-śoka, as, ā, am,* free from sorrow or care.

निःशोध्य *niḥ-śodhya, as, ā, am,* not to be purified, not requiring cleansing; clean, pure.

निःश्मश्रु *niḥ-śmaśru, us, us, u,* beardless; (wrongly read *ni-śmaśru.*)

निःश्रम *niḥ-śrama.* See *ni-śrama.*

निःश्रयणी *niḥ-śrayaṇī* or *niḥ-śrayiṇī,* f. a ladder, a staircase, steps, &c.; [cf. *ni-śrayaṇī, ni-śrayiṇī.*]

Niḥ-śreṇi, is, ī, f. a ladder or staircase, a flight of stairs or steps; the wild date tree.

Niḥśreṇikā, f. a species of grass.

निःश्री *niḥ-śrī, īs, īs, i,* deprived of happiness or prosperity, unfortunate. — *Niḥśrī-kṛita, as, ā, am,* made unfortunate, rendered unhappy.

Niḥśrīka, as, ā, am, deprived of beauty (as a dead body), deprived of happiness, &c.; one whose happiness is destroyed, unhappy, inglorious; (also read *ni-śrīka.*) — *Niḥśrīka-tā,* f. absence of good fortune, want of good luck.

निःश्रेणि *niḥ-śreṇi.* See above.

निःश्रेयस *niḥ-śreyasa, as, ī, am,* having nothing better or superior, the best, most excellent; *(as),* m. an epithet of Śiva; *(am),* n. final beatitude, ultimate bliss or supreme felicity in the life to come, happiness, welfare; knowledge which brings deliverance, learning; belief, faith, devotedness; apprehension, conception.

निःश्वस् *niḥ-śvas,* cl. 2. P. *-śvasiti, -śvasitum,* to breathe out, expire, sigh.

Niḥ-śvasana, am, n. breathing out, sighing.

Niḥ-śvasita, as, ā, am, breathed out, sighed; sighing, breathing out; *(am),* n. sighing, expiration, a sigh.

Niḥ-śvasya, ind. having sighed, sighing, breathing out.

Niḥ-śvāsa, as, m. breathing out, expiration; breath, sighing, a sigh; (often read *ni-śvāsa.*) — *Niḥ-śvāsa-parama, as, ā, am,* chiefly engaged in sighing, melancholy, sorrowful. — *Niḥśvāsa-saṃhitā,* f., N. of a code of laws supposed to have been revealed by Rudra-Śiva.

निःषमम् *niḥ-shamam,* ind. (fr. *nis + samam*), at the wrong time, unseasonably.

निःषिध् *niḥ-shidh, t,* f. (fr. *nis + sidh = sādh*), granting, bestowing; grant, oblation, gift, donation; (Sāy.) hindrance, obstruction; destroying, destructive, adverse.

Niḥ-shidhvan, ā, arī, a (fr. *nis + sidhvan*),

Ved. granting, presenting; (Sāy.) coming to complete perfection.

निःसंशय *niḥ-saṃśaya, as, ā, am,* undoubted, infallible, unerring, certain; not doubting, not doubtful; *(am),* ind. without doubt, doubtless, infallibly, certainly, surely.

निःसङ्कक्ष *niḥ-sankaksha, as, ā, am,* not perplexed, not confused; (also written *ni-sankaksha.*)

निःसङ्ख्य *niḥ-sankhya, as, ā, am,* innumerable, numberless.

निःसङ्ग *niḥ-sanga, as, ā, am,* unattached, unobstructed; not attached, not devoted, regardless, indifferent to (with loc.); free from worldly attachment or selfish desires, unselfish, disinterested; unconnected, separated; *(ena* or *am),* ind. without attachment, without interest, unselfishly, without further reflection; (also written *niḥ-shanga;* cf. *a-sanga.*) — *Niḥsanga-tā,* f. or *niḥsanga-tva, am,* n. absence of attachment, unselfishness, disinterestedness, indifference.

निःसञ्चार *niḥ-sañćāra, as, ā, am,* not moving, not walking about, not leaving one's home.

निःसञ्ज्ञ *niḥ-sañjña, as, ā, am,* senseless, insensible, unconscious.

निःसत्त्व *niḥ-sattva, as, ā, am,* without courage or strength, unenergetic, weak, impotent; insignificant, low, mean; non-existent, unsubstantial; deprived of living beings; *(am),* n. absence of power, want of energy; insignificance; non-existence.

निःसत्य *niḥ-satya, as, ā, am,* untrue, false. — *Niḥsatya-tā,* f. insincerity, falsehood, untruth.

निःसन्तति *niḥ-santati, is, is, i,* destitute of offspring, childless.

Niḥ-santāna, as, ā, am, destitute of posterity, childless.

निःसन्दिग्ध *niḥ-sandigdha, as, ā, am,* undoubted, not doubtful, certain; *(am),* ind. without any doubt, certainly.

Niḥ-sandeha, as, ā, am, free from uncertainty, doubtless, undoubted, certain; *(am),* ind. without any doubt, certainly.

निःसन्धि *niḥ-sandhi, is, is, i,* having no joints, having no joints perceptible, well knit, compact, close, firm.

निःसपत्न *niḥ-sapatna, as, ā, am,* having no rival, not sharing the possession of anything with another; not claimed by another, belonging exclusively to one possessor; having no enemies.

निःसम्पात *niḥ-sampāta, as, ā, am,* affording no passage, blocked up; *(as),* m. thick darkness, midnight.

निःसम्बन्ध *niḥ-sambandha, as, ā, am,* without relatives.

निःसम्बाध *niḥ-sambādha, as, ā, am,* not contracted, large, spacious.

निःसम्भ्रम *niḥ-sambhrama, as, ā, am,* not perplexed or flurried, unembarrassed.

निःसरण *niḥ-saraṇa.* See under *niḥ-sṛi,* col. 2.

निःसलिल *niḥ-salila, as, ā, am,* waterless, having no water.

निःसह *niḥ-saha, as, ā, am,* unable to bear or support or resist, impatient; powerless, weak; intolerable, unbearable, irresistible. — *Niḥsaha-tā,* f. or *niḥsaha-tva, am,* n. inability to bear or support; impatience, unendurance.

निःसहाय *niḥ-sahāya, as, ā, am,* without helpers or associates, unassisted.

निःसाध्वस *niḥ-sādhvasa, as, ā, am,* fearless, bold; *(am),* ind. fearlessly, boldly. — *Niḥsādhvasa-tva, am,* n. fearlessness, boldness.

निःसामर्थ्य *niḥ-sāmarthya, as, ā, am,* unfit, unsuitable.

निःसामान्य *niḥ-sāmānya, as, ā, am,* extraordinary, uncommon, unusual, special.

निःसार 1. *niḥ-sāra, as, ā, am* (for 2. *niḥ-sāra* see under *niḥ-sṛi* below), sapless, pithless, worthless, vain, vapid, unsubstantial; *(as),* m. the plant Trophis Aspera; a kind of time in music; *(ā),* f. the pisang, Musa Sapientum (= *kadalī*). — *Niḥsāra-tā,* f. saplessness, worthlessness, vanity.

निःसाल *niḥ-sāla, as, ā, am,* Ved. being out of the house.

निःसीमन् *niḥ-sīman, ā, ā, a,* immeasurable, having no boundaries or limits.

निःसुख *niḥ-sukha, as, ā, am,* joyless, sad, unhappy; disagreeable, distressing.

निःसृ *niḥ-sṛi* (*nis-s°*), cl. 1. P. *-sarati, -sartum,* to go out, come forth, issue, slip out, depart, withdraw: Caus. *-sārayati, -yitum,* to cause to go out or away, turn out, expel.

Niḥ-sara, as, ā, am, issuing out. — *Niḥsara-tva, am,* n. = *pitta-roga.*

Niḥ-saraṇa, am, n. going forth or out, coming forth, exit; the egress or outlet from a house, market-place, town, &c., the gate, the gate-way; a means or expedient, a remedy; departure, dying, death; final beatitude.

2. *niḥ-sāra, as,* m. (for 1. *niḥ-sāra* see above), going forth or out.

Niḥ-sāraṇa, am, n. driving out, expelling, turning out; the egress or outlet from a building, town, &c., a passage, road of ingress or egress.

Niḥ-sārita, as, ā, am, turned out, made to come out, expelled, dismissed.

Niḥ-sārya, as, ā, am, to be turned out, to be excluded or expelled.

Niḥ-sṛita, as, ā, am, gone forth or out, broken forth; having departed (with abl.).

निःस्तम्भ *niḥ-stambha, as, ā, am,* without posts or columns, having no pillars.

निःस्तुति *niḥ-stuti, is, is, i* (also read *ni-stuti*), praising nothing, without praising (anything).

निःस्नेह *niḥ-sneha, as, ā, am,* without unction, not greasy or unctuous, dry; without love or affection, insensible, cold, unfeeling; not longing for, indifferent; not loved, uncared for, hated; *(ā),* f. linseed, Linum Usitatissimum. — *Niḥsneha-phalā,* f. a species of Solanum with white flowers.

निःस्पन्द *niḥ-spanda, as, ā, am,* motionless.

निःस्पृह *niḥ-spṛiha, as, ā, am* (often written *ni-spṛiha*), free from desire; disregarding, indifferent to (with abl.); content, unenvious.

निःस्यन्द *niḥ-syanda.* See *ni-syanda.*

निःस्रु *niḥ-sru* (*nis-s°*), Caus. *-srāvayati, -yitum,* to cause to flow out or off, to empty.

Niḥ-srava, as, m. remainder, surplus, overplus (with abl.).

Niḥ-srāva, as, m. causing to flow out, expending, expense; the moisture or water of boiled rice; [cf. *ni-srāva.*]

निःस्व *niḥ-sva, as, ā, am,* deprived of one's own, having no property, indigent, poor. — *Niḥsva-tā,* f. poverty. — *Niḥsvi-kṛita* or *niḥsvi-bhūta, as, ā, am,* deprived of one's property, impoverished.

निःस्वन *niḥ-svana, as,* m. (fr. *svan* with *nis*), sound, noise, voice; [cf. *ni-svana.*]

निःस्वभाव *niḥ-svabhāva, as, ā, am,* void of peculiarities, without peculiar properties.

निःस्वादु *niḥ-svādu, us, us* or *dvī, u,* tasteless, void of flavour, insipid, unsavoury.

निःस्वाध्याय *niḥ-svādhyāya, as, ā, am,* not muttering prayers, not repeating texts. — *Niḥsvādhyāya-vashaṭkāra, as, ā, am,* neither repeating holy texts nor sacrificing.

निकक्ष *ni-kaksha, as,* m., Ved. the armpit.

निकट *ni-kaṭa, as, ā, am,* situated at the side, near, proximate, close by; without neighbours, kinless?; *(as, am),* m. n. proximity; *(e),* ind. in the neighbourhood, at hand. — *Nikaṭi-bhūta, as, ā, am,* approached.

निकथित *ni-kathita, as, ā, am,* told, related (?).

Nikathitin, ī, inī, i, one who has told.

निकम् *ni-kam,* cl. 10. A. *-kāmayate, -ća-kame,* &c., to long for, wish for, have a desire for, lust after (with acc.).

Ni-kāma, as, ā, am, Ved. desirous of, longing for, vehemently desiring, (often at the beginning of a comp. in the sense of *ni-kāmam,* ind.); *(as),* m. desire, wish; *(am),* ind. according to wish or desire, willingly, according to pleasure or to one's satisfaction, to one's heart's content; *yadā nikāmam,* if you please, if you like. — *Nikāma-kāma, as, ā, am,* covetous. — *Nikāma-varshin, ī, iṇī, i,* raining according to wish.

Ni-kāman, ā, ā, a, Ved. desirous of, longing for.

Ni-kāmana, am, n. desire, longing after.

Ni-kāmayamāna, as, ā, am, longing for, wishing for.

निकर *ni-kara, as,* m. (fr. rt. 1. *kṛī* with *ni*), a heap, pile; a flock or multitude; a bundle; pith, sap, essence; suitable gift, a honorarium; a treasure, the best of anything, a treasure belonging to Kuvera.

1. *ni-kāra, as,* m. piling up or winnowing corn; tossing or lifting up.

निकष *ni-kasha, as,* m. (fr. rt. *kash* for *karsh* = *kṛish* with *ni*), the touchstone, the streak of gold or test made on it [cf. *ni-kāsha*]; *(ā),* f., N. of the mother of Rāvaṇa or of the mother of the Piśitāśana fiends or imps in general. — *Nikashātmaja* (*°shā-āt°*), *as,* m. a Rākshasa, a sort of demon; [cf. *kashā-putra.*]

Ni-kashaṇa, am, n. (?), the touchstone.

Ni-kashā, ind. near to (with acc.), proximate; in the middle, betwixt, between (with acc.).

Nikashāya, Nom. A. *nikashāyate,* &c., to be used or serve as a touchstone.

निकस *ni-kasa, nikasātmaja* = *ni-kasha* and *nikashātmaja,* q. v.

निकाणम् *ni-kāṇam,* ind. (fr. rt. *kaṇ* with *ni*), having closed the eyes; *nikāṇam akshi jalpati* or *akshi-nikāṇaṃ jalpati,* he speaks with closed eyes.

निकाय *ni-kāya, as,* m. (fr. rt. 1. *ći* with *ni*), a heap, an assemblage, a group, class, association or set of persons who perform like duties; a congregation, a school; a flock, multitude in general; a house, dwelling-place, habitation, hiding-place; the body; (according to Mahī-dhara) the air, wind (Ved.); a butt, aim, mark; the universal Soul, Supreme Being. — *Nikāyāntarīya* (*°ya-an°*), *as, ā, am,* belonging to another assemblage or school.

Ni-kāyin, ī, inī, i, an epithet of particular oblations or sacrifices.

Ni-kāyya, as, am, m. n. (?), a dwelling, house.

निकार 1. and 2. *ni-kāra.* For 1. see above; for 2. see under *ni-kṛi,* p. 483, col. 1.

निकारिन् *ni-kārin.* See p. 483, col. 1.

निकावल्गा *nikāvalgā,* f., N. of a woman, (perhaps rather two names, *nikā* and *valgā.*)

निकाश *ni-kāśa, as,* m. (fr. rt. *kāś* with *ni*),

the horizon; appearance, sight; (at the end of an adj. comp.) having the appearance of, similar, like; [cf. *ni-kāśa.*]

निकाषम् *ni-kāsham*, ind. having pounded or mixed together.

निकास *ni-kāsa* = *ni-kāśa, nī-kāśa.*

निकिल्बिष *ni-kilbisha, am,* n., Ved. freeing from sin, deliverance from evil.

निकुचिति *ni-kućiti, is,* f. (fr. rt. *kuńć* with *ni*), contraction? [cf. Pāṇ. I. 2, 18.]

Nikućya-karṇi, ind. with the ears hanging down.

Ni-kuńćaka, as, m. a measure of capacity equal to ¼ of a Kuḍava; a species of reed (= *vānīra*).

Ni-kuńćita, as, ā, am, contracted.

निकुञ्ज *ni-kuńja, as, am,* m. n. = *kuńja*, an arbour, a bower, a place overgrown with shrubs and creepers, a thicket.

Nikuńjikāmlā (°*kā-am*°), f. a species of plant (= *kuńjikā, kuńja-vallarī*).

निकुम्भ *ni-kumbha, as,* m. the plant Croton Polyandrum; N. of a Dānava who, like Kumbha, was son of Pra-hlāda, (he was father of Sunda and Upa-sunda); N. of a Rakshas; of a son of Kumbha-karṇa; of an attendant of Śiva; of one of Skanda's attendants; N. of one of the Viśve Devāḥ, (also read *viskumbhu*); N. of a hero on the side of the Kurus; N. of a king of Ayodhyā, son of Hary-aśva and father of Saṃhatāśva; (*ī*), f. the plant Croton Polyandrum. — *Nikumbhākhya-jīva* (°*bha-ākh*°), *am,* n. a plant, Croton Jamalgota (= *jaya-pāla*).

Ni-kumbhita, am, n. a kind of time in music.

Ni-kumbhilā, f. (fr. *kumbha*, a jar?), a place where oblations are offered; a grove at the western gate of Laṅkā for the performance of sacrificial rites; (according to another commentator) an image of Bhadra-kālī on the west side of Laṅkā; (also, according to some, *ni-kumbhilas,* m., and *ni-kumbhilam,* n.)

निकुरुम्ब *ni-kurumba* or *ni-kurumbaka, am,* n. a flock, mass, multitude; (also read *ni-kuramba, ni-kurūmba, ni-kurumbha.*)

निकुलीनिका *ni-kulīnikā,* f. a family art or one inherited by birth, any skill or skilful act peculiar to a race.

निकूल *ni-kūla, as, ā, am,* going down hill, (opposed to *ut-kūla*); standing on a declivity or bank.

निकृ *ni-kṛi*, cl. 8. P. A. *-karoti, -kurute, -kartum,* Ved. to put down, bring down, lower, humiliate, subdue, overcome, overpower, depreciate, debase; to act in a low or base manner, to treat ill; (in the post-Vedic literature only occurring in the past part. *ni-kṛita*, q. v.): Desid. *ni-ćikīrshati*, to wish to subdue.

Ni-kartavya, as, ā, am, to be acted badly or basely, to be injured; (*asmākam tair nikartavyam,* a wrong is to be done us by them.)

2. *ni-kāra, as,* m. putting down, bringing down, humiliation, subjugation; injury, insult, wrong, offence; wickedness, malice, abuse, reproach, disrespect; opposition, contradiction.

Ni-kāraṇa, am, n. killing, slaughter.

Ni-kārin, ī, m., Ved. an injurer, oppressor.

Ni-kṛita, as, ā, am, brought down, lowered, cast down, humbled, humiliated; insulted, offended; afflicted; injured; tricked, cheated, deceived; removed, set aside, dismissed; dishonest, wicked, perverse; low, base, vile; (*am*), n. lowering, humbling, humiliation; (also read *ni-kṛiti.*) — *Nikṛita-prajña, as, ā, am,* evil-minded. — *Nikṛita-mati, is, is, i,* depraved in mind.

Ni-kṛiti, is, f. low conduct, baseness, wickedness, dishonest practice, dishonesty, fraud, deception, deceit, cheating; offence, insult; abuse, reproach; rejection, removal; poverty, indigence; wickedness, a wicked person (personified as a daughter of A-dharma and Hiṃsā, or Nirṛiti); (*is, is, i*), base, low, dishonest, wicked; (*is*), m., N. of one of the eight Vasus. — *Nikṛiti-prajña, as, ā, am,* versed in dishonesty, well acquainted with vice.

Nikṛitin, ī, inī, i (fr. *ni-kṛita*), = *ni-kṛiti*, dishonest, low, base, wicked.

Ni-kṛityā, f. wickedness, dishonesty, fraud, &c., = *ni-kṛiti.*

Ni-kṛitvan, ā, arī, a, Ved. acting basely, deceitful.

निकृत् *ni-kṛit*, cl. 6. P. *-kṛintati, -kartitum,* to cut down, hew down, cut away, cut or chop off, cut through, cut asunder, cut to pieces, massacre; tear off, tear away, wear away; A. (*-te*), to cut oneself (or one's nails &c.); to cut down &c.: Caus. *-kartayati*, &c., to cause to cut or cut down.

Ni-kartana, am, n. cutting down, cutting to pieces, cutting off.

Ni-kṛitta, as, ā, am, cut off, cut up. — *Nikṛitta-mūla, as, ā, am,* cut up by the roots.

Ni-kṛintana, as, ī, am, cutting down, cutting off, destroying; (*as*), m., N. of a hell; (*am*), n. massacring, cutting, cutting off, destruction; an instrument for cutting.

निकृष् *ni-kṛish*, cl. 1. 6. P. *-karshati, -kṛishati, -karshṭum* or *-krashṭum,* to draw down, drag down; to tear asunder (?). In Mahā-bh. I. 3616. *ni-kṛishyate* may mean 'is drawn down by the stream of a river.'

Ni-karshaṇa, am, n. an open space for recreation, a sort of play-ground in or near a town; a court at the entrance of a house; a neighbourhood.

Ni-kṛishṭa, as, ā, am, debased, low, base, vile, vulgar; despised, outcast; near; (*am*), n. vicinity, proximity. — *Nikṛishṭāśaya* (°*ṭa-āś*°), *as, ā, am,* having base intentions. — *Nikṛishṭāśaya-tā,* f. the state of one who has base intentions, base disposition of mind; jealousy. — *Nikṛishṭopādhi-tā* (°*ṭa-up*°), f. a state of base or low deception.

निकेचाय *ni-kećāya, as,* m. (fr. rt. 1. *ći* with *ni*), piling or collecting repeatedly.

निकेत *ni-keta* or *ni-ketaka, as,* m. = *ketana*, a house, mansion, habitation; a mark, countersign.

निकेतन *ni-ketana, as,* m. an onion; (*am*), n. = *ni-keta*, a house, mansion, abode, habitation, temple.

निकोचक *ni-koćaka, as,* m. (fr. rt. *kuńć* with *ni*), the tree Alangium Decapetalum; (*am*), n. the fruit of this tree.

Ni-koćana, am, n. contracting, contraction, compression.

निकोठक *ni-koṭhaka, as,* m. = *ni-koćaka* above.

निकोथक *ni-kothaka, as,* m. (fr. rt. *kuth* with *ni*), N. of a teacher with the epithet Bhāyajātya.

निकोश्य *ni-kośya, as* or *am,* m. or n. (?), Ved. a particular part of the entrails of sacrificial animals; [cf. *kośya.*]

निक्तहस्त *nikta-hasta.* See rt. *nij*, p. 485.

निक्रन्द् *ni-krand*, cl. 1. P. *-krandati, -kranditum,* Ved. to utter a cry in a direction downwards (as a bird on a tree): Caus. *-krandayati, -yitum,* Ved. to cause to roar &c.

निक्रम् *ni-kram*, cl. 1. P. *-krāmati, -kramitum,* to set the foot on the ground, put down the feet: to enter; to tread down (with acc.).

Ni-kramaṇa, am, n., Ved. putting down the feet, treading down; the place where the foot is put, foot-step, foot-fall.

निक्रीड् *ni-krīḍ*, Caus. *-krīḍayati*, &c., to play, sport.

Ni-krīḍa, as, m. play, sport; *marutām nikrīḍaḥ,* N. of a Sāman.

निक्वण *ni-kvaṇa* or *ni-kvāṇa, as,* m. a musical tone or sound; any sound.

निक्ष् *niksh*, cl. 1. P. *nikshati*, &c., to pierce (Ved.); to kiss.

Nikshaṇa, am, n. kissing.

निक्षा *nikshā,* f. a nit; (a wrong form for *likshā.*)

निक्षिप् *ni-kship*, cl. 6. P. A. *-kshipati, -te, -ksheptum,* to throw down, cast or put down, throw upon, put or lay down; put in, pour in; to deliver anything (acc.) to a person (loc.); to give or hand over, grant; to deposit, commit, deliver to any one's charge, intrust; to install, appoint, establish; to lay aside, give up, leave off, cast off, repel; to encamp; Caus. *-kshepayati*, &c., to cause to put down, to cause to be set down in writing.

Ni-kshipat, an, antī or *atī, at,* throwing down or on, placing in or upon.

Ni-kshipta, as, ā, am, thrown down or upon, put down, laid down or on, placed into, thrust into; deposited, pawned, pledged; rejected, abandoned, foregone, given or thrown away; sent, sent off or away. — *Nikshipta-vāda, as, ā, am,* one who has ceased talking or left off boasting.

Ni-kshipya, ind. having placed or laid down or upon; having given in charge, having intrusted or deposited in a place of safety.

Ni-kshepa, as, m. throwing upon, casting on (with loc.); a deposit, pledge, trust, anything deposited without a seal in trust or as a compensation, anything pawned; abandoning, parting with, throwing away; sending or putting away; wiping, drying; in *nikshepa-lipi* probably N. of a country; [cf. *ut-kshepa, pra-kshepa, vi-kshepa.*]

Ni-kshepaṇa, am, n. putting down (the feet); a means by which or place in which anything is kept.

Ni-kshepita, as, ā, am, caused to be put down or set down in writing, committed to writing, inscribed.

Ni-ksheptṛi, tā, trī, tṛi, who or what places or deposits, delivers to one's care; (*tā*), m. a depositor, a pawner or pledger.

Ni-kshepya, as, ā, am, to be deposited, to be thrust into.

निक्षुभा *ni-kshubhā,* f. (fr. rt. *kshubh* with *ni*), N. of the mother of Maga.

निखन् *ni-khan*, cl. 1. P. A. *-khanati, -te, -khanitum,* to dig into (the ground), bury; to dig in or up, root up; to infix, pierce (with an arrow &c.), to fix, implant.

Ni-khanana, am, n. digging in, burying.

Ni-khāta, as, ā, am, dug in, buried; dug up, excavated; fixed in the ground as a stake.

Ni-khānita, as, ā, am (fr. the Caus.), infixed, dug in, fixed.

निखर्व *ni-kharba* or *ni-kharva, as, ā, am,* dwarfish, a dwarf; (*am*), n. a billion; [cf. *kharva.*]

Ni-kharvaka, am, n., 1000 millions.

Ni-kharvaṭa, as, m., N. of a Rakshas.

निखिद् *ni-khid*, cl. 6. P., Ved. *-khidati, -khettum,* to press down; (Sāy.) to cut off, remove.

निखिल *ni-khila, as, ā, am* (probably for *niḥ-khila*), complete, all, whole, entire; (*ena*), ind. completely, totally; [cf. *khila, a-kh*°.]

निखुर्यप *nikhurya-pa* (?), *as,* m., Ved. an epithet of Vishṇu.

निगड *ni-gaḍa, as, am,* m. n. (probably fr. rt. *gaḍ* = rt. *gal*; cf. *ni-gala*), an iron chain for the feet, a fetter, especially the chain used to secure the hind feet of an elephant or a noose for catching the feet and throwing an animal down, a fetter or shackle in general, gyves.

Ni-gaḍana, am, n. putting in irons or fetters, binding, fettering.

Nigaḍaya, Nom. P. nigaḍayati, &c., to put in irons or fetters, to bind, fetter.

Nigaḍayitvā, ind. having fettered.

Ni-gaḍita, as, ā, am, chained, bound, tied, &c.

निगण ni-gaṇa, as, m. the smoke of a burnt offering or sacrificial fire; [cf. ni-garaṇa.]

निगद् ni-gad, cl. 1. P. -gadati, &c., to recite, proclaim, declare, communicate, tell, speak, say, shout out; to speak to, address any one (with acc.), to tell anything to any one (with two acc.); to enumerate; to call: Pass. -gadyate, &c., to be recited, to be named or called: Caus. -gādayati, &c., to cause to recite, tell, &c.

Ni-gada or ni-gāda, as, m. reciting, audible recitation of prayers or charms; a prayer or sacrificial formula recited aloud; mention, mentioning; speech, speaking, discourse; N. of a teacher with the epithet Pārṇavalki.

Ni-gadat, an, antī, at, reciting, addressing, speaking, saying, speaking to.

Ni-gadita, as, ā, am, recited, told, said, spoken; (am), n. speech.—Nigadita-vat, ān, atī, at, one who has spoken, having spoken.

Ni-gadya, ind. having told, having declared.

Ni-gāda, as, m. speech, discourse, recitation, &c.

Ni-gādin, ī, inī, i, reciting, telling, speaking, &c.

निगम् ni-gam, cl. 1. P. -gaććhati, -gantum, to settle down upon (Ved.); to enter (acc. or loc.); inire feminam (Ved.); to go to any place or state, to undergo, become (e.g. śāntim ni-gam, to become pacified); to be inserted: Caus. -gamayati, to cause to go in, to insert.

Ni-gama, as, m. insertion, especially of the name of a deity into a liturgical formula; the place or passage in a book where a word occurs, especially a passage of the Vedas or the actual word quoted from such a passage; the Veda or the Vedic text; the root (as the source from which a word comes); a sacred precept, the words of a god or holy man; certainty, assurance; a town, a city; a market, a fair; a road, a market road; trade, traffic; a camp or caravan of itinerant merchants, a merchant; = lunḍī; (am), n. a particular number.

Ni-gamana, am, n. insertion, quotation of words (from the Veda &c.) or the word &c. quoted; the conclusion in a syllogism, the deduction; going in or into.

Nigamin, ī, inī, i, familiar with or versed in the Vedas or in holy writ.

निगर ni-gara, ni-garaṇa, &c. See ni-gṛī.

निगर्ह् ni-garh, cl. 10. P. -garhayati, -yitum, to disdain, despise.

निगल् ni-gal, cl. 1. P. -galati, &c., to fall down (?).

Ni-gala, as, am, m. n. = ni-gaḍa, q. v.

निगा ni-gā, cl. 3. P. -jigāti, &c., to go into, enter, attach one's self to; to come or get into any state &c.; to nestle.

निगु ni-gu, us, m. = manas, the mind, the faculty of feeling and reasoning; (according to others) dirt, excrement [cf. rt. 4. gu]; a root; painting; (us, us, u), pleasing, charming.

निगुत् ni-gut, t, m. (probably fr. rt. 3. gu with ni), Ved. (according to Sāy.) an enemy; [cf. naiguta.]

निगुह् ni-guh, cl. 1. P. A. -gūhati, -te, -gūhitum, to cover, conceal, hide: Caus. -gūhayati, -yitum, to cause to cover or hide.

Ni-gūḍha, as, ā, am, hidden, concealed; profound, recondite, mysterious, obscure; (am), ind. privately, secretly.—Nigūḍha-kārya, as, ā, am, secret in operation.—Nigūḍha-tara, as, ā, am, well concealed or hidden.—Nigūḍha-niśćaya, as, ā, am, whose resolve or determination is concealed.—Nigūḍha-roman, ā, ā, a, having concealed hair.—Nigūḍhārtha (°ḍha-ar°), as, ā, am, having a hidden sense or purpose, difficult to be understood, abstruse, occult.

Ni-gūḍhaka, as, m. a species of wild bean; [cf. vana-mudga.]

Ni-gūhaka, as, ā, am, hiding, concealing.

Ni-gūhana, am, n. hiding, concealing.

Ni-gūhanīya, as, ā, am, to be hidden or concealed; to be covered or protected or defended.

निगृहीत ni-gṛihīta. See ni-grah below.

निगॄ ni-gṛī, cl. 6. P. -girati and -gilati, &c., to swallow, swallow up, swallow down, ingurgitate, devour: Caus. Pass. -gāryate and -gālyate: Intens., Ved. -jegilyate, -galgalīti, to swallow with a gurgling sound.

Ni-gara, as, m. swallowing, devouring.

Ni-garaṇa, am, n. swallowing, devouring, deglutition; (as), m. the throat, the gullet, esophagus; the smoke of a burnt offering; [cf. ni-gaṇa.]

Ni-galana = ni-garaṇa.

Ni-gāra, as, m. swallowing, swallowing down, devouring.

Ni-gāraka, as, ikā, am, = ni-gālaka, swallowing.

Ni-gāla, as, m. the throat or neck of a horse; [cf. gala, ni-garaṇa.]—Nigāla-vat, ān, m. a horse.

Ni-gālaka, as, ā, am, swallowing, devouring.

Ni-gīrṇa, as, ā, am, swallowed; (metaphorically) left out, omitted, not expressed; (a-nigīrṇa, expressed.)

Ni-giryamāṇa, as, ā, am, being swallowed down; (with act. sense?), swallowing, devouring.

निगै ni-gai, cl. 1. P. -gāyati, -gātum, to accompany with song; to sing, chant; to proclaim, announce.

Ni-gīta, as, ā, am, sung, chanted; said.

निग्रन्थ् ni-granth, cl. 9. P. -grathnāti, &c., to intertwine, interweave.

Ni-granthana, am, n. (probably a corruption of ni-kranthana; cf. krath, krathana), killing, destroying, slaughter; [cf. nir-granthana.]

निग्रह् ni-grah, in the older language ni-grabh, cl. 9. P. A. -gṛibhṇāti, -ṇīte, -gṛihṇāti, -ṇīte, -grahītum, to hold down, keep down, depress, keep under, keep in check; to keep back, hold back, stop, obstruct, restrain, suppress, confine; to seize, catch, apprehend, hold, hold fast; to oppress, overpower, subdue, conquer; to chastise, punish, tame; to draw together, contract, close (as the eyes): Caus. -grāhayati, to cause to be apprehended or seized: Caus. of the Desid. -jighṛikshayati, to cause any one to desire to keep under or suppress.

Ni-gṛihīta, as, ā, am, seized, arrested; held back, restrained, confined, subdued, checked; harassed, assailed, attacked.

Ni-gṛihīti, is, f. restraint, check; overpowering.

Ni-gṛihītṛi, wrong form for ni-grahītṛi, q. v.

Ni-gṛihṇat, an, atī, at, seizing, taking; keeping, suppressing, restraining.

1. ni-gṛihya, as, ā, am, to be held back; to be punished, punishable; deserving chastisement or reproof.

2. ni-gṛihya, ind. having taken; having arrested or confined; having restrained or suppressed.

Ni-graha, as, m. keeping down, holding down, keeping under, keeping back, keeping in check, coercion, restraining, binding, restraint, subjugation, subduing, restraint of the appetite &c., abstinence; obstruction, suppression, putting down; seizing, catching, confinement, capture, arrest; the arresting or suppressing of disease, cure; taking down, humbling, punishing, punishment, chastisement, rebuke, rebuff, reprimand, blame; aversion, dislike, disgust; (in the Nyāya phil.) putting down in argument, fault in a syllogism, flaw in an argument, failure in proof; any place for catching hold of, a handle; a boundary, a limit; N. of Śiva and of Vishṇu or Kṛishṇa.—Nigraha-sthāna, am, n. the predicament of rebuke for failure in argument.

Ni-grahaṇa, as, ā, am, holding down, holding back, suppressing; (am), n. subduing, suppression; capture, confinement, prison; defeat, punishment.

Ni-grahītavya, as, ā, am, to be chastised or punished, punishable.

Ni-grahītṛi, tā, trī, tṛi, one who seizes or lays hold of; one who keeps back or prevents; seizing, restraining, binding.

Ni-grābha, as, m., Ved. pressing down; N. of a verse recited when the Soma plants are pressed.

Ni-grābhya, as, ā, am, Ved., with āpas, the water with which the Soma plants are sprinkled before they are pressed.

Ni-grāha, as, m. punishment, chastisement, (used in imprecations, e. g. nigrāhas te bhūyāt, confusion seize thee, &c.)

Ni-grāhya, as, ā, am, to be suppressed or punished, punishable.

निघ ni-gha, as, ā, am (fr. rt. han with ni), as high as broad; (anything) whose height and circumference are equal; a round or circle, a ball; sin.—Nighānigha (°gha-an°), as, ā, am, of different forms or sizes.

निघण्ट ni-ghaṇṭa (said to be fr. rt. gam or han or hṛi with ni; gender doubtful), a word; a glossary or collection of words or names, (in this sense properly pl.); often the collection of Vedic words explained in the Nirukta, see ni-ghaṇṭu below.

Ni-ghaṇṭi, probably only a wrong form for ni-ghaṇṭa or ni-ghaṇṭu.

Ni-ghaṇṭikā, f. a species of bulbous plant (= gulanća-kanda).

Ni-ghaṇṭu, us, m. (or ni-ghaṇṭuka), any vocabulary or collection of words or names, but especially a N. of the Vedic glossary explained by Yāska in his Nirukta, (in this sense usually pl. nighaṇṭavas as embracing five chapters.)—Nighaṇṭu-bhāshya, am, n. 'commentary on part of the Nighaṇṭus,' N. of a work by Deva-rāja on the three chapters of synonyms incompletely treated by Yāska.—Nighaṇṭu-rāja, as, m. 'king of glossaries,' N. of a medical lexicon commonly called Abhidhāna-ćūḍā-maṇi.

निघर्ष ni-gharsha. See ni-ghṛish below.

निघस ni-ghasa, as, m. (fr. rt. ghas with ni), eating; food, victuals.

निघात ni-ghāta, as, m. (fr. the Caus. of rt. han with ni), a blow, stroke; suppression of accent, absence of accent.

Ni-ghātam, ind. having struck.

Ni-ghāti, is, f. an iron club or mace or hammer (?).

Ni-ghātin, ī, inī, i, striking down, killing, destroying.

निघुष् ni-ghush (rt. 2. ghush = ghṛish with ni), Caus. P. -ghoshayati, -yitum, to tread down, trample under foot, crush, pound, grind.

निघुष्ट ni-ghushṭa, am, n. (fr. rt. 1. ghush with ni), sound, noise.

निघृष् ni-ghṛish, cl. 1. P. -gharshati, &c., to rub into, rub down, rub, pound, grind, triturate; graze, chafe, abrade, wear away by rubbing, excoriate.

Ni-gharsha, as, m. rubbing, friction, pounding, crushing.

Ni-gharshaṇa, am, n. rubbing, friction, grinding, trituration; [cf. nir-gharshaṇa.]

Ni-ghṛishṭa, as, ā, am, rubbed, ground; chafed, worn, grazed, abraded, excoriated; subdued.

Ni-ghṛishva, as, ā, am, rubbed off, abraded, excoriated; small, insignificant; (as), m. a hoof; wind; an ass or a mule; a boar; a road; (am), n. the mark of a hoof (?).

निघ्न ni-ghna, as, ā, am (fr. ni-han), dependant, subservient, docile; dependant on a substantive (as an adjective); (after a numeral) multiplied with; (*as*), m., N. of a son of An-araṇya and father of An-amitra; of a son of An-amitra.

Nighna-ka, as, ā, am, = *ni-ghna*, dependant.

Ni-ghnat, an, atī, at, smiting, slaying, killing, destroying, overcoming.

Ni-ghnāna, as, ā, am, slaying, killing.

निचक्र *ni-ćakra, as,* m., N. of a prince.

निचङ्कुण *ni-ćankuṇa* for *ni-ćunkuṇa*, q. v.

निचन्द्र *ni-ćandra, as,* m., N. of a Dānava.

निचमन *ni-ćamana, am,* n. (fr. rt. *ćam* with *ni*), sipping, taking liquid into the mouth.

निचय *ni-ćaya*. See under 1. *ni-ći* below.

निचाङ्कुण *ni-ćānkuṇa* for *ni-ćunkuṇa*, q. v.

निचाय् *ni-ćāy*, cl. 1. P. *-ćāyati*, &c. (occurring only in the form *ni-ćāyya*), Ved. to regard with reverence, honour, worship; to see; [cf. rt. 4. *ći*.]

Ni-ćāyya, ind. having seen, having observed.

निचि 1. *ni-ći*, cl. 5. P. A. *-ćinoti, -ćinute, -ćetum*, to pile up, heap up.

Ni-ćaya, as, m. piling up, heaping up; collection, heap, multitude, quantity, store, stock, provisions (e. g. *shaṇ-māsa-ni-ćaya*, provisioned for six months); assemblage, assemblage or collection of parts constituting a whole (e. g. *śarīra-ni-ćaya*, the assemblage of parts of which the body consists; *vadhū-ni-ćaya*, a collection of women); certainty, ascertainment (in this sense for *niś-ćaya*, q. v.).

Ni-ćayin, ī, inī, i, heaped up, containing a quantity, full of, abounding in.

Ni-ćāya, as, m. a heap (as a measure).

Ni-ćita, as, ā, am, piled up, heaped up, full of, filled; covered, overspread; raised up; (*ās*), m. pl., N. of a warrior-tribe [cf. *naićitya*]; (*ā*), f., N. of a river.

Ni-ćekāya, as, m. (fr. the Intens.), continual or repeated piling up.

Ni-ćeya, as, ā, am, to be piled or heaped up.

निचि 2. *ni-ći*, cl. 3. P. *-ćiketi, -ćikāya*, &c., Ved. to observe, perceive, recognise: Desid., Ved. *-ćikīshate*, to observe, watch, guard.

Ni-ćira, as, ā, am, Ved. attentive, observant, vigilant; (*ā*), m. du. epithet of Mitra-Varuṇa; (Sāy.) excessively ancient (= *nitarām ćirantanau*).

Ni-ćetṛi, tā, trī, tṛi, Ved. an observer; observing, paying attention.

निचिकी *ni-ćikī*, f. an excellent cow (= *naićikī*, q. v.).

निचिर *ni-ćira*. See under 2. *ni-ći* above.

निचुङ्कुण *ni-ćunkuṇa, as, ā, am* (fr. Intens. of rt. *kuṇ*?), Ved. roaring, murmuring; (*as*), m., N. of a Vāruṇi; (often read *ni-ćankuṇa* or *ni-ćānkuṇa*.)

निचुम्पुण *ni-ćumpuṇa, as, ā, am* (rt. *ćup*?), Ved. an epithet of Soma (because, according to Yāska, *nićamanena prīṇāti*); of the Ava-bhṛitha; of the sea (because, according to Yāska, *nićamanena pūryate*); moving about?; (*as*), m., N. of a Śaunaḥśepha.

निचुल *ni-ćula, as,* m. (fr. rt. *ćul* with *ni*), the tree Barringtonia Acutangula, commonly called Hijjal, = *vetasa*; = *ni-ćola*, an upper garment, overcoat; (also read *ni-ćūla*.)

Ni-ćulaka, am, n. an outer garment; a breast-plate, a cuirass.

Ni-ćola, as, m. a cover, wrapper, veil, surtout.

Ni-ćolaka, as, m. a sort of jacket, bodice, mantle, but especially a soldier's jacket serving as a cuirass or breast-plate; (*am*), n. = *ni-ćulaka*.

निचृत् 1. *ni-ćṛit*, cl. 6. P. *-ćṛitati, -ćartitum*, to insert, infix, fix into.

2. *ni-ćṛit, t,* f. a defective metre; [cf. *ati-n°*, *ni-vṛit*.]

निचेरु *ni-ćeru, us, us, u* (fr. rt. *ćar* with *ni*), Ved. gliding; creeping; an epithet of the Ava-bhṛitha.

निच्छवि *niććhavi, is,* f., N. of a district (= *tīra-bhukti*), the modern Tirhut; [cf. *liććhavi*.]

निच्छिद्र *ni-ććhidra* for *niś-ćhidra*, q. v.

निच्छिवि *niććhivi, is,* m., N. of one of the degraded castes sprung from the outcast or Vrātya Kshatriyas (see Manu X. 22; their occupation appears to have been the public exhibition of gymnastic performances &c., as they are classed with the Jhallas, Mallas, and others).

निच्छेद *ni-ćcheda, as,* m. (fr. rt. *ćhid* with *ni*), cutting off; (in arithmetic) leaving no common measure, reduced by the common divisor to the least term so as not to allow of further reduction (in this sense for *niś-ćheda*).

निज् *nij*, cl. 3. P. A. *nenekti* (3rd pl. *nenijati*), *nenikte, nineja, ninije, nektā, nekshyati, -te, anijat, anaikshīt, anikta, nektum*, to wash, clean, cleanse, purify; A. to wash or clean one's self; to nourish: Pass. *nijyate*, &c., to be washed: Caus. *nejayati, -yitum*, Aor. *anīnijat*: Desid. *ninikshati, -te*: Intens. *nenijyate, nenijīti, nenekti*; [cf. rt. *niṅj*: Zend *śnizh*, 'to snow:' Gr. νίζ-ω, νίπ-τ-ω, χέρ-νιβ-α (acc.), νίπ-τρο-ν, νίφ-α (acc.), νιφ-ά(δ)-ς, νίφ-ετό-ς, νίφει; Lat. *Nep-tūnu-s* = νιπτόμενο-ς, 'bathing;' *ning-i-t, ningu-i-t, ningu-i-s, nix*, base *niv* for *nigv*: Goth. *snaivs*, 'snow:' Old Germ. *sneo*, 'snow;' *sniwit*, 'it snows:' Lith. *snig-ti, sning-ti*, 'to snow;' *snēg-a-s*, 'snow;' *snaig-alà*, 'a flake of snow:' Slav. *snēg-ŭ*, 'snow:' Hib. *nigh-im*, 'I wash;' *nigh-te*, 'washed,' = Sanskṛit *nikta*.]

Nikta, as, ā, am, washed, cleaned, cleansed, rinsed; sprinkled. — *Nikta-hasta, as, ā, am,* Ved. clean-handed, having clean hands.

निज *ni-ja, as, ā, am* (fr. rt. *jan* with *ni*), innate, native, congenital, indigenous; own, of one's own party or country; proper, peculiar; continual, perpetual; (*ās*), m. pl. one's own people. *Ni-ja* is used in later Sanskṛit as a reflexive possessive pronoun, like *sva*, for 'my own,' 'his own,' 'our own,' &c.; and frequently for simple 'my,' 'his,' 'our,' &c. — *Nija-karman, a,* n. one's own work, any duty pertaining to one's self. — *Nija-karma-bandhana, as, ā, am,* fettered by one's own works. — *Nija-ghāsa, as,* m. 'devouring his own,' N. of a demon. — *Nija-dhṛiti, is,* f., N. of a river in Śāka-dvīpa. — *Nija-mukta, as, ā, am,* (according to the commentators) = *svabhāva-mukta*, liberated in own nature, essentially liberated (?). — *Nija-lābha-pūrṇa, as, ā, am,* engrossed in self-interest, self-satisfied. — *Nija-sva, am,* n. own property. — *Nijārtham* (°*ja-ar*°), ind. for one's own sake, for one's self.

निजघ्नि *ni-jaghni, is, is, i* (fr. *ni-han*), Ved. striking down, overpowering; [cf. *jaghni*.]

निजानुका *ni-jānukā*, f. (fr. *ni-jānu*), Ved. shaking or trembling of the knees (?).

निजिघृक्षयत् *ni-jighṛikshayat, an, antī, at* (Caus. of Desid. of rt. *grah* with *ni*), causing to be desirous of overpowering or excelling.

निजुर्व् *ni-jurv* or *ni-jūrv*, cl. 1. P. *-jūrvati*, &c., to consume by fire; (Sāy.) to destroy, kill.

Ni-jur, ūr, f., Ved. killing, destroying.

निजुह्नूषु *ni-juhnūshu, us, us, u* (fr. Desid. of rt. *hnu* with *ni*), wishing to conceal or deny.

निञ्ज् *niñj*, cl. 2. A. *nikte*, &c., = rt. *nij*, q. v.

निटल *ni-ṭala* or *ni-ṭāla, am,* n. the forehead. — *Niṭalāksha* (°*la-aksha*), *as,* m. 'having an eye on the forehead,' an epithet of Śiva; (incorrectly spelt *niṭilāksha*.)

निडी *ni-ḍī*, cl. 1. 4. A. *-ḍayate* and *-ḍīyate*, &c., to fly down.

Ni-ḍīna, am, n. the downward flight or swoop of a bird or a peculiar mode of flying.

निणिज् *ni-ṇij, k* (according to Sāy. fr. *ni-nij*, to purify), milk; (according to modern scholars this word may be an adverb related to *ni-ṇya*.)

निण्डिका *niṇḍikā*, f. a species of convolvulus, = *tiṇḍī*; (probably wrongly for *tiṇḍikā*.)

निण्य *ni-ṇya, as, ā, am* (fr. *ni*), Ved. interior, hidden, concealed, secret, mysterious, (in Ṛig-veda I. 32, 10, = *nir-nāmadheya*, nameless, according to Sāy.); (*am*), n. a secret, a mystery; (*am*), ind. secretly, mysteriously.

नितततपम् *nitatatapam*, ind., Ved. an onomatopoetic word to denote the speech of a stutterer.

नितन् *ni-tan*, cl. 8. P. A. *-tanoti, -nute, -tanitum*, Ved. to pervade, penetrate, pierce; to cause to grow downwards (as a shoot, root, &c.).

Ni-tatnī, f., Ved. a species of plant; N. of an Ishṭakā; N. of one of the seven stars of the asterism Kṛittikā.

Ni-tāna, as, m., Ved. the shoot of a plant which grows downwards; N. of a man with the patronymic Māruta.

नितप् *ni-tap*, cl. 1. P. *-tapati, -taptum*, Ved. to emit heat downwards; to consume.

नितम् *ni-tam*, Caus. P. *-tamayati*, &c., Ved. to choke, suffocate.

Ni-tānta, as, ā, am, extraordinary, excessive, exceeding, much, considerable; (*am*), ind. exceedingly, excessively, very, much, in a high degree. — *Nitāntavṛiksha* (°*ta-av*°), *as, ā, am,* excessively treeless.

नितम्ब *ni-tamba, as,* m. (said to be fr. rt. *tamb*, probably connected with rt. *stambh*), the buttocks or posteriors, especially of a woman, (in this sense generally *nitambau*, m. du.); the circumference of the hip and loins; the ridge or side or protuberant flank or swell of a mountain [cf. *giri-nitamba*]; a precipice; the sloping bank or shore of a river; the shoulder; a particular position of the hands in dancing; (*ā*), f. a form of Durgā. — *Ni-tamba-tā*, f. the state of having large hips. — *Ni-tamba-vat, ān, atī, at,* having beautiful buttocks or hips, καλλίπυγος; (*tī*), f. a woman. — *Nitamba-vimba, as, ā, am,* having Vimba-like hips.

Nitambin, ī, inī, i (at the end of a comp.), having buttocks; having beautiful hips; having graceful slopes, having beautiful sides (as a mountain); (*inī*), f. a woman with large and handsome hips.

नितम्भू *nitambhū, ūs,* m., N. of a person mentioned in Mahā-bh. Anuśāsana-p. 1765; (perhaps for *nityam-bhū*.)

नितराम् *ni-tarām*, ind. (fr. *ni* with the comparative affix), downwards, towards the lower part (Ved.); in a low tone (Ved.); completely, wholly, entirely; much, extremely, excessively, in a high degree; in an especial manner, always, continually, eternally; at all events; certainly; [cf. Angl. Sax. *nidher*; Old Germ. *nidar*.]

नितल *ni-tala, am,* n. one of the seven divisions of the lower regions. See *pātāla*.

नितान्त *ni-tānta*. See *ni-tam* above.

नितिक्त *ni-tikta, as, ā, am* (fr. rt. *tij* with *ni*), Ved. excited, roused up.

Ni-tikti, is, f., Ved. excitement, haste, speed; (*i*), ind. quickly, speedily; (Sāy.) = 3rd sing. Pres. of rt. *tij* = *tīkshṇī-karoti*, he sharpens.

नितुद् **ni-tud**, cl. 6. P. A. *-tudati, -te, -tot-tum*, Ved. to pierce, penetrate, pierce into; to goad; (Sāy.) to incite or pain vehemently, or to issue forth (= *nitarām vyathayati* or *nir-gaććhati*).

Ni-toda, as, m. piercing, a prick, puncture, hole.
Ni-todin, ī, inī, i, Ved. piercing, penetrating.

नितृद् **ni-tṛid**, cl. 7. P. A. *-triṇatti, -tṛintte, -tarditum*, Ved. to pierce, penetrate, cleave in two.

नितॄ **ni-tṝi**, cl. 6. P. *-tirati, -taritum, -ta-rītum*, Ved. to dispel, subdue, overpower, obstruct.

नितोशन **ni-tośana**, *as, ā, am* (fr. rt. *tuś* with *ni*), Ved. sprinkling, distributing, granting; (*as*), m. a distributer, granter.

नित्य **nitya**, *as, ā, am* (fr. *ni*), own (Ved.); continual, perpetual, regularly repeated, constant, uninterrupted, endless, eternal, everlasting; invariable, regular, fixed, regularly prescribed, inevitable, not optional, (opposed to *kāmya* &c.); necessary, obligatory, essential; ordinary, usual, (opposed to *naimittika*, unusual, produced by an unusual cause); constantly dwelling in, perpetually engaged in, (often at the end of a comp., e. g. *araṇya-nitya*, constantly dwelling in a forest; *tapo-nitya*, engaged in constant penance); (with *samāsa*) a necessary compound which cannot be resolved without losing its meaning, because the separate ideas have merged in one, as in *Jamad-agni*; (with *svarita*) = *jātya*, the primary or independent Svarita, as opposed to the secondary or dependent; (*as*), m. the ocean; (*ā*), f. an epithet of Durgā; a Śakti or form of Durgā; an epithet of the goddess Manasā; (*am*), n. constant and indispensable rite or act; (*am*), ind. always, ever, daily, constantly, continually, perpetually, everlastingly, eternally; *na nityam*, not always, never, (in Manu VI. 8. *nityam an-ādātā* = never a receiver.) — *Nitya-karman, a*, n. or *nitya-kriyā*, f. constant act or duty, as observance of the five great sacrifices or any daily and necessary rite. — *Nitya-kṛitya, am*, n. regular and necessary act or ceremony; daily or regular act or routine. — *Nitya-gati, is, is, i*, moving continually; (*is*), m. air or wind, the god of wind. — *Nitya-jāta, as, ā, am*, constantly born. — *Nitya-tā*, f. perpetuity, eternity, continuance, continual repetition, (as *maithuna-nityatā*, continually repeated coitus); perseverance; necessity. — *Nitya-tva, am*, n. invariableness, perpetuity, eternity; endurance; inevitableness, necessity. — *Nitya-dā*, ind. always, ever, perpetually, constantly, eternally, at all times. — *Nitya-dāna, am*, n. daily alms-giving. — *Nitya-dhṛit, t, t, t*, constantly bearing or maintaining, observing daily duties (?). — *Nitya-dhṛita, as, ā, am*, constantly maintained or kept up. — *Nitya-nātha-siddha, as*, m., N. of an author. — *Nitya-niyama, as*, m. fixed rule, constant observance. — *Nitya-naimittika, am*, or *nitya-naimittikaṃ karma*, n. any regularly recurring occasional act or ceremony or any rite constantly performed to accomplish some object, as Śrāddhas at fixed lunar periods. — *Nitya-parivṛita, as*, m., N. of a Buddha. — *Nitya-parīkshaṇa, am*, n. constant investigation or inspection. — *Nitya-pūjā-yantra, am*, n. a kind of amulet. — *Nitya-pralaya, as*, m. the constant dissolution of living beings. — *Nitya-bhāva, as*, m. the state of being eternal, eternity. — *Nitya-maya, as, ī, am*, formed of or consisting of anything eternal, eternal. — *Nitya-yukta, as, ā, am*, always busy, ever engaged in. — *Nitya-yauvana, am*, n. perpetual youth; (*as, ī, am*), ever or always young; (*ā*), f. an epithet of Draupadī. — *Nityartu* (°*ya-ṛi*), *us, us, u*, regularly recurring at the seasons, annual. — *Nitya-vatsa, as, ā, am*, Ved. always possessing a calf; (*ā*), f. a particular form of Sāma supplication; (*am*), n., N. of several Sāmans. — *Nitya-vitrasta, as*, m. 'constantly scared,' N. of an antelope. — *Nitya-vaikuṇṭha, as*, m., N. of a particular residence of Vishṇu, the heaven of Vishṇu. — *Nitya-vyaya, as, ā, am*, always expending, constantly disbursing; (*ā*), f. always expending, ever laying out. — *Nitya-śaṅkita, as, ā, am*, perpetually alarmed, always suspicious. — *Nitya-śaya, as, ā, am*, always sleeping or reclining. — *Nitya-śas*, ind. always, continually, constantly, eternally. — *Nitya-saṃhṛishṭa, as, ā, am*, always exulting or triumphant; always rivalling one another, (in this sense *saṃhṛishṭa* = *sanghṛishṭa*.) — *Nitya-sama, as*, m. the assertion that all things remain the same (?). — *Nitya-samāsa*, see *nitya*. — *Nitya-siddha, as, ā, am*, 'ever perfect,' a Jaina predicate of the soul. — *Nitya-stotra, as, ā, am*, Ved. receiving perpetual praise, constantly lauded. — *Nitya-snāyin, ī, inī, i*, constantly bathing or making ablutions. — *Nityānadhyāya* (°*ya-an*°), *as*, m. invariable suspension of repetition of the Vedas, (a term applied to periods when the perusal of the Vedas is invariably prohibited, as the day of full moon, new moon, the eighth and fourteenth days of the half month.) — *Nityānanda* (°*ya-ān*°), *as*, m. eternal happiness. — *Nityānanda-rasodadhi* (°*sa-ud*°), *is*, m. 'ocean of the essence of eternal joy,' God. — *Nityānandāśrama* (°*da-āś*°), *as*, m., N. of a commentator. — *Nityānitya* (°*ya-an*°), *as, ā, am*, eternal and perishable, permanent and temporary. — *Nityāyukta* (°*ya-āy*°), *as*, m., N. of a Bodhi-sattva; (also read *nityoyukta*; cf. *nityodyukta*.) — *Nityāritra* (°*ya-ar*°), *as, ā, am*, Ved. having (its) own oars, ever fitted with oars (i. e. according to Sāy. with priests). — *Nityotkshipta-hasta* (°*ya-ut*°), *as*, m. 'who always raises his hand,' N. of a Bodhi-sattva. — *Nityodita* (°*ya-ud*°), *as*, m., N. of a man. — *Nityodyakta* (°*ya-ud*°), *as*, m., N. of a Bodhi-sattva; [cf. *nityāyukta*.]

नित्यज् **ni-tyaj**, cl. 1. P. *-tyajati, -tyaktum*, Ved. to scare or drive away.

निद् 1. **nid**, cl. 1. P. A. *nedati, nedate, nineda, ninide* or *ninede, neditā*, &c., to be near [cf. rt. *ned, nedīyas, nedishṭha*]; to ridicule, blame, reproach, censure, &c., (in this sense properly a separate rt., the form of which is usually *nind*, q. v.): Desid., Ved. *ninitsati*, to wish to reproach or depreciate; [cf. rt. *nind*; Gr. ὄ-νειδ-ο-ς, probably λοίδ-ο-ρο-ς; Goth. *ga-nait-yan, nai-teins*, probably *neith*; Old Germ. *neiz-yan*; Angl. Sax. *naet-an, naet-ing, nidh, ge-nidhe*, 'hatred;' Mod. Germ. *neid*, 'envy.']

2. *nid, t*, f., Ved. mocking, ridiculing, despising, censure, contempt; (*t*), m. one who ridicules or contemns, a blamer, an enemy.

1. *nidā*, f., Ved. blame, contempt.

1. *nidāna, as, ā, am*, Ved. (= *nidyamāna*), reproached, ridiculed. (For 2. see 3. *ni-dā*, col. 3.)

Nidyamāna, as, ā, am, being reproached, &c.

निद **ni-da**, *am*, n. (said to be fr. *ni-do*), poison, venom.

निदण्ड **ni-daṇḍa**, *as*, m., according to a commentator = *nihita-daṇḍa*, a stick put aside or laid down; (*as, ā, am*), one who has put down a stick (i. e. not using force), one who has laid down a staff.

निदत्त **ni-datta**. See 2. *ni-dā* below.

निदद्रु **nida-dru**, *us*, m. (said to be fr. *nida* + *dru*), a man.

निदर्शन **ni-darśana**. See *ni-dṛiś*, col. 3.

निदह् **ni-dah**, cl. 1. P. *-dahati, -dagdhum*, to burn down, consume by fire.

Ni-dāgha, as, m. (according to native lexicographers also *am*, n.), heat, warmth; the hot season (May and June), summer; internal heat, sweat, perspiration; N. of a man; N. of a son of Pulastya; (*ās*), m. pl. the descendants of the former person. — *Nidāgha-kara, as*, m. 'heat causer' or 'hot-rayed,' the sun. — *Nidāgha-kāla, as*, m. 'the time of heat,' the hot season, two months previous to the rains, about May and June. — *Nidāgha-sindhu, us*, m. a river in hot weather, one nearly dry.

निदा 2. **ni-dā** (rt. 1. *dā*), cl. 3. P. *-dadāti*, &c., Ved. to give. (For 1. *nidā* see above.)

Ni-datta, as, ā, am, given, given absolutely; [cf. *nītta*.]

निदा 3. **ni-dā** (rt. 4. *dā*, to bind), cl. 4. P. *-dyati*, &c., Ved. to fasten.

Ni-dātṛi, tā, trī, tṛi, Ved. one who fastens or ties up; (Sāy.) a restrainer, obstructer, (as if fr. rt. 3. *dā*.)

2. *ni-dāna, am*, n. (for 1. *nidāna* see col. 2), a band, a rope, a halter; a rope for tying up a calf &c.; a first or original cause, a primary or remote cause [cf. *ni-bandhana*]; original form, essence, (*nidānena*, ind. originally, essentially, properly); the cause of a disease, inquiry into the causes of disease, pathology, i. e. study of the symptoms with a view to trace the remote or proximate causes, (regarded as a department of medical science; the sixteen Nidānas being the title of the sixteen divisions into which it is divided; cf. *nidāna-sthāna*); N. of a work on metres and Vedic Stomas (see *nidāna-sūtra*); end, termination, cessation; purification, purity, correctness; claiming the reward of penitential acts. — *Nidāna-vat, ān, atī, at*, Ved. founded on a cause, essential. — *Nidāna-sūtra, am*, n. a work in ten Prapāṭhakas on metres and Vedic Stomas. — *Nidāna-sthāna, am*, n. one of the five departments of medical science, inquiry into the causes of diseases, pathology.

Ni-dita, as, ā, am, Ved. preserved, concealed; (Sāy.) completely bound or fettered (= *nitarām baddha*).

निदाघ **ni-dāgha**. See *ni-dah*, col. 2.

निदिग्ध **ni-digdha**, *as, ā, am* (fr. rt. *dih* with *ni*), smeared, anointed, plastered; clinging to; (*ā*), f. small cardamoms.

Nidigdhikā, f. = *kaṇṭa-kārikā*, a species of prickly nightshade, Solanum Jacquini [cf. *nir-digdhikā, nir-dagdhikā*]; cardamoms.

निदिध्यासन **ni-didhyāsana**, *am*, n. (fr. the Desid. of rt. *dhyai*), profound and repeated meditation.

Ni-didhyāsu, us, us, u, desiring to meditate upon.
Ni-didhyeya, as, ā, am, to be deeply meditated upon.

निदिश् **ni-diś**, cl. 6. P. *-diśati, -deshṭum*, to order, point out, &c.; (perhaps for *nir-diś* and apparently only used in the derivatives below.)

Ni-dishṭa, as, ā, am, ordered, directed; advised, enjoined; explained, pointed out.

Ni-deśa, as, m. order, command, direction, instruction; speech, speaking, narration, conversation; vicinity, proximity, neighbourhood; = *bhājana*, a vessel, vase; (*e*), ind. in the vicinity, near. — *Nideśa-kārin, ī, iṇī, i*, executing orders, obedient, servile.

Ni-deśin, ī, inī, i, showing, directing, ordering, pointing out; (*inī*), f. a region, quarter, point of the compass.

Ni-deśya, as, ā, am, to be ordered, to be told.

Ni-deshṭṛi, ṭā, ṭrī, ṭṛi, who or what points out or orders; explaining, advising, commanding.

निदी **ni-dī**, cl. 3. P. (see rt. 2. *dī*), Ved. to shine down upon; (Sāy. = *nitarām pra-kāś*, to shine exceedingly.)

निदुश **niduśa**, *as*, m. a fish.

निदृश् **ni-dṛiś**, Caus. *-darśayati, -yitum*, to cause to see, to show, point, to point out; to introduce, cause to enter; to impart knowledge, communicate, teach; advise; to appear (in a vision) to any person (acc.).

Ni-darśaka, as, ā, am, seeing into, perceiving; seeing; pointing out, proclaiming, announcing.

Ni-darśana, as, ī, am, pointing to, showing, foreshowing, prognosticating, indicating; proclaiming, announcing, teaching; suiting, pleasing?; (*ā*), f. a simile, a comparison; (*am*), n. seeing, looking into, view, insight, sight, vision (e. g. *svapna-nidarśana*, a vision in sleep); pointing to; showing; evidence; an example or illustration; a designation of the third member of a complete syllogism (usually called *ud-āharaṇa,* q. v.); a foreboding, prognostic, sign, mark, omen; a scheme, system; injunction, precept, ordinance, scriptural authority; authority, text.

Ni-darśita, as, ā, am, illustrated, exemplified.

Ni-darśin, ī, inī, i, seeing, viewing, having an insight into, familiar with, knowing.

निदेश *ni-deśa.* See *ni-diś,* p. 486, col. 3.

निद्रा 1. *ni-drā* or *ni-drai,* cl. 1. 2. P. A. *-drāyati, -te, -drāti,* &c., to fall asleep, sleep.

2. *ni-drā,* f. (said to be fr. rt. *nind* + affix *ra*), sleep, slumber, sleepiness, sloth; (in flowers the budding state is considered as sleep, hence *nidrām tyaj* = to bloom); a mystical N. of the letter *bh.* — *Nidrā-daridra, as,* m., N. of a poet. — *Nidrāndha* (°*rā-an*°), *as, ā, am,* blind with sleep. — *Nidrā-bhanga, as,* m. rousing from sleep, awaking; [cf. *bhagna-nidra.*] — *Nidrā-maya, as, ī, am,* consisting in sleep. — *Nidrā-yoga, as,* m. sleep and deep meditation; [cf. *yoga-nidrā.*] — *Nidrālasa* (°*rā-al*°), *as, ā, am,* slothful from drowsiness, fast asleep, sleepy. — *Nidrā-vṛiksha, as,* m. darkness. — *Nidrā-sañjanana, am,* n. 'producing drowsiness,' phlegm, the phlegmatic humor.

Ni-drāṇa, as, ā, am, sleeping, asleep, sleepy, drowsy; shut up, closed (as a bud or blossom).

Ni-drāt, ān, ātī or *āntī, āt,* sleeping.

Ni-drāyamāṇa, as, ā, am, sleeping, asleep.

Ni-drālu, us, us, u, sleeping, sleepy, drowsy, slothful; (*us*), m. an epithet of Vishṇu; (*us*), f. the plant Solanum Melongena; another plant (= *vana-varvarikā*); a kind of perfume (= *nalī*). — *Nidrālu-tva, am,* n. sleepiness, drowsiness.

Nidrita, as, ā, am, sleeping, asleep. — *Nidrita-vat, ān, atī, at,* having slept.

निधन *ni-dhana, am,* n. (in some senses apparently fr. 1. *ni-dhā* below, but in others more probably fr. *dhan* = rt. *han,* to kill, with *ni;* cf. *pra-dhana*), settling down in a residence, residence, place of residence, domicile, resting-place, receptacle (Ved.); race, family; conclusion, end; dying, death, destruction, loss, disappearance, annihilation, (in these senses also rarely *ni-dhanas,* m., see Hari-vaṇśa 4846); the concluding passage or words at the end of a Sāman which is sung in chorus, (several words are used for this purpose, e. g. *svar-jyotiḥ, vashaṭ, vratam, īm, nām,* &c.); the finale in music; (*am*), n., N. of the eighth mansion; (*as*), m. the head of a family; (*as, ā, am*), without money, poor, (in this sense for *nir-dhana*); [cf. rt. *han;* Gr. θάν-α-το-ς; Hib. *nidh, nith,* 'manslaughter, battle.'] — *Nidhana-kāma, am,* n., Ved., N. of several Sāmans. — *Nidhana-kārin, ī, iṇī, i,* causing death, destroying, destructive. — *Nidhana-kriyā,* f. a funeral ceremony. — *Nidhana-tā,* f. poverty, indigence. — *Nidhana-pati, is,* m., Ved. lord of the end or of destruction. — *Nidhana-bhūta, as, ā, am,* Ved. become final or like a finale in music. — *Nidhana-vat, ān, atī, at,* Ved. having a finale in music.

निधा 1. *ni-dhā,* cl. 3. P. A. *-dadhāti, -dhatte, -dhātum,* to put down, lay down, put or lay into, fix in, deposit, lodge, bury; (with *manas*) to fix or direct the thoughts upon or towards (dat.); resolve, determine; (with *kriyām*) to direct one's labours, use efforts; to appoint; to lay aside, put away, remove, relinquish; lay up, treasure up, put into a safe place; to preserve for one's self (A.); to deliver, intrust, commit, present; (with *hṛidaye* or *manasi*) to keep in mind, bear in mind, remember, lay to heart, keep close; to keep down, keep back, restrain; to end, close; to place in any state, render: Pass. *-dhīyate,* to be placed on or in, to be deposited, be situated in or on, be absorbed into, to rest in: Caus. *-dhāpayati,* &c., to cause to be put or laid on or into, to cause to be deposited or preserved; to appoint: Intens. (?), Ved. 3rd sing. *-dedhyat.*

2. *ni-dhā,* f., Ved. laying snares; a net; a collection of snares, a snare. — *Nidhā-pati, is,* m. the possessor or bearer of snares.

Ni-dhātavya, as, ā, am, to be put down or deposited; to be delivered; to be directed towards; to be concealed.

Ni-dhātṛi, tā, trī, tṛi, Ved. a depositor, one who deposits, keeps, conceals, &c.

Ni-dhāna, am, n. putting down, laying down, depositing, (*daṇḍa-nidhāna,* putting down or laying aside the stick, i. e. not using force, = mildness, clemency); keeping, preserving; a place where anything is laid, a vessel in which anything is deposited, a receptacle; a place of cessation or rest; anything laid up, a treasure, a divine treasure (especially belonging to Kuvera, god of wealth); store, hoard, property, possessions, wealth. — *Nidhāneśa* (°*na-īśa*), *as,* m. 'lord of treasure,' a Yaksha.

Ni-dhānya, as, ā, am, Ved. fit for being laid or put down.

Ni-dhāpaka, as, m. one who causes to be put down or deposited; a weapon (?); burnt timber (?), charcoal (?); the castor-oil plant (?).

Ni-dhāpya, ind. having caused to be placed or fixed in, having installed or appointed.

Ni-dhāya, ind. having fixed or placed in or on, (*manasi nidhāya,* fixing or laying up in the mind, reflecting.)

Ni-dhi, is, m. setting down or serving up food &c. (Ved.); the lower part or bottom of the Ukhā (Ved.); a place where anything is laid or deposited, a receptacle, (*apāṃ nidhiḥ,* the receptacle of waters, the ocean, sea; also N. of a Sāman; sometimes *nidhi* alone stands for 'the ocean'); a place for storing up, a storehouse, treasury, granary, a nest, &c.; (figuratively) a treasure-house of good qualities, a man endowed with many good qualities; a treasure, store, hoard, any collection of wealth or valuables; a divine treasure belonging to Kuvera, (nine of which are enumerated, viz. the Padma, Mahā-padma, Śaṅkha, Makara, Kaććhapa, Mukunda, Nanda, Nīla, and Kharba; their nature is not exactly defined, though some of them appear to be precious gems; according to the Tāntrika system they are personified and worshipped as demi-gods, attendant either upon Kuvera who is sometimes called *Nidhīnam adhipaḥ,* 'lord of the Nidhis,' or upon Lakshmī, the goddess of prosperity); N. of a particular medicinal plant, commonly Jīvikā; a kind of perfume (= *nalikā*); *daivo nidhiḥ,* 'the divine treasure,' N. of a particular philosophical doctrine. — *Nidhi-gopa, as,* m. guardian of treasure. — *Nidhi-nātha, as,* m. or *nidhi-prabhu, us,* m. or *nidhīśvara* (°*dhi-īś*°), *as,* m. 'lord of treasures,' an epithet of Kuvera. — *Nidhi-pa, as,* m. guardian of treasure; [cf. *nidhi-pā.*] — *Nidhi-pati, is,* m. 'lord of treasures,' an epithet of Kuvera; N. of a rich merchant. — *Nidhipati-datta, as,* m., N. of a merchant. — *Nidhi-pā, ās,* Ved., or *nidhi-pāla, as,* m. guardian of treasure. — *Nidhi-pālita, as,* m., N. of a merchant. — *Nidhi-mat, ān, atī, at,* Ved. possessing treasure, forming a store. — *Nidhīśa* or *nidhīśvara* (°*dhi-īś*°), *as,* m. 'lord of treasures,' an epithet of Kuvera. — *Nidhy-arthin, ī, inī, i,* treasure seeking.

Ni-dhīyamāna, as, ā, am, being laid down or deposited, &c.

Ni-dheya, as, ā, am, to be placed in or on, to be deposited.

Ni-hita, as, ā, am, put down, deposited, &c. See s. v.

निधि *ni-dhi.* See above.

निधू *ni-dhū,* cl. 5. 6. P. A. *-dhūnoti, -dhūnute* (in the later language also *-dhunoti, -dhunute*), *-dhuvati, -dhotum, -dhavitum,* to throw down, give or deliver over (Ved.); shake to and fro, agitate.

Ni-dhuvana, am, n. shaking about, agitation, trembling; coition, sexual intercourse; pleasure, enjoyment; sport, play, pastime.

निधृ *ni-dhṛi,* cl. 10. P. *-dhārayati, -yitum* (Ved. *-dīdhar*), to place down or in, deposit in; determine; establish; render (Ved.); to keep, preserve; (Sāy.) to establish firmly; to conceive in the womb: Pass. *-dhāryate* (Ved. *-dadhre*), to be placed in or deposited; to bend down, to stoop (Ved.).

Ni-dhāraya, as, ā, am, Ved. placing in or on, depositing.

Ni-dhārayat, an, antī, at, (Sāy.) abiding in.

Ni-dhṛiti, is, m., N. of a prince, a son of Vṛishṇi; [cf. *nir-vṛiti, ni-vṛitti.*]

निध्यै *ni-dhyai,* cl. 1. P. *-dhyāyati, -dhyātum,* to observe, perceive (Ved.); to meditate on, be absorbed in meditation; to think of, reflect on; remember: Desid. *-didhyāsati, -te,* to wish to meditate on; think of attentively (Ved.).

Ni-didhyāsana, am, n. profound meditation, deep and repeated consideration, thinking of or recalling repeatedly.

Ni-didhyāsitavya, as, ā, am, to be reflected or meditated upon.

Ni-didhyāsu, us, us, u, desirous of meditating on.

Ni-dhyāta, as, ā, am, meditated on, thought on, imagined.

Ni-dhyāna, am, n. intuition, looking at, seeing, beholding, sight.

निध्रुव *ni-dhruva, as,* m., N. of a man; (*ās*), m. pl. his descendants; [cf. *naidhruva, naidhruvi.*]

निध्रुवि *ni-dhruvi, is, is, i,* Ved. constant, persevering, faithful; (*is*), m., N. of a Kāśyapa and author of a Ṛig-veda hymn (IX. 63).

निध्वान *ni-dhvāna, as,* m. (fr. rt. 2. *dhvan* with *ni*), sound.

निनङ्क्षु *ninankshu, us, us, u* (fr. Desid. of rt. 2. *naś*), wishing or expecting to perish or die.

निनद् *ni-nad,* cl. 1. P. *-nadati,* &c., to sound, make a sound, cry out; to resound: Caus. P. *-nādayati, -yitum,* to cause to sound or resound, fill with noise, cries, &c.

Ni-nada or *ni-nāda, as,* m. sound, noise, cry, buzzing, humming, crying.

Ni-nādita, as, ā, am, made to sound, filled with noise or cries; (*am*), n. a sound.

Ni-nādin, ī, inī, i, sounding, resounding, ringing, crying; causing to sound, playing (as a musical instrument).

निनयन *ni-nayana.* See *ni-nī* below.

निनर्तशत्रु *ninarta-śatru, us,* m., N. of a son of An-ādhṛishṭi.

निनर्द् *ni-nard,* cl. 1. P. *-nardati, -narditum,* to sound; prolong a note in chanting; [cf. *ava-nard.*]

Ni-narda, as, m. prolonging a note in chanting, trilling.

Ni-nardat, an, antī, at, sounding; prolonging a cadence.

निनह् *ni-nah,* cl. 4. P. A. *-nahyati, -te, -naddhum,* Ved. to fasten, tie; [cf. *nīnāha.*]

Ni-naddha, as, ā, am, fastened, tied fast.

Ni-nāhya, as, m., Ved. a water-jar; (according to the commentaries) a water-jar put into the ground.

निनित्सु *ninitsu, us, us, u* (fr. Desid. of rt. *nid*), Ved. wishing to censure or blame.

निनी *ni-nī,* cl. 1. P. A. *-nayati, -te, -netum,* to lead to, carry or bring towards, bring near, bring, fetch; to incline, bend; to pour on or into (Ved.); to carry out, perform, accomplish, cause; to spend (time).

Ni-nayana, am, n. carrying out, performing, accomplishing; performance; pouring down.

निनीषा *ninīshā,* f. (fr. Desid. of rt. 1. *nī*), wishing to bring, desire or intention of carrying or taking or leading away.

Ninīshu, us, us, u, desirous to take or lead, wishing to bring; wishing to spend (as time).

निनृत्त *ni-nṛitta, as, ā, am*, repeated (as a portion of a verse or syllable; lit. danced again). — *Ninṛitta-vat, ān, atī, at*, having repetition (as above).

Ni-nṛitti, is, f. repetition.

निन्द् *nind* (sometimes written *nid*, q.v.), cl. 1. P. *nindati* (rarely A. *-te*), *ninindа, nindishyati, anindīt, ninditum*, to blame, censure, reprimand, contemn, despise, ridicule.

Ninda in *ninda-tala, as, ī, am*, = *nindita-hasta*, having a maimed or defective hand; (sometimes read *nimna-tala*.)

Nindaka, as, ā, am, blaming, defaming, reproachful, abusive, scurrilous, censorious; one who ridicules or blames, a scorner.

Nindat, an, antī, at, blaming, censuring, abusing, ridiculing.

Nindana, am, n. reproach, censure, blame.

Nindanīya, as, ā, am, blamable, liable to reproof or censure or blame, reprehensible; [cf. *a-n°*.]

Nindā, f. blame, censure, reproach, reproof, abuse, defamation, scorn, reviling; injury, injuring, wickedness; [cf. *nidā*.] — *Nindā-stuti, is*, f. praise which involves reproof, ironical praise, irony.

Nindita, as, ā, am, blamed, abused, reviled, reproved, despised, rejected; low, despicable, worthy of being reviled; prohibited, forbidden.

Ninditṛi, tā, trī, tṛi, Ved. one who ridicules or blames or despises.

Nindin, ī, inī, i, blaming, censuring, reproaching.

Nindu, us, f. a woman bearing a dead child.

Nindya, as, ā, am, blamable, to be censured or reproached, despicable, reprehensible, bad, vile; forbidden, prohibited; [cf. *a-n*.] — *Nindya-tā*, f. or *nindya-tva, am*, n. blamableness, infamy, contemptibleness.

निन्व् *ninv* (or according to some *sinv*), cl. 1. P. *ninvati*, &c., to wet or sprinkle; or to attend, wait on, worship? (the two meanings have probably arisen from a confusion between *sećane* and *sevane*.)

निप *ni-pa*. See under 2. *ni-pā*, col. 2.

निपक्षति *ni-pakshati, is*, f., Ved. the second rib.

निपठ *ni-paṭha, as*, m. or *nipaṭhana, am*, n. (fr. rt. *paṭh* with *ni*), reading, recitation, studying.

Ni-paṭhita, as, ā, am, read, recited, studied, (hence *nipaṭhitin*, Pāṇ. V. 2, 88.)

Ni-paṭhiti, is, f. reading, recitation, study.

Ni-pāṭha, as, m. = *ni-paṭha*, reading, study of the sacred books or public perusal of popular poems.

निपत् *ni-pat*, cl. 1. P. *-patati, -patitum*, to fly down, fall down, tumble down, settle down, fall, descend, alight, throw one's self down; to fall upon, throw one's self upon, assault, assail, fall into, rush into, rush in, flow in, disembogue into, discharge into; fall into ruin; to fall into (any state or condition); to fall into (a place), enter, insert one's self, become fixed in; to befall, happen, take place; to fall to the share of (with loc.): Caus. *-pātayati, -apīpatat, -yitum*, to cause to fall down, throw down, fell, cast down, cause to fall on (e. g. to cause a stick to fall on any one = strike with a stick); to hurl down; to cast, throw, hurl, throw into; to let in, inlay, emboss; to direct (the eyes &c.) upon; to spit on, spit out; to ruin, kill, destroy (with abl.); to raise or levy a tribute from (with *karān* and abl. c., in Mahā-bh. Śānti-p. 3313); (in grammar) to put down as a special or irregular form, to give as an irregularity, consider as anomalous or irregular; (*nipātyate* is put down or mentioned as a special rule or irregular form.)

Ni-patat, an, antī, at, flying down, falling down, falling, descending, alighting, prostrating one's self, &c.

Ni-patana, am, n. flying down, falling down, falling, descending; alighting, flying.

Ni-patita, as, ā, am, fallen down, fallen; descended, alighted.

Ni-patya, ind. having fallen down, having prostrated one's self, having descended or alighted. — *Ni-patya-rohiṇī*, f. falling and ascending (?).

Ni-patyā, f. any slippery ground; a field of battle.

Ni-pāta, as, m. falling down, falling, descending, coming down, alighting; falling upon, attacking; casting, hurling; death, dying; accidental occurrence or mention; putting down as irregular or exceptional, irregular form, irregularity (e. g. *pūrva-nipāta*, irregular occurrence of a word at the beginning instead of at the end of a compound; *para-nipāta*, irregular placing of a word at the end instead of beginning); the opposite extremity, the lower end; (in grammar) a particle, the term for all adverbs including conjunctions and interjections, (called *nipāta* as falling into the sentence in various senses, i. e. taking their place after other words to modify the sense in various ways.) — *Nipāta-tva, am*, n. the state of being a particle. — *Nipāta-pratīkāra, as*, m. the repelling of assaults.

Ni-pātaka, as, am, m. n. = *pātaka*, a bad deed, a sin.

Ni-pātana, as, ā, am, throwing down, overthrowing, killing, destroying; (*am*), n. causing to descend or fall, throwing down, overthrowing; beating, knocking down; putting on; touching with; killing, destroying; (in grammar) putting down as an irregularity, accidental mention or use of a word; a form which by its rare occurrence shows itself to be irregular; irregularity, exception; falling down, hurrying down, flying down.

Ni-pātanīya, as, ā, am, to be cast down or overthrown, caused to fall (e. g. *daṇḍo nipātanīyas*, the stick must be caused to fall, punishment must be inflicted).

Ni-pātita, as, ā, am, made to fall or descend; beaten down; killed; irregular, excepted.

Ni-pātin, ī, inī, i, falling down, flying down or on, alighting; striking down, destroying, a destroyer.

Ni-pātya, as, ā, am, to be cast down or overthrown; to be put down or mentioned as an irregularity.

Ni-pātyamāna, as, ā, am, being thrown down, being precipitated.

निपलाशम् *ni-palāśam*, ind., Ved. (Sāy.) without speaking, i. e. like a tree without foliage (or as a leafless tree moves without rustling).

निपा 1. *ni-pā*, cl. 2. P. *-pāti, -pātum*, &c., to guard, protect, defend; observe, watch over: Caus. *-pālayati, -yitum*, to protect, guard, govern.

निपा 2. *ni-pā*, cl. 1. and 2. P. *-pibati* or *-pivati, -pātum*, to drink in, imbibe, suck in; to absorb, dry up: Caus. P. *-pāyayati, -yitum*, to cause to imbibe or suck in.

Ni-pa, as, am, m. n. a water-jar; (*as*), m. the Kadamba tree, Nauclea Cadamba (= *kadamba*).

Ni-pāna or *nipānaka, am*, n. drinking, imbibing; any reservoir of water, any place or trough near a well for watering cattle; a well, pool; a milk-pail. — *Nipāna-vat, ān, atī, at*, having reservoirs or ponds, abounding in pools, &c.

Ni-pīta, as, ā, am, drunk in, drunk up, absorbed, imbibed, dried up.

Ni-pīti, is, f. drinking.

Ni-pīyamāna, as, ā, am, being drunk in or imbibed.

निपाक *ni-pāka, as*, m. (fr. rt. *pać* with *ni*), cooking, maturing, ripening.

निपाठ *ni-pāṭha*. See *ni-paṭha*, col. 1.

निपात *ni-pāta*. See above.

निपाद *ni-pāda, as*, m., Ved. low ground, a valley; (Sāy.) high and low ground.

निपिष् *ni-pish*, cl. 7. P., Ved. *-pinashṭi, -peshṭum*, to crush.

निपीड् *ni-pīḍ*, cl. 10. P. *-pīḍayati, -yitum*, to press close to or against, press together, squeeze; to embrace; to impress; to cause pain, afflict, plague, trouble; (in astronomy) to eclipse.

Ni-pīḍana, am, n. squeezing, pressing; hurting, giving pain; (*ā*), f. oppression.

Ni-pīḍayat, an, antī, at, pressing, pressing together; (*dantān dantair nipīḍayan*, gnashing the teeth.)

Ni-pīḍita, as, ā, am, squeezed, pressed, embraced; pained, hurt. — *Nipīḍitālaktaka-vat* (°*ta-al*°), ind. like pressed lac.

Ni-pīḍya, ind. having pressed; having pressed against or upon; having embraced; having hurt.

निपीय् *ni-pīy*, cl. 1. P., Ved. *-pīyati, -yitum*, to revile, abuse, treat with contempt.

निपु *nipu, us*, m., N. of a man.

निपुण *ni-puṇa, as, ā, am* (said to be fr. rt. *puṇ* with *ni*; perhaps fr. rt. *push* + affix *na*, through which dialectically *puṇṇa* = *puṇa*), clever, adroit, skilful, skilled in, conversant with (loc. and gen.); experienced; kind or friendly towards (with loc. or with *prati*); sharp, acute, fine, delicate; complete, perfect, accurate; (*am* or *ena*), ind. skilfully, cleverly, sharply; completely, perfectly, totally, exactly, carefully; in a delicate manner. — *Nipuṇa-tara, as, ā, am*, more clever, perfect, &c.; (*am*), ind. cleverly; perfectly. — *Nipuṇa-tas*, ind. cleverly, skilfully; completely. — *Nipuṇa-tā*, f. skilfulness, cleverness, conversancy, adroitness, versatility; carefulness, accuracy. — *Nipuṇa-dṛiś, k, k, k*, sharp-sighted, clever, knowing.

Nipuṇikā, f. 'the clever one,' N. of a waiting-maid in the Vikramorvaśī.

निपुथ् *ni-puth*, Caus. *-pothayati, -yitum*, to dash down.

निपुर् *ni-pur, ūr*, f., Ved. (according to Mahī-dhara) = *sūkshma-deha*, the subtle body.

निपूत *ni-pūta, as, ā, am*, Ved. strained, filtered, purified.

निप्रहन् *ni-pra-han*, cl. 2. P. *-hanti, -hantum*, to kill (with gen. of the object).

निप्रियाय *nipriyāya* (fr. *ni-priya*), Nom. A. *nipriyāyate*, &c., Ved. to keep in one's possession, not to be willing to give up.

निफला *ni-phalā*, f. the plant Cardiospermum Halicacabum (= *jyotishmatī*).

निफालन *ni-phālana, am*, n. (probably incorrect for *ni-bhālana*), seeing, sight.

निफेन *ni-phena, am*, n. = *a-phena*, opium.

निबद्ध *ni-baddha*. See under *ni-bandh*.

निबन्ध् *ni-bandh*, cl. 9. P. *-badhnāti, -banddhum*, to bind on, bind, tie, fasten, tie together; to fetter, enchain, imprison, ensnare; to attach, to join, unite, connect; compose (in writing), record, write; to construct; to draw together, contract (e. g. *bhru-kuṭīm*, the brow); to fix, hold fast, confine, restrain, obstruct, stop, close up, restrict; to fix on, place or put upon, impose; to put together, form, acquire; (with *padam*) to put the foot upon, i. e. to undertake anything; to fix or direct upon; to appoint, commission, charge; to place, locate; to destroy, (Mahā-bh. Virāṭa-p. 982; cf. rt. *vadh*.)

Ni-baddha, as, ā, am, bound in or on, bound; fastened, tied, connected, bound or sewed together, fastened to; caught (as in a net), fettered, enchained, chained to, dependant on; connected, coherent; shut up, closed, stopped, obstructed; confined, costive; checked, restrained, restricted to; bound over or called as a witness (Manu VIII. 76); composed, written; fixed in, inlaid (as with gold or jewels), enchased, set, inserted; committed, intrusted; enveloped, enclosed, involved, covered with; constructed of, formed of, consisting of; accompanied by, furnished or endowed with; relating to, contained or involved in.

Ni-banddhṛi, dhā, dhrī, dhṛi, who or what ties or binds, a binder, fastener; (*dhā*), m. a composer, writer, author; a commentator; (also written *ni-bandhṛi.*)

Ni-bandha, as, m. binding on, binding, fastening, tying, attachment, attachment to, intentness on; composing, writing down, recording; restraint, obstruction, confinement, constipation, suppression of urine, strangury; a band, bond, fetter; fixed property, not movable or fluctuating; a grant of property, an assignment of cattle or money for support; foundation, origin, root, cause, reason; any literary composition or treatise; a commentary or explanation of technical rules [cf. *grantha*]; N. of a particular work; the plant Azadirachta Indica; (*am*), n. song, singing. —*Nibandha-dāna, am*, n. grant of property, assignment or gift of a corrody. —*Nibandha-saṅgraha, as*, m., N. of a commentary on Su-śruta's medical work.

Ni-bandhana, as, ī, am, binding, fastening, fettering; (*ī*), f. band, bond, fetter; (*am*), n. the act of fastening to, binding together, ligation; constructing, building (as a bridge &c.); checking, restraining, confining; band, fetter; that to which anything is fastened or on which it rests; a receptacle; the part of a lute where the strings are fastened, the tie or peg of a lute; cause, origin, reason, motive, condition; (in grammar) syntax; a composition; a commentary; a grant, an assignment.

Ni-bandhika. See *aśva-n°*.

Ni-bandhita, as, ā, am, bound, fastened, confined, tied.

Ni-bandhin, ī, inī, i, binding, confining; joined or connected by or with, hanging together, cohering; causing, being a cause or having a reason.

निबर्हण *ni-barhaṇa*. See *ni-bṛih* below.

निबल *nibala, as* or *am*, m. or n. (?), a particular number.

निबाध् *ni-bādh*, cl. 1. A. *-bādhate, -bādhitum*, Ved. to press down or together, force in; to cramp, contract, confine, obstruct; to oppress.

Ni-bādha, as, m. obstruction, in *a-n°*, q. v.

निबाळ्ह *ni-bāḷha, as, ā, am* (according to some fr. rt. *baṇh*, according to Sāy. fr. rt. *bāh* = *vāh*, to endeavour), Ved. forced down, thrown into.

निबुध् *ni-budh*, cl. 1. P. A. *-bodhati, -te, -bodhitum*, to learn or hear anything (acc.) from any one (gen. or with *sakāśāt*); to attend to, listen to, (often occurring in the impv. *ni-bodha*); to know, consider: Caus. *-bodhayati*, &c., to cause to know or learn, to inform, give to understand.

Ni-boddhavya, as, ā, am, to be learnt; to be considered or regarded.

निबृह् *ni-bṛih* (also written *ni-vṛih*, q. v.), cl. 1. P. *-barhati, -barhitum, -barhayati, -yitum*, Ved. to throw down, destroy, annihilate, extirpate, eradicate.

Ni-barhaṇa, as, ā, am, destroying, &c.; (*am*), n. destruction, annihilation, &c. See *ni-varhaṇa*.

निभ *ni-bha, as, ā, am* (fr. rt. 1. *bhā* with *ni*), like, resembling, similar, (only at the end of a comp.; sometimes pleonastically after adjectives, e. g. *ćāru-nibhānana*, handsome-faced; and occasionally with another word meaning 'like,' e.g. *naga-nibhopama*, like a mountain); (*as, am*), m. n. appearance, light, manifestation; pretence, pretext, fraud, sham, trick, disguise. —*Nibha-tā*, f. similarity, likeness.

निभञ्ज् *ni-bhañj*, cl. 7. P. *-bhanakti, -bhanktum*, to break or dash to pieces, break asunder.

निभर्त्सन *ni-bhartsana*, wrong reading for *nir-bhartsana*.

निभल् *ni-bhal*, cl. 10. P. A. *-bhālayati, -te, -yitum*, to perceive, see.

Ni-bhālana, am, n. seeing, sight, perception; [cf. *ni-phālana*.]

निभसद् *ni-bhasad* (?), having the hinder parts directed downwards (?). See *bhasad*.

निभिद् *ni-bhid*, cl. 7. P. A. *-bhinatti, -bhintte, -bhettum*, to break or divide asunder: Pass. *-bhidyate*, to be opened, to open.

निभीम *ni-bhīma, as, ā, am*, terrible, frightful. —*Nibhīma-vikrama, as, ā, am*, of terrible valour, of formidable prowess.

निभूत *ni-bhūta, as, ā, am*, past, gone.

निभूयप *nibhūyapa, as*, m., Ved. epithet of Vishṇu, (meaning unknown.)

निभृ *ni-bhṛi*, cl. 1. P. *-bharati, -bhartum*, &c., to bear or put down, (apparently only used in the part. *ni-bhṛita* below.)

Ni-bhṛita, as, ā, am, borne or placed down, deposited in a low place, lowered; concealed, hidden, secret, occult, unperceived, imperceptible; modest, humble, unassuming; mild, gentle; lonely, solitary; still, silent; firm, unmoved, immovable; resolute, decided, firmly attached, faithful; filled with, full of, (Bhāgavata-Purāṇa X. 32, 20, = *pūrṇa, vyāpta*); (*am*), n. humility, modesty, meekness [cf. *naibhṛitya*]; (*am*), ind. covertly, secretly, privately, apart, unobservedly, imperceptibly, in a corner, out of sight. —*Nibhṛitāgata* (°*ta-āg*°), *as, ā, am*, secretly arrived. —*Nibhṛitātman* (°*ta-āt*°), *ā, ā, a*, resolute-minded, resolute. —*Nibhṛitārtha* (°*ta-ar*°), *as, ā, am*, having a secret meaning, occult.

निभ्रंश् *ni-bhraṇś*, Caus. *-bhrāśayati, -yitum*, Ved. to cause to fall off, to strike or break off.

निम *nima, as*, m. a pin, stake (?).

निमज्ज् *ni-majj*, cl. 6. P. *-majjati, -manktum*, to sink into, sink down, dive, plunge into, immerse one's self, bathe, be immersed or submerged (e. g. *akshi nimajjati*, the eye sinks; *ćiram nimamajja*, be remained long under the water); to be drowned; to penetrate into; to disappear, perish; to immerse or submerge in water, cause to sink (e.g. into hell, Mahā-bh. Ādi-p. 4156): Caus. P. *-majjayati, -yitum*, to cause to dive, immerse, dip, plunge (anything) into water, submerge, drown; (figuratively) to cause to plunge or penetrate into a battle, lead into the thick of a fight.

Ni-magna, as, ā, am, plunged or immersed in, dipped into, fallen into (water &c.), submerged, sunk; gone down, set (as the sun); forcibly entered into or penetrated; (with *para-lokāya*) entered into the other world; sunk in, depressed, not prominent; overwhelmed, covered. —*Nimagna-nābhi, is, is, i*, having a depressed navel. —*Nimagna-madhyā*, f. a woman having a depressed (and therefore slender) waist.

Ni-magnaka, as, ā, am, hiding one's self, lurking.

Ni-majjat, an, atī or *antī, at*, bathing, diving, plunging in, sinking.

Ni-majjathu, us, m. the act of diving or entering into, plunging; (with *talpe*) going to bed, sleeping.

Ni-majjana, as, ī, am, causing to enter or plunge into (with gen.), immersing, absorbing; (*am*), n. bathing, diving, immersion, sinking.

Ni-majjamāna, as, ā, am, sinking, plunging into; immersed; being drowned.

Ni-majjita, as, ā, am, plunged into the water, drowned.

निमद् *ni-mad*, Caus. P. *-mādayati, -yitum*, to pronounce distinctly but slowly.

Ni-mada, as, m. pronunciation which is distinct but slow, one of the seven degrees of pronunciation (*vāćaḥ sthānāni*).

निमन्त्र् *ni-mantr*, cl. 10. A. *-mantrayate, -yitum*, to invite, summon, call (to a feast), entertain.

Ni-mantraka, as, m. one who summons or invites, an inviter.

Ni-mantraṇa, am, n. inviting, invitation; summoning, calling; a summons. —*Nimantraṇa-pattra, am*, n. a written summons, a note of invitation.

Ni-mantrita, as, ā, am, invited, summoned, convoked; bidden to a feast, entertained.

Ni-mantrya, as, ā, am, to be invited, to be called.

निमन्यु *ni-manyu, us, us, u*, Ved. not angry, unresentful, appeased.

निमय *ni-maya*. See *ni-me*, p. 490, col. 2.

निमा *ni-mā* [cf. *ni-me*], cl. 2. 3. P. A. *-māti, -mimīte, -mātum*, to measure; to adjust.

1. *ni-mātavya, as, ā, am*, to be measured, &c.; [the *ni-mātavya* which occurs in Manu X. 94. is to be referred to *ni-me*, q. v.]

Ni-māna, am, n. measure. See *a-n°*.

1. *ni-mita, as, ā, am*, measured out. See *dur-n°*.

1. *ni-meya, as, ā, am* (for 2. see *ni-me*), to be measured, measurable, anything the measure or value of which can be fixed.

निमि 1. *nimi, is*, m., N. of several kings of Videha; of a son of Dattātreya; of a son of Ikshvāku, (this Nimi lost his body through the curse of Vaśishṭha, and when the gods were willing to restore it, requested that instead of receiving his former shape he might occupy the eyes of all living creatures; the request was granted, and in consequence of the presence of Nimi, men's eyelids are ever opening and shutting; cf. *ni-misha*, and see Vishṇu-Purāṇa IV. 5); N. of the twenty-first Jaina Arhat of the present Ava-sarpiṇī; of a son of Bhajamāna; of Daṇḍa-pāṇi; of a Dānava; closing or winking of the eyes, twinkling. —*Nimin-dhara, as*, m. (fr. *nimim* acc. sing. + *dhara*), N. of a prince.

निमि 2. *ni-mi*, cl. 5. P. A. *-minoti, -minute*, &c., to fix in, dig in; to fix, erect.

2. *ni-mita, as, ā, am*, fixed in, fixed, erected.

निमित्त *ni-mitta, am*, n. (probably connected with *ni-mā* above), a mark, an aim; an archer's butt, target; sign, token; prognostic, presage, omen [cf. *dur-n°*]; cause, motive, reason, instrumental or efficient cause, (opposed to *upā-dāna*, the material cause); *nimitta* is used at the end of a comp. in the sense 'having as a motive or cause,' 'caused or produced by,' 'occasioned by,' e. g. *visha-nimittā pīḍā*, pain caused by poison; (*am* acc., *ena* inst., *āya* dat., *āt* abl., *asya* gen., *e* loc.), because of, on account of, for the sake of, for the purpose of, through. —*Nimitta-kāraṇa, am*, n. an instrumental or efficient cause, (especially the Deity considered as the agent in creation.) —*Nimitta-kāraṇa-tā*, f. the state of being the efficient cause. —*Nimitta-kāla, as*, m. the period or moment of time which may be regarded as causing any event; any given or specific time. —*Nimitta-kṛit, t*, m. 'omen-maker,' a crow, raven. —*Nimitta-jña, as, ā, am*, acquainted with omens. —*Nimitta-jñāna, am*, n. 'knowledge of causes or signs,' N. of the fifty-eighth chapter of the Kāma-sūtra by Vātsyāyana. —*Nimitta-tas*, ind. by or from a special cause or reason. —*Nimitta-tā*, f. or *nimitta-tva, am*, n. the state of being a cause, causality, instrumentality. —*Nimitta-dharma, as*, m. expiation; any occasional or special penance, rite, or obligation. —*Nimitta-nidāna, am*, n., N. of a work. —*Nimitta-bhūta, as, ā, am*, become a cause or reason, being a cause or means. —*Nimitta-mātra, am*, n. the mere efficient cause or instrument. —*Nimitta-vid, t*, m. 'omen-knower,' an astrologer. — *Nimitta-vedhin, ī, inī, i*, hitting an aim, piercing the mark. —*Nimitta-hetu, us*, m. an efficient cause. —*Nimittahetu-tva, am*, n. the being an instrumental or efficient cause. — *Nimittārtha* (°*ta-ar*°), *as*, m. the infinitive mood (in grammar). — *Nimittāvṛitti* (°*ta-āv*°), *is*, f. dependance upon a special cause or occasion. — *Nimitti-kṛi*, cl. 8. P. A. *-karoti*, *-kurute*, *-kartum*, to make anything a cause, to use as a cause or means. — *Nimitti-bhū*, cl. 1. P. *-bhavati*, *-vitum*, to become a cause or reason for (with loc.).

Ni-mittaka, *as*, *ā*, *am* (at the end of an adj. comp.), caused or occasioned or produced by; (*am*), n. kissing, a kiss.

Nimittāyamāna, *as*, *ā*, *am* (fr. an unused Nominal verb *nimittāya*), causing, producing.

Nimittin, *ī*, *inī*, *i*, operated on or influenced by a cause, having a cause or reason.

निमिश्र *ni-miśra*, *as*, *ā*, *am*, Ved. devoted to, attached to (with loc.); (Sāy.) commixed, commingling, mixing with, being mixed. — *Nimiśla-tama*, *as*, *ā*, *am*, Ved. most attached to (with loc.).

निमिष् 1. *ni-mish*, cl. 6. P. *-mishati*, *-meshitum*, to shut the eyelids, wink, twinkle, blink.

2. *ni-mish*, *t*, f., Ved. winking or twinkling of the eye; shutting the eyes, falling asleep [cf. *nimi*]; *a-nimish*, *t*, *t*, *t*, never closing or winking the eyes; (*t*), m. a god; [cf. Nala V. 24.]

Ni-misha, *as*, m. twinkling, winking, shutting the eye; the twinkling of an eye considered as a measure of time, a moment; morbid twinkling of the eyes; N. of a son of Garuḍa (Mahā-bh. Udyoga-parva 3595); an epithet of Vishṇu, (also *a-nimisha*.) — *Nimishāntara* (°*sha-an*°), *am*, n. the interval of a moment; (*eṇa*), ind. in a twinkling, in the interval of a moment.

Ni-mishat, *an*, *atī* or *antī*, *at*, winking, blinking, closing the eyes.

Ni-mesha, *as*, *am*, m. n. twinkling of the eyes, (opposed to *un-mesha*); a momentary space of time, a moment, a twinkling of the eye considered as a measure of time; morbid twinkling of the eye, morbid closing of the eyelid; N. of a mythical being; *nimesham nimesham*, every moment. — *Nimesha-kṛit*, *t*, f. 'twinkler,' lightning. — *Nimeshatas*, ind., Ved. with regard to the shutting of the eyes, (according to Mahī-dhara gen. sing. of the pres. part.) — *Nimesha-dyut*, *t*, or *nimesha-ruć*, *k*, m. a fire-fly. — *Nimesha-mātra*, *am*, n. only a twinkling, merely an instant; (*eṇa*), ind. in a twinkling, in an instant of time, in barely a moment. — *Nimeshārdhāt* (°*sha-ar*°), ind. in half a twinkling of the eye, i. e. in less than an instant.

Ni-meshaka, *as*, m. twinkling of the eye; a fire-fly.

Ni-meshaṇa, *as*, *ī*, *am*, causing twinkling &c.

निमिह् *ni-mih*, cl. 1. P. *-mehati*, &c., to urine, sprinkle down urine.

निमील् *ni-mīl*, cl. 1. P. *-mīlati*, *-mīlitum*, to shut or close the eyes, fall asleep, sleep; to close (as flowers); to die, disappear: Caus. *-mīlayati*, *-yitum*, to cause (one) to shut the eyes, to close; to kill.

Ni-mīlat, *an*, *antī*, *at*, closing the eyes, winking the eyelids, twinkling.

Ni-mīlana, *am*, n. shutting the eyelids, winking or twinkling of the eyes, winking; closing the eyes in death; (figuratively) dying, death; (in astronomy) immersion, complete obscuration, a total eclipse.

Ni-mīlā, f. shutting the eyes.

Ni-mīlikā, f. shutting the eyes, winking, twinkling, blinking, conniving at anything; fraud, trick.

Ni-mīlita, *as*, *ā*, *am*, closed, shut (as the eye), winked, blinked; blinded, darkened, obscured; [cf. *rajo-nimīlita*.] — *Nimīlitāksha* (°*ta-ak*°), *as*, *ī*, *am*, having the eyes closed.

Ni-mīlin, *ī*, *inī*, *i*, closing the eyes, having the eyelids shut.

निमीव् *ni-mīv*, cl. 1. P. *-mīvati*, &c., to press on, press down.

निमीश्वर *nimīśvara*, *as*, m. (with Jainas) N. of the sixteenth Arhat of the present Ut-sarpiṇī.

निमूलम् *ni-mūlam*, ind. down to the root.

निमृज् *ni-mṛij*, cl. 2. P. *-mārshṭi* (cl. 6. Ved. *-mṛijati*, *-te*), *-mārjitum*, *-mārshṭum*, to rub in, rub upon, wipe, wipe off, wipe away, to cleanse one's self (A.); to lead to, attach to: Intens., Ved. *-māmṛije*, to wipe away, cleanse; to destroy: Desid., Ved. *-mimṛikshati*, (in Ṛig-veda I. 64, 4, Sāy. considers *ni-mimṛikshuḥ* as a Vedic reduplicated perf. = *ni-mṛishṭāḥ sthitā babhūvuḥ*; according to some the meaning is 'to flash down.')

Ni-mṛigra, *as*, *ā*, *am*, Ved. devoted, attached to; (Sāy.) excessively purifying or cleansing.

निमृण् *ni-mṛiṇ*, cl. 6. P. *-mṛiṇati*, &c., to dash down, strike down.

निमृद् *ni-mṛid*, cl. 9. P. *-mṛidnāti*, *-marditum*, to crush, dash to pieces; to rub off.

निमे *ni-me* [cf. *ni-mā*], cl. 1. A. *-mayate*, *-mātum*, to change, exchange for (with inst.), barter.

Ni-maya, *as*, m. barter, change, exchange.

2. *ni-mātavya*, *as*, *ā*, *am* (for 1. see *ni-mā*), to be exchanged or bartered.

2. *ni-meya*, *as*, *ā*, *am* (for 1. see *ni-mā*), to be exchanged; (*as*), m. barter, exchange; [cf. *naimeya*.]

निमेष *ni-mesha*. See under 1. *ni-mish*, col. 1.

निम्न *nimna*, *am*, n. (fr. *ni* or perhaps rather fr. rt. *nam* with *ni* or according to others fr. rt. *man* or rt. *mnā* with *ni*), depth, low ground, lowland; a slope, declivity; gap, chasm or cavity in the ground; a depression, deepening; (*as*, *ā*, *am*), deep, profound (literally or figuratively); low (as ground), depressed, sunk; (*as*), m., N. of a prince. — *Nimna-ga*, *as*, *ā*, *am*, going low or deep, going downwards, descending; (*ā*), f. a river, mountain-stream; [cf. *giri-n*°.] — *Nimna-gata*, *as*, *ā*, *am*, going in deep or low places; (*am*), n. a low place. — *Nimna-tala*, see under *ninda-tala*. — *Nimna-tā*, f. or *nimna-tva*, *am*, n. depth, lowness, profundity. — *Nimna-deśa*, *as*, m. or *nimna-bhāga*, *as*, m. a low or deep place. — *Nimnonnata* (°*na-un*°), *as*, *ā*, *am*, low and high, depressed and elevated, up and down.

Nimnais, ind., Ved. in deep places, low, downwards; [cf. *uććais*, *nīćais*.]

निम्ब *nimba* or *nimbaka*, *as*, m. (said to be fr. rt. *nī*), a tree with bitter fruits, Azadirachta Indica, the Nimb or Neemb tree, (the leaves of this tree are chewed at funeral ceremonies); [cf. *giri-n*°, *tṛiṇa-n*°.] — *Nimba-taru*, *us*, m. the tree Erythrina Fulgens or (according to others) Melia Sempervirens, (it is considered as one of the trees of paradise.) — *Nimba-rajas*, *as*, n. a particular high number; [cf. *mahā-n*°.] — *Nimba-vatī*, f., N. of a woman. — *Nimba-vīja*, *as*, m. a tree (= *rājādanī*). — *Nimbārka-karavīrārćana-vrata* (°*ba-ar*°, °*ra-ar*°), *am*, n., N. of a particular vow; N. of the seventy-seventh chapter of the Bhavishya-Purāṇa.

निम्बूक *nimbūka*, *as*, m. the common lime, Citrus Acida; (also read *nisbū*.)

निम्लुच् *ni-mluć* (Ved. *ni-mruć*), cl. 1. P. *-mloćati*, &c., to set, disappear (as the sun).

Ni-mrukti, Ved., or in later Sanskrit *ni-mlukti*, *is*, f. sunset, setting of the sun, disappearance.

Ni-mruć, *k*, f., Ved. sunset, setting of the sun, evening; (*k*, *k*, *k*), slack, loose.

Ni-mloća, *as*, m. setting of the sun, sunset.

Ni-mloćanī, f. (fr. an unused form *ni-mloćana*), N. of the city of Varuṇa situated on the mountain Mānasottara towards the west.

Ni-mloći, *is*, m., N. of a prince, son of Bhajamāna.

नियत *ni-yata*. See col. 3.

नियन्त्र् *ni-yantr*, cl. 10. P. *-yantrayati*, &c., to restrain, [apparently only used in the derivatives.]

Ni-yantraṇa, *am*, n. the act of restraining, restraint, checking; governing, guiding; defining, definition.

Ni-yantrita, *as*, *ā*, *am*, restrained, curbed, checked; governed, guided.

नियम् *ni-yam*, cl. 1. P. *-yaććhati*, *-yantum*, to check, curb, restrain, hold back, suppress, stop; to hold in (as the breath &c.); govern, control, rule, direct, regulate; to punish; to restrict; to bind, confine, fasten; to conceal; to attain, obtain; to assume; to present, offer; to place or fix upon: Caus. *-yamayati*, *-yitum*, to restrain, curb, check.

Ni-yata, *as*, *ā*, *am*, checked, curbed, restrained, held in; governed, controlled, subdued, submissive, self-governed; abstemious, self-denying, temperate; attentive, intent upon; fixed, constant, steady, permanent, incessant; ascertained, certain, destined, settled, sure; inevitable; positive, definite; permeable, what may be spread through or over?; (*am*), n. elementary or crude matter, the recipient of attributes or properties; (*am*), ind. always, constantly, decidedly, positively, surely, certainly, inevitably; forcibly. — *Niyata-mānasa*, *as*, *ā*, *am*, of subdued mind or spirit. — *Niyata-vishaya-vartin*, *ī*, *inī*, *i*, steadily abiding in one's own sphere. — *Niyatātman* (°*ta-āt*°), *ā*, *ā*, *a*, self-regulated, self-controlled, self-restrained. — *Niyatāhāra* (°*ta-āh*°), *as*, *ā*, *am*, abstemious in food, temperate. — *Niyatendriya* (°*ta-in*°), *as*, *ā*, *am*, having the passions subdued or restrained.

Ni-yati, *is*, f. restraint, restriction; the fixed order of things, necessity, destiny, fate, luck, good or bad fortune; a religious duty or obligation; self-command, self-restraint; (*Niyati* is sometimes personified as a goddess, she and Āyati being regarded as daughters of Meru and wives of Dhātṛi and Vidhātṛi); (*ī*), f. an epithet of Durgā.

Ni-yantavya, *as*, *ā*, *am*, to be restrained, checked, controlled, tamed; to be forced.

Ni-yantu in *dur-n*°, q. v.

Ni-yantṛi, *tā*, *trī*, *tṛi*, who or what holds in, restrains, curbs, governs, guides, tames, &c.; restraining; (*tā*), m. a restrainer, charioteer, driver, coachman; a ruler, governor, master; a punisher. — *Niyantṛi-tva*, *am*, n. restraint, government, ability to rule, power of restraining, controlling faculty.

Ni-yama, *as*, m. restraining, holding back, checking, keeping back; taming, subduing, preventing, confining; restraint, restriction, restriction to (with loc.); limitation; fixing, defining, definition; keeping down, lowering (as the tone of the voice); fixed rule or law, necessity, obligation; rule, precept (e.g. *strīṇām Prākṛita-bhāshaṇam eva niyamaḥ*, the usage of women is to speak only Prākṛit); certainty, ascertainment; agreement, contract, engagement, assent, promise, vow; any self-imposed restraint or religious observance voluntarily practised, as fasting, watching, pilgrimage, praying, &c.; voluntary penance, meritorious or supererogatory piety; a lesser vow, minor observance (as opposed to *yama*, a greater vow which must always be observed); (in rhetoric) a common-place in poetry, any conventional expression or usual comparison (as notice of the birch in describing the Himālaya, of the sandal tree in describing the Malaya mountains, of the peacock's cry in the rains, of the koil in spring, &c.); Necessity or Fixed Law personified as a son of Dharma by Dhṛiti; (*ena* or *āt*), ind. by a fixed rule, necessarily, surely, certainly. — *Niyama-nishṭhā*, f. rigid observance of prescribed rites. — *Niyama-pattra*, *am*, n. a written agreement or stipulation. — *Niyama-para*, *as*, *ā*, *am*, observing fixed rules; relating to or corroborative of a rule. — *Niyama-pāla*, *as*, m. 'observer of vows,' N. of a sage from whom the Nepalese derive the name of their country, (properly Nipāl.) — *Niyama-bhaṅga*, *as*, m. breach of a stipulation or contract. — *Niyama-vat*, *ān*, *atī*, *at*, practising or observing religious observances; (*atī*), f. (a woman) having the monthly courses. — *Niyama-sthiti*, *is*, f. a state of self-restraint, steady observance of religious obligations, asceticism.

Ni-yamana, *as*, *ī*, *am*, regulating, controlling, subduing, taming, overpowering; (*am*), n. subduing, checking, restraining; humiliation, coercion; binding; restriction, limitation; precept, fixed practice or rule.

Ni-yamita, as, ā, am, checked, restrained, suppressed, bound, confined; governed, guided; fixed, regulated, prescribed, stipulated, agreed upon.

1. *ni-yamya, as, ā, am,* to be checked or restrained, restrainable, tamable.

2. *ni-yamya,* ind. having restrained, having guided, &c.

Ni-yāma, as, m. = *ni-yama,* restraint; religious vow, penance, fasting, &c., especially if an act of supererogation; = *ni-yāmaka,* a boatman, sailor; [cf. *nir-yāma.*]

Ni-yāmaka, as, ā, am, restraining, checking, controlling, subduing, suppressing, overpowering; restrictive, limiting; defining more closely; guiding, governing, who or what regulates or restrains; a restrainer, ruler, master; *(as),* m. a charioteer; a boatman, a sailor, but variously applied to one who rows or steers, a pilot, a helmsman; [cf. *nir-yāma.*] — *Niyāmaka-tā,* f. controllership, power of restraining, restraint; exact definition, explanation.

Ni-yāmana, am, n. taming, checking, restraining; (probably incorrectly for *ni-yamana.*)

निययिन् *ni-yayin, ī, inī, i* (fr. rt. *yā* with *ni*), Ved. driving over, passing over (as a carriage).

Ni-yāna, am, n., Ved. way, access.

नियव *ni-yava.* See under 2. *ni-yu* below.

नियातन *ni-yātana, am,* n. causing to fall or descend; (wrong reading for *ni-pātana,* q. v.)

नियु 1. *ni-yu,* cl. 3. P. *-yuyati,* &c., Ved. to repel, keep off.

नियु 2. *ni-yu,* cl. 2. P. *-yauti,* cl. 9. P. A. *-yunāti, -nīte, -yavitum,* to join, yoke, harness; to mix; to bestow.

Ni-yava, as, m. compact order, continuous line or series; (Sāy.) mixing, mixture.

Ni-yut, t, f., Ved. series, line, row; (Sāy.) a horse, steed (as harnessed to a car), especially one of the horses of Vāyu called Niyuts; praise, a praiser; *(as),* f. pl. series of words [cf. *grantha, ni-bandhana*], verses, a poem; (Sāy.) a team of horses, especially the Niyuts or horses of Vāyu; N. of a wife of Rudra in one of his different forms. — *Niyut-vat, ān, atī, at,* Ved. forming a series; flowing continuously, as the Soma; drawn by a line of horses, as Vāyu or Indra, or the Maruts; (Sāy.) possessing the Niyut steeds, possessing horses; containing the word *niyut* or *niyut-vat* (as a verse or hymn). — *Niyud-ratha, as, ā, am,* Ved. one whose car is drawn by a line or team of horses; (Sāy.) having a harnessed chariot.

Ni-yuta, am, n. (according to some lexicographers also m.), a million; a hundred thousand; 100 Ayutas = 10,000 Koṭis.

Ni-yutvatīya, as, ā, am, Ved. belonging to Niyut-vat (Vāyu).

नियुज् *ni-yuj,* cl. 7. P. A. *-yunakti, -yunkte, -yoktum,* to join to, attach or fasten to; to put to (horses), yoke, harness; to place over, appoint, elect or depute any one to any office or duty (with acc. of the person and loc. of the thing or business); to give authority, authorize; to assign, employ, engage; to commit, intrust, commission; to enjoin, order, command; to constrain, urge, coerce, compel; to harass: Caus. (or cl. 10.) *-yojayati, -yitum,* to cause to be attached, cause to be placed or put, to fasten; to appoint, commission, charge, employ; to order, command, direct, prescribe; to urge, instigate, coerce; to perform, make, place in any state (e. g. *sandehe,* in jeopardy); to offer, present with, endow.

Ni-yukta, as, ā, am, fastened to; engaged in, attached to; directed, enjoined, commanded; authorized, appointed; ascertained; *(as),* m. a functionary, official.

Ni-yuktaka, as, ā, am, appointed, elected, placed in authority.

Ni-yukti, is, f. injunction, order, command; appointment, commission, charge, office.

Ni-yujya, ind. having joined or attached; having put to or harnessed; having appointed, &c.

Ni-yujyamāna, as, ā, am, being appointed, being engaged or employed.

Ni-yuñjāna, as, ā, am, appointing, authorizing, enjoining, constituting, appointing to an office.

Ni-yoktavya, as, ā, am, to be appointed or authorized, to be employed, ordered, &c.

Ni-yoktṛi, tā, trī, tṛi, one who joins or fastens or attaches; *(tā),* m. a ruler, lord, master.

Ni-yoga, as, m. attaching or fastening to; application, use, employment, appointment, injunction, direction, order, command, commission, charge, precept; any trust or appointed task or duty, any business or function committed to one's charge; effort, exertion; certainty, ascertainment; necessity; *(āt* or *ena),* ind. according to order or command, necessarily, certainly, surely. — *Niyoga-karaṇa, am,* n. making a command, commanding. — *Niyoga-tas,* ind. according to order or command. — *Niyoga-pāśa, as,* m. a fastening, (probably) a halter. — *Niyoga-prayojana, am,* n. the object or business of any appointment, authorized act or duty. — *Niyoga-vidhi, is,* m. the form or rule of appointing to any act or duty. — *Niyogārtha* (°*ga-ar*°), *as,* m. the object of an authorized act or appointment.

Ni-yogin, ī, inī, i, appointed, authorized, invested with authority, employed, engaged in any duty, attached to any business; *(ī),* m. a functionary, an official, officer, man in office, a minister, a deputy, an agent, &c. — *Niyogy-artha-grahopāya* (°*ha-up*°), *as,* m. the resource of confiscating the property of men in office.

Ni-yogya, as, ā, am, to be enjoined or prescribed; fit to be appointed or authorized, able or qualified for a duty [cf. *ni-yojya*]; *(as),* m. (according to Vopadeva) a master.

Ni-yojana, am, n. tying or fastening (as an animal to the Yūpa or sacrificial post); uniting, attaching to; that with which anything is fastened or tied (Ved.); ordering, prescribing, commanding, directing; urging, impelling; appointing (e. g. *kriyāsu,* to affairs); *(ī),* f. a halter.

Ni-yojanīya, as, ā, am, to be attached or joined to, to be appointed or authorized.

Ni-yojayitavya, as, ā, am (fr. the Caus.), to be appointed, to be commanded or urged or directed.

Ni-yojita, as, ā, am, joined or attached to, connected with, adapted to; appointed, authorized, commissioned; directed, ordered; impelled, urged, instigated.

Ni-yojya, as, ā, am, to be fastened or attached to; fit to be appointed or employed in; to be ordered, commanded, directed, instigated; proper to be enjoined; *(as),* m. a functionary, official, employé, servant.

नियुत *ni-yuta.* See under 2. *ni-yu,* col. 1.

नियुत्सा *ni-yutsā,* f. (fr. Desid. of rt. *yudh* with *ni* without reduplication), N. of the wife of Pra-stāva and mother of Vi-bhu.

Ni-yuddha, am, n. (fr. rt. *yudh* with *ni*), fighting, especially fighting on foot, close fight or combat, personal struggle. — *Niyuddha-bhū, ūs,* f. a battle-field, a place where close fighting has taken place.

Ni-yoddhṛi, dhā, m. a combatant, a wrestler, a boxer; a cock.

Ni-yodhaka, as, m. a fighter, combatant, wrestler, pugilist.

नियोग *ni-yoga.* See under *ni-yuj* above.

निर् *nir* euphonically substituted for *nis,* q. v., before vowels and soft consonants.

निरंश *nir-anśa, as, ā, am,* having no part or fraction remaining, whole. — *Niranśa-tva, am,* n. the state of having no part or fraction over, wholeness, completeness.

निरंशु *nir-anśu, us, us, u,* having no rays, rayless.

निरक्ष *nir-aksha, as, ā, am,* having no dice; having no latitude; *(as),* m. (in astronomy) the place of no latitude, i. e. the terrestrial equator. — *Niraksha-deśa, as,* m. a first meridian, as Lankā; a place where the sun is always vertical and the days and nights are equal; the equatorial region.

निरग्नि *nir-agni, is, is, i,* or *niragnika, as, ā, am,* having no fire, having lost or neglected the consecrated fire.

निरघ *nir-agha, as, ā, am,* sinless, blameless, free from fault or imperfection.

निरङ्कुश *nir-ankuśa, as, ā, am,* unchecked (lit. not held by a hook), uncontrolled, unruly, self-willed, unfettered, independant, completely free; *(am),* ind. freely. — *Nirankuśa-tā,* f. or *nirankuśa-tva, am,* n. unruliness, independance, self-will, wilfulness.

निरङ्ग *nir-anga, as, ā, am,* having no resources, deprived of expedients.

निरज् *nir-aj,* cl. 1. P. *-ajati, -ajitum* (Ved. inf. *-aje*), Ved. to drive or bring out, extricate, remove; to issue out.

निरजिन *nir-ajina, as, ā, am,* without a skin or hide, skinless.

निरञ्छन *ni-rañćhana, am,* n. (fr. *rañćh* = *lañćh* with *ni*), a mark or knot in a measuring line.

निरञ्जन 1. *nir-añjana, as, ā, am,* without collyrium or ointment, unstained, untinged, unblackened, unpainted; free from falsehood; artless; *(as),* m. an epithet of Śiva; N. of one of the attendants of Śiva; *(ā),* f. an epithet of Durgā; the day of full moon.

निरञ्जन 2. *ni-rañjana, as, ā, am,* void of passion or emotion, (applied to the Supreme Being.)

निरण् *ni-raṇ,* cl. 1. P. *-raṇati, -raṇitum,* Ved. to rejoice, delight in.

निरत *ni-rata.* See *ni-ram,* p. 492, col. 2.

निरतिशय *nir-atiśaya, as, ā, am,* unsurpassed. — *Niratiśaya-tva, am,* n. the state of being unsurpassed, unsurpassedness.

निरत्यय *nir-atyaya, as, ā, am,* free from danger, dangerless, secure, infallible, completely successful, faultless, unblamable.

निरधिष्ठान *nir-adhishṭhāna, as, ā, am,* having no fixed resting-place, having no solid basis.

निरध्व *nir-adhva, as, ā, am,* (probably) one who has lost his way.

निरनुक्रोश *nir-anukrośa, as,* m. absence of compassion, hard-heartedness, unmercifulness; *(as, ā, am),* uncompassionate, without pity, pitiless, merciless; hard-hearted towards any person or thing (with loc.). — *Niranukrośa-kārin, ī, iṇī, i,* acting without compassion or pitilessly. — *Niranukrośa-tā,* f. pitilessness, unmercifulness; hard-heartedness, cruelty. — *Niranukrośa-yukta, as, ā, am,* uncompassionate, ruthless, hard-hearted.

निरनुग *nir-anuga, as, ā, am,* unattended, without retinue or followers.

निरनुग्रह *nir-anugraha, as, ā, am,* unfavourable, unkind, ungracious.

निरनुनासिक *nir-anunāsika, as, ā, am,* not marked with the nasal symbol called Anunāsika (Gram. 7), not nasal.

निरनुमान *nir-anumāna, as, ā, am,* without inference, not binding one's self to conclusions or consequences.

निरनुरोध *nir-anurodha, as, ā, am,* unfavourable, unfriendly, unkind, ungracious, unamiable.

निरन्तर *nir-antara, as, ā, am,* without any intermediate space, having no intervening space, granting no room or free space, having no interval, closely contiguous, close; closely connected, continuous; uninterrupted, continual, constant; without interstices, completely filled, compact, dense, coarse, gross; persevering, faithful, true (as a friend); unconcealed, not hidden from view; not other or different, similar, identical; *(am),* ind. without intervening space, without interval, without interruption, constantly, incessantly, continually; closely, tightly, firmly; immediately.—*Nirantarābhyāsa* (°*ra-abh*°), *as,* m. constant repetition or study, continual reading to one's self; diligent and uninterrupted exercise or practice.

निरन्तराल *nir-antarāla, as, ā, am,* without an intervening space, without intervals or interstices; close, contracted, narrow.—*Nirantarāla-tā,* f. close contiguity, closeness, compactness, narrowness.

निरन्धस् *nir-andhas, ās, ās, as,* foodless, without food, hungry.

निरन्न *nir-anna, as, ā, am,* foodless, wanting food, hungry, starving; giving no food.

निरन्वय *nir-anvaya, as, ā, am,* having no offspring or descendants, childless; unconnected with, unrelated; not agreeing with the context (of a sentence); without logical connection, without regular order or sequence, unmethodical; without being seen or observed, out of sight, not visibly committed (Manu VIII. 332).

निरप *nir-apa, as, ā, am,* waterless, destitute of water.

निरपत्रप *nir-apatrapa, as, ā, am,* shameless, impudent; bold, confident.

निरपराध *nir-aparādha, as,* m. faultlessness, innocence; *(as, ā, am),* unoffending, inoffensive, innocent, faultless, guiltless, blameless.—*Nir-aparādha-tā,* f. faultlessness, innocence.—*Nirapa-rādha-vat, ān, atī, at,* faultless, innocent.

निरपवर्त *nir-apavarta, as, ā, am,* not returning or turning back; (in arithmetic) leaving no common measure, not to be divided by a common divisor, reduced to the lowest terms.

निरपवाद *nir-apavāda, as, ā, am,* free from censure, without reproof, blameless.

निरपाय *nir-apāya, as, ā, am,* free from destruction or decay, imperishable, eternal, free from detriment or loss, free from harm or evil; infallible.

निरपेक्ष *nir-apeksha, as, ā, am,* disregarding, not taking notice of (with loc.); careless, negligent, without desire, indifferent; not expecting anything from another; independant of, unconnected or unconcerned with; (often without any object) regardless, indifferent (to praise or blame); without purpose or hope; *(ā),* f. indifference; disregard, the absence of expectation; *(am),* n. without regard, regardlessly, accidentally.—*Nirapeksha-tā,* f. or *nirapeksha-tva, am,* n. disregard, indifference; independance; relationlessness.

Nir-apekshita, as, ā, am, disregarded; regardless.

Nir-apekshin, ī, iṇī, i, disregarding, indifferent, not expecting anything.

Nir-apekshya, as, ā, am, not to be regarded.

निरभिभव *nir-abhibhava, as, ā, am,* not subject to defeat or humiliation, not disgraced; not to be surpassed.

निरभिमान *nir-abhimāna* or *nir-abhīmāna, as, ā, am,* exempt from pride, free from self-conceit, devoid of egotism; unconscious.

निरभिलाप *nir-abhilāsha, as, ā, am,* having no desire for, not intent upon, indifferent.

निरभ्र *nir-abhra, as, ā, am,* cloudless; *(e),* ind. in a cloudless sky, when the sky is unclouded.

निरम् *ni-ram,* cl. 1. A. *-ramate, -rantum,* Ved. to delight in, be delighted; to rest, repose, desist: Caus. *-rāmayati, -yitum,* Aor. *-arīramat,* Ved. to gladden; to cause to rest or abide.

Ni-rata, as, ā, am, engaged or interested in; attached or devoted to; pleased, delighted; rested, ceased.

Ni-rati, is, f. delighting in; attachment to.

Ni-ramaṇa, am, n. delighting in; resting; (in Śata-patha-Brāhmaṇa XIII. 4, 2, 5, *ni-ramaṇa* is by some separated into *nir-amaṇa* and explained to mean 'exhausted,' 'worn out.')

निरमर्ष *nir-amarsha, as, ā, am,* not impatient; patient, apathetic, devoid of energy.

निरमित्र *nir-amitra, as, ā, am,* without foes, free from enemies; *(as),* m., N. of several persons; of a son of Nakula; of a king of Tri-garta; of a son of Khaṇḍa-pāṇi or Daṇḍa-pāṇi, (also *nir-āmitra*); of a son of Ayutāyus; of a sage, considered as a son of Śiva, (also *nir-āmitra.*)

निरम्बर *nir-ambara, as, ā, am,* undressed, naked.

निरम्बु *nir-ambu, us, us, u,* abstaining from water, not drinking; waterless, destitute of water.

निरय *nir-aya, as,* m. 'without happiness,' hell [cf. *tiryan-niraya*]; Niraya or Hell personified as a child of fear and death; (according to some *nir-aya,* in the sense of 'hell,' is fr. *nir-i* and means 'exit,' 'egress from life.')

Nir-ayaṇa, am, n., Ved. egression.

निरर्गल *nir-argala, as, ā, am,* unbarred, without a bolt or hindrance, unobstructed, unrestrained, unimpeded; irresistible; *(am),* ind. without bolt or bar; without restraint or constraint, freely.

निरर्थ *nir-artha, as,* m. loss, detriment; nonsense; *(as, ā, am),* destitute of wealth, poor; useless; meaningless, unmeaning, nonsensical, purposeless, vain; (a consonant is called *nir-artha,* not fulfilling its purpose if it is not followed by a vowel.)—*Nirartha-tā,* f. senselessness, nonsense.

Nir-arthaka, as, ā or *ikā* or *akī* (?), *am,* not fulfilling one's aim or object, purposeless, useless, vain, unprofitable; having no reasonable sense, unmeaning, nonsensical; a consonant which is not followed by a vowel; *(am),* ind. without a purpose, uselessly, in vain.—*Nirarthaka-tva, am,* n. uselessness, vanity.

निरर्द् *nir-ard,* cl. 1. P. *-ardati, -arditum,* Ved. to stream forth, flow out.

निरर्बुद *nir-arbuda, as,* m.? (with Buddhists) N. of a hell in which the wicked are punished by excessive cold.

निरव *nir-ava, as, ā, am?* (occurring only in the gen. sing. *nir-avasya,* which might be the ind. part. of rt. *so* with preps. *nir* and *ava;* said by others to be = *ni* = *nis* + *rava, as,* m. loss of voice; but according to Sāy.) Ved. having no protector or uttering praise.

निरवकाश *nir-avakāśa, as, ā, am,* without free space; having no room for moving freely, wanting an opportunity, without leisure.

निरवग्रह *nir-avagraha, as, ā, am,* without obstruction or obstacle, unrestrained, unchecked, uncontrolled; irresistible; free, independant; self-willed, unmanageable, headstrong.

निरवत्त *nir-ava-tta, nir-ava-tti.* See under *nir-ava-do,* col. 3.

निरवदय् *nir-ava-day,* cl. 1. A. *-dayate,* Ved. to distribute, allot a share or shares.

निरवदो *nir-ava-do* [cf. 3. *dā*], cl. 2. 4. P., Ved. *-dāti* and *-dyati, -dātum,* to distribute, allot a share, give any one his share, to satisfy a claim; to divide completely among.

Nir-ava-tta, as, ā, am, distributed, completely divided or allotted.

Nir-ava-tti, is, f., Ved. allotment or distribution of shares.

निरवद्य *nir-avadya, as, ā, am,* unblamable, blameless, faultless, unobjectionable, unexceptionable; *(am),* n. (or *ā* ?), f. unblamableness, blamelessness, faultlessness; *(as* or *am),* m. or n. (?), a particular high number.—*Niravadya-tva, am,* n. blamelessness, unblamableness, excellence.—*Niravadya-vat, ān, atī, at,* unblamable, blameless.

निरवधि *nir-avadhi, is, is, i,* without bounds or boundaries, unlimited.

निरवयव *nir-avayava, as, ā, am,* without limbs or members, without component parts, not consisting of parts, indivisible.—*Niravayava-tva, am,* n. indivisibility.

निरवरोध *nir-avarodha, as, ā, am,* unrestrained, unobstructed, unopposed.

निरवलम्ब *nir-avalamba, as, ā, am,* having no prop or stay; unsupported; not affording support; not depending or relying on.

Nir-avalambana, am, n. want of a prop, want of reliance, want of a person or thing to depend upon.

निरवशेष *nir-avaśesha, as, ā, am,* without a residue, complete, whole; *(eṇa),* ind. completely, totally, fully, particularly, circumstantially.—*Nir-avaśesha-tas,* ind. completely, &c. (= *niravaśesheṇa*).

निरवसाद *nir-avasāda, as, ā, am,* not cast down, cheerful, good-humoured.

निरवस्कृत *nir-avaskṛita, as, ā, am,* cleansed, clean ?; [cf. *avas-kara, an-avaskara.*]

निरवस्तार *nir-avastāra, as, ā, am,* without a bed or coverlet; not strewn (with leaves &c.), bare.

निरवहालिका *nir-avahālikā,* f. a fence, a hedge, an outer wall; [cf. *avahālikā.*]

निरविन्द *niravinda, as,* m., N. of a mountain.

निरवेक्ष् *nir-aveksh* (*-ava-īksh*), cl. 1. A. *-īkshate, -īkshitum,* to perceive.

Nir-avekshya, ind. having perceived or observed.

निरव्यय *nir-avyaya, as, ā, am,* undecaying, eternal.

निरश् *nir-aś,* cl. 9. P. *-aśnāti,* &c., Ved. to eat up, consume entirely.

Nir-aśita, as, ā, am, eaten up, completely consumed.

निरशन *nir-aśana, as, ā, am,* abstaining from food; *(am),* n. going without food, fasting.

निरष्ट *nir-ashṭa, as, ā, am* (fr. rt. 1. *aś* or *aksh* with *nis*), Ved. deprived of vigour, exhausted; (Sāy.) = *nir-ākṛita,* driven away, scattered, dispersed.

निरस् *nir-as,* cl. 4. P. *-asyati, -asitum,* to cast out, throw away, drive away, banish, expel, evict, drive back, send back; to keep off; to turn out (of doors); to reject, repudiate, decline, refuse; to remove; to tear out, strip off; to stretch out (e. g. *hastau nirasyati* or *-te,* he stretches out the hands); to annihilate, destroy, subdue.

Nir-asana, as, ī, am, expelling, removing, rejecting; vomiting, spitting out; *(am),* n. expelling, ejecting; expulsion, removal, rejection, denial, contradiction, refusal, disallowance; vomiting forth, spitting out; suppressing, checking; killing, destroying, destruction, extermination.

Nir-asanīya, as, ā, am, to be thrown out, to be driven away or expelled.

Nir-asta, as, ā, am, cast out or away, expelled; thrown out or away, cast off; thrown off (as from a horse); driven away, expelled, banished; rejected, repudiated, abandoned, deserted; disallowed; refuted; sent forth, sent away; deprived of, removed; shot off, discharged (as an arrow); spit out; uttered hurriedly or rapidly (as a speech or word); torn out or away; destroyed; broken (as an agreement); suppressed, checked; *(am),* n. rejecting; dropping or leaving out, not pronouncing (regarded as a fault in pronunciation). — *Nirasta-bheda, as, ā, am,* having all difference removed, identical. — *Nirasta-rāga, as, ā, am,* one who has abandoned worldly desires or has devoted himself to religious penance.

1. *nir-asya, as, ā, am,* to be expelled or driven out.

2. *nirasya,* ind. having cast out, thrown out or ejected, having expelled.

Nir-asyat, an, antī, at, ejecting, throwing out; expelling; abandoning, neglecting, scattering, destroying, &c.

Nir-asyamāna, as, ā, am, being thrown out or expelled; being abandoned; being suppressed, &c.

Nir-āsa, as, m. throwing out, casting out, ejection, expulsion, removal, abandonment; dropping (a sound or letter &c.); vomiting; opposing, contradiction, refutation. — *Nirāsa-guṭikā,* f. a pill to produce vomiting; (also written *nirāśa-guṭikā.*)

Nir-āsana, am, n. = *nir-asana,* p. 492, col. 3.

निरस **ni-rasa,** *as, ā, am,* = *nī-rasa,* without flavour, tasteless, insipid, dry; *(as),* m. want of flavour, insipidity; want of juice, dryness; want of passion or feeling; *(ā),* f. a species of grass (= *niḥ-śreṇikā*).

निरस्त्र **nir-astra,** *as, ā, am,* weaponless, unarmed; (fought) without weapons (as a battle).

निरस्थि **nir-asthi,** *is, is, i,* having no bones, boneless.

निरह् **nir-ah,** only in perf. *nir-āha,* Ved. to utter, pronounce, express.

निरहङ्कार **nir-ahankāra,** *as, ā, am,* free from egotism, devoid of selfishness, free from pride, humble, lowly.

Nir-ahankṛita, as, ā, am, having no self-consciousness, without individuality or personality; unselfish.

Nir-ahankṛiti, is, is, i, free from egotism or selfishness.

Nir-ahankriya, as, ā, am, having no individuality or personality, without self-consciousness.

Nir-ahankriyā, f. absence of egotism or selfishness.

निरहम् **nir-aham** or *nir-ahammati, is, is, i,* devoid of self-conceit, free from selfishness.

निराक **nirāka,** *as,* m. cooking; sweat; the recompense of a bad action; (wrong reading for *ni-pāka.*)

निराकरण **nir-ākaraṇa.** See under *nir-ā-kṛi,* col. 2.

निराकाङ्क्ष **nir-ākānksha,** *as, ā, am,* expecting nothing, wishing nothing, free from desire; wanting nothing to fill up or make complete (as the sense of a sentence or word).

Nirākānkshin, ī, iṇī, i, expecting nothing, wishing or wanting nothing.

निराकार 1. **nir-ākāra,** *as, ā, am* (for 2. see *nir-ā-kṛi,* col. 2), devoid of form, deprived of one's natural form; without external appearance; formless, shapeless, deformed; disguised; unassuming; not claiming anything for one's self, modest; *(as),* m. heaven, Vishṇu; Śiva; the universal Spirit, God.

1. *nir-ākṛiti, is, is, i,* formless, shapeless, deformed, ugly; *(is),* m. a person who has not duly gone through a course of study, (especially applied however to the religious student who has not duly read the Vedas); one who neglects the five great religious obligations, who does not worship the gods, &c.; a Brāhman who neglects the duties of his caste (*ākṛiti*) by not going through a regular course of study.

निराकाश **nir-ākāśa,** *as, ā, am,* having no free space, leaving no room, completely filled.

निराकुल **nir-ākula,** *as, ā, am,* unconfused, not disordered; unperplexed; unbewildered; clear; steady, calm; perspicuous; *(am),* n. calmness, perspicuity, clearness.

निराकृ **nir-ā-kṛi,** cl. 8. P. A. *-karoti, -kurute, -kartum,* to separate or divide off (Ved.); to push away, turn or drive away, repudiate, keep away, keep off, banish, expel, eject, remove, reject; to refuse; to oppose, obstruct, contradict; to disallow; to omit, intermit; to frustrate; to contemn, spurn.

Nir-ākaraṇa, am, n. repudiating, expelling, turning out, turning away, throwing off; removing, banishing; repudiation, obstruction, opposition, contradiction, rejection; refutation, reply; contempt, disesteem; forgetting; neglecting the chief sacrificial or religious duties.

Nir-ākarishṇu, us, us, u, expelling, repudiating, a repudiator; obstructive, obstructing, hindering from (with abl.); spurning, disdaining, despising; seeking to remove from (with abl.), envying any person anything (abl.); forgetful. — *Nirākarishṇu-tā,* f. the state of being a repudiator; envy, malevolence.

Nir-ākartṛi, tā, trī, tṛi, a repudiator, repudiating; a despiser, contemner (as of the gods).

2. *nir-ākāra, as,* m. rebuke, reproach, censure, blame. (For 1. *nir-ākāra* see col. 1.)

Nir-ākṛita, as, ā, am, pushed away, driven away, repudiated, expelled, banished, ejected, rejected, removed, set aside, turned away, turned out; thrown off; divorced; refused, denied; refuted, replied to; contemned, despised, spurned, made light of; deprived of. — *Nirākṛitānyottara* (°*ta-anya-ut*°), *as, ā, am,* refuting every answer, irrefutable, irrefragable. — *Nirākṛitānyottara-tva, am,* n. irrefutableness, irrefragableness.

2. *nir-ākṛiti, is,* f. repudiation, rejection; refusal, disallowance; obstruction, obstacle, impediment, interruption; contradiction, opposition; *(is, is, i),* impeding, obstructing; annihilating, destroying; *(is),* m., N. of a son of the first Manu Sāvarṇi.

Nir-ākṛitin, ī, inī, i, (probably) repudiating, impeding, obstructing; avoiding; making no exertion either to do or avoid.

Nir-ākriyā, f. repudiation, expulsion, removal; contradiction, denial, refutation.

निराकृति 1. and 2. **nir-ākṛiti.** See under 1. *nir-ākāra,* col. 1, and under *nir-ā-kṛi* above.

निराक्रन्द **nir-ākranda,** *as, ā, am,* not complaining; a place where no sound can be heard.

निराक्रम् **nir-ā-kram,** cl. 1. P. A. *-krāmati, -kramate, -krāntum* and *-kramitum,* to come forth, to go out of.

निराक्रिया **nir-ākriyā.** See *nir-ā-kṛi* above.

निराक्रोश **nir-ākrośa,** *as, ā, am,* unaccused, unreviled.

निराग **ni-rāga,** *as, ā, am,* passionless, dispassionate.

निरागम **nir-āgama,** *as, ā, am,* not founded on revelation, not resting on scripture.

निरागस् **nir-āgas,** *ās, ās, as,* sinless, faultless, innocent.

निराग्रह **nir-āgraha,** *as, ā, am,* not insisting upon, not peremptory or obstinate.

निराचार **nir-āćāra,** *as, ā, am,* without approved usages or customs, lawless, barbarian, (especially applied to those people who have not the ordinances of the Vedas or distinction of castes.)

निराजीव्य **nir-ājīvya,** *as, ā, am,* not yielding subsistence, not granting a livelihood.

निराडम्बर **nir-āḍambara,** *as, ā, am,* without drums. — *Nirāḍambara-sundara, as, ā* or *ī, am,* (perhaps) beautiful in itself, not requiring a drum to attract attention or not requiring ornaments.

निरातङ्क **nir-ātanka,** *as, ā, am,* not feeling pain or uneasiness, without ailment, well, comfortable; not causing pain or ailment or disagreeable feelings; *(as),* m. an epithet of Śiva.

निरातप **nir-ātapa,** *as, ā, am,* not penetrated by the sun's rays, shady; *(ā),* f. the night.

निरात्मक **nir-ātmaka,** *as, ā, am,* or *nir-ātman, ā, ā, a,* or *nirātma-vat, ān, atī, at,* having no separate soul or no individual existence.

निरादर **nir-ādara,** *as, ā, am,* showing no respect, disrespectful.

निरादान **nir-ādāna,** *as, ā, am,* taking nothing, not taking, one from whom nothing is taken; an epithet of Buddha.

निरादिष्ट **nir-ādishṭa,** *as, ā, am,* paid off (as a debt).

Nir-ādeśa, as, m. complete payment or discharge of a debt.

निराधा **nir-ā-dhā,** cl. 3. P. A. *-dadhāti, -dhatte,* &c., Ved. to take out of, take away.

निराधान **nir-ādhāna,** *as, ā, am,* without a receptacle.

निराधार **nir-ādhāra,** *as, ā, am,* without a receptacle; without a fulcrum or support.

निराधि **nir-ādhi,** *is, is, i,* free from anxiety, undisturbed by care.

निरानन्द **nir-ānanda,** *as, ā, am,* joyless, sad, sorrowful; not delighting. — *Nir-ānanda-kara, as, ī, am,* causing no pleasure, causing care or sorrow.

निरान्त्र **nir-āntra,** *as, ā, am,* Ved. eviscerated, disembowelled; having the entrails hanging out.

निरापद् **nir-āpad,** *t,* f. freedom from misfortune or calamity, a prosperous condition, security; *(t, t, t),* free from calamity or misfortune, prosperous, fortunate.

निराबाध **nir-ābādha,** *as, ā, am,* undisturbed, unmolested, unvexed, secure from disturbance; unobstructed; not disturbing, not molesting, not injuring, not paining; frivolously or not really vexatious. — *Nir-ābādha-kara, as, ā, am,* not causing injury or pain.

निरामय **nir-āmaya,** *as, am,* m. n. freedom from illness, health, happiness, welfare; *(as, ā, am),* free from illness, healthy, well, hale, recovered from sickness, free from disease; free from taint, pure; guileless; free from defects or failings; infallible; not liable to failure or miscarriage; complete, full; *(as),* m. a wild goat; a hog, a boar; N. of a king.

निरामर्द **nir-āmarda,** *as,* m. 'not oppressing,' N. of a king.

निरामालु **nir-āmālu,** *us,* m. (fr. *nirāma-ālu?*), the wood apple, Feronia Elephantum; [cf. *kapittha.*]

निरामित्र **nir-āmitra.** See *nir-amitra.*

निरामिन् **ni-rāmin,** *ī, iṇī, i,* Ved. remaining, staying in; (Sāy.) delighting in.

निरामिष **nir-āmisha,** *as, ā, am,* fleshless, without meat or prey; not receiving wages; having no sensual desires, free from covetousness. — *Nirāmishāśin* (°*sha-āś*°), *ī, inī, i,* not feeding on meat; living without meat; free from sensual desires.

निराय *nir-āya, as, ā, am,* having no income or revenue, profitless, yielding no income or profit. — *Nir-āya-vyaya-vat, ān,* m. having neither income nor expenditure, an idler who lives by clandestine means.

निरायत 1. *nir-āyata, as, ā, am* (fr. rt. *yam* with *ā* and *nis*), stretched out, extended.

निरायत 2. *nir-āyata, as, ā, am,* unextended, contracted, compact.

निरायास *nir-āyāsa, as, ā, am,* not causing trouble, not requiring efforts, not fatiguing; easily attainable, easy.

निरायुध *nir-āyudha, as, ā, am,* weaponless, disarmed, unarmed, defenceless.

निरारम्भ *nir-ārambha, as, ā, am,* not undertaking enterprises, not enterprising, abstaining from all work.

निरालक *nirālaka, as,* m. a species of fish.

निरालम्ब *nir-ālamba, as, ā, am,* having no prop or support, not resting or depending on another, independent, self-supported, not relying on another, standing alone, friendless; *(as),* m., N. of a man mentioned in the Saṅkara-vijaya; *(ā),* f. spikenard, = *ākāśa-māṇsī; (am),* ind. without support, independently. — *Nirālambopanishad* (°*ba-up*°), *t,* f., N. of an Upanishad.

Nir-ālambana, as, ā, am, having no prop, without support, not resting on another.

निरालस्य *nir-ālasya, as, ā, am,* not slothful.

निरालोक *nir-āloka, as, ā, am,* not looking about, not moving the eye, without moving the eyes; deprived of light, dark; invisible, uninvestigable (?); an epithet of Śiva.

निरावर्ष *nir-āvarsha, as, ā, am,* unpenetrated by rain, protecting from rain.

निराश *nir-āśa, as, ā, am* (fr. *nis* + 1. *ā-śā;* cf. *ā-śaṇs*), without hope, hopeless, despairing of (with loc., dat., or with *prati* and acc., e. g. *sva-jīvite* or *sva-jīvitāya* or *sva-jīvitam prati nir-āśaḥ,* despairing of one's own life); depriving of all hope; [cf. *nairāśya.*] — *Nirāśa-tva, am,* n. hopelessness, despair. — *Nirāśī-bhāva, as,* m. hopelessness, despair. — *Nirāśī-bhūta, as, ā, am,* become hopeless; despairing.

Nir-āśaka, as, ā, am, desponding, despairing of (with abl.).

Nir-āśin, ī, inī, i, hopeless. — *Nirāśi-tva, am,* n. = *nirāśa-tva,* hopelessness.

निराशङ्क *nir-āśanka, as, ā, am,* fearless; *(am),* ind. fearlessly, without fear or hesitation.

निराशिस् *nir-āśis, īs, īs, is* (see *ā-śās*), having no wishes or hopes; without a blessing.

निराश्रम *nir-āśrama, as, ā, am,* or *nir-āśramin, ī, iṇī, i,* not being in one of the four periods or orders of a Brāhman's life.

निराश्रय *nir-āśraya, as, ā, am,* supportless, without prop or stay, not resting or depending on, unsupported, self-supported, without shelter or refuge, unprotected, destitute; not deep (as a wound?).

निरास *nir-āsa, as,* m. See under *nir-as* at p. 493, col. 1.

निरासित्व *nirāsi-tva* incorrect reading for *nirāśi-tva.*

निरास्पद *nir-āspada, as, ā, am,* restless, having no place of rest, homeless; portionless.

निरास्वाद *nir-āsvāda, as, ā, am,* tasteless, flavourless, unsavoury, yielding no enjoyment.

Nir-āsvādya, as, ā, am, unsavoury, giving no enjoyment. — *Nirāsvādya-tama, as, ā, am,* most unsavoury.

निराहार *nir-āhāra, as,* m. want of food, not eating, fasting; *(as, ā, am),* foodless, fasting, abstaining from food, without food, having nothing to eat. — *Nirāhāra-tā,* f. foodlessness, fasting.

निराहावत् *nir-āhā-vat, ān, atī, at,* for *nir-āhāva-vat,* without invocation.

निरि *nir-i,* cl. 2. P. *-eti,* &c., *-etum,* to go out, come forth, go off, depart.

निरिङ्ग *nir-inga, as, ā, am,* immovable, not moving to and fro, not flickering.

निरिङ्गिनी *niringinī,* f. a veil.

निरिच्छ *nir-iććha, as, ā, am,* without wish or desire, indifferent.

निरिन्द्रिय *nir-indriya, as, ā, am,* Ved. impotent, destitute of manly vigour or of strength (in general); barren; having lost the use of a limb; imperfect, mutilated, maimed, infirm, weak, frail; (in Manu IX. 18) without evidence or means of certain knowledge (according to Kullūka = *pramāṇa-rahita*).

निरिन्धन *nir-indhana, as, ā, am,* destitute of fuel.

निरी *ni-rī,* cl. 9. P. *-riṇāti, -retum,* Ved. to attack.

निरीक्ष् *nir-īksh,* cl. 1. A. *-īkshate, -īkshitum,* to look at, look towards, behold, gaze at, look about, regard, observe, view, contemplate, perceive.

Nir-īkshaka, as, ā, am, looking at, seeing, viewing, observing, visiting.

Nir-īkshaṇa, as, ā, am, looking at, regarding; *(am),* n. look; looking at, regarding, seeing; expecting; the aspect of the planets.

Nir-īkshat, an, antī, at, or *nir-īkshamāṇa, as, ā, am,* looking at, regarding, expecting, hoping.

Nir-īkshā, f. looking at, regarding; consideration; hope, expectation; *(ayā),* ind. in respect of, in relation to, as to (e. g. *balābala-nirīkshayā,* in respect of strength and weakness; cf. *dur-nirīksha*).

Nir-īkshin, ī, iṇī, i, seeing, looking, viewing; [cf. *nātidūra-n*°.]

1. *nir-īkshya, as, ā, am,* to be looked at or regarded; to be considered; [cf. *dur-n*°.]

2. *nir-īkshya,* ind. having looked at or viewed or scanned.

Nir-īkshyamāṇa, as, ā, am, being looked at or regarded; looking, (Mahā-bh. Ādi-p. 7694.)

निरीति *nir-īti, is, is, i,* free from calamities or afflictions, painless.

Nir-ītika, as, ā, am, not inauspicious, not prognosticating calamity, auspicious.

निरीश *nir-īśa* = *nir-īsha,* q. v.

निरीश्वर *nir-īśvara, as, ā, am,* godless, atheistic. — *Nirīśvara-vāda, as,* m. godlessness, atheism. — *Nirīśvara-vādin, ī, inī, i,* atheistical.

निरीष *nir-īsha, am,* n. the body of a plough (without the pole and ploughshare; also read *nir-īśa*).

निरीह *nir-īha, as, ā, am,* inactive, effortless; desireless, not wishful, indifferent, unanxious. — *Nirīha-tā,* f. or *nirīha-tva, am,* n. or *nir-īhā,* f. indifference, absence of desire or effort. — *Nirīhā-vasthā* (°*hā-av*°), f. a state of indifference.

निरुक्त *nir-ukta, as, ā, am* (fr. rt. *vać* with *nis*), uttered, pronounced, expressed, explained, defined; loud, distinct; *(am),* n. explanation or etymological interpretation of a word; N. of one of the six Vedāṅgas or works considered as connected with the Vedas; glossarial explanation of obscure terms, (especially those occurring in the Vedas); N. of a well-known commentary on the Nighaṇṭus by Yāska; [cf. *nairukta, nairuktika.*] — *Nirukta-kāra, as,* m. 'Nirukta-composer,' N. or epithet of a commentator on Kāli-dāsa's Megha-dūta. — *Nirukta-krit, t,* m. epithet of a pupil of Śāka-pūrṇi. — *Nirukta-ja, as,* m., N. of a class of sons enumerated in Mahā-bh. Anuśāsana-p. 2615. — *Nirukta-pariśishṭa, am,* n., N. of a work supplementary to the Nirukta. — *Nirukta-vat, ān,* m. 'possessing the Nirukta, author of the Nirukta,' an epithet of Yāska. — *Nirukta-vritti, is,* f. 'commentary on the Nirukta,' N. of a commentary on Yāska's Nirukta by Durgāćārya.

Nir-ukti, is, f. explanation, etymological interpretation of words; (in rhetoric) an artificial or poetical explanation of the derivation of a word (e. g. deriving *doshā-kara,* 'the moon,' from *doshā* + *ākara* instead of *doshā* + *kara*); = *nir-ukta,* Yāska's commentary on the Nighaṇṭus.

Nir-ućyamāna, as, ā, am, being uttered or expressed.

निरुक्ष् *nir-uksh,* cl. 6. P. *-ukshati,* &c., Ved. to remove by sprinkling.

निरुच्छ्वास *nir-uććhvāsa, as,* m. absence of breath, not breathing; *(as, ā, am),* without breathing, not breathing, breathless; narrow, contracted, crowded; *(am),* n. (?) a particular hell where the wicked cannot breathe. — *Niruććhvāsa-nipīḍita, as, ā, am,* pained by not breathing (?).

निरुज *ni-ruja, as, ā, am,* for *nī-ruja,* healthy, q. v.

निरुत्तर *nir-uttara, as, ā, am,* having no superior; answerless, without a reply, unable to answer, silenced, posed; *(am),* n., N. of a Tantra. — *Niruttara-tantra, am,* n., N. of a Tantra.

निरुत्पात *nir-utpāta, as, ā, am,* free from portents.

निरुत्सव *nir-utsava, as, ā, am,* without festivals, having no festivities.

निरुत्साह *nir-utsāha, as,* m. absence of exertion, want of energy, indolence, pusillanimity; *(as, ā, am),* without energy, devoid of energy, undertaking nothing, without courage, indolent, indifferent. — *Nirutsāha-tā,* f. want of energy, cowardice.

निरुत्सुक *nir-utsuka, as, ā, am,* careless, indifferent, unconcerned; calm, tranquil, unanxious, unregretful, having no vehement desire for; *(as),* m., N. of a son of Manu Raivata; one of the Saptarshis under the thirteenth Manu.

निरुदक *nir-udaka, as, ā, am,* waterless, devoid of water.

निरुद्यम *nir-udyama, as, ā, am,* effortless, inactive, lazy, at rest.

निरुद्योग *nir-udyoga, as, ā, am,* making no efforts, lazy, listless, idle; disheartened; causeless (?).

निरुद्विग्न *nir-udvigna* or *nir-udvega, as, ā, am,* unexcited, undisturbed, free from perturbation, fearless, sedate, calm. — *Nirudvigna-manas, ās, ās, as,* undisturbed in mind.

निरुध् *ni-rudh,* cl. 7. P. A. *-ruṇaddhi, -runddhe, -roddhum,* to shut in, shut, obstruct, stop, hinder, prevent, restrain, check; to confine; to keep off, remove; to accomplish (?): Caus. *-rodhayati, -yitum,* to cause to be shut or obstructed.

Ni-ruddha, as, ā, am, stopped, obstructed, restrained, checked, hindered, opposed; confined, imprisoned; *(as),* m., N. of a prince. — *Niruddha-kaṇṭha, as, ā, am,* having the breath obstructed, suffocated. — *Niruddha-guda, as,* m. contraction or obstruction of the rectum. — *Niruddha-prakaśa, as,* m. stricture of the urethra. — *Niruddha-śama-vritti, is, is, i,* 'whose state of repose is interrupted,' wearied, tired.

Ni-rundhat, an, atī, at, checking, hindering, suppressing, &c.

Ni-rundhāna, as, ā, am, obstructing, opposing, hindering, preventing; depriving of, &c.

Ni-roddhavya, as, ā, am, to be shut in or confined, to be fenced, to be enclosed with a fence or hedge.

Ni-rodha, as, m. shutting in, confinement, locking up, imprisonment; enclosing, covering up; check, restraint, coercion, suppression, hindrance, prevention, obstruction, opposition; annihilation, destruction; (in dramatic language) disappointment, frustration of hope; hurting, injuring (= *ni-graha*); aversion, disfavour, dislike; (with Buddhists) suppression or annihilation of pain (one of the four principles); N. of a man.

Ni-rodhaka, as, ā, am, obstructive, obstructing, confining, hindering.

Ni-rodhana, as, ī, am, confining, obstructing; (*as*), m. (with *avaṭa*) N. of a hell; (*am*), n. confinement, imprisonment; keeping back, restraining, keeping down, coercion; denying; (in dramatic language) disappointment, frustration of hope.

Ni-rodhin, ī, inī, i, obstructing, hindering.

निरुपक्रम *nir-upakrama, as, ā, am*, having no beginning, without a commencement.

निरुपद्रव *nir-upadrava, as, ā, am*, free from hostile attacks, free from ravages, not visited by calamity or affliction, free from adversity or danger, lucky, happy, undisturbed, unharmed, unmolested; free from national distress, free from tyranny; causing no affliction or adversity; peaceful, secure; not inauspicious (as a star). — *Nirupadrava-tā*, f. absence of calamity or danger, security.

Nir-upadruta, as, ā, am, not visited by calamities; not boding evil (as a star).

निरुपधि *nir-upadhi, is, is, i*, without guile, guileless, honest, secure.

निरुपपत्ति *nir-upapatti, is, is, i*, unfit, unsuitable. — *Nirupapatti-tva, am*, n. unfitness, unsuitableness.

निरुपपद *nir-upapada, as, ā, am*, not connected with a subordinate word; [cf. *upa-pada*.]

निरुपप्लव *nir-upaplava, as, ā, am*, free from calamity or disturbance, free from trouble or alarm; unharmed; not causing adversity; an epithet of Śiva.

निरुपभोग *nir-upabhoga, as, ā, am*, not enjoying, destitute of enjoyment.

निरुपम *nir-upama, as, ā, am*, peerless, matchless, without a compeer or equal, unequalled, incomparable; (*as*), m. a species of poisonous animal (= *gaudheraka*).

निरुपल *nir-upala, as, ā, am*, stoneless, free from stones.

निरुपलेप *nir-upalepa, as, ā, am*, unsmeared, free from ointment.

निरुपसर्ग *nir-upasarga, as, ā, am*, free from portents, not portentous.

निरुपस्कृत *nir-upaskṛita, as, ā, am*, uncorrupted, inartificial, pure.

निरुपहत *nir-upahata, as, ā, am*, unhurt, uninjured, not afflicted; auspicious.

निरुपाख्य *nir-upākhya, as, ā, am*, not perceptible by the eyes, invisible, immaterial; unreal, false, non-existent.

निरुपाधिक *nir-upādhika, as, ā, am*, without attributes or qualities.

निरुपाय *nir-upāya, as, ā, am*, without expedients, remediless, helpless; unsuccessful.

निरुपेक्ष *nir-upeksha, as, ā, am*, not neglectful; free from trick or fraud.

निरुप्ति *nir-upti, is*, f. (fr. rt. *vap* with *nis*), = 1. *nir-vāpa*, q. v.

Nir-upya, as, ā, am, to be scattered or sprinkled.

निरुब्ज् *nir-ubj*, cl. 6. P. *-ubjati*, &c., Ved. to press down, cause to flow down, send down, let loose.

निरुष्णीष *nir-ushṇīsha, as, ā, am*, without a turban or head-dress, bare-headed.

निरूष्मन् *nir-ushman, ā, ā, a*, devoid of heat, cold. — *Nirushma-tva, am*, n. absence of heat, coldness.

निरूढ 1. *ni-rūḍha, as, ā, am* (fr. *ni-ruh*), inherent, conventional, accepted (as the familiar meaning of words in opposition to their etymological sense); (*as*), m. (in rhetoric) the force or application of words according to their natural or received meanings; (in logic) the inherence of any property in the term implying it (as of redness in the word red &c.).

निरूढ 2. *nir-ūḍha, ā*, f. (fr. rt. *vah* with *nis*), unmarried.

निरूप् *ni-rūp*, cl. 10. P. *-rūpayati, -yitum*, to perform; to represent, enact, act dramatically; to see, perceive, look at, look into; to observe, consider, reflect upon; to investigate, examine, look out for, discover, search; to ascertain; to select, choose, appoint; to resolve, determine.

Ni-rūpaṇa, as, ī, am, defining, determining; (*am*), n. form, shape; sight, seeing; looking for, searching; looking into, investigation, determination, definition; ascertaining, defining, (in these senses also *ni-rūpaṇā*.)

Ni-rūpaṇīya, as, ā, am, to be looked for; to be searched into or examined, to be investigated.

Ni-rūpayat, an, antī, at, looking for, investigating, considering.

Ni-rūpita, as, ā, am, seen, beheld; discovered, found; appointed, elected, chosen, deputed; considered, weighed; ascertained, determined, resolved.

Ni-rūpiti, is, f. definition (of an idea), ascertainment.

1. *ni-rūpya, as, ā, am*, to be seen or defined or ascertained.

2. *ni-rūpya*, ind. having seen or considered. — *Nirūpya-tā*, f. or *nirūpya-tva, am*, n. ascertaining, determining.

निरूष्मन् *nir-ūshman*. See *nir-ushman*.

निरूह् *nir-ūh* [cf. rt. 1. *ūh*], cl. 1. P. A. *-ūhati, -te*, &c., Ved. inf. *nir-ūhitavai*, to push out, draw out, remove: Caus. *-ūhayati, -yitum*, to cause to draw out or purge.

3. *nir-ūḍha, as, ā, am*, drawn out, purged, eviscerated; (for 2. *nir-ūḍha* see above.) — *Nirūḍha-paśu-prayoga, as*, m., N. of a treatise on particular sacrifices, (see the next.) — *Nirūḍha-paśu-bandha, as*, m. 'the offering or oblation of an eviscerated animal,' N. of one of the regular Havir-yajñas.

Nir-ūḍhi, is, f. (also to be referred to rt. *vah* with *nis*), fame, celebrity, renown.

1. *nir-ūha, as*, m. a purging clyster; an enema not of an oily kind, = *ni-graha*? (for 2. *nir-ūha* see below.) — *Nirūha-vasti-vidhi, is*, m., N. of the twenty-fifth chapter of the Śārṅga-dhara-saṃhitā, a medical work by Śārṅga-dhara. — *Nirūhādhikāra* (°*ha-adh*°), *as*, m., N. of a chapter of a medical work by Vṛinda.

1. *nir-ūhaṇa, am*, n. causing to purge with a clyster; administering enemas not of an oily kind. (For 2. *nir-ūhaṇa* see below.)

Nir-ūhita, as, ā, am, purged.

निरूह 2. *nir-ūha, as*, m. (fr. rt. 2. *ūh* with *nis*), logic, disputation; certainty, ascertainment. (For 1. *nir-ūha* see above; for 3. see next col.)

2. *nir-ūhaṇa, am*, n. ascertainment.

निरूह 3. *nir-ūha, as*, m. (for 1. and 2. see col. 2), a sentence having no ellipsis, a complete sentence.

निर्ऋ *nir-ṛi*, cl. 3. P. *-iyarti*, &c., Ved. to go out from, depart from, liberate one's self from (with abl.); to be excluded, to become deprived of (with abl.): Caus. *nir-arpayati, -yitum*, to cause to go to pieces or decay, to dissolve.

Nir-ṛita, as, ā, am, dissolved, decaying; debilitated; (*as*), m., N. of a Rudra.

Nir-ṛiti, is, f. decay, dissolution, destruction, annihilation, calamity, evil, adversity; imprecation, curse; Decay or Destruction personified (goddess of death and corruption; she is described as binding mortals with her cords, and is often associated with Mṛityu, A-rāti, and similar beings; she is variously regarded as the wife of A-dharma, mother of Bhaya, Mahā-bhaya, and Mṛityu, or as a daughter of A-dharma and Hiṃsā and mother of Naraka and Bhaya; she is regent of the south-west or south-western quarter and of the asterism Mūla); (*is*), f. the bottom or lower depths of the earth (perhaps regarded as the seat of putrefaction; cf. *nairṛita*); (*is, is, i*), free from adversity, (in this sense *nir* is a privative.)

Nir-ṛitha, as, m. destruction, the Destroyer (i. e. Nirṛitha personified); an epithet of a particular Agni; (according to some) the Sāma-veda.

निर्ऋच्छ् *nir-ṛich*, cl. 6. P. *-ṛiććhati*, &c., Ved. to go out from, fall from, be excluded from (with abl.); to go or cleave asunder.

निरे *nir-e* (*nir-ā-i*), cl. 2. P. *nir-aiti*, Ved. to come forth from, to go off, depart, make way for.

निरेक *ni-reka, as*, m. (fr. rt. *rić* with *ni*), Ved. a lasting possession (?), wealth, property; (*e*), ind. lastingly, for ever; (Sāy.) in poverty or want; in donation or gifts; (according to Mahī-dhara) not empty.

निरेभ *ni-rebha, as, ā, am*, soundless, noiseless.

निरोद्धव्य *ni-roddhavya, ni-rodha*, &c. See col. 1.

निर्गत *nir-gata*. See *nir-gam* below.

निर्गन्ध *nir-gandha, as, ā, am*, inodorous, scentless, unfragrant, void of smell. — *Nirgandha-tā*, f. absence of smell, want of fragrance, scentlessness. — *Nirgandha-pushpī*, f. the silk-cotton tree (= *śālmali*), Bombax Heptaphyllum.

निर्गन्धन *nirgandhana, am*, n. = *nirgranthana*, killing, slaughter.

निर्गम् *nir-gam*, cl. 1. P. *-gaććhati, -gantum*, to go out, come forth, depart from (with abl.), set out; to come out or appear (as a bud); to go away, disappear; to be freed from (with abl.); to enter into any state, undergo (with acc.): Desid. *-jigamishati*, to wish to go out.

Nir-ga, as, m. country, region; place or province.

Nir-gata, as, ā, am, gone out, come forth, come out, appeared; gone away, departed; disappeared, extinct; freed from. — *Nirgata-viśanka, as, ā, am*, freed from fear, fearless.

Nir-gama, as, m. going forth or out, setting out, going away, receding; departure, vanishing; exit, issue, outlet; a door; [cf. *jala-n*°.]

Nir-gamana, am, n. going out or forth.

निर्गर्व *nir-garva, as, ā, am*, free from pride, humble, lowly.

निर्गल् *nir-gal*, cl. 1. P. *-galati*, &c., to trickle or flow out; to dissolve, melt. — *Nir-galita, as, ā, am*, flowed out, poured forth; dissolved, melted.

निर्गवाक्ष *nir-gavāksha, as, ā, am*, windowless, without windows.

निर्गा *nir-gā*, cl. 3. P. *-jigāti* (or *-jagāti*), *-gātum*, Ved. to go out, come forth.

निर्गुण *nir-guṇa, as, ā, am*, stringless (as a bow); devoid of all qualities or properties; without attributes; having no epithet; devoid of good qualities or virtues, bad, worthless, vicious; (*as*), m. the Supreme Being (as without qualities of any kind). — *Nirguṇa-tā*, f. or *nirguṇa-tva, am*, n. absence of qualities, want of properties, freedom from all qualities (as an attribute of the Supreme Being); absence or want of good qualities, wickedness, viciousness, baseness. — *Nirguṇātmaka* (°*ṇa-āt*°), *as, ā, am*, having no qualities.

निर्गुण्टी *nirguṇṭī* or *nirguṇḍī* or *nirguṇḍi, is*, f. the shrub Vitex Negundo; another plant (= *nīla-śephālikā*); the root of a lotus.

निर्गुप् *nir-gup*, cl. 1. P. *-gopāyati*, &c., to guard, protect.

निर्गुल्म *nir-gulma, as, ā, am*, free from bushes, destitute of shrubs.

निर्गूढ *nir-gūḍha, as*, m. (fr. rt. *guh* with *nis*), the hollow of a tree.

निर्गृह *nir-gṛiha, as, ā, am*, houseless, homeless.

निर्गॄ *nir-gṛī*, cl. 6. P. *-girati* or *-gilati*, &c., to vomit forth. — *Nir-gīrṇa, as, ā, am*, vomited forth.

निर्गौरव *nir-gaurava, as, ā, am*, destitute of respect; without dignity, undignified, affable; (*am*), ind. without pride, condescendingly, affably.

निर्ग्रन्थ *nir-grantha, as, ā, am*, freed from all ties or hindrances; a saint, a devotee who has withdrawn from the world and lives either as a hermit or a beggar wandering about naked; possessionless, poor, a pauper, beggar [cf. *grantha*, said to mean 'riches']; (*as*), m. an idiot; a fool; a gambler; N. of a man, son of Jñāti. — *Nirgrantha-śāstra, am*, n., N. of a work.

Nir-granthaka, as, ā, am, unattended, unaccompanied; abandoned, deserted; fruitless; clever, expert, conversant; (*as*), m. a religious mendicant; a naked devotee; a gambler; (*as, am*), m. n. (?), Buddhism (because the Buddhists appeared as religious mendicants, especially as ascetics).

Nir-granthi, is, is, i, free from knots, knotless.

Nir-granthika, as, m. a naked mendicant, an ascetic; (*as, ā, am*), clever, conversant; = *hīna*, destitute (?).

निर्ग्रन्थन *nir-granthana, am*, n. killing, slaughter; [cf. *ni-granthana, ni-gandhana*.]

निर्ग्राह्य *nir-grāhya, as, ā, am*, to be traced or found out, perceivable.

निर्घट *nir-ghaṭa, am*, n. a fair or crowded market, a free market, a wharf or ghaut where no toll is levied, a place where there is no quay or stairs, (in this sense *nir* is a privative.)

निर्घण्ट *nir-ghaṇṭa* or *nir-ghaṇṭaka, as, am*, m. n. a vocabulary, a collection of words, = *ni-ghaṇṭu*, (perhaps for *nir-granthaka*, 'singling out the words of a sentence and writing them down in their independent form.')

निर्घात *nir-ghāta, as*, m. (fr. rt. *han* with *nis*), destruction; a violent gust of wind, hurricane, whirlwind; the noise of contending vapours in the sky; an earthquake; a thunder-stroke; any severe stroke.

Nir-ghātana, am, n. forcing out, bringing out.

Nir-ghātya, as, ā, am, to be forced or brought out.

निर्घुष्ट *nir-ghushṭa, as, ā, am* (fr. rt. *ghush* with *nis*), sounded, resounded.

Nir-ghosha, as, m. sound in general, noise, a loud noise, rattling, trampling; (*as, ā, am*), soundless, noiseless, (in this sense *nir* is a privative.) — *Nirghoshākshara-vimukta* (°*sha-aksh*°), *as*, m., N. of a Samādhi.

निर्घूरिणी *nir-ghūriṇī*, f. a river, (perhaps a wrong reading for *nir-jhariṇī*.)

निर्घृण *nir-ghṛiṇa, as, ā, am*, unmerciful, pitiless, cruel; shameless, immodest; (*am*), ind. without pity, pitilessly. — *Nirghṛiṇa-tā*, f. or *nir-ghṛiṇa-tva, am*, n. pitilessness, unmercifulness, hard-heartedness, cruelty.

Nir-ghṛiṇā, f. unmercifulness, cruelty.

निर्घृष् *nir-ghṛish*, cl. 1. P. *-gharshati*, &c., to rub against or on (with loc.).

Nir-gharshaṇa, am, n. rubbing, friction.

Nirgharshaṇaka, as, ā, am, who or what rubs, a rubber, rubbing, a rubbing, a dentifrice fit for cleaning the teeth.

Nir-ghṛishya, ind. having rubbed, having rubbed on.

निर्घोष *nir-ghosha*. See *nir-ghushṭa* above.

निर्जन *nir-jana, as, ā, am*, unpeopled, depopulated, uninhabited, unfrequented, lonely, deserted, desolate; (*am*), n. a solitude, desert. — *Nir-jana-tā*, f. or *nirjana-tva, am*, n. depopulation, the state of being unpeopled or deserted. — *Nirjana-vana, am*, n. a lonely or unfrequented forest.

निर्जर 1. *nir-jara, as, ā, am* (for 2. see *nir-jṛī*, col. 3), not becoming old, young, fresh; imperishable, immortal, undecaying; (*as*), m. an immortal, a deity, god; (*ā*), f. the plant Cocculus Cordifolius; Anethum Graveolens, = *tattva-bhid*; (*am*), n. ambrosia, the food of the gods. — *Nir-jara-sarshapa, as*, m. a species of mustard (= *deva-sarshapa*).

Nir-jaras, optionally substituted for 1. *nir-jara* in certain cases. (See Pāṇ. VII. 2, 101.)

निर्जरायु *nir-jarāyu, us, us, u*, Ved. skinless (as a snake which has cast its skin).

निर्जर्जल्प *nir-jarjalpa, as, ā, am*, Ved. (according to Mahī-dhara, probably because of its similarity to *jarjara*, =) ragged, tattered; (another reading has *nir-jālmaka*.)

निर्जल *nir-jala, as, ā, am*, waterless, destitute of water, dry, desert; not mixed with water (as buttermilk); (*as*), m. a desert, waste. — *Nirjala-toyadābha* (°*da-ābhā*), *as, ā, am*, of the colour of a waterless cloud, i. e. white, of a fair complexion. — *Nirjalaikādaśī* (°*la-ek*°), f., N. of the eleventh day in the light half of month Jyaishṭha, on which even the drinking of water is forbidden.

निर्जात *nir-jāta, as, ā, am*, come forth, appeared, visible.

निर्जाल्मक *nir-jālmaka*. See *nir-jarjalpa*.

निर्जि *nir-ji*, cl. 1. P. A. *-jayati, -te, -jetum*, to conquer, win, gain, acquire, subdue, vanquish; to overcome in play.

Nir-jaya, as, m. conquest, complete victory, vanquishing, subduing; [cf. *manyu-n*°.]

Nir-jita, as, ā, am, conquered, completely vanquished, thoroughly subdued, overcome; won, acquired, gained; claimed; unconquered. — *Nirjita-varman, ā*, m., N. of a man. — *Nirjitāri-gaṇas* (°*ta-ar*°), *as, ā, am*, one who has conquered hosts of enemies. — *Nirjitendriya* (°*ta-in*°), *as, ā, am*, of subdued passions or feelings. — *Nirjitendriya-grāma, as*, m. 'one who has subdued the whole assemblage of his organs,' a Muni, a saint.

Nir-jiti, is, f. conquest, complete victory, subduing, subjugation.

Nir-jitya, ind. having conquered or won or gained.

Nir-jetṛi, tā, m. a conqueror, vanquisher.

निर्जिह्व *nir-jihva, as, ā, am*, tongueless, without a tongue.

निर्जीव *nir-jīva, as*, m. lifelessness, death; (*as, ā, am*), lifeless, inanimate, dead. — *Nirjīva-kāraṇa, am*, n. a cause of death, a fatal blow.

Nir-jīvita, as, ā, am, lifeless, dead, inanimate.

निर्जुष्ट *nir-jushṭa, as, ā, am* (fr. rt. 1. *jush* with prep. *nis*), frequented, inhabited.

निर्जॄ *nir-jṛī*, Caus. *-jarayati, -yitum*, to wear down, wear away, rub to pieces, crush.

2. *nir-jara, as, ā, am*, completely wearing down or destroying. (For 1. *nir-jara* see col. 2.)

निर्ज्ञाति *nir-jñāti, is, is, i*, destitute of relations; having no kinsfolk.

निर्ज्वर *nir-jvara, as, ā, am*, feverless, healthy.

निर्झर *nir-jhara, as, ī, am*, m. f. n. (perhaps fr. *jhar* for rt. *kshar* with *nis*), a waterfall, cataract, cascade, mountain-torrent, the precipitous descent of water from mountains, &c. [cf. *jhara*]; (*as*), m. burning chaff; an elephant; a horse of the Sun [cf. *nir-ṇara*]; (*ī*), f. a river [cf. *nir-jhariṇī*; cf. also *nilimpa-n*°.]

Nir-jharin, ī, m. a mountain; (*iṇī*), f. a torrent, river.

निर्णय *nir-ṇaya*. See under *nir-ṇī* below.

निर्णर *nir-ṇara, as*, m. one of the horses of the Sun; [cf. *nir-jhara*.]

निर्णाम *nirṇāma, as*, m., Ved. the joint of a wing.

निर्णिज् 1. *nir-ṇij*, cl. 3. P. A. *-ṇenekti, -ṇe-nikte*, Ved. inf. *nir-ṇije, nir-ṇijam*, &c., to wash off, wash, cleanse (A.); to wash one's self; to dress one's self.

Nir-ṇikta, as, ā, am, washed, purified, cleaned, cleansed.

2. *nir-ṇij, k*, f., Ved. a shining dress or ornament, any bright garment [cf. *adhi-n*°, *aśva-n*°, *ghṛita-n*°]; purification, cleansing; (Sāy.) a form, shape; well nourished (m. f. n.).

Nir-ṇeka, as, m. washing, cleansing, cleaning; ablution; expiation, atonement.

Nir-ṇejaka, as, m. a washerman, washer.

Nir-ṇejana, am, n. ablution; expiation, atonement for an offence.

निर्णी *nir-ṇī*, cl. 1. P. A. *-ṇayati, -te, -ṇetum*, to lead or take away, carry away, carry off; to trace out, investigate, find out, ascertain, educe, elicit, to settle, come to a decision, decide.

Nir-ṇaya, as, m. removing, removal; deciding, rendering certain, complete ascertainment, decision, certainty, determination, proof, affirmation, precise definition, settlement; (in logic) deduction, inference, conclusion, demonstration; application of a conclusive argument; (in law) sentence, verdict; (in rhetoric) narration of events; discussion, consideration, investigation. — *Nirṇaya-kamalākara* (°*la-āk*°), *as*, m. 'a lotus-bed of conclusions,' N. of a Mīmāṃsā work. — *Nirṇaya-darpaṇa, am*, n. 'mirror of certainty,' N. of a Vedānta work. — *Nirṇaya-dīpa*, 'lamp of certainty,' N. of a work mentioned in the Śūdra-dharma-tattva by Kamalākara-bhaṭṭa. — *Nirṇaya-dīpikā*, f., N. of a work written about the middle of the seventeenth century. — *Nirṇaya-pāda, as*, m. a sentence, decree, verdict in law. — *Nirṇaya-sindhu*, N. of a Mīmāṃsā work by Kamalākara-bhaṭṭa; (also read *nirṇeya-sindhu*.) — *Nirṇayā-mṛita* (°*ya-am*°), *am*, n. 'nectar of certainty,' N. of a work.

Nir-ṇayat, an, antī, at, concluding, deciding, ascertaining.

Nir-ṇayana, am, n. ascertainment, certainty; positive conclusion.

Nir-ṇāyaka, as, ā, am, causing or leading to certainty, conclusive.

Nir-ṇāyana, am, n. rendering certain; the outer angle of the elephant's eye.

Nir-ṇīta, as, ā, am, deduced, traced out, brought to a conclusion, ascertained, settled, decided, proved.

Nir-ṇetṛi, tā, tṛi, tṛi, decisive, certifying, verifying, leading to certainty, demonstrating, proving; (*tā*), m. one who pronounces a sentence, a judge; a voucher; a guide. — *Nirṇetṛi-tva, am*, n. proof, verification.

Nir-ṇeya, as, ā, am, to be ascertained, to be decided or determined.

निर्णुद् *nir-ṇud*, cl. 6. P. A. (sometimes wrongly *nir-nud*), *-ṇudati, -te, -ṇottum*, to push or drive out; to drive away, expel, reject, remove; to repudiate.

Nir-ṇoda, as, m. removal, banishment.

निर्दंश् *nir-dans*, cl. 1. P. *-daśati* or *-danśati, -danshṭum*, to bite through, bite; (with *dantān*) to gnash the teeth, grind the teeth.

Nir-danśin, ī, inī, i, biting through; not biting, (Ved., in this sense *nir* is a privative.)

Nir-daśat, an, antī, at, biting, biting through; consuming.

Nir-daśamāna, as, ā, am, biting through, biting; gnashing or grinding (the teeth).

Nir-daśya, ind. having bitten, biting through.

निर्दग्ध *nir-dagdha*. See *nir-dah* below.

निर्दंड *nir-daḍa, as, ā, am*, unkind, unfeeling, unmerciful; devoid of pity or charity, rejoicing over the faults of others; envious, slanderous, abusive; useless, unnecessary; mad, intoxicated; violent; (sometimes spelt *nir-daṭa*; cf. *nir-daya*.)

निर्दण्ड *nir-daṇḍa, as, ā, am*, not punishing.

निर्दय *nir-daya, as, ā, am*, pitiless, unmerciful, unkind, cruel, hard-hearted; passionate; excessive, violent; unpitied by any; (*am*), n. without pity, unmercifully; passionately, violently, excessively, much. — *Nirdaya-tva, am*, n. unmercifulness, cruelty.

निर्दर *nir-dara, as*, or *nir-dari, is*, m. = *dara* or *dari*, a cave, cavern; [according to some *nir-dara, as, ā, am*, = *nir-daya*, pitiless, hard; shameless; also *nir-daram*, ind. = excessively, and *nir-dara, am*, n. = pith, essence.] — *Nirdari-vāsin, ī, inī, i*, inhabiting a cave.

निर्दलन *nir-dalana, am*, n. splitting, cleaving asunder, breaking.

निर्दश *nir-daśa, as, ā, am*, more than ten days old, what happened more than ten days ago; [cf. *a-n°*, *nairdaśya*.] — *Nirdaśāha* (°*śa-aha*), see *a-n°*.

निर्दशत् *nir-daśat*, &c. See *nir-dans* above.

निर्दशन *nir-daśana, as, ā, am*, toothless. — *Nirdaśanākshi-jihva* (°*na-aksh*°), *as, ā, am*, deprived of teeth, eyes, and tongue.

निर्दस्यु *nir-dasyu, us, us, u*, free from robbers or bandits.

निर्दह् *nir-dah*, cl. 1. P. *-dahati, -dagdhum*, to burn out, burn up, consume by fire, destroy completely: Caus. *-dāhayati, -yitum*, to cause to burn up or set on fire.

Nir-dagdha, as, ā, am, burnt, burnt up; unburnt, (in this sense *nir* is a privative.)

Nir-dagdhikā, f. = *ni-digdhikā*.

Nir-dahana, as, ī, am, burning, burning up, consuming; (*as*), m. the plant Semecarpus Anacardium; (*ī*), f. the plant Sanseviera Roxburghiana; (*am*), n. burning.

Nir-dāha, as, ā, am, or *nir-dāhuka, as, ā, am*, Ved. burning, consuming by fire.

निर्दातृ *nir-dātṛi, tā*, m. (fr. rt. 3. *dā* or *do* with *nis*), a weeder, digger up of weeds; a reaper, husbandman; [cf. *nir-yātṛi*.]

निर्दारित *nir-dārita*. See *nir-dṛī* below.

निर्दिग्ध *nir-digdha, as, ā, am* (fr. rt. *dih* with *nis*), anointed, smeared; well fed, corpulent, stout, lusty.

Nir-digdhikā, f. a various reading for *nir-dagdhikā* or *ni-digdhikā*.

निर्दिश् *nir-diś*, cl. 6. P. *-diśati, -deshṭum*, to point to, point out, show, direct, declare, announce, tell, enjoin, order; to denote, indicate, mark; to assign, destine; to enumerate, specify, particularize, name; to foretel; to define, determine; to describe; to recommend, advise, suggest; to denounce: Desid. *-didikshati*, to wish to point out or to define more closely.

Nir-diśya, ind. having pointed out, having shown, explained, enjoined, &c.

Nir-dishṭa, as, ā, am, pointed out, shown, specified, particularized; described, depicted; assigned; ordered, directed; asserted, declared; ascertained, determined.

Nir-deśa, as, m. pointing out, directing, ordering, order, command, direction; instruction; saying, telling, declaring; description, designation; depicting, specifying, particularizing, giving particulars or details, specification, special mention; certainty, ascertainment; vicinity, proximity; a particular number; [cf. *ni-deśa*.] — *Nirdeśa-kārin, ī, iṇī, i*, executing orders, obedient.

Nir-deśaka, as, ikā, am, pointing out, showing, describing; ordering.

Nir-deśanīya or *nir-deśya, as, ā, am*, to be pointed out; assignable; to be determined; to be arranged; to be described, to be defined or particularized; to be proclaimed or foretold.

Nir-deshṭṛi, ṭā, ṭrī, ṭṛi, who or what shows, explains, points out, defines, &c.; (*ṭā*), m. an authority, a guide.

निर्दी *nir-dī*, cl. 4. P. *-dīyati*, &c., Ved. to fly away.

निर्दुःख *nir-duḥkha, as, ā, am*, free from pain, painless, not suffering pain; not causing pain. — *Nirduḥkha-tva, am*, n. absence of pain; painlessness.

निर्दुह् *nir-duh*, cl. 2. P. A. *-dogdhi, -dugdhe, -dogdhum*, to milk out, extract, draw out, produce; to withdraw.

Nir-dugdha, as, ā, am, milked out, drawn out, extracted.

निर्दॄ *nir-dṛī*, cl. 9. P. *-dṛiṇāti, -daritum, -darītum*, to tear or rend asunder, tear in pieces, split asunder: Caus. *-dārayati, -yitum*, to tear or split asunder; to root up, cause to be dug up.

Nir-dārita, as, ā, am, torn asunder, rent; split open, opened, unclosed; starting open.

निर्देव *nir-deva, as, ā, am*, Ved. abandoned by the gods, without the gods.

निर्दैन्य *nir-dainya, as, ā, am*, free from misery or wretchedness, happy, comfortable, at ease.

निर्दोष *nir-dosha, as, ā, am*, faultless, without defect or blemish; guiltless, innocent.

Nirdoshī-kṛita, as, ā, am, cleared from guilt.

निर्द्रव्य *nir-dravya, as, ā, am*, immaterial; without property, poor.

निर्द्रु *nir-dru*, cl. 1. P. *-dravati, -drotum*, Ved. to run out, run away.

निर्द्रोह *nir-droha, as, ā, am*, not malevolent, not hostile, friendly; well-disposed; innocent.

निर्द्वन्द्व *nir-dvandva, as, ā, am*, free from either of two alternatives or indifferent in regard to opposite pairs of feelings (as pleasure and pain), neither glad nor sorry, &c.; not standing in mutual relation, not dependant upon another, independant; not striving together, free from envy or jealousy; not causing disputes, uncontested, undisputed; not double; not acknowledging two principles.

निर्धन *nir-dhana, as, ā, am*, without property or money; poor, indigent; (*as*), m. an old ox. — *Nirdhana-tā*, f. or *nirdhana-tva, am*, n. absence of property, poverty, indigence.

निर्धर्म *nir-dharma, as*, m. unrighteousness; (*as, ā, am*), unjust, unrighteous, impious, immoral, void of law, irreligious.

निर्धा *nir-dhā*, cl. 3. P. *-dadhāti, -dhātum*, Ved. to free from; to find out (?).

निर्धार *nir-dhāra*, &c. See *nir-dhṛi* below.

निर्धार्तराष्ट्र *nir-dhārtarāshṭra, as, ā, am*, having no descendants of Dhṛita-rāshṭra, free from them.

निर्धाव् 1. *nir-dhāv*, cl. 1. P. A. *-dhāvati, -te, -dhāvitum*, to stream forth from, spring from; to run out, escape from.

निर्धाव् 2. *nir-dhāv*, cl. 1. P. A. *-dhāvati, -te, -dhāvitum*, to wash off, wash away, cleanse.

Nir-dhauta, as, ā, am, washed off, cleansed, polished, bright.

निर्धू *nir-dhū*, cl. 5. P. A. *-dhūnoti, -dhūnute* (in later language also *-dhunoti, -dhunute*), *-dhotum* and *-dhavitum*, to shake out, shake off, remove; to drive away, expel, banish, repudiate, disown; to shake, agitate, brandish, move about; to harass, distress, torment, pain.

Nir-dhūta or *nir-dhuta, as, ā, am*, shaken off, shaken out, thrown out or off; removed; avoided; departed; deserted, rejected; broken, divided; refuted, destroyed; deprived of, bereft; suffered, undergone; (*as*), m. a man abandoned by his relatives or friends. — *Nirdhūta-pāpa, as, ā, am*, one whose sins are wholly shaken off or removed.

निर्धूम *nir-dhūma, as, ā, am*, smokeless. — *Nirdhūma-tva, am*, n. smokelessness.

निर्धृ *nir-dhṛi*, cl. 1. P. A. *-dharati, -te*, cl. 10. or Caus. *-dhārayati, -yitum*, to take out from; to separate one out of many, particularize; to determine, define, state accurately; to ascertain.

Nir-dhāra, as, m. or *nir-dhāraṇa, am*, n. taking out from, separating or specifying one out of many, particularizing individuals according to their degree of merit; determining, defining, settling; certainty, ascertainment.

Nir-dhāraṇīya or *nir-dhāritavya, as, ā, am*, to be ascertained; irresistible, (in this sense *nir* is a privative.)

Nir-dhārita, as, ā, am, determined, ascertained, settled.

Nir-dhārya, as, ā, am, to be ascertained or determined, ascertainable; not to be restrained, acting resolutely or fearlessly, active, energetic, (in this sense *nir* is a privative.)

Nir-dhāryamāṇa, as, ā, am, being particularized; being determined.

निर्धे *nir-dhe*, cl. 1. P. *-dhayati, -dhātum*, Ved. to drink up, suck up, absorb.

निर्धौत *nir-dhauta*. See 2. *nir-dhāv* above.

निर्ध्मा *nir-dhmā*, cl. 1. P. *-dhamati, -dhmātum*, to blow away, blow out of.

Nir-dhmāpana, am, n. blowing away.

निर्ध्यै *nir-dhyai*, cl. 1. P. *-dhyāyati, -dhyātum*, to think of, reflect upon, meditate about.

Nir-dhyāta, as, ā, am, thought of, reflected upon, meditated.
Nir-dhyāya, ind. having thought of, having reflected.

निर्नमस्कार *nir-namaskāra, as, ā, am,* not respecting any one, uncourteous; unrespected, respected by no one, despised by all.

निर्नर *nir-nara, as, ā, am,* abandoned by men, deserted, desolate.

निर्नाथ *nir-nātha, as, ā, am,* protectorless, without a guardian or master or superior. — *Nirnātha-tā,* f. the being without a master or guardian or protector, want of protection; widowhood; orphanage.

निर्नाभि *nir-nābhi, is, is, i,* without the navel, not reaching to the navel.

निर्नाशन *nir-nāśana, am,* n. (fr. rt. *naś* with *nis*), removing, expelling, banishing.
Nir-nāśin, ī, inī, i (from an unused *nir-nāśa*), removing, expelling, banishing.

निर्निद्र *nir-nidra, as, ā, am,* sleepless. — *Nirnidra-tā,* f. sleeplessness.

निर्निमित्त *nir-nimitta, as, ā, am,* without reason or motive, causeless, groundless; *(am),* n. causelessly, without cause. — *Nirnimitta-kṛita, as, ā, am,* produced without a cause, whose cause is invisible.

निर्निमेष *nir-nimesha, as, ā, am,* not twinkling.

निर्निरोध *nir-nirodha, as, ā, am,* unobstructed.

निर्नीड *nir-nīḍa, as, ā, am,* having no nest.

निर्बद्ध *nir-baddha.* See *nir-bandh* below.

निर्बन्ध् *nir-bandh,* cl. 9. P. *-badhnāti, -banddhum,* to fix or fasten upon, attach one's self to, cling to, to insist upon, persist in; press upon; to urge, importune.
Nir-baddha, as, ā, am, fixed upon, fastened upon; directed on; clung to; pressed hard, urged.
Nir-bandha, as, m. insisting upon (with loc.), persistence, perseverance, pertinacity, intentness; obstinacy; importunity, urgency, pressing or urging anything, (*nirbandhaṃ kṛi,* to urge); accusing, accusation; contest, dispute; caprice, fancy?; [cf. *ni-bandha.*] — *Nirbandha-pṛishṭa, as, ā, am,* urgently asked, importuned.
Nir-bandhanīya, am, n. (perhaps) contest, dispute.
Nir-bandhin, ī, inī, i, insisting upon (with loc.), urgent, persisting in, intent upon.

निर्बन्धु *nir-bandhu, us, us, u,* without relations, without kindred, friendless.

निर्बर्हण *nir-barhaṇa, am,* n. = *ni-varhaṇa,* slaughter, killing, destroying, annihilation.

निर्बल *nir-bala, as, ā, am,* powerless, without strength, impotent, weak, feeble.

निर्बाध् *nir-bādh,* cl. 1. A. *-bādhate, -bādhitum,* Ved. to keep off, ward off, hold back.
Nir-bādha, as, m., Ved. a knob, prominence; (*nirbādhe kṛi* is perhaps a proverbial expression meaning 'to put on one side, set aside, remove.')
Nirbādhin, ī, inī, i, Ved. furnished with knobs or prominences.

निर्बुद्धि *nir-buddhi, is, is, i,* senseless, witless, unwise, ignorant, stupid, out of one's wits.

निर्बुसीकृत *nirbusī-kṛita, as, ā, am,* freed from chaff, husked.

निर्ब्रू *nir-brū,* cl. 2. P. *-bravīti,* &c., Ved. to speak out, pronounce (loud or clearly); to interpret, explain.

निर्भक्त *nir-bhakta.* See *nir-bhaj* below.

निर्भग्न *nir-bhagna.* See *nir-bhañj* below.

निर्भज् *nir-bhaj,* cl. 1. P. A. *-bhajati, -te, -bhaktum,* Ved. to exclude from participation or coparceny (with abl.): Caus. *-bhājayati, -yitum,* to exclude from sharing in, to disinherit.
Nir-bhakta, as, ā, am, excluded from participation in; taken without eating (as medicine; in this sense *nir* is a privative).
Nir-bhājya, as, ā, am, to be excluded from participation in, to be debarred from sharing in.

निर्भञ्ज् *nir-bhañj,* cl. 7. P. *-bhanakti, -bhanktum,* to break asunder, split asunder; to defeat.
Nir-bhagna, as, ā, am, broken in pieces; broken down; bent. — *Nir-bhajyamāna, as, ā, am,* being broken in pieces.

निर्भट *nir-bhaṭa, as, ā, am,* hard, firm, compact; (perhaps a wrong reading.)

निर्भय *nir-bhaya, as, ā, am,* fearless, undaunted; free from danger, secure; *(as),* m., N. of a son of the thirteenth Manu; *(am),* ind. fearlessly, without danger.

निर्भर *nir-bhara, as, ā, am* [cf. *bhara*], excessive, exceeding, vehement, violent; deep, sound (as sleep); ardent; beyond measure, much; (at the end of a comp.) full of, filled with; *(as, am),* m. n. essence?; *(am),* ind. excessively, exceedingly, very much; soundly, deeply.

निर्भर्त्स् *nir-bharts,* cl. 10. P. A. *-bhartsayati, -te, -yitum,* to threaten, menace, abuse, rebuke, reprimand, chide, blame, deride.
Nir-bhartsana, am, ā, n. f. threatening, threat, menace; abuse, reviling, reproach, blame; malignity; red paint, lac. — *Nirbhartsana-daṇḍa-mohita, as, ā, am,* bewildered by the threat of punishment.
Nir-bhartsita, as, ā, am, threatened, menaced; reviled, abused.
Nir-bhartsya, ind. having threatened; having reviled or reproached.

निर्भस् *nir-bhas,* cl. 3. P. *-babhasti, -bapsati,* &c., Ved. to bite off, chew.

निर्भा *nir-bhā,* cl. 2. P. *-bhāti, -bhātum,* to shine forth, appear, arise, proceed.
Nir-bhāta, as, ā, am, shone forth, shining forth, appeared, arisen.

निर्भाग्य *nir-bhāgya, as, ā, am,* unlucky, unfortunate.

निर्भाज्य *nir-bhājya.* See *nir-bhaj* above.

निर्भास् *nir-bhās,* Caus. *-bhāsayati, -yitum,* to illuminate.
Nir-bhāsita, as, ā, am, illuminated, illumined.

निर्भिद् *nir-bhid,* cl. 7. P. A. *-bhinatti, -bhintte, -bhettum,* to cleave or split asunder, break in two, rend, divide, separate, open; to break through, pierce, penetrate, wound; to put out (the eyes); to break down, destroy; to divulge, betray; to find out, detect, discover; to excavate: Pass. *-bhidyate,* to be broken asunder, to cleave or split open (intrans.); to burst asunder.
Nir-bhidya, ind. having broken through, having pierced or penetrated.
Nir-bhinna, as, ā, am, broken asunder, pierced, divided. — *Nirbhinna-tanu, us, us, u,* having the body pierced through or transfixed.
Nir-bheda, as, m. breaking or splitting asunder, bursting, dividing, a split, rent; the bed or channel of a river; the issue or termination of an affair, event.
Nir-bhedin, ī, inī, i, splitting asunder, piercing.
Nir-bhedya, as, ā, am, to be split asunder; having no rent; missing an aim; disappointed; (in the last three senses *nir* is a privative.)

निर्भीत *nir-bhīta, as, ā, am,* fearless, not afraid.

निर्भुज् *nir-bhuj,* cl. 6. P. *-bhujati, -bhoktum,* to bend on one side, bend awry, distort; (*oshṭhau nirbhujati,* he distorts his lips, makes a wry face.)
Nir-bhugna, as, ā, am, bent awry, distorted; not bent, straight, (in this sense *nir* is a privative.)
Nir-bhuja, as, ā, am, a term applied to a kind of Sandhi (or Saṃhitā).

निर्भू *nir-bhū,* cl. 1. P. *-bhavati, -bhavitum,* Ved. to come out, move out, move.
Nir-bhūti, is, f., Ved. disappearing, passing away.

निर्भृ *nir-bhṛi,* cl. 1. 3. P. *-bharati, -bibharti, -bhartum,* to take out, draw out.
Nir-bhṛita, probably a wrong reading for *nibhṛita.*

निर्भृति *nir-bhṛiti, is, is, i,* without wages, hireless.

निर्भेद *nir-bheda, nir-bhedya.* See *nir-bhid.*

निर्भोग *nir-bhoga, as, ā, am,* not devoted to pleasure or enjoyment.

निर्मक्षिक *nir-makshika, as, ā, am,* free from flies, free from tormentors, untroubled; *(am),* n. the being free from flies; *(am),* ind. without flies.

निर्मज् *nir-maj,* Ved. (according to Sāy.) completely pure (as cows).

निर्मज्ज् *nir-majj,* cl. 1. P. *-majjati,* &c., to sink under, sink into; to inundate, deluge.
Nir-magna, as, ā, am, sunk, sunk into, sunk under, (opposed to *un-magna.*)

निर्मज्ज *nir-majja, as, ā, am,* fatless, marrowless, meagre.

निर्मण्डूक *nir-maṇḍūka, as, ā, am,* frogless, destitute of frogs.

निर्मत्सर *nir-matsara, as, ā, am,* without envy, unenvious, free from envy or passion.

निर्मत्स्य *nir-matsya, as, ā, am,* fishless, destitute of fish. — *Nirmatsya-tā,* f. absence of fish, the having no fish.

निर्मथ *nir-matha, nir-mathana.* See under *nir-manth* below.

निर्मद *nir-mada, as, ā, am,* unintoxicated, sober, quiet; not proud, humble; not in rut (as an elephant).

निर्मध्य *nir-madhya, as, ā, am,* having no middle; *(ā),* f. = *nalikā,* a fragrant substance; [cf. *nir-mathyā* below.]

निर्मनस्क *nir-manaska, as, ā, am,* mindless, having no Manas. — *Nirmanaska-tā,* f. the having no Manas.

निर्मनुज *nir-manuja, as, ā, am,* abandoned by men (as a forest), desolate, uninhabited.

निर्मनुष्य *nir-manushya, as, ā, am,* unpeopled, uninhabited, deserted by men, without a man; (*mātaṅgo nirmanushyas,* an elephant without riders.)

निर्मन्त्र *nir-mantra, as, ā, am,* unaccompanied by holy texts or the recitation of sacred verses (as the Gandharva marriage).

निर्मन्थ् *nir-manth* or *nir-math,* cl. 1. 9. P. *-mathati, -manthati, -mathnāti,* &c., to stir about, agitate, churn, shake about, toss about roughly or violently; to rub, elicit fire by rubbing; to strike, beat violently, thresh, bruise, crush, stamp to pieces, grind, break in pieces, destroy.

Nir-matha, as, m. stirring, rubbing. — *Nirmatha-dāru* = *nirmantha-dāru.*

Nir-mathana, am, n. stirring, churning, rubbing, rubbing two pieces of wood together to light a fire.

Nir-mathita, as, ā, am, stirred about, agitated, churned.

1. *nir-mathya, as, ā, am,* to be stirred about or rubbed; (*ā*), f. a kind of fragrant substance, = *nalikā;* [cf. *nir-madhyā* above.]

2. *nir-mathya,* ind. having churned; having ground; having discriminated or particularized.

Nir-mathyamāna, as, ā, am, being shaken or tossed about roughly.

Nir-mantha, as, m. rubbing. — *Nirmantha-dāru, us, u,* m. n. or *nirmantha-kāshṭha, am,* n. the wood used for kindling fire by friction; a churning-stick.

Nir-manthana, am, n. rubbing, churning; separating, distinguishing, discriminating.

Nir-manthya, as, ā, am, to be stirred, to be churned; to be excited by friction (as fire); to be distinguished or discriminated.

Nir-māthin, ī, inī, i, crushing or stamping to pieces, churning, rubbing.

निर्मन्यु **nir-manyu, us, us, u,** free from anger or resentment; (*us*), m., N. of a hunter.

निर्मम **nir-mama, as, ā, am,** unselfish, disinterested; regardless, indifferent to (with loc.); free from all connection with the outer world; an epithet of Śiva; (*as*), m. (with Jainas) N. of the fifteenth Arhat of the future Ut-sarpiṇī. — *Nirmama-tā,* f. or 1. *nirmama-tva, am,* n. unselfishness, disregard of worldly interests, indifference towards (with loc.).

2. *nir-mamatva, as, ā, am,* free from selfishness, indifferent.

निर्मर्याद **nir-maryāda, as, ā, am,** boundless, having no limits, immeasurable, innumerable; transgressing the boundaries of right, unrestrained, unruly, wicked, criminal, sinful, impious; confused; (*am*), n. confusion, disturbance of boundaries or rules; N. of a kind of fight; (*am*), ind. confusedly, topsy-turvy.

निर्मल **nir-mala, as, ā, am,** spotless, free from spots or dirt or impurities, stainless, unsullied, clear, clean, pure, limpid; shining, splendent, bright; virtuous; (*am*), n. talc; the remains of an offering made to a deity. — *Nirmala-gada, as, ā, am,* having a bright mace. — *Nirmala-tā,* f. or *nirmala-tva, am,* n. stainlessness, purity, cleanness (physical or moral). — *Nirmalī-kṛita, as, ā, am,* freed from impurity, cleansed, cleared. — *Nirmalopala* (°*la-up*°), *as,* m. crystal.

Nir-mālya, as, ā, am, stainless, clean, &c., = *nir-mala;* (*ā*), f. a species of medicinal plant, see *pṛikkā;* (*am*), n. stainlessness, purity, cleanness, clearness; the remains of an offering to a deity, flowers left at a sacrificial ceremony; remains in general. — *Nirmālya-tā,* f. = *nirmala-tā.*

निर्मशक **nir-maśaka, as, ā, am,** free from gnats or musquitoes.

निर्मा **1. nir-mā,** cl. 2. P., 3. and 4. A., *-māti, -mimīte, -māyate, -mātum,* to build, make, form, fabricate; to produce, create; to compose; to cause: Caus. *-māpayati, -yitum,* to cause to be made or built.

2. *nir-mā,* f. value, measure, equivalent.

Nir-māṇa, am, n. measuring or meting out, measure; reach, extent, (*eka-nirmāṇa, as, ā, am,* of the same measure; *kakudodagra-nirmāṇa,* as high as the top of a mountain; *avyakta-nirmāṇo bālas,* a boy who has not yet reached his full growth, not yet full grown); forming, making, producing, creating, production, fabrication, manufacture, formation, creation, building; composing, composition, work; a building; a part; (with Buddhists) transformation; the best of anything, pith, marrow, essence; (*ā*), f. propriety, decorum, fitness. — *Nirmāṇa-rata, ās,* m. pl. 'delighting in creating or building,' N. of a particular class of gods. — *Nirmāṇa-rati, is, is, i,* delighting in creating; (*ayas*), m. pl., N. of a class of deities in the eleventh Manvantara; (with Buddhists) delighting in transformation; [cf. *nirvāṇa-ruci.*]

Nir-mātṛi, tā, trī, tṛi, a maker, builder, creator, former, producer; building, fabricating, forming, &c. — *Nirmātṛi-tva, am,* n. creatorship, the condition of a maker or builder or producer.

Nir-mita, as, ā, am, constructed, manufactured, produced, built, fashioned, fabricated, formed, made; artificial; meted out; (*ās*), m. pl. (with Buddhists) N. of a class of deities, 'the transformed.'

Nir-miti, is, f. formation, production, creation, fabrication, manufacture, artificial production; making.

निर्मांस **nir-māṅsa, as, ā, am,** fleshless, emaciated.

निर्माख्य **nir-mākhya, as,** m., N. of a man; (probably a wrong form, also read *tigmātman* and *nirmād.*)

निर्माथिन् **nir-māthin.** See col. 1.

निर्मान **nir-māna, as, ā, am,** without self-confidence, free from pride.

निर्मानुष **nir-mānusha, as, ā, am,** unpeopled, uninhabited, abandoned by men, desolate; (*e*), ind. in a solitary place.

निर्मार्ग **1. nir-mārga, as, ā, am,** roadless, pathless. (For 2. *nir-mārga* see under *nir-mṛij.*)

निर्माली **nir-mālī,** f. = *nir-mālyā.*

निर्माल्य **nir-mālya.** See under *nir-mala,* col. 1.

निर्मुच् **nir-muć,** cl. 6. P. A. *-muñćati, -te, -moktum,* to loosen, free from, liberate.

Nir-mukta, as, ā, am, loosed, set free, liberated, disjoined, sundered, separated, &c.; (*as*), m. a snake which has lately cast his skin.

Nir-mukti, is, f. liberation, deliverance; [cf. *śāpa-n*°.]

Nir-moka, as, m. setting loose or free, liberating; a hide or skin, especially the cast off skin or slough of a snake [cf. *sarpa-n*°]; armour, mail; sky, heaven, atmosphere; N. of a son of the eighth Manu; of one of the Saptarshis under the thirteenth Manu; [cf. *nir-moha.*]

Nir-moktṛi, tā, trī, tṛi, one who solves or liberates, a liberator, looser, solver (of doubts).

Nir-moćana, am, n. liberation, deliverance.

निर्मुट **nir-muṭa, as,** m. a tree bearing large blossoms (= *vanas-pati*); the sun; a rogue; (*as, am*), m. n. a large and free market or fair.

निर्मूल **nir-mūla, as, ā, am,** rootless, deprived of roots (as a tree); baseless, without origin, unfounded; eradicated. — *Nirmūla-tā,* f. rootlessness, baselessness.

Nir-mūlana, am, n. uprooting, eradicating, extirpating.

Nir-mūlaya, Nom. P. *nirmūlayati, -yitum,* to uproot, eradicate, extirpate, annihilate.

निर्मृज् **nir-mṛij,** cl. 2. P. *-mārshṭi, -mārjitum* and *-mārshṭum,* to wipe off, wipe out, rub out, sweep out, strip off.

2. *nir-mārga, as,* m. (for 1. see above), rubbing or stripping off, wiping off; that which is stripped or wiped off, refuse.

Nir-mārguka, as, ā, am, Ved. drawing off, withdrawing, separating.

Nir-mārjana, am, n. wiping off, sweeping, cleaning.

Nir-mṛishṭa, as, ā, am, rubbed out, wiped off or out, swept.

निर्मेघ **nir-megha, as, ā, am,** cloudless. — *Nirmeghāśrama* (°*gha-āś*°), *as,* m., N. of a man.

निर्मेध **nir-medha, as, ā, am,** without understanding, stupid, dull. — *Nirmedhāśrama* (°*dha-āś*°), *as,* m., N. of a man.

निर्मोक **nir-moka, nir-moktṛi,** &c. See under *nir-muć,* col. 2.

निर्मोक्ष **nir-moksha, as,** m. (rt. *moksh*), liberation from, deliverance.

निर्मोह **nir-moha, as, ā, am,** 'free from illusion,' an epithet of Śiva; (*as*), m., N. of a son of the fifth Manu; of one of the Saptarshis under the thirteenth Manu; [cf. *nir-moka.*]

निर्म्रेतुक **nir-mretuka, as, ā, am** (perhaps fr. *mrai* = *mlai* with *nis*), Ved. fading away, withering; (also read *nir-metuka, nir-mṛituka.*)

निर्म्लुक्ति **nir-mlukti.** See *ni-mlukti,* p. 490.

निर्यत् **1. nir-yat, an, atī, at** (fr. *nir-i*), going forth, coming out, issuing.

निर्यत् **2. nir-yat,** cl. 10. P. *-yātayati,* &c., to give back, restore, make restitution; to forgive, pardon, set free.

Nir-yātaka, as, ā, am, bearing away, carrying away, removing.

Nir-yātana, am, n. giving back, returning, delivering, restitution, delivery of a deposit, replacing anything lost; gift, donation; payment of a debt; requital, revenge; killing, slaughter.

Nir-yātita, as, ā, am, restored, given back, retaliated, requited; taken away.

Nir-yātya, as, ā, am, to be given back or restored or delivered (as a deposit &c.).

निर्यत्न **nir-yatna, as, ā, am,** inactive, lazy, listless. — *Niryatna-tā,* f. inactivity.

निर्यन्त्रण **nir-yantraṇa, as, ā, am,** without restraint, unrestrained, unobstructed, uncontrolled, unconfined, unrestricted, self-willed, independant; (*am*), n. absence of restraint, independance; (*am*), ind. without restraint, unrestrainedly. — *Niryantraṇa-pradeśāvasthita* (°*śa-av*°), *as, ā, am,* being at a place where no restraint is needed.

Nir-yantrita, as, ā, am, uncontrolled, unrestrained, self-willed.

निर्यशस्क **nir-yaśaska, as, ā, am,** without fame or reputation, inglorious.

निर्या **1. nir-yā,** f., Ved. any disturbance of the regular course of a rite, any defect.

निर्या **2. nir-yā,** cl. 2. P. *-yāti, -yātum,* to go out, issue, set out: Caus. *-yāpayati, -yitum,* to cause to go out.

Nir-yāṇa, am, n. going forth or out, exit, issue, setting out, departure; vanishing, disappearance; departure from life, dying, death; eternal emancipation, final beatitude, (probably confounded with 1. *nir-vāṇa,* q. v.); the outer corner of an elephant's eye [cf. *nir-ṇayana*]; iron; a rope for tying cattle or for binding a calf's feet, a foot-rope.

Nir-yāta, as, ā, am, gone out, gone forth, issued, departed.

Nir-yāti, is, f. going out, exit, departing, dying.

Nir-yāpaṇa, am, n. (fr. the Caus.), expelling, expulsion, banishing.

Nir-yāya, ind. having gone out or departed.

Nir-yiyāsu, us, us, u (fr. the Desid.), trying or wishing to go out.

निर्यातृ **nir-yātṛi, tā, trī, tṛi,** a husbandman, reaper, weeder; (wrong reading for *nir-dātṛi,* q. v.)

निर्यादव *nir-yādava, as, ā, am,* freed from the Yādavas, without the Yādavas.

निर्याम *niryāma, as,* m. a sailor, pilot, boatman (= *niyāmaka*).

निर्यास *nir-yāsa, as, am,* m. n. (fr. rt. *yas* with *nis*), exudation of trees or plants, juice, gum, resin, milk, &c.; extract, decoction, infusion; any thick fluid substance; [cf. *agni-n°, tantu-n°.*]

निर्युक्ति *nir-yukti, is,* f. disunion; want of connection or government (in grammar); unfitness, inappropriateness, impropriety.

Nir-yuktika, as, ā, am, detached, disunited; unconnected, unmeaning, illogical, not founded on sound reasoning; inappropriate, improper. — *Nir-yuktika-tva, am,* n. inappropriateness; illogicalness.

निर्यूथ *nir-yūtha, as, ā, am,* separated from the herd (as an elephant &c.), strayed from the flock.

निर्यूष *nir-yūsha, as,* m. extract, juice, &c., = *nir-yāsa* = *nir-yūha.*

निर्यूह *nir-yūha, as,* m. (probably for *nir-vyūha*), a prominence, projection (also *am,* n.), perhaps a kind of turret-like ornament on columns or gates, a pinnacle, turret; a chaplet, crest, head-ornament, the crest of a helmet; a peg or bracket projecting from a wall to hang or place anything upon [cf. *nāga-niryūha*]; wood placed in a wall for doves to build their nests upon; a door, gate (also n.); extract, juice, decoction, &c.; [cf. *nir-yāsa, nir-yūsha.*]

निर्योग *nir-yoga, as,* m. (perhaps) a decoration, ornament.

निर्योगक्षेम *nir-yogakshema, as, ā, am,* free from care or anxiety about property.

निर्लक्षण *nir-lakshaṇa, as, ā, am,* having no special marks, undistinguished, unimportant, insignificant; unmarked, unspotted.

निर्लक्ष्य *nir-lakshya, as, ā, am,* not to be observed or perceived, unobservable.

निर्लज्ज *nir-lajja, as, ā, am,* shameless, immodest, impudent, brazen. — *Nirlajja-tā,* f. shamelessness, impudence.

निर्लिङ्ग *nir-linga, as, ā, am,* having no characteristic or distinguishing marks, not to be defined (as *ātman, brahman*).

निर्लिप्त *nir-lipta, as, ā, am* (fr. rt. *lip* with *nis*), unsmeared, unanointed; undefiled, uncontaminated; (*as*), m., N. of Krishṇa; a sage.

Nir-lepa, as, ā, am, unanointed, unsmeared, free from fatty substances; stainless, spotless, sinless; (*as*), m. a sage.

निर्लुञ्चन *nir-luñčana, am,* n. (fr. rt. *luñč* with *nis*), pulling out or off, tearing off, peeling.

निर्लुण्ठन *nir-luṇṭhana, am,* n. (fr. rt. *luṇṭh* with *nis*), robbing, plundering; pulling out, tearing off, (in the latter sense a wrong reading for *nir-luñčana,* q. v.)

निर्लेखन *nir-lekhana, am,* n. (fr. rt. *likh* with *nis*), a scraper, instrument for scraping; [cf. *jihvā-n°.*]

निर्लोभ *nir-lobha, as, ā, am,* free from desire, unavaricious.

निर्लोम *nir-loma, as, ā, am,* devoid of hair, hairless, smooth.

निर्ल्वयनी *nir-lvayanī,* f. the cast off skin of a snake; (wrong reading for *nir-vlayanī,* q. v.)

निर्वंश *nir-vanśa, as, ā, am,* without lineage or posterity, childless.

निर्वक्तव्य *nir-vaktavya, as, ā, am* (fr. rt. *vač* with *nis*), to be interpreted or explained.

1. *nir-vačana, am,* n. (for 2. see below), pronunciation; a proverbial expression, proverb; interpretation, etymological explanation, etymology; vocabulary, index; [cf. 1. *ni-vačana.*]

Nir-vačanīya, as, ā, am, to be defined more closely, to be interpreted or explained, to be described or related.

1. *nir-vāčya, as, ā, am.* = *nir-vačanīya.* (For 2. see under *nir-vākya,* p. 501, col. 1.)

निर्वचन 2. *nir-vačana, as, ā, am* (for 1. see above), not speaking, silent; unobjectionable, unblamable, blameless; (*am*), ind. silently; [cf. 2. *ni-vačana.*]

निर्वण *nir-vaṇa* or *nir-vana, as, ā, am,* being out of a wood, ranging in the open country; free from woods; bare, open, (in this sense *nir* is a privative.)

निर्वत्सशिशुपुङ्गव *nir-vatsa-śiśupungava, as, ā, am,* deprived of calves and young bulls.

निर्वद् *nir-vad,* cl. 1. P. A. *-vadati, -te, -vaditum,* to speak out, to blame; to deny.

1. *nir-vāda, as,* m. (for 2. *nir-vāda* see p. 501, col. 1), obloquy, censure, blame, reproach; rumour, report; asseveration, affirmation, decision of a controversy.

निर्वन *nir-vana.* See *nir-vaṇa* above.

निर्वप् *nir-vap,* cl. 1. P. A. *-vapati, -te, -vaptum,* to pour out, sprinkle, drop, scatter; to offer sacrificial food, present funeral oblations or libations to the Manes of deceased ancestors; to present, deliver; to perform.

Nir-vapaṇa, am, n. pouring out, sprinkling, offering, especially the presentation of funeral offerings to the Manes, libation, oblation; spending, bestowing presents; gift, donation, alms; a ladle or vessel for pouring; (*as, ī, am*), relating to libations; scattering, pouring out, bestowing.

1. *nir-vāpa, as,* m. (for 2. see p. 501, col. 1), scattering, strewing, pouring out; offering, giving, bestowing; offering oblations, especially funeral oblations in honour of a deceased ancestor; gift, alms.

1. *nir-vāpaṇa, am,* n. (for 2. see p. 501, col. 1), scattering, throwing or pouring out, casting in, sowing; offering, presenting funeral oblations; gift, giving.

1. *nir-vāpita, as, ā, am* (for 2. see p. 501, col. 1), offered in oblation, scattered, poured out.

1. *nir-vāpya, as, ā, am* (for 3. see p. 501, col. 1), to be scattered or offered.

2. *nir-vāpya,* ind. having offered funeral cakes.

निर्वयनी *nir-vayanī,* f. the cast off skin of a snake; (a various reading for *nir-vlayanī;* cf. *nir-lvayanī.*)

निर्वर *nir-vara,* a various reading for *nir-dara.*

निर्वरुणता *nirvaruṇa-tā,* f. or *nirvaruṇa-tva, am,* n. deliverance from Varuṇa's power.

निर्वर्ण् *nir-varṇ,* cl. 10. P. *-varṇayati, -yitum,* to look at, contemplate.

Nir-varṇana, am, n. looking at, regarding, sight, seeing.

Nir-varṇanīya, as, ā, am, to be looked at or regarded.

Nir-varṇya, ind. having looked at, having regarded.

निर्वर्तक *nir-vartaka, nir-vartana,* &c. See under *nir-vṛit,* p. 502, col. 1.

निर्वस् *nir-vas,* cl. 1. P. *-vasati, -vastum,* to dwell, finish dwelling; to dwell abroad: Caus. *-vāsayati, -yitum,* to expel from home, banish.

Nir-vāsa, as, m. leaving or abandoning one's home, residing far from one's native place; expulsion, banishment; killing.

1. *nir-vāsana, am,* n. (for 2. *nir-vāsana* see p. 501, col. 1), expelling or driving from home, banishing, banishment, expulsion; hurting, injuring, killing, slaughter, annihilation; [cf. *ud-vāsana, pra-vāsana.*]

Nir-vāsanīya or *nir-vāsya, as, ā, am,* to be expelled or banished.

Nir-vāsita, as, ā, am, expelled, banished, driven from home.

निर्वसु *nir-vasu, us, us, u,* destitute of wealth or property, poor. — *Nirvasu-tva, am,* n. poverty, destitution.

निर्वह् *nir-vah,* cl. 1. P. A. *-vahati, -te, -voḍhum,* to bring or carry out, bring one's self out of, extricate one's self: Caus. P. *-vāhayati, -yitum,* to carry out, carry on, perform, accomplish, effect, fulfil, settle; to pass, spend (time &c.).

Nir-vahaṇa, am, n. end, issue, completion; the closing scene or catastrophe of a drama, the conclusion; carrying on, (for *nir-vāhaṇa.*)

Nir-vahitṛi, tā, tṛī, tṛi, separating, dividing.

Nir-vāha, as, m. carrying on, accomplishing, performing, managing, accomplishment, management; completion, end; narrating, describing; supporting, maintaining; subsisting on; sufficiency, adequacy, competent provision or means of living; steadfastness; [cf. *nairvāhika.*]

Nir-vāhaka, as, ikā, am, accomplishing, performing, effecting; (*am*), n. application or connection of cause and effect (?).

Nir-vāhaṇa, as, ā, am, carrying out, effecting; carrying away, removing; (*am*), n. accomplishment, completion; the catastrophe or closing scene of a drama (= *nir-vahaṇa*).

Nir-vāhin, ī, iṇī, i, leading out, carrying out; discharging (as a wound).

Nir-vāhya, as, ā, am, to be carried on or accomplished or performed.

निर्वा *nir-vā,* cl. 2. P. *-vāti, -vātum,* to cease to blow; (cl. 4. *-vāyati,* &c.), to be extinguished; to be refreshed: Caus. *-vāpayati, -yitum,* to extinguish, put out; to refresh, cool, allay, make happy, delight.

1. *nir-vāṇa, as, ā, am* (for 2. *nir-vāṇa* see p. 501, col. 1), blown out, gone out, put out, extinguished (as a fire); lost, disappeared; liberated from existence (lit. having the fire of life extinguished); dead, deceased, defunct; set (as a planet); calmed, quieted, (*a-nirvāṇa,* an elephant not yet tamed or one just caught and wild); immersed, plunged; (*am*), n. blowing out, extinguishing, extinction, (in this and some of the following senses *nir-vāṇam* is not the neut. of the pass. part. but formed fr. *nir-vā* with affix *ana*), becoming extinguished, disappearance, setting, vanishing from sight, (*nirvāṇam kṛi,* to act as if nothing had happened, not to keep one's promise); extinction of the flame of life, dissolution, liberation, eternal bliss, final emancipation from matter and reunion with the deity, union with the Supreme Spirit; (with Buddhists and Jainas) absolute extinction or annihilation, complete extinction of individual existence; perfect and perpetual calm, repose; complete satisfaction or pleasure, highest felicity; desisting, leaving off, cessation; vacuity, vacuum; union, association, blending, confluence; offering oblations, (perhaps wrongly for 1. *nir-vāpaṇa*); bathing of an elephant (because he draws in water with his trunk and then blows it out over his body); instructing in sciences; 'Deliverance,' N. of an Upanishad; [cf. *apa-n°, pari-n°.*] — *Nirvāṇa-purāṇa, am,* n. offering oblations to the dead. — *Nirvāṇa-prakaraṇa, am,* n., N. of the fourth chapter of the Vāsishṭha-rāmāyaṇa, commonly called Yoga-vāsishṭha. — *Nirvāṇa-bhūyishṭha, as, ā, am,* almost all vanished or departed. — *Nirvāṇa-maṇḍapa,* N. of a temple. — *Nirvāṇa-mantra, am,* n., N. of a mystical formula. — *Nirvāṇa-mastaka, as,* m. liberation, deliverance. — *Nirvāṇa-ruči, ayas,* m. pl. 'delighting in final beatitude,' N. of a class of

deities under the eleventh Manu; [cf. *nirmāṇa-rati.*] — *Nirvāṇa-lakshaṇa, as, ā, am,* having complete felicity as its characteristic mark. — *Nirvāṇa-sūtra, am,* n., N. of certain Buddhist Sūtras.

Nir-vāṇin, ī, m. (with Jainas) N. of the second Arhat of the past Ut-sarpiṇī.

1. *nir-vāta, as, ā, am* (for 2. see below), ceased to blow.

2. *nir-vāpa, as,* m. (for 1. see under *nir-vap,* p. 500, col. 2), putting out, extinguishing (as a fire).

2. *nir-vāpaṇa, am,* n. (for 1. see under *nir-vap,* p. 500, col. 2), putting out (as a fire or light), extinguishing, quenching; extinction, annihilation; slaughter, killing; (in medicine) refrigerant; cooling, refreshing.

Nir-vāpayitṛi, tā, trī, tṛi, extinguishing, refrigerant, one who allays.

2. *nir-vāpita, as, ā, am* (for 1. see under *nir-vap,* p. 500, col. 2), extinguished, put out, quenched; allayed, cooled; killed.

3. *nir-vāpya,* ind. (for 1. and 2. see under *nir-vap,* p. 500, col. 2), having extinguished or quenched; having refreshed or delighted.

निर्वाक **nirvāka,** *as,* m. in *karṇa-nirvāka, as,* m., N. of a man.

निर्वाक्य **nir-vākya,** *as, ā, am,* speechless.

Nir-vāć, k, k, k, silent, mute, dumb.

2. *nir-vāćya, as, ā, am* (for 1. see under *nir-vaktavya,* p. 500, col. 2), improper to be said; unobjectionable, blameless, not to be found fault with or censured.

निर्वाञ्च् **nirvāñć,** *ān, āćī, āk* (according to the commentator fr. *nir-ava-añć*), outward, exterior.

निर्वाण 2. **nir-vāṇa,** *as, ā, am* (for 1. see under *nir-vā,* p. 500, col. 3), having no arrows.

निर्वाणी **nir-vāṇī,** f. (with Jainas) N. of a deity who executes the commands of the sixteenth Arhat of the present Ava-sarpiṇī.

निर्वात 2. **nir-vāta,** *as, ā, am* (for 1. see above), free from wind, sheltered from wind, not windy, calm, still; *(as),* m. a calm, a place sheltered from wind. — *Nirvāta-stha, as, ā, am,* standing sheltered from the wind.

निर्वाद 2. **nir-vāda,** *as,* m. (for 1. *nir-vāda* see under *nir-vad,* p. 500, col. 2), absence of dispute or railing.

निर्वानर **nir-vānara,** *as, ā, am,* free from monkeys.

निर्वाप 1. and 2. **nir-vāpa.** See p. 500, col. 2, and above.

निर्वायस **nir-vāyasa,** *as, ā, am,* free from crows.

निर्वार्य **nir-vārya,** *as, ā, am,* irresistible, not to be opposed or resisted; acting fearlessly or determinedly.

निर्वासन 2. **nir-vāsana,** *as, ā, am* (fr. *nis + vāsanā;* for 1. *nir-vāsana* see under *nir-vas,* p. 500, col. 2), without fancy or imagination.

निर्वाह **nir-vāha, nir-vāhaṇa.** See *nir-vah.*

निर्विकल्प **nir-vikalpa,** *as, ā, am,* not admitting an alternative; recognising no such distinctions as that of subject and object; being without determination; *(am),* ind. without hesitation or vacillation, without wavering, without reflection.

Nir-vikalpaka or *nir-vikalpana, as, ā, am,* not admitting an alternative, free from differences, having no mutual dependence; not capable of mutual relation; undeliberative; conditioned; *(am),* n. knowledge not depending upon or derived from the senses.

निर्विकार **nir-vikāra,** *as, ā, am,* or *nir-vikāra-vat, ān, atī, at,* unchanged, unaltered, unchangeable, immutable, uniform. — *Nirvikāra-tā,* f. unchangeableness, uniformity.

निर्विकास **nir-vikāsa,** *as, ā, am,* not yet opened or expanded (as a blossom), unblown. — *Nirvikāsa-tva, am,* n. the being not yet opened or expanded.

निर्विक्रम् **nir-vi-kram,** cl. 1. P. A. *-krāmati, -kramate, -kramitum,* to go out of, come out of.

निर्विघ्न **nir-vighna,** *as, ā, am,* unobstructed, uninterrupted, untroubled, secure from impediments; *(am),* n. absence of obstruction or impediment; *(am* or *ena),* ind. unobstructedly, freely, securely.

निर्विचार **nir-vićāra,** *as, ā, am,* not reflecting or considering; *(am),* ind. without reflection, without consideration, inconsiderately.

निर्विचिकित्स **nir-vićikitsa,** *as, ā, am,* without reflecting much; *(am),* ind. without much or long reflection.

निर्विचेष्ट **nir-vićeshṭa,** *as, ā, am,* motionless, insensible, unresisting.

निर्वितर्क **nir-vitarka,** *as, ā, am,* unreflecting, inconsiderate.

निर्विद् **nir-vid,** cl. 4. A. *-vidyate,* &c., to be disgusted with one's self, to disparage or despise one's self, to be ashamed of one's self, to be disgusted, to be despondent.

Nir-viṇṇa, as, ā, am, despondent, depressed; disgusted with anything (gen.); loathing; self-disparaged, overcome with fear or sorrow; emaciated with grief; decayed, impaired; abused, degraded; humble; known, certain. — *Nirviṇṇa-ćetas, ās, ās, as,* depressed in mind, broken in spirit, humble-minded, meek, resigned, desponding.

1. *nir-veda, as,* m. disgust, loathing, feeling disgust for (with gen. or loc., e. g. *jīvite nirvedaḥ,* disgust for life); satiety, loathsomeness; despondency, self-disparagement; humility; grief; complete indifference, disregard of worldly objects; despair, desperation; shame. — *Nirveda-vat, ān, atī, at,* disgusted (with worldly concerns); full of despondency; indifferent.

निर्विद्य **nir-vidya,** *as, ā, am,* unlearned, destitute of knowledge, uneducated.

निर्विधित्स **nir-vidhitsa,** *as, ā, am,* not wishing to do, having no designs, free from desire.

निर्विनोद **nir-vinoda,** *as, ā, am,* without amusement, without pastime, void of solace or diversion.

निर्विन्ध्य **nir-vindhya,** *as, ā, am,* living on the outside or other side of the Vindhyas; *(ā),* f., N. of a river rising in the Vindhya hills or of one rising in the Ṛiksha mountains.

निर्विभास् **nir-vi-bhās,** Caus. *-bhāsayati, -yitum,* to illuminate, enlighten.

निर्विमर्श **nir-vimarśa,** *as, ā, am,* not considering, unreflecting, devoid of reflection; (also written *nir-vimarsha.*)

निर्विवर **nir-vivara,** *as, ā, am,* having no opening or rent, without interval or interstice, close, contiguous. — *Nirvivara-tā,* f. want of interstice, contiguousness (as of the female breasts); want of enmity; agreement, understanding.

निर्विवह् **nir-vi-vah,** cl. 1. P. A. *-vahati, -te, -voḍhum,* to carry out, export; to expel.

निर्विवाद **nir-vivāda,** *as, ā, am,* not contending or disagreeing, agreeing with each other; *(am),* n. absence of contention or controversy. — *Nirvivādī-kṛita, as, ā, am,* made to agree.

निर्विवित्सु **nir-vivitsu,** *us, us, u* (fr. the Desid. of rt. *vid* with *nis*), desirous to find (?).

निर्विवेक **nir-viveka,** *as, ā, am,* indiscreet, undiscriminating, wanting discrimination or judgment, foolish. — *Nirviveka-tva, am,* n. want of discrimination or judgment, indiscretion.

निर्विश् **nir-viś,** cl. 6. P. *-viśati, -veshṭum,* to enter into, to meet with, enjoy (with acc., e. g. *madhuṃ nirviviśuḥ,* they enjoyed wine); to experience; to embellish; to reward.

Nir-viśat, an, atī or *antī, at,* entering in or into; attaining, obtaining; engaging in; marrying.

Nir-vishṭa, as, ā, am, attained, arrived at, met with; obtained, gained, experienced, earned, received; engaged in, occupied by, staying in; married.

Nir-veśa, as, m. entering into, gaining, obtaining; wages, hire, employment; payment, returning payment [cf. *ni-veśya*]; expiation, atonement, (*a-nir-veśa,* one who has not expiated his sins); enjoyment, eating; fainting, swooning, syncope.

Nir-veśanīya, as, ā, am, to be gained or enjoyed.

Nir-veshṭavya, as, ā, am, to be entered into; to be rewarded, to be paid; to be embellished.

निर्विशङ्क **nir-viśaṅka,** *as, ā, am,* or *nir-viśaṅkita, as, ā, am,* fearless, undaunted, confident.

निर्विशेष **nir-viśesha,** *as,* m. absence of difference, no difference; *(as, ā, am),* showing no difference, making no difference, not differing, without distinction; undiscriminating; indiscriminate; same, like, (at the end of an adj. comp.; cf. *nilotpala-n°*); *(am* or *eṇa),* ind. without difference, indifferently, indiscriminately, without distinction, equally, (*sva-gṛiha-nirviśesheṇa,* just the same as in one's own house.) — *Nirviśesha-tva, am,* n. absence of difference, want of distinction, indiscriminateness. — *Nirviśesha-vat, ān, atī, at,* showing no difference, undistinguished, indiscriminate. — *Nirviśeshākṛiti* (*°sha-āk°*), *is, is, i,* whose forms are precisely alike.

Nir-viśeshaṇa, as, ā, am, having no attributes.

निर्विष **nir-visha,** *as, ā, am,* without venom, poisonless (as serpents); *(ā* and *ī),* f. a species of grass, Kyllingia Monocephala, used as an antidote.

निर्विषङ्ग **nir-vishaṅga,** *as, ā, am,* not attached to anything, indifferent.

निर्विषय **nir-vishaya,** *as,* m. no residence; any place not deserving the name of a residence; *(as, ā, am),* expelled or driven away from one's residence or home, banished; having no sphere of action, not attached to any object, objectless; separated from sensual objects, not attached to them (as mind). — *Nirvishaya-tva, am,* n. non-attachment to any object. — *Nirvishayākāra* (*°ya-āk°*), *as, ā, am,* not deserving the name of a dwelling-place. — *Nirvishayī-kṛita, as, ā, am,* expelled from one's place of residence. — *Nirvishayoparāga* (*°ya-up°*), *as, ā, am,* unharmed by objects of sense.

निर्विषाण **nir-vishāṇa,** *as, ā, am,* destitute of horns or tusks, tuskless (as an elephant).

निर्विहङ्ग **nir-vihaṅga,** *as, ā, am,* without birds, free from birds.

निर्विहार **nir-vihāra,** *as, ā, am,* having no pleasure, deprived of pleasure.

निर्वीज **nir-vīja,** *as, ā, am,* seedless; impotent; *(ā),* f. a sort of grape without seeds or stones (= *kākalī-drākshā,* commonly called *kishmish*). — *Nirvīja-tva, am,* n. seedlessness, impotence.

निर्वीर **nir-vīra,** *as, ā, am,* deprived of men or heroes; unheroic, cowardly; *(ā),* f. a woman whose husband and children are dead, a childless widow; N. of a river; *(am),* n., N. of a place of pilgrimage.

निर्वीरुध् **nir-vīrudh,** *t, t, t,* deprived of plants.

निर्वीर्य **nir-vīrya,** *as, ā, am,* powerless,

unmanly, without manly courage, spiritless, tame, feeble, impotent. — *Nirvīrya-tā*, f. unmanliness, powerlessness.

निर्वृ *nir-vṛi*, apparently only occurring in the derivatives below.

Nir-vṛita, *as*, *ā*, *am*, satisfied, contented, happy, pleased, enraptured, tranquil, at ease, secure, free from cares, free from anxiety and troubles, free from occupation or interest, emancipated; ended, terminated, ceased.

Nir-vṛiti, *is*, f. complete satisfaction, contentment, tranquillity, bliss, happiness, gladness, pleasure; final emancipation or liberation from existence; freedom; rest, repose; setting, disappearance, death, destruction; completion, accomplishment (for *nir-vṛitti*); ceasing, abstaining from (for *ni-vṛitti*); incivility, impropriety (for *nir-vṛitti*); (*is*), m., N. of a man; of a son of Vṛishṇi; (the forms *nir-vṛiti*, *nir-vṛitti*, and *ni-vṛitti* are often incorrectly confounded together.)

निर्वृक्ष *nir-vṛiksha*, *as*, *ā*, *am*, treeless.

निर्वृत् *nir-vṛit*, cl. 1. A. (also P. in Fut. Cond. and Aor.) *-vartate*, *-vartitum*, to be completed or accomplished, to be effected; to draw back, recede, desist, cease, not to be done, not to take place, (in these senses probably for *ni-vṛit*, q. v.): Caus. *-vartayati*, *-yitum*, to complete, accomplish, finish, perform, produce, create.

Nir-vartaka, *as*, *ikā*, *am* (fr. the Caus.), completing, accomplishing, performing, finishing, ending, executing; desisting; [cf. *ni-vartaka*.]

Nir-vartana, *am*, n. accomplishment, completion, execution; desisting (for *ni-vartana*).

Nir-vartanīya, *as*, *ā*, *am*, to be completed or accomplished.

Nir-vartin, *ī*, *inī*, *i*, accomplishing, performing, executing; behaving rudely or uncivilly, uncivil.

1. *nir-vartya*, *as*, *ā*, *am*, to be accomplished, performable, to be pronounced or uttered, pronounceable. — *Nirvartya-tva*, *am*, n. performableness; pronounceableness.

2. *nir-vartya*, ind. having accomplished, having performed or finished; having ceased, (for *ni-vartya*.)

Nir-vṛitta, *as*, *ā*, *am*, finished, completely done, accomplished. — *Nirvṛitta-śatru*, *us*, m., N. of a prince of the Kaliṅgas; (probably wrongly for *ni-vṛitta-śatru*; cf. *ninarta-śatru*.)

Nir-vṛitti, *is*, f. completion, termination, conclusion; (in grammar) cessation of the influence of one rule over another; result, fruit, reward; impropriety, incivility [cf. *nir-vartin* above]; final beatitude (for *nir-vṛiti*); abstaining from action, inactivity (for *ni-vṛitti*); (*is*, *is*, *i*), having no occupation, destitute, (in this sense *nir* is a privative.)

निर्वृत *nir-vṛita*, *nir-vṛiti*. See under *nir-vṛi* above.

निर्वृष् *nir-vṛish*, cl. 1. P. *-varshati*, *-varshitum*, to cease to rain.

Nir-vṛishṭi, *is*, f. cessation of rain, want of rain.

निर्वृष *nir-vṛisha*, *as*, *ā*, *am*, deprived of bulls.

निर्वेग *nir-vega*, *as*, *ā*, *am*, without violent motion or impetuosity, not waving, quiet, calm.

निर्वेतन *nir-vetana*, *as*, *ā*, *am*, not receiving wages, unsalaried.

निर्वेद 2. *nir-veda*, *as*, *ā*, *am* (for 1. *nir-veda* see under *nir-vid*, p. 501, col. 2), not having the Vedas, infidel, unscriptural.

निर्वेधिम *nir-vedhima* (fr. *vyadh* with *nis*), with *karṇa*, a peculiar deformity of the ear.

निर्वेपन *nir-vepana*, *as*, *ā*, *am*, not trembling, not flickering (as the flame of a lamp).

निर्वेश *nir-veśa*. See under *nir-viś*, p. 501, col. 3.

निर्वेष्टन *nir-veshṭana*, *am*, n. (fr. rt. *veshṭ* with *nis*), a small reed used as a shuttle, a weaver's shuttle.

निर्वैर *nir-vaira*, *am*, n. absence of enmity; (*as*, *ā*, *am*), free from enmity, without enmity, living in peace, peaceable; (*as*), m., N. of a hunter; (*am*), ind. peaceably, without enmity. — *Nirvaira-tā*, f. freedom from enmity, peaceableness, concord.

Nir-vairiṇa, *am*, n. absence of enmity, concord.

निर्वोढृ *nir-voḍhṛi*, *ḍhā*, *ḍhrī*, *ḍhṛi*, carrying or leading away, who or what carries away; separating, dividing; [cf. *nir-vahitṛi*.]

निर्व्यञ्जन *nir-vyañjana*, *as*, *ā*, *am*, without condiment; straightforward; (*e*), ind. in a straightforward or downright manner; plainly, without verbosity; silently (?).

निर्व्यथ *nir-vyatha*, *as*, *ā*, *am*, free from pain; quiet, unmoved, calm.

Nir-vyathana, *am*, n. a hole, chasm (a place of rest); freedom from pain; paining, afflicting, (in this sense *nir* is a prep.)

निर्व्यपेक्ष *nir-vyapeksha*, *as*, *ā*, *am*, disregarding, indifferent to (with loc.).

निर्व्यलीक *nir-vyalīka*, *as*, *ā*, *am*, not causing pain, not hurting, not offending; not feeling pain, without pain, pleased, doing willingly or sincerely, sincere, genuine, undissembling; (*am*), ind. sincerely, readily. — *Nirvyalīka-tas*, ind. sincerely.

निर्व्याकुल *nir-vyākula*, *as*, *ā*, *am*, not troubled or disquieted, not excited, calm. — *Nir-vyākula-tā*, f. freedom from trouble, calmness; (*tayā*), ind. with complete calmness, quite calmly.

निर्व्याघ्र *nir-vyāghra*, *as*, *ā*, *am*, free from tigers, not infested by tigers.

निर्व्याज *nir-vyāja*, *as*, *ā*, *am*, without deceit, candid, upright, straightforward, honest, plain, exact; (*am*), ind. honestly, exactly, plainly. — *Nirvyāja-tā*, f. honesty, plainness, candour. — *Nirvyājī-kṛita*, *as*, *ā*, *am*, made plain, freed from deceit or illusion.

निर्व्याधि *nir-vyādhi*, *is*, *is*, *i*, free from sickness, healthy, strong.

निर्व्यापार *nir-vyāpāra*, *as*, *ā*, *am*, without employment or business, free from occupation, unoccupied, not busy, at leisure.

निर्व्यूह् *nir-vy-ūh*, cl. 1. P. A. *-ūhati*, *-te*, &c., to push out, carry out, lead or bring away, remove; to arrange, put in order, perform, accomplish.

Nir-vyūḍha, *as*, *ā*, *am*, finished, completed; abandoned, left, deserted; (*am*), n. various reading for *nir-vāha*, completion.

Nir-vyūḍhi, *is*, f. end, completion; the top, highest point or degree.

Nir-vyūha, *as*, m. a turret; a helmet or its ornament, a crest; a pinnacle (?); a door, gate; a pin or peg in a wall to hang things upon; decoction; [cf. *nir-yūha*.]

निर्व्रण *nir-vraṇa*, *as*, *ā*, *am*, without wounds, unhurt; undamaged; without notches or rents.

निर्व्रत *nir-vrata*, *as*, *ā*, *am*, neglecting religious observances, not observing vows.

निर्व्रस्क *nir-vraska*, *as*, *ā*, *am* (fr. rt. *vraść* with *nis*), uprooted, extirpated.

निर्व्लयनी *nir-vlayanī*, f. (fr. rt. *vlī* with *nis*). See *nir-lvayanī*, p. 500, col. 1.

निर्हन् *nir-han*, cl. 2. P. *-hanti*, *-hantum*, Ved. to strike out, expel.

निर्हस्त *nir-hasta*, *as*, *ā*, *am*, Ved. handless, without hands; [cf. *nairhasta*.]

निर्हाद *nir-hāda*, *as*, m. (fr. rt. *had* with *nis*), evacuation, voiding excrement; [cf. *nir-hāra*.]

निर्हार *nir-hāra*. See under *nir-hṛi* below.

निर्हिम *nir-hima*, *am*, n. cessation of winter.

निर्हृ *nir-hṛi*, cl. 1. P. A. *-harati*, *-te*, *-hartum*, to draw out from, extract, tear out, pull out, root up; to carry out (a dead body), to carry or take away; to export (goods); to change or mix together (clothes &c.).

Nir-haraṇa, *am*, n. taking forth or out, drawing out, extracting, rooting up, taking away, removing, removal; setting aside, carrying away, carrying out dead bodies to be burnt, carrying a corpse to the funeral pyre.

Nir-haraṇīya or *nir-hartavya*, *as*, *ā*, *am*, to be taken away or removed; to be drawn out, &c.

Nir-hāra, *as*, m. extracting, drawing out, rooting up, destroying, destruction; putting forth or out; carrying away, carrying out a corpse or dead body to the funeral pile to be burnt; taking away, removing, abstracting; setting aside; accumulation of a private store of wealth, a hoard; evacuation of any of the natural excrements of the body, (opposed to *ā-hāra*; cf. *nir-hāda*, *nī-hāra*); giving away (?); diffusive fragrance; completion.

Nir-hāraka, *as*, *ikā*, *am*, carrying out (a dead body to the funeral pile), one who carries out or extracts or removes.

Nir-hāraṇa, *am*, n. (fr. the Caus.), causing (a dead body) to be carried out.

Nir-hārin, *ī*, *iṇī*, *i*, taking forth or out, carrying out; diffusively fragrant, spreading wide (as odour); having wealth.

Nir-hṛita, *as*, *ā*, *am*, extracted, drawn out, taken or carried forth or out.

Nir-hṛiti, *is*, f. bringing away, taking out of one's way, removal.

1. *nir-hṛitya*, *as*, *ā*, *am*, Ved. to be taken out; to be left out or omitted.

2. *nir-hṛitya*, ind. having taken forth or out, having extracted.

निर्हेति *nir-heti*, *is*, *is*, *i*, weaponless, unarmed.

निर्हेतु *nir-hetu*, *us*, *us*, *u*, causeless, reasonless, having no cause or reason. — *Nirhetu-tva*, *am*, n. causelessness.

निर्ह्राद *nir-hrāda* or *ni-hrāda*, *as*, m. (fr. rt. *hrād* with *nis*), a sound in general. — *Nirhrāda-bhīta*, *as*, *ā*, *am*, terrified by a sound or noise.

Nir-hrādin, *ī*, *inī*, *i*, sounding, resounding, roaring.

निर्ह्रास *nir-hrāsa*, *as*, m. abbreviation, shortening (of a vowel).

निर्ह्रीक *nir-hrīka*, *as*, *ā*, *am* (fr. *nis* + *hrī*), not shy, without shame, bold, daring.

निल् *nil*, cl. 6. P. *nilati*, &c., to understand with difficulty, to be impassable or impenetrable; [cf. *ni-lī* below.]

निलय् *nil-ay* (= *nir-ay*), cl. 1. A. *-ayate*, *-yitum*, to go out; [cf. rt. *i* and rt. *ay*.]

1. *nil-ayana*, *am*, n. (for 2. see under *ni-lī* below), the act of going out.

निलिम्प *ni-limpa*, *as*, m. (fr. rt. *lip* with *ni*), Ved., N. of a particular class of supernatural beings; a troop of Maruts; a god in general; (*ā*), f. a cow. — *Nilimpa-nirjharī*, f. the river of the gods, the Gaṅgā.

Nilimpikā, f. a cow.

निली *ni-lī*, cl. 4. A. *-līyate*, *-letum* and *-lātum*, to lie down, settle down, alight; to hide one's self, disappear, conceal one's self from (with abl.); to sink down, perish, (*ni-lilyire*, they perished, Mahā-bh. Sauptika-p. 399.)

Ni-laya, as, m. hiding one's self; a hiding-place; the lair or den of animals, a nest; dwelling, abode, residence, house, habitation; (often at the end of a comp. in the sense of) having one's residence, living, residing in (e.g. *Kailāsa-nilaya*, residing in Kailāsa).

2. *ni-layana, am*, n. (for 1. see p. 502, col. 3), settling in a place, alighting; place of refuge, dwelling-place, dwelling, habitation.

Nilāyi-tā, f. dwelling, residing in, the being domesticated.

Ni-lāyin, ī, inī, i, dwelling in, inhabiting.

Ni-līna, as, ā, am, fused in or into; involved, encompassed, surrounded, shut or wrapt up, embraced, destroyed, perished; transformed, changed; full.

Nilīnaka, as, am, m. n. (?), N. of a village in the north country; [cf. *nailīnaka*.]

Ni-līyamāna, as, ā, am, hiding, lying concealed.

निवक्षस् *ni-vakshas, ās, âs, as*, Ved. (probably) an epithet of the sacrificial animal (implying some peculiarity of colour &c.).

निवचन 1. *ni-vaćana, am*, n. (fr. rt. *vać* with *ni*), Ved. expression, address; a proverbial expression; [cf. 1. *nir-vaćana*.]

निवचन 2. *ni-vaćana, as, ā, am* (*ni* = *nis*), (Pāṇ. I. 4, 76), not speaking; [cf. 2. *nir-vaćana*.] — *Nivaćane-kṛi*, cl. 8. P. *-karoti, -kartum*, to obstruct the speech, to cease to speak. — *Nivaćane-kṛitya* or *nivaćane-kṛitvā*, ind. having ceased to speak.

निवत् *ni-vat, t*, f. (fr. *ni*), Ved. a steep place, a valley; (*tā*), ind. downhill, downwards.

निवध् *ni-vadh*, a defective verb (see *vadh*), to kill.

निवना *ni-vanā*, ind., Ved. downwards, downhill; [cf. *ni-vatā*.]

निवप् *ni-vap*, cl. 1. P. A. *-vapati, -te, -vaptum*, to scatter seed, sow; to offer, make offerings of cakes &c. to the Manes; to kill.

Ni-vapana, am, n. pouring out, scattering or throwing down; sowing; oblations or gifts in honour of deceased ancestors, an offering to the Manes; [cf. *nir-vapaṇa*.]

Ni-vāpa, as, m. seed, grain, seed corn; an oblation or offering to the Manes of deceased parents or relatives, a libation or offering of water &c. at the Srāddha; gift, offering in general.

Ni-vāpaka, as, m. a sower.

Nivāpin, ī, inī, i, pouring out, throwing or scattering down, sowing.

Ny-upta, ny-upya. See s. v.

निवर *ni-vara*. See *ni-vṛi*, p. 504, col. 1.

निवर्त *ni-varta, ni-vartana*, &c. See *ni-vṛit*, p. 504, col. 1.

निवर्हण *ni-varhaṇa*. See *ni-vṛih*, p. 504.

निवस् 1. *ni-vas*, cl. 1. P. *-vasati, -vastum*, to dwell, inhabit, reside, lodge, live in (with loc.); to sojourn, pass time, pass the night; to roost.

Ni-vasat, an, antī, at, dwelling in, inhabiting.

Ni-vasati, is, f. a habitation, abiding, abode, house, residence.

Ni-vasatha, as, f. a village.

1. *ni-vasana, am*, n. a dwelling, house, a habitation. (For 2. see under 2. *ni-vas*, col. 2.)

Ni-vastavya, as, ā, am, to be lived; to be spent.

1. *ni-vāsa, as*, m. (for 2. see under 2. *ni-vas*, col. 2), living, dwelling, residing; passing the night; a place of residence, dwelling-place, abode, house; night-quarters. — *Nivāsa-bhūmi, is*, f. place of residence. — *Nivāsa-bhūya, am*, n. habitation; inhabiting. — *Nivāsa-rājan, ā*, m. the king of the country in which one dwells.

1. *ni-vāsana, am*, n. (for 2. see under 2. *ni-vas* below), living, residing [cf. *jagan-n°*]; sojourn; passing or spending time.

1. *ni-vāsin, ī, inī, i*, dwelling, abiding in, inhabiting, an inhabitant, resident.

निवस् 2. *ni-vas*, cl. 2. A. *-vaste, -vasitum*, to put on or wear (clothes), dress; to change one's clothes: Caus. or cl. 10. P. *-vāsayati, -yitum*, to put on (a garment?).

2. *ni-vasana, am*, n. (for 1. see under 1. *ni-vas*, col. 1), putting on (a garment), cloth, clothes, raiment; an under garment.

2. *ni-vāsa, as*, m. (for 1. see under 1. *ni-vas*, col. 1), dress (e.g. in *ćarma-nivāsa*, dressed in a skin).

2. *ni-vāsana, am*, n. (for 1. see under 1. *ni-vas*, above), (with Buddhists) a kind of raiment.

Ni-vāsaya (fr. 2. *ni-vāsa*), Nom. P. *nivāsayati*, &c., to put on (a garment), to cover.

2. *ni-vāsin, ī, inī, i* (at the end of a comp.), dressed in, wearing, clothed, covered.

निवह् *ni-vah*, cl. 1. P. A. *-vahati, -te, -voḍhum*, to bring or lead near; to carry, to support.

Ni-vaha, as, m. a multitude, quantity, heap, (in this sense also *ās*, m. pl.); N. of one of the seven winds; one of the seven tongues of fire.

Ni-vāha, as, m., Ved. leading down, (opposed to *abhy-avaroha*.)

निवात 1. *ni-vāta, as, ā, am* (*ni* = *nis*), protected against or sheltered from the wind, not reached by the wind, not windy, calm [cf. 2. *nir-vāta*]; (*am*), n. a place sheltered from or inaccessible to the wind, a sheltered spot, (sometimes used at the end of a comp. of which the first member expresses the sheltering object, see Pāṇ. VI. 2, 8); a calm.

निवात 2. *ni-vāta, as, ā, am* (*ni* + *vāta* fr. *van*), unimpeded, unhurt, uninjured; secure, safe (as in an asylum); well armed, accoutred in strong mail; (*as*), m. an asylum, a refuge, a dwelling, &c.; an impenetrable coat of mail; (*am*), n. security, a secure spot; strong armour. — *Nivāta-kavaća, as, ā, am*, whose armour or mail is impenetrable, wearing an impenetrable coat of mail; (*as*), m., N. of a demon, the grandson of Hiraṇya-kaśipu; (*ās*), m. pl., N. of a class of Dānavas or Daityas.

निवाप *ni-vāpa*, &c. See *ni-vap*, col. 1.

निवार *ni-vāra*. See *ni-vṛi*, p. 504, col. 1.

निवाश *ni-vāśa, as, ā, am* (fr. rt. *vāś* with *ni*), Ved. bellowing, roaring, sounding.

निविड *ni-viḍa, as, ā, am* (fr. *viḍa* = *vila*, a hole, with *ni* = *nis*), without spaces or interstices, close, contiguous, coarse, large, bulky; gross, thick, impervious, impenetrable, dense, firm; crooked-nosed; (*as*), m., N. of a mountain.

Niviḍaya, Nom. P. *niviḍayati*, &c., to make tight.

Ni-viḍisa, as, ā, am, compact, close; coarse, gross; crooked-nosed (?).

Ni-virīsa or *ni-viriśa* = *ni-viḍa*.

निविद् 1. *ni-vid*, cl. 2. P. *-vetti, -veda, -veditum*, to tell, communicate, proclaim: Caus. *-vedayati, -yitum*, to make known, tell, communicate, report, represent, betray, relate (with dat., loc., or gen. of the person); to present, offer, give, deliver.

2. *ni-vid, t*, f., Ved. instruction, information, direction, communication, precept, doctrine; invocation; N. of certain sentences or short formularies inserted in a liturgy and containing epithets or short invocations of the gods (e.g. *Agniḥ sushamit, hotā deva-vritaḥ*); (Sāy.) speech, a short text of the Veda. — *Nivid-dhāna, as, ā, am*, Ved. containing the Nivids; (*am*), n. (according to Sāy.) inserting the Nivids. — *Nividdhānīya, as, ā, am*, Ved. containing the Nivids.

Ni-vedaka, as, ā, am, communicating, relating.

Ni-vedana, as, ā, am, proclaiming, announcing; (*as*), m. an epithet of Siva; (*am*), n. making known, proclaiming, apprizing, publishing, relating, communicating, announcement, communication; information; representation; delivering, giving, entrusting; an offering, oblation; dedication.

Ni-vedayishu, us, us, u (fr. the Desid. of the Caus. without reduplication), wishing to make known or report, intending to relate about.

Ni-vedita, as, ā, am, made known, announced, reported, communicated, stated, told; represented; delivered, addressed, entrusted, presented, given.

Ni-vedin, ī, inī, i, communicating, reporting, relating, proclaiming.

1. *ni-vedya, as, ā, am*, to be communicated or related; fit to be reported; (*am*), n. an oblation, offering food to an idol, (probably for *naivedya*.)

2. *ni-vedya*, ind. having respectfully announced or made known.

निविरीस *ni-virīsa*. See *ni-viḍa*, col. 1.

निविवृत्सत् *ni-vivṛitsat, ni-vivṛitsu*. See p. 504, col. 2.

निविश् *ni-viś*, cl. 6. A. *-viśate* (ep. also P. *-viśati*), *-veshṭum*, to enter; to alight, descend; to sit down, take a seat; to lie down; to settle down, to encamp; to settle, take a wife; to be fixed or intent on (with loc.): Caus. *-veśayati, -yitum*, to cause to enter, introduce, place in or on; to cause to sit down; to cause to settle or dwell, cause to lie down or encamp; to cause to marry; to put or place down; to found (a city); to enter (in writing), mark down (letters, lines, &c.), inscribe (on a tablet), depict; (with *manas*) to apply the mind to, fix the mind on (with loc.).

Ni-vishṭa, as, ā, am, entered, gone in or into; seated, sitting upon; situated or placed in or on, fixed on, intent upon; arranged.

Ni-vishṭi, is, f., Ved. entering (a female), copulation.

Ni-veśa, as, m. entering, entrance; settling in a place, encamping, halting; dwelling-place, habitation; halting-place, place of lying, camp, palace, the residence of a king or general, (*niveśaṃ kṛi*, to take up one's residence, settle, encamp); depositing, delivering; founding (a household), settling, marrying, marriage; founding (a town); impression, mark, copy; military array; ornament, dress, decoration. — *Niveśa-deśa, as*, m. a dwelling-place. — *Niveśa-vat, ān, atī, at* (at the end of a comp.), lying in or on, resting on.

Ni-veśana, as, ī, am, entering; placing or laying down, lodging, providing with a resting-place; (*as*), m., N. of a Vṛishṇi; (*am*), n. entering, entrance; sitting down, encamping, settling, putting or laying down, (*niveśanaṃ kṛi*, to settle, encamp); entering (in writing), inscribing; founding (a household), marrying, marriage; resting-place, habitation, dwelling-place, abode, dwelling, house; a nest; a camp; a town or city; [cf. *a-n°*.]

Ni-veśanīya, as, ā, am, to be entered; to be fixed; to be engaged in.

Ni-veśayat, an, antī, at, causing to enter, introducing, sending in or into.

Ni-veśita, as, ā, am, made to enter, introduced; placed in or upon; turned to or towards, fixed upon, directed on; sent into, entered into, engaged in.

Ni-veśin, ī, inī, i, resting in, being in, situated on, lying near; resting on.

1. *ni-veśya, as, ā, am*, to be founded (as a town); to be married (as a man); to be returned or paid.

2. *ni-veśya*, ind. having placed in or on, having made to remain or dwell.

Ni-veshṭavya, as, ā, am, to be married (applied to a man); (*am*), n. to be married, (used impersonally, e.g. *mahākule niveshṭavyaṃ sadṛiśe vā*, one should marry into a high family or an equal).

निविशेष *ni-viśesha, as, ā, am*, not different, alike; (*as*), m. want of difference.

निवीत **ni-vīta**, as, ā, am (fr. rt. vye with ni), having the sacred Brāhmanical thread suspended round the neck; (am), n. wearing the Brāhmanical thread round the neck; the Brāhmanical thread so worn; (as, ā, am), m. f. n. a veil, mantle, a wrapper (=ni-vṛita).

Nivītin, ī, inī, i, wearing the sacred thread suspended round the neck; (ī), m. a Brāhman with the cord so suspended.

निवीर्य **ni-vīrya**, as, ā, am, impotent (= nir-vīrya, q. v.).

निवृ **ni-vṛi**, cl. 5. 9. 1. P. A. -vṛiṇoti, -ṇute, -vṛiṇāti, -ṇīte, -varati, -te, -varitum, -varītum, to surround, defend, restrain: Caus. -vārayati, -yitum, to surround, protect; to keep off, ward off, prohibit, hinder, prevent, hold back from, stop, withhold, forbid, interdict, exclude, obstruct, oppose: Caus. Pass. -vāryate, to be interdicted, to be withheld.

Ni-vara, as, m., Ved. covering, protection, a protector; (Sāy.) a preventer, obstructer; (ā), f. a virgin, an unmarried girl, (in this sense probably fr. ni, 'not,' + vara, 'a husband.')

Ni-vāra, as, m. keeping off, warding off, defending, preventing, hindering, opposition, impediment; (ā), f., N. of a river.

Ni-vāraka, as, ā, am, keeping off, defending, able to keep off.

Ni-vāraṇa, as, ā, am, keeping off, preventing, defending; (am), n. keeping back or off, preventing, defending, hindering, opposing; prohibition, an impediment; contemning (?).

Ni-vāraṇīya, as, ā, am, to be kept off or defended, to be checked or hindered, &c.

Ni-vārayat, an, antī, at, preventing, opposing, hindering.

Ni-vārita, as, ā, am, hindered, forbidden, prevented, checked, opposed.

1. *ni-vārya*=ni-vāraṇīya.

2. *ni-vārya,* ind. having suppressed, having forbidden.

Ni-vāryamāṇa, as, ā, am, being prevented or hindered.

Ni-vṛita, as, ā, am, surrounded, enclosed, encompassed; (as, ā, am), m. f. n. (=ni-vīta), a veil, a mantle, a wrapper.

Ni-vṛiti, is, f. covering, enclosing

निवृज् **ni-vṛij**, cl. 7. 1. P. -vṛiṇakti, -varjati, -varjitum, Ved. to immerse, drown; to overthrow; to pour out; to extirpate.

निवृत् 1. **ni-vṛit**, cl. 1. A. (also P. in Fut. Cond. and Aor.) -vartate, -vartitum, to turn back, return, retreat, retire, go back, turn back or away from (with abl.); to recoil; to escape from (with abl.), run away; to cease from, desist from, abstain or refrain from (with abl.); to refuse, decline; to cease; to come to an end, be accomplished; to be finished, stop, set (as the sun); not to occur; to be withheld; to be forbidden; to be reversed; to be occupied or engaged in: Caus. -vartayati, -yitum, to cause to return; to bring back; to turn away, keep back from, restrain; to cause to desist; to drive back, repel; to accomplish, perform, bring to an end, (for nir-vṛit.)

Ni-varta, as, ā, am, Ved. causing to return or turn back.

Ni-vartaka, as, ikā, am, returning, turning or coming back, flying; desisting from, stopping, ceasing; bringing back, causing to cease, abolishing, expelling, removing. — *Nivartaka-tva, am,* n. the state of one who turns back, &c.

Ni-vartana, as, ā, am, turning back, ceasing, ceasing to exist, disappearing; causing to return; (am), n. returning, turning or coming back, return; ceasing, not happening, not occurring; desisting or abstaining from (with abl.); desisting from work, inactivity, (opposed to pra-vartana); repenting, reforming; causing to come back, bringing back; turning back (the hair); a means of returning (Ved.); keeping back from (with abl.); a measure of land, 20 rods or 200 cubits or 40,000 Hastas square. — *Nivartana-stūpa, as,* m., N. of a Stūpa erected at the spot where the charioteer of Buddha returned.

Ni-vartanīya, as, ā, am, to be brought back; to be made to turn back, to be kept back or diverted or hindered.

Ni-vartamāna, as, ā, am, turning back, returning.

Ni-vartayitavya, as, ā, am, to be kept back, to be restrained, to be diverted.

Ni-vartita, as, ā, am, turned back or away, brought back, made to desist. — *Nivartita-pūrva, as, ā, am,* one who has turned away before.

Ni-vartitavya, as, ā, am, to be brought back.

Ni-vartin, ī, inī, i, turning back, returning, flying, (saṅgrāmād a-nivartin, not turning back from the fight, i. e. not flying); leaving off, abstaining from; allowing to return, causing to turn back.

Ni-vartya, ind. having turned or brought back, having induced to desist; having desisted or refrained from; having repented; having repaid; [cf. dur-n°.]

Ni-vivṛitsat, an, antī, at (fr. the Desid.), wishing to return or desist.

Ni-vivṛitsu, us, us, u, desirous of turning back, wishing to desist.

2. *ni-vṛit,* f.=ni-ćṛit, q. v.; [cf. ati-n°, pāda-n°, atipāda-n°.]

Ni-vṛitta, as, ā, am, returned, returning, turned back; gone, departed; vanished; ceased, refrained from, abstained, stopped, desisted, prohibited; abstaining from worldly acts, &c.; abstaining, abstracted or abstained from or independent of worldly acts or motives, abstracted from this world, quiet; desisting from or repenting of any improper conduct; finished, completed, whole; (am), n. return; [cf. dur-n°.] — *Nivṛitta-kāraṇa, as, ā, am,* without further cause or motive; (as), m. a virtuous man, one uninfluenced by worldly desires. — *Nivṛitta-kṛishi-goraksha, as, ā, am,* ceasing from agriculture and the tending of cattle. — *Nivṛitta-deva-kārya, as, ā, am,* ceasing from sacrificial rites or offerings to the gods. — *Nivṛitta-māṅsa, as, ā, am,* one who abstains from eating meat. — *Nivṛitta-yajña-svādhyāya, as, ā, am,* ceasing from sacrifices and the repetition of prayers. — *Nivṛitta-rāga, as, ā, am,* of subdued appetites or passions. — *Nivṛitta-vṛitti, is, is, i,* quitting any practice or occupation. — *Nivṛitta-hṛidaya, as, ā, am,* with relenting heart. — *Nivṛittātman* (°ta-āt°), ā, m. 'one whose spirit is abstracted,' a sage; an epithet of Vishṇu.

Ni-vṛitti, is, f. returning, return; disappearing, disappearance, ceasing, cessation, suspension, abstaining from action, inactivity, (opposed to pra-vṛitti); ceasing to be active, ceasing to be valid or binding (as a rule); leaving off, desisting from (with abl.); resigning, discontinuance of worldly acts, cessation of emotions, separation from the world, abstinence; repose, rest; felicity, bliss, beatitude, (wrongly for nir-vṛitti); denial, refusal; abolition, prevention; completion; (is), m., N. of a son of Vṛishṇi; of a son of Dharma, king of Magadha; [cf. nir-vṛitti, ni-dhṛiti.]

निवृह् **ni-vṛih** [cf. ni-bṛih], Caus. -varhayati, -yitum, to throw down; to annihilate; to extirpate.

Ni-varhaṇa, as, ā, am, destroying, extirpating, annihilating, removing; (am), n. destruction, eradication, annihilation, killing, removing; [cf. ni-barhaṇa.]

Ni-varhita, as, ā, am, destroyed, annihilated, eradicated.

निवेदक **ni-vedaka, ni-vedana,** &c. See under 1. ni-vid, p. 503, cols. 2, 3.

निवेष्ट **ni-veshṭa**, as, m. (fr. rt. veshṭ with ni), a cover, envelope; Vasishṭhasya niveshṭas, N. of a Sāman.

Ni-veshṭana, am, n. covering, enveloping, clothing.

निवेष्य **ni-veshya**, as, m. (fr. rt. vish with ni), Ved. a whirlpool, a water-spout; a whirlwind or any similar phenomenon [cf. stanayitnu]; a part of the upper or fore-part of an animal, the vertebra?; (according to Mahī-dhara) eddy or hoar-frost; (as, ā, am), whirling, belonging to a whirlpool or eddy.

निव्याध **ni-vyādha**, as, m. (fr. rt. vyadh with ni), Ved. an opening, aperture, a window.

Ni-vyādhin, ī, inī, i, Ved. piercing, opening.

निव्यूढ **ni-vyūḍha**, am, n. perseverance, resolution.

निश् 1. **nis**, euphonically substituted for nis before ć, ćh, &c.

निश् 2. **niś**, cl. 1. P. -neśati, &c., to meditate upon, meditate profoundly, to be absorbed in meditation.

निश् 3. **niś**, f. (perhaps connected with nak fr. rt. 2. naś, or merely a curtailed form of niśā below, which may be connected with ni-śītha and so derived fr. rt. śī with ni; the form niś is defective in nom. voc. sing. du. and pl., acc. sing. du., but may be optionally substituted for niśā in acc. pl. and remaining cases, e. g. niśas or niśās, niśā or niśayā, niḍbhyām [according to some also nijbhyām] or niśābhyām, &c.), night; niśi niśi, every night; mahā-niśi, at midnight.

Niśa, am, n. (at the end of a comp.)=niśā, night (e. g. ahar-niśam, ind. day and night; divā-niśam, ind. day and night; cf. also a-niśa.)

Niśā, f. night; a vision, dream; turmeric, Curcuma (of two species,=haridrā and dāru-haridrā, probably C. Zedoaria and C. Longa; a collective N. of the asterisms Aries, Taurus, Gemini, Cancer, Sagittarius, and Capricorn; cf. niśā-bala.) — *Niśā-kara, as,* m. 'the night-maker,' the moon, (regarded with Divā-kara as a son of Garuḍa); a symbolical expression for the numeral one; a cock. — *Niśā-kara-kalā-mauli, is,* m. 'bearing a crescent as diadem,' an epithet of Śiva. — *Niśā-kāla, as,* m. the time of night. — *Niśā-ketu, us,* m. 'night-sign,' the moon. — *Niśā-kshaya, as,* m. the close of night. — *Niśā-gaṇa, as,* m. a number of nights. — *Niśāgama* (°śā-āg°), as, m. the coming on or commencement of night. — *Niśā-gṛiha, as,* m. a bed-room, sleeping-room. — *Niśā-ćara, as, ā* or *ī, am,* going or moving about by night, nocturnal, night-walking; (as), m. a Rākshasa, a fiend, an imp or goblin; an epithet of Śiva [cf. niśāćara-pati]; a jackal; an owl; a snake; the ruddy goose, Cakravāka; a thief; a ghost, an evil spirit; (ī), f. a she-devil, a female fiend; a woman who goes to an assignation, a harlot, whore; a sort of perfume, (see keśinī.) — *Niśāćara-pati, is,* m. 'lord of night-walkers,' an epithet of Śiva. — *Niśāćareśa* (°ra-īśa), as, m. 'lord of the Rākshasas,' an epithet of Rāvaṇa. — *Niśā-ćarman, a,* n. 'the skin of night,' darkness. — *Niśā-ćhada, as,* m. a species of plant. — *Niśā-jala, am,* n. 'the water of night,' hoar-frost, frost, dew. — *Niśāṭa* (°śā-aṭa), as, m. 'roving by night,' an owl; a demon, a ghost. — *Niśāṭaka, as,* m. bdellium (=guggulu, connected with niśāṭa, an owl; cf. kauśika,=owl and bdellium, ulūkhala, ulūkhalaka). — *Niśāṭana* (°śā-aṭ°), as, m. 'night-rover,' an owl; (ī), f. a species of moth. — *Niśātikrama* (°śā-at°), as, m. the passing away of night. — *Niśātyaya* (°śā-at°), as, m. the close of night, day-break. — *Niśā-darśin, ī,* m. 'seeing at night,' an owl. — *Niśādi* (°śā-ādi), is, f. the beginning of night, evening, twilight. — *Niśādhīśa* (°śā-adh°), as, m. 'lord of night,' the moon. — *Niśā-nātha, as,* m. 'lord of night,' the moon. — *Niśā-nārāyaṇa, as,* m., N. of a poet. — *Niśā-niśam,* ind. night by night, every night, always. — 1. *ni-śānta* (°śā-an°), as, am, m. n. (for 2. ni-śānta see under ni-śam, p. 505, col. 1), the end of night, break of day. — *Niśāndha* (°śā-an°), *as, ā, am,* blind at night; (*ā*), f. a species of creeper (=*jatukā*).—*Niśā-pati, is,* m. 'husband of the night,' the moon; camphor.—*Niśā-putra, ās,* m. pl. 'the sons of night,' N. of certain demons. —*Niśā-pushpa, as,* m. 'the flower of night,' the white water-lily; hoar-frost, dew.—*Niśā-prāneśvara, as,* m. 'husband of night,' the moon. —*Niśā-bala, as,* m. a collective N. of the signs of the zodiac Aries, Taurus, Gemini, Cancer, Sagittarius, and Capricorn.—*Niśā-bhangā,* f. a species of plant (=*dugdha-puććhī*).—*Niśā-maṇi, is,* m. 'jewel of the night,' the moon; [cf. *dhvajāgra-niśāmaṇi.*]—*Niśā-mukha, am,* n. the beginning of night.—*Niśā-mṛiga, as,* m. 'night-animal,' a jackal.—1. *niśā-raṇa, am,* n. a nocturnal battle; (for 2. see *ni-śaraṇa* below.)—*Niśā-ratna, am,* n. (or, according to some, *as,* m.), 'the jewel of the night,' the moon.—*Niśārdhakāla* (°*śā-ardha-k*°), *as,* m. the first part of the night (opposed to the following). —*Niśāvasāna* (°*śā-av*°), *am,* n. the close or end of night, the second part of the night (opposed to the preceding).—*Niśā-vihāra, as,* m. a night-walker, a nocturnal imp or goblin, a Rākshasa. —*Niśā-vṛinda, am,* n. a number of nights.—*Niśā-vedin, ī,* m. 'knowing the night,' a cock.—*Niśā-hasa, as,* m. 'night-smiler,' the white water-lily which opens its petals at night.—*Niśāhvā* (°*śā-āh*°), f. turmeric.—*Niśi-pāla, as,* m. a kind of metre consisting of four lines of fifteen syllables each.—*Niśi-pushpā* or *niśi-pushpī* or *niśipushpikā,* f. the tree Nyctanthes Arbor-Tristis.—*Niśeśa* (°*śa-īśa*), *as,* m. 'lord of night,' the moon.—*Niśaita* (°*śa-eta*), *as,* m. 'shining at night,' the crane, Ardea Nivea.—*Niśotsarga* (°*śā-ut*°), *as,* m. the end of night, day-break.—*Niśopaśāya* (°*śā-up*°), *as,* m. resting at night.

निशठ **ni-śaṭha,** *as, ā, am,* not false, candid, honest; (*as*), m., N. of a Vṛishṇi, a son of Bala-rāma by Revatī; (also written *ni-shaṭha, ni-saṭha, ni-satha.*)

निशद् **ni-śad,** Caus. *-śātayati, -yitum,* Ved. to kill.

निशब्द **ni-śabda,** *as, ā, am,* speechless, silent; [cf. *niḥ-śabda.*]

निशम् **ni-śam,** cl. 4. P. *-śāmyati, -śamitum,* to observe, see; to hear, listen: Caus. *-śāmayati, -yitum,* to observe, perceive, see; to hear, listen.

Ni-śamana, am, n. looking at; seeing, sight; hearing; becoming aware of.

Ni-śamya, ind. having perceived, having heard, hearing.

2. *ni-śānta, as, ā, am* (for 1. *niśānta* see under *niśā,* p. 504, col. 3), tranquillized, quiet, tranquil, patient; (*am*), n. a house, dwelling, habitation. —*Niśānta-nārī,* f. a house-wife.

Niśāntīya, as, ā, am, belonging or relating to a house (?).

Ni-śāma, as, m. observing, perceiving.

Ni-śāmana, am, n. sight, seeing; looking at, beholding; looking at repeatedly; observing, hearing; a shadow, reflection.

Ni-śāmayat, an, antī, at, perceiving, hearing.

Ni-śāmya, ind. having seen; having heard; having tranquillized; having put out (as a light).

निशरण **ni-śaraṇa,** *am,* n. (fr. rt. *śṛī* with *ni*), killing, slaughter.

2. *ni-śāraṇa, am,* n. (fr. *śṛī* with *ni*), killing, slaughter, slaying.

Ni-śāruka, as, m. a kind of Rūpaka (see under *dṛiḍha*); (*am*), n. an air, a sort of musical composition played as an accompaniment to dancing.

निशात **ni-śāta.** See under *ni-śo,* col. 2.

निशाद **ni-śāda,** *as,* m. a man of low caste; (see *nishāda.*)—*Niśāda-tva, am,* n. the state or condition of a man of low caste.—*Niśādā-putra, as,* m. (?), a pestle.—*Niśādā-śilā,* f. a mortar, a slab for grinding.

निशामय **ni-śāmaya**=*śriṇu,* listen, (impv. of Caus. of *ni-śam,* col. 1.)

निशायिन् **ni-śāyin,** *ī, inī, i* (fr. rt. *śī* with *ni*), lying down in, sleeping in (?).

निशावन **niśāvana,** *as,* m. hemp. See *śaṇa.*

निशि **ni-śi** [cf. *ni-śo*], cl. 5. P. A. *-śinoti, -nute, -śetum,* to sharpen; to stimulate, excite; to kill.

Ni-śita, as, ā, am, sharpened, whetted, pointed, stimulated; (*am*), n. iron.

Ni-śiti, is, f., Ved. excitement, stimulation, encouragement.

निशिता **ni-śitā,** f., Ved. night; [cf. *ni-śītha.*]

निशिथ **ni-śitha,** *as,* m. (for *ni-śītha*), N. of one of the three sons of Doshā (Night); (some read this word in Bhāgavata-Purāṇa IV. 13, 14, *ni-śītha.*)

निशीथ **ni-śītha,** *as,* m. (fr. rt. *śī* with *ni*), midnight, the time of sleep, night in general.

Ni-śīthinī, f. night.—*Niśīthinī-nātha, as,* m. 'husband of night,' the moon.

Ni-śīthyā, f. night.

निशुम्भ **ni-śumbha,** *as,* m. (fr. rt. *śumbh* with *ni*), killing, slaughter; N. of a Dānava, brother of Śumbha, slain by Durgā; (also written *nisumbha.*)—*Niśumbha-mathanī,* f. or *niśumbha-mardinī,* f. 'destroyer of Niśumbha,' an epithet of Durgā.

Ni-śumbhana, am, n. killing, slaying, slaughter.

Ni-śumbhin, ī, m. an epithet of Vajra-ṭīka; an inferior deity of the Buddhists.

निशुष्म **ni-śushma,** *as, ā, am,* Ved. not sparkling (as fire), not coruscating, (opposed to *uć-ćhushma.*)

निशृम्भ **ni-śṛimbha,** *as, ā, am* (fr. rt. *śrambh* with *ni*), Ved. stepping firmly? ; (Sāy.) fastened to (a car), harnessed.

निशैत **niśaita.** See under *niśā,* col. 1.

निशो **ni-śo** [cf. *ni-śi*], cl. 4. P. *-śyati, -śātum,* to sharpen, whet, polish.

Ni-śāta, as, ā, am, sharpened, whetted, sharp; polished, burnished, varnished.

Ni-śāna, am, n. sharpening; (also read *ni-śāṇa.*)

निश्चक्षुस् **niś-ćakshus,** *us, us, us,* eyeless, blind.

निश्चत् **niś-ćat** (*nis-ćat*), Caus. A. *-ćātayate, -yitum,* Ved. to scare or drive away.

निश्चत्वारिंश **niś-ćatvāriṅśa,** *as, ī, am,* without forty.

निश्चप्रच **niśća-praća,** (perhaps) backwards and forwards; [cf. *āća-parāća* under 2. *āća.*]

निश्चर् **niś-ćar** (*nis-ćar*), cl. 1. P. *-ćarati, -ćaritum,* to come forth, issue, go out, arise, proceed, appear, be produced; to rise (as sounds): Caus. *-ćārayati, -yitum,* to cause to issue or come forth.

Niś-ćara, as, m., N. of one of the Saptarshis in the eleventh Manv-antara.

Niś-ćāraka, am, n. evacuation by stool; air, wind; obstinacy, wilfulness.

निश्चल **niś-ćala,** *as, ā, am,* immovable, not moving, stock-still, still, fixed, steady; not subject to motion or fluctuation, invariable, unchangeable; (*ā*), f. the earth; Desmodium Gangeticum (=*śāla-parṇī*).—*Niśćala-mati, is, is, i,* steady-minded, of unshaken mind.—*Niśćalāṅga* (°*la-aṅ*°), *as, ā* or *ī, am,* having immovable limbs, firm-bodied, firm; (*as*), m. a species of crane, Ardea Nivea; a rock, mountain.

निश्चि **niś-ći** (*nis-ći,* see rt. 2. *ći*), cl. 3. P. *-ćiketi,* cl. 5. P. A. *-ćinoti, -nute, -ćetum,* Ved. to ascertain, investigate, know thoroughly, arrive at a certain decision, decide, regard as decided, to fix upon, determine, resolve.

Niś-ćaya, as, m. ascertainment, investigation, inquiry, a fixed opinion, a firm conviction, accurate or certain knowledge, certainty, positiveness, positive conclusion, determination, resolution, resolve, decision; settled purpose, fixed intention, design, purpose, aim, (*iti niśćayaḥ,* this is a fixed opinion or established conclusion; *niśćayam jñātum,* to ascertain the certainty; *niśćayaṃ kṛi,* to decide, come to a determination; cf. *pāpa-n*°, *maraṇa-n*°, *eka-n*°); 'removal of fallacy or deception,' N. of a figure in rhetoric; (*ena* or *āt*), ind. certainly.—*Niśćaya-datta, as,* m., N. of a merchant.—*Niśćaya-rūpa, as, ā, am,* having (only) the appearance of certainty, uncertain, wrong.

Niś-ćayin, ī, inī, i, decided, determined, resolved.

Niś-ćāyaka, as, ā, am, who or what ascertains or determines, one who is certain about anything, determining, decisive.

Niś-ćita, as, ā, am, ascertained, determined, settled, concluded, decided, established, certain, one who has come to a conclusion or formed a fixed opinion; sentenced, pronounced; (*am*), n. certainty, decision, conclusion; (*am*), ind. decidedly, positively; (*ā*), f., N. of a river.

Niś-ćiti, is, f. ascertainment, fixing, determining, settling.

Niś-ćitya, ind. having ascertained, having concluded or decided, having made out for certain, having settled or come to a final decision, feeling assured or convinced.

Niś-ćiyamāna, as, ā, am, being in the course of ascertainment, being under investigation, being concluded.

निश्चित्त **niś-ćitta,** *as,* m., N. of a Samādhi.

निश्चिन्त **niś-ćinta,** *as, ā, am,* unthinking, thoughtless, inconsiderate, void of reflection, careless, unconcerned; [cf. *naiśćintya.*]

निश्चुक्कण **niś-ćukkaṇa,** *am,* n. (said to be fr. rt. *ćukk*), a sort of tooth-powder prepared from sulphate of iron &c. which destroys the tartar but blackens the teeth; (also written *niś-ćukvaṇa.*)

निश्चृत् **niś-ćṛit,** cl. 6. P. *-ćṛitati, -ćartitum,* Ved. to loosen, untie.

निश्चेतन **niś-ćetana,** *as, ā, am,* without consciousness, unconscious, unreasonable.

निश्चेतस् **niś-ćetas,** *ās, ās, as,* out of one's mind, not in one's right senses.

निश्चेष्ट **niś-ćeshṭa,** *as, ā, am,* motionless, powerless, helpless; incapable of motion or effort; (*am*), ind. without motion.

Niś-ćeshṭā, f. motionlessness.—*Niśćeshṭā-karaṇa, as, ā, am,* causing motionlessness; epithet of one of the arrows of the god of love.

निश्चौर **niś-ćaura,** *as, ā, am,* free from robbers.

निश्च्यवन **niś-ćyavana,** *as,* m. 'unperishing,' a form of fire; N. of one of the Saptarshis in the second Manv-antara.

निश्छन्दस् **niś-ćhandas,** *ās, ās, as,* not studying holy writ; *niśćhandaḥ kulam,* a family in which the Vedas are not studied.

निश्छिद्र **niś-ćhidra,** *as, ā, am,* having no rent or openings, without holes, having no holes, without weak points or defects, having no weak side; unhurt, uninterrupted.

Niś-ćheda, as, ā, am, indivisible, without division.

निश्रथ्य *ni-śrathya*, ind. having fastened or harnessed.

निश्रम *ni-śrama*, *as*, m. (fr. rt. *śram* with *ni*), labour bestowed upon anything, continued practice.

निश्रयणी *ni-śrayaṇī*, f. (fr. rt. *śri* with *ni*), a ladder, staircase; (also written *niḥ-śrayaṇī*, *niḥ-śrayiṇī*, q. v.)

Ni-śreṇi, f. a ladder, staircase; (other forms of the word are *ni-śreṇī*, f., *niḥ-śreṇi*, and *niḥ-śreṇī*, q. v.)

निश्रीक *ni-śrīka* for *niḥ-śrīka*, q. v.

निश्वस् *ni-śvas*, cl. 2. P. *-śvasiti*, *-śvasitum*, to draw in the breath, inspire; to sigh.

Ni-śvasya, ind. having drawn in the breath, having sighed.

Ni-śvāsa, *as*, m. inspiration, inhaling, sighing. — *Niśvāsa-praśvāsa*, *au*, m. du. inspiration and expiration, respiration.

निष् 1. *nish*, euphonically substituted for *nis* before *k*, *kh*, *ṭ*, &c.

निष् 2. *nish* [cf. rt. *niksh*], cl. 1. P. *neshati*, &c., to moisten, sprinkle.

निषङ्ग *ni-shaṅga*, *as*, m. (fr. rt. *sañj* with *ni*), clinging to, attachment; union, meeting, association; a quiver; a sword (?).

Ni-shaṅgathi, *is*, *is*, *i*, embracing; (*is*), m. embracing, an embrace [cf. *svañj*]; a bowman; a charioteer; a car; grass; the shoulder. — *Nishaṅga-dhi*, *is*, m., Ved. (according to commentators) the sheath of a sword, a scabbard.

Nishaṅgin, *ī*, *inī*, *i*, having a quiver; (*ī*), m. an archer, bowman; N. of one of the hundred sons of Dhṛita-rāshṭra.

निषञ्ज *ni-shañja* in *ku-n°*, q. v.

निषठ *ni-shaṭha*. See *ni-śaṭha*, p. 505.

निषद् 1. *ni-shad* (*ni-sad*), cl. 1. 6. P. *-shīdati*, *-shattum*, to sit down, lie down, recline; to settle down, sink down; to dwell; to be afflicted, suffer pain: Caus. *-shādayati*, *-yitum*, to cause to sit down.

Ni-shaṇṇa, *as*, *ā*, *am*, seated, sitting, perched, placed in or on, rested, reclined, resting or leaning on, reclining; supported; sunk down, afflicted, distressed; gone to.

Ni-shaṇṇaka, *as*, *ā*, *am*, sitting, seated; (*am*), n. a seat; a species of pot-herb, Marsilea Dentata.

Ni-shatti, *is*, f., Ved. sitting down idly, remaining inactive or indifferent, indolence.

Ni-shatsnu, *us*, *us*, *u*, Ved. sitting fast, firmly settled or fixed.

2. *ni-shad*, *t*, *t*, *t*, Ved. sitting inactive; (*t*), f. sitting, especially near the altar at a sacrificial rite; N. of a kind of composition mentioned with Upanishad in Mahā-bh. Śānti-p. 1613.

Ni-shada, *as*, m., N. of an ancient king, (probably a wrong reading for *nishadha*); = *ni-shāda*, a musical note.

Ni-shadana, *am*, n., Ved. sitting down, reclining; dwelling, residing; a seat.

Ni-shadyā, f. a small bed or couch; the hall of a merchant; a market-place.

Ni-shadvara, *as*, *ā*, *am*, Ved. seated (near the altar), sitting lazily; (*as*), m. mud, mire (in which one sinks); the god of love; (*ī*), f. 'the time of rest,' night.

Ni-shāda, *as*, m., N. of certain wild aboriginal tribes in India not belonging to the Āryan race, and described as hunters, fishermen, robbers, &c.; (according to Mahī-dhara) a N. of the Bhillas (a wild mountain tribe whose progenitor is said by a legend to have sprung from the thigh of Vena); a man of a degraded tribe in general, an outcast (especially the son of a Brāhman by a Śūdra woman); the first of the seven musical notes or more properly the last or highest of the scale, corresponding to B of our scale; N. of a Kalpa; [cf. *naishāda*, *naishādaka*, *naishādikā*, *naishādi*.] — *Nishāda-karshu*, *us*, m., N. of a district; [cf. *naishāda-karshuka*.] — *Nishāda-vat*, n., N. of a musical note, = B of our scale.

Ni-shādita, *as*, *ā*, *am* (fr. the Caus.), made to sit down; afflicted.

Ni-shādin, *ī*, *inī*, *i*, sitting down, lying down, reclining, resting; (*ī*), m. an elephant-keeper or driver.

Ni-shīdat, *an*, *antī*, *at*, sitting down, sitting on; settling or sinking down; resting in or on.

Ni-shedivas, *vān*, *dushī*, *vat*, seated in or upon, reclined.

निषध *nishadha*, *as*, m., N. of a mountain or chain of mountains forming one of the principal ranges of the earth, and described as lying immediately south of Ilāvṛita and north of the Himālaya; (*ās*), m. pl., N. of a people and their country governed by Nala; the sovereign of the Nishadhas; N. of a son of Janam-ejaya; of Kuśa the father of Nala; a peculiar position of the closed hand; a musical note [cf. *ni-shāda*]; (*as*, *ā*, *am*), hard, solid; (*ā*), f., N. of Nala's capital, the city of the Nishadhas; N. of a river rising in the Vindhya mountains. — *Nishadha-vaṅśa*, *as*, m. the race of Nishadha. — *Nishadhādhipa* (°*dha-adh*°), *as*, m. or *nishadhādhipati* (°*dha-adh*°), *is*, m. or *nishadheśvara* (°*dha-īś*°), *as*, m. 'lord of Nishadha,' epithet of Nala; [cf. *naishadha*, *naishadhya*.] — *Nishadhāśva* (°*dha-aś*°), *as*, m., N. of a son of Kuru. — *Nishadhendra-kārya*, *am*, n. 'the poem of the prince of the Nishadhas,' N. of a poem.

निषमम् *ni-shamam*, ind. (fr. *ni* + *sama*), see Pāṇ. VI. 2, 121, Schol.

निषर्ग *ni-sharga*, *as*, m. a various reading for *ni-shaṅga*, q. v.

निषाद *ni-shāda*. See 1. *ni-shad*, col. 1.

निषिच् *ni-shić* (*ni-sić*), cl. 6. P. A. *-shińćati*, *-te*, *-shektum*, to sprinkle, pour upon or into, infuse, instil, irrigate: Caus. *-shećayati*, *-yitum*, to cause to sprinkle or irrigate.

Ni-shikta, *as*, *ā*, *am*, sprinkled upon, poured into, infused, instilled, irrigated. — *Nishikta-pā*, *ās*, *ās*, *am*, Ved. protecting the infused (semen).

Ni-sheka, *as*, m. sprinkling, infusion, aspersion; distilling; effusion; seminal infusion, impregnation; the ceremony performed upon impregnation; irrigation; water for washing, (but according to others) seminal impurity; what is poured upon the ground, dirty water, swill.

Ni-shektavya, *as*, *ā*, *am*, to be sprinkled or poured into, to be watered.

Ni-shećana, *am*, n., Ved. pouring out, sprinkling, watering, irrigation.

Ni-shećitṛi, *tā*, *trī*, *tṛi*, one who sprinkles or pours into, an instiller, infuser.

निषिध् *ni-shidh* (*ni-sidh*), cl. 1. P. *-shedhati*, *-sheddhum*, *-shedhitum*, to prohibit, forbid, restrain, keep off, ward off, keep back, prevent, remove: Caus. *-shedhayati*, *-yitum*, to prohibit, keep off.

Ni-shiddha, *as*, *ā*, *am*, prohibited, forbidden, kept back, restrained, warded off, prevented.

Ni-shiddhi, *is*, f. prohibition, warding off, keeping off, defence.

Ni-sheddhavya, *as*, *ā*, *am*, to be kept back or obstructed.

Ni-sheddhṛi, *dhā*, *dhrī*, *dhṛi*, keeping back, obstructing, who or what restrains or prevents or prohibits.

Ni-sheddhra, *as*, *ā*, *am*, in *a-nisheddhra*, having no impeder or subduer.

Ni-shedha, *as*, m. warding off, keeping off, hindering, stopping, obstructing, prevention, prohibition; negation, denial; discontinuance, contrariety to or deviation from rule, exception; N. of several Sāmans.

Ni-shedhaka, *as*, *ā*, *am*, keeping back, obstructing, preventing, prohibiting, forbidding.

Ni-shedhana, *am*, n. the act of warding off or defending, prevention.

Ni-shedhin, *ī*, *inī*, *i*, defending, keeping back; excelling, surpassing.

Ni-shedhya, *as*, *ā*, *am*, to be kept back or prohibited or hindered.

निषिध *ni-shidha*, *ās*, m. pl., N. of a people; (various reading for *nishadha*; cf. *naishidha*.)

निषूद् *ni-shūd* (*ni-sūd*), Caus. *-shūdayati*, *-yitum*, to kill, slay.

Ni-shūdana, *am*, n. killing, slaughter; [cf. *ni-sūdana*.]

निषेव् *ni-shev* (*ni-sev*), cl. 1. A. *-shevate*, *-shevitum*, to wait upon, serve, attend, follow; attach or devote one's self to; to honour, worship, adore; to pursue, practise, perform, observe, cultivate; to frequent, inhabit, visit; to enjoy; to employ.

Ni-sheva, *as*, *ā*, *am*, practising, exercising, following, devoted to [cf. *hrī-n*°]; (*ā*), f. exercising, practice, service; worship, adoration.

Ni-shevaka, *as*, *ā*, *am*, practising, following, devoted to; frequenting, inhabiting; enjoying.

Ni-shevaṇa, *am*, n. waiting on, serving, service, attaching one's self to, worshipping, worship, adoration; practice, performance, adherence to; living in, inhabiting, enjoying, using, use, familiarity with.

Ni-shevaṇīya, *as*, *ā*, *am*, to be served or attended to, to be followed or observed; to be obeyed.

Ni-shevita, *as*, *ā*, *am*, visited, frequented; observed, practised; served, honoured, obeyed.

Ni-shevitavya, *as*, *ā*, *am*, to be practised or observed; to be used or enjoyed; (also read *ni-sevitavya*.)

Ni-shevitṛi, *tā*, *trī*, *tṛi*, one who attaches or devotes himself to anything, an observer, practiser, cultivator, &c.

Ni-shevin, *ī*, *iṇī*, *i*, practising, observing, enjoying.

Ni-shevya, *as*, *ā*, *am*, to be observed, to be honoured, to be visited or frequented; to be enjoyed.

निष्क् *nishk* (probably a Nominal verb artificially formed fr. *nishka* below), cl. 10. A. *nishkayate*, &c., to measure, weigh.

Nishka, *as*, *am*, m. n. (said to be fr. rt. *sad* with preposition *ni* and affix *ka*), a golden ornament for the neck or breast; a golden ornament of a certain weight, used as money; a weight of gold varying in value at different times, = 1 Dīnāra of 32 small or 16 large Rettis, = 1 Karsha or Su-varṇa of 16 Māshas, = 1 Pala of 4 or 5 Su-varṇas, = 1 larger Pala or Dīnāra variously reckoned at 108 or 150 Su-varṇas, = 4 Māshas, = 16 Drammas; a weight of silver of 4 Su-varṇas; gold in general, a golden vessel; (*as*), m. a Ćaṇḍāla; (*ā*), f. a measure of length; [cf. *naishkika*, *naishkaśatika*, *naishka-sahasrika*.] — *Nishka-kaṇṭha*, *as*, *ī*, *am*, wearing a golden ornament round the neck; (*am*), n. a golden ornament of the neck. — *Nishka-grīva*, *as*, *ā*, *am*, Ved. wearing a gold ornament round the neck.

Nishkin, *ī*, *iṇī*, *i*, Ved. having an ornament round the neck.

निष्कण्टक *nish-kaṇṭaka*, *as*, *ā*, *am*, = *a-kaṇṭaka*, thornless, free from thorns or enemies; free from danger or trouble.

निष्कण्ठ *nish-kaṇṭha*, *as*, m. a species of tree, Capparis Trifoliata.

निष्कनिष्ठ *nish-kanishṭha*, *as*, *ā*, *am*, or *nishkanishṭhaka*, *as*, *ā*, *am*, having the little finger stretched out.

निष्कन्द nish-kanda, as, ā, am, without edible or esculent roots, having no bulbous roots.

निष्कपट nish-kapaṭa, as, ā, am, guileless, free from deceit or fraud.

निष्कम्प nish-kampa, as, ā, am, not shaking, not tremulous, motionless, immovable. — Nishkampa-tā, f. motionlessness, immovableness.

निष्कम्भ ni-shkambha in vajra-nishkambha, as, m., N. of one of the sons of Garuḍa.

Ni-shkambhu, us, m., N. of a particular divine being (= Viśva).

निष्करुण nish-karuṇa, as, ā, am, pitiless, unmerciful, merciless, cruel. — Nishkaruṇī-kṛita, as, ā, am, rendered pitiless, made or become heartless or cruel.

निष्करूष nish-karūsha, as, ā, am, not dirty, free from dirt.

निष्कर्तृ nish-kartṛi, tā, m., Ved. = ish-kartṛi, p. 143, col. 1.

निष्कर्मन् nish-karman, ā, ā, a, inactive; exempt from or neglecting religious or worldly acts, &c.

निष्कर्ष nish-karsha, &c. See under nish-kṛish, col. 3.

निष्कल nish-kala, as, ā, am, without parts, undivided, indivisible; waned, diminished, decayed; impotent, seedless, barren; maimed, infirm; (as), m. a receptacle; pudendum muliebre; N. of Brahmā; a fancied personification of Brahmā for religious ceremonies; (ā or ī), f. an elderly woman past childbearing or in whom menstruation has ceased. — Nishkala-tva, am, n. undividedness, indivisibility, the state of the absolute Brahma.

निष्कलङ्क nish-kalanka, as, ā, am, stainless, spotless, sinless, immaculate, unblemished. — Nishkalanka-tīrtha, am, n., N. of a sacred bathing-place.

निष्कल्मष nish-kalmasha, as, ā, am, spotless, sinless. — Nishkalmashī-bhūta, as, ā, am, become spotless or sinless.

निष्कषाय nish-kashāya, as, ā, am, free from dirt or impure passions; (as), m., N. of the thirteenth Arhat of the future Ut-sarpiṇī.

निष्कस् nish-kas (nis-kas; sometimes incorrectly spelt nish-kaś), Caus. -kāsayati, -yitum, to drive out, expel, turn out.

Nish-kāsa, as, m. exit, egress; a portico, veranda, (wrongly spelt nish-kāśa); the day-break; waning, disappearance; (also a wrong reading for nish-kāsha, q. v.)

Nish-kāsita, as, ā, am, expelled, dismissed, turned out; gone forth or out, issued; placed, deposited; placed over, appointed, stationed; reviled, reproached; opened out, blown, expanded.

Nish-kāsin, ī, inī, i, who or what expels; (inī), f. a female slave not restrained by her master.

निष्काम nish-kāma, as, ā, am, desireless, free from wish or desire, disinterested, unselfish; (am), ind. without wish or desire; unwillingly. — Nishkāma-ćārin, ī, iṇī, i, acting disinterestedly or without desire, unselfish in one's conduct.

निष्कारण nish-kāraṇa, as, ā, am, causeless, needless, unnecessary; free from motive, disinterested, groundless, without a reason, not proceeding from any cause; (am), ind. without any special motive, without a reason, causelessly, without any secondary view; [cf. ni-kāraṇa.] — Nishkāraṇa-vairin, ī, iṇī, i, groundlessly hostile.

निष्कारुष nish-kārusha, as, ā, am, of a noble race, not degraded (?).

निष्कालक nish-kālaka, as, m. a penitent shaven and smeared with ghee or clarified butter.

निष्कालन nish-kālana, as, m. (fr. kal with nis), driving away (cattle).

निष्कालिक nish-kālika, as, ā, am, one who has no more time (to live), one whose time is over or whose term of life is elapsed; (am), ind. without delay.

निष्काश nish-kāśa, as, m. issue, egress; a portico, veranda; [cf. nish-kāsa.]

Nish-kāśita, as, ā, am. See nish-kāsita, col. 1.

निष्काष nish-kāsha, as, m. (fr. rt. kash with nis), Ved. the scrapings from a caldron or pan; (also written nish-kāsa.)

निष्किञ्चन nish-kinćana, as, ā, am, having nothing, very poor. — Nishkinćana-tva, am, n. poverty, indigence.

निष्किरीय nish-kirīya, ās, m. pl. (fr. nish-kira, which is fr. rt. 1. kṛī with nis), N. of a race.

निष्किल्विष nish-kilvisha, as, ā, am, sinless, faultless; [cf. ni-kilbisha.]

निष्कुट nish-kuṭa, as, m. a pleasure-grove near a house, (in this sense also am, n.); a field; the hollow of a tree [cf. nish-kuha]; a door; the female apartments, Zenana; N. of a country (?); (am), n., N. of a hole of a peculiar form in the frame of a bedstead; (also read niḥ-kuha.)

Nish-kuṭi, is, ī, f. large cardamoms; [cf. nis-truṭi.]

Nishkuṭikā, f., N. of one of the Mātṛis attending on Śiva.

निष्कुतूहल nish-kutūhala, as, ā, am, having no curiosity, incurious.

निष्कुम्भ nish-kumbha, as, m. = ni-kumbha, Croton Polyandrum; (ā), f., N. of the mother of the Magas.

निष्कुल nish-kula, as, ā, am, having no family or kindred, left alone in the world; nish-kulam kṛi, to make (any one) without family, cut off entirely, exterminate. — Nishkula-tā, f. loss of family, dying out, perishing. — Nishkulā-kṛi or nishkulī-kṛi, cl. 8. P. -karoti, -kartum, to extirminate one's family; to strip off the husk, to husk, shell. — Nishkulā-kṛitya, ind. having stripped off the husk; (also read niḥkulā-kṛitya.) — Nishkulī-kṛitya, ind. having husked or shelled; (also read niḥkulī-kṛitya.)

Nish-kulīna, as, ā, am, of low family, plebeian.

निष्कुष् nish-kush (nis-kush), cl. 9. P. -kushṇāti, -koshitum and -koshṭum, to pull off or out, strip off, tear off or out, extract; to injure or hurt by tearing; to husk, shell.

Nish-kushita, as, ā, am, torn off, stripped off, extracted, forced or drawn out, torn, lacerated; expelled; (as), m., N. of a Marut; (also read nish-karshin.)

Nish-kosha, as, m. tearing out, stripping off the husk, shelling.

Nish-koshaṇa, am, n. tearing off or out, stripping off, drawing out, extracting, extirpating; taking away, husking, shelling.

Nish-koshaṇaka, as, ā, am, fit for picking, used as a picker, serving for a tooth-pick.

Nish-koshitavya, as, ā, am, to be stripped off or extracted, to be forced or drawn out; to be taken away; to be expelled.

निष्कुह nish-kuha, as, m. = nish-kuṭa, the hollow of a tree.

निष्कूज nish-kūja, as, ā, am, noiseless, soundless.

निष्कूट nish-kūṭa, as, ā, am, free from deceit or fraud, guileless.

निष्कृ nish-kṛi (nis-kṛi), cl. 8. P. A. -karoti, -kurute, -kartum, to bring out, extract (Ved.); to take away, do away, remove, expel, exclude, drive away; to break in pieces, destroy; to prepare, equip, arrange, accomplish, finish; to absolve, acquit; to restore, cure.

Nish-kāraṇa, am, n. removing, taking away, doing away; killing, slaughter.

Nish-kṛita, as, ā, am, done away, taken away, removed, expelled; absolved, pardoned, acquitted; disregarded; (am), n. expiation, atonement; a fixed place, place of rendezvous.

Nish-kṛiti, is, f. expiation, atonement; absolution, pardon; acquittance, compensation, discharge of a debt or obligation; removal, doing away; restoration, cure; escaping from, avoiding; disregarding, neglecting; (Nishkṛiti personified is a sister of Lobha and daughter of Dambha by Māyā); bad conduct, roguery, (various reading for ni-kṛiti); (is), m. a form of Agni.

निष्कृत् nish-kṛit (nis-kṛit), cl. 6. P. -kṛintati, -kartitum, to cut off, to cut out; to divide, separate; to cut through, hew asunder, massacre; to loosen.

निष्कृप nish-kṛipa, as, ā, am, pitiless, merciless, cruel.

निष्कृष् nish-kṛish (nis-kṛish), cl. 1. P. -karshati, -karshṭum and -krashṭum, to draw out, extract; to tear out, tear in pieces, rend asunder: Caus. -karshayati, -yitum, to tear in pieces, destroy, annihilate.

Nish-karsha, as, m. drawing out, extracting; the essence of anything, chief point, main point; measuring; certainty, ascertainment; (āt), ind. succinctly.

Nish-karshaṇa, am, n. drawing out, extracting; pulling off, drawing off, taking off; deducting.

Nish-karshin, ī, m., N. of one of the Maruts.

Nish-kṛishṭa, as, ā, am, drawn forth, pulled out, extracted.

निष्केवल nish-kevala, as, ā, am, belonging exclusively.

Nish-kevalya, as, ā, am, belonging exclusively; N. of a particular Uktha (q. v.) connected with the midday oblation and belonging to Indra exclusively.

Nishkaivalya, as, ā, am, mere, pure, absolute.

निष्कौरव nish-kaurava, as, ā, am, deprived of or freed from the Kauravas.

निष्कौशाम्बि nish-kauśāmbi, is, is, i, one who has left Kauśāmbī.

निष्क्रम् nish-kram (nis-kram), cl. 1. P. A. -krāmati, -kramate, -kramitum or -krāmitum, to go out, come forth, go from home, depart; to make an exit from the stage: Caus. -krāmayati, -yitum, to cause to go out or depart, to drive out, expel, to deliver.

Nish-krama, as, m. going out, coming forth; departing from (with abl.); exit; degradation, loss of caste, inferiority of tribe, family, &c.; any intellectual faculty (as intelligence, attention, comprehension, &c.).

Nish-kramaṇa, am, n. going forth or out; taking a child for the first time out of the house in the fourth month after birth to see the sun, (considered as an essential ceremony, Manu II. 34.)

Nish-kramaṇikā, f. the ceremony of taking a child out of the house for the first time in its fourth month to see the sun.

Nish-kramaṇita, as, ā, am, a child taken out for the first time in the fourth month after birth.

Nish-kramya, ind. having gone out, going forth.

Nish-krānta, as, ā, am, gone out, departed, come forth; (in dramatic language) exit, exeunt.

निष्क्रय nish-kraya. See nish-krī, p. 508.

निष्क्रिय nish-kriya, as, ā, am, inactive; abstaining from ceremonial rites, not performing religious ceremonies; (am), n. a term for Brahma or the Supreme Spirit. — Nishkriya-tā, f. inactivity, idleness, negligence. — *Nishkriyātma-tā* (°*ya-āt*°), f. non-performance of appointed acts, habitual neglect of prescribed duties, inactivity, laziness, idleness.

निष्क्री *nish-krī* (*nis-krī*), cl. 9. P. A. *-krīṇāti, -ṇīte, -kretum*, P. to buy off, to redeem or ransom from (with abl.); A. to redeem or ransom one's self.

Nish-kraya, as, m. redemption, ransom; reward; price, hire, wages; acquittance.

Nish-krayaṇa, as, ī, am, redeeming, ransoming; (*am*), n. redemption, ransom.

Nish-krīti, is, f., Ved. redeeming, redemption.

निष्क्रोध *nish-krodha, as, ā, am*, free from wrath, not angry, not angry with (with gen.).

*निष्क्लेश *nish-kleśa, as, ā, am*, (with Buddhists) free from (ten) moral faults. — *Nishkleśa-leśa, as, ā, am*, not suffering the least pain, quite happy.

निष्क्वथ् *nish-kvath* (*nis-kvath*), Caus. *-kvāthayati, -yitum*, to boil down, thicken by boiling.

Nish-kvātha, as, m. a decoction, broth, soup.

निष्खन् *nish-khan* (*nis-khan*), cl. 1. P. A. *-khanati, -te, -khanitum*, to dig out.

निष्खिदम् *nish-khidam*, Ved. probably for *ni-khidam*, an inf. form of *ni-khid*.

निष्टक्वन् *nish-ṭakvan, ā, ari, a* (fr. rt. *tak* with *nis*), Ved. escaping (?).

निष्टप् *nish-ṭap* (*nis-tap*), cl. 1. P. *-ṭapati, -ṭaptum*, to singe, scorch; to heat thoroughly, anneal, to purify by heat, free from impurities; to roast; to fry; to toast.

Nish-ṭapana, am, n. burning.

Nish-ṭapta, as, ā, am, burnished, made bright; well cooked, well dressed or done.

निष्टर्क्य *nish-ṭarkya, as, ā, am* (fr. rt. *tark* with *nis*), Ved. to be opened by unscrewing, to be loosened by untwisting.

निष्टवैश्य *nishṭa-vaiśya, as*, m., N. of a man.

निष्टानक *ni-shṭānaka, as*, m. (fr. rt. *stan* with *ni* = *nis*), roar, murmur, murmuring, rustling; (*as, ā, am*), speaking loud; causing to cry.

निष्टिग्री *nishṭigrī*, f., Ved., N. of the mother of Indra.

निष्टुर् *nish-ṭur, ūr, ūr, ūr* (fr. rt. *tṝ* with *nis*), Ved. one who has no conqueror, unconquered; (Sāy.) an overcomer of enemies.

निष्ट्य *nishṭya, as, ā, am* (fr. *nis*), Ved. external, foreign, strange; exotic, coming from abroad; (*as*), m. a man of one of the outcast or barbarous tribes, a Cāṇḍāla, a Mleććha; (*ā*), f. a particular Nakshatra also called Svātī.

निष्ठ *ni-shṭha, as, ā, am* (fr. rt. *sthā* with *ni* or in some senses with *nis*), staying or being in or on, situated on, grounded on; depending on, resting on, referring to, relating to; intent on, devoted to, attached to, practising; versed in, skilled in; believing in; (1. *ni-shṭhā*), f. position, condition, state, stand-point, basis, foundation; devotion or attachment to, uniform practice or profession; excelling in, conversancy with, skill, eminence, excellence, perfection; believing in, faith; conclusion, end, termination, (sometimes at the end of adj. comp., e.g. *apabhranśa-nishṭha, as, ā, am*, ending in a fall); the end or catastrophe of a drama, conclusion of a fable, accomplishment, completion; culminating point; disappearance, destruction, death, fixed time of life; fixed or certain knowledge, ascertainment, certainty; a technical term for the past participle affixes *ta* and *tavat* (or with their indicatory letters *kta* and *ktavatu*); asking, begging; suffering, trouble, distress, anxiety. — *Nishṭhā-gata, as, ā, am*, gone to perfection, attaining perfection, (a term applied to a class of Buddhist deities.) — *Nishṭhānta* (°*ṭhā-an*°), *as*, m. end, conclusion. — *Nishṭhā-vat, ān, atī, at*, possessed of complete knowledge, perfect, complete, consummate, fulfilling all religious duties.

2. *ni-shṭhā, ās, ās, am* (*ni* for *nis*), Ved. excelling, eminent, leading; staying or being in (= *ni-shṭha*); (*ās*), m. a leader, guide; (Sāy.) station, position.

Ni-shṭhāna, am, n. sauce, condiment.

Nishṭhānaka, as, m., N. of a Nāga.

Ni-shṭhāra, as, ā, am (*ni* for *nis*), Ved. concluding, deciding.

Ni-shṭhita, as, ā, am (*ni* may be for *nis*), staying in, being in or on; engaged in, attached to, devoted to; versed in, skilled in, conversant with; firm, fixed; certain, ascertained.

निष्ठिव् *ni-shṭhiv* or *-shṭhīv*, cl. 1. and 4. P. *-shṭhīvati, -shṭhīvyati, -shṭheritum*, to spit, spit out, eject from the mouth.

Ni-shṭhīva, as, am, m. n. spitting, spitting out.

Ni-shṭhīvana or *ni-shṭhīvita, am*, n. spitting, spitting out, ejecting anything from the mouth. — *Nishṭhīvana-śarāva, as, am*, m. n. a spitting-box, spittoon.

Ni-shṭheva, as, ā, am, m. f. n. or *nishṭhevana, am*, n. spitting, spitting out, ejecting anything from the mouth.

Ni-shṭhyūta, as, ā, am, spit out, ejected from the mouth, cast or thrown out; uttered; directed, despatched (?).

Ni-shṭhyūti, is, f. spitting, spitting out; (less correctly written *ni-shṭhūti*.)

निष्ठुर *ni-shṭhura, as, ā, am* (said to be fr. rt. *sthā*), hard, rough, rugged; harsh, coarse, gruff, cruel, severe, austere; contumelious (as speech). — *Nishṭhura-tā*, f. or *nishṭhura-tva, am*, n. harshness of speech, coarseness, reviling, abuse.

Nishṭhuraka, as, m., N. of a man.

Nishṭhurika, as, m., N. of a Nāga.

Nishṭhūrin, ī, iṇī, i, rough, coarse; [cf. *sthūrin, sthūla*.]

निष्ठ्यूति *ni-shṭhyūti*. See above.

निष्णा *ni-shṇa, as, ā, am* (fr. rt. *snā* with *ni*), clever, skilful, experienced; [cf. *ni-śna, nadī-shṇa*.]

Ni-shṇāta, as, ā, am, deeply versed in, skilful, clever, conversant, learned; perfect, superior; (in law) agreed upon.

निष्पक्व *nish-pakva, as, ā, am* (fr. rt. *pać* with *nis*), decocted, infused, boiled.

निष्पङ्क *nish-panka, as, ā, am*, free from mud or filth, pure.

निष्पत् *nish-pat*, cl. 1. P. *-patati, -patitum*, to fly out of (with abl.), rush out, jump out, hasten out, come forth, issue, depart; to fall out; to fly away; to spring from: Caus. *-pātayati*, &c., to cause to fall out or fly out; to ruin; to destroy.

Nish-patat, an, antī, at, issuing, going forth or out.

Nish-patana, am, n. going quickly forth, rushing out; issuing quickly.

Nish-patishṇu, us, us, u, rushing or running out, hastening out.

निष्पताक *nish-patāka, as, ā, am*, having no flag or banner. — *Nishpatāka-dhvaja, as*, m. a flag-staff without a banner.

निष्पतिसुता *nish-pati-sutā*, f. having no husband and no sons.

निष्पत्ति *nish-patti*. See 2. *nish-pad*, col. 3.

निष्पत्त्र *nish-pattra, as, ā, am*, having no leaves, leafless; without feathers, unfeathered; [cf. *a-nishpattram*]; (*as, am*), m. n. (?), the clove tree.

Nish-pattraka, as, ā, am, leafless; (*ikā*), f. the plant Capparis Aphylla (see *karīra*).

Nish-pattraya, Nom. P. *-pattrayati*, &c., to deprive of leaves, make leafless.

Nishpattrā-kṛi, cl. 8. P. A. *-karoti, -kurute, -kartum*, to pierce with an arrow so that the feathers come through on the other side. — *Nishpattrā-kṛiti, is*, f. causing excessive bodily pain.

निष्पद् 1. *nish-pad* or *nishpād, -pāt, -padī, -pāt*, footless, having no feet.

Nish-pada, as, ā, am, having no feet. — *Nish-pada-yāna, am*, n. a vehicle moving without feet (as a ship &c.).

निष्पद् 2. *nish-pad*, cl. 4. A. *-padyate, -pattum*, to come forth from, issue, spring from, spring up, arise, be produced, be accomplished, be brought about or effected; to be prepared; to become ripe, ripen: Caus. *-pādayati, -yitum*, to produce, bring about, accomplish, effect, perform; to make ripe, cause to ripen.

Nish-patti, is, f. going forth or out, birth, production; completion, conclusion, termination, consummation.

3. *nish-pad, t*, f., Ved. excrement; (according to Sāy. = *nir-gaććhat*.)

Nish-panna, as, ā, am, gone forth or out, sprung up, arisen, born, descended, produced, brought about, effected, completed, concluded, accomplished, done, finished, ready.

Nish-pādaka, as, ikā, am, performing, accomplishing, effective. — *Nishpādaka-tva, am*, n. effectiveness, power of achieving.

Nish-pādana, am, n. doing, effecting, accomplishing; concluding; producing, causing, engendering.

Nish-pādita, as, ā, am, done, effected, made, produced, prepared, achieved.

Nish-pādya or *nish-pādanīya* or *nish-pāditavya, as, ā, am*, to be effected or accomplished, capable of being performed, achievable.

Nish-pādyamāna, as, ā, am, being effected or done, being in the course of accomplishment or completion.

निष्पन्द *ni-shpanda, as, ā, am* (*ni* for *nis* + *spanda*), motionless, immovable.

निष्पराक्रम *nish-parākrama, as, ā, am*, destitute of power or prowess, powerless, weak.

निष्परिकर *nish-parikara, as, ā, am*, without preparations.

निष्परिग्रह *nish-parigraha, as, ā, am*, without property, having no property; (*as*), m. an ascetic without family or dependants.

निष्परिच्छद *nish-pariććhada, as, ā, am*, having no retinue or train, without a court.

निष्परिदाह *nish-paridāha, as, ā, am*, not liable to be burnt, incombustible.

निष्परीक्ष *nish-parīksha, as, ā, am*, not examining or testing accurately.

निष्परीहार *nish-parīhāra, as, ā, am*, not avoiding; not observing caution; (*am*), ind. not so as to avoid.

निष्पर्यन्त *nish-paryanta, as, ā, am*, having no limits, boundless, unbounded.

निष्पवण *nish-pavaṇa*. See *nish-pū*, p. 509.

निष्पा 1. *nish-pā* (*nis-pā*, see rt. 1. *pā*), cl. 1. 2. P. *-pibati* or *-pivati, -pāti, -pātum*, Ved. to drink out, drink up, drink from (with abl.), to empty by drinking, exhaust.

Nish-pāna, am, n. drinking out, drinking up.

Nish-pīta, as, ā, am, drunk up, dried up, sucked up, exhausted.

निष्पा 2. *nish-pā* (*nis-pā*, see rt. 3. *pā*), cl. 2. P. *-pāti, -pātum*, to defend from (with abl.).

निष्पादक *nish-pādaka*, &c. See under 2. *nish-pad*, p. 508, col. 3.

निष्पाप *nish-pāpa*, *as, ā, am*, free from sin, sinless, guiltless.

निष्पार *nish-pāra*, *as, ā, am*, without boundaries, boundless, unlimited.

निष्पालक *nish-pālaka*, *as, ā, am*, without protector or guardian, unprotected.

निष्पिश् *nish-piś* (*nis-piś*), cl. 6. P. A. *-pinśati, -te, -peśitum*, Ved. to tear the flesh of an animal from the skin.

निष्पिष् *nish-pish* (*nis-pish*), cl. 7. P. *-pinashṭi, -peshṭum*, to grind, crush, pound, bruise, triturate; to rub, rub the hands; to gnash the teeth: Caus. *-peshayati, -yitum*, to destroy.

Nish-pishṭa, as, ā, am, ground, pounded, pulverized, bruised, crushed, reduced to dust or powder; beaten, oppressed.

Nish-pesha, as, m. or *nish-peshaṇa, am*, n. rubbing together, grinding, pulverizing, bruising; striking, clashing, hitting or throwing against; the noise or sound produced by striking or clashing; [cf. *naishpeshika*.]

निष्पीड *nish-pīḍa, as, ā, am*, pressed out? (probably incorrect for *nish-pīta*), sucked out.

निष्पीत *nish-pīta*. See 1. *nish-pā*, p. 508.

निष्पुद्गल *nish-pudgala* or *nish-pungala, as, ā, am*, without personality (?); [cf. *pungala, pudgala*.]

निष्पुत्र *nish-putra, as, ā, am*, sonless, childless.

निष्पुराण *nish-purāṇa, as, ā, am*, not existing before, new.

निष्पुरुष *nish-purusha, as, ā, am*, deprived of men, without males, unpeopled, desolate; not having produced male children; not male, feminine, neuter; (*as*), m. a eunuch or impotent man; a coward; [cf. *naishpurushya*.]

निष्पुलाक *nish-pulāka, as, ā, am*, free from chaff or rather from bad or useless grain; (*as*), m., N. of the fourteenth Arhat of the future Utsarpiṇī. — *Nishpulākī-kṛita, as, ā, am*, freed from chaff.

निष्पू *nish-pū* (*nis-pū*), cl. 9. P. A. *-punāti, -punīte, -pavitum*, to cleanse, purify; to winnow, fan.

Nish-pavana, am, n. winnowing, fanning.

Nish-pāva, as, m. fanning, winnowing, cleaning corn, &c.; the wind caused by the winnowing sieve or basket; wind, air; straw, chaff (?) = *kaḍangaka* or *kaḍanga*; a legume, a pod; a species of pulse, Phaseolus Radiatus; Dolichos Sinensis or a similar kind, = *rāja-māsha*, = *valla*, = *sitaśimbika*, = *śimbikā*, = *śveta-śimbī*, = *bola*, = *śimī*, i. e. *śimbī*; (*ī* or *is*), f. a species of pulse, commonly *vāḍā*, of which there are two kinds, a green and a white one; (*as, ā, am*), indubitable, certain.

Nish-pāvaka, as, m. a species of pulse, = *valla* or *śveta-śimbī*; (*ikā*), f., cf. *nakha-n°, vritta-n°*.

Nish-pāvala, an adj. formed fr. *nish-pāva*, Pāṇini V. 2, 97.

निष्पॄ *nish-pṝ* or *nish-pṛi* (*nis-pṝ*), cl. 3. 9. P. *-piparti, -priṇāti, -paritum* or *-parītum*, to bring out, help out, extricate; to fill: Caus. *-pārayati, -yitum*, to lead or bring out, help out, extricate.

Nish-pūrta, as, ā, am, poured out; filled.

निष्पौरुष *nish-paurusha, as, ā, am*, devoid of manhood, unmanly; (also written *niḥ-paurusha*.)

निष्प्रकम्प *nish-prakampa, as, ā, am*, immovable, motionless; (*as*), m., N. of one of the Saptarshis in the thirteenth Manv-antara.

निष्प्रकारक *nish-prakāraka, as, ā, am*, without distinction of species or kind, without specification.

निष्प्रकाश *nish-prakāśa, us, ā, am*, not transparent, not clear, lightless, dark.

निष्प्रचार *nish-praćāra, as, ā, am*, not going or moving away, remaining in one's place; concentrated or fixed upon one point (as mind).

निष्प्रणय *nish-praṇaya, as, ā, am*, without affection, cold.

निष्प्रताप *nish-pratāpa, as, ā, am*, void of dignity, mean, base.

निष्प्रतिकार *nish-pratikāra*. See *nish-pratīkāra* below.

निष्प्रतिक्रिय *nish-pratikriya, as, ā, am*, incurable, irremediable, what cannot be remedied.

निष्प्रतिग्रह *nish-pratigraha, as, ā, am*, not accepting gifts. — *Nishpratigraha-tā*, f. the state of not accepting gifts, not taking presents.

निष्प्रतिघ *nish-pratigha, as, ā, am*, not impeded by obstacles, unhindered, unimpeded.

निष्प्रतिद्वन्द्व *nish-pratidvandva, as, ā, am*, without adversaries or enemies, unopposed; having no match, matchless, unequalled.

निष्प्रतिपक्ष *nish-pratipaksha, as, ā, am*, having no adversary, without an opponent. — *Nishpratipaksha-tā*, f. the state of having no adversary.

निष्प्रतिभ *nish-pratibha, as, ā, am*, having no splendor, deprived of splendor; stupid, frigid, dull, apathetic, ignorant.

निष्प्रतिभान *nish-pratibhāna, as, ā, am*, not bold, cowardly, pusillanimous.

निष्प्रतीकार *nish-pratīkāra, as, ā, am*, without obstacles, unobstructed, uninterrupted; (*am*), ind. unobstructedly, uninterruptedly.

निष्प्रतीप *nish-pratīpa, as, ā, am*, not turned backwards, directed forwards, looking straightforwards; *nishpratīpam darśanam*, an untroubled or unconcerned look.

निष्प्रत्यूह *nish-pratyūha, as, ā, am*, unobstructed, unimpeded, irremediable; (*am*), ind. without hindrance or obstacle, freely.

निष्प्रधान *nish-pradhāna, as, ā, am*, deprived of a chief, destitute of leaders.

निष्प्रपञ्च *nish-prapanća, as, ā, am*, without extension or diffusion; without deceit, pure, honest. — *Nishprapanćātman* (°*ća-āt*°), *ā*, m. an epithet of Śiva.

निष्प्रपतन *nish-prapatana* in *dur-n°*, q. v.

निष्प्रभ *nish-prabha, as, ā, am*, deprived of light or radiance, lustreless; gloomy, dark, obscure; (*as*), m., N. of a Dānava. — *Nishprabha-tā*, f. or *nishprabha-tva, am*, n. obscurity, gloominess, darkness.

निष्प्रभाव *nish-prabhāva, as, ā, am*, powerless. — *Nishprabhāva-tā*, f. or *nishprabhāva-tva, am*, n. powerlessness.

निष्प्रमाणक *nish-pramāṇaka, as, ikā, am*, wanting authority, without authority.

निष्प्रयत्न *nish-prayatna, as, ā, am*, abstaining from exertion or effort, inactive, inert.

निष्प्रयोजन *nish-prayojana, as, ā, am*, without motives, not influenced by any motive; causeless, groundless, reasonless; useless, without an object; needless, unnecessary, uncalled for; (*am*), ind. causelessly, unnecessarily, without reason; (also written *niḥ-prayojana*.) — *Nishprayojana-tā*, f. or *nishprayojana-tva, am*, n. uselessness.

निष्प्रवणि *nish-pravaṇi, is, is, i*, or *nish-pravāṇi, is, is, i*, or *nish-pravāṇa, as, ī, am*, fresh from the loom, quite new and unbleached (as cloth or linen).

निष्प्राण *nish-prāṇa, as, ā, am*, one whose breath has departed, breathless, lifeless, dead, quite exhausted. — *Nishprāṇa-tā*, f. lifelessness.

निष्प्रीति *nish-prīti, is, is, i*, joyless, feeling no pleasure.

निष्प्लाव *nish-plāva* in *kaṭu-n°*, incorrectly for *nish-pāva* under *nish-pū*, col. 1.

निष्फल *nish-phala, as, ā, am*, bearing no fruit, fruitless, unfruitful, barren, useless, unprofitable, vain; meaningless; unproductive, seedless, impotent; (*ā* or *ī*), f. a woman past childbearing or in whom menstruation has ceased, (also read *nishkalā*); (*ā*), f. a species of Momordica. — *Nishphala-tva, am*, n. unfruitfulness, unproductiveness. — *Nishphalī-kṛitya*, ind. having made unfruitful.

Nish-phalaya, Nom. P. *nishphalayati*, &c., to make unfruitful, to render fruitless.

निष्फेन *nish-phena, as, ā, am*, foamless, without foam; (also written *niḥ-phena*.)

निष्यन्द *ni-shyanda, ni-shyandin*. See *ni-syanda, ni-syandin*, p. 510, col. 3.

निष्यूत *ni-shyūta, as, ā, am* (fr. rt. *siv* with *ni*), sewn on.

निष्षपिन् *nishshapin, ī, iṇī, i* (according to the Nirukta fr. *nis* + *sapa* = *pasa*), Ved. libidinous, lustful.

निष्षह् *nish-shah* or *nish-shāh, ṭ, ṭ, ṭ*, Ved. overpowering, expelling; (Sāy. = *niḥsārayitṛi*.)

निस् *nis*, ind. (as a preposition or prefix to verbs and their derivative nouns, expressing) out, forth, outward, out of, out from, away, away from; (*nis* is used as an independent and separable adverb in Atharva-veda VI. 18, 3; VII. 115, 3; XVI. 2, 1.) *Nis* is also prefixed to nouns, not immediately connected with verbs, in the sense 'out of,' 'away from' [cf. *nir-vana*], but more commonly in the sense of a privative or negative adverb = 3. *a*, 'no,' 'not,' 'without.' In this latter signification it may form either negative substantives (e. g. fr. *artha*, advantage, *nir-artha*, disadvantage) or more frequently adjectives (e. g. fr. *mala*, a stain, *nir-mala*, stainless). *Nis* is liable to be euphonically changed to *nir, niḥ, niś, nish* or *nī* [cf. *nī-rasa*, &c.] according to the letter which follows it.

निसङ्कक्ष *ni-sankaksha*. See *niḥ-sankaksha*.

निसञ्ज्ञ *ni-sanjña* for *niḥ-sanjña*, q. v.

निसम्पात *ni-sampāta, as*, m. midnight; (also *niḥ-sampāta*.)

निसर *ni-sara, as*, m., Ved. (according to Mahī-dhara) a noun of agency fr. rt. *sṛi* with *ni*.

निसर्ग *ni-sarga*. See under *ni-sṛij*, p. 510.

निसर्प *ni-sarpa, as*, m. (fr. rt. *sṛip* with *ni*). See *naisarpa*, p. 518, col. 2.

निसिन्धु *ni-sindhu, us*, or *nisindhuka, as*, m. a species of shrub, Vitex Negundo (= *nirguṇḍī*); [cf. *sindhu, sindhuka, sindhu-vāra*.]

निसुन्द *ni-sunda, as*, m., N. of an Asura slain by Kṛishṇa; [cf. *sunda, upa-sunda*.]

निसुम्भ *ni-sumbha*. See *ni-śumbha*, p. 505.

निसुसूष् *ni-susūsh, ūs, ūs, ūs* (fr. the Desid. of rt. *su* with *ni*). See Pāṇini VIII. 3, 117, and cf. *abhi-susūsh*.

निसूदक ni-sūdaka, as, ā, am (fr. rt. sūd with ni), one who kills, a killer, destroyer.

Ni-sūdana, as, ā, am, killing, destroying, a destroyer, (at the end of a comp.); (am), n. killing, destroying, slaughter; (often incorrectly ni-shūdana.)

निसृ ni-sṛi, cl. 1. P. -sarati, -sartum, to go forth, (apparently only occurring in the derivative below.)

Ni-sṛita, as, ā, am, = niḥ-sṛita, q. v., gone forth, gone away, disappeared; (ā), f. the plant Ipomœa Turpethum (= tri-vṛitā); N. of a river; (a various reading for niś-ćitā.)

निसृज् ni-sṛij, cl. 6. P. -sṛijati, -srashṭum, to let go, set free, dismiss, (apparently only used in the derivatives below.)

Ni-sarga, as, m. evacuation, voiding excrement; giving away, presenting, bestowing, granting, showing a favour; a grant; relinquishment, abandoning, setting free; creation; the natural state, nature, natural character, natural condition or form; exchange, barter; nisargeṇa or nisargāt or nisarga-tas, by nature, naturally, from one's natural state or condition. — *Nisarga-ja*, as, ā, am, innate; inborn, produced at creation, natural. — *Nisarga-bhinna*, as, ā, am, naturally distinct. — *Nisarga-vinīta*, as, ā, am, naturally discreet. — *Nisarga-siddha*, as, ā, am, effected by nature, natural.

Ni-sṛishṭa, as, ā, am, dismissed, delivered, deposited, given, bestowed, emancipated; allowed, permitted; central, middle. — *Nisṛishṭārtha* (°ṭa-ar°), as, ā, am, any one to whom the management of an affair is intrusted; (as), m. a chargé d'affaires, envoy, ambassador; messenger, agent, manager.

निसेवितव्य ni-sevitavya for ni-shevitavya, q. v.

निस्तक्ष् nis-taksh, cl. 1. P. -takshati, &c., to form, create.

निस्तत्त्व nis-tattva, as, ā, am, not comprehended in the twenty-four Tattvas or principles, (see tattva.)

निस्तनी ni-stanī, f. (according to some fr. ni + stanī, a small breast), a pill, bolus, a sort of force-meat ball.

निस्तन्तु nis-tantu, us, us, u, having no offspring, childless.

निस्तन्द्र nis-tandra, as, ā, am, or nis-tandri, is, is, i, not lazy or listless, fresh, healthy.

निस्तब्ध ni-stabdha, as, ā, am, paralyzed, numbed, stiffened; stopped, fixed.

Ni-stambha. See niḥ-stambha, p. 482, col. 2.

निस्तमस्क nis-tamaska, as, ā, am, free from darkness, not gloomy, light.

निस्तरण nis-taraṇa, nis-tāra, &c. See under nis-tṛī, col. 2.

निस्तर्क्य nis-tarkya, as, ā, am, unimaginable, inconceivable.

निस्तर्हण nis-tarhaṇa, am, n. (fr. rt. tṛih with nis), crushing, destroying, killing, slaughter.

निस्तल nis-tala, as, ā, am, not flat, round, globular; trembling, shaking, moving; down, below.

निस्तिमिर nis-timira, as, ā, am, free from darkness, clear, light.

निस्तुति ni-stuti. See under niḥ-stuti, p. 482.

निस्तुद् nis-tud, cl. 6. P. A. -tudati, -te, -tottum, to pierce, prick, sting.

Nis-toda, as, m. or nistodana, am, n. pricking, piercing, stinging.

निस्तुष nis-tusha, as, ā, am, freed from chaff or husk; (metaphorically) purified, cleansed; simplified. — *Nistusha-kshīra*, as, m. wheat. — *Nistusha-ratna*, am, n. crystal.

Nis-tushita, as, ā, am, skinned, peeled, shelled, husked, made thin, pared; left, abandoned, deserted.

निस्तृणकण्टक nis-tṛiṇa-kaṇṭaka, as, ā, am, cleared or freed from grass and thorns.

निस्तॄ nis-tṛī, cl. 1. P. -tarati, -taritum, -tarītum,* to come forth from, to rescue or free one's self from, get out of, get clear of, escape, be saved; to pass over, pass, cross; to pass through; to pass or spend time; to accomplish, perform, fulfil, settle; to overcome, overpower, master; to expiate; abhiyogam nis-tṛī, to clear one's self from an accusation: Caus. -tārayati, -yitum, to cause to pass over; to rescue, save, release, deliver, liberate; to overcome, overpower: Desid. -titīrshati, -titarishati, -titarīshati, to wish to cross or pass over. * also nistartum. R.P. 2.575

Nis-taraṇa, am, n. going out or forth, coming out (of danger); crossing over or passing; rescue, releasing, deliverance, getting rid of or free from; means of success or rescue, an expedient, a plan.

Nis-tartavya, as, ā, am, to be overcome or conquered or overpowered.

Nis-tāra, as, m. crossing or passing over or across, getting rid of or away from, release, escape, rescue, preservation; final emancipation, salvation; means, expedient; payment, discharge of a debt, acquittance, requital. — *Nistāra-vīja*, am, n. a means of crossing (the ocean of life), a cause of final liberation.

Nis-tāraka, as, ikā, am, rescuing, delivering; a saviour.

Nis-tāraṇa, am, n. passing or transporting over or across, overcoming, conquering; liberating.

Nis-titīrshat, an, antī, at, desirous or anxious to cross (the ocean of life); wishing for salvation or liberation.

Nis-tīrṇa, as, ā, am, rescued, delivered, saved.

निस्तेजस् nis-tejas, ās, ās, as, deprived of strength or energy, destitute of fire or heat, powerless, impotent; spiritless, dull; obscure.

निस्तोय nis-toya, as, ā, am, deprived or destitute of water, waterless.

निस्त्यज् nis-tyaj, cl. 1. P. -tyajati, -tyaktum, to drive away, expel.

निस्त्रंश nis-traṇśa, as, ā, am, fearless; (probably incorrect for nis-triṇśa below.)

निस्त्रप nis-trapa, as, ā, am, shameless.

निस्त्रिंश nis-triṇśa, as, ā, am (fr. nis + triṇśat), more than thirty; merciless, unfeeling, unpitying, cruel (as a sword); (as), m. a sword, a scimitar, falchion, a sacrificial knife, (so called because more than thirty fingers in length.) — *Nistriṇśa-dhārin*, ī, m. a sword-bearer, a swordsman or soldier armed with a sword. — *Nistriṇśa-pattraka*, as, ikā, m. f. a thorny species of Euphorbia, (Antiquorum or Tortilis). — *Nistriṇśa-bhṛit*, t, t, t, a sword-bearer.

Nistriṇśin, ī, inī, i, bearing a sword, armed with a sword.

निस्त्रुटी nis-truṭī, f. cardamoms; [cf. truṭi, nish-kuṭi.]

निस्त्रैगुण्य nis-traiguṇya, as, ā, am, destitute of the three qualities (viz. sattva, rajas, and tamas; see guṇa).

निस्त्रैणपुष्पक nistraiṇapushpaka, as, m. (fr. nis + straiṇa + pushpa?), a species of thorn-apple.

निस्नाव ni-snāva, as, m. (fr. ni-snu?), residue of articles &c. after a sale or market.

निस्नेहफला nisneha-phalā. See niḥsneha-phalā under niḥ-sneha, p. 482, col. 2.

निस्पन्द 1. ni-spanda, as, m. (fr. rt. spand with ni), throbbing, trembling motion.

निस्पन्द 2. ni-spanda, as, ā, am (fr. ni for nis + spanda), immovable, still, steady; [cf. ni-shpanda.] — *Nispanda-tva*, am, n. immovableness.

निस्पृश् ni-spriś, k, k, k, Ved. confiding; caressing, fondling.

निस्पृह ni-spṛiha. See niḥ-spṛiha, p. 482.

निस्यन्द ni-syanda or ni-shyanda, as, ā, am (fr. rt. syand with ni, or ni for nis), flowing or trickling down, dripping, dropping; (as), m. a trickling or flowing down, oozing, issuing, streaming, dropping, distilling; a discharge (of any fluid), a flux; a stream, any fluid that trickles down or drops; trickling forth from, flowing out, flowing from; necessary consequence or result; uttering.

Ni-syandamāna, as, ā, am, trickling, flowing, oozing, issuing.

Ni-syandin, ī, inī, i, flowing or streaming or trickling down or out.

निस्रव ni-srava, as, m. (fr. rt. sru with ni), flowing down, a stream, torrent; (perhaps for niḥ-srava, flowing forth, streaming out.)

Ni-srāva, as, m. flowing down, a stream, torrent; the scum of boiled rice; [cf. niḥ-srāva.]

Ni-srāvin, ī, iṇī, i, flowing down.

निस्वन 1. ni-svana, as, ā, am, Ved., various reading for ni-svara, q. v.

निस्वन 2. ni-svana, as, m. (fr. rt. svan with ni), noise, sound, voice, (often at the end of comps. when the fem. is nisvanā; cf. ratha-n°, uddhatārṇava-n°); (am), ind. with noise or sound; [cf. niḥ-svana.]

Ni-svanita, am, n. a noise, sound, crying, a cry.

Ni-svāna, as, m. noise, sound; the whistling sound of an arrow.

निस्वर ni-svara, as, ā, am, Ved. soundless, noiseless; (as), m. an epithet of Agni.

निह् nih, Ved. = ni-hantṛi (according to Mahī-dhara).

निहन् 1. ni-han, cl. 2. P. -hanti, -hantum, to strike down, strike, kill, destroy; to strike in, fix in, infix; to disregard, neglect: Caus. -ghātayati, -yitum, to kill, destroy.

Ni-hata, as, ā, am, struck down, stricken, smitten, killed, slain, overcome; struck into, infixed; attached, devoted. — *Nihata-bhūyishṭha*, as, ā, am, having the greater number killed. — *Nihata-sena*, as, ā, am, having (their) armies smitten or destroyed. — *Nihatoshṭra* (°ta-ush°), as, ā, am, having the camels killed, whose camels have been slain.

2. *ni-han*, ā, m. a killer, destroyer.

Ni-hanana, am, n. killing, slaughter, murder.

Ni-hantavya, as, ā, am, to be struck down, to be killed or destroyed.

Ni-hantṛi, tā, trī, tṛi, who or what kills or destroys, a killer; destructive, murderous; one who removes or dispels or hinders.

Ni-hanyamāna, as, ā, am, being struck down or killed.

निहव ni-hava. See ni-hve, p. 511, col. 1.

निहा ni-hā, Pass. -hīyate, &c., to be deprived of.

Nihākā, f., Ved. a storm, whirlwind, &c.; (Sāy.) an iguana, the Gangetic alligator.

Ni-hīna, as, ā, am, low, vile, of low origin; (as), m. a low man, an outcast.

निहिंसन ni-hiṇsana, am, n. killing, slaughter.

निहित ni-hita, as, ā, am (fr. 1. ni-dhā),

placed, laid, fixed, lodged, situated, deposited, delivered, given, intrusted; inserted, infixed, attached; applied to; bestowed upon; treasured up; held; laid (as dust by rain); uttered in a deep tone. — *Nihita-daṇḍa, as, ā, am,* one who lays aside the rod, one who shows clemency. — *Nihita-nayana, as, ā, am,* having the eyes fixed or directed upon (with loc.).

निहीन *ni-hīna.* See under *ni-hā*, p. 510, col. 3.

निहृ *ni-hṛi*, cl. 1. P. A. *-harati, -te, -hartum,* Ved. to offer, give.

Ni-hāra, as, m. = *nī-hāra,* q. v.

Ni-hārin. See *nir-hārin* under *nir-hṛi*, p. 502, col. 3.

निह्नु *ni-hnu*, cl. 2. A. *-hnute, -hnotum,* to disown, deny, dissimulate, conceal, evade.

Ni-hnava, as, m. denial, concealment, hushing up, dissimulation; concealment in general, secrecy; mistrust, doubt, suspicion; a secret; wickedness; atonement, expiation; excuse, exculpation, deprecation; N. of a ceremony; N. of a Sāman. — *Nihnava-vādin, ī,* m. a defendant or witness who prevaricates or tries to hide the truth. — *Nihnavottara* (°*va-ut*°), *am,* n. an evasive reply or defence.

Ni-hnuta, as, ā, am, denied, disowned, evaded; concealed, secreted.

Ni-hnuti, is, f. denial or concealment of knowledge; dissimulation, reserve, secrecy; hiding, concealment.

Ni-hnuvana, am, n. denial or concealment of knowledge; excuse, exculpation.

Ni-hnuvāna, as, ā, am, dissimulating, prevaricating, insinuating, using double entendre.

निह्राद *ni-hrāda, as,* m. (fr. rt. *hrād* with *ni*), sound; (also read *nir-hrāda.*) — *Nihrāda-vat, ān, atī, at,* sounding, making a noise.

Ni-hrādin, ī, inī, i, sounding, pealing.

निह्वे *ni-hve*, cl. 1. P. A. *-hvayati, -te, -hvātum,* to invoke, call.

Ni-hava, as, m. invocation, calling, summoning, calling near; N. of a Sāman, (*vasishṭhasya nihavas* or *vasishṭha-nihavas.*)

नी 1. *nī*, cl. 1. P. A. *nayati, -te, anayat* (ep. also *anayit*), *nayeta* (ep. also *nayīta*), *ninaya* (3rd pl. *ninyus,* anomalous form of Perf. *nayāmāsa*), *ninye, netā* (ep. also *nayitā*), *neshyati, -te* (ep. also *nayishyati*), *anaishīt, aneshṭa* (Ved. forms *neshat, neshati, neshi, naishṭa, neshṭa*), *netum* (ep. also *nayitum*), to lead, guide, conduct, (*vyavahāraṃ nī,* to conduct a process); to direct, govern; to lead or bring away, carry away, to lead or bring away to (with acc., dat., or loc.); to carry off for one's self (A.); to marry; to bring a person (acc.) into any state or condition (acc. or loc., e. g. *nṛipatīn vaśam anayat,* he brought the kings into subjection; *tāṃ duhitṛitve nayati,* he brings her into the state of a daughter: sometimes used with a substantive in the same way as 1. *kṛi,* q. v., e. g. *vināśaṃ nī,* to destroy; *paritoshaṃ nī,* to gratify; *vikrayaṃ nī,* to sell; *duḥkhaṃ nī,* to pain; *sākshyaṃ nī,* to admit as a witness; *ādhānaṃ nī,* to give in pledge; *Śūdratāṃ nī,* to reduce to a Śūdra: or with an adverb ending in *sāt,* e. g. *bhasmasād nī,* to reduce to ashes); to lead away from, exclude from; to draw (a line &c.); to trace, track; to ascertain, investigate; to settle; to pass or spend (time); to carry, bear; (with *daṇḍam*) to bear the rod, inflict punishment; to guide in learning, instruct (A.): Pass. *nīyate,* to be led, &c.: Caus. *nāyayati,* &c., to cause to lead, &c.; to cause to be carried away: Desid. *ninīshati, -te* (Ved. *nineshati*), to wish to lead, &c.; to wish to take away; to wish to bring to a state; to wish to exclude from (with abl.); to wish to trace or ascertain, investigate [cf. *ninīshā, ninīshu*]: Intens. *nenīyate,* to lead as a captive, have in one's power, rule; [cf. Gr. νέ-ο-μαι, νίσσομαι, νῖσομαι; Lith. *neshù;* Slav. *nesun,* 'I bear.']

2. *nī, īs,* m. a leader, a guide, (used at the end of a comp.; cf. *agra-ṇī, agre-ṇī, ṛita-nī, gāthā-nī, grāma-ṇī, pada-nī,* &c.)

Nīka, as, m. a species of tree; (*ā*), f. a channel for irrigation.

1. *nīta, as, ā, am,* led, guided, conducted; brought, reduced; gained, obtained; well-behaved, correct, modest; (*am*), n. wealth; corn, grain; [cf. *asu-n*°, *dur-n*°, &c.]

Nīti, is, f. guiding, guidance, directing, direction, management; manner of conducting one's self, conduct, propriety; right or moral or prudent behaviour, prudent counsel, policy, political wisdom or science, political economy, state policy, statesmanship, the administration of government; moral philosophy, ethics, precepts for prudent and moral behaviour, prudence, Prudence or Polity personified [cf. *naya*]; leading or bringing to, obtaining, acquirement, acquisition; presenting, offering; relation, support; [cf. *agra-ṇīti, adabdha-n*°, *asu-n*°, *ṛiju-n*°, &c.] — *Nīti-kathā,* f. any work on moral or political science, a discourse on political economy. — *Nīti-kuśala, as, ā, am,* conversant with political science, skilful in human affairs, a good statesman. — *Nīti-ghosha, as,* m., N. of the car of Bṛihas-pati. — *Nīti-jña, as, ā, am,* knowing what is right especially in government, sagacious, politic, prudent; (*as*), m. a prudent statesman or soldier, a politician. — *Nīti-dosha, as,* m. error of conduct, mistake in policy. — *Nīti-nishṇa, as, ā, am,* versed in political or moral science. — *Nīti-pradīpa, as,* m. 'the light of prudent behaviour,' N. of a collection of verses attributed to Vetāla-bhaṭṭa. — *Nīti-mañjarī,* f., N. of a work on morality or right behaviour. — *Nīti-mat, ān, atī, at,* knowing the rules of moral or prudent behaviour, moral, prudent, eminent for political wisdom. — *Nīti-ratna, am,* n. 'the jewel of morality,' N. of a collection of verses attributed to Vararuċi. — *Nīti-vākyāmṛita* (°*ya-am*°), *am,* n. 'nectar of discourse on morality or prudent behaviour,' N. of a work. — *Nīti-vid, t,* m. a politician, any one versed in political science, a statesman. — *Nīti-vidyā,* f. moral or political science, political economy; [cf. *nīti-śāstra.*] — *Nīti-vishaya, as,* m. the sphere of morality or prudent conduct. — *Nīti-vīja, am,* n. a germ or source of intrigue. — *Nīti-vedin, ī, inī, i,* knowing policy, a politician. — *Nīti-vyatikrama, as,* m. error of conduct, transgression of the rules of moral or political science. — *Nīti-śataka, am,* n. the hundred verses on morality by Bhartṛi-hari. — *Nīti-śāstra, am,* n. the science of ethics or politics, any work on political ethics or morals. — *Nīti-saṅkalana, am,* n. 'collection of rules for moral conduct or prudent behaviour,' N. of a modern work. — *Nīti-sāra, as,* m. or *am,* n. the essence of political or moral science; (*am*), n. a special work on this subject by Ghaṭa-karpara.

Nītvā, ind. having led or conducted or guided; having taken; having passed or spent (as time).

Nītha, as, m. (Ved. also n.) leading, guiding; a leader, a guider; N. of a man; (*ā*), f., Ved. way, trick; evasion, subterfuge; a mode in music; water; [cf. *dīrgha-n*°, *deva-n*°.] — *Nīthā-vid, t, t, t,* Ved. knowing ways, knowing the musical modes, skilled in sacred song.

Nīthya. See *grāmaṇīthya*, p. 304, col. 2.

Nīyamāna, as, ā, am, being led or conducted or conveyed, being carried or brought, being taken or taken away; being traced or sought or obtained.

Netavya, as, ā, am, to be led or guided or conducted, to be led away, to be taken, to be carried.

Netṛi, tā, trī, tṛi, leading, conducting, guiding, one who brings or leads to; (*tā*), m. a leader, guide, conductor; a chief, master, owner; (with *daṇḍasya*) an inflicter of punishment [cf. *daṇḍa-n*°]; the hero of a drama or play; the plant Azadirachta Indica (= *nimba*); the numeral two; (*trī*), f. a female leader; a river; a vein; an epithet of Lakshmī. — *Netṛi-tva, am,* n. the office or business of a leader &c., leadership. — *Netṛi-mat, ān, atī, at,* containing the word *netṛi.*

Netra, as, ī, am, one who guides or leads, a leader, guide; a substitute for *netṛi* at the end of a comp. (e. g. *bhavan-netra,* having thee as commander); (*as*), m., N. of a son of Dharma and father of Kunti; also a son of Su-mati; (*am*), n. leading, conducting; the eye (as the instrument of leading or guiding); symbolic expression for the number two; the string with which a churning-stick is whirled round; an enema-pipe; the root of a tree; bleached or wove silk; a carriage. — *Netra-kanīnikā,* f. the pupil of the eye. — *Netra-kosha, as,* m. the eyeball; the bud of a flower. — *Netra-goċara, as, ā, am,* within the range of the sight, visible. — *Netra-ċċhada, as,* m. the eyelid. — *Netra-ja, as, ā, am,* 'eye-born,' coming from the eyes; (*am*), n. a tear. — *Netra-jala, am,* n. 'eye-water,' tears. — *Netra-tā,* f. the state of being an eye; *netratāṃ yā,* to become an eye. — *Netra-tribhāga-brahmayaśasvin, ī,* m., N. of an author. — *Netra-paryanta, as, ā, am,* as far as to the eye, up to the eye; (*as*), m. the outer angle of the eye. — *Netra-piṇḍa, as,* m. a cat ('having full eyes'); the eyeball. — *Netra-pushkarā,* f. a species of plant; [cf. *rudra-jaṭā.*] — *Netra-manaḥ-svabhāvās,* m. pl. eyes, mind, and soul. — *Netra-mīnā,* f. a species of plant (= *yava-tiktā*). — *Netra-mush, ṭ, ṭ, ṭ,* stealing or captivating the eye. — *Netra-yoni, is,* m. an epithet of Indra (as covered with marks resembling the female organ, through the curse of Gautama, whose wife Ahalyā he had attempted to seduce; the sage afterwards relenting, changed these disgraceful marks on the body of the deity to as many eyes); the moon (as produced from the eye of Atri). — *Netra-rañjana, am,* n. 'eye-colouring,' collyrium. — *Netra-ruj, k,* f. disease of the eyes. — *Netra-roga, as,* m. disease of the eyes, ophthalmia; (*as, ā, am*), afflicted with disease of the eyes. — *Netraroga-tā,* f. disease of the eyes. — *Netraroga-han, ā,* m. a particular plant used for diseases of the eyes, Tragia Involucrata. — *Netra-roman, a,* n. the eyelash. — *Netra-vasti, is,* m. f. a clyster-pipe with a bag. — *Netra-vastra, am,* n. a veil over the eye. — *Netra-vāri,* n. 'eye-water,' tears. — *Netra-vish, ṭ,* f. excretion of the eyes. — *Netra-visha, as, ā, am,* having poison in the eyes. — *Netra-stambha, as,* m. rigidity of the eyes. — *Netrāñjana* (°*ra-añ*°), *am,* n. 'eye-ointment,' collyrium. — *Netrānta* (°*ra-an*°), *as,* m. the outer corner of the eye. — *Netrābhishyanda* (°*ra-abh*°), *as,* m. running of the eyes. — *Netrāmaya* (°*ra-ām*°), *as,* m. ophthalmia. — *Netrāmbu* (°*ra-am*°) or *netrāmbhas* (°*ra-am*°), *as,* n. 'eye-water,' tears. — *Netrāri* (°*ra-ari*), *is,* m. a species of plant (= *sīhuṇḍa*). — *Netrotsava* (°*ra-ut*°), *am,* n. 'eye-feast,' any pleasing or beautiful object. — *Netropama* (°*ra-up*°), *am,* n. the almond fruit (as resembling eyes). — *Netropama-phala, as,* m. the almond tree. — *Netraushadha* (°*ra-aush*°), *am,* n. medicine for the eyes, collyrium, green sulphate of iron used as collyrium; (*ī*), f. Odina Pinnata (= *ajaśṛiṅgī*).

Netrikā, am, n. a pipe, a clyster-pipe; a ladle.

Neya, as, ā, am, to be guided or led; to be governed; to be passed or spent (as time); to be led away; to be inflicted (e. g. *neyo daṇḍas,* punishment must be inflicted). — *Neya-pāla, as,* m., N. of a prince.

नी 3. *nī* (*ni i*), cl. 2. P. *ny-eti, ny-etum,* Ved. to go into, enter, come or fall into, change to; [cf. *ny-āya.*]

2. *nīta, as, ā, am,* entered, gone to; (Sāy.) = *nitarām prāpta.*

नीकर्षिन् *nī-karshin, ī, iṇī, i* (fr. rt. *kṛish* with *ni*), spreading the tail (as a peacock?).

नीकार *nī-kāra, as,* m. (fr. rt. 1. *kṛi* with *ni*), disrespect, contempt, vilifying, degrading.

नीकाश *nī-kāśa, as,* m. (fr. rt. *kāś* with *ni*),

appearance, look, air, mien; certainty, ascertainment; (*as, ā, am*), like, resembling, (at the end of comps.)

नीकुलक *nīkulaka, as*, m., N. of a man.

नीक्लेद *nī-kleda, as*, m. (fr. rt. *klid* with *ni*), moistening, bedewing (?), Pāṇ. VI. 3, 122, Schol.

नीक्षण *nīkshaṇa, am*, n. (fr. rt. *īksh* with *ni* or rt. *niksh ?*), Ved. a stick for stirring up a caldron, a kind of ladle, (Sāy. = *pāka-parikshā-sādhanam kāshṭham*); [cf. *nekshaṇa*.]

नीच *nīća, as, ā, am* (fr. *ni* + *anć*, cf. *ućća*; said to be fr. rt. *ći* with *ni*), low, not high, short, little, small, dwarfish; deep, lowered (as the voice), pronounced without an accent; situated below, being in a low position; low, vile, insignificant, inferior, base, mean (as a man or action); (*as*), m. a kind of perfume (= *ćoraka*); (*am*), n. (in astrology) the lowest point of a planet (= ταπείνωμα), the seventh house from the highest point; (*āt*), ind. from below, from beneath; [cf. *nīćais, ućća-nīća, ny-anć*.] — *Nīća-kadamba, as*, m., N. of a plant (= *maṇḍīrī*). — *Nīća-kula, am*, n. a low family. — *Nīća-ga, as, ā, am*, going low or downwards, descending (as a river); being in or belonging to a low man or to a low class of men; low, vile, base; (*ā*), f. a river; (*am*), n. water. — *Nīća-gata, as, ā, am* being at the lowest point (as a planet). — *Nīća-gṛiha, am*, n. (in astrology) the house or station of the heavens in which a planet stands at its lowest point. — *Nīća-jāti, is, is, i*, of low birth. — *Nīća-tā*, f. or *nīća-tva, am*, n. (opposed to *ućća-tā*), lowness, meanness, vileness, baseness, humbleness, inferiority, a low situation. — *Nīća-bhojya, as*, m. 'the food of low men,' an onion. — *Nīća-meḍhra, as, ā, am*, Ved. one whose penis hangs low. — *Nīća-yonin, ī, inī, i*, being of low origin, low-born. — *Nīća-rata, as, ā, am*, delighting in mean things. — *Nīćarksha* (°*ća-ṛik*°), *am*, n. (?) = *nīća-gṛiha*, q. v. — *Nīća-vajra, am*, n. an inferior diamond, a sort of gem (= *vaikrānta*). — *Nīća-vayas, ās, ās, as*, Ved. one whose strength has failed; (Sāy.) bending down the body. — *Nīćokti* (°*ća-uk*°), *is*, f. a low or vulgar expression. — *Nīćoćća-vṛitta* (°*ća-uć*°), *am*, n. an epicycle. — *Nīćopagata* (°*ća-up*°), *as, ā, am*, situated low in the sky.

Nīćaka, as, ikā, am, low, short, dwarfish; (low as the voice), soft; vile, mean; (*akā*), f. an excellent cow; (*akī*), f. the head of an ox.

Nīćakin, ī, m. the head or top of anything, the head of an ox; the owner of a good cow; [cf. *naićika*.]

Nīćakais, ind. (diminutive of *nīćais*), low, below, little, &c.

Nīćā, ind. low, below, down, downwards, (this word may be regarded as the inst. c. of *ny-anć*, q.v.)

Nīćāt, ind. from below. See *nīća*.

Nīćāyamāna, as, ā, am, Ved. descending, flying down (as a falcon).

Nīći-kṛi, cl. 8. P. A. *-karoti, -kurute, -kartum*, to lower, to pronounce without an accent.

Nīćīna, as, ā, am, Ved. being low or below, low, directed downwards or underneath, hanging down, flowing down, cast down. — *Nīćīna-bāra, as, ā, am*, Ved. having its opening below (as a cloud).

Nīćais, ind. low, below, down, downwards, underneath, beneath, deeply, deep, in the depths, in a bent or inclined position, bowing low, humbly, modestly; with a low or depressed or deep tone of voice, in a low tone (i. e. *an-udātta*, q. v.), softly; short, small, little, dwarfish; N. of a mountain, also called *Vāmana-giri* and *Kharva* (Dwarfish); [cf. *uććais, nimnais, śanais*.] — *Nīćaiḥ-kara, as, ā* or *ī, am*, causing a low or deep tone, giving depth of voice. — *Nīćair-mukha, as, ī, am*, with downcast countenance. — *Nīćais-tarām*, ind. in a low tone, softly.

1. *nīćya, as, ā, am*, living below; Ved. an epithet of some nations in the West.

2. *nīćya*, Nom. P. *nīćyati*, &c., to be in a low situation, be a slave.

नीड *nīḍa* (Ved. *nīla*), *as, am*, m. n. (perhaps fr. rt. *sad* with *ni*, whence *ni-shada* = *nishḍa* = *niḍḍa* = *nīḍa*, or fr. rt. *il* with *ni*), a resting-place, a place for lying down, a bird's nest; a bed, couch; a lair, den; the interior or seat of a carriage or chariot; a place, abode in general; [cf. Lat. *nidus*; Hib. *nead*; Cambro-Brit. *nyth*; Germ. and Angl. Sax. *nest*.] — *Nīḍa-ja, as*, m. 'nest-born,' a bird. — *Nīḍajendra* (°*ja-in*°), *as*, m. 'chief of the birds,' an epithet of Garuḍa. — *Nīḍodbhava* (°*ḍa-ud*°), *as*, m. 'nest-born,' a bird.

Nīḍaka, as or *am*, m. or n. (?), the nest of a bird.

Nīḍaya or *nīlaya*, Nom. P. *nīḍayati* or *nīlayati, -yitum*, Ved. (according to Sāy.) to bring together, join together, cause to come to close fighting; to bring to rest (?).

Nīḍi or *nīli, is*, m., Ved. one who lives in the same house (?).

नीत *nīta, nīti*, &c. See p. 511, col. 2.

नीतमिश्र *nīta-miśra, as, ā, am* (*nīta* = *nava-nīta*), Ved. not yet become butter, (said of *dadhi*.)

नीत्त *nī-tta, as, ā, am* (for *ni-datta* fr. rt. 1. *dā* with *ni*), Ved. given.

नीध्र *nīdhra, am*, n. the edge of thatch, edge of a roof; a wood; the circumference of a wheel; the moon; the constellation Revatī; (considered by some as a various reading for *nivra*, q. v.)

नीनाह *nīnāha, as*, m., Ved. anything which encircles another (?).

नीप *nīpa, as, ā, am* (fr. *ni-ap*, but said to be fr. rt. 1. *nī*), situated low, deep; (*as*), m. the foot of a mountain; N. of a son of Kṛitin; the tree Nauclea Cadamba (= *kadamba* = *dhārā-kadambaka* = *dharā-kadamba* = *dhūli-kadamba*); the plant Ixora Bandhuca (= *bandhūka*); a species of Aśoka (= *nīlāśoka*); (*am*), n. the fruit of the above plants; (*ās*), m. pl., N. of a regal family descended from Nīpa, son of Pāra. — *Nīpa-rāja, am*, n. (?), the fruit (?) of the Nīpa. — *Nīpātithi* (°*pa-at*°), *is*, m., N. of a descendant of Kaṇva and author of a hymn of the Ṛig-veda (VIII. 34).

Nīpya, as, ā, am, Ved. being low or on the ground.

नीमानुय *nīmānuya, as*, m., N. of a Vaishṇava teacher.

नीयमान *nīyamāna*. See p. 511, col. 2.

नीर् *nīr* (*ni-īr*), Caus. P. *nīrayati, -yitum*, to drive or impel into, urge forwards (to an aim); to send forth, appoint (to a business).

नीर *nīra, am*, n. (said to be fr. rt. 1. *nī*), water; juice, liquor, (sometimes written for *nīḍa, nīla*, q. v.); (*as*), m., N. of a prince; [cf. *kshīra-nīra, nāra*; Gr. νηρός, Νηρεύς.] — *Nīra-graha, as*, m. taking up water in a ladle; see under *graha*. — 1. *nīra-ja, as, ā, am* (for 2. see below), 'water-born,' being in water, aquatic; (*as*), m. an otter; a species of grass, = *uśīrī*; (*as, am*), m. n. (according to the lexicographers only n.), a lotus in general, the water-lily; (*am*), n. a species of Costus, Costus Speciosus (= *kushṭha*); a pearl. — *Nīra-jāta, as, ā, am*, 'water-born,' produced from water, aquatic. — 1. *nīra-da, as*, m. (for 2. see col. 3), 'giving water,' a cloud; a species of Cyperus. — *Nīradin, ī, inī, i*, cloudy. — *Nīra-dhi* or *nīra-nidhi, is*, m. 'the receptacle of waters,' the ocean; [cf. *ab-dhi, toya-dhi*, &c.] — *Nīra-priya, as*, m. a species of reed (*jala-vetasa*). — *Nīra-ruha, am*, n. the water-lily, lotus. — *Nīrākhu* (°*ra-ākhu*), *us*, m. 'water-rat,' an otter.

नीरक्त *nī-rakta, as, ā, am* (fr. *nis* + *rakta*), colourless, faded, having the colour gone.

नीरज 2. *nī-raja, as, ā, am* (fr. *nis* + *raja* for *rajas*), free from dust; devoid of passion; (with *vi-raja*) an epithet of Śiva. (For 1. *nīra-ja* see under *nīra*, col. 2.)

Nī-rajas, ās, ās, as (fr. *nis* + *rajas*), free from dust, having no pollen (as a flower); free from passion; (*ās*), f. a woman not menstruating. — *Nī-rajas-tamasā*, f. absence of passion and darkness.

Nī-rajaska, as, ā, am, free from dust, not accompanied by dust (as wind); free from passion, pure.

Nī-rajasva, as, ā, am, free from dust.

Nīrajī-kṛi, cl. 8. P. A. *-karoti, -kurute, -kartum*, to make free from dust. — *Nīrajī-kārita, as, ā, am*, made free from dust, cleansed.

नीरत *nī-rata, as, ā, am* (fr. *nis* + *rata*), not delighting in, not attached to, indifferent.

नीरद 2. *nī-rada, as, ā, am* (fr. *nis* + *rada*), toothless. (For 1. *nīra-da* see under *nīra*, col. 2.)

नीरन्ध्र *nī-randhra, as, ā, am* (fr. *nis* + *randhra*), having no holes or openings, without apertures or interstices, imperforate, close, uninterrupted; coarse, thick, gross. — *Nīrandhra-tva, am*, n. closeness, close connection.

नीरव *nī-rava, as, ā, am* (fr. *nis* + *rava*), soundless.

नीरस *nī-rasa, as, ā, am* (fr. *nis* + *rasa*), without juice, sapless, dried up, withered; flavourless, unsavoury, tasteless, devoid of taste, flat, dry; insipid; vain; (*as*), m. the pomegranate. — *Nīrasa-tā*, f. the state of being devoid of taste, tastelessness.

नीरसन *nī-rasana, as, ā, am* (fr. *nis* + *rasanā*), having no girdle.

नीराजन *nī-rājana, am, ā*, n. f. (fr. rt. *rāj* with *ni*), lustration of arms (*lustratio exercitus*), a military and religious ceremony held by kings or generals on the nineteenth of Āśvin before taking the field, (it consists in purifying the Puro-hita or chaplain, the king's ministers, and various component parts of the army during the recitation of sacred texts); waving lights before an idol as an act of adoration, (this may also be performed with a lotus, clean cloth, or the leaves of various sacred plants; prostration is considered as a fifth kind of adoration.)

नीरिन्दु *nīrindu, us*, m. a species of plant (= *aśva-śākhoṭa*), Trophis Aspera.

नीरुच् *nī-ruć, k, k, k* (fr. *nis* + *ruć*), lustreless, dull, dim, faded.

नीरुज् *nī-ruj, k, k, k* (fr. *nis* + *ruj*), free from sickness; convalescent, well, in health; painless.

Nī-ruja, as, ā, am, = *nī-ruj*, healthy, in health, well, (sometimes written *ni-ruja*); (*am*), n. a species of Costus, Costus Speciosus (= *kushṭha*).

नीरूप *nī-rūpa, as, ā, am* (fr. *nis* + *rūpa*), formless, shapeless, mis-shapen; (*as*), m. air, wind; a god; (*am*), n. heaven, ether.

नीरेणुक *nī-reṇuka, as, ā, am* (fr. *nis* + *reṇu*), dustless, free from dust.

नीरोग *nī-roga, as, ā, am* (fr. *nis* + *roga*), free from sickness, healthy, well. — *Nīroga-tā*, f. health.

Nīrogya-tā, f. health, freedom from sickness, (perhaps an error for *nīroga-tā*.)

नीरोह *nī-roha, as*, m. (fr. *nis* + *ruh*), Ved. shooting out, growing.

नील् *nīl* (rather a Nom. derived fr. *nīla* below), cl. 1. P. *nīlati*, &c., to be of a dark colour; to dye dark, make or dye blue.

Nīla, as, ā or *ī, am* (probably fr. *niś* + *la* = *niśla* = *nilla* = *nīla*; according to Pāṇ. IV. 1, 42, the fem. form *nīlā* is used in relation to clothes &c., and *nīlī* in relation to plants, animals, &c.; in proper names either form is allowed), of a dark colour, (especially dark-blue or black); dyed with indigo; (*as*), m. dark-blue or black (the colour); a gem, the sapphire; the Indian fig-tree (= *vaṭa*); a species of bird, the blue or hill Maina; an ox or bull of a dark colour; one of the nine Nidhis or divine treasures of Kuvera; N. of a man, the prince of Māhishmatī; of a son of Yadu; of a historian of Kaśmīra; an epithet of Mañju-śrī; N. of a Nāga; of one of the monkey-chiefs attending on Rāma, (said to be a son of Agni); the blue mountain, one of the principal ranges of mountains dividing the world into nine portions and lying immediately north of Ilāvṛita or the central division [cf. *nīlādri*]; (*ā*), f. the indigo plant, Indigofera Tinctoria [cf. *nīlī*]; a species of Boerhavia with blue blossoms (= *nīla-punar-navā*); a species of blue fly [cf. *nīlī*]; the two arteries in front of the neck, (in this sense *nīle*, f. du.); a black and blue mark on the skin (either from a bruise or a disease?); a Rāgiṇī or mode of music, personified as the wife of Rāga Mallāra; (*ī*), f. the indigo plant; another plant, Blyxa Saivala (= *śaivala;* cf. *jala-nīlī*); a species of blue fly; a kind of disease (= *nīlī-roga, nīlikā*); N. of the wife of Aja-mīḍha [cf. *nilinī, nalinī*]; (*am*), n. darkness (Ved.); indigo, the dye; black salt (= *kāća-lavaṇa*); blue vitriol (= *tuttha*); antimony (= *sauvīrāñjana*); poison (= *tālīśa-pattra*); a peculiar position in dancing; a kind of metre consisting of four times sixteen syllables; [cf. Lat. *niger* for *nigro* = *niś-ra*.] — *Nīla-kaṇā*, f. a species of cumin. — *Nīla-kaṇṭha, as, ā, am*, blue-necked; (*as*), m. a peacock; a species of gallinule or water-hen (= *dātyūha*); a wag-tail; a sparrow; a blue-necked jay; the plant Hyperanthera Moringa (= *pīta-sāra*); an epithet of Śiva (as having a black throat, so stained by the acrimony of the poison which he swallowed on its production at the churning of the ocean); N. of several authors and commentators; (*am*), n. a radish; [cf. *kāla-kaṇṭha*.] — *Nīlakaṇṭha-ćampū, ūs*, f., N. of a work by Nīlakaṇṭha Dīkshita. — *Nīlakaṇṭha-tīrtha, am*, n. 'the bathing-place of Śiva,' N. of a sacred Tīrtha. — *Nīlakaṇṭha-bhāratī*, m., N. of an author mentioned in the Sarva-darśana-saṅgraha of Mādhavāćārya. — *Nīlakaṇṭha-stava, as*, m. 'the praise of Śiva,' N. of the fifty-first chapter of the Jñāna-khaṇḍa of the Śiva-Purāṇa. — *Nīlakaṇṭhāksha* (°*ṭha-ak*°), *am*, n. the berry or seed of Elæocarpus Ganitrus. — *Nīla-kanda, as*, m. a species of bulbous plant (= *mahisha-kanda-bheda*). — *Nīla-kamala, am*, n. the blue water-lily. — *Nīla-kāyika, ās*, m. pl. (with Buddhists) 'blue-bodied' or 'dark-bodied,' epithet of a class of deities. — *Nīla-kuntalā*, f., N. of a female friend of Durgā. — *Nīla-kuranṭaka, as*, m. or *nīla-kusumā*, f. or *nīla-kuruṇṭaka*, a species of Barleria with blue blossoms (B. Cœrulea, = *nīla-jhiṇṭī*). — *Nīla-keśī*, f. the indigo plant. — *Nīla-krāntā*, f. a species of plant (= *vishṇu-krāntā*). — *Nīla-krauñća, as*, m. a species of curlew or heron. — *Nīla-gaṅgā*, f., N. of a river. — *Nīla-gaṇeśa, as*, m. the blue Gaṇeśa. — *Nīla-garbha*, a young blue water-lily (?). — *Nīla-giri-karṇikā*, f. a blue variety of Clitoria Ternatea. — *Nīla-grīva, as, ā, am*, blue-necked; (*as*), m. an epithet of Rudra-Śiva or Mahā-deva, (see *nīla-kaṇṭha*); N. of a king. — *Nīla-ghora*, a various reading for *nīla-pora*, q. v. — *Nīla-ćarman, a*, n. the tree Xylocarpus Granatum. — *Nīla-ććhada, as*, m. 'dark-leaved,' the date tree; 'blue-winged,' an epithet of Garuḍa. — *Nīla-ććhavī*, a species of bird (= *kuku;* the right form is probably *nīla-ććhavin, ī*, m.). — *Nīla-ja, as, ā, am*, produced in the blue mountains; (*am*), n. blue steel; (*ā*), f. the river Vitastā. — *Nīla-jhiṇṭī*, f. blue Barleria (= *nīla-kuranṭaka*). — *Nīla-tantra, am*, n., N. of a Tantra. — *Nīla-taru, us*, m. the cocoa-nut tree. — *Nīla-tā*, f. blueness, blackness, a blue or dark colour. — *Nīla-tāla, as*, m. Xanthochymus Pictorius; Phœnix Paludosa. — *Nīla-dūrvā*, f. a species of plant (= *haritā*). — *Nīla-druma, as*, m. a species of tree (= *nīlāsana*). — *Nīla-dhvaja, as*, m. Xanthochymus Pictorius; N. of a prince of Māhishmatī. — *Nīla-nakha, as, ā, am*, Ved. black-clawed, having black claws. — *Nīla-nirguṇḍī*, f. a species of Nirguṇḍī with blue blossoms. — *Nīla-niryāsaka, as*, m. a species of tree (= *nīlāsana*). — *Nīla-nīraja, am*, n. the blue water-lily. — *Nīla-pakshman, ā, ā, a*, having black eyelashes. — *Nīla-paṅka, am*, n. darkness; (*as, am*), m. n. black mud. — *Nīla-paṭala, am*, n. a sort of dark film or membrane over the eye of a blind person; a dark mass, a black coating or covering. — *Nīla-pattra, as, ā, am*, dark-leaved, having black or dark-blue leaves; (*as*), m., N. of several plants, Scirpus Kysoor; the pomegranate tree; (*ā*), f. Premna Herbacea; (*am*), n. the blue water-lily. — *Nīla-padma, am*, n. the blue water-lily. — *Nīla-parṇa, as*, m. Grevia Orientalis; (*ī*), f. Vanda (= *vandā*) Roxburghii. — *Nīla-pāćana, am*, n. steeping or maceration of indigo. — *Nīlapāćana-bhāṇḍa, am*, n. a vessel for steeping indigo, an indigo vat. — *Nīla-piṅgala, as, ā, am*, of a dark-brown colour. — *Nīla-piććha, as*, m. 'black-tailed,' a falcon. — *Nīla-piṭa, as*, m. (with Buddhists) a collection of annals and royal edicts. — *Nīla-pishṭoḍī*, f. a species of shrub (= *nīlāmlī*). — *Nīla-punar-navā*, f. a species of Punar-navā with blue blossoms. — *Nīla-pura, am*, n., N. of a town. — *Nīla-purāṇa, am*, n., N. of a Purāṇa. — *Nīla-pushpa, as*, m. a species of Verbesina with blue flowers; (*ā*), f. a plant (= *vishṇu-krāntā*); (*ī*), f. a plant (= *nīla-vuhnā*); (*am*), n. a species of fragrant plant (= *granthi-parṇa*). — *Nīla-pushpikā*, f. the indigo plant; linseed, Linum Usitatissimum. — *Nīla-pṛishṭha, as, ā, am*, Ved. 'black-backed,' epithet of Agni; (*as*), m. a species of fish, commonly called Rohi, Cyprinus Denticulatus. — *Nīla-pora, as*, m. a species of sugar-cane. — *Nīla-bha, as*, m. 'having a bluish or dark appearance,' the moon; a cloud; a bee; [cf. *nīlābha*.] — *Nīla-bhū, ūs*, f., N. of a river. — *Nīla-bhṛiṅgarāja, as*, m. a species of Verbesina with blue blossoms. — *Nīla-makshā*, f. a species of blue fly or bee. — *Nīla-maṇi, is*, m. a blue gem, the sapphire. — *Nīla-mata, am*, n., N. of a poem in the Pauranic style, celebrating the sacred places of Kaśmīra, and said to have been inspired by Nīla the serpent-king. — *Nīla-mallikā*, f. Ægle Marmelos. — *Nīla-mādhava, as*, m. an epithet of Vishṇu or Kṛishṇa (as being of a dark colour). — *Nīla-māsha, as*, m. Dolichos Catjang. — *Nīla-mīlika, as*, m. a fire-fly. — *Nīla-mṛittikā*, f. iron pyrites; black earth or mould. — *Nīla-mehin, ī, inī, i*, voiding dark or bluish urine. — *Nīla-yashṭikā*, f. a species of dark sugar-cane. — *Nīla-ratna, am*, n. the sapphire. — *Nīla-rāji, is*, f. a dark line, dark row, dark mass. — *Nīla-rudropanishad* (°*ra-up*°), *t*, f., N. of an Upanishad. — *Nīla-rūpaka, as*, m. Thespesia Populneoides. — *Nīla-loha, am*, n. blue steel. — *Nīla-lohita, as, ā, am*, dark-blue mixed with red, purple, of a purple colour, dark-red; (*as*), m., N. of Rudra-Śiva; N. of a Kalpa; a mixture of blue and red, a purple colour; (*ā*), f. a species of vegetable (= *bhūmi-jambu*); N. of a goddess, the wife of Śiva. — *Nīla-vat, ān, atī, at*, Ved. blackish, dark; (*ān*), m., N. of a mountain. — *Nīla-varṇa, as, ā, am*, blue-coloured, blue, of a blue colour; (*as* or *am*), m. n. Grevia Orientalis; radish. — *Nīlavarṇa-śṛigāla-vat*, ind. like the blue jackal. — *Nīla-vallī*, f. Vanda Roxburghii. — *Nīla-vasana, as, ā, am*, wearing dark-blue or black garments; (*as*), m. the planet Saturn. — *Nīla-vastra, am*, n. a blue or dark garment, dark-coloured cloth; (*as, ā, am*), dressed in dark or blue garments; (*as*), m. an epithet of Bala-rāma; (*ā*), f. an epithet of Durgā. — *Nīla-vānara, as*, m. 'the blue monkey,' a species of monkey. — *Nīla-vāsas, ās, ās, as*, dressed in dark-blue clothes; (*ās*), m. the planet Saturn. — *Nīla-vīja, as*, m. a species of tree (= *nīlāsana*). — *Nīla-vuhnā*, f. Convolvulus Argenteus. — *Nīla-vṛiksha, as*, m. a species of plant (= *vātāri*). — *Nīla-vṛinta, as*, m. (?), a fan. — *Nīlavṛintaka, am*, n. cotton. — *Nīla-vṛisha, as*, m. a dark-coloured bull; (*ā*), f. Solanum Melongena. — *Nīla-vrata, am*, n., N. of a kind of religious ceremony. — *Nīla-śikhaṇḍa, as, ā, am*, having black tufts or locks of hair. — *Nīla-śigru, us*, m. Hyperanthera Moringa. — *Nīla-shaṇḍa, as*, m. a dark-coloured bull at liberty. — *Nīla-sandhyā*, f. = *nīla-giri-karṇikā*, q. v. — *Nīla-sarasvatī*, f., N. of a goddess (= *tārā*). — *Nīlasarasvatī-manu*, N. of an incantation or magical formula. — *Nīla-sindu-vāra, as*, m. Vitex Negundo. — *Nīla-skandā* or *nīla-skandhā* or *nīla-spandā*, f. the dark Gokarṇī. — *Nīla-svarūpa, as* or *am*, m. or n. (?), N. of a metre consisting of four lines of eleven syllables each. — *Nīlāksha* (°*la-aksha*), *as*, m. 'blue-eyed,' a goose. — *Nīlāṅkita-dala* (°*la-aṅ*°), *as* or *am*, m. or n. (?), a species of bulbous plant (= *taila-kanda*). — *Nīlāṅga* (°*la-aṅ*°), *as, ā, am*, dark-bodied, having a dark-coloured or dark-blue body; (*as*), m. the Indian crane; the blue jay, Coracias Indica. — *Nīlāñjana* (°*la-añ*°), *am*, n. antimony; blue vitriol; (*ā*), f. lightning; (*ī*), f. a species of shrub (= *kālāñjanī*). — *Nīlāñjasā* (°*la-añ*°), f. lightning [cf. *nīlāñjanā*]; N. of an Apsaras or courtezan of Svarga; N. of a river. — *Nīlādri* (°*la-ad*°), *is*, m. the mountain Nīla. — *Nīlādri-karṇikā*, f. or *nīlāparājitā* (°*la-ap*°), f. = *nīla-giri-karṇikā*. — *Nīlābja* (°*la-ab*°), *am*, n. the blue water-lily, a blue lotus. — *Nīlābha* (°*la-ābhā*), *as, ā, am*, blue-looking, blue; (*as*), m. a cloud; [cf. *nīla-bha*.] — *Nīlābhra* (°*la-abh*°), *as*, m. a dark cloud. — *Nīlābhra-samvṛita* (°*la-abh*°), *as, ā, am*, obscured or concealed by dark clouds. — *Nīlāmbara* (°*la-am*°), *as, ā, am*, dressed in dark-blue cloth, wearing a blue garment; (*as*), m. a demon, a goblin; the planet Saturn; an epithet of Bala-rāma; (*am*), n. black or dark-blue raiment. — *Nīlāmbu-janman* (°*la-am*°), *a*, n. the blue lotus. — *Nīlāmlāna* (°*la-am*°), *as*, m. a species of plant (in Hindī *kālākoraṭhā*) = *dāsī* = *ćhādana*. — *Nīlāmlī* (°*la-am*°), f. a species of shrub. — *Nīlāruṇa* (°*la-ar*°), *as*, m. 'the dark-red' or first dawn of day. — *Nīlāli-kula-saṅkula* (°*la-al*°), 'full of swarms of blue bees,' the plant Rosa Glandulifera. — *Nīlālu* (°*la-ālu*), *us*, m. a species of bulbous plant (= *asitālu*). — *Nīlāśī*, f. the plant Vitex Negundo. — *Nīlāśoka* (°*la-aś*°), *as*, m. an Aśoka with blue blossoms. — *Nīlāśman* (°*la-aś*°), *ā*, m. a blue stone, a sapphire. — *Nīlāśva* (°*la-aś*°), *as*, m., N. of a district. — *Nīlāsana* (°*la-as*°), *as*, m. a species of tree (= *nīla-druma, nīla-niryāsaka*, &c.). — *Nīlāsura* (°*la-as*°), *as*, m., N. of the author of the commentary Nava-kaṇḍikā-bhāshya on Kātyāyana's Śrāddha-sūtras. — *Nīlī-rāga, as*, m. an affection which is unchangeable as the colour of indigo, unalterable attachment; (*as, ā, am*), having the colour of the indigo plant; 'as unchangeable as the indigo colour,' constant in affection; (*as*), m. a firm and constant friend. — *Nīlī-sandhāna, am*, n. fermentation or maceration of indigo. — *Nīlīsandhāna-bhāṇḍa, am*, n. a vessel for steeping indigo, an indigo vat. — *Nīleśvara* (°*la-iś*°), N. of a town on the Malabar shore (Νελκύνδα). — *Nīlotpala* (°*la-ut*°), *am*, n. a blue lotus, the blue water-lily, Nymphæa Cyanea. — *Nīlotpala-maya, as, ī, am*, formed or consisting of blue lotuses. — *Nīlotpalin, ī*, m. an epithet of Mañju-śrī, one of the Jaina saints or teachers. — *Nīloda* (°*la-uda*), *as*, m., N. of an ocean or river with blue water. — *Nīlopala* (°*la-up*°), *am*, n. a blue stone, lapis lazuli.

Nīlaka, as, ā, am, blue, especially an epithet of the third unknown quantity or of its square; (*as*), m. the tree Terminalia Tomentosa (= *asana*); a species of bee (?); a species of antelope, A. Picta; a dark-coloured horse; (*ikā*), f. a species of rank-growing aquatic plant; = *śephālikā*, Nyctanthes Arbor Tristis; = *nīlī*, the indigo plant; = *nīla-sinduvāra*, a species of medicinal plant; a slight malady, black and blue marks on the body from bruises &c.; = *nīlikā-kāća;* N. of a river; (*am*), n. black salt (= *kāća-lavaṇa*); blue steel; blue vitriol; [cf. *kaṇṭha-n*°, *jina-nīlikā*.]

Nīlaṅgu, us, m. (said to be fr. rt. *lag*, to go,

with *nī*), = *nīlāṅgu*, a species of worm growing in the inside of animals; an insect in general; a large bee; a species of fly (= *bhramarālī* or *bhambharālī*); a jackal; = *pra-sūna* or *pra-sūta*, a bud (?).

Nīlāṅgu, us, m. = *nilaṅgu.*

Nīlāya, Nom. P. A. *nīlāyati, -te,* &c., to become blue or dark-coloured.

Nīlikā, see under *nīlaka*, p. 513, col. 3. — *Nīlikā-kāća, as,* m. a disease of the lens or crystalline humor of the eye.

Nīlinī, f. the indigo plant, Indigofera Tinctoria; a species with blue blossoms; N. of the wife of Aja-mīḍha.

Nīliman, ā, m. blueness, blackness, darkness.

नीव् *nīv* [cf. rts. *tīv, pīv, mīv*], cl. 1. P. *nīvati, nīvitum,* to become fat or corpulent.

नीव *nīva, as,* m. a species of tree; [cf. *nīpa.*]

नीवन् *nīvan, ā,* m., N. of one of the ten horses of the Moon.

नीवर *nīvara, as,* m. (said to be fr. rt. 1. *nī*), trade, traffic; a trader; a religious mendicant; a place suitable for the site of a habitation; mud; (*am*), n. water.

नीवाक *nīvāka, as,* m. (fr. *ni-vać*), the increased demand for grain in times of dearth; dearth, scarcity.

नीवार *nīvāra, as,* m. rice growing wild or without cultivation; (*ās*), m. pl. grains of wild rice; (*ā*), f., N. of a river.

Nīvāraka, as, m. rice growing wild or without cultivation.

नीवि *nīvi, is* and *ī*, f. (probably fr. rt. *vye* with *nī*), a cloth worn round a woman's waist or the ends of the cloth passed round the loins so as to hold the whole together; a petticoat; the tie or encircling band of a woman's drawers; the outer tie of a packet in which the offerings of a Śūdra at funeral obsequies are presented; capital, principal, stock; a stake at play, stake, wager. — *Nīvi-bhārya, as, ā, am,* Ved. to be worn in an apron, &c.

नीवृत *nī-vṛit, t, t, t,* m. f. n. (fr. *vṛit* with *ni*), any inhabited country, a realm.

नीव्र *nīvra, am,* n. the edge of a thatch, the edge or side of a sloping roof; a thatch, a roof; a wood; the circumference of a wheel; the constellation Revatī; the moon; [cf. *nīdhra.*]

नीशार *nī-śāra, as,* m. (fr. *śṛī* with *ni*), a warm cloth or outer garment, a blanket; curtains, musquito curtains; an outer tent or screen.

नीषह् *nī-shah, āṭ, āṭ, āṭ* (fr. *sah* with *ni*), Ved. overpowering.

नीहार *nī-hāra, as,* m. (fr. rt. *hṛi* with *ni*?), fog, mist; frost, hoar-frost, heavy dew; evacuation. — *Nīhāra-kara, as,* m. 'dew-maker' or 'cold-rayed,' the moon.

Nīhārāya, Nom. A. *nīhārāyate,* &c., to make frost.

नु 1. *nu,* ind. (perhaps related to 1. *nava;* cf. *nūtana*), written *nū* in Ved. at the beginning of a verse and frequently in other places. (As an adverb of time in Ved.), now, still (e. g. *nū-ća purā-ća,* both now and heretofore; *asti svin nu vīryaṃ tat te,* hast thou still that power?). (As an inferential particle in Ved. often beginning the last sentence of a hymn), now therefore, now then, therefore, then (e. g. *nū no rāsva,* do thou therefore give us): (as an introductory particle, or in encouraging, invoking, inviting, summoning), now, then, pray, come then (e. g. *abhi nu mā ćakshamīthāḥ,* pray now [Sāy. quickly] have compassion upon me). *Nu* is often employed in questions, both in Vedic and classical Sanskṛit, to strengthen an interrogative pronoun or adverb (e. g. *kadā nu,* when indeed? *kathaṃ nu,* how indeed? *kva nu,* where indeed? *kaṃ nu pṛiććhāmi,* whom can I possibly ask? *kiṃ nu syāt,* what can that possibly be? *kiṃ nu khalu,* why in the world?). *Nu* is also used interrogatively in classical Sanskṛit, without an interrogative pronoun, in sentences of two or more clauses (e. g. *svapno nu māyā nu mati-bhramo nu,* was it a dream? or an illusion of magic? or a mental delusion?). *Nu* also serves as a particle of affirmation, to express 'indeed,' 'certainly,' 'surely' (e. g. *ahaṃ nu akārsham,* Yes, I certainly did so), and often gives emphasis to the word it follows without being itself translateable, in which way it is frequently connected in the Veda with other particles (e. g. with *ćid* in *ćin nu;* with *id* in *in nu;* with *adha* in *adha nu;* with *gha* in *ghā nu,* &c.); but in the Veda *nu* sometimes means 'never' (especially in the construction *nū ćit* = never, nevermore; in other passages it is said to = 'from this time forward,' 'for ever'). In classical Sanskṛit *nu* is sometimes found in connection with *vā,* 'or;' and in Rāmāyaṇa II. 72, 27, *nu—nu* may be translated 'either'—'or.' According to native commentators on the Veda *nu* often = *kshipram,* quickly. According to native lexicographers *nu* is used in the following senses: *pṛićchā, vikalpa, vitarka, anunaya, atīta, apamāna, hetu, apadeśa;* [cf. *nū-nam, nū-tana;* Zend *nū,* 'just now;' Gr. νύ, νῦ-νί, νῦν; Lat. *num, nun-c;* Goth. *nu-h;* Old Germ. *nu;* Slav. *nyne,* 'at present.']

नु 2. *nu, us,* m. a weapon; time; a boat; (probably only at the end of a comp.; cf. *nau.*)

नु 3. *nu,* cl. 1. A. *navate,* &c., to go: Caus. *nāvayati,* &c., (probably) to move from a place, remove; (according to a Schol.) to make new.

नु 4. *nu,* cl. 2, or *nū,* cl. 6. P. *nauti, nuvati, nunāva, navishyati, nuvishyati, anāvīt, anuvīt, navitum, nuvitum,* to roar, cry, low, bray, &c.; to sound; to shout; to exult; to praise, commend (with acc.): Caus. *nāvayati, anūnavat:* Desid. *nunūshati:* Intens. *nonūyate, nonoti,* to sound loudly, roar, be tumultuous.

5. *nu, us,* f. praise, eulogium.

Nuta, as, ā, am, praised, commended.

Nuti, is, f. praise, laudation, eulogium, panegyric; worship, reverence.

1. *nūta, as, ā, am,* praised, eulogized, lauded, hymned.

नुड् *nuḍ,* cl. 6. P. *nuḍati,* &c., to hurt, strike, kill.

नुद् 1. *nud,* cl. 6. P. A. *nudati, -te, nunoda, nunude, notsyati, -te, anautsīt, anutta, nottum,* to push, push on, impel, incite, propel, urge on, push away, drive away, repel, banish; to move, remove; to throw, shoot, cast, send; to raise, lift up (Ved.): Caus. *nodayati, -yitum,* to push on, incite, excite: Intens. *nonudyate, nonotti,* to push or impel or drive away repeatedly; [cf. Angl. Sax. *nyd-ian,* 'to compel;' *a-nydan,* 'to repel;' *niot-an:* Goth. *niut-an:* perhaps Gr. νύσσα.]

Nutta, as, ā, am, pushed away, despatched, sent, ordered; (*as*), m. a plant, see *lakuća.*

2. *nud, t, t, t* (at the end of a comp.), driving away, removing, rejecting, repelling.

Nuda, as, ā, am (at the end of a comp.), pushing, impelling, driving away, removing.

Nudat, an, ati or *antī, at,* urging forward.

Nudita, as, ā, am, (ep.) = *nutta, nunna.*

Nunutsu, us, us, u, desirous of impelling or inciting or removing.

Nunna, as, ā, am, pushed, propelled; pushed away; thrown, cast; dismissed, sent, despatched.

2. *nūta, as, ā, am,* = *nutta* or *nunna.*

नूतन *nūtana, as, ā, am* (fr. 1. *nu* and connected with 1. *nava,* q. v.), new, novel, recent, modern, fresh, young, (opposed to *pūrva, purāṇa,* &c.); present; instantaneous, sudden; curious, strange. — *Nūtana-tā,* f. or *nūtana-tva, am,* n. newness, novelty.

Nūtanaya, Nom. P. *nūtanayati,* &c., to make new, renew.

Nūtna, as, ā, am, new, fresh, young, recent. — *Nūtna-vayas, ās, ās, as,* in the bloom of youth, in the spring of life.

नूद *nūda, as,* m. the mulberry tree, Morus Indica.

नूनम् *nūnam,* ind. (fr. 1. *nu*), now, at present (Ved.); just now, just, exactly (Ved.); immediately (Ved.); from this time forward, for the future (Ved.); now then, therefore (Ved.); probably, in all probability, perhaps; without doubt, certainly, assuredly, surely, indeed. — *Nūna-bhāva, as,* m. probability; (*āt*), ind. in all probability, probably, indeed.

नूपुर *nūpura, as, am,* m. n. an ornament for the toes or ancles or feet, an anklet; (*as*), m., N. of a descendant of Ikshvāku. — *Nūpura-vat, ān, atī, at,* adorned with anklets or foot-ornaments.

नृ *nṛi, nā,* m. (said to be fr. rt. 1. *nī,* cf. rt. *nṝ*, see Gram. 128. *b;* the gen. pl. may be *narām* or *nṛiṇām* in Ved., but generally *nṝṇām* in classical Sanskṛit), a leader (said of gods), a man, person, mankind, people (generally pl.); a piece at chess, &c.; the pin or gnomon of a sun-dial; (in grammar) a masculine word; a horse (Ved.); [cf. *nara:* Zend *nar, nara,* 'a man;' *nairya,* 'manly:' Gr. ἀνήρ, ἠνορ-έη, ἀγ-ήνωρ, ἄνθρ-ωπο-ς, 'man's face:' Sabin. *nero,* 'brave;' *ner-io,* 'fortitude:' Hib. *nearth* = Welsh *nerth,* 'virtue.'] — *Nṛi-kukkura, as,* m. 'man-dog,' a dog of a man. — *Nṛi-keśarin* or *nṛi-kesarin, ī,* m. a being, half man and half lion; Vishṇu in his fourth Ava-tāra as man-lion. — *Nṛi-ga, as,* m., N. of several persons; an old king; a grandson of Oghavat; a son of Uśīnara by Nṛigā (he was ancestor of the Yaudheyas); a son of Manu; the father of Sumati; (*ā*), f., N. of the wife of Uśīnara and mother of Nṛiga. — *Nṛiga-śāpa, as,* m. 'the curse of Nṛiga,' N. of the fiftieth chapter of the Uttara-kāṇḍa of the Rāmāyaṇa. — *Nṛigākhyāna* (°*ga-ākh*°), *am,* n. 'the tale of Nṛiga,' an episode of the Mahā-bh. Anuśāsana-p. 3452; N. of the twenty-fourth chapter of the Pārtha Itihāsa-samuććaya. — *Nṛigopākhyāna* (°*ga-up*°), *am,* n. 'the episode of Nṛiga,' N. of the forty-ninth chapter of the Uttara-kāṇḍa of the Rāmāyaṇa. — *Nṛi-ćakshas, ās, ās, as,* Ved. seeing or observing men, (an epithet of the Sun, Savitṛi, Soma, Agni, &c.); leading or guiding men; living among men; (Sāy.) seeing men or injuring men; (*ās*), m. 'waiting for men,' a demon, a Rākshasa, a goblin. — *Nṛi-ćakshus, us, us, us,* seeing with human eyes; (*us*), m., N. of a prince, a grandson or son of Su-nītha. — *Nṛi-ćandra, as,* m. 'man-moon,' N. of a prince, son of Rantināra. — *Nṛi-jagdha, as,* m. 'man-eater,' a cannibal, a Rākshasa. — *Nṛi-jala, am,* n. human urine. — *Nṛi-jāti, is,* f. the human race. — *Nṛi-jit, t, t, t,* Ved. conquering men; (Sāy.) conquering leaders; (*t*), m., N. of an Ekāha. — *Nṛi-tama, as, ā, am,* most manly. — *Nṛi-deva, as,* m. 'man-god,' a god among men, a king. — *Nṛi-dharman, ā, ā, a,* acting as a man, doing a man's duty; (*ā*), m. a N. of Kuvera; (*a*), n. manly quality or duty. — *Nṛi-dhūta, as, ā, am,* Ved. shaken about or stirred by men (as the Soma). — *Nṛi-namana, am,* n. the bending or bowing of men (?). — *Nṛi-pa, as,* m. a protector of men, a warrior, a prince, king, sovereign. — *Nṛipa-kanda, as,* m. a species of onion (= *rāja-palāṇḍu*). — *Nṛipa-kriyā,* f. 'king's act,' government, dominion. — *Nṛipa-gṛiha, am,* n. 'king's house,' the habitation of a prince, a palace. — *Nṛipañ-jaya, as,* m., N. of two princes, a son of Su-vīra and a son of Medhāvin. — *Nṛi-pati, is,* m. 'lord of men,' a king, prince, sovereign, (also applied to gods); an epithet of Kuvera. — *Nṛipati-patha, as,* m. (?), 'king's road,' royal road, chief street. — Nṛipati-vallabha, as, m. 'king's favourite,' a species of medicinal plant. — Nṛipati-śāsana, am, n. a king's order, edict. — Nṛi-patnī, f., Ved. a king's wife, queen. — Nṛipa-tra, am, n. royalty, sovereignty, dominion; nṛipatvaṃ kṛi, to reign. — Nṛipa-dīpa, as, m. 'king-lamp,' a king who is like a lamp. — Nṛipa-druma, as, m. the plant Cathartocarpus (Cassia) Fistula; a species of tree (= rājādanī). — Nṛipa-dvish, ṭ, ṭ, ṭ, king-hating. — Nṛipa-nīti, is, f. royal policy, king-craft. — Nṛipa-priya, as, m. a thorny species of bamboo, Bambusa Spinosa; a variety of Saccharum Sara; rice; a species of onion; the mango tree; (ā), f. the tree Pandanus Odoratissimus; a species of date tree. — Nṛipapriya-phalā, f. Solanum Melongena. — Nṛipa-badara, as, m. a species of jujube; (am), n. its fruit. — Nṛipa-mandira, am, n. a king's residence, a royal palace. — Nṛipa-māngalyaka, am, n. Tabernæmontana Coronaria. — Nṛipa-māna, as, m. (?), music played before kings when eating or feasting; [cf. nṛipābhīra.] — Nṛipa-lakshman, a, n. a mark or symbol of a king, any one of the royal insignia, especially the white umbrella. — Nṛipa-liṅga, am, n. an emblem or mark of royalty. — Nṛipaliṅga-dhara, as, ā, am, assuming the insignia of sovereignty; taking (fraudulently) the emblem or marks of the royal or military caste. — Nṛipa-vallabha, as, ā, am, dear to a king; (as), m. the friend or favourite of a king; a species of mango; (ā), f. a king's wife, a queen; a species of plant. — Nṛipa-vṛiksha, as, m. = rāja-vṛiksha. — Nṛipa-śāsana, am, n. a royal edict. — Nṛi-paśu, us, m. 'man-beast,' a brute of a man; a man serving as a sacrificial victim. — Nṛipa-śreshṭha, as, m. the best of kings. — Nṛipa-saṃśraya, as, m. seeking the protection of kings, service of princes. — Nṛipa-sabha, am, n. an assembly of princes; a royal palace. — Nṛipa-suta, as, m. a king's son, a prince; (ā), f. 'a king's daughter,' the musk-rat. — Nṛipa-snushā, f. the daughter-in-law of a king. — Nṛipāṅśa (°pa-aṅ°), as, m. king's share, royal portion (i. e. a sixth, eighth, or twelfth of grain, a sixth of fruit, a fiftieth of merchandise &c.), royal revenue. — Nṛipākrishṭa (°pa-āk°), a particular favourable position of the pieces in the game Catur-aṅga (a kind of chess). — Nṛipāṅgaṇa and nṛipāṅgana (°pa-aṅ°), am, n. a royal court. — Nṛi-pāṇa, as, ā, am, Ved. giving drink to men. — Nṛi-pātṛi, tā, m., Ved. the protector of men. — Nṛipātmaja (°pa-āt°), as, ā, am, of royal birth; (as), m. a king's son, a prince; (ā), f. a king's daughter, a princess; a bitter gourd. — Nṛipādhama (°pa-adh°), as, m. a bad king. — Nṛipādhvara (°pa-adh°), as, m. a sort of sacrifice (the Rāja-sūya) held by a lord paramount in which all the offices are performed by tributary princes. — Nṛipānućara (°pa-an°), as, m. a king's attendant, a minister. — Nṛipānna (°pa-an°), am, n. 'royal rice,' a sort of rice. — Nṛipānyatva (°pa-an°), am, n. change of government. — Nṛipābhīra (°pa-ābh°), am, n. music played at the royal meals. — Nṛipāmaya (°pa-ām°), as, m. 'king's disease or evil,' consumption. — Nṛi-pāyya, as, ā, am, Ved. protecting men; (Sāy.) to be drunk by the leaders or gods, or to be protected by the leaders of the sacrifice. — Nṛi-pāla, as, m. 'protector of men,' a king. — Nṛipālaya (°pa-āl°), as, m. a king's residence, a palace. — Nṛipāvarta (°pa-āv°), am, n. a kind of gem (= rājāvarta). — Nṛipāsana (°pa-ās°), am, n. the seat of a king, a throne, a chair of state. — Nṛipāspada (°pa-ās°), am, n. a king's residence, a palace. — Nṛipāhvaya (°pa-āh°), as, m. a species of onion (= rāja-palāṇḍu). — Nṛi-pīti, is, f., Ved. the protection of men. — Nṛipećchā (°pa-ić°), f. the royal pleasure. — Nṛi-peśas, ās, ās, as, Ved. (according to Sāy. f.), 'man-shaped,' having the form of men; (probably) formed or decorated by men. — Nṛipoćita (°pa-uć°), as, ā, am, suited to a king, kingly, princely; (as), m. a species of bean (= rāja-māsha). — Nṛi-bāhu, us, m., Ved. a man's arm. — Nṛi-bhartṛi, tā, m. 'lord of men,' a prince, sovereign. — Nṛi-maṇas, ās, ās, as, Ved. propitious or well-disposed towards men, honoured by men; epithet of Indra; (Sāy.) having the mind turned towards men. — Nṛimaṇasya, Nom. A. nṛimaṇasyate, Ved. to be friendly or propitious to men. — Nṛi-maṇi, is, m., N. of a demon said to seize on children; [cf. graha.] — Nṛi-mat, ān, atī, at, abounding in men; (ān), m., N. of a man. — Nṛi-mara, as, ā, am, 'man-destroying,' killing men. — Nṛi-māṅsa, am, n. the flesh of men. — Nṛi-mādana, as, ā, am, Ved. exhilarating or gladdening men. — Nṛi-mithuna, am, n. the sign of the zodiac Gemini. — Nṛi-megha, as, m. 'man-cloud,' a man compared to a cloud or who has qualities like that of a cloud yielding rain. — Nṛi-medha, as, m. 'man-sacrifice' [cf. nṛi-yajña], N. of a man, an Aṅgirasa and author of two hymns of the Ṛig-veda. — Nṛi-yajña, as, m. 'man-offering,' the sacrifice to be offered to men, i. e. hospitality. — Nṛi-yugma, am, n. the sign of the zodiac Gemini. — Nṛi-loka, as, m. the world of men, the earth. — 1. nṛi-vat, ān, atī, at, Ved. having men, manly, belonging to men, fit for men, consisting of men, accompanied by men. — 2. nṛi-vat, ind., Ved. like a man, in a manly way, strongly, powerfully, bravely; in abundance. — Nṛivat-sakhi, is, is, i, Ved. having manly companions. — Nṛi-varāha, as, m. 'man-boar,' Vishṇu in his boar incarnation (with the figure of a man and the head of the wild boar). — Nṛi-vāhana, as, ā, am, or nṛi-vāhas, ās, ās, as, Ved. carrying or bearing men; (Sāy.) conveying leaders or chiefs (i. e. the Aśvins). — Nṛi-vīra, as, m. 'man-hero,' a hero of a man, a hero among men. — Nṛi-veshṭana, as, ā, am, encircled with (the bones of) men; (as), m. an epithet of Śiva. — Nṛi-śaṅsa, as, ā, am, to be desired or praised by men (Ved.); hurting or injuring men, malicious, noxious, cruel, wicked, hurtful, injurious to mankind, mischievous, base, destructive; [cf. Zend nairya śaṅgho.] — Nṛiśaṅsa-tā, f. mischievousness, maliciousness, vileness, baseness. — Nṛiśaṅsa-vat, ān, atī, at, malicious, vile. — Nṛiśaṅsa-vṛitta, as, ā, am, practising mischief. — Nṛiśaṅsya, as, ā, am, malicious, mischievous, vile; (am), n. injury to man, maliciousness, mischievousness, vileness. — Nṛi-śṛiṅga, am, n. 'man's horn,' any chimerical or impossible thing. — Nṛi-shad, t, t, t, Ved. dwelling among men, (in some passages applied to ćaitanya, consciousness, or buddhi, understanding); (t), m., N. of the father of Kaṇva; [cf. nārshada.] — Nṛi-shadana, am, n., Ved. an assemblage of men, residence of men; (Sāy.) the hall of sacrifice, the receptacle of oblations, the house of the sacrificing priest. — Nṛi-shadvan, ā, arī, a, or nṛi-shadman, ā, ā, a, Ved. sitting or living among men. — Nṛi-shah or nṛi-shāh, ṭ, ṭ, ṭ, Ved. overpowering or overcoming men. — Nṛi-shahya or nṛi-shāhya, as, ā, am, Ved. overpowering men; (Sāy.) to be borne by men; (am), n. the overpowering of men; battle (as to be borne by men). — Nṛi-shā, ās, ās, am (fr. nṛi + sā = san), Ved. granting or procuring men. — Nṛi-shāć, k, k, k, Ved. serving men, friendly or benevolent to men; an epithet of the Maruts. — Nṛi-shāti, is, f., Ved. 'capturing or making spoil of men,' i. e. battle, (in Ṛig-veda VII. 27, 1, nṛi-shātā is Ved. loc., but according to Sāy. it is nom. c. of nṛi-shātṛi, benefactor of men.) — Nṛi-shūta, as, ā, am, Ved. impelled or incited by men. — Nṛi-siṅha, as, m. 'man-lion,' a lion among men, a chief, a noble, a great or illustrious man; Vishṇu in his fourth Ava-tāra or incarnation in the shape of a man with the head and claws of a lion [cf. nara-siṅha]; a kind of coitus; N. of several men. — Nṛisiṅha-kavaća, am, n., N. of a chapter of the Tantra-sāra. — Nṛisiṅha-ćaturdaśī, f. the fourteenth day in the light half of the month Vaiśākha (a festival). — Nṛisiṅha-ćampū, ūs, f., N. of a work. — Nṛisiṅha-tāpanīya, as or am, m. or n. (?), N. of an Upanishad. — Nṛisiṅhatāpanīyopanishad-bhāshya, am, n., N. of a commentary on the preceding Upanishad by Śaṅkarāćārya. — Nṛisiṅha-purāṇa, am, n., N. of an Upa-Purāṇa. — Nṛisiṅha-prasāda, as, m., N. of an author mentioned in the Śūdra-dharma-tattva. — Nṛisiṅha-prādurbhāva, as, m. 'the manifestation of the man-lion,' N. of the thirty-ninth to the forty-third chapter of the Narasiṅha-Purāṇa. — Nṛisiṅha-bhaṭṭa, as, m., N. of a man. — Nṛisiṅha-vana, as, m., N. of a district in the north-west of Madhya-deśa. — Nṛisiṅha-sarasvatī, m., N. of a commentator on the Vedānta-sāra. — Nṛisiṅhāćārya (°ha-āć°), as, m., N. of an author. — Nṛisiṅhāśrama (°ha-āś°), as, m., N. of the author of the Prayoga-ratna. — Nṛisiṅhīya, as, ā, am, relating to Nṛi-siṅha; N. of a book. — Nṛi-sena, am, ā, n. f. an army of men. — Nṛi-soma, as, m. 'man-moon,' any illustrious or great man, a prince or chief. — Nṛi-han, ā, ghnī, a, Ved. killing men. — Nṛi-hari, is, m. Vishṇu in his fourth Ava-tāra as the man-lion [cf. nara-siṅha]; N. of a man. — Nṛ-asthi-mālin, ī, inī, i, decorated with a garland of human bones; (ī), m. an epithet of Śiva.

Nṛimṇa, am, n., Ved. manhood (virtus), power, strength, wealth, ability, courage; (as, ā, am), making happy; (as), m. 'giving happiness,' an epithet of Kṛishṇa. — Nṛimṇa-vardhana, as, ā, am, Ved. enhancing courage.

नृत् 1. nṛit, cl. 4. P. nṛityati (ep. also -te), nanarta, nartsyati and nartishyati, anartīt, nartitum, to dance; to act on the stage; represent (as an actor), gesticulate, play: Caus. nartayati, -yitum, to cause to dance: Desid. ninṛitsati and ninartishati: Intens. narnartti, narnṛititi, narinartti, narinṛitīti, narīnartti, narīnṛitīti, narinṛityate, to dance about, dance with vehement gesticulations; (P.) to cause to dance about or to and fro.

2. nṛit, t, f., Ved. dancing, gesticulation, gesture.

Nṛiti, is, f. dancing, acting, playing; (perhaps in Ved.) lovely or grand appearance.

Nṛitu, us, us, u, Ved. dancing, gesticulating, lively, active, (generally as an epithet of Indra); (nṛitū, ūs), m. a dancer, an actor, a mime; the earth; a worm; length.

Nṛitta, am, n. dancing, acting, gesticulation. — Nṛitta-maya, as, ī, am, consisting in dance.

Nṛitya, am, n. dancing, acting, dance, gesticulation, pantomime. — Nṛitya-gīta-vādya, āni, n. pl. dancing, singing, and instrumental music. — Nṛitya-priya, as, ā, am, fond of dancing; (as), m. a peacock; (ā), f., N. of one of the Mātṛis attending on Skanda. — Nṛitya-śālā, f. a dancing-room. — Nṛitya-sarvasva, am, n. 'the whole essence of dancing,' N. of a work. — Nṛitya-sthāna, am, n. a place for dancing, a dancing-room.

Nṛityat, an, antī, at, dancing.

नृपीट nṛipīṭa, am, n., Ved. a various reading (in the Nighaṇṭus) for kṛipīṭa, q. v.

नृमणा nṛimaṇā, f., N. of a river.

नॄ nṝ, cl. 9. P. nṛiṇāti, nanāra, &c., to lead: Caus. narayati, nārayati, &c.

नेक्षण nekshaṇa, am, n., Ved. a sharp stick, a spear, a fork or similar cooking implement; [cf. nīkshaṇa, mekshaṇa.]

नेग nega, ās, m. pl., N. of a school of the Sāma-veda; [cf. naigeya.]

नेजक nejaka, as, m. (fr. rt. nij), a washerman.

Nejana, am, n. washing, cleansing.

नेजमेष nejamesha, as, m., N. of a demon hurtful to children.

नेतव्य netavya, netṛi, &c. See p. 511, col. 2.

नेत्र netra, netrika, &c. See p. 511, col. 3.

नेद् 1. ned or net, ind. (fr. na + id, and regarded in the Pada-pāṭha as two words), Ved. not,

not indeed (Sāy. = *naiva*); that not; (see Pāṇ. VIII. 1, 30; cf. Zend *noiḍ*, 'not.')

नेद् 2. *ned* [cf. rt. 1. *nid*], cl. 1. P. *nedati*, &c., to censure, blame; to be near; to go.

Nedaya (fr. *neda*, see *nedishṭha*), Nom. P. *nedayati*, &c., to bring near.

Nedayat, an, antī, at, bringing near, approximating.

Nedishṭha, as, ā, am (superl. of *neda* which is substituted for *antika*, near; probably allied to *naddha* fr. rt. 1. *nah*), the nearest, next, very near; (*am*), ind. very nearly, next, in the first place; (*āt*), ind. from the neighbourhood; (*as*), m. Alangium Hexapetalum; N. of a son of Manu; [cf. Zend *nazdista*.] — *Nedishṭha-tama, as, ā, am*, Ved. the nearest of all.

Nedishṭhin, ī, inī, i, very near, very nearly related.

Nedīyas, ān, asī, as (compar. of *neda* which is substituted for *antika*), nearer, very near, as near as possible.

नेन्य *nenya, as, ā, am* (fr. Intens. of rt. 1. *nī*), taking or obtaining frequently (?).

नेप *nepa, as*, m. (said to be fr. rt. 1. *nī*), a family priest; (*am*), n. water.

नेपथ्य *nepathya, am*, n. (for *nar-pathya*, i. e. *nṛi-pathya*? cf. *vetana* for *vartana*), an ornament, embellishment, decoration, the costume of an actor, attire, (in this sense said to be also m.); the part of a stage behind the scenes (or rather behind the curtain which was stretched across the stage and served for scenes), the space behind the curtain or scenes where the decorations were kept and where the actors attired themselves; the postscenium; the tiring-room; *nepathye*, loc. sing. (a voice) in the postscenium or behind the scenes, (used in the plays as a stage-direction, where anything is to be said by an actor behind the scenes.)

नेपाल *nepāla, as*, m. (said to be contracted fr. *niyama-pāla*, q. v., the N. of a sage); N. of a country, Nepal; a species of sugar-cane; (*ās*), m. pl., N. of the people inhabiting Nepal; (*ī*), f. red arsenic; the wild date tree or its fruit; (*am*), n. copper. — *Nepāla-jā*, f. or *nepāla-jātā*, f. red arsenic. — *Nepāla-nimba, as*, m. 'the Nepal Nimba,' a species of tree. — *Nepāla-mūlaka, am*, n. a radish.

Nepālaka, am, n. copper; (*ikā*), f. red arsenic.

Naipāla, as, ī, am, produced &c. in Nepal; (*as*), m. a species of sugar-cane; the Nepal Nimba, a species of tree; (*ī*), f. red arsenic; a species of plant, Arabian jasmine, Jasminum Zambac and Nyctanthes Arbor Tristis; the indigo plant.

Naipālika, as, ī, am, produced in or brought from Nepal; (*am*), n. copper.

Naipālīya, as, ī, am, produced in or brought from Nepal. — *Naipālīya-devatā-kalyāṇa-pañća-vinśatikā*, f., N. of a Buddhist work.

नेम *nema, as, ā, am* (fr. rt. *nam* with *e* instead of reduplication, but said to be fr. rt. 1. *nī*; *nema* is one of the *sarvādi* or pronominals according to Pāṇ. I. 1, 27, but the nom. pl. m. is either *neme* or *nemās*), Ved. some, a few, several, (according to Sāy. *nema* = *alpa, katipaya*; *neme* = *ke-ćane*, also = *ete*, these); the one, the other; half; (*as*), m. a part, portion; time, period, season; term, boundary, limit; a fence, enclosure, a boundary wall or hedge; the foundation of a wall; a hole, a chasm; fraud, deceit; acting, dancing; evening; a root; food (Ved.); upper part, above; (*am*), n. a particular number; [cf. Zend *naima*.] — *Nema-ćandra, as*, m. 'the half moon,' N. of a prince of Bengal. — *Nema-dhita, as, ā, am*, Ved. divided, set at variance; (*ās*), m. pl., scil. *saṅgrāmāḥ*, battles in which only some are engaged; (*as*), m., scil. *Indraḥ*, the sharer of half the oblation, the other half going to all the gods; (see Sāy. on Ṛig-veda I. 72, 4.) — *Nema-dhiti, is*, f., Ved. battle, conflict, dispute. — *Nema-nātha, as*, m., N. of a man who is also called Nitya-nātha. — *Nema-sāha, as*, m., N. of a man. — *Nemāditya* (°*ma-āḍ*°), *as*, m., N. of a man, father of Trivikrama-bhaṭṭa, the author of the Damayantī-kathā.

Nemi, is, ī, f. the circumference or ring or felly or outer rim of a wheel; edge, rim; a windlass or frame-work for the rope of a well; a thunderbolt, a circle or circumference in general, the earth; (*is*), m. the plant Dalbergia Ougeinensis; N. of a Daitya; (with Jainas) N. of the twenty-second Arhat of the present Ut-sarpiṇī; N. of a Cakra-vartin; a sacred place, as Mathurā (?). — *Nemi-ćakra, as*, m. a prince descended from Parīkshit, who is said to have removed the capital of India to Kauśāmbi after the inundation of Hāstina-pura. — *Nemin-dhara, as*, m., N. of a mountain.

Nemin, ī, m. the tree Dalbergia Ougeinensis; (with Jainas) N. of the twenty-second Arhat of the present Ut-sarpiṇī.

नेमन्निष् *nemann-ish, ṭ, ṭ, ṭ*, Ved. (perhaps) following guidance?; (according to Sāy. on Ṛig-veda I. 56, 2), moving reverentially or bearing oblations.

नेय *neya*. See p. 511, col. 3.

नेल *nela, as*, or *nelu, us*, or *nevala, as*, m. a particular number.

नेष् *nesh*, cl. 1. A. *neshate, nineshe*, &c., to go, move.

नेष *nesha* (fr. rt. 1. *nī*), forming a superlative *nesha-tama*, occurring in the inst. pl. *nesha-tamais*, used adverbially in Ṛig-veda I. 141, 12, = with the best guidance, by the most effective means; (Sāy.) most conducive.

Neshan, ā or *a*, m. or n. (?), Ved. leading, conducting; (Sāy.) *neshaṇi* = *netarye vishaye*.

Neshṭri, ṭā, m. one of the chief officiating priests at a Soma sacrifice, he who leads forward the wife of the sacrificer and prepares the Surā. In Ṛig-veda I. 15, 3, Neshṭri is said to be another name of Tvashṭri from his having assumed upon some occasion the function of the Neshṭri priest.

Neshṭra, am, n. the Soma vessel of the Neshṭri; the office of the Neshṭri.

Neshṭrīya, as, ā, am, belonging to the Neshṭri priest, relating to him.

नेष्ट *neshṭa, as, ā, am* (fr. *na* + *ishṭa*), not wished for, undesired, disagreeable, unfavourable.

नैःश्रेयस *naiḥśreyasa, as, ī, am* (fr. *niḥ-śreyasa*), leading to happiness or future beatitude; (*am*), n., N. of a wood in the world of Vishṇu; N. of a fabulous forest.

Naiḥśreyasika, as, ī, am, leading to happiness, conducive to future beatitude.

नैःस्नेह्य *naiḥsnehya, am*, n. (fr. *niḥ-sneha*), absence of love, want of affection, coldness.

नैःस्व्य *naiḥsvya, am*, n. (fr. *niḥ-sva*), absence of property, destitution, poverty.

नैक *naika, as, ā, am* (fr. *na* + *eka*), not one, more than one, several, manifold, various, numerous, many. — *Naika-ćara, as, ā* or *ī, am*, going about in troops or flocks, gregarious, living in society, not living alone. — *Naika-duḥkha-dā, ās, ās, am*, causing many sorrows. — *Naika-driś, k*, m., N. of one of the sons of Viśvā-mitra. — *Naika-prishṭha, ās*, m. pl., N. of a people. — *Naika-bhārāśraya* (°*ra-āś*°), *as, ā, am*, 'not abiding in one condition,' changeable, fickle, unsteady. — *Naika-bheda, as, ā, am*, of many kinds, various, multiform, manifold. — *Naika-rūpa, as, ā, am*, multiform, of various kinds, various. — *Naika-varṇa, as, ā, am*, many coloured, of various colours. — *Naika-śastra-maya, as, ī, am*, consisting of a multitude of arrows or of various missiles. — *Naikātman* (°*ka-āt*°), *ā, ā, a*, of manifold nature; (*ā*), m. an epithet of Śiva.

Naikadhā, ind. in many ways, in various ways, manifoldly, in many parts, in many directions, on various sides.

Naikaśas, ind. in great numbers, repeatedly, several times, often.

नैकटिक *naikaṭika, as, ī, am* (fr. *ni-kaṭa*), near, contiguous, neighbouring, living in the neighbourhood.

Naikaṭya, am, n. nearness, proximity, neighbourhood, vicinage.

नैकती *naikatī*, f., N. of a village in the North of India.

नैकषेय *naikasheya, as*, m. a child of Nikashā, a Rākshasa, fiend, goblin; N. of a race of Rākshasas; (also read *naikaseya*.)

नैकृतिक *naikṛitika, as, ī, am* (fr. *ni-kṛiti*), dishonest, wicked, low, vile, morose, harsh spoken; fallacious, (Manu IV. 196.)

नैखान्य *naikhānya, as, ā, am* (fr. *ni-khāna*, see *ni-khan*), liable to be buried.

नैगम *naigama, as, ī, am* (fr. *ni-gama*), relating to Vedic quotations or Vedic words, relating or belonging to the Veda or holy writ, occurring in it, Vedic; (*as*), m. an interpreter of the sacred writings; an Upanishad or portion of the Vedas; a way, road (?); a means, an expedient; prudent conduct; a citizen, a townsman; a trader, a merchant; N. of an ancient teacher. — *Naigama-kāṇḍa*, N. of the second part of the Nirukta, or of the fourth, fifth, and sixth books of that work, where Yāska explains the Nigamas or Vedic words collected in the fourth Adhyāya of the Nighaṇṭus, (also called *Aikapadika*.)

Naigamika, as, ī, am, connected with or peculiar to the Vedas.

नैगमेय *naigameya, as*, m. a form of Skanda, (considered also as his son and play-fellow; cf. *naigamesha*.)

नैगमेष *naigamesha, as*, m., N. of a demon with the head of a ram, (supposed to seize or injure children.)

नैगुत *naiguta, as, ī, am* (fr. *nigut*), Ved. destroying enemies.

नैगेय *naigeya, ās*, m. pl., N. of a school of the Sāma-veda.

नैघण्टुक *naighaṇṭuka, as, ī, am* (fr. *nighaṇṭu*, q. v.), mentioned by the way; (*am*), n. 'a collection of words,' N. of the whole five chapters of the Vedic glossary commented upon by Yāska, but especially of the first three chapters treating of synonyms.

नैचाशाख *naićāśākha, as, ī, am* (fr. *nīćā* + *śākhā*), Ved. belonging to the low branches of the community, i. e. belonging to the lower orders or common people; (*am*), n. (perhaps) low or common people; (Sāy.) N. of a town.

नैचिक *naićika, am*, n. the head of an ox; (*ī*), f. an excellent cow, a cow exhibiting excellent marks on her head.

नैचित्य *naićitya, as*, m. a prince of the Nićitas.

नैचुल *naićula, as, ī, am* (fr. *ni-ćula*), belonging to or produced by the Barringtonia Acutangula.

नैज *naija, as, ī, am* (fr. *ni-ja*), own, one's own.

नैतन्धव *naitandhava, as*, m., N. of a place on the Sarasvatī.

नैतोश *naitośa, as, ī, am* (fr. *ni-tośa*), Ved. (perhaps) granting, giving.

नैत्य *naitya, as, ā* (?), *am* (fr. *nitya*), continual, perpetual, constant, regularly repeated; (*am*), n. eternity, perpetuity.

Naityaka, as, ī, am, to be done always or regularly and not only on certain occasions, (opposed to *naimittika*); regularly recurring, constantly repeated; constant, indispensable, obligatory.
Naityika, as, ī, am, invariable, constant, perpetual, indispensable.

नैदाघ **naidāgha**, *as, ī, am* (fr. *ni-dāgha*), Ved. peculiar or belonging to the hot season, summer-like, scorching; (*as*), m. summer time.
Naidāghika or *naidāghīya, as, ī, am*, peculiar to the summer, summer-like.

नैदान **naidāna**, *as*, m. (fr. *ni-dāna*), an etymologist (who investigates the sources of words).
Naidānika, as, m. a pathologist (who inquires into the causes of diseases).

नैदेशिक **naideśika**, *as, ī, am* (fr. *ni-deśa*), executing orders, a servant.

नैद्र **naidra**, *as, ī, am* (fr. *ni-drā*), sleepy, soporific, somniferous, relating to or occurring in sleep.

नैधन **naidhana**, *as, ī, am* (fr. *ni-dhana*), subject to death, liable to decay, perishable, relating to death, causing death; (in astrology with or without *gṛiha*) the eighth house, the house of death.

नैधान **naidhāna**, *as, ī, am*, relating to a treasure, to a nest, &c.; (*ī*), f. a boundary where articles of value are buried and dug up (?).

नैध्रुवि **naidhruvi**, *is*, m. (patronymic fr. *ni-dhruva*), an epithet of Kāśyapa.

नैप **naipa**, *as, ī, am* (fr. *nīpa*), belonging or relating &c. to the Nauclea Cadamba.

नैपातिक **naipātika**, *as, ī, am* (fr. *ni-pāta*), only mentioned incidentally or by the way.

नैपातिथ **naipātitha**, *am*, n. (fr. *nīpātithi*), N. of a Sāman.

नैपाल **naipāla**. See under *nepāla*, p. 516.

नैपुण **naipuṇa** or *naipuṇya, am*, n. (fr. *ni-puṇa*), dexterity, cleverness, skill; artfulness; experience, exactness, strictness; anything which requires skill, a delicate matter; totality, completeness, completion.

नैबुक **naibuka**, N. of certain rites to be performed at full moon.

नैभृत्य **naibhṛitya**, *am*, n. (fr. *ni-bhṛita*), modesty, humility.

नैमन्त्रणक **naimantraṇaka**, *am*, n. (fr. *ni-mantraṇa*), a banquet, feast.

नैमय **naimaya**, *as*, m. (fr. *ni-maya*), a trader, a merchant.

नैमित्त **naimitta**, *as, ī, am* (fr. *ni-mitta*), relating to or explanatory of signs, tokens, marks, prognostics, &c.
Naimittika, as, ī, am, produced by any cause; connected with any particular cause, dependent on an external cause; (opposed to *nitya*), produced by some cause or by particular and unusual circumstances, unusual, occasional, accidental; (*as*), m. an astrologer, a prophet; (*am*), n. an effect; occasional or periodical act or rite. — *Naimittika-karman, a*, n. or *naimittika-kriyā*, f. an occasional ceremony (as observed on the birth of a child &c.).

नैमिष **naimisha**, *as, ī, am* (fr. *ni-misha*), momentary, transient, lasting for a twinkling; (*am*), n., N. of a forest and sacred Tīrtha celebrated as the residence of certain Ṛishis to whom Sauti related the Mahā-bhārata (Mahā-bh. Ādi-p. 7275, Vana-p. 6079; the district was so called because in it the sage Gaura-mukha destroyed an army of Asuras in a twinkling); (*ās*), m. pl. the inhabitants of the Naimisha wood. — *Naimisha-kānana, am*, n. the Naimisha wood. — *Naimishāraṇya* (°*sha-ar*°), *am*, n. the Naimisha forest. — *Naimishāraṇya-tīrtha, am*, n., N. of a sacred bathing-place.
Naimishāyana, as, ī, am, living in the Naimisha forest.
Naimishīya, ās, m. pl. the inhabitants of the Naimisha forest; (*as, ā, am*), relating to the Naimisha forest.
Naimisheya, as, ī, am, living in the Naimisha forest.

नैमेय **naimeya**, *as*, m. barter, exchange (= *ni-maya* under *ni-me*).

नैम्ब **naimba**, *as, ī, am* (fr. *nimba*), relating to the Azadirachta Indica.

नैयग्रोध **naiyagrodha** or *naiyyagrodha, as, ī, am* (fr. *nyag-rodha*), belonging to or made of the Ficus Indica or Indian fig-tree; (*am*), n. the fruit of the Indian fig-tree.

नैयङ्कव **naiyaṅkava**, *as, ī, am* (fr. *ny-aṅku*), belonging to or coming from the antelope called Nyaṅku, made of its skin, &c.

नैयत्य **naiyatya**, *am*, n. (fr. *ni-yata*), restraint, self-command, self-government.

नैयमिक **naiyamika**, *as, ī, am* (fr. *ni-yama*), according to rule, conformable to precept, regular, enjoined; (*am*), n. regularity.

नैयाय **naiyāya**, *as, ī, am* (fr. *ny-āya*), treating of the Nyāya philosophy (q. v.), explaining it, &c.
Naiyāyika, as, ī, am, knowing the Nyāya philosophy, knowing the laws of logic; (*as*), m. a dialectician, logician (especially a follower of the Nyāya philosophy).

नैरञ्जना **nairañjanā**, f. (fr. *nir-añjana*), N. of a river falling into the Gaṅgā in Magadha (now called Niladyan).

नैरन्तर्य **nairantarya**, *am*, n. (fr. *nir-antara*), absence of interruption or interval, uninterruptedness, close succession, continuousness, contiguity, closeness, compactness; (*eṇa*), ind. without interval or interruption, constantly, incessantly, uninterruptedly.

नैरपेक्ष्य **nairapekshya**, *am*, n. (fr. *nir-apeksha*), disregard, indifference.

नैरयिक **nairayika**, *as*, m. (fr. *nir-aya*), an inhabitant of hell.

नैरर्थ्य **nairarthya**, *am*, n. meaninglessness, senselessness, nonsense.

नैराश्य **nairāśya**, *am*, n. (fr. *nir-āśa*), hopelessness, despair; the absence of wish or expectation, non-expectancy.

नैरास्य **nairāsya**, *as*, m. (fr. *nir-āsa*), N. of a magical formula pronounced over weapons.

नैरुक्त **nairukta**, *as, ī, am* (fr. *nir-ukta*), relating to the Nirukta (q. v.), explaining it; resting on etymology, explained etymologically; (*as*), m. one who knows the etymology or true derivation of words.
Nairuktika, as, ī, am, one who knows the etymology or radical meaning of words, an etymologist.

नैरुज्य **nairujya**, *am*, n. (fr. *nī-ruja*), health.

नैरूहिक **nairūhika**, *as, ī, am* (fr. 1. *nir-ūha*), purging, cleaning out.

नैर्ऋत **nairṛita**, *as, ī, am* (fr. *nir-ṛiti*), belonging &c. to Nir-ṛiti; south-western; belonging to the Rākshasas; relating to the lunar mansion Nairṛita (Mūla); (*as*), m., N. of the ruler of the south-west quarter; a child or offspring of Nir-ṛiti, a demon, imp, goblin, Rākshasa; N. of a Rudra; (*ās*), m. pl., N. of a people; (*ī*), f. an epithet of Durgā; (with or without *diś*) the south-west quarter; (*am*), n. the lunar mansion Mūla.
Nairṛiti, is, m., N. of a demon, a Rākshasa.
Nairṛiteya, as, ī, am, descended from Nir-ṛiti, belonging to or connected with Nir-ṛiti.
Nairṛitya, as, ī, am, relating to Nir-ṛiti; south-western; a sacrifice offered to Nir-ṛiti.

नैर्गन्ध्य **nairgandhya**, *am*, n. (fr. *nir-gandha*), absence of smell or odour, inodorousness.

नैर्गुण्य **nairguṇya**, *am*, n. (fr. *nir-guṇa*), absence of qualities or properties; freedom from qualities; want of excellencies; absence of good qualities; (*as, ī, am*), having no connection with qualities.

नैर्घृण्य **nairghṛiṇya**, *am*, n. (fr. *nir-ghṛiṇa*), pitilessness, unmercifulness, cruelty.

नैर्दश्य **nairdaśya**, *am*, n. (fr. *nir-daśa*), getting over the critical period of the first ten days (of a new-born child), surmounting any dangerous time or bad influence.

नैर्देशिक **nairdeśika**, *as, ī, am*, servant, servile.

नैर्बाध्य **nairbādhya** (fr. *nir-bādha*), Ved. (with *havis*) a sort of oblation.

नैर्मल्य **nairmalya**, *am*, n. (fr. *nir-mala*), stainlessness, spotlessness (physical and moral), cleanness, purity.

नैर्लज्ज्य **nairlajjya**, *am*, n. (fr. *nir-lajja*), shamelessness, impudence.

नैर्वाहिक **nairvāhika**, *as, ī, am* (fr. *nir-vāha*), conducting or leading out, carrying (water &c.) out; (with *dvāra*) a sluice.

नैर्हस्त **nairhasta** (fr. *nir-hasta*), Ved. 'intended for handless demons,' N. of a particular magical missile weapon.

नैल्य **nailya**, *am*, n. (fr. *nīla*), blueness, darkness of colour, blackness, dark-blue (the colour).

नैवसंज्ञानासंज्ञायतन **naivasañjñānāsañjñāyatana**, *am*, n. a place (*āyatana*) where there is no (*na-eva*) thinking (*sañjñāna*) and no (*na*) not-thinking (*a-sañjñā*).
Naiva-sañjñā-samādhi, is, m. meditation in which there is no reflection.

नैवार **naivāra**, *as, ī, am* (fr. *nīvāra*), consisting in or made of wild rice.

नैविड्य **naiviḍya**, *am*, n. (fr. *ni-viḍa*), closeness, denseness, compactness, thickness; substance; a prolonged note or continuous sound.

नैविद **naivida**, *as, ī, am*, having a Nivid (q. v.).

नैवेद्य **naivedya**, *am*, n. (fr. *ni-vedya*), an offering of eatables presented to a deity or idol (which may afterwards be distributed to his ministers or worshippers, especially if presented to any form of Vishṇu).

नैवेशिक **naiveśika**, *am*, n. (fr. *ni-veśa*), any vessel or implement belonging to the furniture of a house; a present to a Brāhman householder, a girl so given, or ornaments with her, &c.

नैश **naiśa**, *as, ī, am* (fr. *niśā*), nocturnal, nightly, relating to the night; a person &c. doing anything by night; done at night; to be observed by night.
Naiśākara, as, ī, am (fr. *niśā-kara*), caused by or belonging to the moon, &c.
Naiśika, as, ī, am, nocturnal, happening at night, obtained in one night, &c.

नैश्चल्य **naiśćalya**, *am*, n. fixedness, fixity, immovableness.

नैश्चित्य *naiśćitya, am,* n. (fr. *niś-ćita*), determination, certainty; a fixed ceremony or festival (as a birth, investiture, marriage, &c.).

नैश्चिन्त्य *naiśćintya, am,* n. (fr. *niś-ćinta*), freedom from anxiety, absence of care.

नैषदिक *naishadika, as, ī, am* (fr. *ni-shad*), sitting, (not lying down.)

नैषध *naishadha, as, ī, am,* relating to Nishadha; *(as),* m. a prince of the Nishadhas, especially an epithet of Nala; *(ās),* m. pl., N. of the people of Nishadha; a species of plant used as food; *(am),* n. or *naishadha-ćarita, am,* n., N. of an artificial epic poem by Srī-harsha, treating of Nala's adventures. — *Naishadhaćarita-bhāva-dyotanikā,* f. 'an explanation of the meaning of the Naishadha-ćarita,' N. of a commentary on the preceding poem. — *Naishadhānveshaṇa* (°*dha-an*°), *am,* n. the seeking or searching for Naishadha, i. e. Nala.

Naishadhīya, as, ī, am, relating to Nala Naishadha; *(am),* n. (with or without *ćarita*) N. of an artificial epic poem on Nala's adventures by Srī-harsha.

Naishadhya, as, ī, am, peculiar or belonging to the Nishadhas; *(as),* m. a prince of the Nishadhas.

Naishidha, as, m. an epithet of Naḍa, (an earlier form of *naishadha* above.)

नैषाद *naishāda, as, ī, am,* belonging to the Nishādas; *(as),* m. a Nishāda; *(ās),* m. pl. the Nishāda people.

Naishādi, is, m. a prince of the Nishādas.

नैष्कर्म्य *naishkarmya, am,* n. (fr. *nish-karman*), idleness, inactivity; abstinence or exemption from acts or their consequences; the salvation obtained by abstraction in opposition to that obtained by works.

नैष्कशतिक *naishkaśatika, as, ī, am* (fr. *nishka-śata*), worth a hundred Nishkas, bought with them, &c.

Naishkasahasrika, as, ī, am (fr. *nishka-sahasra*), worth a thousand Nishkas, bought with them, &c.

Naishkika, as, ī, am (fr. *nishka*), bought with a Nishka, made of a Nishka, &c.; *(as),* m. a Mint-master, superintendent of a Mint.

नैष्किञ्चन्य *naishkinćanya, am,* n. (fr. *nish-kinćana*), absence of property, poverty, destitution.

नैष्कृतिक *naishkritika, as, ī, am,* acting wickedly, wicked, malignant, (probably incorrect for *naikritika*); free from occupation, disengaged.

नैष्क्रमण *naishkramaṇa, as, ī, am* (fr. *nish-kramaṇa*), any oblation offered or rite performed when a new-born child is taken out of the house for the first time.

नैष्ठिक *naishṭhika, as, ī, am* (fr. *ni-shṭhā*), forming the end or conclusion, final, last; conclusive, definitive, decided, accomplished, fixed, firm, constant; highest, perfect, complete; completely versed in or familiar with, conversant; vowing perpetual abstinence and chastity; belonging to the character or office of a perpetual student; *(as),* m. a perpetual religious student or Brāhman who continues with his spiritual preceptor even after the prescribed term of study is expired and observes the vow of chastity.

Naishṭhya, am, n. constancy, steady adherence to rule, firm belief.

नैष्ठुर्य *naishṭhurya, am,* n. (fr. *ni-shṭhura*), severity, cruelty, coarseness, harshness.

नैष्णिह्य *naishṇihya, am,* n. (apparently fr. a form *ni-shṇih = nih-snih*), getting rid of, freeing one's self from anything.

नैष्फल्य *naishphalya, am,* n. (fr. *nish-phala*), unfruitfulness, fruitlessness, absence of fruit or effect, barrenness, unprofitableness.

नैसर्गिक *naisargika, as, ī, am* (fr. *ni-sarga*), natural, innate, inherent, constitutional, original; (with Buddhists) cast off, put off.

नैसर्प *naisarpa, as,* m. (fr. an unused form *ni-sarpa*), N. of one of the nine treasures (with Jainas).

नैस्त्रिंशिक *naistriṇśika, as,* m. (fr. *nis-triṇśa*), a swordsman, a soldier armed with a sword.

नो *no,* ind. (fr. *na-u*), and not (Ved.); not, no (for *na*, but in epic poetry and later literature *no* is generally only used for *na* to suit the verse). *No ćet,* if not; otherwise, else, unless; *no vā,* or not.

नोत् *not* or *nod,* ind., Ved. almost, nearly.

नोदन *nodana, am,* n. (fr. rt. 1. *nud*), pushing, impelling, driving away, removing.

Nodin, ī, inī, i, impelling, driving away, removing.

Nodya, as, ā, am, to be impelled or driven away or removed.

नोधस् *nodhas, ās,* m. (said to be fr. rt. 4. *nu*), N. of a Ṛishi with the epithet Gautama.

नोधा *nodhā,* ind. (contracted fr. *nava-dhā*), ninefold, in nine parts.

नोपस्थातृ *nopasthātṛi* (*na-up*°), *tā, trī, tṛi,* not at hand, absent, remote, far off.

नौ 1. *nau,* the alternative form for the acc., dat., and gen. of the 1st pers. pron., see *asmad*. *Nau* is an enclitic in the Veda.

नौ 2. *nau, ´naus,* f. (fr. rt. 4. *nu*), Ved. speech; [cf. *navish{i*.]

नौ 3. *nau, naus,* f. (probably fr. rt. *snu*, but said to be fr. rt. 1. *nud;* in Ṛig-veda I. 97, 8, *nāvayā* is Vedic inst. for *nāvā*), a ship, a boat, a vessel; (in astrology) N. of a peculiar appearance on the moon; N. of a constellation; [cf. Gr. ναῦς, ναύ-τη-ς, ναυ-τίλο-ς, ναυ-τίλλο-μαι, ναῦ-λο-ν, ναῦ-σθ-λο-ν, ναυ-τία, ναυ-σία, ναυ-τιά-ω, ναυ-σιά-ω; Lat. *nāvis, nau-ta, nāvita, nāv-igare, nav-ig-iu-m;* Old Germ. *nacho;* Angl. Sax. *naca;* Bavarian *naue,* 'a ship;' Old Iceland. *nau-st,* 'a ship station,' *Nōa-tūn;* Hib. *naoi, noi.*] — *Nāv-ākāra, as, ā, am,* boat-shaped, cymbiform. — *Nāv-āroha, as,* m. a passenger on board ship, a sailor. — *Nau-karṇadhāra, as,* m. the steersman of a ship, a helmsman, pilot. — *Nau-karṇī,* f., N. of one of the Mātṛis attending on Skanda. — *Nau-karman, a,* n. 'boat-business,' the occupation or business of a sailor. — *Nau-ćara, as, ā, am,* going in a ship, a sailor. — *Nau-jīvika, as,* m. 'living in ships or boats,' a sailor, boatman. — *Nau-tārya, as, ā, am,* 'passable in a boat,' navigable, to be traversed in a vessel. — *Nau-daṇḍa, as,* m. 'boat-pole,' an oar. — *Nau-bandhana, am,* n. 'ship-binding,' N. of the highest peak of the Himālayas to which in the great flood Manu fastened his ship. — *Nau-bhū,* cl. 1. P. *-bhavati, -bhavitum,* to be a ship, to have been made a ship. — *Nau-yāna, am,* n. going in a ship, navigation. — *Nau-yāyin, ī, inī, i,* going in a boat or vessel, a passenger; freight. — *Nau-vāha, as,* m. 'ship-conductor,' a steersman, pilot, captain. — *Nau-vyasana, am,* n. ship-wreck, naufrage.

Nauka (at the end of an adj. comp.) = 3. *nau; (ā),* f. a small boat or ship; N. of a commentary on the Mantra-mahodadhi by Mahī-dhara. — *Naukākṛishṭa* (°*kā-āk*°), *am,* n., N. of a favourable position of the pieces in the game Ćatur-aṅga; [cf. *nṛipā-kṛishṭa*.] — *Naukā-daṇḍa, as,* m. 'boat-pole,' an oar, a paddle.

नौधस *naudhasa, am,* n., N. of a Sāman.

न्यक्ष *nyak, ny-aksha.* See col. 3.

न्यग्रोध *nyag-rodha.* See under 2. *ny-ańć,* col. 3.

न्यच्छ *nyaććha, am,* n. a mole or spot upon the body.

न्यञ्च् 1. *ny-ańć,* cl. 1. P. A. *-aćati* or *-ańćati, -ańćitum,* Ved. to bend down, curve down.

Nyak-kṛi, cl. 8. P. *-karoti,* &c., to make low, lower, humble, humiliate, degrade, treat with disrespect or contempt, slight. — *Nyak-karaṇa, am,* n. the act of lowering or degrading, treating with disrespect or contempt. — *Nyak-kāra, as,* m. making low, humiliation, humbling, contempt, disregard, disrespect. — *Nyak-kṛita, as, ā, am,* humbled, treated with contempt or contumely.

Ny-akna, as, ā, am, Ved. bent down. — *Nyak-nāṅguli* (°*na-an*°), *is, is, i,* Ved. having the fingers bent.

Ny-aksha, as, ā, am [cf. rt. *aksh*, which may be connected with rt. *ać = ańć*], low, inferior; whole, entire; *(as),* m. a buffalo; an epithet of Paraśu-rāma; *(am),* n. the whole; grass.

Nyag-bhū, cl. 1. P. *-bhavati,* &c., to become low or humble, to humble one's self: Caus. *nyag-bhāvayati,* to cause to become low, humiliate, treat with disrespect. — *Nyag-bhāva, as,* m. humiliation, degradation, debasement, contempt. — *Nyag-bhāvana, am,* n. humbling, degrading, treating with contempt, defiling. — *Nyag-bhāvayitṛi, tā, trī, tṛi,* one who lowers or humbles; humbling.

Ny-aṅka, as, m. a particular part of a carriage.

Ny-aṅku, us, m. a deer, an antelope; N. of a Muni; of a Ćakra-vartin. — *Nyaṅku-bhūruha, as,* m. the tree Calosanthes Indica. — *Nyaṅku-śiras,* scil. *kakubh,* a sort of metre consisting of 11 + 12 + 4 syllables. — *Nyaṅku-sāriṇī,* f., scil. *bṛihatī,* f. a sort of metre, also called *uro-bṛihatī,* consisting of 8 + 12 + 8 + 8 syllables.

2. *ny-ańć, nyaṅ, nīćī, nyak* [cf. *nīća,* p. 512], going downwards, turned or directed downwards, bent down; lying on the face; low, vile, contemptible, base; whole, entire; slow, lazy; *nīćā,* inst. c. on the ground, (see p. 512, col. 1); *(nyak),* ind. downwards, down, humbly. — *Nyag-jāti, is, is, i,* of a low or inferior race, low born. — *Nyag-rodha, as,* m. (= *nyak-roha,* growing downwards), the Indian fig-tree, Ficus Indica; another tree [cf. *śamī*]; a fathom, measured by the arms extended; N. of a son of Ugra-sena; of a Brāhman, of a monastery, of a village; (ī or ā), f. Salvinia Cucculata; a medicinal plant (commonly Mohanā). — *Nyagrodha-parimaṇḍala, as, ā, am,* being a fathom in circumference; *(ā),* f. an elegant woman. — *Nyagrodha-pāda, as,* m., N. of a man.

Ny-ańćana, as, ī, am, Ved. taking on one's lap; (ī), f. the lap; *(am),* n. a curve; a hollow, recess; a hiding-place.

Ny-ańćita, as, ā, am, thrown or cast down, bent down.

न्यञ्ज् *ny-añj,* cl. 7. P. *-anakti* (Ved. also A. *-aṅkte*), *-añjitum* or *-aṅktum,* to anoint, besmear; (A.) to creep in, to conceal or hide one's self.

Ny-akta, as, ā, am, anointed, smeared; mixed up.

Ny-aṅga, as, m. a mark, sign; sort, kind (e. g. *Avabhṛitha-nyaṅga,* a sort of Avabhṛitha); *(am),* n. low abuse (?).

न्यञ्जलिका *ny-añjalikā,* f. an Añjali which is directed downwards.

न्यन्त *ny-anta,* m. n. (?), proximity; *(ena),* ind., Ved. near, near to.

न्यय *ny-aya, as,* m. (fr. 3. *nī,* i. e. rt. 5. *i* with *ni*), destruction, loss, waste.

Ny-ayana, am, n., Ved. entrance or receptacle.

न्यर्ण *ny-arṇa, as, ā, am* (fr. rt. *ard* or rt. 4. *ṛi* with *ni*), dissolved (Ved.); injured; asked, solicited (?); gone (?).

न्यर्थ *ny-artha, am,* n. (fr. rt. 4. *ṛi* with *ni*), Ved. destruction, annihilation; (Sāy. on Ṛig-veda VII. 18, 9) not going in the usual course.

न्यर्पय *ny-arpaya*, Caus. of *ny-ṛi*, q. v.

न्यर्बुद *ny-arbuda, am*, n., Ved. one hundred millions.

न्यर्बुदि *ny-arbudi, is*, m., N. of a divine being described as taking an active part in war.

न्यवग्रह *ny-avagraha, as*, m. the accentless vowel at the end of a Pūrva-pada.

न्यवचर् *ny-ava-ćar*, cl. 1. P. *-ćarati, -ćaritam*, to enter into, penetrate.

न्यस् *ny-as*, cl. 4. P. *-asyati, -asitum*, to throw down, cast down, lay down, set or put down (with loc., e. g. *bhūmau*, on the ground); to lay down, resign, give up (e. g. *jīvitam ny-as*, to lay down one's life); to bring forward, adduce, propound (as an argument &c.); to lay or put down or place upon anything (with loc., e. g. *ćitre ny-as*, to place in a picture, paint, depict; *pathi ny-as*, to lay down on the road, give up an occupation, &c.; *śirasy ājñām ny-as*, to place a command on one's head, i. e. receive a command with due reverence; *śāpam mayi nyasyati*, he lays a curse upon me); to put in, place within (with loc.), to deposit with any one (loc.); to give into any one's keeping, make a deposit, intrust, deliver, consign, commit; to settle, fix, appoint; to support: Caus. *ny-āsayati*, to cause to put or lay down, &c.

Ny-asana, am, n. casting or laying down, depositing; delivering, giving up.

Ny-asta, as, ā, am, thrown or cast down, laid down, placed in or upon, put in, inserted, applied; delivered, deposited, consigned; depicted (e. g. *ćitra-nyasta*, committed to a picture, painted); rested on, leaning, resting; given up, resigned, set aside. — *Nyasta-daṇḍa, as, ā, am*, 'laying down the rod,' giving up all means of punishment. — *Nyasta-deha, as, ā, am*, one who has laid down the body, dead. — *Nyasta-śastra, as, ā, am*, one who has laid down or resigned his weapons, laying down arms; unarmed, defenceless; harmless; epithet of the Manes or deified progenitors.

1. *ny-asya, as, ā, am*, to be deposited; to be appointed to any office (with loc.); to be delivered.

2. *ny-asya*, ind. having put down, having laid down, having deposited, having given up, &c.

Ny-āsa, as, m. putting down, placing, settling, planting or putting down (the feet), stepping, a step; depositing; a deposit, pledge; delivering, intrusting, committing, delivery; putting on colour &c., painting; writing down, writing, impress, stamp, mark; giving up, putting off or away, laying aside; deserting, abandoning; lowering the tone of the voice; bringing forward, adducing; striking or digging in (the claws &c.), seizing (with the claws); consigning or intrusting anything to the mind; mental appropriation or assignment of various parts of the body to tutelary divinities (accompanied with certain prayers and gesticulations); N. of a commentary on the Kāśikā-vṛitti by Jinendra. — *Nyāsa-dhārin, ī*, m. the holder of a deposit, a mortgagee. — *Nyāsāpahnava* (°*sa-ap*°), *as*, m. repudiation of a deposit. — *Nyāsī-kṛi*, cl. 8. P. A. *-karoti, -kurute, -kartum*, to make a deposit, deposit anything with a person. — *Nyāsoddyota* (°*sa-ud*°), *as*, m., N. of a grammatical work.

Ny-āsin, ī, inī, i, one who has abandoned all worldly concerns; (*ī*), m. a Sannyāsī.

न्यह्न *ny-ahna* (?), Ved. the closing day.

न्याकृ *ny-ā-kṛi*, cl. 8. P. *-karoti, -kartum*, Ved. to keep back, hold back.

न्याक्य *nyākya, am*, n. fried rice.

न्याग्रोधमूल *nyāgrodhamūla, as, ī, am* (fr. *nyagrodha-mūla*), being or situated at the roots of the Ficus Indica.

न्याद *nyāda, as*, m. (fr. rt. *ad* with *ni*), eating, feeding.

न्याधा *ny-ā-dhā*, cl. 3. P. *-dadhāti, -dhātum*, to fix in, place in, appoint; to put down.

न्याय *ny-āya, as*, m. (fr. 3. *nī*, i. e. rt. 5. *i* with *ni*), method, way, rule (lit. that to which anything goes back or in which anything goes), model, manner, system, plan, doctrine, right or fit or suitable manner, that which is fitting, fitness, propriety, right, justice, virtue, equity, law, a lawful act; (in gram.) a general or universal rule, an axiom which precedes and must be kept in view in the explanation of special rules; a lawsuit, policy, good government; decision in a lawsuit, judicial sentence, judgment; a celebrated system of Hindū philosophy delivered by Gautama or Gotama in a set of aphorisms divided into five lectures; the proper way of stating an argument, logic, logical philosophy; a logical argument, a complete argument or syllogism (consisting of five members with the Naiyāyikas, viz. *pratijñā, hetu, udāharaṇa, upanaya, nigamana*, and of three members with the Vedāntins); likeness, analogy, apposite illustration; *nyāyena*, in the way of, after the manner of (e. g. *līlā-nyāyena*, by way of sport, as if in sport; cf. *nyāya-tas* below). Placed after a finite verb *nyāyam* is said by Pāṇini (VIII. 1, 27, 57) to express either censure or repetition. — *Nyāya-kalpalatikā*, f., N. of a commentary. — *Nyāya-kusumāñjali, is*, m., N. of the aphorisms of Udayana; [cf. *kusumāñjali*.] — *Nyāya-kokila* (?), *as*, m., N. of a Buddhist teacher. — *Nyāya-kaustubha, am*, n., N. of a general work on the Nyāya philosophy. — *Nyāya-ćūḍā-maṇi*, N. of a confutation of the Nyāya system of philosophy in favour of the Vedānta by Mādhava Sarasvatī. — *Nyāya-ćūḍāmaṇi-prabhā*, f., N. of a commentary on the preceding work by Caṇḍīśvara. — *Nyāya-tas*, ind. in a fitting manner, as is fitting; suitably, justly, fitly, according to right or justice. — *Nyāya-tā*, f. or *nyāya-tva, am*, n. fitness, propriety. — *Nyāya-dvāra-tāraka-śāstra, am*, n., N. of a Buddhist work. — *Nyāya-pañćānana, as*, m. an epithet of Jaya-rāma; [cf. *pañćānana*.] — *Nyāya-bindu*, N. of a commentary on the Mīmāṃsā-sūtras by Vaidya-nātha. — *Nyāya-bodhinī*, f., N. of a commentary on the Tarka-saṅgraha by Go-vardhana Miśra. — *Nyāya-bhāshya, am*, n., N. of a commentary on the Nyāya-sūtras by the Ṛishi Vātsyāyana. — *Nyāya-bhāskara*, N. of a philosophical work. — *Nyāya-bhūshaṇa, am*, n., N. of a work. — *Nyāya-makaranda*, N. of a work on the Nyāya system controverted from the standpoint of the Vedānta. — *Nyāya-mālā-vistara, as*, m., N. of an introduction to the study of the Mīmāṃsā philosophy. — *Nyāya-ratnamālā*, f., N. of a work on the Mīmāṃsā. — *Nyāya-līlāvatī*, N. of an elementary treatise on the Nyāya philosophy. — *Nyāya-vat, ān, atī, at*, acting rightly, behaving properly. — *Nyāya-vartin, ī, inī, i*, well behaved, acting with propriety. — *Nyāya-vāgīśa, as*, m. an epithet of Śrī-kṛishṇa; of Dīkshita-śrī-kaṇṭha-śarman. — *Nyāya-vihita, as, ā, am*, prescribed by rule. — *Nyāya-śāstra, am*, n. the philosophical system of the Nyāya school; logic (as connected with this school). — *Nyāya-saṅkshepa, as*, m. or *nyāya-saṅgraha, as*, m. or *nyāya-sāra, as* or *am*, m. or n., N. of certain compendious works on the Nyāya philosophy. — *Nyāya-sāriṇī*, f. right or fit behaviour; a woman acting or judging rightly. — *Nyāya-siddhānta-pañćānana, as*, m. an epithet of Viśva-nātha. — *Nyāyasiddhānta-mañjarī*, f., N. of a work. — *Nyāya-sūtra, am*, n. the aphorisms of the Nyāya philosophy by Gautama. — *Nyāyāćāra* (°*ya-āć*°), *as, ā, am*, acting justly, virtuous. — *Nyāyādhāra* (°*ya-ādh*°), *as*, m. 'receptacle of justice,' a term applied to any one who is a model of virtue or propriety. — *Nyāyānusāra-śāstra* (°*ya-an*°), *am*, n., N. of a Buddhist work. — *Nyāyāmṛita* (°*ya-am*°), *am*, n. 'nectar of Nyāya,' N. of a Vedānta work by Vyāsa Tīrtha Bindu. — *Nyāyāmṛita-taraṅginī*, f., N. of a commentary on the Nyāyāmṛita by Rāma Āćārya. — *Nyāyārjita* (°*ya-ar*°), *as, ā, am*, obtained in a regular way. — *Nyāyālaṅkāra-bhaṭṭa* (°*ya-al*°), *as*, m. an epithet of Śrī-govinda; also of Śrī-maheśvara. — *Nyāyāvalī-didhiti* (°*ya-āv*°), *is*, f., N. of a commentary on Jaimini. — *Nyāyopeta* (°*ya-up*°), *as, ā, am*, according to rule, right, admitted.

Nyāyin, ī, inī, i, right, fit; logical, rational.

Nyāyya, as, ā, am, regular, proper, just, right, equitable, fit, suitable, adapted, (sometimes giving a passive sense to the infin.); usual, customary. — *Nyāyya-tva, am*, n. fitness, suitableness, propriety.

न्याव्यध् *ny-ā-vyadh*, cl. 4. P. *-vidhyati, -vyaddhum*, to cause to burst forth, let loose, set free.

न्यास *ny-āsa*. See under *ny-as*, col. 1.

न्युङ्ख *nyuṅkha, as*, m. a kind of Sāman, the sixfold repetition of the triliteral name of God or *Om*, [cf. *nyūṅkha*]; (*as, ā, am*), proper, right; pleasing, agreeable.

न्युच् *ny-uć*, cl. 4. P. *-ućyati*, &c., Ved. to rejoice in, delight in, take pleasure in; (Sāy.) to assent to, agree to.

Ny-oćanī, f., Ved. (probably) a kind of woman's ornament; (Sāy.) a female servant or slave.

Ny-oćara, as, ā, am, Ved. (perhaps) belonging to or fit for a place.

न्युत्त *ny-utta, as, ā, am* (fr. rt. 2. *ud* or *und* with *ni*), dipped in, sprinkled.

न्युप्त *ny-upta, as, ā, am* (fr. *ni-vap*, q. v.), offered, presented (to the Manes of deceased ancestors).

Ny-upya, ind. having offered, having presented (cakes &c. to the Manes).

न्युब्ज् *ny-ubj*, cl. 6. P. *-ubjati*, &c., to bend down, press down, throw down.

Ny-ubja, as, ā, am, turned or bent downwards, lying on the face or with the face downwards; looking downwards; bent, crooked; hump-backed, crooked-backed (as the result of disease); convex; (*as*), m. the Nyag-rodha tree; a sort of ladle made of Kuśa grass; (*am*), n. the fruit of the Averrhoa Carambola; a vessel used at Śrāddhas. — *Nyubja-khaḍga, as*, m. a crooked sword, a sabre.

न्युष् *ny-ush* [cf. rt. 1. *ush*], cl. 1. P. *-oshati*, &c., Ved. to burn down; (Sāy.) to consume utterly.

न्यूङ्ख *nyūṅkha, as*, m. the insertion of the sound *o* in different places with variety of prosodial length and accentuation in the recitation of hymns, (this sound may be repeated any number of times in the recitation of Mantras, or may be made long, short, or prolated, or may have different accents.)

Nyūṅkhaya, Nom. P. *nyūṅkhayati, -yitum*, to insert the Nyūṅkha, (occurring in fut. pass. part. *nyūṅkhanīya* and *nyūṅkhya*); (A. *-te*), to make a peculiar sound, to growl.

न्यून *ny-ūna, as, ā, am* (see *ūna*), lessened, diminished, shortened, made smaller, less, inferior, deficient, defective, wanting, destitute, deprived of (e. g. *artha-nyūna*, deprived of property, destitute of wealth); imperfect or defective in some organ (e. g. *pāda-nyūna*, having a defect in the feet); low, vile, wicked, despicable, blamable; (*am*), ind. less; (*am*), n. an euphemistic expression for the vulva. — *Nyūna-tā*, f. or *nyūna-tva, am*, n. inferiority, deficiency, incompleteness. — *Nyūna-dhī, īs, īs, i*, deficient in intellect, ignorant, foolish. — *Nyūna-pañćāśad-bhāva, as*, n. 'having but forty-nine properties of human nature,' an idiot. — *Nyūnākshara* (°*na-ak*°), *as, ā, am*, defective in letters or syllables. — *Nyūnāṅga* (°*na-aṅ*°), *as, ī, am*, defective in a limb or organ, maimed, mutilated, imperfect. — *Nyūnādhika* (°*na-adh*°), *as, ā, am*, less or more, unequal. — *Nyūnādhika-vibhāga, as*, m. unequal partition. — *Nyūnendriya* (°*na-in*°), *as, ā, am*, wanting some organ or sense, deficient, imperfect (as blind, deaf, &c.).

Nyūnaya, Nom. P. *nyūnayati, -yitum*, or *nyūnī-kṛi*, cl. 8. P. A. *-karoti, -kurute, -kartum*, to lessen, diminish, make less.

न्यूह् ny-ūh [cf. rt. 2. ūh], cl. 1. A. -ohate or -ūhate, Ved. to attend to, observe; (Sāy.) to bear up or support completely, (as if fr. rt. 1. ūh.)

न्यृ ny-ṛi [cf. rt. 4. ṛi], cl. 5. P. -ṛiṇoti or -ṛiṇvati, &c., Ved. to put or place in; to infuse: Caus. ny-arpayati, -yitum, to throw down, cast down, overthrow.

न्यृञ्ज् ny-ṛiñj [cf. rt. 2. ṛiñj], cl. 6. A. -ṛiñjate, &c., Ved. to reach, attain, gain, obtain, win; (Sāy.) to propitiate, befriend.

न्यृष् ny-ṛish [cf. rt. 2. ṛish], cl. 6. P. -ṛishati, &c., Ved. to press down or under, suppress, hide, cover; to put in; (Sāy.) to attain to.

Ny-ṛishṭa, as, ā, am, pressed under; (Sāy.) attained to, gained, endowed.

न्ये ny-e (=ny-ā-i), cl. 2. P. ny-aiti, &c., Ved. to come or fall into.

न्योकस् ny-okas, ās, ās, as, Ved. belonging to home or one's native country, domestic, home-bred; (Sāy.) dwelling in an eternal mansion, having an eternal abode.

न्योचनी ny-oćanī, ny-oćara. See ny-uć.

न्योजस् ny-ojas, ās, ās, as, powerful.

नृस्थिमालिन् nr-asthi-mālin. See p. 515, col. 3.

न्वै nvai for nu-vai, ind., Ved. indeed, really, certainly.

प

प 1. pa, the twenty-first consonant of the Nāgarī alphabet and the first letter of the fifth or labial class, having the sound of the English p. — Pa-kāra, as, m. the letter or sound pa. — Pa-varga, as, m. 'the p series,' the labial series of consonants.

प 2. pa, as, ā, am (fr. rt. 1. pā), (at the end of a comp.), drinking; [cf. aneka-pa, ājya-pa, kshīra-pa, &c.]

प 3. pa, as, ā, am (fr. rt. 3. pā), (at the end of a comp.), guarding, protecting, ruling; (ā), f. guarding, protection.

प 4. pa, as, m. air, wind; a leaf; an egg.

पंश् paṅś or paṅs, cl. 1. and 10. P. paṅśati, paṅsati, paṅśayati, paṅsayati, &c., to destroy.

पकथ pakatha, as, m., N. of a man with the patronymic Saubhara.

पक्कटी pakkaṭī, f. the tree Thespesia Populnea.

पक्कण pakkaṇa, as, m. the hut of a Ćaṇḍāla or of any outcast, the abode of a savage or barbarian; (incorrectly read pakvaṇa; cf. pakvaśa.)

पक्तपौड paktapauḍa, as, m. a species of plant (= pańća-kṛitya, pańća-rakshaka, vardhana; in Hindī = pakhaudā).

पक्तव्य paktavya. See rt. 2. pać, p. 521.

पक्ति pakti, pakva. See rt. 2. pać, p. 521.

पक्वश pakvaśa, as, m., N. of a barbarous tribe; a Ćaṇḍāla; [cf. pukkaśa, pukvasa, pakkaṇa.]

पक्वापक्वा pakvāpakvā, an onomatopoetic word imitative of the cry of birds.

पक्ष् paksh [cf. rt. 2. paś], cl. 1. 10. P. pakshati, pakshayati, &c., to take, seize, accept; to take a part or side; [cf. Zend paś, 'to bind:' Gr. πήγ-νυ-μι, ἐ-πάγ-η-ν, πῆγ-μα, πηγ-ό-ς, πάγ-ο-ς, πάχ-νη, πάγ-η, πάσσ-αλο-ς: Lat. pac-i-sc-or, pāx, pac-i-o, pang-o, pig-nus, pā-lu-s: Goth. fah-an, 'to catch:' Mod. Germ. fang-en: Old Germ. fuog-a, ga-fuogi, 'apt;' gafag-yan, 'to satisfy;' fah, 'a shelf:' Bohem. pás, 'a girdle;' pas-mo, 'yarn.']

Paksha, as, m. (probably connected with the preceding, but by some regarded as an unreduplicated Desid. form of an unused rt. paj, fr. which pājas, 'strength,' may be derived; in Uṇādi-s. III. 69. paksha is derived fr. rt. 1. paṇ), a wing, pinion, (in this sense also am, n.); symbolical expression for the number two; a feather, the feathers on both sides of an arrow; the flank or side (of a man &c.), the shoulder; the side of anything (as of a house, carriage, the head, hair, &c.); the wing or flank of an army, &c.; the half of anything; the half of a lunar month, a fortnight comprising fifteen days, (the half from new moon to full moon was called pūrva or āpūryamāṇa, later śukla or śuddha; the other half was called apara or apa-kshīyamāṇa, later kṛishṇa or tāmisra; and every half month is divided into fifteen Tithis, named prathamā, dvitīyā, &c.); a side, party, faction, a partisan, adherent, follower; a class, multitude, host, set, troop, number of adherents or friends (e.g. śatru-paksha, the enemy's side or [as an adj.] being on the enemy's side; mahā-paksha, one who has many adherents; deva-paksha-varāḥ, the most distinguished adherents of the gods; paksha-sammata, approved by a certain set of people); one of two cases, one side of an argument, an alternative, (pakshe, on the other alternative, on the other hand); a case in general, a supposition, (pakshāntare, in the other case, on the other supposition); a thesis, a point under investigation or discussion, a position advanced or argument to be maintained; (in logic) the subject of a syllogism or conclusion or inference; place, position; supposition, view, notion, idea, opinion (e.g. mukhyaḥ pakshaḥ, an excellent idea); state, condition; (in algebra) a primary division or the side of an equation in a primary division. According to the lexicographers the word has also the following meanings: the wall of a house; a wall; an army; favour; contradiction, opposition, rejoinder, reply; the ash-pit of a fire-place, a royal elephant; a limb or member of the body; the feathers of the tail of a peacock, a tail; proximity, neighbourhood; a bracelet; purity, perfection. In composition with words signifying 'hair,' paksha is said to mean 'quantity;' see keśa-paksha; [cf. pūrva-p°, uttara-p°, eka-p°, kāka-p°, kṛishṇa-p°, &c.: cf. probably Gr. πάξ in ἅ-παξ; Goth. fug-ls, 'a bird;' Mod. Germ. Vogel; Lith. panksh-tis; perhaps Lat. passer for paxer.] — Paksha-gama, as, ā, am, moving with or by means of wings, flying. — Paksha-gupta, as, m. 'wing-protected,' a species of bird. — Paksha-grahaṇa, am, n. choosing a party. — Paksha-grāha, as, ā, am, or paksha-grāhin, ī, iṇī, i, one who chooses a party. — Paksha-ghāta = pakshāghāta, q.v. — Paksha-ghna, as, ī, am, a Tri-śālaka having no hall towards the west. — Pakshan-gama, as, ā, am, moving by means of wings, flying. — Paksha-ćara, as, m. an elephant strayed from the herd; the moon; an attendant, a constant companion. — Paksha-ćchid, t, m. 'cutter of the wings' (of the mountains), an epithet of Indra. — Paksha-ja, as, ā, am, or paksha-janman, ā, ā, a, produced in a fortnight; (as or ā), m. the moon. — Paksha-tā, f. or paksha-tva, am, n. partisanship, alliance; adherence to a party; the being a part of; the taking up a side or argument; maintaining or defending a thesis; the essential nature of a proposition; the being the subject of a syllogism. — Paksha-dvaya, am, n. both sides of an argument, &c.; a month (two fortnights). — Paksha-dvāra, am, n. a side door, an inner or back door, a private entrance. — Paksha-dhara, as, ā, am, having a side or wing, winged; taking the side or adhering to the party of any one (gen.); belonging to any party or faction, siding with any one (gen.); (as), m. a bird; a partisan, adherent; the moon; an elephant that has strayed from the herd. — Paksha-nāḍi, f. a quill. — Paksha-pāta, as, m. 'falling of the feathers,' the moulting of birds (considered to proceed from fever); the act of taking the side or adhering to the party of any one (gen.); siding with any one (gen.); adopting a side or argument whether right or wrong, attachment to a party, partisanship, partiality for (with loc. or gen.); a partisan, adherent. — Pakshapāta-kṛita-sneha, as, ā, am, manifesting party attachment, sympathising. — Pakshapāti-tā, f. or pakshapāti-tva, am, n. partisanship, adherence to a side or party, partiality, friendship, fellowship, faction, factiousness. — Paksha-pātin, ī, inī, i, taking the side or adhering to the party (of any one), siding with, favouring a party; (ī), m. a partisan, friend, adherent, follower. — Paksha-pāli, is, m. a private or back door. — Paksha-puṭa, as, m. a wing. — Paksha-poshaṇa, as, ī, am, fostering or favouring a party, factious. — Paksha-pradyota, am, n., N. of a peculiar position of the hands in dancing. — Paksha-bala, am, n. strength of wing. — Paksha-bhāga, as, m. the side or flank, especially the flank of an elephant. — Paksha-bhukti, is, f. the course traversed by the sun in a fortnight. — Paksha-bheda, as, m. distinction between two sides of an argument; the difference between the two halves of a lunar month. — Paksha-mūla, am, n. the root or articulation of a wing. — Paksha-raćanā, f. forming a party or faction. — Paksha-vańćitaka, as, m. a peculiar position of the hands in dancing. — Paksha-vat, ān, atī, at, winged; having flanks; having a side or party, firmly adhering to or having a predilection for any one; belonging to a good family, of good extraction (?). — Paksha-vāda, as, m. expression of opinion, stating a case; ex parte statement. — Paksha-vāhana, as, m. 'whose vehicles are wings,' a bird. — Paksha-vindu, us, m. 'wing-spot,' a heron. — Paksha-vyāpin, ī, inī, i, embracing the whole of an argument or thesis. — Paksha-śas, ind. by or for half months or fortnights. — Paksha-sundara, as, m. a species of tree; [cf. lodhra.] — Paksha-hata, as, ā, am, paralysed on one side. — Paksha-hara, as, m. a bird; (perhaps a wrong reading for paksha-dhara, 'possessing wings.') — Paksha-homa, as, m. (probably) an oblation to be offered every half month. — Pakshākāra (°sha-āk°), as, ā, am, wing-shaped. — Pakshāghāta (°sha-āgh°), as, m. 'side-stroke,' paralysis or palsy of one side, hemiplegia; refutation of an argument or view. — Pakshānta (°sha-an°), as, m. the fifteenth and last day of either half month, new or full moon; the end of the wings of an army arranged in the shape of a bird. — Pakshāntara (°sha-an°), am, n. another side or part, another or different view of an argument, another supposition. — Pakshābhāsa (°sha-ābh°), as, m. a seeming or fallacious argument, a fallacy, a false plaint. — Pakshāvasara (°sha-av°), as, m. the last day of either half month, day of new or full moon. — Pakshāhati (°sha-āh°), is, f. a stroke with the wings. — Pakshāhāra (°sha-āh°), as, ā, am, one who eats food only once in a half month. — Pakshī-kṛi, cl. 8. P. A. -karoti, -kurute, -kartum, to make anything the subject of an argument or syllogism. — Pakshod-grāhin (°sha-ud°), ī, iṇī, i, showing partiality, taking a side or adopting a party.

Pakshaka, as, m. a side door, a private or back door; a side; a sidesman; an associate, a confederate or partisan, (at the end of comps. used for paksha.)

Pakshati, is, f. the root or insertion of a wing, the pit of a bird's wing; the first day of the half month.

Pakshas, as, n. (said to be fr. rt. 1. pać), a wing; the side part of a carriage; the leaf of a door; the wing of an army; a half, a division; a half month; the side or shore of a river; a side.

Pakshālikā, f., N. of one of the Mātṛis attending on Skanda.

Pakshālu, us, m. a bird.

Pakshi, is, m. (curtailed form for pakshin), a bird.

Pakshin, ī, iṇī, i, winged, (figuratively) furnished with wings; taking the side or adhering to the party (of any one); siding with; (ī), m. a day with the two nights enclosing it; the bird Garuḍa as one of the eighteen attendants of the Sun; an arrow; an epithet of S'iva; (ī, iṇī), m. f. a bird; (iṇī), f. (with or without rātri) a night with the two days enclosing it; the day of full moon; N. of a S'ākinī; [cf. Lith. pauksh-tis, 'a bird;' Goth. fug-ls, 'a bird;' Angl. Sax. fug-ul; Mod. Germ. Vogel; probably Lat. passer for paxer.] — Pakshi-kīṭa, as, m. 'bird-insect,' an insect-like bird, an insignificant species of bird. — Pakshi-tīrtha, am, n., N. of a sacred bathing-place. — Pakshi-pati, is, m. 'the prince of birds,' an epithet of Sampāti. — Pakshipānīya-śālikā, f. a trough or reservoir for watering birds, cattle, &c. — Pakshi-pungava, as, m. 'a bull among the birds,' an epithet of Jaṭāyu. — Pakshi-pravara, as, m. 'the most excellent among the birds,' an epithet of Garuḍa. — Pakshi-bālaka, as, m. a young bird. — Pakshi-mṛiga-tā, f. (fr. pakshin and mṛiga), the form or condition of a bird or of a beast. — Pakshi-rāj, ṭ, or pakshi-rāja, as, m. 'king of the birds,' an epithet of Garuḍa or of Jaṭāyu. — Pakshi-rājya, am, n. the sovereignty of the feathered tribes. — Pakshi-śālā, f. 'bird-house,' an aviary, a nest. — Pakshi-śāvaka, as, m. a young bird. — Pakshi-siṅha, as, m. 'lion among the birds,' an epithet of Garuḍa, the bird and vehicle of Vishṇu. — Pakshi-svāmin, ī, m. 'lord or master of the birds,' an epithet of Garuḍa. — Pakshīndra (°shi-in°), as, m. 'prince of the birds,' an epithet of Garuḍa.

Pakshila, as, m. (with svāmin) an epithet of the saint Vātsyāyana. — Pakshila-svāmin, ī, m. an epithet of Vātsyāyana who is identified with Cāṇakya.

Pakshīya, as, ā, am (at the end of a comp.), belonging to a side, siding with, taking the side or adhering to the party of any one.

Pakshman, a, n. an eyelash; the filament of a flower; the point of a thread, a thin thread; the leaf of a flower; a wing; a whisker. — Pakshma-kopa or pakshma-prakopa, as, m. irritation produced in the eye by the eyelashes turning inwards (Entropium). — Pakshmāksha (°ma-aksha), as, ī, am, having an eyelash or eyelashes in the eye (suffering from Entropium).

Pakshmala, as, ā, am, having strong or long eyelashes; having long or thick hair, hairy, shaggy.

Pakshya, as, ā, am, Ved. descended from Paksha (i.e. according to Sāy. the Sun); changing every half month; produced or occurring in a fortnight; belonging to a side, siding with, taking part with; lateral.

पक्ष्णु pakshṇu. See p. 522, col. 1.

पक्ष्मन् pakshman. See above.

पङ्क panka, as, am, m. n. (said to be fr. rt. 1. paċ or pañċ), mud, mire, dirt, clay; a slough, a quagmire; ointment, unguent; moral impurity, sin; [cf. nish-panka, nīla-p°.] — Panka-karvaṭa, as, m. soft mud, especially such as is left by the retiring of floods or on the banks of a river, alluvium, a marsh, a quagmire. — Panka-kīra, as, m. an aquatic bird, a lap-wing. — Panka-krīḍa, as, ā, am, wallowing or sporting in mud; (as), m. a pig; (also panka-krīḍanaka, as, m.) — Panka-gaḍaka, as, m. or panka-gati, is, f. a small fish, Macrognathus Pancalus. — Panka-grāha, as, m. the marine monster Makara, q.v. — Panka-ċċhid, t, m. 'mud-destroyer,' Strychnos Potatorum (the fruit of which is used for purifying foul water). — Panka-ja, am, n. 'mud-born,' a species of lotus, Nelumbium Speciosum (or rather its flower which closes in the evening); (as), m. an epithet of Brahmā, (incorrect for pankaja-ja, 'lotus-born'); (ī), f. an epithet of Durgā. — Pankaja-janman, ā, m. 'sprung from a lotus,' an epithet of Brahmā. — Pankaja-nābha, as, ā, am, 'having a lotus springing from his navel,' an epithet of Vishṇu. — Panka-janman, a, n. = panka-ja. — Pankaja-pattra, am, n. the leaf of a lotus. — Pankajapattra-netra, as, ā, am, having eyes like lotus-leaves. — Pankajāvalī (°ja-āv°), f. a particular metre; [cf. pankāvalī.] — Panka-jit, t, m., N. of a son of Garuḍa. — Pankajinī, f. (fr. pankajin which is fr. panka-ja), Nelumbium Speciosum (the plant itself), a group of such lotuses, a lotus pool, a pool or pond where the lotus grows or a place abounding with that flower; the flexible stalk of a water-lily. — Panka-tā, f. the nature or property of mud, muddiness. — Panka-digdha, as, ā, am, besmeared with mud, soiled with dirt. — Pankadigdha-śarīra, as, m. 'having a mud-smeared body,' N. of a Dānava; (also read as if two names, panka-digdha and śarīra.) — Pankadig-dhānga (°dha-an°), as, m. 'having mud-smeared limbs,' N. of a being attending on Skanda. — Panka-prabhā, f. (with Jainas) N. of one of the seven divisions of hell (where mud or mire takes the place of light). — Panka-bhāj, k, k, k, sunk in the mire. — Panka-bhāraka, as, ā, am, laden with mud, muddy. — Panka-majjana, am, n. immersion in mud. — Panka-maṇḍuka, as, m. a bivalve conch; (also wrongly read -maṇḍūka.) — Panka-maya, as, ī, am, full of mud or mire, muddy. — Panka-ruh, t, or panka-ruha, am, n. 'mud-growing,' a lotus. — Panka-vat, ān, atī, at, muddy, covered with mud. — Panka-vāsa, as, m. 'dwelling in mud,' a crab. — Panka-śukti, is, f. 'mud-shell,' a particular species of muscle or cockle (the stair-case shell, spinnet shell). — Panka-sūraṇa, as, m. 'mud-root,' the fibrous edible root of a lotus; (also written panka-śūraṇa, panka-shūraṇa.) — Panke-ja, am, n. 'born in the mud,' a lotus. — Panke-ruha, am, n. 'growing in mud,' a lotus; (as), m. the Indian crane (as a synonym of pushkara). — Panke-śaya, as, ā, am, resting or dwelling in mud.

Pankāra, as, m. the aquatic plant Blyxa Octandra or Vallisneria (= śaivala); the aquatic plant Trapa Bispinosa (= jala-kubjaka); a dam, dike, or raised bank forming a path amidst inundated fields; stairs, steps, a ladder.

Pankāvalī, f. = pankajāvalī (of which it may be a contraction).

Pankin, ī, inī, i (at the end of a comp.), muddy, filled or covered with mud; [cf. mala-p°.]

Pankila, as, ā, am, muddy, dirty, clayey; (as), m. a boat, canoe.

पङ्कण pankaṇa, wrong form for pakkaṇa, q. v.

पङ्कवारि panka-vāri. See pakva-vāri.

पङ्क्ति pankti, is, ī, f. (connected with pañċan), a row or line or set of five, a collection of five, the number five; a sort of fivefold metre consisting of five Pādas of eight syllables each; (in the later literature) any stanza of four times ten syllables (or of four lines, each line consisting of ten syllables); the number ten, (sometimes in comp., cf. Rāvaṇa-śiraḥ-p°, pankti-grīva, pankti-ratha); a line, range, row, series; a group, flock, troop; a heap; a row of people sitting down to a meal, a company, society, assembly, party; a company of persons of the same caste; the living generation; the earth; cooking, maturing, (incorrectly for pakti); fame, celebrity (for pakti); [cf. akshara-p°, āstāra-p°, pada-p°, prastāra-p°.] — Pankti-kaṇṭaka, 'having rows of thorns (?),' a white-flowering Achyranthes. — Pankti-grīva, as, m. 'ten-necked,' an epithet of Rāvaṇa; [cf. pankti-ratha.] — Pankti-ċara, as, m. 'going in lines,' an osprey. — Pankti-dūsha or -dūshaka, as, ā, am, defiling or contaminating any society or company of persons; (as), m. an improper person with whom to associate, (opposed to pankti-pāvana.) — Pankti-dosha, as, m. a bane of society, anything which defiles or contaminates a company, what spoils a society. — Pankti-pāvana, as, ā, am, purifying a society or company of persons, (opposed to pankti-dūsha); (as), m. a respectable or eminent person. — Pankti-ratha, as, m. 'having ten chariots,' a N. of Daśa-ratha, the father of Rāma-ċandra. — Pankti-rādhas, ās, ās, as, Ved. (a sacrifice) containing fivefold gifts; (Sāy.) abounding in properly presented oblations. — Pankti-vīja, as, m. a species of plant (= varvūra). — Pankti-kṛita, as, ā, am, associated in groups. — Pankty-uttara, as, ā, am, having a Pankti at the end.

Panktikā, f. a row, line, (in akshara-panktikā, a row of letters.)

पङ्गु pangu, us, ūs or vī, u (perhaps fr. apa-anga, said to be connected with rt. 1. khañj), lame, crippled, halt, one who has lost his legs, &c.; (us), m. the planet Saturn (as moving slowly); an epithet of Nirjita-varman. — Pangu-grāha, as, m. the sea-monster Makara, q.v. [cf. panka-grāha]; one of the signs of the zodiac, see makara. — Pangu-tā, f. or pangu-tva, am, n. lameness, deformity, mutilation. — Pangutva-hāriṇī, f. a species of shrub (= śimṛiḍī).

Panguka, as, ā, am, = pangu, lame.

Pangula, as, ā, am, lame, crippled; (as), m. a horse of a glassy or silvery white colour; (amī), n. lameness (?).

पच् 1. paċ or pañċ, cl. 1. P. A. paċati, -te, pañċati, -te, &c., to make clear or evident: Caus. pañċayati, &c., to explain or state fully, amplify; to spread.

Pañċā, f. spreading.

पच् 2. paċ, cl. 1. P. A. paċati, -te, papāċa (papaktha or peċitha), peċe (perf. part. peċivas, f. peċushī), pakshyati, -te, apākshīt, apakta (Vedic forms pakshat, apeċiran, peċiran), paktum (Ved. paktave), to cook, dress food, bake, roast, boil; to melt (metals &c.); to bake or burn (bricks); to digest; to ripen, mature, bring to maturity; (figuratively) to bring to perfection or completion; to develop anything (acc.) into another state (acc.); to cook for one's self (A.): Pass. paċyate, to be cooked; to become ripe or mature, to ripen; to arrive at completion or perfection (Mahā-bh. Anuśāsana-p. 6205); to be developed; to be inflamed: Caus. pāċayati, -yitum, Aor. apīpaċat, to cause to be cooked, to have cooked, have dressed (as food), to cook; to cause to ripen, to bring to maturity or perfection, bring to completion, bring to an end; to cure, heal; (A. -te), to cause to cook for one's self: Pass. of Caus. pāċyate, to be cooked: Desid. pipakshati: Intens. pāpaċyate, pāpaċīti, to be much cooked, to cook very much, burn excessively; (figuratively) to be much afflicted: Desid. of the Intens. pāpaċishati, -te; [cf. Zend paċ, 'to cook:' Gr. πέπ-ων, πεπ-τό-ς, πέψι-ς, πέπ-τω, πέμ-μα, πόπ-ανο-ν, ἕψ-ω for πέψ-ω, ὄψ-ο-ν, ὀπ-τό-ς for ποπ-τό-ς, ὀπτάω, ἀρτο-κόπος, ἀρτο-πόπος, δρυ-πεπής, δρύ-πεψ: Lat. coqu-o, coquu-s, cū-lina, co-quina = pop-īna: Slav. pek-a, 'I cook;' pesh-ti, 'a stove:' Lith. kep-ti, 'to bake.']

Paktavya, as, ā, am, to be cooked or dressed, to be baked; to be matured; to be digested.

Pakti, is, f. cooking, preparing food; food or any dish of cooked food (Ved.); digesting, digestion; the place of digestion; becoming ripe, ripening; development; respectability, dignity, fame. — Pakti-śūla, am, n. violent pain or inflammation of the bowels proceeding from indigestion, colic. — Pakti-sthāna, am, n. the place of digestion.

Paktṛi, tā, trī, tṛi, who or what cooks, cooking, a cook; digestive, promoting digestion; who or what ripens, ripening.

Paktra, am, n. the state of a householder who possesses a sacred fire; the sacred fire perpetually maintained by the householder.

Paktrima, as, ā, am, prepared by cooking, cooked; obtained by boiling (as salt); ripe, ripened, matured.

Paktvā, ind. having cooked or dressed; having matured, &c.

Paktha, as, m., Ved. (according to Sāy.) one who cooks the oblation; N. of a man protected by the Aśvins; (ās), m. pl., N. of a people.

Pakthin, ī, inī, i, Ved. (according to Sāy.) cooking the oblation.

Pakva, as, ā, am (past pass. part.), cooked,

roasted, boiled, prepared on the fire, (opposed to *āma*); warmed, (*dvi-pakva*, warmed up again); baked or burnt (as bricks, porcelain, &c.); digested; mature, ripe, ripened, matured (as fruits or corn or as the milk in an udder); ready to discharge matter or suppurate; ripe (as a boil); grey (as the hair); come to perfection, accomplished, perfect, fully developed (as the understanding, character, &c.), shrewd, experienced; ripe for destruction; on the eve of decay, near to death, perishing, decaying; (*am*), n. cooked food; [cf. *nish-p°*, *pari-p°*, &c.; cf. also Gr. πέπ-ων, πεπ-ανό-ς, πέπ-ειρο-ς.] — *Pakva-kashāya*, *as*, *ā*, *am*, having passion destroyed. — *Pakva-krit*, *t*, *t*, *t*, cooking, maturing, dressing food; (*t*), m. the tree Azadirachta Indica (= *nimba*), the leaves of which are applied to certain swellings to induce suppuration. — *Pakva-keśa*, *as*, *ī*, *am*, grey-haired. — *Pakvatā*, f. ripeness, maturity, greyness (of the hair). — *Pakva-rasa*, *as*, m. wine or any intoxicating liquor. — *Pakva-vat*, *ān*, *atī*, *at*, one who has cooked, &c. — *Pakva-vāri*, n. sour rice-gruel, the water of boiled rice (= *kāñjika*); boiling water; distilled water; (also read *panka-vāri*.) — *Pakvasasyopamonnati* (°*sya-upama-un*°) = *rāja-kadamba*. — *Pakvātisāra* (°*va-at*°), *as*, m. chronic dysentery. — *Pakvādhāna* (°*va-ādh*°), *am*, n. or *pakvāśaya* (°*va-āś*°), *as*, m. the receptacle for digested food, the place of digestion, the stomach, belly, abdomen; [cf. *āmāśaya*.] — *Pakvānna* (°*va-an*°), *am*, n. cooked or dressed food. — *Pakveshṭaka-ćita*, *am*, n. (a building) constructed with burnt bricks, (Pāṇ. VI. 3, 65.) — *Pakveshṭakā* (°*va-ish*°), f. a burnt or baked brick.

Pakshṇu, *us*, *us*, *u*, who or what cooks or matures, cooking, maturing.

3. *pać*, *k*, *k*, *k* (at the end of a comp.), cooking, baking.

Paća, *as*, *ā*, *am*, cooking, baking, roasting; digesting [cf. *alpam-paća*, *ishṭi-p°*, *kim-p°*, *dush-p°*, &c.]; (*as*, *ā*), m. f. cooking, maturing, &c.

Paćaka, *as*, m. a cook, cooking, baking.

Paćat, *an*, *antī*, *at*, cooking, boiling, roasting, ripening, &c. — *Paćat-puṭa*, *as*, m. the tree Hibiscus Phoeniceus.

Paćata, *as*, *ā*, *am*, cooked, dressed, boiled, ripe, mature; (*as*), m. the sun; fire; a N. of Indra; (*am*), n. cooked food. — *Paćata-bhrijjalā*, f. continual baking and roasting.

Paćati-kalpa, *as*, *ā*, *am*, or (*am*), ind. almost cooked or ripened, (also in a similar sense *paćati-deśya* and *paćati-deśīya*.)

Paćatya, *as*, *ā*, *am*, Ved. cooked, dressed (as food), ripe.

Paćana, *as*, *ā*, *am*, cooking, roasting, maturing [cf. *eṇi-p°*]; (*as*), m. fire; (*ā*), f. becoming ripe, ripening; (*ī*), f. the wild citron tree, = *vana-vija-pūraka*; (*am*), n. the act of cooking, a means or instrument for cooking, fuel, a cooking utensil, a vessel, a frying-pan, &c.; cooking, dressing, boiling; ripening, maturing; becoming cooked, becoming ripe.

Paćanikā (gender doubtful), a pan.

Paća-paća, *as*, *ā*, *am*, (probably) 'continually bringing to maturity,' an epithet of Śiva.

Paća-prakūṭā, see Gaṇa Mayūra-vyaṇsakādi to Pāṇ. II. 1, 72.

Paćamāna, *as*, *ā*, *am*, cooking, in the act of cooking or ripening.

Paćam-paćā, f. (reduplicated form fr. rt. 2. *pać*), a species of Curcuma, C. Aromatica or C. Xanthorrhiza.

Paća-lavaṇā, f. constant boiling of salt, (*paća* is 2nd sing. impv., and the comp. belongs to the Gaṇa Mayūra-vyaṇsakādi.)

Paćāna, *as*, *ā*, *am* (anomalous form of the pres. part. A.), cooking, preparing food, (see Mahā-bh. Vana-p. 13239, and cf. *kim-p°*.)

Paći, *is*, m. fire; cooking, maturing.

Paćelima, *as*, *ā*, *am*, being soon cooked, cooking or ripening quickly; fit to cook or ripen, fit to be matured; (*as*), m. Phaseolus Mungo or a similar species of bean; fire; the sun.

Paćeluka, *as*, m. a cook.

Paćya, *as*, *ā*, *am*, becoming ripe, ripening, (see *krishṭa-p°* and cf. *pākya*.)

Paćyamāna, *as*, *ā*, *am*, being cooked, being in the act of ripening, being baked, being melted, being under digestion, being matured.

Pāćyamāna, *as*, *ā*, *am*, being cooked.

पच्छब्द *pać-ćhabda*, *paj-ja*, &c. See under 3. *pad*, p. 529, col. 3.

पज्झटिका *pajjhaṭikā*, f. a kind of metre; a small bell.

पज्र *pajra*, *as*, *ā*, *am*, Ved. (perhaps) stout, fat, corpulent, in good condition, in good plight; wealthy, rich; (Sāy.) powerful, strong, rich in food; *pajrāyā garbhaḥ*, 'the son or child of the fat one,' = the Soma; (*ās*), m. pl. (according to Sāy.) an epithet of the Aṅgirasas or of the family of Kakshīvat; (*am*), n., N. of a Sāman. — *Pajra-hoshin*, *ī*, *iṇī*, *i*, Ved. (perhaps) having rich oblations; (Sāy.) for whom the acclamation of praise (*ghosha*) is prepared.

Pajriya, *as*, m. an epithet of Kakshīvat.

पञ्च् *pańć*. See rt. 1. *pać*, p. 521, col. 3.

पञ्चन् *pańćan*, *a*, m. f. n. pl. (said to be fr. rt. *pańć*; originally the spreading out of the hand to represent the number by the five fingers), five. In the Veda *pańća svasāraḥ*, the five sisters = the fingers; *drih pańća svasāraḥ* = the ten fingers; *pańća kshitīnām*, the five classes of dwellers on the earth = the four castes and the Nishādas, Ṛig-veda I. 7, 9; [cf. 1. *kshiti*, *ćarshaṇi*, *krishṭi*, *jana*; cf. also Ved. *pańća-tha* = Zend *pukh-dha* = Gr. πέμπ-το-ς; Zend *pańćan*; Gr. πέντε, Æol. πέμπε; Lat. *quinque*, *quinc-tu-s* or *quin-tu-s*, *Quinct-īli-s*; Goth. *fimf*; Mod. Germ. *fünf*; Lith. *pan-ti*; Hib. *cuig*; Cambro-Brit. *pump*.] — *Pańća-kapāla*, *as*, *ī*, *am*, Ved. prepared or offered in five cups or bowls, a particular ceremony in which ghee is offered in five cups. — *Pańća-karṇa*, *as*, *ā*, *am*, (perhaps) branded in the ear with the number five (as cattle), see Pāṇ. VI. 3, 115. — *Pańća-karpaṭa*, *ās*, m. pl., N. of a people. — *Pańća-karman*, *a*, n. (in medicine) five kinds of treatment, viz. giving emetics, purging, giving sternutatories, and administering enemas of two kinds, oily and not oily. — *Pańća-kashāya*, *as*, m. (?), a decoction from the fruits of five plants, the Jambu, Sālmali, Vāṭyāla, Vakula, and Badara; (for the five Kashāyas of the Buddhists see under *kashāya*.) — *Pańćakashāya-ja* or *pańća-kashāyottha* (°*ya-ut*°), *as*, *ā*, *am*, produced from the above decoction. — *Pańća-kāpittha*, *as*, *ī*, *am*, prepared with the five products of the Kapittha tree or Feronia Elephantum, (perhaps leaves, blossom, fruit, gum, and bark.) — *Pańća-kritya*, *as*, m. a species of plant (= *pakta-pauḍa*). — *Pańća-kritvas*, ind. five times. — *Pańća-krishṇa*, *as*, m. 'having five black spots,' a species of poisonous insect. — *Pańća-krishṇalaka*, *as*, *ā*, *am*, comprising five Krishṇalas. — *Pańća-koṇa*, *as*, m. 'having five angles,' a pentagon. — *Pańća-kola*, *am*, n. the five spices, viz. long pepper (*kaṇā*), its root (*kaṇā-mūla*), Chai or Piper Chaba (*ćavya*), plumbago (*agni*), and dry ginger (*nāgara*). — *Pańća-kosha*, *ās*, m. pl. the five sheaths or cases supposed to invest the soul; see under *kośa*. — *Pańća-krama*, N. of a work ascribed to Nāgārjuna. — *Pańća-krośa-māhātmya*, *am*, n., N. of a poem. — *Pańća-krośī*, f. (probably) a distance of five Krośas. — *Pańća-kshāra*, *am*, n. = *pańća-lavaṇa*. — *Pańća-khaṭva*, *am*, *ī*, n. f. a collection of five bedsteads. — *Pańća-ganga*, *ās*, m. pl., N. of a place (Mahā-bh. Droṇa-p. 2095). — *Pańća-gaṇa-yoga*, *as*, m. a collective name of the five plants Vidārī-gandhā, Bṛihatī, Pṛiśni-parṇī, Nidigdhikā, and Śva-daṇshṭrā. — *Pańća-gata*, *as*, *ā*, *am*, (in algebra) raised to the fifth power, (lit. arrived at five.) — *Pańća-gava*, *am*, *ī*, n. f. a collection of five cows. — *Pańćagava-dhana*, *as*, *ā*, *am*, whose property consists of five cows. — *Pańća-gavya*, *am*, n. five products of the cow, viz. milk, coagulated or sour milk, butter, urine, and cow-dung. — *Pańća-gu*, *us*, *us*, *u*, bought with five cows. — *Pańća-guṇa*, *as*, *ā*, *am*, five times, fivefold. — *Pańća-gupta*, *as*, *ā*, *am*, covered or protected in a fivefold manner, having five members covered or concealed; (*as*), m. a tortoise, turtle (as drawing in its four feet and head under its shell; cf. *pańćāṅga-gupta*); the materialistic system of the Cārvākas. — *Pańća-gupti-rasā*, f. a species of vegetable, Medicago Esculenta (Trigonella Corniculata). — *Pańća-grihīta*, *as*, *ā*, *am*, Ved. taken or taken up five times. — *Pańća-goṇi*, *is*, *is*, *i*, containing five Droṇas (?), see Pāṇ. I. 2, 50. — *Pańća-grāmī*, f. a collection of five villages. — *Pańća-ćatvāriṇśa*, *as*, *ī*, *am*, the 45th. — *Pańća-ćatvāriṇśat*, *t*, f., 45. — *Pańća-ćandra*, *as*, m., N. of a man. — *Pańća-ćāmara*, *am*, n., N. of a metre consisting of four lines of sixteen syllables each; of another metre of four lines each containing nineteen syllables. — *Pańća-ćitika*, *as*, *ā*, *am*, Ved. piled up in five tiers or layers. — *Pańća-ćīra*, *as*, m. a Buddhist saint and legislator, also named Mañju-śrī, apparently the teacher of Buddhism in Nepal. — *Pańća-ćūḍa*, *as*, *ā*, *am*, 'five-crested,' having five tufts of hair; (*ā*), f., N. of an Apsaras or nymph of heaven. — *Pańća-ćola*, N. of a part of the Himālaya range. — *Pańća-jana*, *ās*, m. pl. the five kinds or classes of beings, viz. gods, men, Gandharvas and Apsarasas, serpents, and Pitṛis; man, mankind; N. of a demon who lived in the sea in the form of a conch shell which was formed of his bones, (he was slain by Krishṇa, who took the conch shell, thence called Pāńćajanya, and used it as his horn, see Vishṇu-Purāṇa V. 21); N. of a son of Saṃhrāda by Kṛiti; of a Prajā-pati; of a son of Sagara by Keśinī; of a son of Sriñjaya and father of Soma-datta; (*ī*), f. an assemblage or aggregate of five persons; N. of a daughter of Viśva-rūpa and wife of Bharata. — *Pańćajanālaya* (°*na-āl*°), *as*, *ā*, *am*, an epithet of the Ābhīras, (perhaps so called as living where the demon Pańća-jana lived.) — *Pańćajanīna*, *as*, *ā*, *am*, devoted to the five races; (*as*), m. an actor, a mimic, a buffoon; the chief of five men. — *Pańća-janīya*, *as*, *ā*, *am*, consecrated to or intended for the five classes of beings. — *Pańća-jñāna*, *as*, m. 'possessing the five kinds of knowledge,' a Buddha or Buddhist sanctified teacher. — *Pańća-taksha*, *am*, *ī*, n. f. a collection of five carpenters. — *Pańća-tattva*, *am*, n. the five elements collectively, see under *tattva*; (in the Tantras) the five essentials (all beginning with *ma*, cf. *pańća-ma-kāra*), viz. wine (*madya*), meat (*māṇsa*), fish (*matsya*), mystic intertwining of the fingers (*mudrā*), and sexual intercourse (*maithuna*). — *Pańća-tantra*, *am*, n., N. of a well-known collection of moral stories and fables in five books or chapters (*tantra*) from which the author of the Hitopadeśa drew a large portion of his materials. — *Pańćatantraka*, *am*, n., N. of a work consisting of five sections, (see the preceding.) — *Pańća-tanmātra*, *am*, n. the five subtile rudiments of the five elements; see *tan-mātra*. — *Pańća-tapas*, *ās*, m. an ascetic who in the hot weather sits between four fires placed towards the four quarters with the burning sun above (Manu VI. 23). — *Pańća-tā*, f. or *pańća-tva*, *am*, n. fivefoldness, fivefold state; the aggregate of five, a collection of five things; the five elements collectively (viz. earth, air, fire, water, and ākāśa); separation into the five elements of which the body consists, death, dissolution. — *Pańća-tāra*, *as*, *ā*, *am*, five-starred. — *Pańća-tikta*, *am*, n. five bitter things (viz. Nimba, Amṛitā, Vṛisha, Paṭola, and Nidigdhikā). — *Pańća-tīrthī*, f. any five principal places of pilgrimage (especially Viśrānti, Saukara, Naimisha, Prayāga, and Pushkara); N. of a sacred bathing-place; bathing on the day of the equinox (?). — *Pańća-triṇśa*, *as*, *ī*, *am*, the 35th. — *Pańća-triṇśat*, *t*, f. or *pańća-triṇśati*, *is*, f., 35. — *Pańća-tva*, see *pańća-tā* above. — *Pańća-daka*, *ās*, m. pl., N. of a people. — *Pańća-daśa*, *as*, *ī*, *am*, the 15th; consisting of 15; joined with or increased by 15 (e. g.

pańća-daśam sahasram, 1015); containing or representing the Pańća-daśa Stoma or connected with it; (*ī*), f., scil. *tithi*, the 15th day of a half month, the day of full or new moon; N. of a book (belonging to the Uttara-mīmāṇsā) consisting of 15 chapters. — *Pańćadaśa-kṛitvas*, ind., 15 times. — *Pańćadaśa-dhā*, ind. in or into 15 parts or ways. — *Pańća-daśan*, *a*, m. f. n. pl., 15. — *Pańćadaśama*, *as*, *ī*, *am*, the 15th. — *Pańćadaśa-vat*, *ān*, *atī*, *at*, possessing the Pańća-daśa Stoma. — *Pańćadaśāha* (°*śa-aha*), *as*, m. a period of 15 days. — *Pańćadaśāhika*, *as*, *ī*, *am*, lasting 15 days. — *Pańćadaśin*, *ī*, *inī*, *i*, consisting of 15, or of 15 parts. — *Pańćadaśī-samāsa*, *as*, m., N. of a work by Rāma-kṛishṇa. — *Pańća-dāman*, *ā*, *mnī*, *a*, Ved. having five cords. — *Pańća-dīrgha*, *am*, n. the five long parts of the body (viz. the arms, eyes, belly [according to the Buddhists, the knees], nose, and breast). — *Pańća-dhā*, ind. in five ways, in five parts, fivefold. — *Pańća-nakha*, *as*, *ā*, *am*, five-clawed, having five nails; (*as*), m. any animal having five claws or toes; an elephant; a tiger; a tortoise. — *Pańća-nada*, *am*, n. (according to Pāṇ. II. 1, 20, an Avyayī-bhāva comp.), the Pañjāb or country of five rivers, viz. the Sata-dru (Sutluj), Vipāśā (Beas), Irā-vatī (Ravee), Candra-bhāgā (Chenab), and Vitastā (Jhelum or Behut); N. of a river produced by the junction of the five rivers of the Pañjāb and which falls into the Sindhu; N. of a Tīrtha near the spot where the Kiraṇā and Dhūta-pāpa fall into the Ganges after the union of the latter river with the Yamunā and Sarasvatī; (*as*), m. a prince of Pańća-nada; N. of an Asura; N. of a preceptor; (*ās*), m. pl. the inhabitants of Pańća-nada. — *Pańća-nada-tīrtha*, *am*, n., N. of a sacred bathing-place. — *Pańćanavata*, *as*, *ī*, *am*, the 95th. — *Pańća-navati*, *is*, f., 95. — *Pańćanavati-tama*, *as*, *ī*, *am*, the 95th. — *Pańća-nāman*, *ā*, *mnī*, *a*, having five names. — *Pańća-nidhana*, *am*, n., N. of a Sāman. — *Pańća-nimba*, *am*, n. the five products of the Azadirachta Indica (viz. the flowers, fruit, leaves, bark, and root). — *Pańća-nīrājana*, *am*, n. waving four things (viz. a lamp, lotus, cloth, mango or betel leaf) before an idol and then falling prostrate. — *Pańća-pakshin*, *ī*, m., N. of a small book ascribed to Śiva containing prophecies, in which the five vowels *a*, *i*, *u*, *e*, *o* are connected with five birds; (also °*pakshi* or °*pakshin*, n.) — *Pańća-pańća-nakha*, *as*, m. five species of animals allowed to be killed and eaten, the hare, porcupine, alligator, rhinoceros, and tortoise. — *Pańća-pańćāśa*, *as*, *ī*, *am*, the 55th. — *Pańća-pańćāśat*, *t*, f., 55. — *Pańća-pańćin*, *ī*, *inī*, *i*, Ved. having five parts, fivefold. — *Pańća-pattra*, *as*, m. 'five-leaved,' a species of Caṇḍāla-kanda. — *Pańća-pad* or *pańća-pād*, *pāt*, *pāt* or *padī*, *pāt*, consisting of five feet, steps, or parts; (*padī*), f., N. of a river in Śāka-dvīpa. — *Pańća-pada*, *as*, *ā*, *am*, Ved. containing five Padas; (*ī*), f. 'only five steps,' a term expressive of a cold unfriendly relationship, (opposed to *sāpta-padīna*, q. v.); the five strong cases (viz. the nom. voc. and acc. sing., the nom. voc. and acc. du., and the nom. and voc. pl.). — *Pańća-parṇikā* or *pańća-parṇī*, f. a species of small shrub (= *go-rakshī*). — *Pańća-parvata*, *am*, n. 'the five mountains,' N. of five peaks of the Himālayas. — *Pańća-pallava*, *am*, n. the aggregate of five sprigs or young shoots of the Āmra, Jambū, Kapittha, Vīja-pūraka, and Vilva; (according to others, of the Āmra, Aśvattha, Vaṭa, Parkaṭī, and Yajñodumbara; or of the Panasa, Āmra, Aśvattha, Vaṭa, and Vakula); Bél or Marmelos, citron, and wood-apple. — *Pańća-pātra*, *am*, n. five cups or vessels collectively; a Śrāddha in which offerings are made in five vessels. — *Pańća-pāda*, *as*, *ā*, *am*, consisting of or containing five feet. — *Pańća-pādikā* or *pańća-pādī*, f., N. of a treatise on the Uṇādi affixes consisting of five sections; N. of a philosophical work by Sa-nandana treating of the first four Brahma-sūtras. — *Pańćapādikā-vivaraṇa*, *am*, n. a commentary by Prakāśātman on Sa-nandana's Pańća-pādī. — *Pańća-pitta*, *am*, n. the gall or bile of five animals (viz. the boar, goat, buffalo, fish, and peacock). — *Pańća-pura*, *am*, n., N. of a city. — *Pańćapushpa-maya*, *as*, *ī*, *am*, formed of five flowers. — *Pańća-prastha*, *as*, *ā*, *am*, having five elevations or rising grounds (as a forest; perhaps N. of a forest). — *Pańća-prāṇa*, *ās*, m. pl. the five vital airs, the five airs supposed to be in the body. — *Pańća-prāsāda*, *as*, m. a temple with four pinnacles and a steeple. — *Pańća-bandha*, *as*, m. a fine equal to the fifth part of anything lost or stolen. — *Pańća-balā*, f. the five plants called Balā (viz. Balā, Nāga-b°, Mahā-b°, Ati-b°, and Rāja-b°). — *Pańća-bāṇa* or *pańća-vāṇa*, *as*, m. 'having five arrows,' epithet of the god of love. — *Pańća-bāhu*, *us*, m. 'five-armed,' N. of one of the attendants of Śiva. — *Pańća-brahma*, *am*, n., N. of an Upanishad. — *Pańća-bhadra*, *as*, *ā*, *am*, having five good qualities; consisting of five good ingredients (as a sauce or a decoction); having five auspicious marks or spotted on the chest, back, face, and flanks (as a horse); vicious. — *Pańća-bhuja*, *as*, *ā*, *am*, five-armed, pentagonal; (*as*), m. a pentagon. — *Pańća-bhūta*, *am*, n. the five elements, earth, air, fire, water, and ākāśa. — *Pańća-bhūta-parityakta*, *as*, *ā*, *am*, deserted by the five elements (as a dead body). — *Pańćabhūtātman* (°*ta-āt*°), *ā*, *ā*, *a*, consisting of the five elements, formed of the five primary elements (as the body). — *Pańća-bhṛiṅga*, epithet of the five plants Deva-dālī, Śamī, Bhaṅgā, Nirguṇḍī, and Tamāla-pattra. — *Pańća-bhautika* incorrect reading for *pāńća-bhautika*. q. v. — *Pańća-ma-kāra*, *am*, n. the five essentials of the left-hand Tantra ritual, the words for which begin with the letter *m*; see *pańća-tattva*. — *Pańća-maya*, *as*, *ī*, *am*, consisting or formed of five, made up or consisting of the five (elements). — *Pańća-mahāpātakin*, *ī*, *inī*, *i*, guilty of the five great sins; see *mahā-pātaka*. — *Pańća-mahāyajña*, *ās*, m. pl. the five great sacrifices of the Hindūs; (see *mahā-yajña*.) — *Pańća-mahisha*, *am*, n. the five products of the buffalo cow; [cf. *pańća-gavya*.] — *Pańća-māshika* or *pańća-māshaka*, *as*, &c., consisting of five Māshas, amounting to five Māshas (as a fine &c.). — 1. *pańća-māsya*, *as*, *ā*, *am* (for 2. see under *pańćama*), happening every five months, containing five months; (*as*), m. the Koil or Indian cuckoo. — *Pańća-mukha*, *as*, *ī*, *am*, five-faced or five-headed, (sometimes applied in the Upanishads to Prajā-pati); (*as*), m. an epithet of Śiva; a lion; an arrow with five points; (*ī*), f. a species of plant, Gendarussa Vulgaris; [cf. *pańća-śikha*, *pańća-vaktra*, *pańćānana*, *pańćāsya*.] — *Pańća-mudrā*, f. five gestures to be made in presenting offerings to an idol. — *Pańća-mushṭi*, *is*, *ī*, f. the plant Trigonella Corniculata. — *Pańća-mūtra*, *am*, n. the urine of five female animals (viz. the cow, goat, sheep, buffalo, and ass). — *Pańća-mūla*, *am*, n. or *pańća-mūlī*, f. a collection or group of five roots or plants with tuberous roots (e. g. Vilva, Agni-mantha, Ṭuṇṭuka, Pāṭala, and Kāśmarī; or Tri-kaṇṭaka, the two Bṛihatīs, Pṛithak-parṇī, and Vidāri-gandha; the first is considered the larger collection, the second the smaller; other groups are also enumerated). — *Pańća-yakshā*, f., N. of a Tīrtha. — *Pańća-yajña*, *ās*, m. pl. the five rites or sacrifices of a house-keeper; [cf. *pańća-mahāyajña*.] — *Pańćayajña-paribhrashṭa*, *as*, m. a Brahman who omits to perform the five great sacrifices. — *Pańća-yāma*, *as*, m., N. of a son of Ātapa (Sun-shine). — *Pańća-yuga*, *am*, n. a cycle of five years, a lustrum. — *Pańća-raksha*, N. of two Prajñā-pāramitās (q. v.) connected with each other. — *Pańća-rakshaka*, *as*, m. a species of plant (= *pakta-pauḍa*). — *Pańća-ratna*, *am*, n. a collection of five jewels or precious things, viz. gold, the diamond, sapphire, ruby, and pearl, or (according to Gaṇḍa) gold, silver, coral, pearl, and Rāga-paṭṭa; N. of a collection of five verses on ethical subjects; (*ānī*), n. pl. the five gems or five most admired episodes of the Mahā-bhārata. — *Pańća-rasā*, f. the Emblic Myrobalan tree (= *āmalakī*). — *Pańća-rātra*, *as*, *ā*, *am*, lasting five nights or days; (*am*), n. a period of five nights, N. of an Ahīna (q. v.) which lasts five days; a general term for the sacred books of various Vaishṇava sects; see *pāńćarātra*. — *Pańća-rātraka*, *as*, *ā*, *am*, lasting five nights (i. e. days). — *Pańćarātra-dīpikā*, f. (probably) N. of a treatise on the fabrication and right dimensions and decoration of idols. — *Pańća-rāśika*, *as*, *ā*, *am*, relating to the five ratios or proportions of numbers; (*am*), n. the rule of five, the rule of proportion with five terms, double rule of three (?). — *Pańćarća* (°*ća-ṛića*), *am*, n., Ved. a stanza consisting of five verses. — *Pańća-lakshaṇa*, *as*, *ā*, *am*, possessing five characteristics (said of the Purāṇas, which ought strictly to comprehend five topics, viz. the creation of the universe, its destruction and renovation, the genealogy of gods and patriarchs, the reigns of the Manus, and the history of the solar and lunar races; but few Purāṇas, except the Vishṇu, conform to this description, and even the Vishṇu-Purāṇa diverges into other topics). — *Pańća-lambaka*, *am*, n., N. of the fourteenth Lambaka in the Kathā-sarit-sāgara. — *Pańća-lavaṇa*, *am*, n. five kinds of salt (viz. Kāća, Saindhava, Sāmudra, Viḍa, and Sauvarćala). — *Pańća-lāṅgalaka*, *am*, n. a gift of as much land as can be cultivated with five ploughs. — *Pańća-loha*, *am*, n. a metallic alloy containing five metals (viz. copper, brass, tin, lead, and iron). — *Pańća-lohaka*, *am*, n. the five metals (viz. gold, silver, copper, tin, and lead). — *Pańća-vaktra*, *as*, *ā*, *am*, five-faced; (*as*), m. epithet of Śiva; N. of one of the attendants of Skanda; a lion; (*ā*), f. epithet of Durgā; [cf. *pańća-mukha*.] — *Pańća-vaṭa*, *as*, m. 'five-threaded,' the Brāhmanical or sacrificial cord worn across the breast or over the shoulder [cf. *pańćā-vaṭa*]; N. of a man; (*ī*), f. the five fig-trees (viz. Aśvattha, Vilva, Vaṭa, Dhātrī, and Aśoka); N. of a part of the great southern forest where the Godāvarī rises and where Rāma resided for a long period of his banishment; (in Rāmāyaṇa I. 3, 18, *pańća-vaṭa*, *am*, n. occurs.) — *Pańća-varga*, *as*, m. a class or group or series of five; the five essential ingredients or constituent elements of the body, (see 1. *dhātu*); the five organs of sense; the five sacrifices, &c., (according to some also *pańća-vargī*, which may mean 'five classes'); (*as*, *ā*, *am*), Ved. proceeding in five lines or at five times. — *Pańća-varṇa*, *as*, *ā*, *am*, five-coloured; (*as*), m., N. of a mountain; (*am*), n., N. of a forest. — *Pańća-vardhana*, *as*, m. = *pańća-rakshaka*. — *Pańća-varshaka-deśīya*, *as*, *ā*, *am*, nearly five years old. — *Pańća-varshīya*, *as*, *ā*, *am*, five years old. — *Pańća-valkala*, *am*, n. a collection of the bark of five kinds of trees, viz. the Indian, glomerous, holy and waved-leaf fig-tree, and Calamus Rotang, a sort of reed, (i. e. Nyag-rodha, Udumbara, Aśvattha, Plaksha, and Vetasa: but other trees are sometimes substituted.) — *Pańća-vāṇa*, *as*, m. 'five-arrowed,' a N. of Kāma-deva, the Indian Cupid. — *Pańća-vātīya*, *am*, n., N. of an oblation offered to the five winds at the Rāja-sūya. — *Pańća-vārshika*, *as*, *ī*, *am*, recurring every five years. — *Pańća-vāhin*, *ī*, *inī*, *i*, yoked with five, drawn by five (as a carriage &c.). — *Pańća-viṇśa*, *as*, *ī*, *am*, the 25th; consisting of 25, containing 25; presenting the Pańća-viṇśa Stoma, belonging to it, celebrated with it; (*as*), m. an epithet of Vishṇu regarded as the 25th Tattva. — *Pańća-viṇśaka*, *as*, *ī*, *am*, the 25th; 25 years old (*vayasā pańća-viṇśakaḥ*); consisting of 25. — *Pańća-viṇśati*, *is*, f., 25. — *Pańćaviṇśatikā*, f. a collection of 25 stanzas or tales, &c.; [cf. *vetāla-p*°.] — *Pańćaviṇśati-tama* or *pańćaviṇśatima*, *as*, *ī*, *am*, the 25th. — *Pańća-vidha* or *pańćavidheya*, *as*, *ā*, *am*, of five kinds, fivefold. — *Pańća-vidhāna-sūtra*, *am*, n., N. of a work belonging to the Sāma-veda. — *Pańća-vindu-prasṛita*, *am*, n., N. of a particular movement in dancing. — *Pańća-vīja*, *am*, n. a collection of five kinds of seeds (viz. of Cardiospermum Halicacabum, Trigonella Fœnum Græcum, Asteracantha Longifolia, Ligusticum Ajowan, and cumin-seed;

or of Trapusa, Karkaṭī, Dāḍima, Padma, and Vānarī; or of Sinapis Racemosa, Ligusticum Ajowan, cumin-seed, sesamum from Chorasan, and poppy). — *Pańća-vīra-goshṭha, am,* n. (perhaps) an assembly-room named 'The Five Heroes,' i. e. the five sons of Pāṇḍu. — *Pańća-vṛit* or *pańća-vṛitam,* ind. fivefold, five times. — *Pańća-śata, am,* n., 105; 500; (*as, ī, am*), amounting to 500 (as a fine); fined 500 (paṇas). — *Pańćaśata-tama, as, ī, am,* the 105th. — *Pańća-śara, as, ā, am,* 'five-arrowed,' armed with five arrows; (*as*), m., N. of Kāma-deva, the god of love. — *Pańća-śas,* ind. by fives, five by five. — *Pańća-śasya, am,* n. (or more correctly *pańća-sasya*), five species of grain, viz. Dhānya, Mudga, Tila, Yava, and Sveta-sarshapa (or Māsha). — *Pańća-śākha, as,* m. 'five-branched,' the hand (πέντοζον). — *Pańća-śāradīya, as,* m., N. of a Pańćāha representing five years. — *Pańća-śikha, as, ā, am,* 'five-crested,' having five tufts of hair on the head; (*as*), m. a lion; N. of a Sāṅkhya teacher (a pupil of Āsuri); N. of an attendant of Śiva; N. of a Gandharva. — *Pańća-śīrsha, as, ā, am,* five-headed; (*as*), m., N. of a mountain. — *Pańća-śukla, as, ā, am,* having five white (spots); (*as*), m. a species of venomous insect. — *Pańća-śūraṇa, am,* n. the five Sūraṇas (Sūraṇa = the bulbous root of Amorphophallus Campanulatus), a collective name of five bulbous plants; (this word may also be used as an adj.) — *Pańća-śairīshaka, am,* n. the five products of the Acacia Sirīsha, leaf, flower, fruit, bark, root. — *Pańća-śaila, as,* m., N. of a mountain. — *Pańća-sha, ās, ās, āni,* pl. (fr. *pańćan + shash*), five or six. — *Pańća-shashṭa, as, ī, am,* the 65th. — *Pańća-shashṭi, is,* f., 65. — *Pańćashashṭi-tama, as, ī, am,* the 65th. — *Pańća-saṭa, as, ā, am,* five-tailed (as a badge of slavery?). — *Pańća-sattra,* N. of a place. — *Pańća-saptata, as, ī, am,* the 75th. — *Pańća-saptati, is,* f., 75. — *Pańćasaptati-tama, as, ī, am,* the 75th. — *Pańća-saptan, a,* m. f. n. pl. five times seven or 35. — *Pańća-sāyaka,* N. of a work. — *Pańća-siddhāntikā,* f., N. of an astronomical work by Varāha-mihira, founded on the five older astronomical works, and called by Varāha-mihira himself Karaṇa. — *Pańća-siddhaushadhika* (°*dha-osh*°), *as, ā, am,* consisting of five kinds of medicinal plants. — *Pańća-sugandhaka, am,* n. a collection of five kinds of aromatic vegetable substances, cloves (*lavanga*), nutmeg (*jāti-phala*), camphor (*karpūra*), aloe wood (*a-guru*), and kakkola (q. v.). — *Pańća-sūtrī,* f. the five Sūtras. — *Pańća-sūnā, ās,* m. pl. the five things in a house by which animal life may be accidentally destroyed, the fire-place, the slab on which condiments are ground, the broom, the pestle and mortar, and the water-pot. — *Pańća-skandhaka,* N. of a work. — *Pańća-srotas,* five streams (probably = *pańća-nada*). — *Pańća-svarā,* f., N. of an astrological work in seven chapters on fortune-telling and the averting of good or bad luck by Prajāpati-dāsa-vaidya. — *Pańća-svarodaya* (°*ra-ud*°), *as,* m., N. of an astronomical work ascribed to Rudra. — *Pańća-svastyayana,* N. of a Vedic work accentuated in an unusual manner and resembling a Brāhmaṇa in its subject-matter. — *Pańća-hasta,* N. of a place. — *Pańća-hāyana, as, ā, am,* five years old. — *Pańća-hotra, as,* m., N. of a son of Manu Rohita. — *Pańća-hrada-tīrtha, am,* n., N. of a place of pilgrimage. — *Pańćāṅśa* (°*ća-aṅ*°), *as,* m. the fifth part, a fifth. — *Pańćākshara* (°*ća-ak*°), *as, ā, am,* consisting of five syllables, five-syllabled. — *Pańćākhyāna* (°*ća-ākh*°), *as, ā, am,* consisting of five tales; (*am*), n. another name of the Pańća-tantra. — *Pańćāgni* (°*ća-ag*°), *i,* n. a collection of five fires, the five sacred fires (viz. Anvāhārya-paćana, Gārhapatya, Āhavanīya, Sabhya, and Āvasathya, generally in comp.); five mystic fires supposed to be present in the body; (*is*), m. a householder who maintains the five sacred fires, one who keeps the five fires constantly burning (= *agni-hotrī,* see Manu III. 185); one who is acquainted with the doctrine of the five mystic fires. — *Pańćāgni-tva, am,* n. a collection or aggregate of five fires or of five passions (which inflame men's minds), &c. — *Pańćāgni-vidyā-prakaraṇa, am,* n., N. of a sacred work of the Vājasaneyins. — *Pańćāṅga, as, ī, am,* five-limbed, five-membered, having five parts or subdivisions, consisting of five members or parts, &c.; *pańćāṅgaḥ praṇāmaḥ,* obeisance made with the arms, knees, head, voice, and look; (*as*), m. a tortoise or turtle [cf. *pańćāṅga-gupta*]; a horse with five spots in various parts of his body (= *pańća-bhadra*); (*ī*), f. a bit for horses; a kind of bandage; (*am*), n. five parts of a tree (viz. root, bark, leaf, flower, and fruit); five limbs or members of the body (in comp.); five modes of devotion, (said to be silent prayer, burnt offerings, libations, bathing idols, and feeding Brāhmans); any aggregate of five parts; a calendar or almanac treating of five things, viz. solar days, lunar days, asterisms, Yogas, and Karaṇas. — *Pańćāṅga-gupta, as,* m. a tortoise or turtle (= *pańća-gupta,* q. v.). — *Pańćāṅga-pattra, am,* n. a calendar or almanac, (see above.) — *Pańćāṅga-śuddhi, is,* f. the propitious or favourable state of five important points, the solar day, lunar day, Nakshatra, Yoga, and Karaṇa. — *Pańćāṅgika* (°*ća-aṅ*°), *as, ā, am,* five-limbed, five-membered. — *Pańćāṅgurī* (°*ća-aṅ*°), *is, is, i,* Ved. five-fingered, having five fingers. — *Pańćāṅgula* (°*ća-aṅ*°), *as, ā* or *ī, am,* five fingers long, measuring five fingers; (*as*), m. the castor-oil plant, Ricinus Communis; (*ī*), f. a species of shrub. — *Pańćāṅguli* (°*ća-aṅ*°), *is, is, i,* five-fingered, having five fingers or finger-like divisions. — *Pańćāja* (°*ća-āja*), *am,* n. the five products of the goat; [cf. *pańća-gavya.*] — *Pańćātapā* (°*ća-āt*°), f. doing penance with five fires or with four fires and the sun, (see under *tapas.*) — *Pańćātmaka* (°*ća-āt*°), *as, ā, am,* consisting of the five elements, (said of the body.) — *Pańćādhikā* (according to the Ṛig-veda Anukramaṇī) = 25 (i. e. 20 + 5). — *Pańćānana* (°*ća-ān*°), *as, ī, am,* five-faced, (hence = *aty-ugra,* very fierce, very passionate, &c.); (*as*), m. an epithet of Śiva; a lion; (often at the end of names of learned men to express respect, e. g. *Nyāya-pańćānana, Nyāya-siddhānta-p*°, &c.); (*ī*), f. an epithet of Durgā. — *Pańćānanda-māhātmya, am,* n., N. of a work. — *Pańćānugāna* (°*ća-an*°), *am,* n., N. of a Sāman. — *Pańćāpsaras* (°*ća-ap*°), *as,* n., N. of a lake or pool supposed to have been produced by an ascetic named Mandakarṇi (Śātakarṇi) through the power of his penance, (so called because under it Mandakarṇi formed a secret chamber for five Apsarasas who had seduced him from his devotions, see Rāmāyaṇa III. 15, 11; Raghu-v. XIII. 38.) — *Pańćābja-maṇḍala* (°*ća-ab*°), *am,* n., N. of a mystical circle. — *Pańćāmṛita* (°*ća-am*°), *am,* n. the five kinds of divine food (viz. milk, coagulated or sour milk, butter, honey, and sugar); the aggregate of any five drugs of supposed efficacy; (*as, ā, am*), consisting of five ingredients (as a medicine); (*am*), n., N. of a Tantra. — *Pańćāmnāya* (°*ća-ām*°), *ās,* m. pl. five Śāstras supposed to have proceeded from the five mouths of Śiva, constituting the basis of the Tantra ritual. — *Pańćāmla* (°*ća-ām*°), *am,* n. the aggregate of five acid plants, the jujube, pomegranate, sorrel, spondias, and citron. — *Pańćārćis* (°*ća-ar*°), *is,* m. the planet Mercury. — *Pańćārtha-bhāshya-dīpikā,* f., N. of a chapter of the Sarva-darśana-saṅgraha by Mādhavāćārya. — *Pańćā-vaṭa, as,* m. the sacrificial cord as worn crossed upon the breast with the ends hanging over the shoulders; [cf. *pańća-vaṭa.*] — *Pańćāratta* (°*ća-av*°), *as, ā, am,* Ved. divided into five parts. — *Pańćāratta-tā,* f. or *pańćāratta-tva, am,* n. fivefold division. — *Pańćārattin, ī, inī, i,* Ved. that which is divided into five parts or has a fivefold division; that which divides into five parts. — *Pańćārattīya, as, ā, am,* Ved. divided into five portions, offered in five portions. — *Pańćāvayava, as, ā, am,* five-limbed, five-membered; *pańćāvayavam vākyam,* a five-membered argument, a syllogism. — *Pańćāvastha* (°*ća-av*°), *as,* m. a corpse (resolved into the five elements). — *Pańćāvi* (°*ća-avi*), *is, ī, i,* Ved. reckoning five lambing times, i. e. five times six months. — *Pańćāvika* (°*ća-āv*°), *am,* n. the five products of the sheep; [cf. *pańća-gavya, pańćāja.*] — *Pańćāśīta* (°*ća-aś*°), *as, ī, am,* the 85th. — *Pańćāśīti* (°*ća-aś*°), *is,* f., 85. — *Pańćāśīti-tama, as, ī, am,* the 85th. — *Pańćāsya* (°*ća-ās*°), *as, ā, am,* five-faced, five-headed; five-pointed (as an arrow); (*as*), m. a lion. — *Pańćāha* (°*ća-aha*), *as,* m. a period of five days; (*as, ā, am*), lasting five days; (*as*), m. a Soma oblation with five Sutyā days. — *Pańćāhika, as, ā, am,* containing five feast days or festivals. — *Pańćī-karaṇa-vārttika, am,* n., N. of a philosophical work by Sureśvara. — *Pańćī-kṛi,* cl. 8. P. A. *-karoti, -kurute, -kartum,* to render fivefold &c., cause anything to contain all the five elements. — *Pańćedhmīya* (°*ća-idh*°), *as, ā, am,* (a nocturnal rite) in which five torches &c. are used. — *Pańćendra* (°*ća-in*°), *as,* m. one who has the five Indrāṇīs as his deity. — *Pańćendra-kalpa, as, ā, am,* like five Indras. — *Pańćendriya* (°*ća-in*°), *am,* n. the five organs of sense (viz. the eye, ear, nose, tongue, and skin) or the five organs of action (viz. hands, feet, larynx, and organs of generation and excretion); (*as, ā, am*), having five organs of sense. — *Pańćeshu* (°*ća-ish*°), *us,* m. 'five-arrowed,' N. of Kāma-deva, the Hindū Cupid. — *Pańćonā* (according to the Ṛig-veda Anukramaṇī) = 15 (i. e. 20 − 5). — *Pańćoshman* (°*ća-ush*°), *āṇas,* m. pl. the five digestive fires supposed to be in the body. — *Pańćaudana* (°*ća-od*°), *as, ā, am,* Ved. prepared with fivefold pulp of mashed grain, &c.

Pańćaka, as, ā, am, consisting of five, relating to five, made of five, bought with five &c., taking five per cent; (*as*), m. any collection or aggregate of five; N. of one of the attendants of Skanda; (*ikā*), f., N. of each book of the Aitareya-Brāhmaṇa (as consisting of five Adhyāyas); N. of a game played with five shells; (*am*), n. an aggregate of five, πεντάς; a field of battle.

Pańćat, t, f. an aggregate of five, πεντάς.

Pańćataya, as, ī, am, fivefold, having five parts or limbs, five.

Pańćatha, as, ā, am, Ved. the fifth.

Pańćathu, us, m. time; the Koïl or Indian cuckoo.

Pańća-dhā, ind. See p. 523, col. 1.

Pańćanī, f. a chequered cloth for playing at draughts, &c.; [cf. *pańćamī, pańćārī, pańćālī.*]

Pańćama, as, ī, am, the fifth; forming the fifth part, constituting a fifth part, beautiful, brilliant, pleasing; dexterous, clever; (*as*), m. the fifth or in later times the seventh note of the Hindū musical scale, (so called because, according to the Hindūs, its tone is produced by air drawn from five parts of the body, the navel, breast, throat, heart, and forehead); one of the Rāgas or musical modes; N. of the twenty-first Kalpa (called after the musical note); the fifth consonant of a Varga, i. e. a nasal; (*ī*), f., scil. *tithi,* the fifth day of the half month; the termination of the fifth or ablative case, a word in the ablative; an epithet of Draupadī, the wife of the five Pāṇḍu princes [cf. *pāńćālī*]; a chequered cloth for playing at draughts &c., a chess-board (= *śāri-śṛiṅkhalā*); N. of a river; (*am*), n. a fifth, the fifth part; copulation as the fifth of the Tattvas of the Tāntrikas, see under *pańća-tattva;* (*am*), ind. for the fifth time, fifthly. — *Pańćama-bhāgīya, as, ā, am,* belonging to the fifth part. — *Pańćama-vat, ān, atī, at,* having the fifth (of anything). — *Pańćama-sāra-saṃhitā,* f., N. of a musical work. — *Pańćamāra* (°*ma-ara*), *as,* m. the fifth spoke in the wheel of time (with Jainas); N. of a son of Bala-deva. — 2. *pańćamāsya* (°*ma-ās*°), *as,* m. (for 1. see p. 523, col. 2), the Indian cuckoo or Koïl (as producing the fifth note of the scale with its mouth or throat).

Pańćamaka, as, ā or *ī* (?), *am,* fifth, the fifth.

Pańćamin, ī, inī, i, being in the fifth year of one's age.

Pańćārī, f. a chequered cloth for playing at draughts; [cf. *pańćanī, pańćamī, pańćālī.*]

Pañćāśa, as, ī, am, the 50th; having 50 added (e. g. *pañćāśam śatam,* 150; *pañćāśam sahasram,* 1050).

Pañćāśaka, as, ikā, am, 50; (*ikā*), f. a collection or aggregate of 50; [cf. *śloka-pañćāśikā.*]

Pañćāśat, t, f., 50; (*ardha-pañćāśat,* 25; *ekona-pañćāśat,* 49; cf. Gr. πεντήκοντα; Lat. *quinquaginta;* Hib. *caogat.*) — *Pañćāśać-ćhas,* ind. (*pañćāśat + śas*), by fifties, fifty by fifty. — *Pañćāśad-bhāga, as,* m. the 50th part.

Pañćāśati, is, f., 50.

Pañćāśatka, as, ā, am, 50 years old.

Pañćāśat-tama, as, ī, am, the 50th.

Pañćāśad-dhā, ind. in 50 parts; *ekona-pañćāśaddhā,* in 49 parts.

Pañćikā, f. a game played with five dice.

Pañćin, ī, inī, i, Ved. divided into five, consisting of five, fivefold.

पञ्चाल *pañćāla, ās,* m. pl. (said to be fr. rt. 1. *pać* or *pañć*), N. of a warrior-tribe and their country in the north of India; (*as*), m. a prince of the Pañćālas; N. of a man brought by Viśvak-sena to the childless Gaṇḍūsha; N. of a Nāga-rāja; a particular venomous insect; (*as, am*), m. n., N. of a metre consisting of twelve syllables; (*ī*), f. a doll, puppet; a style of singing; a chequered cloth for playing at draughts &c. — *Pañćāla-ćaṇḍa, as,* m., N. of a teacher. — *Pañćāla-pada-vṛitti, is,* f., N. of a particular rhythm. — *Pañćāla-rāja, as,* or *pañćāla-rājan, ā,* m. a king of Pañćāla.

Pañćālaka, as, ā, am, relating to the Pañćālas; (*ās*), m. pl. the Pañćālas; (*as*), m. a species of venomous insect; (*ikā*), f. a doll, a puppet; a kind of song.

पञ्छीहिल *pañćhīhila, as,* m., N. of a man.

पञ्ज *pañj,* a Sautra root occurring in grammatical Sūtras only, but not in the Dhātu-pāṭha, said to have the sense of 'enclosing,' and artificially formed on account of *pañjara* below.

Pañjara, am, n. (probably connected with *paj* in Ved. *pajra, pājas*), a cage, an aviary, a dove-cot, &c.; (*as, am*), m. n. a skeleton; the ribs; (*as*), m. the body; the Kali-yuga; a purificatory ceremony performed on cows; (*am*), n. certain prayers and formularies with which a deity is, as it were, caught and confined; [cf. *pāñjarya;* Gr. πήγνυμι, πάγη; Lat. *pango.*] — *Pañjara-śuka, as,* m. a parrot in a cage, a caged parrot. — *Pañjarākheṭa* (°*ra-ākh*°), *as,* m. a sort of basket or wicker trap in which fish are caught.

Pañjaraka, as, am, m. n. a cage, an aviary; (*ikā*), f. peculiar prayers and formularies, (see under *pañjara.*)

पञ्जक *pañjaka, as,* m., N. of a man.

पञ्जल *pañjala, as,* m. a species of bulbous plant (= *kola-kanda*).

पञ्जि *pañji, is, ī,* f. the ball or roll of cotton from which the thread is spun; an almanac, calendar; a journal; (perhaps) a register. — *Pañji-kara, as,* m. a Kāyastha or scribe; an almanac-maker.

Pañjikā, f. the ball or roll of cotton from which the thread is spun; a perpetual commentary which explains and analyses every word; a calendar, an almanac; a journal, a book in which receipts and expenditure are entered; the register or record of human actions kept by Yama (the judge of the dead). — *Pañjikā-kāraka, as,* m. a writer, a man of the Kāyastha tribe; an almanac-maker.

पट् *paṭ,* cl. 1. P. *paṭati, paṭitum,* to go, move: Caus. or cl. 10. P. *pāṭayati, -yitum,* to split, cleave, tear, tear up, tear asunder, tear open, divide, pierce, penetrate; to break, to eradicate, remove; to pluck out; to cause to be torn up; to speak; to shine; *paṭayati, -yitum,* to string; to surround, encircle, encompass, clothe; to distribute (?): Pass. of the Caus. *pāṭyate,* to be split open, cleave asunder (intransitively).

Paṭa, as, am, m. n. (perhaps connected with *pattra,* and usually *paṭas,* m. in the sense of 'cloth,' &c.), woven cloth, cloth, a piece of cloth, a garment, raiment; fine cloth; a veil or screen; a piece of cloth or tablet or plate on which anything may be written or painted [cf. *paṭṭa,* col. 3]; (*as*), m. a species of tree, (see *piyāla*); a species of bird; anything well made or polished, = *puras-kṛita;* (*ī*), f. cloth, a particular sort of cloth, coarse thick cloth, canvas; the curtain of a stage; a screen of cloth surrounding a tent, an outer tent; a coloured or chintz garment (?); (*am*), n. a thatch, a roof (= *paṭala*). — *Paṭa-kāra, as,* m. a weaver; a painter. — *Paṭa-kuṭī,* f. a tent; a tent of woollen cloth. — *Paṭa-ćaura, as,* m. a cloth-stealer, a shop-lifter. — *Paṭa-maṇḍapa, as,* m. 'canvas house,' a tent. — *Paṭa-maya, as, ī, am,* made of cloth; (*am*), n. a tent, a canvas house; a petticoat (?). — *Paṭa-vāpa, as,* m. a tent, (for *paṭa-vāsa.*) — *Paṭa-vāsa, as,* m. a tent; a petticoat; perfumed powder. — *Paṭa-vāsaka, as,* m. perfumed powder. — *Paṭa-veśman, a,* n. a tent. — *Paṭākshepa* (°*ṭa-ak*°), *as,* m. not tossing the stage curtain, not pushing it aside, (probably the correct reading would be *a-paṭī-kshepa.*) — *Paṭī-kshepa, as,* m. tossing aside the stage curtain, (denoting in theatrical language a hurried entrance on the stage.) — *Paṭotaja* (°*ṭa-ut*°), *am,* n. a tent; sunshine (?).

Paṭaka, as, m. cotton cloth; a camp, encampment; the half of a village, (for *pāṭaka.*)

Paṭara, as, am, m. n. (Ved.) a ray (of sunlight); (*as*), m., N. of the third of the seven suns, (see Vishṇu-Purāṇa VI. 3, where the names of the seven suns are given as Ārāga, Bhrāja, Paṭala, Patanga, Svamābhāk, Jyotishmat, and Sa-vibhāsa); an epithet of Varuṇa.

Paṭaraka, as, m. a species of plant (= *gundra*).

Paṭala, am, n. a roof, thatch, (in this sense the fem. form *paṭalī* is also given); a cover, covering, veil, coating, an enclosing or surrounding skin or membrane (especially over the eyes), a film over the eyes; a basket; a heap, mass, number, quantity or multitude, (often at the end of a comp. with words denoting 'cloud,' e. g. *jalada-paṭala,* a mass of clouds; the fem. forms *paṭalī* and *paṭalā* are also given); train, retinue; a mark on the forehead or other parts of the body with sandal-wood (either as an ornament or sectarian mark); a spot, circle, district (?); (*as*), m. 'cataract of the eye,' N. of one of the seven suns at the end of the world; (*as, am*), m. n. a section, chapter, or portion of a book (especially of the Ṛig-veda Prātiśākhya); (*as, ī*), m. f. a tree; a stalk; a book (?); (in law) the filing of suits, (gender doubtful.) — *Paṭala-prānta, as,* m. the edge of a thatch.

Paṭalaka (gender doubtful), a heap, &c. See *paṭala* above.

Paṭi, is, f. (for *paṭī,* cf. *paṭa*), a kind of cloth; a species of aquatic plant (= *kumbhikā*).

Paṭikā, f. woven cloth.

पटच्चर *paṭaććara, as,* m. (probably fr. *paṭat + ćara, paṭ* being an imitative sound, perhaps of creeping stealthily), a thief, a robber [cf. *pāṭaććara*]; (*ās*), m. pl., N. of a people; (*am*), n. old or ragged clothes.

पटत् *paṭat,* ind. the sound *paṭat.*

पटत्ककन्थ *paṭatka-kantha, am,* n., N. of a town, (Pāṇ. VI. 2, 125.)

पटपटा *paṭa-paṭā,* ind. an imitative sound.

पटभाक्ष *paṭabhāksha, as,* m. an instrument for looking (at any object), an optical instrument.

पटह *paṭaha, as, am,* m. n. (but commonly m.; probably fr. *paṭa + ha,* rt. *pan*), a kettle-drum, drum, war-drum, tabor; (*as*), m. beginning, undertaking; hurting, injuring, killing. — *Paṭaha-ghoshaka, as,* m. a crier who beats a drum before making a proclamation. — *Paṭahatā,* f. the noise or function of a drum. — *Paṭaha-dhvani, is,* m. the sound of a drum; (*is, is, i*), sounding like a drum. — *Paṭaha-bhramaṇa, am,* n. going about with a drum to call people together.

पटाक *paṭāka, as,* m. a bird [cf. *paiṭāka*]; (*ā*), f. a flag, banner (= *patākā*).

पटालुका *paṭālukā,* f. a leech; [cf. *jalukā.*]

पटि *paṭi.* See col. 2.

पटिष्ठ *paṭishṭha, paṭīyas.* See *paṭu* below.

पटिस *paṭisa, as,* m. (incorrect for *paṭṭiśa?*), a sort of weapon.

पटीर *paṭīra, as,* m. (said to be fr. rt. *paṭ*), a ball for playing with; the god of love; sandal-wood; (*am*), n. Catechu (= *khadira*); the belly; anything that can be carried off or taken away (= *haraṇīya*); a sieve; height; a radish; a field; a cloud; bamboo manna; rheumatism; catarrh.

पटु *paṭu, us, us* or *vī, u* (said to be fr. rt. *paṭ*), sharp, pointed (as a ray of light); clear, shrill, ringing, sharp-sounding, clear-sounding, crackling, rustling (said of sound); pungent, acid, hot; sharp, clever, smart, dexterous, skilful, crafty, sly, cunning; sensible, intellectual; busy, active, violent, strong, intense; harsh, hard, rough, fierce; hale, healthy; cruel, unmerciful, unfeeling; contumelious (as speech &c.); eloquent, loquacious, talkative [cf. *vāk-paṭu*]; blown, expanded; apt, disposed; (*us*), m. the tree Trichosanthes Diœca; the leaf of the Trichosanthes Diœca; the plant Momordica Charantia; a kind of perfume (= *ćoraka*); N. of a man; (*avas*), m. pl., N. of a people; (*us, u*), m. n. a mushroom; (*u*), n. salt. — *Paṭu-kalpa, as, ā, am,* tolerably clever, pretty skilful. — *Paṭu-jātīya, as, ā, am,* of a clever sort, pretty clever or skilful. — *Paṭu-tara, as, ā, am,* more sharp, sharper, keener, clearer; more clever, &c. — *Paṭu-tā,* f. cleverness; eloquence; [cf. *vāk-p*°.] — *Paṭu-tṛiṇaka, am,* n. a species of pungent grass. — *Paṭu-tva, am,* n. sharpness, keenness (as of sight), cleverness, skilfulness, eloquence. — *Paṭu-deśīya* or *paṭu-deśya, as, ā, am,* tolerably sharp, almost clever, cleverish. — *Paṭu-pattrikā,* f. a species of shrub (= *kshudra-ćañću*). — *Paṭu-parṇikā,* f. a species of plant (= *kshīriṇī*). — *Paṭu-parṇī,* f. Bryonia Grandis, a species of cucurbitaceous plant. — *Paṭu-mat, ān,* m., N. of a prince. — *Paṭu-mitra, as,* m., N. of a prince. — *Paṭu-rūpa, as, ā, am,* very clever.

Paṭiman, ā, m. sharpness, &c. (Pāṇ. V. 1, 122, VI. 4, 155.)

Paṭishṭha, as, ā, am, very sharp or clever, sharpest, &c.

Paṭīyas, ān, asī, as, sharper, more clever.

Paṭuka, as, m. Trichosanthes Diœca.

पटुश *paṭuśa, as,* m., N. of a Rākshasa.

पटुस *paṭusa, as,* m., N. of a prince.

पटोल *paṭola, as,* m. (said to be fr. rt. *paṭ*), a species of cucumber, commonly Palwal, Trichosanthes Diœca, = *paṭu;* (*am*), n. the fruit of the above; a sort of cloth, a kind of chintz [cf. *paṭa*]; (*ī*), f. a small cucumber, either the same as above or another species, Luffa Acutangula (= *kośātakī*).

Paṭolaka, as, m. a muscle or oyster (= *śukti*) compared to the shape of the Trichosanthes; (*ikā*), f. = *paṭolī,* a species of cucumber.

पटौर *paṭaura, as,* m., Ved. (according to the Pada-pāṭha = *paṭa + ūra*), a particular member of the body (?).

पट्ट *paṭṭa, as,* m. (probably for *pattra*), a slab [cf. *śilā-p*°], tablet (for painting), plate (of metal for inscription or engraving royal edicts, grants, &c.); a patent, document, royal grant or order (written on copper, stone, &c. = *nṛipa-śāsana*); a stone for grinding with, a muller (?); = *paṭa*, cloth, coloured cloth, fine cloth, woven silk (= *kausheya*); a strip (e. g. *nirmoka-paṭṭās*, strips of cast off skin); a bandage, ligature, swath, cloth bound round a sore, &c.; a frontlet, fillet or cloth worn round the head, turban, (of which five kinds are enumerated, viz. those of the king, queen, prince, general, and the prasāda-paṭṭa or turban of honour worn as a token of royal favour); a coloured silk turban; a diadem; an upper or outer garment; a plant commonly called Pāt (Corchorus Olitorius) from the fibres of which or jute a coarse sackcloth and cordage are prepared (?); a place where four roads meet (= *ćatush-patha*); a shield (?); a chair, stool (?); N. of various men; (ī), f. an ornament of the forehead; a martingale, horse's girth (= *tala-sāraka*); N. of a certain species of the Lodhra or Lodh plant (= *kramuka, rodhra, lodhra, paṭṭikā-lodhra*); red Lodh, Symplocos Racemosa; (*am*), n. a city, town, village, (probably the Pattah of the South: cf. *paṭṭana, pattana;* cf. also *anśu-p°*.) — *Paṭṭa-ja*, *am*, n. a sort of cloth, probably a kind of canvas or sackcloth. — *Paṭṭa-devī*, f. a queen (decorated with the tiara), the principal wife of a king. — *Paṭṭa-bandha, as*, m. or *paṭṭa-bandhana, am*, n. binding or crowning the head with a fillet or tiara. — *Paṭṭa-mahishī*, f. the principal wife of a king; [cf. *paṭṭa-devī*.] — *Paṭṭa-ranga, am*, n. a plant used in dying, Cæsalpina Sappan. — *Paṭṭa-rañjana* or *paṭṭa-rañjanaka, am*, n. Cæsalpina Sappan. — *Paṭṭa-rājñī*, f. the principal queen. — *Paṭṭa-vastra, as, ā, am*, or *paṭṭa-vāsas, ās, ās, as*, attired in coloured cloth or wove silk. — *Paṭṭa-śāka, as, am*, m. n. a species of pot-herb, commonly also Nālita or Lalita, Corchorus Capsularis. — *Paṭṭa-sūtra-kāra, as*, m. a silk-weaver, (designation of a class of Hindūs who are feeders of silk-worms and silk-twisters.) — *Paṭṭābhisheka* (°*ṭa-abh*°), *as*, m. the consecration of the tiara. — *Paṭṭārhā* (°*ṭa-ar*°), f. 'worthy of the turban,' the principal queen. — *Paṭṭopādhyāya* (°*ṭa-up*°), *as*, m. the writer of royal grants or patents and other similar documents.

Paṭṭaka, as, m. a plate of metal (usually copper) for inscription or engraving royal edicts; a cloth, bandage; a document (said to be also *am*, n.); (*ikā*), f. a tablet, plate; a document; a bandage, frontlet, ribbon, a piece of cloth; a piece of wove silk, cloth used for a turban; a species of tree (= *paṭṭikākhya, paṭṭī*); N. of a woman. — *Paṭṭikākhya* (°*kā-ākh*°), *as*, m. a species of tree (= *paṭṭī*). — *Paṭṭikā-lodhra, as*, m. a species of Lodhra (= *paṭṭī, kramuka*). — *Paṭṭikā-vāyaka, as*, m. a silk-weaver, ribbon-weaver.

Paṭṭi-kāra, as, ī, m. f. a silk-weaver (?).

Paṭṭin, ī, m. red Lodh.

Paṭṭila, as, m. a species of plant (= *pūtika-raja*), Cæsalpina Bonducella.

Paṭṭi-lodhra or *paṭṭi-lodhraka, as*, m. a species of tree, the bark of which is used as an astringent; the red species of Lodh, Symplocos Racemosa.

Paṭṭolikā, f. a title deed, a Paṭṭa, a lease, &c.; a written legal opinion.

पट्टन *paṭṭana, am* and *ī*, n. f. a city; [cf. *pattana;* cf. also *deva-pallī-p°, dharma-p°*.]

पट्टला *paṭṭalā*, f. a district, a community.

पट्टव *paṭṭava* (probably for *paṭṭa-ja*), a kind of cloth.

पट्टार *paṭṭāra*, N. of a district.

पट्टि *paṭṭi, ayas*, m. pl., N. of a people; (also spelt *patti*.)

पट्टिका *paṭṭikā*. See under *paṭṭaka* above.

पट्टिश *paṭṭiśa, as*, m. a sort of weapon, a kind of axe; a spear with a sharp edge.

Paṭṭiśin, ī, inī, i, armed with a Paṭṭiśa.

Paṭṭisa, as, m. a kind of weapon with three points.

Paṭṭīśa, as, m. (probably for *paṭṭiśa*), a kind of weapon used by Śiva; (in Hari-vanśa 10658, Śiva is called Triśūla-paṭṭīśa-dhara.)

पट्टेरक *paṭṭeraka*, the plant Cyperus Hexastachyus Communis.

पठ् *paṭh*, cl. 1. P. (Ved. and ep. also A.) *paṭhati, -te, papāṭha, paṭhishyati, apāṭhīt* or *apaṭhīt, paṭhitum*, to read or repeat aloud, recite in a clear voice, rehearse, speak distinctly, declaim; to repeat or pronounce the name of a god, to invoke (with acc.), to read or recite to one's self, to peruse, study; to teach; to mention (in a book), cite, quote; to express, describe, denote, declare; to learn from (with abl.): Caus. *pāṭhayati, -yitum*, Aor. *apīpaṭhat, apīpaṭhata*, to cause to read; to teach to read or to pronounce; to teach, instruct: Intens. *pāpaṭhyate, pāpaṭhīti*, to recite often or repeatedly, to read diligently, study assiduously.

Paṭhaka, as, m. a reader, reciter.

Paṭhat, an, antī, at, reciting, reading.

Paṭhana, am, n. the act of reciting or reading, mentioning.

Paṭhanīya, as, ā, am, fit to be read or studied, legible, readable.

Paṭha-mañjarī or *paṭha-samañjarī*, f., N. of a Rāginī, one of the wives of Śrī-rāga.

Paṭhi, is, f. reading, reciting, perusal.

Paṭhita, as, ā, am, recited, repeated; read, perused, studied. — *Paṭhitāṅga* (°*ta-an*°), N. of a kind of girdle.

Paṭhitavya, as, ā, am, to be read, what may or ought to be read.

Paṭhiti, is, f., N. of a particular figure of speech.

Paṭhitṛi, tā, trī, tṛi, reciting, reading, a reader.

Paṭhyamāna, as, ā, am, being recited or read.

पठर्वन् *paṭharvan, ā*, m., Ved., N. of a man, (Ṛig-veda I. 112, 17.)

पड् *paḍ* = *pad*, foot, in the inst. pl. *paḍbhis;* and in *paḍ-gribhi, is*, m., N. of a demon or of a man. — *Paḍ-bīśa* or *paḍ-vīśa* or *paḍ-vinśa, am*, n., Ved. a fetter (especially for the foot of a horse); the place of fettering.

पण् 1. *paṇ* (connected with rt. *pan*, q. v.), cl. 1. A. and 10. P. A. *paṇate, paṇāyati, -te, peṇe* or *paṇāyāñ-ćakre, apaṇit, apaṇishṭa* or *apaṇāyishṭa*, to honour, praise.

Paṇasya, Nom. P. *paṇasyati, -yitum*, to honour; [cf. *panasya*.]

Paṇāyita or *paṇita, as, ā, am*, praised.

Paṇitavya, as, ā, am, to be praised.

Paṇya, as, ā, am, to be honoured or praised.

पण् 2. *paṇ* (probably for original *parṇ* fr. rt. *par* or *prī*), cl. 1. A. (ep. also P.) *paṇate, -ti, peṇe, paṇishyate, apaṇishṭa, paṇitum*, to deal in, barter, purchase, buy; to negotiate, bargain, transact business (Ved.); to bet or stake at play (with gen. of the thing staked, e. g. *śatasya paṇate*, he stakes a hundred); to play for (with gen.); to stake anything or any person (acc.) on a game; to risk or hazard (a battle &c.); to win anything (inst.) from any one (acc.) at play; [cf. *baṇij:* Gr. πέρνημι: Lith. *pantas:* Old Germ. *feil; phant.*]

Paṇa, as, m. play, gaming, playing with dice, playing for a stake; a game played for a stake, a bet, a wager, (*paṇam kṛi*, to make a bet); the thing staked or deposited; a sum played for; a compact, contract, agreement; stipulation, treaty; wages, hire; reward; expense of an expedition; a sum (reckoned in coins or shells); a weight of copper (Manu VII. 126); a particular coin (= twenty Māshas = four Kākinīs); a particular measure; a handful of anything; a commodity for sale; price; wealth, property; business; a publican or distiller; a house, dwelling (?). — *Paṇa-kāla, as*, m. gaming-time, time for playing. — *Paṇa-granthi, is*, m. a fair, market. — *Paṇa-tā*, f. or *paṇa-tva, am*, n. the state or condition of a pledge or stake; price, value. — *Paṇa-bandha, as*, m. making a treaty, making peace, pacification. — *Paṇa-strī*, f. or *paṇāṅganā* (°*ṇa-an*°), f. a venal woman, a prostitute, harlot. — *Paṇārpaṇa* (°*ṇa-ar*°), *am*, n. making an agreement, engagement, contract. — *Paṇārha* (°*ṇa ar*°), *as, ā, am*, fit to be laid as a wager. — *Paṇāsthi* (°*ṇa-as*°), *i*, n. Cypræa Moneta, the small shell used as a die and as a coin, a cowrie.

Paṇana, am, n. the act of bartering, purchasing; traffic; sale, selling; betting.

Paṇanīya, as, ā, am, to be laid as a wager, negotiable.

Paṇasa, as, m. a commodity, an article of sale or commerce (= *panasa*, q. v.).

Paṇāyā, f. (probably an incorrect form), business, affair, transaction, buying and selling, &c.; profits and receipts of trade; a market-place.

Paṇi, is, m. (lit. 'a negotiator or tradesman, one who barters and traffics'), a miser, a niggard; one who is sparing of sacrificial oblations; an impious man who gives nothing to the gods, a Śūdra sacrificing priest; N. of a class of envious demons watching over treasures, (they are defeated by the gods and the Angirasas; sometimes the word *paṇi* is only an epithet of the Asuras who are supposed to steal cows and hide them in mountain-caverns.)

Paṇika, as, ā, am, at the end of an adj. comp. (e. g. *pañćāśat-paṇika*, [a fine] consisting of fifty Paṇas).

Paṇita, as, ā, am, transacted as business; betted; (*am*), n. a bet, wager, stake.

Paṇitavya, as, ā, am, to be bought, vendible, fit or intended for sale; to be transacted, negotiable.

Paṇitṛi, tā, trī, tṛi, one who transacts business or traffics or sells; (*tā*), m. a trader, dealer.

Paṇya, as, ā, am, to be sold, saleable, vendible; to be transacted as business; (*am*), n. an article of trade, a ware, commodity; trade, traffic, business; (*ā*), f. heart-pea, Cardiospermum Halicacabum; [cf. *piṇyā*.] — *Paṇya-tā*, f. saleableness, the being an article of trade. — *Paṇyan-dha* or *paṇyan-dhā*, a species of grass, Panicum Verticillatum. — *Paṇya-pati, is*, m. a possessor of many wares, a great merchant, large trader. — *Paṇyapati-tva, am*, n. the state or condition of a great merchant. — *Paṇya-phala-tva, am*, n. prosperity or profit in trade. — *Paṇya-bhūmi, is*, f. a place where goods are stored, a warehouse. — *Paṇya-mūlya, am*, n. the price of a commodity. — *Paṇya-yoshit, t*, f. a venal woman, prostitute, wanton woman, courtezan, harlot, whore. — *Paṇya-vikraya-śālā*, f. a place for buying and selling, a market-place, bazar. — *Paṇya-vikrayin, ī*, m. a seller of goods, a trader, merchant. — *Paṇya-vilāsinī*, f. a venal woman, a harlot; a kind of fragrant substance, the claw of an animal or something similar. — *Paṇya-vīthikā*, f. or *paṇya-vīthī*, f. a place of sale, market; a stall, shop. — *Paṇya-śālā*, f. a market, bazar, shop, a warehouse. — *Paṇya-strī*, f. or *paṇyāṅganā* (°*ya-an*°), f. a venal woman, harlot, courtezan, prostitute. — *Paṇyājira* (°*ya-aj*°), *am*, n. a market. — *Paṇyājīva* (°*ya-āj*°), *as*, m. a trader, tradesman; (*am*), n. a market, fair (?). — *Paṇyājīvaka* (°*ya-āj*°), *am*, n. a market; (also, according to some, *paṇya-jīvaka*.) — *Paṇyān-dhā*, f. = *paṇyan-dhā*, q. v. — *Paṇyārha* (°*ya-ar*°), *as, ā, am*, fit for sale, saleable, vendible.

पणफर *paṇaphara, am*, n. (fr. ἐπαναφορά), the house following upon a Kendra, q. v. (in astrol.).

पणव *paṇava, as*, m. (probably for *praṇava*), a sort of musical instrument, a small drum or tabor or a kind of cymbal, one used to accompany singing; also (*ā*), f. a kind of metre consisting of four lines of ten or five syllables each.

Paṇavin, ī, inī, i, possessing a drum; (*ī*), m. an epithet of Śiva.

पण्ड् *paṇḍ*, cl. 1. A. *paṇḍate*, to go, move; cl. 10. P. *paṇḍayati*, &c., to collect, heap together, pile up; cl. 1. P. *paṇḍati;* cl. 10. P. *paṇḍayati,* to destroy, annihilate.

Paṇḍa, as, or *paṇḍu, us,* m. (said to be fr. rt. 2. *pan*), a eunuch, impotent man [cf. *paṇḍra, shaṇḍa*]; (*ā*), f. wisdom, intelligence, understanding; science, learning. — *Paṇḍāpūrva* (°*ḍa-ap*°), *am,* n. non-occurrence of the results of fate or destiny (?).

Paṇḍaka or *paṇḍaga, as,* m. (probably fr. *paṇḍraka*), a eunuch; N. of one of the sons of the third Manu Sāvarṇa.

Paṇḍita, as, ā, am [cf. *paṇḍā*], learned, wise; shrewd, skilled, clever, educated; (*as*), m. a scholar, learned or wise man, learned Brāhman, teacher, philosopher, Pandit; an adept, proficient; N. of a man; incense. — *Paṇḍita-jātīya, as, ā, am,* somewhat clever, rather learned. — *Paṇḍita-tā,* f. or *paṇḍita-tva, am,* n. learning, knowledge, wisdom, skilfulness, cleverness. — *Paṇḍita-buddhi, is, is, i,* philosophically minded. — *Paṇḍita-maṇḍala, am,* n. an assembly or circle of learned men. — *Paṇḍita-mānika, as, ā, am,* or *paṇḍita-mānin, ī, inī, i,* or *paṇḍitam-manya, as, ā, am,* fancying one's self learned or clever; an ignorant and conceited person, a pedant who thinks himself a Pandit. — *Paṇḍitam-manyamāna, as, ā, am,* Ved. fancying one's self learned. — *Paṇḍita-rāja, as,* m. 'the prince of the learned,' an epithet of a great scholar. — *Paṇḍita-vādin, ī, inī, i,* pretending to be wise. — *Paṇḍita-sabhā,* f. an assembly of Pandits or literati.

Paṇḍitaka, as, ā, am, wise, learned; (*as*), m. a learned man; N. of one of the sons of Dhṛita-rāshṭra.

Paṇḍitāya, Nom. A. *paṇḍitāyate,* &c., to become learned or wise.

Paṇḍitāyamāna, as, ā, am, becoming wise or learned.

Paṇḍitiman, ā, m. wisdom, learning, scholarship.

पण्ड्र *paṇḍra* or *paṇḍraka, as,* m. a eunuch.

पत् 1. *pat,* cl. 4. A. *patyate,* &c., Ved. to share in, partake of (with loc.); to be master of; to rule, control, possess, be in possession of (with acc. or inst.); to be fit for, serve for (with dat.); [cf. Lat. *potior.*]

पत् 2. *pat,* cl. 1. P. (ep. also A.) *patati, -te, papāta* (1st pl. *petima,* Ved. *paptima;* 3rd pl. *petus,* Ved. *paptus;* part. *petivas,* Ved. *paptivas;* fem. *petushī*), *patitā, patishyati, apaptat, patitum,* to fly, soar or move rapidly through the air; to go, move, move downwards, alight, sink down, throw one's self down, to throw or cast one's self at (rarely with acc. for loc., e. g. *papāta ćaraṇau tasyāḥ,* he threw himself at her feet); to sink or set (as the sun); to fall, fall down, fall off, fall away; come down, descend (with loc. or acc., e. g. *papāta narendrāṇām madhye,* he descended in the midst of the princes; *pata bhūmim avāk-śirāḥ,* fall headlong to the earth, Rāmāyaṇa I. 60, 17); to go down into hell (e. g. *narake patanty ete juhvataḥ,* such sacrificers go down into hell, Manu XI. 37); to fall (in a moral sense), lose one's caste, forfeit rank or position (e. g. *para-dharmeṇa jīvan sadyaḥ patati jāti-taḥ,* he who lives by the duties of another class immediately loses caste, Manu X. 97); to fall on, be directed to, light upon (e. g. *prasāda-saumyāni satām suhṛij-jane patanti ćakshūṇshi,* the eyes of the good soft with kindness are directed on a friendly person, S'akuntalā, verse 161); to fall upon, fall or devolve to one's lot or share; to fall in or into, be in, (see *patita*); to fall out, happen, occur, come to pass: Caus. P. *patayati,* &c., Ved. to fly or hasten away; A. *patayate,* &c., Ved. to put to flight, throw down; P. A. *pātayati, -te,* &c., to let fly, fling, hurl; to cause to fall, to fell, cause to sink down or alight, let fall, drop, throw or strike down (e. g. *daṇḍam daṇḍyeshu pātayet,* let him cause punishment to fall on those who deserve it, i. e. let him inflict punishment on the guilty; *vāyuḥ pātayan mahā-drumān,* a wind which throws down lofty trees); to overthrow, ruin; to pour out, shed; to dash out, knock out, strike out; to hew down, lay low (e. g. *pātayishyāmi Rākshasam,* I will lay the Rākshasa low); to throw in, put in or into, cause to enter; to cause to fall (morally), cause to lose caste, cause to sin; (with *pāvakam*) to set on fire; (with *ćakshus, dṛishṭim,* &c.) to cast or direct the eyes, look or glance upon; (with *śāpa, a-yaśas,* &c.) to lay a curse or reproach upon; (with *sthānāt*) to cause any one to lose his rank or position, cause to fall, bring into misfortune; (with *argha-tas*) to depreciate, lower the value of anything; (with or without *ātmānam*) to throw one's self; (in arithmetic) to subtract; to set in motion, set on foot (? see Rāja-taraṅgiṇī V. 173): Desid. *pipatishati, pitsati,* to wish or expect to fall, be about to fall (e. g. *kūlam pipatishati,* the bank is about to fall in): Intens. *panīpatyate, panīpatīti,* see Pāṇ. VII. 4, 84; [cf. Gr. πέτ-ο-μαι, ὠκυ-πέτ-ης, ποτά-ο-μαι, πτε-ρό-ν, πτέρυξ, πτ-ίλο-ν, πί-πτ-ω, πιτ-νέ-ω, πτῶ-μα, πτῶ-σι-ς, πότ-μο-ς, πέτα-λον, ποτή, ἵπταμαι: Lat. *pet-o, im-pet-u-s, penna, acci-pit-er:* Old Germ. *fedara, fedah* or *fetah,* 'wing;' *find-an* = Goth. *finth-an:* Slav. *put-i-ca,* 'a bird;' *pe-ro,* 'a feather:' Hib. *faoth, faodh,* 'a fall:' Cambro-Brit. *pyd-u,* 'to fall.']

3. *pat, t, t, t,* flying, falling; [cf. *akshi-p*°.]

Pata, as, m. flying, flight; going, falling, alighting. — *Pata-ga, as,* m. a winged or flying animal, a bird; N. of one of the five fires in the Svadhākāra. — *Patan-ga, as, ā, am,* flying; (*as*), m. a bird; (according to Naigh. I. 14) a horse; a flying insect, a grasshopper, a butterfly or moth (especially one attracted by a light), a bee; the sun; N. of one of the seven suns; a ball for playing with; (according to Sāy.) a spark; (according to Mahīdhara) a Piśāća; a species of rice; quicksilver; 'the Flier,' a N. of Kṛishṇa; N. of a son of Prajā-pati; N. of a mountain; N. of a village, also called Pataṅga-grāma; (*ās*), m. pl., N. of a caste in Plaksha-dvīpa; (*ī*), f., N. of one of the wives of Tārksha, and mother of the Patagas or flying animals; (*am*), n. quicksilver; a species of sandal-wood. — *Patan-gama, as,* m. a small grasshopper; a butterfly; a bird. — *Patangara, as, ā, am,* Ved. bird-like, like a bird. — *Patanga-vat,* ind. like a bird. — *Patangikā,* f. a small bird; a kind of small bee. — *Patangin, ī, inī,* m. f. a bird.

Pataka, as, ā, am, who or what falls or descends, &c.; (*as*), m. an astronomical table.

Patat, an, antī, at, flying, alighting, descending, coming down, falling, &c.; (*an*), m. a bird. — *Patad-graha, as,* m. 'receiving what falls,' a spittoon; the reserve of an army. — *Patad-grāha, as,* m. a spittoon, spitting-pot. — *Patad-bhīru, us,* m. 'terrible to birds,' a hawk, falcon.

Patatra, am, n. a wing, pinion; a feather; a vehicle; [cf. *pattra.*]

Patatri, is, m. (fr. *patatrin*), a bird; (Ved.) N. of a particular fire; N. of a warrior on the side of the Kurus. — *Patatri-ketana, as,* m. 'characterized by a bird,' Vishṇu. — *Patatri-rāja, as,* m. the king of the birds, Vishṇu's bird Garuḍa.

Patatrin, ī, iṇī, i, winged, feathered, flying; (Ved.) an epithet of a particular form of fire, of the vehicle of the Aśvins, &c.; (*ī*), m. a bird; a horse; the horse in the Aśva-medha sacrifice (Rāmāyaṇa I. 13); an arrow; (*iṇī*), n. du., Ved. day and night; [cf. *pātatriṇa.*]

Patana, as, ā, am, who or what flies, falls, goes down, descends; falling, alighting, &c.; (*as*), m., N. of a Rākshasa; (*am*), n. the act of flying down, falling, alighting, descending, falling down, throwing one's self down or into; setting (as the sun), going down (to hell), slackening, hanging down, becoming flaccid (said of the breasts); falling from dignity, virtue, &c.; neglect of the duties of caste, apostasy; ruin; death; (with *garbhasya*) miscarriage; (in arithmetic) subtraction; the latitude of a planet. — *Patana-dharmin, ī, iṇī, i,* having the quality of or subject to the law of falling.

Patanīya, as, ā, am (fr. *patana*), leading to a fall, causing the loss of caste; (*am*), n. a degrading crime, a crime which causes loss of caste.

Patantaka, as, ā, am, epithet of a kind of Aśva-medha performed in a hurried manner.

Patama, as, m. a bird; a grasshopper; the moon; [cf. *patasa.*]

Patayālu, us, ū, u, flying, falling, liable to fall.

Patayishṇu, us, us, u, or *patayishṇuka, as, ā, am,* Ved. flying.

Patara, as, ā, am, or *pataru, us, us, u,* Ved. flying, fugitive.

Patasa, as, m. a bird; a grasshopper; the moon.

Patāka, as, m. ('flying'), a flag or banner, (perhaps incorrect for *patākā*); a particular position of the hand or of the fingers of the hand; (*ā*), f. a flag, pennant, pennon, banner; a flag-staff; an emblem carried as an ensign or banner, a symbol, sign, mark; a particular high number; an episode or episodical incident in a drama; good fortune, auspiciousness. — *Patāka-dhvaja-mālin, ī, inī, i,* garlanded with flags and banners. — *Patākāṇśuka* (°*kā-aṇ*°), *am,* n. a flag. — *Patākā-sthānaka, am,* n. (in dramatic language) intimation of an episodical incident.

Patākika, as, ā, am, having a flag or banner, carrying a banner.

Patākin, ī, inī, i, having a flag or banner, bearing a flag, adorned with flags; (*ī*), m. an ensign, a standard-bearer, colour-bearer; a figure used in divination, a scheme for casting a nativity; a flag; N. of a warrior on the side of the Kurus; (*inī*), f. an army; N. of a particular divinity.

Patāpata, as, ā, am, going to fall, inclined to fall; going much or frequently.

Patita, as, ā, am, fallen, alighted; dropped, prostrate, sprung from; fallen (in a moral sense), wicked, abandoned, one who has committed a heinous sin; fallen in battle, defeated, overthrown; degraded, outcast; gone; fallen into, occurring in, being in (e. g. *avanśa-patita,* being in a low family; *madhya-patita,* being between); (*am*), n. flying. — *Patita-sāvitrika, as,* m. a man of the first three classes whose investiture with the thread or initiation into sacred knowledge (*upa-nayana*) has not been duly performed or not performed at all, (this can happen to a Brāhman after his sixteenth, to a Kshatriya after his twenty-second, and to a Vaiśya after his twenty-fourth year.) — *Patita-sthita, as, ā, am,* lying on the ground. — *Patitekshita* (°*ta-iksh*°), *as, ā, am,* looked at by an outcast. — *Patitotpanna* (°*ta-ut*°), *as, ā, am,* sprung from an outcast.

Patitavya, am, n. going down to hell.

Patitvā, ind. having flown; having fallen or fallen down or alighted.

Patishṭha, as, ā, am, Ved. flying most or best.

Patīyas, ind. (originally the neut. of a comparative of *pat*), quickly, speedily.

Patera, as, ā, am, flying, falling; going, moving; (*as*), m. a bird; a hole, pit; a particular measure (= *āḍhaka*).

Pattra (sometimes spelt *patra*), *am,* n. (according to some also *as,* m.), the wing of a bird, pinion, feather, the feather of an arrow; a vehicle in general [cf. *patatra*], a chariot, car, cart, horse, camel, &c. (perhaps in these senses connected with 2. *pad*); the leaf of a tree (regarded as its plumage), the leaf of a flower, the leaf of a particular fragrant plant or of a species of plant with fragrant leaves (= *gandha-pattra*); the leaf of the Cassia (= *teja-pattra*); a leaf prepared for writing on, a leaf written on, paper (e. g. *tat pattram āropayati,* he commits that to paper); a letter, any written document, (in the latter sense also *pattrī,* f.); the leaf of a book; gold-leaf, &c., any thin leaf or plate of metal or gold-leaf [cf. *paṭṭa*]; the blade of a sword, knife, &c. [cf. *asi-p*°]; staining the person as a decoration, lines and figures painted on the face by means of musk and other fragrant substances; a knife, dagger; [cf. *aććhinna-p*°, *uktha-p*°, &c.: cf. also Gr. πτε-ρό-ν, πτέρυξ, πτ-ίλο-ν; Old Germ. *fedara, fedah,* 'a wing;' Angl. Sax.

feher; Mod. Germ. *feder;* Eng. *feather.*] — *Pattra-kāhalā,* f. the noise made by the flapping of wings or rustling of leaves. — *Pattra-kriććhra, as,* m. a sort of penance, drinking an infusion of the leaves of various plants and Kuśa grass for a given time; [cf. *parṇa-kriććhra.*] — *Pattra-gupta, as,* m. a kind of bird [cf. *paksha-gupta*]; a species of plant (=*tri-kaṇṭa*). — *Pattra-ghanā,* f. a species of plant with full leaves, Acacia Rugata (=*sātalā*). — *Pattra-ććhedaka, as,* m. a leaf-cutter, a particular trade. — *Pattra-ććhedya, am,* n. (perhaps) plucked feathers. — *Pattra-jhankāra, as,* m. the current of a river (or the rustling of leaves?); other authorities read *pura-sanskāra* and *pattra-sanskāra.* — *Pattra-taṇḍulā,* f. a woman; a species of barley; (*ī*), f. a species of plant (=*taṇḍulī* and *yava-tiktā*). — *Pattra-taru, us,* m. a species of tree (=*dush-khadira*). — *Pattra-dāraka, as,* m. 'leaf-divider,' a saw. — *Pattra-nāḍikā,* f. the fibre or vein of a leaf. — *Pattra-paraśu* or *pattra-parśu, us,* m. a fine file or saw used by silversmiths, &c. — *Pattra-pāṭha, as,* m. the perusal of a writing. — *Pattra-pāla, as,* m. a large knife, a long dagger; (*ī*), f. the feathered part of an arrow. — *Pattra-pāśyā,* f. an ornament on the forehead, a piece of gold-leaf or a painted mark on the forehead. — *Pattra-piśāćikā,* f. a sort of cap or cover for the head made of leaves (used as a protection against rain). — *Pattra-pushpa, as,* m. a species of plant, a red sort of Tulasī or basil, Ocymum Pilosum; (*ā*), f. holy basil, Ocymum Sanctum; holy basil with small leaves. — *Pattra-pushpaka, as,* m. a species of birch; [cf. *bhūrja-pattra.*] — *Pattra-prakāśa, as,* m. a title given to certain astronomical tables. — *Pattra-bandha, as,* m. adorning with leaves, flowers, &c., decorating with nosegays or garlands. — *Pattra-bāla, as,* m. an oar, especially a large one used as a rudder. — *Pattra-bhanga, as,* m. or *pattra-bhangi, is,* f. or *pattra-bhangī,* f. drawing lines or figures on the face and person with fragrant pigments of sandal, musk, &c., as an ornament. — *Pattra-mañjarī,* f. = *pattra-bhanga.* — *Pattra-māla, as,* m. the plant Calamus Rotang (=*vetasa*). — *Pattra-mūlaka, as, ā, am,* resembling leaves and roots. — *Pattra-yauvana, am,* n. a young leaf, sprout. — *Pattra-rañjana, am,* n. embellishing a page, illuminating, gilding. — *Pattra-ratha, as,* m. 'using wings as a vehicle,' a bird. — *Pattraratha-śreshṭha* or *pattrarathendra* (°*tha-in*°), *as,* m. 'chief of birds,' a N. of Garuḍa or the bird of Vishṇu. — *Pattrarathendra-ketu, us,* m. 'characterized by the chief of birds,' an epithet of Vishṇu. — *Pattra-rekhā,* f. = *pattra-lekhā,* q. v. — *Pattra-latā,* f. = *pattra-bhanga,* q. v.; a long knife or poniard. — *Pattra-lavaṇa, am,* n. 'leaf-salt,' a kind of drug made of certain leaves mixed with salt. — *Pattra-lekhā,* f. drawing lines or figures on the face or person by means of fragrant pigments consisting of sandal, saffron, musk, &c.; N. of a woman. — *Pattra-vallarī,* f. = *pattra-bhanga,* q. v. — *Pattra-valli, is* and *ī,* f. = *pattra-bhanga,* q. v.; (*ī*), f., N. of two plants (=*rudra-jaṭā* and *palāśī*). — *Pattra-vāja, as, ā, am,* feathered, furnished with feathers (as an arrow). — *Pattra-vāha, as,* m. 'feather-bearing,' an arrow; a bird ('wing-bearing'); a letter-carrier, postman. — *Pattra-viśeshaka* = *pattra-bhanga,* q. v. — *Pattra-vriśćika, as,* m. a species of venomous reptile. — *Pattra-veshṭa, as,* m. an ornament for the ear, a kind of ear-ring (=*tāṭanka*). — *Pattra-śavara, as,* m. a Savara who decorates himself with feathers, a barbarian or mountaineer who wears peacock feathers as a decoration. — *Pattra-śāka, as,* m. a species of vegetable consisting chiefly of leaves; (*am*), n. leaves and vegetables. — *Pattra-śirā,* f. the vein or fibre of a leaf. — *Pattra-śringī,* f. or *pattra-śreṇi,* f. the plant Anthericum Tuberosum. — *Pattra-śreshṭha, as,* m. the tree Ægle Marmelos (=*vilva*). — *Pattra-sanskāra, as,* m. the current of a river; [cf. *pattra-jhankāra.*] — *Pattra-sundara,* a species of plant (=*tikta-śāka*). — *Pattra-sūći, is,* f. 'leaf-needle,' a thorn. — *Pattra-hima, am,* n. cold, wintry or snowy weather. — *Pattrākhya* (°*ra-ākh*°), *am,* n. Cassia leaf; the leaf of the Flacourtia Cataphracta. — *Pattrānga* (°*ra-an*°), *am,* n. (sometimes written *pattranga*), red sanders, Pterocarpus Santolinus; red or sappan wood; a species of birch (=*bhūrja*); another plant (=*padmaka*). — *Pattrānguli* (°*ra-an*°), *is,* f. drawing lines or figures with the finger on the forehead, throat, neck &c. with coloured sandal, saffron, or any other substance. — *Pattrāñjana* (°*ra-añ*°), *am,* n. ink; blacking. — *Pattrāḍhya* (°*ra-āḍh*°), *am,* n. the root of long pepper; a species of grass. — *Pattrāmlā* (°*ra-am*°), f. a species of sorrel (=*ćukrikā*). — *Pattrālī* (°*ra-ālī*), f. = *pattra-bhanga, pattrāvali,* q. v. — *Pattrālu* (°*ra-ālu*), *us,* m. a species of bulbous plant, = *kāsālu;* a species of sugar-cane (=*ikshu-darbha*). — *Pattrāvali* (°*ra-āv*°), *is,* f. red chalk, a row of leaves; decorating the person with lines of paint, &c.; (*ī*), f. a row or number of leaves; drawing lines or figures on the face or person with coloured and fragrant pigments, as with saffron, sandal, &c.; a mixture of young Aśvattha leaves with barley and honey. — *Pattrāhāra* (°*ra-āh*°), *as,* m. feeding on leaves. — *Pattreśvara-tīrtha* (°*ra-iś*°), *am,* n., N. of a sacred bathing-place. — *Pattropaskara* (°*ra-up*°), *as,* m. the plant Cassia Sophora (=*kāsa-marda*). — *Pattrorṇa* (°*ra-ūr*°), *as,* m. the tree Calosanthes Indica; (*ās*), m. pl., N. of a people; (*am*), n. wove silk, cloth, or a garment made of it; (perhaps also) cotton. — *Pattrollāsa* (°*ra-ul*°), *as,* m. the bud or eye of a plant.

Pattraka, as, m. the plant Achyranthes Triandra the leaves of which are eaten as a vegetable; (*ikā*), f. a leaf for writing upon, a leaf on which anything has been written; a letter, document, &c.; (*am*), n. a leaf; the leaf of the Laurus Cassia; painting lines or figures on the body by way of decoration; (at the end of a comp.) leaf, wing; [cf. *ajina-pattrikā, ali-p*°.] — *Pattrikākhya* (°*kā-ākh*°), *as,* m. a species of camphor. — *Pattrikā-praveśa, as,* m. a festival on the seventh day of the month Aśvina.

Pattraṇā, f. feathering an arrow, putting feathers on an arrow, &c.

Pattraya, Nom. P. *pattrayati,* &c., to feather.

Pattrin, ī, iṇī, i, winged, feathered, having pages or leaves; (*ī*), m. an arrow; a bird, falcon; a mountain; possessing a carriage or driving in one; a chariot; a tree; N. of various plants, the wine-palm (=*gangā-pattrī,* = *śveta-kiṇihī*); (*iṇī*), f. a sprout, shoot. — *Pattri-vāha, as,* m. a bird; [cf. *pattra-vāha.*]

Patman, a, n., Ved. flight.

Patya, (at the end of a comp.) falling.

Patvan, ā, arī, a, Ved. flying; (*a*), n. flying, flight; [cf. *āśu-p*°, *raghu-p*°.]

Patsala, as, m. a way, road.

पत *pata, as, ā, am,* cherished, well fed, protected, (said to = *pushṭa.*)

पतञ्चल *patañćala, as,* m., N. of a man.

पतञ्चिका *patañćikā,* f. a bow-string.

पतञ्जल *patañjala, as,* m., N. of a man; (*ās*), m. pl., N. of his descendants.

पतञ्जलि *patañjali, is,* m. (said to be derived fr. *pata,* falling, and *añjali,* the joined hands; Patañjali, according to a legend, having fallen from heaven in the shape of a small snake into the hands of the saint Pāṇini as he was joining his hands in reverence); N. of a saint or Muni teacher of the Yoga philosophy, (thence called Pātañjala); N. of the celebrated author of the Mahā-bhāshya or great commentary on Pāṇini; a N. of the poet Vara-rući.

पति *pati, is,* m. (said to be fr. rt. 3. *pā,* to protect, but connected with rt. 1. *pat* and probably for original *pātan*), a master, owner, possessor, proprietor, lord, ruler, governor, sovereign; one who presides over, (often applied to tutelary deities or regents, e. g. *oshadhīnām patiḥ,* the Moon as guardian or lord of medicinal plants; *saritām patiḥ,* the Ocean as lord of the rivers; *vaćasām patiḥ,* Bṛihas-pati as lord of speech; sometimes at the end of a comp., cf. *oshadhi-p*°, *bṛihas-p*°, *vāćas-p*°, *ranas-p*°); a husband; a root; going, motion, flight? (in these senses probably connected with rt. 2. *pat*); (*is*), f. a female possessor, mistress (e. g. *grāmasya patiḥ,* the mistress of a village); a wife (at the end of a non-adj. comp., e. g. *vṛiddha-pati* = *vṛiddha-patnī,* the wife of an old man, Pāṇ. IV. 1. 34); [cf. *anśu-p*°, *dam-patī, dvāra-p*°, *nṛi-p*°, *pṛithivī-p*°, *prajā-p*°: cf. also Gr. πόσι-s for πότι-s, δεσπό-τη-s, δεσ-πόσ-υνο-s, δεσ-πόζ-ω: Lat. *com-po(t)-s, im-po(t)-s, pot-is, possum* for *potis-sum, pot-es-tā(t)-s:* Lith. *pat-s,* 'husband;' *vēsz-pat-s,* 'lord, ruler:' Slav. *gos-podju,* 'lord:' Russ. *gos-podin,* 'lord:' Goth. *fath-s,* 'lord;' *bruth-fath-s,* 'bridegroom.'] — *Patiṃ-vara, ā,* f. a woman who chooses her husband for herself, a young woman who has the privilege of choosing her husband [cf. *svayaṃ-vara*]; the plant Nigella Indica. — *Pati-kāma, as, ā, am,* Ved. wishing for a husband. — *Pati-gaṇita-ṭīkā,* f., N. of a commentary on the Līlāvatī. — *Pati-ghātinī,* f., Ved. a woman who murders her husband. — *Pati-ghna, as, ī, am,* killing a husband or surviving him; (*ī*), f. a woman who murders her husband, a husband-killer; a line on the hand indicating that a woman will be faithless or treacherous to her husband. — *Patighnī-lakshaṇa, am,* n. the mark of a husband-killer. — *Pati-tva* or Ved. *pati-tvana, am,* n. mastership, lordship; the conjugal or marital state, wedlock, matrimony, marriage. — *Pati-darśana-lālasa, as, ā, am,* longing to see one's husband. — *Pati-devatā* or *pati-devā,* f. regarding a husband as a divinity, honouring a husband above all others. — *Pati-dvish, ṭ, ṭ, ṭ,* Ved. hating a husband. — *Pati-dharma, as,* m. duty towards a husband. — *Patidharma-vatī,* f. fulfilling duties towards a husband, fulfilling the duties of a wife, faithfully devoted to a husband. — *Pati-prāṇā,* f. a faithful wife ('whose husband is her life'). — *Pati-yāna, as, ā, am,* leading to a husband. — *Pati-rājya-vinākṛita, as, ā, am,* excluded from a husband's kingdom. — *Pati-rip, p, p, p,* Ved. hostile to or hating a husband. — *Pati-langhana, am,* n. injuring a husband; disregarding a former husband by marrying another. — *Pati-lālasa, as, ā, am,* longing for a husband. — *Pati-loka, as,* m. 'husband's world,' the sphere of a husband in a future life. — *Pati-vatī,* f., Ved. a woman who possesses a husband, a married woman. — *Pati-vatnī,* f. a woman who possesses a husband, a married woman, a wife whose husband is living. — *Pati-vidya, am,* n., Ved. finding or procuring a husband. — *Pati-vedana, as, ā, am,* Ved. finding or procuring a husband; (*as*), m. an epithet of Aryaman; (*au*), m. du. a particular part of the body ('attracting a husband?'); (*am*), n. procuring a husband (by means of magical arts). — *Pati-vrata, am,* n. loyalty or fidelity to a husband; (*ā*), f. a devoted and virtuous wife (faithful to her husband). — *Pati-vratā-tva, am,* n. loyalty or fidelity to a husband. — *Pati-śokākula* (°*ka-āk*°), *as, ā, am,* agitated or confounded with grief for a husband. — *Pati-sevā,* f. devotion to a husband.

Patīya, Nom. P. *patīyati,* &c., to wish for a husband; (perhaps also) to become strong.

Patiyantī, f. a woman wishing or fit for a husband.

Patnī, f. (sometimes for the sake of the metre and in a few comps. shortened to *patni*), a female possessor, a mistress (Ved.); a wife (even applied in one or two instances to the female of an animal, as in Ṛig-veda I. 140, 6, to a cow, but according to Sāy. *patnī* here = *pālayitrī*); (in astrology) N. of the seventh house. Adjective comps. ending in *pati* may remain unchanged in the fem. or may substitute *patnī* by Vārt. to Pāṇ. IV. 1, 34 (e. g. *vṛiddha-patnī* or *vṛiddha-pati*, a woman who has an old husband); but the form *patnī* only is allowed in such comps. as *sa-patnī*, a woman who has the same husband with another; *eka-patnī*, a woman who is faithful to one husband; [cf. *jīva-p°;* Gr. πότ-νια, δέσ-ποινα.] — *Patnī-tva, am*, n. wifehood, the condition of a wife, matrimony; (*patnītve grah*, to take as a wife.) — *Patnī-vat, ān, atī, at*, Ved. having a wife or accompanied by wives. — *Patnī-śālā*, f. a hut, tent, or room erected near the place of sacrifice for the wives and domestic use of the sacrificer. — *Patnī-saṃyāja, ās*, m. pl., Ved. the four Ājya oblations offered to Soma, Tvashṭṛi, the wives of the gods, and Agni-gṛihapati. — *Patnī-saṃyājana, am*, n. performing the Patnī-saṃyāja. — *Patnī-sannahana, am*, n. girding a wife; the girdle of a wife. — *Patny-āṭa, as*, m. a gynæceum, the private or women's apartments.

Patnīka, a substitute for *patnī* at the end of a comp.; [cf. *a-p°*, *bahu-p°*, *sa-p°*.]

पत्काषिन् *pat-kāshin.* See 3. *pad*, col. 3.

पत्तङ्ग *pattanga, as, am*, m. n. (probably a corruption of *pattrāṅga*), red sandal or sanders; (*am*), n. Cæsalpina Sappan.

पत्तन *pattana, am*, n. (said to be fr. rt. 1. *pat*), a town, city; [cf. Lat. *op-pidum.*] — *Pattana-baṇij, k*, m. a town-tradesman, one who carries on his business in a town. — *Pattanādhipati* (*°na-adh°*), *is*, m. 'governor of a city,' N. of a prince.

पत्तरङ्ग *patta-ranga* = *paṭṭa-ranga*, q. v.

पत्तला *pattalā*, f. a circuit, district.

पत्तस् *pat-tas*, ind. See 3. *pad*, col. 3.

पत्ति *patti.* See under rt. 2. *pad*, col. 2.

पत्तूर *pattūra, as*, m. a kind of vegetable, Achyranthes Triandra; (*am*), n. red sandal or sanders.

पत्त्र *pattra*, &c. See p. 527, col. 3.

पत्त्राङ्ग *pattranga.* See *pattrāṅga*, p. 528.

पत्त्रल *pattrala, am*, n. thin or skim milk.

पत्नि *patni, is*, f., for *patnī.* See p. 528, col. 3.

पत्मन् *patman, patsala.* See p. 528, col. 2.

पत्सङ्गिन् *pat-sangin, pat-sukha*, &c. See under 3. *pad*, col. 3.

पथ् *path* (connected with rt. *panth*, q. v.), cl. 1. P. *pathati, papātha, apathīt, pathitum*, to go, move; cl. 10. P. *pāthayati*, &c., to throw, cast, send.

Patha, as, m. (said to be fr. rt. 1. *pat;* generally only at the end of a comp.), a path, way, road, course, reach; [cf. *a-patha, aja-p°, adarśana-p°*, &c.; cf. also Zend *pathan*, 'way;' Gr. πάτο-ς, πατέ-ω, πόντο-ς; Lat. *pon(t)-s, ponti-fex;* Slav. *patĭ*, 'way;' Old Germ. *pad, fad, phat;* Angl. Sax. *padh, pād;* Hib. *fath*, 'a district, field.'] — *Patha-kalpanā*, f. juggling tricks, conjuring. — *Patha-darśaka, as*, m. 'way-shower,' a guide, conductor. — *Pathātithi* (*°tha-at°*), *is*, m. a traveller, wayfarer. — *Pathe-shṭhā, ās, ās, am*, Ved. standing in the way or on the road.

Pathaka, as, ā, am, knowing the way, a guide.

Pathat, an, antī, at, going, travelling; (*an*), m. a road.

Pathika, as, ā or *ī, am*, knowing the way, going on a road; (*as*), m. a traveller, wayfarer; a guide, one who knows the way. — *Pathika-santati* or *pathika-saṃhati, is*, f. or *pathika-sārtha, as*, m. a collection or company of travellers, a caravan. — *Pathikāśraya* (*°ka-āś°*), *as*, m. an asylum for travellers, an inn.

Pathikā, f. a kind of vine with red grapes.

Pathin, panthās, m. (nom. voc. sing. *panthās* fr. a base *panthas*, the other strong cases fr. *panthan*, acc. pl. and other weak cases fr. *path*, middle cases fr. *pathin*, see Gram. 162; Ved. acc. sing. is *panthām* for *panthānam*, nom. pl. *panthās* or *panthāsas* or *pathayas* for *panthānas*), a path, way, road, course; a path in morals or religion, sect, doctrine; a division of hell (Manu IV. 90); *panthānaḥ santu te śivāḥ*, may thy ways be happy! a happy journey to thee! *pathi ny-as*, see under *ny-as*). — *Pathan-vat, ān, atī, at*, Ved. containing the word *pathin.* — *Pathi-kāra, as*, m. 'road-maker,' N. of a man (?). — *Pathi-kṛit, t, t, t*, Ved. making a road, constructing a path, preparing a way or ways; guiding, a guide; (*t*), m. an epithet of Agni. — *Pathi-deya, am*, n. a toll levied on public roads. — *Pathi-druma, as*, m. the tree Acacia Catechu. — *Pathi-prajña, as, ā, am*, acquainted with roads. — *Pathi-mat, ān, atī, at*, containing the word *pathin.* — *Pathi-madhye*, ind. in the middle of the road. — *Pathi-rakshi, is, is, i*, Ved. or *pathi-rakshas, ās, ās, as*, Ved. protecting ways or roads. — *Pathi-vāhaka, as*, m. a fowler, bird-catcher; a porter, burden-bearer; (*as, ā, am*), cruel, hard. — *Pathi-shad, t, t, t*, Ved. sitting in the way; an epithet of Rudra; of the dogs of Yama. — *Pathi-shṭhā, ās, ās, am*, Ved. standing in the way or on the road. — *Pathi-stha, as, ā, am*, being on the way, going.

Pathila, as, m. a traveller, wayfarer.

Pathya, as, ā, am (lit. belonging to a road, suitable for the way or course of anything), proper, fit, suitable, salutary, wholesome, agreeing with, (often said in a medical sense of diet, regimen, &c.); according to rule, containing elements or leading forms; (*as*), m. Terminalia Chebula or Citrina; N. of a teacher of the Atharva-veda; (*ā*), f. a path, way, road, (*pathyā revatī*, f., Ved. 'the rich path,' personified as a deity of happiness and welfare); the tree Terminalia Chebula or Citrina; other plants (= *mṛigervāru, ćirbhiṭā, bandhyā, karkoṭakī*); N. of several metres, a sort of Bṛihatī; a kind of Paṅkti; a kind of Āryā; a kind of Vaktra; (*am*), n. a species of salt; [cf. *a-pathya.*] — *Pathya-śāka, as*, m. a species of vegetable. — *Pathyāpathya* (*°ya-ap°*), *am*, n. 'wholesome and unwholesome,' the class of things that are considered beneficial or hurtful in disease. — *Pathyāśin* (*°ya-āś°*), *ī, inī, i*, eating or an eater of wholesome diet.

पद् 1. *pad*, cl. 1. P. *padati*, &c., various reading for rt. *bad*, to stand fast or fixed.

पद् 2. *pad*, cl. 4. A. (ep. also P.) *padyate, pede, patsyate, apādi, pattum*, to fall (Ved.); to fall down or drop with fatigue (Ved.); to perish (Ved.); to fall out (Ved.); to go, to go to (with acc.); to attain, obtain, participate in, gain; to turn one's self towards, observe: Caus. P. A. *pādayati, -te*, to cause to fall (Ved.); to cause to go, &c.; *padayate*, to go: Desid. *pitsate:* Intens. *panīpadyate, panīpadīti;* [cf. Zend *pad*, 'to go;' *padh-a*, 'a foot:' Gr. πέδ-ο-ν, πεδ-ίο-ν, πέδ-η, πέδ-ιλο-ν, πεζό-ς, πέζ-α, πού-ς, base ποδ-, πηδά-ω, ὀ-παδό-ς: Lat. *Ped-u-m, ped-ica, compe(d)-s, ped-ūle, pe(d)-s, ped-e(t)-s, ped-es-ter, tri-pod-are, tri-pud-iu-m:* Old Iceland. *fet-ill*, 'fetter:' Goth. *fōt-u-s*, 'foot:' Old Germ. *fezz-il*, 'fetter;' *fuoz*, 'foot:' Mod. Germ. *fuss:* Eng. *foot:* Lith. *pád-a-s*, 'a sole;' *ped-à*, 'a foot-mark:' Hib. *faoidh-im*, 'I go;' *faidh*, 'departure.']

Patti, is, m. (fr. rt. 2. *pad* or fr. 3. *pad*, col. 3), a footman, foot-soldier, infantry; a pedestrian; a hero; (*ayas*), m. pl., N. of a people [cf. *paṭṭi*]; (*is*), f. the smallest division of an army (= $\frac{1}{3}$ of a *senā-mukha*) or a company consisting of one chariot, one elephant, three horsemen and five foot-soldiers, (according to others = *senā-mukha* = fifty-five foot-soldiers); going, moving, walking. — *Patti-karman, a*, n. the business or operations of infantry. — *Patti-kāya, as*, m. infantry. — *Patti-gaṇaka, as*, m. an officer whose business is to number or muster the infantry. — *Patti-pankti, is*, f. a line of infantry. — *Patti-saṃhati, is*, f. a body of infantry, an assemblage of foot-soldiers; infantry.

Pattika, as, ā, am, going on foot, pedestrian.

Pattin, ī, m. a foot-soldier, footman.

3. *pad* or *pād, pāt*, m. a foot; a step; a fourth part, quarter; [cf. *pāda.*] — *Pać-ćhabda, as*, m. (*pad* + *śabda*), the noise of feet or of footsteps. — *Pać-ćhas*, ind. (*pad* + affix *śas*), Pāda by Pāda, stanza by stanza, foot by foot. — *Pać-ćhauća, am*, n. (*pad* + *śauća*), cleansing or purifying the feet. — *Paj-ja, as*, m. (*pad* + *ja*), 'born from the feet (of Brahmā),' a Śūdra. — *Pat-kāshin, ī, iṇī, i*, rubbing the feet, scratching the feet; going on foot, pedestrian; (*ī*), m. a footman, foot-soldier. — *Pat-tas*, ind., Ved. from the feet; on foot. — *Pat-sangin, ī, inī, i*, Ved. sticking or adhering to the feet. — *Pat-sukha, as, ā, am*, pleasant to the feet. — *Patsutaḥ-śī, īs, īs, i*, Ved. lying at the feet. — *Patsu-tas*, ind. (fr. loc. pl. of 3. *pad* + *tas*), Ved. at the feet. — *Pad-anushanga, as*, m., Ved. anything added or appended to a Pada or quarter of a verse; [cf. *padānushanga.*] — *Padi-baddha, as, ā, am* (fr. loc. sing. of rt. 3. *pad* + *baddha*), tied or bound by the feet. — *Pad-ga, as, ā, am*, going on foot, pedestrian; (*as*), m. a foot-soldier. — *Pad-ghosha, as*, m., Ved. the sound of footsteps. — *Pad-dhati, is, ī*, f. (*pad* + *hati*), a way, path, road; a line, row, range; N. of a class of writings, (described as guide-books or commentaries or a kind of manual detailing the mode of performing certain rites and ceremonies and collecting the texts relating to them); a family name, a surname, title, or perhaps more accurately the characteristic word denoting caste or occupation in comps. which are used as proper names (as *gupta* at the end of Vaiśya names, and *dāsa* at the end of Śūdra names). — *Paddhati-ćintāmaṇi, is*, m. or *paddhati-bhūshaṇa, am*, n., N. of a work on astronomy. — *Pad-dhima, am*, n. (*pad* + *hima*), coldness of the feet. — *Pad-ratha, as*, m. a footman, foot-soldier. — *Pad-vat, ān, atī, at*, having feet; running; (*at*), n. an animal that uses its feet for locomotion. — *Pan-naddhā* or *pan-naddhrī*, f. a shoe, boot. — *Pan-nishka, as*, m. one quarter of a Nishka. — *Pan-nejanī, nyas*, f. pl. (with *āpas*) a bath for the feet. — *Pan-miśra* = *pāda-miśra*, Pāṇ. VI. 3, 56.

Pada, am, n. a step, pace, stride (e. g. *padāt padam ćalitum*, to move on a step from any position; *pade pade*, at every step, everywhere, on every occasion; *madhyamam Vaishṇavam padam*, Vishṇu's middle stride, i. e. the air); a footstep, footprint, footmark, trace, track, vestige, mark (e. g. *Vishṇos trīṇi padāni*, the three footprints of Vishṇu, said to mean the space between the eyebrows, but probably the N. of a constellation; *Vishṇoḥ padam*, 'Vishṇu's footprint,' N. of a place; *kararuha-pada*, the mark of finger-nails, cf. *nakha-p°, daśana-p°; padam anuvidheyam mahatām*, the footsteps of the great are to be followed); a sign, token, characteristic; a particular measure of length (= 12 or 15 fingers' breadth, or $\frac{1}{2}$ or $\frac{1}{3}$ or $\frac{3}{7}$ of a Pra-krama); a footing, stand-point, standing-place, position, station, site (e. g. *bhrāmayitvā padāt padam*, having caused to wander from place to place; *padam ā-tan*, to spread or extend one's position); an abode, home; a place, post, office, rank, degree, dignity (e. g. *ślāghya-padam prāpya*, having obtained an honourable position); a business, affair, matter, (*padam kṛi*, to have dealings with any one, with loc. or acc. of the person or with *prati*); an object, thing; occasion, cause, subject (e. g. *sandeha-padeshu vastushu*, in matters which are subjects of doubt; *ashṭādaśa vyavahāra-padāni*, eighteen titles of law or occasions of litigation); pretext (= *apa-deśa*); a part, portion, division [cf. *tri-pada*]; a plot of ground; a square on a chess-board; a foot, (according to Hemaćandra in this sense also *as*, m.; *padena*, on foot; *padam kṛi*, to set foot in or on; *karishyasi padam punar āśrame*, thou shalt again set foot in the hermitage; *mūrdhni padaṃ kṛi*, to set the foot upon the head of any one, i. e. to conquer or overcome; *hṛidaye* or *ćitte padaṃ kṛi*, to take possession of any one's heart or mind; *padaṃ kṛi* may also mean 'to put confidence in'); a portion of a verse, quarter or line of a stanza, (*Vasishṭhasya padam*, N. of a Sāman); a word; (according to Pāṇini) a complete word, i. e. an inflected word or a *prātipadika*, q. v., with the case-terminations added, (also in Pāṇini's system) the base of a noun before all case-terminations beginning with consonants except those of the strong cases, and before all the Taddhita affixes beginning with consonants except *y;* a mode of writing the Vedas in which the several words are detached from one another [cf. *pada-pāṭha*]; (in arithmetic) any one in a set of numbers the sum of which is required; the last of a series, a period in an arithmetical progression; a square root; a quadrant; protection; (*as*), m. a ray of light. At the end of comps. the fem. form is *padā*; [cf. *a-p°*, *anu-p°*, *dush-p°*, *nish-p°*.] — *Pada-kāra*, *as*, m. the author of the Pada-pāṭha; one who divides or separates compound words. — *Pada-kāla*, *as*, m. = *pada-pāṭha*. — *Pada-kṛit*, *t*, m. = *pada-kāra*. — *Pada-kṛitya*, N. of a commentary on the Tarka-saṅgraha by Ćandraja-siṃha. — *Pada-krama*, *as*, m. a series of steps, pace, walking [cf. *ćitra-pada-kramam*]; a series of quarters of verses; a particular method of reading or writing the Vedas, see *krama*; (*ās*), m. pl. the Pada-pāṭha and the different Krama-pāṭhas. — *Padakramaka*, *am*, n. the Pada-pāṭha and Krama-pāṭha. — *Pada-ga*, *as*, *ā*, *am*, going on foot or with the feet; (*as*), m. a footman, a foot-soldier, &c. — *Pada-gata*, *as*, *ā*, *am*, gone on foot, described or recorded in a line or stanza. — *Pada-gati*, *is*, f. going on foot, manner of going, gait. — *Pada-gotra*, *am*, n. a family supposed to preside over a particular class of words. — *Pada-ćatur-ūrdhva*, *am*, n. a kind of metre in which every Pada is four syllables longer than the preceding. — *Pada-ćandrikā*, f. 'elucidation of words' [cf. *ćandrikā*]; N. of a commentary by Rāja-mukuṭa on the Amara-kosha. — *Pada-ćihna*, *am*, n. a footmark, footprint, footstep. — *Pada-ććheda*, *as*, m. separation of words (in speaking), resolving a sentence into its elementary parts; parsing. — *Pada-ćyuta*, *as*, *ā*, *am*, fallen from a position or office, dismissed from a place or official station. — *Pada-jāta*, *am*, n. a class of words. — *Pada-jña*, *as*, *ā*, *am*, Ved. knowing places, knowing the footmarks (of the cows), knowing degrees. — *Pada-jyotis*, n., N. of a work. — *Pada-tā*, f. the original form of a word. — *Pada-tva*, *am*, n. the state of a word. — *Pada-dārḍhya*, *am*, n. fixedness or security of text. — *Pada-devatā*, f. a deity supposed to preside over a particular class of words. — *Pada-nidhana*, *as*, *ā*, *am*, Ved. having the Nidhana at the end of every quarter of a verse (as a Sāman). — *Pada-nī*, *īs*, *īs*, *i*, Ved. one who guides the steps of another, a guide. — *Pada-nyāsa*, *as*, m. putting down the feet, stepping, step, foot-fall, tread; pace, footmark; position of the feet in a particular attitude; conduct, procedure (?); writing down verses or quarters of verses; the plant Asteracantha Longifolia Nees (= *go-kshura*). — *Pada-pankti*, *is*, f. a series or row of footsteps or footmarks; a kind of metre consisting of five Padas of five syllables each; an Ishṭakā or sacred brick called after this metre; a series of words. — *Pada-paddhati*, *is*, f. a series of footsteps or footmarks. — *Pada-pāṭha*, *as*, m. a particular method of reading and writing the text of the Vedas, by which each word is written and pronounced in its original form, separately and independently, i. e. without regard to its connection with the following or preceding word and without regard to the rules of Sandhi. — *Pada-pāta*, *as*, m. foot-fall, tread, step, pace. — *Pada-pūraṇa*, *as*, *ā*, *am*, filling out a verse, serving to complete a verse. — *Pada-bandha*, *as*, m. a footstep, step. — *Pada-bhañjana*, *am*, n. separating the words of a line or sentence, analysing words, explanation of obscure or obsolete words, etymology. — *Pada-bhañjikā*, f. a commentary which separates the words from each other and analyses the compounds into their parts; a register, a journal, a calendar or almanac. — *Pada-bhraṇśa*, *as*, m. dismissal from an office. — *Pada-mañjarī*, f., N. of a commentary by Haradatta-miśra on the Kāśikā vṛitti; N. of Loka-nātha's commentary on the Amara-kosha. — *Pada-mālā*, f. 'word-wreath,' a form of magical words, a magical formula, an incantation. — *Pada-yopana*, *as*, *ī*, *am*, Ved. stopping or obstructing the steps; (*am*), n. a fetter for the feet. — *Pada-vākya-ratnākara* (°*na-āk*°), *as*, m., N. of a grammatical work by Gokula-nātha. — *Pada-vāya*, *as*, m., Ved. a leader, &c.; [cf. *padavī*.] — *Pada-vikshepa*, *as*, m. step, pace, walking; a horse's paces. — *Pada-vigraha* or *pada-viććheda*, *as*, m. separation of words, dividing words. — *Pada-vid*, *t*, *t*, *t*, Ved. knowing places; familiar with anything. — *Pada-vishṭambha*, *as*, m. tread, step, stamp with the foot. — *Pada-vī*, *īs*, m., Ved. a leader, guide, one who precedes another; (*pada-vī* or according to some also *padavī*, *is*), f. a road, path, way, track (e. g. *moksha-padavī*, the way to final beatitude; *payasaḥ padavī*, a water-course, canal; *artha-padavīṃ gam*, to go the way of profit, to consult one's interest; *smaraṇa-padavīṃ gata*, gone to the way of memory, i. e. living only in the memory, dead; *hāsya-padavīṃ gam*, to go the way of laughter, i. e. to become a subject of ridicule); station, situation, degree, rank, post, office; place, site. — *Pada-vīya*, *am*, n., Ved. seeking for the track or traces of anything. — *Pada-vṛitti*, *is*, f. the hiatus between two words in a sentence. — *Pada-vṛiddhi*, *is*, f. increase of rank or station. — *Pada-vyākhyāna*, *am*, n. the interpretation of words. — *Pada-śas*, ind. step by step, gradually, by degrees. — *Pada-śreṇi*, *is*, f. a series of steps. — *Pada-shṭhīva*, *am*, n. the feet and knees. — *Pada-saṃhitā*, f. = *pada-pāṭha*, q. v. — *Pada-sanghāṭa* or *pada-sanghāta*, *as*, m. connecting those words together which in the Saṃhitā are separated by a kind of refrain; a writer, an annotator, one who collects or classifies words. — *Pada-sadhātu*, *u*, n. a manner of singing. — *Pada-sandhi*, *is*, m. the euphonic combination of words. — *Pada-samūha*, *as*, m. a series of words or parts of verses; = *pada-pāṭha*, q. v. — *Pada-stobha*, N. of a work. — *Pada-stha*, *as*, *ā*, *am*, standing on one's feet, going on foot; being in an official position, having rank, fixed in a station or office. — *Pada-sthāna*, *am*, n. footprint, footmark. — *Pada-sthita*, *as*, *ā*, *am*, standing on one's feet, going on foot. — *Padāṅka* (°*da-aṅ*°), *as*, m. footmark, footprint. — *Padāṅka-dūta*, 'the messenger of the footmark (Kṛishṇa),' N. of a poem. — *Padāṅgī* (°*da-aṅ*°), f. a species of plant (= *haṇsa-padī*). — *Padāṅgushṭha* (°*da-aṅ*°), *as*, m. the great toe; [cf. *pādāṅgushṭha*.] — *Padāji* (°*da-āji*), *is*, m. a footman, foot-soldier. — *Padādi* (°*da-ādi*), *is*, m. the beginning of the line of a stanza; the beginning or first letter of a word. — *Padādyavid*, *t*, m. (either *padādi-avid*, one who does not know the beginning of verses, or *padādya-vid*, one who knows only the first parts of a verse or of a word), a bad student. — *Padādhyayana* (°*da-adh*°), *am*, n. the study of the Vedas according to the Pada-pāṭha. — *Padānuga* (°*da-an*°), *as*, *ā*, *am*, following at one's heels, following closely after (with gen.); suitable, agreeable to; (*as*), m. a companion, follower. — *Padānurāga* (°*da-an*°), *as*, m. a servant; an army. — *Padānuśāsana* (°*da-an*°), *am*, n. the science of words, grammar. — *Padānushanga* (°*da-an*°), *as*, m. anything added or appended to a Pada; [cf. *pad-anushanga*.] — *Padānusvāra* (°*da-an*°), *am*, n., Ved., N. of a Sāman (?). — *Padānta* (°*da-an*°), *as*, m. the end of a line in a stanza; the end of a word; (*as*, *ā*, *am*), having the word Pada at the end, ending in the word Pada. — *Padāntara* (°*da-an*°), *am*, n. an interval of one step (e. g. *padāntare sthitvā*, stopping after taking one step; *a-padāntara*, not having an interval of one step, closely connected; *a-padāntaram*, ind. without any interval, immediately upon, closely, without a pause). — *Padānta-śuddhāśuddhīya* (°*dha-aś*°), *am*, n., N. of a Sāman. — *Padāntīya* or *padāntya*, *as*, *ā*, *am*, being at the end of a word, final. — *Padābhilāshin* (°*da-abh*°), *ī*, *iṇī*, *i*, wishing for an office. — *Padāmbhoja* (°*da-am*°), *am*, n. 'lotus-foot,' the foot of a mistress or divinity; (there are many similar compounds, as *padāravinda*, q. v.) — *Padāyatā* (°*da-āy*°), f. a shoe; [cf. *pan-naddhā*.] — *Padāravinda* (°*da-ar*°), *am*, n. 'lotus-foot,' the foot of a mistress, of a divinity, &c. — *Padārtha* (°*da-ar*°), *as*, m. the meaning of a word, the thing corresponding to a word, a thing, object; a head or topic (of which sixteen are enumerated by the Naiyāyikas, viz. proof, that which is to be known and proven, doubt, motive, example, dogmatic truth, the member of a regular argument or syllogism, reasoning by reductio ad absurdum, ascertainment, disquisition, controversy, cavil, fallacious reason, perversion, futility, and occasion for rebuke); category or predicament in logic (of which seven are enumerated by the Vaiśeshikas, viz. *dravya*, substance; *guṇa*, quality; *karman*, action; *sāmānya*, genus; *viśesha*, difference; *samavāya*, co-inherence; *a-bhāva*, non-existence); the sense of another word which is not expressed but has to be supplied, (see Pāṇ. I. 4, 96.) — *Padārtha-kaumudī*, f., N. of a commentary on the Amara-kosha. — *Padārtha-dīpikā*, f., N. of an introduction to the study of logic by Koṇḍa-bhaṭṭa. — *Padārtha-dharma-saṅgraha*, *as*, m., N. of a work. — *Padārtha-prakāśa*, *as*, m. = *padārtha-mālā*, q. v. — *Padārtha-bodha*, *as*, m., N. of a work on the Nyāya philosophy. — *Padārtha-mālā*, f., N. of an elementary treatise on the Nyāya philosophy. — *Padārthamālā-dīpikā*, f., N. of a Nyāya work. — *Padārtha-viveka*, *as*, m., N. of a work on the categories of the Vaiśeshikas. — *Padāvalī* (°*da-āv*°), f. a series of lines in stanzas, a series of words; N. of a grammar. — *Padāvṛitti* (°*da-āv*°), *is*, f. the repetition of a word. — *Padāsana* (°*da-ās*°), *am*, n. a footstool. — *Padāhata* (°*da-āh*°), *as*, *ā*, *am*, kicked. — *Padodāharaṇa* (°*da-ud*°), *am*, n. an example taken from the Pada-pāṭha. — *Padopahata* (°*da-up*°), see Pāṇ. VI. 3, 52.

Padaka, *am*, n. a step; a position; an office; (*as*), m. a Nishka or weight of gold; an ornament of the neck; (*as*, *ā*, *am*), familiar with the Pada-pāṭha.

Padana, *as*, *ā*, *am*, who or what goes or moves.

Padanīya, *as*, *ā*, *am*, Ved. to be investigated.

Padāta, *as*, m. (properly *pada* + *āta*), a footman, pedestrian.

Padāti, *is*, *is*, *i* (properly *pada* + *āti*), going or being on foot; (*is*), m. a pedestrian, footman, foot-soldier, peon; N. of a son of Janam-ejaya. — *Padāti-jana*, *as*, m. a footman, pedestrian. — *Padātijana-sankula*, *as*, *ā*, *am*, mingled with footmen or pedestrians. — *Padāti-mātra*, *as*, m. only a foot-soldier. — *Padāty-adhyaksha*, *as*, m. the commander-in-chief of the infantry.

Padātika, *as*, m. a footman, foot-soldier, peon.

Padātin, *ī*, *inī*, *i*, having foot-soldiers; going on foot, being on foot; (*ī*), m. a foot-soldier.

Padātīya, *as*, m. a foot-soldier, footman, pedestrian.

Padāra, *as*, m. the dust of the feet; a boat (= *pādālinda*).

Padāsa, *am*, n. (said to be fr. *pada* + 1. *āsa*), with *Vasishṭhasya*, N. of a Sāman.

Padi, *is*, m. (according to the Nirukta = *gantu*), Ved. an animal which uses its feet for locomotion; a bird; a particular kind of animal (?).

Padika, *as*, *ā*, *am*, going on foot, pedestrian; one Pada long; containing only one division; (*as*), m. a footman, foot-soldier; (*am*), n. the point of the foot.

Padeka, *as*, m. a hawk, falcon.

Pade-kṛitya (or *pade kṛitvā*), ind. having placed in a position, (Pāṇ. I. 4, 76.)

Padvan, *ā*, m. a road, path, way.

Panna, as, ā, am, fallen, gone down or downwards, sunk, descended; gone; (*as*), m. downward motion, falling, descent, fall; creeping on the ground. — *Panna-ga, as*, m. 'creeping along the ground,' a snake, serpent, serpent-demon or Nāga; a species of plant (= *padma-kāshṭha*); (*ā*), f. a female serpent, a female serpent-demon; (*ī*), f. a species of shrub (= *sarpiṇī*). — *Pannaga-keśara, as*, m. Mesua Roxburghii. — *Pannaga-nāśana, as*, m. 'serpent-destroyer,' an epithet of Garuḍa, the bird and vehicle of Vishṇu. — *Pannaga-maya, as, ī, am*, formed or consisting of serpents. — *Pannagāri* (°*ga-ari*), *is*, m. 'enemy of serpents,' an epithet of Garuḍa; N. of a teacher; (also read *pannagāni*.) — *Pannagāśana* (°*ga-aś*°), *as*, m. 'serpent-devourer,' an epithet of Garuḍa. — *Pannāgāra* (°*na-ag*° or *āg*°), *as*, m., N. of a man; (*ās*), m. pl., N. of his descendants.

पदवी *pada-vī*. See p. 530, col. 2.

पद्धति *pad-dhati*. See 3. *pad*, p. 529, col. 3.

पद्म *padma, as, am*, m. n. (perhaps for an original *pad-mat*, rich in stalks, but said to be fr. rt. 2. *pad*), a lotus, lotus-flower, especially the Nelumbium Speciosum (not the plant itself, but the flower which closes towards the evening; often confounded with the water-lily or Nymphæa Alba); a lotus-like ornament; the form or figure of a lotus; a N. given by the Tāntrikas to the six divisions of the upper part of the body called Ćakras, (see *ćakra*); a particular mark or mole on the human body; a spot; red or coloured marks on the face and trunk of an elephant; N. of a particular part of a column or pillar; an army arrayed in the form of a lotus; a particular posture of the body in religious meditation; one of the personified treasures of Kuvera as worshipped by the Tāntrikas; a particular high number, 1000 billions; N. of a constellation; (with Buddhists) N. of a particular hell (characterized by coldness); a species of fragrant plant (= *padma-kāshṭha*); the root of the Nelumbium Speciosum; a species of bdellium; a particular fragrant substance; lead; (*as*), m. a kind of temple; a kind of coitus; one of the eight treasures connected with the magical art called Padminī; a species of plant; an elephant; a species of serpent; a Nāga; N. of one of the attendants of Skanda; (with Jainas) N. of the ninth Ćakra-vartin in Bhārata; an epithet of Rāma (the son of Daśa-ratha by his wife Kauśalyā); N. of a prince of Kaśmīra (founder of Padma-pura and of a temple, see *padma-svāmin*); of a man; of a Brāhman; of a mythical elephant [cf. *mahā-padma*]; of a monkey; of a mountain; (*ā*), f. 'the lotus-hued one,' an epithet of Śrī, the goddess of fortune and wife of Vishṇu [cf. *padma-śrī*]; N. of two plants, Clerodendrum Siphonanthus and Hibiscus Mutabilis; cloves; the flower of Carthamus Tinctoria; N. of the mother of Muni-suvrata, the twentieth Arhat of the present Ava-sarpiṇī; N. of a female serpent-demon (= the goddess Manasā, wife of the sage Jarat-kāru; cf. *padma-priyā*); N. of a daughter of king Bṛihad-ratha and wife of Kalki; (*as, ā, am*), lotus-hued, being of the colour of a lotus. — *Padma-kara, as*, m. a lotus-like hand, a hand like a lotus; (*as, ā, am*), having a lotus in the hand, holding a lotus; (*ā*), f. an epithet of Śrī; (*as*), m., N. of the sun. — *Padma-karṇika* (perhaps incorrect for *padma-karṇikā*), the capsule or pericarp of a lotus or the central part of an army arrayed in that form. — *Padma-kalikā*, f. an unblown lotus. — *Padma-kāshṭha, am*, n. a fragrant wood used in medicine and described as cooling and tonic (= *kedāra-ja, padma-vṛiksha*, &c.). — *Padma-kiṭa, as*, m. a species of venomous insect. — *Padma-kūṭa, am*, n. 'lotus-peak,' N. of the palace of Su-bhīmā. — *Padma-ketana, as*, m. 'characterized by a lotus,' N. of a son of Garuḍa. — *Padma-ketu, us*, m., N. of a Ketu. — *Padma-keśara, as, am*, m. n. the filament of a lotus. — *Padma-kośa* or *padma-kosha, as*, m. the calyx of a lotus; a particular position of the fingers resembling the calyx of a lotus. — *Padma-kshetra, am*, n., N. of one of four districts in Orissa held especially sacred. — *Padma-khaṇḍa, am*, n. a quantity of lotuses, a spot abounding with them. — *Padma-gandha, as, ā, am*, or *padma-gandhi, is, is, i*, lotus-scented, smelling like a lotus, fragrant as a lotus. — *Padma-garbha, as, ā, am*, 'lotus-born,' sprung from a lotus; (*as*), m. an epithet of Brahmā; of Vishṇu; of Śiva; the sun; N. of a man; of a Bodhi-sattva; of a Brāhman who was changed into a swan. — *Padma-gṛihā*, f. 'lotus-housed,' 'living in a lotus,' an epithet of Lakshmī. — *Padma-ćāriṇī*, f. a small tree, Hibiscus Mutabilis. — *Padma-ja, as*, m. 'lotus-born,' an epithet of Brahmā. — *Padma-tantu, us*, m. the fibrous stalk of a lotus or the fibre of a lotus-stalk. — *Padma-darśana, as, ā, am*, looking like a lotus; (*as*), m. the resin of the Pinus Longifolia; N. of a man. — *Padma-nandin, ī*, m., N. of an author. — *Padma-nābha*, having a lotus springing from his navel; (*as*), m. an epithet of Vishṇu (so called because the lotus containing Brahmā, the future creator, sprang from his navel); N. of the eleventh month (reckoned from Mārga-śīrsha); N. of a Nāga; of one of the 100 sons of Dhṛita-rāshṭra; of the first Arhat of the future Ut-sarpiṇī; of various other men; of a magical formula pronounced over weapons. — *Padmanābha-datta, as*, m., N. of a grammarian and lexicographer, father of Vijñāneśvara. — *Padmanābha-bīja, am*, n. the algebra of Padma-nābha. — *Padmanābha-bhaṭṭa, as*, m., N. of the father of the commentator Vijñāneśvara. — *Padma-nābhi, is*, m. an epithet of Vishṇu, (see *padma-nābha*.) — *Padma-nāla, am*, n. a lotus-stalk. — *Padma-nibhekshaṇa* (°*bha-īksh*°), *as, ā, am*, having lotus-like eyes, whose eyes are like a lotus. — *Padma-nimīlana, am*, n. the closing of a lotus. — *Padma-netra, as*, m. 'lotus-eyed,' N. of a future Buddha. — *Padma-pattra, am*, n. a lotus-leaf, the petal of a lotus; Costus Speciosus. — *Padmapattra-nibhekshaṇa* (°*bha-īksh*°), *as, ā, am*, having eyes like lotus-leaves. — *Padma-pada* or *padma-pāda, as*, m., N. of an author, the pupil of Śaṅkara. — *Padma-parṇa, am*, n. Costus Speciosus. — *Padma-pāṇi, is*, m. 'lotus-handed,' 'holding a lotus in his hand,' an epithet of Brahmā; of Vishṇu; the sun; N. of a particular Buddha; epithet of the Bodhi-sattva Avalokiteśvara. — *Padma-pādāćārya* (°*da-āć*°), *as*, m., N. of a preceptor. — *Padma-pura, am*, n., N. of a city founded by Padma. — *Padma-purāṇa, am*, n. 'Lotus-purāṇa,' N. of a Purāṇa describing the period during which the world was a lotus. — *Padma-pushpa, as*, m. the plant Pterospermum Acerifolium; a species of small bird (= *pikāṅga*). — *Padma-prabha, as*, m., N. of a future Buddha; of a divine being; (with Jainas) of the sixth Arhat of the present Ava-sarpiṇī. — *Padma-priyā*, f. an epithet of the goddess Manasā, wife of Jarat-kāru. — *Padma-bandha, as*, m. an artificial arrangement of the words of a verse in a figure representing a lotus-flower, (the several syllables being distributed on the eight petals of the flower and a syllable to be repeated before each group of syllables being written on the part representing the pericarp.) — *Padma-bandhu, us*, m. 'friend of the lotus,' an epithet of the Sun; a bee. — *Padma-bīja, am*, n. a lotus-seed, the seed of a lotus. — *Padmabījābha* (°*ja-ābh*°), *am*, n. 'resembling the lotus-seed,' the seed of Euryala Ferox. — *Padma-bhava, as, ā, am*, 'lotus-born,' 'produced from a lotus,' an epithet of Brahmā. — *Padma-bhāsa, as*, m. 'brilliant with a lotus,' or 'bright as a lotus,' an epithet of Vishṇu; [cf. *padma-hāsa*.] — *Padma-bhū, ūs*, m. 'lotus-born,' an epithet of Brahmā. — *Padma-maya, as, ī, am*, made or consisting of lotus-flowers. — *Padma-mālin, ī, inī, i*, 'lotus-garlanded,' wearing a garland of lotuses; (*ī*), m., N. of a Rakshas; (*inī*), f. an epithet of Śrī. — *Padma-mihira, as*, m., N. of the writer of a history of Kaśmīra. — *Padma-mukhī*, f. a species of prickly nightshade, Alhagi Maurorum. — *Padma-yoni, is*, or *padma-yonin, ī*, m. 'lotus-born,' 'sprung from a lotus,' an epithet of Brahmā; N. of a man. — *Padma-ratha, as*, m., N. of two princes. — *Padma-rāga, as, ā, am*, lotus-hued, of the colour of a lotus; (*as*), m. a ruby; (*ī*), f., N. of one of the tongues of Fire. — *Padmarāga-maya, as, ī, am*, made or consisting of rubies. — *Padma-rāja, as*, m., N. of two persons. — *Padma-rūpa, ā*, f. 'lotus-hued,' an epithet of Śrī. — *Padma-rekhā*, f. a line in the palm of the hand indicating the acquisition of great wealth. — *Padma-lāñćhana, as*, m. 'marked or symbolized by a lotus,' a king; an epithet of Brahmā; an epithet of Kuvera; the sun; (*ā*), f. an epithet of the goddess Śrī; an epithet of Sarasvatī; an epithet of Tārā. — *Padma-lekhā*, f., N. of a woman. — *Padma-loćana, as, ā, am*, lotus-eyed. — *Padmavat, ān, atī, at*, full of lotuses, abounding in lotus-flowers; (*atī*), f., N. of a wife of A-śoka. — *Padma-varṇa, as, ā, am*, lotus-hued, lotus-coloured; (*as*), m., N. of a son of Yadu. — *Padmavarṇaka, am*, n. Costus Speciosus. — *Padma-vāsā*, f. 'dwelling in a lotus,' an epithet of Śrī (as having dwelt at the creation within the petals of a lotus). — *Padma-vāhinī*, f., N. of a work. — *Padma-vishaya, as*, m., N. of a country. — *Padma-vṛiksha, am*, n. = *padma-kāshṭha*, q.v. — *Padma-vṛishabha-vikrāmin, ī*, m., N. of a future Buddha. — *Padma-vyūha, as*, m., N. of a Sam-ādhi. — *Padma-śas*, ind. by thousands of billions. — *Padma-śrī, īs*, m., N. of a Bodhi-sattva; (*īs*), f., N. of two princesses. — *Padmaśrī-garbha, as*, m., N. of a Bodhi-sattva. — *Padma-shaṇḍa, am*, n. a quantity or multitude of lotuses; [cf. *padma-khaṇḍa*.] — *Padma-saṅkāśa, as, ā, am*, lotus-like, resembling a lotus. — *Padma-samāsana, as*, m. 'having a seat like a lotus,' an epithet of Brahmā. — *Padma-sambhava, as*, m. 'sprung from a lotus,' an epithet of Brahmā; N. of a Buddhist scholar. — *Padma-saras, as*, n. 'lotus-lake,' N. of various lakes. — *Padma-sūtra, am*, n. a garland of lotuses. — *Padma-sena, as*, m., N. of a man. — *Padma-saugandhika, as, ī, am*, fragrant as a lotus. — *Padma-snushā*, f. 'daughter-in-law of a lotus,' an epithet of Gaṅgā; of Śrī; of Durgā. — *Padma-svastika, as, am*, m. n. a mystical mark consisting of lotus-flowers; (according to the scholiast) a four-cornered sort of painting. — *Padma-svāmin, ī*, m., N. of a sacred edifice built by Padma. — *Padma-hāsa, as*, m. 'smiling like a lotus or with a lotus,' an epithet of Vishṇu; [cf. *padma-bhāsa*.] — *Padmākara* (°*ma-āk*°), *as*, m. a lotus-pool; a large deep tank or pond abounding in lotuses. — *Padmākara-bhaṭṭa, as*, m., N. of a scholar. — *Padmākāra* (°*ma-āk*°), *as, ā, am*, lotus-shaped, shaped like a lotus. — *Padmāksha* (°*ma-aksha*), *as, ī, am*, lotus-eyed, having eyes like a lotus; (*as*), m. an epithet of Vishṇu; N. of a man; (*am*), n. the seed of the lotus. — *Padmāṭa* (°*ma-āṭa*), *as*, m. Cassia Tora. — *Padmāntara* (°*ma-an*°), *as*, m. a lotus-leaf, the petal of a lotus. — *Padmālaya* (°*ma-āl*°), *as*, m. 'dwelling in a lotus,' an epithet of Brahmā; (*ā*), f. an epithet of Śrī. — *Padmāsana* (°*ma-ās*°), *am*, n. a lotus-seat, a seat or throne in the shape of a lotus, especially one on which idols are placed; a particular posture in religious meditation, sitting with the thighs crossed with one hand resting on the left thigh, the other held up with the thumb upon the heart, and with the eyes directed to the tip of the nose; a kind of coitus; (*as, ā, am*), 'sitting in a lotus,' an epithet of Brahmā; of Śiva; of the goddess Manasā; sitting in the position called Padmāsana; (*as*), m. the sun. — *Padmāhvā* (°*ma-āh*°), f. = *padma-ćāriṇī*, q.v. — *Padme-śaya, as, ā, am*, reclining or sleeping on a lotus; (*as*), m. an epithet of Vishṇu. — *Padmottama* (°*ma-ut*°), *as*, m., N. of a future Buddha. — *Padmottara* (°*ma-ut*°), *as*, m. the plant Carthamus Tinctorius; N. of a man; of a Buddha. — *Padmottarātma-ja* (°*ra-āt*°), *as*, m. 'son of Padmottara,' (with Jainas) epithet of the ninth Ćakra-vartin in Bhārata. — *Padmodbhava* (°*ma-ud*°), *as, ā, am*, 'sprung from a lotus,' an epithet of Brahmā, of the goddess Manasā; (*as*), m., N. of a man; origin of the lotus (?). – *Padmodbhava-prādurbhāva* (°*na-ud*°), *as*, m. 'the manifestation of Brahmā on the lotus,' N. of the ninth chapter of the first part of the Kūrma-purāṇa.

Padmaka, as, m. an army arrayed in the form of a lotus-flower; N. of several men; (*as, am*), m. n. red or coloured spots on the skin of an elephant; Costus Speciosus or Arabicus; (*am*), n. a particular posture in sitting; a species of tree and its wood which is used for various purposes (= *padma-kāshṭha* = *kushṭha*, Costus Speciosus or Arabicus). – *Padmakāmalaka-plaksha-kadamboḍumbarā-vṛita* (°*ka-ām*°, °*ba-uḍ*°, °*ra-āv*°), *as, ā, am*, filled with lotuses, Emblic Myrobalans, fig-trees, Nauclea Kadambas and Uḍumbaras (a kind of fig-tree).

Padmakin, ī, m. the Indian birch tree (= *bhūrja*), the bark of which is used for writing upon, &c.

Padmāvata, as, m., N. of a kingdom founded by Padma-varṇa.

Padmāvatī, f. Hibiscus Mutabilis; a kind of Prākṛit metre; an epithet of Lakshmī; N. of one of the Mātṛis attending on Skanda; an epithet of the goddess Manasā; N. of a divine being executing the orders of the twenty-third Arhat of the present Ava-sarpiṇī; N. of a wife of king S'ṛigāla; of a wife of Yudhi-shṭhira, king of Kaśmīra; of the wife of Jaya-deva; of a poetess; of a wife of king Vīra-bāhu; of king Naya-pāla; of a city; of a river; of the seventeenth Lambaka of the Kathā-sarit-sāgara. – *Padmāvatī-priya, as*, m. 'husband of Padmāvatī,' an epithet of Jarat-kāru.

Padmin, ī, inī, i, possessing lotuses; spotted or having coloured marks (as an elephant); (*ī*), m. an elephant; (*inī*), f. a lotus, Nelumbium Speciosum, (the whole plant, whereas *padma* is properly only the flower; the same difference exists between *abja* and *abjinī*, *nalina* and *nalinī*, &c.); a multitude of lotuses or lake abounding in them; a lotus-pool, a pool or pond (especially one deep enough for the growth of the lotus); the fibrous stalk of a lotus; a female elephant; a particular magical art; a woman of the first and most excellent of the four classes into which the sex is distinguished; N. of a woman. – *Padminī-kaṇṭaka, as*, m., N. of a kind of leprosy. – *Padminī-kānta, as*, m. 'beloved of the lotuses,' an epithet of the Sun, (so called because the Nelumbium Speciosum closes towards the evening.) – *Padminī-khaṇḍa, am*, n. a multitude of lotuses, a place abounding in lotuses or district in which they grow. – *Padminī-vallabha, as*, m. 'friend of the lotuses,' an epithet of the Sun. – *Padminīśa* (°*ni-īśa*), *as*, m. 'lord of the lotuses,' the Sun.

पद्य *padya, as, ā, am* (fr. 3. *pad* or *pada*), relating to or belonging to the foot; paining or hurting or coming in contact with the feet; bearing traces of the feet, marked with footprints, measuring a Pada in length, (at the end of a comp. with a preceding numeral, e. g. *daśa-padya*, ten Padas long); consisting of Padas, formed of parts of verses; consisting of one Pada; belonging to a word; final; (*as*), m. a S'ūdra (as sprung from the feet of Brahmā); a part of a word, a verbal element; (*ā*), f. a way, path, road; (*ās*), f. pl., Ved. footsteps, paces; (*am*), n. a verse, metre, poetry. – *Padya-maya, as, ī, am*, consisting of verses. – *Padya-veṇī*, f., N. of a collection of poems by Veṇī-datta. – *Padya-saṅgraha, as*, m. a collection of verses, N. of a collection of twenty verses ascribed to Kavi-bhaṭṭa.

पद्र *padra, as*, m. (said to be fr. rt. 2. *pad*), a village; the entrance into a village; the earth; a particular district.

पद्व *padva, as*, m. (said to be fr. rt. 2. *pad*), the abode or world of human beings; a road; a car; (*nisarga-padva, as, ī, am*, naturally inclined to, feeling attracted towards.)

पद्वन् *padvan*. See p. 530, col. 3.

पन् *pan*, cl. 1. P. A. *panāyati, -te* (Ved. *panayati, -te*), *pene, panitā* or *panāyitā, panitum* or *panāyitum* (mostly Ved.), to be worthy of admiration; to admire; to regard with surprise or wonder; to praise; to acknowledge, recognise; (A.) to rejoice at, be glad of, congratulate one's self upon (with gen.).

Panayāyya, as, ā, am, Ved. worthy of admiration, admirable; astonishing, surprising.

Panasya, Nom. A. *panasyate*, &c., Ved. to show one's self worthy of admiration, be admirable.

Panasyu, us, us, u, Ved. showing one's self worthy of admiration, boasting; an epithet of the Maruts, of Indra, &c.

Panāyita, as, ā, am, praised.

Panāyya, as, ā, am, Ved. worthy of admiration, admirable, surprising.

Panita, as, ā, am, admired, praised.

Panitṛi, tā, trī, tṛi, acknowledging with praise, praising.

Panipnat, at, atī, at (pres. part. of the Intens.), Ved. showing one's self worthy of admiration or praise.

Panishṭama, as, ā, am (perhaps for *panishṭha-tama*, cf. *nedishṭha-tama*), Ved. highly praised; (but Sāy. takes it for 1st pers. pl. = *stumaḥ*.)

Panishṭi, is, f., Ved. (perhaps) admiration, praise.

Panishṭha, as, ā, am, Ved. very wonderful, exceedingly glorious or praiseworthy.

Panīyas, ān, asī, as, Ved. more wonderful or praiseworthy, very wonderful.

Panu, us, or *panū, ūs*, Ved. admiration, praise.

Panya, as, ā, am, Ved. praiseworthy; astonishing.

Panyas, ān, asī, as, Ved. = *panīyas*, more wonderful, very wonderful.

पनस *panasa, as*, m. (said to be fr. rt. *pan*), the bread-fruit or Jaka tree, Artocarpus Integrifolia; a thorn; a species of serpent; N. of a monkey; (*ā* or *ī*), f. a malady, pustular and phlegmonoid inflammation of the skin or external organs; a female monkey; a female demon; (*am*), n. the bread-fruit, fruit of the Jaka tree. – *Panasa-tālikā* or (according to some) *panasa-nālikā*, f. the bread-fruit tree.

Panasikā, f. a kind of disease, pustules on the ears and neck.

पनिष्पद *panishpada, as, ā, am* (fr. Intens. of *spand*), Ved. quivering, palpitating.

पन्थ् *panth*, cl. 1. and 10. P. *panthati, panthayati*, &c., to go, move.

पन्थक *panthaka, as, ā, am*, produced in or on the way; (*as*), m., N. of a Brāhman.

पन्दर *pandara, as*, m., N. of a mountain.

पन्न *panna*. See p. 531, col. 1.

पन्नद्धा *pan-naddhā*. See p. 529, col. 3.

पपि *papi, is, is, i* (fr. rt. 1. *pā*), drinking, who or what drinks; (*is*), m. the moon.

Papīti, is, f. (fr. Intens. of rt. 1. *pā*), mutual or reciprocal drinking, drinking alike or together.

पपी *papī, īs*, m. (fr. rt. 3. *pā*, to cherish), the sun; the moon.

Papu, us, m. a fosterer, protector; (*us*), f. a nurse, foster-mother.

पपुरि *papuri, is, is, i* (fr. rt. *pṛī*), Ved. liberal, giving, granting; abundant.

पपृक्षेण्य *paprikshenya, as, ā, am* (fr. rt. *prać*), Ved. to be wished or longed for, desirable.

पप्रि 1. *papri, is, is, i* (fr. rt. 1. *pṛi*), leading over, delivering, saving.

पप्रि 2. *papri, is, is, i* (fr. rt. 2. *pṛī*), Ved. giving, granting.

पफक *paphaka, as*, m., N. of a man. – *Paphaka-naraka, ās*, m. pl. the descendants of Paphaka and Naraka.

पब्बेक *pabbeka, as*, m., N. of the father of Kedāra who composed the Vṛitta-ratnākara.

पमरा *pamarā*, f. a kind of fragrant substance.

पम्पस्य *pampasya* (probably fr. an unused *pampas*, grief), Nom. P. *pampasyati*, to feel pain.

पम्पा *pampā*, f. (said to be fr. rt. 3. *pā*), N. of a river in the south of India; (according to a Scholiast) N. of a lake.

पम्ब् *pamb*, cl. 1. P. *pambati*, &c., to go, move; [cf. rt. *kamp, bamb, mamb, namb, khamb, gamb, ghamb, ćamb, tamb*.]

पय् *pay*, cl. 1. A. *payate*, &c., to go, move.

पयस् *payas, as*, n. (fr. rt. 1. *pī* or rt. *pinv*; but said to be fr. rt. 1. *pā*, to drink), juice, fluid, vital spirit, power, strength (Ved.); water, rain; milk; semen virile; N. of a Sāman; N. of a Virāj; night (Ved.). – *Payaḥ-kandā*, f. Batatas Paniculata (= *kshīra-vidārī*). – *Payaḥ-payoshṇī*, f. = *payoshṇī*, q. v. – *Payaḥ-pāna, am*, n. drinking milk, a draught of milk. – *Payaḥ-pūra, as*, m. a pool, lake. – *Payaḥ-phenī*, f. a species of small shrub (= *dugdha-phenī*). – *Payaś-ćaya, as*, m. a reservoir, piece of water, lake. – *Payas-pa, as*, m. 'milk-drinker,' a cat; night. – *Payas-pā, ās, ās, am*, Ved. milk-drinking, drinking milk. – *Payas-vat, ān, atī, at*, Ved. full of sap or juice, succulent, juicy, liquid; full of strength or of milk, milky, containing water or milk or semen; (*vatyas*), f. pl. rivers (Ved.). – *Payas-vala, as, ā, am*, rich in milk, yielding milk abundantly; (*as*), m. a goat. – *Payas-vin, ī, inī, i*, abounding in sap or milk, juicy, succulent, milky; (*inī*), f. a milch cow; a she-goat; a river; N. of a river; the night; N. of various plants containing milky juice (= *kākolī, kshīra-kākolī, dugdha-phenī, kshīra-vidārī*); N. of a deity. – *Payo-gaḍa, as*, m. 'water-drop (?),' hail; (*as* or *am*), m. n. an island. – *Payo-graha, as*, m., Ved. an oblation of milk. – *Payo-ghana, as*, m. 'water-lump,' hail. – *Payo-janman, ā*, m. 'birthplace of water,' a cloud. – *Payo-da, as, ā, am*, yielding milk; (*as*), m. 'water-giver,' a cloud; N. of a son of Yadu; (*ā*), f., N. of one of the Mātṛis attending on Skanda. – *Payoda-suhṛid, t*, m. 'friend of the clouds,' the peacock. – *Payo-duh, dhuk, k, k*, Ved. milking; giving semen (?). – *Payo-dhara, as*, m. 'water-holder,' a cloud; 'containing milk,' a woman's breast; an udder; the root of Scirpus Kysoor; a species of sugar-cane (= *kosha-kāra*); the cocoa-nut; a species of Cyperus; (in prosody) an amphibrach. – *Payo-dhas, ās*, m. a rain-cloud; a piece of water, pond, lake; the ocean. – *Payo-dhā, ās, ās, am*, Ved. sucking milk (as a calf). – *Payo-dhārā*, f. a stream of water; N. of a river. – *Payodhārā-gṛiha, am*, n. = *dhārā-gṛiha*, a bath-room with flowing water, shower-bath. – *Payo-dhi, is*, m. 'receptacle of waters,' the ocean. – *Payodhika, am*, n. 'sea-foam,' cuttle-fish bone. – *Payo-nidhana, am*, n., N. of a Sāman. – *Payo-nidhi, is*, m. 'receptacle of waters,' the ocean. – *Payo-mukha, as, ā, am*, having milk on the surface, milk-faced. – *Payo-muć, k, k, k*, yielding or giving milk; (*k*), m. 'water-discharging,' a cloud. – *Payo-'mṛita-tīrtha, am*, n., N. of a Tīrtha. – *Payo-rāśi, is*, m. a piece of water, the ocean. – *Payo-latā*, f. the plant Batatas Paniculata. – *Payo-vāha, as*, m. 'water-bearer,' a cloud. – *Payo-vṛidh, t, t, t*, Ved. full of sap, superabounding with water, overflowing. – *Payo-vrata, am*, n. the act of subsisting on mere milk in consequence of a vow, (regarded as an expiation for receiving an unsuitable present, if continued for a month with prayer and residence in a cow-house); offering milk to Vishṇu and subsisting upon it for twelve days; also for one or for three days as a religious act; (*as, ā, am*), one who subsists upon mere milk in consequence of a vow. — *Payoshṇi-jātā*, f. an epithet of the river Sarasvatī. — *Payoshṇī*, f. (fr. *payas* and *ushṇa*), 'warm as milk,' N. of a river that rises in the Vindhya mountain.

Payasa, as, ā, am, Ved. full of juice or sap; (*am*), n. water; milk.

1. *payasya*, Nom. P. A. *payasyati, -te*, &c., to flow, be fluid.

2. *payasya, as, ā, am*, made of milk (curds, butter, cheese, &c.), milky; watery; (*as*), m. a cat; N. of one of the sons of Aṅgiras; (*ā*), f. coagulated milk, curds (made by mixing sour with hot sweet milk); a shrub, Asclepias Rosea; N. of various plants (= *dugdhikā, kākolī, kshīri-kākolī, svarṇa-kshīrī, arka-pushpikā*, and *kuṭumbinī-kshupa*); any plant yielding a milky sap, as the Euphorbia, the Asclepias, &c.

Payāya, Nom. A. *payāyate*, &c., to be fluid.

Payora, as, m. = *khadira*, Acacia Catechu.

पर *para, as, ā, am* (fr. rt. 1. *pṛi*, or perhaps fr. *apa + ra*; declined optionally as a pronominal in abl. loc. sing. m. n. and nom. voc. pl. m., when it denotes relative position, e. g. abl. *parasmāt* and *parāt*, loc. *parasmin* and *pare*, nom. pl. m. *pare* and *parās*, Ved. *parāsas*, see Gram. 238. *a*), distant, remote, removed; opposite, ulterior, beyond, further, on the other side of (with abl. or rarely with gen., e. g. *Sarayvāḥ pare tīre*, on the opposite or further bank of the Sarayū); past, antecedent, earlier, previous, former (Ved.); long past, ancient; subsequent, succeeding, following, future, next, after (with abl.); added; (at the end of a comp.) having as a following letter or sound (e. g. *ta-para*, having *t* as a following letter, followed by *t*); exceeding, left, remaining; very high or excellent, distinguished, pre-eminent, highest, greatest, longest, most excellent, best, supreme, principal, chief, most complete, utmost (= Lat. *summus*, e. g. *param Brahman*, the Supreme Spirit); highest, latest (e. g. *paraḥ kālaḥ*, the highest or latest times; *param āyuḥ*, the highest or last stage of human life; used at the end of comps. to denote having anything as the highest object, completely devoted to or occupied with or engaged or engrossed in or intent upon, e. g. *ćintā-para*, occupied with reflection; *dhyāna-para*, engaged in meditation, whose highest object is meditation; *sukha-para*, extremely glad or happy; *śoka-para*, filled with grief, whose principal occupation is grief); strange, a stranger, other, another, different, varying, foreign, alien, inimical, hostile, estranged, adverse; exceeding, having a remainder or surplus (e. g. *paraṃ śatam*, more than a hundred); left over, left as a remainder; concerned or anxious for (with loc.); (*as*), m. an enemy, foe, adversary; (sc. *graha*) a subsidiary Soma-graha (Ved.); N. of a king of Kośala with the patronymic Āṭṇāra (Ved.); N. of a prince; (sc. *prāsāda* or *vāsa*) N. of the palace of Mitra-vindā; (*as, am*), m. n. the Supreme, Supreme Spirit, soul of the universe, the Absolute; (*ā*), f., N. of a plant (= *bandhyā-karkoṭakī*); N. of a river; (*am*), n. the highest or culminating point, acme, highest degree; final beatitude; the secondary or more remote meaning of a word; (in logic) one species of common property, that which comprehends many objects, genus; existence (regarded as the common property of all things); (*am*), ind. beyond, over (with abl., e. g. *paraṃ vijñānāt*, beyond human knowledge); after (with abl., e. g. *astamayāt param*, after sunset; *mattaḥ param*, after me; *ataḥ param*, after this, after that, farther from hence, farther from here, farther on, hereupon, hereafter, next; *nāsmāt param*, no more of this, enough; *tataḥ param*, after that, thereupon); thereupon, thereafter (without an abl.); but, however; otherwise; rather; in a high degree, excessively, exceedingly, beyond measure, completely; most willingly; at the most, at the utmost; only; *yadi param*, if at all, perhaps, at any rate; (*eṇa*), ind. farther, beyond (with acc., e. g. *pareṇāsmān paraihi*, pass by us); on the other side, thereupon; afterwards; after (with abl. or gen.); (*pare*), ind. afterwards, in future, farther; thereupon; [cf. *pāra, parā*; Zend *para*, 'before;' Gr. πέρᾶ, πέρας, πέρᾶν, περαίνω, περαῖο-ς, περά-τη, Πειραιεύ-ς, πεῖραρ, ἀ-πειρεσ-ιο-ς; Lat. *peren-die, per-egre, per-per-a-m*; Goth. *fairra*, 'far;' Angl. Sax. *far*; Slav. *pol-ŭ*, 'the opposite border.'] — *Para-karman, a*, n. another's work, service for others. — *Parakarma-nirata, as*, m. engaged in service for another, a servant. — *Para-kalatra, am*, n. another's wife. — *Parakalatrābhigamana* (°*ra-abh*°), *am*, n. approaching the wife of another, intriguing with another man's wife, adultery. — *Para-kārya, am*, n. another's business, the affair of another. — *Para-kṛiti, is*, f. the action or history of another. — *Para-krama, as*, m. Krama of the subsequent or second letter of a conjunction of consonants, (see *krama*.) — *Para-krāthin, ī*, m., N. of a hero in the Mahā-bhārata who fought on the side of the Kurus. — *Para-krānti, is*, f. the greatest declination, inclination of the ecliptic. — *Para-kshudrās*, f. pl. (probably) those verses of the Veda which are the shortest or excessively short. — *Para-kshetra, am*, n. another's field; another man's wife; another's body. — *Para-gata, as, ā, am*, being with another, present with another, relating to another. — *Para-gāmin, ī, inī, i*, belonging or relating to another, beneficial to another. — *Para-guṇa, as, ā, am*, advantageous or beneficial to another or to an enemy. — *Para-gṛiha-vāsa, as*, m. dwelling in the house of another. — *Para-granthi, is*, m. 'the extreme point of a limb,' an articulation, a joint. — *Para-glāni, is*, f. reduction or subjugation of an enemy. — *Para-ćakra, am*, n. the army of an enemy; a hostile prince. — *Para-ćitta-jñāna, am*, n. knowing the thoughts of another. — *Para-ććhanda, as*, m. the will of another; dependance; (*as, ā, am*), depending upon or subject to the will of another, dependant, subjected, subservient. — *Paraććhanda-vat, ān, atī, at*, dependant on the will of another, subjected, subservient. — *Para-ććhidra, am*, n. a fault or flaw or defect in another. — *Para-ja, as, ā, am*, 'born of another,' strange, a stranger, (see *para-jāta*.) — *Para-jana, as*, m. another person, a stranger, (opposed to *sva-jana*.) — *Para-janman, a*, n. a future birth. — *Parajanmika, as, ā, am*, relating to a future birth or life. — *Para-jāta, as, ā, am*, born of another, nourished or maintained by a stranger, dependant on others for sustenance, adopted, fostered by strangers; dependant, servile, subjected; (*as*), m. a servant. — *Para-jita, as, ā, am*, conquered or subdued by another; nourished by a stranger, (for *para-jāta*, q. v.) — *Parañ-ja, as*, m. an oil-press; froth, foam; the blade of a sword or knife, (in these three senses also read *parāñja*, q. v.); a sword or scymitar; (*ā*), f. the sound of instruments at a festival; (*am*), n. Indra's sword. — *Parañ-jana, as*, m. an epithet of Varuṇa, 'regent of the waters.' — *Parañ-jaya, as, ā, am*, foe-conquering; (*as*), m. an epithet of Varuṇa. — *Parataḥ-posha, as, ā, am*, receiving food from another, nourished by another. — *Para-taṅgaṇa, ās*, m. pl., N. of a people. — *Para-tantra, am*, n. a rule, ritual or formula for another rite; (*as, ā, am*), dependant upon another, dependant, subject to another, subservient, obedient. — *Para-tama, as, ā, am*, highest, greatest, most excellent; farthest, &c. — *Para-tara, as, ā, am*, greater, higher, more; farther, &c. — *Para-tas*, ind. through or from another, (often taking the place of the abl. of *para*, e. g. *parato 'pi paraśćāsi*, and thou art greater than the greatest or higher than the highest; *svakāt parato vā gṛihāt*, from his own house or that of another); farther, afterwards, behind, (often used in native grammars after locatives with the omission of the substantive verb, e. g. *śasādau parataḥ* [*sati*], when the termination beginning with *śas* follows); after, over, beyond (with abl.); otherwise, differently. — *Para-tā*, f. comprehensiveness, absoluteness; highest degree. — *Para-tāpana, as*, m. 'paining enemies,' N. of a Marut. — *Para-tīrthika, as*, m., N. of a Brāhman. — *Para-tra*, ind. elsewhere, in another place, in a future state, in another world, in the other or next world; hereafter, in futurity; farther on, in the sequel (of a book). — *Paratra-bhīru, us*, m. 'one who stands in awe of futurity,' a pious or religious man. — *Para-tva, am*, n. the being distant or remote; the state of being consequent, consequence, the following (as of another letter in grammar), posteriority; separateness, difference, distinction; hostility; the being more excellent; (in logic) the nature of common or generic property; priority of place or time, proximity. — *Para-dāra, ās*, m. pl. another's wife. — *Para-dāra-gamana* or *paradārābhigamana* (°*ra-abh*°), *am*, n. approaching the wife of another, adultery, adulterous intercourse or intrigue. — *Paradārābhimarsha* (°*ra-abh*°), *as*, m. contact with the wife of another, intriguing with another's wife. — *Para-dārin, ī*, m. committing adultery with another man's wife, an adulterer. — *Paradāropasevana, am*, n. or *paradāropasevā* (°*ra-up*°), f. intriguing with another's wife. — *Para-duḥkha, am*, n. the pain or sorrow of another. — *Para-devatā*, f. the supreme or highest deity. — *Para-deśa, as*, m. a foreign country, the country of an enemy, (opposed to *sva-deśa*.) — *Paradeśa-sevin, ī, inī, i*, frequenting foreign countries, living abroad, travelling, a traveller. — *Paradeśin, ī, inī, i*, foreign, exotic; (*ī*), m. a foreigner; one residing abroad. — *Para-dosha-kīrtana, am*, n. the proclaiming of others' faults, scandal, calumny, censoriousness. — *Para-dravya, am*, n. another's property, the goods of another. — *Paradravyāpahāraka* (°*ya-ap*°), *as*, m. one who carries off the property of another, a thief, robber. — *Para-droha-karma-dhī, īs, īs, i*, injuring another in deed or thought. — *Para-drohin, ī, iṇī, i*, tyrannizing over another or over others; tyrannical. — *Para-dveshin, ī, iṇī, i*, hating others, hostile to another, inimical, adverse. — *Para-dhana, am*, n. another's wealth. — *Paradhanāsvādana-sukha* (°*na-ās*°), *am*, n. feeding luxuriously at another's expense. — *Para-dharma, as*, m. another's duty or business, the duties of another caste. — *Para-dhyāna, am*, n. intent meditation, absorption or abstraction in contemplation. — *Para-nindā*, f. reviling others. — *Para-nipāta, as*, m. (in gram.) the irregular posteriority of a word in a compound; [cf. *pūrva-nipāta*.] — *Para-nirmita-vaśa-vartin, ī*, m. 'obedient to the will of those who are transformed by others,' an epithet of a class of Buddhist deities. — *Paran-tapa, as, ā, am*, paining enemies, vexing or annoying others, subduing a foe, (said of heroes); (*as*), m. a conqueror; N. of one of the sons of Manu Tāmasa; of a prince of Magadha. — *Para-paksha, as*, m. the side or party of an enemy or adversary, &c.; (*as*), m., N. of a son of Anu. — *Para-patnī*, f. the wife of another or of a stranger. — *Para-pada, am*, n. high station, eminence; final emancipation. — *Para-parigraha, as*, m. 'another's retinue,' the family or dependants of another. — *Para-pāka, as*, m. anything cooked by another, another's food, the meal of a stranger. — *Parapāka-nivṛitta, as*, m. one who cooks his own food without observing the expiatory sacrifice for the five Sūnās or places of destruction of animal life. — *Parapāka-rata, as*, m. 'constant at another's meals,' one who lives upon others but observes the due ceremonies before cooking. — *Parapāka-rući, is*, m. a constant guest at others' tables. — *Para-piṇḍa, am*, n. another's cake, food given by another. — *Parapiṇḍāda* (°*ḍa-āda*), *as, ā, am*, 'taking another's food,' feeding at another's cost or upon another's food; (*as*), m. a servant. — *Para-purañ-jaya, as, ā, am*, 'conquering an enemy's city or cities,' an epithet of heroes. — *Para-purusha, as*, m. 'the Supreme Spirit,' an epithet of Vishṇu; another man, a stranger, the husband of another woman. — *Para-pushṭa, as, ā, am*, fostered or nourished by a stranger; (*as*), m. the Kokila or Indian cuckoo; (*ā*), f. a female cuckoo; a harlot, a whore;

a parasitical plant; N. of a daughter of a king of Kauśāmbī. — *Parapushṭa-mahotsava, as,* m. 'great feast or joy of the cuckoo,' the mango tree. — *Para-pūrvā,* f. a woman who has had a former husband. — *Parapūrvā-pati, is,* m. the husband of a woman who has had a previous husband. — *Para-pauravatantava, as,* m., N. of a son of Viśvāmitra. — *Para-prayojana, as, ā, am,* for the use of others. — *Para-preshya-tva, am,* n. service of another, servitude, slavery. — *Para-brahman, a,* n. the Supreme Spirit or Brahma; N. of an Upanishad. — *Para-bhāga, as,* m. superior merit; good fortune, prosperity; excellence, supremacy; the last part, residue, remainder. — *Parabhāga-tā,* f. superior excellence, supremacy. — *Para-bhāgya, am,* n. another's wealth or prosperity. — *Parabhāgyopajīvin* (°*ya-up*°), *ī, inī, i,* living upon another's fortune. — *Para-bhāshā,* f. a foreign language. — *Para-bhukta, as, ā, am,* possessed or enjoyed by another. — *Para-bhūta, as, ā, am,* following or subsequent, (said of words.) — *Para-bhūmi, is,* f. a foreign or hostile country. — *Parabhūmi-shṭha, as, ā, am,* living or being in a foreign or hostile country. — *Para-bhūshaṇa, am,* n. another's ornament; (*as*), m., scil. *sandhi,* peace purchased by ceding the entire produce of a country; (also a wrong reading for *pari-bhūshaṇa.*) — *Para-bhṛit, t, t, t,* nourishing another; (*t*), m. a crow, (said to nourish the Indian cuckoo.) — *Para-bhṛita, as, ā, am,* cherished or nourished by a stranger, fostered, adopted; (*as*), m. the Indian cuckoo, (supposed to leave its eggs in the nest of the crow to be hatched.) — *Para-bhṛitya, as, ā, am,* to be nourished or supported by another. — *Para-bhedaka, as, ā, am,* 'foe-breaker,' destroying or subduing a foe. — *Para-maṇi, is,* m., N. of a prince. — *Para-mata, am,* n. another's opinion, different opinion or doctrine, heterodoxy, heresy. — *Paramata-kālānala* (°*la-an*°), *as,* m., N. of a pupil of Saṅkara. — *Param-adbhuta, as, ā, am,* very wonderful. — *Para-manyu, us,* m., N. of a son of Kaksheya; (also read *para-manthu.*) — *Para-marma-jña, as, ā, am,* knowing the secret plans or intentions of another, knowing another's character or disposition, able to dive into the recesses of another's heart. — *Para-mātra,* (with Buddhists) a particular high number; (also read *para-mantra.*) — *Para-mṛityu, us,* m. a crow, (probably a corrupt word; cf. *para-bhṛit.*) — *Param-pada, am,* n. final or eternal felicity; a high station; the abode of Vishṇu. — *Param-para, as, ā, am,* one following the other, proceeding from one to another (as from father to son &c.); successive, repeated; (*am*), ind. one after the other, successively, in continuous succession; (*as*), m. a great great-grandson, a great-grandson or one of his descendants; a species of deer; (*ā*), f. an uninterrupted series, a row, regular series, succession, continuous arrangement, order, method; race, progeny, lineage; mediate or indirect condition; injury, killing, hurting. — *Parampara-tas,* ind. successively, in continuous succession, mutually. — *Param-parāka, am,* n. immolating an animal at a sacrifice. — *Paramparā-prāpta, as, ā, am,* received by tradition. — *Param-parīṇa, as, ā, am,* hereditary, obtained by inheritance or descent; traditional. — *Para-ramaṇa, as,* m. 'a strange lover,' a married woman's gallant, a paramour. — *Para-rūpa, am,* n. the following sound, the sound which comes last or in the second place. — *Para-loka, as,* m. the next world, the other world, paradise. — *Paraloka-gama, as,* m. or *paraloka-yāna, am,* n. going to the other world, death, dying. — *Paraloka-bādha, ā,* f. loss of paradise. — *Para-lokārthin* (°*ka-ar*°), *ī, inī, i,* seeking a future state, a candidate for immortality. — 1. *para-vat, ān, atī, at,* dependant upon another, being under the command of another, ready or willing to obey or serve (with inst. or loc., e.g. *bhrātrā* or *bhrātari paravān,* one who obeys his brother); subject to another; deprived of strength; devoted to. — 2. *para-vat,* ind. like a stranger. — *Paravat-tā,* f. submissiveness, obedience. — *Para-vaśa, as, ā, am,* subject to another, depending on the will of another, dependant, subservient, subject; deceived. — *Para-vaśya, as, ā, am,* subject to the will of another, dependant, subservient, subject. — *Paravaśya-tā,* f. dependance on another. — *Para-vāćya, as, ā, am,* blamable by others; (*am*), n. fault, defect. — *Paravāćya-tā,* f. condition of being an object of censure to another. — *Para-vāṇi, is,* m. a judge, ruler; a year; N. of the peacock on which the god Kārttikeya rides. — *Para-vāda, as,* m. 'other's talk,' the statement or speech of others, popular rumour or report, slander; an adverse reason, objection, refutation, controversy. — *Para-vādin, ī,* m. one who makes an adverse statement or raises an objection, a controversialist. — *Para-vīra-han, ā, ghnī, a,* killing hostile heroes, the slayer of the warriors or champions of the enemy, an epithet of brave warriors. — *Para-veśman, a,* n. the dwelling of the Supreme. — *Para-vyūha-vināśana, as,* m. the destroyer of an enemy's ranks. — *Para-vrata, as,* m. an epithet of Dhṛita-rāshṭra. — *Para-śāsana, am,* n. the order of another. — *Para-śući, is,* m., N. of a son of Manu Auttama. — *Para-śvas,* ind. the day after to-morrow; (incorrectly for *paraḥ-śvas;* see *paras.*) — *Para-saṅgata, as, ā, am,* associated with another or with others; fighting or engaged with another. — *Para-saṅćāraka, ās,* m. pl., N. of a people. — *Para-sañjñaka, as,* m. 'called supreme,' the soul. — *Para-sambandha, as,* m. relation or connection with another. — *Para-sambandhin, ī, inī, i,* related to another; belonging to another. — *Para-savarṇa* or *para-sasthāna, as, ā, am,* homogeneous with a following letter. — *Para-sāt,* ind. into the hands of another. — *Parasāt-kṛitā,* f. a woman just given away in marriage. — *Para-sevā,* f. service of another. — *Para-strī,* f. the wife of another, an unmarried woman depending upon another (as upon her father &c.). — *Para-sthāna, am,* n. another or a strange place. — *Paras-para* (sing. only, but without nom. sing.), one another, each other, (often at the beginning of a comp., e.g. *paraspara-sthitau,* m. du. standing opposite to one another); mutual, mutually interchanged or interchangeable; (in Mahā-bh. Śānti-p. 2420. the nom. pl. *parasparās,* like one another, occurs); (*am, eṇa, āt, asya*), ind. one another, each other, with one another, from each other, against one another, to one after another, one after the other, mutually, reciprocally; (*tas*), ind. one another, one after another, mutually, reciprocally. — *Paraspara-jña, as,* m. knowing one another, a friend, an intimate. — *Paraspara-sukhaishin* (°*kha-esh*°), *ī, iṇī, i,* seeking one another's happiness. — *Paraspara-hata, as, ā, am,* killed by one another. — *Parasparānumati* (°*ra-an*°), *is,* f. mutual concurrence or assent. — *Parasparam,* ind. one another, one after another, mutually. — *Paras-paropakāra* (°*ra-up*°), *as,* m. mutual assistance or benefit, offensive and defensive alliance. — *Paras-paropakārin, ī,* m. 'mutually assisting,' an ally; an associate, a helper. — *Parasmai-pada, am,* n. 'word to another' or 'word for another,' the form of a word which relates to another, (a term applied to the terminations of the active verb); the active or transitive verb; [cf. *ātmane-pada.*] — *Parasmaipadin, ī, inī, i,* taking the active terminations. — *Parasmai-bhāshā,* f. = *parasmai-pada,* q. v. — *Para-sva, am,* n. another's property. — *Parasva-tva, am,* n. another's right. — *Parasvatvāpādana* (°*va-āp*°), *am,* n. conferring a right upon another as by gift &c. — *Parasva-haraṇa, am,* n. seizing another's property. — *Parasvādāyin* (°*va-ād*°), *ī, inī, i,* taking or seizing another's property, extortionary, an extortioner. — *Parasvopajīvika* (°*va-up*°), *as, ā, am,* or *parasvopajīvin, ī, inī, i,* living upon the property of others, dependant. — *Para-haṅsa, as,* m. = *parama-haṅsa,* q. v. — *Para-han, ā, ghnī, a,* killing enemies; (*ā*), m., N. of a prince. — *Para-hita, as, ā, am,* friendly to others, benevolent; good or profitable for another; (*am*), n. the welfare of another. — *Parahita-rakshita, as,* m., N. of a commentator on the Pańća-krama. — *Parāgama* (°*ra-āg*°), *as,* m. the arrival or attack of an enemy. — *Parāṅga* (°*ra-aṅ*°), *am,* n. the hinder or back part of the body. — *Parāṅgada, as,* m. (fr. *para-aṅga-da,* giving form to another, Śiva forming with Durgā a deity, half male and half female, or according to others restoring the body of an enemy, i. e. Kāma-deva, to shape, after having reduced it to ashes in a rage), a N. of Śiva. — *Parāćita* (°*ra-āć*°), *as, ā, am,* cherished or fostered by another or by a stranger; (*as*), m. a slave, servant. — *Parāt-para, as, ā, am,* superior to the best. — *Parātman* (°*ra-āt*°), *ā,* m. the Supreme Spirit; (*ā, ā, a*), one who has directed his mind towards the Supreme; (perhaps) one who considers himself the Supreme. — *Parātma-bhūta, as, ā, am,* fixed on the supreme good. — *Parādhikāra* (°*ra-adh*°), *as,* m. another's office or post. — *Parādhikāra-ćarćā,* f. interference with another's concerns, officiousness. — *Parādhīna* (°*ra-ādh*°), *as, ā, am,* depending on another, dependant, subject, subservient. — *Parādhīna-tā,* f. or *parādhīna-tva, am,* n. dependance upon another, subjection. — *Parānta* (°*ra-an*°), *as,* m. the most extreme or remote end, final death; (*ās*), m. pl. 'living at the greatest distance,' N. of a people. — *Parānna* (°*ra-an*°), *am,* n. the food of another, food supplied by or belonging to another; (*as, ā, am*), eating the food of another, living at another's expense, sponging; a servant. — *Parānna-paripushṭa, as, ā, am,* nourished by the food of another. — *Parānnaparipushṭa-tā,* f. living on the food of another. — *Parānna-bhojin, ī, inī, i,* eating the food of another, living at another's cost. — *Parāpara* (°*ra-ap*°), *as, ā, am,* the more distant and near, far and near, remote and proximate, prior and posterior, before and behind, earlier and later (as cause and effect), higher and lower, best and worst; (*as*), m. a Guru of an intermediate class, a term applied in the Tantras to the goddess Durgā; (*am*), n. (in logic) community of property intermediate between the greatest and smallest numbers, species (as being between genus and individual); a species of plant (= *parūshaka*). — *Parāpara-guru, us,* m. a particular Guru; [cf. the preceding.] — *Parāpara-tā,* f. or *parāpara-tva, am,* n. higher and lower degree, absolute and relative state; priority and posteriority; the state of the better and the worse; the state of comprising and not comprising; the condition of being both a genus and a species. — *Parāparaitṛi* (°*ra-et*°), *tā, trī, tṛi,* Ved. going after another, going in a line (to the next world). — 1. *parāmṛita* (°*ra-am*°), *am,* n. rain; (for 2. see s. v. at p. 537, col. 2.) — *Parāyatta* (°*ra-āy*°), *as, ā, am,* dependant upon another, subject to another, subservient. — *Parāyus* (°*ra-āy*°), *us, us, us,* one who has reached the highest age or 100 years; (*us*), m. an epithet of Brahmā. — *Parārtha* (°*ra-ar*°), *as,* m. the highest advantage or interest; the chief meaning or importance; the highest object (euphemistic expression for sexual intercourse); the profit or interest of another; (*am* or *e*), ind. for the sake of another, for the good of another; (*as, ā, am*), having another object or meaning; designed for another, done for another. — *Parārtha-nishṭha, as, ā, am,* fixed on the supreme good. — *Parārtha-vādin, ī, inī, i,* talking of the affairs of others, officious, intermeddling. — *Parārdha* (°*ra-ar*°), *as,* m. the more remote or opposite or other side or half, the ulterior part, the other part; (*as, am*), m. n. the highest number, the number 100,000,000,000,000,000 or a hundred thousand billions; (according to others) a lac of lac of krores or a number equal to half the term of Brahmā's life or as many mortal days as are equal to fifty of his years; (*as, ā, am*), the most excellent, (in this sense incorrectly for *parārdhya.*) — *Parārdhya, as, ā, am,* being on the more remote or opposite or other side, being on the farther side or half, being on the following side or half; most remote, the most distant in number, of the highest possible number or value, highest in rank or quality, most highly esteemed, most costly, most excellent, most beautiful, finest, best; more excellent than (with abl.); (am), n. a maximum; an immense or infinite number; (at the end of a comp.) amounting to an infinite number, amounting at the most to. — Parārbuda (°ra-ar°), as, m. a species of fire-fly. — Parāvajñā (°ra-av°), f. insulting another, indignity offered to another. — Parāvara (°ra-av°), as, ā, am, far and near, distant and near, remote and proximate, earlier and later, prior and subsequent, higher and lower, highest and lowest; handed down from earlier to later times, traditional, each successive or every succeeding (one); all-inclusive, all-including; (ās), m. pl. ancestors and descendants; (am), n. the remote and near, the far and near, the earlier and later, cause and effect, motive and consequence; the whole extent of an idea; totality; the universe. — Parāvara-tva, am, n. state of being higher and lower or superior and inferior. — Parāvara-dṛiś, k, k, k, knowing both the past and the future. — Parāvasatha-śāyin (°ra-av°), ī, inī, i, sleeping in another's house. — Parāviddha (°ra-āv°), as, m. 'pierced or wounded by another,' 'frightened by another' (?), an epithet of Vishṇu; of Kuvera; (perhaps rather parā-viddha fr. parā-vyadh.) — Parāśraya (°ra-āś°), as, m. dependance upon another; the retreat of enemies; (as, ā, am), dependant or relying upon another; (ā), f. a parasitical plant. — Parāśrita (°ra-āś°), as, ā, am, dependant, subject. — Parāsaṅga (°ra-ās°), as, m. dependance on another or on something else, dependance. — Parāskandin (°ra-ās°), ī, m. 'assailing another,' a thief, robber. — Parāha (°ra-aha), as, m. the next day. — Parāhata (°ra-āh°), as, ā, am, struck by another, assailed, attacked. — Parāhṇa (°ra-ah°), as, m. the afternoon, the latter part of the day; (the word is also spelt parāhna.) — Paretara (°ra-it°), as, ā, am, other than hostile, faithful, friendly. — Pare-dyavi or pare-dyus, ind. on the next day, to-morrow. — Pare-prāṇa, as, ā, am, of higher value than life, more precious than life. — Pareśa (°ra-īśa), as, m. 'the supreme or highest lord,' an epithet of Brahmā; of Vishṇu. — Pareshṭi (°ra-ish°), is, m. 'having the highest worship (?),' an epithet of Brahmā. — Paraidhita (°ra-edh°), as, ā, am, nourished by a stranger, maintained by others; (as), m. a servant; the Koïl or Indian cuckoo. — Paroḍhā (°ra-ūḍhā), f. the wife of another. — Parotkarsha (°ra-ut°), as, m. another's superiority. — Parodita (°ra-ud°), as, ā, am, uttered by an enemy, &c.; (am), n. clamour, menace. — Paropakāra (°ra-up°), as, m. the assisting others, doing good to another, beneficence, benevolence, charity. — Paropakārin (°ra-up°), ī, iṇī, i, assisting others, supporting others, beneficent, charitable, kind to others. — Paropakāraikarasa (°ra-ek°), as, ā, am, wholly devoted to the service of another; (ā), f. a wife wholly devoted to her husband. — Paropakṛita (°ra-up°), as, ā, am, helped or befriended by another; brought by another. — Paropajāpa (°ra-up°), as, m. the dissension of enemies, causing dissension among enemies. — Paropadeśa (°ra-up°), as, m. giving advice to others, counselling others, admonishing or instructing another, the instruction of others. — Paroparuddha (°ra-up°), as, ā, am, besieged by an enemy, blockaded, invested.

Paraka, as, ā, am, = para, at the end of an adj. comp. (e.g. iti-śabda-paraka, followed by the word iti).

Parakīya, as, ā, am, belonging to another or to a stranger, another, strange, hostile; (ā), f. the mistress or wife of another, i.e. one of the three objects of love, according to the Sṛiṅgāra or amatory doctrine.

Parama, as, ā, am (superlative of para), most distant, last; highest, first, most excellent or distinguished, best, greatest, chief, primary, principal, superior; exceeding; extreme; worst; more excellent (with abl., Śivāt paramaḥ, more excellent than Śiva); adequate, sufficient; (am), n. the utmost or highest; the chief part, the most prominent part; (at the end of an adj. comp.) amounting at the highest to, consisting chiefly or principally of, occupied only with; (am), ind. (a particle of assent, affirmation, or agreement) yes, very well, well; (in a comp. before an adj. or part.) excessively, extremely, very, much, in the highest degree, to a great degree, excellently; [cf. Lith. pirma, 'the first;' probably Lat. prīmu-s, but cf. pra; Goth. fruma, 'first.'] — Parama-krānti, is, f. = para-krānti. — Paramakrānti-jyā, f. the sine of the greatest declination. — Parama-krodhin, ī, inī, i, extremely angry; (ī), m., N. of one of the Viśve-devas. — Parama-gati, is, f. any chief object or refuge (as a god, a protector); final beatitude. — Parama-gava, as, m. an excellent bull or cow. — Parama-gahana, as, ā, am, very mysterious or profound. — Parama-ćetas, as, n. the entire heart, all the heart. — Parama-jā, f., Ved. (according to the Scholiast) = pra-kṛiti, (probably for parāvataḥ?). — Parama-jyā, ās, ās, am, Ved. 'holding supreme power,' an epithet of Indra. — Parama-tas, ind. in the highest degree, excessively; still worse. — Parama-tā, f. the highest position or rank; highest end or aim. — Parama-dāruṇa, as, ā, am, very dreadful. — Parama-duḥkhita, as, ā, am, deeply afflicted. — Parama-durmedhas, ās, ās, as, exceedingly stupid. — Parama-dru, us, m. Amyris Agallocha. — Parama-nanda, as, m., N. of a teacher; (perhaps a wrong reading for paramānanda.) — Parama-pada, am, n. the highest rank, high station, excellence; final beatitude. — Parama-parama, as, ā, am, highest or most excellent of all. — Parama-purusha, as, m. the Supreme Spirit. — Paramapurusha-prārthanā-mañjarī, f., N. of a collection of prayers addressed to Vishṇu and other deities. — Parama-brahma-ćāriṇī, f. an epithet of Durgā. — Parama-brahman, a, n. the Supreme Spirit. — Parama-bhāsvara, as, ā, am, excessively radiant. — Parama-manyu-mat, ān, atī, at, deeply distressed. — Parama-mahat, ān, atī, at, infinitely great. — Parama-rasa, as, m. 'most excellent beverage,' buttermilk mixed with water. — Parama-rāja, as, m. a supreme monarch. — Paramarshi (°ma-ṛi°), is, m. 'greatest sage,' a Ṛishi or divine sage of a peculiar order or division. — Parama-vismita, as, ā, am, greatly surprized or amazed. — Parama-śobhana, as, ā, am, exceedingly brilliant or beautiful. — Parama-saṃhṛishṭa, as, ā, am, exceedingly rejoiced. — Parama-svadharman, ā, ā, a, most exact in the observance of the duties of one's own (caste or tribe). — Parama-haṇsa, as, m. an ascetic of the highest order, a religious man who has subdued all his senses by abstract meditation. — Paramahaṇsa-priyā, f., N. of a work ascribed to Vopa-deva. — Paramahaṇsopanishad, t, f., N. of an Upanishad. — Paramākhya (°ma-ākh°), as, ā, am, called supreme, considered as the highest. — Paramāṅganā (°ma-an°), f. an excellent woman, a beautiful woman. — Paramāṇu (°ma-aṇ°), us, m. an infinitesimal particle, an atom, the invisible base of all aggregate bodies, (of which thirty are said to form a mote in a sun-beam); the sun's passage past an atom of matter, an infinitesimal division of time; (u), n. the eighth part of a Mātrā. — Paramāṇu-tā, f. infinite minuteness, the state of an atom. — Paramāṇv-aṅgaka, as, m. 'subtle-bodied,' an epithet of Vishṇu (as being smaller than the smallest as well as greater than the greatest). — Paramātmaka (°ma-āt°), as, ikā, am, of the highest nature, the highest, greatest (= summus). — Paramātman (°ma-āt°), ā, m. the Supreme Spirit, soul of the universe. — Paramādvaita (°ma-ad°), as, m. 'the highest without a duplicate,' 'peerless,' an epithet of Vishṇu; (am), n. pure unitarianism. — Paramānanda (°ma-ān°), as, m. supreme felicity, the Supreme Spirit, soul of the universe; N. of the reputed author of the Caitanya-ćandrodaya, (also called Kari-karṇa-pūra or Purī-dāsa.) — Paramānna (°ma-an°), am, n. 'best food,' rice boiled in milk with sugar (offered to gods or to the Manes). — Paramāpakrama (°ma-ap°), as, m. = para-krānti. — Paramāpad (°ma-āp°), t, f. the greatest misfortune. — Paramāpama (°ma-ap°), as, m. 'greatest declination,' the inclination of a planet's orbit to the ecliptic; the sine of the sun's greatest declination. — Paramāyusha (°ma-āy°), as, m. the plant Terminalia Tomentosa. — Paramāyus (°ma-āy°), us, us, us, reaching or attaining to a very advanced age (Ved.); the longest period of life either in men or animals. — Paramārtha (°ma-ar°), as, m. the highest or most sublime truth, the whole truth, real truth, reality, truth; spiritual knowledge; any excellent or important aim or object; the best sense; the best kind of wealth; (āt or ena), ind. in reality. — Paramārtha-tas, ind. in reality, in the true sense of the word. — Paramārtha-tā, f. the highest truth, reality. — Paramārtha-dharma-vijaya, as, m., N. of a Buddhist work. — Paramārtha-nirvṛiti-satya-nirdeśa, as, m., N. of a Buddhist work. — Paramārtha-prapā, f., N. of a commentary by Sūrya-paṇḍita on the Bhagavad-gītā. — Paramārtha-matsya, as, m. a real fish, really a fish. — Paramārtha-vid, t, f. one who knows the highest truth, a philosopher. — Paramārtha-vinda, as, ā, am, acquiring knowledge of truth, obtaining the best kind of wealth, &c. — Paramārtha-satya, am, n. the real truth, the entire or whole truth. — Paramārtha-sāra, as, m., N. of a book. — Paramārtha-supta, as, ā, am, really asleep. — Paramārhata (°ma-ār°), as, m. 'the most excellent follower of Jina,' an epithet of Kumāra-pāla. — Paramāvaṭika (°ma-āv°), ās, m. pl., N. of a school. — Paramāvadhi (°ma-av°), is, m. utmost term or limit. — Paramāha (°ma-aha), as, m. an excellent day. — Paramekshu (°ma-ikshu), us, m., N. of a son of Anu. — Parameśa (°ma-īśa), as, m. 'supreme lord,' an epithet of Vishṇu. — Parameśvara (°ma-īś°), as, m. 'supreme lord,' (said of rich or illustrious men and of princes and of gods); an epithet of Vishṇu; of Indra; of a Jina; (most frequently) of Śiva; the Supreme Being; (ī), f. an epithet of Durgā; (am), n., scil. liṅga, N. of a Liṅga sacred to Śiva. — Parameśvara-tantra, am, n., N. of a work. — Parameshu (°ma-ishu?), us, m., N. of a son of Anu. — Parame-shṭha, as, ā, am, standing at the top, supreme, superior; (as), m. an epithet of Brahmā; a deity. — Parame-shṭhi, is, m. (connected with parame-shṭhin), 'standing at the head,' a superior, a chief god of the Jainas. — Parameshṭhi-tā, f. supremacy, superiority. — Parame-shṭhin, ī, inī, i, standing at the head or top, highest, chief, principal; (ī), m. an epithet of Agni or of any supreme deity; a N. of Prajā-pati; of a son of Prajā-pati; of Brahmā; of Śiva; of Vishṇu; of Garuḍa; of Manu Ćakshus; (with Jainas) an Arhat or superior deity; a Guru or spiritual teacher; N. of a son of Aja-mīḍha; of a son of Indra-dyumna (or of Deva-dyumna); a kind of Virāj; a kind of Śāla-grāma stone; (inau), m. du. an epithet of Vishṇu and Śrī; (inī), f. a species of culinary plant (= brāhmī; cf. pārameshṭhya.) — Parameshṭhina, as, ā, am, Ved. = parame-shṭhin. — Paramaiśvarya (°ma-aiś°), am, n. supremacy.

Paramaka, as, ikā, am, the most excellent, highest, best, greatest, extreme.

Paramika, as, ā, am, = parama, col. 1.

Paras, ind., Ved. beyond, further, (opposed to arvāk), on the other or opposite side, further on, far away, away, at a distance; in future, hereafter, afterwards, after; (with acc.) on the other side, beyond, over against, more than; (with inst.) beyond, away from, higher or more than; (with inst.) without; (with abl.) beyond, on the other side of; without, exclusive of, with the exception of, except. — Para-uru, us, vī, u, Ved. broad on the outside, broad above or at the top. — Para-ṛik-śata-gātha, as, ā, am, Ved. containing in addition 100 verses of the Veda as well as Gāthās. — Paraḥ-kṛishṇa, as, ā, am, more than black or dark, extremely dark. — *Parah-punsā*, f., Ved. a woman who is not satisfied with her husband. — *Parah-purusha, as, ā, am*, higher than a man. — *Parah-śata, as, ā, am*, more than 100; containing more than 100 verses, &c. — *Parah-śvas*, ind. the day after to-morrow. — *Parah-shashṭa, as, ā, am*, Ved. more than 60. — *Parah-sahasra, as, ā, am*, more than 1000. — *Parah-sāman, ā, ā, a*, Ved. 'having super-fluous or surplus Sāmans,' N. of certain sacrificial days. — *Paraś-ćatvārinśa, as, ā, am*, Ved. more than 40. — *Paras-taram* or *paras-tarām*, ind., Ved. further away, further. — *Paras-tāt*, ind. (with gen.) on the other side, beyond, further on, towards, (opposed to *avas-tāt, arvāk*); higher than; from afar off, from above, from before or behind (Ved.); aside, apart; under (Ved.); hereafter, afterwards, later, (opposed to *pūrvam*.) — *Paras-pa, as, ā, am*, Ved. protecting; (*am*), n. protection. — *Paraspa-tra, am*, n. protection. — *Paras-pā, ās*, m. a protector, protecting. — *Paro'nhu* (°*as-an*°), *us, vī, u*, Ved. narrow on the outside or at the top. — *Paro'ksha*, see s. v.

Parārī, ind. the year before last.

Parāritna, as, ā or *ī* (?), *am*, belonging to the year before last.

परण *paraṇa, as, ā, am* (fr. rt. 1. *pṛi*), Ved. crossing [cf. *aritra-paraṇa*]; (*am*), n. reading, (a wrong form for *pāraṇa*); N. of a town.

परतर्कुक *paratarkuka* or *paratarkaka, as*, m., Ved. a beggar; [cf. *tarkuka*.]

परमार *paramāra, as*, m., N. of a son of the Ṛishi Śaunaka (ancestor of Bhoja-deva).

पररु *pararu, us*, m. a species of pot-herb, Eclipta Prostrata; (another reading has *pavaru*.)

परश *paraśa, am*, n. a species of gem.

परशु *para-śu, us*, m. (fr. rt. *śo* and *para*, but said to be fr. rt. *śṛi* and *para*, hurting another), a hatchet, the axe of a wood-cutter, a battle-axe; a thunderbolt; N. of a prince; [cf. *parśu*; Gr. πέλεκυ-ς, πέλεκ-ρα, πέλεκκο-ν, πέλεκκο-ς, πελεκ-ᾶς.] — *Paraśu-dhara, as*, m. a soldier armed with an axe; N. of Gaṇeśa; of Paraśu-rāma. — *Paraśu-pāṇi, is, is, i*, 'axe in hand,' armed with an axe. — *Paraśu-mat, ān, atī, at*, Ved. having an axe. — *Paraśu-rāma, as*, m. 'Rāma with the axe,' an epithet of Rāma, son of the saint Jamad-agni, (the first of the three Rāmas and the sixth Avatāra or descent of the deity Vishṇu who appeared in the world for the purpose of repressing the tyranny and punishing the violence of the Kshatriya or military caste; he seems to typify the tribe of Brāhmans and their contests with the Kshatriyas); N. of a modern prince by whose orders the Paraśurāma-prakāśa was composed. — *Paraśurāma-pratāpa, as*, m., N. of a book mentioned in the Śūdra-dharma-tattva. — *Paraśurāma-prādurbhāva, as*, m. 'the manifestation of Paraśu-rāma,' N. of the forty-fifth chapter of the Narasinha-Purāṇa. — *Paraśurāmāvatāra* (°*ma-av*°), *as*, m. 'the descent of Paraśu-rāma,' i. e. the incarnation of Vishṇu in the form of Paraśu-rāma, N. of a chapter of the Khaṇḍa-praśasti (a poem ascribed to Hanu-mat). — *Paraśurāmāvatāra-kathana, am*, n. 'story of the descent of Paraśu-rāma,' N. of the fiftieth chapter of the Uttara-khaṇḍa or fifth part of the Padma-Purāṇa. — *Paraśu-vana, am*, n. 'forest of axes,' N. of a hell (containing a forest the leaves of which are axes).

Paraśavya, as, ā, am, fit or proper for a hatchet or axe; [cf. *pāraśavya*.]

Paraśvadha, as, m. an axe, a hatchet; [cf. *pāraśvadha, pāraśvadhika*.] — *Paraśvadhāyudha* (°*dha-āy*°), *as, ā, am*, armed with an axe.

Paraśvadhin, ī, inī, i, provided or furnished with an axe.

परश्वध *paraśvadha* or *parasvadha*. See above.

परस्वत् *parasvat, ān*, m., Ved. a species of animal, (perhaps) the wild ass; [cf. *pārasvata*.]

परा *parā* (connected with *para, paras*, and *pra*, probably an old inst. sing. of *para*, and used as an indeclinable and inseparable prefix to verbs and nouns in the sense of) away, off; back, backward; inverted order; aside; to, towards; over, on. According to native lexicographers the senses in which *parā* may be used are expressed by the following Sanskṛit words: *ābhimukhya, prātilomya, gati, vi-krama, dharshaṇa, hinsā* (*vadha*), *vi-moksha, bhṛiśam, pratyā-vṛitti, bhanga, an-ādara*, and *nyag-bhāva*; [cf. *pareṇa, para-tas, pare*: Zend *para*: Gr. παρά, παραί, πάρ, πάλιν: Lat. *per, perco=parā-i, perdo=parā-dā*: Osc. *perum*, 'without:' Goth. *fra-, fair*: Angl. Sax. *for*: Old Germ. *far-, fer*: Mod. Germ. *ver-*: Lith. *par-*, 'back, again;' *per*, 'through:' Hib. *frea, far-*, 'back, again.']

Parā-taram, ind., Ved. further away.

पराक *parāka*. See under *parāñć*, col. 3.

पराकाश *parā-kāśa, as*, m., Ved. distant view, remote expectation.

पराकृ *parā-kṛi*, cl. 8. P. *-karoti, -kartum*, to set aside, reject, disregard.

Parā-karaṇa, am, n. the act of setting aside, rejection, disregarding, disdaining.

Parā-kurvat, an, atī, at, setting aside, throwing off, rejecting, disdaining.

Parā-kṛita, as, ā, am, set aside, rejected, thrown off, disdained.

पराकृष् *parā-kṛish*, cl. 1. P. *-karshati, -karshṭum, -krashṭum*, to draw or drag away; to draw down; to censure, revile.

पराकॄ *parā-kṝi*, cl. 6. P. *-kirati, -karitum, -karītum*, to throw away, lose.

Parā-kīrya, ind. having thrown away; having forfeited.

पराक्रम् *parā-kram*, cl. 1. P. A. *-kramati* (ep. for *-krāmati*), *-kramate, -kramitum, -krāntum*, to march forward, advance; to march against, attack; to turn back; to display courage or spirit, display strength or heroism; show zeal, excel, distinguish one's self.

Parā-krama, as, m. marching or going forth, advancing against, attacking, attack; heroism, prowess, valour, courage, power, strength, forcible means; exertion; attempt, endeavour, effort, enterprise; a N. of Vishṇu; N. of a warrior on the side of the Kurus; of a Vidyā-dhara prince, (associated with Ā-krama, Vi-krama, and San-krama.) — *Parākrama-keśarin, ī*, m., N. of a prince, son of Vikrama-keśarin. — *Parākrama-jña, as, ā, am*, knowing the strength (of an enemy). — *Parākrama-vat, ān, atī, at*, valorous, spirited, heroic, courageous, possessed of power or strength.

Parā-kramin, ī, iṇī, i, spirited, showing or displaying courage or strength, exerting power.

Parā-krānta, as, ā, am, turned back (e. g. *pa-lāyane*, in flight); advanced; valorous, strong, powerful, vigorous, bold, valiant, active, energetic.

Parā-krāntṛi, tā, trī, tṛi, displaying valour, showing courage or strength, exerting power, heroic, a hero.

पराक्षिप् *parā-kship*, cl. 6. P. A. *-kshipati, -te, -ksheptum*, to tear away from, to wrest away, to throw over, upset.

Parā-kshipta, as, ā, am, upset, thrown upside down; wrested away. — *Parākshipta-manas, ās, ās, as*, having the mind carried away or enraptured.

पराख्या *parā-khyā*, cl. 2. P. *-khyāti, -khyātum*, Ved. to see afar off.

पराग *parāga, as*, m. the pollen or farina of a flower; dust in general; fragrant powder used after bathing; sandal; an eclipse of the sun or moon; fame, celebrity; independance, following one's own inclinations; N. of a mountain. — *Parāga-vat, ān, atī, at*, or *parāgin, ī, iṇī, i*, laden with pollen.

परागम् *parā-gam*, cl. 1. P. *-gaććhati, -gantum*, Ved. to go away, pass away, depart; to die.

Parā-gata, as, ā, am, departed, dead; spread, expanded; covered with, filled with, full of.

परागा *parā-gā*, cl. 2. 3. P. *-gāti, -jigāti, -gātum*, Ved. to go away, pass by or on one side, to escape.

पराङ्गव *parāngava, as*, m. the ocean.

पराङ्मुख *parān-mukha*. See under *parāñć*.

पराचर् *parā-ćar*, cl. 1. P. *-ćarati, -ćaritum*, Ved. to go away, depart, retreat, retire.

पराजि *parā-ji*, cl. 1. P. A. *-jayati, -te, -jetum*, to conquer, win, vanquish, overthrow; to defeat in a lawsuit; to lose anything (acc.), be deprived of; to be conquered; to succumb, submit; to be overcome by (with abl., see Pāṇ. I. 4, 26).

Parā-jaya, as, m. conquest, victory, mastering, conquering, overpowering; defeat, being overcome by (with abl.); loss, losing (at play or in a lawsuit); deprivation; turning away from, desertion.

Parā-jayamāna, as, ā, am, overcoming, surpassing, defeating; being deprived of, losing.

Parā-jit, t, m., N. of a son of Rukma-kavaća.

Parā-jita, as, ā, am, conquered, defeated, overcome; overthrown, overpowered, defeated (at play), cast (in a lawsuit), condemned by law.

Parā-jishṇu, us, us, u, victorious; being conquered, defeated.

पराञ्च् *parāñć* or *parāć, ān, āćī, āk* (fr. rt. 1. *añć* with *parā*, opposed to *arvāñć* or *arvāć* and *praty-añć*), directed towards (Ved.); turned away, averted; turning the back upon, having any one behind, standing behind; departing or retiring from (e. g. *parāñćaḥ pitaraḥ*, the departed Manes); not returning, irrevocable, (in these senses generally Ved.); situated beyond or on the other side (e. g. *amushmāt parāñćo lokāḥ*, the worlds situated beyond that); distant; directed outwards or towards the outer world (e. g. *parāñći khāni*, the senses directed outwards); (*āk* or Ved. *ān*), ind. away, away from, in vain, to no purpose; outwards, towards the outer world. — *Parāk-tva, am*, n., Ved. not turning back; non-recurrence. — *Parāk-pushpī*, f. Achyranthes Aspera (= *apāmārga*; cf. *pratya-pushpī*). — *Parāg-driś, k, k, k*, having the eye turned towards the outer world. — *Parān-manas, ās, ās, as*, having the mind or thoughts directed backwards. — *Parān-mukha, as, ī, am*, having the face turned away or averted, turning the back upon; averted, turned away; turning away from, averse from (with loc.); disinclined towards, not caring about, regardless of (with loc. gen. or acc. with *prati*); avoiding, shunning; (*as*), m. a spell or magical formula pronounced over weapons. — *Parānmukha-tā*, f. or *parānmukha-tva, am*, n. turning away or averting the face; disinclination, repugnance, dislike, aversion, disgust. — *Parānmukhaya*, Nom. P. *parānmukhayati*, to turn round, turn back or away. — *Parānmukhī-kṛi*, cl. 8. P. A. *-karoti, -kurute, -kartum*, to cause any one to turn back or avert the face, cause to retreat, put to flight. — *Parānmukhī-bhū*, cl. 1. P. *-bhavati, -bhavitum*, to turn away the face, turn the back upon, take to flight, retreat.

Parāka, distance from, (generally in loc. *parāke*, at a distance, or abl. *parākāt*, from a distance or at a distance); (*as*), m., N. of a Tri-rātra; N. of a sort of penance or religious vow of an expiatory kind, (said to consist in fasting for twelve days and nights and keeping the mind attentive and organs subdued); a sacrificial sword or scimitar; a kind of disease; a species of animal; (*as, ā, am*), small. — *Parākāt-tāt*, ind. from a distance.

Parāćīna, as, ā, am, turned away, turned in an opposite direction, averted, averse from, disinclined to, not minding, not caring about; being on the opposite side, situated on the other side, being beyond; (*am*), ind. away from, beyond, after; more than.

Parāćais, ind., Ved. away, aside, at the side of.

Parāñćana, am, n. turning away from, bending aside.

Parāñćin, ī, inī, i, Ved. not returning, not recurring.

पराञ्ज *parāñja, as*, m. an oil-mill; froth or foam; the blade of a sword or knife; [cf. *parañ-ja*.]

पराण *parāṇa, am*, n., in *vāyoḥ parāṇam*, N. of a Sāman.

पराणी *parā-ṇī* (*parā-nī*), cl. 1. P. A. *-ṇayati, -te, -ṇetum*, to lead back.

पराणुत्ति *parā-ṇutti, is*, f. (fr. rt. *nud* with *parā*), Ved. driving away, expulsion, expelling, removing.

परातंस *parā-taṇsa, as*, m. (fr. rt. *taṇs* with *parā*), the being thrust or pushed aside.

परातरम् *parā-taram*. See *parā*, p. 536.

परात्रस् *parā-tras*, Caus. *-trāsayati, -yitum*, Ved. to scare away, drive away.

परादन *parādana, as*, m. a horse of the Persian breed.

परादा *parā-dā*, cl. 3. P. *-dadāti, -dātum*, Ved. to give up, give over, deliver, surrender, hand over; to give away, throw away, squander; to give away or exchange for (with dat.); to exclude from, (Bhāgavata-Purāṇa IV. 6, 5.)

Parātta, as, ā, am, given over, &c. (See Schol. on Pāṇ. VII. 4, 47.)

Parādadi, is, is, i, Ved. giving up, giving over, delivering over.

Parā-dāna, am, n., Ved. giving up, surrendering, giving away.

परादिश् *parā-diś*, cl. 3. P. *-dideshṭi, -deshṭum*, Ved. to order off or command (anything), to be removed.

परादृश् *parā-dṛiś*, cl. 1. P. *-paśyati, -drashṭum*, Ved. to perceive, observe, behold.

परादु *parā-dru*, cl. 1. P. *-dravati, -drotum*, to run away from, flee away, escape.

पराधि *parādhi, is*, m. hunting, the chase.

पराध्मा *parā-dhmā*, cl. 1. P. *-dhamati, -dhmātum*, Ved. to blow away.

परानसा *parānasā*, f. the practice of medicine, administering remedies, medical treatment.

पराप *parāpa, as, ā, am*, m. f. n. (fr. *parā + ap*), a place &c. whence water has retired; (*am*), n., see Schol. on Pāṇ. VI. 3, 97.

परापत् *parā-pat*, cl. 1. P. *-patati, -patitum*, to fly away, escape; to depart; to fall out; to fail: Caus. *-pātayati*, to chase or drive away.

Parā-patat, an, antī, at, flying away; coming back quickly.

Parā-pātuka, as, ā, am, Ved. miscarrying, abortive.

परापुर् *parā-pur, ūr*, f., Ved. (according to the Commentator) a great body.

परापू *parā-pū*, cl. 9. P. A. *-punāti, -punīte, -pavitum*, Ved. to purify, cleanse away, lustrate.

पराप्रासादमन्त्र *parāprāsāda-mantra, as*, m. = *prāsāda-parāmantra*, N. of a kind of mystical prayer.

पराबव *parābaba, am*, n., N. of a Sāman.

पराभिक्ष *parā-bhiksha, as, ā, am* (probably a wrong reading for *para-bhiksha*), living upon alms received from others.

पराभिद् *parā-bhid*, cl. 7. P. A. *-bhinatti, -bhintte, -bhettum*, to pierce, wound.

पराभू *parā-bhū*, cl. 1. P. *-bhavati, -bhavitum* (Ved. inf. *parā-bhuve*), to pass away, vanish, disappear; to perish, be lost, succumb, yield; to overcome, conquer; to harm, hurt, injure (with acc.): Caus. *-bhāvayati, -yitum*, to overthrow, conquer, subdue, destroy; (A.) to vanish, perish, sustain a loss.

Parā-bhava, as, m. passing away, vanishing, disappearance, coming to an end, dissolution, separation; defeat, discomfiture, overthrow, mortification, humiliation, vexation, injury, contempt, disrespect, disregard; destruction; N. of the fortieth (or fourteenth) year in Jupiter's cycle of sixty years. — *Parābhava-pada, am*, n. an object of contempt.

Parā-bhāva, as, m. defeat, overthrow, discomfiture.

Parā-bhāvuka, as, ā, am, approaching decline or destruction, about to pass away.

Parā-bhūta, as, ā, am, defeated, discomfited, overcome; degraded, humbled, treated with contempt.

Parā-bhūti, is, f. defeat, overthrow, humiliation; injury.

पराभृ *parā-bhṛi*, cl. 3. P. A., Ved. *-bibharti, -bibhṛite*, &c., occurring only in the past pass. part. *parā-bhṛita, as, ā, am*, taken off, put aside, hidden, concealed.

परामृत 2. *parā-mṛita, as, ā, am*, Ved. one who has overcome death or is no longer subject to death. (For 1. *parāmṛita* see p. 534, col. 3.)

परामृश् *parā-mṛiś* (sometimes incorrectly spelt *parā-mṛish*), cl. 6. P. *-mṛiśati, -marshṭum, -mrashṭum*, to stroke, rub, touch, take hold of, grasp, clutch, seize, take; to handle roughly, violate (a woman), ravish, seduce; to have reference, point to: Pass. *-mṛiśyate*, to be touched; to be referred to, to be meant.

Parā-marśa, as, m. (sometimes incorrectly spelt *parā-marsha*), seizing, dragging, pulling (e.g. *keśa-p°*, dragging by the hair); bending or drawing a bow; injuring, any act of violence, violation, assault, attack; affection (by disease &c.); remembering, recollection; reflection, consideration, thought; discrimination, judgment; (in logic) inference, conclusion; drawing conclusions from analogy or experience, knowledge of the minor premiss in its connection with the major.

Parā-marśana, am, n. recollection, remembering; reflection, consideration.

Parā-marśin, ī, inī, i, calling or bringing to mind, reminding, referring to.

Parā-mṛishṭa, as, ā, am, touched, handled, seized, grasped, roughly treated, violated; afflicted by (disease &c.); weighed, considered, judged; connected with, referred to; endured.

परायण *parāyaṇa, am*, n. (fr. rt. 5. *i* with *parā*, or in some senses fr. *para + ayana*), going away, departure (Ved.); way of departure, exit (Ved.); final end or aim, last resort or refuge; principal object, chief aim or purport; essence, sum, summary; *parāyaṇam kṛi*, to do one's utmost, to do all one can; (often at the end of a comp. with fem. *ā*, in the sense of) making anything one's chief object, wholly devoted to, zealously engaged in, wholly occupied with, intent on, affected by, wholly possessed by; (according to some authorities *parāyaṇam*, n., has also the sense of a religious order or division); (*as*), m., N. of a pupil of Yājñavalkya; (*as, ā, am*), principal, being the chief or final end or aim, attached to, adhering to (with acc.); connected with; dependant on, subject to; leading to, conducive to. — *Parāyaṇa-vat, ān, atī, at*, occupying the principal or highest point, most elevated.

परायत्त *parāyatta*. See p. 534, col. 3.

परारु *parāru, us*, m. a species of gourd, Momordica Charantia; [cf. *kāravella*.]

परारुक *parāruka, as*, m. a stone or rock; (another reading has *pavāruka*.)

परार्थ *parārtha, parārdha, parārdhya*. See p. 534, col. 3.

परावच् *parā-vać*, cl. 2. P. *-vakti, -vaktum*, Ved. to contradict.

Parā-vāka, as, m., Ved. contradiction.

Parokta (°*rā-uk*°), *as, ā, am*, Ved. contradicted.

Parośya, as, ā, am, Ved. to be contradicted.

परावत् *parā-vat, t*, f., Ved. distance; (opposed to *arvā-vat*.)

परावत *parāvata, am*, n. a species of plant (= *parūshaka*).

परावर *parāvara*. See p. 535, col. 1.

परावर्त *parā-varta*. See 1. *parā-vṛit*.

परावसु *parā-vasu, us, us, u*, Ved. keeping off wealth; (*us*), m., N. of the fortieth year in Jupiter's cycle of sixty years [cf. *parā-bhava*]; N. of a Gandharva (associated with Viśvā-vasu); also of a son of Raibhya (associated with Arvā-vasu).

परावह *parā-vaha, as*, m. (fr. rt. *vah* with *parā*), N. of one of the seven winds, (the other six being called *ā-vaha, ud-vaha, pari-vaha, pra-vaha, vi-vaha*, and *sam-vaha*.)

परावाक *parā-vāka*. See *parā-vać* above.

परावृज् 1. *parā-vṛij*, cl. 7. 1. P. *-vṛiṇakti, -varjati, -varjitum*, to lose; to depart, depart from life.

2. *parā-vṛij, k*, m., Ved. banished (from society), humbled, miserable, an outcast (?); (according to the Scholiast) N. of a person.

परावृत् 1. *parā-vṛit*, cl. 1. A. (P. in Fut., Cond., and Aor.) *-vartate, -vartitum*, to turn back, return, to turn round.

Parā-varta, as, m. turning back, turning round; retreat; reversal of a sentence; exchange, barter; restoration.

Parā-vartana, am, n. turning back, turning round.

Parā-vartin, ī, inī, i, turning back, turning round, taking to flight (in battle).

Parā-vartya, as, ā, am, to be turned back, to be exchanged; to be reversed (as a sentence); to be given back or restored. — *Parāvartya-vyavahāra, as*, m. appeal (in law).

2. *parā-vṛit, t*, m., N. of a son of Rukma-kavaća.

Parā-vṛitta, as, ā, am, turned back, returned, fled, retreated; turned round, revolved; exchanged; reversed (as a judgment); given back, restored.

Parā-vṛitti, is, f. turning back, turning round, revolving; returning, retreating, return; exchange, barter; reversion of a sentence or judgment; restoration of property; recoiling; not taking effect.

परावेदी *parāvedī*, f. = *bṛihatī*, q. v.

पराव्याध *parā-vyādha, as*, m. (fr. rt. *vyadh* with *parā*), a stone's throw, the range of any missile.

पराशर *parā-śara*. See *parā-śṛī* below.

पराशस् *parā-śas, as*, f. (fr. rt. *śaṇs* with *parā*), Ved. (perhaps) calumny, defamation.

पराशृ *parā-śṛī*, cl. 9. P. *-śṛiṇāti, -śaritum, -śarītum*, to kill, destroy; to repel.

Parā-śara, as, m., Ved. a destroyer; N. of a Nāga; N. of a son of Vasishṭha or of a son of Śakti and grandson of Vasishṭha; (according to the epic poems) the father of Vyāsa, (he was author of certain hymns in the Ṛig-veda [I. 65–73 and part of IX. 97] and is also described as a law-giver.)

— *Parāśara-darśana, am,* n., N. of the 134th chapter of the Kṛīḍā-khaṇḍa of the Gaṇeśa-Purāṇa. — *Parāśara-purāṇa, am,* n., N. of a work. — *Parāśara-bhaṭṭa, as,* m., N. of a poet, author of the Guṇa-ratna-kośa-stotra. — *Parāśara-bhāshya, am,* n., N. of a work mentioned in the Śūdra-dharma-tattva. — *Parāśara-smṛiti, is,* f., N. of a law-book. — *Parāśarasmṛiti-vyākhyā,* f., N. of a commentary on the preceding law-book by Mādhava. — *Parāśareśvara* (°*ra-iś*°), *as,* m., N. of a Liṅga. — *Parāśareśvara-tīrtha, am,* n., N. of a sacred bathing-place mentioned in the Śiva-Purāṇa.

Parāśarin, ī, m. a beggar, a wandering mendicant; [cf. *pārāśarin.*]

पराश्वस् *parā-śvas,* cl. 2. P. *-śvasiti, -śvasitum,* to put trust in, confide in (with loc.).

Parā-śvasya, ind. having put trust or confidence in (with loc.).

परास् *parās* (*parā-as*), cl. 4. P. *parāsyati, parāsitum,* to throw away, cast aside (Ved.); expose (a new-born child, Ved.); to expel; to abandon, leave; to throw back, reject, repudiate.

Parāsa, as, m. the range or distance of anything thrown; (*am*), n. tin.

Parāsana, am, n. killing, slaughter, massacre.

Parāsin, ī, inī, i, throwing, measuring the distance of anything thrown.

Parāsisishu, us, us, u, desirous to throw or cast or send; wishing to overcome.

Parāsta, as, ā, am, thrown; expelled; defeated.

Parāsya, as, ā, am, to be thrown or cast away.

परासु *parāsu* (*parā-asu*), *us, us, u,* one whose vital spirit is departing or departed, dying, at the point of death, expiring, lifeless, dead. — *Parāsu-karaṇa, as, ā, am,* causing death, killing. — *Parāsu-tā,* f. or *parāsu-tva, am,* n. death, extinction; apathy, want of spirit, spiritlessness.

परास्कन्दिन् *parāskandin, ī, inī, i* (fr. *parā* + *āskandin*), a robber, thief.

परास्तोत्र *parā-stotra,* N. of a work.

पराहन् *parā-han,* cl. 2. P. *-hanti, -hantum,* to overthrow, strike down, throw away, cast away, drive away, drive on, impel.

Parā-hata, as, ā, am, struck down or back; driven back, repelled, repulsed; struck, assailed; driven on; (*am*), n. a stroke.

परि *pari* (an indeclinable particle and prefix to verbs and their derivative nouns; often *parī* in composition; allied to *para, parā, pra*), round, around, about, round about; further, in addition to; against, opposite to, in the way; much, excessively.

(As a separable preposition, especially in the Veda), around, about (with acc., e.g. *madhyan-dinam pari,* about midday); against, opposite to, towards, to (with acc., e.g. *vṛiksham pari,* in the direction of a tree; *tvā pari,* against thee); to the share of (with acc., e.g. *yan mām pari syāt,* what may fall to my lot); beyond, more than (with acc., e.g. *daivīm pari vāk,* a voice more than divine); after, successively, severally (with acc. distributively, e.g. *vṛiksham vṛiksham pari siñćati,* he waters tree after tree); from, away from, out of (with abl. after verbs of motion, e.g. *samudrād uta vā divaḥ pari,* out of sea or sky); outside of, except, with exception of (with abl., e.g. *pari Trigartebhyaḥ,* round about or outside Tri-garta); after the lapse or expiration of (with abl., e.g. *pari saṃvatsarāt,* after the lapse of a full year); in consequence of, on account of, for the sake of (with abl., e.g. *Rakshasaḥ pari,* on account of the Rakshas); according to, in accordance with (with abl., e.g. *dharmaṇaḥ pari,* according to the ordinance); above, over (Ved. according to the Scholiast = *adhi, upari*).

(As an adverbial prefix to nouns not immediately connected with verbs), very, excessively (e.g. *pary-aśru,* very tearful; *pari-durbala,* excessively weak). At the beginning of an adverbial comp. *pari* implies outside, without, except, exclusive of (e.g. *pari-trigartam,* outside Trigarta, Pāṇ. II. 1, 12, VI. 2, 33; and according to Pāṇ. II. 1, 10, it may be used in this sense at the end of an adverbial comp., but only after *aksha, śalākā,* and a numeral). At the beginning of an adjective comp., according to Pāṇ. (II. 2, 18, Vārt. 7), *pari* may be used in the sense of *pari-glāna,* exhausted, (but *pary-adhyayana* is said to mean 'one to whom study is repugnant.') Native lexicographers explain the senses of *pari* by the following Sanskṛit words: *ā-liṅgana, doshākhyāna* (*dosha-kīrtana*), *nir-asana* (*nivasana*), *pūjā, bhūshaṇa, vyādhi, vy-āpti, uparama, śoka, śesha, ati-śaya, tyāga, ni-yama;* [cf. Zend *pairi;* Gr. περί, πέριξ, περι-σσό-ς, -περ; Lat. *per-* in adj., e.g. *per-idoneus:* probably Old Germ. *fari;* Old Iceland. *fyri;* Mod. Germ. *für;* Hib. *faoi,* 'about, round.']

परिकथा *pari-kathā,* f. a work of fiction, tale, story, the history or adventures of any fabulous person.

परिकम्प *pari-kampa, as,* m. trembling violently, great fear or terror.

Pari-kampin, ī, inī, i, trembling violently.

परिकर *pari-kara, pari-karman.* See under *pari-kṛi* below.

परिकर्तन *pari-kartana.* See 1. *pari-kṛit.*

परिकर्ष *pari-karsha.* See 1. *pari-kṛish.*

परिकल् 1. *pari-kal* (see rt. 2. *kal*), cl. 10. P. *-kālayati,* &c., to drive about, chase, persecute.

परिकल् 2. *pari-kal* (see rt. 3. *kal*), cl. 10. P. *-kalayati,* &c., to see, observe; to consider as, regard as.

परिकल्कन *pari-kalkana, am,* n. deceit, cheating; [cf. *kalkana.*]

परिकाङ्क्षित *pari-kāṅkshita, as,* m. a devotee, a religious ascetic.

परिकायन *parikāyana* (?), *ās,* m. pl., N. of a school.

परिकीर्ण *pari-kīrṇa.* See *pari-kṛī,* col. 3.

परिकीर्तन *pari-kīrtana.* See *pari-kṛīt.*

परिकुप् *pari-kup,* cl. 4. P. A. *-kupyati, -te,* &c., to become greatly moved or excited, to suffer violent emotion, to be in a rage, be very angry: Caus. *-kopayati, -yitum,* to excite violently; to make very angry.

Pari-kopa, as, m. great or violent anger.

परिकूट *pari-kūṭa, am,* n. a barrier, a trench before the gate of a town forming a sort of covered way; (*as*), m., N. of a Nāga-rāja.

परिकृ *pari-kṛi,* cl. 8. P. A. *-karoti, -kurute, -kartum,* to surround; [cf. *pari-sh-kṛi.*]

Pari-kara, as, ī, am, who or what helps or assists, a helper; (*as*), m. attendants, dependants, retinue, train, followers (in these senses also *ās,* m. pl.); a multitude, crowd; preparation (*parikaram bandh* or *kṛi,* to make preparations); beginning, commencement, effort; a girdle for confining a loose garment, a girth, zone, sash, a cloth worn round the loins; (in dramatic language) covert or indirect intimation of coming events in the plot of a drama, the germ of the Vīja; (in rhetoric) a particular figure, the employment of allusive epithets; discrimination, judgment.

Pari-kartṛi, tā, m. a priest who performs the marriage ceremony for a younger brother whose elder brother is not yet married.

Pari-karman, ā, m. a servant, an assistant, a slave; (*a*), n. the act of surrounding or attending on (any one), worship, adoration; personal decoration, dressing, painting, or perfuming the body; perfuming the person after bathing; cleansing, purifying; a means of purification; preparation; arithmetical computation or operation. — *Parikarmāshṭaka* (°*ma-ash*°), *am,* n. the eight fundamental rules of arithmetic, viz. addition, subtraction, multiplication, division, finding the square, extracting the square root, finding the cube and extracting the cube root.

Pari-karmaya, Nom. P. *parikarmayati,* &c., to anoint, decorate, adorn.

Pari-karmin, ī, iṇī, i, adorning, decorating, &c.; (*ī, iṇī*), m. f. an assistant, a servant, slave.

Pari-kṛita, as, ā, am, surrounded, (Mahā-bh. Anuśāsana-p. 5044.)

Pari-kriyā, f. surrounding, inclosing, inclosing with a fence or ditch, intrenching; attending to (a sacred fire &c.), attention; (in dramatic language) allusion to future action, = *pari-kara.*

परिकृत् 1. *pari-kṛit,* cl. 6. P. *-kṛintati, -kartitum,* to cut round, clip, cut off; to exclude from.

Pari-kartana, as, ā, am, cutting up, cutting to pieces; (*am*), n. cutting, cutting off or round, a circular incision; cutting out, shelling; a shooting pain.

Pari-kartikā, f. sharp shooting pain, especially in the rectum.

परिकृत् 2. *pari-kṛit,* cl. 7. P. *-kṛiṇatti, -kartitum,* to wind round.

परिकृश *pari-kṛiśa, as, ā, am,* very thin, emaciate, wasted.

परिकृष् 1. *pari-kṛish,* cl. 1. P. *-karshati, -karshṭum, -krashṭum,* to draw or drag about, to carry about with one; to lead (an army); to ponder, reflect constantly upon; cl. 6. P. A. *-kṛishati, -te,* (Ved.) to draw or make furrows, to plough: Caus. *-karshayati, -yitum,* to drag to and fro, torment, harass, vex, trouble.

Pari-karsha, as, m. or *pari-karshaṇa, am,* n. dragging about.

Pari-karshita, as, ā, am, dragged about; harassed, tortured (e.g. *kāma-p*°, tortured with love).

Pari-karshin, ī, iṇī, i, dragging away, carrying off, carrying about (to every place).

Pari-kṛishṭa, as, m., N. of a teacher.

परिकॄ *pari-kṝī,* cl. 6. P. *-kirati, -karitum, -karītum,* to scatter or strew about, scatter round, besprinkle; to surround; to deliver over.

Pari-kīrṇa, as, ā, am, spread, diffused, scattered around or about; surrounded, crowded about.

परिकृत् *pari-kṛīt,* cl. 10. P. *-kīrtayati, -yitum,* to proclaim on all sides, announce, relate, communicate; to celebrate, praise, glorify; to propound; to declare, pronounce; to account; to call, name: Pass. *-kīrtyate,* to be called.

Pari-kīrtana, am, n. proclaiming aloud, proclaiming, stating, saying, telling, talking of; boasting; naming.

Pari-kīrtita, as, ā, am, proclaimed, promulgated, announced; vaunted, boasted of; said, declared, called.

परिक्लृप् *pari-klṛip,* cl. 1. A. *-kalpate, -kalpitum, -kalptum* (the simple verb appears only to occur in the part.): Caus. *-kalpayati, -yitum,* to fix, settle, decide, determine; to destine for; to perform, execute, effect, accomplish, make, form, invent; to contrive, arrange; to distribute; to invite.

Pari-kalpana, am, n. deciding, fixing, settling, agreeing upon; making, inventing, forming, contriving, performing; furnishing, providing, dividing, distributing; (*ā*), f. making, forming, assuming a form or shape; contrivance; reckoning.

Pari-kalpita, as, ā, am, settled, decided, agreed upon; made, invented; contrived, arranged; distributed, divided; provided with, furnished with.

Pari-kalpya, as, ā, am, to be settled, to be calculated.

Pari-klṛipta, as, ā, am, existing or occurring here and there, distributed.

परिक्रन्द् *pari-krand,* Caus. P. *-krandayati, -yitum,* Ved. to cry or make a noise round about.

परिक्रम् *pari-kram,* cl. 1. P. *-krāmati, -kramitum, -krāntum,* to step or walk round or about, circumambulate, go round, roam about for pleasure, roam over, walk through, visit (with acc.); to outstrip, overtake: Intens. *-ćankramīti,* to move or walk about continually, turn round perpetually.

Pari-krama, as, m. walking round or about, walking for pleasure, circumambulating, going about, going over, passing over, roaming, walking, going; pervading, penetrating; succession; series, order. — *Parikrama-saha, as,* m. 'one who bears running about,' a goat.

Pari-kramaṇa, am, n., Ved. walking about, going or roaming about.

Pari-kramat, an, antī, at, moving or wandering about.

Pari-kramya, ind. having walked round or about.

Pari-krānta, as, ā, am, walked round, stepped upon; (*am*), n. the place or spot on which any one has walked about or stepped, foot-steps, foot-prints, traces.

Pari-krānti, is, f. moving round, revolution, circumrotation.

Pari-krāmat, an, antī, at, going or moving round or about.

Pari-krāmam, ind., Ved. going about, [cf. *a-parikrāmam.*]

परिक्रिया *pari-kriyā,* f. See *pari-kṛi,* p. 538.

परिक्री 1. *pari-krī,* cl. 9. P. *-krīṇāti, -kretum,* to purchase, buy, give in exchange, acquire, gain (with inst. or dat. of the price, e. g. *śatena* or *śatāya pari-krī,* to buy for a hundred); to hire, engage for hire or for stipulated wages; A. *-krīṇīte, -kretum,* to recompense, reward.

Pari-kraya, as, m. hire, wages; redemption, purchasing or purchasing back, buying off; a particular kind of treaty, a peace purchased with money.

Pari-krayaṇa, am, n. engaging for hire, hiring.

2. *pari-krī,* Ved., N. of the second Sādyaskra.

Pari-krīṇāna, as, ā, am, purchasing, buying.

Pari-krīta, as, ā, am, purchased, bought; hired.

परिक्रीड् *pari-krīḍ,* cl. 1. P. A. *-krīḍati, -te, -krīḍitum,* to play about.

परिक्रुध् *pari-krudh,* cl. 4. P. *-krudhyati, -kroddhum,* to fly into a rage or passion, to become enraged.

परिक्रुश् *pari-kruś,* cl. 1. P. *-krośati, -kroshṭum,* to go about crying, to wail, lament.

परिक्लम् *pari-klam,* cl. 4. P. *-klāmyati, -klamitum,* to be tired out or exhausted.

Pari-klānta, as, ā, am, very tired, tired out, exhausted.

परिक्लिद् *pari-klid,* cl. 4. P. *-klidyati, -kleditum, -klettum,* to be very wet or damp.

Pari-klinna, as, ā, am, very wet, excessively moist or humid.

Pari-kleda, as, m. humidity, wetness, dampness.

Pari-kledin, ī, inī, i, wetting, moistening; wet.

परिक्लिश् *pari-kliś,* cl. 9. P. *-kliśnāti, -kleśitum, -kleshṭum,* to pain, torment, harass, vex; cl. 4. P. A. *-kliśyati, -te,* to suffer, feel pain; to be vexed or troubled or harassed.

Pari-kliśa, as, m. (?), vexation, trouble.

Pari-klishṭa, as, ā, am, much vexed or annoyed, sorely troubled, pained, harassed, exhausted, fatigued; (*am*), n. pain, suffering, vexation; (*am*), ind. with a feeling of uneasiness or reluctance, unwillingly.

Pari-kleśa, as, m. hardship, fatigue.

Pari-kleshṭṛi, ṭā, ṭrī, ṭṛi, causing pain or trouble, a tormentor, torturer.

परिक्वणन *pari-kvaṇana, as, ā, am* (fr. rt. *kvaṇ* with *pari*), loud-sounding, loud.

परिक्षन् *pari-kshan* or *pari-kshaṇ,* cl. 8. P. A. *-kshaṇoti, -kshaṇute, -kshaṇitum,* to wound, hurt, injure.

Pari-kshata, as, ā, am, wounded, hurt, injured, abraded, cut, scratched; killed.

Pari-kshati, is, f. wounding, injury, lesion.

परिक्षय *pari-kshaya.* See *pari-kshi* below.

परिक्षर् *pari-kshar,* cl. 1. P. *-ksharati, -ksharitum,* to stream or flow round, flow or stream towards.

परिक्षल् *pari-kshal,* cl. 10. P. *-kshālayati, -yitum,* to wash out, rinse, wash off.

Pari-kshālana, am, n. water for washing.

परिक्षव *pari-kshava, as,* m. (fr. rt. *kshu* with *pari*), Ved. (ill-omened) sneezing.

परिक्षा *pari-kshā,* f. (fr. rt. *kshai* with *pari*?), clay, mud, dirt.

Pari-kshāṇa, am, n., Ved. that which is charred or burnt to a cinder.

परिक्षाम *pari-kshāma, as, ā, am* (said to be fr. rt. *kshai* with *pari*), excessively emaciated or wasted away, dried up, fallen away.

परिक्षि *pari-kshi* (see rt. 4. *kshi*), cl. 5. 9. P. *-kshiṇoti, -kshiṇāti, -kshetum,* to destroy, put an end to: Pass. *-kshīyate,* to waste away, decay, become exhausted; to be brought low; to become poor.

Pari-kshaya, as, m. disappearing, ceasing, failure, ruin; dissolution, decay, waste, destruction.

Pari-kshīṇa, as, ā, am, vanished, disappeared; quite decayed, wasted, emaciated, worn away; exhausted; brought low; entirely ruined; diminished, decreased; lost, destroyed; (in law) insolvent.

परिक्षित् *pari-kshit* or *parī-kshit* (see rt. 2. *kshi*), Ved. spreading round or about, extending; ('living about or among mankind'), an epithet of Agni; (*au*), du. an epithet of heaven and earth; (*t*), m., N. of an ancient king, a son of Abhi-manyu and father of Janam-ejaya; of a son of Kuru and father of another Janam-ejaya; of a son of A-vīkshit and brother of Janam-ejaya; of a king of A-yodhyā.

परिक्षिप् *pari-kship,* cl. 6. P. A. *-kshipati, -te, -ksheptum,* to throw over or beyond; to put or lay or wind round; to throw about, surround, encircle, embrace; to overlay; to fetter; to throw or put into.

Pari-kshipta, as, ā, am, thrown about, scattered, diffused; surrounded, encircled, intrenched; overspread, overlaid; struck; left, abandoned.

Pari-kshepa, as, m. throwing about, moving to and fro; scattering, spreading, diffusion; surrounding, encircling, circumfluence; an encircling belt or boundary, that by which anything is surrounded; being surrounded; abandoning, leaving.

Pari-kshepaka, as, ā, am, who or what scatters or disperses or surrounds.

Pari-kshepin, ī, iṇī, i, who or what throws about, scatters, or distributes, &c.

परिक्षीव *pari-kshīva, as, ā, am,* drunk, quite intoxicated.

परिखण्डय *pari-khaṇḍaya,* Nom. P. *-khaṇḍayati, -yitum,* to make small, humiliate, conquer.

परिखन् *pari-khan,* cl. 1. P. A. *-khanati, -te, -khanitum,* to dig round, dig up.

Pari-khā, f. a moat, ditch, trench or fosse round a town or fort; N. of a village in the North country. — *Parikhā-sthita, as, ā, am,* secure, impregnable.

Pari-khāta, as, ā, am, dug round; (*as*), m. a furrow, rut.

परिखिद् *pari-khid,* cl. 4. P. *-khidyati, -khettum,* to be depressed, to feel uneasy or disturbed, to be afflicted: Caus. *-khedayati, -yitum,* to trouble, afflict, injure, destroy.

Pari-khinna, as, ā, am, depressed, afflicted, exhausted.

Pari-kheda, as, m. lassitude, fatigue, sleepiness, exhaustion, being worn out.

परिख्या *pari-khyā,* cl. 2. P. (in the non-conjugational tenses also A.) *-khyāti, -khyātum,* to look round or about, look at, perceive (Ved.); to observe, regard, consider; to overlook, disregard (Ved.).

Pari-khyāta, as, ā, am, regarded as; called, named; celebrated, famous.

Pari-khyāti, is, f. reputation, fame, celebrity.

परिगण *pari-gaṇa, as* or *am,* m. or n. (?), a house.

परिगणय *pari-gaṇaya,* Nom. P. *-gaṇayati, -yitum,* to count over, reckon up completely, enumerate one by one; to calculate, reckon, consider, reflect.

Pari-gaṇana, am, n. or *pari-gaṇanā,* f. complete or accurate enumeration, accurate calculation or statement.

Pari-gaṇanīya, as, ā, am, to be enumerated completely, to be stated accurately.

Pari-gaṇita, as, ā, am, enumerated, calculated, reckoned; *a-parigaṇita, as, ā, am,* not counted, innumerable; *a-parigaṇita-tva, am,* n. the state of not being enumerated, innumerableness.

Pari-gaṇya, as, ā, am, calculable, to be calculated or enumerated, to be stated with accuracy.

परिगम् *pari-gam,* cl. 1. P. *-gaćchati, -gantum,* to go round, walk or step round; to wander over; to encircle, surround, embrace, inclose; to spread on all sides, extend everywhere, extend towards; to go away, depart, die; to come to or attain any state or condition (e. g. *śāntim parigam,* to become appeased): Caus. *-gamayati, -yitum,* to cause to go round, to pass or spend (time).

Pari-ga, as, ā, am, going round, surrounding.

Pari-gata, as, ā, am, gone round, encircled, surrounded, encompassed; diffused, spread; overwhelmed, distressed, overcome; filled, possessed of, affected by, afflicted with; known, understood; obtained, gained; performed; forgotten; obstructed.

Pari-gama, as, m. or *pari-gamana, am,* n. going round, surrounding; spreading, extending; knowing, ascertaining; obtaining.

Pari-gamita, as, ā, am, brought, conducted, driven.

परिगर्ज् *pari-garj,* cl. 1. P. *-garjati, -garjitum,* to roar, cry.

परिगर्वित *pari-garvita, as, ā, am,* very proud.

परिगर्ह् *pari-garh,* cl. 1. P. A., cl. 10. P. *-garhati, -te, -garhayati, -garhitum, -garhayitum,* to blame greatly, censure, despise, abuse.

Pari-garhaṇa, am, n. excessive blame, censure.

परिगल् *pari-gal,* cl. 1. P. *-galati, -galitum,* to fall down or drop on all sides; to sink down.

Pari-galita, as, ā, am, tumbled down; sunk; flowing, fluid; melted.

परिगा *pari-gā,* cl. 2. 3. P. *-gāti, -jigāti, -gātum,* to go round, go round in a circle; to spread everywhere or in all directions, permeate, pervade, overspread; to come near, approach, reach, come upon; to go out of the way; to disregard; to investigate, ascertain, obtain knowledge of.

परिगुणय *pari-guṇaya,* Nom. P. *-guṇayati, -yitum,* to repeat, reiterate.

परिगुप् *pari-gup,* cl. 1. P. *-gopāyati, -goptum,* to protect: Desid. A. *-jugupsate,* to beware of, be on one's guard against (with abl.).

परिगै *pari-gai*, cl. 1. P. *-gāyati*, *-gātum*, to go about or walk round singing, to sing or celebrate everywhere, proclaim to all the world.

Pari-gīti, *is*, f. a kind of metre.

परिग्रह् *pari-grah* (Ved. *pari-grabh*), cl. 9. P. A. *-gṛihṇāti*, *-ṇīte* (Ved. *-gṛibhṇāti*, *-ṇīte*), *-grahītum*, to take hold of, lay hold of on both sides; embrace, surround, encircle, enfold, envelop; fence round, hedge round; to wrap round, put round; to put on (as a dress or ornament), to dress; to seize, clutch, hold, grasp, catch, take or carry along with one; to support; to take possession of, master, overpower, overturn; to take (in war); to accept, receive; to conceive, comprehend; to take (food); to take upon one's self, undertake, undergo; to receive (hospitably or kindly); to take (a wife), marry; to take (by the hand), assist; to have regard to, conform to, follow, adopt; to surpass, excel; (in Ved. gram.) to enclose (*iti*) between a word twice repeated, (see under *pari-graha*.)

Pari-gṛihīta, *as*, *ā*, *am*, taken hold of on both sides, grasped, clutched; embraced, surrounded; taken, accepted; admitted, consented to, assented to; followed, obeyed; opposed, checked.

Pari-gṛihīti, *is*, f., Ved. grasping, comprehension; summing up.

Pari-gṛihītṛi, incorrect form for *pari-grahītṛi*.

1. *pari-gṛihya*, *as*, *ā*, *am*, to be taken or accepted, to be regarded, &c.; (*ā*), f. a woman.

2. *pari-gṛihya*, ind. having taken or seized; in company with, together with, along with, along; considering, regarding. — *Parigṛihya-vat*, *ān*, *atī*, *at*, Ved. containing the word *pari-gṛihya*.

Pari-graha, *as*, m. laying hold of, seizing, grasping; surrounding, encircling; embracing, spanning; enclosing, fencing round (the Vedi or sacrificial altar by means of three lines or furrows); wrapping round, putting on (a dress &c.); assuming (a form or shape); comprehension; taking together, summing up, sum, totality; taking, accepting, receiving, acceptance [cf. *a-parigraha*]; anything received, a present; assenting to, assent; taking possession of, attaining, obtaining; possession, property (e. g. *artha-p°*, possession of wealth; *prāṇa-p°*, possession of vital spirit or life; *parigraham pari-tyajya*, having given up all one's property); choosing, selecting; claiming, claim; admitting or receiving any one (into one's house), entertaining; an entertainer; taking the hand, assisting, assistance; taking a wife (lit. taking her by the hand), marrying, marriage; a wife; a husband; honouring, favouring; reverence, homage; grace, favour, patronage, (*tvat-parigrahāt*, by thy favour); apprehending, understanding, comprehension, conception; undertaking, performing; subjugation, making subservient; dominion; chastising, punishing, punishment; connection, concern, relation; adherents, dependants, attendants, train, retinue, family, suite, the seraglio of a prince, household; a house, an abode; taking away, removing; an eclipse of the sun; root, origin; a curse, imprecation, oath; the rear or reserve of an army, (various reading for *prati-graha*); (in Ved. gram.) the double mention of a word both before and after *iti*; the form which precedes the word *iti*. — *Parigraha-tva*, *am*, n. state of a wife, condition of being a wife, marriage. — *Parigraha-dvitīya*, *as*, *ā*, *am*, accompanied by one's wife or family. — *Parigraha-maya*, *as*, *ī*, *am*, consisting of a family. — *Parigraha-vat*, *ān*, *atī*, *at*, possessed of wealth, having property.

Pari-grahaka, *as*, *ā*, *am*, grasping, taking hold of; undertaking.

Pari-grahaṇa, *am*, n. wrapping round, putting on.

Pari-grahin, *ī*, *iṇī*, *i*, possessing, attached to worldly possessions or property.

Pari-grahītṛi, *tā*, *trī*, *tṛi*, taking hold of; one who assists, an assister, assisting; one who receives (another into his house), an adoptive father; (*tā*), m. a husband.

Pari-grāha, *as*, m. the fencing round (of the Vedi or sacrificial altar with three lines or furrows; if of the northern altar, called *uttara-parigrāha*; if of the eastern, *pūrva-parigrāha*).

Pari-grāhya, *as*, *ā*, *am*, to be treated kindly or hospitably, to be addressed with kind words.

परिग्लै *pari-glai*, cl. 1. P. (ep. also A.) *-glāyati* (*-te*), *-glātum*, to be wearied out, be exhausted; to feel repugnance to or aversion from (with dat.).

Pari-glāna, *as*, *ā*, *am*, wearied out, languid, exhausted; averse from.

परिघ *pari-gha*, *as*, m. (fr. rt. *han* with *pari*), an iron beam or bar used for locking or shutting a gate [cf. *argala*]; a bar, obstacle, hindrance (figuratively); an iron bludgeon or stick studded with iron, an iron club; a child which assumes a peculiar cross-position in birth; a line of clouds crossing the sun at sun-rise or sun-set; the gate of a palace, of a town, of a house; (in astron.) N. of the nineteenth Yoga; killing, striking, destroying, a blow; a pitcher, water-jar; a glass pitcher; N. of one of Skanda's attendants; N. of a Cāṇḍāla; of a certain virtuous man; (*au*), m. du. two birds flying one on each side of a traveller (regarded as an omen). — *Parigha-prāṅśu-bāhu*, *us*, m. one whose arm is as long as an iron beam. — *Parigha-bāhu*, *us*, m. one whose brawny arm resembles a knotty club. — *Parighopama* (°*gha-up°*), *as*, *ā*, *am*, resembling an iron club.

Pari-ghāta, *as*, m. killing, striking; removing out of the way, getting rid of; a club, an iron bludgeon.

Pari-ghātana, *am*, n. striking, hurting, killing; a club or bludgeon armed with iron.

Pari-ghātin, *ī*, *inī*, *i*, destroying, annihilating; setting at nought; transgressing (e. g. in *nṛipājñā-parighātin*, transgressing the commands of a king).

परिघट् *pari-ghaṭ*, Caus. P. *-ghāṭayati*, *-yitum*, to strike, sound; to cause to vibrate (as the strings of a musical instrument).

परिघट्ट् *pari-ghaṭṭ*, cl. 10. P. *-ghaṭṭayati*, *-yitum*, to stir round or about; to press or touch on all sides; to rub; to stir up; to open.

Pari-ghaṭṭana, *am*, n. stirring round, stirring up.

Pari-ghaṭṭita, *as*, *ā*, *am*, stirred about, touched or rubbed repeatedly.

परिघर्घर *pari-gharghara* (?), a low murmuring sound.

परिघर्म्य *pari-gharmya*, *as*, m. a vessel for preparing the hot sacrificial beverage.

परिघात *pari-ghāta*. See under *pari-gha*.

परिघूर्ण् *pari-ghūrṇ*, cl. 1. P. A. *-ghūrṇati*, *-te*, *-ghūrṇitum*, to whirl about, shake to and fro, flutter, tremble.

परिघृष् *pari-ghṛish*, cl. 1. P. *-gharshati*, *-gharshitum*, to rub or pound to pieces.

Pari-ghṛishṭika, *as*, *ā*, *am*, (perhaps) one who eats only what is pounded (?).

परिघोष *pari-ghosha*, *as*, m. (fr. rt. *ghush* with *pari*), sound, noise; thunder; improper speech.

परिघ्रा *pari-ghrā*, cl. 1. A. *-jighrate*, *-ghrātum*, to kiss passionately, cover with kisses.

Pari-jighramāṇa, *as*, *ā*, *am* (Mahā-bh. Strī-p. 616), kissing passionately.

परिचक्र *pari-ćakra*, *as*, m., N. of a section of the Dvā-viṅśaty-avadānaka; (*ā*), f., N. of a town.

परिचक्ष् *pari-ćaksh*, cl. 2. A. *-ćashṭe* (see rt. *ćaksh*), to overlook, pass over, despise; to reject; to declare (guilty), report, proclaim; to speak of, mention, relate; to admit, own, acknowledge; to call, name; to address (with acc.); to answer.

Pari-ćakshā, f., Ved. rejection, disapproval, disapprobation.

Pari-ćakshya, *as*, *ā*, *am*, Ved. to be despised or disapproved.

परिचतुर्दश *pari-ćaturdaśa*, *as*, m. or *pari-ćaturdaśan*, *a*, m. f. n. pl. fully fourteen.

परिचपल *pari-ćapala*, *as*, *ā*, *am*, always moving about, very volatile.

परिचर् *pari-ćar*, cl. 1. P. (ep. also A.) *-ćarati* (*-te*), *-ćaritum* (ep. *-ćartum*), to move or walk about, roam about, go round (with acc.); to attend upon, attend to, wait upon, serve, honour (with acc.): Caus. P. *-ćārayati*, *-yitum*, to surround; A. *-ćārayate*, to beset; to be served or waited upon.

Pari-ćara, *as*, *ā*, *am*, roaming about; moving, flowing; movable (as certain verses which may be put at the beginning, middle, or end of a hymn); an attendant, companion, servant, assistant; a guard, patrol, city watchman, body-guard; a commander-in-chief (?); attendance, homage, service.

Pari-ćaraṇa, *as*, m. an assistant, a servant; (*am*), n. going about; serving, attending upon, attention to.

Pari-ćaraṇīya, *as*, *ā*, *am*, to be served or attended on; belonging to attendance, &c.

Pari-ćaritavya, *as*, *ā*, *am*, to be attended on or served or worshipped.

Pari-ćaritṛi, *tā*, *trī*, *tṛi*, one who serves or attends upon, an attendant, servant.

Pari-ćarya, *as*, *ā*, *am*, to be attended upon or served or honoured; (*ā*), f. waiting upon, attendance, service, dependance; devotion, veneration, adoration, worship. — *Paricaryā-vat*, *ān*, *atī*, *at*, attended upon, waited upon, honoured, respected.

Pari-ćāra, *as*, m. attendance, service, homage; a place for walking; an attendant, assistant, a servant.

Pari-ćāraka, *as*, *ikā*, *am*, attending; (*as*), m. an assistant, a servant, attendant, guard; (*ikā*), f. a female attendant, waiting-maid.

Pari-ćāraṇa, *am*, n. attending upon, attendance, serving.

Pari-ćārika, *as*, m. an attendant, assistant, a servant; (*ās*), m. pl. fried grain; (*ikā*), f. a female attendant or servant, a waiting-maid.

Pari-ćārin, *ī*, *iṇī*, *i*, going about in all directions, moving about, movable; attending on, serving, paying homage to; (*ī*), m. an attendant, a servant.

Pari-ćārya, *as*, *ā*, *am*, to be served or obeyed, to be worshipped.

परिचर्तन *pari-ćartana*. See *pari-ćṛit*, p. 541, col. 1.

परिचर्मण्य *parićarmaṇya*, *am*, n. (fr. *pari-ćarman*), a strip of leather.

परिचल् *pari-ćal*, cl. 1. P. *-ćalati*, *-ćalitum*, to move, stir: Caus. *-ćālayati*, *-yitum*, to cause to move round, turn round.

परिचि 1. *pari-ći*, cl. 5. P. A. *-ćinoti*, *-nute*, *-ćetum*, to pile up, heap up, accumulate; to collect; to augment, increase; to gather in, acquire, obtain; to fill with: Pass. *-ćīyate*, to be increased or augmented, to grow.

1. *pari-ćaya*, *as*, m. (for 2. see under 2. *pari-ći*, p. 541, col. 1), heaping up, accumulation. — 1. *pari-ćaya-vat*, *ān*, *ati*, *at*, accumulated, collected; complete, finished.

1. *pari-ćayanīya*, *as*, *ā*, *am*, to be collected or accumulated.

Pari-ćāyya, *as*, m., scil. *agni*, a sacrificial fire arranged in a circle; raising the rent or revenue of land (?).

Pari-ćit, *t*, *t*, *t*, Ved. piling up or arranging all around.

1. *pari-ćita*, *as*, *ā*, *am*, heaped, accumulated, filled with.

1. *pari-ćetavya, as, ā, am,* to be collected together or accumulated.

1. *pari-ćeya, as, ā, am,* to be collected all round or from every side.

परिचि 2. *pari-ći,* cl. 3. P. *-ćiketi, -ćetum,* Ved. to examine, investigate, search; to familiarize one's self with, accustom one's self to, exercise one's self in, practise; to become acquainted with: Caus. A. *-ćāyayate, -yitum,* to search, seek for.

2. *pari-ćaya, as,* m. (for 1. see under 1. *pari-ći,* p. 540, col. 3), acquaintance, familiarity, familiar intercourse, conversancy, intimacy; knowledge; recognition; meeting with a friend; trial, practice, repetition, frequent repetition. — *Parićaya-vat, ān, atī, at,* intimately acquainted, accurately known.

2. *pari-ćayanīya, as, ā, am,* to be known.

2. *pari-ćita, as, ā, am,* known, acquainted or familiar with. — *Parićita-bhū, ūs, ūs, u,* having (its) place well known.

Pari-ćiti, is, f. acquaintance, familiarity.

2. *pari-ćetavya, as, ā, am,* to be known, fit or proper to be known.

2. *pari-ćeya, as, ā, am,* to be known; to be investigated or searched.

परिचिन्त् *pari-ćint,* cl. 10. P. *-ćintayati, -yitum,* to think about, meditate on, reflect, consider well; to call to mind, recollect, remember; to think out, invent, devise.

Pari-ćintaka, as, ā, am, reflecting about, meditating on (with gen.).

परिचिह्नय *pari-ćihnaya,* Nom. P. *-ćihnayati, -yitum,* to mark, sign, subscribe.

Pari-ćihnita, as, ā, am, marked, subscribed.

परिचुद् *pari-ćud,* Caus. P. *-ćodayati, -yitum,* to set in motion, wield, brandish; to drive, impel, urge, incite; to promote, further; to exhort.

Pari-ćodita, as, ā, am, wielded, brandished; impelled, incited.

परिचुम्ब् *pari-ćumb,* cl. 1. P. *-ćumbati, -ćumbitum,* to kiss heartily or passionately, cover with kisses.

Pari-ćumbana, am, n. the act of kissing heartily or passionately.

परिचृत् *pari-ćrit,* cl. 6. P. *-ćritati, -ćartitum,* to wind round; to tie or fasten together.

Pari-ćartana, am, n., Ved. the part of a horse's harness from the girth to the breast and the tail.

परिच्छद् 1. *pari-ććhad (pari-ćhad),* cl. 10. P. *-ććhādayati, -yitum,* to envelop, wrap round, cover, cover up, clothe; to conceal, disguise; to surround with.

2. *pari-ććhad, t,* f. retinue, train, attendants; paraphernalia; (at the end of a comp.) surrounded by, provided with (see *senā-p°*).

Pari-ććhada, as, m. a cover, covering, garment, dress, clothes; surroundings, domestic utensils or implements, goods and chattels, personal property, furniture; court, retinue, train, attendants, family, dependants; necessaries for travelling; paraphernalia, baggage; (at the end of a comp.) furnished or provided with (e.g. *anna-pāna-pariććhada,* provided with food and drink); adorned with.

Pari-ććhanda, as, m. retinue, train, suite, attendants.

Pari-ććhanna, as, ā, am, invested, enveloped, covered, covered over, clothed, clad; overlaid; concealed, disguised; surrounded with (a retinue &c.).

परिच्छिद् *pari-ććhid (pari-ćhid),* cl. 7. P. A. *-ććhinatti, -ććhintte, -ććhettum,* to cut on both sides, clip round, cut through, cut off, cut to pieces; to wound, mutilate; to separate, divide, part; to limit on all sides, define or fix accurately, define, discriminate, decide, determine; to form a just estimate of, weigh duly, assure one's self; to avert, obviate.

Pari-ććhitti, is, f. accurate definition, limiting, limit, measure; partition, separation.

Pari-ććhidya, ind. having cut off; having fixed or defined; having decided.

Pari-ććhinna, as, ā, am, cut off, divided, detached; reaped; confined, limited, small; obviated, remedied.

Pari-ććheda, as, m. cutting, severing, parting, division, separation, discrimination (of false from true), accurate distinction or definition; distinguishing between the good and the bad, the right and the wrong, the expedient and inexpedient; discernment, discretion; exact discrimination, determination, decision; judgment, limit, boundary, moderation; the division of a book, a section or chapter; a segment; obviating, remedying. — *Pariććheda-kara, as,* m., N. of a Sam-ādhi.

Pari-ććhedaka, as, ā, am, separating, defining, determining; *(am),* n. limitation, limit, measure.

Pari-ććhedana, am, n. dividing, division; discriminating; the division of a book; joyful laughter (?).

Pari-ććhedya, as, ā, am, to be accurately defined or limited, definable; to be estimated; to be weighed, to be measured.

परिच्यु *pari-ćyu,* cl. 1. A. *-ćyavate, -ćyotum,* to fly off from (as arrows from a bow); to depart or deviate from, to swerve from or transgress (with abl.); to be displaced or ejected from (with abl.); to be removed from, deprived of, lose, forfeit; to be released or freed from, to escape; to descend or come down; to stream round.

Pari-ćyuta, as, ā, am, fallen from, swerved from; deprived of, lost; ruined; streaming with, surrounded by streams (as of blood).

Pari-ćyuti, is, f. falling down.

परिजन *pari-jana, as,* m. a surrounding company of people, attendants, servants, followers, family; suite, train, court, retinue (especially of females); a single servant.

परिजन्मन् *pari-janman, ā,* m. the moon; fire; [cf. *pari-jman.*]

परिजप् *pari-jap,* cl. 1. P. *-japati, -japitum,* to whisper to, to whisper or mutter (prayers) in a low voice, talk about.

Pari-japita, as, ā, am, muttered, whispered, prayed over in a low voice.

परिजल्प् *pari-jalp,* cl. 1. P. *-jalpati, -jalpitum,* to chatter; prate about, talk about, speak of (with acc.).

Pari-jalpita, am, n. the covert reproaches of a mistress neglected or ill used by her lover.

परिजा *pari-jā,* f. (fr. rt. *jan* with *pari*), Ved. place of origin, source.

परिजाड्य *pari-jāḍya, as, ā, am,* (perhaps) completely rigid or motionless.

परिजातक *pari-jātaka, am,* n., N. of a work on domestic rites.

परिजि *pari-ji,* cl. 1. P. A. *-jayati, -te, -jetum,* to conquer, overpower.

Pari-jayya, as, ā, am, to be conquered, to be mastered.

परिजॄ *pari-jṝ,* cl. 4. P. A. *-jīryati, -te, -jaritum, -jarītum,* to become worn out or old, to wear out; to become withered, to fade; to be digested.

Pari-jīrṇa, as, ā, am, worn out, old; withered.

परिज्ञा 1. *pari-jñā,* cl. 9. P. A. *-jānāti, -jānīte, -jñātum,* to notice, observe, perceive, recognise; to learn, become acquainted with, ascertain, make sure of, know thoroughly, know exactly or accurately, comprehend.

Pari-jñapti, is, f. conversation, discourse; recognition.

2. *pari-jñā,* f. knowledge, accurate ascertainment.

Pari-jñāta, as, ā, am, thoroughly known, ascertained, learnt.

Pari-jñātṛi, tā, trī, tṛi, one who knows or perceives, an observer, knower; wise, intelligent.

Pari-jñāna, am, n. perception, thorough knowledge, learning, complete acquaintance, ascertainment, experience, discrimination.

Pari-jñāya, ind. having fully known or ascertained, having become aware of.

Pari-jñeya, as, ā, am, to be recognised or ascertained; comprehensible; *(a-parijñeya,* incomprehensible.)

परिज्मन् *pari-jman, ā, ā, a* (probably fr. rt. *gam* with *pari*), Ved. running or walking or driving round (said of the sun, of the chariot of the Aśvins, and of the Aśvins themselves, but according to the commentator applied to the wind); *(ā),* m. the moon; fire; *(an),* ind. (Ved. loc. used as adv.), on all sides, round about, everywhere.

परिज्रि *pari-jri, is, is, i,* Ved. running round, hastening about, spreading everywhere.

परिज्वन् *pari-jvan, ā,* m. the moon; a sacrificer; a servant; fire; [? cf. *pari-jman.*]

परिडी *pari-ḍī,* cl. 1. A. *-ḍayate, -ḍīyate, -ḍayitum,* to fly round.

Pari-ḍīna or *pari-ḍīnaka, am,* n. the flight of a bird in circles, flying round.

परिणम् *pari-ṇam,* cl. 1. P. A. *-ṇamati, -te, -ṇantum,* to stoop (as an elephant about to strike), bend down, bend aside; to change into, be transformed into (with inst.); to become ripe or mature, ripen; to be digested; to become old, grow old; to set (as the sun); to elapse (as time): Caus. *-ṇamayati* or *-ṇāmayati,* to make ripe, ripen, mature; to bring to an end, pass (as the night); to bend one's self down, stoop, bend to one side; Pass. of Caus. *-ṇāmyate,* to become ripe, ripen.

Pari-ṇata, as, ā, am, bent down, bowed down, curved, deflected; stooping; changed or transformed into (with inst.); ripened, ripe, mature; digested; full grown, advanced in age, perfected; set (as the sun); elapsed; *(as),* m. an elephant stooping to strike with his tusks or that gives a side blow with the tusks; *(am),* n. capital, wealth accumulated for the sake of profit (?). — *Pariṇata-śarad, t,* f. the latter part of the autumn.

Pari-ṇati, is, f. bending down, bowing; change, alteration, transformation, transmutation; the becoming ripe, ripening, ripeness, maturity; consequence, result, issue, effect; end, close, the last stage or conclusion of anything; fulfilment.

Pari-ṇamana, am, n. change, transformation, changing into (with inst.).

Pari-ṇamayitṛi, tā, trī, tṛi, causing to bend or bow, bending; causing to ripen, bringing to maturity.

Pari-ṇāma, as, m. change, alteration, transformation; alteration of food, digestion; result, consequence, issue, effect, event; end, close, termination, last stage or state, conclusion [cf. *dush-p°*]; advance in age, growing old; lapse (of time); a particular figure of speech by which the properties of any object are transferred to that with which it is compared; *(e),* ind. finally, lastly, in the end, afterwards; at the close of life. — *Pariṇāma-darśin, ī, inī, i,* looking forward to the issue or consequences (of any act or event), prepared for a change, provident; prudent. — *Pariṇāma-drishṭi, is,* f. foresight, providence. — *Pariṇāma-nirodha, as,* m. obstruction (of felicity caused) by human vicissitude, as birth, growth, death, &c. — *Pariṇāma-pathya, as, ā, am,* suited to a future state or condition. — *Pariṇāma-śūla, as,* m. pain resulting from the changes of the food in indigestion, violent and painful indigestion, flatulence with pain, colic.

Pari-ṇāmaka, as, ikā, am, effecting a change, causing vicissitudes (as time).

Pariṇāmika, as, ā, am, resulting from change, produced by alteration.

Pari-ṇāmin, ī, inī, i, changing, altering, subject

to transformation, changeable.—*Pariṇāmi-tva, am,* n. liability to change, mutability.

Pari-ṇinaṅsu, us, us, u, about to stoop, about to make a side thrust (with the tusks, as an elephant).

परिणह *pari-ṇah,* cl. 4. P. A. *-nahyati, -te, -naddhum,* to bind round, tie round, gird, wrap round; to encircle, span, embrace, surround.

Pari-ṇaddha, as, ā, am, bound round, wrapped round; of great span or compass, broad, large.

Pari-ṇahana, am, n. binding round, girding on, wrapping round.

Pari-ṇāha, as, m. compass, circumference, extent, width, breadth, circumference of a circle, periphery; (sometimes spelt *pari-ṇāha,* q. v.)—*Pariṇāha-vat, ān, atī, at,* having a wide compass or circumference, round, large, big.

Pari-ṇāhin, ī, inī, i, having a wide compass or circumference, big, large; (at the end of a comp.) having the circumference of (e. g. *mattebha-kumbha-p°,* q. v.).

Parī-ṇah, t, f., Ved. encompassing, pervading, spreading over; a trunk or chest on a carriage; N. of a place on the Saras-vatī.

Parī-ṇāha, as, m.=*pari-ṇāha* above; a piece of common land encircling a village or city; an epithet of Śiva.

परिणिंसक *pari-ṇiṅsaka, as, ā, am* (fr. rt. *niṅs* with *pari*), tasting, eating; kissing; an eater (=*bhakshayitṛi*).

Pariṇiṅsā, f. tasting, eating; kissing.

परिणिधा *pari-ṇi-dhā,* cl. 3. P. A. *-dadhāti, -dhatte, -dhātum,* Ved. to place or lay round.

परिणिनंसु *pari-ṇinaṅsu.* See above.

परिणिमा *pari-ṇi-mā* (rt. 2. or 4. *mā?*), cl. 3. A. *-mimīte, -mātum,* see Scholiast on Pāṇ. VIII. 4, 17.

परिणिमे *pari-ṇi-me,* cl. 1. A. *-mayate, -mātum,* see Scholiast on Pāṇ. VIII. 4, 17.

परिणिर्मा *pari-ṇir-mā* (rt. 4. *mā*), cl. 2. P., 3. 4. A. *-māti, -mimīte, -māyate, -mātum,* to mark off, to limit; to settle, determine.

परिणिष्ठा *pari-ṇishṭhā,* f. perfect skill or conversancy.

परिणिहन् *pari-ṇi-han,* cl. 2. P. *-hanti, -hantum,* to strike.

Pari-ṇighnat, an, atī, at, striking.

परिणी *pari-ṇī,* cl. 1. P. A. *-ṇayati, -te* (anom. perf. in epic poetry, *pariṇayām-āsa*), *-ṇetum,* to lead about, to lead or conduct round, bear or carry round; (especially) to lead a bride and bridegroom or a bride round the sacrificial fire (with two acc.); to marry, (said of a bridegroom); to lead forward; to trace out, discover, investigate: Caus. *-ṇāyayati, -yitum,* to pass or spend (time).

Pari-ṇaya, as, m. leading round, (especially) leading the bride round the sacred fire, marriage, (*nava-pariṇayā,* a newly married woman.)

Pari-ṇayana, am, n. the act of leading round, (especially) leading round the sacred fire; marrying, marriage.

Pari-ṇāya, as, m. leading round; moving a piece at chess, draughts, &c.; a move (at chess).

Pari-ṇāyaka, as, m. a leader, guide, (*a-pari-ṇāyaka,* being without a guide); a husband.

Pari-ṇīta, as, ā, am, led round; married; (in Mahā-bh. Vana-p. 13739, probably) completed, finished, executed.

Pari-ṇetṛi, tā, m. 'one who leads round,' a husband.

Pari-ṇeya, as, ā, am, to be led round; (*ā*), f. to be led round the fire (as a bride), to be married.

परितकन *pari-takana, am,* n. (fr. rt. *tak* with *pari*), running round or about.

Pari-takmya, as, ā, am, Ved. causing anxiety or uneasiness, insecure, unsafe, perilous, dangerous; (*ā*), f. error; night, darkness.

परितड् *pari-taḍ,* cl. 10. P. *-tāḍayati, -yitum,* to touch, strike against, strike.

परितन् *pari-tan* (see rt. 3. *tan*), cl. 5. P. A. *-tanoti, -tanute, -tanitum,* Ved. to stretch round, clasp round, embrace, surround.

Pari-tatnu, us, us, u, Ved. stretching round, embracing, clasping round, surrounding.

Pari-tat, t, t, t, spread all around, extended in every direction.

परितप् *pari-tap,* cl. 1. P. *-tapati, -taptum,* to burn or scorch all round, burn excessively, set on fire, kindle; to feel or suffer pain; to mortify the body, undergo penance, practise austerities: Pass. *-tapyate* (rarely *-tapyati*), to feel or suffer pain; to undergo penance, mortify the flesh: Caus. *-tāpayati, -yitum,* to scorch; to cause great pain, torment, torture.

Pari-tapta, as, ā, am, surrounded with heat, heated, scorched, burnt; tormented.

Pari-tapti, is, f. great pain or sorrow, anguish, torture.

Pari-tāpa, as, m. glow, heat, scorching heat; pain, anguish, grief, sorrow, affliction; fear, trembling; N. of a particular hell.

Pari-tāpin, ī, inī, i, burning hot, very hot; causing much pain or sorrow, causing anguish, torturing, tormenting.

परितम् *pari-tam,* cl. 4. P. *-tāmyati, -tamitum,* to gasp for breath, to be oppressed.

परितर्क् *pari-tark,* cl. 10. P. (ep. also A.) *-tarkayati, -te, -yitum,* to think about, reflect about, ponder upon; to reflect, consider; to examine (judicially).

Pari-tarkaṇa, am, n. consideration, reflection; pondering upon (with gen.).

Pari-tarkita, as, ā, am, thought about; examined; (*a-paritarkita,* not examined, unexpected.)

परितर्ज् *pari-tarj,* cl. 1. P. (ep. also A.) *-tarjati, -te,* &c., to threaten, menace.

परितस् *pari-tas,* ind. (fr. *pari*), around, round about, all around, on all sides, on every side, to all sides, everywhere, in every direction, from all parts; round (as a prep. with acc. or gen.).

परिताप *pari-tāpa.* See *pari-tap* above.

परितारणीय *pari-tāraṇīya, as, ā, am* (fr. rt. *tṛī* with *pari*), to be delivered or liberated, to be saved or redeemed.

परितिक्त *pari-tikta, as, ā, am,* extremely bitter; (*as, am*), m. or n. (?), Melia Azedarach.

परितुद् *pari-tud,* cl. 6. P. A. *-tudati, -te, -tottum,* to trample down, stamp upon, pound.

परितुष् *pari-tush,* cl. 4. P. (ep. also A.) *-tushyati, -te, -toshṭum,* to be quite satisfied with (with gen. or loc.); to feel complete satisfaction, be much pleased, be very glad: Caus. *-toshayati, -yitum,* to satisfy completely, to please much or gratify; to appease; to flatter.

Pari-tushṭa, as, ā, am, completely satisfied, much pleased, delighted, very glad.—*Paritushṭāt-man* (°*ṭa-āt*°), *ā, ā, a,* contented in mind.

Pari-tushṭi, is, f. complete satisfaction, contentment, delight.

Pari-tosha (rarely *parī-tosha*), *as,* m. complete satisfaction, gratification, contentment, pleasure, delight, glee; delight in (with loc. or gen., e. g. *guṇini paritoshaḥ,* delight in a virtuous person).—*Pari-tosha-vat, ān, atī, at,* satisfied, contented, glad.

Pari-toshaṇa, as, ā, am, satisfying, gratifying, who or what satisfies or makes content; (*am*), n. satisfying, satisfaction, gratification.

Pari-toshayitṛi, tā, trī, tṛi, one who satisfies completely, who or what gratifies, pleasing or making very glad.

Pari-toshin, ī, iṇī, i, completely satisfied, contented.

परितृद् *pari-tṛid,* cl. 7. P. A. *-tṛiṇatti, -tṛintte, -tarditum,* Ved. to pierce through, pierce (with a spear), thrust through.

परितृप् *pari-tṛip,* cl. 4. P. (ep. also A.) *-tṛipyati, -te, -tarpitum, -tarptum, -traptum,* to be completely satisfied or contented: Caus. *-tarpayati, -yitum,* to satiate or satisfy completely, sate; to relish; to refresh.

Pari-tarpaṇa, as, ā, am, satisfying, sating, contenting; (*am*), n. the act of satisfying, gratification.

Pari-tarpita, as, ā, am, satisfied completely, sated; refreshed.

परित्यज् *pari-tyaj,* cl. 1. P. *-tyajati, -tyaktum,* to abandon, forsake, desert, leave, discard, dismiss, repudiate, disown, reject; to quit (a place); to give up, give away, surrender, abdicate, renounce, resign; (with *deham*) to forsake the body, die; (with *prāṇān*) to resign the breath, give up the ghost; (with *nāram*) to disembark; to shake off (as sleep); to leave over, leave a remainder; to leave a space or interval; to let go; to leave out; to put aside, neglect, disregard: Pass. *-tyajyate,* to be deprived of, bereft of (with inst.); to lose: Caus. *-tyājayati, -yitum,* to deprive a person (acc.) of anything (acc.); to rob, take away anything from any one (with two acc.).

Pari-tyakta, as, ā, am, left, quitted, deserted, abandoned; bereft of, deprived of, robbed of (with inst.); left, wanting; let go; let fly or discharged (as an arrow).

Pari-tyaktṛi, tā, trī, tṛi, one who abandons or deserts, leaving, abandoning, a forsaker.

Pari-tyaj, k, k, k, forsaking, deserting, abandoning; giving up, resigning; a forsaker.

Pari-tyajana, am, n. the act of abandoning, giving away, distributing.

1. *pari-tyajya, as, ā, am,* to be abandoned or forsaken or deserted; to be given up or resigned.

2. *pari-tyajya,* ind. having abandoned, &c.; leaving a space, at a distance from (with acc.); with the exception of, excepting.

Pari-tyāga, as, m. abandoning, abandonment, leaving, quitting, desertion, repudiation, divorce, rejection; discarding, resigning, renouncing, renunciation, abdication, letting go, giving up, giving away, liberality; sacrificing, sacrifice; neglecting, neglect, omission; loss, privation; separation from.—*Parityāga-sena, as,* m., N. of a prince.

Parityāgin, ī, inī, i, abandoning, quitting, forsaking, resigning, renouncing.

Pari-tyājana, am, n. causing to abandon or give up.

Pari-tyājya, as, ā, am, to be abandoned or forsaken, to be left or deserted; to be given up or resigned, to be renounced; to be omitted.

परित्रस्त *pari-trasta, as, ā, am* (fr. rt. 2. *tras* with *pari*), terrified, frightened, afraid, much alarmed.

Pari-trāsa, as, m. terror, fright, fear.

परित्रै *pari-trai* (by some written *pari-trā*), cl. 1. A. *-trāyate, -trātum,* to rescue, save, protect, defend; *paritrāyatām* or *paritrāyadhvam,* help! to the rescue!

Pari-trāṇa, am, n. protecting, protection, preserving, rescuing, rescue, deliverance, preservation, defence, means of defence or protection; self-defence; abstaining from; the hair of the body (?).

Pari-trāta, as, ā, am, protected; rescued, saved, preserved.

Pari-trātavya, as, ā, am, to be rescued or preserved, to be protected or defended.

Pari-trātṛi, tā, trī, tṛi, a protector, defender, rescuer.

परित्वर् *pari-tvar*, cl. 1. A. *-tvarate*, *-tva-ritum*, to hasten towards.

परिदंशित *pari-daṅśita*, *as*, *ā*, *am*, completely armed, covered with mail, armed cap-a-pie.

परिदर *pari-dara*. See col. 2.

परिदष्ट *pari-dashṭa*, *as*, *ā*, *am*, bitten to pieces, bitten. — *Paridashṭa-daććhada*, *as*, *ā*, *am*, biting the lips.

परिदह् *pari-dah*, cl. 1. P. *-dahati*, *-dag-dhum*, to burn round, scorch round, burn entirely, consume by fire, to dry up: Pass. *-dahyate*, to be burnt or wholly consumed, to burn.

Pari-dagdha, *as*, *ā*, *am*, burnt, scorched.

Pari-dahana, *am*, n. burning, scorching.

Pari-dāha, *as*, m. burning, combustion; mental anguish, pain, sorrow.

Pari-dāhin, *ī*, *inī*, *i*, burning, scorching, hot.

परिदा 1. *pari-dā*, cl. 3. P. A. *-dadāti*, *-datte*, *-dātum*, to give, give away entirely, surrender, deliver up; to intrust, deposit with (with gen., dat., or loc. of the person); to present; to lend: Caus. *-dāpayati*, *-yitum*, to cause to be delivered or given up.

2. *pari-dā*, f., Ved. giving one's self up to the favour or protection of another; surrender; devotion.

Pari-dāna, *am*, n. devotion; barter, exchange; restitution of a deposit.

Pari-dāya, ind. having given up or surrendered.

Pari-dāyin, *ī*, m. a father (or another relation) who marries his daughter or ward to a man whose elder brother is not yet married.

1. *parī-tta*, *as*, *ā*, *am* (for *pari-datta*), given, given up; entirely given away, delivered up. (For 2. *parī-tta* see *pari-do*, col. 2.)

परिदा 3. *pari-dā*. See *pari-do*, col. 2.

परिदिव् *pari-div* or *pari-dev* (see rts. 1. *div* and *dev*), cl. 1. 10. P. *-devati*, *-devayati* (rarely A. *-te*), *-yitum*, to wail, lament, cry; to bewail, bemoan, weep for (with acc.).

Pari-deva, *as*, m. lamentation, wailing, crying.

Pari-devaka, *as*, *ikā*, *am*, lamenting, who or what laments or complains.

Pari-devana, *am*, *ā*, n. f. lamentation, bewailing, complaint.

Pari-devita, *as*, *ā*, *am*, lamented, bewailed; plaintive, lamenting, miserable; (*am*), n. lamentation, wailing, complaint.

Pari-devin, *ī*, *inī*, *i*, lamenting, bewailing.

Pari-dyūna, *as*, *ā*, *am*, sorrowful, sad, miserable.

परिदिश् *pari-diś*, cl. 3. 6. P. *-dideshṭi*, *-diśati*, *-deshṭum*, to announce, make known; to signify (the existence of anything).

Pari-dishṭa, *as*, *ā*, *am*, made known, known.

परिदिह् *pari-dih*, cl. 2. P. A. *-degdhi*, *-digdhe*, *-degdhum*, Ved. to coat or cover over, smear over.

परिदीन *pari-dīna*, *as*, *ā*, *am*, excessively dejected or downcast, much afflicted. — *Paridīna-sattva*, *as*, *ā*, *am*, distressed in mind.

परिदुर्बल *pari-durbala*, *as*, *ā*, *am*, extremely weak or decrepit.

परिदृश् *pari-dṛiś*, cl. 1. P. *-paśyati*, *-drash-ṭum*, to look at, see, view, look upon, behold, regard, perceive; to regard mentally, consider, investigate, search, find out; to know; to frequent: Pass. *-dṛiśyate*, to be observed or perceived; to appear, become visible: Caus. *-darśayati*, *-yitum*, to show; to set forth, expound, explain.

Pari-drashṭṛi, *ṭā*, *ṭṛī*, *ṭṛi*, a spectator, looker on; perceiver.

परिदॄ *pari-dṛī*, cl. 9. P. A. *-dṛiṇāti*, *-ṇīte*, &c., Ved. to rend or destroy on all sides: Pass. *-dīryate*, to peel or drop off on all sides, to become dropsical (the skin swelling and appearing ready to drop off).

Pari-dara, *as*, m. a disease of the gums in which the skin peels off and bleeds.

Pari-dīrṇa, *as*, *ā*, *am*, rent on all sides.

परिदेव् *pari-dev*. See *pari-div*, col. 1.

परिदो *pari-do* or 3. *pari-dā*, cl. 2. P. *-dāti*, *-dātum*, to cut or clip round.

2. *parī-tta*, *as*, *ā*, *am*, clipped or cut round, incomplete, limited, confined, &c.; see p. 552, col. 1. (For 1. *parī-tta* see under 1. *pari-dā*, col. 1.)

परिद्यून *pari-dyūna*. See *pari-div*, col. 1.

परिद्रु *pari-dru*, cl. 1. P. *-dravati*, *-drotum*, Ved. to run round.

परिद्वीप *pari-dvīpa*, *as*, m., N. of one of the sons of Garuḍa.

परिद्वेषस् *pari-dveshas*, *ās*, *ās*, *as*, Ved. hating, completely hostile.

परिधर्षण *pari-dharshaṇa*, *am*, n. (fr. rt. *dhṛish* with *pari*), assault, attack, injury, abuse, ill-treatment, rough usage.

परिधा *pari-dhā*, cl. 3. P. A. *-dadhāti*, *-dhatte*, *-dhātum*, to lay or put round, place or set round; to put round one's self, wrap round, put on, put on (a garment), dress (without a following acc.); to clothe; to surround, envelop, encompass; to cast (the eyes) round, turn the glance upon; (Ved.) to conclude or close (the recitation of a hymn): Caus. *-dhāpayati*, *-yitum*, to cause to put or wrap round, cause to put on, clothe with (with inst.); clothe any one in (with two acc.): Desid. *-dhitsate*, &c., to be about to put on, to wish to clothe one's self.

Pari-dhāna or *parī-dhāna*, *am*, n. putting round, laying round (Ved.); wrapping round; putting on (a garment), dressing, clothing; that which is put on, a garment, (especially) an under garment, clothes, vesture, (*gagana-paridhāna*, stark naked; cf. *dig-ambara*); closing or concluding (the recitation of a hymn). — *Paridhāna-valkala*, *am*, n. bark for clothing.

Paridhānīya, *as*, *ā*, *am*, Ved. forming the close or conclusion; (*ā*), f., scil. *ṛić*, a concluding or final verse; (*am*), n. an under garment.

Pari-dhāpana, *am*, n. causing to put on (a garment).

Pari-dhāpanīya, *as*, *ā*, *am*, relating to investiture or the causing any one to put on (a garment &c.).

Pari-dhāya, *as*, m. train, retinue, attendants; the hinder parts, posteriors; a receptacle for water, reservoir.

Pari-dhāyaka, *as*, m. a hedge, fence, enclosure.

Pari-dhi, *is*, m. that by which anything is surrounded or enclosed (said of the ocean as surrounding the earth), a fence, hedge, wall; a misty halo or circle round the sun or moon; a circle or disk of light, a glory; the horizon; circumference, compass; the circumference of a circle; the periphery of a wheel; a circle surrounding the globe, a great circle; epicycle; a frame of wood laid round a sacrificial fire to keep it together, (commonly in three pieces, called *madhyama*, *dakshiṇa*, *uttara*); a covering; the branch of the tree to which the victim at a sacrifice is tied (?); N. of a man. — *Pa-ridhi-stha*, *as*, *ā*, *am*, situated on the horizon; (*as*), m. a number of sentinels posted in a circle; a guard, body-guard; an aide-de-camp, an officer attendant on a king or general. — *Paridhi-pati-khećara*, *as*, m. an epithet of Śiva, (perhaps 'the bird presiding over the horizon,' *paridhī* for *pa-ridhi*?).

Pari-dheya, *as*, *ā*, *am*, to be put round, wearable; (*am*), n. an under garment (?).

Pari-hita, *as*, *ā*, *am*, stationed round; placed round, invested, put on, clothed, covered.

परिधारण *pari-dhāraṇa*. See under *pari-dhṛi* below.

परिधाव् *pari-dhāv*, cl. 1. P. (rarely A.) *-dhāvati*, *-te*, *-dhāvitum*, to flow or stream round, to run round or about; go about; (*mṛigayām pari-dhāv*, to go or move about hunting, to hunt); to drive about; to stream through, run through; to run or move round anything (with acc.); to run towards or after, to pursue: Caus. *-dhāvayati*, *-yitum*, to surround, encompass, encircle.

Pari-dhāvin, *ī*, *inī*, *i*, running round; (*ī*), m., N. of the 46th (or 20th) of the 60 years' cycle of Jupiter.

परिधीर *pari-dhīra*, *as*, *ā*, *am*, very deep (as a tone or sound).

परिधूपित *pari-dhūpita*, *as*, *ā*, *am*, richly perfumed or scented.

परिधूसर *pari-dhūsara*, *as*, *ā*, *am*, quite grey.

परिधृ *pari-dhṛi*, cl. 10. P. *-dhārayati*, *-yitum*, to carry about; to support, bear, suffer, endure.

Pari-dhāraṇa, *am*, n. carrying about, supporting, suffering, enduring.

Pari-dhārya, *as*, *ā*, *am*, to be preserved or maintained.

परिध्वंस् *pari-dhvaṇs*, cl. 1. A. *-dhvaṇsate*, *-dhvaṇsitum*, to fall to pieces, fall away, decay; to be destroyed.

Pari-dhvaṇsa, *as*, m. distress, disaster, ruin, trouble, toil; failing, failure; injury, destruction; leaving one's caste, loss of caste, mixture of castes.

Pari-dhvaṇsin, *ī*, *inī*, *i*, falling away, falling off; destroying, ruining.

Pari-dhvasta, *as*, *ā*, *am*, destroyed, ruined; covered.

परिनिन्दा *pari-nindā*, f. strong censure, severe blame.

परिनिम्न *pari-nimna*, *as*, *ā*, *am*, much depressed, deeply hollowed.

परिनिर्जि *pari-nir-ji*, cl. 1. P. A. *-jayati*, *-te*, *-jetum*, to conquer, overpower thoroughly.

परिनिर्वपण *pari-nirvapaṇa*, *am*, n. (fr. rt. *vap* with *pari-nis*), distributing, dispensing, giving.

Pari-nirvivapsā, f. (fr. the Desid.), desire of giving, a disposition to distribute, liberality.

Pari-nirvivapsu, *us*, *us*, *u*, intending to give much, desirous of giving.

परिनिर्वाण *pari-nirvāṇa*, *as*, *ā*, *am*, quite extinguished, quite brought to an end; (*am*), n. the final extinction of the individual; N. of a place where Buddha disappeared.

परिनिर्वृति *pari-nirvṛiti*, *is*, f. final liberation; complete emancipation of the soul from the body and exemption from future transmigration.

परिनिश्चय *pari-niśćaya*, *as*, m. fixed opinion or resolution.

परिनिषद् *pari-ni-shad*, cl. 1. 6. P. (Ved. also A.) *-shīdati*, *-shattum*, to sit round.

परिनिष्ठा *pari-nishṭhā* (fr. rt. *sthā* with *pari* and *ni* or *nis*, see *ni-shṭha*), extreme limit, highest point; complete accomplishment; complete knowledge or acquaintance, familiarity with anything.

Pari-nishṭhita, *as*, *ā*, *am*, completely skilled in or acquainted with.

Pari-naishṭhika, *as*, *ī*, *am*, the highest, utmost, most perfect.

परिन्यस् *pari-ny-as*, cl. 4. P. *-asyati*, *-asi-tum*, to stretch out, extend.

Pari-nyasta, *as*, *ā*, *am*, stretched out, extended.

Pari-nyāsa, *as*, m. completing the sense of a

passage; (in dramatic language) alluding to the development of the so-called seed or origin of the dramatic plot, [cf. *vīja.*]

परिपक्व *pari-pakva, as, ā, am* (fr. rt. 2. *pać* with *pari*), completely cooked or dressed; finally baked; completely burnt (as a brick); digested; quite ripe, mature; highly cultivated or educated, very knowing or shrewd; near death or decay, approaching the end, about to pass away, decaying. — *Paripakva-tā*, f. the state of being completely cooked; digestion; full maturity, perfection; shrewdness.

Pari-pāka, as, m. being completely cooked or dressed; digestion; ripening, maturity, perfection; the fruit or consequence of an action, consequence; cleverness, shrewdness, experience.

Pari-pākin, ī, inī, i, ripening, bringing to maturity; cooking; digesting; (*inī*), f. the plant Ipomœa Turpethum.

Pari-pāćana, as, ā, am, or *pari-pāćayitṛi, tā, trī, tṛi,* cooking, bringing to maturity.

परिपठ् *pari-paṭh,* cl. 1. P. *-paṭhati, -paṭhitum,* to enumerate completely, detail, describe, mention, name, represent.

Pari-pāṭha, as, m. complete enumeration, detail; (*ena*), ind. in detail, completely.

Pari-pāṭhaka, as, ā, am, enumerating in detail, describing the contents.

परिपण *pari-paṇa, am,* n. (fr. rt. 2. *paṇ* with *pari*), capital, principal, stock.

Pari-paṇita, as, ā, am, pledged, plighted, agreed, promised.

परिपत् *pari-pat,* cl. 1. P. *-patati, -patitum,* to fly round or about, to run round or about, run in all directions; to leap down, fall, throw one's self upon, attack: Caus. *-pātayati, -yitum,* to cause to fall down, shoot down, shoot off, throw into.

Pari-patana, am, n. flying round or about.

परिपति *pari-pati, is,* m., Ved. the lord of all around; (Sāy.) a protector; (according to Mahīdhara) flying about.

परिपद् *pari-pad, t,* f., Ved. a snare, trap; walking about; a creature, living being; (Sāy.) a bird (as flying about).

परिपदिन् *paripadin, ī,* m. an enemy; (probably only a wrong reading for *pari-parin.*)

परिपन्थक *pari-panthaka, as,* m. one who obstructs the way, an antagonist, opponent, adversary, enemy.

Pari-pantham, ind. by the way, in the way.

Pari-panthaya, Nom. P. *-panthayati, -yitum,* to obstruct the way, oppose, resist (with acc.).

Pari-panthika, as, m. an adversary, enemy.

Pari-panthin, ī, m. an antagonist, opponent, enemy; a robber, highwayman, bandit. — *Paripanthi-tva, am,* n. obstructing the way.

परिपर *pari-para* (probably fr. *pari* repeated), a tortuous course, roundabout way; [cf. *a-paripara.*]

परिपरिन् *pari-parin, ī,* m. (probably fr. *pari-pari*), Ved. an antagonist, opponent, adversary.

परिपवन *pari-pavana.* See *pari-pū*, col. 3.

परिपशव्य *pari-paśavya, as, ā, am* (fr. *pari-paśu*), Ved. relating to the victim at a sacrifice.

परिपा 1. *pari-pā,* cl. 1. P. *-pibati, -pātum,* to drink before and after any one (Ved.); to drink up, sip up.

Pari-pāna, am, n., Ved. a drink, beverage.

Pari-pīta, as, ā, am, drunk up, sipped up, drunk together with (anything).

परिपा 2. *pari-pā,* cl. 2. P. *-pāti, -pātum,* to protect or defend on every side, to guard, maintain: Caus. *-pālayati,* &c., to protect, guard, govern; to keep, maintain; to wait, expect.

Pari-pāṇa, as, am, m. n., Ved. protection, defence, covert.

Pari-pālaka, as, ikā, am (fr. the Caus.), guarding, protecting, defending, maintaining, supporting, sustaining; taking care of one's property.

Pari-pālana, am, n. protecting, cherishing, defending, maintaining, sustaining, keeping; protection, nurture.

Pari-pālayitṛi, tā, trī, tṛi, a protector, defender.

Pari-pālita, as, ā, am, protected, cherished.

Pari-pālya, as, ā, am, to be protected or defended, to be maintained or observed; to be governed.

Pari-pipālayishā, f. (fr. the Desid. of Caus.), desire of protecting or maintaining or sustaining.

परिपाक *pari-pāka, pari-pākin, pari-pāćana.* See *pari-pakva,* col. 1.

परिपाटल *pari-pāṭala, as, ā, am,* of a pale red colour, pale red.

परिपाटी *pari-pāṭī,* f. succession, order, method, arrangement; arithmetic.

परिपाठ *pari-pāṭha.* See *pari-paṭh,* col. 1.

परिपाण्डु *pari-pāṇḍu, us, us, u,* very light or pale.

परिपाद *pari-pāda.* See Gaṇa to Pāṇ. VI. 2, 184.

परिपार्श्व *pari-pārśva, as, ā, am,* being at or by one's side, at the side, near; [cf. *pārīpārśvika.*] — *Paripārśva-ćara, as, ī, am,* going at or by one's side. — *Paripārśva-tas,* ind. at or by the side, at both sides of (with gen.). — *Paripārśva-vartin, ī, inī, i,* being at the side, standing at or close to one's side.

परिपिञ्जर *pari-piñjara, as, ā, am,* of a brownish red colour.

परिपिष् *pari-pish,* cl. 7. P. *-pinashṭi, -peshṭum,* to crush, trample; to beat, strike.

Pari-pishṭa, as, ā, am, crushed, trampled down.

Pari-pishṭaka, am, n. lead.

परिपीड् *pari-pīḍ,* cl. 10. P. *-pīḍayati, -yitum,* to press all round, press together, compress, squeeze; to hug, embrace; to torment greatly, torture, harass, vex; (in augury) to cover, cover up.

Pari-pīḍana, am, n. squeezing or pressing out, expressing; injuring, prejudicing.

Pari-pīḍā, f. pressing; vexing, torturing, tormenting.

Pari-pīḍita, as, ā, am, pressed; embraced; tormented.

परिपीत *pari-pīta.* See 1. *pari-pā,* col. 1.

परिपुच्छय *pari-pućchaya,* Nom. A. *pari-pućchayate,* &c., to wag the tail.

परिपुट् *pari-puṭ,* Pass. *-puṭyate,* &c., to peel off, lose the bark or skin.

Pari-puṭana, am, n. removing the peel or bark, peeling, desquamation, peeling off; losing the bark or skin. — *Paripuṭana-vat, ān, atī, at,* peeling off, dropping off.

Pari-poṭa, as, m. or *pari-poṭaka, as,* m. peeling off, a particular disease of the ear. — *Paripoṭa-vat, ān, atī, at,* peeling off, losing the skin.

Pari-poṭana, am, n. peeling off, desquamation, losing the bark or skin.

परिपुष् *pari-push,* cl. 10. P. *-poshayati, -yitum,* to cause to be cherished, to nourish, sustain, foster.

Pari-pushṭa, as, ā, am, nourished, cherished; amply provided with, abounding in. — *Paripushṭa-tā,* f. the being nourished or supported, receiving nourishment.

Pari-poshaka, as, ā, am, nourishing, confirming, encouraging, furthering.

Pari-poshaṇa, am, n. the act of nourishing, furthering, promoting.

Pari-poshaṇīya, as, ā, am, to be nourished, to be promoted.

परिपुष्करा *pari-pushkarā,* f. the plant Cucumis Maderaspattanus.

परिपू *pari-pū,* cl. 9. P. A. *-punāti, -nīte, -pavitum,* to purify completely, strain; to lustrate; to become completely purified.

Pari-pavana, am, n. cleaning, winnowing corn; a winnowing-basket.

Pari-pūta, as, ā, am, pure, purified; completely winnowed, threshed, freed from chaff.

परिपूज् *pari-pūj,* cl. 10. P. *-pūjayati, -yitum,* to honour greatly, adore, worship.

Pari-pūjana, am, n. or *pari-pūjā,* f. honouring highly, worshipping, adoring.

Pari-pūjita, as, ā, am, much honoured, served, worshipped, adored.

परिपूर्ण *pari-pūrṇa.* See *pari-pṛī* below.

परिपृ *pari-pṛī,* Pass. *-pūryate,* &c., to fill (intransitively), become completely full: Caus. *-pūrayati, -yitum,* to fill completely (transitively), make full, fill out, completely cover, wholly occupy.

Pari-pūraka, as, ikā, am, filling, fulfilling; causing fulness or prosperity.

Pari-pūraṇa, am, n. the act of filling; perfecting, rendering complete.

Pari-pūrṇa, as, ā, am, quite full, entire, complete, completely filled; fully satisfied, self-satisfied, content. — *Paripūrṇa-ćandra-vimala-prabha, as,* m. 'having the spotless splendor of the full moon,' N. of a Sam-ādhi. — *Paripūrṇa-tā,* f. or *paripūrṇa-tva, am,* n. completion, completeness, entireness, fulness; satiety or satisfaction. — *Paripūrṇa-sahasra-ćandra-vatī,* f. 'possessing a thousand full moons,' an epithet of Indra's wife. — *Paripūrṇāmṛita-raśmi* (°*ṇa-am*°), *is,* m. 'having rays filled with nectar,' the moon. — *Paripūrṇārtha* (°*ṇa-ar*°), *as, ā, am,* full of meaning; (*am*), ind. with deep emotion, affectionately. — *Paripūrṇendu* (°*ṇa-in*°), *us,* m. the full moon.

Pari-pūrti, is, f. fulness, completion.

परिपेलव *pari-pelava, as, ā, am,* very fine or small, very delicate; (*am*), n. a fragrant grass, Cyperus Rotundus.

Pari-pela, am, n. = *pari-pelava,* a fragrant grass, Cyperus Rotundus.

परिपोट *pari-poṭa.* See *pari-puṭ,* col. 2.

परिप्रग्रह् *pari-pra-grah,* cl. 9. P. A. *-gṛihṇāti, -ṇīte, -grahītum,* Ved. to take round, to hand or pass round.

परिप्रछ् *pari-prach,* cl. 6. P. *-pṛićchati, -prashṭum,* to interrogate or ask any one about anything (with two acc. or with acc. of the thing and abl. of the person); to enquire about.

Pari-pṛićchā, f. asking about, question, inquiry, asking for.

Pari-pṛićchya, ind. having inquired about (with two acc.).

Pari-praśna, as, m. question, interrogation, inquiry.

परिप्रमुच् *pari-pra-muć,* cl. 6. A. *-muñćate, -moktum,* Ved. to free one's self from.

परिप्राप्ति *pari-prāpti, is,* f. (fr. rt. *āp* with *pari* and *pra*), acquisition, obtaining.

Pari-prepsu, us, us, u (fr. the Desid.), wishing to reach, desirous of obtaining; wishing to defend; desiring, desirous, seeking.

परिप्रार्ध *pari-prārdha, am,* n., Ved. proximity, nearness.

परिप्री *pari-prī, īs, īs, i* (fr. rt. *prī* with *pari*), Ved. very dear or valued; (Sāy.) gratifying on all sides or in every way (= *paritaḥ priṇayitṛi*).

परिप्रुष् *pari-prush, ṭ, ṭ, ṭ,* Ved. sprinkling, splashing.

परिप्रे *pari-pre* (fr. *pari-pra-i*), cl. 2. P. *-praiti, -praitum,* Ved. to go round, flow round.

परिप्रेष् *pari-presh* (*pari-pra-ish,* see rt. 1. *ish*), Caus. *-praishayati, -yitum,* to send forth, dispatch, send away.

Pari-preshaṇa, am, n. sending forth or away; banishing, abandoning.

Pari-preshita, as, ā, am, sent forth, sent away, dispatched; banished, abandoned.

Pari-preshya, as, m. a servant.

परिप्लु *pari-plu,* cl. 1. A. *-plavate, -plotum,* to swim about, float about, bathe; to flood, inundate; to overwhelm; to hover about, fly or soar through; to jump or spring about; to revolve, move in a circle; to move about, move restlessly; to go astray; to hasten forward: Caus. *-plāvayati, -yitum,* to flood, inundate, bathe, water.

Pari-plava, as, ā, am, swimming about; swaying or moving to and fro, running about, vibrating, oscillating, undulating, waving, shaking, trembling, movable, unsteady, restless; (*as*), m. inundation; bathing, wetting, immersing; a ship, boat; oppression, tyranny; N. of a prince, son of Sukhī-bala (Sukhī-vala, Sukhī-nala); (*ā*), f. a sort of spoon used at sacrifices.

Pari-plavamāna, as, ā, am, swimming about, floating, moving to and fro.

1. *pari-plāvya, as, ā, am,* swimming about, floating around, running (as water).

2. *pari-plāvya,* ind. having flooded or inundated, having bathed.

Pari-pluta, as, ā, am, flooded, inundated; overwhelmed; wetted, bathed, immersed; (*ā*), f. spirituous liquor; (*am*), n. a spring or jump, skipping about.

परिबन्ध् *pari-bandh,* cl. 9. A. *-badhnīte, -banddhum,* to bind together, connect, bind on, bind round one's self, put on (as a girdle); to encircle; to stop, interrupt: Caus. *-bandhayati, -yitum,* to tie round.

Pari-baddha, as, ā, am, bound round, obstructed.

परिबाध् 1. *pari-bādh,* cl. 1. A. *-bādhate, -bādhitum,* to ward off, keep off, to exclude, hinder, obstruct, drive away, (Ved. according to Sāy. = *parito han*); to protect from or defend against (with abl., Ved.); to vex, disturb, annoy, molest, harass, importune, pain: Desid. A. *-bibādhishate,* Ved. to strive to keep or ward off or keep at a distance.

2. *pari-bādh, t,* f., Ved. hindrance, obstruction, check; an obstructor, hinderer.

Pari-bādhā, f. trouble, vexation, worry, annoyance; fatigue, toil, hardship.

परिबृंह् *pari-bṛiṇh* or *pari-bṛih* (also written *pari-vṛiṇh* or *pari-vṛih,* q. v.), cl. 6. P. A. *-bṛiṇhati* or *-bṛihati, -bṛiṇhate* or *-bṛihate, -barhitum,* Ved. to embrace, encircle, surround, encompass; to make strong or compact, fortify, strengthen; to increase: Caus. *-bṛiṇhayati, -yitum,* to make strong, strengthen.

Pari-barha or *pari-varha, as,* m. 'that which surrounds or encompasses,' 'surroundings,' retinue, train, attendants, dependants; royal insignia; furniture, attire, trim; the necessaries of life; wealth, property, substance. — *Paribarha-vat* or *parivarha-vat, ān, atī, at,* having a suitable retinue, possessing a proper train of attendants, provided with suitable furniture, properly furnished.

Pari-barhaṇa or *pari-varhaṇa, am,* n. retinue, train; attire, trim; growth, aggrandizement; worship, adoration.

Pari-bṛiṇhaṇa or *pari-vṛiṇhaṇa, as, ī, am,* augmenting, increasing, enlarging; (*am*), n. prosperity, welfare; an additional work, appendix, supplement.

Pari-bṛiṇhita or *pari-bṛihita* or *pari-vṛiṇhita* or *pari-vṛihita, as, ā, am,* increased, augmented, grown, thriven; strengthened by, connected with, accompanied by, furnished with.

Pari-bṛiḍha or *pari-vṛiḍha, as, ā, am,* firm, fixed, dense, thick, solid, compact, ample, large; the lord of all around, a superior, proprietor, owner. — *Parivṛiḍha-tama, am,* n., Ved., scil. *Brahma,* the Supreme Spirit.

परिब्रू *pari-brū,* cl. 2. P. *-bravīti,* &c., Ved. to utter a spell or charm, lay under a spell, charm, enchant.

परिभक्ष् *pari-bhaksh,* cl. 10. P. *-bhakshayati, -yitum,* Ved. to drink off, drink up; to eat up (what belongs to another), devour, consume.

Pari-bhakshaṇa, am, n. eating up, consuming.

Pari-bhakshita, as, ā, am, drunk up, deprived of food (Ved.); devoured, consumed, gnawed; worn away.

परिभग्न *pari-bhagna, as, ā, am* (fr. rt. *bhañj* with *pari*), broken, interrupted, disturbed, stopped. — *Paribhagna-krama, as, ā, am,* stopped in one's course, checked in one's progress.

Pari-bhanga, as, m. breaking to pieces, shattering.

परिभज् *pari-bhaj,* cl. 1. P. *-bhajati, -bhaktum,* to divide.

Pari-bhajya, ind. having divided.

परिभय *pari-bhaya, as,* m. (fr. rt. 1. *bhī* with *pari*), Ved. apprehension, fear.

परिभर्त्स् *pari-bharts,* cl. 10. P. A. *-bhartsayati, -te, -yitum,* to threaten, menace, treat harshly, rate, scold, chide, reprimand.

Pari-bhartsat, an, antī, at, threatening, chiding; mocking, deriding.

Pari-bhartsana, am, n. threatening, menacing.

Pari-bhartsita, as, ā, am, threatened, chided.

Pari-bhartsyamāna, as, ā, am, being threatened.

परिभाष् *pari-bhāsh,* cl. 1. A. *-bhāshate, -bhāshitum,* to speak to, address, admonish; to declare, teach, explain, interpret, define; to persuade, exhort, encourage.

Pari-bhāshaṇa, as, ā, am, speaking much, declaring, explaining; (*am*), n. speaking, talking, addressing, conversing with, chatting, gossiping; speech, discourse; admonition, expression of censure or contempt, reproof, abuse; rule, precept; agreement (?).

Pari-bhāshaṇīya, as, ā, am, to be addressed or spoken to; reprehensible, liable to censure; deserving reproof.

Pari-bhāshā, f. speech; blame, censure, abuse; an explanation, definition; (in gram.) an explanatory Sūtra or rule mixed with the other rules of Pāṇini and teaching the method of applying them, (these Sūtras are a key to the system and are thought by some to have been interpolated in later times, but by others are ascribed to Pāṇini himself; there are other Paribhāshās by unknown authors); any general definition applicable throughout; a table or list of abbreviations or signs used in any work; (in medicine) prognosis. — *Paribhāshā-prakaraṇa, am,* n., N. of the second chapter of the Prauḍha-manoramā, q. v. — *Paribhāshendu-śekhara* (°*shā-in*°), *as,* m., N. of a grammatical work by Nāgeśa-bhaṭṭa (= *nāgoji-bhaṭṭa*).

Pari-bhāshita, as, ā, am, explained, said; formed or used technically.

Pari-bhāshin, ī, iṇī, i, speaking, explaining.

परिभास् *pari-bhās,* cl. 1. A. *-bhāsate, -bhāsitum,* to appear (Ved.): Caus. *-bhāsayati, -yitum,* to embellish, adorn.

परिभिद् *pari-bhid,* cl. 7. P. A. *-bhinatti, -bhintte, -bhettum,* to split asunder, cleave open, tear or dash to pieces, break through; to change, disfigure, deform.

Pari-bhinna, as, ā, am, split or cleft open, cracked, cut into small pieces; changed, disfigured, deformed.

परिभुज् 1. *pari-bhuj* (see rt. 1. *bhuj*), cl. 6. P. *-bhujati, -bhoktum,* Ved. to span, encompass, embrace.

Pari-bhugna, as, ā, am, bowed, bent.

परिभुज् 2. *pari-bhuj* (see rt. 3. *bhuj*), cl. 7. P. A. *-bhunakti, -bhunkte, -bhoktum,* to eat up, eat, devour; to feed upon; to use, enjoy; to neglect to feed: Caus. *-bhojayati, -yitum,* Ved. to possess, enjoy, govern.

Pari-bhukta, as, ā, am, eaten; enjoyed, possessed.

Pari-bhoktṛi, tā, trī, tṛi, eating, enjoying, possessing, an eater, enjoyer; one who lives at another's cost or uses another's property without his leave.

Pari-bhoga, as, m. enjoyment, especially sexual intercourse, possession, a means of enjoyment; living at another's cost, using another's property without his leave, illegal use of another's goods.

परिभू 1. *pari-bhū,* cl. 1. P. *-bhavati, -bhavitum* (Ved. inf. *-bhve*), to be round or about anything, encompass, surround, embrace, enclose, contain (Ved.); to circle round, go or fly round (Ved.); to accompany (Ved.); to take care of (Ved.); to guide, govern (Ved.); to be superior, surpass, overcome, subdue, conquer; to pass round, pay no attention to, treat with contempt or disrespect, despise; to disgrace; to injure; to grieve; to disappear (= *parā-bhū,* q. v.): Caus. *-bhāvayati, -yitum,* to cause to be surrounded or pervaded; to cause to be saturated or penetrated; to contain, include, comprehend; to conceive, think, reflect, meditate, know, recognise as; to make known.

Pari-bhava, as, m. or *pari-bhavana, am,* n. contumely, insult, injury, humiliation, degradation, disrespect, contempt, disgrace; defeat, discomfiture. — *Paribhava-pada, am,* n. an object or occasion of contempt, a disgraceful situation, disgrace. — *Paribhava-vidhi, is,* m. contumelious or insulting action, humiliation. — *Paribhavāspada* (°*va-ās*°), *am,* n. a position or situation of disgrace, object of contempt.

Pari-bhavanīya, as, ā, am, to be injured or insulted, liable to be humiliated or despised or disgraced.

Pari-bhaviṇ, ī, inī, i, injuring, humiliating, treating with contumely or disrespect, ridiculing; suffering disrespect.

Pari-bhāva, as, m. = *pari-bhava,* q. v.

Pari-bhāvana, am, n. cohesion, union; (*ā*), f. thought.

Pari-bhāvita, as, ā, am, contained, included; penetrated; pervaded; conceived. — *Paribhāvita-tva, am,* n. the state of being included, inclusion.

Pari-bhāvin, ī, inī, i, treating with contempt, slighting, despising; putting to shame, mocking, insulting, outvying, surpassing.

Pari-bhāvuka, as, ī, am, contemning, shaming, humbling.

Pari-bhāvya, ind. having caused to be surrounded; having reflected upon.

2. *pari-bhū, ūs, ūs, u,* Ved. surrounding, embracing, comprehending, pervading; overpowering; surpassing; guiding, governing.

Pari-bhūta, as, ā, am, treated with contempt or disrespect, disregarded, despised; overpowered, conquered. — *Paribhūta-gati-traya, as, ā, am,* surpassing three times the age of man.

Pari-bhūti, is, is, i, Ved. overcoming, overpowering; (*is*), f. superiority, superior power (Ved.); contempt, insult, contumely, humiliation, disrespect, injury.

Pari-bhūya, ind. having treated with contempt, having disgraced or despised; shaming, outvying; experiencing disgrace.

परिभूष् *pari-bhūsh,* cl. 1. 10. P. *-bhūshati, -bhūshayati,* &c., to wait upon, serve, attend; to honour, revere; to take care of; to follow, observe; to furnish, equip, fit out, prepare; to decorate; to be beautiful, to shine.

Pari-bhūshaṇa, as, m., scil. *sandhi,* peace obtained by the cession of the whole revenue of a land.
Pari-bhūshita, as, ā, am, decorated, adorned.

परिभृ *pari-bhṛi,* cl. 3. P. *-bibharti, -bhartum,* Ved. to pass beyond (Sāy. = *ati-kram*); to extend beyond, extend.

परिभेदक *pari-bhedaka, as, ā, am,* breaking through.

परिभ्रंश् *pari-bhraṅś,* cl. 4. P. A. *-bhraśyati, -te, -bhraṅśitum;* cl. 1. A. *-bhraṅśate, -bhraṅśitum,* to fall off, drop off; to fall, be cast down (metaphorically); to run away, escape; to vanish, disappear; to lose, be deprived of (with abl.); to neglect, omit.
Pari-bhraṅśa, as, m. falling from; escape, escaping.
Pari-bhraṅśana, am, n. falling from; losing, loss.
Pari-bhrashṭa, as, ā, am, fallen off, dropped off; fallen, cast down, degraded; escaped; vanished; deprived of, void or devoid of (with abl. or sometimes inst.); lost; neglecting, omitting. — *Paribhrashṭa-sukha, as, ā, am,* fallen from happiness.

परिभ्रज्ज् *pari-bhrajj,* cl. 6. P. *-bhṛijjati, -bhrashṭum, -bharshṭum,* to fry, roast: Caus. *-bharjayati, -yitum,* to fry, roast, parch.
Pari-bhṛishṭa, as, ā, am, fried, roasted, parched.

परिभ्रम् *pari-bhram,* cl. 1. 4. P. (ep. also A.) *-bhramati (-te), bhramyati* or *bhrāmyati, -bhramitum,* to walk round about, wander round, rove or roam about, ramble about, saunter; to fly round about, hover or flutter round; to wander through, rove or roam through, ramble through; to whirl round, wheel or circle round, revolve; to encircle, describe a circle round.
Pari-bhrama, as, ā, am, flying round or about [cf. *khe-p°*]; *(as),* m. wandering, going about; error; circumlocution, rambling discourse.
Pari-bhramaṇa, am, n. turning round, revolving (as of wheels); circumference.
Pari-bhramat, an, antī, at, roaming or wandering about, roving about; turning or whirling round, revolving; describing circles.
Pari-bhramya, ind. having roamed about, having gone to and fro.
Pari-bhrāmyat, an, antī, at, roaming about; flying or fluttering about.

परिभ्राज् *pari-bhrāj,* cl. 1. P. A. *-bhrājati, -te, -bhrājitum,* to shed brilliance all around, become resplendent.

परिमण्डल *pari-maṇḍala, as, ā, am,* round, circular, globular, spherical; *(as),* m., scil. *maśaka,* a venomous species of gnat; *(am),* n. a circle, circumference; a ball, globe, sphere, orb; orbit. — *Parimaṇḍala-tā,* f. or *parimaṇḍala-tva, am,* n. roundness, rotundity, circularity.
Pari-maṇḍalita, as, ā, am, rounded, made round or circular.

परिमण्डित *pari-maṇḍita, as, ā, am,* adorned or decorated all round.

परिमन् *pari-man,* cl. 8. A. *-manute, -manitum,* Ved. to despise, contemn, slight, neglect.

परिमन्त्र् *pari-mantr,* cl. 10. P. *-mantrayati, -yitum,* to charm or consecrate with sacred texts.
Pari-mantrita, as, ā, am, charmed, consecrated, enchanted.

परिमन्थर *pari-manthara, as, ā, am,* extremely slow or tardy.

परिमन्द *pari-manda, as, ā, am,* very dull or faint; very slow; very tired; very little; *(am),* ind. very little, a little, not much. — *Parimanda-tā,* f. fatigue, tiredness, tedium, ennui.

परिमन्यु *pari-manyu, us, us, u,* Ved. wrathful, angry, jealous (Sāy. = *kopa-parivṛita*).

परिमर *pari-mara, as, ā, am,* Ved. (fr. rt. *mṛi* with *pari*), decaying, becoming decrepit; *Brahmaṇaḥ pari-maraḥ,* 'destruction round the Brahman, i. e. the magician' (or, according to Colebrooke, 'around air'), a magical rite for the destruction of adversaries.

परिमर्द *pari-marda, pari-mardana.* See p. 547, col. 1.

परिमल *pari-mala, as,* m. (*mala* perhaps fr. a lost rt. *mal,* to rub), fragrance, perfume, (especially arising from the trituration of fragrant substances); the pounding or trituration of perfumes; a fragrant substance; a fragrant scent diffused during coitus; copulation; a meeting of learned men; soil, stain, dirt; N. of a poet; of a work; of a commentary by Amara-ćandra on the Kāvya-kalpa-latā-vṛitti; of a commentary by Apyāya-dīkshita on the Vedānta-kalpa-taru, (the complete title of which is Vedānta-kalpa-taru-parimala.) — *Parimala-bhṛit, t, t, t,* laden with perfumes, impregnated with sweet odours.
Pari-malita, as, ā, am, perfumed; soiled, despoiled of freshness or beauty.

परिमा *pari-mā* (see rt. 3. *mā*), cl. 2. P., 3. 4. A. *-māti, -mimīte, -māyate, -mātum,* to measure round or about; to mete out; to fulfil (a period or course); to measure, estimate, determine.
Pari-māṇa, am, n. measuring, measure, duration, length of time; compass, weight, number, value (e. g. *pratigraha-parimāṇa,* the value of a gift received). — *Parimāṇa-tas,* ind. by measure; in weight. — *Parimāṇa-vat, ān, atī, at,* capable of being measured, measurable.
Parimāṇaka, am, n. compass, weight, quantity, duration.
Pari-māṇin, ī, inī, i, having measure, measured.
Pari-māṇiya or *pari-mātavya, as, ā, am,* measurable, fit to be measured; requiring to be ascertained as to quantity.
Pari-mita, as, ā, am, measured, meted; circumscribed, limited, adjusted; moderate, sparing; joined; regulated. — *Parimita-katha, as, ā, am,* of measured discourse, seldom speaking, saying little. — *Parimita-tva, am,* n. limitedness, moderation, limited condition. — *Parimita-bhuj, k, k, k,* eating sparingly, abstemious. — *Parimita-bhojana, am,* n. moderation in eating, abstemiousness. — *Parimitābharaṇa* (°*ta-ābh*°), *as, ā, am,* moderately adorned. — *Parimitāyus* (°*ta-āy*°), *us, us, u,* short-lived. — *Parimitāhāra* (°*ta-āh*°), *as, ā, am,* eating little food, eating moderately. — *Parimiteććha-tā* (°*ta-ić*°), f. moderation in desire.
Pari-miti, is, f. measure, quantity, limitation.
Pari-meya, as, ā, am, measurable, to be measured; calculable, capable of being counted, few; finite. — *Parimeya-tā,* f. measurableness, calculableness.

परिमाथिन् *pari-māthin, ī, inī, i* (rt. *math* or *manth* with *pari*), torturing.

परिमाद् *pari-mād, t,* f. or *pari-māda, as,* m. (fr. rt. *mad* with *pari*), Ved., N. of sixteen Sāmans which belong to the Mahā-vrata-stotra.

परिमार्ग् *pari-mārg,* cl. 1. 10. P. *-mārgati, -mārgitum, -mārgayati, -yitum,* to seek or search about, search for, search through, seek, pursue, trace, track, hunt about, investigate, grasp after, seek to gain, ask for, beg for.
1. *pari-mārga, as,* m. (for 2. see under *pari-mṛij*), searching or seeking about; searching for.
Pari-mārgaṇa, am, n. tracing, tracking, searching, seeking or looking for, seeking out.
Pari-mārgitavya, as, ā, am, to be sought after.
Pari-mārgin, ī, iṇī, i, tracing, tracking, seeking for, going after, pursuing, hunting.

परिमि *pari-mi* (see rt. 1. *mi*), cl. 5. P. A. *-minoti, -nute,* &c., Ved. to set or place round, lay round.
Pari-mit, t, f., Ved. the beam of a roof, a connecting beam or rafter (?).

परिमिलन *pari-milana, am,* n. touch, contact, combination.
Pari-milita, as, ā, am, mixed or combined with, pervaded by (with inst.); filled, penetrated.

परिमिह् *pari-mih,* cl. 1. P. *-mehati, -meḍhum,* Ved. to make water against.
Pari-mīḍha, as, ā, am, Ved. sprinkled with urine.
Pari-meha, as, m., Ved. a magical rite in which urine is sprinkled about.

परिमुखम् *pari-mukham,* ind. round or about the face, round, about (any person, &c.; Pāṇ. IV. 4, 29).

परिमुच् *pari-muć,* cl. 6. P. A. *-muñćati, -te, -moktum,* to unloose, unfasten, set free, liberate; to let go, give up, get rid of; to discharge, emit: Pass. *-mućyate,* to loosen or free one's self; to let go, get rid of; to neglect (?).
Pari-mukta, as, ā, am, released, liberated. — *Parimukta-bandhana, as, ā, am,* released from bonds, unbound, unfettered.
Pari-mućya, ind. having released or liberated.

परिमुष् *pari-mush,* cl. 9. 6. P. *-mushṇāti, -mushati, -moshitum,* to steal anything, rob, plunder (with acc.).
Pari-mosha, as, m. stealing, theft, robbing.
Pari-moshaka, as, ā, am, stealing.
Pari-moshin, ī, iṇī, i, stealing; a thief, robber.

परिमुह् *pari-muh,* cl. 4. P. A. *-muhyati, -te, -mohitum, -moḍhum, -mogdhum,* to be bewildered or perplexed, to go astray, fail: Caus. A. *-mohayate* (Pāṇ. I. 3, 89); P. (ep.) *-mohayati, -yitum,* to bewilder, perplex; to fascinate.
Pari-mugdha, as, ā, am, lovely yet simple, fascinating yet foolish. — *Parimugdha-tā,* f. gracefulness or loveliness combined with simplicity.
Pari-mūḍha, as, ā, am, disturbed, perturbed, perplexed, bewildered, troubled. — *Parimūḍha-tā,* f. bewilderment, perplexity, trouble, error.
Pari-mohana, am, n. the act of bewildering, fascination, infatuation, beguiling.
Pari-mohita, as, ā, am, bewildered, deprived of consciousness or recollection.
Pari-mohin, ī, inī, i, perplexing, fascinating, bewitching; perplexed.

परिमूर्णी *pari-mūrṇī,* f. (perhaps fr. rt. *mṛī* with *pari*), Ved. worn out, decrepit (as a cow, according to the commentator = *vṛiddhā*).

परिमृ *pari-mṛi,* cl. 6. A. *-mriyate* (Perf. P. *-mamāra*), *-martum,* Ved. to die (in numbers) round (any one).

परिमृग् *pari-mṛig,* cl. 10. A. *-mṛigayate, -yitum,* to seek, search for, hunt about for.
Pari-mṛigyamāṇa, as, ā, am, being sought for.

परिमृज् 1. *pari-mṛij,* cl. 2. P. *-mārshṭi, -mārjitum, -mārshṭum,* to wipe all round, wipe away, wash, wash away, rinse (the mouth), clean, cleanse, purify; to rub, polish; to wipe off, remove by rubbing, efface, remove; to touch lightly, touch, stroke: Intens. *-marmṛijyate,* Ved. to sweep over; (Sāy. = *tejasā ćhad,* to cover with radiance.)
2. *pari-mārga, as,* m. (for 1. see under *pari-mārg,* col. 2), wiping off, cleaning; friction, touch.
Pari-mārgya, as, ā, am, to be cleaned or cleansed, to be rubbed.
Pari-mārja, as, ā, am, wiping off, cleaning, washing; stroking, rubbing.
Pari-mārjana, am, n. wiping off, cleaning; a dish of honey and oil.
2. *pari-mṛij, k, k, k,* or *pari-mṛija, as, ā, am,* wiping or washing off, cleaning.
1. *pari-mṛijya, as, ā, am,* to be wiped, to be cleansed; to be touched.
2. *pari-mṛijya,* ind. having wiped away, having washed the mouth; having polished; having stroked.
1. *pari-mṛishṭa, as, ā, am,* wiped away, washed,

cleaned, purified; rubbed, stroked. — *Parimṛishṭa-pariććhada, as, ā, am,* trim, neat, spruce.

परिमृद् *pari-mṛid,* cl. 9. P. *-mṛidnāti, -marditum,* to tread or trample down, crush, rub, grind; to wear down, wear out; to rub off, wipe away (as tears); to rub, stroke; cl. 1. P. *-mardati, -marditum,* to excel, surpass.

Pari-marda, as, m. crushing, grinding, wearing out; using up, consuming; destroying, destruction.

Pari-mardana, am, n. rubbing, grinding; trampling, destroying; embracing, pressing.

Pari-mṛidita, as, ā, am, trodden or trampled down; crushed, rubbed, ground; embraced, clasped.

Pari-mṛidnat, an, atī, at, trampling down, crushing; rubbing; wiping away.

परिमृश् *pari-mṛiś,* cl. 6. P. *-mṛiśati, -marshṭum, -mrashṭum,* to touch, handle, stroke, caress; to grasp, seize; to examine, consider, reflect, ponder; to investigate, inquire into, question; to observe, discover: Intens. *-marmarshṭi,* Ved. to encompass, clasp, embrace.

Pari-marśa, as, m. friction; contact; consideration, reflection, examination.

Pari-mṛiśya, ind. having touched or handled; having grasped; having examined or pondered; having found or observed.

Pari-mṛiśyamāna, as, ā, am, being touched; being fanned (by the wind).

2. *pari-mṛishṭa, as, ā, am,* rubbed, touched; embraced, clasped; invested; spread; pervaded.

परिमृष् *pari-mṛish,* cl. 4. P. *-mṛishyati, -marshitum,* to be angry or incensed against (with dat.); to envy.

Pari-marsha, as, m. envy, dislike, anger.

Pari-mṛishyat, an, antī, at, angry, incensed, envying; (according to a Scholiast = *asūyat.*)

परिमोक्ष् *pari-moksh,* cl. 10. P. *-mokshayati, -yitum,* to set free, liberate, let go, discharge.

Pari-moksha, as, m. setting free, liberating; liberation, deliverance; escape; emptying, evacuation.

Pari-mokshaṇa, am, n. liberation, deliverance from (with gen.); untying.

Pari-mokshya, ind. having let go or released.

परिमोटन *pari-moṭana, am,* n. (fr. rt. *muṭ* with *pari*), Ved. snapping, cracking; (according to a Scholiast = *ćaṭāćaṭā-śabda.*)

परिम्लै *pari-mlai,* cl. 1. P. A. *-mlāyati, -te, -mlātum,* to fade or wither away; to wane; to disappear; to faint.

Pari-mlāna, as, ā, am, faded, withered, fainted, fainting; languid; waned; diminished, impaired; soiled, stained; (*am*), n. change of countenance by fear or grief; soil, stain.

Pari-mlāyin, ī, inī, i, fading away; stained, spotted; (*ī*), m., scil. *linga-nāśa,* a kind of disease of the lens or pupil of the eye. — *Parimlāyi-tva, am,* n. fading away, sinking.

परियज्ञ *pari-yajña, as,* m., Ved. a secondary or accompanying rite, one which precedes or follows another in any ritual; (*as, ā, am*), Ved. constituting an accompanying or secondary rite.

परियत्त *pari-yatta, as, ā, am* (fr. rt. *yat* with *pari*), Ved. surrounded.

परियम् *pari-yam,* cl. 1. P. *-yaćchati, -yantum,* to restrain: Caus. *-yamayati, -yitum,* to serve.

परिया *pari-yā,* Caus. P. *-yāpayati, -yitum,* to go round, wait upon (?), circumambulate (as a mark of respect); to protect (Ved.).

परियोग्य *pari-yogya, ās,* m. pl., N. of a school.

परिरक्ष् *pari-raksh,* cl. 1. P. *-rakshati, -rakshitum,* to rescue, save, preserve; to guard well or completely, protect; to govern, restrain; to keep, conceal, keep secret.

Pari-rakshaka, as, ikā, am, guarding, protecting; a guardian, protector, keeper.

Pari-rakshaṇa, as, ī, am, guarding, protecting, a protector; (*am*), n. the act of guarding, defending, preserving, preservation, keeping, protecting, protection, deliverance; saving, rescuing; maintaining; care, caution.

Pari-rakshaṇīya, as, ā, am, to be completely protected or preserved.

Pari-rakshā, f. protection, preservation, keeping, guarding.

Pari-rakshita, as, ā, am, well guarded, well preserved, well kept.

Pari-rakshitavya, as, ā, am, to be protected or guarded, to be kept secret.

Pari-rakshitin, ī, inī, i, keeping, guarding, protecting (with loc., Gaṇa to Pāṇ. V. 2, 88).

Pari-rakshitṛi, tā, trī, tṛi, a protector, guardian; keeping; protecting, &c.

Pari-rakshin, ī, iṇī, i, guarding, protecting, defending; a defender.

Pari-rakshya, as, ā, am, to be guarded or preserved, to be protected, to be kept secret.

Pari-rakshyamāṇa, as, ā, am, being completely defended.

परिरटन *pari-raṭana, am,* n. (fr. rt. *raṭ* with *pari*), crying, crying aloud.

Pari-rāṭin, ī, inī, i, crying, crying aloud, screaming.

परिरथ्य *pari-rathya, am,* n., Ved. or *pari-rathyā,* f. a particular part of a chariot.

परिरन्धित *pari-randhita, as, ā, am,* injured, destroyed.

परिरभ् *pari-rabh,* cl. 1. A. *-rabhate, -rabdhum,* to embrace, clasp: Desid. A. *-ripsate,* to wish or desire to embrace.

Pari-rabdha, as, ā, am, embraced, clasped, encircled.

Pari-rabhamāṇa, as, ā, am, embracing.

Pari-rabhyamāṇa, as, ā, am, being embraced.

Pari-rambha, as, m. embracing, an embrace.

Pari-rambhaṇa, am, n. embracing, clasping.

Pari-rambhin, ī, iṇī, i (at the end of a comp.), clasped, girded, girt.

Pari-ripsamāna, as, ā, am, wishing or trying to embrace.

परिरम् *pari-ram,* cl. 1. P. *-ramati, -rantum,* to be delighted.

परिराज् *pari-rāj,* cl. 1. P. A. *-rājati, -te, -rājitum,* to shine on all sides, be very resplendent.

परिराटिन् *pari-rāṭin.* See *pari-raṭana.*

परिराप् *pari-rāp, p, p, p* (fr. rt. *rap* with *pari*), Ved. crying or talking all round, a reviler (Sāy. = *pari-vadat, nindaka*); (*p*), m. epithet of a demon.

Pari-rāpin, ī, iṇī, i, Ved. whispering to, talking over, persuading.

परिरोध *pari-rodha, as,* m. (fr. rt. *rudh* with *pari*), obstructing, keeping back, resistance.

परिल *parila, as,* m., N. of a man; [cf. *pārila.*]

परिलघु *pari-laghu, us, us, u,* very light, easy to digest.

परिलङ्घ् *pari-laṅgh,* cl. 10. P. *-laṅghayati, -yitum,* to overleap, transgress, overstep.

Pari-laṅghana, am, n. jumping or leaping to and fro, jumping over.

परिलिह् *pari-lih,* cl. 2. P. A. *-leḍhi, -līḍhe, -leḍhum,* to lick all round, lick over, lick: Intens. *-lelihyate, -leleḍhi,* to lick all round, lick repeatedly.

Pari-līḍha, as, ā, am, licked all round, licked over.

Pari-lehin, ī, m. a particular disease of the ear.

परिलुप् *pari-lup,* cl. 6. P. A. *-lumpati, -te, -loptum,* to interrupt, break through, disturb; to suspend, diminish; to dispel.

Pari-lupta, as, ā, am, interrupted, disturbed, diminished, injured, lost. — *Parilupta-sañjña, as, ā, am,* one whose consciousness is suspended, unconscious, senseless.

Pari-lupyamāna, as, ā, am, being interrupted.

Pari-lopa, as, m. injury; neglect, omission.

परिलुभ् *pari-lubh,* Caus. A. *-lobhayate, -yitum,* to entice, allure.

परिलेख *pari-lekha, as,* m. (fr. rt. *likh* with *pari*), outline, delineation, sketch, figure, picture. — *Parilekhādhikāra* (°*kha-adh*°), *as,* m. 'section on delineation,' N. of the sixth chapter of the Sūrya-siddhānta.

Pari-lekhana, am, n., Ved. drawing lines round about.

परिवक्रा *pari-vakrā,* f., Ved. a circular pit; (according to a Scholiast) N. of a town.

परिवञ्च् *pari-vañć,* Caus. P. *-vañćayati, -yitum,* to deceive.

Pari-vañćita, as, ā, am, deceived.

परिवत्सक *pari-vatsaka, ās,* m. pl. (fr. *vatsa* with *pari*), N. of the descendants of Vatsa.

परिवत्सर *pari-vatsara, as,* m. a full year, a year; the second of a cycle of five years.

Pari-vatsarīṇa or *pari-vatsarīya, as, ā, am,* Ved. relating to a full year; lasting a whole year.

परिवद् *pari-vad,* cl. 1. P. A. *-vadati, -te, -vaditum,* to speak ill of, revile, calumniate, slander, accuse.

Pari-vadat, an, antī, at, speaking ill of, reviling, slandering.

Pari-vadana, am, n. reviling, accusing; crying out, clamouring, screaming.

Pari-vāda, as, m. abuse, reproach, reproof, censure, detraction; charge, accusation; an instrument with which the Indian lute is played.

Pari-vādaka, as, m. a complainant, accuser, plaintiff, calumniator; one who plays on the lute.

Pari-vādin, ī, inī, i, speaking ill of, reviling, abusing, slandering, blaming; an accuser; calling out, crying, screaming; censured, abused; (*ī*), m. an accuser, plaintiff, reprover; (*inī*), f. a Vīṇā or lute of seven strings.

परिवर्त *pari-varta.* See p. 548, col. 3.

परिवर्धित 1. *pari-vardhita, as, ā, am* (fr. rt. *vardh,* to cut, with *pari;* for 2. see under *pari-vṛidh,* p. 548, col. 3), cut, excavated.

परिवर्मन् *pari-varman, ā, ā, a,* wearing a coat of mail, clad in mail, armed.

परिवर्ह *pari-varha, pari-varhaṇa.* See *pari-barha, pari-barhaṇa,* p. 545, col. 1.

परिवस् *pari-vas* (see rt. 4. *vas*), cl. 10. P. *-vāsayati, -yitum,* Ved. to split, cut through.

Pari-vāsana, am, n., Ved. a shred, chip.

परिवसथ *pari-vasatha, as,* m. (fr. rt. 6. *vas* with *pari*), a village.

Pari-vāsa, as, m. abode, residence, stay, sojourn; [cf. *kāla-p*°.]

Pari-vāsita, as, ā, am, respectfully attentive to superiors (?).

परिवह् *pari-vah,* cl. 1. P. A. *-vahati, -te, -voḍhum,* to carry round, carry about.

Pari-vaha, as, m., N. of one of the seven winds; one of the seven tongues of fire.

Pari-vāha, as, m. the overflowing of a tank, an inundation, overflow natural or artificial; a water-course or drain to carry off excess of water; [cf. *parī-vāha.*] — *Parivāha-vat, ān,* m. 'having a channel,' a tank, pool.

Pari-vāhita, as, ā, am, drained.

Pari-vāhin, ī, inī, i, overflowing, swimming with.

परिवाप *pari-vāpa, as*, m. (fr. rt. *vap* with *pari*), fried grains of rice; coagulated or thick sour milk (= *dadhi*, Ved.); furniture; a train, retinue; sowing; a reservoir, pool, pond, piece of water; shaving, shearing.

Pari-vāpana, am, n. shaving, shearing.

Pari-vāpita, as, ā, am, shaven, shorn.

Pari-vāpya or *parī-vāpya, as, ā, am*, Ved. having or requiring or deserving fried grains of rice or thickened milk.

परिवार *pari-vāra, pari-vāraṇa*. See under *pari-vṛi*, col. 2.

परिवासस् *pari-vāsas, as*, n., Ved. (probably) an upper garment; *Angirasām abhivāsaḥ-parivāsasī*, N. of two Sāmans.

परिविंशत् *pari-vinśat, t*, f. quite twenty, full twenty, twenty at least.

परिविक्रयिन् *pari-vikrayin, ī, inī, i* (fr. rt. 1. *krī* with *pari-vi*), selling or trading in (with gen.).

परिविक्षत *pari-vikshata, as, ā, am* (fr. rt. *kshan* with *pari-vi*), sorely wounded, much hurt.

परिविक्षोभ *pari-vikshobha, as*, m. (fr. rt. 1. *kshubh* with *pari-vi*), shaking violently, destroying.

परिविचर् *pari-vi-ćar*, cl. 1. P. *-ćarati, -ćaritum*, Ved. to stream forth in all directions.

परिविद् *pari-vid*, cl. 2. P. *-vetti, -veda, -veditum*, Ved. to know thoroughly, understand fully; cl. 6. P. A. *-vindati, -te, -veditum, -vettum*, to marry before an elder brother.

Pari-vinna or *pari-vitta* or *pari-vitti, is*, m. an unmarried elder brother whose younger brother is married. — *Parivitti-tā*, f. the marrying of a younger brother before the elder.

Pari-vindaka, as, m. a younger brother married before the elder.

Pari-vindat, an, m. an unmarried elder brother.

Pari-vividāna, as, m., Ved. a married man whose elder brother is still unmarried.

Pari-vettṛi, tā, m. or *pari-vedaka, as*, m. a younger brother married before the elder.

Pari-veda, as, m. complete or accurate knowledge.

1. *pari-vedana, am*, n. (for 2. see p. 549, col. 1), complete or accurate knowledge; discussion; anguish, pain, misery; the marrying of a younger brother before the elder; marriage; laying the fire on the sacrificial fire-place; gain, acquisition; (*ā*), f. shrewdness, wit; foresight, prudence.

Pari-vedanīyā or *pari-vedinī*, f. the wife of a younger brother who has married before the elder.

Pari-vedin, ī, inī, i, knowing, shrewd.

परिविद्ध *pari-viddha, as*, m. (perhaps fr. *pari-vyadh*), an epithet of Kuvera; [cf. *para-viddha*.]

परिविश् *pari-viś* (often confounded with *pari-vish* below), Caus. *-veśayati, -yitum*, to provide; to offer, present, (probably for *pari-vish*, q. v.)

Pari-veśas, ās, m., Ved. a neighbour.

परिविश्वस् *pari-vi-śvas*, cl. 2. P. *-śvasiti, -śvasitum*, to confide completely, feel secure, be fearless: Caus. *-śvāsayati, -yitum*, to comfort, console.

Pari-śvasta, as, ā, am, feeling secure, confident.

परिविष् *pari-vish*, Caus. P. *-veshayati, -yitum*, to surround; to present, offer, offer food; to wait on; (sometimes erroneously written *pari-viś*, q. v.)

Pari-vishṭa, as, ā, am, surrounded, enclosed; offered, presented.

Pari-vishṭi, is, f., Ved. service, attendance.

Pari-vesha, as, m. (sometimes wrongly spelt *pari-veśa*), preparation (of food); attendance, waiting at meals, distributing food, serving up meals; a circle, circlet, wreath, crown; the circumference of a circle; the disk of the sun or moon; a halo round the sun or moon; anything surrounding or protecting (e. g. *kṛitāngarakshā-p°*, surrounded by a body-guard); putting on, clothing, dressing. — *Parivesha-vat, ān, atī, at*, having a halo, surrounded by a halo.

Pari-veshaka, as, m. (sometimes wrongly *pari-veśaka*), an attendant, waiter, one who serves up meals.

Pari-veshaṇa, am, n. attendance, waiting, serving up meals, distributing food; surrounding, enclosing; circumference; a halo round the sun or moon.

Pari-veshin, ī, iṇī, i, surrounded by a halo.

Pari-veshṭavya or *pari-veshya, as, ā, am*, to be served up; to be offered or presented.

Pari-veshṭṛi, ṭā, ṭrī, ṭṛi, a waiter; one who serves up meals.

परिविष्णु *pari-vishṇu*, ind. = *sarvato Vishṇuḥ*.

परिविहार *pari-vihāra, as*, m. walking or roaming about, walking for pleasure.

परिविह्वल *pari-vihvala, as, ā, am*, extremely agitated, bewildered, beside one's self. — *Parivihvala-tā*, f. bewilderment.

परिवी *pari-vī, pari-vīta*. See under *pari-vye*, p. 549, col. 1.

परिवृ *pari-vṛi*, cl. 5. 9. 1. P. A. *-vṛiṇoti, -ṇute, -vṛiṇāti, -ṇīte, -varati, -te, -varitum, -varītum*, to surround, conceal: Caus. *-vārayati, -yitum*, to surround, cover, clothe.

Pari-vāra, as, m. (also spelt *parī-vāra*), a cover, covering; surroundings, train, suite, retinue, attendants, dependants, subjects, followers; a sheath, scabbard. — *Parivāra-tā*, f. subjection, dependance. — *Parivāra-vat, ān, atī, at*, having a great retinue. — *Parivāra-śobhin, ī, inī, i*, rendered illustrious by a retinue.

Pari-vāraṇa, am, n. a cover, covering, envelope; a train, retinue; keeping or warding off.

Pari-vārita, as, ā, am, encompassed, surrounded, encircled, enclosed, begirt.

Pari-vārya, ind. having surrounded or encompassed.

Pari-vṛita, as, ā, am, encompassed, surrounded, encircled, attended, invested; concealed; overspread, pervaded; entirely gained or received; known; (*am*), n., Ved. a covered place or shed enclosed with walls used as a place of sacrifice.

Pari-vṛiti, is, f. surrounding, standing round.

परिवृंह् *pari-vṛinh* or *pari-vṛih*, also written *pari-bṛinh* or *pari-bṛih*, q. v., p. 545, col. 1.

Pari-vṛinhaṇa. See *pari-bṛinhaṇa*, p. 545.

Pari-vṛinhita or *pari-vṛihita*. See *pari-bṛinhita*, p. 545, col. 1.

Pari-vṛiḍha, as, m. a master, owner, &c. See *pari-bṛiḍha*, p. 545, col. 2.

Pari-vraḍhiman, ā, m. mastery, superiority.

परिवृज् 1. *pari-vṛij*, cl. 7. 1. P. *-vṛiṇakti, -varjati, -varjitum*, to leave, forsake, abandon, shun, avoid, quit, cease, leave off: Caus. *-varjayati, -yitum*, to avoid, shun.

Pari-varga, as, m., Ved. shunning, avoiding, removing, discomfiting; *a-parivargam*, ind. without omission, without intermission, completely.

Pari-vargya, as, ā, am, Ved. to be avoided.

Pari-varjaka, as, ā, am, shunning, avoiding; giving up, resigning, abstaining from.

Pari-varjana, am, n. avoiding, shunning, giving up, resigning, quitting; abstaining from; killing, slaughter.

Pari-varjanīya, as, ā, am, avoidable, to be avoided.

Pari-varjita, as, ā, am, abandoned, shunned; deprived or devoid of.

Pari-vṛikta, as, ā, am, Ved. avoided, disliked, despised; (*ā* and *ī*), f. 'the disliked or despised one,' epithet of a wife lightly esteemed in comparison with the favourite wife (*mahishī, vāvātā*).

2. *pari-vṛij, k*, f., Ved. avoiding, removing, (Sāy. = *paritaḥ sva-sthāna-tyāga*); purification, expiation.

परिवृत् *pari-vṛit*, cl. 1. A. (also P. in Fut., Cond., and Aor.), to turn round, roll or wheel round, revolve; to be whirled; to hasten to and fro, roam or wander about; to change (e. g. *kshaṇena tat parivartate 'nyathā*, that changes or turns out to be different in a moment); to interchange; to become, to be: Caus. *-vartayati, -yitum*, to exchange.

Pari-varta, as, m. revolving, revolution (of a planet &c.); a period or lapse or expiration of time, especially of a Yuga (e. g. *lokānām parivarte*, at the end of the world); a year; going or turning back, flight, retreat, desertion; transmigration, repeated birth; change, exchange, barter (e. g. *anna-parivarta*, change of diet; *samudra-parivarta*, exchange of sealed goods); requital, return; a chapter, section, book, canto; an abode, spot, place; N. of one of the eight sons of Duḥ-saha (son of Mṛityu); N. of a king of the tortoises or the tortoise incarnation.

Pari-vartaka, as, ā, am, turning round, turning back; causing to turn round or flow back; causing to revolve; bringing to a close; requiting, exchanging; leaving off a thing begun for some other object; (*as*), m., N. of a son of Duḥ-saha.

Pari-vartana, as, ī, am, causing to turn round; (*ī*), f. epithet of a particular magical art; (*am*), n. cutting, clipping (the hair, Ved.); (according to a Scholiast) = *preraṇa* (Ved.); turning round, going round, turning back, returning; moving to and fro; whirling round, revolving; revolution, end of a period of time; inverting, taking or putting anything in a wrong direction; change, exchange, barter; requital, return.

Pari-vartanīya, as, ā, am, to be exchanged, capable of being exchanged.

Pari-vartikā, f. contraction of the prepuce, phimosis.

Pari-vartita, as, ā, am, turned round, revolved; returned, retreated; taken or put on in a wrong direction; exchanged.

Pari-vartin, ī, inī, i, moving round, going round, revolving; circling, going in a circle, being constantly renewed, ever recurring; changing, passing into; being or remaining or staying in a place or near a person (e. g. *Sugrīva-parivartin*, being about, i. e. in attendance on Su-grīva); flying, retreating; exchanging, requiting, recompensing; (*inī*), f., scil. *vishṭuti*, a hymn arranged according to the recurring form *abc, abc, abc*.

Pari-vartman, ā, ā, a, Ved. going or extending round.

Pari-vṛitta, as, ā, am, revolved, gone round; turned back, retreated, retired, returned; exchanged, bartered; finished, ended; (*am*), n. an embrace. — *Parivṛittārdha-mukha* (°*ta-ar*°), *as, ī, am*, having the face half turned round.

Pari-vṛitti, is, f. revolution, return; exchange, barter; end, termination; surrounding, encompassing; staying in a place, dwelling; contraction of the prepuce, phimosis; (*tyā*), ind. alternately; (sometimes *pari-vṛitti* is a wrong reading for *pari-vitti*, q. v.)

Pari-vṛitya, ind. having turned round, having revolved; having retreated or retired.

परिवृध् *pari-vṛidh* [cf. *pari-vṛinh*], cl. 1. A. (also P. in Fut., Cond., and Aor.) *-vardhate, -vardhitum*, to grow, grow up, increase: Caus. *-vardhayati, -yitum*, to increase, augment; to bring up, rear.

Pari-vardhana, am, n. increasing, augmenting, enlarging, multiplying; growing; rearing, breeding (as of cattle).

2. *pari-vardhita, as, ā, am*, increased, augmented.

Pari-vṛiddha, as, ā, am, grown, increased. — *Parivṛiddha-tā,* f. increase, extension.

Pari-vṛiddhi, is, f. growth, increase.

परिवृस्ति *pari-vṛisti, is,* m. a wrong reading for *pari-vitti,* q. v.

परिवेदन 2. *pari-vedana, am,* n. (probably a various reading for *pari-devana*), complaining, lamentation. (For 1. see p. 548, col. 1.)

Pari-vedita, as, ā, am (probably for *pari-devita*), lamented; *(am),* n. lamentation.

परिवेष *pari-vesha.* See p. 548, col. 2.

परिवेष्ट् *pari-vesht,* cl. 1. A. *-veshṭate, -veshṭitum,* to surround, encompass, encircle; to wrap up, cover, clothe: Caus. *-veshṭayati, -yitum,* to surround; to wrap up, clothe; to embrace.

Pari-veshṭana, am, n. surrounding, encompassing; circumference; a cover, covering; a ligature, bandage.

Pari-veshṭita, as, ā, am, surrounded, encompassed, enclosed; beset, beleaguered; bound round, covered, veiled, swathed.

Pari-veshṭitṛi, tā, trī, tṛi, Ved. one who surrounds or encompasses.

परिव्यक्त *pari-vyakta, as, ā, am,* very clear or distinct; *(am),* ind. very clearly or distinctly.

परिव्यध् *pari-vyadh,* cl. 4. P. *-vidhyati, -vyaddhum,* to hit, strike, smite, wound.

Pari-vyādha, as, m. a species of reed, Calamus Fasciculatus; a species of tree, Pterospermum Acerifolium; N. of an ancient sage.

परिव्यय *pari-vyaya, as,* m. (fr. rt. 5. *i* with *pari-vi*), expense, cost; condiment, spices.

परिव्ये *pari-vye,* cl. 1. P. A. *-vyayati, -te, -vyātum,* to surround, invest, wrap round, veil, cover, put on, wrap one's self up.

Pari-vī, īs, īs, i, Ved. wound round.

Pari-vīta, as, ā, am, surrounded, encompassed, invested; overspread, pervaded; *(am),* n. the bow of Brahmā.

Pari-vīya, ind. wrapping round.

Pari-vyayaṇa, am, n., Ved. winding round, covering.

Pari-vyayaṇīya, as, ā, am, Ved. relating to wrapping round or binding on (as a verse).

परिव्रज् *pari-vraj,* cl. 1. P. *-vrajati, -vrajitum,* to go or wander about, wander about as a mendicant, lead the life of a religious mendicant.

Pari-vrajya, as, ā, am, to be roamed about or walked for pleasure; *(ā),* f. strolling, wandering about from place to place; religious wandering, leading the life of a religious mendicant; ascetic devotion, religious austerity, abandonment of the world.

Pari-vrāj, ṭ, or *pari-vrāja, as,* m. a vagrant, wandering man, ascetic of the fourth and last religious order, a mendicant devotee.

Pari-vrājaka, as, ikā, m. f. a wandering religious mendicant.

Pari-vrāji, is, f. a species of plant, Sphæranthus Mollis; [cf. *tapo-dhanā, bhikshu.*]

Pari-vrājya, am, n. religious mendicancy.

परिव्रढिमन् *pari-vraḍhiman.* See under *pari-vṛiṅh,* p. 548, col. 2.

परिशङ्क् *pari-śaṅk,* cl. 1. A. *-śaṅkate, -śaṅkitum,* to suspect of (with inst.); to distrust.

Pari-śaṅkanīya, as, ā, am, to be doubted or distrusted; to be feared or apprehended; *pariśaṅkanīyam,* (used impersonally) distrust must be felt.

Pari-śaṅkin, ī, inī, i, fearing, apprehending, having apprehensions.

परिशप् *pari-śap,* cl. 1. 4. P. A. *-śapati, -te, -śapyati, -te, -śaptum,* to curse, execrate.

Pari-śāpa, as, m. cursing, reviling, anathema.

परिशम् *pari-śam,* Caus. P. *-śamayati, -yitum,* to allay, quench; to destroy.

Pari-śamita, as, ā, am, allayed, quenched; destroyed.

परिशाश्वत *pari-śāśvata, as, ī, am,* remaining or continuing for ever, perpetually the same.

परिशिष् *pari-śish,* Caus. P. *-śeshayati, -yitum,* to leave over, leave (as a remainder); to leave (a place), quit; with *na,* to destroy (e. g. *Megha-nādasya dhanur na pary-aśeshayat,* he did not suffer to remain, i. e. he destroyed the bow of Megha-nāda).

Pari-śishṭa, as, ā, am, left, remaining; finished; *(am),* n. a supplement, appendix. — *Pariśishṭa-prakāśa, as,* m., N. of a work by Śrī-nātha-śarman.

Pari-śesha, as, ā, am, left over, remaining (Ved.); *(as, am),* m. n. remnant, remains, remainder, residue, rest; sequel, supplement; conclusion, completion, termination; *(eṇa),* ind. with the residue or conclusion; to the very end, completely, in full. — *Pariśesha-śāstra, am,* n. a supplementary work, an appendix.

Pari-śeshaṇa, am, n. remainder, residue.

परिशीलन *pari-śīlana, am,* n. (fr. rt. *śīl* with *pari*), frequent touch or contact, intercourse, correspondence, constant occupation, fond pursuit of or attachment to (a subject), study.

परिशुच् *pari-śuć,* cl. 1. P. (ep. also A.) *-śoćati (-te), -śoćitum,* to be deeply grieved, mourn, lament, bewail.

परिशुध् *pari-śudh,* Caus. P. *-śodhayati, -yitum,* to clear, clean, purify completely; to solve, explain, clear up.

Pari-śuddha, as, ā, am, completely cleansed, cleaned, purified; acquitted, discharged; cleared off, paid. — *Pariśuddha-bhāva, as,* m. cleansed; discharged, paid.

Pari-śuddhi, is, f. complete purification, becoming perfectly clean; justification, acquittal, proving innocent.

Pari-śodha, as, m. cleansing, purifying, correcting; discharging a debt or obligation, quittance.

Pari-śodhana, am, n. purification; justification; paying, discharging a debt.

परिशुश्रूषा *pari-śuśrūshā.* See under *pari-śru,* col. 3.

परिशुष् *pari-śush,* cl. 4. P. (ep. also A.) *-śushyati (-te), -śoshṭum,* to be thoroughly dried up, become quite dry; to shrivel, wither; to pine, waste away; to be afflicted: Caus. *-śoshayati, -yitum,* to emaciate.

Pari-śushka, as, ā, am, perfectly dried up, thoroughly dried, completely dry or parched; withered, shriveled, shrunk (as a vein); hollow (as the cheeks); *pariśushkam māṅsam,* meat fried in ghee, washed and spiced. — *Pariśushka-tālu, us, us, u,* having the palate dried up. — *Pariśushka-palāśa, as, ā, am,* having withered foliage.

Pari-śushyat, an, antī, at, drying up, evaporating.

Pari-śosha, as, m. becoming completely dried up, dryness, desiccation, evaporation.

Pari-śoshaṇa, as, ā, am, drying up, parching; *(am),* n. drying, parching, emaciating.

Pari-śoshin, ī, iṇī, i, drying up, shriveling up, becoming quite emaciated.

परिशून्य *pari-śūnya, as, ā, am,* quite empty, quite free from, totally devoid of.

परिश्रुत 1. *pari-śrita, as* or *am,* m. or n. (?), ardent spirits; [cf. *pari-srut, pari-srutā.*]

परिशॄ *pari-śṝ,* Pass. *-śīryate,* to be cleft or rent asunder, to be split.

परिश्रम *pari-śrama, as,* m. (fr. rt. *śram* with *pari*), fatigue, distress; fatiguing occupation, labour, exertion, trouble, pain. — *Pariśramāpaha* (°*ma-ap*°), *as, ā, am,* relieving weariness.

Pari-śrānta, as, ā, am, thoroughly fatigued, worn out, exhausted, wearied; one who has performed acts of religious austerity.

Pari-śrānti, is, f. fatigue, exhaustion; labour, trouble.

Pari-śrāma, as, m. fatigue, a fatiguing occupation, exertion, toiling after.

परिश्रय *pari-śraya, as,* m. (fr. rt. *śri* with *pari*), an enclosure, fence (Ved.); a refuge, asylum; an assembly, meeting.

Pari-śrayaṇa, am, n. encompassing, surrounding with a fence.

Pari-śrit, t, f., Ved. 'enclosure,' epithet of certain small stones laid round the hearth and other parts of the altar.

2. *pari-śrita, am,* n., Ved. = *pari-vṛitam,* q. v.

परिश्रु *pari-śru,* cl. 5. P. *-śṛiṇoti, -śrotum,* to hear.

Pari-śuśrūshā, f. complete or implicit obedience.

Pari-śruta, as, ā, am, heard; *(as),* m., N. of one of the attendants of Skanda.

परिश्लिष्ट *pari-ślishṭa, as, ā, am* (fr. rt. *ślish* with *pari*), embraced, clasped.

Pari-ślesha, as, m. embracing, an embrace.

परिषण्ड *pari-shaṇḍa,* a particular part of a house. — *Parishaṇḍa-vārika,* a servant.

परिषद् 1. *pari-shad (pari-sad),* cl. 1. 6. P. *-shīdati, -shattum,* Ved. to sit round.

2. *pari-shad, t, t, t,* Ved. surrounding, besetting; *(t),* f. an assembly, meeting, audience, congregation, council. — *Parishat-tva, am,* n. the state of constituting a legal assembly; a legal assemblage of councillors. — *Parishad-vala, as, ā, am,* surrounded by a council; convoking assemblies; *(as),* m. a member of an assembly, assessor, associate, spectator.

Pari-shada, as, m. (a various reading for *pārishada*), one of an assembly or congregation, a councillor, assessor, a spectator at a play.

Pari-shadya, as, ā, am, to be sought after laboriously (Ved.); to be worshipped (Ved.); to be avoided (Ved.); (according to Mahī-dhara) belonging to an assembly; (according to Sāy. on Ṛig-veda VII. 4, 7, = *pary-āpta*), sufficient, adequate, competent; *(as),* m. a member of an assembly, assessor, hearer, spectator, guest.

Pari-shadvan, ā, arī, a, Ved. surrounding, encompassing, besetting.

परिषह् *pari-shah (pari-sah),* cl. 1. A. *-shahate, -shahitum, -shoḍhum,* to sustain, bear up against.

परिषिच् *pari-shić (pari-sić),* cl. 1. P. A. *-shiñćati, -te, -shektum,* to sprinkle round, scatter about, diffuse: Caus. *-shećayati* (ep. *-shiñćayati*), *-yitum,* to sprinkle round.

Pari-sheka, as, m. sprinkling over, moistening; a bath, bathing apparatus.

Pari-shećaka, as, ā, am, pouring over, sprinkling.

Pari-shećana, am, n. pouring over, sprinkling; water for watering trees.

परिषीवण *pari-shīvaṇa, am,* n. (fr. rt. *siv* with *pari*), Ved. sewing round, winding round.

परिषू *pari-shū (pari-sū,* see rt. 2. *sū*), cl. 6. P. *-shuvati, -shavitum,* Ved. to besiege, beleaguer.

Pari-shūta, as, ā, am, Ved. besieged, beleaguered.

Pari-shūti, is, f., Ved. oppression; (Sāy.) violence (= *paritaḥ preraka upadravaḥ*).

परिषोडश *pari-shoḍaśa, as, ī, am,* full sixteen, quite sixteen.

परिष्कन्द् *pari-shkand* or *pari-skand,* cl. 1. P. *-shkandati, -shkantum,* to leap about, spring round or about.

Pari-shkaṇṇa or *pari-shkanna, as,* m. a foster

or adopted child, one nourished by a stranger; the Koil or Indian cuckoo (?).

Pari-shkanda or *pari-skanda, as,* m. a foster child, one nourished by a stranger; a servant; (*au*), m. du. two servants running by the two sides of a carriage; (*am*), n. going round or about (?).

Pari-shkandat or *pari-skandat, an, antī, at,* leaping about, jumping round, going round or about; surrounding, circumambulating; wandering.

परिष्कृ *pari-sh-kṛi* (*pari-kṛi* with *s* inserted, cf. *pari-kṛi*, p. 538, col. 2), cl. 8. P. A. *-karoti, -kurute, -kartum,* Ved. to prepare, fit out, equip; to adorn, decorate; to polish, perfect; to cleanse.

Pari-sh-kara, as, m. ornament, decoration.

Pari-sh-kāra, as, m. surrounding (?); adorning, ornament, decoration, embellishment; finishing, polishing; cooking, dressing; cleansing, purification by essential rites, initiation; domestic utensils, furniture. — *Parishkāra-ćivara,* a kind of garment.

Pari-sh-kṛita, as, ā, am, surrounded, encompassed (?); prepared, equipped; adorned, decorated, embellished; highly finished, polished; cooked, dressed; cleansed, purified by initiatory rites. — *Parishkṛita-bhūmi, is,* f. an altar or ground prepared for a sacrifice or for the victim and sacrificial utensils.

Pari-sh-kṛiti, is, f. finishing, polishing; cleansing.

Pari-sh-kriyā, f. adorning, decorating; (*agni-p°* is a various reading for *agni-parikriyā,* q. v.)

परिष्टि *pari-shṭi, is,* f. (according to some fr. rt. 1. *as* with *pari,* but more probably fr. *pari-shṭhā* below; cf. *abhi-shṭi, upa-sti*), Ved. obstruction, impediment; distress, dilemma; (Sāy.) searching all round, (as if fr. rt. 3. *ish* with *pari.*)

परिष्टु *pari-shṭu* (*pari-stu*), cl. 2. P. *-stauti, -stotum,* to praise, (Pāṇ. VIII. 3, 70.)

Pari-shṭavanīya, as, ā, am, Ved. intended for the Pari-shṭavana.

Pari-shṭuti, is, f. (fr. *pari-stu*), Ved. praise.

Pari-shṭoma, as, m. an elephant's coloured housings; a coverlet; a cushion; [cf. *pari-stoma.*]

परिष्टुभ् *pari-shṭubh, p, p, p* (fr. rt. *stubh* with *pari*), Ved. uttering joyful cries or exulting on every side; (Sāy.) = *stutibhir yukta,* endowed or glorified with praises; (*p*), f. exultation, acclamation.

Pari-shṭobha, as, m., Ved. embellishing a Sāman with the so-called Stobhas.

परिष्ठल *pari-shṭhala, am,* n. surrounding place or site.

परिष्ठा *pari-shṭhā, ās, ās, am,* Ved. obstructing, hindering, an obstructor; (*ās*), f. obstruction, impediment.

परिष्यन्द *pari-shyanda* or *pari-syanda, as,* m. (fr. rt. *syand* with *pari*), a stream, river; wetness, moisture; a sand-bank, island (Ved.).

Pari-shyandin or *pari-syandin, ī, inī, i,* flowing, streaming.

परिष्वञ्ज् *pari-shvañj* (*pari-svañj*), cl. 1. A. *-shvajate* (rarely P. *-shvajati*), *-shvanktum,* to embrace.

Pari-shvakta, as, ā, am, embraced.

Pari-shvanga, as, m. embracing, an embrace; contact, touch.

Pari-shvajana, am, n. embracing, an embrace.

Pari-shvajāna, as, ā, am, embracing, (Rāmāyaṇa II. 83, 10.)

1. *pari-shvajya, as, ā, am,* to be embraced.

2. *pari-shvajya,* ind. having embraced.

Pari-shvañjana, am, n. embracing, an embrace.

Pari-shvañjalya, as or *am,* m. or n. (?), Ved. a particular domestic utensil.

Pari-shvañjīyas, ān, asī, as, Ved. clasping more firmly.

परिष्वष्कित *pari-shvashkita, am,* n. (fr. rt. *shvashk* with *pari,* probably) the act of leaping about.

परिसंलिह् *pari-saṃ-lih,* cl. 2. P. A. *-leḍhi, -liḍhe, -leḍhum,* to lick all round, lick over, lick.

परिसंवत्सर *pari-saṃvatsara, as,* m. a whole or full year; (*āt*), ind. after the expiration of a whole year; (*as, ā, am*), a whole year old; one who has waited a whole year; (in medicine) chronic.

परिसंस्तु *pari-saṃ-stu,* cl. 2. P. A. *-stauti, -staviti, -stute, -stuvīte, -stotum,* to praise.

Pari-saṃstūyamāna, as, ā, am, being praised.

परिसंस्थित *pari-saṃ-sthita, as, ā, am* (fr. rt. *sthā* with *pari-sam*), standing together on every side.

परिसंस्पृश् *pari-saṃ-spṛiś,* cl. 6. P. *-spṛiśati, -sprashṭum, -sparshṭum,* to touch, stroke.

परिसंहा *pari-saṃ-hā,* cl. 3. A. *-jihīte, -hātum,* Ved. to lay aside, abandon (Sāy. = *pari-tyaj*).

परिसंहृष्ट *pari-saṃ-hṛishṭa, as, ā, am,* very glad, greatly rejoiced.

परिसख्य *pari-sakhya, as, ā, am,* Ved. being on friendly terms.

परिसङ्क्रीड् *pari-san-krīḍ,* cl. 1. P. *-krīḍati, -krīḍitum,* to play about, jest, amuse one's self.

Pari-sankrīḍat, an, antī, at, playing about, indulging in amusements.

परिसङ्क्षिप् *pari-san-kship,* cl. 6. P. A. *-kshipati, -te, -ksheptum,* to encompass, encircle.

परिसङ्ख्या 1. *pari-san-khyā,* cl. 2. P. *-khyāti, -khyātum,* to count over, count up, reckon up, calculate, add together; to enumerate.

2. *pari-sankhyā,* f. enumerating one by one, computation; sum; total, a number; an exhaustive enumeration, exclusive specification, limitation to that which is enumerated or expressly mentioned; recapitulation.

Pari-sankhyāta, as, ā, am, counted, reckoned up; enumerated, specified exclusively.

Pari-sankhyāna, am, n. enumeration; total; a number; exclusive specification; a correct judgment, proper estimate.

परिसङ्घुष् *pari-san-ghush,* cl. 1. P. *-ghoshati, -ghoshitum,* to make to resound on all sides, to fill with cries.

Pari-sanghushṭa, as, ā, am, resonant on all sides.

परिसञ्चक्ष् *pari-sań-ćaksh,* cl. 2. A. *-ćashṭe, -ćashṭum,* to enumerate; to avoid.

Pari-sańćakshya, as, ā, am, to be avoided, avoidable.

परिसञ्चर *pari-sańćara, as,* m. 'a very difficult pass or defile,' a critical period.

परिसञ्चि *pari-sań-ći,* cl. 5. P. A. *-ćinoti, -ćinute, -ćetum,* to collect, accumulate.

Pari-sańćita, as, ā, am, collected, accumulated.

परिसन्तप् *pari-san-tap,* cl. 1. P. *-tapati, -taptum,* to be tormented or afflicted; to scorch, singe.

Pari-santapta, as, ā, am, scorched, singed.

Pari-santapya, ind. having been tormented; having scorched.

परिसन्तान *pari-santāna, as,* m. (fr. rt. 3. *tan* with *pari-sam*), Ved. a string, cord.

परिसभ्य *pari-sabhya, as,* m. (fr. *sabhā* with *pari*), a member of an assembly, an assessor.

परिसमन्त *pari-samanta, as* or *am,* m. or n. (?), circumference, circuit.

परिसमाप् *pari-sam-āp,* Pass. *-āpyate,* to be fully completed, arrive at completion.

Pari-samāpana, am, n. the act of finishing completely.

Pari-samāpta, as, ā, am, fully completed, entirely done or finished.

Pari-samāpti, is, f. entire completion, end, conclusion.

परिसमुत्सुक *pari-samutsuka, as, ā, am,* very anxious, greatly agitated or excited.

परिसमूह् *pari-sam-ūh,* cl. 1. P. A. *-ūhati, -te, -ūhitum,* Ved. to heap or sweep together.

Pari-samūhana, am, n. heaping up or sweeping together.

परिसम्भू *pari-sam-bhū,* cl. 1. P. *-bhavati, -bhavitum,* Ved. to arise, spring, be produced.

परिसर *pari-sara.* See *pari-sṛi* below.

परिसर्प *pari-sarpa.* See *pari-sṛip* below.

परिसहस्र *pari-sahasra, as, ā, am,* Ved. a full thousand, at least a thousand.

परिसाध् *pari-sādh,* Caus. P. *-sādhayati, -yitum,* to finish, complete, settle (a cause).

Pari-sādhana, am, n. accomplishing, effecting, finishing, bringing to a conclusion; arranging, settling; determining, ascertaining.

परिसान्त्वन *pari-sāntvana, am,* n. the act of consoling; conciliation.

परिसामन् *pari-sāman, a,* n., Ved. a Sāman which is occasionally inserted.

परिसिध् *pari-sidh,* cl. 1. P. *-sedhati, -sedhitum,* to go round, go about.

Pari-siddhikā, f. a kind of rice-gruel.

Pari-sedhat, an, antī, at, going round, going about.

परिसीमन् *pari-sīman, ā,* m. a boundary, border, extreme term or limit.

परिसीर्य *pari-sīrya, am,* n. (fr. *pari* + *sīra*), Ved. a leather thong on a plough.

परिसृ *pari-sṛi,* cl. 1. P. *-sarati, -sartum,* to go or flow round.

Pari-sara, as, m. standing-place, position, site; verge, border, proximity, neighbourhood, environs, ground on the border of a river or mountain or contiguous to a town, &c.; width, breadth; death, dying; rule, precept, prescribed mode; a god.

Pari-saraṇa, am, n. running or moving about. — *Parisaraṇa-śīla, as, ā, am,* of a restless disposition, constantly moving about.

Pari-saryā, f. running about, wandering or going about, perambulation, circumambulation; near approach; service.

Pari-sāra, as, m. going round or about, wandering about, perambulation.

Pari-sāraka, am, n., N. of a place near the Sarasvatī.

Pari-sārin, ī, iṇī, i, wandering or running about.

परिसृप् *pari-sṛip,* cl. 1. P. *-sarpati, -sarptum, -sraptum,* to go round, go to and fro.

Pari-sarpa, as, m. going or walking about, perambulation; going about in search of anything, following, pursuing, going after; surrounding, encircling; a species of serpent; a species of worm causing leprosy; N. of a mild form of leprosy.

Pari-sarpaṇa, am, n. creeping about, walking about, running to and fro, constantly changing one's place; a kind of disease (= *vi-sarpa*).

Pari-sarpin, ī, iṇī, i, going or moving or roaming about.

परिस्कन्द् *pari-skand, pari-skanda, pari-skandat, pari-skanna.* See *pari-shkand.*

परिस्तृ *pari-stṛi,* cl. 5. P. A. *-stṛiṇoti, -ṇute,* or *pari-stṝ,* cl. 9. P. A. *-stṛiṇāti, -ṇīte, -startum, -staritum, -starītum,* to spread, extend; to strew round; to arrange; to envelop, cover.

Pari-stara, as, m. strewing round or heaping together, strewing; a cover, covering (?).
Pari-staraṇa, am, n. strewing round, strewing, scattering about; a cover, covering (?).
Pari-stīrya, ind. having strewed around (sacred grass).
Pari-stṛita, as, ā, am, spread over, covered.

परिस्तोम *pari-stoma, as,* m. = *pari-shṭoma.*

परिस्था *pari-sthā,* cl. 1. P. A. *-tishṭhati, -te, -sthātum,* Ved. to stand round, encompass; to obstruct (Sāy. = *pari-vṛitya sthā*).
Pari-sthāna, am, n. or *pari-sthiti, is,* f. abode, dwelling, residence; fixedness, solidity; fortitude, firmness.

परिस्पन्द् *pari-spand,* cl. 1. P. A. *-spandati, -te, -spanditum,* to tremble, throb, quiver, vibrate, totter.
Pari-spanda, as, m. beating, throbbing, vibration; motion, movement; pressure, crush; maintenance, provision; train, retinue (in this sense also spelt *pari-syanda*); decoration of the hair.
Pari-spandat, an, antī, at, trembling, quivering, tottering.
Pari-spandana, am, n. beating, throbbing, vibration, moving about, motion.
Pari-spandamāna, as, ā, am, throbbing, beating; moving tremulously, gently agitated, shaking, trembling.

परिस्पर्धिन् *pari-spardhin, ī, inī, i* (fr. rt. *spardh* with *pari*), vying with, rivalling, emulating.
Pari-spṛidh, t, f., Ved. a rival.

परिस्पृश् *pari-spṛiś,* cl. 6. P. *-spṛiśati, -sparshṭum, -sprashṭum,* to touch.

परिस्फुट *pari-sphuṭa, as, ā, am,* very clear or manifest, quite evident or plain or distinct; fully developed.

परिस्फुर् *pari-sphur,* cl. 6. P. *-sphurati, -sphuritum,* to throb, quiver.
Pari-sphuraṇa, am, n. quivering, glancing, shooting; budding.
Pari-sphurat, an, atī or *antī, at,* quivering; darting, glancing, gleaming, moving quickly or suddenly; budding, expanding; bursting forth.
Pari-sphurita, as, ā, am, quivering, glancing, gleaming; opened, expanded; shot, glanced.

परिस्मापन *pari-smāpana, am,* n. (fr. Caus. of rt. *smi* with *pari*), causing wonder, surprising, outwitting.

परिस्यन्द *pari-syanda, as,* m. (also *pari-shyanda,* q. v.), flow, stream, river; oozing, dropping; train, retinue; decoration of the hair (= *pari-spanda*).
Pari-syandana, am, n. dropping, flowing, oozing.

परिस्रजिन् *pari-srajin, ī, inī, i,* Ved. wearing a garland.

परिस्रसा *pari-srasā,* f. (fr. rt. *sraṃs* with *pari*), Ved. rubbish, lumber.

परिस्रु *pari-sru,* cl. 1. P. *-sravati, -srotum,* to flow round, flow, stream, trickle; to ask (?).
Pari-srava, as, m. (erroneously written *pari-śrava*), flowing, streaming, stream; a river, torrent; birth (of a child); gliding down.
Pari-sravat, an, antī, at, flowing down.
Pari-srāva, as, m. 'flowing,' N. of a morbid state ascribed to the overflowing of the moistures of the body; efflux, effluxion. — *Parisrāva-kalpa,* a kind of straining or filtering vessel.
Pari-srāvaṇa, am, n. a straining or filtering vessel.
Pari-srāvin, ī, iṇī, i, flowing; (*ī*), m., scil. *bhagan-dara,* a form of fistula of the anus; (*i*), n., scil. *udara,* an incurable form of intumescence of the belly.
Pari-srut, t, t, t, Ved. streaming or flowing round or over, foaming, fermenting; (*t*), f. a kind of intoxicating liquor prepared from herbs; dropping, flowing. — *Parisrun-mat, ān, atī, at,* Ved. possessing Pari-srut.
Pari-sruta, as, ā, am, flowed, streamed round; trickled, oozed; (*ā*), f. a kind of intoxicating liquor.

परिस्वार *pari-svāra, as,* m., Ved. a particular kind of singing.

परिहत *pari-hata, as, ā, am* (fr. rt. *han* with *pari*), loosed, loosened.

परिहरण *pari-haraṇa.* See *pari-hṛi* below.

परिहव *pari-hava, as,* m., Ved. (fr. rt. *hve* with *pari*), crying or calling upon (?); invoking (?).

परिहस् *pari-has,* cl. 1. P. *-hasati, -hasitum,* to laugh at, ridicule, deride.
Pari-hasita, as, ā, am, laughed at, ridiculed.
Pari-hāsa, as, m. jesting, joking, mirth, merriment, a jest, joke; laughter; laughing at, deriding, ridiculing. — *Parihāsa-kathā,* f. an amusing story. — *Parihāsa-pura, am,* n. N. of a town. — *Parihāsa-vedin, ī,* m. a jester, a wag, wit. — *Parihāsa-śīla, as, ā, am,* of a gay or joyous disposition. — *Parihāsa-hari, is,* m., N. of a temple of Vishṇu; [cf. *parihāsa-keśava.*]
Pari-hāsya, as, ā, am, laughable, ridiculous.

परिहस्त *pari-hasta, as,* m., Ved. a ring for the hand, an amulet put round the hand to secure the birth of a child.

परिहा *pari-hā,* Pass. *-hīyate,* to wane, fail, waste away, decrease; to be wanting; to want or be deficient in or be destitute of (with abl.); to be deprived of or excluded from (with abl.); to be abandoned; to be avoided or omitted; (in Mahā-bh. Sabhā-p. 1460 the form *pari-hāsyati* occurs, said to mean 'will fail'): Caus. *-hāpayati, -yitum,* to abandon.
Pari-hāna, am, n., Ved. suffering loss, losing; coming short of, being deficient, diminution, decrease.
Pari-hāṇi, is, f. decrease, loss, deficiency.
Pari-hīṇa, as, ā, am, waned, faded, wasted; deserted by; deprived of, destitute of; wanting, deficient in (with abl.).
Pari-hīyamāna, as, ā, am, wasting away, diminishing, becoming emaciated.

परिहाटक *pari-hāṭaka, am,* n. a ring worn round the arm or leg, an armlet, anklet.

परिहार *pari-hāra.* See *pari-hṛi* below.

परिहास *pari-hāsa.* See *pari-has* above.

परिहि *pari-hi,* cl. 5. P. *-hinoti, -hetum,* Ved. to prepare.

परिहित *pari-hita.* See *pari-dhā,* p. 543.

परिहृ *pari-hṛi,* cl. 1. P. A. *-harati, -te, -hartum,* to avoid, shun, pass by; to abandon, desert, leave; to refute; to conceal; to embrace.
Pari-haraṇa, am, n. moving, carrying or placing round or about (Ved.); avoiding; leaving, abandoning; seizing, taking; refuting, repelling; disappearing (?).
Pari-haraṇīya, as, ā, am, to be shunned or avoided, avoidable; to be taken away; to be repelled or refuted or confuted. — *Pariharaṇīya-tā,* f. avoidableness; disappearance, unattainableness; refutation (?).
Pari-harat, an, antī, at, shunning, avoiding, illuding; setting aside, taking away, bumbling.
Pari-haramāṇa, as, ā, am, leaving, quitting; taking, seizing; confuting; concealing.
Pari-hartavya, as, ā, am, to be shunned or avoided, to be abstained from; to be taken away; to be confuted; (in Vedic grammar) to be constructed with the *pari-hāra,* q. v.
Pari-hāra, as, m. leading round; avoiding, shunning, leaving, deserting, abandoning, giving up, resigning; taking away, removing (e. g. *virodha-parihāra,* removing a contradiction); repelling (a charge), confutation; seizing, keeping back; omitting, concealing; reserve, concealment; omitting to mention, leaving out; an extraordinary grant, exemption from taxes, granting privileges, immunity; bounty, largess; a circuit of common land round a village or town; (in grammar) the repetition of a word before and after *iti* (= *pari-graha,* q. v.); contempt, disrespect; any objectionable thing or person; objection; remedying or atoning for any improper action. — *Parihāra-vat, ān, atī, at,* avoidable.
Pari-hāraka, as, ikā, am, repelling, refuting; (*as* or *am*), m. or n.? (a various reading has *pari-haraka*), an armlet; [cf. *pari-hāṭaka.*]
Pari-hārin, ī, iṇī, i, avoiding, shunning.
Pari-hārya, as, ā, am, to be shunned or avoided; to be left undone; to be escaped from; to be taken off or away; to be severed or separated; to be constructed with the *pari-hāra;* (*as*), m. a bracelet.
Pari-hṛita, as, ā, am, avoided, shunned; abandoned, quitted; set aside, removed, rejected; taken away, repelled, refuted; taken, seized.
Pari-hṛiti, is, f. shunning, avoiding, refuting.
Pari-hṛitya, as, ā, am, Ved. to be avoided, avoidable.

परिहृष् *pari-hṛish,* Caus. P. *-harshayati, -yitum,* to delight or gladden greatly, cause to rejoice.
Pari-harshaṇa, as, ī, am, greatly delighting.

परिहृत् *pari-hrut, t, t, t* (fr. rt. *hvṛi* with *pari*), Ved. causing to fall, destroying, injuring, ruining.
Pari-hvṛit, t, f., Ved. falling to the ground, falling down, ruined.
Pari-hvṛiti, is, f., Ved. damage, injury, ruin.

परी *parī* (*pari-i,* see rt. 5. *i*), cl. 2. P. *pary-eti, -etum,* to go about, move in a circle, go or flow round, walk round, circumambulate, roam about; to encompass, encircle, include, grasp, span; to run against; to reach, attain to; (with or without *manasā*) to perceive, ponder: Intens., Ved. *parīyate,* to revolve round, move round, move in a circle.
Parīta, as, ā, am, encircling, surrounding; past, elapsed, expired; departed; surrounded, encompassed; filled; taken possession of, seized. — *Parīta-tā,* f. the being surrounded or filled.
Parītin, ī, inī, i (at the end of a comp.), = *parīta,* filled with, seized by.
Parītya, ind. having passed round or circumambulated; having encompassed.
Parīyamāṇa, as, ā, am, being penetrated or pervaded by.
Pary-aya, as, m. revolution (of time), passing away, lapse, expiration (e. g. *kāla-paryayāt,* after the lapse of a certain time); waste or loss (of time); change, mutation, alteration [cf. *vāsa-p°*]; inversion, irregular or inverted order, confusion; contrariety, opposition; deviation from enjoined or customary observances, neglect of duty.
Pary-ayaṇa, am, n. going round, walking round, circumambulating, roving about; anything wound round (an arrow or other object); a horse's saddle or housings.
Pary-āya, as, m. going or turning round, revolving, winding round; revolution, passing away (of time), course, lapse, expiration; regular recurrence, repetition; succession, turn; regular order, arrangement, methodical disposition, method; a regularly recurring series or formula, especially in the Ati-rātra ceremony (Ved.); a strophe or clause of a hymn (Ved.); a convertible term, synonym; a list of synonyms; N. of a particular figure in rhetoric; way, manner, mode, method of proceeding (e. g. *anena paryāyeṇa,* in this manner); property, quality, generic or specific character; opportunity, occasion; formation, creation, manufacture, preparation, artificial production; comprehensiveness, aggregation; *paryāyeṇa,* in succession, in turn, by turns, by rotation, successively, alternately, (opposed to *yuga-pat.*) — *Paryāya-krama, as,* m. order of

succession, regular rotation or turn. — *Paryāya-ćyuta, as, ā, am,* one who has lost his turn, superseded, supplanted. — *Paryāya-ratna-mālā,* f. 'pearl-string of synonyms,' N. of a lexicon. — *Paryāya-vaćana, am,* n. a convertible term, synonym. — *Paryāya-vāćaka, as, ā, am,* expressing a corresponding notion. — *Paryāya-vritti, is,* f. alternate course or action. — *Paryāya-śabda, as,* m. a convertible term, synonym. — *Paryāya-śayana, am,* n. alternate sleeping and watching. — *Paryāya-śas,* ind. by phrases or sentences, &c. (Ved.); periodically; in succession, by rotation, by turns, seriatim. — *Paryāyānna* (°*ya-an*°), *am,* n. food intended for another, food that should have been given to some one else (as that of a Sūdra to a Brāhman). — *Paryāyārṇava* (°*ya-ar*°), *as,* m. 'ocean of synonyms,' N. of a lexicon. — *Paryāyokta* (°*ya-uk*°), *am,* n., N. of a particular figure in rhetoric.

Paryāyika, as, ā, am, Ved. composed in strophes.

Paryāyin, ī, iṇī, i, Ved. embracing, including; going round, encompassing (in a hostile manner); periodical.

परीक्ष *parīksh* (*pari-īksh*), cl. 1. A. *-īkshate, -īkshitum,* to look round, inspect carefully, examine, investigate, scrutinize; to observe, perceive: Caus. *-īkshayati, -yitum,* to cause to examine or investigate.

Parīkshaka, as, ā, am, trying, testing, examining; (*as*), m. a prover, examiner, experimenter, investigator, judge.

Parīkshaṇa, am, n. trying, testing, experiment, examination, putting to the test, trying, proving.

Parīkshaṇīya, as, ā, am, to be tried or investigated, fit to be brought to the test, to be submitted to ordeal.

Parīkshā, f. investigation, examination, test, trial, experiment, discrimination; trial by ordeal of various kinds; N. of a commentary on Piṅgala's Ćhandaḥ-śāstra.

1. *parīkshita, as, ā, am,* carefully inspected, tried, examined, tested, proved.

Parīkshitavya, as, ā, am, to be tried or tested, to be examined or proved.

Parīkshin, ī, iṇī, i, proving, testing, one who tries or examines, an examiner.

Parīkshya, as, ā, am, to be tried or tested; to be examined or proved.

परीक्षित् *parī-kshit, t,* m. (connected with and frequently written *pari-kshit*), N. of a son of Abhi-manyu and father of Janam-ejaya; of a son of Kuru; of a son of An-aśvan and father of Bhīma-sena; of a king of A-yodhyā.

2. *parī-kshita, as,* m. = *parī-kshit.*

परीज्या *parījyā* (for *pari-ijyā,* fr. rt. *yaj* with *pari*), Ved. an accompanying or secondary rite (= *pari-yajña*).

परीणस् *parīṇas, ās,* m. (probably fr. rt. *pṛī*), Ved. plenty, abundance, wealth; (according to Sāy.) = *parito naddha;* (*asā*), ind. = *bahu,* richly, abundantly.

Parīṇasa, am, n., Ved. plenty, abundance, wealth.

परीणह् *parī-ṇah.* See *pari-ṇah,* p. 542.

Parī-ṇāha = *pari-ṇāha,* q. v.

परीणाम *parī-ṇāma* = *pari-ṇāma,* q. v.

परीणाय *parī-ṇāya* = *pari-ṇāya,* q. v.

परीत *parīta,* &c. See *parī,* p. 551, col. 3.

परीतत् *parī-tat.* See *pari-tan,* p. 542.

परीताप *parī-tāpa, parī-tosha,* = *pari-tāpa, pari-tosha,* q. v.

परीति *parīti* = *pushpāñjana,* q. v.

परीत्त 2. *parī-tta* (fr. *pari-do,* p. 543, col. 2, or identified by some with 1. *parī-tta,* p. 543, col. 1), cut round, incomplete, limited, circumscribed, not too much, little. — *Parītta-śubha, ās,* m. pl. (with Buddhists) N. of the gods of the thirteenth order. — *Parīttābha* (°*ta-ābha*), *ās,* m. pl. (with Buddhists) N. of the gods of the tenth order.

परीदाह *parī-dāha* = *pari-dāha,* q. v.

परीधान *parī-dhāna* = *pari-dhāna,* q. v.

परीधाविन् *parī-dhāvin.* See *pari-dhāvin.*

परीध्य *parīdhya, as, ā, am* (fr. rt. *indh* with *pari*), Ved. to be lighted or kindled.

परीपाक *parī-pāka* = *pari-pāka,* q. v.

परीप्सत् *parīpsat, an, antī, at* (pres. part. of Desid. of rt. *āp* with *pari*), wishing to obtain, striving to reach.

Parīpsamāna, as, ā, am, = *parīpsat.*

Parīpsā, f. the desire of obtaining; the wish to save or maintain or preserve; haste, hurry.

Parīpsu, us, us, u, desirous of obtaining, wishing to save, desirous of maintaining or preserving.

परीभाव *parī-bhāva* = *pari-bhāva,* q. v.

परीमन् *parīman, ā* or *a,* m. or n.? (fr. rt. *pṛī*), Ved. bounty, plenty, plenteousness.

परीमाण *parī-māṇa* = *pari-māṇa,* q. v.

परीयमाण *parīyamāṇa.* See *parī,* p. 551.

परीर *parīra, am,* n. (said to be fr. rt. *pṛī*), fruit.

परीरण *parīraṇa, as,* m. a tortoise; a stick or staff; = *paṭṭa-śāṭaka.*

परीरम्भ *parī-rambha, as,* m. an embrace, &c. See *pari-rambha.*

परीवर्त *parī-varta, as,* m. exchange, barter, &c. See *pari-varta.*

परीवाद *parī-vāda, as,* m. reproof, censure, abuse, &c. See *pari-vāda.*

परीवार *parī-vāra, as,* m. retinue, dependants, family, &c. See *pari-vāra.*

परीवाह *parī-vāha, as,* m. a drain, &c., see *pari-vāha;* a scabbard (?).

परीवेत्तृ *parī-vettṛi* = *pari-vettṛi,* q. v.

परीवेश *parī-veśa* = *pari-vesha,* q. v.

परीशास *parī-śāsa, as,* m. (fr. rt. 1. *śas* with *pari*), Ved. anything cut out, an excision; (*au*), m. du. a kind of tongs used for raising a kettle from the fire.

परीशेष *parī-śesha* = *pari-śesha,* q. v.

परीष् *parīsh* [cf. rt. 3. *ish*], cl. 6. P. *-iććhati, -eshitum, -eshṭum,* Ved. to seek or search about for.

Parishṭi, is, f. investigation, research, inquiry, (especially philosophical); service, attendance, reverence, respect, homage, worship; willingness, readiness, inclination.

परीषेक *parī-sheka* = *pari-sheka,* q. v.

परीसार *parī-sāra, as,* m. = *pari-sāra,* q. v.; near approach (?).

परीहार *parī-hāra* = *pari-hāra,* q. v.

परीहास *parī-hāsa* = *pari-hāsa,* q. v. — *Parīhāsa-keśava, as,* m., N. of a temple of Vishṇu.

परु *paru, us,* m. (said to be fr. rt. *pṛī*), a limb, member; a knot or joint in a reed; a mountain; the ocean; the sky, paradise.

Paru-śas or *paruś-śas,* Ved. limb by limb, member by member.

Parusha, as, ā, am (in the earlier language, f. *parushṇī*), containing knots, knotted (Ved.); spotted, variegated, party-coloured; dirty; rough, rugged, uneven, shaggy; keen, piercing (as the wind); harsh, discordant; unkind, cruel, stern, hard, severe, abusive, contumelious; coarse, gross; churlish, cruel, unkind; (*as*), m. a reed (Ved.); an arrow (Ved.); = *parūsha,* q. v.; (*ā*), f. a kind of riddle; (*shṇī*), f., Ved. 'much indented' or 'winding' or 'reedy,' N. of one of the rivers of the Pañjāb, in later times called Irā-vatī, and at the present day Rāvī; a cloud?; (*am*), n. harsh and contumelious speech, abuse; a species of Barleria with blue flowers; = *parūsha,* q. v.; (*āṇi*), n. pl. rough or harsh or stern words. — *Parusha-tva, am,* n. roughness, harshness. — *Parusha-vaćana, am,* n. harsh language, harsh or contumelious speech, reproach, abuse. — *Parusha-vāć, k, k, k,* harsh-spoken; (*k*), f. harsh or contumelious speech. — *Parushākshara* (°*sha-ak*°), *as, ā, am,* 'harsh-worded,' harsh. — *Parushāhva* (°*sha-āh*°), *as,* m., Ved. a species of reed. — *Parushī-krita, as, ā, am,* spotted, soiled, stained; treated roughly. — *Parushetara* (°*sha-it*°), *as, ā, am,* other than rough, bright, light, beaming, mild. — *Parushokti* (°*sha-uk*°), *is,* f. abusive or harsh language. — *Parushoktika, as,* m. an abuser, one uttering harsh and scurrilous language.

Parushita, as, ā, am, treated roughly or harshly, subjected to rude treatment.

Parushiman, ā, m., Ved. a rough or shaggy appearance.

Parushya, as, ā, am, Ved. party-coloured, variegated, piebald.

Parus, us, n., Ved. a knot or joint of a cane or reed; a member of the body, limb; a joint, junction; a part cut off, portion. — *Paruḥ-sraṇsa, as,* m., Ved. fracture of a joint or limb.

Parūsha or *parūshaka, as,* m. Grewia Asiatica (from the berries of which a cooling beverage is prepared; Bengālī *phalasā;* Hindūstānī پهالسا; according to others) Xylocarpus Granatum = Bengālī, *parusha;* (*am*), n. the fruit of this tree.

परुच्छेप *paru-ććhepa, as,* m. (perhaps irregularly formed fr. *parus* + *kshepa*), N. of a Ṛishi, son of Divo-dāsa and author of the hymns Ṛig-veda I. 127 sqq.

परुत् *parut,* ind. (fr. *para* + *vat?*, occurring only in comp.), last year; [cf. Gr. πέρυσι, Dor. πέρυτι, πέρυτις: Old Germ. *vert, vernent, vern,* 'last year:' Goth. *fairni-s,* 'old;' *fairnyō yēr,* 'the old year.']

परुद्वार *parudvāra* or *parula, as,* m. a horse; [cf. Lat. *paraveredus.*]

परुष *parusha.* See under *paru,* col. 2.

परे *pare* (*parā-i,* see rt. 5. *i*), cl. 2, P. *paraiti, paraitum,* to go away, run away; to go to, set out for, approach; to go to the other world, depart, die.

Pareta, as, ā, am, departed, deceased, defunct, dead; (*as*), m. a kind of spectre; a ghost, spirit. — *Pareta-bhūmi, is,* f. 'place of the departed,' a cemetery. — *Pareta-rāj, ṭ,* m. 'ruler of the dead,' an epithet of Yama.

Pareti, is, f., Ved. departure.

परेक्ष *pareksh* (*parā-īksh*), cl. 1. A. *parekshate, -shitum,* Ved. to look at (anything at one's side).

परेद्यवि *pare-dyavi, pare-dyus, pare-prāṇa.* See under *para.*

परेप *parepa, as, ā, am* (fr. *parā?* + *ap*), (any place) whence water has retired.

परेमन् *pareman,* Ved. (perhaps) = *parīman.*

परेष्टु *pareshṭu, us,* or *pareshṭukā,* f. a cow which has often calved.

परोंहु *paro-'ṇhu.* See under *paras.*

परोक्ष *paro-'ksha, as, ā, am* (fr. *paras* + 4. *aksha,* opposed to *praty-aksha,* q. v.), beyond the range of sight, out of sight, invisible, imperceptible, escaping observation; unknown, strange, unintelligible; absent, past; (*as*), m. an ascetic, religious hermit; N. of one of the sons of Anu; (*ā*), f. past or completed action (in grammar perhaps with *vṛitti*); (*am*), n. invisibility, absence, secrecy; (in grammar) past time or tense. The acc., inst., abl., and loc. cases of *paroksha* are used adverbially, as follow: (*am*), ind. out of sight, behind one's back, in the absence of, without the knowledge of (in the earlier language with inst., in the later with gen.); surreptitiously; (*eṇa*), ind., Ved. out of sight, secretly, mysteriously, surreptitiously; (*āt*), ind., Ved. secretly, without the knowledge of (with inst.); (*e*), ind. behind one's back, in the absence of, imperceptibly, surreptitiously; [cf. *a-paroksha.*] — *Paroksha-kṛitā*, f., Ved., scil. *ṛik*, a hymn or verse in which a deity is spoken of in the third person, the first person being kept out of sight (e. g. 'Indra rules over heaven and earth,' &c.). — *Paroksha-jit, t, t, t*, conquering invisibly, an unseen conqueror. — *Paroksha-tā*, f. or *paroksha-tva, am*, n. the being beyond the sphere of observation, obscurity, invisibility, imperceptibility; keeping one's self as the first person out of sight, speaking of one's self in the third person (Ved.). — *Paroksha-bhoga, as*, m. enjoyment or possession of anything in the absence of the proprietor. — *Paroksha-manmatha, as, ā, am*, inexperienced in love, a stranger to love. — *Paroksha-vṛitti, is, is, i*, whose life is unseen, living out of sight; formed out of sight or unseen, formed in obscurity; (*is*), f. an unseen life. — *Parokshārtha* (°*sha-ar*°), *as, ā, am*, having an unseen meaning, secret, recondite; (*am*), n. an absent or invisible object.

Paro-gavyūti, ind. (fr. *paras + g*°), Ved. beyond or outside the pasture land; (Sāy.) = *krośa-drayād deśāt parastāt*, further than a Gavyūti, q. v.

Paro-bāhu, ind. (fr. *paras + b*°), Ved. beyond the arm or reach.

Paro-mātra, as, ī, am (fr. *paras + m*°), Ved. immense, huge, vast.

Paro-rajas, ās, ās, as (fr. *paras + r*°), Ved. being beyond the dust or above the world (Ved.); untouched by passion.

Paro-laksha, as, ā, am (fr. *paras + l*°), over a lakh, more than 100,000.

Paro-'varam (fr. *paras + av*°), ind., Ved. from top to bottom; from hand to hand; in succession, one after another.

Paro-'varīṇa, as, ā, am (fr. *paras + av*°), having both superior and inferior, prior and subsequent, &c.

Paro-varīyas, ān, asī, as (fr. *paras + v*°), Ved. broader on the outside or at the top; better than good, most excellent of all; (*as*), n. the highest happiness.

Paroshṇih (fr. *paras + ush*°), *k*, f. a kind of metre (consisting of 8 + 8 + 12 syllables).

परोक्त *parokta, parocya.* See *parā-vać.*

परोष्णी *paroshṇī*, f. a cockroach, (sometimes wrongly written *paroshṭī*); N. of a river.

पर्क *parka* in *madhu-p*°, q. v.

पर्कट *parkaṭa, as*, m. a heron [cf. *vakoṭa*]; (*am*), n. regret, anxiety.

Parkaṭin, ī, m. or *parkaṭī*, f. the waved-leaved fig-tree, Ficus Infectoria; a fresh betel-nut.

पर्जनी *parjanī.* See col. 2.

पर्जन्य *parjanya, as*, m. (perhaps fr. *sphurj* for original *sparj*; but said to be fr. rt. *pṛish*; sometimes wrongly written *paryanya*), a rain-cloud, thunder-cloud, cloud; the muttering of clouds or distant thunder; rain; Rain personified; the rain-god, thunderer and fertilizer, i. e. Indra; N. of one of the twelve Ādityas; of a Deva-gandharva; of one of the seven Ṛishis in several Manv-antaras; of a Prajā-pati and father of Hiraṇya-roman; (*ā*), f. = *parjanī*, col. 2. — *Parjanya-krandya, as, ā, am*, Ved. muttering like a rain-cloud or like Parjanya. — *Parjanya-jinvita, as, ā, am*, Ved. animated by Parjanya; (Sāy.) = *Parjanyena prīta*, agreeable to Parjanya. — *Parjanya-nātha, as, ā, am*, Ved. having Parjanya as protector or patron. — *Parjanya-patnī*, f., Ved. having Parjanya for a husband, wedded to Parjanya (said of the earth). — *Parjanya-retas, ās, ās, as*, Ved. generated or growing in the showers or in the rainy season, (said of a reed or arrow; Sāy. = *parjanyo reto yasyāḥ*.) — *Parjanya-vṛiddha, as, ā, am*, Ved. nourished by Parjanya (as the Soma). — *Parjanya-sūkta, am*, n., N. of a hymn contained in the Mantra-saṃhitā.

Parjanī, f. the plant Cucumis Aromatica or Cucumis Xanthorrhiza.

पर्ण् *parṇ* (more properly regarded as a Nom. fr. *parṇa* below), cl. 10. P. *parṇayati, -yitum*, to be green or verdant.

Parṇa, am, n. (said to be fr. rt. *pṛī*), a pinion, feather, wing; the feather of an arrow; a leaf (regarded as the plumage of a tree); the Pān or betel leaf; (*as*), m. Butea Frondosa (a beautiful sacred tree with leaves from eight to sixteen inches in length, of the wood of which particular sacrificial vessels are made, in later times generally called *palāśa*); N. of a man; of a teacher; of a place; (*ī*), f. an aquatic plant, Pistia Stratiotes; the leaf of the Asa Fœtida (?); [cf. *aććhinna-p*°, *aśva-p*°, *uttāna-p*°, &c.; cf. probably Gr. Πάρνης, Παρνασός, Παρνασσός; perhaps Lat. *penna*, if not fr. rt. *pat*, q. v., *frons*; Old Germ. *farn*; Angl. Sax. *fearn*.] — *Parṇa-kāra, as*, m. = *vāra-jīvī* (commonly *vārui*), a vender of betel leaves. — *Parṇa-kuṭikā*, f. or *parṇa-kuṭī*, f. a hut made of leaves. — *Parṇa-kṛićchra, as*, m. 'leaf-penance,' living for a time upon an infusion of leaves and Kuśa grass as a religious observance. — *Parṇa-khaṇḍa, as*, m. a tree without apparent blossoms; a tree in general. — *Parṇa-ćīra-paṭa, as, ā, am*, clad in a garment made of strips of leaves; an epithet of Śiva. — *Parṇa-ćoraka, as*, m. a kind of perfume; [cf. *ćoraka.*] — *Parṇa-dhi, is*, m., Ved. the part of an arrow to which the feathers are fastened. — *Parṇa-dhvas, t, t, t*, causing the falling of leaves. — *Parṇa-nara, as*, m. 'man of leaves,' an effigy stuffed with leaves or the figure of a man made of leaves and burnt in place of a lost corpse. — *Parṇa-nāla, as*, m. a leaf-stalk, petiole. — *Parṇa-prātyika*, N. of a locality (perhaps incorrectly for *parṇa-prāsika*). — *Parṇa-bhedinī*, f. the Priyangu tree. — *Parṇa-bhojana, as, ā, am*, feeding upon leaves; (*as*), m. any animal eating leaves, a goat. — *Parṇa-maṇi, is*, m., Ved. a kind of magical instrument (made of the wood of the Parṇa tree ?). — *Parṇa-maya, as, ī, am*, Ved. made of the wood of the Butea Frondosa. — *Parṇa-māćāla, as*, m. the plant Averrhoa Carambola (= *karmaranga*). — *Parṇa-muć, ṭ, ṭ, ṭ*, causing leaves to fall (as the wind). — *Parṇa-mṛiga, as*, m. 'leaf-animal,' any wild animal lodging in the boughs of trees (as a monkey, sloth, squirrel, &c.). — *Parṇa-ruh, ṭ, ṭ, ṭ*, causing the leaves to grow (as the wind). — *Parṇa-latā*, f. the betel plant. — *Parṇa-vat, ān, atī, at*, abounding in leaves, leafy. — *Parṇa-valka, as*, m., N. of a man. — *Parṇa-vallī*, f. Butea Frondosa (= *palāśi-latā*). — *Parṇa-vādya, am*, n. 'leaf-music,' sounds produced by blowing into a leaf. — *Parṇa-vī, īs, īs, ī*, Ved. 'wing-borne,' carried by wings. — *Parṇa-viṭikā*, f. the Areca nut cut in pieces, sprinkled with spices, and rolled up in betel leaves. — *Parṇa-sada* or *parṇa-śāda, as*, m., Ved. the falling of leaves. — *Parṇa-śadya, as, ā, am*, Ved. relating to the falling of leaves. — *Parṇa-śayyā*, f. a couch of leaves, leafy couch. — *Parṇa-śara, as*, m., Ved. a leaf-stalk, petiole; the stalk of a Parṇa leaf. — *Parṇa-śavara, ās*, m., N. of a people, (Śavaras living upon leaves.) — *Parṇa-śālā*, f. 'leaf-hut,' an arbour or hut made of leaves and grass, hermitage; N. of a great settlement of Brāhmans between the Yamunā and Gangā in Madhya-deśa. — *Parṇaśālāgra* (°*lā-ag*°), *as*, m., N. of a mountain in Bhadrāśva. — *Parṇa-śush, ṭ, ṭ, ṭ*, drying or shriveling the leaves (as the wind). — *Parṇa-saṃstara, as, ā, am*, having leaves for a bed, sleeping on leaves. — *Parṇa-santara, as, ā, am*, having leaves for a bed, sleeping on leaves. — *Parṇāḍhaka* (°*ṇa-āḍh*°), *as*, m., N. of a man; (*ās*), m. pl., N. of his descendants. — *Parṇāda* (°*ṇa-ada*), *as, ā, am*, feeding upon leaves; (*as*), m., N. of an ancient sage; of a Brāhman. — *Parṇāśana* (°*ṇa-aś*°), *am*, n. feeding on leaves; (*as*), m. a cloud. — *Parṇāsi* (°*ṇa-asi*), *is*, m. a species of basil with small leaves, Ocymum Sanctum. — *Parṇāhāra* (°*ṇa-āh*°), *as, ā, am*, feeding upon leaves. — *Parṇoṭaja* (°*ṇa-uṭ*°), *am*, n. 'leaf-hut,' an anchorite's hut or cottage, a hermitage. — *Parṇotsa* (°*ṇa-ut*°), *as*, m., N. of a village.

Parṇaka, as, m., Ved. (according to Mahī-dhara) = *bhilla*, q. v.; N. of a man; (*ās*), m. pl., N. of his descendants; (*ikā*), f. a kind of vegetable; N. of an Apsaras.

Parṇaya, as, m., Ved., N. of an enemy (according to Sāy. an Asura) slain by Indra. — *Parṇaya-ghna, am*, n., Ved. the slaying of Parṇaya.

Parṇala, as, ā, am, abounding in leaves, full of leaves, leafy.

Parṇasi, is, m. (said to be fr. rt. *pṛī*), a house upon or by the water; a summer-house (?); a lotus; a vegetable; adorning, decoration, toilet.

Parṇāśa or *parṇāsa, as*, m. a species of plant, a kind of basil with small leaves, Ocymum Sanctum; (*ā*), f., N. of various rivers; [cf. *pūrṇāśā.*]

Parṇika, as, ā, am, selling or dealing in Parṇī.

Parṇin, ī, inī, i, winged, plumed; leafy, having leaves, leaved; (*ī*), m. a tree; Butea Frondosa; (*inī*), f. a species of plant; N. of an Apsaras.

Parṇila, as, ā, am, abounding in leaves, leafy.

Parṇya, as, ā, am, Ved. relating to leaves, leafy.

पर्णाल *parṇāla, as*, m. a boat; a spade or hoe; single combat.

पर्तृ *partṛi, tā, trī, tṛi* (fr. rt. 1. *pṛi*), Ved. a protector; protection, means of defence, (Sāy. = *pālana-sādhanam.*)

पर्द् *pard*, cl. 1. A. *pardate*, &c., to break wind, fart; [cf. Gr. πέρδ-ω, πέρδ-ο-μαι, ἔ-παρδ-ο-ν, πέ-πορδ-α, πορδ-ή, πέρδ-ιξ; Lat. *pēd-o, pēd-or, pōdex*; Old Germ. *firz-u*; Bohem. *prd-u*; Lith. *perd-z-u, pérs-ti, pìrd-i-s.*]

Parda, as, m. a fart; a quantity of hair, thick hair.

Pardana, am, n. breaking wind, a fart.

पर्प् *parp* (a doubtful rt.; by some regarded as a Sautra rt.; cf. Uṇādi-s. IV. 81), cl. 1. P. *parpati*, &c., to go or move.

Parpa, am, n. (said to be fr. rt. 1. *pṛi*), a wheel-chair, a chair in which a cripple is moved about; young grass; a house.

Parpaṭa, as, m. a species of medicinal plant with bitter leaves (= *bheshajāntara, tiktā kshetra-parpaṭī*, apparently the Oldenlandia Biflora); a kind of thin cake, = *ćarpaṭī*; (*ī*), f. a kind of fragrant earth or a red aluminous earth (apparently a sort of Bol, brought from Surāt or Su-rāshṭra); a sort of fragrant substance or perfume (= *kṛishṇā, ćakra-vartinī, jatukā*, commonly called *paparī*); a thin crisp cake made of any pulse. — *Parpaṭa-druma* or *parpaṭī-druma, as*, m. bdellium.

Parpaṭaka, as, m. a species of medicinal plant with bitter leaves, (probably) Oldenlandia Biflora.

Parpika, as, ī, m. f. a cripple who moves about by the aid of a chair.

पर्परी *parparī*, f. a braid of hair.

पर्परीक *parparīka, as*, m. (said to be fr. rt. *pṛī* with reduplication), the sun; fire; a tank, reservoir, piece of water.

पर्फरीक *parpharīka, as*, m., Ved. one who tears to pieces or fills, (Sāy. = *śatrūṇām vidārayitṛi* or *dhanādi-dānena pūrayitṛī.*)

पर्ब् *parb*, cl. 1. P. *parbati*, &c., to go or move.

7 B

पर्माडि *parmāḍi, is*, m., N. of a prince of Karṇāṭa, (also called Parmāṇḍi.)

पर्यक् *pary-ak*. See 2. *pary-aṅć* below.

पर्यगु *pary-agu* in comp. with *pāramahansya*, Bhāgavata-Purāṇa IV. 21, 40; according to a Scholiast = *parito na gaććhanti gāvo yasmāt*, but variously taken, see *pāramahansya-pari*.

पर्यग्नि *pary-agni, is*, m., Ved. circumambient fire; a torch carried round the sacrificial animal; the ceremony of carrying fire round the sacrificial animal; *paryagni kṛi*, to carry fire round any one (with acc.).

Paryagni-kṛita, as, ā, am, Ved. encircled with fire.

Paryagni-kriyamāṇa, as, ā, am, Ved. being encircled with fire; (*e*), loc. during the encircling with fire.

पर्यङ्क *pary-anka*. See under 1. *pary-aṅć*.

पर्यङ्ख् *pary-ankh*, cl. 10. P. A. *-ankhayati, -te, -yitum*, Ved. to surround, clasp or encircle round.

पर्यङ्ग्य *paryangya, as, ā, am* (fr. *pari* + *anga*), Ved. being about or at the side.

पर्यञ्च् 1. *pary-aṅć* or *pary-ać*, cl. 1. P. A. *-aṅćati, -te, -aṅćitum*, Ved. to turn round, revolve.

Pary-anka, as, m. (fr. *pari* + *anka* or perhaps directly fr. 1. *pary-aṅć* above; also spelt *paly-anka*), a bed, couch, sofa; a litter, palanquin; a cloth thrown over the back, loins and knees while seated on the hams in the Oriental manner; sitting upon the hams (a particular posture especially practised by ascetics in meditation); N. of a mountain (son of Vindhya). — *Paryanka-granthi-bandha, as*, m. or *-°bandhana, am*, n. the bending of the legs in sitting on the hams. — *Paryanka-bandha, as*, m. sitting in the Paryanka posture (= *vīrāsana*). — *Paryanka-bandhana, am*, n. binding a cloth round the back, loins and knees while squatting on the hams. — *Paryanka-bhogin, ī*, m. 'couch-serpent,' a kind of serpent. — *Paryanka-stha, as, ā, am*, sitting on a sofa.

2. *pary-aṅć*, apparently only used in acc. sing. neut. *pary-ak*, ind. round about, all round, in every direction.

पर्यट् *pary-aṭ*, cl. 1. P. A. *-aṭati, -te, -aṭitum*, to roam or wander about, rove about.

Pary-aṭa, ās, m. pl., N. of a people.

Pary-aṭana, am, n. wandering about, peregrination, roaming through.

Pary-aṭita, am, n. wandering about.

पर्यनुबन्ध *pary-anubandha, as*, m. binding round.

पर्यनुयोग *pary-anuyoga, as*, m. asking, inquiring, question; blame, censure, reproach; contesting, disputing (?).

पर्यन्त *pary-anta, as*, m. an encircling boundary, circuit, circumference; limit, edge, skirt, border, verge, extremity; end, termination, close (e. g. *kāla-paryanta*, the end or close of an appointed time; *paryantāt paryantam*, from one end to the other); (*as, ā, am*), bounded, surrounded by a boundary; extending in all directions; (often at the end of comps., e. g. *kshura-paryantaṃ ćakram*, a discus with edges like a razor's; *samudra-paryantā pṛithivī*, the ocean-bounded earth or the earth extending to the ocean.) — *Paryanta-deśa, as*, m. a neighbouring or adjacent district. — *Paryanta-paryantam*, ind. to the end of, as far as. — *Paryanta-parvata, as*, m. an adjoining hill. — *Paryanta-bhū, ūs*, f. ground contiguous to the skirts of a river or mountain. — *Paryanta-stha, as, ā, am*, limitative, confining, adjoining, neighbouring. — *Paryanta-sthita, as, ā, am*, bounding, confining.

Paryantikā, f. loss of all good qualities, depravity.

पर्यन्य *paryanya*, incorrectly for *parjanya*, q. v.

पर्यन्विष् *pary-anv-ish*, cl. 6. P. *-iććhati, -eshṭum, -eshitum*, to seek for, search after.

पर्यय *pary-aya, pary-ayaṇa*. See under *parī*, p. 551, col. 3.

पर्यर्षण *pary-arshaṇa*. See under 2. *pary-ṛish*, p. 555, col. 3.

पर्यवकॄ *pary-ava-kṝ*, cl. 6. P. *-kirati, -karitum, -karītum*, to scatter round or about, shed over.

पर्यवच्छिद् *pary-ava-ććhid* (°*ćhid*), cl. 7. P. A. *-ććhinatti, -ććhintte, -ććhettum*, Ved. to cut off on both sides or all round.

पर्यवदात *pary-avadāta, as, ā, am* (fr. rt. *dai* or 7. *dā* with *pary-ava*), perfectly clean or pure; [cf. 7. *dā, ava-dāta*.]

पर्यवदो *pary-ava-do* or *pary-avadā* (see rt. 3. *dā*), cl. 2. 4. P. *-dāti, -dyati, -dātum*, Ved. to cut off or slice all round.

पर्यवधारण *pary-avadhāraṇa, am*, n. precise determination, refining, subtilizing.

पर्यवरोध *pary-avarodha, as*, m. (fr. rt. *rudh* with *pary-ava*), obstruction, hindrance.

पर्यवशेष *pary-avaśesha, as*, m. end, termination.

Pary-avaśeshita, as, ā, am, regarded as the end of all (i. e. God).

पर्यवष्टम्भ् *pary-ava-shṭambh*, cl. 5. 9. P., 1. A. *-shṭabhnoti, -nāti, -shṭambhate, -shṭambhitum*, to surround; to surround with a view to obstruct.

Pary-avashṭabdha, as, ā, am, surrounded, invested.

Pary-avashṭambhana, am, n. surrounding, investing.

पर्यवसो *pary-ava-so*, cl. 4. P. *-syati, -sātum*, to finish, complete, conclude; to endeavour.

Pary-avasāna, am, n. end, termination, conclusion, issue.

Paryavasānika, as, ā, am, coming to a close, drawing to an end or conclusion.

Pary-avasāyin, ī, inī, i, closing or ending with (often in comps.). — *Paryavasāyi-tva, am*, n. termination, close.

Pary-avasita, as, ā, am, finished, completed, ended, terminated, concluded; perished, lost; resolved; *lokāntaram pary-avasitaḥ*, gone to another world.

पर्यवस्कन्द *pary-avaskanda, as*, m. jumping or leaping down (from a carriage).

पर्यवस्था 1. *pary-ava-sthā*, cl. 1. P. A. *-tishṭhati, -te, -sthātum*, to be present or exist everywhere; to rely upon: Caus. *-sthāpayati, -yitum*, to raise, rouse.

2. *pary-avasthā*, f. or *pary-avasthāna, am*, n. opposition, resistance, contradiction.

Pary-avasthātṛi, tā, trī, tṛi, opposing, obstructing, opposed to or against; (*tā*), m. an antagonist, opponent, adversary, enemy.

Pary-avasthita, as, ā, am, opposed to, siding with an enemy.

पर्यवे *pary-ave* (*pary-ava-i*, see rt. 5. *i*), cl. 2. P. *-avaiti, -avaitum*, Ved. to turn round, turn in the right direction; to pass, elapse.

पर्यवेक्ष् *pary-aveksh* (*pary-ava-īksh*), cl. 1. A. *-avekshate, -kshitum*, to regard from every side, regard (?).

पर्यश् 1. *pary-aś*, cl. 5. P. A. *-aśnoti, -nute, -aśitum*, Ved. to arrive at, reach, attain (Sāy. = *parito vy-āp*).

पर्यश् 2. *pary-aś*, cl. 9. P. *-aśnāti, -aśitum*, to eat.

पर्यश्रु *pary-aśru, us, us, u*, bathed in or suffused with tears, shedding tears, tearful.

पर्यस् 1. *pary-as*, cl. 2. P. *-asti*, Ved. to be in the way; to surpass; to pass or spend (time); (Sāy.) = *parito bhū*, to be everywhere about.

पर्यस् 2. *pary-as*, cl. 4. P. A. *-asyati, -te, -asitum*, to throw or cast round, put or place round, put on, spread round, diffuse; to surround, encircle, encompass; to enchase; to entrap, ensnare; to turn round, turn over; to turn away; to throw down, overturn, upset: Pass. *-asyate*, to fall down, drop, sink down: Caus. to cause to drop, to cause to roll down or shed (as tears).

Pary-asana, am, n. throwing about, moving to and fro, wagging; casting, sending; putting off or away.

Pary-asta, as, ā, am, thrown or cast round, placed round, put on, diffused; surrounded, encompassed, ensnared; thrown off, thrown down; thrown or tossed up; overturned, upset; dismissed, laid aside; struck, killed; bound. — *Paryasta-vat, ān, atī, at*, Ved. containing the notion expressed by the word *pary-asta*. — *Paryasta-vilоćana, as, ā, am*, or *paryastāksha* (°*ta-aksha*), *as, ī, am*, Ved. having the eyes cast or directed round.

Pary-asti, is, f. sitting upon the hams (= *pary-anka*, q. v.).

Paryastikā, f. = *pary-asti* above.

Pary-asyat, an, antī, at, scattering; oversetting, upsetting; investing.

Pary-āsa, as, m. edging, trimming (Ved.); end, conclusion; epithet of particular concluding strophes in certain hymns (Ved.); rotation, revolution; inverted order or position.

Pary-āsana, am, n. revolution, circumvolution.

Pary-āsita, as, ā, am, upset, subverted, reversed.

पर्यस्तमयम् *pary-astamayam*, ind., Ved. about sunset.

पर्याकुल *pary-ākula, as, ā, am*, filled, full; turbid on all sides (as water), turbid; confounded, confused, disordered, beside one's self, excited, agitated, anxious, bewildered, infatuated. — *Paryākula-tva, am*, n. confusion, bewilderment.

पर्याकृ *pary-ā-kṛi*, cl. 8. P. A. *-karoti, -kurute, -kartum*, Ved. to turn round.

पर्याक्षिप् *pary-ā-kship*, cl. 6. P. A. *-kshipati, -te, -ksheptum*, to wind round, turn.

पर्यागम् *pary-ā-gam*, cl. 1. P. *-gaććhati, -gantum*, to go round, perform a revolution, elapse; to last or live through a space of time; to come to an end or conclusion; to surround on every side, encircle, ensnare, get into one's power.

Pary-āgata, as, ā, am, one who has finished the course or career of life.

पर्यागल् *pary-ā-gal*, cl. 1. P. *-galati, -galitum*, to let fall in drops, drop, trickle.

Pary-āgalat, an, antī, at, dropping, falling, trickling.

पर्यागा *pary-ā-gā* (occurring in Aor. *pary-āgāt*, Mahā-bh. Śānti-p. 8157), to perform a revolution, elapse.

पर्याचर् *pary-ā-ćar*, cl. 1. P. *-ćarati, -ćaritum*, Ved. to come near, approach, resort to.

पर्याचान्त *pary-āćānta, as, ā, am*, sipped, rinsed prematurely; (scil. *annam*) food left by a person who has rinsed his mouth out.

पर्याण *paryāṇa, am*, n. (for *pari-yāṇa*), a circuit (Ved.); a saddle, pack-saddle or cloth serving for one.

पर्याणह् *pary-ā-ṇah*, cl. 4. P. A. *-ṇahyati, -te, -ṇaddhum*, Ved. to cover up, cover.

Pary-āṇahana, am, n., Ved. a covering.

पर्याणी pary-ā-ṇī, cl. 1. P. A. -ṇayati, -te, -ṇetum, to lead round; to lead or bring forward.

पर्यातन् pary-ā-tan, cl. 5. P. A. -tanoti, -nute, -tanitum, Ved. to spread round, encompass, surround.

पर्यादा pary-ā-dā, cl. 3. A. -datte, -dātum, to make one's own, appropriate, learn; to take possession of; to take anything (acc.) away from (abl.); to take off, remove; to seize, grasp.

पर्याद्रु pary-ā-dru, cl. 1. P. -dravati, -drotum, to run to and fro, hasten round about.

पर्याधा pary-ā-dhā, cl. 3. P. A. -dadhāti, -dhatte, -dhātum, Ved. to lay round, surround with (fire).

पर्याप् pary-āp, cl. 5. P. -āpnoti, -āptum, to reach, obtain, gain (Ved.); to make an end of; to be content: Desid. parīpsati, &c., to wish to obtain or reach; to try to get at; to ask for, request, desire; to wish to preserve, guard; to lie in wait or ambush.

Pary-āpta, as, ā, am, obtained, gained; finished, ended, completed, complete, large, extensive, spacious; full; able, adequate, enough, sufficient; many; (am), ind. willingly, readily; ably, powerfully; satisfactorily. — Paryāpta-kala, as, ā, am, having full digits (as the moon). — Paryāpta-kāma, as, ā, am, Ved. one whose desires are under control. — Paryāpta-tā, f. satisfaction, gratification. — Paryāpta-dakshiṇa, as, ā, am, accompanied with liberal gifts. — Paryāpta-bhoga, as, ā, am, possessing or enjoying a sufficiency. — Paryāpta-vat, ān, atī, at, able, capable.

Pary-āpti, is, f. attaining, obtaining, acquisition; end, conclusion, close; adequacy, competency, fitness, dexterity; entireness, fulness, sufficiency, enough; satisfaction, repletion, satiety; willingness, readiness; protecting, preserving, guarding, warding off a blow, self-defence; discrimination or distinction of objects according to their natural properties.

पर्यापत् pary-ā-pat, cl. 1. P. -patati, -patitum, to hasten forth, hurry away, run away.

पर्याप्लु pary-ā-plu, cl. 1. A. -plavate, -plotum, to run round, encompass, encircle: Caus. -plāvayati, -yitum, Ved. to cause to float round.

Pary-āplāva, as, m. revolution.

Pary-āpluta, as, ā, am, surrounded, encircled.

पर्याभू pary-ā-bhū, cl. 1. P. -bhavati, -bhavitum, Ved. to turn round.

पर्याभृ pary-ā-bhṛi, cl. 1. P. -bharati, -bhartum, Ved. to extract.

Pary-ā-bhṛita, as, ā, am, Ved. extracted.

पर्यामृश् pary-ā-mṛiś, cl. 6. P. -mṛiśati, -marshṭum, -mrashṭum, to subdue, conquer, overpower.

पर्याय pary-āya. See under parī, p. 551.

पर्यारिन् pary-ārin, ī, iṇī, i (fr. rt. 4. ṛi with pari), Ved. (perhaps) falling away, decaying, decrepit.

पर्यालोच् pary-ā-loć, cl. 10. P. -loćayati, -yitum, to look after, attend to, consider (the interests of another), ponder.

Pary-āloćana, am, n. or pary-āloćanā, f. looking round or about; circumspection, attentive observation, mature consideration or reflection, deliberating; knowing, recognising.

पर्याविल pary-āvila, as, ā, am, very turbid, much soiled.

पर्यावृत् pary-ā-vṛit, cl. 1. A. -vartate, -vartitum, to turn round, return: Caus. P. -vartayati, -yitum, to roll round, turn round: Desid. -vivṛitsati, Ved. to wish to roll round.

Pary-āvarta, as, m. return.

Pary-āvartana, as, m., N. of a hell; (am), n. coming back, returning.

Pary-āvartita, as, ā, am, turned round, subverted, reversed.

Pary-āvivṛitsat, an, antī, at, Ved. wishing to roll round.

पर्याश्वस् pary-ā-śvas, Caus. P. -śvāsayati, -yitum, to comfort, console.

पर्यास् pary-ās, cl. 2. A. -āste, -āsitum, to sit round any one (acc.); to remain sitting, remain inactive; to exclude one's self from (with acc.).

पर्यास pary-āsa, pary-āsana. See under 2. pary-as, p. 554, col. 3.

पर्याहार pary-āhāra, as, m. a yoke worn across the shoulders in carrying a load; conveying, taking; a load; storing hay or grain; a ewer, pitcher.

पर्युक paryuka, as, m., N. of a man.

पर्युक्ष् pary-uksh, cl. 6. P. -ukshati, -ukshitum, Ved. to sprinkle round.

Pary-ukshaṇa, am, n. sprinkling round; sprinkling; (ī), f. a vessel for sprinkling (Ved.).

पर्युत्थान pary-utthāna, am, n. standing up, rising.

पर्युत्सुक pary-utsuka, as, ā, am, afflicted, sad, sorrowful, regretting; eagerly desirous, longing for (with dat.).

पर्युदञ्चन pary-udańćana, am, n. debt.

पर्युदयम् pary-udayam, ind., Ved. about sunrise.

पर्युदस् pary-ud-as, cl. 4. P. -asyati, -asitum, to heap round about, to construct here and there; to prohibit, object to; to expect, exclude.

Pary-udasta, as, ā, am, heaped round; prohibited, objected to (as a ceremony); excepted, excluded.

Pary-udāsa, as, m. or pary-udāsana, am, n. a prohibitive rule or precept, exception.

पर्युद्भृत pary-udbhṛita, as, ā, am, Ved. brought out, extracted; constructed, framed.

पर्युद्विज् pary-ud-vij, cl. 7. P. -vinakti, -vijitum, to suffer pain, suffer.

पर्युपवेशन pary-upaveśana, am, n. sitting about.

पर्युपस्था pary-upa-sthā, cl. 1. P. A. -tishṭhati, -te, -sthātum, to stand round, surround; wait on, serve, minister; to be present.

Pary-upasthāna, am, n. waiting upon, serving, maintaining; rising, elevation.

Pary-upasthita, as, ā, am, drawing nigh, imminent, impending.

पर्युपस्पृश् pary-upa-spṛiś, cl. 6. P. -spṛiśati, -sprashṭum, -sparshṭum, to touch or use for ablution or bathing.

पर्युपास् pary-upās (pary-upa-ās), cl. 2. A. -āste, -āsitum, to sit round, surround, encompass, encircle; to sit on or upon; to live around; to be present at, partake of; to approach as an attendant or worshipper, show reverence, worship.

Pary-upāsaka, as, ā, am, worshipping, honouring, a worshipper, one who honours or respects.

Pary-upāsana, am, n. encamping or sitting round; friendliness, amiability, courtesy; honour, service, worship; joining in or concurrence with any act of reverence.

Pary-upāsitṛi, tā, trī, tṛi, moving round or about; showing respect or honour; a worshipper.

Pary-upāsīna, as, ā, am, seated or sitting upon.

पर्युप्त pary-upta, as, ā, am (fr. rt. vap with pari), sown; set (as a gem in a ring).

Pary-upti, is, f. scattering seed, sowing.

पर्युषण pary-ushaṇa, am, n. (fr. rt. 6. vas with pari or incorrectly for pary-eshaṇa), service, worship, adoration.

Pary-ushita, as, ā, am, having passed the night; stale, not fresh; insipid; stupid, vain. — Paryushita-bhojin, ī, m. the eater of stale food (said to become a maggot or worm in the next birth).

पर्यूह् pary-ūh [cf. rt. 1. ūh], cl. 1. P. A. -ūhati, -te, -ūhitum, Ved. to heap or pile round; to surround or fortify with mounds or embankments.

Pary-ūhaṇa, am, n., Ved. sweeping or heaping together.

पर्यृष् 1. pary-ṛish, cl. 1. P. -arshati, -arshitum, Ved. to flow round, flow into.

पर्यृष् 2. pary-ṛish, cl. 6. P. -ṛishati, -arshitum, Ved. to embrace, clasp round, support.

Pary-arshaṇa, am, n., Ved. clasping round, supporting, making firm.

पर्ये pary-e (pari-ā-i), cl. 2. P. -eti, -etum, Ved. to roam about; to come back, return.

पर्येतृ pary-etṛi, tā, trī, tṛi (fr. parī), Ved, overpowering, mastering; (Sāy.) = nāśaka, a despoiler; = pari-gamayitṛi, a promoter.

पर्येष् pary-esh, cl. 1. P. -eshati, -eshitum, to seek about for.

Pary-eshaṇa, am, n. search, inquiry, investigation; (ā), f. search, inquiry, research, investigation of duty by reasoning; serving, waiting upon, service.

Pary-eshat, an, antī, at, seeking about for.

Pary-eshṭavya, as, ā, am, to be sought after, to be sought.

Pary-eshṭi, is, f. searching for, inquiry.

पर्व् parv, cl. 1. P. parvati, parvitum, to fill; [cf. rts. pṛi, pūrv, marv.]

Parva, as, ā, am, (at the end of a comp.) = parvan, p. 556, col. 1.

Parvaka, am, n. the knee-joint.

Parvaṇa, as, m., N. of a demon; (ī), m. the period of a change of the moon; a festival; (also parvaṇikā and parvaṇīkā), a particular disease of the so-called juncture (sandhi) of the eye; (at the end of a comp.) = parvan, a knot.

Parvata, as, m. (probably connected with parvan, p. 556, col. 1, as 'having crags or elevations'), a mountain, mountain-range, height, hill, elevation, rock, (in Ṛig-veda I. 37. 7, V. 56, 4, parvata is joined as an adj. with giri; and according to Sāy. = jagat-pūrakodaka-vat, laden with water filling the world, or bahuvidha-parva-yukta, shelving, rugged); an artificial mountain or heap (of grain, salt, saffron, sugar, silver or gold presented to the Brāhmans); N. of the presiding genius of the mountains (personified in the Veda with Āptya, Rudra, and Ṛibhu as ruler of the clouds, and associated with Indra, Savitṛi, the Maruts, and other deities; in later times enumerated among the eight Vasus); a fragment of rock, bowlder, stone, (adrayaḥ parvatāḥ, the stones with which the Soma plant is pressed); a cloud (Ved.; in some passages of the Ṛig-veda where parvata is interpreted by adri, the sense 'cloud' seems equally applicable, especially when the battles of Indra or the deeds of the Maruts are described); a N. of the number 7 (from the 7 principal mountains); a tree; a kind of vegetable; a kind of fish (commonly called Pāvdā, the Silurus Pabda); N. of a divine Ṛishi mentioned in several passages of the Mahā-bh. (regarded as a companion of Nārada and messenger of the gods, cf. Nala II. 14; he is the author of Ṛig-veda VIII. 12, IX. 104, 105, where he has the patronymics Kāṇva and Kāśyapa); N. of a son of Paurṇamāsa (a son of Marīći and Sam-bhūti); of a minister of king Purū-ravas; of a grammarian (?); of an ape; (ī), f. (Ved.) a rock, stone; [cf. Serv. brdo, 'a mountain;' perhaps Goth. fairguni.] — Parvata-kāka, as, m. a raven. — Parvata-ćyut, t, t, t, Ved. 'causing mountains (clouds) to totter or fall,' an epithet of the Maruts. — *Parvata-ja, as, ā, am,* mountain-born; (*ā*), f. a river. — *Parvata-triṇa, am,* n. 'mountain-grass,' a species of grass (= *triṇāḍhya*). — *Parvata-pati, is,* m. 'mountain-prince,' lord of the mountains. — *Parvata-moćā,* f. a species of plant (= *giri-kadalī*). — *Parvata-rāj, ṭ,* m. 'mountain-king,' a lofty mountain, 'the highest mountain-range,' the Himālaya. — *Parvata-rāja, as,* m. 'mountain-king,' the Himālaya. — *Parvatarāja-kanyā,* f. 'daughter of the mountain-king,' N. of Pārvatī or Durgā (daughter of Hima-vat, sovereign of the snowy mountains). — *Parvatarāja-putrī,* f. 'daughter of the mountain-king,' an epithet of Durgā. — *Parvata-vāsin, ī, inī, i,* living in the mountains; (*ī*), m. a mountaineer; (*inī*), f. nard, spikenard; a designation of Durgā; of the Gāyatrī. — *Parvata-śreshṭha, as,* m. the best of mountains. — *Parvata-stha, as, ā, am,* situated on a mountain or hill. — *Parvatākāra* (°*ta-āk*°), *as, ā, am,* mountain-shaped, formed like a mountain. — *Parvatātmajā* (°*ta-āt*°), f. 'daughter of the mountain,' an epithet of Durgā. — *Parvatādhārā* (°*ta-ādh*°), f. 'receptacle of mountains,' the earth. — *Parvatāri* (°*ta-ari*), *is,* m. 'enemy of the mountains,' epithet of Indra (who clipped their wings). — *Parvatā-vridh, t, t, t,* Ved. delighting in mountains; (Sāy.) 'delighting in the stones used to press the Soma plant' or 'produced in the mountains,' an epithet of Soma. — *Parvatāśaya* (°*ta-āś*°), *as,* m. 'resting on the mountains,' a cloud. — *Parvatāśraya* (°*ta-āś*°), *as, ā, am,* living on the mountains, a mountaineer; (*as*), m. a fabulous animal, the Śarabha. — *Parvatāśrayin* (°*ta-āś*°), *ī,* m. a dweller on the mountains, mountaineer. — *Parvati-kri,* cl. 8. P. *-karoti, -kartum,* to make into a mountain. — *Parvateśvara* (°*ta-īś*°), *as,* m. a lord of the mountains. — *Parvate-shṭhā, ās, ās, am,* Ved. 'dwelling in the heights,' an epithet of Indra.

Parvataka in *eka-p*°, q. v.

Parvatīya, as, ā, am, relating or belonging to a mountain, mountainous, hilly; a mountaineer.

Parvatya, as, ā, am, Ved. belonging to a mountain or rock; produced in mountains.

Parvan, a, n. (said to be fr. rt. *pṛī*, but connected with *parvata* above), a knot or joint, especially of a cane or other plant; a joint of the body, knuckle, limb, member; a break, pause, division, section; book, chapter; (in Vedic grammar) a member of a compound; a division of time, period, fixed time (especially the Cāturmāsya festival), the days of the four changes of the moon, i. e. the full and change of the moon and the eighth and fourteenth of each half month; the days of conjunction and opposition or eclipse of the sun or moon; a sacrifice performed on the occasion of a change of the moon; a particular period of the year (as the equinox, solstice, &c.); the moment of the sun's entering a new sign; a festival, holiday; opportunity, occasion; a moment, instant; [cf. *parus.*] — *Parva-kāra, as, ā, am,* or *parva-kārin, ī, iṇī, i,* one who works on holidays; (according to others) a Brāhman who for the sake of gain performs on common days such ceremonies as should be performed only on festivals. — *Parva-kāla, as,* m. a periodic change of the moon; the time at which the moon at its conjunction or opposition passes through the node. — *Parva-gāmin, ī,* m. one who has intercourse with his wife on festivals or holidays. — *Parva-gupta, as,* m., N. of a man. — *Parva-dhi, is,* m. 'period-holder,' the moon. — *Parva-nāḍī,* f. 'moment of the Parvan,' moment of opposition or conjunction. — *Parva-pushpī* or *parva-pushpikā,* f. a plant, = *rāma-dūtī,* Tiaridium Indicum (= *nāga-dantī*). — *Parva-pūrṇa-tā,* f. preparations for an assembly or festival; completion of a festival; joining, uniting. — *Parva-bheda, as,* m. the fracture of a joint. — *Parva-mūla, am,* n. the moment at which the fourteenth day passes into the fifteenth day of a month; (*ā*), f. a species of plant (= *śvetā*). — *Parva-yoni, is, is, i,* growing from joints or knots; (*is*), m. a cane or reed, the sugar-cane, &c. — *Parva-ruh, ṭ,* m. a pomegranate tree. — *Parva-varja, as, ā, am,* except the forbidden days of a month. — *Parva-vallī,* f. a species of Dūrvā (= *granthi-dūrvā, mūla-dūrvā*). — *Parva-śarkaraka, as,* m., N. of a man. — *Parva-śas,* ind., Ved. limb by limb, limb from limb, piece by piece; *parvaśaḥ krit,* to cut to pieces. — *Parva-sandhi, is,* m. a joint; the full and change of the moon, the junction of the fifteenth and first of a lunar fortnight or the precise moment of the full and change of the moon. — *Parvāvadhi* (°*va-av*°), *is,* m. a particular period, the end of a Parvan, &c. — *Parvāsphoṭa* (°*va-ās*°), *as,* m. a particular movement of the fingers (regarded as indecorous). — *Parveśa* (°*va-īśa*), *as,* m., Ved. the regent of an astronomical node.

Parvariṇa, as, m. = *parṇa-vrinta-rasa;* = *garva;* = *māruta;* = *parṇa-śirā;* = *mritaka;* = *dyūta-kambala;* = *pattra-ćūrṇa-rasa;* = *parvan.*

पर्वत *parvata, parvan.* See under rt. *parv.*

पर्वित *parvita, as,* m. a species of fish, Silurus Pabda (= *parvata*).

पर्शान *parśāna, as,* m. (probably connected with rts. *parsh* and *prish*), Ved. a precipice, chasm; a well; (Sāy.) = *pārśva-sthāna,* the side; = *pīḍyamāna,* being oppressed; = *sprishyamāna;* = *vimarśana-kshama;* (according to the Naighaṇṭuka I. 10) a cloud.

1. *parśu, us,* m., Ved. a rib; a curved knife, pruning-hook, sickle; N. of a man; (*avas*), m. pl., N. of a warrior-tribe; (*us*), f. (according to the Nirukta IV. 6) the supporting or side wall of a well (Ṛig-veda I. 105, 8, but according to Sāy. = *pārśvāsthi*); N. of a woman. — *Parśu-maya, as, ī, am,* shaped like a curved knife.

Parśukā, f. a rib.

पर्शु 2. *parśu, us,* m. (fr. *pṛī,* substituted for rt. *spriś*), = *paraśu,* an axe, hatchet. — *Parśu-pāṇi, is,* m. 'axe in hand,' an epithet of Gaṇeśa; [cf. *paraśu-dhara.*] — *Parśu-rāma* = *Paraśu-rāma,* q. v.

Parśvadha, as, m. = *paraśvadha,* an axe, hatchet.

पर्ष् *parsh* [cf. rts. *prish, varsh, sparsh*], cl. 1. A. *parshate,* &c., to grow wet, become moist; to delight in, accept (Sāy. = *svī-kri*).

पर्ष *parsha, as,* m. (probably connected with rt. *prish*), a bundle, sheaf.

Parshin, ī, iṇī, i, Ved. in *ishu-p*°, (probably) carrying bundles (of arrows).

पर्षणि *parshaṇi, is, is, i* (fr. rt. 1. *pṛī*), Ved. carrying over or across, ferrying across.

Parshan, a, n. (?), Ved. leading out, delivering.

Parshishṭha, as, ā, am, Ved. most mighty in delivering or rescuing.

पर्षद् *parshad, t,* f. = *parishad,* an assembly, audience. — *Parshad-bhīru, us, us, u,* Ved. shy in society. — *Parshad-vala, as, ā, am,* = *parishad-vala,* surrounded by an assembly; (*as*), m. an assistant at an assembly, a spectator.

पल् *pal,* cl. 1. P. *palati, palitum,* to go, move; cl. 10. *pālayati, -yitum,* see rt. 3. *pā;* [cf. Gr. πάλλω, παλμό-ς, πάλο-ς, παλάσσω, παλ-ύν-ω; Lat. *pello, poll-en, pul-vi-s.*]

Pala, as, m. = *pāla* (Gaṇa Jvalādi to Pāṇ. III. 1, 140); = *palāla,* straw; (*am*), n. a particular weight (= 4 Karshas = $\frac{1}{100}$ of a Tulā); a particular measure of fluids; a particular measure of time (= *vighaṭikā*); flesh, meat; [cf. Lat. *palea;* Angl. Sax. *flesc, flæsc, flec;* Old Germ. *fleisk;* French *paille;* Hib. *feol, feoilc,* 'flesh.'] — *Pala-kshāra, as,* m. 'flesh-fluid,' blood. — *Pala-gaṇḍa, as,* m. a mason, bricklayer, plasterer. — *Palan-kara, as,* m. 'flesh-maker,' gall, bile. — *Palan-kasha, as,* m. 'flesh-hurter,' a Rākshasa, imp, goblin; bdellium; a species of bdellium (= *kaṇa-guggulu*); (*ā*), f., N. of various plants (= *go-kshuraka,* Asteracantha Longifolia; = *kshudra-gokshuraka;* = *kinśuka,* Butea Frondosa; = *muṇḍirī,* a species of climbing plant; = *rāsna;* = *mahā-śrāvaṇī,* bdellium); = *lākshā,* cochineal; a fly. — *Pala-priya, as,* m. 'fond of meat,' a Rākshasa; a raven. — *Pala-bhā* or *pala-vibhā,* f. the equinoctial shadow at midday, the midday shadow of a gnomon when the sun is in the equinoctial points (= *vishuvat-prabhā*). — *Palāgni* (°*la-ag*°), *is,* m. 'flesh-fire,' bile, the bilious humor. — *Palāda* (°*la-ada*), *as,* m. 'flesh-eater,' a Rākshasa; (*ā*), f. a Rākshasī. — *Palādana* (°*la-ad*°), *as,* or 1. *palāśa* (°*la-āś*°), *as,* or 1. *palāśin* (°*la-āś*°), *ī,* m. 'flesh-eater,' a Rākshasa.

Palada, as, m., Ved. a particular material for building, (perhaps) bundles of straw or reeds used for roofing and wainscoting; (*ī*), f., N. of a village.

Palala, as, m. a Rākshasa; ground sesamum seeds, a kind of sweetmeat made of ground sesamum and sugar; mud, mire, clay; = *pala,* flesh, meat; [cf. *palvala;* Gr. πηλό-ς, πήλ-ινο-ς, προ-πηλακ-ίζω; Lat. *pāl-ū(d)s, palus-tri-s;* Hib. *poll,* 'mire, dirt.'] — *Palala-jvara, as,* m. gall, bile; [cf. *palāgni, palan-kara.*] — *Palala-priya, as,* m. 'fond of flesh,' a raven (= *pala-priya*). — *Palalāśaya* (°*la-āś*°), *as,* m. 'flesh-receptacle,' swelled neck, goitre.

Palika, as, ā, am (at the end of a comp. after a numeral), weighing or containing so many Palas.

पलक्या *palakyā,* f. a kind of vegetable (= *pālankya*).

पलक्ष *palaksha, as, ī, am* (a secondary form of *balaksha*), Ved. white.

पलङ्कट *palankaṭa, as, ā, am,* shy, bashful, timid.

पलव *palava, as,* m. (said to be connected with rt. *pal,* probably for *plava* fr. rt. *plu*), a snare or basket of wicker-work for catching fish.

पलस *palasa, as,* m. = *panasa,* the bread fruit tree.

पलस्ति *palasti, is, is, i,* Ved. (according to Sāy.) = *palita,* grey-haired.

पलाङ्ग *palānga, as,* m. Delphinus Gangeticus; (perhaps an error for *ćapalānga.*)

पलाण्डु *palāṇḍu, us, u,* m. n. (said to be fr. rt. *pal*), an onion. — *Palāṇḍu-bhakshita, as, ā* or *ī, am,* one who has eaten onions.

पलाप *palāpa, as,* m. a halter; an elephant's temples.

पलापहा *palāpahā,* f. a kind of collyrium (= *kulatthā;* perhaps only an error for *pralāpa-hā*).

पलाय *palāya* (fr. *ay* = rt. 5. *i* with *palā* = *parā*), cl. 1. A. (ep. also P.) *palāyate (-ti), -yitum,* to flee, run away, make off, take to one's heels, scamper off; to escape; to cease, die away, sink into oblivion.

Palāyaka, as, ā or *ikā* (?), *am,* fleeing, flying, taking to flight; a fugitive, runaway, deserter.

Palāyat, an, antī, at, fleeing, running away.

Palāyana, am, n. fleeing, running away, flight, escape; a saddle (= *palyayana, paryāṇa*). — *Palāyana-parāyaṇa, as, ā, am,* occupied in flight, fugitive. — *Palāyana-manas, ās, ās, as,* thinking of flight. — *Palāyana-vishaya, as, ā, am,* having flight for an object, bent on flight.

Palāyamāna, as, ā, am, fleeing, flying away, taking to flight.

Palāyita, as, ā, am, flown, run away, fled, retreated; defeated.

Palāyin, ī, inī, i, fleeing, flying, running away, taking to flight.

पलाल *palāla, as, am,* m. n. (said to be fr. rt. *pal*), straw; the stalk of the Sorghum,

Indian millet; *(as)*, m., Ved., N. of a demon (associated with Anu-palāla and considered dangerous to children); *(ā)*, f., N. of one of the seven Mātṛis of Skanda; *(ī)*, f. straw.—*Palāla-dohada, as*, m. 'longing for straw,' the mango tree (the fruit of which is sometimes ripened in straw).

पलाव **palāva**, *as*, m., Ved. chaff, husks; [cf. Lat. *palea*.]

पलाश 2. **palāśa**, *am*, n. (for 1. see under *pala*, rt. *pal*, p. 556, col. 2), a leaf, petal, foliage; the blossom of the tree Butea Frondosa; *(as)*, m. Butea Frondosa; Curcuma Zedoaria; a N. of ancient Behar or Magadha; *(ī)*, f. cochineal; a species of climbing plant (=*paṭtra-vallī, parṇa-vallī, palāśikā*); *(as, ā, am)*, green; unfeeling, unmerciful, cruel; (at the end of a comp.) see Gaṇa to Pāṇ. II. 1, 56.—*Palāśa-pattra, am*, n. the leaf of the Butea Frondosa; a single leaf; *(as)*, m., N. of a Nāga.—*Palāśa-parṇī*, f. Physalis Flexuosa (=*aśva-gandhā*).—*Palāśa-śātana, as*, m. an instrument for lopping foliage.—*Palāśākhya* (°*śa-ākh*°), *as*, m.=*nāḍī-hiṅgu*, q. v.; Asa Fœtida.—*Palāśāntā* (°*śa-an*°) or *palāśāmbhā*, f.=*gandha-pattra*, q. v.

Palāśaka, as, m. Butea Frondosa; Curcuma Zedoaria (=*śaṭī*); N. of a place; *(ikā)*, f. a species of climbing plant (=*palāśī*).

2. *palāśin, ī, inī, i* (for 1. see under *pala*, rt. *pal*), leafy, covered with foliage, having luxuriant foliage; *(ī)*, m. a tree; a species of plant (=*kshīra-vṛiksha*); N. of a city or a village (said to be the modern Plassey); *(inī)*, f., N. of a river issuing from the Sukti-mat.

पलिक्नी **paliknī**, f. See *palita* below.

पलिघ **paligha**, *as*, m. a water-pot, pitcher, glass water-vessel; a wall, rampart; the gate-way of a building; an iron club or one studded with iron (=*parigha*).

पलित **palita**, *as, paliknī, am* (said to be fr. rt. *phal* with substitution of *p* for *ph*; a doubtful fem. form *palitā* is also given), grey, grey-haired, hoary, old, aged; *(as)*, m., N. of a mouse in Mahā-bh. Śānti-p. 4933; *(paliknī)*, f. a cow for the first time with calf; *(am)*, n. grey hair; a tuft of hair (=*keśa-pāśa*); much or ornamented hair; mud, mire; heat, burning; benzoin; [cf. Gr. πελ-ό-ς, πελ-ιό-ς, πελ-λό-ς, πελιδνό-ς, πολ-ιό-ς: Lat. *pall-e-o, pall-idu-s, pallu-s*: Old Germ. *falo (fal-wer)*: Angl. Sax. *fealo, falu, fealwe, falewe*: Slav. *plavŭ*, 'white:' Lith. *pàl-va-s*, 'fallow;' *pìl-ka-s*, 'ash-coloured.']—*Palitan-karaṇa, as, ī, am*, rendering grey.—*Palitam-bhavishṇu, us, us, u*, or *palitam-bhāvuka, as, ā, am*, becoming grey.

Palitin, ī, inī, i, having grey hair, grey-haired.

पलियोग **pali-yoga**, *as*, m.=*pari-yoga*.

पलीजक **palījaka**, *as*, m., Ved., N. of a demon.

पल्पूल् **palpūl** (considered by some as a reduplicated form of rt. *pal*), cl. 10. P. *palpūlayati, -yitum*, Ved. to wash in lye or water impregnated with alkaline salt; to wash, cleanse; to tan.

Palpūlana, am, n., Ved. lye, water impregnated with alkaline salt.

Palpūlita, as, ā, am, Ved. curried, tanned; washed (in lye).

पल्य **palya**, *am*, n. (perhaps fr. *pala*), a sack for corn (probably containing a certain measure, Ved.); a particular high number.

पल्यङ्क **paly-aṅka**, *as*, m.=*pary-aṅka*, a bed, couch, bedstead; a cloth thrown round the loins while sitting (=*pary-asti, paryastikā*).

पल्यङ्ग् **paly-aṅg** (for *pary-aṅg*), Caus. P. *-aṅgayati, -yitum*, Ved. to cause to go round, stir round: Pass. *-aṅgyate*, to turn round, revolve.

पल्यय् **paly-ay** (fr. *ay*=rt. 5. *i* with *pali*=*pari*), cl. 1. A. *-ayate*, &c., Ved. to go round.

Paly-ayana, am, n.=*paryāṇa*, a saddle, pack-saddle; a rein, bridle.

पल्युल् **palyul** and **palyūl** (various readings for *palpūl*, q. v.), cl. 10. P. *palyulayati, palyūlayati, -yitum*, to wash, &c.; to cut, cut off (in this sense perhaps for *pari-lū*).

पल्ल् **pall** [cf. rt. *pal*], cl. 1. P. *pallati, pallitum*, to go, move.

Palla, as, m. a large granary, barn.

1. *pallava, as, am*, m. n. a sprout, shoot, twig, sprig, spray, (literally and as a metaphorical expression for the fingers, toes, and lips; cf. *kara-p*°, *oshṭha-p*°); a bud, blossom; a blade of grass; the extremity of a robe, the loose end of a garment or scarf; spreading, expansion; epithet of a particular position of the hands in dancing; the red dye called *a-lakta*; love, affection; a bracelet, armlet; unsteadiness moral or physical (?); strength, power (?); a wood (?); *(as)*, m. a libertine, catamite; *(ās)*, m. pl., N. of a people.—*Pallavagrāhi-tā*, f. the picking up of twigs or straws, the dealing with trifles; superficial or diffusive knowledge.—*Pallava-grāhin, ī, iṇī, i*, putting forth young shoots, sprouting in all directions; twig-picking, straw-gathering; laying hold of trifles; diffusive; superficial; *(ī)*, m., scil. *dosha*, the fault of prolixity or diffusiveness or of mere superficial knowledge.—*Pallava-dru, us*, m. the Aśoka tree.—*Pallava-maya, as, ī, am*, consisting of young shoots or twigs.—*Pallavāṅkura* (°*va-aṅ*°), *as*, m. a leaf-bud.—*Pallavāda* (°*va-ada*), *as*, m. 'eating young shoots,' a deer.—*Pallavādhāra* (°*va-ādh*°), *as*, m. 'receptacle or support of twigs,' a branch.—*Pallavāpīḍita* (°*va-āp*°), *as, ā, am*, bud-laden, loaded with buds.—*Pallavāstra* (°*va-as*°), *as*, m. 'having blossoms for missiles,' an epithet of the god of love.

2. *pallava*, Nom. P. *pallavati, pallavitum*, to put forth young shoots, sprout, bud.

Pallavaka, as, m. a libertine, gallant, the paramour of a harlot; a catamite; a species of fish, Cyprinus Denticulatus; *(ikā)*, f., N. of a female attendant.

Pallavaya, Nom. P. *pallavayati, -yitum*, to put forth young shoots, sprout; to cause to sprout, to make diffuse or prolix (according to a Scholiast =*vistāraya*).

Pallavika, as, m. a libertine, gallant; a catamite; a species of fish, Cyprinus Denticulatus.

Pallavita, as, ā, am, sprouting, having young shoots; spread, extended; dyed red with lac, possessing the red dye; *(as)*, m. the red dye of the lac insect.

Pallavin, ī, inī, i, sprouting, having young shoots; *(ī)*, m. a tree.

Palli, is or *ī*, f. a small village, especially a settlement of wild tribes; a hut, house; any number of houses, a station; a city (or rather an affix to words forming the name of towns; it is especially used in the Dekhan as in Trichinopoly=Triśira-pallī, &c.); a small house-lizard; a creeping plant.

Pallikā, f. a village, station [cf. *ābhīra-p*°]; a small house-lizard.

पल्लि **palli**. See under rt. *pall* above.

पल्लिवाह **pallivāha**, *as*, m. a species of grass.

पल्वल **palvala**, *as*, m. (connected with *palita*; said to be fr. rt. *pal*), a small tank, pond, pool; [cf. Gr. πηλό-ς, πήλ-ινο-ς, προ-πηλακ-ίζω; Lat. *pal-u(d)-s, palus-tri-s*; perhaps Angl. Sax. *pol*, 'a pool.']—*Palvala-tīra, am*, n. the bank or margin of a pool.—*Palvala-paṅka, as*, m. the mud of a pool.—*Palvalāvāsa* (°*la-āv*°), *as*, m. 'living in ponds,' a tortoise.

Palvalya, as, ā, am, Ved. marshy, boggy.

पव् **pav**, cl. 1. A. *pavate, pavitum*, to go; (a various reading for *plav*.)

पव **pava**, *as*, m. (fr. rt. 1. *pū*), purification, purity; winnowing corn; air, wind; a marsh; *(ā)*, f. purification; *(am)*, n. cow-dung.

Pavat, an, antī, at, purifying; pure.

Pavana, am, n. the act of purifying, purification; winnowing; an instrument for purifying, sieve, strainer, &c.; water; *(as)*, m. 'the purifier,' wind, air, the wind of the body; Wind personified (as regent of the Nakshatra Svāti and of the North-west region); a N. of the number five (Ved.); a householder's sacred fire; N. of a son of Manu Uttama; of the author of a Gāndharva-veda; *(as, am)*, m. n. a potter's kiln; *(ī)*, f. a broom; N. of a river; *(as, ā, am)*, clean, pure.—*Pavana-kshipta, as, ā, am*, tempest-tossed.—*Pavana-tanaya, as*, m. 'son of the Wind,' an epithet of Hanu-mat.—*Pavana-vāhana, as*, m. 'having wind as a vehicle,' fire.—*Pavana-vijaya, as*, m. 'victory over the wind or breath,' N. of a mystic work.—*Pavana-vyādhi, is*, m. an epithet of Ud-dhava, the friend and counsellor of Kṛishṇa; morbid condition of wind, rheumatism, &c.—*Pavanātmaja* (°*na-āt*°), *as*, m. 'son of the Wind;' fire; an epithet of Hanumat the monkey-hero.—*Pavanāśa* (°*na-āśa*), or *pavanāśana* (°*na-aś*°), *as*, m. 'feeding on air,' a serpent, snake.—*Pavanāśa-nāśa, as*, m. 'snake-destroyer,' a peacock; Garuḍa the bird and vehicle of Vishṇu.—*Pavanāśin* (°*na-āś*°), *ī*, m. 'feeding on air,' a serpent.—*Pavanāhata* (°*na-āh*°), *as, ā, am*, struck or shaken by the wind; rheumatic.—*Pavanodbhrānta-kārin* (°*na-ud*°), *ī, inī, i*, 'agitating the air,' epithet of a particular mode of fighting.—*Pavanodbhrānta-vīci, is, is*, m. f. a wave tossed up by the winds.

Pavamāna, as, ā, am, being purified, being strained (usually said of the Soma, Ved.); *(as)*, m. wind; N. of a particular Fire (associated with Pāvaka and Śuci, and also regarded as a son of Agni by Svāhā); epithet of the moon; epithet of particular Stotras sung by the Sāma-ga at the Jyotishṭoma (Ved.).—*Pavamāna-vat, ān, atī, at*, Ved. having the Pavamāna-stotra.—*Pavamāna-havis, is*, n. or *pavamāneshṭi* (°*na-ish*°), *is*, f., Ved. offerings to Agni invoked under the title of Pavamāna or Pāvaka or Śuci.

Pavayitṛi, tā, trī, tṛi, Ved. one who purifies or cleans, a purifier, cleanser, cleansing.

Pavākā, f. a storm, whirlwind.

Pavi, is, m., Ved. the tire of a wheel; the metallic point of a spear or arrow; a thunderbolt; an arrow; speech; fire; [cf. *ārdra-p*°, *kṛishṇa-p*°, *kshura-p*°.]—*Pavī-nasa, as, ā, am*, Ved. 'having a nose like a spear-head,' epithet of a demon.

Pavita, as, ā, am, purified, cleansed; *(am)*, n. black pepper.

Pavitṛi or Ved. *pavitṛi, tā, trī, tṛi*, one who purifies or cleanses, a purifier, cleanser.

Pavitra, am, n. a means of purification, instrument for cleansing, filter, strainer, straining-cloth, colander (made of thread or hair or straw plaited or woven, for clarifying fluids, especially the Soma); Kuśa grass (especially a couple of Kuśa leaves a span long used at sacrifices to present offerings upon or to sprinkle and purify ghee, &c.); a ring of Kuśa grass worn on the fourth finger on particular occasions; a purifying prayer or Mantra; water, rain; rubbing, cleansing; the vessel in which the Argha is presented; copper; the sacred thread, Brāhmanical cord; melted butter; honey; any divinity as Agni &c.?; *(as)*, m., N. of a Soma-yāga belonging to the Rāja-sūya; the sesame plant, Nageia Putranjiva; N. of a man (of the family of Aṅgiras and the reputed author of Ṛig-veda IX. 67, 73, 83, 107); *(ās)*, m. pl. epithet of a class of deities in the fourteenth Manv-antara; *(ā)*, f., N. of various plants; basil; Indian saffron, turmeric; =*aśvatthī*, q. v.; N. of a river (the

Pabar, a little to the north-west of Hari-dwār); the twelfth day of the light half of S'rāvaṇa (a festival in honour of Vishṇu); (*as, ā, am*), purifying, cleansing; pure, clean; holy, sinless; averting evil; [cf. Hib. *beathra*, 'water;' *fothragaim*, 'I bathe, cleanse;' *fothragadh*, 'a bath, well of purification.'] — *Pavitra-tā*, f. or *pavitra-tva, am*, n. purity, cleanness. — *Pavitra-dhānya, am*, n. 'pure grain,' barley. — *Pavitra-pati, is*, m., Ved. lord of the Pavitra. — *Pavitra-pāṇi, is, is, i*, 'pure-handed,' having clean hands or holding Darbha grass in the hand; (*is*), m., N. of an ancient sage. — *Pavitra-pūta, as, ā, am*, Ved. clarified with a strainer or colander. — *Pavitra-ratha, as, ā, am*, Ved. having the colander as a chariot (said of the Soma). — *Pavitra-vat, ān, atī, at*, Ved. having an instrument for purifying (as a strainer or Darbha grass); purifying, cleansing; being in the colander; holding Darbha grass; an epithet of Agni; (*atī*), f., N. of a river. — *Pavitrāropaṇa* (°*ra-ār*°), *am*, n. 'putting on the Pavitra,' investiture with the Brāhmanical cord; investing the image of Kṛishṇa with the sacred thread; N. of a festival on the twelfth day of the light half of S'rāvaṇa. — *Pavitrārohaṇa* (°*ra-ār*°), *am*, n. 'putting on the Pavitra,' investing with the sacred thread, N. of a festival in honour of Durgā on the eighth day of the light half of the month S'rāvaṇa or Āshāḍha. — *Pavitrī-karaṇa, am*, n. purification, cleansing; the instrument or means of purifying. — *Pavitrī-kṛi*, cl. 8. P. A. *-karoti, -kurute, -kartum*, to purify, cleanse. — *Pavitrī-kṛita, as, ā, am*, purified, cleansed, cleaned, sanctified. — *Pavitrī-bhū*, cl. 1. P. *-bhavati, -bhavitum*, to become pure or clean.

Pavitraka, am, n. a small strainer or colander, the vessel in which an Argha or oblation is presented (?); pack-thread or a rope or net made of pack-thread; (*as*), m., N. of several sacred plants, Poa Cynosuroides (= *kuśa*); Artemisia Indica (= *damanaka*); Ficus Religiosa; Ficus Glomerata; (at the end of a comp.) = *pavitra*.

Pavitraya, Nom. P. *pavitrayati, -yitum*, to cleanse, purify.

Pavitrita, as, ā, am, cleansed, purified, clean, pure.

Pavitrin, ī, iṇī, i, purifying, cleansing; pure, clean.

Pavira, am, n., Ved. a weapon with a metallic point, a lance, spear. — *Pavira-vat, ān, atī, at*, Ved. armed with a lance or spear; having a goad; having a metallic share (said of a plough).

Pavīrava, as, m., Ved. having a metallic share (said of a plough); (Sāy.) = *kuliśa* or *kuliśa-śabda*, a thunderbolt or the noise of a thunderbolt.

Pavīru, us, m., Ved. (probably) a flash of lightning, a thunderbolt; N. of a man.

Paryā, f., Ved. purification, cleansing.

पवनाल *pavanāla, as*, m. a species of grain, Andropogon Saccharatus (= *deva-dhānya*; incorrectly for *yavanāla*).

पवनेष्ट *pavaneshṭa, as*, m. a large species of Nimba tree; (probably incorrectly for *yavaneshṭa*.)

पवनोम्बुज *pavanombuja, am*, n. = *parūsha*, the Parush tree; (probably an incorrect form.)

पविन्द *pavinda, as*, m., N. of a man.

पवीतृ *pavītṛi*. See *pavitṛi*, p. 557, col. 3.

पवीनस *pavī-nasa*. See under *pavi*, p. 557.

पवीर *pavīra, am*, n. See above.

पश् 1. *paś*, for original *spaś* substituted for rt. 1. *dṛiś*, q. v., 'to see,' in certain tenses; [cf. rt. *spaś, spaśa*: Zend *śpaś*, 'to see, guard;' *śpaś*, 'a spy:' Gr. σκεπ by metathesis for σπεκ in σκέπ-τ-ο-μαι, σκοπ-ή, σκοπιά, σκόπ-ελο-ς, σκοπ-ό-ς, σκώψ: Lat. *spec-i-o, con-spici-o, specula, speculum, specu-s, spec-to*: Old Germ. *speh-ō-m, spāh-i*: Mod. Germ. *späh-en*: Lith. *spega-s*, 'a spy:' Hib. *faic-im*, 'I see;' *feach-aim*, 'I look, view;' *faoch-og*, 'an eye.']

2. *paś*, according to some the form *paḍbhis* in Ṛig-veda IV. 2, 12, may be connected with a base *paś* derived fr. rt. 1. *paś* in the sense of 'sight,' 'look,' 'eye.'

1. *paśu*, ind. see! behold!

1. *paśya*, Ved. or *paśyaka, as, ā, am*, seeing, beholding, surveying, rightly understanding; [cf. *a-p*°, *a-sūryam-paśyā*.]

2. *paśya* (2nd sing. imperative of rt. 1. *dṛiś*), lo! behold! see! (an exclamation of wonder or admiration.)

Paśyat, an, antī, at, seeing, beholding, looking, viewing, observing, remarking; regarding, considering; (*antī*), f. a courtezan, harlot; epithet of a particular sound. — *Paśyato-hara, as, ā, am*, stealing before a person's eyes or in the very sight of the possessor; (*as*), m. a thief, pilferer (a term of reproach proverbially applied to the goldsmith &c.).

Paśyata, as, ā, am, Ved. visible, conspicuous.

Paśyanā, f., in *a-p*°, q. v.

पश् 3. *paś*, cl. 10. P. *pāśayati, -yitum*, to bind; [cf. Zend *paś*, 'to bind;' Gr. πήγ-νυ-μι, ἐ-πάγ-ην, πῆγ-μα, πηγ-ό-ς, πάγ-ο-ς, πάχ-νη, πάγ-η, πάσσ-αλο-ς: Lat. *pac-i-sc-or, pāx, pac-i-o(n), pang-o, pig-nus, pā-lu-s, com-pe-sc-o, dis-pe-sc-o*: Goth. *fah-an*, 'to catch;' *fulla-fahjan*, 'to fulfil;' *fagr-s*: Old Germ. *fuog-a, gafuogi, gafag-jan, fah*: Cambro-Brit. *fasgu*, 'to bind or tie in a bundle;' *fasgiad*, 'a ligation, a tying in a bundle.']

Paśavya, as, ā, am, belonging or relating to cattle, fit or suitable for cattle (as a meadow, pasturage, &c.); relating to a herd or drove; possessed of cattle; brutish; (with *kāma*) sexual love, sexual intercourse; (*am*), n. a herd or drove of cattle; a stall for cattle.

2. *paśu, us*, m. (fr. rt. 3. *paś*, 'to bind,' like Lat. *bestia* fr. rt. *bandh*; also said to be fr. rt. 1. *paś*; Vedic forms are du. *paśvā*, acc. pl. *paśvas*, inst. *paśvā*, dat. *paśve*, gen. *paśvas*), cattle (both singly and collectively), a herd, drove; any smaller animal used as a sacrificial victim, a goat; an animal in general, any domestic animal, (*grāmyāḥ paśavaḥ*, domestic animals, of which five kinds are enumerated, men, kine, horses, goats, and sheep, to which are sometimes added mules and asses or camels and dogs); a brute, beast, (*āraṇyāḥ* or *vanyāḥ paśavaḥ*, wild beasts, beasts of the forest; sometimes said contemptuously of a man; cf. *purusha-p*°); a mere animal in sacred things, an uninitiated person; a victim [cf. *nṛi-p*°]; an oblation; a subordinate deity and one of S'iva's followers; (with Māheśvaras and Pāśupatas) soul, the Supreme Spirit, the divine soul of the universe; Ficus Glomerata; (*u*), n., Ved. cattle; an animal, beast; [cf. Lat. *pecu*; Old Pruss. *pecku*; Goth. *faih-u*; Old Germ. *fih-u*; Mod. Germ. *vieh*, 'cattle;' perhaps Gr. πῶυ.] — *Paśu-karman, a*, n., Ved. the act of offering the victim; sacrifice; copulation. — *Paśu-kalpa, as*, m., Ved. the ritual of animal sacrifice. — *Paśu-kāma, as, ā, am*, Ved. desirous of possessing cattle. — *Paśu-kriyā*, f. the act of animal sacrifice; acting like cattle, copulation. — *Paśu-gāyatrī*, f. a parody of the holy verse of the Vedas whispered into the ear of an animal about to be sacrificed (*paśu-pāśāya vidmahe śiraś-ćhedāya dhīmahi tan naḥ paśuḥ praćodayāt*). — *Paśu-ghāta, am*, n. slaughter of animals for sacrifice. — *Paśu-ghna, as, ī, am*, slaughtering cattle. — *Paśu-ćaryā*, f. acting like cattle; copulation. — *Paśu-ćit, t, t, t*, Ved. piled up with cattle (as a sacrificial fire). — *Paśu-jātīya, as, ā, am*, pertaining to the animal kingdom. — *Paśu-tantra, as*, m. = *paśu-kalpa*, q. v. — *Paśu-tā*, f. or *paśu-tva, am*, n. the condition or nature of an animal, bestiality, brutality; the condition of a sacrificial animal, the being a sacrificial animal; the sacrifice of an animal. — *Paśu-tṛip, p, p, p*, Ved. gratifying one's self with cattle, i. e. stealing cattle; (Sāy.) = *paśūnām tarpayitṛī*, feeding cattle. — *Paśu-da, as, ā, am*, making a grant of cattle; (*ā*), f., N. of one of the Mātṛis attending on Skanda. — *Paśu-dā, ās, ās, am*, making a grant of cattle. — *Paśu-devata, as, ā, am*, Ved. invoking cattle as a deity (said of a formula or ceremony); (*ā*), f. the deity of the victim, i. e. the deity to whom the sacrifice is offered. — *Paśu-dharma, as*, m. the characteristics of cattle, conduct of cattle, treatment of cattle; promiscuous cohabitation; the marrying of widows; (*eṇa*), ind. like a beast. — *Paśu-nātha, as*, m. 'lord of cattle,' an epithet of S'iva. — *Paśu-pa, as, ā, am*, guarding or keeping cattle; (*as*), m. a herdsman. — *Paśu-pati, is*, m. 'lord of the animals' (or according to others 'lord of a servant named Paśu'), an epithet of the later Rudra (Rudra-S'iva) or of a similar deity (often associated in the Veda with Bhava, S'arva, Ugra, Rudra, Mahā-deva, Īśāna, and others, who together with Bhīma are in later times regarded as manifestations of the one deity Rudra); = S'iva; N. of a scholiast; of a lexicographer; of Agni; (according to one legend every deity acknowledged himself to be a mere *paśu* or animal before his lord and master S'iva, when they solicited him to destroy the Asura Tri-pura.) — *Paśupati-śarman, ā*, m., N. of a man. — *Paśupati-śāstra, am*, n. the sacred book of the Pāśupatas revealed by S'iva. — *Paśu-palvala, am*, n. a fragrant grass, Cyperus Rotundus (which grows in pools frequented by cattle). — *Paśu-pā, ās*, m., Ved. a keeper of herds, herdsman; an epithet of Pūshan; (*ā*), m. du. epithet of Pūshan and Revatī. — *Paśu-pāla, as*, m. a keeper of herds, herdsman; (*ās*), m. pl., N. of a people to the N. E. of Madhya-deśa; (*am*), n. the country or kingdom of the Paśupālas; (*as*), m., N. of a king (or perhaps a king of the Paśu-pālas). — *Paśu-pālaka, as*, m. a herdsman; (*ikā*), f. a herdsman's wife. — *Paśu-pālana, am*, n. tending or rearing cattle. — *Paśu-pālya, am*, n. breeding cattle. — *Paśu-pāśa, as*, m. the cord with which the victim is bound, binding the victim at a sacrifice; an animal sacrifice; the chains which fetter the individual soul, the world of sense. — *Paśu-pāśaka, as*, m. a kind of coitus. — *Paśu-preraṇa, am*, n. the driving of cattle. — *Paśu-bandha, as*, m. an animal sacrifice; N. of an Ekāha. — *Paśu-bandhaka, as* or *am*, m. or n. (?), a rope for tethering cattle. — *Paśu-bhartṛi, tā*, m. 'lord of cattle,' an epithet of S'iva. — *Paśu-bheda, as*, m. a class or species of animals. — *Paśu-mat, ān, atī, at*, connected with cattle or animals, relating to cattle or animals; rich in cattle, rich in herds; connected with animal sacrifices; containing the word *paśu*; (*at*), n. possession of cattle. — *Paśu-māra, as*, m. the manner of slaughtering cattle; (*am, eṇa*), ind. according to the manner of slaughtering cattle. — *Paśu-māraka, as, ā, am*, attended with the sacrifice of animals, accompanied by immolation of animals. — *Paśu-mohanikā*, f. 'stupefying animals,' a species of plant (= *kaṭvī*). — *Paśu-yajña, as*, m. an animal sacrifice. — *Paśu-yāga, as*, m. the sacrifice of animals. — *Paśu-rakshaṇa, am*, n. the tending of cattle. — *Paśu-rakshi, is, is, i*, Ved. keeping or tending cattle; (*is*), m. a herdsman. — *Paśu-rakshin, ī*, m. 'tending cattle,' a herdsman, shepherd. — *Paśu-rajju, us*, f. a cord for tethering cattle, a tether for animals. — *Paśu-rāja, as*, m. 'monarch of the beasts,' a lion. — *Paśu-roman, a*, n. the hair of an animal. — *Paśu-vat*, ind. like an animal, brutally; (Ved.) as in an animal (sacrifice). — *Paśu-vardhana, as, ā, am*, Ved. increasing cattle, causing cattle to thrive; (*am*), n. the thriving of cattle. — *Paśu-vid, t, t, t*, Ved. providing cattle. — *Paśu-śīrsha, am*, n. the head of an animal. — *Paśu-śrapaṇa, am*, n., Ved. cooking a sacrificial animal; (*as*), m., scil. *agni*, the fire on which the victim's flesh is cooked. — *Paśu-sha, as, ā, am*, or *paśu-shā, ās, ās, am*, Ved. bestowing cattle. — *Paśu-shṭha, as, ā, am*, Ved. existing or found in cattle. — *Paśu-sakha, as*, m. 'friend of cattle,' N. of a S'ūdra. — *Paśu-sani, is, is, i*, Ved. bestowing cattle.

— *Paśu-samāmnāya, as,* m. 'enumeration of sacrificial animals,' N. of a section of the Vājasaneyi-saṃhitā. — *Paśusamāmnāyika, as, ī, am,* mentioned in books on animal sacrifices. — *Paśu-sambhava, as, ā, am,* produced by animals (as flesh, honey, butter, &c.). — *Paśu-sādhana, as, ī, am,* Ved. leading or guiding cattle. — *Paśu-sūtra, am,* n., N. of a work. — *Paśu-harītakī,* f. the fruit of the Spondias Mangifera. — *Paśu-havya, am,* n. sacrifice of animals. — *Paśū-kṛi,* cl. 8. P. A. *-karoti, -kurute, -kartum,* to transform into an animal; to offer as a victim. — *Paśva-ishṭi, is, is, i* (fr. *paśvas,* acc. pl. of *paśu* and *ishṭi*), Ved. wishing for herds; (*is*), f. desire of cattle; (Sāy.) = *agner ishṭiḥ,* a fire offering, offering by fire. — *Paśv-ayana, am,* n., Ved. a festival attended with animal sacrifices. — *Paśva-yantra, as, ā, am* (fr. *paśva* for *paśvas* + *yantra*), Ved. being within the cattle-fold; (Sāy.) provided with the means of letting out or extricating cattle. — *Paśv-avadāna, am,* n. sacrifice or offering of animals. — *Paśv-āćāra, as,* m., N. of a particular form of the worship of Devī. — *Paśv-ijyā,* f., Ved. animal sacrifice. — *Paśv-ish, ṭ, ṭ, ṭ,* Ved. wishing for cattle; (Sāy.) driving cattle, a cattle-driver. — *Paśv-ishṭakā,* f., Ved. bricks in the shape of animals. — *Paśv-ekādaśinī,* f. an aggregate of eleven sacrificial animals.

Paśukā, f. any small animal.

पश्च *paśća, as, ā, am* (fr. *pas* = *apas* = *apa* + *ća* fr. rt. *anć;* cf. *ućća, nīća, tiraśćīna*), being behind; posterior, later; western, westerly; (*a*), ind., Ved. afterwards; (*ā*), ind., Ved. behind, at the back, abaft, after; afterwards, later; westward; (*āt*), ind. from behind, from the back, behind (*paśćāt-kṛi,* to leave behind, surpass, excel), to or towards the back, backwards (e.g. *paśćād apasarad yānam,* a carriage moving backwards); after, afterwards, subsequently, at a later time, in later times, at last; from the west, westward, to the west of; *tataḥ paśćāt,* thereupon, after that; *uttaratah-paśćāt,* from the north-west. As a prep. *paśćāt* governs the gen. or abl., e.g. *rathasya paśćāt,* behind the chariot; [cf. probably Lat. *post, pone* for *pos-ne, postid-ea:* Gr. ὀπίσσω: Lith. *paskuy,* 'afterwards;' *paskuttinis, paskiausas,* 'last:' Old Pruss. *pansdan,* 'afterwards:' Hib. *feasd, feasda,* 'hereafter, henceforward, forthwith.'] — *Paśćāć-ćara, as, ī, am,* coming or approaching behind. — *Paśćāć-ćhramaṇa, as,* m. a Buddhist priest who walks behind another Buddhist priest in visiting the laity. — *Paśćāt-karṇam,* ind., Ved. behind the ear. — *Paśćāt-kāla, as,* m. subsequent time; (*e*), ind. in later times, afterwards. — *Paśćāt-tap,* cl. 1. P. A. *-tapati, -te, -taptum,* to feel pain after, regret, repent, feel remorse. — *Paśćāt-tara, as, ā, am,* Ved. later, posterior. — *Paśćāt-tāpa, as,* m. 'after-pain,' sorrow, regret, repentance, remorse; *paśćattāpam kṛi,* to feel regret, repent. — *Paśćāt-tāpin, ī, inī, i,* regretting, repenting. — *Paśćāt-sad, t, t, t,* Ved. sitting behind or towards the west. — *Paśćād-aksham,* ind., Ved. behind the axle-tree. — *Paśćād-apavarga, as, ā, am,* Ved. closed or completed behind. — *Paśćād-āgatya,* ind. having returned. — *Paśćād-ayāt, ān, ātī* or *āntī, āt,* coming behind, following. — *Paśćā-dosha, as,* m., Ved. the later part of the evening. — *Paśćād-vartin, ī, inī, i,* remaining behind, following after. — *Paśćād-vāta, as,* m., Ved. a wind from behind, a west wind. — *Paśćānutāpa* (°*ća-an*°), *as,* m. regret, repentance. — *Paśćānupūrvī* (°*ća-an*°), f. a repeated or recurring series. — *Paśćān-nata, as, ā, am,* sunk or depressed behind. — *Paśćān-māruta, as,* m. a wind blowing from behind. — *Paśćārdha* (°*ća-ar*°), *as,* m. the hinder side or part; the remaining half or part; the west side. — *Paśćārdhya, as, ā, am,* Ved. being on the hinder side.

Paśćātāt, ind., Ved. from behind.

Paśćima, as, ā, am, being behind, hinder, hindmost; latter, last (e.g. *paśćimā sandhyā,* the latter, i.e. the evening twilight; *paśćimā kriyā,* the last rite, burning the dead); west, western, westerly; (*ā*), f., scil. *diś,* the west; (*am*), n., N. of a Tantra; (*ena*), ind. behind (with acc.), after; in the west; (*e*), ind. in the west; [cf. *uttara-p*°, *dakshiṇa-p*°.] — *Paśćima-jana, ās,* m. pl., Ved. the people in the west, the inhabitants of the western districts of India. — *Paśćima-tantra, am,* n., N. of a Tantra. — *Paśćima-tas,* ind. from behind. — *Paśćima-darśana, am,* n. a last look; *paśćima-darśanam drashṭum,* to see for the last time. — *Paśćima-deśa, as,* m., N. of a district mentioned in the Romaka-Siddhānta. — *Paśćimānūpaka* (°*ma-an*°), *as,* m., N. of a prince. — *Paśćimābhimukha* (°*ma-abh*°), *as, ā* or *ī, am,* directed towards the west. — *Paśćimārdha* (°*ma-ar*°), *as,* m. the latter half, the hinder part. — *Paśćimottara* (°*ma-ut*°), *as, ā, am,* north-westerly, north-western; (*asyām*), loc. sing. f., scil. *diśi,* Ved. in the north-west; (*e*), ind. in the north-west. — *Paśćimottara-dikpati, is,* m. the regent of the north-west, the god of wind, wind.

पश्य *paśya, paśyat, paśyata.* See under rt. 1. *paś,* p. 558.

पष *pash,* cl. 1. P. A. *pashati, -te, pashitum,* a various reading for rt. *spaś,* q. v.; cl. 10. P. *pashayati, -yitum,* to bind; to hinder; to touch; to go; *pāshayati, -yitum,* a various reading for rt. 3. *paś,* p. 558, col. 2.

पष्ठवाह् *pashṭha-vāh, ṭ,* m. (said to be fr. *pashṭha* = *pṛishṭha* + *vāh*), Ved. a bull four years old; (*pashṭhauhī*), f. a heifer four years old, (probably) a young cow.

पस 1. *pas,* cl. 1. P. A. *pasati, -te, pasitum,* a various reading for rt. *spaś,* q. v.; cl. 10. P. *pāsayati, -yitum,* a various reading for rt. 3. *paś.*

पस 2. *pas,* the pudenda.

Pasas, as, n., Ved. membrum virile; [cf. Gr. πέος, πόσ-θη: Lat. *pēn-is:* Old Germ. *visellin,* 'penis:' Lith. *pis-à,* 'cunnus;' *pìs-ti,* 'coire cum muliere.']

पस्त्य *pastya, am,* n., Ved. habitation, abode, stall, stable; (*ās*), m. pl. a house, dwelling, residence; household, family; (Sāy.) = *daivyaḥ prajāḥ,* divine progeny; = *manushya,* a man; = *ṛitv-ij,* a priest; (*ā*), f. the goddess of domestic affairs; (*as, ā, am*), to be approached by all, venerated (Sāy. = *sarvair gantavyaḥ*). — *Pastya-sad, t,* m., Ved. a member of a family; (Sāy.) = *deva-yajana-lakshaṇe gṛihe nishaṇṇaḥ,* seated in the chamber of divine worship. — *Pastyā-vat, ān, atī, at,* Ved. having a fixed habitation; filled with habitations, abounding in dwellings or sacrificial halls (Sāy. = *gṛiha-vat, yajña-gṛihopeta*); belonging to the Soma press; (*ān*), m. a householder, a wealthy man.

पस्पृश् *paspṛiś,* Ved. in *a-p*°, q. v.

पह्लव *pahlava, ās,* m., N. of a people, the Persians, (also spelt *pahnava;* in the Vishṇu-Purāṇa they are said to be a degraded Kshatriya race conquered by Sagara and sentenced by him to wear beards, see Wilson's Vishṇu-Purāṇa, p. 375.)

पह्लिका *pahlikā,* f. Pistia Stratiotes (= *vāri-praśnī*).

पा 1. *pā,* cl. 1. P. (ep. also A.) *pibati* (in later works generally written *pivati*), *-te* (Ved. *pāti*), *papau, pāsyati, apāt, pātum* (Ved. *pātave, pibadhyai*), to drink, quaff (sometimes with gen. in Ved., e.g. *madhvaḥ pibanti gauryaḥ,* the white cows drink of the sweet Soma juice); to inhale, swallow (dust); to drink in, imbibe (metaphorically, e.g. *piban yaśo mūrtam 'iva,* drinking in as it were embodied glory); to feast on (with the eyes or ears, e.g. *taṃ sā papau loćanābhyām,* she feasted on him with her eyes); to drink up, absorb, swallow up; to drink intoxicating liquors: Caus. *pāyayati, -te, -yitum* (Ved. *-yitavai*), to cause to drink, give to drink; to water (horses or cattle): Desid. *pipāsati* (Ved. *pipīshati*), to wish to drink, thirst, thirst for, thirst after: Desid. of Caus. *pipāyayishati,* to wish or intend to give to drink: Intens. *pepīyate,* to drink greedily or with avidity, drink repeatedly; [cf. Gr. πί-ν-ω, Fut. πί-ομαι, Aor. ἔ-πι-ο-ν, πῖθι, Perf. πέ-πω-κα, πό-το-ς, πό-μα, πῶ-μα, πό-σι-ς, πό-τη-ς, πο-τήρ-ιο-ν, πῖ-νο-ν, πι-πί-σκ-ω, πῖ-σ-ος, Πῖσα, πί-σ-τρα, Æol. πώ-ν-ω: Lat. *po-tu-s, po-ti-o(n), po-tor, po-c-ulu-m, pō-tare, bi-b-o, vini-bu-a* for *vini-bib-a, ex-bu-res, im-bu-o:* Slav. *pi-ti,* 'to drink:' Old Pruss. *pou-ton,* 'to drink:' Lith. *po-tà,* 'tippling;' *pē-na-s,* 'milk;' *pý-va-s,* 'beer:' Angl. Sax. *beor:* Old and Mod. Germ. *bier.*]

2. *pā, ās, ās, am,* (at the end of a comp.) drinking, quaffing; [cf. *agre-pā, añjas-pā, ṛitu-pā.*]

1. *pātavya, as, ā, am,* to be drunk, drinkable.

1. *pātṛi, tā, trī, tṛi,* one who drinks, a drinker.

1. *pātra, am,* n. a drinking-vessel, goblet, bowl, cup, plate, dish, jar, pot; a vessel in general; a utensil; any kind of sacrificial vase or vessel (comprising various forms of cups, plates, spoons, ladles, &c. so used); the channel or bed of a river; a receptacle of any kind, anything which holds or supports; (metaphorically) a receptacle, a recipient or a person in whom any quality is contained [cf. *viśvāsa-p*°]; a fit or competent or worthy person, a person worthy to receive gifts, worthy of, fit for (with gen. or loc. or inf., e.g. *pātram hy eshām asi,* for thou art worthy of these); a king's counsellor or minister; an actor, dramatis persona; a part in a play; propriety, fitness; an order, command; a leaf; (*as*), m. a vessel &c.; a measure of capacity = 1 Āḍhaka; (*ī*), f. a vessel, plate, dish; pot, barrel; a small or portable furnace; an epithet of Durgā; [cf. perhaps Lat. *patera;* Goth. *fōdr;* Hib. *putraice,* 'a vessel, pot.'] — *Pātra-kaṭaka, as* or *am,* m. or n. (?), the ring on which a beggar's alms-dish is carried. — *Pātra-tā,* f. or *pātra-tva, am,* n. the property or capacity of a cup or vessel; the being a receptacle for anything; capacity, fitness; worthiness, merit, desert; dignity, honour; appropriate state or circumstance. — *Pātra-pāṇi, is,* m. 'cup-handed,' N. of a demon hurtful to children. — *Pātra-pāla, as,* m. 'vessel-guiding,' a large paddle used as a rudder (commonly called *pātaluyāra*). — *Pātra-bhūta, as, ā, am,* 'become a recipient,' worthy of receiving anything from any one (gen.); the object of a present or of respectful treatment. — *Pātra-bhṛit, t,* m. 'taking care of utensils,' a servant, scullion. — *Pātra-bheda, as,* m. breaking a drinking-vessel or cup. — *Pātra-melana, am,* n. the bringing together of the characters of a play. — *Pātra-varga, as,* m. a company of actors. — *Pātra-sanskāra, as,* m. the current of a river; the cleaning of a vessel or dish. — *Pātra-sańćāra, as,* m. (perhaps) removing the dishes or arranging them after dinner (or incorrect for *pātra-sanskāra*). — *Pātra-stha, as, ā, am,* being in a dish. — *Pātra-hasta, as, ā, am,* 'cup-handed,' holding a vessel in the hand. — *Pātrī-nirṇejana, am,* n., Ved. water for rinsing a vessel. — *Pātre-bahula, as, ā, am,* constant at meals; a parasite. — *Pātre-samita, as, ā, am,* constant at meals, a parasite; a treacherous or hypocritical person. — *Pātropakaraṇa* (°*ra-up*°), *am,* n. decorations of an inferior class, as bells, chowries, vases, &c.

Pātraka, am, n. a vessel, bowl, bason, dish; (*ikā*), f. a cup, a beggar's bowl or alms-dish.

Pātraṭīra, as, m. an ex-minister; (according to others) an able or competent minister; a vessel of metal; mucus running from the nose; rust of iron; fire; a heron; a crow.

Pātraya, Nom. P. *pātrayati, -yitum,* to use as a drinking-vessel.

Pātrasāt-kṛi, cl. 8. P. *-karoti, -kartum,* to present a worthy person with anything.

Pātrika, as, ī, am, measured out with any vessel or with the measure Pātra; sown with as much as will fill a Pātra; containing it, possessing it; fit, adequate, appropriate; (*am, ī*), n. f. a vessel, cup, dish.

Pātrin, ī, iṇī, i, having a drinking-vessel or provided with a dish; having fit or worthy persons.

Pātriya or *pātrya, as, ā, am,* worthy to partake of a meal.

Pātrī-kṛi, cl. 8. P. *-karoti, -kartum,* to make a fitting receptacle or recipient, to make a worthy object; to dignify, promote to honour.

Pātrīṇa, as, ā, am, measured or sown or cooked with a Pātra.

Pātrī-bhū, cl. 1. P. *-bhavati, -bhavitum,* to become a fitting recipient or worthy object.

Pātrīya, am, n. a sacrificial vessel or utensil.

Pātrīra, as, m. an oblation.

Pātrīva, as, am, m. n. a kind of sacrificial vessel.

1. *pāna, am,* n. (for 2. see col. 2), drinking, drinking spirituous liquors; enjoying; a drink, beverage; a drinking-vessel, cup; a canal; (*as*), m. a distiller, one who sells spirituous liquors, a publican, inn-keeper; [cf. Lith. *pėna-s,* 'milk.'] — *Pāna-kumbha, as,* m. a drinking-vessel. — *Pāna-goshṭhikā* or *pāna-goshṭhī,* f. a drinking-party, drinking-bout; a dram-shop, tavern, place where people drink together. — *Pāna-ja, as, ā, am,* caused by drinking (as a disease). — *Pāna-dosha, as,* m. the vice of drinking, drunkenness. — *Pāna-pa, as, ā, am,* a dram-drinker, drinker of spirituous liquors. — *Pāna-para, as, ā, am,* addicted to drinking. — *Pāna-pātra, am,* n. a drinking-vessel, glass, cup, goblet. — *Pāna-vaṇij, k,* m. a vender of spirits, a distiller. — *Pāna-bhājana, am,* n. a drinking-vessel, glass, goblet. — *Pāna-bhāṇḍa, am,* n. a drinking-vessel. — *Pāna-bhū, ūs,* or *pāna-bhūmi, is* or *ī,* f. a drinking-place, drinking-room, refreshment-room. — *Pāna-maṅgala, am,* n. a drinking-party, drinking-bout. — *Pāna-mada, as,* m. intoxication. — *Pāna-rata, as, ā, am,* addicted to drink, drinking, drunken, a toper. — *Pāna-vat, ān, atī, at,* Ved. abounding in drink, rich in beverages. — *Pāna-vibhrama, as,* m. 'drink-giddiness,' intoxication. — *Pāna-śauṇḍa, as, ā, am,* addicted to intoxication; (*as*), m. a hard drinker. — *Pānāgāra* (°*na-ag*° or *-āg*°), *as,* m. a drinking-house, tavern. — *Pānātyaya* (°*na-at*°), *as,* m. hard drinking, drinking; morbid state after intoxication.

Pānaka, as, am, m. n. a draught, drink, beverage, potion.

Pānika, as, m. a vender of spirituous liquors.

Pānila, am, n. a drinking-vessel.

1. *pānīya, as, ā, am* (for 2. see col. 2), to be drunk, drinkable; (*am*), n. a beverage, drink; water. — *Pānīya-kākikā,* f. 'sea-crow,' the cormorant. — *Pānīya-nakula, as,* m. 'water-ichneumon,' an otter. — *Pānīya-prishṭha-ja, as,* m. 'born on the surface of the water,' an aquatic plant, Pistia Stratiotes. — *Pānīya-phala, am,* n. the seed of Euryala Ferox. — *Pānīya-mūlaka, am,* n. the plant Vernonia Anthelminthica. — *Pānīya-varṇikā,* f. sand (= *bālukā*). — *Pānīya-śālā* or *pānīya-śālikā,* f. a place where water is distributed, a shed on the road-side for providing passengers with water. — *Pānīya-śīta, as, ā, am,* too cold to drink. — *Pānīyādhyaksha* (°*ya-adh*°), *as,* m. a superintendent of the water. — *Pānīyāmalaka* (°*ya-ām*°), *am,* n. a kind of fruit, Flacourtia Cataphracta. — *Pānīyārtham* (°*ya-ar*°), ind. for the sake of water. — *Pānīyālu* (°*ya-ālu*), *us,* m. a species of tuberous plant (= *jalālu, kshupālu*). — *Pānīyāśrā* (°*ya-aś*°), f. a species of grass (= *valvajā, dṛiḍha-kshurā*).

Pānta, as, m., Ved. = 1. *pānīya,* a drink, beverage; (Sāy.) = *pālana-svabhāva,* nutritious (as if fr. rt. 3. *pā*).

पा 3. *pā,* cl. 2. P. *pāti, papau, pāsyati, apāsīt* (Ved. forms *pīpāya* [Sāy. fr. *pyai*], *pāsati*), *pātum,* to watch, keep, preserve, protect, screen, shelter, defend against (with abl.); to rule, govern; to beware of (with abl); to observe, notice, attend to (Ved.); to oversee, take care of, tend (Ved.); to keep, observe (in this sense also A., Ved.): Caus. (or rt. *pal* or *pāl,* cl. 10; or Nom. fr. *pāla*) P. (ep. also A.) *pālayati* (*-te*), *-yitum,* to watch, keep, protect, screen, defend, be a guardian to; to cherish; to rule, govern; to maintain, keep, observe (as a promise or vow): Desid. *pipāsati:* Intens. *pāpāyate, pāpeti, pāpāti;* [cf. Gr. πατ-έομαι, ἐ-πάσάμην, πέ-πᾶμαι, ἄ-πασ-τος, perhaps Πάν, πάτνη, πάθνη, φάτνη, δεσ-πό-της, perhaps ἄνθρω-πος for ἄνδρο-πος = *nṛi-pa*(?): Lat. *pa* in *pā-vi, pa-bulum, pa-sc-or, pas-tor, Pă-le-s, pā-nis, pe-n-us, penātes, penes, pene-tro:* Slav. *pit-a-ti,* 'to nourish:' Russ. *pitáyu,* 'I feed:' Lith. *pō-nas,* 'a lord;' *pė-nas,* 'fodder, food;' *pėnù,* 'I feed;' *pė-mǔ,* 'a shepherd;' *pė-tu-s,* 'midday:' Goth. *fod-yan,* 'to feed;' *fōd-ein-s,* 'food:' Angl. Sax. *fod-a:* Mod. Germ. *futter:* Eng. *food.*]

4. *pā, ās, ās, am,* (at the end of a comp.) keeping, protecting, guarding, screening; [cf. *apāna-pā, āprīta-pā, go-pā, tapush-pā.*]

1. *pāt, ān, ātī* or *āntī, āt* (for 2. see p. 563), guarding, defending, preserving; a guardian, protector.

1. *pāta, as, ā, am* (for 2. *pāta* see under 2. *pāt*), watched, protected, preserved.

2. *pātavya, as, ā, am* (for 1. see p. 559, col. 3), to be guarded or protected.

2. *pātṛi, tā, trī, tṛi* (for 1. see p. 559, col. 3), a defender, protector, defending (with gen. or acc.); (*tā*), m. a species of Ocymum (= *gandha-pattra*).

2. *pātra, am,* n. a preservative from sin.

2. *pāna, as, ā, am,* (for 1. see col. 1) Ved. observing, keeping; (*am*), n. protection, defence; [cf. *tanū-p*°.]

2. *pānīya, as, ā, am* (for 1. see col. 1), to be cherished or protected, to be preserved.

पांशु *pāṅśu, pāṅśana,* &c., = *pāṅsu, pāṅsana,* &c. below.

पांसु *pāṅsu, us,* m. (in later writings mostly spelt *pāṅśu;* probably fr. rt. *paṅs* or *paṅś,* to destroy), crumbling soil, dust, sand; a particle of dust, grain of sand; dung, manure; a species of plant (= *parpaṭa*); a kind of camphor; landed property; [cf. Lat. *pulvis* for *pulcvis;* Cambro-Brit. *pain,* 'pollen, fine powder or dust.'] — *Pāṅsu-kāsīsa, am,* n. sulphate of iron. — *Pāṅsu-kulī,* f. 'multitude of dust,' a high road, highway. — *Pāṅsu-kūla, am,* n. a dust-heap, particularly a collection of rubbish and rags out of which the Buddhist priests make up their clothing; a legal document not made out in any particular person's name. — *Pāṅsukūla-sīvana, am,* n. 'the sewing together of rags from a dust-heap,' N. of the place where Śākya-muni assumed his priestly dress. — *Pāṅsukūlika, as, ā, am,* one who wears clothes made of rags from a dust-heap. — *Pāṅsu-krita, as, ā, am,* covered with dust, dusty. — *Pāṅsu-kshāra* = *pāṅsu-ja,* q. v. — *Pāṅsu-guṇṭhita, as, ā, am,* covered with dust. — *Pāṅsu-ćatvara, am,* n. hail. — *Pāṅsu-ćandana, as,* m. an epithet of Śiva. — *Pāṅsu-ćāmara, as,* m. a heap of dust; a tent; a bank covered with Dūrvā grass; praise; a small cucumber. — *Pāṅsu-ja, am,* n. 'earth-born,' a kind of salt extracted from soil, rock or fossil salt. — *Pāṅsu-jālika, as,* m. an epithet of Vishṇu. — *Pāṅsu-dhūmra, as, ā, am,* dark-red or dark with dust; [cf. *dhūli-dhūmra.*] — *Pāṅsu-dhvasta-śiroruha, as, ā, am,* having the hair soiled with dust. — *Pāṅsu-nipāta, as,* m. a fall of dust. — *Pāṅsu-paṭala, am,* n. a coating or mass of dust. — *Pāṅsu-pattra, am,* n. a kind of vegetable, Chenopodium Album. — *Pāṅsu-bhava, as* or *am,* m. or n. (?) = *pāṅsu-ja,* q. v. — *Pāṅsu-mardana, as,* m. 'dust-destroying,' an excavation for water round the root of a tree. — *Pāṅsu-rāgiṇī,* f. a species of plant (= *mahā-madā*). — *Pāṅsu-rāshṭra, am,* n., N. of a country; (*ās*), m. pl., N. of its inhabitants. — *Pāṅsu-varsha, as,* m. a shower of dust, falling dust. — *Pāṅsu-samūhana, as, ī, am,* collecting or raising dust (as the wind). — *Pāṅsūtkara* (°*su-ut*°), *as,* m., Ved. = *pāṅsu-varsha.*

Pāṅsaka, as, ā, am, vitiating, spoiling; contemptible, vile.

Pāṅsana, as, ā or *ī, am,* (at the end of a comp.) defiling, disgracing, dishonouring; vitiating, spoiling, destructive; contemptible, wicked, bad, infamous; (*am*), n. contempt.

Pāṅsara, as, ā, am, formed or consisting of dust; (*as*), m. a patronymic (Ved.); a kind of salt (in this sense spelt *pāṅśara*).

Pāṅsin, ī, inī, i, = *pāṅsana* (for which it is probably only a wrong reading).

Pāṅsuka, ās, m. pl. dust; (*ā*), f. a menstruous woman; a fragrant plant, Pandanus Odoratissimus.

Pāṅsura, as, ā, am, dusty (Ved.); a gad-fly; a cripple carried or moving about in a chair.

Pāṅsula or *pāṅśula, as, ā, am,* dusty, covered with dust; sullied, defiled, disgraced; defiling, disgracing (e. g. *kula-pāṅsula,* disgracing a family, a disgrace to the family); (*as*), m. a wicked or profligate man, a libertine, paramour, gallant; one of Śiva's weapons (a sort of pole armed at the upper end with transverse pieces representing the breast-bone and adjoining ribs and surmounted by a skull); an epithet of Śiva; a species of tree, Cæsalpinia Bonducella; (*ā*), f. a menstruous woman; a licentious woman, (*a-pāṅśulā,* a chaste woman); the earth; Pandanus Odoratissimus.

पाक 1. *pāka, as, ā, am* (said to be fr. rt. 1. *pā,* to drink), Ved. very young; sincere, simple, genuine, inartificial, honest; ignorant; (*as*), m. the young of animals, a child, an infant; N. of a Daitya slain by Indra; an owl. — *Pāka-trā,* ind., Ved. in a simple or honest way, in simplicity; (Sāy.) = *vipakva-prajñeshu,* towards the sincere-minded. — *Pāka-dūrvā,* f., Ved. a species of plant. — *Pāka-dvish, ṭ,* m. 'the enemy of the Daitya Pāka,' an epithet of Indra. — *Pāka-yajña, as,* m. a simple or domestic sacrifice (an oblation offered on building a house, liberating a bull, &c.; according to Āpastamba this term comprise the Aupāsana-homa, Vaiśvadeva, Pārvaṇa, Ashṭakā, Śrāddha, Sarpa-bali, Īśāna-bali; according to Baudhāyana, the Huta, Pra-huta, Ā-huta, Śūla-gava, Bali-haraṇa, Praty-avarohaṇa, Ashṭakā-homa; according to Gautama, the Ashṭakā, Pārvaṇa, Śrāddha, Śrāvaṇī, Āgrahāyaṇī, Caitrī, Āśva-yujī); N. of a man. — *Pākayajñika, as, ī, am,* relating to the Pāka-yajña; (*as*), m. a performer of the Pāka-yajña ceremony. — *Pākayajñiya, as, ā, am,* relating to the Pāka-yajña. — *Pāka-vat,* ind., Ved. simply, honestly. — *Pāka-śaṅsa, as, ā, am,* Ved. honest-minded; (Sāy.) = *paripakva-vaćana, satya-bhāshin,* speaking sincerely. — *Pāka-śālā,* f. 'cook-house,' a kitchen. — *Pāka-śāsana, as,* m. 'punisher of the Daitya Pāka or instructor of the ignorant,' an epithet of Indra. — *Pākaśāsani, is,* m. (a patronymic fr. the preceding), an epithet of Jayanta; of Arjuna. — *Pāka-saṃsthā,* f. = *pāka-yajña,* q. v. — *Pāka-sutvan, ā, arī, a,* Ved. offering Soma with a simple or sincere mind (Sāy. = *vipakvena manasā Somasyābhishotṛi*). — *Pāka-sthāman, ā,* m., Ved., N. of a man. — *Pāka-hantṛi, tā,* m. 'slayer of the Daitya Pāka,' an epithet of Indra.

Pākya, am, n., Ved. honesty, simplicity; (*ā*), ind. in simplicity, in ignorance.

पाक 2. *pāka, as,* m. (fr. rt. 2. *pać*), cooking, baking, roasting, boiling, dressing food; burning (bricks or earthenware); digestion, assimilation of food; ripening, becoming ripe, ripeness; maturity, perfect development (e. g. *dhiyas,* of the intellect), development of consequences (as of an act done in a former life or of any act); completion, perfection, fulfilment, accomplishment [cf. *phala-p*°]; greyness of the hair, old age; inflammation, suppuration, ripeness of a boil; an abscess, ulcer; a vessel in which anything is cooked or dressed, cooking utensil (a saucepan, boiler, &c.); the domestic fire; general fear and panic resulting in national disaster or revolution; the subversion of a country; [cf. *a-p*°, *ikshu-p*°, *kṛishṇa-p*°.] — *Pāka-kṛishṇa, as,* m. the Caronda tree, Carissa Carondas ('bearing a black fruit when ripe,' also other similar compounds, as *pākakṛishṇa-phala, kṛishṇa-pāka*). — *Pāka-ja, as, ā, am,* caused by cooking or roasting, produced by maturing; (*am*), n. 'obtained by boiling,' black salt; flatulence. — *Pākaja-tva, am*, n. production by warmth, capability of being affected by contact with fire. — *Pāka-pātra, am*, n. a cooking utensil, a boiler, &c. — *Pāka-puṭī*, f. a potter's kiln, pottery. — *Pāka-phala, as*, m. the Caronda tree (= *kṛishṇa-pāka-phala*). — *Pāka-bhāṇḍa, am*, n. a cooking utensil. — *Pāka-matsya, as*, m. a species of fish; a kind of fish-sauce; a species of venomous insect. — *Pāka-rañjana, am*, n. the leaf of the Laurus Cassia. — *Pāka-rājeśvara* (°*ja-ī*s°), *as*, m., N. of a writer on the art of cookery. — *Pāka-śālā*, f. 'hall for cooking,' a kitchen. — *Pāka-śuklā*, f. chalk. — *Pāka-sthāna, am*, n. 'place for cooking,' a kitchen; (scil. *kulālasya*) a potter's kiln. — *Pākāgāra* (°*ka-ag*° or *-āg*°), *as* or *am*, m. or n. (?), 'cooking-room,' a kitchen. — *Pākātīsāra* (°*ka-at*°), *as*, m. chronic dysentery; [cf. *āmātīsāra*.] — *Pākādhyāya* (°*ka-adh*°), *as*, m. 'chapter on cooking,' N. of a chapter of the Sannipāta-kalikā treating of particular medical decoctions. — *Pākāru* (°*ka-aru*), *us*, m., Ved., N. of a particular disease.

Pākala, as, ā, am, bringing to maturity; suppurative, causing suppuration in a boil; (*as*), m. fever in an elephant; fire; wind; = *vodhana-dravya* (probably an error for *rādhana-dravya*); (*ā*), f. Bignonia Suaveolens; (*ī*), f. Cucumis Utilissimus; (*am*), n. Costus Speciosus.

Pākali, is, f. a species of plant (= *rohiṇī*).

Pākin, ī, inī, i, (at the end of a comp.) becoming mature, ripening; being digested.

Pākima, as, ā, am, cooked, dressed, ripened (naturally or artificially); obtained by boiling or evaporation (as salt).

Pākuka, as, m. a cook.

Pākya, as, ā, am, to be cooked or matured; fit to cook, eatable; obtained by cooking or evaporation; (*am*), n. a kind of salt; (*as*), m. saltpetre.

Pāćaka, as, ikā, am, cooking, roasting, baking; causing digestion, digestive, peptic, tonic; maturing, bringing to maturity; (*as, ikā*), m. f. a cook; (*as*), m. fire; (*am*), n. the bile which assists in digestion. — *Pāćaka-strī*, f. a female cook. — *Pāćikā-bhārya, as, ā, am*, having a cook for a wife, married to a cook.

Pāćana, as, ī, am, causing to cook or boil, cooking, ripening; softening, relaxing, digestive; suppurative; (*as*), m. fire; acidity, sourness; a species of plant (= *raktairaṇḍa*); (*ī*), f. a species of Myrobalan, Terminalia Chebula; (*am*), n. the act of cooking or baking; ripening; causing a wound to close; a styptic for closing wounds; a medicinal preparation, infusion, decoction (of various drugs, chiefly carminatives or gentle stimulants given to bring the vitiated humors in fever &c. to maturity); 'extraction by boiling,' eliciting extraneous substances from a wound or ulcer by means of cataplasms &c.; a cataplasm; a sort of diet-drink; dissolving; a dissolvent, digestive; penance, expiation; (*ikā*), f. cooking, maturing.

Pāćanaka, as, m. borax; (*am*), n. a sort of diet-drink; causing a wound to close (by means of styptics &c.).

Pāćanīya, as, ā, am, to be cooked or digested; dissolving, digestive.

Pāćala, as, m. whatever cooks, ripens, causes digestion, &c.; a cook; fire; wind; a thing dressed or matured without the aid of fire; (*am*), n. cooking, maturing.

Pāći or *pāćī, is*, f. cooking, maturing.

Pāćya, as, ā, am, to be cooked; capable of being matured.

पाक्ष *pāksha, as, ī, am* (fr. *paksha*), belonging to a half month, fortnightly, relating to a side or party, &c.

Pākshapātika, as, ī, am (fr. *paksha-pāta*), favouring a party or faction, partial, factious.

Pākshāyaṇa, as, ī, am, belonging to or occurring in a Paksha or fortnight, &c.

Pākshika, as, ī, am (fr. *paksha* or *pakshin*), belonging to a bird; belonging to a fortnight, fortnightly; belonging to an argument, &c.; favouring a party or faction; subject to an alternative, that which may or may not take place, possible but not necessary, contingent, allowed but not prescribed; (*as*), m. a fowler, bird-catcher; an alternative.

पाखण्ड *pākhaṇḍa, as*, m. a heretic, heterodox Hindū (adopting the exterior marks of the classes, but not respecting the ordinances of the Vedas; also *pāshaṇḍa*, q. v.).

पागल *pāgala, as, ā, am*, mad, deranged, demented.

पाङ्क्त *pāṅkta, as, ī, am* (fr. *paṅkti*), consisting of five parts, fivefold (Ved.); relating to or composed in the Paṅkti metre; an epithet of a kind of Soma; (*am*), n., scil. *Sāman*, N. of a Sāman. — *Pāṅkta-tā*, f. or *pāṅkta-tva, am*, n., Ved. fivefoldness, fivefold nature or condition.

Pāṅktakākubha, as, ī, am (fr. *paṅkti-kakubh*), Ved. an epithet of a Pra-gātha consisting of the Paṅkti and Kakubh metres.

Pāṅkteya or *pāṅktya, as, ā, am*, fit to sit in the general row at meals, fit to be associated with, admissible into society, fit for respectable society.

पाङ्क्त्र *pāṅktra, as*, m., Ved. (according to Mahī-dhara) a kind of mouse.

पाङ्गुल्य *pāṅgulya, am*, n. (fr. *paṅgula*), limping, halting, hobbling.

पाचक *pāćaka*. See col. 1.

पाची *pāćī*, f. a species of climbing plant.

पाजस् *pājas, as*, n. (said to be fr. rt. 3. *pā*), Ved. brightness, shining, glimmer, gleam, glitter, sheen [cf. *sahasra-p*°]; cheerfulness, freshness, activity, strength, vigour, impetuosity; a shining surface (said of the sky); (*asī*), n. du. 'the two shining surfaces,' heaven and earth; (Sāy.) = *balavatyau*, powerful (as an epithet of Dyāvā-kshāmā); (*āṅsi*), n. pl. glittering hues, glowing colours; (Sāy.) = *balāni*. — *Pājas-vat, ān, atī, at*, Ved. brilliant, strong.

पाजस्य *pājasya, am*, n., Ved. the region of the belly (of an animal); the flanks, side; [cf. *tri-p*°.]

पाञ्चकपाल *pāñćakapāla, as, ī, am* (fr. *pañća-kapāla*), relating to or forming part of an oblation offered in five cups.

Pāñćagatika, as, ī, am (fr. *pañća-gati*), consisting of five forms of existence.

Pāñćajanī, f. a patronymic of Asiknī the daughter of the Prajā-pati Pañća-jana.

Pāñćajanya, as, ā, am (fr. *pañća-jana*, q. v.), containing or relating to the five classes or races of men, extending over the five races (Ved.); (*as*), m., N. of the conch of Kṛishṇa which was taken by him from the demon Pañća-jana, see *pañća-jana*, p. 522; fire; a species of fish (= *poṭa-gala*); N. of one of the eight Upa-dvīpas in Jambu-dvīpa; (*ā*), f. a patronymic of Asiknī; (*am*), n. (?), N. of a forest. — *Pāñćajanya-dhara, as*, m. 'bearing the conch Pāñćajanya,' an epithet of Kṛishṇa.

Pāñćadaśa, as, ī, am (fr. *pañća-daśī*), relating to the fifteenth day of a month.

Pāñćadaśya, as, śī, am, relating or belonging to the fifteenth day of a month, used on the fifteenth day of a half month; (*am*), n. the aggregate of fifteen.

Pāñćanakha, as, ī, am (fr. *pañća-nakha*), made of the skin of an animal with five claws.

Pāñćanada, as, ī, am (fr. *pañća-nada*), prevailing in the land of the five rivers, observed in Pañća-nada or the Pañjāb; (*as*), m. a prince of the Pañjāb; (*ās*), m. pl. the inhabitants of the Pañjāb.

Pāñćabhautika, as, ī, am (fr. *pañća-bhūta*), composed of or containing the five elements; (with *ā-dāna*) the assumption of the five elements.

Pāñćamāhnika, as, ī, am (fr. *pañćama* + *ahan*), Ved. belonging to the fifth day.

Pāñćamika, as, ī, am, treated of in the fifth (book).

Pāñćayājñika, as, ī, am (fr. *pañća-yajña*), relating or belonging to or included in the five great sacrifices or ceremonies; (*am*), n. any one of the five great sacrifices.

Pāñćarātra, ās, m. pl. (fr. *pañća-rātra*), N. of a Vaishṇava sect following the doctrine of their sacred book called Pañća-rātra. — *Pāñćarātra-rahasya, am*, n., N. of a work mentioned in the Sarva-darśana-saṅgraha by Mādhavāćārya.

Pāñćarātrya-nibarhaṇa, am, n., N. of the eighth chapter of the Saṅkara-vijaya by Anantānanda-giri.

Pāñćavarshika, as, ī, am (fr. *pañća-varsha*), five years old.

Pāñćavāja, am, n. (fr. *pañća-vāja*), N. of a Sāman.

Pāñćavidhya, am, n. (fr. *pañća-vidhi*), N. of a Sūtra treating of the five Vidhis of the Sāman.

Pāñćaśabdika, am, n. (fr. *pañća-śabda*), music of five kinds; musical instruments in general.

Pāñćaśara, as, ī, am (fr. *pañća-śara*), belonging to 'the five-arrowed' or the god of love.

Pāñćārthika, as, m. (fr. *pañćan* + *artha*), a follower or votary of Paśu-pati or Śiva.

पाञ्चाल *pāñćāla, as, ī, am*, relating or belonging to the Pañćālas, dwelling in or ruling over the country of the Pañćālas; (*as*), m. a prince of the Pañćālas; the country of the Pañćālas; (*ās*), m. pl. the people of the Pañćālas; an association of five guilds (viz. those of the carpenter, weaver, barber, washerman, and shoe-maker); (*ī*), f. a princess of the Pañćālas; a N. of Draupadī the wife of the five Pāṇḍu princes; a doll, puppet; scil. *rīti*, epithet of a particular poetical style; the melodious combination of five or six words. — *Pāñćāla-deśa, as*, m. the country of the Pañćālas. — *Pāñćāla-rāja, as*, m. the king of the Pañćālas.

Pāñćālaka, as, ikā, am, belonging to the people of the Pañćālas; (*as*), m. a sovereign of the Pañćālas; (*ikā*), f. a princess of the Pañćālas; a doll, puppet (sometimes written *pāñćalikā*).

Pāñćāleya or *pāñćālya, as, ī, am*, belonging to the Pañćālas; (*as*), m. a prince of the Pañćālas.

पाञ्चि *pāñći, is*, m. (fr. *pañćan*), a patronymic. — *Pāñći-grāma, as*, m., N. of a village.

Pāñćika, as, m., N. of the leader of the Yakshas.

पाट् *pāṭ*, ind. an interjection used in calling (*sambodhane*).

पाट *pāṭa, as*, m. (fr. rt. *paṭ*), breadth, expanse, extension; (in geometry) the intersection of a prolonged side and perpendicular or the figure formed by such intersection; (*ā*), f. regular or successive order, series, succession.

Pāṭaka, as, m. a splitter, divider, one who cleaves or tears asunder; the half of a village, part of a village, a kind of village; a shore, bank; a flight of steps leading to the water; a kind of musical instrument; a long span (= *mahā-kishku*); expense or loss of capital or stock; throwing dice.

Pāṭana, am, n. splitting, cleaving, slitting up, tearing up, breaking, cutting to pieces, destroying. — *Pāṭana-kriyā*, f. lancing an abscess or ulcer.

Pāṭala, as, ā, am (said by some to be connected with *pāṭa* above), pale-red, of a pink or pale-red colour; rose colour; pallid; (*as, ī, am*), m. made of the Pāṭalī or forming a part of it; (*as*), m. a pale-red hue, rose colour, redness; the trumpet-flower, Bignonia Suaveolens (a tree with sweet-scented blossoms); a species of rice ripening in the rains; N. of a man; (*ā*), f. Bignonia Suaveolens (both the tree and its blossom); red Lodhra; a kind of fresh-water fish; an epithet of Durgā; a form of Dākshāyaṇī; (*am, ā*), n. f. the flower of the Bignonia Suaveolens; saffron. — *Pāṭala-gaṇḍa-lekha, as, ā, am*, having the complexion of the cheek reddened. — *Pāṭala-druma, as*, m. a species of tree, Rottleria Tinctoria (= *pun-nāga*). — *Pāṭala-pushpa-sannibha, am*, n. a species of medicinal plant (= *padma-kāshṭha*).

— *Pāṭalā-vatī*, f., N. of a river; an epithet of Durgā. — *Pāṭalopala* (°*la-up*°), *am*, n. a ruby.

Pāṭalaka, as, ā, am, of a pale-red colour, pink.

Pāṭali, is, ī, m. f. the trumpet-flower, Bignonia Suaveolens; a species of rice; (*ī*), f., N. of a city; of a daughter of king Mahendra-varman. — *Pāṭali-putra* or *pāṭali-putraka, am*, n., N. of the capital of Magadha near the confluence of the Śoṇa and the Ganges, supposed to be the ancient Palibothra and the modern Patna. — *Pāṭaliputra-nāmadheya, am*, n., scil. *nagara*, a city called Pāṭali-putra.

Pāṭalika, as, ā, am, knowing the secrets of others; one who knows time and place; (*as*), m. a pupil; (*am*), n., N. of a town (=*pāṭali-putra*).

Pāṭaliman, ā, m. a pale-red or rose colour.

Pāṭalyā, f. a multitude of Pāṭalā flowers.

Pāṭita, as, ā, am, torn, split, broken, divided; epithet of a form of fracture of the leg.

Pāṭī, f. arithmetic; a species of shrub (=*balā*). — *Pāṭī-gaṇita, am*, n. arithmetic.

Pāṭīra, as, m. a field; a pungent root, a kind of radish; the pith or manna of the bamboo; a cloud; a sieve, searce, cribble; tin; disease arising from wind, catarrh; sandal.

पाटच्चर *pāṭaććara, as*, m. (fr. *paṭaććara*), a thief, robber, shop-lifter.

पाटल *pāṭala*. See p. 561, col. 3.

पाटव *pāṭava, as*, m. (fr. *paṭu*), a son or descendant of Paṭu; a pupil of Paṭu; (*as, ī, am*), clever, sharp, dexterous; (*am*), n. sharpness, acuteness, intensity, energy; cleverness, skill, dexterity, talent, eloquence; quickness, rashness, precipitation; health.

Pāṭavika, as, ī, am, clever, adroit, dexterous; cunning, crafty, fraudulent.

पाटहिका *pāṭahikā*, f. a small shrub, Abrus Precatorius; [cf. *guñja*.]

पाटा *pāṭā*, f., Ved. a species of plant (=*pāṭhā*).

पाटिकावाडि *pāṭikāvāḍi*, N. of a village (probably Putcabarry).

पाटिन् *pāṭin, ī*, m. a species of fish described as having many teeth; [cf. *pāṭhīna*.]

पाटूर *pāṭūra, as*, m., Ved. a particular part of an animal near the ribs.

पाट्य *pāṭya, am*, n. a kind of vegetable (=*paṭṭa-śāka*).

पाठ *pāṭha, as*, m. (fr. rt. *paṭh*), recitation, recital; reading, perusal, study; reading sacred texts, studying the Vedas or scriptures; the text of a book. — *Pāṭha-ććheda, as*, m. a break in recitation or in a text; a pause, cæsura. — *Pāṭha-dosha, as*, m. an error in a text, a false reading. — *Pāṭha-niśćiti, is*, f. determining or settling the text (of a passage). — *Pāṭha-bhū, ūs*, f. 'reading-place,' a place where the Vedas are read or studied. — *Pāṭha-mañjarī*, f. a particular small bird, Graculus Religiosa. — *Pāṭha-vat, ān, atī, at*, Ved. well-read, learned. — *Pāṭha-viććheda, as*, m. = *pāṭha-ććheda*. — *Pāṭha-śālā*, f. 'lecture-room,' 'hall of study,' a college, school. — *Pāṭha-śālin, ī, inī*, m. f. a scholar, pupil; (*inī*), f. = *pāṭha-mañjarī*. — *Pāṭhāntara* (°*ṭha-an*°), *am*, n. a variation of reading in a book or manuscript.

Pāṭhaka, as, m. a reciter, reader, one who recites or delivers; a student, pupil; a scholar, a scientific person; a teacher, preceptor, lecturer, public reader (of the Purāṇas or other sacred works), a Paṇḍit who declares what is the law or custom according to the scriptures; a spiritual teacher; the text of a book.

1. *pāṭhana, am*, n. lecturing, teaching.

Pāṭhika, as, ā, am, conformable to the text.

Pāṭhita, as, ā, am, caused or taught to read or recite; instructed, taught, lectured.

Pāṭhin, ī, inī, i, one who has read or studied (any subject), a student; knowing, conversant with; (*ī*), m. a Brāhman, especially one who has finished his studies; Plumbago Zeylanica (also *pāṭhī-kuṭa*).

Pāṭhīna, as, m. a public reader or lecturer (on the Purāṇas &c.); a kind of sheat-fish, Silurus Pelorius or Boalis; a species of Moringa with red blossoms (=*guggalu*).

Pāṭhya, as, ā, am, to be taught, needing instruction.

पाठन 2. *pāṭhana, pāṭhanī*, various readings for *pānaṭha, pānaṭhī*.

पाठा *pāṭhā*, f. a climbing plant possessing various medicinal properties, Clypea Hemandifolia (commonly called *ākanādi*); (according to others) = *pahāḍa-mūla*, the root of Bignonia Suaveolens.

पाडिनी *pāḍinī*, f. an earthen pot; a boiler.

पाण 1. *pāṇa, as*, m. (fr. rt. 2. *paṇ*), a stake at play, a game; trade, traffic; a trader; praise.

पाण 2. *pāṇa*. See col. 3.

पाणि *pāṇi, is*, m. (perhaps akin to *parṇa*; said to be fr. rt. 2. *paṇ*), the hand (in this sense frequently at the end of a comp. describing that which is carried in the hand, e.g. *darbha-pāṇi*, with Kuśa grass in the hand, carrying Kuśa grass; cf. *daṇḍa-p*°, *śastra-p*°, *samit-p*°); a hoof (Ved.); a place of sale, shop, market; *pāṇim grah*, to take the hand of a girl in the marriage ceremony, to marry. — *Pāṇi-kaććhapikā*, f. 'hand-tortoise,' a particular position of the fingers. — *Pāṇi-karṇa, as*, m. 'hand-eared,' 'having hands for ears,' one of the epithets of Śiva. — *Pāṇikūrćan, ā*, m., N. of one of the attendants of Skanda. — *Pāṇi-khāta, as, ā, am*, 'dug with the hand,' N. of a sacred bathing-place. — *Pāṇi-gṛihīta, as, ā, am*, taken by the hand, seized; (*ī*), f. married according to the ritual, a bride, wife. — *Pāṇi-graha, as*, m. or *pāṇi-grahaṇa, am*, n. taking by the hand, taking the hand, marrying, marriage (the joining of the bride and bridegroom's hands forming part of the ceremony). — *Pāṇigraha-kara, as*, m. one who performs (the ceremony of) taking the hand; a lawful husband. — *Pāṇigrahaṇika* or *pāṇigrahaṇīya, as, ī, am*, relating to marriage, matrimonial, nuptial; (*am*), n. a wedding present. — *Pāṇi-grahītṛi, tā*, m. 'hand-taker,' one who has married, a bridegroom, husband. — *Pāṇi-grāha, as*, m. taking the hand, marriage; one who has married, a bridegroom, husband. — *Pāṇi-gha, as*, m. 'striking with the hand,' a drummer, one who plays on a tabor or other hand-instrument; a workman, handicraftsman. — *Pāṇi-ghāta, as*, m. a blow with the hand; striking with the hand, boxing; one who strikes with his hand, a boxer. — *Pāṇi-ghna, as*, m., Ved. clapping the hands. — *Pāṇi-ćandra, as*, m., N. of a prince. — *Pāṇi-ćāpalya, am*, n. fidgeting with the hands, snapping the fingers, &c. — *Pāṇi-ja, as*, m. a finger-nail. — *Pāṇi-tala, am*, n. the palm or flat of the hand; a particular weight (= 2 Tolakas); (*e*), n. du. the two palms. — *Pāṇi-dharma, as*, m. form of marriage, manner of marrying. — *Pāṇin-dhama, as, ā, am*, blowing through the hands; with *adhvan*, a journey in which a person blows into his hands, (perhaps) cold, chilly; obscure, dark (as a path, where a noise is made with the hands to frighten away snakes &c.). — *Pāṇin-dhaya, as, ī, am*, drinking out of the hands. — *Pāṇi-pallava, as, am*, m. n. 'hand-twig,' the fingers. — *Pāṇi-pātra, as, ā, am*, 'hand-cupped,' using the hand as a drinking-vessel, drinking out of the hand. — *Pāṇi-pāda, am*, n. the hands and feet. — *Pāṇi-pīḍana, am*, n. pressing the hand (of a bride), marriage. — *Pāṇi-pūra, as, ā, am*, filling the hand. — *Pāṇipraṇayi-tā*, f. the state of being taken as a wife, wife-hood. — *Pāṇi-praṇayin, ī, inī, i*, loved by the hand, being or resting in the hand; (*inī*), f. 'beloved of the hand,' a wife. — *Pāṇi-pradāna, am*, n. giving the hand (in confirmation of a promise). — *Pāṇi-bandha, as*, m. union or junction of the hands (in marrying). — *Pāṇi-bhuj, k*, m. the glomerous fig-tree, Ficus Glomerata. — *Pāṇi-mat, ān, atī, at*, possessed of hands. — *Pāṇi-marda, as*, m. Carissa Carandas (=*kara-marda*). — *Pāṇi-mukta, am*, n., scil. *astra*, a missile weapon, one thrown with the hand, as a dart, spear. — *Pāṇi-mukha, as, ī, am*, Ved. 'hand-mouthed,' having the hand for a mouth. — *Pāṇi-mūla, am*, n. the root of the hand, the extremity of the arm. — *Pāṇi-ruh, ṭ*, or *pāṇi-ruha, as*, m. a finger-nail. — *Pāṇi-vāda, as*, m. 'playing with the hand,' one who plays a drum or tabour, a drummer; (*am*), n. clapping the hands together. — *Pāṇi-vādaka, as*, m. 'playing with the hand,' one who plays a drum or tabour, a drummer. — *Pāṇi-saṅgrahaṇa, am*, n. clasping the hand (in confirmation of a promise), shaking hands. — *Pāṇi-sargya, as, ā, am*, unwound and let out of the hand (as a rope). — *Pāṇi-saryā* (?), f. a rope or cord. — *Pāṇi-stha, as, ā, am*, being in the hand, held in the hand. — *Pāṇi-svanika, as*, m. one who plays musical instruments with the hands. — *Pāṇi-hatā*, f., scil. *pushkariṇī*, N. of a lake (which the gods created for Śākya-muni with a stroke of the hand). — *Pāṇau-karaṇa, am*, n. marriage. — *Pāṇy-āsya, as, ā, am*, 'hand-mouthed,' having the hand for a mouth; (*as*), m. a Brāhman who reads the Vedas upon receiving a gift at a Śrāddha.

2. *pāṇa, as*, m. = *pāṇi*, the hand.

Pāṇika, as, m. a merchant; N. of one of the attendants of Skanda; (*ā*), f. a kind of song or singing; a sort of spoon or ladle.

Pāṇin, ī, inī, i, at the end of an adj. comp. for *pāṇi* [cf. *śastra-p*°, *śūla-p*°]; (*inas*), m. pl., N. of a family reckoned among the Kauśikas.

Pāṇitala, am, n. a particular measure (= 2 Tolakas).

1. *pāṇya, as, ā, am* (for 2. see p. 563), belonging to the hand (Ved.); a patronymic (=*Kauṇḍinya*).

पाणिन *pāṇina, as*, m. said to = *Pāṇini*, and according to some a patronymic from Paṇin.

Pāṇini, is, m. (probably fr. *pāṇina* above), N. of the most eminent Hindū grammarian (regarded as an inspired Muni; according to one legend his grandfather was an inspired legislator called Devala, and his mother's name was Dākshī, see *dāksheya*; the date at which he lived is a subject of controversy, but he is generally placed in the middle of the fourth century B. C.; from Śalātura, thought to have been the dwelling-place of his ancestors, he is said by some to have been called Śālāturīya; cf. Pāṇ. IV. 3, 94).

Pāṇinīya, as, ā, am, relating to Pāṇini, written or composed by Pāṇini; (*as*), m. a disciple or follower of Pāṇini, one who follows the system of Pāṇini; an adherent or admirer of Pāṇini; (*am*), n. (with or without *vy-ākaraṇa*) the grammar of Pāṇini. — *Pāṇinīya-darśana, am*, n., N. of a chapter of the Sarva-darśana-saṅgraha. — *Pāṇinīya-mata-darpaṇa, am*, n. 'mirror of the system of Pāṇini,' N. of a work.

पाणीतक *pāṇītaka, as*, m., N. of a being attendant upon Skanda; (*ās*), m. pl., N. of a people, (a various reading for *karīti*.)

पाण्डक *pāṇḍaka, as*, m., N. of a teacher.

पाण्डर *pāṇḍara, pāṇḍava*. See p. 563, col. 1.

पाण्डित्य *pāṇḍitya, am*, n. (fr. *paṇḍita*), scholarship, erudition, learning; cleverness, skill, dexterity.

पाण्डु *pāṇḍu, us, us, u* (said to be fr. rt. *paṇḍ*), yellowish white, white, pale; (*us*), m. pale or yellowish white colour; jaundice; N. of two plants, Trichosanthes Diœca (=*pāṇḍura-phalī*); a white elephant; N. of a prince, a son of Vyāsa by the wife of Vićitra-vīrya and brother of Dhṛita-rāshṭra and Vidura; of a son of Janam-ejaya and brother of Dhṛita-rāshṭra; of a son of Dhātṛi by Āyatī (according to others he is called Prāṇa); of an attendant of Śiva; of a Nāga-rāja; of a people in

Madhya-deśa; (*us*), f. a species of plant, Glycine Debilis (commonly called Mashāṇi); [cf. Hib. *buidhe*, 'yellow.'] — *Pāṇḍu-kaṇṭaka*, *as*, m. Achyranthes Aspera (= *apā-mārga*). — *Pāṇḍu-kambala*, *as*, m. a white woollen covering or blanket; a warm upper garment; the housings of a royal elephant; a kind of stone (limestone or marble?). — *Pāṇḍu-kambalin*, *ī*, *inī*, *i*, covered with a white woollen blanket; (*ī*), m. a carriage covered with a sort of blanket; the housings of a royal elephant. — *Pāṇḍu-karaṇa*, *am*, or *pāṇḍu-karman*, *a*, n. (in medicine) making or rendering white. — *Pāṇḍu-taru*, *us*, m. Grislea Tomentosa (= *dhava*). — *Pāṇḍu-tā*, f. or *pāṇḍu-tva*, *am*, n. whitish-yellow colour, paleness. — *Pāṇḍu-tīrtha*, *am*, n., N. of a Tīrtha. — *Pāṇḍu-dukūla*, *am*, n. a white winding-sheet. — *Pāṇḍudukūla-sīvana*, *am*, n. 'sewing of the white winding-sheet,' N. of a place where Śākya-muni made a white winding-sheet. — *Pāṇḍu-nāga*, *as*, m. a white elephant; the plant Rottleria Tinctoria. — *Pāṇḍu-pattra-tā*, f., Ved. the growing yellow of leaves. — *Pāṇḍu-pattrī*, f. = *reṇukā*, a species of fragrant substance. — *Pāṇḍu-putra*, *as*, m. a son of Pāṇḍu, any one of the Pāṇḍava princes; (there are many similar compounds, as *Pāṇḍu-nandana*, &c.) — *Pāṇḍu-pṛishṭha*, *as*, *ā*, *am*, white-backed, having no distinguished or auspicious mark on the body, one from whom nothing great is to be expected. — *Pāṇḍu-phala*, *as*, m. 'having yellow fruit,' Trichosanthes Diœca; (*ā*), f. a species of gourd (= *ćirbhiṭā*); (*ī*), f. = *pāṇḍura-phalī*. — *Pāṇḍu-bhāva*, *as*, m. becoming yellowish-white. — *Pāṇḍu-bhūma*, *as*, *ā*, *am*, having a white, chalky soil; (*as*), m. a country with a light-coloured soil. — *Pāṇḍu-mṛittika*, *as*, *ā*, *am*, having a white, chalky soil, consisting of chalk; (*ā*), f. a pale soil; the opal. — *Pāṇḍu-mṛid*, *t*, f. chalk, a chalky soil, a country in which the soil is of a whitish colour. — *Pāṇḍu-raṅga*, *as*, m. a kind of vegetable (commonly called *pāṭarāṅgā*). — *Pāṇḍu-rāga*, *as*, m. Artemisia Indica; whiteness, pallor. — *Pāṇḍu-roga*, *as*, m. 'yellow disease,' jaundice. — *Pāṇḍurogin*, *ī*, *iṇī*, *i*, suffering from jaundice, jaundiced. — *Pāṇḍu-lekha*, *am*, n. an outline or sketch made with a style or with chalk. — *Pāṇḍu-lomaśā* or *pāṇḍu-lomā*, f. Glycine Debilis. — *Pāṇḍu-varṇa*, *as*, *ā*, *am*, pale-coloured, white; (*as*), m. whiteness. — *Pāṇḍu-varma-deva*, *as*, m., N. of a prince. — *Pāṇḍu-śarkarā*, f. light-coloured gravel (the disease). — *Pāṇḍu-śarmilā*, f. an epithet of Draupadī the wife of the sons of Pāṇḍu. — *Pāṇḍu-sopāka*, *as*, m. a particular mixed caste, the offspring of a Caṇḍāla by a Vaidehī mother (whose occupation, according to Manu X. 37, is working with bamboos and reeds, making baskets, mats, &c.). — *Pāṇḍv-āmaya*, *as*, m. 'yellow disease,' jaundice. — *Pāṇḍvāmayin*, *ī*, *inī*, *i*, suffering from jaundice, jaundiced.

Pāṇḍara, *as*, *ā*, *am*, whitish-yellow, whitish, white; (*as*), m. a species of plant (= *maru-vaka*); N. of a mountain; of a Nāga; of a sect; (*am*), n. the blossom of the jasmine; red chalk, ruddle. — *Pāṇḍura-dvāra-go-pura*, *as*, *ā*, *am*, having white doors and city gates. — *Pāṇḍara-pushpikā*, f. a species of plant (= *śitalā*). — *Pāṇḍara-bhikshu*, *us*, m. 'a white-robed mendicant,' epithet of a particular sect.

Pāṇḍaraka, *as*, m., N. of a Nāga-rāja.

Pāṇḍava, *as*, m. a patronymic, a son or descendant of Pāṇḍu; a partisan of the sons of Pāṇḍu; N. of a mountain; (*ās*), m. pl. the five reputed sons of Pāṇḍu (Yudhi-shṭhira, Bhīma, Arjuna, Nakula, and Saha-deva; cf. *Kuntī* and *Mādrī*); the party or adherents of the sons of Pāṇḍu; (*as*, *ī*, *am*), belonging to the sons of Pāṇḍu, connected with the five Pāṇḍavas. — *Pāṇḍava-nakula*, *as*, m., N. of a poet. — *Pāṇḍava-vahni*, *ayas*, m. pl. 'the Pāṇḍava fires,' a N. applied to the three elder sons of Pāṇḍu ('kindled on the Araṇi, Pṛithā or Kuntī;' cf. *pṛithā-raṇi*). — *Pāṇḍava-śreshṭha*, *as*, m. 'best of the sons of Pāṇḍu,' an epithet of Yudhi-shṭhira. — *Pāṇḍavābhīla* (°*va-ābh*°), *as*, m. an epithet of Kṛishṇa.

Pāṇḍavāyana, *ās*, m. pl. the children of Pāṇḍu; (*as*). m. an epithet of Kṛishṇa the friend and ally of the Pāṇḍu princes.

Pāṇḍavīya, *as*, *ā*, *am*, relating to the children of Pāṇḍu, happening to the Pāṇḍavas.

Pāṇḍaveya = *pāṇḍava*, q. v.

Pāṇḍuka, *as*, *ā*, *am*, = *pāṇḍu*; (*as*), m. a pale or yellowish-white colour; the jaundice; N. of a prince (= *Pāṇḍu*); a species of rice; N. of one of the nine treasures of the Jainas; (*am*), n., N. of a particular forest.

Pāṇḍukin, *ī*, *inī*, *i*, suffering from jaundice, jaundiced.

Pāṇḍura, *as*, *ā*, *am*, whitish, white, pale, yellowish-white; (*as*), m. a form of jaundice; a species of plant (= *maru-vaka*); N. of a being attendant upon Skanda; (*ā*), f. Glycine Debilis (= *māsha-parṇī*); (*am*), n. the white leprosy, vitiligo. — *Pāṇḍura-tā*, f. whiteness, white colour. — *Pāṇḍura-druma*, *as*, m. 'the pale tree,' Wrightia Antidysenterica. — *Pāṇḍura-pṛishṭha*, *as*, *ā*, *am*, = *pāṇḍu-pṛishṭha*, q.v. — *Pāṇḍura-phalī*, f. a species of shrub (= *pāṇḍu-phalī*, *pāṇḍu*, *dhūsarā*, &c.). — *Pāṇḍurekshu* (°*ra-ik*°), *us*, m. 'pale sugar-cane,' a species of sugar-cane (= *śvetekshu*).

Pāṇḍuriman, *ā*, m. pale or white colour, paleness.

Pāṇḍūka, *as*, m., Ved. a species of rice; [cf. *pāṇḍuka*.]

Pāṇḍya, *ās*, m. pl., N. of a people and of the country in the Dekhan inhabited by them; (*as*), m. a prince of the Pāṇḍyas; N. of a son of Ā-krīḍa; N. of the mountain-range in the Pāṇḍya country. — *Pāṇḍya-deśa*, *as*, m. the country of the Pāṇḍyas. — *Pāṇḍya-vāṭa*, Ved., N. of a district in which pearls are found.

Pāṇḍva, *am*, n. an uncoloured woollen garment; (*ās*), m. pl., N. of a people in Madhya-deśa; (a various reading for *pāṇḍu* and *pāṇḍya*.)

पाण्य 2. *pāṇya*, *as*, *ā*, *am* (fr. rt. 1. *paṇ*), praiseworthy, excellent. (For 1. *pāṇya* see p. 562, col. 3.)

पात् 2. *pāt*, m. (fr. rt. 2. *pat*), falling; sin, wickedness. (For 1. see under rt. 3. *pā*.)

2. *pāta*, *as*, m. (for 1. see under rt. 3. *pā*), flying, mode of flying, flight; throwing one's self into or down, falling, fall, downfall; alighting, descending; a cast, throw, shot; a stroke (e.g. *khaḍga-pāta*, a sword-stroke); shedding, discharging, emitting, pouring out; destruction, dissolution; an attack, inroad, incursion; falling out, happening, coming to pass; defect, failing, fault, transgression; (in astrology) a malignant aspect; the node in a planet's orbit; an epithet of Rāhu; (*ās*), m. pl., N. of a school of the Yajur-veda. — *Pātādhikāra* (°*ta-adh*°), *as*, m. 'chapter on malignant aspects,' N. of the eleventh chapter of the Sūrya-Siddhānta and of the thirteenth of the Ārya-Siddhānta. — *Pātotpāta* (°*ta-ut*°), *ās*, m. pl. falls and rises, depressions and elevations, ups and downs.

Pātaka, *as*, *ā*, *am*, causing to fall; (*as*, *am*), m. n. 'that which causes to fall or sink,' sin, crime. — *Pātaka-yoga*, *as*, m. incurring guilt, acting sinfully.

Pātakin, *ī*, *inī*, *i*, guilty of a crime, criminal, wicked, sinful, a sinner.

Pātana, *as*, *ī*, *am*, causing to fall, felling, laying low, cutting down; (*am*), n. causing to fall, felling, bringing down, throwing down, knocking down, laying low, throwing away (as dice); lowering, humbling; removing, bringing away; causing to fall asunder, dividing; nodding (?); (with *daṇḍasya*) causing the rod to fall, chastising, punishing; (with *jalaukasām*) application of leeches; (with *garbhasya*) destroying the fetus, causing an abortion.

Pātanīya, *as*, *ā*, *am*, to be caused to fall or alight, to be discharged or shot off.

Pātayitṛi, *tā*, *trī*, *tṛi*, one who causes to fall, one who throws (dice &c.).

Pātayitvā, ind. having made to fall; having thrown or put down or in.

Pātāla, *am*, n. (probably connected with 2. *pāta*, the termination is compared with *āla* = *ālaya* in *antar-āla*; the names of the other hells point to some connection with *tala*), one of the seven regions under the earth and the abode of the Nāgas or serpents and demons (seven such regions are enumerated, viz. A-tala, Vi-tala, Su-tala, Rasā-tala, Talātala, Mahā-tala, and Pātāla; but Pātāla is sometimes used as a general name for all: according to the Mahā-bhārata, Pātāla is also a town in the world of the serpent-race); an excavation, hole, chasm; submarine fire; (in astrology) the fourth sign from that in which the sun is present, the fourth house; (*as*), m. a sort of apparatus for distillation or for calcining and subliming metals (formed of two earthen pots, the upper one inverted over the lower, and the two joined together by their necks with cement and placed in a hole containing fire); an epithet of Jupiter's year of 361 days; N. of the attendant of the fourteenth Arhat of the present Ava-sarpiṇī. — *Pātāla-ketu*, *us*, m., N. of a Daitya prince. — *Pātāla-khaṇḍa*, *as*, m., N. of the fourth part of the Padma-Purāṇa and of a part of the Skanda-Purāṇa. — *Pātāla-gaṅgā*, f. the Ganges of the lower regions. — *Pātāla-garuḍī*, f. or *pātāla-garuḍāhvaya* (°*ḍa-āh*°), *as*, m. a species of creeper (= *gāruḍī*). — *Pātāla-nilaya*, *as*, or *pātāla-vāsin*, *ī*, or *pātālaukas* (°*la-ok*°), *ās*, m. an inhabitant of the nether world, a demon, Daitya, Asura; a Nāga or serpent-demon. — *Pātāla-bhogi-varga*, *as*, m., N. of a part of the Nāma-liṅgānuśāsana by Amara-siṇha. — *Pātāla-varṇana*, *am*, n. 'description of hell,' N. of the first chapter of the Pātāla-khaṇḍa of the Padma-Purāṇa. — *Pātāla-vijaya*, *as*, m. 'victory over hell,' N. of the twenty-fourth and twenty-fifth chapters of the Uttara-kāṇḍa of the Rāmāyaṇa.

Pātika, *as*, m. the Gangetic porpoise, Delphinus Gangeticus (= *śiśu-māra*).

Pātita, *as*, *ā*, *am*, made to fall, felled, thrown down, cast down, struck down; lowered, depressed, humbled, overthrown.

Pātitya, *am*, n. (fr. *patita*), the state of one who is fallen or sunk, loss of position or caste, degraded condition.

Pātin, *ī*, *inī*, *i*, flying, going to, going, alighting on; falling, sinking; being included or contained in; causing to fall, felling, throwing down; pouring forth, discharging, emitting; [cf. *antaḥ-p*°, *eka-p*°, *garbha-p*°, *daṇḍa-p*°.]

Pātili, f. a trap or snare for catching deer; a small earthen vessel or pot, especially used by religious mendicants; a woman of a particular class.

Pātuka, *as*, *ī*, *am*, falling frequently or habitually, apt or disposed to fall; falling, losing caste; going to hell; (*as*), m. the declivity of a mountain, a precipice; an aquatic animal of a large size; (figuratively) the water-elephant.

1. *pātya*, *as*, *ā*, *am* (for 2. see p. 564, col. 1), to be felled, to be caused to fall, to be precipitated; to be inflicted or imposed (as a penalty).

Pātyamāna, *as*, *ā*, *am*, being caused to fall, being precipitated.

पातङ्ग *pātaṅga*, *as*, *ī*, *am* (fr. *pataṅ-ga*), belonging or peculiar to a grasshopper or moth.

Pātaṅgi, *is*, m. the son of the Sun, Saturn.

पातञ्जल *pātañjala*, *as*, *ī*, *am* (fr. *patañjali*), composed by Patañjali; (*am*), n., scil. *śāstra*, the Yoga system of philosophy (first taught by Patañjali). — *Pātañjala-darśana*, *am*, n. 'the system of Patañjali,' N. of a chapter of the Sarva-darśana-saṅgraha ascribed to Mādhavāćārya. — *Pātañjala-bhāshya*, *am*, n., N. of a philosophical work on the Yoga-sūtras by Vyāsa.

Pātañjali, *is*, m. a various reading for *patañjali*, q. v.

पातत्रिण *pātatriṇa*, *as*, *ī*, *am*, containing the word *patatrin*.

पातल्य *pātalya*, *am*, n., Ved. a particular

part of a carriage; (according to Sāy.) = *kīlaka*, a yoke-pin.

पातव्य 1. and 2. *pātavya*. See under rts. 1. and 3. *pā*, pp. 559, 560.

पातसाह *pātasāha, as*, m. = پادشاه, a king.

पाताण्डिनीय *pātāṇḍinīya, ās*, m. pl., N. of a school of the Yajur-veda.

पाति *pāti, is*, m. (fr. rt. 3. *pā*; but connected with rt. 1. *pat*), a master, lord, owner, possessor; a husband (= *pati*).

Pātivratya, am, n. (fr. *pati-vratā*), devotedness or loyalty to a husband, conjugal fidelity.

Pātnīvata, as, ī, am (fr. *patnī-vat*), Ved. belonging to Agni-patnīvat, i. e. to Agni together with the wives of the gods; containing the word *patnīvat*.

Pātnīśāla, as, ī, am (fr. *patnī-śālā*), Ved. being or contained in the *patnī-śālā*.

2. *pātya, am*, n. dominion. (For 1. *pātya* see p. 563, col. 3.)

पातृ *pātṛi*. See under rts. 1. and 3. *pā*.

पात्यमान *pātyamāna*. See p. 563, col. 3.

पात्र 1. and 2. *pātra*. See under rts. 1. and 3. *pā*, pp. 559, 560.

पात्रट *pātraṭa, as, ā, am*, spare, emaciate, thin; (*as*), m. a cup, pot; ragged garments.

पात्रपाक *pātra-pāka, as*, m. decoction of medicinal herbs; (incorrectly for *pattra-pāka*.)

पाथ *pātha, as*, m. (said to be fr. rt. 1. *pā*), fire; the sun; (*am*), n. water [cf. *pītha*]; N. of a Sāman; = *patha*.

Pāthas, as, n., Ved. a spot, place; food; air; water. — *Pātho-ja, am*, n. 'water-born,' a lotus. — *Pātho-da, as*, m. 'water-giver,' a cloud. — *Pātho-dhara, as*, m. 'water-bearer,' a cloud. — *Pātho-dhi, is*, m. 'receptacle of waters,' the ocean. — *Pātho-nidhi, is*, m. 'treasure-house of waters,' the ocean. — *Pātho-bhāj, k, k, k*, Ved. possessing room or space.

Pāthis, is, m. the sea; the eye; (*is*), n. a blotch, scab; water (?).

Pāthya, as, ā, am, being in a spot or place; (Sāy.) N. of a Ṛishi.

पाथेय *pātheya, am*, n. (fr. *pathin*), provender or provisions &c. for a journey, viaticum; the sign of the zodiac Virgo (= *pāthona*). — *Pātheya-vat, ān, atī, at*, furnished with provisions for a journey, provisioned.

पाथोन *pāthona* (corrupted fr. the Gr. παρθένος), Ved. the sign of the zodiac Virgo.

पाथ्न्य *pāthnya, as*, m., Ved. a patronymic of Dadhīća.

पाद् *pād* (fr. rt. 2. *pad*), see 3. *pad*, p. 529; used at the end of comps., cf. *dvi-pād, tri-pād*, and see Gram. 145.

Pāda, as, m. the foot (of men and animals; sometimes added in token of respect to proper names or titles of address, e. g. *ākarṇayantu deva-pādāḥ*, let your Majesty listen; *Kumārila-pādāḥ*, the venerable Kumārila); the foot or leg of an inanimate object (as of a bedstead); a column, pillar; a foot as a measure (= 12 Aṅgulis); the foot or root of a tree; the foot of a mountain, a hill at the foot of a mountain; the bottom (of a bag); a ray or beam of light (rays being considered as the feet or hands of the heavenly bodies); a quarter, a fourth part (this sense is perhaps derived from the foot of a quadruped being one out of four); a quarter of a weight of gold (= 1¼ Paṇa); the fourth part of a book, (the Adhyāyas in the Saunakīyā Ćatur-adhyāyikā, in the Sārīraka-mīmāṃsā, and in Pāṇini's grammar are divided severally into four Pādas, as also the Dhanur-veda and the Vāyu-Purāṇa; while, on the other hand, the Adhyāyas in Vopa-deva's grammar contain more than four Pādas); the fourth part of a Śloka or of any verse; the line of a hymn or stanza of the Ṛig-veda or of any stanza; the quadrant of a circle; a part in general; [cf. Goth. *fōtu-s*, 'a foot;' Lith. *pėda-s*, 'the sole of the foot;' *pėnda-s*, 'a vestige;' probably Hib. *fadadh*, 'kindling, lighting;' *fadaidhim*, 'I kindle, excite, provoke.'] — *Pāda-kaṭaka, as, am*, m. n. or *pāda-kīlikā*, f. an ornament for the feet or ankles, an anklet. — *Pāda-kṛiććhra, as*, m. 'quarter-penance,' a sort of penance (eating and fasting on alternate nights). — *Pāda-kshepa, as*, m. a footstep. — *Pāda-gaṇḍīra, as*, m. morbid enlargement of the legs and feet. — *Pāda-gṛihya* or *pāde-gṛihya*, ind., Ved., see Gaṇa to Pāṇ. II. 1, 72. — *Pāda-granthi, is*, m. 'foot-knot,' the ankle. — *Pāda-grahaṇa, am*, n. laying hold of or clasping the feet (of a Brāhman or superior as a mark of respectful salutation). — *Pāda-ghṛita, am*, n. melted butter for anointing the feet. — *Pāda-ćatura* or *pāda-ćatvara, as*, m. a slanderer, calumniator; a goat; a sand-bank; hail; the religious fig-tree, Ficus Religiosa. — *Pāda-ćāpalya, am*, n. 'foot-unsteadiness,' fidgeting or shuffling with the feet. — *Pāda-ćāra, as*, m. going on foot, walking; the daily position of the planets; (*eṇa*), ind. on foot. — *Pāda-ćārin, ī, iṇī, i*, going or walking on foot, having feet for locomotion; fighting on foot; (*ī*), m. a footman, pedestrian, a foot-soldier. — *Pāda-ćihna, am*, n. foot-mark, foot-print. — *Pāda-ja, as*, m. 'born from the foot (of Brahmā),' a Śūdra, man of the fourth and servile tribe. — *Pāda-jala, am*, n. water for the feet; water in which the feet have been washed; (*as, ā, am*), that of which a fourth part is water, mixed with one fourth of water. — *Pāda-jāha, am*, n. = *pāda-mūla*, that part of the foot to which the leg is articulated, the tarsus. — *Pāda-tala, am*, n. the sole or lower part of the foot; (*e*), ind. under the feet. — *Pāda-tas*, ind. out of the feet, from the feet, at or near the feet, (*pādataḥ kṛi*, to put down at the feet); at the foot (of a bed); in the south-west (Manu III. 89, according to Kullūka, this may also mean 'at the foot of the bed'); by or with a quarter; after a quarter of a verse (Ved.); step by step, by degrees. — *Pāda-tra, as* or *am*, m. or n. (?), or *pāda-trā*, f. 'foot-covering,' a shoe. — *Pāda-trāṇa, am*, n. 'foot-protecting,' a boot, shoe. — *Pāda-dārī* or *pāda-dārikā*, f. 'foot-rending,' a chap in the feet, a chilblain. — *Pāda-dāha, as*, m. a burning sensation in the feet (said to be in India an excruciating pain difficult to remedy). — *Pāda-dhāraṇa, am*, n. washing the feet. — *Pāda-dhāvanikā*, f. sand used for rubbing the feet. — *Pāda-nakha, as*, m. a toe-nail. — *Pāda-nālikā*, f. an ornament for the feet, an anklet. — *Pāda-nićṛit, t, f.*, scil. *gāyatrī*, a defective metre, in which one syllable is wanting in each Pāda; (also wrongly spelt *pāda-nivṛit*.) — *Pāda-nishka, as*, m. = *pan-nishka*, p. 529. — *Pāda-nyāsa, as*, m. placing the feet, a dance or measured step. — *Pāda-pa, as*, m. 'imbibing nourishment with the foot or root,' a plant, tree; 'protecting the feet,' (fr. rt. 3. *pā*) a foot-stool, cushion for the feet; (*ā*), f. a shoe, slipper. — *Pādapa-khaṇḍa, as*, m. a group or clump of trees. — *Pāda-paddhati, is*, f. a line of footsteps, a track, trail. — *Pāda-padma, as*, m. 'foot-lotus,' a foot beautiful as a lotus. — *Pāda-parighaṭṭana, am*, n. trampling with the feet, treading upon. — *Pādapa-ruhā*, f. a climbing plant, parasitical plant. — *Pāda-pālikā*, f. an ornament for the feet, an anklet. — *Pāda-pāśa, as*, m. a foot-rope for cattle or horses; an anklet of small bells, &c.; (*ī*), f. a chain for the feet, a fetter; a foot-carpet or mat. — *Pāda-pīṭha, am*, n. a foot-stool. — *Pādapīṭhikā*, f. any common or vulgar trade, as that of a barber, &c.; white stone. — *Pāda-pīrī*, f. a shoe; (incorrectly for *pāda-pīṭhī?*). — *Pāda-pūraṇa, as, ā, am*, (Ved.) filling out a part or line of a verse (as a particle), expletive; (*am*), n. the filling out a line or the measure of a verse. — *Pāda-prakshālana, am*, n. 'washing the feet,' N. of a chapter of the Purāṇa-sarva-sva. — *Pāda-praṇāma, as*, m. bowing to the feet, prostration. — *Pāda-pratishṭhāna, am*, n. a foot-stool. — *Pāda-pradhāraṇa, am*, n. 'foot-covering,' a shoe. — *Pāda-prahāra, as*, m. 'foot-blow,' a kick. — *Pāda-baddha, as, ā, am*, bound or held together by quarters of verses (as a metre). — *Pāda-bandha, as*, m. any tie for the foot, a chain or fetter for the feet. — *Pāda-bandhana, am*, n. a fetter for the feet; a stock of cattle (so called from the foot-ropes with which cattle are tied). — *Pāda-bhāga, as*, m. a fourth part, quarter. — *Pāda-bhāj, k, k, k*, possessing a quarter, being only a quarter. — *Pāda-miśra*, see Pāṇ. VI. 3, 56. — *Pāda-mudrā*, f. the impression of a footstep, foot-print, trace. — *Pāda-mūla, am*, n. 'root of the foot,' the part of the foot to which the leg is articulated, tarsus; the sole of the foot; the heel; a polite designation of a person; the foot of a mountain. — *Pāda-yuddha, am*, n. 'foot-fight,' fighting on foot. — *Pāda-raksha, as*, m. a foot-protector, foot-guard; (*ās*), m. pl. armed men who run by the side of an elephant in battle to protect its feet from wounds. — *Pāda-rakshaṇa, am*, n. a cover for the feet; a leather boot or shoe, a stocking. — *Pāda-rajas, as*, n. the dust of the feet. — *Pāda-rajju, us*, f. a tether or rope for the foot of an elephant. — *Pāda-rathī*, f. 'foot-vehicle,' a shoe, boot, slipper. — *Pāda-rohaṇa, as*, m. 'growing from roots,' the Indian fig-tree. — *Pāda-lagna, as, ā, am*, sticking to the foot. — *Pāda-lepa, as*, m. an unguent for the feet. — *Pāda-vat, ān, atī, at*, having feet, possessed of feet. — *Pāda-vandana, am*, n. 'saluting the feet,' respectful salutation. — *Pāda-valmīka, as*, m. morbid enlargement of the legs and feet, elephantiasis. — *Pāda-vigraha, as*, m. (probably) a mode of reading in which the divisions in verses are carefully marked; (*as, ā, am*), having a quarter of the compass or extent. — *Pāda-vidhāna, am*, n. 'the arrangement of the parts of a verse,' N. of a work ascribed to Saunaka. — *Pāda-virajas, ās*, f. a shoe, slipper, stocking (as keeping *rajas* or dust from the feet?). — *Pāda-vīthī*, f. a shoe; (probably an incorrect form, cf. *pāda-pīvī*.) — *Pāda-vṛitta, au*, m. du., Ved. the two component elements of the quarter of a verse, i. e. the long and short syllable; (*as*), m. epithet of a Svarita separated from the preceding Udātta by a hiatus. — *Pāda-veshṭanika, as* or *am*, m. or n. (?), a stocking. — *Pāda-śabda, as*, m. the sound or noise of footsteps (= *pać-ćhabda*). — *Pāda-śas*, ind. foot by foot; verse by verse, stanza by stanza; by a fourth part. — *Pāda-śākhā*, f. 'branch of the foot,' a toe. — *Pāda-śili*, f. an ornament for the feet, an anklet; (probably an incorrect form.) — *Pāda-śuśrūshā*, f. obedience towards the feet (a respectful expression for *śuśrūshā*). — *Pāda-śesha, am*, n. a quarter, fourth part. — *Pāda-śaila, as*, m. a hill at the foot of or near a mountain. — *Pāda-śotha, as*, m. swelling of the feet, gout. — *Pāda-śauća, am*, n. cleaning the feet (= *pać-ćhauća*). — *Pāda-saṃhitā*, f. the union of words in a quarter of a verse. — *Pāda-sevana, am*, n. or *pāda-sevā*, f. 'foot-salutation,' showing respect by touching the feet, service, duty. — *Pāda-stambha, as*, m. a supporting beam, pillar, post. — *Pāda-sphoṭa, as*, m. 'cracking of the feet,' chilblain, a sore or ulcer on the foot. — *Pāda-svedana, am*, n. perspiration of the feet, causing perspiration in the feet. — *Pāda-hata, as, ā, am*, struck with the feet, kicked, trodden on, touched with the feet. — *Pāda-harsha, as*, m. numbness of the feet after pressure upon the crural nerves. — *Pāda-hāraka, as, ā, am*, taken away with the feet; (*as*), m. one who takes away or steals anything with the feet (?). — *Pāda-hīnāt*, ind. without division or transition; on a sudden, all at once. — *Pādākulaka* (°*da-āk*°), *as, am*, m. or n. (?), N. of two kinds of metres. — *Pādāgra* (°*da-ag*°), *am*, n. the point or extremity of the foot. — *Pādāghāta* (°*da-āgh*°), *as* m. 'a blow with the foot,' a kick. — *Pādāṅka* (°*da-aṅ*°), *as*, m. a foot-mark, footstep, foot-print, vestige. — *Pādāṅgada* (°*da-aṅ*°), *am, ī*, n. f.

an ornament for the feet or toes, an anklet. — *Pādāṅguli* (°*da-aṅ*°), *is, ī,* f. 'foot-finger,' a toe. — *Pādāṅguliyaka* (°*da-aṅ*°), *am,* n. a ring worn on one of the toes. — *Pādāṅgushṭha* (°*da-aṅ*°), *as,* m. the great toe. — *Pādāṅgushṭhāśritāvani* (°*ṭha-āś*°, °*ta-av*°), *is, is, i,* 'touching the ground with the toes,' on tiptoe. — *Pādāṅgushṭhikā,* f. a ring worn on the great toe. — *Pādādhyāsa* (°*da-adh*°), *as,* m. treading upon, kicking. — *Pādānata* (°*da-ān*°), *as, ā, am,* bowed or bent down to the feet, prostrate. — *Pādānudhyāta* (°*da-an*°), *as, ā, am,* thought of by the feet of such an one (a respectful expression in inscriptions for 'thought of by such an one'); the son and successor of any one, rightful successor of any one ('thought of by his predecessor'). — *Pādānta* (°*da-an*°), *as,* m. the extremity of the feet; proximity to the feet; (*e*), ind. near the feet. — *Pādāntara* (°*da-an*°), *am,* n. the interval of a step, the distance of a foot; (*e*), ind. in immediate proximity to, close to (with gen.); after the interval of a step. — *Pādāntika* (°*da-an*°), *am,* n. proximity to the feet, the neighbourhood of the feet. — *Pādāmbu* (°*da-am*°), *us, us, u,* containing a fourth part of water. — *Pādāmbhas* (°*da-am*°), *as,* n. 'foot-water,' water in which the feet have been washed. — *Pādāravinda* (°*da-ar*°), *as,* m. 'foot-lotus,' the foot of a deity, lover, &c. — *Pādārghya* (°*da-ar*°), *am,* n. 'offering to the feet,' a donation to Brāhmans or venerable persons. — *Pādārdha* (°*da-ar*°), *am,* n. half a quarter, an eighth; half a line of a stanza. — *Pādārpaṇa* (°*da-ar*°), *am,* n. setting down the feet. — *Pādāvanejana* (°*da-av*°), *as, ī, am,* used for washing the feet (Ved.); washing the feet. — *Pādāvarta* (°*da-āv*°), *as,* m. a wheel worked by the feet for raising water from a well; a square foot. — *Pādāvasećana* (°*da-av*°), *am,* n. washing the feet; water for washing the feet, water in which the feet have been washed. — *Pādāshṭhīla* (°*da-ash*°), *as,* m. the ankle; contusion of the feet (?). — *Pādāsana* (°*da-ās*°), *am,* n. a footstool. — *Pādāsphālana* (°*da-ās*°), *am,* n. trampling or shuffling of the feet, motion of the feet (as in wrestling or struggling), floundering. — *Pādāhata* (°*da-āh*°), *as, ā, am,* 'struck with the foot,' kicked, trodden, touched by the foot. — *Pādāhati* (°*da-āh*°), *is,* f. a blow with the foot, kick; treading, trampling. — *Pāde-gṛihya* = *pāda-gṛihya.* — *Pādotphāla* (°*da-ut*°), *as,* m. shuffling or moving the feet. — *Pādodaka* (°*da-ud*°), *am,* n. 'foot-water,' water for washing the feet, water in which the feet of a Brāhman have been washed, water hallowed by the washing of sacred feet. — *Pādodaka-tīrtha, am,* n., N. of a sacred bathing-place at Benares. — *Pādodara* (°*da-ud*°), *as,* m. a serpent ('using the belly in place of feet').

Pādaka, as, m. a little foot (Ved.); (*as, ikā, am*), making a quarter of anything (Ved.); at the end of a comp. = *pāda;* [cf. *tri-p*°.]

Pādaya, Nom. A. *pādayate, -yitum,* to stretch out the feet.

Pādavika, as, m. a traveller.

Pādāt, t, m. (properly *pāda + at*), a foot-soldier, footman.

Pādāta, as, m. (properly *pāda + āta*), a foot-soldier, footman; (*am*), n. infantry.

Pādāti, is, or *pādātika,* or *pādāvika, as,* m. = *padāti,* a foot-soldier, man on foot, footman.

Pādika, as, ī, am, lasting for a quarter of the time, amounting to a quarter or fourth, a fourth; *pādikam śatam,* one quarter of a hundred, 25 per cent; [cf. *ardha-p*°.]

Pādin, ī, inī, i, footed, having feet; having a fourth part or share, claiming or receiving a fourth part; having four parts, as a stanza &c.; (*ī*), m. a footed aquatic animal, an amphibious animal; the heir to a fourth part of an estate.

Pādina, as, m. a fourth part.

Pādu, us, m., Ved. course, path (Sāy. = *pādenā gamana*).

Pādukā, f. a wooden shoe, shoe, slipper [cf. *ćarma-p*°]; (*as, ā* or *ī, am*), going on foot, going with feet. — *Pādukā-kāra, as,* or *pādukā-kṛit, t,* m. a shoemaker.

Pādū, ūs, f. a shoe. — *Pādū-kṛit, t,* m. a shoemaker; (also spelt *pādu-kṛit.*)

Pādya, as, ā, am, relating or belonging to the foot; (*am*), n. (with or without *udaka*) water for washing the feet. — *Pādya-pātra, am,* n. a metal vessel for washing the feet.

पादक्रमिक *pādakramika, as, ī, am* (fr. *pada-krama*), one who reads or knows the Pada-krama, q. v.

पादप *pāda-pa.* See p. 564, col. 2.

पादारक *pādāraka, as,* m. the knees or ribs of a boat (supporting the deck on each side?).

पादालिन्द *pādālinda, as, ā* or *ī,* m. f. a boat.

पाद्म *pādma, as, ī, am* (fr. *padma*), relating to the lotus, referring to or treating of the lotus; (*as*), m. a patronymic of Brahmā [cf. *padma-garbha, padma-yoni*]; N. of a Mahā-kalpa. — *Pādma-purāṇa, am,* n., N. of a Purāṇa.

पान 1. *pāna, pānīya, pānta.* See p. 560, cols. 1, 2.

पान 2. *pāna, as,* m. = *apāna,* breath, breathing out, expiration.

पानस *pānasa, as, ī, am* (fr. *panasa*), prepared from the fruit of the Jaka or bread-fruit tree; (*am*), n. a spirituous liquor so prepared.

पान्थ *pāntha, as,* m. (fr. *pathin*), a wanderer, traveller; 'the wanderer in the sky,' the sun.

पान्नग *pānnaga, as, ī, am* (fr. *panna-ga*), formed or consisting of snakes, having serpents, snaky.

पान्नेजन *pānnejana, as, ī, am* (fr. 3. *pad + nejana*), Ved. used for washing the feet; (*am*), n. a vessel in which the feet are washed, foot-bath.

पाप *pāpa, as, ā* (or in the earlier language *ī*), *am* (said to be fr. rt. 3. *pā;* according to some for *apāpa* fr. rt. *āp* with *apa*), bad, wicked, vicious, sinful, evil, mischievous, destructive; vile, low, abandoned; (in astrology) boding evil, malignant, inauspicious; (*as*), m. a wicked man, wretch, profligate; N. of a hell; (*am*), n. bad fortune, bad state, unhappiness; evil, sin, vice, crime, wickedness, transgression, guilt (e. g. *pāpam avāpsyasi,* thou wilt incur guilt); (*am*), ind. badly, miserably, wrongly; (*ayā*), ind., Ved. badly, wrongly, wickedly; [cf. Gr. κάκο-ς: Lat. *peccare:* Lith. *pykiù,* 'I am angry;' *paika-s, pikta-s,* 'angry.'] — *Pāpa-kara, as, ā* or *ī, am,* or *pāpa-kartṛi, tā, trī, tṛi,* or *pāpa-karman, ā, ā, a,* or *pāpa-karmin, ī, iṇī, i,* or *pāpa-kārin, ī, iṇī, i,* or *pāpa-kṛit, t, t, t,* 'wrong-doing,' wicked, sinful, criminal, an evil-doer, malefactor, villain. — *Pāpa-kṛita, am,* n. or *pāpa-kṛityā,* f. an evil deed, bad action, sin, crime. — *Pāpa-kshaya, as,* m. the destruction of sin. — *Pāpakshaya-tīrtha, am,* n., N. of a Tīrtha. — *Pāpakshaya-mātra, am,* n. entire destruction (or expiation) of sins. — *Pāpa-gumpa, as,* m. epithet of Bāla-kṛishṇa; (perhaps incorrectly for *pāya-guṇḍa.*) — *Pāpa-goćara, as, ā, am,* evidently involved in (the consequences of) sin. — *Pāpa-graha, as,* m. a planet of evil or malignant aspect (as Mars, Saturn, Rāhu, Ketu); any ill-omened or inauspicious aspect of the stars as the conjunction of the sun or Budha with the moon in its last quarter; calamitous or fatal destiny. — *Pāpa-ghna, as, ī, am,* destroying or removing sin or evil deeds, expiating guilt; (*as*), m. the sesamum plant; (*ī*), f., N. of a river. — *Pāpa-ćara, as,* m. 'walking in sin,' N. of a king. — *Pāpa-ćarya, as,* m. a sinner; a fiend, Rākshasa. — *Pāpa-ćārin, ī, iṇī, i,* doing evil, sinful, wicked, criminal. — *Pāpa-ćetas, ās, ās, as,* evil-minded, being of an evil disposition, wicked, vile. — *Pāpa-ćelī* or *pāpa-ćelikā,* f. the plant Clypea Hernandifolia, a species of creeper (commonly called *ākanādi*). — *Pāpa-ja, as, ā, am,* Ved. springing from evil. — *Pāpa-jīva, as, ā, am,* leading an evil life, wicked, criminal. — *Pāpa-tara, as, ā, am,* worse, more wicked, very evil. — *Pāpa-timira, as, ā, am,* 'sin-bedarkened,' blinded by sin. — *Pāpa-tva, am,* n., Ved. evil condition, misery, poverty. — *Pāpa-da, as, ā, am,* Ved. bringing misfortune, inauspicious. — *Pāpa-darśin, ī, inī, i,* looking at faults, malevolent. — *Pāpa-driśvan, ā, arī, a,* seeing guilt, knowing an act to be wicked. — *Pāpa-dṛishṭi, is, is, i,* evil-eyed. — *Pāpa-dhī, īs, īs, i,* evil-minded. — *Pāpa-nakshatra, am,* n., Ved. an inauspicious constellation. — *Pāpa-nāpita, as,* m. a vile or bad barber. — *Pāpa-nāman, ā, mnī, a,* Ved. having a bad name. — *Pāpa-nāśana, as, ī, am,* destroying the wicked; (*as*), m. an epithet of Śiva; N. of a temple of Vishṇu; (*am*), n., N. of a part of the Brahmāṇḍa-Purāṇa. — *Pāpa-nāśin, ī, inī, i,* sin-destroying, purifying. — *Pāpa-nirati, is, is, i,* wicked, villainous; a wretch; (*is*), f. attachment to evil, wickedness. — *Pāpa-niśćaya, as, ā, am,* having evil designs, malevolent. — *Pāpa-nishkṛiti, is,* f. atonement for sin. — *Pāpa-pati, is,* m. 'sinful master,' a paramour. — *Pāpa-parājita, as, ā, am,* Ved. ignominiously defeated. — *Pāpa-puṇya, āni,* n. pl. vicious or virtuous (deeds). — *Pāpa-purusha, as,* m. a villainous man (a personification of all sin or archetype of a sinner, whose head is Brāhmaṇicide, whose arms are theft, and whose heart is wine-drinking, &c.; also spelt *pāpa-pūrusha*). — *Pāpa-phala, as, ā, am,* having evil consequences, inauspicious. — *Pāpa-buddhi, is, is, i,* evil-minded, wicked; (*is*), m., N. of a man. — *Pāpa-bhakshaṇa, as, ā, am,* devouring the wicked; (*as*), m. an epithet of Kāla-bhairava, a son of Śiva. — *Pāpa-bhañjana, as, ā, am,* breaking or destroying the wicked; (*as*), m., N. of a Brāhman. — *Pāpa-bhāva, as, ā, am,* being of an evil disposition, evil-minded. — *Pāpa-mati, is, is, i,* evil-minded, of a corrupt mind, sinful, graceless, ungodly, depraved. — *Pāpa-mitra, am,* n. friend or companion of sin, bad counsellor, seducer. — *Pāpamitra-tva, am,* n. friendship with the wicked. — *Pāpa-mukta, as, ā, am,* freed from sin, liberated from all crime. — *Pāpa-moćana, am,* n. liberating from sin, remission of guilt. — *Pāpa-yakshma, as,* m., Ved. 'the evil disease,' consumption. — *Pāpa-yoni, is,* f. a bad or low birthplace, birth in an inferior condition (as in that of an animal; considered as the punishment of sin). — *Pāpa-rahita, as, ā, am,* freed from sin, sinless. — *Pāpa-roga, as,* m. any bad disease considered as the penalty of sin in a former life (as leprosy, elephantiasis); small pox. — *Pāparogin, ī, iṇī, i,* suffering from a bad disease as a penalty for sin (committed in a former life). — *Pāparddhi* (°*pa-ṛid*°), *is,* f. 'sin-prosperity,' getting a living by hunting, the chase. — *Pāpa-loka, as,* m., Ved. the evil world, the place of suffering, place of the wicked. — *Pāpalokya, as, ā, am,* belonging to hell or the world of the wicked, fiendish, infernal; belonging to the wicked. — *Pāpa-vasīyas, ān, asī, as,* inverted; confused; (*as*), n. inversion, confusion. — *Pāpa-vasīyasa* or *pāpa-vasyasa, am,* n., Ved. inversion, inverted order, confusion. — *Pāpa-vāda, as,* m., Ved. an inauspicious cry. — *Pāpa-vināśana, as, ī, am,* sin-destroying, destroying transgressions. — *Pāpavināśana-tīrtha, am,* n., N. of a Tīrtha. — *Pāpa-vinigraha, as,* m. restraining or punishing wickedness. — *Pāpa-viniśćaya, as, ā, am,* intending evil, resolved on wickedness or crime. — *Pāpa-śamana, as, ā, am,* palliating or removing crime; (*am*), n. a sin offering; (*ī*), f. a species of tree; [cf. *śamī.*] — *Pāpa-śīla, as, ā, am,* ill-disposed, prone to evil, of bad character, wicked. — *Pāpa-śodhana, as, ā, am,* cleansing or washing away sins; (*am*), n., N. of a Tīrtha. — *Pāpa-saṃśamana, as, ā, am,* removing sin. — *Pāpa-saṅkalpa, as, ā, am,* evil-minded, ill-intentioned. — *Pāpa-sama, am,* n., Ved. a bad year. — *Pāpa-sammita, as, ā, am,* equal in sin, of like guilt. — *Pāpa-sūdana, as, ā, am,* sin-destroying. — *Pāpasūdana-tīrtha, am,* n., N. of a

Tīrtha. — *Pāpa-han, ā, ghnī, a,* sin-destroying, destroying the wicked. — *Pāpa-hara, as, ā, am,* removing evil, destroying sin; *(am),* n. a means of removing evil; *(ā),* f., N. of a river. — *Pāpākhyā* (°*pa-ākh*°), f., scil. *gati,* epithet of one of the seven divisions of the planetary courses (according to the Parāśara-tantra extending over the constellations Hasta, Maitra, and Vi-śākhā). — *Pāpāṅkuśā* (°*pa-an*°), f., N. of the eleventh day in the light half of the month Āśvina. — *Pāpāćāra* (°*pa-āć*°), *as, ā, am,* ill-conducted, following evil courses, practising evil, living an evil life, vicious. — *Pāpātman* (°*pa-āt*°), *ā, ā, a,* evil-minded, wicked; *(ā),* m. a sinner, reprobate, wretch; (opposed to *dharmātman.*) — *Pāpādhama* (°*pa-adh*°), *as, ā, am,* the lowest of the wicked, exceedingly low or wicked. — *Pāpānuvasita* (°*pa-an*°), *as, ā, am,* addicted to sin, sinful. — *Pāpānta* (°*pa-an*°), *am,* n., N. of a Tīrtha ('where sins come to an end'). — *Pāpāpanutti* (°*pa-ap*°), *is,* f. 'removal of sins,' expiation. — *Pāpāvahīyam* (°*pa-av*°), ind., Ved. wrongfully staying away or remaining behind. — *Pāpāśaya* (°*pa-āś*°), *as, ā, am,* evil-intentioned, wicked, sinful. — *Pāpāha* (°*pa-aha*), *am,* n., Ved. an unlucky day. — *Pāpāhi* (°*pa-ahi*), *is,* m. a snake, serpent. — *Pāpokta* (°*pa-uk*°), *as, ā, am,* Ved. addressed in ill-omened words.

Pāpaka, as, ikā or *akī, am,* bad, evil, wicked; *(am),* n. evil, wrong, wickedness, sin; *(as),* m. a wicked person, rascal; an evil or malignant planet.

Pāpala, as, ā, am, imparting or incurring guilt; *(am),* n. a particular measure.

Pāpin, ī, inī, i, wicked, sinful, bad; a sinner, criminal.

Pāpishṭha, as, ā, am, worst, lowest, most wicked; exceedingly bad, very wicked. — *Pāpishṭha-tama, as, ā, am,* worst, most wicked; worse, more wicked. — *Pāpishṭha-tara, as, ā, am,* worse, more wicked; the very worst; exceedingly wicked.

Pāpīya, as, ā, am, worse, &c.; (a contracted form of *pāpīyas* below.)

Pāpīyas, ān, asī, as, worse, worse off, more wretched or miserable; lower, poorer; more wicked; very bad or wicked, very criminal; *māraḥ pāpīyān,* (with Buddhists) the evil spirit, the devil; *(as),* m. a wicked man, wretch, villain. — *Pāpīyas-tara, as, ā, am,* = *pāpīyas.* — *Pāpīyas-tva, am,* n. the state of being very wicked, great wickedness.

Pāpman, ā, m. evil, unhappiness, evil plight, suffering; crime, evil, sin, wickedness; *(ā, ā, a),* injurious, hurtful, evil.

पापापुरी *pāpāpurī,* f. = *pāvāpurī,* f., N. of a town near Rāja-gṛiha.

पामन् *pāman, ā,* m. (fr. rt. *pai*), a kind of skin disease, cutaneous eruption, herpes, scab. — *Pāma-ghna, as, ī, am,* destroying the scab; *(as),* m. sulphur; *(ī),* f. a species of plant (= *kaṭukā*). — *Pāma-vat, ān, atī, at,* diseased with herpes.

Pāmana, as, ā, am, diseased with herpes. — *Pāmanam-bhāvuka, as, ā, am,* Ved. becoming diseased with herpes.

Pāmara, as, ā, am, diseased with herpes, scabby; wicked, vile; low, vulgar, base; stupid; *(as),* m. a man of the lowest extraction, a man engaged in any degrading occupation; an idiot, fool; a wicked man; *(am),* n. evil, bad character, wickedness. — *Pāmaroddharā* (°*ra-ud*°), f. 'removing herpes,' a species of plant (= *guḍūćī*).

Pāmā, f. herpes, scab (enumerated among the forms of so-called mild leprosy). — *Pāmāri* (°*mā-ari*), *is,* m. 'enemy of the scab,' sulphur.

पाम्प *pāmpa, as, ī, am,* belonging to or situated on the river Pampā.

Pāmpana, as, ī, am, belonging or relating to the river Pampā.

पाय *pāya, am,* n. (fr. rt. 1. *pā*), water. — *Pāya-guṇḍa, as,* m., N. of the author of a commentary on the Laghu-śabdendu-śekhara.

Pāyaka, as, ikā, am, drinking; [cf. *taila-pāyikā.*]

Pāyana, am, n. the causing or giving to drink; (Sāy.) = 1. *pāna,* a beverage; *(ā),* f. causing to drink; watering, moistening.

Pāyin, ī, inī, i, (at the end of a comp.) drinking; [cf. *kuṇḍa-p*°, *kshīra-p*°, *ćandrikā-p*°.]

1. *pāyu, us,* m. the anus. — *Pāyu-kshālana-bhūmi, is,* f. or *pāyu-kshālana-veśman, a,* n. a water-closet, privy. — *Pāyu-bheda, as,* m., Ved. (in astrol.) N. of two ways in which an eclipse terminates.

1. *pāyya, as, ā, am,* to be drunk, to be caused to drink; *(am),* n. water; drinking.

पायस *pāyasa, as, ī, am* (fr. *payas*), prepared with or made of milk or water; *(as, am),* m. n. food prepared with milk, rice boiled in milk; an oblation of milk, rice, and sugar; the resin of Pinus Longifolia; turpentine; *(am),* n. milk; a kind of divine beverage, nectar (Rām. I. 15, 8). — *Pāyasa-dagdha, as, ā, am,* scalded by milk-porridge.

Pāyasika, as, ī, am, fond of boiled milk, relating to any mixture of milk, &c.

पायिक *pāyika, as,* m. a foot-soldier, footman; (probably a corruption of *pādātika.*)

पायु 2. *pāyu, us,* m. (fr. rt. 3. *pā;* for 1. see above), Ved. a guard, protector; N. of a man; *(avas),* m. pl. protecting powers or actions.

2. *pāyya* (for 1. see above), protection (at the end of a comp.; cf. *nṛi-p*°).

पाय्य 3. *pāyya, am,* n. measure; practice, profession.

पाय्य 4. *pāyya, as, ā, am,* low, vile, reprehensible, contemptible.

पार *pāra, as,* m. (fr. rt. 1. *pṛi* or rt. *pṝi*), crossing [cf. *dush-p*°]; the further shore or opposite bank of a river; the further side, concluding bound; the end or limit of anything, the utmost reach or extent; quicksilver; N. of a sage, a son of Pṛithu-sheṇa and father of Nīpa; of a son of Samara and father of Pṛithu; of a son of Aṅga and father of Divi-ratha; *(ās),* m. pl., N. of a class of deities under the ninth Manu; *(ā),* f., N. of a river (said to flow from the Pāriyātra mountains or the central and western portion of the Vindhya chain); *(ī),* f. a quantity of water; a small water-jar, drinking-vessel, glass, cup; a milk-pail; a rope for tying an elephant's feet; pollen; *(am),* n. (according to some also *as,* m.), the further or opposite end or bank of a river; the totality of an object, the fullest extent (with gen., e. g. *tamasas,* of darkness; *kāraṇānām,* of tortures); extremity, end, aim (in this sense also m.); *pāraṃ gam,* to cross over; to fulfil (e. g. *pratijñāyāḥ pāraṃ sa gataḥ,* he fulfilled his promise); to become proficient in; *pāraṃ nī,* to bring to a close; [cf. *para, param;* Gr. πόρο-ς, πέρα, πέραν, περαίνω, πείρω, περαῖο-ς, περά-τη, Πειραιεύ-ς, πέρας, πεῖραρ, ἀπειρέσ-ιο-ς; Lat. *per;* Lith. *per,* 'across;' Slav. *polŭ,* 'the opposite bank.'] — *Pāra-kāma, as, ā, am,* desirous of reaching the opposite bank. — *Pāra-ga, as, ā, am,* going to the opposite shore, crossing over, going through or over or across or to the end, ferrying across, intending to cross; one who has arrived at the end, accomplishing, one who has accomplished or completely mastered, completely familiar or conversant with, knowing thoroughly, well versed in (with gen. or loc. or in a comp., e. g. *Vedānām pāragaḥ,* well versed in the Vedas; *pratijñā-p*°, fulfilling or keeping a promise); profoundly learned; going over or beyond the world; *(am),* n. keeping, fulfilling. — *Pāra-gata, as, ā, am,* or *pāra-gāmin, ī, inī, i,* one who has reached the opposite shore, passed over in safety, crossed; passed beyond the world, pure, holy; *(as),* m. (with Jainas) an Arhat or deified saint and teacher. — *Pāra-gati, is,* f. going through, reading, studying through. — *Pāra-gamana, am,* n. reaching the opposite shore, crossing, going to the end. — *Pāra-ćara, as, ī, am,* arriving at the opposite shore, crossing over. — *Pāra-tas,* ind., Ved. on the opposite bank, on the further side. — *Pāra-daṇḍaka, as,* m. (perhaps a Vṛiddhied form fr. *para + daṇḍaka*), N. of a country (part of Orissa). — *Pāra-darśaka, as, ā, am,* showing the opposite bank. — *Pāra-darśana, as, ā, am,* beholding the opposite bank or shore, able to survey all things. — *Pāra-dṛiśvan, ā, arī, a,* one who has seen the opposite bank, completely familiar with, knowing thoroughly; long-sighted, far-seeing, wise. — *Pāra-dhvaja, ās,* m. pl. 'banners of the further shore,' N. of certain banners brought from beyond the sea (from Ceylon) and borne in procession by the kings of Kaśmīra. — *Pāra-netrī, tā, trī, tṛi,* bringing to the further shore. — *Pāram-ita, as, ā, am,* gone to the opposite bank; crossed, traversed; transcendant (as spiritual knowledge); *(ā),* f. (probably a contracted form for *pāramita-tā*), coming to the opposite bank, complete attainment, perfection (the Buddhists enumerate six or sometimes ten Pāramitās or perfections as belonging to a Bodhisattva). — *Pārāpāra* (°*ra-ap*°), *am,* n. = *pārāvāra,* the nearer and further bank, both banks, (a various reading for *pārāvāra,* q. v.); *(as),* m. the sea, ocean. — *Pārāyaṇa* (°*ra-ay*°), *am,* n. going over, going across; reading from one end to the other, reading through, perusing, studying, study; reading a Purāṇa or causing it to be read; the whole, totality, entireness, completeness [cf. *dhātu-p*°, *nāma-p*°]; N. of a grammatical work; *(ī),* f. a N. of the goddess Sarasvatī; an act, action; considering, meditating; light. — *Pārāyaṇa-māhātmya, am,* n., N. of a section of the Pātāla-khaṇḍa of the Pādma-Purāṇa. — *Pārāyaṇika, as, ī, am,* reading to (any one), teaching how to pronounce; *(as),* m. a lecturer, reader of the Purāṇas; a pupil, scholar; *(ās),* m. pl. epithet of a particular school of grammarians. — *Pārāyaṇīya, am,* n., N. of a grammar. — *Pārāvāra* (°*ra-av*°), *am,* n. the further and the nearer bank or shore, the opposite banks (e. g. *pārāvārasya nauḥ,* a boat which plies from one side to the other); *(as),* m. the sea, ocean; [cf. *pārāpāra.*] — *Pārāvāriṇa, as, ā, am,* on both sides of a river, &c., one who goes to both sides. — *Pāre-gaṅgam,* ind. on the other side of the Gaṅgā, beyond the Ganges. — *Pāre-viśoka,* N. of a place. — *Pāre-sindhu,* ind. on the other side of the Sindhu, beyond the Indus.

1. *pāraka, as, ī, am* (for 2. see p. 567, col. 1), carrying over, bearing across, saving, delivering (in *ugra-p*°, q. v.); enabling to cross (a river or the world).

1. *pāraṇa, as, ā, am* (for 2. see p. 567, col. 1), bringing over, carrying across, saving, delivering; *(am),* n. fulfilling, accomplishing; reading through, reading, studying; the complete text (of a book); *(am, ā),* n. f., also *vrata-pāraṇa,* concluding a fast, eating or drinking after a fast, breakfast; [cf. *śoṇita-p*°.] — *Pāraṇa-karman, a,* n. exercise in reading, mode of reading.

Pāraṇīya, as, ā, am, having an attainable end, capable of being completed or brought to an end.

1. *pāraya,* Nom. P. A. *pārayati, -te,* &c., to bring over, lead over; to be able; (this is also regarded as the Caus. of rt. 1. *pṛi,* q. v.)

2. *pāraya, as, ā, am,* able, adequate, fit for.

1. *pārayat, an, antī, at,* being able, competent.

1. *pārayishṇu, us, us, u* (for 2. see s. v.), Ved. bringing to a successful issue, causing to succeed, victorious.

Pārīṇa, as, ā, am, being on the other or opposite side; crossing to the other or opposite side; (at the end of a comp.) completely familiar with, well acquainted with [cf. *trivarga-p*°]; *(as),* m., N. of a man (= *pārīṇa*).

Pārīya, as, ā, am, (at the end of a comp.) completely familiar with, well acquainted with.

Pārya, as, ā, am, Ved. being on the opposite side or bank; upper; last, final; giving the last stroke, decisive (e. g. *pārye dhane,* Ved. in a decisive battle); causing to succeed, helping through; effectual, efficient; *(am),* n. end; decision.

पारक 2. *pāraka, as, ī, am* (fr. rt. *pṛī;* for 1. see p. 566, col. 3), satisfying, pleasing; cherishing.
2. *pāraṇa, as,* m. (for 1. see p. 566, col. 3), satisfying, satisfaction; a cloud.
3. *pāraya, as, ā, am* (for 1. and 2. see p. 566, col. 3), satisfying, filling.
2. *pārayat, an, antī, at,* satisfying, filling.
2. *pārayishṇu, us, us, u,* gratifying, pleasing, satisfying.

पारक्य *pārakya, as, ā, am,* = *parakīya,* belonging to another or a stranger, alien (opposed to *sva*); intended for others, serving others; belonging to an enemy, hostile, inimical; *(as),* m. an enemy; *(am),* n. doing anything for the sake of future happiness, pious conduct.

पारग्रामिक *pāragrāmika, as, ī, am* (fr. *para + grāma*), 'belonging to another village,' hostile, inimical, (*pāragrāmikam vidhim ćikīrshati,* he is about to perform hostile action, i. e. prepares for hostilities.)

पारज् *pāraj, k,* m. (said to be fr. *pāra*), gold.

पारजायिक *pārajāyika, as,* m. (fr. *para + jāyā*), one who intrigues with another's wife, an adulterer.

पारटीट *pāraṭīṭa, as,* m. (connected with *pāra*?), a stone, rock; [cf. *pāraruka.*]

पारणीय *pāraṇīya.* See p. 566, col. 3.

पारत 1. *pārata, as, ī, am* (fr. *para-tas*), see Vārttikā to Pāṇ. IV. 2, 104; (Ved.) N. of a people or country.

पारत 2. *pārata, as,* m. quicksilver; [cf. *pārada.*]
Pārataka, ās, m. pl., N. of a people.

पारतन्त्रिक *pāratantrika, as, ī, am* (fr. *para-tantra*), belonging to or enjoined by the religious treatises of others.
Pāratantrya, am, n. the being subject to another, dependence, subservience, slavery.

पारत्रिक *pāratrika, as, ī, am* (fr. *para-tra*), relating to another world, belonging to the next world, advantageous in the future life.
Pāratrya, as, ā, am, relating to the next world; rewarded in a future state (according to Kullūka = *paraloka-phala*).

पारद *pārada, as,* m. quicksilver; *(ās),* m. pl., N. of a barbarous people (described in Manu X. 44. as a Kshatriya tribe degraded to Sūdras by neglect of duties; cf. 2. *pārata*).

पारदण्डक *pāra-daṇḍaka.* See *pāra,* p. 566.

पारदारिक *pāradārika, as, ī, am* (fr. *para-dāra*), intriguing with another's wife; relating to another's wife; *(as),* m. an adulterer.
Pāradārin, ī, iṇī, i, intriguing with another's wife; (perhaps incorrectly for *para-dārin.*)
Pāradārya, am, n. intriguing with another's wife, adultery.
Pāradeśika, as, ī, am (fr. *para-deśa*), outlandish, foreign, abroad; *(as),* m. a traveller; a foreigner.
Pāradeśya, as, śī, am, belonging to or coming from a foreign country, foreign; *(as),* m. a traveller, one who has gone to a foreign country; a foreigner; [cf. Lat. *per-egrinus.*]
Pāradhenu, us, or *pāradhenuka, as,* m., N. of a low mixed caste, an Āyogava (q. v.).
Pāramparīṇa, as, ī, am (fr. *param-parā*), passing from one to another, handed down from father to son, hereditary.
Pāramparīya, as, ī, am, handed down, traditional.
Pāramparya, as, ī, am, one following the other; *(am),* n. uninterrupted series, continuous order or hereditary succession; traditional instruction, tradition; intercession, intermediation; *(eṇa),* ind. successively. — *Pāramparya-kramāgata* (°*ma-āg*°), or *pāramparyāgata* (°*ya-āg*°), *as, ā, am,* derived from tradition. — *Pāramparyopadeśa* (°*ya-up*°), *as,* m. traditional instruction.
Pāralokya, as, ā, am (fr. *para-loka*), relating to the next world.
Pāralaukika, as, ī, am, relating to the next world (e. g. *sahāyaḥ pāralaukikaḥ,* a companion on the way to the next world); epithet of a place where pearls are found and of the pearls found there (Ved.); *(am),* n. things or circumstances relating to the next world.
Pāravargya, as, ā, am (fr. *para + varga*), belonging to another party, siding with the enemy.
Pāravaśya, am, n. (fr. *para-vaśa*), dependence, dependency.
Pārastraiṇeya, as, m. (fr. *para-strī*), a son by another's wife, an adulterine.
Pārahansya, as, ā, am (fr. *para-hansa*), relating to an ascetic who has subdued all his senses; [cf. *pāramahansya.*]
Pārāvarya, eṇa, ind. (fr. *parāvara*), on all sides, completely.

पारभृत *pārabhṛita, am,* n. a present, offering (incorrectly for *prābhṛita*).
Pārabhṛitīya, as, ī, am, relating or belonging to a present (incorrectly for *prābhṛitīya*); belonging to a cuckoo (fr. *para-bhṛita*).

पारमहंस *pāramahansa, as, ī, am* (fr. *parama-hansa*), relating to Parama-hansa (Brahmā).
Pāramahansya, as, ā, am, relating to the Paramahansas or religious men who have subdued all their senses by abstract meditation; *(am),* n. most sublime ascetism or meditation. — *Pāramahansya-pari,* ind. relating to the most sublime meditation or speculation.
Pāramārthika, as, ī, am (fr. *paramārtha*), relating to a high or spiritual object, relating to supreme truth; real, essential, true; one who cares for truth, loving right; supremely good, excellent, superior.
Pāramika, as, ī, am (fr. *parama*), supreme, chief, best.
Pārameśvara, as, ī, am (fr. *parameśvara*), relating or belonging to the supreme lord (Śiva), coming from the supreme lord.
Pārameshṭha, as, m. a patronymic from Parameshṭhin.
Pārameshṭhya, as, ā, am (fr. *parameshṭhin*), relating or belonging to the highest or supreme god (Brahman), coming from the supreme deity; relating to a king; *(am),* n. highest position, supremacy; royal insignia.

पारमित *pāram-ita.* See under *pāra,* p. 566.

पारय 1. and 2. *pāraya, pārayat, pārayishṇu.* See p. 566, col. 3, and col. 1. of this p.

पारवत *pāravata, as,* m. = *pārāvata,* a pigeon.

पारवश्य *pāravaśya.* See above.

पारशव *pāraśava, as, am,* m. n. (fr. *paraśu*), iron (used for axes), an iron weapon; *(as),* m., N. of a mixed caste, the son of a Brāhman by a Sūdrā woman; a son by another's wife, an adulterine, bastard; *(ās),* m. pl., N. of a people in the south-west of Madhya-deśa; *(as, ī, am),* made of iron; made or derived from an axe; (sometimes written *pārasava.*) — *Pāraśava-tva, am,* n. the state of being born of a Sūdrā woman.
Pāraśarya, as, m., Ved. a patronymic of Tirindira.

पारशीक *pāraśīka* = *pārasika,* q. v.

पारश्वध *pāraśvadha* or *pāraśvadhika, as, ī, am* (fr. *paraśvadha*), armed with an axe; *(as),* m. a man armed with an axe, halbert-man, hatchet-man, pioneer, &c.

पारश्वय *pāraśvaya, as,* m. gold (?).

पारस *pārasa, as, ī, am,* Persian; *(ī),* f. (with or without *bhāshā*) the Persian language.
Pārasika, ās, m. pl. the Persians; *(as, ī, am),* Persian; *(as),* m. Persia (?).
Pārasīka, ās, m. pl. the Persians; *(as),* m. Persia; a Persian horse.
Pārasīkeya, as, ī, am, Persian.

पारसव *pārasava.* See *pāraśava,* col. 2.

पारस्कर *pāraskara, as,* m. (fr. *pāra + kara,* *s* being inserted; or fr. *paras-kara*), N. of the author of certain Gṛihya-sūtras forming a supplement to Kātyāyana's Srauta-sūtras and of a Dharma-śāstra; N. of a district; *(as, ī, am),* composed by Pāraskara. — *Pāraskara-gṛihya-paddhati, is,* f., N. of a work on domestic customs.

पारस्त्रैणेय *pārastraiṇeya, pārahansya.* See col. 2.

पारापत *pārāpata, as,* m. = *pārāvata,* a pigeon.

पारापतक *pārāpataka, as,* m. a kind of rice.

पारायण *pārāyaṇa.* See *pāra,* p. 566.

पारारुक *pāraruka, as,* m. a rock; [cf. *pāraṭīṭa.*]

पारावत *pārāvata, as, ī, am* (fr. *parā-vat*), remote, coming or brought from a distance, of foreign extraction (Ved.); *(as),* m., N. of a tribe on the Yamunā; a turtle-dove, turtle-pigeon, dove, pigeon; a kind of snake; N. of a Nāga of the race of Airāvata; a monkey; a species of tree, Diospyros Embryopteris; a mountain; N. of a class of deities under Manu Svāroćisha; *(ī),* f. the fruit of the Lavalī plant (Annona Reticulata?); a form of song peculiar to cowherds; N. of a river in the peninsula; *(am),* n. the fruit of the tree Diospyros Embryopteris. — *Pārāvata-ghnī,* f., Ved. (according to the Nirukta) destroying both banks (an epithet of the Sarasvatī; Sāy. = *pārāvāra-ghātinī* or = *dūra-deśe vidyamānasyāpi vṛikshāder hantrī;* but the right meaning probably is), hitting the remote (demon), slaying from afar. — *Pārāvata-deśa, as,* m., N. of a district mentioned in the Ratna-kosha. — *Pārāvata-padī,* f. or *pārāvatāṅghri* (°*ta-an*°), 'pigeon's foot,' Cardiospermum Halicacabum (so called from the form of the leaf). — *Pārāvatāṅghri-piććha, as,* m. a pigeon.
Pārāvati, is, m. a patronymic of Vasu-roćis.

पारावद्घ्नी *pārāvada-ghnī,* a wrong reading for *pārāvata-ghnī,* q. v.

पारावर *pārāvara.* See p. 566, col. 3.

पारावर्य *pārāvarya.* See col. 2.

पाराशर *pārāśara, as, ī, am* (fr. *parāśara*), proceeding or derived from Parāśara or from Pārāśarya; *(as),* m. a patronymic from Parāśara and N. of the poet Vyāsa; *(ās),* m. pl., N. of a school; *(ī),* f. a daughter of Parāśara; *(am),* n. the rules of Parāśara for the conduct of the mendicant order. — *Pārāśari-putra, as,* m., Ved., N. of a teacher. — *Pārāśaropapurāṇa* (°*ra-up*°), *am,* n., N. of an Upa-Purāṇa.
Pārāśarakalpika, as, ī, am, one who studies the Parāśara-kalpa; *(as),* m. a follower of Parāśara the institutor of rules for the mendicant order.
Pārāśari, is, m. a patronymic of Vyāsa.
Pārāśarin, ī, m. a mendicant of the school of Parāśara or of Pārāśarya; a religious mendicant in general.
Pārāśarya, as, m. a patronymic of the poet Vyāsa; N. of a teacher.

पारिकर्मिक *pārikarmika, as,* m. (fr. *pari-karman*), one who takes charge of the lesser vessels or utensils.

पारिकाङ्क्षिन् *pārikāṅkshin, ī,* m. an ascetic (who devotes himself to devout contemplation), a contemplative saint, a Brāhman in the fourth period of life, a religious mendicant; (also *pārikāṅkshaka*; cf. *pari-kāṅkshita*.)

पारिकुट *pārikuṭa, as,* m., Ved. an attendant, servant.

पारिक्षित *pārikshita, as, ī, am,* epithet of the verses of the Atharva-veda XX. 127, 7–10; (*as*), m. a patronymic of Janam-ejaya.

Pārikshitīya, as, m., Ved. (according to the commentator) the brother of Pari-kshit.

पारिखेय *pārikheya, as, ī, am* (fr. *pari-khā*), surrounded by a ditch or fosse, belonging to a ditch.

पारिग्रामिक *pārigrāmika, as, ī, am* (fr. *pari-grāmam*), situated round a village.

पारिजात *pārijāta, as,* m. (fr. *pari+jāta*), the coral tree, Erythrina Indica (a splendid tree losing its leaves in June and then covered with large crimson flowers, sometimes identified with the Mandāra); the wood of this tree; N. of one of the five trees of paradise (which was produced at the churning of the ocean and came into the possession of Indra from whom it was afterwards taken by Kṛishṇa); fragrance; N. of a Ṛishi; N. of a Nāga of the race of Airāvata.—*Pārijāta-maya, as, ī, am,* made of flowers of the celestial Pārijāta.—*Pārijāta-vat, ān, atī, at,* possessing the celestial Pārijāta.—*Pārijāta-sarasvatī-mantra, ās,* m. pl., N. of certain magical formulas.—*Pārijāta-haraṇa, am,* n. 'carrying off of the Pārijāta tree,' N. of sections of the Hari-vaṇśa and Vishṇu-Purāṇa (describing the taking of the Pārijāta tree by Kṛishṇa from Indra); N. of a comedy by Gopāla-dāsa.

Pārijātaka, as, m. the coral tree, Erythrina Indica; one of the five trees of paradise; N. of a sage.

पारिण *pāriṇa, as,* m., N. of a man.

पारिणाय्य *pāriṇāyya, as, ā, am* (fr. *pari-ṇāya=pari-ṇaya*), relating to marriage, obtained on the occasion of marriage; (*am*), n. property or paraphernalia received by a woman at the time of marriage; marriage settlement.

पारिणाह्य *pāriṇāhya, am,* n. (fr. *pari-ṇāha*), household furniture and utensils.

पारितथ्या *pāritathyā,* f. (fr. *pari+tathya?*), a string of pearls for binding the hair, a trinket worn on the forehead where the hair is parted.

पारितवत् *pārita-vat, ān, atī, at,* containing the word *pārita* or other forms of the Caus. of rt. 1. *pṛi*.

पारितोषिक *pāritoshika, as, ī, am* (fr. *pari-tosha*), gratifying, delighting, pleasing, making happy, satisfactory, consolatory; (*am*), n. a reward, gratuity (given as a token of satisfaction).

पारिध्वजिक *pāridhvajika, as,* m. (fr. *pari+dhvaja*), a standard-bearer.

पारिन्द्र *pārindra, as,* m. a lion (=*pārīndra*).

पारिपन्थिक *pāripanthika, as,* m. (fr. *pari-pantham*), a highwayman, robber, thief.

पारिपाट्य *pāripāṭya, am,* n. (fr. *pari-pāṭī*), regularity, methodicalness, successiveness.

पारिपात्र *pāripātra, as,* m. (fr. *pari+pātra?*), N. of one of the seven principal mountain ranges of India (the central or western portion of the Vindhya chain which skirts the province of Malwa); N. of a son of Ahīna-gu; (also read *pāriyātra*.)

Pāripātraka or *pāriyātraka, as,* m., N. of a mountain range, the central or western portion of the Vindhya chain.

Pāripātrika or *pāriyātrika, as,* m. an inhabitant of the Pāripātra or Pāriyātra mountain range.

पारिपान्थिक *pāripānthika, as,* m. probably only a wrong reading for *pāripanthika,* q. v.

पारिपार्श्व *pāripārśva, am,* n. (fr. *pari-pārśva*), retinue, attendants, followers.

Pāripārśvaka, as, ikā, am, standing at the side, attending on; (*as*), m. an attendant; an assistant of the manager of a play; an actor who serves in place of a chorus in the drama and is one of the interlocutors in the prologue; (*ikā*), f. a female attendant, a chamber-maid.

Pāripārśvika, as, ī, am, standing at the side, belonging to a retinue; attending on; (*as*), m. an attendant; an assistant of the manager of a play.

पारिपेल *pāripela, am,* n.=*paripelava,* q.v.

पारिप्लव *pāriplava, as, ā, am* (fr. *pari-plava*), swimming; moving to and fro, shaking, unsteady, tremulous, trembling; perturbed, troubled in mind; 'moving in a circle,' epithet of a particular legend recited at the Aśva-medha and repeated at certain intervals throughout the year (Ved.); (*as*), m. a boat; N. of a sage (?) in the fifth Manv-antara; (*am*), n., N. of a Tīrtha.—*Pāriplava-gata, as, ā, am,* being in a boat.—*Pāriplava-netra, as, ā, am,* having tremulous or swimming eyes.

Pāriplavīya, am, n., Ved. an oblation accompanying the recitation of the Pāriplava legend.

Pāriplāvya, as, m. a goose; (*am*), n. perplexity, agitation; tremulousness.

पारिबर्ह *pāribarha* and *pārivarha, as,* m. =*pari-barha* or *pari-varha,* q. v.; a wedding present; N. of one of the sons of Garuḍa.

पारिभद्र *pāribhadra, as,* m. (fr. *pari+bhadra*), the coral tree, Erythrina Indica; the Nimb tree, Azadirachta Indica: a species of pine, Pinus Devadāru; the Saral, Pinus Longifolia; N. of a son of Yajña-bāhu; (*am*), n., N. of a Varsha in Śālmala-dvīpa named after Pāribhadra.

Pāribhadraka, as, m. the tree Erythrina Fulgens; the Nimb tree, Azadirachta Indica; (*am*), n. Costus Speciosus or Arabicus.

पारिभाव्य *pāribhāvya, am,* n. (fr. *pari-bhū*), surety, security, bail (=*prātibhāvya*); a drug, a species of Costus, Costus Speciosus or Arabicus.

पारिभाषिक *pāribhāshika, as, ī, am* (fr. *pari-bhāshā*), universally received, generally current, usual, common; technical (as a term).

पारिमाण्डल्य *pārimāṇḍalya, as, ī, am* (fr. *pari-maṇḍala*), having the measure or being of the size of an atom; (*am*), n. an atom (as a measure of space), a mote in a sun-beam.

पारिमाण्य *pārimāṇya, am,* n. (fr. *pari-māṇa*), circumference, compass.

पारिमित्य *pārimitya, am,* n. (fr. *pari-mita*), the being confined or limited, limitation.

पारिमुखिक *pārimukhika, as, ī, am* (fr. *pari-mukham*), being before or round the face, being near or present.

Pārimukhya, as, ā, am, being before or round the face, being near or present; (*am*), n. the being before the face, presence.

पारियात्र *pāriyātra, as,* m., N. of a mountain; of a country; [cf. *pāripātra*.]

Pāriyātraka, N. of a place mentioned in the Romaka-Siddhānta.

पारियानिक *pāriyānika, as,* m. (fr. *pari+yāna*), a travelling carriage.

पारिरक्षिक *pārirakshika, as,* m. (fr. *pari-rakshā*), a Brāhman in the fourth period of life, an ascetic or religious mendicant.

पारिवत्स *pārivatsa, as,* m. (fr. *pari+vatsa*), a calf belonging (to the cows mentioned in Hari-vaṇśa 11877).

पारिवित्त्य *pārivittya, am,* n. (fr. *pari-vitta*), the being unmarried while a younger brother is married, the condition of an elder brother who is unmarried while the younger is married.

Pārivettrya, am, n. (fr. *pari-vettṛi*), the marrying of a younger brother before the elder; the being unmarried while a younger brother is married.

पारिव्राजक *pārivrājaka, as, ī, am* (fr. *pari-vrājaka*), intended for a religious mendicant; (*am*), n. the wandering life of a religious mendicant.

Pārivrājya, am, n. (fr. *pari-vraj*), the wandering life of a religious mendicant; (also incorrectly written *pārivrajya*.)

पारिश *pāriśa, as,* m. a species of tree (=*phalīśa,* commonly called *palāśa-pipula* and *gaja-haṇḍa*).

पारिशील *pāriśīla, as,* m. a cake (=*apūpa*).

पारिशेष्य *pāriśeshya, am,* n. (fr. *pari-śesha*), that which is left over, a remainder; (*āt*), ind. this alone remaining, there being no alternative.

पारिषद् *pārishad, t, t, t* (fr. *pari-shad*), one who is present at an assembly (?).

Pārishatka, as, ā, am, one who studies or knows what has been settled in an assembly (?).

Pārishada, as, ī, am, belonging to an assembly or council, one who belongs to an assembly or council; (*as*), m. a person present at an assembly or congregation, a spectator; an assessor at a council; a king's companion; (*ās*), m. pl. the retinue or attendants of a god; (*am*), n. taking part in an assembly; (*as, am*), m. or n. (?), N. of a village in the North.

Pārishadaka, as, ī, am, done by an assembly.

Pārishadya, as, ā, am,=*parishadaṃ samavaiti,*=*parishadi sādhuḥ,* one who is present at an assembly, a spectator.

पारिसारक *pārisāraka, as, ī, am,* containing the word *pari-sāraka*.

पारिहारिक *pārihārika, as, ī, am* (fr. *pari-hāra*), taking away, seizing; surrounding; (*as*), m. a maker of garlands; (*ī*), f. a kind of riddle.

Pārihārya, as, m. a bracelet; (*am*), n. taking, seizure.

पारिहास्य *pārihāsya, am,* n. (fr. *pari-hāsa*), jest, joke, fun; (*ena*), ind. in fun.

पारी *pārī,* f. (fr. rt. *pṛī*), a cup, drinking-vessel, &c. See *pāra,* p. 566, col. 2.

पारीक्षित् *pārīkshit, t,* m.=*pārīkshita,* a patronymic of Janam-ejaya.

Pārīkshita, as, ī, am, relating to or treating of Parī-kshit, derived from Parī-kshit; (*as*), m. a patronymic of Janam-ejaya; N. of a sovereign to whom the Bhāgavata-Purāṇa or life of Kṛishṇa is supposed to have been addressed; N. of the successor of the preceding.

पारीण *pārīṇa.* See p. 566, col. 3.

पारीणह्य *pārīṇahya, am,* n. (fr. *parī-ṇah*), household furniture or utensils; [cf. *pāriṇāhya*.]

पारीन्द्र *pārīndra, as,* m. a lion (=*pārindra*); a large snake, boa.

पारीय *pārīya.* See p. 566, col. 3.

पारीरण *pārīraṇa, as,* m.=*parīraṇa,* q. v.

पारु *pāru, us,* m. (said to be fr. rt. 3. *pā*), the sun; fire (=*peru*).

पारुच्छेप *pāruććhepa, as, ī, am,* derived from Paruććhepa; *Bhāradvājam Pāruććhepam,* N. of a Sāman.

Pāruććhepi, is, m. a patronymic from Paruććhepa.

पारूषक *pārushaka, as* or *am,* m. or n. (?), a species of flower; [cf. *parūshaka*.]

पारुषेय *pārusheya, as, ī, am* (fr. *parusha*), Ved. spotted, freckled.

Pārushya, am, n. roughness [cf. *tvak-p°*], harshness; harshness of language, abuse, reproach, contumelious or scurrilous language, opprobrious or unfriendly speech, insult; violence (in word or deed, cf. *daṇḍa-p°*, *vāk-p°*); squalor; the forest or grove of Indra; aloe wood or Agallochum; (*as*), m. a N. of Bṛihas-pati, the planet Jupiter.

पारुष्ण *pārushṇa, as*, m., Ved. a kind of bird.

पारेगङ्गम् *pāre-gangam, pāre-viśoka, pāre-sindhu.* See under *pāra*.

पारेरक *pāreraka, as*, m., a sword, scimitar (?).

पारोक्ष *pāroksha, as, ī, am* (fr. *paroksha*), undiscernible, unintelligible, obscure, mysterious.

Pārokshya, as, ā, am, undiscernible, invisible, hidden; (*am*), n. mysteriousness, mystery.

पारोवर्य *pārovarya, am*, n. (fr. *paro-'varam*), tradition.

पार्घट *pārghaṭa, am*, n. ashes, = *arghaṭa;* [cf. *pārpara*.]

पार्जन्य *pārjanya, as, ā, am* (fr. *parjanya*), belonging to Parjanya.

पार्ण *pārṇa, as, ī, am* (fr. *parṇa*), made or consisting of leaves, leafy; raised from leaves (as a tax); made of the wood of the Butea Frondosa; (*as*), m. a patronymic.

Pārṇavalki, is, m. (fr. *parṇa-valka*), a patronymic of Ni-gada.

पार्थ 1. *pārtha, as, ī, am* (fr. *pṛithi*), Ved. an epithet of twelve sacred texts, ascribed to Pṛithi Vainya, repeated during the ceremony of unction in the Rāja-sūya sacrifice; (*as*), m. a patronymic of Tānva; (*am*), n., N. of several Sāmans.

Pārthya, as, m., Ved. a patronymic from Pṛithi.

पार्थ 2. *pārtha, as*, m. (fr. rt. *prith* for *prath* and connected with *pṛithu*, wide), a prince, king (= *pārthiva*); (fr. *pṛithā*), a metronymic of Yudhi-shṭhira, Bhīma-sena, and Arjuna, especially of the last; N. of a son of Paṇḍu and king of Kaśmīra; N. of a man; the plant Terminalia Arjuna; (*ās*), m. pl. an epithet of the five sons of Pāṇḍu. — *Pārtha-ja, as*, m. the son of Pārtha. — *Pārtha-pura, am*, n., N. of a city near the confluence of the Go-dāvarī and Vi-darbhā. — *Pārtha-maya, as, ī, am*, consisting of sons of Pṛithā. — *Pārtha-sārathi, is*, m., N. of the author of the Tantra-ratna. — *Pārthasārathi-miśra, as*, m., N. of a commentator on Jaimini's Nyāya-sūtras. — *Pārthānuga* (*°tha-an°*), *as, ā, am*, followed by (Pārtha, i. e.) Arjuna.

Pārthava, as, ī, am, belonging or peculiar to Pṛithu; (*am*), n. width, greatness, immensity.

Pārthavi, an earthy substance, rotten wood; (probably a wrong reading for *pārthiva*.)

Pārthiva, as, ī, am (fr. *pṛithivī* for *pṛithvī*, f. of *pṛithu*), earthen, earthly, terrestrial, relating to the earth, springing or derived from the earth, made of earth, earthy; ruling or possessing the earth; fit for kings or princes, royal, princely; *a-pārthiva*, unearthly, i. e. heavenly, celestial; (*as*), m. a dweller on the earth, inhabitant of the earth; a lord of the earth, king, prince, sovereign, warrior; an earthen vessel; the 19th (or 53rd) year in Jupiter's cycle of 60 years; (*ās*), m. pl. a patronymic; (*ī*), f. 'earth-born,' an epithet of Sītā; of Lakshmī; (*am*), n. an earthy substance; (*āni*), n. pl., Ved. the regions of the earth (Sāy. = *pṛithivyām bhavāni sthānāni*). — *Pārthiva-tā*, f. or *pārthiva-tva, am*, n. the dignity or rank of king, royalty. — *Pārthiva-nandinī*, f. the daughter of a king. — *Pārthivarshabha* (*°va-ṛi°*), *as*, m. 'king-bull,' an excellent king. — *Pārthiva-śreshṭha, as*, m. best of kings, an excellent sovereign. — *Pārthiva-sutā* or *pārthivātmajā* (*°va-āt°*), f. the daughter of a king. — *Pārthivādhama* (*°va-adh°*), *as*, m. the lowest or meanest of kings. — *Pārthivendra* (*°va-in°*), *as*, m. the chief or greatest of princes.

पार्थक्य *pārthakya, am*, n. (fr. *pṛithak*), severalty, individuality, separation, separateness, singleness, difference, variety.

पार्थुरश्म *pārthuraśma, am*, n. (fr. *pṛithu-raśmi*), Ved. epithet of various Sāmans.

पार्पर *pārpara, as*, m. a handful of rice; consumption (= *kshaya-roga*); a filament of the Nauclea Cadamba; ashes; = *kīnāśa;* = *gadāntara* (a kind of disease?); a N. of Yama.

पार्य *pārya.* See p. 566, col. 3.

पार्यन्तिक *pāryantika, as, ī, am* (fr. *paryanta*), final, concluding, last.

पार्व *pārva, as, ī, am* (fr. *parvan*), = *pārvaṇa;* (probably an incorrect form.)

Pārvaṇa, as, ī, am, belonging or relating to a division of time or of the month; increasing, waxing full (as the moon); (*as*), m. a kind of deer; the general funeral ceremony to be offered to all the Manes at the Parvan (or conjunction of the sun and moon, at which double oblations are offered, three cakes to the father, paternal grandfather and great-grandfather, and three to the maternal grandfather, his father and grandfather; and the crumbs of each set to the remoter ancestors in each line).

Pārvāyanāntīya, as, ā, am (fr. *parvan* + *ayanānta*), occurring at the end of a Parvan or solstice (as a sacrifice &c.).

पार्वत *pārvata, as, ī, am* (fr. *parvata*), being or living in the mountains, growing on or coming from the mountains, consisting of mountains, mountainous; (*as*), m. the tree Melia Sempervirens (= *mahā-nimba*); (*ī*), f. a mountain stream; a female cowherd or Gopī; a N. of Durgā (as being the daughter of Hima-vat the king of the snowy mountains); N. of a cave in mount Meru; of various women (named after the goddess); an epithet of Draupadī (incorrectly for *pārshatī*); a kind of fragrant earth; a red clay commonly called Saurāshṭrī or Surat earth; N. of various plants; the olibanum tree, Boswellia Thurifera; Grislea Tomentosa; = Celtis Orientalis; = *kshudra-pāshāṇa-bhedā;* = *jīvanī*. — *Pārvatī-kshetra, am*, n. 'district of Pārvatī (Durgā),' N. of one of the four especially sacred districts of Orissa. — *Pārvatī-nandana, as*, m. 'son of Pārvatī,' an epithet of Kārttikeya. — *Pārvatī-paśćāttāpa-varṇana, am*, n., N. of the sixth chapter of the Gīta-gaṅgādhara, a poem by Kalyāṇa. — *Pārvatī-pravartana, am*, n., N. of the ninth chapter of the Gīta-giriśa, a poem by Rāma. — *Pārvatī-prasūdana, am*, n., N. of the fifth chapter of the Gīta-gaṅgādhara. — *Pārvatī-mokshaṇa, am*, n., N. of a chapter of the Gaṇeśa-Purāṇa. — *Pārvatīśvara-linga* (*°tī-īś°*), *am*, n., N. of a Linga. — *Pārvatī-sampradāna, am*, n., N. of a chapter of the Brahma-vaivarta-Purāṇa.

Pārvatāyana, as, m. a patronymic; N. of a chamberlain.

Pārvati, is, m. a patronymic of Daksha.

Pārvatika, am, n. a multitude of mountains, mountain-range.

Pārvatīya, as, ī, am, living or dwelling in the mountains, mountainous; (*as*), m. a mountaineer; epithet of a particular sovereign ruling in the mountains; (*ās*), m. pl., N. of a mountain tribe.

Pārvateya, as, ī, am, belonging or relating to the mountains, mountain-born; (*as*), m., N. of a prince of mountaineers; a species of culinary plant bearing a pungent fruit; (*ī*), f. the smaller or upper mill-stone; (*am*), n. antimony (= *sauvīrāñjana*).

पार्शव 1. *pārśava, as*, m. (fr. 1. *parśu*), a prince of the Parśus.

Pārśukā, f. = *parśukā*, a rib.

Pārśva, as, am, m. n. the region of the ribs or the part of the body below the armpit; the side, flank (either of animate or inanimate objects); a side of any square figure; a curved knife (Ved.); (*as*), m., N. of an ancient Buddhist teacher; (with Jainas) N. of the twenty-third Arhat of the present Ava-sarpiṇī; (*au*), m. du. heaven and earth; (*am*), n. a multitude of ribs, the thorax; the extremity of the fore-axle nearest the wheel to which the outside horses of a four-horse chariot are attached; a fraudulent or crooked expedient, dishonourable means; (*āni*), n. pl. the ribs (Ved.); (*e*), ind. at the side, near, on, upon, (opposed to *dūra-tas, dūre*); aside; (*ayos*), ind. on both sides; (*āt*), ind. away from; (*am*), ind. near to, to, towards; (*as, ā, am*), near, proximate, by the side of. — *Pārśva-ga, as, ā, am*, going at the side (of any one), accompanying, being in close proximity to, an attendant; (*ās*), m. pl. attendants, retinue. — *Pārśva-gata, as, ā, am*, being at the side, attending, accompanying, being close to or beside; sheltered, screening. — *Pārśva-gamana, am*, n. the act of going by the side, accompanying. — *Pārśva-ćara, as*, m. an attendant; (*ās*), m. pl. attendants, retinue. — *Pārśva-tas*, ind. by or from the side, at the side, near, sideways, aside. — *Pārśva-da, as*, m. 'turning the side towards another,' an attendant; (*ās*), m. pl. attendants, retinue. — *Pārśva-dāha, as*, m. a burning pain in the side. — *Pārśva-deśa, as*, m. the region of the ribs, the side. — *Pārśva-druma, ās*, m. pl. the trees at the side, the trees on every side. — *Pārśvanātha, as*, m. (with Jainas) N. of an Arhat; the Jaina pontiff. — *Pārśvanātha-kāvya, am*, n., N. of a poem by Padma-sundara celebrating the preceding Arhat. — *Pārśva-parivartana, am*, n. 'the turning round on the other side or from one side to the other,' epithet of a festival on the eleventh day of the light half of the month Bhādra (Vishṇu being supposed to turn upon the other side in his sleep on this day). — *Pārśva-parivartin, ī, inī, i*, being or going by the side (of any one). — *Pārśva-pippala, am*, n. a species of Harītakī (= Hindī *gajahaḍ*). — *Pārśva-bhāga, as*, m. 'side-portion,' the side, flank (of an elephant). — *Pārśva-ruj, k*, f. pain in the side. — *Pārśva-vaktra, as*, m. whose face is in his side,' N. of a being attendant upon Śiva (Hari-vaṇśa 14851). — *Pārśva-vartin, ī, inī, i*, standing by the side, an attendant; situated at the side, adjacent; (*inas*), m. pl. attendants, retinue. — *Pārśva-vivartin, ī, inī, i*, being by the side of, living with. — *Pārśva-śaya, as, ā, am*, lying or sleeping on the side; sleeping at the side. — *Pārśva-śāyin, ī, inī, i*, 'lying on the side,' epithet of a particular position of the moon. — *Pārśva-śūla, as*, m. a shooting pain in the side, spasm of the chest, stitch; pleurisy. — *Pārśva-saṃstha, as, ā, am*, lying on the side. — *Pārśva-sūtraka, as* or *am*, m. or n. (?), a kind of ornament. — *Pārśva-stha, as, ā, am*, standing at the side or next to, being near or close to, adjacent, proximate; (*as*), m. an associate, companion; a stage manager's assistant (said to serve as a sort of chorus to the Indian drama, being sometimes an actor in the prelude and interpreter of the plot). — *Pārśva-sthita, as, ā, am*, standing at the side, being near or close to. — *Pārśvānućara* (*°va-an°*), *as*, m. 'attending at the side,' an attendant, body-servant, lackey. — *Pārśvāyāta* (*°va-āy°*), *as, ā, am*, one who has approached close to. — *Pārśvāsanna* (*°va-ās°*), *as, ā, am*, standing by the side, standing next, present. — *Pārśvāsīna* (*°va-ās°*), *as, ā, am*, sitting by the side. — *Pārśvāsthi* (*°va-as°*), *i*, n. 'side-bone,' a rib. — *Pārśvaikādaśī* (*°va-ek°*), f., N. of a particular festival (= *pārśva-parivartana*). — *Pārśvodara-priya* (*°va-ud°*), *as*, m. 'fond of (moving) sideways on the belly,' a crab.

Pārśvaka, as, m. a rib; (*as, ā, am*), one who seeks wealth or other objects by dishonest or indirect or side means; a pilferer, swindler.

Pārśvatīya, as, ā, am (fr. *pārśva-tas*), being on or belonging to the side, situated at the side.

Pārśvika, as, ī, am, lateral, belonging to the

side; (*as*), m. a sidesman, partisan; an associate, companion; a juggler; one who seeks money by dishonest means; N. of an ancient Buddhist teacher.

Pārśvya, au, m. du. heaven and earth (a various reading for *pārśvau*).

पार्शव 2. *pārśava, as*, m. a warrior armed with an axe.

पार्श्व *pārśva*. See p. 569, col. 3.

पार्षकि *pārshaki, is*, m. a patronymic.

पार्षत *pārshata, as, ī, am* (fr. *prishata*), belonging to the spotted antelope, made of the skin of the spotted antelope; (*as*), m. a patronymic of Dru-pada and his son Dhrishṭa-dyumna; (*ī*), f. a patronymic of Draupadī; an epithet of Durgā (in this sense a wrong reading for *pārvatī*); N. of two plants, Boswellia Thurifera; = *jīvanī*.

पार्षद् *pārshad, t*, f. (for *pari-shada?*), an assembly; (*das*), m. pl. the attendants or retinue of a god.

Pārshada, as, m. (fr. *parshad*), an associate, companion, attendant; a train, retinue (especially of a god); a person present in a congregation or assembly, a spectator; (perhaps) a councillor, distinguished personage; (*am*), n. a text-book received by any particular grammatical school, a N. given to the Prātiśākhyas; N. of a work on ceremonies. —*Pārshada-tā*, f. the office of an attendant (especially of the attendant of a deity).

Pārshadīya, as, ā, am, conformable to the received text-book of any particular grammatical school.

Pārshadya, as, m. = *pārishadya*, a member of an assembly or council, assessor; (*ās*), m. pl. the attendants or retinue of a god (especially of Śiva).

पार्षद्वाण *pārshadvāṇa, as*, m. (fr. *prishad-vāṇa*), N. of a man.

पार्षिका *pārshikā*, f., N. of a woman.

पार्षी *pārshī* (?), f. dung.

पार्ष्टेय *pārshṭeya, as, ī, am* (fr. *prishṭi*), being within the ribs.

पार्ष्ठिक *pārshṭhika, as, ī, am*, Ved. being after the manner of the Prishṭhya (Shaḍ-aha).

पार्ष्णि *pārshṇi, is*, m. f., rarely *pārshṇī*, f. (said to be fr. rt. *prish*), the heel; the extremity of the fore-axle to which the outside horses of a four-horse chariot are attached (the two inner horses being harnessed to the *dhur* or chariot-pole); the rear of an army; the back; a kick; enquiry, asking (?); (*is*), f. a foolish or licentious woman; a N. of Kuntī the wife of Pāṇḍu. —*Pārshṇi-kshema, as*, m., N. of a divinity. —*Pārshṇi-graha, as, ā, am*, seizing from behind, threatening from behind; (*as*), m. a follower. —*Pārshṇi-grahaṇa, am*, n. attacking or threatening (an enemy) in the rear. —*Pārshṇi-grāha, as, ā, am*, attacking or menacing (an enemy) in the rear; (*as*), m. an enemy in the rear; a commander in the rear of an army; an ally who supports a prince (Manu VII. 207). —*Pārshṇi-tra, am*, n. 'rear-protecting,' a rear-guard, reserve, a body of forces in the rear. —*Pārshṇi-vāh, ṭ, ūhī, ṭ*, or *pārshṇi-vāha, as, ā, am*, drawing (i. e. harnessed to) the extremities of the axle-tree; (*as*), m. an outside horse. —*Pārshṇi-sārathi, is*, m. a charioteer who drives one of the outside horses; (*ī*), m. du. the two charioteers who drive the outer horses attached to the extremities of the axle-tree.

पाल् *pāl*. See Caus. of rt. 3. *pā*.

Pāla, as, m. a guard, guardian, protector, nourisher, keeper; a herdsman; a protector of the earth, a prince; a spitting-pot, spittoon; N. of a Nāga of the race of Vāsuki; of a prince; (*ī*), f. a herdsman's wife; [cf. *pāli*.] —*Pāla-kavi-rāja, as*, m., N. of a poet (also called Śrī-pāla-kavi-rāja). —*Pāla-kārya, am*, n. 'the poem of Pāla,' N. of a work. —*Pāla-ghna, as*, m. a mushroom. —*Pāla-baṇij, k*, m. = *kanyā-pāla*; (a wrong form for *pāna-baṇij*.) —*Pāli-vrata, am*, n., N. of a particular religious observance.

Pālaka, as, ikā, am, guarding, protecting, nourishing; (*as*), m. a guardian, protector, cherisher, nourisher; a foster-father; a prince, ruler, sovereign; a horse-keeper, a groom; one who maintains or observes; N. of several princes; a species of plant with a poisonous bulb, Plumbago Zeylanica; a horse. —*Pālaka-gotra, am*, n. the family or tribe of one's adoptive parents. —*Pālakākhyā* (°*ka-ākh*°), f., N. of the mother of Dhanvantari.

Pālana, as, ī, am, the act of protecting, guarding, fostering, nourishing, cherishing; (*am*), n. guarding, providing with a guardian, protecting, protection, preserving, cherishing, fostering, nourishing; maintaining, keeping, observing; the milk of a cow that has recently calved.

Pālanīya, as, ā, am, to be guarded or protected, to be cherished or nourished; fit to be preserved or maintained; to be observed or respected.

Pālayat, an, antī, at, guarding, protecting, cherishing.

Pālayitṛi, tā, trī, tṛi, protecting, cherishing; a protector, guardian.

Pālita, as, ā, am, guarded, protected, cherished, nourished; (*as*), m. a species of tree (= *śākhoṭa*); N. of a son of Parā-jit (or Parā-vṛit); (*ā*), f., N. of one of the Mātṛis attending on Skanda.

Pālin, ī, inī, i, protecting, guarding, cherishing, nourishing; (*ī*), m., N. of a son of Pṛithu.

Pālya, as, ā, am, to be protected or guarded, to be cherished; being under (any one's) protection or guardianship; to be observed or kept, to be maintained.

पालकाप्य *pālakāpya, as*, m., N. of an ancient sage or Muni; a form of the divine physician Dhanvantari.

पालक्क *pālakka, as* or *am*, m. or n. (?), N. of a country.

पालक्या *pālakyā*, f. the plant Beta Bengalensis.

पालङ्क *pālanka, as*, m. the olibanum tree, Boswellia Thurifera; a species of beet-root, Beta Bengalensis; a hawk; (*ī*), f. the resin of the olibanum tree, incense.

Pālankya, as, ā, m. f. gum olibanum, incense; (*am, ā*), n. f. the plant Beta Bengalensis.

पालङ्गिन् *pālangin, inas*, m. pl., N. of a school called after a disciple of Vaiśampāyana.

पालल *pālala, as, ī, am* (fr. *palala*), made of powdered sesamum seed.

पालवी *pālavī*, f. a kind of vessel.

पालहरि *pālahari, is*, m. (probably a patronymic fr. *palahara*), N. of a man.

पालागल *pālāgala, as*, m., Ved. a runner, messenger; (according to others) a bearer of false tidings; (*ī*), f. the fourth and least respected wife of a prince.

पालाल *pālāla, as, ī, am* (probably incorrectly for *pālvala*), living in a marsh.

पालाश *pālāśa, as, ī, am* (fr. *palāśa*), coming from or belonging to the tree Butea Frondosa, made of the wood of the Butea Frondosa; green; (*as*), m. green (the colour). —*Pālāśa-khaṇḍa* and *pālāśa-shaṇḍa, as*, m. an epithet of Magadha (a country in India, the western part of Behar).

पालि *pāli, is*, f. (fr. Caus. of rt. 3. *pā?*; said to be fr. rt. *pal*), the tip of the ear; an edge, margin; a boundary, limit; the sharp side of anything, the sharp edge or point of a sword or any cutting instrument; a line, row, range; a raised bank, dike, causeway, bridge; the lap, bosom; the hip, haunch; a mark, spot, stain; a particular measure of capacity (= *prastha*); a louse; a woman with a beard; prescribed food, maintenance of a scholar during the period of his studies by his teacher; praise, eulogium; a circumference; (*ī*), f. an edge, margin; the sharp edge of a sword; a line, row, range; a woman with a beard; a louse; a pot, boiler; an oblong pond; a causeway, bridge. —*Pāliṃ-hira, as*, m. a kind of snake, (perhaps a wrong reading for *pāliṃ-hara*, seizing by the tip of the ear.)

Pālikā, f. the tip of the ear; the sharp edge of a cutting instrument; a sort of ladle or knife for skimming milk, curds, &c.; a cheese or butter knife.

पालित्य *pālitya, am*, n. (fr. *palita*), greyness (of age), hoariness.

पालिन्द *pālinda, as*, m. incense; a species of jasmine, Jasminum Pubescens; (*ī*), f. a species of creeper, Ichnocarpus Frutescens; = *pālindhī*.

पालिन्धी *pālindhī*, f. a species of Ipomœa with dark blossoms.

पालीवत *pālīvata, as*, m. a species of tree.

पाल्लवा *pāllavā*, f. (fr. *pallava*), scil. *krīḍā*, a game played with twigs.

पाल्वल *pālvala, as, ī, am* (fr. *palvala*), coming from a tank or pool.

पावक *pāvaka, as, ā, am* (fr. rt. 1. *pū*), (Ved.) pure, clear, bright, shining; (Sāy.) = *śodhaka*, cleansing, purifying (said of Agni, Āditya, Sūrya, and the Maruts; of water, of the dawn, of day and night, &c.); (*as*), m. epithet of a particular Agni (in the Purāṇas said to be a son of Agni Abhi-mānin and Svāhā or of Antar-dhāna and Śikhaṇḍinī; cf. *pava-māna, śući*); fire in general; Agni or the god of fire; social fire, a fire lighted in common; a fire lighted on taking possession of a house; a species of tree, Premna Integrifolia or Spinosa (see *araṇi*); a species of plant, Plumbago Zeylanica (= *ćitraka*); Semecarpus Anacardium; a plant used as a vermifuge, Carthamus Tinctorius (= *viḍanga*); a symbolical expression for the number three (like all other words for 'fire'); epithet of a kind of Ṛishi, a saint, a person purified by religious abstraction, one who purifies from sin; (*ī*), f. the wife of Agni. —*Pāvaka-vat, ān, atī, at*, Ved. 'having the name Pāvaka,' an epithet of Agni; containing the word *pāvaka*. —*Pāvaka-varćas, ās, ās, as*, Ved. brightly resplendent (as Agni). —*Pāvaka-varṇa, as, ā, am*, Ved. being of pure or brilliant aspect; (Sāy.) = *agni-samāna-tejaska*, resembling the brilliance of fire. —*Pāvaka-śoćis, is, is, is*, (voc. anomalously -*će*), Ved. shining brightly. —*Pāvakāraṇi* (°*ka-ar*°), *is*, m. the tree Premna Integrifolia or Spinosa (see *araṇi*). —*Pāvakeśvara* (°*ka-īś*°), *am*, n., N. of a Tīrtha.

Pāvaki, is, m. 'son of Fire,' an epithet of Skanda or Kārttikeya; of Su-darśana; of Hari (?).

Pāvana, as, ī, am, purifying, purificatory, expurgatory, freeing from sin, sanctifying; purified, pure, holy; (*as*), m. fire (generally or for various ceremonial purposes); incense; a species of Verbesina with yellow flowers; a kind of demigod otherwise called a Siddha; N. of one of the Viśve Devāḥ; an epithet of the inspired poet Vyāsa; (*ī*), f. the plant Terminalia Chebula; holy basil; a cow; N. of a river; the Ganges or the goddess Gangā; (*am*), n. the act of cleansing, purifying, sanctifying, expiation, purification (by acts of austerity and devotion); a means of purification; penance; water; cow-dung; the seed of the plant Elæocarpus Ganitrus (of which rosaries are made); a species of grass, Costus Speciosus; a sectarial mark (=*ćitraka*). — *Pāvana-tva, am,* n. the property of cleansing or purifying. — *Pāvana-dhvani, is,* m. a conch-shell.

Pāvamāna, as, ī, am (fr. *pavamāna*), relating to Soma juice while being purified or while passing through the strainer (Ved.); (*ī*), f., scil. *ṛić*, an epithet of particular Vedic hymns (especially of Ṛig-veda IX, Atharva-veda XIX. 71, 1); purificatory water (?).

Pāvita, as, ā, am, cleansed, purified.

Pāvitra, as or *am,* m. or n.? (fr. *pavitra*), N. of a metre, four times – – – – ⏑ ⏑ ⏑ ⏑ –; (perhaps incorrectly for *pavitra*.)

Pāvin, ī, inī, i, cleansing, purifying (Mahā-bh. Vana-p. 10543; perhaps only a wrong reading for *pāranī*).

Pāvya, as, ā, am, to be cleansed or purified.

पावन् 1. *pāvan, ā, arī, a* (fr. rt. 1. *pā*), Ved. (at the end of a comp.) drinking; [cf. *asṛik-p°, gharma-p°, ghṛita-p°*.]

पावन् 2. *pāvan, ā, arī, a* (fr. rt. 3. *pā*), Ved. (at the end of a comp.) protecting; [cf. *tanū-p°*.]

पावर *pāvara, as* or *am,* m. or n. (?), the die or side of a die which is marked with two points (=*dvā-para*, of which it is a corruption).

पावा *pāvā* or *pāvā-purī* (also *pāpā-purī*), f., N. of a city near Rāja-gṛiha.

पावीरव *pāvīrava, as, ī, am* (fr. *pavīru*), Ved. proceeding from or belonging to the thunderbolt; (Sāy.) = *pāvayitrī, śodhayitrī*, purifying; (*ī*), f. 'daughter of lightning,' the noise of thunder.

पाश *pāśa, as,* m. (fr. rt. 3. *paś*), a snare, trap, noose, tie, fastening, cord, chain, fetter (*karaća-p°, jyā-p°*); a net or snare for catching birds and beasts; a string or cord for fastening tame animals [cf. *paśū-p°*]; a noose or lasso employed as a weapon [cf. *dharma-p°*]; a die, dice (=*pāśaka*, Raghu-v. VI. 18); selvage, edge, border (of anything woven); (in astrology) epithet of a particular constellation; (at the end of a comp.) expressive of contempt or depreciation (e. g. *ćhattra-pāśa, as,* m. a bad or shabby umbrella; cf. *bhishak-p°, rakshas-p°, vaiyākaraṇa-p°*); abundance, quantity (after a word signifying 'hair;' cf. *keśa-p°*); expressive of admiration [cf. *karṇa-p°*]. — *Pāśa-krīḍā,* f. play with dice, gambling. — *Pāśa-dyumna, as,* m., Ved., N. of a man. — *Pāśa-dhara, as,* m. 'holding a noose,' an epithet of Varuṇa. — *Pāśa-pāṇi, is, is, i,* noose in hand; (*is*), m. an epithet of Varuṇa (regent of the waters represented as holding in one hand a cord shaped like a sling or noose). — *Pāśa-baddha, as, ā, am,* noosed, snared, entrapped, caught in a net, bound. — *Pāśa-bandha, as,* m. a noose, snare, halter, net. — *Pāśa-bandhaka, as,* m. one who snares birds, a bird-catcher. — *Pāśa-bandhana, am,* n. a snare, fetter; (*as, ā, am*), hanging in a snare. — *Pāśa-bhṛit, t, t, t,* noose-bearing, bearing a noose; (*t*), m. any one armed with a noose; an epithet of Varuṇa. — *Pāśa-rajju, us,* f. a fetter, rope. — *Pāśa-vat, ān, atī, at,* having or possessing a noose. — *Pāśa-hasta, as, ā, am,* 'snare in hand,' holding a snare in the hand; (*as*), m. an epithet of Yama. — *Pāśānta* (°*śa-an*°), *as,* m. the back of a garment, (opposed to *daśā*.) — *Pāśī-krita, as, ā, am,* tied, fettered; snared.

Pāśaka, as, m. (at the end of a comp.) = *pāśa*, a snare, trap, &c. [cf. *kaṇṭha-p°, daṇḍa-p°*]; a die (particularly the long sort used in playing Chaupai). — *Pāśaka-kevalī,* f., N. of a work. — *Pāśaka-pīṭha, am,* n. a gaming-table.

Pāśana, am, n. a noose, lasso, sling; a cord, lash.

Pāśaya, Nom. P. *pāśayati, -yitum,* to bind; [cf. rt. 3. *paś*, to which *pāśayati* is referred by native grammarians.]

Pāśika, as, m. one who snares animals, a bird-catcher (Ved.); N. of a man.

Pāśita, as, ā, am, tied, fettered, bound, snared.

Pāśin, ī, inī, i, having a net or noose, armed with a net or noose, laying snares; a deer-catcher, fowler, trapper; (*ī*), m. an epithet of Varuṇa; of Yama; N. of a son of Dhṛita-rāshṭra. — *Pāśi-vāṭa, ās,* m. pl., N. of a people.

Pāśyā, f. a number or multitude of nooses, a collection of ropes; a net.

पाशव *pāśava, as, ī, am* (fr. *paśu*), derived from or belonging to cattle, relating or belonging to animals (e. g. *pāśavam māṅsam*, animal food); (*am*), n. a flock, herd. — *Pāśava-pālana, am,* n. 'nourishing flocks,' pasturage or meadow grass.

Pāśuka, as, ī, am, Ved. relating or belonging to cattle, relating or belonging to the sacrificial animal.

Pāśupata, as, ī, am, coming from or belonging to Śiva Paśu-pati, relating or sacred to Śiva Paśu-pati; (*as*), m. a follower and worshipper of Śiva in one of his forms as the supreme deity of the Hindū triad; the tree Æschynomene Grandiflora; a species of plant (=*vaka*); N. of a place sacred to Śiva Paśu-pati. — *Pāśupata-yoga-prakaraṇa, am,* n., N. of the eighth chapter of the first part of the Liṅga-Purāṇa. — *Pāśupata-vrata-vivaraṇa, am,* n., N. of the eighteenth chapter of the second part of the Liṅga-Purāṇa. — *Pāśupatāstra* (°*ta-as*°), *am,* n. Śiva's trident.

Pāśupālya, am, n. (fr. *paśu-pāla*), the occupation of a grazier or keeper of cattle, the breeding and rearing of cattle.

Pāśubandhaka, as, ikā, am (fr. *paśu-bandha*), Ved. belonging to the slaughter of a sacrificial animal.

पाशी *pāśī,* f. a stone (perhaps incorrectly for *pāshī*).

पाश्चात्त्य *pāśćāttya* and *pāśćātya, as, ā, am* (fr. *paśćāt*), hinder, behind; western; subsequent; posterior, last; (*am*), n. the hinder part. — *Pāśćāttya-nirṇayāmṛita* (°*ya-am*°), *am,* n., N. of a book on ritual, mentioned in the Saṅskāra-tattva by Raghu-nandana. — *Pāśćāttyākara-sambhava* (°*ya-āk*°), *am,* n., N. of a species of salt coming from the West (=*romaka*).

पाषक *pāshaka, as,* m. an ornament for the feet.

पाषण्ड *pāshaṇḍa, as, ā, am* (sometimes incorrectly spelt *pākhaṇḍa*), heretical, impious; (*as*), m. a heretic, a hypocrite, impostor, any one who not conforming to the orthodox tenets of Hindū faith assumes the external characteristics of tribe or sect, a Jaina, Buddhist; (*as, am*), m. n. false doctrine, heresy. — *Pāshaṇḍa-tā,* f. heresy, heterodoxy, hypocrisy. — *Pāshaṇḍa-patha, as,* m. the way of heretics, false doctrine.

Pāshaṇḍaka or *pāshaṇḍika, as,* m. a heretic.

Pāshaṇḍin, ī, m. a heretic, hypocrite; (also read *pā-hāṇḍin*.)

Pāshāṇḍu, as, m., Ved. a heretic.

पाषाण *pāshāṇa, as,* m. (said to be fr. rt. *pash*), a stone; (*ī*), f. a small stone used as a weight; [cf. Gr. βάσανος; Heb. *bāshān*, 'basalt-land.'] — *Pāshāṇa-gardabha, as,* m. a hard swelling on the maxillary joint. — *Pāshāṇa-ćaturdaśī,* f. the fourteenth day in the light half of the month Mārgaśīrsha (on which a festival of Gaurī is celebrated, when cakes made of rice and shaped like large pebbles are eaten). — *Pāshāṇa-ćaya-nibaddha, as, ā, am,* surrounded with a coping of stone (as a well). — *Pāshāṇa-dāraka* or *pāshāṇa-dāraṇa, as,* m. a sort of hatchet or instrument for cutting stones, a stone-cutter's chisel. — *Pāshāṇa-bheda* or *pāshāṇa-bhedana, as,* or *pāshāṇa-bhedin, ī,* m. the plant Plectranthus Scutellarioides, used as a remedy for stone in the bladder. — *Pāshāṇa-maya, as, ī, am,* consisting of or made of stone. — *Pāshāṇa-sandhi, is,* m. a cave or chasm in a rock. — *Pāshāṇa-setu-bandha, as,* m. a barrier or dam of stone. — *Pāshāṇa-hṛidaya, as, ā, am,* stone-hearted, cruel.

Pāshī, f., Ved. (Sāy.) = *śilā*, a stone; = *śakti*, a spear; [cf. *pāśī*.]

Pāshya, āṇi, n. pl., Ved. stones, a rampart of stones; (*e*), n. du. the two stones for pressing the Soma.

पाष्ठौह *pāshṭhauha, am,* n. (fr. *pashṭha-vāh*), N. of a Sāman.

पास्त्य *pāstya, as, ā, am* (fr. *pastya*), belonging to a house and farm; (Sāy.) = *gṛihe vasat*, dwelling in the house, the master of the house.

पाहणपुर *pāhaṇa-pura,* N. of a place mentioned in the Śrīshavāyaṇa portion of the Romaka-Siddhānta.

पाहात *pāhāta, as,* m. the Indian mulberry tree, Morus Indica (=*brahma-dāru*).

पि 1. *pi,* cl. 6. P. *piyati, petum,* to go, move.

पि 2. *pi.* See under *api.*

पिंस् *pins,* cl. 1. 10. P. *pinsati, pinsitum, pinsayati, -yitum,* to speak; to shine.

पिक *pika, as, ī,* m. f. (probably for *spika*, cf. Gr. σπίζ-ω), the Indian cuckoo, Cuculus Indicus; [cf. Gr. σίττη for σπίττη or ψίττη, σίτταкος, ψίττακος, ψιττάκη, βίττακος; Lat. *pīcus, pīca*; Old Germ. *speh, speht*.] — *Pika-bandhu, us,* m. 'friend of the cuckoo,' the mango tree. — *Pika-bāndhava, as,* m. 'friend of the cuckoo,' the spring. — *Pika-rāga* or *pika-vallabha, as,* m. 'cuckoo's favourite,' the mango tree. — *Pika-vara, as,* m. an excellent cuckoo. — *Pikāksha* (°*ka-aksha*), *as* or *am,* m. or n. (?), 'cuckoo's eye,' a vegetable and perfume (commonly called *roćanī*). — *Pikāṅga* (°*ka-aṅ*°), *as,* m. a small bird, commonly called Ćātakīya. — *Pikānanda* (°*ka-ān*°), *as,* m. 'cuckoo's joy,' the spring. — *Pikekshaṇā* (°*ka-īk*°), f. 'having eyes like the cuckoo's,' the plant Asteracantha Longifolia or Capparis Spinosa (=*kokilāksha*).

पिक्क *pikka, as,* m. an elephant twenty years old (=*vikka*); a young elephant in general.

पिक्का *pikkā,* f., Ved. a collection or string of thirteen pearls weighing a Dharaṇa.

पिङ्ग *piṅga, piṅgara, piṅgala.* See under rt. *piñj*, p. 572.

पिचण्ड *pićaṇḍa, as, am,* m. n. the belly; a particular part or limb of an animal.

Pićaṇḍaka = *pićaṇḍe kuśalaḥ*, see Gaṇa to Pāṇ. V. 2, 64; (*ikā*), f. the calf of the leg; the instep.

Pićaṇḍika, as, ā, am, (probably) big-bellied.

Pićaṇḍin, ī, inī, i, or *pićaṇḍila, as, ā, am,* big-bellied, corpulent.

Pićiṇḍa, as, m. the belly or abdomen; a particular part of an animal. — *Pićiṇḍa-vat, ān, atī, at,* big-bellied, corpulent.

Pićiṇḍikā, f. the calf of the leg; the instep.

Pićiṇḍila, as, ā, am, big-bellied, corpulent.

पिचु *pić u, us,* m. cotton; a sort of grain; the plant Vangueria Spinosa; a Karsha or weight of two Tolas; a kind of leprosy; N. of an Asura; Bhairava or one of the eight faces of Bhairava. — *Pić u-tūla, am,* n. cotton. — *Pić u-manda* or *pić u-marda, as,* m. the Nimb tree, Azadirachta Indica.

Pićarya, as, m. the cotton plant.

Pićuka, as, m. the plant Vangueria Spinosa; a species of tree.

Pićula, as, m. cotton; the tamarisk, Tamarix Indica; another plant, Barringtonia Acutangula; a kind of cormorant or sea crow.

पिच्च् *pićć,* a various reading for rt. *pićh,* q. v.

पिच्चट *piććaṭa, as, ā, am,* pressed flat,

a substance pressed flat, cake [cf. *tila-p°*]; (*as*), m. inflammation of the eyes, ophthalmia; tin, lead.

Piććita, as, ā, am, pressed flat, squeezed; [cf. *ćipiṭa.*]

पिच्चा *piććā*, f. a collection or string of sixteen pearls weighing a Dharaṇa; [cf. *pikkā.*]

पिच्चिट *piććiṭa* or *piććiṭaka, as*, m. a species of venomous insect.

पिच्छोरा *piććhorā*, f., Ved. a pipe, flute.

पिछ् *pićh*, cl. 10. P. *piććhayati, -yitum*, to split, cut, divide; cl. 6. P. *piććhati, piććhitum*, to inflict pain; to obstruct, hinder.

Piććha, am, n. a feather of a tail (especially of a peacock); the tail of a peacock; the feathers of an arrow; a wing; a crest; (*as*), m. a tail in general; (*ā*), f. the scum of boiled rice and of other grain; the gum of the silk-cotton tree; the venomous saliva of a snake; a multitude, heap; the calf of the leg; a sheath, a coat or cover; the areca-nut, betel-nut; a line, row, range; a diseased affection of a horse's feet; a plantain, Musa Sapientum; the Śiśu tree, Dalbergia Sissoo; armour, a sort of cuirass or jacket; = *piććhila*. — *Piććha-bāṇa* or *piććha-vāṇa, as*, m. 'whose feathers are like arrows,' a hawk. — *Piććha-vat, ān, atī, at*, having a tail, tailed.

Piććhaka, am, n. a feather of a tail (at the end of a comp.; cf. *ćitra-p°*); (*ikā*), f. the feathers of a peacock's tail tied in a bunch (used by conjurors).

Piććhala, as, ā, am, slimy, slippery, smeary; (*as*), m., N. of a Nāga of the race of Vāsuki; (*ā*), f., N. of various plants, Dalbergia Sissoo, Bombax Heptaphyllum, Basella Lucida or Rubra; N. of a river; (perhaps an incorrect form for *piććhila*, q. v.) — *Piććhala-dalā*, f. the jujube, Zizyphus Jujuba.

Piććhitikā, f. = *piććhilā*, the Śiśu tree, Dalbergia Sissoo.

Piććhila, as, ā, am, slimy, lubricous, slippery, smeary; having a tail; (*as, ā, am*), m. f. n. sauce mixed with rice-gruel; sauce, gravy or condiments with water or ghee; broth, soup; moist and split pulse; (*as*), m. the plant Cordia Latifolia and Myxa; the tamarisk, Tamarix Indica; (*ā*), f., N. of various plants, Dalbergia Sissoo; Bombax Heptaphyllum, the silk-cotton tree; a pot-herb, Basella Lucida or Rubra; linseed, Linum Usitatissimum; Asteracantha Longifolia; an esculent root, Arum Indicum; N. of a river. — *Piććhila-ććhadā*, f. Basella Cordifolia. — *Piććhila-tvać, k*, m. an orange-tree; orange-peel; a species of fruit tree (= *dhanvana*). — *Piććhila-sāra, as*, m. the gum of Bombax Heptaphyllum.

Piććhilaka, as, m. a species of fruit tree (= *dhanvana*).

Pińćha, am, n. a wing (= *piććha*).

पिजवन *pijavana, as*, m., N. of a man.

पिजूल *pijūla, as*, m., N. of a man.

पिञ्चदेव *pińća-deva, as*, m., N. of a man.

पिञ्ज् *pińj*, cl. 2. A. *pinkte, pipińje, pińjitā, pinktum*, to tinge, dye, colour [cf. rt. 1. *piś*]; to sound; to touch; to join [cf. rt. 1. *prić*]; to adore; cl. 10. P. *pińjayati, -yitum*, to kill, injure; to be strong; to give; to take; to dwell; to shine; to speak; to emit a sound; [cf. Lat. *ping-ere.*]

Pinga, as, ā, am, reddish-brown, tawny, bright red, red, yellow; (*as*), m. tawny colour; (probably) N. of a herb (Ved.); a buffalo; a rat, mouse; N. of a man (Ved., cf. *paingi, paingin*); N. of one of the attendants of the Sun; (*ā*), f. a bow-string (Sāy. = *pinga-varṇā jyā*); a kind of yellow pigment [cf. *go-roćanā*]; the stalk of Ferula Asa Fœtida; bamboo manna; turmeric, Indian saffron; an epithet of Durgā (?); a tubular vessel of the human body which according to the Yoga system is the channel of respiration and circulation for one side; (*ī*), f. a species of Mimosa, Mimosa Suma; (*am*), n. a young animal. — *Pinga-kapiśā*, f. 'tawny-brown,' a species of cockroach. — *Pinga-ćakshus, us*, m. 'tawny-eyed,' a crab. — *Pinga-jaṭa, as*, m. 'having tawny braided hair,' an epithet of Śiva. — *Pinga-tīrtha, am*, n., N. of a Tīrtha. — *Pinga-loćana, as, ā, am*, 'tawny-eyed,' having brown eyes. — *Pinga-sāra, as*, m. yellow orpiment. — *Pinga-sphaṭika, as*, m. 'yellow-crystal,' a kind of gem (= *go-meda*). — *Pingāksha* (°*ga-ak*°), *as, ī, am*, 'tawny-eyed,' having reddish-brown eyes, red-eyed; (*as*), m. an ape; N. of Śiva; of a Rakshas; of a wild man; of a bird; of one of the four sons of Droṇa; (*ī*), f., N. of a divinity; of one of the Mātṛis attending on Skanda. — *Pingāsya* (°*ga-ās*°), *as*, m. 'tawny-faced,' a species of fish, Pimelodius Pangasius. — *Pingekshaṇa* (°*ga-īk*°), *as, ī, am*, 'tawny-eyed,' having reddish-brown eyes; (*as*), m. an epithet of Śiva. — *Pingeśa* (°*ga-īśa*), *as*, m. 'lord of the yellow hue,' an epithet of fire.

Pingara, as, m., N. of a man.

Pingala, as, ā, am, reddish-brown, tawny, brown, yellowish; (*as*), m. tawny colour, a dull brown or yellow hue; fire; a monkey; an ichneumon; a small kind of owl; a species of snake; a particular vegetable poison; (with Jainas) N. of a treasure; N. of one of Kuvera's divine treasures; of an attendant of the Sun; the sun (?); an epithet of Śiva or of a kindred being; N. of a Rudra; of a Yaksha; of an attendant of Śiva; of a Dānava; of a fabulous being in the form of a Nāga (or serpent of the lower regions, the reputed author of the Ćhandas or treatise on prosody, regarded as one of the Vedāngas, and describing Prākṛit as well as Sanskṛit metres; he is identified by some with Patañjali, the author of the celebrated commentary on Pāṇini called the Mahā-bhāshya; by the Hindūs he is considered as a Muni or inspired and divine personage); N. of various ancient sages; N. of the fifty-first (or twenty-fifth) year in a sixty years' cycle of Jupiter; (*ās*), m. pl., N. of a people; (*ā*), f. a species of bird, a kind of owl; the Śiśu tree, Dalbergia Sissoo; a kind of metal; a particular vessel of the body (the right of three canals running from the os coccygis to the head, which according to the anatomy of the Yoga school of philosophy are the chief passages of breath and air); the female elephant of the South quarter; N. of a courtezan who became remarkable for her piety; of an astrological house or period; heart-pea; (*am*), n. a particular metal (= *rāja-rīti*), brass; yellow orpiment. — *Pingala-ćhando-grantha-ṭīkā*, f., N. of a commentary by Ćitra-sena on Pingala's Ćhandaḥ-śāstra. — *Pingala-nāga, as*, m. the serpent-demon Pingala. — *Pingala-vṛitti, is*, f., N. of a commentary on Pingala's Ćhandaḥ-śāstra. — *Pingala-sāra-vikāśinī*, f. 'explaining the substance of Pingala,' N. of a commentary by Ravi-kara on Pingala's Ćhandaḥ-śāstra. — *Pingalāksha* (°*la-ak*°), *as*, m. 'tawny-eyed,' an epithet of Śiva. — *Pingalā-tantra* and *pingalāmṛita* (°*la-am*°), *am*, n., N. of two Tantras. — *Pingaleśvara* (°*la-īś*°), *am*, n., N. of a Linga; (*ī*), f. a form of Dākshāyaṇī. — *Pingaleśvara-tīrtha, am*, n., N. of a sacred bathing-place.

Pingalaka, as, ikā, am, (Ved.) reddish-brown, tawny; (*as*), m., N. of a Yaksha; N. of a man; (*ās*), m. pl., N. of his descendants; (*ikā*), f. a kind of bee; a variety of the owl; a sort of crane; N. of a woman.

Pingalita, as, ā, am, made reddish-brown, become tawny.

Pingāśa, as, m. the chief of a community of wild tribes; the head man or proprietor of a village; a kind of fish, Pimelodius Pangasius (= *pingāsya*); (*ī*), f. the indigo plant; (*am*), n. virgin gold.

Pińja, as, ā, am, confused, confounded, disturbed in mind; (*as*), m. the moon; a species of camphor; killing, slaughter; (*ā*), f. hurting, injuring, injury; turmeric; cotton; a species of tree resembling the vine-palm; a switch; (*am*), n. strength, power.

Pińjaṭa, as, m. the concrete rheum of the eyes.

Pińjana, am, n. a bow or bow-shaped instrument used for cleaning cotton.

Pińjara, as, ā, am, reddish-yellow, yellow or tawny, of the colour of gold; (*as*), m. tawny-brown or reddish-yellow colour, a mixture of red and yellow; a horse (probably a bay or chesnut); N. of a mountain; (*am*), n. gold; yellow orpiment; the flower of Mesua Roxburghii; a cage; the ribs or the cavity formed by them, the thorax; a skeleton; [cf. *pañjara.*] — *Pińjara-tā*, f. yellowish-red (the colour).

Pińjaraka, as, m., N. of a Nāga; (*am*), n. orpiment.

Pińjarita, as, ā, am, coloured reddish-yellow.

Pińjala, as, ā, am, extremely perplexed or confounded, disturbed, overcome with terror or grief; panic-struck, being in great disorder; (*ā*), f., N. of a river; (*ī*), f. two blades of Kuśa grass serving as an implement to hold certain articles at a sacrifice; (*am*), n. the leaf of the Kuśa grass; the plant Curcuma Zerumbet (*haridrābha*); yellow orpiment.

Pińjalaka, as, ā, am, in *ut-pińjalaka*, extremely confounded or disturbed, being in great disorder.

Pińjāna, am, n. gold.

Pińjikā, f. a roll of cotton from which threads are spun.

Pińjūla, am, n., Ved. a bundle of stalks, a bundle of grass, &c.; the wick of a lamp; (sometimes spelt *pińjula.*)

Pińjūlaka, as, m., N. of a man; (*ās*), m. pl., N. of his descendants.

Pińjūsha, as, m. the wax of the ear (= *peńjūsha*).

Pińjeṭa, as, m. the excretion or concrete rheum of the eyes; [cf. *pińjaṭa.*]

पिञ्जोला *pińjolā*, f. the noise or rustling of leaves.

पिट् *piṭ*, cl. 1. P. *peṭati, peṭitum*, to sound; to assemble or heap together.

Piṭa, as, m. a basket for holding grain, a sort of cupboard or granary made of bamboos or canes; a basket, box; (*am*), n. a house, a hovel; a roof.

Piṭaka, as, ā, am, m. f. n. (usually n.), a basket, box; a large basket or receptacle of basket-work for keeping grain &c., a granary; a collection of writings [cf. *tri-p°*]; a boil, blister, ulcer; a kind of ornament on Indra's banner; (*as*), m., N. of a man.

Piṭakyā, f. a multitude of baskets.

Piṭāka, see Gaṇa to Pāṇ. IV. 2, 49; (*as*), m., N. of a man; N. of a sage.

पिटङ्काकी *piṭankākī* or *piṭankokī*, f. the plant Cucumis Colocynthis.

पिटङ्काश *piṭankāśa, as*, m. a kind of fish, a species of pike, Esax Scolopax, Silurus Pabda.

पिट्टक *piṭṭaka, am*, n. the tartar or excretion of the teeth; [cf. *kiṭṭa, kiṭṭaka, pippikā.*]

पिट्टय *piṭṭaya* (fr. *piṭṭa* = *pishṭa*?), Nom. P. *piṭṭayati, -yitum*, Ved. to stamp or press into a solid mass.

Piṭṭita, as, ā, am, stamped into a solid mass, pressed flat.

पिठ् *piṭh*, cl. 1. P. *peṭhati, peṭhitum*, to injure, hurt, kill; to feel pain or affliction.

Piṭha, as, m. pain, distress.

Piṭhara, as, ī, am, m. f. n. a pot, pan; (*as*), m. an addition to a building shaped like a hollow vessel, a hut made of bamboos and mats, or according to some a kind of store-room or scullery; N. of a particular Agni; N. of a Dānava; (*am*), n. a churning-stick; the root of Cyperus Rotundus.

Piṭharaka, as, m. (?), a pot, pan; N. of a Nāga. — *Piṭharaka-kapāla, as, am*, m. n. a fragment of a pot, potsherd.

पिठीनस् *piṭhīnas, ās*, m., N. of a man.

पिडक *piḍaka, as*, m. or *piḍakā*, f. a small boil, pimple, papula, pustule. — *Piḍakā-vat, ān, atī, at*, having boils, pimples, &c.

Piḍakin, ī, inī, i, having boils, &c.

पिण्ड् *piṇḍ* (probably akin to rt. *pish*; considered by some as a Nom. fr. *piṇḍa* below), cl. 1. A., 10. P. *piṇḍate, piṇḍitum, piṇḍayati, -yitum,* to roll into a lump or ball, to put together, join, unite; to accumulate; to assemble.

Piṇḍa, as, am, m. n. (in most senses usually m.), a round mass, ball, globe, lump, knob, clod (e. g. *ayaḥ-piṇḍa,* a ball or lump of iron; *agni-piṇḍau,* the knobs at the end of a pair of tongs; cf. *netra-p°, mṛit-p°*); a roundish lump of food, a bite, morsel, mouthful; a cake or ball of meal offered to the Manes, a ball or lump of meat or rice mixed up with milk, curds, flowers, &c., and offered at the several Śrāddhas to the Manes by the nearest surviving relations (= *ni-vāpa*); food; sustenance, means of living, livelihood, subsistence [cf. *para-piṇḍāda*]; alms; flesh, meat; the embryo or fetus in an early stage of gestation; the body; the projection of an elephant's frontal sinus; a round button; anything roundish, thick, gross, or solid; thickness (one of the three dimensions in geometry); a heap, cluster, quantity, collection; an object; a particular part of a house; a sort of portico or shed in front of the door; myrrh, incense, frankincense; the side immediately below the armpit (?); Vangueria Spinosa; the flower of the China rose; (in arithmetic) sum, total amount; (in astronomy) a sine expressed in numbers [cf. *jyā-p°*]; the twenty-fourth part of the quadrant of a circle, or 3° 45′; N. of a man; (*au*), m. du. the fleshy parts of the shoulder situated above the collar-bone; (*am*), n. power, might; an army; iron; fresh butter; (*ī*), f. a round mass, &c. (= *piṇḍa,* m.); a long gourd, Cucurbita Lagenaria (= *a-lābu*); a species of date tree; the flowering shrub Tabernæmontana Coronaria (= *tagara*); the plant Jonesia Aśoka; a species of palm, Phœnix Dactylifera; the nave of a wheel; performance of certain gesticulations during the silent repetition of prayers while meditating on real or divine knowledge; a house; N. of a woman. – *Piṇḍa-kanda, as,* m. a species of bulbous plant (= *piṇḍālu*). – *Piṇḍa-kharjūra, as,* m. or *piṇḍa-kharjūrikā* or *piṇḍa-kharjūrī,* f. a species of date tree. – *Piṇḍa-gosa, as,* m. gum myrrh. – *Piṇḍa-tarkuka, ās,* m. pl., Ved. the ancestors preceding the great-grandfather (who eat the remnants of the oblations made to the Manes). – *Piṇḍa-tas,* ind. from a ball or lump. – *Piṇḍa-taila, am,* n. or *piṇḍa-tailaka, as,* m. incense, olibanum. – *Piṇḍa-tva, am,* n. the being a lump or ball; *piṇḍatvam gam,* to attain the condition of a lump. – *Piṇḍa-da, as, ā, am,* giving or qualified to give the funeral cake to deceased ancestors; supplying with bread or with the means of subsistence; (*as*), m. the nearest male relation who offers the funeral cake; a patron, master. – *Piṇḍa-dātṛi, tā, trī, tṛi,* one who gives or is qualified to give the funeral cake to deceased ancestors. – *Piṇḍa-dāna, am,* n. offering a cake of meal (especially in the oblation to the Manes); presentation of the obsequial cake; the funeral oblation made to deceased ancestors on the evening of new moon. – *Piṇḍa-nirvapaṇa, am,* n. presenting obsequial cakes to the Manes, the sacrifice to the Manes. – *Piṇḍa-pada, am,* n. a kind of arithmetical calculation. – *Piṇḍa-pāta, as,* m. giving alms. – *Piṇḍapātika, as,* m. one who lives on alms. – *Piṇḍa-pātra, am,* n. the vessel in which the obsequial cakes are offered to the Manes; alms (lit. an alms-dish). – *Piṇḍa-pāda* or *piṇḍa-pādya, as,* m. 'thick-footed,' an elephant. – *Piṇḍa-pitṛi-yajña, am,* n., Ved. the oblation of obsequial cakes to deceased ancestors on the evening of new moon. – *Piṇḍa-pushpa, as,* m. the tree Jonesia Aśoka; the China rose; the pomegranate tree; (*am*), n. the blossom of the Aśoka tree; the flower of the China rose; a lotus; the flower of the plant Tabernæmontana Coronaria. – *Piṇḍapushpaka, as,* m. a kind of vegetable, Chenopodium Album. – *Piṇḍa-phala, as, ā, am,* bearing (long) round fruits; (*ā*), f. a bitter gourd. – *Piṇḍa-bīja* or *piṇḍa-vīja, as,* m. a flowering shrub, Nerium (or Oleander) Odorum. – *Piṇḍabījaka, as,* m. Pterospermum Acerifolium (= *karṇikāra*). – *Piṇḍa-bhāj, k, k, k,* partaking of a funeral oblation, entitled to a share in the funeral cake, eating or receiving the cakes offered at a funeral ceremony; (*jas*), m. pl. deceased ancestors, the Manes. – *Piṇḍa-bhṛiti, is,* f. means of subsistence, livelihood. – *Piṇḍa-maya, as, ī, am,* consisting of a lump (of clay). – *Piṇḍa-mātropajīvin* (°*ra-up*°), *i, inī, i,* subsisting on a mere morsel. – *Piṇḍa-mustā,* f. a species of grass, Cyperus Pertenuis. – *Piṇḍa-mūla* or *piṇḍa-mūlaka, am,* n. a carrot, Daucus Carota (= *garjara*). – *Piṇḍa-yajña, as,* m. the oblation of obsequial cakes to deceased ancestors. – *Piṇḍa-lepa, as,* m. the particles or fragments of the obsequial cakes which cling to the hands, (these are offered to the three ancestors preceding the great-grandfather.) – *Piṇḍa-lopa, as,* m. an interruption in offering the funeral cake; a neglect of the solemn obsequies in honour of deceased ancestors. – *Piṇḍa-vat,* ind. like a lump or ball. – *Piṇḍa-sambandha, as,* m. relationship between a living person and one deceased sufficiently near to qualify the former to offer the obsequial cake to the latter; [cf. *sa-piṇḍa.*] – *Piṇḍa-sambandhin, ī, inī, i,* qualified by near relationship to a living person to receive the obsequial cake from him at the oblation to the Manes. – *Piṇḍa-sektṛi, tā,* m., N. of a Nāga. – *Piṇḍa-stha, as, ā, am,* Ved. 'mingled in a lump,' mixed or intermingled together. – *Piṇḍānvāhārya* (°*ḍa-an*°), *as, ā, am,* to be eaten after the funeral cake has been offered (Manu III. 123). – *Piṇḍānvāhāryaka, am,* n. (with *śrāddha*) a meal in honour of the Manes after offering the funeral cakes. – *Piṇḍābhra* (°*ḍa-abh*°), *am,* n. hail. – *Piṇḍāyasa* (°*ḍa-ay*°), *am,* n. steel. – *Piṇḍālu* (°*ḍa-ālu*), *us,* m., N. of two bulbous plants; = *kanda-guḍūćī;* an esculent medicinal root described as sweet, cooling, and diuretic (= Hindī *peḍālu,* Bengālī *ćuvaḍiālu;* in this sense also *piṇḍāluka, am,* n.). – *Piṇḍāśa* or *piṇḍāśaka* (°*ḍa-aś*°), or *piṇḍāśana* (°*ḍa-aś*°), *as,* or *piṇḍāśin* (°*ḍa-aś*°), *ī,* m. 'eating morsels,' a beggar. – *Piṇḍāhvā* (°*ḍa-āh*°), f. the resin of Gardenia Gummifera (= *nāḍī-hingu*). – *Piṇḍī-khaṇḍa, as* or *am,* m. or n. (?), a small wood of Tabernæmontana Coronaria trees (or of Aśoka trees). – *Piṇḍī-jangha, as,* m., N. of a man or of his descendants. – *Piṇḍī-tagara, as,* m. a species of Tabernæmontana Coronaria (= *kapha-vardhana*). – *Piṇḍītagaraka, as,* m. Tabernæmontana Coronaria. – *Piṇḍī-taru, us,* m. a species of tree (= *mahā-p*°). – *Piṇḍī-pushpa, am,* n. Jonesia Aśoka. – *Piṇḍī-lepa, as,* m. a kind of unguent. – *Piṇḍī-śūra, as,* m. 'a cake-hero,' a cowardly boaster, cotquean, braggart. – *Piṇḍodaka-kriyā* (°*ḍa-ud*°), f. an oblation of obsequial cakes and water. – *Piṇḍoddharaṇa* (°*ḍa-ud*°), *am,* n. participating in funeral offerings, presenting them to common ancestors. – *Piṇḍopanishad* (°*ḍa-up*°), *t,* f., N. of an Upanishad.

Piṇḍaka, as, am, m. n. a lump, lump of food; a round swelling or protuberance [cf. *mastaka-p*°]; the calf of the leg; incense, myrrh; a species of bulbous plant (= *piṇḍālu*); a carrot, Daucus Carota; (in astronomy) a sine expressed in numbers; (*as*), m. a Piśāća, goblin, demon; (*ikā*), f. a globular swelling or protuberance, a fleshy swelling (in the shoulders, arms, legs, &c.), a wen (?); the calf of the leg; the instep; the nave of a wheel; a stool or seat of various shapes and dimensions; a base or pedestal for the image of a deity or for a Linga (Ved.); a kind of shrub (= *śvetāmlī*).

Piṇḍana, am, n. forming globes, taking a globular form (as water); (*as*), m. a mound or bank.

Piṇḍaraka, as or *am,* m. or n. (?), a bridge.

Piṇḍala, as, m. a bridge, causeway, passage over a stream or ravine, a mound, ridge, balk raised to form a path across inundated fields; [cf. *piṇḍana, piṇḍila.*]

Piṇḍasa, as, m. a beggar, mendicant living upon alms; [cf. *piṇḍāśa* under *piṇḍa.*]

Piṇḍāta, as, m. incense.

Piṇḍāra, as, m. a beggar, religious mendicant; a buffalo-herdsman, neatherd, cowherd; a species of tree, Flacourtia Sapida; Trewia Nudiflora; an expression of censure; N. of a Nāga; (*am*), n. a kind of vegetable (= Hindī *piṇḍārā*).

Piṇḍāraka, as, m., N. of a Nāga; N. of a Vṛishṇi; of a son of Vasu-deva and Rohiṇī; of a river considered holy by the Hindūs; (*am*), n., N. of a place of pilgrimage in Guzerat. – *Piṇḍāraka-tīrtha, am,* n., N. of a sacred bathing-place.

Piṇḍi, is, f. the nave of a wheel (= *piṇḍī, piṇḍikā*).

Piṇḍika, as, ā, am, having large calves (?). See *piṇḍikā* under *piṇḍaka,* col. 2.

Piṇḍita, as, ā, am, rolled into a ball or lump, pressed into a solid mass; thick, massy, lumpish; formed into a mass, heaped together, collected; mixed, intermingled with; united; added, multiplied; counted, numbered; (*as*), m. incense.

Piṇḍin, ī, inī, i, possessing a body (= *śarīrin*); receiving cakes of meal (as ancestors &c.); possessing the *piṇḍa* or funeral oblation; (*ī*), m. a beggar; an offerer of obsequial oblations or cakes of meal to the Manes.

Piṇḍila, as, ā, am, having large calves (= *sthūla-jangha*); skilled in calculations; (*as*), m. a skilful calculator or arithmetician, a calculator of nativities, astrologer, astronomer; a bridge, mound, balk, causeway; (*ā*), f. a species of cucumber, Cucumis Maderaspatanus (= *goḍumbā*).

Piṇḍī-kṛi, cl. 8. P. A. *-karoti, -kurute, -kartum,* to make into a lump or ball, press together, unite, join together, mix or intermingle; to concentrate; to identify with (with *saha*). – *Piṇḍī-karaṇa, am,* n. making into a lump or ball, heaping. – *Piṇḍī-kṛita, as, ā, am,* made into a lump or ball. – *Piṇḍī-kṛitya,* ind. having made into a lump or ball; having concentrated.

Piṇḍītaka, as, m. the tree Vangueria Spinosa; a kind of shrub, Tabernæmontana Coronaria; a species of basil (= *phaṇijjhaka*); (*am*), n. the fruit of the tree Vangueria Spinosa.

Piṇḍī-bhū, cl. 1. P. *-bhavati, -bhavitum,* to be made into a lump or ball, to become a solid body. – *Piṇḍī-bhāva, as,* m. the being rolled together into a ball. – *Piṇḍī-bhūta, as, ā, am,* formed into a lump or ball, lumped, heaped.

Piṇḍīra, as, ā, am, sapless, juiceless, arid, dry; (*as*), m. the pomegranate tree [cf. *kṛishṇa-p*°]; cuttle-fish bone; sea foam.

Piṇḍola, as, m., N. of a man.

Piṇḍoli, is, f. leavings of a meal, fragments dropped from the mouth, orts.

पिण्डिपाल *piṇḍipāla, as* or *am,* m. or n. (?), N. of a weapon with a single point; [cf. *bhindipāla.*]

पिण्या *piṇyā,* f. heart-pea, Cardiospermum Halicacabum (= *paṇyā*).

पिण्याक *piṇyāka, as, am,* m. n. (said to be fr. rt. *pish*), the residue of seeds which have been ground for oil; oil-cake; incense; saffron; Asa Fœtida; (*ā*), f. a species of plant.

पितामह *pitā-maha.* See p. 574, col. 1.

पितु *pitu, us,* m., Ved. (fr. rt. *pyai*), juice, drink; nourishment; (Sāy.) = *pālakam annam,* nourishing food. – *Pitu-kṛit, t, t, t,* Ved. bestowing or providing food. – *Pitu-bhāj, k, k, k,* Ved. enjoying or partaking of food; (Sāy.) = *annārthin,* seeking or earning food. – *Pitu-bhṛit, t, t, t,* Ved. bringing food. – *Pitu-mat, ān, atī, at,* Ved. accompanied by food, abounding in food, nourishing. – *Pitu-shaṇi, is, is, i,* Ved. bestowing or granting food. – *Pitu-stoma, as,* m. 'praise of food,' N. of the hymn Ṛig-veda I. 187.

Pitūya, Nom. P. *pitūyati, -yitum,* Ved. to long for food, desire food.

पितृ *pitṛi, tā,* m. (fr. rt. 3. *pā*), a father; (in the Veda *pitṛi* is an epithet of Bṛihas-pati, Varuṇa, Prajā-pati, and especially of heaven or the sky; *antarā pitaram mātaraṅ-ća*, between heaven and earth; according to Sāy. *pitṛi* = *pālaka*, a protector); (*tarau*), m. du. father and mother, parents, (in the Veda an epithet of the Araṇis or two pieces of wood regarded as the parents of Fire, and of heaven and earth regarded as the parents of all beings); (*taras*), m. pl. fathers, forefathers, ancestors; a father and his brothers, father and uncles, paternal ancestors; the spirits of departed ancestors, the Manes or spirits of the dead (they are of two kinds, viz. either the spirits of the father, grandfathers, and great-grandfathers of an individual or the progenitors of mankind generally, to both classes of whom Śrāddhas or obsequial worship is paid and oblations of food called Piṇḍas presented; they inhabit a peculiar region, which, according to some, is the Bhuvas or region of the air, according to others, the orbit of the moon, and are considered as the regents of the Nakshatras Maghā and Mūla); [cf. Zend *pita*, base *pa-tar:* Gr. *πα-τήρ*, *πάτρω-ς*: Lat. *pa-ter*, *Jup-piter:* Goth. *fa-dar:* Old Germ. *fa-tar*, *fa-ter*, 'father;' *fataro*, 'uncle:' Angl. Sax. *faeder*, 'father;' *fadhu*, 'aunt, father's sister:' Hib. *athair*, 'father,' for *pathair*.] — *Pitari-śūra*, *as*, m. 'a hero against his father,' a cowardly boaster. — *Pitā-putra*, *au*, m. du. father and son. — *Pitāputra-virodha*, *as*, m. a contest between father and son. — *Pitāputra-samāgama*, *as*, m., N. of a Buddhist Sūtra. — *Pitāputrīya*, *as*, *ā*, *am*, relating to father and son; containing the words *pitṛi* and *putra;* (with *sampradāna*) the transmission (of bodily capacities and powers) from father to son. — *Pitā-maha*, *as*, m. a paternal grandfather; a N. of Brahmā the great father of all; N. of the author of a Dharma-śāstra; of the author of an astronomical work; (*ās*), m. pl. the ancestors, Manes; (*ī*), f. a paternal grandmother. — *Pitāmaha-saras*, *as*, n. or *pitāmahasya saras*, N. of a place of pilgrimage. — *Pitā-sumati-saṃvāda*, *as*, m., N. of a part of the Brahma-vaivarta-Purāṇa. — *Pituḥ-putra*, *as*, m. a father's son. — *Pituḥ-shvasṛi* or *pituḥ-svasṛi*, *sā*, f. a father's sister. — *Pitṛi-karman*, *a*, or *pitṛi-kārya*, *am*, n. obsequial rites, sacrifice offered to deceased ancestors. — *Pitṛi-kalpa*, *as*, m. (perhaps) legends relating to ancestors; N. of a long period of time, Brahmā's day of new moon. — *Pitṛi-kānana*, *am*, n. 'grove of ancestors,' a cemetery. — *Pitṛi-kulyā*, f. 'rivulet of the Pitṛis,' N. of a river rising in the Malaya mountains. — *Pitṛi-kṛita*, *as*, *ā*, *am*, Ved. committed against parents or ancestors (as sin). — *Pitṛi-kṛitya*, *am*, n. or *pitṛi-kriyā*, f. obsequial rites, oblations offered to the spirits of deceased ancestors. — *Pitṛi-gaṇa*, *as*, m. the whole body of ancestors collectively, a group or class of Manes or deceased progenitors who were sons of the Ṛishis or Prajā-patis, (the principal classes, according to Manu III. 194–199, are the Soma-sads, descended from Vi-rāj, the Agni-shvāttas from Marīći, Barhi-shads from Atri, Soma-pās from Bhṛigu, Havishmats from Aṅgiras, Ājya-pas from Pulastya, and Su-kālins from Vasishṭha; there are also the Agnidagdhas and An-agnidagdhas, Kāvyas and Saumyas.) — *Pitṛi-gaṇā*, f. an epithet of Durgā. — *Pitṛi-gāthā*, *ās*, f. pl. 'songs of the ancestors,' an epithet of particular songs. — *Pitṛi-gāmin*, *ī*, *inī*, *i*, belonging or pertaining to a father. — *Pitṛi-griṇā*, f. probably a wrong reading for *pitṛi-gaṇā*, q. v. — *Pitṛi-gṛiha*, *am*, n. a father's house, paternal mansion; 'house of ancestors,' a burial ground, cemetery. — *Pitṛi-graha*, *as*, m. 'the genius of the Manes,' N. of a demon causing disease. — *Pitṛi-ghātaka*, *as*, or *pitṛi-ghātin*, *ī*, m. 'slaying a father,' a parricide. — *Pitṛi-ćeṭa*, *as*, m., N. of a man. — *Pitṛi-tama*, *as*, m., Ved., in *pitṛitamaḥ pitṛiṇāṃ*, best of the ancestors (Sāy. = *pālakānām madhye atiśayena pālakaḥ*, a defender in the highest degree among defenders). — *Pitṛi-tarpaṇa*, *am*, n. 'refreshing the Manes,' gifts in honour of deceased progenitors, distributed at the Śrāddhas or funeral ceremonies; an oblation to the Manes; the act of throwing water out of the right hand at seasons of ablution as an offering to the Manes or deceased ancestors in general; the part of the hand between the thumb and fore-finger sacred to the Manes; sesamum (= *tila*). — *Pitṛi-tas*, ind., Ved. from the father, on the father's side. — *Pitṛi-tithi*, *is*, f. day of new moon, a day sacred to the Manes of either deceased parent, the day appointed for obsequial rites to deceased ancestors. — *Pitṛi-tīrtha*, *am*, n. 'the place of pilgrimage for progenitors,' epithet of the city called Gayā (where the performance of funeral sacrifices is peculiarly meritorious and efficacious); the part of the hand between the fore-finger and thumb sacred to the Manes. — *Pitṛitīrtha-māhātmya*, *am*, n., N. of a chapter of the Śiva-Purāṇa. — *Pitṛi-tva*, *am*, n. fatherhood, paternity; the state or condition of a Pitṛi or deified progenitor. — *Pitṛi-datta*, *as*, *ā*, *am*, given by a father (a term applied to a woman's peculiar property); (*as*), m., N. of a man. — *Pitṛi-dayitā*, f., N. of a work. — *Pitṛi-dāna* or *pitṛi-dānaka*, *am*, n. a gift in honour of deceased ancestors, an offering to the Manes. — *Pitṛi-dāya*, *as*, m. property inherited from a father, patrimony. — *Pitṛi-deva*, *ās*, m. pl. the Manes and the gods; the divine Manes; (*as*, *ā*, *am*), worshipping a father; relating to the worship of the Manes or deceased ancestors. — *Pitṛi-devata* or *pitṛi-devatya*, *as*, *ā*, *am*, Ved. having the Manes for deities, sacred to the Manes. — *Pitṛi-daivata*, *as*, *ī*, *am*, relating to the worship of the Manes; governed or presided over by the Manes; (*am*), n. epithet of the tenth lunar asterism or Maghā. — *Pitṛi-daivatya*, *as*, *ā*, *am*, relating to the worship of the Manes; (*am*), n., N. of a sacrifice offered to the Manes on the day called Ashṭakā. — *Pitṛi-dravya*, *am*, n. 'father's substance,' patrimony. — *Pitṛi-nāman*, *ā*, *mnī*, *a*, called after the father's name; [cf. *mātṛi-nāman*.] — *Pitṛi-paksha*, *as*, m. paternal side, paternal relationship; the half month of the Manes, N. of the dark half in the Gauṇa Āśvina, so termed as peculiarly appointed for the celebration of obsequial rites to the Pitṛis or Manes; a father's relations, relatives by the father's side; (*as*, *ā*, *am*), being on the father's side. — *Pitṛi-pati*, *is*, m. 'lord of the Manes,' an epithet of Yama, regent of the dead; (*ayas*), m. pl. the Manes and the lords of creatures (Prajā-patis). — *Pitṛi-pada*, *am*, n. the world or state of the Manes. — *Pitṛi-pātra*, *am*, n. a cup or other vessel used at obsequial rites. — *Pitṛi-pitṛi*, *tā*, m. a father's father, paternal grandfather. — *Pitṛi-pīta*, *as*, *ā*, *am*, Ved. drunk by ancestors or deceased progenitors. — *Pitṛi-pūjana*, *am*, n. worship of the Manes. — *Pitṛi-paitāmaha*, *as*, *ī*, *am*, inherited or derived from father and grandfather; (*ās*), m. pl. fathers and grandfathers, ancestors. — *Pitṛipaitāmahika*, *as*, *ī*, *am*, inherited or derived from father and grandfather. — *Pitṛi-prasū*, *ūs*, f. a father's mother; 'mother of the Manes,' twilight (the time when the Manes of departed ancestors are abroad). — *Pitṛi-prāpta*, *as*, *ā*, *am*, received from a father; inherited patrimonially. — *Pitṛi-priya*, *as*, m. 'dear to the Pitṛis,' a species of plant (= *bhṛiṅga-rāja*). — *Pitṛi-bandhu*, *us*, m. a kinsman by the father's side, as the son of the paternal grandfather's sister, of the paternal grandmother's sister, and of the father's maternal uncle; (*u*), n. relationship by the father's side. — *Pitṛi-bāndhava*, *as*, m. a kinsman in the paternal line. — *Pitṛi-bhakta*, *as*, *ā*, *am*, dutifully attached to a father. — *Pitṛi-bhakti*, *is*, f. filial duty to a father. — *Pitṛibhakti-taraṅgiṇī*, f., N. of a work. — *Pitṛi-bhūti*, *is*, m., N. of a commentator on Kātyāyana's Srauta-sūtras. — *Pitṛi-bhojana*, *am*, n. a father's food; food offered to the Manes; (*as*, *am*), m. n. the plant Phaseolus Radiatus (a species of pulse = *māsha*). — *Pitṛi-bhrātṛi*, *tā*, m. a father's brother, paternal uncle. — *Pitṛi-mat*, *ān*, *atī*, *at*, having a father, having an illustrious father; accompanied by the Manes, connected with the Manes (as Soma or Yama); mentioning the Manes or deceased ancestors. — *Pitṛi-mandira*, *am*, n. a father's house, paternal mansion; 'dwelling-place of ancestors,' a cemetery. — *Pitṛi-mātṛi-hīna*, *as*, *ā*, *am*, destitute of father and mother, orphan. — *Pitṛi-medha* or *pitṛi-yajña*, *as*, m. sacrifice offered to the Manes, obsequial offerings. — *Pitṛi-yāṇa*, Ved. or *pitṛi-yāna*, *as*, *ā*, *am*, trodden by the Manes; (*am*), n. the path trodden by the Manes, the way leading to the Manes; the vehicle of the Manes, a car to convey holy persons after their decease to heaven. — *Pitṛi-rāj*, *ṭ*, or *pitṛi-rāja*, *as*, or *pitṛi-rājan*, *ā*, m. 'king of the Manes,' an epithet of Yama. — *Pitṛi-rūpa*, *as*, m., N. of a Rudra. — *Pitṛi-loka*, *as*, m. a father's house, paternal mansion; the world or sphere of the Manes (to which various situations are ascribed, but principally the Bhuvas region or mid-heaven). — *Pitṛi-vaṇśa*, *as*, m. the paternal family. — 1. *pitṛi-vat*, *ān*, *atī*, *at*, having a father, whose father is living. — 2. *pitṛi-vat*, ind. like a father; like the Manes; as if for the Manes; as in the sacrifice offered to the Manes. — *Pitṛi-vana*, *am*, n. 'grove of ancestors,' a cemetery, a place where dead bodies are burnt or buried. — *Pitṛivane-ćara*, *as*, *ī*, *am*, haunting a cemetery; (*as*), m. an epithet of Śiva; a goblin. — *Pitṛi-vartin*, *ī*, m. 'staying or abiding with ancestors,' N. of a Brāhman (= king Brahma-datta). — *Pitṛi-vasati*, *is*, f. 'abode of departed ancestors,' a cemetery. — *Pitṛi-vāk-para*, *as*, *ā*, *am*, attentive to the voice of parents, obedient to parents. — *Pitṛi-vitta*, *as*, *ā*, *am*, Ved. acquired by ancestors; (Sāy.) = *pituḥ sakāśāl labdha*, derived from a father, patrimonial. — *Pitṛi-vrata*, *as*, m. a worshipper of the Manes; (*am*), n. worship of ancestors, obsequial rites. — *Pitṛi-śarman*, *ā*, m., N. of a Dānava. — *Pitṛi-śravaṇa*, *as*, *ā*, *am*, Ved. bringing honour to a father; (Sāy. = *pitā prakhyāyate yena putreṇa tādṛiśaḥ*.) — *Pitṛi-śrāddha*, *am*, n. a funeral ceremony or obsequial rites in honour of a father or deceased ancestor. — *Pitṛi-shad*, *t*, *t*, *t*, Ved. living unmarried with a father or with parents; 'dwelling with the Manes,' an epithet of Rudra. — *Pitṛi-shadana*, *as*, *ā*, *am*, Ved. inhabited by the Manes. — *Pitṛi-shvasṛi*, *sā*, f. a father's sister, paternal aunt (= *pituḥ-shvasṛi*). — *Pitṛi-shvasrīya*, *as*, *ā*, m. f. a father's sister's son or daughter, a paternal aunt's son or daughter. — *Pitṛi-sannibha*, *as*, *ā*, *am*, like a father, fatherly, paternal. — *Pitṛi-sāmānya*, *am*, n. ancestors collectively. — *Pitṛi-sū*, *ūs*, f. a father's mother; 'mother of the Manes,' twilight; [cf. *pitṛi-prasū*.] — *Pitṛi-sūkta*, *am*, n., N. of a Vedic hymn. — *Pitṛi-sthāna*, *as*, m. a guardian; (*am*), n. the sphere of the Manes. — *Pitṛisthānīya*, *as*, m. a guardian (who takes the place of a parent). — *Pitṛi-svasṛi*, *sā*, f. an incorrect form for *pitṛi-shvasṛi*. — *Pitṛisvasrīya*, *as*, *ā*, m. f., see *pitṛishvasrīya*. — *Pitṛi-hatyā*, f. the murder of a father, parricide. — *Pitṛi-han*, *ā*, m. a parricide. — *Pitṛi-hū*, *ūs*, *ūs*, *u*, invoking or dedicated to the Pitṛis; (*ūs*), f., scil. *dvār*, N. of the southern aperture of the human body, i. e. of the right ear; [cf. *deva-hū*.] — *Pitṛi-hūya*, *am*, n., Ved. invoking or summoning deceased ancestors. — *Pitrarjita* (°*tṛi-ar*°), *as*, *ā*, *am*, derived from a father; property originally acquired by a father. — *Pitrartham* (°*tṛi-ar*°), ind. for a father's sake.

Pitṛika, *as*, *ā*, *am*, (at the end of a comp.) paternal, parental, ancestral, relating or belonging to parents or progenitors, obsequial.

Pitṛivya, *as*, m. a father's brother, paternal uncle; any elderly male relation; [cf. Gr. *πάτρω-ς*; Lat. *patruus*.]

Pitrya, *as*, *ā*, *am*, derived from a father, relating to a father, paternal, patrimonial, ancestral, belonging to a father or to progenitors, usual or customary with a father; relating to deceased ancestors, consecrated to the Manes, referring or devoted to the Manes, obsequial; in Manu II. 59. *pitryaṃ tīrtham* = the part of the hand sacred to deified progenitors, i. e. the part between the fore-finger and thumb; (*as*), m. the eldest brother (who takes the place of a father); the month Māgha; (*ā*), f. the Nakshatra Maghā (presided over by the Manes); the day of full moon, the worship of the Manes on the day of full moon; (*am*), n., scil. *karma*, the worship of the Manes; the Nakshatra Maghā; the part of the hand between the fore-finger and thumb. — *Pitryā-vat, ān, atī, at,* Ved. (perhaps) possessing property inherited from a father; (Sāy.) = *pitṛi-mat*, q. v.

पित्त *pitta, am,* n. (etymology doubtful), bile, the bilious humor, one of the three humors of the body (the other two being *vāta* and *kapha*; it is especially secreted between the stomach and bowels, and thence flows through the liver, and distributes itself in the spleen, heart, eyes, and skin; its chief quality is heat); [cf. *kūrma-p°, go-p°, rakta-p°, paittika.*] — *Pitta-kosha, as,* m. the gall-bladder. — *Pitta-kshobha, as,* m. excess and disturbance of the bilious humor. — *Pitta-gadin, ī, inī, i,* suffering from bilious complaints, bilious. — *Pitta-ghna, as, ī, am,* 'bile-destroying,' antibilious; (*am*), n. an antidote to bilious complaints; ghee? ; (*ī*), f. a plant, Cocculus Cordifolius. — *Pitta-jvara, as,* m. bilious fever. — *Pitta-drāvin, ī, iṇī, i,* 'bile-dispersing,' removing bile; (*ī*), m. the sweet citron (= *madhura-jambīra*). — *Pitta-dhara, as, ā, am,* containing bile, bilious. — *Pitta-nivarhaṇa, as, ā, am,* destroying bile. — *Pitta-prakṛiti, is, is, i,* being of a bilious temperament. — *Pitta-prakopa, as,* m. excess and vitiation of the bilious humor. — *Pitta-rakta, am,* n. plethora; [cf. *rakta-pitta.*] — *Pitta-rogin, ī, iṇī, i,* suffering from bilious complaints, bilious. — *Pitta-vat, ān, atī, at,* having bile, bilious. — *Pitta-vāyu, us,* m. flatulence arising from excess and vitiation of the bilious humor. — *Pitta-vidagdha, as, ā, am,* burnt up by bile, impaired or destroyed by bile. — *Pitta-vināśana, as, ī, am,* 'bile-destroying,' antibilious. — *Pitta-śamana, as, ī, am,* 'bile-alleviating,' antibilious. — *Pitta-syanda, as,* m. a bilious form of ophthalmia; [cf. *pittābhishyanda.*] — *Pitta-hara, as, ī, am,* 'bile-removing,' antibilious. — *Pittātīsāra* (°*ta-at*°), *as,* m. 'bile-dysentery,' a bilious form of diarrhœa. — *Pittātīsārin, ī, iṇī, i,* suffering from a bilious form of dysentery. — *Pittābhishyanda* (°*ta-abh*°), *as,* m. a bilious form of ophthalmia; [cf. *pitta-syanda.*] — *Pittāri* (°*ta-ari*), *is,* m. 'enemy of bile,' i. e. anything antibilious; N. of various plants and vegetable substances used to counteract biliousness (= *parpaṭa, lākshā,* and *varvara*). — *Pittopahata* (°*ta-up*°), *as, ā, am,* impaired or destroyed by bile.

Pittala, as, ā, am, bilious, relating to the bilious humor, secreting bile; (*ā*), f. the plant Jussiæa Repens; (*ī*), f., N. of a plant, = *mūrvā*; (*am*), n. brass, bell-metal; a species of birch tree (the bark of which is used for writing upon; cf. *bhūrja-pattra*).

पित्थ *pittha, as,* m., N. of a man.

पित्सत् *pitsat, an, antī, at* (fr. Desid. of rt. 2. *pat*), being about to fly or fall, habitually falling or coming down; (*an*), m. a bird; [cf. Gr. ψίττακος; Lat. *psittacus.*]

Pitsala, am, n. a road, path, way.

Pitsu, us, us, u, being about to fly or fall.

Pipatishat, an, antī, at, about to fly or fall, inclined or addicted to falling repeatedly; (*an*), m. a bird.

Pipatishā, f. wish or inclination to come down or fall.

Pipatishu, us, us, u, being about to fall; (*us*), m. a bird.

पिड्व *pidva, as,* m., Ved. a species of animal.

पिधा *pi-dhā* = *api-dhā*, q. v.

Pi-dadhat, at, atī, at, covering, veiling, hiding.

Pi-dhātavya, as, ā, am, to be covered or hidden; to be stopped up, to be shut or closed.

Pi-dhāna, am, n. covering, stopping up, shutting; (*as* or *am*), m. or n. (?), a covering, cover, concealment; a lid, top, cover; a sheath; a wrapper, cloak; [cf. Cambro-Brit. *fedon,* 'a screen.'] — *Pidhāna-vat, ān, atī, at,* provided with a cover, covered with a lid.

Pidhānaka, as, m. a cover, lid; a sheath, scabbard [cf. *khaḍga-p*°].

Pi-dhāya, ind. having covered.

Pi-dhāyaka, as, ikā, am, covering, hiding, concealing. — *Pidhāyaka-tā,* f. the state or act of covering.

Pi-hita, as, ā, am, shut, covered, hidden, concealed; filled with; (*am*), n. a particular figure of speech, showing any person by insinuation that one knows his secrets.

पिनस *pinasa, as,* m. = *pīnasa,* q. v.

पिनह् *pi-nah* = *api-nah,* q. v.

Pi-naddha, as, ā, am, tied on, put on, fastened, bound; dressed, accoutred; wrapped, covered, concealed; pierced, penetrated.

Pinaddhaka, as, ikā, am, dressed, clothed, covered.

Pi-nahya, ind. having put on or dressed.

पिनाक *pināka, as, am,* m. n. (said to be fr. rt. 3. *pā*), a staff, stick; a bow; the club or bow of Rudra-Śiva; a trident or three-pronged spear; the trident of Śiva; a shower or fall of dust, falling dust; (*as*), m., N. of a man; (*ī*), f. a kind of stringed instrument, a sort of violin. — *Pināka-goptṛī, tā,* m. 'preserver of the Pināka,' an epithet of Śiva. — *Pināka-dhṛik* (see *dhṛik*), or *pināka-bhṛit, t,* m. 'bearer of the Pināka,' an epithet of Śiva. — *Pināka-pāṇi, is,* m. 'Pināka in hand,' an epithet of Śiva.

Pināki, is, is, i (occurring only in acc. sing.), substituted for *pinākin,* q. v.

Pinākin, ī, inī, i, armed with a Pināka; (*ī*), m. an epithet of Rudra-Śiva; N. of one of the eleven Rudras; (*inī*), f., N. of two rivers. — *Pinākinī-māhātmya, am,* n., N. of a part of the Brahmāṇḍa-Purāṇa.

पिन्यास *pinyāsa, am,* n. (said to be fr. rt. 2. *as* with *pi-ni*), Asa Fœtida; [cf. *pinyāka.*]

पिन्व् *pinv,* cl. 1. P. A. *pinvati, -te, pipinva, pipinve, pinvishyati, -te, pinvitum,* Ved. to cause to swell, to distend, to cause to overflow or run over, to cause to abound; to cause to abound in milk (Ṛig-veda I. 112, 3, where, according to Sāy., *pinvathaḥ* = *payasā pūritavantau*); to sprinkle, wet, moisten, water; to discharge, pour forth; to grant, bestow; (A.) to swell, to be distended, to overflow; [cf. rt. *pyai.*]

Pinva, as, ā, am, Ved. causing to swell or flow; [cf. *dānu-p*°.]

Pinvana, am, n., Ved. a particular vessel used in religious ceremonies.

Pinvantyapīyā, f., Ved., scil. *ṛić,* an epithet of the verse beginning *pinvanty apo* (Ṛig-veda I. 64, 6).

Pinvamāna, as, ā, am, Ved. being swollen, swelling, being full or filled.

पिपतिषत् *pipatishat, pipatishā, pipatishu.* See under *pitsat,* col. 1.

पिपविषु *pipavishu, us, us, u* (fr. Desid. of rt. 1. *pū*), wishing to purify.

पिपाठक *pipāṭhaka, as,* m., N. of a mountain.

पिपासत् *pipāsat, an, antī, at* (fr. Desid. of rt. 1. *pā*), thirsting, thirsty.

Pipāsā, f. thirst, desire to drink. — *Pipāsā-vat, ān, atī, at,* thirsting, thirsty.

Pipāsita, as, ā, am, wishing to drink, thirsty, athirst.

Pipāsin, ī, inī, i, wishing to drink, thirsty.

Pipāsu, us, us, u, thirsty, athirst.

पिपिली *pipili,* f. = *pipīlī,* an ant.

पिपिष्वत् *pipishvat, an, antī, at* (fr. a rt. *pi* for *pī*), Ved. (perhaps) swollen, overfull, superabundant; (according to Sāy.) favourable to the husbandman.

पिपीतक *pipītaka, as,* m., N. of a Brāhman who was the first to perform a particular ceremony in honour of Vishṇu on the twelfth day of the light half of the month Vaiśākha; (*ī*), f. the twelfth day of the light half of the month Vaiśākha (when giving away water is an act of merit, so called after the Brāhman Pipītaka).

पिपील *pipīla, as, ī,* m. f. (perhaps a reduplicated form fr. rt. *pīḍ*), an ant.

Pipīlaka, as, m. a large black ant; (*ikā*), f. the common small red ant; a female ant. — *Pipīlikā-parisarpaṇa, am,* n. the running about of ants.

Pipīlika, as, m. an ant; (*am*), n. a kind of gold supposed to be collected by ants. — *Pipīlika-madhya, as, ā, am,* 'thin in the middle like an ant,' N. of any metre the middle Pāda of which is shorter than the preceding and following. — *Pipīlika-madhyamā,* f., N. of a species of the Anushṭubh metre. — *Pipīlikā-madhya, as, ā, am,* a kind of fasting (beginning on the day of full moon with fifteen mouthfuls, decreasing by one daily until the day of new moon, and after that increasing by one daily until the next day of full moon).

पिपृच्छिषु *pipṛiććhishu, us, us, u* (fr. Desid. of rt. *praćh*), about to ask or inquire, wishing to ask.

पिप्पका *pippakā,* f., Ved. a species of bird; [cf. *pippika.*]

पिप्पटा *pippaṭā,* f. a kind of sweetmeat.

पिप्पल *pippala, as,* m. (said to be fr. rt. 3. *pā*), the holy fig-tree, Ficus Religiosa [cf. *aśvattha*]; a kind of bird; a nipple (so called from its similarity to a berry); the sleeve of a jacket or coat; N. of a son of Mitra and Revatī; (*ās*), m. pl., N. of a school of the Atharva-veda; (*ā*), f., N. of a river; (*ī*), f. a berry; long pepper, Piper Longum (both plant and berry; cf. *kapi-p°, jala-p°, toya-p*°); (*am*), n. a berry in general, the berry of the tree Ficus Religiosa; sensual enjoyment; water; the sleeve of a coat; [cf. Gr. πίπερι, πέπερι; Lat. *piper.*] — *Pippalāda* (°*la-ada*), *as,* m. 'eater of berries,' N. of an ancient teacher of the Atharva-veda; (*ās*), m. pl., N. of a school of the Atharva-veda (also *pippalādakās*). — *Pippalāda-tīrtha, am,* n., N. of a sacred bathing-place. — *Pippalāda-śruti, is,* f., N. of a work mentioned in the Parāśara-smṛiti. — *Pippalā-vatī,* f., N. of a river. — *Pippalī-mūla, am,* n. the root of long pepper. — *Pippalī-lavaṇa, e,* n. du. pepper and salt.

Pippalaka, am, n. a nipple; sewing thread.

Pippalāyana, as, m., N. of a man.

Pippali, is, f. long pepper; *Vasishṭhasya pippali,* N. of a Sāman. — *Pippali-śroṇi, is,* f., N. of a river.

Pippalikā, f. a species of plant (= *aśvatthī*).

पिप्पलु *pippalu, ūs,* m. or f. (?), N. of a man (or woman?).

पिप्पिका *pippikā,* f. the tartar of the teeth; [cf. *pițțaka.*]

पिप्पीक *pippīka, as,* m., Ved. a species of animal, probably a bird; [cf. *pippakā.*]

पिप्रीषा *piprīshā,* f. (fr. Desid. of rt. 1. *prī*), Ved. desire of pleasing or showing kindness.

Piprīshu, us, us, u, desirous of pleasing, wishing to give pleasure.

पिप्रु *pipru, us,* m. (fr. rt. *prī?*), Ved., N. of a demon (who was conquered and whose strongholds were destroyed by Indra).

पिप्लु *piplu, us,* m. (perhaps for *api-plu*; said to be fr. rt. *plush* with *api*), a freckle, mark, mole. — *Piplu-karṇa, as, ā, am,* having a mark on the ear. — *Piplu-praććhādana, as, ī, am,* covering or concealing a mole.

पिब *piba* or *piva, as, ā, am* (fr. rt. 1. *pā*),

drinking, who or what drinks; [cf. *tri-p°*.] — *Piba-vat, ān, atī, at*, Ved. containing a form of the verb *pibati*.

Pibat or *pivat, an, antī, at*, drinking, who or what drinks.

पिब्दमान *pibdamāna, as, ā, am* (perhaps fr. a reduplicated form of rt. 2. *pad*), Ved. becoming or being firm or solid, becoming or being hard or compact.

Pibdana, as, ā, am, Ved. firm, hard, solid, compact; (*am*), n. (according to Sāy.) a Rakshas.

पियारु *piyāru, us, us, u* (fr. the Sautra rt. 1. *piy*), Ved. censuring, blaming, deriding, mischievous (Sāy. = *hiṇsaka*).

पियाल *piyāla, as*, m. (= *priyāla*, q. v., but said to be fr. the Sautra rt. 1. *piy*), the tree Buchanania Latifolia (called in Hindī also Chironji, whence it has been named Chironjia Sapida; in Bengal it is commonly called Piya or Piyal); (*am*), n. the fruit of Buchanania Latifolia.

पिल् *pil*, cl. 10. P. *pelayati, -yitum*, to throw, cast; to send; to incite; [cf. rts. *pel, vil*.]

Pilu, us, or *piluka, as*, m. a species of tree (= *pīlu*; cf. *pailava*).

Piluni, f. a species of plant (= *mūrvā*; a wrong form for *pilu-parṇī*; cf. *pīlu-parṇī*).

पिलि *pili, is*, m., N. of a man.

पिलिन्दवत्स *pilinda-vatsa, as*, m., N. of a disciple of Śākya-muni.

पिलिप्पिल *pilippila, as, ā, am*, Ved. slippery.

पिल्ल *pilla, as, ā, am* (said to be a substitute for *klinna*), blear-eyed; (*as*), m. a bleared eye.

Pillakā, f. a female elephant, (the elephant's eye being usually moist.)

पिश् 1. *piś*, cl. 6. P. A. *piṇśati, -te, pipeśa, pipiśe, peśishyati, -te, apeśīt, peśitum*, Ved. to adorn, deck, decorate, embellish; to prepare, make ready (especially meat, by cutting it up and carving it); to shape, fashion, mould, form; to be decomposed, to be reduced to constituent parts; to be organized; to light, enlighten: Caus. *peśayati*, Aor. *apīpiśat*: Desid. *pipiśishati, pipeśishati*: Intens. *pepiśyate, pepeshṭi*, to be richly adorned.

2. *piś*, f. an ornament, decoration; (Sāy.) = *rūpaṃ hiraṇyādi*.

Piśa, as, m., Ved. (according to Sāy.) = *ruru*, a sort of deer (probably so called from its colour).

Piśanga, as, ī, am, reddish, reddish-brown, of a tawny or brown colour; (*as*), m. tawny colour; N. of a serpent-demon. — *Piśanga-tā*, f. or *piśanga-tva, am*, n. the being of a tawny colour, tawniness. — *Piśanga-bhrishṭi, is, is, i*, Ved. (perhaps) having red fangs; (Sāy.) = *ishad-rakta-varṇa*, being of a pale-red hue, tawny-coloured. — *Piśanga-rāti, is, is, i*, Ved. giving reddish (i. e. golden) gifts (said of Indra); (Sāy.) = *bahurūpa-dhanendra*, lord of manifold wealth. — *Piśanga-rūpa, as, ā, am*, Ved. being of a reddish or yellow appearance; (Sāy.) = *hiraṇya-rūpa*, golden-coloured. — *Piśanga-san-dṛiś, k, k, k*, Ved. (according to Mahī-dhara) being of a red or yellow colour; (according to Sāy.) = *nānā-rūpa*, of various kinds. — *Piśangāśva* (°*ga-aś*°), *as, ā, am*, Ved. having reddish or tawny horses (said of the Maruts).

Piśangaka, as, m., N. of an attendant of Vishṇu.

Piśangin, ī, inī, i, brown, tawny.

Piśangila, as, ā, am, Ved., N. of a colour (?); (according to Mahī-dhara) = *piśam* + *gila*.

Piśāća, as, m. (perhaps fr. *piśa* for *piśita*, 'flesh,' and rt. 1. *ańć*), N. of a class of demons (perhaps originally a personification of the ignis fatuus; in the Veda they are enumerated after gods, men, Manes, Asuras, and Rākshasas; in later times they are described as the children of Krodhā); a sprite, fiend, goblin, ogre, malevolent being (something between an infernal imp and a ghost, always described as fierce and malignant); N. of a Rakshas; (*ī*), f. a female imp, a she-demon [cf. *strī-p*°]; N. of a daughter of Daksha and mother of the Piśāćas; a species of Valeriana (= *gandha-māṇsī*). — *Piśāća-tā*, f. or *piśāća-tva, am*, n. the state or condition of a Piśāća. — *Piśāća-dru, us*, m. a species of tree, Trophis Aspera (the favourite haunt of the Piśāćas). — *Piśāća-bādhā*, f. demoniacal possession. — *Piśāća-bhāshā*, f. 'Piśāća language,' a gibberish or corruption of Sanskṛit used in plays. — *Piśāća-moćana, am*, n. 'release of the Piśāća,' N. of a place of pilgrimage. — *Piśāćamoćana-tīrtha, am*, n., N. of a place of pilgrimage. — *Piśāća-vṛiksha, as*, m. a species of tree, Trophis Aspera (= *śākhoṭa*). — *Piśāća-sań-ćāra, as*, m. demoniacal possession. — *Piśāća-sabha, am*, n. an assemblage of goblins or fiends; the place or hall of their assembly, pandemonium. — *Piśāćā-laya* (°*ća-āl*°), *as*, m. 'abode of Piśāćas,' N. of a particular luminous phenomenon, phosphorescence. — *Piśāći-karaṇa, am*, n. transforming into a Piśāća. — *Piśāćoraga-rākshasa* (°*ća-ur*°), *ās*, m. pl. Piśāćas, serpents, and Rākshasas.

Piśāćaka, as, m. a Piśāća; (*ikā*), f. = *piśāći* (at the end of comps., e. g. *gandha-p*°, *dhana-p*°); N. of a river; scil. *bhāshā*, the language of the Piśāćas. — *Piśāćaka-pura, am*, n., N. of a village.

Piśāćakin, ī, m. an epithet of Kuvera the god of wealth (the treasures of this deity being guarded by Piśāćas and other malignant beings).

Piśāći, is, m., Ved. a Piśāća.

Piśita, am, n. flesh which has been cut up or prepared, flesh, meat; a small piece; (*ā*), f. spikenard, Nardostachys Jatamansi (= *jaṭā-māṇsī*). — *Piśita-bhuj, k, k, k*, eating flesh; (*k*), m. one who eats flesh. — *Piśitāśa* (°*ta-āśa*), *as, ā, am*, eating flesh; (*as*), m. an epithet of flesh-eating demons, as Rākshasas or Piśāćas; a fiend; a cannibal. — *Piśitāśana* (°*ta-aś*°), *as, ī, am*, flesh-eating, meat-eating; (*as*), m. a demon, fiend, cannibal, Rakshas, Piśāća (described as a child of Ni-kashā); epithet of a wolf. — *Piśitāśin* (°*ta-āś*°), *ī, inī, i*, eating flesh or meat, carnivorous; (*ī*), m. a demon, goblin, cannibal; N. of an attendant of Śiva. — *Piśitepsu* (°*ta-īp*°), *us, us, u*, desirous of flesh, eager for or greedy after meat.

Piśī, f. spikenard, Nardostachys Jatamansi (= *piśitā*).

Piśuna, as, ā, am, informing against, betraying, treacherous; disparaging, calumniating, backbiting, calumnious, slanderous; cruel, wicked, malignant, mischievous, harsh, unkind; exciting hopes and disappointing them; vile, low, contemptible, infamous; stupid, a fool; making known, indicating, evincing, displaying, reminding, commemorating, memorable for (at the end of comps., e. g. *tulyānurāga-p*°, manifesting an equal attachment; *kshatra-pradhana-p*°, memorable for the conflict of Kshatriyas); (*as*), m. a betrayer, traitor, informer, spy, talebearer, backbiter, calumniator, slanderer; epithet of a goblin dangerous to pregnant women; cotton (which betrays by hanging to the clothes); an epithet of Nārada (the messenger and informant of the gods); a crow; N. of a Brāhman; N. of a minister of Dushyanta; (*ā*), f. a species of plant, Medicago Esculenta; (*am*), n. informing against, betraying, sycophancy; saffron (which betrays an unfaithful lover); [cf. Gr. πικ-ρό-ς, πευκεδανό-ς, πευκάλιμο-ς, ἐχε-πευκές: Lith. pik-ta-s, 'bad;' pýk-ti, 'to be angry;' peik-ti, 'to despise, to blame.'] — *Piśuna-tā*, f. slander, scandal, backbiting, betrayal, sycophancy. — *Piśuna-vaćana* or *piśuna-vākya, am*, n. evil speech, bad report, detraction, slander.

Piśunaya, Nom. P. *piśunayati, -yitum*, to betray, make known, indicate, make manifest.

पिशिक *piśika, ās*, m. pl., N. of a people in the South.

पिशील *piśīla* or *piśīlaka, am*, n., Ved. (a wooden) vessel or dish. — *Piśīla-vīṇā*, f. a kind of stringed instrument or guitar, the strings of which are stretched across a frame (= *śūrpa-vīṇā*).

पिशुन *piśuna*. See col. 2.

पिष् *pish*, cl. 7. P. (ep. also A.) *pinashṭi, pinshṭe* (Impv. 2nd sing. *pinḍhi*), *pipesha, pekshyati, apishat, peshṭum* (ep. Impf. *apinshat*, Pot. *pishet*), to grind, pound, crush; to bruise, hurt, injure, destroy; cl. 10. P. or Caus. *peshayati, -yitum*, Aor. *apīpishat*, to grind, pound; to injure; to give; to be strong; to dwell; cl. 1. 10. P. *peshati, peshayati*, to go, move; [cf. Gr. πτίσσ-ω for πίσσ-ω, πίτυρον, πτίσ-μα, πίσ-ο-ς, πίσ-ινο-ς, πισσο-; Lat. *pins-o, pis-o, pis-tor, pis-tillu-m, pistrīnum, pis-tura, pis-u-m, Piso, pī-lu-m, pī-la, pī-lu-s*; Lith. *pes-tà*, 'a mill.']

Pishṭa, as, ā, am, ground, pounded, crushed, bruised; rubbed together, squeezed, clasped (as the hands); kneaded; (*am*), n. anything ground, any finely ground substance, flour, meal, (*na pishṭam pinashṭi*, he does not grind flour, i. e. he does no useless work or vain repetition); lead; (*as*), m. pastry; N. of a man; (*ās*), m. pl., N. of his descendants. — *Pishṭa-paćana, am*, n. a pan for parching flower; a boiler, seether, sauce-pan. — *Pishṭa-paśu, us*, m. an effigy of a beast or sacrificial victim made with flour or dough. — *Pishṭa-pāka, as*, m. food prepared by baking flour. — *Pishṭapāka-bhṛit, t, t, t*, containing food prepared by baking flour; (*t*), m. a boiler. — *Pishṭa-pāćaka, am*, n. a boiler. — *Pishṭa-pinḍa, as*, m. a cake of meal. — *Pishṭa-pūra, as*, m. meal made up into a sort of cake with clarified butter; [cf. *ghṛita-pūra*.] — *Pishṭa-pesha, as*, m. or *pishṭa-peshaṇa, am*, n. 'grinding flour,' useless labour, vain repetition. — *Pishṭa-maya, as, ī, am*, made of meal or flour, mixed with flour; *jalam pishṭa-mayam*, water sprinkled with meal. — *Pishṭa-meha, as*, m. flour-like diabetes. — *Pishṭamehin, ī, inī, i*, suffering from flour-like diabetes. — *Pishṭa-rasa, as*, m. water mixed with flour. — *Pishṭa-varti*, a small cake made of the meal of barley, rice, or pulse. — *Pishṭa-saurabha, am*, n. (pulverized) sandal-wood. — *Pishṭāda* (°*ṭa-ada*), *as, ā, am*, feeding on meal. — *Pishṭodaka* (°*ṭa-ud*°), *am*, n. water mixed with flour.

Pishṭaka, as, m. a cake made of the flour or meal of any grain, any baked cake, bread; a disease of the eyes, opacity of the cornea; (*ikā*), f. a kind of grits, the meal of pulse steeped in water and peeled and ground; (*am*), n. pounded sesamum seeds, oil-cake.

Pishṭāta, as, m. perfumed powder (for scenting rooms, garments, &c.); scented dust which the Hindūs sprinkle over each other at the Holi or spring festival.

Pishṭika, am, n. a cake made of rice flour.

Pishṭoḍi, f. a species of shrub (= *śvetāmli*).

पिष्टप *pishṭapa, as, am*, m. n. (said to be fr. *piś*, substituted for rt. *viś*), a world, a division of the universe; [cf. *vishṭapa*.]

पिस् *pis*, cl. 4. P. *pisyati, pesitum*, Ved. to go; (perhaps) to extend; cl. 1. P. *pesati, pesitum*, to go, move; cl. 10. P. *pesayati, -yitum*, to go; to hurt, injure; to be strong; to give; to take; to dwell; [cf. rts. *pes, vis, ves, biś, beś*.]

पिस्पृक्षु *pispṛikshu, us, us, u* (fr. Desid. of rt. *spṛiś*), being about to touch; (with *jalam*) being about to enter the water, being about to perform ablutions.

पिहित *pi-hita*. See p. 575, col. 2.

पी 1. *pī* (probably originally Pass. of rt. 1. *pā*, q. v.), cl. 4. A. *pīyate, pipye, peshyati, apeshṭa, petum*, to drink.

पी 2. *pī, īs, īs, i* (fr. rt. *pyai*, q. v.; at the end of a comp.) becoming fat.

पीच *pīća, am,* n. the lower jaw, the chin.

पीटिका *pīṭikā,* a various reading for *piṭhikā,* q. v.

पीठ *pīṭha, am,* n. (thought by some to be a Prākṛit form fr. *pi-sada = pi-shada = pi-shḍa* or connected with rt. *piṭh*), a stool, seat, chair, bench; a religious student's seat made properly of Kuśa grass; the seat of a deity, an altar (according to some native authorities in this and the preceding senses also *as, ī,* m. f.); a basis, basement, pedestal; an epithet of various temples (erected on the fifty-one spots on which, according to tradition, the various members of Pārvatī fell after she had been cut to pieces by the discus of Vishṇu); a kind of ornament; a particular posture in sitting; (in geometry) the complement of a segment; N. of an Asura the minister of Kaṃsa. — *Pīṭha-keli, is,* m. a particular dramatic character, a male confidant, a parasite. — *Pīṭha-ga, as, ā, am,* moving about in a wheel-chair, lame. — *Pīṭha-garbha* or *pīṭha-vivara, as,* m. the cavity in the pedestal of an idol. — *Pīṭha-ćakra, as* or *am,* m. or n. (?), Ved. a chariot with a seat. — *Pīṭha-nāyikā,* f. a girl of fourteen (before menstruation) who impersonates Durgā at the festival of that goddess. — *Pīṭha-nyāsa, as,* m. epithet of a particular mystical ceremony. — *Pīṭha-bhū, ūs,* f. a basis, basement. — *Pīṭha-marda, as, ā, am,* 'rubbing the seat,' (perhaps) riding on horseback, a rider; exceedingly impudent; (*as*), m. the companion of a hero in great undertakings; a companion, parasite; a dancing-master who teaches courtezans. — *Pīṭha-sarpa, as, ā, am,* or *pīṭha-sarpin, ī, iṇī, i,* moving about on a wheel-chair, lame, crippled, a cripple. — *Pīṭha-sthāna, am,* n. a place where one of the limbs of Pārvatī is supposed to have fallen and therefore consecrated to her worship; [cf. *pīṭha.*]

Pīṭhaka, as, am, m. n. a seat, chair, bench; a saddle?; (*ikā*), f. a bench; a base, pedestal; a section, chapter (sometimes wrongly spelt *pīṭikā*).

पीड् *pīḍ* (perhaps connected with rt. *pish*), cl. 1. A. *pīḍate, pīḍitum,* Ved. to be squeezed or pressed out (as Soma): Caus. or cl. 10. P. (ep. also A.) *pīḍayati (-te), -yitum,* to squeeze, pinch, press, oppress, compress, suppress (e. g. *kālaṃ kālena pīḍayan,* Manu I. 51, pressing time against time, or suppressing one period by means of another, according to Kullūka = *sṛishṭi-kālam pralaya-kālena nāśayan*); to overpower; to hurt, harm, injure, pain, vex, harass, annoy, torment; to break, violate (an oath); to beleaguer (a city); to neglect, cause suffering by neglect; to remove; to cover; (in augury) to cover with anything inauspicious; (in astrology) to eclipse; to oppose, resist; to stir, agitate.

Pīḍa, as, am, m. n., in *tila-p°, tṛiṇa-p°,* q. v. — *Pīḍa-yantra-gṛiha, as,* m. a workhouse for criminals, house of correction.

Pīḍaka, as, m. an oppressor; [cf. *tālu-p°.*]

Pīḍana, as, ā, am, molesting, paining, disagreeable; (*am*), n. the act of pressing, squeezing, rubbing; an instrument for pressing, press; oppressing, inflicting pain, paining, distressing; laying a country waste, devastation; (in astrology) the oppression or suppression of a planet &c., i. e. eclipse [cf. *graha-p°*]; suppressing sounds, a fault in the pronunciation of vowels.

Pīḍanīya or *pīḍayitavya, as, ā, am,* to be oppressed or molested, to be pained or harassed; used for pressing, serving for a press.

Pīḍayat, an, antī, at, squeezing, pressing; oppressing, suppressing, harassing, paining; breaking, violating.

Pīḍā, f. pain, suffering, anguish, annoyance; damage, injury, wrong; infraction, violation [cf. *dharma-p°*]; devastation, laying waste; restriction, limitation; the 'pain or calamity' of a planet, eclipse, occultation [cf. *graha-p°*]; compassion, pity, charity; a chaplet, garland for the head; the Saral tree, Pinus Longifolia; a basket (= *piṭaka, peṭā, peḍā*). — *Pīḍā-kara, as, ī, am,* pain-causing, giving pain, afflicting, tormenting. — *Pīḍā-karaṇa, am,* n. the causing of pain, torturing, tormenting. — *Pīḍā-bhāj, k, k, k,* (according to Malli-nātha) = *vimarda-bhāj = bhaṅga-vat.* — *Pīḍā-sthāna, am,* n., Ved. (in astrology) an unlucky position, inauspicious distance (of a planet).

Pīḍ°ya, Nom. A. *pīḍāyate, -yitum,* to feel pain, experience a sense of uneasiness.

Pīḍita, as, ā, am, squeezed, pressed; rubbed, chafed; griped, wrung; oppressed, harassed, distressed, pained, afflicted, suffering pain or distress, injured, impaired; violated, transgressed; destroyed, laid waste, devastated; eclipsed; bound, tied; (*am*), n. injuring, harming, harassing; a kind of coitus; (*am*), ind. closely. — *Pīḍita-tā,* f. or *pīḍita-tva, am,* n. the being squeezed or pressed; the being afflicted or distressed.

Pīḍyamāna, as, ā, am, being squeezed or pressed; being pained or afflicted, suffering.

पीत 1. *pīta, as, ā, am* (fr. rt. 1. *pā*), drunk, quaffed; drunk in, imbibed; soaked, steeped, saturated, filled with; (*am*), n. drinking. — *Pīta-taila, as, ā, am,* one who has drunk oil, filled with oil, = *taila-pīta;* (*ā*), f. a species of creeper; a kind of heart-pea, Cardiospermum Halicacabum (= *jyotish-matī,* = *mahā-jyotishmatī*). — *Pīta-dugdhā,* f. a cow whose milk has been pledged (lit. already drunk); a cow tied up to be milked [cf. *dhenushyā*]; any milch cow. — *Pīta-nidra, as, ā, am,* immersed in slumber. — *Pīta-pratibaddha-vatsa, ā,* f. (a cow) whose calf has drunk milk and been tied up. — *Pīta-madya, as, ā, am,* one who has drunk wine or any other intoxicating liquor. — *Pīta-rasa, as, ā, am,* whose juice is drunk or quaffed. — *Pīta-vat, ān, atī, at,* having drunk or quaffed; containing the verb 1. *pā* (Ved.). — *Pīta-soma, as,* m. a Brāhman by whom the juice of the acid Asclepias is drunk at a ceremony. — *Pītābdhi* (°*ta-ab*°), *is,* m. an epithet of the Muni Agastya ('by whom the ocean was drunk,' this saint having on one occasion swallowed up the sea).

1. *pīti, is,* f. (for 2. and 3. see p. 578, col. 1), drinking, a draught; a tavern, dram-shop.

1. *pītin, ī, inī, i,* (at the end of comps.) drinking, having drunk. (For 2. *pītin* see p. 578, col. 1.)

Pītvā, ind. having drunk or quaffed. — *Pītvā-sthiraka, as, ā, am,* somewhat refreshed by a draught (Gaṇa to Pāṇ. II. 1, 72).

1. *pītha, as,* m. (for 2. and 3. see p. 578, col. 1), a drink, draught [cf. *go-p°*]; (*am*), n. water; melted butter.

Pīthin, ī, inī, i, (at the end of a comp.) drinking; *kośa-p°,* squandering away the treasury.

Pīyamāna, as, ā, am, being drunk or quaffed, being drunk or sucked in.

पीत 2. *pīta, as, ā, am* (probably connected with rt. *pyai,* the colour of butter and oil being yellowish), of a yellow colour, yellow (the colour of the Vaiśyas, white being that of the Brāhmans, red that of the Kshatriyas, and black that of the Śūdras); (*as*), m. yellow colour; a yellow gem, topaz; a yellow pigment prepared from the urine of kine; N. of several plants, Alangium Hexapetalum (= *aṅkoṭha*); safflower, Carthamus Tinctorius; Trophis Aspera (= *śākhoṭa*); (*ā*), f., N. of various plants, turmeric (= *haridrā*); a medical plant, Betula, commonly called Atais; a kind of yellow pigment (= *go-roćanā*); a mystical designation of the letter *sha;* (*am*), n. gold; yellow orpiment. — *Pīta-kadalī,* f. a species of banana (= *svarṇa-kadalī*). — *Pīta-kanda, am,* n. the carrot, Daucus Carota. — *Pīta-karavīraka, as,* m. oleander with yellow flowers. — *Pīta-kāvera, am,* n. saffron; bell-metal. — *Pīta-kāshṭha, am,* n. yellow sanders. — *Pīta-kīlā,* f. a species of plant (= *ā-vartakī*). — *Pīta-kauśeya-vāsas, ās, ās, as,* dressed in yellow silk; (*as*), m. an epithet of Kṛishṇa. — *Pīta-gandha, am,* n. yellow sandal. — *Pīta-ghoshā,* f. yellow Ghoshā, a species of creeper with yellow flowers. — *Pīta-ćandana, am,* n. a yellow fragrant wood considered as a yellow species of sandal-wood; saffron; turmeric. — *Pīta-ćampaka, as,* m. a lamp ('yellow as the Ćampa'). — *Pīta-taṇḍulā,* f. millet, Panicum Italicum; a species of Solanum. — *Pīta-tā,* f. or *pīta-tva, am,* n. yellowness, yellow (the colour). — *Pīta-tuṇḍa, as,* m. 'yellow-beak,' N. of the Sylvia Sutoria (the whole bird being of a light yellow colour). — *Pīta-dāru, us,* m. a species of pine, Pinus Deodora (= *deva-dāru*); Pinus Longifolia; Curcuma Aromatica or Curcuma Xanthorrhiza (= *haridru*). — *Pīta-dru, us,* m. a species of pine, Pinus Longifolia; Curcuma Aromatica or C. Xanthorrhiza. — *Pīta-nīla, as, ā, am,* 'yellow-blue,' green. — *Pīta-parṇī,* f. 'yellow-leaved,' a plant commonly called Bićhati; a N. of the nettle or a plant of the same class, Tragia Involucrata. — *Pīta-pādā,* f. 'yellow-footed,' a small bird, the Maina (Turdus Salica). — *Pīta-pushpa, as,* m., N. of several plants (= *karṇikāra*), Pterospermum Acerifolium, or a species of Karṇikāra; Michelia Champaka; a species of Tabernæmontana Coronaria; a species of Barleria with yellow flowers; (*ā*), f. a species of Coloquintida (= *indra-vāruṇī,* = *jhiñjharishṭā*), Cajanus Indicus (= *āḍhakī*); a species of yellow Barleria; (*ī*), f. Andropogon Acicularis (= *śaṅkha-pushpī, saha-devī, mahā-koshātakī,* and *trapushī*); a species of Barleria with yellow flowers; (*am*), n. Tabernæmontana Coronaria (= *āhulya*). — *Pīta-prasava, as,* m. = *pīta-karavīraka,* q. v. — *Pīta-phala, as,* m. a tree, Trophis Aspera; Averrhoa Carambola. — *Pītaphalaka, as,* m. Trophis Aspera. — *Pīta-bālukā,* f. turmeric; yellow sand. — *Pīta-bījā,* f. Trigonella Fœnum Græcum (= *methikā*). — *Pīta-bhṛiṅga-rāja, as,* m. a species of Verbesina with yellow flowers. — *Pīta-maṇi, is,* m. a yellow gem, a topaz. — *Pīta-mastaka, as,* m. 'yellow-head,' a small bird, Loxia Philippensis (= *kali-kāra;* cf. *pīta-muṇḍa*). — *Pīta-mākshika, am,* n. = *mākshika,* a species of mineral substance. — *Pīta-māñjishṭha, as, ā, am,* yellowish-red. — *Pīta-muṇḍa, as,* m. 'yellow-head,' a bird (= *kali-kāra*), Loxia Philippensis; a kind of gallinule. — *Pīta-mudga, as,* m. a species of bean, a yellow variety of the Phaseolus Mungo. — *Pīta-mūlaka, am,* n. the carrot, Daucus Carota. — *Pīta-yūthī,* f. yellow jasmine. — *Pīta-rakta, as, ā, am,* yellowish-red, orange; (*am*), n. (or according to some *as,* m.), a yellow-coloured gem, perhaps the topaz. — *Pīta-rāga, as, ā, am,* of a yellow colour; (*am*), n. (or according to some *as,* m.), a yellow colour; the fibres of the lotus; wax. — *Pīta-rohiṇī,* f. the plant Gmelina Arborea. — *Pīta-loha, as,* m. yellow metal, queen's metal or a mixed metal resembling gold. — *Pīta-vāsas, ās, as,* dressed in yellow; (*ās*), m. an epithet of Kṛishṇa or Vishṇu. — *Pīta-vṛiksha, as,* m. a species of Syonāka and Pinus Longifolia. — *Pīta-śāla* or *pīta-sāla* or *pīta-sālaka, as,* m. the plant Terminalia Tomentosa. — *Pīta-sāra, as,* m. a yellow gem, a topaz; the sandal tree; the tree Alangium Hexapetalum; Citrus Medica; East-Indian incense, = *turushka;* (*am*), n. a yellow sandal-wood. — *Pīta-sāraka, as,* m. Alangium Hexapetalum; Azadirachta Indica. — *Pīta-sāri, i,* n. antimony. — *Pīta-skandha, as,* m. 'fat-shouldered,' a hog. — *Pīta-sphaṭika, as,* m. 'yellow crystal,' the topaz. — *Pīta-harita, as, ā, am,* yellowish-green. — *Pītāṅga* (°*ta-aṅ*°), *as,* m. a species of Syonāka. — *Pītāmbara* (°*ta-am*°), *as, ā, am,* dressed in yellow clothes, clad in yellow; (*as*), m. a N. of Kṛishṇa or Vishṇu; a dancer or actor; a religious mendicant wearing yellow garments; N. of a man. — *Pītāruṇa* (°*ta-ar*°), *as, ā, am,* yellowish-red; (*as*), m. an epithet of the middle of day-break; [cf. *tāmrāruṇa, nīlāruṇa.*] — *Pītāśman* (°*ta-aś*°), *ā,* m. 'yellow-stone,' a topaz or any yellow gem.

Pītaka, as, ikā, am, of a yellow colour, yellow; (*as*), m. a species of gentian, Gentiana Cherayta; the Tūn tree, Cedrela Toona; (*ikā*), f. saffron; turmeric; yellow jasmine; (*am*), n. yellow orpiment; brass; honey; saffron; yellow sandal; aloe wood, Amyris

Agallocha; a species of Syonāka; = *pita-śāla.* — *Pītaka-druma, as,* m. Curcuma Xanthorrhiza (= *hari-dru*).

Pītana, as, m. the hog-plum, Spondias Mangifera; a tree, Pentaptera Tomentosa; the waved-leaf fig-tree, Ficus Infectoria; (*am*), n. yellow orpiment; saffron; a species of pine (= *deva-dāru*).

Pītanaka, as, m. the hog-plum, Spondias Mangifera.

Pītala, as, ā, am, of a yellow colour; (*as*), m. yellow colour; (*am*), n. brass.

Pītalaka, am, n. brass.

पीति 2. *pīti, is,* f. (fr. rt. 3. *pā;* for 1. see p. 577, col. 2), Ved. protection; [cf. *nṛi-p°*.]

2. *pītha, as,* m. protection; [cf. *go-p°*.]

Pīthya, am, n. protection; [cf. *go-p°*.]

पीति 3. *pīti, is,* m. a horse.

2. *pītin, ī,* m. a horse. (For 1. *pītin* see p. 577, col. 2.)

Pīthi, is, m. a horse.

पीतु *pītu, us,* m. (said to be fr. rt. 1. *pā,* but perhaps fr. rt. *piv*), the sun; fire; the chief elephant of a herd. — *Pītu-dāru, us,* m. = *deva-dāru,* q. v.; (according to others) = *khadira,* a tree related to the Udumbara; (*am*), n. the resin of this tree; [cf. *pūtu-dāru;* Gr. πί-τυ-ς, πίσσα for πι-κ-ια; Lat. *pi-nu-s, pix;* Lith. *pìki-s,* 'pitch.']

3. *pītha, as,* m. the sun; fire; time. (For 1. and 2. *pītha* see p. 577, col. 2, and above.)

पीत्वा *pītvā.* See under 1. *pīta,* p. 577.

पीथि *pīthi, is,* m. See under 3. *pīti* above.

पीथे *pīthe,* m., N. of a chief builder (in an inscription).

पीथ्य *pīthya.* See under 2. *pīti* above.

पीन *pīna, as, ā, am* (fr. rt. *pyai*), fat, fleshy, brawny, muscular; swelling, swollen, large, corpulent, thick, plump; full, round; profuse (e. g. *pīnaḥ svedaḥ,* profuse perspiration); [cf. *pīvara;* Gr. πιαρός, πίας, πίων, πιμελή; Lat. *pinguis;* Iceland. *feit-r,* 'fat;' Angl. Sax. *fætt;* Old Germ. *feizt* = Mod. Germ. *feist, fett.*] — *Pīna-tarala, as, ā, am,* having a large central gem. — *Pīna-tā,* f. fatness, corpulency (opposed to *kṛiśa-tā*). — *Pīna-nitambā,* f. 'having full hips,' N. of a metre, four times ⏑⏑⏑⏑, ⏑ ⏑ ⏑ ⏑ ⏑, ⏑ ⏑ ⏑ ⏑ ⏑ ⏑ ⏑. — *Pīna-vakshas, ās, ās, as,* large-chested, full-breasted, having a large or full breast. — *Pīna-śroṇīpayodharā,* f. having swelling hips and breasts. — *Pīnottuṅga-stanī* (°*na-ut*°), f. (a woman) having a large and prominent breast. — *Pīnodhnī* (°*na-ūdh*°), f. a cow with full or swelling udders (also *pīnodhas, ās,* f.; cf. *ūdhas, ghaṭodhnī*).

Pīpivas, ān, pipyushī, at, Ved. swelling, swollen, distended, overflowing, dropping (Sāy. = *pra-vṛiddha, pīna, vardhayat, ā-pyāyitṛi*).

Pīpyānā, f., Ved. having a full or swelling breast (Sāy. = *putram stanam pāyayantī*).

1. *pīyūsha, as, am,* m. n. (said to be fr. the Sautra rt. 1. *pīy*), the first milk given by a cow after calving, biestings; the milk of a cow during the first seven days after calving; any thick fluid, cream, juice (Sāy. = *rasa-bhūtam payaḥ, abhinavam payaḥ*); the drink of immortality produced at the churning of the ocean of milk, the food of the gods, ambrosia, nectar; milk; [cf. *peyūsha.*] — *Pīyūsha-mahas, ās,* or *pīyūsha-ruci, is,* m. 'bright with nectar,' the moon (whose rays are said to be filled with nectar). — *Pīyūsha-varṇa, as, ā, am,* milk-white, white as milk. — *Pīyūsha-varsha, as, am,* m. n. a shower of nectar or ambrosia. — *Pīyūshavarshāya,* Nom. A. *pīyūshavarshāyate, -yitum,* to become or turn into a shower of nectar.

2. *pīyūsha,* Nom. P. *pīyūshati, pīyūshitum,* to become or turn into nectar.

Pīva, as, ā, am, (according to Sāy.) = *ā-pyāyita,* fat.

Pīvat, an, antī, at, fat; (probably the original form of *pīvan* below.)

Pīvan, ā, arī, a, swelling, full, fat, large; stout, strong, robust; (*ā*), m. wind; (*arī*), f. Asparagus Racemosus, Desmodium Gangeticum (= *śāla-parṇī*); N. of a spiritual daughter of the Barhi-shad Pitṛis; of the wife of Veda-śiras; of a princess of Vi-darbha.

Pīvara, as, ā or *ī, am* (said to be fr. rt. 1. *pā*), fat, stout, large, fleshy, corpulent, plump, thick, dense; (*as*), m. a tortoise; N. of one of the Saptarshis under Manu Tāmasa; (*ā*), f. Physalis Flexuosa, Asparagus Racemosus; N. of a daughter of the Gandharva Huhu; (*ī*), f. a young woman; a cow; [cf. Gr. πιαρό-ς, πιερό-ς, πιαλέο-ς, πίειρα.] — *Pīvara-tva, am,* n. fatness, thickness, largeness, heaviness, density. — *Pīvara-stanī,* f. a woman with large breasts; a cow with a large udder. — *Pīvarī-kṛi,* cl. 8. P. A. *-karoti, -kurute, -kartum,* to fatten, make fat. — *Pīvarī-kṛita, as, ā, am,* fattened.

Pīvas, ān, asī, as (a kindred form to *pīvan*), fat, stout; (*as*), n., Ved. fat; [cf. Zend *pīvanh,* 'fat;' Gr. πῖαρ.] — *Pīva-sphāka, as, ā, am* (for *pīvas-sphāka*), Ved. swelling with fat. — *Pīvas-vat, ān, atī, at,* Ved. abounding with, swollen. — *Pīvo-anna, as, ā, am,* Ved. having rich or abundant food. — *Pīvo-aśva, as, ā, am,* Ved. having fat horses. — *Pīvopavasana* (°*va-up*°), *as, ā, am,* Ved. covered with fat; (according to Mahī-dhara) near to fat or fleshy parts of the body.

Pīvasa, as, ā, am, Ved. abounding with fat, fat, abundant; swelling, swollen, inflated; (Sāy.) = *pīna,* robust; = *a-ććhinna,* untorn.

Pīvishṭha, as, ā, am, extremely fat.

पीनस *pīnasa, as,* m. (probably *api* + *nas* = *nāsā;* by some connected with *pīna*), cough, catarrh; cold affecting the nose, inflammation of the schneiderian membrane [cf. *apī-nasa*]; (*ā*), f. the plant Cucumis Utilissimus (= *karkaṭī*).

Pīnasin, ī, inī, i, having a cold.

पीपरि *pīpari, is,* m. a species of Plaksha of low growth.

पीय् 1. *pīy* (a Sautra rt.), to gladden.

पीय् 2. *pīy,* cl. 1. P. *pīyati,* &c., Ved. to blame, abuse, treat disrespectfully or with contempt; to give pleasure.

Pīyaka, as, m., Ved. 'an abuser,' (probably) N. of a class of demons.

Pīyatnu, us, us, u, Ved. scornful.

Pīyu, us, us, u (said to be fr. rt. 1. *pā*), Ved. scornful, injurious (as an Asura); (*us*), m. an owl; a crow; time; fire; the sun (?); gold.

पीयमान *pīyamāna.* See under 1. *pīta.*

पीयूक्षा *pīyūkshā,* f. a species of plant.

पीयूष 1. 2. *pīyūsha.* See under *pīna,* col. 1.

पील् *pīl,* cl. 1. P. *pīlati, pīlitum,* to check, impede, obstruct; to stop, to cease to be or do; to become stupid.

Pīlaka, as, m. the large black ant; [cf. *pipīla* and *pīluka.*]

Pīlu, us, m. a species of tree, Careya Arborea, (according to others) Salvadora Persica; a flower; the blossoms of the Saccharum Sara; the metacarpus, the central part of the hand; a group of palm trees; the stem of the palm; an arrow; an atom; a worm, an insect; an elephant (Arabic فيل; Persian پيل); (*u*), n. the fruit of the Pīlu tree. — *Pīlu-kuṇa, as,* m. the season of the ripening of the Pīlu fruit. — *Pīlu-pattra, as,* m. the plant Sanseviera Zeylanica (= *mūrvā*). — *Pīlu-parṇī,* f. the plant Sanseviera Zeylanica; Momordica Monadelpha; a kind of drug. — *Pīlu-mat, atī,* f., with *dyaus,* the central or middle region of the sky between Udan-vatī and Pra-dyaus. — *Pīlu-vaha, as* or *am,* m. or n. (?), N. of a district. — *Pīlu-sāra, as,* m., N. of a mountain.

Pīluka, as, m., N. of a tree, Careya Arborea or Salvadora Persica or any other exotic or unknown tree [cf. *kāka-p°, kāla-p°*]; an ant.

Pīlunī, f. the plant Sanseviera Zeylanica (= *mūrvā*).

पीला *pīlā,* f., Ved. epithet of a particular scent; N. of a woman.

पीव *pīv,* cl. 1. P. *pīvati, pīvitum,* to be fat or corpulent, to be thick.

पीव *pīva, pīvan, pīvara, pīvas, pīvasa, pīvishṭha.* See col. 2.

पीवा *pīvā,* f. (said to be fr. rt. 1. *pā*), water.

पुंस् 1. *puṇs* (perhaps a Nom. fr. 2. *puṇs* below), cl. 10. P. *puṇsayati, -yitum,* to crush, grind; to pain, punish.

पुंस् 2. *puṇs, pumān,* m. (voc. *puman,* the strong cases being fr. *pumāṇs,* the middle fr. *pum,* and the weak fr. *puṇs,* but loc. pl. *puṇsu* not *puṇsu* by Pāṇ. VIII. 2, 65; said to be fr. rt. 3. *pā*), a male, male being, man [cf. *na-p°*]; a human being; a servant, attendant; the soul, spirit (= *purusha; paraḥ pumān,* the Supreme Spirit, soul of the universe, Vishṇu); (in grammar) a word in the masculine gender; [cf. *s-tri-pum-napuṇsaka;* Lat. *mas, mar-is* for *mas-is, masculus,* the syllable *pu* being rejected in these words but appearing in *pu-sus, pu-sa, pu-bes* perhaps for *pu-mes.*] — *Pum-yug, k,* or *pum-yoga, as,* m. connection with a man; cohabitation with men. — *Pum-ratna, am,* n. 'a jewel of a man,' an excellent man. — *Pum-rāśi, is,* m. a male sign of the zodiac, an epithet of Aries and the signs following. — *Pum-rūpa, am,* n. the form or shape of a man; *pum-rūpam kṛi,* to assume the form of a man. — *Pum-liṅga, am,* n. the characteristic sign of a man, virility, manhood, the male organ; (in grammar) the masculine gender; (*as, ā, am*), having the characteristics of a man; masculine. — *Pumliṅga-tā,* f. masculineness, the being of the masculine gender. — *Pumliṅga-saṅgraha, as,* m., N. of a part of the Nāma-liṅgānuśāsana by Amara-siṇha. — *Pum-vat,* ind. like a man, as a man, as with a man; like the masculine gender, in the masculine form or gender. — *Pum-vatsa, as,* m. a bull-calf; (*as, ā, am*), having bull-calves, surrounded by bull-calves. — *Pumvad-vidhāna, am,* n. ceremonies as on the birth of a male. — *Pum-vṛisha, as,* m. the musk rat. — *Pum-veśa, as, ā, am,* wearing male attire, dressed like a man. — *Puṇś-ćalī,* f. 'running after men,' a frequenter of men, harlot, an unchaste woman; N. of an Apsaras. — *Puṇśćalīya, as,* m. the son of a harlot. — *Puṇś-ćalū, ūs,* f., Ved. a harlot; (*us*), m. a whoremonger. — *Puṇś-ćihna, am,* n. the characteristic of a male, membrum virile. — *Puṇsa-vat, ān, atī, at* (*puṇsa* substituted for *puṇs*), Ved. having a son. — *Puṃ-sarana, as, ā, am,* bringing forth a male, causing the birth of a male child; (*am*), n. (with or without *vrata*) the first of the essential ceremonies of Hindū initiation, a religious and domestic festival held on the mother's perceiving the first signs of a living conception; a fetus; milk. — *Puṇsānuja* (°*sā-an*°), *as, ā, am,* (perhaps) having an elder brother. — *Pum-suvana, am,* n., Ved. bringing forth a male child. — *Puṇs-kaṭī,* f. a man's hip. — *Puṇs-kāmā,* f. 'desirous of man,' a woman wishing for a lover or husband. — *Puṇs-kokila, as,* m. the male of the Indian cuckoo. — *Puṇskokila-tva, am,* n. the being a male cuckoo, the state or condition of a male cuckoo. — *Puṇs-tva, am,* n. the being a male, the state of a male, masculineness, manhood, virility; semen virile; (in grammar) the masculine gender. — *Puṇs-putra, as,* m. a male child, boy. — *Puṇs-prajanana, am,* n. the male organ of generation. — *Puṇs-pravāda, as,* m. (in Vedic grammar) a masculine base. — *Puṇs-vat, ān, atī, at,* containing the word *puṇs* or the masculine gender. — *Puṅ-khe'ṭa, as,* m. a male planet. — *Puṅ-gava, as,* m. a bull; a kind of drug commonly called Māshāṇī; (at the end of a comp.) a hero or eminent person, chief, best, most excellent [cf. *kuru-p°, gaja-p°, nara-p°.*] — *Puṅgava-ketu, us, us, u,* characterized or symbolized by a bull; (*us*), m. an epithet of Śiva. — *Puṅ-guṇa-jantu-jīva, as,* m. the living or animal soul combined with the qualities of man. — *Puṅ-janma-kara, as* or *am,* m. or n. (?), 'effecting the birth of males,' a constellation under which male children are born. — *Puṅ-janma-da, as* or *am,* m. or n. (?), 'granting the birth of males,' a constellation under which male children are born. — *Puṅ-janman, a,* n. the birth of a male child. — *Puṅjanma-yoga, as,* m. 'star of the birth of males,' a constellation under which male children are born. — *Pun-dāsa, as,* m. a male slave. — *Pun-dhvaja, as,* m. 'having the mark of a male,' the male of any species of animal. — *Pun-nakshatra, am,* n. a Nakshatra regarded as a male, male asterism; an asterism under which males are procreated. — *Pun-nāga, as,* m. 'an elephant among men,' a distinguished man; a white elephant; N. of a tree, Rottleria Tinctoria (from the blossoms of which a yellowish dye is prepared); a white lotus; a nutmeg. — *Pun-nāṭa* or *pun-nāḍa, as,* m. the plant Cassia Tora (= *ćakra-marda*). — *Pun-nāma-dheya, as,* m. 'that which is called man,' one of the male sex, a male. — 1. *pun-nāman, ā, mnī, a* (for 2. see under *put*), having a masculine name; (*ā*), m. the tree Rottleria Tinctoria. — *Pum-anujā,* f. (probably) 'born after a male child,' having an elder brother; born after or like a man. — *Pum-apatya, am,* n. male offspring. — *Pum-artha, as,* m. the aim of man. — *Pum-ākhyā,* f. a name for male beings, a designation of a male being. — *Pum-āćāra, as,* m. the custom or usage of men. — *Pum-bhūman, ā,* m. a word of the masculine gender in the plural number.

Puṇsa (at the end of a comp.) = 2. *puṇs;* [cf. *na-p°, mahā-p°, strī-p°.*]

Puṇsaka in *na-puṇsaka,* q. v.

Puṇska (at the end of an adj. comp.) = 2. *puṇs,* see Gaṇa to Pāṇ. V. 4, 151; [cf. *ukta-p°, bhūshita-p°.*]

पुंस्ति *puṇsti,* N. of a Sāman.

पुक्कश *pukkaśa* or *pukkasa, as,* m. epithet of a degraded mixed caste (erroneously identified by lexicographers with the Ćaṇḍālas), the offspring of a Ni-shāda by a Śūdrā female, a man of an impure or degraded tribe or occupation; (*ī*), f. a woman of the Pukkaśa caste; a bud, blossom; the indigo plant; (*as, ī, am*), low, vile.

Pukkaśaka, as, m. a man of the Pukkaśa caste; (*as, ā, am*), low, vile.

पुङ्ख *puṅkha, as,* m. the feathered part of an arrow, the lower part of an arrow which comes in contact with the bow-string and contains the feathers and shaft; a hawk, falcon (= *maṅgalāćāra,* q. v.).

Puṅkhita, as, ā, am, furnished with a Puṅkha.

पुङ्खिलतीर्थ *puṅkhila-tīrtha, am,* n., N. of a place of pilgrimage (= *Rāma-tīrtha*).

पुङ्ग *puṅga, as, am,* m. n. a heap, collection, quantity; [cf. *puñja.*]

पुङ्गल *puṅgala, as,* m. the soul; [cf. *pudgala.*]

पुङ्गव *puṅ-gava.* See under 2. *puṇs.*

पुच्छ *puććha, as, am,* m. n. a tail; the hinder part; the tail of a peacock; a horse's tail; any hairy tail; the end of anything; [cf. probably Gr. πυγή, perhaps πύματος.] — *Puććha-jāha, am,* n. the root of the tail. — *Puććha-dā,* f. a bulbous plant used as a remedy for sterility, = *lakshmaṇā-kanda;* (probably a corruption of *putra-dā.*) — *Puććha-dhi, is,* m., Ved. the root of the tail. — *Puććha-mūla* or *puććhāgra* (°*ćha-ag*°), *am,* n. the tip of the tail. — *Puććhāṇḍaka* (°*ćha-aṇ*°), *as,* m., N. of a Nāga of the race of Takshaka. — *Puććheśvara* (°*ćha-īś*°), *as* or *am,* m. or n. (?), N. of a place or of a temple.

Puććhaya in *ut-puććhaya,* q. v.

Puććhikā in *kroshṭu-p°, kroshṭuka-p°,* q. v.

Puććhin, ī, inī, i, having a tail, tailed; a cock; Calotropis Gigantea (= *arka*).

पुच्छटि *puććhaṭi, i,* n. snapping or cracking the fingers; [cf. *mućuṭī.*]

पुछ् *pućh* [cf. *yućh*], cl. 1. P. *puććhati, pupuććha, puććhitum,* to be careless or inattentive.

पुञ्ज *puñja, as,* m. (perhaps for *api* + *yuñja* fr. rt. *yuj*), a heap, lump, mass, quantity, collection, multitude; [cf. *nakha-puñja-phalā, puṅga, pūga;* Gr. πύξ perhaps an abbreviated dat. pl., πύκ-τη-ς, πύγ-μαχ-ο-ς, πυγ-μή, πυγ-ών, πυκ-νό-ς, πυκ-ι-νό-ς; Lat. *pug-nu-s, pug-na, pug-nā-re, pug-io, pug-il, pugillu-s, pugillaris;* Old Germ. *fū-st;* Old Slav. *pę-stĭ.*] — *Puñja-rāja, as,* m., N. of a grammarian and author of a commentary on the Sarasvatī-prakriyā. — *Puñja-śas,* ind. in heaps. — *Puñjī-kṛi,* cl. 8. P. A. *-karoti, -kurute, -kartum,* to heap, lay in a heap.

Puñjaya, Nom. P. *puñjayati, -yitum,* to heap, heap up, heap together.

Puñjātuka (?), *as,* m. = *phalelāṅku* (?).

Puñji, is, f. a heap, quantity, collection. — *Puñji-shṭha, as, ā, am,* heaped, accumulated; (*as*), m., Ved. a fisherman; (according to Mahī-dhara) a birdcatcher.

Puñjika, as, m. hail. — *Puñjika-sthalā* or *puñjikā-sthalā* or *puñjikā-stanā,* f. an allegorical N. of an Apsaras; (scil. *bhūmi,* ground thrown up in digging or having such ground?).

Puñjita, as, ā, am, piled up, heaped, heaped together; made up into a ball, pressed or put together.

पुञ्जन्मन् *puṅ-janman.* See under 2. *puṇs.*

पुञ्जील *puñjīla, am,* n., Ved. = *piñjūla,* q. v.

पुट् *puṭ,* cl. 6. P. *puṭati, puṭitum,* to embrace, clasp, fold; to intertwine; cl. 1. P. *poṭati,* to rub, to press, to grind or pound, (perhaps an incorrect form for *muṭ*); cl. 10. P. *puṭayati, -yitum,* to be in contact with; to bind together, fasten, string; *poṭayati, -yitum,* to reduce to powder, grind; to be or become small or shallow; to shine; to speak; [cf. rts. *paṭ, paṭh, puṭṭ, puth, muṭ, muṇṭ, puṇṭ, puṇḍ.*]

Puṭa, as, ī, am, m. f. n. a fold, pocket; a tubular or hollow space, cavity, concavity [cf. *kaksha-p°, karṇa-p°, gaja-p°*]; a cup or concavity made of a leaf folded or doubled; a basket or vessel or dish made of leaves (Manu VI. 28; cf. *pattra-p°, parṇa-p°, palāśa-p°*); the pod or capsule which envelops young shoots; a shallow cup or receptacle (as the hollow of the hand); an eyelid; a cover, covering, wrapper, cloth worn round the middle of the body to cover the privities; (*as, am*), m. n. a horse's hoof; (*as*), m. a casket (= *sam-puṭa*); a narrowing or contracting of anything; a folding or doubling of anything so as to form a cup or concavity; N. of a man; (*am*), n. a nutmeg; two vessels joined together (the upper one being inverted, for the sublimation of medicinal substances). — *Puṭa-kanda, as,* m. a species of bulbous plant (= *kola-kanda*). — *Puṭa-grīva, as,* m. 'hollow-necked,' a pot, jar, pitcher, vessel for butter; a copper vessel. — *Puṭa-pāka, as,* m. a particular method of preparing drugs (the various substances being wrapped up in leaves, covered with clay, and roasted in the fire); digesting, subliming. — *Puṭa-bhid, t, t, t,* Ved. causing to break through, opening (said of a rock under which a spring is discovered). — *Puṭa-bheda, as,* m. (probably) the fountain-head of a river; the bend of a river (?); the mouth of a river (?); a city, town; a kind of musical instrument. — *Puṭa-bhedaka, as, ikā, am,* Ved. = *puṭa-bhid,* q. v. — *Puṭa-bhedana, am,* n. a town, city. — *Puṭāhvaya* (°*ṭa-āh*°), *as,* m. = *puṭa-pāka,* q. v. — *Puṭoṭaja* (°*ṭa-uṭ*°), *am,* n. a white umbrella or parasol. — *Puṭodaka* (°*ṭa-ud*°), *as,* m. 'having water in its hollow or interior,' a cocoa-nut.

Puṭaka, am, n. a fold, pocket, &c. [cf. *puṭa*]; any shallow cup or concavity (also *pattra-p°*), a bag or vessel made of a leaf doubled over in a funnel-like shape; a lotus; a nutmeg; (*as*), m. a particular position of the hands; (*ikā*), f. cardamoms.

Puṭakinī, f. a lotus; a group of lotuses.

Puṭita, as, ā, am, rubbed, ground; split, torn up; contracted; sewn, stitched; (*am*), n. closing or shutting the hands to hold anything, the hollow of the hands.

पुट्ट् *puṭṭ,* cl. 10. P. *puṭṭayati, -yitum,* to decrease, diminish; to be or become small, be or become low or shallow.

पुड् *puḍ,* cl. 6. P. *puḍati, puḍitum,* to leave, quit; to dismiss; to emit; to cover; cl. 1. P. *poḍati,* &c., to grind; [cf. rts. *puṭ,* 1. *puṇs, buḍ, muḍ, muṇṭ, muṭ.*]

पुण् *puṇ* (connected with *puṇya,* q. v.), cl. 6. P. *puṇati, puṇitum,* to be pure or virtuous; to do a pious or holy act; cl. 10. P. *poṇayati, -yitum,* to collect, heap up, accumulate.

पुणतामकर *puṇatāmakara, as,* m., N. of the author of the Ātmatva-jāti-vićāra and Sādṛiśya-vāda, (also called Mahā-deva.)

पुण्ट् *puṇṭ,* cl. 10. P. *puṇṭayati, -yitum,* to speak; to shine.

पुण्ड् *puṇḍ,* cl. 1. P. *puṇḍati, puṇḍitum,* to rub, grind, pound, reduce to dust or powder.

पुण्ड *puṇḍa, as,* m. = *puṇḍra,* a mark, sign. — *Puṇḍa-vardhana* = *puṇḍra-vardhana,* q. v.

पुण्डरीक *puṇḍarīka, am,* n. (said to be fr. rt. *puṇ*), a lotus-flower, especially a white lotus, (used at the end of an adj. comp. as expressive of beauty, see Gaṇa Vyāghrādi to Pāṇ. II. 1, 56); a white umbrella; a kind of drug; a mark on the forehead (in this sense perhaps also m.); N. of a sacred bathing-place; (*as*), m. a kind of sacrifice; a species of rice; a fragrant kind of mango; Artemisia Indica (= *damanaka*); a variety of the sugar-cane; a silk-worm (?); a kind of leprosy; fever in an elephant; white (the colour); a tiger; a kind of serpent; N. of a Nāga; a pitcher, student's water-pot; N. of the elephant of the south-east quarter; N. of an ancient king; of a son of Nabha or Nabhas; (with Jainas) N. of a Gaṇa-dhara; N. of a hermit the son of Śveta-ketu and Lakshmī; of a mountain; (*ā*), f., N. of an Apsaras; of a daughter of Vasishṭha and wife of Prāṇa or Pāṇḍu. — *Puṇḍarī-srajā,* f. (*puṇḍarī* substituted for *puṇḍarīka*), Ved. a wreath or garland of lotuses. — *Puṇḍarīka-nārada-saṃvāda, as,* m., N. of the thirty-second chapter of the Pārtha Itihāsa-samuććaya. — *Puṇḍarīka-palāśāksha* (°*śa-aksha*), *as, ī, am,* having eyes like the petals of a lotus. — *Puṇḍarīka-pura, am,* n., N. of a city. — *Puṇḍarīka-plava, as,* m. a kind of bird. — *Puṇḍarīka-mukhī,* f. a kind of leech. — *Puṇḍarīkāksha* (°*ka-aksha*), *as,* m. 'lotus-eyed,' an epithet of Vishṇu; a kind of drug (= *puṇḍarya, pra-pauṇḍarīka*). — *Puṇḍarīkāta-patra* (°*ka-āt*°), *as, ā, am,* having the lotus for an umbrella (said of the autumn). — *Puṇḍarīkāva-taṇsa* (°*ka-av*°), *as, ā, am,* having white lotus-flowers for ear ornaments. — *Puṇḍarīkodara-prabha* (°*ka-ud*°), *as, ā, am,* resplendent as the interior of a white lotus.

Puṇḍarīyaka, as, m., N. of a divinity enumerated among the Viśve Devāḥ; (*am*), n. Ketmia Mutabilis (= *sthala-padma*); a kind of drug (commonly called *puṇḍarīya*).

Puṇḍarya, am, n. a creeper; a medicinal plant used as a remedy for diseased eyes (=*pra-pauṇḍarīka*).

पुण्ड्र *puṇḍra, as,* m. a red variety of the common sugar-cane, Saccharum Officinarum; a white lotus, a lotus in general; a species of tree (=*hrasva-plaksha*); a kind of creeper, Gærtnera Racemosa (=*ati-muktaka, vāsantī*); a mark or line made on the forehead with sandal &c., sectarial mark; a worm; N. of a Daitya or Infernal being considered incarnate in Śiśu-pāla; N. of a son of Bali; (*ās*), m. pl., N. of a people and of their country (the modern Bengal and Behar, 'the country of the sugar-cane'); N. of a mythical city between the mountains Hima-vat and Hema-kūṭa. — *Puṇḍra-keli, is,* m. an elephant. — *Puṇḍra-deśa, as,* m., N. of a district. — *Puṇḍra-nagara, am,* n. 'city of the Puṇḍras,' N. of a town; [cf. *pauṇḍranāgara.*] — *Puṇḍra-vardhana, am,* n., N. of a town in Gauḍa; (also spelt *puṇḍa-vardhana.*)

Puṇḍraka, as, m. a red variety of the common sugar-cane, Saccharum Officinarum; a kind of creeper, Gærtnera Racemosa; a species of tree; a mark on the forehead, sectarial mark; one who lives by breeding silk-worms; N. of a man (?).

Puṇḍhra, as or *am,* m. or n. (?), a mark, sign, sectarial mark; [cf. *puṇḍra.*]

पुण्य *puṇya, as, ā, am* (said to be fr. rt. 1. *pū;* according to others fr. rt. 1. *push* or rt. *puṇ;* not met with in the earliest language), good, pure, holy, right, righteous, virtuous, just, sacred; happy, prosperous, favourable, propitious, auspicious, lucky; bright, fine, beautiful, pleasing; sweet, fragrant (as an odour); solemn, festive, ferial; (*am*), n. good, right, virtue, moral or religious merit; a good or meritorious act; purity, purification; a religious ceremony, especially one performed by a wife in order to retain her husband's affections and to obtain a son; a brick trough for watering cattle, = *koshṭhaka;* (*as*), m., N. of a man; of a lake (in this sense perhaps n.); (*ā*), f. holy basil, Ocymum Sanctum; N. of a daughter of Kratu and San-natī. — *Puṇya-kartṛi, tā,* m. 'right-doer,' an upright or virtuous man. — *Puṇya-karman, a,* n. a virtuous or meritorious act; (*ā, ā, a*), whose actions are holy or meritorious, doing good works, upright, righteous, virtuous, pious; [cf. *puṇyaika-karman.*] — *Puṇya-kāla, as,* m. an auspicious time. — *Puṇyakāla-tā,* f. a propitious period. — *Puṇya-kīrtti, is, is, i,* bearing a good name, famous, celebrated; N. of a Buddhist (whose form was assumed by Vishṇu). — *Puṇya-kṛit, t, t, t,* 'right-doing,' upright, virtuous; N. of a divinity enumerated among the Viśve Devāḥ. — *Puṇya-kṛityā,* f. a good action. — *Puṇya-kshaya, as,* m. decay or loss of religious merit. — *Puṇya-kshetra, am,* n. a holy place or district, a place by visiting which merit is acquired, a place of pilgrimage. — *Puṇya-gandha, as, ā, am,* sweet-scented, fragrant; (*as*), m. the Campaka, Michelia Champaka. — *Puṇya-gandhi, is, is, i,* or *puṇya-gandhin, ī, inī, i,* sweet-scented, fragrant. — *Puṇya-gṛiha, am,* n. a house of charity, an alms-house; a temple. — *Puṇya-jana, as,* m. a good or pious or virtuous man; N. of a class of supernatural beings; a Yaksha or attendant of Kuvera the god of wealth; a fiend, goblin, Rākshasa. — *Puṇyajaneśvara* (°*na-iś*°), *as,* m. 'lord of the Yakshas,' Kuvera the Hindū deity of wealth. — *Puṇya-jala, as, ā, am,* containing pure water. — *Puṇya-jita, as, ā, am,* gained or attained by good works. — *Puṇya-tara, as, ā, am,* purer, holier. — *Puṇyatarī-kṛi,* cl. 8. P. *-karoti, -kartum,* to make purer or cleaner. — *Puṇya-tā,* f. or *puṇya-tva, am,* n. purity, holiness. — *Puṇya-tīrtha, am,* n. a holy shrine or place of pilgrimage. — *Puṇya-tṛiṇa, am,* n. holy grass; N. of the white variety of Kuśa grass. — *Puṇya-darśana, as, ā, am,* of beautiful appearance, beautiful; (*as*), m. the blue jay, = *ćāsha;* (*am*), n. visiting holy shrines. — *Puṇya-duh, -dhuk, k, k,* yielding or granting happiness or beatitude. — *Puṇya-nātha, as,* m., N. of a grammarian. — *Puṇya-nāman, ā,* m., N. of one of the attendants of Skanda. — *Puṇya-puṇya-tā,* f. perfect holiness. — *Puṇya-purusha, as,* m. a godly or good man, a man rich in moral merit. — *Puṇya-pratāpa, as,* m. the might and efficacy of virtue or of the merit acquired by a course of virtuous acts. — *Puṇya-prada, as, ā, am,* conferring merit, meritorious. — *Puṇya-prasava, ās,* m. pl. (with Buddhists) N. of a class of deities. — *Puṇya-phala, am,* n. the fruit or reward of good works or meritorious actions; (*as*), m. 'having good fruit,' the garden of Lakshmī; a grove. — *Puṇya-bala, as,* m., N. of a king of Puṇya-vatī. — *Puṇya-bharita, as, ā, am,* extremely blessed, abounding in holiness or bliss. — *Puṇya-bhāj, k, k, k,* or *puṇya-bhājin, ī, inī, i,* possessing happiness, partaker of bliss, happy; possessing merit, virtuous. — *Puṇya-bhū, ūs,* f. the holy land of the Hindūs (bounded on the north by the Himālayas, on the south by the Vindhya mountains, and on the east and west by the sea, = Āryāvarta). — *Puṇya-bhūmi, is,* f. the holy land of the Hindūs [cf. *puṇya-bhū* above]; the mother of a male child. — *Puṇya-maya, as, ī, am,* formed or consisting of good. — *Puṇya-mitra, as,* m., N. of a Buddhist patriarch. — *Puṇya-yoga, as,* m. the influence or effect of virtuous actions done in a former life. — *Puṇya-rātra, as,* m. a good or auspicious night; a night on which any religious commemoration or ceremony is held; [cf. *puṇyāha.*] — *Puṇya-rāśi, is,* m., N. of a man; N. of a mountain. — *Puṇya-labdha, as, ā, am,* attained by good works (as a reward in heaven). — *Puṇya-loka, as, ā, am,* belonging to a better world, sharing in a better world (Ved.); (*as*), m. heaven, paradise. — *Puṇyaloka-tra,* ind., Ved. in a better world. — *Puṇya-vat, ān, atī, at,* possessing merit, meritorious, pure, holy, righteous, pious, virtuous; pleasing, beautiful; fortunate, lucky, auspicious; happy; (*atī*), f., N. of a country. — *Puṇya-vardhana, am,* n., N. of a town; (probably a wrong reading for *puṇḍra-vardhana.*) — *Puṇya-varman, ā,* m., N. of a prince of Vi-darbha. — *Puṇya-vāg-buddhi-karmin, ī, iṇī, i,* pure in word, thought, and deed. — *Puṇya-vijita, as, ā, am,* acquired by merit, merited. — *Puṇya-śakuna, as,* m. a bird of good omen. — *Puṇya-śālā,* f. a house of charity, alms-house. — *Puṇya-śīla, as, ā, am,* being of a virtuous disposition, disposed to virtuous acts, virtuous, pious, righteous. — *Puṇya-śrī-garbha, as,* m., N. of a Bodhi-sattva. — *Puṇya-śloka, as, ā, am,* 'well spoken of,' of good fame or reputation; (*as*), m. an epithet of Nala; of Yudhi-shṭhira; of Kṛishṇa; (*ā*), f. an epithet of Draupadī; of Sītā. — *Puṇyaśloka-didṛikshā,* f. the desire of seeing Nala. — *Puṇya-śloka-parāṅmukha, as, ī, am,* having the face averted from Nala. — *Puṇya-sañćaya, as,* m. a store of virtue or religious merit. — *Puṇya-sama, am,* n. a good year. — *Puṇya-sāra, as,* m., N. of a prince. — *Puṇya-sundara, as,* m., N. of a grammarian who arranged the Dhātu-pāṭha of Hemaćandra's grammar in alphabetical order. — *Puṇya-sena, as,* m., N. of a man; of a prince of Ujjayinī. — *Puṇya-stambha-kara, as,* m., N. of a man. — *Puṇya-sthāna, am,* n. a sacred place, consecrated ground. — *Puṇyātman* (°*ya-āt*°), *ā, ā, a,* pure-souled, righteous, virtuous, pious, holy. — *Puṇyālankṛita* (°*ya-al*°), *as, ā, am,* adorned by virtue; (*as*), m., N. of a demon. — *Puṇyāha* (°*ya-aha*), *am,* n. a good or happy or auspicious day, holiday; *puṇyāhaṃ vać* in Caus., to wish any one a happy or pleasant day. — *Puṇyāhan* (°*ya-ahan*), *a,* n., Ved. = *puṇyāha* above. — *Puṇyāha-vāćana, am,* n. the declaration of a holiday, repeating at sacrifices &c. 'this is a holiday' three times, wishing any one a happy day. — *Puṇyaika-karman* (°*ya-ek*°), *ā, ā, a,* one whose actions are only virtuous. — *Puṇyodakā* (°*ya-ud*°), f. 'having sacred waters,' N. of a river in the next world. — *Puṇyodaya* (°*ya-ud*°), *as,* m. the resulting of good fortune (as the effect of virtuous acts done in a former life). — *Puṇyodyāna* (°*ya-ud*°), *as, ā, am,* having beautiful gardens.

Puṇyaka, am, n. a religious ceremony, festival; a meritorious act or obligation of a religious nature (as fasting, praying, &c.); a ceremony performed by a woman in order to retain her husband's affections and to obtain a son; the observance of this ceremony; the present made to a wife on that occasion. — *Puṇyaka-vrata, am,* n. the worship of Kṛishṇa for a year, with daily presents, to be performed by a woman desirous of a son.

पुत् *put* or *pud,* n. hell, a particular hell to which the childless are condemned, a division of the infernal regions considered to be the abode of those who die childless; (a word invented to explain *putra;* see Manu IX. 138.) — 2. *pun-nāman, ā, mnī, a* (for 1. see under 2. *puṃs*), having the name Put, called Put.

पुत *puta, au,* m. du. the buttocks; *puta* and *śrī-puta,* a kind of metre consisting of four times ⏑⏑⏑⏑⏑⏑ – –, – ⏑ – –.

पुतारिका *putārikā* (?), f. the navel.

पुतीसृञ्जय *putī-sṛiñjaya, ās,* m. pl., N. of a people; (a wrong reading for *pūti-sṛiñjaya.*)

पुत्तल *puttala, puttalaka, puttikā.* See p. 581, cols. 1, 2.

पुत्र *putra, as,* m. (perhaps connected with *pitṛi;* said to be fr. rt. 1. *pū,* but according to others fr. rt. 1. *push;* traditionally said to be a comp. *put-tra,* 'preserving from the hell called Put,' Manu IX. 138), a son, child, the young of an animal; (at the end of a comp.) used as a diminutive to express 'any little thing of its kind' [cf. *śilā-p*°]; the fifth mansion from the point of conjunction of the sun and a zodiacal sign (in astrol.), the fifth house; N. of a son of Brahmishṭha; of a son of Priya-vrata; of a son of a Brāhman; (*au*), m. du. two sons, a son and daughter; (*ī*), f. a daughter; a doll [cf. *dāru-p*°]; (at the end of a comp.) used as a diminutive to express 'any little thing of its kind' [cf. *asi-p*°]; an epithet of Pārvatī; a species of plant. *Putra* in the voc. sing. is sometimes used as a mode of addressing young persons, 'my son,' 'my child;' [cf. Pers. *pusr,* 'a son;' Gr. πῶλο-ς, πωλ-ίο-ν; Lat. *pullu-s,* (*Marci-*)*por, pu-er, puera, pu-su-s, pusa, pū-pu-s, pū-pa, pūpilla, putu-s;* Goth. *fula*(*n*) = Old Germ. *folo,* 'a foal;' Armor. *paotr,* 'a boy.'] — *Putra-kandā,* f. a bulbous plant supposed to cause fecundity (= *lakshmaṇā-kanda*). — *Putra-karman, a,* n. a ceremony or sacrifice on the birth of a son. — *Putra-kalatra-nāśa-bhīta, as, ā, am,* fearful or apprehensive of the destruction of wife and children. — *Putra-kāma, as, ā, am,* Ved. desirous of sons or children. — *Putrakāmeshṭi* (°*ma-ish*°), *is,* f., Ved. an oblation or sacrifice made by one desirous of offspring. — *Putrakāmya,* Nom. P. *putrakāmyati,* &c., to wish for or be desirous of a son. — *Putrakāmyā,* f., Ved. wish for sons or children, affection for progeny. — *Putra-kārya, am,* n. a ceremony relating to a son. — *Putra-kṛit, t, t,* m. f. an adopted child. — *Putra-kṛitaka, as, ā, am,* adopted as a child or son. — *Putra-kṛitya, am,* n. the duty of a son. — *Putra-kṛitha, as* or *am,* m. or n. (?), Ved. the bringing forth or procreation of children. — *Putra-krama-dīpikā,* f., N. of a work by Rāma-bhadra on the law of inheritance. — *Putra-ghna, as, ī, am,* child-killing; scil. *yoni,* in which the fetus dies. — *Putra-jagdhī,* f. 'one who has devoured her children,' an unnatural mother. — *Putra-jāta, as, ā, am,* one to whom a son is born, having a son. — *Putra-jīva* or *putrañ-jīva* or *putrañ-jīvaka, as,* m. 'giving life to children,' the tree Putranjiva Roxburghii (from the fruit of which necklaces are made, supposed to be of prolific efficacy, and when worn by children to keep them in good health). — *Putra-tā,* f. or *putra-tva, am,* n. sonship, filial relation. — *Putra-tīrtha, am,* n., N. of the 119th and 120th chapters of the Bhūmi-khaṇḍa or